S0-BWN-905

FILM & VIDEO FINDER VOL. III

Published by Access Innovations, Inc., Albuquerque, New Mexico 87196.

ISBN: 0-89320-110-3
First Edition, 1987. 3 volumes.

TITLE SECTION

K

K Of C Is You And Me, The C 28 MIN
16MM FILM - 3/4 IN VIDEO
Recreates the founding of the Knights of Columbus. Uses cinema verite interviews. Shows the scope of programs available to members and their families.
Prod-KNICOL Dist-MTP

K Or Hard 'C' Sound, The - Caroline Cat's Cough C 15 MIN
2 INCH VIDEOTAPE P
Introduces some of the consonant sounds met in early reading. Identifies the written letter with the spoken sound.
From The Listen And Say Series.
Prod-MPATI Dist-GPITVL

K Sound, The C 15 MIN
3/4 INCH VIDEO CASSETTE P
Describes the production of the k sound.
From The New Talking Shop Series.
Prod-BSPTV Dist-GPITVL 1978

K-9000 - A Space Oddity C 10 MIN
16MM FILM OPTICAL SOUND K-C
Presents a cartoon spoof on '2001 - A SPACE ODDYSEY.'
Prod-CFS Dist-CFS 1969

K, G, T, D, N C
3/4 OR 1/2 INCH VIDEO CASSETTE
See series title for descriptive statement.
From The Educational Video Concepts For Early Childhood Language Development Series.
Prod-ECCOAZ Dist-ECCOAZ

K, M, N, U C 15 MIN
3/4 OR 1/2 INCH VIDEO CASSETTE P
Presents techniques of handwriting, focusing on the capital letters K, M, N and U.
From The Cursive Writing Series.
Prod-WHROTV Dist-GPITVL 1984

Ka Rorn - Southern Village C 18 MIN
16MM FILM, 3/4 OR 1/2 IN VIDEO J-C A
Depicts life in a small village community in southern Thailand. Explains that on an island which few villagers will ever leave, the community is self-sufficient and is supported by farming and fishing.
Prod-FLMAUS Dist-SF 1973

Kabuki - Classic Theatre Of Japan C 30 MIN
16MM FILM OPTICAL SOUND
Shows how Kabuki actors create dramatic effects of extraordinary intensity using elaborate costumes, vivid makeup, exaggerated vocalization, picturesque settings and wonderful music.
Prod-MTP Dist-MTP

Kabylia B 10 MIN
16MM FILM OPTICAL SOUND
Depicts the Kabyles, or Berbers, ancestors of modern day North Africans cultivating their land in semi-primitive methods and fashioning handicrafts with skill and beauty.
Prod-FILIM Dist-RADIM 1947

Kachinas C 29 MIN
3/4 INCH VIDEO CASSETTE
Examines the importance of Kachinas in Pueblo religions, their use in teaching the young, the Kachina ceremonial calendar and the Kachina as an art form. Also available in two-inch quad and one-inch videotape.
From The Indian Arts At The Phoenix Heard Museum Series.
Prod-KAETTV Dist-NAMPBC

Kaddish C 92 MIN
3/4 INCH VIDEO CASSETTE
Portrays a young Jewish activist coming to terms with his father's traumatic history. Reveals how a young man's world view was principally shaped by the Holocaust which took place before he was born.
Prod-FIRS Dist-FIRS

Kafiristan - Hedningernes Land (They Were Kafirs) C 45 MIN
16MM FILM OPTICAL SOUND
A Danish language film. Presents the everyday life of the Kafirs, which amazingly resembles what we know about our own past. Points out that the Kafirs do not look like the neighboring peoples, and there are many indications that they are remnants of the original Indo-European tribes who have become isolated here, and thus have been able to preserve their culture almost unchanged through thousands of years.
Prod-STATNS Dist-STATNS 1958

Kai C 10 MIN
16MM FILM, 3/4 OR 1/2 IN VIDEO I-H
Focuses on a young boy with a cleft lip and palate, and shows how he has learned to cope with his disability.
From The People You'd Like To Know Series.
Prod-WGBHTV Dist-EBEC 1978

Kaibab Bucks C 13 MIN
16MM FILM OPTICAL SOUND
An account of the first bow and arrow season in Arizona's Kaibab forest showing some of the largest mule deer bucks ever taken.
Prod-SFI Dist-SFI

Kailash At Ellora B 19 MIN
16MM FILM OPTICAL SOUND I-C A
Explains how the architectural marvel of Kailash Temple could have been cut out of the rocks at Ellora.
Prod-INDIA Dist-NEDINF

Kainai C 27 MIN
16MM FILM OPTICAL SOUND
Reports on a new development in the history of the Blood Indian Reserve in Alberta.
LC NO. 75-701474
Prod-CDIAND Dist-CDIAND Prodn-NFBC 1974

Kakapo - The Night Parrot C 25 MIN
16MM FILM, 3/4 OR 1/2 IN VIDEO P A
Presents a true nature story told as a fairy tale. Portrays the Kakapo, the largest type of parrot, in the rain forests of New Zealand where it had no predators and ceased being able to fly. Shows how man arrived, introducing predators and causing the Kakapo to become almost extinct. Documents efforts to locate, photograph and save this parrot.
Prod-NWDIMF Dist-NWDIMF

Kakeya Problem, The C 60 MIN
16MM FILM OPTICAL SOUND H-C
Professor A S Besicovitch presents a proof, using charts and animation, that there is no minimum area in which a unit horizontal line segment may be rotated so that its direction is reversed.
From The MAA Individual Lecturers Series.
LC NO. FIA63-465
Prod-MAA Dist-MLA 1962

Kalahari Desert People, The C 24 MIN
16MM FILM, 3/4 OR 1/2 IN VIDEO J-C A
A shorter version of the 1974 film Bushmen of the Kalahari. Examines the social and cultural changes being made by three groups of Bushmen in southern Africa's Kalahari Desert as they become farmer-herders after thousands of years of being hunter-gatherers.
LC NO. 80-706335
Prod-NGS Dist-NGS Prodn-WOLPER 1975

Kaleidoscope Bargello C 30 MIN
3/4 OR 1/2 INCH VIDEO CASSETTE
Shows how to use Bargello, the classic flame embroidery stitch. Shows firescreens, seat covers and still lifes made with this pattern.
From The Erica Series.
Prod-WGBHTV Dist-KINGFT

Kaleidoscope Geometry C 20 MIN
3/4 OR 1/2 INCH VIDEO CASSETTE H
Presents teachers Beth McKenna and David Edmonds exploring kaleidoscope geometry with designs reflected in two or three mirrors. Uses various special triangles to generate semiregular and demiregular tesselations, stellar polygons and solids.
From The Shapes Of Geometry Series. Pt 5
LC NO. 82-707391
Prod-WVIZTV Dist-GPITVL 1982

Kaleidoscope Orissa C 37 MIN
16MM FILM, 3/4 OR 1/2 IN VIDEO H-C A
Explores the culture of Orissa, one of the states of India, rich in artistic tradition. From early childhood, the people of Orissa are introduced to the primitive instruments of the family craft, tools which they will use all their lives.
Prod-PILGRM Dist-IFB 1967

Kaleidoscope—A Series

Explores art in the Santa Clara Valley, in the Bay area of San Francisco.
Prod-KTEHTV Dist-SCCOE

Art And Community	060 MIN
Art And The Three R's	030 MIN
Children's Theatre	030 MIN
Electric Weasel/Museums	030 MIN
Galleries Role, The/And All That Jazz	030 MIN
Literary Arts	030 MIN
Los Lupenos/Freimark	030 MIN
Middlebrook/Bluegrass	030 MIN
Montalvo/Battenburg/Lord	030 MIN
Opera	030 MIN
Paper Art/Cartooning	030 MIN
Peoples Theatre, The	030 MIN
Reflections - A Cultural History	030 MIN
San Jose Theatre/Sam Richardson Profile	030 MIN
Symphony, The	030 MIN
Theatre	060 MIN
Three Black Artists	030 MIN
Watercolor Society, The/Lou Harrison	030 MIN
Young Audiences/Muralist	030 MIN

Kalulu And The Leopard C 15 MIN
3/4 OR 1/2 INCH VIDEO CASSETTE K-P
See series title for descriptive statement.
From The Gather Round Series.
Prod-CTI Dist-CTI

Kama Sutras B 10 MIN
16MM FILM, 3/4 OR 1/2 IN VIDEO A
Presents soloists Diana Russell and Raymond Evans in Marks' choreographed work inspired by the Indian book of love.
Prod-SFCT Dist-CNEMAG 1965

Kamakura And Enoshima C 25 MIN
16MM FILM OPTICAL SOUND
A Japanese language film. Introduces the unique islet of Enoshima and Kamakura, noted for its fine beach and many temples and shrines. Explains that since Japan's feudal government was set up in this city in the century, it had its prosperous age for 150 years as the center of the military administration and culture. Shows the Daibutsu (great Buddha), Hase Kannon, the gilded goddess of mercy and Yabusame, ancient archery from horse-back.
Prod-UNIJAP Dist-UNIJAP 1969

Kameleon C 10 MIN
16MM FILM, 3/4 OR 1/2 IN VIDEO C A
Uses animation to tell a story in which a demagogue standing on a speaker's platform offers convincing arguments on topics ranging from religion to the women's movement. Shows how the speaker is interrupted by arty images and finally reveals his true parrot-like nature.
LC NO. 80-707373
Prod-ZAGREB Dist-IFB 1975

Kameradschaft B 80 MIN
3/4 OR 1/2 INCH VIDEO CASSETTE
Shows French miners who are buried in a shaft explosion and the German co-workers who struggle to free them.
Prod-IHF Dist-IHF

Kami, The C 6 MIN
16MM FILM OPTICAL SOUND
Demonstrates the vanishing art of making a water powered lathe and using it to manufacture traditional water jugs of wood.
LC NO. 80-700819
Prod-STEVNT Dist-TASCOR 1979

Kamikaze B 89 MIN
3/4 OR 1/2 INCH VIDEO CASSETTE
Documents the war in the Pacific. Introduces proof that the U S received warnings of impending Japanese aggression in 1941. Follows the declaration of war after Pearl Harbor.
Prod-IHF Dist-IHF

Kamikaze - Flower Of Death C 30 MIN
3/4 OR 1/2 INCH VIDEO CASSETTE H-C A
See series title for descriptive statement.
From The World War II - GI Diary Series.
Prod-TIMLIF Dist-TIMLIF 1980

Kampuchea - The Past And The Future C 24 MIN
3/4 OR 1/2 INCH VIDEO CASSETTE H-C A
Presents the history, people and problems facing Kampuchea in the aftermath of the ravages of the Vietnam war.
Prod-JOU Dist-JOU

Kandinsky (1866 - 1944) C 15 MIN
16MM FILM OPTICAL SOUND
Discusses how Kandinsky gave birth to modern art by an almost accidental discovery of the freedom of pure form.
Prod-ROLAND Dist-ROLAND

Kangaroo Island C 17 MIN
16MM FILM, 3/4 OR 1/2 IN VIDEO I-H A
Shows a wildlife sanctuary in Australia. Views the activities of opossum, pelicans, seals, emus, kangaroos, black swans and koalas. Captures the tranquil beauty of the island's wide beaches, fields and woods, exotic flowering plants and bright-colored birds.
Prod-LUF Dist-LUF 1978

Kangaroos, Pt 1 - Biography C 13 MIN
16MM FILM OPTICAL SOUND J-C A
Describes the life cycle of the kangaroo, discussing mating habits, birth and the development of the young in the pouch.
LC NO. 70-713555
Prod-ANAIB Dist-AUIS 1970

Kangaroos, Pt 2 - Varieties C 12 MIN
16MM FILM OPTICAL SOUND J-C A
Shows various types of kangaroos in their habitats.
LC NO. 74-713556
Prod-ANAIB Dist-AUIS 1970

Kangra And Kulu C 16 MIN
16MM FILM OPTICAL SOUND I-C A
Explains that the two valleys of Kangra and Kulu, in the Himalayan range, are not only famous for their natural beauty, but also for the festivals and colorful marriages of the people who live there.
Prod-INDIA Dist-NEDINF

Kansas Circa '90 C 26 MIN
16MM FILM OPTICAL SOUND
Uses the activities of a young boy to show life in Kansas around 1890.
LC NO. 74-702653
Prod-UKANS Dist-UKANS 1974

Kansas City Jazz C 30 MIN
3/4 OR 1/2 INCH VIDEO CASSETTE
Presents an interview with Jay 'Hootie' McShann, who played with big bands and his own jazz group around the country. Mixes stories with jazz, featuring drummer Paul Gunther and bassman Bill Britto.
Prod-NETCHE Dist-NETCHE 1974

Kansas School Days C 5 MIN
16MM FILM SILENT I-H A S
Describes in American sign language early school days in a little red schoolhouse in Kansas and the lives of two poor families who made up the student body. Signed for the deaf by Carolyn Larson.

LC NO. 76-701686
Prod-JOYCE Dist-JOYCE 1975

Kaposi's Sarcoma C 20 MIN
3/4 OR 1/2 INCH VIDEO CASSETTE
Discusses the so-called 'gay cancer,' including the history, extent, symptoms and treatments.
Prod-NOTTH Dist-UWISC 1982

Karate C 10 MIN
16MM FILM, 3/4 OR 1/2 IN VIDEO J-C A
Gives a brief history of karate, observing some of its basic procedure demonstrated by a group of experts from the age of five on up.
Prod-PFP Dist-PFP 1972

Karate - Art Or Sport C 20 MIN
16MM FILM, 3/4 OR 1/2 IN VIDEO J-C A
Demonstrates the philosophy underlying a sport that is better understood as a 'MARTIAL ART' - karate. Features six black belts demonstrating body discipline, mental concentration, choreographed exercises and regulated breathing necessary for maximum coordination and harmony between mind and body to achieve maximum physical powers.
Prod-ACI Dist-AIMS 1974

Karate And Self-Defense For Women C 30 MIN
3/4 INCH VIDEO CASSETTE
Demonstrates the basic techniques and skills of self-defense for women.
Prod-WMENIF Dist-WMENIF

Karate Kid Show C 24 MIN
3/4 OR 1/2 INCH VIDEO CASSETTE
Features a 15-year-old black belt in karate who also has farm chores and a dirt bike racing hobby. Shows a young peoples' band, an ice skating team, a dance group and a visit to the Free Wheel Bike co-op.
Prod-WCCOTV Dist-WCCOTV 1981

Karate—A Series

A series of 14 videocassettes. Explores karate as an art form, a sport and a self-defense technique. Provides instruction leading toward attainment of the yellow belt, the first step in the six-step stairway to the black belt. Hosted by the brothers Sin The and Hiang The.
Prod-KYTV Dist-KYTV 1982

Karate, Pt 1 C 60 MIN
1/2 IN VIDEO CASSETTE BETA/VHS
Introduces Karate as it was before it became a sport. Deals with self defense as well as the disciplines associated with the martial arts.
Prod-MOHOMV Dist-MOHOMV

Karate, Pt 2 C 60 MIN
1/2 IN VIDEO CASSETTE BETA/VHS
Demonstrates the moves of attack and defense in Karate.
Prod-MOHOMV Dist-MOHOMV

Karba's First Years B 19 MIN
16MM FILM OPTICAL SOUND H-C
Considers the life of a Balinese child of seven months. Shows his relationships to others. Illustrates the Balinese child's lack of responsiveness because of unresponsive parents.
From The Character Formation In Different Cultures Series.
Prod-MEAD Dist-NYU 1950

Karel Shock And Joe Nash C 30 MIN
3/4 OR 1/2 INCH VIDEO CASSETTE
Presents historical perspectives on black dancers in the United States. Hosted by Julinda Lewis.
From The Eye On Dance - Third World Dance, Beyond The White Stream Series.
Prod-ARTRES Dist-ARTRES

Karen C 30 MIN
16MM FILM OPTICAL SOUND H-C A R
Uses a dramatization about a teen-age girl and her unwanted pregnancy and the assurance she receives from her pastor of God's forgiveness and love in order to provide a basis for discussing the question of abortion and the pressures placed on the unmarried pregnant woman.
LC NO. 78-715499
Prod-CONCOR Dist-CPH 1969

Karen Bernard, Mimi Garrard And Susan Salinger C 30 MIN
3/4 OR 1/2 INCH VIDEO CASSETTE
Focuses on the impact of light, sculpture and film in conjunction with dance. Features 'Esoterica' with Gwen Krause. Hoseted by Celia Ipiotis.
From The Eye On Dance - Dance And The Plastic Art Series.
Prod-ARTRES Dist-ARTRES

Karen Goes Political C 30 MIN
3/4 OR 1/2 INCH VIDEO CASSETTE
Dramatizes the classic debate between monetary and fiscal policy as alternative ways of stabilizing the economy.
From The Money Puzzle - The World Of Macroeconomics Series. Module 12
Prod-MDCC Dist-MDCC

Karen Kain, Ballerina C 53 MIN
16MM FILM OPTICAL SOUND
Provides an in-depth study of Canadian ballerina Karen Kain, with a behind-the-scenes view of her preparation for a cross-Canada tour with the Ballets de Marseille.
LC NO. 77-702930
Prod-NIELSE Dist-NIELSE 1977

Karen's Magic Flute C 30 MIN
3/4 OR 1/2 INCH VIDEO CASSETTE
Takes the viewer through the phase of business organizations. Covers sole proprietorship to incorporation.
From The Money Puzzle - The World Of Macroeconomics Series. Module 5
Prod-MDCC Dist-MDCC

Karius And Bactus C 16 MIN
16MM FILM OPTICAL SOUND P-I
Uses animated puppets to illustrate to children the importance of regularly brushing their teeth and having periodic dental checkups.
LC NO. 72-701334
Prod-CAPRIN Dist-MLA 1968

Karl A Folkers C
3/4 OR 1/2 INCH VIDEO CASSETTE
Discusses the broad spectrum of Dr Karl A Folkers' accomplishments in both the industrial and academic setting, including his contributions to the development of B-6 and B-12, penicillin and most recently, co-enzyme Q.
From The Eminent Chemists - The Interviews Series.
Prod-AMCHEM Dist-AMCHEM 1984

Karl Hess - Toward Liberty C 26 MIN
16MM FILM, 3/4 OR 1/2 IN VIDEO
Presents a tribute to former conservative speechwriter Karl Hess, who became a spokesman for a social philosophy called appropriate technology. Shows how he encourages his audiences to examine social issues and to think of society as people rather than institutions.
Prod-HALLAD Dist-DIRECT 1980

Karl Marx - The Massive Dissent C 60 MIN
16MM FILM, 3/4 OR 1/2 IN VIDEO H-C A
Investigates the impact of Karl Marx and other Socialist leaders on later economic interpretations of society. Based on the book The Age Of Uncertainty by John Kenneth Galbraith.
From The Age Of Uncertainty Series.
LC NO. 77-700663
Prod-BBCL Dist-FI 1977

Karl Menninger Looks At Psychiatric History C 21 MIN
16MM FILM OPTICAL SOUND
Presents Dr Karl Menninger looking back at the early roots of psychiatric discipline, encompassing a span from prehistory to one hundred years ago.
LC NO. FIA66-129
Prod-ROCHEL Dist-AMEDA Prodn-VISPRJ 1966

Karl Menninger, Psychiatry, Education C 29 MIN
3/4 OR 1/2 INCH VIDEO CASSETTE A
See series title for descriptive statement.
From The Quest For Peace Series.
Prod-AACD Dist-AACD 1984

Karl Shapiro's America C 13 MIN
16MM FILM, 3/4 OR 1/2 IN VIDEO
Uses photographs, collage animation, paintings and live action to illuminate the ideas and images of the poetry of Karl Shapiro.
Prod-HOYLEA Dist-PFP 1976

Kasa Twene - The Drum That Talks C 29 MIN
3/4 INCH VIDEO CASSETTE
Features Ghanese drummer Kwasi Aduonum as he demonstrates the drums of Africa. Includes dancers performing African dances.
Prod-UMITV Dist-UMITV 1975

Kasak C 9 MIN
16MM FILM OPTICAL SOUND
Documents the story of a race car driver leading to the final race in an endurance series in Canada.
LC NO. 76-703778
Prod-CONCRU Dist-CONCRU 1975

Kaseki C 213 MIN
16MM FILM OPTICAL SOUND
A Japanese language film. Centers around Itsuki, the aging head of a large Japanese construction company who is beginning to feel an emptiness in his life as he leaves Japan on a business trip to Europe. Follows him as he learns he is dying of cancer and has only a year to live.
Prod-NYFLMS Dist-NYFLMS 1974

Kashia Men's Dances - Southwestern Pomo Indians C 40 MIN
16MM FILM, 3/4 OR 1/2 IN VIDEO J-C A
Four authentic Pomo dances are performed by Indians in elaborate dance costumes and body paint on the Kashia Reservation near Stewart's Point on the northern California coast. Photographs made before 1900 show the history of the development of the dance.
From The American Indian Series.
Prod-UCEMC Dist-UCEMC Prodn-UCEMC 1963

Kasmir C 14 MIN
16MM FILM OPTICAL SOUND
Presents a travelog on Kasmir, India.
From The Journal Series.
LC NO. 74-701971
Prod-FIARTS Dist-CANFDC 1973

Kasrilevka On The Mississippi B 30 MIN
16MM FILM OPTICAL SOUND
Mark Twain's Huckleberry Finn meets Sholom Aleichem's motel, the cantor's son in the play 'KASRILEVKA ON THE MISSISSIPPI,' which illustrates the resemblance between the two authors. (Kinescope)
Prod-JTS Dist-NAAJS Prodn-NBCTV 1955

Kate Chopin - The Joy That Kills C 56 MIN
3/4 OR 1/2 INCH VIDEO CASSETTE
Presents an adaptation of The Joy That Kills, a short story by late 19th century American writer Kate Chopin.
Prod-FOTH Dist-FOTH

Kate Chopin's The Story Of An Hour C 24 MIN
16MM FILM OPTICAL SOUND
Relates that upon hearing of the death of her husband, Mrs Mallard looks inside herself and discovers her own freedom in a shocking awakening. Based on the short story The Story Of An Hour by Kate Chopin.
Prod-ISHTAR Dist-ISHTAR

Kate Millett - Women And Violence C 60 MIN
3/4 INCH VIDEO CASSETTE
Presents Kate Millett discussing the nature of violence against women. Gives an overview of how rape in patriarchal society was and continues to be used as a weapon of fear to control women.
Prod-WMENIF Dist-WMENIF

Kate, A Two Year Old In Foster Care B 33 MIN
16MM FILM OPTICAL SOUND C T
Discusses the responses of young children of previous good experience to Foster care and residential nursery care.
From The Young Children In Brief Separation Series.
LC NO. FIA68-639
Prod-TVKI Dist-NYU 1968

Katei Seikatsu C 28 MIN
16MM FILM OPTICAL SOUND
Depicts the activities of a Japanese family living in Alberta, Canada, as they prepare for the Obon ceremony, a religous celebration. Another version issued under the title Alberta's Japanese Community.
From The Family Life Series.
LC NO. 76-703063
Prod-ASB Dist-CFPRO Prodn-CNTLN 1975

Kathakali C 22 MIN
16MM FILM OPTICAL SOUND I-C A
Introduces the dance-drama of Kerala. Traces the history and background of Kathakali and reveals the many unique features of this dance. Includes visits to a Kathakali school and to the green-room, where the elaborate make-up is created.
Prod-INDIA Dist-NEDINF

Kathe Kollwitz B 19 MIN
16MM FILM OPTICAL SOUND
Describes the life and work of Kathe Kollwitz, the most powerfully emotional German artist of the 20th century. Shows how her work portrays the suffering of Berliners during the 1890's, the cruelty and senselessness of World War I and the agony of World War II.
Prod-ROLAND Dist-ROLAND

Katherine - Air-Conditioned Frontier C 17 MIN
16MM FILM OPTICAL SOUND J-C A
Explores life in the northern Australian town of Katherine. Shows ranching activities in the surrounding area and follows tourists as they see the cliffs of an inland river gorge.
LC NO. 75-702388
Prod-FLMAUS Dist-AUIS 1974

Katherine Densford - Nursing Highlights C 4 MIN
3/4 OR 1/2 INCH VIDEO CASSETTE
Contains four half-hour videotapes on the nursing profession.
Prod-TELSTR Dist-TELSTR

Kathy C 27 MIN
16MM FILM OPTICAL SOUND
Follows Kathy, a three-foot-high girl who is confined to a wheelchair, as she goes through her senior year, graduates and prepares to enter college.
LC NO. 81-700217
Prod-CLNTCR Dist-FILMID 1981

Kathy C 15 MIN
3/4 OR 1/2 INCH VIDEO CASSETTE J-H
Shows how Kathy starts skipping school for a thrill, becomes chronically truant, and finds herself in deep trouble with school authorities.
From The Changing Series.
Prod-WGTETV Dist-AITECH 1980

Kathy C 27 MIN
3/4 OR 1/2 INCH VIDEO CASSETTE P-C A
Captures the life and spirit of a handicapped teenager who shows that a positive attitude, determination and enthusiasm can help eliminate barriers the handicapped must face.
Prod-FILMID Dist-FILMID

Kathy Bernson And Stormy Mullis C 30 MIN
3/4 OR 1/2 INCH VIDEO CASSETTE
See series title for descriptive statement.
From The Partners In Dance Series.
Prod-ARCVID Dist-ARCVID

Kathy Bernson And Stormy Mullis C 30 MIN
3/4 OR 1/2 INCH VIDEO CASSETTE
See series title for descriptive statement.
From The Eye On Dance - Partners In Dance Series.
Prod-ARTRES Dist-ARTRES

Kathy, Mike And Alcohol C 13 MIN
16MM FILM, 3/4 OR 1/2 IN VIDEO H-C A
Points out the dangers of misusing or overusing alcohol with a case study of two teenagers who have a drinking problem. Presents a counselor discussing their problem with them after a serious car accident, emphasizing that the cause of alcoholism is more often to be found in the reason for drinking than in the amount consumed.
Prod-DAVP Dist-AIMS 1977

Kathy's Dance C 28 MIN
16MM FILM, 3/4 OR 1/2 IN VIDEO
Follows several months in the life of dancer Kathy Posin as she choreographs a new dance for her troupe, gives solo performances as an affiliate artist and prepares to open the new dance in New York.

From The Bravo Series.
Prod-AAI Dist-DIRECT Prodn-DREWAS 1977

thy's Pacing Horse C 25 MIN
16MM FILM, 3/4 OR 1/2 IN VIDEO J-C A
Introduces an Australian girl who is training her trotting horse.
From The World Cultures And Youth Series.
Prod-SUNRIS Dist-CORF 1981

tika's Dearest Wish - A Hungarian Folk Tale C 7 MIN
16MM FILM, 3/4 OR 1/2 IN VIDEO K-I
Tells the story of a young girl who solves three seemingly impossible riddles and becomes a queen.
From The Folk Tales From Around The World Series.
Prod-ADPF Dist-SF 1980

tmai C 15 MIN
16MM FILM - 3/4 IN VIDEO A
Focuses on the remote Katmai region in Alaska. Enters the timeless world of this area and shows some of the hazards and rewards of meeting the land on its own terms.
LC NO. 79-706132
Prod-USNPS Dist-USNAC Prodn-MCBRID 1979

tmai - Astronaut Field Trip To Mt Katmai Area, Alaska C 19 MIN
16MM FILM OPTICAL SOUND
Describes the geology of Katmai National Monument in Alaska. Presents a geologic interpretation of the ash flow of the Valley of Ten Thousand Smokes.
LC NO. 74-706372
Prod-USGEOS Dist-USNAC 1969

tnips Of 1940 C 8 MIN
16MM FILM OPTICAL SOUND
Presents Krazy Kat as the manager of a musical comedy with an unforgettable comedy.
Prod-TIMLIF Dist-TIMLIF 1940

tura And The Cat C 11 MIN
16MM FILM, 3/4 OR 1/2 IN VIDEO K-I
Presents an animated Halloween fairy tale of a young girl who defeats an evil forest witch, rescues a prince from an imprisoning enchantment, and finds true love.
Prod-PAJON Dist-CORF 1982

tutura C 37 MIN
16MM FILM, 3/4 OR 1/2 IN VIDEO
Analyzes the problems and conflicts in South Africa.
Prod-PHENIX Dist-PHENIX 1974

ty C 17 MIN
16MM FILM, 3/4 OR 1/2 IN VIDEO
Questions the extent to which sexual sterotypes limit aspirations of females by telling about a girl who is faced with the prejudice of the boys and the route manager when she takes over her brother's paper route.
Prod-BFA Dist-PHENIX 1974

tyn Forest Massacre B 19 MIN
3/4 OR 1/2 INCH VIDEO CASSETTE
Documents the discovery by the Germans on April 13, 1943, of the mass graves of several thousand officers of the former Polish Army murdered on Stalin's orders, then buried in Katyn Forest near Smolensk. Uses the Germans' own film records to depict the investigation of the massacre by an international commission.
Prod-IHF Dist-IHF

tzelmacher B 88 MIN
16MM FILM OPTICAL SOUND
A German language film. Delineates the life of the youth in a provincial German town as they sleep together, play cards, beat their women and drink at the local pub. Shows how their life changes with the arrival of a Greek immigrant.
Prod-NYFLMS Dist-NYFLMS 1969

waida, When / South Carolina Sea Islands C 29 MIN
3/4 INCH VIDEO CASSETTE
Presents a two-part program which investigates black-white relationships in Newark and which looks at the lifestyles on the islands of the South Carolina coast.
From The Interface Series.
Prod-WETATV Dist-PUBTEL

wartha Cup C 24 MIN
16MM FILM OPTICAL SOUND
Depicts three snowmobile races.
LC NO. 77-702932
Prod-YAMAHA Dist-CHET Prodn-CHET 1976

yak C 8 MIN
16MM FILM, 3/4 OR 1/2 IN VIDEO J A
Depicts the joy man can find in nature through sport, following a kayak trip down a river.
Prod-PFP Dist-PFP 1971

yaking And Hiking Fun C 30 MIN
1/2 IN VIDEO CASSETTE BETA/VHS
Provides a refresher course on strokes and paddles for kayak cruising. Presents a hike along the Appalachian Trail's Springer Mountain and a raft ride down the Trisuli River.
From The Great Outdoors Series.
Prod-WGBHTV Dist-MTI

yaking And Rafting C 30 MIN
3/4 OR 1/2 INCH VIDEO CASSETTE
Discusses kayaking and rafting as outdoor activities that require 'roughing it.'
From The Roughing It Series.
Prod-KYTV Dist-KYTV 1984

zablan C
16MM FILM OPTICAL SOUND

Features Menachem Golan, producer of Israel's first important motion picture musical based on conflicts between Oriental and European Jews, who explains these relationships and plays some music from the film.
From The Dateline Israel, 1973 Series.
Prod-ADL Dist-ADL

Kebekio - Ali Baba C 14 MIN
16MM FILM OPTICAL SOUND P-I
A French-language film which employs a clever collage of puppets and cartoons to show that children should respect their patrimony and develop an intelligent sense of what is worth buying.
Prod-QDTFG Dist-MTP

Keds Commercial C 1 MIN
3/4 OR 1/2 INCH VIDEO CASSETTE
Shows a classic television commercial with Keso the clown and the Keds theme song.
Prod-BROOKC Dist-BROOKC

Keen Machines C 13 MIN
16MM FILM, 3/4 OR 1/2 IN VIDEO K-I
Uses lyrics set to original music to introduce the six basic simple machines.
Prod-ERICP Dist-AIMS 1971

Keen Machines (Spanish) C 13 MIN
16MM FILM, 3/4 OR 1/2 IN VIDEO K-I
Uses lyrics set to original music to introduce the six basic simple machines.
Prod-ERICP Dist-AIMS 1971

Keeneland C 22 MIN
1/2 IN VIDEO CASSETTE BETA/VHS
Features Keeneland and its record-breaking yearlings.
Prod-KEENE Dist-EQVDL

Keeneland Story, The C 18 MIN
16MM FILM OPTICAL SOUND
Shows racing and sales at Keeneland, the accomplishments of some noted Keeneland Sales alumni at other tracks and Keeneland's role in the community as a contributor to charitable and educational causes.
Prod-KEENE Dist-KEENE

Keep A 'Knockin' C 5 MIN
3/4 OR 1/2 INCH VIDEO CASSETTE
Gives the comical side of what can happen when mothers leave children at home alone.
Prod-NOVID Dist-NOVID

Keep A Safe Bike C 19 MIN
16MM FILM, 3/4 OR 1/2 IN VIDEO I-H
Shows different kinds of bicycles and emphasizes the importance of good maintenance in operating them safely. Demonstrates in detail how to make many adjustments and repairs at home using ordinary tools.
Prod-CUNIV Dist-CUNIV 1975

Keep An Open Mind C 30 MIN
3/4 OR 1/2 INCH VIDEO CASSETTE K-P
See series title for descriptive statement.
From The Villa Alegre Series.
Prod-BCTV Dist-MDCPB

Keep It Clean B 15 MIN
2 INCH VIDEOTAPE P-I
Discusses the importance of keeping your teeth clean the reasons why you should, what happens when you don't and the best way in which you can. Covers dental plaque and its cause and prevention.
From The Dental Health Series.
Prod-GPITVL Dist-GPITVL

Keep It Clear C 15 MIN
2 INCH VIDEOTAPE J
Discusses methods of achieving clarity.
From The From Me To You...In Writing, Pt 1 Series
Prod-DELE Dist-GPITVL

Keep It Going C 9 MIN
16MM FILM OPTICAL SOUND
Discusses America's critical highway needs and presents a history of American transportation and a montage of highway use.
LC NO. 76-702829
Prod-HUF Dist-HUF Prodn-CAS 1976

Keep It Green C 8 MIN
16MM FILM OPTICAL SOUND
Presents an edited combination of all six animated Sniff and Snuff TV spots.
Prod-FILCOM Dist-FILCOM

Keep It Green C 10 MIN
16MM FILM OPTICAL SOUND H-C A
Shows the methods used to protect Australian agriculture and forestry against the accidental introduction of new pests and diseases.
LC NO. 71-709829
Prod-ANAIB Dist-AUIS 1970

Keep It In Balance C 16 MIN
16MM FILM OPTICAL SOUND
Features a group of high school students, who, unimpressed by a film shown in class about nutrition, are challenged by the teacher to make their own movie. In arranging interviews with professionals for their class project, they are shown the hazards of fad diets while learning that they can eat a variety of foods as long as they balance their food intake with proper exercise.
Prod-WSTGLC Dist-WSTGLC

Keep It Running Safely - The Reliability Approach C
16MM FILM - 3/4 IN VIDEO A
Shows workers how the reliability approach to safety works and how they can make it a success.
Prod-BNA Dist-BNA 1983

Keep It Running–A Series

Provides a basic understanding of the automobile and the functions of its operating systems. Details the many maintenance and repair jobs which can be done in the owner's driveway or garage. Emphasizes safety and good work habits.
Prod-NETCHE Dist-NETCHE 1982

Basic Systems Of The Automobile	030 MIN
Basic Tool Kit For Weekend Mechanics	030 MIN
Battery And Electrical System, Pt I	030 MIN
Battery And Electrical System, Pt II	030 MIN
Brake System Checks And Adjustments	030 MIN
Car Cosmetics	030 MIN
Cooling System Checks And Services	030 MIN
Course Introduction	030 MIN
Diagnosing Emergency Problems	030 MIN
Garages And Mechanics	030 MIN
Lubrication Checks And Services	030 MIN
Safety Precautions And Work Habits	030 MIN
Summary	030 MIN
Taking Care Of The Engine	030 MIN
Tune-Up, Pt I	030 MIN
Tune-Up, Pt II	030 MIN
Tune-Up, Pt III	030 MIN
Vehicle Safety And Maintenance Checks	030 MIN
Wheel Bearings And Lubrication	030 MIN
Wheels And Tires	030 MIN

Keep Off The Grass C 20 MIN
16MM FILM OPTICAL SOUND J-H
Questions a group of teenager's about experimentation with marijuana.
From The Family Life Education And Human Growth Series.
Prod-SF Dist-SF 1969

Keep Off The Grass C 20 MIN
16MM FILM, 3/4 OR 1/2 IN VIDEO J-C A
Presents unadulterated facts about the smoking of marijuana. States facts in an honest manner telling a dramatic story.
Prod-DAVP Dist-AIMS 1970

Keep On Rockin' C 95 MIN
16MM FILM OPTICAL SOUND
Presents Chuck Berry, Little Richard, Jerry Lee Lewis, and Bo Diddley at the Toronto Rock and Roll Revival concert in 1969. By D A Pennebaker.
Prod-PENNAS Dist-PENNAS

Keep Reaching - The Power Of High Expectations C 30 MIN
3/4 OR 1/2 INCH VIDEO CASSETTE
Offers a step-by-step approach to increasing personal motivation and motivating others, and develops a better understanding of expectations, how a person's attitude and opinions affect all aspects of life, how to give others support and how working relationships can be enhanced by understanding and acceptance of others. Includes a discussion leader's guide, a self-discovery handbook, a poster and student handouts.
Prod-CREMED Dist-DELTAK

Keep The Coal Rollin' C 30 MIN
16MM FILM OPTICAL SOUND
Documents the coal industry.
LC NO. 81-701179
Prod-WJLATV Dist-WJLATV 1981

Keep Them Alive C 11 MIN
3/4 OR 1/2 INCH VIDEO CASSETTE IND
Portrays a step-by-step instruction on the primary and secondary surveys in looking for the killer conditions in accident victims.
From The Emergency Medical Training Series. Lesson 3
Prod-LEIKID Dist-LEIKID

Keep Them Alive C 11 MIN
3/4 OR 1/2 INCH VIDEO CASSETTE
Shows how to conduct a primary survey to determine if a victim is breathing, has a heartbeat and exhibits severe bleeding. Shows how to begin emergency treatment for any of these life-threatening conditions, conduct a second survey to examine the victim from head to toe for injuries which could cause serious complications and begin emergency care management for any such injuries.
From The Emergency Medical Training Series.
Prod-VTRI Dist-VTRI

Keep Track C 29 MIN
2 INCH VIDEOTAPE
See series title for descriptive statement.
From The Our Street Series.
Prod-MDCPB Dist-PUBTEL

Keep Your Car Cool C 60 MIN
1/2 IN VIDEO CASSETTE BETA/VHS
Demonstrates the proper way to service a car's cooling system.
From The Car Care Series.
Prod-MOHOMV Dist-MOHOMV

Keep Your Cool C 14 MIN
16MM FILM, 3/4 OR 1/2 IN VIDEO S
Uses a TV game show format to show ways of keeping anger under control.
From The Good Life Series.
LC NO. 81-706174
Prod-DUDLYN Dist-HUBDSC 1981

Keep Your Cool C 14 MIN
3/4 OR 1/2 INCH VIDEO CASSETTE S
Shows ways to keep anger under control. Includes how to handle disappointments.

From The Good Life Series.
Prod-HUBDSC Dist-HUBDSC

Keep Your Eyes Moving X 10 MIN
16MM FILM OPTICAL SOUND
Shows how to avoid the 'FIXED STARE' and stay alert.
From The Expert Seeing Series.
Prod-NSC Dist-NSC

Keep Your Mind On The Job C 16 MIN
16MM FILM, 3/4 OR 1/2 IN VIDEO A
Examines the fact that the major cause of mistakes, accidents and lost time on the job is lack of concentration. Dramatizes common working situations showing the various types of interference that inhibit our ability to concentrate. Shows how to recognize the reasons for lack of concentration and how to take simple steps to eliminate it.
Prod-CENTRO Dist-CORF 1983

Keeper Of The Glades, The C 23 MIN
3/4 OR 1/2 INCH VIDEO CASSETTE
Goes to the Florida Everglades where alligators create the water holes that keep all the creatures of the swamp alive through the drought.
Prod-NWLDPR Dist-NWLDPR

Keepers Of Wildlife C 21 MIN
16MM FILM, 3/4 OR 1/2 IN VIDEO J-C A
Examines Canada's programs to protect its wildlife.
Prod-NFBC Dist-NFBC 1972

Keeping A Record C 25 MIN
16MM FILM, 3/4 OR 1/2 IN VIDEO J-C A
Explores the principles involved in the microcomputer's ability to control and search through a data base.
From The Making The Most Of The Micro Series. Episode 5
Prod-BBCTV Dist-FI 1983

Keeping Busy C 15 MIN
16MM FILM, 3/4 OR 1/2 IN VIDEO S
Uses a TV game show format to suggest several activities appropriate for leisure time.
From The Good Life Series.
LC NO. 81-706178
Prod-DUDLYN Dist-HUBDSC 1981

Keeping Busy C 15 MIN
3/4 OR 1/2 INCH VIDEO CASSETTE S
Shows activities appropriate for free time. Includes jogging and playing games. Focuses on persons with special development needs.
From The Good Life Series.
Prod-HUBDSC Dist-HUBDSC

Keeping Fit C 1 MIN
3/4 OR 1/2 INCH VIDEO CASSETTE
Features Farah Fawcett expressing personal concerns about fitness and health. Shows her advising viewers that not smoking, doing monthly breast self-examinations and getting regular cancer checkups are good ways to stay healthy. Uses TV spot format.
Prod-AMCS Dist-AMCS 1980

Keeping Fit C 12 MIN
3/4 OR 1/2 INCH VIDEO CASSETTE P
See series title for descriptive statement.
From The Strawberry Square Series.
Prod-NEITV Dist-AITECH 1982

Keeping Friends C 15 MIN
3/4 OR 1/2 INCH VIDEO CASSETTE P
Explains that Sam and Sally have trouble discussing the neighborhood picnic while Molly and Sara tussle and argue after Molly paints on Sara's pictures. Reveals that eventually all four apologize and reestablish their friendships.
From The Out And About Series.
Prod-STSU Dist-AITECH Prodn-WETN 1984

Keeping In Place C 20 MIN
3/4 OR 1/2 INCH VIDEO CASSETTE H-C A
See series title for descriptive statement.
From The Engineering Crafts Series.
Prod-BBCTV Dist-FI 1981

Keeping In Proportion C 30 MIN
3/4 OR 1/2 INCH VIDEO CASSETTE A
Shows how to handle ratios, proportion problems and some elementary algebra as done by adult math students.
From The Adult Math Series.
Prod-KYTV Dist-KYTV 1984

Keeping My Job - Habits That Help C
3/4 OR 1/2 INCH VIDEO CASSETTE
Shows how to identify specific on-the-job problems that could lead to losing or leaving a job. Identifies good work habits that can help to avoid or minimize specific on-the-job problems.
From The Employability Skills Series.
Prod-ILCS Dist-CAMB

Keeping Of The Green, The C 30 MIN
16MM FILM - 3/4 IN VIDEO J-C A
Explains that although by the end of the century two-thirds of humanity will be living in cities, there still remains a strong drive for the simpler rural life of ancient generations. Visits some cities with green belts - London, Vienna, Denver - and some cities without them.
From The Man Builds - Man Destroys Series.
Prod-UN Dist-GPITVL 1973

Keeping Our Economy Healthy, Pt 1 C 20 MIN
2 INCH VIDEOTAPE J-H
Introduces the idea of stability and poses the possibility that wild surges in the economy may be lessened by appropriate government action.
From The Our World Of Economics Series.
Prod-MPATI Dist-GPITVL

Keeping Our Economy Healthy, Pt 2 C 20 MIN
2 INCH VIDEOTAPE J-H
Discusses monetary and fiscal policy as it interrelates the actions of the Federal reserve board, the U S Treasury and Congress.
From The Our World Of Economics Series.
Prod-MPATI Dist-GPITVL

Keeping Safe C 28 MIN
16MM FILM, 3/4 OR 1/2 IN VIDEO S
Focuses on the concepts of personal safety by presenting examples of potential hazards at home, at work and while commuting.
From The Learning To Live On Your Own Series.
Prod-LINCS Dist-JOU 1979

Keeping Speech Stutter-Free - A Case Study C 20 MIN
3/4 OR 1/2 INCH VIDEO CASSETTE
Presents the Meyer Children's Rehabilitation Institute's speech Pathology Department's use of the Stutter-Free speech program developed by George Shames.
Prod-UNEBO Dist-UNEBO

Keeping The Mailman From Disturbing Crystal During Piano Practice C 8 MIN
16MM FILM OPTICAL SOUND K-P
Shows how Alistair tries all sorts of ways to keep out the mailman while Crystal practices the piano.
From The Crystal Tipps And Alistair Series.
LC NO. 73-700455
Prod-BBCTV Dist-VEDO 1972

Keeping The Old Game Alive C 60 MIN
16MM FILM, 3/4 OR 1/2 IN VIDEO C A
Considers how the next war might unfold. Looks at the annual elaborate dress rehearsals for World War III as the combined forces of the fifteen member countries of NATO meet to conduct war games in central Europe. Points out that on either side of the heavily patrolled border between East and West Germany, the site of more than six wars in the last three centuries, lie half the world's conventional and non-nuclear armed forces with 10,000 nuclear warheads.
From The War Series.
Prod-NFBC Dist-FI

Keeping Track - Data Base Management And Microcomputers C 30 MIN
3/4 OR 1/2 INCH VIDEO CASSETTE
See series title for descriptive statement.
From The Promedia - Microcomputer Applications Series.
Prod-DSIM Dist-DSIM

Keeping Your Balance C 20 MIN
3/4 OR 1/2 INCH VIDEO CASSETTE
Deals with increasing employee self-confidence by exploring individual rights and responsibilities in the work environment, the use of power in the work environment, and job-related self-assessment.
From The Confidence Game Series.
Prod-ERF Dist-DELTAK

Keeping Your Car Fit B 12 MIN
16MM FILM OPTICAL SOUND
Explains the necessity of a checkup on automobile tires, battery, engine, oil and radiator.
From The Automotive Operation And Maintenance Series. Automobile Operation, No. 3
LC NO. FIE52-344
Prod-USOE Dist-USNAC Prodn-HANDY 1945

Keeping Your Health C 29 MIN
3/4 OR 1/2 INCH VIDEO CASSETTE
Presents scenes from a doctor's examining room portraying what happens during male and female physical exams. Shows women how to perform breast self-examination. Features Milton Diamond, Ph D, a biologist at the University of Hawaii, talking with several people about the general reluctance to get periodic health checks and with physicians about sexual problems connected with alcoholism, diabetes and heart problems.
From The Human Sexuality Series.
Prod-KHETTV Dist-PBS

Keeping Your Houseplants Happy C 30 MIN
3/4 OR 1/2 INCH VIDEO CASSETTE
Discusses the care of houseplants.
From The Even You Can Grow Houseplants Series.
Prod-WGTV Dist-MDCPB

Keeping Your Teeth Healthy (Spanish) C 8 MIN
16MM FILM, 3/4 OR 1/2 IN VIDEO P
Prod-EBEC Dist-EBEC 1981

Keeping Your Teeth Healthy (2nd Ed) C 8 MIN
16MM FILM, 3/4 OR 1/2 IN VIDEO P
Illustrates routine procedures to protect teeth and prevent decay, and explains the relationship between good nutrition and healthy teeth. Shows how the necessary visits to the dentist's office can be a less-frightening experience than usually imagined.
Prod-EBEC Dist-EBEC 1981

Keepsake, Keepsafe C
16MM FILM - 3/4 IN VIDEO A
Uses humor to drive home off-the-job safety by following two couples through four seasons during which they get involved in several near-misses and experience their share of accidents.
Prod-BNA Dist-BNA 1983

Kei Takei C 30 MIN
3/4 OR 1/2 INCH VIDEO CASSETTE
Captures the essence of dance and brings vivid awareness of movement.
From The Doris Chase Dance Series.
Prod-CHASED Dist-CHASED

Keiko C 60 MI
3/4 OR 1/2 INCH VIDEO CASSETTE J
Recounts how a Japanese-American teenager learns a valuab lesson in ethnic pride from her culturally conscious Puerto R can roommate during a summer camp program for the pe forming arts.
From The Rainbow Movie Of The Week Series.
Prod-RAINTV Dist-GPITVL 198

Keio Plaza, The - A Story In Modern Design C 20 MI
16MM FILM OPTICAL SOUND
Presents an experiment in expressing, in line with the thought c the designers, the impression of the interior design prepare and incorporated in the spaces and walls of the lobby, gues rooms, imperial room and the tapestry restaurant of the Kei Plaza Hotel.
Prod-KAJIMA Dist-UNIJAP 197

Keith C 9 MI
16MM FILM OPTICAL SOUND
Presents a mime in which a man's fear and terror reduce him t a meek, robot-like existence.
LC NO. 73-702031
Prod-BBF Dist-BBF 197

Keith - A Second Grader B 23 MI
16MM FILM OPTICAL SOUND C
Depicts a second grade pupil in various school situations bot in and out of the classroom. Provides data regarding his activi ties and behavior for observation and analysis.
From The Four Students Series.
LC NO. FIA67-2367
Prod-INSITE Dist-IU Prodn-IU 1966

Keith Sonnier - Animation I C 14 MIN
3/4 OR 1/2 INCH VIDEO CASSETTE
Explores the formal properties of computer-generated video.
Prod-ARTINC Dist-ARTINC

Keith Sonnier - Animation II C 25 MIN
3/4 OR 1/2 INCH VIDEO CASSETTE
Explores the formal properties of computer-generated video.
Prod-ARTINC Dist-ARTINC

Keith Sonnier - TV In And TV Out C 10 MIN
3/4 OR 1/2 INCH VIDEO CASSETTE
Deals with television.
Prod-ARTINC Dist-ARTINC

Keith Turns 18 C 18 MIN
16MM FILM OPTICAL SOUND
Pictures various activities in the life of an 18-year-old black student, showing him jazz dancing as well as ballet dancing, with his family and friends, and as he talks about his reasons for wanting to become a ballet dancer.
From The Exploring Human Nature Series.
LC NO. 74-702485
Prod-EDC Dist-EDC 1974

Keller On PSI C 27 MIN
16MM FILM OPTICAL SOUND H-C A
Presents psychologist Fred S Keller introducing his personalized system of instruction, showing the application of the Psi teaching method to several curriculums at the University of Texas at Austin.
LC NO. 76-701102
Prod-UTEX Dist-UTEX 1975

Kellogg Dream, The C 27 MIN
1/2 IN VIDEO CASSETTE BETA/VHS
Traces the history of the Kellogg Ranch. Features Arabian horses including Pep, Raseyn and Ferdona.
Prod-CSPC Dist-EQVDL

Kelly C 9 MIN
16MM FILM OPTICAL SOUND I-H
Emphasizes the need for personal discipline and provides an example of strong leadership by showing Kelly Robinson, a nine-year-old black girl from Watts, Los Angeles, as she tells about her personal growth as a member of the world's only all-black trapeze troupe, The Flying Souls.
From The Rebop Series.
LC NO. 79-700475
Prod-WGBHTV Dist-IU 1979

Kelly C 27 MIN
16MM FILM OPTICAL SOUND
Shows the integration of a young girl with cerebral palsy into a day-care center with nonhandicapped children. Shows her development over two years, the problems she encounters, the role of the teacher and her acceptance by the other children.
LC NO. 77-702096
Prod-OPEN Dist-EDC 1977

Keltie's Beard C 9 MIN
16MM FILM, 3/4 OR 1/2 IN VIDEO
Interviews a woman who is defying the typical feminine image by growing a beard.
Prod-MARTNB Dist-FLMLIB 1982

KemMurch And Women's Workshop C 27 MIN
3/4 OR 1/2 INCH VIDEO CASSETTE
Provides an experiential look at pre-trades and technology training programs for women as well as a first hand account of the women who enter them. Explores the process a woman goes through physically and psychologically from the time she decides to train for a job in the skilled trades or technology until her graduation from the program with new skills and confidence.
Prod-CANFDW Dist-CANFDW

Ken Feingold - Irony C 28 MIN
3/4 OR 1/2 INCH VIDEO CASSETTE
Catalogs images and Sounds from around the world and off the air.
Prod-CAT Dist-ARTINC

Ken Feingold - New Building Under The Water C 12 MIN
3/4 OR 1/2 INCH VIDEO CASSETTE
Assembles images and sounds from around the world.
Prod-ARTINC Dist-ARTINC

Ken Feingold - The Double C 29 MIN
3/4 OR 1/2 INCH VIDEO CASSETTE
Collects images and sounds from around the world and off the air.
Prod-ARTINC Dist-ARTINC

Ken Feingold - Vito Acconci, In And Out Of Performance C 40 MIN
3/4 OR 1/2 INCH VIDEO CASSETTE
Deals with Vito Acconci.
Prod-ARTINC Dist-ARTINC

Ken Feingold - 5dim, MIND C 29 MIN
3/4 OR 1/2 INCH VIDEO CASSETTE
Features various images and sounds.
Prod-ARTINC Dist-ARTINC

Ken Hoyt Comments I C 20 MIN
3/4 OR 1/2 INCH VIDEO CASSETTE
Offers comments by Ken Hoyt on the processes of 'infusion' and 'collaboration', and explains why the cost of career education can be incredibly low.
From The School Board Debates - Career Education Series.
Prod-NSBA Dist-SWRLFF

Ken Hoyt Comments II C 20 MIN
3/4 OR 1/2 INCH VIDEO CASSETTE
Offers comments by Ken Hoyt on the processes of 'infusion' and 'collaboration', and explains why the cost of career education can be incredibly low.
From The School Board Debates - Career Education Series.
Prod-NSBA Dist-SWRLFF

Ken Hoyt Comments, Pt 1 C 20 MIN
16MM FILM OPTICAL SOUND
Presents Ken Hoyt, director of the U S Office of Career Education, offering his views on comprehensive career education and telling why education should be linked with preparation for work.
From The School Board Debates - Career Education Series.
LC NO. 79-700357
Prod-NSBA Dist-SWRLFF 1978

Ken Hoyt Comments, Pt 2 C 20 MIN
16MM FILM OPTICAL SOUND
Presents Ken Hoyt of the U S Office of Career Education discussing the economic realities of career education.
From The School Board Debates - Career Education Series.
LC NO. 79-700357
Prod-NSBA Dist-SWRLFF 1978

Kennedy - Years Of Charisma C 24 MIN
16MM FILM, 3/4 OR 1/2 IN VIDEO H-C A
Explains that during his life John Kennedy experienced both popularity and hostility. States that after his death he became a hero, wrapped suddenly in mythology and sentimentality. Originally shown on the Canadian television program Portraits Of Power.
From The Leaders Of The 20th Century - Portraits Of Power Series.
Prod-NIELSE Dist-LCOA 1980

Kennedy And Cohen Interview With The President B 30 MIN
3/4 OR 1/2 INCH VIDEO CASSETTE
Explains the principles of retail management, financing, purchasing, marketing and after-the-sale service.
Prod-HBS Dist-IVCH

Kennedy And Confrontation B 16 MIN
16MM FILM, 3/4 OR 1/2 IN VIDEO H-C A
Documents Kennedy's handling of major foreign policy issues, such as the Bay Of Pigs invasion, the Cuban missile crisis, the Berlin crisis and the growing conflicts in Southeast Asia.
From The American Foreign Policy Series.
Prod-EBEC Dist-EBEC 1981

Kennedy Family, The C 52 MIN
3/4 OR 1/2 INCH VIDEO CASSETTE A
Looks at a handicapped child and his needs that affect all the relationships in a professional family in Albuquerque. Shows the engineer father who is a crusader for the rights of the mentally retarded but who travels extensively because of his work. Looks at the mother who begins to resent his absences and sees them as an escape from the difficult situation at home.
From The Six American Families Series.
Prod-GROUPW Dist-ECUFLM Prodn-UCHC 1976

Kennedy/Humphrey Presidential Primary B 55 MIN
3/4 OR 1/2 INCH VIDEO CASSETTE
Highlights views of Kennedy and Humphrey, candidates for the presidential primary in 1960. Presents a candidate's view of the frantic process of campaigning.
Prod-IHF Dist-IHF

Kennedys Don't Cry C 100 MIN
16MM FILM, 3/4 OR 1/2 IN VIDEO
Documents the life and politics of the Kennedy family and their influence during the 1960's.
Prod-HOBLEI Dist-CNEMAG Prodn-DOCUA 1975

Kennedys Of Albuquerque, The C 59 MIN
16MM FILM, 3/4 OR 1/2 IN VIDEO H-C A
Focuses on an upper-middle-class professional family. Explains how their retarded child affects their life.
From The Six American Families Series.
Prod-GROUPW Dist-CAROUF

Kennel Murder Case, The B 76 MIN
16MM FILM OPTICAL SOUND
Stars William Powell as Philo Vance, an urbane detective. Directed by Michael Curtiz.
Prod-WB Dist-KITPAR 1933

Kennen Sie Meinen Sohn C 15 MIN
16MM FILM, 3/4 OR 1/2 IN VIDEO
See series title for descriptive statement.
From The Guten Tag Wie Geht's Series. Part 1
Prod-BAYER Dist-IFB 1973

Kenneth B Clark, Psychology C 29 MIN
3/4 OR 1/2 INCH VIDEO CASSETTE A
See series title for descriptive statement.
From The Quest For Peace Series.
Prod-AACD Dist-AACD 1984

Kenneth King And Robert Dunn C 30 MIN
3/4 OR 1/2 INCH VIDEO CASSETTE
See series title for descriptive statement.
From The Experimentalists Series.
Prod-ARCVID Dist-ARCVID

Kenneth King And Robert Dunn C 30 MIN
3/4 OR 1/2 INCH VIDEO CASSETTE
See series title for descriptive statement.
From The Eye On Dance - The Experimentalists Series.
Prod-ARTRES Dist-ARTRES

Kenny Davern C 30 MIN
3/4 INCH VIDEO CASSETTE
Features Kenny Davern, Art Hodes, Truck Parham and Red Maddock performing such songs as C C Rider, My Blue Heaven, and That's A Plenty.
From The After Hours With Art Hodes Series.
Prod-FAJAZZ Dist-FAJAZZ

Kensho C 7 MIN
16MM FILM OPTICAL SOUND
Deals with man's relationship to his primal nature versus his role in his contemporary environment.
LC NO. 79-701371
Prod-MARGAR Dist-MARGAR 1978

Kent State - May 1970 C 23 MIN
16MM FILM, 3/4 OR 1/2 IN VIDEO J-C A
Re-creates the events at Kent State University following President Nixon's invasion of Cambodia which resulted in the death of four students and injury to nine others.
Prod-SYNES Dist-MGHT 1972

Kentucky - The Ultimate Equestrian Trial C 58 MIN
1/2 IN VIDEO CASSETTE BETA/VHS
Documents the 1982 Rolex Three-Day Event at the Kentucky Horse Park.
Prod-EQVDL Dist-EQVDL

Kentucky Green—A Series

Deals with indoor and outdoor planting, lawn and garden care and equipment maintenance.
Prod-EASTKU Dist-EASTKU

Kentucky Pioneers (2nd Ed) X 29 MIN
16MM FILM, 3/4 OR 1/2 IN VIDEO I-J
Explains why the pioneers moved out to settle the frontier wilderness. Shows the type of community that existed among the pioneers and some of the hardships they endured.
Prod-EBEC Dist-EBEC 1969

Kenya Beekeeping With The Top Bar Hive C 18 MIN
16MM FILM OPTICAL SOUND
Discusses beekeeping, showing traditional hives in treetops, night collection of honey and practices developed by University of Guelph scientists which are now being taught throughout Kenya by the Kenyan government and the Canadian International Development Agency.
LC NO. 76-702439
Prod-CIDA Dist-CIDA Prodn-UGUEL 1975

Kenya Boran I C 33 MIN
16MM FILM OPTICAL SOUND
Shows how a growing town and a new road encroaches on the the territory of a once-isolated Kenyan people. Demonstrates how two fathers and their sons confront difficult choices between old and new ways.
From The Faces Of Change - Kenya Series.
Prod-AUFS Dist-WHEELK

Kenya Boran II C 33 MIN
16MM FILM OPTICAL SOUND
Focuses on the life of Peter Boru, a 16-year-old former herdsboy who has become a boarding school student. Shows how tradition and modern forces common to the developing areas make the economic outlook bleak for such young people in Kenya.
From The Faces Of Change - Kenya Series.
Prod-AUFS Dist-WHEELK

Kenya-Uganda Safari C 26 MIN
16MM FILM OPTICAL SOUND I-C A
Familiarizes the viewer with the greatest possible number of east African animals, as the camera ranges over the varied landscape of Kenya-Uganda. Portrays animal life in the marshes, on the plains, in the forests, in the Uganda highlands, in the game parks and on the river.
From The Audubon Wildlife Theatre Series.
Prod-AVEXP Dist-AVEXP

Kenya, Israel, Arizona-Nevada C 27 MIN
16MM FILM OPTICAL SOUND P-I
Explores the daily activities of children in Kenya, Israel and the American Southwest. Presents a Japanese folk tale about a goddess who proves that honesty is the best policy.
From The Big Blue Marble - Children Around The World Series. Program W
LC NO. 76-700615
Prod-ALVEN Dist-VITT 1975

Kenyatta C 28 MIN
16MM FILM, 3/4 OR 1/2 IN VIDEO H-C
An abridged version of the motion picture Kenyatta. Presents a case study of colonialism in Africa that begins with the emergence of the independence movement and ends with the contemporary politics of Jomo Kenyatta.
Prod-ADP Dist-FI 1973

Kenyatta C 51 MIN
16MM FILM, 3/4 OR 1/2 IN VIDEO H-C
Presents a case study of colonialism in Africa that begins with the emergence of the independence movement and ends with the contemporary politics of Jomo Kenyatta.
Prod-FI Dist-FI 1973

Kepler Problem, The C 30 MIN
16MM FILM, 3/4 OR 1/2 IN VIDEO C A
Presents the Kepler problem as the task of deducing all three of Kepler's laws from Newton's universal law of gravitation.
From The Mechanical Universe Series.
Prod-ANNCPB Dist-FI

Kepler's Three Laws C 30 MIN
16MM FILM, 3/4 OR 1/2 IN VIDEO C A
Discusses Kepler's three laws which described the motion of heavenly bodies with unprecedented accuracy.
From The Mechanical Universe Series.
Prod-ANNCPB Dist-FI

Keratin - The Protein That Is Hair C
3/4 OR 1/2 INCH VIDEO CASSETTE
Shows hair-care professionals the role proteins play in the proper development of all living organisms. Explains how the polypeptide chain and amino acids combine to form different types of protein, and focuses on the protein which represents hair. Presents information concerning nutrition and sources of A- and B-grade proteins.
Prod-MPCEDP Dist-MPCEDP 1984

Keratoplasty, Penetrating And Lamellar C 20 MIN
16MM FILM OPTICAL SOUND
Illustrates the repair of a chemical burn by penetrating keratoplasty and a virus scar by Lamellar graft. Shows a fiber optic light source and edge-to-edge sutures with fine silk. Demonstrates the Martinez method of splitting the cornea with a semi-sharp spatula for the lamellar graft.
LC NO. FIA66-878
Prod-ACYDGD Dist-ACY 1963

Kerepe's House - A House Building In New Guinea C 50 MIN
16MM FILM OPTICAL SOUND H-C
Describes in detail the construction of a house from the vines, leaves and trees found in the forest by members of the Fungai tribe of New Guinea. Discusses the history and social customs of the tribe.
Prod-PSUPCR Dist-PSUPCR 1966

Kernel, The B
16MM FILM OPTICAL SOUND
Shows how the ideal of kernel and morphism can link different types of math problems, and suggests methods of solution for each problem.
Prod-OPENU Dist-OPENU

Kerouac C
1/2 IN VIDEO CASSETTE BETA/VHS
Presents an award-winning documentary about the King of the Beat Generation, featuring interviews with Lawrence Ferlinghetti and others.
Prod-GA Dist-GA

Ketut Di Bali C 50 MIN
16MM FILM - 1/2 IN VIDEO
Presents a meditation on life in Bali by musician Serge Raoul.
Prod-RHPSDY Dist-RHPSDY

Kevin B 30 MIN
16MM FILM OPTICAL SOUND J-H
Presents a case study of a four-year-old boy afficted with cerebral palsy and athetosis, a nervous disorder marked by peculiar movements of the fingers and toes. Demonstrates the Else Haeussermann techniques for testing children with multiple handicaps.
LC NO. FIA67-5315
Prod-HAEUS Dist-UCPA Prodn-NEWF 1965

Kevin Alec C 17 MIN
16MM FILM, 3/4 OR 1/2 IN VIDEO I-J
Introduces Kevin Alec, who lives on the Fountain Indian Reservation in British Columbia. Glimpses his way of life which preserves many of the old ways of Indian life. Concludes that no matter where Kevin spends his adult life, he will always take pride in his Indian heritage.
Prod-NFBC Dist-MEDIAG 1978

Kevin Is Four - The Early Development Of A Child Amputee C 27 MIN
16MM FILM OPTICAL SOUND H-C A
Traces the early development of a child amputee. Shows how the child is fitted for artificial limbs. Pictures him in therapy sessions, nursery school, at home and at play.
LC NO. FIA66-450
Prod-OSUMPD Dist-OSUMPD 1965

Kevin's Story C 19 MIN
16MM FILM OPTICAL SOUND

Presents the story of Kevin Tunell, aged 18, who was convicted of manslaughter and drunk driving for the death of an 18 year old girl. Shows how, as an alternative form of punishment, he was sentenced to speak about his accident for one year.
Prod-DURRIN Dist-NEWDAY

Key Direct Mail Letter Concepts C 30 MIN
3/4 OR 1/2 INCH VIDEO CASSETTE
Explains key letter concepts in direct mail.
From The Business Of Direct Mail Series.
Prod-KYTV Dist-KYTV 1983

Key Elements C 60 MIN
3/4 OR 1/2 INCH VIDEO CASSETTE IND
See series title for descriptive statement.
From The Quality Circle Concepts Series.
Prod-NCSU Dist-AMCEE

Key Elements In The Decision Making Process B 29 MIN
16MM FILM OPTICAL SOUND IND
See series title for descriptive statement.
From The Quantitative Approaches To Decision Making Series.
LC NO. 74-703326
Prod-EDSD Dist-EDSD 1969

Key Goal To Winning Soccer, The C 17 MIN
3/4 OR 1/2 INCH VIDEO CASSETTE
Designed to provide an understanding of the rules and officiating procedures used in soccer by focusing on such topics as substitution, player violations and assessed penalties.
Prod-NFSHSA Dist-NFSHSA Prodn-ATHI 1979

Key Goals To Winning Soccer, The C 17 MIN
16MM FILM OPTICAL SOUND
Explains the rules and correct officiating procedures as written by the National Federation Soccer Rules Committee. Demonstrates such points as pre-match responsibilities of officials, player violations and penalty kick.
From The National Federation Sports Films Series.
LC NO. 79-701267
Prod-NFSHSA Dist-NFSHSA Prodn-TWCF 1979

Key Is Understanding, The C 15 MIN
16MM FILM, 3/4 OR 1/2 IN VIDEO C A
Assists law enforcement officers in their encounters with the handicapped.
Prod-NIMR Dist-STNFLD

Key Largo B 101 MIN
16MM FILM OPTICAL SOUND
Features the story of fugitives from the world, in a run-down Florida Keys resort isolated by a hurricane, enacting a stark political drama.
Prod-UAA Dist-UAE 1948

Key Man—A Series

Illustrates the important message that the foreman's role in accident prevention is made up of 'LITTLE THINGS' which, taken together, comprise good supervision.
Prod-NSC Dist-NSC

It's The Little Things That Count 10 MIN
People Are The Puzzle 10 MIN
Point Of No Return 10 MIN
You're The Key Man 10 MIN

Key Man, The C 14 MIN
16MM FILM, 3/4 OR 1/2 IN VIDEO
Orients field training officer candidates by describing the range of challenges and satisfactions they will likely experience.
Prod-JOU Dist-JOU 1981

Key Of His Own, A C 9 MIN
16MM FILM, 3/4 OR 1/2 IN VIDEO I-J
Depicts a child who balances his independence against loneliness. Non-narrated, it begins by showing Jeff's house dark. Jeff comes home and finds a note and money to buy his own dinner. Finally comes to a realization that despite his solitude, he is a valued member of the family.
Prod-EVANS Dist-PHENIX 1969

Key To Cleanliness C 21 MIN
16MM FILM, 3/4 OR 1/2 IN VIDEO
Introduces sanitary work habits for restaurant employees. Demonstrates how germs get into food and points out their breeding grounds.
Prod-WALGRV Dist-IFB

Key To Corn Profits C 15 MIN
16MM FILM OPTICAL SOUND
Interviews an Iowa farmer who tells how he tried to increase his corn yields, failed, tried again and succeeded, even with unfavorable weather conditions.
Prod-FUNKBS Dist-VENARD

Key To Innerspace C 19 MIN
16MM FILM OPTICAL SOUND
Presents a special report on the contributions of Skylab 4 to oceanography.
LC NO. 75-704045
Prod-USN Dist-USNAC 1975

Key To Mastery Of Environment, The B 30 MIN
2 INCH VIDEOTAPE PRO
Helps nursing students understand how self-understanding can prove the key to a mastery of the environment and a help for their abilities in treating patients.
From The Mental Health Concepts For Nursing, Unit 1 - Self-Understanding Series.
Prod-GPITVL Dist-GPITVL

Key To Power C 24 MIN
16MM FILM OPTICAL SOUND
Examines the manufacture, testing and use of fuel pumps in the modern automobile.
Prod-GM Dist-GM

Key To Productivity, A - Human Capital C 15 MIN
3/4 OR 1/2 INCH VIDEO CASSETTE J-H
Relates that while working in Mr Reilly's locksmith shop, Brett and Carl develop new job skills. Tells that when the competition comes looking for skilled workers, Carl quits school but Brett plans to get even more training. Raises questions about labor productivity.
From The Give And Take Series. Pt 6
LC NO. 83-706374
Prod-AITV Dist-AITECH 1982

Key To The Universe C 120 MIN
16MM FILM, 3/4 OR 1/2 IN VIDEO C A
Reports on theories and scientific breakthroughs concerning the links between the macro-world of stars and galaxies and the micro-world of atoms and their components. Explores the composition of matter and the bizarre rules that govern its behavior on a subatomic scale.
Prod-BBCTV Dist-FI 1977

Key To Understanding B 30 MIN
2 INCH VIDEOTAPE T
Dr Dreikurs discusses the ability of a teacher or parent to exert influence on a child by utilizing the principles of logical consequences. (Broadcast quality)
From The Dynamics Of Classroom Behavior Series.
Prod-VTETV Dist-GPITVL Prodn-WETKTV

Key West - Outpost In Time C 19 MIN
16MM FILM OPTICAL SOUND
Presents Key West, the southernmost city in Florida.
Prod-FLADC Dist-FLADC

Key West Picture Show, The C 40 MIN
16MM FILM OPTICAL SOUND
Depicts the lifestyles of the people of Key West, Florida, in a parody of the travelogues of the 1950's.
LC NO. 79-700449
Prod-SOUFI Dist-SOUFI 1978

Key Women At International Women's Year C 28 MIN
3/4 INCH VIDEO CASSETTE J-C
Features women leaders attending the 1975 Women's Year Conference talking about equality for women. Emphasizes the importance of educating rural women on such issues as family planning and women's rights. Describes the difficulty of convincing male-dominated national governments to act in ways that benefit women.
From The Are You Listening Series.
LC NO. 80-707403
Prod-STURTM Dist-STURTM 1975

KEY-TV Interview By Tony Perino C 30 MIN
3/4 OR 1/2 INCH VIDEO CASSETTE
Shows an interview with Sri Gurudev by Tony Perino of KEY-TV Santa Barbara, California.
Prod-IYOGA Dist-IYOGA

Keyboard And Percussion C 30 MIN
3/4 OR 1/2 INCH VIDEO CASSETTE
Looks at the history of such rarities as the hurdy-gurdy and the dulcimer, as well as better-known keyboard and percussion instruments such as the organ, harpsichord and kettledrums.
From The Early Musical Instruments Series.
Prod-GRATV Dist-FOTH

Keyboard Family, The C 14 MIN
3/4 OR 1/2 INCH VIDEO CASSETTE P-I
Discusses the keyboard family of musical instruments.
From The Music And Me Series.
Prod-WDCNTV Dist-AITECH 1979

Keyboard Styles - Mass, Resistance, Distance, Space, Clarity B 45 MIN
2 INCH VIDEOTAPE C
See series title for descriptive statement.
From The General Humanities Series. Unit 3 - The Auditory Arts
Prod-CHITVC Dist-GPITVL Prodn-WTTWTV

Keyboard, The C 29 MIN
3/4 INCH VIDEO CASSETTE H A
Introduces two new pieces to play. Gives the names of white keys. Begins to demonstrate playing with both hands.
From The Beginning Piano - An Adult Approach Series. Lesson 2
Prod-COAST Dist-CDTEL

Keyhole Of Eternity, The C 27 MIN
16MM FILM, 3/4 OR 1/2 IN VIDEO H
Looks at basic scientific research and some of the people involved. Covers a wide array of scientific studies, including physics, earth sciences, biochemistry, animal behavior and astronomy.
Prod-DYP Dist-IU Prodn-NSF 1980

Keyhole Of Eternity, The C 27 MIN
16MM FILM, 3/4 OR 1/2 IN VIDEO
Takes a look at the wide array of basic scientific research and at the people involved.
LC NO. 81-706420
Prod-NSF Dist-USNAC 1981

Keymaker, The C 18 MIN
16MM FILM OPTICAL SOUND H-C A
Studies an old man's search to find life in a world lost in its loneliness. Shows the old man, alone and reminiscent of his departed wife, seeking to amuse his peers, but without success. Pictures his attempt to recapture his youth.
Prod-USC Dist-USC

Keys Of Paradise, The C 57 MIN
16MM FILM, 3/4 OR 1/2 IN VIDEO H-C A
Describes endorphins, the powerful and complex pain-killing drugs manufactured by the human brain.
From The Nova Series.
LC NO. 80-706218
Prod-BBCTV Dist-TIMLIF 1979

Keys To Fishing Fun C 10 MIN
16MM FILM OPTICAL SOUND
Shows an airline pilot taking his boat to the Florida Keys to fish for the many varieties of game fish that abound in the area.
Prod-MERMAR Dist-TELEFM

Keys To Keeping A Good Thing Going C 28 MIN
16MM FILM, 3/4 OR 1/2 IN VIDEO A
See series title for descriptive statement.
From The Care And Maintenance Of A Good Marriage Series. Program 6
Prod-UMCOM Dist-ECUFLM 1982

Keys To Success, The C 15 MIN
16MM FILM, 3/4 OR 1/2 IN VIDEO J-C A
Presents a story about a boy with a reading disability who learns to type. Shows the typewriter, not as a solution, but depicts the typewriting learning process in a new light that could be valuable to adults who are involved with children with reading and writing problems.
Prod-KLEINW Dist-KLEINW 1978

Keystone For Education C 28 MIN
16MM FILM OPTICAL SOUND
Shows many ways in which to approach the teaching of religion using both interviews and examples. Includes ideas expressed by top religious educators from all faiths.
LC NO. 70-706367
Prod-ECA Dist-SMUSA 1969

Keystone Of Competence C 22 MIN
16MM FILM OPTICAL SOUND
Describes sheltered workshops for the mentally retarded in Europe.
LC NO. 74-704989
Prod-GWASHU Dist-USNAC

KGB Connections, The C 100 MIN
16MM FILM - VIDEO, ALL FORMATS A
Investigates Soviet espionage activities in North America. Bases its findings on interviews with KGB officers and Communist agents.
Prod-CFW Dist-CFW

Khajuraho Eternal C 11 MIN
16MM FILM OPTICAL SOUND H-C A
Presents a study of the cycle of creation and destruction expressed through the use of sculptures from the temples of Khajuraho built 1000 years ago during the Hindu period of India.
LC NO. FIA66-1840
Prod-FILMAS Dist-FILMAS Prodn-CHAUDH 1966

Khan Du II - Chris C 30 MIN
3/4 OR 1/2 INCH VIDEO CASSETTE
Tells how a deaf child learns that interesting careers and a challenging life are possible even with a disability.
LC NO. 81-706275
Prod-USDED Dist-USNAC Prodn-KRLNTV 1981

Khan Du II - Jean C 30 MIN
3/4 OR 1/2 INCH VIDEO CASSETTE
Explains how a child with a visual impairment meets adults with the same disability and learns that handicapped people can have rewarding careers.
LC NO. 81-706476
Prod-USDED Dist-USNAC Prodn-KRLNTV 1981

Khan Du II - Joe C 30 MIN
3/4 OR 1/2 INCH VIDEO CASSETTE
Tells how a boy with a learning disability finds out that this handicap does not prevent him from having a good career.
LC NO. 81-706477
Prod-USDED Dist-USNAC Prodn-KRLNTV 1981

Khan Du II - Kate C 30 MIN
3/4 OR 1/2 INCH VIDEO CASSETTE
Focuses on Kate, a girl with a physical disability who learns that she will be able to choose a rewarding career.
LC NO. 81-706478
Prod-USDED Dist-USNAC Prodn-KRLNTV 1981

Khan Du—A Series

Depicts various handicapped young people and shows how they meet a magical creature named Khan Du, who explains that disabled people can do many things.
Prod-USOE Dist-USNAC Prodn-KRLNTV 1978

David Takes Off 30 MIN
Robert's Second Chance 30 MIN
Shelley Finds Her Way 30 MIN

Kheturni Bayo - North Indian Farm Women C 19 MIN
3/4 OR 1/2 INCH VIDEO CASSETTE
Examines the roles and duties of the women in a typical extended family of land-owning peasants in Gujarat, India. Shows the women have an opportunity for a tolerable and even enjoyable life through the feelings of affection developed from working and living together. Discusses arranged marriages.
Prod-PSU Dist-PSU 1984

Khomeini Profile C 17 MIN
3/4 OR 1/2 INCH VIDEO CASSETTE H-C A
Looks at the Ayatollah Khomeini, mastermind of the Iranian revolution in 1979. Examines the man, his country and the events that made news.
Prod-JOU Dist-JOU

Khrushchev - The Bear's Embrace C 24 MIN
16MM FILM, 3/4 OR 1/2 IN VIDEO H-C A
Documents Russian premier Nikita Khrushchev's political evolution from advocating world domination to promoting detente. Narrated by Henry Fonda.
From The Leaders Of The 20th Century - Portraits Of Power Series.
Prod-NIELSE Dist-LCOA 1980

Kiai - Women In Self-Defense C 28 MIN
16MM FILM, 3/4 OR 1/2 IN VIDEO
Shows women gathering at the Brooklyn Women's Martial Arts Center to learn the skill of self-defense based on karate. Describes some of the traumatic experiences some of the women have had with domestic violence or street crime.
Prod-PILCHR Dist-FLMLIB 1982

Kialoa To Jamaica C 31 MIN
16MM FILM, 3/4 OR 1/2 IN VIDEO
Joins Jim Kilroy and his crack crew on board the 79-foot maxi boat Windward Passage for the 1975 Miami to Montego Bay race.
Prod-OFFSHR Dist-OFFSHR 1975

Kibbutz C 28 MIN
16MM FILM OPTICAL SOUND
Shows how members of kibbutz Afikm and Eliot live, work and enjoy their unique way of life.
Prod-ALDEN Dist-ALDEN

Kibbutz C 30 MIN
3/4 INCH VIDEO CASSETTE I-J
Examines the changing aspirations of second and third generation kibbutz dwellers in Israel.
From The Project Middle East Series.
Prod-UNICEF Dist-GPITVL

Kibbutz Care And Family Care, Pt 1 - Two Climates Of Childhood In Israel C 32 MIN
16MM FILM OPTICAL SOUND
Shows a typical day of a Kibbutz child and his age mates, all three and one-half years of age. Shows how they rise in the morning, dress themselves with minimum help of the caretaker, play, eat, nap, walk to their parents' house without escort and return, each with one of their parents for the night. Portrays a typical day of a town child, including his experiences in his family and in his play group.
Prod-NYU Dist-NYU

Kibbutz Care And Family Care, Pt 2 - Patterns Of Parenting In Israel C 32 MIN
16MM FILM OPTICAL SOUND
Shows a Kibbutz and a town child, who are both three and a half years old, with each of the significant adults in their lives. Points out the striking differences between child-adult relationships as each child-adult pair goes through the same specified activities.
Prod-VASSAR Dist-NYU

Kibbutz Daphna C 26 MIN
16MM FILM OPTICAL SOUND K-C A
Explains how the Kibbutz settlements of Israel are organized as agricultural communities to serve all the people living there. Show how the Kibbutz society has been brought to fulfillment at Dafna in northern Galilee.
LC NO. 74-701198
Prod-GARNER Dist-ALDEN 1968

Kibbutz, A B 40 MIN
16MM FILM OPTICAL SOUND
Presents a visit to a Kibbutz, an Israeli collective village, and looks at its way of life.
Prod-ALDEN Dist-ALDEN

Kick Me C 8 MIN
16MM FILM, 3/4 OR 1/2 IN VIDEO
Uses animation to tell a story about a pair of legs, a baseball and a nest of spiders.
Prod-SWARR Dist-LRF 1976

Kicking C 15 MIN
3/4 OR 1/2 INCH VIDEO CASSETTE T
Explains how to teach primary students about foot dribbling, stopping the ball, the place kick pattern, place kicking for distance and accuracy and kicking a pitched ball, punting and making up a game.
From The Leaps And Bounds Series. No. 15
Prod-HSDE Dist-AITECH 1984

Kicking The Loose Gravel Home - A Portrait Of Richard Hugo C 56 MIN
3/4 OR 1/2 INCH VIDEO CASSETTE
Portrays the American poet Richard Hugo. Follows him from his childhood home in Seattle to his teaching post in Missoula, from tavern to picnic and from highway to lecture hall.
Prod-MEDIPR Dist-MEDIPR 1977

Kicking Tires Is Not Enough - Or, How To Buy A Used Car C 16 MIN
16MM FILM, 3/4 OR 1/2 IN VIDEO H-C A
Contains research in testing cars and monitoring their performance and repair records. Provides instructions for testing cars and discusses selling tactics and other problems to be surmounted when shopping for a used car.
From The Consumer Reports Series.
Prod-CU Dist-FI Prodn-BFD 1977

Kicks - A Formula For Control C 29 MIN
16MM FILM, 3/4 OR 1/2 IN VIDEO IND
Follows a derrickman's progress as he encounters kicks. Shows how he studies the nature of the oil field hazards, and learns to control them on both land and offshore drilling rigs.
Prod-HYDRIL Dist-UTEXPE 1982

Kicks While Drilling C 27 MIN
3/4 OR 1/2 INCH VIDEO CASSETTE IND
Shows causes of kicks and blowouts, kick warning signs while drilling, flow check while drilling, shut-in procedure while drilling and crew drill.
From The Blowout Prevenion And Well Control Series.
Prod-CAODC Dist-GPCV

Kicks while Out Of The Hole C 7 MIN
3/4 OR 1/2 INCH VIDEO CASSETTE IND
Speaks on kick warning signs while out of the hole, flow check while out of the hole, shut-in procedure while out of the hole and crew drill.
From The Blowout Prevention And Well Control Series.
Prod-CAODC Dist-GPCV

Kicks while Tripping C 10 MIN
3/4 OR 1/2 INCH VIDEO CASSETTE IND
Relates kick warning signs while tripping, flow check while tripping and crew drill.
From The Blowout Prevention And Well Control Series.
Prod-CAODC Dist-GPCV

Kid C 5 MIN
16MM FILM OPTICAL SOUND
Uses animation and live action to depict a couple who imagine themselves in a scene from the motion picture Casablanca.
LC NO. 76-703843
Prod-CONCRU Dist-CONCRU 1976

Kid Brother, The B 84 MIN
16MM FILM, 3/4 OR 1/2 IN VIDEO
Features Harold Lloyd in a comedy about a tough sheriff's weak son who fantasizes about being a hero. Issued in 1927 as a silent motion picture.
From The Harold Lloyd Series.
LC NO. 79-707443
Prod-LLOYDH Dist-TIMLIF 1976

Kid From Borneo, The B 19 MIN
16MM FILM OPTICAL SOUND
Tells how the Little Rascals go to the sideshow to visit their uncle and mistake him for the Wildman from Borneo.
Prod-ROACH Dist-BHAWK 1933

Kid From Left Field, The C 99 MIN
3/4 OR 1/2 INCH VIDEO CASSETTE
Introduces J R Cooper, a ten-year-old whose father is a has-been San Diego Padres second-baseman who teaches him all he knows about the game. Reveals that when J R passes on what he knows to the Padres, they become World Series contenders. Stars Gary Coleman, Ed McMahon and Tab Hunter.
Prod-TIMLIF Dist-TIMLIF 1982

Kid Thomas And The Preservation Hall Band C 58 MIN
3/4 OR 1/2 INCH VIDEO CASSETTE I-C A
Presents footage of Kid Thomas and his band playing in New Orleans, the birthplace of jazz. Gives an understanding of this band's particular type of music as well as the social culture behind it.
Prod-COLBYC Dist-PHENIX

Kid Who Couldn't Miss, The C 80 MIN
3/4 OR 1/2 INCH VIDEO CASSETTE J-C A
Combines footage and newly created film with a historical look to provide an imaginative portrait of Canadian World War I flying ace, Billy Bishop.
LC NO. 84-707240
Prod-COWAP Dist-NFBC 1983

Kid, You've Got A Dirty Mouth B 15 MIN
2 INCH VIDEOTAPE P-I
Presents general information about dental disease including the bacteria that cause trouble and the various forms of disease. Covers the prevalence of dental problems in the United States and the role of diet and dental hygiene.
From The Dental Health Series.
Prod-GPITVL Dist-GPITVL

Kiddie Kaleidoscope C 6 MIN
16MM FILM OPTICAL SOUND K-I
A teacher shows a boy and a girl a kaleidoscope, explains how its designs are formed by mirrors and bits of colored glass and suggests they make their own designs by placing paper cutouts on a paper background.
Prod-MMP Dist-MMP 1959

Kidnap - Executive Style C 25 MIN
16MM FILM OPTICAL SOUND
Shows several varieties of kidnapping, including abduction by revolutionaries, abduction for ransom and abduction by a psychopath. Dramatizes the need for effective executive protection against kidnapping.
From The Urban Crisis Series.
LC NO. 75-700450
Prod-BROSEB Dist-BROSEB 1975

Kidnapped C 94 MIN
16MM FILM OPTICAL SOUND
Presents the story of David Balfour and his attempts to regain his rightful inheritance, the house and lands of Shaws of Scotland.
Prod-DISNEY Dist-UAE 1965

Kidnapped C 105 MIN
16MM FILM OPTICAL SOUND K A
Tells the story of a young boy who is sold by his wicked uncle as a slave and is helped by an outlaw. Based on the Robert Louis Stevenson novel. Stars Michael Caine, Trevor Howard and Donald Pleasance.
Prod-OMNISA Dist-TIMLIF 1971

Kidnapped C 28 MIN
16MM FILM, 3/4 OR 1/2 IN VIDEO J-H
Presents an excerpt from the motion picture Kidnapped, which tells of the efforts of David Balfour to regain his inherited property. Stars James MacArthur. Based on the novel KIDNAPPED by Robert Louis Stevenson.
From The Film As Literature, Series 1 Series.
Prod-DISNEY Dist-WDEMCO Prodn-WDEMCO

Kidney Failure C 29 MIN
3/4 OR 1/2 INCH VIDEO CASSETTE
Looks at the causes, symptoms and treatment of kidney disease. Shows a kidney machine in action and interviews a kidney patient.
From The Daniel Foster, MD Series.
Prod-KERA Dist-PBS

Kidney Function Tests B 43 MIN
16MM FILM, 3/4 OR 1/2 IN VIDEO
Disucsses renal function tests, including the blood urea nitrogen and the creatinine clearance tests. Underlines the usefulness of the albumin-to-creatinine clearance ratio in relation to the nephrotic syndrome.
From The Clinical Pathology Series.
Prod-NMAC Dist-USNAC 1969

Kidney Transplant B 50 MIN
16MM FILM OPTICAL SOUND PRO
Shows the first kidney transplant, performed at the Stanford University Medical Center on twin brothers.
Prod-CMA Dist-LAWREN

Kidney Transplant C 20 MIN
16MM FILM, 3/4 OR 1/2 IN VIDEO
Shows a kidney transplant operation, as Dr Michael Robinette and his surgical team connect a donated kidney in time to keep it functioning. Explores the emotional factors of donation by family members.
Prod-CANBC Dist-FLMLIB

Kidney Transplant Using An Ileal Conduit C 20 MIN
16MM FILM OPTICAL SOUND PRO
Demonstrates the use of intestinal conduits in kidney transplantation and shows their value.
LC NO. 80-701413
Prod-EATONL Dist-EATONL Prodn-AEGIS 1980

Kidney Transplantation C 11 MIN
3/4 OR 1/2 INCH VIDEO CASSETTE PRO
Presents criteria for evaluating the suitability of kidney transplant donors and recipients. Categorizes tests performed during the evaluation. Presents survival data comparing related and cadaver kidney transplant.
Prod-UMICHM Dist-UMICHM 1977

Kidney Transplantation - An Approach To A Complicated Subject C 33 MIN
16MM FILM OPTICAL SOUND PRO
Reviews the entire conduct of a kidney transplantation, including certain points relative to the decision to perform this operation, the choice of patients and the technique of the operation itself.
Prod-ACYDGD Dist-ACY 1965

Kidney Transplants And Hemodialysis B 44 MIN
16MM FILM OPTICAL SOUND PRO
Discusses criteria for patient selection both for kidney transplant and dialysis and procedures for preparation of cadaver and living donor for transplant. Describes the process of rejection of a transplanted kidney and methods of treatment. Stresses nursing care of children undergoing either procedure and attitudes of the children.
From The Pediatric Nursing Series.
LC NO. 75-703416
Prod-VDONUR Dist-AJN Prodn-WTTWTV 1967

Kidneys C 11 MIN
16MM FILM, 3/4 OR 1/2 IN VIDEO J-H
See series title for descriptive statement.
From The Exploring The Body Series.
Prod-IFFB Dist-FI 1972

Kids C 12 MIN
16MM FILM OPTICAL SOUND
Follows a day in the life of an 11-year-old deaf boy who can talk but is hard of hearing.
Prod-USC Dist-USC

Kids And Alcohol Don't Mix C 14 MIN
16MM FILM - VIDEO, ALL FORMATS K-J
Presents a Fat Albert cartoon about a young soccer player with a drinking problem.
From The Fat Albert And The Cosby Kids IV Series.
Prod-BARR Dist-BARR Prodn-FLMTON

Kids And Birds And European Winter C 10 MIN
16MM FILM, 3/4 OR 1/2 IN VIDEO I-H
Shows children as they make unusual containers, hang them from the snow-covered evergreens in their garden and watch different kinds of birds respond to their efforts.
Prod-IFFB Dist-FI 1972

Kids And Cash—A Series
P-J
Prod-COUNFI Dist-COUNFI

Money Magic 11 MIN
Once Upon A Dime 11 MIN

Kids And Conflict C 12 MIN
3/4 OR 1/2 INCH VIDEO CASSETTE T
Designed for teachers. Illustrates how to use the conflict curriculum.
From The Magic Circle Series.
Prod-HDI Dist-UMCOM Prodn-UMCOM

Kids And Conflicts C 12 MIN
16MM FILM OPTICAL SOUND

Presents teachers discussing problems they have encountered when conflict in the classroom has interrupted their teaching. Demonstrates a process which they can use with their students to assist them in discovering alternatives to conflict.
From The Magic Circle Series.
LC NO. 75-703080
Prod-UMCH Dist-MMA 1975

Kids And Drugs - The Reasons Why C 15 MIN
16MM FILM, 3/4 OR 1/2 IN VIDEO I
Shows how elementary students can have fun and win social acceptance through more positive ways than drugs and alcohol use.
Prod-WDEMCO Dist-WDEMCO 1983

Kids And Matches C 10 MIN
16MM FILM SILENT H-C A S
Describes in American sign language what happens when a deaf boy and his brother try to make a kiln like the one they read about in school. Relates graphically the damage and punishment that results when the boys swipe matches to start a fire in an oven. Signed for the deaf by Ted Supalla.
LC NO. 76-701687
Prod-JOYCE Dist-JOYCE 1975

Kids Are People, Too C 29 MIN
2 INCH VIDEOTAPE
See series title for descriptive statement.
From The That's Life Series.
Prod-KOAPTV Dist-PUBTEL

Kids At Camp C 25 MIN
3/4 INCH VIDEO CASSETTE K-H
Gives true-life picture of disabled children taking part in activities at Easter Seal Society's Woodeden Camp near London. Reveals positive feelings about programs by campers, parents and staff.
Prod-ESST Dist-ESST 1983

Kids At Play C 28 MIN
16MM FILM OPTICAL SOUND P-I
Follows the origin and development of various games that children have played since ancient times. States that such games as Ring Around The Rosy and London Bridge Is Falling Down are probably based on real events in British history.
Prod-CANBC Dist-FI

Kids For Sale C 22 MIN
16MM FILM OPTICAL SOUND A
Looks at the state of children's TV with a sampling of commercials and programs as well as parent's and children's comments. Includes strategies for guiding family TV viewing.
Prod-ACTV Dist-MMM 1979

Kids Ill, The C 4 MIN
3/4 OR 1/2 INCH VIDEO CASSETTE
Offers a portrait of the filmmakers unusual family based upon his child's scrawls and his wife's picture of herself quilting in a field. Uses animation.
Prod-MEDIPR Dist-MEDIPR 1982

Kids In Conflict C 12 MIN
16MM FILM OPTICAL SOUND T
Presents a step-by-step illustration of how to use the Magic Circle Conflict Curriculum.
From The Magic Circle Series.
Prod-TRAFCO Dist-ECUFLM 1975

Kids On Smoking C 10 MIN
16MM FILM, 3/4 OR 1/2 IN VIDEO I-H
Presents four young children exploring the grown-up world of cigarette smoking and deciding it is not for them. Looks at peer pressure and behavior examples displayed by adults regarding smoking.
From The Life And Breath Series.
Prod-JOU Dist-JOU 1978

Kids On Smoking C 10 MIN
16MM FILM, 3/4 OR 1/2 IN VIDEO I-J
Explores the full range of young people's attitudes on smoking and delivers the message not to get hooked on cigarettes.
Prod-PELICN Dist-PELICN 1978

Kids Playing With Fire - The Clarke Family Tragedy C 22 MIN
16MM FILM, 3/4 OR 1/2 IN VIDEO A
Presents reporter Mike Botula interviewing the Clarks, whose six-year-old son started a fire in their home which led to the deaths of four other children. Features fire officials and others who tell how parents can deal with a fire-curious, problem child and how to teach their children the correct use of fire.
LC NO. 82-706410
Prod-JEWELR Dist-FILCOM 1981

Kids With Problems - One Community's Response B 29 MIN
16MM FILM OPTICAL SOUND C A
Shows the work of the Centre County, Pennsylvania Youth Service Bureau, an agency comprised of citizen volunteers which offers alternatives to institutional confinement of youthful offenders by placing emphasis on prevention of delinquency and a cooperative learning process rather than an authoritative punitive process.
LC NO. 76-703205
Prod-WPSXTV Dist-PSU 1973

Kids, Courts And Corrections C 29 MIN
3/4 INCH VIDEO CASSETTE
Discusses problems of adolescents. Questions the United States juvenile court system and the concept of equal justice for young people.
From The Issue At Hand Series.
Prod-UMITV Dist-UMITV 1976

Kids' Stuff C 29 MIN
2 INCH VIDEOTAPE
See series title for descriptive statement.
From The Maggie And The Beautiful Machine - Shape-Up Now For Kids Series.
Prod-WGBHTV Dist-PUBTEL

Kiel Canal, The C 5 MIN
16MM FILM, 3/4 OR 1/2 IN VIDEO
Describes the importance and operation of the Kiel Canal, the shortest connection between the North and Baltic Seas.
From The European Studies - Germany Series. Part 4
Prod-BAYER Dist-IFB 1973

Kiel Olympiad C 27 MIN
16MM FILM, 3/4 OR 1/2 IN VIDEO J-C A
Records the major parts of the 1972 Olympic yachting races held in the North Sea, off Kiel Harbor, Germany, where men are seen gathering from all over the world, hoping to win one of the coveted gold medals.
Prod-OFFSHR Dist-OFFSHR 1973

Kifaru - The Black Rhinoceros C 51 MIN
16MM FILM, 3/4 OR 1/2 IN VIDEO J-H A
Tells how Canadian biologist John Goddard, convinced that the black rhino was doomed to extinction, spent six years in a thorough investigation of the animal and its habits.
Prod-MGMD Dist-FI 1972

Kikiriki C 12 MIN
3/4 INCH VIDEO CASSETTE
Presents artistic video techniques forming a composite portrait of the alien and the displaced of U S society, underscored by struggle and confusion. By Tony Labat.
Prod-EAI Dist-EAI

Kilauea Speaks C 8 MIN
16MM FILM OPTICAL SOUND J-C A
Uses the Hawaiian volcano, Kilauea, to show how volcanic activity can affect the lives of people and their land. Uses animation to describe the origin and the products of a volcano.
Prod-WSU Dist-WSU 1962

Kilimanjaro C 50 MIN
3/4 OR 1/2 INCH VIDEO CASSETTE H-C A
Explores Mount Kilimanjaro, on the edge of east Africa's Great RifValley and close to the Kenyan border, its craters, mysterious melting glaciers, a volcano and the distinct ecozones ranging from the plains to the summit with their differing types of vegetation and wildlife.
Prod-WNETTV Dist-FI

Kilimanjaro Mission C 30 MIN
16MM FILM OPTICAL SOUND J-C A
Shows the life of a missionary priest in Kenya aiding the sick, educating the young and teaching trades.
Prod-SMUSA Dist-SMUSA

Kiliwa - Hunters And Gatherers Of Baja California C 14 MIN
16MM FILM, 3/4 OR 1/2 IN VIDEO J-C
Documents aspects of hunting and gathering, food preparation and shelter construction by a group of Baja California Indians. Illustrates the cultural and ecological adaptation of the population to the high desert country and the intrusion of technology on traditional modes of subsistence.
Prod-UCEMC Dist-UCEMC 1975

Killer Arson C 40 MIN
16MM FILM, 3/4 OR 1/2 IN VIDEO
Shows how deadly and devastating the act of arson can be. Considers some victims of arson and suggests how arson may be prevented.
Prod-FILCOM Dist-FILCOM 1981

Killer Bees - Fact Or Fantasy C 14 MIN
16MM FILM - 3/4 IN VIDEO
Documents the African bees which are said to be a threat to the United States. Discusses the exaggeration of the problem and ways to diminish the bees' aggressive qualities.
LC NO. 79-706102
Prod-USDA Dist-USNAC 1979

Killer Force C 110 MIN
16MM FILM OPTICAL SOUND H A
Tells an adventure story about crooks who try to smuggle diamonds from a formidably defended South African mine. Stars Peter Fonda, Telly Savalas and Maud Adams.
Prod-AIP Dist-TIMLIF 1976

Killer In The Village C 56 MIN
16MM FILM, 3/4 OR 1/2 IN VIDEO A
Looks at the impact of Acquired Immune Deficiency Disease by interviewing patients, potential victims, physicians and medical researchers and graphic documentation of medical investigations as well as using animated sequences to clarify the operation of the human immune system.
LC NO. 84-707241
Prod-BBCTV Dist-TEXFLM 1983

Killer Is A Softie, The C 7 MIN
16MM FILM OPTICAL SOUND
Features Hugo, a young killer whale who is brought to the Miami Seaquarium and taught to perform.
LC NO. 76-700700
Prod-MIAMIS Dist-MIAMIS Prodn-TELAIR 1975

Killer Leopard B 70 MIN
16MM FILM OPTICAL SOUND I-C A
See series title for descriptive statement.
From The Bomba, The Jungle Boy Series.
Prod-CINEWO Dist-CINEWO 1954

Killer Of Sheep B 84 MIN
16MM FILM OPTICAL SOUND
Tells the story of a man who works in a slaughterhouse in Los Angeles and whose job conditions cause him to lose touch with his family. Shows him being offered alternatives, including crime, which he finds morally unacceptable.
Prod-BLKFMF Dist-BLKFMF

Killers And The Killed B 27 MIN
16MM FILM, 3/4 OR 1/2 IN VIDEO J-H
Shows how final victory was gained in the Atlantic during World War II between 1943 and 1945.
From The Victory At Sea Series.
Prod-NBCTV Dist-LUF

Killers, The—A Series

Explores in depth the five major causes of premature non- accidental death, including heart disease, genetic defects, pulmonary disease, trauma from accident or violent crime, and cancer.
Prod-TRAINX Dist-TRAINX

Cancer - The Cell That Won't Die 090 MIN
Genetic Defects - The Broken Code 090 MIN
Heart Disease - The 20th Century Epidemic 090 MIN
Pulmonary Disease - The Hidden Enemy 090 MIN
Trauma - It's An Emergency 090 MIN

Killing Fields, The C
1/2 IN VIDEO CASSETTE BETA/VHS
Presents the Oscar-winning drama of friendship and courage played against the harsh backdrop of the Khmer Rouge takeover of Cambodia. Starring Sam Waterston and Dr Haing S Ngor.
Prod-GA Dist-GA

Killing Ground, The C 52 MIN
16MM FILM, 3/4 OR 1/2 IN VIDEO H-C
Reveals what toxic chemical wastes have done to communities across the United States. Examines confidential files, interviews corporate executives, and questions public officials.
Prod-ABCNEW Dist-MTI 1979

Killing Of An Egg C 3 MIN
16MM FILM, 3/4 OR 1/2 IN VIDEO J-C A
Presents an animated fable of a man who destroys an egg, only to become a victim himself.
LC NO. 78-700693
Prod-DRIESP Dist-PFP Prodn-CRAMAN 1978

Killing Of Bacteria By Antibotics, The C 21 MIN
3/4 OR 1/2 INCH VIDEO CASSETTE PRO
Understanding the mechanism of action of various types of antimicrobial agents provides a guide to their therapeutic use.
Prod-WFP Dist-WFP

Killing The Golden Goose - The Poisoning Of America's Farms and Foods C 20 MIN
3/4 OR 1/2 INCH VIDEO CASSETTE
Describes contamination problems caused by the use of agrichemicals. Examines the conflict between the demands for ever greater agricultural productivity and the need to protect the quality of our drinking water and food.
Prod-DCTVC Dist-DCTVC

Killing Time B 9 MIN
16MM FILM OPTICAL SOUND
Portrays, in an off-beat and humorous manner, a day in the life of a woman who is determined to commit suicide in style.
Prod-BLKFMF Dist-BLKFMF

Killing Time B 9 MIN
16MM FILM OPTICAL SOUND
Provides a suicide's guide on how to live forever. Depicts one day of the life of Sage Brush, a woman determined to die in style if it kills her.
LC NO. 80-701229
Prod-WIC Dist-WIC 1979

Killing Time C 54 MIN
16MM FILM OPTICAL SOUND
Looks at the correctional system in Massachusetts through the eyes of correctional officers, inmates and administrators.
Prod-KBP Dist-KBP

Killing Us Softly - Advertising's Image Of C 30 MIN
16MM FILM - 3/4 IN VIDEO H-C A
Analyzes the fifty billion dollar industry that preys on fears and insecurities of every consumer in America. Reveals how advertising's messages degrade, trivialize and straight-jacket women.
Prod-CMBRD Dist-CMBRD 1979

Killington Winter Holiday C 22 MIN
16MM FILM OPTICAL SOUND
Presents the accelerated ski method and the Killington Ski Resort. Shows living accomodations, dining and night life as well as scenes of the Vermont countryside.
LC NO. 78-700374
Prod-KSR Dist-MTP Prodn-PERRYB 1977

Kiln Atmospheres And Temperatures For Glaze Firing C 28 MIN
2 INCH VIDEOTAPE
Features Mrs Peterson describing certain ceramic processes for her classroom at the University of Southern California. Explains appropriate kiln atmospheres and temperatures for glaze firing.
From The Wheels, Kilns And Clay Series.
Prod-USC Dist-PUBTEL

Kilns And Glazes C 29 MIN
2 INCH VIDEOTAPE
Features Mrs Vivika Heino introducing and demonstrating basic techniques in using kilns and glazes.

From The Exploring The Crafts - Pottery Series.
Prod-WENHTV Dist-PUBTEL

Kilns For Firing C 28 MIN
2 INCH VIDEOTAPE
Features Mrs Peterson describing certain ceramic processes for her classroom at the University of Southern California. Shows kilns for firing.
From The Wheels, Kilns And Clay Series.
Prod-USC Dist-PUBTEL

Kilo Sounds Greek To Me C 15 MIN
3/4 INCH VIDEO CASSETTE J-C A
Introduces metric prefixes and their values.
From The Measure To Measure Series.
Prod-WCVETV Dist-GPITVL 1975

Kilogram, The C 20 MIN
3/4 INCH VIDEO CASSETTE I
Explains the difference between mass and weight. Demonstrates several types of scales and shows how to construct a hand-held scale.
From The Metric Marmalade Series.
Prod-WCVETV Dist-GPITVL 1979

Kilometres And Seconds C 20 MIN
3/4 INCH VIDEO CASSETTE I
Demonstrates that 1,000 meters equal one kilometer. Introduces various metric symbols and shows how to convert between meters and kilometers.
From The Metric Marmalade Series.
Prod-WCVETV Dist-GPITVL 1979

Kilometro Lanciato C 28 MIN
16MM FILM OPTICAL SOUND
Explains that the kilometro Lanciato Race was held on the glacier of Plato Rosa at Cervinia in Italy in July of 1970, in which five Japanese ski-racers took part and came in first, second and third. Describes the world of men who are possessed with speed.
Prod-UNIJAP Dist-UNIJAP 1970

Kilowatt Kaper, The C 8 MIN
16MM FILM OPTICAL SOUND
Uses animation to tell the story of a man who wastes electrical power by misusing his appliances. Shows how the appliances hold a midnight meeting and decide not to cooperate with his wasteful habits.
LC NO. 78-701556
Prod-LADWP Dist-NTN Prodn-NTN 1978

Kilowatt Kaper, The C 8 MIN
3/4 OR 1/2 INCH VIDEO CASSETTE K A
Shows an animated story of a man who misuses applicances and wastes electricity. Can be used for non-English audiences.
Prod-SUTHRB Dist-SUTHRB

Kilowatts From Cowpies - The Methane Option C 25 MIN
16MM FILM, 3/4 OR 1/2 IN VIDEO J-C A
Shows how biogas can be created from the waste products of farm animals.
LC NO. 82-707097
Prod-MAYRH Dist-BULFRG 1982

Kimosomiunawak, The Time Of The Cree C 26 MIN
16MM FILM OPTICAL SOUND
Shows the relationship between an Indian family and a group of diggers who are investigating an ancient tribe.
LC NO. 76-702083
Prod-CANFDC Dist-CANFDC 1975

Kimray Glycol Pump—A Series
IND
Introduces workers to the Kimray Glycol Pump. Covers basic information, operation and dismantling the pump.
Prod-UTEXPE Dist-UTEXPE 1981

Kimray Pump, Pt 1 - Introduction 008 MIN
Kimray Pump, Pt 2 - Operation 012 MIN
Kimray Pump, Pt 3 - Tear-Down 019 MIN

Kimray Pump, Pt 1 - Introduction C 8 MIN
3/4 OR 1/2 INCH VIDEO CASSETTE IND
Provides a basic introduction to the opeation of glycol dehydration system and to the inner workings of the pump itself.
From The Kimray Glycol Pump Series.
Prod-UTEXPE Dist-UTEXPE 1981

Kimray Pump, Pt 2 - Operation C 12 MIN
3/4 OR 1/2 INCH VIDEO CASSETTE IND
Examines the pump's critical operating parameters. Shows how to properly start up the pump, identify malfunctionS and apply troubleshooting procedures.
From The Kimray Glycol Pump Series.
Prod-UTEXPE Dist-UTEXPE 1981

Kimray Pump, Pt 3 - Tear-Down C 19 MIN
3/4 OR 1/2 INCH VIDEO CASSETTE IND
Gives step-by-step procedures for dismantling a Kimray 4015 glycol pump.
From The Kimray Glycol Pump Series.
Prod-UTEXPE Dist-UTEXPE 1981

Kinabulu, The Summit Of Borneo C 50 MIN
3/4 OR 1/2 INCH VIDEO CASSETTE H-C A
Presents Kinabulu, the highest peak in southeast Asia and a mountain of legend and fable, believed to be the abode of 'the spirits of the dead' and of a giant dragon guarding a priceless pearl. Features the bizarre plant life found there, carnivorous plants, 1,500 kinds of orchids and the largest flower in the world that stinks of rotten meat.
Prod-WNETTV Dist-FI Prodn-BBCTV

Kind Of Seeing, A - The Colour Of Scotland C 13 MIN
16MM FILM, 3/4 OR 1/2 IN VIDEO J-H
Presents an invitation to visual pleasure through images drawn from natural life. Views daffodils in the grounds of a ruined Abbey, azaleas in a wild garden, the patterns of reeds, wind-blown flower seeds, lakes, mountains and the setting sun.
Prod-FOSCOT Dist-IFB 1971

Kindergarten Puppy Training C 15 MIN
16MM FILM, 3/4 OR 1/2 IN VIDEO
Provides examples of obedience instruction given to young dogs, including instruction in walking on a lead.
From The Dog Obedience Training Series.
Prod-KLEINW Dist-KLEINW 1974

Kindest Cut, The - Story Of A Sawmill C 26 MIN
3/4 INCH VIDEO CASSETTE J-C A
Shows how wood is processed, from the felling of a tree through treatment in a lumber mill.
Prod-PRFLM Dist-LAWREN

Kindest Cut, The - The Story Of A Sawmill C 26 MIN
16MM FILM OPTICAL SOUND I-H A
Shows the process of cutting wood and producing lumber in a sawmill. Examines processes which cut waste and offer a use for wood materials formerly burned or thrown away.
LC NO. 76-700377
Prod-LAWREN Dist-LAWREN Prodn-JOHNLM 1976

Kindness Week Or The Seven Capital Elements (Max Ernst) B 19 MIN
16MM FILM OPTICAL SOUND
Presents an animated film collage mimicking and mocking the sentimental style of Victorian engravings.
Prod-ROLAND Dist-ROLAND

Kinds Of Plants C 15 MIN
3/4 OR 1/2 INCH VIDEO CASSETTE I-J
Investigates the two groups of plants. Includes those with chlorophyll and those without.
From The Animals And Such Series. Module Green - Animals And Plants
Prod-WHROTV Dist-AITECH 1972

Kinesics B 70 MIN
16MM FILM OPTICAL SOUND C A
Presents a lecture by Raymond L Birdwhistell of the Eastern Pennsylvania Psychiatric Institute on Linguistic Kinesics. Describes system of categorizing and defining facial expressions, posturing and gestures of humans in terms of communicative meaning.
LC NO. 73-712162
Prod-PSUPCR Dist-PSUPCR 1964

Kinesics - Motion And Meaning C 30 MIN
3/4 OR 1/2 INCH VIDEO CASSETTE C
See series title for descriptive statement.
From The Language And Meaning Series.
Prod-WUSFTV Dist-GPITVL 1983

Kinesiology C 30 MIN
3/4 OR 1/2 INCH VIDEO CASSETTE
Deals with kinesiology, the science of studying muscle movement and leverage, in terms of both anatomy and physiological processes. Discusses the various procedures and results of the study of movement.
Prod-NETCHE Dist-NETCHE 1969

Kinesis C 6 MIN
16MM FILM OPTICAL SOUND
Examines kinesis, an art film which features rapidly changing computer-generated images resembling forms designed by the graphic artist M C Escher.
LC NO. 75-703104
Prod-LILYAN Dist-LILYAN 1975

Kinestasis 60 C 4 MIN
16MM FILM OPTICAL SOUND J A
Reviews the socio-political events of the 1960's in America.
LC NO. 72-712360
Prod-BRAMAN Dist-BRAMAN 1970

Kinetic Karnival Of Jearl Walker—A Series
H
Presents a number of physics experiments presented in a non-laboratory environment.
Prod-WVIZTV Dist-GPITVL 1982

Fluid Flow And Friction 030 MIN
Forces And Collisions 030 MIN
Leidenfrost Effect, The 030 MIN
Rotation 030 MIN
Science Of Cooking, The 030 MIN
Viscosity 030 MIN

Kinetic Sculpture Of Gordon Barlow C 7 MIN
16MM FILM, 3/4 OR 1/2 IN VIDEO H A
Demonstrates the kinetic art of Gordon Garlow. Shows dominoes falling and apparently rising again.
Prod-MTOLP Dist-MTOLP 1974

Kinetic Theory By Computer Animation—A Series
H-C A
Prod-KALMIA Dist-KALMIA 1973

Avogadro's Principle 3 MIN
Brownian Motion And Random Walk 3 MIN
Dalton's Law 2 MIN
Deviations From Ideal Gas 3 MIN
Graham's Law 3 MIN
Gravitational Distribution 4 MIN
Heating, Cooling And Charles' Law 4 MIN
Ideal Gas Law 3 MIN
Maxwell-Boltzmann Distribution 4 MIN
Pressure, Volume And Boyle's Law 4 MIN
Temperature, Energy And Thermal Equilibrium 3 MIN

Kinetics And Orthotics For Function B 25 MIN
16MM FILM OPTICAL SOUND
Covers the four aspects of the rehabilitation program.
Prod-NYU Dist-NYU

Kinetics Of Flocculation C 57 MIN
3/4 OR 1/2 INCH VIDEO CASSETTE
See series title for descriptive statement.
From The Colloid And Surface Chemistry - Lyophobic Colloids Series.
Prod-KALMIA Dist-KALMIA

Kinetics Of Flocculation B 57 MIN
3/4 OR 1/2 INCH VIDEO CASSETTE
See series title for descriptive statement.
From The Colloid And Surface Chemistry - Lyophobic Colloids Series.
Prod-MIOT Dist-MIOT

King - Montgomery To Memphis B 103 MIN
16MM FILM, 3/4 OR 1/2 IN VIDEO
Documents the civil rights movement led by Dr Martin Luther King right up to his death in Memphis in 1968.
Prod-KINGML Dist-TEXFLM

King And I, The C 133 MIN
16MM FILM, 3/4 OR 1/2 IN VIDEO
Relates the clash of temperaments which occurs when an English widow travels to Bangkok in 1862 to tutor the wives and children of a king. Stars Yul Brynner and Deborah Kerr.
Prod-TWCF Dist-FI 1956

King And The Sprite, The C 10 MIN
16MM FILM OPTICAL SOUND I-C A
Uses puppets to present a variation on the King Midas legend.
LC NO. 83-700164
Prod-KRATKY Dist-MOKIN 1983

King And The Sprite, The C 10 MIN
3/4 OR 1/2 INCH VIDEO CASSETTE I-C A
Uses puppets to present a variation on the King Midas legend.
Prod-SFSP Dist-MOKIN Prodn-TRNKAJ 1983

King Arthur C 24 MIN
16MM FILM, 3/4 OR 1/2 IN VIDEO P-J
Presents an animated adaptation of the legend of King Arthur and the Knights of the Round Table featuring Mr Magoo in the role of King Arthur.
Prod-UPAPOA Dist-MCFI 1976

King Edward VIII - For Love Of A Woman B 15 MIN
1/2 IN VIDEO CASSETTE BETA/VHS
Tells the story of King Edward VIII, who gave up a kingdom for the love of a woman.
Prod-STAR Dist-STAR

King Football B 28 MIN
16MM FILM OPTICAL SOUND
Defines and illustrated football terms and some of the problems and methods used by the officials in a game. Sponsored by General Mills and Wilson Sporting Goods.
Prod-OSFS Dist-OSFS 1949

King Henry IV, Pt 1 - Historical Background Of The War Of Roses B 45 MIN
2 INCH VIDEOTAPE C
See series title for descriptive statement.
From The Shakespeare Series.
Prod-CHITVC Dist-GPITVL Prodn-WTTWTV

King Henry IV, Pt 1 - Shakespeare's Theme, Evil Of Civil War - Maturity Of Plot B 45 MIN
2 INCH VIDEOTAPE C
See series title for descriptive statement.
From The Shakespeare Series.
Prod-CHITVC Dist-GPITVL Prodn-WTTWTV

King Henry IV, Pt 2 - Falstaff At Work B 45 MIN
2 INCH VIDEOTAPE C
See series title for descriptive statement.
From The Shakespeare Series.
Prod-CHITVC Dist-GPITVL Prodn-WTTWTV

King Henry IV, Pt 2 - Machiavellian Politics, Rejection Of Falstaff C 45 MIN
2 INCH VIDEOTAPE C
See series title for descriptive statement.
From The Shakespeare Series.
Prod-CHITVC Dist-GPITVL Prodn-WTTWTV

King In New York, A B 105 MIN
1/2 IN VIDEO CASSETTE (BETA)
Tells how the deposed king of a European mini-monarchy comes to America to make a new life. Stars Charlie Chaplin.
Prod-UNKNWN Dist-BHAWK 1957

King John C 120 MIN
3/4 OR 1/2 INCH VIDEO CASSETTE H-C A
Presents a dramatization of Shakespeare's play King John which unenthusiastically depicts the king and shows his wickedness and weaknesses at the same time as raising Faulconbridge, the bastard, from swaggerer to clear-eyed champion of England.
From The Shakespeare Plays Series.
Prod-BBCTV Dist-TIMLIF 1981

King Kane C 5 MIN
3/4 OR 1/2 INCH VIDEO CASSETTE J-H
Consists of a lesson on misplaced modifiers.
From The Write On, Set 1 Series.
Prod-CTI Dist-CTI

King Khalid Military City C 19 MIN
16MM FILM OPTICAL SOUND
Looks at an architectural simulation of a city which was designed for the Government of Saudi Arabia by architects Brown, Daltas and Associates. Focuses on the city's design, pointing out that it is in the middle of the Arabian Desert and must hold 70,000 people.
LC NO. 79-700845
Prod-GOVSA Dist-FLECKG Prodn-FLECKG 1978

King Kong B 18 MIN
16MM FILM OPTICAL SOUND H-C A
Presents an excerpt from the motion picture King Kong, issued in 1933. Shows the attempts to rescue a young actress from a giant ape who has taken her as his bride. Exemplifies the horror film genre.
From The American Film Genre - The Horror Film Series.
LC NO. 77-701144
Prod-RKOP Dist-FI 1975

King Kung C 25 MIN
16MM FILM OPTICAL SOUND
Presents correspondent Michael Maclear's travels to Hong Kong, where he looks into the action films of the Orient, which involve flashing swords, flying limbs and rolling heads.
LC NO. 77-702514
Prod-CTV Dist-CTV 1976

King Lear C 29 MIN
2 INCH VIDEOTAPE
Features Alan Levitan, associate professor of English at Brandeis University discussing King Lear by Shakespeare.
From The Feast Of Language Series.
Prod-WGBHTV Dist-PUBTEL

King Lear C 30 MIN
3/4 OR 1/2 INCH VIDEO CASSETTE J-C A
Presents an adaptation of Shakespeare's King Lear, which is the story of the sins that are committed through lust of possession and of the cruelties that the young inflict on the old. Includes the plays A Midsummer's Night Dream, The Tempest and As You Like It on the same tape.
From The Shakespeare In Perspective Series.
LC NO. 84-707155
Prod-FI Dist-FI 1984

King Lear C 158 MIN
3/4 OR 1/2 INCH VIDEO CASSETTE
Offers a presentation of King Lear with Laurence Olivier in the starring role.
Prod-FOTH Dist-FOTH 1984

King Lear C 186 MIN
3/4 OR 1/2 INCH VIDEO CASSETTE H-C A
Presents William Shakespeare's play about a foolish king who divides his realm between two ungrateful daughters.
From The Shakespeare Plays Series.
LC NO. 82-707041
Prod-BBCTV Dist-TIMLIF 1981

King Lear - An Introduction C 28 MIN
16MM FILM, 3/4 OR 1/2 IN VIDEO J-C A
Presents scenes of Shakespeare's play King Lear. Attempts to preserve the continuity of the comedy and suggests to the first-time reader its prevailing mood and rhythm, the tone and manner of expression of the characters and an idea of Elizabethan costuming.
From The Shakespeare Series.
Prod-SEABEN Dist-PHENIX 1970

King Lear - Shakespeare's Blending And Transfiguration Of Source Materials B 45 MIN
2 INCH VIDEOTAPE C
See series title for descriptive statement.
From The Shakespeare Series.
Prod-CHITVC Dist-GPITVL Prodn-WTTWTV

King Lear - Shakespeare's Conception Of Poetic Justice B 45 MIN
2 INCH VIDEOTAPE C
See series title for descriptive statement.
From The Shakespeare Series.
Prod-CHITVC Dist-GPITVL Prodn-WTTWTV

King Lear - The Most Profound Of Shakespeare's Plays - The Nature Of Tragedy B 45 MIN
2 INCH VIDEOTAPE C
See series title for descriptive statement.
From The Shakespeare Series.
Prod-CHITVC Dist-GPITVL Prodn-WTTWTV

King Lear, Shakespeare C 158 MIN
3/4 OR 1/2 INCH VIDEO CASSETTE H-C A
Presents the Shakespeare tragedy King Lear. Stars Sir Laurence Olivier as Lear.
Prod-GRATV Dist-FOTH

King Midas C 5 MIN
16MM FILM, 3/4 OR 1/2 IN VIDEO P-I
Presents the fable story of King Midas, interpreted through modern crayon and watercolor resist. Stresses that monetary values alone are not the most important.
Prod-AIMS Dist-AIMS 1968

King Midas C 15 MIN
3/4 INCH VIDEO CASSETTE K-P
See series title for descriptive statement.
From The Storytime Series.
Prod-WCETTV Dist-GPITVL 1976

King Midas' Golden Touch C 8 MIN
16MM FILM OPTICAL SOUND K-I
Uses animation to tell the story of King Midas who wished for the power to turn everything he touched into gold.
From The Language Arts Series.
LC NO. FIA68-1043
Prod-NBC Dist-GRACUR 1968

King Of Sports C 50 MIN
1/2 IN VIDEO CASSETTE BETA/VHS
Provides an orientation to horse racing. Covers riding styles to racing luck.
Prod-TBRDRA Dist-EQVDL

King Of The Beasts C 26 MIN
16MM FILM, 3/4 OR 1/2 IN VIDEO
Uses animation to explain how the animals elected the King of the Beasts.
Prod-WESFAL Dist-LUF 1976

King Of The Block X 15 MIN
16MM FILM OPTICAL SOUND P-I R
Tells a story about a boy who learns that selfish actions lead to unhappiness and loneliness.
From The Our Children Series.
Prod-FAMF Dist-FAMF

King Of The Cats C 5 MIN
16MM FILM, 3/4 OR 1/2 IN VIDEO K-P
Recounts the encounter between Tom the Cat and the gravedigger.
Prod-SCHNDL Dist-WWS 1984

King Of The Game Birds C 15 MIN
16MM FILM OPTICAL SOUND
Presents an unusual study of a German short hair pointer in the field grouse hunt.
Prod-SFI Dist-SFI

King Of The Hill C 13 MIN
16MM FILM, 3/4 OR 1/2 IN VIDEO I-C A
Uses analogy, based upon a child's game, to analyze the consideration of an array of concepts concerning individual and group interaction. Motivates thought and discussion rather than explaining or defining relationships.
Prod-BARR Dist-BARR 1971

King Of The Minors C 36 MIN
16MM FILM OPTICAL SOUND
Introduces Stan Wasiak, a minor league baseball manager for 30 years.
LC NO. 81-700417
Prod-UCLA Dist-UCLA 1980

King Of The Penny Arcade X 27 MIN
16MM FILM, 3/4 OR 1/2 IN VIDEO J-C A
Offers a look at alcoholism and loneliness by telling the story of an 18-year-old penny arcade operator.
Prod-PAULST Dist-MEDIAG

King Of The Roaring Twenties B 106 MIN
16MM FILM OPTICAL SOUND C A
Presents a drama starring David Janssen, Mickey Rooney and Jack Carson.
Prod-CINEWO Dist-CINEWO 1961

King Of The World C 58 MIN
1/2 IN VIDEO CASSETTE BETA/VHS
Originally shown as The Other Side Of The Track. Presents an insider's look at the 'sport of Kings,' horse racing, visiting places such as Belmont in New York, where the rich indulge their interest in racing, and Great Barrington in Massachusetts, where infirm horses run for purses that can barely pay feed bills.
From The Frontline Series.
Prod-DOCCON Dist-PBS

King Rat B 134 MIN
16MM FILM OPTICAL SOUND H-C A
Stars George Segal in a study of human existence under the most adverse conditions and a prisoner-of-war con artist who manipulates the other prisoners for his own benefit.
Prod-CPC Dist-TIMLIF 1965

King Rollo And King Frank C 5 MIN
16MM FILM, 3/4 OR 1/2 IN VIDEO K-I
See series title for descriptive statement.
From The King Rollo Series.
Prod-PERSPF Dist-CORF 1981

King Rollo And The Balloons C 5 MIN
16MM FILM, 3/4 OR 1/2 IN VIDEO K-I
See series title for descriptive statement.
From The King Rollo Series.
Prod-PERSPF Dist-CORF 1981

King Rollo And The Bath C 5 MIN
16MM FILM, 3/4 OR 1/2 IN VIDEO K-I
See series title for descriptive statement.
From The King Rollo Series.
Prod-PERSPF Dist-CORF 1981

King Rollo And The Birthday C 5 MIN
16MM FILM, 3/4 OR 1/2 IN VIDEO K-I
See series title for descriptive statement.
From The King Rollo Series.
Prod-PERSPF Dist-CORF 1981

King Rollo And The Bread C 5 MIN
16MM FILM, 3/4 OR 1/2 IN VIDEO K-I
See series title for descriptive statement.
From The King Rollo Series.
Prod-PERSPF Dist-CORF 1981

King Rollo And The Breakfast C 5 MIN
16MM FILM, 3/4 OR 1/2 IN VIDEO K-I
See series title for descriptive statement.
From The King Rollo Series.
Prod-PERSPF Dist-CORF 1981

King Rollo And The Comic C 5 MI
16MM FILM, 3/4 OR 1/2 IN VIDEO K
See series title for descriptive statement.
From The King Rollo Series.
Prod-PERSPF Dist-CORF 198

King Rollo And The Dishes C 5 MI
16MM FILM, 3/4 OR 1/2 IN VIDEO K
See series title for descriptive statement.
From The King Rollo Series.
Prod-PERSPF Dist-CORF 198

King Rollo And The Dog C 5 MI
16MM FILM, 3/4 OR 1/2 IN VIDEO K-
See series title for descriptive statement.
From The King Rollo Series.
Prod-PERSPF Dist-CORF 198

King Rollo And The New Shoes C 5 MI
16MM FILM, 3/4 OR 1/2 IN VIDEO K-
See series title for descriptive statement.
From The King Rollo Series.
Prod-PERSPF Dist-CORF 198

King Rollo And The Playroom C 5 MIN
16MM FILM, 3/4 OR 1/2 IN VIDEO K-I
See series title for descriptive statement.
From The King Rollo Series.
Prod-PERSPF Dist-CORF 1981

King Rollo And The Search C 5 MIN
16MM FILM, 3/4 OR 1/2 IN VIDEO K-I
See series title for descriptive statement.
From The King Rollo Series.
Prod-PERSPF Dist-CORF 1981

King Rollo And The Tree C 5 MIN
16MM FILM, 3/4 OR 1/2 IN VIDEO K-I
See series title for descriptive statement.
From The King Rollo Series.
Prod-PERSPF Dist-CORF 1981

King Rollo—A Series
16MM FILM, 3/4 OR 1/2 IN VIDEO K-I
Presents the adventures of King Rollo and his cohorts, including Queen Gwen, the Magician, the Cook and Hamlet the Cat.
Prod-PERSPF Dist-CORF 1981

King Rollo And King Frank 005 MIN
King Rollo And The Balloons 005 MIN
King Rollo And The Bath 005 MIN
King Rollo And The Birthday 005 MIN
King Rollo And The Bread 005 MIN
King Rollo And The Breakfast 005 MIN
King Rollo And The Comic 005 MIN
King Rollo And The Dishes 005 MIN
King Rollo And The Dog 005 MIN
King Rollo And The New Shoes 005 MIN
King Rollo And The Playroom 005 MIN
King Rollo And The Search 005 MIN
King Rollo And The Tree 005 MIN

King Tut Exhibition, The C 10 MIN
3/4 OR 1/2 INCH VIDEO CASSETTE
Tours the King Tut exhibit and gives background on the items viewed.
Prod-UPI Dist-JOU

King Vat - Introduction To Decimals C 13 MIN
16MM FILM, 3/4 OR 1/2 IN VIDEO I-J
Uses animation to discuss the metric system and decimal notation.
From The Math That Counts Series.
Prod-DAVFMS Dist-EBEC

King's Hunchback, The B 30 MIN
16MM FILM OPTICAL SOUND
Dramatizes episodes in the life of German-Jewish philosopher Moses Mendelssohn, who, in 1760, challenged Frederick the Great of Prussia on the question of freedom of religion. (Kinescope)
Prod-JTS Dist-NAAJS Prodn-NBCTV 1952

King's Mountain C 28 MIN
16MM FILM, 3/4 OR 1/2 IN VIDEO I-H
Presents a re-creation of the bitter struggles of southern colonists during the Revolutionary War. Deals with one group of militia from North Carolina, known as the Overmountain Men. Focuses on their leaders' decision of whether to seek revenge on the British. Explains that he must take into consideration that many of his men had brothers fighting on the British side.
From The Decades Of Decision - The American Revolution News.
LC NO. 80-706342
Prod-NGS Dist-NGS 1975

King's New Suit, The C 14 MIN
16MM FILM OPTICAL SOUND
A Japanese language film. Uses puppets and animation to tell the Hans Christian Andersen story of 'THE EMPEROR'S NEW CLOTHES.'
Prod-UNIJAP Dist-UNIJAP 1968

King's Secret, The C 12 MIN
16MM FILM OPTICAL SOUND
Tells the story of a king who tried to hide the fact that he had long ears.
From The Animatoons Series.
LC NO. FIA67-5709
Prod-ANTONS Dist-RADTV 1968

Kingdom Come School, The C 22 MIN
16MM FILM - 3/4 IN VIDEO H A
Teacher Harding Ison employs temporary teaching methods to

instruct pupils in a one room schoolhouse in eastern Kentucky. His views are contrasted with the county's rationale for consolidation.
Prod-APPAL Dist-APPAL 1973

Kingdom Of Bronze C 52 MIN
16MM FILM, 3/4 OR 1/2 IN VIDEO
Traces the development of bronze casting techniques practiced by the Beni tribe of Nigeria. Shows examples of Beni bronze artifacts and explains the lost wax process used by Nigerians in bronze casting in the 1970's.
From The Tribal Eye Series.
LC NO. 79-707113
Prod-BBCTV Dist-TIMLIF 1976

Kingdom Of Could Be You—A Series
16MM FILM, 3/4 OR 1/2 IN VIDEO K-I
Deals with children's aspirations and abilities to become problem-solvers and doers in society. Introduces the wizard, who helps the animated children to try out many adult-world activities as they set about helping the wizard solve the problems of his kingdom.
Prod-EBEC Dist-EBEC

Agribusiness	6 MIN
Business And Office	6 MIN
Communication	6 MIN
Construction	6 MIN
Consumer Homemaking	6 MIN
Environment	6 MIN
Fine Arts And Humanities	6 MIN
Health	6 MIN
Kingdom Of Could Be You, The	6 MIN
Manufacturing	6 MIN
Marine Science	6 MIN
Marketing And Distribution	6 MIN
Personal Service	6 MIN
Public Service	6 MIN
Recreation - Hospitality - Tourism	6 MIN
Transportation	6 MIN

Kingdom Of Could Be You, The C 6 MIN
16MM FILM, 3/4 OR 1/2 IN VIDEO K-I
Presents an animated film showing a wide variety of occupations, including marine science, public service and communications.
From The Kingdom Of Could Be You Series.
Prod-EBEC Dist-EBEC 1974

Kingdom Of Kite—A Series
16MM FILM, 3/4 OR 1/2 IN VIDEO P-J
Uses animation to illustrate how knowledge is interrelated as the heroes of Kite are forced to combine their specialized skills in order to solve the emergencies oppressing this little monarchy.
Prod-KINGSP Dist-PHENIX 1971

Big Is Lots Of Things	11 MIN
How Hot Is A Dragon	11 MIN
Numbskulls And Crossbones	11 MIN
One, Two, Plop	11 MIN

Kingdom Of Mocha C 27 MIN
16MM FILM OPTICAL SOUND J-H
Offers an introduction to the important economic concepts that have shaped the free enterprise society. Presents Mocha, a mythical island whose delightful inhabitants experience rapid change as their economy develops from primitive barter to complex modern day problems.
Prod-STOIND Dist-MTP

Kingdom Of The Crooked Mirrors C 80 MIN
16MM FILM OPTICAL SOUND P-I
Prod-FI Dist-FI

Kingdoms Of The Western Sudan B 30 MIN
16MM FILM OPTICAL SOUND J-C A
Professor Joseph E Harris surveys the development of political structures, economic systems, and intellectual currents in the kingdoms of Ghana, Mali, and SonGhai, and assesses the impact of Islam on these kingdoms. Points out the use of various trade routes and describes how they affected the various people who lived along them.
From The Black History Series.
LC NO. 70-704034
Prod-WCBSTV Dist-HRAW 1969

Kingfisher C 20 MIN
16MM FILM, 3/4 OR 1/2 IN VIDEO I-H
Deals with the kingfisher, looking at its technique for capturing fish, mating and nesting behavior, domestic arrangements, and the hazards it faces in summer and winter.
From The RSPB Collection Series.
LC NO. 83-707234
Prod-RSFPB Dist-BCNFL 1983

Kings Mountain - Turning Point Of The South C 19 MIN
16MM FILM - 3/4 IN VIDEO A
Tells how the Blue Ridge Mountain men thwarted a British thrust through the western part of the Carolinas during the American Revolution. Issued in 1975 as a motion picture.
LC NO. 79-706133
Prod-USNPS Dist-USNAC Prodn-VISION 1979

Kings Of Beasts C 25 MIN
16MM FILM OPTICAL SOUND
Shows how the lion became known as 'the king of the beasts.'
LC NO. 77-702935
Prod-WESFAL Dist-MARMO 1976

Kings, Fools And Liars C 35 MIN
1/2 IN VIDEO CASSETTE (VHS) P-I
Features storyteller Carolyn Horovitz presenting two traditional folktales called The King Who Was A Gentleman, and The Jolly Tailor.
LC NO. 80-706113
Prod-BLUHER Dist-BLUHER 1980

Kings' Accordion, The B 22 MIN
16MM FILM OPTICAL SOUND H-C A
Explores the part played by primitive rituals within the social framework of life in Madagascar. Asks if they are mere entertainment or if they represent a resistance to the processes of evolution.
Prod-NYFLMS Dist-NYFLMS

Kingsnake Predation On Rattlesnakes C 9 MIN
16MM FILM, 3/4 OR 1/2 IN VIDEO I-C A
Records the attack and eating of a sidewinder rattlesnake by a kingsnake. Demonstrates the immunity of kingsnakes to rattlesnake venom and examines the process of subduing the prey by constriction.
From The Aspects Of Animal Behavior Series.
Prod-UCLA Dist-UCEMC 1978

Kingston Olympiad C 57 MIN
16MM FILM, 3/4 OR 1/2 IN VIDEO
Looks at the first appearance of the dramatic Tornado catamaran at the 1976 Canadian Olympic games.
Prod-OFFSHR Dist-OFFSHR 1976

Kinsey Reports, The C
3/4 OR 1/2 INCH VIDEO CASSETTE PRO
See series title for descriptive statement.
From The Independent Study In Human Sexuality Series.
Prod-MMRC Dist-MMRC

Kinship And Descent, Pt 1 C 30 MIN
3/4 INCH VIDEO CASSETTE C A
Reviews some of the ways our culture incorporates kinship and descent considerations. Focuses on some ways in which other cultures are organized around descent patterns.
From The Faces Of Culture - Studies In Cultural Anthropology Series. Lesson 11
Prod-COAST Dist-CDTEL Prodn-HRAW

Kinship And Descent, Pt 2 C 30 MIN
3/4 INCH VIDEO CASSETTE C A
Considers whether or not there is a relationship between subsistence patterns and the degree of importance placed on kinship and descent. Diagrams and illustrates some of the six major systems of classifying kin.
From The Faces Of Culture - Studies In Cultural Anthropology Series. Lesson 12
Prod-COAST Dist-CDTEL Prodn-HRAW

Kinships C 11 MIN
16MM FILM, 3/4 OR 1/2 IN VIDEO J-C A
Probes various values in the parent-teenager relationship.
From The Vignettes Series.
Prod-PAULST Dist-PAULST 1973

Kipnuk - Moving Forward C 30 MIN
16MM FILM OPTICAL SOUND
Gives an account of the village and people of Kipnuk, Alaska, in terms of the children and activities of the Kipnuk Village School. Shows the role of the Parent Advisory Council and its success in getting parents involved in all phases of their children's education.
LC NO. 77-700061
Prod-USBIA Dist-BAILYL Prodn-BAILYL 1976

Kipps B 86 MIN
16MM FILM OPTICAL SOUND
Stars Michael Redgrave as a draper's assistant who becomes wealthy through an inheritance. Directed by Carol Reed.
Prod-TWCF Dist-KITPAR 1937

KIPS-TV Interview By Roger Allen C 60 MIN
3/4 OR 1/2 INCH VIDEO CASSETTE
Tells about Sri Gurudev's life and shows him answering questions.
Prod-IYOGA Dist-IYOGA

Kirby Stanat On Jobs—A Series
H-C A
Presents Kirby Stanat giving advice on job hunting. Covers such topics as resumes, cover letters, question answering techniques in job interviews and etiquette.
Prod-SUMITP Dist-GPITVL 1983

Avenues To Interviews	030 MIN
Interview, The, Pt 1	030 MIN
Interview, The, Pt 2 And Beyond	030 MIN
Job Hunting Tips And Review	030 MIN
Tools Of Job Hunting	030 MIN

Kirk - American Furniture—A Series

Focuses on the American furniture created between the 17th and 19th centuries. Explains how and why different pieces were made, where the ideas originated, how the pieces serve as documents of past lifestyles, and the importance of aesthetic judgment about furniture.
Prod-WGBHTV Dist-PUBTEL

Dating And Style	029 MIN
High Style, Country, Primitive, Rustic	029 MIN
In The Beginning	028 MIN
Quality In Design	029 MIN

Kirkpatrick Plays Bach C 60 MIN
3/4 INCH VIDEO CASSETTE
Presents harpsichordist Ralph Kirkpatrick giving a recital of music by Johann Sebastian Bach.
Prod-MDCPB Dist-MDCPB

Kirtland's Warbler Bird Of Fire, The C 10 MIN
3/4 OR 1/2 INCH VIDEO CASSETTE J-C A
Illustrates how the Kirtland Warbler is an endangered species, and how management programs protect the very existence of this little warbler found nesting exclusively in Jack Pine forests in Michigan.
Prod-BERLET Dist-BERLET

Kiruna C 15 MIN
16MM FILM OPTICAL SOUND
Shows Kiruna, Sweden's largest mining center above the Arctic circle, in its magnificent natural surroundings.
Prod-ASI Dist-AUDPLN

Kisan B 10 MIN
16MM FILM OPTICAL SOUND I-C A
Presents the Indian farmer in the age-long historical perspective and explains how he becomes the very pivot of the national economy.
Prod-INDIA Dist-NEDINF

Kishan Who Dreamed Of Flying C 13 MIN
16MM FILM, 3/4 OR 1/2 IN VIDEO P-I
Tells the story of a young East Indian boy named Kishan who studies and plans to make an airplane and endures the punishments of a stern teacher for his inattention. Shows that in the end, it is the teacher who learns a lesson.
LC NO. 82-706567
Prod-CENTET Dist-CF 1980

Kiss Me Petruchio C 58 MIN
16MM FILM, 3/4 OR 1/2 IN VIDEO J-C A
Goes behind the scene of the New York Shakespeare Festival production of The Taming Of The Shrew starring Meryl Streep and Raul Julia. Discusses what makes a 400-year-old play relevant to a modern audience.
LC NO. 84-706184
Prod-NYSF Dist-FI 1982

Kiss Of Death, The B 4 MIN
3/4 OR 1/2 INCH VIDEO CASSETTE
Presents a gangster spoof, includes a don, his moll, hit-men, chase scenes and a zany rubout.
Prod-DENONN Dist-DENOPX

Kiss The Animals Goodbye C 20 MIN
16MM FILM, 3/4 OR 1/2 IN VIDEO H-C A
Presents a realistic picture of what happens inside a large animal shelter where caring shelter workers must dispose of 40,000 abandoned dogs and cats each year. Discusses the tragic results of uncontrolled breeding and irresponsible human behavior.
Prod-FRIEDL Dist-PFP

Kiss The Girls - Make Them Cry C 7 MIN
3/4 OR 1/2 INCH VIDEO CASSETTE
See series title for descriptive statement.
From The Five Short Works By Dana Birnbaum Series.
Prod-EAI Dist-EAI

Kiss The Girls - Make Them Cry C 7 MIN
3/4 OR 1/2 INCH VIDEO CASSETTE
Extracts 'iconic women' and 'receding men' from television's game show, Hollywood Squares.
Prod-KITCHN Dist-KITCHN

Kisses C 55 MIN
16MM FILM OPTICAL SOUND
Uses a collage of footage from feature films, newsreels and old television serials in a humorous study of the kiss in film.
LC NO. 76-703064
Prod-CANFDC Dist-CANFDC 1975

Kissimmee C 15 MIN
16MM FILM OPTICAL SOUND
Features the community of Kissimmee, Florida.
Prod-FLADC Dist-FLADC

Kissinger In Retrospect C 89 MIN
3/4 OR 1/2 INCH VIDEO CASSETTE
Analyzes the diplomatic approach of former Secretary of State Henry Kissinger. Includes comment from the leaders of France, Egypt, and Israel.
Prod-WETATV Dist-PBS

Kissinger Profile, The C 27 MIN
3/4 OR 1/2 INCH VIDEO CASSETTE H-C A
Follows the career of Henry Kissinger, who drastically changed American foreign policy during the 1970's.
Prod-UPI Dist-JOU

Kit Car - Final Inspection C 30 MIN
1/2 IN VIDEO CASSETTE BETA/VHS
Checks out a kit car before it is test driven. Considers whether door guards are necessary to protect against scratches. Features an AMC Encore.
From The Last Chance Garage Series.
Prod-WGBHTV Dist-MTI

Kit Carson B 20 MIN
2 INCH VIDEOTAPE I
See series title for descriptive statement.
From The Americans All Series.
Prod-DENVPS Dist-GPITVL Prodn-KRMATV

Kita, Or, What Have You Done For Me Lately C 25 MIN
16MM FILM - 3/4 IN VIDEO IND
Explains in details the motivation-hygiene theory with an in-depth analysis of hygiene—what it is, why it escalates, why it does not motivate and how to manage it as a necessary part of the work environment. Shows typical employee reactions to management's efforts to use hygiene as a motivator.
From The Motivation To Work Series.
Prod-BNA Dist-BNA 1969

Kitchen Cocktail Party C 29 MIN
3/4 OR 1/2 INCH VIDEO CASSETTE
See series title for descriptive statement.
From The Julia Child And Company Series.
Prod-WGBHTV Dist-PBS

Kitchen Crafts C 29 MIN
2 INCH VIDEOTAPE

See series title for descriptive statement.
From The Commonwealth Series.
Prod-WITFTV Dist-PUBTEL

Kitchen Equipment C
3/4 INCH VIDEO CASSETTE H A
Helps viewer develop guidelines for assembling a functional and economic collection of kitchen equipment. Stresses choosing quality equipment.
From The Matter Of Taste Series. Lesson 2
Prod-COAST Dist-CDTEL

Kitchen Fire Safety (Rev Ed) C
16MM FILM, 3/4 OR 1/2 IN VIDEO
Provides housekeeping and basic fire safety knowledge in preventing the start and spread of kitchen fires. Reviews common hazards emphasizing grease fires and the cleaning of the hood and duct system, and shows how to use fire extinguishers and fire alarms.
From The Professional Food Preparation And Service Programs Series.
Prod-NEM Dist-NEM 1983

Kitchen Knives - Safe And Efficient Use C 11 MIN
16MM FILM, 3/4 OR 1/2 IN VIDEO
Shows how to handle knives to speed and simplify cutting of a wide variety of foods. Demonstrates the use of the chef's knife for chopping, dicing and slicing and of the paring knife for peeling and other small cutting tasks. Covers critical hand coordination skills, and the care and cleaning of knives.
From The Professional Food Preparation And Service Programs Series.
Prod-NEM Dist-NEM 1983

Kitchen Management Principles C 13 MIN
16MM FILM OPTICAL SOUND I-C A
Presents five concepts dealing with kitchen management --the kitchen, planning for efficiency, cleanliness and safety, setting the table and washing up. The projector may be stopped after each concept.
From The Cooking, Home Economics Series.
LC NO. FIA68-1373
Prod-MORLAT Dist-SF 1968

Kitchen Physics C 30 MIN
16MM FILM OPTICAL SOUND T
Follows a sixth-grade class in Vermont as they use an elementary science study unit. Shows their activities with their teacher in exploring the behavior of water, designing experiments and predicting scientific findings.
From The Elementary Science Study Series.
LC NO. 75-701393
Prod-NSF Dist-EDC 1971

Kitchen Remodeling - Kitchen Cabinets, Counter Tops C 30 MIN
1/2 IN VIDEO CASSETTE BETA/VHS
See series title for descriptive statement.
From The Wally's Workshop Series.
Prod-KARTES Dist-KARTES

Kitchen Safety - Preventing Cuts And Strains C 8 MIN
16MM FILM, 3/4 OR 1/2 IN VIDEO J A
Shows safety rules as the use of the right tool for the job, procedures of sharpening and cutting, storage and maintenance of cutlery. Includes the proper methods for lifting and carrying.
From The Professional Food Preparation And Service Program Series.
Prod-NEM Dist-NEM 1969

Kitchen Safety - Preventing Falls C 8 MIN
16MM FILM, 3/4 OR 1/2 IN VIDEO J-C A
Shows simple rules for safety in the kitchen, including care of floor and stairs and safe use of ladders.
From The Professional Food Preparation And Service Program Series.
Prod-NEM Dist-NEM 1967

Kitchen Safety - Preventing Machine Injuries C 8 MIN
16MM FILM, 3/4 OR 1/2 IN VIDEO J A
Demonstrates safe methods of operating and cleaning equipment.
From The Professional Food Preparation And Service Program Series.
Prod-NEM Dist-NEM 1969

Kitchen Safety - Preventing Machine Injuries (French) C 8 MIN
16MM FILM, 3/4 OR 1/2 IN VIDEO J A
Demonstrates safe methods of operating and cleaning equipment.
From The Professional Food Preparation And Service Program (French) Series.
Prod-NEM Dist-NEM 1969

Kitchen Safety - Preventing Machine Injuries (German) C 8 MIN
16MM FILM, 3/4 OR 1/2 IN VIDEO J A
Demonstrates safe methods of operating and cleaning equipment.
From The Professional Food Preparation And Service Program (German) Series.
Prod-NEM Dist-NEM 1969

Kitchen Safety - Preventing Machine Injuries (Spanish) C 8 MIN
16MM FILM, 3/4 OR 1/2 IN VIDEO J A
Demonstrates safe methods of operating and cleaning equipment.
From The Professional Food Preparation And Service Program (Spanish) Series.
Prod-NEM Dist-NEM 1969

Kitchen Tools C 30 MIN
3/4 OR 1/2 INCH VIDEO CASSETTE
Presents guests who are experts in their respective fields who share tips on collecting and caring for antique kitchen tools.
From The Antique Shop Series.
Prod-WVPTTV Dist-MDCPB

Kitchen Utensil Identification C 11 MIN
3/4 OR 1/2 INCH VIDEO CASSETTE PRO
Shows how to extract the garlic clove and demonstrates the proper use of the chef's knife and paring knife to prepare the clove for use in different recipes.
Prod-CULINA Dist-CULINA

Kite Magic C 9 MIN
16MM FILM OPTICAL SOUND
Encourages the sport of kite flying by explaining the construction of three different kites, including a simple plastic kite, a bird kite and a box kite.
LC NO. 75-701974
Prod-FLMART Dist-FLMART 1976

Kite Story, A C 25 MIN
16MM FILM, 3/4 OR 1/2 IN VIDEO P-I
A story about a boy, two kites, and the stranger who makes the kites.
Prod-CF Dist-CF 1969

Kite Tale, A C 16 MIN
16MM FILM, 3/4 OR 1/2 IN VIDEO K-I
Presents a story about a boy who has trouble flying a kite and a man who shows the boy how to build a kite using materials they find around them.
Prod-MINTZM Dist-PHENIX 1975

Kite, The C 10 MIN
16MM FILM OPTICAL SOUND
Presents a story about a boy and his frustrations and eventual success as he designs and builds a kite.
LC NO. 75-701587
Prod-IBMSGC Dist-MTP Prodn-CORWNR 1975

Kitemen C 15 MIN
16MM FILM OPTICAL SOUND
Follows the competition at the National Delta Wing Kite Tournament in Cypress Gardens, Florida.
Prod-FLADC Dist-FLADC

Kites - A Collage Of Kites And Kiteflyers C 28 MIN
16MM FILM, 3/4 OR 1/2 IN VIDEO I-C A
Places the craft of kite making in different cultural and historical contexts. Shows that kite building and flying is a skilled craft and always a source of great pleasure.
Prod-COMPSS Dist-LUF 1983

Kites Are Quadrilaterals C 14 MIN
16MM FILM OPTICAL SOUND I-H
Shows one of the possible developments arising from the order of generality of the quadrilaterals. Begins with the general quadrilateral and proceeds to trapezoids, parallelograms and kites, their meaning and their properties.
LC NO. FIA67-54
Prod-MMP Dist-MMP 1964

Kites To Capsules C 5 MIN
16MM FILM, 3/4 OR 1/2 IN VIDEO A
Shows in fast moving humor the contrasts of early flying attempts with modern, successful commercial and general aviation.
Prod-FAAFL Dist-AVIMA 1969

Kitkatla - A Community Involvement In Education C 28 MIN
16MM FILM OPTICAL SOUND H-C A
Presents a documentary about the interaction and mutual involvement of school and community in British Columbia Indian culture.
LC NO. 74-703080
Prod-SFRASU Dist-SFRASU 1972

Kittens Are Born C 10 MIN
16MM FILM, 3/4 OR 1/2 IN VIDEO I-J
Follows a mother cat from her pregnancy through labor and the birth of three kittens. Emphasizes the birth process and the postnatal care.
Prod-JHNSTN Dist-MGHT 1971

Kittens Grow Up C 10 MIN
16MM FILM, 3/4 OR 1/2 IN VIDEO I-J
Follows the development of kittens from the time immediately after birth before their eyes are open, through learning to walk, to their mature coordination. Emphasizes the stages of development and how the mother cat encourages their development.
Prod-JHNSTN Dist-MGHT 1971

Kitty - A Return To Auschwitz C 90 MIN
16MM FILM, 3/4 OR 1/2 IN VIDEO H-C A
Introduces Kitty Felix Hart, who spent her teen years as an inmate in the Auschwitz death camp and remembers her experiences there.
Prod-TRIDNT Dist-FI 1981

Kitty - Return To Auschwitz C
1/2 IN VIDEO CASSETTE BETA/VHS
Presents a documentary about a concentration-camp survivor who returns to Auschwitz so that 'we will never forget'.
Prod-GA Dist-GA

Kitty Hawk To Paris - The Heroic Years C 30 MIN
16MM FILM, 3/4 OR 1/2 IN VIDEO J-H A
Recalls the early years of American aviation in the exploits of its heroes, including the Wright Brothers, pilots of World War I, barnstormers, airmail flyers and Charles Lindbergh. Edited from the 1970 film Kitty Hawk To Paris - The Heroic Years.
Prod-SCNDRI Dist-LCOA 1976

Kitty Hawk To Paris - The Heroic Years C 54 MIN
16MM FILM, 3/4 OR 1/2 IN VIDEO J-H A
Depicts the first chapter in the continuing story of men who fly--their successes, failures and sacrifices which blazed the trail that leads from Kitty Hawk to Paris.
Prod-SCNDRI Dist-LCOA 1970

Kiwanis Convention C 20 MIN
16MM FILM OPTICAL SOUND
Depicts the 56th annual kiwanis convention held in San Francisco which features Dr Billy Graham as the speaker. Features Dr Graham's address on 'AMERICA AND ITS ROLE IN SHAPING THE WORLD'S DESTINY.'
Prod-WWP Dist-NINEFC

Klaipedos Atvadavimas (Lithuanian) B 20 MIN
3/4 OR 1/2 INCH VIDEO CASSETTE
Offers original newsreel footage of the military seizure of Klaipeda by Lithuanian rebels in 1923.
Prod-IHF Dist-IHF

Klan Youth Corps C 11 MIN
16MM FILM, 3/4 OR 1/2 IN VIDEO H-C A
Reveals how Ku Klux Klan leaders are reaching out to recruit young people. Originally shown on the CBS television show 30 Minutes.
LC NO. 81-706837
Prod-CBSNEW Dist-CAROUF 1980

Klan, The - A Legacy Of Hate In America C 30 MIN
16MM FILM, 3/4 OR 1/2 IN VIDEO H-C A
Shows that despite its efforts to change its image, the Ku Klux Klan's traditions of lynching, bigotry and intimidation continue in the 1980s against Vietnamese and Mexicans as well as Blacks.
LC NO. 84-706064
Prod-GUG Dist-FI 1982

Kleenex C 1 MIN
3/4 OR 1/2 INCH VIDEO CASSETTE
Shows a classic television commercial in which Manners the butler saves the day.
Prod-BROOKC Dist-BROOKC

Kluane, Yukon Territory C 15 MIN
16MM FILM OPTICAL SOUND
Presents examples of the wildlife of the Canadian Yukon Territory.
LC NO. 74-701185
Prod-WILFGP Dist-WILFGP 1973

Klyde - Recurvirostra (Avocet) C 4 MIN
16MM FILM OPTICAL SOUND
Presents a description of the avocet in its natural surroundings. Includes sound effects.
Prod-STATNS Dist-STATNS 1965

Klystrons B 34 MIN
16MM FILM - 3/4 IN VIDEO
Shows the purpose of components and operation of a two-cavity klystron. Traces a signal through the circuit and points out the difference between velocity and density modulation. Demonstrates the operation of the klystron as an amplifier and oscillator.
LC NO. 79-707772
Prod-USAF Dist-USNAC 1979

Knacky People C 24 MIN
16MM FILM, 3/4 OR 1/2 IN VIDEO J-C A
Looks at the work of blacksmiths.
Prod-GARNIA Dist-WOMBAT

Knaves And Fools C 30 MIN
3/4 OR 1/2 INCH VIDEO CASSETTE C
See series title for descriptive statement.
From The Art Of Being Human Series. Module 8
Prod-MDCC Dist-MDCC

Knee And Ankle Injuries C 17 MIN
3/4 OR 1/2 INCH VIDEO CASSETTE
Discusses knee and ankle injuries, emergency evaluation and treatment.
From The Emergency Management - The First 30 Minutes, Vol II Series.
Prod-VTRI Dist-VTRI

Knee Joint, The C 16 MIN
16MM FILM, 3/4 OR 1/2 IN VIDEO PRO
Details the articulation between the femur and tibia as demonstrated with dry bones. Shows the menisci with their ligaments on a wet specimen.
From The Cine-Prosector Series.
Prod-AVCORP Dist-TEF

Knee, The C 30 MIN
3/4 OR 1/2 INCH VIDEO CASSETTE
Explains how a damaged knee can cut short an athletic career, and discusses how, with proper protection and rehabilitation, an athlete can realize his or her full potential and avoid the hazards of damaged cartilage.
From The Athletic Trainer Series.
Prod-NETCHE Dist-NETCHE 1972

Knee, The C 30 MIN
3/4 OR 1/2 INCH VIDEO CASSETTE
Examines the knee for rheumatoid arthritis, meniscus, medial collaterial ligaments, cruciate ligaments coronary ligaments and quadriceps.
From The Cyriax On Orthopaedic Medicine Series.
Prod-VTRI Dist-VTRI

Knees C 29 MIN
2 INCH VIDEOTAPE
See series title for descriptive statement.

From The Maggie And The Beautiful Machine - Feet And Legs Series.
Prod-WGBHTV Dist-PUBTEL

Knife Edge Of Deterrence, The C 60 MIN
16MM FILM, 3/4 OR 1/2 IN VIDEO C A
Serves as companion piece to the War Series. Contains alternate, authoritative points of view on the most salient issues. Features government figures, defense strategists, military specialists, political scientists, historians and philosophers focusing primarily on deterrence viewed as the central strategic idea of this time.
Prod-KCTSTV Dist-FI

Knife In The Head (German) C 108 MIN
16MM FILM OPTICAL SOUND
Tells how a scientist is accidentally shot in the head during a police raid at a radical hangout. Describes his struggle to overcome brain damage and shows how both the police and the radicals try to manipulate him for their own purposes. Directed by Reinhard Hauff. With English subtitles.
Prod-UNKNWN Dist-NYFLMS 1978

Knife In The Water (Polish) B 94 MIN
16MM FILM OPTICAL SOUND
Presents a study of three characters in the confining setting of a sailboat on one of the lovely but littleknown Polish lakes. Includes English subtitles.
Prod-UNKNWN Dist-KITPAR 1962

Knight's Tale, The B 30 MIN
1 INCH VIDEOTAPE A
See series title for descriptive statement.
From The Canterbury Tales Series.
Prod-UMITV Dist-UMITV 1967

Knights Of The Round Table C
1/2 IN VIDEO CASSETTE BETA/VHS
Tells the story of King Arthur and his sword Excalibur. Stars Robert Taylor and Ava Gardner.
Prod-GA Dist-GA

Knitting C
3/4 OR 1/2 INCH VIDEO CASSETTE
See series title for descriptive statement.
From The ITMA 1983 Review Series.
Prod-NCSU Dist-NCSU

Knitting C 14 MIN
2 INCH VIDEOTAPE
Shows how to knit a small sample called a gauge. Explains how to use a gauge in determining how many stitches to knit per inch. Gives information on casting on, knitting, purling and binding off.
From The Living Better II Series.
Prod-MAETEL Dist-PUBTEL

Knitting - Beginning With Kay Blanck C 93 MIN
1/2 INCH VIDEOTAPE J-H A
Introduction to knitting. Instruction and advice about needles, yarns and stitches.
From The Knitting Series.
LC NO. 84-706660
Prod-ANVICO Dist-ANVICO 1984

Knitting—A Series
J-H A
Introduces beginning knitting technique, carrying on for intermediate abilities, ends with the circular method.
Prod-ANVICO Dist-ANVICO 1984

Beginning Knitting	093 MIN
Circular Method Sweater	118 MIN
Intermediate Knitting	094 MIN

Knock At The Door C 18 MIN
16MM FILM OPTICAL SOUND
Shows what some state highway departments, union organizations and highway construction contractors are doing to train minority group persons to operate heavy highway construction equipment. Tells that there are opportunities for those who will seek training to improve their positions in the working force of the nation as well as their social standing.
LC NO. 74-704994
Prod-USDTFH Dist-USNAC 1970

Knock On Any Door B 100 MIN
16MM FILM OPTICAL SOUND J-C A
Stars Humphrey Bogart and John Derek in a drama of a sensitive youngster who dreams of escaping his slum environment.
Prod-CPC Dist-NAFVC

Knock On The Door, The C 60 MIN
16MM FILM OPTICAL SOUND
Relates that when Steven Cooper is arrested for an unspecified crime, his lawyer's defense is to call various members of the town as witnesses to testify as to how they have or have not helped Steven as he grew up. Shows that responsibility for his crime must be shared.
Prod-NBCTV Dist-CCNCC

Knockout, The B 23 MIN
16MM FILM OPTICAL SOUND
Presents a story about a boxer. Stars Fatty Arbuckle and Charlie Chaplin.
Prod-MSENP Dist-BHAWK 1914

Knots For Restraint C 31 MIN
1/2 IN VIDEO CASSETTE BETA/VHS
Demonstrates how to tie knots, including the double half hitch, the square knot and the hondu.
Prod-COLOSU Dist-EQVDL

Know And Think C 15 MIN
3/4 OR 1/2 INCH VIDEO CASSETTE
See series title for descriptive statement.
From The Children In Action Series.
Prod-LVN Dist-LVN

Know Exactly What To Do C 15 MIN
16MM FILM, 3/4 OR 1/2 IN VIDEO
Presents crime prevention techniques for bank tellers and other employees of financial institutions who might be involved in a robbery. Details how to act in a robbery, how to handle a note and how to activate several types of alarms. Stresses the importance of obtaining an immediate and accurate description of the robber and protecting fingerprints.
Prod-MTI Dist-MTI

Know Exactly What To Do (Spanish) C 15 MIN
16MM FILM, 3/4 OR 1/2 IN VIDEO
Provides instruction procedures to follow in case of a robbery. Helps reduce the possibility of personal injury. Stresses obtaining an accurate description of the robber and protecting fingerprints.
Prod-MTI Dist-MTI

Know The Facts C 16 MIN
3/4 OR 1/2 INCH VIDEO CASSETTE J A
Presents facts and definitions of alcoholism. Shows vignettes of drinking situations.
Prod-SUTHRB Dist-SUTHRB

Know The Land And The People—A Series

Explores the relationship between what people know, see and do and the environment around them. Presents the views of meteorologists, paleontologists, dolphin trainers, mining engineers, museum curators and maple syrup makers.
Prod-EKC Dist-MDCPB

Air	030 MIN
Desert, The	030 MIN
Mountains	030 MIN
Plains, The	030 MIN
Sea, The	030 MIN
Water	030 MIN

Know The Score C 11 MIN
3/4 OR 1/2 INCH VIDEO CASSETTE T
Tells how to interpret the many different kinds of standardized tests.
From The Tests Series.
Prod-WTVITV Dist-AITECH 1980

Know Thy Exit C 11 MIN
3/4 OR 1/2 INCH VIDEO CASSETTE
Emphasizes the importance of knowing where the exits are in a building in case of fire. Describes how to check for alternative exits if you are in a strange building.
Prod-FILCOM Dist-FILCOM

Know Thyself Road C 20 MIN
3/4 OR 1/2 INCH VIDEO CASSETTE
Focuses on finding out what kind of reader one is.
From The Efficient Reading - Instructional Tapes Series. Tape 1
Prod-TELSTR Dist-TELSTR

Know Your Air Rescue Service B 31 MIN
16MM FILM OPTICAL SOUND
Illustrates four phases of rescue operations notification, search, aid and rescue. Explains the work of the U S Air Rescue Service.
LC NO. FIE55-121
Prod-USAF Dist-USNAC 1954

Know Your Ally - Britain B 43 MIN
16MM FILM, 3/4 OR 1/2 IN VIDEO
Presents a film produced by Frank Capra for the Signal Corps in World War II. Helps improve the American soldier's understanding of the British and their habits and customs.
Prod-USAPS Dist-USNAC

Know Your Antiques I—A Series

Reveals displays of aging treasures, presented by nationally syndicated columnists, Ralph and Terry Kovel.
Prod-WVIZTV Dist-PUBTEL

Know Your Antiques III—A Series

Features Ralph and Terry Kovel appealing to the established antique collector and those people who are interested in antiques who would like to learn how to become wise collectors themselves.
Prod-WVIZTV Dist-PUBTEL

Know Your Antiques III, Program 19	30 MIN
Know Your Antiques III, Program 20	30 MIN
Know Your Antiques III, Program 21	30 MIN
Know Your Antiques III, Program 22	30 MIN
Know Your Antiques III, Program 23	30 MIN
Know Your Antiques III, Program 24	30 MIN
Know Your Antiques III, Program 25	30 MIN
Know Your Antiques III, Program 26	30 MIN

Know Your Antiques III, Program 19 C 30 MIN
2 INCH VIDEOTAPE
See series title for descriptive statement.
From The Know Your Antiques III Series.
Prod-WVIZTV Dist-PUBTEL

Know Your Antiques III, Program 20 C 30 MIN
2 INCH VIDEOTAPE
See series title for descriptive statement.
From The Know Your Antiques III Series.
Prod-WVIZTV Dist-PUBTEL

Know Your Antiques III, Program 21 C 30 MIN
2 INCH VIDEOTAPE
See series title for descriptive statement.
From The Know Your Antiques III Series.
Prod-WVIZTV Dist-PUBTEL

Know Your Antiques III, Program 22 C 30 MIN
2 INCH VIDEOTAPE
See series title for descriptive statement.
From The Know Your Antiques III Series.
Prod-WVIZTV Dist-PUBTEL

Know Your Antiques III, Program 23 C 30 MIN
2 INCH VIDEOTAPE
See series title for descriptive statement.
From The Know Your Antiques III Series.
Prod-WVIZTV Dist-PUBTEL

Know Your Antiques III, Program 24 C 30 MIN
2 INCH VIDEOTAPE
See series title for descriptive statement.
From The Know Your Antiques III Series.
Prod-WVIZTV Dist-PUBTEL

Know Your Antiques III, Program 25 C 30 MIN
3/4 OR 1/2 INCH VIDEO CASSETTE
See series title for descriptive statement.
From The Know Your Antiques III Series.
Prod-WVIZTV Dist-PBS

Know Your Antiques III, Program 26 C 30 MIN
2 INCH VIDEOTAPE
See series title for descriptive statement.
From The Know Your Antiques III Series.
Prod-WVIZTV Dist-PUBTEL

Know Your Baseball X 27 MIN
16MM FILM OPTICAL SOUND J-H
Demonstrates the rules of baseball through play situations and through split-screen and stop action photography.
LC NO. FIA68-1952
Prod-OSFS Dist-OSFS 1968

Know Your Basketball X 27 MIN
16MM FILM OPTICAL SOUND J-C
Presents various rules and infractions to rules for the game of basketball. Shows rule changes as advocated by various interscholastic physical education associations.
LC NO. FIA67-5035
Prod-NFSHSA Dist-OSFS Prodn-CALVIN 1967

Know Your Car B 15 MIN
16MM FILM OPTICAL SOUND
Explains how gasoline is converted into power and how brakes stop a car. Examines the electrical and coiling systems, the clutch, transmission and rear axle, various gages on the instrument panel and chassis construction.
LC NO. FIE52-317
Prod-USOE Dist-USNAC 1945

Know Your Clouds C 16 MIN
16MM FILM, 3/4 OR 1/2 IN VIDEO
Describes the development of the ten basic kinds of clouds, their principle characteristics, their relative positions and average attitudes and their flight hazards.
LC NO. 81-706648
Prod-USA Dist-USNAC 1967

Know Your Enemy - Japan B 63 MIN
3/4 OR 1/2 INCH VIDEO CASSETTE
Acquaints the American soldier with the fighting characteristics of the Japanese counterpart. Explores the reasons for Japan's rise to power.
Prod-IHF Dist-IHF

Know Your Enemy - Japan B 63 MIN
16MM FILM, 3/4 OR 1/2 IN VIDEO
Presents a documentary about Japan which was intended to show American servicemen during World War II the fighting characteristics of their Japanese counterparts. Directed by Frank Capra.
LC NO. 79-706579
Prod-USDD Dist-USNAC Prodn-USASC 1945

Know Your Enemy - The Viet Cong B 22 MIN
3/4 OR 1/2 INCH VIDEO CASSETTE
Shows captured newsreel produced by the Central Office of South Vietnam. Provides a comprehensive report on Vietcong activity in South Vietnam.
Prod-IHF Dist-IHF

Know Your Facts C 9 MIN
16MM FILM OPTICAL SOUND H-C A
Dramatizes the selling power of accurate and authoritative merchandise information. Provides a pattern for determining facts about merchandise and shows how these facts can be translated into performance benefits that represent buying appeals.
From The Professional Selling Practices Series 1 Series.
LC NO. 77-702359
Prod-SAUM Dist-SAUM Prodn-CALPRO 1967

Know Your Library (3rd Ed) C 13 MIN
16MM FILM, 3/4 OR 1/2 IN VIDEO J-C
Presents an knowledgeable and helpful librarian who guides three young people through the exciting possibilities in a library. Demonstrates reference materials, various guides and directories, books and magazines and a multitude of special collections and services.
Prod-CORF Dist-CORF 1983

Know Your Sprinkler System C 15 MIN
3/4 OR 1/2 INCH VIDEO CASSETTE
Examines basic sprinkler system design and outlines inspection and maintenance procedures.
Prod-NFPA Dist-NFPA

Knowing How To Drive Is Not Enough C 22 MIN
16MM FILM - 3/4 IN VIDEO
Shows the Liberty Mutual Insurance Company's driver safety program. Covers common emergency driving situations. Not available to elementary and junior high schools.
Prod-LIBMIC Dist-MTP Prodn-HALMIR 1977

Knowing One - Sophocles C 45 MIN
2 INCH VIDEOTAPE
See series title for descriptive statement.
From The Humanities Series. Unit II - The World Of Myth And Legend
Prod-WTTWTV Dist-GPITVL

Knowing The Prospect C 13 MIN
3/4 OR 1/2 INCH VIDEO CASSETTE
Shows the relationship of product or service benefits to the prospect's personal goals and illustrates the value of knowing a prospect's needs.
From The Basic Sales Series.
Prod-RESEM Dist-RESEM

Knowing The Rules C 30 MIN
3/4 OR 1/2 INCH VIDEO CASSETTE H-C A
Focuses on the rules that govern the structure of language, the sounds and letters, the formation of words and the structure of sentences. Emphasizes the relationship between rules and meaning.
From The Principles of Human Communication Series.
Prod-UMINN Dist-GPITVL 1983

Knowing Where You Stand C 15 MIN
16MM FILM, 3/4 OR 1/2 IN VIDEO
Explains effective and alternative inventory management control systems for small businesses.
Prod-USSBA Dist-USNAC

Knowing Where You're Going C 20 MIN
3/4 INCH VIDEO CASSETTE I-J
Explains the directions north, south, east and west.
From The Project Survival Series.
Prod-MAETEL Dist-GPITVL

Knowing Who You Are C 30 MIN
3/4 OR 1/2 INCH VIDEO CASSETTE
See series title for descriptive statement.
From The Rebop Series.
Prod-WGBHTV Dist-MDCPB

Knowing Your Employees - Individuals C 23 MIN
3/4 OR 1/2 INCH VIDEO CASSETTE
Shows supervisors how to become better leaders by teaching them why people behave as they do. Explains how supervisors can deal with, motivate, counsel and discipline subordinates.
Prod-AMA Dist-AMA

Knowing's Not Enough C 28 MIN
16MM FILM OPTICAL SOUND H-C A
Presents a safety film produced with the realization that knowledge of safety practices alone is just not enough, and that knowledge must be put into practice.
Prod-USSC Dist-USSC

Knowledge Acquisition Using Tieresias C 45 MIN
3/4 OR 1/2 INCH VIDEO CASSETTE PRO
Deals with errors of if-then rule systems, debugging, interpreting, second guessing, and final reviewing.
From The Artificial Intelligence - Pt 2, Expert Systems Series.
Prod-MIOT Dist-MIOT

Knowledge Acquisition Using Tieresias C 60 MIN
3/4 OR 1/2 INCH VIDEO CASSETTE C
See series title for descriptive statement.
From The Artificial Intellience, Pt II - Expert Systems Series.
Prod-MIOT Dist-AMCEE

Knowledge Bank, The C 25 MIN
3/4 INCH VIDEO CASSETTE
Shows how the tools in near-Earth space research have progressed since Benjamin Franklin's time to the sounding rockets and unmanned Earth-orbiting satellites of the 1970's. Pictures the type of data that is being collected by the U S National Aeronautics and Space Administration. Issued in 1971 as a motion picture.
From The Space In The 70's Series.
LC NO. 79-706965
Prod-NASA Dist-USNAC 1979

Knowledge Engineering C 45 MIN
3/4 OR 1/2 INCH VIDEO CASSETTE PRO
Features expert programs, questions of domain, system organization, and level of performance. Covers the tradeoff between generality and high performance, and The General Problem Solver versus systems based on if-then rules.
From The Artificial Intelligence - Pt 2, Expert Systems Series.
Prod-MIOT Dist-MIOT

Knowledge Engineering C 57 MIN
3/4 OR 1/2 INCH VIDEO CASSETTE C
See series title for descriptive statement.
From The Artificial Intelligence, Pt II - Expert Systems Series.
Prod-MIOT Dist-AMCEE

Knowledge Or Certainty C 52 MIN
16MM FILM, 3/4 OR 1/2 IN VIDEO J-C A
Considers the moral dilemma that confronts today's scientists. Contrasts the humanist tradition in science with some results that seem inhuman.
From The Ascent Of Man Series. No. 11
LC NO. 79-707234
Prod-BBCTV Dist-TIMLIF 1973

Known And The Unknown, The C 57 MIN
16MM FILM, 3/4 OR 1/2 IN VIDEO H-C A
Highlights the musical forms which emerged between the World Wars, especially jazz which was popularized by Louis Armstrong, Count Basie and George Gershwin. Views the works of Aaron Copland, who helped mature American music, and Martha Graham, who created a new dance form. Analyzes the effects of music and radio on American musical forms.
From The Music Of Man Series.
Prod-CANBC Dist-TIMLIF 1981

Knurling C 12 MIN
1/2 IN VIDEO CASSETTE BETA/VHS IND
See series title for descriptive statement.
From The Machine Shop - Engine Lathe Series.
Prod-RMI Dist-RMI

Knurling On The Lathe C
3/4 OR 1/2 INCH VIDEO CASSETTE
See series title for descriptive statement.
From The Basic Engine Lathe Series.
Prod-VTRI Dist-VTRI

Knurling On The Lathe C 15 MIN
3/4 OR 1/2 INCH VIDEO CASSETTE
See series title for descriptive statement.
From The Machine Technology I - Basic Machine Technology Series.
Prod-CAMB Dist-CAMB

Knurling On The Lathe C 15 MIN
3/4 OR 1/2 INCH VIDEO CASSETTE IND
See series title for descriptive statement.
From The Machining And The Operation Of Machine Tools, Module 2 - Engine Lathe Series.
Prod-LEIKID Dist-LEIKID

Knurling On The Lathe (Spanish) C
3/4 OR 1/2 INCH VIDEO CASSETTE
See series title for descriptive statement.
From The Basic Engine Lathe (Spanish) Series.
Prod-VTRI Dist-VTRI

Knute Rockne B 23 MIN
3/4 OR 1/2 INCH VIDEO CASSETTE
Presents the legendary football coach of Notre Dame and tells how he left an indelibe mark on American sports development. Features pictures, sound and special narration by Pat O'Brien reviewing the people and the games who made collegiate football history.
Prod-KINGFT Dist-KINGFT

Knute Rockne B 26 MIN
16MM FILM, 3/4 OR 1/2 IN VIDEO I-C
Uses rare actuality footage to portray the personal life and history-making deeds of Knute Rockne.
From The Biography Series.
Prod-WOLPER Dist-SF 1965

Knute Rockne - The Rock Of Notre Dame B 15 MIN
1/2 IN VIDEO CASSETTE BETA/VHS
Documents the football career of Knute Rockne, who played for Notre Dame.
Prod-STAR Dist-STAR

Koala C 21 MIN
16MM FILM OPTICAL SOUND I-C A
Portrays the unique koala bear, a marsupial who sustains himself on eucalyptus leaves and lives in treetops. Presents the life history of this strange little bear with sequences from birth to maturity, including the unusual sequence of a new-born koala, weighing one-eightieth of an ounce, crawling to his mother's upside-down pouch.
From The Australian Wildlife Series.
Prod-AVEXP Dist-AVEXP

Koalas C 11 MIN
16MM FILM, 3/4 OR 1/2 IN VIDEO P-J
Looks at Australia's unique marsupial, the koala, discussing its habits, habitat, and name origin. Offers a glimpse at other rare Australian mammals.
Prod-FLMAUS Dist-FLMFR

Koan C 3 MIN
3/4 OR 1/2 INCH VIDEO CASSETTE
Appears like a motion oil painting made with an electronic pallette knife.
From The TeleVisions Series.
Prod-WTV Dist-EAI

Kodak Ektagraphic 210 (Sound/Slide/Project/Viewer) C 11 MIN
3/4 OR 1/2 INCH VIDEO CASSETTE
See series title for descriptive statement.
From The Audio-Visual Skills Modules Series.
Prod-MDCC Dist-MDCC

Kodiak Island C 16 MIN
16MM FILM, 3/4 OR 1/2 IN VIDEO
Describes the bears, eagles and salmon of Kodiak Island in Alaska. Explains how predators and prey live in the roles assigned them by nature. Edited from the television program Wild, Wild World Of Animals.
From The Wild, Wild World Of Animals Series.
LC NO. 79-707919
Prod-TIMLIF Dist-TIMLIF 1976

Koen Og Kamelen (The Cow And The Camel) C 26 MIN
16MM FILM OPTICAL SOUND
A Danish language film. Describes everyday life on a farm which has been made a zoological park and where ordinary Danish domestic animals live side by side with many different animals from far-off countries. Shows the farmer's children helping to look after all the animals.
Prod-STATNS Dist-STATNS 1963

Koko - A Talking Gorilla C 85 MIN
16MM FILM OPTICAL SOUND
Looks at an experiment in primate communication. Shows how a San Francisco psychologist has taught sign language to Koko, a seven-year-old gorilla. Directed by Barbet Schroeder.
Prod-UNKNWN Dist-NYFLMS 1978

Kokoschka (1886-1977) C 11 MIN
16MM FILM OPTICAL SOUND
Presents the early paintings of Kokoschka from 1910 to 1940, showing the many changes through which his tortured soul struggled.
Prod-ROLAND Dist-NEW

Kol Nevelu (Lithuanian) B 95 MIN
3/4 OR 1/2 INCH VIDEO CASSETTE
A Lithuanian language film version of Before It's Too Late, a romantic comedy filmed on location in the Lithuanian fishing village of Palanga.
Prod-IHF Dist-IHF

Kolberg C 118 MIN
3/4 OR 1/2 INCH VIDEO CASSETTE
A German language motion picture. Re-creates the true story of a Prussian town's rebellion against Napoleon's army of occupation. Mirrors Hitler Germany's own war for survival. Reflects the spirit of fanatical resolve to fight on that Nazi propaganda was attempting to instill in the German people during the final years of World War II. With English Subtitles.
Prod-IHF Dist-IHF

Koltanowski On Chess—A Series

Offers anecdotes, combinations and tips drawn from host George Koltanowski's many years in the world of international chess.
Prod-KQEDTV Dist-PUBTEL

And Then There Were None	30 MIN
Baby Loves War, The	30 MIN
Blindfold Chess	29 MIN
Carlos Torre - The Fallen Eagle	29 MIN
Dark Victory	29 MIN
Drawing Master, The	29 MIN
Euwe And Najdorf - Take Two	30 MIN
From Russia With Talent	30 MIN
From The Palace To The People	30 MIN
Game At The Opera, The	29 MIN
Game Of Kings, The	30 MIN
Gentleman From Amsterdam, The	30 MIN
Loose Screw, A	29 MIN
Luck Is A Lady	29 MIN
Mikhail Tahl	29 MIN
Musician And The General, The	29 MIN
Numbers Racket, The	29 MIN
Steinitz Style, The	30 MIN
Strength Through Weakness	30 MIN
When Kings Were Champagne	30 MIN

Komo Mai - The House Is Yours C 30 MIN
16MM FILM OPTICAL SOUND H-C
Shows the new state capitol building of Hawaii, and the process by which state laws are enacted.
Prod-CINEPC Dist-CINEPC

Kompani Bilong Yumi C 27 MIN
16MM FILM OPTICAL SOUND H A
Presents the story of a cooperative company in Papua and New Guinea which is largely owned and operated by the indigenous people of Papua and New Guinea. Kompani bilong yumi is pidgin English for company belonging to you and me.
LC NO. 70-710751
Prod-AUSCG Dist-AUIS 1971

Kon-Tiki B 75 MIN
16MM FILM OPTICAL SOUND
Presents the story of the famous voyage from South America to Polynesia by six Scandinavian scientists on a balsa raft bound by ropes. Thor Heyerdahl, expedition leader and author of 'KON-TIKI,' narrates.
LC NO. FIA67-1029
Prod-RKOP Dist-KITPAR 1951

Koniec C 10 MIN
16MM FILM OPTICAL SOUND C A
Presents an absurdist incident about a meaningless ritual on a desolate slagheap.
Prod-VIERAD Dist-CANCIN 1974

Konrad C 15 MIN
3/4 OR 1/2 INCH VIDEO CASSETTE I
Presents a satire about a 'factory-made' seven-year-old boy. From the book by Christine Nostlinger.
From The Storybound Series.
Prod-CTI Dist-CTI

Konrad Adenauer B 26 MIN
16MM FILM, 3/4 OR 1/2 IN VIDEO H-C A
Uses rare actuality footage to portray the personal life and history-making deeds of Konrad Adenauer.
From The History Makers Of The 20th Century Series.
Prod-WOLPER Dist-SF 1965

Konrad Lorenz - Of Geese And Men C 25 MIN
16MM FILM, 3/4 OR 1/2 IN VIDEO
Presents Nobel Prize winner Konrad Lorenz telling how he developed his central concepts on imprinting, domestication and aggression. Relates his findings to human behavior.
LC NO. 80-706231
Prod-PHILBT Dist-MEDIAG 1979

Konrad Lorenz - Science Of Animal Behavior C 15 MIN
16MM FILM, 3/4 OR 1/2 IN VIDEO I-H
Documents the work of Konrad Lorenz in animal behavior, describing his studies with geese and his findings on the function of rank and order in animal social structure.

From The Animal Behavior Series.
LC NO. 80-706271
Prod-NGS Dist-NGS 1975

Kontakion - A Song Of Praise C 26 MIN
16MM FILM, 3/4 OR 1/2 IN VIDEO J-C A
Presents a modern ballet which tells the story of Jesus' birth, baptism, ministry, healing, crucifixion and resurrection. Choreographed by Barry Loreland and danced by William Louther to music arranged by Peter Maxwell Davis.
Prod-THAMES Dist-MEDIAG 1973

Kontakte—A Series
16MM FILM, 3/4 OR 1/2 IN VIDEO
Presents twenty-five 25-minute programs which provide enough language to survive in a German-speaking country. Assumes no previous knowledge of the language.
Prod-FI Dist-FI 1982

Kontiki Kids B 17 MIN
16MM FILM OPTICAL SOUND P-I
Shows how the magnificent six-and-a-half gang builds a raft to reach its home base when a canal lock is closed for repairs. Depicts their adventures when the raft, built with wheels, careens out of control through the local streets.
From The Magnificent 6 And 1/2 Series.
Prod-CHILDF Dist-LUF 1970

Kool Cigarettes With Singing Penguin C 1 MIN
3/4 OR 1/2 INCH VIDEO CASSETTE
Shows a classic television commercial.
Prod-BROOKC Dist-BROOKC

Kopje - A Rock For All Seasons C 60 MIN
16MM FILM, 3/4 OR 1/2 IN VIDEO H-C A
Describes Kopjes, which are massive outcrops of Africa's ancient bedrock that sit like island's in Tanzania's Serengeti plain. Shows that they provide shelter, shade and a source of water to an incredible array of plant and animal life.
Prod-WNETTV Dist-FI 1982

Korea - Land Of The Morning Calm C 22 MIN
16MM FILM OPTICAL SOUND
Presents a travelog on the Republic of Korea.
From The Journey To Adventure Series.
LC NO. 78-700426
Prod-KORGOV Dist-GLLTV Prodn-SECOM 1978

Korea - Overview, The Face Of Korea C 23 MIN
16MM FILM, 3/4 OR 1/2 IN VIDEO J-C A
Introduces the geography, history, education, agriculture and industry of Korea. Contrasts the quiet contemplative philosophy of traditional Korean culture and the brisk, efficient aspects of life in the industrialized cities.
LC NO. 80-706822
Prod-CENTRO Dist-CORF 1980

Korea - Performing Arts, The Wonderful World Of Kim Sung Hee C 21 MIN
16MM FILM, 3/4 OR 1/2 IN VIDEO J-C A
Focuses on Kim Sung Hee, a professional dancer at the National Theater in Seoul, Korea.
LC NO. 80-706466
Prod-CENTRO Dist-CORF 1979

Korea - Reflections On The Morning Calm C 29 MIN
16MM FILM, 3/4 OR 1/2 IN VIDEO J-C A
Merges views of the Korean countryside and buildings with artworks ranging from pieces 5,000 years old to modern works. Includes scenes of the excavated tomb in the ancient kingdom of Paekche and the distinctive Koryo Celadon.
LC NO. 84-706393
Prod-CHAPA Dist-EBEC 1980

Korea - Rich Heritage, Land Of Morning Calm C 19 MIN
16MM FILM, 3/4 OR 1/2 IN VIDEO J-C A
Delves into the cultural heritage of Korea.
LC NO. 80-706467
Prod-CENTRO Dist-CORF 1979

Korea - The Circle Of Life, Traditional Customs And Rituals C 35 MIN
16MM FILM, 3/4 OR 1/2 IN VIDEO H-C A
Depicts Korean social patterns and customs, studying the major events in the cycle of life. Examines the Confucian heritage on which the traditional Korean society is based and shows the rituals related to birth, marriage and death.
LC NO. 80-706874
Prod-KORNFU Dist-CORF 1980

Korea - The Family C 18 MIN
16MM FILM, 3/4 OR 1/2 IN VIDEO J-C A
Discusses the typical young urban family in Korea.
LC NO. 80-707321
Prod-CENTRO Dist-CORF 1980

Korea, Land Of The Morning Calm C
3/4 OR 1/2 INCH VIDEO CASSETTE
Introduces Korea, an important region. Focuses on themes of family, education, religion and modern industrial development.
Prod-CEPRO Dist-CEPRO

Korean Court Music C 25 MIN
16MM FILM, 3/4 OR 1/2 IN VIDEO J-C A
Presents musicians performing different court music of Korea.
Prod-UWASH Dist-UWASHP 1971

Korean Folk Dances C 25 MIN
16MM FILM, 3/4 OR 1/2 IN VIDEO J-C A
Presents a variety of Korean folk dances.
Prod-UWASH Dist-UWASHP 1971

Korean People, The C 11 MIN
16MM FILM, 3/4 OR 1/2 IN VIDEO I-H
Discusses the geography and traditions of Korea.
Prod-IFB Dist-IFB 1961

Korean Vocal Music C 14 MIN
16MM FILM, 3/4 OR 1/2 IN VIDEO J-C A
Presents two prominent vocal forms of the Korean traditional music.
Prod-UWASH Dist-UWASHP 1971

Korek Frame Repair Equipment C 17 MIN
1/2 IN VIDEO CASSETTE BETA/VHS
Deals with auto body repair.
Prod-RMI Dist-RMI

Korochan, The Little Bear B 11 MIN
16MM FILM, 3/4 OR 1/2 IN VIDEO P
A Japanese fairy tale about a little bear who can't keep out of trouble. After experiencing a series of mishaps, he realizes that mischief doesn't pay.
Prod-EBF Dist-EBEC 1959

Korochan, The Little Bear (Spanish) B 11 MIN
16MM FILM, 3/4 OR 1/2 IN VIDEO P
A Spanish language version of the film and video recording Korochan, The Little Bear.
Prod-EBF Dist-EBEC

Koryo Celadon C 17 MIN
16MM FILM OPTICAL SOUND
Compares the nearly 1,000-year-old, jade-green, Koryo celadon ceramics with newly created works of potter Yoo Kun-Hyong. Shows the entire process used in making celadon pottery.
LC NO. 80-700208
Prod-KORIO Dist-CHAPA Prodn-CHAPA 1979

Kosciuszko - An American Portrait C 21 MIN
16MM FILM, 3/4 OR 1/2 IN VIDEO
Documents the accomplishments of Thaddeus Kosciuszko, a young Polish officer whose ideals and actions contributed greatly to the American Revolution.
Prod-READER Dist-PFP 1976

Kosciuszko - An American Portrait C 58 MIN
16MM FILM, 3/4 OR 1/2 IN VIDEO
Traces the life of Thaddeus Kosciuszko, the foreign officer who aided the American Continental Army during the Revolutionary War.
Prod-READER Dist-PFP 1976

Kosher Dietary Laws C 11 MIN
3/4 OR 1/2 INCH VIDEO CASSETTE PRO
Explains kosher dietary laws and tells how a modern kosher kitchen may enhance its menu with the addition of synthetically produced foods.
Prod-CULINA Dist-CULINA

Kotex-Kleenex Saga, Kimberly-Clark Co. C 20 MIN
3/4 OR 1/2 INCH VIDEO CASSETTE
Reveals true marketing case history of the introduction and ultimate success of Kotex and Kleenex.
Prod-HBS Dist-IVCH

Koto, The C 30 MIN
3/4 OR 1/2 INCH VIDEO CASSETTE
Provides an introduction to the ancient Japanese stringed instrument, the koto, and its music. Traces the evolution of the koto from its introduction in 800 AD to the present. Features Ms Noriko Sato giving both solo and duet performances and demonstrating how to tune the koto.
Prod-OHUTC Dist-OHUTC

Kottar - Model For Development C 18 MIN
16MM FILM OPTICAL SOUND
Portrays Catholic Relief Services efforts to help Indian fisherman, weavers, potters and other craftspeople join in cooperative ventures to increase their incomes and improve their stations in life.
Prod-CATHRS Dist-MTP

Koumiko Mystery, The C 60 MIN
16MM FILM OPTICAL SOUND
Describes the nature of women through the mystery of Koumiko, a girl Chris Marker met at the Olympic games.
Prod-UNKNWN Dist-NYFLMS 1965

Kpix Reports—A Series

Prod-KPIXTV Dist-WEBC

Division In His House 30 MIN
Taste Of A Millionaire 30 MIN

Kraft Pulping, Pt 1 C
3/4 OR 1/2 INCH VIDEO CASSETTE IND
Includes chemistry, sulphidity, concentration, penetration, diffusion and variations due to types of wood and tree growth.
From The Pulp And Paper Training, Module 1 - Kraft Pulping Series.
Prod-LEIKID Dist-LEIKID

Kraft Pulping, Pt 2 C
3/4 OR 1/2 INCH VIDEO CASSETTE IND
Covers wood preparation, cooking time and temperature, variable factors and the pulping process.
Prod-LEIKID Dist-LEIKID

Kraft Pulping, Pt 3 C
3/4 OR 1/2 INCH VIDEO CASSETTE IND
Focuses on the continuous process. Covers types of digesters, kamyr, presteaming chips, cooling, washing and blowing pulp, and control.
From The Pulp And Paper Training, Module 1 - Kraft Pulping Series.
Prod-LEIKID Dist-LEIKID

Kraft Pulping, Pt 4 C
3/4 OR 1/2 INCH VIDEO CASSETTE IND
Deals with the batch process in wood pulping. Includes direct and indirect digester, loading, cooking blow tank and digester control.
From The Pulp And Paper Training, Module 1 - Kraft Pulping Series.
Prod-LEIKID Dist-LEIKID

Krakonos - The Mountain King And The Castle Governor C 18 MIN
16MM FILM, 3/4 OR 1/2 IN VIDEO P-J
Presents animated puppets who tell the story of how true love, though temporarily thwarted by greed and a malicious parent, runs its course when assisted by the spirit of Good residing in the person of the humble Mountain King, who helps the just in need and always finds a suitable reward for wrong doers.
LC NO. 84-706790
Prod-KRATKY Dist-PHENIX

Krakonos - The Mountain King And The Ghost C 15 MIN
16MM FILM, 3/4 OR 1/2 IN VIDEO I
Tells how a young man disguises himself as a ghost in order to scare wealthy travelers into giving him their money. The Mountain King, Krakonos takes matters in hand by dressing as a skeleton to scare the ghost right out of his sheet and out of the village he's plagued.
LC NO. 84-706791
Prod-KRATKY Dist-PHENIX

Krakonos - The Mountain King And The Glassmaker C 15 MIN
16MM FILM, 3/4 OR 1/2 IN VIDEO I-J
Presents an industrious young glassmaker who falls into company with a no-account fellow who persuades the glassmaker to stop at a tavern enroute to market with his wares. Tells how after robbing an old man, who turns out to be Krakonos, justice prevails once again.
LC NO. 84-706792
Prod-KRATKY Dist-PHENIX

Kramer Vs Kramer C 105 MIN
16MM FILM OPTICAL SOUND
Tells the story of parents entangled in a legal and emotional tug-of-war for their child. Stars Dustin Hoffman and Meryl Streep.
Prod-CPC Dist-SWANK

Krasner, Norman C 6 MIN
16MM FILM, 3/4 OR 1/2 IN VIDEO
Shows Norman's humorous battle with a men's room.
Prod-MTI Dist-MTI

Krasner, Norman - Beloved Husband Of Irma B 7 MIN
16MM FILM OPTICAL SOUND H-C
Presents a comedy about a man who has to borrow a dime for a pay toilet, who must substitute the pages of an expensive art book for lack of toilet paper and who is forced to suffer the consequences of a clogged drain and a door that will not unlock and let him out.
LC NO. 73-700015
Prod-CFS Dist-CFS 1972

Kreinik And Bosworth Families, The C 7 MIN
16MM FILM, 3/4 OR 1/2 IN VIDEO H-C A
Focuses on two single people who have adopted children.
From The American Family - An Endangered Species Series.
Prod-NBC Dist-FI 1979

Kremlin, The C 54 MIN
16MM FILM, 3/4 OR 1/2 IN VIDEO H-C A
Re-creates events that took place in the Kremlin, the seat of Russian authority, during many centuries--from the early Moscow princes to the Soviet Era.
Prod-NBCTV Dist-MGHT 1963

Kremlin, The, Pt 1 C 27 MIN
16MM FILM, 3/4 OR 1/2 IN VIDEO H-C A
Re-creates events that took place in the Kremlin, the seat of Russian authority, during many centuries--from the early Moscow princes to the Soviet era.
Prod-NBCTV Dist-MGHT 1963

Kremlin, The, Pt 2 C 27 MIN
16MM FILM, 3/4 OR 1/2 IN VIDEO H-C A
Re-creates events that took place in the Kremlin, the seat of Russian authority, during many centuries--from the early Moscow princes to the Soviet Era.
Prod-NBCTV Dist-MGHT 1963

Kriegsmarine, Die B 45 MIN
3/4 OR 1/2 INCH VIDEO CASSETTE
Presents two films on Germany's famous battlecruisers and Q-Boats. Battleship On A Voyage and Auxiliary Cruiser in All the Seas of the World are Germany's wartime documentaries.
Prod-IHF Dist-IHF

Kroger Eggs With The Perfect Shape C 1 MIN
3/4 OR 1/2 INCH VIDEO CASSETTE
Shows a classic animated television commercial.
Prod-BROOKC Dist-BROOKC

Krugers, The - Texas Immigrants C 28 MIN
3/4 OR 1/2 INCH VIDEO CASSETTE
Features first generation American Texan Bert Kruger Smith relating the lives, immigration, and successes of her Russian Jewish parents who moved to Wichita Falls, Texas. Emphasizes how this ethnicity has affected the narrator's life and the lives of other Texans.
Prod-UTXITC Dist-UTXITC 1980

Ksan C 27 MIN
16MM FILM OPTICAL SOUND
Chronicles the downfall of the Gitksan people, a northwest coast

Indian tribe in British Columbia. Shows their successful efforts to re-establish their folk arts and culture at 'Ksan, the re-creation of an Indian village at the confluence of the Skeena and Bulkley Rivers.
LC NO. 74-701973
Prod-BCDTI Dist-CTFL 1973

Ku Klux Klan - The Invisible Empire B 47 MIN
16MM FILM, 3/4 OR 1/2 IN VIDEO J-C A
Uses interviews and newsreel footage to depict Ku Klux Klan activities in the United States. Reveals how the Klan's use of violence contradicts the American concepts of justice and human rights.
Prod-CBSTV Dist-CAROUF 1965

Ku-Damm In Berlin, The C 5 MIN
16MM FILM, 3/4 OR 1/2 IN VIDEO
Shows West Berlin's shopping areas, architectural attractions, cafes and restaurants.
From The European Studies - Germany Series. Part 16
Prod-BAYER Dist-IFB 1973

Kuala Lampur C 11 MIN
16MM FILM, 3/4 OR 1/2 IN VIDEO J-C A
Visits the Malaysian capital of Kuala Lumpur, which produces tin and rubber. Analyzes the city's history, its modern growth and future hopes.
Prod-LUF Dist-LUF 1980

Kuala Lumpur C 10 MIN
16MM FILM OPTICAL SOUND
Shows Kuala Lumpur, the federal capital and the seat of the federal government of Malaysia. Includes the Batu Caves and the Merdeka Stadium.
Prod-FILEM Dist-PMFMUN 1975

Kuboto C 20 MIN
16MM FILM, 3/4 OR 1/2 IN VIDEO
Features Kuboto, a musician whose imagination stretches far beyond the confines of conventional musical instrumentation. Records a performance in which Kuboto converts the most ordinary and unlikely objects into sound-making devices.
LC NO. 84-706146
Prod-NFBC Dist-NFBC 1983

Kudamm Berlin C 5 MIN
16MM FILM, 3/4 OR 1/2 IN VIDEO H-C A
A German-language version of the motion picture The Ku-Damm In Berlin. Shows scenes of West Berlin's version of Fifth Avenue, the Ku-Damm, with its shops, architectural attractions, cafes and restaurants.
From The European Studies - Germany (German) Series.
Prod-MFAFRG Dist-IFB Prodn-BAYER 1973

Kudzu C 16 MIN
16MM FILM, 3/4 OR 1/2 IN VIDEO I-C A
Examines the tropical vine kudzu and its damaging effects in the southern region of the United States. Dramatizes cultural traditions that have grown up around planting the vine with a story that features a cast of characters and appearances by President Jimmy Carter and American poet James Dickey, who recites stanzas of his poem called Kudzu.
LC NO. 77-701093
Prod-SHORTM Dist-PFP 1977

Kujichagulia C 6 MIN
16MM FILM, 3/4 OR 1/2 IN VIDEO K-I
Shows how two young kangaroos in the Australian outback find themselves living in a village of platypuses. Averts near disaster when, emulating the animals around them, they forget how to hop but don't learn to swim. Notes how, when danger struck, they barely survived and were told by their rescuer to be what they are, not what they are not.
From The Nguzo Saba-Folklore For Children Series.
Prod-NGUZO Dist-BCNFL 1981

Kukurantumi - The Road To Accra C 83 MIN
16MM FILM OPTICAL SOUND
Tells the story of a lorry driver in a small village in Ghana who loses his job. Shows what happens to his traditional lifestyle when he moves to the city of Accra.
Prod-BLKFMF Dist-BLKFMF

Kul-Tur (Coal Trip) C 11 MIN
16MM FILM OPTICAL SOUND
Explains that from the turn of the century until 1969 a real train was running daily with coal from the Copenhagen free port to the neighboring gas-works, a journey of only about one kilometer, which ended in a chugging final trip up the slope of the gas-works. Includes sound effects.
Prod-STATNS Dist-STATNS 1969

Kulturlandschaft Rheinland C 20 MIN
16MM FILM OPTICAL SOUND H-C A
Deals with the 2,000-year history of the Rhineland, and provides a tour of fourteen cities and towns of the region, with its rich artistic tradition, from the artifacts of the ancient Romans and German tribes to the bright aggressive paintings of the expressionists.
Prod-WSTGLC Dist-WSTGLC

Kum Ba Yah C 19 MIN
3/4 OR 1/2 INCH VIDEO CASSETTE P-I
Shows how melodies consist of skips, stepwise movements and repeated tones.
From The USS Rhythm Series.
Prod-ARKETV Dist-AITECH 1977

Kundalini And Therapeutic Yoga C 60 MIN
1/2 IN VIDEO CASSETTE (BETA)
Presents a complete Kundalini yoga exercise sequence and shows specific yoga positions, breathing and chanting.
Prod-UNKNWN Dist-HOMET

Kung Bushmen Hunting Equipment C 37 MIN
3/4 INCH VIDEO CASSETTE
Details all the pieces of the hunting kit of Kung bushmen in Namibia. Includes preparation of poison arrows.
From The San (Bushmen) Series.
Prod-DOCEDR Dist-DOCEDR Prodn-MRSHL

Kung-Fu Master - Gin Foon Mark C 17 MIN
16MM FILM OPTICAL SOUND J-C A
Presents a biography of Gin Foon Mark, master of the southern praying mantis style of kung-fu. Illustrates the self-defense technique and philosophy of kung-fu.
LC NO. 77-703282
Prod-SPMKFH Dist-FLMART Prodn-FLMART 1977

Kunstigt Andedraet Ved Indblaesningsmetoden (Expired Air Resuscitation) C 10 MIN
16MM FILM OPTICAL SOUND
A Danish language film. Describes Danish artificial respiration methods, including the mouth-to-mouth and the mouth-to-nose methods. Gives precise instructions as to the application of these methods pointing out the difference between the two systems.
Prod-STATNS Dist-STATNS 1961

Kupecky C 11 MIN
16MM FILM, 3/4 OR 1/2 IN VIDEO H-C A
Depicts the life of Jan Kupecky, an early 18th-century Czech artist. Tells how he was persecuted because of his Prostestant faith and examines his portrait paintings in detail.
Prod-IFB Dist-IFB 1974

Kurelek C 10 MIN
16MM FILM, 3/4 OR 1/2 IN VIDEO J-H
Paintings of the self-taught painter William Kurelek tells the story of his father who left his village in the Ukraine and immigrated to Canada. Pictures the life of the artist and his family on a prairie homestead as well as present-day life in Ontario.
Prod-NFBC Dist-IFB 1967

Kurelek The Ukrainian Pioneer C 14 MIN
16MM FILM OPTICAL SOUND
Features Canadian artist William Kurelek in his studio, describing in his sketches the history of his grandparents' exodus from the Ukraine to western Canada in the 1900's.
From The Journal Series.
LC NO. 76-702084
Prod-FIARTS Dist-CANFDC 1975

Kurt - A Retarded Child In The Family B 11 MIN
16MM FILM OPTICAL SOUND J-C A S
Features a mother of a retarded child who talks about her feelings about having the child in the family.
LC NO. 74-703075
Prod-WITFTV Dist-POLYMR 1974

Kurt Carlsen - Man Against The Sea B 15 MIN
1/2 IN VIDEO CASSETTE BETA/VHS
Tells the story of a man - Kurt Carlsen - whose heroism at sea wonhim world wide acclaim.
Prod-STAR Dist-STAR

Kurt Vonnegut, Jr - A Self-portrait C 29 MIN
16MM FILM, 3/4 OR 1/2 IN VIDEO J-C A
Features Kurt Vonnegut, Jr discussing his development as a writer, his themes and their meaning, his relationship to other writers and his future. Includes photographs which chronicle the author's life and selections from home movies taken during his youth.
Prod-MANTLH Dist-FOTH 1975

Kurt Vonnegut, Jr - Deadeye Dick C 60 MIN
16MM FILM, 3/4 OR 1/2 IN VIDEO J-C A
Offers an interview with author Kurt Vonnegut, Jr which crosses from reality to fiction by having the author's own characters interview him.
LC NO. 84-706165
Prod-BBCTV Dist-WOMBAT 1983

Kurtis, Hollywood Stuntboy C 25 MIN
16MM FILM, 3/4 OR 1/2 IN VIDEO J-C A
Introduces Kurtis, who works as a stuntboy for movies and television.
From The World Cultures And Youth Series.
Prod-SUNRIS Dist-CORF 1981

Kuru Mystery, The C 60 MIN
3/4 OR 1/2 INCH VIDEO CASSETTE
Details Nobel Prize-winning pediatrician Carleton Gajdusek's search for the cause of the slow virus kuru, which is decimating a tribe of stone age people in the Eastern Highlands of Papua New Guinea. Relates the kuru virus to Alzheimer's Disease.
From The Quest For The Killers Series.
Prod-PBS Dist-PBS

Kuumba C 8 MIN
16MM FILM OPTICAL SOUND I
Uses animation to tell the story of a young boy who is searching for a new instrument with which to celebrate Trinidad's pre-Easter Carnival. Shows his success in fabricating a steel drum from the carefully indented bottom of an oildrum.
LC NO. 78-701258
Prod-NGUZO Dist-NGUZO 1978

Kuumba - Simon's New Sound C 8 MIN
16MM FILM, 3/4 OR 1/2 IN VIDEO K-I
Tells how a young boy in Trinidad created a new musical instrument, a drum, by listening to rain drops striking an old metal oil drum during a down pour. Noting that rain drops hitting dents produced high notes, and big dents low notes, he fashioned a drum that became the national instrument of Trinidad.
From The Nguzo Saba-Folklore For Children Series.
Prod-NGUZO Dist-BCNFL 1979

Kuwait C 12 MIN
3/4 OR 1/2 INCH VIDEO CASSETTE H-C A
Documents Kuwait's accumulation of oil resources and wealth.
Prod-UPI Dist-JOU

Kvindegymnastikkens Udvikling I Danmark (The Development Of Women's Gymnastics In Denmark) B 22 MIN
16MM FILM SILENT
A Danish language film. Presents a reconstruction of the most important exercises within the four most common systems of women's gymnastics during the period from 1865 to 1912. Includes the Drachman, the Poul Petersen, the Ling and Bjorksten systems.
Prod-STATNS Dist-STATNS 1952

Kwakiutl of British Columbia, The B 55 MIN
16MM FILM, 3/4 OR 1/2 IN VIDEO
Depicts traditional Kwakiutl dances, crafts, games, oratory and the actions of the shaman.
Prod-BOASF Dist-UWASHP

Kwame Nkrumah - The Fallen Idol B 15 MIN
16MM FILM OPTICAL SOUND
Presents an analysis of the rise and fall of Kwame Nkrumah from the time of Ghana's independence in 1957 to the military coup which forced Nkrumah from power.
From The Screen News Digest Series. Vol 8, Issue 10
Prod-HEARST Dist-HEARST 1966

Kwame's Gang C 30 MIN
3/4 OR 1/2 INCH VIDEO CASSETTE I-J
Presents a story designed to help Black students remember and explore the Black folklore that is their heritage.
From The Gettin' To Know Me Series.
Prod-CTI Dist-MDCPB 1979

Kwanzaa - An Afro-American Festival C 29 MIN
3/4 OR 1/2 INCH VIDEO CASSETTE
Prod-RCOMTV Dist-SYLWAT 1982

Kwanzaa - The Gathering Of A People C 47 MIN
16MM FILM OPTICAL SOUND
Documents an Afro-American holiday celebrated from December 26 to January 1 each year.
Prod-BLKFMF Dist-BLKFMF

Kwegu, The C 52 MIN
3/4 OR 1/2 INCH VIDEO CASSETTE A
Uses subtitles, interviews and cinema verite to document the life of the Kwegu, a sedentery Ethiopian tribe of boatmen and farmers. Shows how the Kwegu live in clientlike dependency on their more numerous neighbors, the cattle-herding Mursi.
From The Disappearing World Series.
LC NO. 82-707384
Prod-GRATV Dist-FLMLIB 1982

Kyocera Equipment, The C 30 MIN
16MM FILM, 3/4 OR 1/2 IN VIDEO C A
Shows how theory Z comes alive in the United States as the American employees of San Diego's Kyocera Company productively adapt to the owners' thoroughly Japanese brand of management. Tells how there is tension, particularly between Japanese managers and American salesmen whose styles are different, at this company which makes computer chips and chip holders.
From The Enterprise Series.
LC NO. 81-707542
Prod-WGBHTV Dist-LCOA Prodn-DORSOL 1981

Kyogen Drama Kirokuda, The C 46 MIN
16MM FILM OPTICAL SOUND
A Japanese language film. Tells the story of an inhabitant of Okutamba, deep in the mountains northeast of Kyoto who has ordered his servant to deliver to his uncle in Kyoto six horseback loads of firewood and a cask of sake. Explains that the heavy snowfall and accompanying severe coldness encountered on his way caused the servant to drink the whole cask of sake at a teahouse on a mountain pass and when he reaches his destination he must explain the difference between what was shown on the invoice and what he carried.
Prod-IWANMI Dist-UNIJAP 1970

Kypseli - Women And Men Apart, A Divided Reality C 40 MIN
16MM FILM, 3/4 OR 1/2 IN VIDEO C A
Presents a film essay on the peasant society of Kipseli, a small isolated Greek village on the island of Thira. Depicts how the people of Kipseli divide time, space, material possessions and activities according to an underlying pattern based on the separation of the sexes and shows how this division determines the village social structure.
Prod-UCEMC Dist-UCEMC 1976

L

L A Backwater - The Venice Canals C 15 MIN
16MM FILM OPTICAL SOUND
Profiles the community of Venice, California, and its struggle to preserve its unique rural identity in the face of encroaching development and the spread of urban progress.
LC NO. 75-703265
Prod-USC Dist-USC 1975

L A Too Much C 12 MIN
16MM FILM, 3/4 OR 1/2 IN VIDEO
Takes a look at the American past, symbolized by the long life and violent death of a Victorian house. Criticizes the American tendency to casually destroy old values to make way for a modern present.
Prod-ROSOW Dist-UCEMC 1969

. I G H T C 15 MIN
16MM FILM, 3/4 OR 1/2 IN VIDEO I-C A
Offers a tribute to Thomas A Edison and a brief history of light which culminates with the invention of the incandescent light bulb and the machinery for its mass production.
Prod-MIDMAR Dist-DIRECT 1981

. I USA C 31 MIN
16MM FILM OPTICAL SOUND
Pictures life in Long Island as a microcosm of America. Focuses on life in suburbia with its problems of pollution, planning, housing, health care, education and transportation.
LC NO. 72-702393
Prod-AVON Dist-AVON 1972

. Sound C 14 MIN
3/4 OR 1/2 INCH VIDEO CASSETTE K
See series title for descriptive statement.
From The I-Land Treasure Series.
Prod-UWISC Dist-AITECH 1980

L Sound, The C 15 MIN
3/4 INCH VIDEO CASSETTE P
Discusses the proper production of the l sound and uses riddles to illustrate this sound.
From The New Talking Shop Series.
Prod-BSPTV Dist-GPITVL 1978

L Sound, The - The Leaning Ladder C 15 MIN
2 INCH VIDEOTAPE P
Introduces some of the consonant sounds met in early reading. Identifies the written letter with the spoken sound.
From The Listen And Say Series.
Prod-MPATI Dist-GPITVL

L-Blends - Climbing The Cliff C 20 MIN
3/4 OR 1/2 INCH VIDEO CASSETTE J-H
See series title for descriptive statement.
From The Getting The Word Series. Unit II
Prod-SCETV Dist-AITECH 1974

L-Dopa And Parkinsonism C 18 MIN
3/4 INCH VIDEO CASSETTE PRO
Discusses indications for treating Parkinsonism with L-dopa. Describes dosage and possible side effects.
LC NO. 76-706052
Prod-WARMP Dist-USNAC 1970

L-Four--A Series
I
Explores earth science and space science. Emphasizes the interrelationships in nature and shows that man is a catalyst in the precarious balance of nature.
Prod-CTI Dist-CTI

Atmosphere	015 MIN
Changing Earth, The	015 MIN
Cycles	015 MIN
Earth Limits	015 MIN
Earth Measurement	015 MIN
Energy	015 MIN
Gravity	015 MIN
Human Communications	015 MIN
Human Life Support	015 MIN
Order Of Nature, The	015 MIN
Reach Far Out	015 MIN
Reach Out	015 MIN
Reach Up	015 MIN
Soil	015 MIN
Things In Motion	015 MIN
Water	015 MIN

L-I-G-H-T C 15 MIN
16MM FILM OPTICAL SOUND
Traces the history of lighting, from the Sun as man's only source of light through the invention of the light bulb and the manufacture of the Corning ribbon machine.
LC NO. 80-701236
Prod-CORGLW Dist-CORGLW Prodn-MIDMAR 1979

L-4 Earth Science--A Series

Prod-IITC Dist-IITC 1977

Changing Earth, The 14 MIN

L/R Time Constants C
3/4 OR 1/2 INCH VIDEO CASSETTE
See series title for descriptive statement.
From The Basic DC Circuits Series.
Prod-VTRI Dist-VTRI

L/R Time Constants C 15 MIN
3/4 OR 1/2 INCH VIDEO CASSETTE
See series title for descriptive statement.
From The Basic Electricity And D.C. Circuits, Laboratory Series.
Prod-TXINLC Dist-TXINLC

L, T And E C 15 MIN
3/4 INCH VIDEO CASSETTE P
From The Writing Time Series.
Prod-WHROTV Dist-GPITVL

L'Adaptation A La Survie - Les Oiseaux C 14 MIN
16MM FILM, 3/4 OR 1/2 IN VIDEO J-H
A French language version of the videocassette Adaptations For Survival - Birds. Illustrates structural and behavioral adaptations of birds to their environments.
Prod-IFB Dist-IFB 1969

L'Amour Fou B 252 MIN
16MM FILM OPTICAL SOUND
A French language film. Portrays a young Paris theater director and his actress wife. Follows the couple's personal ups and downs and underscores the conflict between the theater and life.
Prod-NYFLMS Dist-NYFLMS 1968

L'Appapartement B 13 MIN
16MM FILM OPTICAL SOUND J-C
See series title for descriptive statement.
From The En France Avec Jean Et Helene Series.
LC NO. 73-700110
Prod-PEREN Dist-CHLTN 1967

L'Art Et La Vie C 9 MIN
16MM FILM, 3/4 OR 1/2 IN VIDEO H-C
A French language film. Presents examples of French contributions to art and traces the steps by which contemporary French artists gain recognition for their work. Examines recent efforts by the French government to bring the general public into closer contact with the work of modern artists.
From The La France Contemporaine Series.
Prod-EBEC Dist-EBEC 1971

L'Aube De L'Histoire - The Dawn Of History--A Series

Traces the development of ancient civilization from its beginning to the birth of modern France using ancient artifacts and actual geographic locations.
Prod-FACSEA Dist-FACSEA

L'Automne Est Une Aventure C 11 MIN
16MM FILM, 3/4 OR 1/2 IN VIDEO --H
French version of 'AUTUMN IS AN ADVENTURE.' Depicts and narrates in simple French leaf raking, a marshmallow roast and a hike through the woods. Introduces a poem in French to encourage pupils to try their abilities in creative writing.
Prod-CORF Dist-CORF 1960

L'Aviateur B 13 MIN
16MM FILM OPTICAL SOUND I-H
See series title for descriptive statement.
From The Les Francais Chez Vous Series. Set III, Lesson 32
Prod-PEREN Dist-CHLTN 1967

L'Ecluse B 13 MIN
16MM FILM OPTICAL SOUND J-C
See series title for descriptive statement.
From The En France Avec Jean Et Helene Series.
LC NO. 73-704507
Prod-PEREN Dist-CHLTN 1967

L'Ennui B 18 MIN
16MM FILM OPTICAL SOUND
Presents three short sequences with and without narration which create a synthesis of the real and the unreal.
LC NO. 74-702740
Prod-ONCA Dist-CANFDC 1973

L'Epopee Canadienne De L'energie C 25 MIN
16MM FILM OPTICAL SOUND
A French language version of Great Canadian Energy Saga. Looks at the special importance of energy and energy resources.
LC NO. 76-701328
Prod-IMO Dist-IMO

L'Ere Des Revolutions C 26 MIN
16MM FILM, 3/4 OR 1/2 IN VIDEO H-C
A French-language version of the motion picture An Age Of Revolutions. Focuses on the French and Industrial Revolutions, ending with the Franco-Prussian War.
LC NO. 83-706815
Prod-IFB Dist-IFB 1976

L'Etang C 20 MIN
16MM FILM, 3/4 OR 1/2 IN VIDEO I-H
A French language version of the videocassette The Pond. Examines the interdependent members of the community in a pond, pointing out that the pond provides an environment containing sunlight, minerals and permanent water of relatively constant temperature.
Prod-IFB Dist-IFB 1961

L'Europe De L'An Mil - Europe In The Year 1000 C 52 MIN
16MM FILM OPTICAL SOUND
Looks at Western Europe during the year 1000 through views of the Abbey Of Tournus, the tapestries of Bayeaux and the bronze door of the church Saint-Michel.
From The Le Temp Des Cathedrales Series.
Prod-FACSEA Dist-FACSEA 1979

L'Halterophile Industriel C 12 MIN
16MM FILM, 3/4 OR 1/2 IN VIDEO H A
A French-language version of the motion picture The Industrial Weightlifter. Presents a flexible model to illustrate how discs are pinched when weights are lifted when the backbone is curved. Demonstrates the correct method of lifting heavy objects and shows good posture, positioning and smooth application of lifting power. Emphasizes that extremely heavy items can be handled only with a special lifting device.
Prod-IAPA Dist-IFB Prodn-RUDFLM 1965

L'Hopital's Rule C
3/4 INCH VIDEO CASSETTE
See series title for descriptive statement.
From The Calculus Series.
Prod-MDDE Dist-MDCPB

L'Idee B 27 MIN
16MM FILM OPTICAL SOUND
Presents a film by Berthold Bartosch, based on a book of 83 woodcuts by the Belgian artist, Frans Masereel, which was published in Germany in 1927, with a preface by Hermann Hesse. Makes a strong political statement about Europe just prior to the rise of Nazism, with the leading character, a slender, nude female figure, symbolizing the universal idealistic spirit in a world where good and evil constantly battle. Includes Arthur Honegger's score, thought to be the first to contain electronic instrumentation, which was created for the finished film in 1932.
Prod-STARRC Dist-STARRC

L'ile De La Cite C 12 MIN
16MM FILM, 3/4 OR 1/2 IN VIDEO
See series title for descriptive statement.
From The Sejour En France Series.
Prod-SEABEN Dist-IFB 1970

L'Immortelle B 95 MIN
16MM FILM OPTICAL SOUND C A
A mystery-drama in which a French professor goes in search of a woman with whom he once had a brief affair.
LC NO. 75-707876
Prod-COMOF Dist-GROVE 1969

L'Impressionnisme Et Le Neo-Impressionnisme C 22 MIN
16MM FILM, 3/4 OR 1/2 IN VIDEO H-C
A French language version of Impressionism And Neo-Impressionism. Explores the birth of impressionist painting in the works of Constable, Turner, Delacroix, Boudin, Jongkind, Corot, Rousseau and Courbet, followed by those of Manet, Monet, Degas, Cezanne, Guillaumain, Sisley, Morisot, Pissarro, Renoir and Seurat.
Prod-IFB Dist-IFB 1971

L'Oiseau C 4 MIN
16MM FILM OPTICAL SOUND
Transforms, enhances and interprets the force and beauty of a single bird in flight to present a unique visual experience.
Prod-LILYAN Dist-LILYAN

L'Or Bleu Du Quebec C 11 MIN
16MM FILM OPTICAL SOUND
A French-language film which looks at the St Lawrence River and its many ports, each with its own personality. Shows that the river is one of the major reasons Quebec finds itself at the center of world commerce.
Prod-QDTFG Dist-MTP

La Abuela Chicana (English) C 30 MIN
3/4 OR 1/2 INCH VIDEO CASSETTE H-C A
Depicts what happens when the grandmother of a Mexican-American family moves to Texas. Uses the story to try to reduce the minority isolation of Mexican-American students by showing the teenager as an individual, as a member of a unique cultural group and as a member of a larger complex society.
From The La Esquina (English) Series.
Prod-SWEDL Dist-GPITVL 1976

La Acequia C 10 MIN
16MM FILM OPTICAL SOUND J-C A
Depicts the cleaning of rural irrigation ditches in New Mexico, an annual tradition practiced since the arrival of the Spanish settlers in the 16th century.
From The Lifeways Series.
LC NO. 79-7018247
Prod-BLUSKY Dist-BLUSKY 1980

La Acequia C 14 MIN
16MM FILM, 3/4 OR 1/2 IN VIDEO
Portrays the traditional Hispanic agrarian practices and way of life of the people of the villages of northern New Mexico. Shows the gathering of the men of the village in early spring to clean the acequia, or water ditch so that the farmers can irrigate their crops.
Prod-BLUSKY Dist-ONEWST

La Alfombra Roja C 9 MIN
16MM FILM, 3/4 OR 1/2 IN VIDEO
A Spanish version of 'THE RED CARPET.' Shows that when the doorman of a hotel rolls out the red carpet for the arrival of a Duke, the carpet keeps rolling through the streets and attracts a number of motorcycle policemen who pursue it to the dock where the titled visitor receives an impressive reception.
Prod-WWS Dist-WWS 1960

La Belle Au Bois Dormant C 3 MIN
16MM FILM OPTICAL SOUND
Presents Sleeping Beauty, one of the first commercials filmed in Gasparcolor, made with Jean Aurenche for Nicolas Wines, and contains Alexander Alexeieff's only example of puppet animation.
Prod-STARRC Dist-STARRC 1934

La Bellicosa C 5 MIN
3/4 OR 1/2 INCH VIDEO CASSETTE J-H
Consists of a lesson on adverbs.
From The Write On, Set 1 Series.
Prod-CTI Dist-CTI

La Boheme C 110 MIN
3/4 OR 1/2 INCH VIDEO CASSETTE A
Portrays a tale of love in the garretts of the Latin Quarter in Pucci-ni's opera, La Boheme.
Prod-EDDIM Dist-EDDIM

La Bonne Aventure--A Series
P-I
Consists of 20 bilingual programs, in French and English. Deals with French-American culture, heritage, language and traditions. Uses puppets.
Prod-MPBN Dist-GPITVL 1976

Aurevoir Is Not Goodbye	015 MIN
Bazaar, The	015 MIN
Christmas Eve Celebration	015 MIN
Clock, The	015 MIN

Commercial, The 015 MIN
Deportation, The 015 MIN
Explorers, The 015 MIN
Good Adventure, The 015 MIN
Invention, The 015 MIN
Laughter 015 MIN
Legend, The 015 MIN
Lucky Find, The 015 MIN
Mistake, The 015 MIN
New Friends 015 MIN
Our Place 015 MIN
Plans, The 015 MIN
Prize, The 015 MIN
Problem Of Feelings, A 015 MIN
Quest, The 015 MIN
Work 015 MIN

La Carrera C 10 MIN
16MM FILM OPTICAL SOUND
Shows the 1978 Clasico del Caribe horserace, one of the most elegant horseraces in the world.
LC NO. 79-701313
Prod-PHILMO Dist-PHILMO 1979

La Casa De Maria Retreat—A Series

Presents Sri Gurudev speaking on Shan Karacharya and Adwaita philosophy, how all is changing, abortion and when life begins.
Prod-IYOGA Dist-IYOGA

La Cathedrale, La Ville, L'Ecole - Cathedral, City, School C 52 MIN
16MM FILM OPTICAL SOUND
Explains the urban renaissance of the 13th century during which cathedral art and schools blossom. Analyzes the concepts of cathedrals as homes of the people and cities as one big castle.
From The Le Temp Des Cathedrales Series.
Prod-FACSEA Dist-FACSEA 1979

La Celula - Una Estructura En Funcionamiento, Pt 1 C 29 MIN
16MM FILM, 3/4 OR 1/2 IN VIDEO H-C A
A Spanish language version of The Cell - A Functioning Structure, Pt 1. Describes the structure and functions of the living cell. Illustrates the processes by which cells nourish themselves and reproduce. Reveals the key functions of DNA and protein enzymes.
Prod-KATTNS Dist-MGHT 1978

La Celula - Una Estructura En Funcionamiento, Pt 2 C 30 MIN
16MM FILM, 3/4 OR 1/2 IN VIDEO H-C A
A Spanish language version of The Cell - A Functioning Structure, Pt 2. Explores the chemistry of the cell, showing how the cell manufactures proteins. Discusses how plant cells convert solar energy into chemical energy and how proteins are exported from the cell.
Prod-KATTNS Dist-MGHT 1978

La Cena C 22 MIN
16MM FILM OPTICAL SOUND
Shows how 11-year-old Pedrito works to buy medicine and a Christmas dinner for his sick mother, but loses his money to a gambler posing as a policeman. Explains how Pedrito then steals some food and is hit by a car as he flees from the police. Tells how the police promise to take Christmas dinner to Pedrito's mother while he is in the hospital.
LC NO. 78-700194
Prod-VALENJ Dist-VALENJ 1977

La Chambre C 6 MIN
16MM FILM, 3/4 OR 1/2 IN VIDEO J-C A
Uses animation, to show the frustration and confusion of a person trapped in a room. Shows how, as he tries to escape, the walls move and his tension increases. Reflects the feeling experienced when one is caught in a dilemma and there appears to be no way out. Without narration.
Prod-IFB Dist-IFB 1971

La Chasse A Mort C 15 MIN
16MM FILM, 3/4 OR 1/2 IN VIDEO C A
See series title for descriptive statement.
From The La Maree Et Ses Secrets Series.
Prod-FI Dist-FI

La Chinoise C 95 MIN
16MM FILM OPTICAL SOUND H-C A
A French language film director by Jean-Luc Godard. Examines the militant New Left and the lives of five young Maoists plotting revolution from a Paris suburb.
Prod-PENBAK Dist-NYFLMS 1973

La Classification Animale C 13 MIN
16MM FILM, 3/4 OR 1/2 IN VIDEO I-J
A French language version of the videocassette Putting Animals In Groups. Explains how animals are classified according to their structure. Points out the distinctive characteristics of mammals, birds, reptiles, amphibians, fishes and insects.
Prod-IFB Dist-IFB 1956

La Colonia Tovar C 13 MIN
16MM FILM, 3/4 OR 1/2 IN VIDEO J-C
Examines the process and effects of change in Colonia Tovar, a small village in the coastal mountains of Venezuela. Shows how the community, settled more than 100 years ago by immigrants from southern Germany, adapted slowly until in 1940 a road linked the village with Caracas and how cultural changes swiftly accelerated after the road was built.
Prod-UCEMC Dist-UCEMC 1975

La Couleur De La Forme C 7 MIN
16MM FILM OPTICAL SOUND H-C
Presents a collage film.
Prod-CFS Dist-CFS 1969

La Divina C 8 MIN
16MM FILM OPTICAL SOUND
Uses a juxtaposition of transcendental paintings and the activities in a car-washing establishment to satirize the preoccupation of the American people with cleanliness.
LC NO. 76-702332
Prod-USC Dist-USC 1968

La Dolce Festa - Little Italy, New York C 31 MIN
16MM FILM OPTICAL SOUND H-C A
Documents the 10-day San Gennaro Festival, held each September in New York City's Little Italy to celebrate the liquification of the martyred saint's blood.
LC NO. 77-703179
Prod-CECROP Dist-CECROP 1977

La Esquina (English)—A Series
H-C A
Uses stories to try to reduce the minority isolation of Mexican-American students by showing the teenager as an individual, as a member of a unique cultural group and as a member of a larger complex society.
Prod-SWEDL Dist-GPITVL 1976

Cada Quien Hace Su Parte (English) 030 MIN
Coconuts 030 MIN
El Chicano (English) 030 MIN
Encounter, The 030 MIN
La Abuela Chicana (English) 050 MIN
Last Hurrah, The 030 MIN
Rollos / Roles 030 MIN
Roots / Raices 030 MIN
Superstar 030 MIN
Walkout That Never Was, The 030 MIN

La Estrella Del Carnival (Cuba) C 10 MIN
16MM FILM OPTICAL SOUND
Shows a nurse in Havana being chosen as the carnival queen. Presents one of the eclectic aspects of Cuba's revolutionary culture.
Prod-NEWSR Dist-NEWSR 1965

La Estructura (Cuba) C 12 MIN
16MM FILM OPTICAL SOUND
Gives a lyrical and impressionist treatment of the thermoelectric plant construction. Uses an unusual electric music track to complement the images.
Prod-NEWSR Dist-NEWSR

La Familia Silvestre Encuentra Hogar C 11 MIN
16MM FILM, 3/4 OR 1/2 IN VIDEO
A Spanish version of 'MAKE WAY FOR DUCKLINGS.' Follows Mrs Mallard as she leaves her home on an island in the Charles River and escorts her eight ducklings through hazardous Boston traffic to the public gardens where Mr Mallard is waiting for his family to join him.
Prod-WWS Dist-WWS 1960

La Fantaisie De Melies B 8 MIN
16MM FILM SILENT H-C A
Shows how special effects and camera tricks, such as stop photography and double exposures, were used in early films. Provides samples of phantasmagoria using three films--extraordinary illusions, the enchanted well and the apparition--copied from 35mm positives. A silent film.
LC NO. FI68-7
Prod-BHAWK Dist-BHAWK 1963

La Femme Infidele C 102 MIN
16MM FILM OPTICAL SOUND C A
A French language film. Presents a suspense drama. Includes English subtitles.
Prod-CINEWO Dist-CINEWO 1969

La Flor Y La Colmena C 15 MIN
16MM FILM, 3/4 OR 1/2 IN VIDEO I-C A
A Spanish language version of the videocassette The Flower And The Hive. Examines the relationship between the activities of bees and the fertility of fields.
Prod-NFBC Dist-IFB 1961

La France Contemporaine—A Series
16MM FILM, 3/4 OR 1/2 IN VIDEO H-C
Explores the geography, people and culture of France.
Prod-EBEC Dist-EBEC 1971

L'Art Et La Vie 9 MIN
Loin De Paris 10 MIN
Loisirs Et Vacances 11 MIN
Rythmes De Paris 9 MIN
Vivre Mieux, Demain 10 MIN

La France Telle Qu'Elle Est—A Series
16MM FILM, 3/4 OR 1/2 IN VIDEO H-C
Each film in this series has three parts - a documentary about one aspect of French life, role playing dialogue and a personal interview with a French national.
Prod-THAMES Dist-MEDIAG 1977

Le Tourisme 019 MIN
Paris, Aujourd' Hui 019 MIN
Paris, Hier 019 MIN
Un Hypermarche 019 MIN
Une Vile De Province 019 MIN

La Frontera C 28 MIN
16MM FILM OPTICAL SOUND
Views the border zone between the United States and Mexico. Portrays the meeting of two worlds with two standards of living through interviews with people living along the border zone.
Prod-HUDRIV Dist-HUDRIV

La Frontera (Spanish) C 28 MIN
16MM FILM OPTICAL SOUND
Views the border zone between the United States and Mexic
Portrays the meeting of two worlds with two standards of livin
through interviews with people living along the border zone
Prod-HUDRIV Dist-HUDRIV

La Frustration - Est-Ce Que Je Finirai Par L'avoir C 7 MI
16MM FILM OPTICAL SOUND
A French version of Frustration - How Can I Get It Right. Deal with a student's frustration caused by his inability to remembe the lines of a play.
From The Emotions (French) Series.
LC NO. 75-704305
Prod-MORLAT Dist-MORLAT 197

La Gallinita Roja C 16 MI
16MM FILM, 3/4 OR 1/2 IN VIDEO I-
A Spanish version of The Little Red Hen.
Prod-FA Dist-PHENIX 196

La Gallinita Sabia B 11 MI
16MM FILM, 3/4 OR 1/2 IN VIDEO I-
Spanish version of 'THE LITTLE RED HEN.' Combines art wor and live action to depict the story. Narration is designed to pro vide frequent repetition.
Prod-CORF Dist-CORF 196

La Gare C 18 MI
16MM FILM, 3/4 OR 1/2 IN VIDEO J-
Features the rail station at Chateau-du-Loir, that serves bot main and local lines. Shows how to buy a ticket, inquire abou train times and for la consigne. Linguistically explains ho changing the intonation of a question beginning 'Est-ce-que can produce a statement.
From The Comment Dit-On Series.
Prod-THAMES Dist-MEDIAG 197

La Garonne C 7 MI
16MM FILM, 3/4 OR 1/2 IN VIDEO H-C
A French language videocassette. Follows the course of the rive Garonne.
From The Chroniques De France Series.
LC NO. 81-706548
Prod-ADPF Dist-IFB 198

La Grande Breteche C 25 MI
16MM FILM, 3/4 OR 1/2 IN VIDEO H-
Presents a mystery story set in France during the Napoleoni wars. Involves the revenge taken by a one-time criminal in re turn for the infidelity of his wife and her lover. Televised on CB in the Orson Wells Great Mystery Series.
From The Orson Welles Great Mysteries Series.
Prod-ANGLIA Dist-EBEC 197

La Grande Vitesse - The Work Of Alexander Calder C 16 MI
16MM FILM OPTICAL SOUND
Shows American sculptor Alexander Calder as he complete work on stabiles, several large forty ton steel environmenta sculptures.
LC NO. 72-702308
Prod-GVSC Dist-GVSC 197

La Guarda Cuidadosa C 28 MI
16MM FILM, 3/4 OR 1/2 IN VIDEO H-
Presents a version of the novel La Guarda Cuidadosa, by Cervantes, which tells how the guarda protects the house of the girl he hopes to marry. Includes scenes of the village of Nuevo Bastan which dates back to the time of Cervantes.
Prod-EBEC Dist-EBEC 196

La Guitarra Espanola C 10 MIN
16MM FILM, 3/4 OR 1/2 IN VIDEO J-C A
A Spanish-language beginning level version adapted from the motion picture I Am A Guitar. Shows how Ignacio Fleta and his sons lovingly shape and sand classical guitar frames, apply the inlaid rosette that is their trademark and polish the well-seasoned Cuban cedar, German spruce, Brazilian rosewood and hard African ebony that comprise the kind of instrument Andres Segovia or John Williams would wait a decade to play.
Prod-IFB Dist-IFB 1973

La Habanera (Captioned) C 108 MIN
16MM FILM, 3/4 OR 1/2 IN VIDEO A
Portrays modern Cuba through the story of the mid-life crisis of a female psychiatrist who is dedicated to her professional life as well as to her home and family. Spanish dialog with English subtitles.
Prod-CNEMAG Dist-CNEMAG 1983

La Historia De Las Aztecas C 19 MIN
16MM FILM, 3/4 OR 1/2 IN VIDEO
A Spanish language version of The Story Of The Aztecs. Presents the accomplishments of the Aztecs, showing ruins of the Aztec empire. Points out their relationship to the Mexican people.
From The Mexican Heritage (Spanish) Series.
Prod-STEXMF Dist-FI 1976

La Historia De Un Nino Esquimal C 31 MIN
16MM FILM, 3/4 OR 1/2 IN VIDEO I-C A
A Spanish language version of the motion picture Angotee. Presents an account of an Eskimo boy's life from infancy to maturity.
Prod-NFBC Dist-IFB 1953

La Historia Romantica Del Tranporte Canadiense C 11 MIN
16MM FILM, 3/4 OR 1/2 IN VIDEO
A Spanish language version of The Romance Of Transportation. Uses animation to show the growth of transportation in North America. Comments on the development of the canoe, oxcart, barge, steamboat, railroad, automobile, and airplane.
Prod-NFBC Dist-IFB 1954

La Idea De Los Numeros C 14 MIN
16MM FILM, 3/4 OR 1/2 IN VIDEO I-H
A Spanish language version of the videocassette The Idea Of Numbers - An Introduction To Number Systems. Describes various number systems, including the decimal system, arabic numbers, and binary notation.
Prod-IFB Dist-IFB 1961

La Jaconde - The Smile Of The Mona Lisa C 16 MIN
16MM FILM, 3/4 OR 1/2 IN VIDEO J-C
Presents the story of an obsession held since the creation of Portrait Of Mona Lisa by Leonardo De Vinci.
Prod-ARGOS Dist-TEXFLM 1970

La Jetee B 29 MIN
16MM FILM, 3/4 OR 1/2 IN VIDEO H-C A
A French language film. Presents survivors of an atomic war who try by telepathy to establish contact with the past. Includes English subtitles.
Prod-ARGOS Dist-TEXFLM 1973

La Leyenda Del Alcalde de Zalamea (Spanish) C 120 MIN
3/4 OR 1/2 INCH VIDEO CASSETTE
Offers a retelling of the story of the alcalde of Zalamea based on the plays of Lope and Calderon with its emphasis on the concepts of honor and loyalty.
Prod-FOTH Dist-FOTH 1984

La Lucha Contra Los Microbios C 29 MIN
16MM FILM, 3/4 OR 1/2 IN VIDEO H-C
A Spanish language version of the videocassette The Fight Against Microbes. Traces the development of methods for combating pathogenic bacteria, including the contributions of Leeuwenhoek, Jenner, Pasteur, Koch, Behring, Lister, Ehrlich, Domagh and Fleming.
Prod-IFB Dist-IFB 1966

La Maison C 18 MIN
16MM FILM, 3/4 OR 1/2 IN VIDEO J-H
Presents a French family sunbathing, playing table tennis and tending flowers in the garden of a large house at Chateau-du-Loir. Linguistically shows that a question involving the inversion of verb and subject pronoun is answered by re-inversion of verb and pronoun.
From The Comment Dit-On Series.
Prod-THAMES Dist-MEDIAG 1977

La Mal Vie - Algerian Migrants C 58 MIN
3/4 OR 1/2 INCH VIDEO CASSETTE
Profiles two Algerian migrant laborers who are part of a rootless population working in menial jobs in Europe.
From The World Series.
Prod-WGBHTV Dist-PBS 1980

La Mandragola B 97 MIN
16MM FILM OPTICAL SOUND C A
An Italian language film with English subtitles about a husband who makes his wife take various fertility potions in order for her to provide him with an heir. Details how Gallimaco, a worldly blade and admirer of feminine beauty, conceives of a way by which he may possess the wife.
Prod-TRANSW Dist-TRANSW 1967

La Maree Et Ses Secrets—A Series
C A
Presents beginning French language combined with a continuing mystery story set in Brittany.
Prod-FI Dist-FI

Chez Keravec 015 MIN
La Chasse A Mort 015 MIN
Les Choux-Fleurs De Saint-Brieuc 015 MIN
Les Surprises 015 MIN
Une Ombre Du Passe 015 MIN

La Mauricie C 14 MIN
16MM FILM OPTICAL SOUND
Depicts the pulp mills and the giant hydro works of the region of Quebec through which the St Maurice River flows. Shows the annual canoe classic that tests paddlers' skill one hundred miles downstream.
Prod-QUEBEC Dist-CTFL 1964

La Meilleure Occasion B 13 MIN
16MM FILM OPTICAL SOUND I-H
See series title for descriptive statement.
From The Les Francais Chez Vous Series. Set III, Lesson 34
Prod-PEREN Dist-CHLTN 1967

La Mort Du Rat C 7 MIN
3/4 OR 1/2 INCH VIDEO CASSETTE
Tells of a French factory worker who loses his job, returns home, and passes his anger along to his wife.
Prod-FLOWER Dist-FLOWER

La Mosca De La Fruta C 21 MIN
16MM FILM, 3/4 OR 1/2 IN VIDEO H-C A
A Spanish language version of The Fruit Fly - A Look At Behavior Biology. Examines the relationship of genes to behavior, using the fruit fly as a microcosm of life.
Prod-KATTNS Dist-MGHT 1978

La Moto C 7 MIN
16MM FILM, 3/4 OR 1/2 IN VIDEO H-C A
A French language videocassette. Shows the two-day long motorcycle rally that begins at Val d'Isere.
From The Chroniques De France Series.
LC NO. 81-706552
Prod-ADPF Dist-IFB 1980

La Mujer En Los Negocios C 30 MIN
16MM FILM, 3/4 OR 1/2 IN VIDEO H-C A
A Spanish language version of Women In Management - Threat Or Opportunity. Examines the effect of the women's liberation movement in several organizations and shows how leaders and managers are dealing with the situation.
Prod-MGHT Dist-MGHT 1976

La Muralla Invisible B 107 MIN
16MM FILM OPTICAL SOUND
A Spanish version of the English language film, Question 7.
Prod-LUTHER Dist-LUTHER

La Musica De La Gente - The Music Of The People C 28 MIN
16MM FILM, 3/4 OR 1/2 IN VIDEO
Features the popular music of Hispanic people of the Southwest. Presents the music against the social and environmental background from which it developed.
Prod-BLUSKY Dist-ONEWST

La Musica De Los Viejos - Music Of The Old Ones C 28 MIN
16MM FILM, 3/4 OR 1/2 IN VIDEO
Features the Hispanic folk music of the Southwest and the old musicians who preserve it.
Prod-PMEDA Dist-ONEWST

La Musique C 13 MIN
16MM FILM OPTICAL SOUND I-C
See series title for descriptive statement.
From The En Francaise, Set 2 Series.
Prod-PEREN Dist-CHLTN 1969

La Naissance Du Kangourou Rouge C 21 MIN
16MM FILM, 3/4 OR 1/2 IN VIDEO J-H
A French language version of the videocassette The Birth Of The Red Kangaroo. Traces the development of the Australian red kangaroo from conception through the first year of life. Illustrates the unique features of marsupial development.
Prod-CSIROA Dist-IFB 1966

La Naturaliez De La Materia C 24 MIN
16MM FILM, 3/4 OR 1/2 IN VIDEO H-C A
A Spanish language version of The Nature Of Matter. Probes the nature of atomic and subatomic particles. Discusses the concepts which led to the quantum theory. Emphasizes the particle-like and wave-like characteristics of the atomic constituents.
From The Physical Science (Spanish) Series.
Prod-KATTNS Dist-MGHT 1978

La Navidad En Oaxaca C 14 MIN
16MM FILM, 3/4 OR 1/2 IN VIDEO
A Spanish language version of Christmas In Oaxaca. Shows Christmas celebrations in the Oaxaca region of Mexico, including folkloric dancers in vivid costumes, various customs of the region, students and a marimba band.
From The Mexican Heritage (Spanish) Series.
Prod-STEXMF Dist-FI 1975

LA Nickel C 9 MIN
3/4 INCH VIDEO CASSETTE
Presents a video verite record of the interactions of the street bums and LA police. A night drive blocked by a police car suggests a metaphor of social confinement.
Prod-EAI Dist-EAI

La Notte Brava B 96 MIN
16MM FILM, 3/4 OR 1/2 IN VIDEO A
Portrays contemporary life among aimless youth in Rome. English dubbed version.
Prod-CNEMAG Dist-CNEMAG 1961

La Operacion C 40 MIN
16MM FILM, 3/4 OR 1/2 IN VIDEO
Begins by noting that Puerto Rico has the world's highest incidence of female sterilization, with one-third of all Puerto Rican women of childbearing age having been sterilized. Documents the social, moral and religious issue as a means of population control with interviews of women, physicians, politicians and others.
Prod-CNEMAG Dist-CNEMAG 1982

La Peau De Chagrin C 10 MIN
16MM FILM, 3/4 OR 1/2 IN VIDEO H A
Uses animation to tell the story of a poor and unhappy man who leaves his love to try his luck at gambling, loses his last penny, and then is given a magic skin which fulfills all wishes, but grows shorter as it is used.
Prod-ZAGREB Dist-IFB 1971

La Perichole C 30 MIN
16MM FILM, 3/4 OR 1/2 IN VIDEO J-C A
Features Joan Sutherland singing selected arias from the opera La Pericole.
From The Who's Afraid Of Opera Series.
Prod-PHENIX Dist-PHENIX 1973

La Petite Ferme C 12 MIN
16MM FILM OPTICAL SOUND I-C A
A French language film. Pictures the daily activities of a peasant family, living in the farm area of Etampes (Seine-et-Oise.)
From The Voix Et Images De France Series.
Prod-PEREN Dist-CHLTN Prodn-CRDDF 1962

La Petite Poule Rouge C 16 MIN
16MM FILM, 3/4 OR 1/2 IN VIDEO I-H A
A French version of The Little Red Hen.
Prod-FA Dist-PHENIX 1961

La Pinata C 11 MIN
16MM FILM, 3/4 OR 1/2 IN VIDEO H-C
A Spanish language film. Uses animation to tell the story of Pepe, who works in a Mexican pinata factory. Designed for first-year Spanish classes.
Prod-SIGMA Dist-FILCOM 1964

La Piscine B 13 MIN
16MM FILM OPTICAL SOUND J-C
See series title for descriptive statement.
From The En France Avec Jean Et Helen Series. Set 1, Lesson 5
LC NO. 70-704512
Prod-PEREN Dist-CHLTN 1967

La Place C 18 MIN
16MM FILM, 3/4 OR 1/2 IN VIDEO J-H
Describes a visit to some of the businesses in the small town of Bauge on market day. Includes a boulangerie, a charcuterie, and a marchand de primeurs. Linguistically reviews how a change of intonation transforms a question into an affirmative answer.
From The Comment Dit-On Series.
Prod-THAMES Dist-MEDIAG 1977

La Plage C 4 MIN
16MM FILM, 3/4 OR 1/2 IN VIDEO H-C A
Presents an animated tale in which a man foresees the drowning of a woman who was sailing alone.
Prod-NFBC Dist-PHENIX 1981

La Plage C 18 MIN
16MM FILM, 3/4 OR 1/2 IN VIDEO J-H
Looks at the sandy beaches of les Sables-d'Olonne, which every summer attract thousands of children and adults to the seaside. Linguistically explains the principles governing the use of perfect and imperfect tense, matching the tense of an answer to a question to avoid confusion and error.
From The Comment Dit-On Series.
Prod-THAMES Dist-MEDIAG 1977

La Pomme B 15 MIN
16MM FILM OPTICAL SOUND C A
A French language film. Presents an informal, impressionistic record of a contemporary artist's happy life with painting, love, people and the city. Includes English subtitles.
Prod-UWFKD Dist-UWFKD

La Poulette Grise C 6 MIN
16MM FILM, 3/4 OR 1/2 IN VIDEO
Presents an adaptation of a French lullaby.
Prod-NFBC Dist-IFB

La Premiere Soiree C 8 MIN
16MM FILM OPTICAL SOUND H-C A
Uses experimental techniques to create the moods and feelings of the poem La Premiere Soiree by Rimbaud.
Prod-VIERAD Dist-VIERAD 1979

La Primera Ciudad De Las Americas - Teotihuacan C 18 MIN
16MM FILM, 3/4 OR 1/2 IN VIDEO
A Spanish version of America's First City - Teotihuacan. Visits the pyramids of Teotihuacan, 25 miles from Mexico City, pointing out the skills and artistry of the early Mexican people who built this city about 2,000 years ago. Notes that Teotihuacan was the first city built in the Americas.
From The Mexican Heritage (Spanish) Series.
Prod-STEXMF Dist-FI 1975

La Princesse C 5 MIN
16MM FILM OPTICAL SOUND K-I
A story about two farm children who meet a princess who changes their bread and leaves to cake and flowers.
From The Bonjour Line Series. Part 1.
Prod-PEREN Dist-CHLTN 1962

La Proprete - Si Vous Ne Pouvez Pas Vous Laver Les Mains, Mettez Un Pansement C 9 MIN
16MM FILM OPTICAL SOUND
A French language version of the motion picture Cleanliness - If You Can't Wash Your Hands Wear A Band-Aid. Explores the world of germs, including where they live, what they do and how some of them get inside the human body and cause illness.
From The Health (French) Series.
LC NO. 76-700122
Prod-MORLAT Dist-MORLAT 1974

La Quete De Dieu - The Quest Of God C 52 MIN
16MM FILM OPTICAL SOUND
Analyzes the importance of monasteries among peasants and knights in the 11th century. Views Gerone's Apocalypse paintings of Saint-Vincent of Cardona and Tahull's frescoes.
From The Le Temp Des Cathedrales Series.
Prod-FACSEA Dist-FACSEA 1979

La Quinceanera C 30 MIN
3/4 OR 1/2 INCH VIDEO CASSETTE P-I
See series title for descriptive statement.
From The Sonrisas Series.
Prod-KRLNTV Dist-MDCPB

La Region Centrale C 180 MIN
16MM FILM OPTICAL SOUND
A French language film. Uses a specially designed camera mount in order to provide a new perspective on the scenery of the wilderness of northern Quebec.
LC NO. 74-701608
Prod-CFDEVC Dist-CANFDC 1971

La Rentree (The Return To School) C 15 MIN
16MM FILM OPTICAL SOUND J-C A
A French language film. Tells the adventure of Caroline's and Victor's trip to a shop to buy their school supplies which brought Caroline's teacher's reprimands for wearing make-up.
From The Toute La Bande Series. No. 6
LC NO. 75-715482
Prod-SCHMAG Dist-SCHMAG 1970

La Reproduccion De La Plantas C 14 MIN
16MM FILM, 3/4 OR 1/2 IN VIDEO

A Spanish language film. Shows the difference between sexual and asexual reproduction of plants and explains the processes involved in both methods. Describes self-pollination, cross-pollination and the improvement of plant strains by selective breeding.
Prod-CORF Dist-CORF 1958

La Reunion B 11 MIN
16MM FILM OPTICAL SOUND J-C A
A Spanish language film. See series title for annotation.
From The Beginning Spanish Series. No. 3
Prod-CBF Dist-AVED 1960

La Robe De Chambre De Georges Bataille (French) C 70 MIN
3/4 OR 1/2 INCH VIDEO CASSETTE
Features the 1983 Paris production by Foreman's Ontological/Hysterical Theatre.
Prod-KITCHN Dist-KITCHN

La Salamandre B 125 MIN
16MM FILM OPTICAL SOUND
An English subtitle version of the French language, Swiss-made film. Follows incidents in the life of a young working-class Swiss girl, Rosemonde, who works at one job after another whenever the spirit and her sinking finances move her. Tells how she seeks out men who please her and sheds them when they start weighing her down.
Prod-NYFLMS Dist-NYFLMS 1971

La Salud Mental Y La Communidad B 31 MIN
16MM FILM, 3/4 OR 1/2 IN VIDEO H-C
A Spanish film. Dramatizes the process of developing and operating a community--based mental health center whose function extends far beyond the diagnostic and treatment services of the traditional clinic. Traces the developments of the clinic and some of the problems that arise.
Prod-MHFB Dist-IFB 1931

La Sculpture Du Cuivre Au Chalumeau C 14 MIN
16MM FILM, 3/4 OR 1/2 IN VIDEO H-C A S
A French-language version of the motion picture Sculpturing Copper With A Torch. Shows the use of copper tube, wire, sheets and pipes in sculpturing. Explains the processes of forming, patching, enameling, brazing, cleaning and oxidation.
Prod-MOTIVF Dist-IFB 1965

La Sopa De Piedras C 11 MIN
16MM FILM, 3/4 OR 1/2 IN VIDEO
A Spanish version of 'STONE SOUP.' Shows how three famished soldiers satisfy their hunger by tricking a group of gullible French peasants into supplying meat and vegetables for a pot of stone soup.
Prod-WWS Dist-WWS 1960

La Sorpresa C 30 MIN
3/4 OR 1/2 INCH VIDEO CASSETTE P-I
See series title for descriptive statement.
From The Sonrisas Series.
Prod-KRLNTV Dist-MDCPB

La Soufriere C 30 MIN
16MM FILM OPTICAL SOUND
Shows what happened when an earthquake was predicted on the island of Guadeloupe and all the residents, except for one, left. Directed by Werner Herzog.
Prod-UNKNWN Dist-NYFLMS 1977

La Superficie De La Tierra En Mapas C 16 MIN
16MM FILM, 3/4 OR 1/2 IN VIDEO
A Spanish language film. Explains the process of mapmaking from the establishment of a network of control points, through the collection of detailed information, to final compilation and printing.
Prod-CORF Dist-CORF 1969

La Tapisserie De Bayeux C 7 MIN
16MM FILM, 3/4 OR 1/2 IN VIDEO H-C A
A French language videocassette. Shows the Bayeux Tapestry.
From The Chroniques De France Series.
LC NO. 81-706546
Prod-ADPF Dist-IFB 1980

La Television - Linea Por Linea C 11 MIN
16MM FILM, 3/4 OR 1/2 IN VIDEO H-C
A Spanish language version of the videocassete Television - Line By Line. Uses animation to explain the principles of television.
Prod-IFB Dist-IFB 1970

La Tercera Palabra B 110 MIN
16MM FILM OPTICAL SOUND A
A Spanish language film. Tells the story of an aunt who hires a beautiful woman to teach her uneducated nephew.
Prod-TRANSW Dist-TRANSW

La Terre Est Une Femme C 28 MIN
16MM FILM OPTICAL SOUND
A French-language version of the motion picture The Land Is A Woman. Looks at the activities inherent in grape-growing and wine making in Virginia plus the romance they inspire in a vintner and his wife.
Prod-SCHDRC Dist-SCHDRC 1981

La Tete Et Les Jambes C 13 MIN
16MM FILM OPTICAL SOUND J A
From The En Francais, Set 1 Series.
Prod-PEREN Dist-CHLTN 1969

La Traversee De L'Atlantique A La Rame - Crossing The Atlantic In A Small Boat C 22 MIN
16MM FILM OPTICAL SOUND
Takes an improbable news item about a married couple's strange odyssey in a small boat and turns it into a narrative as the years pass and the journey continues.
Prod-FWRGHT Dist-FWRGHT 1978

La Traviata C 30 MIN
16MM FILM, 3/4 OR 1/2 IN VIDEO J-C A
Features Joan Sutherland singing selected arias from the opera 'LA TRAVIATA.'
From The Who's Afraid Of Opera Series.
Prod-PHENIX Dist-PHENIX 1973

La Traviata C 130 MIN
3/4 OR 1/2 INCH VIDEO CASSETTE
Presents the Augusta Opera's production of La Traviata at Columbus' Springer Opera House.
Prod-GPTV Dist-MDCPB

La Ultima Descarga C 21 MIN
16MM FILM, 3/4 OR 1/2 IN VIDEO IND
A Spanish-language version of the motion picture One Last Shock. Dramatizes the events leading to an electrical accident. Outlines the misuses of electrical equipment in the factory and office.
Prod-MILLBK Dist-IFB 1980

La Vida Es Sueno (Spanish) C 55 MIN
3/4 OR 1/2 INCH VIDEO CASSETTE
Presents an example of the Spanish form of literature known as the auto written by Pedro Calderon De La Barca
Prod-FOTH Dist-FOTH 1984

La Vie Dans La Foret Feuillue C 19 MIN
16MM FILM, 3/4 OR 1/2 IN VIDEO I-H
A French language version of the videocassette Life In The Deciduous Forest. Discusses life in the deciduous forest, tracing variations in temperature, moisture and light.
Prod-IFB Dist-IFB 1962

La Vie Tient A Plus D'Un Fil C 12 MIN
16MM FILM, 3/4 OR 1/2 IN VIDEO
A French language videocassette. Includes sequences on the history of puppets, how marionettes and their costumes are made, and a puppeteer at work.
Prod-INTNEW Dist-IFB 1978

La Viejecita Del Zapato C 11 MIN
16MM FILM, 3/4 OR 1/2 IN VIDEO I
A Spanish language film. Uses the nursery rhyme about the old woman and the shoe to develop beginning number vocabulary in Spanish.
Prod-CORF Dist-CORF 1966

La Vita (Life In A Tin) C 7 MIN
16MM FILM SILENT J-C A
Philosophizes about twentieth century man who is so caught up in the business of living that he forgets the meaning of life.
Prod-UWFKD Dist-UWFKD

La Voix Humaine C 57 MIN
16MM FILM OPTICAL SOUND
Offers an adaptation of the Cocteau-Poulenc opera La Voix Humaine, utilizing the capabilities of film to go in and out of space and time.
LC NO. 79-700406
Prod-APRO Dist-PBS 1979

LA 53 C 10 MIN
16MM FILM, 3/4 OR 1/2 IN VIDEO I-H
Captures the sights, sounds, rhythms and feelings of railroading by following a freight train from Chicago to Los Angeles.
Prod-ALTPRO Dist-JOU 1970

LA, LA, Making It In Los Angeles C 58 MIN
16MM FILM, 3/4 OR 1/2 IN VIDEO H-C A
Focuses on the search for show business fame and fortune in the Los Angeles entertainment industry.
Prod-MOURIS Dist-DIRECT 1979

Lab Safety C
3/4 OR 1/2 INCH VIDEO CASSETTE
See series title for descriptive statement.
From The Basic AC Circuits Series.
Prod-VTRI Dist-VTRI

Lab Safety C 12 MIN
16MM FILM, 3/4 OR 1/2 IN VIDEO H-C A
Outlines safety procedures to follow when accidents occur in a chemistry laboratory. Demonstrates extinguishers for four different types of fires and shows procedures for using a fire blanket and for washing harmful chemicals out of the eyes and off the body.
LC NO. 80-706096
Prod-NET Dist-IU 1975

Lab Safety C 13 MIN
3/4 OR 1/2 INCH VIDEO CASSETTE C A
Highlights rules and procedures that help to prevent serious accidents in the laboratory. Through the use of staged accidents, shows the proper steps to take in case of an accident.
From The Chemistry - Master Apprentice Series. Program 13
LC NO. 82-706030
Prod-CUETV Dist-CUNIV 1981

Lab Studies Of Development C 45 MIN
3/4 OR 1/2 INCH VIDEO CASSETTE C
Shows lab studies of development.
From The Biology I Series.
Prod-MDCPB Dist-MDCPB

Label Logic C 18 MIN
16MM FILM, 3/4 OR 1/2 IN VIDEO H-C A
Shows just exactly what the label should tell the consumer under the provisions of the Food and Drug Act and Fair Packaging and Labeling Act. Points out what the consumer should look for in particular and where he may possibly be misled or misguided.
Prod-AIMS Dist-AIMS 1968

Label Logic (Spanish) C 18 MIN
16MM FILM, 3/4 OR 1/2 IN VIDEO J-C A
Informs buyer to read labels in order that he can make better judgments before making purchases. Discusses standards of quality and fill of container as checked scientifically by the food and drug administration.
Prod-ASSOC Dist-AIMS 1968

Label The Behavior C 30 MIN
3/4 OR 1/2 INCH VIDEO CASSETTE T
Discusses physical, emotional and mental characteristics of exceptional children.
From The Stretch Concepts For Teaching Handicapped Children Series.
Prod-HUBDSC Dist-HUBDSC

Label The Behavior, Not The Child C 30 MIN
16MM FILM OPTICAL SOUND T
Depicts physical, emotional and mental characteristics of exceptional children and describes behavior patterns.
From The Project STRETCH Series. Module 12
LC NO. 80-700619
Prod-METCO Dist-HUBDSC Prodn-GAEDTN 1980

Label To Table, Pt 1 C 29 MIN
3/4 OR 1/2 INCH VIDEO CASSETTE H-C A
Looks at the information found on food labels, the coming of metric weight, open dating, drained weight labeling, universal product code and label graphics.
From The Be A Better Shopper Series. Program 5
LC NO. 81-707305
Prod-CUETV Dist-CUNIV 1978

Label To Table, Pt 2 C 29 MIN
3/4 OR 1/2 INCH VIDEO CASSETTE H-C A
Explores the legal aspects of food labeling, such as ingredient lists, federal standards and imitation and artificial products.
From The Be A Better Shopper Series. Program 6
LC NO. 81-707306
Prod-CUETV Dist-CUNIV 1978

Labeling C 30 MIN
3/4 OR 1/2 INCH VIDEO CASSETTE
See series title for descriptive statement.
From The Food For Life Series.
Prod-MSU Dist-MSU

Labels C 13 MIN
2 INCH VIDEOTAPE
See series title for descriptive statement.
From The Living Better I Series.
Prod-MAETEL Dist-PUBTEL

Labels - If You Label It This, It Can't Be That C 14 MIN
16MM FILM, 3/4 OR 1/2 IN VIDEO
Explains how labels can perpetuate misconceptions and stereotypes. Uses candid interviews with children to illustrate the extent to which labels about people are erroneous.
Prod-FLMFR Dist-FLMFR

Labels And Distortion C 30 MIN
3/4 OR 1/2 INCH VIDEO CASSETTE C
See series title for descriptive statement.
From The Language And Meaning Series.
Prod-WUSFTV Dist-GPITVL 1983

Labor C 30 MIN
2 INCH VIDEOTAPE
Examines the problems labor faced in its struggle to organize.
From The American History II Series.
Prod-KRMATV Dist-GPITVL

Labor - Its History C 30 MIN
3/4 INCH VIDEO CASSETTE
See series title for descriptive statement.
From The It's Everybody's Business Series. Unit 4, Managing A Business
Prod-DALCCD Dist-DALCCD

Labor And Delivery C 14 MIN
3/4 OR 1/2 INCH VIDEO CASSETTE
Defines stages of labor and discusses what the mother can expect physically and emotionally during these stages. Details cervical dilation and effacement, and explains medication before and during delivery, defines episiotomy and actual delivery of the baby followed by the placenta.
LC NO. 77-73135
Prod-TRAINX Dist-TRAINX

Labor And Delivery C 19 MIN
16MM FILM, 3/4 OR 1/2 IN VIDEO H-C A
Examines the stages of labor and shows the actual birth of a baby in the delivery room. Includes scenes of hospital care of the mother after delivery, care of the newborn and the first few days at home.
From The Pregnancy And Childbirth Series.
Prod-DALHSU Dist-IFB Prodn-CRAF 1977

Labor And Delivery C 29 MIN
3/4 OR 1/2 INCH VIDEO CASSETTE H-C A
Describes the three main stages of childbirth and shows how these stages can be assisted by various techniques.
From The Tomorrow's Families Series.
LC NO. 81-706903
Prod-MSDOE Dist-AITECH 1980

Labor And Delivery (Spanish) C 14 MIN
3/4 OR 1/2 INCH VIDEO CASSETTE
Defines stages of labor and discusses what the mother can expect physically and emotionally during these stages. Details cervical dilation and effacement, and explains medication before and during delivery, defines episiotomy and actual delivery of the baby followed by the placenta.
LC NO. 77-73135
Prod-TRAINX Dist-TRAINX

Labor And Management - How Do They Come To Terms C 30 MIN
3/4 OR 1/2 INCH VIDEO CASSETTE C
See series title for descriptive statement.
From The Economics USA Series.
Prod-WEFA Dist-ANNCPB

Labor And Social Security B 20 MIN
16MM FILM OPTICAL SOUND J-H A
Traces the background of economic conditions which led to the enactment of the Social Security Act. States that security and human dignity have replaced the degradation of poverty and dependence which old people faced before 1935.
Prod-AFLCIO Dist-AFLCIO

Labor Bosses Of Texas B 28 MIN
16MM FILM OPTICAL SOUND
Gives some answers to the charge that officers of the State Federation and State Council are 'LABOR BOSSES' and not representing the union membership. Emphasizes the Democratic structure of the labor movement and the way its members make decisions which are carried out.
Prod-AFLCIO Dist-AFLCIO 1956

Labor Day C 15 MIN
3/4 INCH VIDEO CASSETTE P
See series title for descriptive statement.
From The Celebrate Series.
Prod-KUONTV Dist-GPITVL 1978

Labor In The Promised Land C 52 MIN
3/4 OR 1/2 INCH VIDEO CASSETTE
Profiles union members who pride themselves on their skills, discipline and professionalism, while looking at the growth of non-union construction in the sunbelt. Presents angry, poverty-level working people who are embracing unionism as a means of solving their economic problems.
Prod-NBCNEW Dist-FI

Labor Movement, The Beginnings And Growth In America C 14 MIN
16MM FILM, 3/4 OR 1/2 IN VIDEO J-C
Traces the growth of organized labor, focusing on events and personalities, from the end of the Civil War to World War I. Considers the methods labor used to achieve its goals against a background of labormanagement relations and changing economic conditions.
Prod-CORF Dist-CORF 1959

Labor Of Love - Childbirth Without Violence C 27 MIN
16MM FILM, 3/4 OR 1/2 IN VIDEO H-C A
Focuses on the radically new method of birth popularized by Dr Frederick Leboyer. Contrasts the traditional method of delivery with the Leboyer method and shows the predelivery activities of a woman who is planning to delivery by this method.
Prod-MENTA Dist-PEREN

Labor Of Thy Hands, The B 30 MIN
16MM FILM OPTICAL SOUND H-C A
Traces the development of contemporary labor legislation from its origins in Jewish teachings. (Kinescope)
From The Eternal Light Series.
LC NO. 75-700970
Prod-JTS Dist-NAAJS 1968

Labor Reform Act Of 1978, The - Should Congress Provide More Protection For... C 59 MIN
3/4 INCH VIDEO CASSETTE
Presents Stephen I Schlossberg and Vincent J Atruzze debating Congress's role in providing protection for union organizing.
From The Advocates Series.
Prod-WGBHTV Dist-PUBTEL

Labor Relations--A Series

Looks at the various stages in a labor conflict.
Prod-IVCH Dist-IVCH

Anatomy Of A Grievance	030 MIN
Arbitration Of A Grievance	030 MIN
Buttons...Buttons	030 MIN
Dimensions Of Bargaining	030 MIN
Harmonics Of Conflict	030 MIN
Scenes From The Workplace	030 MIN
Waldenville I	030 MIN
Waldenville II	030 MIN

Labor Songs B 30 MIN
3/4 INCH VIDEO CASSETTE
Features labor song writer Joe Glazer as he talks about how and why he writes labor songs.
From The Folklore - U S A Series.
Prod-UMITV Dist-UMITV 1967

Labor Turnover I C 30 MIN
3/4 OR 1/2 INCH VIDEO CASSETTE
See series title for descriptive statement.
From The Effective Supervision Series.
Prod-ERF Dist-DELTAK

Labor Turnover II C 30 MIN
3/4 OR 1/2 INCH VIDEO CASSETTE
See series title for descriptive statement.
From The Effective Supervision Series.
Prod-ERF Dist-DELTAK

Labor Unions C 30 MIN
3/4 INCH VIDEO CASSETTE
See series title for descriptive statement.
From The It's Everybody's Business Series. Unit 4, Managing A Business
Prod-DALCCD Dist-DALCCD

Labor Unions - A Question Of Violence C 15 MIN
16MM FILM, 3/4 OR 1/2 IN VIDEO H-C A
Documents the confrontation between a successful, independent non-union building contractor in Philadelphia and the construction union. Originally shown on the CBS television program 60 Minutes.
Prod-CBSNEW Dist-CAROUF

Labor Unions In Japan C 30 MIN
3/4 OR 1/2 INCH VIDEO CASSETTE A
See series title for descriptive statement.
From The Business Nippon Series.
LC NO. 85-702161
Prod-JAPCTV Dist-EBEC 1984

Labor-Management Relations C 23 MIN
3/4 INCH VIDEO CASSETTE
Gives an overview of the provisions of Title II and their implications for federal managers. Covers changes in administrative bodies, scope of negotiations, grievance arbitration procedures, and employee representational rights.
From The Launching Civil Service Reform Series.
LC NO. 79-706274
Prod-USOPMA Dist-USNAC 1978

Labor-Management Relations In Japan C 30 MIN
3/4 OR 1/2 INCH VIDEO CASSETTE A
See series title for descriptive statement.
From The Business Nippon Series.
LC NO. 85-702160
Prod-JAPCTV Dist-EBEC

Labor/Management EAP C 17 MIN
3/4 OR 1/2 INCH VIDEO CASSETTE
Trains supervisors of union production workers in the techniques of employee assistance program (EAP) referral.
Prod-WHITEG Dist-WHITEG

Labor's Turning Point C 44 MIN
3/4 OR 1/2 INCH VIDEO CASSETTE
Conveys the upheaval created by a strike of Local 574, International Brotherhood of Teamsters. Gives a visual description of the socio-economic trauma of the Great Depression as it impacted on Minnesota's workers, businesses, banks and politics.
Prod-TCPT Dist-NFPS

Laboratory Aspects Of Diseases Of The Testicle, The B 35 MIN
16MM FILM OPTICAL SOUND PRO
Discusses testicular physiology and biochemistry. Points out factors in the assessment of testicular function, Leydig cell failure, sperm production, testicular biopsy evaluation, karyotyping analysis, and plasmatestosterone levels. Provides detailed information concerning pituitary involvement, LSH, FSH, use of radioactive isotopes in determination of malfunctions of testes, and Klinefelters syndrome. (Kinescope)
From The Clinical Pathology Series.
LC NO. 74-704997
Prod-NMAC Dist-USNAC 1969

Laboratory Design For Microbiological Safety C 35 MIN
16MM FILM - 3/4 IN VIDEO
Points out problems concerning safety and functional use of microbiological laboratories. Describes some of the principal features and devices used to provide effective microbiological containment. Issued in 1966 as a motion picture.
LC NO. 80-736279
Prod-USNCI Dist-USNAC Prodn-USPHS 1980

Laboratory Design For Microbiological Safety, M-1091 C 35 MIN
16MM FILM OPTICAL SOUND
Approaches safety problems in the design and construction of a microbiological laboratory from an engineering standpoint and describes the primary and secondary barrier concept for the containment of microorganisms.
Prod-DUART Dist-NMAC

Laboratory Diagnosis Of Rabies In Animals C 30 MIN
3/4 INCH VIDEO CASSETTE
Demonstrates laboratory techniques for examination of animals in the diagnosis of rabies. Shows the preparation of brain impressions, the inoculation of animals, the serum neutralization test and the flourescent antibody test. Issued in 1961 as a motion picture.
LC NO. 78-706275
Prod-USPHS Dist-USNAC Prodn-NMAC 1978

Laboratory High Vacuum Technique, Using Solder Glass, The B 30 MIN
16MM FILM OPTICAL SOUND C
Demonstrates techniques for producing various electrode structures and mounting them onto regular glass headers.
From The College Physics Film Program Series.
LC NO. FIA68-1427
Prod-EDS Dist-MLA 1968

Laboratory In The Desert C 23 MIN
16MM FILM OPTICAL SOUND
Outlines living conditions in Las Vegas, Nevada. Shows a day in the life of technical personnel who commute daily from Las Vegas to Tonopah Test Range. Illustrates the capabilities of the range and the special techniques used to meet unique testing problems.
LC NO. 75-701180
Prod-USAEC Dist-USNAC 1969

Laboratory Methods For Airborne Infection, Pt 2, The Henderson Apparatus C 34 MIN
16MM FILM OPTICAL SOUND
Discusses aerosols and their use in studying diseases transmitted by air. Uses diagrams to explain the animal exposure chamber. Discusses the Henderson apparatus, which is especially useful in development of vaccine and drugs used in the treatment of respiratory diseases. Shows how laboratory workers are protected.
LC NO. FIE65-87
Prod-USACC Dist-USNAC Prodn-USPHS 1959

Laboratory Of The Body C 30 MIN
3/4 OR 1/2 INCH VIDEO CASSETTE PRO
Describes the multi-discipline approach to modern dental research. Demonstrates a typical research problem, such as the effect of collagenase on collagen.
Prod-WFP Dist-WFP

Laboratory Procedures For Complete Dentures, Pt 1 - Waxing And Flasking C 12 MIN
16MM FILM, 3/4 OR 1/2 IN VIDEO PRO
Demonstrates the steps of waxing and flasking dentures. Shows the anatomical considerations of shaping the wax, and discusses investing procedures using artificial stone in sections. Illustrates removal of the wax, followed by sprinkling a characterizing veneer into the mold.
LC NO. 81-707196
Prod-VADTC Dist-USNAC 1981

Laboratory Procedures For Complete Dentures, Pt II - Processing And Finishing C 16 MIN
16MM FILM, 3/4 OR 1/2 IN VIDEO
Shows the handling and packing of the flasked molds for dentures with methylmethacrylate resin, followed by recovery of the processed dentures and their correction for processing errors.
Prod-VADTC Dist-AMDA 1980

Laboratory Procedures For Complete Dentures, Pt 2 - Processing And Finishing C 16 MIN
16MM FILM, 3/4 OR 1/2 IN VIDEO PRO
Shows the handling and packing of flasked molds with methylmethacrylate resin, followed by recovery of the processed dentures. Illustrates finishing the dentures with polishing elements, and gives attention to preserving orientation indices to facilitate delivery of the dentures.
LC NO. 81-707197
Prod-VADTC Dist-USNAC 1981

Laboratory Safety C
3/4 OR 1/2 INCH VIDEO CASSETTE
See series title for descriptive statement.
From The Basic DC Circuits Series.
Prod-VTRI Dist-VTRI

Laboratory Safety C 15 MIN
3/4 OR 1/2 INCH VIDEO CASSETTE
See series title for descriptive statement.
From The Basic Electricity And D.C. Circuits, Laboratory Series.
Prod-TXINLC Dist-TXINLC

Laboratory Safety C 30 MIN
3/4 OR 1/2 INCH VIDEO CASSETTE
See series title for descriptive statement.
From The Basic AC Circuits, Laboratory--Sessions--A Series.
Prod-TXINLC Dist-TXINLC

Laboratory Safety Basics C 55 MIN
3/4 OR 1/2 INCH VIDEO CASSETTE H-C A
Includes basics of laboratory safety, and signs of life which examines the way symbols, color codes and number codes are employed to signal danger. Features also electrical and radiation hazards and biohazards which illustrate basic procedures and precautions related to dissection, live animals and microorganisms.
Prod-CMLMS Dist-MOKIN

Laboratory Technique For Darkfield Microscopy B 16 MIN
16MM FILM OPTICAL SOUND
Explains the theory of darkfield microscopy, the preparation of slides and the use of a darkfield microscope.
Prod-USN Dist-USNAC 1953

Laboratory Techniques C 9 MIN
3/4 INCH VIDEO CASSETTE
Demonstrates laboratory techniques including bending glass to make a wash bottle. Introduces the pipette and the volumetric flask.
From The Chemistry Videotapes Series.
Prod-UMITV Dist-UMITV

Laboratory Tests For Asphaltic Concrete B 60 MIN
3/4 OR 1/2 INCH VIDEO CASSETTE
See series title for descriptive statement.
From The Bases For Several Pavement Design Methods Series. Pt 4
Prod-UAZMIC Dist-UAZMIC 1977

Laborers Of India C 11 MIN
16MM FILM, 3/4 OR 1/2 IN VIDEO I-J
Depicts the life of 13-year-old boy and his family who live in a village of laborers in India. Shows typical daily activities of different members of the family.
Prod-WULFFR Dist-AIMS 1975

Labrador - Land Out Of Time C 30 MIN
3/4 OR 1/2 INCH VIDEO CASSETTE
Documents the problems in Labrador, where progress was long in coming and where the heritage of fishing and hunting has been replaced by forced government relocation and welfare.
Prod-UPI Dist-JOU

Labyrinth C 14 MIN
16MM FILM, 3/4 OR 1/2 IN VIDEO H-C
Combines animated cartoons, cutouts of graphic art, and photographic montage to portray a desolate urban world and the loneliness of the individual who is trapped among its frightening inhabitants.
Prod-CELHLD Dist-TEXFLM Prodn-LENICA 1969

Labyrinths C 28 MIN
16MM FILM OPTICAL SOUND

Depicts five astronauts, trapped in space, participating in a collective hallucination involving existential love, a planet and its dying sun, and a time traveler.
LC NO. 80-700645
Prod-MINEM Dist-MINEM 1979

Lacemaker, The (French) C 108 MIN
16MM FILM OPTICAL SOUND
Describes the ill-fated love affair between an awkward bourgeouis student and an inexperienced shop girl. Directed by Claude Goretta. With English subtitles.
Prod-UNKNWN Dist-NYFLMS 1977

Laceration - Principles And Techniques Of Management C 14 MIN
3/4 INCH VIDEO CASSETTE PRO
Takes the student through the entire process of laceration management in the emergency room. Uses medical graphics, actual surgical film segments and discussion. Shows how to anesthesize and cleanse traumatic wounds, debride wounds prior to closure, suture wounds and manage the closed wound.
Prod-UNM Dist-UNM

Lacrosse, Little Brother Of War C 14 MIN
16MM FILM OPTICAL SOUND
Traces the history of lacrosse from its origins as an Indian game of skill and bloodshed to its growing popularity today as an amateur sport and as a professional spectator sport.
LC NO. 75-704314
Prod-CANFDC Dist-CANFDC 1974

Lad In The Lamp, A C 16 MIN
16MM FILM OPTICAL SOUND K-I
Presents the magnificent 'SIX AND 1/2' who find a lamp which they believe resembles a legendary one. When strange happenings take place, the small fry are convinced that it has magic powers.
From The Magnificent 6 And 1/2 Series.
Prod-CHILDF Dist-LUF 1970

Ladder Of Creation, The C 52 MIN
16MM FILM, 3/4 OR 1/2 IN VIDEO J-C A
Explores the controversy around the theory of evolution developed simultaneously by Alfred Wallace and Charles Darwin.
From The Ascent Of Man Series. No. 9
LC NO. 77-707235
Prod-BBCTV Dist-TIMLIF 1973

Ladder Of Creation, The (Spanish) C 52 MIN
16MM FILM OPTICAL SOUND H-C A
Explores the controversy around the theory of evolution developed simultaneously by Alfred Wallace and Charles Darwin.
From The Ascent Of Man Series. No. 9
Prod-BBCTV Dist-TIMLIF 1973

Ladder, The C 6 MIN
16MM FILM, 3/4 OR 1/2 IN VIDEO J-C A
Offers a symbolic tale about a man who climbs an actual ladder by going over and around those already on the ladder. Reveals him later at the bottom of the ladder writing his memoirs.
Prod-SFTB Dist-PHENIX 1981

Ladders B 29 MIN
16MM FILM, 3/4 OR 1/2 IN VIDEO H-C A
Demonstrates the standard procedures for carrying, footing, spotting, raising, securing and lowering straight and extension hand ladders from 14 feet to 50 feet in length.
Prod-LACFD Dist-FILCOM 1954

Ladders C 30 MIN
3/4 OR 1/2 INCH VIDEO CASSETTE PRO
Shows crews using various ladders up to 35 ft to move both personnel and equipment. Stresses individual and team effort while demonstrating fire fighting from ladders using hoses and other equipment.
Prod-IFSTA Dist-IFSTA

Ladders And Linemen C 10 MIN
16MM FILM, 3/4 OR 1/2 IN VIDEO IND
Points out how accidents can be avoided when using a ladder. Stresses the importance of selecting the right ladder for the job, especially when electricity is involved.
Prod-EUSA Dist-IFB Prodn-KROSTR 1974

Ladders And Lines - Number Line Concepts B 20 MIN
3/4 INCH VIDEO CASSETTE P
See series title for descriptive statement.
From The Let's Figure It Out Series.
Prod-WNYETV Dist-NYSED 1968

Ladders And Scaffolds C 60 MIN
3/4 OR 1/2 INCH VIDEO CASSETTE IND
See series title for descriptive statement.
From The Mechanical Equipment Maintenance, Module 1 - Rigging And Lifting Series.
Prod-LEIKID Dist-LEIKID

Ladies In Retirement B 97 MIN
16MM FILM OPTICAL SOUND
Describes a woman who will do anything to prevent her two sisters from being put into a mental institution, even if it means doing something grisly to her employer. Stars Ida Lupino and Elsa Lanchester.
Prod-CPC Dist-KITPAR 1941

Ladies In Waiting C 11 MIN
16MM FILM OPTICAL SOUND J-C A
Emphasizes the importance during pregnancy of balancing activity with rest and of practicing controlled relaxation and correct posture. Demonstrates breathing exercises to aid rest and ease labor.
From The Family Life Education And Human Growth Series.
LC NO. FIA66-1177
Prod-MORLAT Dist-SF 1966

Ladies Of Leisure B 98 MIN
16MM FILM OPTICAL SOUND
Tells how a wealthy young man falls in love with a street-smart girl. Depicts her attempted suicide after his parents refuse to let him marry her. Stars Barbara Stanwyck. Directed by Frank Capra.
Prod-CPC Dist-KITPAR 1930

Ladies Wear The Blue C 29 MIN
16MM FILM OPTICAL SOUND
Traces the history of Navy women from 1917 to the present. Stresses the importance of equal employment opportunity and highlights the changes the Navy has made to offer a more satisfying and rewarding career for women in naval service.
LC NO. 74-706481
Prod-USN Dist-USNAC 1974

Lady And The Owl, The C 28 MIN
16MM FILM, 3/4 OR 1/2 IN VIDEO C A
Tells how Kay McKeever and her husband help restore injured owls to health and then release them.
Prod-NFBC Dist-WOMBAT

Lady And The Tramp - A Lesson In Sharing Attention C 8 MIN
16MM FILM, 3/4 OR 1/2 IN VIDEO P-I
Tells how a young boy fears the loss of attention that may accompany his parents having another child. Uses a scene from the animated film Lady And The Tramp to show that there is plenty of love to share when new people enter the scene.
From The Disney's Animated Classics - Lessons In Living, Series 1 Series.
Prod-DISNEY Dist-WDEMCO Prodn-WDEMCO 1978

Lady Beware C 17 MIN
16MM FILM, 3/4 OR 1/2 IN VIDEO
Demonstrates techniques that women can use to protect themselves from the growing menace of personal assault. Includes details of security for home, car and phone, precautions for avoiding danger when out at night, the wisdom of flight, and what to do if escape isn't possible.
Prod-PFP Dist-PFP

Lady Called Camille, A C 28 MIN
16MM FILM OPTICAL SOUND P-H
Tells the story of the most devastating hurricane that swept through the gulf coast.
LC NO. 74-704999
Prod-USOCD Dist-USNAC 1971

Lady Called Camille, A C 29 MIN
3/4 INCH VIDEO CASSETTE
Documents the devastation caused by Hurricane Camille. Tells how thousands of lives were saved because of emergency plans, trained rescue teams and help from thousands in volunteer groups and the military. Issued in 1971 as a motion picture.
LC NO. 79-706663
Prod-USOCD Dist-USNAC 1979

Lady Called Camille, A (Spanish) C 27 MIN
16MM FILM OPTICAL SOUND
Tells the dramatic story of Hurricane Camille. Depicts the disaster, the advance warnings and evacuation efforts that saved thousands of lives before the storm and the relief and rescue operations which followed.
LC NO. 74-705000
Prod-USOCD Dist-USNAC 1971

Lady Elaine Discovers Planet Purple C 25 MIN
16MM FILM OPTICAL SOUND K-P S
Presents Mr Rogers talking, singing and using puppets to tell a story about Lady Elaine's arrival home from Jupiter and her discovery of Planet Purple on the return trip. Discusses individual differences, handicaps, uniqueness and change.
From The Purple Adventures Of Lady Elaine Fairchilde Series. Program 2
LC NO. 80-700581
Prod-FAMCOM Dist-HUBDSC 1979

Lady Elaine Discovers Planet Purple C 25 MIN
3/4 OR 1/2 INCH VIDEO CASSETTE K-P
Presents Mr Rogers talking and singing about how being different is what makes each person special. Describes Lady Elaine Fairchilde's trip home from Jupiter during which she discovers Planet Purple.
From The Purple Adventures Of Lady Elaine Fairchilde Series. Program 2
LC NO. 80-706562
Prod-FAMCOM Dist-HUBDSC 1979

Lady Elaine Flies For Jupiter C 29 MIN
3/4 OR 1/2 INCH VIDEO CASSETTE K-P
Presents Mr Rogers discussing and singing about similarities and differences. Begins the story of Lady Elaine Fairchilde and her voyage to Jupiter.
From The Purple Adventures Of Lady Elaine Fairchilde Series. Program 1
LC NO. 80-706562
Prod-FAMCOM Dist-HUBDSC 1979

Lady Elaine Flies To Jupiter C 29 MIN
16MM FILM OPTICAL SOUND K-P S
Presents Mr Rogers talking, singing and using puppets to tell a story about Lady Elaine getting ready for her trip into space. Discusses individual differences, handicaps, uniqueness and change.
From The Purple Adventures Of Lady Elaine Fairchilde Series. Program 1
LC NO. 80-700581
Prod-FAMCOM Dist-HUBDSC 1979

Lady Elaine Wants Everything To Be As It Is On Planet Purple C 24 MIN
16MM FILM OPTICAL SOUND K-P S
Presents Mr Rogers talking, singing and using puppets to tell a story about Lady Elaine's attempts to make her neighborhood just like Planet Purple, where everything and everyone is the same. Discusses individual differences, including handicaps, uniqueness and change.
From The Purple Adventures Of Lady Elaine Fairchilde Series. Program 3
LC NO. 80-700581
Prod-FAMCOM Dist-HUBDSC 1979

Lady Elaine Wants Everything To Be As It Is On Planet Purple C 24 MIN
3/4 OR 1/2 INCH VIDEO CASSETTE K-P
Presents Mr Rogers talking and singing about being liked for oneself. Continues the story of Lady Elaine Fairchilde, who tries to make her neighborhood like Planet Purple where everyone and everything are the same. Reveals that she meets resistance from her friends.
From The Purple Adventures Of Lady Elaine Fairchilde Series. Program 3
LC NO. 80-706562
Prod-FAMCOM Dist-HUBDSC 1979

Lady Fishbourne's Complete Guide To Better Table Manners C 6 MIN
16MM FILM, 3/4 OR 1/2 IN VIDEO
Uses animation to describe the do's and don'ts of table manners. Demonstrates how to hold a fork, how to handle a knife, and what not to do when a parrot lands on one's plate.
Prod-NFBC Dist-CAROUF

Lady From Montreal B 24 MIN
16MM FILM OPTICAL SOUND
Tells a tale of a detective with something to hide.
LC NO. 76-703842
Prod-CCAAT Dist-CCAAT 1975

Lady From Shanghai, The B 87 MIN
16MM FILM OPTICAL SOUND C A
Stars Orson Welles, Rita Hayworth and Everett Sloane in the story of murder on a leisurely pleasure cruise.
Prod-CPC Dist-TIMLIF 1948

Lady In The Lincoln Memorial, The C 18 MIN
16MM FILM OPTICAL SOUND I-C A
Portrays the life of Marian Anderson as a struggling Negro singer in a prejudiced world through dramatized situations in her childhood and young adult years and through authentic photographs of her vocal and social triumphs. Includes photographs of her European tours and her historic concert at the Lincoln Memorial in 1939.
LC NO. 70-709231
Prod-NYT Dist-SF

Lady In The Lincoln Memorial, The C 18 MIN
3/4 OR 1/2 INCH VIDEO CASSETTE I-C A
Portrays the life of Marian Anderson as a struggling Negro singer in a prejudiced world through dramatized situations in her childhood and young adult years and through authentic photographs of her vocal and social triumphs. Includes photographs of her European tours and her historic concert at the Lincoln Memorial in 1939.
Prod-NYT Dist-SF

Lady Is Willing, The B 92 MIN
16MM FILM OPTICAL SOUND
Stars Marlene Dietrich as an actress who finds an abandoned baby and insists on keeping it, hiring her own pediatrician (Fred MacMurray) and installing him in her hotel suite.
Prod-CPC Dist-KITPAR 1942

Lady Named Baybie, A C 58 MIN
16MM FILM OPTICAL SOUND
Shows the daily life of 64-year-old Baybie Hoover, a blind gospel singer who earns her living performing on the street corners of New York City.
LC NO. 81-700509
Prod-STURTM Dist-DIRECT 1980

Lady Named Baybie, A C 58 MIN
3/4 OR 1/2 INCH VIDEO CASSETTE
Shows the daily life of 64-year-old Baybie Hoover, a blind gospel singer who earns her living performing on the street corners of New York City.
Prod-STURTM Dist-DIRECT 1980

Lady Of The Rapids C 11 MIN
16MM FILM OPTICAL SOUND
Follows the adventures of Georgie White as she shoots the rapids of the Colorado river on its course through the Grand Canyon.
From The Movietone Sports Series.
LC NO. FI68-1545
Prod-TWCF Dist-TWCF 1962

Lady Of The Sea C 20 MIN
16MM FILM, 3/4 OR 1/2 IN VIDEO I-C
Presents the saga of a two-year journey around the world aboard a square-rigged sailing ship. Includes footage of the San Bias Islands, Pitcairn Island, Tahiti and Bali.
Prod-JONESF Dist-MGHT 1978

Lady On The Lower C 13 MIN
16MM FILM OPTICAL SOUND
Depicts the barge-lining activites of a towboat which hauls agricultural commodities on the Mississippi River.
LC NO. 77-702402
Prod-UMCSN Dist-UMCSN 1977

Lady Sings The Blues C 144 MIN
16MM FILM, 3/4 OR 1/2 IN VIDEO
Features Diana Ross as the immortal blues singer Billie Holiday.
Prod-PARACO Dist-FI 1972

Lady Vanishes, The B 99 MIN
16MM FILM OPTICAL SOUND
Tells how a middle-aged governess vanishes from a train and how the other passengers deny she was ever there. Directed by Alfred Hitchcock.
Prod-UNKNWN Dist-REELIM 1938

Lady Vanishes, The - Where Are The Women In Film C 29 MIN
3/4 INCH VIDEO CASSETTE
Assesses the role of women in film. States that films have not reflected the struggle and changing status of American women, but have relegated them to secondary roles as victims of violence or on the brink of madness.
From The Woman Series.
Prod-WNEDTV Dist-PUBTEL

Lady Without Camelias, The (Captioned) B 106 MIN
16MM FILM, 3/4 OR 1/2 IN VIDEO A
Portrays the story of the discovery of a young salesgirl by a film producer, their collaboration and eventual marriage, their failure together in their careers, their separation and her inability to find a new lover or a renewed career. Italian dialog with English subtitles.
Prod-CNEMAG Dist-CNEMAG 1953

Lady, Or The Tiger By Frank Stockton, The C 16 MIN
16MM FILM, 3/4 OR 1/2 IN VIDEO J-C
Resets a story of the 1800's, The Lady, Or The Tiger, in the space age, adding helicopters, sportscars, penthouses and other touches.
From The Humanities - Short Story Showcase Series.
Prod-EBEC Dist-EBEC 1970

Ladybug, Ladybug C 11 MIN
16MM FILM, 3/4 OR 1/2 IN VIDEO P
Presents a series of word-filled vignettes of ladybugs, flying squirrels and boys and girls to reinforce the words jump, fly, from, away, house, home and if.
From The Reading And Word Play Series.
Prod-PEDF Dist-AIMS 1976

Ladybug, Ladybug, Winter Is Coming C 10 MIN
16MM FILM, 3/4 OR 1/2 IN VIDEO K-P
Uses a nature story about safe animal habitats for winter to introduce language-arts and science.
Prod-CORF Dist-CORF 1976

Ladykillers, The C 90 MIN
16MM FILM OPTICAL SOUND
Features Alec Guinness as the head of a motley group of thieves planning the robbery of an armored truck. Shows how they plan to use an old lady's house as their base of operations, but how things go awry when she finds out about their plans. Directed by Alexander Mackendrick.
Prod-CONPIC Dist-LCOA 1955

Lafayette C 99 MIN
16MM FILM OPTICAL SOUND I-C A
Stars Orson Welles, Jack Hawkins and Michael Le Royer as Lafayette, the young French nobleman who spent his personal fortune and risked his life helping our country win its independence.
Prod-UNKNWN Dist-TWYMAN 1962

Lafcadio, The Lion Who Shot Back C 15 MIN
3/4 OR 1/2 INCH VIDEO CASSETTE P
Presents librarian Phyllis Syracuse reading from Shel Silverstein's story Lafcadio, The Lion Who Shot Back. Relates how a circus lion learns to become a trick shooter and becomes more and more like a person. Shows how a crisis forces him to decide whether he is a man or a lion.
From The Through The Pages Series. No. 10
LC NO. 82-707378
Prod-WVIZTV Dist-GPITVL 1982

Lafcadio, The Lion Who Shot Back B 24 MIN
16MM FILM, 3/4 OR 1/2 IN VIDEO I-C A
Tells the story of a young lion, Lafcadio, who fails to make friends with hunters, then decides to become the world's greatest marksman, only to discover he has lost his own identity.
Prod-LCOA Dist-LCOA 1979

Laffin' Gas B 7 MIN
16MM FILM SILENT K-C A
Presents a comedy about a dental assistant who takes over when the dentist steps out, thus causing a free-for-all. Features Charlie Chaplin.
Prod-SENN Dist-TWYMAN 1914

Lagrimas De Apache C 30 MIN
3/4 OR 1/2 INCH VIDEO CASSETTE P-I
See series title for descriptive statement.
From The Sonrisas Series.
Prod-KRLNTV Dist-MDCPB

Laguardia Story, The C 25 MIN
16MM FILM, 3/4 OR 1/2 IN VIDEO I-C
Laguardia sustained himself, through three terms as a Republican mayor in a Democratic city, by making zany public appearances and radio talks and by ballyhooing his accomplishments.
Prod-SF Dist-SF 1965

Laguna Beach Festival Of Arts C 10 MIN
16MM FILM, 3/4 OR 1/2 IN VIDEO J-C A
Presents the Laguna Beach Festival Of Arts, where living models replicate famous works of art.
Prod-IFADV Dist-MCFI 1980

Lahaul And Spiti C 20 MIN
16MM FILM OPTICAL SOUND I-C A
Documents the scenic grandeur and life of the colorful people of lahaul and Spiti, up in the Himalayas. Explains that the area remains snowbound and cut off from the rest of the world for six months, but that in spring, life is stirred into activity.
Prod-INDIA Dist-NEDINF

Laila C 12 MIN
16MM FILM, 3/4 OR 1/2 IN VIDEO I-C A
Shows the lifestyle and work of Laila Paatinen, a handicapped person who is the only female carpenter in Nova Scotia.
Prod-NFBC Dist-PHENIX 1981

Lake And River Kayaking C 14 MIN
16MM FILM, 3/4 OR 1/2 IN VIDEO
Demonstrates the handling of paddle and kayak in smooth water and white water.
From The Outdoor Education White Water Paddling Series.
Prod-MORLAT Dist-SF 1973

Lake Bonneville - History's High-Water Mark C 19 MIN
3/4 OR 1/2 INCH VIDEO CASSETTE I
Creates an evolutionary picture of Lake Bonneville, a prehistoric lake, including the explorers and geologists who have studied its shoreline and fossils.
From The Natural Science Specials Series. Module Green
Prod-UNPRO Dist-AITECH 1973

Lake Community, A C 15 MIN
3/4 OR 1/2 INCH VIDEO CASSETTE P-I
Discusses the living things found in a lake.
From The Why Series.
Prod-WDCNTV Dist-AITECH 1976

Lake Erie C 22 MIN
16MM FILM OPTICAL SOUND
Shows Roland Martin bass fishing in Lake Erie. Depicts how a dying lake was scientifically rehabilitated to restore one of the world's most productive freshwater fishing areas.
Prod-BRNSWK Dist-KAROL

Lake Michigan Coho-DDT Story, The C 13 MIN
16MM FILM OPTICAL SOUND
Shows why coho salmon were introduced into Lake Michigan, and how they were commercially marketed. Traces the discovery of DDT in the fish, the research that was done as a result, and the outcome of that research.
From The Environmental Science Series.
LC NO. 72-700193
Prod-CIASP Dist-CIASP 1971

Lake Of Perch—A Series
16MM FILM, 3/4 OR 1/2 IN VIDEO P-I
Looks at life cycles and ecosystems in a lake.
Prod-FISYNG Dist-CORF 1981

Food Chain, The 012 MIN
Winter 011 MIN
Young Perch, The 013 MIN

Lake Placid '80 C 4 MIN
3/4 INCH VIDEO CASSETTE
Presents portions from the 1980 Winter Olympic Games at Lake Placid, New York.
LC NO. 81-706560
Prod-PAIKNJ Dist-EAI 1980

Lake Poets, The - Wordsworth And Coleridge C 30 MIN
3/4 INCH VIDEO CASSETTE H-C A
Presents a tour of the Lake District of England and features the First Poetry Quartet reading selections from the works of William Wordsworth and Samuel Taylor Coleridge.
From The Anyone For Tennyson Series.
Prod-NETCHE Dist-GPITVL

Lake Superior - The Region Till Now C 22 MIN
16MM FILM, 3/4 OR 1/2 IN VIDEO I-C A
Provides general information on the people, economy, industry and geography of the Lake Superior region. Shows the people, industries and natural beauty in the watersheds of Michigan, Wisconsin, Minnesota and Ontario.
Prod-UWISC Dist-MCFI 1972

Lakemont High School C 18 MIN
16MM FILM OPTICAL SOUND C T
Presents eight problem incidents which confront teachers in multi-ethnic schools. The viewers assume the role of a new teacher who is confronted and must deal with these problems.
From The Solving Multi-Ethnic Problems - A Simulation Game For School Teacher Series.
LC NO. 75-707080
Prod-UTENN Dist-ADL 1969

Lakes C 9 MIN
16MM FILM, 3/4 OR 1/2 IN VIDEO P-I
Characterizes, defines and describes the physical features of lakes, how they are created and destroyed and their uses.
Prod-IU Dist-IU 1969

Lakes - Aging And Pollution C 15 MIN
16MM FILM, 3/4 OR 1/2 IN VIDEO P-J
Explains the aging process of lakes and investigates the changing water quality and the succession of organisms in lakes as they age.
Prod-CENTRO Dist-CORF

Lakes, Rivers And Other Water Sources C 17 MIN
16MM FILM, 3/4 OR 1/2 IN VIDEO J-H
Discusses the fresh water system consisting of lakes, rivers and underground water supplies. Deals with the origins of the water, the action of rivers, the ways a lake dies and forces that create the underground water supply. Introduces the concept of the continental divide and reviews the idea of the water cycle.
From The Natural Phenomena Series.
Prod-JOU Dist-JOU 1982

Lakeside Habitat C 15 MIN
16MM FILM, 3/4 OR 1/2 IN VIDEO J-C A
Shows how the birds living at the lakeside return in spring.
From The Animals And Plants Of North America Series.
Prod-KARVF Dist-LCOA 1980

Lakota, The - One Nation On The Plains C 30 MIN
16MM FILM, 3/4 OR 1/2 IN VIDEO H-C
See series title for descriptive statement.
From The Great Plains Experience Series.
Prod-UMA Dist-GPITVL 1976

Lamar Dodd - A Great Georgian C 29 MIN
16MM FILM OPTICAL SOUND
Presents a biographical study of artist and art educator Lamar Dodd, showing the relationship between his life-philosophy and his art.
From The Great Georgians Series.
LC NO. 75-703105
Prod-GCCED Dist-UGA Prodn-UGSYFL 1974

Lamb And Pork C 29 MIN
2 INCH VIDEOTAPE
Features gourmet-humorist Justin Wilson showing ways to cook lamb and pork with various ingredients.
From The Cookin' Cajun Series.
Prod-MAETEL Dist-PUBTEL

Lamb Slaughter Technique C 25 MIN
16MM FILM, 3/4 OR 1/2 IN VIDEO C A
Close-up photography shows step-by-step the modern methods used in the killing, skinning, evisceration and inspection of lambs.
Prod-NYSCAG Dist-CUNIV Prodn-CUNIV 1966

Lambchop And The Professor C 24 MIN
3/4 OR 1/2 INCH VIDEO CASSETTE K-J
Features Shari Lewis and Lambchop on a visit to a physics professor. Shows Lambchop helping the professor with several classroom experiments.
Prod-SUTHRB Dist-SUTHRB

Lambert And Company B 15 MIN
16MM FILM OPTICAL SOUND
Presents Dave Lambert, of Lambert, Hendricks and Ross, with his newly formed quintet auditioning for RCA in 1964, shortly before his death. By D A Pennebaker.
Prod-PENNAS Dist-PENNAS

Lambert, The Sheepish Lion C 8 MIN
16MM FILM, 3/4 OR 1/2 IN VIDEO K-I
Presents a story about a lion cub that the stork delivered by mistake to a flock of lambs.
Prod-DISNEY Dist-WDEMCO 1971

Lambeth Walk, Nazi Style B 4 MIN
16MM FILM OPTICAL SOUND
Offers a satiric view of Hitler and his elite guard marching and dancing to the popular World War II song The Lambeth Walk.
Prod-UNKNWN Dist-REELIM 1944

Lamellar Keratoprosthesis C 7 MIN
16MM FILM OPTICAL SOUND
Shows a research operation for replacing part of the opaque cornea by means of an optical prosthesis constructed of plastic and gold mesh.
LC NO. FIA66-877
Prod-ACYDGD Dist-ACY 1962

Lameness Of Both Fore And Hindlimb C 53 MIN
1/2 IN VIDEO CASSETTE BETA/VHS
Deals with the wobbler syndrome, compressed spinal cord, cut flexor tendons and other causes of lameness in horses. Covers the fundamentals of wound therapy.
Prod-EQVDL Dist-EQVDL

Lameness Of The Forelimb, Pt 1 C 30 MIN
1/2 IN VIDEO CASSETTE BETA/VHS
Illustrates cases of forelimb lameness, including septic arthritis, hygroma and fractures.
Prod-EQVDL Dist-EQVDL

Lameness Of The Forelimb, Pt 2 C 36 MIN
1/2 IN VIDEO CASSETTE BETA/VHS
Centers on the treatment of lameness occurring below the fetlock joint on the forelimb.
Prod-EQVDL Dist-EQVDL

Lameness Of The Forelimb, Pt 3 C 46 MIN
1/2 IN VIDEO CASSETTE BETA/VHS
Deals with forelimb lameness between the shoulders of a horse in conjunction with prognosis and treatment of carpus.
Prod-EQVDL Dist-EQVDL

Lameness Of The Forelimb, Pt 4 C 42 MIN
1/2 IN VIDEO CASSETTE BETA/VHS
Shows treatment techniques for the areas on a horse below the carpus down through fractures of the sesamoid bone.
Prod-EQVDL Dist-EQVDL

Lameness Of The Forelimb, Pt 5 C 40 MIN
1/2 IN VIDEO CASSETTE BETA/VHS
Covers conditions and treatment of the forelimb of a horse. Discusses pastern joint subluxation, hoof wall loss, laminitis and more.
Prod-EQVDL Dist-EQVDL

Lameness Of The Hindlimb, Pt 1 C 35 MIN
1/2 IN VIDEO CASSETTE BETA/VHS
Discusses hindlimb lameness in a horse. Includes diagnosis of wobbler syndrome and Achilles tendons.
Prod-EQVDL Dist-EQVDL

Lameness Of The Hindlimb, Pt 2 C 23 MIN
1/2 IN VIDEO CASSETTE BETA/VHS

Covers signs of lameness in a horse's hock and below. Discusses bone spavin, weak flexor tendons and more.
Prod-EQVDL Dist-EQVDL

Lameness Of The Hindlimb, Pt 3 C 42 MIN
1/2 IN VIDEO CASSETTE BETA/VHS
Reviews the causes of hindlimb lameness in a horse. Describes the joints and ligaments.
Prod-EQVDL Dist-EQVDL

Lament Of The Reservation C 24 MIN
16MM FILM, 3/4 OR 1/2 IN VIDEO H-C
Presents an uncompromising record of life on an Indian reservation - a life plagued by poverty, unemployment, hunger and infant mortality.
From The North American Indian Series. Part 3
Prod-MGHT Dist-MGHT 1971

Lamp At Midnight C 76 MIN
3/4 OR 1/2 INCH VIDEO CASSETTE
Deals with three critical moments in the life of Galileo Galilei, the great astronomer whose physical observations of the universe by means of a telescope conflicted with the teachings of his church. Stars Melvyn Douglas and David Wayne.
Prod-FOTH Dist-FOTH 1984

Lamps C 15 MIN
2 INCH VIDEOTAPE
Shows how to make a lamp from a half-gallon bottle and a shade from heavy paper. Explains basic information for replacing cords, plugs and sockets.
From The Living Better II Series.
Prod-MAETEL Dist-PUBTEL

Lamps And Electrical Outlets - Lamps And Chandeliers, Adding Electrical Outlets C 30 MIN
1/2 IN VIDEO CASSETTE BETA/VHS
See series title for descriptive statement.
From The Wally's Workshop Series.
Prod-KARTES Dist-KARTES

LAN Technology, Pt I - Transmission And Media C 45 MIN
3/4 OR 1/2 INCH VIDEO CASSETTE C
Covers transmission technology, baseband and broadland, channel bandwith allocation, multiplexing techniques, ring networks and token passing, contention, Local Area Network (LAN) media, twisted pair, coaxial cable, fiber optics, radio and infrared.
From The Local Area Networks Series.
Prod-AMCEE Dist-AMCEE

LAN Technology, Pt II - Interfaces And Protocol C 45 MIN
3/4 OR 1/2 INCH VIDEO CASSETTE C
Goes into protocol functions, network architecture, OSI reference model, Bus Interface Unit (BIU) organization, network interconnection Local Area Network (LAN) standards.
From The Local Area Networks Series.
Prod-AMCEE Dist-AMCEE

Lance C 4 MIN
16MM FILM OPTICAL SOUND P-C
Presents a story about a young boy's fantasy involving an imaginary tiger and lion. Uses a technique in which the screen is split into three vertically parallel rectangles, with each section containing a different scene that unites with the others to form a full image.
LC NO. 72-700566
Prod-PFIELO Dist-CFS 1971

Lancelot Of The Lake (French) C 83 MIN
16MM FILM OPTICAL SOUND
Features the Knights of the Round Table returning from an unsuccessful quest for the Holy Grail. Shows how they have also failed individually in their personal vows of purity. as exemplified by Lancelot.
Prod-NYFLMS Dist-NYFLMS 1974

Lancez C 10 MIN
3/4 OR 1/2 INCH VIDEO CASSETTE
Focuses on sports and command forms.
From The Salut - French Language Lessons Series.
Prod-BCNFL Dist-BCNFL 1984

Land - With Love And Respect C 26 MIN
16MM FILM - 3/4 IN VIDEO H-C A
Explores social and economic conflicts related to land-use decisions. Introduces information tools, such as topographic maps, air photos, soil studies, and resource inventories.
LC NO. 81-706235
Prod-CUETV Dist-CUNIV 1979

Land Along The Water, The X 10 MIN
16MM FILM, 3/4 OR 1/2 IN VIDEO I-J
Characterizes the land that lies along oceans and large lakes in terms of its physical features and uses. Explains that differences in the physical appearance of land near shorelines may be caused by natural forces or by man building inland waterways and constructing recreational facilities.
Prod-NET Dist-IU 1969

Land And Sea C 24 MIN
16MM FILM OPTICAL SOUND
Examines the effects of mountains, the sea and barren soil on the three most important city-states that existed before and during the classical period Sparta, Corinth and Athens. Uses archeological evidence to recreate city life at that time.
Prod-BBCTV Dist-OPENU 1981

Land And Sea C 24 MIN
16MM FILM, 3/4 OR 1/2 IN VIDEO
Examines the effects of mountains, the sea and barren soil on the three most important city-states that existed before and during the classical period Sparta, Corinth and Athens. Uses archeological evidence to recreate city life at that time.
Prod-OPENU Dist-MEDIAG Prodn-BBCTV 1981

Land And Sea—A Series
P
Supplements a variety of science curricula by providing resources not usually available in the classroom. Presents experiences with the processes and procedures in science rather than facts alone. Encourages the student to search, to critically observe his findings and to evaluate his accumulated evidence.
Prod-TTOIC Dist-GPITVL Prodn-WGBHTV

Edge Of The Sea, The	15 MIN
Face Of The Earth, The	15 MIN
Forces That Change The Earth - Glaciers	15 MIN
Forces That Change The Earth - Water	15 MIN
Forces That Change The Earth - Wind	15 MIN
Life And Death In The Sea	15 MIN
Mountains And Volcanoes	15 MIN
Pond, The	15 MIN
Rocks	15 MIN
Rotation Of The Earth, The	15 MIN
Sea Animals	15 MIN
Sea, The	15 MIN
Shape Of The Earth, The	15 MIN
Soil	15 MIN
World Was Once Very Different, The	15 MIN

Land And The People C 57 MIN
16MM FILM, 3/4 OR 1/2 IN VIDEO H-C A
Focuses on the role of land in determining wealth and poverty and its effect on social and foreign policies. Based on the book The Age Of Uncertainty by John Kenneth Galbraith.
From The Age Of Uncertainty Series.
LC NO. 77-701488
Prod-BBCL Dist-FI 1977

Land And The Pursuit Of Happiness C 32 MIN
16MM FILM OPTICAL SOUND
Discusses the use of land on a global scale, moving from an era of abundance to scarity. Focuses on the devastated forest land of the Olympic Peninsula in Washington State, the Rio Grande Valley, New Mexico, where water resources are scarce and the Waiahole-Waikane Valley in Hawaii, whose farmers fight against housing developments. Explains the reason for the downfall of the Anasazi Indians in Chaco Canyon, New Mexico.
Prod-UCLA Dist-UCLA 1975

Land And Water C 25 MIN
16MM FILM OPTICAL SOUND H-C
Shows the differences between peasant and plantation agriculture in a Mexican valley. Examines human ecology in relation to crops grown under conditions of drought, erosion and winter frost.
Prod-PSUPCR Dist-PSUPCR 1961

Land And Water In Iraq C 14 MIN
16MM FILM OPTICAL SOUND I-H
Provides a fragmentary view of some of the aspects of ecology of modern Iraq, dealing in particular with Mesopotamia and emphasizing those aspects of life between the Tigris and Euphrates that have probably remained unchanged since the time of the Sumerians. Dr Robert Adams explains with the aid of maps and diagrams the annual cycle of flooding and drought on the alluvial plains.
From The Social Studies Program Series.
LC NO. FIA65-356
Prod-EDS Dist-EDC 1964

Land Below The Sea C 20 MIN
3/4 INCH VIDEO CASSETTE I
Visits Holland and looks at its dunes, dikes and polders. Explains why and how they were built.
From The Understanding Our World, Unit III - Living In Other Lands Series.
Prod-KRMATV Dist-GPITVL

Land Beneath The Sea C 58 MIN
16MM FILM OPTICAL SOUND
Follows three dives by French and American deep-sea submersibles over the Rift Valley in the mid-Atlantic and uses the dives as a narrative device to explain plate tectonics theory.
LC NO. 76-702833
Prod-MAETEL Dist-MAETEL 1976

Land Beneath The Sea, The C 24 MIN
16MM FILM - 3/4 IN VIDEO
Describes the origins and development of the sea floor. Discusses how the study of submarine and relief features, sediments, and the general nature of marine geology is vital to naval operations and economic exploitation of the ocean.
LC NO. 76-706179
Prod-USN Dist-USNAC 1972

Land Burns, The B 12 MIN
16MM FILM, 3/4 OR 1/2 IN VIDEO P-I
Discusses the northeastern 'DROUGHT REGION' in Brazil. Presents the story of Juan Amaro, a man who six years ago founded and settled on an abandoned ranch, with his wife and 11 children. Explains that today only four children survive, as a result of the sufferings in the droughts. Concludes with the realization that the family can no longer survive on the dried out ranch, so they decide to leave and go to the big city, where they hope things will be better.
Prod-PIC Dist-CNEMAG

Land Dayaks Of Borneo C 38 MIN
16MM FILM OPTICAL SOUND C T
Depicts life in Mentu Tapuh village, a border region between Indonesia and Malaysia. Pictures activities of Borneo's 50,000 land dayaks, including harvesting, dancing and canoe-making. Shows religious ceremonies, the harvest festival and games.
LC NO. FIA65-1667
Prod-GEDDES Dist-NYU 1965

Land Divers Of Melanesia C 30 MIN
16MM FILM, 3/4 OR 1/2 IN VIDEO J-C A
Depicts the men of Pentecost Island who anchor their feet with vines and dive head-first from a wooden tower over 100 feet high.
Prod-HUFSC Dist-PHENIX 1974

Land Divided, A - India And Pakistan At War B 15 MIN
16MM FILM OPTICAL SOUND J-H
Examines in depth the smouldering hatreds that triggered war between India and Pakistan and led to the creation of the Bangladesh Republic.
From The Screen News Digest Series. Vol 14, Issue 5
LC NO. 72-702748
Prod-HEARST Dist-HEARST 1972

Land Drainage C 25 MIN
16MM FILM, 3/4 OR 1/2 IN VIDEO J-C A
Explains that system drainage may be the solution to late planting and reduced crop yields. Discusses machines for laying plastic tile, the importance of adequate outlet systems, the treatment of fine-textured soils, and land smoothing.
Prod-CUETV Dist-CUNIV 1978

Land For Life C 25 MIN
16MM FILM OPTICAL SOUND
Discusses the problem of population growth in the Lower Mainland of British Columbia in Canada. Explains what has been done to accomodate this growth without destroying the quality of life.
LC NO. 76-703065
Prod-BCDA Dist-BCDA 1974

Land For People, Land For Bears C 15 MIN
3/4 OR 1/2 INCH VIDEO CASSETTE
Presents an example of LANDSAT multi-spectral scanning in the planning and mapping of land use for people in Florida and for wildlife in its native habitat.
From The LANDSAT Series.
Prod-IVCH Dist-IVCH

Land For People, Land For Bears C 15 MIN
16MM FILM - 3/4 IN VIDEO
Looks at how satellites help supply a new kind of data for land use mapping and wildlife habitat mapping. Shows biologists using data to identify habitat for the relocations of endangered animal species.
From The Environmental Series - Landsat - Satellite For All Seasons Series.
Prod-NASA Dist-USNAC 1972

Land From The North Sea C 17 MIN
16MM FILM, 3/4 OR 1/2 IN VIDEO P-C
Shows how man re-shapes his environment by use of sedimentation, dike construction and use of plant life. Teaches how man reclaims land from the sea.
From The Man And His World Series.
Prod-IFFB Dist-FI 1969

Land Images C 20 MIN
16MM FILM, 3/4 OR 1/2 IN VIDEO
Considers natural images as a source of ideas for artists. Shows how several people respond to the same natural setting and how they express their varied responses.
From The Images And Things Series.
LC NO. 73-702101
Prod-NITC Dist-AITECH

Land Is A Woman, The C 28 MIN
16MM FILM OPTICAL SOUND
Looks at the activities inherent in grape-growing and wine making in Virginia plus the romance they inspire in a vintner and his wife.
Prod-SCHDRC Dist-SCHDRC 1981

Land Is Life C 30 MIN
3/4 OR 1/2 INCH VIDEO CASSETTE
Deals with the history of the land problems of the Oneida Indians of Wisconsin. Shows how the Oneidas are trying to recover land they lost and improve land which they control.
From The Forest Spirits Series.
Prod-NEWIST Dist-GPITVL

Land Is Rich, The B 40 MIN
16MM FILM OPTICAL SOUND
Traces the development of the Delano grape strike and documents the efforts of the workers to organize.
Prod-RICHA Dist-SFN 1967

Land Landing Operations C 17 MIN
3/4 INCH VIDEO CASSETTE
Describes the testing of the parawing - terminal landing system and the progress made in developing a ground control capability for advanced landing systems. Depicts, by animation, the theoretical aspects of the program.
Prod-NASA Dist-NASA 1972

Land Like No Other, A - Alaska C 22 MIN
16MM FILM OPTICAL SOUND
Depicts the diversity of Alaska and the reactions of its visitiors. Includes views of 30 different localities.
LC NO. 76-702834
Prod-WESTRS Dist-WESTRS Prodn-SUNSET 1975

Land Lives On, The C 20 MIN
16MM FILM OPTICAL SOUND
Describes soil stewardship as the sense of responsibility for preserving the resources of air, land and water. Illustrates how soil stewards work effectively on farms, in urban areas and in industry.
LC NO. 78-700391
Prod-NACD Dist-FINLYS Prodn-FINLYS 1978

Land Meets Sea C 28 MIN
3/4 INCH VIDEO CASSETTE J
Explores shorelines around the world. Examines a barrier island,

showing how the ecosystems of the island vary from beach to salt marsh.
From The What On Earth Series.
Prod-NCSDPI Dist-GPITVL 1979

Land Of Buddha, The C 17 MIN
16MM FILM OPTICAL SOUND I-C A
Uses 200-year-old sculptures of the Ghuandara civilization, which are now lying in the northwestern part of Pakistan, to tell the story of the Gautama Buddha.
LC NO. FIA65-1859
Prod-FILMAS Dist-FILMAS Prodn-CHAUDH 1965

Land Of Endeavor C 29 MIN
16MM FILM OPTICAL SOUND J-C A
Shows developments in South Africa in the last two decades. Describes how the people have contributed to the country's development.
Prod-SMUSA Dist-SMUSA

Land Of Enlightenment B 11 MIN
16MM FILM OPTICAL SOUND I-C A
Presents the route of a Chinese pilgrim through Bihar, 'THE LAND OF ENLIGHTENMENT.' Features all the places venerated by Buddhists.
Prod-INDIA Dist-NEDINF

Land Of Frost And Fire C 15 MIN
3/4 OR 1/2 INCH VIDEO CASSETTE P
Pictures the Icelandic countryside.
From The Other Families, Other Friends Series. Brown Module - Iceland
Prod-WVIZTV Dist-AITECH 1971

Land Of Gold C 13 MIN
16MM FILM OPTICAL SOUND
Chronicles the process of wheat farming and, through images of relics from years past, explores the relationship of humans to the land.
LC NO. 79-701372
Prod-MARTSS Dist-ESSIA 1979

Land Of Hawaii C 15 MIN
3/4 INCH VIDEO CASSETTE
Presents a geological background of Hawaii and its soil and erosion problems. Outlines conservation programs and their relation to the economy of the islands and to the many crops.
Prod-USDA Dist-USDA 1972

Land Of Heart's Desire, The C 29 MIN
16MM FILM, 3/4 OR 1/2 IN VIDEO H-C A
Shows how retirement's looming causes a New York couple to explore Ireland as a return home.
Prod-CULLEN Dist-CEPRO

Land Of Immigrants (2nd Ed) C 16 MIN
16MM FILM, 3/4 OR 1/2 IN VIDEO P-J
Uses animation to trace the waves of immigration to the United States. Shows how the quality of this nation has been molded by many cultures.
LC NO. 82-706538
Prod-CF Dist-CF 1981

Land Of Liberty, Pt 1 B 22 MIN
16MM FILM OPTICAL SOUND I-C
Early colonial history and the development of the republic to 1805. A pictorial history of the United States originally prepared for exhibition at the NewYork World's Fair.
Prod-MPAA Dist-IU 1943

Land Of Liberty, Pt 2 B 22 MIN
16MM FILM OPTICAL SOUND I-C
A pictorial history of the United States from 1805 to 1860.
Prod-MPAA Dist-IU 1943

Land Of Liberty, Pt 3 B 22 MIN
16MM FILM OPTICAL SOUND I-C
A pictorial history of the United States from 1860 to 1890.
Prod-MPAA Dist-IU 1943

Land Of Liberty, Pt 4 B 22 MIN
16MM FILM OPTICAL SOUND I-C
A pictorial history of the United States from 1890 to 1938.
Prod-MPAA Dist-IU 1943

Land Of Liberty, Pt 5 B 22 MIN
16MM FILM OPTICAL SOUND I-C
Depicts the developments in the U S during the years 1939-1958. Includes the significant events of World War II, of the Atomic Age and of the Cold War. Discusses domestic problems and describes the progress in scientific research, education and welfare.
Prod-MPAA Dist-IU 1959

Land Of Lost Borders - The Chihuahuan Desert, Pt 1 C 27 MIN
16MM FILM OPTICAL SOUND
Studies the characteristics of the Chihuahuan Desert, with particular emphasis on the plants, animals and biomes.
LC NO. 82-700297
Prod-GRDNH Dist-ADAMSF 1982

Land Of Muck And Money C 25 MIN
16MM FILM OPTICAL SOUND
Presents correspondent Michael Maclear's examination of the phenomenon of mainstreeting in Canada. Notes that crime, fighting, alcoholism and related social problems can be seen on the streets of any urban center.
LC NO. 77-702515
Prod-CTV Dist-CTV 1976

Land Of Mystery C 13 MIN
16MM FILM OPTICAL SOUND
An exciting jaunt through Yellowstone National Park, showing different views of canyon and falls.

From The Travelbug Series.
Prod-SFI Dist-SFI

Land Of Opportunity C 26 MIN
16MM FILM, 3/4 OR 1/2 IN VIDEO H-C A
Shows the adaptation of plant reproductive systems in New Zealand, a botanically unique enclave of flora and fauna without large predators and herbivores. The land was isolated in the south seas by the continental drift, explained by the plate tectonic theory.
From The Botanic Man Series.
Prod-THAMES Dist-MEDIAG 1978

Land Of Opportunity–A Series

Prod-REP Dist-REP

American Rodeo 10 MIN
Sponge Divers 10 MIN

Land Of Our Fathers B 30 MIN
16MM FILM OPTICAL SOUND
States that the reasons for the biblical names of American towns and cities can be found in the Biblical roots of American civilization. (Kinescope)
Prod-JTS Dist-NAAJS Prodn-NBCTV 1954

Land Of Our Fathers C 60 MIN
3/4 OR 1/2 INCH VIDEO CASSETTE J-C A
Presents flutist James Galway discussing the renewed interest in the folk song and attempts to express in music the sense of homeland. Includes the song Londonderry Air and Dvorak's New World Symphony and Quartet in E-Flat.
From The James Galway's Music In Time Series.
Prod-POLTEL Dist-FOTH 1982

Land Of Promise B 28 MIN
16MM FILM OPTICAL SOUND J-H A
Explains the role of labor in social, economic and political history and traces the history of industry in America.
Prod-AFLCIO Dist-AFLCIO 1960

Land Of Silence And Darkness C 108 MIN
16MM FILM OPTICAL SOUND
Focuses on a woman who became blind and deaf in her youth, went into depression for 20 years, and emerged to become a tireless organizer of assistance to others in her situation. Directed by Werner Herzog. In English and German with English subtitles.
Prod-UNKNWN Dist-NYFLMS 1971

Land Of Smiles C 25 MIN
16MM FILM OPTICAL SOUND
Shows the beauty of Thailand, including her people and her temples.
From The Eye Of The Beholder Series.
LC NO. 75-701891
Prod-RCPDF Dist-VIACOM 1972

Land Of The Bible–A Series
I-H T R

Prod-FAMF Dist-FAMF

Dead Sea Scrolls 14 MIN
Exploring Ancient Cities 14 MIN
Jerusalem, The Sacred City 14 MIN
Life And Customs 14 MIN
Pictorial Geography, A 14 MIN

Land Of The Big Blue Sky C 29 MIN
16MM FILM OPTICAL SOUND
Shows many of the vacation attractions of southern Alberta, including local rodeos, historical mementos such as Indian picture writing, a wooden Mormon temple and Waterton Lakes National Park.
LC NO. 79-700884
Prod-SATC Dist-CTFL Prodn-CANAW 1967

Land Of The Big Ice C 55 MIN
16MM FILM OPTICAL SOUND
Looks at the more than 8,000 square miles of Baffin Island's Cumberland Peninsula that have been set aside as the world's first arctic national park.
From The To The Wild Country Series.
LC NO. 75-703400
Prod-CANBC Dist-KEGPL Prodn-KEGPL 1974

Land Of The Bighorn C 12 MIN
16MM FILM - 3/4 IN VIDEO
Reports the attitudes of the Crow Indians towards the land behind the dam on the Bighorn River. Includes glimpses of water sports. Issued in 1973 as a motion picture.
LC NO. 79-706134
Prod-USNPS Dist-USNAC 1979

Land Of The Book C 28 MIN
16MM FILM OPTICAL SOUND H-C
Brings alive the life and times of thousands of years ago in ancient Israel. Depicts the beauty of the land which gave birth to three great religions, the sites where heroic deeds took place and the towering splendor of the ancient works.
LC NO. 78-701199
Prod-GARNER Dist-AVED 1967

Land Of The Book, The B 30 MIN
16MM FILM OPTICAL SOUND
Ralph Bellamy shows how the Bible can be viewed as a guide book to Israel–it presents the past, present and future. Biblical sites shown include Solomon's mines, the plains of Armageddon, the River Jordan, Mt Tabor, Mt Zion, Galilee, Jerusalem, Carmel, Caesarea, Beersheba, the Negev and Acre. A companion film to 'THE PEOPLE OF THE BOOK.' (Kinescope)
Prod-JTS Dist-NAAJS Prodn-NBCTV 1959

Land Of The Brahmaputra B 12 MIN
16MM FILM OPTICAL SOUND I-C A
Follows the River Brahmaputra and its vagaries, which flow through Assam alternately ravaging and helping Assam to reap rich harvests. Includes view of the land and the people.
Prod-INDIA Dist-NEDINF

Land Of The Brave C 8 MIN
16MM FILM OPTICAL SOUND J-C A
Reveals the spiritual and physical courage of Americans who live in poverty as the poor speak out on the issues of hunger, housing, employment and education.
LC NO. 75-712176
Prod-CHD Dist-FRACOC 1970

Land Of The Dragon–A Series
H-C A
Describes the changes that have taken place over the centuries in the Himalayan Kingdom of Bhutan.
Prod-NOMDFI Dist-LANDMK 1983

Man Of The Forest 025 MIN
Man Of The People 025 MIN
Mountain Of The Goddess 025 MIN
Tiger's Nest, The 025 MIN

Land Of The Dragon–A Series

Describes the Kingdom of Bhutan, which remains a profoundly traditional society despite the changes which transformed it from an isolated feudal state into a developing member of the world community.
Prod-NOMDFI Dist-LANDMK

Man Of The Forest 025 MIN
Man Of The People 025 MIN
Mountain Of The Goddess 025 MIN
Tiger's Nest, The 025 MIN

Land Of The Drowned River C 26 MIN
16MM FILM OPTICAL SOUND P A
An ecological survey of the Del Mar Via Peninsula.
From The Audubon Wildlife Theatre Series.
LC NO. 76-710202
Prod-KEGPL Dist-AVEXP 1968

Land Of The Friendly Animals C 11 MIN
16MM FILM, 3/4 OR 1/2 IN VIDEO P-J
Features the animals, people and the islands of the Galapagos. Emphasizes the many interesting animals including the giant tortoises, blue footed boobies, iguanas, great blue herons, sea lions, pelicans and flamingoes.
Prod-EBEC Dist-EBEC 1972

Land Of The Kapriska Purara C 15 MIN
3/4 OR 1/2 INCH VIDEO CASSETTE P
Pictures a park, a market and the Presidential Palace in Managua, Nicaragua.
From The Other Families, Other Friends Series. Brown Module - Nicaragua
Prod-WVIZTV Dist-AITECH 1971

Land Of The Loon C 26 MIN
16MM FILM OPTICAL SOUND P A
Examines the mood of a wilderness park through close-ups of many birds and animals in Algonquin Park in Ontario.
From The Audubon Wildlife Theatre Series.
LC NO. 70-710203
Prod-KEGPL Dist-AVEXP 1969

Land Of The Loon (2nd Ed) C 26 MIN
16MM FILM OPTICAL SOUND
Shows the wilderness of a Canadian wildlife sanctuary, Algonquin Park, its lakes and trails.
LC NO. 76-702023
Prod-GIB Dist-KEGPL 1975

Land Of The Peacock Throne, The C 14 MIN
16MM FILM, 3/4 OR 1/2 IN VIDEO I-H
Describes 40 years of crises and unrest in Iran. Includes information on the rise of the Ayatollah Khomeini and the taking of American hostages.
From The Screen News Digest Series. Volume 23, Issue 7
Prod-HEARST Dist-HEARST 1981

Land Of The Pineapple C 15 MIN
3/4 OR 1/2 INCH VIDEO CASSETTE P
Pictures a pineapple field, a sugar cane field and the Polynesian Cultural Village in Hawaii.
From The Other Families, Other Friends Series. Green Module - Hawaii
Prod-WVIZTV Dist-AITECH 1971

Land Of The Sea C 26 MIN
16MM FILM OPTICAL SOUND P-C A
Explores the Canadian province of Nova Scotia and studies the famous tides of the Minas Basin with time-lapse photography. Describes the various underwater life and the Bay of Fundy tides.
From The Audubon Wildlife Theatre Series.
LC NO. 70-709405
Prod-KEGPL Dist-AVEXP 1969

Land Of The Silver Birch C 15 MIN
3/4 OR 1/2 INCH VIDEO CASSETTE P-I
See series title for descriptive statement.
From The Ready, Sing Series.
Prod-ARKETV Dist-AITECH 1979

Land Of The Sleeping Mountains, The C 60 MIN
16MM FILM, 3/4 OR 1/2 IN VIDEO H-C A
Reveals that the Great Basin was formed when the floor of the Pacific Ocean slid under the continent, pushing up the Sierra Nevada and cutting off the moisture from the west. Shows how the plants and creatures responded to this upheaval.

From The Making Of A Continent Series.
Prod-BBCTV Dist-FI 1983

Land Of The Tiger C 25 MIN
16MM FILM OPTICAL SOUND H-C A
Follows Fred Bear as he travels to India in search of Sher Kan, the great Bengal tiger. Portrays his experiences in the magnificent palace of his highness the Maharaja of Bundi and on the surrounding game trails. Shows him hunting the sambur, nilgai and axis deer.
Prod-GFS Dist-GFS

Land Of The Tiger C 59 MIN
16MM FILM, 3/4 OR 1/2 IN VIDEO J-H A
Presents an intimate portrait of the tiger, filmed in two national reserves in India throughout the seasons. Shows the predator stalking, capturing and devouring its prey, mating, caring for its cubs and marking territorial boundaries.
Prod-NGS Dist-NGS

Land Of Their Own - The Face Of Courage C 30 MIN
3/4 OR 1/2 INCH VIDEO CASSETTE
Presents an 'original cast' western based on letters, diaries and photographs of the people who settled Nebraska. Includes photographs from the collection of the Nebraska Historical Society, many taken by Solomon D Butcher, Nebraska's pre-eminent pioneer photographer. Narrated by the late John G Neihardt, Nebraska's poet laureate.
Prod-NETCHE Dist-NETCHE 1982

Land Of Third, The C 15 MIN
3/4 OR 1/2 INCH VIDEO CASSETTE P
Employs a magician named Amazing Alexander and his assistants to reinforce learning the letters of the alphabet.
From The Magic Shop Series. No. 1
LC NO. 83-706146
Prod-CVETVC Dist-GPITVL Prodn-WCVETV 1982

Land Of 10,000 Dumps C 40 MIN
3/4 OR 1/2 INCH VIDEO CASSETTE
Takes a worrisome look at waste disposal in Minnesota.
Prod-WCCOTV Dist-WCCOTV 1981

Land Pollution - A First Film C 8 MIN
16MM FILM, 3/4 OR 1/2 IN VIDEO
Tells how the American people can best use the land resources. Lists the many uses made of the land and explains that good land is not unlimited.
Prod-BEAN Dist-PHENIX 1974

Land Speaks Out, The C 12 MIN
16MM FILM OPTICAL SOUND
Points out that Israel is a modern country, rooted deeply in its historic past. Shows convenient vacation facilities at sea resorts and camping grounds combined with unique archaeological sites and beautiful scenery of the countryside.
Prod-ALDEN Dist-ALDEN

Land Surveying-A Series
C
Uses classroom format to videotape 30 one-hour lectures. Covers original surveys, retracement of original surveys, legal aspects of property surveys and writing property descriptions. Goes into history and development, related laws, subdivision planning and method for property surveys.
Prod-UIDEEO Dist-AMCEE

Land That Came In From The Cold, The C 13 MIN
16MM FILM, 3/4 OR 1/2 IN VIDEO J-C A
Explores the glaciers of Glacier National Monument, showing how they have changed over the past 200 years. Points out that a glacier can be seen as a geological and zoological time line.
From The Natural Phenomenon Series.
Prod-JOU Dist-JOU 1980

Land That Time Forgot C 90 MIN
16MM FILM OPTICAL SOUND I A
Based on the book by Edgar Rice Burroughs. Set in 1916, survivors from a torpedoed ship find themselves on a legendary island full of prehistoric monsters. Stars Doug McClure.
Prod-AMICP Dist-TIMLIF 1974

Land The Landing Force C 29 MIN
16MM FILM OPTICAL SOUND
Shows operations of the naval amphibious forces.
LC NO. 74-706483
Prod-USN Dist-USNAC 1967

Land The Landing Force - The History Of Marine Amphibious Operations C 28 MIN
16MM FILM OPTICAL SOUND
Explains the development of the amphibious doctrine and its use in vertical assault.
LC NO. FIE62-30
Prod-USMC Dist-USNAC 1960

Land Use And Misuse C 13 MIN
16MM FILM, 3/4 OR 1/2 IN VIDEO J-H
Describes malpractice in the use of land surfaces without regard for erosion by wind and water, alteration of hydrologic cycle, contamination of ground water by irrigation and resulting changes in climate. Discusses phenomena, problems, effects, causes and possible solutions.
From The Environmental Sciences Series.
Prod-DAVFMS Dist-LCOA 1975

Land Use And Misuse (Captioned) C 13 MIN
16MM FILM, 3/4 OR 1/2 IN VIDEO J-C A
Demonstrates why careful use of our land surface is essential to human existence.
Prod-LCOA Dist-LCOA 1975

Land Use In The City C 30 MIN
3/4 OR 1/2 INCH VIDEO CASSETTE C
Discusses efficient use of land for the city and the countryside. Includes urban sprawl, zoning, subdivision regulation, environmental impact of population and industrial growth and the need for master planning.
From The Living Environment Series.
Prod-DALCCD Dist-DALCCD

Land Use On The Flood Plains C 16 MIN
16MM FILM, 3/4 OR 1/2 IN VIDEO J-C
Examines the relationship between flooding and land use. Explains that the proximity to transportation, energy and fertile soil has often outweighted the dangers of flood and offers dams, levies and flood-plan zoning as methods of controlling land use of flood plains.
LC NO. 80-707097
Prod-IU Dist-IU 1976

Land Use Planning In The Town Of Dunn B 45 MIN
3/4 OR 1/2 INCH VIDEO CASSETTE
Explores the negative and positive effects of land use planning in the town of Dunn.
Prod-UWISC Dist-UWISC 1981

Land Vs Sea - The Interface C 21 MIN
3/4 INCH VIDEO CASSETTE J
Examines the disappearing world of the sailing clippers. Looks at the mechanics of waves and the morphology of a sand beach.
From The What On Earth Series.
Prod-NCSDPI Dist-GPITVL 1979

Land Where The Blues Began C 59 MIN
16MM FILM, 3/4 OR 1/2 IN VIDEO
Presents a documentary about the culture of the Mississippi hill country.
Prod-MAETEL Dist-PHENIX Prodn-LOMCAR 1980

Land Without Bread / Housing Problems B 43 MIN
3/4 OR 1/2 INCH VIDEO CASSETTE
Presents a documentary on the impoverished people living in the Las Hurdes region of Spain. Directed by Luis Bunuel. Explores the horrors and evils of the urban housing of the '30s through interviews with slum dwellers. Directed by Arthur Elton and Edgar Anstey.
Prod-IHF Dist-IHF

Land, Labor And Capital C 10 MIN
16MM FILM, 3/4 OR 1/2 IN VIDEO P-I
Introduces the student to the farmer to discover the importance of land, the mill foreman who emphasizes capital and a designer at a clothing factory who points out the merits of labor.
From The Economics For Elementary Series.
Prod-EVANSA Dist-AIMS 1971

Land, The C 30 MIN
16MM FILM, 3/4 OR 1/2 IN VIDEO H-C
See series title for descriptive statement.
From The Great Plains Experience Series.
Prod-UMA Dist-GPITVL 1976

Land, The B 44 MIN
16MM FILM - 3/4 IN VIDEO
Portrays American agriculture during the Depression decade. Issued in 1941 as a motion picture.
LC NO. 79-706463
Prod-USAGA Dist-USNAC 1979

Land, The Sea, The Children There, The C 24 MIN
3/4 OR 1/2 INCH VIDEO CASSETTE
Gives a lifestyle portrayal of two children, one from Maine and one from Nebraska.
From The Young People's Specials Series.
Prod-MULTPP Dist-MULTPP

Land's Edge C 28 MIN
3/4 OR 1/2 INCH VIDEO CASSETTE
Shows human, animal and plant life along the ocean shore near Newport, Oregon. Features the natural beauty and the buildup of a storm.
Prod-MEDIPR Dist-MEDIPR 1974

Landbased Helicopter Operations - Functions B 10 MIN
16MM FILM OPTICAL SOUND
Describes to helicopter pilots the many duties which they will be expected to perform in landbased helicopter operations and points out the versatility of the helicopter.
LC NO. FIE59-237
Prod-USN Dist-USNAC 1952

Landbased Helicopter Operations - Precautions B 11 MIN
16MM FILM OPTICAL SOUND
Stresses the need for pilot alertness in helicopter operation and demonstrates night and rough-terrain operations.
LC NO. FIE59-236
Prod-USN Dist-USNAC 1952

Landet De Vandt (Conquered Land) C 35 MIN
16MM FILM OPTICAL SOUND
A Danish language film. Presents interviews with old Moorland farmers who tell about their strenuous efforts to realize Enrico Dalgas' dream of fertilizing the moors of Jutland. Aims at proving that the history of the Danish health society reflects Denmark's development. Documents their work since 1866.
Prod-STATNS Dist-STATNS 1966

Landfall No. 1 C 6 MIN
16MM FILM OPTICAL SOUND
Presents a seascape film made on Prince Edward Island.
LC NO. 76-701022
Prod-CANFDC Dist-CANFDC 1974

Landfill C 12 MIN
16MM FILM OPTICAL SOUND
Proves that solid waste disposal need not be damaging to the environment. Depicts a regional transfer and landfill operation which serves a big city and several nearby suburban communities. Shows that it is designed to do a big job without the truck traffic, dust, noise and health problems which so often disturb citizens and arouse protest elsewhere.
Prod-FINLYS Dist-FINLYS

Landforms - What They Are And How They Are Shaped C
3/4 OR 1/2 INCH VIDEO CASSETTE J-H
Discusses the major landforms on earth - seacoasts, deserts, streams and river valleys, and glaciers and glaciated landscapes. Explains plate tectonics and illustrates the interaction of lifting, sculpting and eroding forces.
Prod-CRYSP Dist-GA

Landforms Of Washington C 15 MIN
16MM FILM OPTICAL SOUND I A
Shows typical geography from each of the major regions of the state of Washington, coastal, lowlands of Puget Sound, Cascade Mountains, central and Inland Empire. Points out climatic differences between western and eastern regions.
LC NO. 75-704199
Prod-SAMSHL Dist-HLSPRO 1975

Landing - Weather Minimums Investigation C 21 MIN
16MM FILM OPTICAL SOUND
Examines problems faced by pilots making approaches under low visibility conditions. Depicts landings in deep, shallow and cloud base fog, in drizzle with and without windshield wipers and with misaligned instruments.
LC NO. 75-700562
Prod-USAF Dist-USNAC 1967

Landing - Weather Minimums Investigation C 21 MIN
3/4 OR 1/2 INCH VIDEO CASSETTE
Examines problems faced by pilots making approaches under low visibility conditions. Depicts landings in deep, shallow and cloud base fog, in drizzle with and without windshield wipers and with misaligned instruments.
LC NO. 81-706649
Prod-USAF Dist-USNAC 1967

Landing Illusions - Short Landings C 10 MIN
16MM FILM, 3/4 OR 1/2 IN VIDEO
Discusses optical illusions which can cause pilot error. Shows visibility restrictions on the glidepath caused by changing weather conditions.
LC NO. 82-707217
Prod-USAF Dist-USNAC 1969

Landing On The Moon B 20 MIN
16MM FILM - 3/4 IN VIDEO
Takes the viewers inside the lunar module and simulates a ride to the surface of the moon. Includes details of the lunar module landing and lift-off from the moon.
Prod-USNAC Dist-USNAC 1972

Landing Team, The C 10 MIN
16MM FILM OPTICAL SOUND H-C A
Emphasizes the skill, safe working procedures and productive operations of the landing team. Shows professional landing teams at work in various conditions, terrains and locations.
From The Logging Safety Series.
Prod-RARIG Dist-RARIG 1968

Landlord And Tenant C 22 MIN
16MM FILM OPTICAL SOUND J-C A
Takes a cinema-verite look at the opinions and attitudes held by landlords and tenants. Considers views from landlords, a welfare family with housing problems and a group of people responsible for organizing a tenant's union in a large housing project.
LC NO. 76-700674
Prod-OHHUM Dist-OSUMPD Prodn-OSUPD 1974

Landlord-Tenant Law C 23 MIN
16MM FILM, 3/4 OR 1/2 IN VIDEO J-C A
Discusses the rights of tenants and landlords and raises questions concerning the landlords' obligation to maintain their apartments at legally imposed levels of habitability. Discusses the question of whether tenants should be allowed to deduct repair costs from the rent.
From The Law And The Citizen Series.
Prod-WILETS Dist-BARR 1978

Landlords And Tenants C 29 MIN
3/4 INCH VIDEO CASSETTE C A
Discusses legal right and responsiblities that exist between landlords and tenants. Focuses on terms and basic clauses found in a typical lease.
From The You And The Law Series. Lesson 16
Prod-COAST Dist-CDTEL Prodn-SADCC

Landman, The C 16 MIN
16MM FILM, 3/4 OR 1/2 IN VIDEO IND
Explains common roles of a landman as a member of an exploration team.
Prod-UTEXPE Dist-UTEXPE

Landmark C 14 MIN
16MM FILM OPTICAL SOUND
Traces the development of nuclear power reactors in the United States and shows how their increased use in the future could ease the current energy crisis.
LC NO. 74-700711
Prod-ANL Dist-USNAC 1973

Landmark In Beta-Blocker Research - Findings Of The Norwegian Multicenter Study Group C 13 MIN
3/4 OR 1/2 INCH VIDEO CASSETTE PRO
Reports on the use of Timolol Maleate, a beta blocker, in a study population of nearly 2000 patients, which showed the effectiveness of the drug in reducing the risk of death and reinfarc-

tion in those who have survived the acute phase of a myocardial infarction.
Prod-WFP Dist-WFP

andmarks To Remember C 20 MIN
3/4 INCH VIDEO CASSETTE I
Highlights America's national monuments. Features the Washington Monument, the Jefferson Memorial, the Gettysburg battlefield, the Gateway Arch at St Louis, and Ft Laramie.
From The Exploring Our Nation Series.
Prod-KRMATV Dist-GPITVL 1975

ands And Waters Of Our Earth C 11 MIN
16MM FILM, 3/4 OR 1/2 IN VIDEO P
Shows the many kinds of land and water forms on the earth's surface, such as hills, mountains, valleys and rivers.
Prod-CORF Dist-CORF 1956

ands Of Promise C 30 MIN
3/4 OR 1/2 INCH VIDEO CASSETTE
Shows how many nations are overcoming complex agricultural, social, political and economic problems to bring arid or jungle-choked areas into productivity, and thus make themselves more self-sufficient.
Prod-IVCH Dist-IVCH

ands Of The Falling Waters, The X 10 MIN
16MM FILM OPTICAL SOUND
Pictures scenes of South America including a flight to the world's highest waterfalls, Angle Falls, in Venezuela, Georgetown, capital of British Guiana and the Kaietur Falls.
Prod-MILWOD Dist-PLP 1958

andsat - Satellite For All Seasons—A Series
J-H
Shows how scientist and researchers use information transmitted by NASA's satellite to solve environmental problems.
Prod-NASA Dist-AITECH

ANDSAT—A Series

Depicts the non-military functions of the earth's orbiting satellites. Combines earth resources management with four natural disasters.
Prod-IVCH Dist-IVCH

Earthquake Below 015 MIN
Flood Below 015 MIN
Hurricane Below 015 MIN
Land For People, Land For Bears 015 MIN
Pollution Solution 015 MIN
Remote Possibilities 015 MIN
Tornado Below 015 MIN
Wet Look, The 015 MIN

andsbykirken (The Danish Village Church) B 10 MIN
16MM FILM SILENT
Presents the history of Danish country church architecture by showing how the church is used by the congregation, beginning with the celebration of Mass in a small and simple wooden church 800 years ago, and ending with the congregation singing in a village church of today. Shows the development and growth of the pattern of church architecture. Includes Danish subtitles.
Prod-STATNS Dist-STATNS 1947

andscape C 37 MIN
16MM FILM OPTICAL SOUND J-C A
Presents an adaptation of the Royal Shakespeare Company production of Harold Pinter's play, Landscape, staring Dame Peggy Ashcroft and David Waller.
Prod-CANTOR Dist-CANTOR

andscape C 6 MIN
3/4 INCH VIDEO CASSETTE
Transforms a single illuminated hand through movement and scale into a sculptural landscape.
From The Nan Hoover - Selected Works 2 Series.
Prod-EAI Dist-EAI

Landscape C 8 MIN
16MM FILM, 3/4 OR 1/2 IN VIDEO H-C A
Uses experimental animation techniques to depict one man's dreams and fantasies.
Prod-HUFSC Dist-PHENIX 1975

Landscape - A Pattern Of Change C 19 MIN
16MM FILM OPTICAL SOUND J-C A
Traces the changing patterns of land use as they affect a typical Australian town, using the example of Mudgee in New South Wales.
LC NO. 76-700566
Prod-FLMAUS Dist-AUIS 1975

Landscape After Battle (Polish) C 110 MIN
16MM FILM OPTICAL SOUND
Presents a love story set in a displaced persons camp in Poland after World War II. Directed by Andrzej Wajda. With English subtitles.
Prod-UNKNWN Dist-NYFLMS 1970

Landscape And Cityscape C 30 MIN
3/4 OR 1/2 INCH VIDEO CASSETTE
See series title for descriptive statement.
From The Photographic Vision - All About Photography Series.
Prod-COAST Dist-CDTEL

Landscape And Light C 30 MIN
3/4 OR 1/2 INCH VIDEO CASSETTE H-C A
Discusses the practicalities of landscape photography and how to capture mood and atmosphere through viewpoint, composition and the quality of light.
From The What A Picture - The Complete Photography Course By John Hedgecoe Series. Program 5
Prod-THREMI Dist-FI

Landscape Artistry C 30 MIN
1/2 IN VIDEO CASSETTE BETA/VHS
Discusses planting on a deck. Pictures some landscape artistry in Boston and Lexington.
From The Victory Garden Series.
Prod-WGBHTV Dist-MTI

Landscape Design C 30 MIN
1/2 IN VIDEO CASSETTE BETA/VHS
Considers gardening possibilities for a renovated house.
From The This Old House, Pt 1 - The Dorchester Series.
Prod-WGBHTV Dist-MTI

Landscape In Painting C 19 MIN
16MM FILM, 3/4 OR 1/2 IN VIDEO H-C
Traces the history of landscape painting, from the examples unearthed at Pompeii to the 20th century.
Prod-SEABEN Dist-IFB 1972

Landscape Of Pleasure, The C 52 MIN
16MM FILM, 3/4 OR 1/2 IN VIDEO C A
Discusses the liberation of color which began in the late 19th century and which was amplified by Matisse and Derain. Points out the increasing personalization of art as seen in the work of Braque and Picasso.
From The Shock Of The New Series.
LC NO. 80-706952
Prod-BBCTV Dist-TIMLIF 1980

Landscape With Boots And Child C 9 MIN
16MM FILM OPTICAL SOUND
Attempts to re-create the story behind a photograph that was found in Europe during World War II.
LC NO. 79-700233
Prod-POORI Dist-POORI 1978

Landscape, The C 30 MIN
3/4 OR 1/2 INCH VIDEO CASSETTE
Discusses the scope of architecture, which has expanded in recent years to include a consciousness of the entire ecological system of the planet and how this concern is now considered fundamental to good design.
From The Designing The Environment Series.
Prod-NETCHE Dist-NETCHE 1971

Landslides - Descriptive C 47 MIN
3/4 OR 1/2 INCH VIDEO CASSETTE IND
See series title for descriptive statement.
From The Basic And Petroleum Geology For Non-Geologists - Landforms Series.
Prod-PHILLP Dist-GPCV

Langevin Equation, Distribution Function And Boltzmann Equation C
3/4 OR 1/2 INCH VIDEO CASSETTE IND
Describes the Langevin equation for electron motion which includes both the driving term from the electric field force and the opposing momentum-loss collisions between electrons and atoms, and their terminal velocities. Includes calculation of distribution function.
From The Plasma Process Technology Fundamentals Series.
Prod-COLOSU Dist-COLOSU

Langston Hughes C 20 MIN
3/4 INCH VIDEO CASSETTE I
See series title for descriptive statement.
From The Truly American Series.
Prod-WVIZTV Dist-GPITVL 1979

Langston Hughes C 24 MIN
16MM FILM, 3/4 OR 1/2 IN VIDEO J-C A
Describes the life and work of poet Langston Hughes.
Prod-WCAUTV Dist-CAROUF

Language B 28 MIN
16MM FILM OPTICAL SOUND
Demonstrates the direct teaching method for disadvantaged children, developed at the University of Illinois by Dr Carl Bereiter and Siefgried Englemann, with a class of four-year-olds, who have never been in school.
Prod-ADL Dist-ADL

Language C 30 MIN
16MM FILM, 3/4 OR 1/2 IN VIDEO H-C A
Probes the impact of language on culture including a rehearsal and performance with the National Theatre of the Deaf, a look at the influence that the woman's movement has had on the newest Barnhart Dictionary, a seminar with the world's leading authority on abusive language and an animated Doonesbury strip extolling the virtues of California's Mellow-Speak. Hosted by Victor Borge.
From The Media Probes Series.
Prod-LAYLEM Dist-TIMLIF 1982

Language C 30 MIN
3/4 OR 1/2 INCH VIDEO CASSETTE C
Discusses how the black community has changed and adapted language.
From The Afro-American Perspectives Series.
Prod-MDDE Dist-MDCPB

Language C 60 MIN
3/4 OR 1/2 INCH VIDEO CASSETTE A
Presents biologist Humberto Maturana discussing language.
From The Biology Of Cognition And Language Series. Program 12
Prod-UCEMC Dist-UCEMC

Language (Interaction - Human Concerns In The Schools) C 30 MIN
3/4 OR 1/2 INCH VIDEO CASSETTE T
Analyzes the importance of language in an educational setting.
From The Interaction - Human Concerns In The Schools Series.
Prod-MDDE Dist-MDCPB

Language - A Sign And Symbol System C 30 MIN
3/4 OR 1/2 INCH VIDEO CASSETTE C
See series title for descriptive statement.
From The Language And Meaning Series.
Prod-WUSFTV Dist-GPITVL 1983

Language - The Social Arbiter—A Series
H-C T
Prod-FINLYS Dist-FINLYS

English Teaching Tomorrow 24 MIN
Language And Integration 28 MIN
Language Problems In The Schools 26 MIN
Linguistics And Education 22 MIN
Nature Of Language, The 28 MIN
Regional Variations 28 MIN
Social Variations 28 MIN

Language - Thinking, Writing, Communicating—A Series

Offers an overall view of language and communication. Features linguist Walt Wolfman from the Center for Applied Linguistics; Ellen Goodman, Pulitzer Prize-winning columnist; and advertising professional and former Senator Eugene McCarthy discussing dialects, jargon, good writing techniques, linguistics and the history of the English language.
Prod-MDCPB Dist-MDCPB

Apes And Language 030 MIN
Communities Of Speech 030 MIN
Just Plain English 030 MIN
Language, Learning And Children 030 MIN
Men, Women, And Language 030 MIN
Rhyme And Reason Of Politics, The 030 MIN
Shape Of Language, The 030 MIN
State Of English, The 030 MIN
Written Word, The 030 MIN

Language And Character C 51 MIN
3/4 OR 1/2 INCH VIDEO CASSETTE
Discusses the Elizabethan relish of words - their resonances, onomatopeia, alliteration and antithesis. Deals with how Shakespeare uses language to define character and how his characters use heightened language to achieve their intentions. Includes examples from Love's Labour's Lost, Henry V, Julius Caesar and Hamlet.
From The Royal Shakespeare Company Series.
Prod-FOTH Dist-FOTH 1984

Language And Communication C 30 MIN
3/4 INCH VIDEO CASSETTE PRO
Suggests ways of ensuring clarity and comprehension in attorneys' communications with jurors.
From The Picking And Persuading A Jury Series. Program 5
LC NO. 81-706170
Prod-ABACPE Dist-ABACPE 1980

Language And Communication C 30 MIN
3/4 INCH VIDEO CASSETTE C A
Introduces some key terms for understanding the structure of language. Includes paralanguage, historical linguistics and nonverbal communication.
From The Faces Of Culture - Studies In Cultural Anthropology Series. Lesson 6
Prod-COAST Dist-CDTEL Prodn-HRAW

Language And Hearing-Impaired Children C 15 MIN
3/4 OR 1/2 INCH VIDEO CASSETTE PRO
Explains differences between normal language development and that of the hearing-impaired child. Delineates how to overcome the obstacles of teaching language skills.
Prod-HSCIC Dist-HSCIC 1984

Language And Integration C 28 MIN
16MM FILM OPTICAL SOUND
A bi-racial panel of linguistic specialists discusses how language complicates and seems to interfere with the process of integration.
From The Language - The Social Arbiter Series.
LC NO. FIA67-463
Prod-FINLYS Dist-FINLYS Prodn-CALING 1966

Language And Meaning—A Series
C
Features Robert O'Hara, professor of linguistics at the University of South Florida exploring such topics as the nature of language as a uniquely human phenomenon, misconceptions about language, language as metaphor, how/why meanings change, language taboos and euphemisms.
Prod-WUSFTV Dist-GPITVL 1983

Dominant Metaphor And Perception 030 MIN
English Language - Racist And Sexist 030 MIN
Euphemism - Telling It Like It Is 030 MIN
Euphemism And Social Change 030 MIN
Function Of Language, The - Perception 030 MIN
Function Of Language, The - The Social 030 MIN
How Meanings Change 030 MIN
Kinesics - Motion And Meaning 030 MIN
Labels And Distortion 030 MIN
Language - A Sign And Symbol System 030 MIN
Language As A Metaphor 030 MIN
Language Taboos - Cultural 030 MIN
Language Taboos - Grammatical 030 MIN
Levels Of Abstraction And Meaning 030 MIN
Manipulation Of Language And Meaning, The 030 MIN
Nature Of Language, The - Brain And Mind 030 MIN
Nature Of Language, The - The Linguistic 030 MIN
Nature Of Signs, The 030 MIN
Nature Of Symbols, The 030 MIN
Past In Our Words, The 030 MIN
Proxemics - Distance 030 MIN
Some Misconceptions About Language, Pt 1 030 MIN

Some Misconceptions About Language, Pt 2 030 MIN
Standards, Styles And Keys 030 MIN
Tunes Of Language Intonation And Meaning, The 030 MIN
What Do We Mean By Meaning 030 MIN
Why Meanings Change 030 MIN
Words - They Come And Go 030 MIN

Language And The Aphasic Child C 108 MIN
3/4 OR 1/2 INCH VIDEO CASSETTE
Discusses issues relevant to childhood aphasia.
Prod-PUAVC Dist-PUAVC 1972

Language And The Disadvantaged Child C 110 MIN
3/4 OR 1/2 INCH VIDEO CASSETTE
Relates a brief history of black Americans with particular attention to the translocation of blacks from their native country to America and two theories which attempt to explain the origin of black speech differences.
From The Mainstreaming Secondary Special Vocational Needs Student Series.
Prod-PUAVC Dist-PUAVC

Language And The Retarded Child C 108 MIN
3/4 OR 1/2 INCH VIDEO CASSETTE
Describes the speech and language functions of the mentally retarded child, and demonstration problems in hearing, speech, language, cognition and general motor development.
Prod-PUAVC Dist-PUAVC 1972

Language Arts - Literature—A Series
16MM FILM, 3/4 OR 1/2 IN VIDEO
Prod-BFA Dist-PHENIX

Cat In The Hat, The
Dragon Stew
Evan's Corner
Gabrielle And Selena
Lorax, The
Possum That Didn't

Language Arts - Motivation—A Series
16MM FILM, 3/4 OR 1/2 IN VIDEO
Prod-BFA Dist-PHENIX

Children's Chants And Games
Craftsman, The
Fence, The
Junkyard
Log Raft, The - A Norwegian Summer Story
Rock In The Road, A
Violin Maker, The (In Praise Of Hands)

Language Arts Holidays—A Series

Prod-MORLAT Dist-MORLAT 1973

Christmas In Pioneer Times 15 MIN

Language As Metaphor C 30 MIN
3/4 OR 1/2 INCH VIDEO CASSETTE C
See series title for descriptive statement.
From The Language And Meaning Series.
Prod-WUSFTV Dist-GPITVL 1983

Language Assessment And Programming C 29 MIN
3/4 OR 1/2 INCH VIDEO CASSETTE T
Discusses language assessment and programming in a mainstreaming situation.
From The Mainstreaming The Exceptional Child Series.
Prod-MFFD Dist-FI

Language At Twelve C 28 MIN
16MM FILM OPTICAL SOUND C A
Shows a group of twelve-year-olds as they participate in a language project. Points out differences in communication with parents, teachers and peers.
LC NO. 79-700525
Prod-FLMAUS Dist-AUIS 1976

Language Corner—A Series
P
Features Mrs Hope Mitchell stressing the spoken and written language of words, phrases and sentences, facial expressions, bodily movements, voice quality, rate of speed, pitch, emphasis, phrasing and drama. (Broadcast quality)
Prod-CVETVC Dist-GPITVL Prodn-WCVETV

Autobiography 15 MIN
Being Friendly And Kind 15 MIN
Biography 15 MIN
Book Review, A 15 MIN
Communicating Through Art 15 MIN
Communicating Through Poetry And Monologues 15 MIN
Communicating With Your Body 15 MIN
Fairy Tales 15 MIN
Fun Of Reading, The 15 MIN
Hands Communicate 15 MIN
Imagination Can Be Many Things 15 MIN
Letter Writing 15 MIN
Library, The 15 MIN
Listening 15 MIN
Magic And Mystery 15 MIN
Observation And Conversation 15 MIN
Poetry Out Loud 15 MIN
Puppet Show 15 MIN
Review Of The Course, A - Language Corner 15 MIN
Sharing Effectively 15 MIN
Speech And Telephone 15 MIN
Speech Lesson 15 MIN
Story By The Teacher 15 MIN
Synonyms 15 MIN
Telling A Story 15 MIN
Vocabulary - Language Corner 15 MIN
Walk In The Woods, A 15 MIN

Write Stories Aobut Daydreams 15 MIN
Writing On An Interesting And Complete Thought 15 MIN

Language Development C 20 MIN
16MM FILM OPTICAL SOUND C S
Illustrates the child's language process in the first four years, beginning with the development of phonemes, syntax and semantics - the process by which language is acquired and how that acquisition can be influenced.
From The Child Development Series.
LC NO. 72-712596
Prod-HRAW Dist-HRAW Prodn-BAY 1971

Language Development B 44 MIN
16MM FILM OPTICAL SOUND
Discusses processes involved in the child's acquisition of speech and language skills.
From The Man - His Growth And Development, Birth Through Adolescence Series.
LC NO. 78-703682
Prod-VDONUR Dist-AJN Prodn-WTTWTV 1967

Language Development C 20 MIN
16MM FILM, 3/4 OR 1/2 IN VIDEO H-C A
Shows the most current research being done on language development, such as Dr David Premack's work at the University of California teaching language to chimpanzees.
From The Developmental Psychology Today Film Series.
Prod-CRMP Dist-CRMP 1973

Language Experience Approach C 20 MIN
16MM FILM, 3/4 OR 1/2 IN VIDEO T
Focuses on literacy instruction techniques involving the use of one's own words and experiences as reading material. Shows a student using his many successes in life to learn how to read.
From The Literacy Instructor Training Series.
LC NO. 80-706060
Prod-IU Dist-IU 1978

Language Experience Approach C 30 MIN
3/4 OR 1/2 INCH VIDEO CASSETTE T
Emphasizes starting to teach reading at students' present levels and proceeding through activities centered on their progressing interests.
From The Stretch Subject Matter Materials For Teaching Handicapped Children Series.
Prod-HUBDSC Dist-HUBDSC

Language Experience Approach C 30 MIN
16MM FILM, 3/4 OR 1/2 IN VIDEO T S
Shows a kindergarten teacher demonstrating the principles of the Language Experience Approach as the children in her class record events and create stories about those events.
From The Project STRETCH (Strategies To Train Regular Educators To Teach Children With...) Series. Module 11
LC NO. 80-706647
Prod-METCO Dist-HUBDSC 1980

Language Features, Pt 2 C 30 MIN
3/4 OR 1/2 INCH VIDEO CASSETTE IND
Discusses programming language features for scope control, exception handling, data encapsulation and structured central flow. Reviews and summarizes concepts of structured coding.
From The Software Engineering - A First Course Series.
Prod-COLOSU Dist-COLOSU

Language Features, Pt 3 C 30 MIN
3/4 OR 1/2 INCH VIDEO CASSETTE IND
Goes into structural programming concepts of single entry-single exit, 'structured' violations to single entry-single exit, the GOTO statement and uses of recursion.
From The Software Engineering - A First Course Series.
Prod-COLOSU Dist-COLOSU

Language In Life C
3/4 OR 1/2 INCH VIDEO CASSETTE
Prod-MSTVIS Dist-MSTVIS

Language Instruction At The USAF Academy C 25 MIN
16MM FILM OPTICAL SOUND
Illustrates progressive methods of teaching foreign languages at the Air Force Academy.
LC NO. 74-706123
Prod-USAF Dist-USNAC 1962

Language Is Sound And Sense B 15 MIN
2 INCH VIDEOTAPE I
Shows how sounds are used to communicate thoughts and feelings from the moment of birth. Describes how the printed word means nothing unless associated with appropriate sentence sounds. Features selections such as The Kind Of Bath For Me by Sir Edward Parry, Susie Moriar and a Carolina mountain song. (Broadcast quality)
From The Bill Martin Series. No. 1
Prod-BRITED Dist-GPITVL Prodn-KQEDTV

Language Lane—A Series
P
Explores various ways of expressing one's thoughts, viewpoints and desires. Helps one develop and use all communicative skills at his command in making his ideas known to others, in listening to the thoughts and ideas of others, in ably expressing his thoughts through written word and in reading and understanding the written words of others. (Broadcast quality)
Prod-CVETVC Dist-GPITVL Prodn-WCVETV

All Yours 20 MIN
As Easy As ABC 20 MIN
Building Better Paragraphs 20 MIN
Building Better Sentences 20 MIN
Canine Corps Communicates, The 20 MIN
Choral Reading Takes Team Work 20 MIN
Creating A Poem 20 MIN
Dance A Story 20 MIN
Face Plus Hands Equal Story 20 MIN
First Things First 20 MIN
Flavor In Your Stories 20 MIN
Fun With Marionettes 20 MIN
Give A Little Talk 20 MIN
Happy Holiday 20 MIN
I Beg Your Pardon, What Did You Say 20 MIN
Imagination Is Funny 20 MIN
Interesting Conversation 20 MIN
On Stage 20 MIN
Poet Speaks, The 20 MIN
Reading With Sparkle 20 MIN
Right Book For You, The 20 MIN
Seven Ways Of Communicating News 20 MIN
Share That Book 20 MIN
Sincerely Yours, Mrs Mitchell 20 MIN
So Many Ways To Communicate 20 MIN
Storytelling Time 20 MIN
Tongue, Teeth, Jaws And Lips 20 MIN
We Speak 'American' 20 MIN
Word Parade, The 20 MIN
Writing About You 20 MIN
Your Voice Is A Gift 20 MIN

Language Of Algebra C 16 MIN
16MM FILM, 3/4 OR 1/2 IN VIDEO
Defines symbols, surveys applications in a modern world, and illustrates their role in mathematics. Uses animation to explain the solution of various algebraic problems.
Prod-IFB Dist-IFB 196

Language Of Business, The C 15 MIN
16MM FILM OPTICAL SOUND
Dramatizes the need for being able to analyze facts and problem areas in a business so that decisions can be made. Shows the value of records in business management.
LC NO. 74-705002
Prod-USSBA Dist-USNAC

Language Of Business, The C 15 MIN
3/4 OR 1/2 INCH VIDEO CASSETTE
Depicts the owner of a radio and TV retail and service shop who wants to open a branch store and asks his accountant to interpret his records to illustrate danger areas.
From The Small Business Administration Series.
Prod-IVCH Dist-IVCH

Language Of Dance, The B 29 MIN
16MM FILM, 3/4 OR 1/2 IN VIDEO C A
Explains the basic element of emotion and shows how it can be transformed into a dance movement for one person, a group of dancers and an entire company. Presents the modern dance There Is A Time.
From The Time To Dance Series.
LC NO. 80-707033
Prod-NET Dist-IU Prodn-WGBHTV 1960

Language Of Education, The C 60 MIN
3/4 INCH VIDEO CASSETTE
Lectures on language as the medium of education. Includes how language imposes a point of view and how culture is constantly created and negotiated.
Prod-OHC Dist-HRC

Language Of Faces C 20 MIN
16MM FILM OPTICAL SOUND J-H A
Presents the problems of survival in an age of materialism, arms races and fear of total annihilation. Suggests certain action of responsible citizenship.
Prod-YALEDV Dist-YALEDV

Language Of Graphs, The (2nd Ed) C 15 MIN
16MM FILM, 3/4 OR 1/2 IN VIDEO J-H
Depicts Skip and Bill making graphs to show the school paper staff why they should raise the price of the paper. Discusses the construction of a bar graph, a line graph, a circle graph, and an equation graph.
Prod-CORF Dist-CORF

Language Of Maps, The B 30 MIN
16MM FILM OPTICAL SOUND T
Discusses the use of maps in the classroom.
From The Starting Tomorrow Series. Unit 2 - Understanding The School's Neighborhood
LC NO. 75-702435
Prod-EALING Dist-WALKED Prodn-MIFE 1969

Language Of Maps, The X 11 MIN
16MM FILM, 3/4 OR 1/2 IN VIDEO I-H
Uses aerial photography, topographic models and maps to show that the language of maps is composed of symbols representing natural and man-made features of the earth's surface.
Prod-EBF Dist-EBEC 1964

Language Of Medicine, The C 12 MIN
3/4 OR 1/2 INCH VIDEO CASSETTE
Twelve quarter hour videos which train medical secretaries, nurse's aides, technicians and other medical-related personnel.
Prod-CAMB Dist-CAMB

Language Of Music, The C 15 MIN
16MM FILM, 3/4 OR 1/2 IN VIDEO I-J
Introduces musical notation using both live action and animation. Traces the history of musical notation, demonstrates pitch and duration, explains notes and the musical scale and discusses the bass and treble clefs.
Prod-NAF Dist-MCFI 1977

Language Of Poetry C 30 MIN
3/4 OR 1/2 INCH VIDEO CASSETTE C
See series title for descriptive statement.
From The Communicating Through Literature Series.
Prod-DALCCD Dist-DALCCD

Language Of The Bee C 15 MIN
16MM FILM, 3/4 OR 1/2 IN VIDEO J-H
Dr Karl Von Frisch performs some experiments which led to his discovery of the language of the bees. The importance of an active, disciplined curiosity in scientific research is emphasized.
Prod-MIS Dist-MIS 1965

Language Of The Camera Eye, The B 29 MIN
16MM FILM, 3/4 OR 1/2 IN VIDEO H-C A
Presents Ansel Adams and Beaumont Newhall as they analyze the photographs of Edward Weston, CartierBresson, Edward Steichen, Alfred Stieglitz and others.
From The Photography - The Incisive Art Series.
LC NO. 80-707009
Prod-NET Dist-IU Prodn-KQEDTV 1962

Language Of The Deaf C 16 MIN
16MM FILM, 3/4 OR 1/2 IN VIDEO J-C A
Explores the many ways in which deaf people enjoy all facets of life, and deals with the social implications of being deaf. Highlights the role of Gallaudet College. Originally shown on the CBS television program 60 Minutes.
Prod-CBSNEW Dist-CAROUF

Language Of The Mute Swan X 14 MIN
16MM FILM, 3/4 OR 1/2 IN VIDEO I-H
Tells the story of the swan from the ritual of courtship and nest building to the emergence of the first cygnet. Includes allusions to the works of Molnar, Hans Christian Anderson and Tchaikovsky.
Prod-JOU Dist-JOU 1965

Language Options C 30 MIN
3/4 OR 1/2 INCH VIDEO CASSETTE C
See series title for descriptive statement.
From The Writing For A Reason Series.
Prod-DALCCD Dist-DALCCD

Language Power For Peace C 29 MIN
16MM FILM OPTICAL SOUND
Details the story of the Defense Language Institute.
From The Big Picture Series.
LC NO. 74-705003
Prod-USA Dist-USNAC

Language Preschool C 19 MIN
16MM FILM OPTICAL SOUND
Depicts preschool activities of the Regional Intervention Program, particularly those associated with language. Shows how the developmentally-delayed child is exposed to group activities and is forced to interact with other children in a variety of work and play situations.
From The Regional Intervention Program Series.
LC NO. 75-702410
Prod-USBEH Dist-USNAC 1973

Language Problems In The Schools C 26 MIN
16MM FILM OPTICAL SOUND H-C T
English and linguistic educators outline problems faced by teachers in helping children to communicate well in spoken and written standard English.
From The Language - The Social Arbiter Series.
LC NO. FIA67-5262
Prod-FINLYS Dist-FINLYS Prodn-CALING 1966

Language Taboos - Cultural C 30 MIN
3/4 OR 1/2 INCH VIDEO CASSETTE C
See series title for descriptive statement.
From The Language And Meaning Series.
Prod-WUSFTV Dist-GPITVL 1983

Language Taboos - Grammatical C 30 MIN
3/4 OR 1/2 INCH VIDEO CASSETTE C
See series title for descriptive statement.
From The Language And Meaning Series.
Prod-WUSFTV Dist-GPITVL 1983

Language Teaching In Context C 25 MIN
16MM FILM OPTICAL SOUND C T
Demonstrates a new method of language teaching which associates objects, actions and events with the words. The context is a simulated foreign world of foreign people going about their affairs.
Prod-WSU Dist-WSU 1959

Language Techniques For The Multi-Handicapped Learner C 6 MIN
16MM FILM, 3/4 OR 1/2 IN VIDEO
Shows how deaf children learn to speak one syllable at a time until they have mastered a short phrase. Illustrates methods involving repetition and the associaton of pictures with words. Describes the use of tapes and films for individualized instruction.
LC NO. 80-707417
Prod-USBEH Dist-USNAC 1980

Language Therapy C 112 MIN
3/4 OR 1/2 INCH VIDEO CASSETTE
Discusses the clinical description of the typical preschool child manifesting a language disorder and clinical observations that should be made by the clinician.
Prod-PUAVC Dist-PUAVC 1971

Language Through Sight And Sound C 18 MIN
16MM FILM, 3/4 OR 1/2 IN VIDEO C A
Looks at the total communications (T.C.) philosophy of teaching hearing impaired children language, which advocates that hearing impaired children be encouraged to use all forms of communication in order to develop both receptive and expressive langauge. Includes sign language and fingerspelling along with auditory-oral training.
From The Ways Of Hearing Series.
Prod-BCNFL Dist-BCNFL

Language To Share C 30 MIN
3/4 OR 1/2 INCH VIDEO CASSETTE
See series title for descriptive statement.
From The Rebop Series.
Prod-WGBHTV Dist-MDCPB

Language Without Words C 9 MIN
16MM FILM, 3/4 OR 1/2 IN VIDEO
Examines a variety of nonverbal methods of communication used by animals, such as wolves, grouse, beavers and Siamese fighting fish.
From The BSCS Behavior Film Series.
Prod-BSCS Dist-PHENIX 1974

Language Works In Chunks Of Meaning B 15 MIN
2 INCH VIDEOTAPE I
Explains the use of punctuation marks as used by writers to convey meaning and by poets in natural linguistic clusters. Features selections such as Calico Pie by Edward Lear, Circus by Eleanor Farjeon and The Big Cheese by Mirian Schlein. (Broadcast quality)
From The Bill Martin Series. No. 3
Prod-BRITED Dist-GPITVL Prodn-KQEDTV

Language-Experience Approach To Teaching Reading, The - Grades 1-6 C 48 MIN
16MM FILM OPTICAL SOUND C A
Offers scenes from selected classroom sessions in which elements of the language-experience approach are being used in first, second and third grade classes. Helps teachers become acquainted with the language-experience system of reading instruction.
LC NO. 76-700039
Prod-UDEL Dist-UDEL 1975

Language, Learning And Children C 30 MIN
3/4 OR 1/2 INCH VIDEO CASSETTE
See series title for descriptive statement.
From The Language - Thinking, Writing, Communicating Series.
Prod-MDCPB Dist-MDCPB

LANL Underground Testing C 18 MIN
16MM FILM OPTICAL SOUND
Shows how data is collected from underground nuclear detonation tests.
LC NO. 81-700290
Prod-LASL Dist-LASL 1980

Laos - Crossroads Of Conflict C 19 MIN
16MM FILM, 3/4 OR 1/2 IN VIDEO H-C A
Discusses the geography, living habits, culture, history and present-day political conflicts of Laos and its people. Explains that the internationalism of Laos has been going for almost 100 years. Contrasts a legacy from the past with the anxieties of the present.
Prod-SIGMA Dist-FILCOM 1970

Laos - Outpost In Peril B 5 MIN
16MM FILM OPTICAL SOUND
Explains in depth the free world's stake in the fate and future of Laos. Shows Laotian troops overlooking a bridge blown up by communist rebel guerillas.
From The Screen News Digest Series. Vol 3, Issue 10
Prod-HEARST Dist-HEARST 1961

Lap Joint C 4 MIN
1/2 IN VIDEO CASSETTE BETA/VHS IND
See series title for descriptive statement.
From The Welding Training (Comprehensive) - Basic Shielded Metal Arc Welding Series.
Prod-RMI Dist-RMI

Lap Joint V-Down C 2 MIN
1/2 IN VIDEO CASSETTE BETA/VHS IND
See series title for descriptive statement.
From The Welding Training (Comprehensive) - Metal Inert Gas (M I G) Welding Series.
Prod-RMI Dist-RMI

Lap Weld C 7 MIN
1/2 IN VIDEO CASSETTE BETA/VHS IND
See series title for descriptive statement.
From The Welding Training (Comprehensive) — Oxy-Acetylene Welding Series.
Prod-RMI Dist-RMI

Lap Weld A1 C 3 MIN
1/2 IN VIDEO CASSETTE BETA/VHS IND
See series title for descriptive statement.
From The Welding Training (Comprehensive) - Tungsten Inert Gas (T I G) Welding Series.
Prod-RMI Dist-RMI

Lap Weld E6011 Electrode C 6 MIN
1/2 IN VIDEO CASSETTE BETA/VHS IND
See series title for descriptive statement.
From The Arc Welding And M I G Welding Series.
Prod-RMI Dist-RMI

Lap Weld E7024 Electrode C 5 MIN
1/2 IN VIDEO CASSETTE BETA/VHS IND
See series title for descriptive statement.
From The Arc Welding And M I G Welding Series.
Prod-RMI Dist-RMI

Laparoscopy - Refinements In Technique And Anesthesia C 16 MIN
16MM FILM OPTICAL SOUND PRO
Depicts cold-light laparoscopy performed under local anesthesia plus neuroleptanalgesia, a state of psychic indifference.
Prod-SCITIF Dist-SCITIF 1970

Lapis C 10 MIN
16MM FILM OPTICAL SOUND J-C A
Presents an abstract art film composed of images produced by an analog computer. Explains the shifting kaleidoscopic patterns, mandalas and starbursts tracing a pattern of mystic meditation, accompanied by the sitar music of Ravi Shankar.
LC NO. 75-701555
Prod-WHITNY Dist-CFS 1966

Laplace Transforms B
16MM FILM OPTICAL SOUND
Defines Laplace transforms and explains how they can be used to solve differential equations with zero initial conditions.
Prod-OPENU Dist-OPENU

Laplace Transforms B 38 MIN
3/4 OR 1/2 INCH VIDEO CASSETTE
See series title for descriptive statement.
From The Calculus Of Differential Equations Series.
Prod-MIOT Dist-MIOT

Lapland Journey C 13 MIN
16MM FILM OPTICAL SOUND
Portrays Sweden's unspoiled wilderness, showing the rich possibilities for relaxation which Norrland offers.
Prod-SWNTO Dist-SWNTO

Laplanders, The C 18 MIN
16MM FILM, 3/4 OR 1/2 IN VIDEO P-I
Demonstrates how important reindeer are to the economy of the Lapps, providing food, shelter and income. Reveals how the animals still respond to ancient migratory instincts and cover great distances.
Prod-LUF Dist-LUF 1979

Lappedykker - Podiceps (Grebe) C 5 MIN
16MM FILM OPTICAL SOUND
Presents a description of the grebe in its natural surroundings, accompanied by sound effects.
Prod-STATNS Dist-STATNS 1965

Lapplandia C 20 MIN
16MM FILM OPTICAL SOUND
Shows the rich possibilities of recreation offered to tourists by Lapland's mountains.
Prod-SWNTO Dist-SIS 1964

Large And Growly Bear, The C 6 MIN
16MM FILM, 3/4 OR 1/2 IN VIDEO P
Presents the story of a bear who can't scare anyone no matter how hard he tries until one day he scares himself.
From The Golden Book Storytime Series.
Prod-MTI Dist-MTI 1977

Large Angles And Coordinate Axes B 30 MIN
16MM FILM OPTICAL SOUND H
Describes trigonometric value of angles larger than 90 degrees. Discusses positive and negative angles, four quadrants of a circle and coordinates of a point. Explains methods of reducing large angles to equivalent smaller ones for use in trigonometric tables.
From The Trigonometry Series.
Prod-CALVIN Dist-MLA Prodn-UNIVFI 1959

Large Animals Of The Arctic (Dutch) C 22 MIN
16MM FILM, 3/4 OR 1/2 IN VIDEO I-H
Shows the relationship between the Arctic grass-eaters and the carnivores who prey on them.
From The White Wilderness (Dutch) Series.
Prod-WDEMCO Dist-WDEMCO 1963

Large Animals Of The Arctic (French) C 22 MIN
16MM FILM, 3/4 OR 1/2 IN VIDEO I-H
Shows the relationship between the Arctic grass-eaters and the carnivores who prey on them.
From The White Wilderness (French) Series.
Prod-WDEMCO Dist-WDEMCO 1963

Large Animals Of The Arctic (German) C 22 MIN
16MM FILM, 3/4 OR 1/2 IN VIDEO I-H
Shows the relationship between the Arctic grass-eaters and the carnivores who prey on them.
From The White Wilderness (German) Series.
Prod-WDEMCO Dist-WDEMCO 1963

Large Animals Of The Arctic (Norwegian) C 22 MIN
16MM FILM, 3/4 OR 1/2 IN VIDEO I-H
Shows the relationship between the Arctic grass-eaters and the carnivores who prey on them.
From The White Wilderness (Norwegian) Series.
Prod-WDEMCO Dist-WDEMCO 1963

Large Animals Of The Arctic (Portuguese) C 22 MIN
16MM FILM, 3/4 OR 1/2 IN VIDEO I-H
Shows the relationship between the Arctic grass-eaters and the carnivores who prey on them.
From The White Wildernes (Portuguese) Series.
Prod-WDEMCO Dist-WDEMCO 1963

Large Animals Of The Arctic (Swedish) C 22 MIN
16MM FILM, 3/4 OR 1/2 IN VIDEO I-H
Shows the relationship between the Arctic grass-eaters and the carnivores who prey on them.
From The White Wilderness (Swedish) Series.
Prod-WDEMCO Dist-WDEMCO 1963

Large Animals That Once Roamed The Plains (French) C 12 MIN
16MM FILM, 3/4 OR 1/2 IN VIDEO I-H
Glimpses the pronghorn antelope, bighorn sheep, cougar and other large animals that once roamed the American plains in large numbers but have now virtually disappeared.
From The Vanishing Prairie (French) Series.
Prod-WDEMCO Dist-WDEMCO 1963

Large Animals That Once Roamed The Plains (German) C 12 MIN
16MM FILM, 3/4 OR 1/2 IN VIDEO I-H

Glimpses the pronghorn antelope, bighorn sheep, cougar and other large animals that once roamed the American plains in large numbers but have now virtually disappeared.
From The Vanishing Prairie (German) Series.
Prod-WDEMCO Dist-WDEMCO 1963

Large Animals That Once Roamed The Plains (Norwegian) C 12 MIN
16MM FILM, 3/4 OR 1/2 IN VIDEO I-H
Glimpses the pronghorn antelope, bighorn sheep, cougar and other large animals that once roamed the American plains in large numbers but have now virtually disappeared.
From The Vanishing Prairie (Norwegian) Series.
Prod-WDEMCO Dist-WDEMCO 1963

Large Animals That Once Roamed The Plains (Swedish) C 12 MIN
16MM FILM, 3/4 OR 1/2 IN VIDEO I-H
Glimpses the pronghorn antelope, bighorn sheep, cougar and other large animals that once roamed the American plains in large numbers but have now virtually disappeared.
From The Vanishing Prairie (Swedish) Series.
Prod-WDEMCO Dist-WDEMCO 1963

Large Appliances C 30 MIN
3/4 OR 1/2 INCH VIDEO CASSETTE
Presents tips on the purchase and care of large appliances.
From The Consumer Survival Series. Homes
Prod-MDCPB Dist-MDCPB

Large Bowel Obstruction C 22 MIN
16MM FILM OPTICAL SOUND PRO
Discusses the problem of large bowel obstruction due primarily to carcinoma. Presents the indications for the various forms of treatment in relation to the site of obstruction, the competence or incompetence of the ileocecal valve and other pertinent factors.
Prod-ACYDGD Dist-ACY 1960

Large Group Instruction C 28 MIN
16MM FILM OPTICAL SOUND
Dr Dwight Allen, professor of education at Stanford University, analyzes the effective use of large group instruction, discussing techniques, types and presentation modes.
From The Innovations In Education Series.
Prod-STNFRD Dist-EDUC 1966

Large Numbers C 15 MIN
3/4 OR 1/2 INCH VIDEO CASSETTE I-J
Explains how to write and punctuate large numbers correctly.
From The Math Matters Series. Blue Module
Prod-STETVC Dist-AITECH Prodn-KLRNTV 1975

Large Passion B 14 MIN
16MM FILM OPTICAL SOUND J-C A
Presents the works of Albrecht Durer which depict the final episodes in the life of Christ on earth, the entombment and the symbol of his return on earth. Taken from 12 original woodcuts at the Albertina Museum in Vienna.
Prod-FILIM Dist-RADIM 1957

Large Passion, The B 14 MIN
16MM FILM OPTICAL SOUND
Features the final episodes of the life of Christ as it is captured by Albrecht Durer who grasped the importance of the medium of copperplate engraving, which was the artistic equivalent of printing.
Prod-FILIM Dist-RADIM

Large Toys C 25 MIN
3/4 OR 1/2 INCH VIDEO CASSETTE H-C A
Shows how to build a wagon and introduces a handbuilt rocking animal and a large toy crane.
From The Blizzard's Wonderful Wooden Toys Series.
Prod-BBCTV Dist-FI

Large Transformers, Tape 1 - Protective Devices And Routine Maintenance C 60 MIN
3/4 OR 1/2 INCH VIDEO CASSETTE IND
See series title for descriptive statement.
From The Electrical Equipment Maintenance Series.
Prod-ITCORP Dist-ITCORP

Large Transformers, Tape 1 - Protective-Devices And Routine Maintenance (Spanish) C 60 MIN
3/4 OR 1/2 INCH VIDEO CASSETTE IND
See series title for descriptive statement.
From The Electrical Equipment Maintenance (Spanish) Series.
Prod-ITCORP Dist-ITCORP

Large Utility, A - Indiana Bell Telephone Company C 20 MIN
3/4 OR 1/2 INCH VIDEO CASSETTE C A
Presents an interview with a representative from Indiana Bell Telephone Company. Enumerates the various jobs available to college graduates with liberal arts backgrounds in large, specialized companies.
From The Clues To Career Opportunities For Liberal Arts Graduates Series.
LC NO. 79-706054
Prod-IU Dist-IU 1978

Large White Butterfly, The C 9 MIN
16MM FILM, 3/4 OR 1/2 IN VIDEO I-J
Uses close-up photography to present the life cycle of the butterfly. Shows egg laying, the emergence of the larva, feeding on cabbage leaves, shedding of skin and pupation. Emergence of the adult insect from the chrysalis is shown twice and is followed by detailed shots of the uncoiling of the proboscis.
Prod-GATEEF Dist-AIMS 1968

Laroussie The Saddlemaker C 25 MIN
16MM FILM, 3/4 OR 1/2 IN VIDEO J-C A
Introduces a Moroccan boy named Laroussie who works as a brass and copper apprentice in his father's shop in the city of Fez. Reveals that the boy's true love is horses and that when an uncle provides him with the opportunity to make a saddle for an upcoming festival, Laroussie's father permits him to learn this new craft.
From The World Cultures And Youth Series.
Prod-SUNRIS Dist-CORF 1981

Larry - An Amputee's Story C 57 MIN
3/4 OR 1/2 INCH VIDEO CASSETTE PRO
Helps amputees, families and their health care providers cope with the special problems amputation brings.
Prod-HSCIC Dist-HSCIC 1984

Larry Fagin C 29 MIN
3/4 INCH VIDEO CASSETTE
See series title for descriptive statement.
From The Poets Talking Series.
Prod-UMITV Dist-UMITV 1975

Larry Hagman C 1 MIN
3/4 INCH VIDEO CASSETTE
Uses television star Larry Hagman to discuss prejudice. Set in a television spot announcement form.
From The ADL Celebrity Spot Series.
Prod-ADL Dist-ADL

Larry P Case, The C 30 MIN
3/4 OR 1/2 INCH VIDEO CASSETTE C A
Reviews the background, content and progress of the Larry P versus Riles case, a class action suit brought by parents of Black children in the San Francisco school district to end the use of culturally biased IQ testing for placement.
From The Law And Handicapped Children In School Series.
LC NO. 79-706358
Prod-IU Dist-IU 1979

Larry, Mr Jenkins And The Antique Car C 15 MIN
16MM FILM, 3/4 OR 1/2 IN VIDEO I-J
Presents three totally different stories about the same characters to provide a base for introducing story evaluation, as well as training in effective listening and speaking.
From The Creative Writing Series.
Prod-MORLAT Dist-AIMS 1972

Laryngectomy - What It Means To You C 34 MIN
3/4 OR 1/2 INCH VIDEO CASSETTE A
Discusses the implications of a total laryngectomy, including Medical and Surgical Aspects, Speech Without A Larynx, Physical Changes, Social And Emotional Adjustment and Marital and Family Adjustment.
Prod-VAMCNY Dist-USNAC 1984

Laryngectomy And Neck Dissection (2nd Ed) C 22 MIN
16MM FILM OPTICAL SOUND C
Demonstrates operative techniques of laryngectomy and radical neck dissection. Shows new closure and drainage procedures on dogs and humans. Closes with a dialogue between two laryngectomy patients using esophageal speech.
LC NO. FIA65-814
Prod-OSUMPD Dist-OSUMPD 1964

Larynx - Unit 7 C 11 MIN
3/4 OR 1/2 INCH VIDEO CASSETTE PRO
Discusses the intrinsic muscles of the larynx including the arytemoideus, aryepiglotticus, cricoarytenoideus, thyroarytenoideus, cricothyroideus, thyroepiglotticus, as well as the folds in the mucosa of the larynx.
From The Gross Anatomy Prosection Demonstration Series.
Prod-HSCIC Dist-HSCIC

Larynx And Voice—A Series

Prod-ILAVD Dist-ILAVD

Function Of The Normal Larynx, The 21 MIN
Function Of The Pathologic Larynx, The 24 MIN
Physiology Of The Larnyx Under Daily Stress 23 MIN

Larynx And Voice, The - Physiology Of The Larynx Under Daily Stress C 23 MIN
16MM FILM OPTICAL SOUND PRO
Demonstrates the complex pattern of laryngeal function during everyday life. Photographs the larynx at up to 5000 frames per second to reveal new and hitherto unreported phenomena concerning its biology and physiology.
Prod-VLEMOO Dist-ILAVD

Larynx And Voice, The - The Function Of The Pathologic Larynx C 24 MIN
16MM FILM OPTICAL SOUND PRO
Describes the functional adjustment of the larynx to pathology. Presents patients with different laryngeal diseases, featuring the clinical appearance of the larynx and the related voice, and examples of the underlying physiology photographed in ultra slow motion. Includes information of value in planning therapy.
Prod-VLEMOO Dist-ILAVD

Larynx, The C 13 MIN
16MM FILM, 3/4 OR 1/2 IN VIDEO C A
Focuses on the head and neck. Demonstrates the dissection of the larynx.
From The Guides To Dissection Series.
Prod-UCLA Dist-TEF

Larynx, The C 15 MIN
3/4 OR 1/2 INCH VIDEO CASSETTE PRO
Reviews, using animation, the mechanics of speech and how certain disorders affect it. Portrays changes in voice quality and tone. Views physical examination of patients with laryngeal disorders.
Prod-PRIMED Dist-PRIMED

Larynx, The C 86 MIN
3/4 INCH VIDEO CASSETTE PRO
Explains the larynx and surrounding structures, including voc cords, internal anatomy, arteries, veins and fascia. Discusse the function of deglutition and phonation in health and diseas
From The Head And Neck Anatomy Series.
LC NO. 78-706038
Prod-NMAC Dist-USNAC 197

Las Invenciones C 30 MI
3/4 OR 1/2 INCH VIDEO CASSETTE K-
See series title for descriptive statement.
From The Villa Alegre Series.
Prod-BCTV Dist-MDCPB

Las Muchas Caras De Mexico C 17 MI
16MM FILM, 3/4 OR 1/2 IN VIDEO
A Spanish language version of The Many Faces of Mexic Shows facets of the Mexican land and people.
From The Mexican Heritage (Spanish) Series.
Prod-STEXMF Dist-FI 197

Las Vegas, Your Best Bet C 14 MI
16MM FILM OPTICAL SOUND
Discusses the advantages of Las Vegas and of holding conver tions there.
LC NO. 75-703106
Prod-MCDO Dist-MCDO 197

LaSalle String Quartet—A Series

Presents the LaSalle String Quartet, which was formed in 194 at the Julliard School of Music in New York.
Prod-NETCHE Dist-NETCHE 197

LaSalle String Quartet, Pt I, The 030 MI
LaSalle String Quartet, Pt II, The 030 MI

LaSalle String Quartet, Pt I, The C 30 MI
1/2 INCH VIDEOTAPE
Presents the LaSalle String Quartet using a set of instrument built by Nicolo Amati in the 1600s and performing Penderecki' 'Quartetto per archi', a composition which alters the norma sound of the instruments.
From The LaSalle String Quartet Series.
Prod-NETCHE Dist-NETCHE 197

LaSalle String Quartet, Pt II, The C 30 MI
1/2 INCH VIDEOTAPE
Uses Penderecki's 'Quartetto per archi', as a starting point for fur ther exploration of modern composition.
From The LaSalle String Quartet Series.
Prod-NETCHE Dist-NETCHE 197

Lascaux - Cradle Of Man's Art C 17 MIN
16MM FILM, 3/4 OR 1/2 IN VIDEO I-C A
Explores the prehistoric wall paintings in the Lascaux cave o France.
Prod-IFB Dist-IFB 1952

Lascaux Treasures C 15 MIN
3/4 OR 1/2 INCH VIDEO CASSETTE H-C A
Uses documentary footage of the original prehistoric cave-paintings at Lascaux in southwest France to explain the importance of the site of an exact replica which is being buil by international art experts.
Prod-JOU Dist-JOU

Laser C 11 MIN
16MM FILM OPTICAL SOUND
Enumerates the various ways in which lasers are used in communication, medicine and other fields.
LC NO. 79-701044
Prod-ATAT Dist-MGS Prodn-CUNLIM 1979

Laser - Miracles With Light B 24 MIN
3/4 INCH VIDEO CASSETTE
Defines what a laser is, how it works and how it is being applied in the army and in medicine and scientific research.
Prod-USNAC Dist-USNAC 1972

Laser - The Light Of The Future X 30 MIN
16MM FILM, 3/4 OR 1/2 IN VIDEO J-C A
Illustrates theoretical principles involved in laser light and documents how these principles were applied by scientists to produce the first laser. Demonstrates working lasers and their uses.
From The Experiment Series.
Prod-PRISM Dist-IU 1966

Laser Beam, The (2nd Ed) C 20 MIN
16MM FILM, 3/4 OR 1/2 IN VIDEO H-C A
Uses animation to explain the laser process. Shows some of the applications of lasers in medicine, industry, communications, space exploration and holograms.
Prod-HANDEL Dist-HANDEL 1982

Laser Drilling C 8 MIN
3/4 OR 1/2 INCH VIDEO CASSETTE
Shows how laser drilling works, the components, advantages and disadvantages.
From The Manufacturing Materials And Processes Series.
Prod-GE Dist-WFVTAE

Laser Fusion C 18 MIN
16MM FILM OPTICAL SOUND
Explains the techniques and principles of the laser fusion program under development at the Los Alamos Scientific Laboratory. Discusses high-power lasers and describes future laser systems and conceptual laser fusion generating stations.
LC NO. 78-700288
Prod-LASL Dist-LASL 1977

Laser Images Demonstration, A C 10 MIN
16MM FILM OPTICAL SOUND H-C
Uses argon, krypton and helium neon gas lasers to create mul-

ti-colored abstract patterns that flow to the accompaniment of electronic, rock and classical music.
LC NO. 77-714318
Prod-LASER Dist-CFS 1971

Laser Light Therapy C 11 MIN
16MM FILM, 3/4 OR 1/2 IN VIDEO A
Describes how photocoagulation assists in treatment of diabetic and vascular retinopathies and macular diseases. Emphasizes general principles, benefits, limitations and complications.
Prod-PRORE Dist-PRORE

Laser Physics B 30 MIN
16MM FILM OPTICAL SOUND H-C A
Features Dr Marvin Hass, a research physicist at the U S Naval Research Laboratory in Washington, DC, who discusses the fundamentals of laser operation and simulated emission of radiation. Presents experiments using a high-power continuous argonion laser and a high resolution double grating spectrometer.
LC NO. 74-700173
Prod-UNL Dist-UNEBR 1970

Laser Safety C 11 MIN
16MM FILM, 3/4 OR 1/2 IN VIDEO
Describes hazards involved in the use of lasers. Shows how an eye injury can result either from direct or reflected exposure to laser beams and how fires result when flammable materials are pierced by laser beams. Explains safety precautions to be exercised by technicians using lasers.
LC NO. 82-707219
Prod-NASA Dist-USNAC Prodn-MIFE 1973

Laser Safety C 18 MIN
16MM FILM, 3/4 OR 1/2 IN VIDEO H-C A
Illustrates hazards involved in using lasers, and shows what can be done to prevent injury to eyes and skin. Explains four properties that make the laser a useful tool, but can also combine to destroy biological tissue. Demonstrates various precautions and safety devices.
Prod-STNFRD Dist-UCEMC 1971

Laser Scanning Of Active Semiconductor Devices C 55 MIN
3/4 INCH VIDEO CASSETTE
Presents new and powerful applications for laser scanning in semiconductor device design and reliability work.
Prod-USNBOS Dist-MTP

Laser, The C 12 MIN
16MM FILM OPTICAL SOUND I-C A
Explains the physics of light - the atom which emits it, radian energy and wave lengths and frequencies. Uses a solid-state ruby laser to demonstrate how it can generate an intense coherent beam of monochromatic light.
Prod-SF Dist-SF 1967

Laser, The - A Light Fantastic C 21 MIN
16MM FILM, 3/4 OR 1/2 IN VIDEO J-C A
Shows the laser and explains how all the light waves travel simultaneously in exactly the same direction and at exactly the same frequency. Discusses the functions of the laser, such as making precise measurements, melting and welding metals, diamonds and other materials, communication, surgery and even to produce a new sort of three-dimensional image, called a hologram.
Prod-CBSTV Dist-PHENIX 1968

Laser, The - A Light Fantastic C 30 MIN
1 INCH VIDEOTAPE
Shows how the laser beam will some day be used as often and as easily as 20th century man now uses electricity.
From The Twenty-First Century Series.
Prod-UCC Dist-MTP

Laserimage C 10 MIN
16MM FILM OPTICAL SOUND P-C A
Introduces a new visual medium in which organic images generated from helium-neon and argon gas lasers convolute, evolve, burst and fuse into rhythms. Depicts cosmic flowers, electronic plasmas, cellular galaxies and primordial atoms.
LC NO. 77-701094
Prod-DRYER Dist-CFS 1972

Lasers - An Introduction C 13 MIN
16MM FILM, 3/4 OR 1/2 IN VIDEO J
Illustrates principles of laser operation, including concepts of coherent and incoherent light, continuous and discrete spectra, stimulation of atoms and resonance. Shows gaseous and crystalline lasers to be valuable tools in holography, communications, medicine and industry.
Prod-CORF Dist-CORF 1970

Lasers - The Light Fantastic C 30 MIN
3/4 OR 1/2 INCH VIDEO CASSETTE
Describes the variety of uses for lasers. Shows physicians using lasers to perform delicate eye surgery and discusses the scores of industrial uses.
From The Innovation Series.
Prod-WNETTV Dist-WNETTV 1985

Lasers And Your Eyes C 12 MIN
16MM FILM OPTICAL SOUND IND
Uses animation to explain lasers and their danger to the eyes. Describes the proper protective eye wear to be used in laser laboratories.
LC NO. 79-700052
Prod-LASL Dist-LASL 1979

Lassa Fever C 57 MIN
3/4 OR 1/2 INCH VIDEO CASSETTE H-C A
Tells about a medical missionary in Nigeria who died of an unknown fever which began to spread among the hospital staff and seemed immune to all treatment. Follows the efforts of a Yale research team as they discovered an effective treatment for the new tropical disease Lassa fever.
From The Nova Series.
LC NO. 83-707208
Prod-WGBHTV Dist-TIMLIF 1982

Last Act For An Actor B 20 MIN
16MM FILM OPTICAL SOUND H-C A
Shows the stages of rehabilitation that a troubled persons undergoes following a suicide attempt. Examines the effect of psychiatric interviews on the progress of the patient. Includes a discussion on the motives for suicide.
From The Doctors At Work Series.
LC NO. FIA65-1348
Prod-CMA Dist-LAWREN Prodn-LAWREN 1962

Last And First Frontier, The C 20 MIN
16MM FILM OPTICAL SOUND C A
Shows how a governor's science advisory council is formed and how it assists government. Gives interpretation for governors, legislators and national and city governments.
LC NO. 76-703206
Prod-PSU Dist-PSU 1972

Last Angry Man, The B 100 MIN
16MM FILM OPTICAL SOUND
Contrasts an elderly doctor who is primarily concerned in curing people with a doctor interested in money.
Prod-CPC Dist-TIMLIF 1959

Last Barrier, The - Crossing The Rhine C 30 MIN
3/4 OR 1/2 INCH VIDEO CASSETTE H-C A
See series title for descriptive statement.
From The World War II - GI Diary Series.
Prod-TIMLIF Dist-TIMLIF 1980

Last Boat Home, The C 59 MIN
16MM FILM OPTICAL SOUND
Shows how citizens fought to preserve the Delta Queen, America's last riverboat, from Federal efforts intended to withdraw her from service.
LC NO. 75-700451
Prod-LAGORC Dist-LAGORC 1975

Last Bomb, The C 35 MIN
16MM FILM, 3/4 OR 1/2 IN VIDEO
Describes the bombing of Japan by B-29 airplanes and the dropping of the first atomic bomb on Japan.
Prod-USAF Dist-USNAC

Last Call For Union Station C 10 MIN
16MM FILM OPTICAL SOUND
Presents a documentary using the architecture of Union Station in Los Angeles to recall the heyday of the 1930's and 1940's using old stills and motion pictures.
LC NO. 82-700331
Prod-USC Dist-USC 1981

Last Case Of Polio, The C 20 MIN
16MM FILM OPTICAL SOUND
Contains a number of episodes, including an animated one, showing how polio viruses are transmitted and their primary effect in humans. Traces recent trends in poliomyelitis incidence and demonstrates the care, precision and skill required to produce Orimune oral polio vaccine.
Prod-ACYLLD Dist-LEDR 1962

Last Case, The C 14 MIN
16MM FILM OPTICAL SOUND
Urges employees of small soft-drink bottling firms to oppose an FTC ruling through political activism.
LC NO. 79-700234
Prod-PEPSI Dist-PEPSI 1978

Last Chance For The Navajo C 27 MIN
16MM FILM, 3/4 OR 1/2 IN VIDEO J-C A
Examines the human rights issues in the struggle of the Navajo Indians to preserve their culture and land and at the same time cope with the realities of the economy.
Prod-ABCF Dist-MGHT 1978

Last Chance Garage—A Series

Reviews how to purchase, maintain and repair a car.
Prod-WGBHTV Dist-MTI

Air, Water And Fuel Lines	030 MIN
Brake Installation	030 MIN
Car Designs And The '40s	030 MIN
Cooling Systems, Thermostats, Exhausts	030 MIN
Filters To Fiero	030 MIN
Fuel System - How It Works	030 MIN
Kit Car - Final Inspection	030 MIN
Motorcycles And Helmets	030 MIN
Reading Your Tires	030 MIN
Right Hose And Fuel Tanks	030 MIN
Suspension Test	030 MIN
Winter Wipers	030 MIN
Wiring, Batteries, Coolant And Upholstery	030 MIN

Last Chance, The C 28 MIN
16MM FILM, 3/4 OR 1/2 IN VIDEO J-C A
Tells how 3,000 acres of grasslands in Front Royal, Virginia, were dedicated in 1974 to the preservation of exotic animals threatened with extinction. Shows that human contact with the animals is minimal.
Prod-FNZOO Dist-BULFRG 1979

Last Chance, The C 29 MIN
16MM FILM - 3/4 IN VIDEO
Focuses on poverty by showing a black psychiatrist's interview with a white school dropout. Presents a community worker in the ghetto talking about his job.
From The To Live Again Series.
LC NO. 80-706858
Prod-USSRS Dist-USNAC 1980

Last Chapter, The B 21 MIN
16MM FILM OPTICAL SOUND I-C A
Presents the last six months from the life of Jawaharlal Nehru, including his sudden illness, his recovery, his death and the funeral procession as well as the immersion of his ashes at the Holy Sangam. Provides intimate glimpses of the life of the late Prime Minister.
Prod-INDIA Dist-NEDINF

Last Cry For Help, A C 33 MIN
16MM FILM, 3/4 OR 1/2 IN VIDEO H-C
Tells how a girl who appears to have everything going for her attempts suicide. Explains that her pschiatrist helps her realize that she must take control of her life.
Prod-ABCTV Dist-LCOA 1980

Last Days Of Living C 58 MIN
16MM FILM, 3/4 OR 1/2 IN VIDEO H-C A
Documents the efforts of the medical staff and volunteers at a special unit of Montreal's Royal Victoria Hospital as they tend to the special needs of the terminally ill. Explores the patients' evolving philosophies about their illnesses and impending deaths.
Prod-NFBC Dist-NFBC 1980

Last Days Of Living, The C 58 MIN
3/4 OR 1/2 INCH VIDEO CASSETTE
Shares advanced and humanitarian methods of caring for the dying, including pain management and basic, creative techniques such as touching, music therapy and more.
Prod-NFBC Dist-AJN

Last Epidemic, The C 21 MIN
3/4 OR 1/2 INCH VIDEO CASSETTE
A shortened version of the 1981 film and videotape The Last Epidemic. Documents a 1981 conference of the Physicians for Social Responsibility. Describes the effect of a nuclear attack on human life and on the environment. Argues for the necessity of ending the arms race.
Prod-PSR Dist-PSR

Last Epidemic, The C 22 MIN
16MM FILM, 3/4 OR 1/2 IN VIDEO J-C A
Conveys the effects of one or more nuclear weapons on a civilian population. Describes the drastic damage to the environment and the long range devastation to the planet.
Prod-EFVP Dist-EFVP 1981

Last Epidemic, The C 36 MIN
3/4 OR 1/2 INCH VIDEO CASSETTE
Documents a 1981 conference of the Physicians for Social Responsibility. Describes the effect of a nuclear attack on human life and on the environment. Argues for the necessity of ending the arms race.
Prod-PSR Dist-PSR 1981

Last Epidemic, The - Medical Consequences Of Nuclear War C 36 MIN
16MM FILM, 3/4 OR 1/2 IN VIDEO
Presents the speeches of Dr H Jack Geiger and others at the conference of Physicians for Social Responsibility which describe the probable medical consequences of nuclear attack on an American city.
Prod-RCN Dist-RCN 1980

Last Epidemic, The - The Medical Consequences Of Nuclear Weapons And Nuclear War C 47 MIN
3/4 OR 1/2 INCH VIDEO CASSETTE
Presents a series of excerpts from the conference on the medical consequences of nuclear weapons and nuclear war. Includes documentary footage, illustrations and demonstrations.
Prod-PSR Dist-UWISC 1980

Last Fishermen, The C 29 MIN
3/4 INCH VIDEO CASSETTE
Profiles the commercial fishermen of the Great Lakes, focusing on their heritage of hard work and individualism and on the future of their industry.
Prod-UWISCA Dist-PUBTEL

Last Flight B 21 MIN
16MM FILM OPTICAL SOUND H-C A
A brain tumor is confirmed and located by skull films, EEG and arteriogram. Describes the symptoms and shows details of surgery for meningioma.
From The Doctors At Work Series.
LC NO. FIA65-1349
Prod-CMA Dist-LAWREN Prodn-LAWREN 1963

Last Flower, The B 5 MIN
16MM FILM OPTICAL SOUND
Presents an animated short story based on the story The Last Flower by James Thurber.
LC NO. 76-701463
Prod-QUEENU Dist-QUEENU 1975

Last Flower, The C 60 MIN
3/4 OR 1/2 INCH VIDEO CASSETTE J-C A
Focuses on efforts to save plants, animals and precious objects. Includes efforts to restore Leonardo da Vinci's The Last Supper, a study of the herbal cures of tribal medicine in Kenya and the task of saving the golden lion tamarin monkey from extinction.
From The Smithsonian World Series.
Prod-WETATV Dist-WETATV Prodn-SMITHS

Last Freak In The World, The C 25 MIN
16MM FILM OPTICAL SOUND
Presents a story about the relationship between a disenchanted young woman and an old-time carnival man she befriends.

LC NO. 75-704315
Prod-CANFDC Dist-CANFDC 1974

Last Frontier, The - Indians And Farmers C 30 MIN
2 INCH VIDEOTAPE
Concerns the end of the long struggle between Indian and settler. Deals with the problems in settling the Great Plains.
From The American History II Series.
Prod-KRMATV Dist-GPITVL

Last Frontier, The - The Miners C 30 MIN
2 INCH VIDEOTAPE
Introduces the postwar West, specifically the 'frontier theory' of history, and the development of mining in Colorado, Nevada and South Dakota.
From The American History II Series.
Prod-KRMATV Dist-GPITVL

Last Great Race On Earth, The C 53 MIN
16MM FILM, 3/4 OR 1/2 IN VIDEO J-C A
Documents the 1979 Iditarod Trail Race from Anchorage to Nome, Alaska. Shows the 55 mushers as they participate in 15-day-long dogsled race of over 1,000 miles. Talks with leading contenders during the race.
LC NO. 82-706968
Prod-BBCTV Dist-FI 1982

Last Holiday B 89 MIN
16MM FILM OPTICAL SOUND
Presents a story of a little man struggling cleverly with ingenuity against the odds of modern life. Stars Alec Guinness.
Prod-STRAT Dist-LCOA

Last Hour Clash C 58 MIN
16MM FILM, 3/4 OR 1/2 IN VIDEO C T
Presents a classroom situation of frustration in which a teacher sees one of the students as disruptive while the student feels the teacher is picking on him. Focuses on the dynamics of classroom management and control of the learning environment.
From The Heart Of Teaching Series.
LC NO. 80-706428
Prod-AITV Dist-AITECH Prodn-KETCTV 1976

Last Hunger Strike, The C 60 MIN
3/4 OR 1/2 INCH VIDEO CASSETTE
Relates how in the spring and summer of 1981 fifteen young men, prisoners in Northern Ireland, decided as a final form of protest to begin a hunger strike. Notes how over four months, ten of these men starved to death. Focuses on Michael James Devine, the last of the hunger strikers to die, and explores the day-to-day reality which compels a man to voluntarily surrender his life as a form of protest.
Prod-TAMERP Dist-TAMERP

Last Hunger Strike, The - Ireland, 1981 C 56 MIN
3/4 OR 1/2 INCH VIDEO CASSETTE A
Highlights the political and social agony of Northern Ireland through a biographical sketch of Michael James Devine, an Irish Republican Army supporter who died in a hunger strike in 1981. Shows scenes of street violence and interviews with other IRA sympathizers.
LC NO. 83-707211
Prod-SEVDAY Dist-ICARUS 1982

Last Hurrah, The B 121 MIN
16MM FILM OPTICAL SOUND
Examines the vanishing American tradition of the big city political 'Boss.' Stars Spencer Tracy and Pat O'Brien.
Prod-CPC Dist-TIMLIF 1958

Last Hurrah, The C 30 MIN
3/4 OR 1/2 INCH VIDEO CASSETTE H-C A
Presents a story centering on school politics. Uses the story to try to reduce the minority isolation of Mexican-American students by showing the teenager as an individual, as a member of a unique cultural group and as a member of a larger complex society.
From The La Esquina (English) Series.
Prod-SWEDL Dist-GPITVL 1976

Last Journey To Jerusalem X 20 MIN
16MM FILM OPTICAL SOUND J-H T R
Jesus tells the disciples of His coming death and Resurrection. James and John make their selfish ambitions known and Jesus rebukes them. In Jericho Jesus heals blind Bartinaeus. Jesus and his followers form the procession into Jerusalem.
From The Living Bible Series.
Prod-FAMF Dist-FAMF

Last Journey, The C 24 MIN
16MM FILM OPTICAL SOUND C A
Traces the dying traces of Jewish life in Russia through pictures taken by Nodar, a Jew about to leave the Soviet Union for the final time. Shows Russian Jews in synagogues, Jewish cemeteries and the scene of the Babi Yar massacre.
Prod-NJWB Dist-NJWB 1980

Last Laugh, The (German) B 70 MIN
3/4 OR 1/2 INCH VIDEO CASSETTE
Relates the story of an elderly man who as the doorman of a great hotel, has been demoted to washroom attendant due to his age. Directed by F W Murnau.
Prod-IHF Dist-IHF

Last Man On Earth C 86 MIN
16MM FILM OPTICAL SOUND H A
Tells the story of the sole survivor of plague who is besieged by victims who arise at night thirsting for his blood. Stars Vincent Price.
Prod-AIP Dist-TIMLIF 1964

Last March, The C 60 MIN
3/4 OR 1/2 INCH VIDEO CASSETTE C A
Describes how Alexander the Great tries to further unity among his kingdoms by having his Greek officers marry Persian women. Shows how he resumes his search for the ends of the world which he continues until he dies in the year 323 BC.
From The Search For Alexander The Great Series.
LC NO. 82-707383
Prod-TIMLIF Dist-TIMLIF 1981

Last Menominee, The B 30 MIN
16MM FILM OPTICAL SOUND H-C A
Menominee Indians state their opinions concerning the termination of their reservation status. Though they are now citizens, they have lost their hunting and fishing rights, doctors and hospital facilities, and educational and employment opportunities.
From The Local Issue Series.
LC NO. 72-702889
Prod-NET Dist-IU Prodn-WHATV 1966

Last Meow, The - Sibelius' Valse Triste C 7 MIN
16MM FILM OPTICAL SOUND J-C
Uses animation to tell the story of a scrawny cat who prowls the crumbling ruins of an abandoned house.
From The Animations From Allegro Non Troppo Series.
LC NO. 80-700526
Prod-BOZETO Dist-TEXFLM 1978

Last Metro, The C 133 MIN
16MM FILM OPTICAL SOUND
A French language motion picture. Depicts life in the French theater during the Nazi occupation in World War II. Stars Catherine Deneuve and Gerard Depardieu. Directed by Francois Truffaut.
Prod-UAA Dist-UAE 1980

Last Movement Of A New World Symphony C 10 MIN
16MM FILM OPTICAL SOUND
Presents a cinematic joke in which a man is trying to put money into a parking meter before the time on it expires. Includes background music by Dvorak.
LC NO. 73-700487
Prod-TEMPLU Dist-TEMPLU 1972

Last Nazi, The C 72 MIN
16MM FILM, 3/4 OR 1/2 IN VIDEO J-C A
Features an interview between Canadian reporter Patrick Watson and Adolf Hitler's architect and Minister of War Armaments, Albert Speer, who responds calmly to questions about his 20-year jail sentence for war crimes, his inclusion in Hitler's circle, his early years and his memoirs.
Prod-GLOBTV Dist-LCOA 1977

Last Novelist, The C 60 MIN
3/4 OR 1/2 INCH VIDEO CASSETTE C
Presents Fitzgerald kept alive by his dream of success in movies, while the romantic world of Hollywood kept a depressed nation's hopes alive in this dramatization of a Fitzgerald story.
From The World Of F Scott Fitzgerald Series.
Prod-DALCCD Dist-DALCCD

Last Of Life, The C 28 MIN
16MM FILM, 3/4 OR 1/2 IN VIDEO H-C A
Examines the physiological causes of aging and points out the problems that the elderly face in trying to function in a fast-paced, youth-oriented society.
Prod-CANBC Dist-FLMLIB 1978

Last Of The Blue Devils, The C 90 MIN
3/4 OR 1/2 INCH VIDEO CASSETTE
Tells the story of the music that came out of Kansas City during the 1920s and 1930s. Includes examples of the music of Count Basie, Lester Young, Buster Smith, Eddie Durham, Jimmy Rushing, Walter Page, Hot Lips Page, Ernie Williams, Bernie Moten, Big Joe Turner and Jay McShann.
Prod-RICKRR Dist-DIRECT 1980

Last Of The Caddoes, The C 29 MIN
16MM FILM, 3/4 OR 1/2 IN VIDEO J-C
Presents a story about a young boy, living in rural Texas in the 1930's, who discovers that he is part Indian. Despite his parent's disapproval, he immerses himself in the folklore of the Caddo tribe and enters into a summer of self-discovery.
LC NO. 83-706410
Prod-HARK Dist-PHENIX 1982

Last Of The Giants C 23 MIN
16MM FILM OPTICAL SOUND I-C A
Shows a parade of locomotves commemorating a romantic era of railroading when steam was King of the iron trail. Stars 'BIG BOY,' the largest of its type ever built, at work and in the roundhouse.
Prod-UPR Dist-UPR 1960

Last Of The Great Male Chauvinists C 28 MIN
16MM FILM, 3/4 OR 1/2 IN VIDEO
Presents a story dealing with feminine fulfillment.
Prod-PAULST Dist-PAULST

Last Of The Incas, The C 28 MIN
16MM FILM, 3/4 OR 1/2 IN VIDEO H-C A
Focuses on the High Andes of Peru, the region that spawned the Inca civilization. Discusses the social organization and art of the Incas and shows the lost city of Machu Picchu.
Prod-FRUCTN Dist-JOU 1979

Last Of The Jacks C 15 MIN
16MM FILM OPTICAL SOUND
Uses archival photographs, old motion picture footage and filmed interviews with lumberjacks to describe logging operations in northern Minnesota after the turn of the century.
LC NO. 78-700427
Prod-MINHS Dist-MINHS Prodn-FIARTS 1977

Last Of The Karaphuna C 30 MIN
16MM FILM, 3/4 OR 1/2 IN VIDEO A
Presents the plight of the Carib Indians who once dominated the West Indies and are now reduced in numbers to 2800. Discusses their efforts to preserve their ethnic and cultural identity.
Prod-CNEMAG Dist-CNEMAG 1983

Last Of The Log Drives C 28 MIN
3/4 OR 1/2 INCH VIDEO CASSETTE
Documents the log drive of the North Fork of the Clearwater River, as this logging practice comes to an end. Using authentic background sound and voices, portrays the life of lumberjacks on a log drive. Includes musical soundtrack of lumberjack tunes.
Prod-POTFOR Dist-FO Prodn-FO

Last Of The Mayas C 27 MIN
16MM FILM, 3/4 OR 1/2 IN VIDEO
Discusses the Mayan civilization which flourished in Central America from the 10th through the 14th centuries.
Prod-HANDEL Dist-HANDEL 1981

Last Of The Mohicans, The B 91 MIN
16MM FILM OPTICAL SOUND
Features Randolph Scott in an adaptation of James Fenimore Cooper's novel THE LAST OF THE MOHICANS.
Prod-UAA Dist-KITPAR 1936

Last Of The Mohicans, The C 46 MIN
16MM FILM, 3/4 OR 1/2 IN VIDEO J-H
Presents the story of the Indian scout Hawkeye and his Mohican companions, Chingachnook and his son Uncas. Based on the novel THE LAST OF THE MOHICANS by James Fenimore Cooper.
From The Classic Stories Series.
Prod-LUF Dist-LUF 1980

Last Of The Mohicans, The C 99 MIN
16MM FILM, 3/4 OR 1/2 IN VIDEO J-H
Presents the story of the Indian scout Hawkeye and his Mohican companions, Chingachnook and his son Uncas. Based on the novel THE LAST OF THE MOHICANS by James Fenimore Cooper.
Prod-LUF Dist-LUF 1980

Last Of The Monsters, The C 23 MIN
3/4 OR 1/2 INCH VIDEO CASSETTE
Focuses on the octopus and its survival skills. Shows it in its fascinating environment as it displays a variety of tricks to stay alive.
Prod-NWLDPR Dist-NWLDPR

Last Of The Red Hot Dragons, The C 27 MIN
16MM FILM, 3/4 OR 1/2 IN VIDEO P-I
Features King Lion and his followers who attempt to help the last dragon on earth who is trapped at the North Pole.
Prod-LUF Dist-LUF 1980

Last Outcasts, The C 60 MIN
3/4 OR 1/2 INCH VIDEO CASSETTE
Deals with the work of doctors and scientists in the remote hilltop villages of Nepal to overcome superstition and the longstanding stigmatization of leprosy, a disease many still believe to be a punishment from the gods.
From The Quest For The Killers Series.
Prod-PBS Dist-PBS

Last Paragraph C 30 MIN
3/4 OR 1/2 INCH VIDEO CASSETTE
Focuses on ending a business letter. Includes closing the sale, getting the check and avoiding trouble.
From The Better Business Letters Series. Lesson 4
Prod-TELSTR Dist-TELSTR

Last Paragraph - The Gimmick C 30 MIN
3/4 OR 1/2 INCH VIDEO CASSETTE
See series title for descriptive statement.
From The Better Business Letters Series.
Prod-TELSTR Dist-DELTAK

Last Patterns C 29 MIN
2 INCH VIDEOTAPE
See series title for descriptive statement.
From The Busy Knitter II Series.
Prod-WMVSTV Dist-PUBTEL

Last Pony Mine, The C 23 MIN
16MM FILM OPTICAL SOUND J-C A
Examines the operation of the last pony coal mine in Iowa, and the feelings of its miners as the mine is threatened with closing.
LC NO. 72-702154
Prod-IOWA Dist-IOWA 1972

Last Prom, The C 24 MIN
3/4 OR 1/2 INCH VIDEO CASSETTE I A
Tells the story of four teens on prom night and what occurs when drinking and driving are mixed.
Prod-SUTHRB Dist-SUTHRB

Last Rabbi, The B 30 MIN
16MM FILM OPTICAL SOUND
Portrays the heroism and courage of the victims of the Warsaw ghetto as evidenced in documents left by Jews in that ghetto. Relates how the last surviving rabbi refused to accept an opportunity to escape at the hands of the Nazis.
LC NO. FIA64-1146
Prod-JTS Dist-NAAJS Prodn-NBC 1955

Last Rally, The B 31 MIN
3/4 OR 1/2 INCH VIDEO CASSETTE
Chronicles the passing of a great American rite, the anti-Vietnam Rally. Interviews lawyer William Kunstler.
Prod-EAI Dist-EAI

Last Reflections On A War B 44 MIN
16MM FILM OPTICAL SOUND H-C A

Presents the critical comments and philosophies of Asian scholar and war correspondent, Bernard B Fall. Shows combat scenes in South Vietnam and illustrates the war's effect upon the people of Vietnam. Includes the comments which fall was recording when he was killed.
LC NO. FIA68-1938
Prod-NET Dist-IU 1968

Last Refuge, The C 29 MIN
16MM FILM OPTICAL SOUND
Studies Al Oeming's game farm in Alberta, a 16-hundred-acre outdoor laboratory for the breeding of threatened and endangered species. Focuses on the long vigil and treatment of a young wolf that is badly hurt.
From The Al Oeming - Man Of The North Series.
LC NO. 77-702868
Prod-NIELSE Dist-NIELSE 1977

Last Resort, The C 60 MIN
16MM FILM, 3/4 OR 1/2 IN VIDEO
Presents the human side of the confrontation at Seabrook, New Hampshire, where construction of a nuclear power project sparked opposition of local communities. Balances the arguments of the strongly pronuclear Governor Meldrim Thomson and nuclear utility officials against those of local citizens and project opponents.
Prod-GMPF Dist-GMPF

Last Rite, The B 15 MIN
16MM FILM OPTICAL SOUND C A
Follows a young girl's gradual descent into schizophrenia.
Prod-UWFKD Dist-UWFKD

Last Rites C 30 MIN
16MM FILM OPTICAL SOUND
Presents the story of a young boy who is unable to accept his mother's death and tries to bring her back through magic rites. Shows how he finds solace from an unexpected source after his efforts to bring her back fail.
LC NO. 79-700060
Prod-THOMAC Dist-FLMLIB 1979

Last Round, The C 10 MIN
16MM FILM, 3/4 OR 1/2 IN VIDEO
Follows a supervisor as he is confronted with evidence of one of his workers drinking on the job. Demonstrates how in-plant supervisors can recognize and deal with employees who have a drinking problem.
From The Alcohol Abuse Series.
Prod-NSC Dist-JOU Prodn-ALTSUL 1976

Last Sailors, The C
3/4 OR 1/2 INCH VIDEO CASSETTE
Captures some of the last sailing ships still in practical use during their final voyages. Ponders crafts and sailors with equal perception, focusing on the durable metal of both that allows them to survive the rugged life. Narrated by Orson Welles.
LC NO. 84-706220
Prod-ADFIPR Dist-ADFIPR 1984

Last Salmon Feast Of The Celilo Indians C 18 MIN
16MM FILM OPTICAL SOUND I-C A
Features scenes of Indians fishing for salmon, preparing the fish for the feast, partaking in the feast and dancing after the meal. Includes interviews with the participants.
LC NO. FIA63-68
Prod-OREGHS Dist-OREGHS 1955

Last Scale, The C 29 MIN
3/4 INCH VIDEO CASSETTE H A
Focuses on presentation of the scale and chords of F major. Reviews earlier scales and chords. Introduces Beethoven's 'Waltz In F,' the longest and most complex in the telecourse.
From The Beginning Piano - An Adult Approach Series. Lesson 28
Prod-COAST Dist-CDTEL

Last Space Voyage Of Wallace Ramsel, The C 59 MIN
3/4 OR 1/2 INCH VIDEO CASSETTE
Presents a fictional television play which achieves a blend of fact and fiction.
Prod-EAI Dist-EAI

Last Stand C 20 MIN
16MM FILM, 3/4 OR 1/2 IN VIDEO J-H
Examines the conditions that led to the mass martyrdom of Jews at Masasa in the first century A D. Shows a trip to the mountain of Masads and studies ancient Jerusalem.
From The Matter Of Fact Series.
LC NO. 74-703196
Prod-NITC Dist-AITECH Prodn-WETATV 1973

Last Stand Farmer C 25 MIN
16MM FILM OPTICAL SOUND H-C A
Shows how an old Vermont farmer attempts to keep his farm operating in the face of rising taxes and lower farm output. Contrasts his philosophy with that of mass production on farms run by agribusiness enterprises.
LC NO. 75-701414
Prod-SILO Dist-SILO 1975

Last Stand In Eden C 59 MIN
16MM FILM, 3/4 OR 1/2 IN VIDEO
Shows how drought and poachers have forced the elephants of East Africa to migrate to new areas, where they have come into direct conflict with man.
LC NO. 80-706363
Prod-NGS Dist-NGS 1979

Last Straw B 20 MIN
16MM FILM, 3/4 OR 1/2 IN VIDEO H-C A
Explains how a bumbling, unhappy young man seeks help from a doctor who turns out to be even more maladjusted than he is himself.
Prod-PHENIX Dist-PHENIX 1976

Last Stronghold Of The Eagles C 30 MIN
16MM FILM, 3/4 OR 1/2 IN VIDEO J-C A
Explores the life cycle of the bald eagle, from courtship, through mating, to the raising and fledging of young eaglets. Culminates in the winter gathering of thousands of eagles in southeast Alaska, where human development now threatens their habitat.
LC NO. 81-707589
Prod-NAS Dist-LCOA Prodn-BENETJ 1981

Last Summer C 97 MIN
16MM FILM OPTICAL SOUND J-C A
Examines the lives of four young people during a single summer. Stars Richard Thomas and Barbara Hershey.
Prod-CINEWO Dist-CINEWO 1969

Last Summer Won't Happen C 60 MIN
16MM FILM, 3/4 OR 1/2 IN VIDEO
Traces the development of a group of individuals on the Lower East Side of New York from individual isolation and alienation to the beginnings of a sense of community and political activity.
Prod-GESHUR Dist-CNEMAG 1968

Last Taboo, The C 28 MIN
16MM FILM, 3/4 OR 1/2 IN VIDEO H-C A
Explores the feelings of six people who were sexually abused as children.
Prod-CAVPIC Dist-MTI 1977

Last Tasmanian, The C 101 MIN
16MM FILM OPTICAL SOUND
Follows the quest of two men to uncover the story of the Tasmanian aborigines. Offers an account of total genocide.
LC NO. 80-700820
Prod-ARTIS Dist-TASCOR 1977

Last Tasmanian, The - Ancestors C 17 MIN
16MM FILM, 3/4 OR 1/2 IN VIDEO H-C A
Examines the geographical origin of Tasmania, describing how it became physically separated from Australia. Discusses how the resulting isolation affected the culture and lifestyle of the Tasmanian Aborigines through the years.
LC NO. 80-707175
Prod-ARTIS Dist-CRMP 1980

Last Tasmanian, The - Extinction C 63 MIN
16MM FILM, 3/4 OR 1/2 IN VIDEO H-C A
Tells the story of a Tasmanian people, focusing on the British colonization of the island of Tasmania which began in 1803. Describes its use as a penal colony after which came the colonization which resulted in the extinction of the native inhabitants.
LC NO. 80-707176
Prod-ARTIS Dist-CRMP 1980

Last Thing On My Mind B 39 MIN
3/4 INCH VIDEOTAPE
Shows residents of two homes for the aging, one urban and one rural, telling what it means to spend one's last years in a home for the elderly.
Prod-CUETV Dist-CUNIV 1972

Last Thursday Night B 14 MIN
16MM FILM OPTICAL SOUND
Tells the love story of young nonconformists who are part of a motorcycle crowd.
Prod-NYU Dist-NYU

Last To Know, The C 45 MIN
16MM FILM OPTICAL SOUND
Discusses women's problems with alcohol and prescribed drugs.
Prod-FRIEDB Dist-NEWDAY

Last Trail, The B 58 MIN
16MM FILM SILENT
Shows how Tom Dane rides to the rescue of an old friend's daughter and young son to help them save their stagecoach line from the bad guys. Stars Tom Mix and directed by Louis Seiler.
Prod-FOXFC Dist-KILLIS 1927

Last Tree C 10 MIN
16MM FILM, 3/4 OR 1/2 IN VIDEO
Presents an ecological parable which traces the evolution of matter from the first amorphous blob right up to the emergence of man.
Prod-PHENIX Dist-PHENIX 1975

Last Tribes Of Mindanao, The C 52 MIN
16MM FILM, 3/4 OR 1/2 IN VIDEO J-C A
Takes a glimpse of a Stone Age tribe of Mindanao Island. Shows a people unknown to the outside world until June, 1971.
LC NO. 80-706397
Prod-NGS Dist-NGS 1971

Last Unicorn, The C
1/2 IN VIDEO CASSETTE BETA/VHS
Tells the story of the last unicorn.
Prod-EQVDL Dist-EQVDL

Last Videotapes of Marcel Duchamp, The C 32 MIN
3/4 OR 1/2 INCH VIDEO CASSETTE
Presents a fantasy of historical and artistic coincidence. Shot by Videoartist John Sanborn for Marcel Duchamp.
Prod-EAI Dist-EAI

Last Vikings, The C 52 MIN
16MM FILM, 3/4 OR 1/2 IN VIDEO P-C A
Explains that the Scandinavians of ten centuries ago were pirates and plunderers and points out that today their descendents are still masters of the sea, harvesting a rich crop of fish from their ancient enemy and only provider.
LC NO. 80-706391
Prod-NGS Dist-NGS 1972

Last Wagon, The C 29 MIN
16MM FILM OPTICAL SOUND H A
Traces the authentic music of the American cowboy to its actual source. Features the Western musicologist and folksigner, Katie Lee, who introduces a pair of original cowboy composers whose songs, philosophies, humor and anecdotes provide a glimpse into our vanished West.
LC NO. 70-715321
Prod-UARIZ Dist-UARIZ 1971

Last Wagon, The C 29 MIN
2 INCH VIDEOTAPE
Traces the authentic music of the American cowboy, neither Hollywood nor Nashville, to its actual source. Features Western musicologist and folk singer Katie Lee introducing a pair of original cowboy composers, both born in the last century and both natives of Arizona.
Prod-KUATTV Dist-PUBTEL

Last Waltz, The C 117 MIN
16MM FILM OPTICAL SOUND
Records The Band's farewell concert, given in San Francisco in 1976. Directed by Martin Scorsese.
Prod-UNKNWN Dist-UAE 1978

Last Whalers, The C 20 MIN
16MM FILM OPTICAL SOUND J-C
Studies the simple European life of a group of whalers. Focuses on the customs and traditions of the Pico Island villagers, who are seen going to market, painting their homes, sweeping the streets, attending church and religious festivals and laughing, singing and drinking.
LC NO. 73-701920
Prod-NEUF Dist-IFF 1973

Last Whalers, The (Portugal) C 20 MIN
3/4 OR 1/2 INCH VIDEO CASSETTE
Focuses on the lives of a group of whalers and on the customs and traditions of the villagers. Filmed on Pico Island off the coast of Portugal.
Prod-IFF Dist-IFF

Last Wild Virus, The C 60 MIN
3/4 OR 1/2 INCH VIDEO CASSETTE
Deals with the efforts of the World Health Organization to marshal its resources and manpower to eliminate smallpox from Bangladesh.
From The Quest For The Killers Series.
Prod-PBS Dist-PBS

Last Winters, The C 23 MIN
16MM FILM, 3/4 OR 1/2 IN VIDEO
Focuses on an episode in the love life of 84-year-old Charles and 79-year-old Marguerite. Shows how Charles becomes anxious and jealous when he cannot find Marguerite.
Prod-PERSPF Dist-CORF

Last Words B 12 MIN
16MM FILM OPTICAL SOUND
Presents a Crete dialect motion picture with English subtitles. Focuses on a Cretan hermit forcibly brought back to society. Directed by Werner Herzog.
Prod-UNKNWN Dist-NYFLMS 1967

Last Years Of The Tsars B 19 MIN
16MM FILM, 3/4 OR 1/2 IN VIDEO H-C
Presents the story of tsarist Russia in the early years of the 20th century when the pleas of the millions of peasants and workers for mild reforms went unheard by the aristocracy but heard by others including a young revolutionary named Lenin.
From The Russian Revolution Series.
Prod-GRANOV Dist-FI 1971

Last-State Collections B 45 MIN
2 INCH VIDEOTAPE C
See series title for descriptive statement.
From The Business Writing Series. Unit III - Persuasive Messages
Prod-CHITVC Dist-GPITVL Prodn-WTTWTV

Latch/D-Type Flip-Flops And Registers C
3/4 OR 1/2 INCH VIDEO CASSETTE
See series title for descriptive statement.
From The Digital Techniques Video Training Course Series.
Prod-VTRI Dist-VTRI

Latch, D-Type Flip-Flop And Registers C
3/4 OR 1/2 INCH VIDEO CASSETTE
See series title for descriptive statement.
From The Digital Techniques Series.
Prod-HTHZEN Dist-HTHZEN

Late Autumn (Japanese) C 127 MIN
16MM FILM OPTICAL SOUND
Relates the story of a young woman who announces that she is not ready for marriage. Shows the shocked reaction of her elders who are determined that she find a husband at once.
Prod-NYFLMS Dist-NYFLMS 1960

Late Eye Report B 6 MIN
16MM FILM OPTICAL SOUND
Features an experimental film which presents a collage of realities which end up at zero.
LC NO. 74-702997
Prod-LICLIP Dist-CANFDC 1973

Late For Dinner - Was Dawn Right X 8 MIN
16MM FILM, 3/4 OR 1/2 IN VIDEO P
Presents the story of Dawn who is scolded by her mother for coming home late to dinner. Features Dawn's side of the situation--on the way home she bumped into a woman who dropped a five dollar bill and she tried to catch up with the woman on a bus in an effort to return the money.
Prod-EBEC Dist-EBEC 1970

Late Great God, The X 28 MIN
16MM FILM, 3/4 OR 1/2 IN VIDEO J-C A
Describes a beach party at which God is put on trial.
From The Insight Series.
Prod-PAULST Dist-PAULST

Late Great God, The C 28 MIN
3/4 OR 1/2 INCH VIDEO CASSETTE J A
Tells the story of God being put on trial at a Malibu Beach party and a girl who defends him.
Prod-SUTHRB Dist-SUTHRB

Late Great God, The (Spanish) X 28 MIN
16MM FILM, 3/4 OR 1/2 IN VIDEO J-C A
Describes a beach party at which God is put on trial.
From The Insight Series.
Prod-PAULST Dist-PAULST

Late Great God, The (Spanish) C 28 MIN
3/4 OR 1/2 INCH VIDEO CASSETTE J A
Tells the story of God being put on trial at a Malibu Beach party and a girl who defends him.
Prod-SUTHRB Dist-SUTHRB

Late Great Me, The - Story Of A Teenage Alcoholic C 71 MIN
16MM FILM OPTICAL SOUND I-C A
Recounts how an emotionally troubled girl is led down the path to alcoholism by a boy who is equally emotionally disturbed. Shows how her life becomes one of deception, escape from reality and loss of responsibility. Reveals that she has a frightening accident which forces her to face her situation and, with the help of a teacher, attempt to overcome her illness.
LC NO. 82-700563
Prod-WILSND Dist-WILSND 1982

Late Great Planet Earth, The C 46 MIN
16MM FILM OPTICAL SOUND R
Examines the prophecies of the ancient Hebrew seers as described in the book, THE LATE GREAT PLANET EARTH, by Hal Lindsey.
Prod-GF Dist-GF

Late Sequelae Of Nonpenetrating Abdominal Trauma C 27 MIN
16MM FILM OPTICAL SOUND PRO
Explains that visceral damage resulting from blunt trauma may initially escape detection because of minimal findings, diagnostic oversight and overshadowing injuries. Demonstrates the clinical radiologic and surgical aspects of the late sequelae of injuries to the liver, pancreas, spleen and intestine.
Prod-ACYDGD Dist-ACY 1963

Late Spring (Japanese) B 107 MIN
16MM FILM OPTICAL SOUND
Relates the story of an aging professor, a widower who lives outside Tokyo with his unmarried daughter, in perfect harmony and contentment that he knows cannot last. Shows how he arranges his daughter's marriage.
Prod-NYFLMS Dist-NYFLMS 1949

Latent Heat B 22 MIN
16MM FILM OPTICAL SOUND H
Demonstrates that a change of phase is brought about by the release or absorption of energy. Compares the quantity of energy involved in a change with the specific heat of the substance. Explains that this energy is known as 'LATENT' heat because no change of temperature occurs during the change of phase.
From The Heat Series.
Prod-CETO Dist-GPITVL

Later Years Of The Woodleys, The B 30 MIN
16MM FILM OPTICAL SOUND
Illustrates the relationship between the aging process and ill health and shows how the social worker can be indispensable to appropriate medical care. Depicts the supervisory process and group supervision.
LC NO. 74-705006
Prod-USSRS Dist-USNAC

Later Years, The C 9 MIN
16MM FILM, 3/4 OR 1/2 IN VIDEO H-C A
Deals with old age as the sum of all preceding stages, hopefully culminating in contentment and a healthy acceptance of death.
Prod-HUBLEY Dist-PFP

Later Years, The C 30 MIN
3/4 INCH VIDEO CASSETTE H-C A
Examines the interaction of physical, psychological and socio-economic factors which can threaten the nutritional status of older adults.
From The Changing Nutritional Needs Series.
Prod-UWISCA Dist-GPITVL 1976

Lateral Cerebral Ventricle And The Fornix - A Self-Evaluation Exercise C 18 MIN
3/4 OR 1/2 INCH VIDEO CASSETTE C A
From The Neuroanatomy Series.
Prod-UWO Dist-TEF

Lateral Cerebral Ventricles And The Fornix C 20 MIN
3/4 OR 1/2 INCH VIDEO CASSETTE C A
From The Neuroanatomy Series.
Prod-UWO Dist-TEF

Lateral Corner Drop (Modified Sumi-Gaeshi) B 3 MIN
16MM FILM OPTICAL SOUND
Demonstrates the lateral corner drop in judo and shows how to use this drop against attack.
From The Combative Measures - Judo Series. Part 3K
LC NO. 75-700837
Prod-USAF Dist-USNAC 1955

Lateral Flap Cleft Lip Surgery Technique C 18 MIN
16MM FILM OPTICAL SOUND PRO
Demonstrates an original method for closure of cleft lip through diagrams, actual technique and case results. Points out that the method can be adapted to use in both single and double cleft lip.
Prod-ACYDGD Dist-ACY 1962

Lateral Neck Superficial Structures C 9 MIN
16MM FILM - 3/4 IN VIDEO PRO
Uses diagrams to present a dissection of superficial structures of the anterior and lateral neck. Shows the vessels and nerves transversing the external cervical fascia.
From The Anatomy Of The Head And Neck Series.
LC NO. 78-706248
Prod-USVA Dist-USNAC Prodn-VADTC 1978

Lateral Penile Curvature - Etiology And Management C 16 MIN
16MM FILM OPTICAL SOUND PRO
Explains the anatomy and etiology of an erect penis with congenital lateral curvature. Demonstrates x-ray techniques for diagnosis and techniques for surgical correction and discusses postoperative results.
LC NO. 77-700738
Prod-KPLAMC Dist-BURKEB 1977

Lateral Sliding Flap C 15 MIN
16MM FILM, 3/4 OR 1/2 IN VIDEO PRO
Demonstrates the lateral sliding flap operation for the correction of labial gingival recession on a central incisor. Discusses the rationale for this surgical procedure.
LC NO. 81-706826
Prod-USVA Dist-USNAC 1971

Laterally Positioned Flap In Periodontics C 15 MIN
16MM FILM, 3/4 OR 1/2 IN VIDEO
Shows how laterally positioned flaps are used to cover the denuded roots of a mandibular central incisor and maxillary molar. Shows how a partial or split thickness dissection is performed in order to leave periosteum at the donor sites.
LC NO. 81-706824
Prod-USVA Dist-USNAC 1968

Latex Test For Fibrin Degradation Products / Protamine Sulfate Paracoagulation... C 14 MIN
3/4 OR 1/2 INCH VIDEO CASSETTE
Demonstrates a convenient assay for fibrin degradation products and how to measure fibrin degradation products and monomers by dissociating the fibrin monomer complexes with protamine complexes.
From The Blood Coagulation Laboratory Techniques Series.
LC NO. 79-707604
Prod-UMICH Dist-UMICH 1977

Latex, The Market Builder C 22 MIN
16MM FILM OPTICAL SOUND
Depicts the extent of production, technical service and new product development for Dow latexes. Depicts the Dow research commitment in latexes for the paper, textile, coatings and adhesives markets.
Prod-DCC Dist-DCC

Lathe - Chuck Work C 13 MIN
16MM FILM, 3/4 OR 1/2 IN VIDEO I-C A
Parts of the lathe, mounting chucks and types, chucking work, taper turning and drilling, filing and polishing.
From The Metalwork - Machine Operation Series.
Prod-MORLAT Dist-SF 1967

Lathe - Work Between Centers C 13 MIN
16MM FILM, 3/4 OR 1/2 IN VIDEO I-C A
Setting up and turning work between centers, knurling, taper turning, filing and polishing.
From The Metalwork - Machine Operation Series.
Prod-MORLAT Dist-SF 1967

Lathe Of Heaven, The C 120 MIN
3/4 OR 1/2 INCH VIDEO CASSETTE
Presents an adaptation of Ursula K LeGuin's futuristic novel THE LATHE OF HEAVEN.
Prod-WNETTV Dist-WNETTV

Lathe Tools C 11 MIN
3/4 OR 1/2 INCH VIDEO CASSETTE IND
Focuses on types of lathe cutting tools and their uses. Includes high speed, insert type, parting tools, forming tools, boring tools and knurling tools.
From The Introduction To Machine Technology, Module 2 Series.
Prod-LEIKID Dist-LEIKID

Lathe, The B 15 MIN
16MM FILM, 3/4 OR 1/2 IN VIDEO
Describes the characteristics and basic operations of the engine lathe.
From The Machine Shop Work - Basic Machines Series.
Prod-USOE Dist-USNAC Prodn-LNS 1942

Lathe, The C 17 MIN
3/4 OR 1/2 INCH VIDEO CASSETTE
Covers major components of a lathe and its major functions.
From The Manufacturing Materials And Processes Series.
Prod-GE Dist-WFVTAE

Lathe, The (Spanish) B 15 MIN
16MM FILM OPTICAL SOUND
Describes the characteristics and basic operations of the engine lathe.
From The Machine Shop Work Series.
LC NO. 74-705010
Prod-USOE Dist-USNAC 1942

Latin America B 20 MIN
16MM FILM OPTICAL SOUND
Analyzes the political, social and economic factors affecting South American countries and their 200 million inhabitants. Pictures the development of South America and explains communist infiltration in Latin America.
LC NO. 72-701049
Prod-USDD Dist-USNAC 1961

Latin America - Intervention In Our Own Backyard C 26 MIN
16MM FILM, 3/4 OR 1/2 IN VIDEO H-C
Examines diplomatic relations between the United States and Latin America from the 19th century until 1933.
From The Between The Wars Series.
Prod-LNDBRG Dist-FI 1978

Latin America - The Dead Hand Of The Past C 20 MIN
3/4 INCH VIDEO CASSETTE H-C
See series title for descriptive statement.
From The Geography For The '70's Series.
Prod-KLRNTV Dist-GPITVL

Latin America—A Series

Examines various social issues in Latin America.
Prod-OECA Dist-OECA 1972

Chile Nuevo	23 MIN
Hospital Amazonico	23 MIN

Latin American Cooking C 22 MIN
16MM FILM OPTICAL SOUND
Introduces Latin American cooking using modern cooking equipment, and discusses the Indian and Spanish heritage in Latin American cooking. Shows the preparation of tortillas, tamales, enchiladas, Argentine beef roll stuffed with vegetables and eggs, anticuchos, mole poblano and other dishes popular in Latin American countries.
LC NO. 70-706044
Prod-BUGAS Dist-BUGAS Prodn-BAILYB 1969

Latin American Cooking C 25 MIN
3/4 OR 1/2 INCH VIDEO CASSETTE
Brings to life the romance and excitement of 'South of the Border' cooking.
From The Magical Cook's Tour Series.
Prod-IVCH Dist-IVCH

Latin American Overview C 25 MIN
16MM FILM, 3/4 OR 1/2 IN VIDEO I-H
Provides information about South America, Central America, Mexico and the Caribbean Islands. Covers a broad range of topics, including the people, culture, religion, geography and economics.
LC NO. 82-706881
Prod-BIBICF Dist-CRMP 1982

Latin American Series - A Focus On People—A Series
3/4 OR 1/2 INCH VIDEO CASSETTE I-H
Prod-CLAIB Dist-SF 1973

Bolivia, Peru And Ecuador	20 MIN
Caribbean, The	21 MIN
Central America	16 MIN
Chile And Argentina	20 MIN
Colombia And Venezuela	18 MIN
Mexico	18 MIN
North Brazil	18 MIN
South America - Overview	17 MIN
South Brazil	19 MIN

Latin Splendor - Spain And Portugal C 20 MIN
3/4 OR 1/2 INCH VIDEO CASSETTE J-C A
Gives an overview of Majorca and the Spanish cities of Madrid and Barcelona. Shows Portugal's beaches, port towns, Lisbon and the Catholic religious procession at Fatima.
LC NO. 82-706766
Prod-AWSS Dist-AWSS 1980

Latino Profiles - Living In The U S Today C 18 MIN
16MM FILM, 3/4 OR 1/2 IN VIDEO J-C
Takes a look at the lives and work of a variety of Latinos in the United States. Presents Latino people as they discuss their work their leisure, their goals and heritage and their pride in being Latinos.
Prod-BFA Dist-PHENIX 1976

Latissimus Dorsi Flap For Modified Radical Mastectomy, The C 22 MIN
3/4 OR 1/2 INCH VIDEO CASSETTE PRO
Demonstrates a surgical technique for breast reconstruction which utilizes a latissimus dorsi musculocutaneous flap to give additional skin and cover for a breast implant.
Prod-WFP Dist-WFP

Latitude And Longitude C 9 MIN
16MM FILM, 3/4 OR 1/2 IN VIDEO I-H
Demonstrates that the location of a point on earth can be determined by using angular distances of measurement called latitude and longitude. Uses a globe to demonstrate the various relationships between latitude and longitude.
Prod-LUF Dist-LUF 1983

Latitude And Longitude (Spanish) C 14 MIN
16MM FILM, 3/4 OR 1/2 IN VIDEO I-J
A Spanish language version of the film and videorecording Latitude And Longitude.
Prod-EBEC Dist-EBEC 1981

Latitude Zero C 26 MIN
16MM FILM, 3/4 OR 1/2 IN VIDEO H-C A
Demonstrates that the adaptation and exploitation of plants and animals to their environments takes place in nature wherever there is any potential. Shows a tremendous variation in vegetation zones along the equator in Ecuador, high in the Andes and not far from the sea.

From The Botanic Man Series.
Prod-THAMES Dist-MEDIAG 1978

Latitude, Longitude And Time Zones (Rev Ed) C 13 MIN
16MM FILM, 3/4 OR 1/2 IN VIDEO I-J
Illustrates the development and use of the system of locating places on earth using latitude and longitude. Shows how world time zones are established.
Prod-CORF Dist-CORF 1979

Laton - A Handicapped Child In Need C 15 MIN
16MM FILM OPTICAL SOUND
Shows the services provided for the handicapped by Head Start programs. Examines Head Start programs for physical and mental evaluation, dental care and hygiene.
LC NO. 76-702599
Prod-CFDC Dist-CFDC 1976

Laton Goes To School C 15 MIN
16MM FILM OPTICAL SOUND A
Focuses on Laton, a symbolic handicapped child involved with the Head Start program. Shows the transition made by handicapped children from the Head Start program to the public school system.
LC NO. 81-701205
Prod-CALVIN Dist-CALVIN 1978

Latvia C 29 MIN
2 INCH VIDEOTAPE
Features home economist Joan Hood presenting a culinary tour of specialty dishes from around the world. Shows the preparation of Latvian dishes ranging from peasant cookery to continental cuisine.
From The International Cookbook Series.
Prod-WMVSTV Dist-PUBTEL

Laudate C 11 MIN
16MM FILM OPTICAL SOUND J-C A
Presents the celebration of the Eucharist to stimulate a reverie in a young monk that incorporated all of life into the Eucharistic event, from the moment of birth to the experiences of an average day.
LC NO. 74-701709
Prod-FRACOC Dist-FRACOC 1974

Laugh And Cry C 15 MIN
3/4 OR 1/2 INCH VIDEO CASSETTE
See series title for descriptive statement.
From The Children In Action Series.
Prod-LVN Dist-LVN

Laugh Lines - A Profile Of Kaj Pindal C 27 MIN
16MM FILM OPTICAL SOUND J-C A
Offers a portrait of animator Kaj Pindal. Shows him at work creating zany cartoon characters, teaching students of animation and at home enjoying a full-size street car that tours his backyard.
Prod-NFBC Dist-NFBC 1979

Laughing Alligator C 21 MIN
3/4 OR 1/2 INCH VIDEO CASSETTE
Conveys the personal experiences of which the primitive landscape is composed. Juxtaposes sequences of body movements.
Prod-KITCHN Dist-KITCHN

Laughing Gravy B 19 MIN
16MM FILM OPTICAL SOUND
Describes the havoc which ensues when Laurel and Hardy try to sneak an orphan puppy into their room.
Prod-ROACH Dist-BHAWK 1931

Laughter C 15 MIN
3/4 OR 1/2 INCH VIDEO CASSETTE K-P
Deals with French-American children. Shows that differences make the world interesting.
From The La Bonne Aventure Series.
Prod-MPBN Dist-GPITVL

Laughter Is Holy B 30 MIN
16MM FILM OPTICAL SOUND
Portrays a chapter from Joe E. Brown's diary written during his personal appearances before American troops during World War II. Shows him battling a physical affliction as he performs, as well as the bombings and blackouts of many performances.
Prod-GUIDAS Dist-WWPI 1959

Launch Control Center C 5 MIN
16MM FILM - 3/4 IN VIDEO
Explains control launch operations at the Kennedy Space Center. Shows the evolution of space control facilities, including close-up views of the complex array of equipment used to control a Saturn launch. Issued in 1969 as a motion picture.
From The Apollo Digest Series.
LC NO. 79-706979
Prod-NASA Dist-USNAC 1979

Launch Of The Saturn 5 C 4 MIN
16MM FILM - 3/4 IN VIDEO
Shows a typical launch of the Saturn 5, including assembly and transport to the launch pad preceding launching. Includes footage of separation of the first stage, taken from a mounted camera inside the second stage. Issued in 1969 as a motion picture.
From The Apollo Digest Series.
LC NO. 78-706980
Prod-NASA Dist-USNAC 1979

Launch Site To The Moon C 3 MIN
16MM FILM - 3/4 IN VIDEO
Shows the Kennedy Space Center's facilities for launching the Apollo and Saturn moon flights. Includes scenes of the vehicle assembly building, the launch control center and the launch pads. Issued in 1969 as a motion picture.
From The Apollo Digest Series.
LC NO. 79-706981
Prod-NASA Dist-USNAC 1979

Launch Windows For Lunar Landing C 20 MIN
3/4 INCH VIDEO CASSETTE
Describes the planning of a lunar mission with trajectories and physical capabilities which define these trajectories. Emphasizes the importance of the launch windows and earth reentry.
Prod-NASA Dist-NASA 1972

Launching Civil Service Reform–A Series

Describes the changes brought about by the Civil Service Reform Bill.
Prod-USOPMA Dist-USNAC 1978

Labor-Management Relations 23 MIN
Merit Pay 18 MIN
New Framework For Federal Personnel 30 MIN
Orientation To Civil Service Reform - A 31 MIN
Performance Appraisal And Workforce Discipline 22 MIN
Program Development Conference 29 MIN
Senior Executive Service, The 30 MIN

Launching Of The Bicentennial C 28 MIN
16MM FILM OPTICAL SOUND
Looks at America's then upcoming 200th anniversary. Features former President Nixon, Chief Justice Burger, former Speaker of the House Carl Albert and the U S Army Chorus. Narrated by actor James Stewart.
Prod-NBCTV Dist-AMRC 1971

Launching The New Government (1789-1800) (Rev Ed) C 10 MIN
16MM FILM, 3/4 OR 1/2 IN VIDEO I-H
Dramatizes crucial events of the first 12 years of constitutional government in the United States.
Prod-CORF Dist-CORF

Laundry Syndrome, The C 23 MIN
16MM FILM OPTICAL SOUND H
Provides instruction in proper laundry techniques by telling a story about a woman who is a laundry junkie.
LC NO. 80-701231
Prod-USBCC Dist-MTP Prodn-HEN 1980

Laundry Tips C 13 MIN
2 INCH VIDEOTAPE
See series title for descriptive statement.
From The Living Better I Series.
Prod-MAETEL Dist-PUBTEL

Laura Reitman And Nancy Reynolds C 30 MIN
3/4 OR 1/2 INCH VIDEO CASSETTE
See series title for descriptive statement.
From The Second Time Around - Career Options For Dancers Series.
Prod-ARCVID Dist-ARCVID

Laura Reitman And Nancy Reynolds C 30 MIN
3/4 OR 1/2 INCH VIDEO CASSETTE
See series title for descriptive statement.
From The Eye On Dance - Second Time Around, Career Options For Dancers Series.
Prod-ARTRES Dist-ARTRES

Laurel And Hardy Compendium B 16 MIN
16MM FILM OPTICAL SOUND H-C A
Presents excerpts from two Laurel and Hardy films, Air Raid Wardens, issued in 1943, and Hollywood Party, issued in 1934. Features a series of misadventures and mishaps as Laurel and Hardy try to contribute to the World War II war effort by volunteering as air raid wardens, and then attend a glamorous party in Hollywood. Exemplifies the comedy film genre.
From The American Film Genre - The Comedy Film Series.
LC NO. 77-701136
Prod-MGMA Dist-FI 1975

Laurel And Hardy Murder Case, The B 28 MIN
16MM FILM OPTICAL SOUND
Relates how Stan Laurel is mistaken for a missing heir. Shows how he and Oliver Hardy go to a creepy old house to claim his inheritance.
Prod-ROACH Dist-BHAWK 1930

Laurel And Hardy Mystery Case, The B 28 MIN
16MM FILM OPTICAL SOUND
Tells how Ollie becomes convinced that Stan is the long-lost heir of the late tycoon Ebenezeer Laurel, which causes the pair to become involved with a strange butler, the police, heirs, black cats, a stormy night, murder and an assortment of suspects.
Prod-ROACH Dist-BHAWK 1930

Laurie C 14 MIN
16MM FILM OPTICAL SOUND I-J
Shows how Laurie, a blind girl, works to maintain her independence.
From The Feeling Free Series.
LC NO. 79-700430
Prod-WOCA Dist-SCHMAG Prodn-BRIGHA 1978

Laurie C 14 MIN
3/4 OR 1/2 INCH VIDEO CASSETTE J-H
Tells how a chronic runaway begins experimenting with drugs at the age of 11 and lives the life of a burnt-out drifter.
From The Changing Series.
Prod-WGTETV Dist-AITECH 1980

Laurie McDonald–A Series

Series of four videotapes which satirize dance.
Prod-WMENIF Dist-WMENIF

Deux Pieds 004 MIN
Duet For Tap And Galoshes 003 MIN
Dying Swan, The 003 MIN
Minute Waltz 003 MIN

Laurie Simmons, A Teaser C 5 MIN
3/4 OR 1/2 INCH VIDEO CASSETTE
See series title for descriptive statement.
From The Cross-Overs - Photographers Series.
Prod-ARTINC Dist-ARTINC

Lautrec In Paris C 29 MIN
2 INCH VIDEOTAPE
See series title for descriptive statement.
From The Museum Open House Series.
Prod-WGBHTV Dist-PUBTEL

Lava And The River C 20 MIN
16MM FILM OPTICAL SOUND I-C
A story of the numerous lava flows which have made the Columbia Plateau, showing how they entombed plant and animal life. Points out the effects of the glacial melt-water action.
Prod-MMP Dist-MMP 1959

Lava Beds National Monument C 12 MIN
16MM FILM, 3/4 OR 1/2 IN VIDEO
Presents animation intercut with recent volcanic activity to trace the history of the Lava Beds National Monument in northern California. Describes shield volcanoes, lava tubes, pahoehoe lava and spatter cones, and traces the slow return of life to the area.
Prod-USNPS Dist-USNAC 1981

Lavas Of Etna C 24 MIN
16MM FILM, 3/4 OR 1/2 IN VIDEO
Examines the form and structural complexity of Mount Etna, Europe's largest and most contemporary volcano, as well as the historic evolution of lava and ash types comprising the mountain's mantle. Demonstrates scientific analyses of the distribution of lava flows through chemical and X-ray analysis and mapping.
Prod-OPENU Dist-MEDIAG Prodn-BBCTV 1982

Lavinia Moyer And The Attic Theater C 22 MIN
3/4 OR 1/2 INCH VIDEO CASSETTE
Traces the Attic Theater's production of Wings, a play about stroke victims. Shows Lavinia Moyer, founder, involved in auditions, rehearsals, staging, comedy workshops and other activities.
From The Working Artist Series.
Prod-MARXHA Dist-MARXS

Lavinia Moyer And The Attic Theater C 22 MIN
16MM FILM, 3/4 OR 1/2 IN VIDEO H-C A
Documents the work of stage designer, artistic director, and actor Lavinia Moyer of the Attic Theater. Shows the Attic Theater Ensemble Group preparing the play Wings, about a former aeronautic acrobat who suffers a disabling stroke.
Prod-MIFA Dist-LRF Prodn-MARXS 1982

Law - A System Of Order C 18 MIN
16MM FILM, 3/4 OR 1/2 IN VIDEO J-H
Provides an introduction into the field of law.
From The Humanities Series.
Prod-MGHT Dist-MGHT Prodn-TMP 1972

Law And Handicapped Children In School–A Series
16MM FILM, 3/4 OR 1/2 IN VIDEO C A
Assesses the history and applicability of PL94-142 (the Education For All Handicapped Children Act of 1975) and PL93-112, section 504, of the Rehabilitation Act of 1973. Consists of testimony and interpretations by legal and special education experts, simulations, analysis of procedures required by the law, and documentary footage of instructional settings and approaches for educating the handicapped.
Prod-IU Dist-IU 1978

Annual Review 030 MIN
Assessment 030 MIN
Due Process Hearing, The 030 MIN
Due Process Panel, The 030 MIN
Educating The Severely And Profoundly 030 MIN
Including Me, Pt 1 030 MIN
Including Me, Pt 2 030 MIN
Individualized Education Program Case 030 MIN
Individualized Education Program, The 030 MIN
Integrating Handicapped Children In The 030 MIN
Larry P Case, The 030 MIN
Law And Handicapped Children In School, 030 MIN
Least Restrictive Environment - Resource 030 MIN
Least Restrictive Environment - Special Day 030 MIN
Least Restrictive Environment Panel 030 MIN

Law And Handicapped Children In School, The - Overview C 30 MIN
3/4 OR 1/2 INCH VIDEO CASSETTE C A
Reviews the provisions and background of the Education For All Handicapped Children Act of 1975 and the Rehabilitation Act of 1973.
From The Law And Handicapped Children In School Series.
LC NO. 79-706361
Prod-IU Dist-IU 1979

Law And Justice C 30 MIN
3/4 INCH VIDEO CASSETTE
Discusses the many fluctuations within Chinese politics. Points to different bases of Chinese and western law and justice.
From The China After Mao Series.
Prod-UMITV Dist-UMITV 1980

Law And Liability - A Security Perspective C 15 MIN
3/4 OR 1/2 INCH VIDEO CASSETTE
Defines legal powers and limitations of the security officer with emphasis on search, arrest and use of physical force.

From The Health Care Security Training Series.
Prod-GREESM Dist-MTI 1984

Law And Order C 81 MIN
16MM FILM, 3/4 OR 1/2 IN VIDEO
Surveys the wide range of work the police are asked to perform, such as enforcing the law, maintaining order and providing general social services. Illustrates how training, community expectations, socio-economic status of the subject, threat of violence and discretion affect police behavior.
Prod-WISEF Dist-ZIPRAH

Law And The Citizen—A Series
16MM FILM, 3/4 OR 1/2 IN VIDEO J-C A
Reviews legal rights of citizens.
Prod-WILETS Dist-BARR 1978

Contract Law 023 MIN
Landlord-Tenant Law 023 MIN

Law And The Juvenile—A Series
16MM FILM, 3/4 OR 1/2 IN VIDEO J-H A
Explores the law and how it affects the lives of teenagers. Includes views of teens in detention in a juvenile facility and others receiving protection in a small claims court.
Prod-BARR Dist-BARR

It's The Law 017 MIN
Joy Ride - An Auto Theft 013 MIN
Juvenile Delinquency - It's Up To You 019 MIN

Law And The Prophets, The C 51 MIN
16MM FILM, 3/4 OR 1/2 IN VIDEO H A R
Presents a biblical account of the Creation, the high points of the history of the Hebrew people and the developing of their faith through the time of the prophets. The prologue recounts the sin of Adam and Eve and closes with their banishment from the Garden of Eden.
Prod-NBC Dist-MGHT 1968

Law And The Prophets, The, Pt 1 C 27 MIN
16MM FILM, 3/4 OR 1/2 IN VIDEO H-C R
Presents a biblical account of the creation, the high points of the history of the Hebrew people and the development of their faith through the time of the prophets. Recounts the sin of Adam and Eve and their banishment from the Garden of Eden. Depicts sacred themes by means of artwork.
Prod-NBCTV Dist-MGHT 1968

Law And The Prophets, The, Pt 2 C 24 MIN
16MM FILM, 3/4 OR 1/2 IN VIDEO H-C R
Presents a biblical account of the creation, the high points of the history of the Hebrew people and the development of their faith through the time of the prophets. Recounts the sin of Adam and Eve and their banishment from the Garden of Eden. Depicts sacred themes by means of artwork.
Prod-NBCTV Dist-MGHT 1968

Law Enforcement - Patrol Officers C 19 MIN
3/4 OR 1/2 INCH VIDEO CASSETTE H
Dramatizes typical police officer problem situations. Presents discussions with former and present patrol officers.
From The Ways Of The Law Series.
Prod-SCITV Dist-GPITVL 1980

Law Enforcement - The Citizen's Role C 19 MIN
3/4 OR 1/2 INCH VIDEO CASSETTE H
Discusses the citizen's role in law enforcement with county, state, city and national police.
From The Ways Of The Law Series.
Prod-SCITV Dist-GPITVL 1980

Law Enforcement Equipment Standards C 7 MIN
16MM FILM OPTICAL SOUND H-C A
Describes standards being developed for equipment used in the protection and safety of a policeman and patrol car, and communications and standards for new equipment under the National Institute of Law Enforcement and Criminal Justice.
LC NO. 73-702596
Prod-USNBOS Dist-USNBOS 1972

Law Ethics And Love Of God C 15 MIN
3/4 OR 1/2 INCH VIDEO CASSETTE
Explains Maimonides' two concepts of law, civil and Torah. Explores the potential of a Maimonidian society.
From The Tradition And Contemporary Judaism - Maimonides - Torah And Philosophic... Series.
Prod-ADL Dist-ADL

Law In The Schools C 30 MIN
16MM FILM, 3/4 OR 1/2 IN VIDEO PRO
Examines law enforcement in relation to school campuses. Outlines the role of the police on school premises and suggests greater protection to curb violence and abate crime in schools.
From The Legal Information For Law Enforcement Series.
Prod-CAGO Dist-AIMS 1974

Law Machine, The C 29 MIN
16MM FILM OPTICAL SOUND
Discusses the steps through which a bill must pass before it becomes law. Points out the problems and strategies of leadership in steering a bill through Congress and the effect of individual personalities on passage of legislation.
From The Government Story Series. No. 9
LC NO. 70-707166
Prod-WBCPRO Dist-WBCPRO 1968

Law Of Armed Conflict, The C 21 MIN
16MM FILM, 3/4 OR 1/2 IN VIDEO
Presents an overview of laws of armed conflict in the air, on the sea and on the ground. Covers treaties and conventions and how they apply to members of the Air Force.
Prod-USAF Dist-USNAC

Law Of Cosines B 30 MIN
16MM FILM OPTICAL SOUND H
Derives the law of cosines and uses it to solve a problem in which either two sides and the included angle or three sides of a triangle are known.
From The Trigonometry Series.
Prod-CALVIN Dist-MLA Prodn-UNIVFI 1959

Law Of Falling Bodies, The C 30 MIN
16MM FILM, 3/4 OR 1/2 IN VIDEO C A
Demostrates Galileo's experiments proving that all bodies fall with the same constant acceleration.
From The Mechanical Universe Series.
Prod-ANNCPB Dist-FI

Law Of Gravitation, The - An Example Of Physical Law B 56 MIN
3/4 INCH VIDEOTAPE
Describes the history of the law of gravity, the method and its limitations.
From The Feynman Lectures - The Character Of Physical Law Series.
Prod-EDC Dist-EDC

Law Of Sines B 30 MIN
16MM FILM OPTICAL SOUND H
Derives the law of sines and uses it to solve a problem in which two angles and the included side of a triangle are known. Describes a problem in which two sides and the angle opposite one of them are given and either of two solutions is possible.
From The Trigonometry Series.
Prod-CALVIN Dist-MLA Prodn-UNIVFI 1959

Law Of Tangents B 28 MIN
16MM FILM OPTICAL SOUND H
Derives the law of tangents and explains that it is significant because its ratio form is suitable to the use of logarithms for calculation. Shows a problem in which the law is utilized.
From The Trigonometry Series.
Prod-CALVIN Dist-MLA Prodn-UNIVFI 1959

Law Of The Land, The C 20 MIN
3/4 OR 1/2 INCH VIDEO CASSETTE I
Deals with the meaning and significance of the Constitution of the United States. Focuses on the Bill of Rights.
From The Exploring Our Nation Series.
Prod-KRMATV Dist-GPITVL 1975

Law Of The Land, The C 26 MIN
16MM FILM, 3/4 OR 1/2 IN VIDEO J-C A
Looks at the use and misuse of land and what can be done to manage it more efficiently in the wake of urban sprawl, strip mining, leap-frog development, grotesque commercial districts and ruined scenery.
Prod-UFLA Dist-MCFI 1980

Law Of The Sea C 29 MIN
16MM FILM OPTICAL SOUND
Illustrates various legal problems that can arise at sea and their solutions.
LC NO. 74-705014
Prod-USN Dist-USNAC 1970

Law Of The Sea C 28 MIN
16MM FILM, 3/4 OR 1/2 IN VIDEO J-C A
Examines the state of maritime laws as related to Iceland, Ecuador, Alaska, England, the Netherlands, Denmark, Norway and the North Sea. Deals with off-shore fishing and mineral rights and discusses the concepts of freedom of the seas and the common heritage approach.
Prod-UN Dist-JOU 1974

Law Office Management C 160 MIN
3/4 OR 1/2 INCH VIDEO CASSETTE PRO
Discusses how to improve the efficiency and profitability of a law practice through recruiting, selecting and training personnel, jury and docket control and use of stored materials.
Prod-CCEB Dist-ABACPE

Lawn And Garden—A Series

Demonstrates gardening and lawn care.
Prod-MOHOMV Dist-MOHOMV

Annuals / Hanging Baskets 038 MIN
Basic Gardening 059 MIN
Ground Covers 060 MIN
Grow Your Own Vegetables 055 MIN
Pruning 047 MIN
Success With Indoor Plants 057 MIN
Your Beautiful Lawn 048 MIN
Your Beautiful Roses 056 MIN

Lawn And Vacant Lot Community, The C 15 MIN
3/4 OR 1/2 INCH VIDEO CASSETTE P-I
Discusses the living things found on lawns and vacant lots.
From The Why Series.
Prod-WDCNTV Dist-AITECH 1976

Lawn Care C 30 MIN
3/4 OR 1/2 INCH VIDEO CASSETTE C A
Examines selection and use of mowers, mowing techniques and schedules and types of equipment for spreading fertilizer.
From The Home Gardener With John Lenanton Series. Lesson 19
Prod-COAST Dist-CDTEL

Lawn Care C 48 MIN
1/2 IN VIDEO CASSETTE BETA/VHS
Explains how to seed a lawn and how to maintain it. Includes liming, moss control, raking, thatching, mowing and trimming.
Prod-RMI Dist-RMI

Lawn Equipment And Mowing Operations C 29 MIN
3/4 INCH VIDEO CASSETTE
Describes various types of mowers and lawn care equipment. Illustrates their use, maintenance care and safety precautions.
From The Grounds Maintenance Training Series.
Prod-UMITV Dist-UMITV 1978

Lawn Installation C 30 MIN
3/4 OR 1/2 INCH VIDEO CASSETTE C A
Explains and demonstrates four methods of establishing a lawn. Suggests planting times and methods. Shows proper techniques of preparing the ground for planting.
From The Home Gardener With John Lenanton Series. Lesson 11
Prod-COAST Dist-CDTEL

Lawns And Groundcovers C 30 MIN
3/4 OR 1/2 INCH VIDEO CASSETTE C A
Designed to help home gardener decide which type of grass or groundcover to use for a particular landscape purpose. Describes qualities and growing habits of most widely used grasses.
From The Home Gardener With John Lenanton Series. Lesson 10
Prod-COAST Dist-CDTEL

Lawrence Of Arabia C 18 MIN
16MM FILM OPTICAL SOUND
An abridged version of the motion picture Lawrence Of Arabia. Tells the true story of T E Lawrence, the World War I British officer who united the Arabs against the Turks. Stars Peter O'Toole and Alec Guinness.
Prod-CPC Dist-TIMLIF 1982

Lawrence Of Arabia C 185 MIN
16MM FILM OPTICAL SOUND
Offers a biography of T E Lawrence, recounting his spectacular career and battles. Stars Peter O'Toole and Omar Sharif.
Prod-CPC Dist-TIMLIF 1962

Lawrence Raab C 29 MIN
3/4 INCH VIDEO CASSETTE
See series title for descriptive statement.
From The Poets Talking Series.
Prod-UMITV Dist-UMITV 1975

Lawrence University C 10 MIN
16MM FILM OPTICAL SOUND J-H A
Portrays Lawrence University, a small selective private liberal arts college of 750 men and 650 women located in Appleton, Wisconsin. Explains that Lawrence University is well known for its dedication to excellence, small classes and close student-faculty relationships.
Prod-CAMPF Dist-CAMPF

Lawrence Weiner - Affected And Or Effected C 20 MIN
3/4 OR 1/2 INCH VIDEO CASSETTE
Presented by Lawrence Weiner.
Prod-ARTINC Dist-ARTINC

Lawrence Weiner - Green As Well As Blue As Well As Red C 20 MIN
3/4 OR 1/2 INCH VIDEO CASSETTE
Presented by Lawrence Weiner.
Prod-ARTINC Dist-ARTINC

Lawrence Weiner - Shifted From Side To Side B 1 MIN
3/4 OR 1/2 INCH VIDEO CASSETTE
Offers illustrations of possibility.
Prod-ARTINC Dist-ARTINC

Lawrence Weiner - There But For C 20 MIN
3/4 OR 1/2 INCH VIDEO CASSETTE
Presented by Lawrence Weiner.
Prod-ARTINC Dist-ARTINC

Lawrence Weiner - To And Fro And Fro And To And To And Fro And Fro And To B 1 MIN
3/4 OR 1/2 INCH VIDEO CASSETTE
Presents a comic introduction to the institution of conceptual art.
Prod-ARTINC Dist-ARTINC

Lawrence Welk And His Champagne Music C 10 MIN
16MM FILM OPTICAL SOUND
Presents Lawrence Welk and his orchestra playing his famous Champagne Music.
Prod-UNKNWN Dist-BHAWK

Laws And Labels C 30 MIN
3/4 OR 1/2 INCH VIDEO CASSETTE C A
See series title for descriptive statement.
From The Pests, Pesticides And Safety Series.
Prod-UMA Dist-GPITVL 1976

Laws Of Motion B 45 MIN
2 INCH VIDEOTAPE C
See series title for descriptive statement.
From The Physical Science Series. Unit 4 - Motion, Work And Energy
Prod-CHITVC Dist-GPITVL Prodn-WTTWTV

Laws Of Motion, Pt 1, The C 18 MIN
16MM FILM, 3/4 OR 1/2 IN VIDEO J-C
Illustrates Newton's Laws of Motion as well as the principle of Conservation Of Momentum. Continued in the Laws of Motion, Pt 2.
From The Physics In Action Series.
Prod-LUF Dist-LUF

Laws Of Motion, Pt 2, The C 18 MIN
16MM FILM, 3/4 OR 1/2 IN VIDEO J-C
Illustrates Newton's Laws of Motion as well as the principle of Conservation of Momentum. Continued from the Laws of Motion, Pt 1.
From The Physics In Action Series.
Prod-LUF Dist-LUF

Laws Of Motion, The C 29 MIN
2 INCH VIDEOTAPE
See series title for descriptive statement.
From The Observing Eye Series.
Prod-WGBHTV Dist-PUBTEL

Laws Of Nature C 5 MIN
16MM FILM OPTICAL SOUND J
Shows how the traffic engineer applies his knowledge of nature's laws and forces in determining safe speeds for vehicles to round curves.
From The Driver Education Series.
LC NO. FIA66-1004
Prod-AMROIL Dist-AMROIL 1964

Laws Of Nature And Driving C 20 MIN
3/4 OR 1/2 INCH VIDEO CASSETTE
Deals with the natural laws of gravity, friction, inertia and the force of impact, which affect drivers, and explains how these 'laws' affect vehicle performance and control in order to make driving safer and more enjoyable.
Prod-BUMPA Dist-BUMPA

Laws Of Sliding Friction, The B 6 MIN
16MM FILM OPTICAL SOUND C
Demonstrates the effects of both static and kinetic friction. Measures the forces required to start and maintain the motion of a block on a uniform surface.
Prod-PUAVC Dist-PUAVC 1961

Lawyer From Boston B 30 MIN
16MM FILM OPTICAL SOUND R
Tells the story how Supreme Court Justice and Zionist Louis D Brandeis came to discover his Jewish heritage. (Kinescope)
Prod-JTS Dist-NAAJS Prodn-NBCTV 1956

Lawyer, The C 29 MIN
3/4 INCH VIDEO CASSETTE C A
Discusses several aspects of the lawyer. Includes training and qualifications necessary to be a lawyer, expected ethical principles and major forms of specialization.
From The You And The Law Series. Lesson 3
Prod-COAST Dist-CDTEL Prodn-SADCC

Lawyering Skills—A Series
PRO
Traces stages of the lawyer-client relationship through demonstrations of interviewing, counseling and negotiation meetings.
Prod-ABACPE Dist-ABACPE

Business Planning 047 MIN
Business Transaction, The 030 MIN
Dispute Resolution 047 MIN

Lawyers C 30 MIN
3/4 OR 1/2 INCH VIDEO CASSETTE
Presents tips on using lawyers.
From The Consumer Survival Series. Personal Planning
Prod-MDCPB Dist-MDCPB

Laxmi Bomb, The C 15 MIN
16MM FILM, 3/4 OR 1/2 IN VIDEO I-J
Presents an Indian fairy tale about a young boy who discovers a magical firecracker named after the goddess of good luck, Laxmi. Describes an adventure during which the boy overcomes the demon firecrackers with the help of Laxmi and saves other children who were captured by the demon.
LC NO. 82-706946
Prod-KELTCS Dist-PHENIX 1982

Lay It On The Line C 22 MIN
16MM FILM, 3/4 OR 1/2 IN VIDEO
Discusses campaign fire management. Tells the story of a fire suppression organization set up for an all out campaign fire effort.
Prod-PUBSF Dist-FILCOM

Lay Lady Lay C 6 MIN
16MM FILM, 3/4 OR 1/2 IN VIDEO
Shows how a hen is sent to the company psychiatrist after she loses pride in her work. Illustrates aspects of morale and production.
Prod-KRATKY Dist-PHENIX 1978

Lay My Burden Down B 60 MIN
16MM FILM, 3/4 OR 1/2 IN VIDEO H-C A
Illustrates the arduous work and poverty of the Negro tenant farmers of the Southern United States and documents the debt cycle and inadequate schools which perpetuate the poverty. Comments on the hope aroused by the recently obtained right to vote.
From The N E T Journal Series.
Prod-NET Dist-IU 1966

Lay My Burden Down B 60 MIN
16MM FILM, 3/4 OR 1/2 IN VIDEO
Documents black tenant farmers in Alabama in 1966.
Prod-NEWTIM Dist-NEWTIM

Lay Therapy B 30 MIN
3/4 OR 1/2 INCH VIDEO CASSETTE
Uses excerpts from a regular meeting of lay therapists to help introduce the responsibilities of a lay therapist as a loving friend and link between the family and professional service agencies.
Prod-NCCAN Dist-UWISC

Layered Silicone Mold Technique For Processing Dentures, The C 30 MIN
16MM FILM OPTICAL SOUND
Presents a technique for processing mold in the upper half of the flask. Explains that this new method of processing produces extremely accurate dentures, free of adhering calcium sulphate film or particles and with the surfaces as smooth as the polished wax of the trial dentures.
LC NO. 74-705015
Prod-USVA Dist-USVA

Layering, Trimming, Clipping And Notching Seam Allowances C 3 MIN
16MM FILM SILENT J-C A
Illustrates techniques of layering, trimming, clipping and notching. Suggests where each technique would be used.
From The Clothing Construction Techniques Series.
LC NO. 77-701181
Prod-IOWA Dist-IOWASP 1976

Laying Concrete Block C 15 MIN
3/4 OR 1/2 INCH VIDEO CASSETTE IND
Illustrates the importance of good mortar when used in masonry construction. Shows how the first course is laid in a full mortar bed and how vital the corner blocks and first course are in laying the succeeding courses.
From The Marshall Maintenance Training Programs Series. Tape 16
Prod-LEIKID Dist-LEIKID

Laying Concrete Block C 15 MIN
16MM FILM, 3/4 OR 1/2 IN VIDEO IND
Stresses the importance of good mortar when used in masonry construction. Shows how the first course is laid in a full mortar bed and how vital the corner blocks and the first course are in laying the succeeding courses.
Prod-MOKIN Dist-MOKIN

Laying Down Pipe C 11 MIN
3/4 OR 1/2 INCH VIDEO CASSETTE IND
Shows how drill pipe and drill collars should be layed down, inspected and prepared for transport to the next location. Designed for entry-level rotary drill helpers.
From The Roughneck Training Series.
Prod-UTEXPE Dist-UTEXPE 1983

Laying It On The Line C 28 MIN
16MM FILM - 3/4 IN VIDEO IND
Gives an overview of the planning, laying and testing of stoneware and PVC pipes.
LC NO. 81-706509
Prod-VICCOR Dist-TASCOR 1981

Laying Out And Forming Plywood B 21 MIN
16MM FILM OPTICAL SOUND
Demonstrates how to lay out plywood using blueprint and templates, form plywood in a press, reinforce plywood and apply glue and varnish.
LC NO. FIE52-313
Prod-USOE Dist-USNAC 1944

Laying Out And Installing Compartment Fixtures B 12 MIN
16MM FILM OPTICAL SOUND
Explains how to locate installations on a planview blueprint, lay out ceiling fixtures and studs, lay out and burn a hole for the passage of cable and install ceiling fixtures.
LC NO. FIE52-209
Prod-USOE Dist-USNAC 1945

Laying Out And Installing Hangers B 19 MIN
16MM FILM OPTICAL SOUND
Explains how to measure and cut hanger legs to length, and how to install stool, angle iron bracket, strap, rod and saddle hangers.
From The Shipbuilding Skills Series. Pipefitting, No. 5
LC NO. FIE52-201
Prod-USOE Dist-USNAC Prodn-WALKER 1944

Laying Out And Installing Hangers B 19 MIN
3/4 INCH VIDEO CASSETTE
Demonstrates how to measure and cut hanger legs and how to install stool, strap, saddle and angle iron bracket hangers. Issued in 1944 as a motion picture.
From The Shipbuilding Skills - Pipefitting Series. Number 5
LC NO. 80-707272
Prod-USOE Dist-USNAC Prodn-WALKER 1980

Laying Out And Installing Kickpipes And Stuffing Tubes B 16 MIN
16MM FILM OPTICAL SOUND
Shows how to locate the kickpipe or stuffing tube area, lay out the penetration area, cut or burn the penetration area and install the kickpipe or stuffing tube.
LC NO. FIE52-212
Prod-USOE Dist-USNAC 1945

Laying Out And Installing Main Wireway B 21 MIN
16MM FILM OPTICAL SOUND
Explains how to determine from the blueprint the route which cables are to follow and the size of the hangers to be used. Shows how to lay out the raceways, install flat bars and hangers and how to lay out penetration holes to but.
LC NO. FIE52-211
Prod-USOE Dist-USNAC 1945

Laying Out Small Castings B 16 MIN
16MM FILM - 3/4 IN VIDEO IND
Shows how to lay out holes for drilling, locate a reference point, and use hermaphrodite callipers, combination square, and surface gauge. Issued in 1942 as a motion picture.
From The Machine Shop Work - Bench Work Series. Number 6
LC NO. 80-706753
Prod-USOE Dist-USNAC Prodn-CALVCO 1980

Laying Out, Drilling And Tapping Flanges On Sea Chest B 19 MIN
16MM FILM OPTICAL SOUND
Points out the component parts of a sea chest. Explains how locations of flanges are checked, flanges leveled, stud hold centers laid out and stud holes drilled and tapped.
LC NO. FIE52-215
Prod-USOE Dist-USNAC 1944

Laying Pipe The Reel Way C 24 MIN
16MM FILM OPTICAL SOUND
Describes the advantages of laying pipe on the ocean floor using the reel system operated from a ship.
LC NO. 80-701237
Prod-SFINTL Dist-SFINTL Prodn-MARTB 1980

Laying The Foundation For Exhibits And Witnesses At Trial C 49 MIN
3/4 OR 1/2 INCH VIDEO CASSETTE PRO
Establishes a basic checklist for the advocate to follow in laying foundations. Includes witness qualifications, relevance, the hearsay rule and 'magic words.'
From The Training The Advocate Series.
Prod-AMBAR Dist-ABACPE

Laying, Pinning And Cutting A Pattern C 4 MIN
16MM FILM SILENT J-C A
Shows how to prepare the fabric for pattern layout. Demonstrates pinning the pattern on the correct grainline and cutting out the garment.
From The Clothing Construction Techniques Series.
LC NO. 77-701169
Prod-IOWA Dist-IOWASP 1976

Layout And Drilling Operations C 60 MIN
3/4 OR 1/2 INCH VIDEO CASSETTE IND
See series title for descriptive statement.
From The Mechanical Maintenance Basics, Module C - General Shop Practices Series.
Prod-LEIKID Dist-LEIKID

Layout Cutting C 29 MIN
2 INCH VIDEOTAPE
Features Mrs Ruth Hickman demonstrating layout cutting.
From The Sewing Skills - Tailoring Series.
Prod-KRMATV Dist-PUBTEL

Layout No. 1 - Hole Location C 19 MIN
1/2 IN VIDEO CASSETTE BETA/VHS IND
Explains how to layout hole locations using basic layout tools (combination square, scriber, dividers, prick punch and center punch). Stresses the importance of working from proper reference points.
From The Machine Shop - Layout Series.
Prod-RMI Dist-RMI

Layout No. 2 - Contours And Angles C 19 MIN
1/2 IN VIDEO CASSETTE BETA/VHS IND
Explains how to layout an irregular part from horizontal and vertical centerlines. Includes methods of laying out contours and angles.
From The Machine Shop - Layout Series.
Prod-RMI Dist-RMI

Layout No. 3 - Surface Plate C 14 MIN
1/2 IN VIDEO CASSETTE BETA/VHS IND
Demonstrates tools and procedures used when laying out work on the surface plate. Covers use of angle plate, surface gauge and vernier height gauge.
From The Machine Shop - Layout Series.
Prod-RMI Dist-RMI

Layout Tools For Metal Work C 13 MIN
16MM FILM, 3/4 OR 1/2 IN VIDEO I-C A
Measuring and marking tools - try squares, dividers, calipers, scribers and punches, transferring design to metal and the use of layout fluids.
From The Metalwork - Hand Tools Series.
Prod-MORLAT Dist-SF 1967

Lazy Days B 29 MIN
16MM FILM OPTICAL SOUND
Explains that for Farina a shady tree on a summer day is hard to resist, even though a 50 dollar prize is at stake. A Little Rascals film.
Prod-ROACH Dist-BHAWK 1929

Lazy Eye, The C 14 MIN
16MM FILM OPTICAL SOUND
Emphasizes the importance of early eye examinations for children. Presents the true stories of how unsuspected eye problems were detected in preschoolers in time to restore good vision.
LC NO. 78-700290
Prod-NSPB Dist-NSPB Prodn-NOWAKA 1977

Lazy Fox, The / Senor Fox And Senor Coyote C 15 MIN
3/4 OR 1/2 INCH VIDEO CASSETTE P-I
Tells Argentinian tale of the fox who can't outfox the slow, hard-working armadillo and northern Mexican tale of Senor Fox who leaves Senor Coyote holding up a cliff.
From The Sixteen Tales Series.
Prod-KLCSTV Dist-AITECH

Lazybones B 79 MIN
16MM FILM SILENT
Follows the circuitous love affair of Agnes and Lazybones, from the time he saves Agnes' sister from suicide, adopts the sister's daughter, returns from World War I and falls for his adopted daughter. Stars Buck Jones and Madge Bellamy. Directed by Frank Borzage.
Prod-FOXFC Dist-KILLIS 1925

LBJ (Luther, Bobby, Jack) C 15 MIN
16MM FILM OPTICAL SOUND
Presents a cultural assault on LBJ'S America, or, 'DR STRANGELOVE - FACT OR FICTION.'
Prod-SFN Dist-SFN

LBJ - The Last Interview C 43 MIN
16MM FILM, 3/4 OR 1/2 IN VIDEO H-C A

Presents an interview with Lyndon Johnson filmed ten days before his death.
Prod-CBSNEW Dist-CAROUF

LBJ Goes To War, 1964-1965 C 60 MIN
3/4 OR 1/2 INCH VIDEO CASSETTE H-C A
Reveals that after Kennedy's assassination in 1963, Lyndon Johnson inherited revolving door coups in South Vietnam as none of Diem's successor's was able to control the area. Shows that increasingly the NLF guerillas controlled the countryside as the national army disintegrated. States that secretly, Johnson approved open-ended deployment of U S troops.
From The Vietnam - A Television History Series. Episode 4
Prod-WGBHTV Dist-FI 1983

LCA Short Story Library--A Series
16MM FILM, 3/4 OR 1/2 IN VIDEO
Presents adaptations of various short stories.
Prod-LCOA Dist-LCOA 1982

All Summer In A Day 025 MIN
Antaeus 020 MIN
Butch Minds The Baby 030 MIN
Chapparral Prince, The 020 MIN
Cop And The Anthem, The 023 MIN
Invisible Boy, The 020 MIN
Luck Of Roaring Camp, The 027 MIN
Monkey's Paw, The 027 MIN
Pardon Me For Living 030 MIN
Robbers, Rooftops And Witches 046 MIN
Split Cherry Tree 026 MIN

Le Bonheur Et La Mort - Happiness And Death C 52 MIN
16MM FILM OPTICAL SOUND
Demonstrates how the 14th century's secularization of art contrasts the anguish of death with the refined, festive life of hunting and princely pleasures.
From The Le Temp Des Cathedrales Series.
Prod-FACSEA Dist-FACSEA 1979

Le Bourdon C 11 MIN
16MM FILM, 3/4 OR 1/2 IN VIDEO J-C A
A French language version of the videocassette The Bumblebee. Examines the life of the bumblebee.
Prod-DEU Dist-IFB 1956

Le Cafe C 18 MIN
16MM FILM, 3/4 OR 1/2 IN VIDEO J-H
Shows drinks and a meal being ordered at the cafe Le Commerce, a typical cafe-restaurant at its busiest on market day. Linguistically looks at questions that require information in addition to that which is already present in the question itself.
From The Comment Dit-On Series.
Prod-THAMES Dist-MEDIAG 1977

Le Chagrin Et La Pitie C 260 MIN
16MM FILM OPTICAL SOUND H-C A
Examines the occupation of France by the Germans during World War II using reminiscences of individuals and officials involved in the events at the time. Concentrates on the themes of collaboration and resistance.
LC NO. 76-702631
Prod-NPSSRT Dist-CINEMV 1972

Le Chantier B 13 MIN
16MM FILM OPTICAL SOUND J-C
See series title for descriptive statement.
From The En France Avec Jean Et Helen Series. Set 1, Lesson 9
LC NO. 73-704505
Prod-PEREN Dist-CHLTN 1967

Le Chat VA Tomber B 13 MIN
16MM FILM OPTICAL SOUND I-H
See series title for descriptive statement.
From The Les Francais Chez Vous Series. Set II, Lesson 16
LC NO. 72-704466
Prod-PEREN Dist-CHLTN 1967

Le Choc Septique C 21 MIN
3/4 OR 1/2 INCH VIDEO CASSETTE PRO
A French language version of Septic Shock. Discusses the general pathophysiology of shock, the nine basic parts of evaluation (which include vital signs, cultures, CBC differential and a coagulation screen), chronologic treat- ment (which includes fluid therapy, pharmacologic agents and antibiotics) and differentiation of septic shock from hypovolemia.
Prod-UMICHM Dist-UMICHM 1976

Le Cirque C 8 MIN
16MM FILM, 3/4 OR 1/2 IN VIDEO H-C A
A French language videocassette. Looks at the lives of circus performers.
From The Chroniques De France Series.
LC NO. 81-706554
Prod-ADPF Dist-IFB 1980

Le Coche D'Eau B 13 MIN
16MM FILM OPTICAL SOUND I-H
See series title for descriptive statement.
From The Les Francais Chez Vous Series. Set II, Lesson 24
LC NO. 76-704467
Prod-PEREN Dist-CHLTN 1967

Le Cocktail C 29 MIN
2 INCH VIDEOTAPE
A French language videotape. Features Julia Child of Haute Cuisine au Vin demonstrating how to make a cocktail. With captions.
From The French Chef (French) Series.
Prod-WGBHTV Dist-PUBTEL

Le Compartif (French) C
3/4 OR 1/2 INCH VIDEO CASSETTE
See series title for descriptive statement.
From The French Language Videotapes (French) Series.
Prod-UCEMC Dist-UCEMC

Le Conte Stewart, Landscape Painter C 23 MIN
16MM FILM OPTICAL SOUND
Presents the historical and philosophical background of American painter Le Conte Stewart. Includes scenes of Stewart working outdoors and shows a large collection of his work in pastels, prints and oils as well as some of his drawings.
LC NO. 77-702268
Prod-SISEMF Dist-SISEMF 1977

Le Corbeau B 92 MIN
16MM FILM OPTICAL SOUND
A French language motion picture with English subtitles. Tells how secretly circulated poison pen letters accuse a town doctor of incompetence and possibly murder.
Prod-UNKNWN Dist-KITPAR 1943

Le Cycle De Reproduction De L'Ange De Mer C 10 MIN
16MM FILM, 3/4 OR 1/2 IN VIDEO H-C
A French language version of the videocassette Reproductive Cycle Of Angel Fish. Details the reproduction of the angel fish. Documents the development of the fish during the six weeks they remain under their parents' care.
Prod-IFB Dist-IFB 1971

Le Cycliste C 5 MIN
16MM FILM OPTICAL SOUND J-C A
Presents Le Cycliste, the great master of all cycles, in a mime.
LC NO. 73-701225
Prod-ALBM Dist-MARALF 1973

Le Facteur Qui S'Envole Et La Fleur C 22 MIN
16MM FILM OPTICAL SOUND K-I
A French language film. Two children decide to play a joke on the postman by hoisting him on a bicycle into the air with a hook and pulley from the barn and two little girls take a walk in the garden and pick a flower only to be chased by the watchman.
From The Bonjour Line Series. Part 1.
Prod-PEREN Dist-CHLTN 1962

Le Farfalle (The Butterflies) C 5 MIN
16MM FILM OPTICAL SOUND
Uses live action, special effects and animation, intergrated with music, to give symbolic hints to the concept that women are like butterflies whose beauty is functional and that they can make butterflies with their sewing machines.
LC NO. FIA65-1011
Prod-SINGER Dist-SVE Prodn-TORCEL 1965

Le Fauvisme C 17 MIN
16MM FILM, 3/4 OR 1/2 IN VIDEO H-C
A French-language version of the motion picture Fauvism. Points out that the main contribution to modern painting of the Fauves was their use of color to express form, light and volume independent of subject matter or a given light. Includes examples from work by Vlaminck, Duchamp, Matisse and Dufy.
Prod-LFLMDC Dist-IFB 1972

Le Foyer International D'Accueil De Paris C 7 MIN
16MM FILM, 3/4 OR 1/2 IN VIDEO H-C A
A French language videocassette. Presents a summary of the facilities and activities available to foreign and provincial students in Paris.
From The Chroniques De France Series.
LC NO. 81-706551
Prod-ADPF Dist-IFB 1980

Le Geant De La Prairie C 21 MIN
16MM FILM, 3/4 OR 1/2 IN VIDEO J-H
A French language version of the videocassette Prairie Giant. Introduces the giant Canada goose in its natural habitat of prairies and tall grass plains.
Prod-COTTER Dist-IFB 1968

Le Haut De Cagnes C 10 MIN
16MM FILM OPTICAL SOUND H-C
A French language film. Shows life in the old medieval town of Cagnes, situated on a hill above the Mediterranean. Points out that artists go there for inspiration from the quaint old homes.
From The Aspects De France Series.
Prod-WSU Dist-MLA Prodn-BORGLM 1952

Le Journaliste B 13 MIN
16MM FILM OPTICAL SOUND J-C
See series title for descriptive statement.
From The En France Avec Jean Et Helen Series. Set 1, Lesson 8
LC NO. 78-704509
Prod-PEREN Dist-CHLTN 1967

Le Magasin C 5 MIN
16MM FILM OPTICAL SOUND K-I
A French language film. A merchant sells various objects to his patrons.
From The Bonjour Line Series. Part 2
Prod-PEREN Dist-CHLTN 1962

Le Mans - The Grand Prize C 17 MIN
16MM FILM OPTICAL SOUND
Records the thrills, disappointments and rewards of the 24-hour 1973 Grand Prix at Le Mans.
Prod-GC Dist-MTP

Le Marais C 13 MIN
16MM FILM, 3/4 OR 1/2 IN VIDEO
See series title for descriptive statement.
From The Sejour En France Series.
Prod-SEABEN Dist-IFB 1970

Le Marche C 11 MIN
16MM FILM OPTICAL SOUND I-C A
A French language film. Depicts marketing on a Sunday morning in one of the workers' districts of Paris.
From The Voix Et Images De France Series.
Prod-PEREN Dist-CHLTN Prodn-CRDDF 1962

Le Merle C 5 MIN
16MM FILM, 3/4 OR 1/2 IN VIDEO H-C
A French language film. Visualizes an old FrenchCanadian nonsense song. Simple white cut-outs on pastel backgrounds provide illustrations as the song relates how a blackbird loses parts of his body and then regains them two-and-three fold.
Prod-NFBC Dist-IFB Prodn-MCLN 1959

Le Monde Sonore Des Sauterelles (The Musical World Of Grasshoppers) C 38 MIN
16MM FILM OPTICAL SOUND C
A French language film. Demonstrates certain experiments based on the presumption that locusts might be attracted by sound signals or ultra-sound signals. Uses this method for the destruction of migratory locusts.
Prod-SFRS Dist-PSUPCR 1958

Le Mont Saint-Michel C 12 MIN
16MM FILM OPTICAL SOUND H-C
A French language film. Explores life in the islet community of Le Mont Saint-Michel with its gothic architecture that reflects the Middle Ages. Visitors come daily to see 'LA MERVEILLE DE L'OUEST.'
From The Aspects De France Series.
Prod-WSU Dist-MLA Prodn-BORGLM 1955

Le Mouvement C 14 MIN
16MM FILM OPTICAL SOUND
Presents a French version of the 1967 motion picture 'MOTION.' Illustrates man in motion, showing such scenes as a small boy sliding down a bannister, an astronaut walking in space and free-falling parachutists.
LC NO. FIA67-2356
Prod-CNR Dist-CRAF 1967

Le Moyen Age C 31 MIN
16MM FILM, 3/4 OR 1/2 IN VIDEO H-C A
A French-language version of the motion picture The Middle Ages. Traces the social, economic and cultural development of western Europe, emphasizing the life of the people during the middle ages.
LC NO. 83-706816
Prod-IFB Dist-IFB 1975

Le Musee Grevin C 12 MIN
16MM FILM, 3/4 OR 1/2 IN VIDEO
See series title for descriptive statement.
From The Sejour En France Series.
Prod-SEABEN Dist-IFB 1970

Le Musee Rodin B 13 MIN
16MM FILM OPTICAL SOUND J-C
See series title for descriptive statement.
From The En France Avec Jean Et Helen Series. Set 1, Lesson 4
LC NO. 72-704510
Prod-PEREN Dist-CHLTN 1967

Le Mystere Kuomiko - The Kuomiko Mystery C 47 MIN
16MM FILM OPTICAL SOUND H-C A
A French language film with English subtitles. Features an interview with a young girl concerning her likes and dislikes and her feelings toward herself and the world. Reveals the mystery of individuality and the social mood of acceptance of estrangement characteristic of children of the atomic bomb era.
LC NO. 75-704370
Prod-MARKC Dist-NYFLMS 1975

Le Nez B 11 MIN
16MM FILM OPTICAL SOUND
Presents Gogol's celebrated short story, The Nose, animated without words in fantastic moving pictures that capture the scene and spirit of 19th century Russia. Produced by Alexander Alexeieff and Claire Parker.
Prod-STARRC Dist-STARRC 1963

Le Noir Et Le Blanc C 13 MIN
16MM FILM OPTICAL SOUND J A
From The En Francais, Set 1 Series.
Prod-PEREN Dist-CHLTN 1969

Le Pari B 13 MIN
16MM FILM OPTICAL SOUND J-C
See series title for descriptive statement.
From The En France Avec Jean Et Helen Series. Set 1, Lesson 1
LC NO. 76-704511
Prod-PEREN Dist-CHLTN 1967

Le Parrain C 30 MIN
3/4 OR 1/2 INCH VIDEO CASSETTE I
Dramatizes family tradition in contemporary Franco-American life.
From The Franco File Series.
Prod-WENHTV Dist-GPITVL

Le Partage Des Eaux C 13 MIN
16MM FILM OPTICAL SOUND J A
From The En Francais, Set 2 Series.
Prod-PEREN Dist-CHLTN 1969

Le Partitif (French) C
3/4 OR 1/2 INCH VIDEO CASSETTE
See series title for descriptive statement.
From The French Language Videotapes (French) Series.
Prod-UCEMC Dist-UCEMC

Le Pere C 13 MIN
16MM FILM OPTICAL SOUND K-P

A French language version of the motion picture Call Me Dad. Provides an explanation of family relations.
From The Family Relations (French) Series.
LC NO. 76-700119
Prod-MORLAT Dist-MORLAT 1974

Le Perroquet C 11 MIN
16MM FILM, 3/4 OR 1/2 IN VIDEO H-C
A French language film. Uses animation to present the story of a parrot for beginning language students. Tells how Pedrito, a clever parrot, is kidnapped by a magician and then returned to his owners after a circus performance. Narration is by a native speaker.
Prod-SIGMA Dist-FILCOM 1966

Le Petit Chaperon Rouge C 14 MIN
16MM FILM, 3/4 OR 1/2 IN VIDEO A
A French version of Little Red Riding Hood. Shows an object or action as it is being described. Uses repetition, recapitulation and visual aids to promote learning.
Prod-FA Dist-PHENIX 1967

Le Petit Coq Qui Reveille Le Soleil B 11 MIN
16MM FILM, 3/4 OR 1/2 IN VIDEO I-H
French version of 'THE LITTLE ROOSTER WHO MADE THE SUN RISE.' Animated story of the rooster who discovers that his crowing does not make the sun rise, but who acquires pride in doing his job of waking his farmyard friends.
Prod-CORF Dist-CORF 1962

Le Pink Grapefruit C 27 MIN
16MM FILM, 3/4 OR 1/2 IN VIDEO H-C A
Presents a portrait of the Spanish artist, Salvador Dali. Shows how his surrealism is carried over into his home and lifestyle. Includes a tour of the Salvador Dali Museum in Figueras, Spain, in which the artist discusses the building and collection.
Prod-YUNGLI Dist-PHENIX 1976

Le Pique-Nique C 15 MIN
16MM FILM, 3/4 OR 1/2 IN VIDEO
See series title for descriptive statement.
From The Lettres D'un Ami Francais Series.
Prod-SEABEN Dist-IFB 1962

Le Plan Americain - The American Shot C 16 MIN
16MM FILM OPTICAL SOUND
Tells how a young man who has stolen books from a bookstore in order to donate them to a public library meets and befriends a French-speaking young lady in a New York bookshop.
LC NO. 80-701232
Prod-WASSS Dist-WASSS 1979

Le Plat Du Jour C 13 MIN
16MM FILM, 3/4 OR 1/2 IN VIDEO
Offers a humorous look at Parisian eating habits, focusing on a cafe between the hours of noon and two.
Prod-CECILE Dist-CAROUF

Le Plus Petit Ange B 14 MIN
16MM FILM, 3/4 OR 1/2 IN VIDEO I-C
French version of 'THE LITTLEST ANGEL.' Presents the story of a little angel who gave his most prized possessions to the baby Jesus and how God chose that gift to shine as an inspiration for all men.
Prod-CORF Dist-CORF 1962

Le Pont C 13 MIN
16MM FILM OPTICAL SOUND J A
From The En Francais, Set 1 Series.
Prod-PEREN Dist-CHLTN 1969

Le Poulet B 16 MIN
16MM FILM, 3/4 OR 1/2 IN VIDEO
A French language motion picture. Tells the story of a boy who tries to save his pet chicken from becoming the family lunch.
Prod-FI Dist-TEXFLM

Le Printemps Est Une Aventure B 11 MIN
16MM FILM, 3/4 OR 1/2 IN VIDEO I-H
French version of 'SPRING IS AN ADVENTURE.' Shows changes and activities which come with spring, such as flowers budding and blooming, eggs hatching and the planting of a garden.
Prod-CORF Dist-CORF 1962

Le Pronom Relatif C
3/4 OR 1/2 INCH VIDEO CASSETTE
See series title for descriptive statement.
From The French Language Videotapes (French) Series.
Prod-UCEMC Dist-UCEMC

Le Quatorze Juillet C 15 MIN
16MM FILM, 3/4 OR 1/2 IN VIDEO
See series title for descriptive statement.
From The Lettres D'un Ami Francais Series.
Prod-SEABEN Dist-IFB 1962

Le Quebec Au Temps Des Froidures C 15 MIN
16MM FILM OPTICAL SOUND
A French language version of Quebec In The Colder Months. Depicts winter sports in Canada.
LC NO. 76-702047
Prod-QDTFG Dist-CTFL Prodn-SDAPRO 1975

Le Restaurant B 13 MIN
16MM FILM OPTICAL SOUND J-C
See series title for descriptive statement.
From The En France Avec Jean Et Helen Series. Set 1, Lesson 10
LC NO. 77-704514
Prod-PEREN Dist-CHLTN 1967

Le Retour D'Afrique B 109 MIN
16MM FILM OPTICAL SOUND
An English subtitle version of the French language, Swiss-made film. Presents a political parable about a young Swiss couple with radical leanings who find themselves on the brink of settling into a bourgeois life in Geneva. Includes screwball comedy elements as the couple decides to move to Algeria, but are stranded midway between the two continents.
Prod-NYFLMS Dist-NYFLMS 1973

Le Rhin C 7 MIN
16MM FILM, 3/4 OR 1/2 IN VIDEO H-C A
A French language videocassette. Presents the different faces of the Rhine river.
From The Chroniques De France Series.
LC NO. 81-706547
Prod-ADPF Dist-IFB 1980

Le Socrate C 90 MIN
16MM FILM OPTICAL SOUND
A French language film. Deals with a poor wandering philosopher in a crisis who is being followed around the countryside by a police inspector.
Prod-NYFLMS Dist-NYFLMS 1969

Le Subjonctif C
3/4 OR 1/2 INCH VIDEO CASSETTE
See series title for descriptive statement.
From The French Language Videotapes (French) Series.
Prod-UCEMC Dist-UCEMC

Le Tambou, The Drum Of Haiti C 19 MIN
16MM FILM OPTICAL SOUND
Shows the crafting of Haiti's unique tambou, a drum used in religious and cultural activities on the island, and points out its special place in the lives of the people.
LC NO. 74-700513
Prod-NLC Dist-NLC 1973

Le Telephone B 6 MIN
16MM FILM OPTICAL SOUND I-C A
A French language film. Pictures Monsieur Brun waiting his turn at the telephone booth. Captures the changing intonations from mild irritation to despair.
From The Voix Et Images De France Series.
Prod-PEREN Dist-CHLTN Prodn-CRDDF 1962

Le Temps Des Cathedrales—A Series

Explores Western Christian civilization and its evolution from the 11th to the 14th centuries by viewing cathedrals, sites and art objects.
Prod-FACSEA Dist-FACSEA 1979

Dieu Est Lumiere - God Is Light 052 MIN
L'Europe De L'An Mil - Europe In The Year 1000 052 MIN
La Cathedrale, La Ville, L'Ecole - Cathedral, 052 MIN
La Quete De Dieu - The Quest For God 052 MIN
Le Bonheur Et La Mort - Happiness And Death 052 MIN
Le Tournant Du 14e Siecle - The Turn Of The 052 MIN
Les Nations S'Affirment - Nations Assert 052 MIN
Roi, Chavalier Et Saint - King, Knight And 052 MIN
Vers Des Temps Nouveaux - Toward New Times 052 MIN

Le Theatre Des Jeunes B 13 MIN
16MM FILM OPTICAL SOUND J-C
See series title for descriptive statement.
From The En France Avec Jean Et Helen Series. Set 1, Lesson 7
LC NO. 70-704515
Prod-PEREN Dist-CHLTN 1967

Le Tourisme C 19 MIN
16MM FILM, 3/4 OR 1/2 IN VIDEO H-C
Includes requesting a hotel room, ordering breakfast, asking for a campsite and visiting a Syndical d'Initiative. Shows tourist attractions around Saumer, interviews with a hotel proprietor and the director of a youth sports center.
From The La France Telle Qu'Elle Est Series.
Prod-THAMES Dist-MEDIAG 1977

Le Tournant De 14e Siecle - The Turn Of The 14th Century C 52 MIN
16MM FILM OPTICAL SOUND
Shows that although Western Europe is ravaged by famine and black plague during the 14th century, spotty prosperity still occurs. Reveals that statesman patronize artists while the works of Dante and Giotto mingle the profane with the religious.
From The Le Temp Des Cathedrales Series.
Prod-FACSEA Dist-FACSEA 1979

Le Vieux Paris (The Latin Quarter) C 15 MIN
16MM FILM OPTICAL SOUND J-C
A French language film. Presents the adventures of Caroline, Elisabeth and Jacques as they travel through the Ile de la Cite and the Palace des Vosges.
From The Toute La Bande Series. No. 12
LC NO. 73-715479
Prod-SCHMAG Dist-SCHMAG 1970

Le Vilain Caneton X 11 MIN
16MM FILM, 3/4 OR 1/2 IN VIDEO I-H
French version of 'THE UGLY DUCKLING.' Follows the misfortunes of the unwanted Ugly Duckling who grows into a beautiful swan.
Prod-CORF Dist-CORF 1960

Le Village, Un Village (France) C 22 MIN
16MM FILM, 3/4 OR 1/2 IN VIDEO
Views life in Le Village, Sainte Alvere in the Dordogne region of France. Describes the annual village festival and shows the marriage of the town's motor mechanic to a girl from a smaller nearby town.
From The Village Life Series.
Prod-JOU Dist-JOU 1979

Le Vin Rose C 13 MIN
16MM FILM OPTICAL SOUND J A
From The En Francais, Set 1 Series.
Prod-PEREN Dist-CHLTN 1969

Lead In Motion C 20 MIN
16MM FILM OPTICAL SOUND
A revised version of The Lead Matrix. Documents the use of lead from Biblical times to the present, discussing the location of lead deposits, refining techniques, characteristics of lead and its use in industry.
Prod-USDIBM Dist-USDIBM

Lead In Motion C 22 MIN
16MM FILM OPTICAL SOUND
Discusses lead energy in one of its most dense arrangements. Explains that lead, when refined, is one of the purest raw materials known to man. It resists vibrations and blocks radiation. Shows lead being mined and refined, with the careful extraction of such precious metals as copper, zinc and silver.
Prod-WSTGLC Dist-WSTGLC

Lead Paint Poisoning C 5 MIN
16MM FILM OPTICAL SOUND H-C A
Overviews the lead paint problem and some of the steps being taken by the Federal government, particularly the Department of Housing and Urban Development and the National Bureau of Standards, to overcome it.
LC NO. 73-702597
Prod-USNBOS Dist-USNBOS 1972

Lead Poisoning C 1 MIN
16MM FILM OPTICAL SOUND
Warns parents of children living in older homes and apartments of the dangers of lead poisoning. Uses cinema verite showing children playing in areas where cracked and peeling paint and plaster are obvious.
LC NO. 74-700347
Prod-NPVLA Dist-WSTGLC 1973

Lead Poisoning - The Hidden Epidemic C 10 MIN
16MM FILM OPTICAL SOUND J-C A
Discusses the causes, testing and preventative methods of childhood lead poisoning.
LC NO. 72-701738
Prod-LIFLMS Dist-LIFLMS 1972

Lead Poisoning Could Strike Your Child C 22 MIN
16MM FILM, 3/4 OR 1/2 IN VIDEO J-C A
Reveals the most common source of lead poisoning, the life-saving medical treatment applied to children who have eaten lead-contaminated paint and the steps to decontaminate, walls, ceilings and woodwork.
Prod-SPCTRI Dist-MCFI 1980

Lead Shoes, The B 18 MIN
16MM FILM OPTICAL SOUND C A
Sidney Peterson, who deals with parricide and the compulsive efforts to undo the deed.
Prod-GROVE Dist-GROVE

Lead Your Horse C 61 MIN
1/2 IN VIDEO CASSETTE BETA/VHS
Demonstrates the steps in training a horse to lead. Shows how to train horses from ten-day-old foals to mature adults.
From The Horse Care And Training Series.
Prod-MOHOMV Dist-MOHOMV

Lead, Nickel, Tin And Zinc C 12 MIN
3/4 OR 1/2 INCH VIDEO CASSETTE
Covers the use, production and properties of lead, nickel, tin and zinc.
From The Working With Metals In The Plant Series.
Prod-TPCTRA Dist-TPCTRA

Leadbelly C 52 MIN
3/4 OR 1/2 INCH VIDEO CASSETTE
Presents a solo performance by Pete Seeger in which he sings some of the songs composed by the famous black folksinger Hudie Ledbetter.
From The Rainbow Quest Series.
Prod-SEEGER Dist-CWATER

Leader Of The People, The C 23 MIN
16MM FILM, 3/4 OR 1/2 IN VIDEO J-C A
Records the reactions of a little boy and his family as they listen to their grandfather's tales of his adventures as a wagon leader during the westward migrations on the American frontier. Based on the story The Leader Of The People by John Steinbeck.
Prod-WILETS Dist-BARR 1979

Leaders C 11 MIN
16MM FILM OPTICAL SOUND H-C A
Uses split-screen techniques in order to show the multi-disciplinary career opportunites available to officers in Australia's modern army.
LC NO. 76-700567
Prod-FLMAUS Dist-AUIS 1975

Leaders In American Medicine - A Mc Gehee Harvey, MD C 60 MIN
16MM FILM - 3/4 IN VIDEO PRO
Presents an interview with Dr A Mc Gehee Harvey, who discusses the role of the physician in problem solving and explains his interest in the application of the scientific method to clinical problem solving.
LC NO. 78-706147
Prod-NMAC Dist-USNAC Prodn-AOMA 1977

Leaders In American Medicine - Abraham White, Ph D, D Sc C 60 MIN
3/4 INCH VIDEO CASSETTE PRO
Presents an interview with Dr Abraham White, consulting professor of biochemistry at Stanford University School of Medicine, who describes his research in the field of biochemistry and dis-

cusses changes in laboratories, equipment and grants during the 30 years of his career.
LC NO. 79-706863
Prod-NMAC Dist-USNAC Prodn-NMAC 1979

Leaders In American Medicine - Albert Baird Hastings, Ph D, Sc D B 66 MIN
16MM FILM - 3/4 IN VIDEO PRO
Discusses major research being done by Dr Albert Hastings while at Harvard University. Recounts his interest and research in electrolyte composition, tetany and parathyroid tetany, intermediary metabolism of lactic acid in the liver, the effect of chemicals on the mechanical work of the heart and other applications of biochemistry.
LC NO. 76-706155
Prod-NMAC Dist-USNAC 1971

Leaders In American Medicine - Alexander D Langmuir, MD C 60 MIN
3/4 OR 1/2 INCH VIDEO CASSETTE
Presents Dr Alexander D Langmuir, former Chief Epidemiologist of the Center for Disease Control, discussing his career in epidemiology and his contributions at the Center for Disease Control.
LC NO. 80-706828
Prod-NMAC Dist-USNAC 1979

Leaders In American Medicine - Cecil J Watson, MD C 58 MIN
16MM FILM - 3/4 IN VIDEO PRO
Presents Dr Cecil J Watson discussing his career as a clinician, teacher and investigator. Stresses the need for a closer tie between medicine, research and teaching.
LC NO. 76-706132
Prod-NMAC Dist-USNAC Prodn-AOMA 1977

Leaders In American Medicine - Charles Huggins, MD C 60 MIN
16MM FILM - 3/4 IN VIDEO PRO
Recounts the life of Dr Charles Huggins and his research in endocrinology and prostatic cancer. Includes his work on bone marrow, his interest and work in the physiology and control of disease with the introduction of chemotherapy and his views on medical education and the future role of medicine.
LC NO. 76-706133
Prod-NMAC Dist-USNAC 1972

Leaders In American Medicine - David Seegal, MD C 37 MIN
16MM FILM - 3/4 IN VIDEO PRO
Provides insight into the teaching methods used by Dr David Seegal at Columbia University. Examines the reasons for his effectiveness in motivating his students.
LC NO. 77-706201
Prod-NMAC Dist-USNAC Prodn-AOMA

Leaders In American Medicine - Dorothy M Horstmann, MD C 60 MIN
3/4 INCH VIDEO CASSETTE PRO
Presents Dr Dorothy M Horstmann, professor of epidemiology and pediatrics at Yale University School of Medicine, discussing her interest in infectious diseases, her work in testing polio virus, her interest in rubella and future problems relating to infectious diseases.
LC NO. 79-706864
Prod-NMAC Dist-USNAC 1979

Leaders In American Medicine - Dwight L Wilbur, MD C 59 MIN
16MM FILM - 3/4 IN VIDEO PRO
Presents an interview with Dr Dwight L Wilbur. Describes his family background and tells why he became a doctor. Examines his schooling at Stanford University and the University of Pennsylvania and his position at the Mayo Clinic. Explores his work with the American Medical Association.
LC NO. 77-706196
Prod-NMAC Dist-USNAC Prodn-AOMA

Leaders In American Medicine - Emile Holman, MD C 51 MIN
16MM FILM - 3/4 IN VIDEO PRO
Presents Dr Emile Holman discussing his career in medicine at Stanford University, his experience as a Rhodes scholar and his research contributions in cardiovascular physiology and surgery with special emphasis on arteriovenous fistulae.
LC NO. 76-706156
Prod-NMAC Dist-USNAC Prodn-AOMA 1974

Leaders In American Medicine - Franz J Ingelfinger, MD B 59 MIN
16MM FILM OPTICAL SOUND PRO
Describes the success of Dr Franz J Ingelfinger in two separate areas of medicine. Discusses his research accomplishments in gastroenterology and reviews the nine years he spent as editor of the New England Journal Of Medicine.
LC NO. 77-703507
Prod-NMAC Dist-USNAC Prodn-AOMA

Leaders In American Medicine - Franz J Ingelfinger, MD C 39 MIN
3/4 INCH VIDEO CASSETTE PRO
Describes the success of Dr Franz J Ingelfinger in two separate areas of medicine. Discusses his research accomplishments in gastroenterology and reviews the nine years he spent as editor of the New England Journal Of Medicine.
LC NO. 77-706202
Prod-NMAC Dist-USNAC Prodn-AOMA

Leaders In American Medicine - George L Engel, MD C 61 MIN
16MM FILM - 3/4 IN VIDEO PRO
Presents Dr George L Engel discussing the influence of his family and the strong need for self-identity which led to his dual specialization in internal medicine and psychiatry. Tells about his studies of the use of EEG on delirious patients, high altitude decompression and the psychosomatic factors of pain.
LC NO. 76-706134
Prod-NMAC Dist-USNAC Prodn-AOMA 1974

Leaders In American Medicine - George W Corner, MD C 57 MIN
16MM FILM - 3/4 IN VIDEO PRO
Presents an interview with Dr George W Corner, who speaks of his early days at Johns Hopkins and the people who influenced his career in medicine. Includes comments on his studies of the menstrual cycle, its causes and effects and the discovery of the corpus luteum hormone later termed progesterone.
LC NO. 76-706135
Prod-NMAC Dist-USNAC Prodn-AOMA 1974

Leaders In American Medicine - Grace A Goldsmith, MD C 58 MIN
16MM FILM - 3/4 IN VIDEO PRO
Presents an interview with Dr Grace A Goldsmith, who discusses her interest in nutritional and metabolic diseases. Recalls her research on drugs and diet and their effect on lipid metabolism and chronic cardiovascular diseases. Discusses her research on niacin, vitamin C and riboflavin which led to the establishment of minimum daily requirement standards.
LC NO. 76-706136
Prod-NMAC Dist-USNAC Prodn-AOMA 1974

Leaders In American Medicine - H W Magoun, MD C 60 MIN
3/4 OR 1/2 INCH VIDEO CASSETTE
Presents H W Magoun, professor emeritus at the University of California at Los Angeles Brain Research Institute, discussing his career and his research in the field of poliomyelitis and electroencephalography.
LC NO. 80-706810
Prod-NMAC Dist-USNAC 1979

Leaders In American Medicine - Helen B Taussig, MD C 50 MIN
16MM FILM - 3/4 IN VIDEO PRO
Presents Dr Helen B Taussig discussing her medical education at Johns Hopkins, where she later became the first woman to be appointed a full professor. Discusses her pediatric internship, her interest in congenital heart deformations and her research on pediatric malformations due to the use of thalidomide, which led to the warning of American officials of the dangers of the drug.
LC NO. 76-706137
Prod-NMAC Dist-USNAC Prodn-AOMA 1973

Leaders In American Medicine - Henry G Schwartz, MD C 59 MIN
16MM FILM - 3/4 IN VIDEO PRO
Interviews Dr Henry G Schwartz, Professor of Neurological Surgery at Washington University School of Medicine. Describes his years in medical school and explains how a project on the regeneration of earthworms led him to specialize in anatomy and the physiology of the nervous system.
LC NO. 77-706203
Prod-NMAC Dist-USNAC Prodn-AOMA

Leaders In American Medicine - Howard C Taylor, Jr, MD C 57 MIN
16MM FILM - 3/4 IN VIDEO PRO
Presents Dr Howard C Taylor describing the early days of internships in surgery and gynecology prior to the initiation of National Board exams. Discusses his papers in the areas of family planning, psychosomatic uterine congestion and endometrial hyperplasia.
LC NO. 76-706138
Prod-NMAC Dist-USNAC Prodn-AOMA 1974

Leaders In American Medicine - Irvine H Page, MD C 60 MIN
3/4 INCH VIDEO CASSETTE PRO
Presents an interview with Dr Irvine H Page, director emeritus, Research Division, Cleveland Clinic, who discusses his life and work in the field of hypertension.
LC NO. 79-706865
Prod-NMAC Dist-USNAC Prodn-NMAC 1979

Leaders In American Medicine - Jacques Genest, MD, CC C 51 MIN
16MM FILM - 3/4 IN VIDEO PRO
Presents an interview with Dr Jacques Genest. Discusses his medical education and numerous awards. Highlights the beginning of the Clinical Research Institute in Montreal.
LC NO. 77-706139
Prod-NMAC Dist-USNAC Prodn-AOMA

Leaders In American Medicine - James V Warren, MD C 60 MIN
3/4 OR 1/2 INCH VIDEO CASSETTE
Presents James V Warren, MD, discussing the circumstances that led him to a career in academic medicine at Ohio State University, Department of Medicine. Describes his use of the cardiac catheter and his thoughts on medical education and the future of internal medicine.
LC NO. 80-706811
Prod-NMAC Dist-USNAC 1979

Leaders In American Medicine - John F Enders, Ph D And Frederick C Robbins, MD B 34 MIN
16MM FILM - 3/4 IN VIDEO
Presents Drs John F Enders and Frederick C Robbins discussing the discovery of the capacity of the poliomyelitis virus to grow in cultures of various tissues in vitro. Points out their contributions as part of a three-man team that won the 1954 Nobel Prize for medicine and physiology.
LC NO. 76-706140
Prod-NMAC Dist-USNAC 1974

Leaders In American Medicine - John P Hubbard, MD C 58 MIN
16MM FILM - 3/4 IN VIDEO PRO
Presents Dr John P Hubbard, who tells why he decided to study medicine and describes his activities during World War II. Discusses his contribution as the Executive Director of the National Board of Medical Examiners.
LC NO. 78-706148
Prod-NMAC Dist-USNAC Prodn-AOMA 1978

Leaders In American Medicine - Jonathan E Rhoads, MD C 57 MIN
16MM FILM - 3/4 IN VIDEO PRO
Highlights the significant achievements of Dr Jonathan E Rhoads' medical career at the University of Pennsylvania. Describes his early schooling and his college years. Examines his years in medical school and his decision to pursue a career in surgery.
LC NO. 77-706198
Prod-NMAC Dist-USNAC Prodn-AOMA

Leaders In American Medicine - Joseph T Wearn, MD B 48 MIN
16MM FILM - 3/4 IN VIDEO
Presents Dr Joseph Wearn discussing his career, philosophy and experience as an educator with Dr Thomas Hale Ham, with whom he was associated in an experiment in medical education. Recalls how a young faculty was organized and a new curriculum adopted at Case Western Reserve University.
LC NO. 76-706141
Prod-NMAC Dist-USNAC 1973

Leaders In American Medicine - Karl F Meyer, MD C 59 MIN
16MM FILM - 3/4 IN VIDEO PRO
Presents Dr Karl F Meyer discussing his work in the field of microbiology and immunology. Covers his work in setting standards for quality control in the canning industry, his research efforts in the development of a vaccine against plague and his work in psittacosis, brucellosis, relapsing fever, valley fever and the toxic effects of shellfish poisoning.
LC NO. 76-706142
Prod-NMAC Dist-USNAC Prodn-AOMA 1974

Leaders In American Medicine - L T Coggeshall, MD C 55 MIN
16MM FILM - 3/4 IN VIDEO PRO
Discusses the career of Dr L T Coggeshall as a teacher and researcher. Covers his studies and research in malaria immunology and chemotherapy as well as his role in helping to establish the University of Chicago School of Medicine.
LC NO. 77-706143
Prod-NMAC Dist-USNAC Prodn-AOMA

Leaders In American Medicine - Leo G Rigler, MD B 60 MIN
16MM FILM - 3/4 IN VIDEO
Presents Dr Leo G Rigler highlighting his lifetime experience and research in the science of radiology. Comments on the foundation of professional societies concerned with radiology and on residency programs in Minnesota.
LC NO. 76-706144
Prod-NMAC Dist-USNAC 1973

Leaders In American Medicine - Lester R Dragstedt, Ph D, MD C 60 MIN
16MM FILM - 3/4 IN VIDEO PRO
Features Dr Lester Dragstedt and his first research on gastric ulcers and the cause of pain. Discusses his later research on physiology and peptic ulcers, which led to the introduction of vagotomy as a surgical technique for duodenal ulcers. Highlights Dragstedt's experiences in Europe, where he studied abdominal surgery.
LC NO. 76-706145
Prod-NMAC Dist-USNAC 1972

Leaders In American Medicine - Martin M Cummings, MD C 45 MIN
16MM FILM - 3/4 IN VIDEO PRO
Presents Dr Martin M Cummings, Director of the National Library of Medicine, giving a brief autobiographical profile and an historical review of the founding of the library. Emphasizes the role played by Dr John Shaw Billings in the development of the institution.
LC NO. 76-706146
Prod-NMAC Dist-USNAC Prodn-AOMA 1973

Leaders In American Medicine - Matthew Walker, MD C 56 MIN
16MM FILM - 3/4 IN VIDEO PRO
Discusses the medical career of Dr Matthew Walker. Tells about his efforts to train more surgeons, his responsibility for the success or failure of his students and his concern for the delivery of comprehensive health care to ghettos and rural areas.
LC NO. 77-706147
Prod-NMAC Dist-USNAC Prodn-AOMA

Leaders In American Medicine - Maxwell Finland, MD B 58 MIN
16MM FILM - 3/4 IN VIDEO PRO
Presents Dr Maxwell Finland discussing his medical career, his interest in infectious diseases, his scientific insights in observation of patients and the use of clinical drugs.
LC NO. 78-706085
Prod-NMAC Dist-USNAC Prodn-AOMA 1977

Leaders In American Medicine - Maxwell M Wintrobe, MD C 57 MIN
16MM FILM - 3/4 IN VIDEO PRO
Presents Dr Maxwell M Wintrobe reviewing some of the major contributions in the area of hemotology which bear his credits. Discusses his contribution in effecting a classification system for the anemias and his role in the development of more precise laboratory procedures and equipment.

LC NO. 76-706148
Prod-NMAC Dist-USNAC Prodn-AOMA 1974

Leaders In American Medicine - Medical Teaching Philosophies B 30 MIN
16MM FILM - 3/4 IN VIDEO PRO
Expresses scientists' philosophies of medical education with excerpts from interviews with several leaders in the field.
LC NO. 76-706254
Prod-NMAC Dist-USNAC 1976

Leaders In American Medicine - Owen H Wangensteen, MD C 60 MIN
16MM FILM - 3/4 IN VIDEO PRO
Describes the career of Dr Owen Wangensteen, including his work as a surgeon and his research experiments on the etiology of appendicitis and the etiology and surgical treatment of peptic ulcers and esophagitis. Emphasizes the importance of the history of medicine in medical education and the importance of encouraging and sharing opportunities with students.
LC NO. 76-706150
Prod-NMAC Dist-USNAC 1972

Leaders In American Medicine - Owsei Temkin, MD C
3/4 OR 1/2 INCH VIDEO CASSETTE PRO
Presents an interview with Dr Owsei Temkin in which he recounts his arrival in the United States from Leipzig and his work at Johns Hopkins University with such personalities as Osler and Welch. Discusses the role of the sciences in the evolution of medicine as a profession.
LC NO. 81-707186
Prod-NMAC Dist-USNAC 1979

Leaders In American Medicine - Paul B Besson, MD And Eugene A Stead, Jr, MD C 60 MIN
16MM FILM - 3/4 IN VIDEO PRO
Presents an interview between Dr Paul B Besson, distinguished physician at the U S veterans Administration, and Dr Eugene A Stead, Jr, professor of medicine at Duke University Medical Center. Discusses their separate careers as well as their previous work together.
LC NO. 78-706112
Prod-NMAC Dist-USNAC Prodn-AOMA 1977

Leaders In American Medicine - Robert H Williams, MD C 60 MIN
16MM FILM - 3/4 IN VIDEO PRO
Presents Dr Robert H Williams discussing his activities in the field of endocrinology, his philosophy of life, his teaching techniques and his views on patient care, the role of the administrator and the politics of medicine.
LC NO. 78-706149
Prod-NMAC Dist-USNAC Prodn-AOMA 1978

Leaders In American Medicine - Russell V Lee, MD C 57 MIN
16MM FILM - 3/4 IN VIDEO PRO
Examines the medical career of Dr Russell V Lee. Describes his change from chemistry to medicine during his years at Stanford University. Examines his efforts to raise the standards of medical care in Palo Alto through the formation of a group medical clinic.
LC NO. 77-706197
Prod-NMAC Dist-USNAC Prodn-AOMA

Leaders In American Medicine - Shields Warren, MD C 61 MIN
16MM FILM - 3/4 IN VIDEO PRO
Presents Dr Shields Warren discussing his academic career, his research in the pathology of diabetes, his association with the Atomic Energy Commission, his research in radiation pathology and the introduction of the use of isotopes in the biomedical field.
LC NO. 76-706151
Prod-NMAC Dist-USNAC Prodn-AOMA 1973

Leaders In American Medicine - T R Harrison, MD C 55 MIN
16MM FILM - 3/4 IN VIDEO PRO
Discusses the career of Dr T R Harrison. Examines his years at Johns Hopkins, Vanderbilt and Peter Bent Brigham Hospital. Highlights his tenure as chairman of the Department of Medicine at the University of Alabama.
LC NO. 77-706152
Prod-NMAC Dist-USNAC Prodn-AOMA

Leaders In American Medicine - W Montague Cobb, MD B 58 MIN
16MM FILM - 3/4 IN VIDEO
Discusses the influence of parents and teachers on the goals and ideals of Dr W Montague Cobb. Recounts his professional training, his work at Howard University and his role in helping to gain equal rights for Black physicians.
LC NO. 76-706255
Prod-NMAC Dist-USNAC 1976

Leaders In American Medicine - Walsh Mc Dermott, MD B 60 MIN
16MM FILM - 3/4 IN VIDEO PRO
Presents the views of Dr Walsh Mc Dermott on the state of American medicine and on the future of medical education. Discusses Mc Dermott's early research on infectious diseases and his experimentation with laboratory animals in field testing the antimicrobial drugs streptomycin and isoniazid. Recalls the development of a research program for the prevention and control of tuberculosis in Navaho Indians and tells about the problems that were solved.
LC NO. 76-706154
Prod-NMAC Dist-USNAC 1971

Leaders In American Medicine - William Barry Wood, Jr, MD C 60 MIN
16MM FILM - 3/4 IN VIDEO PRO
Presents Dr William Barry Wood, Jr giving highlights of his early years at Harvard College and Johns Hopkins University. Describes his work with mechanisms of disease, pneumococcal pneumonia and the pathogenesis of fever.
LC NO. 76-706153
Prod-NMAC Dist-USNAC 1971

Leaders In American Medicine - William P Longmire, Jr, MD And Francis D Moore, MD C 60 MIN
3/4 INCH VIDEO CASSETTE PRO
Presents an interview between Dr William P Longmire, Jr, professor of surgery at the University of California at Los Angeles School of Medicine, and Dr Francis D Moore, professor of surgery at Harvard Medical School. Discusses their early careers in medicine and the discoveries in the field of surgery that became milestones during their careers.
LC NO. 79-706866
Prod-NMAC Dist-USNAC Prodn-AOMA 1979

Leaders Of The 20th Century - Portraits Of Power—A Series
16MM FILM, 3/4 OR 1/2 IN VIDEO H-C A
Presents eight portraits of leaders, described by journalists who had first-hand experience with their subjects.
Prod-NIELSE Dist-LCOA 1979

Adenauer - Germany Reborn 024 MIN
Ben-Gurion - One Place, One People 024 MIN
Churchill - Voice Of A Lion 024 MIN
Churchill - Voice Of A Prophet 024 MIN
De Gaulle - Force Of Character 024 MIN
De Gaulle - Republican Monarch 024 MIN
Eisenhower - Years Of Caution 024 MIN
Elizabeth II - Winds Of Change 024 MIN
End Of The Old Order, The - 1900-1918 024 MIN
Franco - Caudillo Of Spain 024 MIN
Hirohito - The Chrysanthemum Throne 024 MIN
Hitler - Revenge To Ruin 024 MIN
Hitler - The Road To Revenge 024 MIN
Kennedy - Years Of Charisma 024 MIN
Khrushchev - The Bear's Embrace 024 MIN
Mahatma Gandhi - Soul Force 024 MIN
Mao - Long March To Power 024 MIN
Mao - Organized Chaos 024 MIN
Mohammed Reza Pahlavi - Politics Of Oil 024 MIN
Nasser - People's Pharaoh 024 MIN
Roosevelt - Hail To The Chief 024 MIN
Roosevelt - Manipulator-In-Chief 024 MIN
Stalin - Man And Image 024 MIN
Stalin - The Power Of Fear 024 MIN
Tito - Power Of Resistance 024 MIN
Truman - Years Of Decision 024 MIN

Leaders Of Tomorrow B 20 MIN
16MM FILM OPTICAL SOUND
Portrays Japanese teen-age boys and girls learning the principles of democracy at the Youth Training Centers sponsored in Japan by the American Red Cross and the Allied Powers.
LC NO. FIE52-1946
Prod-USA Dist-USNAC 1949

Leadership C 18 MIN
16MM FILM, 3/4 OR 1/2 IN VIDEO
Uses dramatic re-creations of actual situations to illustrate the impact of various leadership styles and the effectiveness of the supervisor. Points out that leadership can be learned and that there is no absolutely right way to lead.
From The Supervisory Development For Law Enforcement Series. Part 1
Prod-HAR Dist-MTI

Leadership C 20 MIN
3/4 OR 1/2 INCH VIDEO CASSETTE
See series title for descriptive statement.
From The Effective Manager Series.
Prod-DELTAK Dist-DELTAK

Leadership C 30 MIN
3/4 OR 1/2 INCH VIDEO CASSETTE
See series title for descriptive statement.
From The Effective Supervision Series.
Prod-ERF Dist-DELTAK

Leadership - Let's Get Started—A Series
A
Presents in a series of four videocassettes of 74 minutes Brownie and Junior Girl Scout leaders' instruction on how to structure a meeting and explains recognition awards. Shows Girl Scout leaders sharing their experiences.
LC NO. 84-706025
Prod-GSUSA Dist-GSUSA 1980

Leadership - Style Or Circumstance C 30 MIN
16MM FILM, 3/4 OR 1/2 IN VIDEO H-C A
Identifies and differentiates two diverse types of leaders, the relationship-oriented leader and the task-oriented leader. Shows how each type of leader can work effectively depending on the job situation.
Prod-CRMP Dist-CRMP 1975

Leadership - Working With People C
3/4 OR 1/2 INCH VIDEO CASSETTE
Stresses the importance of a manager in assessing and developing a philosophy of management as the basis for leadership. Identifies and analyzes the various leadership styles.
From The Principles Of Management Series.
Prod-RMI Dist-RMI

Leadership And Growth C 30 MIN
3/4 OR 1/2 INCH VIDEO CASSETTE
See series title for descriptive statement.
From The You - The Supervisor Series.
Prod-PRODEV Dist-DELTAK

Leadership And Small Work Group Dynamics C 27 MIN
16MM FILM, 3/4 OR 1/2 IN VIDEO
Presents Dr Verne J Kallejian who offers a chalkboard lecture in which he describes how to integrate the needs of people within an organization. Cites the family and the military as classic examples of need-oriented and task-oriented institutions and defines organizational efficiency as the optimization of the two factors.
From The Management Development Series.
Prod-UCLA Dist-UCEMC 1976

Leadership Issues - Theoretical And Pragmatic C 30 MIN
16MM FILM - 3/4 IN VIDEO PRO
Describes different approaches to leadership in nursing. Includes case studies which identify leadership behavior and skills. Defines leadership as a process rather than authority or power of position, emphasizing the interpersonal nature of leadership.
From The Dimensions Of Leadership In Nursing Series.
LC NO. 77-702472
Prod-AJN Dist-AJN Prodn-CATTN 1977

Leadership Link - Fundamentals Of Effective Supervision—A Series
Deals with the role of the supervisor, which has increased in importance and is expected to continue to grow. Includes a two-part program, with the manager completing the first part and the participant completing the second part. Includes a student text, a student handout and a personal resource handbook.
Prod-CHSH Dist-DELTAK

Managing Energy, Effort, Time, And Money 014 MIN
Peermanship 010 MIN
Role Of The Supervisor, The 017 MIN
Solid Performance Leadership 018 MIN
Straightforward Communication 019 MIN

Leadership Roles - First Line To Executive C 45 MIN
3/4 OR 1/2 INCH VIDEO CASSETTE PRO
Describes the role of nurse as a leader and presents principles of effective management. Outlines the philosophical and detailed process of management practices for top leadership positions.
From The Nursing Career Development Series. Pt 3
LC NO. 81-707109
Prod-USVA Dist-USNAC 1981

Leadership Styles C 20 MIN
3/4 OR 1/2 INCH VIDEO CASSETTE
Offers a dramatization showing how to work well with any type of boss, including the authoritarian boss, the humanitarian boss and the 'little bit of both' boss.
Prod-AMA Dist-AMA

Leadership—A Series
Looks at collective skills of leadership. Uses participative techniques, examines traits of leadership and how they are acquired and then applies sound leadership skills to a variety of on-the-job situation.
Prod-RESEM Dist-RESEM

Applied Leadership 018 MIN
Nature Of Leadership 015 MIN
Styles Of Leadership 018 MIN

Leadfoot C 27 MIN
16MM FILM, 3/4 OR 1/2 IN VIDEO J-H A
Shows how Tom is so proud of his first car that he ignores the efforts of the police to get him to drive carefully. Explains that he eventually tumbles into a ravine while driving carelessly and kills his girlfriend. Stars Philip McKeon and Peter Barton.
Prod-PAULST Dist-MEDIAG 1984

Leading C 50 MIN
3/4 OR 1/2 INCH VIDEO CASSETTE PRO
Surveys alternative organizational options. Stresses coordination, time management and motivation.
From The Project Management For Engineers Series.
Prod-AMCEE Dist-AMCEE

Leading A First Group Session C 88 MIN
3/4 INCH VIDEO CASSETTE C A
Explores some of the skills involved in leading a group session. Discusses clarifying purpose and role for group members, reaching for feedback, encouraging interaction, evaluating the first session, and other skills.
From The Skills Of Helping Series. Program 2
LC NO. 80-707459
Prod-MCGILU Dist-SYRCU 1980

Leading Application C 20 MIN
1/2 IN VIDEO CASSETTE BETA/VHS
Deals with auto body repair. Covers cleaning, tinning, applying, and paddle finishing lead fill.
Prod-RMI Dist-RMI

Leading Discussions, Whole Class C 49 MIN
3/4 OR 1/2 INCH VIDEO CASSETTE T
Shows ways of stimulating different kinds of discussions and explains how to give directions and vary discussion format.
From The Strategies In College Teaching Series.
LC NO. 79-706291
Prod-IU Dist-IU 1977

Leading Effectively C
3/4 OR 1/2 INCH VIDEO CASSETTE
See series title for descriptive statement.
From The Management Training Series.
Prod-THGHT Dist-DELTAK

Leading Group Discussions C 27 MIN
16MM FILM OPTICAL SOUND C T

Demonstrates techniques for leading effective classroom discussions, including the abilities to respond to feelings, to clarify and summarize content, to pair feelings or content, to formulate stimulating questions and to provide feedback. Based on the book Facilitative Teaching - Theory And Practice by Joe Wittmer and Robert D Myrick.
LC NO. 77-703458
Prod-EDMDC Dist-EDMDC 1977

Leading Skills C 45 MIN
3/4 OR 1/2 INCH VIDEO CASSETTE IND
Discusses motivation theories, what managers can and can't do to improve motivations, the Pygmalion Principle, assessing personal strengths and weaknesses, communication and basic guides to help in working with people.
From The Basic Management Skills For Engineers And Scientists Series.
Prod-USCITV Dist-AMCEE

Leading The Parade C 13 MIN
16MM FILM OPTICAL SOUND
Features baton twirling performances by leading high school and college majorettes.
Prod-FLADC Dist-FLADC

Leadville C 5 MIN
16MM FILM OPTICAL SOUND
Shows the dance-theatre of Alex Hay, in which man is portrayed as a machine.
Prod-VANBKS Dist-VANBKS

Leaf C 8 MIN
16MM FILM OPTICAL SOUND I-C A
Presents an artistic expression of a leaf.
Prod-HRAW Dist-HRAW

Leaf C 15 MIN
16MM FILM OPTICAL SOUND
Discusses the impact of leaf tobacco on the economic and social life of the United States.
LC NO. 75-703516
Prod-TOBCCO Dist-MTP Prodn-CNCPTF 1974

Leaf From Nature, A, Pt 1 C 30 MIN
3/4 OR 1/2 INCH VIDEO CASSETTE J-H
Introduces the process of photosynthesis and the nature of catalytic reactions. Tells how the secret of the earth's energy production cycle is unlocked by a piece of cake and a blade of grass.
From The Natural History Of A Sunbeam Series.
Prod-KINGFT Dist-KINGFT

Leaf From Nature, A, Pt 2 C 30 MIN
3/4 OR 1/2 INCH VIDEO CASSETTE J-H
Presents Professor Porter probing the mysteries of photosynthesis by means of a photochemical reaction sunlight hitting a chlorophyll molecule.
From The Natural History Of A Sunbeam Series.
Prod-KINGFT Dist-KINGFT

Leaf Prints C 11 MIN
16MM FILM, 3/4 OR 1/2 IN VIDEO I-C A
Demonstrates a variety of print designs made with leaves.
Prod-ACORN Dist-LUF 1973

League Of Arab States C 28 MIN
3/4 INCH VIDEOTAPE
Interviews Ambassador Clovis Maksoud, permanent observer of the League of Arab States to the United Nations. Focuses on the objectives of the League.
From The International Byline Series.
Prod-PERRYM Dist-PERRYM

League Of Nations, The - The Hope Of Mankind C 52 MIN
16MM FILM - 1/2 IN VIDEO
Discusses the aftermath of World War I, including the creation of the League of Nations, the problems of the Weimar Republic, the establishment of dictatorships in Poland, Yugoslavia and Hungary, and Mussolini's rise to power in Italy.
From The Europe, The Mighty Continent Series. No. 7
LC NO. 79-707422
Prod-BBCTV Dist-TIMLIF 1976

League School For Seriously Disturbed Children—A Series

Prod-USBEH Dist-USNAC 1973

No Two Of These Kids Are Alike 28 MIN
One Hour A Week 18 MIN
Psycho-Educational Assessment 24 MIN
Teacher Support 15 MIN

Leak Surveys—A Series
IND
Designed to train new employees of a leak detection department about the types of leak surveys, the tools and equipment that are used and the methods employed in locating gas leaks.,
Prod-UTEXPE Dist-UTEXPE 1983

Leak Surveys, Pt 1 - Introduction 022 MIN
Leak Surveys, Pt 2 - Tools And Equipment 020 MIN
Leak Surveys, Pt 3 - Field Operations 024 MIN

Leak Surveys, Pt 1 - Introduction C 22 MIN
3/4 OR 1/2 INCH VIDEO CASSETTE IND
Describes what leak surveys are and their purpose. Explains components and properties of natural gas. Discusses the use of maps and recordkeeping and the three classes of gas leaks.
From The Leak Surveys Series.
Prod-UTEXPE Dist-UTEXPE 1983

Leak Surveys, Pt 2 - Tools And Equipment C 20 MIN
3/4 OR 1/2 INCH VIDEO CASSETTE IND
Discusses the combustible gas indicator, the flame pack, pipe locators and ethane detectors, all of which are used extensively in leak survey work.
From The Leak Surveys Series.
Prod-UTEXPE Dist-UTEXPE 1983

Leak Surveys, Pt 3 - Field Operations C 24 MIN
3/4 OR 1/2 INCH VIDEO CASSETTE IND
Covers the three methods of leak surveys, including vegetation, mobile and walking. Explains techniques unique to each method. Describes bar-hole tests and the use of probe bars in pinpointing a leak. Reviews the three classes of leaks and steps needed to classify a particular type of leak.
From The Leak Surveys Series.
Prod-UTEXPE Dist-UTEXPE 1983

Leak Test For Direct Reading Instruments C 5 MIN
1/2 IN VIDEO CASSETTE BETA/VHS
Discusses manometers and water analysis experiments.
Prod-RMI Dist-RMI

Leakey C 23 MIN
16MM FILM, 3/4 OR 1/2 IN VIDEO J-C A
Provides an intimate portait of Louis S B Leakey from his youth in Africa through his education at Cambridge to his seminal discoveries at Olduvai Gorge. Describes the work of his wife and son and the other scientists Leakey inspired, such as Jane Goodall, Dian Fossey and Birute Galdikas.
Prod-NGS Dist-NGS 1983

Leanne And Wayne C 8 MIN
16MM FILM OPTICAL SOUND
Presents two examples of the care offered to socially disadvantaged children in Australia.
LC NO. 80-700907
Prod-TASCOR Dist-TASCOR 1977

Leap, The C 7 MIN
16MM FILM OPTICAL SOUND J-C A
Presents a videographic film in which an ordinary man seems to interact physically with videographic apparitions, moving in and out of different space-time realities, fluctuating between the physical and the metaphysical with each stride of his leap toward freedom.
Prod-UWFKD Dist-UWFKD

Leaping Silver C 13 MIN
16MM FILM OPTICAL SOUND
Describes the fishing skills of expert Joan Salvato as she combats the powerful Atlantic salmon of Newfoundland with the lightest of tackle. Shows the use of equipment and demonstrates fishing techniques.
LC NO. 73-706952
Prod-CTFL Dist-CTFL 1969

Leaps And Bounds—A Series
T
Explains how primary students can be taught movement skills and an awareness of what they can do with their bodies.
Prod-HSDE Dist-AITECH 1984

Apparatus 015 MIN
Body Awareness And Control I 015 MIN
Body Awareness And Control II 015 MIN
Body Awareness And Control III 015 MIN
Creative Movement 015 MIN
Kicking 015 MIN
Locomotor Skills I 015 MIN
Locomotor Skills II 015 MIN
Locomotor Skills III 015 MIN
Overhand Throw And Ball Dodging 015 MIN
Projecting The Ball 015 MIN
Rope Jumping 015 MIN
Striking 015 MIN
Tumbling I 015 MIN
Tumbling II 015 MIN
Underhand Throw And Catching 015 MIN

Learn CPR C 28 MIN
3/4 OR 1/2 INCH VIDEO CASSETTE
Explains and demonstrates the basic skills of cardiopulmonary resuscitation. Covers such topics as heart attack symptoms, how to recognize cardiac arrest and how to perform CPR as a single rescuer.
Prod-AJN Dist-AJN

Learn From Criticism Game, The C 11 MIN
16MM FILM, 3/4 OR 1/2 IN VIDEO P
Presents a story about a little boy who is unhappy when his friends criticize him. Shows how children can evaluate and deal with criticism.
From The Learning Responsibility Series.
Prod-HIGGIN Dist-HIGGIN 1979

Learn From Disappointments Game, The C 11 MIN
16MM FILM, 3/4 OR 1/2 IN VIDEO P
Tells how a young girl learns that understanding disappointments often leads to something better.
From The Learning Responsibility Series.
Prod-HIGGIN Dist-HIGGIN 1979

Learn Not To Burn C 9 MIN
16MM FILM OPTICAL SOUND I-H A
A revised edition of the 1975 film Learn Not To Burn. Shows some common fire hazards around the house, including smoking in bed, the kitchen stove and improper house wiring. Illustrates proper emergency escape procedures and shows what to do when one's clothing catches fire.
LC NO. 76-701792
Prod-NFPA Dist-NFPA Prodn-TALDKR 1976

Learn Not To Burn (2nd Ed) C 9 MIN
3/4 INCH VIDEO CASSETTE I-H A
Shows some common fire hazards around the house, including smoking in bed, the kitchen stove and improper house wiring. Illustrates proper emergency escape procedures and shows what to do when one's clothing catches fire.
LC NO. 76-701792
Prod-NFPA Dist-NFPA Prodn-TALDKR 1976

Learn Not To Burn - Wherever You Are C 10 MIN
16MM FILM, 3/4 OR 1/2 IN VIDEO
Takes a new look at fire safety. Demonstrates how one can prevent and survive fire by practicing simple fires safety lessons.
Prod-NFPA Dist-NFPA

Learn PC Video Systems Introduction To Lotus 1-2-3 C
3/4 OR 1/2 INCH VIDEO CASSETTE A
Shows a complete training program for the Lotus 1-2-3 that is self paced. Explains which keys to press and what appears on the computer monitor.
Prod-DSIM Dist-DSIM

Learn To Deal C 30 MIN
3/4 OR 1/2 INCH VIDEO CASSETTE
See series title for descriptive statement.
From The Rebop Series.
Prod-WGBHTV Dist-MDCPB

Learn To Live With Stress - Programming The Body For Health C 19 MIN
16MM FILM, 3/4 OR 1/2 IN VIDEO
Explains that stress can cause heart problems, hypertension and a host of other threats to life. Describes the use of meditation to treat people with high blood pressure.
Prod-DOCUA Dist-CNEMAG

Learn To Ski—A Series

Prod-SFI Dist-SFI

Ski Classic
Ski Esta
Ski Moderne
Skiing

Learner-Controlled Instruction C 14 MIN
3/4 OR 1/2 INCH VIDEO CASSETTE
Introduces the technique of learner-controlled instruction which allows the teacher and student to 'contract' on learning goals. Gives do's and don'ts, successes and failures.
From The Dynamic Classroom Series.
Prod-RESEM Dist-RESEM

Learners With Problems C 30 MIN
3/4 OR 1/2 INCH VIDEO CASSETTE T
Shows how to cope with learners with problems when teaching adult basic education classes.
From The Basic Education - Teaching The Adult Series.
Prod-MDDE Dist-MDCPB

Learning B 10 MIN
16MM FILM OPTICAL SOUND
See series title for descriptive statement.
From The Parent Education - Attitude Films Series.
Prod-TC Dist-TC

Learning B 29 MIN
3/4 OR 1/2 INCH VIDEO CASSETTE
See series title for descriptive statement.
From The One Strong Link Series.
Prod-CUETV Dist-CUNIV 1971

Learning C 30 MIN
16MM FILM, 3/4 OR 1/2 IN VIDEO H-C A
Shows experiments in learning. B F Skinner and Richard Malott deal with operant conditioning. Nathan Azrin demonstrates aversive conditioning. Jack Hailman deals with sign stimuli, and G P Baerends demonstrates super-normal conditioning. Explains the work of David Mc Clelland on motivation training and the work of Lewis Lipsitt on infant learning.
From The Psychology Today Films Series.
Prod-CRMP Dist-CRMP 1971

Learning C 30 MIN
3/4 OR 1/2 INCH VIDEO CASSETTE C
See series title for descriptive statement.
From The Artificial Intelligence, Pt 1 - Fundamental Concepts Series.
Prod-MIOT Dist-AMCEE

Learning C 45 MIN
3/4 OR 1/2 INCH VIDEO CASSETTE PRO
Discusses learning by being told and learning by examples and near misses. Features modeling, teaching, and an illustration.
From The Artificial Intelligence - Pt 1, Fundamental Concepts Series.
Prod-MIOT Dist-MIOT

Learning - A Happy Experience C 16 MIN
16MM FILM, 3/4 OR 1/2 IN VIDEO C A
Explains that elementary grade students with positive feelings toward school are happier and more receptive to learning. Demonstrates classroom techniques for creating a stimulating atmosphere.
Prod-BENSNS Dist-FLMFR 1979

Learning - A Happy Experience (Spanish) C 16 MIN
16MM FILM, 3/4 OR 1/2 IN VIDEO C A
Explains that elementary grade students with positive feelings toward school are happier and more receptive to learning. Demonstrates classroom techniques for creating a stimulating atmosphere.
Prod-BENSNS Dist-FLMFR 1979

Learning - Classical C 19 MIN
2 INCH VIDEOTAPE C A

Features a humanistic psychologist who, by analysis and examples, discusses learning in the classical sense of the word.
From The Interpersonal Competence, Unit 05 - Learning Series.
Prod-MVNE Dist-TELSTR 1973

Learning - How It Occurs C 30 MIN
3/4 OR 1/2 INCH VIDEO CASSETTE T
Discusses the learning process. Tells how to identify and accommodate different learning styles.
From The Training The Trainer Series.
Prod-ITCORP Dist-ITCORP

Learning - Operant C 22 MIN
2 INCH VIDEOTAPE C A
Features a humanistic psychologist who, by analysis and examples, discusses learning by its operant definition.
From The Interpersonal Competence, Unit 05 - Learning Series.
Prod-MVNE Dist-TELSTR 1973

Learning A Living C 20 MIN
3/4 OR 1/2 INCH VIDEO CASSETTE J-H A
Shows how, behind the prosperity of the big cities of Bangkok, Lima and New York lies a distinct undergrowth of poverty. Demonstrates how the people are rectifying the situation by building schools, beauty shops and studios in Bangkok, performing street theater and doing handicrafts in Lima, providing paramedical training in the Bronx and building a recording studio in the Bedford-Stuyvesant area of New York.
From The Urban Challenge Series. Pt 3
LC NO. 83-706586
Prod-NYSED Dist-GPITVL 1981

Learning About Air C 11 MIN
16MM FILM, 3/4 OR 1/2 IN VIDEO P
Presents a mime representing air appearing and disappearing as children experiment with soapbubbles, balloons, straws and a small windmill, demonstrating that air has weight, takes up space, exerts pressure and is a source of energy when in motion.
From The Learning About Science Series.
Prod-ACI Dist-AIMS 1976

Learning About Bears X 11 MIN
16MM FILM, 3/4 OR 1/2 IN VIDEO P-I
Identifies black bears, brown bears, grizzly bears and polar bears, showing what bears eat, where they live, and how they behave. Explains that although bears are by nature timid, they are 'WILD' animals and potentially dangerous.
Prod-EBF Dist-EBEC 1960

Learning About Cells C 16 MIN
16MM FILM, 3/4 OR 1/2 IN VIDEO J
Presents an introduction to the biological study of cell structure and function and examines the principles of cell growth and differentiation.
Prod-EBEC Dist-EBEC 1976

Learning About Computers C 11 MIN
16MM FILM, 3/4 OR 1/2 IN VIDEO
Shows an elementary school student doing a report on computers as a homework assignment. Shows that a computer, receives, stores and processes information very quickly.
Prod-NGS Dist-NGS 1984

Learning About Deer C 13 MIN
16MM FILM, 3/4 OR 1/2 IN VIDEO P-I
Examines the habits and behavior of deer, focusing on a doe and her fawns. Follows the animals from birth in late spring to their retreat to the forest for winter, showing how the doe nurtures her young and the ways in which the fawns are naturally protected.
LC NO. 82-706147
Prod-BTHFLM Dist-EBEC 1981

Learning About Electric Current (2nd Ed) C 15 MIN
16MM FILM, 3/4 OR 1/2 IN VIDEO I-J
Examines the basic characteristics of electric current. Shows how electric current consists of a flow of electrons under the influence of an electric field and demonstrates the relationship between electric current and magnetism.
From The Introduction To Physical Science Series.
Prod-EBEC Dist-EBEC 1974

Learning About Fire C 12 MIN
16MM FILM, 3/4 OR 1/2 IN VIDEO P-I
Reveals the mystery of fire and shows how to use it safely. Illustrates the difference between 'good fires' and 'bad fires', fireplace and campfire safety, and emphasizes that fire is a tool, not a toy.
Prod-FILCOM Dist-FILCOM

Learning About Flowers And Their Seeds (Spanish) C 14 MIN
16MM FILM, 3/4 OR 1/2 IN VIDEO P
A Spanish language version of the film and videorecording Learning About Flowers And Their Seeds.
Prod-EBEC Dist-EBEC 1983

Learning About Flowers And Their Seeds (2nd Ed) C 14 MIN
16MM FILM, 3/4 OR 1/2 IN VIDEO P
Introduces the concept of the flower as a functioning plant mechanism. Examines the various parts of a typical flower and describes how each contributes to the production and dispersal of seeds. Emphasizes the role of seeds as an important factor in the food supply and traces the progress of grain and fruit shipments from the produce market to local grocers.
LC NO. 83-706925
Prod-EBEC Dist-EBEC 1983

Learning About Fruits We Eat C 11 MIN
16MM FILM, 3/4 OR 1/2 IN VIDEO P-I
Discusses fruits from the tree, bush and vine to the market and to the tables and explains their remarkable variety in appearance and taste.
Prod-CORF Dist-CORF 1970

Learning About Heat (Spanish) C 15 MIN
16MM FILM, 3/4 OR 1/2 IN VIDEO I-J
A Spanish language version of the film and videorecording Learning About Heat.
Prod-EBEC Dist-EBEC

Learning About Heat (2nd Ed) C 15 MIN
16MM FILM, 3/4 OR 1/2 IN VIDEO I-J
Uses animation and live action demonstrations in examining the physics of heat. Shows its properties, its effects on matter and its travel by conduction, convection and radiation.
From The Introduction To Physical Science Series.
Prod-EBEC Dist-EBEC 1974

Learning About Human Behavior C 11 MIN
16MM FILM, 3/4 OR 1/2 IN VIDEO J-C
Shows different approaches to the study of human behavior as scientists describe current studies in physical development, perception, learning, emotions, intelligence, aptitudes and social behavior.
Prod-CORF Dist-CORF 1971

Learning About Incentive Spirometry C 11 MIN
3/4 OR 1/2 INCH VIDEO CASSETTE
Illustrates and explains the effects of deep breathing, then explains role of incentive spirometry in respiratory care. Emphasizes need for patient cooperation for best results.
LC NO. 79-731359
Prod-TRAINX Dist-TRAINX

Learning About Learning - Learning Research B 29 MIN
16MM FILM, 3/4 OR 1/2 IN VIDEO H-C A
Explores the different strategies employed in developing new theoretical concepts about man's ability to learn. These studies conducted with human beings and animals have already led to changes in methods of instruction in schools and colleges.
From The Focus On Behavior Series.
Prod-NET Dist-IU 1963

Learning About Leaves C 11 MIN
16MM FILM, 3/4 OR 1/2 IN VIDEO P
Investigates leaves on trees, bushes and other plants to see how they differ in size, shape, edges and veins.
Prod-CORF Dist-CORF 1968

Learning About Leaves X 11 MIN
16MM FILM, 3/4 OR 1/2 IN VIDEO I
Identifies pine needles, vegetable leaves, blades of grass and many deciduous leaves. Uses animation and time-lapse photography to show photosynthesis and the life cycle of leaves. Explains that leaves are essential to all life forms.
Prod-EBF Dist-EBEC 1958

Learning About Leaves (Spanish) C 11 MIN
16MM FILM, 3/4 OR 1/2 IN VIDEO I
Identifies pine needles, vegetable leaves, blades of grass and deciduous leaves. Demonstrates how leaves synthesize sugar and illustrates the life cycle of leaves.
Prod-EBEC Dist-EBEC

Learning About Light C 8 MIN
16MM FILM, 3/4 OR 1/2 IN VIDEO P
Explains some of the characteristics and properties of light. Shows how light rays may be reflected or refracted by transparent media and proves that light may be produced by the process of burning.
From The Learning About Science Series.
Prod-ACI Dist-AIMS Prodn-GORKER 1975

Learning About Light (Spanish) C 15 MIN
16MM FILM, 3/4 OR 1/2 IN VIDEO I-J
A Spanish language version of the film and videorecording Learning About Light.
Prod-EBEC Dist-EBEC 1976

Learning About Light (2nd Ed) C 15 MIN
16MM FILM, 3/4 OR 1/2 IN VIDEO J-H
Shows experiments which illustrate the way in which light normally moves, how it bends and is refracted, how a prism separates white light into its component colors and various applications of lasers.
From The Introduction To Physical Science Series.
Prod-EBEC Dist-EBEC 1976

Learning About Liquids, Solids And Gases C 11 MIN
16MM FILM, 3/4 OR 1/2 IN VIDEO P
Shows a group of children enjoying winter sports before moving indoors to pop corn, make taffy and perform some simple, easily-duplicated experiments which show the properties of and the differences among the three states of matter.
From The Learning About Science Series.
Prod-ACI Dist-AIMS 1976

Learning About Magnetism (Spanish) C 14 MIN
16MM FILM, 3/4 OR 1/2 IN VIDEO I-J
A Spanish language version of the film and videorecording Learning About Magnetism.
Prod-EBEC Dist-EBEC 1975

Learning About Magnetism (2nd Ed) C 14 MIN
16MM FILM, 3/4 OR 1/2 IN VIDEO I-J
Uses animation and practical demonstrations to explore the physical characteristics of magnetism. Shows that magnetism is ultimately associated with the movements of charged particles within atoms.
From The Introduction To Physical Science Series.
Prod-EBEC Dist-EBEC 1975

Learning About Metric Measures C 16 MIN
16MM FILM, 3/4 OR 1/2 IN VIDEO P-J
Introduces the basic concepts of the metric system. Identifies and defines the units of the metric stick. Uses the terms decimeter, centimeter, millimeter and meter. Shows the relationship of the meter and decimal systems.
Prod-BOUNDY Dist-PHENIX 1970

Learning About Nuclear Energy C 15 MIN
16MM FILM, 3/4 OR 1/2 IN VIDEO I-J
Prod-EBEC Dist-EBEC 1975

Learning About Nuclear Energy (Spanish) C 15 MIN
16MM FILM, 3/4 OR 1/2 IN VIDEO I-J
A Spanish language version of the film and videorecording Learning About Nuclear Energy.
Prod-EBEC Dist-EBEC 1975

Learning About Reptiles C 12 MIN
16MM FILM, 3/4 OR 1/2 IN VIDEO K-I
Offers information on alligators, crocodiles, turtles, lizards and snakes, showing how they have adapted to their environments and how they take care of themselves.
LC NO. 80-706250
Prod-NGS Dist-NGS 1979

Learning About Science—A Series
16MM FILM, 3/4 OR 1/2 IN VIDEO P
Prod-ACI Dist-AIMS 1976

Learning About Air	11 MIN
Learning About Light	8 MIN
Learning About Liquids, Solids And Gases	11 MIN
Learning About Solar Energy	12 MIN
Learning About Sound	8 MIN
Learning About Water	8 MIN

Learning About Solar Energy C 12 MIN
16MM FILM, 3/4 OR 1/2 IN VIDEO P
Shows a group of children as they experiment with energy from the Sun. Includes cooking on a solar cooker, playing with different colored paints to examine the relationship between color and heat and experiments with solar panels and solar cells.
From The Learning About Science Series.
Prod-ACI Dist-AIMS Prodn-COURTR 1975

Learning About Sound C 8 MIN
16MM FILM, 3/4 OR 1/2 IN VIDEO P
Explains some of the characteristics and properties of sound. Shows the different ways in which sound travels through solid, liquid and gaseous media and describes other phenomena such as echoes and the character of sound vibrations.
From The Learning About Science Series.
Prod-ACI Dist-AIMS Prodn-GORKER 1975

Learning About Sound (Spanish) C 17 MIN
16MM FILM, 3/4 OR 1/2 IN VIDEO I-J
A Spanish language version of the film and videorecording Learning About Sound.
Prod-EBEC Dist-EBEC 1974

Learning About Sound (2nd Ed) C 17 MIN
16MM FILM, 3/4 OR 1/2 IN VIDEO J-H
Demonstrates what sound is, how sound is made, how it travels and how it is perceived. Shows and analyzes the three common methods of making sound.
From The Introduction To Physical Science Series.
Prod-EBEC Dist-EBEC 1974

Learning About Stroke C 19 MIN
16MM FILM, 3/4 OR 1/2 IN VIDEO A
Explains what happens when an individual suffers a stroke. Shows how the three types of cerebral vascular accidents affect blood supply to the brain. Discusses the major disabilities, both physical and emotional, that may result from stroke. Stresses the importance of beginning rehabilitation and retraining for the stroke patient immediately.
Prod-EBEC Dist-EBEC 1981

Learning About The Cameroon B 60 MIN
3/4 OR 1/2 INCH VIDEO CASSETTE
Features a lecture on the Cameroon by a former diplomat to Africa.
From The Black Studies Series. Pt 3
Prod-UAZMIC Dist-UAZMIC 1979

Learning About The Gambia B 60 MIN
3/4 OR 1/2 INCH VIDEO CASSETTE
Features a lecture by a native of Gambia.
From The Black Studies Series. Pt 2
Prod-UAZMIC Dist-UAZMIC 1979

Learning About The Reader C 29 MIN
3/4 OR 1/2 INCH VIDEO CASSETTE T
See series title for descriptive statement.
From The Reading Comprehension Series.
Prod-IU Dist-HNEDBK

Learning About Time In The Preschool Years B 37 MIN
3/4 OR 1/2 INCH VIDEO CASSETTE PRO
Helps children understand concepts of times. Illustrates strategies for encouraging children to recall the past, anticipate the future and observe and represent temporal sequences and intervals.
Prod-HSERF Dist-HSERF

Learning About Water C 8 MIN
16MM FILM, 3/4 OR 1/2 IN VIDEO P
Helps children understand the many ways in which water affects life on earth. Shows how water can be both a constructive force in helping man do work and a destructive force in destroying crops, land and livestock.
From The Learning About Science Series.
Prod-ACI Dist-AIMS Prodn-COURTR 1975

Learning About Your Colostomy C 16 MIN
3/4 OR 1/2 INCH VIDEO CASSETTE

Introduces the patient to the function of the digestive tract and colon. Shows events which take place in the hospital, and uses color graphics to explain the surgical procedure.
LC NO. 79-730905
Prod-TRAINX Dist-TRAINX

Learning About Your Ileostomy C 16 MIN
3/4 OR 1/2 INCH VIDEO CASSETTE
Notes intent to show patient before surgery, and introduces the function of the digestive tract and small intestine. Shows hospital events taking place before surgery, and uses color graphics to explain the procedure.
LC NO. 78-730905
Prod-TRAINX Dist-TRAINX

Learning About Your Urostomy C 13 MIN
3/4 OR 1/2 INCH VIDEO CASSETTE
Introduces the patient to the function of the urinary system. Discusses events which take place in the hospital before surgery, and uses color graphics to explain one type of surgical procedure, the ileal conduit.
LC NO. 79-730905
Prod-TRAINX Dist-TRAINX

Learning Alternatives Through Instructional Media, Pt 1 C 30 MIN
16MM FILM OPTICAL SOUND C A
Features James G Buterbaugh, who establishes for educators of nursing a basic rationale for instructional development. Points out advantages of overhead projection, with a demonstration of a number of presentation models. Emphasizes elements which generally have been determined to improve instruction.
LC NO. 74-700165
Prod-NTCN Dist-UNEBR 1973

Learning Alternatives Through Instructional Media, Pt 2 C 30 MIN
16MM FILM OPTICAL SOUND C A
Features James G Buterbaugh, who discusses for educators in nursing various instructional media, including videotape, recording systems, audio systems and others. Emphasizes the use of learning indexes for the selection of materials.
LC NO. 74-700167
Prod-NTCN Dist-UNEBR 1973

Learning And Behavior C 27 MIN
16MM FILM OPTICAL SOUND
Shows how learning and conditioning are measured in the laboratory, uncovering important knowledge about the most fundamental processes in behavior.
Prod-CBSTV Dist-CCNY

Learning And Behavior (The Teaching Machine) B 26 MIN
16MM FILM, 3/4 OR 1/2 IN VIDEO H-C A
Shows how Drs B F Skinner and R J Herrnstein measure the learning process.
Prod-CBSTV Dist-CAROUF

Learning And Earning C 20 MIN
3/4 OR 1/2 INCH VIDEO CASSETTE
Illustrates the principle of systematic decision making by presenting the story of family members who must decide whether or not to take a course.
From The Trade-Offs Series.
LC NO. 79-706204
Prod-OECA Dist-AITECH Prodn-EDFCEN

Learning And Earning - Investment In Human Capital C 20 MIN
16MM FILM OPTICAL SOUND I-J
Relates how Judy and Andrea take a course which will enable them to be junior playground supervisors. Discusses whether their investment will pay off.
From The Trade-Offs Series. No. 8
LC NO. 79-700548
Prod-OECA Dist-AITECH 1978

Learning And Liking It—A Series
T
Designed to help any person who care for or instructs children. Uses televised media to facilitate the viewer's learning of the materials. Introduces the application of positive reinforcement, shaping, differential reinforcement and extinction techniques as well as other aspects of behavioral learning theory.
Prod-MSU Dist-MSU

Classical Conditioning	045 MIN
Classroom Environment	051 MIN
Extinction And Differential Reinforcement	042 MIN
Introduction	040 MIN
Motivation	041 MIN
Positive Refinforcement	040 MIN
Punishment	044 MIN
Shaping And Scheduling	042 MIN
Use Of Positive Reinforcement	049 MIN
Why Use Positive Reforcement?	033 MIN

Learning And Memory C 60 MIN
3/4 INCH VIDEO CASSETTE PRO
Treats learning that begins prenatally in relation to the 'pre-programmed nervous system,' learning and memory during the first six months, trial and error learning, and how young, mature and older individuals think in relation to environmental stimuli and the maturing nervous system.
From The Nonbehavioral Sciences And Rehabilitation Series. Part X
Prod-AOTA Dist-AOTA 1980

Learning And Memory C 60 MIN
3/4 OR 1/2 INCH VIDEO CASSETTE C A
Discusses the mystery of memory.
From The Brain, Mind And Behavior Series.
Prod-WNETTV Dist-FI

Learning And Teaching Of Concepts And Principles - Learning And Teaching Of... C
3/4 OR 1/2 INCH VIDEO CASSETTE T
Discusses learning and teaching of concepts and principles, and learning and teaching of problem solving.
From The Learning System Design Series. Unit 5
Prod-MSU Dist-MSU

Learning Booths C 17 MIN
16MM FILM OPTICAL SOUND
Describes the use of learning booths in the responsive environment education program at the New Nursery School, Greeley, Colorado, operated by Colorado State University. Shows how the program aids disadvantaged children to improve language, learn problem-solving techniques, self-concepts, interpersonal relations and self-control.
From The New Nursery School Series.
LC NO. 75-700791
Prod-USDHEW Dist-USNAC 1969

Learning By Experience C 10 MIN
3/4 OR 1/2 INCH VIDEO CASSETTE H A
Points out that finding the right job takes time and persistence. Shows Steve and his wife Ann reviewing his efforts and finding some things he could do better to improve his chances next time.
From The Making It Work Series.
Prod-ERF Dist-AITECH 1983

Learning Centers C 30 MIN
3/4 OR 1/2 INCH VIDEO CASSETTE T
Introduces concepts and skills needed to design and implement learning centers.
From The Stretch Strategies For Teaching Handicapped Children Series.
Prod-HUBDSC Dist-HUBDSC

Learning Centers C 30 MIN
16MM FILM, 3/4 OR 1/2 IN VIDEO T S
Demonstrates how to acquire the concepts and skills necessary for designing and implementing learning centers.
From The Project STRETCH (Strategies To Train Regular Educators To Teach Children With...) Series. Module 2
LC NO. 80-706638
Prod-METCO Dist-HUBDSC 1980

Learning Concept - Introduction To Personal Computers C 53 MIN
3/4 OR 1/2 INCH VIDEO CASSETTE
Demonstrates how easy personal computers are to use and introduces such common terms as RAM, DOS, run, load and save. Shows the variety of computer applications such as data bases, word processing, spreadsheets and graphics.
Prod-GA Dist-GA 1984

Learning Concept - The VisiCalc Program C 58 MIN
3/4 OR 1/2 INCH VIDEO CASSETTE A
Shows how to set up and utilize VisiCalc. Contains keyboard and screen reference charts, as well as descriptions and VisiCalc command instructions.
Prod-DSIM Dist-DSIM

Learning Concept - The VisiCalc Program C 58 MIN
3/4 OR 1/2 INCH VIDEO CASSETTE
Takes a step-by-step tour through the VisiCalc program. Explains what the program can and can't do, and how to apply its functions to specific needs.
Prod-GA Dist-GA 1984

Learning Disabilities C 34 MIN
3/4 OR 1/2 INCH VIDEO CASSETTE
Shows teacher Beverly Doyle administering the Keywath Diagnosis Arithmetic Test.
Prod-UNEBO Dist-UNEBO

Learning Disabilities (Gates-McKillop Diagnostic Reading Test) C 34 MIN
3/4 OR 1/2 INCH VIDEO CASSETTE
Shows teacher Beverly Doyle administering the Gates-McKillop Diagnostic Reading Test.
Prod-UNEBO Dist-UNEBO

Learning English - It's Harder Than You Think C 13 MIN
16MM FILM OPTICAL SOUND
Probes the reasons why some Australian migrants do not attempt to learn English.
LC NO. 80-700821
Prod-NSWF Dist-TASCOR 1979

Learning Environment, The B 30 MIN
2 INCH VIDEOTAPE
See series title for descriptive statement.
From The Program Development In The Kindergarten Series.
Prod-GPITVL Dist-GPITVL

Learning For A Lifetime - The Academic Club Method—A Series

Explains the Academic Club Method developed by Sally L Smith, Director of the Kingsbury Center Lab School.
Prod-KINGS Dist-KINGS

Developing Reading Readiness Skills	28 MIN
Learning For A Lifetime - The Academic Club	28 MIN
Setting Up Of A Club, The	28 MIN
Teacher As Club Leader, The	25 MIN
Teaching History, Geography And Civics	27 MIN

Learning For A Lifetime - The Academic Club Method, Introduction C 28 MIN
16MM FILM OPTICAL SOUND
Presents an overview of the Academic Club Method used at the Kingsbury Center Lab School. Shows how the traditional school day is transformed through the formation of clubs.
From The Learning For A Lifetime - The Academic Club Method Series. Part 1
Prod-KINGS Dist-KINGS

Learning For Earning - A Montage C 10 MIN
16MM FILM OPTICAL SOUND J-H
Uses case history interviews to illustrate the major advantages of vocational education and describes 24 occupational courses with the accent on individualized learning.
LC NO. 73-700528
Prod-PART Dist-PART 1972

Learning For Life C 30 MIN
16MM FILM OPTICAL SOUND
Shows how, through public school programs, adults are learning skills of citizenship and personal growth. Shows adults exploring community issues, learning to become more efficient executives and better informed voters, and studying astronomy, government and Russian
Prod-NEA Dist-NEA 1961

Learning From Experience C 20 MIN
16MM FILM, 3/4 OR 1/2 IN VIDEO
Shows that the difference between a good salesman and a bad one is the ability to analyze and learn from experiences.
Prod-RANKAV Dist-DARTNL

Learning From Film And Television C 27 MIN
3/4 OR 1/2 INCH VIDEO CASSETTE C A
Shows an opening film and TV research quiz that immediately involves the audience and demonstrates how each medium can be used effectively to expand learning experiences. Reviews disastrous ways to project a film. Depicts a teacher illustrating the importance of student involvement via media learning through preparation before viewing and planned follow-up activities.
From The Instructional Technology Introduction Series.
Prod-MCGILU Dist-BCNFL

Learning From Pets In The Classroom X 15 MIN
16MM FILM, 3/4 OR 1/2 IN VIDEO P-I
Shows how to organize the classroom for science and how to keep animals for observation. Views various classrooms where children are caring for pets, such as amphibians, insects and mannals.
Prod-ALTSUL Dist-JOU 1961

Learning In Kindergarten B 39 MIN
16MM FILM OPTICAL SOUND
Presents key concepts of its innovative program, showing all phases of the program stimulated to direct involvement.
Prod-ADL Dist-ADL

Learning Infant, The C 30 MIN
3/4 INCH VIDEO CASSETTE
Discusses the mental development of the child from birth to age three.
From The Growing Years Series.
Prod-COAST Dist-CDTEL

Learning Is Searching - A Third Grade Studies Man's Early Tools B 30 MIN
16MM FILM OPTICAL SOUND C
A third grade studies tools and their origins. The process of search is stressed. Shows the relation of these studies to the group's other school activities.
From The Studies Of Normal Personality Development Series.
Prod-NYU Dist-NYU 1955

Learning Laws - Respect For Yourself, Others And The Law—A Series
16MM FILM, 3/4 OR 1/2 IN VIDEO I
Discusses such topics as television viewing habits, respecting other people and their possessions, child abuse and resisting peer pressure to take drugs or alcohol.
Prod-WDEMCO Dist-WDEMCO 1982

High Road, The	013 MIN
That's My Bike	012 MIN
Too Much Of A Good Thing	013 MIN
What's Wrong With Me	016 MIN
Who Will Be The Teacher	016 MIN

Learning Management C 28 MIN
3/4 OR 1/2 INCH VIDEO CASSETTE T
See series title for descriptive statement.
From The Next Steps With Computers In The Classroom Series.
Prod-PBS Dist-PBS

Learning Means Feeling As Well As Knowing B 45 MIN
3/4 OR 1/2 INCH VIDEO CASSETTE
Discusses affective learning, how attitudes about a subject influence the ability to comprehend it. Discusses the evaluatiion of affective objectives and methods for changing attitudes.
Prod-BU Dist-BU

Learning Objectives/Evaluating Learning Systems C
3/4 OR 1/2 INCH VIDEO CASSETTE T
See series title for descriptive statement.
From The Learning System Design Series. Unit 2
Prod-MSU Dist-MSU

Learning Of Love, The C 30 MIN
3/4 OR 1/2 INCH VIDEO CASSETTE C A
Investigates the multitude of forms, developmental stages and feelings encompassed by the emotions of love. Charts love experiences from infancy to aging. Discusses love in a paired relationship.
From The Family Portrait - A Study Of Contemporary Lifestyles Series. Lesson 2
Prod-SCCON Dist-CDTEL

Learning Our Language, Unit III - Creative Writing—A Series
P
Introduces creative writing as an outlet for self-expression. Suggests familiar topics for writing, stimulates imagination, and motivates the writing which should follow the telecast.
Prod-MPATI Dist-GPITVL

Delicious, Fragrant, Colorful Bang, A 20 MIN
Fur And Feathers 20 MIN
I Wish I Had Known 20 MIN
If I Were 20 MIN
It's All The Weather We Got 20 MIN
Loveliness Of Words, The 20 MIN
Out Of This World 20 MIN
Pictures With Words 20 MIN
Ring-A-Jing-Jing 20 MIN
Talking Mailbox, The 20 MIN
This Is My Life 20 MIN
Why Of It, The 20 MIN

Learning Our Language, Unit IV - Speaking And Spelling—A Series
P
Provides an opportunity to learn, practice, and begin to establish careful habits of visual and auditory discrimination and distinct utterance. Shows the relationship of phonetics to spelling and speaking.
Prod-MPATI Dist-GPITVL

Big Difference, A 20 MIN
Breaking Up Words 20 MIN
Discovering Problems 20 MIN
Doing Away With Demons 20 MIN
How It Came About 20 MIN
Influencing Each Other 20 MIN
It Takes Two 20 MIN
More About Stopping Sounds 20 MIN
Say What You Mean 20 MIN
Starting And Stopping Sounds 20 MIN
Word Arithmetic 20 MIN
Word Surprises 20 MIN

Learning Our Language, Unit V - Exploring With Books—A Series
P-I
Presents stories, poems and books that are planned to encourage viewers to extend their reading interests. Includes both modern and classical works.
Prod-MPATI Dist-GPITVL

Adventure Is Yours 20 MIN
Fairies And Giants And Elves And Such 20 MIN
Friends Around The World 20 MIN
Friends Here And There 20 MIN
Funnybone Ticklers 20 MIN
Here Comes The Parade 20 MIN
Meet The Author 20 MIN
Really And Truly 20 MIN
Right Book For You, The 20 MIN
Singing Words 20 MIN
Tales Your Grandpa Heard 20 MIN
They Made Our Country Great 20 MIN
When America Was Young 20 MIN

Learning Our Language, Unit 1 - Listening Skills—A Series
P
Introduces listening skills, moving from the simple to the highly complex. Includes getting the main idea, noticing important details, arranging ideas in the proper order, following directions, predicting an outcome, enriching the vocabulary, and enjoying listening experiences.
Prod-MPATI Dist-GPITVL

Are You Listening 20 MIN
Big Idea, The 20 MIN
Do You Follow Me 20 MIN
Hear And Know 20 MIN
Listen And Laugh 20 MIN
Listen To Ask 20 MIN
My Very Own Ears 20 MIN
Now What 20 MIN
Picture Words 20 MIN
Then What Happened 20 MIN
Wiggle Your Ears 20 MIN
Words Make The Difference 20 MIN

Learning Our Language, Unit 2 - Dictionary Skills—A Series
P
Introduces a new skill which aids in using the dictionary efficiently as a source of word meaning, spelling and pronunciation.
Prod-MPATI Dist-GPITVL

Alphabet Goes To Work, The 20 MIN
Another Clue 20 MIN
Are You A Word Detective 20 MIN
Can You Divide 20 MIN
Do You Mean It 20 MIN
Exchange Words 20 MIN
Let's Get To The Root Of It 20 MIN
Little Mark Or Two, A 20 MIN
Meeting A New Friend 20 MIN
More Changes 20 MIN
More Than One 20 MIN
Spell It Right 20 MIN
They Change Their Tune 20 MIN
Two Words For One 20 MIN
When Two Makes One 20 MIN

Learning Path, The C 30 MIN
3/4 OR 1/2 INCH VIDEO CASSETTE
Shows the conflicts Native Americans have with white school systems and how the conflicts are resolved.
From The Forest Spirits Series.
Prod-NEWIST Dist-GPITVL

Learning Problem, A B 30 MIN
2 INCH VIDEOTAPE
Presents the case of Christopher, age ten, who is hyperactive, has difficulties in reading and spelling, tends to forget and is messy. Analyzes his personal and family life and explains this as a typical case where behavior and learning problems go hand-in-hand.
From The Motivating Children To Learn Series.
Prod-VTETV Dist-GPITVL

Learning Process, The C 25 MIN
3/4 INCH VIDEO CASSETTE PRO
Demonstrates general biofeedback learning strategies and discusses the external loop neurophysiological basis. Shows the frustrations and rewards of using biofeedback to elicit motor control that could not otherwise be used.
From The Biofeedback Strategies Series. Pt I
Prod-AOTA Dist-AOTA 1981

Learning Responsibility—A Series
16MM FILM, 3/4 OR 1/2 IN VIDEO
Describes how responsible attitudes make daily life more organized and more pleasant.
Prod-HIGGIN Dist-HIGGIN

Being On Time Game, The 011 MIN
Common Sense Game, The 011 MIN
Following Instructions Game, The 011 MIN
Getting Organized Game 011 MIN
Golden Rule Game, The 011 MIN
Good Manners Game, The 013 MIN
Good Sport Game, The 011 MIN
Learn From Criticism Game, The 011 MIN
Learn From Disappointments Game, The 011 MIN
Respecting Others Game, The 011 MIN
Sharing And Not Sharing Game, The 011 MIN

Learning Society, The C 21 MIN
16MM FILM OPTICAL SOUND C A
Examines the educational needs of nontraditional students who enter colleges after experiences in the world of work, including the military, the blue-collar work force or other institutions. Shows how colleges are being encouraged to meet the needs of nontraditional students in order to help them attain their goals.
LC NO. 74-703707
Prod-AMAHE Dist-AMAHE Prodn-VISEDC 1973

Learning Strategies X 11 MIN
16MM FILM, 3/4 OR 1/2 IN VIDEO T
Depicts a human relations program at a Cleveland, Ohio, school.
From The One To Grow On Series.
LC NO. 80-706188
Prod-NIMH Dist-USNAC Prodn-UCLA 1979

Learning Styles C 30 MIN
3/4 OR 1/2 INCH VIDEO CASSETTE T
Develops awareness of and sensitivity to children's learning styles. Gives specific ways to adapt to them.
From The Stretch Concepts For Teaching Handicapped Children Series.
Prod-HUBDSC Dist-HUBDSC

Learning Styles C 30 MIN
3/4 OR 1/2 INCH VIDEO CASSETTE T
Discusses the learning styles of children with special needs.
From The Teaching Children With Special Needs Series.
Prod-MDDE Dist-MDCPB

Learning Styles C 30 MIN
16MM FILM, 3/4 OR 1/2 IN VIDEO T S
Shows a group of college students who, for a final examination in their course, must 'release' a young girl from an enclosure, representing her environment, by determining what is her dominant learning style.
From The Project STRETCH (Strategies To Train Regular Educators To Teach Children With...) Series. Module 15
LC NO. 80-706651
Prod-METCO Dist-HUBDSC 1980

Learning System Design—A Series
T
Provides basic information on learning system design. Covers learning objectives, task analysis and system approach to instruction. Permits active practice of skills.
Prod-MSU Dist-MSU

General Principles Of Learning And Motivation
Learning And Teaching Of Concepts And
Learning Objectives/Evaluating Learning System
Perceptual-Motor Skills/System Approach
Preview/Overview Of Learning System Design
Task Descriptions/Task Analysis

Learning The Backstroke B 11 MIN
16MM FILM, 3/4 OR 1/2 IN VIDEO I-C
Illustrates techniques of the backstroke—position of body, timing, use of the flutterkick, starts, turns and practice. Uses slow motion underwater shots.
Prod-BHA Dist-IFB 1965

Learning The Breast Stroke B 11 MIN
16MM FILM, 3/4 OR 1/2 IN VIDEO I-C
Shows the three basic steps of the breast stroke—the pull, kick and glide. Draws attention to arm and leg movements, position of body, proper breathing and practice methods.
Prod-BHA Dist-IFB 1965

Learning The Butterfly Stroke C 11 MIN
16MM FILM, 3/4 OR 1/2 IN VIDEO J-H
Demonstrates body positions for leg kick, arm action, breathing and turning in the butterfly stroke. Uses underwater photography to illustrate specific movements. Shows proper starting position, the grab turn and the tumble.
Prod-BHA Dist-IFB 1968

Learning The Crawl Stroke B 16 MIN
16MM FILM, 3/4 OR 1/2 IN VIDEO I-C
Gives instruction in the techniques of the crawl, showing body position, leg and arm movement, proper breathing, timing, starts, turns and practice methods.
Prod-BHA Dist-IFB 1965

Learning The Process C 30 MIN
3/4 OR 1/2 INCH VIDEO CASSETTE H-C A
Focuses on defining the basic principles of the nature of communication by presenting examples of the various components and explaining how they interrelate.
From The Principles of Human Communication Series.
Prod-UMINN Dist-GPITVL 1983

Learning Through Movement B 32 MIN
16MM FILM OPTICAL SOUND C A S
Explores learning concepts a child can experience in a creative dance class.
LC NO. 70-711460
Prod-BARLEN Dist-SLFP 1968

Learning Through Play - Modules—A Series
C
Presents views of children at play.
Prod-UTORMC Dist-UTORMC 1976

Adult Role In Play, The 026 MIN
Children's Playspace 027 MIN
Coping With Problems 026 MIN
Dramatic Play 026 MIN
Pliable Materials 027 MIN
Social Development 027 MIN
Waterplay 023 MIN

Learning Through Play - Programs—A Series
C
Traces child development from infancy to pre-teens indicating how play furthers physical, emotional, cognitive and social development. Provides examples of appropriate play environments and suitable playthings and illustrates how values are communicated to children through play.
Prod-UTORMC Dist-UTORMC 1976

I And The Others, The 026 MIN
Playspace 027 MIN
Rhyme And Reason 028 MIN
Toying With Reality 027 MIN

Learning Through Play—A Series
H-C A
Shows scenes of spontaneous, undirected children's play with interpretive narrative and commentary on the importance of play in child development.
Prod-UTORMC Dist-UTORMC 1980

Adult Role In Play, The 030 MIN
Children's Playspace 030 MIN
Coping With Problems 030 MIN
Dramatic Play 030 MIN
I And The Others, The 027 MIN
Playspace 028 MIN
Pliable Materials 030 MIN
Rhyme And Reason 029 MIN
Social Development 030 MIN
Toying With Reality 028 MIN
Waterplay 030 MIN

Learning Through Problems: A Baby's Point Of View B 10 MIN
3/4 OR 1/2 INCH VIDEO CASSETTE PRO
Observes events and problems from a baby's point of view. Shows how reaching, holding, moving and pulling can be complex for an infant. Suggests how baby's sensory-motor explorations can be turned into learning experiences.
Prod-HSERF Dist-HSERF

Learning To Be C 20 MIN
3/4 OR 1/2 INCH VIDEO CASSETTE P
Presents folk stories that contain morals.
From The Folk Book Series.
LC NO. 80-706747
Prod-UWISC Dist-AITECH 1980

Learning To Be In East Africa C 20 MIN
3/4 OR 1/2 INCH VIDEO CASSETTE P
Presents East African folk stories that contain morals.
From The Folk Book Series.
Prod-UWISC Dist-AITECH 1980

Learning To Breastfeed C 22 MIN
16MM FILM, 3/4 OR 1/2 IN VIDEO
Deals with initial nursing experiences, differences among babies at birth, differences among mothers, and what can be done if nursing does not seem to be going well.
Prod-POLYMR Dist-POLYMR Prodn-CHEDAS

Learning To Cope C 14 MIN
16MM FILM OPTICAL SOUND H-C A
Presents Dr Hans Selye, who offers suggestions on avoiding stress and provides insights on human's abilities to handle problems.
From The Stress And You Series.
LC NO. 78-701902
Prod-MAWBYN Dist-AMEDFL Prodn-AMEDFL 1978

Learning To Cope C 25 MIN
16MM FILM, 3/4 OR 1/2 IN VIDEO
Depicts how seven people cope with the everyday problems of life.
Prod-MEHA Dist-MTI Prodn-SCRESC 1978

Learning To Dive C 16 MIN
16MM FILM OPTICAL SOUND I-C A
Includes basics in learning to dive, safety data, diving competitions, champion divers and a diving sequence to music.
LC NO. 73-702467
Prod-CRECP Dist-CRECP 1973

Learning To Enjoy C 28 MIN
16MM FILM OPTICAL SOUND
Looks at some elderly people who have discovered that their later years can be satisfying if they make their own choices, take risks, and allow themselves to pursue the things that bring enjoyment.
From The Prime Time Series.
LC NO. 79-701485
Prod-SEARS Dist-MTP Prodn-UPCI 1979

Learning To Learn In Infancy B 30 MIN
16MM FILM OPTICAL SOUND C T
Stresses the essential role of curiosity and exploration in learning and points to the kinds of experience that cultivate and stimulate an eager approach to the world. Suggests ways in which adults can help infants make approaches, differentiate between objects and develop the earliest communication skills.
From The Head Start Training Series.
LC NO. 74-701436
Prod-VASSAR Dist-NYU 1970

Learning To Live On Your Own—A Series
16MM FILM, 3/4 OR 1/2 IN VIDEO S
Provides information on various aspects of independent living.
Prod-LINCS Dist-JOU 1979

Keeping Safe 028 MIN
Most For Your Money, The 028 MIN
Where Your Money Goes 028 MIN

Learning To Live Together B 10 MIN
16MM FILM OPTICAL SOUND
See series title for descriptive statement.
From The Parent Education - Attitude Films Series.
Prod-TC Dist-TC

Learning To Live With Fear C 5 MIN
16MM FILM, 3/4 OR 1/2 IN VIDEO H-C A
Highlights the types of fears that are imaginary and those that are real and suggests how to deal with them.
From The Communicating From The Lectern Series.
Prod-METAIV Dist-AIMS 1976

Learning To Live—A Series
A
Uses the increasingly popular approach of transactional analysis to deal with human relationship in conflict resolution as well as growth and development as persons. Shows how this method translates complex psychological concepts into language which lay persons can understand and implement. Provides a positive approach by which persons can understand their own feelings and behavior and that of others.
Prod-UMCOM Dist-ECUFLM 1974

Acquiring Life Scripts 030 MIN
Changing Life Scripts 030 MIN
Ego States 030 MIN
Feelings 030 MIN
Games 030 MIN
Strokes 030 MIN
Time Structures 030 MIN
Transactions 030 MIN

Learning To Look At Hands C 8 MIN
16MM FILM, 3/4 OR 1/2 IN VIDEO P
Takes a close look at hands, showing that the way a hand is held may say something about what a person is thinking. Depicts fingers and thumbs in action.
From The Learning To Look Series.
Prod-MGHT Dist-MGHT Prodn-CENTRO 1969

Learning To Look—A Series
16MM FILM, 3/4 OR 1/2 IN VIDEO P
Teaches children about the size, shape, color, texture, identity and totality of the world around them. Explores the concepts of visual literacy through familiar objects.
Prod-MGHT Dist-MGHT 1969

All Kinds Of Buildings 8 MIN
Just Like In School 8 MIN
Learning To Look At Hands 8 MIN
Let's Find Some Faces 9 MIN
Movement Movie, A 9 MIN
On Your Way To School 8 MIN
What Is A Family 7 MIN
What Makes A Home A Home 9 MIN

Learning To Massage C 60 MIN
1/2 IN VIDEO CASSETTE (BETA)
Shows how to give an expert massage, focusing on intricate Swedish and Japanese accupressure massage.
Prod-UNKNWN Dist-HOMET

Learning To Observe C 7 MIN
16MM FILM, 3/4 OR 1/2 IN VIDEO I-J
Suggests ways in which we can improve our abilities to observe. Shows how viewers can strengthen skills in observing as they watch the antics of interesting animated characters.
Prod-LEARN Dist-PHENIX 1972

Learning To Read Maps (2nd Ed) C 12 MIN
16MM FILM, 3/4 OR 1/2 IN VIDEO P-I
Explains how maps are pictorial representations of real places, how physical features are represented as symbols on a map, how to find directions and how to calculate the distance to a destination.
Prod-EBEC Dist-EBEC 1980

Learning To Read Music C 29 MIN
2 INCH VIDEOTAPE
See series title for descriptive statement.
From The Playing The Guitar I Series.
Prod-KCET Dist-PUBTEL

Learning To Say No C
3/4 OR 1/2 INCH VIDEO CASSETTE I-J
Teaches assertiveness techniques. Emphasizes the sense of accomplishment, increased self-respect and admiration of others that result when young people are able to say 'No.'
Prod-SUNCOM Dist-SUNCOM

Learning To See C 15 MIN
16MM FILM, 3/4 OR 1/2 IN VIDEO P-I
Employs animation to show how light enters the eye and creates an upside-down image on the retina which the brain interprets. Presents optical illusions and lists the factors which affect what is seen.
From The Human Senses Series.
LC NO. 82-706605
Prod-NGS Dist-NGS 1982

Learning To See Color C 20 MIN
2 INCH VIDEOTAPE I
Helps the student explore the world of color and to grasp meanings and significance in the use of color.
From The Creating Art, Pt 1 - Learning To See Series.
Prod-GPITVL Dist-GPITVL

Learning To See Line And Shape C 20 MIN
2 INCH VIDEOTAPE I
Helps the student learn about line and shape and exposes him to these art elements as they appear in his visual world.
From The Creating Art, Pt 1 - Learning To See Series.
Prod-GPITVL Dist-GPITVL

Learning To See Space And Movement C 20 MIN
2 INCH VIDEOTAPE I
Helps the student sense various motions which occur and to see the relationships of space and motion to visual expression.
From The Creating Art, Pt 1 - Learning To See Series.
Prod-GPITVL Dist-GPITVL

Learning To See Texture C 20 MIN
2 INCH VIDEOTAPE I
Helps the student see texture and become aware of actual as well as created textures.
From The Creating Art, Pt 1 - Learning To See Series.
Prod-GPITVL Dist-GPITVL

Learning To See The Subjects Of Art C 20 MIN
2 INCH VIDEOTAPE I
Shows the student the sources and inspiration for subject matter for visual expression.
From The Creating Art, Pt 1 - Learning To See Series.
Prod-GPITVL Dist-GPITVL

Learning To See The Visual Environment C 20 MIN
2 INCH VIDEOTAPE I
Helps strengthen the student's awareness to his visual world and to sharpen sensitivity to people, objects and things.
From The Creating Art, Pt 1 - Learning To See Series.
Prod-GPITVL Dist-GPITVL

Learning To Speak, Pt 1 C 20 MIN
16MM FILM, 3/4 OR 1/2 IN VIDEO
Treats the characteristics of intonation, pitch, articulation, and vocal quality requisite to the deaf child's attainment of intelligible speech within the phonological language system.
LC NO. 80-707415
Prod-USBEH Dist-USNAC 1980

Learning To Speak, Pt 2 C 20 MIN
16MM FILM, 3/4 OR 1/2 IN VIDEO
Treats the perception of intonation patterns in the deaf child's attainment of intellectual speech within the phonological language system. Discusses how meaning is affected by stress, pitch, and phrasing, and by developing and improving speech rhythm.
LC NO. 80-707416
Prod-USBEH Dist-USNAC 1980

Learning To Swim With Artificial Aids B 10 MIN
16MM FILM, 3/4 OR 1/2 IN VIDEO I-H
Presents the primary stages of beginner swimming using artificial aids. Emphasizes free movement and confidence, then proceeds to basic strokes. Underwater photography clarifies movements and demonstrates buoyancy.
Prod-BHA Dist-IFB 1968

Learning To Swim—A Series
16MM FILM, 3/4 OR 1/2 IN VIDEO
Prod-IFB Dist-IFB 1965

Back Stroke, The 9 MIN
Breast Stroke, The 11 MIN
Crawl, The 11 MIN

Learning To Think Like A Manager C 25 MIN
16MM FILM, 3/4 OR 1/2 IN VIDEO H-C A
Chronicles the experiences of two new managers during their first three months on the job. Discusses the mistakes each makes, how to avoid these common pitfalls and suggests an active role for upper management in training new managers.
LC NO. 83-706392
Prod-CRMP Dist-CRMP 1983

Learning To Travel C 22 MIN
16MM FILM OPTICAL SOUND I-H
Lays out the principles of trip-planning and trip-taking for handicapped passengers including how to choose the best transportation, how to find out trip information, what to take, how to find addresses and good travel behavior.
Prod-PARPRO Dist-PARPRO

Learning To Use Money C 10 MIN
16MM FILM, 3/4 OR 1/2 IN VIDEO I
Follows three children as they learn to shop for the best price, check sizes and compare quality on making decisions about how much money to spend.
Prod-CORF Dist-CORF 1973

Learning To Use Your Senses X 11 MIN
16MM FILM, 3/4 OR 1/2 IN VIDEO K-P
Encourages children to verbalize sensory perceptions. Points out that people use their five senses automatically and explains how to learn about the environment by using the senses.
Prod-EBEC Dist-EBEC 1968

Learning To Walk C 8 MIN
16MM FILM, 3/4 OR 1/2 IN VIDEO H-C A
Tells the story of a lone figure who sets out on a purposeful stroll, only to be accosted by experts who demonstrate their ideas of the proper way he should walk.
Prod-ZAGREB Dist-IFB 1980

Learning Values With Fat Albert And The Cosby Kids, Set I—A Series
16MM FILM, 3/4 OR 1/2 IN VIDEO K-I
Presents Bill Cosby and the animated Fat Albert and the Cosby Kids telling stories with lessons in living.
Prod-FLMTON Dist-MGHT 1975

Check It Out 13 MIN
Do Your Own Thing 13 MIN
Dope Is For Dopes 14 MIN
Hospital, The 12 MIN
Lying 13 MIN
Runt, The 14 MIN
Summer Camp 13 MIN
What Is A Friend 13 MIN

Learning Values With Fat Albert And The Cosby Kids, Set II—A Series
16MM FILM, 3/4 OR 1/2 IN VIDEO P-I
Presents Bill Cosby and the animated Fat Albert and the Cosby Kids telling stories with lessons in living.
Prod-FLMTON Dist-MGHT

Animal Lover 14 MIN
Junk Food 14 MIN
Ounce Of Prevention, An 14 MIN
Smoke Gets In Your Hair 14 MIN
Take Two, They're Small 14 MIN
Uncle Monty's Gone 14 MIN
What's Say 14 MIN
You Have Something To Offer 14 MIN

Learning With Film and Video C 15 MIN
16MM FILM, 3/4 OR 1/2 IN VIDEO A
Shows how good teachers use film and video as an essential tool to provide learning experiences not otherwise available.
Prod-CF Dist-CF

Learning With Film And Video C 15 MIN
16MM FILM - 1/2 IN VIDEO, VHS
Discusses film and video as essential tools of learning and explains how film can bring the world into the classroom, motivate children to read, enhance basic skills development and enrich their learning experiences with exciting visual images. A live action film.
Prod-FAC Dist-WWS

Learning With Today's Media C 35 MIN
16MM FILM, 3/4 OR 1/2 IN VIDEO C A
Describes the role of media centers in educational programs. Tells how media centers can be organized to provide the framework and resources that will enable students to discover new areas of information on their own.
Prod-EBEC Dist-EBEC 1974

Learning With Today's Media (Spanish) C 35 MIN
16MM FILM, 3/4 OR 1/2 IN VIDEO C A
Defines and describes the role of the media center at elementary, junior high, senior high and college levels. Presents four case studies which reveal ways in which media centers may be equipped to serve classroom needs.
Prod-EBEC Dist-EBEC

Learning With Your Ears C 11 MIN
16MM FILM, 3/4 OR 1/2 IN VIDEO P
Pictures a game of blind man's buff to illustrate that the loudness, pitch and tone of sounds convey information about the size, power, speed and distance of objects. Demonstrates instruments such as the stethoscope, megaphone and tape recorder which act as extensions of the ear.
Prod-CORF Dist-CORF 1967

Learning With Your Eyes C 11 MIN
16MM FILM, 3/4 OR 1/2 IN VIDEO P
Utilizes a variety of scenes to highlight the value of sight and the importance of looking carefully at things. Points out the use of binoculars and magnifying glasses in extending the range of the eyes and explains how to judge sizes, shapes and colors.
Prod-CORF Dist-CORF 1967

Learning With Your Senses C 11 MIN
16MM FILM, 3/4 OR 1/2 IN VIDEO P
Focuses on sight, hearing, smell, taste, and touch, and the different information derived from each. Explains how all five senses can be used together to bring more knowledge and appreciation of the world.
Prod-CORF Dist-CORF 1967

Learning—A Series

Prod-ANDRA Dist-ANDRA

I'm Not Too Famous At It - A Definition Of

Old Enough But Not Ready - Early Recognition 28 MIN

Lease Safety Tips For New Employees C 23 MIN
3/4 OR 1/2 INCH VIDEO CASSETTE IND
Illustrates the more common potential hazards that a person may face on the lease and suggests ways to work safely and overcome these hazards.
Prod-UTEXPE Dist-UTEXPE 1978

Least Likely C 20 MIN
16MM FILM OPTICAL SOUND
Presents a story about a man who was considered a loser in high school. Reveals that when he returns to the school for his class's tenth reunion as a rich and famous cartoonist, his calculated plan for revenge takes an unexpected turn and has unpredictable and humorous results.
LC NO. 82-700332
Prod-USC Dist-USC 1981

Least Restrictive Environment - Resource Rooms And Special Classes C 30 MIN
3/4 OR 1/2 INCH VIDEO CASSETTE C A
Presents two teaching situations which illustrate the use of a multipurpose resource room for mildly retarded and/or learning disabled children, and special classes for hearing handicapped children.
From The Law And Handicapped Children In School Series.
LC NO. 79-706363
Prod-IU Dist-IU 1979

Least Restrictive Environment - Special Day And Residential Schools C 30 MIN
3/4 OR 1/2 INCH VIDEO CASSETTE C A
Illustrates three educational alternatives for severely handicapped children, including a day school featuring specialized instruction, a residential school through personalized living environments and self-help facilities, and an innovative recreation camp.
From The Law And Handicapped Children In School Series.
LC NO. 79-706365
Prod-IU Dist-IU 1979

Least Restrictive Environment Panel C 30 MIN
3/4 OR 1/2 INCH VIDEO CASSETTE C A
Presents a panel discussion on the requirements prescribed by PL94-142, the Education For All Handicapped Children Act of 1975, for providing the least restrictive educational environment for handicapped students.
From The Law And Handicapped Children In School Series.
LC NO. 79-706362
Prod-IU Dist-IU 1979

Least Upper Bounds B
16MM FILM OPTICAL SOUND
Relates the global properties of continuous functions to the underlying axioms of the real number system. Shows how a problem can be tackled using these properties.
Prod-OPENU Dist-OPENU

Leather C 15 MIN
16MM FILM, 3/4 OR 1/2 IN VIDEO I-C A
Shows a leather craftsman using a variety of tools and several kinds of leather to make a simple pouch and belt and a more complicated shoulder bag and sandals. Includes basic instructions for making leather articles.
From The Rediscovery - Art Media Series.
Prod-ACI Dist-AIMS 1971

Leather (Spanish) C 15 MIN
16MM FILM, 3/4 OR 1/2 IN VIDEO I-C A
Demonstrates the basic techniques of an ancient craft that has undergone a recent renaissance. Reveals the skills and procedures of an expert as he fashions belts, handbags and apparel. Shows methods for preparing, cutting, gluing and stitching hides, as well as proper use of tools.
From The Rediscovery - Art Media (Spanish) Series.
Prod-ACI Dist-AIMS 1971

Leather I - Layout And Cutting C 30 MIN
3/4 OR 1/2 INCH VIDEO CASSETTE H A
Describes different types, grades, thicknesses, and uses of leather. Includes a demonstration of the fundamental techniques needed for developing a pattern, laying out the pattern on the leather stock and cutting out the item.
From The Arts And Crafts Series.
LC NO. 81-706989
Prod-GPITVL Dist-GPITVL 1981

Leather II - Assembly And Lacing C 30 MIN
3/4 OR 1/2 INCH VIDEO CASSETTE H A
Describes and demonstrates how to create leather articles using rivets, snaps, and sewing.
From The Arts And Crafts Series.
LC NO. 81-706992
Prod-GPITVL Dist-GPITVL 1981

Leather III - Carving And Finishing C 30 MIN
3/4 OR 1/2 INCH VIDEO CASSETTE H A
Describes abd demonstrates leather tooling, dying, finishing techniques and design transfer techniques.
From The Arts And Crafts Series.
LC NO. 81-706994
Prod-GPITVL Dist-GPITVL 1981

Leather In Your Life C 23 MIN
16MM FILM OPTICAL SOUND
Tells the story of the processing and tanning of leather. Shows the many important uses of this material.
Prod-LIA Dist-CCNY

Leather Series - Leather Finishing C 6 MIN
3/4 OR 1/2 INCH VIDEO CASSETTE
Shows how to apply four different leather finishes and explains when to use each one. Part five in a series of seven programs designed to acquaint occupational therapy students with leather activities.
Prod-HSCIC Dist-HSCIC

Leather Series - Leather Lacing C 21 MIN
3/4 OR 1/2 INCH VIDEO CASSETTE
Covers the four types of stitches used to lace leather pieces together. Last in a series of seven programs designed to acquaint occupational therapy students with leather activities.
Prod-HSCIC Dist-HSCIC

Leather Series - Leather Tooling C 8 MIN
3/4 OR 1/2 INCH VIDEO CASSETTE
Teaches techniques for decorating leather by tooling parts of the design. Part four in a series of seven programs designed to acquaint occupational therapy students with leather activities.
Prod-HSCIC Dist-HSCIC

Leather Series - Setting An Eyelet, A Rivet, And A Snap C 9 MIN
3/4 OR 1/2 INCH VIDEO CASSETTE
Demonstrates the setting of three types of leather fasteners, an eyelet, a rivet, and a snap. Part six in a series of seven programs designed to acquaint occupational therapy students with leather activities.
Prod-HSCIC Dist-HSCIC

Leather, Pt 2 - Leather Carving C 11 MIN
3/4 OR 1/2 INCH VIDEO CASSETTE
Introduces leather-carving techniques.
Prod-HSCIC Dist-HSCIC

Leather, Pt 3 - Leather Stamping C 8 MIN
3/4 OR 1/2 INCH VIDEO CASSETTE
Explains and demonstrates different types of leather-stamping tools.
Prod-HSCIC Dist-HSCIC

Leathercraft Video Tape C 41 MIN
3/4 OR 1/2 INCH VIDEO CASSETTE
Shows leather master Joey Smith's demonstration and explanation of everything from casing leather to the completion of a leather bag. Second lesson by master leathercrafter Al Stohlman shows secrets of carving and most effective dyeing methods.
Prod-TANDY Dist-TANDY

Leathercraft, Pt 1 - Pattern Construction And Layout C 27 MIN
3/4 OR 1/2 INCH VIDEO CASSETTE
Shows how to make a pattern for a leather item and how to cut out and prepare leather pieces for assembly.
Prod-HSCIC Dist-HSCIC

Leatherneck Ambassadors C 15 MIN
16MM FILM - 3/4 IN VIDEO
Features the performance of the Marine Corps in the International Festival of Music, Edinburgh, Scotland, 1958.
Prod-USNAC Dist-USNAC 1972

Leatherstocking Tales - New Perspectives, The C 30 MIN
1/2 INCH VIDEOTAPE
Deals with James Fenimore Cooper's LEATHERSTOCKING TALES, in which he expresses the transcendence of the woodman.
Prod-NETCHE Dist-NETCHE 1970

Leave 'Em Laughing B 30 MIN
16MM FILM SILENT P A
Presents a Laurel and Hardy comedy in which Stan and Ollie muddle through the complications of a toothache, laughing gas and an eviction notice. Includes Edgar Kennedy as a police officer.
From The Laurel And Hardy Comedy Series.
LC NO. 78-711883
Prod-ROACH Dist-BHAWK 1927

Leave Herbert Alone C 8 MIN
16MM FILM, 3/4 OR 1/2 IN VIDEO P-I
Presents a story about a young child who tries to play with her next door neighbor's cat. Shows how she disturbs the cat by constantly pursuing it, until she finds that if she is quiet and still the cat will come to her.
Prod-MORLAT Dist-AIMS 1974

Leave It To You - OK C
16MM FILM - 3/4 IN VIDEO A
Explores the skills of delegation, what it is, how it is done, what can and cannot be delegated, the barriers and benefits.
Prod-BNA Dist-BNA 1983

Leave Me Alone, God C 25 MIN
16MM FILM, 3/4 OR 1/2 IN VIDEO H-C A
Explains how a college professor who had denied the existence of God changes his mind after one of his students overdoses as a result of what he has taught her. Stars Richard Jordan.
From The Insight Series.
Prod-PAULST Dist-PAULST

Leave Me Alone, God C 27 MIN
3/4 OR 1/2 INCH VIDEO CASSETTE J A
Tells the story of a philosophy professor who denies the reality of God.
Prod-SUTHRB Dist-SUTHRB

Leave Your Shoes Outside The Door B 15 MIN
2 INCH VIDEOTAPE P
Explains how clothing is worn according to tradition and custom. (Broadcast quality)
From The Around The Corner Series. No. 24
Prod-FWCETV Dist-GPITVL Prodn-WEDUTV

Leave Yourself An Out X 10 MIN
16MM FILM OPTICAL SOUND
Shows how to plan for emergencies and how to provide an 'ESCAPE ROUTE.'
From The Expert Seeing Series.
Prod-NSC Dist-NSC

Leave-Taking, The C 15 MIN
3/4 OR 1/2 INCH VIDEO CASSETTE I
Presents a Bedouin wedding ceremony. Ends a story of western visitors learning about the Bedouin way of life.
From The Encounter In The Desert Series.
Prod-CTI Dist-CTI

Leaves C 13 MIN
16MM FILM, 3/4 OR 1/2 IN VIDEO P-I
Tells the story of a six year old boy's efforts to assist nature by replacing fallen leaves with his own creations made with construction paper, marking crayons and scissors. Portrays the mixture of reality and fantasy that is the child's world. With an original music score, but no narration.
Prod-PHILLR Dist-AIMS 1968

Leaves Of Grass, Continued B 10 MIN
16MM FILM OPTICAL SOUND
Contrasts Walt Whitman's optimism for the future, in which he tried to foresee a great new life for the American city, with the congestion, squalor and filth produced by a city grown too big.
Prod-UPENN Dist-UPENN 1961

Leaves Take Leave, The C 20 MIN
16MM FILM, 3/4 OR 1/2 IN VIDEO J-H
States that the idea of recycling is a relatively new idea among humans, but an old idea in nature. There are excellent examples of recyclers in nature. One of man's recycling problems is permanent rubbish, which cannot be recycled.
From The Biology - It's Life Series.
Prod-THAMES Dist-MEDIAG 1980

Leaving And Coming Back C 18 MIN
16MM FILM, 3/4 OR 1/2 IN VIDEO K-P S
Presents Mr Rogers exploring the feelings children have when separated from things and people they love.
From The I Am, I Can, I Will, Level II Series.
LC NO. 80-706547
Prod-FAMCOM Dist-HUBDSC 1979

Leaving For The Sea B 30 MIN
1/2 INCH VIDEOTAPE
Portrays women's friendships in a dream-like fiction.
Prod-WMENIF Dist-WMENIF

Leaving Home - A Family In Transition C 28 MIN
16MM FILM, 3/4 OR 1/2 IN VIDEO H-C A
Employs cinema verite techniques to show what happens when two young sisters decide to move away from home. Profiles the girls' desires for independence as well as for parental acceptance and approval.
LC NO. 81-706984
Prod-PNTNGL Dist-DIRECT Prodn-BARIL 1980

Leaving Home, Going Home C 30 MIN
3/4 OR 1/2 INCH VIDEO CASSETTE
See series title for descriptive statement.
From The Rebop Series.
Prod-WGBHTV Dist-MDCPB

Leaving The Twentieth Century C 3 MIN
3/4 OR 1/2 INCH VIDEO CASSETTE
Creates a stylized landscape of the future and a high-fashion couple in flight from the mundanities of post-modern society.
Prod-EAI Dist-EAI

Leaving The 20th Century—A Series

Calls attention to the fact that we are approaching a point of departure in history. Covers concepts and technologies which will define the future. By Max Almy.
Prod-KITCHN Dist-KITCHN

Arrival
Countdown
Departure

Lebanon C 28 MIN
3/4 INCH VIDEOTAPE
Interviews Ambassador Ghassan Tueni, permanent representative to the United Nations on Lebanon yesterday, today and tomorrow. Presents films on Lebanon. Hosted by Marilyn Perry.
From The International Byline Series.
Prod-PERRYM Dist-PERRYM

Lebanon - Land Of Survivors C 16 MIN
3/4 INCH VIDEO CASSETTE
Illustrates Beirut during the summer of 1982, focusing on the devastation of the city and the nonpartisan aid given by Catholic Relief Services. Narrated by Joseph Curtin, Catholic Relief Services Program Director in Lebanon.
Prod-CATHRS Dist-MTP

Lebanon And The Crusades C 12 MIN
16MM FILM, 3/4 OR 1/2 IN VIDEO I-H A
Chronicles the three year campaign of the crusaders of Christian Europe to remove the Holy City of Jerusalem from the bonds of the Muslims. Looks at the fortresses the crusaders built along the Lebanese coast.
Prod-LUF Dist-LUF 1981

Lebanon Valley College - Guest Dan Smith, Program A C 29 MIN
2 INCH VIDEOTAPE
Features French folk singer Sonia Malkine and her special guest Dan Smith visiting Lebanon Valley College in Pennsylvania.
From The Sonia Malkine On Campus Series.
Prod-WITFTV Dist-PUBTEL

Lebanon Valley College - Guest Dan Smith, Program B C 29 MIN
2 INCH VIDEOTAPE
Features French folk singer Sonia Malkine and her special guest Dan Smith visiting Lebanon Valley College in Pennsylvania.
From The Sonia Malkine On Campus Series.
Prod-WITFTV Dist-PUBTEL

Lebanon, Israel And The PLO C 28 MIN
3/4 OR 1/2 INCH VIDEO CASSETTE H-C A
Examines the history that led to the confrontation between Israeli troops and the PLO in West Beirut.
Prod-JOU Dist-JOU

Lebesgue Integral On RK, The B
16MM FILM OPTICAL SOUND
Deals with the four-stage definition of the Lebesgue integral on RK. Discusses Fubini's theorem, which relates this integral to the integrals on lower dimensions.
Prod-OPENU Dist-OPENU

Lebesgue Integration, Pt 1 B
16MM FILM OPTICAL SOUND
Presents Lebesgue integration as an extension of Riemann integration, motivated by the desire to be able to integrate limit functions of sequences of integrable functions.
Prod-OPENU Dist-OPENU

Lebesgue Integration, Pt 2 B
16MM FILM OPTICAL SOUND
Discusses the individual ingredients in the third stage of the definition of the Lebesgue integral.
Prod-OPENU Dist-OPENU

Lectra Nancy Side A, Side B C 7 MIN
3/4 OR 1/2 INCH VIDEO CASSETTE
Produces dissonant images which are high gloss, confrontational and anti-authoritarian. Presented by Beth Berolzheimer, Wayne Fielding and Karl Hauser.
Prod-ARTINC Dist-ARTINC

Lecture And Role-Playing Strategy, The B 30 MIN
16MM FILM OPTICAL SOUND C A
Dramatizes principles for presenting meaningful lectures and demonstrations.
From The Nursing - Where Are You Going, How Will You Get There Series.
LC NO. 74-700179
Prod-NTCN Dist-NTCN 1971

Lecture Eight, FORTRAN C 30 MIN
3/4 OR 1/2 INCH VIDEO CASSETTE
Talks about one dimensional arrays - array subscripts, a new statement DIMENSION, and Slash on Input FORMAT.
From The FORTRAN Series.
Prod-COLOSU Dist-COLOSU

Lecture Five, FORTRAN C 30 MIN
3/4 OR 1/2 INCH VIDEO CASSETTE
Discusses statement components logical variables and constants and logical format descriptor, plus header data.
From The FORTRAN Series.
Prod-COLOSU Dist-COLOSU

Lecture Four, FORTRAN C 30 MIN
3/4 OR 1/2 INCH VIDEO CASSETTE
Discusses real and integer types, statement components AND, OR and NOT, the order of operations, and using counter to terminate loop.
From The FORTRAN Series.
Prod-COLOSU Dist-COLOSU

Lecture Nine, FORTRAN C 30 MIN
3/4 OR 1/2 INCH VIDEO CASSETTE
Shows two-dimensional arrays, and searching for subscript pattern.
From The FORTRAN Series.
Prod-COLOSU Dist-COLOSU

Lecture On Theory Of Memory Association Techniques, Master Chain System, Exercise On... C 60 MIN
3/4 OR 1/2 INCH VIDEO CASSETTE
Lecture on theory of memory association techniques. Master Chain System. Exercise on memorizing 14 cabinet positions of the government.
From The Memory Improvement Series. Pt 3
Prod-UAZMIC Dist-UAZMIC

Lecture Seven, FORTRAN C 30 MIN
3/4 OR 1/2 INCH VIDEO CASSETTE
Shows new statement DO and nested DO loops.
From The FORTRAN Series.
Prod-COLOSU Dist-COLOSU

Lecture Six, FORTRAN C 30 MIN
3/4 OR 1/2 INCH VIDEO CASSETTE
Shows new statement - Computed GO TO, predefined subprograms and labeled output.
From The FORTRAN Series.
Prod-COLOSU Dist-COLOSU

Lecture Ten, FORTRAN C 30 MIN
3/4 OR 1/2 INCH VIDEO CASSETTE
Discusses user-defined subprograms, new statements CALL and SUBROUTINE, and subprogram use.
From The FORTRAN Series.
Prod-COLOSU Dist-COLOSU

Lecture Three, FORTRAN C 30 MIN
3/4 OR 1/2 INCH VIDEO CASSETTE
Shows new statements GO TO and Logical IF. Lists statement components, relational operators and logical expression, attacking a problem, carriage control and debugging.
From The FORTRAN Series.
Prod-COLOSU Dist-COLOSU

Lee Baltimore - 99 Years, What Makes A Poor Man Rich C 17 MIN
16MM FILM, 3/4 OR 1/2 IN VIDEO J-C
Records the reminiscenses of Lee Baltimore, a 99-year-old ex-slave who is still a working farmer in Jasper County, Texas. Shows him plowing his fields with a horse and hand plow and demonstrates his interest in God and music.
From The American Character Series.
Prod-ODYSSP Dist-EBEC 1976

Lee Krasner - The Long View C 30 MIN
16MM FILM OPTICAL SOUND
Portrays abstract expressionist artist Lenore Krasner, focusing on her life, her studies and her marriage to Jackson Pollock. Shows the artist at work.
LC NO. 79-700392
Prod-ROSEBA Dist-AFA 1978

Lee Strasberg C 28 MIN
3/4 OR 1/2 INCH VIDEO CASSETTE
Profiles the late Lee Strasberg, recognized actor and legendary acting teacher of Dustin Hoffman, Jane Fonda, Al Pacino, Marlon Brando and Marilyn Monroe.
From The Old Friends - New Friends Series.
Prod-FAMCOM Dist-PBS 1981

Lee Suzuki - Home In Hawaii C 19 MIN
16MM FILM, 3/4 OR 1/2 IN VIDEO I-J
Presents a simple episode in the life of a 14-year-old Hawaiian boy to provide a view of the island people whose multi-ethnic society makes them unique among our states. Provides glimpses of the human and social geography of Hawaii.
From The Many Americans Series.
Prod-LCOA Dist-LCOA 1973

Lee Theodore, Buzz Miller And Barbara Naomi CohenêStratyner C 30 MIN
3/4 OR 1/2 INCH VIDEO CASSETTE
Focuses on the development of theatre dance.
From The Eye On Dance - Broadway Dance Series.
Prod-ARTRES Dist-ARTRES

Lee's Parasol C 25 MIN
16MM FILM, 3/4 OR 1/2 IN VIDEO I-J A
Introduces Lee, a Thai girl who is making a beautiful parasol for her cousin, a Buddhist monk. Shows her in the process of constructing the parasol and then presenting it to her cousin as part of the ceremonies at the colorful Buddhist festival.
From The World Cultures And Youth Series.
Prod-CORF Dist-CORF 1980

Leeks - Trimming, Washing, Slicing, Dicing And Cutting For Julienne C 8 MIN
3/4 OR 1/2 INCH VIDEO CASSETTE PRO
Prod-CULINA Dist-CULINA

Leenya - Daughter Of The Noble Blacks Of Surinam C 11 MIN
16MM FILM, 3/4 OR 1/2 IN VIDEO I-J
Looks at the life of Leenya, a young Bush Negro of Surinam.
Prod-GORDAJ Dist-IFB 1973

Leenya - Daughter Of The Noble Blacks Of Surinam (Captioned) C 11 MIN
16MM FILM, 3/4 OR 1/2 IN VIDEO I-J
Looks at the life of Leenya, a young Bush Negro of Surinam.
Prod-GORDAJ Dist-IFB 1973

Left Atrial Myxoma Excision Using The Superior Approach C 9 MIN
3/4 OR 1/2 INCH VIDEO CASSETTE PRO
Shows the left atrial myxoma excision using the superior approach.
Prod-WFP Dist-WFP

Left Brain, Right Brain C 56 MIN
16MM FILM, 3/4 OR 1/2 IN VIDEO H-C A
Presents and demonstrates theories about the development of specialized roles within the human brain.
From The Nature Of Things Series.
Prod-CANBC Dist-FLMLIB 1980

Left Colectomy For Carcinoma Of The Rectosigmoid C 15 MIN
3/4 OR 1/2 INCH VIDEO CASSETTE PRO
Describes left colectomy for carcinoma of the rectosigmoid.
Prod-WFP Dist-WFP Prodn-UKANMC

Left Ventricle Catheterization C 14 MIN
16MM FILM - 3/4 IN VIDEO PRO
Shows the fundamental physiological relationships involved in left ventricle catheterization using the retrograde technique.
LC NO. 76-706953
Prod-NMAC Dist-USNAC 1973

Left Ventricular Hypertrophy C 49 MIN
3/4 OR 1/2 INCH VIDEO CASSETTE PRO
Teaches criteria for the diagnosis of left ventricular hypertrophy. Discusses increased magnitude of the mean QRS vector, ventricular repolarization abnormalities, and left axis deviation.
From The Electrocardiogram Series.
Prod-HSCIC Dist-HSCIC 1982

Left Wall Of Cenotaph Corner, The C 14 MIN
16MM FILM - 3/4 IN VIDEO J-C A
Traces the development of the chock or nut as an alternative to the hammered piton. Includes historical footage of two climbers ascending the Left Wall of Cenotaph Corner in North Wales in 1964, using engineering nuts for direct aid.
Prod-OAKCRK Dist-CRYSP

Left-Handed Woman, The (German) C 119 MIN
16MM FILM OPTICAL SOUND
Focuses on a German housewife, living in Paris, who decides to become unmarried. Records her quiet 'war with the world' over three months of loneliness, near-breakdown, and adjustment. Directed by Peter Handke. With English subtitles.
Prod-UNKNWN Dist-NYFLMS 1978

Left, Right Movie, The C 7 MIN
16MM FILM OPTICAL SOUND K-P S
Teaches and reinforces the concepts of left and right.
LC NO. 73-701041
Prod-FILMSM Dist-FILMSM 1972

Leg Med Musik Og Sang (Music And Games) B 18 MIN
16MM FILM OPTICAL SOUND
A Danish language film. Presents an on-the-spot report from various educational situations. Contributes to the debate about the teaching of music and singing in the kindergarten and the first school years.
Prod-STATNS Dist-STATNS 1968

Leg, Ankle And Foot, The C 29 MIN
3/4 OR 1/2 INCH VIDEO CASSETTE
Examines the leg, ankle and foot for Achillis, tennis leg, sprained ankle, peroneal tendons, talocalcaean joint arthritis, loose body, dancer's heel, plantar fascitis and hallux.
From The Cyriax On Orthopaedic Medicine Series.
Prod-VTRI Dist-VTRI

Legacies C 60 MIN
3/4 OR 1/2 INCH VIDEO CASSETTE H-C A
Discusses the legacies of the Vietnamese war including delayed stress syndrome and the effects of Agent Orange. Shows that the volume of boat people demonstrated that a portion of the Vietnamese were so unable to relate to the victors that they risked their lives to escape.
From The Vietnam - A Television History Series. Episode 13
Prod-WGBHTV Dist-FI 1983

Legacies Of The Depression On The Great Plains—A Series

Explores the impact of the Depression on those who lived through it and its vestiges in the lives of their progeny. Describes both the economic and human conditions of the Depression through still photos and motion pictures from the past and present from the Farm Security Administration's archives.
Prod-NETCHE Dist-NETCHE 1978

Farm, Pt I, The 030 MIN
Small Town, Pt II, The 030 MIN

Legacies Of The Ice Age C 12 MIN
16MM FILM, 3/4 OR 1/2 IN VIDEO I-H
Describes the formation and movement of different types of glaciers and shows their effects on the land. Discusses how glaciers benefit man.
LC NO. 80-707087
Prod-IU Dist-IU 1979

Legacy C 4 MIN
16MM FILM OPTICAL SOUND
Presents an overview of the development of the Earth's natural resources.
LC NO. 80-701233
Prod-VINTN Dist-BBF 1979

Legacy - A Very Short History Of Natural Resources C 5 MIN
16MM FILM OPTICAL SOUND J-C A
Uses claymation to recount the origins of the Earth's key energy resources.
LC NO. 80-701079
Prod-BBF Dist-BBF 1979

Legacy For A Loon C 20 MIN
16MM FILM, 3/4 OR 1/2 IN VIDEO J-C A
Illustrates the life history of the common loon, including courtship, mating, and nesting. Shows the aquatic nature of this diving bird through underwater scenes, and notes that acid rain is a present threat to the survival of this species.
Prod-BERLET Dist-BERLET 1982

Legacy Of A Dream B 29 MIN
16MM FILM, 3/4 OR 1/2 IN VIDEO J-C A
Presents a compilation of newsreel and videotape footage showing the events that secured the vote for American Blacks and ultimately led to the death of Martin Luther King, Jr. Includes a sketch of King's career and statements by Coretta King and Andrew Young on voter registration and the need for Blacks to be informed on exercising their right to vote.
Prod-KAP Dist-TEXFLM 1974

Legacy Of Anne Frank, The C 29 MIN
16MM FILM, 3/4 OR 1/2 IN VIDEO H A
Presents a portrayal of Anne Frank, using photographs of the house she lived in, her school and the Annex where she and her family were confined. Interviews her teacher and her father, emphasizing how their love and hope survived.
Prod-NBCTV Dist-MGHT Prodn-NBCTV 1967

Legacy Of Anne Sullivan, The C 28 MIN
16MM FILM OPTICAL SOUND K-C A
Demonstrates the work being done today to teach and rehabilitate deaf-blind children and adults. Describes the pioneering work of Anne Sullivan with Helen Keller.
LC NO. 79-702444
Prod-PERKNS Dist-CAMPF Prodn-CAMPF 1968

Legacy Of Currier And Ives, The C 23 MIN
16MM FILM MAGNETIC SOUND I-H A
Surveys 19th century American life with Currier and Ives lithographs and period memorabilia. Includes such categories as

general history, farming life, city life, sports and pastimes, riverlife, war scenes, life in the West, trains and patriotism.
LC NO. 76-701611
Prod-ESMARK Dist-ESMARK Prodn-CREATW

Legacy Of Gemini C 18 MIN
3/4 OR 1/2 INCH VIDEO CASSETTE
Traces the major accomplishments of the Gemini manned spaceflight program and their relationships to the Apollo lunar landing program. Presents the 12 Gemini flights as a single composite flight. Issued in 1967 as a motion picture.
LC NO. 80-707381
Prod-NASA Dist-USNAC Prodn-AVCORP 1980

Legacy Of Gemini C 30 MIN
16MM FILM - 3/4 IN VIDEO
Discusses the legacy of the Gemini space program.
From The History Of Space Travel Series.
Prod-NASAC Dist-MDCPB

Legacy Of Genius - The Story Of Thomas Alva Edison C 59 MIN
3/4 INCH VIDEO CASSETTE
Examines the extraordinary life and career of Thomas Alva Edison, America's most prolific inventor.
Prod-SCETV Dist-PUBTEL

Legacy Of L S B Leakey, The C 59 MIN
16MM FILM, 3/4 OR 1/2 IN VIDEO
Documents the life and career of anthropologist Louis Leakey.
LC NO. 80-706375
Prod-NGS Dist-NGS 1977

Legacy Of Rome, The C 52 MIN
16MM FILM, 3/4 OR 1/2 IN VIDEO J-C A
Describes the grandeur and imperial power of ancient Rome. Examines the influence on civilization of Roman achievements in the arts, the sciences, jurisprudence, and politics. Includes sequences filmed in Italy and in outposts of the Roman Empire from Libya to Scotland and from Jordan to the south of France.
From The Saga Of Western Man Series.
Prod-ABCTV Dist-MGHT 1966

Legacy Of Rome, The, Pt 1 C 22 MIN
16MM FILM, 3/4 OR 1/2 IN VIDEO J-C A
Describes the grandeur and imperial power of ancient Rome. Examines the influence on civilization of Roman achievements in the arts, the sciences, jurisprudence, and politics. Includes sequences filmed in Italy and in outposts of the Roman Empire from Libya to Scotland and from Jordan to the south of France.
From The Saga Of Western Man Series.
Prod-ABCTV Dist-MGHT 1966

Legacy Of Rome, The, Pt 2 C 30 MIN
16MM FILM, 3/4 OR 1/2 IN VIDEO J-C A
Describes the grandeur and imperial power of ancient Rome. Examines the influence on civilization of Roman achievements in the arts, the sciences, jurisprudence, and politics. Includes sequences filmed in Italy and in outposts of the Roman Empire from Libya to Scotland and from Jordan to the south of France.
From The Saga Of Western Man Series.
Prod-ABCTV Dist-MGHT 1966

Legacy Of The Mountain Men C 29 MIN
16MM FILM OPTICAL SOUND J-C A
Shows modern day mountain men re-creating the spirit and activities of 19th century fur trappers at an annual gathering in the western United States. Depicts people using period tools and participating in hatchet-throwing and shooting contests while other members of the group explain why they enjoy re-enacting the harsh and often lonely life of the trapper.
LC NO. 80-701985
Prod-BYU Dist-BYU 1980

Legacy Of The Mountainmen, The C 29 MIN
16MM FILM, 3/4 OR 1/2 IN VIDEO J-H A
Tells the story of 19th century mountainmen who roamed the western wilderness in search of valuable, fur-bearing animals.
Prod-BYU Dist-EBEC 1980

Legacy Of The New Deal, The C 30 MIN
3/4 OR 1/2 INCH VIDEO CASSETTE C
Discusses the legacy of FDR and the New Deal, which created the expectation that the national government can respond to national concerns.
America - The Second Century Series.
Prod-DALCCD Dist-DALCCD

Legacy Of Wings C 40 MIN
3/4 OR 1/2 INCH VIDEO CASSETTE
Recounts the pioneering work performed by Harold F Pitcairn. Shows how Pitcairn's work with autogyros led to the development of the modern helicopter. Chronicles the events that led to the establishment of Eastern Airlines.
Prod-MIRABC Dist-MIRABC 1983

Legacy Restored, A C 10 MIN
16MM FILM, 3/4 OR 1/2 IN VIDEO
Recounts the history of the California State Capitol and its recent restoration.
Prod-UCEMC Dist-UCEMC

Legacy, The C 28 MIN
16MM FILM, 3/4 OR 1/2 IN VIDEO
Explains the total systems approach to fire safety and building protection. Focuses on the first GSA high-rise structure to include a total fire safety system, including a total sprinkler system, two-way voice communications, smoke detection equipment and other fire safety devices.
LC NO. 81-707713
Prod-USGSA Dist-USNAC 1975

Legacy, The - Children Of Holocaust Survivors C 23 MIN
16MM FILM OPTICAL SOUND H-C A
Presents interviews with five children of holocaust survivors, who explain how their parents' wartime experiences have affected their own lives.
LC NO. 80-700044
Prod-ROSEMS Dist-ROSEMS 1979

Legacy, The - Children Of Holocaust Survivors C 23 MIN
16MM FILM, 3/4 OR 1/2 IN VIDEO
Explores the painful experiences of those whose lives were touched by the Holocaust. Focuses on the children of the survivors.
Prod-JANUS Dist-FI 1980

Legal Affairs C 30 MIN
3/4 OR 1/2 INCH VIDEO CASSETTE
Contains information concerning contracts, buying, selling and renting. Includes estate planning and other obligations. Presented by David Ralston.
From The How People Age Fifty And Up Can Plan For A More Successful Retirement Series.
Prod-RCOMTV Dist-SYLWAT

Legal Aspects Of Marriage C 30 MIN
3/4 OR 1/2 INCH VIDEO CASSETTE C A
Describes basic legal requirements and some differences between state's laws. Presents common-law marriages and marriage contracts as variations of the traditional ceremony.
From The Family Portrait - A Study Of Contemporary Lifestyles Series. Lesson 10
Prod-SCCON Dist-CDTEL

Legal Bibliography C 52 MIN
3/4 OR 1/2 INCH VIDEO CASSETTE
Helps social workers feel more comfortable in the courtroom setting and helps develop their legal skills.
From The Legal Training For Children Welfare Workers Series. Pt I
Prod-UWISC Dist-UWISC 1975

Legal Discussion Of A Hit And Run, A B 28 MIN
3/4 INCH VIDEO CASSETTE
Discusses the legal points about the police investigation and interrogation and the rights of witnesses or suspects appearing in the film Investigation Of A Hit And Run. Features Professor James Vorenberg of Harvard Law School.
From The Pittsburgh Police Series.
Prod-DOCEDR Dist-DOCEDR Prodn-MSHLLJ

Legal Ethics - Applying The Model Rules—A Series
PRO
Dramatizes attorneys making ethical decisions. Comments on the propriety or impropriety of the decisions in light of the Model Rules.
Prod-ABACPE Dist-ABACPE

Advocacy	040 MIN
Counseling	034 MIN
Interviewing And The Lawyer-Client Relationship	043 MIN
Investigation	032 MIN
Negotiation	035 MIN

Legal Implications, Communication And Family Living Styles C 30 MIN
16MM FILM - 3/4 IN VIDEO J-C A
See series title for descriptive statement.
From The Middle Road Traveler Series.
Prod-BAYUCM Dist-GPITVL 1979

Legal Issues, Processes And Roles In Foste Care, Pt I B 60 MIN
3/4 OR 1/2 INCH VIDEO CASSETTE
Discusses various aspects of legal and judicial matters in foster care, including provisions of the Children's Code, juvenile court procedures, attorney and social worker roles, legal rights of children/parents/foster parents and issues arising from dealing with family matters.
Prod-UWISC Dist-UWISC 1978

Legal Issues, Processes And Roles In Foster Care, Pt II B 60 MIN
3/4 OR 1/2 INCH VIDEO CASSETTE
Continues discussion of various aspects of legal and judicial matters in foster care.
Prod-UWISC Dist-UWISC 1978

Legal Issues, Processes And Roles In Foster Care, Pt III B 33 MIN
3/4 OR 1/2 INCH VIDEO CASSETTE
Concludes discussion of various aspects of legal and judicial matters in foster care.
Prod-UWISC Dist-UWISC 1978

Legal Or Illegal C 20 MIN
3/4 OR 1/2 INCH VIDEO CASSETTE J-H
See series title for descriptive statement.
From The Contract Series.
Prod-KYTV Dist-AITECH 1977

Legal Reference Materials C 24 MIN
3/4 OR 1/2 INCH VIDEO CASSETTE
Discusses Maryland legal reference materials. Describes statutory and administrative law in terms of the library patron's reference questions.
Prod-BCPL Dist-LVN

Legal Requirements For Boatmen B 18 MIN
16MM FILM - 3/4 IN VIDEO
Lists the state and Federal legal requirements for boat numbering and documenting, lifesaving devices, fire extinguishers, horns and whistles, lights and accident reports.
Prod-USNAC Dist-USNAC 1968

Legal Rights C 30 MIN
3/4 OR 1/2 INCH VIDEO CASSETTE
See series title for descriptive statement.
From The Rights And Citizenship Series.
Prod-MAETEL Dist-CAMB

Legal System, The C 30 MIN
3/4 OR 1/2 INCH VIDEO CASSETTE C
Dramatizes vignettes to explain and illustrate many types of law. Clarifies many ways Americans settle their legal disputes through constitutional, administrative, statutory, criminal and civil laws.
From The American Government 2 Series.
Prod-DALCCD Dist-DALCCD

Legal Training For Children Welfare Workers—A Series
Presents a series on various legal aspects of dealing with children as welfare cases.
Prod-UWISC Dist-UWISC 1975

Children's Code	058 MIN
Delinquency	058 MIN
General Court Strategy	055 MIN
Grantsmanship And Funding	060 MIN
Innovative Services For Children And Youth	058 MIN
Legal Bibliography	052 MIN
Protective Services	058 MIN
Termination Of Parental Rights	059 MIN

Legal Typing - A Lawyer Defines A Good Legal Secretary C 11 MIN
1/2 IN VIDEO CASSETTE BETA/VHS
From The Typing - Legal Series.
Prod-RMI Dist-RMI

Legal Typing - Course introduction C 17 MIN
1/2 IN VIDEO CASSETTE BETA/VHS
From The Typing - Legal Series.
Prod-RMI Dist-RMI

Legate, The B 30 MIN
16MM FILM OPTICAL SOUND
A drama of the Jewish struggle for religious freedom in Jerusalem in the middle of the second century B C. Describes the role of a Roman legate in making treaty arrangements with Simon Maccabeus, victorious leader of the Jewish movement. Features the celebration of the festival of Hanukkah.
LC NO. FIA65-1100
Prod-JTS Dist-NAAJS Prodn-NBC 1965

Legend At Big Sur, A C 15 MIN
16MM FILM OPTICAL SOUND C A
Presents a surrealistic cinepoem on Big Sur, California.
Prod-CFS Dist-CFS

Legend Days Are Over C 5 MIN
16MM FILM, 3/4 OR 1/2 IN VIDEO
Presents in kinestasis animation various aspects of the life of the American Indian, conveying the human impact of the cultural change from the world of legend to modern life.
Prod-PFP Dist-PFP 1973

Legend Of Corn, The C 26 MIN
16MM FILM, 3/4 OR 1/2 IN VIDEO
Dramatizes an Ojibway Indian legend telling how the Great Manitou sent corn to keep the people from hunger.
Prod-FOTH Dist-FOTH

Legend Of Duncan Falls, The C 22 MIN
3/4 INCH VIDEO CASSETTE
Dramatizes the story of David Duncan, one of the first white explorers of the Muskingum River in Ohio.
Prod-OHC Dist-HRC

Legend Of El Dorado C 25 MIN
16MM FILM, 3/4 OR 1/2 IN VIDEO
Relates the myth and reality of gold as viewed through the pre-Columbian treasure of Bogota's Gold Museum.
Prod-MOMALA Dist-MOMALA

Legend Of El Dorado (Spanish) C 25 MIN
16MM FILM, 3/4 OR 1/2 IN VIDEO
Relates the myth and reality of gold as viewed through the pre-Columbian treasure of Bogota's Gold Museum.
Prod-MOMALA Dist-MOMALA

Legend Of Harriet Tubman, The C 15 MIN
3/4 OR 1/2 INCH VIDEO CASSETTE I-C
See series title for descriptive statement.
From The Juba Series.
Prod-WETATV Dist-WETATV

Legend Of John Henry, The C 11 MIN
16MM FILM OPTICAL SOUND I-C A
Presents the ballad of John Henry, the greatest steel-driving man of them all. Portrays strength, courage and perseverance in the face of overwhelming odds.
Prod-NWMA Dist-NWMA 1974

Legend Of John Henry, The C 11 MIN
16MM FILM, 3/4 OR 1/2 IN VIDEO P-J
Features Roberta Flack singing the scored narrative describing John Henry's stubborn refusal to allow a mechanized steam drill win the Chesapeake and Ohio railroad's drive through the big bend tunnel in West Virginia, in 1873. Explains that John Henry, fictionalized for his prowess and stamina as a steel driver, died beating the steam drill through the mountain.
Prod-BOSUST Dist-PFP 1974

Legend Of Johnny Appleseed C 20 MIN
16MM FILM, 3/4 OR 1/2 IN VIDEO I-H A
Presents legend of John Chapman, Johnny Appleseed, in verse and in music sung by Dennis Day.
Prod-DISNEY Dist-WDEMCO 1958

Legend Of Lake Titicaca C 22 MIN
16MM FILM, 3/4 OR 1/2 IN VIDEO I-C
A shortened version of Legend Of Lake Titicaca. Features Jacques Cousteau and his divers in search of Inca treasure in Lake Titicaca, 12,000 feet above sea level. Shows how they discover a unique species of aquatic frog instead of the treasure.
From The Undersea World Of Jacques Cousteau Series.
Prod-METROM Dist-CF 1971

Legend Of Lake Titicaca C 52 MIN
16MM FILM, 3/4 OR 1/2 IN VIDEO
Reports on Jacques Cousteau's investigation of Lake Titicaca's legend of Inca treasure. Shows that the treasure proves not to exist, but that ancient pottery and a unique species of aquatic frog are found.
From The Undersea World Of Jacques Cousteau Series.
Prod-METROM Dist-CF 1971

Legend Of Lobo, The C 68 MIN
16MM FILM OPTICAL SOUND
Presents the true story of Lobo the wolf, who leads his family and the wolf pack into lands uninvaded by man.
Prod-DISNEY Dist-TWYMAN 1962

Legend Of Mark Twain, The C 32 MIN
16MM FILM, 3/4 OR 1/2 IN VIDEO I-H A
Traces Samuel Clemen's remarkable life and writing career concerning America and dramatizes selections from two of his well-known classics 'THE ADVENTURES OF HUCKLEBERRY FINN' and 'THE CELEBRATED JUMPING FROG OF CALAVERAS COUNTY.'
Prod-ABCTV Dist-BNCHMK 1969

Legend Of Old Bill C 9 MIN
16MM FILM OPTICAL SOUND
Presents Willard Madsen, who relates in American sign language his story about a town hermit called Old Bill.
LC NO. 76-701688
Prod-JOYCE Dist-JOYCE 1973

Legend Of Old Bill, The C 9 MIN
16MM FILM SILENT I-C A
Presents Willard Madsen relating, in American sign language for the deaf, his own story about a town hermit called Old Bill.
LC NO. 76-701688
Prod-JOYCE Dist-JOYCE 1975

Legend Of Paul Bunyan, The C 13 MIN
16MM FILM, 3/4 OR 1/2 IN VIDEO I-C A
Depicts Paul Bunyan, who was no ordinary man. Points out that embodied in him are the qualities of the early pioneers who helped to fashion the character of America.
Prod-BOSUST Dist-PFP 1973

Legend Of Paul Bunyan, The C 15 MIN
16MM FILM, 3/4 OR 1/2 IN VIDEO P
Presents an adaptation of the legend of Paul Bunyan.
From The Magic Carpet Series.
Prod-SDCSS Dist-GPITVL 1977

Legend Of Paulie Green, The C 29 MIN
16MM FILM - 3/4 IN VIDEO H
Features a problem drinker and a young woman who has an alcoholic mother. Shows, through the use of flashbacks, events that triggered the drinker's problem and demonstrates how a hotline assists the girl to cope with her mother's problem.
From The Dial Alcohol Series.
LC NO. 76-704026
Prod-USOLLR Dist-USNAC Prodn-NVETA 1976

Legend Of Paulie Green, The C 30 MIN
3/4 OR 1/2 INCH VIDEO CASSETTE H
Shows the progress of an advisor with a drinking problem. Introduces the daughter of an alcoholic mother to Alateen, an organization for children of alcoholics.
From The Dial A-L-C-O-H-O-L Series.
Prod-EFLMC Dist-GPITVL

Legend Of Rockmonotone C 15 MIN
16MM FILM OPTICAL SOUND H-C A
Recaptures the great days of the silent melodrama through the story of hero Rockmonotone, his sweetheart Lotta Passionata and the villian Dudley Dagger.
Prod-UWFKD Dist-UWFKD

Legend Of Rudolph Valentino, The B 71 MIN
16MM FILM, 3/4 OR 1/2 IN VIDEO H-C A
Explores the life of Rudolph Valentino.
Prod-JANUS Dist-TEXFLM

Legend Of Salt, The - A South East Asian Folk Tale C 7 MIN
16MM FILM, 3/4 OR 1/2 IN VIDEO P-I
Tells how the greed of an evil brother and a magic salt jar turned the ocean salty.
From The Folk Tales From Around The World Series.
Prod-ADPF Dist-SF 1980

Legend Of Sleepy Hollow, The C 13 MIN
16MM FILM, 3/4 OR 1/2 IN VIDEO P-C
Presents an animated film based on The Legend Of Sleepy Hollow, by Washington Irving. Illustrates the spectral spirits and twilight superstitions that haunt the town of Sleepy Hollow.
Prod-BOSUST Dist-PFP 1972

Legend Of Sleepy Hollow, The C 20 MIN
16MM FILM, 3/4 OR 1/2 IN VIDEO I-H
Uses animation to tell Washington Irving's tale about a gangly schoolmaster and a headless ghost who haunts the Hudson River region.
Prod-DISNEY Dist-WDEMCO 1974

Legend Of Sleepy Hollow, The C 46 MIN
16MM FILM, 3/4 OR 1/2 IN VIDEO I-H
Portrays the story of the Headless Horseman which haunts the Hudson Valley near Tarrytown, New York. Based on the story The Legend Of Sleepy Hollow by Washington Irving.
From The Classic Stories Series.
Prod-LUF Dist-LUF 1979

Legend Of Sleepy Hollow, The C 99 MIN
16MM FILM, 3/4 OR 1/2 IN VIDEO I-H
Portrays the story of the Headless Horseman which haunts the Hudson Valley near Tarrytown, New York. Based on the story The Legend Of Sleepy Hollow by Washington Irving.
Prod-LUF Dist-LUF 1979

Legend Of Sleepy Hollow, The (Spanish) C 13 MIN
16MM FILM, 3/4 OR 1/2 IN VIDEO I-C A
A Spanish language version of the film, The Legend of Sleepy Hollow. Relates Washington Irving's classic American folk tale and the story of Ichabod Crane in an animated film which retains the richness of Irving's original language.
Prod-PFP Dist-PFP

Legend Of The Birds C 22 MIN
16MM FILM OPTICAL SOUND H-C A
A narrator uses the natural rhythm of Longfellow's 'HIAWATHA' to describe the habits of New Zealand's birds and to tell the many Maori legends about birds.
LC NO. 72-706200
Prod-NZNFU Dist-NZNFU 1960

Legend Of The Boy And The Eagle, The C 21 MIN
16MM FILM, 3/4 OR 1/2 IN VIDEO P-J
Presents an adaptation of the Legend of The Boy And The Eagle, a drama story about a young Hopi Indian boy who suffers grave consequences after he frees the sacred eagle of his tribe.
Prod-DISNEY Dist-WDEMCO 1976

Legend Of The Cruel Giant, The C 11 MIN
16MM FILM, 3/4 OR 1/2 IN VIDEO K-P
Tells what happens when a fisherman releases a genie from a bottle.
Prod-SYZMT Dist-CAROUF

Legend Of The Ilima Blossoms C 11 MIN
16MM FILM OPTICAL SOUND I-C A
Presents the Hawaiian legend telling how the ilima blossoms appeared and why they could be worn only by those of royal lineage.
Prod-CINEPC Dist-CINEPC

Legend Of The Magic Knives C 11 MIN
16MM FILM, 3/4 OR 1/2 IN VIDEO I-H
Portrays an ancient Indian legend in the setting of a totem village in the Pacific Northwest. Deals with an old chief who realizes that the carvings of an apprentice are superior to his and decides to knife him.
Prod-EBEC Dist-EBEC 1971

Legend Of The Paramo, The C 22 MIN
16MM FILM, 3/4 OR 1/2 IN VIDEO J-C A
Describes how a 12-year-old boy in Colombia meets a phantom mule-driver and manages to conquer his fear.
Prod-SAMPER Dist-PHENIX 1977

Legend Of The Paramo, The (Spanish) C 22 MIN
16MM FILM, 3/4 OR 1/2 IN VIDEO J-C A
A Spanish language videocassette. Describes the cultural identity of South American people through the fantasy of a 12-year-old boy in Colombia, who recalls the legend of the Paramo, a desolate highland region near Caldas, Columbia.
Prod-SAMPER Dist-PHENIX 1977

Legend Of The Stick Game C 30 MIN
3/4 INCH VIDEO CASSETTE
Explores the functions of myth and legend in American Indian culture. Describes the role of the oral tradition.
From The Real People Series.
Prod-KSPSTV Dist-GPITVL 1976

Legend, The C 15 MIN
2 INCH VIDEOTAPE I
Examines the legendary stories of Paul Bunyan, John Henry and Sleepy Hollow.
From The Images Series.
Prod-CVETVC Dist-GPITVL

Legend, The C 15 MIN
3/4 OR 1/2 INCH VIDEO CASSETTE K-P
Examines the history of French-Americans.
From The La Bonne Aventure Series.
Prod-MPBN Dist-GPITVL

Legendary West, The C 53 MIN
16MM FILM, 3/4 OR 1/2 IN VIDEO J-H A
Uses Hollywood motion pictures and archive material to trace the creation of the legend of the West. Compares the popular image of bandits, badmen, law officers and the American Indian with respect to the way it really was.
From The American Documents Series.
Prod-LUF Dist-LUF 1976

Legendary Women In Dance - Syvilla Fort And Thelma Hill C 30 MIN
3/4 OR 1/2 INCH VIDEO CASSETTE
See series title for descriptive statement.
From The Third World Dance - Tracing Roots Series.
Prod-ARCVID Dist-ARCVID

Legislative Branch, The C 26 MIN
16MM FILM, 3/4 OR 1/2 IN VIDEO J-C A
A shortened version of the motion picture The Legislative Branch. Analyzes how the United States Congress works by presenting interviews with several senators and congressmen. Narrated by Jack Anderson.
From The Government As It Is Series.
Prod-EMLEN Dist-PFP

Legislative Branch, The C 58 MIN
16MM FILM, 3/4 OR 1/2 IN VIDEO J-C A
Analyzes how the United States Congress works by presenting interviews with several senators and congressmen. Narrated by Jack Anderson.
From The Government As It Is Series.
Prod-EMLEN Dist-PFP

Legislative Fight For Metrication C 20 MIN
3/4 INCH VIDEO CASSETTE
Illustrates the simplicity of the metric system and explains action the government has taken toward conversion to the metric system. Notes the feelings of the general public toward such conversion.
From The Metric Marmalade Series.
Prod-WCVETV Dist-GPITVL 1979

Legislative Game, The - Government Relations, Political Action C 40 MIN
1/2 INCH VIDEOTAPE A
Provides instructions to allow AACD members to exercise political influence. Shows, in two parts, how to become involved in grassroots legislative action.
Prod-AACD Dist-AACD

Legislative Report C 29 MIN
3/4 INCH VIDEO CASSETTE
Covers legislation that would benefit women, including child care credit, national health insurance, displaced homemakers' legislation, and the Humphrey-Hawkins Bill.
From The Woman Series.
Prod-WNEDTV Dist-PUBTEL

Legislative Report Update C 29 MIN
3/4 INCH VIDEO CASSETTE
Discusses attempts to lobby for women's issues.
From The Woman Series.
Prod-WNEDTV Dist-PUBTEL

Lehman Caves National Monument C 13 MIN
16MM FILM - 3/4 IN VIDEO
Focuses on the formation of limestone caves by highlighting the Lehman Caves National Monument in Nevada. Issued in 1971 as a motion picture.
LC NO. 79-706135
Prod-USNPS Dist-USNAC Prodn-BARBRE 1979

Leiden Connection C 20 MIN
16MM FILM, 3/4 OR 1/2 IN VIDEO
Explains the trade opportunity program administered by the U S Industry and Trade Administration, which provides a computer matching service bringing together U S sellers with foreign buyers. Issued in 1978 as a motion picture.
From The Export Development Series.
LC NO. 80-706631
Prod-USIATA Dist-USNAC 1980

Leidenfrost Effect, The C 30 MIN
3/4 OR 1/2 INCH VIDEO CASSETTE H
Presents physics professor Jearl Walker offering graphic and unusual demonstrations exemplifying the principles of the Leidenfrost effect, in which rapid evaporation prevents the immediate transfer of heat.
From The Kinetic Karnival Of Jearl Walker. Pt 5
LC NO. 83-706119
Prod-WVIZTV Dist-GPITVL 1982

Leisure C 14 MIN
16MM FILM, 3/4 OR 1/2 IN VIDEO
Surveys man's encounter with the idea that what he does with his leisure time may become the determining factor in society's system of values. Traces the history of leisure, from the play of cavemen to modern times.
Prod-FLMAUS Dist-PFP

Leisure And Pursuit Of Happiness C 20 MIN
3/4 INCH VIDEO CASSETTE J-H
Looks at young people who, through their skills, imagination and creative ability, are deriving real pleasure from their leisure time.
From The Dollar Data Series.
LC NO. 81-707358
Prod-WHROTV Dist-GPITVL 1974

Leisure And Recreation C 30 MIN
3/4 OR 1/2 INCH VIDEO CASSETTE C A
Presents travel and vacation options such as trip insurance, time-sharing arrangements, and home exchange programs. Discusses precautions to take before leaving on a vacation.
From The Personal Finance Series. Lesson 7
Prod-SCCON Dist-CDTEL

Leisure And Vacations C 11 MIN
16MM FILM, 3/4 OR 1/2 IN VIDEO I-H
Examines how the French spend their leisure time, including such activities as soccer, rugby, sailing, mountain climbing and touring.
From The Life In Modern France Series.
Prod-EBEC Dist-EBEC 1971

Leisure Planning - A Gerontological Approach C 22 MIN
3/4 OR 1/2 INCH VIDEO CASSETTE
Tells how to identify and manage problems in leisure planning for the elderly. Presents objective and subjective observations, and addresses twenty problems, psychological needs and goal statements.
Prod-USVA Dist-USNAC

Leisure Time Photography C 20 MIN
16MM FILM, 3/4 OR 1/2 IN VIDEO J-C A
Shows world class photographer Freeman Patterson conducting

a course in 'making pictures,' the medium he considers to be the most accessible for leisure time pursuits and one offering unlimited opportunities for self-expression.
Prod-HARDAP Dist-BCNFL 1981

Leisure Time, U.S.S.R. C 12 MIN
16MM FILM, 3/4 OR 1/2 IN VIDEO J-C A
See series title for descriptive statement.
From The Russia Today Series.
Prod-IFF Dist-IFF

Lemmings And Arctic Bird Life, The (Dutch) C 21 MIN
16MM FILM, 3/4 OR 1/2 IN VIDEO I-H
Documents the lemmings' mass march into the sea during times of famine. Looks at Arctic birds.
From The White Wilderness (Dutch) Series.
Prod-WDEMCO Dist-WDEMCO 1964

Lemmings And Arctic Bird Life, The (French) C 21 MIN
16MM FILM, 3/4 OR 1/2 IN VIDEO I-H
Documents the lemmings' mass march into the sea during times of famine. Looks at Arctic birds.
From The White Wilderness (French) Series.
Prod-WDEMCO Dist-WDEMCO 1964

Lemmings And Arctic Bird Life, The (German) C 21 MIN
16MM FILM, 3/4 OR 1/2 IN VIDEO I-H
Documents the lemmings' mass march into the sea during times of famine. Looks at Arctic birds.
From The White Wilderness (German) Series.
Prod-WDEMCO Dist-WDEMCO 1964

Lemmings And Arctic Bird Life, The (Norwegian) C 21 MIN
16MM FILM, 3/4 OR 1/2 IN VIDEO I-H
Documents the lemmings' mass march into the sea during times of famine. Looks at Arctic birds.
From The White Wilderness (Norwegian) Series.
Prod-WDEMCO Dist-WDEMCO 1964

Lemmings And Arctic Bird Life, The (Portuguese) C 21 MIN
16MM FILM, 3/4 OR 1/2 IN VIDEO I-H
Documents the lemmings' mass march into the sea during times of famine. Looks at Arctic birds.
From The White Wilderness (Portuguese) Series.
Prod-WDEMCO Dist-WDEMCO 1964

Lemmings And Arctic Bird Life, The (Swedish) C 21 MIN
16MM FILM, 3/4 OR 1/2 IN VIDEO I-H
Documents the lemmings' mass march into the sea during times of famine. Looks at Arctic birds.
From The White Wilderness (Swedish) Series.
Prod-WDEMCO Dist-WDEMCO 1964

Lemonade Stand, The - What's Fair C 14 MIN
16MM FILM, 3/4 OR 1/2 IN VIDEO P-I
Focuses on the meaning of commitment, obligation and responsibility to others and introduces some basic principles of economics, such as the investment of time and money the boys made to set up a lemonade stand.
Prod-EBEC Dist-EBEC 1970

Lemonade Suite C 30 MIN
3/4 OR 1/2 INCH VIDEO CASSETTE H-C A
Employs rhythmic instrumental compositions and fluid modern-dance movements to interpret selected poems by Gwendolyn Brooks. Relates the story of a girl who lusts for adventure, gets pregnant, suffers an abortion, then renews her vigor for life.
LC NO. 83-706042
Prod-WINNER Dist-IU 1981

Len Chandler C 52 MIN
3/4 OR 1/2 INCH VIDEO CASSETTE
Features Pete Seeger and Len Chandler trading songs they have written including 'Keep On Keeping On,' and 'Beans in my Ears.'
From The Rainbow Quest Series.
Prod-SEEGER Dist-CWATER

Lena The Glassblower C 25 MIN
16MM FILM, 3/4 OR 1/2 IN VIDEO J-C A
Introduces Lena Sundberg who is glassblowing at the Orresfors Glassworks in Sweden. Follows her through her work at the factory as she learns the difficult breath control and dexterity needed to produce fine glasswork. Shows how she pursuades her parents to let her forego college for glassblowing.
From The World Cultures And Youth Series.
Prod-SUNRIS Dist-CORF 1981

Lend A Paw C 8 MIN
16MM FILM, 3/4 OR 1/2 IN VIDEO P-I
Shows conflict between good and evil in the individual and poses typical dilemmas about self-worth and personal denial by presenting a story about Pluto's problem with a new kitten.
Prod-DISNEY Dist-WDEMCO 1975

Length C 25 MIN
3/4 OR 1/2 INCH VIDEO CASSETTE
Discusses the most common metric units of length and presents guidelines for relating these lengths to everyday use.
From The Metric Education Video Tapes For Pre And Inservice Teachers (K-8) Series.
Prod-PUAVC Dist-PUAVC

Length C 30 MIN
3/4 INCH VIDEO CASSETTE T
Discusses length measurement with the metric system. Shows classroom activities which can show length measurement to children.
From The Measure For Measure Series.
Prod-UWISCM Dist-GPITVL 1979

Length Of A Plane Curve C
3/4 INCH VIDEO CASSETTE
See series title for descriptive statement.
From The Calculus Series.
Prod-MDDE Dist-MDCPB

Length 1 - Who Measures C 15 MIN
16MM FILM, 3/4 OR 1/2 IN VIDEO I-J
Explores metric measurement in downtown Toronto with two teenage boys. Demonstrates proper length-measuring techniques, using the zero point, recording results with proper symbols, using the appropriate measurement instrument and learning the linear equivalents.
From The Measuremetric Series.
LC NO. 80-706495
Prod-AITV Dist-AITECH Prodn-OECA 1977

Length 2 - A Thousand Clicks C 15 MIN
16MM FILM, 3/4 OR 1/2 IN VIDEO I-J
Explores metric measurement in downtown Toronto with two teenage boys. Demonstrates how to measure circular objects and record the answers using decimal notation, how to measure lengths that are more than one meter and how to use the trundle wheel to measure a kilometer.
From The Measuremetric Series.
LC NO. 80-706496
Prod-AITV Dist-AITECH Prodn-OECA 1977

Length 3 - The Final Test C 15 MIN
16MM FILM, 3/4 OR 1/2 IN VIDEO I-J
Explores metric measurement in downtown Toronto with two teenage boys. Demonstrates estimation, measurement, recording, selection of an appropriate instrument and the use of equivalents and decimal notation.
From The Measuremetric Series.
LC NO. 80-706497
Prod-AITV Dist-AITECH Prodn-OECA 1977

Lengthened Maxim, The - Formal Satire C 30 MIN
2 INCH VIDEOTAPE J-H
See series title for descriptive statement.
From The From Franklin To Frost - Benjamin Franklin Series.
Prod-MPATI Dist-GPITVL

Lengths And Angles B
16MM FILM OPTICAL SOUND
Discusses the possibility of generalizing the concepts of length and angle to non-geometric vector spaces, using the idea of an inner product.
Prod-OPENU Dist-OPENU

Lenin B 39 MIN
16MM FILM, 3/4 OR 1/2 IN VIDEO J-C A
Documents the life and times of Lenin. Includes archival footage.
Prod-GRANDA Dist-LCOA 1978

Lenin And The Great Ungluing C 57 MIN
16MM FILM, 3/4 OR 1/2 IN VIDEO H-C A
Focuses on the breakup of the old political order in Soviet Russia under Lenin. Based on the book The Age Of Uncertainty by John Kenneth Galbraith.
From The Age Of Uncertainty Series.
LC NO. 77-701489
Prod-BBCL Dist-FI 1977

Lenin Prepares For Revolution B 22 MIN
16MM FILM, 3/4 OR 1/2 IN VIDEO
Traces the role of Lenin as a revolutinary in his early life. Conveys the feeling of popularity he had with the masses and constant harassment from the government which was caused by his unswerving devotion to the overthrow of the Tsar. Portrays Lenin's leadership not as the cause of the revolution, but as an imprint on the revolution and modern Russia.
From The Russian Revolution Series.
Prod-GRATV Dist-FI 1971

Leningrad Mint, The C 15 MIN
16MM FILM, 3/4 OR 1/2 IN VIDEO J-C A
Offers a history of Russian coins and medals beginning with the birth of the ruble in 1724. Visits the Leningrad Mint to show the different phases of coin-making.
Prod-LENPSF Dist-CAROUF

Lenny Bruce On TV B 35 MIN
16MM FILM OPTICAL SOUND H-C A
Presents the late comic Lenny Bruce as he appeared on two Steve Allen shows and in an unaired pilot for a show of his own. Asks if he was a sinner with a dirty mouth or a saint with a rusty halo.
Prod-NYFLMS Dist-NYFLMS

Lenny Moore C 20 MIN
16MM FILM OPTICAL SOUND I-J
Shows how Lenny Moore's speed and pass-receiving ability made him a football great. Follows his career from his days at Penn State University through all the years with the Baltimore Colts and Johnny Unitas. Features Lenny talking about film footage of some of his games.
From The Sports Legends Series.
Prod-COUNFI Dist-COUNFI

Lenses On Nature C 27 MIN
3/4 OR 1/2 INCH VIDEO CASSETTE K A
Features nature photographers Len and Maria Zorn showing their techniques photographing birds, insects and flowers.
Prod-SUTHRB Dist-SUTHRB

Lenses, Pt 1 B 22 MIN
16MM FILM OPTICAL SOUND H
Begins with a comparison of the virtual images formed by other convex and concave lenses and then shows their opposing properties in relation to parallel incident rays. Includes how a lens works and spherical aberration as well as the formation of a real image by a convex lens.
From The Optics Series.
Prod-CETO Dist-GPITVL

Lenses, Pt 2 B 22 MIN
16MM FILM OPTICAL SOUND H
Continues the study of the formation of images both real and virtual by a convex lens. Includes the virtual image formed by a concave lens, application of principles to a camera, the action of the lens of the human eye, and defects of vision and their correction.
From The Optics Series.
Prod-CETO Dist-GPITVL

Lentil B 9 MIN
16MM FILM, 3/4 OR 1/2 IN VIDEO K-P
An iconographic motion picture, using the original illustrations and story from the children's picture book by Robert Mc Closkey, about a boy who couldn't whistle and saved the day with his harmonica.
Prod-WWS Dist-WWS 1957

Leo - A Dream About A Lion C 16 MIN
16MM FILM, 3/4 OR 1/2 IN VIDEO
Tells how a toy stuffed lion comes to life as a real lion cub in a little girl's dream.
Prod-FLMFR Dist-FLMFR

Leo At The Photgrapher C 8 MIN
16MM FILM, 3/4 OR 1/2 IN VIDEO P-I
Presents an animated tale about Leo the Lion and his adventures at a photographic studio.
Prod-KRATKY Dist-PHENIX

Leo Beuerman C 13 MIN
16MM FILM, 3/4 OR 1/2 IN VIDEO I-C A
Documents the life of Leo Beuerman, an unusual man physically handicapped since birth, describing his ability to overcome diversity and his philosophy of life.
Prod-CENTRO Dist-CORF 1969

Leo Beuerman (French) C 13 MIN
16MM FILM, 3/4 OR 1/2 IN VIDEO I-C A
Documents the life of Leo Beuerman, a man with multiple handicaps. Describes his outlook on life and his attitude toward his fellow man.
Prod-CENTRO Dist-CORF 1969

Leo Beuerman (German) C 13 MIN
16MM FILM, 3/4 OR 1/2 IN VIDEO I-C A
Documents the life of Leo Beuerman, a man with multiple handicaps. Describes his outlook on life and his attitude toward his fellow man.
Prod-CENTRO Dist-CORF 1969

Leo Beuerman (Spanish) C 13 MIN
16MM FILM, 3/4 OR 1/2 IN VIDEO I-C A
Documents the life of Leo Beuerman, a man with multiple handicaps. Describes his outlook on life and his attitude toward his fellow man.
Prod-CENTRO Dist-CORF 1969

Leo Buscaglia C 60 MIN
3/4 OR 1/2 INCH VIDEO CASSETTE
See series title for descriptive statement.
From The John Callaway Interviews Series.
Prod-WTTWTV Dist-PBS 1981

Leo Buscaglia–A Series

Presents noted educator and lecturer, Dr Leo Buscaglia, a leading figure in the human potential movement, who believes that all people have an infinite capacity for growth. Encourages staff to examine work relationships, why they work and why they don't, and decide what can be done to make these relationships succeed.
Prod-PBS Dist-DELTAK

Art Of Being Fully Human, The	058 MIN
Love Class, A	046 MIN
Speaking Of Love	054 MIN
Time To Live, A	050 MIN
Together	052 MIN

Leo Claws C 5 MIN
3/4 OR 1/2 INCH VIDEO CASSETTE J-H
Deals with writing the business letter.
From The Write On, Set 2 Series.
Prod-CTI Dist-CTI

Leo On Vacation C 11 MIN
16MM FILM, 3/4 OR 1/2 IN VIDEO K-I
Uses animation to tell how a hard-working circus lion plans for a vacation.
Prod-KRATKY Dist-PHENIX 1975

Leo Tolstoy C 57 MIN
16MM FILM, 3/4 OR 1/2 IN VIDEO
Discusses the life and thought of Leo Tolstoy. Includes rare archival material. Written and narrated by Malcolm Muggeridge.
From The Third Testament Series.
LC NO. 79-707922
Prod-CANBC Dist-TIMLIF Prodn-RAYTAF 1976

Leon 'Peck' Clark - Basketmaker C 15 MIN
16MM FILM - 3/4 IN VIDEO H-C A
Peck Clark, a Black Mississippi farmer, describes how he learned to make white oak baskets. Shows Mr. Clark gathering materials and creating a basket.
LC NO. 81-707514
Prod-SOFOLK Dist-SOFOLK 1981

Leon Garfield C 8 MIN
16MM FILM OPTICAL SOUND I-J T
Leon Garfield discusses how and why he writes and describes the research that goes into his books of high adventure.

LC NO. 78-704568
Prod-PENGIN Dist-CONNF 1969

Leonard Easter, Rachal Harms And Nicholas Arcomano C 30 MIN
3/4 OR 1/2 INCH VIDEO CASSETTE
Discusses developing and protecting artistic assets.
From The Eye On Dance - The Business And Law Of Dance Series.
Prod-ARTRES Dist-ARTRES

Leonard Henny, How Nations Televise Each Other, Or Ronald Gone Dutch C 28 MIN
3/4 OR 1/2 INCH VIDEO CASSETTE
Attacks the ideology and economics of mass media. Presented by Paper Tiger Television.
Prod-ARTINC Dist-ARTINC

Leonard Unterberger, MA - Director, Family Workshop, Chicago C 60 MIN
3/4 OR 1/2 INCH VIDEO CASSETTE PRO
Presents a young therapist who has trained probation officers and street workers based on an approach derived from the social awareness of the 1960's.
From The Perceptions, Pt B - Dialogues With Family Therapists Series. Vol II, Pt B4
Prod-BOSFAM Dist-BOSFAM

Leonard Unterberger, MA - Just Making It - On Being White And Poor C 60 MIN
3/4 OR 1/2 INCH VIDEO CASSETTE PRO
Elicits from a young, low-income Chicago family its struggle to make their way in the world. Explores the family in its socio-economic context after a course of therapy.
From The Perceptions, Pt B - Interventions In Family Therapists Series. Vol II Pt A4.
Prod-BOSFAM Dist-BOSFAM

Leonard Z Lion Presents Learning About Your Heart Operation (Spanish) C 14 MIN
3/4 OR 1/2 INCH VIDEO CASSETTE K-I
Designed to be shown to parents and their children (ages 3- 12) and features a lion. Shows what occurs before and after a heart operation. Focuses on the sights, sounds and sensations experienced during hospitalization for heart surgery.
Prod-UMICHM Dist-UMICHM 1981

Leonard Z Lion Presents Learning About Your Heart Catheterization (Spanish) C 16 MIN
3/4 OR 1/2 INCH VIDEO CASSETTE K-I
Designed to be shown to parents and their children (ages 3- 12) and features a lion. Explains the events that take place during cardiac catheterization. Prepares the child for the sights, sounds and sensations experienced.
Prod-UMICHM Dist-UMICHM 1981

Leonard Z Lion Presents...Learning About Your Operation C 13 MIN
3/4 OR 1/2 INCH VIDEO CASSETTE K-I A
Features Leonard Z Lion showing friend Peter what occurs before and after an operation. Focuses on the sights, sounds and sensations experienced during hospitalization.
Prod-UMICHM Dist-UMICHM 1983

Leonard Z Lion Presents...Learning About Your Heart Operation (Spanish) C 14 MIN
3/4 OR 1/2 INCH VIDEO CASSETTE K-I
Explains, in Spanish, what occurs before and after a heart operation. Uses animated characters to illustrate the events associated with hospitalization for heart surgery.
Prod-UARIZ Dist-UARIZ

Leonard Z Lion Presents..Learning About Your Heart Catheterization (Spanish) C 16 MIN
3/4 OR 1/2 INCH VIDEO CASSETTE K-I
Explains, in Spanish, the events of a cardiac catheterization. Prepares the child for the sights and sounds associated with this diagnostic procedures.
Prod-UARIZ Dist-UARIZ

Leonardo - To Know How To See C 55 MIN
16MM FILM OPTICAL SOUND J-C A
A documentary on the life and works of Leonardo da Vinci, including both his artistic and scientific achievements.
LC NO. 72-702400
Prod-USNGA Dist-USNGA 1972

Leonardo Da Vinci - Giant Of The Renaissance X 25 MIN
16MM FILM, 3/4 OR 1/2 IN VIDEO J-C
Da Vinci is revealed as a master painter and sculptor, architect and inventor and author of a scientific method that foreshadowed modern research. Examples of his paintings and amazing notebooks are shown.
Prod-EBF Dist-EBEC 1957

Leonardo Da Vinci - Giant Of The Renaissance (Spanish) C 25 MIN
16MM FILM, 3/4 OR 1/2 IN VIDEO J-C
Presents the life and work of Leonardo da Vinci. Shows examples of his art and scientific research.
Prod-EBEC Dist-EBEC

Leonardo Da Vinci And His Art C 14 MIN
16MM FILM, 3/4 OR 1/2 IN VIDEO J-C
Provides a basis for appreciating the style and beauty of Leonardo da Vinci's art by examining his famous works. His versatility as an artist, mathematician, anatomist and architect is also pictured.
Prod-CORF Dist-CORF 1957

Leonid Brezhnev - The Rise To The Top B 14 MIN
16MM FILM, 3/4 OR 1/2 IN VIDEO J-H
Presents a graphic study of the men and events that have shaped the growth of Soviet rulers Lenin, Stalin and Khruschev, along with the rise to power of Leonid Brezhnev.
Prod-HEARST Dist-HEARST 1977

Leontyne Price C 60 MIN
3/4 OR 1/2 INCH VIDEO CASSETTE
See series title for descriptive statement.
From The John Callaway Interviews Series.
Prod-WTTWTV Dist-PBS 1981

Leopold Allen, Brian Dube And Raymond Serrano C 30 MIN
3/4 OR 1/2 INCH VIDEO CASSETTE
From The Eye On Dance - Behind The Scenes Series.
Prod-ARTRES Dist-ARTRES

Leopold Sedar Senghor B 30 MIN
16MM FILM, 3/4 OR 1/2 IN VIDEO H-C A
Introduces Leopold Sedar Senghor, his poetry and the environment which his poems reflect. President Senghor also discusses his philosophy towards the blending of African and Western culture.
From The Creative Person Series.
Prod-NET Dist-IU 1967

Leopold, The See-Through Crumbpicker C 9 MIN
16MM FILM, 3/4 OR 1/2 IN VIDEO K-P
Illustrates a story by James Flora about Leopold, the invisible crumbpicker and how he finally becomes visible.
Prod-FIRE Dist-WWS 1971

Leopold, The See-Through Crumbpicker C 15 MIN
3/4 INCH VIDEO CASSETTE P
Presents the children's story Leopold, The See-Through Crumbpicker.
From The Tilson's Book Shop Series.
Prod-WVIZTV Dist-GPITVL 1975

Leptospirosis C 16 MIN
16MM FILM, 3/4 OR 1/2 IN VIDEO
Explains the different phases of leptospirosis. Discusses the possibility of human infection and points out the various aspects of the disease. For professional and laboratory personnel.
Prod-USPHS Dist-USNAC 1960

Leroy C 25 MIN
16MM FILM, 3/4 OR 1/2 IN VIDEO J-C A
Tells the story of a poor, illiterate couple who lose their home because of an unpaid medical bill. Relates that the man is jailed when he threatens the speculator who bought the house. Shows that when the man tells his story on television, he finds out that people do care.
From The Insight Series.
Prod-PAULST Dist-PAULST 1977

Leroy Jenkens - Solo Violin C 29 MIN
16MM FILM - 1/2 IN VIDEO
Presents solos by jazz violinist Leroy Jenkens.
Prod-RHPSDY Dist-RHPSDY

LeRoy Walker Track And Field - Men—A Series
16MM FILM, 3/4 OR 1/2 IN VIDEO J-C
Discusses running, jumping and throwing in track and field events.
Prod-ATHI Dist-ATHI 1976

Fundamentals Of Running - Men 017 MIN
Jumping Events, The - Men 021 MIN
Running Events, The - Men 021 MIN
Throwing Events, The - Men 021 MIN

LeRoy Walker Track And Field - Women—A Series
16MM FILM, 3/4 OR 1/2 IN VIDEO J-C
Provides coaching, training and instructional material for women.
Prod-ATHI Dist-ATHI 1976

Fundamentals Of Running - Women 017 MIN
Jumping Events, The - Women 015 MIN
Running Events, The - Women 021 MIN
Throwing Events, The - Women 020 MIN

Les Amis (Friends) C 14 MIN
3/4 OR 1/2 INCH VIDEO CASSETTE C A
Documents the intimacy between an older man and a younger women. Emphasizes mutual responsibility for contraception.
Prod-NATSF Dist-MMRC

Les Animaux C 13 MIN
16MM FILM OPTICAL SOUND J A
From The En Francais, Set 2 Series.
Prod-PEREN Dist-CHLTN 1969

Les Antiquites C 13 MIN
16MM FILM OPTICAL SOUND J A
From The En Francais, Set 2 Series.
Prod-PEREN Dist-CHLTN 1969

Les Aventures De Monsieur Carre—A Series
16MM FILM, 3/4 OR 1/2 IN VIDEO
A French language series. Uses animation to describe the adventures of Monsieur Carre and his family.
Prod-HALAS Dist-IFB 1978

Dans Le Parc 008 MIN
En Retard Au Bureau 008 MIN
Une Soiree Chez Les Carre 010 MIN

Les Baux De Provence C 10 MIN
16MM FILM OPTICAL SOUND H-C
A French language film. Depicts the remains of the castle of Les Baux.
From The Aspects De France Series.
Prod-WSU Dist-MLA Prodn-BORGLM 1956

Les Belles Couleurs C 10 MIN
3/4 OR 1/2 INCH VIDEO CASSETTE
Focuses on colors, sizes, masculine and feminine adjectives, and demonstrative adjectives.
From The Salut - French Language Lessons Series.
Prod-BCNFL Dist-BCNFL 198

Les Blank's Blues And Cajun—A Series

Prod-FLOWER Dist-FLOWER 197

Dry Wood 37 MI
Spend It All 30 MI

Les Blues De Balfa C 28 MI
16MM FILM, 3/4 OR 1/2 IN VIDEO H-C
Presents Cajun fiddler Dewey Balfa who with his late brother Rodney and Will made up the Balfa Brothers. Features Cajun music by the Balfa Brothers, the late Nathan Abshire, Allie Young, Rockin' Dopsie, Raymond Francois and the Cajun Playboys.
Prod-AGINP Dist-AGINP

Les Blues De Balfa C 28 MI
3/4 OR 1/2 INCH VIDEO CASSETTE
Features Louisiana's most renown Cajun musician, Dewey Balfa and his brothers with other Cajun greats.
Prod-FLOWER Dist-FLOWER

Les Bons Debarras - Good Riddance (French) C 114 MIN
16MM FILM OPTICAL SOUND
A French-language film with English subtitles. Tells the story of Manon, a precocious 13-year-old girl who quietly and subtly rids her life of every deterrent to be the sole object of her mother's love.
Prod-PRISMA Dist-IFEX 1981

Les Cafes B 13 MIN
16MM FILM OPTICAL SOUND J-C
See series title for descriptive statement.
From The En France Avec Jean Et Helen Series. Set 1, Lesson 2
LC NO. 70-704504
Prod-PEREN Dist-CHLTN 1967

Les Castors Au Travail C 10 MIN
16MM FILM, 3/4 OR 1/2 IN VIDEO I-J
A French language version of the videocassette Beavers At Work. Shows how beavers are suited to the environment and their work. Depicts baby beavers at play and adult beavers building homes.
Prod-IFB Dist-IFB 1964

Les Chansons De Bilitis C 30 MIN
3/4 OR 1/2 INCH VIDEO CASSETTE
Presents a dance and reading set to music of the French poet Pierre Louys' series of poems which he claimed were inspired by ancient Greek verse. Uses the musical score of Claude Debussy who featured the delicate sounds of harp, flute and celeste woven into the narrative text of the poems. Shows a modern-day woman who studies her image in the waters of a pond and is transformed into the Grecian courtesan Bilitis.
Prod-OHUTC Dist-OHUTC

Les Chateaux C 16 MIN
16MM FILM OPTICAL SOUND H-C
A French language film. Examines the architectural evolution of the chateaux, relating them to the life and times of their occupants.
From The Aspects De France Series.
Prod-WSU Dist-MLA Prodn-BORGLM 1966

Les Chevaux B 13 MIN
16MM FILM OPTICAL SOUND J-C
See series title for descriptive statement.
From The En France Avec Jean Et Helen Series. Set 1, Lesson 12
LC NO. 77-704506
Prod-PEREN Dist-CHLTN 1967

Les Choux-Fleurs De Saint-Brieuc C 15 MIN
16MM FILM, 3/4 OR 1/2 IN VIDEO C A
See series title for descriptive statement.
From The La Maree Et Ses Secrets Series.
Prod-FI Dist-FI

Les Cles C 14 MIN
16MM FILM OPTICAL SOUND
A French language version of Wrenches. Illustrates the versatilities and practicalities of a variety of wrenches.
From The Hand Operations - Woodworking (French) Series.
LC NO. 75-704363
Prod-MORLAT Dist-MORLAT 1974

Les Crepes C 5 MIN
16MM FILM OPTICAL SOUND K-I
A French language film. A little girl is making pancakes while her young brother secretly eats them one by one.
From The Bonjour Line Series. Part 1
Prod-PEREN Dist-CHLTN 1962

Les Dangers Du Travail En Espace Reduit C 16 MIN
16MM FILM, 3/4 OR 1/2 IN VIDEO H A
A French-language version of the motion picture Confined Space Hazards. Stressses the correct procedure for working safely in confined spaces or areas. Shows a worker preparing to enter a tank as others take such safety precautions as blocking off intake and outlet pipes, locking and tagging all electrical switches, eliminating vapors from the space and testing the oxygen supply. Emphasizes the recognition of the hazardous space, planning for every eventuality and precision in remedial procedures.
Prod-IAPA Dist-IFB 1971

Les Dents - Les Gens Peuvent Vaincre Les Microbes C 10 MIN
16MM FILM OPTICAL SOUND
A French language version of the motion picture Teeth - People

Are Smarter Than Germs. Demonstrates how people who are taking care of their teeth are also looking after their health.
From The Health (French) Series.
LC NO. 75-704341
Prod-MORLAT Dist-MORLAT 1974

Les Femmes Connaissent La Mecanique C 13 MIN
16MM FILM OPTICAL SOUND J A
From The En Francais, Set 1 Series.
Prod-PEREN Dist-CHLTN 1969

Les Francais Chez Vous—A Series
I-H
Presents well-known French television personalities in sketches which portray various aspects of French life and at the same time emphasize a point of French grammar.
Prod-PEREN Dist-CHLTN 1967

A Nous Les Bijoux 13 MIN
Alice Vient D'arriver 13 MIN
Aujourd'hui Friture 13 MIN
Ce Cavalier Qui Vient 13 MIN
Chasser Est Un Plaisir 13 MIN
Dans Deux Heures 13 MIN
Dites-Le Avec Des Fleurs 13 MIN
Elle Lui Sourit 13 MIN
Est-Ce Que C'est Ta Veste 13 MIN
Fenetre Sur Jardin 13 MIN
Georges Epousera 13 MIN
Il Donne Ses Croissants Aux Diseaux 13 MIN
Il Faut Tout Lui Enseigner 13 MIN
Il Me Regarde 13 MIN
Il N'en Reste Plus 13 MIN
Il Y A Beaucoup De Place 13 MIN
J'y Vais 13 MIN
Je N'ai Rien A Declarer 13 MIN
Je Prends Un Tournevis 13 MIN
Je Suis Arrive Avant Vous 13 MIN
L' Aviateur 13 MIN
La Meilleure Occasion 13 MIN
Le Chat VA Tomber 13 MIN
Le Coche D'eau 13 MIN
Mon Ticket S'il Vous Plait 13 MIN
Nous Avons Faim 13 MIN
Nous Irons Peut-Etre En Chine 13 MIN
Nous Sommes Seuls 13 MIN
Operation Biberon 13 MIN
Ou VA-T-Il. D'ou Vient-Il 13 MIN
Pourquoi N'est-Il Pas La 13 MIN
Qu'est-Ce Qu'il Y A 13 MIN
Qu'est-Ce Que C'est 13 MIN
Qui Est-Ce 13 MIN
Soudain Le Paradis 13 MIN
Symphonie Realiste 13 MIN
Vendons Ces Meubles 13 MIN
Voila Gilbert, Le Voila 13 MIN
Vous, Encore Vous 13 MIN

Les Gardes De Caserne C 4 MIN
16MM FILM OPTICAL SOUND
A French language version of the motion picture The Quarters Guard. Demonstrates the military drill known as the Quarters Guard.
From The Ceremonial Drill (French) Series.
LC NO. 77-702844
Prod-CDND Dist-CDND Prodn-FLMSMI 1976

Les Grecs C 29 MIN
16MM FILM, 3/4 OR 1/2 IN VIDEO H-C A
A French-language version of the motion picture The Greeks. Surveys Greek history and culture from the early Aegean civilizations to the conquests of Alexander.
Prod-IFB Dist-IFB 1975

Les Insectes Sont Interessantes C 11 MIN
16MM FILM, 3/4 OR 1/2 IN VIDEO I-J
A French language version of the videocassette Insects Are Interesting. Examines the life histories, biologies and adaptations of insects. Stresses the importance of insects to man.
Prod-DEU Dist-IFB 1956

Les Jeux Sont Faits B 105 MIN
16MM FILM OPTICAL SOUND H-C A
A French language motion picture illustrating Jean-Paul Sartre's idea that man must exercise his free will and that to do so he must not depend on the past.
Prod-IFB Dist-TRANSW 1947

Les Lunettes Astronomiques C 13 MIN
16MM FILM OPTICAL SOUND J A
From The En Francais, Set 2 Series.
Prod-PEREN Dist-CHLTN 1969

Les Maitres Fous (The Mad Masters) C 35 MIN
3/4 INCH VIDEO CASSETTE
Summarizes the Hauka religious movement in Ghana between the 1920's and 1950's. Portrays the end of the Hauka development after independence from France in 1957. Filmed by Jean Rouch.
Prod-DOCEDR Dist-DOCEDR Prodn-LESFMP

Les McCann - Makin' It Real C 29 MIN
3/4 INCH VIDEO CASSETTE
Features musician-composer Les McCann singing, playing and talking about his music.
From The Interface Series.
Prod-WETATV Dist-PUBTEL

Les McCann Trio C 29 MIN
16MM FILM - 1/2 IN VIDEO
See series title for descriptive statement.
From The Jazz On Stage Series.
Prod-RHPSDY Dist-RHPSDY

Les Mistons B 18 MIN
16MM FILM, 3/4 OR 1/2 IN VIDEO J-C A
A French language film. A short masterpiece by the new wave director Francoise Truffaut. Tells of five very young boys who view a Parisian romance from afar and in confusion, react to it by becoming 'LES MISTONS' (BRATS.)
Prod-PFP Dist-TEXFLM

Les Nations S'Affirment - Nations Assert Themselves C 52 MIN
16MM FILM OPTICAL SOUND
Reveals how Gothic art meets with political and cultural resistance in Sicily and Spain while there is a renewal of Catholic spirituality in southern Italy. Shows examples of architectural rigidity including the cathedrals of Salisbury, Ely and Gloucester.
From The Le Temp Des Cathedrales Series.
Prod-FACSEA Dist-FACSEA 1979

Les Ordres C 107 MIN
16MM FILM OPTICAL SOUND
A French language film with English subtitles. Describes the 1970 arrest and incarceration of 450 French Canadians without charges or explanation. Directed by Michel Brault.
Prod-UNKNWN Dist-NYFLMS 1974

Les Parfums C 13 MIN
16MM FILM OPTICAL SOUND J A
From The En Francais, Set 2 Series.
Prod-PEREN Dist-CHLTN 1969

Les Passagers B 90 MIN
16MM FILM OPTICAL SOUND
A French language motion picture. Presents the problems of Algerian emigrants working in France. Focuses on the problems of an Algerian youth from the time he leaves Algeria, through two years in Paris, to the time he decides to return to Algeria.
LC NO. 74-702328
Prod-CADI Dist-TRIFC 1972

Les Petites Fugues C 137 MIN
16MM FILM OPTICAL SOUND
A French language film with English subtitles. Describes the adventures of a 66-year-old farmhand who buys a motorbike. Directed by Yves Yersin.
Prod-UNKNWN Dist-NYFLMS 1979

Les Pinces C 12 MIN
16MM FILM OPTICAL SOUND
A French language version of Pliers. Describes common types of pliers.
From The Hand Operations - Woodworking (French) Series.
LC NO. 76-700147
Prod-MORLAT Dist-MORLAT 1974

Les Precurseurs - Cezanne, Gauguin, Van Gogh C 26 MIN
16MM FILM, 3/4 OR 1/2 IN VIDEO H-C
A French language version of the videocassette The Precursors - Cezanne, Gauguin, Van Gogh. Explains how Cezanne, Gauguin and Van Gogh contributed to the development of modern painting. Studies the artistic influences they received from other painters and looks at the development of their own personalities.
Prod-IFB Dist-IFB 1971

Les Prisonnieres C 44 MIN
16MM FILM OPTICAL SOUND
Shows how a 15-year-old American girl discovers her Huguenot heritage while attending school in France. Tells how she learns about Marie Durand, who was imprisoned for 38 years because of her beliefs.
LC NO. 80-700306
Prod-ADVENT Dist-ADVENT Prodn-MARTC 1979

Les Pronoms Personnels Direct Et Indirect (French) C 15 MIN
3/4 OR 1/2 INCH VIDEO CASSETTE
A French language videotape of The Direct And Indirect Personal Pronouns, Presents a lesson on various pronouns in French.
From The French Language Videotapes (French) Series.
Prod-UCEMC Dist-UCEMC

Les Radio-Taxis B 13 MIN
16MM FILM OPTICAL SOUND J-C
See series title for descriptive statement.
From The En France Avec Jean Et Helen Series. Set 1, Lesson 6
LC NO. 73-704513
Prod-PEREN Dist-CHLTN 1967

Les Romains C 23 MIN
16MM FILM, 3/4 OR 1/2 IN VIDEO H-C
A French-language version of the motion picture The Romans which surveys the political history of Rome from the Etruscans to Caesar, the unification of the peninsula and the growth of the empire.
LC NO. 83-706817
Prod-DOOLYJ Dist-IFB 1983

Les Saisons C 14 MIN
16MM FILM, 3/4 OR 1/2 IN VIDEO
A French language videocassette. Looks at the changing seasons in France.
Prod-SEABEN Dist-IFB 1969

Les Surprises C 15 MIN
16MM FILM, 3/4 OR 1/2 IN VIDEO C A
See series title for descriptive statement.
From The La Maree Et Ses Secrets Series.
Prod-FI Dist-FI

Les Trois Ours X 15 MIN
16MM FILM, 3/4 OR 1/2 IN VIDEO A
A French version of The Three Bears with simple beginning French narration. Visualizes nouns, adjectives and verbs by the appropriate object or action on the screen.
Prod-FA Dist-PHENIX 1960

Les Vedettes C 26 MIN
16MM FILM OPTICAL SOUND
French version of the 'THE ENTERTAINERS.' Presents a summary of the highlights of the 1966 Canadian Open Golf Championship, which was played in Vancouver from September 29th to October 3rd.
LC NO. FIA67-2235
Prod-HSEGRM Dist-MTP Prodn-CRAF 1966

Les Verbes Pronominaux (French) C 10 MIN
3/4 OR 1/2 INCH VIDEO CASSETTE
A French language videotape. Presents an intermediate French lesson. Illustrates the different uses of reflexive pronouns.
From The French Language Videotapes (French) Series.
Prod-UCEMC Dist-UCEMC

Les Voyageurs C 30 MIN
3/4 OR 1/2 INCH VIDEO CASSETTE I
Dramatizes cooperation in contemporary Franco-American life.
From The Franco File Series.
Prod-WENHTV Dist-GPITVL

Lesbian Mothers B 26 MIN
3/4 INCH VIDEO CASSETTE
Explores the social stigmas of being a lesbian mother in modern society through interviews with young people and their lesbian mothers.
Prod-WMENIF Dist-WMENIF

Lesbian Mothers And Child Custody, Pt 1 C 29 MIN
3/4 INCH VIDEO CASSETTE
Discusses lesbian mothers' struggle for custody of their children. Explains the controversy surrounding the question of parental fitness and its relationship to sexual preference.
From The Woman Series.
Prod-WNEDTV Dist-PUBTEL

Lesbian Mothers And Child Custody, Pt 2 C 29 MIN
3/4 INCH VIDEO CASSETTE
Presents Mary Jo Risher and Ann Foreman describing their efforts to reclaim custody of Mary Jo's 10-year-old son, who was taken from the Risher-Foreman home and placed under his father's guardianship. Points out that Mary Jo's lesbianism was the central issue in the trial.
From The Woman Series.
Prod-WNEDTV Dist-PUBTEL

Lesbians Against The Right C 45 MIN
3/4 INCH VIDEO CASSETTE
Discusses the attempts of the New Right to blame the ills of this society on the breakdown of the family, immigration and abortion. Discusses attempts which have been made to combat the New Right.
Prod-AMELIA Dist-WMENIF

Lesions Of The Brain, Pt A - Stroke B 41 MIN
16MM FILM OPTICAL SOUND PRO
Presents Dr Michael E De Bakey of the Baylor University College of Medicine demonstrating his surgical treatment for cerebral vascular insufficiency caused by occlusive lesions in the arteries supplying the brain. Discusses the status of anticoagulants in the treatment of a stroke.
Prod-UPJOHN Dist-UPJOHN 1961

Lesions Of The Brain, Pt B - Head Injury B 34 MIN
16MM FILM OPTICAL SOUND PRO
Presents a panel of doctors discussing a skull fracture complicated by blood clots at successive stages of the case history. Examines the panelists' recommended course of therapy and emphasizes the cardinal signs of impending danger in the patient with a head injury.
Prod-UPJOHN Dist-UPJOHN 1961

Lesions Of The Brain, Pt C - Parkinsonism B 27 MIN
16MM FILM OPTICAL SOUND PRO
Presents Dr Irving S Cooper of the New York University School of Medicine demonstrating his technique for relieving Parkinsonism by freezing the ventral lateral region of the thalamus by means of a cannula and liquid hydrogen. Includes Dr Mac Donald Critchely of the National Hospital Queen Square, London, presenting two patients that illustrate the difference between Parkinsonian tremor and ideopathic or familial tremor.
Prod-UPJOHN Dist-UPJOHN 1961

Lesions Of The Fallopian Tube C 31 MIN
16MM FILM OPTICAL SOUND PRO
Shows various conditions which arise in the fallopian tubes including inflammatory diseases of acute, subacute and chronic stages. Illustrates diagnosis and treatment of tubal pregnancy.
Prod-ACYDGD Dist-ACY 1957

Leslie Jane Pessemier, Mark Kloth And Rika Burnham C 30 MIN
3/4 OR 1/2 INCH VIDEO CASSETTE
See series title for descriptive statement.
From The Collaborations Series.
Prod-ARCVID Dist-ARCVID

Leslie Jane Pessemier, Mark Kloth And Rika Burnham C 30 MIN
3/4 OR 1/2 INCH VIDEO CASSETTE
Features a performance of 'Esoterica' with Domy Reiter-Sofer, choreographer with the Bat-Dor Dance Company of Israel. Hosted By Celia Ipiotis.
From The Eye On Dance - Collaborations Series.
Prod-ARTRES Dist-ARTRES

Less And More C 20 MIN
3/4 OR 1/2 INCH VIDEO CASSETTE

Provides information on economic productivity, using as an example a small restaurant where changes are made that increase productivity with the result that some workers must be laid off.
From The Trade-Offs Series.
LC NO. 79-706205
Prod-OECA Dist-AITECH 1978

Less And More - Increasing Productivity C 20 MIN
16MM FILM OPTICAL SOUND I-J
Discusses economic productivity. Uses as an example a small restaurant where changes are made that increase productivity with the result that some workers must be laid off.
From The Trade-Offs Series. No. 5
LC NO. 79-700549
Prod-OECA Dist-AITECH 1978

Less Is More C 14 MIN
16MM FILM, 3/4 OR 1/2 IN VIDEO H-C
Examines the premise that a minimal use of natural resources can potentially produce large amounts of energy.
Prod-DURCEL Dist-AIMS 1975

Less Stress C 14 MIN
16MM FILM, 3/4 OR 1/2 IN VIDEO I-J
Introduces the concept of stress. Explains how stress affects the body and behavior. Includes vignettes that demonstrate ways of reducing stress.
LC NO. 82-706560
Prod-KLINGL Dist-CF 1979

Less Stress In Five Easy Steps C
1/2 IN VIDEO CASSETTE BETA/VHS
Presents a 'right brain' approach to stress managements, and provides techniques for recognizing stress, and integrating habitual and new stress reduction mechanisms, including breathing, exercise, imaging and music-video meditation. Emphasizes flexibility of response within a progressive framework of skills. Features Ed Asner.
Prod-BRUMAZ Dist-BRUMAZ

Less Than A Minute C 6 MIN
16MM FILM OPTICAL SOUND
Examines the effect of noise on people and shows how earplugs can be used to help prevent hearing loss due to exposure to excessive noise.
LC NO. 80-700386
Prod-LEOARB Dist-LEOARB 1979

Lesson And Analysis C 29 MIN
3/4 OR 1/2 INCH VIDEO CASSETTE
Identifies skills needed by the beginning teacher.
From The Working With The Beginning Teacher - Teaching Story Analysis Series.
Prod-SPF Dist-SPF

Lesson Doesn't End, A B 30 MIN
16MM FILM OPTICAL SOUND T
Describes classroom techniques dealing with science investigations using batteries, bulbs and wire.
From The Starting Tomorrow Series. Unit 4 - New Ways In Elementary Science
Prod-EALING Dist-WALKED

Lesson In Learning, A C 45 MIN
16MM FILM OPTICAL SOUND T
Presents spontaneous and unrehearsed classroom activity. Capsules a semester's curriculum.
Prod-YALEDV Dist-YALEDV

Lesson In Microcomputers, A - Hardware And Software C
3/4 OR 1/2 INCH VIDEO CASSETTE
Gives a complete introduction to computer basics and helps review terms, functions and basic troubleshooting.
Prod-GA Dist-GA

Lesson In The Symphony, A B 7 MIN
16MM FILM OPTICAL SOUND
A 1951 screen news digest excerpt shows a film lesson on the functions of the symphonic orchestra, the strings, the woodwinds, brass winds, and percussion.
From The News Magazine Of The Screen Series. Vol 2, No. 5
Prod-PATHE Dist-HEARST 1951

Lesson On Change, A C 12 MIN
16MM FILM OPTICAL SOUND C A
Presents a model of good teaching. Emphasizes the importance of taking advantage of teachable moments with children. Shows a teacher as she explains spontaneously to her second grade class the death of Dr Martin Luther King, Jr and the changes for which he gave his life.
LC NO. 72-702445
Prod-COLPS Dist-OSUMPD Prodn-OSUMPD 1969

Lesson, The B 67 MIN
16MM FILM OPTICAL SOUND H-C A
Eugene Ionesco's play, 'THE LESSON,' which satirizes the interaction between pupil and professor.
LC NO. 79-700913
Prod-GROVE Dist-GROVE 1966

Lesson, The C 30 MIN
3/4 OR 1/2 INCH VIDEO CASSETTE I-H
See series title for descriptive statement.
From The Gettin' To Know Me Series.
Prod-CTI Dist-MDCPB 1979

Lessons Learned From Aircraft Accidents - Know Your Aircraft B 21 MIN
16MM FILM OPTICAL SOUND
Discusses the problem of aircraft accidents resulting from aviators' lack of knowledge or disregard of aircraft limitations.
LC NO. 74-705021
Prod-USA Dist-USNAC 1967

Lessons On A Mannequin Series C
3/4 OR 1/2 INCH VIDEO CASSETTE
Includes six tapes which are generally used in sequence. Begins with starting the first lesson with a mannequin having fairly long hair. Shows through the sequence of haircuts the hair becoming shorter until it finally reaches a length it can no longer be cut. Shows various styling techniques and a permanent wave is given.
Prod-MPCEDP Dist-MPCEDP 1984

Lester Wilson, Bernice Johnson C 30 MIN
3/4 OR 1/2 INCH VIDEO CASSETTE
Focuses on Black dancers and choreography in films. Features Roberto Gautier on Lower East Side clubs in New York. Hosted by Celia Ipiotis.
From The Eye On Dance - Popular Culture And Dance Series.
Prod-ARTRES Dist-ARTRES

Let 'Er Buck C 20 MIN
3/4 OR 1/2 INCH VIDEO CASSETTE
Documents the history of rodeos in Oregon, the transition from the range to the arena and the competition of the Pendleton Round-Up.
Prod-KOAPTV Dist-MEDIPR 1976

Let A Song Be A Friend C 15 MIN
3/4 OR 1/2 INCH VIDEO CASSETTE P
See series title for descriptive statement.
From The Strawberry Square Series.
Prod-NEITV Dist-AITECH 1982

Let Everybody Help B 10 MIN
16MM FILM OPTICAL SOUND
Shows how to get employees talking about safety.
From The Communications For Safety Series.
Prod-NSC Dist-NSC

Let Freedom Ring B 24 MIN
16MM FILM OPTICAL SOUND H-C A
Deals with a nationwide network of anonymously recorded phone messages known as 'LET FREEDOM RING.' These messages spread a radical right wing brand of 'FEAR AND SMEAR.' Features Wyoming's Senator Gale Mc Gee, Mrs Jennelle Moorehead, president of the National Congress of Parents and Teachers, and William Pinsley of the Anti-Defamation League.
Prod-ADL Dist-ADL

Let Go C 10 MIN
2 INCH VIDEOTAPE
See series title for descriptive statement.
From The Janaki Series.
Prod-WGBHTV Dist-PUBTEL

Let Habit Help B 10 MIN
16MM FILM OPTICAL SOUND
Stresses developing safe habits and breaking unsafe habits.
From The Personal Side Of Safety Series.
Prod-NSC Dist-NSC

Let His Blood Fall On Our Heads C
2 INCH VIDEOTAPE
See series title for descriptive statement.
From The Jesus Trial Series. Program 2
LC NO. 79-706738
Prod-TVOTAR Dist-TVBUS 1979

Let It Bee - Vivaldi's Concerto In C-Dur C 4 MIN
16MM FILM OPTICAL SOUND I-C
Tells the story of an elegantly domestic honeybee whose attempts to prepare a picnic are interrupted by a human couple.
From The Animations From Allegro Non Troppo Series.
LC NO. 80-700527
Prod-BOZETO Dist-TEXFLM 1978

Let Katie Do It B 28 MIN
16MM FILM SILENT
Presents a recently discovered film by D W Griffith, set in rural Maine in 1915.
From The Movies - Our Modern Art Series.
Prod-SPCTRA Dist-STRFLS 1973

Let Me Count The Ways I Know Me C 15 MIN
3/4 INCH VIDEO CASSETTE H
Describes the personal data sheet and the resume. Explores ways of gaining experience or specific skills in order to acquire desired jobs.
From The Success In The Job Market Series.
Prod-KUONTV Dist-GPITVL 1980

Let Me Count The Ways, Baby C 29 MIN
2 INCH VIDEOTAPE
See series title for descriptive statement.
From The Our Street Series.
Prod-MDCPB Dist-PUBTEL

Let Me Destroy My Own Life C 21 MIN
3/4 INCH VIDEO CASSETTE H-C
Portrays Gary Gerbev, a rock and roll drummer, in striving for success in the music business. Explores his unique lifestyle on Long Island while he talks candidly and humorously about himself, his problems and his goals.
LC NO. 83-706243
Prod-ZUBLIL Dist-ZUBLIL 1981

Let Me Say This - Reflections On Living In The Nuclear Age C 30 MIN
16MM FILM, 3/4 OR 1/2 IN VIDEO
Examines the energy and enthusiasm with which many groups and individuals are working to avert nuclear disaster. Looks at four different groups, including children and teenagers, grassroots activists and politicians, academicians and professionals, and performing artists.
Prod-DISARM Dist-CNEMAG 1984

Let Me See C 20 MIN
16MM FILM OPTICAL SOUND
Shows the nursery school for visually handicapped children in Los Angeles, California. Asks what can parents do to help a blind child, should he be treated like any normal-sighted child and will he ever really become a useful member of society.
LC NO. FI54-131
Prod-USC Dist-USC 1951

Let Me See—A Series

Encourages the use of the powers of observation and reasoning to understand such things and events as pendulums, forces magnets, the sun, water, rain and soil.
Prod-WETN Dist-AITECH Prodn-STSU 1981

Air And Wind 015 MIN
Ants And Worms 015 MIN
Birds 015 MIN
Forces 015 MIN
Insects 015 MIN
Magnets 015 MIN
Pendulums 015 MIN
Plants 015 MIN
Pond, The 015 MIN
Soil 015 MIN
Sun 015 MIN
Water And Rain 015 MIN

Let Me Try - A Mentally Retarded Child C 6 MIN
16MM FILM, 3/4 OR 1/2 IN VIDEO K-P
Tells the story of Wendy, a mentally retarded child whose grandmother wants to shield her from other children.
From The Like You, Like Me Series.
Prod-EBEC Dist-EBEC 1977

Let Me Try Please B 15 MIN
2 INCH VIDEOTAPE K-P
Encourages children to tell stories before the group, stressing the use of flannel boards, masks and puppets. (Broadcast quality)
From The Magic Of Words Series.
Prod-GWTVAI Dist-GPITVL Prodn-WETATV

Let My People Go B 54 MIN
16MM FILM, 3/4 OR 1/2 IN VIDEO J-C A
Describes the difficulties encountered by the Jews in their search for a homeland. Tells about the efforts of Theodore Herzl, the beginning of Zionism and the
Prod-PMI Dist-FI 1965

Let Nature Work For You C 12 MIN
16MM FILM, 3/4 OR 1/2 IN VIDEO
Illustrates how natural plant regeneration can be used to assist highway maintenance engineers in beautifying the right-of-way, after construction has been completed. Encourages maintenance crews to keep mowing operations to a minimum by not mowing the complete right-of-way, giving nature a chance to revegetate the areas with natural growth.
LC NO. 82-706165
Prod-USDTFH Dist-USNAC 1969

Let No Man Put Asunder C 25 MIN
16MM FILM OPTICAL SOUND
Shows how three divorced women have dealt with the problems of child rearing, loneliness, finances, employment and adjustment to the life of a single parent.
From The Perspective Series.
LC NO. 73-702324
Prod-WRCTV Dist-WRCTV 1973

Let No Man Regret C 11 MIN
16MM FILM, 3/4 OR 1/2 IN VIDEO I-C A
Shows how the unspoiled beauty of nature is being endangered by man's pollution and uncontrolled development by illustrating the phrase, 'Let no man regret that I passed here.'
Prod-HIGGIN Dist-HIGGIN 1973

Let The Church Say Amen C 75 MIN
16MM FILM OPTICAL SOUND
Follows the travels of a young Black minister just out of the seminary in order to illustrate the state of the Black religious experience.
LC NO. 74-700101
Prod-UMCH Dist-UMCH 1973

Let The Church Say Amen C 58 MIN
16MM FILM, 3/4 OR 1/2 IN VIDEO A
Portrays the travels of a young Black student through the South as he prepares to become a minister. Shows the Black church from the inside and how it affects Black life in both urban and rural America. Explores a specific segment of the Black American experience while treating the larger theme of a young man seeking his role in life.
Prod-BRNSTC Dist-CHAMBA

Let The Church Say, Amen C 60 MIN
16MM FILM OPTICAL SOUND
Presents a documentary about the Black church in such diverse places as Mound Bayou, Mississippi and in the urban north side of Chicago. Tells the story through the eyes of a young black seminarian, who is struggling with his blackness and the new black interpretation of Christian theology. Focuses on the black church as the most stable and most representative community organization that Black people have in the United States.
Prod-UCBHM Dist-ECUFLM

Let The Current Do The Work C 20 MIN
3/4 OR 1/2 INCH VIDEO CASSETTE J-C A
Considers rafts, canoes, and kayaks as alternatives to motor-powered excursions. Focuses on techniques, waterproof packing, loading, rigging 'for a flip' and 'after a flip' along with rescue techniques for boat and passenger.
LC NO. 82-706769
Prod-AWSS Dist-AWSS 1981

Let The Fabric Do The Work, Pt 1 C 29 MIN
2 INCH VIDEOTAPE
See series title for descriptive statement.
From The Designing Women Series.
Prod-WKYCTV Dist-PUBTEL

Let The Fabric Do The Work, Pt 2 C 29 MIN
2 INCH VIDEOTAPE
See series title for descriptive statement.
From The Designing Women Series.
Prod-WKYCTV Dist-PUBTEL

Let The Good Times Roll C 99 MIN
16MM FILM OPTICAL SOUND H-C A
Tells the story of rock and roll, the popular music of the 1950s, through a compilation of footage of performers of the day. Features Chuck Berry, Chubby Checker, Bo Diddley, Little Richard, The Five Satins, The Shirelles, The Coasters, and Bill Haley and The Comets.
Prod-CPC Dist-TIMLIF 1973

Let The Student Come First C 7 MIN
3/4 OR 1/2 INCH VIDEO CASSETTE
Points out that the teacher's goal is to see that students learn and therefore everything in the classroom should be directed toward the student's learning needs.
From The Producing Better Learning Series. Module 1
Prod-RESEM Dist-RESEM

Let The Waters Run Free C 22 MIN
16MM FILM OPTICAL SOUND
Explores one of the last natural stretches of the Missouri River and the free-flowing little White River of South Dakota. Shows the wildlife which flourishes there, the recreational use of the rivers and the effects of channelization and dam building on natural rivers.
LC NO. 73-702327
Prod-SDDGFP Dist-SDDGFP 1973

Let Them Come With Rain C 20 MIN
16MM FILM, 3/4 OR 1/2 IN VIDEO J-C A
Discusses the problems of life and the potential for development in Botswana, a country in Southern Africa.
Prod-UN Dist-JOU 1975

Let Them Know C 10 MIN
16MM FILM OPTICAL SOUND
See series title for descriptive statement.
From The Safety Management Series.
Prod-NSC Dist-NSC

Let Them Learn C 27 MIN
16MM FILM, 3/4 OR 1/2 IN VIDEO A
Examines the characteristics of educational films which make them significant teaching materials. Illustrates the ways a film can be sued in a planned manner for a spontaneous teaching situation.
From The Project Discovery II Series.
Prod-PORTA Dist-EBEC 1967

Let There Be Light C 29 MIN
3/4 OR 1/2 INCH VIDEO CASSETTE
Shows that light does more than just expose film, its presence can be the reason you are taking the shot.
From The Photo Show Series.
Prod-WGBHTV Dist-PBS 1981

Let There Be Light B 58 MIN
3/4 OR 1/2 INCH VIDEO CASSETTE
Concerns the rehabilitation of returning World War II soldiers suffering psychosomatic disabilities from the effects of battle fatigue. Reveals the disabilities not as symptoms of abnormalities but as the response of sound minds to the unendurable. Directed by John Huston. Made for the government and banned for many years.
Prod-IHF Dist-IHF

Let There Be Light B 58 MIN
16MM FILM, 3/4 OR 1/2 IN VIDEO
Shows the treatment of combat neuropsychiatric patients in an Army hospital. Demonstrates narcosynthesis, hypnosis and psychiatric therapy for individuals and for groups.
LC NO. 81-706530
Prod-USASC Dist-USNAC 1981

Let There Be Music C 24 MIN
16MM FILM OPTICAL SOUND T
Documents a variety of programs designed to introduce a wider range of musical learning opportunities in the primary grades of elementary school. Explains the goal of improving the quality of musical experience available to all children by tracing such innovative musical resources for teachers as concerts by musicians-in-residence, special projects of school authorities and television programming.
Prod-BBCTV Dist-OPENU 1982

Let There Be Music C 24 MIN
16MM FILM, 3/4 OR 1/2 IN VIDEO T
Documents a variety of programs designed to introduce a wider range of musical learning opportunities in the primary grades of elementary school. Explains the goal of improving the quality of musical experience available to all children by tracing such innovative musical resources for teachers as concerts by musicians-in-residence, special projects of school authorities and television programming.
Prod-OPENU Dist-MEDIAG Prodn-BBCTV 1982

Let Us Teach Guessing C 61 MIN
16MM FILM OPTICAL SOUND H-C
Professor George Polya is shown guiding an undergraduate class to discover the number of parts into which 3-space is divided by five arbitrary planes. He also identifies the steps in plausible reasoning and points out that they are relevant in attacking any mathematical problem.
From The MAA Individual Lecturers Series.
LC NO. FIA66-1276
Prod-MAA Dist-MLA 1966

Let Your Child Help You B 11 MIN
16MM FILM OPTICAL SOUND C T
Shows how young children may help at home and achieve a sense of accomplishment and responsibility as well as increased skill.
From The Parent-Child Relations In The Early Years Series.
Prod-NYU Dist-NYU 1947

Let's All Sing—A Series
P-I
Includes 32, 15-minute music lessons given by folk singer Tony Saletan. Invites children to experience the joys of making music and to listen sensitively to music through a variety of songs and instruments, largely selected from our folk heritage. Encourages children to sing along, participate in rythmic movement and improvise with words tunes and simple instruments. Introduces the ideas of tone, rhythm, pitch, form and other concepts.
Prod-WESTEL Dist-WESTEL

Let's Be Flexible C 15 MIN
3/4 OR 1/2 INCH VIDEO CASSETTE P
See series title for descriptive statement.
From The Strawberry Square Series.
Prod-NEITV Dist-AITECH 1982

Let's Be Frank About Pork Show C 30 MIN
3/4 OR 1/2 INCH VIDEO CASSETTE
Presents basically crazy cooks Larry Bly and Laban Johnson who offer recipes, cooking and shopping tips.
From The Cookin' Cheap Series.
Prod-WBRATV Dist-MDCPB

Let's Be Friends - An Emotionally Disturbed Child C 6 MIN
16MM FILM, 3/4 OR 1/2 IN VIDEO K-P
Shows how a group of children decide to help one of their friends, a little girl with an emotional problem.
From The Like You, Like Me Series.
Prod-EBEC Dist-EBEC 1977

Let's Be Rational About Fractions C 30 MIN
3/4 OR 1/2 INCH VIDEO CASSETTE A
Shows adult math students what fractions are and how they are used.
From The Adult Math Series.
Prod-KYTV Dist-KYTV 1984

Let's Build A City—A Series

Prod-WVIZTV Dist-GPITVL

Elect A Leader	15 MIN
Hand-Made	15 MIN
Help	15 MIN
Introducing A City	15 MIN
Is Jack A Dull Boy	15 MIN
Let's Eat	15 MIN
Long, Long Ago	15 MIN
Mass Production	15 MIN
Monsters Of The City	15 MIN
School Days	15 MIN
Stay Healthy	15 MIN
Talk To Everyone	15 MIN
Talk To Me	15 MIN
Travel Time	15 MIN
Where Do You Live	15 MIN
Why A City	15 MIN

Let's Build A Mountain B 30 MIN
16MM FILM OPTICAL SOUND
Explains the life zones of a mountain in relation to climate and altitude. Shows a trip up Mt Washington. Discusses the Canadian life zone at the foot of the presidential range in New Hampshire, the Hudsonian zone and the Arctic-Alpine region.
From The Discovery II Series.
Prod-NET Dist-WNETTV 1956

Let's Carve B 10 MIN
16MM FILM OPTICAL SOUND
Shows examples of sculpture and the kind of stone used for each. Also demonstrates how students can create their own material for carving.
LC NO. 75-703194
Prod-USC Dist-USC 1966

Let's Count (2nd Ed) C 14 MIN
16MM FILM, 3/4 OR 1/2 IN VIDEO K-P
Follows the adventures of a little girl as she learns to count.
Prod-CORF Dist-CORF

Let's Create A Play C 15 MIN
2 INCH VIDEOTAPE I
Discusses a play created by youngsters.
From The Images Series.
Prod-CVETVC Dist-GPITVL

Let's Dance (French) C 14 MIN
3/4 OR 1/2 INCH VIDEO CASSETTE H-C A
Features a folklore dance company and a rehearsal at the Maison de Culture at Grenoble.
From The En Francais Series. Part 2 - Temporal Relationships, Logical Relationships
Prod-MOFAFR Dist-AITECH 1970

Let's Dance With Arthur Murray C 120 MIN
3/4 OR 1/2 INCH VIDEO CASSETTE H-C A
Presents basic ballroom etiquette and shows how to perform the waltz, the cha cha, the foxtrot, the samba, the rumba and disco.
Prod-TIMLIF Dist-TIMLIF 1982

Let's Decorate B 15 MIN
2 INCH VIDEOTAPE P
Discusses decorations and gifts for the holiday season.
From The Art Corner Series.
Prod-CVETVC Dist-GPITVL Prodn-WCVETV

Let's Draw—A Series
P
Explains that drawing is a way of communicating one's thoughts and feelings to others and sometimes, to one's self.
Prod-OCPS Dist-AITECH Prodn-KOKHTV 1976

Birds (Let's Draw)	015 MIN
Boats - Water	015 MIN
Cars (Let's Draw)	015 MIN
Cartoon Bodies	015 MIN
Cartoon Faces (Let's Draw)	015 MIN
Cats	015 MIN
Christmas (Let's Draw)	015 MIN
Deer (Let's Draw)	015 MIN
Dinosaurs (Let's Draw)	015 MIN
Distance In Pictures	015 MIN
Elephants (Let's Draw)	015 MIN
Faces - Expressions	015 MIN
Forest - Outdoor Scene, Cabin	015 MIN
Halloween - Haunted House	015 MIN
Halloween - Symbols	015 MIN
Hats	015 MIN
Horses (Let's Draw)	015 MIN
Lions (Let's Draw)	015 MIN
Outer Space	015 MIN
Ovals	015 MIN
People	015 MIN
People - Figures In Action	015 MIN
Rabbits	015 MIN
Santa Claus	015 MIN
Shadows	015 MIN
Shapes, Pt 1	015 MIN
Shapes, Pt 2	015 MIN
Shapes, Surface	015 MIN
Small Animals	015 MIN
Squiggles	015 MIN
Thanksgiving (Let's Draw)	015 MIN
Trees	015 MIN
Underwater	015 MIN
Wild Animals	015 MIN

Let's Eat C 15 MIN
2 INCH VIDEOTAPE
Creates an awareness of the difficulties of feeding a city and gives a brief outline of the progression of food from the farmer to the market.
From The Let's Build A City Series.
Prod-WVIZTV Dist-GPITVL

Let's Eat Food C 35 MIN
16MM FILM, 3/4 OR 1/2 IN VIDEO H-C A
Examines the relationship between diet and health in the United States. Looks at the roles of sugar and excess cholesterol, eating habits, and dental hygiene. Narrated by Tony Randall.
Prod-CAPCI Dist-CRMP 1976

Let's Evaluate Our Work C 25 MIN
2 INCH VIDEOTAPE I
Evaluates student art work.
From The Art For Every Day Series.
Prod-CVETVC Dist-GPITVL

Let's Experiment With Water Colors B 15 MIN
2 INCH VIDEOTAPE P
Shows how to manipulate paint and water to mix light and dark shades.
From The Art Corner Series.
Prod-CVETVC Dist-GPITVL Prodn-WCVETV

Let's Explore Science—A Series
I
Prod-GPITVL Dist-GPITVL

Crystal Clear	15 MIN
Drawing A Picture Of Nature	15 MIN
Exploring Gases	15 MIN
Exploring Plants	15 MIN
Extending Our Senses	15 MIN
Hot And Cold	15 MIN
How Do You Know	15 MIN
Hunches And Guesses	15 MIN
Magnet Earth, The	15 MIN
Push And Pull	15 MIN
Seesaws, Slides And Swings	15 MIN
Sorting Things	15 MIN
What Do You Do With Numbers	15 MIN
What Do You Think	15 MIN

Let's Explore Science—A Series
I
Presents a science instruction telecourse employing the inquiry approach. (Broadcast quality)
Prod-POPS Dist-GPITVL Prodn-KOAPTV

Crystal Clear	15 MIN
Drawing A Picture Of Nature	15 MIN
Exploring Gases	15 MIN
Exploring Plants	15 MIN
Extending Our Senses	15 MIN
Hot And Cold	15 MIN
How Do You Know	15 MIN
Hunches And Guesses	15 MIN
Magnet Earth, The	15 MIN
Push And Pull	15 MIN
Seesaws, Slides And Swings	15 MIN
Sorting Things	15 MIN
What Do You Do With Numbers	15 MIN
What Do You Think	15 MIN

Let's Figure It Out—A Series
P
Shows a young woman whose interest in mathematics prompts her to write to a 'math company' for puzzles, problems and games. Explains how she solves these activities in her math lab.
Prod-WNYETV Dist-NYSED 1968

Changes And Exchange - Addition With Exchange 020 MIN
Constructing Houses - Facts About Threes 020 MIN
Doubles - Multiples Of Two 020 MIN
Guess Again - Algebraic Concepts And The 020 MIN
Half 'N Half - Operations, Fractional Numbers 020 MIN
How Many Beans - Averages In General 020 MIN
Hurry Up - Patterns In Multiplication 020 MIN
Ladders And Lines - Number Line Concepts 020 MIN
Mirror Images - Figures And Symmetry 020 MIN
Patterns - Aids In Generalization 020 MIN
Ready, Get Set, Go - Subtraction Via Time 020 MIN
Take A Guess - Estimation And Problem Solving 020 MIN
What's Missing - Missing Addends 020 MIN
What's The Rule - Concepts From Algebra 020 MIN
Wheels And Things - Linear Measurement 020 MIN

Let's Find Life C 8 MIN
16MM FILM, 3/4 OR 1/2 IN VIDEO P-I
Describes the natural habitats of various animals that can be found in the urban environment.
From The Wonder Walks Series.
Prod-EBEC Dist-EBEC 1971

Let's Find Out C 15 MIN
16MM FILM OPTICAL SOUND P-I T
Shows how the local environment can be used to teach science in creative ways. Presents students of a primary class in Tanzania who are involved in using local insects to sharpen observation of questioning skills.
From The African Primary Science Program Series.
LC NO. 70-713891
Prod-EDC Dist-EDC 1971

Let's Find Some Faces C 9 MIN
16MM FILM, 3/4 OR 1/2 IN VIDEO P
Presents a look at faces and their many expressions and shapes.
From The Learning To Look Series.
Prod-MGHT Dist-MGHT 1973

Let's Find Something Better To Do C 16 MIN
16MM FILM, 3/4 OR 1/2 IN VIDEO P-I
Examines vandalism at the grade shcool level by illustrating with puppets and live action. Stresses alternate behavior and responsibility for one's own actions.
Prod-BORTF Dist-BCNFL 1983

Let's Finish The Job C 11 MIN
16MM FILM OPTICAL SOUND A
Shows the many breeding areas of the Aedes aegypti mosquito in the modern city. Discusses the life cycle of the mosquito and describes steps necessary of eradicate it.
LC NO. 74-705025
Prod-USPHS Dist-USNAC Prodn-NMAVF 1967

Let's Get Away From It All C 14 MIN
16MM FILM OPTICAL SOUND
Follows several visitors on their vacation in Pompano Beach, Florida.
Prod-FLADC Dist-FLADC

Let's Get It Back, America C 29 MIN
16MM FILM OPTICAL SOUND
Presents George Washington, James Madison, Ben Franklin and Alexander Hamilton returning to Washington, DC and offering advice to an America whose government has grown far beyond what they envisioned.
Prod-CCUS Dist-CCUS 1980

Let's Get To The Root Of It C 20 MIN
2 INCH VIDEOTAPE P
See series title for descriptive statement.
From The Learning Our Language, Unit 2 - Dictionary Skills Series.
Prod-MPATI Dist-GPITVL

Let's Get To Work C 20 MIN
16MM FILM, 3/4 OR 1/2 IN VIDEO I-J
Presents ideas for aiding students in choosing a career.
From The Whatcha Gonna Do Series.
Prod-NVETA Dist-EBEC 1974

Let's Get Together - Culture (Anthropology-Sociology) C 15 MIN
3/4 OR 1/2 INCH VIDEO CASSETTE P
Shows Stuart, a Winnebago Indian, teaching his friend Chip about the colorful ceremonial dances his family does to make a living.
From The Two Cents' Worth Series.
Prod-WHATV Dist-AITECH Prodn-WIEC 1976

Let's Go Golfing B
16MM FILM OPTICAL SOUND
Bryon Nelson gives golf lesson in 13 segments.
Prod-SFI Dist-SFI

Let's Go Out Together C 13 MIN
16MM FILM, 3/4 OR 1/2 IN VIDEO P
Presents children experiencing the diversity of city life through visits to an open market, a firehouse, a zoo and a construction site.
From The Visit To Series.
Prod-CCPEP Dist-JOU 1977

Let's Go Sciencing, Unit I - Matter—A Series
K
Revolves around the properties or characteristics common to all matter.
Prod-DETPS Dist-GPITVL

Colors 15 MIN
Matter 15 MIN
Odors 15 MIN
Our Senses 15 MIN
Shapes 15 MIN
Size And Weight 15 MIN
Sounds 15 MIN
Tastes 15 MIN
Textures 15 MIN
Weight 15 MIN

Let's Go Sciencing, Unit II - Energy—A Series
K
Allows children to investigate the forces such as, gravity and magnetic force, that initiates, retards or changes the direction of motion.
Prod-DETPS Dist-GPITVL

Gravity 15 MIN
Gravity And Friction 15 MIN
Levers 15 MIN
Lift 15 MIN
Magnets 15 MIN
Starting 15 MIN
Stopping 15 MIN

Let's Go Sciencing, Unit III - Life—A Series
K
Uses both animal and plant materials to enable children to become aware of both differences in structure and similarities in the life activities of living things. Emphasizes the differences among those things that are living and those that are not.
Prod-DETPS Dist-GPITVL

Amphibians 15 MIN
Animals 15 MIN
Birds 15 MIN
Children 15 MIN
Fish 15 MIN
Grouping Animals 15 MIN
Insects 15 MIN
Living Together 15 MIN
Mammals 15 MIN
Mollusks 15 MIN
Plants 15 MIN
Reptiles 15 MIN
Seed Plants 15 MIN
Seeds 15 MIN
Trees 15 MIN
Water Plants 15 MIN

Let's Go There Together C 18 MIN
16MM FILM OPTICAL SOUND
Shows the ski areas of British Columbia.
LC NO. 77-700296
Prod-PETRIC Dist-PCFCWA 1976

Let's Help Recycle C 11 MIN
16MM FILM, 3/4 OR 1/2 IN VIDEO P-I
Depicts a group of school children who come to a city council meeting to present a report on the need to stop waste and recycle materials. Shows that each child has conducted a study of one aspect of the problem and has a solution for it. Describes the recycling of paper, bottles and cans.
From The Caring About Our Community Series.
Prod-GORKER Dist-AIMS 1973

Let's Keep In Touch C 28 MIN
16MM FILM OPTICAL SOUND
Describes how Medicare, with recommended supplementary insurance, can serve the needs of senior citizens.
Prod-BALIN Dist-MTP

Let's Lip Read—A Series
Teaches lip reading to hard-of-hearing adults and secondary school age children who would not otherwise have instruction available to them.
Prod-WETATV Dist-PUBTEL

Let's Listen B 15 MIN
2 INCH VIDEOTAPE P
See series title for descriptive statement.
From The Sounds Like Magic Series.
Prod-MOEBA Dist-GPITVL Prodn-KYNETV

Let's Look At Castles C 19 MIN
16MM FILM, 3/4 OR 1/2 IN VIDEO H-C
Traces the development of the castle in England from the 11th century to the beginning of the 14th century.
Prod-ATTICO Dist-IFB 1969

Let's Look At Levers X 10 MIN
16MM FILM, 3/4 OR 1/2 IN VIDEO P-I
Presents an introduction to levers. Shows how a lever works with examples of nail pulling and other common household uses.
Prod-JOU Dist-JOU 1961

Let's Look At New Zealand C 15 MIN
16MM FILM OPTICAL SOUND I-H
Discusses the history, geography, culture, economic development and farm exports of New Zealand. Depicts the cities of Wellington and Auckland. Shows North Island's geysers and pools of hot mud and water.
LC NO. FIA67-5305
Prod-TEXTBK Dist-SF 1966

Let's Look Back C 15 MIN
2 INCH VIDEOTAPE P
Provides an enrichment program utilizing many of the communicative skills.
From The Word Magic (2nd Ed) Series.
Prod-CVETVC Dist-GPITVL

Let's Make A Deal - Cable Vs Dance C 30 MI
3/4 OR 1/2 INCH VIDEO CASSETTE
See series title for descriptive statement.
From The Business And Law Of Dance Series.
Prod-ARCVID Dist-ARCVID

Let's Make A Film C 13 MI
16MM FILM OPTICAL SOUND P-C
Explores the activities of the yellow ball workshop, Newto Mass., Which involves young people from the ages of eig through eighteen who create their own films. Individual stu dents demonstrate and discuss the steps involved in preparin their films and show the finished product.
LC NO. 79-714171
Prod-YELLOW Dist-VANREN 197

Let's Make A Map X 11 MI
16MM FILM, 3/4 OR 1/2 IN VIDEO P
Describes how the physical world is represented on a map. Illus trates comparative size and distance, and shows how a ma can help us find our way from one place to another.
Prod-WILETS Dist-PHENIX 196

Let's Make A Musical C 29 MI
3/4 INCH VIDEO CASSETTE
Features Jerry Bilik as he composes a musical comedy on th spot to show how it's done.
From The Music Shop Series.
Prod-UMITV Dist-UMITV 197

Let's Make A Print C 25 MI
2 INCH VIDEOTAPE
Illustrates linoleum and cardboard printing.
From The Art For Every Day Series.
Prod-CVETVC Dist-GPITVL

Let's Make Up A Story C 11 MI
16MM FILM, 3/4 OR 1/2 IN VIDEO P-
Shows how you can use your imagination to make up your own stories with your own characters, settings and plots.
Prod-CORF Dist-CORF 1972

Let's Measure - Inches, Feet And Yards C 11 MIN
16MM FILM, 3/4 OR 1/2 IN VIDEO P
A young boy, endeavoring to estimate distances, is taught by his father to use a ruler and a yardstick to find the length of familiar objects.
Prod-CORF Dist-CORF 1953

Let's Measure - Ounces, Pounds And Tons C 11 MIN
16MM FILM, 3/4 OR 1/2 IN VIDEO P
Two small boys learn to use the scales by weighing a pound of cotton and a pound of iron bolts. They observe the use of scales for weighing meat and vegetables, and learn to estimate the weight of common objects in ounces, pounds and fractions of pounds.
Prod-CORF Dist-CORF 1956

Let's Measure - Pints, Quarts And Gallons C 11 MIN
16MM FILM, 3/4 OR 1/2 IN VIDEO P
A small boy discovers the relationship of pints, quarts and gallons, learns to identify the symbols used to designate liquid content, and observes the use of liquid measures in the dairy, in the gasoline station and in the home.
Prod-CORF Dist-CORF 1956

Let's Measure - Using Standard Units C 13 MIN
16MM FILM, 3/4 OR 1/2 IN VIDEO P
Describes Jimmy's visit to Measuring Land, where he learns to understand standard units.
From The Let's Measure Series.
Prod-CORF Dist-CORF

Let's Measure—A Series
16MM FILM, 3/4 OR 1/2 IN VIDEO P
Discusses metric measurement.
Prod-CORF Dist-CORF

Let's Measure - Using Centimeters, Meters 010 MIN
Let's Measure - Using Grams And Kilograms 010 MIN
Let's Measure - Using Milliliters And Liters 012 MIN
Let's Measure - Using Standard Units 013 MIN

Let's Play Hospital C 53 MIN
16MM FILM OPTICAL SOUND
Correlates a child's experiences in the hospital with what he feels about it. Shows how the hospital staff helps the children deal with their anxious feelings and describes a program of hospital-related play.
LC NO. 74-706373
Prod-USOE Dist-USNAC

Let's Play Safe C 10 MIN
16MM FILM, 3/4 OR 1/2 IN VIDEO K-P
Illustrates incidents that commonly cause accidents at play. Shows how these situations can be changed to avoid accidents. Combines animation and live action.
Prod-PORTAP Dist-AIMS 1974

Let's Pretend B 15 MIN
3/4 OR 1/2 INCH VIDEO CASSETTE P
Shows how to create puppets using cardboard or paper plates.
From The Art Corner Series.
Prod-CVETVC Dist-GPITVL Prodn-WCVETV

Let's Pretend C 15 MIN
3/4 OR 1/2 INCH VIDEO CASSETTE K-P
Develops the communication skills desirable for successful creative dramatics.
From The Magic Of Words Series.
Prod-GWTVAI Dist-GPITVL Prodn-WETATV

Let's Pretend C 25 MIN
16MM FILM, 3/4 OR 1/2 IN VIDEO J-C A

Explores the computers ability to be an accurate model or simulation of the real thing.
From The Computer Programme Series. Episode 7
Prod-BBCTV Dist-FI 1982

Let's Pretend It C 10 MIN
3/4 OR 1/2 INCH VIDEO CASSETTE K-P
Deals with the skills to create stories from a variety of sources.
From The Book, Look And Listen Series.
Prod-MDDE Dist-AITECH 1977

Let's Read Together B 20 MIN
2 INCH VIDEOTAPE I
Explores the enjoyment of reading aloud. (Broadcast quality)
From The Quest For The Best Series.
Prod-DENVPS Dist-GPITVL Prodn-KRMATV

Let's Really Look B 15 MIN
3/4 OR 1/2 INCH VIDEO CASSETTE P
Searches for beauty and ideas for art in nature and man-made things. Looks at patterns and colors in shifting clouds, falling rain, specks of dust, cobblestones, old houses, chairs and television towers. Shows works by Nicolas De Stael, Henri Mousseau, Georgia Okeefe and Mc Donald-Wright.
From The Primary Art Series.
Prod-WETATV Dist-AITECH

Let's Rejoice C 10 MIN
16MM FILM, 3/4 OR 1/2 IN VIDEO H-C A
Profiles the residents of an old people's home who face personal adversity but who belong to a choir that affirms life.
Prod-WOMBAT Dist-WOMBAT

Let's Save - Opportunity Cost C 15 MIN
3/4 OR 1/2 INCH VIDEO CASSETTE J-H
Tells of three boys who want to enter their rock and roll trio in a talent contest and give up nonessentials to save for new outfits that could help them win. Reveals that when one boy needs part of their savings, the group is faced with a new decision. Deals with saving and opportunity cost.
From The Give And Take Series. Pt 3
LC NO. 83-706371
Prod-AITV Dist-AITECH 1982

Let's Shape Up C
3/4 OR 1/2 INCH VIDEO CASSETTE
Provides a base upon which dietitians can build a personal diet plan. Stresses exercise.
Prod-MEDFAC Dist-MEDFAC

Let's Sing Smokey's Song C 3 MIN
16MM FILM, 3/4 OR 1/2 IN VIDEO
Presents picnickers who sing along with Smokey Bear. Cautions against carelessness with fire in the forest.
Prod-FILCOM Dist-FILCOM

Let's Split (Inner Thighs II) C 29 MIN
2 INCH VIDEOTAPE
See series title for descriptive statement.
From The Maggie And The Beautiful Machine - Feet And Legs Series.
Prod-WGBHTV Dist-PUBTEL

Let's Start At The Very Beginning C 6 MIN
16MM FILM, 3/4 OR 1/2 IN VIDEO H-C A
Suggests that it is not necessary to recognize every person in the room before beginning the body of the speech. Shows effective and ineffective speech openings and notes how extensive background is not necessary when using quotes.
From The Communicating From The Lectern Series.
Prod-METAIV Dist-AIMS

Let's Take The Mystery Out Of Power Brakes C 22 MIN
16MM FILM OPTICAL SOUND H-C A
Presents an analysis of power brake malfunctions and illustrates their correction by the installation of a replacement unit.
LC NO. 73-703375
Prod-BENDIX Dist-BENDIX 1971

Let's Talk About Safety B 10 MIN
16MM FILM OPTICAL SOUND C A
Offers an approach to the universal problem of getting ideas across. Shows foremen how to use plain talk to put safety across, how to talk safety as easily as they talk bowling or baseball.
From The Communication For Safety Series.
Prod-DUNN Dist-NSC 1959

Let's Talk About Surgery C 30 MIN
3/4 OR 1/2 INCH VIDEO CASSETTE
Considers medical versus surgical procedures. Looks at who really makes the decision to have surgery. Examines the idea of whether or not there is ever such a thing as 'minor surgery.'
Prod-UILCCC Dist-AL

Let's Talk About The Hospital (Spanish)–A Series

Features Mister Rogers in four video programs which provide basic information and reassurance about hospital experiences.
Prod-FAMCOM Dist-FAMCOM

Going To The Hospital (Spanish)
Having An Operation (Spanish)
Visit To The Emergency Department, A (Spanish)
Wearing A Cast (Spanish)

Let's Talk About The Hospital–A Series

Features Mister Rogers in four video programs which provide basic information and reassurance about hospital experiences.
Prod-FAMCOM Dist-FAMCOM

Going To The Hospital
Having An Operation
Visit To The Emergency Department, A
Wearing A Cast

Let's Talk It Over - A Child With Epilepsy C 6 MIN
16MM FILM, 3/4 OR 1/2 IN VIDEO K-P
Presents a story about Sandy, an epileptic child who is afraid of telling the other children about her condition.
From The Like You, Like Me Series.
Prod-EBEC Dist-EBEC 1977

Let's Think And Be Safe C 10 MIN
16MM FILM, 3/4 OR 1/2 IN VIDEO K-P
Dramatizes seven episodes around the major causes of accidents in schools. Shows what can happen and suggests ways to avoid these accidents. Combines animation and live action.
Prod-PORTAP Dist-AIMS 1975

Let's Think Fat C 15 MIN
2 INCH VIDEOTAPE
See series title for descriptive statement.
From The Umbrella Series.
Prod-KETCTV Dist-PUBTEL

Let's Try Communicating C 13 MIN
16MM FILM OPTICAL SOUND
Depicts how a simple three-part tag system benefits mechanics in railroad diesel repair shops in maintaining a replacement component inventory.
LC NO. 76-702297
Prod-UPR Dist-UPR 1976

Let's Visit–A Series
P-I
Extends the student's experience from the world of the family into the community. Shows how familiar items are produced and how each community distributes its goods.
Prod-BCNFL Dist-BCNFL

Books - From Start To Finish 015 MIN
How To Make A Truck 009 MIN
Market Gardening 009 MIN
Sandwich Stuff 015 MIN

Let's Walk Together C 29 MIN
3/4 OR 1/2 INCH VIDEO CASSETTE J-H A
Shows how abusive parents can develop more positive relationships with their children.
LC NO. 85-703548
Prod-BYU Dist-EBEC 1981

Let's Watch Plants Grow C 10 MIN
16MM FILM, 3/4 OR 1/2 IN VIDEO P-I
A class watches plants grow. It learns that plants need water, minerals and sunlight.
Prod-CORF Dist-CORF 1962

Let's Work With Clay B 20 MIN
2 INCH VIDEOTAPE P-I
Teaches awareness of clay products, bricks, pottery and tiles. Demonstrates the construction of well-designed and decorated pinch pots.
From The Art Adventures Series.
Prod-CVETVC Dist-GPITVL Prodn-WCVETV

Let's Write A Story C 15 MIN
3/4 OR 1/2 INCH VIDEO CASSETTE T
Uses the adventures of a pirate and his three friends to explore the many facets of language arts. Focuses on punctuation and illustrates its use in reading and writing.
From The Hidden Treasures Series. No. 5
LC NO. 82-706529
Prod-WCVETV Dist-GPITVL 1980

Let's Write A Story (2nd Ed) C 11 MIN
16MM FILM, 3/4 OR 1/2 IN VIDEO P-I
Presents three episodes as the basis for creative writing exercises.
Prod-CF Dist-CF 1978

Lethal Arrhythmias C 19 MIN
16MM FILM OPTICAL SOUND PRO
Discusses lethal arrhythmias, including ventricular fibrillation, ventricular tachycardia and ventricular standstill. Describes pathophysiology, electrocardiographic pattern, clinical picture and treatment given.
From The Intensive Coronary Care Multimedia Learning System (ICC/MMLS) Series.
LC NO. 73-701774
Prod-SUTHLA Dist-SUTHLA 1969

Lets Teach Signs C 7 MIN
16MM FILM SILENT H-C A S
Presents Herb Larson giving his views on teaching sign language to deaf students. Speaking as a deaf adult he advocates improving sign language skills as a means of acquiring a better understanding of English.
LC NO. 76-701689
Prod-JOYCE Dist-JOYCE 1975

Letter C, The C 15 MIN
3/4 INCH VIDEO CASSETTE P
See series title for descriptive statement.
From The I Need To Read Series.
Prod-WCETTV Dist-GPITVL 1975

Letter From A Mother B 10 MIN
16MM FILM OPTICAL SOUND
Shows an American mother's understanding of the role her son must play in defense of his country.
LC NO. FIE55-80
Prod-USA Dist-USNAC 1955

Letter From An Airman C 17 MIN
16MM FILM OPTICAL SOUND
Presents an airman's thoughts as he writes his brother about Air Force basic training.
LC NO. 74-706124
Prod-USAF Dist-USNAC 1964

Letter From An Unknown Woman B 89 MIN
16MM FILM OPTICAL SOUND
Stars Joan Fontaine as a woman who reveals her lifetime love for a concert pianist who fathered her child years ago and now can't even remember her. Tells how Fontaine's present husband challenges the pianist to a duel. Directed by Max Ophuls.
Prod-UPCI Dist-KITPAR 1948

Letter From Siberia (French) C 60 MIN
16MM FILM OPTICAL SOUND
Parodies the standard travelogue in its presentation of Siberia. Features an animated segment in which mammoths are described as a fashionable feature of Siberian life. Converts the Siberian gold rush into a full-blown Western, complete with Indians, cowboys rustlers, trappers and gunfights.
Prod-NYFLMS Dist-NYFLMS 1957

Letter G And Review, The C 15 MIN
3/4 INCH VIDEO CASSETTE P
See series title for descriptive statement.
From The I Need To Read Series.
Prod-WCETTV Dist-GPITVL 1975

Letter Of Application And The Application Form, The C 15 MIN
3/4 INCH VIDEO CASSETTE H-C A
Tells how to use letters of application and application forms.
From The Job Seeking Series.
Prod-WCETTV Dist-GPITVL 1979

Letter Of Application, The C 30 MIN
3/4 OR 1/2 INCH VIDEO CASSETTE C
See series title for descriptive statement.
From The Writing For A Reason Series.
Prod-DALCCD Dist-DALCCD

Letter R After Vowels, The - And Review C 15 MIN
3/4 INCH VIDEO CASSETTE P
See series title for descriptive statement.
From The I Need To Read Series.
Prod-WCETTV Dist-GPITVL 1975

Letter Reports B 45 MIN
2 INCH VIDEOTAPE C
See series title for descriptive statement.
From The Business Writing Series. Unit IV - Letters About Employment - Reports
Prod-CHITVC Dist-GPITVL Prodn-WTTWTV

Letter T, The C 15 MIN
3/4 INCH VIDEO CASSETTE P
See series title for descriptive statement.
From The I Need To Read Series.
Prod-WCETTV Dist-GPITVL 1975

Letter To A Friend B 20 MIN
16MM FILM OPTICAL SOUND
Explains how Japanese boys and girls correspond, as pen pals, with boys and girls of their own ages in the United States.
LC NO. FIE52-1945
Prod-USA Dist-USNAC 1951

Letter To Amy, A C 7 MIN
16MM FILM, 3/4 OR 1/2 IN VIDEO K-P
Tells the story of Peter who is having a birthday party and although he has asked all his friends in person, he decides to write out one special invitation to a girl. Shows what happens before he reaches the mailbox, leaving him very mixed-up and worried about whether or not she will come to the party.
Prod-WWS Dist-WWS Prodn-SCHNDL 1970

Letter To Jane B 55 MIN
16MM FILM OPTICAL SOUND
Studies the social issues raised by actress Jane Fonda and looks at her films and those of her father. Produced in France with English narration. Directed by Jean-Luc Godard and Jean-Pierre Gorin.
Prod-NYFLMS Dist-NYFLMS 1972

Letter To Nancy, A C 80 MIN
16MM FILM OPTICAL SOUND H-C A
Deals with a romance between Carol Reed, daughter of a family of comfortable means, and the minister of a church serving mixed races in an underprivileged city area, which introduces young Nancy to the Reed family. Shows how through Nancy's plight, the family's selfcentered, complacent attitudes are jarred.
Prod-CONCOR Dist-CPH

Letter To Write, A C 15 MIN
2 INCH VIDEOTAPE I
Discusses business and personal letter writing and shows excerpts from letters of well-known people.
From The Images Series.
Prod-CVETVC Dist-GPITVL

Letter V And Syllables, The C 15 MIN
3/4 INCH VIDEO CASSETTE P
See series title for descriptive statement.
From The I Need To Read Series.
Prod-WCETTV Dist-GPITVL 1975

Letter Writing B 15 MIN
2 INCH VIDEOTAPE P
See series title for descriptive statement.
From The Language Corner Series.
Prod-CVETVC Dist-GPITVL Prodn-WCVETV

Letter Writing At Work C 19 MIN
16MM FILM, 3/4 OR 1/2 IN VIDEO

Reviews letter writing skills for all employees who write letters as part of their job. Shows how the business letter can be made to fulfill its two main functions of messenger as well as ambassador.
LC NO. 74-700687
Prod-RANKAV Dist-RTBL 1972

Letter Y, The C 15 MIN
3/4 INCH VIDEO CASSETTE P
See series title for descriptive statement.
From The I Need To Read Series.
Prod-WCETTV Dist-GPITVL 1975

Letter, The C 15 MIN
16MM FILM, 3/4 OR 1/2 IN VIDEO K-P
Tells of Toad's sadness that he has never received a letter. Reveals that Frog attempts to correct this by sending him a letter, but that Toad has a long wait when the letter is delivered by a snail.
From The Words And Pictures Series.
Prod-FI Dist-FI

Lettering Instructional Materials X 22 MIN
16MM FILM, 3/4 OR 1/2 IN VIDEO H-C T
Shows many types of letters and lettering devices, such as rubber stamps, stencil letters and mechanical scribers, which may be used to produce effective printing on display materials.
From The Preparation Of Audio-Visual Materials Series.
Prod-IU Dist-IU 1955

Letters C 9 MIN
16MM FILM, 3/4 OR 1/2 IN VIDEO J-C A
Shows how a new school in a rural village in Brazil brings opportunity and work for children and adults who cannot read.
Prod-SLUIZR Dist-PHENIX 1974

Letters B And L, The C 15 MIN
3/4 INCH VIDEO CASSETTE P
See series title for descriptive statement.
From The I Need To Read Series.
Prod-WCETTV Dist-GPITVL 1975

Letters F And D, The C 15 MIN
3/4 INCH VIDEO CASSETTE P
See series title for descriptive statement.
From The I Need To Read Series.
Prod-WCETTV Dist-GPITVL 1975

Letters From Morazan C 55 MIN
16MM FILM, 3/4 OR 1/2 IN VIDEO
Tells the story of a guerilla offensive in the Morazan province of El Salvador. Shows preparation for battle and meetings of FMLN leaders and two remarkably filmed battles.
Prod-RADIOV Dist-ICARUS 1982

Letters From Viet Nam C
16MM FILM, 3/4 OR 1/2 IN VIDEO
Views 60 helicopter combat missions flown by a young American pilot in Vietnam.
Prod-DREWAS Dist-DIRECT 1965

Letters H, W And R, The C 15 MIN
3/4 INCH VIDEO CASSETTE P
See series title for descriptive statement.
From The I Need To Read Series.
Prod-WCETTV Dist-GPITVL 1975

Letters J And K, The C 15 MIN
3/4 INCH VIDEO CASSETTE P
See series title for descriptive statement.
From The I Need To Read Series.
Prod-WCETTV Dist-GPITVL 1975

Letters M And S, The C 15 MIN
3/4 INCH VIDEO CASSETTE P
See series title for descriptive statement.
From The I Need To Read Series.
Prod-WCETTV Dist-GPITVL 1975

Letters P And N, The C 15 MIN
3/4 INCH VIDEO CASSETTE P
See series title for descriptive statement.
From The I Need To Read Series.
Prod-WCETTV Dist-GPITVL 1975

Letters To The World - Emily Dickinson And Walt Whitman C 20 MIN
3/4 OR 1/2 INCH VIDEO CASSETTE H-C A
Offers a dramatization which presents interviews between a journalist and Emily Dickinson and Walt Whitman. Includes a conversation with students interested in their poems.
From The American Literature Series.
LC NO. 83-706255
Prod-AUBU Dist-AITECH 1983

Letting Go Of Grief And Pain - Looking Ahead To The Future C 90 MIN
3/4 OR 1/2 INCH VIDEO CASSETTE A
See series title for descriptive statement.
From The Growing Through Loss - A Howard Clinebell Resource Series. Session 6
Prod-UMCOM Dist-ECUFLM 1982

Lettre De Suisse, Une C 10 MIN
16MM FILM, 3/4 OR 1/2 IN VIDEO H-C
Prod-EBEC Dist-EBEC 1974

Lettres D'un Ami Francais—A Series
16MM FILM, 3/4 OR 1/2 IN VIDEO
A French language videocassette series. Describes the life of a typical French teenager.
Prod-SEABEN Dist-IFB 1962

Chez Nous 012 MIN
Le Pique-Nique 015 MIN
Le Quatorze Juillet 015 MIN
Un Journee Au Lycee 016 MIN

Leukemia B 14 MIN
16MM FILM OPTICAL SOUND H-C A
Discusses three main forms of leukemia. Describes the incidence of leukemia in patients at various age levels.
From The Doctors At Work Series.
LC NO. FIA65-1350
Prod-CMA Dist-LAWREN Prodn-LAWREN 1963

Leukemia C 29 MIN
3/4 OR 1/2 INCH VIDEO CASSETTE
Focuses on treatments for leukemia and describes how the disease affects adults and children.
From The Daniel Foster, MD Series.
Prod-KERA Dist-PBS

Levels Of Abstraction And Meaning C 30 MIN
3/4 OR 1/2 INCH VIDEO CASSETTE C
See series title for descriptive statement.
From The Language And Meaning Series.
Prod-WUSFTV Dist-GPITVL 1983

Levels Of Contrast - Levels Of Context B 45 MIN
2 INCH VIDEOTAPE C
See series title for descriptive statement.
From The General Humanities Series. Unit 3 - The Auditory Arts
Prod-CHITVC Dist-GPITVL Prodn-WTTWTV

Levels Of Human Need B 29 MIN
16MM FILM OPTICAL SOUND IND
See series title for descriptive statement.
From The Supervisory Leadership Series.
LC NO. 72-703320
Prod-EDSD Dist-EDSD

Levels Of Learning C 24 MIN
16MM FILM OPTICAL SOUND I-C
Examines ways in which different animals learn. Points out that an understanding of the way the minds of animals work may provide information about the human mind.
From The Animal Secrets Series.
LC NO. FIA68-1036
Prod-NBC Dist-GRACUR 1967

Lever - A Simple Machine C 15 MIN
3/4 OR 1/2 INCH VIDEO CASSETTE P-I
Discusses the characteristics of a lever.
From The Why Series.
Prod-WDCNTV Dist-AITECH 1976

Levers C 15 MIN
2 INCH VIDEOTAPE K
Illustrates the one function of a lever is to change the direction of a force.
From The Let's Go Sciencing, Unit II - Energy Series.
Prod-DETPS Dist-GPITVL

Levi's For Feet C 9 MIN
16MM FILM OPTICAL SOUND
Shows the joint development of Levi's for Feet by the Brown Shoe Company and Levi Strauss and Company. Explains their selling method.
LC NO. 76-702658
Prod-BRNSHO Dist-BRNSHO Prodn-COMPIX 1975

Levitation C 6 MIN
3/4 OR 1/2 INCH VIDEO CASSETTE
Shows a man trying to fly like a bird who becomes half-bird himself. Includes mime by Yass Hakoshima.
From The Three Works By Ian Hugo Series.
Prod-EAI Dist-EAI

Lew Mathe C 30 MIN
3/4 OR 1/2 INCH VIDEO CASSETTE A
Presents bridge master Lew Mathe discussing bidding, dummy play and defensive problems.
From The Play Bridge With The Experts Series. Pt 14
Prod-KUHTTV Dist-GPITVL 1980

Lewis And Clark C 15 MIN
3/4 OR 1/2 INCH VIDEO CASSETTE P
Tells how Indian maiden Sacajawea helped Lewis and Clark cross the Rocky Mountains.
From The Stories Of America Series.
Prod-OHSDE Dist-AITECH Prodn-WVIZTV 1976

Lewis And Clark B 20 MIN
2 INCH VIDEOTAPE I
See series title for descriptive statement.
From The Americans All Series.
Prod-DENVPS Dist-GPITVL Prodn-KRMATV

Lewis And Clark At The Great Divide C 22 MIN
16MM FILM, 3/4 OR 1/2 IN VIDEO I-J
Portrays the background, purposes and drama of the Lewis and Clark Expedition, concentrating on the events of 1805.
From The You Are There Series.
Prod-CBSNEW Dist-PHENIX 1971

Lewis And Clark Journey, The C 16 MIN
16MM FILM, 3/4 OR 1/2 IN VIDEO I-J
Traces the expedition of Lewis and Clark using authentic records and pictures taken along the route.
Prod-CORF Dist-CORF 1968

Lexington, Concord And Independence C 17 MIN
16MM FILM, 3/4 OR 1/2 IN VIDEO I-J
Presents the battles between the royal forces of King George who meant to teach the young colonial upstarts a lesson and the forces of the colonial Minutemen.

From The American History - Birth Of A Nation Series.
Prod-AIMS Dist-AIMS 196

Liang And The Magic Paintbrush C 30 MI
3/4 OR 1/2 INCH VIDEO CASSETTE
Presents an old Chinese legend about a boy who finds a paintbrush that magically brings brings pictures to life. Shows LeVa Burton participating in a lion dance in New York's Chinatown and exploring the world of computer art.
From The Reading Rainbow Series. No. 7
Prod-WNEDTV Dist-GPITVL 198

Liberal Arts College For Men, A C 18 MI
16MM FILM OPTICAL SOUND J-H A
Students at Davidson College, an academically selective school located in a rural area in North Carolina, point out that selective admissions does not mean a constant struggle to remain in good standing if reasonable effort is exerted. Notes that students must travel to cities or to girls' schools in the area for an active social life.
From The College Selection Film Series.
LC NO. 74-713111
Prod-VISEDC Dist-VISEDC 1971

Liberalism And Conservatism C
3/4 OR 1/2 INCH VIDEO CASSETTE H
Traces the formation of liberal and conservative alliances from the post-Civil War period through the present and studies the positions of each on a variety of issues.
Prod-GA Dist-GA

Liberated Tops C 15 MIN
2 INCH VIDEOTAPE
See series title for descriptive statement.
From The Umbrella Series.
Prod-KETCTV Dist-PUBTEL

Liberation Of Paris B 34 MIN
16MM FILM OPTICAL SOUND C
A documentary of the August, 1944, seige of Paris by the resistance movement. Begins in Nazi-controlled Paris one week before the arrival of allied troops. Shows the allies' arrival and the welcome given them.
Prod-LCFRCI Dist-RADIM 1944

Liberation Of Soviet Byelorussia C 30 MIN
3/4 OR 1/2 INCH VIDEO CASSETTE
Presents a review of the defeat of Germany's Center Army Group and the liberation of Soviet Byelorussia during World War II.
Prod-IHF Dist-IHF

Liberation Of Zoospores In The Alga Basicladia C 4 MIN
16MM FILM OPTICAL SOUND H-C
Identifies the 'MOSS' on a 'MOSS-BACK' turtle as the Alga basicladia. An examination of filaments under a microscope shows darkening as zoospores mature, an exit pore forming and the escape of zoospores after the pore membrane bursts.
From The Plant Science Series.
LC NO. FIA65-823
Prod-IOWA Dist-MLA 1964

Liberation Of Zoospores In The Alga Oedogonium C 4 MIN
16MM FILM OPTICAL SOUND H-C
Shows asexual reproduction in the Alga oedogonium. Pictures cells in a filament which has modified to form zoospores, breaking of the filament, emergence of zoospores into a vesicle and the zoospores swimming after leaving the vesicle.
From The Plant Science Series.
LC NO. FIA65-926
Prod-IOWA Dist-MLA 1964

Liberation—A Series

Deals with various aspects of liberation.
Prod-OHC Dist-HRC

Free For All 059 MIN
Good Grief 060 MIN
She, He Shall Overcome 060 MIN
When Will We Ever Learn 060 MIN

Liberator, The B 30 MIN
16MM FILM OPTICAL SOUND R
Presents narration and choral and solo music to explain songs traditionally associated with Hanukkah and to explain other music influenced by the holiday theme. (Kinescope)
Prod-JTS Dist-NAAJS Prodn-NBCTV 1957

Libertarians, The B 29 MIN
16MM FILM, 3/4 OR 1/2 IN VIDEO
Investigates the development of an urban working class in Brazil around the turn of the century. Shows how these immigrant laborers, confronted by brutal working conditions and poor wages, were instrumental in building a labor movement with a strong anarchist orientation.
Prod-FIHOL Dist-CNEMAG

Liberty B 22 MIN
16MM FILM SILENT
Relates the comic adventures of two men who try to escape from prison while simultaneously trying to get into the right pair of pants. Stars Stan Laurel and Oliver Hardy.
Prod-ROACH Dist-BHAWK 1929

Liberty C 60 MIN
3/4 OR 1/2 INCH VIDEO CASSETTE A
Presents Dr Mortimer J Adler who declares that there is no such thing as liberty in itself. Points out that virtue and wisdom, circumstance and political forces each contain a singular aspect of freedom. Traces the thread that leads from one to the other.
From The Six Great Ideas Series.
Prod-WNETTV Dist-FI 1982

Liberty In A Featherbed - The Story Of Thomas Kennedy B 30 MIN
16MM FILM OPTICAL SOUND
Tells the story of Thomas Kennedy, dramatizing the struggle in the legislature of Maryland to remove civil and political inequalities. (Kinescope)
Prod-JTS Dist-NAAJS Prodn-NBCTV 1953

Liberty's Booty C 50 MIN
3/4 OR 1/2 INCH VIDEO CASSETTE
Views middle-class, white prostitution. Concerns sexual demystification. Provides an ironic exposition of American 'permissivenss.'
Prod-KITCHN Dist-KITCHN

Libra C 39 MIN
16MM FILM, 3/4 OR 1/2 IN VIDEO
Presents the story of Libra, a privately owned space habitat whose primary industry is the development and delivery of cheap, safe solar energy to earth, bringing reaction from the energy monopolies of earth.
Prod-WORLDR Dist-WORLDR

Librarians Communicate C 51 MIN
3/4 INCH VIDEO CASSETTE
Discusses verbal and nonverbal communication used by library reference and public service staffs.
LC NO. 78-706316
Prod-USDHEW Dist-USNAC Prodn-UARIZ 1977

Libraries And The Pursuit Of Happiness C 29 MIN
16MM FILM, 3/4 OR 1/2 IN VIDEO
Describes the services provided by libraries and dispels some popular misconceptions as to what the library environment is really like. Discusses the role played by libraries and librarians in local communities.
Prod-EBEC Dist-EBEC 1981

Libraries Are Kid Stuff C 14 MIN
16MM FILM, 3/4 OR 1/2 IN VIDEO C A
Services of the Myers Demonstration Library, Tucson, Arizona, are shown through the eyes of the children who use the elementary school library.
Prod-UARIZ Dist-WWS 1970

Libraries For Louisiana C 20 MIN
16MM FILM OPTICAL SOUND T
Shows the value of Louisiana's library service. Presents librarians doing the job they love most, bringing books and other related materials to people wherever they are.
LC NO. FIA60-3458
Prod-LASLIB Dist-RAMSEY

Libraries For The Kid In All Of Us C 1 MIN
3/4 INCH VIDEO CASSETTE
Features children's comments about why they like the public library.
Prod-MDPL Dist-LVN

Libraries Without Bars B 25 MIN
16MM FILM, 3/4 OR 1/2 IN VIDEO
Shows modern improvements being made in Japanese libraries to stimulate interest in reading and to encourage appreciation of art, music and literature.
LC NO. 82-706344
Prod-USA Dist-USNAC 1951

Library Lens Sampler C 10 MIN
3/4 OR 1/2 INCH VIDEO CASSETTE
Contains a sampler of the Baltimore County Public Library weekly five-minute news programs.
Prod-BCPL Dist-LVN

Library Lobbying - A Primer For Trustees C 15 MIN
3/4 OR 1/2 INCH VIDEO CASSETTE
Discusses the role of trustees in lobbying at the state level for library legislation.
Prod-LVN Dist-LVN

Library Media Center, The C 20 MIN
3/4 INCH VIDEO CASSETTE I
Introduces basic library activities, focusing on classification, the card catalog and reference.
From The Study Skills Series.
Prod-WCVETV Dist-GPITVL 1979

Library Of Career Counseling Films—A Series
J-H
Prod-COUNFI Dist-COUNFI 1971

How A Career Develops 15 MIN
Is A Career As A Technician For You 14 MIN
Is A Career In Agri-Business For You 15 MIN
Is A Career In Atomic Energy For You 15 MIN
Is A Career In Banking For You 14 MIN
Is A Career In Bench Work For You 15 MIN
Is A Career In Business Administration For You 16 MIN
Is A Career In Civil Aviation For You 15 MIN
Is A Career In Clerical Work For You 16 MIN
Is A Career In Electronics Manufacturing For 16 MIN
Is A Career In Finance, Insurance Or Real 16 MIN
Is A Career In Fishing Or Forestry For You 15 MIN
Is A Career In Food Preparation For You 15 MIN
Is A Career In Government For You 15 MIN
Is A Career In Industrial Chemicals For You 15 MIN
Is A Career In Iron Steel For You 15 MIN
Is A Career In Machining For You 16 MIN
Is A Career In Management For You 15 MIN
Is A Career In Mining, Petroleum Or Gas 15 MIN
Is A Career In Motor Freight Transportation 15 MIN
Is A Career In Motor Vehicle Or Equipment 16 MIN
Is A Career In Processing For You 15 MIN
Is A Career In Radio Or Television For You 15 MIN
Is A Career In Structural Work For You 15 MIN
Is A Career In The Aero-Space Industry For You 15 MIN
Is A Career In The Apparel Industry For You
Is A Career In The Electric Power Industry 15 MIN
Is A Career In The Health Services For You 14 MIN
Is A Career In The Hotel Or Motel Business 14 MIN
Is A Career In The Natural Sciences For You 15 MIN
Is A Career In The Performing Arts For You 15 MIN
Is A Career In The Professions For You 15 MIN
Is A Career In The Pulp And Pater Industry 15 MIN
Is A Career In The Restaurant Business For You 14 MIN
Is A Career In The Service Industries For You 15 MIN
Is A Career In The Social Sciences For You 14 MIN
Is A Career In The Telephone Business For You 15 MIN
Is A Career In The Textile Or Apparel 15 MIN
Is A Railroad Career For You 15 MIN
Is Sales A Career For You 15 MIN
World Of Work, The (Overview) 14 MIN

Library Of Congress X 23 MIN
16MM FILM, 3/4 OR 1/2 IN VIDEO H A
Shows the variety of services offered by the Library of Congress and how important documents are stored on films, maps, Braille and recordings. Describes two typical research projects at the library, one related to the possibilities of using the moon as an exploration base, and the other for a biography on one of the signers of the Declaration of Independance.
Prod-EBEC Dist-EBEC 1969

Library Of Congress, The B 21 MIN
16MM FILM - 3/4 IN VIDEO
Explains the resources and services of the U S Library of Congress. Issued in 1949 as a motion picture.
From The American Scene Series. No. 11
LC NO. 79-700698
Prod-USOWI Dist-USNAC 1979

Library Of Congress, The C 90 MIN
16MM FILM, 3/4 OR 1/2 IN VIDEO H-C A
Looks at the collections and activities of the Library of Congress. Tells how the library serves Congress, scholars, other libraries, and copyright applicants.
Prod-WNETTV Dist-FI Prodn-BBCTV 1990

Library Organization - Introduction B 60 MIN
3/4 OR 1/2 INCH VIDEO CASSETTE
See series title for descriptive statement.
From The Library Organization Series. Pt 1
Prod-UAZMIC Dist-UAZMIC 1977

Library Organization—A Series

Explains how to organize a library.
Prod-UAZMIC Dist-UAZMIC 1977

Description - Monograph 060 MIN
Description - Non-Book 060 MIN
Entry 060 MIN
Library Organization - Introduction 060 MIN
Preparation Of Cards And Labels 060 MIN
Subject Headings Classification 060 MIN

Library Reference Information - How To Locate And Use It C
3/4 OR 1/2 INCH VIDEO CASSETTE J-H A
Presents an introductory course on library usage. Includes locating information, using reference books, compiling a working bibliography, and using the card catalog.
Prod-EDUACT Dist-EDUACT

Library Reference Section C 15 MIN
16MM FILM, 3/4 OR 1/2 IN VIDEO I-J
Shows a school librarian demonstrating how to use basic reference tools to learn more about a subject.
Prod-PERSPE Dist-PHENIX 1979

Library Report C 25 MIN
16MM FILM, 3/4 OR 1/2 IN VIDEO I-H
Presents the steps for researching, organizing and writing a library report. Discusses choosing and narrowing down a topic, finding information sources in the library, taking notes, organizing and outlining before writing and revising a rough draft.
LC NO. 84-706384
Prod-UNDERR Dist-BARR 1983

Library Show, The - Merchandise It C 19 MIN
3/4 OR 1/2 INCH VIDEO CASSETTE
Offers display and merchandising techniques for the library.
Prod-LVN Dist-LVN

Library Skills Tapes—A Series

Presents the necessary library skills all students need for course work and research papers. Employs actual library use and hands-on student learning.
Prod-MDCC Dist-MDCC

Almanacs, Yearbooks, And Handbooks 004 MIN
Atlases And Gazetteers 004 MIN
Biographical Tools 004 MIN
Book Index 007 MIN
Card Catalog, The 007 MIN
How To Use Dictionaries 008 MIN
How To Use Encyclopedias 006 MIN
New York Times Index, The 006 MIN
Reader's Guide To Periodical Literature 007 MIN
Reviews And Criticisms 006 MIN
Special Periodical Index, 006 MIN
Special Reference Material 007 MIN
Writing A Research Paper 007 MIN

Library Skills—A Series
16MM FILM, 3/4 OR 1/2 IN VIDEO P-J
Discusses the use of certain sections of the library such as the reference section, the card catalog, the Reader's Guide and the dictionary.
Prod-BARR Dist-BARR

Dictionary - The Adventure Of Words 016 MIN
Library World 016 MIN
Reference Section, The 022 MIN

Library World C 16 MIN
16MM FILM, 3/4 OR 1/2 IN VIDEO I-J
Presents two children visiting their local public library and learning about the library's many resources, including the card catalog, Reader's guide, microfilm collection, reference collection and audiovisual collection.
From The Library Skills Series.
Prod-BARR Dist-BARR Prodn-UNDERR 1977

Library Zone - Where Every Patron Is A VIP, The C 9 MIN
3/4 OR 1/2 INCH VIDEO CASSETTE
Emphasizes the need for all library employees to give patrons courteous and good quality library service.
Prod-PRATTE Dist-LVN

Library, The B 15 MIN
2 INCH VIDEOTAPE P
See series title for descriptive statement.
From The Language Corner Series.
Prod-CVETVC Dist-GPITVL Prodn-WCVETV

Library, The - A Place For Discovery X 17 MIN
16MM FILM, 3/4 OR 1/2 IN VIDEO I
Illustrates services, materials and facilities of public and school libraries. Shows students how to use the card catalog and locate books. Explains vertical picture files and those for other A-V materials.
Prod-EBF Dist-EBEC 1966

Library, The - A Place For Discovery (Spanish) C 17 MIN
16MM FILM, 3/4 OR 1/2 IN VIDEO I
Highlights the services, materials and resources of public and school libraries. Explains how to use the card catalog, find books on the shelves and use the vertical files for pictures.
Prod-EBEC Dist-EBEC

Library, The - Morning Moon And Night B 25 MIN
16MM FILM OPTICAL SOUND C
Points out specific library services and research techniques through the experiences of various students and librarians during the course of an ordinary day in a university.
LC NO. FIA66-410
Prod-PUAVC Dist-PUAVC Prodn-PUAVC 1966

Libya C 28 MIN
3/4 INCH VIDEOTAPE
Interviews Ambassador Mansur Rashid Kikhia on Libya's political position. Hosted by Marilyn Perry. Includes a film clip on Libya.
From The International Byline Series.
Prod-PERRYM Dist-PERRYM

Libya (International Byline) C 28 MIN
3/4 INCH VIDEOTAPE
Interviews Mr Ahmed Shahati, Special Envoy of the Foreign Liaison Bureau in Tripoli, Libya, who was on a mission from the Socialist People's Libyan Arab Jamahiriya. Presents the Libyan view of relations between Libya and the United States.
From The International Byline Series.
Prod-PERRYM Dist-PERRYM

Libya (Marilyn's Manhatten) C 28 MIN
3/4 INCH VIDEOTAPE
Features an interview with Mr Ibrahim Dharat, Counsellor for Economic Affairs, on the economic development of Libya. Includes a film clip on Libya's development. Hosted by Marilyn Perry.
From The Marilyn's Manhatten Series.
Prod-PERRYM Dist-PERRYM

License Plate Traffic Survey C 12 MIN
16MM FILM OPTICAL SOUND
Demonstrates a method of conducting a traffic survey to obtain origination and destination information using motion picture photography and a computer.
LC NO. 74-705028
Prod-USDTFH Dist-USNAC 1968

License To Kill C 28 MIN
16MM FILM, 3/4 OR 1/2 IN VIDEO A
Examines the worldwide use of the death penalty, methods and reasons for its use, and arguments for and against it.
Prod-CNEMAG Dist-CNEMAG 1984

Licensing And Traffic Laws C 29 MIN
3/4 OR 1/2 INCH VIDEO CASSETTE
Discusses traffic laws, vehicle registration laws, vehicle inspection and equipment and maintenance laws.
From The Right Way Series.
Prod-SCETV Dist-PBS 1982

Lickety-Split Licorice C 8 MIN
16MM FILM, 3/4 OR 1/2 IN VIDEO
Tells a story about a boy and girl making licorice in their kitchen in order to stimulate the imagination of young people for writing, role playing and art work and to encourage recognition of differences between actuality and fantasy. Suggests that such common activities as making licorice can form the basis for engaging stories.
Prod-MORLAT Dist-SF 1972

Licorice Train C 7 MIN
3/4 OR 1/2 INCH VIDEO CASSETTE
Delineates a ghetto youth's journey, via elevated train, into neighborhoods greatly different from his own, and indulges in various fantasies about what life is and might be like. Uses sweet background music to make an ironic contrast to the grim realities of the boy's existence.
Prod-IFF Dist-IFF

Lid Reconstruction In Thermal Burns C 11 MIN
16MM FILM OPTICAL SOUND

Demonstrates the surgical correction of the cicatrical ectropion caused by a severe unilateral radiation burn.
LC NO. FIA66-880
Prod-ACYDGD Dist-ACY 1962

Lidded Pots C 28 MIN
2 INCH VIDEOTAPE
Features Mrs Peterson describing certain ceramic processes for her classroom at the University of Southern California. Illustrates lidded pots.
From The Wheels, Kilns And Clay Series.
Prod-USC Dist-PUBTEL

Liderazgo C 30 MIN
16MM FILM, 3/4 OR 1/2 IN VIDEO H-C A
A Spanish version of Leadership - Style Or Circumstance. Shows that the effectiveness of different types of leadership depends upon the specific situation. Points out ways of developing leadership and insuring the effectiveness of such leaders once they are on the job.
Prod-MGHT Dist-MGHT 1977

Liebesspiel (A Song Without Words) B 2 MIN
16MM FILM SILENT I-C A
Uses animation to express the poetry of movement.
LC NO. 72-703163
Prod-FISCHF Dist-GRAF 1931

Lies C 30 MIN
3/4 OR 1/2 INCH VIDEO CASSETTE
Uses cost accounting to emphasize the spoken lie.
From The Doris Chase Concepts Series.
Prod-CHASED Dist-CHASED

Lietuviskos Dainos Svente (Lithuanian) C 20 MIN
3/4 OR 1/2 INCH VIDEO CASSETTE
Shows the first postwar traditional song and dance festival in Vilnius, Lithuania.
Prod-IHF Dist-IHF

Lietuvos Dainu Svente (Lithuanian) C 20 MIN
3/4 OR 1/2 INCH VIDEO CASSETTE
Features a song festival held in Vilnius, Lithuania, with dancing and singing groups from various parts of the country.
Prod-IHF Dist-IHF

Life C 15 MIN
3/4 OR 1/2 INCH VIDEO CASSETTE I-H
Tells how Howard Carter and his team of archaeologists discovered the tomb of Tutankhamun. Describes the objects placed in the tomb which where buried for the king to use in the afterlife.
From The Tutankhamun - Life And Death Series.
LC NO. 80-706751
Prod-KCPQTV Dist-AITECH 1979

Life C 15 MIN
16MM FILM, 3/4 OR 1/2 IN VIDEO
Stresses the importance of establishing the characteristics of life on Earth before searching for it on other planets. Describes life and nonlife similarities and adaptations to Earth conditions and shows how certain life forms are able to tolerate environmental hardships.
LC NO. 78-706263
Prod-NASA Dist-USNAC Prodn-WHROTV 1978

Life - Patent Pending C 57 MIN
16MM FILM, 3/4 OR 1/2 IN VIDEO H-C A
Presents breakthroughs in gene engineering and describes how scientists go about creating new forms of life. Tells how the impact of the gene bonanza affects industry, medicine and the scientific community.
From The Nova Series.
LC NO. 83-706028
Prod-WGBHTV Dist-TIMLIF 1982

Life After Death C 30 MIN
16MM FILM, 3/4 OR 1/2 IN VIDEO H-C A
Discusses the expenses involved in American funerals.
From The Enterprise Series.
Prod-MTI Dist-MTI

Life After Death C 30 MIN
3/4 OR 1/2 INCH VIDEO CASSETTE H-C A
Follows the Telophase Corporation's multi-million dollar venture to market cremation to the general public and change 'the American way of death.'
From The Enterprise III Series.
Prod-WGBHTV Dist-KINGFT

Life After Death C 35 MIN
16MM FILM, 3/4 OR 1/2 IN VIDEO
Deals with the question of the persistence of consciousness after biological death.
Prod-HP Dist-HP

Life After 60 - The Old Dream/New Dilemma C 30 MIN
3/4 OR 1/2 INCH VIDEO CASSETTE
Looks into the lives of some Wisconsin elderly citizens, their needs and the care they receive. Talks about the necessity of community and government support ot help them continue to have choices and options concerning their care.
Prod-WMTVTV Dist-UWISC

Life And Adventures Of Nicholas Nickleby, The C 479 MIN
3/4 OR 1/2 INCH VIDEO CASSETTE
Presents the Royal Shakespeare Company's production of Charles Dickens' novel THE LIFE AND ADVENTURES OF NICHOLAS NICKLEBY.
Prod-FOTH Dist-FOTH

Life And Assassination Of The Kingfish, The C
1/2 IN VIDEO CASSETTE BETA/VHS
Presents a portrayal by Ed Asner of the flamboyant and controversial Louisiana politician Huey Long.
Prod-GA Dist-GA

Life And Assassination Of The Kingfish, The C 97 MIN
16MM FILM, 3/4 OR 1/2 IN VIDEO H-C A
Examines the life and career of Louisiana Governor Huey Long, telling how he was idealized by some and despised by others. Explains how he changed the face of his State during his tempestuous political career and that he was preparing to run for the Presidency when he was assassinated in 1935.
Prod-TOMENT Dist-LCOA 1979

Life And Breath C 15 MIN
16MM FILM OPTICAL SOUND
Describes the disease emphysema, and points out that it is the fastest growing lung ailment today.
LC NO. FIA68-2430
Prod-CTRDA Dist-AMLUNG Prodn-CRAF 1968

Life And Customs X 14 MIN
16MM FILM OPTICAL SOUND I-H T R
Shows many of the customs and practices of the people of the Bible lands. Emphasizes the relationship between the teachings of Jesus and the life and customs of the people.
From The Land Of The Bible Series.
LC NO. FIA67-1925
Prod-FAMF Dist-FAMF 1960

Life And Death C 30 MIN
3/4 OR 1/2 INCH VIDEO CASSETTE
See series title for descriptive statement.
From The Health, Safety And Well-Being Series.
Prod-MAETEL Dist-CAMB

Life And Death - Dawson, Georgia C 27 MIN
3/4 INCH VIDEO CASSETTE
Documents the trial of five black men charged with the murder of a white man during a store robbery. Paints a picture of life and conflicting racial attitudes in a small Georgia town.
Prod-KANDIN Dist-PUBTEL

Life And Death In A Pond C 15 MIN
16MM FILM, 3/4 OR 1/2 IN VIDEO H-C
Describes the struggle for survival which occurs in the waters of a pond from the fertilization of eggs through the quest for food to the eventual death of such creatures as frogs, newts, diving beetles and dragonfly nymphs.
Prod-CORF Dist-CORF 1981

Life And Death In The Sea B 15 MIN
2 INCH VIDEOTAPE P
Examines the food chain and some animals' natural defense systems. (Broadcast quality)
From The Land And Sea Series.
Prod-TTOIC Dist-GPITVL Prodn-WGBHTV

Life And Death Of A Cell C 20 MIN
16MM FILM, 3/4 OR 1/2 IN VIDEO H-C A
Uses an amoeba proteus to illustrate that the cell embodies all the functions and properties common to living things. Illustrates cell habitat, digestion and division, and explains the cause of cell death.
Prod-UCB Dist-UCEMC 1959

Life And Death Of A Tree C 20 MIN
16MM FILM, 3/4 OR 1/2 IN VIDEO H-C A
Explores the contributions of an oak tree to the ecology of other plants and animals.
LC NO. 80-706293
Prod-NGS Dist-NGS 1979

Life And Death Of An African Pan C 25 MIN
3/4 OR 1/2 INCH VIDEO CASSETTE J-H
Tells the story of the creation, existence, and ultimate destruction of the shallow water-filled depressions called pans on the fringe of the Kalahari desert in Africa.
LC NO. 84-706733
Prod-CEPRO Dist-CEPRO 1982

Life And Liberty - For All Who Believe C 30 MIN
16MM FILM, 3/4 OR 1/2 IN VIDEO J-C A
Debates whether religious groups can use their freedom of religion to ban books and thus curtail other people's freedom of speech. Demonstrates how difficult it is to differentiate between parental discipline and child abuse.
LC NO. 84-707506
Prod-PAMWAY Dist-FI 1983

Life And Livelihood In The Bible B 30 MIN
16MM FILM OPTICAL SOUND H-C A
Features Maurice Samuel and Mark Van Doren, discussing and comparing practical day-to-day aspects of life in Bible times with their parallels in modern times. (Kinescope)
From The Eternal Light Series.
LC NO. 72-700972
Prod-JTS Dist-NAAJS 1966

Life And Message Of Swami Vivekananda B 22 MIN
16MM FILM OPTICAL SOUND I-C A
Presents the biography of Swami Vivekananda, who, as the ardent disciple of Sri Ramakrishna Paramahamsa, made a deep impression at the Chicago Conference of World Religions. Portrays him as a humanist, patriot and exponent of Hindu philosophy.
Prod-INDIA Dist-NEDINF

Life And Poetry Of Julia De Burgos, The (Captioned) C 28 MIN
16MM FILM, 3/4 OR 1/2 IN VIDEO A
Portrays the life and work of the Puerto Rican poet Julia De Burgos. Spanish dialog with English subtitles.
Prod-CNEMAG Dist-CNEMAG 1979

Life And The Structure Of Hemoglobin C 28 MI
16MM FILM, 3/4 OR 1/2 IN VIDEO C
Describes the structure and mechanism of hemoglobin, as pres ented by Linus Pauling and other scientists, using compute animation.
Prod-PAROX Dist-AIMS 197

Life And Times Of Judge Roy Bean, The C 124 MI
16MM FILM OPTICAL SOUND
Stars Paul Newman as a slightly crazy judge who decides to re store law and order to his town, all for the love of Lily Langtry Directed by John Huston.
Prod-UNKNWN Dist-TWYMAN 197

Life And Times Of Rosie The Riveter, The C 65 MIN
16MM FILM, 3/4 OR 1/2 IN VIDEO J-C
Presents five women who movingly recall their experiences dur ing World War II when women gained entry into major industri al plants for the first time. Interweaves their testimony with rare archival recruiting films, posters and music of the period.
Prod-CLARTY Dist-DIRECT 198

Life And Work Of Sir James Hutton C 28 MIN
3/4 OR 1/2 INCH VIDEO CASSETTE
Focuses on the development of the theory of uniformitarianism with field visits illustrating how geologists reconstruct the history of an area. Filmed in Scotland.
From The Earth Explored Series.
Prod-BBCTV Dist-PBS

Life Another Way C 55 MIN
3/4 INCH VIDEO CASSETTE
Gives the story of a courageous woman who fought back from disabilities to become one of Canada's foremost crusaders for the rights of the disabled.
Prod-LAURON Dist-LAURON

Life Around Us (Spanish)—A Series
16MM FILM, 3/4 OR 1/2 IN VIDEO
Prod-TIMLIF Dist-TIMLIF 1971

After The Whale (Spanish) 30 MIN
Animal Communication (Spanish) 30 MIN
How Old Is Old (Spanish) 30 MIN
Life In A Tropical Forest (Spanish) 30 MIN
Look At Sound, A (Spanish) 30 MIN
Lopsided Wheel, The (Spanish) 30 MIN
Losers, The (Spanish) 30 MIN
More Than Meets The Eye (Spanish) 30 MIN
Not-So-Solid Earth, The (Spanish) 30 MIN
Other Planets - No Place Like Earth (Spanish) 30 MIN
Rock-a-Bye Baby (Spanish) 30 MIN
Should Oceans Meet (Spanish) 30 MIN
Small Wilderness (Spanish) 30 MIN
Ultimate Machine, The (Spanish) 30 MIN

Life Around Us—A Series
16MM FILM, 3/4 OR 1/2 IN VIDEO
Examines topics in the field of science.
Prod-TIMLIF Dist-TIMLIF

After The Whale 30 MIN
Animal Communication 30 MIN
How Old Is Old 30 MIN
Life In A Tropical Forest 30 MIN
Look At Sound, A 30 MIN
Lopsided Wheel, The 30 MIN
Losers, The 30 MIN
More Than Meets The Eye 30 MIN
Not-So-Solid Earth, The 30 MIN
Other Planets - No Place Like Earth 30 MIN
Rock-A-Bye Baby 30 MIN
Should Oceans Meet 30 MIN
Small Wilderness 30 MIN
Ultimate Machine, The 30 MIN

Life At Salt Point - Salt Water Ecology C 15 MIN
16MM FILM, 3/4 OR 1/2 IN VIDEO J-C A
Uses the natural laboratory of the California coast to study three salt water ecosystems. Examines habitat, adaption, food chains, filter feeding, and species interaction in each ecosystem through the use of underwater photography and photomicrography.
Prod-CORF Dist-CORF Prodn-BIOMED 1978

Life At The Top C 24 MIN
16MM FILM, 3/4 OR 1/2 IN VIDEO J-C
Examines population and national development patterns in industrialized France, Romania and the United Kingdom. Focuses on the question of family planning.
Prod-UN Dist-SF 1975

Life Between The Tides C 20 MIN
16MM FILM, 3/4 OR 1/2 IN VIDEO I-C A
Portrays the diversity of animal life in the intertidal zone. Uses macro- and micro-cinematography to portray these animals in their natural environment.
From The Natural Phenomena Series.
Prod-CINEM Dist-JOU 1977

Life Between Tides X 11 MIN
16MM FILM, 3/4 OR 1/2 IN VIDEO I
Pictures inter-tidal life. Shows the variety of animals and plants on a stretch of shoreline . points out the relationships among the plants and animals and their marine environment.
Prod-EBF Dist-EBEC 1963

Life Beyond Earth And The Mind Of Man C 25 MIN
16MM FILM - 3/4 IN VIDEO
Presents a symposium held at Boston University in November, 1972, in which participants explored the implications of the possible existence of extraterrestrial life within the galaxy and the universe.
LC NO. 78-706264
Prod-NASA Dist-USNAC Prodn-DREWAS 1978

Life Changes C 29 MIN
3/4 OR 1/2 INCH VIDEO CASSETTE
Illustrates changes in human sexuality during different life stages, including childhood to puberty, puberty to adolescence, maturity and senescence by talking with people who have reached these stages. Features Milton Diamond, Ph D, a biologist at the University of Hawaii, who debunks some of the myths about each life stage.
From The Human Sexuality Series.
Prod-KHETTV Dist-PBS

Life Cycle Of A Bacteriophage B 1 MIN
16MM FILM, 3/4 OR 1/2 IN VIDEO H-C A
A virus particle attacks a host bacterial cell and replicates. Its progeny is released as the cell bursts.
From The Microbiology Teaching Series.
Prod-UCEMC Dist-UCEMC 1961

Life Cycle Of A Fish C 13 MIN
16MM FILM, 3/4 OR 1/2 IN VIDEO J-H
Focuses on the killifish, showing the process by which a fertilized egg develops into an approximate copy of its parents.
Prod-MACMFL Dist-FI

Life Cycle Of A Flowering Plant—A Series
16MM FILM, 3/4 OR 1/2 IN VIDEO
Uses the apple tree as a model to examine plant cells, genes, DNA and reproductive parts, meiosis and mitosis.
Prod-SCHLAT Dist-LUF 1971

Meiosis 7 MIN
Mitosis 11 MIN
Plant Cell And Male And Female Flower Parts 11 MIN

Life Cycle Of A Yeast Cell B 17 MIN
16MM FILM OPTICAL SOUND
Demonstrates the operation of the De Fonbrune pneumatic micro-manipulator and the making of microtools. Shows by diagram or microphotograph the sexual reproduction of yeast cells, asci and fusion of ascopores.
Prod-SILLU Dist-SIUFP 1952

Life Cycle Of Bass C 22 MIN
16MM FILM OPTICAL SOUND
Introduces little-knows facts about the life cycle of the large-mouth bass, now considered the world's most popular fresh-water game fish. Explains how these patterns of courtship, spawning, habit and habitat affect the angler.
Prod-BRNSWK Dist-KAROL

Life Cycle Of Diphyllobothrium Latum B 17 MIN
16MM FILM - 3/4 IN VIDEO
Depicts the life cycle of the broad tapeworm in a fish and a human host. Issued in 1950 as a motion picture.
LC NO. 79-706021
Prod-USPHS Dist-USNAC Prodn-NMAC 1978

Life Cycle Of Endamoeba Histolytica In Dysenteric And Nondysenteric Amoebiasis C 18 MIN
16MM FILM SILENT
Shows the parasites as cysts in an ulcerated colon. Demonstrates by animation how the amoeba divides into eight amoebulae which move about, and how the amoebae enter the blood. For medical personnel.
LC NO. FIE52-1124
Prod-USN Dist-USNAC 1948

Life Cycle Of Endamoeba Histolytica In Dysenteric And Nondysenteric Amoebiasis C 11 MIN
3/4 INCH VIDEO CASSETTE PRO
Shows the parasites as cysts in an ulcerated colon and uses animation to demostrate how the amoeba divides into eight amoebulae which move and enter the blood. Issued in 1943 as a motion picture.
LC NO. 78-706102
Prod-USN Dist-USNAC 1978

Life Cycle Of Insects, The - Complete Metamorphosis C 20 MIN
16MM FILM, 3/4 OR 1/2 IN VIDEO J-H
Examines the egg-larva-pupa-adult cycle of insect life, known as complete metamorphosis.
From The Insect Series.
LC NO. 80-706707
Prod-BHA Dist-IFB 1977

Life Cycle Of Insects, The - Incomplete Metamorphosis C 17 MIN
16MM FILM, 3/4 OR 1/2 IN VIDEO J-H
Explains the incomplete metamorphosis of various insects.
From The Insect Series.
LC NO. 80-706708
Prod-BHA Dist-IFB 1977

Life Cycle Of The Honeybee C 13 MIN
16MM FILM, 3/4 OR 1/2 IN VIDEO
Shows the organization and specialization of the honeybee, including views of the new hive and the various activities of the workers, foragers, queen and young bees.
From The Bio-Science Series.
LC NO. 80-706307
Prod-NGS Dist-NGS 1976

Life Cycle Of The Jew, The B 30 MIN
16MM FILM OPTICAL SOUND
Discusses Jewish moral and ethical values and shows how these values are reflected in rituals related to birth, education, marriage and family.
Prod-ADL Dist-ADL

Life Cycle Of The Malaria Parasite, The C 12 MIN
16MM FILM, 3/4 OR 1/2 IN VIDEO H-C A
Sexual and asexual cycles, including exorythrocytic stages, are depicted through the use of animation.
From The Microbiology Teaching Series.
Prod-UCEMC Dist-UCEMC 1961

Life Cycle Of The Silk Moth C 11 MIN
16MM FILM, 3/4 OR 1/2 IN VIDEO
Uses closeups and slow-motion photography in presenting the silk moth's life cycle. Follows various moth species in the act of mating and egglaying, egghatching and metamorphosis from caterpillar to pupa to adult moth.
From The Bio-Science Series.
LC NO. 80-706315
Prod-NGS Dist-NGS 1976

Life Cycle Of The Stars, The C 26 MIN
16MM FILM, 3/4 OR 1/2 IN VIDEO J-H
Discusses the building blocks of matter and explains the anatomy of stars and the forces that act on stellar interiors. Edited from an episode of the Cosmos series.
From The Cosmos (Edited Version) Series.
Prod-SAGANC Dist-FI Prodn-KCET 1980

Life Cycle Of Trichinella Spiralis, The C 10 MIN
16MM FILM SILENT
Discusses the parasite which causes trichinosis.
Prod-UR Dist-UR

Life Cycles C 20 MIN
3/4 INCH VIDEO CASSETTE T
Shows how games, competition and class goal-setting can be effectively incorporated into life science lessons.
From The Science In The Elementary School - Life Science Series.
Prod-UWKY Dist-GPITVL 1980

Life Cycles, The - Aging C 30 MIN
3/4 OR 1/2 INCH VIDEO CASSETTE C
Discusses the realities and stereotypes of aging.
From The Focus On Society Series.
Prod-DALCCD Dist-DALCCD

Life Endeath C 7 MIN
16MM FILM OPTICAL SOUND H-C
Presents an experimental film study of the obstract forms found in the flames of a fire to represent the cyclical nature of life from birth to death. Photographed by Erik Shiozaki.
LC NO. FIA67-5188
Prod-KAPR Dist-RADIM

Life Force - A Salute To America's Most Productive Industry - Agriculture C 24 MIN
16MM FILM OPTICAL SOUND
Portrays the strength and closeness of farm families, their bond with the land and each other and how farmers combine business management, science, technology and plain hard work to make American agriculture the envy and wonder of the world.
LC NO. 82-700738
Prod-FARMCB Dist-MTP 1982

Life From Life C 10 MIN
16MM FILM OPTICAL SOUND K-P
Examines plants and trees producing the seeds for new life. Explains that all living things come from other living things of the same kind. Shows the mating, egg-laying, fertilization, hatching and early growth of angel fish and leopard frogs.
From The Family Life And Sex Education Series.
Prod-SF Dist-SF 1968

Life From The Dead Sea C 14 MIN
16MM FILM OPTICAL SOUND
Shows how the rich mineral resources from the Dead Sea, the lowest spot on earth, are extracted and processed.
Prod-ALDEN Dist-ALDEN

Life From The Sea C 26 MIN
16MM FILM OPTICAL SOUND
Demonstrates Japan's efforts to protect its fishery resources while endeavoring to develop inland and coastal supplies.
Prod-MTP Dist-MTP

Life Games C 8 MIN
16MM FILM OPTICAL SOUND
Focuses on attitudes toward life.
LC NO. 80-700874
Prod-VICCOR Dist-TASCOR 1979

Life Goes To The Movies—A Series
16MM FILM, 3/4 OR 1/2 IN VIDEO
Presents a compilation of feature film clips, news photographs and narrative that examines the development of 20th century American popular culture as reflected in motion pictures. Narrated by Henry Fonda, Shirley Mac Laine and Liza Minnelli.
LC NO. 79-707671
Prod-TIMLIF Dist-TIMLIF 1976

Fifties, The - Television And A New Hollywood 27 MIN
Golden Age Of Hollywood, The - The Depression 35 MIN
Movies Today, The - A New Morality 37 MIN
Post-War Era, The - Film Noir And The 20 MIN
War Years, The - Fabulous 1939, Then Global 35 MIN

Life Habits C 17 MIN
3/4 OR 1/2 INCH VIDEO CASSETTE
Focuses on important life habits such as exercise, nutrition, stress management, alcohol, smoking and safety in an interesting manner. Emphasizes that health control is an individual responsibility.
Prod-MTAUBH Dist-AHOA 1980

Life History Of The Rocky Mountain Wood Tick C 18 MIN
16MM FILM - 3/4 IN VIDEO
Depicts the two-year life cycle of the Rocky Mountain wood tick, major vector of Rocky Mountain spotted fever. Illustrates the various stages of its development and discusses its adaptability to environment, host requirements and natural controlling factors. Issued in 1969 as a motion picture.
LC NO. 79-706022
Prod-USNIAI Dist-USNAC Prodn-NMAC 1978

Life In A Drop Of Water (2nd Ed) C 10 MIN
16MM FILM, 3/4 OR 1/2 IN VIDEO I-J
Uses photomicrography to reveal the amoeba, spirogyra, paramecium, volvox, hydra, rotifer and other living forms carrying on the basic life processes of moving, reacting, obtaining food and reproducing.
Prod-CORF Dist-CORF 1973

Life In A Garden C 13 MIN
16MM FILM OPTICAL SOUND
Shows insects, mammals and birds to be seen in a suburban or rural garden. Includes magnified photography.
Prod-FENWCK Dist-FENWCK

Life In A Medieval Town C 16 MIN
16MM FILM, 3/4 OR 1/2 IN VIDEO J-H
Pictures daily life in a medieval town, showing activity in the town square and guild workshops. Gives a background for understanding the influence of trade and the role of the merchant and craft guilds in the rise of towns in Europe.
Prod-CORF Dist-CORF 1965

Life In A Medieval Town (Captioned) C 16 MIN
16MM FILM, 3/4 OR 1/2 IN VIDEO J-H
Pictures daily life in a medieval town, showing activity in the town square and guild workshops. Gives a background for understanding the influence of trade and the role of the merchant and craft guilds in the rise of towns in Europe.
Prod-CORF Dist-CORF 1965

Life In A Pond (2nd Ed) C 11 MIN
16MM FILM, 3/4 OR 1/2 IN VIDEO
On a field trip, high school boys and girls study life in a fresh water pond. They see a self-sustaining group of plants and animals sharing the problems of obtaining sunlight, food and water.
Prod-CORF Dist-CORF 1970

Life In A Tropical Forest C 30 MIN
16MM FILM, 3/4 OR 1/2 IN VIDEO
Visits the jungles of Cambodia, the Amazon and the island of Barro Colorado to investigate the various forms of life in tropical rain forests. Originally shown on the television series The World We Live In.
From The Life Around Us Series.
LC NO. 79-707831
Prod-TIMLIF Dist-TIMLIF 1971

Life In A Tropical Forest (Spanish) C 30 MIN
16MM FILM OPTICAL SOUND
Surveys the jungles of Cambodia, the Amazon and the island of Barro Colorado to investigate various forms of animals and plant life found in tropical rain forests.
From The Life Around Us (Spanish) Series.
LC NO. 78-700067
Prod-TIMLIF Dist-TIMLIF 1971

Life In A Tropical Rainforest C 14 MIN
16MM FILM, 3/4 OR 1/2 IN VIDEO I-H
Documents life in a tropical rainforest, where warm weather and heavy rainfall encourage a wide variety of unique plant and animal life.
Prod-BFA Dist-PHENIX Prodn-BAYERW 1977

Life In A Tropical Rainforest (Dutch) C 14 MIN
16MM FILM, 3/4 OR 1/2 IN VIDEO I-H
Documents life in a tropical rainforest, where warm weather and heavy rainfall encourage a wide variety of unique plant and animal life.
Prod-BFA Dist-PHENIX Prodn-BAYERW 1977

Life In A Vacant Lot X 10 MIN
16MM FILM, 3/4 OR 1/2 IN VIDEO I
Discusses the interrelationships of organisms living in an urban vacant lot. Studies environmental factors influencing the balance of life in a vacant lot.
Prod-EBF Dist-EBEC 1966

Life In A Weaverbird Colony C 20 MIN
16MM FILM OPTICAL SOUND H-C T
Illustrates the breeding behavior of weaverbirds, including weaving of the nests by the male, territorial defense, courtship and pair formation, copulation, female behavior in lining the nest and feeding nestlings and the development of the young and their behavior.
Prod-UCLA Dist-UCLA 1971

Life In Ancient Rome X 14 MIN
16MM FILM, 3/4 OR 1/2 IN VIDEO I-H
Re-creates typical scenes in Rome during the reign of Emperor Trajan. Examines characteristics and achievements of the Roman Empire at the height of its power, points out some of the weaknesses in Roman society and considers the ways in which Roman ideas and culture influenced the development of Western civilization.
Prod-EBF Dist-EBEC 1964

Life In Ancient Rome (Captioned) C 14 MIN
16MM FILM, 3/4 OR 1/2 IN VIDEO I-H
Re-creates typical scenes in Rome during the reign of Emperor Trajan. Examines characteristics and achievements of the Roman Empire at the height of its power, points out some of the weaknesses in Roman society and considers the ways in which Roman ideas influenced the development of Western civilization.
Prod-EBEC Dist-EBEC 1964

Life In Ancient Rome (Spanish) C 14 MIN
16MM FILM, 3/4 OR 1/2 IN VIDEO I-H
Re-creates scenes and activities in Rome during the reign of Em-

peror Trajan. Examines the characteristics and achievements of the Roman Empire. Considers how Roman ideas and culture influenced the development of Western civilization.
Prod-EBEC Dist-EBEC

Life In China - Agricultural Worker In The Commune C 28 MIN
16MM FILM OPTICAL SOUND J-C A
Relates to the common man in China and his place within the social structure of which he is a part. Portrays the communal structure of rural China today and reveals the place of the individual citizen within it.
Prod-UHAWAI Dist-UHAWAI 1972

Life In China - Industry B 28 MIN
16MM FILM OPTICAL SOUND H
Stresses the importance of industry in the development of mainland China, showing the operation of fertilizer and ceramics factories, a textile mill and a commune tea factory. Reviews the life of an industrial worker, including his living conditions, educational and health programs and the part which workers play in political and cultural demonstrations in the People's Republic of China.
LC NO. 73-700264
Prod-OSUPD Dist-OSUMPD 1972

Life In China - Mill Worker's Family B 17 MIN
16MM FILM OPTICAL SOUND
A view of life in the People's Republic of China, as revealed in the daily activities of the members of the family of a worker in a state-operated cotton mill.
LC NO. 72-713593
Prod-OSUPD Dist-OSUMPD 1971

Life In Colombia—A Series
P-H
Follows a still photographer as he tries to capture the essence of Colombia's capital city, Bogota, and village life in the remote mountain village of Roguira. Shows contrasts and comparisons of city and village life and the impact of modernization in Colombia.
Prod-IFF Dist-IFF

Bogota - Fragments Of A City 015 MIN
Raguira 009 MIN

Life In Lost Creek - Fresh Water Ecology C 15 MIN
16MM FILM, 3/4 OR 1/2 IN VIDEO J-C A
Uses the natural laboratory of a small mountain stream which flows into a peaceful pond to study three fresh water ecosystems. Examines habitat, adaptation, ecological niche, population and species interaction in each ecosystem through the use of underwater photography and photomicrography.
Prod-CORF Dist-CORF Prodn-BIOMED 1978

Life In Mediterranean Lands (2nd Ed) (Revised) C 13 MIN
16MM FILM, 3/4 OR 1/2 IN VIDEO I-J
Focuses on the Mediterranean climate and explains how it affects the agricultural activities and lifestyles of people around the world.
Prod-CORF Dist-CORF 1978

Life In Modern France—A Series
16MM FILM, 3/4 OR 1/2 IN VIDEO I-H
Explores the geography, people and culture of France.
Prod-EBEC Dist-EBEC 1971

Art And Life 9 MIN
Better Life Tomorrow, A 10 MIN
Far From Paris 10 MIN
Leisure And Vacations 11 MIN
Rhythms Of Paris 9 MIN

Life In Soviet Asia - 273 Days Below Zero C 11 MIN
16MM FILM, 3/4 OR 1/2 IN VIDEO I-H
Looks at the transformation of wasteland to agricultural and industrial complexes in Soviet Asia.
From The Man And His World Series.
Prod-POLSKI Dist-FI 1974

Life In The City C 30 MIN
3/4 OR 1/2 INCH VIDEO CASSETTE C
Talks of urban change, its cause and effects in St Louis.
From The Focus On Society Series.
Prod-DALCCD Dist-DALCCD

Life In The Colonies C 30 MIN
3/4 OR 1/2 INCH VIDEO CASSETTE C
See series title for descriptive statement.
From The American Story - The Beginning To 1877 Series.
Prod-DALCCD Dist-DALCCD

Life In The Deciduous Forest C 19 MIN
16MM FILM, 3/4 OR 1/2 IN VIDEO I-H
Discusses life in the deciduous forest, tracing variations in temperature, moisture and light.
From The Living Science Series.
Prod-IFB Dist-IFB 1962

Life In The Desert - The American Southwest (2nd Ed) C 11 MIN
16MM FILM, 3/4 OR 1/2 IN VIDEO I-J
Examines the physical characteristics and ecology of the American Southwest desert. Focuses on the ways flora and fauna have adapted to the desert environment.
Prod-EBEC Dist-EBEC Prodn-AFAI

Life In The Developing World—A Series
H-C A
Makes clear the relationship between the national economies of many developing countries and problems in such areas as discrimination, education, urban migration and basic health care.
Prod-UNICEF Dist-GPITVL Prodn-NHK 1982

Bolivia - Indians Of The Andes 030 MIN
Haiti - Education For The Future 030 MIN
India - Migration To The City 030 MIN
Zaire - Health Care 030 MIN

Life In The English Colonies C 30 MIN
2 INCH VIDEOTAPE
Emphasizes the social history of the New England, Middle and Southern colonies. Compares such facets as way of life, education, and religion.
From The American History I Series.
Prod-DENVPS Dist-GPITVL

Life In The Grasslands (2nd Ed) C 11 MIN
16MM FILM, 3/4 OR 1/2 IN VIDEO I-J
Gives an overview of life on the American prairie, examining plants, animals and weather.
Prod-EBEC Dist-EBEC

Life In The High Country C 12 MIN
3/4 OR 1/2 INCH VIDEO CASSETTE
Looks at mountains as a storehouse of minerals, trees, wildlife and water. Covers life zones and the mountains' impact on weather.
Prod-CBSC Dist-CBSC

Life In The Ocean C 16 MIN
16MM FILM, 3/4 OR 1/2 IN VIDEO I-H
Illustrates many plants and animals of shore, shallow water and ocean depths relating them to each other, to their environment and to similar forms of life found on land.
Prod-FA Dist-PHENIX 1955

Life In The Past C 15 MIN
16MM FILM, 3/4 OR 1/2 IN VIDEO I-H
Deals with the formation of the Grand Canyon. Shows different types of fossils from the Canyon's bands of rock.
From The Place To Live Series.
Prod-GRATV Dist-JOU

Life In The Quick Lane C 25 MIN
16MM FILM OPTICAL SOUND
Looks at the sport of drag racing which was once just a backyard hobby and is now a multi-million dollar business in which races are won and lost in the blink of an eye.
Prod-SEARS Dist-MTP

Life In The Sahara C 15 MIN
16MM FILM, 3/4 OR 1/2 IN VIDEO I-H
Reviews important aspects of life, habits and customs of people living in the Sahara Desert.
Prod-EBF Dist-EBEC 1953

Life In The Sahara (Spanish) C 15 MIN
16MM FILM, 3/4 OR 1/2 IN VIDEO I-H
Chronicles patterns of life in the desert. Emphasizes the importance of water, oasis vegetation and camels in the desert economy. Contrasts nomadic life-styles with Arab and Berber settlements.
Prod-EBEC Dist-EBEC

Life In The Sea X 11 MIN
16MM FILM, 3/4 OR 1/2 IN VIDEO I-H
Divides sea life into three groups—plankton, bottom dwellers and free swimmers. Shows how various animals capture food and protect themselves against natural enemies. Explains how sea life must depend upon a process of photosynthesis.
Prod-EBF Dist-EBEC 1958

Life In The Thirties B 52 MIN
16MM FILM, 3/4 OR 1/2 IN VIDEO H-C A
Focuses on the critical years of the early 1930's and the leadership of Franklin Roosevelt in enacting measures to meet the challenge of the Great Depression.
From The Project 20 Series.
Prod-NBC Dist-CRMP 1965

Life In The Trees, A C 58 MIN
3/4 OR 1/2 INCH VIDEO CASSETTE J-C A
Explores the evolution of primates in a wide range of geographic areas and explains the significance of binocular vision and grasping hands in successful adaptation to life in the trees.
From The Life On Earth Series. Program 12
LC NO. 82-706503
Prod-BBCTV Dist-FI 1981

Life In The Valley C 15 MIN
16MM FILM, 3/4 OR 1/2 IN VIDEO I-H
Describes the formation of valleys. Illustrates the plant and animal life and rock formations that are characteristic of valleys.
From The Place To Live Series.
Prod-GRATV Dist-JOU

Life In The Womb - The First Stages Of Human Development C 40 MIN
1/2 IN VIDEO CASSETTE (VHS) J-C A
Chronicles the course of human development from fertilization through the birth of a human being. Looks at both genetic and environmental influences on prenatal growth.
LC NO. 85-703930
Prod-HRMC Dist-HRMC

Life In The Woodlot C 17 MIN
16MM FILM, 3/4 OR 1/2 IN VIDEO I-C
Reveals the complex pattern in which the seasons and the life cycles of man, animals and plants are interrelated.
Prod-NFBC Dist-NFBC 1960

Life In Your Hands, A C 15 MIN
16MM FILM OPTICAL SOUND
Dramatizes the effectiveness of cardiopulmonary resuscitation and how it can be used by laypersons to save thousands of lives each year. Concentrates on the use of cardiopulmonary resuscitation for heart attack victims.

LC NO. 75-703023
Prod-ACTF Dist-WSTGLC Prodn-SUTHLA 197

Life Insurance C 14 MI
2 INCH VIDEOTAPE
Discusses the different kinds of life insurance and explains some common insurance terms. Explains the qualifications and requirements of an insurance agent and then compares the rate of term and straight life policies.
From The Living Better II Series.
Prod-MAETEL Dist-PUBTEL

Life Insurance C 29 MI
3/4 INCH VIDEO CASSETTE C
Studies life insurance policies and the effects of their legal elements. Describes some of the legal rights and obligations of the parties to a life insurance contract.
From The You And The Law Series. Lesson 14
Prod-COAST Dist-CDTEL Prodn-SADCC

Life Insurance C 29 MI
3/4 INCH VIDEO CASSETTE
See series title for descriptive statement.
From The You Owe It To Yourself Series.
Prod-WITFTV Dist-PUBTEL

Life Insurance C 30 MI
3/4 OR 1/2 INCH VIDEO CASSETTE C
Explores the basic elements of life insurance, including the kinds of companies that sell life insurance and the various plans and policies that are available. Provides guidelines to assist in determining how much individual life insurance is needed.
From The Personal Finance Series. Lesson 20
Prod-SCCON Dist-CDTEL

Life Is Fragile C 5 MIN
16MM FILM OPTICAL SOUND
Examines awareness of the value of human life and of the need for personal safety through an aesthetic theme without narration.
LC NO. 76-700185
Prod-SWBELL Dist-SWBELL 1976

Life Is Like A Domino C 5 MIN
16MM FILM OPTICAL SOUND
Gives a demonstration of a domino design stunt and relates it to everyday life.
LC NO. 80-700360
Prod-CORPOR Dist-CORPOR 1980

Life Is Precious - Buckle Them In C 14 MIN
3/4 OR 1/2 INCH VIDEO CASSETTE J-C A
Explains the need to use such restraining devices as seat belts and child car seats for children riding in automobiles. Shows the four development stages during which children need different kinds of protection.
LC NO. 84-700432
Prod-CMT Dist-FIESTF 1983

Life Is Worth The Living C 22 MIN
16MM FILM, 3/4 OR 1/2 IN VIDEO H-C
Examines the high number of traffic accidents involving teenage drivers and insists on the need for driver training by professional instructors. Demonstrates many traffic violations and etiquette common among all drivers.
Prod-CHET Dist-IFB 1968

Life Of A Butterfly, The C 18 MIN
16MM FILM OPTICAL SOUND P-J
Pictures the life cycle of a black swallowtail butterfly. Begins with an adult feeding on flowers, then laying its eggs. The eggs hatch—the emerging caterpillars, or larvae, eat, crawl about and molt. Finally they go through their elaborate preparations for pupation, which involve attaching themselves to a twig with silk threads. The pupa remains dormant and then suddenly the adult butterfly emerges, its wings expand and dry and the cycle is complete.
From The Butterflies Series.
LC NO. FIA67-2431
Prod-EDS Dist-EDC 1966

Life Of A Logo C 23 MIN
16MM FILM OPTICAL SOUND
Follows the evolution of a live product logo using the stag which is a symbol of the Hartford Insurance group as an example.
Prod-HFI Dist-MTP

Life Of A Plant C 11 MIN
16MM FILM, 3/4 OR 1/2 IN VIDEO I-H
Portrays the growth of a flowering pea plant by means of time-lapse photography. Close-ups of the seed, germination and the growth of stem and roots are shown.
Prod-EBF Dist-EBEC 1950

Life Of A Red Cell, The C 10 MIN
3/4 OR 1/2 INCH VIDEO CASSETTE I-J
Uses animation and humor to introduce the blood circulatory system. Shows how a new red blood cell is made in the bone marrow and joins others in a blood vein. Follows its adventures through the entire system and back to the beginning of its path revealing the cyclic nature of the blood system.
Prod-EDMI Dist-EDMI 1983

Life Of Abraham Lincoln, The B 16 MIN
16MM FILM SILENT
Presents highlights from the life of Abraham Lincoln, beginning with his years in the Senate and ending with his death at Ford's Theater.
LC NO. 74-713154
Prod-EDISOT Dist-BHAWK 1960

Life Of Buffalo Bill B 28 MIN
16MM FILM SILENT
A biographical film about Buffalo Bill, featuring William F Cody in the prolog and epilog.

LC NO. 70-713153
Prod-BBPBFC Dist-BHAWK

Life Of Christ As Seen By A Puerto Rican Woodcarver, The C 47 MIN
16MM FILM OPTICAL SOUND
Focuses on the work of a little-known Puerto Rican woodcarver whose creations depict the life of Christ from birth to crucifixion and resurrection.
From The Puerto Rican Folkart Expression - Las Artesanias De Puerto Rico Series.
LC NO. 79-701046
Prod-CASPRC Dist-CASPRC 1979

Life Of Christ As Seen By A Puerto Rican Woodcarver, The (Spanish) C 47 MIN
16MM FILM OPTICAL SOUND
Focuses on the work of a little-known Puerto Rican woodcarver whose creations depict the life of Christ from birth to crucifixion and resurrection.
From The Puerto Rican Folkart Expression - Las Artesanias De Puerto Rico Series.
LC NO. 79-701046
Prod-CASPRC Dist-CASPRC 1979

Life Of Elizabeth B 10 MIN
16MM FILM OPTICAL SOUND
Presents a 1952 Screen News Digest excerpt showing the English royal couple's visit to Canada and the United States in 1952. Shows briefly Queen Elizabeth's early life. Shows colorful crown jewels in preparation for Queen Elizabeth's coronation in 1953. Covers the historic coronation and pagentry.
From The News Magazine Of The Screen Series.
Prod-PATHE Dist-HEARST 1953

Life Of Emile Zola, The B 32 MIN
16MM FILM OPTICAL SOUND H-C
An excerpt from the feature film of the same title. Depicts the trial of Emile Zola for slander and libel upon his exposure of the injustice of the French Army high command in condemning Dreyfus to Devil's Island.
Prod-WB Dist-IU Prodn-WB 1946

Life Of Emile Zola, The B 110 MIN
16MM FILM OPTICAL SOUND
Traces the career of prolific French novelist Emile Zola, centering on his heroic defense of the unjustly persecuted Captain Dreyfus. Stars Paul Muni.
Prod-WB Dist-UAE 1937

Life Of Mahatma Gandhi C 28 MIN
16MM FILM OPTICAL SOUND H-C A
A documentary account of the life of Gandhi, using newsreel footage.
LC NO. 70-705737
Prod-BAGAI Dist-FINDIA 1963

Life Of Mahatma Gandhi C 80 MIN
16MM FILM OPTICAL SOUND H-C A
A documentary account of the life of Gandhi, using newsreel footage.
LC NO. 70-705737
Prod-BAGAI Dist-FINDIA 1950

Life Of Oharu, The (Japanese) B 133 MIN
16MM FILM OPTICAL SOUND
Covers several decades in the life of a Japanese courtesan, tracing her progress from innocent youth to an old woman begging through the streets. Examines the lifestyles to be found in feudal Japan.
Prod-NYFLMS Dist-NYFLMS 1952

Life Of The Bighorn Sheep C 16 MIN
16MM FILM, 3/4 OR 1/2 IN VIDEO J-C A
Depicts four rams involved in a head butting contest in a test of dominance. Shows how the sheep adapt to the hardships of extreme temperatures and the natural danger posed by their natural predators.
Prod-BERLET Dist-BERLET

Life Of The Hermit Crab C 24 MIN
16MM FILM OPTICAL SOUND
Explains that the hermit crab is grouped into the category of crustancea and describes its form and way of living.
Prod-TOEI Dist-UNIJAP 1970

Life Of The Honeybee (2nd Ed) C 24 MIN
16MM FILM, 3/4 OR 1/2 IN VIDEO I-C A
Looks inside a beehive to observe the functions of the cells and the roles of the bees.
LC NO. 81-706864
Prod-EBEC Dist-EBEC 1980

Life Of The Honeybee, The (Spanish) C 24 MIN
16MM FILM, 3/4 OR 1/2 IN VIDEO J-H
A Spanish language version of the film and videorecording Life Of The Honeybee.
Prod-EBEC Dist-EBEC

Life Of The Sockeye Salmon C 25 MIN
16MM FILM, 3/4 OR 1/2 IN VIDEO I-C A
Highlights spring in the Pacific Northwest, the season when the salmon eggs in river beds are beginning to hatch. Traces the development of the sockeye salmon as it completes a 6,000-mile roundtrip journey.
Prod-WILFGP Dist-JOU 1977

Life Of The Spadefoot Toad X 13 MIN
16MM FILM OPTICAL SOUND
Introduces the World Outdoors series. Tennessee Charlie relates the life of the spadefoot toad.
From The World Outdoors Series. No. 1
Prod-TGAFC Dist-TGAFC

Life Of Thomas Jefferson, The C 15 MIN
16MM FILM OPTICAL SOUND P-H S
Presents in American sign language the life of Thomas Jefferson. Filmed at Independence Hall, Monticello, the University of Virginia and the Library of Congress. Signed by Louie J Fant, Jr.
LC NO. 76-701095
Prod-JOYCE Dist-JOYCE 1976

Life Offshore C 16 MIN
3/4 OR 1/2 INCH VIDEO CASSETTE IND
Serves as a preview for the new employee about to work on an offshore production platform for the first time.
Prod-UTEXPE Dist-UTEXPE

Life On A Dead Tree C 11 MIN
16MM FILM, 3/4 OR 1/2 IN VIDEO P-I
Dave and Tommy have found an old dead tree in the woods. As they explore it, they find that it is the home of many different plants and animals such as lizards, beetles, crickets, slugs, fungus plants, tree salamanders, ants and gopher snakes.
Prod-FA Dist-PHENIX 1957

Life On A Rotting Log C 15 MIN
3/4 OR 1/2 INCH VIDEO CASSETTE I-J
Examines a rotting log as the habitat of countless creatures, each with its own means of survival.
From The Animals And Such Series. Module Blue - Habitats
Prod-WHROTV Dist-AITECH 1972

Life On A Silken Thread C 60 MIN
16MM FILM - 3/4 IN VIDEO
Focuses on the world of spiders, showing a closeup look at the processes of molting, web spinning and prey catching.
From The Nova Series.
LC NO. 79-708088
Prod-WGBHTV Dist-PBS 1979

Life On Earth–A Series
16MM FILM, 3/4 OR 1/2 IN VIDEO J-C A
Presents the story of the development of life on earth.
Prod-BBCTV Dist-FI 1981

Building Bodies	058 MIN
Compulsive Communicators, The	058 MIN
Conquest Of The Waters, The	058 MIN
First Forests, The	058 MIN
Hunters And The Hunted, The	058 MIN
Infinite Variety, The	058 MIN
Invasion Of The Land, The	058 MIN
Life In The Trees, A	058 MIN
Lords Of The Air	058 MIN
Rise Of The Mammals, The	058 MIN
Swarming Hordes, The	058 MIN
Theme And Variations	058 MIN
Victors Of The Dry Land	058 MIN

Life On Other Planets C 18 MIN
16MM FILM OPTICAL SOUND J-C A
A revised version of the 1964 film Of Stars And Men. Tells the story of a man who gives up his hum-drum existence to seek truth through a philosophical quest. Based on the book OF STARS AND MEN by Dr Harlow Shapley.
From The Of Stars And Men (2nd Ed) Series.
LC NO. 76-701274
Prod-HUBLEY Dist-RADIM 1976

Life On Other Planets C 24 MIN
16MM FILM OPTICAL SOUND I-C
Studies the biochemical origins of life. Analyzes the possibility of life existing on other planets in the universe.
From The Animal Secrets Series.
LC NO. FIA68-1041
Prod-NBC Dist-GRACUR 1967

Life On Seashores C 24 MIN
16MM FILM OPTICAL SOUND
Uses close-up and microscopic photography to compare and contrast the most common plant and animal organisms living in rocky and sandy seashores. Looks at such plants and animals as lichen, wrack, alga, periwinkle, limpets, barnacles, diatoms and crustaceans.
Prod-BBCTV Dist-OPENU 1982

Life On Seashores C 24 MIN
16MM FILM, 3/4 OR 1/2 IN VIDEO
Uses close-up and microscopic photography to compare and contrast the most common plant and animal organisms living in rocky and sandy seashores. Looks at such plants and animals as lichen, wrack, alga, periwinkle, limpets, barnacles, diatoms and crustaceans.
Prod-OPENU Dist-MEDIAG Prodn-BBCTV 1982

Life On The Forest Floor - A First Film C 10 MIN
16MM FILM, 3/4 OR 1/2 IN VIDEO I-J
Explains that the forest floor is sheltered from strong sunlight and it is moist. Shows that the falling leaves and rotting stumps provide food and shelter for many kinds of animals and plants in this unique habitat.
Prod-NELLES Dist-PHENIX 1972

Life On The Forest Floor - A First Film (French) C 10 MIN
16MM FILM, 3/4 OR 1/2 IN VIDEO I-J
Explains that the forest floor is sheltered from strong sunlight and it is moist. Shows that the falling leaves and rotting stumps provide food and shelter for many kinds of animals and plants in this unique habitat.
Prod-NELLES Dist-PHENIX 1972

Life On The Great Plains C 20 MIN
3/4 INCH VIDEO CASSETTE I
Visits a small town. Includes the largest cattle feedlot in the world, riding a combine at wheat harvest, going to a consolidated school and drilling for oil.
From The Understanding Our World, Unit II - Geography We Should Know Series.
Prod-KRMATV Dist-GPITVL

Life On The Limit C 26 MIN
16MM FILM, 3/4 OR 1/2 IN VIDEO H-C A
Tells how the agricultural revolution enabled society to develop communities and cultures and also created the first man-made ecological disaster. Discusses how Hillong, in Assam, India, the wettest place on earth, became barren by such carelessness. New ecological disasters are created with concrete, asphalt, waste and poison.
From The Botanic Man Series.
Prod-THAMES Dist-MEDIAG 1978

Life On The Macon Plateau C 12 MIN
16MM FILM, 3/4 OR 1/2 IN VIDEO
Features the Indian cultures of the Macon Plateau, particularly the Mississippian culture. Displays archeological evidence, pottery, tools, mound construction and grave goods at the Ocmulgee National Monument.
Prod-USNPS Dist-USNAC

Life On The Mississippi C 47 MIN
3/4 OR 1/2 INCH VIDEO CASSETTE
Takes an expedition of the Mississippi River and the lives it touches through the narration of Mark Twain (Warren Frost). Reveals the story about today in terms of what survives of yesterday.
Prod-WCCOTV Dist-WCCOTV 1978

Life On The Mississippi C 54 MIN
16MM FILM, 3/4 OR 1/2 IN VIDEO H-C A
An abridged version of the motion picture Life On The Mississippi. Presents an account of a young man's apprenticeship on the Mississippi River. Based on the book Life On The Mississippi by Mark Twain.
Prod-WNETTV Dist-FI 1980

Life On The Mississippi C 120 MIN
3/4 OR 1/2 INCH VIDEO CASSETTE H-C A
Dramatizes 18 months in the life of Mark Twain when, as a young man, he fulfilled his dream of becoming a river pilot.
LC NO. 81-707230
Prod-GREAM Dist-FI 1980

Life On The Tundra C 14 MIN
16MM FILM, 3/4 OR 1/2 IN VIDEO I
Studies the tundra regions of the Canadian Arctic. Reveals the activities of various types of animal life such as nesting birds, musk-oxen and herds of caribou between the winter and spring seasons.
Prod-NFBC Dist-EBEC 1965

Life Or Breath C 30 MIN
3/4 OR 1/2 INCH VIDEO CASSETTE I-J
Relates how relaxation exercises save a life when an ambassador's son is kidnapped.
From The Powerhouse Series.
LC NO. 83-707179
Prod-EFCVA Dist-GA 1982

Life Or Death C 25 MIN
16MM FILM, 3/4 OR 1/2 IN VIDEO
Contrasts the right and wrong ways of performing extrication, body survey, first aid and patient transport through the discussion of two ghosts concerning the emergency medical treatment they received at their fatal automobile accident.
Prod-FILCOM Dist-FILCOM 1977

Life Planning C 18 MIN
2 INCH VIDEOTAPE C A
Features a humanistic psychologist who, by analysis and examples, discusses life planning.
From The Interpersonal Competence, Unit 09 - Growth Series.
Prod-MVNE Dist-TELSTR 1973

Life Safety In High Rise Fires C 21 MIN
16MM FILM, 3/4 OR 1/2 IN VIDEO A
Describes a fire safety plan for high rise building occupants.
Prod-AREASX Dist-SF

Life Science C 30 MIN
3/4 OR 1/2 INCH VIDEO CASSETTE H-C A
Dramatizes the experiences of the staff of a high school newspaper. Focuses on marriage.
From The New Voice Series.
Prod-WGBHTV Dist-GPITVL

Life Science For Elementary–A Series
16MM FILM, 3/4 OR 1/2 IN VIDEO P-I
Prod-PEDF Dist-AIMS 1976

Predators And Prey	9 MIN
Wild Animals Adapt	9 MIN
Wild Animals Catch Fish	9 MIN
Wildlife Families	9 MIN
Wildlife Mothers	9 MIN

Life Science–A Series
16MM FILM, 3/4 OR 1/2 IN VIDEO P-I
Prod-ALTSUL Dist-JOU

Adapting To Changes In Nature	10 MIN
Animal Predators And The Balance Of Nature	10 MIN
Animal Reproduction	17 MIN
Instincts In Animals	10 MIN
Learning From Pets In The Classroom	15 MIN
Spring Is A Season	11 MIN

Life Space And Life Style B 30 MIN
16MM FILM OPTICAL SOUND C
Shows the effect of life space and life style upon the aging individual and the way in which he functions in society.

From The Growth And Development, The Adult Years Series.
LC NO. 70-706816
Prod-VDONUR Dist-AJN Prodn-WTTWTV 1969

Life Span - How Long Do We Live And Why C 13 MIN
16MM FILM, 3/4 OR 1/2 IN VIDEO I-J
Compares the life span of an interest that may only live for a few days with that of other animals that may live for many years. Analyzes why there is such a difference in life span and how humans have increased their life span far beyond that of most animals.
Prod-GLDWER Dist-JOU 1972

Life Span - How Long Do We Live And Why (Captioned) C 13 MIN
16MM FILM, 3/4 OR 1/2 IN VIDEO I-J
Compares the life span of an interest that may only live for a few days with that of other animals that may live for many years. Analyzes why there is such a difference in life span and how humans have increased their life span far beyond that of most animals.
Prod-GLDWER Dist-JOU 1972

Life Stances Genogram, Pt 7 C 41 MIN
3/4 OR 1/2 INCH VIDEO CASSETTE
Shows how to make life stance genograms of the family, enabling one to better understand behavior in personal encounters.
From The Relationship Growth Group Series.
Prod-WRAMC Dist-UWISC 1979

Life Stances, Pt 6 C 45 MIN
3/4 OR 1/2 INCH VIDEO CASSETTE
Features lecture by Dr Donald R Bardill on life stances, the manner in which an individual approaches personal encounters. Discusses disfunctional, functional and and irrational life stances.
From The Relationship Growth Group Series.
Prod-WRAMC Dist-UWISC 1979

Life Story Of A Moth - The Silkworm C 11 MIN
16MM FILM, 3/4 OR 1/2 IN VIDEO I
Illustrates the structural and behavioral changes which occur during the process of metamorphosis in the silkworm moth. Includes close-ups of the molting process, the complex behavior of the larva, the emergence of the silkworm moth, its mating and the laying of eggs.
Prod-EBEC Dist-EBEC 1964

Life Story Of A Moth - The Silkworm (Captioned) C 11 MIN
16MM FILM, 3/4 OR 1/2 IN VIDEO I
Illustrates the structural and behavioral changes which occur during the process of metamorphosis in the silkworm moth. Includes close-ups of the molting process, the complex behavior of the larva, the emergence of the silkworm moth, its mating and the laying of eggs.
Prod-EBEC Dist-EBEC 1964

Life Story Of A Plant - About Flowers C 7 MIN
16MM FILM, 3/4 OR 1/2 IN VIDEO P
Follows the life cycle and processes of a plant. Shows how seeds develop and then are scattered to make new plants.
Prod-NFBC Dist-EBEC 1965

Life Story Of A Snake X 11 MIN
16MM FILM, 3/4 OR 1/2 IN VIDEO I
Uses close-ups and live-action sequences to examine the physical characteristics, life cycle and behavior of the North American blacksnake. Shows how snakes move, obtain food, reproduce, protect themselves and adapt to their environment.
Prod-EBF Dist-EBEC 1964

Life Story Of A Social Insect - The Ant X 11 MIN
16MM FILM, 3/4 OR 1/2 IN VIDEO I
Explains why ants are considered social insects. Shows how a new ant colony begins and the ways in which each ant works for the benefit of the colony. Identifies the three sections of an ant's body.
From The Basic Life Science Program Series.
Prod-EBEC Dist-EBEC 1968

Life Story Of A Water Flea - Daphnia X 10 MIN
16MM FILM, 3/4 OR 1/2 IN VIDEO I
Uses microphotography to demonstrate the importance of the daphnia for observing biological functions. Follows the life cycle of the daphnia and explores its role in the fresh-water food chain.
Prod-EBF Dist-EBEC 1966

Life Story Of The Crayfish X 10 MIN
16MM FILM, 3/4 OR 1/2 IN VIDEO I
Shows the life cycle of crayfish from fertilized egg to adult. Demonstrates how it is adapted to live in water. Photographed in the Louisiana bayou country.
Prod-EBF Dist-EBEC 1963

Life Story Of The Crayfish (Captioned) C 10 MIN
3/4 OR 1/2 INCH VIDEO CASSETTE I
Shows the life cycle of crayfish from the fertilized seed to adult. Demonstrates how it is adapted to live in water. Photographed in the Louisiana bayou country.
Prod-EBEC Dist-EBEC 1963

Life Story Of The Earthworm X 10 MIN
16MM FILM, 3/4 OR 1/2 IN VIDEO I
Studies how the earthworm moves, feeds, reproduces and reacts to stimuli. Demonstrates the relationship of the earthworm to the leech, sandworm and other annelids. Stresses its importance in improving the soil.
Prod-EBF Dist-EBEC 1963

Life Story Of The Earthworm (Spanish) C 10 MIN
16MM FILM, 3/4 OR 1/2 IN VIDEO I
Shows how the earthworm moves, feeds, reproduces and reacts to various stimuli. Demonstrates the relationship of the earthworm to the leech, sandworm and other annelids. Points out the worm's importance in improving the soil.
Prod-EBEC Dist-EBEC

Life Story Of The Grasshopper X 11 MIN
16MM FILM, 3/4 OR 1/2 IN VIDEO I
Shows the grasshopper's structure and relates it to his ability to survive. Compares the life cycle of other insects to that of the grasshopper, whose metamorphosis is incomplete.
Prod-EBF Dist-EBEC 1966

Life Story Of The Hummingbird X 16 MIN
16MM FILM, 3/4 OR 1/2 IN VIDEO I
Shows physical characteristics and feeding, mating and nesting habits of hummingbirds. Depicts the care and growth of young birds. Uses high speed photography to reveal the hummingbird's unusual wing movement.
Prod-EBF Dist-EBEC 1963

Life Story Of The Ladybird Beetle X 10 MIN
16MM FILM, 3/4 OR 1/2 IN VIDEO I
Depicts the complete life cycle of a ladybird beetle. Shows structural and behavioral characteristics at each of the four stages of development.
Prod-EBF Dist-EBEC 1966

Life Story Of The Oyster X 11 MIN
16MM FILM, 3/4 OR 1/2 IN VIDEO I
Demonstrates how the oyster develops into an adult and how the adult feeds, grows and reproduces. Shows the place of this mollusk in the marine food cycle.
Prod-EBF Dist-EBEC 1963

Life Story Of The Paramecium X 11 MIN
16MM FILM, 3/4 OR 1/2 IN VIDEO I
Depicts the life functions of the paramecium, showing how it feeds, grows, breathes, moves, reproduces, reacts to stimuli and gives off wastes. Explains that the basic unit of life is the individual cell.
Prod-EBF Dist-EBEC 1963

Life Story Of The Red-Winged Blackbird X 11 MIN
16MM FILM, 3/4 OR 1/2 IN VIDEO I
Uses close-up photography to reveal the redwing's typical activities and behavior during the nesting season. Views the mass migration of red-winged blackbirds to their winter ranges in the south.
Prod-EBF Dist-EBEC 1964

Life Story Of The Sea Star X 11 MIN
16MM FILM, 3/4 OR 1/2 IN VIDEO I
Depicts the life cycle of the starfish, showing its adaptations to intertidal zone environment. Demonstrates characteristics which brittle stars, sand dollars and sea urchins have in common with starfish.
Prod-EBF Dist-EBEC 1963

Life Story Of The Snail X 11 MIN
16MM FILM, 3/4 OR 1/2 IN VIDEO I
Presents a photographic study of the characteristics, behavior patterns and life cycle of a freshwater snail. Shows examples of different types of snails and snail's mollusk relatives. Indicates that they have adapted to a wide variety of environments.
Prod-EBF Dist-EBEC 1963

Life Story Of The Toad X 10 MIN
16MM FILM, 3/4 OR 1/2 IN VIDEO I
Introduces the metamorphosis of a toad, explaining how toads reproduce, feed and move. Shows the position of the toad in the food cycle. Photographed in Louisiana bayou country.
Prod-EBF Dist-EBEC 1963

Life That's Left, The C 29 MIN
16MM FILM, 3/4 OR 1/2 IN VIDEO H-C A
Offers a study of bereavement that focuses upon the personal experiences of ordinary people. Features interviews with people who have gone through the sudden severance of a close relationship.
Prod-CHERIO Dist-GPITVL 1979

Life Through Fire C 15 MIN
3/4 INCH VIDEO CASSETTE I-C A
Documents a new technique which uses fire productivity to improve wildlife habitat, water production and rangeland.
Prod-CSDWR Dist-CALDWR

Life Times Nine C 15 MIN
16MM FILM, 3/4 OR 1/2 IN VIDEO I-C A
Presents Commercials for Life, a series of nine short films made by children ages 11 to 16.
Prod-INST Dist-PFP 1974

Life Transitions C 30 MIN
3/4 OR 1/2 INCH VIDEO CASSETTE A
Features panels who relate moments of personal discovery and insight which evolved from their life transitions. Focuses on work, family and social changes which contributed to their learning. Includes such changes as employment and unemployment, aging, marriage and divorce.
From The Transitions Series. Program 101
Prod-OHUTC Dist-OHUTC

Life Under Pressure C 30 MIN
3/4 OR 1/2 INCH VIDEO CASSETTE
Focuses on the three deep ocean zones and the basic physical water conditions within these zones. Discusses deep-water life forms.
From The Oceanus - The Marine Environment Series. Lesson 23
Prod-SCCON Dist-CDTEL

Life Under The Sea C 16 MIN
16MM FILM, 3/4 OR 1/2 IN VIDEO I
Reveals the colorful life on reefs in shallow areas of the sea. Shows pictures of hermit crabs, starfish, sea urchins, lobsters, octopus and eels.
Prod-PARACO Dist-AIMS 197

Life With Father B 118 MIN
16MM FILM OPTICAL SOUND
Looks at life in the Day household in 1883 New York, emphasizing the bond of love which holds the children and parents together. Stars William Powell, Irene Dunne and Elizabeth Taylor. Directed by Michael Curitz. Based on the book Life With Father by Clarence Day.
Prod-UNKNWN Dist-REELIM 194

Life With Father C 118 MIN
16MM FILM OPTICAL SOUND
Presents a story of family life about author Clarence Day's youth in 1883 New York. Stars William Powell, Irene Dunne and Elizabeth Taylor. Directed by Michael Curitz.
Prod-WB Dist-TWYMAN 1947

Life With Hypertension - Practical Approaches To Therapy (Focus On Prazosin) B 24 MIN
16MM FILM OPTICAL SOUND PRO
Demonstrates practical approaches to therapy for hypertension patients.
LC NO. 80-701234
Prod-PFIZLB Dist-PFIZLB Prodn-EFFCOM 1980

Life With St Helens C 29 MIN
3/4 OR 1/2 INCH VIDEO CASSETTE
Presents a documentary on the eruption of Mount St Helens in 1980 from the viewpoint of the citizens in the vicinity of the volcano. Includes film footage of the eruption and the commentary of geologists, who offer the prospect of future eruptions.
LC NO. 82-706226
Prod-KSPSTV Dist-PBS 1980

Life You Save, The C 30 MIN
3/4 OR 1/2 INCH VIDEO CASSETTE C A
Focuses on the cause and prevention of accidents. Offers first aid information.
From The Contemporary Health Issues Series. Lesson 28
Prod-SCCON Dist-CDTEL

Life You Save, The (First Aid) C 17 MIN
16MM FILM, 3/4 OR 1/2 IN VIDEO J-C A
Presents four true cases where knowledge of basic first aid saved lives. Features Tim Donnelly of the 'EMERGENCY' TV series, describing the first aid method of each case.
Prod-BURKSA Dist-FLMFR 1973

Life You Save, The (First Aid) (Captioned Version) C 17 MIN
16MM FILM, 3/4 OR 1/2 IN VIDEO J-C A
Presents four true cases where knowledge of basic first aid saved lives. Features Tim Donnelly of the 'EMERGENCY' TV series, describing the first aid method of each case.
Prod-BURKSA Dist-FLMFR 1973

Life-Force C 25 MIN
16MM FILM OPTICAL SOUND
Presents a documentary on Canadian painter Jack Chambers, exploring the creative energy which motivates the artist and his work.
LC NO. 75-701893
Prod-MELFIL Dist-CANFDC 1974

Life-Lifting Language B 15 MIN
2 INCH VIDEOTAPE I
Defines life-lifting language as any bit or unit of language, such as a story, poem or expression that is so memorable that it tends to impress itself indelibly on the mind and thereby becomes part of the culture's cherished language ways. Features selections Winter Wind and One Misty, Moisty Morning both Mother Goose Rhymes by Randall Jarrell and Come Dance With Me by Bill Martin. (Broadcast quality)
From The Bill Martin Series. No. 13
Prod-BRITED Dist-GPITVL Prodn-KQEDTV

Life-Long Rechargeable Pacemaker, The C 9 MIN
3/4 OR 1/2 INCH VIDEO CASSETTE PRO
Describes how a new type rechargeable, implanted pacemaker regulates the rhythm of the heart. (Also available in Spanish).
Prod-WFP Dist-WFP

Life, A C 10 MIN
16MM FILM OPTICAL SOUND
Shows an abandoned log cabin in winter and summer.
LC NO. 76-703066
Prod-MEDCS Dist-VIP 1975

Life, Death And Recovery Of An Alcoholic, The C 26 MIN
16MM FILM - 3/4 IN VIDEO
Traces the normal course of alcoholism from the first drink to alcohol addiction. Shows the psychological relationships which exist between an alcoholic and his employer, family and friends, the medical profession and the legal system.
LC NO. 79-706854
Prod-FMSP Dist-FMSP 1977

Life, Death And Taxes—A Series

Deals with estate planning. Offers the layman a comprehensive overview of the complicated legal issues that are central to understanding the workings of estate planning.
Prod-UMITV Dist-UMITV 1977

Chosen Devices	029 MIN
Exchangeable Value, An	029 MIN
First And Great Rule	029 MIN
Fleeting Estate, The	029 MIN
More Than A Contract	029 MIN

Most Efficient Instrument	029 MIN
Shifting Of Risk, A	029 MIN
Specified Perils	029 MIN

Life, Death And The American Woman C 52 MIN
16MM FILM OPTICAL SOUND J-C A
Covers causes, consequences and cures of common health problems experienced by American women.
LC NO. 78-701503
Prod-LNDBRG Dist-BESTF 1978

Life, Liberty And The Pursuit Of Happiness - A Celebration C 21 MIN
16MM FILM OPTICAL SOUND
Presents examples of nonacademic art from the early days of America as seen in an exhibition staged by Marcel Breuer at the Whitney Museum Of American Art in New York.
LC NO. 75-702229
Prod-PHILMO Dist-MTP Prodn-FRMART 1975

Life? / Mars - Is There Life? C 30 MIN
3/4 OR 1/2 INCH VIDEO CASSETTE
Compares life forms with non-life similarities. Explores the Martian environment.
From The Reaching For The Stars, And Life Beyond Earth Series.
Prod-IVCH Dist-IVCH

Life's Higher Goals C 29 MIN
16MM FILM OPTICAL SOUND H-C
Shows Bob Richards, twice Olympic pole vault champion, giving one of his inspiring messages on living your life to the fullest. Illustrates persons who have overcome obstacles to become 'CHAMPIONS OF LIFE.'
Prod-GEMILL Dist-NINEFC

Lifeboats Under Gravity Davits - Launching Boats B 25 MIN
16MM FILM OPTICAL SOUND
Shows the method of launching the merchant marine type of nested lifeboats using the 'WELIN GRAVITY DAVIT.' Demonstrates methods of launching at dockside and while underway at sea.
LC NO. FIE54-362
Prod-USN Dist-USNAC 1954

Lifeboats Under Gravity Davits - Recovering Boats B 25 MIN
16MM FILM OPTICAL SOUND
Shows the single method of recovering the Merchant Marine type of nested lifeboats using the Welin Gravity Davit. Illustrates an actual recovery.
LC NO. FIE54-363
Prod-USN Dist-USNAC 1954

Lifeclimb C 22 MIN
16MM FILM, 3/4 OR 1/2 IN VIDEO C A
Presents a documentary in which 64-year-old Stan Zundell describes how he has faced the difficulties and challenges of aging.
LC NO. 77-703265
Prod-PFP Dist-PFP Prodn-ZUNDEL 1977

Lifeline - Dispatcher Communications C 16 MIN
16MM FILM, 3/4 OR 1/2 IN VIDEO
Presents the working dispatcher/communications environment in which a variety of complainant calls are received and proper dispatcher field responses are shown.
Prod-MTI Dist-MTI

Lifeline In Space C 14 MIN
16MM FILM OPTICAL SOUND P-H
Presents a fictionalized account of the many roles man will be playing in space in the near future.
LC NO. 70-712362
Prod-NOVLES Dist-GRAF 1971

Lifeline To Learning C 27 MIN
16MM FILM OPTICAL SOUND
Illustrates the special requirements of transporting handicapped school children and includes examples of how various school bus drivers encounter and respond to the needs of handicapped student passengers.
LC NO. 77-701440
Prod-VISUCP Dist-VISUCP 1977

Lifelines - A Career Profile Study C 26 MIN
16MM FILM, 3/4 OR 1/2 IN VIDEO
Discusses career formation, describing five patterns by which individuals discover what they are good at and what they would like to do for the rest of their lives.
From The Human Resources And Organizational Behavior Series.
Prod-DOCUA Dist-CNEMAG

Lifelines—A Series

Deals with various aspects of the medical field including folk medicine, medicine on television, sports medicine and pain treatment.
Prod-UGATV Dist-MDCPB

Childbirth	030 MIN
Emergency Medical Care	030 MIN
Folk Medicine	030 MIN
Forensic Medicine	030 MIN
It's All In Your Mind	030 MIN
Medicine On The Tube	030 MIN
Nursing As A Profession	030 MIN
Sports Medicine	030 MIN
Treatment Of Pain, The	030 MIN

Lifesavers - Fitness And Nutrition C 20 MIN
16MM FILM, 3/4 OR 1/2 IN VIDEO
Illustrates how sedentary lifestyles and improper eating habits take their toll on an individual's physical and emotional well-being. Shows how a properly balanced diet and regular fitness activity can help people work and play more effectively and enjoyably.
From The Stress Management System Series.
Prod-MITCHG Dist-MTI

Lifesaving And Water Safety—A Series
I-C A
Prod-AMRC Dist-AMRC

Boating Safety And Rescues	10 MIN
Defenses, Releases And Escapes	7 MIN
Nonswimming Rescues	7 MIN
Preventive Lifeguarding	9 MIN
Removal From The Water	6 MIN
Snorkelling Skills And Rescue Techniques	13 MIN
Special Equipment Rescues	9 MIN
Survival Swimming	7 MIN
Swimming Rescues	8 MIN

Lifesaving And Water Safety—A Series

Presents a series on lifesaving and water safety.
Prod-AMRC Dist-AMRC 1975

Boating, Safety And Rescues	010 MIN
Boating, Safety And Rescues (Spanish)	010 MIN
Defenses, Releases And Escapes	007 MIN
Non-Swimming Rescues	007 MIN
Non-Swimming Rescues (Spanish)	007 MIN
Preventive Lifeguarding	009 MIN
Removal From The Water	006 MIN
Snorkeling Skills And Rescue Techniques	013 MIN
Special Equipment Rescues	009 MIN
Survival Swimming	007 MIN
Swimming Rescues	008 MIN

Lifestream - Collecion, Preparation And Administration Of Blood And Its Components C 26 MIN
3/4 OR 1/2 INCH VIDEO CASSETTE PRO
Shows how modern techniques make it possible to greatly extend the collection and therapeutic use of blood and its components.
Prod-WFP Dist-WFP

Lifestyle C 30 MIN
3/4 INCH VIDEO CASSETTE
Discusses experiences and observations of modern China.
From The China After Mao Series.
Prod-UMITV Dist-UMITV

Lifestyles/Lifestages C 30 MIN
3/4 OR 1/2 INCH VIDEO CASSETTE C A
Focuses on lifestage theory and choosing lifestyles. Shows lifestyle and career changers talking about the momentum behind their decisions.
From The Making A Living Work Series. Program 102
Prod-OHUTC Dist-OHUTC

Lifestyles, The B 22 MIN
16MM FILM, 3/4 OR 1/2 IN VIDEO I-H
Uses newsreel footage to show how the average American citizen worked and played during the first half of the 20th century.
From The Eyewitness To History Series.
Prod-WDEMCO Dist-WDEMCO 1978

Lifetime Employment C 28 MIN
16MM FILM, 3/4 OR 1/2 IN VIDEO H-C A
Shows how Japan must rely on imports for its economic survival and focuses on the Theory Z methods used to ensure a consistently high level of quality and productivity.
From The Human Face Of Japan Series.
LC NO. 82-707049
Prod-FLMAUS Dist-LCOA 1982

Lifetime In Photography, A C 30 MIN
3/4 OR 1/2 INCH VIDEO CASSETTE
See series title for descriptive statement.
From The Photographic Vision - All About Photography Series.
Prod-COAST Dist-CDTEL

Lifetime Of Learning, A C 28 MIN
3/4 OR 1/2 INCH VIDEO CASSETTE PRO
Depicts role of the University of Kansas Medical Center in the continuing education of the physician and surgeon in Kansas.
Prod-WFP Dist-WFP

Lifetime Protection C 20 MIN
16MM FILM OPTICAL SOUND
Shows how styrofoam is finding wide use as a perimeter insulation and combination building insulation and plaster base for masonry residential construction. Explains the qualities of styrofoam and shows proper methods of installation.
Prod-DCC Dist-DCC 1956

Lifetimes Of Change - Development And Growth C 18 MIN
3/4 OR 1/2 INCH VIDEO CASSETTE I-H A
Illustrates how all living creatures, whether plants, animals or human beings, experience growth, development and change. Shows how man ages by a series of 15 portraits from infancy to old age. Cites three other examples for further exposition, including life-changes in toadstools, frog, and flowering plants.
Prod-EDMI Dist-EDMI 1983

Lifewalks C
16MM FILM - 3/4 IN VIDEO A
Alerts people to the danger of being a pedestrian, gives safety tips and encourages people to walk safely.
Prod-BNA Dist-BNA 1983

Lifeways—A Series

Documents various aspects of life and culture in the Southwestern United States.
Prod-BLUSKY Dist-BLUSKY

La Acequia	010 MIN
Los Tejedores	028 MIN

Lifework C
1/2 IN VIDEO CASSETTE BETA/VHS
Explores the role of work in adult lives, and discusses the new work ethic. Includes comments by a real estate agent, an executive, a factory worker, and the manager of a fast food restaurant.
From The Adult Years - Continuity And Change Series.
Prod-OHUTC Dist-OHUTC

Lift C 15 MIN
2 INCH VIDEOTAPE K
Involves a force acting in a direction opposite to the pull of gravity.
From The Let's Go Sciencing, Unit II - Energy Series.
Prod-DETPS Dist-GPITVL

Lift Truck Safety C 12 MIN
3/4 OR 1/2 INCH VIDEO CASSETTE IND
Looks at the professional way to operate a lift truck. Stresses pre-shift inspection. Discusses proper driving techniques.
From The Steel Making Series.
Prod-LEIKID Dist-LEIKID

Lift, The B 8 MIN
16MM FILM OPTICAL SOUND
Explains how a man loses control of the machines in his mechanized world when an old elevator refuses to respond to his commands and eventually causes his death.
LC NO. 72-702398
Prod-USC Dist-USC 1972

Lifting - A Weight, A Way C 10 MIN
16MM FILM, 3/4 OR 1/2 IN VIDEO
Illustrates proper methods of lifting parcels and sacks to reduce back injuries among postal employees. Features an olympic weightlifting champion applying proper techniques to actual postal operation.
LC NO. 82-706294
Prod-USPOST Dist-USNAC 1970

Lifting - Man's Age Old Problem C 14 MIN
16MM FILM OPTICAL SOUND J-C A
Utilizes special photographic techniques to dramatize the functions of the back muscles and spine and to illustrate the efects of both correct and incorrect lifting methods. Suggests guidelines for use in establishing individual strength limits and offers advice on proper lifting techniques.
Prod-AETNA Dist-AETNA 1964

Lifting And Analysis C 17 MIN
3/4 OR 1/2 INCH VIDEO CASSETTE A
Discusses how to calculate parameters for safe lifting activity in specific situations. Intended for managers, supervisors, safety specialists and loss controllers.
Prod-USPHS Dist-USNAC 1981

Lifting Equipment C 10 MIN
16MM FILM, 3/4 OR 1/2 IN VIDEO
Emphasizes safe operation of cranes and lifting equipment. Stresses the need to train operators in safe operations.
From The Safety In Construction Series.
Prod-NFBTE Dist-IFB

Lifting Safety C 9 MIN
16MM FILM OPTICAL SOUND
Shows the proper technique for lifting heavy or bulky objects safely to avoid back and other injuries.
Prod-RARIG Dist-RARIG

Lifting Techniques And Body Mechanics C 20 MIN
3/4 OR 1/2 INCH VIDEO CASSETTE
Describes in non-technical terms what happens to the back when an object is lifted. Visualizes the spine with simple diagrams and a split-screen technique. Cites dangers to the back when an object is lifted incorrectly.
Prod-FAIRGH Dist-FAIRGH

Lifting Templates For A Foundation B 23 MIN
16MM FILM OPTICAL SOUND
Tells how to lift a template within the hull of a ship, and transfer the shape of the hull by use of measurements and cardboard.
LC NO. FIE52-1210
Prod-USN Dist-USNAC 1944

Lifting The Shadows C 27 MIN
16MM FILM OPTICAL SOUND
Features four doctors discussing the effects of marijuana, alcohol and tobacco on sexual libido. Highlights the emotional impact on social and family relationships.
Prod-NARCED Dist-NARCED

Lifting The Veil - The Tuskegee Tradition C 14 MIN
16MM FILM, 3/4 OR 1/2 IN VIDEO I-C A
Presents a documentary about the Tuskegee Institute in Alabama, established in 1885. Discusses Booker T Washington, George Washington Carver, Theodore Roosevelt, Andrew Carnegie and other persons important to the Institute, as well as historical events, places and facts.
From The Screen News Digest Series.
Prod-HEARST Dist-HEARST 1976

Lifting Weight C 10 MIN
16MM FILM, 3/4 OR 1/2 IN VIDEO P-I
Views Grandpa and Boy hard at work lifting heavy sacks of grain and carrying them to the barn loft. Reveals that a dangling spider gives Boy the idea of pulling up the sacks with a rope and pulley. Demonstrates the concept of mechanical advantage.

From The Inventive Child Series.
Prod-POLSKI Dist-EBEC 1983

Ligado Technique C 29 MIN
2 INCH VIDEOTAPE
See series title for descriptive statement.
From The Playing The Guitar I Series.
Prod-KCET Dist-PUBTEL

Ligaments Of The Knee Joint, The Pathophysiology C 20 MIN
3/4 OR 1/2 INCH VIDEO CASSETTE
Demonstrates the origins of knew instability preceded by explanation of the control functions of ligaments and semilunar cartilages.
Prod-SPRVER Dist-SPRVER

Ligation And Stripping Of Varicose Veins C 23 MIN
16MM FILM OPTICAL SOUND PRO
Demonstrates a malleable stripper with detachable stripper heads. Illustrates the normal venous return and the disturbance found in varicose veins.
Prod-ACYDGD Dist-ACY 1961

Ligation And Stripping Treatment Of Varicose Veins, The C 22 MIN
16MM FILM OPTICAL SOUND PRO
Shows the operative technique of the high sapheno femoral ligation together with the actual stripping technique.
Prod-ACYDGD Dist-ACY 1952

Light C 10 MIN
16MM FILM, 3/4 OR 1/2 IN VIDEO I-C A
Explains that light is the phenomenon which makes visual experience possible. Shows how different kinds of light can change people's perceptions of the world. Discusses light as an important element in art. Illustrates ways in which artists have used light to achieve their expressive purposes.
From The Art Of Seeing Series.
Prod-AFA Dist-FI 1969

Light C 15 MIN
3/4 OR 1/2 INCH VIDEO CASSETTE K-J
See series title for descriptive statement.
From The Arts Express Series.
Prod-KYTV Dist-KYTV 1983

Light C 18 MIN
1 INCH VIDEOTAPE
Features the world of light--its uses, beauty and effect on man.
Prod-GE Dist-MTP

Light - A First Film C 13 MIN
16MM FILM, 3/4 OR 1/2 IN VIDEO P-I
Explores the pervasiveness of light as the basic form of energy, including its manifestations and transformations.
Prod-BFA Dist-PHENIX 1982

Light - Light And Shadows C 15 MIN
3/4 OR 1/2 INCH VIDEO CASSETTE P
Presents Mr Featherby who tells a story about a town that thought it was being terrorized by monsters. Shows how Captain Light finds that the culprits are shadows.
From The Featherby's Fables Series.
Prod-WVUTTV Dist-GPITVL 1983

Light - Play Black, White, Gray B 6 MIN
16MM FILM OPTICAL SOUND
Illustrates the forms and relationships of the constructivist art of Moholy-nagy, leading exponent of modern design for architecture, painting, typography and theatre.
Prod-MOHOLY Dist-RADIM

Light - The Sun Is The Source C 15 MIN
3/4 OR 1/2 INCH VIDEO CASSETTE P
Presents Captain Light who explains why plants need sunlight and comes to the rescue of campers and miners with his flashlight and candle.
From The Featherby's Fables Series.
Prod-WVUTTV Dist-GPITVL 1983

Light - Transparent, Translucent, Opaque C 15 MIN
3/4 OR 1/2 INCH VIDEO CASSETTE P
Tells how Captain Light is called upon to apprehend whoever has been stealing all man-made light sources in the Kingdom of Lightonia.
From The Featherby's Fables Series.
Prod-WVUTTV Dist-GPITVL 1983

Light - Wave And Quantum Theories C 13 MIN
16MM FILM, 3/4 OR 1/2 IN VIDEO J-H
Introduces the accepted theory of light as consisting of both a wave motion and of discrete bundles or quanta of energy. Performs the Young's double-slit experiment to show the wave character of light. Discusses the photoelectric and Compton effects.
Prod-CORF Dist-CORF 1961

Light All About Us (2nd Ed) C 10 MIN
16MM FILM, 3/4 OR 1/2 IN VIDEO P-I
Presents everyday and decorative uses of light to stimulate youngsters to follow an inductive path of discovery about the sources of light beams and their behavior.
Prod-CORF Dist-CORF 1972

Light And Color C 14 MIN
16MM FILM, 3/4 OR 1/2 IN VIDEO I
Shows how some colors seem to soak up light while others reflect it. A color wheel is used to illustrate the difference between light and color. Explains how scientists use color to identify elements.
Prod-EBF Dist-EBEC 1961

Light And Color C 15 MIN
3/4 OR 1/2 INCH VIDEO CASSETTE P-I
Discusses light and color.
From The Why Series.
Prod-WDCNTV Dist-AITECH 1976

Light And Color (Spanish) C 14 MIN
16MM FILM, 3/4 OR 1/2 IN VIDEO I-J
Explains what color is, how color is related to light, why a certain color looks the way it does, and the role color plays in the identification of chemical elements.
Prod-EBEC Dist-EBEC

Light And Easy, Pt 1 - A Measure Of Responsibility C 20 MIN
3/4 OR 1/2 INCH VIDEO CASSETTE J-H A
Presents Graham Kerr of 'Galloping Gourmet' fame, highlighting four factors he believes should be considered in planning menus. Includes aroma and emotion, nutrition, budget and effort.
Prod-CUETV Dist-CUNIV 1975

Light And Easy, Pt 2 - Elegant Low-Calorie Foods C 30 MIN
3/4 OR 1/2 INCH VIDEO CASSETTE J-H A
Presents Graham Kerr demonstrating techniques used to achieve specific nutrition and low-calorie dishes that have a gourmet touch.
Prod-CUETV Dist-CUNIV 1975

Light And Heat C 15 MIN
3/4 OR 1/2 INCH VIDEO CASSETTE P-I
Discusses the characteristics of light and heat.
From The Why Series.
Prod-WDCNTV Dist-AITECH 1976

Light And Its Relation To Color C 20 MIN
16MM FILM OPTICAL SOUND
Demonstrates different sources of light and how light can be modified by transparent, translucent, or opaque materials or by reflection, transmission or absorption. Visualizes the wave theory of light and shows how light is refracted when it enters a transparent material denser than air.
LC NO. 77-700049
Prod-ACA Dist-ACA 1977

Light And Lenses C 10 MIN
16MM FILM, 3/4 OR 1/2 IN VIDEO J-C
Uses diagrams and everyday examples from experience in order to show the basic properties of light and to describe how the application of various optical systems is used for photographic purposes.
Prod-KVH Dist-JOU 1973

Light And Life, Pt 1 C 30 MIN
3/4 OR 1/2 INCH VIDEO CASSETTE J-H
Presents Professor Porter, using ancient fossil-bearing rocks, demonstrating that living organisms existed as long as three billion years ago.
From The Natural History Of A Sunbeam Series.
Prod-KINGFT Dist-KINGFT

Light And Life, Pt 2 C 30 MIN
3/4 OR 1/2 INCH VIDEO CASSETTE J-H
States that from the simplest bacterium to the largest elephant, the nature of every organism is determined by a mere 24 molecules. Explains why living things were finally able to crawl out of the sea.
From The Natural History Of A Sunbeam Series.
Prod-KINGFT Dist-KINGFT

Light And Objects C 10 MIN
3/4 OR 1/2 INCH VIDEO CASSETTE
From The Nan Hoover - Selected Works I Series.
Prod-EAI Dist-EAI

Light And Shadow B 22 MIN
16MM FILM OPTICAL SOUND H
Examines the assumption that light travels in straight lines and shows how sharp and diffuse shadows are formed and their relevance to the eclipse of the sun. Shows the construction and action of a pinhole camera and the construction and purpose of a simple ray-box.
From The Optics Series.
Prod-CETO Dist-GPITVL

Light And Shadow C 7 MIN
16MM FILM, 3/4 OR 1/2 IN VIDEO K-I
Experiments with shadows explain where the earth gets its light, what daytime and nighttime are, and the nature of a shadow.
From The Science Series.
Prod-MORLAT Dist-SF 1967

Light And Shadow Techniques C 15 MIN
2 INCH VIDEOTAPE
See series title for descriptive statement.
From The Charlie's Pad Series.
Prod-WSIU Dist-PUBTEL

Light And Shadows C 14 MIN
3/4 OR 1/2 INCH VIDEO CASSETTE P
Gives experience in observing light and shadows.
From The Hands On, Grade 2 - Lollipops, Loops, Etc Series. Unit 1 - Observing
Prod-WHROTV Dist-AITECH 1975

Light And Sight B 22 MIN
16MM FILM OPTICAL SOUND H
Shows what happens when we 'SEE' an object and explains the difference between luminous and non-luminous objects. Presents the student with an overall view of the general properties of light including the concept of light as a form of energy.
From The Optics Series.
Prod-CETO Dist-GPITVL

Light And What It Does X 11 MIN
16MM FILM, 3/4 OR 1/2 IN VIDEO P
Demonstrates how light is reflected and refracted, how it travels, how it is affected by different materials and how it is used in daily activities. Shows boys experimenting with a camera.
Prod-EBF Dist-EBEC 1963

Light And What It Does (Spanish) C 11 MIN
16MM FILM, 3/4 OR 1/2 IN VIDEO P
Demonstrates how light travels, how it is affected by different materials, what causes reflection and refraction and how light is used in many activities.
Prod-EBEC Dist-EBEC

Light Beam Named Ray, A C 20 MIN
16MM FILM, 3/4 OR 1/2 IN VIDEO
Uses an animated light beam 'RAY' to explain the fundamentals of light, color and optics. Discusses the invisible neighbors of light and introduces the superlight and the laser beam. Covers sources of light, reflection, heliograph, refraction, shortsightedness and farsightedness, prisms, the color spectrum, the color wheel and white light.
Prod-HANDEL Dist-HANDEL 1973

Light Beam Named Ray, A (Captioned) C 20 MIN
16MM FILM, 3/4 OR 1/2 IN VIDEO
Uses an animated light beam 'RAY' to explain the fundamentals of light, color and optics. Discusses the invisible neighbors of light and introduces the superlight and the laser beam. Covers sources of light, reflection, heliograph, refraction, shortsightedness and farsightedness, prisms, the color spectrum, the color wheel and white light.
Prod-HANDEL Dist-HANDEL 1973

Light Bulb, The C 5 MIN
16MM FILM, 3/4 OR 1/2 IN VIDEO K-C A
See series title for descriptive statement.
From The How It's Made Series.
Prod-HOLIA Dist-LUF

Light Bulbs And The American Consumer C 15 MIN
16MM FILM, 3/4 OR 1/2 IN VIDEO
Tells how to select the proper light bulbs for each residential application.
Prod-KLEINW Dist-KLEINW

Light Energy B 30 MIN
2 INCH VIDEOTAPE J
See series title for descriptive statement.
From The Investigating The World Of Science, Unit 1 - Matter And Energy Series.
Prod-MPATI Dist-GPITVL

Light Experiments B 15 MIN
2 INCH VIDEOTAPE P
See series title for descriptive statement.
From The Just Inquisitive Series. No. 28
Prod-EOPS Dist-GPITVL Prodn-KOACTV

Light Fantastick, The C 58 MIN
16MM FILM OPTICAL SOUND J-C A
Discusses the use of animation and animation techniques.
LC NO. 76-702442
Prod-NFBC Dist-NFBC 1974

Light For Debra, A C 27 MIN
3/4 INCH VIDEO CASSETTE
Presents an overview of the use of behavior modification through reinforcement as a tool to aid in concept, academic task and social development of the severely mentally retarded child.
LC NO. 79-706103
Prod-USBEH Dist-USNAC Prodn-USBEH 1979

Light For John, A B 22 MIN
16MM FILM OPTICAL SOUND
Two days in the lives of a stout, retarded man and his worrying mother are revealed. Shows the Depression and the hopelessness faced by both parties.
LC NO. FIA59-308
Prod-USC Dist-USC 1956

Light From Heaven X 17 MIN
16MM FILM OPTICAL SOUND J-H T R
Presents the story of Saul of Tarsus and the stoning of Stephen. Reassures Christians on the firmness of their hope in Christ and shows sinners that everyone can be saved by Christ.
From The Book Of Acts Series.
Prod-BROADM Dist-FAMF 1957

Light From The North - Durer And Bosch, Religious Paintings C 45 MIN
2 INCH VIDEOTAPE
See series title for descriptive statement.
From The Humanities Series. Unit III - The Realm Of Idea And Speculation
Prod-WTTWTV Dist-GPITVL

Light From Within C 30 MIN
3/4 OR 1/2 INCH VIDEO CASSETTE J-H
Examines the trend toward graphic experimentation in photography.
From The Developing Image Series.
Prod-CTI Dist-CTI

Light Here Kindled, The C 26 MIN
16MM FILM, 3/4 OR 1/2 IN VIDEO I-H
Re-creates the Pilgrims' journey to the New World and their struggle for survival after they arrive.
Prod-IFB Dist-IFB 1966

Light In The Darkness, A B 33 MIN
16MM FILM OPTICAL SOUND
Presents the story of Red Cross peacetime activities around the world.
Prod-LRCSF Dist-AMRC 1964

Light In The Sea C 30 MIN
3/4 OR 1/2 INCH VIDEO CASSETTE
Discusses the importance of the light that penetrates the ocean to life on earth. Looks at the physical factors that influence the penetration of light in the sea.
From The Oceanus - The Marine Environment Series. Lesson 21
Prod-SCCON Dist-CDTEL

Light Is Many Things C 12 MIN
16MM FILM, 3/4 OR 1/2 IN VIDEO P-J
Shows a group of children experimenting, observing and discovering light in classroom and outdoor activities. Explores the dimensions of light.
Prod-FILLIP Dist-BARR 1977

Light Motif C 4 MIN
16MM FILM OPTICAL SOUND
Shows light patterns which are variations of the sphere.
LC NO. 76-703067
Prod-CANFDC Dist-CANFDC 1975

Light Of Day, The C 9 MIN
16MM FILM OPTICAL SOUND
Shows how color and daylight change in the environment from dawn through evening, in the city and the country.
LC NO. 73-701040
Prod-FILMSM Dist-FILMSM 1972

Light Of Experience, The C 52 MIN
16MM FILM, 3/4 OR 1/2 IN VIDEO J-C A
Surveys the development of Western civilization during the 17th century. Points out that the works of the Dutch painters, including Rembrandt, Frans Hals, Vermeer and Saenredam, show the revolutionary change in thought that replaced divine authority with experience, experiment and observation.
From The Civilisation Series. No. 8
LC NO. 79-707048
Prod-BBCTV Dist-FI 1970

Light Of Faith C 33 MIN
16MM FILM, 3/4 OR 1/2 IN VIDEO J-C A
Stars Lon Chaney and Hope Hampton in an updated variation of the Holy Grail legend.
Prod-HHP Dist-PHENIX 1922

Light Of India B 80 MIN
16MM FILM OPTICAL SOUND
Presents the story of Gyandev, an outcast child who became one of India's great religious teachers. Features Indian spiritual music and religious songs.
Prod-FINDIA Dist-FINDIA

Light Of The 21st Century C 57 MIN
16MM FILM, 3/4 OR 1/2 IN VIDEO H-C A
Investigates the use of lasers in the fields of medicine, dentistry, construction and communication. Explores possible developments in the use of lasers.
From The Nova Series.
LC NO. 79-708135
Prod-WGBHTV Dist-TIMLIF 1978

Light On Lasers C 24 MIN
3/4 OR 1/2 INCH VIDEO CASSETTE H-C
Defines the theory and construction of lasers in terms of the physical transitions or changes of the energy states of the atoms of lasing material and the optical geometry of the laser itself. Describes wide range of laser applications. Uses animated and computer graphics.
From The Discovering Physics Series.
Prod-BBCTV Dist-MEDIAG Prodn-OPENU 1983

Light On The Mountain C 20 MIN
16MM FILM OPTICAL SOUND J-C A
Shows senior Girl Scouts from all over the United States at a roundup in Idaho. A cinema verite presentation of the behavior, the attitudes and the conversation of senior Girl Scouts from all over the United States. Without narration.
LC NO. FIA66-357
Prod-GSUSA Dist-GSUSA 1965

Light Opera C 3 MIN
16MM FILM OPTICAL SOUND H-C A
Presents an experiment in the manipulation of light over a mylar surface in relation to a musical score.
LC NO. 79-700121
Prod-USC Dist-USC 1979

Light Relections C 15 MIN
16MM FILM OPTICAL SOUND
Studies the unusual effects obtained by moving, changing patterns of multi-colored lights and abstract mobiles.
Prod-DAVISJ Dist-RADIM

Light Scattering C 39 MIN
3/4 OR 1/2 INCH VIDEO CASSETTE
See series title for descriptive statement.
From The Colloid And Surface Chemistry - Lyophilic Colloids Series.
Prod-KALMIA Dist-KALMIA

Light Scattering B 39 MIN
3/4 OR 1/2 INCH VIDEO CASSETTE
See series title for descriptive statement.
From The Colloids And Surface Chemistry - Lyophilic Colloids Series.
Prod-MIOT Dist-MIOT

Light Shines In The Darkness, A C 22 MIN
16MM FILM OPTICAL SOUND I A
Portrays the events from the Crucifixion through the Ascension climaxing the day of the Pentecost.
Prod-CAFM Dist-CAFM

Light Stage, Cinema, Radio, TV C 30 MIN
3/4 OR 1/2 INCH VIDEO CASSETTE C
Discusses black trends on the light stage, cinema, radio and television.
From The Afro-American Perspectives Series.
Prod-MDDE Dist-MDCPB

Light To Freedom, A C 20 MIN
16MM FILM OPTICAL SOUND
Examines how the Canadian Salvation Army deals with juvenile delinquency, alcoholism, old age and prostitution.
LC NO. FIA68-1374
Prod-SALVA Dist-SALVA Prodn-MORLAT

Light Waltz, A C 5 MIN
16MM FILM OPTICAL SOUND
Shows the manufacture of lights, accompanied by the music of Strauss.
LC NO. 78-701491
Prod-WEBC Dist-WEBC Prodn-SCRESC 1978

Light Waves B 22 MIN
16MM FILM OPTICAL SOUND H
Offers the student some evidence that light does travel as waves. Shows the reflection of waves in a ripple tank to be in accordance with the laws of reflection derived from the observed behavior of light. Includes demonstrations of the diffraction of light and young's fringes to show that the behavior of light accords with the demonstrations of diffraction and interference in the ripple tank.
From The Optics Series.
Prod-CETO Dist-GPITVL

Light-Play, Black-White-Gray B 6 MIN
16MM FILM OPTICAL SOUND C
Moholy-nagy, an exponent of modern design, illustrates the forms and relationships of his constructivist art. Figures of glass, steel and wire move, merge and dissolve in interrelated shapes and patterns.
Prod-MOHOLY Dist-RADIM 1951

Light-Sensitive Materials C 22 MIN
16MM FILM OPTICAL SOUND
Discusses physics of light and color, and the classification and composition of light-sensitive materials.
From The Fundamentals Of Photography Series.
LC NO. FIE52-1352
Prod-USN Dist-USNAC Prodn-LNS 1948

Light, Dark And Daumier C 29 MIN
2 INCH VIDEOTAPE
See series title for descriptive statement.
From The Museum Open House Series.
Prod-WGBHTV Dist-PUBTEL

Light, Lenses And The Image C 17 MIN
3/4 OR 1/2 INCH VIDEO CASSETTE PRO
Presents basic properties of lenses and their effects upon light in order to form an image on the retina. Explains the concepts of convergence and divergence. Discusses the effects of convex and concave lenses upon light rays and the ability of the lens to increase its power through the process of accomodation.
Prod-UMICHM Dist-UMICHM 1976

Light, Part 5 C 20 MIN
16MM FILM OPTICAL SOUND H-C A
Presents a 1971 dance choreographed by Kei Takei in which a trio performs slow, liquid movements in an isolated pool of light.
LC NO. 78-701820
Prod-DANCE Dist-DANCE 1976

Lighter Than Air C 14 MIN
16MM FILM OPTICAL SOUND
Focuses on the history of balloons and dirigibles. Shows how they are used in the 1980's.
From The Screen News Digest Series. Volume 23, Issue 4
Prod-HEARST Dist-HEARST 1980

Lighter-Than-Air History - The Rigid Airship B 45 MIN
3/4 OR 1/2 INCH VIDEO CASSETTE
Examines the development of the airship between 1900 and 1947.
Prod-IHF Dist-IHF

Lighthouse That Never Fails, The C 8 MIN
16MM FILM OPTICAL SOUND
Uses comedy to describe space flight.
Prod-THIOKL Dist-THIOKL 1961

Lighting C 30 MIN
3/4 OR 1/2 INCH VIDEO CASSETTE
Demonstrates how to repair lighting.
From The You Can Fixit Series.
Prod-WRJATV Dist-MDCPB

Lighting And Composition C 30 MIN
3/4 OR 1/2 INCH VIDEO CASSETTE H-C A
Explains the principles of composition in photographing still-life subjects in a controlled studio situation. Demonstrates the concept of depth of focus at a Normandy chateau and the challenge of photographing a wedding at an English village church.
From The What A Picture - The Complete Photography Course By John Hedgecoe Series. Program 3
Prod-THREMI Dist-FI

Lighting And Staging Techniques For Television C 100 MIN
3/4 OR 1/2 INCH VIDEO CASSETTE
Provides step-by-step instruction to visually exemplify the most current lighting and staging techniques essential for top quality television pictures.
Prod-FIOREN Dist-FIOREN

Lighting Application For Video C 30 MIN
3/4 OR 1/2 INCH VIDEO CASSETTE
Provides the theory, rules and principles of video lighting. Demonstrates the creative use of backlighting, proper placement of lights and subjects on location and in the studies. Questions 'flat video lighting' precepts.
From The Video - A Practical Guide...and More Series.
Prod-VIPUB Dist-VIPUB

Lighting Techniques For New Sets C 50 MIN
3/4 OR 1/2 INCH VIDEO CASSETTE
Demonstrates how to meet the special needs of TV sets specifically designed for news and weather programming.
Prod-FIOREN Dist-FIOREN

Lightning And Precipitation Static - Causes And Effects On Aircraft - Damage And Protection C 15 MIN
16MM FILM OPTICAL SOUND
Deals with the causes of lightning and precipitation static and tells their effect on aircraft. Focuses on damage and protection.
LC NO. 74-706484
Prod-USN Dist-USNAC 1972

Lightning And Precipitation Static - Causes And Effects On Aircraft - Flash And Glow C 19 MIN
16MM FILM OPTICAL SOUND
Deals with the causes of lightning and precipitation static and tells their effect on aircraft. Focuses on flash and glow.
LC NO. 74-706485
Prod-USN Dist-USNAC 1972

Lightning And Precipitation Static - Causes And Effects On Aircraft - Future Aircraft... C 6 MIN
16MM FILM OPTICAL SOUND
Deals with the causes of lightning and precipitation static and tells their effect on aircraft. Focuses on aircraft design problems.
LC NO. 74-706486
Prod-USN Dist-USNAC 1972

Lightning And Precipitation Static - Causes And Effects On Aircraft - Research... C 9 MIN
16MM FILM OPTICAL SOUND
Deals with the causes of lightning and precipitation static and tells their effect on aircraft. Focuses on research development and testing.
LC NO. 74-706487
Prod-USN Dist-USNAC 1972

Lightning And Thunder C 14 MIN
16MM FILM, 3/4 OR 1/2 IN VIDEO I
Demonstrates the time lapse between a lightning flash and the thunder that follows. Uses experiments with static electricity to show the cause of lightning. Shows safety practices against injury by lightning.
Prod-CORF Dist-CORF 1967

Lightning And Thunder Case, The C 14 MIN
16MM FILM, 3/4 OR 1/2 IN VIDEO P
Demystifies the often-terrifying electrical storm and offers a set of safety rules for avoiding the dangers of lightning and thunder.
From The Simply Scientific Series.
Prod-LCOA Dist-LCOA Prodn-MBROS 1981

Lightning Does Strike Twice C 24 MIN
3/4 OR 1/2 INCH VIDEO CASSETTE H-C
Describes some of the physical mechanisms responsible for the electrostatic charging of thunderclouds and the resulting precipitation and electrical lightning discharges. Uses animation to show conducting paths preceding lightning strikes and what to do about lightning.
From The Discovering Physics Series.
Prod-BBCTV Dist-MEDIAG Prodn-OPENU 1983

Lightning Rod Man, The C 16 MIN
16MM FILM, 3/4 OR 1/2 IN VIDEO J-C A
Presents an adaptation of the short story by Herman Melville.
Prod-DECHJ Dist-PFP 1975

Lightning Rod Thief, The C 10 MIN
16MM FILM, 3/4 OR 1/2 IN VIDEO K-P
Uses animation to tell the story of a thief who only steals lightning rods.
Prod-CAROUF Dist-CAROUF

Lightning War In The Middle East B 14 MIN
16MM FILM OPTICAL SOUND
Traces the roots of unrest that burst into conflict between Israel and Egypt in the lightning war of 1967.
From The Screen News Digest Series. Vol 10, Issue 1
LC NO. FIA68-1654
Prod-HEARST Dist-HEARST 1967

Lights Have Limits B 5 MIN
16MM FILM OPTICAL SOUND J
Shows the blinding effect of high beam lights and the limitation of low beam lights. Tackles the problem of overdriving the headlights.
From The Driver Education Series.
LC NO. FIA66-1005
Prod-AMROIL Dist-AMROIL 1964

Lights Running And Anchor B 18 MIN
16MM FILM OPTICAL SOUND
Shows inland and international rules for color of lights, position and visibility for masthead, side, range and anchor lights and lights displayed by vessels being overtaken.
LC NO. FIE52-933
Prod-USN Dist-USNAC 1944

Lights, Action, Africa C 55 MIN
16MM FILM, 3/4 OR 1/2 IN VIDEO

Portrays how photographers Joan and Alan Root photograph such unpredictable animals as cobras, wildebeests and hippos.
Prod-ROOTA Dist-BNCHMK 1983

Lights, Action, Camera B 15 MIN
2 INCH VIDEOTAPE K-P
See series title for descriptive statement.
From The Magic Of Words Series.
Prod-GWTVAI Dist-GPITVL Prodn-WETATV

Lights, Camera, Lettuce C 28 MIN
16MM FILM OPTICAL SOUND
Deals with the growing, harvesting, packing, care, preparation and varied uses of lettuce.
LC NO. 74-700546
Prod-MTP Dist-MTP 1973

Lights, Vessels Being Towed C 10 MIN
16MM FILM OPTICAL SOUND
Gives inland light rules for barges and canal boats, scow barges, scows and nondescript vessels in New York harbor area and dump scows in new York harbor.
LC NO. FIE52-936
Prod-USN Dist-USNAC 1943

Like A Rose B 23 MIN
16MM FILM OPTICAL SOUND
Focuses on the lonely and frustrating existence of two women currently serving 25-year sentences in the Missouri State Penitentiary.
LC NO. 75-703518
Prod-TOMATO Dist-TOMATO 1975

Like Any Child Only More So C 29 MIN
16MM FILM, 3/4 OR 1/2 IN VIDEO C A
Profiles three families with children labeled as hyperactive. Presents the complex emotional, medical and environmental possibilities that may influence a child's behavior. Shows troublesome symptoms of hyperactivity as well as problems resulting from misunderstanding and mistreating the symptoms.
Prod-ALLORN Dist-UCEMC 1978

Like Cats And Dogs C 23 MIN
3/4 OR 1/2 INCH VIDEO CASSETTE
Focuses on bobcats and coyotes and how different they are from domestic pets, but how much they are the same.
Prod-NWLDPR Dist-NWLDPR

Like Coming To A New World C 17 MIN
16MM FILM OPTICAL SOUND
Presents post-war migrants describing their lives in Australia.
LC NO. 80-701570
Prod-NESWE Dist-TASCOR 1979

Like Everybody Else C 32 MIN
16MM FILM, 3/4 OR 1/2 IN VIDEO H-C A S
Documents the life of the retarded adult in the community, showing a model program for achieving integration of retarded adults in society.
Prod-JLA Dist-STNFLD 1976

Like Father, Like Son C 15 MIN
3/4 OR 1/2 INCH VIDEO CASSETTE I-J
Tells the story of a boy whose father is a problem drinker.
From The Jackson Junior High Series.
Prod-EFLMC Dist-GPITVL

Like Father, Like Son C 15 MIN
16MM FILM, 3/4 OR 1/2 IN VIDEO J
Shows how a son tries to approach the problem of alcoholism with his father, who is a problem drinker. Suggests methods of rehabilitation and sources of help.
From The Jackson Junior High Series.
Prod-USOLLR Dist-USNAC Prodn-NVETA 1976

Like It Is - The Environment Of Poverty, Pt 1 B 30 MIN
16MM FILM OPTICAL SOUND T
Depicts the degenerating environment of poverty and how it warps and eventually destroys the human resources trapped in it. Reveals that a fouled environment not only impairs the physical fate of future generations, but also systematically infests and rots hearts, minds, values and hopes, dooming the poor even before they are born.
Prod-MLA Dist-MLA

Like It Is - The Environment Of Poverty, Pt 2 B 30 MIN
16MM FILM OPTICAL SOUND T
Depicts the degenerating environment of poverty and how it warps and eventually destroys the human resources trapped in it. Reveals that a fouled environment not only impairs the physical fate of future generations, but also systematically infests and rots hearts, minds, values and hopes, dooming the poor even before they are born.
Prod-MLA Dist-MLA

Like It Is - The Environment Of Poverty, Pt 3 B 23 MIN
16MM FILM OPTICAL SOUND T
Depicts the degenerating environment of poverty and how it warps and eventually destroys the human resources trapped in it. Reveals that a fouled environment not only impairs the physical fate of future generations, but also systematically infests and rots hearts, minds, values and hopes, dooming the poor even before they are born.
Prod-MLA Dist-MLA

Like It Is—A Series

Deals with various issues involving minorities.
Prod-OHC Dist-HRC

Assertive Learning 029 MIN
Brown, Tony - Black Perspective On The News 030 MIN
Carmichael, Stokely 029 MIN
Cunningham, Reverend J F 029 MIN
Evans, Dr Thurman, M D 029 MIN
Gillespie, Marcia Ann 028 MIN
Green, Dr Robert 029 MIN
Hollis, Meldon 030 MIN
Johnson, Minnie 029 MIN
Jones, Dr Johnny 029 MIN
McGee, James / Dale Bertch 029 MIN
Mitchell, Parren 029 MIN
Moss, Reverend Otis 029 MIN
Page, Dr Joyce 029 MIN
Poussaint, Alvin 030 MIN
Robinson, Wilhemena 029 MIN
Survival Of The Black College 029 MIN
Wesley, Charles 029 MIN
Whitley, Joyce 029 MIN
Williams, Robert 029 MIN

Like Ordinary Children C 25 MIN
16MM FILM, 3/4 OR 1/2 IN VIDEO H-C A
Presents the viewpoint of a normal fourteen-year-old girl who visits handicapped children each week and contrasts it with those of a bright thirteen-year-old girl who has been handicapped since birth with a spinal deformity, Spina Bifida. Conveys the feelings and difficulties of the handicapped and of those who meet them.
Prod-THAMES Dist-MEDIAG 1973

Like Other People C 37 MIN
16MM FILM, 3/4 OR 1/2 IN VIDEO H-C A
Deals with the sexual and emotional needs of the physically and mentally handicapped, especially with sexual sensitivities. Raises questions about the quality of life for the handicapped, about privacy and about understanding other people.
LC NO. 74-702340
Prod-DIDTFL Dist-PEREN 1973

Like The Wind C 59 MIN
3/4 INCH VIDEO CASSETTE
Examines individual religious experience in America. Presents the stories of five people from different religious backgrounds who all share a deep spiritual commitment.
Prod-PPTN Dist-PUBTEL

Like You, Like Me—A Series
16MM FILM, 3/4 OR 1/2 IN VIDEO K-P
Presents animated short stories about events in the lives of handicapped children.
Prod-EBEC Dist-EBEC 1977

Doing Things Together - A Child With A 006 MIN
Everyone Needs Some Help - A Child With 007 MIN
I Can Do It - A Child With Double Braces 006 MIN
It's Up To Me - A Child With Asthma 007 MIN
Let Me Try - A Mentally Retarded Child 006 MIN
Let's Be Friends - An Emotionally Disturbed 006 MIN
Let's Talk It Over - A Child With Epilepsy 006 MIN
See What I Feel - A Blind Child 006 MIN
When I Grow Up - Career Aspirations 006 MIN
Why Me - An Orthopedically Handicapped Child 007 MIN

Like-Getting Out C 19 MIN
16MM FILM OPTICAL SOUND H
Points out that getting out of high school and getting a job does not release a young person from supervision and routine. Stresses the importance of further education or training in order to achieve a challenging and interesting life.
Prod-OSSHE Dist-OSSHE

Liking Me - Building Self-Confidence C
3/4 OR 1/2 INCH VIDEO CASSETTE I-J
Examines the concept of self-esteem and its importance in school performance, in resisting peer pressure, and in coping with life. Includes teacher's guide.
Prod-SUNCOM Dist-SUNCOM

Lila C 28 MIN
16MM FILM OPTICAL SOUND
Examines the life of Lila Bonner-Miller, who at 80 is still active as a church leader, psychiatrist, artist and great-grandmother.
LC NO. 80-701329
Prod-IDIM Dist-IDIM 1980

Lilac Time B 27 MIN
16MM FILM OPTICAL SOUND
Presents Colleen Moore and Gary Cooper in a melodrama of World War I pilots.
From The History Of The Motion Picture Series.
Prod-SF Dist-KILLIS

Lilies Grow Wild C 16 MIN
16MM FILM OPTICAL SOUND
Presents a drama about the unsuccessful effort of a new teacher to impose discipline on an unruly student. Relates her discovery that love and personal attention are stronger than force.
LC NO. 80-700426
Prod-BYU Dist-BYU 1980

Lilies Of Japan C 28 MIN
16MM FILM OPTICAL SOUND
Explains that the Japanese have always felt a close affinity with nature and this is especially true with flowers. Points out that the lily is one flower which grows in abundance throughout Japan. Depicts the many different kinds of lilies which grow in Japan and the significance of this flower in the daily lives of the people.
Prod-UNIJAP Dist-UNIJAP 1969

Lillehei On Stagnant Shock C 21 MIN
16MM FILM OPTICAL SOUND PRO
Presents visual evidence to support the concept of treating shock with vasodilators, rather than vasopressors, by utilizing cinemicrography of the mesentary microcirculation in living animals. Includes a demonstration of the step-by-step management of a patient in stagnant endotoxin shock secondary t abortion.
From The Upjohn Vanguard Of Medicine Series.
LC NO. 73-702448
Prod-UPJOHN Dist-UPJOHN Prodn-UTEXMB 196

Lillies Grow Wild C 16 MI
16MM FILM OPTICAL SOUND J-H
Emphasizes that everyone is important. Shows how a rebelliou boy is affected positively by the love and attention of a teache
LC NO. 80-700426
Prod-BYU Dist-EBEC 198

Lillith Summer C
16MM FILM, 3/4 OR 1/2 IN VIDEO I
Tells the story of an unlikely friendship between a young girl an an old woman. Shows their developing understanding and ac cetance of the many stages of life. Based on the novel by Irwi Hadley.
Prod-PAR Dist-AIMS 198

Lily - A Story About A Girl Like Me C 14 MI
16MM FILM, 3/4 OR 1/2 IN VIDEO
Portrays a Downs Syndrome child who has been mainstreame in regular classrooms.
From The Special Education Series.
Prod-DAVFMS Dist-DAVFMS

Lima Family B 19 MI
16MM FILM OPTICAL SOUND
Depicts a day in the lives of the members of an upper class famil of Lima, capital of Peru. Points out similarities to a family of th same class in the United States.
LC NO. FIE52-719
Prod-UWF Dist-USOIAA 194

Limbic System, The, Pt I C 60 MI
3/4 INCH VIDEO CASSETTE PR
Presents terminology, major structures of the limbic lobe and as sociated structures composing the limbic system.
From The Nonbehavioral Sciences And Rehabilitation Series. Part VIII
Prod-AOTA Dist-AOTA 198

Limbic System, The, Pt II C 60 MI
3/4 INCH VIDEO CASSETTE PR
Shows limbic circuitry and function including behavioral sub strates and major limbic system syndromes.
From The Nonbehavioral Sciences And Rehabilitation Series. Part VIII
Prod-AOTA Dist-AOTA 198

Limelight B 145 MI
1/2 IN VIDEO CASSETTE (BETA)
Features Charlie Chaplin as an aging music hall star who be friends a suicidal young dancer.
Prod-UNKNWN Dist-BHAWK 1952

Limericks And Haiku To Share C 15 MI
2 INCH VIDEOTAPE
Recites haiku and limericks and discusses their forms and pat terns.
From The Images Series.
Prod-CVETVC Dist-GPITVL

Limericks For Laughs C 15 MI
3/4 OR 1/2 INCH VIDEO CASSETTE
Uses the limerick to demonstrate the uses of meter, rhyme, repe tition and rhythm in poetry.
From The Tyger, Tyger Burning Bright Series.
Prod-CTI Dist-CTI

Limericks, Epigrams And Occasional Verse C 30 MI
3/4 INCH VIDEO CASSETTE H-C A
Presents George Plimpton and the First Poetry Quartet in a romp through the world of humorous rhyme. Includes works by Dorothy Parker, Hilarie Belloc, Edward Lear, John Betjeman and others.
From The Anyone For Tennyson Series.
Prod-NETCHE Dist-GPITVL

Limestone C 13 MI
16MM FILM, 3/4 OR 1/2 IN VIDEO I-J
Explains and simulates the formation of sedimentary rock, focusing on the importance of limestone as a natural resource. Shows how the rock is quarried and enumerates its major uses.
LC NO. 80-706010
Prod-IU Dist-IU 1978

Limestone - Iowa's Buried Treasure C 26 MI
16MM FILM OPTICAL SOUND
Explains the origin of limestone and shows mining and processing methods. Contrasts present rehabilitation methods with earlier practices, emphasizing the economic importance of limestone and suggesting the compatibility of mining and agriculture.
LC NO. 74-700413
Prod-IOWALP Dist-IOWA 1974

Limestone Legacy, Nature's Gift To Mankind, The C 27 MI
16MM FILM OPTICAL SOUND
Shows the many uses of limestone in construction, agriculture and industry, as well as in the home. Describes the geology and mining of limestone.
LC NO. 76-700378
Prod-MOLPA Dist-UMO Prodn-UMO 1975

Limit C 10 MI
16MM FILM OPTICAL SOUND H-C
Defines limit by the use of neighborhoods and illustrates use of the definition with examples of real valued functions of a single real variable in both continuous and discontinuous cases. An animated film narrated by Robert C Fisher.

From The MAA Calculus Series.
LC NO. 72-703521
Prod-MAA Dist-MLA 1967

Limit Curves And Curves Of Infinite Length C 14 MIN
16MM FILM, 3/4 OR 1/2 IN VIDEO
See series title for descriptive statement.
From The Topology Short Film Series.
LC NO. 81-706245
Prod-NSF Dist-IFB 1979

Limit Surfaces And Space Filling Curves C 11 MIN
16MM FILM, 3/4 OR 1/2 IN VIDEO
See series title for descriptive statement.
From The Topology Short Films Series.
LC NO. 81-706247
Prod-NSF Dist-IFB 1979

Limit Switches, Torque Switches C 60 MIN
3/4 OR 1/2 INCH VIDEO CASSETTE IND
See series title for descriptive statement.
From The Electrtical Maintenance Training, Module 1 - Control Equipment Series.
Prod-LEIKID Dist-LEIKID

Limit Theorems C
3/4 INCH VIDEO CASSETTE
See series title for descriptive statement.
From The Calculus Series.
Prod-MDDE Dist-MDCPB

Limitations C 30 MIN
3/4 OR 1/2 INCH VIDEO CASSETTE H-C A
Reviews the primary problem areas that first-time Pascal users encounter. Goes over list of reasons for choosing Pascal along with major limitations in using Pascal in serious programming environments.
From The Pascal, Pt 2 - Intermediate Pascal Series.
LC NO. 81-706049
Prod-COLOSU Dist-COLOSU 1980

Limitations Of Heat Treatment C 50 MIN
3/4 OR 1/2 INCH VIDEO CASSETTE PRO
Considers the limitations of heat treatment, including cracking and distortion. Explores causes and prevention.
From The Heat Treatment - Metallurgy And Application Series.
Prod-AMCEE Dist-AMCEE

Limited Offer To Purchase C 7 MIN
16MM FILM OPTICAL SOUND
Gives an explanation of the Australian Wool Corporation's 'Limited Offer to Purchase' scheme.
LC NO. 80-700909
Prod-TASCOR Dist-TASCOR 1977

Limits B
16MM FILM OPTICAL SOUND
Discusses aspects of mathematical limits.
Prod-OPENU Dist-OPENU

Limits And Infinity C
3/4 INCH VIDEO CASSETTE
See series title for descriptive statement.
From The Calculus Series.
Prod-MDDE Dist-MDCPB

Limits Of Physical Force C 19 MIN
16MM FILM, 3/4 OR 1/2 IN VIDEO
Explains how, when, and to what extent a police officer may use physical force. Covers topics such as the use and abuse of the police baton, flashlight and gunbelt.
From The Police Civil Liability Series. Part 3
Prod-HAR Dist-MTI Prodn-BAY 1979

Limits To Growth C 30 MIN
16MM FILM, 3/4 OR 1/2 IN VIDEO J-C A
Explores the fact that unless we control our world's population growth, its energy use, food in the Third World and pollution, a catastrophe will occur within this century. According to this study of world economic development, stability can be achieved only when economic growth is ended.
Prod-THAMES Dist-MEDIAG 1972

Limits To Growth, The C 30 MIN
16MM FILM, 3/4 OR 1/2 IN VIDEO J-C A
Explains that overlapping environmental problems have made it almost essential to plan in large units with a strong interdisciplinary approach. Discusses a recent decision by Nassau and Suffolk counties in New York to pool their water-quality information and share computer resources.
From The Man Builds - Man Destroys Series.
Prod-UN Dist-GPITVL

Limits, A Formal Approach C
3/4 INCH VIDEO CASSETTE
See series title for descriptive statement.
From The Calculus Series.
Prod-MDDE Dist-MDCPB

Limits, An Informal Approach C
3/4 INCH VIDEO CASSETTE
See series title for descriptive statement.
From The Calculus Series.
Prod-MDDE Dist-MDCPB

Lincoln C 15 MIN
3/4 INCH VIDEO CASSETTE P
See series title for descriptive statement.
From The Celebrate Series.
Prod-KUONTV Dist-GPITVL 1978

Lincoln - New Capital City, The B 30 MIN
16MM FILM OPTICAL SOUND J-C A
Portrays Nebraska's political and social history epitomized in the development of the city of Lincoln. Discusses the state's internal strife, its admission to the Union in 1867, and Lincoln's 'GOLDEN YEARS.' Shows Lincoln as the home of nationally prominent people.
From The Great Plains Trilogy, 3 Series. Explorer And Settler - The White Man Arrives
Prod-KUONTV Dist-UNEBR 1954

Lincoln - The Kentucky Years C 18 MIN
16MM FILM - 3/4 IN VIDEO
Focuses on Lincoln's birthplace, emphasizing how his background shaped the future President's character. Issued in 1972 as a motion picture.
LC NO. 79-706136
Prod-USNPS Dist-USNAC Prodn-IA 1979

Lincoln - Trial By Fire C 52 MIN
16MM FILM OPTICAL SOUND H-C
Examines the first two years of Abraham Lincoln's Civil War administration. Includes his disagreement with generals over military strategy, a hostile Congress and other problems.
Prod-WOLPER Dist-FI 1974

Lincoln - Trial By Fire, Pt 1 - The Union Besieged (1861-1862) C 26 MIN
16MM FILM OPTICAL SOUND H-C
Examines the first two years of Lincoln's Civil War administration.
Prod-WOLPER Dist-FI 1974

Lincoln - Trial By Fire, Pt 2 - Emancipation Proclamation (1862-1863) C 26 MIN
16MM FILM OPTICAL SOUND H-C
Examines the first two years of Lincoln's Civil War administration.
Prod-WOLPER Dist-FI 1974

Lincoln Center B 12 MIN
16MM FILM OPTICAL SOUND
Explains how 35,000 Puerto Rican families in New York City are driven from their homes to provide a cultural playground for the city's upper classes.
Prod-SFN Dist-SFN

Lincoln Conspiracy, The C 91 MIN
16MM FILM, 3/4 OR 1/2 IN VIDEO J-H A
Provides a step-by-step account of a conspiracy by high level government officials to forcefully remove President Lincoln from office and the successful cover-up of that conspiracy after the assassination. Stars Bradford Dillman and John Dehner.
Prod-LUF Dist-LUF 1979

Lincoln Heritage Trail, The C 28 MIN
16MM FILM OPTICAL SOUND I-C A
Describes scenic highlights of the Lincoln heritage trail, a 993 mile trail through Illinois, Indiana and Kentucky. Shows where Lincoln lived, worked and traveled before he became President. Old photos, daguerrotypes, pen-and-ink sketches, water colors, drawings and modern photos show what life along the trail was like in Lincoln's time and today.
Prod-AMROIL Dist-AMROIL 1964

Lincoln Speeches C 58 MIN
2 INCH VIDEOTAPE
Features Dean Robert A Goldwin of St John's College of Annapolis and three of his students discussing Lincoln Speeches with a special guest.
From The Dialogue Of The Western World Series.
Prod-MDCPB Dist-PUBTEL

Lincoln 200M I G Welding Machine Set-Up C 20 MIN
1/2 IN VIDEO CASSETTE BETA/VHS IND
Explains the set-up for an Air Products M I G 150 wire feed machine.
Prod-RMI Dist-RMI

Lincoln's Gettysburg Address C 15 MIN
16MM FILM, 3/4 OR 1/2 IN VIDEO I-C
Features Charlton Heston.
From The Great American Patriotic Speeches Series.
Prod-EVANSA Dist-AIMS 1973

Linda C 15 MIN
3/4 OR 1/2 INCH VIDEO CASSETTE J-H
Explains how Linda rebels against her family and ends up a fugitive faced with multiple arrest warrants.
From The Changing Series.
Prod-WGTETV Dist-AITECH 1980

Linda - Encounters In The Hospital C 29 MIN
16MM FILM OPTICAL SOUND PRO
Uses the case of a four-year-old girl as she prepares to have major surgery to illustrate how play therapy as instituted at the UCLA Center For The Health Sciences has strong, positive effects on children who suffer emotional stress when coming to the hospital.
LC NO. 75-703048
Prod-UCLA Dist-UCLA 1974

Linda And Billy Ray From Appalachia B 14 MIN
16MM FILM, 3/4 OR 1/2 IN VIDEO I-J
Presents the story of a family who moves from Appalachia to Cincinnati for better job opportunities. Shows how the family has a hard time adjusting to the ways of a big city.
From The Newcomers To The City Series.
Prod-EBEC Dist-EBEC 1970

Linda And Richie's Choice C 15 MIN
3/4 OR 1/2 INCH VIDEO CASSETTE J-C A
Features interviews with kids recovering from drug and alcohol abuse. Stresses standing up to peer pressure.
From The Chemical People Educational Modules Series.
Prod-MTI Dist-MTI

Linda Bechtold, Marlin MacKenzie, Howard Siegal C 30 MIN
3/4 OR 1/2 INCH VIDEO CASSETTE
Focuses on the psychological aspects of dance performance and competition. Features Michael Vernon discussing Beryl Grey. Hosted By Irene Dowd.
From The Eye On Dance - Dancers' Bodies Series.
Prod-ARTRES Dist-ARTRES

Linda Lavin C 1 MIN
3/4 INCH VIDEO CASSETTE
Uses television star Linda Lavin to pose questions about race, religion and ethnicity. Made in a television spot announcement format.
From The ADL Celebrity Spot Series.
Prod-ADL Dist-ADL

Linda Montano C 26 MIN
3/4 OR 1/2 INCH VIDEO CASSETTE
Features an interview with Linda Montano. Presented by Kate Horsfield and Lyn Blumenthal.
Prod-ARTINC Dist-ARTINC

Linda Roberts And Jessica Wolf C 30 MIN
3/4 OR 1/2 INCH VIDEO CASSETTE
Looks at the role of everyday movement habits in chronic injuries.
From The Eye On Dance - Care And Feeding Of Dancers Series.
Prod-ARTRES Dist-ARTRES

Linda Velzey Is Dead C 13 MIN
16MM FILM, 3/4 OR 1/2 IN VIDEO H-C A
Examines the dangers of hitchhiking by telling the story of one hitchhiker who was killed. Originally shown on the CBS television program 60 Minutes.
Prod-CBSNEW Dist-MTI 1979

Linda's Film On Menstruation C 18 MIN
16MM FILM, 3/4 OR 1/2 IN VIDEO J-H
Presents the story of a fifteen-year-old girl who experiences her menstrual period, describing the reaction of the girl and her sixteen-year-old boyfriend as they learn more about the subject of menstruation.
Prod-PHENIX Dist-PHENIX 1974

Line C 15 MIN
3/4 OR 1/2 INCH VIDEO CASSETTE K-J
See series title for descriptive statement.
From The Arts Express Series.
Prod-KYTV Dist-KYTV 1983

Line And Form B 20 MIN
2 INCH VIDEOTAPE I
Shows how by shaping, defining and creating dimensions line carries our eye through all the vast experiences we share in painting, drawing, architecture and nature.
From The For The Love Of Art Series.
Prod-GWTVAI Dist-GPITVL Prodn-WETATV

Line Driver And Receiver Applications, I Basic Systems C 30 MIN
3/4 OR 1/2 INCH VIDEO CASSETTE PRO
Defines various data transmission systems and when and where used. Discusses single ended systems with available integrated circuits.
From The Linear And Interface Circuits, Part II - Interface Integrated Circuits Series.
Prod-TXINLC Dist-TXINLC

Line Drivers And Receivers Applications, II Advanced Systems C 30 MIN
3/4 OR 1/2 INCH VIDEO CASSETTE PRO
Continues applications examples with differential and party-line systems, and advantages and disadvantages of using particular integrated circuits.
From The Linear And Interface Circuits, Part II - Interface Integrated Circuits Series.
Prod-TXINLC Dist-TXINLC

Line Is A Line Is A Line, A B 6 MIN
16MM FILM, 3/4 OR 1/2 IN VIDEO J-C A
Uses lines to create different images while J S Bach's Toccata and Fuge in D Minor is played on a powerful organ. Outlines hundreds of everyday objects, which become witty by being set to overly grand music and by merging into surprisingly dissimilar, yet seemingly logical shapes.
Prod-IFB Dist-IFB 1972

Line Of Apogee C 46 MIN
16MM FILM OPTICAL SOUND
This experimental film pictures the images that occur during a dream.
LC NO. FIA68-149
Prod-WILMLM Dist-FMCOOP 1967

Line Of Balance C 14 MIN
16MM FILM, 3/4 OR 1/2 IN VIDEO IND
Explains the principles and applications of the Line of Balance programming method for the planning and control of production. Shows how the method applies to any production process that involves repetitive or sequential operation.
Prod-WWP Dist-IFB 1973

Line Prints C 15 MIN
3/4 OR 1/2 INCH VIDEO CASSETTE P-I
See series title for descriptive statement.
From The Young At Art Series.
Prod-WSKJTV Dist-AITECH

Line-Up Procedures For Tactical Telegraph Carrier Equipment B 8 MIN
16MM FILM OPTICAL SOUND
Demonstrates the procedures for setting up tactical telegraph carrier equipment for two wire operations and emphasizes various tests to determine its operating efficiency.
LC NO. FIE53-604
Prod-USA Dist-USNAC 1953

Line, The C 13 MIN
16MM FILM OPTICAL SOUND H-C A
Views the first crossing of Australia by the New Standard Gauge Railway Line between Sydney and Perth. Natural sounds and folk music replace narration.
LC NO. 78-709548
Prod-ANAIB Dist-AUIS 1970

Linea De Balance C 14 MIN
16MM FILM, 3/4 OR 1/2 IN VIDEO IND
A Spanish-language version of the motion picture Line Of Balance. Explains the principles and applications of the Line of Balance programming method for the planning and control of production. Shows how the method applies to any production process that involves repetitive or sequential operation.
Prod-WWP Dist-IFB 1973

Lineage, The C 29 MIN
2 INCH VIDEOTAPE
See series title for descriptive statement.
From The Our Street Series.
Prod-MDCPB Dist-PUBTEL

Linear Accelerators In Radiation Therapy, Theory And Operation, Pts 1, 2 And 3 C 42 MIN
3/4 OR 1/2 INCH VIDEO CASSETTE
Introduces the basic components of the Linear Accelerator (LINAC), discusses their functions and describes the technical operation of the LINAC, including microwave cavities.
LC NO. 82-706636
Prod-USDHEW Dist-USNAC 1982

Linear Algebra—A Series
C A
Includes linear equations, matrices, linear transformations, eigenvalues and diagonalization. Emphasizes applications. Contains 35 fifty-minute lectures.
Prod-UIDEEO Dist-UIDEEO

Linear Analog Integrated Circuits Fundamentals And Applications—A Series
IND
Discusses in four modules, including 19 videotapes and 11 demonstrations, basics of complicated linear analog integrated circuits. Provides fundamental building blocks of circuit design as one useful circuit after another is analyzed and discussed.
Prod-COLOSU Dist-COLOSU

Module A - Bipolar Transistor Fundamentals	
Module B - Current Sources And Applications	045 MIN
Module C - The Differential Amplifier	045 MIN
Module D - Class A, B, and AB Output Stages	045 MIN

Linear And Angular Measure C 30 MIN
16MM FILM OPTICAL SOUND C
Introduces fundamental concepts of geometry. Indicates that it is a deductive system. To be used following 'METRIC PROPERTIES OF FIGURES.'
From The Mathematics For Elementary School Teachers Series. No. 16
Prod-SMSG Dist-MLA 1963

Linear And Interface Integrated Circuits, Part I - Linear Integrated Circuits—A Series
PRO
Shows systems designer how to better apply linear and interface circuits technology to his own problems. Discusses circuit technology, defines characteristic and examines advantages and limitations of particular integrated circuits. Provides effective communication of balance, internal matching and compact characteristics of IC technology.
Prod-TXINLC Dist-TXINLC

Comparator Applications	030 MIN
Comparator Design	030 MIN
Linear I/C Techology	030 MIN
New Developments In Operational Amplifiers	030 MIN
Operational Amplifier Applications - I	030 MIN
Operational Amplifier Applications - II	030 MIN
Operational Amplifier Design - I	030 MIN
Operational Amplifier Design - II	030 MIN
Power Amplifier IC Applications	030 MIN
Video And IF Amplifiers	030 MIN

Linear And Interface Integrated Circuits, Part II - Interface...Circuits—A Series
PRO
Shows systems designer how to better apply linear and interface circuits technology to his own problems. Discusses circuit technology, defines characteristics and examines advantages and limitations of particular integrated circuits. Provides effective communication of balance, internal matching and compact characteristics of IC Technology.
Prod-TXINLC Dist-TXINLC

Core Memory Driver Applications	030 MIN
DC Voltage Regulator Design	030 MIN
General Purpose Driver Circuits	030 MIN
Line Driver And Receiver Applications, I	030 MIN
Line Drivers And Receivers Applications, II	030 MIN
Linear IC Technology - I	030 MIN
Linear IC Technology - II	030 MIN
Semiconductor Memory Driver Applications	030 MIN
Sense Amplifiers	030 MIN
Translator Circuits	030 MIN
Voltage Regulator Applications	030 MIN

Linear Circuit Design—A Series
PRO
Covers design of discrete and integrated solid-state circuits for small-signal applications, flow graphs analysis, DC operational and wide-band amplifier design and power amplifier design. Uses classroom format to videotape three one-hour lectures weekly for 15 weeks and 42 cassettes.
Prod-UAZMIC Dist-AMCEE

Linear Continuous Time Dynamical Systems C 42 MIN
3/4 OR 1/2 INCH VIDEO CASSETTE
See series title for descriptive statement.
From The Modern Control Theory - Systems Analysis Series.
Prod-MIOT Dist-MIOT

Linear Differential Equations B
16MM FILM OPTICAL SOUND
Explains how the analogue computer solves a simple differential equation. Discusses the existence and uniqueness theorem for solutions of differential equations.
Prod-OPENU Dist-OPENU

Linear Differential Equations B 35 MIN
3/4 OR 1/2 INCH VIDEO CASSETTE
See series title for descriptive statement.
From The Calculus Of Differential Equations Series.
Prod-MIOT Dist-MIOT

Linear Equations C 30 MIN
3/4 INCH VIDEO CASSETTE C
See series title for descriptive statement.
From The Introduction To Mathematics Series.
Prod-MDCPB Dist-MDCPB

Linear Equations In One Unknown B 30 MIN
16MM FILM OPTICAL SOUND H
Solves two word problems—finding the point of no return in an airplane flight and computing the amount of alcohol needed to produce a certain percentage mixture in an automobile radiator.
From The Advanced Algebra Series.
Prod-CALVIN Dist-MLA Prodn-UNIVFI 1960

Linear Estimation B 44 MIN
3/4 OR 1/2 INCH VIDEO CASSETTE PRO
Introduces linear estimation. Discusses mean-square estimators in this light.
From The Probability And Random Processes - Statistical Averages Series.
Prod-MIOT Dist-MIOT

Linear Fantasy, A C 6 MIN
16MM FILM OPTICAL SOUND
Features a geometric scratch film with designs drawn directly on the surface film and color added.
LC NO. 76-700134
Prod-ABOT Dist-ABOT 1974

Linear First-Order Equations B
16MM FILM OPTICAL SOUND
Shows how the ideas of vector space and vector space morphism can help solve an important problem in calculus.
Prod-OPENU Dist-OPENU

Linear Functions - Rate Of Change Of A Linear Function C 45 MIN
2 INCH VIDEOTAPE
See series title for descriptive statement.
From The Fundamentals Of Mathematics (2nd Ed.) Unit III - Linear And Quadratic Functions Series.
Prod-CHITVC Dist-GPITVL

Linear I/C Technology C 30 MIN
3/4 OR 1/2 INCH VIDEO CASSETTE PRO
Covers general overall technology considerations for all linear IC's including types of devices commonly used, their structures and characteristics.
From The Linear And Interface Integrated Circuits, Part I - Linear Integrated Circuits Series.
Prod-TXINLC Dist-TXINLC

Linear IC Technology - II C 30 MIN
3/4 OR 1/2 INCH VIDEO CASSETTE PRO
Provides background for application of linear art and interface integrated circuits. Includes extension of first session for common devices, more exotic devices such as FET's, current source structures and dialectric isolation structures for complementary devices.
From The Linear And Interface Circuits, Part II - Interface Integrated Circuits Series.
Prod-TXINLC Dist-TXINLC

Linear IC Techology - I C 30 MIN
3/4 OR 1/2 INCH VIDEO CASSETTE PRO
Includes this lesson as a repeat of Part I and should be used by engineers catering the Interface Circuits portion only.
From The Linear And Interface Integrated Circuits, Part II - Interface Integrated Circuits Series.
Prod-TXINLC Dist-TXINLC

Linear Induction Motor Field Tested C 2 MIN
16MM FILM OPTICAL SOUND
Shows how the linear induction motor field is tested for high speed ground transportation.
Prod-ALLFP Dist-NSTA 1973

Linear Inequalities C 30 MIN
3/4 INCH VIDEO CASSETTE C
See series title for descriptive statement.
From The Introduction To Mathematics Series.
Prod-MDCPB Dist-MDCPB

Linear Measurement C 10 MIN
16MM FILM OPTICAL SOUND P-I
Introduces the metric system of measurement. Discusses the shape of the earth, using the earth as a standard, why the metric system is a better system of measuring and the difficulties involved with people in changing to the metric system.
From The Metric System Series.
Prod-SF Dist-SF

Linear Measurement C 12 MIN
3/4 OR 1/2 INCH VIDEO CASSETTE
Covers linear measurement, error, tolerances, measuring devices, scales and rules, scribers and dividers, using and reading a micrometer.
From The Making Measurements Series.
Prod-TPCTRA Dist-TPCTRA

Linear Measurement B 15 MIN
2 INCH VIDEOTAPE P
See series title for descriptive statement.
From The Just Inquisitive Series. No. 7
Prod-EOPS Dist-GPITVL Prodn-KOACTV

Linear Measurement C 15 MIN
3/4 INCH VIDEO CASSETTE P
Tells how to make linear measurement in both non-standard units and metric units.
From The Studio M Series.
Prod-WCETTV Dist-GPITVL 1979

Linear Programming B
16MM FILM OPTICAL SOUND
Discusses linear programming and presents a simple problem of the type commonly found in refinery operation.
Prod-OPENU Dist-OPENU

Linear Programming B 60 MIN
3/4 OR 1/2 INCH VIDEO CASSETTE
See series title for descriptive statement.
From The Engineering Design Optimization I Series. Pt 15
Prod-UAZMIC Dist-UAZMIC

Linear Programming - Theory B
16MM FILM OPTICAL SOUND
Discusses a linear programming problem and investigates whether it is possible to restrict the values that the solution can take by considering positive linear combinations of the problem's inequalities.
Prod-OPENU Dist-OPENU

Linear Programming In Structures B 60 MIN
3/4 OR 1/2 INCH VIDEO CASSETTE
See series title for descriptive statement.
From The Engineering Design Optimization I Series. Pt 16
Prod-UAZMIC Dist-UAZMIC

Linear Programming, Pt 1 C 30 MIN
3/4 INCH VIDEO CASSETTE C
See series title for descriptive statement.
From The Introduction To Mathematics Series.
Prod-MDCPB Dist-MDCPB

Linear Programming, Pt 2 C 30 MIN
3/4 INCH VIDEO CASSETTE C
See series title for descriptive statement.
From The Introduction To Mathematics Series.
Prod-MDCPB Dist-MDCPB

Linear Regression B
16MM FILM OPTICAL SOUND
Discusses the normal bivariate model of heights and weights of the adult population.
Prod-OPENU Dist-OPENU

Linear System Descriptions B 40 MIN
3/4 OR 1/2 INCH VIDEO CASSETTE PRO
Discusses the characterization of a linear time-invariant (LTI) system in the time domain by its impulse response.
From The Probability And Random Processes - Linear Systems Series.
Prod-MIOT Dist-MIOT

Linear System Theory—A Series
C A
Introduces state space concepts for control of dynamic systems. Consists of 38 fifty-minute videotape lectures.
Prod-UIDEEO Dist-UIDEEO

Linear Time Invariant Dynamical Systems C 52 MIN
3/4 OR 1/2 INCH VIDEO CASSETTE
See series title for descriptive statement.
From The Modern Control Theory - Systems Analysis Series.
Prod-MIOT Dist-MIOT

Linear Transformations B 36 MIN
3/4 OR 1/2 INCH VIDEO CASSETTE
See series title for descriptive statement.
From The Calculus Of Linear Algebra Series.
Prod-MIOT Dist-MIOT

Linear-motion Saws C 12 MIN
3/4 OR 1/2 INCH VIDEO CASSETTE
Covers linear-motion saws including band saws, saber saws, blades and techniques.
From The Using Portable Power Tool Series.
Prod-TPCTRA Dist-TPCTRA

Linear-motion Saws (Spanish) C 12 MIN
3/4 OR 1/2 INCH VIDEO CASSETTE
Covers linear-motion saws including band saws, saber saws, blades and techniques.
From The Using Portable Power Tool Series.
Prod-TPCTRA Dist-TPCTRA

Linearity Revisited B 47 MIN
3/4 OR 1/2 INCH VIDEO CASSETTE
See series title for descriptive statement.
From The Calculus Of Several Variables - Matrix- Algebra Series.
Prod-MIOT Dist-MIOT

Linearization Methods, Pt 1 B 60 MIN
3/4 OR 1/2 INCH VIDEO CASSETTE
See series title for descriptive statement.
From The Engineering Design Optimization I Series. Pt 23
Prod-UAZMIC Dist-UAZMIC

Linearization Methods, Pt 2 B 60 MIN
3/4 OR 1/2 INCH VIDEO CASSETTE
See series title for descriptive statement.
From The Engineering Design Optimization I Series. Pt 24
Prod-UAZMIC Dist-UAZMIC

Linearization Methods, Pt 3 B 60 MIN
3/4 OR 1/2 INCH VIDEO CASSETTE
See series title for descriptive statement.
From The Engineering Design Optimization I Series. Pt 25
Prod-UAZMIC Dist-UAZMIC

Linearization Methods, Pt 4 B 60 MIN
3/4 OR 1/2 INCH VIDEO CASSETTE
See series title for descriptive statement.
From The Engineering Design Optimization I Series. Pt 26
Prod-UAZMIC Dist-UAZMIC

Lineman, The C 14 MIN
16MM FILM, 3/4 OR 1/2 IN VIDEO IND
Explains why people become electrical linemen and what is involved in the job. Stresses that doing the job safely is the hallmark of the professional lineman.
Prod-KROSTR Dist-IFB 1975

Liner And Piston B 20 MIN
16MM FILM OPTICAL SOUND
Tells how to inspect liner, disassemble piston rod assembly, inspect slipper rod assembly, inspect piston assembly and piston, and replace rings.
LC NO. FIE52-1365
Prod-USN Dist-USNAC 1945

Liner Cementing C 30 MIN
3/4 OR 1/2 INCH VIDEO CASSETTE IND
Defines liners used in drilling. Describes why they are used and the tools needed to set them. Discusses problems encountered and how to overcome or minimize them.
Prod-UTEXPE Dist-UTEXPE 1980

Lines C 15 MIN
3/4 INCH VIDEO CASSETTE P
See series title for descriptive statement.
From The Is The Sky Always Blue Series.
Prod-WDCNTV Dist-GPITVL 1979

Lines - Vertical And Horizontal C 13 MIN
16MM FILM, 3/4 OR 1/2 IN VIDEO I-C
Presents pure non-objective art in which design and music are inseparable, as created by Norman McLaren and Evelyn Lambart.
Prod-NFBC Dist-IFB 1963

Lines And Dots C 7 MIN
16MM FILM OPTICAL SOUND P-H
Shows blue dashes and red dots fighting each other whey they are brought in close contact with an unknown third power, which destroys the embattled signs and spreads over the screen like spilled paint.
Prod-SF Dist-SF 1970

Lines In Relief - Woodcut And Block Printing C 11 MIN
16MM FILM, 3/4 OR 1/2 IN VIDEO I-C
Reviews the history of woodcuts and block printing from the Middle Ages to the present. Shows how a fine woodcut is made. Pictures the selection of tools and materials, transfer of design and techniques used in cutting the block.
Prod-EBF Dist-EBEC 1964

Lines Of Force C 10 MIN
3/4 INCH VIDEO CASSETTE H-C A
Presents an abstract montage of forms, colors and sounds. Utilizes split screen, live television and synthesized audio visual techniques.
LC NO. 81-706007
Prod-SYNAPS Dist-SYNAPS 1980

Lines To Find C 20 MIN
2 INCH VIDEOTAPE I-J
Points out that the entire grid system must be used to locate exact places. Shows how to locate places using latitude and longitude. Illustrates the correct order when writing latitude and longitude.
From The Project Survival Series.
Prod-GPITVL Dist-GPITVL

Lines To Find C 20 MIN
3/4 INCH VIDEO CASSETTE I-J
Shows that the entire grid system must be used to locate exact places. Discusses latitude and longitude.
From The Project Survival Series.
Prod-MAETEL Dist-GPITVL

Lingering Depression, The C 28 MIN
3/4 OR 1/2 INCH VIDEO CASSETTE
See series title for descriptive statement.
From The All About Welfare Series.
Prod-WITFTV Dist-PBS

Lingo C 32 MIN
16MM FILM OPTICAL SOUND
Features a profile of T D Lingo and his unique theories about the mechanisms and potentials of the human brain.
LC NO. 80-700300
Prod-TENST Dist-TENST 1979

Lingua - Alveloars C 10 MIN
1/2 IN VIDEO CASSETTE BETA/VHS A
See series title for descriptive statement.
From The Speech Reading Materials Series.
Prod-RMI Dist-RMI

Lingual Delivery Of Impacted Mandibular Third Molars C 9 MIN
16MM FILM - 3/4 IN VIDEO PRO
Shows a lingual delivery technique for removal of unerupted third molars. Issued in 1977 as a motion picture.
LC NO. 79-707998
Prod-VADTC Dist-USNAC 1979

Linguistic Domains C 60 MIN
3/4 OR 1/2 INCH VIDEO CASSETTE A
Presents biologist Humberto Maturana discussing linguistic domains.
From The Biology Of Cognition And Language Series. Program 11
Prod-UCEMC Dist-UCEMC

Linguistics C 30 MIN
2 INCH VIDEOTAPE T
Focuses on the linguistic approach to the teaching of reading and some of the many linguistically-oriented materials available today.
From The Child Reads Series.
Prod-WENHTV Dist-GPITVL

Linguistics And Education C 22 MIN
16MM FILM OPTICAL SOUND H-C T
Three linguistics educators discuss the proposition that most laymen and some educators hold certain views about language which limit their effectiveness in teaching children standard English.
From The Language - The Social Arbiter Series.
LC NO. FIA67-5263
Prod-FINLYS Dist-FINLYS Prodn-CALING 1966

Lining And Finishing The Details C 29 MIN
2 INCH VIDEOTAPE
Features Mrs Ruth Hickman demonstrating how to line a coat and how to finish the details on it.
From The Sewing Skills - Tailoring Series.
Prod-KRMATV Dist-PUBTEL

Lining Techniques C 4 MIN
16MM FILM SILENT J-C A
Illustrates putting a separate lining in a skirt. Shows stitching lining, joining lining to fashion fabric at the waistline and zipper, completing the hem and anchoring the lining to the garment with crocheting.
From The Clothing Construction Techniques Series.
LC NO. 77-701175
Prod-IOWA Dist-IOWASP 1976

Lining The Coat C 29 MIN
2 INCH VIDEOTAPE
Features Mrs Ruth Hickman demonstrating how to line a coat.
From The Sewing Skills - Tailoring Series.
Prod-KRMATV Dist-PUBTEL

Link And The Chain, The C 28 MIN
16MM FILM OPTICAL SOUND
Prod-WAORT Dist-WAORT 1980

Link Between Us, The...Electronics C 28 MIN
16MM FILM, 3/4 OR 1/2 IN VIDEO
Documents the daily influences of electronics products in people's lives. Features appearances by Eugene Fodor, Jim Henson, Lorin Maazel, Kenny Rogers, Eric Sevareid and Stevie Wonder.
Prod-ELECTR Dist-MTP

Link Control Procedures C 45 MIN
3/4 OR 1/2 INCH VIDEO CASSETTE C
Includes link configurations, data versus control signalling, stages and types of link control and procedures, both character and bit-oriented, control functions such as framing, transparency, data transfer, flow and error control plus examples.
From The Telecommunications And The Computer Series.
LC NO. 81-707502
Prod-AMCEE Dist-AMCEE 1981

Link Control Procedures C 56 MIN
3/4 OR 1/2 INCH VIDEO CASSETTE
Discusses types of link control procedures.
From The Telecommunications And The Computer Series.
Prod-MIOT Dist-MIOT

Link Sextant, Air, The B 16 MIN
16MM FILM, 3/4 OR 1/2 IN VIDEO
Explains the operating principle of the sextant and the reading of the vernier scale. Shows two ways of making observations and how to grip the sextant when making observations.
From The Navigation Series.
LC NO. 81-706346
Prod-USN Dist-USNAC 1943

Link, The C 19 MIN
16MM FILM OPTICAL SOUND
Provides an introduction to the work of the armed forces reporting unit - a vital link between the serviceman and his family. Follows a newly assigned Afru Correspondent at National Headquarters during her first days on the job.
Prod-AMRC Dist-AMRC 1971

Linkage - Population Genetics C 20 MIN
16MM FILM OPTICAL SOUND
Describes linkage, genetic mapping, the Hardy-Weinberg principle and factors which disturb the Hardy-Weinberg principle.
From The General Genetics Series.
Prod-MIFE Dist-MIFE 1972

Linkage - Population Genetics C 20 MIN
16MM FILM OPTICAL SOUND
Depicts a variety of linkage relations, including Lutheran and secretor loci, elliptocytosis and Rh loci, and ABO and nail patella loci. Illustrates the Hardy-Weinberg law and shows segregation analysis and ascertainment of bias in collecting data.
From The Human Genetics Series. No. 5
LC NO. 75-700021
Prod-NFMD Dist-MIFE Prodn-MIFE 1968

Linkage - Population Genetics (Spanish) C 20 MIN
16MM FILM OPTICAL SOUND
Depicts a variety of linkage relations, including Lutheran and secretor loci, elliptocytosis and Rh loci, and ABO and nail patella loci. Illustrates the Hardy-Weinberg law and shows segregation analysis and ascertainment of bias in collecting data.
From The Human Genetics (Spanish) Series. No. 5
LC NO. 75-700021
Prod-NFMD Dist-MIFE Prodn-MIFE 1968

Linked Lists B
16MM FILM OPTICAL SOUND
Illustrates the linked list structure and the additional storage locations which are required to implement the insertion flow-chart. Examines the role of the computer in carrying out these steps in the computer store.
Prod-OPENU Dist-OPENU

Linking Arms C 22 MIN
16MM FILM OPTICAL SOUND
Documents the work of Toronto sculptror Colette Whiten. Shows how she conceived the idea to link the arms of five men in one of her works.
LC NO. 76-703240
Prod-CANFDC Dist-CANFDC 1975

Linking Writing To Reading B 15 MIN
2 INCH VIDEOTAPE I
Lists three basic questions posed by independent writing--what shall I write about, how shall I frame the ideas and sentences and how do I edit my writing. Suggests that books and illustrations may stimulate story subjects and ideas. (Broadcast quality)
From The Bill Martin Series. No. 14
Prod-BRITED Dist-GPITVL Prodn-KQEDTV

Linnaeus C 18 MIN
16MM FILM OPTICAL SOUND
Presents the life of Sweden's great botanist, Carl Linnaeus, who devised the system of botanical classification and describes his contribution to science.
Prod-SIS Dist-SIS 1957

Lino Manocchia, Ralph Marino And Federico Picciano C 52 MIN
3/4 OR 1/2 INCH VIDEO CASSETTE
Presents Italian folk music and a film of a group sing in an Italian village. Features Linco Manocchia, Ralph Marino and Federico Picciano.
From The Rainbow Quest Series.
Prod-SEEGER Dist-CWATER

Lintola - Addition With Carrying C 9 MIN
16MM FILM, 3/4 OR 1/2 IN VIDEO P-I
Uses a story about aliens and space travel to illustrate the theory behind two-digit addition with carrying.
From The Math That Counts Series.
Prod-DAVFMS Dist-EBEC

Lion C 11 MIN
16MM FILM, 3/4 OR 1/2 IN VIDEO I-H
Shows the lion as he eats, sleeps and plays with females and cubs in his natural habitat.
From The Magic Moments, Unit 6 - Silent Safari Series.
Prod-EBEC Dist-EBEC 1972

Lion C 22 MIN
16MM FILM, 3/4 OR 1/2 IN VIDEO P-I
Explores the lion and his dazzling role in art from the Alhambra to the Great Pyramid of Khufu to Rousseau's The Dream. Includes the story Androcles And The Lion. Hosted by Hal Linden.
From The Animals, Animals, Animals Series.
Prod-ABCNEW Dist-MEDIAG 1977

Lion And The Eagle, The B 60 MIN
16MM FILM OPTICAL SOUND J-C A
Uses film clips to document from the point of view of the anglo-American alliance, the main events and personalities of the era from 1939 to the Vietnam War.
From The Intertel Series.
Prod-NET Dist-IU Prodn-REDFTV 1966

Lion And The Horse, The C 83 MIN
16MM FILM OPTICAL SOUND
Presents the story of Wildfire, a wild horse that is sold to a cruel rodeo owner and freed by a sympathetic cowpoke.
Prod-WB Dist-TWYMAN 1952

Lion And The Mouse, The C 5 MIN
16MM FILM, 3/4 OR 1/2 IN VIDEO K-P
Presents an animated version of Aesop's fable about a mouse who saves a lion by chewing through the rope in which the lion is trapped.
Prod-NFBC Dist-BNCHMK 1977

Lion And The Mouse, The C 10 MIN
16MM FILM, 3/4 OR 1/2 IN VIDEO P
Cartoon story of a mouse who helps remove a speck of dirt from a lion's eye.
Prod-FCHILD Dist-CORF 1959

Lion Country Safari C 15 MIN
16MM FILM OPTICAL SOUND
Shows a 640-acre preserve in Florida where wild animals from Africa live freely in their natural habitat.
Prod-FENWCK Dist-FENWCK

Lion Dance C 3 MIN
16MM FILM OPTICAL SOUND
Offers a graphic interpretation of the traditional Chinese lion dance utilizing traditional music. Employs visuals which are simple brush drawings and colors painted directly on the film.
Prod-USC Dist-USC 1981

Lion Game, The C 4 MIN
3/4 INCH VIDEO CASSETTE
Shows a lion hunt game played by bushmen in Namibia.
From The San (Bushmen) Series.
Prod-DOCEDR Dist-DOCEDR Prodn-MRSHL

Lion Has Seven Heads (German) C 97 MIN
16MM FILM OPTICAL SOUND
Tells the story of revolution in Africa and Third World exploitation involving the CIA and the Portuguese.
Prod-NYFLMS Dist-NYFLMS 1970

Lion Has Seven Heads (Spanish) C 97 MIN
16MM FILM OPTICAL SOUND
Tells the story of revolution in Africa and Third World exploitation involving the CIA and the Portuguese.
Prod-NYFLMS Dist-NYFLMS 1970

Lion Has Seven Heads, The (French) C 97 MIN
16MM FILM OPTICAL SOUND
Tells the story of revolution in Africa and Third World exploitation involving the CIA and the Portuguese.
Prod-NYFLMS Dist-NYFLMS 1970

Lion Has Seven Heads, The (Italian) C 97 MIN
16MM FILM OPTICAL SOUND
Tells the story of revolution in Africa and Third World exploitation involving the CIA and the Portuguese.
Prod-NYFLMS Dist-NYFLMS 1970

Lion Has Seven Heads, The (Portuguese) C 97 MIN
16MM FILM OPTICAL SOUND
An English subtitle version of the Portuguese language film. Tells the story of revolution in Africa and Third World exploitation involving the CIA and the Portuguese.
Prod-NYFLMS Dist-NYFLMS 1970

Lion Head C 29 MIN
2 INCH VIDEOTAPE
Features Joyce Chen showing how to adapt Chinese recipes so they can be prepared in the American kitchen and still retain the authentic flavor.
From The Joyce Chen Cooks Series.
Prod-WGBHTV Dist-PUBTEL

Lion Hunters, The C 68 MIN
3/4 INCH VIDEO CASSETTE
Shows several lion hunts in northern Niger and Mali, Africa. Explains how and why Gao tribesmen hunt lions. Filmed by Jean Rouch over a seven-year period in the 1950's and 1960's.
Prod-DOCEDR Dist-DOCEDR Prodn-LESFMP

Lion Roars, The C 10 MIN
2 INCH VIDEOTAPE
See series title for descriptive statement.
From The Janaki Series.
Prod-WGBHTV Dist-PUBTEL

Lion, The C 19 MIN
16MM FILM, 3/4 OR 1/2 IN VIDEO P-J
Features the relationship of a lion family, as well as its relationship to other animals. Highlights the ways in which the lioness cares for and caters to her cubs, the imperious nature of the father lion and the playfulness of the baby cubs.
Prod-CFD Dist-LUF 1971

Lion's Cub, The C 90 MIN
16MM FILM, 3/4 OR 1/2 IN VIDEO
Portrays young Queen Elizabeth I during the brief reigns of her brother Edward and her sister Mary. Dramatizes her exile to the Tower because of her suspected relationship with courtier and political intriguer Thomas Seymour.
From The Elizabeth R Series. No. 1
LC NO. 79-707278
Prod-BBCTV Dist-FI 1976

Lion's Roar, The C 50 MIN
3/4 OR 1/2 INCH VIDEO CASSETTE C A
Presents the belief system of Tibetan Buddhism by following the living embodiment of human compassion and enlightenment, the Karmapas, on his journey from Sikkim in the Indian Himalayas to the U.S. and Europe.
Prod-CEPRO Dist-CEPRO

Liona Boyd C 58 MIN
3/4 OR 1/2 INCH VIDEO CASSETTE
See series title for descriptive statement.
From The Evening At Pops Series.
Prod-WGBHTV Dist-PBS 1978

Lionel's Problem - Estimation C 15 MIN
3/4 OR 1/2 INCH VIDEO CASSETTE P
Explains how Lionel must decode word problems and estimate outcomes in order to effectively use a calculator.
From The Math Country Series.
Prod-KYTV Dist-AITECH 1979

Lions C 15 MIN
3/4 OR 1/2 INCH VIDEO CASSETTE I-J
Gives a simple step-by-step approach for drawing a lion's head. Suggests ways of completing a wildlife picture.
From The Draw Man Series.
Prod-OCPS Dist-AITECH 1975

Lions (Let's Draw) C 15 MIN
3/4 OR 1/2 INCH VIDEO CASSETTE P
See series title for descriptive statement.
From The Let's Draw Series.
Prod-OCPS Dist-AITECH Prodn-KOKHTV 1976

Lions And Tigers C 6 MIN
16MM FILM, 3/4 OR 1/2 IN VIDEO K-P
Depicts the characteristics of lions and tigers who spend most of their day fighting, and caring for their young.
From The Zoo Animals In The Wild Series.
LC NO. 81-707454
Prod-CORF Dist-CORF 1981

Lions Den, The B 10 MIN
16MM FILM OPTICAL SOUND
Presents a middle aged failure who looks at himself and his past. Explores the concept of frustration, and depicts a rather subtle form of self-delusion. Portrays the man talking about his parents, his past life as a Pimp, his clothes and his way of life.
Prod-UPENN Dist-UPENN 1967

Lions Love C 110 MIN
16MM FILM OPTICAL SOUND
Offers a free-form look at the culture of the 1960's.
Prod-UNKNWN Dist-TWYMAN

Lipid Storage Disease - Past, Present And Future C 60 MIN
3/4 OR 1/2 INCH VIDEO CASSETTE
Discusses the clinical and metabolic aspects of lipid storage diseases, emphasizing diagnosis and carrier detection as well as therapeutic approaches. Includes Gaucher's, Niemann-Pick, Fabry's and Tay-Sachs Diseases.
Prod-USDHEW Dist-USNAC

Lipswitch Mandibular Labial Vestibuloplasty C 10 MIN
16MM FILM, 3/4 OR 1/2 IN VIDEO
Describes the lipswitch vestibuloplasty, a procedure to correct an inadequate mandibular labial sulcus. Explains that it is a relatively simple surgical procedure and can be done on an outpatient basis under local anesthesia.
LC NO. 80-707611
Prod-VADTC Dist-USNAC 1980

Liquid Crystals C 29 MIN
2 INCH VIDEOTAPE
See series title for descriptive statement.
From The Interface Series.
Prod-KCET Dist-PUBTEL

Liquid Fire, The B 30 MIN
16MM FILM OPTICAL SOUND H-C A
Portrays the adult life of Samuel Gompers, who served as President of the American Federation of Labor. (Kinescope)
From The Eternal Light Series.
LC NO. 79-700963
Prod-JTS Dist-NAAJS 1967

Liquid Junction Potentials / The pH And Its Measurement / Buffer Solutions / Non-Aqueous... C 56 MIN
3/4 OR 1/2 INCH VIDEO CASSETTE
Discusses liquid junction potentials, the pH and its measurement, buffer solutions and non-aqueous solvents.
From The Electrochemistry, Pt III - Thermodynamics Of Galvanic Cells Series.
Prod-MIOT Dist-MIOT

Liquid Junction Potentials, The Ph And Its Measurement, Buffer Solutions, Non-Aqueous... C 56 MIN
3/4 OR 1/2 INCH VIDEO CASSETTE
Discusses liquid junction potentials, the pH and its measurement, buffer solutions and non-aqueous solvents.
From The Electrochemistry Series.
Prod-KALMIA Dist-KALMIA

Liquid Measure C 20 MIN
2 INCH VIDEOTAPE P
See series title for descriptive statement.
From The Mathemagic, Unit VI - Measurement Series.
Prod-WMULTV Dist-GPITVL

Liquid Natural Gas C 16 MIN
16MM FILM OPTICAL SOUND
Introduces and explains the science of cryogenics as applied to natural gas. Shows how liquid natural gas can be transported safely by truck and ship and how it may power a new generation of pollution free cars and buses.
LC NO. 74-706048
Prod-BUGAS Dist-BUGAS Prodn-BAILYB 1969

Liquid Natural Gas C 15 MIN
3/4 OR 1/2 INCH VIDEO CASSETTE
Explores natural gas and its characteristics as both a gas and a liquid.
Prod-IVCH Dist-IVCH

Liquid Penetrant Testing C 55 MIN
3/4 OR 1/2 INCH VIDEO CASSETTE PRO
Reviews the basic principles, history and development of liquid penetrant testing. Shows how to interpret test results.
From The Fundamentals Of Nondestructive Testing Series.
Prod-AMCEE Dist-AMCEE

Liquid Show, The C 25 MIN
16MM FILM, 3/4 OR 1/2 IN VIDEO I-H
Features experiments that demonstrate the remarkable properties of ordinary liquids.
From The Start Here - Adventure Into Science Series.
Prod-LANDMK Dist-LANDMK

Liquid Volume C 15 MIN
3/4 INCH VIDEO CASSETTE P
Focuses on the proper use of the one-half liter and the one-fourth liter.
From The Studio M Series.
Prod-WCETTV Dist-GPITVL 1979

Liquids Can Burn C 13 MIN
16MM FILM, 3/4 OR 1/2 IN VIDEO I-C A
Uses demonstrations and laboratory experiments to show the flammability of various liquids found in the home.
Prod-HIGGIN Dist-HIGGIN 1973

Lisa - Pay Attention C 22 MIN
16MM FILM OPTICAL SOUND C A
Presents everyday situations in order to see how a child with a hearing impairment reacts to and may be hampered in the events that she and her teacher experience. Helps teachers become more aware of children's hearing problems.
LC NO. 71-709400
Prod-PLATTS Dist-AVEXP 1970

Lisa - The Legacy Of Sandra Blain C 22 MIN
16MM FILM, 3/4 OR 1/2 IN VIDEO H A
Relates the story of a young woman who almost dies after taking pills and alcohol three months after her alcoholic mother's funeral. Relates how she is saved when she enters an alcohol recovery program.
LC NO. 81-706722
Prod-CAHILL Dist-AIMS 1979

Lisa Steele - Some Call It Bad Luck C 47 MIN
3/4 OR 1/2 INCH VIDEO CASSETTE
Examines the process of interrogation in the format of a cop show.
Prod-ARTINC Dist-ARTINC

Lisa Steele - The Gloria Tapes C 12 MIN
3/4 OR 1/2 INCH VIDEO CASSETTE
Depicts Gloria, who lacks the ability to speak on her own behalf. Uses the soap opera format.
Prod-ARTINC Dist-ARTINC

Lisa's World C 30 MIN
3/4 INCH VIDEO CASSETTE J A
Focuses on a family with a mildly-retarded seven-year-old child. Discusses the difficulties and rewards of raising the child in a normal home setting and the effects on other members of the family.
Prod-UMITV Dist-UMITV 1969

LISP C 60 MIN
3/4 OR 1/2 INCH VIDEO CASSETTE C
Introduces main programming language of AI. Includes objects, atoms and lists, functions, symbol manuipulating and evaluation functions (CAR, CDR, APPEND, CONS, QUOTE, EVAL). Gives assignment functions (SET and SETQ, predicates, LIST, the branching function COND, DEFINE and LAMBDA.
From The Introduction To Artificial--Intelligence Series.
Prod-UAZMIC Dist-AMCEE

Lissajous Figures B 27 MIN
16MM FILM OPTICAL SOUND
Shows lissajous figures on an oscilloscope. Discusses them in terms of their general use of phase and frequency determinations, and demonstrates their use. (Kinescope)
LC NO. 74-705037
Prod-USAF Dist-USNAC 1963

Listen C 42 MIN
16MM FILM OPTICAL SOUND J-C A
Shows the problems created for paper workers and their families by industrial noise pollution.
LC NO. 76-701161
Prod-UPIU Dist-UPIU Prodn-GOROH 1974

Listen C 10 MIN
16MM FILM, 3/4 OR 1/2 IN VIDEO
Explains how to 'see' the images created by music.
Prod-FLMFR Dist-FLMFR

Listen C 19 MIN
3/4 OR 1/2 INCH VIDEO CASSETTE
Demonstrates that listening is a valuable skill and shares a number of listening techniques. Suggests exercises to heighten skills.
Prod-MELROS Dist-VISUCP

Listen (Captioned) C 30 MIN
3/4 OR 1/2 INCH VIDEO CASSETTE
Presents a documentary on hearing loss, its causes, its psychological meaning and what can be done to cope with the problem.
From The Western Maryland College Series.
Prod-WMARYC Dist-USNAC 1973

Listen (Spanish) C 10 MIN
16MM FILM, 3/4 OR 1/2 IN VIDEO
Explains how to 'see' the images created by music.
Prod-FLMFR Dist-FLMFR

Listen And Laugh C 20 MIN
2 INCH VIDEOTAPE P
See series title for descriptive statement.
From The Learning Our Language, Unit 1 - Listening Skills Series.
Prod-MPATI Dist-GPITVL

Listen And Say - Consonants And Digraphs—A Series
P
Helps children become aware of some of the consonant sounds they will meet in early reading. Teaches identification of the written letter which represents the spoken sound.
Prod-GPITVL Dist-GPITVL

B Sound, The - Betty's Bonnet	15 MIN
Ch Sound, The - Charlie, The Chubby Chipmunk	15 MIN
D Sound, The - Dick's Dog	15 MIN
F Sound, The - Fifi Is Frightened	15 MIN
H Sound, The - Hannah's New Hat	15 MIN
K Or Hard C Sound, The - Caroline Cat's Cough	15 MIN
L Sound, The - The Leaning Ladder	15 MIN
M Sound, The - Maybe The Mouse Might	15 MIN
N Sound, The - Nobody's Nose	15 MIN
R Sound, The - Reddy Rooster's New Tail	15 MIN
S Sound, The - Mr Sam's Little Tire	15 MIN

Sh Sound, The - Sherman's Wish 15 MIN
T Sound, The - The Tiniest Tick 15 MIN
Th Sound, The - Thimble, Thimble Is My Name 15 MIN
W Sound, The - Willie Watermelon 15 MIN
Wh Sound, The - Whoo-Oo-Oo, I Want To Go 15 MIN

Listen And Say - Vowels—A Series P

Introduces the concept that letters have more than one sound, teaches the letter names of the vowels and presents the long and short sound for each vowel.
Prod-GPITVL Dist-GPITVL

Carl And The Corner Market 15 MIN
How The Lazy E Ranch Got Its Name 15 MIN
Introduction To The Vowels - The Five Magic 15 MIN
Long A - April's Apron 15 MIN
Long And Short Of It, The 15 MIN
Long E - The Teeny Weeny Eel 15 MIN
Long I - Ida's Ice Cream 15 MIN
Long O - Ole's Old Overalls 15 MIN
Long U - The Unicorn In The Uniform 15 MIN
Short A - Andy And The Apple 15 MIN
Short E - The Elephant Who Wanted To Go 15 MIN
Short I - Inky The Imp 15 MIN
Short O - The Ox In The Box 15 MIN
Short U - Uncle Umber's Umbrella 15 MIN
Sometimes Vowel, A 15 MIN
When Two Vowels Go Walking 15 MIN

Listen And Say—A Series P

Prod-MPATI Dist-GPITVL

B Sound, The - Betty's Bonnet 15 MIN
Carl And The Corner Market 15 MIN
Ch Sound, The - Charlie, The Chubby Chipmunk 15 MIN
D Sound, The - Dick's Dog 15 MIN
F Sound, The - Fifi Is Frightened 15 MIN
H Sound, The - Hannah's New Hat 15 MIN
How The Lazy 'E' Ranch Got Its Name 15 MIN
Introduction To The Vowels - The Five Magic 15 MIN
K Or Hard C Sound, The - Caroline Cat's 15 MIN
L Sound, The - The Leaning Ladder 15 MIN
Long 'A' - April's Apron 15 MIN
Long 'E' - The Teeny Weeny Eel 15 MIN
Long 'I' - Ida's Ice Cream 15 MIN
Long 'O' - Ole's Old Overalls 15 MIN
Long 'U' - The Unicorn In The Uniform 15 MIN
Long And Short Of It, The 15 MIN
M Sound, The - Maybe The Mouse Might 15 MIN
N Sound, The - Nobody's Nose 15 MIN
R Sound, The - Reddy Rooster's New Tail 15 MIN
S Sound, The - Mr Sam's Little Tire 15 MIN
Sh Sound, The - Sherman's Wish 15 MIN
Short 'A' - Andy And The Apple 15 MIN
Short 'E' - Elephant Who Wanted To Go Upstairs 15 MIN
Short 'I' - Inky The Imp 15 MIN
Short 'O' - The Ox In The Box 15 MIN
Short 'U' - Uncle Umber's Umbrella 15 MIN
Sometimes Vowel, A 15 MIN
T Sound, The - The Tiniest Tick 15 MIN
W Sound, The - Willie Watermelon 15 MIN
Wh Sound, The - Whoo-Oo-Oo, I Want To Go 15 MIN
When Two Vowels Go Walking 15 MIN

Listen Caracas C 19 MIN
16MM FILM, 3/4 OR 1/2 IN VIDEO
Offers insights into the process of cultural genocide by presenting the last surviving Yecuana chief in the Amazon region who, with great dignity and urgency, describes the disrespectful attitude of colonizers and missionaries toward his people's beliefs and way of life.
Prod-AZPURC Dist-CNEMAG

Listen Caracas (Spanish) C 19 MIN
16MM FILM, 3/4 OR 1/2 IN VIDEO
Offers insights into the process of cultural genocide by presenting the last surviving Yecuana chief in the Amazon region who, with great dignity and urgency, describes the disrespectful attitude of colonizers and missionaries toward his people's beliefs and way of life.
Prod-AZPURC Dist-CNEMAG

Listen Cindy C 18 MIN
16MM FILM, 3/4 OR 1/2 IN VIDEO I-J
Teaches the importance of developing good listening skills through the story of a girl who violates most of the rules of being a good listener in order to win a gold star for her paper on the subject.
LC NO. 81-707576
Prod-CF Dist-CF 1981

Listen Hear C 15 MIN
16MM FILM, 3/4 OR 1/2 IN VIDEO P-I
Deals with the causes of sound, how the brain receives and recognizes sounds and the effects of sound on people. Uses animation to identify the parts of the ear and shows what happens when sound waves enter human ears.
From The Human Senses Series.
LC NO. 82-706606
Prod-NGS Dist-NGS 1982

Listen To Ask C 20 MIN
2 INCH VIDEOTAPE P
See series title for descriptive statement.
From The Learning Our Language, Unit 1 - Listening Skills Series.
Prod-MPATI Dist-GPITVL

Listen To Communicate C 40 MIN
16MM FILM, 3/4 OR 1/2 IN VIDEO C A
Presents the concepts and skills of listening.
LC NO. 80-707318
Prod-MGHT Dist-CRMP 1980

Listen To The Kid - Adolescents Talk About Diabetes C 15 MIN
3/4 OR 1/2 INCH VIDEO CASSETTE PRO
Designed to help health professionals and parents understand the special problems facing the adolescent with a chronic illness like diabetes. Includes interviews with teenagers about how diabetes affects their lives.
Prod-UMICHM Dist-UMICHM 1982

Listen To The Mountains C 22 MIN
16MM FILM, 3/4 OR 1/2 IN VIDEO H-C A
Follows two couples on a three-week ski mountaineering expedition to California's Sierra Nevada.
Prod-JONESD Dist-PFP 1977

Listen Well, Learn Well (2nd Ed) C 11 MIN
16MM FILM, 3/4 OR 1/2 IN VIDEO P-I
Shows listening problems and how to solve them.
Prod-CORF Dist-CORF 1974

Listen While You Can C 21 MIN
16MM FILM, 3/4 OR 1/2 IN VIDEO J-C A
Uses animation to define sound and to illustrate the construction of the ear. Explains types of ear damage and kinds of noise conditions that are dangerous.
Prod-UKMD Dist-IFB Prodn-HARDY 1972

Listen, Listen C 18 MIN
16MM FILM, 3/4 OR 1/2 IN VIDEO
Presents an unusual and highly symbolic film, which shows real-life situations in which people are enjoying fulfilled lives. Motivates viewers to consider positive alternatives in their own lives.
Prod-FORDFL Dist-FORDFL

Listen, Look And Learn C 15 MIN
3/4 OR 1/2 INCH VIDEO CASSETTE P
Points out the different parts of the eye and describes the function of each. Illustrates how sound travels through the ear. Explains why some people must wear hearing aids and glasses.
From The All About You Series.
Prod-WGBHTV Dist-AITECH Prodn-TTOIC 1975

Listen, Please C 12 MIN
16MM FILM - 3/4 IN VIDEO IND
Shows an audience of supervisors that they often think they're better listeners than they really are. Emphasizes the importance of listening in a supervisory job.
From The Modern Management Series.
Prod-BNA Dist-BNA 1960

Listening B 20 MIN
16MM FILM OPTICAL SOUND C A
See series title for descriptive statement.
From The All That I Am Series.
Prod-MPATI Dist-NWUFLM

Listening B 29 MIN
16MM FILM OPTICAL SOUND IND
See series title for descriptive statement.
From The Developing Communication Skills Series.
LC NO. 70-703322
Prod-EDSD Dist-EDSD

Listening C 14 MIN
16MM FILM, 3/4 OR 1/2 IN VIDEO
Examines a typical day of a middle manager who does not listen to the people with whom he works. Demonstrates the importance of good listening habits to open up the half-way communication that blocks managerial input.
LC NO. 74-700688
Prod-RANKAV Dist-RTBL 1972

Listening B 15 MIN
2 INCH VIDEOTAPE P
See series title for descriptive statement.
From The Language Corner Series.
Prod-CVETVC Dist-GPITVL Prodn-WCVETV

Listening - A Key To Problem-Solving C 22 MIN
16MM FILM, 3/4 OR 1/2 IN VIDEO H-C A
Identifies causes of poor listening habits and ways to improve those habits. Shows how improved listening reduces problems, improves working relationships, and increases productivity. Discusses the need for sensitivity to both the facts and the feelings in oral messages and how to increase understanding of implied messages.
Prod-AIMS Dist-AIMS

Listening - The Forgotten Skill—A Series

Provides a foundation for effective communication and professional development, and teaches a variety of skills and concepts to improve listening skills. Assumes the student has a familiarity with basic communication concepts. Includes textbook, Listening - The Forgotten Skill, and reference cards.
Prod-DELTAK Dist-DELTAK

Techniques For Handling Difficult People And Understanding The Listening Process 011 MIN

Listening - The Problem Solver C 20 MIN
16MM FILM, 3/4 OR 1/2 IN VIDEO H-C A
Focuses on creative, critical and sympathetic listening.
Prod-BARR Dist-BARR 1981

Listening And Singing C 15 MIN
3/4 OR 1/2 INCH VIDEO CASSETTE K-P
Discusses musical instruments, clapping patterns and the differences between soft and loud.
From The Pass It On Series.
Prod-WKNOTV Dist-GPITVL 1983

Listening And Speaking C 30 MIN
3/4 OR 1/2 INCH VIDEO CASSETTE T
Deals with listening and speaking when teaching adult basic education students.
From The Basic Education - Teaching The Adult Series.
Prod-MDDE Dist-MDCPB

Listening And You C 30 MIN
3/4 OR 1/2 INCH VIDEO CASSETTE
Demonstrates skills to become a good listener. Focuses on becoming aware of listening styles. Shows how to make a personal profile.
From The Effective Listening Series. Tape 1
Prod-TELSTR Dist-DELTAK

Listening Between The Lines C 16 MIN
16MM FILM, 3/4 OR 1/2 IN VIDEO I-H
Examines obstacles which interfere with listening, such as distractions and personal prejudices which color what a person hears. Explores the issues of interpretation and evaluation and shows how listening is an acquired ability.
Prod-HIGGIN Dist-HIGGIN 1975

Listening Beyond Words C 21 MIN
16MM FILM OPTICAL SOUND
Revised edition of 'ARE YOU LISTENING.' Presents several brief sketches showing communication problems in a family, in a business and in school in order to analyze and correct failures in interpersonal relations.
LC NO. 74-700705
Prod-BYU Dist-BYU 1973

Listening Emotions C 30 MIN
3/4 OR 1/2 INCH VIDEO CASSETTE
Explores emotional triggers and how they interfere with listening.
From The Effective Listening Series. Tape 7
Prod-TELSTR Dist-TELSTR

Listening Eyes C 19 MIN
16MM FILM OPTICAL SOUND
Demonstrates how a deaf child and her classmates are taught by tutors of the deaf to listen with their eyes and speak almost as well as normal hearing children.
LC NO. FIA52-324
Prod-USC Dist-USC 1947

Listening For Language C 22 MIN
16MM FILM, 3/4 OR 1/2 IN VIDEO C A
Introduces two auditory methods of teaching hearing impaired children language, the auditory-oral and the auditory-verbal. Strives in both methods to teach the child listening skills which will enable him/her to communicate and function in a hearing world.
From The Ways Of Hearing Series.
Prod-BCNFL Dist-BCNFL

Listening For More Sales C 10 MIN
16MM FILM, 3/4 OR 1/2 IN VIDEO A
Shows an unsuccessful sales effort and analyzes the various reasons why the effort broke down. Shows how to apply successful listening techniques to close a deal.
Prod-SANDYC Dist-RTBL

Listening For More Sales (Dutch) C 10 MIN
16MM FILM, 3/4 OR 1/2 IN VIDEO A
Shows an unsuccessful sales effort and analyzes the various reasons why the effort broke down. Shows how to apply successful listening techniques to close a deal.
Prod-SANDYC Dist-RTBL

Listening For More Sales (Portuguese) C 10 MIN
16MM FILM, 3/4 OR 1/2 IN VIDEO A
Shows an unsuccessful sales effort and analyzes the various reasons why the effort broke down. Shows how to apply successful listening techniques to close a deal.
Prod-SANDYC Dist-RTBL

Listening For More Sales (Spanish) C 10 MIN
16MM FILM, 3/4 OR 1/2 IN VIDEO A
Shows an unsuccessful sales effort and analyzes the various reasons why the effort broke down. Shows how to apply successful listening techniques to close a deal.
Prod-SANDYC Dist-RTBL

Listening For Results C 10 MIN
16MM FILM, 3/4 OR 1/2 IN VIDEO A
Shows a salesman and manager attempting to plan a sales campaign and committing such listening errors as interrupting, failing to pay attention, making assumptions and jumping to conclusions. Reveals how these problems could have been avoided.
Prod-SANDYC Dist-RTBL 1982

Listening For The Sale C 19 MIN
16MM FILM, 3/4 OR 1/2 IN VIDEO
Presents humorous vignettes which are designed to show salespeople how to direct a customer simply by listening.
Prod-CRMP Dist-MGHT 1981

Listening For The Sale C 20 MIN
16MM FILM, 3/4 OR 1/2 IN VIDEO H-C A
Demonstrates that listening is an acquired skill that salespeople must develop in order to be successful. Shows obstacles to listening and illustrates time-proven techniques for successful listening.
LC NO. 81-706212
Prod-CRMP Dist-CRMP 1982

Listening For The TH Sounds C 15 MIN
3/4 INCH VIDEO CASSETTE P
Demonstrates the use of the TH sound.
From The New Talking Shop Series.
Prod-BSPTV Dist-GPITVL 1978

Listening Makes A Difference C 7 MIN
16MM FILM, 3/4 OR 1/2 IN VIDEO A

Demonstrates the importance of active listening. Shows that by listening to prospective customers and asking questions, a salesman can discover a customer's needs and wants.
Prod-SALENG Dist-SALENG

Listening Skills C 30 MIN
3/4 OR 1/2 INCH VIDEO CASSETTE A
Emphasizes active listening - listening that entails specific skills to promote a desired outcome. Presents host Paula Prentiss stressing the need for a listener to be receptive, while Richard Benjamin talks about the two parts of active listening, taking it in and checking it out.
From The Communication Skills For Managers Series.
Prod-TIMLIF Dist-TIMLIF 1981

Listening Skills - How To Be An Active Listener C
3/4 OR 1/2 INCH VIDEO CASSETTE H-C
Demonstrates techniques for improving listening skills in interpersonal, school and job situations.
Prod-GA Dist-GA

Listening Skills - The Art Of Active Listening C 56 MIN
1/2 IN VIDEO CASSETTE (VHS) J-C
Tells how listening affects work, study and social relationships. Describes major listening faults and explains the techniques of good listening and how to improve comprehension.
LC NO. 85-703928
Prod-HRMC Dist-HRMC

Listening With A Third Ear C 30 MIN
3/4 INCH VIDEO CASSETTE PRO
Highlights an interview between a psychiatric nurse and patient in order to create an awareness of unrecognized interactional dynamics operative in professional relationships.
LC NO. 80-706505
Prod-VAHSL Dist-USNAC 1978

Listening With The Third Ear B 20 MIN
16MM FILM OPTICAL SOUND C A
See series title for descriptive statement.
From The All That I Am Series.
Prod-MPATI Dist-NWUFLM

Listening, Discrimination, Association, Memory, Description, Pt 1 C 14 MIN
3/4 OR 1/2 INCH VIDEO CASSETTE K
See series title for descriptive statement.
From The I-Land Treasure Series.
Prod-NETCHE Dist-AITECH 1980

Listening, Discrimination, Association, Memory, Description, Pt 2 C 13 MIN
3/4 OR 1/2 INCH VIDEO CASSETTE K
See series title for descriptive statement.
From The I-Land Treasure Series.
Prod-NETCHE Dist-AITECH 1980

Listening, Discrimination, Association, Memory, Description, Pt 3 C 15 MIN
3/4 OR 1/2 INCH VIDEO CASSETTE K
See series title for descriptive statement.
From The I-Land Treasure Series.
Prod-NETCHE Dist-AITECH 1980

Listening, Speaking And Nonverbal Language Skills C 15 MIN
16MM FILM, 3/4 OR 1/2 IN VIDEO P-I
Identifies, through a series of humorous skits, abuses and misuses of listening, speaking and nonverbal language skills. Describes and demonstrates correct and appropriate ways of using these skills.
From The Communication Skills Series.
Prod-MOCEP Dist-PHENIX 1976

Lists C 50 MIN
3/4 OR 1/2 INCH VIDEO CASSETTE
Discusses programming techniques for list processing functions in computer languages.
From The Computer Languages - Pt 1 Series.
Prod-MIOT Dist-MIOT

Liszt, The Piano, And Craig Sheppard C 26 MIN
16MM FILM, 3/4 OR 1/2 IN VIDEO J-C A
Presents Hungarian pianist and composer Franz Liszt (1811-1886) who is regarded as the greatest pianist of his age. Features professional pianist Craig Sheppard performing some of Liszt's most famous compositions in a theater where Liszt himself once played concerts.
From The Musical Triangles Series.
Prod-THAMES Dist-MEDIAG 1975

Lisztomania C 105 MIN
16MM FILM OPTICAL SOUND
Portrays Franz Liszt as a 19th century pop star who wavers between the pleasures of the flesh and an almost religious devotion to his music. Directed by Ken Russell.
Prod-WB Dist-TWYMAN 1975

Litany Of Breath C 7 MIN
16MM FILM OPTICAL SOUND
Analyzes the question whether a person can remain silent during fascist-style repression.
Prod-SFN Dist-SFN

Literacy Instructor Training—A Series
16MM FILM, 3/4 OR 1/2 IN VIDEO T
Discusses various aspects of teaching adult nonreaders.
Prod-IU Dist-IU 1978

Comprehension 020 MIN
Language Experience Approach 020 MIN
Patterns In Language 020 MIN
Talking It Over 020 MIN
Word Analysis Skills 020 MIN

Literary Essay 1 C 30 MIN
3/4 OR 1/2 INCH VIDEO CASSETTE C
See series title for descriptive statement.
From The Communicating Through Literature Series.
Prod-DALCCD Dist-DALCCD

Literary Essay 2 C 30 MIN
3/4 OR 1/2 INCH VIDEO CASSETTE C
See series title for descriptive statement.
From The Communicating Through Literature Series.
Prod-DALCCD Dist-DALCCD

Literature C 15 MIN
3/4 OR 1/2 INCH VIDEO CASSETTE K-P
Identifies rhyming words and ways that poems and stories are different.
From The Pass It On Series.
Prod-WKNOTV Dist-GPITVL 1983

Literature C 30 MIN
3/4 OR 1/2 INCH VIDEO CASSETTE C
Discusses black trends in literature.
From The Afro-American Perspectives Series.
Prod-MDDE Dist-MDCPB

Literature - Behind The Words C 30 MIN
3/4 INCH VIDEO CASSETTE C A
Discusses some questions and topics basic to the critical, analytical approach to literature. Explores nature of creative process, writers' inspiration, role of rhythm in poetry and reasons for popularity of some modern fiction over others.
From The Humanities Through The Arts With Maya Angelou Series. Lesson 17
Prod-COAST Dist-CDTEL Prodn-CICOCH

Literature - From Words, Truth C 30 MIN
3/4 INCH VIDEO CASSETTE C A
Traces evolution of the alphabet as the essential tool in written literature. Surveys characteristics of literature in each of the major periods of Western literature. Notes how various types of literature have portrayed humankind differently.
From The Humanities Through The Arts With Maya Angelou Series. Lesson 14
Prod-COAST Dist-CDTEL Prodn-CICOCH

Literature - Legacy For The Future C 18 MIN
16MM FILM, 3/4 OR 1/2 IN VIDEO J-C
An introduction to the study of literature.
From The Humanities Series.
Prod-MGHT Dist-MGHT Prodn-JOSHUA 1971

Literature - The Story Beyond C 30 MIN
3/4 INCH VIDEO CASSETTE C A
Defines good fiction and gives an overview of the history of fiction. Examines the basic elements of fiction through film and narrative of The Lottery read by Maya Angelou.
From The Humanities Through The Arts With Maya Angelou Series. Lesson 16
Prod-COAST Dist-CDTEL Prodn-CICOCH

Literature - The Synthesis Of Poetry C 30 MIN
3/4 INCH VIDEO CASSETTE C A
Centers on elements of poetry and on how those elements are fused to create a form that conveys the poet's meaning. Analyzes rhythm, imagery, repetition, meaning and rhyme.
From The Humanities Through The Arts With Maya Angelou Series. Lesson 15
Prod-COAST Dist-CDTEL Prodn-CICOCH

Literature Appreciation - Analyzing Characters C 13 MIN
16MM FILM, 3/4 OR 1/2 IN VIDEO J-C
Presents literary characters who come to life to explains themselves, appear in dramatizations of stories they are in and rate themselves in terms of development and complexity.
From The Literature Appreciation Series.
Prod-CORF Dist-CORF 1970

Literature Appreciation - How To Read Biographies C 14 MIN
16MM FILM, 3/4 OR 1/2 IN VIDEO J-H
Presents passages from outstanding biographies and autobiographies to show how these literary forms contribute to an understanding of history and give an insight into the character and philosophies of men and women—Washington, Lincoln, Michelangelo, Helen Keller, Charles Lindbergh and Babe Ruth. Illustrates the biography as a form of entertainment in a book by George and Helen Papshivily.
From The Literature Appreciation Series.
Prod-CORF Dist-CORF 1965

Literature Appreciation - How To Read Novels C 14 MIN
16MM FILM, 3/4 OR 1/2 IN VIDEO J-H
Encourages high school students to find out about the author, to study characterizations, and to visualize the setting and action in order to gain pleasure in novel reading and to give better oral and written book reports.
From The Literature Appreciation Series.
Prod-CORF Dist-CORF 1953

Literature Appreciation - How To Read Poetry C 10 MIN
16MM FILM, 3/4 OR 1/2 IN VIDEO J-C
Shows how understanding a poet, looking for experiences the poet is sharing and recognizing word devices used to convey these experiences will increase the pleasures of reading poetry.
From The Literature Appreciation Series.
Prod-CORF Dist-CORF 1952

Literature Appreciation - Stories C 14 MIN
16MM FILM, 3/4 OR 1/2 IN VIDEO J-C
Explains how to analyze stories by studying plot development, characters, setting and author's style.
From The Literature Appreciation Series.
Prod-CORF Dist-CORF 195

Literature Appreciation—A Series
16MM FILM, 3/4 OR 1/2 IN VIDEO
Prod-CORF Dist-CORF

Literature Appreciation - Analyzing Characters 013 MIN
Literature Appreciation - How To Read 014 MIN
Literature Appreciation - How To Read Novels 014 MIN
Literature Appreciation - How To Read Poetry 010 MIN
Literature Appreciation - Stories 014 MIN

Literature For Children C 29 MIN
3/4 OR 1/2 INCH VIDEO CASSETTE C A
Presents a noted children's librarian and educator exploring the place of books and literature in general in the live of young people from infancy to adolescence.
From The Focus On Children Series.
LC NO. 81-707451
Prod-IU Dist-IU 1981

Literature In The Kindergarten B 30 MIN
2 INCH VIDEOTAPE
See series title for descriptive statement.
From The Program Development In The Kindergarten Series.
Prod-GPITVL Dist-GPITVL

Literature Of Science Fiction—A Series
H-C T
From The Literature Of Science Fiction Series.
Prod-UKANBC Dist-UKANS

History Of Science Fiction From 1938 To The
Lunch With John Campbell, Jr - An Editor At 28 MIN
New Directions In Science Fiction 25 MIN
Plot In Science Fiction 25 MIN
Science Fiction Films 30 MIN

Literature Of Sports, The C 29 MIN
2 INCH VIDEOTAPE
From The One To One Series.
Prod-WETATV Dist-PUBTEL

Literature, Pt 1 C 30 MIN
3/4 OR 1/2 INCH VIDEO CASSETTE H-C A
Examines the literature in Japan.
From The Japan - The Living Tradition Series.
Prod-UMA Dist-GPITVL 1976

Literature, Pt 2 C 30 MIN
3/4 OR 1/2 INCH VIDEO CASSETTE H-C A
Examines the literature in Japan.
From The Japan - The Living Tradition Series.
Prod-UMA Dist-GPITVL 1976

Lithography C 25 MIN
3/4 OR 1/2 INCH VIDEO CASSETTE H-C A
Shows a lithographer drawing directly onto lithographic zinc plates using a detailed drawing in colored pencils. Shows another lithographer spraying lithographic ink through masks onto his plates to build up the image in tones after which the plates are processed and proofed.
From The Artist In Print Series.
Prod-BBCTV Dist-FI

Lithuanian Ethnographic Ensemble, The C 30 MIN
3/4 OR 1/2 INCH VIDEO CASSETTE
Shows actors, musicians and other artists of the renowned Lithuanian Ethnographic Ensemble combine their talents to perform Lithuanian polyphonic folks songs throughout scenic locations in their native land.
Prod-IHF Dist-IHF

Litres And Millilitres C 20 MIN
3/4 INCH VIDEO CASSETTE
Shows the relationship between liters and milliliters and demonstrates the making of a cubic decimeter model.
From The Metric Marmalade Series.
Prod-WCVETV Dist-GPITVL 1979

Litter Monster, The C 17 MIN
16MM FILM, 3/4 OR 1/2 IN VIDEO I-J
Presents an overview of the litter problem indicating the dollar costs per year to clean up littered areas. Points out that this money could be better used to support medical research or to fund better housing projects. Shows a variety of projects across the nation where young people have recognized the litter problem and are doing something about it.
Prod-HIGGIN Dist-HIGGIN 1972

Litterbug C 5 MIN
16MM FILM OPTICAL SOUND K-I
Depicts an insect community in puppet animation.
From The Adventures In The High Grass Series.
LC NO. 74-702130
Prod-MMA Dist-MMA 1972

Litterbug, The C 8 MIN
16MM FILM, 3/4 OR 1/2 IN VIDEO P-C A
Donald Duck appears in the role of the litterbug, public nuisance number one, the most comtemptible pest known to mankind.
Prod-DISNEY Dist-WDEMCO 1962

Litterbug, The (Italian) C 8 MIN
16MM FILM, 3/4 OR 1/2 IN VIDEO P
Discourages littering. Hosted by Donald Duck.
Prod-WDEMCO Dist-WDEMCO 1962

Litterbug, The (Spanish) C 8 MIN
16MM FILM, 3/4 OR 1/2 IN VIDEO P
Discourages littering. Hosted by Donald Duck.
Prod-WDEMCO Dist-WDEMCO 1962

Litterbug, The (Swedish) C 8 MIN
16MM FILM, 3/4 OR 1/2 IN VIDEO P
Discourages littering. Hosted by Donald Duck.
Prod-WDEMCO Dist-WDEMCO 1962

Litters C 9 MIN
16MM FILM, 3/4 OR 1/2 IN VIDEO
Tells what happens when a horde of rampaging letters lays waste to Coney Island by obstructing traffic, scattering litter, spray painting graffiti and harassing people. Shows how they are forced to rectify their damage and are imprisoned once again in trash barrels.
Prod-MOURIS Dist-DIRECT

Little Airplane That Grew, The C 9 MIN
16MM FILM, 3/4 OR 1/2 IN VIDEO P-I
Tells a story of a little boy who daydreams when he should be studying. Presents the universal human qualities of joy, boredom, imagination and sheds light on the pros and cons of self-indulgence.
Prod-LCOA Dist-LCOA 1969

Little Airplane That Grew, The (French) C 8 MIN
16MM FILM, 3/4 OR 1/2 IN VIDEO P-I
Features an imaginative schoolboy who realizes his dream of flying his airplane.
Prod-LCOA Dist-LCOA 1969

Little Annie Rooney B 97 MIN
16MM FILM SILENT
Reveals that Little Annie Rooney, the daughter of a policeman, divides her time between getting into mischief and caring for her father and her brother, Tim. Reveals that when Annie's father is killed, Annie and Tim become intent on revenge. Stars Mary Pickford and William Haines. Directed by William Beaudine.
Prod-PICKFO Dist-KILLIS 1925

Little Bear Keepers, The C 51 MIN
16MM FILM, 3/4 OR 1/2 IN VIDEO I-J
Presents the story of Pepiko, whose father is a zoo keeper. Tells how Pepiko learns that his favorite bear cub, Bruno, is about to be traded to another zoo and how Pepiko 'cub-naps' Bruno, embarking on a series of wild adventures.
From The Featurettes For Children Series.
Prod-AUDBRF Dist-FI

Little Big Land C 29 MIN
16MM FILM - 3/4 IN VIDEO
Examines the American commodity of land and looks at the utilization of resources and tools to do away with Mother Earth.
From The Earthkeeping Series.
Prod-WTTWTV Dist-PUBTEL

Little Big Top C 9 MIN
16MM FILM OPTICAL SOUND K
Uses a circus put on by life game players to teach mathematical concepts to pre-school children. Shows the children as they enjoy discovering geometric shapes in everything around them.
From The Amazing Life Games Theater Series.
LC NO. 72-701751
Prod-HMC Dist-HMC 1971

Little Big Top C 10 MIN
16MM FILM, 3/4 OR 1/2 IN VIDEO I-C A
Takes a behind-the-scenes look at the everyday life of a small traveling circus troupe.
Prod-NFBC Dist-NFBC 1978

Little Bit More Pregnant, A C 29 MIN
2 INCH VIDEOTAPE
See series title for descriptive statement.
From The Maggie And The Beautiful Machine - Pregnancy Series.
Prod-WGBHTV Dist-PUBTEL

Little Bit Of Everything, A C 15 MIN
3/4 OR 1/2 INCH VIDEO CASSETTE J-H
Shows Hansel and Gretel teaching the witch about empty calories and the need for a balanced diet. Presents private eye Max Lionel discussing the Case of the Neglected Nutrients.
From The Soup To Nuts Series.
Prod-GSDE Dist-AITECH 1980

Little Bit Of Paris, A C 15 MIN
3/4 OR 1/2 INCH VIDEO CASSETTE P
Pictures the Notre Dame Cathedral, Montmartre and the Eiffel Tower in Paris, France.
From The Other Families, Other Friends Series. Red Module - France
Prod-WVIZTV Dist-AITECH 1971

Little Bit Pregnant, A C 29 MIN
2 INCH VIDEOTAPE
See series title for descriptive statement.
From The Maggie And The Beautiful Machine - Pregnancy Series.
Prod-WGBHTV Dist-PUBTEL

Little Black Puppy, The C 6 MIN
16MM FILM, 3/4 OR 1/2 IN VIDEO P
Presents the story of a puppy who is disliked by a boy's family until it grows up.
From The Golden Book Storytime Series.
Prod-MTI Dist-MTI 1977

Little Blocks C 8 MIN
16MM FILM OPTICAL SOUND J-C A
Presents a situation in which a teenager has difficulty in working with a shy young boy. Shows the boy discussing the situation with his classmates.
From The Exploring Childhood Series.
LC NO. 76-701888
Prod-EDC Dist-EDC Prodn-FRIEDJ 1976

Little Blue And Little Yellow C 10 MIN
16MM FILM, 3/4 OR 1/2 IN VIDEO P-I
An animated version of Leo Lionni's book in which Little Blue and Little Yellow turn green to the amazement of their friends and parents.
Prod-HILBER Dist-MGHT 1962

Little Bluebird's Valley, The C 11 MIN
16MM FILM, 3/4 OR 1/2 IN VIDEO P
Introduces conservation concepts in an animated cartoon in the little bluebird's valley where humans come to build a dam that prevents floods and produces electricity.
Prod-CORF Dist-CORF 1970

Little Boat, A (French) C 14 MIN
3/4 OR 1/2 INCH VIDEO CASSETTE H-C A
Contrasts a pond on the Ile de-France and a school near Grenoble where the world's most unnavigable waterways are reconstructed in miniature.
From The En Francais Series. Part 2 - Temporal Relationships, Logical Relationships
Prod-MOFAFR Dist-AITECH 1970

Little Boy Lost C 11 MIN
16MM FILM OPTICAL SOUND
Uses the experiences of a young husband who tours the agencies of United Way and subsequently adopts a small boy to point out the work of the United Way of America.
LC NO. 74-702486
Prod-UWAMER Dist-UWAMER 1974

Little Brother Montgomery C 30 MIN
3/4 INCH VIDEO CASSETTE
Features blues piano player and singer Little Brother Montgomery. Includes the songs Mule Face Blues, Cow Cow Blues, Gonna Move On The Outskirts Of Town, and others.
From The After Hours With Art Hodes Series.
Prod-FAJAZZ Dist-FAJAZZ

Little Brown Burro, The C
1/2 IN VIDEO CASSETTE BETA/VHS
Tells the story of a little brown burro.
Prod-EQVDL Dist-EQVDL

Little Brown Burro, The C 23 MIN
16MM FILM, 3/4 OR 1/2 IN VIDEO P-I
Presents the tale of a little donkey, belittled as useless, who comes to realize that by doing his best he can make his own special contributions.
Prod-ATKINS Dist-LCOA 1979

Little Businessman C 28 MIN
16MM FILM OPTICAL SOUND K-I
Reveals that Luke's uncle wants to do away with Luke's pet dog. Describes an agreement which is reached wherein Luke pays his uncle to allow the old dog to live out his days in his uncle's house.
Prod-CANBC Dist-FI

Little By Little C 14 MIN
3/4 OR 1/2 INCH VIDEO CASSETTE P
See series title for descriptive statement.
From The Strawberry Square Series.
Prod-NEITV Dist-AITECH 1982

Little Chimney Sweep B 10 MIN
16MM FILM OPTICAL SOUND K-I
Shows the fairy tale 'LITTLE CHIMNEY SWEEP' in animated form based on the live shadow plays L Reiniger produced for BBC television.
From The Lotte Reiniger's Animated Fairy Tales Series.
Prod-PRIMP Dist-MOMA 1956

Little Church Around The Corner B 60 MIN
16MM FILM SILENT
A drama concerning an orphan who is reared to be a minister in a small mining town, but later becomes torn between his duty to the people of the town and his love for the mine owner's daughter, who wants him to preach in New York.
LC NO. 72-709612
Prod-WB Dist-WB 1923

Little City C 31 MIN
16MM FILM, 3/4 OR 1/2 IN VIDEO T
Shows the learning activities and social interaction of retarded, emotionally handicapped and blind individuals living at Little City Foundation residential training community.
Prod-LICIFO Dist-FLMLIB Prodn-DACHA 1980

Little Computers - See How They Run—A Series
J-C A
Studies the small computer and explains how the computer receives, processes, stores and transmits the range and quantity of information it does.
Prod-ELDATA Dist-GPITVL 1980

Character I/O Devices	018 MIN
CPU And Memory	018 MIN
Data Communication	018 MIN
Inside The Computer	018 MIN
Making Things Happen	018 MIN
Mass Storage Devices	018 MIN
Meet The Computer	018 MIN
Speech, Music And Graphics	018 MIN

Little Death, A C 30 MIN
16MM FILM, 3/4 OR 1/2 IN VIDEO H-C A
Tells how a woman and a priest concoct a plan for teaching her husband a lesson. Based on Giovanni Boccaccio's Tales Of The Decameron.
Prod-PHENIX Dist-PHENIX 1979

Little Dog And The Bees, The C 7 MIN
16MM FILM, 3/4 OR 1/2 IN VIDEO K-P
Presents an animated story in which a little dog and a kitten cross paths with a greedy alley cat when trying to keep him from taking some honeycomb from their friends the bees. Shows how the dog and the kitten come out ahead through ingenuity and teamwork.
From The Little Dog Series.
Prod-ROMAF Dist-PHENIX Prodn-ANIMAF 1982

Little Dog And The Chicks, The C 8 MIN
16MM FILM, 3/4 OR 1/2 IN VIDEO I-J
Tells the story about Little Dog and his friend Kitten being mistakenly identified as their mother by a group of newborn chicks. They devise a clever plan to get the chicks back into their shells to be greeted by their real mother when they are 'born' a second time.
From The Little Dog Series.
LC NO. 84-706793
Prod-KRATKY Dist-PHENIX

Little Dog And The Goat, The C 8 MIN
16MM FILM, 3/4 OR 1/2 IN VIDEO K-P
Presents the story of Little Dog and his friend Kitten helping a baby goat who has a bump on his head and thinks it was caused by Friend Squirrel carelessly throwing acorns. Explains that the real reason for the bump is that the goat is growing his first set of horns.
From The Little Dog Series.
Prod-ROMAF Dist-PHENIX

Little Dog Goes Fishing C 8 MIN
16MM FILM, 3/4 OR 1/2 IN VIDEO I
Tells how several fish, too clever to allow themselves to be caught, come to the aid of their would-be captors when they fall into the river. The fishes' act of kindness makes the fishermen abandon fishing and they all part as friends.
From The Little Dog Series.
LC NO. 84-706794
Prod-KRATKY Dist-PHENIX

Little Dog Goes Skiing, The C 8 MIN
16MM FILM, 3/4 OR 1/2 IN VIDEO I
Describes how Little Dog and Kitten make themselves comfortable in a warm, seemingly unoccupied cabin after a day of skiing until the irritable owner returns to evict them. Tells that when, as a result of his bad temper, the owner gets into trouble, Little Dog and Kitten rescue him and find themselves welcome in the cabin.
From The Little Dog Series.
LC NO. 84-706795
Prod-KRATKY Dist-PHENIX

Little Dog Lost C 6 MIN
16MM FILM, 3/4 OR 1/2 IN VIDEO P
Relates that while searching for their lost dog, Tim and Jody visit all kinds of neighborhood stores.
From The Golden Book Storytime Series.
Prod-MTI Dist-MTI 1977

Little Dog Lost C 48 MIN
16MM FILM, 3/4 OR 1/2 IN VIDEO
Presents the story of Candy, a Welsh Cordy, who becomes lost from his master.
From The Animal Featurettes, Set 1 Series.
Prod-DISNEY Dist-WDEMCO

Little Dog—A Series
16MM FILM, 3/4 OR 1/2 IN VIDEO K-P
Presents a series about Little Dog, a friendly black and white pup who likes to help his friends out of difficulties, and his faithful companion, Kitten.
Prod-ROMAF Dist-PHENIX

Christmas Party, The	006 MIN
Halloween Dream	007 MIN
Little Dog And The Bees, The	007 MIN
Little Dog And The Chicks, The	008 MIN
Little Dog And The Goat, The	008 MIN
Little Dog Goes Fishing	008 MIN
Little Dog Goes Skiing, The	008 MIN
Little Pig, The	008 MIN
Pancakes With Surprises	009 MIN
Turtle, The	008 MIN
Who's The Cleanest	007 MIN

Little Dog's Adventures, The - A Story To Finish C 14 MIN
16MM FILM, 3/4 OR 1/2 IN VIDEO P
Invites pupils to tell stories of their own about a little dog's adventures with other animals as she looks for her master. Provides a background for language arts activities such as story-telling, creative dramatics and reading.
Prod-CORF Dist-CORF 1970

Little Drummer Boy, The C 25 MIN
16MM FILM OPTICAL SOUND K-H A
Presents the story of the little orphan who shares his gift of music with the infant Jesus. Uses puppet animation. The television special of the Little Drummer Boy.
Prod-CORF Dist-CORF

Little Drummer Boy, The C 7 MIN
16MM FILM, 3/4 OR 1/2 IN VIDEO
Shows the excitement felt by all who came to witness the birth in Bethlehem. Expresses the spirit of Christmas and inspires good will throughout the year.
Prod-WWS Dist-WWS 1968

Little Drummer Boy, The - Book II C 24 MIN
16MM FILM, 3/4 OR 1/2 IN VIDEO
Presents Greer Garson narrating a puppet-animated story of how the Little Drummer Boy helped spread the word of the first Christmas.
Prod-PERSPF Dist-CORF 1982

Little Dutch Boy C 3 MIN
16MM FILM SILENT P-H S
Tells in American sign language the story of the little Dutch boy who became a national hero when he saved his country from flooding by blocking a leak in a dyke with his hands. Signed for the deaf by Jack Burns.
LC NO. 76-701691
Prod-JOYCE Dist-JOYCE 1976

Little Dutch Island C 15 MIN
3/4 OR 1/2 INCH VIDEO CASSETTE P
Presents various features of the island of Aruba.
From The Other Families, Other Friends Series. Blue Module - Aruba
Prod-WVIZTV Dist-AITECH 1971

Little Engine That Could, The C 10 MIN
16MM FILM, 3/4 OR 1/2 IN VIDEO K-P
Animated story of the little engine that pulled a trainload of toys to the children on the other side of the mountain.
Prod-CORF Dist-CORF 1963

Little Extra Work, A B 9 MIN
16MM FILM - 3/4 IN VIDEO
Examines the emotional conflicts involved in the working relationship between local and state health departments.
Prod-USNAC Dist-USNAC 1972

Little Flame, A C 28 MIN
16MM FILM OPTICAL SOUND
Shows the dangers of fires carelessly caused by trash burning, smoking, brush and grass burning, campfires, and children playing with matches. Shows how John Weaver, a public spirited insurance man, helps to lick the fire problems in his community.
LC NO. 74-705039
Prod-USDA Dist-USNAC 1965

Little Forest C 8 MIN
16MM FILM OPTICAL SOUND P-C
Explores the nature of the essence of the forest. Examines the timelessness, the small and quiet phenomena and the equalness of all that occurs in the forest, from a deer being eaten away to a butterfly caught in a spider's web.
LC NO. 72-703328
Prod-ALBM Dist-MARALF 1972

Little Foxes, The B
1/2 IN VIDEO CASSETTE BETA/VHS
Presents Lillian Hellman's drama of a Southern matriarch and the family she drives mercilessly. Starring Bette Davis.
Prod-GA Dist-GA

Little Giants, The - The Inside Story Of Your Glands C 14 MIN
3/4 OR 1/2 INCH VIDEO CASSETTE P-I
Explores the electrical and chemical partnership between the brain and the endocrine system. Explains the functions and importance of the thyroid, pituitary, adrenal, the sex glands and the hypothalmus.
From The Inside Story With Slim Goodbody Series.
Prod-GBCTP Dist-AITECH Prodn-WETN 1981

Little Girl And A Gunny Wolf, A C 6 MIN
16MM FILM, 3/4 OR 1/2 IN VIDEO P-I
Tells of a little girl who, in spite of her mother's warning, goes to pick flowers in the forest where she encounters a fabulous animal known as the Big, Bad Gunny Wolf.
From The Children's Storybook Theater Series.
Prod-ACI Dist-AIMS 1971

Little Girl And The Tiny Doll, The C 15 MIN
3/4 OR 1/2 INCH VIDEO CASSETTE K-P
Tells the story of a little girl with her mother in a grocery store who discovers a tiny doll among the frozen food in the freezer. Reveals that over several days she brings the doll warm clothes, plays with it and finally is given permission by the clerk to take the doll home to live in a beautiful doll house. Emphasizes the letter d.
From The Words And Pictures Series.
Prod-FI Dist-FI

Little Gray Neck C 18 MIN
16MM FILM OPTICAL SOUND
Fantasy of a little gray-necked duck which, because of a hurt wing, is left behind when the other ducks fly South. A family of rabbits and an eagle help him escape the red fox.
Prod-SYZMT Dist-TEXFLM 1955

Little Help From My Friends, A - Friendship C 15 MIN
16MM FILM, 3/4 OR 1/2 IN VIDEO J-H
Tells how Hector covers for his friend Beto while Beto flirts with women and avoids work. Describes the confrontation which changes their relationship.
From The On The Level Series.
LC NO. 81-706933
Prod-EDFCEN Dist-AITECH 1980

Little Hiawatha C 8 MIN
16MM FILM, 3/4 OR 1/2 IN VIDEO K-J
Shows 'MIGHTY LITTLE HIAWATHA' who goes hunting but is too fainthearted to kill a rabbit. His kindness is returned when the animals help him escape from a bear.
Prod-DISNEY Dist-WDEMCO 1954

Little Hiawatha C 8 MIN
16MM FILM, 3/4 OR 1/2 IN VIDEO P
Shows how to win support by playing fair. Focuses on the qualities of true friendship. An animated international version.
Prod-WDEMCO Dist-WDEMCO 1954

Little Hiawatha (Spanish) C 8 MIN
16MM FILM, 3/4 OR 1/2 IN VIDEO P
Shows how to win support by playing fair. Focuses on the qualities of true friendship.
Prod-WDEMCO Dist-WDEMCO 1954

Little House In The Big Woods C 15 MIN
3/4 OR 1/2 INCH VIDEO CASSETTE I
Presents selections from Laura Ingalls Wilder's story of family life on the frontier.
From The Book Bird Series.
Prod-CTI Dist-CTI

Little Injustices - Laura Nader Looks At The Law C 58 MIN
3/4 OR 1/2 INCH VIDEO CASSETTE
Presents anthropologist Laura Nader as she compares the Mexican and American legal systems and how they resolve consumer complaints.
From The Odyssey Series.
LC NO. 82-706986
Prod-PBA Dist-PBS

Little League Baseball's Official Instruction Video C
3/4 OR 1/2 INCH VIDEO CASSETTE
Prod-MSTVIS Dist-MSTVIS

Little Lie That Grew B 30 MIN
16MM FILM OPTICAL SOUND P-I
Presents a nine-year-old boy who learns that telling the truth is always best when a little white lie grows until it is out of control.
LC NO. 72-701647
Prod-CONCOR Dist-CPH 1956

Little Lord Fauntleroy B 102 MIN
16MM FILM OPTICAL SOUND P-I
Portrays a boy growing up in Brooklyn in the 1880's.
Prod-FI Dist-FI

Little Lost Blue Rock C 8 MIN
16MM FILM OPTICAL SOUND
Contrasts environmental conditions on Earth with those on the moon, emphasizing the difference made by the availability of water on Earth.
LC NO. 79-700236
Prod-GROENG Dist-GROENG 1978

Little Lost Burro, The C 9 MIN
16MM FILM OPTICAL SOUND K-I
Tells how Blanco, the little white burro, sets out to find his mother who has been captured and taken away by men who sell wild burros to prospectors. Describes his adventures with a friendly rabbit, a ghost town and a hungry bobcat, and shows how he finds his mother after giving up all hope.
Prod-CORF Dist-CORF 1982

Little Lost Burro, The C 9 MIN
16MM FILM, 3/4 OR 1/2 IN VIDEO K-I
Tells how Blanco, the little white burro, sets out to find his mother who has been captured and taken away by men who sell wild burros to prospectors. Describes his adventures with a friendly rabbit, a ghost town and a hungry bobcat, and shows how he finds his mother after giving up all hope.
Prod-CORF Dist-CORF 1982

Little Lulu C 24 MIN
16MM FILM, 3/4 OR 1/2 IN VIDEO
Presents a live action story on equal rights, featuring the comic strip character Little Lulu. Illustrates the changing perceptions of male and female roles in society. Originally shown on the television series ABC Weekend Specials.
LC NO. 79-707131
Prod-ABCTV Dist-MTI Prodn-ABCCIR 1979

Little Mariner, The - A True Fairy Tale X 20 MIN
16MM FILM, 3/4 OR 1/2 IN VIDEO P-I
Describes the port of Long Beach, California, from the point of view of a small boy who sails into the port an enchanted sailboat. Formerly titled 'LE PETIT MARINER.'
Prod-TIGERF Dist-EBEC 1966

Little Mark Or Two, A C 20 MIN
2 INCH VIDEOTAPE P
See series title for descriptive statement.
From The Learning Our Language, Unit 2 - Dictionary Skills Series.
Prod-MPATI Dist-GPITVL

Little Mary - America's Sweetheart B 12 MIN
16MM FILM SILENT J A
Tells about the career of Mary Pickford. In June of 1909, young Gladys Smith applied for work at the Biograph Studio. As Mary Pickford, the 16-year-old girl had acquired an impressive list of credits in her 11 years on the stage. But stage roles for the young ingenue were scarce in the spring of 1909 when D W Griffith gave her her first bit role in films. Includes All On Account Of The Milk (1910) Ever Again (1910) The New York Hat (1912) and The Mender Of Nets (1912).
Prod-BHAWK Dist-BHAWK

Little Match Girl, The C 9 MIN
16MM FILM, 3/4 OR 1/2 IN VIDEO P-I
Presents an adaptation of Hans Christian Andersen's tale about a little girl who is sent out on a bitterly cold Christmas Eve to sell her basket of matchsticks.
Prod-BFA Dist-PHENIX 1976

Little Match Girl, The C 17 MIN
16MM FILM, 3/4 OR 1/2 IN VIDEO P
Uses puppet animation to tell the story of a ragged child who sells matches on the cold streets of a city. Based on the story The Little Match Girl by Hans Christian Andersen.
Prod-CORF Dist-CORF

Little Match Girl, The C 24 MIN
3/4 OR 1/2 INCH VIDEO CASSETTE
Tells Hans Christian Andersen's classic story of a little girl's search for love at Christmas. Presented in a contemporary setting.
From The Young People's Specials Series.
Prod-MULTPP Dist-MULTPP

Little Match Girl, The (Captioned) C 17 MIN
16MM FILM, 3/4 OR 1/2 IN VIDEO P
Uses puppet animation to tell the story of a ragged child who sells matches on the cold streets of a city. Based on the story The Little Match Girl by Hans Christian Andersen.
Prod-CORF Dist-CORF

Little Men Of Chromagnon, The C 8 MIN
16MM FILM, 3/4 OR 1/2 IN VIDEO I-C A
An animated film which introduces the primary colors and their combinations.
Prod-NFBC Dist-IU 1971

Little Mermaid, The C 25 MIN
16MM FILM, 3/4 OR 1/2 IN VIDEO
Presents Hans Christian Andersen's fairy story 'THE LITTLE MERMAID' about a little mermaid and her love for a prince.
Prod-READER Dist-PFP 1974

Little Mermaid, The (French) C 25 MIN
16MM FILM, 3/4 OR 1/2 IN VIDEO P-I
A French language version of the film, The Little Mermaid, an animated version of Hans Christian Anderson's story. Tells the story of a young mermaid who falls in love with a prince, sacrifices her voice to be with him in human form, and, when the prince marries another, nearly loses her soul, but instead is rewarded with everlasting happiness. Narrated by actor Richard Chamberlain.
Prod-HUBLEY Dist-PFP

Little Mermaid, The (Spanish) C 25 MIN
16MM FILM, 3/4 OR 1/2 IN VIDEO P-I
A Spanish language version of the film, The Little Mermaid, an animated version of Hans Christian Anderson's story. Tells the story of a young mermaid who falls in love with a prince, sacrifices her voice to be with him in human form, and, when the prince marries another, nearly loses her soul, but instead is rewarded with everlasting happiness. Narrated by actor Richard Chamberlain.
Prod-HUBLEY Dist-PFP

Little Miseries C 27 MIN
16MM FILM, 3/4 OR 1/2 IN VIDEO H-C A
Dissects the relationship between a young man and his overbearing aunt who raised him after his parents died. Shows that the aunt's behavior is really due to loneliness and the need for the young man's love. Stars John Ritter and Audra Lindley.
From The Insight Series.
Prod-PAULST Dist-PAULST

Little People Clothes C 15 MIN
2 INCH VIDEOTAPE
See series title for descriptive statement.
From The Umbrella Series.
Prod-KETCTV Dist-PUBTEL

Little Phantasy On A 19th Century Painting, A B 4 MIN
16MM FILM, 3/4 OR 1/2 IN VIDEO P-H T
Based on a nineteenth-century painting, 'ISLE OF THE DEAD,' by Arnold Boecklin. Animation artist Norman Mc Laren captures the mood of the original painting through light and movement. The island wakes to mysterious life and fades again into the dark.
Prod-NFBC Dist-IFB Prodn-MCLN 1947

Little Pig, The C 8 MIN
16MM FILM, 3/4 OR 1/2 IN VIDEO K-P
Presents the story of Little Dog and Kitten trying to prevent a little pig from playing in a mud puddle and always getting dirty. Shows that their efforts are to no avail.
From The Little Dog Series.
Prod-ROMAF Dist-PHENIX

Little Players, The C 59 MIN
16MM FILM OPTICAL SOUND
Focuses on the Little Players, a five-member theatrical troupe created by artists Frank Peschka and Bill Murdock.
LC NO. 81-700418
Prod-OPUS Dist-OPUS 1981

Little Players, The C 27 MIN
16MM FILM, 3/4 OR 1/2 IN VIDEO J-C A
Introduces the Little Players, a puppet troupe whose repertoire is drawn from Shakespeare, Oscar Wilde and Noel Coward.
LC NO. 83-706166
Prod-LEHWIL Dist-WOMBAT 1982

Little Plover (River) Project, A Study In Sand Plains Hydrology C 35 MIN
16MM FILM OPTICAL SOUND
Shows how geologists and engineers collect and interpret data to determine the occurrence, movement and amount of water available in a particular area, how ground water and surface water are inter-related and how the effects of various water uses on stream flows and ground-water levels may be predicted.
Prod-USGEOS Dist-USGEOS 1963

Little Prince, The C 27 MIN
16MM FILM OPTICAL SOUND P-J
Uses the technique of clay animation to tell the story of a little prince who lives on a tiny planet and who travels to Earth to find the secret of happiness. Based on the book The Little Prince by Antoine de Saint-Exupery.
LC NO. 79-701069
Prod-BBF Dist-BBF 1979

Little Prince, The C 27 MIN
16MM FILM OPTICAL SOUND
Tells the story of The Little Prince who lived on a tiny planet watching over his three volcanoes and tending a single rose

of great beauty. Reveals that his interplanetary travels took him to earth where he made friends with a fox who shared with him the secret of happiness.
Prod-VINTN Dist-FACSEA

Little Princess, The C 92 MIN
3/4 OR 1/2 INCH VIDEO CASSETTE
Stars Shirley Temple as the Little Princess.
Prod-ADVCAS Dist-ADVCAS

Little Rascals' Christmas Special, The C 24 MIN
16MM FILM OPTICAL SOUND K-I A
Uses animation to present a Christmas story featuring the Little Rascals. Shows how Spanky and Porky's mother buys them a train for Christmas with money she saved to buy a winter coat. Tells how her sacrifice and the boys' realization of it eventually involve a street-wise sidewalk Santa and the rest of the Little Rascals.
Prod-CORF Dist-CORF 1982

Little Red Circle, The C 8 MIN
16MM FILM OPTICAL SOUND P
Uses animation to introduce the principles of classification by physical attribute. Shows the basic attributes of objects, including color, shape and size.
Prod-RAMFLM Dist-SUTHRB 1977

Little Red Fire Engine, The C 15 MIN
3/4 INCH VIDEO CASSETTE K-P
See series title for descriptive statement.
From The Storytime Series.
Prod-WCETTV Dist-GPITVL 1976

Little Red Hen, The C 11 MIN
16MM FILM, 3/4 OR 1/2 IN VIDEO P
Uses both art and live action to retell the fable The Little Red Hen.
Prod-CORF Dist-CORF 1950

Little Red Lighthouse X 9 MIN
16MM FILM, 3/4 OR 1/2 IN VIDEO K-P
An iconographic motion picture based on the children's book of the same title by Hildegarde Swift. Tells the story of a lighthouse who learns he is still useful even if a more powerful light has been installed on the great bridge.
Prod-WWS Dist-WWS 1956

Little Red Lightouse, The - The Great Gray Bridge C 15 MIN
3/4 INCH VIDEO CASSETTE K-P
See series title for descriptive statement.
From The Storytime Series.
Prod-WCETTV Dist-GPITVL 1976

Little Red Riding Hood C 9 MIN
16MM FILM, 3/4 OR 1/2 IN VIDEO P-I A
Re-creates the story book tale of Little Red Riding Hood.
Prod-HARRY Dist-PHENIX 1958

Little Red Riding Hood C 13 MIN
16MM FILM, 3/4 OR 1/2 IN VIDEO P-I
Tells the story of Little Red Riding Hood and her adventures and dangers on the way to visit Grandmother.
Prod-DEFA Dist-LCOA 1979

Little Red Riding Hood C 17 MIN
16MM FILM, 3/4 OR 1/2 IN VIDEO P
Offers an animated version of the story of Little Red Riding Hood, adding some 20th century twists.
Prod-CORF Dist-CORF 1978

Little Red Riding Hood C 17 MIN
16MM FILM, 3/4 OR 1/2 IN VIDEO I-J
Uses Balinese masks and mime to tell the story of Little Red Riding Hood.
LC NO. 81-706024
Prod-SONNED Dist-TEXFLM 1980

Little Richard B 30 MIN
16MM FILM OPTICAL SOUND
Relates how Little Richard, a blue-tick hound, became trapped in a practically inaccessible hole while he was hunting raccoons and how he was rescued with the help of his owner, the neighbors and the phone and utility companies.
LC NO. FI67-114
Prod-GE Dist-WB 1963

Little Rivers, The C 20 MIN
16MM FILM OPTICAL SOUND J A
Describes the difficulties which plague little urban streams such as the small creeks in the Buffalo metropolitan area. Explains the comprehensive planning program which proposes to provide a modern water resources system for this urban area.
LC NO. 74-714056
Prod-FINLYS Dist-FINLYS 1969

Little Romance, A, Part I C 30 MIN
3/4 OR 1/2 INCH VIDEO CASSETTE
See series title for descriptive statement.
From The Up And Coming Series.
Prod-KQEDTV Dist-MDCPB

Little Romance, A, Part II C 30 MIN
3/4 OR 1/2 INCH VIDEO CASSETTE
See series title for descriptive statement.
From The Up And Coming Series.
Prod-KQEDTV Dist-MDCPB

Little Rooster Who Made The Sun Rise, The C 11 MIN
16MM FILM, 3/4 OR 1/2 IN VIDEO P
Animated story of the rooster who discovers that his crowing does not make the sun rise, but who acquires pride in doing his job of waking his farmyard friends.
Prod-CORF Dist-CORF 1961

Little School In The Desert C 15 MIN
3/4 OR 1/2 INCH VIDEO CASSETTE I
Deals with the education of Bedouin children.
From The Encounter In The Desert Series.
Prod-CTI Dist-CTI

Little Shepherd And The First Christmas, The C 19 MIN
16MM FILM, 3/4 OR 1/2 IN VIDEO P-H
Tells of a certain night in Judea 2,000 years ago, when shepherds followed a star and found a new-born child. Uses animation to tell the story of one of the shepherds, an orphan boy, and the gift he brought to Bethlehem. The little shpherd's journey of faith proves his own worth and brings wondrous joy to the foster father and brother he loves.
Prod-CORF Dist-CORF 1967

Little Shop Of Horrors, The B 76 MIN
16MM FILM OPTICAL SOUND C A
Tells of a simple-minded florist's helper who in an effort to impress his girlfriend, develops a hybrid plant which rejects ordinary plant foods and demands blood.
Prod-CORMAN Dist-KITPAR 1960

Little Sinners B 17 MIN
16MM FILM OPTICAL SOUND
Explains how Spanky learns a morality lesson and gets a spiritual scare when he chooses fishing over Sunday school. A Little Rascals film.
Prod-ROACH Dist-BHAWK 1935

Little Sister C 45 MIN
16MM FILM OPTICAL SOUND
Tells how a reunion of friends evolves into an emotional test for Ellen. Shows that the group's dynamic force threatens to clamp off her connection to an idealized past, impelling her to a painful confrontation with her oldest and most cherished friend.
LC NO. 80-700068
Prod-BRIMED Dist-BRIMED 1977

Little Slow, A C 14 MIN
16MM FILM - 3/4 IN VIDEO
Features two young adults as they discuss the issue of legal rights for retarded citizens, using flashbacks to their problems as children. Portrays several forms of discrimination that retarded persons encounter. Issued in 1974 as a motion picture.
LC NO. 79-706093
Prod-USPCMR Dist-USNAC Prodn-PRODH 1979

Little Soot Slayer, The C 10 MIN
16MM FILM, 3/4 OR 1/2 IN VIDEO P-I
Presents a story of a little girl and her ingenious way of cleaning up the air.
Prod-SF Dist-SF 1980

Little Story, A Negligible Story, The C 7 MIN
16MM FILM, 3/4 OR 1/2 IN VIDEO J-C
Presents an animated tale, based on a story by Ambrose Bierce, about a starving orphan girl who is showered with an assortment of delights on Christmas night. Shows how shopkeepers rush for the delights at dawn and find the orphan dead.
LC NO. 77-701523
Prod-LESFG Dist-TEXFLM 1977

Little Sunshade, The (Umbrella) C 32 MIN
16MM FILM, 3/4 OR 1/2 IN VIDEO K-I
Presents a puppet film about a little old man who flies into a nursery on an umbrella, bringing all the toys to life and putting them in a circus show.
Prod-PHENIX Dist-PHENIX 1973

Little Swelling, A C 56 MIN
3/4 OR 1/2 INCH VIDEO CASSETTE H-C A
Shows a 16-year old girl who becomes pregnant and how she deals with it.
Prod-MMRC Dist-MMRC

Little Tadpole Who Grew, The C 10 MIN
16MM FILM, 3/4 OR 1/2 IN VIDEO P-I
Uses a story about a tadpole to motivate reading and language expression.
Prod-CORF Dist-CORF 1976

Little Theater Of Jean Renoir, The C 100 MIN
16MM FILM, 3/4 OR 1/2 IN VIDEO H-C A
Presents The Last Christmas Dinner, The Electric Floorwaxer, Le Belle Epoque, and The King Of Yvetot, four short subjects directed by Jean Renoir.
Prod-JANUS Dist-TEXFLM 1969

Little Theatre Of The Deaf C 29 MIN
3/4 INCH VIDEO CASSETTE
Features a children's play performed by the Little Theatre of the Deaf.
Prod-NETCHE Dist-PUBTEL

Little Thing Like Security, A C 22 MIN
16MM FILM OPTICAL SOUND
Illustrates the time and effort spent to recover a document lost by a subcontractor. Shows how a single lapse in security consciousness can hurt a company.
LC NO. 74-706374
Prod-USDD Dist-USNAC 1972

Little Things C 10 MIN
16MM FILM OPTICAL SOUND
Features an employee motivation film which presents a series of animated vignettes to show how good and bad habits can affect the employee.
LC NO. 75-703598
Prod-IBMSGC Dist-IBM 1975

Little Tiger, The C 11 MIN
16MM FILM, 3/4 OR 1/2 IN VIDEO P-I
Presents an animated story of a young tiger's search for true courage.
Prod-KRATKY Dist-PHENIX

Little Tim And The Brave Sea Captain C 11 MIN
16MM FILM, 3/4 OR 1/2 IN VIDEO
Tells the story of Tim, a stowaway on an ocean liner who braves a storm alongside the ship's captain. Uses illustrations to capture the rigors of shipboard life.
Prod-WWS Dist-WWS

Little Tom Thumb C 8 MIN
16MM FILM, 3/4 OR 1/2 IN VIDEO
An adaptation of the English fairy tale about Tom Thumb, the miller's miniature son who slept in a thimble.
From The Halas And Batchelor Fairy Tale Series.
Prod-HALAS Dist-EBEC 1969

Little Tom Thumb (Spanish) C 8 MIN
16MM FILM, 3/4 OR 1/2 IN VIDEO P
Shows how Tom Thumb becomes a hero by saving his six brothers and returning home with treasure and magic boots.
Prod-HALAS Dist-EBEC

Little Toot C 9 MIN
16MM FILM, 3/4 OR 1/2 IN VIDEO P-I
A story about a mischievous tugboat whose antics get it banished beyond the 12-mile limit until its heroic efforts during a storm bring it back to the harbor.
Prod-DISNEY Dist-WDEMCO 1971

Little Train Of The Caipira, The C 14 MIN
16MM FILM, 3/4 OR 1/2 IN VIDEO P-I
Uses animation and photography to introduce Brazilian composer, Villalobos and his work. Features 'The Little Train Of The Caipira' suite.
From The Music Experiences Series.
Prod-STEVNS Dist-AIMS 1971

Little Train Of The Caipira, The (Spanish) C 14 MIN
16MM FILM, 3/4 OR 1/2 IN VIDEO P-I
Uses animation and photography to introduce Brazilian composer, Villalobos and his work. Features 'The Little Train Of The Caipira' suite.
From The Music Experiences Series.
Prod-STEVNS Dist-AIMS 1971

Little Train, The C 11 MIN
16MM FILM OPTICAL SOUND K-P
Describes how a small old-fashioned steam locomotive tries to prove its worth by racing a modern diesel engine.
Prod-ZAGREB Dist-RADIM 1972

Little Train, The C 14 MIN
16MM FILM, 3/4 OR 1/2 IN VIDEO P-I
Presents the story of a little train to show how easy it is to underrate the value of one's position. Tells how the little train, who shuttles coal continuously to the big long-distance trains, longs to see the world outside the train yards and finally jumps the tracks to have a merry time until his fuel runs out. Shows how he realizes the importance of his job when he is rescued and returns to see how the long distance trains were stranded because he was not there to bring them fuel.
Prod-BFA Dist-PHENIX 1969

Little Tree That Had A Dream, The C 11 MIN
16MM FILM OPTICAL SOUND P-I
A nature-study film about a little Joshua tree that dreamed of the far-away places he wanted to see.
From The Inspirations From Nature Series.
LC NO. 79-702452
Prod-ALEF Dist-ALEF Prodn-FORF 1969

Little Tummy, The C 15 MIN
16MM FILM, 3/4 OR 1/2 IN VIDEO P-H A
Presents Chef Bernard Collot of Le Petit Bedon, a tiny Paris restaurant where kings dine.
Prod-KLEINW Dist-KLEINW

Little Twelvetoes C 4 MIN
3/4 OR 1/2 INCH VIDEO CASSETTE P-I
Uses songs and cartoons to explore the mathematical possibilities of the number twelve.
From The Multiplication Rock Series.
Prod-ABCTV Dist-GA

Little Wars B 20 MIN
16MM FILM OPTICAL SOUND
Takes a satirical look at a group of men who re-enact Civil War battles.
LC NO. 79-701292
Prod-USC Dist-USC 1978

Little White Line That Cried, The X 5 MIN
16MM FILM OPTICAL SOUND K-P
Otto the Auto and two animated white crosswalk lines join to emphasize that everyone should cross at the corner, in the crosswalk.
From The Otto The Auto Series.
Prod-AAAFTS Dist-AAAFTS 1957

Little Women C 60 MIN
3/4 OR 1/2 INCH VIDEO CASSETTE P-J
Dramatizes Louisa May Alcott's classic LITTLE WOMEN in an animated video in the field of language arts.
Prod-BRENTM Dist-BRENTM

Little Yellow Fur C 15 MIN
3/4 OR 1/2 INCH VIDEO CASSETTE P
Focuses on a young homesteader who makes friends with her Sioux neighbors.
From The Stories Of America Series.
Prod-OHSDE Dist-AITECH Prodn-WVIZTV 1976

Littleford Implant Film C 8 MIN
16MM FILM OPTICAL SOUND PRO
Shows the use of the Subclavian Stick Sheath and the proper technique for implanting a pacer using this approach.
Prod-CORDIS Dist-CORDIS

Littlest Angel, The C 14 MIN
16MM FILM OPTICAL SOUND P-H
Presents the story of a little child who loses his way among the fluffy clouds. Explains that this little angel gives his dearest possession for love of the Christ child.
Prod-CORF Dist-CORF 1950

Littlest Hobo B 77 MIN
16MM FILM OPTICAL SOUND I-J
Tells of a hobo German Shepherd dog and a wooly lamb rescued from the slaughterhouse who bring happiness to a broken-hearted boy and the will to walk to a little girl.
Prod-CINEWO Dist-CINEWO 1958

Littlest Outlaw, The C 75 MIN
16MM FILM OPTICAL SOUND
Illustrates the fact that nothing can defeat a small boy armed with great personal courage and a deep devotion to a heroic horse.
Prod-DISNEY Dist-TWYMAN 1956

Liturgy Of Foundation Laying And The Use Of Exhibits C 87 MIN
3/4 OR 1/2 INCH VIDEO CASSETTE PRO
Describes the major evidentiary considerations relevant to exhibits and steps in the proper procedure for introduction and use of exhibits in trials.
From The Exhibit Series.
Prod-ABACPE Dist-ABACPE

Live A Little X 30 MIN
16MM FILM OPTICAL SOUND J-H T R
Rick, a young radio disc jockey, has a swinging glib patter that appeals to a large teenage following. He is not conscious of the real problems of the teenagers until one of his listeners is involved with a serious problem. He begins to examine his own goals for life.
LC NO. FIA67-5779
Prod-FAMF Dist-FAMF 1967

Live And Learn C 28 MIN
16MM FILM OPTICAL SOUND C A
Describes the process approach of the Kansas plan for educating special students. Explains how problem solving in daily living is incorporated into instruction and how students are taught to understand their own actions and the steps they must take to achieve their own goals.
LC NO. 76-701599
Prod-UKANS Dist-UKANS 1974

Live At Preservation Hall C 28 MIN
3/4 OR 1/2 INCH VIDEO CASSETTE
Features a performance of the Kid Thomas Band at the famous Preservation Hall jazz club in New Orleans' French Quarter.
Prod-NOVID Dist-NOVID

Live Contortions B 30 MIN
3/4 OR 1/2 INCH VIDEO CASSETTE
Presents one shot from below the belt at Max's Kansas City.
Prod-KITCHN Dist-KITCHN

Live Ghost B 20 MIN
16MM FILM SILENT P A
Features Laurel and Hardy as fish market employees who collaborate with the captain of a ghost ship in shanghaiing a crew. Shows how they are shanghaied themselves and suffer many ghostly experiences.
Prod-ROACH Dist-BHAWK 1934

Live Line Maintenance—A Series
IND
Presents a variety of maintenance tasks in a step-by-step procedure. Shows linemen under actual working conditions. Deals specifically with live line maintenance procedures for distribution lines.
Prod-LEIKID Dist-LEIKID

Care And Maintenance Of Tools And Protective
Cutting In Disconnect Switches, Pt 1
Cutting In Disconnect Switches, Pt 2
Deadend Insulator Replacement, Pt 1
Deadend Insulator Replacement, Pt 2
Insulator And Cross Arm Changeout, Pt 1
Insulator And Cross Arm Changeout, Pt 2
Insulator And Cross Arm Changeout, Pt 3
Insulator And Cross Arm Changeout, Pt 4
Pole Replacement, Pt 1
Pole Replacement, Pt 2
Reconductoring Or Upgrading Voltage
Single Insulator Changeout
Temporary Grounding For De-Energized

Live Lobster C 24 MIN
16MM FILM, 3/4 OR 1/2 IN VIDEO
Presents a lobster fisherman as he opens his traps and sorts out the sea life. Shows the life cycle of the lobster, including the moulting of its bursting shell as it grows larger.
Prod-DICEP Dist-BODFIL

Live Or Die C 28 MIN
3/4 OR 1/2 INCH VIDEO CASSETTE PRO
Reconstructs through the autopsy findings of an unrelated 47 year old man and woman the life styles which led to their premature deaths. Shows how each person is responsible for his own health.
Prod-WFP Dist-WFP

Live Or Die C 29 MIN
16MM FILM, 3/4 OR 1/2 IN VIDEO
Tells how a pathologist uses autopsy findings to reconstruct the lifestyles of two people who died prematurely. Points out that each individual is responsible for his or her own health and well-being.
From The Life And Breath Series.
Prod-BROWN Dist-JOU Prodn-WFP 1978

Live Or Die (Captioned) C 29 MIN
16MM FILM - VIDEO, ALL FORMATS
Deals with taking responsibility for living in ways that make our bodies healthy. Dramatizes the lives of two people who both died at age 47. Shows that the effects of our life habits determine our health.
Prod-BROWN Dist-PEREN Prodn-WFP

Live Teddy Bears - The Koala B 11 MIN
16MM FILM, 3/4 OR 1/2 IN VIDEO P-I
Depicts the habits, characteristics and habitat of the koala bear as seen in an Australian park and in the bush country.
Prod-EBF Dist-EBEC 1947

Live Test Of Westinghouse Washing Machines C 7 MIN
3/4 OR 1/2 INCH VIDEO CASSETTE
Shows a classic television commercial in two segments, clothes being put into the washer and clothes being taken out.
Prod-BROOKC Dist-BROOKC

Live To Tell About It C 40 MIN
3/4 OR 1/2 INCH VIDEO CASSETTE
Examines in detail the most common hazards causing lateral lift truck tipovers. Introduces the Clark safety seat and explains to lift truck operators how to protect themselves from serious injury in the event of a tipover.
Prod-CLARKV Dist-CLARKV

Live Westinghouse Commercial For Refrigerators With Betty Furness C 3 MIN
3/4 OR 1/2 INCH VIDEO CASSETTE
Shows a classic television commercial with Furness having problems opening the refrigerator door.
Prod-BROOKC Dist-BROOKC

Live With It C 25 MIN
3/4 INCH VIDEO CASSETTE
Presents an informative commentary on what it's like to have diabetes. Focuses on the more subtle psychological aspects of the disease, on the mental outlook of those who've just learned they have it, rather than showing the diabetic how to take insulin or how to regulate his/her diet.
Prod-WAHC Dist-TEACHM

Live, Learn And Teach C 24 MIN
16MM FILM OPTICAL SOUND
Shows an eight-week summer teacher training program run by the University of New Hampshire Department of Education.
LC NO. 77-702097
Prod-SEJW Dist-EDC 1976

Liveliest Wire, The C 59 MIN
2 INCH VIDEOTAPE
Features Ed Baumeister, supported by animation and filmed interviews, surveying the cable, its origins, current uses and forecasts for growth.
Prod-WGBHTV Dist-PUBTEL

Lively Art Of Picture Books C 57 MIN
16MM FILM, 3/4 OR 1/2 IN VIDEO C A
Examines the qualities that lend vitality to good picture books through interviews with Barbara Cooney, Robert Mc Closkey and Maurice Sendak. Exhibits samples of the works of 36 illustrators plus the complete films 'TIME OF WONDER' and 'A SNOWY DAY.'
Prod-WWS Dist-WWS 1964

Liver C 8 MIN
16MM FILM OPTICAL SOUND H-C A
Uses animation to depict the various stages and symptoms of liver deterioration caused by alcohol abuse. Emphasizes the liver's regenerative powers, explaining that by ending alcohol abuse, an individual can regain much of his original liver capacity.
LC NO. 79-700994
Prod-HUBLEE Dist-FMSP Prodn-FMSP 1979

Liver Resection C 18 MIN
16MM FILM OPTICAL SOUND PRO
Illustrates thoracoabdominal laparotomy with left hepatic lobectomy for a huge echinococcus cyst. Shows that the procedure involved partial evacuation and sterilization of the cyst with formaldehyde followed by mobilization of the cyst and the left lobe of the liver from multiple adherent adjacent organs and finally, resection through the left lobe of the liver.
Prod-ACYDGD Dist-ACY 1969

Liver Scan C
3/4 OR 1/2 INCH VIDEO CASSETTE
See series title for descriptive statement.
From The X-Ray Procedures In Layman's Terms Series.
Prod-FAIRGH Dist-FAIRGH

Liver, Pancreas, And Spleen C 14 MIN
16MM FILM, 3/4 OR 1/2 IN VIDEO C A
Demonstrates the dissection of the liver, pancreas and spleen.
From The Guides To Dissection Series.
Prod-UCLA Dist-TEF

Liver, The C 15 MIN
16MM FILM, 3/4 OR 1/2 IN VIDEO
Discusses the structure and functions of the liver, including regulation of blood sugar level, metabolic activities involving amino acid linkage, excretion of poisons and storage of vitamins.
LC NO. 80-706176
Prod-IFFB Dist-IFB 1979

Liverwort - Alternation Of Generations C 16 MIN
16MM FILM, 3/4 OR 1/2 IN VIDEO H
Shows alternation of generations in close-up and timelapse photography. Explains that liverworts need a damp environment and are dependent on water for their reproductive processes.
Prod-CORF Dist-CORF 1965

Lives C 27 MIN
16MM FILM OPTICAL SOUND
Looks at the lives of five people who were affected by NATO. Stresses the resonance and textures of these lives in a free and democratic way of life.
LC NO. 79-701234
Prod-NATO Dist-VISION Prodn-VISION 1979

Lives (Danish) C 27 MIN
16MM FILM OPTICAL SOUND
Looks at the lives of five people who were affected by NATO. Stresses the resonance and textures of these lives in a free and democratic way of life.
LC NO. 79-701234
Prod-NATO Dist-VISION Prodn-VISION 1979

Lives (Dutch) C 27 MIN
16MM FILM OPTICAL SOUND
Looks at the lives of five people who were affected by NATO. Stresses the resonance and textures of these lives in a free and democratic way of life.
LC NO. 79-701234
Prod-NATO Dist-VISION Prodn-VISION 1979

Lives (French) C 27 MIN
16MM FILM OPTICAL SOUND
Looks at the lives of five people who were affected by NATO. Stresses the resonance and textures of these lives in a free and democratic way of life.
LC NO. 79-701234
Prod-NATO Dist-VISION Prodn-VISION 1970

Lives (German) C 27 MIN
16MM FILM OPTICAL SOUND
Looks at the lives of five people who were affected by NATO. Stresses the resonance and textures of these lives in a free and democratic way of life.
LC NO. 79-701234
Prod-NATO Dist-VISION Prodn-VISION 1979

Lives (Italian) C 27 MIN
16MM FILM OPTICAL SOUND
Looks at the lives of five people who were affected by NATO. Stresses the resonance and textures of these lives in a free and democratic way of life.
LC NO. 79-701234
Prod-NATO Dist-VISION Prodn-VISION 1979

Lives (Norwegian) C 27 MIN
16MM FILM OPTICAL SOUND
Looks at the lives of five people who were affected by NATO. Stresses the resonance and textures of these lives in a free and democratic way of life.
LC NO. 79-701234
Prod-NATO Dist-VISION Prodn-VISION 1979

Lives And Lifestyles C 12 MIN
16MM FILM OPTICAL SOUND
Presents representatives of four generations of people living in Maine, including a lobsterman, a great-grandmother, the young members of a commune and a dairy farming family who speak of change and how it is affecting their lives.
LC NO. 79-700914
Prod-POLYMR Dist-POLYMR

Lives Of The Stars, The C 60 MIN
16MM FILM, 3/4 OR 1/2 IN VIDEO J-C A
Discusses molecules, atoms, and subatomic particles and explains the anatomy of stars and the forces acting on stellar interiors. Deals with stellar evolution, supernovae, and neutron stars. Uses an Alice In Wonderland sequence to explain gravitational effects. Based on the book Cosmos by Carl Sagan. Narrated by Carl Sagan.
From The Cosmos Series. Program 9
LC NO. 81-707180
Prod-KCET Dist-FI 1980

Lives We Touch, The C 30 MIN
16MM FILM, 3/4 OR 1/2 IN VIDEO H A
Documents the Reform Jewish movement in America. Demonstrates unusual new community service programs.
Prod-KLEINW Dist-KLEINW

Livestock Farmer And The Four Flies, The C 22 MIN
16MM FILM OPTICAL SOUND J
Describes distinctive habits of the horn fly, the stable fly, the house fly and the face fly, showing the relationship of the life cycle and control methods for each.
LC NO. FIA67-469
Prod-AMROIL Dist-AMROIL Prodn-IOWA 1967

Livin' In The City C 30 MIN
3/4 OR 1/2 INCH VIDEO CASSETTE
See series title for descriptive statement.
From The Rebop Series.
Prod-WGBHTV Dist-MDCPB

Living C 10 MIN
16MM FILM OPTICAL SOUND
Offers an interpretation of the poem Living by Denise Levertov.
LC NO. 80-701617
Prod-LYTM Dist-LYTM 1980

Living C 57 MIN
16MM FILM, 3/4 OR 1/2 IN VIDEO H-C A
Visits Maoping village in Zhejiang province in China, focusing on local peasants and their way of life. Follows the day-to-day life

of one village family as they tend the land allocated to them by the state under the new 'responsibility' system and their own private plot.
From The Heart Of The Dragon Series. Pt 7
Prod-ASH Dist-TIMLIF 1984

Living - Nonliving C 15 MIN
3/4 OR 1/2 INCH VIDEO CASSETTE P
Gives experience in classifying living versus nonliving things.
From The Hands On, Grade 2 - Lollipops, Loops, Etc Series. Unit 3 - Classifying
Prod-WHROTV Dist-AITECH 1975

Living Africa - A Village Experience C 34 MIN
16MM FILM, 3/4 OR 1/2 IN VIDEO J-C A
Portrays the daily experinces and concerns of the people of Wassetake, a small village on the Senegal River in West Africa, emphasizing changes taking place within and outside the community.
LC NO. 84-706392
Prod-IU Dist-IU 1984

Living American Theater Dance C 11 MIN
16MM FILM, 3/4 OR 1/2 IN VIDEO I-C A
Shows how the American Dance Machine, under the direction of Leo Theodore, performs show-stopping numbers from musical plays. Presents interviews with Theodore and teacher Ann Reinking, as well as chats with troupe members about the company's purpose.
Prod-MAYQEN Dist-PHENIX 1982

Living And Income For Older Adults C 14 MIN
2 INCH VIDEOTAPE
Explains the qualifications and procedure for applying for social security, Medicare, Medicaid and food stamps and tells how older adults use them for financial security when they retire. Suggests that an older adult may either live in a variety of facilities or at home with other family members.
From The Living Better II Series.
Prod-MAETEL Dist-PUBTEL

Living And Non-Living Things (2nd Ed) C 11 MIN
16MM FILM, 3/4 OR 1/2 IN VIDEO P
Surveys a variety of plants, animals and objects in order to clarify the differences between things that are alive and things that are not alive.
Prod-CORF Dist-CORF 1978

Living And Non-Living Things (2nd Ed) (Captioned) C 11 MIN
16MM FILM, 3/4 OR 1/2 IN VIDEO P
Surveys a variety of plants, animals and objects in order to clarify the differences between things that are alive and things that are not alive.
Prod-CORF Dist-CORF 1978

Living Archeology C 10 MIN
16MM FILM, 3/4 OR 1/2 IN VIDEO P-I
Demonstrates the value of archeology through the discovery of artifacts and views the lives of ancient people through the use of Indian hunting implements and stone tools.
Prod-ATLAP Dist-ATLAP

Living Arrangements And Services C 15 MIN
3/4 INCH VIDEO CASSETTE
Traces the historical development of specialized housing. Illustrates older people adapting to the rising costs of housing.
From The Aging In The Future Series.
Prod-UMITV Dist-UMITV 1981

Living Arts Of Japan C 30 MIN
16MM FILM OPTICAL SOUND
Shows Japanese artisans at work, including an internationally known potter, a ceramic artist, Yuzen dyeing of kimono fabrics, a master of lacquer art, a bamboo weaver and an outstanding woodblock artist.
Prod-CONSUJ Dist-MTP 1964

Living Below The Line C 60 MIN
3/4 OR 1/2 INCH VIDEO CASSETTE
Presents an in-depth study of the U S welfare state, with fifteen and two-tenths percent of the American population trying to survive with some form of government assistance, and thirty-five million people trying to use various agencies and services, while trying to subsist during economic hard times.
From The Frontline Series.
Prod-DOCCON Dist-PBS

Living Better I—A Series

Shows ways to improve family and home life among the disadvantaged, including those who have little income and/or little formal education. Presents tips to the frugal housekeeper who wants to stretch dollars.
Prod-MAETEL Dist-PUBTEL

Bathing Baby 14 MIN
Breakfast 14 MIN
Building A Sleeping Area 12 MIN
Canisters 14 MIN
Choosing Baby Clothes 13 MIN
Cleaning House 14 MIN
Closet Space 13 MIN
Clothing For Preschool Children 14 MIN
Day Care Centers 13 MIN
Decorating Closets 14 MIN
Developing An Infant's Basic Skills 13 MIN
Footstools 14 MIN
Free Form Papier Mache 13 MIN
Good Grooming 14 MIN
Labels 13 MIN
Laundry Tips 13 MIN
Making A Table 15 MIN
More Storage Space In The Kitchen 13 MIN
Nonfat Dry Milk 14 MIN
Patchwork Cover And Pillows 14 MIN
Selecting And Buying Clothes 13 MIN
Shoes For Children 13 MIN
Supermarket Dollar 14 MIN
Toys And Games For Five Years And Older 14 MIN
Toys And Games For Preschoolers 14 MIN
Using Gift Paper 15 MIN

Living Better II—A Series

Presents practical advice in the fields of health education, home furnishings, clothing, money management, food and nutrition, housing and equipment and child development for low-income women.
Prod-MAETEL Dist-PUBTEL

Chicken I 15 MIN
Chicken II 14 MIN
Credit 14 MIN
Curtains I 12 MIN
Curtains II 13 MIN
Dashikis 13 MIN
Dental Care 14 MIN
Draped Papier Mache 14 MIN
Envelope Purses 14 MIN
Food And Exercise For Older Adults 14 MIN
Found Things 13 MIN
Homemaker As Manager 13 MIN
Knitting 14 MIN
Lamps 15 MIN
Life Insurance 14 MIN
Living And Income For Older Adults 14 MIN
Molded Papier Mache 14 MIN
Rag Rugs 14 MIN
Scrambled Eggs And Canned Meat 14 MIN
Shopping For Insurance 14 MIN
Slip Covering Wooden Chairs 13 MIN
Spending Plan, A 14 MIN
Things Of Value 14 MIN
Variety Meats 14 MIN
Ways With Pork 14 MIN
When Your Baby Needs A Doctor 14 MIN

Living Bible—A Series

I-H T R
Prod-FAMF Dist-FAMF

And The Fishermen 15 MIN
Before Abraham Was, I Am 20 MIN
Betrayal In Gethsemane 15 MIN
Birth Of John The Baptist 20 MIN
Birth Of The Savior 15 MIN
Childhood Of Jesus 15 MIN
Crucifixion, The 20 MIN
First Disciples 15 MIN
I Am The Resurrection 20 MIN
Jesus And The Lepers 15 MIN
Jesus At Nazareth And Capernaum 15 MIN
Jesus Before The High Priest 15 MIN
Jesus Heals The Man Born Blind 20 MIN
Jesus Teaches Forgiveness 15 MIN
Jesus, Lord Of The Sabbath 15 MIN
Last Journey To Jerusalem 20 MIN
Lord Is Risen, The 15 MIN
Lord's Ascension, The 15 MIN
Ministry Of John The Baptist 20 MIN
Nicodemus 20 MIN
Thirty Pieces Of Silver 15 MIN
Thy Sins Are Forgiven 15 MIN
Transfiguration, The 20 MIN
Trial Before Pilate 15 MIN
Upper Room, The 15 MIN
Woman At The Well 15 MIN

Living Bible, The C 25 MIN
16MM FILM OPTICAL SOUND R
Explains how the Bible was made available and understandable to the common man. Traces the development of the English Bible.
Prod-GF Dist-GF

Living Bird, The C 14 MIN
16MM FILM, 3/4 OR 1/2 IN VIDEO I-J
Examines the physiology and metabolism of birds. Discusses migration, courtship and territorial warning songs. Focuses on nest building, the hatching of eggs and the protection and feeding of the young.
Prod-DEU Dist-IFB 1956

Living Body - An Introduction To Human Biology—A Series

Uses cinemicrography, x-ray scanners, nuclear magnetic resonance Schlieren and thermography to show the functions and designs of the major systems in the human body.
Prod-FOTH Dist-FOTH 1985

Aging 026 MIN
Cell Duplication - Growth And Change 026 MIN
Circulatory System, The - Breath Of Life 026 MIN
Circulatory System, The - Hot And Cold 026 MIN
Circulatory System, The - Life Under Pressure 026 MIN
Circulatory System, The - Two Hearts That 026 MIN
Hormones - Messengers 026 MIN
Introduction To Human Biology - Landscapes 026 MIN
Lower Digestive Tract, The - Breakdown 026 MIN
Mechanisms Of Defense - Accident 026 MIN
Mechanisms Of Defense - Internal Defenses 026 MIN
Muscles And Joints - Moving Parts 026 MIN
Muscles And Joints - Muscle Power 026 MIN
Nervous System, The - Decision 026 MIN
Nervous System, The - Nerves At Work 026 MIN
Nervous System, The - Our Talented Brain 026 MIN
Reproduction - A New Life 026 MIN
Reproduction - Coming Together 026 MIN
Reproduction - Into The World 026 MIN
Reproduction - Shares In The Future 026 MIN
Review Of Human Biology - Design For Living 026 MIN
Senses, The - Eyes And Ears 026 MIN
Senses, The - Skin Deep 026 MIN
Sleep - Dream Voyage 026 MIN
Upper Digestive Tract, The - Eating To Live 026 MIN
Urinary Tract, The - Water 026 MIN

Living Cell, The C 28 MIN
16MM FILM OPTICAL SOUND J-C A
Presents an overview of the structure and function of living plant and animal cells, showing how different aspects of cell structure and function are best studied in selected cells of different kinds of organisms.
LC NO. 72-701877
Prod-HAR Dist-HAR 1972

Living Cell, The - An Introduction C 20 MIN
16MM FILM, 3/4 OR 1/2 IN VIDEO H
Introduces the fundamental principles of cell biology, examining the various structures and biochemical processes that occur in all living cells. Provides a brief historical background to the discovery of the cell and relates this discovery to the development of the microscope.
From The Biology Series. Unit 3 - The Cell
Prod-EBEC Dist-EBEC 1974

Living Cell, The - An Introduction (Spanish) C 20 MIN
16MM FILM, 3/4 OR 1/2 IN VIDEO H
A Spanish language version of the film and videorecording The Living Cell - An Introduction.
Prod-EBEC Dist-EBEC 1974

Living Cell, The - DNA (Spanish) C 20 MIN
16MM FILM, 3/4 OR 1/2 IN VIDEO H-C
A Spanish language version of the film and videorecording The Living Cell - DNA.
Prod-EBEC Dist-EBEC 1976

Living Cell, The - DNA (2nd Ed) C 20 MIN
16MM FILM, 3/4 OR 1/2 IN VIDEO H-C
Illustrates how genetic information contained in the DNA molecule directs the synthesis of proteins in the cell and how information in the DNA molecule is duplicated and passed on to new cells.
From The Biology Series.
Prod-EBEC Dist-EBEC 1976

Living Cells C 14 MIN
3/4 OR 1/2 INCH VIDEO CASSETTE H-C
Shows there is much activity within a living cell. Illustrates modern film techniques which reveal that all parts of a living cell are in constant motion as compared to static nature shown in prepared microscopic slides.
Prod-EDMI Dist-EDMI 1983

Living Christ—A Series

J A
Prod-CAFM Dist-ECUFLM

Boyhood And Baptism 30 MIN
Challenge Of Faith 30 MIN
Conflict 30 MIN
Crucifixion And Resurrection 30 MIN
Discipleship 30 MIN
Escape To Egypt 30 MIN
Fate Of John The Baptist 30 MIN
Holy Night 30 MIN
Men Of The Wilderness 30 MIN
Retreat And Decision 30 MIN
Return To Nazareth 30 MIN
Triumph And Defeat 30 MIN

Living Constitution, A C 24 MIN
16MM FILM OPTICAL SOUND J A
Shows how Pennsylvania modernized its archaic state constitution through a constitutional convention.
LC NO. 70-714055
Prod-FINLYS Dist-FINLYS 1968

Living Constitution, The C 16 MIN
16MM FILM, 3/4 OR 1/2 IN VIDEO I-J
Describes the development of the Constitution by the famous and capable individuals present at the Constitutional Convention, the American people's desire for a Bill of Rights, the ratification of the Constitution and the eventual inauguration of George Washington as the first President of the new nation.
From The American History - Birth Of A Nation Series.
Prod-AIMS Dist-AIMS 1967

Living Constitution, The C 30 MIN
3/4 OR 1/2 INCH VIDEO CASSETTE C
Furnishes an in-depth look at the amendments, customs, usage and interpretation of the U S Constitution, with special attention to the 25th Amendment, the Child Labor Act and the Fair Labor Standards Act, to provide a better appreciation for a document that still works after 200 years.
From The American Government 1 Series.
Prod-DALCCD Dist-DALCCD

Living Constitution, The (Spanish) C 16 MIN
16MM FILM, 3/4 OR 1/2 IN VIDEO I-H A
Describes the Constitutional Convention of 1787. Portrays how after months of argument and debate, a constitution presented by James Madison was signed by the delegates. Explains why this plan did not become law until the states were guaranteed a Bill of Rights, which became the first ten amendments to the Constitution in 1791.
From The American History - Birth Of A Nation Series. No. 7
Prod-CAHILL Dist-AIMS 1967

Living Creatures C 15 MIN
3/4 OR 1/2 INCH VIDEO CASSETTE K-J
See series title for descriptive statement.
From The Arts Express Series.
Prod-KYTV Dist-KYTV 1983

Living Cytology B 16 MIN
16MM FILM OPTICAL SOUND
Demonstrates, by means of phase-contrast cinemicrography and time-lapse photography, the various functions and organelles of living cells.
LC NO. 73-700732
Prod-BURTNA Dist-UTXHSA 1972

Living Desert (French)–A Series
I-H
Focuses on some of the survival patterns that plants and creatures inhabiting the American desert have adopted. Explains the geographic and weather patterns that create deserts.
Prod-WDEMCO Dist-WDEMCO

Animals At Home In The Desert (French) 023 MIN
Predators Of The Desert (French) 022 MIN
What Is A Desert (French) 013 MIN

Living Desert–A Series
16MM FILM, 3/4 OR 1/2 IN VIDEO I-H
Looks at the inhabitants and environment of the desert.
Prod-WDEMCO Dist-WDEMCO

Animals At Home In The Desert 023 MIN
Predators Of The Desert 022 MIN
What Is A Desert 013 MIN

Living Domiciliary Style C 27 MIN
3/4 OR 1/2 INCH VIDEO CASSETTE
Illustrates domiciliary lifestyle, rehabilitative and therapeutic programs, recreational activities, rules and regulations in a VA domiciliary.
Prod-VAMCSL Dist-USNAC

Living Environment–A Series
C
Introduces a college credit overview of environmental studies. Asks questions about human survival in the face of an advanced technology and a declining environment Provides a survey of critical ecological issues from a variety of perspectives. Focuses on the physical, biological and social preservation of planet earth.
Prod-DALCCD Dist-DALCCD

Air Pollution 030 MIN
Antecedents of Contemporary Problems 030 MIN
Conservation Of Vital Resources 030 MIN
Ecology Concepts 1 030 MIN
Ecology Concepts 2 030 MIN
Economic Geology (Living Environment) 030 MIN
Energy Alternatives 030 MIN
Energy Problems 030 MIN
Environmental Imperatives 030 MIN
Environmental Perception 030 MIN
Food Resources 030 MIN
Forest And Man 030 MIN
Human Population Growth 030 MIN
Impact Of Economic Systems 030 MIN
Impact Of Political Systems 030 MIN
Individual Involvement 030 MIN
Land Use In The City 030 MIN
Myths Of Technology 030 MIN
Population Growth 030 MIN
Solid Waste 030 MIN
Solutions And Projections 030 MIN
Water Pollution 030 MIN
Water Resources 030 MIN
Wildlife Management 030 MIN

Living Eucharist C 10 MIN
3/4 OR 1/2 INCH VIDEO CASSETTE J-C A
Uses the celebration of Sunday Mass in a typical parish as the framework for the short stories. Explains the human dimension of the Eucharist.
Prod-FRACOC Dist-FRACOC

Living Every Minute C 12 MIN
16MM FILM, 3/4 OR 1/2 IN VIDEO H-C A
Highlights the ways in which Carole Soucaze, a disabled woman, goes about her daily life and activities in her home in Nashville. Shows her working with the handicapped in her community while voicing her observations about the anger she experienced as she initially recuperated from her illness and the empathy she now feels toward her students and other students who are coping with physical disabilities.
LC NO. 83-706205
Prod-CBSNEW Dist-LAWREN 1982

Living Free C 92 MIN
16MM FILM OPTICAL SOUND
Tells what happens when Elsa the Lioness goes back to the jungle and gives birth to three cubs.
Prod-CPC Dist-TIMLIF 1972

Living Goddess, The C 30 MIN
16MM FILM, 3/4 OR 1/2 IN VIDEO H-C A
Explores the practice among the Newar people of Nepal of deifying selected female children as living representatives of ancient goddesses.
LC NO. 79-706910
Prod-CINETF Dist-WOMBAT 1979

Living In A Nightmare C 30 MIN
16MM FILM, 3/4 OR 1/2 IN VIDEO H-C A
Studies Alzheimer's Disease using a nationwide survey of the illness, a look at two research projects in progress and candid interviews with patients of the disease and family members who care for them.
Prod-WXYZTV Dist-MTI 1983

Living In A Nuclear Age–A Series
I-J
Examines the benefits, dangers and safeguards of the nuclear age. Probes the role of nuclear energy in current social issues now prominent in the news.
Prod-GPITVL Dist-GPITVL

Bombarding Things 30 MIN
Discovering The Atom 30 MIN
Nuclear Energy And Living Things 30 MIN
Power From The Atom 30 MIN
Radioisotopes 30 MIN
Society And Things Nuclear 30 MIN

Living In Space C 8 MIN
16MM FILM - 3/4 IN VIDEO
Reports on the problems and solutions of astronauts taking oxygen, water and food in space. Deals with how astronauts have adjusted to weightlessness. Issued in 1969 as a motion picture.
From The Apollo Digest Series.
LC NO. 79-706664
Prod-NASA Dist-USNAC 1979

Living In Space, Pt 1 - The Case For Regeneration B 12 MIN
16MM FILM OPTICAL SOUND
Introduces the concept of regenerative life support. Shows what is needed to provide men with clean fresh air, drinkable water, food, personal hygiene, waste disposal and temperature and humidity control.
Prod-NASA Dist-NASA 1967

Living In Space, Pt 2 - Regenerative Processes C 20 MIN
16MM FILM OPTICAL SOUND
Shows the principles of physics, chemistry and mechanics employed in a regenerative life support system. Includes oxygen recovery, water purification, food and waste management, humidity and temperature control.
LC NO. FIE67-118
Prod-NASA Dist-NASA 1966

Living In Space, Pt 3 - A Technology For Spacecraft Design C 12 MIN
16MM FILM OPTICAL SOUND
Shows the features that must be incorporated into a spacecraft intended for long duration manned space flight and the technology that is being developed to solve the numerous problems.
LC NO. 74-705042
Prod-NASA Dist-NASA 1966

Living In The Future - Chips C 15 MIN
16MM FILM, 3/4 OR 1/2 IN VIDEO I-J
Describes a computer as a machine that processes information by performing a series of tasks according to a set of instructions. It works very fast, can make logical decisions, and is adaptable to a wide variety of processes and applications.
From The Living In The Future Series.
Prod-THAMES Dist-MEDIAG 1983

Living In The Future - Energy C 15 MIN
16MM FILM, 3/4 OR 1/2 IN VIDEO I-J
Shows how modern society depends upon a great deal of energy, and such natural resources as coal, gas and oil are being used up at an ever-increasing rate and are becoming harder to find and more expensive to produce. Describes how electricity can be produced from the sun, wind or ocean tides or even in space.
From The Living In The Future Series.
Prod-THAMES Dist-MEDIAG 1983

Living In The Future - Evolution C 15 MIN
16MM FILM, 3/4 OR 1/2 IN VIDEO I-J
States that the rapid changes the world has recently undergone were made possible by the use of the modern computer. Tells how it has evolved into an electronic tool that is more powerful, smaller, less expensive, more widely available and uses less energy than its predecessor, primarily because of the silicon chip.
From The Living In The Future Series.
Prod-THAMES Dist-MEDIAG 1983

Living In The Future - Health C 15 MIN
16MM FILM, 3/4 OR 1/2 IN VIDEO I-J
Describes how computers can be used to greatly increase human life expectancy. Patients interviews during routine checkups can be conducted by computer in order to save doctor's time. Tells how storage and retrieval of detailed and extensive medical records is enhanced by computers and artificial limbs are designed and controlled with microchips.
From The Living In The Future Series.
Prod-THAMES Dist-MEDIAG 1983

Living In The Future - Home C 15 MIN
16MM FILM, 3/4 OR 1/2 IN VIDEO I-J
Presents a tour of a specially equipped house in which a computer can control such activities as heating, lighting and cooking, while linking its residents with information sources and businesses outside to obtain services and merchandise.
From The Living In The Future Series.
Prod-THAMES Dist-MEDIAG 1983

Living In The Future - Learning C 15 MIN
16MM FILM, 3/4 OR 1/2 IN VIDEO I-J
Shows how the computer is used as an educational tool to mediate or assist with training and instruction for learners of all ages and in all fields. Tells how schools will become activity and resource centers for individuals, families and work groups who learn from video and computer programs.
From The Living In The Future Series.
Prod-THAMES Dist-MEDIAG 1983

Living In The Future - Working C 15 MIN
16MM FILM, 3/4 OR 1/2 IN VIDEO I-J
States that in a post-industrial society, computers will influence the working lives of most people. Describes robotics in industry, controls in manufacturing, information processing in offices and inventory and customer service in businesses will require a new knowledge of computers.
From The Living In The Future Series.
Prod-THAMES Dist-MEDIAG 1983

Living In The Future - World C 15 MIN
16MM FILM, 3/4 OR 1/2 IN VIDEO I-J
Describes how computers make it possible to communicate around the world, translating information in many different languages and dialects at the touch of a button. Tells how this capability makes it possible to observe the need to effectively distribute resources to those in need.
From The Living In The Future Series.
Prod-THAMES Dist-MEDIAG 1983

Living In The Future–A Series
16MM FILM, 3/4 OR 1/2 IN VIDEO I-J
Presents a series about computers, how they work and their impact on modern life, accelerated by the silicon chip. Shows computer applications in a variety of settings, such as education and training, the work place, medicine, utilities and at home.
Prod-THAMES Dist-MEDIAG 1983

Living In The Future - Chips 015 MIN
Living In The Future - Energy 015 MIN
Living In The Future - Evolution 015 MIN
Living In The Future - Health 015 MIN
Living In The Future - Home 015 MIN
Living In The Future - Learning 014 MIN
Living In The Future - Working 015 MIN
Living In The Future - World 015 MIN

Living In The Middle Atlantic States - Urban Complex (2nd Ed) C 15 MIN
16MM FILM, 3/4 OR 1/2 IN VIDEO I-H
The second edition of Geography Of The Middle Atlantic States. Shows the land and the people of New York, Pennsylvania, New Jersey, Delaware, Maryland and West Virginia.
From The Living In The United States (2nd Ed) Series.
Prod-CORF Dist-CORF

Living In The Midwestern States - The Nation's Heartland C 13 MIN
16MM FILM, 3/4 OR 1/2 IN VIDEO I-H
Surveys the geographic, economic and cultural activities of the Midwestern states of Ohio, Michigan, Indiana, Wisconsin and Illinois.
From The Living In The United States Series.
Prod-CORF Dist-CORF 1974

Living In The New England States - Birthplace Of A Nation (2nd Ed) C 13 MIN
16MM FILM, 3/4 OR 1/2 IN VIDEO I-H
The second edition of Geography Of The New England States. Shows the land, the heritage and the people of the New England states.
From The Living In The United States (2nd Ed) Series.
Prod-CORF Dist-CORF

Living In The Pacific States - Variety And Change (2nd Ed) C 14 MIN
16MM FILM, 3/4 OR 1/2 IN VIDEO I-H
The second edition of Geography Of The Pacific States. Shows the land, the heritage and the people of Washington, Oregon and California.
From The Living In The United States (2nd Ed) Series.
Prod-CORF Dist-CORF

Living In The Plain States - Meat And Grain (2nd Ed) C 13 MIN
16MM FILM, 3/4 OR 1/2 IN VIDEO I-H
The second edition of Geography Of The North Central States. Shows the land and the people of the plains states. Includes North Dakota, South Dakota, Nebraska, Kansas, Minnesota, Iowa and Missouri.
From The Living In The United States Series.
Prod-CORF Dist-CORF

Living In The Rocky Mountain States - Changing Frontier Lands (2nd Ed) C 15 MIN
16MM FILM, 3/4 OR 1/2 IN VIDEO I-H
The second edition of Geography Of The Rocky Mountain States. Shows the land and the people of Montana, Idaho, Wyoming, Colorado, Utah and Nevada.
From The Living In The United States (2nd Ed) Series.
Prod-CORF Dist-CORF

Living In The Soil C 20 MIN
16MM FILM, 3/4 OR 1/2 IN VIDEO J-H
Discusses the creatures that live just above and below the earth's surface, showing that the great majority are less than one-fourth inch long.
From The Exploring Science Series.
Prod-BBCTV Dist-FI 1982

Living In The Southern States - Historic Lands, New Ideas (2nd Ed) C 14 MIN
16MM FILM, 3/4 OR 1/2 IN VIDEO I-H
The second edition of Geography Of The Southern States. Shows the land, the heritage, and the people of the South.
From The Living In The United States (2nd Ed) Series.
Prod-CORF Dist-CORF

Living In The Southwestern States - Growth In The Desert (2nd Ed) C 15 MIN
16MM FILM, 3/4 OR 1/2 IN VIDEO I-H
The second edition of Geography Of The Southwestern States. Shows the land and people of Arizona, New Mexico, Texas and Oklahoma.
From The Living In The United States (2nd Ed) Series.
Prod-CORF Dist-CORF

Living In The United States (2nd Ed) C 13 MIN
16MM FILM, 3/4 OR 1/2 IN VIDEO I-H
The second edition of Geography of The United States An Introduction. Gives an overview of the United States and its people. Introduces each of the state groupings treated in depth in the series.
From The Living In The United States Series.
Prod-CORF Dist-CORF

Living In The United States (2nd Ed)—A Series
I-H
Shows the geography, heritage and people of different sections of the United States.
Prod-CORF Dist-CORF

Living In The Middle Atlantic States - Urban	
Living In The Midwestern States - The	013 MIN
Living In The New England States - Birthplace	013 MIN
Living In The Pacific States - Variety And	014 MIN
Living In The Plain States - Meat And Grain	013 MIN
Living In The Rocky Mountain States	015 MIN
Living In The Southern States - Historic	014 MIN
Living In The Southwestern States - Growth In	015 MIN
Living In The United States (2nd Ed)	013 MIN

Living Jungle, The C 26 MIN
16MM FILM OPTICAL SOUND P-C A
Shows unique jungle life in Panama. Explores the intricate relationships between the plants and animals in this tropical rainforest.
From The Audubon Wildlife Theatre Series.
LC NO. 73-709406
Prod-KEGPL Dist-AVEXP 1969

Living Language (French) C 60 MIN
3/4 OR 1/2 INCH VIDEO CASSETTE
Presents an introductory course in French. Introduces the viewer to the language through situational usage.
Prod-KARLVI Dist-KARLVI 1984

Living Language (Spanish) C 60 MIN
3/4 OR 1/2 INCH VIDEO CASSETTE
Presents an introductory course in Spanish. Introduces the viewer to the language through situational usage.
Prod-KARLVI Dist-KARLVI 1984

Living Language French Video C 60 MIN
1/2 IN VIDEO CASSETTE BETA/VHS
Provides instruction in conversational French.
Prod-CROWNP Dist-CROWNP

Living Language German Video C 92 MIN
1/2 IN VIDEO CASSETTE BETA/VHS
Provides instruction in conversational German.
Prod-CROWNP Dist-CROWNP

Living Language Spanish Video C 77 MIN
1/2 IN VIDEO CASSETTE BETA/VHS
Provides instruction in conversational Spanish.
Prod-CROWNP Dist-CROWNP

Living Language Video - French C 60 MIN
1/2 IN VIDEO CASSETTE BETA/VHS
Teaches the basics of French. Features real-life situations with English subtitles.
Prod-NORTNJ Dist-NORTNJ

Living Life Fully With Leo Buscaglia C 58 MIN
3/4 OR 1/2 INCH VIDEO CASSETTE
Reveals that Dr Buscaglia's message of accepting yourself using love as a force, was even more pertinent than usual because just a few months before this program, Buscaglia had open heart surgery.
Prod-PBS Dist-PBS 1982

Living Lightning C
3/4 OR 1/2 INCH VIDEO CASSETTE
Focuses on a season in the lives of a breeding pair of peregrine falcons. Follows them and their young into both triumph and tragedy.
Prod-NWLDPR Dist-NWLDPR

Living Machine, The C 60 MIN
16MM FILM, 3/4 OR 1/2 IN VIDEO C A
Explores plate tectonics with scientists on location at Kilanea Volcano during an eruption, aboard a submersible craft as it dives to the bottom of the Atlantic, in pursuit of the causes of the worst earthquakes in American history.
From The Planet Earth Series.
Prod-ANNCPB Dist-FI

Living Machine, The, Pt 1 B 29 MIN
16MM FILM OPTICAL SOUND I-C A
Demonstrates the artificial intelligence of machines. Shows a chess game between an IBM computer and a champion player. Pictures simultaneous language translations in English and Russian done by computers.
Prod-NFBC Dist-SF 1963

Living Machine, The, Pt 2 B 30 MIN
16MM FILM OPTICAL SOUND I-C A
Explores the impact of computer technology on our society. Shows experiments in duplicating, electronically, our sensory perceptions. Provides the example of an artificial eye. Presents Dr Warren Mc Culloch and Dr Margaret Mead who give their views.
Prod-NFBC Dist-SF 1963

Living Machines C 57 MIN
16MM FILM, 3/4 OR 1/2 IN VIDEO H-C A
Focuses on the work of a group of biologists called natural engineers. Examines their methods of studying phenomena in nature, such as the aerodynamics of insects in flight or the feeding habits of marauding crabs. Looks at the reasons for particular designs in plants and animals.

LC NO. 80-706261
Prod-BBCTV Dist-FI 1980

Living Mammal, The C 17 MIN
16MM FILM, 3/4 OR 1/2 IN VIDEO J-H
Shows common characteristics of all mammals. Presents various adaptations which enable mammals to live in air, in water, in treetops and on the ground. Examines the highly developed senses of sight, smell, touch and hearing. Shows adaptations of teeth.
Prod-DEU Dist-IFB 1961

Living Maya—A Series

Documents the ancient agricultural and religions practices that ground contemporary Maya life in traditional values. Shows how these values underlie the spirit of amiable cooperation that characterizes Maya family and community life.
Prod-UCEMC Dist-UCEMC

Living Maya, Program 1, The	058 MIN
Living Maya, Program 2, The	058 MIN
Living Maya, Program 3, The	058 MIN
Living Maya, Program 4, The	058 MIN

Living Maya, Program 1, The C 58 MIN
3/4 OR 1/2 INCH VIDEO CASSETTE
Introduces the Maya village of Chican. Witnesses the Maya's to resolve the many problems that beset them.
From The Living Maya Series.
Prod-UCEMC Dist-UCEMC

Living Maya, Program 2, The C 58 MIN
3/4 OR 1/2 INCH VIDEO CASSETTE
Shows the strength and resourcefulness of a Maya family.
From The Living Maya Series.
Prod-UCEMC Dist-UCEMC

Living Maya, Program 3, The C 58 MIN
3/4 OR 1/2 INCH VIDEO CASSETTE
Focuses on the relationships Between Maya culture and religion and the cultivation of corn.
From The Living Maya Series.
Prod-UCEMC Dist-UCEMC

Living Maya, Program 4, The C 58 MIN
3/4 OR 1/2 INCH VIDEO CASSETTE
Explores assumptions, priorities and social values of the Mayas.
From The Living Maya Series.
Prod-UCEMC Dist-UCEMC

Living Metric C 20 MIN
3/4 INCH VIDEO CASSETTE
See series title for descriptive statement.
From The Enter - Metrics Series.
Prod-MDDE Dist-MDCPB

Living Metrics - Count Me In C 13 MIN
16MM FILM, 3/4 OR 1/2 IN VIDEO T
Explains how teachers can create a total metric environment within their classroom and within their school. Tells how to integrate metrics into each subject area.
Prod-JOU Dist-JOU

Living Music For Golden Mountains C 27 MIN
16MM FILM, 3/4 OR 1/2 IN VIDEO
Documents the efforts of Leo Lew, a Chinese immigrant to America, to pass on the deep-rooted Cantonese folk music to new generations of Chinese-Americans. Traces Lew's life in America and shows some of the many problems facing the elderly in San Francisco's Chinatown. Presented in both English and Chinese with subtitles.
Prod-DNGMEY Dist-UCEMC 1982

Living Objects B 15 MIN
2 INCH VIDEOTAPE P
See series title for descriptive statement.
From The Just Wondering Series.
Prod-EOPS Dist-GPITVL Prodn-KOACTV

Living Off The Land C 30 MIN
16MM FILM - 3/4 IN VIDEO J-C A
Contrasts the ecological problems of a developing nation with those of one which has already developed. Cites an irrigation project in Madagascar to use arable land, a canal project in India to provide an irrigation network, construction of the Volta Dam in Ghana and the growing urban slums throughout the world. Emphasizes the need for careful study and planning in rural as well as industrial development in such nations.
From The Man Builds - Man Destroys Series.
Prod-UN Dist-GPITVL

Living On Our Changing Planet C 23 MIN
16MM FILM, 3/4 OR 1/2 IN VIDEO J-C A
Shows earthquake detectives, volcano watchers and disaster experts at work. Depicts an earthquake drill in Japan and scientists using lasers and computers to probe the earth.
Prod-NGS Dist-NGS 1984

Living On The Salmon Run C
3/4 OR 1/2 INCH VIDEO CASSETTE
Takes a look at commercial fishing in Alaska, the state's biggest industry. Shows a tough and bitter lifestyle through the eyes of a 17-year-old boy.
From The Alaska Series.
Prod-WCCOTV Dist-WCCOTV 1982

Living Past, The, Pt 1 B 15 MIN
16MM FILM OPTICAL SOUND I-C T
Includes scenes of important events in American life between 1896 and 1905.
LC NO. FIA56-886
Prod-FCE Dist-FCE

Living Past, The, Pt 2 B 15 MIN
16MM FILM OPTICAL SOUND I-C T
Includes the early days of the horseless carriage, Columbus Circle 1900, Fifth Avenue in 1900, Spanish American War films, Duke of Windsor as a child, return of the Spanish War veterans, Dewey Flagship, Coney Island, death of President Mc Kinley, Theodore Roosevelt takes oath of office, Justice Holmes.
LC NO. FIA56-1249
Prod-FCE Dist-FCE

Living Past, The, Pt 3 B 15 MIN
16MM FILM OPTICAL SOUND I-C T
Includes President Throdore Roosevelt, the changing scene, New York's finest (police,) Rough Riders, Roosevelt's Conservation policies.
LC NO. FIA56-1250
Prod-FCE Dist-FCE

Living Past, The, Pt 4 B 15 MIN
16MM FILM OPTICAL SOUND I-C T
Includes New York Giants (1905,) Bennett Cup Race (1905,) Roosevelt visits San Francisco, Gans-Nelson fight, nickelodeon movie from France, San Francisco earthquake, (unusual and complete coverage by cameramen from the Thomas A Edison studios.)
LC NO. FIA56-1251
Prod-FCE Dist-FCE

Living Planet—A Series
16MM FILM, 3/4 OR 1/2 IN VIDEO H-C A
Traces the changing face of the earth over the millenia in cycles of creation and destruction. Introduces organisms, relationships and landscapes, studying especially how organisms adapt to their physical environment.
Prod-BBCTV Dist-TIMLIF 1984

Baking Deserts, The	055 MIN
Building Of The Desert, The	055 MIN
Community Of The Skies, The	055 MIN
Frozen World, The	055 MIN
Jungle	055 MIN
Margins Of The Land, The	055 MIN
New Worlds	055 MIN
Northern Forests, The	055 MIN
Oceans	055 MIN
Seas Of Grass	055 MIN
Sweet Fresh Water	055 MIN
Worlds Apart	055 MIN

Living Reef, The C 22 MIN
3/4 OR 1/2 INCH VIDEO CASSETTE I-J A
Reveals some of the teeming life on, under and behind Australia's Great Barrier Reef, one of the world's most remarkable collections of living things. Shows the reef's main structures, including gutters and caves along the sheltered edge, the shallow lagoon behind the crests of the reef, and an island formed from coral sand. Exhibits all kinds and shapes of coral, all kinds and shapes of fish, sponges, sea-squirts, tubeworms, stingrays, turtles and sharks.
Prod-EDMI Dist-EDMI 1976

Living River C 21 MIN
16MM FILM OPTICAL SOUND I-C A
Presents an ecological story of a Pacific slope river and the life which it supports. Follows a river as it winds its way to the ocean, showing how the environment, both in and near the river, is shaped and influenced by its existence. Pictures the life cycle of the Pacific salmon from egg through alevin and fry to adult fish. Includes views of wildlife as well as underwater photography of salmon and trout. Filmed on Vancouver Island.
LC NO. 74-702803
Prod-MMP Dist-MMP 1974

Living Sands Of Namib, The C 59 MIN
16MM FILM, 3/4 OR 1/2 IN VIDEO
Documents the animals of Africa's Namib Desert.
LC NO. 80-706370
Prod-NGS Dist-NGS 1978

Living Science—A Series
16MM FILM, 3/4 OR 1/2 IN VIDEO I-H
Considers various aspects of biology and ecology.
Prod-IFB Dist-IFB

Around A Big Lake	017 MIN
Boreal Forest, The	019 MIN
Conservation And Balance In Nature	018 MIN
Life In The Deciduous Forest	019 MIN
Pond, The	020 MIN
Prairie, The	018 MIN
Stream, The	015 MIN
Vacant Lot	021 MIN

Living Sculpture C 22 MIN
16MM FILM OPTICAL SOUND H-C A
Introduces sculptor Hart Tavel Goodman, who presents the intellectual and physical work involved in stone carving as exemplified by his own sculpture and that of other famous sculptors.
LC NO. 77-700731
Prod-WETFP Dist-WETFP 1976

Living Sober - The Class Of '76 C 28 MIN
16MM FILM OPTICAL SOUND C A
Introduces recovered alcoholics of all ages who tell their stories of the pain of addiction and the freedom of recovery.
Prod-TRIAD Dist-FMSP 1976

Living Soil, The C 9 MIN
3/4 OR 1/2 INCH VIDEO CASSETTE
Illustrates, using time-lapse photography, the forces which create the soil and the many organisms which use and enrich it. Shows how rock is weathered by water, wind and sun's heat to produce soil, which then is brought to life by rain.
Prod-CSIROA Dist-EDMI 1982

Living Stone, The C 33 MIN
16MM FILM, 3/4 OR 1/2 IN VIDEO J A
Pictures many aspects of Eskimo life and explains the Eskimo's belief in the legend that a spirit exists in every stick and stone, bird and beast. An elderly grandfather carves an image and relates its legend.
Prod-NFBC Dist-NFBC 1959

Living Sun, The B 30 MIN
16MM FILM OPTICAL SOUND H-C A
Depicts activities involved in outfitting and executing an expedition which uses aircraft in flight as platforms from which to observe a solar eclipse. Shows scientists at work before and during the expedition as they prepare and use equipment for recording the eclipse. Shows several views of the eclipse.
From The Spectrum Series.
Prod-NET Dist-IU Prodn-KNMETV 1967

Living Systems C 60 MIN
3/4 OR 1/2 INCH VIDEO CASSETTE A
Presents biologist Humberto Maturana discussing living systems.
From The Biology Of Cognition And Language Series. Program 4
Prod-UCEMC Dist-UCEMC

Living The Good Life With Helen And Scott Nearing C 30 MIN
16MM FILM, 3/4 OR 1/2 IN VIDEO J-C A
Shows that homesteading is not only viable in modern America, but beneficial to the individuals and society as well. Views Helen and Scott Nearing, who 45 years ago quit city life and went back to the land.
LC NO. 82-707171
Prod-BULFRG Dist-BULFRG 1977

Living The Second Time Around C 25 MIN
16MM FILM, 3/4 OR 1/2 IN VIDEO PRO
Presents a story of the aging process and of Miriam Akins, depressed and lonely, who finds new values and goals for living. Shows the interaction between Miriam and her new employer.
Prod-FEIL Dist-FEIL

Living Things And Their Environment C 15 MIN
3/4 OR 1/2 INCH VIDEO CASSETTE P-I
Discusses living things and their environment.
From The Why Series.
Prod-WDCNTV Dist-AITECH 1976

Living Things Are All Around Us C 4 MIN
16MM FILM, 3/4 OR 1/2 IN VIDEO K-I
Follows as Johnny Running Bear learns to appreciate the living things of nature and finds it easier to make a friend at the day care center.
From The Most Important Person - Getting Along With Others Series.
Prod-EBEC Dist-EBEC 1972

Living Things Are Everywhere X 11 MIN
16MM FILM, 3/4 OR 1/2 IN VIDEO P
Illustrates that living things may be found almost anywhere through the story of a young boy's discovery of various living things along a river bank.
Prod-EBF Dist-EBEC 1963

Living Things Can Break Too C 8 MIN
16MM FILM OPTICAL SOUND P
Shows that the human body is a fragile machine and that the balance of what it takes to make the mechanism run smoothly is delicate. Portrays two children who discover how quickly living things can be killed by ordinary things found inside a house.
LC NO. 76-703635
Prod-MENKNS Dist-MALIBU

Living Things Depend On Each Other X 11 MIN
16MM FILM, 3/4 OR 1/2 IN VIDEO K
Reveals how many different living things humanity depends on. Presents a montage of cattle, chickens, pigs, oranges, grapes and the wheat harvest to show the sources of breakfast foods. Points out that many plants and animals furnish food, clothing and shelter.
From The Basic Life Science - The World Of Living Things Series.
Prod-ANDERS Dist-EBEC 1967

Living Things Grow And Change C 15 MIN
3/4 OR 1/2 INCH VIDEO CASSETTE I-J
Shows how insects develop through a series of stages and how markings reveal age in trees and clam shells.
From The Animals And Such Series. Module Red - Life Processes
Prod-WHROTV Dist-AITECH 1972

Living Things Grow, Pt 1 C 15 MIN
2 INCH VIDEOTAPE P
Shows the limitation of size and structure of an organism through heredity.
From The Science Is Searching Series.
Prod-DETPS Dist-GPITVL

Living Things Grow, Pt 2 C 15 MIN
2 INCH VIDEOTAPE P
Shows the development of all organisms and how they are determined by heredity and environment.
From The Science Is Searching Series.
Prod-DETPS Dist-GPITVL

Living Things In A Drop Of Water X 10 MIN
16MM FILM, 3/4 OR 1/2 IN VIDEO P
Pictures many living things too small to be seen with the naked eye. Explains that cells are the smallest units of life and the building blocks for all large living things, both plant and animal.
Prod-EBF Dist-EBEC 1965

Living Things In A Drop Of Water (2nd Ed) C 12 MIN
16MM FILM, 3/4 OR 1/2 IN VIDEO I
Allows young science students to look through the microscope' at a drop of pond water and see a variety of one-celled organisms called protists.
Prod-EBEC Dist-EBEC 1985

Living Things In The Classroom B 30 MIN
2 INCH VIDEOTAPE
Explains to the science teacher that the study of living things may enable children to better understand how other species manage to survive and through this understanding be better able to make its critical decisions that will insure their own survival.
From The Science In Your Classroom Series.
Prod-WENHTV Dist-GPITVL

Living Things Reproduce C 15 MIN
3/4 OR 1/2 INCH VIDEO CASSETTE I-J
Observes how living things reproduce and compares simple and complex methods of reproduction.
From The Animals And Such Series. Module Red - Life Processes
Prod-WHROTV Dist-AITECH 1972

Living Through It C 27 MIN
16MM FILM, 3/4 OR 1/2 IN VIDEO H-C A
Presents teacher and author Laura Knox interviewing Carole Soucaze, a young woman who suffered a catastrophic disability. Shows Miss Soucaze, a therapist herself, discussing her emotional reactions and growth through her illness and challenging those in the helping professions to consider how they behave toward disabled individuals.
Prod-PRNTIP Dist-LAWREN 1982

Living Time - Sarah Jesup Talks On Dying C 15 MIN
16MM FILM OPTICAL SOUND
Presents Sarah Jesup, an articulate and attractive woman in her last two months of life, who discusses the issues dying people face.
Prod-COFODY Dist-COFODY

Living Together B 28 MIN
16MM FILM OPTICAL SOUND
Features three collective groups who discuss their experiences, and the rewards and drawbacks of communal living. Includes a statement by Margaret Mead on the value of these social experiments.
LC NO. 72-702205
Prod-GSHDME Dist-GSHDME 1972

Living Together C 15 MIN
2 INCH VIDEOTAPE K
Shows plants and animals sharing common environment which provide the things needed to carry on their life activites.
From The Let's Go Sciencing, Unit III - Life Series.
Prod-DETPS Dist-GPITVL

Living Together C 30 MIN
3/4 OR 1/2 INCH VIDEO CASSETTE
Defines symbiosis. Gives several examples of direct and indirect symbiosis. Discusses mutualism, commensalism and parasitism with the ocean world.
From The Oceanus - The Marine Environment Series. Lesson 20
Prod-SCCON Dist-CDTEL

Living Together C 60 MIN
3/4 OR 1/2 INCH VIDEO CASSETTE J-C A
Portrays the work of Thorlief Schjelderup-Ebbe, Solly Zuckerman, Clarence Ray Carpenter, Frank Fraser Darling, William Hamilton and Amotz Zahavi who studied the communal living patterns of animals.
From The Discovery Of Animal Behavior Series.
Prod-WNETTV Dist-FI 1982

Living Tradition, The C 20 MIN
3/4 OR 1/2 INCH VIDEO CASSETTE H-C
Features 19th Century etchings and readings from Whitman's Leaves of Grass by Allen Ginsberg. Chronicles the poet's life.
Prod-CEPRO Dist-CEPRO

Living Traditions - Five Indian Women Artists C 27 MIN
3/4 OR 1/2 INCH VIDEO CASSETTE J-C A
Examines the relationship between traditional Indian values and the handiwork of five Indian women artists from Minnesota. Focuses on the role of culture handed down from generation to generation.
Prod-UCV Dist-UCV

Living Treasures Of Japan C 59 MIN
16MM FILM, 3/4 OR 1/2 IN VIDEO
Introduces nine Japanese artisans who are highly valued in Japan because of their particular skills. Looks at a potter, a dollmaker, a bellmaker, a swordmaker, a weaver-dyer, a papermaker, a Kabuki theatre actor, a musician and a puppeteer.
LC NO. 81-707373
Prod-NGS Dist-NGS 1981

Living Under Water C 20 MIN
16MM FILM, 3/4 OR 1/2 IN VIDEO J-H
Shows that most of the ocean floor is covered by green plant life, floating pastures of microscopic single celled phytoplankton which are the feeding ground of the scarcely larger zooplankton.
From The Exploring Science Series.
Prod-BBCTV Dist-FI 1982

Living Up North C 24 MIN
16MM FILM OPTICAL SOUND
Discusses living in the Canadian North.
LC NO. 76-702086
Prod-PARA Dist-PARA 1974

Living Water C 26 MIN
16MM FILM, 3/4 OR 1/2 IN VIDEO H-C A
Describes a complete food chain, from microscopic, single-celled plankton through anchovies harvested by humans, and is supported in a confined environment 6,000 meters under the ocean in the Peruvian Trench. Marine plants are perfectly adapted to water but useless on land.
From The Botanic Man Series.
Prod-THAMES Dist-MEDIAG 1978

Living Waters Of The Big Cypress C 14 MIN
16MM FILM, 3/4 OR 1/2 IN VIDEO
Presents an introduction to the Big Cypress National Preserve in Florida. Explains the role of water in the life cycle of this unique swamp and shows the wilderness habitats and plants and animals which inhabit them.
LC NO. 80-707449
Prod-USNPS Dist-USNAC 1980

Living Waters Of The Colorado C 22 MIN
16MM FILM, 3/4 OR 1/2 IN VIDEO
Portrays life along the Colorado River and its tributaries. Examines the effects of man's activities in this area, concentrating on wildlife and recreational benefits of the Colorado River Storage Project. Includes scenes of Lake Powell and reservoirs at Flaming Gorge, Blue Mesa and Navajo.
Prod-USBR Dist-USNAC 1981

Living Way Out C 25 MIN
16MM FILM OPTICAL SOUND H A
Depicts life in Shay Gap, a remote mining town in Western Australia. Presents residents and a social planner speaking on the problems of isolation and how they attempt to resolve them.
LC NO. 78-701230
Prod-FLMAUS Dist-AUIS 1976

Living Wilderness, The C 26 MIN
16MM FILM OPTICAL SOUND P A
Studies the animals in the Rocky Mountains and how they adapt themselves to the changing environment of the mountains as winter turns to spring.
From The Audubon Wildlife Theatre Series.
LC NO. 73-710204
Prod-KEGPL Dist-AVEXP 1970

Living With An Alcoholic Parent C
3/4 OR 1/2 INCH VIDEO CASSETTE J-H
Presents young people revealing the fear, confusion, disappointment and anger they feel over their parents' drinking, and tell what crises prompted them to seek outside help. Encourages contacting Alateen and outlines their approach to dealing with alcoholism in the family.
Prod-AVNA Dist-GA

Living With Antabuse Therapy C 18 MIN
3/4 OR 1/2 INCH VIDEO CASSETTE A
Discusses the effects, risks and problems of taking Antabuse and defines some restrictions for patients registered as veterans in the program.
Prod-VAMSLC Dist-USNAC 1984

Living With Cancer - A Conversation With Six Adolescent Cancer Patients C 25 MIN
3/4 OR 1/2 INCH VIDEO CASSETTE PRO
Features six adolescent cancer patients describing their reactions to cancer. Includes the effect of illness on the family and friends, impact of chemotherapy and amputation, changes in personal relationships, self concept and dating.
Prod-UARIZ Dist-UARIZ

Living With Change C 10 MIN
16MM FILM, 3/4 OR 1/2 IN VIDEO P-I
Encourages the development of a positive and flexible attitude toward change.
From The Skills For The New Technology - What A Kid Needs To Know Today Series.
Prod-EPCOT Dist-EPCOT 1983

Living With Change C 10 MIN
16MM FILM, 3/4 OR 1/2 IN VIDEO I
Emphasizes developing a positive and flexible attitude toward change.
From The Skills For The New Technology - What A Kid Needs To Know Today Series.
Prod-WDEMCO Dist-WDEMCO

Living With Chronic Illness C 29 MIN
3/4 OR 1/2 INCH VIDEO CASSETTE A
Presents Dr Salk investigating how children who have chronic illness deal with their problems, their friends and their families, as he talks to three 12-year-olds.
From The Feelings Series.
Prod-SCETV Dist-PBS 1979

Living With Computers C 10 MIN
16MM FILM, 3/4 OR 1/2 IN VIDEO P-I
Points out the importance of computer literacy.
From The Skills For The New Technology - What A Kid Needs To Know Today Series.
Prod-EPCOT Dist-EPCOT 1983

Living with Computers C 10 MIN
16MM FILM, 3/4 OR 1/2 IN VIDEO I
Points out the importance of computer literacy.
From The Skills For The New Technology - What A Kid Needs To Know Today Series.
Prod-WDEMCO Dist-WDEMCO

Living With Cystic Fibrosis C 36 MIN
16MM FILM - 3/4 IN VIDEO PRO
Presents an overview of cystic fibrosis, the leading genetic killer of young people in the United States. Emphasizes its complications, diagnosis, personal and familiar impact, and the team approach for support.
Prod-CYSFIB Dist-MTP

Living With Death C 53 MIN
3/4 OR 1/2 INCH VIDEO CASSETTE

Reports on four months of research on the various aspects of death and how people deal with it.
Prod-WCCOTV Dist-WCCOTV 1973

Living With Death - Unfinished Business C 30 MIN
16MM FILM, 3/4 OR 1/2 IN VIDEO
From The Perspectives On Death And Dying Series. Presents Dr Elisabeth Kubler-Ross showing how dying patients can be assisted in accepting death. Includes scenes from Dr Kubler-Ross' workshops in which terminally ill people are counseled.
From The Death And Dying Series.
LC NO. 83-707100
Prod-CBSNEW Dist-MTI 1983

Living With Diabetes C 11 MIN
16MM FILM OPTICAL SOUND
Stresses the importance of exercise in the control of diabetes.
LC NO. 76-702443
Prod-QUEENU Dist-QUEENU 1974

Living With Diabetes - Anything You Can Get, I Can Get Better C 21 MIN
3/4 INCH VIDEO CASSETTE
Explains the importance of personal hygiene and other preventive measures in living with diabetes.
LC NO. 80-706506
Prod-VAHSL Dist-USNAC 1979

Living With Diabetes - Meal Planning - Eat Right, Live Well C 30 MIN
3/4 OR 1/2 INCH VIDEO CASSETTE A
Discusses the concept of meal planning in a diabetic diet for proper control of diabetes.
Prod-VAMCSL Dist-USNAC 1984

Living With Diabetes - The Exchange Lists, The Spice Of Life C 26 MIN
3/4 OR 1/2 INCH VIDEO CASSETTE A
Discusses food exchange lists and how to use them to maintain a proper diabetic diet.
Prod-VAMCSL Dist-USNAC 1984

Living With Diabetes - Your Future With A Difference C 40 MIN
3/4 INCH VIDEO CASSETTE
Features a doctor explaining treatments and probable lifestyle changes to a recently diagnosed diabetic and his family.
LC NO. 80-706507
Prod-VAHSL Dist-USNAC 1979

Living With Disaster C 24 MIN
16MM FILM OPTICAL SOUND J-C A
Emphasizes the need for long-term psychological and physical after-care of natural disaster victims.
LC NO. 79-700526
Prod-FLMAUS Dist-AUIS 1975

Living With Dust C 15 MIN
16MM FILM OPTICAL SOUND
Presents causes of dust in nature and industry and gives methods of controlling these conditions. Tells how different dusts affect the worker and what can be done to protect him.
LC NO. 75-700356
Prod-MMAMC Dist-MMAMC Prodn-VIBFI 1974

Living With Dying C 19 MIN
16MM FILM, 3/4 OR 1/2 IN VIDEO
Presents four patients who discuss the emotional, social and medical problems which frequently accompany a life-threatening illness and how they have learned to cope with these problems.
Prod-FILMA Dist-PRORE 1975

Living With Dying C 30 MIN
3/4 OR 1/2 INCH VIDEO CASSETTE C A
Looks at attitudes toward death that have led to the rejection and isolation of the elderly and the institutionalization of the dying. Examines the ways in which people cope with impending death.
From The Contemporary Health Issues Series. Lesson 11
Prod-SCCON Dist-CDTEL

Living With Grace, Alzheimer's Disease C 28 MIN
3/4 OR 1/2 INCH VIDEO CASSETTE
Focuses on the life of one woman suffering from Alzheimer's disease, loss of memory, emotional swings, catastrophic reactions and confusion.
Prod-UMDSM Dist-UMDSM

Living With Heat C 29 MIN
16MM FILM, 3/4 OR 1/2 IN VIDEO IND
Explains the precautions man must take if he is to survive in very hot environments, whether natural or manmade. Points out that in order to avoid hypothermia, a balance must be maintained between heat production and heat loss.
Prod-UKMD Dist-IFB

Living With Love C 15 MIN
16MM FILM, 3/4 OR 1/2 IN VIDEO
Stresses the benefits that love produces and shows how to cope with a lack of love in life. Explains the different ways in which love can be expressed.
From The Inside-Out Series.
Prod-NITC Dist-AITECH

Living With Nebraska's Water C 27 MIN
16MM FILM OPTICAL SOUND H-C A
Illustrates natural water quality and pollution in Nebraska. Describes how nature creates the basic characteristics of the earth's surface and ground water and reviews the bacterial and chemical quality of both.
From The Nebraska Water Resources Series.
LC NO. 74-700162
Prod-UNEBR Dist-UNEBR 1971

Living With Peter C 22 MIN
16MM FILM OPTICAL SOUND J-C A
Explores the issue of living together without marriage.
LC NO. 74-702017
Prod-WEINSM Dist-WEINSM 1973

Living With Stress C
3/4 OR 1/2 INCH VIDEO CASSETTE
Provides an overview on the subtle pressures of daily stress. Explains the primitive flight or fight response and the need to modify the way we cope with our individual stressors today. Presents techniques to control stress.
Prod-MIFE Dist-MIFE

Living With Stress C 16 MIN
16MM FILM, 3/4 OR 1/2 IN VIDEO A
Describes what stress is. Shows how the body reacts to stressors - events that produce change.
Prod-MIFE Dist-EBEC 1981

Living With Stress C 22 MIN
3/4 INCH VIDEO CASSETTE A
Looks at typical daily stress-producing situations. Emphasizes that stress is a problem that each person must first understand and then deal with in an individual way.
Prod-XEROXF Dist-GA

Living With Stress (Arabic) C
3/4 OR 1/2 INCH VIDEO CASSETTE
Provides an overview on the subtle pressures of daily stress. Explains the primitive flight or fight response and the need to modify the way we cope with our individual stressors today. Presents techniques to control stress.
Prod-MIFE Dist-MIFE

Living With Stress (Spanish) C
3/4 OR 1/2 INCH VIDEO CASSETTE
Provides an overview on the subtle pressures of daily stress. Explains the primitive flight or fight response and the need to modify the way we cope with our individual stressors today. Presents techniques to control stress.
Prod-MIFE Dist-MIFE

Living With Technology C 20 MIN
3/4 OR 1/2 INCH VIDEO CASSETTE J-H
Portrays the everyday, commonplace uses of technology through the familiar encounters of a fictitious suburban family with the clothing, communications, transportation and food industries. Uses dramatizations, archival artwork and stills to depict the development of technology. Emphasizes the trade-offs modern persons accept when they choose to use technology.
From The You, Me, And Technology Series.
LC NO. 83-707177
Prod-TEMPLU Dist-AITECH Prodn-NJN 1983

Living With The City C 24 MIN
16MM FILM OPTICAL SOUND H-C A
Discusses developments in the preservation and rehabilitation of inner city areas of Sydney, Melbourne and Adelaide, Australia. Highlights the need for strong relationships between communities and government.
LC NO. 78-701231
Prod-FLMAUS Dist-AUIS 1975

Living With The Work Ethic C 30 MIN
3/4 INCH VIDEO CASSETTE
See series title for descriptive statement.
From The Growing Old In Modern America Series.
Prod-UWASHP Dist-UWASHP

Living With Tradition C 30 MIN
3/4 OR 1/2 INCH VIDEO CASSETTE
Shows the struggles of the Menominee Indians and the tradition they attempt to keep alive after loss of tribal status.
From The Forest Spirits Series.
Prod-NEWIST Dist-GPITVL

Living With Trouble - Crisis In The Family C
3/4 OR 1/2 INCH VIDEO CASSETTE J-C
Dramatizes the stories of three teenagers who cope with the task of carrying on their lives despite trouble in their families. Promotes understanding of family crises and how to take steps to make life personally rewarding. Includes teacher's guide.
Prod-SUNCOM Dist-SUNCOM

Living With Wildlife C 26 MIN
16MM FILM, 3/4 OR 1/2 IN VIDEO
Illustrates how people can best live with and preserve the natural heritage of wildlife. Highlighted by time-lapse sequences.
Prod-STOUFP Dist-STOUFP

Living With Your Back C 16 MIN
3/4 OR 1/2 INCH VIDEO CASSETTE
Describes the intervertebral disks, their function and their relationship to the vertebrae. Includes demonstrations of good posture and proper body mechanics as they apply to helping the patient protect his/her back from further stress and strain. Demonstrates exercises designed to strengthen and tone the back-supporting muscles.
LC NO. 72-736646
Prod-TRAINX Dist-TRAINX

Living With Your Back (French) C 16 MIN
3/4 OR 1/2 INCH VIDEO CASSETTE
Describes the intervertebral disks, their function and their relationship to the vertebrae. Includes demonstrations of good posture and proper body mechanics as they apply to helping the patient protect his/her back from further stress and strain. Demonstrates exercises designed to strengthen and tone the back-supporting muscles.
LC NO. 72-736646
Prod-TRAINX Dist-TRAINX

Living Wood - African Masks And Myths C 12 MIN
16MM FILM OPTICAL SOUND I-H A
Explains that to the African Black, the tree is a living thing and the masks he carves from the tree have a special power, a vital force. Attempts to reveal this vital force by showing the masks of Africa, as a tribesman relates the tales and myths of his people.
LC NO. 73-701042
Prod-GRADYM Dist-FILMSM 1973

Living Yoga C 20 MIN
3/4 OR 1/2 INCH VIDEO CASSETTE
Introduces the paths and practices that lead to the realization that living Yoga is living peacefully, healthfully and joyfully in all conditions.
Prod-IYOGA Dist-IYOGA

Living Yoga C 22 MIN
3/4 OR 1/2 INCH VIDEO CASSETTE
Shows four classic pathways of 'union' (yoga) through the lives of disciples of Swami Satchidananda: hatha, the yoga of physical postures and breathing techniques; raja, the path of meditation and introspection; Karma, the way of selfless service; and bhakti, the yoga of love and devotion.
Prod-HP Dist-HP

Living Yoga - Four Yokes To God C 20 MIN
16MM FILM OPTICAL SOUND J-C A
Discusses the everyday practices of Hatha, Raja, Bhakti and Karma Yoga. Explains various Yoga postures, correct breathing, diet, meditation and the concepts of selfless service and true devotion.
LC NO. 77-700747
Prod-HP Dist-HP 1977

Living/Non-Living/Once Lived - Evidence Of Past Life C 15 MIN
3/4 OR 1/2 INCH VIDEO CASSETTE P
Tells how Mr Featherby's fossil center display at the library is being stolen, piece by piece. Shows how a newspaper reporter catches the thief.
From The Featherby's Fables Series.
Prod-WVUTTV Dist-GPITVL 1983

Living/Non-Living/Once Lived - Grouping C 15 MIN
3/4 OR 1/2 INCH VIDEO CASSETTE P
Presents TV game show contestants who demonstrate how being able to group like objects develops skill in the area of organizing information.
From The Featherby's Fables Series.
Prod-WVUTTV Dist-GPITVL 1983

Living/Non-Living/Once Lived - Identification C 15 MIN
3/4 OR 1/2 INCH VIDEO CASSETTE P
Shows a summer camp which provides the setting for a scavenger hunt during which living and non-living things are sought.
From The Featherby's Fables Series.
Prod-WVUTTV Dist-GPITVL 1983

Living, The B 3 MIN
16MM FILM OPTICAL SOUND I-C A
Issues an anti-war statement by blending scenes of statues coming alive, young girls dancing merrily to Pan's flute and the silent screams of bursting bullets.
Prod-WOLMAN Dist-NJWB 1981

Liz Sits The Schlegels C 26 MIN
16MM FILM, 3/4 OR 1/2 IN VIDEO I-J
Tells the story of Liz who gets a job sitting for three children. Describes Liz's difficulty in dealing with the oldest child who resents Liz's presence but comes to accept her when he almost endangers the lives of his younger brother and sister.
Prod-PLAYTM Dist-BCNFL 1985

Liza Bear - Earthglow C 8 MIN
3/4 OR 1/2 INCH VIDEO CASSETTE
Visualizes phrases of a narrative poem. Involves indoor and outdoor sounds.
Prod-ARTINC Dist-ARTINC

Liza Bear - Lost Oasis C 10 MIN
3/4 OR 1/2 INCH VIDEO CASSETTE
Centers around the search for a lost oasis.
Prod-ARTINC Dist-ARTINC

Liza Bear - Oned Nefifik, A Foreign Movie C 28 MIN
3/4 OR 1/2 INCH VIDEO CASSETTE
Shows that the relation between the fact and experience of an event can be fluently and responsibly articulated.
Prod-ARTINC Dist-ARTINC

Liza Bear - Polisario, Liberation Of The Western Sahara C 29 MIN
3/4 OR 1/2 INCH VIDEO CASSETTE
Deals with communications technology and production.
Prod-ARTINC Dist-ARTINC

Liza Bear - Title Advance, Les Conditions Du Travail C 20 MIN
3/4 OR 1/2 INCH VIDEO CASSETTE
Deals with communications technology and production.
Prod-ARTINC Dist-ARTINC

Liza Bear - Towards A New World Information Order C 60 MIN
3/4 OR 1/2 INCH VIDEO CASSETTE
Deals with communications technology and production.
Prod-ARTINC Dist-ARTINC

Lizard C 11 MIN
16MM FILM, 3/4 OR 1/2 IN VIDEO K-I
Shows the lizard as it drinks dew from the grass and feeds on insects and spiders, sheds its skin and mates.
From The See 'N Tell Series.
Prod-PMI Dist-FI 1970

Lizard Music C 15 MIN
3/4 OR 1/2 INCH VIDEO CASSETTE I
Presents a satire on modern culture and science fiction fantasy. From the book by D Manus Pinkwater.
From The Storybound Series.
Prod-CTI Dist-CTI

Lloyd J Reynolds - William M Geer B 59 MIN
16MM FILM OPTICAL SOUND C T
Focuses on William Geer, lecturer in modern civilization and history at the University of North Carolina and Lloyd Reynolds, calligrapher and art historian, Reed College, portland, Oregon. Samples their lectures, their counseling methods and their philosophies. Interviews present and former students.
From The Men Who Teach Series.
LC NO. FIA68-2615
Prod-NET Dist-IU 1968

Lloyds Of London B 117 MIN
16MM FILM OPTICAL SOUND
Tells the story of the founding of the world's most famous insurance company, and of two boyhood friends, Johnathan Blake and Horatio Nelson. Re-enacts the Battle of Trafalgar. Stars Freddie Bartholomew, Tyrone Power and Madeleine Carroll.
Prod-TWCF Dist-TWCF 1936

Lo-Cal Banquet C 29 MIN
3/4 OR 1/2 INCH VIDEO CASSETTE
See series title for descriptive statement.
From The Julia Child And Company Series.
Prod-WGBHTV Dist-PBS

Loaded Voltage Dividers B 33 MIN
16MM FILM - 3/4 IN VIDEO
Shows how to determine voltage and current through loads and voltage dividers. Outlines the solution of a problem involving the calculation of voltage and current through a loaded voltage divider. Explains how the direction of current flow and the polarity of the voltages across from each resistor is determined.
LC NO. 79-707773
Prod-USAF Dist-USNAC 1979

Loaders In The News C 15 MIN
16MM FILM OPTICAL SOUND
Shows the advantages of a new utility loader in a variety of situations.
LC NO. 75-700078
Prod-SPRYNH Dist-SRCNHD 1974

Loading And Firing A Bisque Kiln C 28 MIN
2 INCH VIDEOTAPE
Features Mrs Peterson describing certain ceramic processes for her classroom at the University of Southern California. Demonstrates how to load and fire a bisque kiln.
From The Wheels, Kilns And Clay Series.
Prod-USC Dist-PUBTEL

Loading And Operating The Autoclave In The Dental Office C 8 MIN
1/2 IN VIDEO CASSETTE BETA/VHS PRO
Prod-RMI Dist-RMI

Loading And Transporting The Horse C 13 MIN
1/2 IN VIDEO CASSETTE BETA/VHS
Demonstrates how to load and transport a horse.
Prod-EQVDL Dist-EQVDL

Loading And Unloading Heavy Equipment On A Trailer C 13 MIN
16MM FILM, 3/4 OR 1/2 IN VIDEO H-C A
Shows checks and safety precautions to follow when transporting heavy equipment on the highway. Demonstrates procedures for loading, unloading and transporting a backhoe and a bulldozer.
Prod-CUETV Dist-CUNIV 1979

Loading And Unloading Poles B 21 MIN
16MM FILM OPTICAL SOUND
Shows procedures for loading poles on and unloading from a flatcar or trailer. Stresses safety precautions.
LC NO. 74-705044
Prod-USA Dist-USNAC 1944

Loads And Loading Of General Transport Vehicles B 18 MIN
16MM FILM OPTICAL SOUND
Shows characteristics of the five types of military cargo transported via vehicle and the prescribed loading procedures for each. Emphasizes maximum authorized load, proper vehicle for given load and safety precautions.
LC NO. 74-705045
Prod-USA Dist-USNAC 1954

Loans And Credit C 15 MIN
3/4 OR 1/2 INCH VIDEO CASSETTE
See series title for descriptive statement.
From The Consumer Education Series.
Prod-MAETEL Dist-CAMB

Lob And Drop Shot C 29 MIN
3/4 OR 1/2 INCH VIDEO CASSETTE
See series title for descriptive statement.
From The Vic Braden's Tennis For The Future Series.
Prod-WGBHTV Dist-PBS 1981

Lob And The Smash, The C 29 MIN
3/4 OR 1/2 INCH VIDEO CASSETTE
Features Lew Gerrard and Don Candy giving tennis instructions, emphasizing the lob and the smash.
From The Love Tennis Series.
Prod-MDCPB Dist-MDCPB

Lobbying - A Case History (2nd Ed) C 18 MIN
16MM FILM, 3/4 OR 1/2 IN VIDEO J-H
Presents a revised version of the 1952 motion picture Pressure Groups. Uses a case study to illustrate the legislative lobbying activities of various interest groups in conflict over a single issue.
Prod-EBEC Dist-EBEC Prodn-OLINC 1977

Lobbying Congress - Lobbying Congress / Influences And Interests, Pt 1 C 30 MIN
3/4 OR 1/2 INCH VIDEO CASSETTE
Illustrates different types of interest groups and their strategies and tactics, the mutual interdependence of Congress and interest groups, and congressional regulation of interest groups.
From The Congress - We The People Series.
Prod-WETATV Dist-FI 1984

Lobbying Congress - Lobbying Congress / Influences And Interests, Pt 2 C 30 MIN
3/4 OR 1/2 INCH VIDEO CASSETTE
Illustrates different types of interest groups and their strategies and tactics, the mutual interdependence of Congress and interest groups, and congressional regulation of interest groups.
From The Congress - We The People Series.
Prod-WETATV Dist-FI 1984

Lobectomy Techniques In The Dog B 20 MIN
16MM FILM OPTICAL SOUND C A
Discusses the three primary indications for performing lobectomy in the dog. Shows equipment necessary for the operation and schematic drawings to illustrate anatomy of the area and the proper identification of arterial, vein, and broncus. (Kinescope)
Prod-AMVMA Dist-AMVMA

Lobster C 29 MIN
2 INCH VIDEOTAPE
Features Joyce Chen showing how to adapt Chinese recipes so they can be prepared in the American kitchen and still retain the authentic flavor. Demonstrates how to prepare lobster.
From The Joyce Chen Cooks Series.
Prod-WGBHTV Dist-PUBTEL

Lobster, The C 20 MIN
3/4 OR 1/2 INCH VIDEO CASSETTE PRO
Shows a live lobster dismembered, prepared, and served on a a small table resembling a sandy beach surrounded by cucumber waves and black pebbles.
From The Japanese Cuisine Series.
Prod-CULINA Dist-CULINA

Lobsterman C 15 MIN
3/4 OR 1/2 INCH VIDEO CASSETTE P
Describes how lobster is caught, cooked and sold in Maine.
From The Other Families, Other Friends Series. Blue Module - Maine
Prod-WVIZTV Dist-AITECH 1971

Local Area Networks C 55 MIN
3/4 OR 1/2 INCH VIDEO CASSETTE C
Covers economics and connectivity issues for local area networks, local area network configurations, pros and cons of various topologies, broadland/baseland comparison and vendor configurations and products.
From The Distributed Telecommunications Networks Series.
Prod-AMCEE Dist-AMCEE

Local Area Networks And Office Automation—A Series

Presents an introduction to local area networks and presents management's perspective of this concept. Defines a local area network, identifies important applications, discusses key management issues, examines the fundamental local area network technologies and shows how these technologies have been incorporated into five existing local area network designs.
Prod-DELTAK Dist-DELTAK

Access And Use 030 MIN
Components And Organization 030 MIN
Designs And Implementations 030 MIN
Impact And Issues 030 MIN

Local Area Networks—A Series

PRO
Introduces the various types of local networks, baseband and broadband transmission, interfaces and protocols, bus and non-bus systems, message and circuit switched networks, Ethernet Wangnet and GEnet, managing local area networks, and market and and technology forecasts.
Prod-AMCEE Dist-AMCEE

Implementations, Pt I - Non-Bus Oriented
Implementations, Pt II - Bus Oriented Systems 045 MIN
Introduction To Local Area Networks 045 MIN
LAN Technology, Pt I - Transmission And Media 045 MIN
Managing Local Area Networks 045 MIN

Local Color B
3/4 OR 1/2 INCH VIDEO CASSETTE
Pictures a deep, sculptural space taking America into past and future worlds. Uses essayistic language.
From The Red Tapes Series.
Prod-KITCHN Dist-KITCHN

Local Color B 116 MIN
3/4 INCH VIDEO CASSETTE C A
Presents humorous explorations into such topics as sexual frustration, fear of aging, unsatisfactory relationships and contemplated suicide. Interplays eight characters to create a kind of modernist melodrama.
Prod-FIRS Dist-FIRS

Local Color - Bret Harte And Mary Wilkins Freeman C 20 MIN
3/4 OR 1/2 INCH VIDEO CASSETTE H-C A
Offers dramatizations of two short stories, Bret Harte's Tennessee's Partner and Mary Wilkins Freeman's One Good Time.
From The American Literature Series.
LC NO. 83-706256
Prod-AUBU Dist-AITECH 1983

Local Government C 30 MIN
3/4 OR 1/2 INCH VIDEO CASSETTE C
Compares and contrasts many different forms of local government and ways people come into contact with them on a daily basis, often without realizing it. Examines the multiple layers of government - federal, state, county, city, special districts and specified authority.
From The American Government 1 Series.
Prod-DALCCD Dist-DALCCD

Local Infiltration Anesthesia C 9 MIN
3/4 OR 1/2 INCH VIDEO CASSETTE PRO
See series title for descriptive statement.
From The Medical Skills Films Series.
Prod-WFP Dist-WFP

Local Networks - Access Control C 50 MIN
3/4 OR 1/2 INCH VIDEO CASSETTE PRO
Describes medium access control techniques of local networks. Highlights performance and capacity issues.
From The Communication Networks Series.
Prod-AMCEE Dist-AMCEE

Local Networks - Technology C 50 MIN
3/4 OR 1/2 INCH VIDEO CASSETTE PRO
Describes the technology of local networks, including transmission media, topologies and repeaters. Stresses benefits and problems.
From The Communication Networks Series.
Prod-AMCEE Dist-AMCEE

Locale C 30 MIN
3/4 INCH VIDEO CASSETTE
Presents dance choreographed by Merce Cunningham with the camera as a moving element around and among the dancers.
Prod-CUNDAN Dist-CUNDAN

Localized Corrosion - Pitting And Crevice Corrosion C 59 MIN
3/4 OR 1/2 INCH VIDEO CASSETTE PRO
See series title for descriptive statement.
From The Corrosion Engineering Series.
Prod-GPCV Dist-GPCV

Localized Corrosion - Pitting And Crevice Corrosion C 59 MIN
3/4 OR 1/2 INCH VIDEO CASSETTE
Discusses the pitting resistance of metals such as Al, Ni, Zr, Cr and Ti and their alloys in terms of critical pitting and repassivation potentials.
From The Corrosion Engineering Series.
Prod-MIOT Dist-MIOT

Locate Yourself - Are You Spiritual Or Are You Carnal C 28 MIN
16MM FILM OPTICAL SOUND
Features personal and marriage counselor Henry Brandt who discusses the differences between those individuals who are guided by carnal drives and those who are spiritually directed in love, joy, peace, patience and the other gifts of the spirit. Presents a challenge for each person to find where they stand.
From The Christian Home Series. No. 1
LC NO. 73-701552
Prod-CCFC Dist-CCFC 1972

Locate Yourself In Space And Time C 30 MIN
2 INCH VIDEOTAPE J
See series title for descriptive statement.
From The Summer Journal, Unit 1 - You Are What You Feel Series.
Prod-WNINTV Dist-GPITVL

Locating And Repairing Leaks B 17 MIN
16MM FILM, 3/4 OR 1/2 IN VIDEO
Shows how to test for sulphur dioxide and methyl chloride leaks, use the halide torch to locate freon leaks and repair several types of leaks.
From The Refrigeration Service - Domestic Units Series. No. 3
LC NO. 81-707335
Prod-USOE Dist-USNAC Prodn-ROCKT 1945

Locating Buttons And Buttonholes C 4 MIN
16MM FILM SILENT J-C A
Presents a step-by-step procedure for proper location of buttons and buttonholes. Includes an explanation of why certain button placements are made.
From The Clothing Construction Techniques Series.
LC NO. 77-701198
Prod-IOWA Dist-IOWASP 1976

Locating Holes, Drilling And Tapping In Cast Iron B 18 MIN
16MM FILM, 3/4 OR 1/2 IN VIDEO
Shows how to lay out a bolt circle having eight holes, to use the center punch as centers for drilling and to use a tapping chuck for set screws.
From The Machine Shop Work - Operations On The Drill Press - Vertical Drill Series. No. 1
Prod-USOE Dist-USNAC Prodn-WCSS 1942

Locating Information C 20 MIN
3/4 INCH VIDEO CASSETTE I
Explains the process of locating information. Deals with finding data in books.
From The Study Skills Series.
Prod-WCVETV Dist-GPITVL 1979

Locating Objects By Coordinates C 20 MIN
3/4 INCH VIDEO CASSETTE T

Focuses on the role of time/space relationships in the science curriculum and placement of this relationship in child development theory. Uses classroom scenes to illustrate the concepts of polar and rectangular coordinates.
From The Science In The Elementary School - Physical Science Series.
Prod-UWKY Dist-GPITVL 1979

Locating Points Along A Line B 15 MIN
2 INCH VIDEOTAPE P
See series title for descriptive statement.
From The Just Curious Series. No. 16
Prod-EOPS Dist-GPITVL Prodn-KOACTV

Locating Points, Using Intersecting Lines B 15 MIN
2 INCH VIDEOTAPE P
See series title for descriptive statement.
From The Just Curious Series. No. 17
Prod-EOPS Dist-GPITVL Prodn-KOACTV

Locating Rinciples And Feature Controls C 22 MIN
3/4 OR 1/2 INCH VIDEO CASSETTE IND
Presents elements within a feature control, as well as the 3-2-1 locating principle which is applied through simple drawings.
From The Geometric Dimensioning And Tolerancing Series.
Prod-GMIEMI Dist-AMCEE

Location And Time C 24 MIN
3/4 INCH VIDEO CASSETTE J
Examines the Earth's network of latitude and longitude. Discusses the relationship of the Earth's rotation and longitude to time. Discusses geodetic markers and benchmarks.
From The What On Earth Series.
Prod-NCSDPI Dist-GPITVL 1979

Location Of Decks And Compartments B 17 MIN
16MM FILM OPTICAL SOUND
Explains number and letter designations and deck and compartment arrangement aboard ship.
Prod-USN Dist-USNAC 1948

Loch Ness Monster C 4 MIN
16MM FILM OPTICAL SOUND
Depicts a fast-moving ride aboard the loop coaster ride at the Old Country Busch Gardens amusement park in Williamsburg, Virginia.
LC NO. 79-700134
Prod-AROWDV Dist-BRAVFI Prodn-BRAVFI 1978

Lock Former Machine Acme Or Pipelock Seam C 11 MIN
1/2 IN VIDEO CASSETTE BETA/VHS IND
See series title for descriptive statement.
From The Metal Fabrication - Lock Former Machine Series.
Prod-RMI Dist-RMI

Lock Former Machine Pittsburgh Seam C 14 MIN
1/2 IN VIDEO CASSETTE BETA/VHS IND
See series title for descriptive statement.
From The Metal Fabrication - Lock Former Machine Series.
Prod-RMI Dist-RMI

Lock Welt And Self-Lock Window Installation C 12 MIN
1/2 IN VIDEO CASSETTE BETA/VHS
Deals with auto body repair. Describes the step-by-step installation of stationary glass, using locking weatherstrips.
Prod-RMI Dist-RMI

Lock-Hold-Step C
3/4 OR 1/2 INCH VIDEO CASSETTE IND
Discusses proper method for getting in, on and around large trucks. Increases driver awareness on the importance of this method.
From The Driving Safety Series.
Prod-DCC Dist-GPCV

Lock-Out C 8 MIN
3/4 OR 1/2 INCH VIDEO CASSETTE IND
Details the procedures to be followed when performing maintenance or repair on electrically-driven equipment.
From The Take Ten For Safety Series.
Prod-OLINC Dist-MTI

Locked Inside C 14 MIN
16MM FILM OPTICAL SOUND
Satirizes a man's obsession with the contents of a suitcase which his neighbor constantly carries.
LC NO. 79-701373
Prod-SIDCIN Dist-SIDCIN 1979

Lockheed L-1011 Tristar C 42 MIN
3/4 OR 1/2 INCH VIDEO CASSETTE
Traces the history of the development of a great passenger plane from drawing board to actual test flights, including spectacular footage of assembly production techniques.
Prod-IHF Dist-IHF

Lockout For Safety C 14 MIN
16MM FILM - 3/4 IN VIDEO
Points out that failure to guard against power being turned on during repair or maintenance operations on electrically driven machinery or equipment has caused many deaths and injuries. Presents a fail-safe system for locking out electrical power during repair and maintenance work.
Prod-ALLIED Dist-BNA

Locks And Garage Door Openers - Installing Door Locks, Garage Door Opener C 30 MIN
1/2 IN VIDEO CASSETTE BETA/VHS
See series title for descriptive statement.
From The Wally's Workshop Series.
Prod-KARTES Dist-KARTES

Locomotion Of Cancer Cell In Vivo Compared With Normal Cells (Time-Lapse Cinemicrography) C 21 MIN
16MM FILM OPTICAL SOUND PRO
Examines the locomotion of cancer cells in the blood stream and shows a single cancer cell engulfing three lymphocytes, while a second cancer cell ingests an erythrocyte.
Prod-UPJOHN Dist-UPJOHN 1967

Locomotion Of Cancer Cells In Vivo Compared With Normal Cells C 21 MIN
16MM FILM OPTICAL SOUND PRO
Uses time-lapse cinemicrography to show how rapidly cancer cells move in respect to normal cells and pictures cancer cells engulfing and ingesting red and white blood cells.
From The Upjohn Vanguard Of Medicine Series.
LC NO. FIA68-150
Prod-UPJOHN Dist-UPJOHN Prodn-JHU 1967

Locomotion Of Four-Footed Animals B 15 MIN
16MM FILM, 3/4 OR 1/2 IN VIDEO
Shows all of the major animal gaits including walk, pace, single-foot, trot, bound, pronk, gallop, bipedal run and bipedal hop. Documents the type of locomotion with unique footage of a variety of mammals and reptiles.
From The Aspects Of Animal Behavior Series.
Prod-UCLA Dist-UCEMC 1980

Locomotion Of The Horse C 19 MIN
1/2 IN VIDEO CASSETTE BETA/VHS
Describes the Thoroughbred walk, trot, canter and gallop, as well as the Standardbred amble, pace and trot.
Prod-MSU Dist-EQVDL

Locomotions And Skeletons C 29 MIN
3/4 INCH VIDEO CASSETTE C A
Describes varied movements of animals and how these movements are made possible. Details functions of the skeleton. Examines structure and function of the Haversian systems.
From The Introducing Biology Series. Program 12
Prod-COAST Dist-CDTEL

Locomotor Skills I C 15 MIN
3/4 OR 1/2 INCH VIDEO CASSETTE T
Demonstrates how to explain to primary students about walking, running, leaping, hopping, parts of the leg and foot, pushing, kinesthetic awareness, step size and cooperation in physical activities.
From The Leaps And Bounds Series. No. 4
Prod-HSDE Dist-AITECH 1984

Locomotor Skills II C 15 MIN
3/4 OR 1/2 INCH VIDEO CASSETTE T
Explains how primary students can be taught about various types of jumping, developing force, pushing off and cooperating on the schoolyard.
From The Leaps And Bounds Series. No. 5
Prod-HSDE Dist-AITECH 1984

Locomotor Skills III C 15 MIN
3/4 OR 1/2 INCH VIDEO CASSETTE T
Demonstrates how to explain to primary students about slides, gallops, skips, body part relationships and awareness, recognition of skills by their rhythmic pattern, dodging moving objects and people.
From The Leaps And Bounds Series. No. 6
Prod-HSDE Dist-AITECH 1984

Locus C 20 MIN
3/4 OR 1/2 INCH VIDEO CASSETTE J-C
See series title for descriptive statement.
From The Math Topics - Geometry Series.
Prod-BBCTV Dist-FI

Locusts - The Now And Ancient Plague C 9 MIN
16MM FILM, 3/4 OR 1/2 IN VIDEO I-J
Shows locusts mating and laying eggs. Views the developing nymphs which turn into swarming, destroying hordes. Gives examples of the coordinating efforts of the United Nations' Food and Agriculture Organization to control the locust population and prevent the damage they can cause.
From The Real World Of Insects Series.
Prod-LCOA Dist-LCOA 1973

Locusts - The Now And Ancient Plague (Captioned) C 10 MIN
16MM FILM, 3/4 OR 1/2 IN VIDEO P-C A
Explores the behavior pattern of the locust, who has created critical food shortages over centuries. Discusses worldwide efforts to control this natural phenomenon.
From The Real World Of Insects Series.
Prod-PEGASO Dist-LCOA 1973

Locusts - The Now And Ancient Plague (Spanish) C 10 MIN
16MM FILM, 3/4 OR 1/2 IN VIDEO P-C A
Explores the behavior pattern of the locust, who has created critical food shortages over centuries. Discusses worldwide efforts to control this natural phenomenon.
From The Real World Of Insects Series.
Prod-PEGASO Dist-LCOA 1973

Locusts - War Without End C 57 MIN
16MM FILM, 3/4 OR 1/2 IN VIDEO H-C A
Shows how locusts can transform themselves from a group of harmless insects to a voracious swarm, capable of destroying all vegetation in their path. Depicts a frightening surge of a billion locusts, carpeting the ground and moving like a single, monstrous animal.
From The Nova Series.
Prod-WGBHTV Dist-TIMLIF 1982

Lodge Night B 29 MIN
16MM FILM SILENT
Tells how the black and white members of the Gang join the Cluck Cluck Klan. A Little Rascals film.
Prod-ROACH Dist-BHAWK 1923

Lodger, The B 66 MIN
16MM FILM SILENT
Focuses on a boarding house tenant whose mysterious life causes him to be suspected as Jack the Ripper. Directed by Alfred Hitchcock.
Prod-UNKNWN Dist-KITPAR 1926

Log Driver's Waltz C
16MM FILM, 3/4 OR 1/2 IN VIDEO I-C A
Presents an animated tale about a young girl who loves to dance and marries a log driver over his well-to-do landloving competition. Shows that driving logs down the river has made the young man the best dancing partner to be found.
Prod-NFBC Dist-NFBC

Log House (Cabane De Rondins) C 28 MIN
16MM FILM, 3/4 OR 1/2 IN VIDEO J-C A
A French language motion picture. Observes a group of men as they build a log house. Follows the year-long process from the felling of pine trees to the installation of handmade kitchen counters.
Prod-NFBC Dist-BULFRG 1976

Log Of Mariner IV C 27 MIN
16MM FILM OPTICAL SOUND H A
A documentary account of the successful and rewarding Mariner 1964-65 fly-by mission to the planet Mars. Contains the first close-ups of Mars and planetary scientific conclusions resulting from the flight.
LC NO. FIE67-96
Prod-NASA Dist-NASA Prodn-JETPL 1966

Log Raft, The - A Norwegian Summer Story C 25 MIN
16MM FILM, 3/4 OR 1/2 IN VIDEO I-J
Shows the activities of three young children who spend the summer at an island cabin in the Norwegian fjords.
Prod-BFA Dist-PHENIX Prodn-SVEK 1972

Log Splitter B 15 MIN
2 INCH VIDEOTAPE P
See series title for descriptive statement.
From The Children's Literature Series. No. 17
Prod-NCET Dist-GPITVL Prodn-KUONTV

Log 43 B 15 MIN
16MM FILM OPTICAL SOUND
Presents a re-enactment based upon the Algier's Motel incident in which three people were killed during the Detroit riots in 1967.
LC NO. 75-703197
Prod-USC Dist-USC 1969

Logarithmic Decades, The C 50 MIN
3/4 OR 1/2 INCH VIDEO CASSETTE
Gives a brief historical overview of energy growth in the United States. Covers potential consequences if growth is continued.
From The Energy Issues And Alternatives Series.
Prod-UIDEEO Dist-UIDEEO

Logarithmic Functions C 30 MIN
3/4 INCH VIDEO CASSETTE C
See series title for descriptive statement.
From The Introduction To Mathematics Series.
Prod-MDCPB Dist-MDCPB

Logarithms And The Slide Rule, Lesson 1 B 30 MIN
16MM FILM, 3/4 OR 1/2 IN VIDEO H-C
Traces the history of logarithms and the slide rule. Compares 'LONGHAND' multiplication and the exponential method. Defines logarithm and shows how to determine the characteristic of the logarithm of a number when the number is greater than or equal to unity.
Prod-IFB Dist-IFB 1960

Logarithms And The Slide Rule, Lesson 2 B 30 MIN
16MM FILM, 3/4 OR 1/2 IN VIDEO H-C
Emphasizes the mantissa. Explains the use of the 'NINE MINUS TEN' convention when dealing with negative characteristics. Gives formal proof of the theorem 'THE LOGARITHM OF A QUOTIENT IS EQUAL TO THE LOGARITHM OF THE DIVIDEND MINUS THE LOGARITHM OF THE DIVISOR.' Applies this to an example.
Prod-IFB Dist-IFB 1960

Logarithms And The Slide Rule, Lesson 3 B 30 MIN
16MM FILM, 3/4 OR 1/2 IN VIDEO H-C
Solves a problem requiring fourth power of the product of two numbers. Explains the method of computing mantissae. Explains and illustrates the technique of 'INSERTING A GEOMETRIC MEAN BETWEEN TWO NUMBERS.'
Prod-IFB Dist-IFB 1960

Logarithms And The Slide Rule, Lesson 4 B 30 MIN
16MM FILM, 3/4 OR 1/2 IN VIDEO H-C
Uses close-up photography to illustrate the use of a table of logarithms. Explains the method of looking up logarithms and antilogarithms.
Prod-IFB Dist-IFB 1960

Logarithms And The Slide Rule, Lesson 5 B 30 MIN
16MM FILM, 3/4 OR 1/2 IN VIDEO H-C
Explains the method of designing the slide rule. Illustrates logarithmic division of the scales and the basic use of the 'C' and 'D' scales for multiplication. Defines 'LOGARITHM.'
Prod-IFB Dist-IFB 1960

Logarithms And The Slide Rule, Lesson 6 B 30 MIN
16MM FILM, 3/4 OR 1/2 IN VIDEO H-C
Describes division, using the 'C' and 'D' scales. Explains the principle of proportion in use of the slide rule. Demonstrates solving of 'COMBINED MULTIPLICATION AND DIVISION' problems using the principle of proportion.
Prod-IFB Dist-IFB 1960

Logarithms And The Slide Rule, Lesson 7 B 30 MIN
16MM FILM, 3/4 OR 1/2 IN VIDEO H-C
Explains the 'C1' scale and shows its use for reciprocals, multiplication and division. Demonstrates the use of the 'A' and 'B' scales for squares and square roots. Shows how to determine which end of the 'A' scale to use in extracting square roots.
Prod-IFB Dist-IFB 1960

Logarithms And The Slide Rule, Lesson 8 B 30 MIN
16MM FILM, 3/4 OR 1/2 IN VIDEO H-C
Illustrates finding the area of a circle using the 'A' and 'B' scales. Explains cubes and cube roots, use of the 'S' scale for finding sines and cosines of angles, and use of 'T' scale for finding tangents of angles.
Prod-IFB Dist-IFB 1960

Logdrivers C 17 MIN
16MM FILM, 3/4 OR 1/2 IN VIDEO
Follows the spring log drive from timber stand to sawmill down the Coulouge River in Quebec, comparing the axes and horse-drawn sleds of the 1920s to modern equipment used today. A former logdriver recalls his days on the rivers and tells how this once common activity is rarer, though still carried on today.
Prod-BARNEM Dist-BCNFL 1982

Logic Arrays C 55 MIN
3/4 OR 1/2 INCH VIDEO CASSETTE PRO
Deals with the topics of logic minimization, AND and OR gates for Sum-of-Products implementation, the programmed logic array (PLA), and two-input decoding.
From The Introduction To VLSI Design Series.
Prod-MIOT Dist-MIOT

Logic Building Blocks C 12 MIN
3/4 OR 1/2 INCH VIDEO CASSETTE
Covers logic circuits, logic gates, AND gates, OR gates, NAND gates, NOR gates, operations of typical logic gates in a circuit and other gates and circuits.
From The Industrial Electronics - Logic Circuits Series.
Prod-TPCTRA Dist-TPCTRA

Logic Building Blocks (Spanish) C 12 MIN
3/4 OR 1/2 INCH VIDEO CASSETTE
Covers logic circuits, logic gates, AND gates, OR gates, NAND gates, NOR gates, operations of typical logic gates in a circuit and other gates and circuits.
From The Industrial Electronics - Logic Circuits (Spanish) Series.
Prod-TPCTRA Dist-TPCTRA

Logic Circuit Characteristics C
3/4 OR 1/2 INCH VIDEO CASSETTE
See series title for descriptive statement.
From The Digital Techniques Series.
Prod-HTHZEN Dist-HTHZEN

Logic Circuit Characteristics C
3/4 OR 1/2 INCH VIDEO CASSETTE
See series title for descriptive statement.
From The Digital Techniques Video Training Course Series.
Prod-VTRI Dist-VTRI

Logic Circuit Operation B 21 MIN
16MM FILM, 3/4 OR 1/2 IN VIDEO A
Discusses the circuit operations of the various logic gates found in basic computers.
Prod-USAF Dist-USNAC 1970

Logic Concepts C 48 MIN
3/4 OR 1/2 INCH VIDEO CASSETTE PRO
See series title for descriptive statement.
From The Digital Electronics Series.
Prod-MIOT Dist-MIOT

Logic Design Of Digital Systems—A Series
C
Uses classroom format to videotape two 75-minute lectures weekly on 56 cassettes. Reviews switching algebra, gates and logic modules, map simplification techniques, multiple output systems, large switching systems, iterative networks, sample designs, computer oriented simplification algorithms, state assignment, partition techniques and sequential system decompositions.
Prod-UMD Dist-AMCEE

Logic Elements B 60 MIN
3/4 OR 1/2 INCH VIDEO CASSETTE
See series title for descriptive statement.
From The Understanding Microprocessors Series. Pt 2
Prod-UAZMIC Dist-UAZMIC 1979

Logic I B
16MM FILM OPTICAL SOUND
Tells how to define binary operations on the set (0.1).
Prod-OPENU Dist-OPENU

Logic II - Proof B
16MM FILM OPTICAL SOUND
Presents examples where proof is not an absolute quality. Investigates scientific and mathematical proof by looking at angles, triangles and axiomatics.
Prod-OPENU Dist-OPENU

Logic Modules - Task Description Using An Algorithm C 30 MIN
3/4 OR 1/2 INCH VIDEO CASSETTE IND
Introduces general block structure for digital systems, including block modules. Shows concept of using algorithms to design tasks and uses Euclid's algorithm as example.
From The Microprocessors For Monitoring And Control Series.
Prod-COLOSU Dist-COLOSU

Logical Consequences And Punishment B 30 MIN
2 INCH VIDEOTAPE
Presents a discussion centered around the basic principle of applying logical consequences and how to distinguish them from punishment. Explains that applying logical consequences and avoiding punishment provides an atmosphere in which children can grow without fighting and without feeling subdued.
From The Motivating Children To Learn Series.
Prod-VTETV Dist-GPITVL

Logical Controls C 30 MIN
3/4 OR 1/2 INCH VIDEO CASSETTE
Describes logical controls that can be designed into the computer system, including identification of system elements, authorization to perform transactions, surveillance of system activities and encryption of data.
From The Computer Security Techniques Series.
Prod-DELTAK Dist-DELTAK

Logical Data Base Design - The Key To Success C 60 MIN
3/4 OR 1/2 INCH VIDEO CASSETTE
Examines the methods used to develop a logical data base model, the most important step in the development of the data base system.
From The Managing The Data Base Environment Series.
Prod-DELTAK Dist-DELTAK

Logical Or Boolean Expressions - Table Representations, Map Representations C 30 MIN
3/4 OR 1/2 INCH VIDEO CASSETTE IND
Gives sufficient introduction to Boolean Algebra for viewers to learn how to represent logical functions through algebraic equations and maps.
From The Microprocessors For Monitoring And Control Series.
Prod-COLOSU Dist-COLOSU

Logical Power Of Computing Schemes C 50 MIN
3/4 OR 1/2 INCH VIDEO CASSETTE
Lectures on the theoretical notions of computability and universality in computer languages.
From The Computer Languages - Pt 1 Series.
Prod-MIOT Dist-MIOT

Logistic Support Management For Advanced Weapons C 20 MIN
16MM FILM OPTICAL SOUND
Defines the mission of a ballistic missile squadron and shows the component parts of weapon systems. Discusses the role of logistic support management in supplying prompt and accurate data, the role of an electronic data processing center and the procedures used in management by exception.
LC NO. FIE61-60
Prod-USDD Dist-USNAC 1960

Logistics For A Microteaching Clinic C 28 MIN
16MM FILM OPTICAL SOUND T
Presents alternatives to the establishment of a pre-service or in-service microteaching clinic.
Prod-EDUC Dist-EDUC

Lognormal And Normal Times-To-Restore Distributions, Their Central Tendencies, And... C 60 MIN
3/4 OR 1/2 INCH VIDEO CASSETTE C
Covers lognormal and normal times-to-restore distributions, their central tendencies, and calculation of maintainability.
From The Maintainability Operational Availability, And Preventive Maintenance Of...Series. Pt 2
Prod-UAZMIC Dist-UAZMIC

Logo - The Computer As An Intellectual Tool C 27 MIN
3/4 OR 1/2 INCH VIDEO CASSETTE J-C A
Discusses computer literacy and the basis of LOGO, a computer educational language. Demonstrates the use of LOGO, including some student programming projects.
From The New Technology In Education Series.
LC NO. 84-706536
Prod-USDOE Dist-USNAC 1983

Logos C 2 MIN
16MM FILM OPTICAL SOUND H-C
Combines non-objective visuals and electronic music to produce optical illusions and a distortion of time perception.
Prod-CONGER Dist-CFS

Loin De Paris C 10 MIN
16MM FILM, 3/4 OR 1/2 IN VIDEO H-C
A French language film. Explores the lives of the four-fifths of the French population that live and work in the provinces. Shows the way environmental factors affect the various lifestyles. Examines the forces of change at work in the provinces of France.
From The La France Contemporaine Series.
Prod-EBEC Dist-EBEC 1971

Lois Gould On Women Writers C 29 MIN
3/4 OR 1/2 INCH VIDEO CASSETTE
Features novelist Lois Gould explaining some traditional assumptions about women writers and describing the limitations they impose on writers of fiction. Discusses her feelings about the responsibility of women writers.
From The Woman Series.
Prod-WNEDTV Dist-PBS

Lois Jaffe, MSW - A Need To Know - A Family Faces Death C 60 MIN
3/4 OR 1/2 INCH VIDEO CASSETTE PRO
Focuses on the effect of a terminal illness on the family. Features interviews with the family of a boy dying of acute myelogenous leukemia conducted by Lois Jaffe, who suffers from the same disease.
From The Perceptions, Pt A - Interventions In Family Therapy Series. Vol IV, Pt A8.
Prod-BOSFAM Dist-BOSFAM

Lois Jaffe, MSW - Associate Professor, University Of Pittsburgh School Of Social Work C 60 MIN
3/4 OR 1/2 INCH VIDEO CASSETTE PRO
Interviews Lois Jaffe, Who became a family therapist and social worker after raising a family. Reveals how contracting acute myelogenous leukemia focused her work on the seriously ill and dying.
From The Perceptions, Pt B - Dialogues With Family Therapists Series. Vol IV, Pt B8.
Prod-BOSFAM Dist-BOSFAM

Loisirs Et Vacances C 11 MIN
16MM FILM, 3/4 OR 1/2 IN VIDEO H
A French language film. Examines how the French spend their leisure time, paying special attention to the interests of the young.
From The La France Contemporaine Series.
Prod-EBEC Dist-EBEC 1971

Lokmanya Tilak B 23 MIN
16MM FILM OPTICAL SOUND I-C A
Presents the life story of Lokmanya Tilak. Discusses the Indian struggle for independence.
Prod-INDIA Dist-NEDINF

Lollipop Opera, The C 9 MIN
16MM FILM, 3/4 OR 1/2 IN VIDEO K-C A
Don Freeman, cartoonist and illustrator, uses colored chalks to present an account of a young boy's visit to a barber shop.
Prod-JOHNGL Dist-PFP 1971

Lolly, Lolly, Lolly - Get Your Adverbs Here C 3 MIN
3/4 OR 1/2 INCH VIDEO CASSETTE P
Uses a story about a special kind of store in order to demonstrate the function of adverbs as parts of speech.
From The Grammar Rock Series.
Prod-ABCTV Dist-GA Prodn-SCOROC 1974

Lombardi - Commitment To Excellence C 20 MIN
16MM FILM, 3/4 OR 1/2 IN VIDEO
Uses Vince Lombardi's gift for getting people to do better than they believed they could to leave a lasting impression on every employee.
Prod-BBP Dist-BBP

Lomvie - Uria Aalge (Guillemot) C 6 MIN
16MM FILM OPTICAL SOUND
Presents a description of the guillemot in its natural surroundings, accompanied by sound effects.
Prod-STATNS Dist-STATNS 1965

London C 3 MIN
16MM FILM OPTICAL SOUND P-I
Discusses the city of London in England.
From The Of All Things Series.
Prod-BAILYL Dist-AVED

London C 40 MIN
16MM FILM, 3/4 OR 1/2 IN VIDEO
Shows the sights of London, including the London Zoo, Portobello Road, the Tower of London and a Tower guard.
From The Touring Great Cities Series.
LC NO. 78-700486
Prod-BBCTV Dist-FI 1977

London - Center Of The World's Art Trade (1970) C 27 MIN
16MM FILM OPTICAL SOUND
Takes a shrewd look behind the scenes of one of the major art centers, where masterpieces are traded daily by laconic experts.
Prod-ROLAND Dist-ROLAND

London Bridge Is Falling Down C 9 MIN
16MM FILM OPTICAL SOUND K-P
Uses illustrations by Peter Spier from the book 'LONDON BRIDGE IS FALLING DOWN' to show the life and activity on the famous bridge as it appeared in the 18th century.
LC NO. 71-703005
Prod-CONNF Dist-CONNF 1969

London Of William Hogarth, The C 27 MIN
16MM FILM, 3/4 OR 1/2 IN VIDEO H-C A
Uses the satirical engravings of William Hogarth to depict 18th century London life.
LC NO. 80-706718
Prod-BCF Dist-IFB 1977

Lone Eagle, The B 13 MIN
16MM FILM OPTICAL SOUND J-C A
Documents the unforgettable flight of Charles Augustus Lindbergh from New York to Paris in 1927.
From The Screen News Digest Series.
LC NO. 77-701296
Prod-HEARST Dist-HEARST 1977

Lone Star Trail C 18 MIN
3/4 OR 1/2 INCH VIDEO CASSETTE P-I
Reviews melodic contour and shows phrases on the musical staff.
From The USS Rhythm Series.
Prod-ARKETV Dist-AITECH 1977

Loneliness - And Loving C 17 MIN
16MM FILM, 3/4 OR 1/2 IN VIDEO J-C A
Tells how a young man, estranged from his family, his past, and himself, returns home to face emotions and conflicts he has chosen to keep suppressed.
From The Searching For Values - A Film Anthology Series.
Prod-LCOA Dist-LCOA 1972

Loneliness - The Empty Tree House C 10 MIN
3/4 INCH VIDEO CASSETTE I-J

Tells how John's best friend moves away and leaves him reluctant to make friends with other children.
Prod-GA Dist-GA

Lonely Are The Brave B 107 MIN
16MM FILM OPTICAL SOUND
Pits a cowboy-outlaw against a sheriff in a flight for freedom. Stars Kirk Douglas and Walter Matthau.
Prod-UPCI Dist-TWYMAN 1962

Lonely Boy B 27 MIN
16MM FILM, 3/4 OR 1/2 IN VIDEO H-C A
Uses the song 'I'M JUST A LONELY BOY' sung by Paul Anka, teenage idol of the fifties as the theme of a classic film in direct cinema about the 'POP' singer image. Emphasizes the creation of an 'IMAGE' that sells and the people who buy it.
Prod-NFBC Dist-NFBC 1962

Lonely Crime, The C 48 MIN
16MM FILM OPTICAL SOUND
Probes the difficulties in applying legal and medical procedures to the crime of rape. Explains that rape is one of the hardest crimes to prove in court. Interviews women who have been raped, a convicted rapist and representatives of the police, prosecution and medical establishments.
From The Perspective Series.
LC NO. 73-700733
Prod-WRCTV Dist-WRCTV 1972

Lonely Dorymen, The C 51 MIN
16MM FILM, 3/4 OR 1/2 IN VIDEO I-H
Tells the story of the Portuguese cod fishing fleet which uses outmoded methods and traditions, including use of one-man dories, but competes against modern Russian and U S fleets.
LC NO. 80-706384
Prod-NGS Dist-NGS 1968

Lonely Dove, The C 12 MIN
3/4 OR 1/2 INCH VIDEO CASSETTE P-I
See series title for descriptive statement.
From The Ready, Sing Series.
Prod-ARKETV Dist-AITECH 1979

Lonely Hunter, The C 6 MIN
16MM FILM, 3/4 OR 1/2 IN VIDEO K-P
Tells the story of an Inuit boy who lives alone, and befriends a baby seal. Relates how, although they enjoy each other's companionship, the seal senses the boy's need for human friends and calls on help from the Queen of the Sea, who finds a kayak with a young companion.
From The Inuit Legends Series.
Prod-ANIMET Dist-BCNFL 1982

Lonely Island C 7 MIN
16MM FILM OPTICAL SOUND P-J
Describes the animal and bird life of the Antarctic.
Prod-ANAIB Dist-AUIS 1971

Lonely Office, The C 29 MIN
16MM FILM OPTICAL SOUND
Explains how and why the decision-making responsibility in every area of national life falls ultimately on the President, giving examples which illustrate the President's duties.
From The Government Story Series. No. 26
LC NO. 74-707167
Prod-WBCPRO Dist-WBCPRO 1968

Lonely Scarecrow, The C 11 MIN
16MM FILM, 3/4 OR 1/2 IN VIDEO P
Tells a story about a talking scarecrow to present some basic concepts on cornfield ecology.
Prod-CORF Dist-CORF 1970

Loner, The C 30 MIN
3/4 OR 1/2 INCH VIDEO CASSETTE
Features the slightly pornographic adventures of a mean-minded but likeable character.
Prod-EAI Dist-EAI

Loner, The C 32 MIN
3/4 OR 1/2 INCH VIDEO CASSETTE
Shows that we all have a little loner in us whom we both love and hate.
Prod-KITCHN Dist-KITCHN

Lonesome Ghosts C 8 MIN
16MM FILM, 3/4 OR 1/2 IN VIDEO
Shows what happens when the Ajax Ghost Exterminators consisting of Mickey Mouse, Donald Duck and Goofy encounter some lonesome ghosts.
From The Gang's All Here Series.
Prod-DISNEY Dist-WDEMCO

Lonesome Train, The C 21 MIN
16MM FILM, 3/4 OR 1/2 IN VIDEO I-C A
Uses etchings and photographs from the late 19th century to portray the progress of Abraham Lincoln's funeral train from Washington D C to Springfield, Illinois. Uses history, anecdote and legend to show the problems of the times and the powerful symbol of freedom Lincoln represented.
Prod-FLMFR Dist-FLMFR

Long 'A' - April's Apron C 15 MIN
2 INCH VIDEOTAPE P
Develops auditory awareness and discrimination of vowel sounds. Introduces a few common vowel generalizations which are an aid in learning to read.
From The Listen And Say Series.
Prod-MPATI Dist-GPITVL

Long 'E' - The Teeny Weeny Eel C 15 MIN
2 INCH VIDEOTAPE P
Develops auditory awareness and discrimination of vowel sounds. Introduces a few common vowel generalizations which are an aid in learning to read.
From The Listen And Say Series.
Prod-MPATI Dist-GPITVL

Long 'I' - Ida's Ice Cream C 15 MIN
2 INCH VIDEOTAPE P
Develops auditory awareness and discrimination of vowel sounds. Introduces a few common vowel generalizations which are an aid in learning to read.
From The Listen And Say Series.
Prod-MPATI Dist-GPITVL

Long 'O' - Ole's Old Overalls C 15 MIN
2 INCH VIDEOTAPE P
Develops auditory awareness and discrimination of vowel sounds. Introduces a few common vowel generalizations which are an aid in learning to read.
From The Listen And Say Series.
Prod-MPATI Dist-GPITVL

Long 'U' - The Unicorn In The Uniform C 15 MIN
2 INCH VIDEOTAPE P
Develops auditory awareness and discrimination of vowel sounds. Introduces a few common vowel generalizations which are an aid in learning to read.
From The Listen And Say Series.
Prod-MPATI Dist-GPITVL

Long A - April's Apron B 15 MIN
2 INCH VIDEOTAPE P
See series title for descriptive statement.
From The Listen And Say - Vowels Series.
Prod-GPITVL Dist-GPITVL

Long And Short A C 15 MIN
3/4 INCH VIDEO CASSETTE P
See series title for descriptive statement.
From The I Need To Read Series.
Prod-WCETTV Dist-GPITVL 1975

Long And Short E C 15 MIN
3/4 INCH VIDEO CASSETTE P
See series title for descriptive statement.
From The I Need To Read Series.
Prod-WCETTV Dist-GPITVL 1975

Long And Short O C 15 MIN
3/4 INCH VIDEO CASSETTE P
See series title for descriptive statement.
From The I Need To Read Series.
Prod-WCETTV Dist-GPITVL 1975

Long And Short Of It, The C 15 MIN
3/4 OR 1/2 INCH VIDEO CASSETTE P
Employs a magician named Amazing Alexander and his assistants to explore vowel sounds.
From The Magic Shop Series. No. 3
LC NO. 83-706148
Prod-CVETVC Dist-GPITVL Prodn-WCVETV 1982

Long And Short Of It, The B 15 MIN
2 INCH VIDEOTAPE P
See series title for descriptive statement.
From The Listen And Say - Vowels Series.
Prod-GPITVL Dist-GPITVL

Long And Short Of It, The C 15 MIN
2 INCH VIDEOTAPE P
Develops auditory awareness and discrimination of vowel sounds. Introduces a few common vowel generalizations which are an aid in learning to read.
From The Listen And Say Series.
Prod-MPATI Dist-GPITVL

Long And Short Of It, The C 15 MIN
3/4 OR 1/2 INCH VIDEO CASSETTE P
Tells how a space robot helps his puppet assistant and her friends understand and use standard units of measure, including the inch, foot, yard, centimeter, and meter. Shows how the puppet and her friends then measure things in the robot's spaceship with a ruler, yardstick and meter stick.
From The Math Mission 2 Series.
LC NO. 82-706353
Prod-WCVETV Dist-GPITVL 1980

Long And Short Of Shadows, The C 14 MIN
16MM FILM OPTICAL SOUND K-I
Features Yoffy telling the story of villagers who exchange shadows for a day.
From The Fingermouse, Yoffy And Friends Series.
LC NO. 73-700440
Prod-BBCTV Dist-VEDO 1972

Long And Short U C 15 MIN
3/4 INCH VIDEO CASSETTE P
See series title for descriptive statement.
From The I Need To Read Series.
Prod-WCETTV Dist-GPITVL 1975

Long Beach Community Arts C 53 MIN
3/4 OR 1/2 INCH VIDEO CASSETTE A
Features a series of mini-documentaries involving community and art activities in Long Beach.
From The Shared Realities Series.
Prod-LBMART Dist-LBMART 1983

Long Beach Museum Of Art - Video C 56 MIN
3/4 OR 1/2 INCH VIDEO CASSETTE A
Presents an outline of the historical development of video at Long Beach, focusing on its origins and major activities.
From The Shared Realities Series.
Prod-LBMART Dist-LBMART 1983

Long Beach Olympiad C 50 MIN
16MM FILM - 1/2 IN VIDEO
Deals with the U S Olympic sailing team.
Prod-OFFSHR Dist-OFFSHR

Long Beach Operation Readiness C 29 MIN
16MM FILM OPTICAL SOUND
Documents the largest training exercise in the history of Naval Reserve forces.
LC NO. 74-706488
Prod-USN Dist-USNAC 1973

Long Cast, The B 30 MIN
16MM FILM OPTICAL SOUND
Dramatizes the life of Adolph Ochs, who published the Chattanooga Times until he became affiliated with the New York Times, which he published from 1896 to 1935. (Kinescope)
Prod-JTS Dist-NAAJS Prodn-NBCTV 1963

Long Chain, The B 20 MIN
16MM FILM OPTICAL SOUND
Examines the effects of multi-national corporations establishing branches in Third World countries. Interviews construction workers on buildings for U S companies in Bombay.
Prod-NEWTIM Dist-NEWTIM

Long Chain, The C 52 MIN
16MM FILM, 3/4 OR 1/2 IN VIDEO
Traces the connection between mercantile competition between the British and Dutch in the 17th century, the development of a coal-tar pitch to protect ship hulls, and the creation of waterproofed clothing, gaslight lamps and nylon.
From The Connections Series. No. 7
LC NO. 79-700862
Prod-BBCTV Dist-TIMLIF 1979

Long Childhood, The C 52 MIN
16MM FILM, 3/4 OR 1/2 IN VIDEO J-C A
Surveys the complex roles of science in the cultural evolution of man.
From The Ascent Of Man Series. No. 13
LC NO. 79-707232
Prod-BBCTV Dist-TIMLIF 1973

Long Childhood, The (Spanish) C 52 MIN
16MM FILM OPTICAL SOUND H-C A
Surveys the complex role of science in the cultural evolution of man.
From The Ascent Of Man Series.
Prod-BBCTV Dist-TIMLIF 1973

Long Christmas Dinner, The C 37 MIN
16MM FILM, 3/4 OR 1/2 IN VIDEO H-C A
Presents The Long Christmas Dinner by Thornton Wilder, an example of the modern trend toward non-representational, symbolic theater. Represents 90 Christmas dinners in the Bayard household. Expresses the view that life is cyclical and that ordinary existence repeats itself.
From The Humanities - Short Play Showcase Series.
Prod-EBEC Dist-EBEC 1976

Long E - The Teeny Weeny Eel B 15 MIN
2 INCH VIDEOTAPE P
See series title for descriptive statement.
From The Listen And Say - Vowels Series.
Prod-GPITVL Dist-GPITVL

Long Fist, The C 24 MIN
3/4 INCH VIDEO CASSETTE J A
Highlights episodes from a Hong King visit of Canadian kung fu devotees Gary Bush and Dennis Crawford. Shows viewers an open-air market, scenes of the city from a double-decker bus, visits to a restaurant and to Show Studios, the Hollywood of kung fu movies, and a demonstration of long fist techniques. Narrated by Bush and Crawford.
Prod-MOBIUS Dist-MOBIUS 1982

Long Haul Men, The C 17 MIN
16MM FILM, 3/4 OR 1/2 IN VIDEO I-J A
Documents the experiences of a two-man driving team freighting produce from Mexico to the Canadian border. Shows glimpses of the changing terrain as the truck rolls on through day and night.
Prod-NFBC Dist-NFBC 1966

Long Haul, The B 14 MIN
3/4 INCH VIDEO CASSETTE
Describes the fisherman's efforts to provide for his family after a crippling accident. Explains the protection provided by Social Securtiy.
Prod-USNAC Dist-USNAC 1965

Long Haul, The C 30 MIN
16MM FILM, 3/4 OR 1/2 IN VIDEO C A
See series title for descriptive statement.
From The Case Studies In Small Business Series.
Prod-UMA Dist-GPITVL 1979

Long I - Ida's Ice Cream B 15 MIN
2 INCH VIDEOTAPE P
See series title for descriptive statement.
From The Listen And Say - Vowels Series.
Prod-GPITVL Dist-GPITVL

Long Island, The C
3/4 OR 1/2 INCH VIDEO CASSETTE
From The Antartica Series.
Prod-EAI Dist-EAI

Long John C 15 MIN
3/4 OR 1/2 INCH VIDEO CASSETTE P-I
See series title for descriptive statement.
From The Ready, Sing Series.
Prod-ARKETV Dist-AITECH 1979

Long Journey B 29 MIN
16MM FILM OPTICAL SOUND H-C A

Depicts the story of the long journey of the Korean people from the battlefields back to life in a land being rehabilitated. Tells the postwar life of Kim Tai Yung, a farmer from North Korea who made his way south to freedom in the winter of 1951.
LC NO. FIA57-1131
Prod-UN Dist-UN 1955

Long Journey West - 1820 C 15 MIN
16MM FILM, 3/4 OR 1/2 IN VIDEO I-J
Portrays highlights of a journey from Massachusetts to Illinois in the 1800's. Stresses hardships and shows the different types of transportation.
From The Pioneer Life Series.
Prod-IU Dist-IU 1960

Long Journey, The C 12 MIN
16MM FILM OPTICAL SOUND
Designed to motivate audiences to contribute to charitable causes. Tells about a man who is concerned about people in need. Showing flashbacks in his life when he came in contact with Combined Federal Campaign agencies and services. Shows how he later is helped to face serious illness and overcome problems.
LC NO. 74-702487
Prod-UWAMER Dist-UWAMER 1974

Long Journey, The B 29 MIN
16MM FILM OPTICAL SOUND H-C A
Presents the story of the long journey of the Korean people from the battlefields back to life in a land being rehabilitated. Focuses on the postwar life of Kim Tai Yung, a farmer from North Korea who made his way south to freedom in the winter of 1951.
LC NO. FIA57-1131
Prod-UN Dist-UN 1955

Long Jump C 4 MIN
16MM FILM SILENT
Presents male athletes competing in the long jump, including Lewis, Myricks, Grimes, Conley, Lauterbach, Abbyasov, Benson, Leitner and Samarin.
Prod-TRACKN Dist-TRACKN 1982

Long Jump C 46 MIN
1/2 IN VIDEO CASSETTE BETA/VHS
See series title for descriptive statement.
From The Women's Track And Field Series.
Prod-MOHOMV Dist-MOHOMV

Long Jump C 46 MIN
1/2 IN VIDEO CASSETTE BETA/VHS A
Deals with the long jump, a demanding event in Women's Track and Field. Demonstrates the step-by-step procedure used to train a beginning long jumper. Features Olympic Games veteran Martha Watson and Coach Ken Foreman.
Prod-RMI Dist-RMI

Long Jump (Women) C 4 MIN
16MM FILM SILENT
Presents female athletes competing in the long jump, including Lewis, Anderson, McMillan, Johnson, Loud, Wlodarczyk, Skachko, Wujak, Kolpakova, Nygrynova, Joyner and Zorina.
Prod-TRACKN Dist-TRACKN 1982

Long Jump, The C 11 MIN
16MM FILM, 3/4 OR 1/2 IN VIDEO H-C A
Shows an international competition in the long jump. Discusses training exercises and depicts critical phases of the jump.
From The Athletics Series.
LC NO. 80-706583
Prod-GSAVL Dist-IU 1980

Long Lasting Blossoming Plants C 29 MIN
2 INCH VIDEOTAPE
See series title for descriptive statement.
From The Making Things Grow III Series.
Prod-WGBHTV Dist-PUBTEL

Long Life, A C 1 MIN
3/4 OR 1/2 INCH VIDEO CASSETTE
Uses TV spot format and panning technique to show a woman as she might look at 50, 40, 30, and 20 years of age. Encourages viewers to know which tests are necessary and when to take them for a long, healthy life.
Prod-AMCS Dist-AMCS 1981

Long Live C 29 MIN
2 INCH VIDEOTAPE
See series title for descriptive statement.
From The Maggie And The Beautiful Machine - Easy Does It Series.
Prod-WGBHTV Dist-PUBTEL

Long Live The Heart C 25 MIN
3/4 OR 1/2 INCH VIDEO CASSETTE
Shows how the heart works, the sophisticated diagnostic measures doctors have of looking at it, what happens when doctors have a heart attack and how heart attacks can be avoided. Features an actual cardio-catheterization procedure, in which one can see the patient's heart pumping through sophisticated X-ray techniques.
Prod-TRAINX Dist-TRAINX

Long March Of The Suffragists, The C 50 MIN
16MM FILM, 3/4 OR 1/2 IN VIDEO H-C A
Recounts how women demonstrated to get the vote in 1916 by picketing the White House, being imprisoned, going on hunger strikes and being forcibly fed. Presents six suffragists who relate the final, dramatic years of their battle for the vote which culminated in victory in 1920.
From The Yesterday's Witness In America Series.
Prod-BBCTV Dist-TIMLIF 1982

Long Night, The C 15 MIN
16MM FILM OPTICAL SOUND J-C A
Presents the drama of a young man as he faces the reality of having tuberculosis. Provides information on the disease and explains how to prevent it.
Prod-WSU Dist-WSU 1959

Long Night, The X 87 MIN
16MM FILM OPTICAL SOUND
Tells the story of a twelve-year-old boy in Harlem. Presents his search for money that was stolen from him, money which his mother desperately needs. Shows him finding his father on his search into the night. Based on the novel by Julian Mayfield.
Prod-BLKFMF Dist-BLKFMF

Long O - Ole's Old Overalls B 15 MIN
2 INCH VIDEOTAPE P
See series title for descriptive statement.
From The Listen And Say - Vowels Series.
Prod-GPITVL Dist-GPITVL

Long Pants B 60 MIN
16MM FILM SILENT J-C A
Stars Harry Langdon as a country boy pitted against city slickers in a series of adventures as he pursues a femme fatale.
Prod-MGM Dist-TWYMAN 1927

Long Road Home C 27 MIN
3/4 OR 1/2 INCH VIDEO CASSETTE J A
Tells the story of a young man who panics the night before his wedding and learns about love and fidelity from God. Stars Harold Gould and Martin Sheen.
Prod-SUTHRB Dist-SUTHRB

Long Road Home, The C 27 MIN
16MM FILM OPTICAL SOUND
Traces the history of the Muscogee, or Creek, Indian nation from their prehistoric migration from the Northwestern Rockies to the southeast and their removal to Indian territory in the 19th century. Includes an account of the contemporary cultural and social conditions of the tribe.
LC NO. 74-701143
Prod-LODSTR Dist-LODSTR 1973

Long Road Home, The C 27 MIN
16MM FILM, 3/4 OR 1/2 IN VIDEO H-C A
Tells how a young man leaves his fiancee on the night before their wedding, heads for Canada, and meets a gentleman who claims he is God. Examines the issue of godly and human fidelity. Stars Martin Sheen and Harold Gould.
From The Insight Series.
Prod-PAULST Dist-PAULST

Long Rope Jumping C 17 MIN
16MM FILM OPTICAL SOUND P-H
Promotes the physical education objectives of agility, rhythm, timing and alertness.
Prod-MMP Dist-MMP 1967

Long Search - A Study Of Religions—A Series

Includes 13 videotapes that survey the world's religions. Traces the global journey of Ronald Eyre, London Playwright and director, as he examines the role of religion today. Examines the ability of each religion to satisfy the spiritual needs of its followers.
Prod-MDCC Dist-MDCC

Long Search—A Series
16MM FILM, 3/4 OR 1/2 IN VIDEO
Presents theater director Ronald Eyre discussing religions of the world.
Prod-BBCTV Dist-TIMLIF

African Religions - Zulu Zion 52 MIN
Alternative Lifestyles In California - West 52 MIN
Buddhism - Footprint Of The Buddha - India 52 MIN
Buddhism - The Land Of The Disappearing 52 MIN
Catholicism - Rome, Leeds And The Desert 52 MIN
Hinduism - 330 Million Gods 52 MIN
Islam - There Is No God But God 52 MIN
Judaism - The Chosen People 52 MIN
Orthodox Christianity - The Rumanian Solution 52 MIN
Protestant Spirit USA 52 MIN
Reflections On The Long Search 52 MIN
Religion In Indonesia - The Way Of The 52 MIN
Taoism - A Question Of Balance 52 MIN

Long Shadow, The C 32 MIN
16MM FILM OPTICAL SOUND
Presents the early years of Abraham Lincoln's life showing the places of his birth, childhood, schooling, his work as a farmer, as a river boat pilot and as a surveyor, his study of law and politics and his early legislative years.
LC NO. FIA68-216
Prod-USC Dist-USC 1968

Long Straight, The C 60 MIN
16MM FILM, 3/4 OR 1/2 IN VIDEO J-C A
Travels the longest railroad line without a curve through Australia's Nullarbor Plain. Traces the Australian dream of a transcontinental railroad and rides on the antique Ghan train at a top speed of 17 miles per hour.
From The Great Railway Journeys Of The World Series.
Prod-BBCTV Dist-FI 1979

Long Tidal River C 30 MIN
16MM FILM OPTICAL SOUND
Prod-FENWCK Dist-FENWCK

Long Time Ago, A C 1 MIN
3/4 OR 1/2 INCH VIDEO CASSETTE
Shows Larry Hagman turning the anti-smoking message into a family affair by warning his daughter against smoking. Uses TV spot format.
Prod-AMCS Dist-AMCS 1983

Long Time Intervals C 25 MIN
16MM FILM OPTICAL SOUND H-C
Discusses the significance of long time intervals. Describes the radioactive dating process used in estimating the age of the earth.
From The PSSC Physics Films Series.
Prod-PSSC Dist-MLA 1959

Long Time To Grow, Pt 1 - Two- And Three-Year-Olds In Nursery School C 35 MIN
16MM FILM OPTICAL SOUND
Follows the activities and learning behavior of nursery school children throughout the day and various seasons of the year. Shows how teachers offer help by setting limits as well as discussing the necessary support, encouragement and the amount of supervision.
From The Studies Of Normal Personality Development Series.
Prod-NYU Dist-NYU 1951

Long Time To Grow, Pt 2 - Four And Five Year Olds In School B 40 MIN
16MM FILM OPTICAL SOUND
Presents children ages four and five at work and play at the Vassar College Nursery School and the Poughkeepsie Day School.
From The Studies Of Normal Personality Development Series.
Prod-NYU Dist-NYU 1954

Long Time To Grow, Pt 3 - Six-, Seven- And Eight-Year-Olds - Society Of Children C 30 MIN
16MM FILM OPTICAL SOUND
Documents the entrance of children into a world of tradition, magic and customs that are resistant to change. Shows the growth of group cohesion leading toward cliques, peer groups and cleavages on the basis of interest and sex.
From The Studies Of Normal Personality Development Series.
Prod-NYU Dist-NYU 1957

Long U - The Unicorn In The Uniform B 15 MIN
2 INCH VIDEOTAPE P
See series title for descriptive statement.
From The Listen And Say - Vowels Series.
Prod-GPITVL Dist-GPITVL

Long Valley, The - A Study Of Bereavement C 50 MIN
16MM FILM, 3/4 OR 1/2 IN VIDEO H-C A
States that bereaved people usually experience shock and numbness, a search for the dead person, depression, and, finally, acceptance. Emphasizes that these normal reactions to loss must not be suppressed.
LC NO. 79-707823
Prod-BBCTV Dist-FI 1980

Long Vowel Sounds, The C 15 MIN
16MM FILM, 3/4 OR 1/2 IN VIDEO P-I
Reviews the long and short vowel sounds. Shows through illustration and example three rules for long vowel sounds in long words.
From The Reading Skills, Set 2 Series. No. 1
Prod-GLDWER Dist-JOU 1972

Long Vowels With Silent E C 15 MIN
3/4 INCH VIDEO CASSETTE P
See series title for descriptive statement.
From The I Need To Read Series.
Prod-WCETTV Dist-GPITVL 1975

Long Vowels With Two Vowels Together C 15 MIN
3/4 INCH VIDEO CASSETTE P
See series title for descriptive statement.
From The I Need To Read Series.
Prod-WCETTV Dist-GPITVL 1975

Long Voyage Home, The - Donne's Religious Poetry C 45 MIN
3/4 OR 1/2 INCH VIDEO CASSETTE
Looks at John Donne's religious poetry
From The Survey Of English Literature I Series.
Prod-MDCPB Dist-MDCPB

Long Walk Of Fred Young, The C 49 MIN
16MM FILM OPTICAL SOUND H-C A
Deals with the struggle of Fred Young, a Navaho Indian, to move from the poverty of his childhood to his position as a laser fusion researcher. Shows that for Young and others like him survival means accomodation to an alien culture and the loss of native identity. Deals with the lives of his relatives who have not been able to bridge the two cultures.
From The Nova Series.
Prod-BBCTV Dist-KINGFT 1979

Long Walk Of Fred Young, The C 60 MIN
3/4 INCH VIDEO CASSETTE H-C A
Deals with the struggle of Fred Young, a Navaho Indian, to move from the poverty of his childhood to his position as a laser fusion researcher. Shows that for Fred and others like him survival means accomodation to an alien culture and the loss of native identity. Deals with the lives of his relatives who have not been able to bridge the two cultures.
From The Nova Series.
LC NO. 79-706417
Prod-WGBHTV Dist-PBS 1979

Long Way From Home, A C 15 MIN
3/4 OR 1/2 INCH VIDEO CASSETTE P
Visits Acapulco and Teotihuacan in Mexico.
From The Other Families, Other Friends Series. Blue Module - Mexico
Prod-WVIZTV Dist-AITECH 1971

Long Way To Go, A B 26 MIN
16MM FILM OPTICAL SOUND
Examines the 1969 AFL-CIO convention. Includes addresses by former Vice President Hubert Humphrey, Israeli Prime Minister Golda Meir and astronaut Edwin Aldrin.
Prod-AFLCIO Dist-AFLCIO 1969

Long Weekend, The - The Odds Get Shorter C 23 MIN
16MM FILM OPTICAL SOUND
Dramatizes the risk of driving long distances on weekend trips. Depicts a professional gambler who relates the theories of gambling to a weekend fling of four Las Vegas-bound airmen.
LC NO. 74-706130
Prod-USAF Dist-USNAC 1968

Long Years Of Experiment, The - 1844-1920 C 16 MIN
16MM FILM OPTICAL SOUND
See series title for descriptive statement.
From The Twelve Decades Of Concrete In American Architecture Series.
Prod-PRTLND Dist-PRTLND 1965

Long- And Short-Line Catheters - The Paths Of Chemotherapy C 12 MIN
3/4 INCH VIDEO CASSETTE
Describes the indications for employing indwelling silicone central-venous catheters and then demonstrates the technique and locations for inserting both short-line and long-line catheters.
Prod-UTAHTI Dist-UTAHTI

Long-Term Psychiatric Patient, The C 40 MIN
16MM FILM - 3/4 IN VIDEO PRO
Presents a case study concerning a nurse's relationship with a long-term patient to demonstrate the principles, concepts and skills essential to therapeutic outcomes and rehabilitation. Shows opportunities for helping in patterns of social isolation, withdrawal and chronicity and methods for helping a patient move from very dependent to more independent modes of relating.
LC NO. 76-701619
Prod-AJN Dist-AJN Prodn-WGNCP 1976

Long-Term Stress Management C 15 MIN
16MM FILM, 3/4 OR 1/2 IN VIDEO A
Compares cause and effect with management of trauma stress cases.
From The Stress Management System Series. Film 3
Prod-MTI Dist-MTI 1983

Long, Long Ago B 15 MIN
2 INCH VIDEOTAPE P
See series title for descriptive statement.
From The Children's Literature Series. No. 21
Prod-NCET Dist-GPITVL Prodn-KUONTV

Long, Long Ago C 15 MIN
2 INCH VIDEOTAPE
Provides a basis for the study of contributions made to America by people from all countries.
From The Let's Build A City Series.
Prod-WVIZTV Dist-GPITVL

Longest River, The C 29 MIN
3/4 OR 1/2 INCH VIDEO CASSETTE
Accompanies three young Americans as they raft down one of the world's most dangerous rivers, the Bio Bio in the Chilean Andes.
Prod-WINGS Dist-FLMLIB 1984

Longest Wave, The C 25 MIN
16MM FILM OPTICAL SOUND
Discusses the complexities of the absorption of the longest wave of Russian immigration to Israel.
Prod-UJA Dist-ALDEN

Longevity - To Live To Be 140 C 20 MIN
16MM FILM, 3/4 OR 1/2 IN VIDEO
Focuses on the Andean village of Vilcabamba, where there is a high percentage of people over 100 years old. Looks at the differences between this society and American society. Examines the factors leading to a long life and raises questions about American attitudes towards the old.
Prod-DOCUA Dist-CNEMAG

Longfellow - A Rediscovery C 30 MIN
3/4 INCH VIDEO CASSETTE H-C A
Presents Will Geer and the First Poetry Quartet reading the poetry of Henry Longfellow.
From The Anyone For Tennyson Series.
Prod-NETCHE Dist-GPITVL

Longhorns B 6 MIN
16MM FILM OPTICAL SOUND
Shows the graceful rhythms of longhorns in motion.
Prod-HARH Dist-RADIM

Longhouse People, The C 24 MIN
16MM FILM, 3/4 OR 1/2 IN VIDEO J-C A
Pictures the life and religious ceremonies of the Longhouse People--Iroquois Indians who adhere to the old religion. Shows their rain dances and healing ceremony performed by men of the false-face society.
Prod-NFBC Dist-NFBC 1950

Longine-Wittnauer Interviews - Lapp, McCarthy X 26 MIN
3/4 OR 1/2 INCH VIDEO CASSETTE H A
Discusses topics contained in 'The Longine-Wittnauer Chronoscope,' a series of 15-minute television interviews broadcast between 1951 and 1955. Includes interviews with Senator Joseph R McCarthy and Dr Ralph E Lapp (nuclear physicist).
Prod-NA Dist-USNAC

Longine-Wittnauer Television Interviews- Senator Joseph R McCarthy And Dr Ralph E Lapp B 26 MIN
3/4 OR 1/2 INCH VIDEO CASSETTE
Presents two interviews from the Longine-Wittnauer Chronoscope broadcast on TV between 1951 and 1955. Features Senator Joseph R McCarthy and nuclear physicist Dr Ralph E Lapp discussing the term 'McCarthyism' and the rationale behind the development of thehydrogen bomb.
Prod-IHF Dist-IHF

Longines-Wittnauer Interviews - Adam Clayton Powell, Jr B 11 MIN
3/4 OR 1/2 INCH VIDEO CASSETTE J A
Portrays Congressman Adam Clayton Powell Jr in this interview first aired on CBS-TV on June 7, 1954. Powell, whose commentary in the 1950's following the 'Brown vs Board of Education' Supreme Court decision helped clarify the Negro community's hopes and goals. Discusses prejudice, integration in schools, churches, and the armed forces, interracial marriage and the Supreme Court decision.
Prod-CBSNEW Dist-USNAC 1954

Look Ahead, A B
16MM FILM OPTICAL SOUND
Illustrates what to look for when analyzing fresh data. Discusses the need for so-called 'robust' statistics in the analysis of data from non-normal distributions.
Prod-OPENU Dist-OPENU

Look And A Closer Look--A Series
P-I
Shows how various places, such as farms and beaches, have inspired artists of the past and present. Demonstrates techniques of working with various art materials.
Prod-WCVETV Dist-GPITVL 1976

Animals	15 MIN
Beach, The	15 MIN
Block Printing, Outdoor Sketching And	15 MIN
City, The	15 MIN
Clay Shaping, Clay Decoration And Papier	15 MIN
Construction	15 MIN
Farm, The	15 MIN
Media	15 MIN
Patterns	15 MIN
Puppetry	15 MIN
Salvage Printing, Collage And Care Of	15 MIN
Slides, Film Animations	15 MIN
Stick Puppets, Hand Puppets And Papier	15 MIN
Vegetable Printing, Mosaics And Drawing	15 MIN
Wire Sculpture, Crayon Batik And Figures	15 MIN

Look And See C 15 MIN
2 INCH VIDEOTAPE P
Provides an enrichment program in the communitive arts area by observing and conversing.
From The Word Magic (2nd Ed) Series.
Prod-CVETVC Dist-GPITVL

Look Around Us B 29 MIN
2 INCH VIDEOTAPE K-P
See series title for descriptive statement.
From The Children's Fair Series.
Prod-WMVSTV Dist-PUBTEL

Look Around You C 15 MIN
3/4 INCH VIDEO CASSETTE P
Discusses the function of expressions, movement, clothing and body-talk.
From The Becoming Me, Unit 1 - Physical Identity Series.
Prod-KUONTV Dist-GPITVL 1974

Look Around You C 15 MIN
3/4 OR 1/2 INCH VIDEO CASSETTE P
Shows how information can be acquired by observing the places and things in one's environment.
From The Spinning Stories Series.
Prod-MDDE Dist-AITECH 1977

Look Around You B 15 MIN
2 INCH VIDEOTAPE P
See series title for descriptive statement.
From The Children's Literature Series. No. 28
Prod-NCET Dist-GPITVL Prodn-KUONTV

Look Around You In Autumn C 17 MIN
16MM FILM, 3/4 OR 1/2 IN VIDEO I-H
Focuses on some of the taken-for-granted and unobserved events associated with the arrival of autumn.
From The Look Around You Series.
Prod-DEU Dist-MCFI 1978

Look Around You In Autumn (Captioned) C 17 MIN
16MM FILM, 3/4 OR 1/2 IN VIDEO I-H A
Focuses on some of the taken-for-granted and unobserved events associated with the arrival of autumn.
From The Look Around You Series.
Prod-DEU Dist-MCFI 1978

Look Around You In Spring C 17 MIN
16MM FILM, 3/4 OR 1/2 IN VIDEO I-H
Focuses on some of the taken-for-granted and unobserved events associated with the arrival of spring.
From The Look Around You Series.
Prod-DEU Dist-MCFI 1978

Look Around You In Spring (Captioned) C 17 MIN
16MM FILM, 3/4 OR 1/2 IN VIDEO I-H A
Focuses on some of the taken-for-granted and unobserved events associated with the arrival of spring.
From The Look Around You Series.
Prod-DEU Dist-MCFI 1978

Look Around You In Summer C 17 MIN
16MM FILM, 3/4 OR 1/2 IN VIDEO I-H
Describes taken-for-granted and unobserved events associated with the arrival of summer.
From The Look Around You Series.
Prod-DEU Dist-MCFI 1978

Look Around You In Summer (Captioned) C 17 MIN
16MM FILM, 3/4 OR 1/2 IN VIDEO I-H A
Focuses on some of the taken-for-granted and unobserved events associated with the arrival of summer.
From The Look Around You Series.
Prod-DEU Dist-MCFI 1978

Look Around You In The Desert C 18 MIN
16MM FILM, 3/4 OR 1/2 IN VIDEO I-J
Shows what a desert is and how one is created. Introduces four distinctly different deserts that occupy the southwestern part of the United States and reveals how plants adapt to life in an arid land.
From The Look Around You Series.
Prod-DEU Dist-MCFI

Look Around You In The Everglades C 19 MIN
16MM FILM, 3/4 OR 1/2 IN VIDEO I-J
Observes wildlife in the everglades in both the wet and dry seasons and explains how the mammals, birds and reptiles have adapted in remarkable ways to the harsh demands of survival.
From The Look Around You Series.
Prod-DEU Dist-MCFI

Look Around You In The Zoo C 17 MIN
16MM FILM, 3/4 OR 1/2 IN VIDEO P-J
Introduces animals from North America, Africa, Asia and the Far East, South America, Australia and other parts of the world.
From The Look Around You Series.
Prod-DEU Dist-MCFI 1984

Look Around You In Winter C 17 MIN
16MM FILM, 3/4 OR 1/2 IN VIDEO I-H
Focuses on some of the taken-for-granted and unobserved events associated with the arrival of winter.
From The Look Around You Series.
Prod-DEU Dist-MCFI 1978

Look Around You In Winter (Captioned) C 17 MIN
16MM FILM, 3/4 OR 1/2 IN VIDEO I-H A
Focuses on some of the taken-for-granted and unobserved events associated with the arrival of winter.
From The Look Around You Series.
Prod-DEU Dist-MCFI 1978

Look Around You--A Series
16MM FILM, 3/4 OR 1/2 IN VIDEO
Discusses life in the wild during the four seasons and in the desert and everglades.
Prod-DEU Dist-MCFI 1978

Look Around You In Autumn	017 MIN
Look Around You In Spring	017 MIN
Look Around You In Summer	017 MIN
Look Around You In The Desert	018 MIN
Look Around You In The Everglades	019 MIN
Look Around You In The Zoo	017 MIN
Look Around You In Winter	017 MIN

Look At A Book, A B 15 MIN
2 INCH VIDEOTAPE K-P
Explores the world within a book from cover to cover with an explanation of the various aids and directives. (Broadcast quality)
From The Magic Of Words Series.
Prod-GWTVAI Dist-GPITVL Prodn-WETATV

Look At A Community, A - The Dismal Swamp C 15 MIN
3/4 OR 1/2 INCH VIDEO CASSETTE I
Looks at the community of life within a swamp.
From The Hands On, Grade 5 - Our Environment Series.
Prod-WHROTV Dist-AITECH 1975

Look At Chemical Change, A C 15 MIN
16MM FILM, 3/4 OR 1/2 IN VIDEO I-J A
Shows that different materials have different chemical reactions, using as an example a banana which has turned brown after having been left out on a table for several days.
Prod-HANBAR Dist-MGHT 1970

Look At Greek-American Women--A Series

Prod-MOSESD Dist-MOSESD

Village In Baltimore, A	058 MIN

Look At Growing Up, A - The Adolescent Years C 30 MIN
3/4 OR 1/2 INCH VIDEO CASSETTE C T
Points out that teenagers are caught in a biological 'squeeze play.' Shows they are neither child nor adult. Offers advice to parents and teenagers on ways to resolve their differences through negotiation. Talks to teen- agers about sex, peer acceptance and their attitudes towards adults.
From The Here's To Your Health Series.
Prod-DALCCD Dist-DALCCD

Look At Growing Up, A - The Early Years C 30 MIN
3/4 OR 1/2 INCH VIDEO CASSETTE C T
Shows a straightforward look at the common physical and emotional problems faced by children in the early years of life. Features a visit to a pediatric clinic. Discusses ways to help children cope with the divorce of their parents in this first of a two-part program on pediatrics.
From The Here's To Your Health Series.
Prod-DALCCD Dist-DALCCD

Look At Leaders, A C 29 MIN
3/4 INCH VIDEO CASSETTE
Focuses on personalities, talents and foibles of world political leaders.
From The Conversations With Allen Whiting Series.
Prod-UMITV Dist-UMITV 1979

Look At Lines C 15 MIN
3/4 OR 1/2 INCH VIDEO CASSETTE P-I

Discusses lines in art.
From The Young At Art Series.
Prod-WSKJTV Dist-AITECH 1980

Look At Liv, A C 67 MIN
16MM FILM, 3/4 OR 1/2 IN VIDEO H-C A
Looks at the life of Norwegian actress Liv Ullmann, who discusses her work, her role as a woman in a shifting society, and her relationship with her daughter.
Prod-MACMFL Dist-TEXFLM

Look At Local Government, A B 20 MIN
16MM FILM OPTICAL SOUND H-C A
Dr Charles Adrian, director, Institute for Community Development and Services, Michigan State University, describes conflicts between groups and between the central city and suburbs.
From The Government And Public Affairs Films Series.
Prod-RSC Dist-MLA 1960

Look At Local Government, A - Dr Charles Adrian B 20 MIN
16MM FILM OPTICAL SOUND H-C
See series title for descriptive statement.
From The Building Political Leadership Series.
Prod-RCS Dist-MLA 1960

Look At Log Island C 12 MIN
16MM FILM OPTICAL SOUND
Portrays the swinging Swedish capital at Stockholm, which originally was built on logs in the Stockholm archipelago.
Prod-SWNTO Dist-SWNTO 1965

Look At Me—A Series
A
Emphasizes three basic concepts for parents who are looking for new ways to enjoy being with their children.
Prod-PARLTF Dist-USNAC 1975

Child-Parent Relationships	28 MIN
Everyday Parenting	28 MIN
Fun With Dad	28 MIN
Grandmother And Leslie	28 MIN
Single Parent, The	28 MIN
Working Mother, The	28 MIN

Look At Me—A Series
16MM FILM, 3/4 OR 1/2 IN VIDEO
Shows parents and children having fun together and learning at the same time.
Prod-PEREN Dist-PEREN

Child/Parent Relationships	028 MIN
Everday Parenting	028 MIN
Fun With Dad	028 MIN
Grandmother And Leslie	028 MIN
Single Parent, The	028 MIN
Working Mother, The	028 MIN

Look At Me—A Series
16MM FILM, 3/4 OR 1/2 IN VIDEO C A
Examines the challenges, frustrations, and joy faced by parents of young children. Presents real families coping with aspects of rearing children. Narrated by Phil Donahue.
Prod-WTTWTV Dist-FI 1980

Building Family Relationships	030 MIN
Discipline	030 MIN
Exploring And Accepting Individual Traits	030 MIN
Exploring The World Together	030 MIN
Responsibilities And Rewards of Parenting	030 MIN
Separation	030 MIN
Understanding Sexuality	030 MIN

Look At Money, A C 20 MIN
2 INCH VIDEOTAPE P
See series title for descriptive statement.
From The Mathemagic, Unit VII - Money Series.
Prod-WMULTV Dist-GPITVL

Look At Percussion, A B 29 MIN
2 INCH VIDEOTAPE
See series title for descriptive statement.
From The American Band Goes Symphonic Series.
Prod-WGTV Dist-PUBTEL

Look At Rheumatoid Arthritis, A C 30 MIN
3/4 INCH VIDEOTAPE
Explains the medical multidisciplinary approach for care of the Rheumatoid arthritis patient. Shows patients in physical therapy, occupational therapy and joint replacement surgery.
Prod-UNDMC Dist-UNDMC

Look At Science Fiction, A C 30 MIN
3/4 OR 1/2 INCH VIDEO CASSETTE C
See series title for descriptive statement.
From The Communicating Through Literature Series.
Prod-DALCCD Dist-DALCCD

Look At Sound, A C 30 MIN
16MM FILM, 3/4 OR 1/2 IN VIDEO
Shows what causes sound, how it travels, how we hear it and the effect it has on man and animals in an increasingly noisy world. Explains how the human ear receives sound-wave vibrations and reacts to them.
From The Life Around Us Series.
LC NO. 79-707830
Prod-TIMLIF Dist-TIMLIF 1971

Look At Sound, A (Spanish) C 30 MIN
16MM FILM OPTICAL SOUND
Probes into the phenomenon of sound. Explains what causes it, how it travels, how we hear it and the effect it has on people and animals in an increasingly noisy world.
From The Life Around Us (Spanish) Series.
LC NO. 78-700068
Prod-TIMLIF Dist-TIMLIF 1971

Look At Southern China, A C 20 MIN
3/4 OR 1/2 INCH VIDEO CASSETTE J-C A
Visits Kunming and other cities and scenic landmarks in the southern part of China.
LC NO. 82-706770
Prod-AWSS Dist-AWSS 1980

Look At That C 11 MIN
16MM FILM, 3/4 OR 1/2 IN VIDEO P-I
Defines and studies the basic art elements of line, form, pattern, texture and color. Emphasizes the discovery of these elements in a child's everyday life.
Prod-FILMSM Dist-PHENIX 1968

Look At The Equipment, A C 26 MIN
16MM FILM OPTICAL SOUND H
Focuses on the motor vehicle with emphasis on good and bad automobile design.
From The To Get From Here To There Series.
Prod-PROART Dist-PROART

Look At The Lives Of Others, The C 15 MIN
2 INCH VIDEOTAPE I
Reviews GULLIVER'S TRAVELS by Jonathan Swift. Discusses literary forms and writing purposes.
From The Images Series.
Prod-CVETVC Dist-GPITVL

Look At The Wild Side, A C 22 MIN
16MM FILM OPTICAL SOUND
Shows two faces of Tasmania, the fertile land of the East and North and the wild mountainous land of the West and Central Plateau.
Prod-TASCOR Dist-TASCOR 1968

Look At Us B 20 MIN
2 INCH VIDEOTAPE P-I
Discusses students' observations of themselves and their friends as subject matter for two-or threedimensional portraits, using salvage, paint or a variety of other materials.
From The Art Adventures Series.
Prod-CVETVC Dist-GPITVL Prodn-WCVETV

Look At You Now C 15 MIN
3/4 OR 1/2 INCH VIDEO CASSETTE P
Shows the growth and development of babies, emphasizing their capabilities at various stages.
From The All About You Series.
Prod-WGBHTV Dist-AITECH Prodn-TTOIC 1975

Look At You—A Series
P-I
Prod-ECI Dist-ECI

Look At You, A	13 MIN
Look At You, A - Health	13 MIN
Look At You, A - On The Bus	9 MIN
Look At You, A - The Body	8 MIN
Look At You, A - The Muscles	8 MIN

Look At You, A C 13 MIN
16MM FILM OPTICAL SOUND
Features two puppets, Orsen the dog and Webster the owl, who present concepts of the face and senses.
From The Look At You Series.
Prod-ECI Dist-ECI

Look At You, A - On The Bus C 9 MIN
16MM FILM OPTICAL SOUND P-I
Features two puppets, Orsen the dog and Webster the owl, who demonstrate correct ways to safely board, ride and exit a school bus.
From The Look At You Series.
Prod-ECI Dist-ECI

Look At You, A - The Body C 8 MIN
16MM FILM OPTICAL SOUND P-I
Discusses physical components of the body. Includes discussion of all of the parts of the body individually and repeats them several times using different visuals each time, both abstract and real. Demonstrates the concepts of the whole versus parts, the self as an entity and the sense of touch.
From The Look At You Series.
Prod-ECI Dist-ECI

Look At You, A - The Muscles C 8 MIN
16MM FILM OPTICAL SOUND P-I
Introduces concepts such as brain impulses to the muscles, admitting one's mistakes, group activities, colors, right and left and numbers.
From The Look At You Series.
Prod-ECI Dist-ECI

Look At Zoos C 12 MIN
16MM FILM, 3/4 OR 1/2 IN VIDEO P-I
Presents a visit to some of the world's major zoos, with a special attention to unusual animals and the different manner in which animals are housed at each zoo.
LC NO. 80-706254
Prod-NGS Dist-NGS 1978

Look Back In Anger B
1/2 IN VIDEO CASSETTE BETA/VHS
Presents John Osborne's play about an angry young man fighting the Establishment. Stars Richard Burton and Claire Bloom.
Prod-GA Dist-GA

Look Back In Sorrow C 18 MIN
16MM FILM, 3/4 OR 1/2 IN VIDEO
Tells the story of Samuel Curwen of Salem, Massachussetts, who is harrassed by his fellow citizens for his loyalty to the King. Reveals that when he flees to England, he is beset by financial problems and homesickness and begins to doubt the wisdom of his decision to leave.
From The Decades Of Decision - The American Revolution Series.
LC NO. 80-706347
Prod-NGS Dist-NGS 1975

Look Before And After, A C 15 MIN
2 INCH VIDEOTAPE J
Explores the necessity of orderly arrangement in a compositon.
From The From Me To You...In Writing, Pt 2 Series.
Prod-DELE Dist-GPITVL

Look Before You Eat C 22 MIN
16MM FILM, 3/4 OR 1/2 IN VIDEO J-C A
Looks at the relationship between eating habits and health by showing students who volunteer to reduce the amount of sugar, salt and fat in their diets and then report the results. Examines the roles of the food industry, fast food chains and vending machines in determining what foods are available.
Prod-CF Dist-CF 1978

Look Before You Leap C 15 MIN
3/4 INCH VIDEO CASSETTE J-C A
Tells how to recognize hazards on an ocean beach.
From The Afloat And Aboat Series.
Prod-MDDE Dist-GPITVL 1979

Look Beyond The Disability C 29 MIN
16MM FILM OPTICAL SOUND C A
Highlights 16 services provided in Kansas for people who may be considered developmentally disabled.
LC NO. 78-701600
Prod-UKANS Dist-UKANS 1974

Look Both Ways C 19 MIN
16MM FILM, 3/4 OR 1/2 IN VIDEO
Follows aircraft through normal and emergency air traffic activities. Emphasizes the importance of the air traffic controller viewing a situation both from his position and that of the pilot.
Prod-USAF Dist-USNAC

Look Closely B 15 MIN
2 INCH VIDEOTAPE P
Creates awareness of pattern in nature through collecting nature objects and making crayon rubbings.
From The Art Corner Series.
Prod-CVETVC Dist-GPITVL Prodn-WCVETV

Look Further Than Tomorrow B 34 MIN
16MM FILM OPTICAL SOUND
Discusses the pros and cons of summer youth involvement programs in Washington, DC.
LC NO. 74-705047
Prod-USOJD Dist-USNAC 1967

Look In The Answer Book C 11 MIN
16MM FILM, 3/4 OR 1/2 IN VIDEO P
Shows students that answers to their many questions are held in the 'ANSWER BOOK,' represented by all books in a library.
Prod-EBEC Dist-EBEC 1972

Look Inside Russia C 22 MIN
16MM FILM OPTICAL SOUND H-C A
This is a film of pictures taken in Russia by an U S Agriculture delegation that visited there in 1955.
Prod-UNL Dist-UNEBR 1956

Look Inside Yourself C 30 MIN
16MM FILM OPTICAL SOUND I
Explains the reasons for eating breakfast and describes the digestive system.
From The Mulligan Stew Series.
Prod-GPITVL Dist-GPITVL

Look Inside Yourself - 4 4 3 2 C 30 MIN
2 INCH VIDEOTAPE I
Explains the reasons for eating breakfast and describes the digestive system.
From The Mulligan Stew Series.
Prod-GPITVL Dist-GPITVL

Look Into The Brain, A C 18 MIN
16MM FILM, 3/4 OR 1/2 IN VIDEO J A
Introduces the study of the brain and examines what researchers are discovering about its formation and function. Discusses the developmental stages of the brain, the traffic of electrical impulses and memory.
Prod-IFB Dist-IFB

Look It Up C 15 MIN
3/4 OR 1/2 INCH VIDEO CASSETTE P
Focuses on the variety of resources available for the pursuit of special interests.
From The Spinning Stories Series.
Prod-MDDE Dist-AITECH 1977

Look Me In The Eye C 30 MIN
2 INCH VIDEOTAPE
See series title for descriptive statement.
From The Unconscious Cultural Clashes Series.
Prod-SCCOE Dist-SCCOE

Look Of America, 1750-1800, The C 26 MIN
16MM FILM, 3/4 OR 1/2 IN VIDEO J-C A
Depicts the early years of the United States, describing the arts and crafts brought to the new world by British colonists. Reveals the lives of early Americans through historical artwork, maps, stills of homes, cities and tools of the era, and narration from colonists' writings.
Prod-EAMES Dist-PFP 1977

Look To The Children C 10 MIN
16MM FILM OPTICAL SOUND

Surveys the various types of educational programs offered at the Rochester School for the Deaf. With captions.
LC NO. 79-700238
Prod-ROCHDF Dist-ROCHDF Prodn-SMITJA 1978

Look To The Sun C 12 MIN
16MM FILM, 3/4 OR 1/2 IN VIDEO
Explains how sunlight collectors and solar heat systems function. Discusses solar heat in terms of business, education, research and construction.
LC NO. 79-706023
Prod-UDEN Dist-USNAC 1978

Look To Tomorrow C 28 MIN
16MM FILM OPTICAL SOUND PRO
Motivates the newly disabled serviceman to plan his vocational future by using the Veterans Administration vocational counselors.
LC NO. FIE68-71
Prod-VA Dist-USVA 1968

Look What I Can Do / Can't Do It Yet / Worrying C 15 MIN
3/4 OR 1/2 INCH VIDEO CASSETTE P
Presents stories presented by Muppet-like Clyde Frog presenting stories emphasizing positive self-images, feelings of optimism and self-confidence.
From The Clyde Frog Show Series.
Prod-MAETEL Dist-GPITVL 1977

Look What We've Done To This Land C 22 MIN
16MM FILM OPTICAL SOUND I-C A
Shows the effects of strip mining and production of electricity on the people and land of the Four Corners area of the Southwest United States.
LC NO. 74-701070
Prod-CCHSE Dist-BLUSKY 1974

Look Where You Are Going C 17 MIN
16MM FILM OPTICAL SOUND
Features the cartoon character Popeye showing groups of city school children that policemen are their friends and are around to help them and that each traffic sign has a different shape and different meaning.
Prod-KINGFT Dist-KINGFT

Look Who's Coming To Dinner C 27 MIN
16MM FILM OPTICAL SOUND
Explains the environmental requirements in devastating a termite invasion. Discusses various insecticides.
Prod-VELSIC Dist-MTP

Look Who's Driving C 8 MIN
16MM FILM OPTICAL SOUND H-C A
Uses animation to show a normally careful driver who loses control of himself and his car when angered by another driver. Emphasizes the importance of good judgment and courtesy on the road.
Prod-UPA Dist-AETNA 1953

Look Who's Living Next Door C 30 MIN
16MM FILM OPTICAL SOUND H-C T
Pictures Mike and Jerry, moving into an off-campus trailer court to explore their own ideas of morality. Portrays their neighbors who are a young doctoral candidate clergyman and his wife. Shows Mike living with a girl and Jerry finding no meaning in life. Presents Roy, a Black neighbor, unloading his feelings about racism. Challenges the young Christian couple to minister effectively to their various neighbors.
Prod-FAMF Dist-FAMF

Look With Pride C 5 MIN
16MM FILM OPTICAL SOUND C A
Reviews the scope of scientific investigation and credits the American Cancer Society volunteer for his vital role in helping to win the battle.
Prod-AMCS Dist-AMCS

Look, Listen, And Lead C 30 MIN
16MM FILM, 3/4 OR 1/2 IN VIDEO
Discusses supervision, leadership, decision making, planning and performance appraisal. Suggests that managers should remain aware of and sensitive to the needs of their employees. Formerly titled The Goya Effect.
Prod-RANKAV Dist-RTBL

Look, Listen, And Lead (Captioned) C 30 MIN
16MM FILM, 3/4 OR 1/2 IN VIDEO
Discusses supervision, leadership, decision making, planning and performance appraisal. Suggests that managers should remain aware of and sensitive to the needs of their employees. Formerly titled The Goya Effect.
Prod-RANKAV Dist-RTBL

Look, We Have Come Through B 11 MIN
16MM FILM, 3/4 OR 1/2 IN VIDEO H-C A
Uses experimental techniques to depict a dancer in motion.
Prod-ELDERB Dist-PHENIX 1977

Lookback - A Musical Fantasy C 54 MIN
16MM FILM OPTICAL SOUND
Presents a fantasy which reviews some of the common experiences of growing up, such as high school, friends, teachers and music.
LC NO. 74-703601
Prod-MLYNJ Dist-CFDEVC 1973

Looking Ahead C 30 MIN
3/4 OR 1/2 INCH VIDEO CASSETTE C
See series title for descriptive statement.
From The In Our Own Image Series.
Prod-DALCCD Dist-DALCCD

Looking Ahead C 30 MIN
3/4 OR 1/2 INCH VIDEO CASSETTE A
Examines physical fitness and nutritional awareness as they dovetail with effective stress management. Presents how the skills of day-to-day stress management transfer to the larger issues of life.
From The Stress Management - A Positive Strategy Series. Pt 5
LC NO. 82-706501
Prod-TIMLIF Dist-TIMLIF 1982

Looking At A Larger System B 15 MIN
2 INCH VIDEOTAPE P
See series title for descriptive statement.
From The Just Curious Series. No. 7
Prod-EOPS Dist-GPITVL Prodn-KOACTV

Looking At Amphibians X 11 MIN
16MM FILM, 3/4 OR 1/2 IN VIDEO P
Uses frogs, toads and salamanders to show how amphibians are adapted to spend their early life in water and their adult life on land. Compares adaptations among different kinds of amphibians.
Prod-EBF Dist-EBEC 1964

Looking At Amphibians (Captioned) C 11 MIN
16MM FILM, 3/4 OR 1/2 IN VIDEO P
Uses frogs, toads and salamanders to show how amphibians are adapted to spend their early life in water and their adult life on land. Compares adaptations among different kinds of amphibians.
Prod-EBEC Dist-EBEC 1964

Looking At Amphibians (Spanish) C 11 MIN
16MM FILM, 3/4 OR 1/2 IN VIDEO P
Shows how amphibians spend their early life in water and their adult life on land. Compares frogs', toads' and salamanders' adaptations to land living.
Prod-EBEC Dist-EBEC

Looking At Animals—A Series
16MM FILM, 3/4 OR 1/2 IN VIDEO P-I
Provides information about animals in their natural habitats.
Prod-IFB Dist-IFB

Animals That Gnaw And Burrow	013 MIN
Bears	017 MIN
Cat Family, The	010 MIN
Cattle	016 MIN
Deer And Antelope	011 MIN
Dog Family, The	010 MIN
Elephants	010 MIN
Horse Family, The	010 MIN
Insect Eaters	010 MIN
Monkeys	009 MIN
Pigs And Hippos	013 MIN
Rabbits And Hares	010 MIN
Rhinos	008 MIN
Sheep And Goats	012 MIN

Looking At Art C 20 MIN
2 INCH VIDEOTAPE
See series title for descriptive statement.
From The Art Has Many Forms Series.
Prod-CVETVC Dist-GPITVL

Looking At Birds X 10 MIN
16MM FILM, 3/4 OR 1/2 IN VIDEO P
Illustrates the ways in which birds differ from other animals in appearance, body structure and behavior. Shows how they adapt to various places and conditions.
Prod-EBF Dist-EBEC 1964

Looking At Birds (Captioned) C 10 MIN
16MM FILM, 3/4 OR 1/2 IN VIDEO P
Illustrates the ways in which birds differ from other animals in appearance, body structure and behavior. Shows how they adapt to various places and conditions.
Prod-EBEC Dist-EBEC 1964

Looking At Birds - An Introduction To Birdwatching C 15 MIN
16MM FILM OPTICAL SOUND
Provides basic training in how to look at birds, to identify them and to begin to understand their behavior. Explains grouping of birds by habitat and family.
Prod-ACORN Dist-ACORN

Looking At Children C 24 MIN
16MM FILM OPTICAL SOUND T
Portrays the early signs of health problems and conditions in children as seen frequently in the classroom by observant teachers. Depicts the important interactions of the teacher with parents and the school nurse to obtain appropriate remedial action.
Prod-MLIC Dist-MTP 1969

Looking At Fishes X 11 MIN
16MM FILM, 3/4 OR 1/2 IN VIDEO P
Underwater photography and animation reveal the structure of a fish and how it lives and breathes. The development of fresh-water fish is shown from the hatching eggs to the migration of the young fish.
Prod-NFBC Dist-EBEC 1965

Looking At Fishes (Spanish) C 11 MIN
16MM FILM, 3/4 OR 1/2 IN VIDEO P
Observes the basic life process of the fish, including reproduction, growth, nutrition, excretion, respiration and behavior. Points out the specific structural adaptations the fish has made to survive in an aquatic environment.
Prod-NFBC Dist-EBEC

Looking At Mammals X 11 MIN
16MM FILM, 3/4 OR 1/2 IN VIDEO P
Illustrates the importance of animal classification and shows the difference between birds, amphibians, reptiles and mammals.
Prod-EBF Dist-EBEC 1967

Looking At Mammals (Captioned) C 11 MIN
16MM FILM, 3/4 OR 1/2 IN VIDEO P
Illustrates the importance of animal classification and shows the difference between birds, amphibians, reptiles and mammals.
Prod-EBEC Dist-EBEC 1967

Looking At Objects From Different Positions C 13 MIN
3/4 OR 1/2 INCH VIDEO CASSETTE I
Shows Kaylin and Chenetta helping the police outsmart a crook who realized that the appearance of a three-dimensional object may change as an observer changes his position. Includes an animated segment in which Tom Thumb stumps the king on three riddles based on changing points of view.
From The It Figures Series. No. 9
Prod-AITV Dist-AITECH Prodn-NJN 1982

Looking At Ourselves C 8 MIN
2 INCH VIDEOTAPE C A
Features a humanistic psychologist who, by analysis and examples, discusses self-image.
From The Interpersonal Competence, Unit 01 - The Self Series.
Prod-MVNE Dist-TELSTR 1973

Looking At Plants—A Series
16MM FILM, 3/4 OR 1/2 IN VIDEO I-J
Shows how plants grow and reproduce.
Prod-IFB Dist-IFB 1975

How Plants Climb	011 MIN
How Plants Move	011 MIN
How Seeds Are Made	015 MIN
How Seeds Are Scattered	015 MIN
How Seeds Sprout	016 MIN

Looking At Processes C
3/4 OR 1/2 INCH VIDEO CASSETTE
Shows how to determine the capabilities and characteristics of a manufacturing process. Explains how to identify and control production process variations.
From The Organizational Quality Improvement Series.
Prod-BNA Dist-BNA

Looking At Reptiles X 11 MIN
16MM FILM, 3/4 OR 1/2 IN VIDEO P
Defines reptiles in terms of body structure, respiratory system and manner of egg laying. Discusses the diversity of adaptation in the five kinds of reptiles.
Prod-EBF Dist-EBEC 1965

Looking At Reptiles (Spanish) C 11 MIN
16MM FILM, 3/4 OR 1/2 IN VIDEO P
Differentiates reptiles from other creatures by comparing body structure, respiratory system and manner of egg laying. Emphasizes the fact that reptiles were the first vertebrates to adopt a terrestrial life.
Prod-EBEC Dist-EBEC

Looking At Systems B 15 MIN
2 INCH VIDEOTAPE P
See series title for descriptive statement.
From The Just Curious Series. No. 6
Prod-EOPS Dist-GPITVL Prodn-KOACTV

Looking At Systems Of Objects, Pt 1 B 15 MIN
2 INCH VIDEOTAPE P
See series title for descriptive statement.
From The Just Curious Series. No. 4
Prod-EOPS Dist-GPITVL Prodn-KOACTV

Looking At Systems Of Objects, Pt 2 B 15 MIN
2 INCH VIDEOTAPE P
See series title for descriptive statement.
From The Just Curious Series. No. 5
Prod-EOPS Dist-GPITVL Prodn-KOACTV

Looking At Tomorrow - Thinking And Acting In The Real World C 15 MIN
16MM FILM OPTICAL SOUND J-H
Introduces the concepts of critical thought and action. Emphasizes the importance of critical thought to help people achieve the kind of future they want.
Prod-EPCOT Dist-EPCOT 1983

Looking Back B 15 MIN
2 INCH VIDEOTAPE K-P
Provides a culmination of the year's experiences for review and evaluation. (Broadcast quality)
From The Magic Of Words Series.
Prod-GWTVAI Dist-GPITVL Prodn-WETATV

Looking Back C 15 MIN
3/4 INCH VIDEO CASSETTE P
Studies the various animals in the world from the simple ones to the more complex.
From The Tell Me What You See Series.
Prod-WVIZTV Dist-GPITVL

Looking Back C 30 MIN
3/4 OR 1/2 INCH VIDEO CASSETTE C
See series title for descriptive statement.
From The In Our Own Image Series.
Prod-DALCCD Dist-DALCCD

Looking Backward C 30 MIN
16MM FILM OPTICAL SOUND I-C A
Gives a brief overview of activities and programs of the Oregon Historical Society. Focuses on the Society's collection of early motion picture films.
LC NO. 77-700448
Prod-OREGHS Dist-OREGHS 1973

Looking Backwards X 28 MIN
3/4 OR 1/2 INCH VIDEO CASSETTE

Presents footage from the Oregon Historical Society's collection documenting such phenomena from the past as an eastern Oregon wheat harvest with a 38-horse team, President Harding dedicating the Oregon Trail Marker and salmon fishing with horse-drawn nets in the Columbia River. Utilizes early newsreels.
Prod-MEDIPR Dist-MEDIPR 1973

Looking For A Grant? Here's What You Should Know–A Series

Provides assistance in preparing proposals, understanding proposal guidelines, translating ideas into measurable goals and researching grants resources. Presented as a workshop by the Opportunities For Women program at the University of Arizona.
Prod-UAZMIC Dist-UAZMIC 1978

Basics Of Proposals	050 MIN
Budget Preparation	050 MIN
Looking For A Grant? Here's What You Should	050 MIN
Management Plan	050 MIN
Review Process, Policies Of Grants	050 MIN

Looking For A Grant? Here's What You Should Know - Bibliography B 50 MIN
3/4 OR 1/2 INCH VIDEO CASSETTE
See series title for descriptive statement.
From The Looking For A Grant? Here's What You Should Know Series. Pt 1
Prod-UAZMIC Dist-UAZMIC 1978

Looking For A Job? C 30 MIN
3/4 INCH VIDEO CASSETTE
Offers practical advice, including a 7-step formula, to aid women in getting the job they want. Gives special advice to women seeking a job in an alternative, non-traditional, field.
Prod-WMENIF Dist-WMENIF

Looking For Aquarius - California's Quest For Water C 30 MIN
3/4 OR 1/2 INCH VIDEO CASSETTE
Examines the options open to a state when its thirst outstrips available water resources. Discusses conservation, dams, ocean desalting and a scheme to import water from the Pacific Northwest.
From The Synthesis Series.
Prod-KPBS Dist-KPBS 1978

Looking For Love - Teenage Parents C
3/4 OR 1/2 INCH VIDEO CASSETTE H
Presents teenage mothers discussing their ambivalent feelings, from loving and worrying about their children to longing for lost adolescence and opportunities they might have had.
Prod-EDCC Dist-GA

Looking For Love - Teenage Parents C 30 MIN
3/4 OR 1/2 INCH VIDEO CASSETTE J-H R
Presents the impact of teenage pregnancy on the young parents. Traces the choices and decisions caused by pregnancy.
From The Vital Link Series.
Prod-EDCC Dist-EDCC

Looking For Mao C 58 MIN
3/4 OR 1/2 INCH VIDEO CASSETTE
Features a journey through modern day China, looking at some of the startling changes that have taken place six years after the death of Mao.
From The Frontline Series.
Prod-DOCCON Dist-PBS

Looking For Me B 29 MIN
16MM FILM OPTICAL SOUND
Investigates the therapeutic benefits of patterned movement in working with different types of students, including normal preschool children aged four and five, emotionally disturbed children, two autistic children and a group of adult teachers.
Prod-NYU Dist-NYU

Looking For Me B 29 MIN
16MM FILM, 3/4 OR 1/2 IN VIDEO H-C A
Introduces Janet Adler, a young movement therapist in Philadelphia, who works with normal and emotionally disturbed children and with teachers. Supports her belief that an over-intellectualized society destroys the basic sense of the body, and that the reduction of conflict between body language and verbal language encourages honesty with oneself and others.
Prod-MAUFMF Dist-UCEMC 1970

Looking For Me B 29 MIN
16MM FILM, 3/4 OR 1/2 IN VIDEO C A
Demonstrates how 'body language' can be the first means of communicating with psychotic persons and how freedom of body movement can be beneficial to normal people in this overly intellectualized society.
Prod-MMRC Dist-MMRC

Looking For Mr Goodjob C 29 MIN
3/4 OR 1/2 INCH VIDEO CASSETTE
Profiles three people who traded in their old careers, for new vocations, discussing their fears and anxieties in making the switch.
Prod-WHATV Dist-PBS 1980

Looking For Organic America C 28 MIN
16MM FILM, 3/4 OR 1/2 IN VIDEO J-C A
Presents a picture of the organic farming movement in America today. Emphasizes the difference between conventional commercial farms and organic farms, and reveals the roles played by legislators, scientists, merchants and distributors in the development of organic farming.
LC NO. 82-707172
Prod-RPFD Dist-BULFRG 1972

Looking For Yesterday C 30 MIN
16MM FILM, 3/4 OR 1/2 IN VIDEO
Shows senior citizens talking about their feelings, fantasies, and need to relive the past when the present becomes unbearable.
Prod-NCBA Dist-FEIL Prodn-FEIL 1978

Looking For Yesterday C 30 MIN
16MM FILM - 3/4 IN VIDEO
Illustrates why reality orientation doesn't help severely disoriented aged patients. Suggests an alternative therapy.
Prod-OHC Dist-HRC

Looking For–A Series
K-P
Helps children understand means of transportation and getting from one place to another.
Prod-FILMID Dist-FILMID

Looking Forward To The Future C 30 MIN
3/4 OR 1/2 INCH VIDEO CASSETTE
See series title for descriptive statement.
From The Rebop Series.
Prod-WGBHTV Dist-MDCPB

Looking Glass, The - Juan Downing C 28 MIN
3/4 INCH VIDEO CASSETTE A
Prod-AFA Dist-AFA 1981

Looking Good C 19 MIN
16MM FILM, 3/4 OR 1/2 IN VIDEO S
Uses a TV game show format to show appropriate grooming habits, including bathing, showering, brushing teeth and combing hair.
From The Good Life Series.
LC NO. 81-706175
Prod-DUDLYN Dist-HUBDSC 1981

Looking Good - A Guide To Personal Grooming C
3/4 OR 1/2 INCH VIDEO CASSETTE J-H
Discusses body language as a prelude to tips on selection and maintenance of clothing. Advises on skin care and cleanliness and stresses the importance of good eating habits, sufficient sleep and exercise, and the fact that a pleasing appearance helps develop a positive image.
Prod-GA Dist-GA

Looking Good On Paper C
3/4 OR 1/2 INCH VIDEO CASSETTE
Shows how to prepare thoroughly for and complete an employment application form which will make a favorable impression on a prospective employer.
From The Employability Skills Series.
Prod-ILCS Dist-CAMB

Looking In On Sunset C 27 MIN
16MM FILM OPTICAL SOUND
Traces the history of Sunset Magazine from 1898 to modern times. Shows editors at work scouting and developing stories on travel, gardening, homes and food - the four subjects which set the West apart from the rest of the country.
Prod-MTP Dist-MTP

Looking Into Things C 13 MIN
16MM FILM, 3/4 OR 1/2 IN VIDEO P-I
Tells how some common scientific instruments are used to extend the human senses. Shows how the length and mass of a fly is measured with various magnifiers and microscopes.
From The Scientific Fact And Fun Series.
Prod-GLDWER Dist-JOU 1979

Looking Northward C 20 MIN
3/4 INCH VIDEO CASSETTE I-J
Recognizes that the earth's axis points toward the North Star. Identifies ways of finding the northward direction to explain that a compass always points north. Explains the value of using a compass.
From The Project Survival Series.
Prod-MAETEL Dist-GPITVL

Looking Out Is In–A Series
I-J
Prod-WHATV Dist-GPITVL

How Do Some Cultures Meet Their Need For Food	15 MIN
How Do The Methods Of Gathering Food	15 MIN
How Is Culture Learned	15 MIN
What Caused Agrarian Cultures	15 MIN
What Caused Industrial Complexes	15 MIN
What Is An Agrarian Culture	15 MIN
What Is An Industrial Complex	15 MIN
What Is Anthropology	15 MIN
What Is Culture	15 MIN
What Is Enculturation	15 MIN
Why Is Culture Changing	15 MIN
Why Is Man A Social Animal	15 MIN

Looking Up To Your Aviation Career C 14 MIN
16MM FILM, 3/4 OR 1/2 IN VIDEO
Explores more than 60 career specialties in the field of aviation.
LC NO. 81-706384
Prod-USFAA Dist-USNAC 1979

Looks - How They Affect Your Life C 51 MIN
3/4 OR 1/2 INCH VIDEO CASSETTE H-C A
Illustrates the social and psychological impact of fulfilling and not fulfilling the American standards of beauty.
Prod-GANNET Dist-MTI

Loom In Essence C 4 MIN
16MM FILM OPTICAL SOUND
A non-narrative study of a weaver at her loom.
LC NO. 70-711309
Prod-UMD Dist-UMD 1970

Loom Weaving C 6 MIN
16MM FILM, 3/4 OR 1/2 IN VIDEO J-C
Illustrates how to build a loom from a broom and a few pieces of wood. Shows how to thread the warp through the heddle, how to wind and use the bobbin, and the proper use of wool, cotton and other threads in making useful objects.
From The Creative Hands Series.
Prod-CRAF Dist-IFB 1951

Loon's Necklace, The (Restored Version) C 11 MIN
16MM FILM, 3/4 OR 1/2 IN VIDEO I-C
A restored version of the 1949 motion picture The Loon's Necklace. Tells an Indian legend which explains how the loon, a water bird, received his distinguished neckband. Uses authentic ceremonial masks, carved by Indians of British Columbia, to portray the Indian's sensitivity to the moods of nature.
Prod-EBEC Dist-EBEC

Loons Of Amisk C 15 MIN
16MM FILM, 3/4 OR 1/2 IN VIDEO J-C A
Describes the habitats, nesting and feeding of the common loon.
From The Animals And Plants Of North America Series.
Prod-KARVF Dist-LCOA 1980

Loons, The C 18 MIN
16MM FILM - VIDEO, ALL FORMATS
Tells the story of six children who find success through the pursuit of positive, health-conscious lifestyles. Emphasizes the importance of diet and exercise.
Prod-SCCL Dist-PEREN

Loop, The B 14 MIN
16MM FILM OPTICAL SOUND
Instructs in the procedure of making the loop and the precautions to take before leaving the ground.
From The Intermediate Acrobatics Series. Part 1
LC NO. FIE52-1006
Prod-USN Dist-USNAC 1943

Loopholes C 30 MIN
3/4 OR 1/2 INCH VIDEO CASSETTE
Takes a broad view of our taxation system. Illustrates to the viewer that though far from perfect the system contains mechanisms which serve as investment incentives.
From The Money Puzzle - The World Of Macroeconomics Series. Module 4
Prod-MDCC Dist-MDCC

Looping C 15 MIN
3/4 OR 1/2 INCH VIDEO CASSETTE PRO
See series title for descriptive statement.
From The Numerical Control/Computer Numerical Control, Part 2 - Advanced Programming Series.
Prod-ICSINT Dist-ICSINT

Loopings C 16 MIN
3/4 OR 1/2 INCH VIDEO CASSETTE IND
Covers aspects of a loop statement and writing a program that contains a nested loop.
From The Numerical Control/Computerized Numerical Control - Advanced Programming Series. Module 2
Prod-LEIKID Dist-LEIKID

Loops C
3/4 OR 1/2 INCH VIDEO CASSETTE
Describes loops and nested looping. Includes commands FOR, DO, WHILE, DO and REPEAT UNTIL.
From The PASCAL - A Modern Programming Language Series
Prod-EDUACT Dist-EDUACT

Loops C 3 MIN
16MM FILM, 3/4 OR 1/2 IN VIDEO C
An experimental film by Norman McLaren in which sound and visuals are created entirely by drawing upon film.
Prod-NFBC Dist-IFB Prodn-MCLN 194

Loose Bolts C 29 MIN
16MM FILM, 3/4 OR 1/2 IN VIDEO
Deals with work on assembly lines. Interviews employees at a Ford automobile plant in order to show their reactions to this well-paid but potentially dehumanizing type of work.
Prod-SCHLP Dist-RBFLM 197

Loose Ends B 108 MIN
16MM FILM OPTICAL SOUND
Focuses on two buddies with a terminal case of blue-collar blues.
Prod-UNKNWN Dist-TWYMAN 197

Loose Screw, A C 29 MIN
2 INCH VIDEOTAPE
See series title for descriptive statement.
From The Koltanowski On Chess Series.
Prod-KQEDTV Dist-PUBTEL

Loosening The Grip–A Series
C
Uses documentary, drama and interview formats to examine a variety of topics regarding the history of alcoholism and its prevention. Hosted by E G Marshall.
Prod-UMA Dist-GPITVL 198

Ain't Goin' Away	030 MIN
Alcohol And The Body	030 MIN
Alcoholics Anonymous	030 MIN
End, The Beginning, The	030 MIN
Experts On The Causes, The	030 MIN
Family Matter, A	030 MIN
First Step, The	030 MIN
Louder Than Words	030 MIN
Ounce Of Prevention, An	030 MIN
Picking Up The Tab	030 MIN
Special Treatment	030 MIN

Lope De Vega - Fuenteovejuna (Spanish) C 142 MIN
3/4 OR 1/2 INCH VIDEO CASSETTE

Offers an adaptation of Lope De Vega's play Fuenteovejuna.
Prod-FOTH Dist-FOTH 1984

Lopsided Wheel, The C 30 MIN
16MM FILM, 3/4 OR 1/2 IN VIDEO
Explains that although the wheel is a symbol of man's evolutionary process and is responsible for much of his progress, it has carried him to the brink of overdevelopment and world-wide traffic jams.
From The Life Around Us Series.
LC NO. 79-707832
Prod-TIMLIF Dist-TIMLIF 1971

Lopsided Wheel, The (Spanish) C 30 MIN
16MM FILM OPTICAL SOUND
Traces the development of the wheel from its invention to its use in computer machinery. Shows various machines containing wheels and explains how the laws of energy apply to both simple and complex machines.
From The Life Around Us (Spanish) Series.
LC NO. 78-700070
Prod-TIMLIF Dist-TIMLIF 1971

Lopsideland C 5 MIN
16MM FILM, 3/4 OR 1/2 IN VIDEO K-I
Shows children the way the world would look upside-down. Explains how to look at things from a different perspective.
From The Magic Moments Series.
Prod-EBEC Dist-EBEC 1969

Lorang's Way (Turkana) C 69 MIN
16MM FILM, 3/4 OR 1/2 IN VIDEO
Offers a multifaceted portrait of Lorang, the head of a Turkana tribal homestead. Shows that Lorang has seen the outside world and thinks his tribe's traditions will be affected by it. Presented in Turkana with English subtitles.
From The Turkana Conversations Trilogy Series.
Prod-MCDGAL Dist-UCEMC 1980

Lorax, The C 25 MIN
16MM FILM, 3/4 OR 1/2 IN VIDEO P-J
Introduces the Dr Seuss character known as the Lorax in a fanciful tale with a serious theme - clean up the environment before it's too late.
From The Dr Seuss Series.
Prod-CBSTV Dist-PHENIX 1972

Lord And Father C 45 MIN
16MM FILM - 3/4 IN VIDEO H A
Examines the tension between a Kentucky tobacco farmer, Joe Gray, Sr, who defends his way of life as landlord to tenant farmers, and his son, Joe Gray, Jr, who questions its morality. Examines the son's objections to the growing of tobacco and the social system of sharecrop tenancy used to cultivate it.
LC NO. 83-706756
Prod-APPAL Dist-APPAL 1983

Lord Is My Shepherd, The B 5 MIN
16MM FILM OPTICAL SOUND P-J
Presents a modern interpretation of Psalm 22 using animated figures drawn on a blackboard.
From The Song Of The Ages Series.
LC NO. 70-702124
Prod-FAMLYT Dist-FAMLYT 1964

Lord Is Risen, The X 15 MIN
16MM FILM OPTICAL SOUND I-H T R
Pictures the events of the resurrection, the placing of the special guard at the tomb, the rolling away of the stone, the discovery by the three women, Peter and John at the tomb, the two women and Jesus' appearance to Mary.
From The Living Bible Series.
Prod-FAMF Dist-FAMF

Lord Jim C 154 MIN
16MM FILM OPTICAL SOUND
Based on the novel of the same name by Joseph Conrad. Tells the story of Jim, an officer in the 19th century British merchant marine, a man with such a powerful sense of guilt that he gives his life to atone for a single act of cowardice.
Prod-CPC Dist-TIMLIF 1964

Lord Of Asia C 60 MIN
3/4 OR 1/2 INCH VIDEO CASSETTE C A
Shows Alexander the Great at the peak of his power as he becomes the ruler of Asia, subdues his longtime foe and overtakes Babylon and Persepolis. Reveals that although he marries, he soon returns to his first love - conquering the world.
From The Search For Alexander The Great Series. Pt 3
LC NO. 82-707382
Prod-TIMLIF Dist-TIMLIF 1981

Lord Of The Flies B 90 MIN
16MM FILM OPTICAL SOUND I-C A
Presents a dramatization of the novel, 'LORD OF THE FLIES,' by William Golding about the society which is set up and destroyed by a group of middle class English school boys whose plane crashes on an uninhabited island.
LC NO. 71-707615
Prod-HODGAP Dist-KITPAR 1963

Lord Of The Jungle B 69 MIN
16MM FILM OPTICAL SOUND I-C A
See series title for descriptive statement.
From The Bomba, The Jungle Boy Series.
Prod-CINEWO Dist-CINEWO 1955

Lord Of The Universe B 60 MIN
3/4 OR 1/2 INCH VIDEO CASSETTE
Covers the national gathering in the Houston Astrodome of the followers of 16-year-old Guru Mahara Ji.
Prod-TOPTV Dist-EAI

Lord's Ascension, The X 15 MIN
16MM FILM OPTICAL SOUND I-H T R
Shows the appearances Jesus made on earth after His Crucifixion. Includes Jesus walking with the two on the road to Emmaus, appearing to the disciples, later again appearing before the disciples when Thomas was present, meeting the disciples at the Sea of Galilee, his appearance on the Mount of Olives and his Ascension to His Father.
From The Living Bible Series.
Prod-FAMF Dist-FAMF

Lord's Prayer, The C 27 MIN
16MM FILM OPTICAL SOUND H-C A
Combines music and panoramic views of nature with the narration of Ralph W Sockman to interpret the Lord's Prayer. Filmed in Sequoia and King's Canyon National Parks.
Prod-CCNCC Dist-CCNCC

Lords Of Flatbush, The C 85 MIN
16MM FILM OPTICAL SOUND
Presents a comedy about growing up in lower middle-class Brooklyn in the 1950's. Stars Sylvester Stallone and Henry Winkler.
Prod-CPC Dist-TWYMAN 1974

Lords Of The Air C 58 MIN
3/4 OR 1/2 INCH VIDEO CASSETTE J-C A
Describes the evolution of bird feathers as well as territorial behavior, courtship display, navigation and migration. Speculates on the extinction of the dinosaurs and why birds failed to inherit the earth.
From The Life On Earth Series. Program 8
LC NO. 82-706680
Prod-BBCTV Dist-FI 1981

Lords Of The Forest C
16MM FILM OPTICAL SOUND J-C A
Shows animal life and ethnology of the Congo.
Prod-TWCF Dist-TWCF

Lords Of The Labyrinth, The C 54 MIN
16MM FILM, 3/4 OR 1/2 IN VIDEO H-C A
Visits the ruins of the city of Chan Chan in Peru which was once the greatest city in the Americas. Looks at the massive pyramids, huge courtyards, maze-like passages and thousands of cell-like buildings huddled inside walled compounds.
Prod-BBCTV Dist-FI 1976

Lords Of The Sea C 26 MIN
16MM FILM, 3/4 OR 1/2 IN VIDEO H-C A
Looks at the shark's nature and abilities.
Prod-CTV Dist-MTI

Lorelie Called Sleep, A C
3/4 OR 1/2 INCH VIDEO CASSETTE IND
Looks at sleep while driving, how sleep-related accidents are a major cause of serious accidents, and what to do if you become drowsy while driving.
From The Driving Safety Series.
Prod-DCC Dist-GPCV

Loren Maciver, Pt 1 C 23 MIN
16MM FILM SILENT
Presents paintings by an American comtemporary painter, Loren Maciver. Reveals the transposition of objects, movement and color in city and country.
Prod-FILIM Dist-RADIM

Loren Maciver, Pt 2 C 23 MIN
16MM FILM SILENT
Presents paintings by an American comtemporary painter, Loren Maciver. Reveals the transposition of objects, movement and color in city and country.
Prod-FILIM Dist-RADIM

Loretta Abbott And Al Perryman C 30 MIN
3/4 OR 1/2 INCH VIDEO CASSETTE
See series title for descriptive statement.
From The Partners In Dance Series.
Prod-ARCVID Dist-ARCVID

Loretta Abbott And Al Perryman C 30 MIN
3/4 OR 1/2 INCH VIDEO CASSETTE
See series title for descriptive statement.
From The Eye On Dance - Partners In Dance Series.
Prod-ARTRES Dist-ARTRES

Lori - Art Therapy And Self Discovery C 31 MIN
16MM FILM OPTICAL SOUND PRO
Demonstrates the use of art therapy in mental health rehabilitation based on a clinical case history by therapist Helen B Landgarten. Dramatizes the case of an emotionally disturbed 15-year-old girl whose art therapy sessions help her emerge from depression and regain contact with herself and the world around her.
LC NO. 78-700692
Prod-FILCOA Dist-FILCOA 1978

Lorin Hollander C 28 MIN
3/4 OR 1/2 INCH VIDEO CASSETTE
Presents internationally acclaimed classical pianist Lorin Hollander talking with Fred Rogers about his deep concerns for both child prodigies and prison inmates.
From The Old Friends - New Friends Series.
Prod-FAMCOM Dist-PBS 1981

Lorraine Hansberry - The Black Experience In The Creation Of Drama C 35 MIN
16MM FILM, 3/4 OR 1/2 IN VIDEO J-C A
Traces the artistic growth and vision of the black playwright Lorraine Hansberry, largely in her own words and in her own voice. Describes the author's childhood in Chicago, student days at the University of Wisconsin, work as a journalist in Harlem, life as a housewife in Greenwich Village and success on Broadway.
Prod-MANTLH Dist-FOTH 1975

Lorraine, Pays Du Fer C 11 MIN
16MM FILM OPTICAL SOUND H-C
A French language film. Presents a close-up of a middle class Lorraine family.
From The Aspects De France Series.
Prod-WSU Dist-MLA Prodn-BORGLM 1966

Los Alamos Computing Network C 24 MIN
16MM FILM OPTICAL SOUND
Uses layman's terms to describe the Los Alamos Computing Network which deals with scientific calculations.
LC NO. 82-700062
Prod-LASL Dist-LASL 1982

Los Angeles C 3 MIN
16MM FILM OPTICAL SOUND P-I
Discusses the city of Los Angeles, California.
From The Of All Things Series.
Prod-BAILYL Dist-AVED

Los Axiomas En Algebra C 13 MIN
16MM FILM, 3/4 OR 1/2 IN VIDEO H
A Spanish language version of the videocassette Axioms In Algebra. Presents the idea that an axiom is a statement accepted as true without proof. Demonstrates the addition, subtraction, multiplication and division axioms as applied to solving practical problems.
Prod-IFB Dist-IFB 1960

Los Campesinos C 60 MIN
3/4 OR 1/2 INCH VIDEO CASSETTE
Presents a look at Mexican farmers.
From The Bill Moyers' Journal Series.
Prod-WNETTV Dist-WNETTV 1975

Los Cinco Hermanos Chinos C 10 MIN
16MM FILM, 3/4 OR 1/2 IN VIDEO
A Spanish version of the 'THE FIVE CHINESE BROTHERS.' Tells the story of five Chinese brothers who elude execution by virtue of their extraordinary individual qualities.
Prod-WWS Dist-WWS 1960

Los Estados De La Materia C 18 MIN
16MM FILM, 3/4 OR 1/2 IN VIDEO H-C A
A Spanish language version of The States Of Matter. Examines the characteristics of the states of matter and the atomic and molecular movements within solids, liquids and gases.
From The Physical Science (Spanish) Series.
Prod-LOGANL Dist-MGHT 1978

Los Four C 22 MIN
16MM FILM, 3/4 OR 1/2 IN VIDEO
Shows how four Mexican American artists reach back into their cultural roots for their artistic inspiration and expression. Introduces the philosophy behind their work and their own individual and unique style.
Prod-LACFU Dist-IA

Los Fresnos Detention Center C 17 MIN
3/4 INCH VIDEO CASSETTE J-H A
Shows the Immigration and Naturalization Service's detention facility at Los Fresnos, Texas, where illegal immigrants are held. Includes interviews with officials and detainees and tells what happens there. Discusses the increasing problem of illegal aliens from Latin America.
LC NO. 82-707077
Prod-SWINS Dist-SWINS 1982

Los Gamines - Colombia C 28 MIN
16MM FILM OPTICAL SOUND
Tells the story of Father Xavier, a missionary working in with the street children of Bogota, Colombia. Shows how he converts them from thieving scavengers into hard-working, law-abiding citizens.
Prod-SCC Dist-MTP

Los Habladores X 17 MIN
16MM FILM, 3/4 OR 1/2 IN VIDEO H-C
A Spanish language film. Dramatizes Cervantes' droll comedy about a talkative man who is invited to the home of another to break his wife of the same habit. Use in fourth year Spanish class or above.
Prod-EBF Dist-EBEC 1966

Los Indios C 25 MIN
16MM FILM OPTICAL SOUND
Examines a group of South American Indians who are having difficulties in coping with modernization.
From The Eye Of The Beholder Series.
LC NO. 75-701472
Prod-RCPDF Dist-VIACOM 1972

Los Mamiferos Vivientes C 17 MIN
16MM FILM, 3/4 OR 1/2 IN VIDEO I-J
A Spanish language version of the videocassette The Living Mammal. Discusses characteristics of mammals, including physiology and adaptive techniques.
Prod-DEU Dist-IFB 1961

Los Nietos Kindergarten - A Camera Visit B 25 MIN
16MM FILM OPTICAL SOUND
Describes a Head Start-like program for disadvantaged children operated by a special public school kindergarten for Mexican-American children. Follows the childrens' unrehearsed activities while the director of the program is being interviewed.
Prod-VASSAR Dist-NYU 1965

Los Novios C 30 MIN
3/4 OR 1/2 INCH VIDEO CASSETTE
See series title for descriptive statement.
From The Que Pasa, U S A Series.
Prod-WPBTTV Dist-MDCPB

Los Que Dan Carino B 23 MIN
16MM FILM, 3/4 OR 1/2 IN VIDEO C A

A Spanish language film. Depicts a typical family home as parents share work and play with the children and shows them at a family picnic where everyone has a chance to help, to be needed, to do something new and to be part of an exciting outing.
Prod-MHFB Dist-IFB 1963

Los Salvajes B 83 MIN
16MM FILM OPTICAL SOUND A
A Spanish language film. Reveals how a young girl is forced to marry a man of violent and brutal character and traces the problems that ensue.
Prod-TRANSW Dist-TRANSW

Los Santeros C 27 MIN
16MM FILM - 3/4 IN VIDEO J-C A
Focuses on the traditional New Mexican form of art creations known as santos, saints' figures carved from wood. Discusses the artistic origins of the figures, the symbols and attributes typical of santos, and the resurgence in interest and support of this craft in recent decades.
LC NO. 79-707341
Prod-BLUSKY Dist-BLUSKY 1979

Los Santeros C 28 MIN
16MM FILM, 3/4 OR 1/2 IN VIDEO
Deals with the folk art of santos, wood carvings of saints, in northern New Mexico. Shows the work of contemporary santeros and examines the heritage of the craft.
Prod-BLUSKY Dist-ONEWST

Los Siete De La Raza (English) B 30 MIN
16MM FILM OPTICAL SOUND
Presents seven Latino youths recruiting street kids into a College Brown studies program, who are charged with killing a plain clothesman. Explains that while they become victims of a press and police campaign to clean up the Latino community, their defense becomes the foundation of a revolutionary community organization.
Prod-SFN Dist-SFN

Los Sures C 58 MIN
16MM FILM, 3/4 OR 1/2 IN VIDEO A
Focuses upon the throbbing, thriving albeit poverty-ridden area in Brooklyn known as Los Sures. Examines the life of poor Hispanics, mostly Puerto Rican, struggling to successfully integrate themselves into mainstream America. Follows activities of auto-strippers, welfare permanents, advocates of strange cults and religions as well as street musicians, break dancers and card players.
Prod-ECHDIX Dist-CNEMAG 1983

Los Tejedores C 28 MIN
16MM FILM, 3/4 OR 1/2 IN VIDEO
Portrays the craft and traditions of weavers of Hispanic and Navajo descent in the Southwest.
Prod-BLUSKY Dist-ONEWST

Los Tres Osos C 15 MIN
16MM FILM, 3/4 OR 1/2 IN VIDEO I-H
A Spanish language version of The Three Bears. Uses simple Spanish narration to relate the story as cartoons depict the scenes. Reviews basic sentences and the audience is asked to repeat them.
Prod-FA Dist-PHENIX 1960

Los Vendidos C 30 MIN
16MM FILM OPTICAL SOUND H-C A
Features El Teatro Campesino, discussing the evolution of the group, presenting a one-act play and performing a musical number which summarizes the group's aspirations and life work.
Prod-KNBCTV Dist-ETCO

Lose Weight With Alf Fowles C 60 MIN
1/2 IN VIDEO CASSETTE BETA/VHS
Presents a program for weight loss based on deep relaxation and visual messages directed at the subconscious.
Prod-MOHOMV Dist-MOHOMV

Loser Take All C 15 MIN
16MM FILM, 3/4 OR 1/2 IN VIDEO
Tells how a 14-year-old Chicano boy is challenged to a bike race during which an accident occurs and how he must decide whether to win the race or keep his challenger from being hurt.
From The Reflections Series.
LC NO. 79-706603
Prod-PAULST Dist-MEDIAG 1978

Loser, The C 15 MIN
16MM FILM OPTICAL SOUND I-C A
Illustrates the drug problem among youths of Waianae in the Hawaiian Islands.
Prod-CINEPC Dist-CINEPC

Loser, The C 20 MIN
16MM FILM OPTICAL SOUND J-C
Edited from the motion picture The Luck Of Ginger Coffey. Tells a story about a man's job difficulties which result when he lies about abilities he does not have and refuses to accept the kind of position for which he is qualified. Focuses on the conflict that arises when people are overly optimistic, while failing to grasp reality.
From The Patterns Series.
LC NO. 77-701383
Prod-SF Dist-SF 1977

Loser, The C 20 MIN
3/4 OR 1/2 INCH VIDEO CASSETTE J-C
Edited from the motion picture The Luck Of Ginger Coffey. Tells a story about a man's job difficulties which result when he lies about abilities he does not have and refuses to accept the kind of position for which he is qualified. Focuses on the conflict that arises when people are overly optimistic, while failing to grasp reality.
From The Patterns Series.
Prod-SF Dist-SF 1977

Losers, The C 19 MIN
16MM FILM MAGNETIC SOUND IND
Dramatizes two case histories which show how store employees who steal merchandise from their employer cause irreparable damage to their own security, self-respect, family and future.
From The Positive Shortage Prevention Series.
LC NO. 77-702199
Prod-SAUM Dist-SAUM Prodn-CALVIN 1972

Losers, The C 30 MIN
16MM FILM, 3/4 OR 1/2 IN VIDEO
Traces the history of the horse, from the time when it was a terrier-sized creature to its current status as a thoroughbred.
From The Life Around Us Series.
Prod-TIMLIF Dist-TIMLIF

Losers, The (Spanish) C 30 MIN
16MM FILM OPTICAL SOUND
Explores the historical relationship between horses and humans. Shows how the horse has served humans in work, war and play, but points out that the horse's usefulness is becoming limited.
From The Life Around Us (Spanish) Series.
LC NO. 78-700080
Prod-TIMLIF Dist-TIMLIF 1971

Losing - A Conversation With Parents C 20 MIN
3/4 OR 1/2 INCH VIDEO CASSETTE
Examines the relationship between anorexia and forced starvation in third world countries where food is a weapon of political subjugation.
Prod-KITCHN Dist-KITCHN

Losing A Conversation With The Parents C 20 MIN
3/4 INCH VIDEO CASSETTE
Shows parent's trying to deal with their daughter's death related to anorexia nervosa. Handles two widespread problems, namely, anorexia nervosa and starvation because of poverty.
Prod-WMENIF Dist-WMENIF

Losing Just The Same B 60 MIN
16MM FILM, 3/4 OR 1/2 IN VIDEO H-C A
The story of a Negro mother and her ten children who live on welfare but who dream of a world of Cadillac prestige and middle class status. A commentary on poverty in a Negro urban ghetto.
Prod-NET Dist-IU Prodn-KQEDFU 1966

Loss And Grieving - You And Your Patient C 120 MIN
3/4 OR 1/2 INCH VIDEO CASSETTE PRO
Presents a study of death, dying and grief. Includes a discussion of the rights of the dying patient and guidelines for individuals working with the patient.
LC NO. 81-706293
Prod-USVA Dist-USNAC 1980

Loss Control, Impact 1980 C 40 MIN
3/4 OR 1/2 INCH VIDEO CASSETTE IND
Presents a panel discussion on a variety of loss control issues.
From The Safety, Health, and Loss Control - Managing Effective Programs Series.
LC NO. 81-706527
Prod-AMCEE Dist-AMCEE 1980

Loss On Innocence C 30 MIN
3/4 OR 1/2 INCH VIDEO CASSETTE
See series title for descriptive statement.
From The Up And Coming Series.
Prod-KQEDTV Dist-MDCPB

Loss Prevention For Business - Internal Crime C 20 MIN
16MM FILM, 3/4 OR 1/2 IN VIDEO
Discusses methods of preventing employee pilferage and theft, including persecution. Covers white collar crime including fraud, embezzlement, expense account cheating and computer data bank security breaches.
Prod-JACSTO Dist-MTI

Loss Prevention For Business - Intrusion And Access Control C 20 MIN
16MM FILM, 3/4 OR 1/2 IN VIDEO A
Shows methods for preventing a wide variety of externally perpetuated thefts. Stresses the need to identify and secure problem areas and demonstrates security training for key personnel.
Prod-HAR Dist-MTI Prodn-JACSTO 1978

Loss Prevention—A Series
16MM FILM - 3/4 IN VIDEO C A
Prod-ABA Dist-BNA 1972

Checks - What To Cash	015 MIN
Checks - When To Cash	015 MIN
Holdups - What To Do	015 MIN
Nine Dollars Plus One Dollars Equals 20	027 MIN

Lost C 15 MIN
16MM FILM, 3/4 OR 1/2 IN VIDEO S
Uses a TV game show format to demonstrate what to do when lost.
From The Good Life Series.
LC NO. 81-706183
Prod-DUDLYN Dist-HUBDSC 1981

Lost C 15 MIN
3/4 OR 1/2 INCH VIDEO CASSETTE S
Emphasizes what to do if lost. Shows how to get help.
From The Good Life Series.
Prod-HUBDSC Dist-HUBDSC

Lost C 15 MIN
16MM FILM, 3/4 OR 1/2 IN VIDEO
Depicts a young boy who becomes lost at the zoo when his sister stops to talk to a friend. Shows how he searches frantically in a sea of legs for his guardian and then finally pauses and begins to think his way out of his problem.
From The Ripples Series.
LC NO. 73-702144
Prod-NITC Dist-AITECH

Lost - Magician's Rabbit C 15 MIN
3/4 OR 1/2 INCH VIDEO CASSETTE P
Employs a magician named Amazing Alexander and his assistants to explore the use of descriptive words.
From The Magic Shop Series. No. 8
LC NO. 83-706153
Prod-CVETVC Dist-GPITVL Prodn-WCVETV 1982

Lost And Found C 12 MIN
16MM FILM, 3/4 OR 1/2 IN VIDEO P-I
Discusses what one should do when one finds something that is lost and may be valuable to someone else. Gives children the opportunity to examine their own feelings both as finders and as losers.
Prod-YEHU Dist-PHENIX 1969

Lost And Found C 29 MIN
2 INCH VIDEOTAPE
See series title for descriptive statement.
From The That's Life Series.
Prod-KOAPTV Dist-PUBTEL

Lost And Found - Spatial Relationships (Geography) C 14 MIN
3/4 OR 1/2 INCH VIDEO CASSETTE P
Shows that with help from a mime, Tracy and Ronnie learn to locate their favorite carnival rides using spatial directions.
From The Two Cents' Worth Series.
Prod-WHATV Dist-AITECH Prodn-WIEC 1976

Lost And Lucky C 60 MIN
3/4 OR 1/2 INCH VIDEO CASSETTE C
Examines the expatriate set that steamed to Europe in the 1920's in flight from 'Main Street' in this dramatization of a Fitzgerald story.
From The World Of F Scott Fitzgerald Series.
Prod-DALCCD Dist-DALCCD

Lost Cities Of Copan And Tikal C 14 MIN
16MM FILM OPTICAL SOUND
Explores the Mayan cities of Copan and Tikal and attempts to gain an insight into the characteristics of Mayan civilization through an examination of the ruins of their cities.
LC NO. 74-703076
Prod-CRTVLC Dist-CRTVLC 1974

Lost Continent B 92 MIN
16MM FILM OPTICAL SOUND
Relates the experience of a group of scientist who land on a Pacific island searching for a stray missile and encounter prehistoric animals instead. Stars Cesar Romero and Hillary Brooke.
Prod-LIPPRT Dist-REELIM 1951

Lost Days Of Glory, The, Pt 1 C 29 MIN
2 INCH VIDEOTAPE
See series title for descriptive statement.
From The Our Street Series.
Prod-MDCPB Dist-PUBTEL

Lost Days Of Glory, The, Pt 2 C 29 MIN
2 INCH VIDEOTAPE
See series title for descriptive statement.
From The Our Street Series.
Prod-MDCPB Dist-PUBTEL

Lost Generation, The C 20 MIN
16MM FILM OPTICAL SOUND
Shows the effects of the atomic bombing of Japan. Uses footage from the U S government and the Hiroshima-Nagasaki Publishing Committee.
Prod-PSR Dist-PSR

Lost Generations, The C 20 MIN
16MM FILM, 3/4 OR 1/2 IN VIDEO A
Offers a verbal and visual diary of the bombing of Hiroshima and Nagasaki, revealing the effects on the populations of both cities.
LC NO. 84-706065
Prod-FI Dist-FI 1983

Lost Horizon B 118 MIN
16MM FILM OPTICAL SOUND
Tells how a group of people find themselves in the miraculous world of Shangri-La. Directed by Frank Capra.
Prod-CPC Dist-TIMLIF 1937

Lost Hunter C 22 MIN
3/4 OR 1/2 INCH VIDEO CASSETTE J-C A
Emphasizes importance of proper preparation and equipment as safety measures in the event of getting lost. Depicts through a personal narration how a hunter got lost, the mistakes he made, what he did right, and how he was found.
Prod-FO Dist-FO

Lost In Death Valley C 47 MIN
16MM FILM, 3/4 OR 1/2 IN VIDEO I-H
Reveals what happens when five young members of a high school marching band are stranded in the desert when their single-engine plane crashes. Shows that traditional roles for male and females come into question as a shy girl who is the only one who knows how to deal with the dangers they face, shrinks from asserting herself, while an aggressive boy leads them on a trail headed for certain disaster.
From The Teenage Years Series.
Prod-ALAMAR Dist-TIMLIF 1984

Lost In Space C 15 MIN
3/4 OR 1/2 INCH VIDEO CASSETTE I-J
Shows how future societal alternatives may be predicted by a better understanding of the present society.
From The It's All Up To You Series.
Prod-COOPED Dist-AITECH Prodn-WHATV 1978

Lost In The Barrens C 15 MIN
3/4 OR 1/2 INCH VIDEO CASSETTE I
Tells of two boys lost in the subarctic forests of northern Canada. From the book by Farley Mowatt.
From The Book Bird Series.
Prod-CTI Dist-CTI

Lost In The Crowd C 43 MIN
16MM FILM OPTICAL SOUND
Portray's God's search for the lost soul by showing how Easter vacation triggers the invasion of the beaches by thousands of high school and college young people in a frenzied search for sun, sand, surf, suds and sex. They soon lose their identity in a carnival of night clubs, go-go girls, bright lights and beer cans.
LC NO. FIA67-474
Prod-YOUTH Dist-GF 1966

Lost In The Mish-Mosh - Area Measure C 13 MIN
3/4 INCH VIDEO CASSETTE P
Tells how a famous detective selects the appropriate unit of measure in order to save a kidnapped professor.
Prod-DAVFMS Dist-GA

Lost In The Translation C 10 MIN
3/4 INCH VIDEO CASSETTE
Presents a highly-structured, fragmented narrative about the elusive and the subliminal, by Tony Labat.
Prod-EAI Dist-EAI

Lost In The Woods C 23 MIN
16MM FILM, 3/4 OR 1/2 IN VIDEO P-I A
Tells the story of a six-year-old boy who becomes lost in the woods while camping with his parents. Since he had previously learned about survival, he knows just what to do. Emphasizes simple survival techniques.
Prod-CASSB Dist-BCNFL 1984

Lost In The Woods C 30 MIN
3/4 OR 1/2 INCH VIDEO CASSETTE I-J
Focuses on farming and the identification of edible foods in the wild.
From The High Feather Series. Pt 6
LC NO. 83-706052
Prod-NYSED Dist-GPITVL 1982

Lost Is A Feeling C 15 MIN
16MM FILM, 3/4 OR 1/2 IN VIDEO I
Helps children understand how persons can feel lost and threatened in new situations by introducing Amadore, a Puerto Rican who moves to Washington, DC, and attempts to make friends with a group of boys playing baseball. Shows how his efforts are marred by his inability to speak English.
From The Inside-Out Series.
LC NO. 73-702444
Prod-NITC Dist-AITECH 1973

Lost Love - Another Senseless Tragedy C 11 MIN
3/4 OR 1/2 INCH VIDEO CASSETTE C A
A light-hearted approach to the break-up of a love affair. Addresses romantic depression, rejection, loss, coping methods.
Prod-MMRC Dist-MMRC

Lost Mission, The C 19 MIN
3/4 OR 1/2 INCH VIDEO CASSETTE I A
Shows an archaeological discovery being made that establishes evidence of a culture that existed 3500 years ago.
Prod-SUTHRB Dist-SUTHRB

Lost Mixing Time Of Dual-Drum Paver C 30 MIN
16MM FILM OPTICAL SOUND
Highlights the importance of the simultaneous mixing interval in meeting mixing time specifications with dual-drum pavers. Shows some trouble spots and emphasizes the significance of proper adjustments to the batchmeter.
Prod-USDTFH Dist-USNAC 1959

Lost Pharaoh, The - The Search For Akhenaten C 67 MIN
3/4 OR 1/2 INCH VIDEO CASSETTE H-C A
Tells the fascinating story of an ancient pharaoh who was almost lost to history and the archeological sleuthing which went into piecing together information about him.
Prod-NFBC Dist-NFBC

Lost Phoebe, The C 30 MIN
16MM FILM, 3/4 OR 1/2 IN VIDEO
Shows how an old, senile man searches for his dead wife. Based on the short story The Lost Phoebe by Theodore Dreiser.
Prod-AMERFI Dist-CORF

Lost Pigeon C 15 MIN
16MM FILM, 3/4 OR 1/2 IN VIDEO
Deals with the concept of ownership and responsibility for one's actions by telling a story about a boy who lost one of his homing pigeons. Tells how the pigeon is injured by a group of boys and that one of the boys nurses it back to health. Raises the question of ownership of a bird.
Prod-BARR Dist-BARR 1974

Lost Pigeon (Captioned) C 15 MIN
16MM FILM - VIDEO, ALL FORMATS I-J
Tells the story of a boy taking care of an injured homing pigeon. Deals with what happens when the pigeon's owner puts up a sign describing his lost bird.
Prod-BARR Dist-BARR

Lost Pigeon (Spanish) C 15 MIN
16MM FILM - VIDEO, ALL FORMATS I-J
Tells the story of a boy taking care of an injured homing pigeon. Deals with what happens when the pigeon's owner puts up a sign describing his lost bird.
Prod-BARR Dist-BARR

Lost Pilgrim, The B 45 MIN
16MM FILM OPTICAL SOUND
Describes the adventures of a lost pilgrim in a forest in 16th century France. Studies peasant life in a medieval village in a time of ignorance and religious obsession.
Prod-FILIM Dist-RADIM

Lost Production Highway Construction C 30 MIN
16MM FILM OPTICAL SOUND
Examines minor delays that affect the production rates of key units of highway construction equipment, including power shovels, scrapers, hot-mix bituminous plants and concrete paver.
LC NO. 74-705049
Prod-USDTFH Dist-USNAC 1957

Lost Puppy C 14 MIN
16MM FILM, 3/4 OR 1/2 IN VIDEO P
An open-end film about a young girl's responsibility to obey her mother.
From The Values For Grades K-3 Series.
Prod-CF Dist-CF 1969

Lost Sheep, The C 15 MIN
16MM FILM OPTICAL SOUND P-H
Uses puppets to tell the parable of the lost sheep.
Prod-YALEDV Dist-YALEDV

Lost Sheep, The C 13 MIN
3/4 OR 1/2 INCH VIDEO CASSETTE K-P
Uses cell and puppet animation to tell the story of a young shepherd who stumbles upon a mysterious underground kingdom while searching for his sheep. Shows how his kindness to his flock and loyalty to his job are rewarded.
LC NO. 83-706400
Prod-CFET Dist-MOKIN 1983

Lost Sun, The C 12 MIN
16MM FILM OPTICAL SOUND
The story of the barnyard trio-a rabbit, a pussy cat, and a dauntless duck-who search the skies for the sun which has disappeared. Relates how they find the sun and discover that those who want bright days must search for the sun.
From The Animatoons Series.
LC NO. FIA67-5512
Prod-ANTONS Dist-RADTV 1968

Lost To The Revolution C 28 MIN
16MM FILM, 3/4 OR 1/2 IN VIDEO
Looks at the final years of Imperial Russia through the legacy of Peter Carl Faberge, the renowned jeweler who created many fabulous designs for the Romanovs during the reigns of Czar Alexander III and Czar Nicholas II.
Prod-FORBES Dist-PHENIX Prodn-SEVSEA 1981

Lost Wax C 9 MIN
16MM FILM, 3/4 OR 1/2 IN VIDEO J-C A
Illustrates the lost wax process of casting metal images--an ancient art still practiced today in India by itinerant craftsmen.
Prod-KAP Dist-AIMS 1969

Lost World Of The Maya, The C 36 MIN
16MM FILM, 3/4 OR 1/2 IN VIDEO H-C A
Follows Eric Thompson, an authority on Mayan civilization, as he travels through Central America. Presents theories that have been used to explain the decline of the Mayan culture.
From The Nova Series.
LC NO. 79-707814
Prod-BBCTV Dist-TIMLIF 1974

Lost World Of The Medusa C 50 MIN
3/4 OR 1/2 INCH VIDEO CASSETTE H-C A
Explores the labyrinthine limestone islands of Palau in the Pacific, a lake filled with millions of medusa jellyfish, rain forests sprouting from coral rubble and vast caves haunted by whip scorpions, giant crickets and bats.
Prod-WNETTV Dist-FI Prodn-BBCTV

Lost World Revisited, The B 28 MIN
16MM FILM, 3/4 OR 1/2 IN VIDEO J-C A
Discusses the 1925 motion picture 'THE LOST WORLD,' based on a novel by Sir Arthur Conan Doyle, about the discovery of a river inhabited by gigantic pre-historic animals and which featured Lewis Stone, Wallace Beery, Bessie Love and Lloyd Hughes in the cast. Tells how Willis H O'brien used stop-motion photography in order to bring the pre-historic monsters to life.
From The Movies - Our Modern Art Series.
Prod-SPCTRA Dist-SF 1967

Lost 600, The C 18 MIN
16MM FILM OPTICAL SOUND
Emphasizes the dangers associated with foolish, unsafe and reckless behavior in and on the water. Covers still-water drownings, surfing, boating, yachting, water skiing, rock fishing, and swimming in home pools.
LC NO. 80-700822
Prod-NSWF Dist-TASCOR 1978

Lostine C 30 MIN
3/4 INCH VIDEO CASSETTE
Presents video art by Willard Rosenquist.
Prod-EAI Dist-EAI

Lot Acceptance Sampling C 30 MIN
3/4 OR 1/2 INCH VIDEO CASSETTE IND
Describes content and application of Military Standard 781C, 'Reliability Design Qualification and Product Acceptance Tests - Exponential Distribution.'
From The Reliability Engineering Series.
Prod-COLOSU Dist-COLOSU

Lot In Sodom B 27 MIN
16MM FILM OPTICAL SOUND J-C A
A lyrical interpretation of the biblical story based on rhythmical arrangements of symbols rather than on chronological development of action.
Prod-WATWEB Dist-TWYMAN 1934

Lot Of Living Things, A C 15 MIN
3/4 OR 1/2 INCH VIDEO CASSETTE K-P
Explains diversity in living things.
From The Dragons, Wagons And Wax, Set 1 Series.
Prod-CTI Dist-CTI

Lots Of Kids Like Us C 28 MIN
16MM FILM, 3/4 OR 1/2 IN VIDEO
Presents a dramatization of children living in a home where a parental drinking problem exists. Explores healthy ways for children to deal with alcoholism in the family.
Prod-MTI Dist-MTI

Lots Of Kids Like Us C 28 MIN
3/4 OR 1/2 INCH VIDEO CASSETTE I
Tells of two children as they try to cope with their father's alcoholism. Dramatizes specific problem-solving techniques as well as basic information about how alcoholism affects a family.
Prod-ROGRSG Dist-ROGRSG

Lotte Eisner In Germany C 34 MIN
16MM FILM OPTICAL SOUND H-C A
Presents noted film critic Lotte Eisner, German born but long a resident of France, who offers her memoirs on film. Shows her reminiscing about meeting such greats as Eisenstein, Murnau and Pabst. Tells of her influence on various filmmakers.
LC NO. 81-701028
Prod-NYFLMS Dist-NYFLMS 1980

Lotte Goslar And Bertram Ross C 30 MIN
3/4 OR 1/2 INCH VIDEO CASSETTE
See series title for descriptive statement.
From The Great Performers Series.
Prod-ARCVID Dist-ARCVID

Lotte Goslar And Bertram Ross C 30 MIN
3/4 OR 1/2 INCH VIDEO CASSETTE
See series title for descriptive statement.
From The Eye On Dance - Great Performers Series.
Prod-ARTRES Dist-ARTRES

Lotte Jacobi, A Film Portrait C 24 MIN
16MM FILM OPTICAL SOUND
Examines the life of Lotte Jacobi, a noted portrait photographer.
LC NO. 79-701174
Prod-UNH Dist-UNH 1979

Lottery And Informaion Prices, Risk Aversion C 56 MIN
3/4 OR 1/2 INCH VIDEO CASSETTE
See series title for descriptive statement.
From The Decision Analysis Series.
Prod-MIOT Dist-MIOT

Lottery By Shirley Jackson, The C 18 MIN
16MM FILM, 3/4 OR 1/2 IN VIDEO J-C
Presents Shirley Jackson's short story 'THE LOTTERY.'
From The Humanities - Short Story Showcase Series.
Prod-EBEC Dist-EBEC 1970

Lotus In The West C 28 MIN
16MM FILM, 3/4 OR 1/2 IN VIDEO J-C A
Explores the lives of two young Americans who have taken up residence in a Buddhist meditation center near downtown Los Angeles.
LC NO. 80-707719
Prod-BONTEJ Dist-CAROUF 1980

LOTUS Plans 1978 C 60 MIN
3/4 OR 1/2 INCH VIDEO CASSETTE
Explains the plans for the Light Of Truth Universal Shrine (LOTUS) by architect Vishwanath Watson.
Prod-IYOGA Dist-IYOGA

Lotus 1-2-3 C
3/4 OR 1/2 INCH VIDEO CASSETTE
Shows how to use Lotus 1-2-3- program efficiently and how to use the most frequently used commands.
Prod-LANSFD Dist-ANDRST

Lou Gehrig B 20 MIN
2 INCH VIDEOTAPE I
See series title for descriptive statement.
From The Americans All Series.
Prod-DENVPS Dist-GPITVL Prodn-KRMATV

Lou Gehrig - King Of Diamonds B 15 MIN
1/2 IN VIDEO CASSETTE BETA/VHS
Documents the sportsmanship, character and courage of baseball player Lou Gehrig.
Prod-STAR Dist-STAR

Lou Rawls C 28 MIN
2 INCH VIDEOTAPE
Presents the jazz music of Lou Rawls. Features host Jim Rockwell interviewing the artist.
From The People In Jazz Series.
Prod-WTVSTV Dist-PUBTEL

Louder Than Our Words - Women And Civil Disobedience C 36 MIN
3/4 OR 1/2 INCH VIDEO CASSETTE
Follows the experience of one womens' affinity group, from their

discussions through their arrests at the June 14, 1982, peace action during the United Nations Special Session on Disarmament. Addresses the historical use of civil disobedience by women to gain political rights.
Prod-GMPF Dist-GMPF

Louder Than Words C 30 MIN
3/4 OR 1/2 INCH VIDEO CASSETTE C A
See series title for descriptive statement.
From The Loosening The Grip Series.
Prod-UMA Dist-GPITVL 1980

Louie C 28 MIN
16MM FILM OPTICAL SOUND H-C A
Presents a portrait of 80-year-old shopkeeper Louie Gzinterman, a strong-willed, independent individual with a desire to help others. Shows that his age has not limited him or his vision of life.
LC NO. 80-700741
Prod-IMGLNK Dist-IMGLNK 1979

Louie C 28 MIN
3/4 OR 1/2 INCH VIDEO CASSETTE
Provides a portrait of 80-year-old shopkeeper Louis Gzinterman, a strong-willed independent individual with a desire to help others. Shows how his age has not limited his image of life.
LC NO. 80-706741
Prod-LOWSUL Dist-PBS

Louis Armstrong C 12 MIN
16MM FILM OPTICAL SOUND
Portrays Louis Armstrong, whose musical innovations, influence and inspiration changed and enriched the course of American music.
Prod-HEARST Dist-COUNFI

Louis Armstrong B 30 MIN
16MM FILM OPTICAL SOUND
Presents a jazz concert in which Louis Armstrong is accompanied by other jazz greats.
Prod-GOODYR Dist-REELIM 1962

Louis Armstrong C
16MM FILM, 3/4 OR 1/2 IN VIDEO
Offers reflections on Louis Armstrong's personality as reflected through his music.
Prod-DREWAS Dist-DIRECT 1968

Louis Armstrong C 13 MIN
3/4 OR 1/2 INCH VIDEO CASSETTE
Records the career and life of jazz immortal Louis Armstrong. Includes Billy Taylor, Peggy Lee, Fred Robbins and Al Hibbler, who participate in this tribute.
Prod-KINGFT Dist-KINGFT

Louis Armstrong C 20 MIN
3/4 INCH VIDEO CASSETTE I
See series title for descriptive statement.
From The Truly American Series.
Prod-WVIZTV Dist-GPITVL 1979

Louis Armstrong - The Gentle Giant Of Jazz C 29 MIN
16MM FILM OPTICAL SOUND
Examines the life of Louis Armstrong and his accomplishments as a jazz musician. Includes newsreel footage and archival photographs.
From The American Life Style Series.
LC NO. 79-700068
Prod-USFGC Dist-SHOWCO Prodn-COMCO 1978

Louis Comfort Tiffany - Artist In Glass C 30 MIN
3/4 OR 1/2 INCH VIDEO CASSETTE
Looks at the glass sculpture of Louis Comfort Tiffany, most of which is housed at the Chrysler Museum in Norfolk, VA. Explores the cultural development of Art Nouveau and Art Deco.
Prod-WHROTV Dist-MDCPB

Louis I Kahn - Architect C 28 MIN
16MM FILM OPTICAL SOUND
Describes architect Louis I Kahn's early rebellion against the Bauhaus and the classical clarity of his later works. Shows his gradual mastery of interior light effects as he talks of the building's slice of the sun. Presents examples of his works, including the Yale University Art Gallery, the Salk Institute in San Diego, the Olivetti plant in Pennsylvania and the Kimball Art Museum in Texas.
Prod-MUSLAR Dist-MUSLAR 1977

Louis James Hates School C 12 MIN
16MM FILM, 3/4 OR 1/2 IN VIDEO P-I
Tells how Louis James hates everything about school and decides he doesn't need to read or spell in order to find a job and make lots of money. Traces his misadventures and describes his realization of the real values of reading and spelling.
Prod-ARTASI Dist-LCOA 1980

Louis P Hammett C 45 MIN
3/4 OR 1/2 INCH VIDEO CASSETTE
Provides a tour of Dr Louis P Hammett's career and accomplishments as an industrial chemist and long-time professor at Columbia University. Reviews the evolution of physical organic chemistry.
From The Eminent Chemists - The Interviews Series.
Prod-AMCHEM Dist-AMCHEM 1982

Louis Pasteur C 24 MIN
16MM FILM, 3/4 OR 1/2 IN VIDEO H A
Presents Professor Richard Eakin of the department of Zoology, University of California giving a lecture in which he impersonates Louis Pasteur in the words, dress and manner of his time. Recounts Pasteur's study of right-handed and left-handed molecules of tartic acid, fermentation, spontaneous generation and different kinds of disease-producing bacteria.
From The Great Scientists Speak Again Series.
Prod-QUICK Dist-UCEMC Prodn-UCB 1975

Louis Pasteur - Man Of Science B 30 MIN
16MM FILM, 3/4 OR 1/2 IN VIDEO I-H A
Presents a biography of Louis Pasteur from 1857, when he discovered that microbes caused fermentation, to his death in 1865. Describes his contribution to pasteurization and the development of the vaccine.
Prod-SF Dist-SF 1959

Louis Simpson C 29 MIN
3/4 INCH VIDEO CASSETTE
See series title for descriptive statement.
From The Poets Talking Series.
Prod-UMITV Dist-UMITV 1975

Louis The Fish C 30 MIN
3/4 OR 1/2 INCH VIDEO CASSETTE P
Presents Vincent Gardenia narrating the story Louis The Fish about a man who turns into a fish and leading LeVar Burton on an exploration of exotic marine life, tide pools and dolphins.
From The Reading Rainbow Series. No. 5
Prod-WNEDTV Dist-GPITVL 1982

Louise Burns, Kate Johnson And Jennifer Way C 30 MIN
3/4 OR 1/2 INCH VIDEO CASSETTE
See series title for descriptive statement.
From The Great Performers Series.
Prod-ARCVID Dist-ARCVID

Louise Burns, Kate Johnson And Jennifer Way C 30 MIN
3/4 OR 1/2 INCH VIDEO CASSETTE
Looks at 'Esoterica' with Mama Lou Parks. Hosted by Celia Ipiotis.
From The Eye On Dance - Great Performers Series.
Prod-ARTRES Dist-ARTRES

Louise Nevelson C 25 MIN
16MM FILM OPTICAL SOUND C A
Features sculptress Louise Nevelson commenting on her art and telling of the development of the various periods in her work.
LC NO. 73-701406
Prod-CONNF Dist-CONNF 1971

Louise Torres C 43 MIN
3/4 OR 1/2 INCH VIDEO CASSETTE H-C A
Follows the Hispanic traditions of the mountain folk of northern New Mexico through the eyes of a 79-year-old woman going about her simple tasks. Presents medicinal native plants and the casket she made for herself to spare her family the burden.
Prod-BLUSKY Dist-CEPRO

Louisiana Bass Champ C 25 MIN
16MM FILM OPTICAL SOUND
Focuses on the Atchfalaya Basin in Louisiana, discussing its early settlement by French Canadians and showing the various types of wildlife found in the area.
LC NO. 79-701048
Prod-VICFIP Dist-VICFIP 1978

Louisiana Plantation C 15 MIN
16MM FILM, 3/4 OR 1/2 IN VIDEO I
Depicts the early exploration of the southern United States. Discusses farming, slave labor and the eventual establishment of the large, self-sufficient plantations of the region.
From The American Scrapbook Series.
Prod-WVIZTV Dist-GPITVL 1977

Louisiana Purchase - America's Best Buy B 30 MIN
16MM FILM OPTICAL SOUND H-C A
Describes the role of the Mississippi Valley in world diplomacy, pointing out the details and significance of the Louisiana Purchase. Traces the Lewis and Clarke expedition, their first camp in Nebraska, their council with the Indians and the significance of the expedition.
From The Great Plains Trilogy, 3 Series. Explorer And Settler - The White Man Arrives
Prod-KUONTV Dist-UNEBR 1954

Louisiana Story B 77 MIN
16MM FILM OPTICAL SOUND
Tells the story of a young Cajun boy who plays, hunts, fishes, battles a giant alligator and follows the drama of a monster oil derrick probing for petroleum far below the water's surface in the Louisiana Bayou. Music score by Virgil Thompson.
Prod-CON Dist-TEXFLM Prodn-FLAH 1948

Louisiana's Fabled Plantations C 28 MIN
16MM FILM OPTICAL SOUND
Shows 22 Louisiana plantations which are open to the public.
From The Tour Louisiana Travel Series.
LC NO. 78-701559
Prod-LATPA Dist-RAMSEY Prodn-RAMSEY 1978

Louisville C 13 MIN
16MM FILM OPTICAL SOUND
Tours the International Harvester Company's manufacturing plant at Louisville, including coverage of employee participation in its open house activities.
LC NO. 75-703519
Prod-IH Dist-IH Prodn-IPHC 1975

Loulou C 110 MIN
16MM FILM OPTICAL SOUND
A French language motion picture with English subtitles. Tells how a middle class woman leaves her husband for a leather-jacketed Romeo. Directed by Maurice Pialat.
Prod-UNKNWN Dist-NYFLMS 1980

Louvre, The C
1/2 IN VIDEO CASSETTE BETA/VHS
Tours the Louvre and explores both its collection of masterpieces and its dramatic history. Hosted by Charles Boyer.
Prod-GA Dist-GA

Louvre, The C 45 MI
16MM FILM, 3/4 OR 1/2 IN VIDEO H-
Traces the evolution of the Louvre in terms of the historical and cultural growth of France from the Renaissance. Provides close-ups of paintings and sculptures in this museum, which was once the residence of French kings. Narrated by Charles Boyer.
From The Humanities - The Fine Arts Series.
Prod-NBCTV Dist-EBEC 196

Lovable Lyle C 15 MI
3/4 OR 1/2 INCH VIDEO CASSETTE
Presents the children's story Lovable Lyle by Bernard Waber.
From The Picture Book Park Series. Red Module
Prod-WVIZTV Dist-AITECH 197

Love C 2 MI
16MM FILM OPTICAL SOUND I-H A
Creates a mood for discussion, thought, prayer or meditation on the subject of God is love.
From The Meditation Series.
LC NO. 80-700752
Prod-IKONOG Dist-IKONOG 197

Love C 11 MI
16MM FILM, 3/4 OR 1/2 IN VIDEO J-
Presents the question of definition and responsibilities of love as opposed to the feelings of sex.
From The Family Life Education And Human Growth Series.
Prod-SF Dist-SF 197

Love C 29 MI
3/4 OR 1/2 INCH VIDEO CASSETTE
Discusses whether parents and children have to love one another, and can children love and hate parents at the same time.
From The Feelings Series.
Prod-SCETV Dist-PBS 197

Love - Myth And Mystery C 30 MI
3/4 OR 1/2 INCH VIDEO CASSETTE C
See series title for descriptive statement.
From The Art Of Being Human Series. Module 10
Prod-MDCC Dist-MDCC

Love - The Ultimate Affirmation C 58 MI
3/4 OR 1/2 INCH VIDEO CASSETTE
Presents Dr Leo Buscaglia who offers a challenge to those who seek happiness and fulfillment in a relationship.
Prod-STSU Dist-PBS 1979

Love Among The Mutants C 29 MI
3/4 OR 1/2 INCH VIDEO CASSETTE
Features a science fiction comedy about a female vacuum cleaner transplanted into a human body and her adventures through a world populated with biological and electronic hybrids.
Prod-EAI Dist-EAI

Love And Adventure - Hamilton C 45 MI
2 INCH VIDEOTAPE
See series title for descriptive statement.
From The Humanities Series. Unit II - The World Of Myth And Legend
Prod-WTTWTV Dist-GPITVL

Love And Anarchy C 108 MI
16MM FILM OPTICAL SOUND H-C A
Tells the story of shy country peasant who goes to the city with a plan to assassinate Benito Mussolini. Shows how his underground contact in the network of anarchists offers him a hideout in her brothel where he meets a young prostitute and falls in love.
LC NO. 76-702145
Prod-CARDAR Dist-CINEMV 1975

Love And Intimacy C 29 MI
3/4 OR 1/2 INCH VIDEO CASSETTE
Presents a dance sequence, folk singing and poetry readings to set a mood of love, warmth and intimacy. Features Milton Diamond, Ph D, a biologist at the University of Hawaii, who uses these techniques to support his point that love is not synonymous with sex or marriage and defies strict definition.
From The Human Sexuality Series.
Prod-KHETTV Dist-PBS

Love And Learn C 10 MIN
3/4 INCH VIDEO CASSETTE
Depicts the interaction between six preschoolers and six nursing home grandmothers who have been teamed for a weekly sharing of stories, games and affection.
LC NO. 81-706222
Prod-ADELPH Dist-ADELPH 1980

Love And Loneliness C 29 MIN
3/4 OR 1/2 INCH VIDEO CASSETTE H-C A
Explores the satisfactions of love and the anguish of absence.
From The Young And Old - Reaching Out Series.
LC NO. 80-707180
Prod-CRFI Dist-PBS 1979

Love And Marriage C
1/2 IN VIDEO CASSETTE BETA/VHS
Attempts to answer the question of love and marriage through a look at newlyweds, a Golden Wedding Anniversary couple, and a remarried couple.
From The Adult Years - Continuity And Change Series.
Prod-OHUTC Dist-OHUTC

Love At First Bite C 96 MIN
16MM FILM OPTICAL SOUND H-C
Presents the comedy about New York which has become so jaded, even Dracula doesn't scare its inhabitants. Stars Susan St James, George Hamilton and Richard Benjamin.
Prod-AIP Dist-TIMLIF 1979

Love Carefully C 17 MIN
16MM FILM, 3/4 OR 1/2 IN VIDEO A
Presents information about such birth control methods as the pill, withdrawal, condoms, foam, the diaphragm, the IUD, rhythm, abortion and voluntary sterilization.
Prod-PPSY Dist-PEREN

Love Class With Leo Buscaglia, A C 45 MIN
3/4 OR 1/2 INCH VIDEO CASSETTE
Presents Dr Leo Buscaglia in a question and answer session with a group of his students and friends in which he probes the dynamics of love and relationships.
Prod-KVIETV Dist-PBS 1980

Love Class, A C 46 MIN
3/4 OR 1/2 INCH VIDEO CASSETTE
See series title for descriptive statement.
From The Leo Buscaglia Series.
Prod-PBS Dist-DELTAK

Love Conquers All C 30 MIN
3/4 INCH VIDEO CASSETTE H-C A
Explores the many moods of love as depicted by 16 poets.
From The Anyone For Tennyson Series.
Prod-NETCHE Dist-GPITVL

Love Conquers All - Love, Human, Divine Unlawful And Domesticated In The Canterbury... C 45 MIN
3/4 OR 1/2 INCH VIDEO CASSETTE
Looks at the different types of love depicted in Chaucer's Canterbury Tales.
From The Survey Of English Literature I Series.
Prod-MDCPB Dist-MDCPB

Love Goddesses, The B 87 MIN
16MM FILM, 3/4 OR 1/2 IN VIDEO
Shows the changing role of the 'LOVE GODDESS' as a reflection of fluctuating American morality. Includes scenes with Pola Negri, Gloria Swanson, Theda Bara, Marlene Dietrich, Clara Bow, Jean Harlow, Mae West, Claudette Colbert, Bette Davis, Betty Grable, Rita Hayworth, Sophia Loren, Elizabeth Taylor, Simone Signoret, Marilyn Monroe and many others.
Prod-JANUS Dist-TEXFLM

Love In Later Life C 30 MIN
3/4 OR 1/2 INCH VIDEO CASSETTE C A
Affirms physical love as a life-long source of strength and pleasure. Shows a couple as they grew and changed through the years.
Prod-MMRC Dist-MMRC

Love In The Afternoon B 126 MIN
16MM FILM OPTICAL SOUND J-C A
Presents Audrey Hepburn, Gary Cooper and Maurice Chevalier in the Billy Wilder story of the romance between a naive young music student and an aging millionaire swinger.
Prod-CINEWO Dist-CINEWO 1957

Love Is C 1 MIN
16MM FILM OPTICAL SOUND
Presents an animated short-short, utilizing creative typography and colorful backgrounds to express the facetious concept that love may not always live up to its romantic reputation.
LC NO. 72-702550
Prod-USC Dist-USC 1972

Love Is Beautiful C 15 MIN
16MM FILM OPTICAL SOUND R
Deals with the proper attitude toward sex, love and marriage in light of Christian scripture.
Prod-OUTRCH Dist-OUTRCH

Love Is The Answer C 20 MIN
16MM FILM OPTICAL SOUND
Presents a story which compares the way a girl makes her husband's life better with the way silicones improve products.
LC NO. 74-700351
Prod-GE Dist-GE 1973

Love Is To Grow On C 24 MIN
16MM FILM OPTICAL SOUND
Shows the progress of Down's Syndrome children from birth through employment under a specialized and integrated educational system involving home, school and community environment.
LC NO. 77-701810
Prod-HCINST Dist-MVI Prodn-MVI 1977

Love Is... C 15 MIN
3/4 INCH VIDEO CASSETTE P-I
Explains that a family is a close-knit group that will stick together.
From The Can You Imagine Series.
Prod-WVIZTV Dist-GPITVL

Love It Like A Fool C 28 MIN
3/4 INCH VIDEO CASSETTE
Follows Malvina Reynolds as she composes, records and performs. Reveals an artist of true integrity who unites her talents, insights and humanism in song.
Prod-FIRS Dist-FIRS

Love It Like A Fool - A Film About Malvina Reynolds C 28 MIN
16MM FILM OPTICAL SOUND H-C A
Presents a biographical portrait of Malvina Reynolds, songwriter, performer, political activist and philosopher. Conveys her exuberance and enthusiasm for life through segments of her live performances, personal conversations and recordings of her songs.
LC NO. 78-701586
Prod-WNGRF Dist-NEWDAY 1977

Love Letter To Maryland C 45 MIN
3/4 OR 1/2 INCH VIDEO CASSETTE
Tours the state of Maryland, visiting such locales as Deal Island, a quaint fishing village and Applegarth's boatyard in the beautiful town of Oxford.
Prod-MDCPB Dist-MDCPB

Love Me And Leave Me C 30 MIN
16MM FILM - 3/4 IN VIDEO
Focuses on the relationship between parent and child, showing how this bond forms and how it affects the development of the child. Offers suggestions for making separations between parent and child easier.
From The Footsteps Series.
LC NO. 79-707628
Prod-USOE Dist-USNAC 1978

Love Of Life C 30 MIN
16MM FILM, 3/4 OR 1/2 IN VIDEO H-C A
Tells the story of a man's struggle for survival after he is deserted by his partner in the Canadian Klondike. Based on the story Love Of Life by Jack London. Narrated by Orson Welles.
Prod-NORCOM Dist-LCOA 1981

Love Of Life (French) C 91 MIN
16MM FILM OPTICAL SOUND
Celebrates the life and work of pianist Arthur Rubenstein. Directed by Francois Reichenbach and S G Patris. With English subtitles.
Prod-UNKNWN Dist-NYFLMS 1968

Love Seen C 12 MIN
16MM FILM OPTICAL SOUND
Presents an analytic exercise in the ontology of the cinematic sex-scene.
LC NO. 75-704319
Prod-CANFDC Dist-CANFDC 1974

Love Somebody C 21 MIN
3/4 OR 1/2 INCH VIDEO CASSETTE P-I
Compares the same rhythm pattern in two songs. Introduces the half note.
From The USS Rhythm Series.
Prod-ARKETV Dist-AITECH 1977

Love Story C 20 MIN
16MM FILM, 3/4 OR 1/2 IN VIDEO H-C A
Shows how the media perpetuate and reinforce stereotyped roles in society. Contrasts the media treatment of relationships between men and women with alternative possible treatments.
From The Viewpoint Series.
Prod-THAMES Dist-MEDIAG 1975

Love Story (And I Want Time) C 28 MIN
16MM FILM, 3/4 OR 1/2 IN VIDEO J A
Edited from the motion picture Love Story. Traces the life of a young couple from their marriage to the untimely death of the young wife. Shows the needs of the dying and the grieving. Stars Ali McGraw and Ryan O'Neil.
Prod-PAR Dist-AIMS 1977

Love Story - Donne's Love Poetry C 45 MIN
3/4 OR 1/2 INCH VIDEO CASSETTE
Provides examples of John Donne's love poetry.
From The Survey Of English Literature I Series.
Prod-MDCPB Dist-MDCPB

Love Story, A C 15 MIN
3/4 OR 1/2 INCH VIDEO CASSETTE I
Tells of marital customs among the Bedouins.
From The Encounter In The Desert Series.
Prod-CTI Dist-CTI

Love Story, A - The Canada Goose C 23 MIN
3/4 OR 1/2 INCH VIDEO CASSETTE K-C A
Visits the land of the Giant Canada Goose. Shows them raise their young in the face of constant danger from racoons, mink and man.
Prod-NWLDPR Dist-NWLDPR

Love Talks, Pt 1 C 30 MIN
3/4 OR 1/2 INCH VIDEO CASSETTE
Presents Dr Leo Buscaglia and a group of high school students who discuss the meaning of love and its risks. Emphasizes the idea that sharing love requires tolerance, compromise, respect and honesty.
Prod-PBS Dist-PBS

Love Talks, Pt 2 C 30 MIN
3/4 OR 1/2 INCH VIDEO CASSETTE
Presents Dr Leo Buscaglia and a group of high school students who discuss the meaning of love and its risks. Emphasizes the idea that sharing love requires tolerance, compromise, respect and honesty.
Prod-PBS Dist-PBS

Love Tapes - An Interactive Video Art Process B 40 MIN
3/4 INCH VIDEO CASSETTE A
Presents eight individuals of various ages and lifestyles who are allowed three minutes each to express his or her perceptions and feelings about love.
LC NO. 81-706189
Prod-CLARKW Dist-FLMLIB 1981

Love Tapes - Series 16 C 25 MIN
3/4 OR 1/2 INCH VIDEO CASSETTE
Collection of self-interviews on 'love' from a widely diverse group of individuals. Becomes a revelation through a shared experience.
Prod-EAI Dist-EAI

Love Tapes - Series 18 B 58 MIN
3/4 OR 1/2 INCH VIDEO CASSETTE
Presents haunting portraits of ordinary people. Collection of self-interviews on 'love' from a widely diverse group of individuals.
Prod-EAI Dist-EAI

Love Tapes - Series 19 B 28 MIN
3/4 INCH VIDEO CASSETTE
Presents a collection of statements on love from a diverse group of individuals, each talking alone and spontaneously for three minutes.
Prod-EAI Dist-EAI

Love Tapes In New York B 46 MIN
3/4 INCH VIDEO CASSETTE A
Shows eight people facing a video camera and expressing their perceptions of love.
LC NO. 80-707696
Prod-CLARKW Dist-KINHOL 1980

Love Tennis—A Series

Features Lew Gerrard and Don Candy giving tennis instructions.
Prod-MDCPB Dist-MDCPB

Backhand, The 29 MIN
Doubles Strategy 29 MIN
Forehand, The 29 MIN
Interviews 29 MIN
Jargon, Scoring And Answers 29 MIN
Lob And The Smash, The 29 MIN
Return Of The Serve, The 29 MIN
Serve, The 29 MIN
Singles Strategy 29 MIN
Volley, The 29 MIN

Love That Car C 10 MIN
16MM FILM, 3/4 OR 1/2 IN VIDEO H A
Presents a humorous approach to the importance of automobile maintenance.
Prod-AIMS Dist-AIMS 1967

Love That Car (Spanish) C 10 MIN
16MM FILM, 3/4 OR 1/2 IN VIDEO H-C A
Presents a 'kidding-on-the-square' approach to the importance of car maintenance. Depicts the dilemmas in which several victims of carelessness find themselves.
Prod-PART Dist-AIMS 1967

Love Those Trains C 59 MIN
16MM FILM, 3/4 OR 1/2 IN VIDEO
Takes trips on famous trains such as Europe's Orient Express and the Salad Bowl Express which takes lettuce from California to New York. Interviews hoboes who use trains as their main method of transportation.
Prod-NGS Dist-NGS 1984

Love Thy Customer C 26 MIN
16MM FILM OPTICAL SOUND
Uses a kidding approach to show service writers how to better their relationship with the customers by doing things right the first time. Shows the customers as the service writers see them and the service writers and mechanics as the customers see them.
LC NO. FIA66-1283
Prod-FMCMP Dist-PART Prodn-PART 1966

Love To Kill C 15 MIN
16MM FILM, 3/4 OR 1/2 IN VIDEO J-C A
Tells how six young boys, repulsed by their encounter with 'KILLING FOR SPORT' take action and become the victims themselves of society's violence. Explains that the boys free buffalo at a commercial buffalo preserve and that hunters, attempting to stop them, shoot and kill one of the boys.
From The Searching For Values - A Film Anthology Series.
Prod-LCOA Dist-LCOA 1972

Love Toad C 2 MIN
16MM FILM, 3/4 OR 1/2 IN VIDEO
Shows two-colorful beanbag frogs engage in animated sexual activity.
Prod-MMRC Dist-MMRC

Love, Family In The Community C 30 MIN
3/4 OR 1/2 INCH VIDEO CASSETTE K-P
See series title for descriptive statement.
From The Villa Alegre Series.
Prod-BCTV Dist-MDCPB

Love, Hatred, Friendship And God C 120 MIN
3/4 OR 1/2 INCH VIDEO CASSETTE
Shows Sri Gurudev at Yogaville East where he answers questions on love, hatred, friendship and God.
Prod-IYOGA Dist-IYOGA

Love, Susan C 15 MIN
16MM FILM, 3/4 OR 1/2 IN VIDEO I
Helps children deal with the misunderstandings and conflicts that arise within even a loving family. Explains what happens when Susan's father arrives home from work, exhausted and troubled and rejects her pleas to look at the portrait that she has just painted. Depicts Susan's hurt and confusion.
From The Inside-Out Series.
LC NO. 73-702445
Prod-NITC Dist-AITECH 1973

Love's Labour's Lost C 29 MIN
2 INCH VIDEOTAPE
Features Alan Levitan, associate professor of English at Brandeis University discussing Love's Labour's Lost by Shakespeare.
From The Feast Of Language Series.
Prod-WGBHTV Dist-PUBTEL

Love's Labour's Lost C 120 MIN
3/4 OR 1/2 INCH VIDEO CASSETTE H-C A
Offers a satire directed against intellectual pride and pedantry in which the king of Navarre and three of his lords vow to spend three years in study and not to see any women. Reveals that when the Princess of France arrives on a diplomatic mission with her three ladies, the men break their vow and fall in love with them.

From The Shakespeare Plays Series.
Prod-BBCTV Dist-TIMLIF 1984

Love's Lesson Learned C 30 MIN
3/4 OR 1/2 INCH VIDEO CASSETTE
See series title for descriptive statement.
From The Up And Coming Series.
Prod-KQEDTV Dist-MDCPB

Love's Sweet Song C 29 MIN
2 INCH VIDEOTAPE
See series title for descriptive statement.
From The Our Street Series.
Prod-MDCPB Dist-PUBTEL

Love's Tough Reach C 30 MIN
3/4 OR 1/2 INCH VIDEO CASSETTE J-H A
Tells the story of a father's love, understanding and respect for his wild daughter.
LC NO. 85-703549
Prod-BYU Dist-EBEC 1983

Loved, Honored And Bruised C 25 MIN
16MM FILM, 3/4 OR 1/2 IN VIDEO H-C A
Documents the true story of Jeannie, beaten by her husband throughout the thirteen years of her marriage, who was too ashamed to ask for help. Tells how Jeannie and her five children were finally given shelter in a home for battered women and received counseling, financial aid, social support and legal aid to divorce her husband and start a new life.
Prod-NFBC Dist-MEDIAG 1982

Lovejoy's Nuclear War C 60 MIN
16MM FILM, 3/4 OR 1/2 IN VIDEO J-C A
Describes how Sam Lovejoy burned a weather tower in Massachusetts which had been built prior to erecting a nuclear power plant. Explains that he took this action to protect other citizens from possible radioactive waste. Discusses the legal aspects of such a decision.
LC NO. 82-707173
Prod-GMPF Dist-BULFRG 1975

Loveliness Of Words, The C 20 MIN
2 INCH VIDEOTAPE P
See series title for descriptive statement.
From The Learning Our Language, Unit III - Creative Writing Series.
Prod-MPATI Dist-GPITVL

Lovely Lady B 15 MIN
2 INCH VIDEOTAPE P
See series title for descriptive statement.
From The Children's Literature Series. No. 29
Prod-NCET Dist-GPITVL Prodn-KUONTV

Lovely, Lively Bavaria C 23 MIN
16MM FILM OPTICAL SOUND
Records the changes that have turned parts of Bavaria into bustling centers of new industry and crafts. Describes Bavaria as taking its place in the mainstream of modern life while not seeming to change at all.
Prod-WSTGLC Dist-WSTGLC

Lovemaking C 13 MIN
16MM FILM OPTICAL SOUND
Presents two persons making love in a sauna.
Prod-MMRC Dist-MMRC

Lover's Quarrel With The World, A B 40 MIN
16MM FILM, 3/4 OR 1/2 IN VIDEO J-C A
Presents a portrait of the American poet Robert Frost, revealing his key philosophic and artistic views.
Prod-PFP Dist-PHENIX Prodn-WGBH 1970

Lovers Of Language C 15 MIN
2 INCH VIDEOTAPE J-H
Shows how command of a second language can be a valuable asset in the international world of work.
From The Work Is For Real Series.
Prod-STETVC Dist-GPITVL

Lovers, The (French) B 90 MIN
16MM FILM OPTICAL SOUND
Focuses on a provincial wife whose shallow life is changed by a night of love. Directed by Louis Malle. With English subtitles.
Prod-UNKNWN Dist-NYFLMS 1958

Lovesick B 28 MIN
16MM FILM, 3/4 OR 1/2 IN VIDEO H-C A
Describes how a naive young man tries to win the heart of a neighborhood prostitute.
Prod-DNBAUM Dist-PHENIX 1976

Lovey - A Circle Of Children II C 120 MIN
16MM FILM, 3/4 OR 1/2 IN VIDEO H-C A
Tells the story of Mary McCracken, a special education teacher who must try to reach a little girl who has been diagnosed as schizophrenic or brain-damaged. Views Mary's personal life and shows how she must get over her divorce to venture forth with romance and a new life. Stars Jane Alexander.
Prod-TIMLIF Dist-TIMLIF 1982

Loving Couples C 97 MIN
16MM FILM, 3/4 OR 1/2 IN VIDEO H-C A
Tells the stories of two couples, one married and one unmarried who regroup in rather unconventional ways. Stars Shirley MacLaine, James Coburn, Susan Sarandon and Stephen Collins.
Prod-TIMLIF Dist-TIMLIF 1982

Loving Hands C 23 MIN
16MM FILM OPTICAL SOUND
Shows how a mother can transmit love, energy, and well-being to her infant through massage. Directed by Frederick Leboyer.
Prod-UNKNWN Dist-NYFLMS 1976

Loving Me Is Loving You C 15 MIN
3/4 INCH VIDEO CASSETTE H
Shows a young man settling into his new job, explaining that he must learn to adapt to the change.
From The Success In The Job Market Series.
Prod-KUONTV Dist-GPITVL 1980

Loving Parents C 24 MIN
16MM FILM, 3/4 OR 1/2 IN VIDEO J-C A
Uses short, open-ended dramatic sequences to illustrate questions of concern to parents about their children's sexuality. Features a group of parents discussing their own attitudes, experiences and concerns.
Prod-ENGLE Dist-TEXFLM 1978

Loving Relationships With Leo Buscaglia C 50 MIN
3/4 OR 1/2 INCH VIDEO CASSETTE
Provides an affectionate trip through Leo Buscaglia's rich repertoire of warm family stories and personal experiences.
Prod-PBS Dist-PBS

Loving Young Company C 16 MIN
16MM FILM OPTICAL SOUND
Shows groups of American teenagers visiting Israel in the summer time. Follows their tour through the country, creating new friendships, acquainting themselves with the country and its people and having fun.
Prod-ALDEN Dist-ALDEN

Lovins On The Soft Path - An Energy Future With A Future C 36 MIN
16MM FILM, 3/4 OR 1/2 IN VIDEO H-C A
Presents energy analysts Amory and Hunter Lovins who argue that the only long-term solution to the energy crisis lies in using energy efficiently and adopting appropriate renewable energy sources as opposed to nuclear power and coal.
LC NO. 82-707096
Prod-ECECF Dist-BULFRG Prodn-ENVIC 1982

Lovis James Hates School (Captioned) C 11 MIN
16MM FILM, 3/4 OR 1/2 IN VIDEO P-I
Tells the story of young boy who decides to quit school for adventure, only to learn he needs to be back in school.
Prod-ARTASI Dist-LCOA 1980

Low Back Pain C
3/4 OR 1/2 INCH VIDEO CASSETTE
Explains how easy it is to overstress the lower back in a variety of ways. Discusses the proper treatment for a typical back episode and recovery. Includes a list of dos and don'ts on how to maintain a strong, healthy back.
Prod-MIFE Dist-MIFE

Low Back Pain C 14 MIN
16MM FILM, 3/4 OR 1/2 IN VIDEO H-C A
Shows that low back pain is a common problem which can be caused by muscle strain, fatigue, certain chronic diseases and aging.
From The Health Awareness Series.
Prod-PRORE Dist-JOU 1975

Low Back Pain C 17 MIN
3/4 OR 1/2 INCH VIDEO CASSETTE PRO
Identifies the symptoms of degenerative disc disease. Differentiates the cause of low back pain using a standard evaluation form (included with the program). Determines an appropriate treatment regimen for acute and chronic cases. Includes a discussion of several experimental treatment modalities.
Prod-UMICHM Dist-UMICHM 1976

Low Back Pain C 24 MIN
16MM FILM, 3/4 OR 1/2 IN VIDEO
Examines low back pain as a major cause of lost production days, impaired work capacity, and pain-related distractions, errors and accidents. Presents Dr Hans Kraus, a noted orthopedic surgeon, who introduces five exercises to alleviate and prevent back pain.
Prod-SPORP Dist-MTI

Low Back Pain (Arabic) C
3/4 OR 1/2 INCH VIDEO CASSETTE
Explains how easy it is to overstress the lower back in a variety of ways. Discusses the proper treatment for a typical back episode and recovery. Includes a list of dos and don'ts on how to maintain a strong, healthy back.
Prod-MIFE Dist-MIFE

Low Back Pain (Spanish) C
3/4 OR 1/2 INCH VIDEO CASSETTE
Explains how easy it is to overstress the lower back in a variety of ways. Discusses the proper treatment for a typical back episode and recovery. Includes a list of dos and don'ts on how to maintain a strong, healthy back.
Prod-MIFE Dist-MIFE

Low Back Pain (Spanish) C 14 MIN
16MM FILM, 3/4 OR 1/2 IN VIDEO H-C A
Shows that low back pain is a common problem which can be caused by muscle strain, fatigue, certain chronic diseases and aging.
Prod-PRORE Dist-JOU 1975

Low Back Pain - Exercise And Lifestyle Management C
3/4 OR 1/2 INCH VIDEO CASSETTE
Introduces the importance of proper muscle tone to minimize low back pain. Demonstrates an exercise program and techniques to limit the stresses and strains of physical activity on the lower back.
Prod-MIFE Dist-MIFE

Low Choke Method C 11 MIN
3/4 OR 1/2 INCH VIDEO CASSETTE IND
Shows conditions under which this variation of the Low Choke Method is used, the formation leak-off test and overview of Low Choke Method procedure.
From The Blowout Prevention And Well Control Series.
Prod-CAODC Dist-GPCV

Low Cost Energy Now C 20 MIN
16MM FILM OPTICAL SOUND
Investigates the history of mankind's long search for new, clean and renewable sources of energy, and offers a low cost energy solution.
Prod-KEITHA Dist-KEITHA

Low Fat Meat Preparation C 13 MIN
16MM FILM - 3/4 IN VIDEO
Shows how to use the leaner cuts of beef with emphasis on the selection of meat, proper trimming and boning, and preparation techniques that greatly reduce saturated fats and calorie intake.
From The Eat Right To Your Heart's Delight Series.
Prod-IPS Dist-IPS 1976

Low Fire - Enamel On Copper C 28 MIN
2 INCH VIDEOTAPE
Features Mrs Peterson describing certain ceramic processes for her classroom at the University of Southern California. Discusses appropriate temperatures for enamel on copper.
From The Wheels, Kilns And Clay Series.
Prod-USC Dist-PUBTEL

Low Frequency Navigation C 29 MIN
3/4 OR 1/2 INCH VIDEO CASSETTE A
Explains navigation by VLF or very low frequency signals. Includes nature of VLF waves, signal generation, waveguide theory, advantages of VLF signals and receiving antennas. Discusses omega VLF transmission system and uses for navigation including system problem areas.
Prod-FAAFL Dist-AVIMA

Low Level Air Navigation C 22 MIN
16MM FILM OPTICAL SOUND
Demonstrates flight planning and flight techniques to be used by carrier attack pilots in the navigation portion of the low level attack mission.
LC NO. FIE61-88
Prod-USN Dist-USNAC 1960

Low Level Wind Shear C 16 MIN
16MM FILM, 3/4 OR 1/2 IN VIDEO
Describes research to refine airborne and ground-based wind shear detection techniques.
LC NO. 81-707207
Prod-USFAA Dist-USNAC 1978

Low Reynolds Number Flows C 33 MIN
16MM FILM, 3/4 OR 1/2 IN VIDEO H-C
Shows 'INERTIA-FREE' flows, in which every element of fluid is nearly in equilibrium under the influence of forces due to viscosity, pressure and gravity, the forces required to produce acceleration being comparatively very small.
From The Fluid Mechanics Series.
Prod-NCFMF Dist-EBEC 1967

Low Ride C 3 MIN
3/4 INCH VIDEO CASSETTE
Shows the New Mexican landscape as seen from a few inches off the ground on the front of a car.
From The South-Western Landscapes Series.
Prod-EAI Dist-EAI

Low Rider (Spanish) C 22 MIN
3/4 OR 1/2 INCH VIDEO CASSETTE J A
Discusses drinking, driving and youth. Depicts a typical situation in the Chicano community when two friends purchase a 'low rider.'
Prod-SUTHRB Dist-SUTHRB

Low Riders C 22 MIN
16MM FILM, 3/4 OR 1/2 IN VIDEO
Features two teenagers who work hard to customize a car only to have one of them wreck it during a drunk driving spree. Deals with suitable alternatives to drinking and driving.
Prod-LACFU Dist-IA

Low Riders C 23 MIN
3/4 OR 1/2 INCH VIDEO CASSETTE
Describes low riders - the cars and drivers that flourish in Mexican-American communities.
From The Images / Imagenes Series.
Prod-TUCPL Dist-LVN

Low Salt, Low Fat Cooking C 30 MIN
1/2 IN VIDEO CASSETTE BETA/VHS
Demonstrates how to cook and dine avoiding salt and animal fat. Includes fish sauces, chicken thighs and herb and spice blends.
From The Frugal Gourmet Series.
Prod-WTTWTV Dist-MTI

Low Side-To-End Colorectal Anastomosis C 28 MIN
16MM FILM OPTICAL SOUND PRO
Presents a technique for a low side-to-end colorectal anastomosis which offers greater technical ease, a more secure anastomosis and a larger anastomotic lumen than the conventional end-to-end anastomosis.
Prod-ACYDGD Dist-ACY 1968

Low Speed Car Crash Costs C 22 MIN
16MM FILM OPTICAL SOUND J-C A
Uses actual crash test scenes, charts, and chalkboard to demonstrate costs for 1969 standard automobiles.
LC NO. 72-700543
Prod-IIHS Dist-HF Prodn-HF 1970

Low View From A Dark Shadow C 29 MIN
2 INCH VIDEOTAPE

See series title for descriptive statement.
From The Synergism - In Today's World Series.
Prod-WMVSTV Dist-PUBTEL

Low Water Safeguards For Boiler Operation C
16MM FILM - 3/4 IN VIDEO
Discusses the reasons for boiler failure, including failure to check monitoring devices, neglecting or overriding warning signals given by monitoring devices, poor maintenance and failure to keep records. Illustrates the quick-drain and slow-drain tests for checking proper opperation of low-water detection devices and offers a five-point program to assure safe boiler operations.
Prod-ALLIED Dist-BNA

Low-Fat Diet, The C 10 MIN
3/4 OR 1/2 INCH VIDEO CASSETTE
Illustrates process of atherosclerosis and its development and emphasizes importance of low-fat diet, suggesting foods to be included and those to be avoided in well-balanced, low-fat diets.
LC NO. 77-730426
Prod-TRAINX Dist-TRAINX

Low-Level Wind Shear C 16 MIN
3/4 OR 1/2 INCH VIDEO CASSETTE A
Defines wind shear as any change, gradual or abrupt, in wind speed and direction in a thin layer of the atmosphere. Notes danger potential of wind shear for aircraft takeoffs and landings. Describes research and detection techniques of Federal Government.
Prod-FAAFL Dist-AVIMA

Lowdown On High Blood Pressure C 10 MIN
3/4 OR 1/2 INCH VIDEO CASSETTE
Stresses the importance of controlling blood pressure. Useful as an aid in blood pressure screening, referral, follow-up and education.
Prod-AMRC Dist-AMRC

Lowell Herrero - The Graphic Process C 28 MIN
16MM FILM OPTICAL SOUND
Presents Lowell Herrero, the creator of the calendarschedule of the San Francisco Giants baseball team for the 1972 season. Shows all phases of the work involved in graphics and printing.
LC NO. 73-701039
Prod-FILMSM Dist-FILMSM 1973

Lowell Thomas Remembers 1932 B 28 MIN
16MM FILM OPTICAL SOUND J-H
Looks at the major news events of the year 1932.
Prod-BHAWK Dist-BHAWK 1976

Lowells, The - An American Family Of Poets C 30 MIN
3/4 INCH VIDEO CASSETTE H-C A
Presents poetry by three generations of the Lowell family of Massachusetts. Looks at the works of James Russell Lowell, Amy Lowell and Robert Lowell.
From The Anyone For Tennyson Series.
Prod-NETCHE Dist-GPITVL

Lowen And Bioenergetic Therapy C 48 MIN
16MM FILM OPTICAL SOUND H-C A
Features Dr Alexander Lowen describing his key ideas of bioenergetic therapy and demonstrating them in his work with a young female patient. Shows that Dr Lowen's theory is that the unconscious really exists in the muscle constrictions of the body and that therapy requires working with the body as opposed to the mind.
LC NO. 75-701106
Prod-PSYCHD Dist-PSYCHD 1973

Lowen And Bioenergetic Therapy, Pt 1 C 24 MIN
16MM FILM OPTICAL SOUND
Features Dr Alexander Lowen, the foremost exponent of incorporating direct work with the body in the therapeutic process, who describes his key ideas of bioenergetic therapy and demonstrates them in his work with a young female patient. Describes Lowen's theory that the unconscious really exists in the muscle constrictions of the body and that therapy requires working with the body as opposed to the mind.
Prod-PSYCHF Dist-PSYCHD

Lowen And Bioenergetic Therapy, Pt 2 C 24 MIN
16MM FILM OPTICAL SOUND
Features Dr Alexander Lowen, the foremost exponent of incorporating direct work with the body in the therapeutic process, who describes his key ideas of bioenergetic therapy and demonstrates them in his work with a young female patient. Describes Lowen's theory that the unconscious really exists in the muscle constrictions of the body and that therapy requires working with the body as opposed to the mind.
Prod-PSYCHF Dist-PSYCHD

Lower Digestive Tract, The - Breakdown C 26 MIN
3/4 OR 1/2 INCH VIDEO CASSETTE
Traces food as it enters the mouth and the process of breakdown and transformation occurs. Follows the food through the entire alimentary tract, showing how it is dissolved in acid, how the liver and gall bladder work, and how digestion and absorption work.
From The Living Body - An Introduction To Human Biology Series.
Prod-FOTH Dist-FOTH 1985

Lower Extremity, Pt 1 C
3/4 OR 1/2 INCH VIDEO CASSETTE PRO
Introduces manipulative procedures for the foot and ankle with identification of bony landmarks and an outline of the arch mechanism. Uses asymmetry of positional and tissue findings within the ankle and arch to direct the testing of mobility of local joints for dysfunction. Employs motion findings as a basis for treatment of foot and ankle dysfunction by manipulative procedures using the principles of direct technique.
From The Osteopathic Examination And Manipulation Series.
Prod-MSU Dist-MSU

Lower Plant Forms, The C 15 MIN
3/4 OR 1/2 INCH VIDEO CASSETTE I
See series title for descriptive statement.
From The Discovering Series. Unit 7 - Plants
Prod-WDCNTV Dist-AITECH 1978

Lower South, The C 25 MIN
16MM FILM, 3/4 OR 1/2 IN VIDEO I-J
Surveys the diversity of the lower south, including Arkansas, Alabama, Mississippi, Louisiana, Georgia, Florida and South Carolina.
From The United States Geography Series.
Prod-NGS Dist-NGS 1983

Lower Than The Angels C 52 MIN
16MM FILM, 3/4 OR 1/2 IN VIDEO J-C A
Explores the anatomical and intellectual changes which gave rise to man's superiority among the animals.
From The Ascent Of Man Series. No. 1
LC NO. 79-707218
Prod-BBCTV Dist-TIMLIF 1973

Lower Than The Angels (Spanish) C 52 MIN
16MM FILM OPTICAL SOUND H-C A
Explores the anatomical and intellectual changes which gave rise to man's superiority among the animals.
From The Ascent Of Man Series. No. 1
Prod-BBCTV Dist-TIMLIF 1973

Lower Urinary Tract Infections In Women C
3/4 OR 1/2 INCH VIDEO CASSETTE
Explains the major causes of lower urinary tract infections in women along with a discussion of diagnosis and treatment. Emphasizes personal cleanliness as the best precaution against recurring or new infections.
Prod-MIFE Dist-MIFE

Lower Urinary Tract Infections In Women (Arabic) C
3/4 OR 1/2 INCH VIDEO CASSETTE
Explains the major causes of lower urinary tract infections in women along with a discussion of diagnosis and treatment. Emphasizes personal cleanliness as the best precaution against recurring or new infections.
Prod-MIFE Dist-MIFE

Lower Urinary Tract Infections In Women (Spanish) C
3/4 OR 1/2 INCH VIDEO CASSETTE
Explains the major causes of lower urinary tract infections in women along with a discussion of diagnosis and treatment. Emphasizes personal cleanliness as the best precaution against recurring or new infections.
Prod-MIFE Dist-MIFE

Lozanov Language Class B 30 MIN
3/4 OR 1/2 INCH VIDEO CASSETTE T
Includes remarks from Georgi Lozanov and clips from Evelina Gatora on teaching a beginning Italian class.
LC NO. 84-707263
Prod-LLI Dist-LLI 1984

LSD B 28 MIN
16MM FILM - 3/4 IN VIDEO
Outlines how LSD was discovered, the dangers of its misuse and its effects on brain and body.
Prod-USNAC Dist-USNAC 1972

LSD - Insight Or Insanity (2nd Ed) C 28 MIN
16MM FILM, 3/4 OR 1/2 IN VIDEO J-C A
Doctors, scientists and geneticists discuss the possible effects of LSD on the chromosomes. Examines the psychological and physiological effects of LSD use.
Prod-MILLRM Dist-PHENIX 1968

LSD - Insight Or Insanity (2nd Ed) (French) C 28 MIN
16MM FILM, 3/4 OR 1/2 IN VIDEO J-C A
Presents doctors, scientists and geneticists discussing the possible effects of LSD on the chromosomes. Examines the psychological and physiological effects of LSD use.
Prod-MILLRM Dist-PHENIX 1968

LSD - Insight Or Insanity (2nd Ed) (Portuguese) C 28 MIN
16MM FILM, 3/4 OR 1/2 IN VIDEO J-C A
Presents doctors, scientists and geneticists discussing the possible effects of LSD on the chromosomes. Examines the psychological and physiological effects of LSD use.
Prod-MILLRM Dist-PHENIX 1968

LSD - Insight Or Insanity (2nd Ed) (Spanish) C 28 MIN
16MM FILM, 3/4 OR 1/2 IN VIDEO J-C A
Presents doctors, scientists and geneticists discussing the possible effects of LSD on the chromosomes. Examines the psychological and physiological effects of LSD use.
Prod-MILLRM Dist-PHENIX 1968

LSD - Insight Or Insanity (2nd Ed) (Swedish) C 28 MIN
16MM FILM, 3/4 OR 1/2 IN VIDEO J-C A
Presents doctors, scientists and geneticists discussing the possible effects of LSD on the chromosomes. Examines the psychological and physiological effects of LSD use.
Prod-MILLRM Dist-PHENIX 1968

LSD - The Other Side Of Reality C 21 MIN
16MM FILM OPTICAL SOUND C A
Examines the effects of LSD and its potential therapeutic uses in the field of mental health, featuring interviews with California researchers, clinicians and a rabbi.
Prod-KRONTV Dist-KRONTV 1964

LSD Trip - Or Trap C 20 MIN
16MM FILM, 3/4 OR 1/2 IN VIDEO J-C A
Presents facts about LSD, illustrating its use and tragic consequences when a teenage boy and a friend become involved in a car accident.
Prod-DAVP Dist-AIMS 1968

LSD-25 C 27 MIN
16MM FILM OPTICAL SOUND J-C A
Explains what LSD is and what it does. Begins with an LSD 'MOLECULE' saying, 'I AM A COMPLICATED THING, HERE IN COMPLICATED TIMES AND IN COMPLICATED PLACES. BUT NOW LET ME TELL YOU WHAT I REALLY AM AND WHAT I REALLY DO.'
LC NO. FIA68-148
Prod-PROART Dist-PROART 1967

LTA History - Balloons B 27 MIN
16MM FILM, 3/4 OR 1/2 IN VIDEO
Traces the history of balloon experimentation covering problems discovered by outstanding men. Describes the modern uses of balloons.
LC NO. 82-706706
Prod-USN Dist-USNAC

Lubba Dubba - The Inside Story Of Your Heart And Blood C 15 MIN
3/4 OR 1/2 INCH VIDEO CASSETTE P-I
Presents Slim Goodbody introducing the circulatory system.
From The Inside Story With Slim Goodbody Series.
Prod-UWISC Dist-AITECH 1981

Lubricating Ball Bearings C 6 MIN
3/4 OR 1/2 INCH VIDEO CASSETTE IND
Illustrates a technique for ball bearing maintenance showing the proper procedure for removing deteriorated lubricant and replacing with fresh grease.
From The Marshall Maintenance Training Programs Series. Tape 14
Prod-LEIKID Dist-LEIKID

Lubricating Ball Bearings C 6 MIN
16MM FILM, 3/4 OR 1/2 IN VIDEO IND
Demonstrates a technique for ball bearing maintenance showing the proper procedure for removing deteriorated lubricant and replacing with fresh grease.
Prod-MOKIN Dist-MOKIN

Lubrication C 5 MIN
16MM FILM, 3/4 OR 1/2 IN VIDEO H-C A
Focuses on checking and changing oil, and lubricating cables on a motorcycle.
From The Basic Motorcycle Maintenance Series.
LC NO. 81-706497
Prod-PACEST Dist-IFB 1980

Lubrication (1) C 43 MIN
3/4 OR 1/2 INCH VIDEO CASSETTE
Discusses fluid lubrication, boundary lubrication and the types of lubrication in between.
From The Tribology 1 - Friction, Wear, And Lubrication Series.
Prod-MIOT Dist-MIOT

Lubrication (2) C 45 MIN
3/4 OR 1/2 INCH VIDEO CASSETTE
Discusses effect of reduction of surface energy on wear and types of lubricants which are effective in this regard.
From The Tribology 1 - Friction, Wear, And Lubrication Series.
Prod-MIOT Dist-MIOT

Lubrication - The Automobile C 44 MIN
3/4 OR 1/2 INCH VIDEO CASSETTE
Discusses the automobile and ways in which friction causes energy dissipation.
From The Tribology 2 - Advances In Friction, Wear, And Lubrication Series.
Prod-MIOT Dist-MIOT

Lubrication Checks And Services C 30 MIN
3/4 OR 1/2 INCH VIDEO CASSETTE
Identifies the components of the engine's lubrication system and describes their functions. Explains the functions of lubricating oil, service requirements and how to change the oil.
From The Keep It Running Series.
Prod-NETCHE Dist-NETCHE 1982

Lubrication In Healthy And Arthritic Joints C 15 MIN
16MM FILM OPTICAL SOUND
Illustrates how joints are lubricated and explains the roles of articular cartilage and synovial fluid. Describes what happens when nature fails to lubricate joints, as in arthritis. Explains the difference between inflammatory and degenerative arthritis and explores various therapies.
Prod-UPJOHN Dist-UPJOHN 1970

Lubrication Of Electronic Equipment C 9 MIN
16MM FILM OPTICAL SOUND
Explains the importance of routine and methodical lubrication of electronic equipment according to recommended procedures.
LC NO. FIE56-58
Prod-USN Dist-USNAC 1953

Lucia (Spanish) C 160 MIN
16MM FILM OPTICAL SOUND
Dramatizes three separate periods in the Cuban struggle for liberation, showing the participation of Cuban women in that fight. Uses English subtitles.
Prod-TRIFC Dist-TRIFC Prodn-CUBAFI 1969

Lucia Celebration C 10 MIN
16MM FILM OPTICAL SOUND
Shows candle making, preparing for Christmas and Lucia Day celebration in Sweden.
Prod-ASI Dist-AUDPLN

Lucia Di Lammermoor C 30 MIN
16MM FILM, 3/4 OR 1/2 IN VIDEO J-C A
Features Joan Sutherland singing the opera 'LUCIA DI LAMMERMOOR.' Features puppets in an opera box acting as a reviewing audience, conversing with the performers as they enter or leave front stage.
From The Who's Afraid Of Opera Series.
Prod-PHENIX Dist-PHENIX 1973

Luck Is A Lady C 29 MIN
2 INCH VIDEOTAPE
See series title for descriptive statement.
From The Koltanowski On Chess Series.
Prod-KQEDTV Dist-PUBTEL

Luck Of Laura Tedesco C 27 MIN
2 INCH VIDEOTAPE
Explains that in April, 1972, Laura Tedesco, a waitress, won 50,000 dollars in Pennsylvania's lottery. Explores the fact that Laura and others who won big in 1970's lotteries have continued to win regularly in drawings and pools elsewhere.
Prod-WQED Dist-PUBTEL

Luck Of Roaring Camp, The C 27 MIN
16MM FILM, 3/4 OR 1/2 IN VIDEO J-C A
Tells of the birth of a baby in a mining camp who is soon orphaned. Shows that the miners band together to raise the baby and he brings them luck in finding gold. Relates that their belief in him is so strong that they risk injury and death to save him from drowning. Based on the short story The Luck Of Roaring Camp by Bret Harte.
From The LCA Short Story Library Series.
LC NO. 82-706847
Prod-LCOA Dist-LCOA Prodn-KIMLAN 1982

Luck Of The Stiffhams, The C 30 MIN
3/4 OR 1/2 INCH VIDEO CASSETTE C A
Presents an adaptation of the short story The Luck Of The Stiffhams by P G Wodehouse.
From The Wodehouse Playhouse Series.
Prod-BBCTV Dist-TIMLIF 1980

Luckey C 15 MIN
3/4 OR 1/2 INCH VIDEO CASSETTE J-H
Focuses on a talented young musician who nearly wrecks his life in a spiral of crime that begins with shoplifting and grows to include auto theft.
From The Changing Series.
Prod-WGTETV Dist-AITECH 1980

Lucky Corner, The B 17 MIN
16MM FILM OPTICAL SOUND
Explains how a pretentious diner operator and his bratty son run Grandpa's lemonade stand off the block. Shows how Spanky and the Gang stage a parade which leads potential customers to the stand's new location. A Little Rascals film.
Prod-ROACH Dist-BHAWK 1936

Lucky Find, The C 15 MIN
3/4 OR 1/2 INCH VIDEO CASSETTE K-P
Deals with French-American culture. Focuses on the theme of honesty.
From The La Bonne Aventure Series.
Prod-MPBN Dist-GPITVL

Lucky Seven Sampson C 4 MIN
3/4 OR 1/2 INCH VIDEO CASSETTE P-I
Uses songs and cartoons to explore the mathematical possibilities of the number seven.
From The Multiplication Rock Series.
Prod-ABCTV Dist-GA 1974

Lucky Strike (LSMFT) C 1 MIN
3/4 OR 1/2 INCH VIDEO CASSETTE
Shows a classic television commercial with dancing cigarettes doing a square dance.
Prod-BROOKC Dist-BROOKC

Lucky You C 15 MIN
16MM FILM OPTICAL SOUND I-C A
Points out the hazards involved in approaching railroad grade crossings without caution. Joins a motorist whose luck runs out at a grade crossing.
LC NO. 75-700332
Prod-UPR Dist-PCF 1974

Lucretia C 5 MIN
3/4 OR 1/2 INCH VIDEO CASSETTE J-H
Shows the correct use of the words 'Like' and 'As' in writing.
From The Write On, Set 1 Series.
Prod-CTI Dist-CTI

Lucy - A Teenage Pregnancy C 10 MIN
16MM FILM, 3/4 OR 1/2 IN VIDEO J-C
Looks at the life of a 15-year-old mother who is trying to make a life for herself and her baby in a crowded apartment in the projects with her nine siblings.
Prod-PPSPRN Dist-PEREN

Lucy Covington - Native American Indian C 16 MIN
16MM FILM, 3/4 OR 1/2 IN VIDEO J-C
Presents Lucy Covington, a grandchild of the last recognized chief of the Colville Indians. Tells how she led her people in a successful fight against the government's threat to close reservation.
Prod-EBEC Dist-EBEC Prodn-ODYSSP 1978

Luis Llongueras (Spain), Tape A, No. 17 C
3/4 OR 1/2 INCH VIDEO CASSETTE
Shows two cuts in one, upside-down cuts, programmed cuts, sectioning techniques and the frizzy 'disc' look.
Prod-MPCEDP Dist-MPCEDP 1984

Luisa Tenia Razon C 11 MIN
16MM FILM OPTICAL SOUND A
A Spanish language film. Tells how a young medical technician allays her mother-in-law's needless shame about the subject of uterine cancer. Makes it clear that cancer is nothing to be ashamed of, and that cancer of the uterus is a very curable cancer if detected early by a pap test and treated in time.
LC NO. 72-700667
Prod-AMCS Dist-AMCS 1968

Luisa Torres C 43 MIN
16MM FILM, 3/4 OR 1/2 IN VIDEO
Portrays 79-year-old Luisa Torres and her husband Eduardo, 83. Deals with their way of life in a small village near Mora, New Mexico.
Prod-BLUSKY Dist-ONEWST

Luke - The Theological Historian—A Series
A
Features Dr James A Sanders, theologian, as he presents a different approach to the study of the Gospel of Luke and the Acts. Focuses on God as the center of the scriptures.
Prod-UMCOM Dist-UMCOM 1981

Birth Of The Church And The Conversion	
Eyewitnesses And Servants Of The Word	030 MIN
Grumbling Of The Faithful, The	030 MIN
Jesus' Way Of Teaching And Preaching Scriptures	030 MIN
Luke, The Christian Deuternomist	030 MIN
Luke's Account Of Holy Week	030 MIN
Luke's Way Of Reading His Scriptures, The Old	030 MIN

Luke Was There C 32 MIN
16MM FILM, 3/4 OR 1/2 IN VIDEO P-C A
A shortened version of the motion picture Luke Was There. Tells the story of a boy whose disillusioning experiences with the adult world make him a runaway, until he learns the meaning of trust from a perceptive counselor at a children's shelter. An NBC Special Treat program.
Prod-LCOA Dist-LCOA 1976

Luke Was There C 47 MIN
16MM FILM, 3/4 OR 1/2 IN VIDEO P-C A
Tells the story of a boy whose disillusioning experiences with the adult world make him a runaway, until he learns the meaning of trust from a perceptive counselor at a children's shelter. An NBC Special Treat Program.
Prod-LCOA Dist-LCOA 1976

Luke Was There (Captioned) C 32 MIN
16MM FILM, 3/4 OR 1/2 IN VIDEO P-J A
Tells about a young troubled ghetto youth and a perceptive black counselor named Luke. Edited version.
Prod-LCOA Dist-LCOA 1977

Luke Was There (Captioned) C 47 MIN
16MM FILM, 3/4 OR 1/2 IN VIDEO P-J A
Tells about a young, troubled ghetto boy and a perceptive black counselor named Luke. Full version.
Prod-LCOA Dist-LCOA 1977

Luke Was There (French) C 32 MIN
16MM FILM, 3/4 OR 1/2 IN VIDEO P-J A
Tells about a young troubled ghetto youth and a perceptive black counselor named Luke. Edited.
Prod-LCOA Dist-LCOA 1977

Luke Was There (French) C 47 MIN
16MM FILM, 3/4 OR 1/2 IN VIDEO P-J A
Tells about a young troubled ghetto youth and a perceptive black counselor named Luke. Full version.
Prod-LCOA Dist-LCOA 1977

Luke Was There (Spanish) C 32 MIN
16MM FILM, 3/4 OR 1/2 IN VIDEO P-J A
Tells the story of a young troubled ghetto youth and a perceptive black counselor named Luke. Edited.
Prod-LCOA Dist-LCOA 1977

Luke Was There (Spanish) C 47 MIN
16MM FILM, 3/4 OR 1/2 IN VIDEO P-J A
Tells the story of a young troubled ghetto youth and a perceptive black counselor named Luke. Full version.
Prod-LCOA Dist-LCOA 1977

Luke, The Christian Deuteronomist C 30 MIN
3/4 OR 1/2 INCH VIDEO CASSETTE A
Discusses Luke's keen interest in the book of Deuteronomy and how this earlier book helped him. Discusses the historical context in which Deuteronomy was written. Covers Luke's scriptural interpretation of Jesus' ministry.
From The Luke - The Theological Historian Series.
Prod-UMCOM Dist-UMCOM 1981

Luke's Account Of Holy Week C 30 MIN
3/4 OR 1/2 INCH VIDEO CASSETTE A
Explains why the watching Pharisees felt that Jesus' entry into Jerusalem was blasphemous. Discusses the significance of the Last Supper. Explains the concepts of anamnesis and transubstantiation.
From The Luke - The Theological Historian Series.
Prod-UMCOM Dist-UMCOM 1981

Luke's Way Of Reading His Scriptures, The Old Testament C 30 MIN
3/4 OR 1/2 INCH VIDEO CASSETTE A
Introduces the series and gives background information on Luke, the writer. Explains the 'septuagint' which Luke used for his scripture and how he used it. Concludes with a discussion of Luke's purposes for writing his scripture.
From The Luke - The Theological Historian Series.
Prod-UMCOM Dist-UMCOM 1981

Lull By Saki, The C 15 MIN
16MM FILM, 3/4 OR 1/2 IN VIDEO J-C A
Tells about a politician who, seeking a respite from campaigning, ends up tending barnyard animals in his room due to a mischievously arranged misunderstanding. Based on the short stories The Lull and Louise by Saki.
From The Short Story Series.
LC NO. 83-706177
Prod-IITC Dist-IU 1978

Lullaby B 6 MIN
16MM FILM OPTICAL SOUND C A
Presents a hilarious look at marriage several years after the vows have been taken.
Prod-UWFKD Dist-UWFKD

Lullaby C 5 MIN
16MM FILM, 3/4 OR 1/2 IN VIDEO K-I
Uses intricate dough sculptures, folded paper and textured fabrics blended together to tell the animated story of a little dove.
Prod-GOTWAF Dist-PHENIX

Lullaby (Altato) C 4 MIN
16MM FILM, 3/4 OR 1/2 IN VIDEO P-I
Offers an interpretation of a lullaby, showing pinwheels spinning, clocks, butterflies and balloons.
LC NO. 83-707091
Prod-PANNOF Dist-IFB 1977

Lumaaq - An Eskimo Legend C 8 MIN
16MM FILM, 3/4 OR 1/2 IN VIDEO J-C A
Tells the story of a legend widely believed by the Povungnitik Inuit Eskimos.
Prod-NFBC Dist-NFBC 1975

Lumbar Puncture C 4 MIN
3/4 OR 1/2 INCH VIDEO CASSETTE PRO
See series title for descriptive statement.
From The Medical Skills Films Series.
Prod-WFP Dist-WFP

Lumbar Puncture C 8 MIN
3/4 OR 1/2 INCH VIDEO CASSETTE PRO
Lists indications and contraindications for the procedure, contains graphics showing a step-by-step analysis and shows a 16mm film sequence of an actual lumbar puncture.
Prod-UWASH Dist-UWASH

Lumbar Region, Pt 1 C 17 MIN
3/4 OR 1/2 INCH VIDEO CASSETTE PRO
Discusses the principle of introducing motion into the lumbar spine through the lower extremities in preparation for its use in the diagnosis of segmental dysfunction in the lumbar spine. Illustrates this principle further by the three direct manipulative techniques which are demonstrated.
From The Osteopathic Examination And Manipulation Series.
Prod-MSU Dist-MSU

Lumbar Region, Pt 2 C 10 MIN
3/4 OR 1/2 INCH VIDEO CASSETTE PRO
Demonstrates palpatory examination and manipulative procedures for the lumbar spine with the patient in the seated position. Places emphasis on diagnostic information leading to improve localization of operator forces. Demonstrates both rotary and translatory types of motion testing.
From The Osteopathic Examination And Manipulation Series.
Prod-MSU Dist-MSU

Lumbar Spine I, The C 25 MIN
3/4 OR 1/2 INCH VIDEO CASSETTE
Offers 11 manipulative techniques for the treatment of the lumbar spine.
From The Cyriax On Orthopaedic Medicine Series.
Prod-VTRI Dist-VTRI

Lumbar Spine II, The C 22 MIN
3/4 OR 1/2 INCH VIDEO CASSETTE
Presents a non-manipulative treatment of disc lesions, including epidural local anaesthesia, traction and sclerosants.
From The Cyriax On Orthopaedic Medicine Series.
Prod-VTRI Dist-VTRI

Lumiere Years, The B 93 MIN
16MM FILM OPTICAL SOUND H-C A
Presents rare film footage of such historical events as the coronation of Czar Nicholas II, President McKinley preparing to invade Cuba and the Paris Exposition. Includes sequences from Europe, Africa, The Americas, Asia and India.
Prod-FI Dist-FI 1974

Luminare C 7 MIN
3/4 INCH VIDEO CASSETTE
Presents a visual tribute to video artist Ed Emshwiller that includes a surreal landscape, digitally transformed dancers, and a central scene that traces the history of art through a computerized gallery.
From The John Sanborn And Dean Winkler - Selected Works Series.
Prod-EAI Dist-EAI

Luminescence And Incandescence X 20 MIN
2 INCH VIDEOTAPE I
See series title for descriptive statement.
From The Process And Proof Series. No. 13
Prod-MCETV Dist-GPITVL Prodn-WVIZTV

Luminous Image, The C 56 MIN
3/4 OR 1/2 INCH VIDEO CASSETTE
Documents an international exhibition of video installations held in the fall of 1984 in Amsterdam. Presented by the Stedelijk Museum.
Prod-ARTINC Dist-ARTINC

Lumpy And Bumpy C 14 MIN
16MM FILM OPTICAL SOUND K-I
Follows Yoffy and his friends as they collect objects that are soft and objects that are hard.

From The Fingermouse, Yoffy And Friends Series.
LC NO. 73-700432
Prod-BBCTV Dist-VEDO 1972

Luna The Lovely C 18 MIN
16MM FILM, 3/4 OR 1/2 IN VIDEO J
Demonstrates basic laws of relativity and of physics with a story about a filmmaker who learns about time lapse in communications across great distances, spaceship power devices and travel at or near the speed of light, while making a science fiction movie.
From The Universe And I Series.
LC NO. 80-706483
Prod-KYTV Dist-AITECH 1977

Lunar Aspects C 29 MIN
3/4 INCH VIDEO CASSETTE C A
Explains the phases of the moon. Reviews basic data such as moon's size and distance from earth. Describes lunar and solar eclipses.
From The Project Universe - Astronomy Series. Lesson 3
Prod-COAST Dist-CDTEL Prodn-SCCON

Lunar Geology C 29 MIN
3/4 INCH VIDEO CASSETTE C A
Contrasts data about the moon gathered by telescope and by space programs. Describes types of rock found on the moon.
From The Project Universe - Astronomy Series. Lesson 7
Prod-COAST Dist-CDTEL Prodn-SCCON

Lunar Geology C 30 MIN
3/4 OR 1/2 INCH VIDEO CASSETTE C
Illustrates advances in lunar geology.
From The Earth, Sea And Sky Series.
Prod-DALCCD Dist-DALCCD

Lunar Landing - The Mission Of Surveyor 1 C 16 MIN
16MM FILM OPTICAL SOUND
Presents a documentary account of the Surveyor I mission to land on the moon and send back close-up photographs of the lunar terrain. Shows the launching and the method by which the photographs were received.
LC NO. 75-701346
Prod-NASA Dist-USNAC 1967

Lunar Landing 1 - The Eagle Has Landed C 55 MIN
3/4 INCH VIDEO CASSETTE J-C A
Presents archival footage of Neil Armstrong's landing on and exploration of the moon's surface.
From The NASA Tapes Series.
LC NO. 80-706111
Prod-NASA Dist-ASTROV 1979

Lunar Module, The C 5 MIN
16MM FILM - 3/4 IN VIDEO
Offers interior and exterior closeup views of the vehicle which was used in exploring the lunar surface. Issued in 1969 as a motion picture.
From The Apollo Digest Series.
LC NO. 79-706982
Prod-NASA Dist-USNAC 1979

Lunar Orbit Rendezvous C 21 MIN
16MM FILM OPTICAL SOUND
Discusses the groundwork conducted by the Mission Planning and Analysis Division in perfecting lunar rendezvous techniques.
Prod-NASA Dist-NASA

Lunar Receiving Lab C 8 MIN
3/4 INCH VIDEO CASSETTE
Shows the laboratory facilities of the Manned Spacecraft Center. Issued in 1969 as a motion picture.
From The Apollo Digest Series.
LC NO. 79-706984
Prod-NASA Dist-USNAC 1979

Lunar Samples Of Apollo Eleven C 8 MIN
3/4 INCH VIDEO CASSETTE
Examines results of the preliminary investigation of the lunar samples. Includes biological and chemical studies and the distribution of the lunar material.
Prod-NASA Dist-NASA 1972

Lunch Money C 6 MIN
16MM FILM, 3/4 OR 1/2 IN VIDEO I-J
Represents the problem of finding an article and assuring its return to the rightful owner.
From The What Should I Do Series.
Prod-DISNEY Dist-WDEMCO 1970

Lunch Money, The (French) C 6 MIN
16MM FILM, 3/4 OR 1/2 IN VIDEO P
Illustrates the disappearance of Susie's purse. Shows the need for personal integrity and honesty.
From The What Should I Do (French) Series.
Prod-WDEMCO Dist-WDEMCO 1970

Lunch Time With Babies C 13 MIN
3/4 INCH VIDEO CASSETTE C A
Observes children between the ages of three and 24 months of age as they eat lunch in a day care center. Discusses food preparation and nutritional information and describes how children play with food and utensils.
LC NO. 81-706223
Prod-CUETV Dist-CUNIV 1981

Lunch With John Campbell, Jr - An Editor At Work C 28 MIN
16MM FILM OPTICAL SOUND C A
John W Campbell, Jr, late editor of Analog, discusses with Gordon Dickson and Harry Harrison the development of plot, theme and characters of a new story.
From The Literature Of Science Fiction Series.
LC NO. 72-700537
Prod-UKANBC Dist-UKANS 1972

Lunchroom Etiquette (2nd Ed) C 10 MIN
16MM FILM, 3/4 OR 1/2 IN VIDEO I
Shows a variety of lunchroom situations and a variety of responses. Contrasts the positive and the not-so-positive responses to demonstrate the advantages of good manners. Deals with washing hands before eating, orderliness in line, carrying trays carefully, keeping the noise level low, and cleaning up after oneself.
Prod-AIMS Dist-AIMS 1982

Lung Cancer - Early Diagnosis And Management C 18 MIN
16MM FILM OPTICAL SOUND PRO
Shows physicians the preventive, diagnostic, and therapeutic measures by which they can help reduce the rising rates of morbidity and mortality from lung cancer.
LC NO. 72-700666
Prod-AMCS Dist-AMCS 1969

Lung Scanning In Pulmonary Disease C 35 MIN
16MM FILM OPTICAL SOUND PRO
Demonstrates lung scanning as a valuable new diagnostic tool. Shows it aiding the radiologist in the interpretation of chest films and angiograms and serving as a screening procedure for routine or selective pulmonary angiography.
LC NO. 77-707689
Prod-SQUIBB Dist-SQUIBB Prodn-BURKEB 1967

Lung Scanning In Pulmonary Diseases C 38 MIN
3/4 OR 1/2 INCH VIDEO CASSETTE PRO
Prod-PRIMED Dist-PRIMED

Lung Ventilation Scan C
3/4 OR 1/2 INCH VIDEO CASSETTE
See series title for descriptive statement.
From The X-Ray Procedures In Layman's Terms Series.
Prod-FAIRGH Dist-FAIRGH

Lungless Salamanders, The C 16 MIN
16MM FILM, 3/4 OR 1/2 IN VIDEO J-C
Examines the adaptive features of the lungless salamanders. Demonstrates the respiratory pattern of a typical lunged salamander and describes the probable events which led to the loss of lungs in plethodontids.
From The Aspects Of Animal Behavior Series.
Prod-UCLA Dist-UCEMC 1979

Lungs C 10 MIN
3/4 OR 1/2 INCH VIDEO CASSETTE H-C
Covers a step by step study of the lung in which the commentary points out important features as they are revealed by the scientist doing the dissection. Shows sequence of lungs of a living animal filmed by x-ray photography.
Prod-EDMI Dist-EDMI 1982

Lungs And Removal Of The Heart C 10 MIN
16MM FILM, 3/4 OR 1/2 IN VIDEO C A
Focuses on the thoracic region. Demonstrates the dissection of the lungs and the removal of the heart.
From The Guides To Dissection Series.
Prod-UCLA Dist-TEF

Lungs And Respiratory System, The C 17 MIN
16MM FILM, 3/4 OR 1/2 IN VIDEO I-J
Describes the structure and functions of the human respiratory system and explains how the exchange of oxygen and carbon dioxide gases takes place in the lungs.
Prod-EBEC Dist-EBEC 1975

Lungs, The - An Inside Story C 11 MIN
16MM FILM, 3/4 OR 1/2 IN VIDEO J
Uses models and endoscopic photography within a human lung to reveal the structure of the lungs and how it affects their efficiency.
Prod-CORF Dist-CORF 1976

Lupinek Case, The C 51 MIN
16MM FILM, 3/4 OR 1/2 IN VIDEO I-J
Tells how four talented children, guided by adults, operate a successful hand puppet theater. Shows how, when the puppets are stolen, the kids organize a search for the puppets, using techniques they remember from detective stories.
From The Featurettes For Children Series.
Prod-AUDBRF Dist-FI

Lupus - Wolf In Disguise C 25 MIN
3/4 OR 1/2 INCH VIDEO CASSETTE
Explores ways to diagnose and treat the unusual disease of Lupus.
Prod-TRAINX Dist-TRAINX

Lure Of Empire, The - America Debates Imperialism C 27 MIN
16MM FILM, 3/4 OR 1/2 IN VIDEO J-H A
Gives an account of the annexation of the Philippines. Shows the debate on the floor of Congress over these islands, gained by chance during the United States' war with Spain to free Cuba.
Prod-LCOA Dist-LCOA 1974

Lure Of Empire, The - America Debates Imperialism (Spanish) C 27 MIN
16MM FILM, 3/4 OR 1/2 IN VIDEO J-C A
Recreates the agony and self-searching that preceded America's turn to expansionism. Tells of the annexation of the Philippines.
Prod-LCOA Dist-LCOA 1974

Lure Of The Everest C 30 MIN
16MM FILM OPTICAL SOUND I-C A
Records the attempts made by the Indian expedition of 1960 to conquer Everest. Highlights the elaborate preliminary arrangements and the camps set up at various heights.
Prod-INDIA Dist-NEDINF

Lure Of The Lakes C
16MM FILM OPTICAL SOUND
Shows Roger Latham fishing the TVA Kentucky Lakes.
Prod-WMC Dist-WMC

Lure Of Water, The C 11 MIN
3/4 INCH VIDEO CASSETTE
Illustrates the dangers associated with recreation along the California State Water Project. Shows some of the more scenic places to enjoy while encouraging the safe use of the Project's many lakes and miles of aqueduct and bicycle trails.
Prod-CSDWR Dist-CALDWR

Lures Of Death, The C 15 MIN
16MM FILM, 3/4 OR 1/2 IN VIDEO P-C A
Examines the deceptive lures child killers use to entice their victims into a trap of kidnapping, sexual abuse, torture or even death.
Prod-ABCTV Dist-MTI

Lures Of The Market Place C 18 MIN
16MM FILM OPTICAL SOUND
Examines a variety of advertising practices.
From The Consumer Game Series.
LC NO. 74-701193
Prod-OECA Dist-OECA 1972

Luristan C 14 MIN
16MM FILM OPTICAL SOUND
A Danish language film. Presents an example of a half-nomadic civilization. Shows that the people live in a small village during the winter but during the summer the village is deserted, man and beast are on the plateau where they move from place to place to find pasture.
Prod-STATNS Dist-STATNS 1966

Lusers, The C 15 MIN
16MM FILM, 3/4 OR 1/2 IN VIDEO J-C A
Presents Peter Hackes who reveals how to make a diet a real success by changing eating habits and increasing physical exercise. Discusses antistress foods, the memory diet, and creativity in dieting.
Prod-KLEINW Dist-KLEINW 1977

Luther And The Reformation C 60 MIN
3/4 OR 1/2 INCH VIDEO CASSETTE J-C A
Presents flutist James Galway discussing the impact of the reformation on the history of music, focusing on the work of J S Bach and the importance of church organs and chorale singing.
From The James Galway's Music In Time Series.
LC NO. 83-706261
Prod-POLTEL Dist-FOTH 1982

Luther Burbank B 5 MIN
16MM FILM OPTICAL SOUND
Presents a 1954 Screen News Digest excerpt to recall the genius of Luther Burbank, after his death. Depicts many results of his experimentation--the spineless cacti, the Burbank potatoe and pollination of flowers.
From The News Magazine Of The Screen Series. Vol 5, No. 3
Prod-PATHE Dist-HEARST 1954

Luther Metke At 94 C 27 MIN
16MM FILM, 3/4 OR 1/2 IN VIDEO
Profiles Luther Metke, who has lived in the Cascade Mountains of Oregon since 1907. Tells how he was a veteran of the Spanish American War, an early labor organizer, and a builder. Explains that he is an example of the rural ethic in America.
Prod-UCLA Dist-NWDIMF 1979

Lutherans And Jews - A Dialogue C
3/4 OR 1/2 INCH VIDEO CASSETTE J A
Presents a discussion between Rabbi Marc Tanenbaum and Luther scholar Dr George Forell. Discusses how Lutheran and Jewish scholars are dealing with Luther's often vitriolic attitudes toward Jews and how religious groups are helping to bring about greater tolerance today.
Prod-ABCVID Dist-ECUFLM 1983

LVN Public Service Announcement Sampler C
3/4 INCH VIDEO CASSETTE
Presents a sampler for preview of the public service announcements produced for Maryland libraries. Updated regularly.
Prod-LVN Dist-LVN

Lycidas C 18 MIN
16MM FILM, 3/4 OR 1/2 IN VIDEO
Presents an adaptation of the elegy Lycidas by John Milton. Combines paintings and music with a dramatic reading of the poem.
Prod-BIERJH Dist-UCEMC 1977

Lying C 13 MIN
16MM FILM, 3/4 OR 1/2 IN VIDEO P-I
Tells how the gang learns that Eddie is a liar. Points out how lying can spoil friendships.
From The Learning Values With Fat Albert Series.
Prod-FLMTON Dist-CRMP 1977

Lying And Cheating C 29 MIN
3/4 OR 1/2 INCH VIDEO CASSETTE A
Discusses the problems that parents and schools face with dishonesty. Features Dr Salk's discussions with six graders regarding their ideas about lying and its relationship to self-respect.
From The Feelings Series.
Prod-SCETV Dist-PBS 1979

Lyman H Howe's High Class Moving Pictures C 28 MIN
16MM FILM, 3/4 OR 1/2 IN VIDEO A
Portrays the career of Lyman H Howe, a travelling exhibitor who brought motion pictures to America's towns and cities in the infancy of movies. Includes excerpts from some of Howe's own productions.
Prod-CNEMAG Dist-CNEMAG 1983

Lymphatic System, The C 15 MIN
16MM FILM, 3/4 OR 1/2 IN VIDEO
Discusses the relationship between the circulatory and the lymphatic systems. Describes the nature of lymph and how it moves through the body. Explains the function of the lymphatic system and shows the flow of lymph through the lymphatic vessels.
LC NO. 80-706177
Prod-IFFB Dist-IFB 1979

Lymphography In Female Genital Cancer C 25 MIN
16MM FILM OPTICAL SOUND
Follows the diagnosis and treatment of genital malignancy in patients at the University of Miami School of Medicine. Demonstrates the application of direct lymphography in the treatment of carcinoma of the vulva and relates the results of the lymphadenectomy operation.
LC NO. FIA66-52
Prod-EATONL Dist-EATONL Prodn-AVCORP 1964

Lymphoproliferative Lesions Of Salivary Glands And Upper Airways C 55 MIN
3/4 INCH VIDEO CASSETTE
Presents lymphoproliferative lesions, their systemic consequences and lymphomas of the head and neck.
Prod-UTAHTI Dist-UTAHTI

Lyn Blumenthal - Social Studies, Pt 1, Horizontes C 20 MIN
3/4 OR 1/2 INCH VIDEO CASSETTE
Presents a Cuban soap opera.
Prod-ARTINC Dist-ARTINC

Lyn Blumenthal - Social Studies, Pt 2, The Academy C 18 MIN
3/4 OR 1/2 INCH VIDEO CASSETTE
Suggests aggression, sexism and bigotry, Pictures an Academy Award stage.
Prod-ARTINC Dist-ARTINC

Lynda Benglis - Female Sensibility C 14 MIN
3/4 OR 1/2 INCH VIDEO CASSETTE
Challenges patriarchal standards.
Prod-ARTINC Dist-ARTINC

Lynda Benglis - Mumble B 20 MIN
3/4 OR 1/2 INCH VIDEO CASSETTE
Presented by Lynda Benglis.
Prod-ARTINC Dist-ARTINC

Lyndon B Johnson B 17 MIN
3/4 OR 1/2 INCH VIDEO CASSETTE
Traces the life of Lyndon Baines Johnson from his humble birth in 1908 to the beginning of his Presidency in 1963.
Prod-KINGFT Dist-KINGFT

Lyndon Johnson And The Tragedy Of Vietnam C 29 MIN
2 INCH VIDEOTAPE
See series title for descriptive statement.
From The Course Of Our Times II Series.
Prod-WGBHTV Dist-PUBTEL

M

M (German) B 95 MIN
3/4 OR 1/2 INCH VIDEO CASSETTE
Presents Peter Lorre as a notorious child killer hunted by the police and the underworld. Directed by Fritz Lang.
Prod-IHF Dist-IHF

M (Searching For A Victim) B 12 MIN
16MM FILM OPTICAL SOUND J-C A
Presents an excerpt from the 1931 motion picture M. Depicts the child murderer, played by Peter Lorre, whistling obsessively as he stalks his new victim. Directed by Fritz Lang.
From The Film Study Extracts Series.
Prod-UNKNWN Dist-FI

M A R C C 14 MIN
16MM FILM OPTICAL SOUND
Describes research being performed at the United States Meat Animal Research Center, whose goal is the development of new technology to increase the supply of high-quality red meats.
LC NO. 80-700766
Prod-USDA Dist-USNAC 1979

M I G-Fillet-Vert-Down Fillet And Butt Welds C 8 MIN
1/2 IN VIDEO CASSETTE BETA/VHS IND
See series title for descriptive statement.
From The Arc Welding And M I G Welding Series.
Prod-RMI Dist-RMI

M Machine Language C 50 MIN
3/4 OR 1/2 INCH VIDEO CASSETTE
Discusses addressing modes, instruction formats and types of instructions.
From The Computer Languages - Pt 1 Series.
Prod-MIOT Dist-MIOT

M R - Mental Retardation C 50 MIN
16MM FILM OPTICAL SOUND
Presents a survey of Wisconsin's mental retardation program, which demonstrates ways of coping with the condition of mental retardation and its many problems. Shows techniques of PKU testing and research in genetics, a multidisciplined approach to diagnosis and management, examples of severe retardation and recent advances in treatment. Depicts methods of handling the trainable and educable retarded, with emphasis on keeping the children at home.
Prod-VASSAR Dist-NYU

M Sound C 14 MIN
3/4 OR 1/2 INCH VIDEO CASSETTE K
See series title for descriptive statement.
From The I-Land Treasure Series.
Prod-NETCHE Dist-AITECH 1980

M Sound, The - Maybe The Mouse Might C 15 MIN
2 INCH VIDEOTAPE P
Introduces some of the consonant sounds met in early reading. Identifies the written letter with the spoken sound.
From The Listen And Say Series.
Prod-MPATI Dist-GPITVL

M-Sixty-Eight Hundred Hardware - ACIA, PIA B 60 MIN
3/4 OR 1/2 INCH VIDEO CASSETTE
See series title for descriptive statement.
From The Understanding Microprocessors Series. Pt 10
Prod-UAZMIC Dist-UAZMIC 1979

M-Sixty-Eight Hundred Hardware - MPU, RAM, ROM B 60 MIN
3/4 OR 1/2 INCH VIDEO CASSETTE
See series title for descriptive statement.
From The Understanding Microprocessors Series. Pt 9
Prod-UAZMIC Dist-UAZMIC 1979

Ma Liang And The Magic Brush C 15 MIN
3/4 OR 1/2 INCH VIDEO CASSETTE P-I
Tells The Chinese tale of how Ma Liang, rewarded for his hard work with a brush that makes everything he paints become real, outsmarts a greedy emperor and uses his magic brush for the good of his people.
From The Sixteen Tales Series.
Prod-KLCSTV Dist-AITECH

Ma Province, Mes Chansons C 14 MIN
16MM FILM OPTICAL SOUND
A French language film. Jacques Labrecque, one of Quebec's best-known folksingers, sings folksongs of French Canada which reflect the spirit and traditions of the province and village life.
Prod-CTFL Dist-CTFL 1964

Ma'bugi' - Trance Of The Toraja C 21 MIN
16MM FILM, 3/4 OR 1/2 IN VIDEO H-C
Documents a religious trance ritual practiced in the Toraja highlands of Indonesia in order to restore health and prosperity to an afflicted village community.
Prod-CRYRHD Dist-UCEMC 1974

Ma's Motors C 28 MIN
16MM FILM OPTICAL SOUND
Portrays a disabled boy's struggle in Taiwan for a chance to learn auto mechanics at Ma's Motors.
Prod-MARYFA Dist-MTP 1982

MAA Calculus—A Series

Prod-MAA Dist-MLA 1967

Area Under A Curve	10 MIN
Continuity Of Mappings	10 MIN
Definite Integral As A Limit, The	10 MIN
Definite Integral, The	21 MIN
Function Is A Mapping, A	10 MIN
Fundamental Theorem Of The Calculus	10 MIN
I Maximize	10 MIN
Infinite Acres	10 MIN
Limit	10 MIN
Newton's Method	10 MIN
Theorem Of The Mean, The	10 MIN
Volume By Shells	8 MIN
Volume Of A Solid Of Revolution	8 MIN
What Is Area	20 MIN

MAA Elementary Arithemtic—A Series

Designed for use with a college course in arithmetic for prospective elementary school teachers. Can also be used for in-service teacher training and for instruction of children in arithmetic classes. Uses animation and music to show relationships between abstract arithmetic ideas and situations in daily life.
Prod-MAA Dist-MLA 1967

Addition And Subtraction	7 MIN
Counting	9 MIN
Multiplication And Division	7 MIN
One To One Correspondence	10 MIN
Sets - Union And Intrasection	7 MIN
What Is A Set, Pt 1	7 MIN
What Is A Set, Pt 2	7 MIN

MAA Individual Lecturers—A Series

Consists of lectures on mathematical concepts of use to those with little mathematical knowledge, college under-graduates and advanced mathematicians. The intended audience for each title is indicated in the individual annotation.
Prod-MAA Dist-MLA 1966

Applications Of Group Theory In	60 ...
Can You Hear The Shape Of A Drum	49 MIN
Can You Hear The Shape Of A Drum	67 MIN
Challenge In The Classroom - The Methods Of	55 MIN
Challenging Conjectures	40 MIN
Classical Groups As A Source Of	65 MIN
Differential Topology, Lecture 1	60 MIN
Differential Topology, Lecture 2	60 MIN
Differential Topology, Lecture 3	60 MIN
Fixed Points	60 MIN
Gottingen And New York - Reflections On A	43 MIN
John Von Neumann	63 MIN
Kakeya Problem, The	60 MIN
Let Us Teach Guessing	61 MIN
Mathematical Induction, Pt 1	30 MIN
Mathematical Induction, Pt 2	30 MIN
Measure And Set Theory	47 MIN
Mr Simplex Saves The Aspidistra	33 MIN
Nim And Other Oriented Graph Games	63 MIN
Pits, Peaks And Passes, A Lecture On Critical	48 MIN
Pits, Peaks And Passes, A Lecture On Critical	26 MIN
Predicting At Random	43 MIN
Search For Solid Ground, The	62 MIN
Theory Of Limits, Pt 1, Limits Of Sequences	34 MIN
Theory Of Limits, Pt 2, Limits Of Functions	25 MIN
Theory Of Limits, Pt 3, The Cauchy Criterion	13 MIN
Topology	30 MIN
What Is An Integral, Pt 1, Integrals	29 MIN
What Is An Integral, Pt 2, Averages	29 MIN
What Is Mathematics And How Do We Teach It	60 MIN

MAA Mathematics—A Series
C A
Prod-MAA Dist-MLA 1974

Applications Of The Marriage Theorem	47 MIN
Matching Theory - The Marriage Theorem	46 MIN
Singular Perturbation Theory	50 MIN

Mac Donald's Farm - Animals Go To School C 11 MIN
16MM FILM, 3/4 OR 1/2 IN VIDEO P-I
Show two children on a farm who see animals performing unusual demonstrations of the behavior concept of learning based on the stimulus-response-reward principle.
Prod-AIMS Dist-AIMS 1971

Mac Remembers Place Value - Place Value C 15 MIN
3/4 OR 1/2 INCH VIDEO CASSETTE I
Tells the story of Alice's race to restore her computer friend's memory. Introduces the significance of place value and the meaning of the digit's location in a number.
From The Figure Out Series.
Prod-MAETEL Dist-AITECH 1982

Mac Subtracts In Jail - Subtraction Of Hundreds, Single Regrouping C 15 MIN
3/4 OR 1/2 INCH VIDEO CASSETTE I
Demonstrates subtraction with only one regrouping, using the story of Mac's undercover venture to capture a computer embezzler.
From The Figure Out Series.
Prod-MAETEL Dist-AITECH 1982

Mac's Fame Is Multiplied - Multiplication, Two Digits Times Three Digits C 15 MIN
3/4 OR 1/2 INCH VIDEO CASSETTE I
Uses the story of Mac's campaign for mayor to introduce the hand-held calculator and explain how to estimate the answer before using a calculator.
From The Figure Out Series.
Prod-MAETEL Dist-AITECH 1982

Mac's Mill C 12 MIN
16MM FILM, 3/4 OR 1/2 IN VIDEO J-C A
Focuses on a New Brunswick resident who runs a waterpowered mill built in 1909. Discusses balanced ecology, intelligent use of natural resources, and the possibility of earning a living without the aid of 20th century technology.
LC NO. 83-706291
Prod-NFBC Dist-BULFRG 1976

Macaroni, Nutrition And Numbers C 13 MIN
16MM FILM OPTICAL SOUND J-C A
Demonstrates the process of labeling the nutritional content of various foods.
Prod-NMI Dist-MTP

Macbeth C 11 MIN
16MM FILM, 3/4 OR 1/2 IN VIDEO H-C
See series title for descriptive statement.
From The Shakespeare Series.
Prod-IFB Dist-IFB 1974

Macbeth C 30 MIN
3/4 OR 1/2 INCH VIDEO CASSETTE J-C A
Presents an adaptation of Shakespeare's play Macbeth, the tragic story of an upright man, goaded by his ambition, and of the mental torment resulting from his crime. Includes the plays Julius Caesar, Romeo And Juliet and Hamlet on the same tape.
From The Shakespeare In Perspective Series.
Prod-FI Dist-FI 1984

Macbeth C 36 MIN
16MM FILM, 3/4 OR 1/2 IN VIDEO
Presents an adaptation of William Shakespeare's play Macbeth
From The World Of William Shakespeare Series.
LC NO. 80-706323
Prod-NGS Dist-NGS 1978

Macbeth C 60 MIN
3/4 OR 1/2 INCH VIDEO CASSETTE H-C A
Explores methods of character development. Uses the play Macbeth as an example.
From The Drama - Play, Performance, Perception Series. Dramatis Personae
Prod-BBCTV Dist-FI 1978

Macbeth C 148 MIN
3/4 OR 1/2 INCH VIDEO CASSETTE H-C A
Presents the play Macbeth by William Shakespeare about a warrior who is told by a trio of witches that he is fated to become King of Scotland and, therefore, with the aid of his wife, murders the king and assumes his throne. Reveals that the new king and his wife embark on a guilt-ridden reign of terror, murdering former friends and striking down the families of their adversaries.
From The Shakespeare Plays Series.
Prod-BBCTV Dist-TIMLIF 1984

Macbeth C 148 MIN
3/4 OR 1/2 INCH VIDEO CASSETTE
Presents an American production of the Shakespearean play Macbeth, directed by Sarah Caldwell and starring Philip Anglim.
Prod-FOTH Dist-FOTH 1984

Macbeth - Act I, Scene VII C 8 MIN
16MM FILM, 3/4 OR 1/2 IN VIDEO I-C A
Presents a lively form of entertainment which enables the viewer to focus on the atmosphere and theme of Shakespeare's Macbeth.
From The Great Scenes From Shakespeare Series.
Prod-SEABEN Dist-PHENIX 1971

Macbeth - An Introduction C 26 MIN
16MM FILM, 3/4 OR 1/2 IN VIDEO J A
Presents a version of Shakespeare's play 'MACBETH' Used narration to help bridge the transitions between the main sequences in the play.
From The Shakespeare Series.
Prod-SEABEN Dist-PHENIX 1968

Macbeth, Pt 1 - The Politics Of Power C 28 MIN
16MM FILM, 3/4 OR 1/2 IN VIDEO H-C
Interprets and points out the relationships of the characters in the play Macbeth. Discusses the witches and the Monarch Duncan and considers how it is possible to portray Macbeth as a brutal murderer who remains a tragic hero. Narrated by Douglas Campbell.
From The Humanities - The Drama Series.
Prod-EBF Dist-EBEC 1964

Macbeth, Pt 2 - The Themes Of Macbeth C 28 MIN
16MM FILM, 3/4 OR 1/2 IN VIDEO H-C
Studies how the entire play is built on the paradox, 'Nothing is but what is not.' Explains that the world of Macbeth is one in which appearances cannot be trusted. Narrated by Douglas Campbell.
From The Humanities - The Drama Series.
Prod-EBF Dist-EBEC 1964

Macbeth, Pt 3 - The Secret'st Man C 33 MIN
16MM FILM, 3/4 OR 1/2 IN VIDEO H-C
Emphasizes the capacity for good and evil within the same human heart. Macbeth reiterates that 'everyman is the secret'st man of blood.' Narrated by Douglas Campbell.
From The Humanities - The Drama Series.
Prod-EBF Dist-EBEC 1964

Macedonia Baptist Choir C 29 MIN
2 INCH VIDEOTAPE
Presents the Macedonia Baptist Choir performing God Is, Blessed Be The Name, I'll Do His Will and We've Come A Long Way.
From The Changing Rhythms Series.
Prod-KRMATV Dist-PUBTEL

Mache Sculpture C 13 MIN
16MM FILM OPTICAL SOUND I-C A
Shows the techniques which can be used to create a variety of objects using papier-mache.
LC NO. 74-703049
Prod-AVED Dist-AVED 1974

MacHenry C 5 MIN
3/4 OR 1/2 INCH VIDEO CASSETTE J-H
Presents a lesson in diction. Discusses the use of 'Awful' and 'Terrible' and 'Nice'.
From The Write On, Set 2 Series.
Prod-CTI Dist-CTI

Machinability, No. 1 C 30 MIN
2 INCH VIDEOTAPE IND
Illustrates how to turn fixtures and check and cut.
From The Basic Machine Shop Practices Series.
Prod-VTETV Dist-GPITVL

Machinability, No. 2 C 30 MIN
2 INCH VIDEOTAPE IND
Illustrates milling, milling fixtures, checking tools, cutting tools and operator steps.
From The Basic Machine Shop Practices Series.
Prod-VTETV Dist-GPITVL

Machinability, No. 3 C 30 MIN
2 INCH VIDEOTAPE IND
Illustrates grinding, grinding fixtures, checking tools, cutting tools and operator tools.
From The Basic Machine Shop Practices Series.
Prod-VTETV Dist-GPITVL

Machinability, No. 4 C 30 MIN
2 INCH VIDEOTAPE IND
Illustrates drilling and reaming, fixture, checking tools, cutting tools and operator steps.
From The Basic Machine Shop Practices Series.
Prod-VTETV Dist-GPITVL

Machine C 10 MIN
16MM FILM SILENT J A
A deftly animated allegory on man and his inventions.
LC NO. 70-712365
Prod-JANUS Dist-VIEWFI 1966

Machine - Master Or Slave B 14 MIN
16MM FILM OPTICAL SOUND H-C T
Uses a factory to illustrate problems management faces with the human and financial factors of technology. Asks such questions as, how can management coordinate its own self-interest with the needs of employees and consumers.
Prod-NYU Dist-NYU 1941

Machine Age, The C 28 MIN
16MM FILM, 3/4 OR 1/2 IN VIDEO J-H
Tells the story of a rookie policeman escorting a runaway back to her orphanage. Describes how the policeman is torn between his responsibility and his growing attachment for the girl.
LC NO. 82-706208
Prod-NFBC Dist-FI 1978

Machine At Work, The C 14 MIN
3/4 OR 1/2 INCH VIDEO CASSETTE
Explains how the computer can handle the basic record-keeping functions of any business. Shows examples such as invoicing, inventory control, financial planning, graphics and word processing.
From The You And Your Personal Computer Series. Pt II
Prod-VISUCP Dist-VISUCP

Machine Drawings C 12 MIN
3/4 OR 1/2 INCH VIDEO CASSETTE
Covers clutch-brake control, assembly drawing, drafting technique for gear trains and other aspects of machine tools.
From The Reading Blueprints Series.
Prod-TPCTRA Dist-TPCTRA

Machine Drawings (Spanish) C 12 MIN
3/4 OR 1/2 INCH VIDEO CASSETTE
Covers clutch - brake control, assembly drawing, drafting technique for gear trains and other aspects of machine tools.
From The Reading Blueprints Series.
Prod-TPCTRA Dist-TPCTRA

Machine For Living B 29 MIN
2 INCH VIDEOTAPE
See series title for descriptive statement.
From The Design 2000 Series.
Prod-WITFTV Dist-PUBTEL

Machine Keyways On The Vertical Milling Machine (Straight And Woodruff) C
3/4 OR 1/2 INCH VIDEO CASSETTE
See series title for descriptive statement.
From The Milling And Tool Sharpening (Spanish) Series.
Prod-VTRI Dist-VTRI

Machine Keyways On The Vertical Milling Machine (Straight And Woodruff) (Spanish) C
3/4 OR 1/2 INCH VIDEO CASSETTE
See series title for descriptive statement.
From The Milling And Tool Sharpening Series.
Prod-VTRI Dist-VTRI

Machine Language C 55 MIN
3/4 OR 1/2 INCH VIDEO CASSETTE
See series title for descriptive statement.
From The Computer Languages - Pt 2 Series.
Prod-MIOT Dist-MIOT

Machine Language Programming, Pt 1 B 45 MIN
2 INCH VIDEOTAPE
See series title for descriptive statement.
From The Data Processing, Unit 3 - Instructing The Computer Series.
Prod-GPITVL Dist-GPITVL

Machine Language Programming, Pt 2 B 45 MIN
2 INCH VIDEOTAPE
See series title for descriptive statement.
From The Data Processing, Unit 3 - Instructing The Computer Series.
Prod-GPITVL Dist-GPITVL

Machine Language Programming, Pt 3 B 45 MIN
2 INCH VIDEOTAPE
See series title for descriptive statement.
From The Data Processing, Unit 3 - Instructing The Computer Series.
Prod-GPITVL Dist-GPITVL

Machine Operations - Sheet Metal C 13 MIN
16MM FILM, 3/4 OR 1/2 IN VIDEO J-H
Sheet metal work--the bar folder, slip-role former, standard brake and box, pan brake and hand forming.
From The Metalwork - Machine Operation Series.
Prod-MORLAT Dist-SF 1967

Machine Parts C 12 MIN
3/4 OR 1/2 INCH VIDEO CASSETTE
Shows six simple machines and a variety of machine parts including heads, rivets, welds, pins and others.
From The Reading Blueprints Series.
Prod-TPCTRA Dist-TPCTRA

Machine Parts (Spanish) C 12 MIN
3/4 OR 1/2 INCH VIDEO CASSETTE
Shows six simple machines and a variety of machine parts including heads, rivets, welds, pins and others.
From The Reading Blueprints Series.
Prod-TPCTRA Dist-TPCTRA

Machine Setup And Safety C 14 MIN
3/4 OR 1/2 INCH VIDEO CASSETTE IND
Covers cold start procedures, safety practices and features of the machine, establishing an origin point and determining tool length offsets.
From The Numerical Control/Computerized Numerical Control, Module 1 - Fundamentals Series.
Prod-LEIKID Dist-LEIKID

Machine Shop - Bandsaw—A Series
IND
Provides individualized training units on measurement and layout, and operational procedures on the bandsaw, drill press, engine lathe, surface grinder and milling machine. Assists the student in obtaining the necessary skills needed to qualify for employment as a machine operator, machine apprentice and tool and die apprentice. Teaches proper machine operation and relevant safety procedures.
Prod-RMI Dist-RMI

Safety And Familiarization On The	
Safety And Familiarization On The Vertical	025 MIN
Welding Bandsaw Blades	022 MIN

Machine Shop - C N C Machine Operations—A Series
IND
Provides individualized training units on measurement and layout and operational procedures on the bandsaw, drill press, engine lathe, surface grinder, and milling machine. Assists the student in obtaining the necessary skills needed to qualify for employment as a machine operator, machine apprentice, and tool and die apprentice. Teaches proper machine operation and relevant safety procedures.
Prod-RMI Dist-RMI

Bridgeport Series I, C N C Basic Set-Up And	
Bridgeport Series I, C N C Familiarization	029 MIN
Bridgeport Series II Milling Machine	021 MIN
Numerical Control No. 1 - Introduction To A	008 MIN
Numerical Control No. 2 - Setup Of Machine	019 MIN
Numerical Control No. 3 - Tape Controlled	005 MIN
Programming C N C - Absolute	014 MIN
Programming C N C - Incremental	023 MIN
Programming C N C, Circular Interpolation	020 MIN
Programming C N C, Drilling Cycles	019 MIN
Programming C N C, Special Milling Cycles	016 MIN
Repetitive Programming	015 MIN

Machine Shop - Cylindrical Grinder—A Series
IND
Provides individualized training units on measurement and layout, and operational procedures on the bandsaw, drill press, engine lathe, surface grinder and milling machine. Assists the student in obtaining the necessary skills to qualify for employment as a machine operator, machine apprentice and tool and die apprentice. Teaches proper machine operation and relevant safety procedures.
Prod-RMI Dist-RMI

Cylindrical Grinder No. 1 - Basic Setup	
Cylindrical Grinder No. 2 - Shoulder Grinding	014 MIN

Machine Shop - Drill Press, Radial Drill, Drill Grinder—A Series
IND
Provides individualized training units on measurement and layout, and operational procedures on the bandsaw, drill press, engine lathe, surface grinder and milling machine. Assists the student in obtaining the necessary skills needed to qualify for employment as a machine operator, machine apprentice and tool and die apprentice. Teaches proper machine operation and relevant safety procedures.
Prod-RMI Dist-RMI

Drill Grinder No. 1, Block Diamond Model 0	012 MIN
Hand Sharpening A Drill	016 MIN
Radial Drill No. 1, Familiarization And Basic	022 MIN
Radial Drill No. 2, Production, Drilling,	022 MIN
Safety And Familiarization On Radial Arm	026 MIN
Sharpening A Drill On The Drill Grinder	016 MIN

Machine Shop - Engine Lathe—A Series
IND
Provides individualized training units on measurement and layout, and operational procedures on the bandsaw, drill press, engine lathe, surface grinder and milling machine. Assists the student in obtaining the necessary skills needed to qualify for employment as a machine operator, machine apprentice and tool and die apprentice. Teaches proper machine operation and relevant safety procedures.
Prod-RMI Dist-RMI

Cutting External Threads On The Engine Lathe	039 MIN
Cutting Tapers Using The Compound Rest	021 MIN
Cutting Tapers Using The Tailstock Offset	023 MIN
Cutting Tapers Using The Taper Attachment	020 MIN
Drilling On The Lathe	018 MIN
Engine Lathe No. 14, Cutting Threads With A	012 MIN
Engine Lathe No. 16, Cutting Internal Threads	021 MIN
Engine Lathe No. 17, Aligning The Tailstock	013 MIN
Engine Lathe No. 19, Mounting Cylindrical	013 MIN
Engine Lathe No. 20, Mounting Rectangular	016 MIN
Engine Lathe No. 21, Measuring Screw Threads	010 MIN
Engine Lathe No. 22, Principles Of Cutting-Off	015 MIN
Facing And Center Drilling	017 MIN
Grinding A Right-Hand Turning Tool	026 MIN
Grinding Lathe Centers With The Tool Post	021 MIN
Knurling	012 MIN
Safety And Familiarization On The Clausing	025 MIN
Safety And Familiarization On The LeBlond	022 MIN
Safety And Familiarization On The South	030 MIN
Tapping Threads On The Engine Lathe	022 MIN
Turning Between Centers	040 MIN
Using The Four-Jaw Chuck	013 MIN
Using The Three-Jaw Chuck	026 MIN

Machine Shop - Jig Boring Operation—A Series
IND
Provides individualized training units on measurement and layout, and operational procedures on the bandsaw, drill press, engine lathe, surface grinder and milling machine. Assists the student in obtaining the necessary skills needed to qualify for employment as a machine operator, machine apprentice and tool and die apprentice. Teaches proper machine operation and relevant safety procedures.
Prod-RMI Dist-RMI

Jig Boring Operation No. 1 - Locating Lines	
Jig Boring Operation No. 2 - Locating From	019 MIN
Jig Boring Operation No. 3 - Locating From	022 MIN
Jig Boring Operation No. 4 - Locating Holes	022 MIN
Jig Boring Operation No. 5 - Boring Head	019 MIN

Jig Boring Operation No. 6 - Precise Edge 014 MIN

Machine Shop - Layout—A Series
IND
Provides individualized training units on measurement and layout, and operational procedures on the bandsaw, drill press, engine lathe, surface grinder and milling machine. Assists the student in obtaining the necessary skills needed to receive employment as a machine operator, machine apprentice and tool and die apprentice. Teaches proper machine operation and relevant safety procedures.
Prod-RMI Dist-RMI

Basic Layout Procedures 012 MIN
Layout No. 1 - Hole Location 019 MIN
Layout No. 2 - Contours And Angles 019 MIN
Layout No. 3 - Surface Plate 014 MIN

Machine Shop - Measurement—A Series
IND
Provides individualized training units on measurement and layout, and operational procedures on the bandsaw, drill press, engine lathe, surface grinder and milling machine. Assists the student in obtaining the necessary skills needed to receive employment as a machine operator, machine apprentice and tool and die apprentice. Teaches the proper machine operational practices and relevant safety information.
Prod-RMI Dist-RMI

Geometric Form And Positional Tolerancing 020 MIN
How To Read A Metric Micrometer 020 MIN
How To Read A Vernier Caliper 016 MIN
Use And Care Of The Micrometer 019 MIN

Machine Shop - Milling Machine—A Series
IND
Provides individualized training units on measurement and layout and operational procedures on the bandsaw, drill press, engine lathe, surface grinder, and milling machine. Assists the student in obtaining the necessary skills needed to qualify for employment as a machine operator, machine apprentice, and tool and die apprentice. Teaches proper machine operation and relevant safety procedures.
Prod-RMI Dist-RMI

Basic Mill Setup No. 1 - Clamping Procedures 010 MIN
Basic Mill Setup No. 2 - Casting And 010 MIN
Basic Milling Procedures 053 MIN
Cutting A Keyway 026 MIN
Cutting A Woodruff Keyseat 030 MIN
Drilling On The Bridgeport Milling Machine 027 MIN
Finding The Center Of A Shaft On The 016 MIN
Horizontal Mill No. 2 - Milling Steps And 021 MIN
Horizontal Mill No. 4 - Straddle Milling 020 MIN
Horizontal Mill No. 5 - Milling A 90 Degree 021 MIN
Safety And Familiarization On The 024 MIN
Safety And Familiarization On The Bridgeport 023 MIN
Safety And Familiarization On The Bridgeport I- 021 MIN
Safety And Familiarization On The Kearney 022 MIN
Safety And Familiarization On The Kearney I- 017 MIN
Squaring A Block 039 MIN
Using A Boring Head 022 MIN
Using The Index Head 029 MIN

Machine Shop - Surface Grinder—A Series
IND
Provides individualized training units on measurement and layout, and operational procedures on the bandsaw, drill press, engine lathe, surface grinder and milling machine. Assists the student in obtaining the necessary skills needed to qualify for employment as a machine operator, machine apprentice and tool and die apprentice. Teaches proper machine operation and relevant safety procedures.
Prod-RMI Dist-RMI

Inspecting 'V' Blocks 010 MIN
Safety And Familiarization On The Surface 033 MIN
Surface Grinder No. 1 - Mounting Work On A 016 MIN
Surface Grinder No. 2 - Mounting And 010 MIN
Surface Grinder No. 3 - Grinding Flat 014 MIN
Surface Grinder No. 4 - Squaring Up A Block 018 MIN
Surface Grinder No. 5 - Grinding To Remove Warp 019 MIN
Surface Grinder No. 6 - Grinding A Vertical 016 MIN
Surface Grinder No. 7 - Grinding A 90 Degree 025 MIN
Surface Grinder No. 8 - Surface Grinding 012 MIN

Machine Shop - Turret Lathe—A Series
IND
Provides individualized training units on measurement and layout, and operational procedures on the bandsaw, drill press, engine lathe, surface grinder and milling machine. Assists the student in obtaining the necessary skills needed to qualify for employment as a machine operator, machine apprentice and tool and die apprentice. Teaches proper machine operation and relevant safety procedures.
Prod-RMI Dist-RMI

Turret Lathe No. 1 - Familiarization 017 MIN
Turret Lathe No. 2 - Drilling, Tapping, 021 MIN
Turret Lathe No. 3 - Plunge Forming And 012 MIN
Turret Lathe No. 4 - Bar Turner Setup And 018 MIN

Machine Shop Safety C 14 MIN
16MM FILM, 3/4 OR 1/2 IN VIDEO J-H
Deals With protective procedures to prevent injury, respiratory protection, maintenance and correct handling of power and hand tools. Shows safety expert and accident victim stressing need to be safety conscious.
Prod-BORTF Dist-BCNFL 1983

Machine Shop Safety C 17 MIN
3/4 OR 1/2 INCH VIDEO CASSETTE IND
Demonstrates safe operation of machine tools such as lathes, presses and grinds. Discusses housekeeping, personal safety and electrical lockouts.
From The Safety Action For Employees Series.
Prod-GPCV Dist-GPCV

Machine Shop Work - Basic Machines—A Series

Prod-USOE Dist-USNAC

Drill Press, The 010 MIN
Lathe, The 015 MIN
Milling Machine, The 015 MIN
Shaper, The 015 MIN

Machine Shop Work - Bench Work—A Series

Prod-USOE Dist-USNAC

Centering Small Stock 12 MIN
Fitting And Scraping Small Bearings 24 MIN
Laying Out Small Castings 16 MIN
Reaming With Straight Hand Reamers 20 MIN
Reaming With Taper Hand Reamers 15 MIN
Scraping Flat Surfaces 14 MIN

Machine Shop Work - Bench Work—A Series

Prod-USOE Dist-USNAC Prodn-RAYBEL

Centering Small Stock 012 MIN
Cutting Threads With Taps And Dies 019 MIN
Fitting And Scraping Small Bearings 024 MIN
Fundamentals Of Filing 012 MIN
Laying Out Small Castings 016 MIN
Reaming With Straight Hand Reamers 020 MIN
Reaming With Taper Hand Reamers 015 MIN
Scraping Flat Surfaces 014 MIN

Machine Shop Work - Cutting Tools—A Series

Prod-USOE Dist-USNAC

Brazing Carbide Tools 18 MIN
Cutting With Carbide Tools, Pt 1, Single Point 19 MIN
Grinding Multiple-Point Carbide Tools 20 MIN
Grinding Single-Point Carbide Tools 26 MIN

Machine Shop Work - Fundamentals Of Blueprint Reading—A Series

Prod-USOE Dist-USNAC

Principal Dimensions - Reference Surfaces,
Reading A Drawing Of A Valve Bonnet 020 MIN
Reading A Three-View Drawing 010 MIN
Sectional Views And Projections - Finish 015 MIN
Visualizing An Object 009 MIN

Machine Shop Work - Operation On The Planer—A Series

Prod-USOE Dist-USNAC

Planing A Flat Surface 22 MIN
Planing A Flat Surface (Spanish) 22 MIN

Machine Shop Work - Operation On The Shaper—A Series

Prod-USOE Dist-USNAC

Machining A Cast Iron Rectangular Block 25 MIN
Machining A Tool Steel V Block 21 MIN

Machine Shop Work - Operations Of A Broaching Machine—A Series

Prod-USOE Dist-USNAC

Broaching An Internal Keyway 23 MIN
Single Ram Vertical Surface Broaching 28 MIN

Machine Shop Work - Operations Of The Centerless Grinding Machine—A Series

Prod-USOE Dist-USNAC

Infeed Grinding Shouldered Work 23 MIN
Thrufeed Grinding A Straight Pin, Pt 1 29 MIN
Thrufeed Grinding A Straight Pin, Pt 2 28 MIN

Machine Shop Work - Operations Of The Vertical Milling Machine—A Series

Prod-USOE Dist-USNAC

Milling A Circular T-Slot 22 MIN
Milling A Helical Groove 28 MIN
Using A Shell End Mill 21 MIN

Machine Shop Work - Operations Of The Center Type Grinder—A Series

Prod-USOE Dist-USNAC

Grinding A Plain Pin, Pt 1, The Grinding Wheel 17 MIN
Grinding A Plain Pin, Pt 2, Grinding Operations 17 MIN
Grinding A Slender Shaft With Back Rest 17 MIN
Plunge Cut Grinding 15 MIN

Machine Shop Work - Operations Of The Cutter Grinder—A Series

Prod-USOE Dist-USNAC

Sharpening A Form Relieved Cutter 18 MIN
Sharpening A Shell End Mill 17 MIN
Sharpening A Side Milling Cutter 23 MIN

Machine Shop Work - Operations Of The Drill Press Radial Drill—A Series

Prod-USOE Dist-USNAC

Countersinking, Counterboring And Spot Facing 20 MIN
Drilling And Tapping Cast Steel 19 MIN
Locating Holes, Drilling And Tapping In 18 MIN

Machine Shop Work - Operations Of The Surface Grinder—A Series

Prod-USOE Dist-USNAC

Grinding A Parallel Bar, Pt 1, Setting Up
Grinding A Parallel Bar, Pt 2, 15 MIN
Grinding A V Block 22 MIN
Grinding Thin Discs 15 MIN

Machine Shop Work - Operations Of The Turret Lathe —A Series

Prod-USOE Dist-USNAC

Bar Work - Magnesium, Pt 3, Necking And Setting Up And Machining Bar Stock 34 MIN

Machine Shop Work - Operations On A Broaching Machine—A Series

Prod-USOE Dist-USNAC

Broaching An Internal Keyway 023 MIN
Double Ram Vertical Surface Broaching 028 MIN
Single Ram Vertical Surface Broaching 028 MIN

Machine Shop Work - Operations On The Centerless Grinding Machine—A Series

Prod-USOE Dist-USNAC

Endfeed Grinding A Tapered Pin 026 MIN
Infeed Grinding A Shaft Of Two Diameters 031 MIN
Infeed Grinding Shouldered Work 023 MIN
Thrufeed Grinding A Straight Pin, Pt 1 029 MIN
Thrufeed Grinding A Straight Pin, Pt 2 028 MIN

Machine Shop Work - Operations On The Cutter Grinder—A Series

Prod-USOE Dist-USNAC

Sharpening A Form Relieved Cutter 018 MIN
Sharpening A Plain Helical Milling Cutter 016 MIN
Sharpening A Shell End Mill 017 MIN
Sharpening A Side Milling Cutter 023 MIN
Sharpening An Angular Cutter 018 MIN

Machine Shop Work - Operations On The Drill Press - Radial Drill—A Series

Prod-USOE Dist-USNAC

Drilling And Tapping Cast Steel 019 MIN
Drilling To A Layout And Spotfacing Cast Iron 015 MIN

Machine Shop Work - Operations On The Drill Press - Vertical Drill—A Series

Prod-USOE Dist-USNAC

Countersinking, Counterboring And Spot Facing 020 MIN
Locating Holes, Drilling And Tapping In 018 MIN

Machine Shop Work - Operations On The Engine Lathe—A Series

Prod-USOE Dist-USNAC

Boring To Close Tolerances 017 MIN
Cutting A Taper With The Compound Best And 011 MIN
Cutting An External Acme Thread 016 MIN
Cutting An External National Fine Thread 012 MIN
Cutting An Internal Acme Thread 022 MIN
Cutting An Internal Taper Pipe Thread 020 MIN
Drilling, Boring and Reaming Work Held In 011 MIN
Machine Work Held In Chuck - Use Of 024 MIN
Rough Turning Between Centers 015 MIN
Turning A Taper With The Tailstock Set Over 017 MIN
Turning Work Held On A Fixture 021 MIN
Turning Work Held On A Mandrel 020 MIN
Turning Work On Two Diameters 014 MIN
Using A Boring Bar Between Centers - Work 022 MIN
Using A Follower Rest 021 MIN
Using A Steady Rest 025 MIN
Using A Steady Rest When Boring 021 MIN

Machine Shop Work - Operations On The Gear Hobbing Machine—A Series

Prod-USOE Dist-USNAC

Hobbing A Helical Gear - Two Cuts,
Hobbing A Spur Gear, Pt 1 - Setting Up The 015 MIN
Hobbing A Spur Gear, Pt 2 - Setting Up And 024 MIN
Hobbing A Square Tooth Spline Shaft 017 MIN
Hobbing A Worm Gear - Infeed Method 018 MIN

Machine Shop Work - Operations On The Horizontal Boring Mill—A Series

Prod-USOE Dist-USNAC

Contour Face Milling 017 MIN
Drilling, Tapping, Stub-Boring, And Reaming 022 MIN
Face Milling With A Fixture 016 MIN
Setup For Face Milling With A Fixture 020 MIN
Setup For Rough Line-Boring 015 MIN

Machine Shop Work - Operations On The Internal Grinder–A Series

Prod-USOE Dist-USNAC

Grinding A Deep Hole 018 MIN
Grinding And Facing A Blind Hole 017 MIN

Machine Shop Work - Operations On The Horizontal Boring Mill-A Series

Prod-USOE Dist-USNAC

Drilling, Tapping, Stub-Boring And Reaming 22 MIN
Setup For Face Milling With A Fixture 20 MIN

Machine Shop Work - Operations On The Metal Cutting Band Saw–A Series

Prod-USOE Dist-USNAC

Filing An Internal Irregular Shape 027 MIN
Sawing An Internal Irregular Shape 032 MIN

Machine Shop Work - Operations On The Milling Machine–A Series

Prod-USOE Dist-USNAC

Boring Holes With Offset Boring Head 028 MIN
Cutting A Short Rack 018 MIN
Cutting Keyways 015 MIN
Cutting Teeth On A Worm Gear 017 MIN
Milling A Helical Cutter 018 MIN
Milling A Template 017 MIN
Milling Machine, The 008 MIN
Plain Indexing And Cutting A Spur Gear 026 MIN
Straddle And Surface Milling To 027 MIN
Straddle Milling 017 MIN

Machine Shop Work - Operations On The Planer–A Series

Prod-USOE Dist-USNAC

Planing A Dovetail Slide 028 MIN
Planing A Flat Surface 022 MIN

Machine Shop Work - Operations On The Shaper–A Series

Prod-USOE Dist-USNAC

Cutting A Keyway On End Of A Finished Shaft 013 MIN
Machining A Cast Iron Rectangular Block 025 MIN
Machining A Tool Steel V Block 021 MIN

Machine Shop Work - Operations On The Surface Grinder–A Series

Prod-USOE Dist-USNAC Prodn-WFC

Grinding A Parallel Bar - Grinding Operations 015 MIN
Grinding A Parallel Bar - Setting Up The 014 MIN
Grinding A Template 015 MIN
Grinding A V-Block 022 MIN
Grinding Thin Discs 015 MIN

Machine Shop Work - Operations On The Turret Lathe–A Series

Prod-USOE Dist-USNAC

Bar Work, Magnesium - Necking And Threading
Bar Work, Magnesium - Setting Up Bar 018 MIN
Bar Work, Magnesium - Setting Up Multiple 017 MIN
Chuck Work - Setting Up Hexagon Turret Tools 022 MIN
Chuck Work - Setting Up Tools For Combined Cuts 016 MIN
Setting Up And Machining Bar Stock 034 MIN
Turret Lathe, The - An Introduction 017 MIN

Machine Shop Work - Operations On The Vertical Boring Mill–A Series

Prod-USOE Dist-USNAC

Facing, Turning, Boring, Grooving, And
Rough-Facing, Boring And Turning A Shoulder 022 MIN
Rough-Facing, Turning And Drilling 031 MIN

Machine Shop Work - Operations On The Vertical Milling Machine–A Series

Prod-USOE Dist-USNAC

Cutting A Dovetail Taper Slide 026 MIN
Cutting A Round End Keyway 022 MIN
Milling A Circular T-Slot 022 MIN
Milling A Helical Groove 028 MIN
Using A Shell End Mill 021 MIN

Machine Shop Work - Operations On The Drill Press Sensitive Drill–A Series

Prod-USOE Dist-USNAC

Drilling A Hole In A Pin 10 MIN

Machine Shop Work - Operations On The Engine Lathe–A Series

Prod-USOE Dist-USNAC

Boring To Close Tolerances 17 MIN
Cutting A Taper With The Compound Rest And 11 MIN
Cutting An External Acme Thread 16 MIN
Cutting An External National Fine Thread 12 MIN
Cutting An Internal Acme Thread 22 MIN
Cutting An Internal Taper Pipe Thread 20 MIN
Drilling, Boring And Reaming Work Held 11 MIN
Machining Work Held In Chuck - Use Of 24 MIN
Rough Turning Between Centers 15 MIN
Turning A Taper With The Tailstock Set Over 17 MIN
Turning Work Held On A Fixture 21 MIN
Turning Work Held On A Mandrel 20 MIN
Using A Boring Bar Between Centers - Work 22 MIN
Using A Follower Rest 21 MIN
Using A Steady Rest 25 MIN
Using A Steady Rest When Boring 21 MIN

Machine Shop Work - Operations On The Gear Hobbing Machine–A Series

Prod-USOE Dist-USNAC

Hobbing A Spur Gear, Pt 1, Setting Up The
Hobbing A Spur Gear, Pt 2, Setting Up And 24 MIN

Machine Shop Work - Operations On The Milling Machine–A Series

Prod-USOE Dist-USNAC

Boring Holes With Offset Boring Head 28 MIN
Cutting Teeth On A Worm Gear 17 MIN
Milling A Helical Cutter 18 MIN
Milling A Template 17 MIN
Straddle And Surface Milling To 27 MIN

Machine Shop Work - Precision Measurement– A Series

Prod-USOE Dist-USNAC

Gage Blocks And Accessories 23 MIN
Precision Gage Blocks 18 MIN
Verniers 19 MIN

Machine Shop Work - Precision Measurement–A Series

Discusses various aspects of precision measurement in machine shop work.
Prod-USOE Dist-USNAC 1979

Bevel Protractor, The 015 MIN
Fixed Gages 017 MIN
Gage Blocks And Accessories 023 MIN
Height Gages And Test Indicators 012 MIN
Micrometer, The 015 MIN
Precision Gage Blocks 018 MIN
Steel Rule, The 014 MIN

Machine Shop Work - Single Point Cutting Tools (Spanish)–A Series

IND
A Spanish language series. Discusses end- and side-cutting machine shop tools.
Prod-USOE Dist-USNAC

Fundamentals Of End Cutting Tools (Spanish) 012 MIN
Fundamentals Of Side Cutting Tools (Spanish) 011 MIN

Machine Shop-Shaper–A Series

IND
Provides individualized training units on measurement and layout and operational procedures on the bandsaw, drill press, engine lathe, surface grinder, and milling machine. Assists the student in obtaining the necessary skills needed to qualify for employment as a machine operator, machine apprentice, and tool and die apprentice. Teaches proper machine operation and relevant safety procedures.
Prod-RMI Dist-RMI

Shaper No. 2 - Squaring A Block 020 MIN
Shaper No. 3 - Machining Angles 011 MIN

Machine Stitching Techniques C 5 MIN
16MM FILM SILENT J-C A
Describes four machine stitching techniques. Illustrates their correct location and possible uses. Shows the understitch, topstitch, stitch in the ditch and blind hemming stitch.
From The Clothing Construction Techniques Series.
LC NO. 77-701182
Prod-IOWA Dist-IOWASP 1976

Machine Story C 4 MIN
16MM FILM, 3/4 OR 1/2 IN VIDEO
Offers an animated history of technology from the invention of the inclined plane, circa 8000 BC to the Saturn probe developed in 1980.
Prod-MILLRD Dist-PFP

Machine Technology I - Basic machine Technology–A Series

Presents a hands-on approach to vocational training with lessons in the basics of machine technology, including equipment and safety measures.
Prod-CAMB Dist-CAMB

Cutting Speeds And Feeds For The Engine
Drilling, Boring, And Reaming Work Held In A 015 MIN
Engine Lathe Accessories 015 MIN
Filing And Polishing On The Engine Lathe 015 MIN
Grinding A Right-Hand Roughing Tool 015 MIN
Grinding A Round Nose Finishing Tool 015 MIN
Identification Of Parts And Care Of The 015 MIN
Knurling On The Lathe 015 MIN
Mounting And Truing In The 4-Jaw Independent 015 MIN
Straight Turning Between Centers 015 MIN
Straight Turning Work Of Two Diameters 015 MIN
Taper Turning On A Lathe 015 MIN
Three Methods Of Facing Work To Length 015 MIN
Turning A Radius 015 MIN

Machine Technology II - Engine Lathe Accessories–A Series

Presents hands-on approach to vocational training in engine lathe and accessories, safety procedures and techniques.
Prod-CAMB Dist-CAMB

Butt Welding Saw Blades 015 MIN
Drill Presses (Sensitive And Radial) 015 MIN
Hand Hacksaw And Filing Procedures 015 MIN
Hand Tools And Their Use In Machine Technology 015 MIN
Micrometer (Telescope Gages, Caliper, Hole 015 MIN
Operations Frequently Performed On The Drill 015 MIN
Pedestal Grinder, The 015 MIN
Safety Procedures And Guidelines For Machine 015 MIN
Setting The Bandsaws Up For Sawing And Use Of 015 MIN
Sharpening Drill Bits By Hand And Machine 015 MIN
Use Of Layout Tools In Machine Technology 015 MIN
Use Of Measuring Tools In Machine Technology 015 MIN
Vernier Scale And Vernier Caliper (Inside, 015 MIN
Vertical Bandsaws - Parts And Accessories 015 MIN

Machine Technology III - Intermediate Engine Lathe–A Series

Presents hands-on training on the intermediate level of the engine lathe, safety procedures and techniques.
Prod-CAMB Dist-CAMB

Machine Technology IV - Milling–A Series

Presents hands-on aproach to vocational training in use of the vertical and horizontal milling machines.
Prod-CAMB Dist-CAMB

Cutters And Machining Operations For The
Gouging Of End Mills, 2 And 4 Flute 015 MIN
Identification Of Parts And Operation Of A 015 MIN
Identification Of Parts And Operation Of A 015 MIN
Machining Keyways On The Vertical Milling 015 MIN
Reamer Sharpening Between Centers 015 MIN
Setup For Holding Work To Be Milled 015 MIN
Sharpening Ends Of End Mills 015 MIN
Sharpening Lathe Tools Including N/C Lathe 015 MIN
Sharpening Side Milling Cutters, Slitting 015 MIN
Sharpening The Periphery Of End Mills 015 MIN
Use Of Dividing Head And Rotary Table 015 MIN
Use Of Face Milling Cutters On The Horizontal 015 MIN
Use Of Plain And Side Milling Cutters On The 015 MIN

Machine Tools And Motions B 22 MIN
16MM FILM OPTICAL SOUND
Shows how the design of a machine's controls can improve the operator's efficiency and how operating levers can be extended and controls relocated so that the machine operator can load and unload the machine and manipulate the necessary controls with the least amount of effort and motion.
LC NO. FIA53-1132
Prod-GM Dist-GM 1951

Machine Trades C 7 MIN
16MM FILM, 3/4 OR 1/2 IN VIDEO
Describes job opportunities that are available for entry-level workers. Stresses good pay and career ladder potential in the machine trades. Issued in 1968 as a motion picture.
From The Career Job Opportunity Film Series.
LC NO. 79-707880
Prod-USDLMA Dist-USNAC Prodn-DEROCH 1979

Machine Transcription - Transcription Technique B 15 MIN
16MM FILM OPTICAL SOUND
Tells how to phrase dictation at various speeds, prepare for a day's work, compose a letter and correct errors in the transcriptions on the cylinder.
LC NO. FIE52-73
Prod-USN Dist-USNAC 1943

Machine Vision C 45 MIN
3/4 OR 1/2 INCH VIDEO CASSETTE PRO
Features understanding constraints on observed intensity, history of machine vision, determinations, and manufacturing surface shading for synthetic images.
From The Artificial Intelligence - Pt 3, Computer Vision Series.
Prod-MIOT Dist-MIOT

Machine Vision C 56 MIN
3/4 OR 1/2 INCH VIDEO CASSETTE C
See series title for descriptive statement.
From The Artificial Intelligence, Pt III - Computer Vision Series.
Prod-MIOT Dist-AMCEE

Machine Vision Technology C 35 MIN
3/4 OR 1/2 INCH VIDEO CASSETTE
Explains the current types of machine vision systems in operation and how they can be used with welding, assembly and inspection applications. Demonstrates visual sensing, computer analysis and interpretation of critical factory data.
Prod-SME Dist-SME

Machine, The C 12 MIN
3/4 OR 1/2 INCH VIDEO CASSETTE
Looks at the hardware which makes up the personal computer and shows what each part does and how it interrelates with each other part. Explains the logic, memory and control functions and what software is and how it's used.
From The You And Your Personal Computer Series. Part I
Prod-VISUCP Dist-VISUCP

Machinery Set-Up And Safety C 15 MIN
3/4 OR 1/2 INCH VIDEO CASSETTE PRO
See series title for descriptive statement.
From The Numerical Control/Computer Numerical Control, Pt 1 - Fundamentals Series.
Prod-ICSINT Dist-ICSINT

Machines That Move People C 15 MIN
3/4 OR 1/2 INCH VIDEO CASSETTE I
Visits Transpo '72 to see past, present and future modes of transportation.
From The Matter And Motion Series. Module Green
Prod-WHROTV Dist-AITECH 1973

Machines That Think C 30 MIN
3/4 OR 1/2 INCH VIDEO CASSETTE
Discusses the next generation of computers which will be the first to have true 'artificial intelligence.'
From The Innovation Series.
Prod-WNETTV Dist-WNETTV 1983

Machines, Engines And Motors C 13 MIN
16MM FILM, 3/4 OR 1/2 IN VIDEO
Defines machines, engines and motors and relates them to everyday items. Discusses their interrelationships and discusses the research process.
From The Scientific Fact And Fun Series.
Prod-GLDWER Dist-JOU 1980

Machines, Engines And Motors (Captioned) C 13 MIN
16MM FILM, 3/4 OR 1/2 IN VIDEO
Defines machines, engines and motors and relates them to everyday items. Discusses their interrelationships and describes the research process.
From The Scientific Fact And Fun Series.
Prod-GLDWER Dist-JOU 1980

Machining A Cast Iron Rectangular Block B 21 MIN
16MM FILM, 3/4 OR 1/2 IN VIDEO
Shows several processes, such as how to set the shaper ram stroke, adjust the shaper table, vise, vertical feed, head feed and crossfeed, and set up a rectangular cast iron block.
From The Machine Shop Work - Operations On The Shaper Series. No. 2
Prod-USOE Dist-USNAC Prodn-YORKES 1942

Machining A Cast Iron Rectangular Block (Spanish) B 25 MIN
16MM FILM OPTICAL SOUND
Shows several processes, such as how to set the shaper ram stroke. Tells how to adjust the shaper table, vice vertical feed, head feed and crossfeed and set up a rectangular cast iron block.
From The Machine Shop Work Series. Operations On The Shaper, No. 3
LC NO. FIE62-64
Prod-USOE Dist-USNAC 1942

Machining A Cast Iron Rectangular Block (Spanish) B 25 MIN
3/4 OR 1/2 INCH VIDEO CASSETTE
Shows several processes, such as how to set the shaper ram stroke. Tells how to adjust the shaper table, vice vertical feed, head feed and crossfeed and set up a rectangular cast iron block.
From The Machine Shop Work Series. Operations On The Shaper, No. 3
Prod-USOE Dist-USNAC 1942

Machining A Tool Steel V Block B 21 MIN
16MM FILM, 3/4 OR 1/2 IN VIDEO
Shows how to lay out work for machining on a shaper, set up and position the ram stroke, and machine 'V' grooves and rectangular slots.
From The Machine Shop Work - Operations On The Shaper Series. No. 3
Prod-USOE Dist-USNAC Prodn-YORKES 1942

Machining And The Operation of Machine Tools, Module 1 - Basic Machine Technology—A Series
IND
Presents a comprehensive skills training program for machinists. Designed to teach proper and safe machine shop practice and machine tool operation. Looks at basic machine technology.
Prod-LEIKID Dist-LEIKID

Butt Welding Saw Blades 015 MIN
Contour Band Machine Set-up And Use Of 015 MIN
Contour Hand Machines - Parts And Accessories 015 MIN
Drill Presses - Sensitive And Radial 015 MIN
Hand Hacksaw And Filing Procedures 015 MIN
Handtools And Their Use In Machine Technology 015 MIN
Micrometer 015 MIN
Operations Frequently Performed On The Drill 015 MIN
Pedestal Grinder, The 015 MIN
Safety Procedures And Guidelines For Machine 015 MIN
Sharpening Drill Bits By Hand And Machine 015 MIN
Use Of Layout Tools In Machine Technology, The 015 MIN
Use Of Measuring Tools In Machine Technology 015 MIN
Vernier Scale And Vernier Caliper 015 MIN

Machining And The Operation Of Machine Tools, Module 2 - Engine Lathe—A Series
IND
Presents a comprehensive skills training program for machinists. Designed to teach proper and safe machine shop practice and machine tool operation. Focuses on the engine lathe.
Prod-LEIKID Dist-LEIKID

Cutting Speeds And Feeds For The Engine Lathe 015 MIN
Drilling, Boring And Reaming Work Held In A 015 MIN
Engine Lathe Accessories 015 MIN
Filing And Polishing On The Engine Lathe 015 MIN
Grinding A Right-Hand Roughing Tool 015 MIN
Grinding A Round-Nose Finishing Tool 015 MIN
Identification Of Parts And Care Of The 015 MIN
Knurling On The Lathe 015 MIN
Mounting And Truing Work In The 4-Jaw 015 MIN
Straight Turning Between Centers 015 MIN
Straight Turning Work Of Two Diameters 015 MIN
Taper Turning On A Lathe 015 MIN
Three Methods Of Facing Work To Length 015 MIN
Turning A Radius 015 MIN

Machining And The Operation Of Machine Tools, Module 3 - Intermediate Engine Lathe—A Series
IND
Presents a comprehensive skills training program for machinists. Designed to teach proper and safe machine shop practice and machine tool operation. Focuses on the engine lathe.
Prod-LEIKID Dist-LEIKID

Chasing External Threads And Finishing With A
Chasing Tapered Pipe Threads On The Lathe 015 MIN
Cutting Acme Threads 015 MIN
Cutting Internal Threads On The Lathe 015 MIN
Grinding Forming Tools And Machine Forms 015 MIN
Matching Offset Holes - Face Plate And 4-Jaw 015 MIN
Matching Shoulders And Corners On The Lathe 015 MIN
Measuring External And Internal Threads 015 MIN
Roughing And Finishing External Threads On 015 MIN
Spring Winding On The Lathe 015 MIN
Tap And Die Threading On The Lathe 015 MIN
Using The Cutoff Tool On The Lathe 015 MIN
Using The Steady Rest And Follower Rest To 015 MIN
Using The Toolpost Grinder On The Lathe 015 MIN

Machining And The Operation Of Machine Tools, Module 4 - Milling And Tool...—A Series
IND
Presents a comprehensive skills training program for machinists. Designed to teach proper and safe machine shop practice and machine tool operation. Deals with aspects of milling and tool sharpening.
Prod-LEIKID Dist-LEIKID

Cutters And Machining Operations For The
Gougings Of 2- And 4-Flute End Mills 015 MIN
Identification Of Parts And Operation Of 015 MIN
Identification Of Parts And Operation Of 015 MIN
Machining Keyways On The Vertical Milling 015 MIN
Set-Up For Holding Work To Be Milled 015 MIN
Sharpening A Reamer Between Centers 015 MIN
Sharpening Brazed Carbide Lathe Tools Using A 015 MIN
Sharpening Ends Of End Mills 015 MIN
Sharpening The Periphery Of An End Mill 015 MIN
Sharpening The Periphery Of Plain Milling 015 MIN
Use Of Dividing Head And Rotary Table 015 MIN
Use Of Plain And Side Milling Cutters On The 015 MIN
Use Of The Face Milling Cutter On The 015 MIN

Machining Keyways On The Vertical Milling Machine (Straight And Woodruff) C 15 MIN
3/4 OR 1/2 INCH VIDEO CASSETTE
See series title for descriptive statement.
From The Machine Technology IV - Milling Series
Prod-CAMB Dist-CAMB

Machining Keyways On The Vertical Milling Machine (Straight And Woodruff) C 15 MIN
3/4 OR 1/2 INCH VIDEO CASSETTE IND
See series title for descriptive statement.
From The Machining And The Operation Of Machine Tools, Module 4 - Milling And Tool...Series.
Prod-LEIKID Dist-LEIKID

Machining Laminated Plastics B 19 MIN
16MM FILM, 3/4 OR 1/2 IN VIDEO
Shows how to machine a typical laminated part, cut the tube stock to length on a circular saw, turn the outside diameters on a lathe, machine inside diameters by boring with a lathe and finish on a milling machine.
From The Plastics Series. No. 10
Prod-USOE Dist-USNAC Prodn-CARFI 1945

Machining Offset Holes - Face Plate And 4-Jaw Chuck C 15 MIN
3/4 OR 1/2 INCH VIDEO CASSETTE
See series title for descriptive statement.
From The Machine Technology III - Intermediate Engine Lathe Series.
Prod-CAMB Dist-CAMB

Machining Offset Holes - Face Plate and 4-Jaw Chuck C
3/4 OR 1/2 INCH VIDEO CASSETTE
See series title for descriptive statement.
From The Intermediate Engine Lathe Operation Series.
Prod-VTRI Dist-VTRI

Machining Offset Holes - Face Plate And 4-Jaw Chuck (Spanish) C
3/4 OR 1/2 INCH VIDEO CASSETTE
See series title for descriptive statement.
From The Intermediate Engine Lathe Operation (Spanish) Series.
Prod-VTRI Dist-VTRI

Machining On The Lathe And Machining Offset Diameters On The Lathe C 15 MIN
3/4 OR 1/2 INCH VIDEO CASSETTE
See series title for descriptive statement.
From The Machine Technology III - Intermediate Engine Lathe Series.
Prod-CAMB Dist-CAMB

Machining Shoulders And Corners On The Lathe C
3/4 OR 1/2 INCH VIDEO CASSETTE
See series title for descriptive statement.
From The Intermediate Engine Lathe Operation Series.
Prod-VTRI Dist-VTRI

Machining Shoulders And Corners On The Lathe (Spanish) C
3/4 OR 1/2 INCH VIDEO CASSETTE
See series title for descriptive statement.
From The Intermediate Engine Lathe Operation (Spanish) Series.
Prod-VTRI Dist-VTRI

Machining Shoulders On The Lathe C 15 MIN
3/4 OR 1/2 INCH VIDEO CASSETTE
From The Machine Technology III - Intermediate Engine Lathe Series.
Prod-CAMB Dist-CAMB

Machining Work Held In Chuck - Use Of Reference Surfaces B 24 MIN
16MM FILM - 3/4 IN VIDEO
Shows how to select and machine surfaces to be used for reference, how to set up a workpiece accurately to the reference surfaces in a lathe chuck and how to use a boring bar to machine several internal surfaces.
From The Machine Shop Work - Operations On The Engine Lathe Series. No. 12
LC NO. 79-707088
Prod-USOE Dist-USNAC Prodn-ATLAS 1979

Machining Work Held In Chuck - Use Of Reference Surfaces (Spanish) B 24 MIN
16MM FILM OPTICAL SOUND
Explains how to select and machine surfaces to be used for reference, how to set up a workpiece accurately to the reference surfaces in a lathe chuck and how to use a boring bar to machine several internal surfaces.
From The Machine Shop Work Series. Operations On The English Lathe, No. 12
LC NO. FIE62-88
Prod-USOE Dist-USNAC 1944

Machining Work Held In Chuck - Use Of Reference Surfaces (Spanish) B 24 MIN
3/4 OR 1/2 INCH VIDEO CASSETTE
Explains how to select and machine surfaces to be used for reference, how to set up a workpiece accurately to the reference surfaces in a lathe chuck and how to use a boring bar to machine several internal surfaces.
From The Machine Shop Work Series. Operations On The English Lathe, No. 12
Prod-USOE Dist-USNAC 1944

Machinist's Vice C 15 MIN
3/4 OR 1/2 INCH VIDEO CASSETTE IND
Shows how to read an assembly line drawing and a bill of material. Demonstrates how to interpret cross-sectioned views.
From The Blueprint Reading For Machinists Series.
Prod-LEIKID Dist-LEIKID

Machorka-Muff B 18 MIN
16MM FILM OPTICAL SOUND
Attacks West Germany's rearmament and revival of its militaristic tradition in the Adenauer era. Spotlights a former Nazi officer working his way back to society and official good standing. Based on a story by Heinrich Boll.
Prod-NYFLMS Dist-NYFLMS

Macintosh And TJ C 96 MIN
16MM FILM OPTICAL SOUND P-I
Prod-FI Dist-FI

Mackinac Bridge Diary C 27 MIN
16MM FILM OPTICAL SOUND H-C A
Describes the story of the conversion of steel, wire and concrete into the world's longest suspension bridge, spanning the Straits of Mackinac.
Prod-USSC Dist-USSC

Maclarification C 4 MIN
16MM FILM OPTICAL SOUND
Presents fluid lines, patterns, colors and lively music in a style similar to the experimental films of Canadian film artist Norman Mc Laren.
LC NO. 75-703199
Prod-USC Dist-USC 1966

Macmillan Video Almanac For Kids, The C 60 MIN
1/2 IN VIDEO CASSETTE BETA/VHS K-I
Presents eight subjects - soap bubble magic, a journey into space, a secret language, body talk, kite flying, volcanoes, drawing faces and string figures. Based on The Macmillan Illustrated Almanac For Kids.
Prod-MACLS Dist-CARAVT

Macrame C 15 MIN
16MM FILM, 3/4 OR 1/2 IN VIDEO I-C A
Points out that the ancient art of knotting known as macrame has had a great revival in recent years and shows how to make the few basic knots, how to combine them to form simple and useful objects and how to create various effects.
From The Rediscovery - Art Media Series.
Prod-ACI Dist-AIMS 1972

Macrame C 30 MIN
3/4 OR 1/2 INCH VIDEO CASSETTE H A
Demonstrates and explains the basics of macrame construction, from cutting the cord to whipping and knotting techniques. Shows artistic macrame creations such as wall hangings, necklaces, and plant hangings.
From The Arts And Crafts Series.
LC NO. 81-706190
Prod-GPITVL Dist-GPITVL 1981

Macrame (Spanish) C 15 MIN
16MM FILM, 3/4 OR 1/2 IN VIDEO I-C A
Shows how to make the few basic knots which comprise the art of macrame, and how to combine them to form simple and useful objects.
From The Rediscovery - Art Media (Spanish) Series.
Prod-ACI Dist-AIMS 1972

Macroeconomic Performance C 45 MIN
3/4 OR 1/2 INCH VIDEO CASSETTE
Discusses various aspects of macroeconomic performance.
From The Economic Perspectives Series.
Prod-MDCPB Dist-MDCPB

Macroeconomics C 45 MIN
3/4 OR 1/2 INCH VIDEO CASSETTE
Discusses various aspects of macroeconomics.
From The Economic Perspectives Series.
Prod-MDCPB Dist-MDCPB

Macromolecules - Polymerization Thermoplastics C 60 MIN
3/4 OR 1/2 INCH VIDEO CASSETTE IND
Discusses fibers formed from macromolecules, polymerization of ethylene at high pressure, polystyrene, macromolecules of different shapes, modification with acrylonnitrile and the extrusion of thermoplastics.
From The Chemistry Training Series.
Prod-ITCORP Dist-ITCORP

Macros And Other Advanced Features Of Lotus 1-2-3 - Learn-PC Video Systems C
3/4 OR 1/2 INCH VIDEO CASSETTE
Covers spreadsheet consolidation and macros in a self-paced training program.
Prod-DSIM Dist-DSIM

Macular Degeneration C
3/4 OR 1/2 INCH VIDEO CASSETTE
Helps the patient understand how central vision is lost as macular degeneration progresses. Includes a review of the eye's anatomy, process of sight, and the areas affected. Explains follow-up monitoring using the Amsler Grid.
Prod-MIFE Dist-MIFE

Macular Degeneration C 4 MIN
3/4 OR 1/2 INCH VIDEO CASSETTE
Discusses one of the conditions of aging which seriously impairs vision. Explains the human eye, and how macular degeneration occurs when cells in the macula begin to die. Reassures patient that macula degeneration while serious, will not cause total blindness.
Prod-TRAINX Dist-TRAINX

Mad Bomber, The C 5 MIN
3/4 OR 1/2 INCH VIDEO CASSETTE J-H
Deals with the use of the phrases 'Is where' and 'Is when' in writing.
From The Write On, Set 1 Series.
Prod-CTI Dist-CTI

Mad Chemist, The C 10 MIN
16MM FILM OPTICAL SOUND P-I
Shows how a 'mad chemist' creates a green-skinned Frankenstein monster which he hooks up to a 'happiness machine.' Demonstrates the futility of finding happiness through chemical means.
Prod-PROART Dist-PROART 1969

Mad Dog C 5 MIN
16MM FILM OPTICAL SOUND
Tells how a doll comes to life to seek retribution against a playful dog who tore apart her fellow stuffed animals.
LC NO. 79-701374
Prod-ADELPH Dist-ADELPH 1978

Mad River C 58 MIN
16MM FILM OPTICAL SOUND
Presents a portrait of a rural community caught in a crossfire between demands for increased protection of the environment and concern for jobs and economic development. Focuses on a coalition of displaced workers, their unions, and community groups, which joined together to reopen a closed plywood mill as a community-owned cooperative.
Prod-FINLIN Dist-CANCIN

Mad River - Plant Closures In The Redwoods C 55 MIN
3/4 OR 1/2 INCH VIDEO CASSETTE H A
Uses the example of a timber community near California's Mad River to examine the use of natural resources and the conflict between those who desire increased protection of the environment and those who are concerned with jobs and economic development.
LC NO. 81-707596
Prod-FINLIN Dist-FINLIN 1982

Mad Whirl, The C 71 MIN
2 INCH VIDEOTAPE
See series title for descriptive statement.
From The Toys That Grew Up II Series.
Prod-WTTWTV Dist-PUBTEL

Madame Bovary B
1/2 IN VIDEO CASSETTE BETA/VHS
Presents Flaubert's story about a young woman trapped in an unhappy marriage. Stars Jennifer Jones, Van Heflin, James Mason and Louis Jourdan.
Prod-GA Dist-GA

Madame Butterfly (Italian) C 140 MIN
3/4 OR 1/2 INCH VIDEO CASSETTE A
Presents Puccini's tragedy, Madame Butterfly, in a production which tranforms the Arena di Verona into a magical setting of Japanese gardens and cherry trees.
Prod-EDDIM Dist-EDDIM

Madame Chiang Kai-shek B 26 MIN
16MM FILM, 3/4 OR 1/2 IN VIDEO J-H A
Uses rare actuality footage to portray the personal life and history-making deeds of Madame Chiang Kai-Shek.
From The History Makers Of The 20th Century Series.
Prod-WOLPER Dist-SF 1965

Madame Dubarry B 85 MIN
16MM FILM SILENT
A silent motion picture with German subtitles. Tells the story of Madame Dubarry, who advanced from seamstress to become the mistress of Louis XV. Hated by the people for her lavishness, after the king's death is brought before the revolutionary court, sentenced and executed. Influenced by Max Reinhardt's monumental stage productions.
Prod-WSTGLC Dist-WSTGLC 1919

Made In Barbados C 20 MIN
16MM FILM, 3/4 OR 1/2 IN VIDEO J-H
Shows how some Caribbean islands must choose to use available labor to manufacture goods from imported raw materials.
From The One World Series.
Prod-BBCTV Dist-FI 1982

Made In Britain C 52 MIN
16MM FILM, 3/4 OR 1/2 IN VIDEO J-C A
Describes how the British, highly skilled and seeking prosperity, were model immigrants. Interviews and historic pictures portray what life in America was like for the English and Welsh who were able to reap the material rewards of America's expanding economy.
From The Destination America Series.
Prod-THAMES Dist-MEDIAG 1976

Made In Japan C 30 MIN
3/4 OR 1/2 INCH VIDEO CASSETTE H-C A
See series title for descriptive statement.
From The Japan - The Changing Tradition Series.
Prod-UMA Dist-GPITVL 1978

Made In Japan - Ukiyo-E Prints C 29 MIN
2 INCH VIDEOTAPE
See series title for descriptive statement.
From The Museum Open House Series.
Prod-WGBHTV Dist-PUBTEL

Made In Japan, Pt 1 - Cultural Influences On Industry C 16 MIN
16MM FILM, 3/4 OR 1/2 IN VIDEO H-C A
Delineates the integral link between Japan's cultural tradition and its modern corporate structure. Discusses family and educational values that shape Japanese attitudes toward work. Explains why the intense loyalty between employer and employee has done so much to promote industrial productivity in Japan.
Prod-WABCTV Dist-MTI 1982

Made In Japan, Pt 2 - Business Practices And Changing Lifestyles C 22 MIN
16MM FILM, 3/4 OR 1/2 IN VIDEO H-C A
Examines the business practices responsible for Japan's booming economy. Looks at the way Japan views management, research, long-range planning, re-investment, profit-making and training. Interviews corporate heads, the head of the Japanese Productivity Center, government leaders and workers.
Prod-WABCTV Dist-MTI 1982

Made In Mississippi - Black Folk Art And Crafts C 20 MIN
16MM FILM - 3/4 IN VIDEO
Looks at black folk arts and the people of rural Mississippi who make them. Discusses how seven unique folk artists do their work.
Prod-SOFOLK Dist-SOFOLK

Made In Sweden C 26 MIN
16MM FILM OPTICAL SOUND
Shows how the natural resources of Sweden are used, pointing out that modern industrialism helps to give Sweden a high standard of living.
LC NO. FIA66-1389
Prod-SWEDIN Dist-SWNTO 1957

Made In The Bronx C 30 MIN
16MM FILM, 3/4 OR 1/2 IN VIDEO A
Tells about a workshop in creativity which was organized in the Bronx for adults who work with children in neighborhood community centers. Shows the workshop members participating in exercises designed to familiarize them with various aspects of creativity.
LC NO. 81-701072
Prod-SULANI Dist-SULANI 1981

Made To Wear - Wool's A Natural C 15 MIN
16MM FILM OPTICAL SOUND
Describes, in chronological order, how the fashion trends set by couturiers are translated into clothing. Discusses the interaction of the fashion designer and fabric designer, and includes the charting of sample fabrics. Shows the mechanical process of cutting and manufacturing garments. Conveys wool's quality and versatility while emphasizing the importance of 'investment' dressing in today's economy. Narrated by Orson Welles.
Prod-WSTGLC Dist-WSTGLC

Madeira C 15 MIN
16MM FILM OPTICAL SOUND
Describes the Portuguese island of Madeira, whose inhabitants remain almost untouched by western technology. Pictures the age-old methods and practices which are still maintained in farming, in growing and processing grapes for wine, in fishing and in embroidery. Includes views of the mountainous island and of the relaxed amusements available to the tourist. Filmed in Madeira.
LC NO. FIA65-1871
Prod-MACKIN Dist-RADIM 1965

Madeleines C 29 MIN
2 INCH VIDEOTAPE
A French language videotape. Features Julia Child of Haute Cuisine au Vin demonstrating how to prepare madeleines. With captions.
From The French Chef (French) Series.
Prod-WGBHTV Dist-PUBTEL

Madeline C 7 MIN
16MM FILM, 3/4 OR 1/2 IN VIDEO
Uses animation to describe the adventures of an irrepressible French school girl and her life in boarding school. Based on the book Madeline by Ludwig Bemelman.
Prod-BOSUST Dist-CF 1969

Madeline C 8 MIN
3/4 OR 1/2 INCH VIDEO CASSETTE
Uses animation to describe the adventures of an irrepressible French school girl and her life in boarding school. Based on the book Madeline by Ludwig Bemelman.
Prod-BOSUST Dist-LCOA

Madeline (Spanish) C 7 MIN
16MM FILM, 3/4 OR 1/2 IN VIDEO P-I
Tells the story of a young french girl in Paris who goes to the hospital to have her appendix removed.
Prod-RANK Dist-LCOA 1969

Madeline And The Bad Hat C 8 MIN
16MM FILM OPTICAL SOUND P-I
Presents an animated story about Madeline and her friends. Introduces Pepito who is named a 'BAD HAT' by Madeline because of his distressing habit of caging up frogs, birds, bugs, bats and cats. Shows how he learns his lesson and delights Madeline by freeing his menagerie.
From The Madeline Series.
LC NO. 73-701756
Prod-REMBRT Dist-TEXFLM

Madeline And The Gypsy C 7 MIN
16MM FILM OPTICAL SOUND P-I
Presents an animated story about Madeline and her friends. Tells of Madeline and Pepito's adventures while stranded at a gypsy carnival and visiting some of the most beautiful places in France.
From The Madeline Series.
LC NO. 73-701757
Prod-REMBRT Dist-TEXFLM

Madeline—A Series
16MM FILM, 3/4 OR 1/2 IN VIDEO P-I
Uses animation to tell the story of Madeline, Miss Clavel, director of Madeline's boarding school, Pepito, the Spanish ambassador's son who lives next door, and a dog named Genevieve. Based on the books by Ludwig Bemelmans.
Prod-AUDBRF Dist-TEXFLM

Madeline And The Bad Hat	008 MIN
Madeline And The Gypsy	007 MIN
Madeline's Rescue	007 MIN

Madeline's Dream C 20 MIN
16MM FILM, 3/4 OR 1/2 IN VIDEO H-C
Using the Gestalt method, a young girl re-lives a repetitive dream and discovers some basic truths about herself.
From The Gestalt Series.
Prod-PMI Dist-FI 1969

Madeline's Rescue C 7 MIN
16MM FILM OPTICAL SOUND
Presents an animated version of Ludwig Bemelman's picture book Madeline's Rescue, utilizing the original artwork and story about '12 little girls in two straight lines.' Tells how the 12 nearly become 11 when Madeline falls into the Seine. Shows how she is rescued by a dog that they keep as a pet.
From The Madeline Series.
LC NO. FIA65-1779
Prod-RFL Dist-TEXFLM 1966

Madera-Plastico - Una Nueva Dimension C 12 MIN
16MM FILM, 3/4 OR 1/2 IN VIDEO H-C
A Spanish-language version of the motion picture Wood Plastic - A New Dimension. Demonstrates the use of the catalyst heat system in making wood plastic. Shows how the usual disadvantages of wood are minimized by this process and presents a commercial use for the new material.
Prod-HOLTMB Dist-IFB 1969

Madina Boe B 40 MIN
16MM FILM OPTICAL SOUND
Explains how the people of Guinea Bissau have liberated two-thirds of their country. Describes a people's war fought by a people's army, where poets, peasants and doctors fight side-by-side.
Prod-SFN Dist-SFN

Madison Artists—A Series

Presents a magazine format concerning accomplishments of east Kentucky artists.
Prod-EASTKU Dist-EASTKU

Madison School Plan, The C 18 MIN
16MM FILM, 3/4 OR 1/2 IN VIDEO C
Describes an innovative learning center concept providing for the education of exceptional children in a setting allowing the free flow of children between the regular classes and the specialized faculty.
Prod-AIMS Dist-AIMS

Madison School Plan, The (Spanish) C 18 MIN
16MM FILM, 3/4 OR 1/2 IN VIDEO C A
Presents a plan for intergrating exceptional children into the regular school program. Explains that children are allowed to take part in regular classes as well as being instructed by the specialized faculty of a learning center.
Prod-SMUSD Dist-AIMS 1971

Madmax C 93 MIN
16MM FILM OPTICAL SOUND H A
Tells the story of a desolate, lawless future where leather suited cops protect highways from suicidally daring drivers and roving motorcycle gangs. Stars Mel Gibson.
Prod-AIP Dist-TIMLIF 1980

Madness C 60 MIN
3/4 OR 1/2 INCH VIDEO CASSETTE C A
Discusses schizophrenia.
From The Brain, Mind And Behavior Series.
Prod-WNETTV Dist-FI

Madness And Medicine C 49 MIN
16MM FILM, 3/4 OR 1/2 IN VIDEO J-C A
Explores the quality of mental institutions. Examines the relatively radical therapies of drugs, electroshock therapy, and psychosurgery.
Prod-ABCTV Dist-CRMP 1977

Madness And Method - The Play Within The Play - Hamlet As Playwright C 45 MIN
3/4 OR 1/2 INCH VIDEO CASSETTE
Looks at the play within a play in Shakespeare's work Hamlet.
From The Survey Of English Literature I Series.
Prod-MDCPB Dist-MDCPB

Madrid - Capital De Espana C 18 MIN
16MM FILM, 3/4 OR 1/2 IN VIDEO J-C
A Spanish language film for first year Spanish students. Views Madrid, Spain--the principle streets, the airport, Spain's tallest building, monuments and statues, the bull ring and a bull fight. Visits the Prado Museum featuring the paintings of El Greco, Goya and Velasquez.
From The Spanish Language Series.
Prod-IFB Dist-IFB 1969

Madrid, N M C 9 MIN
16MM FILM OPTICAL SOUND I-C A
Uses poetry, music and scenes of empty houses and sunrises to present a portrait of a ghost town in New Mexico.
LC NO. 79-700760
Prod-BLUSKY Dist-BLUSKY 1978

Maelstrom C 1 MIN
16MM FILM OPTICAL SOUND
Presents an old woman who takes a ride on the carousel of life and is flooded with memories of her past.
LC NO. 72-702401
Prod-USC Dist-USC 1972

Maestros De La Pintura X 9 MIN
16MM FILM, 3/4 OR 1/2 IN VIDEO H-C
A Spanish language film. Camon Aznar gives historical and cultural backgrounds of important painters of the golden age of Spain. Includes El Greco, Murillo, Velasquez, Zurbaran, Goya and Ribera.
From The Rasgos Culturales Series.
Prod-EBF Dist-EBEC 1965

Maggie And The Beautiful Machine - Backs--A Series

Features Maggie Lettvin offering physical fitness exercises for improvement of the back.
Prod-WGBHTV Dist-PUBTEL

Back, The, Pt 1 29 MIN
Back, The, Pt 2 29 MIN
Maintenance 29 MIN
Posture 29 MIN
Upper Back, The 29 MIN

Maggie And The Beautiful Machine - Bellies--A Series

Features Maggie Lettvin offering physical fitness exercises for improvement of the abdomen.
Prod-WGBHTV Dist-PUBTEL

Abdominals 29 MIN
Basics (Abdominals) 29 MIN
Breathe 29 MIN
Pot Bellies 29 MIN
Side Abdominals 29 MIN

Maggie And The Beautiful Machine - Easy Does It--A Series

Features Maggie Lettvin offering physical fitness exercises for improvement of the human body.
Prod-WGBHTV Dist-PUBTEL

Chairs, Pt 1 29 MIN
Chairs, Pt 2 29 MIN
Flexibility 29 MIN
Long Live 29 MIN
Slow And Easy 29 MIN

Maggie And The Beautiful Machine - Eating --A Series

Features Maggie Lettvin offering physical fitness as a means for removal of unwanted weight.
Prod-WGBHTV Dist-PUBTEL

Dieting 29 MIN
Goodies 29 MIN
I Never See Maggie Alone 29 MIN
Ten Ugly Pounds 29 MIN
Thoroughbreds 29 MIN

Maggie And The Beautiful Machine - Feet And Legs--A Series

Features Maggie Lettvin offering physical fitness exercises for the improvement of the feet and legs.
Prod-WGBHTV Dist-PUBTEL

Basics (Thighs) 29 MIN
Feet, The 29 MIN
Inner Thighs, The 29 MIN
Knees 29 MIN
Let's Split (Inner Thighs II) 29 MIN

Maggie And The Beautiful Machine - General Shape-Up--A Series

Features Maggie Lettvin offering physical fitness exercises for improvement of the human body.
Prod-WGBHTV Dist-PUBTEL

Best Ones, The 29 MIN
Combinations 29 MIN
Maintenance 29 MIN
Test, Pt 1 29 MIN
Test, Pt 2 29 MIN

Maggie And The Beautiful Machine - Hips And The Bottom--A Series

Features Maggie Lettvin offering physical fitness exercises for improvement of hips and the bottom.
Prod-WGBHTV Dist-PUBTEL

Basics (Thighs) 29 MIN
Four Walls 29 MIN
Hips And Bottom, Pt 1 29 MIN
Hips And Bottom, Pt 2 29 MIN
Inner Thighs, The 29 MIN

Maggie And The Beautiful Machine - Maggie And Her Willing Accomplices--A Series

Features Maggie Lettvin offering physical fitness exercises for improvement of the human body.
Prod-WGBHTV Dist-PUBTEL

Chest, The 29 MIN
Chin And Neck 29 MIN
Face, The 29 MIN
Hips And Bottom, Pt 1 29 MIN
When In Rome 29 MIN

Maggie And The Beautiful Machine - Pregnancy --A Series

Features Maggie Lettvin offering physical fitness exercises for improvement of health and figure during pregnancy.
Prod-WGBHTV Dist-PUBTEL

Babies And Bellies 29 MIN
Delivery 29 MIN
Little Bit More Pregnant, A 29 MIN
Little Bit Pregnant, A 29 MIN
Round Seven Months, A 29 MIN

Maggie And The Beautiful Machine - Shape-Up Now For Kids--A Series

Features Maggie Lettvin offering physical fitness exercises for improvement of the human body.
Prod-WGBHTV Dist-PUBTEL

Circulation 29 MIN
Dieting 29 MIN
Kids' Stuff 29 MIN
Test, Pt 2 29 MIN
When You And I Were Young Maggie 29 MIN

Maggie Kuhn - Wrinkled Radical C 27 MIN
16MM FILM, 3/4 OR 1/2 IN VIDEO H-C A
Profiles Gray Panthers leader Maggie Kuhn and her efforts in protecting the rights of the elderly. Shows her being interviewed in her home, working in the Panthers' Philadelphia offices and speaking with groups about discrimination against the aged.
Prod-WNDTTV Dist-IU 1977

Maggie, A Girl Of The Streets - A Novel By Stephen Crane C 15 MIN
16MM FILM, 3/4 OR 1/2 IN VIDEO J-C A
Presents the story of an impoverished young woman living a life of violence, cruelty and despair in New York City's Lower East Side in the 1890's. Based on the novel MAGGIE, A GIRL OF THE STREETS by Stephen Crane.
From The Novel Series.
LC NO. 83-706269
Prod-IITC Dist-IU 1982

Maggie's Farm C 5 MIN
16MM FILM OPTICAL SOUND
Deals with a woman who makes pottery for a living.
LC NO. 78-701311
Prod-LCSDNO Dist-LCSDNO Prodn-VOGELP 1978

Magic And Catholicism C 34 MIN
16MM FILM OPTICAL SOUND
Shows how the people of the Bolivian highlands blend in thought and practice the religion of their ancestors and their conquerors. Demonstrates how a fatal automobile accident provides occasion for expressions of both faiths in an effort to influence events.
Prod-AUFS Dist-WHEELK

Magic And Motion C 20 MIN
3/4 INCH VIDEO CASSETTE I
Presents a lesson in psychomotor development. Depicts characters in a school classroom to illustrate a series of motor skills activities.
From The Wonderama Of The Arts Series.
Prod-WBRATV Dist-GPITVL 1979

Magic And Music C 17 MIN
16MM FILM, 3/4 OR 1/2 IN VIDEO P-C A
Uses animation to depict modern and classical music. Enacts Rimsky-Korsakoff's Flight of the Bumblebee and excerpts from Beethoven's Sixth Symphony.
Prod-DISNEY Dist-WDEMCO 1974

Magic Balloons, The C 16 MIN
16MM FILM, 3/4 OR 1/2 IN VIDEO P-I
Presents an art film without narration about a little boy on the beach who sells balloons which become real people to him.
Prod-LCOA Dist-LCOA 1969

Magic Bill C 7 MIN
16MM FILM, 3/4 OR 1/2 IN VIDEO I-H A
Presents Magic Bill, a sweet-talking drug dealer and Bruce Weitz from Hill Street Blues. Discusses how not to be fooled into thinking drugs are harmless.
Prod-WQED Dist-MTI

Magic Brew Of L-L-L-L, The B 15 MIN
2 INCH VIDEOTAPE P
See series title for descriptive statement.
From The Sounds Like Magic Series.
Prod-MOEBA Dist-GPITVL Prodn-KYNETV

Magic Brew Of R-R-R-R, The B 15 MIN
2 INCH VIDEOTAPE P
See series title for descriptive statement.
From The Sounds Like Magic Series.
Prod-MOEBA Dist-GPITVL Prodn-KYNETV

Magic Brew Of S-S-S-S, The B 15 MIN
2 INCH VIDEOTAPE P
See series title for descriptive statement.
From The Sounds Like Magic Series.
Prod-MOEBA Dist-GPITVL Prodn-KYNETV

Magic Bullet, The C 27 MIN
16MM FILM, 3/4 OR 1/2 IN VIDEO J-C A
Discusses the medical uses of isolated individual antibodies.
From The Perspective Series.
Prod-LONTVS Dist-STNFLD

Magic Carpet--A Series
P
Presents folk tales from around the world.
Prod-SDCSS Dist-GPITVL 1977

Aesop And His Fables 015 MIN
Aladdin And His Magic Lamp 015 MIN
Butterfly Tray, The 015 MIN
Legend Of Paul Bunyan, The 015 MIN
Monkey And The Crocodile, The 015 MIN
Paul Revere's Ride 015 MIN
Princess Of The Full Moon, The 015 MIN
Rip Van Winkle 015 MIN
Story Of John Henry, The 015 MIN
Story Of Molly Pitcher, The 015 MIN
Three Billy Goats Gruff, The 015 MIN
Why Rabbits Have Long Ears 015 MIN
Why Spiders Hide In Dark Corners 015 MIN

Magic Circle--A Series

Provides a behavioral model for classroom children to discover the power of creative alternatives. Teaches children to share their feelings and to realize that other children have similar problems.
Prod-TRAFCO Dist-ECUFLM 1975

Bleacher Feature 12 MIN
Kids In Conflict 12 MIN
Pinch, The 12 MIN

Magic Circle--A Series

Prod-UMCH Dist-MMA 1975

Kids And Conflicts 12 MIN

Magic Circle--A Series
K A
Designed to teach children about conflict and feelings. Encourages children to discuss their feelings.
Prod-HDI Dist-UMCOM Prodn-UMCOM 1975

Bleach Feature, The 012 MIN
Kids And Conflict 012 MIN
Pinch, The 012 MIN

Magic Day C 22 MIN
16MM FILM OPTICAL SOUND H-C A
Shows how such public agencies as transportation, police, fire and public health departments work to protect a teen-age girl during one day. Also explains the protective services of volunteer agencies.
Prod-WSU Dist-WSU 1954

Magic Endings B 15 MIN
2 INCH VIDEOTAPE P
See series title for descriptive statement.
From The Sounds Like Magic Series.
Prod-MOEBA Dist-GPITVL Prodn-KYNETV

Magic Fishbone, The C 11 MIN
16MM FILM, 3/4 OR 1/2 IN VIDEO I-J
Relates what happens when a good fairy aids an impoverished family with a magic fishbone that may only be used once. Based on a story by Charles Dickens.
Prod-KRATKY Dist-PHENIX 1982

Magic Flute, The C 8 MIN
16MM FILM OPTICAL SOUND
Offers a Fox and Crow satire on the foibles of mankind.
Prod-TIMLIF Dist-TIMLIF 1982

Magic Flute, The C 8 MIN
16MM FILM - 3/4 IN VIDEO
Presents an animated story about a boy whose mundane life is filled with enchantment when he finds an abandoned flute and begins to play magical melodies.
LC NO. 79-706254
Prod-THOMG Dist-NFBC 1979

Magic Flute, The C 10 MIN
16MM FILM, 3/4 OR 1/2 IN VIDEO K-P
Uses animation to tell how a minstrel inspires the wrath of a lord who hates music.
Prod-CAROUF Dist-CAROUF

Magic Gift Of Rongo X 11 MIN
16MM FILM OPTICAL SOUND J-H
A story of an inept young fisherman who becomes skillful after he learns net making from a demigod, which he captured by chance.
Prod-CINEPC Dist-CINEPC

Magic Grandpa C 8 MIN
16MM FILM, 3/4 OR 1/2 IN VIDEO I-J
Uses puppet animation to tell a story about a lazy brother who is tricked into learning industrious habits.
Prod-KRATKY Dist-PHENIX 1980

Magic Hands C 7 MIN
16MM FILM, 3/4 OR 1/2 IN VIDEO K-I
Shows four make-believe sequences in which children use their hands to make wishes come true.
From The Magic Moments Series.
Prod-EBEC Dist-EBEC 1969

Magic Harp, The C 26 MIN
16MM FILM, 3/4 OR 1/2 IN VIDEO
Dramatizes a story from the Llanos country of southern Venezuela about a boy who saved his family from destitution through the power and beauty of his music.
Prod-FOTH Dist-FOTH

Magic Hat, The C 23 MIN
16MM FILM, 3/4 OR 1/2 IN VIDEO P-I
Presents a contemporary story, based on the fairy tale The Emperor's New Clothes, about a young boy who is having difficulties making friends in a new city and receives a magic hat guaranteed to make everyone like him. Shows how he learns some truths about friendships and the powers of the special hat.
From the Unicorn Tales Series.
LC NO. 80-706518
Prod-MGHT Dist-MGHT Prodn-DENOIA 1980

Magic Horse, The C 57 MIN
16MM FILM OPTICAL SOUND P-I
Presents the first full-length Russian color cartoon in an English language version.
Prod-FI Dist-FI

Magic Horse, The C 56 MIN
3/4 OR 1/2 INCH VIDEO CASSETTE
Features a Russian cartoon based on one of the most popular children's folk tales about a boy who befriends a magical horse.
Prod-IHF Dist-IHF

Magic House, The C 17 MIN
16MM FILM, 3/4 OR 1/2 IN VIDEO P-I
Presents a modern fantasy about children who are unhappy with household chores and the family pecking order. Reveals what happens when their wishes come true and they discover a difference between getting what they wished for and getting what they wanted. Provides insight into the idea of mutual responsibility in society.
Prod-KINGSP Dist-PHENIX 1970

Magic In The Fingers B 16 MIN
16MM FILM OPTICAL SOUND I-C A
Presents child maestros who perform on different musical instruments with considerable talent.
Prod-INDIA Dist-NEDINF

Magic In The Sky C 57 MIN
16MM FILM, 3/4 OR 1/2 IN VIDEO
Presents a documentary that investigates the impact of U S and Canadian television on Eskimos in the Arctic and their struggle to establish their own network. Provides examples of the effects television can have on any culture.
LC NO. 83-707220
Prod-NFBC Dist-NFBC 1983

Magic Lantern Movie, The C 9 MIN
16MM FILM OPTICAL SOUND
Traces the Magic Lantern's history and shows slides depicting travel scenes, familiar stories, jokes and tricks. Illustrates the basic principles of all future projection of slides, as well as movies. Includes scenes from George Melies' 1903 film, The Magic Lantern, with music selected from works played on antique music boxes which were used with slide presentations of the 19th century. Produced by Maxine Haleff, with narration written by Cecile Starr and animation by Bob Fontana.
Prod-STARRC Dist-STARRC

Magic Lantern Show, The - And How It Grew - A History Of Movies B 14 MIN
16MM FILM OPTICAL SOUND I-C A
Focuses on the birth and growth of the art of cinema. Includes film clips from early classics, both silent and sound. Explains the development of color film, high speed photography and sophisticated cameras.
From The Screen News Digest Series. Vol 17, Issue 6
LC NO. 76-701236
Prod-HEARST Dist-HEARST 1975

Magic Letters C 16 MIN
16MM FILM OPTICAL SOUND K-I
Demonstrates the teaching formation of letters and the relationship of the capital and small letter. Includes the letters A, B, C, D, E, F and G.
Prod-SF Dist-SF 1968

Magic Machines, The C 14 MIN
16MM FILM, 3/4 OR 1/2 IN VIDEO J-H
Documents the lifestyle and art of Robert Gilbert, a sculptor who transforms society's junk into magic machines that bring fantasy to life.
Prod-PFP Dist-PFP 1970

Magic Man C 24 MIN
16MM FILM, 3/4 OR 1/2 IN VIDEO P-J
Shows Nicholas preferring to perform magic with his uncle rather than studying for school. Reveals that he soon discovers that both learning magic and school require study and imagination.
From The World According To Nicholas Series.
Prod-LUF Dist-LUF 1980

Magic Moments At Magic Mountain C 16 MIN
16MM FILM OPTICAL SOUND
Gives a guided tour of the various attractions at Magic Mountain amusement park.
LC NO. 79-701107
Prod-MAGMOU Dist-CALCOM Prodn-CALCOM 1978

Magic Moments—A Series
16MM FILM, 3/4 OR 1/2 IN VIDEO K-I
Presents stories and games designed to stimulate language skills.
Prod-EBEC Dist-EBEC 1969

Bang	003 MIN
Choosing Up	007 MIN
Clap	005 MIN
Fantasy Of Feet	008 MIN
Follow Me	006 MIN
Getting Along	003 MIN
Getting Even	004 MIN
Guessing Game	007 MIN
Hands Grow Up	004 MIN
Holding On	005 MIN
Join Hands, Let Go	009 MIN
Lopsideland	005 MIN
Magic Hands	007 MIN
Magic Sneakers	009 MIN
Matching Up	005 MIN
Me, Too	004 MIN
Toes Tell	007 MIN
What If	004 MIN
What's Happening	005 MIN
Whose Shoes	004 MIN

Magic Moth, The C 22 MIN
16MM FILM, 3/4 OR 1/2 IN VIDEO P-C A
Presents a film version of the book THE MAGIC MOTH. Depicts the death of a child, the reactions of the other family members and the process which the family goes through during this crisis. Deals realistically with death from the point of view of a young boy.
Prod-CENTRO Dist-CORF 1976

Magic Moth, The (Captioned) C 22 MIN
16MM FILM, 3/4 OR 1/2 IN VIDEO P-C A
Presents a film version of the book The Magic Moth. Depicts the death of a child, the reactions of the other family members and the process which the family goes through during this crisis. Deals realistically with death from the point of view of a young boy.
Prod-CENTRO Dist-CORF 1976

Magic Movies Of Georges Malies, The C 56 MIN
2 INCH VIDEOTAPE
See series title for descriptive statement.
From The Toys That Grew Up II Series.
Prod-WTTWTV Dist-PUBTEL

Magic Numbers C 20 MIN
16MM FILM OPTICAL SOUND K-I
Demonstrates the teaching formation of numbers. Shows the relationship between a numeral, its name and its meaning. Includes the numbers 1, 2, 3, 4, 5, 6, 7, 8, 9 and 10.
Prod-SF Dist-SF 1968

Magic Of A Counter, The C 14 MIN
16MM FILM, 3/4 OR 1/2 IN VIDEO P-J
Introduces the basic concepts of decimal numeration through the use of blocks and a large counter.
Prod-BOUNDY Dist-PHENIX 1969

Magic Of Color C 15 MIN
3/4 OR 1/2 INCH VIDEO CASSETTE P-I
Discusses color in art.
From The Young At Art Series.
Prod-WSKJTV Dist-AITECH 1980

Magic Of Dance—A Series
16MM FILM, 3/4 OR 1/2 IN VIDEO J-C A
Presents Dame Margot Fonteyn offering a look at the world of ballet.
LC NO. 80-706668
Prod-BBCTV Dist-TIMLIF 1980

Ebb And Flow, The	052 MIN
Magnificent Beginning, The	052 MIN
Out Of The Limelight, Home In The Rain	052 MIN
Romantic Ballet, The	052 MIN
Scene Changes, The	052 MIN
What Is New	052 MIN

Magic Of Disneyland C 21 MIN
16MM FILM, 3/4 OR 1/2 IN VIDEO I-H
Shows the revised version of 'GALA DAY AT DISNEYLAND A VISIT TO THE HAPPIEST PLACE ON EARTH.'
Prod-DISNEY Dist-WDEMCO 1970

Magic Of Fire, The C 23 MIN
16MM FILM, 3/4 OR 1/2 IN VIDEO
Illustrates how fires and explosions occur and describes the safe use and control of commonly used gases and flammable liquids by tabletop displays and laboratory demonstrations. Points out the various industrial fires and fire hazards in the home with instruction on their prevention.
Prod-USBM Dist-USNAC 1965

Magic Of Ireland, The C 12 MIN
16MM FILM, 3/4 OR 1/2 IN VIDEO J-H
Offers an introduction to the history, literature, countryside and people of Ireland.
LC NO. 80-707500
Prod-SPECTR Dist-MTI 1978

Magic Of Manatee C 15 MIN
16MM FILM OPTICAL SOUND
Presents a scenic tour of Manatee County, Florida.
Prod-FLADC Dist-FLADC

Magic Of Model Railroading, The C 15 MIN
16MM FILM OPTICAL SOUND
Discusses the joys of model railroading.
Prod-MORAIL Dist-MORAIL

Magic Of Oil Painting—A Series

Presents California artist William Alexander sharing his oil painting techniques and discussing his philosophy of art.
Prod-KOCETV Dist-PUBTEL

Floral	029 MIN
Morning Scene	029 MIN
Seascape	029 MIN
Still Life	029 MIN
Summer Landscape	029 MIN
Sunset	029 MIN

Magic Of Refining, The C 17 MIN
3/4 OR 1/2 INCH VIDEO CASSETTE
Illustrates what goes on inside the metal walls of strange vessels and mazes of pipes in an oil refinery.
Prod-HBS Dist-IVCH

Magic Of The Atom—A Series
16MM FILM, 3/4 OR 1/2 IN VIDEO
Prod-HANDEL Dist-HANDEL

Atom And Archaeology, The	025 MIN
Atom And the Environment, The	022 MIN
Atom In The Hospital, The	013 MIN
Atom Smashers (2nd Ed)	018 MIN
Atom, The - Underground	020 MIN
Atomic Energy For Space	017 MIN
Atomic Fingerprint, The	013 MIN
Atomic Power Production	014 MIN
Radioisotope Scanning In Medicine	016 MIN
Riddle Of Photosynthesis, The (2nd Ed)	015 MIN

Magic Of The Atom, The - The Riddle Of Photosynthesis C 15 MIN
16MM FILM OPTICAL SOUND J-C A
Explains the role of photosynthesis in the production of food in nature. Details the complex sequence of chemical processes that occur and identifies some of the intermediary compounds formed by plants in the process of producing food stuffs.
Prod-ATOMEC Dist-USERD

Magic Of The Mountains C 11 MIN
16MM FILM OPTICAL SOUND I-C A
Studies the color and splendor investing the beautiful valley of Kashmir as spring gives place to summer and again as autumn lights up the valley in gorgeous tints of fascinating beauty which slowly fade out with the advent of winter.
Prod-INDIA Dist-NEDINF

Magic Of TV, The C 12 MIN
16MM FILM, 3/4 OR 1/2 IN VIDEO I-J
Shows how special effects and slow-motion photography are used to enhance television programming and explains the techniques behind various special effects. Helps children distinguish between fantasy and reality.
From The Getting The Most Out Of TV Series.
LC NO. 81-706059
Prod-TAPPRO Dist-MTI 1981

Magic Of Virginia, The C 14 MIN
16MM FILM OPTICAL SOUND
Tells the importance of proper public relations training, particularly when attracting out-of-state visitors.

LC NO. FIA67-2146
Prod-VADE Dist-VADE 1966

Magic Of Walt Disney World, The C 25 MIN
16MM FILM OPTICAL SOUND
Features a tour of Walt Disney World, a vacation kingdom of entertainment for the whole family.
Prod-FLADC Dist-FLADC

Magic Of Walt Disney World, The C 30 MIN
16MM FILM, 3/4 OR 1/2 IN VIDEO
Provides a tour of the unique vacation destination area of Disneyland. Shows the aesthetics which are achievable with careful and innovative community planning.
Prod-DISNEY Dist-WDEMCO 1973

Magic Of Water, The C 25 MIN
16MM FILM OPTICAL SOUND
Shows the techniques of irrigation.
LC NO. 76-701466
Prod-CENTWO Dist-CENTWO 1975

Magic Of Words—A Series
K-P
Encourages us to engage in individual activities which will further widen our appreciation of and interest in the various language arts. Explores storytelling, creative writing, dramatics, poetry reading and writing, expression through puppetry, reading of books, language of words and music and the art of cartooning. (Broadcast quality)
Prod-GWTVAI Dist-GPITVL Prodn-WETATV

Alphabet 15 MIN
Art Of Story Telling, The 15 MIN
Classroom Dramatics 15 MIN
Enjoying Poetry Together 15 MIN
Finding The Right Book For You 15 MIN
From The Author To You 15 MIN
Giving A Talk 15 MIN
Has Your Writing Improved 15 MIN
It's Poetry Time 15 MIN
Let Me Try Please 15 MIN
Let's Pretend 15 MIN
Lights, Action, Camera 15 MIN
Look At A Book, A 15 MIN
Looking Back 15 MIN
Play For Television, A 15 MIN
Poet's World, The 15 MIN
Sound Of Words, The 15 MIN
Speak Up Please 15 MIN
Stories In Picture 15 MIN
Talking Hands 15 MIN
Tell Us A Story 15 MIN
Unspoken Word, The 15 MIN
Villains And Heroes 15 MIN
What To Do With An Old Sock 15 MIN
Words And Music 15 MIN

Magic Pages—A Series
P
Presents a series of children's stories.
Prod-KLVXTV Dist-AITECH 1976

Adventures Of Egbert The Easter Egg, The 015 MIN
Aminal, The 014 MIN
Bears On Hemlock Mountain 015 MIN
Billy Goat In The Chili Patch 015 MIN
Book Of Giant Stories, The 015 MIN
Case Of The Hungry Stranger, The 012 MIN
Dragon In The Clock Box, The 015 MIN
Duchess Bakes A Cake, The 015 MIN
Eggs And Three Gold Pieces, The 015 MIN
Fish From Japan, The 015 MIN
Five Chinese Brothers, The 015 MIN
Green Machine By Polly Cameron, The 015 MIN
Hansel And Gretel 015 MIN
How Six Found Christmas 015 MIN
Ira Sleeps Over 013 MIN
Jim And The Beanstalk 015 MIN
Messy Sally 013 MIN
My Father's Dragon And The Hundred Dresses 015 MIN
Pair Of Red Clogs, A 015 MIN
Seamstress Of Salzburg, The 015 MIN
Selection Of Fables, A 015 MIN
Singing Trilogy, The 015 MIN
Sometimes It's Turkey, Sometimes It's 014 MIN
Sphero, The Reluctant Snowball 015 MIN
Stone Soup, The 015 MIN
Troll Music, The 015 MIN
Twice Upon A Time 015 MIN
You Look Ridiculous Said The Rhinocerus To 015 MIN

Magic Pipes, The C 15 MIN
16MM FILM, 3/4 OR 1/2 IN VIDEO P-I
Shows that the town of Kufstein, Austria, runs by the knowledge that every day its famous organ will play beautiful music. Tells that one day, however, something very mysterious and funny happens to the organ and the town.
Prod-DOKUMP Dist-SF 1977

Magic Pipes, The (German) C 15 MIN
16MM FILM OPTICAL SOUND
Shows that the town of Kufstein, Austria, runs by the knowledge that every day its famous organ will play beautiful music. Tells that one day, however, something very mysterious and funny happens to the organ and the town.
LC NO. 77-701813
Prod-DOKUMP Dist-SF 1977

Magic Pipes, The (Spanish) C 15 MIN
16MM FILM OPTICAL SOUND
Shows that the town of Kufstein, Austria, runs by the knowledge that every day its famous organ will play beautiful music. Tells that one day, however, something very mysterious and funny happens to the organ and the town.

LC NO. 77-701813
Prod-DOKUMP Dist-SF 1977

Magic Pony Ride, The C 23 MIN
16MM FILM, 3/4 OR 1/2 IN VIDEO P-I
Presents a contemporary story, based on the fairy tale The Ugly Duckling, about a lonely little girl and a weary pony who meet a magic man. Tells how he transforms the street into a technicolor playground and the pony into a unicorn which the little girl rides with joy.
From the Unicorn Tales Series.
LC NO. 80-706520
Prod-MGHT Dist-MGHT Prodn-DENOIA 1980

Magic Pony, The C 80 MIN
16MM FILM OPTICAL SOUND P-I
Prod-FI Dist-FI

Magic Pony, The - A Russian Fairy Tale C 11 MIN
16MM FILM, 3/4 OR 1/2 IN VIDEO K-P
Presents the Russian fairy tale The Magic Pony. Shows how a strange looking pony uses his magic to help his young master, Ivan, find a marvelous sun bird and an enchanted ring for a cruel czar. Tells how the ponu uses his magic again when the wicked ruler demands to be made young again and Ivan becomes ruler.
From The Favorite Fairy Tales And Fables Series.
Prod-CORF Dist-CORF 1980

Magic Powder Called Portland Cement C 27 MIN
3/4 OR 1/2 INCH VIDEO CASSETTE
Discusses what portland cement is, how it works and how it is made. Describes the cement hydration process, and the production of portland cement from raw materials to finished product. Covers the wet, semi-dry and dry processes of manufacturing with emphasis on the new technology such as preheaters, precalciners, roller mills and pollution-control devices.
Prod-PRTLND Dist-PRTLND

Magic Powder Called Portland Cement, The C 27 MIN
16MM FILM, 3/4 OR 1/2 IN VIDEO IND
A revised version of the motion picture From Mountains To Microns. Describes the cement hydration process and the production of Portland cement from raw materials to the finished product. Includes scenes from various cement plants which show the use of new technology to conserve fuel and control pollution and describes the work of the Portland Cement Association.
LC NO. 82-706081
Prod-PRTLND Dist-PRTLND 1979

Magic Prison - A Dialogue Set To Music C 36 MIN
16MM FILM, 3/4 OR 1/2 IN VIDEO H-C
Presents a dramatized dialogue of letters between Emily Dickinson and a stranger, Colonel T W Higginson, revealing the unique qualities of mind and character of this American poet. Dramatizes some of the most moving moments in the poet's life.
From The Humanities - Poetry Series.
Prod-EBEC Dist-EBEC 1969

Magic Rectangle, The - Short Multiplication C 11 MIN
16MM FILM, 3/4 OR 1/2 IN VIDEO P-I
Tells how a little pig explores the relationship between area and perimeter, thereby learning how to create the maximum protective area to keep the wolf away.
From The Math That Counts Series.
Prod-DAVFMS Dist-EBEC

Magic Rites - Divination By Animal Tracks - Dogon C 7 MIN
16MM FILM OPTICAL SOUND C
See series title for descriptive statement.
From The African Village Life In Mali Series.
Prod-BRYAN Dist-IFF 1967

Magic Rites - Divination By Chicken Sacrifice - Dogon C 7 MIN
16MM FILM OPTICAL SOUND C
See series title for descriptive statement.
From The African Village Life In Mali Series.
Prod-BRYAN Dist-IFF 1967

Magic Rolling Board, The C 15 MIN
16MM FILM, 3/4 OR 1/2 IN VIDEO
Takes a look at the joys and pleasures of skateboarding.
Prod-MCGIF Dist-PFP 1976

Magic Scarab, The (Superstition) C 12 MIN
16MM FILM, 3/4 OR 1/2 IN VIDEO K-P
Uses a puppet story to explore the fallacy of belief in superstition, emphasizing self-reliance. Shows how Oni and the other puppets find out whether or not a good luck charm really works when Oni reluctantly enters the spelling contest without it.
From The Forest Town Fables Series.
Prod-CORF Dist-CORF 1974

Magic Sense, The C
3/4 OR 1/2 INCH VIDEO CASSETTE
Explores the mystery and beauty of the body's living camera, the eye, showing how an image is formed and work of an eye surgeon including that of a cataract that must be shattered and clouded fluid removed to restore vision to a 30-year-old, blind from diabetes, of spastic eye muscles that keep a thirteen-month-old boy with a giant retinal tear. Illustrates how a man, tragically blinded, overcame his blindness using remembered images to interpret information from his other senses.
From The Body Human Series.
Prod-TRAINX Dist-TRAINX

Magic Shapes C 10 MIN
16MM FILM OPTICAL SOUND K-I
Reinforces the learning of basic shapes as readiness for reading, writing and mathematics. Includes the circle, square, triangle, rectangle, diamond and cross.
Prod-SF Dist-SF 1968

Magic Shop—A Series
P
Uses a magician to present selected language arts concepts.
Prod-CVETVC Dist-GPITVL Prodn-WCVETV 1982

Action Words 015 MIN
Capital Idea 015 MIN
Divide And Conquer 015 MIN
End It Right 015 MIN
Land Of Third, The 015 MIN
Long And Short Of It, The 015 MIN
Lost - Magician's Rabbit 015 MIN
Magic Shop, The - In-Service 015 MIN
Name It 015 MIN
One Plus One Equals New 015 MIN
Opposite / Same Machine, The 015 MIN
Quote, Unquote 015 MIN
Rhyming Words 015 MIN
Who, What, When, Where And Why 015 MIN
Yours Truly 015 MIN

Magic Shop, The C 12 MIN
16MM FILM, 3/4 OR 1/2 IN VIDEO J-H
Presents a story about a father who takes his son to the Genuine Magic Shop, where they encounter surprises and some unusual disappearances. Based on the short story The Magic Shop by H G Wells.
From The Humanities - Short Story Classics Series.
Prod-EBEC Dist-EBEC 1980

Magic Shop, The - In-Service C 15 MIN
3/4 OR 1/2 INCH VIDEO CASSETTE T
Presents an overview designed to acquaint teachers with the use of the 14 Magic Shop programs, which teach language arts concepts.
From The Magic Shop Series.
LC NO. 83-706145
Prod-CVETVC Dist-GPITVL Prodn-WCVETV 1982

Magic Sneakers C 8 MIN
16MM FILM, 3/4 OR 1/2 IN VIDEO K-I
Tells the story of a boy who finds a pair of magic sneakers and outwits an evil monster who wants to take the shoes away from him.
From The Magic Moments Series.
Prod-EBEC Dist-EBEC 1969

Magic Square, The C 8 MIN
16MM FILM OPTICAL SOUND P
See series title for descriptive statement.
From The Mathematics For Elementary School Students - Whole Numbers Series.
LC NO. 73-701844
Prod-DAVFMS Dist-DAVFMS 1974

Magic Stick, The C 12 MIN
16MM FILM OPTICAL SOUND K-I
Dramatizes a story about a hedgehog who finds a stick, and a rabbit who believes it has magical powers.
LC NO. 71-700760
Prod-RADTV Dist-RADTV 1969

Magic Touch, The B 12 MIN
16MM FILM OPTICAL SOUND I-C A
Shows some of the exquisite arts and crafts India's artisans produce all over the country.
Prod-INDIA Dist-NEDINF

Magic Tree, The C 10 MIN
16MM FILM, 3/4 OR 1/2 IN VIDEO P A
Presents a tale from the Congo about an unloved boy, a lonely river and a magic tree whose leaves become people. Explains how the boy finds a secret paradise, but loses it when he reveals its mystery.
Prod-LAEM Dist-TEXFLM 1970

Magic Vine, The C 15 MIN
3/4 OR 1/2 INCH VIDEO CASSETTE P
Encourages children to respond to the parts of a song - words, rhythm and melody through body movement.
From The Stepping Into Rhythm Series.
Prod-WVIZTV Dist-AITECH

Magic Water, The C 7 MIN
16MM FILM, 3/4 OR 1/2 IN VIDEO K-P
Tells how an Eskimo boy has learned to hunt and fish although blind. Cites how he catches fish to feed hungry baby seals leaving the mother seal to help him. Highlights how she visits the Queen of the Sea who rewards the youngster by restoring his sight.
From The Inuit Legends Series.
Prod-ANIMET Dist-BCNFL 1982

Magic Way Of Going, A - The Thoroughbred C 50 MIN
16MM FILM, 3/4 OR 1/2 IN VIDEO I-C A
Analyzes the thoroughbred racehorse's ability to run using the comments of expert researchers, reproductions of art masterpieces and examinations of museum specimens.
LC NO. 84-706166
Prod-CANBC Dist-WOMBAT 1983

Magic Weapons For Healthy Teeth C 15 MIN
16MM FILM, 3/4 OR 1/2 IN VIDEO P-I
Presents a dentist who uses magic to teach facts about dental hygiene to a young boy. Explains how plaque builds up on teeth and the values and techniques of proper brushing and flossing.
Prod-AIMS Dist-AIMS 1978

Magic Well, The C 14 MIN
16MM FILM, 3/4 OR 1/2 IN VIDEO P-I
Presents an adaptation of the Grimm brothers' fairytale entitled Frau Holle, in which two sisters journey to an enchanted land where kindness is rewarded by Mother Holle. Shows how the girls' journeys have very different results.
Prod-CORF Dist-CORF 1976

Magic Well, The (Captioned) C 14 MIN
16MM FILM, 3/4 OR 1/2 IN VIDEO P-I
Presents an adaptation of the Grimm Brothers' fairytale entitled Frau Holle, in which two sisters journey to an enchanted land where kindness is rewarded by Mother Holle. Shows how the girls' journeys have very different results.
Prod-CORF Dist-CORF 1976

Magic Wheel C 6 MIN
16MM FILM OPTICAL SOUND
Tells the story of Henry Joliff and the business machines he helped to make. Shows how these machines are made and used. Presents a trip to the famous school of business developed by the National Cash Register Company for the purpose of training its representatives.
Prod-NCR Dist-CCNY

Magic Window C 18 MIN
16MM FILM OPTICAL SOUND
Illustrates the operations and functions of the various IBM business machines.
Prod-IBUSMA Dist-IBUSMA

Magic Words C 10 MIN
16MM FILM, 3/4 OR 1/2 IN VIDEO P-I
Humorously portrays the joys and sorrows of languages, the function of written words, and the quirks of rhyme, synonyms, and alliteration.
Prod-KINGSP Dist-PHENIX 1971

Magic Work-Shop Of Reveron C 23 MIN
16MM FILM, 3/4 OR 1/2 IN VIDEO
Shows the fantastic life of the Venezuelan painter Armando Reveron through his objects and dolls at his studio.
Prod-MOMALA Dist-MOMALA

Magic Work-Shop Of Reveron (Spanish) C 23 MIN
3/4 OR 1/2 INCH VIDEO CASSETTE
Shows the fantastic life of the Venezuelan painter Armando Reveron through his objects and dolls at his studio.
Prod-MOMALA Dist-MOMALA

Magic Workshop Of Reveron, The (Spanish) C 23 MIN
16MM FILM OPTICAL SOUND J-C A
Details the fantastic life of the Venezuelan painter Reveron through the objects and dolls at his studio.
LC NO. 82-700847
Prod-OOAS Dist-MOMALA 1982

Magical Cook's Tour—A Series

Offers a magical tour of cooking that includes American, European, South American and Chinese delicacies and how to prepare, serve and enjoy them at home.
Prod-IVCH Dist-IVCH

Art Of French Cooking, The	020 MIN
Cooking Of German, The	025 MIN
Cooking Of Italy	020 MIN
Cooking Of Scandinavia	020 MIN
Latin American Cooking	025 MIN
New England Cooking	020 MIN
Of Course You Can	020 MIN
Outdoor Cooking	015 MIN
Pennsylvania Country Cooking	020 MIN
Pleasure Of Chinese Cooking	020 MIN

Magical Death C 29 MIN
16MM FILM - 3/4 IN VIDEO
Portrays shamanic activity and explores the connection between politics and shamanism in Yanamamo culture. Filmed in 1970 by Timothy Asch and Napoleon Chagnon.
Prod-PSU Dist-DOCEDR

Magical Disappearing Money C 11 MIN
16MM FILM, 3/4 OR 1/2 IN VIDEO J-C A
Portrays a cheerful, slightly scatterbrained 'food expert witch' appearing in a supermarket and working her magic to draw the customers around her. Shows her explaining with accompanying magic why certain purchases of the customers are unwise. Pictures the wiser customers returning to their shopping.
From The Consumer Education Series.
Prod-LEARN Dist-FLMFR 1972

Magical Disappearing Money (Spanish) C 11 MIN
16MM FILM, 3/4 OR 1/2 IN VIDEO J-C A
Provides information on how to shop wisely for food, taking into account what one gets for the money spent.
Prod-LEARN Dist-FLMFR 1972

Magical Malaysia C 25 MIN
16MM FILM, 3/4 OR 1/2 IN VIDEO H-C A
Visits the verdant jungles, exotic creature and striking religious shrines of Malaysia together with the cities of Kuala Lampur and Penang. Shows traditional dances, shadow puppets, cottage industries and small-scale farms.
LC NO. 84-706253
Prod-POLNIS Dist-IFB 1984

Magical Mystery Coat B 13 MIN
16MM FILM OPTICAL SOUND
Tells how a budding young composer is unable to write a song for the high school variety show because he lacks confidence in himself. Shows how the gift of Paul Mc Cartney's overcoat inspires him.
LC NO. 79-701177
Prod-KINGCH Dist-KINGCH 1979

Magical Wonderful What, The C 15 MIN
3/4 INCH VIDEO CASSETTE P
Discusses the human body, pointing out the analogies between mechanical and human instruments.
From The Becoming Me, Unit 1 - Physical Identity Series.
Prod-KUONTV Dist-GPITVL 1974

Magician, The C 20 MIN
16MM FILM OPTICAL SOUND P-I
Tells the story of a magician who was invited to a surprise party by some children who experiment with the star performer's equipment.
From The Magnificent 6 And 1/2 Series.
Prod-CHILDF Dist-LUF 1970

Magician, The B 13 MIN
16MM FILM, 3/4 OR 1/2 IN VIDEO I-H
Presents an anti-war film in the form of allegory about a magician who attracts a group of children at the beach. Shows how he begins by amusing them with innocent tricks, then leads them in playing with toy guns and finally, has them playing with real guns.
Prod-LUF Dist-LUF

Magician, The B 13 MIN
16MM FILM, 3/4 OR 1/2 IN VIDEO I-C A
An anti-war film in the form of an allegory. A magician attracts a group of children at a beach with amusing and innocent tricks. Gradually, however, they are led into playing with real guns.
Prod-SF Dist-SF 1963

Magician, The C 30 MIN
3/4 OR 1/2 INCH VIDEO CASSETTE P-I
See series title for descriptive statement.
From The Sonrisas Series.
Prod-KRLNTV Dist-MDCPB

Magit - A 17-Year-Old On A Kibbutz C 22 MIN
16MM FILM OPTICAL SOUND
Presents an interview with a typical Kibbutz teenager while she goes about her work in an orange grove. Features the girl speaking about life, family, sex, work and marriage.
From The Exploring Human Nature Series.
LC NO. 73-702035
Prod-EDC Dist-EDC 1973

Magna Carta, Pt 1, Rise Of The English Monarchy C 16 MIN
16MM FILM, 3/4 OR 1/2 IN VIDEO J-C
Traces the history of England from the Norman invasion in 1066 to the crowning of King John in 1199. Discusses the concept of feudalism and the conflict between the English kings and barons.
Prod-EBF Dist-EBEC 1959

Magna Carta, Pt 2, Revolt Of The Nobles And The Signing Of The Charter C 16 MIN
16MM FILM, 3/4 OR 1/2 IN VIDEO J-C
Dramatizes the events after the crowning of King John which brought the conflict between kings and barons to a climax, leading to the drafting of the Magna Carta.
Prod-EBF Dist-EBEC 1959

Magnasync Story, The C 8 MIN
16MM FILM OPTICAL SOUND J-C T
Discusses magnasync motion picture sound recording equipment which is available to film producers.
Prod-MAGSYN Dist-RVIERA 1959

Magnesium And Titanium C 12 MIN
3/4 OR 1/2 INCH VIDEO CASSETTE
Covers the production, extraction, melting, refinement and alloying of magnesium. Deals with the properties of titanium.
From The Working With Metals In The Plant Series.
Prod-TPCTRA Dist-TPCTRA

Magnesium Oxide-Sulfur Dioxide Recovery Process C 12 MIN
16MM FILM OPTICAL SOUND
Describes the magnesium oxide-sulfur dioxide recovery process used in two power stations. Provides an overview of the sulfur dioxide control problem, discusses possible solutions and examines the chemistry and equipment involved in the process.
LC NO. 78-701895
Prod-USEPA Dist-USNAC Prodn-TEKNI 1978

Magnet Earth C 50 MIN
16MM FILM, 3/4 OR 1/2 IN VIDEO H-C A
Explores current research into the earth's magnetic field and examines the effects it has on living organisms.
Prod-BBCTV Dist-FI 1982

Magnet Earth, The B 15 MIN
2 INCH VIDEOTAPE I
Explains the ways to interpret data.
From The Let's Explore Science Series.
Prod-GPITVL Dist-GPITVL

Magnet Earth, The B 15 MIN
2 INCH VIDEOTAPE I
Explains the way to interpret data. (Broadcast quality)
From The Let's Explore Science Series. No. 9
Prod-POPS Dist-GPITVL Prodn-KOAPTV

Magnet Laboratory, A B 20 MIN
16MM FILM OPTICAL SOUND H-C
Shows equipment used in producing strong magnetic fields. Demonstrates magnetic effects of currents and the magnetism of iron.
From The PSSC Physics Films Series.
Prod-PSSC Dist-MLA 1960

Magnetic Amplifiers C 39 MIN
16MM FILM, 3/4 OR 1/2 IN VIDEO
Discusses the use and advantages of magnetic amplifiers in controlling electric power. Uses schematics and graphs of the ideal hysteresis loop to illustrate the theory behind the operation and construction of saturable reactors and self-saturating reactors.
Prod-USAF Dist-USNAC 1963

Magnetic Bubble Memories (MBM) C 30 MIN
3/4 OR 1/2 INCH VIDEO CASSETTE IND
Shows magnetic bubble memory (MBM) features, MBM technology and device organization, operation of an MBM system, inter- facing MBM with microprocessors and design examples.
From The Microcomputer Memory Design Series.
Prod-COLOSU Dist-COLOSU

Magnetic Confinement C 24 MIN
3/4 OR 1/2 INCH VIDEO CASSETTE H-C
Explores plasma which can be contained and controlled by magnetic force fields at very hot temperatures. Shows how collisions of plasma molecules cause fusion. Uses models, demonstrations, and animation to illustrate behavior of charge particles in various magnetic field geometrics.
From The Discovering Physics Series.
Prod-BBCTV Dist-MEDIA Prodn-OPENU 1983

Magnetic Cores, Pt 1 - Properties B 29 MIN
16MM FILM, 3/4 OR 1/2 IN VIDEO
Depicts properties of magnetic cores and their application in data processing systems. Shows how information is stored and transferred from one core to another.
Prod-USA Dist-USNAC 1962

Magnetic Cores, Pt 2 - Basic Circuits B 30 MIN
16MM FILM, 3/4 OR 1/2 IN VIDEO
Describes the features and functions of single-diode, split-winding and inhibit transfer loops. Shows the application of these loops singly or in combination.
Prod-USA Dist-USNAC 1962

Magnetic Disc Interfacing, Pt 1 C 48 MIN
3/4 OR 1/2 INCH VIDEO CASSETTE
See series title for descriptive statement.
From The Microprocessor Interfacing Series.
Prod-MIOT Dist-MIOT

Magnetic Disk Interfacing, Part 1 C 45 MIN
3/4 OR 1/2 INCH VIDEO CASSETTE IND
See series title for descriptive statement.
From The Microprocessor Interfacing Series.
Prod-ICSINT Dist-ICSINT

Magnetic Disk Interfacing, Part 2 C 45 MIN
3/4 OR 1/2 INCH VIDEO CASSETTE IND
See series title for descriptive statement.
From The Microprocessor Interfacing Series.
Prod-ICSINT Dist-ICSINT

Magnetic Disk Interfacing, Pt 1 C 35 MIN
3/4 INCH VIDEO CASSETTE C
See series title for descriptive statement.
From The Microprocessor Interfacing Series. Part 11
LC NO. 81-706199
Prod-AMCEE Dist-AMCEE 1980

Magnetic Disk Interfacing, Pt 1 C 43 MIN
3/4 OR 1/2 INCH VIDEO CASSETTE PRO
Describes disk storage techniques. Deals with bit-shifting problems.
From The Microprocessing Interfacing Series.
Prod-AMCEE Dist-AMCEE

Magnetic Disk Interfacing, Pt 2 C 35 MIN
3/4 INCH VIDEO CASSETTE C
See series title for descriptive statement.
From The Microprocessor Interfacing Series. Part 12
LC NO. 81-706199
Prod-AMCEE Dist-AMCEE 1980

Magnetic Disk Interfacing, Pt 2 C 43 MIN
3/4 OR 1/2 INCH VIDEO CASSETTE PRO
Discusses floppy disk controller implementation techniques, delineator controller functions. Considers timing.
From The Microprocessing Interfacing Series.
Prod-AMCEE Dist-AMCEE

Magnetic Disk Interfacing, Pt 2 C 44 MIN
3/4 OR 1/2 INCH VIDEO CASSETTE
See series title for descriptive statement.
From The Microprocessor Interfacing Series.
Prod-MIOT Dist-MIOT

Magnetic Effects In Space C 14 MIN
16MM FILM, 3/4 OR 1/2 IN VIDEO
Illustrates basic principles of science by utilizing film footage from Skylab in-flight science demonstrations. Shows astronaut Owen K Garriott discussing experiments in which magnetic effects in space are shown from Skylab television transmission and demonstration equipment. Issued in 1975 as a motion picture.
From The Skylab Science Demonstrations Series.
LC NO. 80-706412
Prod-NASA Dist-USNAC Prodn-AVCORP 1980

Magnetic Fields - Lines Of Force C 20 MIN
2 INCH VIDEOTAPE I
See series title for descriptive statement.
From The Exploring With Science, Unit VII - Magnetism Series.
Prod-MPATI Dist-GPITVL

Magnetic Fields And Electric Currents, Pt 1 C 14 MIN
16MM FILM, 3/4 OR 1/2 IN VIDEO I-H
Explores the magnetic properties associated with a wire carrying a direct electric current. Uses models to demonstrate the existence of a magnetic field in the vicinity of a current-carrying conductor. Establishes properties of the magnetic field, such as direction and strength by experimentation.
Prod-BFA Dist-PHENIX 1972

Magnetic Fields And Electric Currents, Pt 2 C 13 MIN
16MM FILM, 3/4 OR 1/2 IN VIDEO
Investigates what happens when magnetic fields interact. Studies

the effect by observing the magnetic fields of permanent magnets which are attracting and repelling other magnets. Shows that similar effects occur when the interacting fields are produced by electric currents. Uses the principles demonstrated to explain the operation of a simple electric motor.
Prod-BFA Dist-PHENIX 1973

Magnetic Force C 15 MIN
2 INCH VIDEOTAPE P
Demonstrates magnetic force that can counteract the force of gravity.
From The Science Is Searching Series.
Prod-DETPS Dist-GPITVL

Magnetic Highway C 28 MIN
16MM FILM OPTICAL SOUND
Demonstrates the sophistication reached by modern motor carrier operations, looks at career opportunities available in the trucking industry, and provides a view of electronic communications and motor freight management.
Prod-ATA Dist-MTP

Magnetic Memory C 25 MIN
16MM FILM OPTICAL SOUND
Explains how magnetic tape has added a new dimension to the memory of man. Outlines many uses of magnetic tape, describes the manufacturing process and discusses the controls exercised to produce tape.
Prod-MMAMC Dist-MMAMC 1961

Magnetic North B 27 MIN
16MM FILM, 3/4 OR 1/2 IN VIDEO J-H
Documents World War II battles in the Polar region from Murmansk to Alaska.
From The Victory At Sea Series.
Prod-NBCTV Dist-LUF

Magnetic Particle And Radiographic Inspection C
3/4 OR 1/2 INCH VIDEO CASSETTE IND
Covers magnetic particle inspection, type of magnetizing current, demagnetization equipment, interpretation of patterns, nonrelevant indications, radiographic sources, foundamentals, technique, detectable discontinuities and interpretation and standards.
From The Welding Inspection And Quality Control Series.
Prod-AMCEE Dist-AMCEE

Magnetic Particle Testing C 55 MIN
3/4 OR 1/2 INCH VIDEO CASSETTE PRO
Recounts the history and development of magnetic particle testing. Describes test procedures and evaluation.
From The Fundamentals Of Nondestructive Testing Series.
Prod-AMCEE Dist-AMCEE

Magnetic Removal Of Foreign Bodies From The Bovine Reticulum C 24 MIN
16MM FILM OPTICAL SOUND PRO
Demonstrates the removal of a foreign body from the bovine animal and discusses the equipment used. (Kinescope)
Prod-CIBA Dist-AMVMA

Magnetic Tape Interfacing, Part 1 C 45 MIN
3/4 OR 1/2 INCH VIDEO CASSETTE IND
See series title for descriptive statement.
From The Microprocessor Interfacing Series.
Prod-ICSINT Dist-ICSINT

Magnetic Tape Interfacing, Part 2 C 45 MIN
3/4 OR 1/2 INCH VIDEO CASSETTE IND
See series title for descriptive statement.
From The Microprocessor Interfacing Series.
Prod-ICSINT Dist-ICSINT

Magnetic Tape Interfacing, Pt 1 C 35 MIN
3/4 INCH VIDEO CASSETTE C
See series title for descriptive statement.
From The Microprocessor Interfacing Series. Part 9
LC NO. 81-706199
Prod-AMCEE Dist-AMCEE 1980

Magnetic Tape Interfacing, Pt 1 C 43 MIN
3/4 OR 1/2 INCH VIDEO CASSETTE PRO
Describes magnetic tape storage techniques. Highlights the Kansas City Standard.
From The Microprocessing Interfacing Series.
Prod-AMCEE Dist-AMCEE

Magnetic Tape Interfacing, Pt 1 C 45 MIN
3/4 OR 1/2 INCH VIDEO CASSETTE
See series title for descriptive statement.
From The Microprocessor Interfacing Series.
Prod-MIOT Dist-MIOT

Magnetic Tape Interfacing, Pt 2 C 35 MIN
3/4 INCH VIDEO CASSETTE C
See series title for descriptive statement.
From The Microprocessor Interfacing Series. Part 10
LC NO. 81-706199
Prod-AMCEE Dist-AMCEE 1980

Magnetic Tape Interfacing, Pt 2 C 43 MIN
3/4 OR 1/2 INCH VIDEO CASSETTE PRO
Features design techniques for phase-locked wops in data and clock recovery.
From The Microprocessing Interfacing Series.
Prod-AMCEE Dist-AMCEE

Magnetic Tape Interfacing, Pt 2 C 45 MIN
3/4 OR 1/2 INCH VIDEO CASSETTE
See series title for descriptive statement.
From The Microprocessor Interfacing Series.
Prod-MIOT Dist-MIOT

Magnetic, Electric And Gravitation Fields (Spanish) C 11 MIN
16MM FILM, 3/4 OR 1/2 IN VIDEO I-J
Illustrates a magnetic field's properties by showing what happens when a magnet is placed next to a compass.
Prod-EBEC Dist-EBEC

Magnetic, Electric And Gravitational Fields B 11 MIN
16MM FILM, 3/4 OR 1/2 IN VIDEO I-J
Through demonstrations and drawings, shows characteristics of magnetic, electric and gravitational fields. Defines field as an area in which a force can be felt. Shows how the earth's gravitational field affects objects on the earth.
Prod-EBF Dist-EBEC 1962

Magnetism C 7 MIN
16MM FILM, 3/4 OR 1/2 IN VIDEO H-C A
Describes the uses of magnetism, the kinds of magnets, the magnetic field, lines of force, polarity, the concentration of lines of force at the poles, induced magnetism, temporary and permanent magnets, polar attraction and repulsion.
From The Basic Electricity Series.
Prod-STFD Dist-IFB 1979

Magnetism C 13 MIN
16MM FILM, 3/4 OR 1/2 IN VIDEO J-H A
Magnetism--North and South poles, magnetic fields and lines of force, the compass, electrons and magnetic field, electromagents and solenoids.
From The Electricity Series.
Prod-MORLAT Dist-SF 1967

Magnetism B 21 MIN
16MM FILM, 3/4 OR 1/2 IN VIDEO
Discusses aspects of magnetism.
LC NO. 79-707509
Prod-USAF Dist-USNAC 1979

Magnetism And Electricity C 15 MIN
3/4 OR 1/2 INCH VIDEO CASSETTE I
Considers the relationship between magnets and electricity.
From The Matter And Motion Series. Module Green
Prod-WHROTV Dist-AITECH 1973

Magnetism And Electricity C 60 MIN
3/4 OR 1/2 INCH VIDEO CASSETTE IND
See series title for descriptive statement.
From The Electrical Maintenance Training, Module A - AC And DC Theory Series.
Prod-LEIKID Dist-LEIKID

Magnetism And Fields Of Force C 14 MIN
16MM FILM, 3/4 OR 1/2 IN VIDEO P-I
Investigates a variety of substances, including the Earth itself, to find which ones may have magnetic properties.
From The Physical Science Learning Lab Series.
Prod-BARR Dist-BARR 1981

Magnetism At Work C 12 MIN
16MM FILM OPTICAL SOUND J-C
Provides a brief history of magnetism, from discovery through compasses, magnetic fields, and electromagnetics. Demonstrates important points by actual laboratory experiments. Explains what magnetism is, covering diamagnetism, paramagnetism, ferromagnetism and domains. Presents a series of modern applications, including a simplified demonstration of one of magnetism's roles in medicine.
LC NO. 75-707624
Prod-GE Dist-GE 1970

Magnetism In Space C 19 MIN
16MM FILM, 3/4 OR 1/2 IN VIDEO
Describes basics of magnetism through demonstrations on Earth and in space on board Skylab. Shows astronaut Owen K Garriott reviewing familiar magnetic effects and applications of magnets on Earth and shows how these effects are observable in space. Issued in 1975 as a motion picture.
From The Skylab Science Demonstrations Series.
LC NO. 80-706413
Prod-NASA Dist-USNAC Prodn-AVCORP 1980

Magnetism, Pt A B 34 MIN
16MM FILM OPTICAL SOUND
Defines magnets and explains the difference between natural and artificial magnets. Discusses the characteristics of magnetic lines of force about a magnet and the laws of repulsion and attraction. Explains the theory of molecular arrangement in a magnet. (Kinescope)
LC NO. 74-705062
Prod-USAF Dist-USNAC

Magnetism, Pt B B 34 MIN
16MM FILM OPTICAL SOUND
Discusses magnetic terms - permeability, retentivity, flux, reluctance, residual magnetism and magnetic shielding. Explains the characteristics of temporary and permanent magnets, concluding with a presentation of the basic shapes in which magnets are generally found. (Kinescope)
LC NO. 74-705063
Prod-USAF Dist-USNAC

Magnetism, Pt 1 C 15 MIN
3/4 INCH VIDEO CASSETTE I
Presents an explanation of the nature of magnetism.
From The Search For Science (2nd Ed,) Unit V - Electricity Series.
Prod-WVIZTV Dist-GPITVL

Magnetism, Pt 2 C 15 MIN
3/4 INCH VIDEO CASSETTE I
Shows how man's knowledge of magnetism allowed him to produce an electric motor.
From The Search For Science (2nd Ed,) Unit V - Electricity Series.
Prod-WVIZTV Dist-GPITVL

Magnetisme (Magnetic Field,) Pt 1 B 3 MIN
16MM FILM SILENT
Shows that in a magnet the molecules lie in a certain order, whereas in a piece of iron they lie in a disorderly way, but will become ordered if a magnet is brought near to the iron. Includes Danish subtitles.
Prod-STATNS Dist-STATNS 1950

Magnetisme (Magnetic Field,) Pt 2 B 3 MIN
16MM FILM SILENT
Shows the movements of free electrons in a magnetic field. Includes Danish subtitles.
Prod-STATNS Dist-STATNS 1950

Magneto Ignition C 6 MIN
16MM FILM, 3/4 OR 1/2 IN VIDEO J-C A
See series title for descriptive statement.
From The Power Mechanics Series.
Prod-THIOKL Dist-CAROUF

Magnetohydrodynamics X 27 MIN
16MM FILM, 3/4 OR 1/2 IN VIDEO PRO
Shows by experiments with incompressible conducting fluids the three-dimensional interaction between electromagnetic and velocity fields. Explanations based on simple flux-linkage arguments. Stresses rotationality of force fields and thus on vorticity, its suppression, creation and propagation.
From The Fluid Mechanics Series.
Prod-EDC Dist-EBEC 1967

Magnetron B 40 MIN
16MM FILM - 3/4 IN VIDEO
Explains how the traveling wave magnetron operates. Discusses the filters that exist in the magnetron and their effects on electron motion. Describes the basic requirements of an oscillator and points out factors that determine power and frequency, as well as the effects of varying magnetic field.
LC NO. 79-707774
Prod-USAF Dist-USNAC 1979

Magnetron Sputtering C 35 MIN
3/4 OR 1/2 INCH VIDEO CASSETTE IND
Compares normal discharge and magnetron-enhanced sputtering in terms of deposition rate, film adhesion, stress and step coverage.
From The Plasma Sputtering, Deposition And Growth Of Microelectronic Films For VLSI Series.
Prod-COLOSU Dist-COLOSU

Magnets B 10 MIN
3/4 INCH VIDEO CASSETTE P
Offers a basic introductory approach to the study of magnetism.
From The Two For Tomorrow Series.
Prod-BEOC Dist-GPITVL

Magnets C 15 MIN
2 INCH VIDEOTAPE K
Illustrates a magnet exerting a pulling and pushing force.
From The Let's Go Sciencing, Unit II - Energy Series.
Prod-DETPS Dist-GPITVL

Magnets C 15 MIN
3/4 OR 1/2 INCH VIDEO CASSETTE P
Presents Pocus showing that magnets can attract things and repel other magnets, even from a distance. Shows Myrtle and Hocus determining whether a lodestone is a magnet and which of two magnets is stronger.
From The Let Me See Series. No. 3
Prod-WETN Dist-AITECH Prodn-STSU 1982

Magnets - The Dragon's Secret C 15 MIN
16MM FILM, 3/4 OR 1/2 IN VIDEO K-P
Uses the story of a knight in clanking armor to demonstrate what magnets are, how they work and their many uses.
LC NO. 82-706655
Prod-EBEC Dist-EBEC 1981

Magnets And Their Uses X 10 MIN
16MM FILM, 3/4 OR 1/2 IN VIDEO P-I
Uses animation to illustrate the characteristics and properties of magnets. Demonstrates that a magnet has two poles and shows every-day use of magnets.
Prod-KAHANA Dist-PHENIX 1964

Magnets For Beginners C 11 MIN
16MM FILM, 3/4 OR 1/2 IN VIDEO P
Shows what materials magnets attract, what a magnetic field is, what poles are and how magnetic force can pass through objects. Uses iron filings suspended in glycerin to show magnetic field in three dimensions.
Prod-CORF Dist-CORF 1965

Magnets, Magnetism And Electricity C 9 MIN
16MM FILM, 3/4 OR 1/2 IN VIDEO P-J
Describes the major characteristics of magnets and shows how compasses and magnets are used to detect a magnetic field. Includes an animated sequence to show the relation of the electron spin in atoms in a magnet to the electron flow in a current of electricity.
Prod-MGHT Dist-MGHT Prodn-CLAIB 1970

Magnificence In Trust (Rev Ed) C 28 MIN
16MM FILM, 3/4 OR 1/2 IN VIDEO
Shows Glacier Bay National Monument, Katmai National Monument and Mount McKinley in Alaska.
Prod-USNPS Dist-USNAC

Magnificent Adventure B 28 MIN
16MM FILM OPTICAL SOUND H-C A
A feature-length version of the Life of Paul series. Tells the story of Saul of Tarsus, Saint Paul.
Prod-CAFM Dist-ECUFLM

Magnificent Adventure, The B 80 MIN
16MM FILM OPTICAL SOUND J-C A
Witnesses an adventure from the book of Acts and the life of St

Paul. Includes the stoning of Stephen, the vision of St Paul on the Damascus Road, his missionary journeys and other significant events.
Prod-CAFM Dist-CAFM

Magnificent Ambersons, The B
1/2 IN VIDEO CASSETTE BETA/VHS
Presents a story about Victorian America based on Booth Tarkington's novel THE MAGNIFICENT AMBERSONS, directed by Orson Welles.
Prod-GA Dist-GA

Magnificent Beginning, The C 52 MIN
16MM FILM, 3/4 OR 1/2 IN VIDEO J-C A
Describes the first real ballet school, founded by King Louis XIV of France. Tells how the courtly dances of 17th century France eventually led to the worldwide phenomenon of ballet.
From The Magic Of Dance Series.
Prod-BBCTV Dist-TIMLIF 1980

Magnificent Century, A C 29 MIN
16MM FILM OPTICAL SOUND
Deals with the consequences of the industrial revolution for the people who went through it.
From The Industrial Revolution Series. Film 3
Prod-LIBFUN Dist-MTP

Magnificent Ditch, The C 28 MIN
16MM FILM OPTICAL SOUND
Dramatizes an old muleskinner describing life on the Chesapeake and Ohio Canal at the turn of the twentieth century. Includes scenes of the Potomac Valley, Harper's Ferry, Salty Dog Tavern, Paw Paw Tunnel and the Canal Museum at Great Falls.
LC NO. FIA66-742
Prod-WMALTV Dist-WMALTV 1966

Magnificent Heritage C 55 MIN
16MM FILM OPTICAL SOUND J-C A
Dramatizes John Leland's role in the struggle for religious liberty in America.
LC NO. FIA65-831
Prod-BROADM Dist-BROADM 1964

Magnificent Major, The C 23 MIN
16MM FILM, 3/4 OR 1/2 IN VIDEO P-I
Presents a contemporary story, based on the children's book The Wizard Of Oz, about a little girl who hates to read, is transported to a society of non-readers and suddenly finds herself on trial for having a book. Shows how when she is forced to defend herself she reads aloud, enchanting both the court and herself, and returns with a different outlook on reading.
From the Unicorn Tales Series.
LC NO. 80-706516
Prod-MGHT Dist-MGHT Prodn-DENOIA 1980

Magnificent Moose, The C 16 MIN
16MM FILM, 3/4 OR 1/2 IN VIDEO P-J
Follows the events of a moose year, from the birth of calves, the attack of a predatory wolf pack, the training of young to feed and swim, the growing of antlers, to the climactic autumn encounters between male bulls.
From The North American Species Series.
Prod-KARVF Dist-BCNFL 1984

Magnificent Music Machines, The C 15 MIN
16MM FILM, 3/4 OR 1/2 IN VIDEO J-C A
Traces the history of mechanical music makers, from the first tiny music boxes invented in 1750 to the popular playing piano. Explains that with the coming of the phonograph and radio, the era of music machines was over.
Prod-SWAIN Dist-MCFI 1979

Magnificent 6 And 1/2–A Series
16MM FILM, 3/4 OR 1/2 IN VIDEO K-I
Prod-CHILDF Dist-LUF 1970

Astronoughts, The	021 MIN
Billy The Kid	018 MIN
Bob A Job	016 MIN
Five Survive	015 MIN
Ghosts And Ghoulies	021 MIN
Good Deed In Time, A	018 MIN
It's Not Cricket	016 MIN
Kontiki Kids	017 MIN
Lad In The Lamp, A	016 MIN
Magician, The	020 MIN
Peewee Had A Little Ape	020 MIN
Peewee's Pianola	016 MIN
Ski Wheelers, The	014 MIN
That's All We Need	016 MIN
Time Flies	015 MIN
Up For The Cup	015 MIN
Up The Creek	017 MIN
When Knights Were Bold	017 MIN

Magnolia Gardens - Charleston C 30 MIN
1/2 IN VIDEO CASSETTE BETA/VHS
Presents the Magnolia Gardens in Charleston.
From The Victory Garden Series.
Prod-WGBHTV Dist-MTI

Magoo's Puddle Jumper C 7 MIN
16MM FILM, 3/4 OR 1/2 IN VIDEO K-J
A reissue of the 1956 motion picture Magoo's Puddle Jumper. Shows how Mr Magoo accidentally drives his new automobile under water. Shows that Mr Magoo fails to realize that he is surrounded by marine life.
From The Mister Magoo Series.
Prod-BOSUST Dist-CF 1978

Magpie Lays An Egg C 17 MIN
16MM FILM OPTICAL SOUND P-I
Relates what happens when the circus comes to town and the star penguin disappears. Tells what occurs when the Chiffy kids and one goose egg enter the picture.
Prod-LUF Dist-LUF 1979

Magpie's Talking Duck C 17 MIN
16MM FILM OPTICAL SOUND P-I
Covers what happens when the Chiffy Kids enter a duck in a pet show and convince the judges that it can really talk.
Prod-LUF Dist-LUF 1979

Magritte C 14 MIN
16MM FILM OPTICAL SOUND
Presents an interview with painter Rene Magritte as he discusses his rarely seen modern works and the values of modern art.
Prod-GROVE Dist-GROVE

Magritte - The False Mirror C 22 MIN
16MM FILM, 3/4 OR 1/2 IN VIDEO J A
Discusses the Belgian painter, Rene Magritte, using an assemblage of the painter's images. The spoken commentary is confined to a few of Magritte's own statements about his intentions and an occasional pertinent anecdote from his close friends, Mesens and Scutenaire.
Prod-FI Dist-FI 1971

Magritte Sur La Plage C 14 MIN
3/4 OR 1/2 INCH VIDEO CASSETTE
Focuses on Surrealist painter Magritte.
Prod-WGBHTV Dist-EAI

Maguindanao Kulintang Ensembles From Mindanao, The Philippines C 16 MIN
16MM FILM, 3/4 OR 1/2 IN VIDEO
Shows the complex and highly developed style of the Maguindanao of northern Mindanao of gong music.
Prod-UWASHP Dist-UWASHP

Mahalia Jackson C 34 MIN
16MM FILM, 3/4 OR 1/2 IN VIDEO J-C A
Presents a portrait of Mahalia Jackson, who spread the religious music of American blacks throughout the world.
LC NO. 81-706854
Prod-SCHWEJ Dist-PHENIX 1974

Mahalia Jackson Sings Spirituals C
3/4 OR 1/2 INCH VIDEO CASSETTE
Prod-MSTVIS Dist-MSTVIS

Maharajas, The - Imperialism By Conspiracy C 25 MIN
16MM FILM, 3/4 OR 1/2 IN VIDEO H-C A
Describes the 200-year reign of the Indian Maharajas. Explains the inevitability of their downfall.
Prod-CFDLD Dist-CORF

Mahatma Gandhi - Silent Revolution C 38 MIN
16MM FILM, 3/4 OR 1/2 IN VIDEO H-C
Documents Gandhi's plan for basic education and shows this plan operating in South India.
Prod-PFMP Dist-IFB 1970

Mahatma Gandhi - Soul Force C 24 MIN
16MM FILM, 3/4 OR 1/2 IN VIDEO H-C A
Explores Mahatma Gandhi's philosophy of non-violence. Narrated by Henry Fonda.
From The Leaders Of The 20th Century - Portraits Of Power Series.
Prod-NIELSE Dist-LCOA 1980

Mai Zetterling's Stockholm C 25 MIN
16MM FILM, 3/4 OR 1/2 IN VIDEO H-C A
A shortened version of the motion picture Mai Zetterling's Stockholm. Presents actress-writer-director Mai Zetterling on a tour of Stockholm, Sweden.
From The Cities Series.
Prod-NIELSE Dist-LCOA Prodn-MCGREE 1980

Mai Zetterling's Stockholm C 50 MIN
16MM FILM, 3/4 OR 1/2 IN VIDEO I-C A
Presents Swedish actress Mai Zetterling as she takes Stockholm.
From The Cities Series.
Prod-NIELSE Dist-LCOA Prodn-MCGREE 1978

Mai Zetterling's Stockholm (Spanish) C 25 MIN
16MM FILM, 3/4 OR 1/2 IN VIDEO H-C A
Presents an image of the city Stockholm through the eyes of Queen Christina and August Strindberg. Edited version.
Prod-NIELSE Dist-LCOA Prodn-MCGREE 1980

Mai Zetterling's Stockholm (Spanish) C 50 MIN
16MM FILM, 3/4 OR 1/2 IN VIDEO H-C A
Presents an image of the city Stockholm through the eyes of Queen Christina and August Strindberg. Full version.
Prod-NIELSE Dist-LCOA Prodn-MCGREE 1978

Mail And Female B 11 MIN
16MM FILM OPTICAL SOUND
Explains that when Alfalfa is made president of the He-Man Woman Haters' Club, he must rush after Darla to retrieve a love letter he has sent her. A Little Rascals film.
Prod-ROACH Dist-BHAWK 1937

Mail Distribution Clerk, The C 15 MIN
16MM FILM OPTICAL SOUND
Tells what the duties of a mail distribution clerk are and demonstrates the inside work at a post office.
LC NO. 74-705065
Prod-USPOST Dist-USNAC

Mail Handler, The C 12 MIN
16MM FILM OPTICAL SOUND
Demonstrates the responsibilities of the mail handler at a large post office.
LC NO. 74-705066
Prod-USPOST Dist-USNAC

Mail It Right C 12 MIN
16MM FILM OPTICAL SOUND H A
Shows secretarial practices which save time and money for businesses and get the best service at the post office. Gives the recommended methods for preparing first-class mail and introduces the correct address format for mechanized sorting in post offices.
LC NO. 76-701591
Prod-USPS Dist-USNAC 1975

Mail Order Sales C 30 MIN
3/4 OR 1/2 INCH VIDEO CASSETTE
Presents tips on purchasing something by mail order.
From The Consumer Survival Series. Shopping
Prod-MDCPB Dist-MDCPB

Mailbox, The C 24 MIN
16MM FILM OPTICAL SOUND J-H A
Tells the story of an elderly widow who waits and waits for a letter from her children. Relates that when the letter finally arrives, the woman dies before she can read it.
LC NO. 77-702102
Prod-BYU Dist-EBEC 1977

Main Idea Road C 20 MIN
3/4 OR 1/2 INCH VIDEO CASSETTE
Shows how to learn the ways to find key words and ideas and how to read for the main idea.
From The Efficient Reading - Instructional Tapes Series. Tape 8
Prod-TELSTR Dist-TELSTR

Main Street C 29 MIN
16MM FILM OPTICAL SOUND A
Focuses on the economic and esthetic plight of Main Street, America. Describes how concerned merchants and consulting preservationists have joined forces in many cities and towns to revitalize the commercial and architectural advantages of downtown business areas.
LC NO. 79-701275
Prod-NTHP Dist-NTHP 1979

Main Street Gym B 6 MIN
16MM FILM OPTICAL SOUND
A study of an old boxing gym in the Los Angeles area.
Prod-USC Dist-USC 1968

Main Street U S A - Today C 22 MIN
1 INCH VIDEOTAPE
Presents the story of progress in this country through steel research. Contrasts the life of a Main Street family 30 years ago and the life today. Presents the great improvements through the wonders of modern steel. Prizewinner.
Prod-ARMCO Dist-MTP

Mainly Math–A Series
H-C
Discusses basic math principles.
Prod-WCVETV Dist-GPITVL 1977

Common Fractions	20 MIN
Decimal Fractions	20 MIN
Directed Numbers, Pt 1	20 MIN
Directed Numbers, Pt 2	20 MIN
Geometric Formulas	20 MIN
Motion Geometry	20 MIN
Number Patterns	20 MIN
Percentages	20 MIN
Plane Geometry	20 MIN
Probabilities, Pt 1	20 MIN
Probabilities, Pt 2	20 MIN
Ratios And Proportions	20 MIN
Scientific Notation	20 MIN
Statistics And Graphs, Pt 1	20 MIN
Statistics And Graphs, Pt 2	20 MIN

Mainstay Of The Mails, The C 13 MIN
16MM FILM OPTICAL SOUND
Shows the complexity and importance of maintaining the equipment and buildings of today's postal system. Illustrates the latest mechanization equipment and stresses the need for highly skilled maintenance employees.
LC NO. 74-705068
Prod-USPOST Dist-USNAC

Mainstream C 30 MIN
3/4 INCH VIDEO CASSETTE
Focuses on the resurgence of pride in tribal values among the Indians of the Northwestern United States.
From The Real People Series.
Prod-KSPSTV Dist-GPITVL 197

Mainstreaming C 26 MIN
3/4 INCH VIDEO CASSETTE H
Provides information concerning the real-life integration of a number of disabled children into public schools.
Prod-ESST Dist-ESST 1980

Mainstreaming C 30 MIN
3/4 OR 1/2 INCH VIDEO CASSETTE T
Provides awareness of reasons for mainstreaming handicapped children. Discusses major service models.
From The Stretch Concepts For Teaching Handicapped Children Series.
Prod-HUBDSC Dist-HUBDSC

Mainstreaming C 30 MIN
16MM FILM, 3/4 OR 1/2 IN VIDEO T S
Presents three special educators discussing the reasons for the movement towards mainstreaming handicapped children and the major models of service to the children and their teachers.
From The Project STRETCH (Strategies To Train Regular Educators To Teach Children With...) Series. Module 7
LC NO. 80-706643
Prod-METCO Dist-HUBDSC 1980

Mainstreaming C 30 MIN
3/4 OR 1/2 INCH VIDEO CASSETTE
Presents answers to questions regarding Public Law 94-142, which mandates comprehensive programming for public school services to children with handicaps. Focuses on least restrictive alternatives, mainstreaming, and the rights of handicapped citizens.
Prod-UNEBO Dist-UNEBO

Mainstreaming In Action C 27 MIN
16MM FILM, 3/4 OR 1/2 IN VIDEO T
Shows several elementary and secondary classrooms in public schools as teachers work with handicapped students as part of regular classroom sessions. Discusses solutions to problems teachers may encounter, the practicality of mainstreaming, what it means, and how it affects teachers and students.
LC NO. 80-706407
Prod-TOGGFI Dist-EBEC 1979

Mainstreaming Techniques - Life Science And Art C 12 MIN
16MM FILM, 3/4 OR 1/2 IN VIDEO T
Illustrates the involvement activities, interactions and responses of handicapped children in a mainstreamed life science and art program. Features classroom experiments with live organisms, including suggestions for adaptation in teaching strategy and equipment modification to provide for individual modes of learning. Based on the book Laboratory Science And Art For Blind, Deaf, And Emotionally Handicapped Children by Doris Hadary.
From The Special Education Curriculum Design - A Multisensory Approach Series.
LC NO. 80-706558
Prod-MGHT Dist-MGHT Prodn-HADDOR 1979

Mainstreaming The Exceptional Child—A Series
16MM FILM, 3/4 OR 1/2 IN VIDEO T
Discusses how the mainstreaming of handicapped children into regular schools should work in accordance with Public Law 94-142, focusing on classroom techniques for teachers and administrators who must learn how best to implement the law.
Prod-MFFD Dist-FI

Behavior - Assessment And Programming 029 MIN
Delivery Systems 029 MIN
Human Relations In The Classroom 029 MIN
Introduction To Exceptionality, Pt 1 029 MIN
Introduction To Exceptionality, Pt 2 029 MIN
Language Assessment And Programming 029 MIN
Mathematics - Assessment And Programming 029 MIN
Overview Of Mainstreaming 029 MIN
Parent Involvement 029 MIN
Reading - Assessment And Programming 029 MIN
School And Classrooms 029 MIN
Whither The Mainstream 029 MIN

Mainstreet Soldier C 36 MIN
16MM FILM OPTICAL SOUND
Documents the life of a 48-year-old alcoholic who has spent the last 28 years on and around Winnipeg's Main Street Skid Row district. Follows him to his favorite haunts and listens to what he has to say about himself and his life.
LC NO. 77-702955
Prod-YAKIR Dist-CANFDC 1972

Maintainability Engineering C 28 MIN
3/4 OR 1/2 INCH VIDEO CASSETTE
Covers Maintainability Engineering principles, corrective and preventive maintenance practices, equipment operating and downtime categories, maintenance personnel factors and safety factors.
Prod-UAZMIC Dist-UAZMIC

Maintainability, Operational Availability And Preventive Maintenance Of...—A Series

Discusses maintainability, operational availability, and preventive maintenance of equipment and systems with applications. Presents the methodologies involved and illustrates with examples. Spoken by Dimitri Kececioglu, Professor of Aerospace and Mechanical Engineering at the University of Arizona.
Prod-UAZMIC Dist-UAZMIC 1981

Course Objecives, Downtimes And Their
Design Practices For Better Maintainability, 060 MIN
Spares Provisioning At A Desired Assurance 060 MIN
Steady State Availability Applications, 060 MIN

Maintaining A Lawn C 29 MIN
2 INCH VIDEOTAPE
Features Tom Lied offering tips for keeping a lawn healthy and problem-free and suggesting ways to get rid of problems that may occur.
From The Dig It Series.
Prod-WMVSTV Dist-PUBTEL

Maintaining A Winning Team C 30 MIN
3/4 OR 1/2 INCH VIDEO CASSETTE
Emphasizes on pulling back at agreed-to intervals to review how plans are working. Stresses the role of leadership. Shows how to maintain a winning team by keeping their attention directed to operating problems rather than problem personalities.
From The Managerial Game Plan - Team Building Through MBO Series. Session 5
Prod-PRODEV Dist-PRODEV

Maintaining Fruit Quality C 43 MIN
16MM FILM OPTICAL SOUND
Discusses methods of keeping fruit healthy until it reaches the consumer.
LC NO. 77-702856
Prod-BCDA Dist-BCDA 1977

Maintaining Good Working Conditions B 9 MIN
16MM FILM - 3/4 IN VIDEO
Dramatizes a discussion in which two supervisors describe methods which they use to improve working conditions. Issued in 1944 as a motion picture.
From The Problems In Supervision Series.
LC NO. 79-706511
Prod-USOE Dist-USNAC Prodn-MODART 1979

Maintaining Good Working Conditions (Spanish) B 9 MIN
16MM FILM OPTICAL SOUND
Shows two supervisors describing specific ways they improved working conditions.
From The Problems In Supervision Series.
LC NO. FIE62-55
Prod-USOE Dist-USNAC 1944

Maintaining Ideal Weight, Avoiding Excess Fat, Saturated Fat And Cholesterol C 28 MIN
3/4 OR 1/2 INCH VIDEO CASSETTE H-C A
Introduces guidelines Nos. 2 and 3 - Maintain Ideal Weight And Avoid Too Much Fat, Saturated Fat and Cholesterol. Explores the effects of fat types on the body and alerts us to the dangers of obesity.
From the Eat Well, Be Well Series.
Prod-JOU Dist-JOU 1983

Maintaining Quality Standards B 10 MIN
16MM FILM - 3/4 IN VIDEO
Tells how a supervisor learns that quality as well as quantity is necessary in production. Explains how quality standards can be achieved and maintained. Issued in 1944 as a motion picture.
From The Problems In Supervision Series.
LC NO. 79-706512
Prod-USOE Dist-USNAC Prodn-MODART 1979

Maintaining Quality Standards (Spanish) B 10 MIN
16MM FILM OPTICAL SOUND
Tells how a supervisor learns that quality as well as quantity production is necessary and how such quality standards can be achieved and maintained.
From The Problems In Supervision Series.
LC NO. 74-705069
Prod-USOE Dist-USNAC 1944

Maintaining Quality Standards (Spanish) B 10 MIN
3/4 INCH VIDEO CASSETTE
Tells how a supervisor learns that quality as well as quantity is necessary in production. Explains how quality standards can be achieved and maintained. Issued in 1944 as a motion picture.
From The Problems In Supervision (Spanish) Series.
LC NO. 79-706957
Prod-USOE Dist-USNAC 1979

Maintaining The Deep Fat Fryer C 20 MIN
1/2 IN VIDEO CASSETTE BETA/VHS
Details steps used to clean, filter and fill the deep fat fryer.
Prod-RMI Dist-RMI

Maintaining The Hub Service Type Helicopter - Rotor Systems And Related Controls B 16 MIN
16MM FILM OPTICAL SOUND
Illustrates basic steps in the removal of rotor blades and hub, snubbers, flap restrainers and dampers. Shows procedures for setting blade angle of incidence and checking control cable tensions.
LC NO. FIE60-30
Prod-USN Dist-USNAC 1952

Maintaining The Organization - How Far Should I Trust You C 33 MIN
16MM FILM - 3/4 IN VIDEO IND
Discusses costs and benefits of personal trust in an organization. Points out why personal relationships and personal trust are not enough to manage a complex organization.
From The Two-Person Communication Series.
Prod-BNA Dist-BNA 1975

Maintaining Workers' Interest B 13 MIN
16MM FILM - 3/4 IN VIDEO
Portrays employees doing poor work because their jobs do not interest them. Explains what the supervisor should do to detect and remedy such situations. Issued in 1944 as a motion picture.
From The Problems In Supervision Series.
LC NO. 79-706513
Prod-USOE Dist-USNAC Prodn-CARFI 1979

Maintaining Workers' Interest (Spanish) B 13 MIN
16MM FILM OPTICAL SOUND
Dramatizes instances of employees doing poor work because their jobs do not interest them and shows what the supervisor should do to detect and remedy such situations.
From The Problems In Supervision Series.
LC NO. FIE62-58
Prod-USOE Dist-USNAC 1944

Maintaining Your Motivation C 20 MIN
16MM FILM - 3/4 IN VIDEO
Presents Dr Saul Gellerman's motivation maintenance suggestions for salespeople. Shows the importance of analyzing every sales call immediately, seeking feedback and looking for clues to identify causes of poor performance. Discusses why the customer's motivation is a key factor.
From The Self-Motivation In Selling Series.
Prod-BNA Dist-BNA

Maintenance C 26 MIN
3/4 OR 1/2 INCH VIDEO CASSETTE
Describes basic car care and maintenance.
From The Right Way Series.
Prod-SCETV Dist-PBS 1982

Maintenance C 29 MIN
2 INCH VIDEOTAPE
See series title for descriptive statement.
From The Maggie And The Beautiful Machine - Backs Series.
Prod-WGBHTV Dist-PUBTEL

Maintenance And Exterior Repairs - Household Maintenance, Exterior Repairs C 30 MIN
1/2 IN VIDEO CASSETTE BETA/VHS
See series title for descriptive statement.
From The Wally's Workshop Series.
Prod-KARTES Dist-KARTES

Maintenance And Inspection Of The Float And Pressure Type Carburetors B 28 MIN
16MM FILM, 3/4 OR 1/2 IN VIDEO IND
Shows visual inspection, adjustment, removal and replacement of carburetors installed in Army aircraft.
Prod-USA Dist-USNAC

Maintenance And Repair Of Steam Condensers - Circulating Water Side B 17 MIN
16MM FILM - 3/4 IN VIDEO
Explains the principles and operation of the steam condenser and demonstrates procedures for preparing, cleaning, inspecting, repairing and testing a condenser. Issued in 1952 as a motion picture.
LC NO. 79-707967
Prod-USN Dist-USNAC Prodn-DFC 1979

Maintenance And Show Grooming C 72 MIN
1/2 IN VIDEO CASSETTE BETA/VHS
Covers horse grooming techniques. Includes body clipping, mane and tail care and hoof preparation.
Prod-CSPC Dist-EQVDL

Maintenance Management—A Series

Provides maintenance management instruction. Includes student workbooks, instructor's guides and overhead transparencies.
Prod-ITCORP Dist-ITCORP

Computerized Maintenance Systems 030 MIN
Evaluating The Maintenance Program 030 MIN
Maintenance Organization, The 030 MIN
Maintenance Safety And Efficiency 030 MIN
Maintenance Systems And Documentation 030 MIN
Parts And Materials 030 MIN
Planning 030 MIN
Preventive And Predictive Maintenance 030 MIN
Scheduling 030 MIN
Work Execution 030 MIN

Maintenance Of Energized Circuits - Use Of Hot Line Tools On Circuits Of Over 5,000 Volts C 20 MIN
16MM FILM, 3/4 OR 1/2 IN VIDEO IND
Outlines specific tasks in maintenance of energized circuits carrying over 5,000 volts. Emphasizes personal safety in use of high voltage equipment and ground and pole-top work.
Prod-USAF Dist-USNAC

Maintenance Of Energized Circuits - Use Of Rubber Protective Equipment C 19 MIN
16MM FILM, 3/4 OR 1/2 IN VIDEO IND
Outlines work tasks in maintenance of energized high voltage circuits. Covers hazards and countermeasures, protective equipment, work crew safety, use of high voltage maintenance equipment and pole-top safety procedures.
Prod-USAF Dist-USNAC

Maintenance Of Microwave Power Tubes C 34 MIN
16MM FILM, 3/4 OR 1/2 IN VIDEO A
Outlines procedures for the care and handling of the magnetron and kleptron power tubes used in radar and tropospheric communications equipment.
Prod-USAF Dist-USNAC 1959

Maintenance Organization, The C 30 MIN
3/4 OR 1/2 INCH VIDEO CASSETTE
Discusses maintenance management goals and process. Describes leadership and time management techniques. Deals with centralized and decentralized shops.
From The Maintenance Management Series.
Prod-ITCORP Dist-ITCORP

Maintenance Painting C 26 MIN
16MM FILM OPTICAL SOUND
Shows pictorially what all parties concerned, from the designer to the man with the paint brush, should know about maintenance painting.
Prod-HERC Dist-HERC

Maintenance Safety And Efficiency C 30 MIN
3/4 OR 1/2 INCH VIDEO CASSETTE
Examines plant, shop and field safety. Pursues shop and field efficiency.
From The Maintenance Management Series.
Prod-ITCORP Dist-ITCORP

Maintenance Safety In Aviation - Murphy's Law B 17 MIN
16MM FILM OPTICAL SOUND
Tells how improper installation of aircraft equipment can cause accidents.
LC NO. 74-705070
Prod-USN Dist-USNAC

Maintenance Systems And Documentation C 30 MIN
3/4 OR 1/2 INCH VIDEO CASSETTE
Defines the functions of documentation. Describes work request systems and maintenance history files. Discusses evaluating contractor performance.
From The Maintenance Management Series.
Prod-ITCORP Dist-ITCORP

Maintenance Tank Cleaning - Butterworth Method B 31 MIN
16MM FILM OPTICAL SOUND
Explains how purposes govern procedures to be followed and shows basic techniques in applying the Butterworth method.
LC NO. FIE52-1264
Prod-USN Dist-USNAC 1950

Maintenance, Lubrication And Troubleshooting C 29 MIN
3/4 INCH VIDEO CASSETTE C
Presents guidelines for the maintenance and lubrication of automatic radiographic processors.
From The Radiographic Processing Series. Pt 14
LC NO. 77-706135
Prod-USVA Dist-USNAC 1975

Maitre C 11 MIN
16MM FILM OPTICAL SOUND I-C A
Uses animation, without narration, to present an abstract expression of the dilemma of an artist in search of success and recognition.
LC NO. 78-701050
Prod-CITE Dist-SIM 1967

Maitre De L'Ungava C 28 MIN
16MM FILM OPTICAL SOUND
A French-language film which shows the caribou in his courageous struggle for life in Quebec.
Prod-QDTFG Dist-MTP

Maize In Metal C 15 MIN
3/4 OR 1/2 INCH VIDEO CASSETTE P-I
Visits a food canning company to show the complexity of the food industry.
From The Explorers Unlimited Series.
Prod-WVIZTV Dist-AITECH 1971

Majestic Brass, Pt 1 C 15 MIN
3/4 OR 1/2 INCH VIDEO CASSETTE
See series title for descriptive statement.
From The Musical Instruments Series.
Prod-WWVUTV Dist-GPITVL

Majestic Brass, Pt 2 C 16 MIN
3/4 OR 1/2 INCH VIDEO CASSETTE
See series title for descriptive statement.
From The Musical Instruments Series.
Prod-WWVUTV Dist-GPITVL

Majestic Canadian Rockies, The C 20 MIN
3/4 OR 1/2 INCH VIDEO CASSETTE J-C A
Shows the Canadian Rockies and discusses the mountains in reference to the park areas in Jasper, Banff, Alberta, and Calgary.
LC NO. 82-706771
Prod-AWSS Dist-AWSS 1980

Majestic Clockwork, The C 52 MIN
16MM FILM, 3/4 OR 1/2 IN VIDEO J-C A
Focuses on the contributions of Newton and Einstein to the evolution of physics. Explores the revolution that ensued when Einstein's theory of relativity upset Newton's description of the universe.
From The Ascent Of Man Series. No. 7
LC NO. 79-707220
Prod-BBCTV Dist-TIMLIF 1973

Majestic Clockwork, The (Spanish) C 52 MIN
16MM FILM OPTICAL SOUND H-C A
Focuses on the contributions of Newton and Einstein to the evolution of physics. Explores the revolution that ensued when Einstein's theory of relativity upset Newton's description of the universe.
From The Ascent Of Man Series. No. 7
Prod-BBCTV Dist-TIMLIF 1973

Majestic Eagles Of North America, The C 12 MIN
16MM FILM OPTICAL SOUND P-I
Presents the story of the American eagle.
LC NO. 85-703606
Prod-EBEC Dist-EBEC 1985

Majestic Wapiti, The C 16 MIN
16MM FILM, 3/4 OR 1/2 IN VIDEO P-J
Depicts the successful adaptation of the Wapiti (elk or red deer) to the open western woods.
From The North American Species Series.
Prod-KARVF Dist-BCNFL 1984

Major Amputations For Arteriosclerosis - Technic And Rehabilitation C 13 MIN
16MM FILM OPTICAL SOUND PRO
Shows the importance of simple techniques of amputation and early provision of temporary limbs in patients receiving amputations for above-knee and below knee amputation. Illustrates the methods for measuring the artificial limbs and constructing them.
Prod-ACYDGD Dist-ACY 1959

Major Barbara B 121 MIN
16MM FILM OPTICAL SOUND
Features Wendy Hiller as an idealistic Salvation Army soldier dedicated to saving the poor from the abuses of the rich. Shows her conflict with her father, a wealthy munitions manufacturer who believes that the poor can be saved through intelligent manipulation of money. Features Rex Harrison as a lovestruck intellectual caught in the middle of the conflict. Directed by Gabriel Pascal. Based on the play Major Barbara by George Bernard Shaw.
Prod-UAA Dist-LCOA 1941

Major Burns C
3/4 OR 1/2 INCH VIDEO CASSETTE
Focuses on the appropriate care for major burn patients in the field and in the emergency department. Explains illustrates and simulates each step. Discusses various physical and medical ramifications to further aid in determining proper emergency care.
From The Burns - Emergency Management Series.
Prod-VTRI Dist-VTRI

Major Burns C 20 MIN
3/4 OR 1/2 INCH VIDEO CASSETTE PRO
Teaches how to recognize and initiate treatment for patients suffering with major burns. Discusses how to direct the activity of paramedics at the scene, how to stabilize patients, anticipation of post-burn complications and provision of initial therapy.
From The Medical Crisis Intervention Series.
Prod-LEIKID Dist-LEIKID

Major Divisions And Areas Of Function C 19 MIN
3/4 OR 1/2 INCH VIDEO CASSETTE PRO
Identifies by means of brain specimens and diagrams the anatomical landmarks of the cerebral hemispheres, the lobes of the brain and their subdivisions, and the functional areas related to the cerebrocortical structure.
From The Neurobiology Series.
Prod-HSCIC Dist-HSCIC

Major Environments Of North America Set C
3/4 OR 1/2 INCH VIDEO CASSETTE
Discusses the interaction of plants and animals with their environment. Includes spectacular photography of the prairie, mountains, desert, seashore, forest and the Everglades.
Prod-CBSC Dist-CBSC

Major Medical Syndromes—A Series
PRO
Prod-NMAC Dist-USNAC 1979

Acute Myocardial Infarction	020 MIN
Cirrhosis	020 MIN
Congestive Heart Failure	020 MIN
Dissecting Aortic Aneurysm	020 MIN
Meningitis	020 MIN

Major Or Minor C 14 MIN
3/4 OR 1/2 INCH VIDEO CASSETTE P
Encourages children to distinguish between major and minor modes through ear training.
From The Stepping into Rhythm Series.
Prod-WVIZTV Dist-AITECH

Major Phyla—A Series
16MM FILM, 3/4 OR 1/2 IN VIDEO J-C
Studies the variety of plants and animals that inhabit the earth, from bacteria to vertebrates.
Prod-CORF Dist-CORF

Arthropods - Insects And Their Relatives	011 MIN
Chordates, The - Diversity In Structure	014 MIN
Classifying Plants And Animals	011 MIN
Echinoderms And Mollusks	015 MIN
Fungi - The One Hundred Thousand	007 MIN
Invertebrates	013 MIN
Liverwort, The - Alternation Of Generations	016 MIN
Mosses, Liverworts And Ferns	013 MIN
Protozoa - Structures And Life Functions	017 MIN
Simple Organisms - Algae And Fungi	014 MIN
Simple Organisms - Bacteria	015 MIN
Spirogyra - Structure And Life Functions	014 MIN
Sponges And Coelenterates - Porous And	011 MIN
Worms - Flat, Round And Segmented	016 MIN

Major Religions Of The World - Development And Rituals X 20 MIN
16MM FILM, 3/4 OR 1/2 IN VIDEO J-C
Surveys the origins, ritual and symbols of the major religions of the world—Hinduism, Buddhism, Judaism, Christianity and Islam. Stresses the need for toleration and respect for the different religious faiths.
Prod-EBF Dist-EBEC 1954

Major Structural Repairs Of Plastic Boats C 20 MIN
16MM FILM OPTICAL SOUND
Shows the methods and materials used for repairing major structural damage to fiberglass reinforced plastic boats.
LC NO. 74-706489
Prod-USN Dist-USNAC 1972

Major Venereal Disease C 24 MIN
3/4 OR 1/2 INCH VIDEO CASSETTE
Illustrates the symptoms, diagnosis and treatment of gonorrhea and syphilis.
From The Emergency Management - The First 30 Minutes, Vol III Series.
Prod-VTRI Dist-VTRI

Makai - The Documentary Of An Open Ocean Dive C 28 MIN
16MM FILM, 3/4 OR 1/2 IN VIDEO
Shows the preparation and employment of a mobile saturation dive off the coast of Oahu, Hawaii. Combines underwater photography with descriptions of diving research sponsored by the Bureau of Medicine and Surgery, the Office of Naval Research, and the Navy Supervisor of Diving.
LC NO. 80-707640
Prod-USN Dist-USNAC 1980

Make A Deal With Yourself C 15 MIN
16MM FILM, 3/4 OR 1/2 IN VIDEO I
Tells how Duncan rewards himself for practicing his music diligently, and soon makes real progress.
From The Thinkabout Series. Judging Information
LC NO. 81-706102
Prod-UNIT Dist-AITECH 1979

Make A Joyful Sound B 54 MIN
16MM FILM OPTICAL SOUND
Shows how teachers affect the musical interests of 450 youngsters chosen for the New Jersey All-State High School Chorus and Orchestra. Includes sequences of their concert at Symphony Hall, Newark, New Jersey.
LC NO. FIA66-841
Prod-WCBSTV Dist-CBSF 1965

Make A Noise! C 25 MIN
16MM FILM, 3/4 OR 1/2 IN VIDEO I-H
Explains what sound is, why some sounds are musical, how to experiment with vibrations.
From The Start Here - Adventure Into Science Series.
Prod-LANDMK Dist-LANDMK

Make A Present For The Future C 15 MIN
16MM FILM, 3/4 OR 1/2 IN VIDEO I
Tells how a boy and girl living in the future find a time capsule created by children of the 1970's.
From The Thinkabout Series. Giving And Getting Meaning
LC NO. 81-706103
Prod-SCETV Dist-AITECH 1979

Make A Print B 15 MIN
2 INCH VIDEOTAPE P
Describes manipulating objects such as fingers or salvage shapes to make a print.
From The Art Corner Series.
Prod-CVETVC Dist-GPITVL Prodn-WCVETV

Make A Print - With A Potato Or Tomato C 60 MIN
1/2 IN VIDEO CASSETTE BETA/VHS K-P
Demonstrates making prints with fruits and vegetables and objects such as kitchen tools and old toys.
From The Children's Crafts Series.
Prod-MOHOMV Dist-MOHOMV

Make A Puppet - Make A Friend C 56 MIN
1/2 IN VIDEO CASSETTE BETA/VHS K-P
Demonstrates how to make a puppet out of a paper bag, how to make clothes for paper dolls and how to make snowflakes by cutting and folding paper.
From The Children's Crafts Series.
Prod-MOHOMV Dist-MOHOMV

Make A Stencil Print B 20 MIN
2 INCH VIDEOTAPE P-I
Presents simplifying shapes in nature as the basis for designing a stencil print for use in daily life. Emphasizes relating shape to the area to be decorated.
From The Art Adventures Series.
Prod-CVETVC Dist-GPITVL Prodn-WCVETV

Make A Wish C 5 MIN
16MM FILM OPTICAL SOUND C A
Attempts to give insight into some of the physical, social and psychological problems generated by sensory deprivation in the elderly. Depicts a family birthday party for the the grandmother who is 75 and the granddaughter who is five, using audio and visual simulation techniques to approximate restricted sensory capabilities of the grandmother.
LC NO. 76-703728
Prod-PSU Dist-PSU 1973

Make A Wish B 15 MIN
2 INCH VIDEOTAPE P
See series title for descriptive statement.
From The Children's Literature Series. No. 3
Prod-NCET Dist-GPITVL Prodn-KUONTV

Make Believe Fun B 15 MIN
2 INCH VIDEOTAPE P
Discusses the important need of having fun in the daily existence. (Broadcast quality)
From The Around The Corner Series. No. 31
Prod-FWCETV Dist-GPITVL Prodn-WEDUTV

Make Believe, No. 1 B 15 MIN
2 INCH VIDEOTAPE P
See series title for descriptive statement.
From The Children's Literature Series. No. 15
Prod-NCET Dist-GPITVL Prodn-KUONTV

Make Believe, No. 2 C 15 MIN
2 INCH VIDEOTAPE P
See series title for descriptive statement.
From The Children's Literature Series. No. 16
Prod-NCET Dist-GPITVL Prodn-KUONTV

Make Fewer Motions - Motion Economy C 18 MIN
16MM FILM, 3/4 OR 1/2 IN VIDEO
Shows principles of motion economy which enables workers to perform tasks with less fatigue and increased output. Shows how to select a job for analysis and how to use a motion economy chart.
Prod-USA Dist-USNAC 1973

Make Germany Pay C 20 MIN
16MM FILM, 3/4 OR 1/2 IN VIDEO H-C A
Presents a portrait of life in Germany after its defeat in World War I. Shows the serious financial inflation and the problems caused by French and Belgian occupation of the Ruhr. Ends with Germany joining the League Of Nations in 1926.
From The Twentieth Century History Series.
Prod-BBCTV Dist-FI 1981

Make It Easy On Yourself C 30 MIN
3/4 OR 1/2 INCH VIDEO CASSETTE A
Explains cancellation and some of the rules about how fractions fit together.
From The Adult Math Series.
Prod-KYTV Dist-KYTV 1984

Make It Fit C 29 MIN
2 INCH VIDEOTAPE

See series title for descriptive statement.
From The Designing Women Series.
Prod-WKYCTV Dist-PUBTEL

Make It Happen C 22 MIN
16MM FILM, 3/4 OR 1/2 IN VIDEO J-H
Suggests that women should strive for respect rather than approval in their work and personal lives. Shows women in various careers and home environments and tells about the planning, retraining and rethinking they went through to attain their current satisfying jobs.
Prod-MOBIUS Dist-MOBIUS

Make It Happen C 30 MIN
16MM FILM, 3/4 OR 1/2 IN VIDEO PRO
No descriptive information available.
Prod-DARTNL Dist-DARTNL 1969

Make It Lamb, 1,2,3 C 32 MIN
3/4 OR 1/2 INCH VIDEO CASSETTE PRO
Presents facts about lamb and its desirability as a restaurant menu item. Demonstrates cooking methods, including roasting, sauteing and pan broiling, and making an aromatic stew from the shank.
Prod-CULINA Dist-CULINA

Make It Move C 32 MIN
16MM FILM OPTICAL SOUND
Presents an original 'documentary' musical comedy. Satirizes student life in the Department of Cinema of the University of Southern California. Contains such original songs as Make It Move, A Splice Is Nice, Kodachrome Blues, Patio Patter, My Star and Love Laughed. (A USC Cinema Graduate Workshop production.)
LC NO. 75-703202
Prod-USC Dist-USC 1965

Make It Your Way C 15 MIN
3/4 OR 1/2 INCH VIDEO CASSETTE P
Explains that no two persons express themselves artistically in the same way and that there is strength in diversity and dissimilarity. Scans art from prehistoric times to present day showing the variety of artistic form and expression.
From The Primary Art Series.
Prod-WETATV Dist-AITECH

Make Light Of Lifting C 17 MIN
16MM FILM, 3/4 OR 1/2 IN VIDEO
Presents various manual lifting techniques designed to prevent back injury.
Prod-MILLBK Dist-IFB

Make Math Work For You C 15 MIN
3/4 INCH VIDEO CASSETTE I
Discusses the reading and writing of large numbers. Tells how to determine the total value of each digit in a number.
From The Math - No Mystery Series.
Prod-WCETTV Dist-GPITVL 1977

Make Mine Metric C 13 MIN
16MM FILM, 3/4 OR 1/2 IN VIDEO
Introduces the metric system, using animation and live action sequences. highlights the adjustments that must be made when confronted with a new system of measurement.
Prod-BRAVC Dist-PFP

Make Money Picking Berries C 10 MIN
16MM FILM OPTICAL SOUND J-H
Discusses the need for strawberry pickers in western Oregon, with an overview of the job and its rewards.
Prod-OSSHE Dist-OSSHE 1958

Make Room For Dad C 15 MIN
3/4 OR 1/2 INCH VIDEO CASSETTE
Helps parents expecting to face cesarean section know what to expect by following an expectant couple from their classes and into the delivery room. Shows actual delivery of their little girl.
LC NO. 79-730076
Prod-TRAINX Dist-TRAINX

Make Room For Daddy C 23 MIN
3/4 OR 1/2 INCH VIDEO CASSETTE
Presents a four-part series on the changing role of fatherhood.
Prod-WCCOTV Dist-WCCOTV 1982

Make Something New C 14 MIN
16MM FILM, 3/4 OR 1/2 IN VIDEO I
Shows young people using objects, machines, words, and their imaginations to make new things.
From The Thinkabout Series. Communicating Effectively
LC NO. 81-706104
Prod-EDFCEN Dist-AITECH 1979

Make Sure They See You X 10 MIN
16MM FILM OPTICAL SOUND
Shows how to communicate with other drivers and pedestrians.
From The Expert Seeing Series.
Prod-NSC Dist-NSC

Make Up Your Mind C 29 MIN
2 INCH VIDEOTAPE
See series title for descriptive statement.
From The That's Life Series.
Prod-KOAPTV Dist-PUBTEL

Make Way For Ducklings B 11 MIN
16MM FILM, 3/4 OR 1/2 IN VIDEO K-P
The picture book classic by Robert McCloskey. Iconographic filming with original score by Arthur Kleiner.
Prod-WWS Dist-WWS 1955

Make Way For The Past C 28 MIN
16MM FILM OPTICAL SOUND
Tells the stories of five people who have restored almost forgotten 18th-century houses.
LC NO. 77-700384
Prod-RIC Dist-WSTGLC Prodn-BRIAN 1976

Make Your Blood Do Double Duty C 14 MIN
16MM FILM OPTICAL SOUND
Stresses the need for a continuous supply of volunteer blood donors within the U S Navy.
LC NO. 75-702473
Prod-USN Dist-USNAC 1973

Make Your Investigation Count C 11 MIN
3/4 OR 1/2 INCH VIDEO CASSETTE
Provides supervisors with solid, hands-on experience in accident investigation.
Prod-EDRF Dist-EDRF

Make Your Own Arrangement C 30 MIN
2 INCH VIDEOTAPE C A
Discusses selecting adaptable furnishings for smaller environments such as apartments and condominiums.
From The Designing Home Interiors Series. Unit 13
Prod-COAST Dist-CDTEL Prodn-RSCCD

Make Your Own Identikit C 20 MIN
16MM FILM, 3/4 OR 1/2 IN VIDEO J-H
States that measurement is necesssary in science to make accurate observations and to record them for interpretation. Demonstrates a kit of simple measuring tools. Explains how to decide which measurements to take and defines range of variation, using averages and norms.
From The Biology - It's Life Series.
Prod-THAMES Dist-MEDIAG 1980

Make Your Own Wine C 60 MIN
1/2 IN VIDEO CASSETTE BETA/VHS
Provides step-by-step instruction in the techniques of wine making.
Prod-MOHOMV Dist-MOHOMV

Make Yourself Comfortable C 20 MIN
16MM FILM, 3/4 OR 1/2 IN VIDEO
Examines modern and ancient solutions to the problems of chair design. Looks at the relationship of design to materials, purpose, comfort and style.
From The Images And Things Series.
LC NO. 73-702102
Prod-NITC Dist-AITECH

Make-Believe Marriage C 33 MIN
16MM FILM, 3/4 OR 1/2 IN VIDEO J-C A
A shortened version of the motion picture Make-Believe Marriage. Presents a classroom experiment in marriage. Shows how the teenagers in Mr Webster's high school marriage class are paired off, take vows, draw up a budget, have make-believe babies, learn to deal with unemployment and eventually decide whether to continue the marriage or get a divorce. An ABC After School Special.
Prod-LCOA Dist-LCOA 1979

Make-Believe Marriage C 49 MIN
16MM FILM, 3/4 OR 1/2 IN VIDEO J-C A
Presents a classroom experiment in marriage. Shows how the teenagers in Mr Webster's high school marriage class are paired off, take vows, draw up a budget, have make-believe babies, learn to deal with unemployment and eventually decide whether to continue the marriage or get a divorce. An ABC After School Special.
Prod-LCOA Dist-LCOA 1979

Make-Believe Marriage (Captioned) C 33 MIN
16MM FILM, 3/4 OR 1/2 IN VIDEO J-H A
Tells the story of high school students who try their hand at make-believe marriage for a short time as a school project. Edited.
Prod-LCOA Dist-LCOA 1979

Make-Believe Marriage (Captioned) C 50 MIN
16MM FILM, 3/4 OR 1/2 IN VIDEO J-H A
Tells the story of high school students who try their hand at make-believe marriage for a short time as a school project. Unedited version.
Prod-LCOA Dist-LCOA 1979

Make-Believe Marriage (Spanish) C 33 MIN
16MM FILM, 3/4 OR 1/2 IN VIDEO J-H A
Features high school students who try their hand at make-believe marriage. Edited version.
Prod-LCOA Dist-LCOA 1979

Make-Believe Marriage (Spanish) C 50 MIN
16MM FILM, 3/4 OR 1/2 IN VIDEO J-H A
Features high school students who try their hand at make-believe marriage. Unedited version.
Prod-LCOA Dist-LCOA 1979

Make-Up And Juggling C 30 MIN
3/4 OR 1/2 INCH VIDEO CASSETTE
See series title for descriptive statement.
From The Behind The Scenes Series.
Prod-ARCVID Dist-ARCVID

Make-Up For The Theater C 20 MIN
16MM FILM, 3/4 OR 1/2 IN VIDEO
Demonstrates the application of stage make-up. Shows how to account for differences in sexes and stage lighting.
Prod-UCEMC Dist-UCEMC

Make-up For Women C 60 MIN
1/2 IN VIDEO CASSETTE (BETA)
Explains how women can enhance their natural beauty through make-up.
Prod-CINAS Dist-HOMET

Make-Up For Women C 60 MIN
1/2 IN VIDEO CASSETTE BETA/VHS
Shows how to apply make-up properly and effectively.
Prod-MOHOMV Dist-MOHOMV

Make-Up, Pt 1 B 25 MIN
16MM FILM OPTICAL SOUND
Discusses the basic rules of make-up for black and white television. Demonstrates the initial stages, cleansing, applying the foundation, shading, lighting, and powdering. Shows special treatment for the eyes, lips, hair and hands.
From The CETO Television Training Films Series.
Prod-CETO Dist-GPITVL

Make-Up, Pt 2 B 33 MIN
16MM FILM OPTICAL SOUND
Deals with the basic techniques used in character make-up to show youth and age. Points out make-up problems involved in the aging of historical characters.
From The CETO Television Training Films Series.
Prod-CETO Dist-GPITVL

Makeshift Solutions C 18 MIN
16MM FILM, 3/4 OR 1/2 IN VIDEO
Uses animation to look at economic trends during the last half of the 19th century, including the formation of trade unions and the influence of Karl Marx. Discusses the colonization of Africa.
From The History Book Series. Volume 6
Prod-STATNS Dist-CNEMAG

Makin' Hole In The Eighties C 31 MIN
16MM FILM, 3/4 OR 1/2 IN VIDEO
Introduces today's drilling industry from seismic exploration to action on the rig floor. Designed for nontechnical audiences.
Prod-UTEXPE Dist-UTEXPE 1981

Makin' Sweet Harmony C 14 MIN
3/4 OR 1/2 INCH VIDEO CASSETTE
Introduces the concept of harmony through participation, listening and learning a song about harmony.
From The Music And Me Series.
LC NO. 80-706748
Prod-WDCNTV Dist-AITECH 1979

Making A Book C 15 MIN
3/4 OR 1/2 INCH VIDEO CASSETTE P
See series title for descriptive statement.
From The Word Shop Series.
Prod-WETATV Dist-WETATV

Making A Choice B 10 MIN
16MM FILM OPTICAL SOUND S
Describes the procedure for selecting and teaching the second lip-reading word.
From The Parent Education - Information Films Series.
Prod-TC Dist-TC

Making A Cold Bend On A Hand Powered Machine B 13 MIN
16MM FILM - 3/4 IN VIDEO
Discusses the importance of bends in marine pipe installations. Shows how to measure pipe for bends and how to operate a hand powered bending machine. Issued in 1944 as a motion picture.
From The Shipbuilding Skills - Pipefitting Series. Number 4
LC NO. 80-707271
Prod-USOE Dist-USNAC Prodn-PHOTOS 1980

Making A Connection C
3/4 OR 1/2 INCH VIDEO CASSETTE IND
Covers procedures for making up a joint of pipe including getting the joint ready, placing it in the mousehole, cleaning and doping threads, unlatching the kelly on the new joint, stabbing and making up the new joint and other roughneck duties in making a connection.
From The Working Offshore Series.
Prod-GPCV Dist-GPCV

Making A Connection C 12 MIN
3/4 OR 1/2 INCH VIDEO CASSETTE IND
Identifies points that the drilling crew should be aware of when adding a mousehole joint to the drill string. Includes inspection, preparation and procedures.
From The Roughneck Training Series.
Prod-UTEXPE Dist-UTEXPE 1983

Making A Continuous Lapped Placket C 5 MIN
16MM FILM SILENT J-C A
Illustrates how to prepare the placket area by marking and reinforcing stitching. Presents the option of using a bias or straight grain placket strip, and shows how to reinforce the placket at the point of strain.
From The Clothing Construction Techniques Series.
LC NO. 77-701206
Prod-IOWA Dist-IOWASP 1976

Making A Core Box For A Flanged Pipe Elbow B 21 MIN
16MM FILM OPTICAL SOUND
Explains how to use a pattern layout in making a core box, design a core box, lay out a curved core piece, turn the core cavity in a curved piece, assemble a core box having a curved core piece and finish the core box.
LC NO. FIE52-126
Prod-USOE Dist-USNAC 1945

Making A Core Box For A Machine Base B 12 MIN
16MM FILM OPTICAL SOUND
Shows how a patternmaker, working from a casting, goes about the job of designing a core box, examines the casting, visualizes the problem, makes the layout and constructs the pattern and core boxes.
LC NO. FIE52-130
Prod-USOE Dist-USNAC 1945

Making A Core Box For A Tail Print B 18 MIN
16MM FILM OPTICAL SOUND
Explains how to use dry sand cores in molding holes in castings, use a pattern layout to make a core box, distinguish between core and core print, add the core and determine the parting line of a core box.
LC NO. FIE52-135
Prod-USOE Dist-USNAC 1945

Making A Core Box For A Vertical Core B 19 MIN
16MM FILM OPTICAL SOUND
Explains the function of the sand core. Depicts how to make a half box, use parted boxes, use a layout pattern in making a core box, prepare core box pieces and assemble a core box.
LC NO. FIE52-125
Prod-USOE Dist-USNAC 1945

Making A Decision Is C 19 MIN
16MM FILM, 3/4 OR 1/2 IN VIDEO J-C
Examines the decision-making skill in the making of decisions varying from trivial to life's choices. Explores key considerations in helping to arrive at decisions.
Prod-CF Dist-CF 1974

Making A Difference C 14 MIN
16MM FILM, 3/4 OR 1/2 IN VIDEO J A
Focuses on the nature of the ministry. Shows the daily tasks of serving a local church as three ministers explain and illustrate what he or she feels to be the nature of their work. Indicates both the joys and frustrations of the ministry through glimpses into a suburban church, an urban church and a small town church.
Prod-TRAFCO Dist-ECUFLM 1971

Making A Difference C 27 MIN
16MM FILM - 3/4 IN VIDEO
Shows occupational therapists working with clients with a variety of physical and psychosocial dysfunctions.
Prod-AOTA Dist-AOTA 1972

Making A Fabric Covered Belt C 5 MIN
16MM FILM SILENT J-C A
Shows making a professional-looking, fabric-covered belt using commercial belting. Describes a method for achieving the desired length and shows using the belting as a guide for achieving the correct size fabric tube.
From The Clothing Construction Techniques Series.
LC NO. 77-701217
Prod-IOWA Dist-IOWASP 1976

Making A Faced Opening For A Pleated Sleeve Closure C 4 MIN
16MM FILM SILENT J-C A
Shows how to make a faced opening and how to attach the cuff to a sleeve that has this type of opening.
From The Clothing Construction Techniques Series.
LC NO. 77-701210
Prod-IOWA Dist-IOWASP 1976

Making A Five Tuck Splice B 26 MIN
16MM FILM OPTICAL SOUND
Pictures the preparation of a cable for splicing. Shows how to make the first tuck and the four succeeding tucks.
LC NO. FIE52-24
Prod-USOE Dist-USNAC 1944

Making A Flat Position Open Butt Weld/ Making A Flat Position Closed Butt... C 22 MIN
3/4 OR 1/2 INCH VIDEO CASSETTE H-C A
Describes how to make a flat position open butt weld, a flat position closed butt weld and butt welding steel rods end to end.
From The Arc Welding Series.
Prod-CUETV Dist-CUNIV 1981

Making A Good Impression C 15 MIN
3/4 OR 1/2 INCH VIDEO CASSETTE PRO
Presents the steps involved in making a custom ear mold for an air-conduction hearing aid.
LC NO. 80-706812
Prod-BRENTW Dist-USNAC 1976

Making A Good Thing Better C 11 MIN
16MM FILM OPTICAL SOUND PRO
Shows how use of a tamper-resistant package of Tubex narcotics and barbiturates helps strengthen drug security programs in hospitals and clinics.
LC NO. 74-703662
Prod-WYETH Dist-WYLAB 1970

Making A Half-Slip C 13 MIN
16MM FILM OPTICAL SOUND J-H A
Shows the procedure of making a half-slip, analyzing the marking and measuring, sewing the pieces together and adding the waistband and the lace.
From The Home Economics - Clothing Series.
LC NO. 79-709993
Prod-MORLAT Dist-SF 1968

Making A Horizontal Tee Weld C 10 MIN
3/4 OR 1/2 INCH VIDEO CASSETTE H-C A
See series title for descriptive statement.
From The Arc Welding Series.
LC NO. 81-707041
Prod-CUETV Dist-CUNIV 1981

Making A Living B 8 MIN
16MM FILM SILENT
Tells the story of man who tries to get a job on a newspaper by stealing a rival's camera and racing to the newspaper's office with pictures of an auto accident. Stars Charlie Chaplin.
Prod-MSENP Dist-TWYMAN 1914

Making A Living Work—A Series
C A
Examines adult life/work planning. Presents interviews, montages and spontaneous on-the-street conversations. Features adults asking important questions about their own life and career goals and identifies some strategies to help adults reach those goals. Encourages adults to look at their lifestyle needs and career aspirations in order to achieve a workable blend of work, education and leisure time.
Prod-OHUTC Dist-OHUTC

Change	030 MIN
Decision Making	030 MIN
Lifestyles/Lifestages	030 MIN
Making Change	030 MIN
Occupational Research	030 MIN
Skills	030 MIN
Values	030 MIN
World Of Work	030 MIN

Making A Mask C 6 MIN
16MM FILM, 3/4 OR 1/2 IN VIDEO I-C
Shows how to make two kinds of masks--tie-on and slipover--out of wet paper and paste.
From The Creative Hands Series.
Prod-CRAF Dist-IFB 1951

Making A Master Developed Layout, Pt 1 B 20 MIN
16MM FILM OPTICAL SOUND
Demonstrates how to make the complete pattern or master developed layout for a bulkhead in an airplane fin, using a master contour template.
LC NO. FIE52-13
Prod-USOE Dist-USNAC 1944

Making A Master Developed Layout, Pt 2 - And Making The Form Block B 16 MIN
16MM FILM OPTICAL SOUND
Explains how to complete the master developed layout by calculating and scribing the form block lines. Shows how to make the form block.
LC NO. FIE52-11
Prod-USOE Dist-USNAC 1944

Making A Matchboard Pattern B 21 MIN
16MM FILM OPTICAL SOUND
Shows how to sketch a matchboard, make patterns, prepare gates to connect patterns, prepare the runner for the cope side, assemble the matchboard, turn a draft taper on a hole and attach flask fixtures.
From The Precision Wood Machining Series. Fundamentals Of Patternmaking, No. 8
LC NO. FIE52-124
Prod-USOE Dist-USNAC Prodn-RCM 1945

Making A Melody C 29 MIN
3/4 INCH VIDEO CASSETTE
Shows composer Jerry Bilik as he examines five sets of lyrics, chooses one, and, at the end of 29 minutes, has written a tune.
From The Song Writer Series.
Prod-UMITV Dist-UMITV 1977

Making A Mosaic X 10 MIN
16MM FILM OPTICAL SOUND I-H A
Demonstrates the making of a mosaic by ADA Korsakaite from sketch to completion by the use of ceramic tile and commercial tessary. Shows examples of work done by Juan O' Gorman, Millard Sheets and Chavez Morado.
Prod-ALLMOR Dist-AVED 1955

Making A Neckband Collar C 5 MIN
16MM FILM SILENT J-C A
Demonstrates making a shirt-type collar that has the neckband cut in one with the collar. Illustrates stitching the front edges of the collar and band accurately, clipping and notching where appropriate.
From The Clothing Construction Techniques Series.
LC NO. 77-701193
Prod-IOWA Dist-IOWASP 1976

Making A Newspaper C 13 MIN
3/4 OR 1/2 INCH VIDEO CASSETTE P
Shows Ruth's grandfather, a newspaper editor, showing her the steps in putting out a newspaper for the Animal Lover's Club.
From The Under The Yellow Balloon Series.
Prod-SCETV Dist-AITECH 1980

Making A One-Piece Flat Pattern B 22 MIN
16MM FILM OPTICAL SOUND
Shows how to identify the parts of the molding flask, to use shrinkage rules, to prepare the pieces, to make identical castings and to finish the patterns.
From The Precision Wood Machining Series. Fundamentals Of Pattern Making, No. 1
LC NO. FIE52-118
Prod-USOE Dist-USNAC Prodn-RCM 1945

Making A Pattern For A Flanged Pipe Elbow B 18 MIN
16MM FILM OPTICAL SOUND
Illustrates how to make a right-angle layout, turn out separate core prints, make split flanges, set flanges into core prints, assemble half the pattern on the layout, dowel an elbow pattern and apply leather fillets.
LC NO. FIE52-123
Prod-USOE Dist-USNAC 1945

Making A Pattern For A Machine Molded Steel Globe And Angle Valve B 14 MIN
16MM FILM OPTICAL SOUND
Explains how machine molding affects pattern design and how a patternmaker designs and constructs a pattern for a valve body, including the gating system.
From The Precision Wood Machining Series. Problems In patternmaking
LC NO. FIE52-134
Prod-USOE Dist-USNAC Prodn-HANDY 1945

Making A Pattern For A Three-Part Mold B 20 MIN
16MM FILM OPTICAL SOUND
Discusses the reasons for the three-part pattern. Shows how to make the layout, segment the body or center section, eliminate the end grain on large flanges and turn large work on the end of the lathe.
LC NO. FIE52-122
Prod-USOE Dist-USNAC 1945

Making A Pattern Requiring A Cover Core B 14 MIN
16MM FILM OPTICAL SOUND
Explains how molding and coring problems lead to the choice of a cover core, and shows how a pattern-maker designs patterns and core boxes requiring a cover core.
LC NO. FIE52-128
Prod-USOE Dist-USNAC 1945

Making A Pattern Requiring Box Construction B 17 MIN
16MM FILM OPTICAL SOUND
Explains how the patternmaker approaches the task of making a pattern for a duplicate of a casting, examines and measures the casting, visualizes the problem and constructs the pattern.
Prod-USOE Dist-USNAC

Making A Pattern Requiring Segmental Construction B 13 MIN
16MM FILM OPTICAL SOUND
Explains why segmental construction is a preferred method for some patterns and shows how a patternmaker designs and constructs a pattern for a gear blank which requires segmental construction.
From The Precision Wood Machining Series. Problems In patternmaking
LC NO. FIE52-89
Prod-USOE Dist-USNAC Prodn-HANDY 1945

Making A Pattern Using A Green And A Dry Sand Core B 14 MIN
16MM FILM OPTICAL SOUND
Illustrates how a green sand core is molded. Tells how a patternmaker determines when to allow for a green sand core, how he designs a pattern allowing for a green sand core and how he visualizes and constructs a particular pattern.
LC NO. FIE52-127
Prod-USOE Dist-USNAC 1945

Making A Pattern With A Horizontal Core B 14 MIN
16MM FILM OPTICAL SOUND
Explains when a horizontal core is used and how to allow for shrinkage in bronze. Shows how to lay out fillets, make horizontal core prints, true up a parting plane, dowel a pattern with a horizontal core and turn.
LC NO. FIE52-121
Prod-USOE Dist-USNAC 1945

Making A Pattern With A Tail Print B 19 MIN
16MM FILM OPTICAL SOUND
Shows how to mold castings with holes, make a rough sketch for visualizing the actual casting, use a dry sand core, form core cavities by using tail prints and make a layout including tail prints.
LC NO. FIE52-120
Prod-USOE Dist-USNAC 1945

Making A Pattern With A Vertical Core B 14 MIN
16MM FILM OPTICAL SOUND
Points out the importance of making a preliminary sketch. Explains how to make the layout, allow for shrinkage and finish, lay out the core prints, use the layout, assemble the pattern, allow for draft and shellac the pattern.
LC NO. FIE52-117
Prod-USOE Dist-USNAC 1945

Making A Picture C 30 MIN
3/4 OR 1/2 INCH VIDEO CASSETTE H-C A
Introduces the working principles of a camera and encourages an understanding of the basic elements of light, shape, form and pattern in the setting of a small family circus.
From The What A Picture - The Complete Photography Course By John Hedgecoe Series. Program 1
Prod-THREMI Dist-FI

Making A Pinata C 11 MIN
16MM FILM - 3/4 IN VIDEO I-J
Shows how a pinata is made of paper mache formed around a balloon and decorated with tissue paper ruffles.
Prod-ATLAP Dist-ATLAP 1969

Making A Pointed Collar (With Seam On Outer Three Sides) C 5 MIN
16MM FILM SILENT J-C A
Illustrates a technique in which the upper and under collars are stitched from the same pattern piece. Shows how the outer seam is stitched and understitched before the end seams, thus keeping the under collar from showing.
From The Clothing Construction Techniques Series.
LC NO. 77-701192
Prod-IOWA Dist-IOWASP 1976

Making A Presentation C 15 MIN
16MM FILM, 3/4 OR 1/2 IN VIDEO I
Tells how a young Navajo girl polishes her oral presentation skills, wins the school speech contest, and shames local bigots with her speech on her proud heritage.
From The Thinkabout Series. Communicating Effectively
LC NO. 81-706105
Prod-UNIT Dist-AITECH 1979

Making A Recovery Bed B 10 MIN
16MM FILM OPTICAL SOUND
Demonstrates the procedure to be followed and the equipment and supplies needed to arrange a bed unit in the hospital ward or room to ensure a safe, warm, comfortable bed for the patient returning from surgery.

LC NO. FIE59-133
Prod-USN Dist-USNAC 1957

Making A Revolution C 52 MIN
16MM FILM, 3/4 OR 1/2 IN VIDEO J-C A
Describes how the diverse colonies joined together in common complaints against the mother country. Presents Alistair Cooke who traces the American tradition of turning to arms in the face of trouble.
From The America - A Personal History Of The United States Series. No. 3
LC NO. 79-707153
Prod-BBCTV Dist-TIMLIF 1972

Making A Revolution (Spanish) C 52 MIN
16MM FILM OPTICAL SOUND J-C A
Describes how the diverse colonies grew together in common complaints against the mother country. Presents Alistair Cooke who traces the American tradition of turning to arms in the face of trouble.
From The America - A Personal History Of The United States Series. No. 3
Prod-BBCTV Dist-TIMLIF 1972

Making A Round Collar C 4 MIN
16MM FILM SILENT J-C A
Illustrates a technique in which the upper and under collars are from the same pattern piece. Shows how the under collar is extended one-eighth inch beyond the upper collar, thus preventing it from showing.
From The Clothing Construction Techniques Series.
LC NO. 77-701191
Prod-IOWA Dist-IOWASP 1976

Making A Segmented Pattern B 22 MIN
16MM FILM OPTICAL SOUND
Explains how to plan segmentation of the pattern, lay out the segments and web, assemble the pattern, prepare a recessed hub and finish the pattern.
LC NO. FIE52-119
Prod-USOE Dist-USNAC 1945

Making A Simple Core B 15 MIN
16MM FILM OPTICAL SOUND
Demonstrates how to prepare sand for coremaking, make a small cylindrical core in either one or two pieces, assemble a two-piece core and locate a vertical core in a mold to provide necessary venting. Shows how core gases escape when a mold is poured.
From The Foundry Practice Series. Bench Molding, No. 2
LC NO. FIE52-107
Prod-USOE Dist-USNAC Prodn-ATLAS 1944

Making A Sound Decision C 28 MIN
16MM FILM OPTICAL SOUND
Shows the craftsmanship needed to design, manufacture and install a Reuter pipe organ.
LC NO. FIA66-484
Prod-REUTER Dist-REUTER Prodn-CENTRO 1965

Making A Sound Film C 13 MIN
16MM FILM, 3/4 OR 1/2 IN VIDEO J-C A
Demonstrates the recording, editing and mixing of various types of sound with the visual images of a film. Describes the equipment used, the techniques involved, the procedures for synchronized dialog, voice over, music and sound effects.
From The Films About Filmmaking Series.
Prod-IFB Dist-IFB 1973

Making A Table C 15 MIN
2 INCH VIDEOTAPE
See series title for descriptive statement.
From The Living Better I Series.
Prod-MAETEL Dist-PUBTEL

Making A Thread Pouch C 13 MIN
16MM FILM OPTICAL SOUND J-H A
Reviews the threading of the bobbin and straightening of the material. Shows the pinning of the thread pouch, the sewing of the seams and the finishing of the seams.
From The Home Economics - Clothing Series.
LC NO. 71-709991
Prod-MORLAT Dist-SF 1968

Making A Trip C 18 MIN
3/4 OR 1/2 INCH VIDEO CASSETTE IND
Points out factors rotary helpers should consider in order to make a round trip in a proper and safe manner.
From The Roughneck Training Series.
Prod-UTEXPE Dist-UTEXPE 1983

Making A Vinyl Repair Grain Matrix C 9 MIN
1/2 IN VIDEO CASSETTE BETA/VHS
Deals with auto body repair. Shows the fabrication of a graining matrix, using Uticolor and a heat gun to cure.
Prod-RMI Dist-RMI

Making A Wire Template B 19 MIN
16MM FILM OPTICAL SOUND
Shows how to draw lay-out measurements with blueprints, transfer blueprints, find the radius with a beam compass and bend a template.
LC NO. FIE52-1190
Prod-USN Dist-USNAC 1944

Making A Work Sampling Study C 23 MIN
16MM FILM, 3/4 OR 1/2 IN VIDEO H-C A
Shows the steps used in making the work sampling study, including definition of the problem, preparatory steps, designing the study, making the observations, analyzing and summarizing the data, and reporting the results.
Prod-UCB Dist-UCEMC 1957

Making A Wrapped And Soldered Splice B 15 MIN
16MM FILM OPTICAL SOUND
Demonstrates how to make a ball soldered terminal, prevent the wires from unlaying when cut, fit a cable to a thimble and make the wire wrap.
From The Aircraft Work Series. Control Cables, No. 1
LC NO. FIE52-35
Prod-USOE Dist-USNAC Prodn-BRAY 1944

Making An Occupied Bed B 28 MIN
16MM FILM OPTICAL SOUND PRO
Discusses the source and collection of clean linen and demonstrates a method of making an occupied bed.
From The Directions For Education In Nursing Via Technology Series. Lesson 5
LC NO. 74-701778
Prod-DENT Dist-WSU 1974

Making An Occupied Bed C 19 MIN
3/4 OR 1/2 INCH VIDEO CASSETTE PRO
See series title for descriptive statement.
From The Basic Nursing Skills Series.
Prod-BRA Dist-BRA

Making An Occupied Bed C 19 MIN
3/4 OR 1/2 INCH VIDEO CASSETTE PRO
See series title for descriptive statement.
From The Basic Nursing Skills Series. Tape 2
Prod-MDCC Dist-MDCC

Making An Operational Analysis B 29 MIN
16MM FILM OPTICAL SOUND IND
See series title for descriptive statement.
From The Job Instructor Training Series.
LC NO. 77-703324
Prod-EDSD Dist-EDSD

Making An Unoccupied Bed B 14 MIN
16MM FILM OPTICAL SOUND
Demonstrates the procedures to be followed and the equipment and supplies needed to arrange a unit in a hospital ward or room.
LC NO. FIE59-134
Prod-USN Dist-USNAC 1957

Making An Unoccupied Bed B 22 MIN
16MM FILM OPTICAL SOUND PRO
Discusses the source and collection of clean linen and demonstrates a method for making an unoccupied bed. Shows the use of a contour sheet and draw sheet.
From The Directions For Education In Nursing Via Technology Series. Lesson 3
LC NO. 74-701776
Prod-DENT Dist-WSU 1974

Making An Unoccupied Bed C 13 MIN
3/4 OR 1/2 INCH VIDEO CASSETTE PRO
See series title for descriptive statement.
From The Basic Nursing Skills Series.
Prod-BRA Dist-BRA

Making An Unoccupied Bed C 13 MIN
3/4 OR 1/2 INCH VIDEO CASSETTE PRO
See series title for descriptive statement.
From The Basic Nursing Skills Series. Tape 3
Prod-MDCC Dist-MDCC

Making And Cutting The Lining C 29 MIN
2 INCH VIDEOTAPE
Features Mrs Ruth Hickman demonstrating how to make and cut lining.
From The Sewing Skills - Tailoring Series.
Prod-KRMATV Dist-PUBTEL

Making And Repairing Tubing Connections B 18 MIN
16MM FILM OPTICAL SOUND
Shows how to straighten copper tubing, how to work, cut and dress copper tubing, how to make a flare for various sizes of tubing and how to sweat in a connector to cover a break.
From The Refrigeration Service Series. Commercial Systems, No. 5
LC NO. FIE52-263
Prod-USOE Dist-USNAC Prodn-BONDP 1944

Making And Sterilization Of An Innoculating Loop, The/Development Of Aseptic... C 32 MIN
1/2 INCH VIDEO CASSETTE
Includes three presentations titled The Making And Sterlization Of An Innoculating Loop, The Development Of Aseptic Technique and Pure Culture Techniques. Covers characteristics of a well-made inocculating loop and techniques for making the loops, the use and development of aseptic technique to maintain purity during the transfer of stock cultures and isolated colonies and the concept of a pure culture as well as a demonstration of two isolation techniques typically employed in the microbiology laboratory.
Prod-AMSM Dist-AVMM

Making And Using A Light Exposure Scale B 15 MIN
2 INCH VIDEOTAPE P
See series title for descriptive statement.
From The Just Inquisitive Series. No. 27
Prod-EOPS Dist-GPITVL Prodn-KOACTV

Making And Using Bias Strips C 6 MIN
16MM FILM SILENT J-C A
Demonstrates how to cut, shape and join bias strips and shows where and how to use bias. Includes piping and bias facings.
From The Clothing Construction Techniques Series.
LC NO. 77-701229
Prod-IOWA Dist-IOWASP 1976

Making Appraisals Effective C 30 MIN
3/4 OR 1/2 INCH VIDEO CASSETTE
See series title for descriptive statement.
From The Management For Engineers Series.
Prod-UKY Dist-SME

Making Arrangements C 29 MIN
3/4 INCH VIDEO CASSETTE
Shows how songs can be improved by a group working together.
From The Song Writer Series.
Prod-UMITV Dist-UMITV 1977

Making Basic Plumbing Repairs C 60 MIN
1/2 IN VIDEO CASSETTE (BETA)
Shows how to repair problems with faucets, toilets, drains and showers.
Prod-CINAS Dist-HOMET

Making Basic Plumbing Repairs C 60 MIN
1/2 IN VIDEO CASSETTE BETA/VHS
Explains how to make basic plumbing repairs and the tools to use for each job. Demonstrates how to tackle the problems that can occur with a toilet, and how to install a new shower head.
Prod-RMI Dist-RMI

Making Baskets - An Art Adventure C 11 MIN
16MM FILM, 3/4 OR 1/2 IN VIDEO
Shows how handsome baskets can be made from a variety of materials.
From The Art Adventure Series.
Prod-EASY Dist-CORF

Making Behavioral Objectives Meaningful—A Series
T
Presents lectures by Dr Madeline Hunter, principal of University Elementary School and lecturer at the University of California at Los Angeles Graduate School of Education.
Prod-SPF Dist-SPF

Behavioral Objectives And Accountability 30 MIN
Objectives In The Affective Domain 30 MIN
Objectives In The Cognitive Domain 30 MIN

Making Bound Buttonholes C 6 MIN
16MM FILM SILENT J-C A
Demonstrates a method of making bound buttonholes which is suitable for a wide variety of fabrics. Shows how the buttonhole location is marked and illustrates how a fabric piece is attached to form the lips of the buttonhole.
From The Clothing Construction Techniques Series.
LC NO. 77-701199
Prod-IOWA Dist-IOWASP 1976

Making Bound Buttonholes C 29 MIN
2 INCH VIDEOTAPE
Features Mrs Ruth Hickman demonstrating how to make bound buttonholes.
From The Sewing Skills - Tailoring Series.
Prod-KRMATV Dist-PUBTEL

Making Bread C 6 MIN
3/4 OR 1/2 INCH VIDEO CASSETTE
Shows the machinery and the machinations of a bread making factory. Uses wit in its presentation.
Prod-MEDIPR Dist-MEDIPR 1979

Making Button Loops C 5 MIN
16MM FILM SILENT J-C A
Shows preparing button loops from bias fabric strips and using lined or graph paper as an aid for getting the loops evenly spaced and the same size.
From The Clothing Construction Techniques Series.
LC NO. 77-701201
Prod-IOWA Dist-IOWASP 1976

Making Change C 9 MIN
16MM FILM, 3/4 OR 1/2 IN VIDEO P
Teaches the names, values and relationships of coins, how to make change and the use of decimals in money notation.
Prod-BFA Dist-PHENIX 1977

Making Change C 20 MIN
2 INCH VIDEOTAPE P
See series title for descriptive statement.
From The Mathemagic, Unit VII - Money Series.
Prod-WMULTV Dist-GPITVL

Making Change C 30 MIN
3/4 OR 1/2 INCH VIDEO CASSETTE C A
Offers portraits of two families, one a man legally blind since birth, and the other a couple on the verge of separation who changed their lifestyle in order to keep their marriage. Shows two kinds of change, reacting and adapting and planning and moving towards a new life.
From The Making A Living Work Series. Program 108
Prod-OHUTC Dist-OHUTC

Making Change For A Dollar (2nd Ed) C 13 MIN
16MM FILM, 3/4 OR 1/2 IN VIDEO P
Tells how a cash register named Ka-Ching comes to life and teaches Chris how to make change.
Prod-CORF Dist-CORF

Making Change Work C 9 MIN
3/4 OR 1/2 INCH VIDEO CASSETTE
Offers five simple steps to avoid the major pitfalls of introducing change. Covers timing, preparation and the actual implementation.
From The Introduction Of Change Series.
Prod-RESEM Dist-RESEM

Making Choices B 15 MIN
2 INCH VIDEOTAPE I
Explains that through books, the readers' choices in art and literature and language and ideas will be changing constantly. (Broadcast quality)
From The Bill Martin Series. No. 15
Prod-BRITED Dist-GPITVL Prodn-KQEDTV

Making Composite Color Slides With A Rear Projection System C 8 MIN
3/4 INCH VIDEO CASSETTE
Discusses equipment, materials and procedures used for making composite slides.
LC NO. 77-706052
Prod-NMAC Dist-USNAC 1976

Making Contact - A Beginning In Speech And Language Therapy C 9 MIN
16MM FILM OPTICAL SOUND
Provides an introduction to the field of speech pathology. Concentrates on the role of the clinician in relation to children who do not communicate or relate.
LC NO. 74-705072
Prod-USDHEW Dist-USNAC 1971

Making Contacts C 29 MIN
3/4 OR 1/2 INCH VIDEO CASSETTE
Features an introduction to the darkroom, including photograms and how to take processed film and make a contact sheet, and prepare it for printing.
From The Photo Show Series.
Prod-WGBHTV Dist-PBS 1981

Making Cuffs C 6 MIN
16MM FILM SILENT J-C A
Illustrates attaching a cuff to the lower edge of a gathered sleeve. Discusses both one-piece and two-piece cuffs and shows the different techniques for applying interfacing for the two cuff constructions.
From The Clothing Construction Techniques Series.
LC NO. 77-701207
Prod-IOWA Dist-IOWASP 1976

Making Dance Films C 30 MIN
3/4 OR 1/2 INCH VIDEO CASSETTE
See series title for descriptive statement.
From The Dance On Television And Film Series.
Prod-ARCVID Dist-ARCVID

Making Dances C 90 MIN
16MM FILM OPTICAL SOUND
Includes interviews, rehearsal and performance sequences with choreographers Trisha Brown, Lucinda Childs, David Gordon, Douglas Dunn, Kenneth King, Meredith Monk and Sara Rudner.
LC NO. 81-700433
Prod-BLACKW Dist-BLACKW 1980

Making Dances - 7 Post-Modern Choreographers C 90 MIN
3/4 OR 1/2 INCH VIDEO CASSETTE
Reflects the diversity of contemporary dance. Documents the work and ideas of Trisha Brown, Lucinda Childs, David Gordon, Douglas Dunn, Kenneth King, Meredith Monk and Sara Rudner.
Prod-BLACKW Dist-BLACKW

Making Darts, Tucks And Pleats C 5 MIN
16MM FILM SILENT J-C A
Shows stitching darts and securing threads with a tailor's knot. Illustrates making regular tucks, narrow pin tucks and pleats.
From The Clothing Construction Techniques Series.
LC NO. 77-701177
Prod-IOWA Dist-IOWASP 1976

Making Decisions C 15 MIN
3/4 OR 1/2 INCH VIDEO CASSETTE H
Presents a model for thoughtful decision-making in the political process.
From The By The People Series.
Prod-CTI Dist-CTI

Making Decisions C 15 MIN
3/4 OR 1/2 INCH VIDEO CASSETTE P
Uses the format of a television program to explain the basic economic principle that wants are unlimited and resources are limited. Demonstrates that satisfying our wants calls for analyzing alternatives based on setting priorities and considering values.
From The Pennywise Series. No. 2
LC NO. 82-706005
Prod-MAETEL Dist-GPITVL 1980

Making Decisions / Doing What You Think Is Right / Why Am I Punished C 15 MIN
3/4 OR 1/2 INCH VIDEO CASSETTE P
Presents stories presented by Muppet-like Clyde Frog presenting stories emphasizing positive self-images, feelings of optimism and self-confidence.
From The Clyde Frog Show Series.
Prod-MAETEL Dist-GPITVL 1977

Making Decisions About Sex C 25 MIN
16MM FILM, 3/4 OR 1/2 IN VIDEO J-H
Presents a group of teenagers who candidly assess their decisions and the circumstances that influenced them to either have or refrain from sex.
LC NO. 81-707577
Prod-CF Dist-CF 1981

Making Delegation Work For You C
3/4 OR 1/2 INCH VIDEO CASSETTE
Sharpens the manager's ability to make appropriate delegation decisions through group sessions, activities and self-assessment exercises.
Prod-AMA Dist-AMA

Making Dew C 15 MIN
1/2 IN VIDEO CASSETTE BETA/VHS I-J
Describes how the shipwrecked crew puts survival skills into action and solves their first life-threatening challenge by making a solar still to provide drinking water. Provides a look at water, its physical properties, pollution and natural purification techniques.
From The Voyage Of The Mimi Series.
Prod-HRAW Dist-HRAW

Making Discoveries In A Museum B 15 MIN
2 INCH VIDEOTAPE P
Features a visit to a museum to look at paintings and discusses the artists' inspirations for the paintings. (Broadcast quality)
From The Art Discoveries Series. Lesson 10
Prod-CVETVC Dist-GPITVL Prodn-WCVETV

Making Ends Meet C 11 MIN
16MM FILM OPTICAL SOUND
Shows, via film-a-graph technique, the successful operation of a day-care center in Perry, Georgia, where limited funds are available.
LC NO. 74-705997
Prod-USSRS Dist-USNAC 1969

Making Eye Glass Lenses C 5 MIN
16MM FILM, 3/4 OR 1/2 IN VIDEO
Examines the German eyeglass manufacturing industry.
From The European Studies - Germany Series. Part 6
Prod-BAYER Dist-IFB 1973

Making Felt Rugs (Pushtu) C 9 MIN
16MM FILM, 3/4 OR 1/2 IN VIDEO
See series title for descriptive statement.
From The Mountain Peoples Of Central Asia (Afghanistan) Series.
Prod-IFF Dist-IFF

Making Folded And Fake Cuffs C 6 MIN
16MM FILM SILENT J-C A
Shows how to make a fake cuff which achieves the effect of a regular cuff cut, but eliminates bulk. Includes the more conventional folded cuff, with a formula for achieving the desired width and length.
From The Clothing Construction Techniques Series.
LC NO. 77-701212
Prod-IOWA Dist-IOWASP 1976

Making French And Flat Fell Seams C 5 MIN
16MM FILM SILENT J-C A
Defines French and flat fell seams and identifies where they might be used. Illustrates steps in making both types of seams.
From The Clothing Construction Techniques Series.
LC NO. 77-701183
Prod-IOWA Dist-IOWASP 1976

Making Friends C 15 MIN
3/4 OR 1/2 INCH VIDEO CASSETTE P
Depicts Molly's difficulties in making new friends at school after her best friend moves away. Explains that at first she meets rejection, but that a fable about a rhinoceros and a tickbird encourages her to keep trying.
From The Out And About Series.
Prod-STSU Dist-AITECH Prodn-WETN 1984

Making Friends C 29 MIN
2 INCH VIDEOTAPE
See series title for descriptive statement.
From The Our Street Series.
Prod-MDCPB Dist-PUBTEL

Making Gathers C 3 MIN
16MM FILM SILENT J-C A
Illustrates the use of gathering threads and suggests stitch length. Shows pinning and stitching the gathered layer to the ungathered layer, finishing with two rows of stitching and trimming to reduce bulk in the finished hem.
From The Clothing Construction Techniques Series.
LC NO. 77-701178
Prod-IOWA Dist-IOWASP 1976

Making Gunpowder (Tajik) B 10 MIN
16MM FILM, 3/4 OR 1/2 IN VIDEO
See series title for descriptive statement.
From The Mountain Peoples Of Central Asia (Afghanistan) Series.
Prod-IFF Dist-IFF

Making Haiku C 8 MIN
16MM FILM, 3/4 OR 1/2 IN VIDEO P-J
Introduces and explains the form of haiku and presents scenes from nature which inspire haiku. Emphasizes the simplicity and beauty of this form of poetry and encourages students' creativity in composing their own.
Prod-EBEC Dist-EBEC 1972

Making Hay C 10 MIN
16MM FILM OPTICAL SOUND H-C A
Features modern methods of putting up hay. Emphasizes the quantity and quality of hay and explains that modern machinery which enables hay to be cut and stacked within 48 hours has done much to improve its quality.
Prod-UPR Dist-UPR 1964

Making Human Resources Productive C 30 MIN
16MM FILM - 3/4 IN VIDEO PRO
Defines 'job enrichment' as altering the relationship of the individual employee to the authority structure of the organization. Explains why work is not meaningful under authoritarian supervision.
From The Effective Organization Series.
Prod-BNA Dist-BNA 1971

Making Ideas Happen C 22 MIN
16MM FILM OPTICAL SOUND
Provides a look at aluminum production facilities in many parts of the United States as well as in France and Australia, showing how it is made and the markets it serves.
LC NO. 81-700560
Prod-MTP Dist-MTP Prodn-VISION 1981

Making Inferences C 30 MIN
3/4 OR 1/2 INCH VIDEO CASSETTE
See series title for descriptive statement.
From The General Reading Series.
Prod-CAMB Dist-CAMB

Making Inferences (Practical Reading) C 30 MIN
3/4 OR 1/2 INCH VIDEO CASSETTE
See series title for descriptive statement.
From The Practical Reading Series.
Prod-CAMB Dist-CAMB

Making Inferences (Prose Literature) C 30 MIN
3/4 OR 1/2 INCH VIDEO CASSETTE
See series title for descriptive statement.
From The Prose Literature Series.
Prod-CAMB Dist-CAMB

Making It C 18 MIN
16MM FILM OPTICAL SOUND
Discusses the role of sex in personal relationships.
LC NO. 76-703324
Prod-MORLAT Dist-MORLAT 1975

Making It C 18 MIN
3/4 OR 1/2 INCH VIDEO CASSETTE H-C A
Tells how Margaret Gibson wrote a short story about her battle against schizophrenia, aided by a hairdresser who dreamed of fame as a female impersonator. Explains how the story was turned into a movie with a large cult following and examines the two people and their battles to achieve success.
Prod-CANBC Dist-JOU

Making It - They Tell Their Stories C 30 MIN
3/4 OR 1/2 INCH VIDEO CASSETTE
See series title for descriptive statement.
From The Rebop Series.
Prod-WGBHTV Dist-MDCPB

Making It Better - How Everyone Can Create A Safer Workplace C
16MM FILM - 3/4 IN VIDEO A
Shows how to motivate workers to make their workplace safer for themselves and others.
Prod-BNA Dist-BNA 1983

Making It Come Alive C 15 MIN
16MM FILM, 3/4 OR 1/2 IN VIDEO I
Shows how Heather, a dedicated ballet dancer, learns that creative expression is a form of communication and depends on the artist's sincere involvement.
From The Thinkabout Series. Communicating Effectively
LC NO. 81-706085
Prod-SCETV Dist-AITECH 1979

Making It Count--A Series
H-C A
Presents a broad overview of data processing concepts and problems. Covers the fundamentals of hardware and software, programming languages and programming logic. Introduces and defines data processing terms. Examines topics such as computer applications, how a computer system is developed to solve a typical user problem, word processing, microcomputers, distributed processing and future developments in data processing.
Prod-BCSC Dist-BCSC 1980

Acquiring Computer Systems	30 MIN
Additional Programming Capabilities	30 MIN
Batch Processing	30 MIN
Computer Aids To Management	30 MIN
Computer Languages	30 MIN
Computer Operations Centers	30 MIN
Computers And Society	30 MIN
Evaluating Computer Resources	30 MIN
Hardware And Software	30 MIN
History Of Computing	30 MIN
Information Representation	30 MIN
Introduction And Preview	30 MIN
Introduction To Programming, An	30 MIN
Microcomputers	30 MIN
Multiprogramming And Multiprocessing	30 MIN
Networks And Distributed Data Processing	30 MIN
Online Processing	30 MIN
Review And Preview	30 MIN
Review And The Future	30 MIN
System Analysis - Design	30 MIN
System Analysis - Development And	30 MIN
System Analysis - Problem Definition	30 MIN
Word Processing In Office Systems	30 MIN

Making It Happen C 17 MIN
3/4 INCH VIDEOTAPE
Focuses on whether or not winning is a 'feminine' attribute. Explores the lives of three sportswomen. Highlights women's major contributions to sports history.
Prod-EDC Dist-EDC

Making It In Hollywood C 30 MIN
3/4 OR 1/2 INCH VIDEO CASSETTE
Presents actors and actresses giving hints on what to do and what not to do in order to 'Make It In Hollywood.'
Prod-EAI Dist-EAI

Making It In The Organization C 18 MIN
16MM FILM, 3/4 OR 1/2 IN VIDEO
A revised version of the Canadian videorecording Living In The Company. Shows how an employee's attitude toward his work, his supervisor, his reponsibility and his organization affect job performance and satisfaction.
LC NO. 80-706184
Prod-WILCOD Dist-SALENG 1980

Making It In The World Of Work C 26 MIN
16MM FILM, 3/4 OR 1/2 IN VIDEO J-C

Presents nine graduates describing the work they are doing, why they chose it, its benefits to them, and their personal goals in relation to it. Emphasizes choosing work which one enjoys.
Prod-FLMFR Dist-FLMFR

Making It Live C 14 MIN
3/4 OR 1/2 INCH VIDEO CASSETTE
Demonstrates that knowing the product or service being sold and being able to tell about it with enthusiasm and conviction is a key to sale success.
From The Basic Sales Series.
Prod-RESEM Dist-RESEM

Making It Move C 10 MIN
16MM FILM, 3/4 OR 1/2 IN VIDEO
Follows the development of an animated film from the animator's search for an idea to his final preparation of the animation cels.
Prod-HALAS Dist-PHENIX 1979

Making It On Your Own - Building A Private Law Practice C 50 MIN
3/4 OR 1/2 INCH VIDEO CASSETTE PRO
Designed for the lawyer considering going into solo practice or already in independent practice. Focuses on problems of law office management, financing, time management, counseling and client relations.
Prod-ABACPE Dist-ABACPE

Making It On Your Own—A Series
16MM FILM, 3/4 OR 1/2 IN VIDEO H-C
Discusses problems of moving out on one's own for the first time and suggests ways to cope with these problems.
Prod-BARR Dist-BARR 1979

Managing Your Money	23 MIN
On Your Own	21 MIN
Your Own Place	21 MIN

Making It Work B 20 MIN
16MM FILM OPTICAL SOUND I-C A
Illustrates the techniques in the work of the church press secretary.
LC NO. FIA59-812
Prod-ADVENT Dist-ADVENT 1960

Making It Work—A Series

Presents an 18-module course for young adults and adults entering or re-entering the job force. Discusses job keeping skills in eight modules: First Impressions, Practical Planning, I'm Here To Work, The Supervisor And Me, Say That One More Time, Working Together, What About My Money? and How Am I Doing? Discusses job seeking skills in ten modules: How Do I Find A Job?, Opening Doors, The Application, Who Gets Fired, Tests And Stress, The Interview (Getting Ready), The Interview, You Have A Job Offer (Now What?), Learning By Experience and Making The Most Of Yourself.
Prod-EDRF Dist-EDRF

Making It Work—A Series
H A
Focuses on the characteristics employers consider most important in hiring and keeping employees. Deals with topics such as dependability, getting along with co-workers, cooperation with supervisors, accepting responsibility and effective communication.
Prod-ERF Dist-AITECH 1983

Application, The	011 MIN
How Am I Doing	015 MIN
How Do I Find A Job	015 MIN
I'm Here To Work - Now What	012 MIN
Interview, The	011 MIN
Learning By Experience	010 MIN
Making The Most Of Yourself	014 MIN
Opening Doors	013 MIN
Practical Planning	015 MIN
Say That One More Time	014 MIN
Tests And Stress	012 MIN
You Have A Job Offer - Now What	013 MIN

Making It Young C 28 MIN
16MM FILM, 3/4 OR 1/2 IN VIDEO
Encourages children to explore the world's unlimited possibilities. Explains that children's senses are keenest, enthusiasm is abundant and limitations are untested. Hosted by 15-year-old actress Cree Francks.
From The Youth Lifeskills Series.
Prod-SCCL Dist-JOU

Making Judgments C 15 MIN
3/4 OR 1/2 INCH VIDEO CASSETTE H
Provides criteria which can be used in making judgments about political issues.
From The By The People Series.
Prod-CTI Dist-CTI

Making Learning Its Own Reward C 18 MIN
3/4 OR 1/2 INCH VIDEO CASSETTE
Depicts motivational problems of a student who lacks the intrinsic motivation to pass spelling. Shows how together he and his teacher decide on an appropriate motivational reward.
Prod-UNEBO Dist-UNEBO

Making Liberal Arts A Plus C 30 MIN
3/4 OR 1/2 INCH VIDEO CASSETTE
Deals with opportunities of interest to arts and science graduates.
From The Where The Jobs Are Series.
Prod-IVCH Dist-IVCH

Making Light Work, Pt 1 C 30 MIN
3/4 OR 1/2 INCH VIDEO CASSETTE J-H
Studies the science of thermodynamics - turning heat into work. Features Sir George Porter who reveals how the random motion of molecules can be converted into an efficient source of power.
Prod-KINGFT Dist-KINGFT

Making Light Work, Pt 2 C 30 MIN
3/4 OR 1/2 INCH VIDEO CASSETTE J-H
Looks at the various kinds of solar collectors, explains what they are made of and why some materials are better than others for absorbing the sun's radiation.
From The Natural History Of A Sunbeam Series.
Prod-KINGFT Dist-KINGFT

Making Line Graphs C 14 MIN
3/4 OR 1/2 INCH VIDEO CASSETTE I
Gives experience in making line graphs.
From The Hands On, Grade 4 - Cars, Cartoons, Etc Series. Unit 2 - Measuring
Prod-WHROTV Dist-AITECH 1975

Making Map Plans C 15 MIN
2 INCH VIDEOTAPE P-I
Demonstrates that map symbols show the locations of various places and things on maps. Explains that maps help show someone what an area looks like. Shows how to make simple maps.
From The B B's Cover The Globe Series.
Prod-GPITVL Dist-GPITVL

Making Map Plans C 15 MIN
3/4 INCH VIDEO CASSETTE P-I
Demonstrates that map symbols show the locations of various places and things on maps. Explains that maps help show someone what an area looks like. Shows how to make simple maps.
From The B B's Cover The Globe Series.
Prod-MAETEL Dist-GPITVL

Making Maps C 14 MIN
3/4 OR 1/2 INCH VIDEO CASSETTE I
Gives experience in making maps.
From The Hands On, Grade 4 - Cars, Cartoons, Etc Series. Unit 2 - Measuring
Prod-WHROTV Dist-AITECH 1975

Making Measurments—A Series

Covers all units of measurement used in industrial applications. Examines metric and linear measurement. Explains the theories and techniques of measuring.
Prod-TPCTRA Dist-TPCTRA

Comparison And Surface Measurement	012 MIN
Linear Measurement	012 MIN
Measuring Bulk Materials	012 MIN
Measuring Electricity	012 MIN
Measuring Fluids	012 MIN
Measuring Forces	012 MIN
Measuring Motion	012 MIN
Measuring Temperature	012 MIN
Metric Measurement	012 MIN
Units Of Measurement	012 MIN

Making Meetings Count C
16MM FILM - VIDEO, ALL FORMATS C A
Dramatizes ways that business meetings can go wrong and shows how to prepare and run an effective meeting.
Prod-BFA Dist-BFA

Making Meetings Count C 15 MIN
16MM FILM, 3/4 OR 1/2 IN VIDEO H-C A
Shows a young business woman presenting a new idea and failing to convince her boss of its worthiness. Provides relevant business instruction while pointing out what went wrong with her presentation and what steps to take to run an effective presentation.
LC NO. 84-706796
Prod-MATVCH Dist-PHENIX 1983

Making Meetings Work C 18 MIN
16MM FILM - VIDEO, ALL FORMATS A
Introduces five basic steps that will lead to meetings that produce results, build team trust, increase creative thinking and encourage commitment to team decisions.
Prod-EBEC Dist-EBEC 1983

Making Memories C 25 MIN
3/4 OR 1/2 INCH VIDEO CASSETTE
Probes the many mystifying aspects of memory with aid of leading experts and a quiz testing viewers on their recall. Includes a segment with two amnesia patients, one who has regained his memory and one who is still trying. Features memory feats by mathematical genius 'Willie the Wizard' and former basketball star Jerry Lucas.
Prod-TRAINX Dist-TRAINX

Making Models To Explain Ideas B 15 MIN
2 INCH VIDEOTAPE P
See series title for descriptive statement.
From The Just Inquisitive Series. No. 12
Prod-EOPS Dist-GPITVL Prodn-KOACTV

Making Moods C 15 MIN
3/4 OR 1/2 INCH VIDEO CASSETTE P
Illustrates a wide variety of moods in literature.
From The Spinning Stories Series.
Prod-MDDE Dist-AITECH 1977

Making More Effective Presentations, Ward V Speaker C
3/4 OR 1/2 INCH VIDEO CASSETTE PRO
See series title for descriptive statement.
From The Management Skills Series.
Prod-AMCEE Dist-AMCEE

Making More Effective Technical Presentations—A Series
PR
Covers both the art and the science of proper communicatio. Outlines the 'tools of the public speaking trade' and develop them for the specific needs of technical presentations by eng neers and others.
Prod-ICSINT Dist-ICSINT

Audience Analysis	045 MI
Audience As Listeners, The	045 MI
Audience Characteristics	045 MI
Basics, The	045 MI
Fielding Questions	045 MI
Graphics - The Tools, Part 1	045 MI
Graphics - The Tools, Part 2	045 MI
Graphics - Why And What	045 MI
Making The Presentation	045 MI
Presentation Design	045 MI

Making More Effective Technical Presentations—A Series
IN
Tells how to improve the way one makes technical presentations practical techniques to apply when in front of an audience, how to size up an audience, use graphics and how to field difficul questions. Concentrates on attitudes, preparation, organiza tion, tools and techniques.
Prod-UMCEES Dist-AMCEE

Audience Analysis	036 MIN
Audience As Listeners, The	029 MIN
Audience Characteristics, The	033 MIN
Basic Principles, The	035 MIN
Design	032 MIN
Graphics - The Tools, Pt I	037 MIN
Graphics - The Tools, Pt II	036 MIN
Graphics - Why And What	036 MIN
Making The Presentation	035 MIN
Questions And Answers	029 MIN

Making Movie Music C 29 MIN
3/4 INCH VIDEO CASSETTE
Discusses how Jerry Bilik makes music for movies.
From The Music Shop Series.
Prod-UMITV Dist-UMITV 1974

Making Music C 12 MIN
3/4 OR 1/2 INCH VIDEO CASSETTE P-I
Presents Michael Small who guides the viewer through the fun and hard work of writing and playing music for a living.
Prod-SF Dist-SF 1972

Making Music - The Emerson String Quartet C 28 MIN
3/4 OR 1/2 INCH VIDEO CASSETTE
Provides a close look at the personal and musical qualities tha must combine to make an ensemble of excellence.
Prod-VINEVI Dist-VINEVI

Making Numbers Work C 24 MIN
16MM FILM, 3/4 OR 1/2 IN VIDEO
Shows how to use numbers more effectively. Explains how to work with numbers quickly as well as how to present or read data mentally in such a way as to highlight significant trends in such a way as to highlight significant trends.
Prod-MELROS Dist-VISUCP

Making Of 'The Frog King,' The C 9 MIN
3/4 OR 1/2 INCH VIDEO CASSETTE
Tells how the Frog King was brought to life with real people and live frogs.
From The Children's Folktales Series.
Prod-FILMID Dist-FILMID

Making Of A Ballet, The C 38 MIN
3/4 OR 1/2 INCH VIDEO CASSETTE I A
Focuses on choreographer Rudi van Dantzig who spends most of his life in theaters and at rehearsals where he creates most of his ballets.
Prod-SUTHRB Dist-SUTHRB

Making Of A Clinician - Teaching The Medical Student To Teach C 86 MIN
3/4 OR 1/2 INCH VIDEO CASSETTE PRO
Presents a discussion between Dr David Seegal and four medical students about teaching methods.
LC NO. 77-706200
Prod-NMAC Dist-USNAC 1977

Making Of A Clinician, Pts 1 And 2 B 86 MIN
16MM FILM OPTICAL SOUND PRO
Presents a discussion between Dr David Seegal and four medical students about teaching methods. Includes his decalogue of nonprofessional virtues and describes the self-evaluation recommended for students.
LC NO. 77-703505
Prod-NMAC Dist-USNAC 1977

Making Of A Community, The B 30 MIN
16MM FILM OPTICAL SOUND H-C A
John Henrik Clarke lectures on the Afro-American in New York, the role of Harlem in the Black revolution, and the contribution of such leaders as Dubois, Garvey, Malcolm X, Adam Clayton Powell, Jr and Father Divine.
From The Black History, Section 14 - Harlem Renais- Sance Series.
LC NO. 70-704082
Prod-WCBSTV Dist-HRAW 1969

Making Of A Continent—A Series
16MM FILM, 3/4 OR 1/2 IN VIDEO H-C A
Describes and shows the traumatic geological events which led to the shaping of the North American continent. Reveals that large areas of land have been rafted on the ocean floor to their

present position and could conceivably leave again at some time in the future.
Prod-BBCTV Dist-FI 1983

Eighteen Corridors Of Time 060 MIN
Land Of The Sleeping Mountains 060 MIN
Price Of Gold, The 060 MIN

Making Of A Decision, The C 32 MIN
16MM FILM, 3/4 OR 1/2 IN VIDEO J-C A
Suggests various techniques for managers in decision making coaching, planning, interviewing and performance appraisal.
LC NO. FIA68-569
Prod-RTBL Dist-RTBL 1968

Making Of A Decision, The (Arabic) C 32 MIN
16MM FILM, 3/4 OR 1/2 IN VIDEO J-C T
Suggests various techniques for managers in decision-making, coaching, planning, interviewing and performance appraisal.
Prod-RTBL Dist-RTBL 1968

Making Of A Decision, The (Dutch) C 32 MIN
16MM FILM, 3/4 OR 1/2 IN VIDEO J-C T
Suggests various techniques for managers in decision-making, coaching, planning, interviewing and performance appraisal.
Prod-RTBL Dist-RTBL 1968

Making Of A Decision, The (French) C 32 MIN
16MM FILM, 3/4 OR 1/2 IN VIDEO J-C T
Suggests various techniques for managers in decision-making, coaching, planning, interviewing and performance appraisal.
Prod-RTBL Dist-RTBL 1968

Making Of A Decision, The (German) C 32 MIN
16MM FILM, 3/4 OR 1/2 IN VIDEO J-C T
Suggests various techniques for managers in decision-making, coaching, planning, interviewing and performance appraisal.
Prod-RTBL Dist-RTBL 1968

Making Of A Decision, The (Japanese) C 32 MIN
16MM FILM, 3/4 OR 1/2 IN VIDEO J-C T
Suggests various techniques for managers in decision-making, coaching, planning, interviewing and performance appraisal.
Prod-RTBL Dist-RTBL 1968

Making Of A Decision, The (Spanish) C 32 MIN
16MM FILM, 3/4 OR 1/2 IN VIDEO J-C T
Suggests various techniques for managers in decision-making, coaching, planning, interviewing and performance appraisal.
Prod-RTBL Dist-RTBL 1968

Making Of A Decision, The (Swedish) C 32 MIN
16MM FILM, 3/4 OR 1/2 IN VIDEO J-C T
Suggests various techniques for managers in decision-making, coaching, planning, interviewing and performance appraisal.
Prod-RTBL Dist-RTBL 1968

Making Of A Documentary, The C 21 MIN
16MM FILM, 3/4 OR 1/2 IN VIDEO J-C A
Presents a behind-the-scenes look at the preparation of a documentary television film.
Prod-CBSNEW Dist-CAROUF

Making Of A Film, The C 30 MIN
3/4 OR 1/2 INCH VIDEO CASSETTE C
See series title for descriptive statement.
From The Communicating Through Literature Series.
Prod-DALCCD Dist-DALCCD

Making Of A Fire Fighter, The C 16 MIN
16MM FILM, 3/4 OR 1/2 IN VIDEO IND
Presents a brief history of fire fighting, along with modern training methods. Introduces prospective recruits to the techniques of the profession.
Prod-LAFD Dist-FILCOM

Making Of A Live TV Show, The C 24 MIN
16MM FILM, 3/4 OR 1/2 IN VIDEO
Looks at the preparation and televising of the annual Emmy Awards show. Moves from rehearsal halls and production meetings to the actual events. Uses split screen effects to emphasize the parts played by all members of the production company.
Prod-BRAVC Dist-PFP

Making Of A Natural History Film, The C 52 MIN
16MM FILM, 3/4 OR 1/2 IN VIDEO H-C A
Follows naturalists and biologists as they film a variety of biological phenomena.
From The Nova Series.
LC NO. 79-707824
Prod-BBCTV Dist-TIMLIF 1974

Making Of A Natural History Film, The (Spanish) C 52 MIN
16MM FILM OPTICAL SOUND J-C A
Follows naturalists and biologists as they use modern film techniques and technology to film a variety of biological phenomena.
From The Nova Series.
Prod-BBCTV Dist-TIMLIF 1974

Making Of A Package Deal, The C 30 MIN
16MM FILM, 3/4 OR 1/2 IN VIDEO C A
Shows how various entertainment industries join forces to create properties which have huge potential for profits in various media.
From The Enterprise Series.
Prod-WGBHTV Dist-LCOA Prodn-DORSOL 1981

Making Of A Plague, The C 13 MIN
16MM FILM OPTICAL SOUND
Documents the damage created by the gypsy moth caterpillar, a voracious pest that is a threat to all living trees. Records this severe plague and shows control efforts to stop its rapid spread across the United States and Canada.
Prod-CHEVRN Dist-CHEVRN 1971

Making Of A Quarterback, The (With Roger Staubach) C 30 MIN
16MM FILM, 3/4 OR 1/2 IN VIDEO
Presents former Dallas Cowboys quarterback Roger Staubach and Cowboys assistant coach, Dan Reeves, employing close-up demonstrations, scrimmage plays and NFL game footage to illustrate the fundamental skills of quarterbacking and training. Includes scenes of Staubach executing specific conditioning exercises, ball handling and passing techniques, and huddle leadership, and shows the importance of a winning philosophy of leadership.
Prod-INVISN Dist-LCOA 1981

Making Of A Salesman—A Series

Uses the training technique of discovery-based learning. Utilizes role models to create situations as 'trigger' devices for the development of 'think' and 'do' problem solving professionals. Provides step-by-step information to enable in-house trainers and district sales managers to get up to speed quickly as program facilitators.
Prod-PRODEV Dist-PRODEV

Closings - Techniques And Characteristics Of
Communication And Listening Skills/Logical
Developing Effective Presentation Skills/Who
Dual Channel Communication - Psychology Of
Motivational Selling/What Motivates You?
Problem Solving Selling
Real World Of Selling, The
Selling Strategies - Steps To Sale
Time And Territory Management

Making Of An Alcoholic, The C 28 MIN
3/4 OR 1/2 INCH VIDEO CASSETTE J A
Shows a chart on the making of an alcoholic that looks at how one person might become an alcoholic.
Prod-SUTHRB Dist-SUTHRB

Making Of Bronco Billy B 11 MIN
16MM FILM SILENT H-C A
Features G M Anderson in the role he made famous, Bronco Billy. A silent film.
Prod-SPOOR Dist-BHAWK 1913

Making Of Butch Cassidy And The Sundance Kid C 40 MIN
16MM FILM OPTICAL SOUND
Traces the development of the major scenes in the feature film, Butch Cassidy and the Sundance Kid, showing sets, staging of action and casting of characters. Leading characters Paul Newman and Robert Redford, and Director George Roy Hill comment on personal relationships between actors and directors.
LC NO. 76-706051
Prod-CRAR Dist-TEXFLM 1970

Making Of Flaws, The C 5 MIN
3/4 OR 1/2 INCH VIDEO CASSETTE J-H
Teaches the active and passive voice.
From The Write On, Set 1 Series.
Prod-CTI Dist-CTI

Making Of Letters, The C 28 MIN
16MM FILM OPTICAL SOUND
Shows how early records were kept on clay and wax tablets and discusses heiroglyphics, the making of papyrus, the cutting of a reed pen, the development of the alphabet and Roman lettering.
From The Alphabet - The Story Of Writing Series.
Prod-CFDLD Dist-FILAUD 1982

Making Of Letters, The C 30 MIN
3/4 OR 1/2 INCH VIDEO CASSETTE
Deals with the making of the first paper in Egypt, the creation of the reed pen, how letters emerged from symbols, and the Roman letter.
From The Alphabet - The Story Of Writing Series.
Prod-WSTGLC Dist-WSTGLC

Making Of Mankind—A Series
16MM FILM, 3/4 OR 1/2 IN VIDEO H-C A
Traces the origins of the human species. Explores clues that lie buried in fossil records and interprets, through these long-hidden clues, how humans developed their edge over animals. Hosted by Richard Leakey.
Prod-BBCTV Dist-TIMLIF 1982

Beyond Africa 055 MIN
Human Way Of Life, A 055 MIN
In The Beginning 055 MIN
New Era, A 055 MIN
One Small Step... 055 MIN
Settling Down 055 MIN
Survival Of The Species, The 055 MIN

Making Of Mind And Power, The - The Naval War College C 19 MIN
16MM FILM OPTICAL SOUND
Looks at the Naval War College as an educational institution, developing new concepts and original free-world maritime strategic thought.
LC NO. 74-706492
Prod-USN Dist-USNAC 1970

Making Of Raiders Of The Lost Ark, The C 58 MIN
16MM FILM, 3/4 OR 1/2 IN VIDEO I-C A
Shows how colorful stunts from the motion picture Raiders Of The Lost Ark were created for the screen. Includes interviews with the stars Harrison Ford and Karen Allen, the director Steven Spielberg, the producers, the cinematographer, the stunt director and others.
Prod-LUCAS Dist-DIRECT 1982

Making Of Star Wars, The C 52 MIN
16MM FILM, 3/4 OR 1/2 IN VIDEO H-C A
Offers a behind-the-scenes look at the making of Star Wars. Features visits to location sets in Tunisia and appearances by Mark Hamill, Carrie Fisher, Sir Alec Guinness, and Harrison Ford.
Prod-KURTZG Dist-FI 1979

Making Of The Frog King, The C 12 MIN
16MM FILM, 3/4 OR 1/2 IN VIDEO P-H A
Shows the making of a short film from an American version of the Grimm Brother's tale, The Frog King.
From The Brothers Grimm Folktales Series.
LC NO. 81-706632
Prod-DAVT Dist-DAVT

Making Of The President, The - 1972 C 90 MIN
16MM FILM, 3/4 OR 1/2 IN VIDEO H-C A
Tells the story of Richard Nixon and his men, including the campaign, the convention, the Eagleton Affair, the Committee to Re-Elect the President, the Plumbers, Colson, E Howard Hunt, G Gordon Liddy, M Cord, John Erlichman and Bob Haldeman. Traces Nixon's political career from his early political days to his communist witchhunt. Based on the book The Making Of The President - 1972 by Theodore White.
LC NO. 79-707820
Prod-TIMLIF Dist-TIMLIF 1973

Making Of The President, The, 1960 B 80 MIN
16MM FILM, 3/4 OR 1/2 IN VIDEO I-J
Analyzes the campaign for President in 1960 as cameras follow John F Kennedy and Richard Nixon. Based on the book by Theodore H White.
Prod-METROM Dist-FI 1964

Making Of The President, The, 1964 B 80 MIN
16MM FILM, 3/4 OR 1/2 IN VIDEO
Outlines events in the presidential campaign of 1964, beginning with the early efforts of Barry Goldwater and ending with Johnson's victory.
Prod-METROM Dist-FI

Making Of The President, The, 1972 (Spanish) C 90 MIN
16MM FILM OPTICAL SOUND
Documents the 1972 Presidential campaign which resulted in the landslide reelection of Richard Nixon.
LC NO. 78-700038
Prod-TIMLIF Dist-TIMLIF 1972

Making Of The President, 1964 B 79 MIN
16MM FILM OPTICAL SOUND
Describes the 1964 political conventions and the presidental campaigns, beginning with John F Kennedy's death and ending with Lyndon B Johnson's election. Based on the book of the same title by Theordore H White.
LC NO. FIA66-462
Prod-XEROX Dist-WOLPER Prodn-WOLPER 1965

Making Pattern, Core Boxes And Assembling Core For A Water-Cooled Motor Block B 15 MIN
16MM FILM OPTICAL SOUND
Explains how a patternmaker constructs the pattern and master core boxes, checks the working core boxes, and pastes up and assembles test cores.
LC NO. FIE52-133
Prod-USOE Dist-USNAC 1945

Making Points C 11 MIN
16MM FILM, 3/4 OR 1/2 IN VIDEO J-C A
Shows adolescent boys being interviewed by a television reporter about their plans for the future, but giving answers actually offered by girls. Examines differences in the behavior of men and women.
Prod-MIDMAR Dist-DIRECT 1980

Making Producing And Trading Easier - Transportation C 20 MIN
2 INCH VIDEOTAPE J-H
Introduces the concept of transportation and examines what kinds exist, where each kind performs best and what common elements are found in each kind.
From The Our World Of Economics Series.
Prod-MPATI Dist-GPITVL

Making Producing And Trading Easier - Capital C 20 MIN
2 INCH VIDEOTAPE J-H
Shows the importance of investments.
From The Our World Of Economics Series.
Prod-MPATI Dist-GPITVL

Making Producing And Trading Easier - Money C 20 MIN
2 INCH VIDEOTAPE J-H
Examines what money is, how it helps the economy work better and how much money society needs.
From The Our World Of Economics Series.
Prod-MPATI Dist-GPITVL

Making Producing And Trading Easier - Savings And Investment C 20 MIN
2 INCH VIDEOTAPE J-H
Introduces the idea of savings and examines what happens when people, businesses or governments do not spend all of their income.
From The Our World Of Economics Series.
Prod-MPATI Dist-GPITVL

Making Product Recommendations And Closing The Call C 15 MIN
3/4 OR 1/2 INCH VIDEO CASSETTE
See series title for descriptive statement.

From The Telemarketing For Better Business Results Series.
Prod-COMTEL Dist-DELTAK

Making Sense C 25 MIN
16MM FILM, 3/4 OR 1/2 IN VIDEO H-C A
Demonstrates how a child sees and makes sense of the world.
From The Children Growing Up Series.
Prod-BBCTV Dist-FI 1981

Making Sense Of A Big Number C 14 MIN
3/4 OR 1/2 INCH VIDEO CASSETTE I
Shows that Zeke plans to collect a hundred thousand bottle caps until he learns to picture how many that would be. Includes an animated segment in which the Duke of York's baker needs help thinking about ten thousand muffins.
From The It Figures Series. No. 21
Prod-AITV Dist-AITECH Prodn-NJN 1982

Making Sense Of It C 13 MIN
16MM FILM, 3/4 OR 1/2 IN VIDEO P-I
Takes a trip through a wooded area in order to illustrate the human senses. Explains how a scientist identifies and classifies living things.
From The Scientific Fact And Fun Series.
Prod-GLDWER Dist-JOU 1979

Making Sense Of The Real World C 25 MIN
3/4 OR 1/2 INCH VIDEO CASSETTE H-C A
Examines the range of sensors available for getting information into the computer and discusses the difference between the analog and digital world.
From The Computers In Control Series.
Prod-BBCTV Dist-FI 1984

Making Sense Out Of Nonsense C 29 MIN
3/4 OR 1/2 INCH VIDEO CASSETTE T
See series title for descriptive statement.
From The Coping With Kids Series.
Prod-MFFD Dist-FI

Making Sense Out Of Nonsense C 30 MIN
3/4 OR 1/2 INCH VIDEO CASSETTE
Identifies basic assumptions underlying Adler's approach and how a child's position in the family affects behavior.
From The Coping With Kids Series.
Prod-OHUTC Dist-OHUTC

Making Sense With Outlines (2nd Ed) C 10 MIN
16MM FILM, 3/4 OR 1/2 IN VIDEO I-J
Presents the basic structure and benefits of using outlines to organize ideas with an example of how a student uses an outline in writing about glass recycling.
Prod-CORF Dist-CORF 1977

Making Sense With Sentences (2nd Ed) C 16 MIN
16MM FILM, 3/4 OR 1/2 IN VIDEO I
Shows how to state ideas in complete sentences.
Prod-CORF Dist-CORF 1975

Making Shadows With Pierrot C 6 MIN
16MM FILM, 3/4 OR 1/2 IN VIDEO P
Shows how Pierrot makes hand shadows on the wall to amuse his noisy little brother, and how the shadows come alive and put on a show of their own.
From The Pierrot Series.
Prod-CORF Dist-CORF

Making Sheet Metal Repairs B 19 MIN
16MM FILM - 3/4 IN VIDEO IND
Explains how to remove a damaged area around a hole in an airplane and how to lay out trim lines. Shows how to prepare the hole to receive a patch, how to bump out the plug and doubler, how to mark and drill the plug and doubler, and how to rivet the completed patch to the part. Issued in 1945 as a motion picture.
From The Aircraft Work - Aircraft Maintenance Series.
LC NO. 79-706787
Prod-USOE Dist-USNAC Prodn-TRADEF 1979

Making Soft Dolls C 60 MIN
1/2 IN VIDEO CASSETTE BETA/VHS
Demonstrates body construction of five different soft dolls.
From The Crafts And Decorating Series.
Prod-MOHOMV Dist-MOHOMV

Making Soft Dolls C 60 MIN
1/2 IN VIDEO CASSETTE BETA/VHS
Provides step-by-step instruction on body construction of five different dolls. Explains how to make contour dolls.
Prod-RMI Dist-RMI

Making Square Or V-Shaped Corners C 5 MIN
16MM FILM SILENT J-C A
Demonstrates reinforcing the inside corner, clipping to stitching, pinning and stitching two layers together and finishing to reduce bulk. Includes reinforcement of the corner with fusible interfacing.
From The Clothing Construction Techniques Series.
LC NO. 77-701184
Prod-IOWA Dist-IOWASP 1976

Making T-Joint, Lap Joint And Outside Corner Welds All Positions With Aluminum, Steel C 15 MIN
3/4 OR 1/2 INCH VIDEO CASSETTE
See series title for descriptive statement.
From The Welding III - TIG and MIG (Industry) Welding series.
Prod-CAMB Dist-CAMB

Making The American Scrape Oboe Reed C 27 MIN
16MM FILM OPTICAL SOUND H
A musician demonstrates the detailed steps that are necessary for making a good oboe reed.
LC NO. 73-711315
Prod-UILL Dist-UILL 1971

Making The Boss Look Good C 10 MIN
3/4 OR 1/2 INCH VIDEO CASSETTE
Stresses the importance of assisting the manager or supervisor in many different ways. Offers tips on handling mail, visitors, appointments, phone calls and travel.
From The Effective Office Worker Series
Prod-RESEM Dist-RESEM

Making The Desert Green (3rd Ed) C 16 MIN
16MM FILM, 3/4 OR 1/2 IN VIDEO I
Presents a case study for the Pacific Southwest region introducing the concept of water management and scientific farming. Shows the method used in the Coachella Valley, California which has changed this dry soil into the richest farm land acre for acre in the world today.
Prod-EBEC Dist-EBEC

Making The Difference C 14 MIN
16MM FILM OPTICAL SOUND
Uses six short segments to show how General Aviation airplanes serve the public every day in both critical and common situations.
LC NO. 77-700170
Prod-GEAVMA Dist-MTP Prodn-AMESP 1976

Making The Difference C 5 MIN
16MM FILM, 3/4 OR 1/2 IN VIDEO H-C A
Instructs police officers in proper conduct on the witness stand. Shows how to prepare and review notes, have a pretrial conference with the prosecutor, present a professional appearance, speak clearly and conversationally, and avoid distractions.
Prod-KLEINW Dist-KLEINW 1978

Making The Difference C 14 MIN
3/4 OR 1/2 INCH VIDEO CASSETTE A
Stresses contributions of general aviation, and indicates growing importance of and opportunities related to its future.
Prod-FAAFL Dist-AVIMA

Making The Future Work C 22 MIN
3/4 OR 1/2 INCH VIDEO CASSETTE C A
Focuses upon the need for creative leadership and forward thinking as the means to shape America's social, economic and political future.
Prod-MTI Dist-MTI

Making The Interview Work - Five Ways To Improve Interviewing C 25 MIN
3/4 OR 1/2 INCH VIDEO CASSETTE
See series title for descriptive statement.
From The Videosearch Employment Interview Series.
Prod-DELTAK Dist-DELTAK

Making The Most Of On-The-Job Changes C
3/4 OR 1/2 INCH VIDEO CASSETTE
Explores the nature of organizational change and the employee's role in adapting to and suggesting changes. Shows how chance can play a positive role in the work environment.
From The Team Building For Administrative Support Staff Series.
Prod-AMA Dist-AMA

Making The Most Of The Micro—A Series
16MM FILM, 3/4 OR 1/2 IN VIDEO
Looks at the principles behind the use of microcomputers in a range of applications and offers examples of its use.
Prod-BBCTV Dist-FI 1983

At The End Of The Line	025 MIN
Everything Is Under Control	025 MIN
Getting Down To BASIC	025 MIN
Getting Down To Business	025 MIN
Introducing Graphics	025 MIN
Keeping A Record	025 MIN
Moving Pictures	025 MIN
Sounds Interesting	025 MIN
Strings And Things	025 MIN
Versatile Machine, The	025 MIN

Making The Most Of Your Money C
3/4 OR 1/2 INCH VIDEO CASSETTE J-H
Teaches young consumers the skills of using and spending money wisely, and how to avoid the common problems that beset the economically unwary. Includes saving, buying a car, understanding contracts, and budget dating.
Prod-EDUACT Dist-EDUACT

Making The Most Of Yourself C 14 MIN
3/4 OR 1/2 INCH VIDEO CASSETTE H A
Explains that Bill is willing to take additional training, adjust his schedule as needed and fulfill his commitment when tired, while Bobby isn't. Dramatizes how body language, choice of words and tone of voice are important to effective communication.
From The Making It Work Series.
Prod-ERF Dist-AITECH 1983

Making The Occupied Bed B 15 MIN
16MM FILM OPTICAL SOUND
Demonstrates the procedure to be followed and the supplies and equipment needed to arrange a bed unit in the hospital room or ward while the bed is occupied by a patient.
LC NO. FIE59-135
Prod-USN Dist-USNAC 1957

Making The Presentation B 35 MIN
3/4 OR 1/2 INCH VIDEO CASSETTE IND
Relates the techniques of delivery, notes, stance, voice, word choice and gesturing for effective communication.
From The Making More Effective Technical Presentations Series.
Prod-UMCEES Dist-AMCEE

Making The Presentation C 45 MIN
3/4 OR 1/2 INCH VIDEO CASSETTE PRO
See series title for descriptive statement.
From The Making More Effective Technical Presentations Series.
Prod-ICSINT Dist-ICSINT

Making The Scene C 15 MIN
3/4 OR 1/2 INCH VIDEO CASSETTE
Shows the need to establish a strong story to set the mood and enhance the plot.
From The Tyger, Tyger Burning Bright Series.
Prod-CTI Dist-CTI

Making The Surgical (Postoperative) Bed C 19 MIN
16MM FILM - 3/4 IN VIDEO H-C A
Demonstrates procedures to be followed in making a safe surgical/postoperative bed.
From The Nurse's Aide, Orderly And Attendant Series.
Prod-COPI Dist-COPI 1969

Making The Things We Need - Division Of Labor X 14 MIN
16MM FILM, 3/4 OR 1/2 IN VIDEO P
Introduces the concept of division of labor and shows that division of labor and specialization account for the difference between underdeveloped and technologically advanced societies.
Prod-EBEC Dist-EBEC 1969

Making The Transition To Training C
3/4 OR 1/2 INCH VIDEO CASSETTE IND
Shows how the former field hand must become acquainted with the tools of training to be an effective trainer. Teaches how to motivate, how to use visual instructional aids, how to ask and answer questions, how to promote interaction and how evaluation can be used to both trainer and trainee advantage.
Prod-GPCV Dist-GPCV

Making The Unoccupied (Closed) Bed C 13 MIN
16MM FILM - 3/4 IN VIDEO H-C A
Demonstrates how to make an unoccupied bed, emphasizing quick, easy, safe and sanitary procedures.
From The Nurse's Aide, Orderly And Attendant Series.
Prod-COPI Dist-COPI 1969

Making The Unseen Visible C 20 MIN
16MM FILM, 3/4 OR 1/2 IN VIDEO
Looks at the aesthetic contributions of instruments of technology that make visible what is generally unseen. Considers various kinds of photography and cinematography as used for scientific research and as a source of imagery for the artist.
From The Images And Things Series.
LC NO. 72-700283
Prod-NITC Dist-AITECH

Making The World Safe For Democracy B 30 MIN
16MM FILM OPTICAL SOUND H-C A
Dr St Clair Drake describes the struggle of Afro-Americans against white bigots during the period from 1915 through World War I, their participation in the war, and the effect of the war on the labor market.
From The Black History, Section 12 - World War I And The Post War Series.
LC NO. 77-704076
Prod-WCBSTV Dist-HRAW 1969

Making Things Grow I—A Series

Features Thalassa Cruso discussing different aspects of gardening.
Prod-WGBHTV Dist-PUBTEL

Displaying House Plants	30 MIN
Dutch Bulbs	30 MIN
Easy Bulbs	30 MIN
Gesneriads	30 MIN
Holiday Decorations	30 MIN
Horticultural Presents	30 MIN
Plants For Dim Places	30 MIN
Pot Problem, The	30 MIN
Potting	30 MIN
Questions And Answers - Making Things Grow 1	30 MIN
Soils	30 MIN
Succulents, The	30 MIN
Watering	30 MIN

Making Things Grow II—A Series

Features Thalassa Cruso discussing different aspects of gardening.
Prod-WGBHTV Dist-PUBTEL

Accent Plants	30 MIN
Artificial Lighting	30 MIN
Bonsai	30 MIN
Bromeliads	30 MIN
Cool Window, The	30 MIN
Dividing	30 MIN
Ferns	30 MIN
Forcing Bulbs	30 MIN
Hanging Plants	30 MIN
Indoor Topiary	30 MIN
Massing A Window	30 MIN
Questions And Answers - Making Things Grow II	30 MIN
Short Day Problems	30 MIN

Making Things Grow III—A Series

Features Thalassa Cruso discussing different aspects of gardening.
Prod-WGBHTV Dist-PUBTEL

Arranging	29 MIN

Children's Show, A	29 MIN
Dormancy	29 MIN
Fall Duties	29 MIN
Geraniums	29 MIN
Gifts That Grow	29 MIN
Have You Ever Been To Kew	29 MIN
Herbs And Scented Plants	29 MIN
High Summer	29 MIN
Long Lasting Blossoming Plants	29 MIN
Mea Culpa	29 MIN
More Cuttings	29 MIN
Moving On	29 MIN
Portable Garden, The	29 MIN
Pruning And Pinching Out	29 MIN
Questions And Answers III - Making Things	29 MIN
Questions And Answers IV - Making Things	29 MIN
Seeds	29 MIN
Short Cuts	29 MIN
Softwood Cuttings	28 MIN
Starting From Scratch	29 MIN
Summer Hanging Plants	29 MIN
Summering House Plants	29 MIN
Supermarket - Ten Cent Store	29 MIN
Variety	29 MIN
Window Boxes	29 MIN

Making Things Happen C 18 MIN
3/4 OR 1/2 INCH VIDEO CASSETTE J-C A
Goes step-by-step through the process of developing a program that will make a toy mouse move on command. Reviews the application of similar systems to control mechanisms such as sensors that keep track of time, count and respond to pressure and temperature changes.
From The Little Computers - See How They Run Series.
LC NO. 81-706846
Prod-ELDATA Dist-GPITVL 1980

Making Things Move X 11 MIN
16MM FILM, 3/4 OR 1/2 IN VIDEO P
Uses machinery and other farm objects to introduce concepts of force and motion. Illustrates forces that make things move, forces that keep things from moving, and forces that make things more difficult to move, such as gravity and friction.
Prod-EBF Dist-EBEC 1962

Making Things Move C 25 MIN
3/4 OR 1/2 INCH VIDEO CASSETTE H-C A
Discusses the application of computer technology to electric motors. Features a new growth industry called animatronics, which uses computers and small motors to make lifelike statues that talk and move.
From The Computers In Control Series.
Prod-BBCTV Dist-FI 1984

Making Things Move (Spanish) C 11 MIN
16MM FILM, 3/4 OR 1/2 IN VIDEO P
Shows examples of forces that make things move, forces that keep things from moving and forces that make things more difficult to move.
Prod-EBEC Dist-EBEC

Making Things To Learn B 11 MIN
16MM FILM OPTICAL SOUND T
Shows people working to build educational materials and children using the materials in their classrooms. Filmed at several public and private schools and head start classrooms in the Boston area.
From The Early Childhood Educational Study Series.
LC NO. 73-705608
Prod-EDS Dist-EDC 1970

Making Things Work--A Series

Features Thalassa Cruso giving advice on small household problems.
Prod-WGBHTV Dist-PUBTEL

Battered Pictures	15 MIN
Care Of Birds	15 MIN
Chair Problems	15 MIN
Cut Christmas Trees	15 MIN
Furniture Stains	15 MIN
Glass	15 MIN
Household Smells	15 MIN
Mending Books	15 MIN
Mending China And Glass	15 MIN
Pewter	15 MIN
Rug Spots	15 MIN
Small Electrical Repairs	15 MIN
Waste Not	15 MIN
Window Problems	15 MIN
Wrappings	15 MIN

Making Up The Room C 9 MIN
16MM FILM, 3/4 OR 1/2 IN VIDEO J-C A
Shows proper responsibilities of a maid making up a check-out room with special emphasis given to thoroughness in cleaning.
From The Professional Hotel And Tourism Programs Series.
Prod-NEM Dist-NEM 1970

Making Vertical Butt, Overhead Butt Welds With Aluminum, Steel And Stainless Steel C 15 MIN
3/4 OR 1/2 INCH VIDEO CASSETTE
See series title for descriptive statement.
From The Welding III - TIG and MIG (Industry) Welding series.
Prod-CAMB Dist-CAMB

Making Work Easier C 15 MIN
3/4 OR 1/2 INCH VIDEO CASSETTE P-I
Discusses the characteristics of work.
From The Why Series.
Prod-WDCNTV Dist-AITECH 1976

Making Your Case C 24 MIN
3/4 OR 1/2 INCH VIDEO CASSETTE
Stresses the importance of preliminary research, making proper notes and rehearsing before making a presentation.
Prod-VIDART Dist-VISUCP

Making Your Case C 27 MIN
3/4 OR 1/2 INCH VIDEO CASSETTE A
Illustrates the principles of effective presentation through the use of a dream technique. Shows Alice, pension plan presenter, dreaming she is presenting pensions to the Queen of Hearts and her court and doing a poor job of it. Presents the Mad Hatter and the March Hare rescuing her and teaching her how to be more effective.
Prod-XICOM Dist-XICOM

Making Your Money Grow C 30 MIN
3/4 OR 1/2 INCH VIDEO CASSETTE C A
Offers an introduction to investments, including federal and state laws governing investments. Describes some sources for investment information.
From The Personal Finance Series. Lesson 15
Prod-SCCON Dist-CDTEL

Making Your Point C 16 MIN
16MM FILM, 3/4 OR 1/2 IN VIDEO I
Shows how Flash and TJ use a well-organized oral presentation to convince the basketball coach that Flash should be on the team.
From The Thinkabout Series. Communicating Effectively
LC NO. 81-706086
Prod-EDFCEN Dist-AITECH 1979

Making, Shaping And Treating Of Steel--A Series
H-C A
Shows the development and treating of steel as a product of a major industry.
Prod-USSC Dist-USSC

Blast Furnace, The	8 MIN
Chemistry Of Iron And Steel	14 MIN
Electric Arc Furnace, The	7 MIN
Hot Rolling Of Steel Sheets	7 MIN
Open Hearth Furnace, The	7 MIN
Semi-Finished Steel	8 MIN

Mako C 30 MIN
3/4 INCH VIDEO CASSETTE H-C A
Presents a Hollywood actor discussing the world of Asian movie stereotypes.
From The Pearls Series.
Prod-EDFCEN Dist-GPITVL 1979

Malakapalakadoo, Skip Two C 10 MIN
16MM FILM, 3/4 OR 1/2 IN VIDEO J-C A
Introduces imaginative approaches to problem solving. Presents two children disguised as beanbags entering into the magical land of Malakapalakadoo and meeting a kindly but helpless king.
Prod-EBEC Dist-EBEC 1977

Malaria - Images Of A Reality C 13 MIN
16MM FILM OPTICAL SOUND
Examines the worldwide resurgence of malaria, discussing the disease, its cause, how it affects victims, and what can be done about it.
LC NO. 78-701126
Prod-UNEP Dist-DYP Prodn-DYP 1978

Malas Companias C 30 MIN
3/4 OR 1/2 INCH VIDEO CASSETTE
See series title for descriptive statement.
From The Que Pasa, U S A Series.
Prod-WPBTTV Dist-MDCPB

Malay Fisherman Of Sabak C 11 MIN
16MM FILM OPTICAL SOUND I-C A
Depicts the fishing village of Sabak, located along the shores of the China Sea in Malaysia. Explains that the Sabak fishermen form into small groups or associations. Tells the story of Ismail Bin Awang, the leader of one of these associations, and his family.
From The Human Family, Pt 1 - South And Southeast Asia Series.
Prod-AVED Dist-AVED 1972

Malaysia C 10 MIN
16MM FILM OPTICAL SOUND
Describes Malaysia, with emphasis on the east coast.
Prod-FILEM Dist-PMFMUN 1975

Malaysia In Brief C 26 MIN
16MM FILM OPTICAL SOUND
Describes the main industries of Malaysia.
Prod-FILEM Dist-PMFMUN 1973

Malaysian Parliament B 9 MIN
16MM FILM OPTICAL SOUND
Shows the formal opening of the new Parliament building in Malaysia by His Majesty and the first ceremonial meetings of the House of Representatives and the Senate.
Prod-FILEM Dist-PMFMUN 1964

Malaysian Village C 18 MIN
3/4 OR 1/2 INCH VIDEO CASSETTE I-J
Visits a tranquil Malaysian village family of husband, wife and six children. Reveals that father, a former fisherman, now drives a school bus. Shows food preparation, school, traditional wedding, games, sports and church.
Prod-EDMI Dist-EDMI 1974

Malbangka Country C 30 MIN
16MM FILM, 3/4 OR 1/2 IN VIDEO
Portrays an Aboriginal family that has moved back to its original homestead following unsuccessful government attempts at resettlement in small towns with missionary schools.
From The Australian Institute Of Aboriginal Studies Series.
Prod-AUSIAS Dist-UCEMC 1979

Malcolm Brewer - Boat Builder C 18 MIN
16MM FILM, 3/4 OR 1/2 IN VIDEO J-C
Focuses on Malcolm Brewer, a 77-year-old resident of Camden, Maine, who still builds boats by hand with the tools he has used for years. Tells of his life built on self-reliance and joy in hard work.
From The American Character Series.
Prod-ODYSSP Dist-EBEC 1976

Malcolm Campbell - Man Against Time B 15 MIN
1/2 IN VIDEO CASSETTE BETA/VHS
Portrays Malcolm Campbell, who drove 302 mph in 1935.
Prod-STAR Dist-STAR

Malcolm Decides C 20 MIN
3/4 OR 1/2 INCH VIDEO CASSETTE
Tells how a young boy faces some economic decision making after receiving a gift certificate for being chosen paperboy of the month.
From The Trade-Offs Series.
LC NO. 79-706194
Prod-EDFCEN Dist-AITECH 1978

Malcolm Decides - Personal Decision-Making C 20 MIN
16MM FILM OPTICAL SOUND I-J
Tells the story of a boy who utilizes the five steps in the decision-making process when he decides how to use his gift certificate.
From The Trade-Offs Series. No. 2
LC NO. 79-700551
Prod-EDFCEN Dist-AITECH 1978

Malcolm X C 23 MIN
16MM FILM, 3/4 OR 1/2 IN VIDEO J-C A
Looks at the life of black activist Malcolm X.
Prod-WCAUTV Dist-CAROUF

Malcolm X - Struggle For Freedom B 22 MIN
16MM FILM OPTICAL SOUND J-C A
Portrays Malcolm X at a time when his views were changing to include the world situation with regard to the race problem. Includes interviews filmed during Malcolm X's trip to Europe and Africa shortly before his assassination in the United States, interspaced with scenes of African rebellion.
LC NO. 73-700845
Prod-GROVE Dist-GROVE 1966

Malcolm X Speaks B 44 MIN
16MM FILM OPTICAL SOUND I-C A
Documents the life and thought of Malcolm X. Includes his most important speeches, seminar interviews and dialogues with those who knew him best (including his wife and children.)
LC NO. 73-701013
Prod-ABCM Dist-GROVE 1970

Maldives And Fiji Islands C 28 MIN
3/4 INCH VIDEOTAPE
Interviews the ambassadors from the Maldives and Fiji Islands. Includes slides and a short film clip on both countries. Presents a special program on island nations.
From The International Byline Series.
Prod-PERRYM Dist-PERRYM

Male And Female - God Created Us C 45 MIN
3/4 OR 1/2 INCH VIDEO CASSETTE
Features Ralph and Mary Cline Detrick in a three act 'dialog-drama' that humorously documents their personal struggle to become equal partners in marriage. Discusses their ongoing effort to bring biblical values to bear on their life together.
Prod-FRACOC Dist-FRACOC

Male And Female Homosexuality And Bisexuality C
3/4 OR 1/2 INCH VIDEO CASSETTE PRO
See series title for descriptive statement.
From The Independent Study In Human Sexuality Series.
Prod-MMRC Dist-MMRC

Male And Female In Plants And Animals C 10 MIN
16MM FILM, 3/4 OR 1/2 IN VIDEO P-I
Introduces the concept of male and female and shows that the physiology and functions of each are similar in the majority of plants and animals.
Prod-CORF Dist-CORF 1973

Male Cartoon Figure C 15 MIN
2 INCH VIDEOTAPE
See series title for descriptive statement.
From The Charlie's Pad Series.
Prod-WSIU Dist-PUBTEL

Male Catheterization, Pt 1 C 9 MIN
16MM FILM MAGNETIC SOUND
Explains the purpose of catheterization and shows the techniques involved in preparing a male patient for the procedure. Describes the essential functions of the organs of the urinary system and the two basic types of catheterization.
From The Urological Nursing Series.
LC NO. 76-712980
Prod-TRNAID Dist-TRNAID 1969

Male Catheterization, Pt 2 C 11 MIN
16MM FILM MAGNETIC SOUND
Describes the techniques involved in using a simple catheter and a foley retention catheter for male patients. Emphasizes the importance of minimizing patient discomfort and trauma.
From The Urological Nursing Series.
LC NO. 70-712981
Prod-TRNAID Dist-TRNAID 1969

Male Genital-Rectal Examination C 12 MIN
3/4 OR 1/2 INCH VIDEO CASSETTE PRO

Outlines systematic approach to the male genital-rectal examination.
Prod-HSCIC Dist-HSCIC 1984

Male Genitalia, Anus And Hernias (2nd Ed) C 12 MIN
16MM FILM - 3/4 IN VIDEO PRO
Demonstrates the physical examination of the male genitalia, anus and hernias, showing necessary procedures, manipulations, pacing, positions and patient-examiner interaction.
From The Visual Guide To Physical Examination (2nd Ed) Series.
LC NO. 81-707473
Prod-LIP Dist-LIP Prodn-JACSTO 1981

Male Genitourinary Examination C 24 MIN
3/4 OR 1/2 INCH VIDEO CASSETTE PRO
Demonstrates techniques used in examining the male genitourinary system and how to differentiate normal from abnormal findings.
Prod-HSCIC Dist-HSCIC 1982

Male Health Profile C 30 MIN
3/4 OR 1/2 INCH VIDEO CASSETTE
Discusses the reasons for the male's shorter life expectancy. Includes such destructive health habits as heavy smoking, drinking and negative effects of the male sex hormone, testosterone. Examines the relationship between male behavior and male health.
From The Here's To Your Health Series.
Prod-KERA Dist-PBS 1979

Male Health Profile C 30 MIN
3/4 OR 1/2 INCH VIDEO CASSETTE
See series title for descriptive statement.
From The Here's To Your Health Series.
Prod-PBS Dist-DELTAK

Male Health Profile, The C 30 MIN
3/4 OR 1/2 INCH VIDEO CASSETTE C T
Traces male development from the fetus through old age. Examines biological and cultural factors that influence male behavior.
From The Here's To Your Health Series.
Prod-DALCCD Dist-DALCCD

Male Involvement Project Trigger Film C 3 MIN
16MM FILM, 3/4 OR 1/2 IN VIDEO
Attempts to give young men the realization that they should examine the potential effects that sexual activity can have on their lives and encourages them to seek information or advice from their local family or health clinic.
Prod-PEREN Dist-PEREN 1983

Male Makeover C
3/4 OR 1/2 INCH VIDEO CASSETTE
Demonstrates the intricacies of pointing and other methods of hair shaping and beard trimming.
Prod-MPCEDP Dist-MPCEDP 1984

Male Masturbation C 6 MIN
3/4 OR 1/2 INCH VIDEO CASSETTE C A
Portrays male masturbation in terms of realistic gratification and tension release.
Prod-MMRC Dist-MMRC

Male Menopause C 29 MIN
3/4 INCH VIDEO CASSETTE
Focuses on the real and imagined sexual problems of the middle-aged American male as seen by a physician and a sociologist.
Prod-UMITV Dist-UMITV 1974

Male Menopause - The Pause That Perplexes C 59 MIN
3/4 OR 1/2 INCH VIDEO CASSETTE
Examines the problems of the middle-aged male, dealing with the reality and myths surrounding the mid-life crisis of mind and spirit.
Prod-NPACT Dist-PBS

Male Pelvis - Unit 20 C 24 MIN
3/4 OR 1/2 INCH VIDEO CASSETTE PRO
Describes the arteries, muscles, and nerves of the pelvic wall. Discusses structures which pass from the posterior abdominal wall into the pelvis, the major structures of the pelvis and structures related to them, the blood vessels of the pelvis, and structures related to the prostate.
From The Gross Anatomy Prosection Demonstration Series.
Prod-HSCIC Dist-HSCIC

Male Pelvis, The C 15 MIN
16MM FILM, 3/4 OR 1/2 IN VIDEO C A
Focuses on the pelvis and perineum. Demonstrates the dissection of the male pelvis.
From The Guides To Dissection Series.
Prod-UCLA Dist-TEF

Male Perineum C 19 MIN
16MM FILM, 3/4 OR 1/2 IN VIDEO PRO
Examines the parts and planes of the bony pelvis.
From The Cine-Prosector Series.
Prod-AVCORP Dist-TEF

Male Perineum - Unit 22 C 15 MIN
3/4 OR 1/2 INCH VIDEO CASSETTE PRO
Discusses the male penis, the layers of the perineum and its vessels and nerves, and the deeper aspect of the perineum, which is divided into two regions, the aval triangle and the U G triangle.
From The Gross Anatomy Prosection Demonstration Series.
Prod-HSCIC Dist-HSCIC

Male Perineum, The C 16 MIN
16MM FILM, 3/4 OR 1/2 IN VIDEO C A
Focuses on the pelvis and perineum. Demonstrates the dissection of the male perineum.
From The Guides To Dissection Series.
Prod-UCLA Dist-TEF

Male Physician And The Female Patient, The C 15 MIN
3/4 OR 1/2 INCH VIDEO CASSETTE PRO
Dramatizes encounters between female patients and male physicians, and accuses some doctors of sexism.
Prod-HSCIC Dist-HSCIC 1977

Male Radical Mastectomy C 20 MIN
3/4 OR 1/2 INCH VIDEO CASSETTE
See series title for descriptive statement.
From The Breast Series.
Prod-SVL Dist-SVL

Male Reproductive System - Pt 1 - Testis, Epididymis, Vas Deferens, Ampulla C 39 MIN
3/4 OR 1/2 INCH VIDEO CASSETTE PRO
Covers anatomy, functions, and histological organizations of the testis, epididymis, vas deferens, and ampulla.
From The Histology Review Series.
Prod-HSCIC Dist-HSCIC

Male Reproductive System - Pt 2 - Accessory Organs - Prostate, Seminal Vesicle, Cowper's... C 36 MIN
3/4 OR 1/2 INCH VIDEO CASSETTE PRO
Presents the following organs of the male reproductive system including the seminal vesicle, prostate gland, Cowper's gland, and penis.
From The Histology Review Series.
Prod-HSCIC Dist-HSCIC

Male Sexuality - Infancy To Old Age C
3/4 OR 1/2 INCH VIDEO CASSETTE PRO
See series title for descriptive statement.
From The Continuing Medical Education - Basic Sexology Series.
Prod-TIASHS Dist-MMRC

Male, The C 29 MIN
3/4 INCH VIDEO CASSETTE C A
Discusses role of male in human reproduction. Provides basic overview of anatomy of male reproductive system. Covers birth control and venereal disease.
From The Introducing Biology Series. Program 28
Prod-COAST Dist-CDTEL

Malice In Bigotland (Industry Version) C 21 MIN
16MM FILM OPTICAL SOUND A
Deals with the destructive force of prejudice through the story of an executive who, having revealed his prejudices while interviewing potential employees, goes home and dreams about a sinister carnival called Bigotland where prejudice and hatred are sold. Introduced by Charlton Heston.
LC NO. 78-700999
Prod-ESMRDA Dist-ESMRDA 1978

Malice In Bigotland (School Version) C 21 MIN
16MM FILM OPTICAL SOUND J-C A
Deals with the destructive force of prejudice through the use of a fantasy in which a class of students are transported to a carnival playground where the main attraction is the House of Racial Stereotypes. Introduced by Charlton Heston.
LC NO. 78-700991
Prod-ESMRDA Dist-ESMRDA 1978

Maligne C 9 MIN
16MM FILM OPTICAL SOUND
Depicts Lake Maligne in Jasper National Park, Alberta, Canada.
Prod-CTFL Dist-CTFL

Mallet Of Luck, A C 55 MIN
3/4 OR 1/2 INCH VIDEO CASSETTE PRO
Demonstrates the preparation of a Mallet of Luck broiled sea bream between cedar chips, shaped rice, a ribbon box of pressed egg white, yolk, and seaweed, and other garde-manger work.
From The Japanese Cuisine Series.
Prod-CULINA Dist-CULINA

Mallet, The C 11 MIN
16MM FILM, 3/4 OR 1/2 IN VIDEO J-C A
Presents a story about a futuristic, antiseptic food factory where workers select healthy chicks, while rejects are carried along a conveyor belt until they are crushed by a mallet and dropped into a garbage bin. Tells how a single black chick rebels against his fate before the mallet strikes.
Prod-DUNAV Dist-IFB 1978

Mallorca - An Island Paradise C 15 MIN
16MM FILM OPTICAL SOUND C A
Explains that Mallorca lies in the blue Mediterranean just off the coast of Spain, and has a deeply penetrating history. Points out that some of its cities were founded before the time of Christ and this sun-splashed island was known to the Phoenicians, Greeks and Carthaginians, and yet today, the island offers elegant hotels, villas and beaches that lure vacationers from all over the world.
Prod-MCDO Dist-MCDO 1965

Malmo - Gateway To The North C 13 MIN
16MM FILM OPTICAL SOUND
Points that because of its location, on the southern coast of Sweden, the city of Malmo has become one of the most important industrial centers in the country and is presently in the midst of a tremendous Industrial expansion.
Prod-ASI Dist-AUDPLN

Malnala (Captioned) C 103 MIN
16MM FILM, 3/4 OR 1/2 IN VIDEO A
Portrays the runaway African slaves in Cuba in the 19th century who were political rebels in the war of independence against the Spanish. Third part of a trilogy (includes 'The Other Francisco' and 'The Bount Hunter'). Spanish dialog with English subtitles.
Prod-CNEMAG Dist-CNEMAG 1979

Malnutrition - Diagnosis And Therapeutic Alternatives C 40 MIN
3/4 OR 1/2 INCH VIDEO CASSETTE PRO
Covers types and causes of malnutrition, assessment of nutritionalstatus and therapeutic techniques in the treatment of malnutrition.
From The Nutrition And Health Series.
Prod-HSCIC Dist-HSCIC 1983

Malnutrition In A Third World Community C 23 MIN
16MM FILM OPTICAL SOUND C
Studies malnutrition in the Philippines. Covers infant feeding practices, breast feeding and supplements, and the problems of poverty.
LC NO. 80-701545
Prod-PSUPCR Dist-PSUPCR 1980

Malocclusion C 15 MIN
16MM FILM, 3/4 OR 1/2 IN VIDEO
Defines the problem and examines causes and effects. Includes bruxism and TMJ syndrome. Explains diagnosis and treatment, including splints and equilibration.
Prod-PRORE Dist-PRORE

Malocclusion - Causes And Effects C 9 MIN
16MM FILM, 3/4 OR 1/2 IN VIDEO A
Defines malocclusion and examines the causes and effects. Presents information on bruxism, results of not replacing missing teeth, high spots and TMJ syndrome.
Prod-PRORE Dist-PRORE

Malocclusion - Diagnosis And Treatment C 7 MIN
16MM FILM, 3/4 OR 1/2 IN VIDEO PRO
Discusses the need for early diagnosis and treatment of malocclusion. Stresses the role the patient can play in correction of the disorder.
Prod-PRORE Dist-PRORE

Malpractice C 30 MIN
16MM FILM - 3/4 IN VIDEO PRO
Explains the elements and legal procedures of malpractice as they apply to nursing personnel. Describes professional negligence, proximate cause, damage sustained by the patient and situations in which a nurse could be held negligent.
From The Nurse And The Law Series.
LC NO. 76-701549
Prod-AJN Dist-AJN Prodn-WGNCP 1974

Malta C 28 MIN
3/4 INCH VIDEOTAPE
Interviews Ambassador Victor Gauci, permanent representative of Malta to the United Nations. Discusses the conference on the Law of the Sea. Describes the attractions of his country. Includes film clips.
From The International Byline Series.
Prod-PERRYM Dist-PERRYM

Maltese Falcon, The B 100 MIN
16MM FILM OPTICAL SOUND
Presents a crime film with Sam Spade as the private detective.
Prod-UNKNWN Dist-UAE

Maltese Unicorn, The C 23 MIN
16MM FILM, 3/4 OR 1/2 IN VIDEO P-I
Presents a contemporary story, based on the fairy tale The Boy Who Cried Wolf, about a mischievous boy who who tries to prove he didn't break the Maltese Unicorn. Shows how with the help of a famous detective, he discovers the guilty party and the learns the value of being a man of his word.
From the Unicorn Tales Series.
LC NO. 80-706514
Prod-MGHT Dist-MGHT Prodn-DENOIA 1980

Malvina Reynolds And Jack Elliot C 52 MIN
3/4 OR 1/2 INCH VIDEO CASSETTE
Presents Malvina Reynolds singing her famous 'Little Boxes.' Presents Jack Elliott singing some of Woody Guthrie's songs.
From The Rainbow Quest Series.
Prod-SEEGER Dist-CWATER

Mama's Little Pirate B 19 MIN
16MM FILM OPTICAL SOUND
Tells how dreams of a pirate's treasure lead the Little Rascals into a huge underground room with a giant footprint on the muddy floor.
Prod-ROACH Dist-BHAWK 1934

Mambush C 13 MIN
16MM FILM OPTICAL SOUND I-C A
Examines the philosophy and artistry of Mambush, a master craftsman who transfers paintings to the medium of tapestry.
LC NO. 74-703686
Prod-IFF Dist-IFF 1974

Mame C 131 MIN
16MM FILM OPTICAL SOUND
Tells the story of a youngster who comes to live with his bohemian aunt.
Prod-WB Dist-TWYMAN 1974

Mammal Fossils C 15 MIN
2 INCH VIDEOTAPE P
Reconstructs the life in the past from fossil remains and artifacts.
From The Science Is Searching Series.
Prod-DETPS Dist-GPITVL

Mammal Young C 15 MIN
2 INCH VIDEOTAPE P
Shows mammals having special characteristics.
From The Science Is Searching Series.
Prod-DETPS Dist-GPITVL

Mammalian Heart, The C 15 MIN
3/4 OR 1/2 INCH VIDEO CASSETTE H-C
Reveals parts of the heart in a laboratory dissection carried out by a skilled veterinarian. Shows the heart in action, too, during a routine surgical operation.
Prod-EDMI Dist-EDMI 1982

Mammals C 3 MIN
16MM FILM OPTICAL SOUND P-C A
Presents a vignette picturing classes of mammals.
From The Of All Things Series.
LC NO. FIA65-1431
Prod-BAILYL Dist-AVED 1961

Mammals C 10 MIN
16MM FILM, 3/4 OR 1/2 IN VIDEO P
Illustrates the characteristics of familiar and exotic mammals.
From The All About Animals Series.
Prod-BURGHS Dist-AIMS 1978

Mammals C 12 MIN
16MM FILM, 3/4 OR 1/2 IN VIDEO K-I
Identifies the characteristics of mammals. Shows that household pets may be relatives of large, wild animals.
LC NO. 80-706249
Prod-NGS Dist-NGS 1979

Mammals C 15 MIN
2 INCH VIDEOTAPE K
Shows various mammals.
From The Let's Go Sciencing, Unit III - Life Series.
Prod-DETPS Dist-GPITVL

Mammals C 15 MIN
3/4 OR 1/2 INCH VIDEO CASSETTE I
See series title for descriptive statement.
From The Discovering Series. Unit 1 - Vertebrate Animals
Prod-WDCNTV Dist-AITECH 1978

Mammals B 30 MIN
2 INCH VIDEOTAPE J
See series title for descriptive statement.
From The Investigating The World Of Science, Unit 3 - Animals And Their Adaptations Series.
Prod-MPATI Dist-GPITVL

Mammals - A First Film C 11 MIN
16MM FILM, 3/4 OR 1/2 IN VIDEO P-I
Describes the similarities that mammals have in common and also shows the many different places in the world where mammals live. Includes discussion of the beautiful, unusual and sometimes comic shapes that mammals have.
Prod-BFA Dist-PHENIX 1982

Mammals - Characteristics C 20 MIN
2 INCH VIDEOTAPE I
See series title for descriptive statement.
From The Exploring With Science, Unit XI - Vertebrates series.
Prod-MPATI Dist-GPITVL

Mammals - Seals And Otters C 30 MIN
3/4 OR 1/2 INCH VIDEO CASSETTE
Discusses the ancestry of marine mammals. Looks at the three main groups of marine mammals and compares their basic characteristics. Differentiates between seals and sea lions.
From The Oceanus - The Marine Environment Series. Lesson 18
Prod-SCCON Dist-CDTEL

Mammals - Whales C 30 MIN
3/4 OR 1/2 INCH VIDEO CASSETTE
Focuses on a typical marine mammal, the whale. Distinquishes between cetaceans. Explains functions of odontoceti sonar. Discusses current states of whaling and its effect on existing whale populations.
From The Oceanus - The Marine Environment Series. Lesson 19
Prod-SCCON Dist-CDTEL

Mammals And Milk C 14 MIN
16MM FILM, 3/4 OR 1/2 IN VIDEO P-I
Shows that, although animals are different, they are all alike in one respect - they have mammary glands and they all produce milk to feed their young.
Prod-AIMS Dist-AIMS 1971

Mammals And Milk (Captioned) C 11 MIN
16MM FILM, 3/4 OR 1/2 IN VIDEO K-I
Shows that animals are all alike in the respect that they produce milk to feed their young. Also useful in early sex education and to stimulate language arts discussion.
Prod-ASSOCF Dist-AIMS 1971

Mammals Are Interesting C 12 MIN
16MM FILM, 3/4 OR 1/2 IN VIDEO I-J
Views of many different animals are included to illustrate the distingushing characteristics of mammals.
Prod-EBF Dist-EBEC 1953

Mammals Of The Sea C 29 MIN
3/4 OR 1/2 INCH VIDEO CASSETTE
Examines the biological role and importance of Pacific marine mammals and the controversies that surround them.
Prod-OSU Dist-PBS 1980

Mammals With Hoofs C 11 MIN
16MM FILM, 3/4 OR 1/2 IN VIDEO I-J
Surveys the hoofed mammals, called ungulates, including those which are even-toed, such as hippopotami, pigs and deer and those which are odd-toed, such as rhinoceroses and horses. Describes their diets, feeding habits, special adaptations and usefulness to man.
Prod-CORF Dist-CORF 1977

Mammary Augmentation And Construction With Omentum C 19 MIN
16MM FILM OPTICAL SOUND PRO
Shows the technique for one-stage subcutaneous mastectomy and reconstruction, mammary augmentation and delayed mammary construction with re-located omentum. Discusses the indications, feasibility and limitations.
From The Cine Clinic Series.
Prod-ACYDGD Dist-NMAC 1970

Mammography C
3/4 OR 1/2 INCH VIDEO CASSETTE
See series title for descriptive statement.
From The X-Ray Procedures In Layman's Terms Series.
Prod-FAIRGH Dist-FAIRGH

Mammography Technique B 27 MIN
16MM FILM OPTICAL SOUND
Details the radiographic procedure for detection of breast cancer. Emphasizes positioning of the patient, coning procedures and film exposure and development. Restricted to radiologists. (Kinescope)
LC NO. 74-733992
Prod-USPHS Dist-USNAC 1965

Mammoth And Mastodon - Elephants On The Plains B 30 MIN
16MM FILM OPTICAL SOUND H-C A
Traces the development and migration of the enormous old world mammoths and mastodons of the Ice Age. Describes the hunting of them by early man on the great plains and their extinction during the Ice Age.
From The Great Plains Trilogy, 1 Series. In The Beginning - The Primitive Man
Prod-KUONTV Dist-UNEBR 1954

Man B 30 MIN
2 INCH VIDEOTAPE J
See series title for descriptive statement.
From The Investigating The World Of Science, Unit 3 - Animals And Their Adaptations Series.
Prod-MPATI Dist-GPITVL

Man - Friend And Enemy Of Nature C 20 MIN
16MM FILM, 3/4 OR 1/2 IN VIDEO
Explores the wonders of the natural world as depicted by artists. Considers how man has changed the natural environment, for better or worse, through industry, farming, land development and his own habits.
From The Images And Things Series.
LC NO. 73-702103
Prod-NITC Dist-AITECH

Man - His Growth And Development, Birth Through Adolescence—A Series

Prod-VDONUR Dist-AJN Prodn-WTTWTV 1967

Adolescence - A Cultural Phenomenon	44 MIN
Adolescent Idealism And Realism	44 MIN
Adolescent Sexuality	44 MIN
Cognitive Functioning - Ages 6-13	44 MIN
Consolidation And Growth	44 MIN
Coping With The Toddler	44 MIN
Emerging Consciousness	44 MIN
Emotional Development Of The Infant	44 MIN
Heredity And Behavior	44 MIN
Infant And Society, The	44 MIN
Intellectual Development - Ages 6-13	44 MIN
Language Development	44 MIN
Man - His Growth And Development, Birth	44 MIN
Path To Adulthood	44 MIN
Peer Groups - Ages 3-13	44 MIN
Play Activities - Ages 6-13	44 MIN
Preschooler - Concept Development	44 MIN
Preschooler - Psycho-Sexual Development	44 MIN
Rudiments Of Self Concept	44 MIN
School And The Child	44 MIN
Sex Roles - Ages 3-13	44 MIN
Toddler, The - Origins Of Independence	44 MIN
Understanding Infant Behavior	44 MIN
Unfolding Infant Behavior	44 MIN

Man - The Incredible Machine C 28 MIN
16MM FILM, 3/4 OR 1/2 IN VIDEO J-C A
Uses photographs and recording techniques in examining the human body, including the heart, lungs, blood vessels, skeleton and joints, muscles, ears, skin, eyes and brain.
LC NO. 80-706291
Prod-NGS Dist-NGS 1975

Man - The Measure Of All Things C 52 MIN
16MM FILM, 3/4 OR 1/2 IN VIDEO J-C A
Surveys the development of Western civilization during the 15th century as evidenced in the works of Botticelli, Masaccio, Bellini, Giorgione, Van Eyck and Alberti.
From The Civilisation Series. No. 4
LC NO. 79-707044
Prod-BBCTV Dist-FI 1970

Man Abuses Man - Lifestyle Abuses C 30 MIN
3/4 OR 1/2 INCH VIDEO CASSETTE
Reveals facts about how the American lifestyle has incorporated health abuses without much regard for the grave consequences. Discusses importance of restructuring lives and relates how the pregnant woman should care for herself, thus giving a better health start to her unborn child.
Prod-FAIRGH Dist-FAIRGH

Man Against Fire C 28 MIN
16MM FILM, 3/4 OR 1/2 IN VIDEO
Tells of man's fight to save forest resources from destruction by fire. Recounts how Federal, State and local cooperative fire-control measures protect America's water supply, timber, wildlife, recreation areas and scenic spots. Issued in 1969 as a motion picture.
LC NO. 79-706665
Prod-USDA Dist-USNAC 1979

Man Against Fire (Spanish) C 28 MIN
16MM FILM, 3/4 OR 1/2 IN VIDEO
Tells the story of man's fight to save forest resources from destruction by wildfire by the use of stamina, technology and strategy. Tells how federal, state and local cooperative fire control measures protect our nation's water supply, timber, wildlife, recreation areas and scenic wonders of the forests.
Prod-USDA Dist-USNAC 1969

Man Alive C 12 MIN
16MM FILM OPTICAL SOUND C A
Illustrates the importance of seeking competent medical advice when cancer is suspected. Uses animation to humorously draw a parallelism between the problems of physical symptoms and the symptoms of an automobile.
Prod-AMCS Dist-AMCS 1952

Man Amplifiers C 29 MIN
2 INCH VIDEOTAPE
See series title for descriptive statement.
From The Interface Series.
Prod-KCET Dist-PUBTEL

Man And A River, A C 15 MIN
16MM FILM, 3/4 OR 1/2 IN VIDEO
Tells the story of Thomas Hart Benton, famous painter, author, conservationist and raconteur, and his great love for the Buffalo River, a clear-running waterway that winds through the Ozark Hills of northwestern Arkansas.
LC NO. 81-707199
Prod-EPA Dist-USNAC 1973

Man And His Art—A Series
H-C A
Shows works of art that man has produced and aids the viewer in relating to works of art, both past and present. Explores various styles of artistic creation and with the help of each of the artists, teaches the viewer to 'SEE' and appreciate them.
Prod-WTTWTV Dist-GPITVL

And There Was Light	45 MIN
Non-Western	30 MIN
Painter's Eye, The	45 MIN
Reflections Of Reality	45 MIN
Shape Of Our Vision, The	45 MIN
Style - The Man And His Work	45 MIN

Man And His Environment B 30 MIN
16MM FILM - 3/4 IN VIDEO PRO
See series title for descriptive statement.
From The Public Health Science Series. Unit V - Introduction To Bioenvironmental Health
Prod-TEXWU Dist-GPITVL Prodn-KUHTTV

Man And His Environment I - Rainforest Family C 17 MIN
16MM FILM, 3/4 OR 1/2 IN VIDEO I-H
Shows the Choco Indians of Central and South America who are typical of the hunting and gathering societies explains that because of their extreme isolation, each child is taught by his parents the many skills necessary to live in the forest. Shows how they adapt to the forest environment by using available forest materials to make their houses, clothing, tools and utensils.
From The Man And His Environment Series.
Prod-MITC Dist-PHENIX 1971

Man And His Environment II - Food From The Rainforest C 17 MIN
16MM FILM, 3/4 OR 1/2 IN VIDEO I-H
Shows how the Choco Indians of Central and South America supply most of their own food by hunting, fishing, gathering and simple agriculture. Tells how boys hunt and fish with their fathers while girls learn to gather and prepare food with their mothers. Shows how surplus products are taken away by canoe to to the trading post which is several days journey away.
From The Man And His Environment Series.
Prod-MITC Dist-PHENIX 1971

Man And His Environment—A Series
16MM FILM, 3/4 OR 1/2 IN VIDEO
Describes the lifestyle of the Choco Indians of Central and South America.
Prod-MITC Dist-PHENIX

Man And His Environment I - Rainforest Family	017 MIN
Man And His Environment II - Food From The	017 MIN

Man And His Gold C 28 MIN
16MM FILM OPTICAL SOUND
Shows the many and varied roles that gold has played and continues to play for man. Demonstrates gold's unique properties which make it both desirable and useful.
LC NO. 79-701375
Prod-GOLDIC Dist-MTP Prodn-PTRSEN 1979

Man And His Habits C 13 MIN
16MM FILM, 3/4 OR 1/2 IN VIDEO
Shows how man's habits endanger his safety by becoming routine when carried over to his work. Shows the worker how to acquire safe work habits by practicing safety at home and on the job.
From The Foremanship Training Series.
LC NO. 82-706277
Prod-USBM Dist-USNAC 1969

Man And His Men, A C 30 MIN
16MM FILM OPTICAL SOUND R
Takes a look at the life of a professional football player. Spotlights Tom Landry, coach of the Dallas Cowboys and how his Christian faith affects his work.
Prod-YOUTH Dist-GF

Man And His Sport—A Series
H-C A
Prod-ANAIB Dist-AUIS 1970

Soccer 27 MIN
Sports Medicine 28 MIN
Swimmer 26 MIN

Man And His Wife Make A Hammock, A C 9 MIN
16MM FILM OPTICAL SOUND H-C A
Features a Yanomama Indian headman in Venezuela weaving a hammock while his wife and baby watch.
From The Yanomama Series.
LC NO. 75-702184
Prod-DOCEDR Dist-PSUPCR 1975

Man And His Wife Weave A Hammock, A C 12 MIN
3/4 INCH VIDEO CASSETTE
Shows a Yanamamo man weaving a hammock as his wife teases him. Filmed by Timothy Asch and Napoleon Chagnon.
Prod-DOCEDR Dist-DOCEDR

Man And His World C 22 MIN
16MM FILM, 3/4 OR 1/2 IN VIDEO I-J
A provoking film that creates a metaphorical portrait of the inhabitants of the earth. Shows a group of Negro teen-agers playing with a soccer ball as titles appear on the screen which tell of the vulnerable suspension of the planet in time and space. The admonishment to people is 'DO NOT BLOW' its chances for survival.
Prod-GROENG Dist-AIMS 1969

Man And His World—A Series
16MM FILM, 3/4 OR 1/2 IN VIDEO
Prod-FI Dist-FI 1970

Bangkok 018 MIN
Bargemen Of The Rhine 013 MIN
Coffee Planters Near Kilimanjaro 014 MIN
Cooperative Farming In East Germany 015 MIN
Cork From Portugal 014 MIN
Dairy Farming In The Alps 016 MIN
Deep Sea Trawler 018 MIN
Diamond Mining In East Africa 009 MIN
Egyptian Villages 014 MIN
Favela - Diary Of A Slum 017 MIN
Highland Indians Of Peru 018 MIN
Indian Villagers In Mexico 012 MIN
Industrial Beginnings In West Pakistan 017 MIN
Industrial Region In Sweden 018 MIN
Industrial Worker In Kenya 013 MIN
Israeli Kibbutz 019 MIN
Japanese Farmers 017 MIN
Land From The North Sea 017 MIN
Life In Soviet Asia - 273 Days Below Zero 011 MIN
Man Changes The Nile 013 MIN
Masai In Tanzania 014 MIN
Miners Of Bolivia 015 MIN
New Life For A Spanish Farmer 018 MIN
North Sea Islanders 019 MIN
Norwegian Fjord, A 013 MIN
Oasis In The Sahara 016 MIN
Oil In Libya 015 MIN
Over The Andes In Ecuador 018 MIN
Plateau Farmers In France 015 MIN
Rainy Season In West Africa 014 MIN
Ranchero And The Gauchos In Argentine 017 MIN
Rice Farmers In Thailand 019 MIN
River Journey On The Upper Nile 018 MIN
River People Of Chad 020 MIN
Romania 018 MIN
Sugar In Egypt 013 MIN
Three Brothers In Haiti 017 MIN
Timber In Finland 015 MIN
Tokyo Industrial Worker 017 MIN
Two Brothers In Greece 015 MIN
Venezuela 014 MIN
Winemakers In France 015 MIN
Wool In Australia 019 MIN
Yugoslavian Coastline 014 MIN

Man And Nature C 45 MIN
3/4 OR 1/2 INCH VIDEO CASSETTE C
Discusses the relationship between man and nature.
From The Biology I Series.
Prod-MDCPB Dist-MDCPB

Man And Radiation C 29 MIN
16MM FILM OPTICAL SOUND
Discusses the discovery of radiation, the different types, and its beneficial applications in medicine, industry, agriculture, power and research.
LC NO. FIE64-193
Prod-USAEC Dist-USERD Prodn-USA 1963

Man And Safety - Communications C 30 MIN
16MM FILM, 3/4 OR 1/2 IN VIDEO
Discusses the need for better communication and its importance in preventing accidents. Reenacts several accidents to show the consequences of too much or too little information, unclear messages and emotional difficulties.
Prod-USAF Dist-USNAC 1983

Man And Safety - Physical Limitations C 23 MIN
3/4 OR 1/2 INCH VIDEO CASSETTE
Describes man's physical limitations and relates them to human error accidents. Reconstructs several accidents to show the consequences of exceeding one's physical capabilities.
LC NO. 82-706286
Prod-USAF Dist-USNAC 1963

Man And Safety - Physiological Limitations C 26 MIN
16MM FILM, 3/4 OR 1/2 IN VIDEO J-H
Discusses the boundaries beyond which human efficiency breaks down and accidents occur. Considers the added complexity of equipping man to survive environments of outer space.
LC NO. 82-706287
Prod-USAF Dist-USNAC 1963

Man And Safety - Supervision C 26 MIN
16MM FILM, 3/4 OR 1/2 IN VIDEO
Discusses supervision and its role in human failure accidents. Dramatizes several accidents to show the consequences of poor supervision and illustrates the role of positive supervision in preventing a major catastrophe.
Prod-USAF Dist-USNAC 1983

Man And Safety - Tools C 28 MIN
16MM FILM OPTICAL SOUND
Enacts accidents on the ground, in the air and in the mountains to show how misuse of tools can lead to disaster. Points out the importance of selecting and correctly using proper tools for specific purposes.
LC NO. 81-700788
Prod-USAF Dist-USNAC 1981

Man And Safety-Physical Limitations C 23 MIN
16MM FILM OPTICAL SOUND
Describes man's physical limitations and relates them to human error accidents. Reconstructs several accidents to show the consequences of exceeding one's physical capacities.
LC NO. 73-702416
Prod-USAF Dist-USNAC 1963

Man And The 'Second' Industrial Revolution C 19 MIN
16MM FILM, 3/4 OR 1/2 IN VIDEO J-C A
Shows how man is using new technological knowledge to change the world and to reach out to new worlds. Poses the problems that have come with this knowledge, overpopulation, pollution and the ability to destroy the environment. Provides a point of departure for discussion on how the future history of man will be written.
From The History Of Man Series.
Prod-MGHT Dist-MGHT Prodn-ABCTV 1970

Man And The Atom - Challenge Of Our Times, The B 17 MIN
16MM FILM OPTICAL SOUND
Uses historic films to illustrate the crises and challenges of the Atomic Age.
LC NO. FIA68-1655
Prod-HEARST Dist-HEARST 1967

Man And The Atom, Pt 1 B 30 MIN
3/4 INCH VIDEO CASSETTE
Surveys the role of the Atomic Energy Commission in the nation's atomic energy program. Reviews the atom's place in national defense and the peaceful use of nuclear explosives. Surveys radioisotopes and their many applications.
Prod-USNAC Dist-USNAC 1972

Man And The Atom, Pt 2 B 30 MIN
3/4 INCH VIDEO CASSETTE
Surveys the role of the Atomic Energy Commission and their guidance of research for both defense and research purposes.
Prod-USNAC Dist-USNAC 1972

Man And The Changing Earth - Science, Social Studies C
3/4 OR 1/2 INCH VIDEO CASSETTE
Provides the necessary background for understanding current problems. Discusses forces that change our environment, the balance of the ecosystem, effects, the beginning of the industrial revolution, and the rise and problems of cities.
Prod-EDUACT Dist-EDUACT

Man And The FBM C 28 MIN
16MM FILM OPTICAL SOUND
Shows the U S Navy's fleet ballistic missile submarine and discusses the recruitment and training of the personnel who will operate the nuclear weapons system.
LC NO. FIE61-90
Prod-USN Dist-USNAC 1960

Man And The Forest—A Series
I-C A
Prod-MMP Dist-MMP 1969

Cedar Tree, The 11 MIN
Decorative Foliage 20 MIN
Decorative Woods And Fuel 20 MIN
Native Transplants And Crude Drugs 18 MIN
Red Man And The Red Cedar 12 MIN
Seed Cones And Reforestation 23 MIN

Man And The Giant, The C 8 MIN
16MM FILM, 3/4 OR 1/2 IN VIDEO H-C A
Shows Inuit Indians acting out a legend about a captured hunter.
Prod-NFBC Dist-PHENIX 1978

Man And The Industrial Revolution C 20 MIN
16MM FILM, 3/4 OR 1/2 IN VIDEO J-C A
Describes the beginnings of the first industrial revolution in Europe, its spread and its social, political and technological implications.
From The History Of Man Series.
Prod-MGHT Dist-MGHT Prodn-ABCTV 1970

Man And The Land, The C 28 MIN
16MM FILM OPTICAL SOUND
Shows how American farmers, using up-to-date agricultural techniques, feed the people of the United States and provide food for millions of people overseas.
LC NO. 74-701771
Prod-INDIFB Dist-INDIFB Prodn-SCENE 1974

Man And The Rise Of Civilization C 19 MIN
16MM FILM, 3/4 OR 1/2 IN VIDEO J-C A
Deals with the general process of becoming civilized. Shows how urbanization and specialization of functions occurred within civilizations. Emphasizes that great civilizations grew at various times in all parts of the world, among all men.
From The History Of Man Series.
Prod-MGHT Dist-MGHT Prodn-ABCTV 1970

Man And The Rocket, The B
16MM FILM OPTICAL SOUND H
Presents a report on the Grissom flight and the earlier launchings of the Discoverer XXVI, Tiros III, and Midas III.
From The Screen News Digest Series. Vol 4, Issue 1
Prod-HEARST Dist-HEARST 1961

Man And The Sea C 24 MIN
3/4 INCH VIDEO CASSETTE J
Describes how erosion and deposition occur on beaches and dunes. Takes a look at the eastern coastline of North Carolina.
From The What On Earth Series.
Prod-NCSDPI Dist-GPITVL 1979

Man And The Snake, The C 26 MIN
16MM FILM, 3/4 OR 1/2 IN VIDEO
Features the short story by Ambrose Bierce about a young man's visit to the home of a zoologist who keeps and studies snakes with the locale changed from post-Civil War America to Victorian England.
Prod-JOCF Dist-PFP 1975

Man And The State - Burke And Paine On Revolution C 28 MIN
16MM FILM, 3/4 OR 1/2 IN VIDEO
Features Thomas Paine who was a leading radical and revolutionary in 1792. Presents Edmund Burke who is a most articulate conservative. Shows Burke and Paine debating their conflicting views of man, political change and liberty while elements of the French Revolution are acted out in microcosm before them. Explains the government of the United States as related to the ideas under discussion.
From The Man And The State Series.
Prod-WILETS Dist-BARR 1974

Man And The State - Hamilton And Jefferson On Democracy C 26 MIN
16MM FILM, 3/4 OR 1/2 IN VIDEO J-C A
Discusses Alexander Hamilton's and Thomas Jefferson's differing views of democracy.
From The Man And The State Series.
Prod-WILETS Dist-BARR 1975

Man And The State - Machiavelli On Political Power C 28 MIN
16MM FILM, 3/4 OR 1/2 IN VIDEO J-C A
Presents the political ideas of Niccolo Machiavelli, which have had a tremendous impact on society. Machiavelli is forced to debate his ideas. Questions if his politics is a politics of realism, and does he show the world as it is today. An open ended film.
From The Man And The State Series.
Prod-WILETS Dist-BARR 1972

Man And The State - Marx And Rockefeller On Capitalism C 26 MIN
16MM FILM, 3/4 OR 1/2 IN VIDEO J-H
Features Karl Marx and John D Rockefeller, who are temporarily brought back to life by a future society in order to debate the basic ideas of communism and capitalism as they evolved up to the last quarter of the 20th century. Shows how the conflict between these ideas is reflected in the main social and economic tensions in the world today.
From The Man And The State Series.
Prod-WILETS Dist-BARR 1977

Man And The State - Roosevelt And Hoover On The Economy C 25 MIN
16MM FILM, 3/4 OR 1/2 IN VIDEO J-C A
Explores what would happen if Herbert Hoover and Franklin Roosevelt were forced to confront one another and debate their reasons for acting or failing to act during the Great Depression. Evaluates the conflicting views of both men on deficit financing bureaucracy and the role the federal government plays in people's lives.
From The Man And The State Series.
Prod-WILETS Dist-BARR 1976

Man And The State - The Trial Of Socrates C 29 MIN
16MM FILM, 3/4 OR 1/2 IN VIDEO J-C A
Explains the significance of the trial and death of Socrates in the history of Western civilization as reflected in the works of Plato, Xenophon and Aristophanes, as well as in other Greek sources.
From The Man And The State Series.
Prod-WILETS Dist-BARR 1971

Man And The State—A Series
16MM FILM, 3/4 OR 1/2 IN VIDEO
Examines the relationship between man and government in a historical context, presenting famous statesmen from history debating their various political philosophies.
Prod-WILETS Dist-BARR

Man And The State - Burke And Paine On
Man And The State - Hamilton And Jefferson 26 MIN
Man And The State - Machiavelli On Political 28 MIN
Man And The State - Marx And Rockefeller On 25 MIN
Man And The State - Roosevelt And Hoover On 25 MIN
Man And The State - The Trial Of Socrates 29 MIN

Man And Water C 28 MIN
16MM FILM OPTICAL SOUND
Offers a look at a river system and concludes that the farmer, rancher and environmentalist must work together to prevent degradation of the river.
LC NO. 78-701697
Prod-CONICO Dist-CONICO 1978

Man And Woman C 33 MIN
16MM FILM, 3/4 OR 1/2 IN VIDEO J-C A
Presents an edited version of Franco Zeffirelli's film The Taming Of The Shrew, which is based on Shakespeare's play. Features Richard Burton as the clever and boisterous Petruchio, who woos and weds the flamboyant and resistant Katherine, played by Elizabeth Taylor.
From The Great Themes Of Literature Series.
Prod-LCOA Dist-LCOA 1973

Man And Woman's Guide To Breast Examination, A C 5 MIN
16MM FILM, 3/4 OR 1/2 IN VIDEO
Uses live action and animation in presenting a guide to breast examination. Shows how a husband learns to examine his wife for the early detection of breast cancer.
Prod-RTOMP Dist-UCEMC 1976

Man As He Behaves B 30 MIN
16MM FILM OPTICAL SOUND
Outlines lab research concerning human behavior and explains the need for methods to gauge human behavior indirectly and objectively. Demonstrates how cooperation and competition are tested by observing subjects operating machines. Suggests that research leads to an understanding of mental health.
From The Science Reporter Series.
LC NO. FIA65-1665
Prod-MIOT Dist-IU Prodn-WABHTV 1967

Man As Hunter And Food Gatherer C 19 MIN
16MM FILM, 3/4 OR 1/2 IN VIDEO
Discusses hunters and gatherers, the type of man who has occupied the planet for a longer period of time than any other. Describes the problems faced by scientists who seek to describe early hunter bands.
Prod-MGHT Dist-MGHT

Man Behind The Gavel, The C 29 MIN
16MM FILM OPTICAL SOUND
Discusses the role of the speaker of the House of Representatives, pointing out that he is the second most powerful elected official in the United States. Shows how individual speakers from Henry Clay to Sam Rayburn have interpreted and wielded that power.
From The Government Story Series. No. 6
LC NO. 70-707171
Prod-WBCPRO Dist-WBCPRO 1968

Man Behind The Gun B 12 MIN
16MM FILM OPTICAL SOUND
Presents gun safety, emphasizing the importance of safe handling of firearms. Depicts humorously some ways not to handle firearms.
Prod-TGAFC Dist-TGAFC

Man Behind The Mask, The C 50 MIN
3/4 OR 1/2 INCH VIDEO CASSETTE J-C A
Reviews the life of Heinrich Schiemann, the man who was long recognized as the Father of Archeology until it was discovered that virtually all his achievements were fakery.
LC NO. 84-706202
Prod-BBCTV Dist-FI 1982

Man Belongs To The Earth C 22 MIN
16MM FILM, 3/4 OR 1/2 IN VIDEO
Deals with the natural environment of cities, the desert, the oceans and the mountains. Shows the dread waste and destruction threatening the environment and points out natural wonders that should be preserved. Presents the problems and some solutions. Includes scenes photographed throughout the 50 states.
LC NO. 80-707743
Prod-USBIC Dist-USNAC Prodn-PAR 1974

Man Between, The B 104 MIN
16MM FILM OPTICAL SOUND
Features James Mason as a shadowy figure who becomes caught between West and East Berlin when he falls in love with a woman. Directed by Sir Carol Reed.
Prod-UNKNWN Dist-KITPAR 1953

Man Blong Custom C 52 MIN
16MM FILM, 3/4 OR 1/2 IN VIDEO
Examines the tribal sculpture from the islands of the Western Pacific, including Malekula in the New Hebrides, the Solomon Islands and Southern Guadalcanal.
From The Tribal Eye Series.
LC NO. 79-707115
Prod-BBCTV Dist-TIMLIF 1976

Man Builds - Man Destroys—A Series
J-C A
Explains that man destroys what he builds but also has the ability to restore. Looks at environmental problems and their possible solutions.
Prod-UN Dist-GPITVL

Air We Breathe, The	30 MIN
All The Fish In The Sea	30 MIN
Among The Living	30 MIN
Car In The City, The	30 MIN
City With A Future, The	30 MIN
Day After Tomorrow, The	30 MIN
Everyone Talks About It	30 MIN
Flow Gently	30 MIN
Home To The Sea	30 MIN
It Can Be Done	30 MIN
Keeping Of The Green, The	30 MIN
Limits To Growth, The	30 MIN
Living Off The Land	30 MIN
Nor Any Drop To Drink	30 MIN
Numbers Game, The	30 MIN
Only One Earth	30 MIN
Place To Live, A	30 MIN
Power To The People	30 MIN
Saving A Big Land	30 MIN
Scars On The Surface	30 MIN
Seamless Web, The	30 MIN
Six Fathoms Deep	30 MIN
Striking A Balance	30 MIN
Things Worth Keeping	30 MIN
Through The Mill Once More	30 MIN
Traffic Or Transit	30 MIN
Under New Management	30 MIN
Vanishing Breed, The	30 MIN
Waste Not	30 MIN
You Can Help - Throw It Here	30 MIN

Man Called 'Bee' - Studying The Yanamamo C 40 MIN
3/4 INCH VIDEO CASSETTE
Explores the relationship between anthropologist Napoleon Chagnon and his Yanamamo subjects. Touches on issues of mutual exploitation and reciprocity.
Prod-DOCEDR Dist-DOCEDR

Man Called 'Duce,' A - Benito Mussolini In Perspective B 15 MIN
16MM FILM OPTICAL SOUND J-H
Documents the rise and fall of Benito Mussolini.
From The Screen News Digest Series. Vol 14, Issue 7
Prod-HEARST Dist-HEARST 1972

Man Called Bee, A - Studying The Yanomamo C 40 MIN
16MM FILM OPTICAL SOUND
Follows anthropologist Napoleon Chagnon as he collects anthropological field data among the Yanoama Indians of southern Venezuela.
From The Yanomamo Series.
LC NO. 75-702654
Prod-DOCEDR Dist-DOCEDR 1974

Man Called Bogart, The B 26 MIN
16MM FILM OPTICAL SOUND
Follows the career of Humphrey Bogart, from his unsuccessful early films and his gangster films, to his greatest films, including 'TREASURE OF THE SIERRA MADRE,' 'THE AFRICAN QUEEN' and 'THE CAINE MUTINY.'
LC NO. FI68-174
Prod-WOLPER Dist-WOLPER 1963

Man Called Edison, A B 28 MIN
16MM FILM, 3/4 OR 1/2 IN VIDEO I A
Presents the contributions of Thomas A Edison to the motion picture through his early kinetoscope films. Provides a vivid panorama of early moviemaking.
Prod-SPCTRA Dist-SF 1970

Man Called Flintstone, A C 87 MIN
16MM FILM OPTICAL SOUND J-C
Presents an animated feature, starring Fred Flintstone and the whole Flintstone gang as Fred impersonates a well known secret agent and pursues his mission of tracking down the enemy operative.
Prod-HANBAR Dist-TIMLIF 1966

Man Changes The Nile C 13 MIN
16MM FILM, 3/4 OR 1/2 IN VIDEO P-C
Explains how man uses his ingenuity to take advantage of the Nile River for both power and irrigation.
From The Man And His World Series.
Prod-FI Dist-FI 1969

Man Dies, A C 45 MIN
16MM FILM OPTICAL SOUND H
Features the teenagers of the Bristol Church Youth Club in England who present a contemporary form of the medieval mystery play, using drama, 'ROCK AND ROLL' music and dancing, and modern dress to tell the story of the Passion of Christ and its meaning for today.
Prod-YALEDV Dist-YALEDV

Man Escaped, A (French) B 100 MIN
16MM FILM OPTICAL SOUND
Tells how French resistance leader Andre Devigny escaped from a Nazi prison in Lyon just hours before he was to be executed.
Prod-NYFLMS Dist-NYFLMS 1956

Man From Deer Creek, The, The Story Of Ishi C
3/4 OR 1/2 INCH VIDEO CASSETTE
Tells the story of Ishi, a Yahi Indian who was the last Indian in America to grow up without contact with 'American civilization.'
Prod-MMPRO Dist-MMPRO

Man From Inner Space, The X 27 MIN
16MM FILM, 3/4 OR 1/2 IN VIDEO H-C A
Features a parable about God-man interaction. Relates what happens when a spaceship arrives on Earth and a black man emerges. Describes his ability to work miracles and tells how his growing following eventually leads to problems. Stars James Franciscus and Lou Gossett.
From The Insight Series.
Prod-PAULST Dist-PAULST

Man From Laramie, The C 104 MIN
16MM FILM OPTICAL SOUND
Tells how Will Lockhart travels to the sunbaked wasteland of New Mexico to find and kill the man who sold guns to the Apaches who killed his brother. Stars James Stewart.
Prod-CPC Dist-TIMLIF

Man From Maisinicu, The (Captioned) B 117 MIN
16MM FILM, 3/4 OR 1/2 IN VIDEO A
Presents espionage and counter intelligence activity during the early years of the Cuban revolution. Spanish dialog with English subtitles.
Prod-CNEMAG Dist-CNEMAG 1973

Man From NECA, The C 20 MIN
16MM FILM OPTICAL SOUND J-C
Narration and a series of episodes document the variety of services provided to members of NECA, and emphasizes the chapter manager's role and status in chapter activities.
LC NO. 71-704743
Prod-NECA Dist-FINLYS Prodn-FINLYS 1967

Man From Nowhere C 58 MIN
16MM FILM OPTICAL SOUND I-J
Tells how Alice's life with her great-uncle is disrupted when a sinister man appears to tell her that her life is in danger. Describes how four local urchins befriend her by setting a trap for the stranger.
Prod-LUF Dist-LUF 1978

Man From Snowy River C
1/2 IN VIDEO CASSETTE BETA/VHS
Tells the story of the man from Snowy River.
Prod-EQVDL Dist-EQVDL

Man Hunt C 31 MIN
3/4 OR 1/2 INCH VIDEO CASSETTE A
Employs humorous examples to demonstrate effective and ineffective techniques for drawing out a candidate during a job interview. Emphasizes preparation and good questions.
Prod-XICOM Dist-XICOM

Man Hunters, The C 52 MIN
16MM FILM, 3/4 OR 1/2 IN VIDEO I A
Explores the time and the place where man first walked on the earth.
Prod-FI Dist-FI 1971

Man In A Paper Boat C 20 MIN
16MM FILM, 3/4 OR 1/2 IN VIDEO J-H
Presents interviews with Dr Heyerdahl, who organized the Kon Tiki and Ra II expeditions, and his crewmate, the late Erik Hesselberg, explaining their motives, discoveries and experiences.
From The Matter Of Fact Series.
LC NO. 74-703200
Prod-NITC Dist-AITECH Prodn-WETATV 1973

Man In Charge, The C 18 MIN
16MM FILM OPTICAL SOUND
Discusses the problems of leadership on the small unit level in the Marine Corps. Emphasizes the importance of identifying the overall concepts of leadership by the individual Marine.
LC NO. 74-706493
Prod-USN Dist-USNAC 1973

Man In Command C 29 MIN
16MM FILM OPTICAL SOUND
Shows training career opportunities offered to line officers in the U S Navy.
LC NO. 75-700792
Prod-USN Dist-USNAC 1968

Man In Flight C 19 MIN
16MM FILM OPTICAL SOUND
Depicts the research being carried on at the School Of Aviation Medicine, Brooks Air Force Base, Texas, to insure man's comfort and safety in flight.
LC NO. FIE61-91
Prod-USAF Dist-USNAC 1945

Man In Green, The C 19 MIN
16MM FILM OPTICAL SOUND
Tells the story of the state forestry organizations. Shows the different kinds of foresters and where they function.
LC NO. 74-705080
Prod-USDA Dist-USNAC 1970

Man In His Environment C 29 MIN
16MM FILM, 3/4 OR 1/2 IN VIDEO I-C A
Presents a film essay on the checks and balances of the natural cycle, showing how the processes that regulate other forms of life ultimately regulate humans as well. Explores ramifications of human overpopulation, wastefulness of modern industrial society and disruption caused by many agricultural methods.
Prod-FMNH Dist-UCEMC Prodn-SOSHI 1976

Man In Society C 36 MIN
3/4 OR 1/2 INCH VIDEO CASSETTE
Includes 36 half-hour videotapes.
Prod-TELSTR Dist-TELSTR

Man In Space B 30 MIN
2 INCH VIDEOTAPE J
See series title for descriptive statement.
From The Investigating The World Of Science, Unit 5 - Life In The Universe Series.
Prod-MPATI Dist-GPITVL

Man In Space, The Second Decade C 28 MIN
3/4 INCH VIDEO CASSETTE
Reviews achievements of manned space flight during the 1960's and shows programs for manned flight during the 1970's. Describes programs that are technically feasible and desirable beyond 1980. Issued in 1971 as a motion picture.
From The Space In The 70's Series.
LC NO. 79-706964
Prod-NASA Dist-USNAC 1979

Man In The Cast Iron Suit, The C 25 MIN
16MM FILM, 3/4 OR 1/2 IN VIDEO
Shows how three generations of a family struggle to fulfill themselves. Points out that loving relationships will lead to fulfillment.
From The Insight Series.
LC NO. 79-706587
Prod-PAULST Dist-PAULST 1976

Man In The Desert C 19 MIN
16MM FILM OPTICAL SOUND J-C A

Examines the human and environmental effects of man's use of the Australian desert.
LC NO. 72-702257
Prod-ANAIB Dist-AUIS 1970

Man In The Fifth Dimension C 33 MIN
16MM FILM OPTICAL SOUND
Features Billy Graham who guides the viewer through space and time into the realm of the fifth dimension, the spirit.
Prod-WWP Dist-NINEFC

Man In The Iron Mask, The B 113 MIN
16MM FILM OPTICAL SOUND
Tells what happens when twin Dauphins are born to Louis XIII of France and one of them is spirited away to be raised by the Three Musketeers. Stars Louis Hayward and Joan Bennett. Based on the novel THE MAN IN THE IRON MASK by Alexandre Dumas.
Prod-UAA Dist-KITPAR 1939

Man In The Ironic Mask, The - Jonathan Swift - The Modest Proposal And The Second... C 45 MIN
3/4 OR 1/2 INCH VIDEO CASSETTE
Analyzes Jonathan Swift's Modest Proposal and the Second Voyage Of Gulliver.
From The Survey Of English Literature I Series.
Prod-MDCPB Dist-MDCPB

Man In The Middle C 22 MIN
16MM FILM, 3/4 OR 1/2 IN VIDEO
Discusses the role of the supervisor who is sandwiched between the need for full production and the health and safety needs of his employees. Discusses attitudes toward safety.
Prod-MILLBK Dist-IFB

Man In The Middle, The C 25 MIN
16MM FILM, 3/4 OR 1/2 IN VIDEO J-C A
Records the daily efforts to seek an elusive peace in Lebanon as seen through the eyes of members of the multinational peacekeeping body stationed in the country. Shows that since 1978, the force has had to cope not only with the problem of maintaining a stable buffer zone between Lebanese guerillas and Christian militia, but also with separating Israeli soldiers and PLO members.
Prod-LUF Dist-LUF 1982

Man In The Mirror, The C 25 MIN
16MM FILM - 3/4 IN VIDEO PRO
Discusses a manager's behavior off the job as well as on the job.
From The Tough-Minded Management Series.
Prod-BNA Dist-BNA 1969

Man In The Moon Remembers, The C 5 MIN
16MM FILM, 3/4 OR 1/2 IN VIDEO
Uses animation and film footage from the Apollo moon landings to depict the history of the moon.
Prod-NASM Dist-USNAC

Man In The Sea - The New Frontier B 14 MIN
16MM FILM OPTICAL SOUND J-H
Presents a study of man's attempts to push back the frontiers of the sea.
LC NO. 70-703536
Prod-HEARST Dist-HEARST 1969

Man In The Sea - The Story Of Sea Lab II C 28 MIN
3/4 INCH VIDEO CASSETTE
Describes the U S Navy's Sea Lab II experiment. Includes underwater photography inside in the vehicle and of the sea around it. Issued in 1966 as a motion picture.
LC NO. 79-708130
Prod-USN Dist-USNAC 1979

Man In The White Suit, The B 85 MIN
16MM FILM OPTICAL SOUND
Presents a comedy about a young man whose discovery of a miracle fabric leads him to discover some contradictions upon which society is based. Features Alec Guinness.
Prod-EALPRO Dist-LCOA 1952

Man In The White Suit, The (Captioned) B 85 MIN
16MM FILM OPTICAL SOUND H-C A
Features Alec Guinness as an impassioned scientist intent on giving humanity a fabric that repels dirt and lasts forever.
Prod-EALPRO Dist-LCOA 1952

Man In The Wilderness C 105 MIN
16MM FILM OPTICAL SOUND
Presents the story of a trapper who is mauled by a grizzly bear and left for dead by his companions. Tells how he sets out to recover his furs and to wreak revenge.
Prod-WB Dist-TWYMAN 1968

Man Into Space - The Story Of Rockets And Space Science—A Series
16MM FILM, 3/4 OR 1/2 IN VIDEO I-C A
Documents a sequence in the total space drama placing important scientific developments in proper historical perspective. Deals with future possibilities—interplanetary flights to mars, space probes to the outer planets and the development of the nuclear rocket engine.
Prod-ACI Dist-AIMS 1970

Early Rockets And Dreams Of Space	024 MIN
Exploring The Planets	024 MIN
Pioneers And Modern Rockets	024 MIN
Satellites And Men In Orbit (2nd Ed)	024 MIN
Target - Moon (2nd Ed)	024 MIN

Man Is His Own Worst Enemy C 12 MIN
16MM FILM, 3/4 OR 1/2 IN VIDEO I-C A
Features cartoon character Professor Von Drake discussing the struggle between reason and emotion in man. Emphasizes the need to seek a balance between the two and the desirability of emotional responses when directed toward worthwhile goals.
Prod-DISNEY Dist-WDEMCO 1975

Man Is His Own Worst Enemy (Arabic) C 12 MIN
16MM FILM, 3/4 OR 1/2 IN VIDEO I-C A
Features cartoon character Professor Von Drake discussing the struggle between reason and emotion in man. Emphasizes the need to seek a balance between the two.
Prod-WDEMCO Dist-WDEMCO 1975

Man Is His Own Worst Enemy (French) C 12 MIN
16MM FILM, 3/4 OR 1/2 IN VIDEO I-C A
Features cartoon character Professor Von Drake discussing the struggle between reason and emotion in man. Emphasizes the need to seek a balance between the two.
Prod-WDEMCO Dist-WDEMCO 1975

Man Is His Own Worst Enemy (Spanish) C 12 MIN
16MM FILM, 3/4 OR 1/2 IN VIDEO I-C A
Features cartoon character Professor Von Drake discussing the struggle between reason and emotion in man. Emphasizes the need to seek a balance between the two.
Prod-WDEMCO Dist-WDEMCO 1975

Man Is Responsible To The Earth C 15 MIN
16MM FILM, 3/4 OR 1/2 IN VIDEO
Explains that pesticides have been an invaluable aid for improving quantity and quality in crops, but that they have been used incorrectly and unnecessarily in some instances. Presents insect scouting as a tool for determining the need for insecticide use, including an example of the control and savings realized with pea growing.
LC NO. 82-706235
Prod-USEPA Dist-USNAC 1975

Man Isn't Dying Of Thirst C 22 MIN
16MM FILM OPTICAL SOUND
Explains the effects of LSD on the body, based on scientific research done in Czechoslovakia.
Prod-DANPRO Dist-DANPRO

Man Looks At The Moon X 15 MIN
16MM FILM, 3/4 OR 1/2 IN VIDEO I-H
Presents line drawings, rare photographs taken through telescopes, and dramatic films taken both in mission control rooms and by astronauts to show what is currently known about the moon's geology.
Prod-EBEC Dist-EBEC 1971

Man Makes A Desert X 11 MIN
16MM FILM, 3/4 OR 1/2 IN VIDEO I-H A
Illustrates the changes that can occur when man upsets the delicate balance between the plants and animals that inhabit an area. Explains that through scientific study man is attempting to reclaim the land by reversing the changes he made.
Prod-FA Dist-PHENIX 1964

Man Makes A Desert (Spanish) C 11 MIN
16MM FILM, 3/4 OR 1/2 IN VIDEO I-H A
Illustrates the changes that can occur when man upsets the delicate balance between the plants and animals that inhabit an area. Explains that through scientific study man is attempting to reclaim the land by reversing the changes he made.
Prod-FA Dist-PHENIX 1964

Man Management And Rig Management—A Series
IND
Designed for first-line supervisors in the oil patch but can be used in any industry to help personnel become effective managers. Covers several aspects of management including personnel problems, a description of basic management techniques, training and organization.
Prod-UTEXPE Dist-UTEXPE

How Can Work Be Done More Efficiently?	024 MIN
How Do You Handle Personnel Problems?	014 MIN
How Do You Plan And Organize Work?	021 MIN
How Do You Start Out A New Hand?	020 MIN
How Do You Train Employees?	021 MIN
Introduction	025 MIN
What Is Leadership?	014 MIN
What Is Management?	023 MIN
Where Do You Fit Into The Organization?	020 MIN

Man Must Work C 15 MIN
16MM FILM OPTICAL SOUND
Describes the work therapy program called 'CHIRP' (Community Hospital Industrial Rehabilitation Program) being conducted at the Veterans' Administration Hospital in Brockton, Massachusetts. Shows how patients are assigned to jobs which enable them to participate in one of society's basic economic functions - productive work.
Prod-HOFLAR Dist-AMEDA

Man Named Lincoln, A C 15 MIN
3/4 INCH VIDEO CASSETTE P
Presents the children's story A Man Named Lincoln by Gertrude Norman.
From The Tilson's Book Shop Series.
Prod-WVIZTV Dist-GPITVL 1975

Man Named Lombardi, A C 55 MIN
16MM FILM, 3/4 OR 1/2 IN VIDEO J-C A
Reveals the total commitment of Vince Lombardi both as a player and as a coach. Narrated by George C Scott.
Prod-LUF Dist-LUF 1972

Man Of Aran B 62 MIN
16MM FILM OPTICAL SOUND J-C A
Depicts the meaning of man's struggle against the elements for his existence on the barren island of Aran, off the coast of Western Ireland.
Prod-MGHT Dist-TEXFLM

Man Of Aran, Pt 1 B 35 M
16MM FILM OPTICAL SOUND J-C
Depicts the meaning of man's struggle against the elements f his on the barren island of Aran, off the coast of Western Ir land.
Prod-MGHT Dist-TEXFLM

Man Of Aran, Pt 2 B 40 M
16MM FILM OPTICAL SOUND J-C
Depicts the meaning of man's struggle against the elements f his on the barren island of aran, off the coast of Western Ir land.
Prod-MGHT Dist-TEXFLM

Man Of Consciousness - Dostoevsky, Notes From The Underground C 45 M
2 INCH VIDEOTAPE
See series title for descriptive statement.
From The Humanities Series. Unit III - The Realm Of Idea An Speculation
Prod-WTTWTV Dist-GPITVL

Man Of Faith B 22 MI
16MM FILM OPTICAL SOUND J-C
Dramatizes Mark's account of Christ healing the man who is pa alyzed. Shows how many came to follow Jesus and depic Jesus' great influence through His teachings and ministry.
Prod-CAFM Dist-CAFM

Man Of La Mancha C 121 MI
16MM FILM OPTICAL SOUND
Stars Peter O'Toole in a musical version of Don Quixote.
Prod-UAA Dist-UAE 197

Man Of Leather (Captioned) C 20 MI
16MM FILM, 3/4 OR 1/2 IN VIDEO
Portrays the life of the 'vaquero', the cowboy of the Brazilia Northeast. Portuguese dialog with English subtitles.
Prod-CNEMAG Dist-CNEMAG

Man Of Letters—A Series

Presents Malcolm Muggeridge discussing W Somers Maugham, D H Lawrence, George Orwell and Graham Green Includes the views of people who knew the authors and deal with what their works said about each man.
Prod-SCETV Dist-MDCPB

D H Lawrence	060 MI
George Orwell	060 MI
Graham Greene	060 MI
W Somerset Maugham	060 MI

Man Of Lightning C 29 MI
3/4 INCH VIDEO CASSETTE
Presents a drama of the long-vanished world of the Cherokee i the years before European contact. Explores the demandin morality and complex spirit world of the earliest American Also available in two-inch quad and one-inch videotape.
Prod-GASU Dist-NAMPBC

Man Of The Forest C 25 MI
16MM FILM, 3/4 OR 1/2 IN VIDEO
Features a forest ranger, who along with others, patrols and pro tects the jungle, forest and grassland areas of the Mana Game Sanctuary, inhabited by elephants, tigers, buffalo, bisor rhinoceros and many species of deer.
From The Land Of The Dragon Series.
Prod-NOMDFI Dist-LANDMK

Man Of The House, The C 8 MI
3/4 OR 1/2 INCH VIDEO CASSETTE
Concerns the problems of four-year-old David, who tries to tak on the role of grown-up protector of the house while his fathe is on a business trip. Depicts David promising to protect hi mother against all sorts of monsters. Portrays his reconciliatio with reality as resolving the problems of wrestling with impos sible goals while maintaining self-respect.
Prod-PRIMED Dist-PRIMED

Man Of The House, The C 29 MI
2 INCH VIDEOTAPE
See series title for descriptive statement.
From The Our Street Series.
Prod-MDCPB Dist-PUBTEL

Man Of The People C 25 MI
16MM FILM, 3/4 OR 1/2 IN VIDEO
Features a moderately wealthy farmer and his family in the leas elevated of Bhutan's central valleys who devotes much of hi time taking care of the needs of his villagers.
From The Land Of The Dragon Series.
Prod-NOMDFI Dist-LANDMK

Man Of The Serengeti C 52 MI
16MM FILM, 3/4 OR 1/2 IN VIDEO J-C A
Presents the Masai, warriors and herdsmen who share the Ser engeti Plain in northern Tanzania with African animals. Show how civilization is impinging on their ancient way of life an threatening the animals.
LC NO. 80-706399
Prod-NGS Dist-NGS 1972

Man Of The Trees C 25 MI
16MM FILM, 3/4 OR 1/2 IN VIDEO
Recounts Richard St Barbe-Baker's efforts to bring world attention to the alarming rate at which trees are being felled and the dangers of overgrazing. Shows Baker's 1952 Sahara crossing and ecological survey. Sketches his early life in the forests o Canada, colonial Kenya and Nigeria. Reveals his support of the Chipko people of India and explores his involvement in New Zealand.
Prod-JOU Dist-JOU 1982

an Of Wheat - The Saga Of Glen Miller C 28 MIN
16MM FILM, 3/4 OR 1/2 IN VIDEO
Introduces Glen Miller, a wheat farmer in eastern Washington state who started a small farm in 1943 that has now expanded to include thousands of acres of wheat. Recounts Miller's life and shows how his farm has grown into a business which includes sons and grandsons, who man more than a dozen great harvesting tractors.
LC NO. 82-706489
Prod-MARTSS Dist-PFP 1981

an On A Skateboard C 20 MIN
16MM FILM OPTICAL SOUND J-H T R
A study of the attitudes of a church and a community toward a severely handicapped man, a multiple amputee. Shows him with his family, driving a car, operating a newsstand and being ignored by modern church people in his own community.
LC NO. 70-702458
Prod-JONY Dist-FAMF 1969

an On The Flying Trapeze, The C 8 MIN
16MM FILM OPTICAL SOUND
Presents an animated version of the song The Man On The Flying Trapeze.
Prod-TIMLIF Dist-TIMLIF 1982

an On The Hot Seat - Explosives Safety, Egress Systems C 29 MIN
16MM FILM OPTICAL SOUND
Explains the egress team concept and shows how to maintain and inspect aircraft explosive egress systems. Simulates two fatal accidents caused by careless repair of the egress systems. Stresses the importance of effective and safe maintenance procedures and delineates appropriate guidelines.
LC NO. 80-701138
Prod-USAF Dist-USNAC 1963

an Or Woman For The Job, The C 15 MIN
16MM FILM OPTICAL SOUND
Points out the importance of effective employee recruitment and selection procedures through the experiences of a small print shop owner who learns the hard way that such procedures are necessary. Shows various sources of employees.
LC NO. 74-705084
Prod-USSBA Dist-USNAC

an Or Woman For The Job, The C 15 MIN
3/4 OR 1/2 INCH VIDEO CASSETTE
Dramatizes the importance of effective employee recruitment and selection procedures through the experiences of a small print shop owner.
From The Small Business Administration Series.
Prod-IVCH Dist-IVCH

an Overboard C 23 MIN
16MM FILM OPTICAL SOUND J-C A
Presents the difficulties involved in finding and retrieving a person overboard. Describes preventive measures and rescue procedures and stresses the need for man overboard drills on all vessels.
LC NO. 80-700141
Prod-HISEAS Dist-HISEAS 1980

an Overboard C 30 MIN
1/2 IN VIDEO CASSETTE BETA/VHS
Tells what to do when someone falls overboard, when a line gets caught in the propeller and when a boat capsizes. Introduces sailboat racing.
From The Under Sail Series.
Prod-WGBHTV Dist-MTI

an That Corrupted Hadleyburg, The C 40 MIN
16MM FILM, 3/4 OR 1/2 IN VIDEO J-C A
Reveals how a visitor to a small town concocts a scheme to test the honesty of the town's leading citizens. Based on the short story The Man That Corrupted Hadleyburg by Mark Twain.
From The American Short Story Series.
LC NO. 80-706664
Prod-LEARIF Dist-CORF 1979

an That Corrupted Hadleyburg, The (Spanish) C 40 MIN
16MM FILM, 3/4 OR 1/2 IN VIDEO J-C
Presents an adaptation of Mark Twain's short story The Man That Corrupted Hadleyburg. Tells about a small town that is visited by a stranger who concocts a scheme to test the honesty of the town's leading citizens.
From The American Short Story Series.
Prod-LEARIF Dist-CORF 1980

an That Gravity Forgot, The C 9 MIN
16MM FILM, 3/4 OR 1/2 IN VIDEO P-I
Uses animation to present the extraordinary life of Bram, the only man in the world who is not affected by the force of gravity. Illustrates the zany things that happen when you weigh nothing at all and reveals the important role that gravity plays in our lives.
Prod-CORF Dist-CORF 1979

an The Creator B 13 MIN
16MM FILM OPTICAL SOUND I-C A
Depicts the art and craft of pottery since ancient times. Reveals the many changes effected in recent times in regard to the wheel and firing methods.
Prod-INDIA Dist-NEDINF

an To Ride The River With, A C 15 MIN
16MM FILM, 3/4 OR 1/2 IN VIDEO I
Traces the life and explorations of Juan Bautiste de Anza, who led an expedition in 1774 through the desert to San Francisco.
From The American Scrapbook Series.
Prod-WVIZTV Dist-GPITVL 1977

an Upstairs, The B 6 MIN
16MM FILM OPTICAL SOUND
Shows a meeting between skid row alcoholics and Bible-thumping evangelists.
LC NO. 76-703783
Prod-YORKU Dist-YORKU 1975

Man Who Brought Happiness, The C 5 MIN
16MM FILM OPTICAL SOUND I-C A
Provides a modern restatement of the parable of the talents. Tells the story of a stranger who shares his happiness with villagers who see it only as bread and how a little child leads them to see that only when they use their happiness will they know it.
LC NO. 80-700859
Prod-ALBA Dist-ALBA 1977

Man Who Can't Stop, The C 58 MIN
16MM FILM OPTICAL SOUND H-C
Documents the story of Francis Sutton and his flight to save the Australian coastline from sewage pollution. Shows the struggle for a personal ideal, as an individual against the establishment.
LC NO. 75-701045
Prod-NFBD Dist-AUIS 1974

Man Who Dances - Edward Villella C 54 MIN
16MM FILM, 3/4 OR 1/2 IN VIDEO
Depicts the dancer's exhausting world of classes, rehearsals and performances as revealed through the experiences of one of America's bravura dancers, Edward Villella. Includes scenes from performances of George Balanchine's Tarantella, Glinkiana and the Rubies section of The Jewels.
From The Bell Telephone Hour Series.
Prod-ATAT Dist-DIRECT Prodn-DREW 1968

Man Who Didn't Belong, The C 7 MIN
16MM FILM OPTICAL SOUND IND
Presents an incident illustrating results of a communications breakdown with a new employee. Answers questions of how much orientation is enough, how much initial break-in and training is enough and where to find the explanations of a high rate of turnover of employees.
From The Human Side Of Supervision Series.
LC NO. 73-701930
Prod-VOAERO Dist-VOAERO 1972

Man Who Digs For Fish, The C 13 MIN
16MM FILM, 3/4 OR 1/2 IN VIDEO J-C A
Reveals the conservation methods of Frank Jenkinson, who digs up newly-hatched salmon in the Jarvis Inlet to protect them from dying before reaching maturity. Shows how his methods have increased the salmon population from 500 to 25,000.
Prod-NFBC Dist-NFBC 1979

Man Who Had No Dream, The C 7 MIN
16MM FILM, 3/4 OR 1/2 IN VIDEO K-I
Tells an animated story about wealthy Mr Oliver who couldn't sleep or dream until he found an injured bird and repaired its wing. Emphasizes the need to work for others and the importance of being needed. Illustrates that money alone cannot buy happiness and that satisfaction comes from setting goals and working to achieve them. Based on the book The Man Who Had No Dream by Adelaide Holl.
LC NO. 81-707558
Prod-BOSUST Dist-CF 1981

Man Who Had To Sing, The C 10 MIN
16MM FILM OPTICAL SOUND J-C A
A story about the life of a man who was pushed, shoved, kicked and bounced around because, during all of his life, he expressed himself in a fashion that did not harmonize with those around him.
LC NO. 72-700418
Prod-ZAGREB Dist-MMA 1971

Man Who Kept House, The C 15 MIN
3/4 INCH VIDEO CASSETTE K-P
See series title for descriptive statement.
From The Storytime Series.
Prod-WCETTV Dist-GPITVL 1976

Man Who Knew How To Fly, The C 10 MIN
16MM FILM, 3/4 OR 1/2 IN VIDEO I-C A
Tells of a man who discovers that he has the power to fly and shows how earthbound scholars demand that he make so many changes in his takeoff and landing procedures that he finds that he no longer can fly.
Prod-KRATKY Dist-PHENIX 1982

Man Who Knew Too Much, The B 77 MIN
16MM FILM OPTICAL SOUND
Tells how a vacationing British family learns of an assassination plot, and shows what happens when the teenage daughter is kidnapped. Directed by Alfred Hitchcock.
Prod-UNKNWN Dist-KITPAR 1934

Man Who Left His Will On Film, The (Japanese) B 93 MIN
16MM FILM OPTICAL SOUND
Traces the life of a filmmaker who commits suicide by studying the meaning of the last footage he shot. Presents numerous scenes of Japanese cities and countryside in an effort to find out more about the young man.
Prod-NYFLMS Dist-NYFLMS 1970

Man Who Loved Bears, The C 50 MIN
16MM FILM, 3/4 OR 1/2 IN VIDEO
Presents the true story of a man and a bear which was thought to be extinct in the state.
Prod-STOUFP Dist-STOUFP

Man Who Loved Machines, The C 9 MIN
16MM FILM, 3/4 OR 1/2 IN VIDEO I-C A
Introduces the concepts of energy forms and energy conservation using the animated story of a man who loves machines. Looks at the law of entropy which states that when energy is converted to power, a certain amount is lost to heat.
Prod-NFBC Dist-BULFRG Prodn-GOLDS 1984

Man Who Mugged God, The C 28 MIN
16MM FILM, 3/4 OR 1/2 IN VIDEO H-C A
Shows what happens when a desperate drug addict mugs a blind old beggar who turns out to be God. Stars Warren Oates and Harold Gould.
From The Insight Series.
Prod-PAULST Dist-PAULST

Man Who Mugged God, The C 28 MIN
16MM FILM, 3/4 OR 1/2 IN VIDEO J A
Tells the story of a mugger who learns about God's love from a 'beggar.'
Prod-SUTHRB Dist-SUTHRB

Man Who Needed Nobody, The C 30 MIN
3/4 OR 1/2 INCH VIDEO CASSETTE
Illustrates the meaning of comparative advantage as a crucial element in trading. Looks at international trade.
From The Money Puzzle - The World Of Macroeconomics Series. Module 14
Prod-MDCC Dist-MDCC

Man Who Needs No Introduction, A C 5 MIN
16MM FILM, 3/4 OR 1/2 IN VIDEO H-C A
Shows proper forms of guest introduction and describes how to give a speech of thanks.
From The Communicating From The Lectern Series.
Prod-METAIV Dist-AIMS 1976

Man Who Read Books, The C 17 MIN
16MM FILM OPTICAL SOUND
Presents a speculative fantasy about a meek librarian who loves and understands books and is fighting a new process that will eliminate all printed matter.
LC NO. 79-701293
Prod-USC Dist-USC 1979

Man Who Shot The Pope, The C 52 MIN
3/4 OR 1/2 INCH VIDEO CASSETTE H-C A
Discusses the findings of a nine-month investigation of the shooting of Pope John Paul II by terrorist Mehmet Ali Agca. Traces Agca's life from his boyhood in Turkey to the present, building a case for the theory that he was employed by the Soviet Union to slay the pope.
LC NO. 83-706305
Prod-NBCNEW Dist-FI 1982

Man Who Talks To Water, The C 29 MIN
16MM FILM OPTICAL SOUND
Discusses the importance of long-range water planning. Surveys man's efforts to put water to his uses and shows major water-moving projects in the Western United States.
LC NO. 78-701560
Prod-AMERON Dist-MTP Prodn-FPA 1978

Man Who Tried To Kill The Pope, The C 16 MIN
3/4 OR 1/2 INCH VIDEO CASSETTE H-C A
Examines the life Of Mehmet Ali Agca, the man who attempted to assasinate Pope John Paul II in St Peter's Square in Rome on May 13, 1981. Looks at the political atmosphere in Turkey, which it is believed gives rise to terrorists and their activities.
Prod-JOU Dist-JOU

Man Who Wanted To Fly, The - A Japanese Tale C 11 MIN
16MM FILM, 3/4 OR 1/2 IN VIDEO P
Presents a story about a man who seemed to learn how to fly, but who had good reason to keep the secret to himself.
Prod-CORF Dist-CORF 1969

Man Who Would Be King, The C 129 MIN
16MM FILM OPTICAL SOUND H-C
Presents the adventures of two men in British-controlled India in the 19th century. Stars Sean Connery and Michael Caine. Based on the work by Rudyard Kipling.
Prod-CPC Dist-CINEWO 1975

Man With A Movie Camera, A B 69 MIN
3/4 OR 1/2 INCH VIDEO CASSETTE
Offers a classic experimental Russian film directed by Dziga Vertov.
Prod-IHF Dist-IHF

Man With A Problem B 17 MIN
16MM FILM OPTICAL SOUND C T
Shows the admission of an alcoholic to a clinic, Describes the etiology, follows the diagnosis and treatment of the case and discusses the team approach by psychiatrists and psychologists. Demonstrates the treatment of alcoholism by aversion and relaxation techniques and illustrates the learning of new habit patterns based on a system of operant conditioning.
LC NO. 72-700825
Prod-UADEL Dist-PSUPCR 1967

Man With A Suitcase B 30 MIN
16MM FILM OPTICAL SOUND
Accounts the experiences of a West German citizen who smuggled his fiancee out of East Germany by carrying her through the border check-station in a suitcase. Includes commercials from the original telecast.
LC NO. FI67-113
Prod-GE Dist-WB Prodn-WB 1962

Man With Not Time For Beauty C 30 MIN
3/4 OR 1/2 INCH VIDEO CASSETTE C
See series title for descriptive statement.
From The Art Of Being Human Series. Module 1
Prod-MDCC Dist-MDCC

Man With The Torque Wrench, The B 10 MIN
16MM FILM - 3/4 IN VIDEO
Demonstrates the proper use of torquing equipment, emphasizing the importance of torquing and the serious consequences that can arise from improper torquing. Shows the different

types of torque wrenches used by the U S Air Force. Issued in 1958 as a motion picture.
LC NO. 80-706612
Prod-USAF Dist-USNAC 1980

Man Without A Country, The B 25 MIN
16MM FILM, 3/4 OR 1/2 IN VIDEO I-H
Based on the book The Man Without A Country by Edward Everett Hale. Portrays a judge, swearing in new American citizens, as he relates the story of an American naval officer who rejected and damned his country in a burst of anger.
Prod-CROSBY Dist-MGHT 1953

Man Writes To A Part Of Himself, A C 58 MIN
3/4 OR 1/2 INCH VIDEO CASSETTE J-C A
Portrays poet Robert Bly. Shows him at his northern Minnesota farm. Recounts his early struggles in New York City.
Prod-UCV Dist-UCV

Man-Flying-Mountain-Kite C 11 MIN
16MM FILM OPTICAL SOUND
Presents a visual essay of mountain hang gliders in Montana and Idaho, filmed from a balloon, helicopter and glider.
LC NO. 76-700381
Prod-BITROT Dist-BITROT 1975

Man-Made Diamond C 11 MIN
16MM FILM OPTICAL SOUND J-C
Describes the study, research and technology involved in the process of producing industrial diamonds. Provides a survey of the earth's elements and how they vary in abundance. Follows the problem of how to reproduce and accelerate nature's process of changing carbon into diamonds.
LC NO. 79-707625
Prod-GE Dist-GE 1968

Man-Made Diamond C 12 MIN
16MM FILM OPTICAL SOUND
Demonstrates the process of producing industrial diamonds. Shows how to accelerate nature's process of changing carbon into diamonds.
Prod-GE Dist-GE

Man-Made Land - Mizushima Coastal Industrial Area C 27 MIN
16MM FILM OPTICAL SOUND
Explains that Mizushima is a typical country town near the sea in Japan. Shows what happens when next to an old market town a whole new industrial complex rises. Points out that here we have things Japanese, things Western, the traditional and the new all fused into a new kind of place to live, modernized by industrial transformation.
Prod-KAJIMA Dist-UNIJAP 1965

Man-Made Macromolecules - Polymers C 25 MIN
3/4 OR 1/2 INCH VIDEO CASSETTE H-C
Describes the discovery and laboratory polymerization of three man-made plastics - polyethylene, propylene and nylon 6-6. Shows the industrial manufacture of two of them - polyethlene and nylon.
Prod-BBCTV Dist-OPENU 1982

Man-Sized Job C 28 MIN
16MM FILM OPTICAL SOUND
Deals with the recruitment of newspaper carrier boys. Shows how newspaper carrier boys form a vital link between the newspaper and its readers, and tells the importance of providing youngsters with a challenging job that rewards them for their personal effort, and gives them a sense of responsibility and accomplishment.
LC NO. 72-702405
Prod-NYT Dist-AVON 1972

Man, A B 5 MIN
16MM FILM OPTICAL SOUND H-C A
Shows a modern interpretation of Psalm 138 using a dramatization about a fool who flees an angry crowd and takes refuge in a church.
From The Song Of The Ages Series.
LC NO. 75-702139
Prod-FAMLYT Dist-FAMLYT 1964

Man, Animal, Climate And Earth B 30 MIN
16MM FILM OPTICAL SOUND J-C A
Discusses discovery of early human camp sites in southwestern Nebraska. Describes what is known about the climate, the behavior of streams and the animals and men.
From The Great Plains Trilogy, 2 Series. Nomad And Indians - Early Man On The Plains
Prod-UNEBR Dist-UNEBR 1954

Man, Monsters And Mysteries C 25 MIN
16MM FILM, 3/4 OR 1/2 IN VIDEO I-H
Tells the story of famous 'monster' Nessie of Loch Ness from 1933 to the present. Reveals the existence of ancient legends and writings concerning the Scottish monster.
Prod-DISNEY Dist-WDEMCO 1973

Man, The Esthetic Being C 60 MIN
3/4 OR 1/2 INCH VIDEO CASSETTE H-C A
Discusses the esthetic aspects of man.
From The Art Of Being Human Series.
Prod-FI Dist-FI 1978

Man, The Manager C 15 MIN
2 INCH VIDEOTAPE J-H
Points out that one of the fastest growing occupational fields in the country is business management.
From The Work Is For Real Series.
Prod-STETVC Dist-GPITVL

Man, The Snake And The Fox, The C 12 MIN
16MM FILM, 3/4 OR 1/2 IN VIDEO P-I
Relates the Indian story of a man who is saved from a snake by a fox. Shows that although the grateful man promises to share his food with the fox whenever the animal is hungry, when the fox does partake of the food the man kills him.
LC NO. 81-706910
Prod-NFBC Dist-MOKIN 1980

Man, The Symbol Maker C 25 MIN
16MM FILM OPTICAL SOUND J-C A
Discusses nonverbal human communication and examines the difference between animal signals and symbols. Shows how a chimpanzee was taught to symbolize and looks at the possible dangers of the symbolic process.
From The Science Of Life Series.
LC NO. 81-700848
Prod-CRIPSE Dist-WARDS 1981

Man, Tools And The Necessary Nuisance C 33 MIN
16MM FILM OPTICAL SOUND
Traces the long and relentless search of man, his discovery of tools, basic machines, machine tools and the intricate advancements of technology. Spans the distance from primitive paleolithic times to the explorations of Apollo, the first lunar landing and the age of Skylab. Delves into the beginnings, in the early 1800's, of the search for and refinement of various compounds that have led to the extremely sophisticated cutting fluids used in today's high speed metalworking operations. Narrated by Lowell Thomas.
Prod-MASTER Dist-MASTER

Man's A Man For All That, A C 14 MIN
16MM FILM OPTICAL SOUND
Tells a story set in a small diner during World War II in which a recently discharged soldier brings unexpected rivalry between four women.
Prod-USC Dist-USC

Man's Basic Need - Natural Resources X 11 MIN
16MM FILM, 3/4 OR 1/2 IN VIDEO P-I
Shows the use and misuse of natural resources, as demonstrated in a study of two towns in the desert region of New Mexico—one a deserted mining town, and the other a rich farming community, which has prospered through the use of dams and irrigation.
From The Social Studies Series.
Prod-EBEC Dist-EBEC 1969

Man's Best Friend C 15 MIN
3/4 OR 1/2 INCH VIDEO CASSETTE K-P
Discusses pets and caring for pets.
From The Pass It On Series.
Prod-WKNOTV Dist-GPITVL 1983

Man's Best Friends C 58 MIN
1/2 IN VIDEO CASSETTE BETA/VHS
Discusses the issue of the use of animals for laboratory experiments in U S laboratories, hospitals, and medical schools. Describes the emerging animal movement which has challenged the right of man to 'oppress' other species, equating 'specieism' to racism, while scientists claim that laboratory animals are well cared for.
From The Frontline Series.
Prod-DOCCON Dist-PBS

Man's Best Friends C 60 MIN
16MM FILM, 3/4 OR 1/2 IN VIDEO A
Examines the needs of animals used in research in relation to the needs of science. Discusses the views of animal lovers, who maintain that far too many animals are consumed in medical research, and such research is not only cruel but mostly unnecessary. Notes that the issue has not been realistically addressed by all parties but does require considered study, and soon.
Prod-PACSFM Dist-CNEMAG 1985

Man's Effect On The Environment C 14 MIN
16MM FILM, 3/4 OR 1/2 IN VIDEO J-H
Shows some of the effects of man's exploitation of natural resources from the time of the earliest colonists. Raises questions as to the quality of life such environmental changes might produce.
Prod-BFA Dist-PHENIX Prodn-CHANGW 1970

Man's Experience Of The World C 25 MIN
16MM FILM OPTICAL SOUND
Presents interviews with a business executive and with a young man involved in the organization of a rural commune near York, England. Illustrates their career timetables and their notions of advancement and improvement, occupational consciousness, privacy, leisure and religion.
From The Social Psychology Series.
LC NO. 78-700329
Prod-OPENU Dist-OPENU 1977

Man's Hand, A B 21 MIN
16MM FILM OPTICAL SOUND H-C A
Shows how a finger crippled in an accident is examined and treated in an operation. Discusses the anatomy and functioning of the hand.
From The Doctors At Work Series.
LC NO. FIA65-1351
Prod-CMA Dist-LAWREN Prodn-LAWREN 1962

Man's Hands, A C 5 MIN
16MM FILM OPTICAL SOUND I A
Dramatizes man's favorite appendage squeezing, poking, playing, fixing and touching.
LC NO. 72-711722
Prod-PROKP Dist-VIEWFI 1970

Man's Impact On The Environment C 20 MIN
16MM FILM OPTICAL SOUND J-C A
Discusses ecological and social consequences of a fuel-intensive economy for agriculture, population, urbanization, production and marketing, and resources.
From The Science Of Life Series.
LC NO. 81-700849
Prod-CRIPSE Dist-WARDS 198

Man's Impact On The Environment C 23 MI
16MM FILM OPTICAL SOUND H-
Reveals how man has caused dangerous changes in his enviror ment. Shows that man is the single most important factor a fecting the 'BALANCE OF NATURE.' Explains the tragic cor sequences of man's almost complete encroachment upon h environment.
Prod-MLA Dist-MLA

Man's Inhumanity C 10 MI
16MM FILM, 3/4 OR 1/2 IN VIDEO J-
Explores the qualities of people who lived humanely through th horrors of concentration camps and other tortures of war.
From The Matter Of Fact Series.
LC NO. 74-703199
Prod-NITC Dist-AITECH Prodn-WETATV 197

Man's Interdependence With Other Organisms C 14 MI
3/4 OR 1/2 INCH VIDEO CASSETTE
See series title for descriptive statement.
From The Discovering Series. Unit 8 - Ecology
Prod-WDCNTV Dist-AITECH 197

Man's Material Welfare C 30 MI
3/4 OR 1/2 INCH VIDEO CASSETTE
Features president of Amway Corporation addressing Do Chemical executives on the fundamentals of the free ente prise economic system as contrasted to socialistic systems.
From The Small Business Administration Series.
Prod-IVCH Dist-IVCH

Man's Place In The Universe C 30 MI
3/4 OR 1/2 INCH VIDEO CASSETTE H-C
Presents George Abell, author and astronomy professor, tracin the origin of the solar system through photographic slides. Fo cuses on the need for continuing space exploration, the pros pects for life in outer space and the ethical issue involved i possible encounters with other human beings.
From The Ethics In America Series.
Prod-AMHUMA Dist-AMHUMA

Man's Place, A C 25 MI
16MM FILM, 3/4 OR 1/2 IN VIDEO J-C
Presents four men who are pursuing nontraditional male roles and their families, who tell how the men enjoy roles as home maker, worker in a traditionally female job, parenting, and shar ing family responsibilities.
LC NO. 81-706004
Prod-CUNY Dist-CUNY Prodn-TVGDAP 197

Man's Reach Should Exceed His Grasp C 30 MI
3/4 OR 1/2 INCH VIDEO CASSETTE
Presents the story of man's efforts to escape the surface of th earth. Narration by Burgess Meredith.
From The Reaching For The Stars, And Life Beyond Earth Series.
Prod-IVCH Dist-IVCH

Man's Reach Should Exceed His Grasp, A C 24 MI
16MM FILM, 3/4 OR 1/2 IN VIDEO
Presents the history of flight and man's reach for a new freedom through aviation and the exploration of space, recounting de velopments from the Wright Brothers' flight to the landing o the Moon and plans for future missions to other planets. Em phasizes the creative role of research and cites statements by scientists, writers, poets and philosophers which documen man's search for knowledge. Narrated by Burgess Meredith.
LC NO. 77-706031
Prod-NASA Dist-USNAC 1972

Man's Reach, A B 33 MIN
16MM FILM OPTICAL SOUND J-C
Describes the functions and responsibilities of a school superintendent and points up his relationship to the school system. Reveals the demanding nature of the position.
LC NO. FIA65-835
Prod-OSUMPD Dist-OSUMPD 1964

Man's Search For Identity C
3/4 OR 1/2 INCH VIDEO CASSETTE
Explains that the struggle for identity is life-long and that it may be shaped publicly or privately. Describes the awakening of self using passages from The Catcher In The Rye, The Red Badge Of Courage, The Lord Of The Flies, The Diary Of Anne Frank, Black Boy and The Invisible Man.
Prod-CHUMAN Dist-GA

Man's Shortcomings C 13 MIN
16MM FILM, 3/4 OR 1/2 IN VIDEO
Shows how man's personality quirks may endanger his and other workers' safety. Gives suggestions to avoid or change this mental attitude and prevent these nonsensical actions.
From The Foremanship Training Series.
LC NO. 82-706278
Prod-USBM Dist-USNAC 1969

Man's Thumb On Nature's Balance C 51 MIN
16MM FILM OPTICAL SOUND J-C A
Explains that animals live in nature in a relationship of predator and prey keeping their numbers in balance until man gets involved in the equation. Shows that man brings about profound changes in the total environment that often lead the other animals to the danger of extinction. Examines the weeding out of deer herds, the regulation of bird species and the selective 'HARVESTING' of the seal crop.
Prod-NBCEE Dist-NBC 1971

Man's Thumb On Nature's Balance B 51 MIN
16MM FILM OPTICAL SOUND
Examines whether man has the right to regulate or protect or

'FARM' his fellow creatures, while showing scenes of weeding out of deer herds, regulation of bird species, and harvesting of seal crops.
LC NO. 72-700080
Prod-NBCTV Dist-NBC 1971

Man's Thumb On Nature's Balance, Pt 1 C 23 MIN
16MM FILM OPTICAL SOUND J-C A
Explains that animals live in nature in a relationship of predator and prey keeping their numbers in balance until man gets involved in the equation. Shows that man brings about profound changes in the total environment that often lead the other animals to the danger of extinction. Examines the weeding out of deer herds, the regulation of bird species and the selective 'HARVESTING' of the seal crop.
Prod-NBCEE Dist-NBC 1971

Man's Thumb On Nature's Balance, Pt 2 C 28 MIN
16MM FILM OPTICAL SOUND J-C A
Explains that animals live in nature in a relationship of predator and prey keeping their numbers in balance until man gets involved in the equation. Shows that man brings about profound changes in the total environment that often lead the other animals to the danger of extinction. Examines the weeding out of deer herds, the regulation of bird species and the selective 'HARVESTING' of the seal crop.
Prod-NBCEE Dist-NBC 1971

Manabu Mabe Paints A Picture C 13 MIN
16MM FILM, 3/4 OR 1/2 IN VIDEO J-C A
Presents Japanese-Brazilian artist Mabe creating an abstract painting.
LC NO. 82-707008
Prod-MOMALA Dist-MOMALA

Manage Your Career - The U S Army Civilian Career Management Program B 30 MIN
16MM FILM OPTICAL SOUND
Explains the objectives, principles and benefits of the U S Army Civilian Career Management Program, which is designed to provide formalized education or training, self-development activities and appropriate experience.
Prod-USA Dist-USNAC

Manage Your Stress C 52 MIN
16MM FILM, 3/4 OR 1/2 IN VIDEO C A
Presents a program of stress management.
LC NO. 80-707245
Prod-MGHT Dist-CRMP 1980

Managed Forest, The C 26 MIN
16MM FILM OPTICAL SOUND
Presents the problems of multiple land use and vanishing wildlife habitat.
LC NO. 77-702956
Prod-MEPHTS Dist-MEPHTS 1976

Management C 30 MIN
3/4 INCH VIDEO CASSETTE
See series title for descriptive statement.
From The It's Everybody's Business Series. Unit 4, Managing A Business
Prod-DALCCD Dist-DALCCD

Management C 45 MIN
3/4 OR 1/2 INCH VIDEO CASSETTE
Explores the reasons that executives and managers must get involved in decisions concerning the communications networks that are springing up in corporations.
From The Corporate Network Strategy Series.
Prod-DELTAK Dist-DELTAK

Management - A Joint Venture C 8 MIN
3/4 OR 1/2 INCH VIDEO CASSETTE
Contains eight half-hour videotapes on business management.
Prod-TELSTR Dist-TELSTR

Management And Business Games C 12 MIN
3/4 OR 1/2 INCH VIDEO CASSETTE
Shows how to use complex and simple management games, group and individual games. Points out the purpose, definition and uses of games and cautions of dangers in overusing.
From The Dynamic Classroom Series.
Prod-RESEM Dist-RESEM

Management And Motivation, Version I - Management And Motivation, Pt 1 C
3/4 OR 1/2 INCH VIDEO CASSETTE
Offers a basic framework for organizing thoughts and perceptions about people and how to develop one's self-perception in management.
Prod-AMA Dist-AMA

Management And Motivation, Version I - Management And Motivation, Pt 2 C
3/4 OR 1/2 INCH VIDEO CASSETTE
Begins a presentation on understanding what it is that different types of personalities want in a job and what they need in a job if they are to be successful.
Prod-AMA Dist-AMA

Management And Motivation, Version I - Management And Motivation, Pt 4 C
3/4 OR 1/2 INCH VIDEO CASSETTE
Applies the theory and the system for specific techniques for applying knowledge about personal behavior styles.
Prod-AMA Dist-AMA

Management And Motivation, Version I - Management And Motivation, Pt 5 C
3/4 OR 1/2 INCH VIDEO CASSETTE
Demonstrates how behavioral styles affect day-to-day business situations. Discusses what can go wrong and how to prevent it.
Prod-AMA Dist-AMA

Management And Motivation, Version II - Personality Styles C
3/4 OR 1/2 INCH VIDEO CASSETTE
Offers a five-part series on improving sales performances with effective management of different personality styles.
Prod-AMA Dist-AMA

Management And Motivaton, Version I - Management And Motivation, Pt 3 C
3/4 OR 1/2 INCH VIDEO CASSETTE
Concludes a presentation on understanding what it is that different types of personalities want in a job and what they need in a job if they are to be successful.
Prod-AMA Dist-AMA

Management And Ownerships Options For Independent Hospitals—A Series

Explores the alternative management options available to independent hospitals and the advantages and disadvantages of each arrangement in two video tapes.
Prod-AHOA Dist-AHOA

Management And Treatment Of The Violent Patient—A Series

Presents a series on management and treatment of the violent patient by John R Lion, MD, director of the Clinical Research Program for Violent Behavior and professor of psychiatry at the University of Maryland School of Medicine.
Prod-HEMUL Dist-HEMUL

Assaultive Patient, The	030 MIN
Calming And Medicating Violent Patients In	030 MIN
Differentiating Personality, Psychodynamic	030 MIN
Overview Of Management And Treatment Issues	030 MIN
Prediction Of Dangerousness	030 MIN
Psychotherapy And Medication	030 MIN
Restraints, Seclusion And A Demonstration Of	030 MIN
Victims - Their Circumstances, Management And	030 MIN

Management Basics In Action—A Series

Shows how to handle management problems. Dramatizes responses to particular situations.
Prod-MTI Dist-MTI

Conducting A Performance Appraisal	013 MIN
Conducting A Salary Discussion	010 MIN
Conducting A Termination	008 MIN
Defining The Job	009 MIN
Discussing Career Goals	011 MIN
Giving Positive Feedback	007 MIN
Handling Personal Problems	011 MIN
Improving Employee Performance	011 MIN
Taking Disciplinary Action	010 MIN

Management By Example C 24 MIN
16MM FILM - 3/4 IN VIDEO PRO
Explains that a tough-minded manager is not solely a disciplinarian, but one whose primary drive is to build himself, his subordinates and his organization.
From The Tough-Minded Management Series.
Prod-BNA Dist-BNA 1969

Management By Motivation C 12 MIN
3/4 OR 1/2 INCH VIDEO CASSETTE
Offers a comprehensive list of ways to motivate workers on almost any job and an introduction to job enrichment.
From The Improving Managerial Skills Series.
Prod-RESEM Dist-RESEM

Management By Objectives C 8 MIN
16MM FILM OPTICAL SOUND J-C A
Examines, through the use of animation, the process of management by objectives. Defines four basic stages that can be used as guidelines in achieving better management and personal fulfillment.
LC NO. 76-704019
Prod-NILCOM Dist-BESTF 1973

Management By Objectives C 30 MIN
16MM FILM - 3/4 IN VIDEO PRO
Defines the basic philosophy of 'management by objectives' and demonstrates how clearly-defined company objectives, once established, are integrated with individual manager development programs.
From The Management By Objectives Series.
Prod-BNA Dist-BNA 1969

Management By Objectives - An Overview C 9 MIN
3/4 OR 1/2 INCH VIDEO CASSETTE
Introduces management by objectives (MBO) by identifying its component parts and by briefly describing the process of the MBO system. Discusses the relationship of MBO to the overall management process and its dependency upon participative management.
From The Management By Objectives Series. Module 1
Prod-RESEM Dist-RESEM

Management By Objectives—A Series
IND
Trains individuals in mbo concepts and assists management in actually installing an MBO program.
LC NO. 70-703325
Prod-EDSD Dist-EDSD

Applying Management By Objectives	29 MIN
Establishing Performance Criteria	29 MIN
Innovation By Objectives	29 MIN
Job Responsibilities And Measurement	29 MIN
Organizational Goal-Planning	29 MIN
Problem Solving By Objectives	29 MIN

Management By Objectives—A Series
16MM FILM - 3/4 IN VIDEO PRO
Prod-BNA Dist-BNA 1969

Colt - A Case History	025 MIN
Defining The Manager's Job	021 MIN
Focus The Future	027 MIN
Management By Objectives	030 MIN
Management Training	024 MIN
Performance And Potential Review	021 MIN

Management By Objectives—A Series
16MM FILM, 3/4 OR 1/2 IN VIDEO A
Presents animated vignettes which delineate various aspects of management by objectives.
Prod-BOSUST Dist-CRMP 1981

MBO I - What Is MBO	013 MIN
MBO II - Developing Objectives	014 MIN
MBO III - Performance Appraisal	014 MIN

Management By Objectives—A Series

Instructs all levels of management in any organization that is implementing or seeking to improve a management by objectives program.
Prod-RESEM Dist-RESEM

Goal Setting	010 MIN
Installing Management By Objectives	010 MIN
Management By Objectives - An Overview	009 MIN

Management By Participation C 30 MIN
16MM FILM - 3/4 IN VIDEO PRO
Discusses organizational climate, leadership style and participation as a total systems approach.
From The Effective Organization Series.
Prod-BNA Dist-BNA 1971

Management By Responsibility—A Series

Focuses on responsibility as the ultimate factor for success in management and personal endeavors, and teaches the concept that each individual is 100 percent responsible for his or her actions and reactions. Includes a facilitator's guide, a participant's manual and copies of Management By Responsibility (MBR).
Prod-TRAINS Dist-DELTAK

Achievement Level, The	060 MIN
Conformist Level (Section A), The	048 MIN
Conformist Level (Section B), The	020 MIN
Implementation Of MBR Process - Feedback	028 MIN
Implementation Of MBR Process - Feedback	030 MIN
Implementation Of MBR Process - Goal Setting	038 MIN
Implementation Of MBR Process - Phase I -	035 MIN
Implementation Of MBR Process - Phase I -	025 MIN
Implementation Of MBR Process - Phase II -	054 MIN
Introduction To Responsible Management	040 MIN
Introduction To Responsible Management	028 MIN
Process Of Growth (Section A), The	028 MIN
Process Of Growth (Section B), The	028 MIN
Responsible Level, The	040 MIN
Self-Protective Level (Section A), The	028 MIN
Self-Protective Level (Section B), The	040 MIN
Unconscious Level (Section A), The	025 MIN
Unconscious Level (Section B), The	033 MIN

Management Challenges C 20 MIN
3/4 OR 1/2 INCH VIDEO CASSETTE
See series title for descriptive statement.
From The Effective Manager Series.
Prod-DELTAK Dist-DELTAK

Management Change - The People Issues C 45 MIN
3/4 OR 1/2 INCH VIDEO CASSETTE
Discusses the organizational impacts of office automation, the importance of preparing the organization for change and strategies for doing that.
From The Management Strategies For Office Automation Series.
Prod-DELTAK Dist-DELTAK

Management Control Of System Schedule And Cost C 55 MIN
3/4 OR 1/2 INCH VIDEO CASSETTE
Presents program management techniques. Illustrates the application of PERT for controlling schedule.
From The Systems Engineering And Systems Management Series.
Prod-MIOT Dist-MIOT

Management Controls C 11 MIN
16MM FILM OPTICAL SOUND
Outlines how to get the most useful help out of accountancy. Summarizes the essential ingredients of the proper uses of accounting.
From The Running Your Own Business Series.
Prod-EFD Dist-EFD

Management Development—A Series

Deals with management development.
Prod-UCEMC Dist-UCEMC

Constructive Use Of The Emotions	022 MIN
Effective Leadership	032 MIN
Emotional Styles In Human Behavior	024 MIN
Group Leadership - The History Of The Group	028 MIN
Human Considerations In Management	029 MIN
Human Skills Of Management	029 MIN
Importance Of Relationships In Organizational	016 MIN
Leadership And Small Work-Group Dynamics	027 MIN
Managerial Grid, The	035 MIN

Organizational Development 030 MIN
Problem Solving In Groups 025 MIN
Some Personal Learnings About Interpersonal 033 MIN
Theory Of Management Development 028 MIN
War On Bureaucracy - A New Way Of Looking At 030 MIN
Ways Of Dealing With Conflict In Organizations 027 MIN

Management Diagnostic—A Series

Assesses personal management skills, organizational effectiveness, and personal style of interaction. Includes a student text and a set of diskettes.
Prod-THGHT Dist-DELTAK

Assessing Personal Management Skills
Evaluating Organizational Effectiveness
Understanding Personal Interaction Styles

Management Emergency Medical Priorities C 14 MIN
3/4 OR 1/2 INCH VIDEO CASSETTE IND
Teaches importance and procedures for setting priorities of treatment of an individual who has suffered multiple injuries.
From The Emergency Medical Training Series. Lesson 22
Prod-LEIKID Dist-LEIKID

Management Faces The Waves Of Change C 30 MIN
3/4 OR 1/2 INCH VIDEO CASSETTE
See series title for descriptive statement.
From The Third Wave Series.
Prod-TRIWVE Dist-DELTAK

Management For Engineers—A Series

Presents a series on management for engineers, based on experience from a decade of teaching hundreds of engineers at Fortune 500 companies to manage. Provides knowledge and techniques necessary for becoming a more effective manager.
Prod-UKY Dist-SME

Control Techniques For The Engineer Manager 030 MIN
Creating An Effective Team 030 MIN
Decision Making Techniques 030 MIN
Effective Communication 030 MIN
Making Appraisals Effective 030 MIN
Motivational Techniques For Engineers 030 MIN
Organizing Technical Activities 030 MIN
Participative Management 030 MIN
Planning Technical Activities 030 MIN
Role Of The Engineer Manager 030 MIN
Selecting And Managing Projects 030 MIN
Time Management 030 MIN

Management For The '90s - Quality Circles—A Series

Deals with productivity, a responsibility of every employee in an organization from the chief executive officer to the janitor. Includes a participant's resource book.
Prod-TELSTR Dist-DELTAK

How Do You Start 030 MIN
Should We 030 MIN
What Are They 030 MIN

Management Implications Of SQL/DS C 30 MIN
3/4 OR 1/2 INCH VIDEO CASSETTE
Addresses some of the basic concerns about relational data base and SQL/DS. Focuses on such topics as conversion, implementation and performance associated with SQL/DS.
From The SQL/DS And Relational Data Base Systems Series.
Prod-DELTAK Dist-DELTAK

Management Improvement - It's Your Business C 16 MIN
16MM FILM OPTICAL SOUND
Shows through the use of animation that good management means effective use of men, money, materials and facilities.
LC NO. FIE61-93
Prod-USN Dist-USNAC 1959

Management Issues C 11 MIN
16MM FILM, 3/4 OR 1/2 IN VIDEO
Contrasts indifferent and concerned attitudes displayed by a nursing home admissions officer toward a prospective patient. Shows why nursing home menus should be varied and nutritious. Examines the dubious use of sedatives to maintain a quiet atmosphere.
From The It Can't Be Home Series.
Prod-USDHEW Dist-USDHEW

Management Issues C 28 MIN
3/4 INCH VIDEO CASSETTE
Pulls together various issues and topics which should be considered by health care professionals when working with clients.
From The Psychotropic Drugs And The Health Care Professional Series.
Prod-UWASHP Dist-UWASHP

Management Of Abnormal Tone In Head Trauma Patients - Strategies For Occupational... C 25 MIN
3/4 INCH VIDEO CASSETTE PRO
Complete title is Management Of Abnormal Tone In Head Trauma Patients - Strategies For Occupational Therapists. Demonstrates three major reflex patterns in the lower level head trauma patient and techniques used to facilitate more normal positions for functions. Identifies high level balance and postural problems which inhibit function in the ambulatory patient with head trauma. Describes improved postural adaptations.
Prod-RICHGO Dist-RICHGO

Management Of Acute Renal Failure, The C 12 MIN
3/4 OR 1/2 INCH VIDEO CASSETTE PRO
Provides a succinct analysis of management of fluid and electrolyte problems in acute renal failure.
Prod-UMICHM Dist-UMICHM 1978

Management Of Acute Upper Gastrointestinal Bleeding C 30 MIN
3/4 OR 1/2 INCH VIDEO CASSETTE
Describes dignostic and therapeutic approach for management of patients bleeding from the upper gastrointestinal tract.
Prod-ROWLAB Dist-ROWLAB

Management Of Advanced And Neglected Surgical Lesions C 25 MIN
16MM FILM OPTICAL SOUND PRO
Portrays the treatment of numerous advanced surgical lesions from patients in Eastern Kentucky (Appalachia.) Emphasizes technical operative features.
Prod-ACYDGD Dist-ACY 1964

Management Of Airway Obstruction C 11 MIN
3/4 OR 1/2 INCH VIDEO CASSETTE PRO
Shows how to successfully manage airway obstruction whether victim is conscious, becomes unconscious, or is found unconscious and whether the blockage is caused by an anatomical structure or a foreign body, such as food.
From The Cardiopulmonary Resuscitation Series.
Prod-HSCIC Dist-HSCIC 1984

Management Of Alcohol Dependency In The Medical Patient C 27 MIN
16MM FILM - 3/4 IN VIDEO PRO
Discusses the disease concept of alcoholism. Demonstrates specific techniques for drawing up an alcoholic patient profile.
Prod-AYERST Dist-AYERST

Management Of Angina Pectoris By Coronary Angioplasty C 32 MIN
3/4 OR 1/2 INCH VIDEO CASSETTE PRO
Describes coronary angioplasty - a recent approach in the management of angina pectoris. Discusses criteria used for the selection of patients, preparations prior to the procedure and management following the procedure. Uses a cineradiograph to illustrate balloon dilatation of arterial blockage.
Prod-UMICHM Dist-UMICHM 1982

Management Of Breast Feeding B 15 MIN
16MM FILM, 3/4 OR 1/2 IN VIDEO
Provides simple answers to the expectant mother's questions. Demonstrates the technique of manual expression of breast milk.
Prod-UWASHP Dist-UWASHP

Management Of Bronchial Asthma C 20 MIN
3/4 OR 1/2 INCH VIDEO CASSETTE PRO
Presents the physiologic processes which influence the patency of the airway. Divides the management of asthma into three treatment phases including treatment of an acute attack, treatment of chronic asthma and treatment of ventilatory failure.
Prod-UMICHM Dist-UMICHM 1974

Management Of Burn Trauma Wounds C 29 MIN
3/4 OR 1/2 INCH VIDEO CASSETTE PRO
Details management of burn trauma wounds in terms of three major objects - adequate nutrition for tissue regeneration, prevention of invesive wound infection, and removal of necrotic tissue. Leads to successful wound closure when each objective is achieved.
From The Burn Trauma Series.
Prod-BRA Dist-BRA

Management Of Burns, Pt 1 - Supportive Care B 18 MIN
16MM FILM OPTICAL SOUND
Explains the diagnosis, care and treatment of patients suffering from burn injuries.
Prod-USA Dist-USNAC 1958

Management Of Burns, Pt 2 - Local Care B 15 MIN
16MM FILM OPTICAL SOUND
Describes procedures followed in the dressing and operating rooms, including cleansing the wound, debridement of the skin, occlusive dressing treatment, air treatment and skin grafting.
Prod-USA Dist-USNAC 1958

Management Of Child Behavior In The Dental Office B 38 MIN
16MM FILM, 3/4 OR 1/2 IN VIDEO
Shows how to guide a child's behavior in ways that will help him accept dental care in his early years and allow the dentist to treat him efficiently and safely.
Prod-IU Dist-USNAC

Management Of Classroom Environment C 30 MIN
3/4 OR 1/2 INCH VIDEO CASSETTE
Revues student behavior and gives suggestions for creating a positive teaching-learning environment in the classroom.
From The Teaching Students With Special Needs Series.
Prod-MSITV Dist-PBS 1981

Management Of Cleft Lip And Cleft Palate Deformities C 11 MIN
16MM FILM - 3/4 IN VIDEO PRO
Shows when a primary care physician should refer patients to specialists of the ongoing care team.
LC NO. 76-703700
Prod-NMAC Dist-USNAC 1976

Management Of Compound Fractures, The C 17 MIN
16MM FILM OPTICAL SOUND PRO
Demonstrates the first aid, resuscitation and definitive treatment of compound tibial fractures. Illustrates wound excision with primary closure and wound excision with delayed primary closure.
Prod-ACYDGD Dist-ACY 1961

Management Of Conflict C 20 MIN
16MM FILM OPTICAL SOUND J-C A
Presents a police training film which explains certain principles for managing various forms of interpersonal conflict encountered by officers. Emphasizes management of domestic disturbances and encourages officers to maintain a neutral position for conflict management.
LC NO. 75-702164
Prod-IACP Dist-IACP Prodn-UNCMID 1974

Management Of Conflict In Business—A Series

A

Shows how to identify kinds of conflict in business and to understand their causes. Presents five modes of coping with specific situations. Consists of four untitled video tapes.
Prod-XICOM Dist-XICOM

Management Of Data Communications C 42 MIN
3/4 OR 1/2 INCH VIDEO CASSETTE
Discusses planning functions and implementation and operations in data communications.
From The Telecommunications And The Computer Series.
Prod-MIOT Dist-MIOT

Management Of Data Communications C 45 MIN
3/4 OR 1/2 INCH VIDEO CASSETTE C
Includes planning functions like regulatilon financing, security, traffic, costs, implementing and operations like multivendor coordination, network control center, and user support, with types of users and support required.
From The Telecommunications And The Computer Series.
LC NO. 81-707502
Prod-AMCEE Dist-AMCEE 1981

Management Of Domestic Violence C 17 MIN
3/4 OR 1/2 INCH VIDEO CASSETTE PRO
Illustrates on-the-scene management of a spouse-beating situation by both emergency medical technicians and police.
From The Crisis Intervention Series.
Prod-SBG Dist-GPITVL 1983

Management Of Drug Overdose C 10 MIN
3/4 OR 1/2 INCH VIDEO CASSETTE PRO
Discusses the five basic principles in the management of drug overdose, recognition of respiratory depression, support of respiration and circulation, identification of the causative agent, elimination of the causative agent and psychiatric support of the patient.
Prod-UMICHM Dist-UMICHM 1973

Management Of Esophageal Carcinoma C 36 MIN
16MM FILM OPTICAL SOUND PRO
Outlines one method of managing carcinoma of the esophagus. Includes staging of the operation, preliminary bypass of esophagus with colon to relieve obstruction, irradiation before resection and total thoracic esophagectomy.
Prod-ACYDGD Dist-ACY 1969

Management Of Fresh Water Near Drowning C 13 MIN
3/4 OR 1/2 INCH VIDEO CASSETTE PRO
Discusses the phenomenon of the near drowning victim with emphasis on the initial and delayed effects of immersion. Shows the importance of obtaining an appropriate history and x-ray and of observing the near drowning victim for cardiac dysrhythmias, hyperbolemia and pulmonary edema. Includes ten necessary elements to be used in the manage- ment of near drowning patients and difficulties which may arise during management.
Prod-UMICHM Dist-UMICHM 1973

Management Of Gallstones Outside The Gallbladder C 30 MIN
3/4 OR 1/2 INCH VIDEO CASSETTE
Discusses the management of retained or newly formed calculi in the bileducts of patients who had undergone cholecystectomy.
Prod-ROWLAB Dist-ROWLAB

Management Of Gastrointestinal Tubes C 21 MIN
16MM FILM OPTICAL SOUND PRO
Demonstrates the insertion, care and types of gastro-intestinal tubes as well as indications for use.
Prod-ACYDGD Dist-ACY 1970

Management Of Heparin Therapy (2nd Ed) C 20 MIN
3/4 OR 1/2 INCH VIDEO CASSETTE PRO
Considers the questions of how heparin should be administered, by what route, for how long and how it should be monitored. Compares heparin with oral anticoagulants and gives reasons why one is more appropriate than the other in certain situations. Discusses common laboratory assays for heparin measurement including the Thrombin Clotting Time.
Prod-UMICHM Dist-UMICHM 1977

Management Of Human Assets, The C 28 MIN
16MM FILM - 3/4 IN VIDEO IND
Dr Rensis Likert, director of the Institute for Social Research at the University of Michigan, summarizes the years of research and activity he has directed at the institute. Discusses his keen understanding of supervision and leadership to bear on the training and direction a company must take to obtain high-producing management.
From The Motivation And Productivity Series.
Prod-BNA Dist-BNA 1967

Management Of Hydrocephalus With The Denver Shunt C 19 MIN
3/4 OR 1/2 INCH VIDEO CASSETTE PRO
Demonstrates how to surgically implant a Denver Shunt in an infant in order to drain excess fluid from the brain.
Prod-WFP Dist-WFP

Management Of Hyperuricemia And Gout C 28 MIN
3/4 OR 1/2 INCH VIDEO CASSETTE PRO
Covers the management of the patient with acute gout, how the diagnosis is substanstiated and currently accepted therapy. Discusses the standard approach to the management of the patient with asymptomatic hyperuricemia.
Prod-UMICHM Dist-UMICHM 1981

Management Of Interfering And Annoying Behavior - Normalization C 129 MIN
3/4 OR 1/2 INCH VIDEO CASSETTE
Discusses the humane and ethical techniques available for reducing or eliminating the interfering and annoying behaviors of severely and profoundly handicapped persons.
From The Meeting The Communications Needs Of The Severely/Profoundly Handicapped 1980 Series.
Prod-PUAVC Dist-PUAVC

Management Of Interfering And Annoying Behavior - Normalization C 154 MIN
3/4 OR 1/2 INCH VIDEO CASSETTE
Addresses four areas included in elimination of inappropriate behaviors which interfere with language acquisition.
From The Meeting The Communication Needs Of The Severely/Profoundly Handicapped 1981 Series.
Prod-PUAVC Dist-PUAVC

Management Of Malignant Melanoma Of The Trunk C 37 MIN
16MM FILM OPTICAL SOUND PRO
Presents rationale of regional node dissection for melanoma of the trunk. Demonstrates anatomic choice of appropriate lymph node basic and techniques of dissection.
Prod-ACYDGD Dist-ACY 1970

Management Of Mass Casualties, Pt 6 - Sorting C 13 MIN
16MM FILM OPTICAL SOUND
Discusses problems concerning the identification of various types of casualties likely to be encountered in nuclear weapon warfare, where the medical personnel and facilities available are inadequate to meet the medical requirements.
LC NO. FIE59-205
Prod-USA Dist-USNAC 1959

Management Of Massive Hemorrhage From The Lower Gastrointestinal Tract C 21 MIN
16MM FILM OPTICAL SOUND PRO
Points out that massive bleeding from the lower gastrointestinal tract presents both internist and surgeon with an exceedingly difficult problem in diagnosis and treatment. Discusses diagnostic and therapeutic measures.
Prod-ACYDGD Dist-ACY 1966

Management Of Maturity Onset Diabetes Mellitus, The C 117 MIN
3/4 OR 1/2 INCH VIDEO CASSETTE PRO
Discusses managing patients with maturity onset diabetes.
LC NO. 81-706294
Prod-USVA Dist-USNAC 1980

Management Of Microprocessor Technology—A Series
IND
Introduces technical background and language of this relatively new field of technology. Shows how information is made practical through application examples, and explores potential impact on operational and marketing functions.
Prod-ICSINT Dist-ICSINT

Advanced Software	045 MIN
Basic Software For Product Development	045 MIN
Developing The Microprocessor Based Product	045 MIN
Management Of Microprocessor Technology -	045 MIN
Microprocessor Architecture I	045 MIN
Microprocessor Architecture II	045 MIN
Microprocessor Based Product Opportunities	045 MIN
Planning For The Future - New Microprocessor	045 MIN
Real Time Systems	045 MIN
Strategic Impact Of Technology	045 MIN

Management Of Microprocessor Technology—A Series

Introduces the language and applications of microprocessor technology.
Prod-MIOT Dist-MIOT

Advanced Software	053 MIN
Basic Software For Product Development	048 MIN
Future Trends	056 MIN
Introduction	057 MIN
Microprocessor Architecture I	050 MIN
Microprocessor Architecture II	049 MIN
Microprocessor-Based Product Opportunities	056 MIN
Product Development	058 MIN
Real Time Systems	057 MIN
Strategic Impact Of Technology	044 MIN

Management Of Microprocessor Technology - Introduction C 45 MIN
3/4 OR 1/2 INCH VIDEO CASSETTE IND
See series title for descriptive statement.
From The Management Of Microprocessor Technology Series.
Prod-ICSINT Dist-ICSINT

Management Of Open Traumatic Dislocation, The C 11 MIN
16MM FILM OPTICAL SOUND PRO
Shows that open wounds of joints must be treated promptly and the positioning and draping of the extremity must be such so that manipulation can be carried out as necessary.
Prod-ACYDGD Dist-ACY 1962

Management Of Organic Headache C 23 MIN
3/4 INCH VIDEO CASSETTE PRO
Describes how headaches can be signals which alert physicians to the possibility of organic disease. Discusses various tests which verify the physician's diagnosis.
LC NO. 76-706054
Prod-WARMP Dist-USNAC 1970

Management Of Pain—A Series
PRO
Tells how nurses can assess and manage their patients' pain. Includes information on the use of behavior modification to control pain.
LC NO. 80-707393
Prod-BRA Dist-BRA 1980

Assessment Of Pain	021 MIN
Neurophysiology Of Pain	024 MIN
Pain Control Through Behavior Modification	023 MIN
Physiologic Modulation Of Pain	028 MIN
Psychodynamics Of Pain	019 MIN

Management Of Peptic Ulcer Disease C 30 MIN
3/4 OR 1/2 INCH VIDEO CASSETTE
Discusses the pathophysiology of duodenal ulcer, the basis for selecting specific treatments for short term and long term healing of duodenal ulcer and the result of these treatments.
Prod-ROWLAB Dist-ROWLAB

Management Of Postdate Pregnancy C
3/4 OR 1/2 INCH VIDEO CASSETTE PRO
Discusses management of pregnancies which remain undelivered for two weeks or more beyond the estimated date of confinement. Presents guidelines for precise pregnancy dating, screening for complications, fetal assessment tests, use of real-time ultrasonography and delivery of the postmature infant. Outlines fetal and neonatal risks associated with postdate delivery. Emphasizes careful monitoring and conservative management.
Prod-UMICHM Dist-UMICHM 1983

Management Of Premature Labor C 9 MIN
3/4 OR 1/2 INCH VIDEO CASSETTE PRO
Includes considerations for consultation, proper techniques of monitoring during delivery, means of minimizing trauma and the organization of personnel and equipment for the preterm infant.
Prod-UMICHM Dist-UMICHM 1983

Management Of Processors C 60 MIN
3/4 OR 1/2 INCH VIDEO CASSETTE IND
See series title for descriptive statement.
From The Microprocessor Fundamentals For Decision Makers Series.
Prod-NCSU Dist-AMCEE

Management Of School Disruption And Violence—A Series
16MM FILM, 3/4 OR 1/2 IN VIDEO T
Presents a series consisting of eight elements considered critical to the control of school disruption.
Prod-BFA Dist-PHENIX 1984

Conflict Management - Youth	012 MIN
Constitutional Issues And Liability	018 MIN
Management System For School Disruption	026 MIN
Police/School Relations	028 MIN

Management Of Severe Burns In Children, The C 20 MIN
16MM FILM OPTICAL SOUND PRO
Discusses and illustrates the care given severely burned children at Children's Hospital, Columbus, Ohio. Focuses on the coordinated efforts of physicians, nurses, physiotherapists, social workers, dietitians and ancillary personnel.
LC NO. FIA66-53
Prod-EATONL Dist-EATONL Prodn-AVCORP 1965

Management Of Technological Innovation—A Series

Examines the results of a decade long MIT research program on management of technological innovation. Includes areas such as motivating innovation, understanding user's needs, determining venture strategies, communicating in organizations and interfacing technological innovation with the market.
Prod-MIOT Dist-MIOT

Communication In Science And Technology	048 MIN
Corporate/R And D Interface Management	034 MIN
Innovation In Industrial Organizations	049 MIN
Motivating Scientists And Engineers	045 MIN
Technical Venture Strategies	049 MIN
User Needs And Industrial Innovation	042 MIN

Management Of Technological Corporations—A Series
PRO
Uses classroom format to videotape 16 one hundred minute lectures on 32 cassettes. Gives overview of management issues characteristic of technological corporations, including development of corporate goals and objectives, costs of capital, investment analysis, selection of product mix, solving production problems, technological marketing, planning for growth and working with government and international market environments.
Prod-USCITV Dist-AMCEE

Management Of The Above Knee Amputee B 25 MIN
3/4 OR 1/2 INCH VIDEO CASSETTE
Shows a 60-year-old man demonstate the bandaging of his unshaped stump, measuring and applying a shrinker sock, applying an above knee prosthesis and ambulating with a prosthesis and crutches.
Prod-BU Dist-BU

Management Of The Adult Respiratory Distress Syndrome C 30 MIN
3/4 OR 1/2 INCH VIDEO CASSETTE PRO
Discusses the adult pathophysiological abnormalities underlying the adult respiratory distress syndrome. Presents variables involved in the treatment of this disease and in maximizing the oxygen delivery to the tissues.
Prod-UMICHM Dist-UMICHM 1982

Management Of The Below Knee Amputee B 17 MIN
3/4 OR 1/2 INCH VIDEO CASSETTE
Demonstrates bandaging a mature below knee stump and measuring and applying a shrinker sock. Shows the components of a PTS prothesis with a medical wedge while the subject is attaching the prosthesis and then walking with a walker.
Prod-BU Dist-BU

Management Of The Crushed Chest C 13 MIN
3/4 OR 1/2 INCH VIDEO CASSETTE PRO
Reviews pathological changes occurring in crushing injuries of the chest and illustrates the principles of management.
Prod-PRIMED Dist-PRIMED

Management Of The Drug Dependent Person - Heroin B 30 MIN
16MM FILM OPTICAL SOUND PRO
Discusses a program established at a methadone clinic in an outpatient department of a private hospital. Describes the program of a nonsubstitute protected environment approach to treatment of heroin addiction.
From The Directions For Education In Nursing Via Technology Series. Lesson 91
LC NO. 74-701870
Prod-DENT Dist-WSU 1974

Management Of The Leprosy Patient C 19 MIN
16MM FILM OPTICAL SOUND
Discusses the work done with leprosy patients at the Public Health Service Hospital at Carville, Louisiana. Shows the effectiveness of sulfone drugs in treatment. Explains the importance of rehabilitation, which includes restoring muscular function, teaching vocational skills and building self-confidence.
LC NO. FIE61-49
Prod-USPHS Dist-USNAC 1960

Management Of The Tuberosity Area In Periodontics C 12 MIN
16MM FILM OPTICAL SOUND
Demonstrates the use of an internal beveled flap procedure in the treatment of an infrabony pocket involving a maxillary molar. Explains the rationale of this procedure and postoperative results are shown.
LC NO. 74-705088
Prod-USVA Dist-USNAC 1968

Management Of The Tuberosity Area In Periodontics C 12 MIN
3/4 OR 1/2 INCH VIDEO CASSETTE
Demonstrates the use of an internal beveled flap procedure in the treatment of an infrabony pocket involving a maxillary molar. Explains the rationale of this procedure.
Prod-VADTC Dist-AMDA 1969

Management Of Third Degree Burns In A Newborn C 16 MIN
16MM FILM OPTICAL SOUND
Provides a clinical demonstration of the management of third degree burns of the genitalia and lower extremities suffered by a male infant within an hour after birth.
LC NO. 74-706133
Prod-USA Dist-USNAC 1969

Management Of Thoracic Injuries C 29 MIN
16MM FILM OPTICAL SOUND PRO
Demonstrates the basic principles underlying the treatment of thoracic injuries by model and animal demonstrations and shows application of these principles in the care of patients. Emphasizes practical measures for maintenance of uninterrupted respiratory function in the presence of severe trauma.
Prod-ACYDGD Dist-ACY 1962

Management Of Thoracic Trauma C 26 MIN
3/4 OR 1/2 INCH VIDEO CASSETTE PRO
Discusses the more common surgical thoracic emergencies in the categories of penetrating and non-penetrating trauma. Presents the pathophysiology of thoracic trauma, the evaluation of patients with chest trauma, the initiation of appropriate therapy and some of the life- threatening injuries which may occur with little, or no, external evidence.
Prod-UMICHM Dist-UMICHM 1977

Management Of Time—A Series

Helps supervisors to identify and reduce unproductive time-wasting activities.
Prod-RESEM Dist-RESEM

Analyzing Our Time Usage	010 MIN
Our Time Is Our Time	013 MIN
Time Of Our Lives, The	012 MIN
Using Others To Save Time	010 MIN

Management Of Time, The C 10 MIN
16MM FILM OPTICAL SOUND
Shows how a successful businessman organizes his time to his best advantage in order to educate middle management executives on methods of utilizing time.
LC NO. 74-700545
Prod-NILCOM Dist-NILCOM 1974

Management Of Upper Airway Obstruction C 12 MIN
3/4 OR 1/2 INCH VIDEO CASSETTE PRO
Outlines the indications and the steps in management of upper airway obstruction from various causes. Points out error in improper techniques and demonstrates proper approaches for oral airways, bronchoscopy, naso and oro-tracheal intubation and tracheostomy.
Prod-PRIMED Dist-PRIMED

Management Of Upper And Lower Gastrointestinal Bleeding C 30 MIN
3/4 OR 1/2 INCH VIDEO CASSETTE
Discusses the management of upper and lower gastrointestinal

bleeding. Considers the resuscitation and examination of the bleeding patient, diagnosis of the cause of bleeding and therapy.
Prod-ROWLAB Dist-ROWLAB

Management Of Vesicant Extravasation C 53 MIN
3/4 INCH VIDEO CASSETTE
Shows how to care for the relatively rare phenomenon of vesicant extravasation resulting from drug injection and infiltration into surrounding skin.
Prod-UTAHTI Dist-UTAHTI

Management Of Viral Hepatitis C 19 MIN
3/4 OR 1/2 INCH VIDEO CASSETTE PRO
Describes the overlap of hepatitis A and hepatitis B and the differential diagnosis of acute viral hepatitis in the pre-icteric and icteric phases of viral hepatitis. Covers the specific points in the management of viral hepatitis, the approach in evaluating and managing patients with hepatitis B antigen and the indications for gamma globulin prophylaxis.
Prod-UMICHM Dist-UMICHM 1974

Management Of Work—A Series

Helps build key management skills such as the ability to plan, organize and direct.
Prod-RESEM Dist-RESEM

Controlling 013 MIN
Directing 014 MIN
Organizing 012 MIN
Planning 009 MIN
Successful Manager, The 010 MIN

Management Organization And Critical Job Elements C 120 MIN
3/4 OR 1/2 INCH VIDEO CASSETTE
Describes the principles on which successful organizations are based, and the contribution of accurate statements of critical job elements to the smooth functioning of a management unit and to the clarification of management goals.
From The AMA's Program For Performance Appraisal Series.
Prod-AMA Dist-AMA

Management Organization And Position Description C 28 MIN
2 INCH VIDEOTAPE A
Features James L Hayes, president of the American Management Associations, exploring nine principles on which successful organizations are based. Shows the contribution made by accurate position descriptions to the smooth functioning of a management unit.
From The How To Improve Managerial Performance - The AMA Performance Standards Program Series.
LC NO. 75-704233
Prod-AMA Dist-AMA 1974

Management Organization And Position Descriptions C 29 MIN
3/4 OR 1/2 INCH VIDEO CASSETTE
Shows how to bypass the morass of 'organizational layering,' avoid the confusion of corporate relationships and bring the basics of responsibility and accountability into sharp focus.
Prod-AMA Dist-AMA

Management Perspective Of Office Automation C 45 MIN
3/4 OR 1/2 INCH VIDEO CASSETTE
Provides an overview of the justifications, benefits, tools and organizational issues associated with the introduction of office automation.
From The Management Strategies For Office Automation Series.
Prod-DELTAK Dist-DELTAK

Management Plan B 50 MIN
3/4 OR 1/2 INCH VIDEO CASSETTE
See series title for descriptive statement.
From The Looking For A Grant? Here's What You Should Know Series. Pt 3
Prod-UAZMIC Dist-UAZMIC 1978

Management Practice—A Series
16MM FILM - 3/4 IN VIDEO A
Discusses management theories and their application in solving problems regarding information systems, marketing and long-range planning.
Prod-BNA Dist-BNA 1972

What Every Manager Needs To Know About
What Every Manager Needs To Know About 034 MIN
What Every Manager Needs To Know About 023 MIN
What Every Manager Needs To Know About 033 MIN
What Every Manager Needs To Know About 024 MIN
What Every Manager Needs To Know About 034 MIN

Management Presentation C
3/4 OR 1/2 INCH VIDEO CASSETTE
Examines the ways to present a solution to management. Covers assembling data and using visual aids. Lists pitfalls.
From The Implementing Quality Circles Series.
Prod-BNA Dist-BNA

Management Skills For Supervisors—A Series
16MM FILM, 3/4 OR 1/2 IN VIDEO A
Emphasizes understanding the function, role, key responsibilities and skill requirements of a supervisor or first level manager, meeting the complex challenge of problem-solving and creating a climate that keeps motivation high and productivity up.
Prod-TIMLIF Dist-TIMLIF 1984

Manager's Role And Function Unit, A
Motivation Unit
Problem-Solving Unit

Management Skills—A Series
PRO
Features 14 of the nation's leading management consultants speaking on management skills.
Prod-AMCEE Dist-AMCEE

Clear Writing, Pt 1 And Pt 2, Anne H Carlisle
Communication Skills, Joseph A Robinson
Competitive Analysis, Victor H Prushan
Conducting A Performance Appraisal, James F
Conducting Effective Meetings, David B Norris
Effective Management Style, Arnold Ruskin
Engineer As Businessperson, David B Norris, The
Estimating Time And Cost, Ward V Speaker
Information Systems For Technical Managers,
Interviewing Techniques, Richard J Pinsker
Making More Effective Presentations, Ward V
Marketing New Products, Victor H Prushan
Motivation And Team Building, Susan Pistone
Negotiating Techniques, Arnold Ruskin
Recruiting Talented People, J Kenneth Lund
Salary Administration, James F Carey
Strategic Planning, William S Birnbaum
Time Management, E Byron Chew
Your Career, J Kenneth Lund

Management Strategies For Office Automation—A Series

Addresses the management implications of office automation and presents strategies for a coherent approach to implementation.
Prod-DELTAK Dist-DELTAK

Getting Started - The Pilot Application
Management Change - The People Issues 045 MIN
Management Perspective Of Office Automation 045 MIN
Office Automation Game Plan 045 MIN
Survey Of Office Automation Applications 045 MIN

Management Style C 45 MIN
3/4 OR 1/2 INCH VIDEO CASSETTE PRO
Deals with making decisions. Covers leadership, conflict, change and ethics.
From The Advanced Project Management Series.
Prod-AMCEE Dist-AMCEE

Management System For School Disruption And Violence C 26 MIN
16MM FILM, 3/4 OR 1/2 IN VIDEO T
Presents a profile of basic management skills at work in four schools that have been turned around from a pattern of disruption and violence.
Prod-BFA Dist-PHENIX 1984

Management Technique C 30 MIN
3/4 OR 1/2 INCH VIDEO CASSETTE
Discusses the agricultural calendar and management problems in beekeeping.
From The Bees And Honey Series.
Prod-WGTV Dist-MDCPB

Management Theories X And Y C 10 MIN
16MM FILM OPTICAL SOUND PRO
Features Dr Warren Schmidt who presents a distillation of Douglas Mc Gregor's key concepts on managerial assumptions.
Prod-UCLA Dist-UCLA 1970

Management Training C 24 MIN
16MM FILM - 3/4 IN VIDEO
Explains how a training program is devised for the 'problem' employee, how to prevent a future mishap and how to improve his skills.
From The Management By Objectives Series.
Prod-BNA Dist-BNA 1971

Management Training—A Series

Meets the specific training needs identified in the Management Diagnostic Series, with each unit containing one or more activities, such as self-assessments, graphic presentations, readings, case studies and simulations. Includes a student text and a set of diskettes.
Prod-THGHT Dist-DELTAK

Conducting Successful Meetings
Defining Goals And Objectives
Improving Employee Performance
Leading Effectively
Managing By Exception
Managing Stress
Managing Time Effectively
Motivating To Achieve Results
Performance Appraisal

Management View Of Structured Techniques C 30 MIN
3/4 OR 1/2 INCH VIDEO CASSETTE
Discusses structured techniques from a management viewpoint. Focuses on how structured techniques can be used to combat many serious software problems, such as poor program quality and low productivity.
From The Structured Techniques - An Overview Series.
Prod-DELTAK Dist-DELTAK

Management View Of Structured Techniques, A C 30 MIN
3/4 OR 1/2 INCH VIDEO CASSETTE
Discusses structured techniques from a management viewpoint, focusing on how structured techniques can be used to combat many serious software problems, such as poor program quality and low productivity.
From The Structured Techniques - An Overview Series.
Prod-DELTAK Dist-DELTAK

Management, Impact 1980 C 40 MIN
3/4 OR 1/2 INCH VIDEO CASSETTE IND
Shows business executives Lawrence Miller and Frank Bird answering questions on management issues relating to occupational health and safety and on the topic of loss control.
From The Safety, Health, and Loss Control - Managing Effective Programs Series.
LC NO. 81-706528
Prod-AMCEE Dist-AMCEE 1980

Management, Pt 1 - Listening For Understanding C 30 MIN
16MM FILM, 3/4 OR 1/2 IN VIDEO C
Dramatizes the importance of effective communication for managers.
Prod-UMA Dist-GPITVL 1981

Management, Pt 2 - Work Redesign C 30 MIN
16MM FILM, 3/4 OR 1/2 IN VIDEO C
Introduces the recent and highly respected Hackman/Oldham model of work design.
Prod-UMA Dist-GPITVL 1981

Management's Five Deadly Diseases - A Conversation With Dr W Edwards Deming C 16 MIN
16MM FILM, 3/4 OR 1/2 IN VIDEO C A
Describes aspects of American management style that are adversely affecting productivity and diminishing American capacity for competitiveness.
Prod-EBEC Dist-EBEC 1984

Management's Role In Health And Safety C 15 MIN
16MM FILM OPTICAL SOUND
Defines management's responsibility for the health and safety of the men working in our nation's mines. Points out various environmental health problems, safety hazards, and offers possible solutions, with emphasis on effective safety training.
LC NO. 74-705089
Prod-USDA Dist-USNAC 1972

Management's Safety Mirror C 40 MIN
3/4 OR 1/2 INCH VIDEO CASSETTE IND
Shows Frank Bird, who expresses the view that increasing risk factors require a more comprehensive safety management system and that such a system is avilable using ISMEC. He also describes the components of this system, which begins with identification of work required to achieve safety objectives and ends with evaluation and correcting safety hazards.
From The Safety, Health, and Loss Control - Managing Effective Programs Series.
LC NO. 81-706526
Prod-AMCEE Dist-AMCEE 1980

Manager And The Law, The C 19 MIN
16MM FILM, 3/4 OR 1/2 IN VIDEO J-C A
Uses a series of short dramatizations to present six guidelines based on general principles of law to assist managers in reducing legal risks to themselves and their organizations.
From The Professional Management Program Series.
Prod-NEM Dist-NEM 1975

Manager And The Law, The (Spanish) C 19 MIN
16MM FILM, 3/4 OR 1/2 IN VIDEO
Examines the responsibilities of managers toward laws and regulations. Offers guidelines for avoiding legal problems in business.
From The Professional Management Program (Spanish) Series.
Prod-NEM Dist-NEM

Manager And The Organization (Portuguese)—A Series

Reveals steps for managers to upgrade their performance, improve relations and motivate people to greater productivity.
Prod-BNA Dist-BNA

Helping People Perform, What Managers Are
How To Make The Organization Work For You
How To Manage The Boss (Portuguese)
How To Take The Right Risks, The Manager As
How to Work With Your Fellow Managers
Planning And Goal Setting, Time-Waste Or

Manager And The Organization (Spanish)—A Series

Reveals steps for managers to upgrade their performance, improve relations and motivate people to greater productivity.
Prod-BNA Dist-BNA

Helping People Perform, What Managers Are
How To Make The Organization Work For You
How To Manage The Boss (Spanish)
How To Take The Right Risks, The Manager As
How To Work With Your Fellow Managers (Spanish)
Planning And Goal Setting, Time-Waste Or

Manager And The Organization (French)—A Series

Reveals steps for managers to upgrade their performance, improve relations and motivate people to greater productivity.
Prod-BNA Dist-BNA

Helping People Perform, What Managers Are
How To Make The Organization Work For You
How To Manage The Boss (French)
How To Take The Right Risks, The Manager As
How To Work With Your Fellow Managers (French)
Planning And Goal Setting, Time-Waste Or

Manager And The Organization (German)—A Series

Reveals steps for managers to upgrade their performance, improve relations and motivate people to greater productivity.
Prod-BNA Dist-BNA

Helping People Perform, What Managers Are
How To Make The Organization Work For You
How To Manage The Boss (German)
How To Take The Right Risks, The Manager As
How To Work With Your Fellow Managers (German)
Planning And Goal Setting, Time-Waste Or

Manager And The Organization—A Series
16MM FILM - 3/4 IN VIDEO IND
Uses vignettes of situations in the fictitious General Pipe and Plumbing Supply Company to illustrate problems of middle management which Peter F Drucker discusses and for which he offers solutions
Prod-BNA Dist-BNA

Helping People Perform, What Managers Are 13 ..
How To Make The Organization Work For You 22 MIN
How To Manage The Boss 24 MIN
How To Take The Right Risks, The Manager 23 MIN
How To Work With Your Fellow Managers 21 MIN
Planning And Goal Setting, Time-Waste Or 22 MIN

Manager As Entrepreneur, The C 31 MIN
16MM FILM - 3/4 IN VIDEO PRO
Describes the entrepreneurial manager as one who takes risks to support genuine innovation and continuing self-renewal.
From The Managing Discontinuity Series.
Prod-BNA Dist-BNA 1971

Manager In The Automated Office, The C 30 MIN
3/4 OR 1/2 INCH VIDEO CASSETTE
Examines the impact of office automation on the manager and the adaptations the manager will have to make in this new office environment.
From The Impact Of Office Automation On People Series.
Prod-DELTAK Dist-DELTAK

Manager Under Pressure C 17 MIN
16MM FILM, 3/4 OR 1/2 IN VIDEO A
Demonstrates in a humorous manner five basic patterns for coping with pressure in a business setting. Emphasizes the fifth pattern, seeking perspectives and alternatives.
Prod-XICOM Dist-XICOM Prodn-BOSUST

Manager Wanted C 28 MIN
16MM FILM, 3/4 OR 1/2 IN VIDEO H-C
Stresses the importance of training subordinates to handle a supervisor's work so that the supervisor may be elevated when the opportunity arises.
Prod-RTBL Dist-RTBL 1964

Manager Wanted (Danish) C 28 MIN
16MM FILM, 3/4 OR 1/2 IN VIDEO H-C
Stresses the importance of training subordinates to handle a supervisor's work so that the supervisor may be elevated when the opportunity arises.
Prod-RTBL Dist-RTBL 1964

Manager Wanted (Dutch) C 28 MIN
16MM FILM, 3/4 OR 1/2 IN VIDEO H-C
Stresses the importance of training subordinates to handle a supervisor's work so that the supervisor may be elevated when the opportunity arises.
Prod-RTBL Dist-RTBL 1964

Manager Wanted (French) C 28 MIN
16MM FILM, 3/4 OR 1/2 IN VIDEO H-C
Stresses the importance of training subordinates to handle a supervisor's work so that the supervisor may be elevated when the opportunity arises.
Prod-RTBL Dist-RTBL 1964

Manager Wanted (German) C 28 MIN
16MM FILM, 3/4 OR 1/2 IN VIDEO H-C
Stresses the importance of training subordinates to handle a supervisor's work so that the supervisor may be elevated when the opportunity arises.
Prod-RTBL Dist-RTBL 1964

Manager Wanted (Japanese) C 28 MIN
16MM FILM, 3/4 OR 1/2 IN VIDEO H-C
Stresses the importance of training subordinates to handle a supervisor's work so that the supervisor may be elevated when the opportunity arises.
Prod-RTBL Dist-RTBL 1964

Manager Wanted (Norwegian) C 28 MIN
16MM FILM, 3/4 OR 1/2 IN VIDEO H-C
Stresses the importance of training subordinates to handle a supervisor's work so that the supervisor may be elevated when the opportunity arises.
Prod-RTBL Dist-RTBL 1964

Manager Wanted (Portuguese) C 28 MIN
16MM FILM, 3/4 OR 1/2 IN VIDEO H-C
Stresses the importance of training subordinates to handle a supervisor's work so that the supervisor may be elevated when the opportunity arises.
Prod-RTBL Dist-RTBL 1964

Manager Wanted (Swedish) C 28 MIN
16MM FILM, 3/4 OR 1/2 IN VIDEO H-C
Stresses the importance of training subordinates to handle a supervisor's work so that the supervisor may be elevated when the opportunity arises.
Prod-RTBL Dist-RTBL 1964

Manager's Environment, The C
3/4 OR 1/2 INCH VIDEO CASSETTE
Discusses internal and external influences on the manager's job and how these influences determine which managerial actions may or may not be acceptable.
From The Principles Of Management Series.
Prod-RMI Dist-RMI

Manager's Job Responsibilities C 3 MIN
2 INCH VIDEOTAPE
Shows office employees that they share some of the same overall organizational responsibilities with their supervisors. Suggests that employees should recognize the many different roles they have in meeting these responsibilities.
From The SUCCESS, The AMA Course For Office Employees Series.
LC NO. 75-704219
Prod-AMA Dist-AMA 1972

Manager's Operating Realities C 10 MIN
2 INCH VIDEOTAPE
Presents an instructional course for office employees. Provides insights into the problems and pressures with which today's managers must deal. Offers a definition of management, identifies three major managerial activities and uses dramatized examples in order to show the five basic operating realities faced by managers.
From The SUCCESS, The AMA Course For Office Employees Series.
LC NO. 75-704209
Prod-AMA Dist-AMA 1972

Manager's Role And Function Unit, A C
3/4 OR 1/2 INCH VIDEO CASSETTE A
Covers the basic responsibilities, roles and skills expected of those in the beginning ranks of management. Shows how managers function within the organization, their relationship to upper management, peers and employees, and their effects on productivity and the organization at large.
From The Management Skills For Supervisors Series.
Prod-TIMLIF Dist-TIMLIF 1984

Managerial Control C 20 MIN
16MM FILM, 3/4 OR 1/2 IN VIDEO A
Reveals how simple control procedures help supervisors and managers keep their operations within budget and on schedule without losing sight of their goals. Deals with standards, measurement and corrective action.
Prod-NEM Dist-NEM

Managerial Control (Spanish) C 20 MIN
16MM FILM, 3/4 OR 1/2 IN VIDEO
Dramatizes the importance of establishing and maintaining control for managers and supervisors.
From The Professional Management Program (Spanish) Series.
Prod-NEM Dist-NEM

Managerial Decision Making C
3/4 OR 1/2 INCH VIDEO CASSETTE
Defines decision making, and explores the parameters of the decision-making environment.
From The Principles Of Management Series.
Prod-RMI Dist-RMI

Managerial Game Plan - Team Building Through MBO—A Series

Demonstrates an atmosphere of interaction through the demonstration of an operations group developing team building, sharpening their skills and becoming aware of their interdependency. Presents analogies drawn from the world of professional football. Useful as a starter program or in determining systematic steps to take in reaching a desired goal.
Prod-PRODEV Dist-PRODEV

Developing The Plan, Pt 1 030 MIN
Developing The Plan, Pt 2 030 MIN
Gaining Commitment 030 MIN
Maintaining A Winning Team 030 MIN
Name Of The Game, The 030 MIN

Managerial Grid In Action, The C 33 MIN
16MM FILM - 3/4 IN VIDEO
Shows the styles of various managers before they learn about the grid, their mixed reactions to it and how they come to feel that it may offer a solution to their current problem, an across-the-board budget cut.
From The Managerial Grid Series. No. 1
Prod-BNA Dist-BNA 1977

Managerial Grid—A Series
16MM FILM - 3/4 IN VIDEO IND
Introduces and applies the Grid approach to industrial management.
Prod-BNA Dist-BNA 1974

Grid Approach To Conflict Solving 33 MIN
Managerial Grid In Action, The 33 MIN

Managerial Grid, The B 35 MIN
16MM FILM, 3/4 OR 1/2 IN VIDEO C A
Explains a useful system for evaluating management methods. Shows the system applied to various situations in order to determine the attitudes, values, degree of commitment, creativity and conflict that can be expected under different management methods.
From The Management Development Series.
Prod-UCLA Dist-UCEMC 1963

Managerial Stress C 30 MIN
3/4 OR 1/2 INCH VIDEO CASSETTE C A
Interviews managers as they discuss personal sources of stress and the steps they take to alleviate it. Looks at the direct action large corporations have taken to reduce employee stress.
From The Business Of Management Series. Lesson 23
Prod-SCCON Dist-SCCON

Managerial World, The C 30 MIN
3/4 OR 1/2 INCH VIDEO CASSETTE C A
Features working managers and professors of management as they explore the five inter-dependent functions that represent the heart of management.
From The Business Of Management Series. Lesson 1
Prod-SCCON Dist-SCCON

Managing A Structured Programming Project C 15 MIN
16MM FILM OPTICAL SOUND
Explains how data processing managers can develop and evaluate programs using the structured approach.
From The Structured Program Design Series.
LC NO. 81-700499
Prod-EDTRCS Dist-EDTRCS 1981

Managing And Implementing C 30 MIN
3/4 OR 1/2 INCH VIDEO CASSETTE
Focuses on preparing advertising and evaluating the results. Introduces several approaches to ad preparation, and discusses resources that might help small business operators understand how different media develop ads.
From The Advertising The Small Business Series.
Prod-NETCHE Dist-NETCHE 1981

Managing And Using The Data Resource C 20 MIN
3/4 OR 1/2 INCH VIDEO CASSETTE
Presents the concepts of data management and user application development. Discusses data base concepts and explores the structures and techniques which must support it for data base to be an effective tool for the user.
From The User-Directed Information Systems Series.
Prod-DELTAK Dist-DELTAK

Managing Application Development C 30 MIN
3/4 OR 1/2 INCH VIDEO CASSETTE
Suggests goals for DP management and new methodologies for achieving those goals to capitalize on new techniques for application development.
From The Application Development Without Programmers Series.
Prod-DELTAK Dist-DELTAK

Managing Behavior In School C 30 MIN
3/4 OR 1/2 INCH VIDEO CASSETTE T
Presents the principal, a classroom teacher, the counselor, a librarian and a student from the Vandenberg Middle School who speak to the value and impact of the discipline program described in the Developing Discipline series.
From The Developing Discipline Series.
Prod-SDPT Dist-GPITVL 1983

Managing Business Organization C 29 MIN
3/4 OR 1/2 INCH VIDEO CASSETTE
See series title for descriptive statement.
From The Business File Series.
Prod-PBS Dist-PBS

Managing By Decision-Making C 11 MIN
3/4 OR 1/2 INCH VIDEO CASSETTE
Offers an easy-to-follow set of rules for increasing a supervisor's decision-making skills.
From The Improving Managerial Skills Series.
Prod-RESEM Dist-RESEM

Managing By Exception C
3/4 OR 1/2 INCH VIDEO CASSETTE
See series title for descriptive statement.
From The Management Training Series.
Prod-THGHT Dist-DELTAK

Managing Change C 23 MIN
16MM FILM, 3/4 OR 1/2 IN VIDEO A
Illustrates and suggests solutions to some of the special problems that confront managers when it is their responsibility to manage change. Shows how, when a new assembly line is installed and new products are introduced in an English laminating factory, unexpected problems arise.
LC NO. 81-707626
Prod-MILLBK Dist-IFB 1981

Managing Change C 30 MIN
3/4 OR 1/2 INCH VIDEO CASSETTE C A
Focuses on the need for sound planning by managers when dealing with change.
From The Business Of Management Series. Lesson 22
Prod-SCCON Dist-SCCON

Managing Change, The Human Dimension C 33 MIN
3/4 OR 1/2 INCH VIDEO CASSETTE PRO
Helps managers understand why people resist change, and how to manage it more effectively and help people see change as an opportunity, not a threat.
Prod-GOODMI Dist-GOODMI

Managing Computer Enhanced Training C 25 MIN
3/4 OR 1/2 INCH VIDEO CASSETTE
Describes the criteria that will help organizations implement the computer enhanced training system of their choice. Covers hardware, delivery system software and courseware for both those who decide to purchase courseware and those who opt to create their own training material in-house.
From The Implementing Computer Enhanced Training Series.
Prod-DELTAK Dist-DELTAK

Managing Conflict C 13 MIN
3/4 OR 1/2 INCH VIDEO CASSETTE
See series title for descriptive statement.
From The Applied Management Series Series.
Prod-ORGDYN Dist-DELTAK

Managing Conflict - How To Make Conflict Work For You C 15 MIN
16MM FILM, 3/4 OR 1/2 IN VIDEO H-C A
Illustrates several strategies for dealing with conflict, discussing both advantages and disadvantages of each strategy.
Prod-SALENG Dist-SALENG 1978

Managing Conflict Productively C 120 MIN
3/4 OR 1/2 INCH VIDEO CASSETTE
Provides insights into strategies to turn conflict into a positive force, contributing to efficiency and stimulating problem solving and innovation.
Prod-UNIVAS Dist-UNIVAS

Managing Creatively C 21 MIN
16MM FILM, 3/4 OR 1/2 IN VIDEO
Encourages managers to take an imaginative approach and recognize barriers to creativity. Tells the story of a manager who has fallen into a stagnant routine and copes with crises in a piecemeal manner while exhibiting dynamic leadership and resourcefulness in his private life. Shows how he changes his approach to management.
LC NO. 83-706706
Prod-MILLBK Dist-IFB 1982

Managing Cultural Differences—A Series
A
Uses lecture format for in-depth look at how cultural differences can affect business and management practices inside and outside the US. Utilizes Dr Philip R Harris of La Jolla, CA and Dr Robert T Moran of Glendale, AZ as content consultants.
Prod-GPCV Dist-GPCV

Cosmopolitan Manager, The
Family Relocation Coping Skills
Improving The Productivity Of International
Transnational Managers As Cultural Change
Transnational Managers As Intercultural
Understanding Cultural Differences

Managing Dancers C 30 MIN
3/4 OR 1/2 INCH VIDEO CASSETTE
See series title for descriptive statement.
From The Business And Law Of Dance Series.
Prod-ARCVID Dist-ARCVID

Managing Discontinuity—A Series
16MM FILM - 3/4 IN VIDEO PRO
Challenges managers in all kinds of organizations to look at the problems of today and tomorrow in a realistic, innovative and far-seeing way.
Prod-BNA Dist-BNA 1971

Coping With Technological Change 032 MIN
Future Of Technology, The 028 MIN
Innovative Organization, The 035 MIN
Manager As Entrepreneur, The 031 MIN
Multinational Corporation, The 032 MIN
Pollution Control - The Hard Decisions 028 MIN
Social Needs As Business Opportunities 033 MIN
Tomorrow's Customers 034 MIN
Who's Gonna Collect The Garbage 044 MIN

Managing Emergency Medical Priorities C 14 MIN
3/4 OR 1/2 INCH VIDEO CASSETTE
Defines priority injuries and shows how to determine and establish priorities and how to treat brain, chest and abdominal emergencies as priorities.
From The Emergency Medical Training Series.
Prod-VTRI Dist-VTRI

Managing Employee Morale C 25 MIN
3/4 OR 1/2 INCH VIDEO CASSETTE
Discusses methods for improving employee morale including fact-finding, letting people participate in decisions and using channels of upward communication.
From The Motivation And Productivity Series.
Prod-BNA Dist-BNA

Managing Energy, Effort, Time, And Money C 14 MIN
3/4 OR 1/2 INCH VIDEO CASSETTE
See series title for descriptive statement.
From The Leadership Link - Fundamentals Of Effective Supervision Series.
Prod-CHSH Dist-DELTAK

Managing Financial Resources - Long Term Funds C 29 MIN
3/4 OR 1/2 INCH VIDEO CASSETTE
See series title for descriptive statement.
From The Business File Series.
Prod-PBS Dist-PBS

Managing Financial Resources - Short Term Funds C 29 MIN
3/4 OR 1/2 INCH VIDEO CASSETTE
See series title for descriptive statement.
From The Business File Series.
Prod-PBS Dist-PBS

Managing For Productivity C 30 MIN
3/4 OR 1/2 INCH VIDEO CASSETTE C A
Examines the various aspects of the Japanese approach to management. Looks at whether or not the techniques that work in Japan would have the same result in the United States. Looks at ways a manager can coordinate productivity efforts.
From The Business Of Management Series. Lesson 26
Prod-SCCON Dist-SCCON

Managing For Results C 10 MIN
3/4 OR 1/2 INCH VIDEO CASSETTE
Shows how to create a goal-setting environment and how to manage it. Develops techniques for helping supervisors bring employee goals and organization goals closer together.
From The Human Side Of Management Series.
Prod-RESEM Dist-RESEM

Managing For Tomorrow (Dutch)—A Series

Teaches managers to give their organizations increased productivity, financial stability and flexibility to meet growth objectives.
Prod-BNA Dist-BNA

Challenge Of Productivity, The (Dutch)
Managing Innovation And Growth (Dutch)
Managing The Knowledge Worker (Dutch)
New Employees And The New Customers, The
Where Do I Belong (Dutch)

Managing For Tomorrow (German)—A Series

Teaches managers to give their organizations increased productivity, financial stability and flexibility to meet growth objectives.
Prod-BNA Dist-BNA

Challenge Of Productivity, The (German)
Managing Innovation And Growth (German)
Managing The Knowledge Worker (German)
New Employees And The New Customers, The
Where Do I Belong (German)

Managing For Tomorrow—A Series
16MM FILM - 3/4 IN VIDEO
Presents basic skills for managers and supervisors. Based on the book Managing In Turbulent Times by Peter F Drucker.
Prod-BNA Dist-BNA

Challenge Of Productivity, The
Managing Innovation And Growth
Managing The Knowledge Worker
New Employee And The New Customers, The
Where Do I Belong

Managing Hemorrhoids C
3/4 OR 1/2 INCH VIDEO CASSETTE
Explains how over-strained blood vessels can result in hemorrhoids (both internal and external) and how proper diet and bowel habits can alleviate the discomfort. Discusses surgery as a possible but unlikely option.
Prod-MIFE Dist-MIFE

Managing Hemorrhoids (Arabic) C
3/4 OR 1/2 INCH VIDEO CASSETTE
Explains how over-strained blood vessels can result in hemorrhoids (both internal and external) and how proper diet and bowel habits can alleviate the discomfort. Discusses surgery as a possible but unlikely option.
Prod-MIFE Dist-MIFE

Managing Human Resources C 29 MIN
3/4 OR 1/2 INCH VIDEO CASSETTE
See series title for descriptive statement.
From The Business File Series.
Prod-PBS Dist-PBS

Managing In A Crisis C 28 MIN
16MM FILM - 3/4 IN VIDEO
Shows how the supervisor can actually use a crisis to strengthen his team.
From The Advanced Supervision Series.
Prod-BNA Dist-BNA 1973

Managing Information C 29 MIN
3/4 OR 1/2 INCH VIDEO CASSETTE
See series title for descriptive statement.
From The Business File Series.
Prod-PBS Dist-PBS

Managing Information Technology C 30 MIN
3/4 OR 1/2 INCH VIDEO CASSETTE
Discusses the problems and implications of information technology from a top management viewpoint. Outlines considerations for planning and implementing information technology.
From The Strategic Impact Of Information Technology Series.
Prod-DELTAK Dist-DELTAK

Managing Innovation And Growth C
16MM FILM - 3/4 IN VIDEO
Examines the role of the manager and supervisor in the motivation and growth of the organization. Tells how to gain budgetary approval for long-range projects, implement a growth strategy, and provide interim financial returns on long-range projects.
From The Managing For Tomorrow Series. Unit 2
Prod-BNA Dist-BNA

Managing Innovation And Growth (Dutch) C
16MM FILM, 3/4 OR 1/2 IN VIDEO
Shows that innovation and growth require focused planning and hard work. Tells how to implement a growth strategy.
From The Managing For Tomorrow (Dutch) Series.
Prod-BNA Dist-BNA

Managing Innovation And Growth (German) C
16MM FILM, 3/4 OR 1/2 IN VIDEO
Shows that innovation and growth require focused planning and hard work. Tells how to implement a growth strategy.
From The Managing For Tomorrow (German) Series.
Prod-BNA Dist-BNA

Managing Interruptions C 30 MIN
3/4 OR 1/2 INCH VIDEO CASSETTE A
Explains that one key to managing interruptions effectively is to anticipate them whenever possible. Shows how to block out time on daily calendars for anticipated or routine matters and how to establish policies with secretaries or assistants for handling unexpected interruptions.
From The Time Management For Management Series. Pt 5
Prod-TIMLIF Dist-TIMLIF 1981

Managing Job Related Stress C 30 MIN
16MM FILM, 3/4 OR 1/2 IN VIDEO PRO
Emphasizes the importance of helping employees who are undergoing stress. Presents vignettes of four stressful situations.
From The Dimensions Of Leadership In Nursing Series.
LC NO. 81-706081
Prod-CATTN Dist-AJN Prodn-AJN 1979

Managing Local Area Networks C 45 MIN
3/4 OR 1/2 INCH VIDEO CASSETTE C
Covers Local Area Network (LAN) selection criteria, functionality, interfaces, availabilty, cost, support, baseland versus broadband, PABX as an Structural, LAN market forecasts, technology forecasts and what to do now.
From The Local Area Networks Series.
Prod-AMCEE Dist-AMCEE

Managing Meetings C 30 MIN
3/4 OR 1/2 INCH VIDEO CASSETTE A
Presents hosts Richard Benjamin and Paula Prentiss giving guidelines on when to call a meeting, how to prepare for it, how to establish leadership and how to stick to the agenda.
From The Communication Skills For Managers Series.
Prod-TIMLIF Dist-TIMLIF 1981

Managing Microcomputers - The Microcomputer Game C 30 MIN
3/4 OR 1/2 INCH VIDEO CASSETTE
Stresses the idea of determining what needs and groups of students will be served by microcomputers.
From The Ready Or Not Series.
Prod-NCSDPI Dist-PCATEL

Managing Motivation C 11 MIN
16MM FILM, 3/4 OR 1/2 IN VIDEO A
Illustrates how to increase employee motivation.
LC NO. 81-706184
Prod-SALENG Dist-SALENG 1981

Managing People For Project Success C 30 MIN
3/4 OR 1/2 INCH VIDEO CASSETTE
Tells how to motivate a project team. Demonstrates leadership styles. Deals with conflict resolution.
From The Project Management Series.
Prod-ITCORP Dist-ITCORP

Managing Production - Automotive Industry, Combining Resources On A Grand Scale C 20 MIN
2 INCH VIDEOTAPE J-H
Examines the automobile industry and discusses the inputs and outputs of the industry as well as how it is managed.
From The Our World Of Economics Series.
Prod-MPATI Dist-GPITVL

Managing Production - How To Bake A Cake, The Recipe Of Production C 20 MIN
2 INCH VIDEOTAPE J-H
Generalizes the economics of decision-making in an enterprise. Shows how resources are combined and what happens when too much of a certain resource is used.
From The Our World Of Economics Series.
Prod-MPATI Dist-GPITVL

Managing Production - Junior Achievement, Combining Resources On A Small Scale C 20 MIN
2 INCH VIDEOTAPE J-H
Presents a group of youngsters in a Junior Achievement company and examines the inputs and outputs of the business and how it is managed.
From The Our World Of Economics Series.
Prod-MPATI Dist-GPITVL

Managing Risk C 29 MIN
3/4 OR 1/2 INCH VIDEO CASSETTE
See series title for descriptive statement.
From The Business File Series.
Prod-PBS Dist-PBS

Managing Safety Yourself C 15 MIN
3/4 OR 1/2 INCH VIDEO CASSETTE IND
Reviews nine 'how to' principles of good supervision for promoting safe workmanship. Contains an exercise of seven observation examples in which the foreman must detect an unsafe act or condition.
From The Foreman's Accident Prevention Series.
Prod-GPCV Dist-GPCV

Managing Secretions In Chronic Lung Disease - Emphysema C
3/4 OR 1/2 INCH VIDEO CASSETTE
Shows how failure of ciliary action and the cough mechanisms in chronic lung disease, such as asthma, chronic bronchitis or emphysema, can be managed by means of bronchodilators, expectorants and postural drainage.
Prod-MIFE Dist-MIFE

Managing Secretions In Chronic Lung Disease - Emphysema (Arabic) C
3/4 OR 1/2 INCH VIDEO CASSETTE
Shows how failure of ciliary action and the cough mechanisms in chronic lung disease, such as asthma, chronic bronchitis or emphysema, can be managed by means of bronchodilators, expectorants and postural drainage.
Prod-MIFE Dist-MIFE

Managing Secretions In Chronic Lung Disease - Emphysema (Spanish) C
3/4 OR 1/2 INCH VIDEO CASSETTE
Shows how failure of ciliary action and the cough mechanisms in chronic lung disease, such as asthma, chronic bronchitis or emphysema, can be managed by means of bronchodilators, expectorants and postural drainage.
Prod-MIFE Dist-MIFE

Managing Stress C
3/4 OR 1/2 INCH VIDEO CASSETTE
See series title for descriptive statement.
From The Management Training Series.
Prod-THGHT Dist-DELTAK

Managing Stress C 33 MIN
16MM FILM, 3/4 OR 1/2 IN VIDEO H-C A
Explores different types of stress and discusses stress reactions. Shows techniques for alleviating stress.
Prod-CRMP Dist-CRMP 1979

Managing Stress And Anger C
3/4 OR 1/2 INCH VIDEO CASSETTE A
Shows experts telling how to make stress a positive influence if one recognizes and manages it. Looks at causes of stress, importance of self-talk to reduce it and steps involved in conflict resolution.
From The Administrative Woman Series.
Prod-GPCV Dist-GPCV

Managing Stress—A Series
16MM FILM, 3/4 OR 1/2 IN VIDEO H-C A
Presents a series on the handling of stress.
Prod-CENTRO Dist-CORF 1984

Time Bomb Within, The 014 MIN
What The World Dishes Out 015 MIN
What You Bring On Yourself 015 MIN

Managing Stress, Anxiety And Frustration C 55 MIN
1/2 IN VIDEO CASSETTE (VHS) H-C
Defines stress, analyzes its causes and effects, and provides stress managing techniques including biofeedback, meditation, progressive relaxation and guided imagery.
LC NO. 85-703931
Prod-HRMC Dist-HRMC

Managing The Data Base Environment—A Series

Presents an overview of the data base environment, concentrating on the advantages and problems of converting from a file system to a data base system. Examines the methods that a data administrator uses to develop a logical data base design and explores the process of data administration and the types of people involved in this process.
Prod-DELTAK Dist-DELTAK

Concerns Of End Users 060 MIN
Data Administration 060 MIN
Data Base Is A Change In Management 060 MIN
Logical Data Base Design - The Key To Success 060 MIN
View From The Top, The 060 MIN

Managing The Decision C 60 MIN
3/4 OR 1/2 INCH VIDEO CASSETTE
See series title for descriptive statement.
From The Missiles Of October - A Case Study In Decision Making Series.
Prod-LCOA Dist-DELTAK

Managing The Executive Branch C 60 MIN
3/4 OR 1/2 INCH VIDEO CASSETTE I
Explores how a president gets things done. Examines the growth in presidential staff and the ways modern presidents have worked with their staff members.
From The Every Four Years Series.
LC NO. 81-706957
Prod-WHYY Dist-AITECH 1980

Managing The Fire Risk C
3/4 OR 1/2 INCH VIDEO CASSETTE
See series title for descriptive statement.
From The Fire Away Series.
Prod-NFPA Dist-NFPA

Managing The Information Resource C 45 MIN
3/4 OR 1/2 INCH VIDEO CASSETTE
Defines and explains information management and its implications for organizations of today and tomorrow.
From The Information Resource Management - Challenge For The 1980s Series.
Prod-DELTAK Dist-DELTAK

Managing The Job C 10 MIN
3/4 OR 1/2 INCH VIDEO CASSETTE
Looks at the five 'w's' of organization and offers 13 ways to better organization.
From The Effective Office Worker Series
Prod-RESEM Dist-RESEM

Managing The Knowledge Worker C
16MM FILM - 3/4 IN VIDEO
Shows how a manager or supervisor should deal with expert, professional and semiprofessional subordinates who may know more about their specialties than the manager or supervisor. Discusses how to obtain top performance from them and use their talents more effectively.
From The Managing For Tomorrow Series. Unit 1
Prod-BNA Dist-BNA

Managing The Knowledge Worker (Dutch) C
16MM FILM, 3/4 OR 1/2 IN VIDEO
Examines how to manage a work force characterized by experts who know more than their managers.
From The Managing For Tomorrow (Dutch) Series.
Prod-BNA Dist-BNA

Managing The Knowledge Worker (German) C
16MM FILM, 3/4 OR 1/2 IN VIDEO
Examines how to manage a work force characterized by experts who know more than their managers.
From The Managing For Tomorrow (German) Series.
Prod-BNA Dist-BNA

Managing The Overseas Assignment C 29 MIN
3/4 OR 1/2 INCH VIDEO CASSETTE A
Explains cultural and business practices in various foreign countries, such as Japan, Saudi Arabia, Venezuela, India, England and Mexico in order to help American families adjust to living abroad.
From The Going International Series.
LC NO. 84-706118
Prod-COPGRG Dist-COPGRG 1983

Managing The Transition C 30 MIN
3/4 OR 1/2 INCH VIDEO CASSETTE
See series title for descriptive statement.
From The Third Wave Series.
Prod-TRIWVE Dist-DELTAK

Managing The Transition To IRM C 45 MIN
3/4 OR 1/2 INCH VIDEO CASSETTE
Examines the critical issues of information management and discusses what organizations can do today to implement it.
From The Information Resource Management - Challenge For The 1980s Series.
Prod-DELTAK Dist-DELTAK

Managing The Troubled Employee C 24 MIN
3/4 OR 1/2 INCH VIDEO CASSETTE A
Provides managers with an approach to the detection and confrontation of the troubled employee.
Prod-SUTHRB Dist-SUTHRB

Managing Time C 11 MIN
3/4 OR 1/2 INCH VIDEO CASSETTE
See series title for descriptive statement.
From The Applied Management Series.
Prod-ORGDYN Dist-DELTAK

Managing Time C 25 MIN
16MM FILM - 3/4 IN VIDEO IND
Explains how time is inevitably wasted when an executive must spend much of his time on things that are not important.
From The Effective Executive Series.
Prod-BNA Dist-BNA 1968

Managing Time - Professional And Personal C 30 MIN
3/4 OR 1/2 INCH VIDEO CASSETTE A
Shows managers how they can make use of all their time, personal as well as professional, and balance demands in both spheres. Details how to define and accomplish their free time activities, relating each to long-term goals.
From The Time Management For Management Series. Pt 6
Prod-TIMLIF Dist-TIMLIF 1981

Managing Time Effectively C
3/4 OR 1/2 INCH VIDEO CASSETTE
See series title for descriptive statement.
From The Management Training Series.
Prod-THGHT Dist-DELTAK

Managing To Survive C 28 MIN
16MM FILM, 3/4 OR 1/2 IN VIDEO A
Dramatizes the events which lead to the bankruptcy of an English furniture-manufacturing firm. Designed to promote discussion of general financial principles and specific problems related to roles of managers and the development of supporting skills and attitudes.
LC NO. 81-707642
Prod-LOYDSB Dist-IFB Prodn-MILLBK 1980

Managing To Win C 23 MIN
3/4 OR 1/2 INCH VIDEO CASSETTE A
Shows former University of Arkansas football coach Lou Holtz explaining how he motivates and manages his teams to win, just as a businessmen must motivate and manage his employees. Treats related issues that bear on both sports and business success. Narrated by Pat Summerall.
Prod-SFTI Dist-SFTI

Managing Value Engineering C 60 MIN
3/4 OR 1/2 INCH VIDEO CASSETTE IND
See series title for descriptive statement.
From The Value Engineering Series.
Prod-NCSU Dist-AMCEE

Managing Volunteer Fire Departments C
3/4 OR 1/2 INCH VIDEO CASSETTE
See series title for descriptive statement.
From The Fire Away Series.
Prod-NFPA Dist-NFPA

Managing Wildlife Resources C 14 MIN
16MM FILM OPTICAL SOUND
Profiles the need for effective programs to manage the Earth's wildlife, a source of food and knowledge.
Prod-ALLFP Dist-NSTA 1975

Managing With Alzheimer's Disease C 30 MIN
3/4 OR 1/2 INCH VIDEO CASSETTE
Focuses on solutions to the problems encountered by anyone caring for a person with this Alzheimer's disease. Includes information on when and how to choose a nursing facility.
Prod-GSHDME Dist-GSHDME Prodn-ADACW

Managing Your High Blood Pressure With Drugs C 4 MIN
3/4 OR 1/2 INCH VIDEO CASSETTE
Explains necessity for controlling high blood pressure, or hypertension, which if untreated can damage the blood circulatory system and lead to kidney failure, stroke, heart disease or other complications Describes benefits and possible side effects of physician-prescribed drugs and cites importance of developing habit of taking medication regularly and keeping a record of it.
Prod-TRAINX Dist-TRAINX

Managing Your Law Firm—A Series

Gives attorneys practical suggestions on how to manage a law firm better. Shows how to analyze a firm's operations, isolate the weaknesses and establish effective business procedures.
Prod-ABACPE Dist-ABACPE

Basic Financial Management 040 MIN
How To Avoid Self-Malpractice 040 MIN
Winning Isn't Everything - Improving Client 035 MIN

Managing Your Molecule C 15 MIN
3/4 OR 1/2 INCH VIDEO CASSETTE
See series title for descriptive statement.
From The Time Management For Managers And Professionals Series.
Prod-DELTAK Dist-DELTAK Prodn-ONCKEW

Managing Your Money C 23 MIN
16MM FILM, 3/4 OR 1/2 IN VIDEO H-C
Suggests ways of managing money.
From The Making It On Your Own Series.
Prod-BARR Dist-BARR 1979

Managing Your Motivation C 20 MIN
16MM FILM - 3/4 IN VIDEO
Presents Dr Saul Gellerman and salespeople who discuss the two faces of success, the dangers of too much success, what a slump is and how to get out of it, the derailing sequence, early warning signals of an impending slump, how they should feel when people don't buy and the two biggest motivational dangers salespeople face.
From The Self-Motivation In Selling Series.
Prod-BNA Dist-BNA

Managing Your Time C 9 MIN
3/4 OR 1/2 INCH VIDEO CASSETTE
Shows office workers more than 20 ways to manage their time more effectively. Offers tips for saving time in typing, filing and dictation.
From The Effective Office Worker Series
Prod-RESEM Dist-RESEM

Managing Yourself C 30 MIN
3/4 OR 1/2 INCH VIDEO CASSETTE A
Studies how to manage anxiety through the management of thoughts, feelings and reactions to stress by using relaxation skills and behavioral techniques.
From The Stress Management - A Positive Strategy Series. Pt 3
LC NO. 82-706501
Prod-TIMLIF Dist-TIMLIF 1982

Manassas C 15 MIN
3/4 OR 1/2 INCH VIDEO CASSETTE J A
Portrays the first (Bull Run) and second battles of Manassas. Illustrates the consequences paid by both North and South in the Civil War.
Prod-USNPS Dist-USNAC 1983

Mandabi C 90 MIN
16MM FILM OPTICAL SOUND I-C A
A story about a man who receives a money order that threatens to destroy the traditional fabric of his life is used to point out the problems of modern Africa as a civilization struggling to recapture its own rich heritage after colonial corruption.
LC NO. 76-707580
Prod-DOMIR Dist-GROVE 1969

Mandarin Pancakes C 29 MIN
2 INCH VIDEOTAPE
Features Joyce Chen showing how to adapt Chinese recipes so they can be prepared in the American kitchen and still retain the authentic flavor. Demonstrates how to prepare mandarin pancakes.
From The Joyce Chen Cooks Series.
Prod-WGBHTV Dist-PUBTEL

Mandarin Revolution, The C 57 MIN
16MM FILM, 3/4 OR 1/2 IN VIDEO H-C A
Focuses on the worldwide slump that threatened economic disaster after World War I and the role of economist John Maynard Keynes' ideas on saving the West. Based on the book The Age Of Uncertainty by John Kenneth Galbraith.
From The Age Of Uncertainty Series.
LC NO. 77-701490
Prod-BBCL Dist-FI 1977

Mandibular Block Anesthesia - Gow-Gates Techniques C 9 MIN
16MM FILM - 3/4 IN VIDEO PRO
Describes the Gow-Gates method of mandibular block anesthesia, which uses the condylar neck as the target area for the injection, as well as extra- and intra-oral landmarks. Reviews the anatomy of this area and demonstrates injection procedures.
LC NO. 79-706838
Prod-VADTC Dist-USNAC 1978

Mandibular Prognathism C 43 MIN
16MM FILM OPTICAL SOUND
Demonstrates the two-stage operation for the correction of a mandibular prognathism. Shows in considerable detail preoperative and postoperative studies as well as the two stages of the operation. Includes inserts of X-ray studies and medical sketches demonstrating various stages in the surgical procedure.
LC NO. FIE56-30
Prod-USVA Dist-USNAC 1956

Mandibular Reconstruction - Cancellous Bone From The Iliac Crest In An Alloplastic Mesh... C 21 MIN
3/4 OR 1/2 INCH VIDEO CASSETTE PRO
Shows an implantable material, 'alloplastic mesh,' which can be

easily molded and cut, used to reconstruct osseous contour defects. Demonstrates the technique to reconstruct a large section of a patient's mandible which had been resected to remove a tumor.
Prod-WFP Dist-WFP

Mandibular Vestibuloplasty With Skin Graft C 18 MIN
16MM FILM, 3/4 OR 1/2 IN VIDEO PRO
Demonstrates the surgical procedure for increasing the quantity of the mandibular denture bearing area by lowering the buccal, labial and lingual muscular attachments and introducing a skin graft.
LC NO. 81-706361
Prod-VADTC Dist-USNAC 1977

Mandy's Checkup C 15 MIN
16MM FILM, 3/4 OR 1/2 IN VIDEO K
Uses clowns to show what a physical checkup is like. Points out that it is not painful or unpleasant, and that just because a person feels fine does not mean that he or she is healthy.
LC NO. 81-707658
Prod-USDHHS Dist-USNAC 1981

Mandy's Grandmother C 30 MIN
16MM FILM, 3/4 OR 1/2 IN VIDEO I-J
Presents a story about a young tomboy and her prim grandmother who quickly forget the disappointment of their first meeting and become friends. Based on the book Mandy's Grandmother by Liesel Skorpen. Features Maureen O'Sullivan and Amy Levitan.
Prod-SUGERA Dist-PHENIX 1978

Manejando El Cambio C 23 MIN
16MM FILM, 3/4 OR 1/2 IN VIDEO A
A Spanish-language version of the motion picture Managing Change. Illustrates and suggests solutions to some of the special problems that confront managers when it is their responsibility to manage change. Shows how, when a new assembly line is installed and new products are introduced in an English laminating factory, unexpected problems arise.
Prod-MILLBK Dist-IFB 1981

Manet, An Innovator In Spite Of Himself C 15 MIN
16MM FILM OPTICAL SOUND
Reveals that Manet's paintings were the harbingers of modern art even though the were ridiculed by critics of his time. Shows that his Olympia was called the first truly modern painting and his works inspired such impressionists as Renoir and Monet.
Prod-LEEN Dist-FACSEA 1980

Manhattan B 96 MIN
16MM FILM OPTICAL SOUND
Stars Woody Allen as a television writer whose quest for the perfect woman leads him through a variety of relationships. Features Meryl Streep, Diane Keaton, Mariel Hemingway and Michael Murphy.
Prod-UNKNWN Dist-UAE 1979

Manhattan Street Band C 24 MIN
16MM FILM, 3/4 OR 1/2 IN VIDEO J-C A
Tells how inner-city youth transcend cultural and racial barriers through the formation of a band.
Prod-EQINOX Dist-CAROUF

Manic Depressive Illness C 17 MIN
3/4 OR 1/2 INCH VIDEO CASSETTE PRO
Discusses disturbances in mood which may reach from mania to severe depression. Discusses the classification of manic-depression and explains the types, manic, depressed and circular. Reviews lithium carbonate, a drug frequently considered in the care of patients with manic-depressive illness.
LC NO. 77-730522
Prod-TRAINX Dist-TRAINX

Manifest Destiny C 30 MIN
3/4 OR 1/2 INCH VIDEO CASSETTE C
See series title for descriptive statement.
From The American Story - The Beginning To 1877 Series.
Prod-DALCCD Dist-DALCCD

Manifest Destiny C 30 MIN
2 INCH VIDEOTAPE
Discusses the Turner frontier theory. Covers the events of the war between Texas and Mexico and the Mexican War.
From The American History I Series.
Prod-DENVPS Dist-GPITVL

Manifold Controversy B 3 MIN
3/4 INCH VIDEO CASSETTE
Shows a customer trying to explain to police why he feels he has been cheated out of an exhaust system by a garage owner.
From The Pittsburgh Police Series.
Prod-DOCEDR Dist-DOCEDR

Manifold II C 10 MIN
3/4 OR 1/2 INCH VIDEO CASSETTE PRO
Shows how to assemble and use a new manifold which helps simplify multiple pressure lines used in hemodynamic monitoring.
Prod-WFP Dist-WFP

Manila C 11 MIN
16MM FILM, 3/4 OR 1/2 IN VIDEO J-C A
Explores the city of Manila, from Rizal Park to Port Santiago in the old Spanish City. Views the Chinese district, the churches, shopping centers, modern office buildings and traffic.
Prod-LUF Dist-LUF 1979

Manimals C 29 MIN
16MM FILM, 3/4 OR 1/2 IN VIDEO
Explores the world of exotic pets and the emotions surrounding them, ranging from love and ego to comedy and tragedy.
Prod-OPUS Dist-PHENIX 1978

Manioc Bread C 11 MIN
16MM FILM, 3/4 OR 1/2 IN VIDEO
See series title for descriptive statement.
From The Indians Of The Orinoco (Venezuela) - The Makiritare Series.
Prod-IFF Dist-IFF

Manipulation And Actualization C 30 MIN
3/4 INCH VIDEO CASSETTE
Illustrates eight different manipulative techniques which are predominately used by people today. Discusses recent developments in the 'Manipulation and Actualization' theory.
Prod-PSYCHD Dist-PSYCHD

Manipulation Of Language And Meaning, The C 30 MIN
3/4 OR 1/2 INCH VIDEO CASSETTE C
See series title for descriptive statement.
From The Language And Meaning Series.
Prod-WUSFTV Dist-GPITVL 1983

Manipulative Client, The C 30 MIN
16MM FILM - 3/4 IN VIDEO PRO
Presents course instructors Grayce Sills and Doreen James Wise and guest Mary R Bock reviewing the psychodynamics underlying manipulative behavior. Discusses nursing intervention with emphasis on consistency and communication. Presents everyday situations demonstrating manipulative behavior.
LC NO. 77-700135
Prod-AJN Dist-AJN Prodn-WGNCP 1977

Manipulative Techniques To Assist Fluid Flow C 14 MIN
3/4 OR 1/2 INCH VIDEO CASSETTE PRO
Applies principles of manipulation to treatment of somatic findings common in patients with upper respiratory infections. Directs palpatory examination for disturbances in tissue fluid flow to related areas of tissue tension and congestion. Demonstrates soft tissue and articulatory techniques in the cervical and thoracic spinal regions, the anterior cervical compartment and the thoracic cage.
From The Osteopathic Examination And Manipulation Series.
Prod-MSU Dist-MSU

Manitoba - Everyman's Wilderness C 14 MIN
16MM FILM OPTICAL SOUND
Depicts the 100,000 lakes and unspoiled wilderness of Manitoba, Canada. Portrays recreation areas, a train journey to the seaport of Churchill, northern mining towns and a summer cruise down Lake Winnipeg.
Prod-CTFL Dist-CTFL

Manitoba - Everyman's Wilderness C 27 MIN
16MM FILM OPTICAL SOUND
Depicts the 100,000 lakes and unspoiled wilderness of Manitoba, Canada. Portrays recreation areas, a train journey to the seaport of Churchill, northern mining towns and a summer cruise down Lake Winnipeg.
Prod-CTFL Dist-CTFL

Manitoba Fish Tale C 30 MIN
16MM FILM OPTICAL SOUND
Shows three fishermen traveling to the the remote lakes of Manitoba to catch the fighting smallmouth bass, northern pike, Winnipeg perch and walleye pike.
Prod-BRNSWK Dist-KAROL

Manitoba In The Wintertime C 12 MIN
16MM FILM OPTICAL SOUND
Portrays winter activities in Manitoba, showing a dog derby, sleigh rides, a ballet concert, snowmobile races and swimming.
LC NO. 73-714309
Prod-MDTR Dist-CTFL 1971

Mankind And The Atom B 20 MIN
16MM FILM OPTICAL SOUND
Illustrates the birth and history, crises and challenges of the Atomic Age.
From The Screen News Digest Series. Vol 10, Issue 2
Prod-HEARST Dist-HEARST 1967

Manloading And Budgeting In Project Planning C 30 MIN
3/4 OR 1/2 INCH VIDEO CASSETTE
Describes manload charts. Covers resource allocation and budget formats. Explores the use of computers in project management.
From The Project Management Series.
Prod-ITCORP Dist-ITCORP

Manly Bacon, Unholey And Two-Minute Mousse C 15 MIN
2 INCH VIDEOTAPE
See series title for descriptive statement.
From The Umbrella Series.
Prod-KETCTV Dist-PUBTEL

Manmade Extinction C 15 MIN
16MM FILM OPTICAL SOUND C
Deals with the efforts of ecologists and research scientists to stave off and control the extermination of the many species imperiled by modern civilization.
From The Science In Action Series.
Prod-ALLFP Dist-COUNFI

Manna Of The South Seas C 20 MIN
16MM FILM OPTICAL SOUND I-H
Shows the many uses of the coconut in the Fiji Islands--for food, to make baskets and for trade in the form of copra.
Prod-MMP Dist-MMP 1954

Manne And Jazz B 21 MIN
16MM FILM OPTICAL SOUND
Presents a documentary depicting the professional and private life of Shelly Manne, a jazz musician.
LC NO. 75-703204
Prod-USC Dist-USC 1965

Manned Space Flight - New Goals, New Challenges C 19 MIN
16MM FILM OPTICAL SOUND
Shows where we stand today in manned space flight and where we will be in the future if present capability is applied to such imminent developments as Skylab, space stations and space shuttles.
Prod-NASA Dist-NASA

Manned Space Flight 1964 C 14 MIN
16MM FILM OPTICAL SOUND
Reports NASA'S manned flight programs. Includes the two-man Gemini earth-orbital and the three-man Apollo lunar landing missions.
Prod-NASA Dist-THIOKL 1964

Manned Spacecraft Center, The - Where Tomorrow Begins C 30 MIN
16MM FILM OPTICAL SOUND
Depicts the role of the NASA Manned Spacecraft Center in the nation's space flight programs from Mercury, Gemini and Apollo through Skylab and programs of the future.
Prod-NASA Dist-NASA

Mannerisms Displayed By Gestures C 30 MIN
3/4 OR 1/2 INCH VIDEO CASSETTE
Explains that gestures from a boss, spouse or good friend have distinct meaning to a person.
From The Nonverbal Communication Series.
Prod-IVCH Dist-IVCH

Manners And Morals Of High Capitalism, The C 60 MIN
16MM FILM, 3/4 OR 1/2 IN VIDEO H-C A
Looks at the robber baron industrial capitalists of the late 19th century. Based on the book The Age Of Uncertainty by John Kenneth Galbraith.
From The Age Of Uncertainty Series.
LC NO. 77-700662
Prod-BBCL Dist-FI 1977

Mannikin, The C 28 MIN
16MM FILM, 3/4 OR 1/2 IN VIDEO
Presents a supernatural story by Robert Bloch about a young singer who is possessed by a demon. Features Ronee Blakley and Keir Dullea.
From The Classics, Dark And Dangerous Series.
Prod-LCOA Dist-LCOA 1977

Mannikin, The (Spanish) C 28 MIN
16MM FILM, 3/4 OR 1/2 IN VIDEO P-C A
Tells the horror story of a young woman with a back ailment who is healed when she goes to her former home, where evil rituals are taking place. Based on story by Robert Bloch.
From The Classics Dark And Dangerous (Spanish) Series.
Prod-LCOA Dist-LCOA 1977

Manoeuvre C 115 MIN
16MM FILM, 3/4 OR 1/2 IN VIDEO
Follows an infantry tank company from the US through the various stages of a NATO training exercise in West Germany, showing the defensive and offensive tactics and the hypothetical wins and losses of a company fighting a simulated, conventional ground and air war.
Prod-WISEF Dist-ZIPRAH

Manon Lescaut C 126 MIN
3/4 OR 1/2 INCH VIDEO CASSETTE A
Presents the story of an obsessive love that begins in pre-revolutionary France in the always popular Puccini opera, Manon Lescaut.
Prod-EDDIM Dist-EDDIM

Manos A La Obra - The Story Of Operation Bootstrap - Pt I (Captioned) C 28 MIN
16MM FILM - 3/4 IN VIDEO
Chronicles Puerto Rico's history from the peaceful revolution and U S invasion in 1898 when its peaceful and natural state was changed forever. Reveals how the contradictory historical forces led to the industrialization and transformation of Puerto Rican society. In English and Spanish with English subtitles.
From The Presente Series.
Prod-KCET Dist-KCET

Manos A La Obra - The Story Of Operation Bootstrap C 59 MIN
16MM FILM, 3/4 OR 1/2 IN VIDEO H-C A
Looks at Puerto Rico's Operation Bootstrap, the highly vaunted economic development plan undertaken in the Fifties that was to provide a role model for economic development throughout the Americas. Surveys Puerto Rican history from the 1930s through the 1980s when Fortune Magazine has labeled Puerto Rico's economy as Operation Welfare.
Prod-CPRS Dist-CNEMAG

Manos A La Obra - The Story Of Operation Bootstrap - Pt II (Captioned) C 29 MIN
16MM FILM - 3/4 IN VIDEO
Chronicles the history of U S involvement in the underdeveloped country of Puerto Rico. Uses filmclips, archival newspapers, government propaganda films and candid interviews with key figures in recent Puerto Rican history to emphasize the purpose of Operation Bootstrap to attract U S capital to Puerto Rico by offering tax-free earnings and calling the island the 'showcase of the Americas.' Reveals the industrialization experience in a land that was free. In English and Spanish with English subtitles.
From The Presente Series.
Prod-KCET Dist-KCET

Manpower C 7 MIN
3/4 OR 1/2 INCH VIDEO CASSETTE
See series title for descriptive statement.
From The Five Short Works by Janice Tanaka Series.
Prod-EAI Dist-EAI

Mansion Of The Doomed C 93 MIN
16MM FILM OPTICAL SOUND
Focuses on a scientist who will do anything to restore his daughter's sight, including using the eyeballs from her fiancee and other unlucky victims.
Prod-UNKNWN Dist-TWYMAN 1975

Manson's Blood Fluke B 16 MIN
16MM FILM OPTICAL SOUND
Uses primarily animation photomicography to demonstrate stages in the life cycle of schistosoma mansoni in secondary and primary hosts, to depict the biologic relationships between the blood fluke and its hosts, man and snail, and to explain the pathology of Manson's schistosomiasis in man. For professional use.
LC NO. FIE53-290
Prod-USPHS Dist-USNAC 1948

Mansube Machlidar B 11 MIN
16MM FILM OPTICAL SOUND I-C A
Illustrates the development of fisheries in village ponds which have enabled the village panchayats to earn revenue.
Prod-INDIA Dist-NEDINF

Mantle Of Protection, The B 29 MIN
16MM FILM OPTICAL SOUND PRO
Aims to heighten awareness of the importance of the early diagnosis, treatment and prevention of rheumatic fever. Depicts the great advances made in research and treatment and in antibiotic prophylaxis, at Irvington house, helping to return sick children to health and normal lives.
Prod-DOCF Dist-WYLAB 1956

Manton Plan, The C 13 MIN
16MM FILM OPTICAL SOUND
Shows how a local municipality in Australia goes about establishing a Disaster Plan.
LC NO. 80-700910
Prod-TASCOR Dist-TASCOR 1977

Manual Alphabet C 16 MIN
16MM FILM MAGNETIC SOUND K-C A S
See series title for descriptive statement.
From The PANCOM Beginning Total Communication Program For Hearing Parents Of... Series. Level 2
LC NO. 77-700504
Prod-CSDE Dist-JOYCE Prodn-CSFDF 1977

Manual Cutting A Bevel - Freehand B 13 MIN
16MM FILM, 3/4 OR 1/2 IN VIDEO
Shows how to select a tip for bevel cutting, clean a tip, adjust oxygen and acetylene pressure for bevel cutting and cut a bevel with minimum drag.
From The Welding Procedures - Oxygen Cutting Series. No. 2
LC NO. 82-706088
Prod-USOE Dist-USNAC Prodn-DEFREN 1944

Manual Cutting A Shape - Freehand Guided B 16 MIN
16MM FILM, 3/4 OR 1/2 IN VIDEO
Shows how to make plywood template for cutting, make a tip guide device, position a template for cutting, use the guide device and use a circle cutting device.
From The Welding Procedures - Oxygen Cutting Series. No. 3
Prod-USOE Dist-USNAC 1944

Manual Cutting To A Line - Freehand B 21 MIN
16MM FILM, 3/4 OR 1/2 IN VIDEO
Shows how to assemble an oxyacetylene cutting outfit, select proper cutting tip, adjust oxygen and acetylene delivery pressures, adjust the preheating cutting flames, make a 90 degree free-hand cut and disassemble the cutting outfit.
From The Welding Procedures - Oxygen Cutting Series. No. 1
LC NO. 82-706087
Prod-USOE Dist-USNAC Prodn-DEFREN 1944

Manual Data Input C 15 MIN
3/4 OR 1/2 INCH VIDEO CASSETTE PRO
See series title for descriptive statement.
From The Numerical Control/Computer Numerical Control, Part I - Fundamentals Series.
Prod-ICSINT Dist-ICSINT

Manual Data Input C 17 MIN
3/4 OR 1/2 INCH VIDEO CASSETTE IND
Examines the parts of the manual data input keyboard. Discusses entering and storing programs and entering tool length offsets.
From The Numerical Control/Computerized Numerical Control, Module 1 - Fundamentals Series.
Prod-LEIKID Dist-LEIKID

Manual English Vocabularies C 100 MIN
3/4 OR 1/2 INCH VIDEO CASSETTE S
Demonstrates Signing Exact English (SEE) vocabulary words. Presents fingerspelling, signing, and usage of words in a sentence.
Prod-GALCO Dist-GALCO Prodn-GALCO 1975

Manual Lifting C 19 MIN
3/4 OR 1/2 INCH VIDEO CASSETTE IND
Describes and demonstrates correct manual lifting techniques and how unsafe lifting can lead to serious injury.
From The Safety Action For Employees Series.
Prod-GPCV Dist-GPCV

Manual Positive Pressure Ventilation C 9 MIN
3/4 OR 1/2 INCH VIDEO CASSETTE PRO
See series title for descriptive statement.
From The Medical Skills Films Series.
Prod-WFP Dist-WFP

Manuel From Puerto Rico X 14 MIN
16MM FILM, 3/4 OR 1/2 IN VIDEO P-I
Describes the difficulties of a boy from Puerto Rico in adjusting to metropolitan surroundings when he moves with his family to New York City.
From The Newcomers To The City Series.
Prod-EBEC Dist-EBEC 1968

Manuel Jimenez - Artesano En Madera C 22 MIN
16MM FILM OPTICAL SOUND
A Spanish language version of the motion picture Manuel Jimenez - Woodcarver. Shows how a rural Mexican woodcarver represents the sights and scenes of his daily life. Recounts how he begins his sculptures by striking swiftly at the green branches of the wood with an ordinary farmer's machete, finishing the work with a common kitchen knife and completing the piece in a wild whimsy of character and color.
From The Artesanos Mexicanos Series.
Prod-WORKS Dist-WORKS 1977

Manuel Jimenez - Woodcarver C 22 MIN
16MM FILM OPTICAL SOUND
Shows how a rural Mexican woodcarver represents the sights and scenes of his daily life. Recounts how he begins his sculptures by striking swiftly at the green branches of the wood with an ordinary farmer's machete, finishing the work with a common kitchen knife and completing the piece in a wild whimsy of character and color.
From The Mexico's Folk Artists Series.
Prod-WORKS Dist-WORKS 1977

Manuel Jimenez - Woodcarver C 29 MIN
16MM FILM - 3/4 IN VIDEO
Profiles the life of Manuel Jimenez, the woodcarver whose dream came true. Shows how he became interested in the art after years of herding animals and plowing the fields. Follows the woodcarver's process from selecting a tree to adding the finishing touches. In Spanish with English voice-over. Filmed in Arrazola, Oaxaca, Mexico.
From The Presente Series.
Prod-KCET Dist-KCET

Manufacture Of Planet Pinions C 14 MIN
16MM FILM OPTICAL SOUND
Examines the machining and inspection processes of planet pinions.
Prod-GM Dist-GM

Manufactured Epidemic, The C 30 MIN
3/4 OR 1/2 INCH VIDEO CASSETTE C A
Identifies smoking as a contributing factor in a number of disease processes. Examines the characteristics of smokers and describes the nature of the drug nicotine. Discusses the difficulty of breaking the smoking habit in light of national economic interests.
From The Contemporary Health Issues Series. Lesson 20
Prod-SCCON Dist-CDTEL

Manufacturing C 6 MIN
16MM FILM, 3/4 OR 1/2 IN VIDEO K-I
See series title for descriptive statement.
From The Kingdom Of Could Be You Series.
Prod-EBEC Dist-EBEC 1974

Manufacturing C 10 MIN
3/4 INCH VIDEO CASSETTE P
Takes a tour of the Hershey chocolate factory to show how a candy bar is produced. Examines the entire manufacturing process, from raw materials to finished product.
Prod-MINIP Dist-GA

Manufacturing C 30 MIN
3/4 OR 1/2 INCH VIDEO CASSETTE
See series title for descriptive statement.
From The Videosearch Performance Appraisal (Case Studies) Series.
Prod-DELTAK Dist-DELTAK

Manufacturing - IBM C 20 MIN
3/4 OR 1/2 INCH VIDEO CASSETTE
Interviews a representative of IBM and enumerates the jobs available in large corporations for college graduates with liberal arts backgrounds.
From The Clues To Career Opportunities For Liberal Arts Graduates Series.
LC NO. 79-706055
Prod-IU Dist-IU 1978

Manufacturing And Industry B 15 MIN
2 INCH VIDEOTAPE P-I
See series title for descriptive statement.
From The Our Changing Community Series.
Prod-VITA Dist-GPITVL 1967

Manufacturing Automation - A Key To Productivity—A Series

Points out that the manufacturing environment is undergoing dramatic change and the result of this change will be the creation of a new manufacturing environment, calling for the use of such tools as robots, programmed controllers and computer numerical control within the context of computer-aided design and computer-aided manufacturing to improve productivity.
Prod-DELTAK Dist-DELTAK

CAD/CAM - The Computer In Manufacturing	030 MIN
Implementation, Impact And Change	030 MIN
Implications For MIS	030 MIN
New Manufacturing Environment, The	030 MIN
Using Industrial Robots	030 MIN

Manufacturing Automation—A Series
PRO
Covers general principles of CAD/CAM integration, engineer- ing databases, computer process control, group technology concepts and applications and flexible manufacturing systems. Uses classroom format to videotape 30 hours of on 20 cassettes.
Prod-NCSU Dist-AMCEE

Manufacturing Engineering—A Series
C
Relates manufacturing concepts stressing the inter-relationships of materials and processes used to develop finished products. Emphasizes metals and provides a broad perspective of major machining processes involved in goods manufacture. Focuses on scope and impact of automation, especially areas likely to be replaced by computer oriented systems.
Prod-NCSU Dist-AMCEE

Manufacturing Materials And Processes—A Series

Explains production machinery and demonstrates process of manufacturing.
Prod-GE Dist-WFVTAE

Abrasive Flow Machine	011 MIN
Abrasive Machining	011 MIN
Broaching And Shaping	016 MIN
Casting	028 MIN
Chemical Milling	011 MIN
Cleaning	015 MIN
Computer Applications In Industry	017 MIN
Drilling And Boring	025 MIN
Electrical Discharge Machining	017 MIN
Electrochemical Grinding	014 MIN
Electrochemical Machining	013 MIN
Electroplating	017 MIN
Finishing And Deburring	016 MIN
Forging	019 MIN
Gages And Measurements	015 MIN
Heat Treating	015 MIN
Interactive Graphics	010 MIN
Introduction To Coatings And Painting	015 MIN
Introduction To Joining	009 MIN
Introduction To Metallurgy	011 MIN
Introduction To Sheet Metal	009 MIN
Laser Drilling	008 MIN
Lathe, The	017 MIN
Materials Testing	010 MIN
Milling	009 MIN
Non-Destructive Testing	016 MIN
Powder Metallugy	014 MIN
Rolling	011 MIN
Sheet Metal Processing	019 MIN
Soldering And Brazing	017 MIN
Welding	015 MIN

Manufacturing Midwest, The C 15 MIN
16MM FILM, 3/4 OR 1/2 IN VIDEO J
Examines the manufacturing resources of the Midwest region of the United States.
From The U S Geography Series.
Prod-MGHT Dist-MGHT 1976

Manufacturing Processes C 12 MIN
3/4 OR 1/2 INCH VIDEO CASSETTE
Covers sand casting, permanent-mold, centrifugal and die casting. Deals with forging, extrusion and powder metal forming as well as other manufacturing processes.
From The Working With Metals In The Plant Series.
Prod-TPCTRA Dist-TPCTRA

Manufacturing Team, The C 20 MIN
16MM FILM OPTICAL SOUND H
Points out that industry requires a multitude of men and women working together to produce the hundreds of thousands of products that consumers use everyday. Views this teamwork in action at a large rubber company.
From The Career Guidance Series.
Prod-KRMATV Dist-GPITVL

Manufacturing The Ducor Catheter C 10 MIN
16MM FILM OPTICAL SOUND PRO
Illustrates the manufacturing and quality control of the Ducor catheter.
Prod-CORDIS Dist-CORDIS

Manufacturing With Plastics C 25 MIN
3/4 OR 1/2 INCH VIDEO CASSETTE H-C A
Discusses manufacturing with plastics.
From The Technical Studies Series.
Prod-BBCTV Dist-FI 1981

Manure Storage C 16 MIN
3/4 OR 1/2 INCH VIDEO CASSETTE
Focuses on gases as often being the major concern in rescues from manure storage facilities. Stresses the importance of restraint and personal protection.
From The Agricultural Accidents And Rescue Series.
Prod-PSU Dist-PSU

Manxmen, The C 25 MIN
16MM FILM OPTICAL SOUND
Surveys the Isle of Man, a little known island set in the midst of the Irish Sea. Points out that it is all that remains of an ancient Norse Kingdom and contains a wealth of stories.
From The Eye Of The Beholder Series.
LC NO. 75-701896
Prod-RCPDF Dist-VIACOM 1974

Many Adventures Of Winnie The Pooh—A Series
16MM FILM, 3/4 OR 1/2 IN VIDEO K-I
Presents three adventures based on the book Winnie-The-Pooh by A A Milne.
Prod-WDEMCO Dist-WDEMCO 1981

Winnie The Pooh And The Blustery Day	025 MIN
Winnie The Pooh And The Honey Tree	026 MIN
Winnie The Pooh And Tigger Too	026 MIN

Many Americans—A Series
16MM FILM, 3/4 OR 1/2 IN VIDEO J-H
Prod-LCOA Dist-LCOA 1970

Felipa - North Of The Border 17 MIN
Geronimo Jones 21 MIN
Lee Suzuki - Home In Hawaii 19 MIN
Matthew Aliuk - Eskimo In Two Worlds 18 MIN
Miguel Up From Puerto Rico 15 MIN
Siu Mei Wong - Who Shall I Be 18 MIN
Todd - Growing Up In Appalachia 14 MIN
William - From Georgia To Harlem 15 MIN

Many Cities Of Boston, The C 17 MIN
16MM FILM OPTICAL SOUND J-C A
Features Daniel P Moynihan and Charles V Hamilton who discuss the new period in our national history when, for many, confrontation is replacing the democratic process, when established institutions are being questioned and found wanting. Studies Boston as representative of any city in the United States, its black ghetto, Roxbury, which is raging with violence and Dover, white and prosperous, which is help ing Roxbury to help itself. Concludes with the statement that the cities are our civilization, they are in trouble now, but these troubles must be worked out in order to survive.
LC NO. 75-709034
Prod-NBCTV Dist-NBC 1969

Many Different Gifts C 50 MIN
16MM FILM OPTICAL SOUND
Focuses on the planning and preparation by the Nova Community for a liturgy for the second Sunday in Advent and shows how each element is incorporated in the finished liturgy.
LC NO. 74-703215
Prod-NOVAC Dist-MMM 1974

Many Faces Of Argonne C 60 MIN
16MM FILM OPTICAL SOUND
Depicts the Argonne National Laboratory in Argonne, Illinois, showing objectives, methods and hardware of the broad range of nuclear research conducted by a national laboratory of the U S Atomic Energy Commission.
LC NO. FIE64-167
Prod-ANL Dist-USERD 1963

Many Faces Of Mexico, The C 29 MIN
16MM FILM OPTICAL SOUND I-C A
Shows how medical assistance and spiritual hope are brought to an underprivileged people by U S physicians and dentists, who fly their own planes into remote Mexican areas.
Prod-CAFM Dist-CAFM

Many Faces Of Mexico, The C 30 MIN
16MM FILM OPTICAL SOUND C A
Illustrates attractions and activities of Mexico, ranging from ancient ruins to modern industrial facilities. Includes views of Guaymas, Mazatlan, Guadalajara, Acapulco, Taxco and Mexico City.
LC NO. FIA65-836
Prod-DAC Dist-MCDO 1964

Many Faces Of Mexico, The C 17 MIN
16MM FILM, 3/4 OR 1/2 IN VIDEO
Shows facets of the Mexican land and people.
From The Mexican Heritage Series.
Prod-STEXMF Dist-FI 1976

Many Faces Of Television, The C
3/4 INCH VIDEO CASSETTE T
Presents television professionals discussing why television has been so successful.
From The Visual Learning Series. Session 2
Prod-NYSED Dist-NYSED

Many Faces Of Visual Aids, The C 20 MIN
3/4 OR 1/2 INCH VIDEO CASSETTE H-C A
Explores ways to use 16mm films, transparencies for overhead projectors, videotapes, 3-D models, film loops and charts, graphs and maps. Classroom visits show students and teachers using and in some cases producing their own visual aids.
LC NO. 85-702563
Prod-IFB Dist-IFB Prodn-ICEM

Many Faces, Many Meanings C 29 MIN
16MM FILM OPTICAL SOUND
Asks what is big business and what is a big company. Shows how both are more than jobs, products, profits and inventories. Suggests that a concern for people, including employees, stockholders and customers, also plays a part.
Prod-FTARC Dist-FTARC

Many Happy Returns C 10 MIN
16MM FILM OPTICAL SOUND I-J
Presents an animated film outlining basic principles of reincarnation through the adventures of a child.
LC NO. 76-703109
Prod-JDDS Dist-ASSRE 1972

Many Happy Returns C 15 MIN
3/4 OR 1/2 INCH VIDEO CASSETTE K-P
Shows how people change physically as they grow older.
From The Dragons, Wagons And Wax, Set 2 Series.
Prod-CTI Dist-CTI

Many Hear - Some Listen C 12 MIN
16MM FILM, 3/4 OR 1/2 IN VIDEO H-C A
Examines several listening styles and points out that effective listening involves the listener as well as the speaker.
From The Art Of Communication Series.
Prod-CENTRO Dist-CORF

Many Men Say... B 5 MIN
16MM FILM OPTICAL SOUND H-C A
Presents a modern interpretation of Psalm 4 using the dramatization about a scrubwoman who, while cleaning a newsroom, hears the sounds of the happenings of the world and sweeps these absurdities away.
From The Song Of The Ages Series.
LC NO. 77-702118
Prod-FAMLYT Dist-FAMLYT 1964

Many Moons C 10 MIN
16MM FILM OPTICAL SOUND P-I
Shows how a court jester finds a way to bring Princess Lenore the moon.
Prod-REMBRT Dist-TEXFLM

Many Races Hopemobile C 58 MIN
16MM FILM OPTICAL SOUND P-C
Presents the story of the many races hopemobile, a motorized library distributing literature on black heritage and culture.
Prod-GCCED Dist-GCCED 1971

Many Voices C 10 MIN
16MM FILM OPTICAL SOUND
Shows ethnic and racial participation in the Bicentennial. Discusses cultural pluralism and intergroup cooperation in American society, showing the wide variety of people who have contributed to the building of the nation. Offers a sampling of ethnic and multicultural Bicentennial projects across the country.
LC NO. 76-703434
Prod-USARBA Dist-USNAC Prodn-COMCOR 1976

Many Worlds Of Carlos Fuentes, The, Pt 1 C 60 MIN
3/4 OR 1/2 INCH VIDEO CASSETTE
Presents an interview with Carlos Fuentes, the Mexican author and authority on Third World countries.
From The Bill Moyers' Journal Series.
Prod-WNETTV Dist-WNETTV 1980

Many Worlds Of Carlos Fuentes, The, Pt 2 C 60 MIN
3/4 OR 1/2 INCH VIDEO CASSETTE
Presents an interview with Carlos Fuentes, the Mexican author and authority on Third World countries.
From The Bill Moyers' Journal Series.
Prod-WNETTV Dist-WNETTV 1980

Many Worlds Of Childhood–A Series

Highlights the many facets of childhood.
Prod-OECA Dist-OECA 1972

Discovering The Many Worlds 28 MIN
Shaping The Many Worlds 28 MIN
World Of Feelings, The 28 MIN
World Of People, The 28 MIN
World Of Things, The 28 MIN

Many Worlds Of Nature–A Series
16MM FILM, 3/4 OR 1/2 IN VIDEO
Prod-MORALL Dist-MTI 1975

Adaptation 011 MIN
Bird's Year, The - Variety And Change 012 MIN
Birds' Nest, The 012 MIN
Environment Manipulation 012 MIN
Evergreens 014 MIN
Flowers 013 MIN
Marsh, The 012 MIN
Monarch And The Milkweed, The 011 MIN
Oak, The 012 MIN
Of Birds, Beaks And Behavior 011 MIN
Partners 013 MIN
Patterns 012 MIN
Pollination Mechanisms 012 MIN
Protective Coloration 013 MIN
Seed Dispersal 012 MIN
Surviving The Cold 012 MIN
Tree Blossoms 012 MIN
Winter 011 MIN

Manzana Por Manzana C 35 MIN
3/4 OR 1/2 INCH VIDEO CASSETTE
Introduces the vast process of reconstruction in Northern Nicaragua. Explains the Nicaraguan revolution through songs, statements and views of local Nicaraguan activities.
Prod-YASHGR Dist-ICARUS

Manzana Por Manzana (Spanish) C 35 MIN
3/4 OR 1/2 INCH VIDEO CASSETTE
Introduces the vast process of reconstruction in Northern Nicaragua. Explains the Nicaraguan revolution through songs, statements and views of local Nicaraguan activities.
Prod-YASHGR Dist-ICARUS

Mao - Long March To Power C 24 MIN
16MM FILM, 3/4 OR 1/2 IN VIDEO H-C A
Portrays Mao Tse-Tung's rise to power as he competed against nationalist rival Chiang Kai-Shek.
From The Leaders Of The 20th Century - Portraits Of Power Series.
Prod-NIELSE Dist-LCOA 1979

Mao - Long March To Power (Danish) C 24 MIN
16MM FILM, 3/4 OR 1/2 IN VIDEO H-C A
Focuses on Mao's revolutionary victory.
Prod-NIELSE Dist-LCOA 1979

Mao - Long March To Power (Spanish) C 24 MIN
16MM FILM, 3/4 OR 1/2 IN VIDEO H-C A
Focuses on Mao's revolutionary victory.
Prod-NIELSE Dist-LCOA 1979

Mao - Organized Chaos C 24 MIN
16MM FILM, 3/4 OR 1/2 IN VIDEO H-C A
Shows the philosophy of Mao's Little Red Book, and how the chaos of the cultural revolution produced the greatest order China had ever known.
From The Leaders Of The 20th Century - Portraits Of Power Series.
Prod-NIELSE Dist-LCOA 1979

Mao - Organized Chaos (Danish) C 24 MI
16MM FILM, 3/4 OR 1/2 IN VIDEO H-C
Focuses on the Red Guards and the little red book.
Prod-NIELSE Dist-LCOA 197

Mao - Organized Chaos (Spanish) C 24 MI
16MM FILM, 3/4 OR 1/2 IN VIDEO H-C
Focuses on the Red Guards and the little red book.
Prod-NIELSE Dist-LCOA 197

Mao By Mao C 28 MI
3/4 OR 1/2 INCH VIDEO CASSETTE
Offers an autobiography of Chinese leader Mao Tse-Tung draw from his writings, diaries, speeches and personal notes. Includes the first photos in which Mao appeared as well as a look at the 1949 Shanghai victory parade, filmed by Henri Cartier-Bresson
Prod-FOTH Dist-FOTH 198

Mao To Mozart - Isaac Stern In China C
1/2 IN VIDEO CASSETTE BETA/VHS
Provides insights into east and west through Isaac Stern's tou of China and the resulting cultural exchange.
Prod-GA Dist-GA

Mao Tse Tung Profile C 17 MI
3/4 OR 1/2 INCH VIDEO CASSETTE H-C
Documents the life of Mao Tse-tung, from his role in the overthrow of the Man Chu dynasty to the opening of China to the Western nations.
Prod-UPI Dist-JOU

Mao Tse-tung - Life And Legacy B 13 MI
16MM FILM, 3/4 OR 1/2 IN VIDEO J-C
Examines the life and times of Mao Tse-Tung, architect of the Peoples Republic Of China. Deals with persons, places, facts and events related to China and the history of the People's Republic.
From The Screen News Digest Series.
Prod-HEARST Dist-HEARST 197

Mao Tse-Tung Remakes China C 29 MI
2 INCH VIDEOTAPE
See series title for descriptive statement.
From The Folk Guitar Plus Series.
Prod-WGBHTV Dist-PUBTEL

Maori C 22 MI
16MM FILM, 3/4 OR 1/2 IN VIDEO J
Presents a comprehensive look at the past, present and future of the Maori people, descendants of the original inhabitants of New Zealand. Portrays the stresses and pulls of this rural, traditional people as they move to the cities for jobs and urban lifestyles.
Prod-NFUNZ Dist-NWDIMF

Maori Arts And Culture C 29 MI
16MM FILM OPTICAL SOUND J A
Shows the magnificent carving of the early Maori and explains the reasons for the decline and renaissance of Maori art. Points out that in the decoration of some new meeting houses, Maori artists and craftsmen are again producing fine work.
Prod-NFUNZ Dist-NWDIMF

Map And Globe Skills - Introduction C 20 MIN
3/4 OR 1/2 INCH VIDEO CASSETTE I-J
Provides information on maps and globes by showing visits to the Library of Congress map division and to the American Automobile Association's cartographic department.
From The Map And Globe Skills Series.
Prod-WCVETV Dist-GPITVL 1978

Map And Globe Skills–A Series
I-J
Explains the use of maps and globes. Features professionals who use maps in their work.
Prod-WCVETV Dist-GPITVL 1979

Earth, Direction And Time 020 MIN
Geographical Forms 020 MIN
Map And Globe Skills - Introduction 020 MIN
Map Reading 020 MIN
Map Usage 020 MIN
Types Of Maps 020 MIN

Map Collectors, The C 30 MIN
3/4 INCH VIDEO CASSETTE
Gives an historical review of map societies of cartographers and collectors. Looks at examples of rare maps.
From The Maps - Horizons To Knowledge Series.
Prod-UMITV Dist-UMITV 1980

Map Film, The C
16MM FILM, 3/4 OR 1/2 IN VIDEO
Shows children how to make a map of their home, then a map of the neighborhood. Surveys the importance of maps to one's state, the nation and the world.
Prod-HIGGIN Dist-HIGGIN

Map Making Skills C 15 MIN
2 INCH VIDEOTAPE P-I
Reinforces the interpretation of map symbols. Shows that map symbols are standard and that different maps may use symbols to represent different things. Stresses the correct use of the map key.
From The B B's Cover The Globe Series.
Prod-GPITVL Dist-GPITVL

Map Making Skills C 15 MIN
3/4 INCH VIDEO CASSETTE P-I
Reinforces the interpretation of map symbols. Shows that map symbols are standard and that different maps may use various symbols to mean different things. Stresses the correct use of the map key.

From The B B's Cover The Globe Series.
Prod-MAETEL Dist-GPITVL

Map Of California - Agricultural Uses Of Lowlands In Coastal Valleys C 18 MIN
16MM FILM OPTICAL SOUND I-H
Shows how the lowland coastal valleys are used to grow many of the products, such as apples, pears, lettuce and prunes, which California exports to other parts of the nation and the world.
LC NO. FIA67-7
Prod-ACA Dist-ACA 1966

Map Of California - Highlands And Their Uses C 18 MIN
16MM FILM OPTICAL SOUND I-H
Shows how the highlands, ranging from 1,000 to 14,000 feet above sea level, are used to grow apricots and peaches, to raise sheep and cattle, to mine ore, to provide lumbering and military bases and to serve as recreation sites for national and state parks.
LC NO. FIA67-8
Prod-ACA Dist-ACA 1966

Map Of California - The Central Valley And How Man Uses The Land For Agriculture C 18 MIN
16MM FILM OPTICAL SOUND I-H
Shows how the rich soil of the central valley is used to raise crops, such as potatoes, cotton, barley and alfalfa, as well as dairy and beef cattle. Tells how irrigation water is brought in and how new machines increase production.
LC NO. FIA67-9
Prod-ACA Dist-ACA 1966

Map Of California - The Desert And How Man Uses Desert Valleys For Agriculture C 18 MIN
16MM FILM OPTICAL SOUND I-H
Discusses the nature of California deserts and shows how canals and irrigations ditches have been used to change some desert land into rich farm land for crops as well as for livestock.
LC NO. FIA67-10
Prod-ACA Dist-ACA 1966

Map Of Hawaii - Hawaii's Land And Its Uses C 18 MIN
16MM FILM OPTICAL SOUND I-H
Discusses the climate and land form variations in Hawaii and how they influence the land usage at different elevations. Ranges from the growing of taro in the valley bottoms and lowlands to the volcanic national parks in the over 10,000 feet elevations.
LC NO. FIA64-1451
Prod-ACA Dist-ACA 1964

Map Of Hawaii - Hawaii's Origin, Land And Climate C 18 MIN
16MM FILM OPTICAL SOUND I-H
Explains the importance of volcanic eruptions in the formation of Hawaii. Shows the many land forms, including the eroding domes, sand beaches, canyons and high mountain palis. Discusses the influence of trade winds on the climate.
LC NO. FIA64-1452
Prod-ACA Dist-ACA 1964

Map Projection In The Computer Age (2nd Ed) C 11 MIN
16MM FILM, 3/4 OR 1/2 IN VIDEO I-H
The second edition of Global Concepts In Maps. Shows how computers are used in mapmaking.
Prod-CORF Dist-CORF

Map Reading C 16 MIN
16MM FILM, 3/4 OR 1/2 IN VIDEO
Presents a boy trying to find a present hidden in a park. Tells how he learns from his father about directions, the use of a compass, scales for distances and map symbols.
Prod-HANDEL Dist-HANDEL 1981

Map Reading C 20 MIN
3/4 INCH VIDEO CASSETTE I-J
Imparts basic map reading information. Explains distance determination and scales and symbols interpretation.
From The Map And Globe Skills Series.
Prod-WCVETV Dist-GPITVL 1979

Map Reading C 25 MIN
2 INCH VIDEOTAPE I
Examines map reading skills.
From The Images Series.
Prod-CVETVC Dist-GPITVL

Map Reading And Trip Planning B 30 MIN
16MM FILM - 3/4 IN VIDEO C A
See series title for descriptive statement.
From The Sportsmanlike Driving Series.
Prod-AAAFTS Dist-GPITVL Prodn-SCETV

Map Scales C 15 MIN
2 INCH VIDEOTAPE P-I
Shows that a map scale measures distance on a map in relation to distance on the earth. Points out that a scale is necessary to determine distance because most maps cannot be drawn full scale.
From The B B's Cover The Globe Series.
Prod-GPITVL Dist-GPITVL

Map Scales C 15 MIN
3/4 INCH VIDEO CASSETTE P-I
Shows that a map scale measures distance in relation to distance on the earth.
From The B B's Cover The Globe Series.
Prod-MAETEL Dist-GPITVL

Map Scales - How And Why C 20 MIN
2 INCH VIDEOTAPE I-J
Explains that a map scale relates distance on a map to distance on earth. Shows how to measure and relate the measurement of the land area to the map scale. Demonstrates how to draw simple maps to scale.
From The Project Survival Series.
Prod-GPITVL Dist-GPITVL

Map Scales - How And Why C 20 MIN
3/4 INCH VIDEO CASSETTE I-J
States that a map scale relates distance on a map to distance on earth. Recognizes that not all maps use the same scale. Explains that to be able to compute distance on maps one must measure and relate the measurement of the land area to the map scale. Demonstrates how to draw simple maps to scale and how to compute distance on maps.
From The Project Survival Series.
Prod-MAETEL Dist-GPITVL

Map Skills - Recognizing Physical Features C 11 MIN
16MM FILM, 3/4 OR 1/2 IN VIDEO I-J
Compares map symbols with physical features, shows how colors represent elevation and defines physical features, such as gulf, peninsula, island, strait, channel, tributary, plain and plateau.
From The Map Skills Series.
Prod-CORF Dist-CORF 1969

Map Skills - Understanding Latitude C 11 MIN
16MM FILM, 3/4 OR 1/2 IN VIDEO
Traces the development of latitude in exploration and map-making. Introduces tropic, temperate and frigid climate zones; and shows the relationship between latitude and climate.
From The Map Skills Series.
Prod-CORF Dist-CORF 1971

Map Skills - Understanding Longitude C 11 MIN
16MM FILM, 3/4 OR 1/2 IN VIDEO
Shows how meridians are drawn, how longitude and time are related, and how to use longitude with latitude to pinpoint the exact locations of places.
From The Map Skills Series.
Prod-CORF Dist-CORF 1971

Map Skills - Using Different Maps Together C 11 MIN
16MM FILM, 3/4 OR 1/2 IN VIDEO I-J
Maps of the same scale and projection are combined to reveal relationships between natural features of the earth, human use and social and political features. Animation is used.
From The Map Skills Series.
Prod-CORF Dist-CORF 1966

Map Skills - Using Scale C 11 MIN
16MM FILM, 3/4 OR 1/2 IN VIDEO I-J
Compares scale models with actual objects to define scale. Introduces the main types of scales and shows how to use them to estimate distances.
From The Map Skills Series.
Prod-CORF Dist-CORF 1971

Map Skills—A Series
16MM FILM, 3/4 OR 1/2 IN VIDEO I-J
Introduces basic concepts in understanding maps. Describes latitude, longitude, scales, map comparison and recognizing physical features.
Prod-CORF Dist-CORF

Map Skills - Recognizing Physical Features	011 MIN
Map Skills - Understanding Latitude	011 MIN
Map Skills - Understanding Longitude	011 MIN
Map Skills - Using Different Maps Together	011 MIN
Map Skills - Using Scale	011 MIN

Map Usage C 20 MIN
3/4 INCH VIDEO CASSETTE I-J
Explains important map elements, including grid, index systems and legends. Features a taxi driver discussing the importance of maps in his work.
From The Map And Globe Skills Series.
Prod-WCVETV Dist-GPITVL 1979

Mapandangare, The Great Baboon C 10 MIN
16MM FILM, 3/4 OR 1/2 IN VIDEO P-J
Provides a basic introduction to African musical instruments and shows how they are made. Features musicologist Andrew Tracy, who illustrates the role of music in African storytelling by having children chant responses as he relates a tale of a brave baboon.
Prod-TEGNID Dist-FLMFR 1978

Maple C 4 MIN
16MM FILM OPTICAL SOUND K-P
Presents a story about a sad child who is offered a variety of material things, but only becomes happy when she receives the gift of friendship.
LC NO. 80-700759
Prod-IKONOG Dist-IKONOG 1976

Maple Leaf Forever, The C 10 MIN
16MM FILM, 3/4 OR 1/2 IN VIDEO I-H
Uses authentic costumes, buildings and language to re-create the life of a small Canadian town in the middle of the 19th century, the time of the celebration of that country's nationhood.
Prod-TFW Dist-JOU 1977

Maple Spring C 14 MIN
16MM FILM, 3/4 OR 1/2 IN VIDEO P-J
Illustrates how a family works together, when the spring thaw begins in the north, to harvest the sap from the sugar maple trees on their farm. Shows many uses they make from the syrup, on fresh bread, butter-raisin tarts, and finally, a 'sugaring off' party to celebrate the end of harvest.
Prod-NELVNA Dist-BCNFL 1979

Maple Sugar Farmer, The C 29 MIN
16MM FILM, 3/4 OR 1/2 IN VIDEO I-C A
Portrays Sherman Graff, a 72-year-old maple sugar farmer who lives in Southern Illinois. Features Graff explaining how to make both maple syrup and maple sugar the way his ancestors did six generations ago.
From The Yesterday And Today Series.
Prod-HINDAV Dist-AIMS 1973

Maple Syrup C 13 MIN
16MM FILM, 3/4 OR 1/2 IN VIDEO I-H A
Shows how maple syrup is produced, from the sapping of trees to the treatment and storage of sap.
Prod-UWISC Dist-MCFI 1978

Mapping - Exploring The Globe C 30 MIN
3/4 INCH VIDEO CASSETTE
See series title for descriptive statement.
From The Of Earth And Man Series.
Prod-MDCPB Dist-MDCPB

Mapping - Round World, Flat Maps C 30 MIN
3/4 INCH VIDEO CASSETTE
See series title for descriptive statement.
From The Of Earth And Man Series.
Prod-MDCPB Dist-MDCPB

Mapping Australia C 21 MIN
16MM FILM OPTICAL SOUND
Describes the mapping of Australia, from the initial aerial and ground surveys to the final printing of the completed sheet. Illustrates the importance of cartography in the nation's development.
LC NO. FIA68-1741
Prod-ANAIB Dist-AUIS 1968

Mapping For Defense C 14 MIN
16MM FILM OPTICAL SOUND
Explains the method by which maps are developed from initial survey information.
LC NO. 79-707416
Prod-CDND Dist-CDND Prodn-NFBC 1968

Mapping It Out C 30 MIN
2 INCH VIDEOTAPE C A
Shows the drawing of a floor plan to enable students to better understand the concept of scale, placement of windows and doors, and architectural symbols.
From The Designing Home Interiors Series. Unit 6
Prod-COAST Dist-CDTEL Prodn-RSCCD

Mapping Of History - The History Of Mapping C 30 MIN
3/4 INCH VIDEO CASSETTE
Describes the earliest maps, showing cultural and political influences of the time. Explores modern map making techniques.
From The Maps - Horizons To Knowledge Series.
Prod-UMITV Dist-UMITV 1980

Mapping The Earth's Resources C 22 MIN
3/4 INCH VIDEO CASSETTE J
Shows how geologists work and discusses the problems of diminishing mineral resources.
From The What On Earth Series.
Prod-NCSDPI Dist-GPITVL 1979

Mapping The Earth's Surface C 16 MIN
16MM FILM, 3/4 OR 1/2 IN VIDEO I-H
Studies the process of mapmaking from the establishment of a network of control points, through the collection of detailed information by ground teams and stereoscopic aerial photography, to final compilation and printing. Shows how triangulation, distance measuring devices and computers are used.
Prod-CORF Dist-CORF 1969

Mapping The Products Of The Human Genome C 59 MIN
3/4 INCH VIDEO CASSETTE
Discusses the anatomy of the cell and its molecular constituents.
Prod-UTAHTI Dist-UTAHTI

Mappings And Functions B
16MM FILM OPTICAL SOUND
Shows how a graph can be used to represent a particular situation. Defines abstract mappings and functions.
Prod-OPENU Dist-OPENU

Maps - Horizons To Knowledge—A Series

Discusses the map making process. Describes and illustrates the origins of maps, how map information is gathered and the modern methods of map production. Hosted by Dr Douglas Marshall, Curator of Maps at the University of Michigan Clements Library.
Prod-UMITV Dist-UMITV 1980

Map Collectors, The	030 MIN
Mapping Of History - The History Of Mapping	030 MIN
New Horizons, The	029 MIN
New Horizons, The (Spanish)	029 MIN
Production And Printing	030 MIN
To Measure The Earth	030 MIN

Maps - How To Read Them C 14 MIN
16MM FILM, 3/4 OR 1/2 IN VIDEO I-J
Uses the legend of the map along with its scale and compass rose to show how maps help locate important places, trace routes from place to place and calculate distance.
Prod-BFA Dist-PHENIX 1982

Maps - Know Where You're Going C 16 MIN
16MM FILM - VIDEO, ALL FORMATS P-I
Teaches the fundamentals of map reading.
Prod-SAIF Dist-BARR

Maps - Land Symbols And Terms (2nd Ed) C 20 MIN
16MM FILM OPTICAL SOUND I-J
Uses aerial photography to show the actual land forms, boundary

lines, major water courses, rail terminals, bodies of water, large cities, locks, dams and waterfalls of the United States.
From The Know America Series.
LC NO. 71-712447
Prod-ACA Dist-ACA 1969

Maps - Symbols And Terms C 15 MIN
16MM FILM, 3/4 OR 1/2 IN VIDEO I
Discusses map symbols, common and practical uses of maps, and the concepts and related language of direction, scale and projection.
LC NO. 83-706223
Prod-AIMS Dist-AIMS 1983

Maps - Where Am I (3rd Ed) C 12 MIN
16MM FILM, 3/4 OR 1/2 IN VIDEO P
Takes a helicopter ride over a neighborhood and translates the vertical view into a flat map. Discusses the use of colors, symbols, map scale, distance scale, and direction.
LC NO. 83-706314
Prod-AIMS Dist-AIMS 1982

Maps And Globes - An Introduction C 17 MIN
16MM FILM, 3/4 OR 1/2 IN VIDEO P-J
Introduces basic map reading skills and indicates the diversity of information available from maps.
LC NO. 80-707728
Prod-FLMFR Dist-FLMFR 1980

Maps And Landmarks C 11 MIN
16MM FILM, 3/4 OR 1/2 IN VIDEO P-I
Tells how children use objects in their environment as landmarks to help them find their way. Traces a family's trip to grandmother's house and back, first showing the real objects used as landmarks, then a model of the area and a simple pictorial map. Provides an opportunity to apply the basic understandings to major landmarks on a physical map of the United States.
Prod-BFA Dist-PHENIX Prodn-BRUNOS 1971

Maps And Models C 15 MIN
16MM FILM, 3/4 OR 1/2 IN VIDEO I
Tells how the members of a club use a contour map and a scale model to rescue the club's cherished emblem.
From The Thinkabout Series. Reshaping Information
LC NO. 81-706106
Prod-EDFCEN Dist-AITECH 1979

Maps And Their Meaning (2nd Ed) C 20 MIN
16MM FILM OPTICAL SOUND I-J
Describes how a system of colors is used to denote the varying water and land areas represented on maps of the United States. Views the land areas for which the colors stand. Discusses land and water usage.
From The Know America Series.
LC NO. 70-712441
Prod-ACA Dist-ACA 1969

Maps And Weather Vanes C 6 MIN
16MM FILM, 3/4 OR 1/2 IN VIDEO P-I
Describes the making of maps and weather vanes.
From The Basic Facts About The Earth, Sun, Moon And Stars Series.
Prod-MORLAT Dist-SF 1967

Maps Are Fun (2nd Ed) C 11 MIN
16MM FILM, 3/4 OR 1/2 IN VIDEO P-I
Shows a cartographer as he helps a young boy prepare a map of his paper route. Defines legend, scale and grid. Discusses the use of color in maps and exhibits some different types of maps.
Prod-CORF Dist-CORF 1963

Maps For A Changing World (3rd Ed) C 18 MIN
16MM FILM, 3/4 OR 1/2 IN VIDEO I-J
Discusses the history of mapmaking. Explores the problems of depicting accurate representations of a round earth. Offers information on symbols, legends and scales, and takes a look at aerial photography.
LC NO. 81-706862
Prod-EBEC Dist-EBEC 1980

Maps For Man C 26 MIN
3/4 INCH VIDEO CASSETTE J
Focuses on a topographic map and shows how high altitude aircraft and satellites are used to map from space.
From The What On Earth Series.
Prod-NCSDPI Dist-GPITVL 1979

Maps Show Our Earth C 10 MIN
16MM FILM, 3/4 OR 1/2 IN VIDEO P
Explains how colors and key symbols are used on maps, how maps can be used together and how they relate to a globe.
Prod-CORF Dist-CORF 1973

Maps, Charts, And Tables C 14 MIN
16MM FILM, 3/4 OR 1/2 IN VIDEO H
Tells how maps, charts and tables help a floral delivery business. Shows how Cynthia uses charts to plan a strategy for a boat race.
From The Math Wise Series. Module 3 - Locating/Interpreting
Prod-KOCETV Dist-AITECH 1981

Mara-Mara-Marathon C 3 MIN
3/4 OR 1/2 INCH VIDEO CASSETTE P-I
Shows how Meter Man uses a track meet to explain kilometers and other metric distances.
From The Metric Marvels Series.
Prod-NBCTV Dist-GA 1978

Marathon C 8 MIN
16MM FILM OPTICAL SOUND
Shows the running of the New York Marathon.
LC NO. 78-700429
Prod-MHT Dist-COMCOR Prodn-COMCOR 1977

Marathon C 10 MIN
16MM FILM OPTICAL SOUND
Documents the progress of a 52-hour dance marathon which was held by students at the University of Maryland to raise money for the Muscular Dystrophy Association of America.
LC NO. 73-700735
Prod-UMD Dist-UMD 1972

Marathon Challenge, The C 60 MIN
1/2 IN VIDEO CASSETTE BETA/VHS
Presents instruction and advice for the runner training for a marathon.
Prod-MOHOMV Dist-MOHOMV

Marathon Fever C 24 MIN
16MM FILM OPTICAL SOUND
Follows a marathon race from start to finish.
LC NO. 81-700396
Prod-ALPERT Dist-CANTOR 1979

Marathon Woman - Miki Gorman C 28 MIN
16MM FILM, 3/4 OR 1/2 IN VIDEO H-C A
Presents Miki Gorman, twice winner of both the New York and Boston marathons, who describes her metamorphosis from sports observer to dedicated runner.
Prod-FLMLIB Dist-FLMLIB 1982

Marathon, The C 50 MIN
16MM FILM OPTICAL SOUND
Presents a television special from the CTV program Olympiad which highlights dramatic moments in the history of the Olympic marathon competitions. Includes newsreel footage from 1908 to 1976.
LC NO. 77-702541
Prod-CTV Dist-CTV 1976

Marble Game B 12 MIN
16MM FILM OPTICAL SOUND T
Focuses on a group of pre-school children at Cambridge Neighborhood House playing an impromptu game of marbles.
From The Vignette Series.
LC NO. 73-707933
Prod-EDS Dist-EDC 1969

Marbleized Paper, Crayons And Paint, And Other Fascinations C 56 MIN
1/2 IN VIDEO CASSETTE BETA/VHS K-P
Shows how to make marbleized paper. Demonstrates art projects such as cards and booklets.
From The Children's Crafts Series.
Prod-MOHOMV Dist-MOHOMV

Marbury V Madison C 36 MIN
16MM FILM - 3/4 IN VIDEO
Presents a dramatization of the landmark Supreme Court decision of Marbury versus Madison, which established the Supreme Court's responsibility to review the constitutionality of acts of Congress.
From The Equal Justice Under Law Series.
LC NO. 78-706017
Prod-USJUDC Dist-USNAC Prodn-WQED 1977

Marbury Vs Madison C
3/4 OR 1/2 INCH VIDEO CASSETTE H
Describes the decision that clarified the power of the judiciary.
From The Supreme Court Decisions That Changed The Nation Series.
Prod-GA Dist-GA

Marc Chagall C 25 MIN
16MM FILM, 3/4 OR 1/2 IN VIDEO H-C A
Explores the life and work of Marc Chagall, depicting his works on canvas, in sculpture and in stained glass.
LC NO. 81-706534
Prod-AUERBH Dist-CRMP 1965

Marc Chagall - The Colours Of Passion C 24 MIN
16MM FILM, 3/4 OR 1/2 IN VIDEO
Focuses on the diverse artistic achievements of Marc Chagall. Includes examples of his work and a discussion of his background. Points out the influences of impressionism, cubism and Russia on his art.
LC NO. 79-707197
Prod-IFB Dist-IFB 1979

Marceau On Mime C 22 MIN
16MM FILM, 3/4 OR 1/2 IN VIDEO I-C A
Presents mime artist Marcel Marceau discussing the history of mime and his personal credo as a mime artist.
Prod-GOULDP Dist-AIMS 1973

Marcel A Paris C 24 MIN
16MM FILM, 3/4 OR 1/2 IN VIDEO
A French language videocassette. Follows the adventures of nine-year-old Marcel as he tries to earn money in Paris.
Prod-IFB Dist-IFB 1969

Marcel Breuer Video Portrait B 30 MIN
3/4 OR 1/2 INCH VIDEO CASSETTE
Profiles the late Marcel Breuer, student and teacher at the Bauhaus who designed the Whitney Museum and the Grand Coulee Dam.
Prod-EAI Dist-EAI

Marcel Duchamp - Interviewed By Russell Connor B 30 MIN
3/4 OR 1/2 INCH VIDEO CASSETTE
Interviews Dada artist Marcel Duchamp by Russell Connor. Duchamp expresses his views on art and society.
Prod-EAI Dist-EAI

Marcel Duchamp And John Cage C 25 MIN
3/4 OR 1/2 INCH VIDEO CASSETTE
Records the well-known chess match between Marcel Duchamp and John Cage, where the chess board was wired for sound so that it became a musical instrument.
Prod-EAI Dist-EAI

Marcel In Paris C 10 MIN
16MM FILM, 3/4 OR 1/2 IN VIDEO P-H
Follows a small boy as he explores the streets of Paris and witnesses the wonders of the city. Portrays the Eiffel Tower, Champs d'elysee and the Tuileries.
Prod-FI Dist-FI 1972

Marcel Proust C 15 MIN
16MM FILM, 3/4 OR 1/2 IN VIDEO
Offers a biography of Marcel Proust.
Prod-JANUS Dist-CORF

Marcello, I'm So Bored C 8 MIN
16MM FILM OPTICAL SOUND
Combines modern music and pop-art style to mirror the contemporary American social landscape with its growing lack of sincere human feeling and emotional involvement.
LC NO. 75-703205
Prod-USC Dist-USC 1967

Marcelo Ramos - Artesano Pirotecnico C 23 MIN
16MM FILM OPTICAL SOUND
A Spanish language version of the motion picture Marcelo Ramos - The Firework Maker's Art. Documents the care that goes into the construction of Mexican firework displays by following Mexican firework maker Marcelo Ramos during a typical day. Shows his fireworks ending a traditional Mexican village fiesta.
From The Artesanos Mexicanos Series.
Prod-WORKS Dist-WORKS 1980

Marcelo Ramos - The Firework Maker's Art C 23 MIN
16MM FILM OPTICAL SOUND
Documents the care that goes into the construction of Mexican firework displays by following Mexican firework maker Marcelo Ramos during a typical day. Shows his fireworks ending a traditional Mexican village fiesta.
From The Mexico's Folk Artists Series.
LC NO. 81-700537
Prod-WORKS Dist-WORKS 1980

March Of The Wooden Soldiers B 70 MIN
16MM FILM OPTICAL SOUND
Stars Laurel and Hardy in an adaptation of Victor Herbert's operetta Babes In Toyland. Shows how Laurel and Hardy try to help Bo Peep save her home from the evil Barnaby.
Prod-ROACH Dist-FI 1934

March Of Time—A Series

Prod-WOLPER Dist-WOLPER

Frontiers Of The Mind 60 MIN
Seven Days In The Life Of The President 60 MIN

March Of Time—A Series
16MM FILM, 3/4 OR 1/2 IN VIDEO
Presents excerpts from The March Of Time newsreel series of the 1930's and 1940's.
Prod-TIMLIF Dist-TIMLIF 1974

Demagogues And Do-Gooders 20 MIN
Exits And Entrances 20 MIN
Is Everybody Listening 20 MIN
Movies March On, The 20 MIN
Under The Clouds Of War 20 MIN

March On Paris 1914 Of Generaloberst Alexander Von Kluck And His Memory Of Jessie... C 75 MIN
16MM FILM OPTICAL SOUND
Dramatizes the reminiscences of German General Alexander von Kluck concerning the campaign of his army from the Belgian border to the Battle of the Marne and his romance with Jessie Holladay.
LC NO. 77-701814
Prod-HAWKSP Dist-FMCOOP 1977

March On Washington - The Bonus Marches C 15 MIN
16MM FILM OPTICAL SOUND
Examines tactics of rebellion groups, pointing out that today's rebels against the establishment don't deserve credit for inventing protest, but are merely refining a process that has been characteristic of the means by which much progress has been achieved in the United States.
Prod-INTEXT Dist-REAF

March Or Die C 106 MIN
16MM FILM OPTICAL SOUND
Presents an adventure story about the French Foreign Legion.
Prod-CPC Dist-SWANK

Marching - Rifles Section C 12 MIN
16MM FILM OPTICAL SOUND
Offers information on rifle handling, spinning and tossing for the marching band show.
Prod-MCCRMK Dist-MCCRMK 1978

Marching Mizzou C 11 MIN
16MM FILM OPTICAL SOUND
Portrays the color, pageantry and precision of the University of Missouri's marching band. Includes behind-the-scenes preparation and a halftime show.
LC NO. 76-702845
Prod-UMO Dist-UMO 1976

Marching Percussion C 11 MIN
16MM FILM OPTICAL SOUND J-H
Covers the elements involved in building a championship marching percussion section, including the precision method, tonality in percussion, selecting instruments, mallets, carrying devices,

timptoms and how to write for them, scoring music, field positioning and visual presentation.
From The How To Series.
Prod-MCCRMK Dist-MCCRMK Prodn-COSTEL 1974

Marching Show Design C 12 MIN
16MM FILM OPTICAL SOUND
Shows the Bridgemen approach to planning and designing a field marching show.
Prod-MCCRMK Dist-MCCRMK 1978

Marching The Colours C 3 MIN
16MM FILM, 3/4 OR 1/2 IN VIDEO P-C
An experiment in film animation, made by Guy Glover without a camera, visualizing a military march in geometric, abstract patterns of color.
Prod-NFBC Dist-IFB 1942

Marciano-Charles B 30 MIN
16MM FILM OPTICAL SOUND
See series title for descriptive statement.
From The IBC Championship Fights, Series 1 Series.
Prod-SFI Dist-SFI

Marciano-Louis B 30 MIN
16MM FILM OPTICAL SOUND
See series title for descriptive statement.
From The IBC Championship Fights, Series 1 Series.
Prod-SFI Dist-SFI

Marciano-Moore B 29 MIN
16MM FILM OPTICAL SOUND
See series title for descriptive statement.
From The IBC Championship Fights, Series 1 Series.
Prod-SFI Dist-SFI

Marciano-Moore B 30 MIN
16MM FILM OPTICAL SOUND
From The IBC Championship Fights, Series 2 Series.
Prod-SFI Dist-SFI

Marco Polo C 22 MIN
16MM FILM, 3/4 OR 1/2 IN VIDEO I-J
Presents an animated version of the adventures of Marco Polo who traveled across Europe and Asia to secure the overland route to Cathay.
Prod-LUF Dist-LUF 1979

Marco Polo's Travels B 19 MIN
16MM FILM, 3/4 OR 1/2 IN VIDEO I-H
Re-creates adventures that Marco Polo described in his book about his travels. Differences between Eastern and Western cultures are shown. Indicates the impact upon medieval Europe of Marco Polo's account.
Prod-EBF Dist-EBEC 1955

Marco Polo's Travels (Spanish) B 19 MIN
16MM FILM, 3/4 OR 1/2 IN VIDEO I-H
Re-creates the adventures that Marco Polo described in his book. Dramatizes the differences between Eastern and Western cultures by showing scenes in Kubla Khan's court.
Prod-EBEC Dist-EBEC

Marcus Garvey - Toward Black Nationhood C 42 MIN
3/4 OR 1/2 INCH VIDEO CASSETTE J-C A
Combines archival material and live interviews with Marcus Garvey, Jr and others to introduce the life and work of the pioneer Black nationalist leader Marcus Garvey.
LC NO. 84-706039
Prod-WGRMTV Dist-FOTH 1983

Marcus Garvey And His Time B 30 MIN
16MM FILM OPTICAL SOUND H-C A
Dr E U Essien-udom lectures on the life and times of Marcus Garvey, the Pan-African Nationalist leader, stressing the problem of the identity dilemma which was gradually becoming problematic for the Black Freedom Movement, and explaining that Garvey sought to consolidate the national consciousness of the Black masses in the United States as the basis for the establishment of an independent nation in Africa.
From The Black History, Section 13 - Marcus Garvey And his Movement Series.
LC NO. 72-704080
Prod-WCBSTV Dist-HRAW 1969

Marcus Garvey And The UNIA Papers C 28 MIN
3/4 OR 1/2 INCH VIDEO CASSETTE
Prod-RCOMTV Dist-SYLWAT 1984

Mare Nostrum B 27 MIN
16MM FILM, 3/4 OR 1/2 IN VIDEO J-H
Describes the military command of the Mediterranean from 1940 to 1942.
From The Victory At Sea Series.
Prod-NBCTV Dist-LUF

Mare Tranquillitatis - Flagstaff, Arizona C 12 MIN
16MM FILM OPTICAL SOUND
Documents the construction of an area simulating a lunar crater field. Shows how the site near Sunset Crater in Arizona was prepared by using explosives and compares the aerial photographs of the completed construction to those of the lunar surface.
LC NO. 74-706375
Prod-USGS Dist-USNAC 1969

Margaret B 13 MIN
16MM FILM OPTICAL SOUND J-C A
Tells about a mildly retarded girl who, apart from a short period in an institution, has lived happily at home with her family. Shows how, now that she is 14 years old, she appears to be unaware that she is different although her parents worry about the future.
LC NO. 76-701866
Prod-AUSDSS Dist-AUIS Prodn-FLMAUS 1975

Margaret Atwood - An Interview C 28 MIN
3/4 INCH VIDEO CASSETTE
Presents Margaret Atwood discussing the writing process, poetry poetry and the special problems of women writers, such as learning to be persistent in order to get published. Explains some of the reasons behind Canadian Nationalism.
Prod-WMENIF Dist-WMENIF

Margaret Beals And Dr Jay Adlersberg C 30 MIN
3/4 OR 1/2 INCH VIDEO CASSETTE
See series title for descriptive statement.
From The Dancers' Health Alert Series.
Prod-ARCVID Dist-ARCVID

Margaret Mead B 30 MIN
16MM FILM OPTICAL SOUND H-C A
Anthropologist Margaret Mead appraises human values with relation to man's potential for complete selfannihilation. She explains that an understanding of human traditions, philosophy and action is necessary to give the future a meaningful value. (Kinescope)
LC NO. FIA67-5107
Prod-USC Dist-MLA 1964

Margaret Mead - An Interview C 20 MIN
3/4 INCH VIDEO CASSETTE
Features anthropologist and author Margaret Mead talking about the influence of women in her life, her own work and experiences.
Prod-WMENIF Dist-WMENIF

Margaret Mead - Cultural Factors In Population Control B
3/4 OR 1/2 INCH VIDEO CASSETTE
Discusses the cultural factors in population control in a talk by Dr Margaret Mead.
Prod-VRL Dist-UWISC 1970

Margaret Mead - Taking Note C 58 MIN
3/4 OR 1/2 INCH VIDEO CASSETTE
Presents a biographical tribute to anthropologist Margaret Mead. Tells how she entered her career at a time when it was a rarity for women.
From The Odyssey Series.
LC NO. 82-706987
Prod-PBA Dist-PBS

Margaret Sloan On Black Sisterhood C 29 MIN
3/4 INCH VIDEO CASSETTE
Presents Margaret Sloan discussing sexism and feminism and how they relate to black women in the movement.
From The Woman Series.
Prod-WNEDTV Dist-PUBTEL

Margia Kramer - Freedom Of Information Tape 3, The CIA Guerrilla Manual C 4 MIN
3/4 OR 1/2 INCH VIDEO CASSETTE
Deals with First Amendment rights.
Prod-ARTINC Dist-ARTINC

Margia Kramer - Freedom Of Information Tape 2 - Progress And Access C 36 MIN
3/4 OR 1/2 INCH VIDEO CASSETTE
Tells how computerization contributes to the isolating tendencies of capitalist culture.
Prod-ARTINC Dist-ARTINC

Margia Kramer - Freedom Of Information Tape-1, Jean Seberg C 18 MIN
3/4 OR 1/2 INCH VIDEO CASSETTE
Documents the FBI's surveillance and harassment of Jean Seberg. Conveys contradictions between her public and private personas.
Prod-ARTINC Dist-ARTINC

Margia Kramer - No More Witchhunts, A Street Festival C 17 MIN
3/4 OR 1/2 INCH VIDEO CASSETTE
Focuses on a New York City street festival protesting the rise of neo-McCarthyism.
Prod-ARTINC Dist-ARTINC

Margia Kramer - Progress, Memory C 5 MIN
3/4 OR 1/2 INCH VIDEO CASSETTE
Deals with First Amendment rights.
Prod-ARTINC Dist-ARTINC

Margin Of Safety C 4 MIN
16MM FILM OPTICAL SOUND H-C
Discusses the distance that should be maintained between vehicles going in the same direction. Stresses the importance of looking well ahead of one's own car.
From The Driver Education Series.
LC NO. FIA66-1006
Prod-AMROIL Dist-AMROIL 1964

Margin Of Safety - Psychological Distance Under Danger B 16 MIN
16MM FILM SILENT H-C
Reports on an experiment showing that subjects (college students) allow greater margins of safety under dangerous conditions and that they change to a slower pace than is characteristic under conditions of no danger. Provides an illustration of how an experiment of this kind is conducted.
Prod-PSUPCR Dist-PSUPCR 1955

Marginal People C 28 MIN
16MM FILM, 3/4 OR 1/2 IN VIDEO J-C A
Depicts the plight of the newly independent country of Bangladesh in terms of the need to establish a new international order.
Prod-LUF Dist-LUF 1979

Margins Of The Land, The C 55 MIN
16MM FILM, 3/4 OR 1/2 IN VIDEO H-C A
Looks at life along the coastlines and shows how mangroves with their roots help to expand the coastline.
From The Living Planet Series. Pt 9
Prod-BBCTV Dist-TIMLIF 1984

Margo C 11 MIN
16MM FILM, 3/4 OR 1/2 IN VIDEO C A
Shows a woman stimulate herself to orgasm.
Prod-NATSF Dist-MMRC

Marguerite C 30 MIN
3/4 OR 1/2 INCH VIDEO CASSETTE H-C A
Dramatizes the investigations of the staff of a high school newspaper. Focuses on prostitution.
From The New Voice Series.
Prod-WGBHTV Dist-GPITVL

Maria And The Coconuts C 15 MIN
3/4 OR 1/2 INCH VIDEO CASSETTE P
Visits Mexico City, Tula and Taxco.
From The Other Families, Other Friends Series. Blue Module - Mexico
Prod-WVIZTV Dist-AITECH 1971

Maria Montessori, Follow The Child C 49 MIN
16MM FILM OPTICAL SOUND
Documents the life of Maria Montessori, physician and educator in the field of early childhood development. Includes accounts by individuals who worked with her and scenes from Montessori classrooms.
LC NO. 79-700393
Prod-DCASS Dist-DCASS 1978

Maria Morzeck C 101 MIN
16MM FILM OPTICAL SOUND
A German language film with English subtitles. Tells the story of Maria Morzeck, a coy and progressive girl in East Berlin whose brother is involved in broadcasting a taped Adenauer speech on a factory announcement system and is subsequently arrested and imprisoned. Continues as Maria meets Paul Dreister, the judge who sentenced her brother, who admires her, and with whom she plays along even though she despises him in hopes of obtaining a reduced prison term for her brother.
Prod-WSTGLC Dist-WSTGLC 1976

Maria Of The Pueblos C 15 MIN
16MM FILM, 3/4 OR 1/2 IN VIDEO I-C
Presents Indian philosophy on art through the life of Maria Martinez, a Pueblo Indian and probably the world's most famous and successful Indian potter. Shows the step-by-step process she uses in creating her pottery. Tells how she has helped the people of her impoverished village become financially independent and points out that she has perhaps done more to elevate the state and success of Indian art than any other person in history.
Prod-CFE Dist-CORF 1971

Maria Of The Pueblos (Captioned) C 15 MIN
16MM FILM, 3/4 OR 1/2 IN VIDEO I-C
Presents Indian philosophy on art through the life of Maria Martinez, a Pueblo Indian and probably the world's most famous and successful Indian potter. Shows the step-by-step process she uses in creating her pottery. Tells how she has helped the people of her impoverished village become financially independent and points out that she has perhaps done more to elevate the state and success of Indian art than any other person in history.
Prod-CFE Dist-CORF 1971

Mariachi - The Music, The Spirit C 28 MIN
16MM FILM - 3/4 IN VIDEO
Gives an account of the first Tucson International Mariachi Conference, a five-day celebration of Mexican music and culture where people compete and learn. Features discussions by participants explaining the difficulty in learning the techniques and the years of training required to master mariachi music. Includes appearances by Don Silvestre Vargas giving the history of the music and Lola Beltran, one of Mexico's mariachi singers. In Spanish and English with English voice-over.
Prod-KUATTV Dist-KCET

Marian Anderson C 20 MIN
3/4 INCH VIDEO CASSETTE I
See series title for descriptive statement.
From The Truly American Series.
Prod-WVIZTV Dist-GPITVL 1979

Marie Curie - A Love Story C 32 MIN
16MM FILM, 3/4 OR 1/2 IN VIDEO
Recounts the life of Nobel Prize winner Marie Curie. Tells of her marriage to Dr Pierre Curie and of the couple's dedication to scientific research. Focuses on Curie's continued work after the death of her husband.
From The Nobel Prizewinners Series.
Prod-CFDLD Dist-CORF

Marie Curie - A Love Story (Captioned) C 32 MIN
16MM FILM, 3/4 OR 1/2 IN VIDEO
Recounts the life of Nobel Prize winner Marie Curie. Tells of her marriage to Dr Pierre Curie and of the couple's dedication to scientific research. Focuses on Curie's continued work after the death of her husband.
From The Nobel Prizewinners Series.
Prod-CFDLD Dist-CORF

Marie Et Le Cure B 30 MIN
16MM FILM OPTICAL SOUND C A
A French language film. Tells the story of a country girl whose arrival leads to tragedy.
Prod-UWFKD Dist-UWFKD

Marie-Claire Blais - An Interview C 30 MIN
3/4 INCH VIDEO CASSETTE
Presents Marie-Claire Blais talking about herself and her writing.

Tells of the barriers that confronted women writers as evidenced by the long historical tradition of women's adopting male pseudonyms in order to get published and gain acceptance as authors.
Prod-WMENIF Dist-WMENIF

Marihuana C 5 MIN
3/4 OR 1/2 INCH VIDEO CASSETTE
Explains sources of marihuana and its effects on the individual personality, admitting that the drug has not yet been fully researched. Issued in 1971 as a motion picture.
From The Single Concept Drug Film Series.
LC NO. 80-706846
Prod-NIMH Dist-USNAC 1980

Marijuana C 10 MIN
16MM FILM, 3/4 OR 1/2 IN VIDEO
Discusses the characteristics of marijuana. Identifies the signs of use and abuse, the pharmacological and behavioral effects, and the shortand long-term dangers.
From The Drug Information Series.
LC NO. 84-706154
Prod-MITCHG Dist-MTI 1982

Marijuana C 34 MIN
16MM FILM, 3/4 OR 1/2 IN VIDEO J-H A
Discusses the physical dangers, emotional dependency and legalities of using marijuana. Interviews users and non-users. Narrated by singer Sonny Bono.
Prod-AVANTI Dist-PHENIX 1968

Marijuana (French) C 34 MIN
16MM FILM, 3/4 OR 1/2 IN VIDEO J-H A
Discusses the physical dangers, emotional dependency and legalities of using marijuana. Interviews users and non-users. Narrated by singer Sonny Bono.
Prod-AVANTI Dist-PHENIX 1968

Marijuana (Spanish) C 34 MIN
16MM FILM, 3/4 OR 1/2 IN VIDEO J-H A
An action-packed narrative in which a young drag racing enthusiast and his girl friend believable portray the dangers involved in smoking marijuana.
Prod-AVANTI Dist-PHENIX 1968

Marijuana - Facts, Myths, And Decisions C 45 MIN
3/4 OR 1/2 INCH VIDEO CASSETTE I-H
Describes the chemical properties of marijuana and explains the way it affects the human body. Presents arguments for and against its use and legalization, and points to the possibility of psychological addiction. Encourages students to base their decisions on facts about the drug and not on peer pressure.
LC NO. 81-706152
Prod-GA Dist-GA 1981

Marijuana - The Great Escape C 20 MIN
16MM FILM, 3/4 OR 1/2 IN VIDEO I-H
Presents the story of George Willis, a young drag racer, who uses marijuana. Shows that not everyone will die as a result of using marijuana but every user sacrifices control of his own will, judgement and perception. Demonstrates the established effects of marijuana and emphasizes the possibility of psychological dependence.
Prod-BFA Dist-PHENIX 1970

Marijuana - The Hidden Danger C 30 MIN
3/4 OR 1/2 INCH VIDEO CASSETTE J-C
Explains what marijuana does to the mind, body and behavior of those who smoke it.
LC NO. 80-707446
Prod-WABCTV Dist-MTI 1979

Marijuana - Up Close C 30 MIN
3/4 OR 1/2 INCH VIDEO CASSETTE I-C A
Dispels common myths about the use of marijuana. Discusses its wide use and details its physical effects.
LC NO. 82-706436
Prod-WVIZTV Dist-GPITVL 1981

Marijuana Alert C 20 MIN
16MM FILM, 3/4 OR 1/2 IN VIDEO J-H
Looks at the effects of marijuana on the human body, including the reproductive organs, lungs, heart and brain.
Prod-GREENF Dist-PHENIX 1982

Marijuana In Medicine C 32 MIN
3/4 INCH VIDEO CASSETTE
Explains the program at the University of Texas M D Anderson Hospital for using marijuana in medicine.
Prod-UTAHTI Dist-UTAHTI

Marijuana, Driving, And You C 13 MIN
16MM FILM, 3/4 OR 1/2 IN VIDEO J-C A
Investigates the psychological and motor-response effects of marijuana. Tells how marijuana use affects driving.
LC NO. 81-706592
Prod-PORTA Dist-AIMS 1980

Marilyn And Orrin C
3/4 OR 1/2 INCH VIDEO CASSETTE A
Looks at a couple who divorce after 13 years of marriage. Looks at the wife's feelings of guilt, anger and helplessness and the husband's struggle to overcome his own guilt and adjust to his life as a bachelor.
From The Portraits Of Goodbye Series.
Prod-UMCOM Dist-ECUFLM 1980

Marilyn Monroe C
1/2 IN VIDEO CASSETTE (VHS)
Portrays Marilyn Monroe, a special woman who wanted most of all to find love and good feelings but seldom found either. Includes exclusive news clips.
Prod-KARLVI Dist-KARLVI

Marilyn Schorin And Wendy Banker C 30 MIN
3/4 OR 1/2 INCH VIDEO CASSETTE
Focuses on two differing perspectives of dancers' nutrition. Includes 'Esoterica' with Harvy Lichtenstein. Hosted by Irene Dowd.
From The Eye On Dance - Dancers' Health Series.
Prod-ARTRES Dist-ARTRES

Marilyn's Manhatten—A Series

Features Marilyn Perry, host of International Byline, as she talks with representatives of United Nations member nations. Discusses the historical, social, political and economic aspects of each country.
Prod-PERRYM Dist-PERRYM

Arab League 028 MIN
Austria 028 MIN
Buhtan 028 MIN
Ecuador 028 MIN
German Democratic Republic - Tape 1 (Leipzig) 028 MIN
German Democratic Republic - Tape 2 028 MIN
Jordan (Marilyn's Manhatten) 028 MIN
Libya (Marilyn's Manhatten) 028 MIN
Philippines 028 MIN
Saudi Arabia (Marilyn's Manhatten) 028 MIN
Special - Cyprus 028 MIN
Under-Secretary General Of U N For The Office 028 MIN
United Nations Chief Of Protocol 028 MIN
Yugoslavia 028 MIN
Zambia (Marilyn's Manhatten) 028 MIN

Marimba Music Of Mexico C 8 MIN
16MM FILM, 3/4 OR 1/2 IN VIDEO
Presents marimba music of southern Mexico played on a single five-and-one-half-octave instrument by four men.
Prod-UWASHP Dist-UWASHP

Marina Holiday - West Coast Style C 19 MIN
16MM FILM OPTICAL SOUND H-C
Follows the cruise of three Vancouver sailors traveling by cabin boat toward the port of Prince Rupert, 400 miles north of Vancouver. Views lumber industry, Indian relics and the hydro-aluminum development at Kitimat.
LC NO. FIA67-134
Prod-MWSTBR Dist-CTFL Prodn-CHET 1966

Marina Popovich C 20 MIN
3/4 OR 1/2 INCH VIDEO CASSETTE
Features Lieutenant Colonel Marina Popovich, the Soviet test pilot and engineer who set 13 world records. Begins with the romantic aspects of flying which had been primarily a man's profession and follows with a biography of Marina illustrated by interviews and off-screen commentary.
Prod-IHF Dist-IHF

Marine Animals Of The Open Coast - A Story Of Adaptation C 22 MIN
16MM FILM OPTICAL SOUND I-C A
Shows the interrelationships between sea anemone, sea urchin, barnacle, other marine animals and their surroundings. Describes the five general types of food on which they depend.
Prod-MMP Dist-MMP 1963

Marine Biologist C 15 MIN
3/4 OR 1/2 INCH VIDEO CASSETTE I
Explains the qualifications and personal qualities required for a successful career as a marine biologist.
From The Career Awareness Series.
Prod-KLVXTV Dist-GPITVL 1973

Marine Biology - Life In The Tropical Sea C 11 MIN
16MM FILM, 3/4 OR 1/2 IN VIDEO I-H
Presents a documentary by Jacques Cousteau about the many marine animal groups living in tropical waters, largely within coral reefs. Emphasizes the need to preserve the delicate balance of this environment.
Prod-LIVDC Dist-PHENIX 1975

Marine Corps Junior ROTC C 20 MIN
16MM FILM OPTICAL SOUND
Shows how the students, in uniforms, participate in drill team and drum and bugle corps activities, sanctioned rifle matches and other appropriate activities.
LC NO. 74-705093
Prod-USN Dist-USNAC 1972

Marine Delicacies B 9 MIN
16MM FILM OPTICAL SOUND I-C A
Shows how the abundant quantity of fish along the Indian coastline is caught with modern equipment and how it is processed and scientifically canned.
Prod-INDIA Dist-NEDINF

Marine Diesel Engines For Power Boats B 16 MIN
16MM FILM OPTICAL SOUND
Shows the BUDA marine diesel engines DA, DB and DD. Explains the mechanical operation of the DB and its points of difference from the Dd.
LC NO. FIE52-1070
Prod-USN Dist-USNAC 1942

Marine Dynamics C 28 MIN
16MM FILM OPTICAL SOUND
Presents a look at the phenomenon of marine dynamics and examines the workings of a marine laboratory.
From The Education Showcase Series.
LC NO. 74-701200
Prod-OECA Dist-OECA 1972

Marine Firefighting (Italian)—A Series
IND
Covers in five videotapes the rudiments of fires, fire safety and training on board ships at sea. Includes nature of fires, extinguishers, water and fire, the use of foam and interior firefighting. Developed with the Marine Fire Safety Division of Texas A And M University, and endorsed by the American Institute of Merchant Shipping.
Prod-GPCV Dist-GPCV

Exploring Fire's Chemistry (Italian)
Interior Firefighting (Italian)
Portable Extinguishers (Italian)
Use of Foam (Italian)
Water And Fire (Italian)

Marine Firefighting (Korean)—A Series
IND
Covers in five videotapes the rudiments of fires, fire safety and training on board ships at sea. Includes nature of fire, extinguishers, water and fire, the use of foam and interior firefighting. Developed with the Marine Fire Safety Division of Texas A & M University, and endorsed by the American Institute of Merchant Shipping.
Prod-GPCV Dist-GPCV

Exploring Fire's Chemistry (Korean)
Interior Firefighting (Korean)
Portable Extinguishers (Korean)
Use Of Foam (Korean)
Water And Fire (Korean)

Marine Firefighting—A Series
IND
Covers in five videotapes the rudiments of fires, fire safety and training on board ships at sea. Includes nature of fires, extinguishers, water and fire, the use of foam and interior firefighting. Developed with the Marine Fire Safety Division of Texas A And M University, and endorsed by the American Institute of Merchant Shipping.
Prod-GPCV Dist-GPCV

Exploring Fire's Chemistry
Interior Firefighting
Portable Extinguishers
Use Of Foam
Water And Fire

Marine Flowers C 31 MIN
16MM FILM, 3/4 OR 1/2 IN VIDEO C
Studies the structure, behavior and life cycle of coelenterates, including jellyfish, hydroids, sea anemones, and corals.
LC NO. 80-706178
Prod-TOKYO Dist-IFB 1977

Marine Gas Turbine Engines - Principles Of Operation C 19 MIN
16MM FILM OPTICAL SOUND
Explains the basic principles of the gas turbine engine, some variations in the design of turbines currently in use and the applications of the gas turbine in the operation of pumps, boats, trucks and helicopters.
LC NO. FIE53-153
Prod-USN Dist-USNAC 1953

Marine Gas Turbine Engines - The Boeing 502-10c Engine C 22 MIN
16MM FILM OPTICAL SOUND
Demonstrates the construction, operation and maintenance of the 502-10c engine.
Prod-USN Dist-USNAC 1960

Marine Gas Turbine Engines - The Solar T-45 Engine C 23 MIN
16MM FILM OPTICAL SOUND
Discusses the basic concept behind the gas turbine engine, its assembly and operation, unit accessories and their functions and how to operate the unit.
LC NO. FIE61-94
Prod-USN Dist-USNAC 1960

Marine Gas-Turbine Engine - Trouble Shooting C 16 MIN
16MM FILM OPTICAL SOUND
Describes the general procedure for locating the cause of trouble when a gas-turbine engine fails to start, to attain power, to keep oil pressure or to maintain performance.
LC NO. FIE58-16
Prod-USN Dist-USNAC 1954

Marine Highway (2nd Ed) C 14 MIN
16MM FILM OPTICAL SOUND J-C A
Takes the viewer on a tour of Nova Scotia's seacoast along Highway No 7. Visits the Institute of Oceanography at Dartmouth, the golf courses and the ships at anchor in Bedford Basin. Includes the annual regatta, a display of water sports including tub rowing to schooner racing.
LC NO. 76-700886
Prod-NFBC Dist-CTFL 1968

Marine Invertebrates Of The Chesapeake Bay C 9 MIN
16MM FILM OPTICAL SOUND I-H
Shows shallow water invertebrates from the low order hydroid to high order crab in their natural habitat.
Prod-VADE Dist-VADE 1963

Marine Marvels B 11 MIN
16MM FILM OPTICAL SOUND I-C A
Shows the large variety of fish that exists in the Indian marine world and covers the two aquariums at Bombay and Trivandrum.
Prod-INDIA Dist-NEDINF

Marine Meteorology C 30 MIN
3/4 OR 1/2 INCH VIDEO CASSETTE
Traces the fundamental change in the composition of the earth's atmosphere since its formation. Discusses weather and the cause of the seasons.
From The Oceanus - The Marine Environment Series. Lesson 11
Prod-SCCON Dist-CDTEL

Marine Pollution C 30 MIN
3/4 OR 1/2 INCH VIDEO CASSETTE
Focuses on pollution of oceans. Explains problems that exist in determining pollution levels in the ocean. Discusses some of the effects of specific pollutants.
From The Oceanus - The Marine Environment Series. Lesson 28
Prod-SCCON Dist-CDTEL

Marine Scene With Herb Olsen, The C 19 MIN
16MM FILM, 3/4 OR 1/2 IN VIDEO
Presents marine watercolorist Herb Olsen demonstrating some of his techniques.
From The Watercolor Painting Series.
Prod-ELCORP Dist-CORF

Marine Science C 6 MIN
16MM FILM, 3/4 OR 1/2 IN VIDEO K-I
See series title for descriptive statement.
From The Kingdom Of Could Be You Series.
Prod-EBEC Dist-EBEC 1974

Marine Science C 10 MIN
3/4 INCH VIDEO CASSETTE P
Focuses on the role played by marine scientists in safeguarding the resources of the sea.
Prod-MINIP Dist-GA

Mariner - Mars 1969 C 21 MIN
16MM FILM OPTICAL SOUND J-C A
Reviews the principal facts known, and theories held, about Mars prior to 1969. Presents the scientific information obtained from the two Mariner spacecraft that passed close by it in 1969. Incorporates numerous photographs of the Martian surface.
LC NO. 75-710695
Prod-NASA Dist-NASA 1971

Mariner Mars Space Probe - President Kennedy Remembered - Focus On The Aswan Dam B 20 MIN
16MM FILM OPTICAL SOUND H-C
Focuses on the events of 1964. Shows the preparation and launching of the Mariner spacecraft for a journey to Mars. Recalls the death of President Kennedy. Shows the Aswan Dam in Egypt, pointing out its value.
From The Screen News Digest Series. Vol 7, Issue 5
Prod-HEARST Dist-HEARST 1965

Marines - 65 C 25 MIN
3/4 OR 1/2 INCH VIDEO CASSETTE
Highlights the activities under President Johnson of the U S Marine Corps, who fought in two hemispheres the Dominican Republic and Vietnam.
Prod-IHF Dist-IHF

Marines In Perspective C 8 MIN
16MM FILM OPTICAL SOUND
Shows prospective Marine recruits the types of duties available to them while serving in the Marine Corps.
LC NO. 76-702711
Prod-USMC Dist-USNAC 1975

Marines, 1965 C 15 MIN
16MM FILM, 3/4 OR 1/2 IN VIDEO
Highlights Marine Corps activities during 1965, including battle operations and civic action in the Dominican Republic and Vietnam.
LC NO. 81-706612
Prod-USMC Dist-USNAC 1966

Marinos, The C 9 MIN
16MM FILM, 3/4 OR 1/2 IN VIDEO H-C A
Focuses on a divorcing couple in the middle of a bitter custody fight.
From The American Family - An Endangered Species Series.
Prod-NBC Dist-FI 1979

Mario And The Marvelous Gift C 20 MIN
16MM FILM OPTICAL SOUND K-I
Relates the story of a marvelous gem which spread happiness until it was broken by the henchmen of a wicked witch.
From The Animatoons Series.
LC NO. FIA68-1535
Prod-ANTONS Dist-RADTV 1968

Mario Sanchez - Painter Of Memories C 17 MIN
16MM FILM OPTICAL SOUND J-C A
Presents a study of the life and work of Cuban-American wood painter Mario Sanchez. Includes the artist's reminiscences about his family and old neighborhood, as well as his commentary on the techniques and subject matter typifying his work.
From The American Folk Artists Series.
LC NO. 78-700604
Prod-BOWGRN Dist-BOWGRN 1978

Marionette Theatre C 29 MIN
3/4 INCH VIDEO CASSETTE
Focuses on adaptations of Greek plays by a puppeteer who uses as many as 18 figures at once.
From The Off Stage Series.
Prod-UMITV Dist-UMITV 1975

Marionettes C 15 MIN
2 INCH VIDEOTAPE P
Provides an enrichment program in the communitive arts area through imaginative communication.
From The Word Magic (2nd Ed) Series.
Prod-CVETVC Dist-GPITVL

Mariposa C 60 MIN
3/4 OR 1/2 INCH VIDEO CASSETTE J A
Shows how the son of a Mexican tenant farmer rescues his own dreams and those of his neighbors when he devises a plan to raise enough money to save their land and secure their financial future.
From The Rainbow Movie Of The Week Series.
Prod-RAINTV Dist-GPITVL 1981

Marisa And The Mermaid - Florida's War On Water Weeds C 14 MIN
16MM FILM OPTICAL SOUND I-C
Employs underwater photography to demonstrate the central and southern Florida Flood Control District's war on aquatic weeds. Explains the importance of placing sea cows and marisa snails in weed-infested areas to eat the weeds.
LC NO. FIA66-744
Prod-CSFFCD Dist-FDC Prodn-GOODWY 1965

Marist College C 5 MIN
16MM FILM OPTICAL SOUND J-H A
Depicts Marist College, located on the Hudson River outside of Poughkeepsie, Illinois. Explains that Marist College is a co-ed liberal arts college of 1400 students which recently adopted an innovative program which enables students to begin their major program in their freshman year.
Prod-CAMPF Dist-CAMPF

Marital Dance, The - A Study Of Movement In Therapy, Pt 1 C 52 MIN
3/4 OR 1/2 INCH VIDEO CASSETTE PRO
Uses the movements of dance to illustrate the predictable patterns of a marital relationship. Presents a series of edited interview sequences with a married couple. Shows how the therapist demonstrates the recurrent dysfunctional patterns and how the couple comes to recognize the roles they play.
Prod-PSU Dist-PSU

Marital Dance, The - A Study Of Movement In1 Therapy, Pt 2 C 32 MIN
3/4 OR 1/2 INCH VIDEO CASSETTE PRO
Uses the movements of dance to illustrate the predictable patterns of a marital relationship. Presents a series of edited interview sequences with a married couple. Shows how the therapist demonstrates the recurrent dysfunctional patterns and how the couple comes to recognize the roles they play. Comprises the second of two parts.
Prod-PSU Dist-PSU

Mark B 11 MIN
16MM FILM OPTICAL SOUND J-C A
Tells about a young quadriplegic who is confined to a wheelchair after an accident. Shows how he is concerned about his studies and prospects for employment while his family worries about the future when they will not be around to care for him.
LC NO. 76-701868
Prod-AUSDSS Dist-AUIS Prodn-FLMAUS 1975

Mark C 10 MIN
16MM FILM, 3/4 OR 1/2 IN VIDEO I-H
Tells the story of 14-year-old Mark, who has a reading problem but who is working to overcome it.
From The People You'd Like To Know Series.
Prod-WGBHTV Dist-EBEC 1978

Mark Of A Man C 17 MIN
16MM FILM OPTICAL SOUND
Presents an anti-recruiting film. Shows how the Army trains its men to fight against the people of Vietnam. Presents recent veterans of the Vietnamese war who describe their experiences.
Prod-NEWSR Dist-NEWSR

Mark Of Excellence, The C 11 MIN
16MM FILM - 3/4 IN VIDEO
Compares the oil field fire fighters to astronaut Neil Armstrong, as care is exercised by all men who live with danger. Includes a message from astronaut Armstrong about the manned flight awareness program.
Prod-NASA Dist-NASA 1972

Mark Of Quality, A C 14 MIN
3/4 INCH VIDEO CASSETTE
A tour for the housewife from feedlot to pack plant to supermarket and back into her own kitchen. Tells how the Federal Meat Grading Service helps the shopper by providing a guide to buying quality meat.
Prod-USDA Dist-USDA 1972

Mark of Quality, The - Case C 13 MIN
16MM FILM OPTICAL SOUND
Offers a look behind the scenes in research and manufacturing at J I Case Company, one of the world's largest makers of agricultural and construction equipment.
LC NO. 80-700359
Prod-CASE Dist-CORPOR Prodn-CORPOR 1980

Mark Of The D P Professional, The C 30 MIN
3/4 OR 1/2 INCH VIDEO CASSETTE
See series title for descriptive statement.
From The Recruiting And Developing The D P Professional Series.
Prod-DELTAK Dist-DELTAK

Mark Of Zorro, The B 77 MIN
16MM FILM SILENT
Presents the first of the swashbuckler costume films Douglas Fairbanks Sr made.
Prod-UAA Dist-KITPAR 1920

Mark Of Zorro, The B 91 MIN
16MM FILM - 1/2 IN VIDEO, BETA
Stars Douglas Fairbanks as Zorro, the crusader for the rights of the Mexican people.
Prod-UNKNWN Dist-BHAWK 1920

Mark Of Zorro, The (Silent) B 121 MIN
1/2 IN VIDEO CASSETTE BETA/VHS
Stars Douglas Fairbanks as the heroic Zorro.
Prod-UNKNWN Dist-VIDIM 1920

Mark Tobey Abroad C 30 MIN
16MM FILM, 3/4 OR 1/2 IN VIDEO H-C A
Offers an interview with painter Mark Tobey.
Prod-HUFSC Dist-PHENIX 1973

Mark Twain C 20 MIN
3/4 OR 1/2 INCH VIDEO CASSETTE H-C A
Presents dramatized sketches of Mark Twain's life and discusses various selections from his works including The Celebrated Jumping Frog Of Calaveras County, The Adventures of Huckleberry Finn and The Innocents Abroad.
From The American Literature Series.
LC NO. 83-706258
Prod-AUBU Dist-AITECH 1983

Mark Twain B 20 MIN
2 INCH VIDEOTAPE I
See series title for descriptive statement.
From The Americans All Series.
Prod-DENVPS Dist-GPITVL Prodn-KRMATV

Mark Twain - Background For His Works (2nd Ed) C 14 MIN
16MM FILM, 3/4 OR 1/2 IN VIDEO J-C A
Uses rare motion picture footage to introduce Mark Twain and show scenes from his boyhood home in Hannibal, Missouri, and from locations in the East where he wrote the recollections of his life. Dramatizes excerpts from many of his works.
Prod-CORF Dist-CORF 1978

Mark Twain - Beneath The Laughter C 58 MIN
16MM FILM, 3/4 OR 1/2 IN VIDEO
Presents dramatic re-creations showing Mark Twain as a somber old man of 74, mourning his daughter's death.
Prod-FALM Dist-PFP 1979

Mark Twain - Critical Theory B 30 MIN
2 INCH VIDEOTAPE J-H
From The Franklin To Frost Series.
Prod-GPITVL Dist-GPITVL

Mark Twain - Frogs, Jays And Humor B 30 MIN
2 INCH VIDEOTAPE J-H
From The Franklin To Frost Series.
Prod-GPITVL Dist-GPITVL

Mark Twain - Huck Finn - Character And Growth B 30 MIN
2 INCH VIDEOTAPE J-H
From The Franklin To Frost Series.
Prod-GPITVL Dist-GPITVL

Mark Twain - HUCKLEBERRY FINN C 29 MIN
2 INCH VIDEOTAPE
Presents readings from HUCKLEBERRY FINN by Mark Twain.
From The One To One Series.
Prod-WETATV Dist-PUBTEL

Mark Twain - The Adventures Of Huckleberry Finn B 30 MIN
2 INCH VIDEOTAPE J-H
From The Franklin To Frost Series.
Prod-GPITVL Dist-GPITVL

Mark Twain - When I Was A Boy C 25 MIN
16MM FILM, 3/4 OR 1/2 IN VIDEO
Portrays Mark Twain's life along the Mississippi River, as a boy growing up, later as a young cub and pilot on the glamorous stern-wheeled steamboats and finally as a world-renowned writer reflecting back on those days.
LC NO. 80-706339
Prod-NGS Dist-NGS 1977

Mark Twain And The Automated Office C 12 MIN
16MM FILM OPTICAL SOUND
Uses the personage of Mark Twain to underscore Commercial Union Leasing Corporation's human approach to computers. Emphasizes the flexibility and importance of time, time-saving and time-stretching.
LC NO. 79-700728
Prod-CULC Dist-CULC Prodn-WINGS 1978

Mark Twain And Tom Sawyer C 11 MIN
16MM FILM, 3/4 OR 1/2 IN VIDEO J-H
Illustrates elements in the life of Samuel Clemens by describing incidents in his books.
Prod-IFB Dist-IFB

Mark Twain Gives An Interview C 14 MIN
16MM FILM OPTICAL SOUND I-C
Re-creates an interview with Mark Twain, portrayed by Hal Holbrook.
Prod-CORF Dist-CORF 1961

Mark Twain's 'Connecticut Yankee' C
3/4 OR 1/2 INCH VIDEO CASSETTE
Prod-MSTVIS Dist-MSTVIS

Mark Twain's America B 54 MIN
16MM FILM, 3/4 OR 1/2 IN VIDEO H-C A
Re-creates the life of Mark Twain and the age in which he lived. Describes frontier towns, Manhattan in the gay 90's, and Twain's stagecoach ride across the wild western plains.
From The Project 20 Series.
Prod-NBC Dist-CRMP 1961

Mark Twain's Hartford Home C 24 MIN
16MM FILM, 3/4 OR 1/2 IN VIDEO I-H
Features E G Marshall touring the home of Mark Twain.
From The American Lifestyle - Cultural Leaders Series.
Prod-COMCO Dist-AIMS 1978

Mark Van Doren - Poems And Criticism C 29 MIN
2 INCH VIDEOTAPE
Presents the poetry of Mark Van Doren.
From The One To One Series.
Prod-WETATV Dist-PUBTEL

Mark Waters Story, The C 29 MIN
3/4 OR 1/2 INCH VIDEO CASSETTE
Presents the true story of a Honolulu newsman who wrote his own obituary as he lay dying of lung cancer induced by cigarette smoking. Stars Richard Boone.
From The Synergism - In Today's World Series.
Prod-KHETTV Dist-PBS

Mark-Up C 90 MIN
16MM FILM, 3/4 OR 1/2 IN VIDEO
Covers the frantic lobbying through the final test vote of the congressional struggle over President Carter's energy proposal.
From The Energy War Series.
Prod-PBS Dist-PENNAS

Marked For Failure B 60 MIN
16MM FILM OPTICAL SOUND C A
Examines the situation in New York City's Harlem section, revealing the profound handicaps to learning and efforts being made to overcome these disadvantages.
From The America's Crises Series.
LC NO. FIA66-824
Prod-NET Dist-IU 1965

Marken (The Field) C 18 MIN
16MM FILM OPTICAL SOUND
Depicts animal life in the open field, accompanied by sound effects.
Prod-STATNS Dist-STATNS 1962

Market Clearing Price C 23 MIN
16MM FILM, 3/4 OR 1/2 IN VIDEO H A
Explains how the price of a good equates the amount of that good demanded with the amount supplied. Explains how inventories help to provide reliable supply at more predictable prices.
From The People On Market Street Series.
Prod-FNDREE Dist-WDEMCO Prodn-KAHNT 1977

Market Economy Of The United States C 15 MIN
16MM FILM, 3/4 OR 1/2 IN VIDEO J-H
Defines the concept of limited resources and outlines the features of traditional, market, and command economies. Shows freedom of choice, competition, and the profit motive to be the major components of a market economy and illustrates how these principles work in real life.
Prod-GREENF Dist-PHENIX 1980

Market Gardening C 15 MIN
16MM FILM, 3/4 OR 1/2 IN VIDEO P-I
Shows how Wing Lee and his family supply fresh produce for the city's supermarkets and greengrocers from their six-acre market garden. Describes traditional methods of Chinese cultivation. Explains the steps in raising vegetables and how Lee works to keep labor and profit within the family unit.
From The Let's Visit Series.
Prod-BCNFL Dist-BCNFL 1984

Market In Berlin B 15 MIN
16MM FILM SILENT
Shows the routine activities at the weekly farmers' market on Wittenberg Square, the idyllic small-town life amidst the Berlin metropolis.
Prod-WSTGLC Dist-WSTGLC 1929

Market Place In Mexico C 13 MIN
16MM FILM, 3/4 OR 1/2 IN VIDEO P-J
Examines socioeconomic conditions in a rural Mexican marketplace. Shows how people, such as a serape maker, a potter and a rope maker, are dependent on one another's skills. Points out the similarities and differences between the contemporary market and its ancestor, the Aztec market of 500 years ago.
Prod-FLMFR Dist-FLMFR Prodn-PEREZ 1974

Market Place In Mexico (Captioned Version) C 13 MIN
16MM FILM, 3/4 OR 1/2 IN VIDEO P-J
Examines socioeconomic conditions in a rural Mexican marketplace. Shows how people, such as a serape maker, a potter and a rope maker, are dependent on one another's skills. Points out the similarities and differences between the contemporary market and its ancestor, the Aztec market of 500 years ago.
Prod-FLMFR Dist-FLMFR Prodn-PEREZ 1974

Market Prices - Supply And Demand C 15 MIN
3/4 OR 1/2 INCH VIDEO CASSETTE J-H
Uses documentary and dramatic vignettes to explore the effects of a drastically reduced overseas sugar crop, including the prices of sugar and sugar products going up, people substituting other goods, and producers and sellers facing declining income.
From The Give And Take Series. Pt 9
LC NO. 83-706307
Prod-AITV Dist-AITECH 1982

Market Research C 30 MIN
3/4 OR 1/2 INCH VIDEO CASSETTE
Gives marketing information systms and their components, primary and secondary data, traditional methods of information gathering and test marketing as an information method.
From The Marketing Perspectives Series.
Prod-MATC Dist-WFVTAE

Market, The B 29 MIN
16MM FILM, 3/4 OR 1/2 IN VIDEO H-C A
Presents supermarket chain owner Sam Steinberg, who discusses the three main forces in the battle of the marketplace, including suppliers, competitors and consumers.
From The Corporation Series.
Prod-NFBC Dist-NFBC 1973

Market, The C 45 MIN
3/4 OR 1/2 INCH VIDEO CASSETTE IND
Compares market need versus technological capacity. Shows a case history, market research method and sources of information, four key technology and marketing issue, on-line information retrieval and case history, conjoint analysis, sales forecasting and problems with market research.
From The New Product Development Series.
Prod-AMCEE Dist-AMCEE

Market, The - Allocating A Surplus C 10 MIN
16MM FILM, 3/4 OR 1/2 IN VIDEO
Shows the possible solutions to the problem of allocating the surplus created by the division of labor and mechanization.
From The Foundations Of Wealth Series.
Prod-FOTH Dist-FOTH

Marketeers, The - Careers In Marketing C 13 MIN
16MM FILM OPTICAL SOUND I-H
Explores the variety of careers available in marketing and distribution.
From The Working Worlds Series.
LC NO. 75-701545
Prod-OLYMPS Dist-FFORIN 1974

Marketing C
3/4 INCH VIDEO CASSETTE H A
Shows that the modern cook has virtually unlimited choices of fresh, nutritious foods all year round. Discusses how to have a successful marketing trip, from weekly menu plans to buying according to season.
From The Matter Of Taste Series. Lesson 1
Prod-COAST Dist-CDTEL

Marketing C 30 MIN
3/4 INCH VIDEO CASSETTE
See series title for descriptive statement.
From The It's Everybody's Business Series. Unit 5, Operating A Business
Prod-DALCCD Dist-DALCCD

Marketing And All You Ever Wanted To Know About Accounting C 47 MIN
3/4 OR 1/2 INCH VIDEO CASSETTE
Presents the basis of the profit and loss statement from the standpoint of how a retailer might cheat on his income tax.
From The Introduction To Marketing, A Lecture Series.
Prod-IVCH Dist-IVCH

Marketing And Distribution C 6 MIN
16MM FILM, 3/4 OR 1/2 IN VIDEO K-I
See series title for descriptive statement.
From The Kingdom Of Could Be You Series.
Prod-EBEC Dist-EBEC 1974

Marketing And Distribution C 10 MIN
3/4 INCH VIDEO CASSETTE P
Shows the many careers involved in designing, researching, testing, marketing, advertising and distributing a product.
Prod-MINIP Dist-GA

Marketing And The Law - An Introduction C 35 MIN
3/4 OR 1/2 INCH VIDEO CASSETTE PRO
Outlines the legal counsel's role in marketing decision-making and discusses the nature of marketing, the marketing concept and the product life cycle.
From The Antitrust Counseling And The Marketing Process Series.
Prod-ABACPE Dist-ABACPE

Marketing Communications C 30 MIN
3/4 OR 1/2 INCH VIDEO CASSETTE
Shows basic processes of communication in sales skills, steps in the sales process, importance of personal motivation to a salesperson, factors to be assessed in establishing sales territories and methods of organizing a sales force.
From The Marketing Perspectives Series.
Prod-MATC Dist-WFVTAE

Marketing Concepts C 29 MIN
3/4 OR 1/2 INCH VIDEO CASSETTE
See series title for descriptive statement.
From The Business File Series.
Prod-PBS Dist-PBS

Marketing Distribution C 29 MIN
3/4 OR 1/2 INCH VIDEO CASSETTE
See series title for descriptive statement.
From The Business File Series.
Prod-PBS Dist-PBS

Marketing In The Modern Economy C 53 MIN
3/4 OR 1/2 INCH VIDEO CASSETTE
Explores the question as to where the future force of progress lies, in production, marketing or consumer demand.
From The Introduction To Marketing, A Lecture Series.
Prod-IVCH Dist-IVCH

Marketing Management C 30 MIN
3/4 OR 1/2 INCH VIDEO CASSETTE
Covers the efforts of the marketing concept of goal-setting by corporations, role of market information in the decision making process and other aspects of marketing management.
From The Marketing Perspectives Series.
Prod-MATC Dist-WFVTAE

Marketing New Products, Victor H Prushan C
3/4 OR 1/2 INCH VIDEO CASSETTE PRO
See series title for descriptive statement.
From The Management Skills Series.
Prod-AMCEE Dist-AMCEE

Marketing Perspectives—A Series

Emphasizes the fundamentals of marketing and the profitable operation of a business enterprise. Gives attention to the middleman, evaluation of consumer needs and other situations.
Prod-MATC Dist-WFVTAE

Advertising - Broadcast	030 MIN
Advertising - Print	030 MIN
Agents and Brokers	030 MIN
Channels Of Distribution	030 MIN
Communications Management	030 MIN
Consumer Buying Behavior	030 MIN
Consumerism	030 MIN
Direct Marketing	030 MIN
Future Trends	030 MIN
Government And Its Influences	030 MIN
Industrial Markets	030 MIN
International Marketing	030 MIN
Market Research	030 MIN
Marketing Communications	030 MIN
Marketing Management	030 MIN
Marketing Strategies	030 MIN
Marketing Today	030 MIN
Marketing Variables	030 MIN
Packaging And Labeling	030 MIN
Physical Distribution	030 MIN
Pricing Strategies	030 MIN
Pricing Theories	030 MIN
Product Development	030 MIN
Product Management	030 MIN
Retail Location	030 MIN
Retailing	030 MIN
Service Marketing	030 MIN
Target Markets	030 MIN
Wholesalers And Distributors	030 MIN

Marketing Pricing Strategy C 29 MIN
3/4 OR 1/2 INCH VIDEO CASSETTE
See series title for descriptive statement.
From The Business File Series.
Prod-PBS Dist-PBS

Marketing Product Strategy C 29 MIN
3/4 OR 1/2 INCH VIDEO CASSETTE
See series title for descriptive statement.
From The Business File Series.
Prod-PBS Dist-PBS

Marketing Promotional Strategy C 29 MIN
3/4 OR 1/2 INCH VIDEO CASSETTE
See series title for descriptive statement.
From The Business File Series.
Prod-PBS Dist-PBS

Marketing Real Estate And Resorts In The 1980's C 34 MIN
3/4 OR 1/2 INCH VIDEO CASSETTE
Describes product positioning, target market segmentation, advertising, sales promotion and free publicity in marketing real estate projects nationally.
From The Contemporary Issues In Marketing Series.
Prod-CANTOR Dist-IVCH

Marketing Research Pays Off C 13 MIN
16MM FILM OPTICAL SOUND
Tells the story of agricultural marketing research, showing USDA scientists at work improving marketing methods, reducing processing and handling costs and expanding the market for farm products.
LC NO. FIE59-192
Prod-USDA Dist-USNAC 1959

Marketing Strategies C 30 MIN
3/4 OR 1/2 INCH VIDEO CASSETTE
Shows how to develop marketing strategies, the importance of technological changes on product lines management and how the shortage of products affects marketing management.
From The Marketing Perspectives Series.
Prod-MATC Dist-WFVTAE

Marketing Strategies And Tactics For The Dominant Product C 39 MIN
3/4 OR 1/2 INCH VIDEO CASSETTE PRO
Raises questions concerning permissable strategies and tactics for marketing a dominant product, especially with reference to pricing, meeting competition, advertising intensity and the introduction of flanking or blocking brands.
From The Antitrust Counseling And The Marketing Process Series.
Prod-ABACPE Dist-ABACPE

Marketing Strategies And Tactics For The Aging Product C 60 MIN
3/4 OR 1/2 INCH VIDEO CASSETTE PRO
Discusses alternatives available to a company manager charged with the responsibility of reducing a product's cost by recasting the distribution system. Evaluates the risks.
From The Antitrust Counseling And The Marketing Process Series.
Prod-ABACPE Dist-ABACPE

Marketing Techniques C 20 MIN
3/4 OR 1/2 INCH VIDEO CASSETTE
Illustrates marketing techniques and the steps consumers can take to counteract them.
From The Consumer Squad Series.
Prod-MSITV Dist-PBS 1982

Marketing The Myths C 25 MIN
16MM FILM, 3/4 OR 1/2 IN VIDEO H-C A
Presents 24 television commercials which show how advertising reflects the cultural forces used to sell a sponsor's product.
Prod-PHENIX Dist-PHENIX 1977

Marketing Today C 30 MIN
3/4 OR 1/2 INCH VIDEO CASSETTE
Points out the benefits of marketing in the U S economic system and to the individual firm. Shows marketing functions, differentiating between marketing and selling.
From The Marketing Perspectives Series.
Prod-MATC Dist-WFVTAE

Marketing Variables C 30 MIN
3/4 OR 1/2 INCH VIDEO CASSETTE
Shows how to control variables in the marketing mix and addresses the external factors which affect the marketing mix.
From The Marketing Perspectives Series.
Prod-MATC Dist-WFVTAE

Marketing Your Records Management Programs C
3/4 OR 1/2 INCH VIDEO CASSETTE
Presents a records management program, and explains how to show the high-cost impact of current records handling practices, set up a short and long-term plan, develop cost and savings projections, develop a productivity measurement scenario, and present plans to management. Features Dennis F Morgan, a nationally recognized leader in the records management field.
Prod-CAPVID Dist-CAPVID

Marketplace In The Port Of Barcelona, The C 15 MIN
16MM FILM, 3/4 OR 1/2 IN VIDEO
See series title for descriptive statement.
From The Rudolf Nureyev's Film Of Don Quixote Series.
Prod-WRO Dist-SF Prodn-IARTS 1978

Marketplace—A Series
16MM FILM, 3/4 OR 1/2 IN VIDEO P-I
Discusses basic economic concepts.
Prod-EBEC Dist-EBEC 1977

Choosing What To Buy 15 MIN
Choosing What To Make 16 MIN
Money, Money, Money 15 MIN

Marketplace, The C 15 MIN
16MM FILM, 3/4 OR 1/2 IN VIDEO
Explains how local weights and measures officials ensure accuracy in the marketplace. Follows an inspector through a typical workday, observing as he tests scales in a produce market, checks the accuracy of gasoline pumps, and verifies the weights of prepackaged foods.
LC NO. 81-707694
Prod-USNBS Dist-USNAC 1978

Marketplace, The C 30 MIN
3/4 OR 1/2 INCH VIDEO CASSETTE
See series title for descriptive statement.
From The Photographic Vision - All About Photography Series.
Prod-COAST Dist-CDTEL

Marketplaces, The C 55 MIN
1/2 IN VIDEO CASSETTE BETA/VHS
Discusses the investment opportunities in a range of markets, from the American Stock Exchange and the Commodities Market to the Penny Market.
From The Investing Series.
Prod-MOHOMV Dist-MOHOMV

Marketplaces, The C 55 MIN
1/2 IN VIDEO CASSETTE BETA/VHS
Discusses opportunities to invest, and explores arenas for investing from the most conservative to the riskiest, New York Stock Exchange, American Stock Exchange, Over-The-Counter Market, Penny Market, and Commodities Market. Details financial vocabulary, the broker-dealer's role, and some of the rules and protections of each market.
Prod-RMI Dist-RMI

Markets And Prices - Do They Meet Our Needs C 30 MIN
3/4 OR 1/2 INCH VIDEO CASSETTE C
See series title for descriptive statement.
From The Economics USA Series.
Prod-WEFA Dist-ANNCPB

Markets, Prices And Equilibrium I C 45 MIN
3/4 OR 1/2 INCH VIDEO CASSETTE
Discusses the economic concepts of markets, prices and equilibrium.
From The Economic Perspectives Series.
Prod-MDCPB Dist-MDCPB

Markets, Prices And Equilibrium II C 45 MIN
3/4 OR 1/2 INCH VIDEO CASSETTE
Discusses the economic concepts of markets, prices and equilibrium.
From The Economic Perspectives Series.
Prod-MDCPB Dist-MDCPB

Marking C 17 MIN
3/4 OR 1/2 INCH VIDEO CASSETTE A
Discusses how National Security Information should be marked in regard to classification. Presents how derivative classification must be marked. Discusses use of acronyms, abbreviations and special markings.
From The Information Security Briefing Series.
Prod-USISOO Dist-USNAC 1983

Marking Symbols And Applications C 16 MIN
1/2 IN VIDEO CASSETTE BETA/VHS IND
Explains the marking symbols used in various sheet metal shops, which help to eliminate the possibility of making mistakes in layout assembly and fabrication of various fittings and metal fabrications.
Prod-RMI Dist-RMI

Marking Time C 28 MIN
16MM FILM, 3/4 OR 1/2 IN VIDEO
Explains Einstein's theory of relativity as meaning that space and time are relative, depending on the motion of the observer. Uses an imaginary space voyage to demonstrate how 50 years and a vast distance to one person may be a few weeks and a much shorter distance to another.
From The Understanding Space And Time Series.
Prod-BBCTV Dist-UCEMC 1980

Marlboro - The Type Of Man Who Smokes Marlboro C 1 MIN
3/4 OR 1/2 INCH VIDEO CASSETTE
Shows a classic television commercial relating smoking and working.
Prod-BROOKC Dist-BROOKC

Marlene B 27 MIN
16MM FILM OPTICAL SOUND
Features Marlene, an adopted 15 year old from a broken home, who is committed to a youth services institution for being a stubborn child. Follows her through placements, interviews with social workers, arguments with friends, discussions with her mother and confrontations with probation officers after being accused of stealing a car.
Prod-HALLM Dist-IMAGER

Marlin To The Fly C 23 MIN
2 INCH VIDEOTAPE
Tells the story of the late Dr Webster Robinson's history-making achievement of catching a striped marlin with a fly rod, caught off Baja California, Mexico.
Prod-WPBTTV Dist-PUBTEL

Marloo - The Red Kangaroo C 22 MIN
16MM FILM OPTICAL SOUND I-C A
Presents the life history of Marloo, the red kangaroo. Explains that this marsupial is in danger of extinction due to droughts and man's progress. Follows the daily activities of the female, the male and their young.
From The Australian Wildlife Series.
Prod-AVEXP Dist-AVEXP

Marmes Archaeological Dig, The C 18 MIN
16MM FILM, 3/4 OR 1/2 IN VIDEO
Presents the oldest fully-documented discovery of early man in the Western Hemisphere, the remains of the 'Marmes Man' found in the hot dry scrublands of southeast Washington.
Prod-UWASHP Dist-UWASHP

Marmots Of The Pacific Northwest C 18 MIN
16MM FILM OPTICAL SOUND I-H A
Examines the hibernation, reproduction, feeding and social interaction of the Olympic marmot in his natural environment.
LC NO. 72-701379
Prod-KIRL Dist-UWASHP 1972

Marooned C 134 MIN
16MM FILM OPTICAL SOUND
Describes the plight of American astronauts who are trapped in an orbiting spacecraft. Stars Gregory Peck, Richard Crenna, and David Janssen.
Prod-CPC Dist-TWYMAN 1969

Marquee Mystery, The - Using Structural Analysis C 9 MIN
3/4 INCH VIDEO CASSETTE
Tells how a movie house employee almost loses his job when the letters on the marquee tumble down. Shows how Alexander and his friends save the day by using structural analysis.
From The Alexander Hawkshaw's Language Arts Skills Series.
Prod-LUMIN Dist-GA

Marquette And Jolliet - Voyage Of Discovery C 14 MIN
16MM FILM, 3/4 OR 1/2 IN VIDEO I-J
Recounts the exploration of French explorers Marquette and Jolliet from Lake Michigan through Wisconsin rivers and down the Mississippi.
Prod-CORF Dist-CORF 1975

Marquette Park C 62 MIN
3/4 OR 1/2 INCH VIDEO CASSETTE
Presents the issues and emotions involved in the American Nazi Party's radical confrontations against integrationists, communists and police in Chicago's Marquette Park in the 1970s. Shows a march into a Black neighborhood halted by police in October 1975, Nazi efforts to inflame angry whites opposed to a black civil rights march in June 1976 and a Nazi rally at the peak of the organization's visibility in June 1978. Not recommended for young or impressionable audiences.
Prod-IHF Dist-IHF

Marriage C
3/4 INCH VIDEOTAPE
Focuses on a young couple who feel, despite the woman's earlier failed marriage and an increasing trend toward informal relationships, that their commitment to each other can best be expressed by a traditional wedding.
From The Home Series. Pt 3
Prod-EDC Dist-EDC

Marriage C 14 MIN
16MM FILM, 3/4 OR 1/2 IN VIDEO J-H A
Contrasts the lives of two couples, one marrying right out of high school and the other who waited.
From The Family Life Education And Human Growth Series.
Prod-SF Dist-SF 1970

Marriage C 17 MIN
3/4 OR 1/2 INCH VIDEO CASSETTE
Looks at various aspects of marriage from the wedding to the golden anniversary.
Prod-PEREN Dist-PEREN

Marriage C 20 MIN
3/4 OR 1/2 INCH VIDEO CASSETTE J-H
See series title for descriptive statement.
From The Contract Series.
Prod-KYTV Dist-AITECH 1977

Marriage C 25 MIN
16MM FILM, 3/4 OR 1/2 IN VIDEO H-C
Using two married couples, Dr Frederick Perls demonstrates the Gestalt method of achieving achieving a more honest communication in marriage.
From The Gestalt Series.
Prod-PMI Dist-FI 1969

Marriage C 30 MIN
3/4 INCH VIDEO CASSETTE
Examines some of the marital problems that may hit hard at mid-life.
From The Transitions - Caught At Midlife Series.
Prod-UMITV Dist-UMITV 1980

Marriage - Is It A Health Hazard C 30 MIN
16MM FILM, 3/4 OR 1/2 IN VIDEO H-C A
Points out that married women make up the largest percentage of first admissions to psychiatric hospitals suffering from depression. Reveals that they also consume the greatest quantity of tranquilizers and sleeping pills. Shows how this can result from a seemingly happy marriage as many women come to feel devoured by their dependents.
From The Women Series.
Prod-LUF Dist-LUF 1979

Marriage And After B 14 MIN
16MM FILM OPTICAL SOUND J-C A
Explains that the happiness of the married couple is quite often marred when the family grows into unmanageable proportions. Emphasizes the plea for family planning.
Prod-INDIA Dist-NEDINF

Marriage And Divorce Test C 60 MIN
1/2 IN VIDEO CASSETTE (VHS)
Presents some answers to the multitude of questions surrounding the topic of divorce and marriage.
Prod-KARLVI Dist-KARLVI

Marriage And The Family C 30 MIN
3/4 INCH VIDEO CASSETTE C A
Reviews various forms of marriage and family structure. Introduces some of the terms used to distinguish marriage and family patterns and demonstrates these concepts in their specific cultural contexts.
From The Faces Of Culture - Studies In Cultural Anthropology Series. Lesson 9
Prod-COAST Dist-CDTEL Prodn-HRAW

Marriage Circle, The B 86 MIN
16MM FILM SILENT
Tells the story of a five-way love affair in Vienna. Directed by Ernst Lubitsch.
Prod-UNKNWN Dist-KITPAR 1923

Marriage Game, The C 90 MIN
16MM FILM, 3/4 OR 1/2 IN VIDEO
Dramatizes Queen Elizabeth I's romance with the Earl of Leicester, who became her constant companion but who never succeeded in becoming her husband.
From The Elizabeth R Series. No. 2
LC NO. 77-701549
Prod-BBCTV Dist-FI 1976

Marriage In The Middle Years C 30 MIN
3/4 OR 1/2 INCH VIDEO CASSETTE C A
Deals with recognition of physiological and psychological changes in the years when children leave home. Evaluates resources that aid in adjustment.
From The Family Portrait - A Study Of Contemporary Lifestyles Series. Lesson 28
Prod-SCCON Dist-CDTEL

Marriage Is For Keeps X 30 MIN
16MM FILM OPTICAL SOUND J-H T R
A young married couple becomes increasingly aware that communication is breaking down between them. Arguments and misunderstandings are frequent. With the help of their pastor-counselor, each learns to see himself through the other's eyes, and they begin to find answers to their problems.
LC NO. FIA67-5777
Prod-FAMF Dist-FAMF 1966

Marriage Mixup C 30 MIN
16MM FILM OPTICAL SOUND H-C A
Formerly titled 'LOVE IS FOR THE BYRDS.' Studies the problems of communication in marriage. Dramatizes the solution found by a young couple.
LC NO. FIA66-1502
Prod-BYU Dist-CAFM 1966

Marriage Of Figaro B 25 MIN
16MM FILM OPTICAL SOUND J-C A
Presents a condensed version of Mozart's comic opera The Marriage Of Figaro as performed by the Metropolitan Opera Company. Uses English narration.
Prod-OFF Dist-SELECT

Marriage Of Hamey, The C 20 MIN
16MM FILM, 3/4 OR 1/2 IN VIDEO J-C A
Studies the marriage ceremony of the Wogo people in Nigeria.
Prod-JAMPH Dist-CAROUF

Marriage Of Maria Braun, The (German) C 120 MIN
16MM FILM OPTICAL SOUND
Tells the story of a German woman whose husband is missing in the Second World War and who mobilizes herself upward while waiting for him to return. Directed by Rainer Werner Fassbinder. With English subtitles.
Prod-UNKNWN Dist-NYFLMS 1978

Marriage Of Siva And Parvathi, The C 40 MIN
3/4 OR 1/2 INCH VIDEO CASSETTE
Presents a contemporary play portraying the Yogic approach to training the mind.
Prod-IYOGA Dist-IYOGA

Marriage Savers, The C 29 MIN
3/4 INCH VIDEO CASSETTE
Offers advice on choosing a marriage counselor.
From The Woman Series.
Prod-WNEDTV Dist-PUBTEL

Marriage Story, A C 29 MIN
3/4 OR 1/2 INCH VIDEO CASSETTE
Profiles a couple who have weathered 26 years of marriage through some difficult times, including a fight with alcoholism.
From The Tom Cottle Show Series.
Prod-WGBHTV Dist-PBS 1981

Marriage—A Series
H-C
Prod-FRACOC Dist-FRACOC 1970

We Do, We Do 11 MIN
Weekend 15 MIN
You Haven't Changed A Bit 15 MIN

Marriage/Family/Self C 30 MIN
3/4 OR 1/2 INCH VIDEO CASSETTE
See series title for descriptive statement.
From The Health, Safety And Well-Being Series.
Prod-MAETEL Dist-CAMB

Married Lives Today C 19 MIN
16MM FILM, 3/4 OR 1/2 IN VIDEO I-C
Shows glimpses of three couples which survey the range of interpersonal experiences and reactions in various contemporary marriage relationships.
Prod-SILSHA Dist-PHENIX 1975

Marrieds, The C 29 MIN
3/4 OR 1/2 INCH VIDEO CASSETTE
Features Milton Diamond, Ph D, a biologist at the University of Hawaii, defining a traditional marriage. Depicts several different types of marriages. Includes a young, swinging couple discussing their sexual activities and interviews two marriage counselors about some of the problems they encounter. Presents columnist Ann Landers divulging some of the most common marital questions she is asked.
From The Human Sexuality Series.
Prod-KHETTV Dist-PBS

Marriott At Kennedy C 13 MIN
3/4 OR 1/2 INCH VIDEO CASSETTE PRO
Gives a view of the operation of the Marriott flight kitchen at Kennedy Airport in New York. Shows the management, control systems, kitchens, storerooms and offices, and details food preparation and presentation.
Prod-CULINA Dist-CULINA

Marry Me, Marry Me (French) C 87 MIN
16MM FILM OPTICAL SOUND C A
Presents a comedy about a man who turned everything he touched to marriage. Includes English subtitles.
Prod-AA Dist-CINEWO 1969

Marrying C 57 MIN
16MM FILM, 3/4 OR 1/2 IN VIDEO H-C A
Examines the central role of the family in Chinese society, the changing status of women and the reactions of a rural community to the government policy of birth control, which seeks to limit children to one per family.
From The Heart Of The Dragon Series. Pt 8
Prod-ASH Dist-TIMLIF 1984

Mars C 29 MIN
3/4 INCH VIDEO CASSETTE C A
Reviews overall characteristics of Mars. Presents historical perspective on the interest which Mars has generated during the past century. Shows some of the findings of Mariner explorations.
From The Project Universe - Astronomy Series. Lesson 9
Prod-COAST Dist-CDTEL Prodn-SCCON

Mars - Chemistry Looks For Life C 26 MIN
16MM FILM, 3/4 OR 1/2 IN VIDEO
Shows how the Viking Mission facilitated the study of life on Mars.
Prod-CHEMED Dist-WARDS Prodn-WFP 1978

Mars - Is There Life C 15 MIN
16MM FILM - 3/4 IN VIDEO
Discusses the possible history of Mars and its present surface topography of volcanoes, ice caps and canyons. Discusses the Viking lander and its biology experiments in relation to the search for life on Mars.
LC NO. 78-706267
Prod-NASA Dist-USNAC Prodn-WHROTV 1978

Mars - New Laboratory For Science C 13 MIN
16MM FILM OPTICAL SOUND
States that Mars has become a planetary laboratory for studying soil chemistry, geology, weather and other processes.
Prod-ALLFP Dist-NSTA 1980

Mars - The Search Begins C 29 MIN
16MM FILM - 3/4 IN VIDEO
Examines the planet Mars, using pictures taken by the Mariner 9 spacecraft.
LC NO. 79-706058
Prod-NASA Dist-USNAC 1979

Mars - The Search For Life Begins C 15 MIN
16MM FILM OPTICAL SOUND C
Investigates some of the attempts of scientists to determine whether or not there is life beyond the earth. Includes one of the space probes sent to Mars in the 1970's, Mariner 9, which photographed the entire Martian surface in nearly a year of operation and provided material for much experimentation and speculation.
From The Science In Action Series.
Prod-ALLFP Dist-COUNFI

Mars And Beyond C 15 MIN
16MM FILM - 3/4 IN VIDEO
Deals with the Viking Mission to Mars to explore the biochemical components of life. Demonstrates the chemical conditions involved and discusses the potential significance of the biochemical findings in relation to theories concerning Martian life.
LC NO. 78-706265
Prod-NASA Dist-USNAC Prodn-WHROTV 1978

Mars In 3-D - Images From The Viking Mission C 32 MIN
16MM FILM OPTICAL SOUND
Presents images of the Martian surface photographed from various angles by the Viking orbiter and its two test landers.
LC NO. 79-701441
Prod-NASA Dist-NASA 1979

Mars Minus Myth (2nd Ed) C 22 MIN
16MM FILM, 3/4 OR 1/2 IN VIDEO J-C
Presents pictures and data from the Mariner Nine and Viking missions to Mars. Discusses origins of land forms, the discovery of water ice in the polar caps and the improbability of life.
Prod-CF Dist-CF 1977

Marsch Zum Fuehrer, Der B 50 MIN
3/4 OR 1/2 INCH VIDEO CASSETTE
Tells of the Hitler Youth who traveled from their home towns each summer to Nuremburg to participate in the annual Nazi Party Congress. Climaxes in the colorful cereomonies during the Nuremburg congress as they parade before their Fuehrer.
Prod-IHF Dist-IHF

Marsh Community, The X 11 MIN
16MM FILM, 3/4 OR 1/2 IN VIDEO I
Explains why the marsh is changing, illustrates living things and their adaptations to the marsh environment and asks what will become of these plants and animals as the marsh continues to fill in.
Prod-EBF Dist-EBEC 1966

Marsh Treasures C 13 MIN
16MM FILM OPTICAL SOUND I-J
Points out the vast treasures of oil, salt and sulfur found along the gulf coast marsh lands. Shows special machines and mining processes used to overcome the hazards of mining in water and swamp land.
Prod-DAGP Dist-MLA 1961

Marsh, The C 12 MIN
16MM FILM, 3/4 OR 1/2 IN VIDEO I-H A
Explores the habitat and food chains of the marsh.
From The Many Worlds Of Nature Series.
Prod-SCRESC Dist-MTI

Marsha C 24 MIN
3/4 OR 1/2 INCH VIDEO CASSETTE J-C A
Presents a story of a mentally retarded teenage girl, exploring her conflict at home and her relationship with the community. Provides a personal glimpse of her problems as well as her achievements.
Prod-ATLAP Dist-ATLAP

Marsha And Harry C 10 MIN
3/4 OR 1/2 INCH VIDEO CASSETTE H-C A
Presents a humorous look at the trials, tribulations and joys of first time sexual intercourse. Introduces topics essential to all sexuality discussion groups.
Prod-SFTCEN Dist-MMRC

Marshall Maintenance Training Programs—A Series
IND
Presents a series of videotapes shot in actual work situations to demonstrate correct procedures for performing specific maintenance tasks.
Prod-LEIKID Dist-LEIKID

Anchoring, Shimming, Grouting 011 MIN
Anti-Friction Bearings 020 MIN
Basic Hand Tools 011 MIN
Basic Motor Controls 026 MIN
Basic Pipefitting 025 MIN
Belt Conveyors 021 MIN
Boiler Operation, Fireside 016 MIN
Boiler Operation, Waterside 020 MIN
Calculating Pipe Lengths 011 MIN
Centrifugal Pump Maintenance 023 MIN
Concrete Core Drill, The 010 MIN
Concrete Finishing 012 MIN
Concrete Saw, The 013 MIN
Connecting Welding Machines 010 MIN
Coupling Alignment 018 MIN
Drill Sharpening 010 MIN
Flashing Roof Openings 013 MIN
Hydraulic Fittings 019 MIN
Installing Conduit And Cable 025 MIN
Insulation - Covering Hot Piping 030 MIN
Joining Plastic Pipe 019 MIN
Laying Concrete Block 015 MIN
Lubricating Ball Bearings 006 MIN
Mechanical Seal Installation 020 MIN
Metric Micrometer, The 009 MIN
Optical Alignment 034 MIN
Oxyacetylene Cutting 012 MIN
Pipefitting/Cutting/Reaming/Threading 018 MIN
Pipefitting, Bell And Spigot 019 MIN
Planning And Scheduling Of Maintenance 013 MIN
PM Of Hydraulic Systems 013 MIN
PM Of Mobile Equipment 010 MIN
Pouring Babbitt Bearings 017 MIN
Pump Packing 007 MIN
Reading Piping Drawings 017 MIN
Rigging - Wire Rope Slings 018 MIN
Rigging Equipment Over The Floor 016 MIN
Rotary Gear Pumps 1 014 MIN
Rotary Gear Pumps 2 014 MIN
Rotary Joints - Installation And Maintenance 013 MIN
Safety For The New Employee 020 MIN
Soldering And Brazing Copper Tubing 013 MIN
Taper Key, Installation And Removal 014 MIN
Theodolite, The 013 MIN
Torquing 011 MIN
V-Belts Proper Care 015 MIN

Marshall-Marchetti Cysto-Urethropexy For The Correction Of Stress Incontinence, The C 20 MIN
16MM FILM OPTICAL SOUND PRO
Illustrates Dr Spellman's adaptation of the MarshallMarchetti cysto-urethropexy procedure and defines his recommendations for incontinence tests and procedural application.
LC NO. FIA66-54
Prod-EATONL Dist-EATONL Prodn-AVCORP 1963

Marshall-Marchetti-Krantz Procedure C 9 MIN
3/4 OR 1/2 INCH VIDEO CASSETTE
See series title for descriptive statement.
From The Gynecologic Series.
Prod-SVL Dist-SVL

Marshall, Texas - Marshall, Texas C 90 MIN
3/4 OR 1/2 INCH VIDEO CASSETTE
Describes the small town of Marshall, Texas, which in the past has been resistant to change but now is moving forward at a faster pace.
From The Walk Through The 20th Century With Bill Moyers Series.
Prod-CORPEL Dist-PBS 1982

Marshes Of 'Two' Street, The C 29 MIN
2 INCH VIDEOTAPE
See series title for descriptive statement.
From The Synergism - In Today's World Series.
Prod-KVIETV Dist-PUBTEL

Marshes Of The Mississippi C 13 MIN
16MM FILM OPTICAL SOUND I-J
Shows the land building work of the Mississippi River along the Gulf of Mexico, the daily spreading and development of some three million tons of sediment into spongy land. Points out the dependence of animal life on specific plants of the area.
Prod-DAGP Dist-MLA 1960

Marshland Is Not Wasteland C 14 MIN
16MM FILM OPTICAL SOUND P-H
Explains that marshlands are among the most productive lands on earth, pointing out that marsh grasses provide food for the growth of organisms, that algae become food for tiny water animals, which are then eaten by the larger animals and fish. Discusses the wide spread annihilation of coastal marshes, pointing out that their destruction also means the destruction of spawning and nursery grounds of many species of Commercial and sports fishes.
LC NO. FIA63-1055
Prod-WILCOX Dist-FENWCK 1962

Marshlands - Where The Action Is C 20 MIN
3/4 OR 1/2 INCH VIDEO CASSETTE I
Examines the interrelationships and interdependencies of plants and animals within the marsh community. Suggests improving marshland management.
From The Natural Science Specials Series. Module Green
Prod-UNPRO Dist-AITECH 1973

Marsupialization Of A Hydatid Cyst Of Echinococcus Granulosus In The Liver C 14 MIN
16MM FILM, 3/4 OR 1/2 IN VIDEO PRO
Demonstrates the serologic and radiologic findings confirming the diagnosis of hydatid cyst in a 21-yearold white male. Shows the surgical treatment of the patient leading to complete recovery.
Prod-USPHS Dist-USNAC 1963

Marsupialization Of An Anterior Maxillary Residual Cyst C 7 MIN
16MM FILM - 3/4 IN VIDEO PRO
Illustrates a surgical technique for the marsupialization of a maxillary cyst. Explains the advantages and indications for this procedure.
LC NO. 76-706220
Prod-USVA Dist-USNAC Prodn-VADTC 1968

Martha C 9 MIN
16MM FILM, 3/4 OR 1/2 IN VIDEO P-I
Introduces Martha Ann Rudolph who has suffered from epilepsy since birth. Shows her ice skating with friends, sledding, volunteering at a hospital and sharing her feelings with her peers who also have epilepsy.
From The Zoom Series.
Prod-WGBHTV Dist-FI 1978

Martha Ann And The Mother Store C 7 MIN
16MM FILM, 3/4 OR 1/2 IN VIDEO J-H
Uses animation to tell the story of Martha Ann who does not want to pick up her toys, go to bed early, or clean her shoes as her mother requires. Shows how she goes to the Mother Store for a trade-in, but after trying out several new mothers, she discovers that her own is the best of all. Based on the book Martha Ann And The Mother Store by Nathaniel and Betty Jo Charnley.
From The Wrong Way Kid Series.

LC NO. 83-707025
Prod-BOSUST Dist-CF 1983

Martha Bowers, Myrna Renaud C 30 MIN
3/4 OR 1/2 INCH VIDEO CASSETTE
Discusses contemporary dancers' social and political concerns. Features 'Esoterica' with William Starrett. Looks at a humorous escapade in Dublin.
From The Eye On Dance - Politics And Comment In-- Dance Series.
Prod-ARTRES Dist-ARTRES

Martha Clarke C 54 MIN
16MM FILM, 3/4 OR 1/2 IN VIDEO
Portrays artist Martha Clarke as she creates an evening of original theatrical dance.
Prod-CHOPRA Dist-PHENIX 1980

Martha Clarke and Senta Driver C 30 MIN
3/4 OR 1/2 INCH VIDEO CASSETTE
See series title for descriptive statement.
From The Comedy And Outrage In Dance Series.
Prod-ARCVID Dist-ARCVID

Martha Clarke And Senta Driver C 30 MIN
3/4 OR 1/2 INCH VIDEO CASSETTE
See series title for descriptive statement.
From The Eye On Dance - Comdey And Outrage In Dance Series.
Prod-ARTRES Dist-ARTRES

Martha Graham Dance Company, The C 90 MIN
16MM FILM, 3/4 OR 1/2 IN VIDEO H-C A
Focuses on Martha Graham and her influence on modern dance.
From The Dance In America Series.
Prod-WNETTV Dist-IU 1976

Martha Mitchell C 29 MIN
2 INCH VIDEOTAPE
Presents vocalist Martha Mitchell, backed by the Billy Wallace Trio. Interviews songwriter Rudy Jackson talking about the problems of publishing a song.
From The Changing Rhythms Series.
Prod-KRMATV Dist-PUBTEL

Martha Rosler C 56 MIN
3/4 OR 1/2 INCH VIDEO CASSETTE
Features an interview with Martha Rosler. Presented by Kate Horsfield and Lyn Blumenthal.
Prod-ARTINC Dist-ARTINC

Martha Rosler - A Simple Case For Torture, Or How To Sleep At Night C 62 MIN
3/4 OR 1/2 INCH VIDEO CASSETTE
Makes explicit references to historical and political events.
Prod-ARTINC Dist-ARTINC

Martha Rosler - Domination And The Everyday C 32 MIN
3/4 OR 1/2 INCH VIDEO CASSETTE
Includes both images and texts. Contains a social framework.
Prod-ARTINC Dist-ARTINC

Martha Rosler - If It's Too Bad To Be True, It Could Be Disinformation C 17 MIN
3/4 OR 1/2 INCH VIDEO CASSETTE
Combines facts, figures, newspaper reports, anecdotes, autobiographical material, mass media images and questions in a social framework.
Prod-ARTINC Dist-ARTINC

Martha Schlamme C 52 MIN
3/4 OR 1/2 INCH VIDEO CASSETTE
Features German-born Martha Schlamme singing several songs in German while accompanied by Abraham Stockman on piano.
From The Rainbow Quest Series.
Prod-SEEGER Dist-CWATER

Martial Arts - Fun, Protection And Self-Improvement C 25 MIN
3/4 OR 1/2 INCH VIDEO CASSETTE J-C A
Features a visit with two of the most respected martial arts instructors and practitioners in the world, Master Yoshimitsu Yamada and Professor Ronald Duncan.
Prod-SIRS Dist-SIRS

Martian In Moscow—A Series
16MM FILM, 3/4 OR 1/2 IN VIDEO H-C A
Presents Russian-language motion pictures which visit various locales in Moscow.
Prod-HALAS Dist-IFB

Martian In Moscow, Film 1 009 MIN
Martian In Moscow, Film 2 010 MIN
Martian In Moscow, Film 3 010 MIN
Martian In Moscow, Film 4 011 MIN

Martian In Moscow, Film 1 C 9 MIN
16MM FILM, 3/4 OR 1/2 IN VIDEO H-C A
A Russian-language motion picture which deals with shopping for clothes and toys in Moscow.
From The Martian In Moscow Series.
Prod-HALAS Dist-IFB 1977

Martian In Moscow, Film 2 C 10 MIN
16MM FILM, 3/4 OR 1/2 IN VIDEO H-C A
A Russian-language motion picture which deals with visiting the cafeteria, the river and the health centern Moscow.
From The Martian In Moscow Series.
Prod-HALAS Dist-IFB 1977

Martian In Moscow, Film 3 C 10 MIN
16MM FILM, 3/4 OR 1/2 IN VIDEO H-C A
A Russian-language motion picture dealing with such topics as a balloon chase over Moscow and a visit to the Kremlin and the Bolshoi Ballet School.
From The Martian In Moscow Series.
Prod-HALAS Dist-IFB 1977

Martian In Moscow, Film 4 C 11 MIN
16MM FILM, 3/4 OR 1/2 IN VIDEO H-C A
A Russian-language motion picture dealing with a ride on the Moscow underground and an outing in Gorki Park.
From The Martian In Moscow Series.
Prod-HALAS Dist-IFB 1977

Martian Investigators, The C 28 MIN
16MM FILM OPTICAL SOUND I-C A
Presents the team of scientists who built and controlled the experiments of Mariners 6 and 7 that passed close to Mars in July and August 1969, and sent back photographs of the Martian surface and scientific data that expanded our knowledge of the planet. Gives the preliminary results of the missions.
LC NO. 70-705153
Prod-NASA Dist-NASA 1969

Martin And Abraham Lincoln C 15 MIN
3/4 OR 1/2 INCH VIDEO CASSETTE P
Recounts a Civil War incident involving Abraham Lincoln and the son of an Andersonville prisoner.
From The Stories Of America Series.
Prod-OHSDE Dist-AITECH Prodn-WVIZTV 1976

Martin Chuzzlewit C 29 MIN
3/4 INCH VIDEO CASSETTE
Examines Dickens' problems of learning to deal with rascals and with the world around him.
From The Dickens World Series.
Prod-UMITV Dist-UMITV 1973

Martin Kahan, Rodney Nugent And Louis Falco C 30 MIN
3/4 OR 1/2 INCH VIDEO CASSETTE
Looks at dance and new music videos. Hosted by Celia Ipiotis.
From The Eye On Dance - Dance On TV And Film Series.
Prod-ARTRES Dist-ARTRES

Martin Lutero B 103 MIN
16MM FILM OPTICAL SOUND
A Spanish version of the English language film, Martin Luther.
Prod-LUTHER Dist-LUTHER

Martin Luther B 100 MIN
16MM FILM OPTICAL SOUND H-C
Depicts the life of Martin Luther, including his acceptance into the Augustinian Order. Part 1 discusses his questioning of accepted teaching and the posting of the 95 theses. Part 2 tells about Luther's trial where he refused to recant his writings. Part 3 describes his life at Wartburg Castle and his marriage.
Prod-LUTHER Dist-CPH 1953

Martin Luther - Excerpt B 29 MIN
16MM FILM OPTICAL SOUND C
Presents the life work of Luther from the time of his views as Augustinian monk, through his ordination as a priest, his self doubts, opposition to sales of indulgences, posting of the 95 theses, debate with eck, excommunication, burning of papal decree and refusal to recant before a diet of worms.
Prod-TFC Dist-IU 1971

Martin Luther King B 28 MIN
16MM FILM OPTICAL SOUND
Dr Martin Luther King explains the Negro non-violent resistance movement being practiced in the South. A discussion with Ned Brooks, moderator, Mae Craig, Anthony Lewis, Lawrence Spivak and Frank Van Der Linden.
From The Meet The Press Series.
LC NO. 72-701448
Prod-NBCTV Dist-NBC 1960

Martin Luther King C 15 MIN
3/4 INCH VIDEO CASSETTE P
See series title for descriptive statement.
From The Celebrate Series.
Prod-KUONTV Dist-GPITVL 1978

Martin Luther King C 103 MIN
3/4 OR 1/2 INCH VIDEO CASSETTE
Examines Martin Luther King's life.
Prod-NORTNJ Dist-NORTNJ

Martin Luther King - The Man And The March B 83 MIN
16MM FILM OPTICAL SOUND C A
Records the history of the late Dr Martin Luther King's 'POOR PEOPLE'S MARCH,' shows Dr King conferring with aides, speaking at rallies and visiting schools.
LC NO. FIA68-1939
Prod-NET Dist-IU 1968

Martin Luther King And The Civil Rights Movement B 30 MIN
2 INCH VIDEOTAPE H-C A
See series title for descriptive statement.
From The Americans From Africa - A History Series. No. 29
Prod-CVETVC Dist-GPITVL Prodn-WCVETV

Martin Luther King Jr - The Assassin Years C 26 MIN
16MM FILM, 3/4 OR 1/2 IN VIDEO J-C A
Uses dramatized sequences and historical newsreel footage to recapture the great crusade of Martin Luther King, Jr.
From The Nobel Prizewinners Series.
Prod-CFDLD Dist-CORF

Martin Luther King, Jr (2nd Ed) C 24 MIN
16MM FILM, 3/4 OR 1/2 IN VIDEO J-H A
Examines Martin Luther King, Jr's career, his belief in the non-violent protest and the impact of his leadership on the civil rights movement using documentary footage and the voices of people in the most prominent issues of his life. Demonstrates how King helped establish the Public Accomodations Act, the Voting Rights Act and the Open Housing Act.
From The Great Americans Series.
LC NO. 82-706657
Prod-EBEC Dist-EBEC Prodn-OLINC 1981

Martin Luther King, Jr - A Man Of Peace B 30 MIN
16MM FILM, 3/4 OR 1/2 IN VIDEO J-C A
Dr Martin Luther King discusses contemporary questions—the role of organized religion as an instrument to bring social change, the future of the civil rights movement and the possibility of his own violent death.
Prod-JOU Dist-JOU 1968

Martin Luther King, Jr - A New Dawn - A New Day C 29 MIN
3/4 OR 1/2 INCH VIDEO CASSETTE
Depicts events in the life of Martin Luther King, Jr. Presented in a montage by artist Melusena Carl Whitlock.
Prod-RCOMTV Dist-SYLWAT 1985

Martin Luther King, Jr - From Montgomery To Memphis B 27 MIN
16MM FILM, 3/4 OR 1/2 IN VIDEO J-C A
Traces the life of Martin Luther King when he first rose to national prominence as a result of his leadership in a struggle against bus segregation in Montgromery, Alabama—his civil rights campaigns in Albany, Georgia and Birmingham, Alabama, and the massive march in Washington, helped bring about meaningful civil rights legislation—he was awarded the Nobel Peace Prize in 1964 and he was assassinated In Memphis, on April 4, 1968.
Prod-FA Dist-PHENIX 1969

Martin Luther, His Life And Time (Silent) B 101 MIN
1/2 IN VIDEO CASSETTE BETA/VHS
Traces the life and work of Martin Luther, focusing on his early years.
Prod-UNKNWN Dist-VIDIM 1924

Martin Luther, Pt 1 - The Ninety-Five Thesis B 40 MIN
16MM FILM OPTICAL SOUND H-C A
Portrays Luther's acceptance into the Augustinian order, his inner spiritual turmoil, journey to Rome, appointment as Professor of Theology at Wittenberg University, questioning of the accepted teaching and interpretations of scripture, preaching against indulgences and posting of the ninety-five thesis on the eve of All Saints Day, October 31, 1517.
Prod-CONCOR Dist-CPH

Martin Luther, Pt 2 - By Faith Alone B 30 MIN
16MM FILM OPTICAL SOUND H-C A
Portrays the early attempts by the church to link Luther with John Hus, the Leipzig debates with John Eck, Luther's release from the vows of the Augustinian order, his condemenation by Pope Leo X, and burning of the Papal Bull on December 10, 1520. Shows Luther's trial.
Prod-CONCOR Dist-CPH

Martin Luther, Pt 3 - Champions Of The Faith B 30 MIN
16MM FILM OPTICAL SOUND H-C A
Shows Luther taken by friends to Wartburg Castle, after he is condemend by both Pope and Emperor and under sentence of death, where he completes translation of the New Testament. Closing scene is back at the castle church in Wittenberg with Luther standing before his congregation. Closes to the rousing strains of 'A MIGHTY FORTRESS IS OUR GOD.'
Prod-CONCOR Dist-CPH

Martin Meets The Pirates C 26 MIN
16MM FILM, 3/4 OR 1/2 IN VIDEO I-J
Presents the story of Martin who is tempted to join a street gang until he learns the gang has demanded 'protection money' from his younger sister and her friend. Shows brother and sister rallying the neighborhood to scare off the gang.
Prod-PLAYTM Dist-BCNFL 1985

Martine Van Hamel, Hector Mercado C 30 MIN
3/4 OR 1/2 INCH VIDEO CASSETTE
Discusses physical and emotional changes as the dance artist matures. Features 'Esoterica' with costume designer Willa Kim. Hosted by Irene Dowd.
From The Eye On Dance - Dancers' Bodies Series.
Prod-ARTRES Dist-ARTRES

Marusska And The Wolf Castle C 15 MIN
16MM FILM, 3/4 OR 1/2 IN VIDEO I-C
Presents an animated version of the Moravian tale of Marusska, a poor mountain girl, and the consequences that befall her later in her life as a result of trying to free a duchess imprisoned in a castle she happens upon as a girl.
Prod-KUBRIC Dist-PHENIX 1982

Marva C 17 MIN
16MM FILM, 3/4 OR 1/2 IN VIDEO A
Shows teacher Marva Collins at her one-and-a-half-room West Side Preparatory School in Chicago's West Side as she succeeds in challenging her students beyond the expectations of the statistically unsuccessful public schools. Originally shown on the television program 60 Minutes.
LC NO. 80-706154
Prod-CBSNEW Dist-CAROUF 1979

Marvel - A Jakarta Boy C 17 MIN
16MM FILM OPTICAL SOUND H-C A
Examines the life of a young migrant boy in Jakarta, Indonesia. Shows how he works hard so that he can fulfill his life's goal of getting an education.
From The Asian Neighbors - Indonesia Series.
LC NO. 75-703583
Prod-FLMAUS Dist-AVIS 1975

Marvella Bayh Story, The C 10 MIN
16MM FILM OPTICAL SOUND H-C A

Presents Marvella Bayh, who encourages women to have medical checkups and breast examinations by telling how she faced having breast cancer and how she returned to a full, active life.
LC NO. 77-701312
Prod-AMCS Dist-AMCS 1973

Marvelous Machines - Expendable People C 48 MIN
3/4 OR 1/2 INCH VIDEO CASSETTE H-C A
Visits the Monongahela Valley to study the depressed steel industry that once was the region's lifeblood. Probes the causes and senses the multi-faceted effects of steel's decline in the U S.
LC NO. 84-706264
Prod-NBCNEW Dist-FI 1983

Marvelous March Of Jean Francois, The C 18 MIN
16MM FILM, 3/4 OR 1/2 IN VIDEO P-I
Presents the adventures of Jean Francois, a small drummer boy in Napoleon's Grande Armee.
Prod-SF Dist-SF 1970

Marvelous Math Caper, The C 11 MIN
16MM FILM, 3/4 OR 1/2 IN VIDEO P-I
Tells how a superhuman being named Dory learns that she doesn't need her special arm calculator to solve a simple math problem.
Prod-BARR Dist-BARR

Marvelous Mousetrap, The C 24 MIN
16MM FILM - 3/4 IN VIDEO IND
Presents a dramatization which explains the basic principles of the American capitalist system. Shows how profits arise and how they are used to insure employee job security - explains the necessity for careful work by each employee in order to protect a company's continuity.
Prod-BNA Dist-BNA Prodn-NRWOOD 1963

Marvels In Miniature C 15 MIN
16MM FILM OPTICAL SOUND J-C A
Shows underwater life of the barrier reef under the magnifying glass, depicting the thousands of small particles that go to make up the plankton upon which the smallest of fishes feed. Features sea creatures, from the smallest of diatoms to the ghost shrimp and the sea worm.
Prod-ANAIB Dist-AUIS 1950

Marvels of Industrial Robots, The C 36 MIN
3/4 OR 1/2 INCH VIDEO CASSETTE H-C A
Shows the newest of the industrial robots - precision work-robots that locate, lift, sort, weld, assemble and package in light or darkness, cold or heat. Recognizes the inevitability and potentialities of industrial robots.
Prod-CENTRO Dist-CORF 1983

Marvels Of The Mind C 23 MIN
16MM FILM, 3/4 OR 1/2 IN VIDEO
Explores the complex structures and processes of the human brain. Pictures extremely thin sections of brain tissue and uses computer simulation.
LC NO. 80-706292
Prod-NGS Dist-NGS 1980

Marvin Bell C 29 MIN
3/4 INCH VIDEO CASSETTE
See series title for descriptive statement.
From The Poets Talking Series.
Prod-UMITV Dist-UMITV 1975

Marx Brothers Mosaic B 27 MIN
16MM FILM OPTICAL SOUND
Presents the Marx Brothers' one-reel shorts 'The Incredible Jewel Robbery,' 'Pigskin Capers' and 'This Is War' mounted onto a single reel.
Prod-CFS Dist-CFS

Marx For Beginners C 7 MIN
16MM FILM, 3/4 OR 1/2 IN VIDEO
Presents an animated motion picture which highlights the major philosophical and economic theories of Karl Marx.
LC NO. 83-706824
Prod-CUCMBR Dist-ICARUS 1983

Marx, Pt 1 - His Life, His Work As Official Doctrine C 30 MIN
3/4 INCH VIDEO CASSETTE
Traces the life of Karl Marx and examines his work as official doctrine.
From The From Socrates To Sartre Series.
Prod-MDCPB Dist-MDCPB

Marx, Pt 2 - Metaphysics, Dialectical Materialism C 30 MIN
3/4 INCH VIDEO CASSETTE
Discusses metaphysics and dialectical materialism in the work of Marx.
From The From Socrates To Sartre Series.
Prod-MDCPB Dist-MDCPB

Marx, Pt 3 - Class Conflict, Withering Away Of The State C 30 MIN
3/4 INCH VIDEO CASSETTE
Examines Marx's ideas on class conflict and the withering away of the state.
From The From Socrates To Sartre Series.
Prod-MDCPB Dist-MDCPB

Marx, Pt 4 - Ethics, Marxism As Ideology, Leninism C 30 MIN
3/4 INCH VIDEO CASSETTE
Discusses the Marxist theory of ethics and focuses on Marxism as ideology. Offers a look at Leninism.
From The From Socrates To Sartre Series.
Prod-MDCPB Dist-MDCPB

Marxism - The Theory That Split A World C 25 MIN
16MM FILM, 3/4 OR 1/2 IN VIDEO H-C A
Explores the historical and current dimensions of Karl Marx through dramatized interviews with those who knew him, animated explanations of his major tenets and documentary treatment of the monumental changes wrought in his name.
Prod-INCC Dist-LCOA 1970

Marxism - The Theory That Split A World (Spanish) C 26 MIN
16MM FILM, 3/4 OR 1/2 IN VIDEO H-C A
Outlines the history and significance of Marxism by interviews witpeople who knew Karl Marx or were influenced by his ideas.
Prod-INCC Dist-LCOA 1970

Mary C 10 MIN
16MM FILM, 3/4 OR 1/2 IN VIDEO I-H
Focuses on an 11-year-old girl who was born deaf. Shows how she uses a hearing aid and reads lips and how she is working with a speech therapist to learn how to speak.
From The People You'd Like To Know Series.
Prod-WGBHTV Dist-EBEC 1978

Mary B 30 MIN
2 INCH VIDEOTAPE
Presents an interview with a 13-year-old girl and her mother. Includes problems of staying out late at night and other misbehavior.
From The Counseling The Adolescent Series.
Prod-GPITVL Dist-GPITVL

Mary Anthony And Bettie deJong C 30 MIN
3/4 OR 1/2 INCH VIDEO CASSETTE
Looks at the roots of dance on television and in film. Presents an excerpt from 'Nine Variations on a Dance Theme,' a film by Hilary Harris. Features Birgit Cullberg in 'Esoterica.'
From The Eye On Dance - Dance On TV Series.
Prod-ARTRES Dist-ARTRES

Mary Baldwin College C 5 MIN
16MM FILM OPTICAL SOUND J-C A
Explains that Mary Baldwin College is a private liberal arts college for women located on a ten-acre campus in Staunton, Virginia, in the Shenandoah Valley. Points out that their AB-3 program makes it possible to complete college in three years.
Prod-CAMPF Dist-CAMPF

Mary Cassatt - Impressionist From Philadelphia C 30 MIN
16MM FILM, 3/4 OR 1/2 IN VIDEO H-C A
Discusses the work of 19th century impressionist painter Mary Cassatt.
From The Originals - Women In Art Series.
Prod-WNETTV Dist-FI 1977

Mary Daly Presents Gyn/Ecology B 80 MIN
3/4 INCH VIDEO CASSETTE
Features Mary Daly discussing the liberation of women. Focuses on the global dimension of atrocities against women. Celebrates the becoming of the radical feminist.
Prod-WMENIF Dist-WMENIF

Mary Hinkson And Zachary Solov C 30 MIN
3/4 OR 1/2 INCH VIDEO CASSETTE
Discusses dancers' changing attitudes. Looks at 'Esoterica' with Frederick Franklin. Hosted by Celia Ipiotis.
From The Eye On Dance - Update, Topics Of Current Concern Series.
Prod-ARTRES Dist-ARTRES

Mary Kate's War C 25 MIN
16MM FILM, 3/4 OR 1/2 IN VIDEO
Recreates Mary Katherine Goddard's efforts to uphold the freedom of the press when she refused the Baltimore Whig Club's demand that she reveal the author of an unsigned article that she had published in the Maryland Journal.
From The Decades Of Decision - The American Revolution Series.
LC NO. 80-706345
Prod-NGS Dist-NGS 1975

Mary Kingsley C 52 MIN
16MM FILM, 3/4 OR 1/2 IN VIDEO
Dramatizes Mary Kingsley's 1893 journey along the Ogowe and Rembwe Rivers of Africa's West Coast, where she studied the native cultures of the cannibalistic tribes.
From The Ten Who Dared Series.
LC NO. 79-707387
Prod-BBCTV Dist-TIMLIF 1976

Mary Kingsley - West Africa, 1893, Pt 1 C 26 MIN
16MM FILM OPTICAL SOUND I A
Special classroom version of the film and videorecording Mary Kingsley - West Africa, 1893.
From The Ten Who Dared Series.
Prod-BBCTV Dist-TIMLIF 1977

Mary Kingsley - West Africa, 1893, Pt 2 C 26 MIN
16MM FILM OPTICAL SOUND I A
Special classroom version of the film and videorecording Mary Kingsley - West Africa, 1893.
From The Ten Who Dared Series.
Prod-BBCTV Dist-TIMLIF 1977

Mary Lou At Saratoga C 29 MIN
3/4 OR 1/2 INCH VIDEO CASSETTE
Follows Mary Lou Vanderbilt Whitney through the social whirl of Saratoga's racing season.
Prod-KITCHN Dist-KITCHN

Mary McLeod Bethune C 30 MIN
3/4 OR 1/2 INCH VIDEO CASSETTE
Discusses why Mary McLeod Bethune was memorialized with a conmemorative postage stamp, a memorial statue, the Bethune Museum-Archives National Historic Site, and the Bethune-Cookman College.
Prod-RCOMTV Dist-SYLWAT 1985

Mary Of Mile 18 C 12 MIN
16MM FILM, 3/4 OR 1/2 IN VIDEO I-J
Describes the life of a young girl growing up on a farm in a remote Mennonite community. Includes full animation of visuals.
LC NO. 83-706653
Prod-NFBC Dist-NFBC 1982

Mary S McDowell B 51 MIN
16MM FILM, 3/4 OR 1/2 IN VIDEO I-H
Dramatizes the pacifist stand taken by Mary McDowell, a Quaker teacher in a New York school during World War I. Based on book Profiles In Courage by John F Kennedy. Stars Rosemary Harris.
From The Profiles In Courage Series.
LC NO. 83-706540
Prod-SAUDEK Dist-SSSSV 1964

Mary Wigman - When The Fire Dances Between The Two Poles B 43 MIN
16MM FILM, 3/4 OR 1/2 IN VIDEO
Reveals the work and philosophy of choreographer Mary Wigman. Shows highlights of Wigman's performances from 1923 through her final solo in 1942. Describes her work with students following her retirement from the stage.
LC NO. 84-706014
Prod-MACSNY Dist-UCEMC 1982

Maryon Kantaroff B 18 MIN
16MM FILM OPTICAL SOUND
Visits Canadian sculptor Maryon Kantaroff in her studio and observes as she creates a sculpture. Shows a wide variety of her works.
LC NO. 77-702960
Prod-RYALLS Dist-CANFDC 1974

Masada C 12 MIN
16MM FILM OPTICAL SOUND
Depicts Professor Yigael Hadin leading the excavations at Masada, the last Jewish stronghold against the Roman legions in the first millennium. Shows the hundreds of volunteers from all over the world who participate.
Prod-ALDEN Dist-ALDEN

Masada B 30 MIN
16MM FILM OPTICAL SOUND H-C A
Presents a documentary filmed in Israel, showing the excavations on the site of the ancient rock-fortress of Masada. Includes an interview of Dr Yigael Yadin, Israeli archeologist in charge of these excavations. Discusses the significance of the discoveries at Masada, indicating that it was valiantly defended as the last outpost of resistance to Roman tyranny, in 73 C E. (Kinescope)
From The Eternal Light Series.
LC NO. 72-700964
Prod-JTS Dist-NAAJS 1967

Masai In Tanzania C 14 MIN
16MM FILM, 3/4 OR 1/2 IN VIDEO
Shows the life styles and dress of the African tribe, the Masai. Emphasizes the economy and social attitudes of this tribe and its relationship with neighboring tribes.
From The Man And His World Series.
Prod-PMI Dist-FI 1969

Masai Manhood C 53 MIN
16MM FILM OPTICAL SOUND A
Looks at the seven-year period in the life of Masai men during which they serve as warriors.
From The Disappearing World Series.
LC NO. 80-701658
Prod-GRATV Dist-INSHI 1980

Masai Women C 52 MIN
16MM FILM OPTICAL SOUND A
Looks at the women of the Masai tribe, tracing their passage into womanhood and examining their daily lives.
From The Disappearing World Series.
LC NO. 80-701666
Prod-GRATV Dist-INSHI 1980

Masajes Cardiacos C 11 MIN
16MM FILM, 3/4 OR 1/2 IN VIDEO C A
A Spanish-language version of the motion picture Closed Chest Cardiac Massage. Introduces the technique of closed chest cardiac massage.
From The Emergency Resuscitation (Spanish) Series.
Prod-UKMD Dist-IFB

Masculin Et Feminin C 13 MIN
16MM FILM OPTICAL SOUND J A
From The En Francais, Set 2 Series.
Prod-PEREN Dist-CHLTN 1969

Masculine And Feminine (French) C 14 MIN
3/4 OR 1/2 INCH VIDEO CASSETTE H-C A
Presents two humorous sketches involving the opposite sexes.
From The En Francais Series. Part 2 - Temporal Relationships, Logical Relationships
Prod-MOFAFR Dist-AITECH 1970

Masculine Or Feminine - Your Role In Society C 19 MIN
16MM FILM, 3/4 OR 1/2 IN VIDEO J A
Shows that society defines the roles of male and female and considers the effect of these stereotypes on individual development.
Prod-CORF Dist-CORF 1971

Masculine, Feminine And Androgyny C 29 MIN
3/4 OR 1/2 INCH VIDEO CASSETTE
Discusses the meaning of an androgynous personality and its significance to the women's movement.

From The Woman Series.
Prod-WNEDTV Dist-PBS

Mashi Warak And Mashi Kussa C 26 MIN
3/4 OR 1/2 INCH VIDEO CASSETTE PRO
Demonstrates stuffing and how it is used in Middle Eastern cuisine. Grape leaves are stuffed with a lamb and rice filling and steamed, and squash is stuffed with a similar filling and cooked with a Marinara sauce.
Prod-CULINA Dist-CULINA

Mashpee Wamponogs, The C 30 MIN
3/4 INCH VIDEO CASSETTE
See series title for descriptive statement.
From The People Of The First Light Series.
Prod-WGBYTV Dist-GPITVL 1977

Mask C 30 MIN
3/4 OR 1/2 INCH VIDEO CASSETTE
Charts the subsconcious journey of a black woman, unravelling history, and discovering her true source of strength.
From The Doris Chase Concepts Series.
Prod-CHASED Dist-CHASED

Mask Layout C 55 MIN
3/4 OR 1/2 INCH VIDEO CASSETTE PRO
Deals with transformation of a circuit design to a geometrical layout, using the design rules. Gives detailed example and shows influence of design rules on the order of design.
From The Introduction To VLSI Design Series.
Prod-MIOT Dist-MIOT

Mask Layout C 59 MIN
3/4 OR 1/2 INCH VIDEO CASSETTE PRO
See series title for descriptive statement.
From The Introduction To VLSI Design Series.
Prod-MIOT Dist-AMCEE

Mask Patterns And Their Constraints C 55 MIN
3/4 OR 1/2 INCH VIDEO CASSETTE PRO
Covers shapes for mask patterns, formal languages, student design examples, design rules, and classes of design.
From The Introduction To VLSI Design Series.
Prod-MIOT Dist-MIOT

Mask, The C 4 MIN
16MM FILM OPTICAL SOUND P
Presents a story about two African boys, various comical animals and a mask.
LC NO. 77-702961
Prod-CANFDC Dist-CANFDC 1976

Mask, The B 5 MIN
16MM FILM OPTICAL SOUND J-C A
Presents a modern interpretation of Psalm 61, using scenes of a circus clown applying his make-up.
From The Song Of The Ages Series.
LC NO. 72-702130
Prod-FAMLYT Dist-FAMLYT 1964

Mask, The B 34 MIN
16MM FILM OPTICAL SOUND
Explains that alcohol may mask symptoms of both physical and mental disorders and suggests a system of observation for police. Emphasizes the significance of alcoholism as a problem confronted most frequently by policemen and stresses the increasingly humanitarian role of the police.
LC NO. FIA65-3427
Prod-LAAMH Dist-USPHS Prodn-STONEY 1964

Mask, The C 35 MIN
16MM FILM, 3/4 OR 1/2 IN VIDEO
Describes how alcohol may mask symptoms of both physical and mental disorders. Suggests a system of observation used by the police and general public in detecting the signs of alcoholism.
LC NO. 80-706834
Prod-USPHS Dist-USNAC 1972

Masked Dance (Dogon People) C 6 MIN
3/4 OR 1/2 INCH VIDEO CASSETTE
See series title for descriptive statement.
From The African Village Life (Mali) Series.
Prod-IFF Dist-IFF

Maskerade B 10 MIN
16MM FILM OPTICAL SOUND J-C A
Shows African masks photographed to the rhythm of native music.
Prod-RFL Dist-RFL

Masking C 13 MIN
1/2 IN VIDEO CASSETTE BETA/VHS
Deals with auto body repair.
Prod-RMI Dist-RMI

Maskmaker, The C 9 MIN
16MM FILM, 3/4 OR 1/2 IN VIDEO J-C
Explains that for Marcel Marceau, the Maskmaker is one who represents humanity, with all the faces humanity can possess. Includes the classic symbols for comedy and tragedy.
From The Humanities - The Performing Arts, Art Of Silence, Pantomimes With Marcel Marceau Series.
Prod-EBEC Dist-EBEC 1975

Masks C 12 MIN
16MM FILM, 3/4 OR 1/2 IN VIDEO J-C A
Displays a collection of primitive and modern masks. Discusses the role of masks in the cultural and artistic life of various peoples. Explains how masks are used in rituals and in dramatizing myths and legends.
Prod-PEGF Dist-PHENIX 1962

Masks B 20 MIN
2 INCH VIDEOTAPE I
Shows how masks can delight or frighten the observer and how they can be made from a variety of materials, including papier-mache, paper bags, or by paper sculpture.
From The For The Love Of Art Series.
Prod-GWTVAI Dist-GPITVL Prodn-WETATV

Maslow And Self-Actualization, No. 1 C 30 MIN
16MM FILM OPTICAL SOUND C T
Dr Abraham Maslow discusses the dimensions of selfactualization and elaborates on recent research and theory related to honesty, awareness, freedom and trust.
LC NO. FIA68-1961
Prod-PSYCHF Dist-PSYCHD 1968

Maslow And Self-Actualization, No. 2 C 30 MIN
16MM FILM OPTICAL SOUND C
Dr Abraham Maslow discusses the dimensions of selfactualization and elaborates on recent research and theory related to honesty, awareness, freedom and trust.
LC NO. FIA68-1961
Prod-PSYCHF Dist-PSYCHD 1968

Maslow's Hierarchy Of Needs C 15 MIN
16MM FILM, 3/4 OR 1/2 IN VIDEO A
Presents Abraham Maslow's analysis of the role of needs in human motivation and indicates its relevance to supervisors, managers and students.
Prod-SALENG Dist-SALENG 1975

Masonry, Plastering And Glazing Tools C 12 MIN
3/4 OR 1/2 INCH VIDEO CASSETTE
Covers masonry, plastering and glazing tools for edging, jointing and finishing.
From The Using Hand Tools Series.
Prod-TPCTRA Dist-TPCTRA

Masonry, Plastering And Glazing Tools (Spanish) C 12 MIN
3/4 OR 1/2 INCH VIDEO CASSETTE
Covers masonry, plastering and glazing tools for edging, jointing and finishing.
From The Using Hand Tools Series.
Prod-TPCTRA Dist-TPCTRA

Masque B 25 MIN
16MM FILM OPTICAL SOUND
Tells how a girl has a profound effect on the relationship of two guys who live together.
LC NO. 78-711327
Prod-USC Dist-USC 1970

Masque Of The Red Death C 88 MIN
16MM FILM OPTICAL SOUND H A
Describes a medieval Italian prince who practices devil worship while the plague rages outside. When he holds a ball, death is an uninvited guest. Directed by Roger Corman. Stars Vincent Price.
Prod-AIP Dist-TIMLIF 1964

Masque Of The Red Death C 10 MIN
16MM FILM, 3/4 OR 1/2 IN VIDEO H-C
An adaptation of the story Masque Of The Red Death by Edgar Allan Poe, about a count who locks himself and his court inside his castle in order to avoid the plague only to be destroyed by the plague masquerading as a seductive woman.
Prod-ZAGREB Dist-MGHT 1970

Masque Of The Red Death, The C 90 MIN
16MM FILM OPTICAL SOUND
Concerns a 12th century Italian prince whose masked ball is visited by the Red Death, the plague that is decimating the population of the countryside. Based on the short story The Masque Of The Red Death by Edgar Allan Poe.
Prod-AIP Dist-TWYMAN 1964

Masquerade C 27 MIN
16MM FILM, 3/4 OR 1/2 IN VIDEO
Presents the inhabitants of an imaginary planet as they prepare for a masquerade. Focuses on the importance of creativity. From the studio of Co Hoedeman, creator of the Claymation technique.
Prod-NFBC Dist-MEDIAG 1985

Masqueraders, The B 10 MIN
16MM FILM SILENT J-C A
Charlie Chaplin, Charlie Chase and Minta Durfee star in the comic story of a male actor who, after being fired, returns to the movie studio disguised as a woman. A silent film.
Prod-SENN Dist-BHAWK 1914

Mass (Weight) C 30 MIN
3/4 INCH VIDEO CASSETTE T
Explores the use of grams and kilograms and shows classroom activities which deal with the concept of metric measurement.
From The Measure For Measure Series.
Prod-UWISCM Dist-GPITVL 1979

Mass And Volume C 15 MIN
3/4 OR 1/2 INCH VIDEO CASSETTE P-I
Introduces concepts of mass and volume. Demonstrates that objects can have the same volume but different masses and the same mass but different volumes.
From The First Films On Science Series.
Prod-MAETEL Dist-AITECH 1975

Mass And Weight C 11 MIN
16MM FILM, 3/4 OR 1/2 IN VIDEO J-H
Shows the behavior of a bowling ball in a real bowling alley and in imaginary ones at the North pole, at the equator, on the moon and in intergalactic space to explore the concepts of mass and weight. Explains the relationship between gravitational and inertial mass.
Prod-CORF Dist-CORF 1966

Mass And Weight C 24 MIN
3/4 OR 1/2 INCH VIDEO CASSETTE
Presents the most common units of mass and relates this to everyday objects. Includes activities such as finding the mass of an object, matching containers of equal mass and distinguishing between mass and weight.
From The Metric Education Video Tapes For Pre And Inservice Teachers (K-8) Series.
Prod-PUAVC Dist-PUAVC

Mass And Weight In Orbit C
3/4 OR 1/2 INCH VIDEO CASSETTE
Distinguishes weight from mass. Depicts astronauts lifting weights in space.
From The Experiments In Space Series.
Prod-EDMEC Dist-EDMEC

Mass Communications - Effects B 30 MIN
2 INCH VIDEOTAPE C T
Describes the difficulties facing the social scientist in communications research--each method of communication has a different influence on different people, and how the effects of mass communications can be isolated from other influences. Effects are dependent on who says when to whom, how, when and in what. (Broadcast quality)
From The Communications And Education Series. No. 17
Prod-NYSED Dist-GPITVL Prodn-WNDTTV

Mass Feeding (Rev Ed) C 17 MIN
3/4 OR 1/2 INCH VIDEO CASSETTE
Presents an updated version of the 1976 disaster mass feeding program. Discusses mobile and fixed feeding facilities, the importance of pre-planning, assembling and organizing community resources and other assistance.
Prod-AMRC Dist-AMRC 1981

Mass Of Atoms, The, Pt 1 B 20 MIN
16MM FILM OPTICAL SOUND J-C
Depicts the first part of an experiment to determine the masses of a helium atom and a polonium atom. Shows the various laboratory techniques involved and necessary precautions to take during the experiment.
From The PSSC Physics Films Series.
LC NO. FIA67-5928
Prod-PSSC Dist-MLA 1967

Mass Of Atoms, The, Pt 2 B 27 MIN
16MM FILM OPTICAL SOUND J-C
Depicts the last part of an experiment to determine the masses of a helium atom and a polonium atom. Shows the various laboratory techniques involved and necessary precautions to take during the experiment.
From The PSSC Physics Films Series.
LC NO. FIA67-2929
Prod-PSSC Dist-MLA 1967

Mass Of The Electron B 18 MIN
16MM FILM OPTICAL SOUND H-C
Shows the steps involved in calculating the mass of an electron, using a cathode ray tube encircled by a current-carrying loop of wire. Reference is made to the millikan experiment.
From The PSSC Physics Films Series.
Prod-PSSC Dist-MLA 1959

Mass Preschool Testing C 30 MIN
3/4 OR 1/2 INCH VIDEO CASSETTE
Discusses mass preschool testing, the most promising method to detect hearing difficulties while they can still be treated with reasonable success. Presents a scenario for the organization and implementation of such a program.
From The Hearing Screening Series.
Prod-NETCHE Dist-NETCHE 1971

Mass Production C 15 MIN
2 INCH VIDEOTAPE
Establishes an understanding of the basic principles of mass production and shows how industry forces houses from the core of the city to establish neighborhoods in the suburban areas.
From The Let's Build A City Series.
Prod-WVIZTV Dist-GPITVL

Mass Spectrometry C 33 MIN
16MM FILM, 3/4 OR 1/2 IN VIDEO C
Introduces the techniques of mass spectrometry, shows how the spectrometer operates and describes the kinds information that the instrument yields.
Prod-WILEYJ Dist-MEDIAG 1971

Mass Storage Devices C 18 MIN
3/4 OR 1/2 INCH VIDEO CASSETTE J-C A
Takes a practical look at problems and solutions in the area of information storage and retreival. Covers the relative cost of various options and describes the advantages and disadvantages of a number of storage methods.
From The Little Computers - See How They Run Series.
LC NO. 81-706844
Prod-ELDATA Dist-GPITVL 1980

Mass Transit - Up, Up, And Away C 20 MIN
16MM FILM, 3/4 OR 1/2 IN VIDEO
Examines methods of handling city traffic, presenting the possibilities for capsule cars, jet belts and high-speed monorails.
Prod-DOCUA Dist-CNEMAG

Mass 1 - The Case Of The Disappearing Mass C 15 MIN
16MM FILM, 3/4 OR 1/2 IN VIDEO I-J
Presents a girl and a famous retired French detective who solve the mystery of a disappearing mass, an elephant, using metric measurement. Demonstrates milligrams, grams, kilograms and tonnes.
From The Measuremetric Series.
LC NO. 80-706498
Prod-AITV Dist-AITECH 1977

Mass 2 - The Case Of The Disappearing Mass C 15 MIN
16MM FILM, 3/4 OR 1/2 IN VIDEO I-J
Presents a girl and a famous retired French detective solving the mystery of a disappearing mass, an elephant, using metric measurement. Demonstrates milligrams grams, kilograms and tonnes.
From The Measuremetric Series.
LC NO. 80-706498
Prod-AITV Dist-AITECH 1977

Massachusetts Story C 58 MIN
16MM FILM OPTICAL SOUND H-C A
Examines the issues relating to off-shore oil drilling in Massachusetts, using the comments of local businesspeople, regional political figures, ecological experts and oil industry spokespersons.
LC NO. 78-701435
Prod-MASHAM Dist-MASHAM 1977

Massachusetts Story C
3/4 OR 1/2 INCH VIDEO CASSETTE
Examines the way people live, work and play on Cape Cod, the Islands and New Bedford and the challenge to that way of life by the plans to exploit energy resources on the Georges Bank.
Prod-LAWDET Dist-LAWDET

Massage C 48 MIN
3/4 OR 1/2 INCH VIDEO CASSETTE C A
Combines a complete instruction unit on the art of giving relief and pleasure through touch with analysis of cultural taboos concerning touch.
Prod-MMRC Dist-MMRC

Massage - Back, Feet And Basic Strokes C 60 MIN
3/4 OR 1/2 INCH VIDEO CASSETTE
Teaches massage.
Prod-BULFRG Dist-BULFRG

Massage Of The Lower Extremity B 34 MIN
3/4 OR 1/2 INCH VIDEO CASSETTE
Demonstrates massage of the lower extremity, review of the anatomy of leg muscles and lists the equipment needed.
Prod-BU Dist-BU

Massage Of The Upper Extremity C 40 MIN
3/4 OR 1/2 INCH VIDEO CASSETTE
Demonstrates massage of the upper extremity, including a list of equipment needed and a review of the anatomy.
Prod-BU Dist-BU

Masses And The Millionaires, The - The Homestead Strike C 26 MIN
16MM FILM, 3/4 OR 1/2 IN VIDEO J-C A
Presents a dramatization of the strike at the homestead steel mills in 1892 which ended in violence and bloodshed. Emphasizes the hostile attitude of the mill's manager, Henry Clay Fricks and epitomizes the decisive beginnings of America's management with labor union dealings. Explains the outcome of the strike which was to paralyze the progress of organized labor for decades to come.
Prod-LCOA Dist-LCOA 1974

Masses And The Millionaires, The - The Homestead Strike (Spanish) C 26 MIN
16MM FILM, 3/4 OR 1/2 IN VIDEO J-C A
Recreates the bloody strike at the Carnegie Steel Company in 1892
Prod-LCOA Dist-LCOA 1974

Masseter And Temporal Muscles C 14 MIN
16MM FILM - 3/4 IN VIDEO PRO
Presents the anatomy of the lateral aspect of the head, including deep dissection views of the muscles, tissue spaces and associated nerves and vessels of the temporal and masseter areas.
From The Anatomy Of The Head And Neck Series.
LC NO. 78-706249
Prod-USVA Dist-USNAC Prodn-VADTC 1978

Massey Tapes—A Series
A
Presents Dr Morris Massey, author of The People Puzzle, discussing the different values, attitudes and world views people have developed. Shows how these differences have come about.
Prod-CBSFOX Dist-CBSFOX

What You Are Is Where You See 075 MIN
What You Are Is Where You Were When 090 MIN
What You Are Is..., Pt 1 030 MIN
What You Are Is..., Pt 2 060 MIN
What You Are Is..., Pt 3 060 MIN
What You Are Isn't Necessarily What You Will Be 060 MIN

Massing A Window C 30 MIN
2 INCH VIDEOTAPE
See series title for descriptive statement.
From The Making Things Grow II Series.
Prod-WGBHTV Dist-PUBTEL

Massive Pulmonary Embolism - Surgical Treatment C 14 MIN
16MM FILM OPTICAL SOUND
Portrays the emergency surgical management treatment of otherwise lethal massive pulmonary emboli. Demonstrates pulmonary embolectomy using cardio pulmonary bypass. Shows methods of temporary circulatory support with a portable heart-lung machine.
LC NO. FIA68-760
Prod-UMIAMI Dist-GENT Prodn-UMIAMI 1967

MAST - Military Assistance To Safety And Traffic C 19 MIN
16MM FILM OPTICAL SOUND
Introduces MAST, a program dedicated to providing military medical assistance to civilians in need by utilizing helicopters and medical corpsmen during emergencies. Outlines the capabilities of aeromedical evacuation helicopters and crews.
LC NO. 75-702411
Prod-USA Dist-USNAC 1974

Mast Bumping - Causes And Prevention C 20 MIN
16MM FILM, 3/4 OR 1/2 IN VIDEO A
Offers instruction to helicopter pilots on excessive rotor flopping, explains in-flight conditions which precede mast bumping and shows actions pilots must take to avoid accidents.
Prod-USA Dist-USNAC 1982

Mast-Making For The King C 17 MIN
16MM FILM OPTICAL SOUND J-H A
Presents the history of mast-making in New England which goes back to 1634, when a shipment of pines was sent to England to be hewn into masts for the ships of the king's navy. Shows the process of selecting a mast tree, preparing the bed, building a platform for choppers, felling the tree and hauling the 80-foot log with many yokes of oxen.
Prod-UNH Dist-UNH 1977

Master Bathroom C 30 MIN
1/2 IN VIDEO CASSETTE BETA/VHS
Features remodeling a master bathroom. Shows how to build kitchen cabinets.
From The This Old House, Pt 2 - Suburban '50s Series.
Prod-WGBHTV Dist-MTI

Master Class I C 30 MIN
3/4 OR 1/2 INCH VIDEO CASSETTE
Presents Grant Johannesen with his master class of students at the University of Nebraska-Lincoln.
From The Grant Johannesen - Pianist Series.
Prod-NETCHE Dist-NETCHE 1973

Master Class II C 30 MIN
3/4 OR 1/2 INCH VIDEO CASSETTE
Continues Grant Johannesen's work with his class, stressing concentration before an audience and the need to explore a piece.
From The Grant Johannesen - Pianist Series.
Prod-NETCHE Dist-NETCHE 1973

Master Hook System, Master Exchange System, Memorizing The Ten Most Populous Cities In... C 60 MIN
3/4 OR 1/2 INCH VIDEO CASSETTE
Covers the Master Hook System and the Master Exchange System. Focuses on Memorizing the Ten Most Populous Cities in the world for the year 2000 and their population.
From The Memory Improvement Series. Pt 2
Prod-UAZMIC Dist-UAZMIC

Master Musicians Of Jahjouka, The C 58 MIN
3/4 OR 1/2 INCH VIDEO CASSETTE
Documents the rich musical history of a remote Moroccan village that has been unusually affected by westernization. Shows people who believe their music to possess healing powers. Shows the musicians performing as ancient ceremonies are described.
Prod-MENASS Dist-MENASS 1983

Master Musicians Of Jahjouka, The (Dutch) C 58 MIN
3/4 OR 1/2 INCH VIDEO CASSETTE
Documents the rich musical history of a remote Moroccan village that has been unusually affected by westernization. Shows people who believe their music to possess healing powers. Shows the musicians performing as ancient ceremonies are described.
Prod-MENASS Dist-MENASS 1983

Master Musicians Of Jahjouka, The (German) C 58 MIN
3/4 OR 1/2 INCH VIDEO CASSETTE
Documents the rich musical history of a remote Moroccan village that has been unusually affected by westernization. Shows people who believe their music to possess healing powers. Shows the musicians performing as ancient ceremonies are described.
Prod-MENASS Dist-MENASS 1983

Master Of Ballantrae, The C 89 MIN
16MM FILM OPTICAL SOUND
Offers an adaptation of Robert Louis Stevenson's novel THE MASTER OF BALLANTRAE. Stars Errol Flynn.
Prod-WB Dist-TWYMAN 1953

Master Of Light, The - A Biography Of Albert A Michelson C 25 MIN
16MM FILM, 3/4 OR 1/2 IN VIDEO H A
Depicts the life of Albert A Michelson, with the aid of computer graphics, archival stills and historic film footage. Describes him as America's first Nobel Prize winner in physics, and artist and musician as well as a scientist who pioneered in light research.
Prod-ONEPAS Dist-CNEMAG 1984

Master Of The Art C 30 MIN
3/4 OR 1/2 INCH VIDEO CASSETTE I-J
Shows how some kids use self-discipline to restore a security director's job.
From The Powerhouse Series.
LC NO. 83-707180
Prod-EFCVA Dist-GA 1982

Master Race, The C 20 MIN
3/4 OR 1/2 INCH VIDEO CASSETTE
Discusses the Nazi concept of racial superiority and their attempts to achieve it. Deals with the secret police and the German concentration camps.
From The History In Action Series.
Prod-FOTH Dist-FOTH 1984

Master Singers Of Nuremberg, The B 20 MIN
16MM FILM OPTICAL SOUND
Presents Franco Farrara directing the Radio Philharmonic Orchestra of Italy playing 'PRELUDE, THIRD ACT OVERTURE' from Wagner's 'THE MASTER SINGERS OF NUREMBERG.'
From The Musical Masterpieces Series.
Prod-SG Dist-SG

Master Thief, The C 15 MIN
16MM FILM, 3/4 OR 1/2 IN VIDEO P-I
Presents an animated puppet film based upon a fairy tale by the Grimm brothers. Shows a count who tells a master thief that he will remain free if he can steal the count's favorite horse while it is being guarded. Follows the thief as he is given another challenge by the count after he is successful with the horse.
LC NO. 80-707062
Prod-NET Dist-IU 1970

Master Touch, The C 18 MIN
16MM FILM OPTICAL SOUND
Combines live action and animation and stars Captain Silversides, who not only drives cars and sailboats but owns and operates a Gleaner Combine on his farm. Explains the different efficiency features on his Gleaner.
Prod-ALLISC Dist-IDEALF

Master Weavers Of The Andes C 15 MIN
16MM FILM, 3/4 OR 1/2 IN VIDEO J-C A
Examines the craft of weaving as practiced by the Quechua Indians near Cuzco, Peru. Points out that, except for the use of chemical dyes, the processes of spinning and weaving are practiced as they have been for centuries.
Prod-CINECO Dist-EBEC Prodn-PILAF 1978

Master's Figure Drawing Class - Composition/Anatomy, Male And Female C 20 MIN
3/4 INCH VIDEO CASSETTE H-C
Shows the composition and anatomy of male and female figures.
LC NO. 79-706395
Prod-EDDIM Dist-EDDIM 1979

Master's Figure Drawing Class - Female Gesture C 20 MIN
3/4 INCH VIDEO CASSETTE J-H
Shows how to draw the female gesture.
LC NO. 79-706389
Prod-EDDIM Dist-EDDIM 1979

Master's Figure Drawing Class - Female Proportions C 20 MIN
3/4 INCH VIDEO CASSETTE J-C
Shows how to draw female proportions.
LC NO. 79-706390
Prod-EDDIM Dist-EDDIM 1979

Master's Figure Drawing Class - Female Quick Sketch C 20 MIN
3/4 INCH VIDEO CASSETTE H-C
Shows how to draw a quick sketch of the female figure.
LC NO. 79-706393
Prod-EDDIM Dist-EDDIM 1979

Master's Figure Drawing Class - Male Gesture C 20 MIN
3/4 INCH VIDEO CASSETTE J-C
Shows how to draw the male gesture.
LC NO. 79-706391
Prod-EDDIM Dist-EDDIM 1979

Master's Figure Drawing Class - Male Proportions C 20 MIN
3/4 INCH VIDEO CASSETTE H-C
Shows how to draw male proportions.
LC NO. 79-706392
Prod-EDDIM Dist-EDDIM 1979

Master's Figure Drawing Class - Male Quick Sketch C 20 MIN
3/4 INCH VIDEO CASSETTE H-C
Shows how to draw a quick sketch of the male figure.
LC NO. 79-706394
Prod-EDDIM Dist-EDDIM 1979

Master's Figure Drawing Class - Review Female, Seated C 20 MIN
3/4 INCH VIDEO CASSETTE H-C
Offers a review of drawing the seated female figure.
LC NO. 79-706396
Prod-EDDIM Dist-EDDIM 1979

Masterbuilders, The C 15 MIN
16MM FILM, 3/4 OR 1/2 IN VIDEO I-H
Exhibits what is considered the most intelligent of all birds, the weaverbird of Africa. Shows its nest-building techniques that involve actual tying of the first knot in its woven nest. Discloses male birds, after nest building, in the display ritual to attract female birds.
From The RSPB Collection Series.
LC NO. 84-707100
Prod-RSFPB Dist-BCNFL 1983

Mastering Grammar C 30 MIN
3/4 OR 1/2 INCH VIDEO CASSETTE
Deals with the mastering of grammar as part of improving business writing skills.
From The Business Of Better Writing Series.
Prod-KYTV Dist-KYTV 1983

Mastering Job Safety Analysis C 15 MIN
3/4 OR 1/2 INCH VIDEO CASSETTE IND
Teaches first-line supervisors how to develop a step-by-step procedure for breaking down the elements of a job so it can be performed with maximum safety.
From The Foreman's Accident Prevention Series.
Prod-GPCV Dist-GPCV

Mastering Math Skills C 29 MIN
3/4 OR 1/2 INCH VIDEO CASSETTE

Presents a program for elementary school children with learning disabilities and behavioral problems. Emphasizes long-term memory, progression from concrete to abstract ideas and visual-spatial problems. Provides lessons in mathematics.
From The Integration Of Children With Special Needs In A Regular Classroom Series.
Prod-LPS Dist-AITECH Prodn-WGBHTV 1975

Mastering Mechanics C 30 MIN
3/4 OR 1/2 INCH VIDEO CASSETTE
Deals with the mastering of mechanics as part of improving business writing skills.
From The Business Of Better Writing Series.
Prod-KYTV Dist-KYTV 1983

Mastering Punctuation C 30 MIN
3/4 OR 1/2 INCH VIDEO CASSETTE
Deals with the mastering of punctuation as part of improving business writing skills.
From The Business Of Better Writing Series.
Prod-KYTV Dist-KYTV 1983

Mastering Spelling C 30 MIN
3/4 OR 1/2 INCH VIDEO CASSETTE
Deals with the mastering of spelling as part of improving business writing skills.
From The Business Of Better Writing Series.
Prod-KYTV Dist-KYTV 1983

Mastering The Bow And Arrow Sports C 10 MIN
16MM FILM, 3/4 OR 1/2 IN VIDEO I-C A
Focuses on mastering the sport of archery.
From The Archery Series. No. 5
Prod-ATHI Dist-ATHI 1978

Masterpiece C 26 MIN
16MM FILM OPTICAL SOUND
Presents an imaginative look at the future.
LC NO. 76-702448
Prod-ATFICO Dist-CANFDC 1975

Masterpiece Of Spanish Painting, A C 25 MIN
16MM FILM OPTICAL SOUND C T
Shows 26 large panels of a Spanish masterpiece--The Retablo of Ciudad Rodrigo by Fernando Gallego. Gives a stylistic and iconographic explanation of this Hispano-Flemish masterpiece which was presented to the University of Arizona by the Kress Foundation in 1960.
Prod-ATWOOD Dist-UARIZ Prodn-ATWOOD 1962

Masterpieces Of Chinese Art C 28 MIN
16MM FILM OPTICAL SOUND H-C A
Uses interpretive Chinese music and narration to show the beauty of 16 pieces of traditional Chinese bronze, jade, porcelain and vertical hand scroll painting on exhibit since 1949 in the Taiwan National Palace Museum.
LC NO. 73-702039
Prod-MASCOM Dist-MASCOM 1973

Masterpieces Of Chinese Art C 28 MIN
16MM FILM, 3/4 OR 1/2 IN VIDEO H-C A
Exhibits some 50 pieces of Chinese art including ancient bronzes from the Shang dynasty, jade articles spanning some 3,000 years of artistic development and porcelain wares including Ju ware. Covers carved lacquer and calligraphy.
Prod-LUF Dist-LUF 1974

Masters Of Disaster, The C 30 MIN
16MM FILM, 3/4 OR 1/2 IN VIDEO I-C A
Shows how a caring, creative teacher motivates black elementary school kids to organize a championship chess team.
Prod-IU Dist-IU 1985

Masters Of Hang Gliding C 28 MIN
16MM FILM OPTICAL SOUND
Shows hang gliding as it is practiced in various parts of the United States and at the Master of Hang Gliding Championship at Grandfather Mountain, North Carolina.
LC NO. 79-700394
Prod-MORTON Dist-MORTON 1978

Masters Of Modern Sculpture--A Series

Prod-BLACKW Dist-BLACKW 1978

Beyond Cubism	059 MIN
New World, The	059 MIN
Pioneers, The	059 MIN

Masters Of Modern Sculpture, Pt 1 - The Pioneers C 58 MIN
3/4 OR 1/2 INCH VIDEO CASSETTE
Introduces the major sculptors of the 20th century and looks closely at their works. Includes Rodin, Degas, Rosso, Bourdelle, Maillol, Lehmbruck, Matisse, Picasso, Lipchitz, Laurens, Epstein, Boccioni, Duchamp-Villon, Gonzales and Brancusi.
Prod-BLACKW Dist-BLACKW

Masters Of Modern Sculpture, Pt 2 - Beyond Cubism C 58 MIN
3/4 OR 1/2 INCH VIDEO CASSETTE
Introduces the major sculptors of the 20th century and looks closely at their works. Includes Vladimir Tatlin, Naum Gabo, Antoine Pevsner, Marcel Duchamp, the Dada Artists, Man Ray, Joan Miro, Jean Arp, Max Ernst, Alexander Calder, Alberto Giacometti, Henry Moore, Barbara Hepworth, Germaine Richier, Cesar, Gunther Uecker, Heinz Mack, Otto Piene, Joseph Beuys, Arman, Yves Klein, Daniel Spoerri, Jean Tinguely, Anthony Caro and Gilbert & George.
Prod-BLACKW Dist-BLACKW

Masters Of Modern Sculpture, Pt 3 - The New World C 58 MIN
3/4 OR 1/2 INCH VIDEO CASSETTE
Introduces the major sculptors of the 20th century and looks closely at their works. Includes David Smith, Louise Nevelson, David Hare, Ibram Lassaw, Theodore Roszak, Herbert Ferber, Louise Baurgeois, John Chamberlain, Mark Di Suvero, Isamu Noguchi, George Rickey, Barnett Newman, Tony Smith, George Segal, Donald Judd, Claes Oldenburg, Robert Morris, Richard Serra, Carl Andre, Edward Kienholz, Christo, Michael Heizer and Robert Smithson.
Prod-BLACKW Dist-BLACKW

Masters Of Murano C 17 MIN
16MM FILM OPTICAL SOUND H-C A
Portrays three master glass blowers on the Island of Murano in Italy, where they follow a 600-year old tradition of craft and technique.
Prod-ARNSNR Dist-LANDMK 1983

Masters Of Our Musical Heritage C 8 MIN
3/4 OR 1/2 INCH VIDEO CASSETTE
Contains eight half-hour videotapes on the history of music.
Prod-TELSTR Dist-TELSTR

Masters Of Our Musical Heritage--A Series
P-I
Prod-KTCATV Dist-GPITVL

Composer With A Cause - The Howard Hanson	
Fourth 'B,' The - The Bela Bartok Story	30 MIN
From Triumph To Tragedy - The Wolfgang	30 MIN
German Giant, The - The Johann Sebastian	30 MIN
Pride Of Norway - The Edvard Grieg Story	30 MIN
Prince Of The Piano, The - Frederic Chopin	30 MIN
Sorcerer Of Sounds - The Claude Debussy Story	30 MIN
Two Hearts - The Ludwig Van Beethoven Story	30 MIN

Masters Of The Congo Jungle C 88 MIN
16MM FILM, 3/4 OR 1/2 IN VIDEO J-C A
Looks at African flora, fauna and native life.
Prod-STORCH Dist-PHENIX 1975

Masters Of The Wok C 29 MIN
16MM FILM, 3/4 OR 1/2 IN VIDEO J-C A
See series title for descriptive statement.
From The Taste Of China Series.
LC NO. 84-707744
Prod-UCEMC Dist-UCEMC 1984

Masterworks Of Painting C 51 MIN
3/4 OR 1/2 INCH VIDEO CASSETTE A
Introduces the principles of great painting through the art of European and American masters. Views the great movements up to the recent past.
Prod-EDDIM Dist-EDDIM

Mastery At Sea B 30 MIN
16MM FILM OPTICAL SOUND
Traces the development of modern seapower, using historical footage showing great batteships from World War I, aircraft carriers, submarines and missile-bearing vessels, including Polaris submarines.
LC NO. FIE65-103
Prod-NATO Dist-USDS

Mastery Of Space, The C 58 MIN
16MM FILM - 3/4 IN VIDEO
Traces the development of the Project Mercury program, showing scenes of the flight of Freedom 7 and the orbital flight of Friendship 7 in 1962. Discusses Project Gemini, Project Apollo, and the Saturn booster. Issued in 1962 as a motion picture.
LC NO. 79-708024
Prod-NASA Dist-USNAC 1979

Mastoidectomy And Tympanoplasty C
3/4 OR 1/2 INCH VIDEO CASSETTE
Shows how the normal ear works, how chronic middle ear infections can lead to ruptured ear drum or begin to invade and destroy bone.
Prod-MIFE Dist-MIFE

Mastri - A Balinese Woman C 18 MIN
16MM FILM OPTICAL SOUND H-C A
Explores the lives of a Balinese couple in their village. Contrasts their day-to-day activities and religious beliefs with the Bali known to tourists.
From The Asian Neighbors - Indonesia Series.
LC NO. 75-703583
Prod-FLMAUS Dist-AVIS 1975

Masturbation - Men C 18 MIN
3/4 OR 1/2 INCH VIDEO CASSETTE C A
Men between the ages of 20 and 50 share their patterns of masturbation. Provides insight and reassurance about a topic rarely discussed openly by men.
Prod-MMRC Dist-MMRC

Masturbatory Story, A C 15 MIN
16MM FILM, 3/4 OR 1/2 IN VIDEO J-H
Appraises and explains the needs and desires involved with male masturbation. Destroys the serious fallacies that have surrounded masturbation for centuries.
Prod-DOOMOR Dist-PEREN

Masuo Ikeda - Printmaker C 14 MIN
16MM FILM, 3/4 OR 1/2 IN VIDEO J-H
Features Masuo Ikeda, a modern Japanese artist who lives in New York. Observes as he creates a color print from copper plates and explains how he finds ideas and how he creates his prints. Shows his procedure and tools in close-up detail as he makes the plates, pulls proofs, checks and corrects the proofs, makes corrections on the plates and pulls the finished prints.
Prod-ACI Dist-AIMS 1973

Matches C 9 MIN
16MM FILM, 3/4 OR 1/2 IN VIDEO P-I
Explains the dangers of playing with fire and points out that grown-ups as well as children have to obey the rules.
Prod-BELLDA Dist-FLMFR

Matching B 75 MIN
3/4 OR 1/2 INCH VIDEO CASSETTE
See series title for descriptive statement.
From The Analog IC Layout Design Considerations Series. Pt 5
Prod-UAZMIC Dist-UAZMIC

Matching - Greater Than, Less Than C 15 MIN
3/4 INCH VIDEO CASSETTE P
Explains how to match numerals to given sets of objects with up to nine elements. Shows the order of the numbers one to nine.
From The Measure Up Series.
Prod-WCETTV Dist-GPITVL 1977

Matching Of Sally Dean, The C 11 MIN
3/4 OR 1/2 INCH VIDEO CASSETTE
Inspires voluntary blood donations. Concentrates on various types of people who help save the life of a young advertising artist injured in an accident.
Prod-AMRC Dist-AMRC 1979

Matching Offset Holes - Face Plate And 4-Jaw Chuck C 15 MIN
3/4 OR 1/2 INCH VIDEO CASSETTE IND
See series title for descriptive statement.
From The Machining And The Operation Of Machine Tools, Module 3 - Intermediate Engine Lathe Series.
Prod-LEIKID Dist-LEIKID

Matching People And Positions C 10 MIN
3/4 OR 1/2 INCH VIDEO CASSETTE
Shows how employee evaluation can be made easier and more effective through careful analysis of job requirement and the qualifications of the person being considered.
From The Assessing Employee Potential Series.
Prod-RESEM Dist-RESEM

Matching Plaids In Darts And Seams By Slip Stitching C 29 MIN
2 INCH VIDEOTAPE
Features Mrs Ruth Hickman demonstrating how to match plaids in darts and seams by slip stitching.
From The Sewing Skills - Tailoring Series.
Prod-KRMATV Dist-PUBTEL

Matching Seams And Pleats In Plaid C 29 MIN
2 INCH VIDEOTAPE
Features Mrs Ruth Hickman showing how to match seams and pleats in plaid.
From The Sewing Skills - Tailoring Series.
Prod-KRMATV Dist-PUBTEL

Matching Shoulders And Corners On The Lathe C 15 MIN
3/4 OR 1/2 INCH VIDEO CASSETTE IND
See series title for descriptive statement.
From The Machining And The Operation Of Machine Tools, Module 3 - Intermediate Engine Lathe Series.
Prod-LEIKID Dist-LEIKID

Matching Theory - The Marriage Theorem B 46 MIN
16MM FILM OPTICAL SOUND C A
Contains an extended introduction to the marriage theorem and some of its elementary consequences, shifting to a proof of the theorem and a separate result, Sperner's Theorem.
From The MAA Mathematics Series.
LC NO. 74-702787
Prod-MAA Dist-MLA 1974

Matching Up C 4 MIN
16MM FILM, 3/4 OR 1/2 IN VIDEO K-I
Uses a split-screen technique to match pairs of feet with the rest of the body.
From The Magic Moments Series.
Prod-EBEC Dist-EBEC 1969

Mate Location By A Moth C 5 MIN
3/4 OR 1/2 INCH VIDEO CASSETTE J-C
Shows how a male moth can locate a female moth in complete darkness by scent and touch. Provides a useful case study of scientific method, and illustrates how a special camera was used that amplified dim light to avoid disturbing the moths.
Prod-EDMI Dist-EDMI 1977

Mate Selection And Marriage Readiness C 30 MIN
3/4 OR 1/2 INCH VIDEO CASSETTE C A
Discusses the selection of a mate and the factors governing that decision. Covers exogamy and endogamy and the process of mate selection as a multi-stage development. Includes values that figure in marriage readiness such as age, education, religion and personality.
From The Family Portrait - A Study Of Contemporary Lifestyles Series. Lesson 9
Prod-SCCON Dist-CDTEL

Mateo C 17 MIN
16MM FILM, 3/4 OR 1/2 IN VIDEO I-H
Relates the story of a young farm boy who runs away from home and goes to a large city where he learns some valuable, but painful, lessons before he is reunited with his parents.
Prod-PHENIX Dist-PHENIX 1980

Material Handling Principles In Transportation B 20 MIN
16MM FILM OPTICAL SOUND
Shows the deplorable waste of money, time and manhours when material handling and loading prqctices are faulty. Emphasizes the importance of using the right equipment to transport items. Demonstrates right and wrong methods of handling cargo.
Prod-USDD Dist-USNAC 1960

Material Removal C 30 MIN
3/4 OR 1/2 INCH VIDEO CASSETTE
Discusses the elctrochemical discharge machining methods as they are applied to exotic metals. Explains the advantages and disadvantages of electrochemical grinding and machining.
Prod-CONNTV Dist-SME Prodn-SME

Material Removal - Principles C 20 MIN
3/4 OR 1/2 INCH VIDEO CASSETTE H-C A
See series title for descriptive statement.
From The Engineering Crafts Series.
Prod-BBCTV Dist-FI 1981

Material That Can Do Almost Anything, The 1950-1964 C 21 MIN
16MM FILM OPTICAL SOUND
See series title for descriptive statement.
From The Twelve Decades Of Concrete In American Architecture Series.
Prod-PRTLND Dist-PRTLND 1965

Materials C 15 MIN
16MM FILM, 3/4 OR 1/2 IN VIDEO I-J
Points out that of all the materials suitable for workshops, plastic is more versatile than wood, metal or clay, even though a large quantitiy of energy is required to extract each. Plastic can be produced by chemists from petroleum so that it possesses properties designed to suit specific applications.
From The Craft, Design And Technology Series.
Prod-THAMES Dist-MEDIAG 1983

Materials - Key To Progress C 17 MIN
16MM FILM OPTICAL SOUND
Portrays the over-all technical mission of the USAF materials research and development program and emphasizes the important contributions of industry and science to its progress.
LC NO. FIE59-226
Prod-USDD Dist-USNAC 1958

Materials Handling C
3/4 OR 1/2 INCH VIDEO CASSETTE IND
Covers transport and handling of chips in a typical system from the chip receiving end through to the chip bin. Demonstrates different methods of conveying, such as belt, screw, chip washing, safety arrangements and operating variables.
From The Pulp And Paper Training - Thermo-Mechanical Pulping Series.
Prod-LEIKID Dist-LEIKID

Materials Handling C 12 MIN
3/4 OR 1/2 INCH VIDEO CASSETTE
Shows how to forklift, dolly and hand-truck materials from place to place and how to move materials without getting hurt.
Prod-FILCOM Dist-FILCOM

Materials Handling C 16 MIN
3/4 OR 1/2 INCH VIDEO CASSETTE IND
Discusses how to load pallets and trucks, safe use of two-wheel hand trucks and forklift trucks, safe use of gravity conveyors and power conveyors and working on a hook-on team. Includes working with different types of ladders and mobile scaffolding.
From The Industrial Safety Series.
Prod-LEIKID Dist-LEIKID

Materials Handling Equipment Operation - Gantry Truck And Warehouse Cranes B 21 MIN
16MM FILM OPTICAL SOUND
Shows the uses and operations of gantry truck and warehouse cranes and discusses safety precautions.
LC NO. FIE55-206
Prod-USN Dist-USNAC 1953

Materials Testing C 10 MIN
3/4 OR 1/2 INCH VIDEO CASSETTE
Covers types of metal testing.
From The Manufacturing Materials And Processes Series.
Prod-GE Dist-WFVTAE

Maternal Behavior In The Female Rat And Its Modification By Cortical Injury B 10 MIN
16MM FILM SILENT
Presents studies of animal behavior from the American Museum of Natural History in New York.
Prod-PSUPCR Dist-PSUPCR

Maternal Deprivation In Young Children B 30 MIN
16MM FILM OPTICAL SOUND C T
The first part shows some of the disorders caused by prolonged maternal deprivation. The second part shows the progress of children under psychotherapy.
Prod-ASSM Dist-NYU Prodn-AUBRY 1953

Maternity Care - Medical Examinations During Pregnancy C 28 MIN
16MM FILM OPTICAL SOUND
Explains the nature and purpose of medical examinations given prospective mothers during pregnancy.
LC NO. 74-706494
Prod-USN Dist-USNAC 1963

Maternity Hospital Routine C 15 MIN
16MM FILM OPTICAL SOUND J-C A
Shows the hospital maternity ward and labor room including pre-delivery tests, the work of doctors and nurses during delivery, methods of baby identification and the care given in the recovery room.
From The Family Life Education And Human Growth Series.
Prod-MORLAT Dist-SF 1967

Maternity Nursing—A Series
PRO
Prod-VDONUR Dist-AJN Prodn-WTTWTV 1966

Antepartum Care 44 MIN
Chromosomal Aberrations 44 MIN
Complications Of Pregnancy 44 MIN
Complications Of The Third Trimester 44 MIN
Family Mores And Attitudes 44 MIN
Hemolytic Diseases Of The Newborn 44 MIN
Hospital Care - Admission And Delivery 44 MIN
Hospital Care Of The Newborn 44 MIN
Infertility And Sterility 44 MIN
Neonate, The 44 MIN
Normal Labor And Delivery 44 MIN
Normal Pregnancy 44 MIN
Normal Puerperium 44 MIN
Nurse Midwifery 44 MIN
Postpartum Care - Hospital To Home 44 MIN
Premature Infant 44 MIN
Preparation For Parenthood 44 MIN
Trends In Maternal And Infant Care 44 MIN
Unwed Families 44 MIN

Mates, Martyrs And Masters C 27 MIN
16MM FILM, 3/4 OR 1/2 IN VIDEO A
Dramatizes methods of improving performance by not letting emotional needs conflict with supervisory responsibilities. Includes establishing priorities, delegating tasks, taking risks and initiating change.
Prod-SEVDIM Dist-SEVDIM

Math - All Skill Areas And Problem Types C 120 MIN
3/4 OR 1/2 INCH VIDEO CASSETTE
See series title for descriptive statement.
From The SAT Exam Preparation Series.
Prod-KRLSOF Dist-KRLSOF 1985

Math - No Mystery—A Series
I
Presents the fundamental concepts of mathematics.
Prod-WCETTV Dist-GPITVL 1977

Decimals To The Point 15 MIN
Divide And Conquer 15 MIN
Division - Round Two 15 MIN
Doggone Word Problems 15 MIN
Escape From Dullsville 15 MIN
Fractions 15 MIN
Fractions For Dollars 15 MIN
Group And Regroup 15 MIN
Make Math Work For You 15 MIN
Math-Possible 15 MIN
Maxi Multiplication 15 MIN
Multiplication And Division 15 MIN
Operations With Fractions 15 MIN
Patterns In Multiplication 15 MIN
Points In The News 15 MIN
Renaming Olympics 15 MIN
Round Up 15 MIN
Strategies 15 MIN
Subtraction 15 MIN
Sum And Difference 15 MIN

Math - Quantitative Comparison C 120 MIN
3/4 OR 1/2 INCH VIDEO CASSETTE
See series title for descriptive statement.
From The SAT Exam Preparation Series.
Prod-KRLSOF Dist-KRLSOF 1985

Math Anxiety C 29 MIN
16MM FILM OPTICAL SOUND
Highlights a course for math-anxious adults.
LC NO. 81-700538
Prod-JASON Dist-EDC 1980

Math Anxiety - We Beat It, So Can You C 29 MIN
3/4 OR 1/2 INCH VIDEO CASSETTE
Focus on math anxiety experienced by students of all ages. Discusses the nature and pervasive effects of math anxiety. Demonstrates one method to control the anxiety through a supportive, non-threatening teaching style. Shows scenes from a math anxiety classroom.
Prod-EDC Dist-EDC

Math Country—A Series
P
Uses stories about a young widow and her two children to offer information about arithmetic. Features Ray Walston as a mysterious old man with wonderful tricks up his sleeve.
Prod-KYTV Dist-AITECH 1979

And In The First Place - Counting, Number
Bigger Fish, The - Comparing 014 MIN
Checkerboard Multiplication 014 MIN
Count Your Chickens - Addition, Pt 1 014 MIN
Division Place, The - Division 014 MIN
Easy Go - Addition And Subtraction 014 MIN
Farm For Sale - Review 014 MIN
For Clocks And Cornerstones - Expressing 014 MIN
Ghostly Number, The - Addition, Pt 2 014 MIN
Hot And Heavy - Temperature And Weight 014 MIN
How Many Seeds - Problem Solving And 014 MIN
Lionel's Problem - Estimation 014 MIN
Math Rally, The - Place Value And Expanded 014 MIN
Matter Of Time 014 MIN
Meter The Liter - Linear Measure 014 MIN
Pattern Fixer, The - Word Problems And 014 MIN
Pieces Of Numbers - Fractions 014 MIN
Playing With Patterns - Geometric Patterns 014 MIN
Problem With Bears, The - Number Patterns 014 MIN
Shape Of Things, The - Geometry 014 MIN
Skip Some - Skip Counting 014 MIN
Subtraction Gang, The - Subtraction, Pt 1 014 MIN
Subtraction Squadron - Subtraction, Pt 3 014 MIN
Subtractor, The - Subtraction, Pt 2 014 MIN
Tanks, But No Thanks - Measuring Volume 014 MIN
Tencan, The - Grouping And Regrouping 014 MIN
This Little Penny Went To Market - Money 014 MIN
Too Many Geeziks - Problem Solving And 014 MIN
Welcome To The Farm 014 MIN
What Am I Bid - Equal And Unequal 014 MIN

Math Cycle—A Series
P
Presents mathematic skills commonly found in the first semester, third grade skills curriculum.
Prod-WDCNTV Dist-GPITVL 1983

Addition Facts 015 MIN
Checking Addition And Subtraction 015 MIN
Computers 015 MIN
Division 015 MIN
Equality And Inequality 015 MIN
Fractions 015 MIN
Graphs 015 MIN
Measurement - Introduction To Distance, Mass 015 MIN
Measurement - Time And Temperature 015 MIN
Money 015 MIN
Multiplication 015 MIN
Parts And Wholes 015 MIN
Place Value 015 MIN
Renaming In Addition 015 MIN
Renaming In Subtraction 015 MIN
Subtraction Facts 015 MIN

Math Factory, Module I - Sets—A Series
P
Prod-MAETEL Dist-GPITVL

Introducing Sets 15 MIN
Joining Sets - Addition 15 MIN
Nonequivalent Sets - Inequalities 15 MIN
Separating Sets 15 MIN
Set Numeration 15 MIN

Math Factory, Module II - Geometry—A Series
P
Prod-MAETEL Dist-GPITVL

Angles And Other Figures 15 MIN
Circles 15 MIN
Curves 15 MIN
Great Game Contest, The 15 MIN
Points And Line Segments 15 MIN

Math Factory, Module III - Number Patterns—A Series
P
Prod-MAETEL Dist-GPITVL

Addition With Zero And One 15 MIN
Attention To Tens 15 MIN
Beginning Concepts In Multiplication 15 MIN
Building Number Patterns 15 MIN
Place Value, Face Value 15 MIN

Math Factory, Module IV - Problem Solving—A Series
P
Prod-MAETEL Dist-GPITVL

Addition Of Tens And Ones 15 MIN
Relating Multiplication And Division 15 MIN
Renaming In Addition 15 MIN
Subtraction Of Tens And Ones 15 MIN
Writing Number Sentences 15 MIN

Math Factory, Module V - Fractions—A Series
P
Prod-MAETEL Dist-GPITVL

Following With Fractions 15 MIN
Fraction Action 15 MIN
Fraction Magic 15 MIN
Presenting One-Third 15 MIN
What's Half, What's A Fourth 15 MIN

Math Factory, Module VI - Money—A Series
P
Prod-MAETEL Dist-GPITVL

Dollar Scholar 15 MIN
Money Business 15 MIN
Sets Of Coins 15 MIN
Solving Money Problems 15 MIN
What Buys More 15 MIN

Math For Beginners (3rd Ed)—A Series
P
Uses animation to teach addition, subtraction, multiplication and division.
Prod-CORF Dist-CORF

Addition (3rd Ed) 012 MIN
Division (3rd Ed) 012 MIN
Multiplication (3rd Ed) 012 MIN
Subtraction (3rd Ed) 012 MIN

Math For Medications C 7 MIN
3/4 OR 1/2 INCH VIDEO CASSETTE
Focuses on the mathematics necessary for pharmacists and physicians.
Prod-TELSTR Dist-TELSTR

Math For Us Moderns C 15 MIN
2 INCH VIDEOTAPE J-H
Covers jobs that apply mathematics and technology to industrial problems and jobs that use math and science to explore unknown regions of pure research.
From The Work Is For Real Series.
Prod-STETVC Dist-GPITVL

Math Matters—A Series I-J
Focuses on mathematical concepts in the context of concrete situations.
Prod-STETVC Dist-AITECH Prodn-KLRNTV 1975

Area I 014 MIN
Area II 014 MIN
Data Graphs 015 MIN
Doing And Undoing 015 MIN
Estimation 015 MIN
Fractions I 015 MIN
Fractions II 015 MIN
Large Numbers 015 MIN
Metric System - Linear Measurement 015 MIN
Metric System - Weight And Capacity 015 MIN
Percent 015 MIN
Probability I 014 MIN
Probability II 014 MIN
Properties Of One And Zero 015 MIN
Quadrilaterals 015 MIN
Symmetry 015 MIN
Triangles 015 MIN
Unit Pricing 015 MIN
Volume I 015 MIN
Volume II 015 MIN

Math Minus Mystery C 6 MIN
16MM FILM, 3/4 OR 1/2 IN VIDEO T
Explains a teacher education program to train undergraduate college students to teach elementary school mathematics.
Prod-NSF Dist-AMEDFL 1975

Math Mission 2 - Overview C 15 MIN
3/4 OR 1/2 INCH VIDEO CASSETTE T
Shows selected segments from programs in the Math Mission 2 series. Demonstrates the format used, explains the philosophy of the program, and gives a preview of the content.
From The Math Mission 2 Series.
LC NO. 82-706319
Prod-WCVETV Dist-GPITVL 1981

Math Mission 2—A Series P
Tells how a robot comes to Earth to help students with math problems.
Prod-WCVETV Dist-GPITVL

Characteristic Characters 015 MIN
Everything In Its Place 015 MIN
Graphic Graphs 015 MIN
It's Time 015 MIN
Long And Short Of It, The 015 MIN
Missing Addends, The 015 MIN
Money Matters 015 MIN
Overview 015 MIN
Part Of Something 015 MIN
Pints, Quarts And Pottles 015 MIN
Place For Everything, A 015 MIN
Plus And Minus 015 MIN
Predictions And Reflections 015 MIN
Puzzling Problems 015 MIN
Shape Of Things, The 015 MIN
Shapes And More Shapes 015 MIN

Math Rally, The - Place Value And Expanded Notation C 14 MIN
3/4 OR 1/2 INCH VIDEO CASSETTE P
Explains how place value and expanded notation help contestants in a Math Rally.
From The Math Country Series.
Prod-KYTV Dist-AITECH 1979

Math Readiness - This One With That One - One-To-One Matching C 10 MIN
3/4 OR 1/2 INCH VIDEO CASSETTE
Focuses on the world's unluckiest fisherman in order to discuss one-to-one correspondence.
From The Math Readiness Series.
Prod-CORF Dist-CORF

Math Readiness - Up, Down, All Around - Directional Relationships C 10 MIN
3/4 OR 1/2 INCH VIDEO CASSETTE
Tells how Mr Lion learns about spatial directions as he builds his house.
From The Math Readiness Series.
Prod-CORF Dist-CORF

Math Readiness - Which Go Together - Set Building C 10 MIN
3/4 OR 1/2 INCH VIDEO CASSETTE
Illustrates the fundamentals of set-building by showing toy blocks regrouping.
From The Math Readiness Series.
Prod-CORF Dist-CORF

Math Readiness—A Series
16MM FILM, 3/4 OR 1/2 IN VIDEO K-P
Presents basic mathematical concepts.
Prod-CORF Dist-CORF

Math Readiness - This One With That One 010 MIN
Math Readiness - Up, Down, All Around 010 MIN
Math Readiness - Which Go Together 010 MIN

Math Review And Math Shortcuts C
3/4 OR 1/2 INCH VIDEO CASSETTE IND
See series title for descriptive statement.
From The Drafting - Blueprint Reading Basics Series.
Prod-GPCV Dist-GPCV

Math Review, Pt 1 C
3/4 OR 1/2 INCH VIDEO CASSETTE IND
Focuses on basic mathematics for the shop operator. Includes numbers, addition, subtraction, multiplication and division.
From The Industrial Training, Module 1 - Plant Principles Series.
Prod-LEIKID Dist-LEIKID

Math Review, Pt 2 C
3/4 OR 1/2 INCH VIDEO CASSETTE IND
Studies averages, fractions, decimals and percentages.
From The Industrial Training, Module 1 - Plant Principles Series.
Prod-LEIKID Dist-LEIKID

Math Review, Pt 3 C
3/4 OR 1/2 INCH VIDEO CASSETTE IND
Includes algebra, the equation and symbols.
From The Industrial Training, Module 1 - Plant Principles Series.
Prod-LEIKID Dist-LEIKID

Math Show, The C 20 MIN
3/4 INCH VIDEO CASSETTE I
Introduces the basic fundamentals of mathematics.
From The Wonderama Of The Arts Series.
Prod-WBRATV Dist-GPITVL 1979

Math That Counts—A Series
16MM FILM, 3/4 OR 1/2 IN VIDEO
Uses animation to explain key mathematical concepts.
Prod-DAVFMS Dist-EBEC

Artimus And Old Laces - Long 013 MIN
Banana Fever - Short Division 011 MIN
Caretaker's Dilemma, The - Place Value 010 MIN
Filbert And The Melon Cheater - 010 MIN
Ghost Of Captain Peale - Linear 011 MIN
Great Diamond, The - Long Division 010 MIN
King Vat - Introduction To Decimals 013 MIN
Lintola - Addition With Carrying 009 MIN
Magic Rectangle, The - Short 011 MIN
Tree Of Truth, The - Relationship 009 MIN

Math Topics - Geometry—A Series
16MM FILM, 3/4 OR 1/2 IN VIDEO J-C
Covers various aspects of geometry requiring an ability to construct drawings of what is viewed and take them as starting points for exploration by generalizing or specializing the results found.
Prod-BBCTV Dist-FI

Circles 020 MIN
Exterior Angles 020 MIN
Grids 020 MIN
Locus 020 MIN
Points And Line 020 MIN

Math Topics - Statistics—A Series
16MM FILM, 3/4 OR 1/2 IN VIDEO J-C
Demonstrates concepts and techniques that have a practical application both within society at large and within various school subjects.
Prod-BBCTV Dist-FI

Data Collection 020 MIN
Data Reduction 020 MIN
Data Representation 020 MIN
Probability I 020 MIN
Probability II 020 MIN

Math Topics - Trigonometry—A Series
16MM FILM, 3/4 OR 1/2 IN VIDEO J-C
Introduces trigonometry with the functions being defined either as projections or as ratios.
Prod-BBCTV Dist-FI

Scale Factor 020 MIN
Similar Shapes 020 MIN
Sine Graph 020 MIN
Sine Of Obtuse Angles 020 MIN
Turning 020 MIN

Math Wise—A Series H
Introduces math skills and presents vignettes illustrating these skills.
Prod-KOCETV Dist-AITECH 1981

Averages 015 MIN
Choosing A Sample 014 MIN
Finding A Common Unit 015 MIN
Formulas 015 MIN
Graphs 014 MIN
Maps, Charts, And Tables 014 MIN
Measuring Instruments 015 MIN
Numerical Comparisons 014 MIN
Organizing Information 000 MIN
Percent 015 MIN
Probability 000 MIN
Proportion 000 MIN

Math Works—A Series I
Extends mathematics instruction begun in fourth-grade series It Figures to fifth-graders as part of the Mathematics for the '80s project. Uses dramatic vignettes, animation and documentary illustrations to teach estimation, mental computation and problem-solving strategies and show how they apply to real life.
Prod-AITECH Dist-AITECH

Decimals - Comparing Decimals 015 MIN
Decimals - Place Value In Decimals 015 MIN
Decimals - Relating Fractions And Decimals 015 MIN
Decimals - Understanding The Placement Of The 015 MIN
Estimating - Estimating By Rounding 015 MIN
Estimating - Other Estimation Strategies 015 MIN
Fractions - Adding And Subtracting Fractions 015 MIN
Fractions - Adding And Subtracting Fractions 015 MIN
Geometry - Exploring Geometric Shapes 015 MIN
Geometry - Exploring The Movement Of Objects 015 MIN
Measurement - Dividing Regions Into 015 MIN
Measurement - Finding Areas Of Rectangles 015 MIN
Measurement - The Difference Between 015 MIN
Mental Computation - Using Mental Computation 015 MIN
Mental Computation - Using Mental Computation 015 MIN
Place Value - Place Value Of Large Numbers 015 MIN
Probability - Possible Outcomes 015 MIN
Problem Solving - Identifying The Problem 015 MIN
Problem Solving - Looking For A Pattern 015 MIN
Problem Solving - Simplifying The Problem 015 MIN
Problem Solving - Using Diagrams And Models 015 MIN
Problem Solving - Using Graphs 015 MIN
Problem Solving - Using Maps 015 MIN
Problem Solving - Using Tables 015 MIN
Ratio - Forming Ratios 015 MIN
Statistics - Analyzing Data 015 MIN
Statistics - Collecting Data 015 MIN
Statistics - Sampling 015 MIN

Math 01 C 30 MIN
3/4 OR 1/2 INCH VIDEO CASSETTE
Presents lessons in mathematics dealing with fractions.
From The Mathematics Series.
Prod-KYTV Dist-CAMB

Math 02 C 30 MIN
3/4 OR 1/2 INCH VIDEO CASSETTE
Presents lessons in mathematics dealing with fractions and production to decimals.
From The Mathematics Series.
Prod-KYTV Dist-CAMB

Math 03 C 30 MIN
3/4 OR 1/2 INCH VIDEO CASSETTE
Presents lessons in mathematics dealing with decimals.
From The Mathematics Series.
Prod-KYTV Dist-CAMB

Math 04 C 30 MIN
3/4 OR 1/2 INCH VIDEO CASSETTE
Presents lessons in Mathematics dealing with rounding off, ratios, proportions and conversions of measurements.
From The Mathematics Series.
Prod-KYTV Dist-CAMB

Math 05 C 30 MIN
3/4 OR 1/2 INCH VIDEO CASSETTE
Presents lessons in mathematics dealing with percents.
From The Mathematics Series.
Prod-KYTV Dist-CAMB

Math 06 C 30 MIN
3/4 OR 1/2 INCH VIDEO CASSETTE
Presents lessons in mathematics dealing with percents and interest, simple and compound interest.
From The Mathematics Series.
Prod-KYTV Dist-CAMB

Math 07 C 30 MIN
3/4 OR 1/2 INCH VIDEO CASSETTE
Presents lessons in mathematics dealing with reading graphs such as bar, line and circle.
From The Mathematics Series.
Prod-KYTV Dist-CAMB

Math 08 C 30 MIN
3/4 OR 1/2 INCH VIDEO CASSETTE
Presents lessons in mathematics dealing with angles.
From The Mathematics Series.
Prod-KYTV Dist-CAMB

Math 09 C 30 MIN
3/4 OR 1/2 INCH VIDEO CASSETTE
Presents lessons in mathematics dealing with perimeter and area.
From The Mathematics Series.
Prod-KYTV Dist-CAMB

Math 10 C 30 MIN
3/4 OR 1/2 INCH VIDEO CASSETTE
Presents mathematics lessons dealing with circumference, area and volume.
From The Mathematics Series.
Prod-KYTV Dist-CAMB

Math 11 C 30 MIN
3/4 OR 1/2 INCH VIDEO CASSETTE
Presents lessons in mathematics dealing with algebra.
From The Mathematics Series.
Prod-KYTV Dist-CAMB

Math-Possible C 15 MIN
3/4 INCH VIDEO CASSETTE I
Discusses renaming in mathematics.
From The Math - No Mystery Series.
Prod-WCETTV Dist-GPITVL 1977

Math/Science Encounter, The C 25 MIN
16MM FILM, 3/4 OR 1/2 IN VIDEO P-J
Shows how math and science is an important part of everyday life.
LC NO. 84-706385
Prod-DONMAC Dist-BARR 1984

Math's Alive C
16MM FILM OPTICAL SOUND
Explains the ways in which a teacher can make the study of mathematics more real and alive for the student.
Prod-SUTHP Dist-SUTHLA

Mathemagic, Unit I - Place Value—A Series
P
Increases the depth of understanding of a mathematical concept through visual concrete experiences before individual or independent mathematical involvement. Develops problem solving ability through interchange of mathematical and verbal language. Provides a sample copy of a teacher's guide.
Prod-WMULTV Dist-GPITVL

Cardinal Numbers 20 MIN
Equalities And Inequalities 20 MIN
Expanded Numerals 20 MIN
One-To-One Correspondence 20 MIN
Ones And Tens 20 MIN
Ordinal Numbers 20 MIN
Subsets 20 MIN
What Is A Set 20 MIN

Mathemagic, Unit II - Addition And Subtraction—A Series
P
Increases the depth of understanding of a mathematical concept through visual concrete experiences before individual or independent mathematical involvement. Develops problem solving ability through interchange of mathematical and verbal language. Provides a sample copy of a teacher's guide.
Prod-WMULTV Dist-GPITVL

Adding And Subtracting Tens 20 MIN
Addition Using Expanded Notation 20 MIN
Associative Property Of Addition 20 MIN
Commutative Property Of Addition 20 MIN
Partitioning Sets, Pt 1 20 MIN
Partitioning Sets, Pt 2 20 MIN
Problem Solving 20 MIN
Problem Solving 20 MIN
Regrouping Tens In Subtraction 20 MIN
Renaming Numbers 20 MIN
Renaming Ones In Addition 20 MIN
Subtraction Using Expanded Notation 20 MIN
Union Of Disjoint Sets, Pt 1 20 MIN
Union Of Disjoint Sets, Pt 2 20 MIN

Mathemagic, Unit III - Geometry—A Series
P
Increases the depth of understanding of a mathematical concept through visual concrete experiences before individual or independent mathematical involvement. Develops problem solving ability through interchange of mathematical and verbal language. Provides a sample copy of a teacher's guide.
Prod-WMULTV Dist-GPITVL

Circles 20 MIN
Points And Line Segments 20 MIN
Polygons (Geometric Figures) 20 MIN
Rays And Angles 20 MIN
Rectangles And Right Angle 20 MIN
Squares And Triangles 20 MIN

Mathemagic, Unit IV - Fractions—A Series
P
Increases the depth of understanding of a mathematical concept through visual concrete experiences before individual or independent mathematical involvement. Develops problem solving ability through interchange of mathematical and verbal language. Provides a sample copy of a teacher's guide.
Prod-WMULTV Dist-GPITVL

Fourths 20 MIN
Halves 20 MIN
Problem Solving 20 MIN
Thirds 20 MIN

Mathemagic, Unit V - Addition And Subtraction—A Series
P
Increases the depth of understanding of a mathematical concept through visual concrete experiences before individual or independent mathematical involvement. Develops problem solving ability through interchange of mathematical and verbal language. Provides a sample copy of a teacher's guide.
Prod-WMULTV Dist-GPITVL

Adding Expanded Numerals 20 MIN
Adding In Column Form 20 MIN
Expanding A Three-Digit Numeral 20 MIN
Problem Solving 20 MIN
Subtracting Expanded Numerals 20 MIN
Subtracting In Column Form 20 MIN

Mathemagic, Unit VI - Measurement—A Series
P
Increases the depth of understanding of a mathematical concept through visual concrete experiences before individual or independent mathematical involvement. Develops problem solving ability through interchange of mathematical and verbal language. Provides a sample copy of a teacher's guide.
Prod-WMULTV Dist-GPITVL

Hour Hand, The 20 MIN
Liquid Measure 20 MIN
Measuring 20 MIN
Minute Hand, The 20 MIN
Reading A Thermometer 20 MIN
Simple Linear Measure 20 MIN
Telling Time 20 MIN
Time 20 MIN
Using Liquid Measure 20 MIN
Weight 20 MIN

Mathemagic, Unit VII - Money—A Series
P
Presents concepts through visual concrete experiences before individual or independent mathematical involvement. Develops problem solving ability through interchange of mathematical and verbal language.
Prod-WMULTV Dist-GPITVL

Look At Money, A 20 MIN
Making Change 20 MIN
Using Money 20 MIN

Mathemagic, Unit VIII - Multiplication And Division—A Series
P
Increases the depth of understanding of a mathematical concept through visual concrete experiences before individual or independent mathematical involvement. Develops problem solving ability through interchange of mathematical and verbal language. Provides a sample copy of a teacher's guide.
Prod-WMULTV Dist-GPITVL

Equivalent Sets - Joining 20 MIN
Equivalent Sets - Partitioning 20 MIN
More Multiplication 20 MIN
Multiplication 20 MIN
Problem Solving 20 MIN
Problem Solving 20 MIN
Properties Of I And 0 In Multiplication And 20 MIN
Relating Addition To Multiplication 20 MIN
Relating Division To Multiplication 20 MIN
Relating Subtraction To Division 20 MIN
Review Of Addition 20 MIN
Review Of Subtraction 20 MIN
Using Mathematics 20 MIN

Mathematical Calculations Of Glaze Formulas C 28 MIN
2 INCH VIDEOTAPE
Features Mrs Peterson describing certain ceramic processes for her classroom at the University of Southern California. Shows how to use mathematical calculations of glaze formulas.
From The Wheels, Kilns And Clay Series.
Prod-USC Dist-PUBTEL

Mathematical Curves C 10 MIN
16MM FILM, 3/4 OR 1/2 IN VIDEO I-C
Presents an animated montage of the names and shapes of 14 mathematical curves.
Prod-WATSOC Dist-CF 1977

Mathematical Induction C
16MM FILM OPTICAL SOUND
Presents an example of proof by induction.
Prod-OPENU Dist-OPENU 1979

Mathematical Induction C 60 MIN
16MM FILM OPTICAL SOUND J-H
Professor Leon Henkin develops the principle of mathematical induction through a number of simple examples.
From The Maa Individual Lecturers Series.
Prod-MAA Dist-MLA 1960

Mathematical Induction, Pt 1 C 30 MIN
16MM FILM OPTICAL SOUND H-C
Professor Leon Henkin develops the principle of mathematical induction through a number of simple examples.
From The MAA Individual Lecturers Series.
LC NO. FIA63-464
Prod-MAA Dist-MLA 1960

Mathematical Induction, Pt 2 C 30 MIN
16MM FILM OPTICAL SOUND H-C
Professor Leon Henkin develops the principle of mathematical induction through a number of simple examples and proves the principle using the axiom that states that the positive integers are well-ordered.
From The MAA Individual Lecturers Series.
LC NO. FIA63-464
Prod-MAA Dist-MLA 1960

Mathematical Methods In Engineering And Science—A Series
C
Discusses matrices, determinants, bounds and approximations to eigenvalues, introduction to linear operator theory and inner product spaces, orthogonal expansions and Fourier transforms, systems of differential equations and stability and linearication.
Prod-UILU Dist-AMCEE

Mathematical Peep Show C 12 MIN
16MM FILM, 3/4 OR 1/2 IN VIDEO I-J
Illustrates the basic principles of abstract measurement of the Earth, functions, exponents, topology, and symmetry.
Prod-EAMES Dist-EBEC

Mathematical Problems I C 30 MIN
3/4 OR 1/2 INCH VIDEO CASSETTE T
Discusses the teaching of mathematical problem-solving skills to children with special needs.
From The Teaching Children With Special Needs Series.
Prod-MDDE Dist-MDCPB

Mathematical Problems II C 30 MIN
3/4 OR 1/2 INCH VIDEO CASSETTE T
Discusses the teaching of mathematical problem-solving skills to children with special needs.
From The Teaching Children With Special Needs Series.
Prod-MDDE Dist-MDCPB

Mathematics B 150 MIN
3/4 OR 1/2 INCH VIDEO CASSETTE PRO
See series title for descriptive statement.
From The Professional Engineer's Exam Refresher Course Series.
Prod-UMICE Dist-AMCEE

Mathematics (GMAT), Lesson 3 C
3/4 OR 1/2 INCH VIDEO CASSETTE C A
See series title for descriptive statement.
From The GMAT/Graduate Management Admission Test Series.
Prod-COMEX Dist-COMEX

Mathematics (GRE), Lesson 3 C
3/4 OR 1/2 INCH VIDEO CASSETTE H A
See series title for descriptive statement.
From The GRE/Graduate Record Examination Series.
Prod-COMEX Dist-COMEX

Mathematics - An Animated Approach To Fractions—A Series
16MM FILM, 3/4 OR 1/2 IN VIDEO
Presents an erudite, well-read pigeon named Checkoff who tries to help his New York friend Googol out of his difficulties with fractions. Covers addition, subtraction, multiplication, division of fractions and mixed numbers.
Prod-FI Dist-FI

Familiarity With Fractions And Multiplication
Renaming Fractions And Addition Of Fractions 012 MIN
Subtraction, Division And Mixed Numbers 012 MIN

Mathematics - Assessment And Programming C 29 MIN
3/4 OR 1/2 INCH VIDEO CASSETTE T
Discusses mathematics assessment and programming in a mainstreaming situation.
From The Mainstreaming The Exceptional Child Series.
Prod-MFFD Dist-FI

Mathematics - Graphing—A Series
J-H
Prod-UNISYS Dist-PHM 1972

Four Quadrant 13 MIN
Graphing An Equation 14 MIN
Point Coordinates - Quadrant One 13 MIN

Mathematics - Life's Number Game C 20 MIN
16MM FILM, 3/4 OR 1/2 IN VIDEO I-H
Shows different people solving job-related and everyday problems with mathematics. Illustrates the great number of situations that require a thorough knowledge of basic math.
Prod-CORF Dist-CORF

Mathematics - Unending Search For Excellence B 25 MIN
16MM FILM OPTICAL SOUND T
Reports on the current audio-visual aids used in teaching new mathematics.
LC NO. FIE63-347
Prod-USDHEW Dist-USNAC 1962

Mathematics And Physics—A Series
IND
Covers high school and vocational school subjects from measurement to energy, work and power to Newton's Law, temperature, pressure and fluids (liquids and gases) to Bernoulli's Principle, airplane flight, to sound and its effects.
Prod-AVIMA Dist-AVIMA

Bernoulli's Principle - Why An Airplane Flies 015 MIN
Energy, Work, Power And Force 031 MIN
Measurement Of Area And Volume 023 MIN
Newton's Law Of Motion 031 MIN
Sound And Its Effects 022 MIN
Temperature, Pressure And Fluids, Pt 1 030 MIN
Temperature, Pressure And Fluids, Pt 2 016 MIN

Mathematics And The Special Child C 29 MIN
16MM FILM OPTICAL SOUND T
Demonstrates how to use concrete, manipulative materials to teach abstract concepts.
From The Project STRETCH Series. Module 20
LC NO. 80-700627
Prod-METCO Dist-HUBDSC Prodn-GAEDTN 1980

Mathematics And The Special Student C 30 MIN
3/4 OR 1/2 INCH VIDEO CASSETTE T
Identifies specific learning problems in mathematics. Shows how to correct them.
From The Stretch Subject Matter Materials For Teaching Handicapped Children Series.
Prod-HUBDSC Dist-HUBDSC

Mathematics And The Special Student C 30 MIN
3/4 OR 1/2 INCH VIDEO CASSETTE T S
Demonstrates how to use concrete, manipulative materials to teach abstract concepts.
From The Project STRETCH (Strategies To Train Regular Educators To Teach Children With...) Series. Module 20
LC NO. 80-706656
Prod-METCO Dist-HUBDSC 1980

Mathematics For Elementary School Teachers— A Series

A sequentially arranged series for teacher training.
Prod-SMSG Dist-MLA

Pre-Number Ideas 30 MIN
Whole Numbers 30 MIN
Names For Numbers 30 MIN
Numeration Systems 30 MIN
Place Value And Addition 30 MIN
Addition And Subtraction 30 MIN
Addition And Subtraction Techniques 30 MIN
Multiplication 30 MIN
Division 30 MIN
Multiplication Techniques 30 MIN
Division Techniques 30 MIN
Sentences, Number Line 30 MIN
Points, Lines, Planes 30 MIN

Polygons And Angles	30 MIN
Metric Properties Of Figures	30 MIN
Linear And Angular Measure	30 MIN
Factors And Primes	30 MIN
Introducing Rational Numbers	30 MIN
Equivalent Fractions	30 MIN
Addition And Subtraction Of Rational Numbers	30 MIN
Multiplication Of Rational Numbers	30 MIN
Division Of Rational Numbers	30 MIN
Decimals	30 MIN
Ratio, Rate, Percent	30 MIN
Congruence And Similarity	30 MIN
Solid Figures	30 MIN
Area	30 MIN
Measurement Of Solids	30 MIN
Negative Rational Numbers	30 MIN
Real Numbers, The	30 MIN

Mathematics For Primary (Spanish)—A Series
16MM FILM, 3/4 OR 1/2 IN VIDEO P-I
Presents basic math concepts through animation.
Prod-PARACO Dist-AIMS Prodn-LEVKEA 1977

Mathematics For Primary - Addition (Spanish)	9 MIN
Mathematics For Primary - Division (Spanish)	8 MIN
Mathematics For Primary - Multiplication	7 MIN
Mathematics For Primary - Subtraction (Spanish)	8 MIN

Mathematics For Primary - Addition C 9 MIN
16MM FILM, 3/4 OR 1/2 IN VIDEO P-I
Uses bunnies, boats, helicopters and roller skates to illustrate the operation of addition.
From The Mathematics For Primary Series.
Prod-PARACO Dist-AIMS Prodn-LEVKEA 1977

Mathematics For Primary - Addition (Spanish) C 9 MIN
16MM FILM, 3/4 OR 1/2 IN VIDEO P-I
Illustrates the operation of addition as sets of bunnies, boats, helicopters, desk lamps and roller skates join together to make new groups, and arrange themselves to exemplify the commutative property of addition.
From The Mathematics For Primary (Spanish) Series.
Prod-PARACO Dist-AIMS Prodn-LEVKEA 1977

Mathematics For Primary - Division C 8 MIN
16MM FILM, 3/4 OR 1/2 IN VIDEO P-I
Illustrates the concept of division by depicting animated shoes, balls, cards and chairs.
From The Mathematics For Primary Series.
Prod-PARACO Dist-AIMS Prodn-LEVKEA 1977

Mathematics For Primary - Division (Spanish) C 8 MIN
16MM FILM, 3/4 OR 1/2 IN VIDEO P-I
Illustrates the concept of division as animated tennis shoes, dancing chairs, bouncing balls and shuffled cards divide themselves into groups of varying sizes, often involving a remainder.
From The Mathematics For Primary (Spanish) Series.
Prod-PARACO Dist-AIMS Prodn-LEVKEA 1977

Mathematics For Primary - Multiplication C 7 MIN
16MM FILM, 3/4 OR 1/2 IN VIDEO P-I
Discusses the operation of multiplication by showing bottles in rows, socks in pairs, cars in columns, and pencils in jars.
From The Mathematics For Primary Series.
Prod-PARACO Dist-AIMS Prodn-LEVKEA 1977

Mathematics For Primary - Multiplication (Spanish) C 7 MIN
16MM FILM, 3/4 OR 1/2 IN VIDEO P-I
Presents the operation of multiplication as animated pop bottles line up in rows, socks in pairs, toy cars in columns and pencils in jars.
From The Mathematics For Primary (Spanish) Series.
Prod-PARACO Dist-AIMS Prodn-LEVKEA 1977

Mathematics For Primary - Subtraction C 8 MIN
16MM FILM, 3/4 OR 1/2 IN VIDEO P-I
Uses animated objects to illustrate the concept of subtraction.
From The Mathematics For Primary Series.
Prod-PARACO Dist-AIMS Prodn-LEVKEA 1977

Mathematics For Primary - Subtraction (Spanish) C 8 MIN
16MM FILM, 3/4 OR 1/2 IN VIDEO P-I
Introduces and illustrates the concept of subtraction by showing hot dogs, fried eggs, cupcakes, ice cream and apples as they appear on the screen and then disappear. Superimposes mathematical sentences on the screen to express the subtraction operation.
From The Mathematics For Primary (Spanish) Series.
Prod-PARACO Dist-AIMS Prodn-LEVKEA 1977

Mathematics For Primary—A Series
16MM FILM, 3/4 OR 1/2 IN VIDEO P-I
Prod-PARACO Dist-AIMS Prodn-LEVKEA 1977

Mathematics For Primary - Addition	9 MIN
Mathematics For Primary - Division	8 MIN
Mathematics For Primary - Multiplication	7 MIN
Mathematics For Primary - Subtraction	8 MIN

Mathematics For Technical Personnel, Pt 1—A Series

Discusses basic mathematical operations, including fractions, decimals, algebra, and geometry.
Prod-RCAHSS Dist-RCAHSS

Mathematics For Technical Personnel, Pt 2—A Series

Discusses basic mathematical tools related to quadratic equations, simultaneous equations, trigonometry, exponents, logarithms, elementary vector analysis and complex notation.
Prod-RCAHSS Dist-RCAHSS

Mathematics For Tomorrow's World, Part I-Thinking, Learning, Living C
3/4 OR 1/2 INCH VIDEO CASSETTE
Points out the changing role of mathematics in the classroom. Presents the challenging implications for today's mathematics teacher.
Prod-FILMID Dist-FILMID 1983

Mathematics For Tomorrow's World, Part II-The Shape Of Things To Come C
3/4 OR 1/2 INCH VIDEO CASSETTE
Offers an opportunity to explore and utilize geometry at the elementary level.
Prod-FILMID Dist-FILMID 1983

Mathematics In Music C 30 MIN
3/4 INCH VIDEO CASSETTE
See series title for descriptive statement.
From The Changing Music Series.
Prod-WGBHTV Dist-PUBTEL

Mathematics In The Kindergarten, Pt 1 B 30 MIN
2 INCH VIDEOTAPE
See series title for descriptive statement.
From The Program Development In The Kindergarten Series.
Prod-GPITVL Dist-GPITVL

Mathematics In The Kindergarten, Pt 2 B 30 MIN
2 INCH VIDEOTAPE
See series title for descriptive statement.
From The Program Development In The Kindergarten Series.
Prod-GPITVL Dist-GPITVL

Mathematics Of Choice And Chance, Pgm 1 - Overview C 30 MIN
3/4 OR 1/2 INCH VIDEO CASSETTE C A
Introduces the major themes of statistics collecting, organizing and picturing data and drawing conclusions from data. Explains bias and randomness by looking at formal and informal public opinion polls and examining a major medical experiment. Presents inference as a tour through a telephone factory and games of chance in a visit to a casino.
From The For All Practical Purposes - Fundamentals Of Mathematics Series.
Prod-ANNCPB Dist-FI

Mathematics Of Choice And Chance, Pgm 2 - Behind The Headlines C 30 MIN
3/4 OR 1/2 INCH VIDEO CASSETTE C A
Explores how surveys and public opinion polls work. Examines how the unemployment rate is determined and what statistical evidence means. Explains the difference between a survey and an experiment and how chance is used in random sampling.
From The For All Practical Purposes - Fundamentals Of Mathematics Series.
Prod-ANNCPB Dist-FI

Mathematics Of Choice And Chance, Pgm 3 - Picture This C 30 MIN
3/4 OR 1/2 INCH VIDEO CASSETTE C A
Focuses on exploratory data analysis, emphasizing the human eye and brain as the best devices for seeing and recognizing patterns. Introduces histograms, medians, quartiles and the concept of an outlier with one variable and moves to situations with two variables to introduce scatterplots and box plots.
From The For All Practical Purposes - Fundamentals Of Mathematics Series.
Prod-ANNCPB Dist-FI

Mathematics Of Choice And Chance, Pgm 4 - Odds-On Favorite C 30 MIN
3/4 OR 1/2 INCH VIDEO CASSETTE C A
Analyzes how long-term patterns of chance events can be predicted by observing the operation of a casino. Introduces elementary probability concepts and analyzes normal curves, standard deviation and expected value. Demonstrates use of the Central Limit Theorem.
From The For All Practical Purposes - Fundamentals Of Mathematics Series.
Prod-ANNCPB Dist-FI

Mathematics Of Choice And Chance, Pgm 5 - Confident Conclusions C 30 MIN
3/4 OR 1/2 INCH VIDEO CASSETTE C A
Focuses on the concept of a confidence interval and describes what opinion polls do and do not reveal. Explains formula for computing confidence intervals, how confidence in statistical conclusion is related to sample size and how to analyze a sampling distribution.
From The For All Practical Purposes - Fundamentals Of Mathematics Series.
Prod-ANNCPB Dist-FI

Mathematics Of Finance, Pt I C 30 MIN
3/4 OR 1/2 INCH VIDEO CASSETTE PRO
Presents mathematics of finance, also referred to as Time Value Of Money. Illustrates and develops basic formula for equating the future value of the dollar.
From The Analysis Of Appropriations Series.
Prod-GMIEMI Dist-AMCEE

Mathematics Of Finance, Pt II C 30 MIN
3/4 OR 1/2 INCH VIDEO CASSETTE PRO
Explains concept of Present Value. Shows how Present Value is used in making investment decisions.
From The Analysis Of Appropriations Series.
Prod-GMIEMI Dist-AMCEE

Mathematics Of Personal Finance C 30 MIN
3/4 INCH VIDEO CASSETTE C
See series title for descriptive statement.
From The Introduction To Mathematics Series.
Prod-MDCPB Dist-MDCPB

Mathematics Of The Honeycomb (2nd Ed) C 13 MIN
16MM FILM, 3/4 OR 1/2 IN VIDEO
States that the elegance of the honeycomb, admired by the Greek mathematician Pappus, was not fully appreciated until modern mathematical methods were applied. Shows a historical and analytical approach to the honeycomb problem leading to an appreciation of the importance of mathematics in science and engineering.
Prod-MIS Dist-MIS 1977

Mathematics Review, Tape 1 C 45 MIN
3/4 OR 1/2 INCH VIDEO CASSETTE H A
Reviews basic math skills to prepare the SAT/ACT examination.
From The SAT/ACT Examination Video Review Series.
Prod-COMEX Dist-COMEX

Mathematics Review, Tape 2 C 45 MIN
3/4 OR 1/2 INCH VIDEO CASSETTE H A
Includes percentage problems, tax, interest formula and percent increase and decrease problems similar to the ones on the SAT/ACT examination.
From The SAT/ACT Examination Video Review Series.
Prod-COMEX Dist-COMEX

Mathematics Review, Tape 3 C 45 MIN
3/4 OR 1/2 INCH VIDEO CASSETTE H A
Includes basic algebra skills as tested on the SAT/ACT examination.
From The SAT/ACT Examination Video Review Series.
Prod-COMEX Dist-COMEX

Mathematics Review, Tape 4 C 45 MIN
3/4 OR 1/2 INCH VIDEO CASSETTE H A
Includes problems involving prime numbers, and simple and weighted averages as tested on the SAT/ACT examination.
From The SAT/ACT Examination Video Review Series.
Prod-COMEX Dist-COMEX

Mathematics Review, Tape 5 C 45 MIN
3/4 OR 1/2 INCH VIDEO CASSETTE H A
Includes problems involving radicals, properties and symbolic algebra as tested on the SAT/ACT examination.
From The SAT/ACT Examination Video Review Series.
Prod-COMEX Dist-COMEX

Mathematics Review, Tape 6 C 45 MIN
3/4 OR 1/2 INCH VIDEO CASSETTE H A
Includes word problems, consecutive integer problems and age problems as tested on the SAT/ACT examination.
From The SAT/ACT Examinatlion Video Review Series.
Prod-COMEX Dist-COMEX

Mathematics Review, Tape 7 C 45 MIN
3/4 OR 1/2 INCH VIDEO CASSETTE H A
Includes basic geometry problems and problems involving different relationships between figures as tested on the SAT/ACT examination.
From The SAT/ACT Examination Video Review Series.
Prod-COMEX Dist-COMEX

Mathematics Review, Tape 8 C 45 MIN
3/4 OR 1/2 INCH VIDEO CASSETTE H A
Includes solid geometry problems, analytical geometry problems and chart and graph problems as tested on the SAT/ACT examination.
From The SAT/ACT Examination Video Review Series.
Prod-COMEX Dist-COMEX

Mathematics Through Discovery B 25 MIN
16MM FILM OPTICAL SOUND T
Shows how skilled instructors use a learner discovery method to teach new concepts in mathematics at elementary and secondary school levels.
LC NO. FIE63-346
Prod-USOE Dist-USNAC 1963

Mathematics Today—A Series

Prod-WNDTTV Dist-MLA

Search For Solid Ground, The	45 MIN
Topology With Raoul Bott And Marston Morse	30 MIN

Mathematics—A Series

Presents lessons in mathematics including fractions, percents, graphs and angles.
Prod-KYTV Dist-CAMB

Math 01	030 MIN
Math 02	030 MIN
Math 03	030 MIN
Math 04	030 MIN
Math 05	030 MIN
Math 06	030 MIN
Math 07	030 MIN
Math 08	030 MIN
Math 09	030 MIN
Math 10	030 MIN
Math 11	030 MIN

Mathematics, Tape 1 C
3/4 OR 1/2 INCH VIDEO CASSETTE H A
Reviews material for the high school equivalency examination (GED). Explains the GED mathematics examination. Covers fractions.
From The New GED Examinations Series.
Prod-COMEX Dist-COMEX

Mathematics, Tape 1 C 45 MIN
3/4 OR 1/2 INCH VIDEO CASSETTE H A
Prepares students for the College Level Examination Program (CLEP) tests in Mathematics. Gives an introduction to CLEP mathematics and basic arithmetic.

From The CLEP General Examinations Series.
Prod-COMEX Dist-COMEX

Mathematics, Tape 1 (Spanish) C
3/4 OR 1/2 INCH VIDEO CASSETTE H A
Reviews material for the high school equivalency examination (GED). Explains the GED mathematics examination and covers fractions.
From The New GED Examination Series.
Prod-COMEX Dist-COMEX

Mathematics, Tape 1 (Spanish) C 45 MIN
3/4 OR 1/2 INCH VIDEO CASSETTE H A
Prepares students for the College Level Examination Program (CLEP) tests in Mathematics. Gives an introduction to CLEP mathematics and basic arithmetic.
From The CLEP General Examinations Series.
Prod-COMEX Dist-COMEX

Mathematics, Tape 2 C
3/4 OR 1/2 INCH VIDEO CASSETTE H A
Reviews material for the high school equivalency examination (GED). Discusses fractions, ratios and proportions.
From The New GED Examination Series.
Prod-COMEX Dist-COMEX

Mathematics, Tape 2 C 45 MIN
3/4 OR 1/2 INCH VIDEO CASSETTE H A
Prepares students for the College Level Examination Program tests in Mathematics. Covers basic algebra, factoring and solving equations and inequalities.
From The CLEP General Examinations Series.
Prod-COMEX Dist-COMEX

Mathematics, Tape 2 (Spanish) C
3/4 OR 1/2 INCH VIDEO CASSETTE H A
Reviews material for the high school equivalency examination (GED). Discusses fractions, ratios and proportions.
From The New GED Examination Series.
Prod-COMEX Dist-COMEX

Mathematics, Tape 2 (Spanish) C 45 MIN
3/4 OR 1/2 INCH VIDEO CASSETTE H A
Prepares students for the College Level Examination Program tests in Mathematics. Covers basic algebra, factoring and solving equations and inequalities.
From The CLEP General Examinations Series.
Prod-COMEX Dist-COMEX

Mathematics, Tape 3 C
3/4 OR 1/2 INCH VIDEO CASSETTE H A
Reviews material for the high school equivalency examination (GED). Focuses on decimals.
From The New GED Examination Series.
Prod-COMEX Dist-COMEX

Mathematics, Tape 3 C 45 MIN
3/4 OR 1/2 INCH VIDEO CASSETTE H A
Prepares students for the College Level Examination Program tests in Mathematics. Focuses on modern mathematics, probability and statistics.
From The CLEP General Examinations Series.
Prod-COMEX Dist-COMEX

Mathematics, Tape 3 (Spanish) C
3/4 OR 1/2 INCH VIDEO CASSETTE H A
Reviews material for the high school equivalency examination (GED). Focuses on decimals.
From The New GED Examination Series.
Prod-COMEX Dist-COMEX

Mathematics, Tape 3 (Spanish) C 45 MIN
3/4 OR 1/2 INCH VIDEO CASSETTE H A
Prepares students for the College Level Examination Program tests in Mathematics. Focuses on modern mathematics, probability and statistics.
From The CLEP General Examinations Series.
Prod-COMEX Dist-COMEX

Mathematics, Tape 4 C
3/4 OR 1/2 INCH VIDEO CASSETTE H A
Reviews material for the high school equivalency examination (GED). Covers percentages.
From The New GED Examination Series.
Prod-COMEX Dist-COMEX

Mathematics, Tape 4 C 45 MIN
3/4 OR 1/2 INCH VIDEO CASSETTE H A
Prepares students for the College Level Examination Program tests in Mathematics. Focuses on geometry.
From The CLEP General Examinations Series.
Prod-COMEX Dist-COMEX

Mathematics, Tape 4 (Spanish) C
3/4 OR 1/2 INCH VIDEO CASSETTE H A
Reviews material for the high school equivalency examination (GED). Covers percentages.
From The New GED Examination Series.
Prod-COMEX Dist-COMEX

Mathematics, Tape 4 (Spanish) C 45 MIN
3/4 OR 1/2 INCH VIDEO CASSETTE H A
Prepares students for the College Level Examination Program tests in Mathematics. Focuses on geometry.
From The CLEP General Examinations Series.
Prod-COMEX Dist-COMEX

Mathematics, Tape 5 C
3/4 OR 1/2 INCH VIDEO CASSETTE H A
Reviews material for the high school equivalency examination (GED). Focuses on several aspects of geometry.
From The New GED Examination Series.
Prod-COMEX Dist-COMEX

Mathematics, Tape 5 C 45 MIN
3/4 OR 1/2 INCH VIDEO CASSETTE H A
Prepares students for the College Level Examination Program tests in Mathematics. Covers number systems, functions, symbolic algebra and radicals.
From The CLEP General Examinations Series.
Prod-COMEX Dist-COMEX

Mathematics, Tape 5 (Spanish) C
3/4 OR 1/2 INCH VIDEO CASSETTE H A
Reviews material for the high school equivalency examination (GED). Focuses on several aspects of geometry.
From The GED Examination Series.
Prod-COMEX Dist-COMEX

Mathematics, Tape 6 C
3/4 OR 1/2 INCH VIDEO CASSETTE H A
Reviews material for the high school equivalency examination (GED). Reviews test taking. Covers charts and graphs.
From The New GED Examination Series.
Prod-COMEX Dist-COMEX

Mathematics, Tape 6 (Spanish) C
3/4 OR 1/2 INCH VIDEO CASSETTE H A
Reviews material for the high school equivalency examination (GED). Reviews test taking. Covers charts and graphs.
From The New GED Examination Series.
Prod-COMEX Dist-COMEX

Mathematics, Tapes 5 (Spanish) C 45 MIN
3/4 OR 1/2 INCH VIDEO CASSETTE H A
Prepares students for the College Level Examination Program tests in Mathematics. Covers number systems, functions, symbolic algebra and radicals.
From The CLEP General Examinations Series.
Prod-COMEX Dist-COMEX

Mathew Brady B 13 MIN
16MM FILM, 3/4 OR 1/2 IN VIDEO H-C
Documents the work of Mathew Brady, the first United States combat photographer.
Prod-USDD Dist-TEXFLM 1957

Mathilde Mohring C 40 MIN
16MM FILM OPTICAL SOUND
A German language film with English subtitles. Tells the story of Mathilde, who manipulates the student Hugo Grassman into marrying her and procures a mayor's position for him. Continues as Hugo, unable to fulfill all of Mathilde's expectations, falls sick and dies. Ends with Mathilde realizing her selfishness and becoming a better person as a result of it.
Prod-WSTGLC Dist-WSTGLC 1977

Mathscore One—A Series
16MM FILM, 3/4 OR 1/2 IN VIDEO I-J
Discusses various aspects of mathematics, including place value, fractions, angles, decimals, graphs, symmetry and shapes.
Prod-BBCTV Dist-FI

Angles - A Good Turn	020 MIN
Axes And Grids - Get Coordinated	020 MIN
Capacity, Volume And Mass - Fill It Up	020 MIN
Decimals - Get The Point	020 MIN
Fractions - Bits And Pieces	020 MIN
Graphs - Graphic Description	020 MIN
Place Value - Know Your Place	020 MIN
Sequences - What Next	020 MIN
Symmetry And Shapes - Mirror Image	020 MIN
Tesselations And Area - A Cover Up	020 MIN

Mathscore Two—A Series
16MM FILM, 3/4 OR 1/2 IN VIDEO I-J
Discusses different mathematical concepts such as place value, fractions, angles, decimals, graphs, tesselations and area, capacity, volume and area.
Prod-BBCTV Dist-FI

Angles - A Matter Of Degree	020 MIN
Axes And Grids - Graphs Rule, OK	020 MIN
Capacity, Volume And Mass - Massive Ending	020 MIN
Decimals - Fine Adjustment	020 MIN
Fractions - Half And Half	020 MIN
Graphs - Picture Story	020 MIN
Place Value - Take It Away	020 MIN
Sequences - Numbers Growing	020 MIN
Symmetry And Shapes - S For Symmetry	020 MIN
Tesselations And Area - Space Count	020 MIN

Mathways—A Series
I-J
Offers information on mathematics.
Prod-STSU Dist-AITECH 1980

Areas Of Circles And Cylinders	015 MIN
Decimal Point, The	015 MIN
Percent	015 MIN
Volumes	015 MIN

Matina Horner - Portrait Of A Person C 16 MIN
16MM FILM, 3/4 OR 1/2 IN VIDEO H-C A
Discusses Matina Horner's concerns as sixth president of Radcliffe College. Presents, in humorous cartoon form with her own narration, her famous research on the expectations of women and their apparent fear of success.
Prod-PHENIX Dist-PHENIX 1975

Matinee At The Bijou, No. 01 C 90 MIN
3/4 INCH VIDEO CASSETTE
Includes a cartoon, a short subject, a segment of a serial, a coming attraction, and the 1935 feature film The Lost City.
Prod-BIJOU Dist-PUBTEL

Matinee At The Bijou, No. 02 C 90 MIN
3/4 INCH VIDEO CASSETTE
Includes a cartoon, a short subject, a segment of a serial, a coming attraction, and the 1937 feature film Movie Struck.
Prod-BIJOU Dist-PUBTEL

Matinee At The Bijou, No. 03 C 90 MIN
3/4 INCH VIDEO CASSETTE
Includes a cartoon, a short subject, a segment of a serial, a coming attraction, and the feature film West Of The Divide.
Prod-BIJOU Dist-PUBTEL

Matinee At The Bijou, No. 04 C 90 MIN
3/4 INCH VIDEO CASSETTE
Includes a cartoon, a short subject, a segment of a serial, a coming attraction, and the 1934 feature film The Lost Jungle.
Prod-BIJOU Dist-PUBTEL

Matinee At The Bijou, No. 05 C 90 MIN
3/4 INCH VIDEO CASSETTE
Includes a cartoon, a short subject, a segment of a serial, a coming attraction, and the 1932 feature film Winds Of The Wasteland.
Prod-BIJOU Dist-PUBTEL

Matinee At The Bijou, No. 06 C 90 MIN
3/4 INCH VIDEO CASSETTE
Includes a cartoon, a short subject, a segment of a serial, a coming attraction, and the 1934 feature film Polooka.
Prod-BIJOU Dist-PUBTEL

Matinee At The Bijou, No. 07 C 90 MIN
3/4 INCH VIDEO CASSETTE
Includes a cartoon, a short subject, a segment of a serial, a coming attraction, and the 1938 feature film The Man From Music Mountain.
Prod-BIJOU Dist-PUBTEL

Matinee At The Bijou, No. 08 C 90 MIN
3/4 INCH VIDEO CASSETTE
Includes a cartoon, a short subject, a segment of a serial, a coming attraction, and the 1939 feature film Flying Deuces.
Prod-BIJOU Dist-PUBTEL

Matinee At The Bijou, No. 09 C 90 MIN
3/4 INCH VIDEO CASSETTE
Includes a cartoon, a short subject, a segment of a serial, a coming attraction, and the 1934 feature film Submarine Alert.
Prod-BIJOU Dist-PUBTEL

Matinee At The Bijou, No. 10 C 90 MIN
3/4 INCH VIDEO CASSETTE
Includes a cartoon, a short subject, a segment of a serial, a coming attraction, and the 1943 feature film Million Dollar Kid.
Prod-BIJOU Dist-PUBTEL

Matinee At The Bijou, No. 11 C 90 MIN
3/4 INCH VIDEO CASSETTE
Includes a cartoon, a short subject, a segment of a serial, a coming attraction, and the 1942 feature film Wildcat.
Prod-BIJOU Dist-PUBTEL

Matinee At The Bijou, No. 12 C 90 MIN
3/4 INCH VIDEO CASSETTE
Includes a cartoon, a short subject, a segment of a serial, a coming attraction, and the feature films Yellow Rose Of Texas and Song Of Texas.
Prod-BIJOU Dist-PUBTEL

Matinee At The Bijou, No. 13 C 90 MIN
3/4 INCH VIDEO CASSETTE
Includes a cartoon, a short subject, a segment of a serial, a coming attraction, and the 1943 feature film Gung Ho.
Prod-BIJOU Dist-PUBTEL

Matinee At The Bijou, No. 14 C 90 MIN
3/4 INCH VIDEO CASSETTE
Includes a cartoon, a short subject, a segment of a serial, a coming attraction, and the 1947 feature film It's A Joke, Son.
Prod-BIJOU Dist-PUBTEL

Matinee At The Bijou, No. 15 C 90 MIN
3/4 INCH VIDEO CASSETTE
Includes a cartoon, a short subject, a segment of a serial, a coming attraction, and the 1944 feature film Cowboy Commandos.
Prod-BIJOU Dist-PUBTEL

Matinee At The Bijou, No. 16 C 90 MIN
3/4 INCH VIDEO CASSETTE
Includes a cartoon, a short subject, a segment of a serial, a coming attraction, and the 1947 feature film Philo Vance Returns.
Prod-BIJOU Dist-PUBTEL

Mating Behavior Of The Honey Bee C 13 MIN
16MM FILM OPTICAL SOUND C A
Documents research methods for studying mating behavior of the honey bee. Shows reactions of drones to the tethered queen, to the queen confined in a small cage, to the odor of the queen, to the queen bee suspended at various altitudes, and to artificial models of queen bees with various characteristics.
LC NO. 74-713860
Prod-NSF Dist-PSUPCR 1971

Mating Season, The C 96 MIN
1/2 IN VIDEO CASSETTE BETA/VHS P-C A
Features a romantic comedy about a high-strung lawyer and a laid-back laundromat owner. Stars Lucie Arnaz and Laurence Lockinbill.
Prod-LCOA Dist-LCOA

Matisse - A Sort Of Paradise C 30 MIN
16MM FILM, 3/4 OR 1/2 IN VIDEO I A
Takes the viewer on a lyrical trip through the world of Matisse as seen in his painting. Reveals the idyllic quality of his works.
Prod-BCACGB Dist-FI 1969

Matisse And The Fauves C 20 MIN
16MM FILM, 3/4 OR 1/2 IN VIDEO H-C
Offers a survey of Fauvism, exploring the works of Matisse, Derain, de Vlaminck, Braque, Dufy, Marguet and Rouault.
Prod-IFB Dist-IFB 1970

Matrices C 30 MIN
3/4 INCH VIDEO CASSETTE C
See series title for descriptive statement.
From The Introduction To Mathematics Series.
Prod-MDCPB Dist-MDCPB

Matrioska C 5 MIN
16MM FILM, 3/4 OR 1/2 IN VIDEO K-P A
An animated film which shows enamelled wooden Russian dolls performing a Russian folk dance.
Prod-NFBC Dist-MGHT 1970

Matrix C 6 MIN
16MM FILM, 3/4 OR 1/2 IN VIDEO I A
Presents horizontal and vertical lines, squares and cubes where all motion is a long closed invisible pathway.
Prod-WHIT Dist-PFP 1970

Matrix Structural Analysis—A Series
PRO
Uses classroom format to videotape three 50-minute lectures per week for 15 weeks and 40 cassettes. Discusses a systematic approach to formulation of force and displacement method of analysis, representation of structures as assemblages of elements and computer solution of structural systems.
Prod-SMUITV Dist-AMCEE

Matrix Structural Analysis—A Series

Covers the formulation of the analysis of trusses, beams and frames using the stiffness method of matrix structural analysis, development of element properties, coordinate transformations and global analysis theory and special topics such as initial loads. Contains 40 one-hour tapes.
Prod-UIDEEO Dist-UIDEEO

Matt And The Missing Parts C 8 MIN
16MM FILM OPTICAL SOUND IND
Studies human motives, how they can be misunderstood, how they affect all layers of supervision, how they are symptoms of even deeper personal and company problems and how significant they can be to the welfare of any company.
From The Human Side Of Supervision Series.
LC NO. 73-701931
Prod-VOAERO Dist-VOAERO 1972

Mattehw Geller - Everglades City C 98 MIN
3/4 OR 1/2 INCH VIDEO CASSETTE
Features a fairy tale. Gives equal weight to characters, plot and environment.
Prod-ARTINC Dist-ARTINC

Matteo And Alan Lynes C 30 MIN
3/4 OR 1/2 INCH VIDEO CASSETTE
Focuses on the cultural experience reflected in dance. Looks at a performance of 'Esoterica' with Robert Cohan. Hosted by Julinda Lewis.
From The Eye On Dance - Dance In Religion And Ritual Series.
Prod-ARTRES Dist-ARTRES

Matter C 15 MIN
2 INCH VIDEOTAPE K
Illustrates materials having various properties. Uses our senses to determine these properties.
From The Let's Go Sciencing, Unit I - Matter Series.
Prod-DETPS Dist-GPITVL

Matter C 15 MIN
3/4 OR 1/2 INCH VIDEO CASSETTE P-I
Focuses on the three states of matter which are solid, liquid and gas. Illustrates that all matter, regardless of its state, has weight, takes up space and is composed of the small particles called molecules.
From The First Films On Science Series.
Prod-MAETEL Dist-AITECH 1975

Matter - Science Is Searching C 15 MIN
2 INCH VIDEOTAPE P
Shows matter existing in various states.
From The Science Is Searching Series.
Prod-DETPS Dist-GPITVL

Matter And Energy C 11 MIN
16MM FILM OPTICAL SOUND J-C A
A revised version of the 1964 film Of Stars And Men Tells the story of a man who gives up his hum-drum existence to seek truth through a philosophical quest. Discusses man's place in the universe through an examination of time, one of life's basic elements. Based on the book OF STARS AND MEN by Dr Harlow Shapley.
From The Of Stars And Men (2nd Ed) Series.
LC NO. 76-701274
Prod-HUBLEY Dist-RADIM 1976

Matter And Energy (2nd Ed) C 14 MIN
16MM FILM, 3/4 OR 1/2 IN VIDEO J-H
Presents properties and states of matter, potential and kinetic energy and the rule of energy in chemical changes.
Prod-CORF Dist-CORF 1972

Matter And Minerals C 30 MIN
3/4 OR 1/2 INCH VIDEO CASSETTE C
Explores the history and make-up of matter. Concentrates on minerals, the basic building blocks of the earth and of many astronomical bodies.
From The Earth, Sea And Sky Series.
Prod-DALCCD Dist-DALCCD

Matter And Motion—A Series
I
Prod-WHROTV Dist-AITECH 1973

About Christmas Trees	015 MIN
About Energy	015 MIN
Days And Seasons	015 MIN
Earth Resources	015 MIN
Earth's Past, The	015 MIN
It's About Time	015 MIN
Machines That Move People	015 MIN
Magnetism And Electricity	015 MIN
Our Polluted Waters	015 MIN
Radioactivity And The Environment	015 MIN
Simple Machines	015 MIN
Solar System, The	015 MIN
Something In The Air	015 MIN
Sounds Around Us	015 MIN
States Of Matter, The	015 MIN
Thinking About Rocks	015 MIN
Weather	015 MIN

Matter And The Molecular Theory C 13 MIN
16MM FILM, 3/4 OR 1/2 IN VIDEO J
Presents inductive demonstrations and experiments to show evidences for the existence of atoms and molecules. Shows how crystal lattices, individual crystallites, diffusion in solids, liquids and gases, Brownian movement and electron micrographs add support to the molecular theory.
Prod-CORF Dist-CORF 1970

Matter Changes C 14 MIN
16MM FILM, 3/4 OR 1/2 IN VIDEO P-I
Shows how electrons govern chemical change and illustrates molecular motion in solids, liquids and gases.
From The Physical Science Learning Lab Series.
Prod-BARR Dist-BARR 1981

Matter Into Energy (2nd Ed) C 10 MIN
16MM FILM, 3/4 OR 1/2 IN VIDEO I-J
Introduces nuclear energy, explaining protons, neutrons, nuclear binding energy, chain reactions, and the conversion of mass into energy in nuclear reactions.
Prod-CENTRO Dist-CORF

Matter Is Everything C 12 MIN
16MM FILM, 3/4 OR 1/2 IN VIDEO P-I
Shows the relationships among matter, mass, properties, elements, compounds, molecules, atoms, protons, neutrons and electrons.
From The Physical Science Learning Lab Series.
Prod-BARR Dist-BARR 1981

Matter Is Made Of C 15 MIN
3/4 OR 1/2 INCH VIDEO CASSETTE P-I
Discusses the properties of molecules. Shows how, with different arrangement of molecules, matter takes different forms. Includes experiments that show how to detect very large molecules and that demonstrate molecular motion.
From The First Films On Science Series.
Prod-MAETEL Dist-AITECH 1975

Matter Of Air, The B 30 MIN
16MM FILM OPTICAL SOUND T
Shows how elementary science lessons that are activity oriented can be undertaken using the simplest materials, even in a highly formal classroom.
From The Starting Tomorrow Series. Unit 4 - New Ways In Elementary Science
Prod-EALING Dist-WALKED

Matter Of Balance, A C 12 MIN
16MM FILM OPTICAL SOUND
Examines inflation and the goals of Phase 2 of the Economic Stabilization Program by comparing the economy to a set of scales. Explains administrative responsibilities, methods and results.
LC NO. 76-703436
Prod-USOPA Dist-USOPA Prodn-METVIP 1972

Matter Of Balance, A C 12 MIN
16MM FILM - 3/4 IN VIDEO
Exposes situations and actions that cause falls, pointing out that falls account for about 20 percent of industrial accidents. Sets forth an action plan for preventing falls while presenting case studies of actual accidents.
Prod-ALLIED Dist-BNA

Matter Of Chance C 28 MIN
3/4 INCH VIDEO CASSETTE A
Features a hospital-based sickle-cell anemia counseling program. Differentiates sickle cell disease from sickle cell trait and discusses the chances of hereditary transmission.
LC NO. 77-703362
Prod-VADTC Dist-USNAC 1977

Matter Of Choice, A C 28 MIN
16MM FILM OPTICAL SOUND
Looks at far-reaching prospects of nuclear development and its benefits and consequences.
LC NO. 76-703246
Prod-TETRA Dist-CANFDC 1975

Matter Of Choice, A C 20 MIN
3/4 INCH VIDEO CASSETTE J-H
Presents teen-agers in buying situations illustrating the impact of youthful consumers on our economy.
From The Dollar Data Series.
LC NO. 81-707349
Prod-WHROTV Dist-GPITVL 1974

Matter Of Concern, A - Organizing Emergency Field Care Of Athletes C 12 MIN
16MM FILM, 3/4 OR 1/2 IN VIDEO I-H
Explains emergency treatment of the injured football player, with instructions for the person assigned first aid responsibility, including how to recognize and handle serious injuries.
From The Football Injury Prevention Series.
Prod-ATHI Dist-ATHI

Matter Of Conscience, A C 29 MIN
16MM FILM OPTICAL SOUND H-C A
Tells the story of two draft resisters.
LC NO. 72-703357
Prod-CAFM Dist-CAFM 1970

Matter Of Conscience, A - Henry VIII And Thomas More C 30 MIN
16MM FILM, 3/4 OR 1/2 IN VIDEO H-C A
Accentuates the historic clash between Henry VIII and Sir Thomas More as More as a prototypical confrontation between state policy and an individual who is living in opposition to it.
From The Western Civilization - Majesty And Madness Series.
Prod-CPC Dist-LCOA 1972

Matter Of Contamination Sense, A B 10 MIN
16MM FILM OPTICAL SOUND PRO
Discusses the hazards present when handling radioactive substance and the principles and practice of contamination drills.
Prod-UKAEA Dist-UKAEA 1958

Matter Of David J, The C 16 MIN
16MM FILM, 3/4 OR 1/2 IN VIDEO I-C
Tells a story about a boy who agrees to drive a getaway truck in a robbery to raise money to pay for a motorcycle. Shows how he must accept responsibility for the consequences of the robbery when it results in a shooting.
From The Under The Law, Pt 2 Series.
Prod-USNEI Dist-WDEMCO 1975

Matter Of Degree, A C 30 MIN
3/4 OR 1/2 INCH VIDEO CASSETTE C A
Examines the stress that is characteristic of life in twentieth-century America. Focuses on three sources of stress and looks at specific means by which individuals can combat the effects of stress.
From The Contemporary Health Issues Series. Lesson 4
Prod-SCCON Dist-CDTEL

Matter Of Doing Something To Live, A B 20 MIN
3/4 INCH VIDEO CASSETTE
Documents the life and work experiences of women in the Thompson/Nicola region of British Columbia, a northern farming area, from the 19th to the mid-20th centuries. Looks at the work options available to women during this period, links these choices to the economic system and Canadian society's expectations of women and examines the effects of the work options upon women's lives.
Prod-WMENIF Dist-WMENIF

Matter Of Fact—A Series
J-H
Presents analyses of factual books by interviewing authors and exploring the subjects of their books.
Prod-NITC Dist-AITECH Prodn-WETATV 1973

Action / Reaction	20 MIN
And There Were No More	20 MIN
As The World Plays	20 MIN
Black Wealth	20 MIN
Creative Person, The	20 MIN
Diggers And Finders	20 MIN
In A Violent Time	20 MIN
It Will Happen Again	20 MIN
Last Stand	20 MIN
Man In A Paper Boat	20 MIN
Man's Inhumanity	20 MIN
Search And Serendipity	20 MIN
To A Different Drum	20 MIN
Trail Of Tears	20 MIN
White Magic, Black Magic	20 MIN

Matter Of Fat, A C 99 MIN
16MM FILM, 3/4 OR 1/2 IN VIDEO H-C A
Examines several aspects of the problem of over-weight in a documentary about the ordeal of a fat man and his struggle to lose weight.
Prod-NFBC Dist-NFBC 1969

Matter Of Fiction—A Series
J-H
Provides a perspective of students through an involvement with books concerned with young people in problem situations and reveals the differences and similarities of various cultures by using books from different countries. (Broadcast quality)
Prod-WETATV Dist-AITECH

Across Five Aprils	20 MIN
All The Dark Places And Five Boys In A Cave	20 MIN
Ash Road	20 MIN
Bookbag	20 MIN
Day Of The Bomb And The Little Fishes, The	20 MIN
Donbas And The Endless Steppe	20 MIN
Durango Street	20 MIN
Faraway Lurs, The	20 MIN
Innocent Wayfaring And A Traveler In Time, The	20 MIN
Outsiders, The	20 MIN
Pit And Smoke, The	20 MIN
Slave's Tale, A	20 MIN
Undertow And Count Me Gone	20 MIN
White Mountains And The City Of Gold And Lead	20 MIN
Year Of The Jeep, The	20 MIN

Matter Of Hope, A C 23 MIN
16MM FILM OPTICAL SOUND
Tells what happened in several communities when natural disasters struck and shows how the Red Cross responded. Focuses on small local disasters.
Prod-AMRC Dist-AMRC 1973

Matter Of Identity, A C 30 MIN
3/4 OR 1/2 INCH VIDEO CASSETTE
See series title for descriptive statement.
From The Mundo Real Series.
Prod-CPT Dist-MDCPB

Matter Of Inconvenience, A C 10 MIN
16MM FILM, 3/4 OR 1/2 IN VIDEO A
Depicts a group of young skiers on the slopes of Lake Tahoe, Nevada. Explains that they are either blind or amputees, showing that a disability does not have to be a handicap, but only a matter of inconvenience.
Prod-STNFLD Dist-STNFLD 1974

Matter Of Independence, A C 16 MIN
16MM FILM OPTICAL SOUND
Discusses the experiences of handicapped students at St Andrew's Presbyterian College. Shows their lives in mobile home units adapted to accommodate individuals in wheelchairs.
LC NO. 77-703225
Prod-STANPC Dist-USNAC Prodn-DUMEPR 1976

Matter Of Indifference, A B 48 MIN
16MM FILM, 3/4 OR 1/2 IN VIDEO H-C A
Presents a critique of society's ambivalence toward the aged. Includes an interview with Maggie Kuhn, founder of the Gray Panther movement.
Prod-PHENIX Dist-PHENIX 1974

Matter Of Insurance, A C 52 MIN
16MM FILM, 3/4 OR 1/2 IN VIDEO
Recounts an incident involving a slave captain who murdered 130 Africans by throwing them overboard and who was then brought to trial, not on a murder charge but for an insurance claim. Shows how this dramatically changed public opinion on slavery.
From The Fight Against Slavery Series. No. 3
LC NO. 79-707669
Prod-BBCTV Dist-TIMLIF 1977

Matter Of Job Protection C 12 MIN
16MM FILM OPTICAL SOUND
Presents an animated story of the last day in the career of a letter carrier.
LC NO. 74-700823
Prod-CRAF Dist-CRAF 1972

Matter Of Life And Death, A C 30 MIN
16MM FILM, 3/4 OR 1/2 IN VIDEO J-H A
Demonstrates how students face the possibility of losing a teacher they idolize when he suffers a stroke. Shows that as they learn to come to terms with the inevitability of death, they help the teacher begin his recovery.
From The Moving Right Along Series.
LC NO. 84-706558
Prod-WQED Dist-MTI 1983

Matter Of Opportunity, A C 27 MIN
16MM FILM OPTICAL SOUND J-H
Focuses on the many opportunities available to students who decide on a career in medicine.
Prod-AMEDA Dist-AMEDA

Matter Of Perspective, A B 8 MIN
16MM FILM - 3/4 IN VIDEO
Illustrates the difficulties of a young mother in having her children vaccinated at a county clinic. Presents this problematical situation intended as a stimulus to guide group discussion.
Prod-USNAC Dist-USNAC 1972

Matter Of Protection, A C 28 MIN
16MM FILM OPTICAL SOUND A
Shows how the public health service helped to combat the Asian flu epidemic of 1957, how it seeks causes and cures of many diseases and how it helps to safeguard the nation's health. Explains how the nation's resources are mobilized.
LC NO. FIE64-115
Prod-USPHS Dist-USNAC Prodn-DEROCH 1963

Matter Of Respect, A C 18 MIN
16MM FILM, 3/4 OR 1/2 IN VIDEO H
Uses the dramatization of a teen love affair to emphasize male sexual responsibility.
Prod-USDHEW Dist-USNAC

Matter Of Seconds, A X 30 MIN
16MM FILM OPTICAL SOUND C T
Concerns three elderly people who had accidents in the home as a result of a lack of safety measures.
Prod-CFDC Dist-CFDC

Matter Of Size, A C 29 MIN
3/4 INCH VIDEO CASSETTE
Examines the effects of bigness and smallness on American life. Surveys the growing frustration felt by many as the result of big business and big government.
Prod-WMHTTV Dist-PUBTEL

Matter Of Size, A - Power And People C 29 MIN
3/4 OR 1/2 INCH VIDEO CASSETTE
Considers questions of size, power, politics, economics and culture. Presents divergent views. Originally aired on PBS.
Prod-KITCHN Dist-KITCHN

Matter Of Survival, A - Toxic Solvents C 9 MIN
16MM FILM OPTICAL SOUND H-C
Demonstrates the safety precautions technical assistants should observe when handling toxic solvents.
LC NO. FIA65-1064
Prod-CSIROA Dist-CSIROA Prodn-CSIRFU 1963

Matter Of Taste—A Series
H A
Introduces the scientific principles of food nutrition and preparation. Shows esthetic methods of presenting prepared food.
Prod-COAST Dist-CDTEL

Beverages
Bread
Cheese And Milk
Eggs
Fish
Fruit
Grains And Legumes
Herbs, Spices, And Oils
Kitchen Equipment
Marketing
Meat
Pasta
Pastry
Poultry
Presentation
Salads
Soups
Sugar
Varietal Meats
Vegetables

Matter Of Taste, A C 14 MIN
16MM FILM, 3/4 OR 1/2 IN VIDEO P-I
Employs animation to show how taste information is sent from cells in taste buds on the tongue along nerve pathways to the brain. Describes the four common tastes and shows that what people eat depends on where they live and their personal experiences.
From The Human Senses Series.
LC NO. 82-706607
Prod-NGS Dist-NGS 1982

Matter Of Time - Time C 14 MIN
3/4 OR 1/2 INCH VIDEO CASSETTE P
Describes how a dream convinces Lionel that understanding time measurement is important.
From The Math Country Series.
Prod-KYTV Dist-AITECH 1979

Matter Of Time, A C 22 MIN
16MM FILM OPTICAL SOUND
Deals with the safe operation of large construction machines. Shows a series of accident vignettes, some described by the actual operators involved and others by witnesses.
LC NO. 77-701815
Prod-CLARK Dist-PILOT Prodn-PILOT 1976

Matter Of Time, A B 22 MIN
16MM FILM OPTICAL SOUND
Follows the drama of life through the activities of an ordinary French citizen. Reflects the problems faced by a barge skipper and his family in taking a cargo to Belgium.
Prod-VICASV Dist-RADIM

Matter Of Time, A C 97 MIN
16MM FILM OPTICAL SOUND H A
Tells the story of a chambermaid in pre-WWI Europe who is taught to love life by an eccentric contessa. Stars Liza Minnelli, Ingrid Bergman, Charles Boyer. Directed by Vincent Minnelli.
Prod-FWTVP Dist-TIMLIF 1976

Matter Of Time, A C 15 MIN
16MM FILM, 3/4 OR 1/2 IN VIDEO I
Tells how a light plane crashes, injuring one of the passengers. Explains that the other passengers and pilot are forced to do some fast decision-making.
From The Thinkabout Series. Solving Problems
LC NO. 81-706107
Prod-KOCETV Dist-AITECH 1979

Matter Of Time, A C 20 MIN
3/4 OR 1/2 INCH VIDEO CASSETTE P-I
Presents literary selections that deal with adventures in time and space and looks at the world of tomorrow.
From The Once Upon A Time Series.
Prod-MDDE Dist-AITECH 1977

Matter Of Time, A C 30 MIN
16MM FILM, 3/4 OR 1/2 IN VIDEO J-H A
Chronicles the painful period of growth which occurs for Lisa when she discovers that her mother has a malignant tumor and only a few months to live. Shows the girl emerging from her mother's shadow and discovering her own special talent.
LC NO. 81-707015
Prod-TAHSEM Dist-LCOA

Matter Of Understanding, A - The Coyote, His Story C 27 MIN
16MM FILM - 3/4 IN VIDEO
Examines the life and habits of coyotes and explains why they are misunderstood by humans. Discusses various methods of coyote control, encouraging selective removal of only killer coyotes.
LC NO. 79-706024
Prod-USEPA Dist-USNAC 1978

Matter Waves B 28 MIN
16MM FILM OPTICAL SOUND H-C
Presents a modern version of the original experiment which showed the wave behavior of the electron. Shows electron diffraction patterns on a flourescent screen and discusses the electron diffraction experiments of G p Thomson.
Prod-PSSC Dist-MLA 1962

Matter With Me, The C 15 MIN
16MM FILM, 3/4 OR 1/2 IN VIDEO H-C A
Follows the movements of a twelve-year-old Black boy through two worlds - one White, one Black. Shows the boy in various places in these two worlds and presents both worlds through the boy's eyes.
Prod-MONWIL Dist-AIMS 1972

Matter, Matter Everywhere - How Materials Change C 11 MIN
16MM FILM, 3/4 OR 1/2 IN VIDEO P
Shows that some changes in materials result in new materials with different characteristics.
From The Matter, Matter Everywhere Series.
Prod-CORF Dist-CORF 1970

Matter, Matter Everywhere - Its Smallest Parts C 14 MIN
16MM FILM, 3/4 OR 1/2 IN VIDEO P
Shows how the concept of atoms and molecules accounts for the three forms of matter. Children discover what molecules might be like and how they are believed to behave.
From The Matter, Matter Everywhere Series.
Prod-CORF Dist-CORF 1970

Matter, Matter Everywhere - Mixing And Dissolving C 11 MIN
16MM FILM, 3/4 OR 1/2 IN VIDEO P
Introduces the characteristics of mixtures and solutions. Shows children combining familiar materials and then try to separate them in order to learn about mixtures and solution.
From The Matter, Matter Everywhere Series.
Prod-CORF Dist-CORF 1970

Matter, Matter Everywhere - Solids, Liquids And Gas C 11 MIN
16MM FILM, 3/4 OR 1/2 IN VIDEO P
Explores ways of describing matter and explains how the three states of matter differ.
From The Matter, Matter Everywhere Series.
Prod-CORF Dist-CORF 1970

Matter, Matter Everywhere—A Series
16MM FILM, 3/4 OR 1/2 IN VIDEO P-I
Prod-CORF Dist-CORF 1970

Matter, Matter Everywhere - How Materials
Matter, Matter Everywhere - Its Smallest Parts 014 MIN
Matter, Matter Everywhere - Mixing And 011 MIN
Matter, Matter Everywhere - Solids, Liquids 011 MIN

Matter, The C 4 MIN
3/4 OR 1/2 INCH VIDEO CASSETTE
See series title for descriptive statement.
From The Four Short Programs By Woody Vasulka Series.
Prod-EAI Dist-EAI

Matters Of The Heart C 30 MIN
3/4 OR 1/2 INCH VIDEO CASSETTE
Looks at the research effort underway to combat heart disease. Discusses new diagnostic techniques as well as experimental methods of treatment.
From The Innovation Series.
Prod-WNETTV Dist-WNETTV 1983

Matthew C 6 MIN
16MM FILM OPTICAL SOUND
Follows a three-year-old child's exploration of a meadow.
LC NO. 77-700385
Prod-ASPTEF Dist-ASPTEF Prodn-HARDRM 1976

Matthew C 15 MIN
3/4 OR 1/2 INCH VIDEO CASSETTE J-H
Looks at Matthew, a wild brawler whose violent behavior culminates in attempted suicide after he is arrested for robbing a gas station.
From The Changing Series.
Prod-WGTETV Dist-AITECH 1980

Matthew Aliuk - Eskimo In Two Worlds C 18 MIN
16MM FILM, 3/4 OR 1/2 IN VIDEO I-J
Tells the story of Matthew, an Eskimo boy assimilated into the city life of Anchorage and his Uncle Isak, from a hunting village in the north, who represents a different tradition.
From The Many Americans Series.
LC NO. 73-701259
Prod-LCOA Dist-LCOA 1973

Matthew Manning - A Study Of A Psychic C 27 MIN
16MM FILM OPTICAL SOUND
Describes the experiences of Matthew Manning, a young British psychic.
LC NO. 75-704205
Prod-RAYMDB Dist-USCAN 1975

Matthew Manning - Study Of A Psychic C 30 MIN
3/4 OR 1/2 INCH VIDEO CASSETTE
Shows the life of English psychic Matthew Manning including his work with scientists trying to discover what produces his talent.
Prod-HP Dist-HP

Matthew Merian - European Engraver And Historian (1593 - 1650) B 14 MIN
16MM FILM OPTICAL SOUND
Presents the photo-journalism of the troubled age during the 17th century, showing the engraving of large and crowded scenes of city and country life in war and peace by Merian.
Prod-ROLAND Dist-ROLAND

Matthew 5.5 C 5 MIN
16MM FILM OPTICAL SOUND H-C A
Discusses chapter five, verse five of the gospel of Matthew, in the New Testament. Juxtaposes views of argumentative, 'INVOLVED' humanity with the poor, the derelict and the oppressed. Poses the question, 'WHO IS THE MEEK.' Views a grave, its preparation and closing as one suggestion of 'INHERITING THE EARTH.'
LC NO. 73-702538
Prod-FRACOC Dist-FRACOC 1973

Matthew, Your Mother Is Calling You - Marcel, Ta Mere T'Appelle C 9 MIN
16MM FILM, 3/4 OR 1/2 IN VIDEO J-C
Presents an animated story, without narration, in which two characters, formed from colored papers in a kaleidoscope, enjoy a world of fantasy that becomes disrupted by the conventions of life.

LC NO. 77-701525
Prod-LESFG Dist-TEXFLM 1977

Matthew's Broken Arm - First Visit To The Hospital C 12 MIN
16MM FILM, 3/4 OR 1/2 IN VIDEO P
Shares Matthew's experiences as he breaks his arm, is rushed to the hospital, has a cast applied and is introduced to the daily routines of a hospital.
Prod-IFB Dist-IFB

Maturational Lag And Specific Language Disabilities B 30 MIN
16MM FILM OPTICAL SOUND
Discusses maturational lag and Specific Language Disability as well as those borderline children who might be regarded as 'high risk' for failure. Explains the purpose of the Slingerland screening tests.
From The Slingerland Screening Tests For Identifying Children With Specific Language...series. Part A
Prod-EDPS Dist-EDPS

Mature Woman, The C 30 MIN
16MM FILM OPTICAL SOUND C A
Explains how myths, stereotypes and the media influence society's attitudes toward aging, especially aging women.
LC NO. 79-700916
Prod-AMERGA Dist-AACD 1976

Maturing Female, The C 14 MIN
16MM FILM OPTICAL SOUND J-H
Shows through a story that the teenager is rarely experienced enough to know her friends or herself as well as she think she does.
From The Family Life Education And Human Growth Series.
Prod-SF Dist-SF 1970

Maturing Market, The C 30 MIN
3/4 OR 1/2 INCH VIDEO CASSETTE
Explores the maturing of the marketplace and the resulting restructuring among information services, two of the top change issues facing information industry strategists.
From The Information Industry - Strategic Planning Considerations Series.
Prod-DELTAK Dist-DELTAK

Maturing Patterns In A Dancer's Life C 30 MIN
3/4 OR 1/2 INCH VIDEO CASSETTE
See series title for descriptive statement.
From The Dancers' Health Alert Series.
Prod-ARCVID Dist-ARCVID

Mau Mau C 28 MIN
16MM FILM, 3/4 OR 1/2 IN VIDEO H-C
An edited version of the motion picture Mau Mau. Analyzes the history of post World War II political events in Kenya. Documents how British over-reaction to a movement for native representation in the Kenyan colonial government led to repression and persecution. Presents a narrative account of how white settlers in Kenya responded to the nationalistic aspirations expressed through the Mau Mau movement.
Prod-FI Dist-FI 1973

Mau Mau C 51 MIN
16MM FILM, 3/4 OR 1/2 IN VIDEO H-C
Analyzes the history of post World War II political events in Kenya. Documents how British over-reaction to a movement for native representation in the Kenyan colonial government led to repression and persecution. Presents a narrative account of how white settlers in Kenya responded to the nationalistic aspirations expressed through the Mau Mau movement.
Prod-FI Dist-FI 1973

Maud Hart Lovelace 1892-1980 - A Minnesota Childhood C 14 MIN
3/4 OR 1/2 INCH VIDEO CASSETTE P-J
Portrays Lovelace's childhood in relation to her well-known Betsy-tacy books. Includes historical photographs and illustrations from the books. Explains the concept of historical fiction.
LC NO. 84-730300
Prod-HERPRO Dist-HERPRO 1984

Maud Lewis - A World Without Shadows C 10 MIN
16MM FILM, 3/4 OR 1/2 IN VIDEO J-C A
Presents a posthumous tribute to Maud Lewis, an untutored Nova Scotia painter.
Prod-NFBC Dist-PHENIX 1978

Maui And His Kite C 11 MIN
16MM FILM OPTICAL SOUND I-C A
Tells the story of Maui, demi-god hero of Polynesia, who assembles a kite of bamboo and tapa cloth and with a magic wind Calabash given to him by wind boy makes a flying machine.
Prod-CINEPC Dist-CINEPC

Maurice C 27 MIN
16MM FILM, 3/4 OR 1/2 IN VIDEO A
Examines the events of Oct 19, 1983 when members of Grenada's Provisional Revolutionary Government were assassinated. Portrays the following US invasion.
Prod-CNEMAG Dist-CNEMAG 1984

Maurice Hines, Mercedes Ellington, Dean Badolato And Valarie Pettiford C 30 MIN
3/4 OR 1/2 INCH VIDEO CASSETTE
Looks at today's 'Broadway gypsies.'
From The Eye On Dance - Broadway Dance Series.
Prod-ARTRES Dist-ARTRES

Maurice Sendak C 14 MIN
16MM FILM, 3/4 OR 1/2 IN VIDEO C A
Maurice Sendak, in his studio apartment, speaks of his favorite composers and expresses his admiration for painters and illustrators of the past. He discusses ways these artists have influenced his own work and traces the development of the book 'WHERE THE WILD THINGS ARE.'
Prod-WWS Dist-WWS Prodn-SCHNDL 1966

Mauritius C 28 MIN
3/4 INCH VIDEOTAPE
Interviews Sir Harold Walter, Minister of External Affairs of Mauritius. Shows the beauty of Mauritius and the lifestyles of its people. Hosted by Marilyn Perry.
From The International Byline Series.
Prod-PERRYM Dist-PERRYM

Maurits Escher - Painter Of Fantasies C 27 MIN
16MM FILM, 3/4 OR 1/2 IN VIDEO H-C
Shows how the works of this graphic artist are a curious blend of fact and fancy, with mirror images and interlocking figures flowing from symmetrical shapes. He discusses his art and philosophy, and the camera explores such works as 'DAY AND NIGHT' and 'ASCENDING AND DESCENDING.'
Prod-CORF Dist-CORF 1970

Mauro The Gypsy C 43 MIN
16MM FILM OPTICAL SOUND P-I
Tells about Mauro and his gypsy family having to move on.
Prod-LUF Dist-LUF

Maury Wills On Baserunning C 60 MIN
16MM FILM, 3/4 OR 1/2 IN VIDEO I-H
Presents baseball great Maury Will demonstrating good baserunning from the time the batter-runner leaves home plate until he scores or the inning ends. Includes tips on leading off, base stealing, sliding, the hit-and-run play and stretching an extra base out of a hit.
Prod-ATHI Dist-ATHI 1981

Maury Wills On Baserunning C 60 MIN
1/2 IN VIDEO CASSETTE BETA/VHS
Demonstrates baserunning techniques, from the time the batter-runner leaves home plate until he scores or the inning ends. Features Maury Wills, the man who broke Ty Cobb's base-stealing record.
Prod-MOHOMV Dist-MOHOMV

Maury Wills On Baserunning C 60 MIN
1/2 IN VIDEO CASSETTE BETA/VHS A
Presents Maury Wills, who demonstrates good baserunning techniques from the time the batter-runner leaves homeplate until he scores or the inning ends. Includes tips on leading off, base stealing, sliding, the hit and run play, stretching an extra base out of a hit and other items.
Prod-RMI Dist-RMI

Max C 20 MIN
16MM FILM, 3/4 OR 1/2 IN VIDEO
Presents a story about an aspiring actress who stays late one night to work on her performance in a Broadway show. Tells how she meets the night watchman, an ex-vaudevillian, who, after hearing her emote, says that she would be better off marrying a doctor. Concludes with her insisting on pursuing her acting career.
LC NO. 79-706429
Prod-GILLAX Dist-CAROUF 1979

Max Adrian As George Bernard Shaw C 90 MIN
16MM FILM OPTICAL SOUND J-C A
Features British actor Max Adrian in a one-man show as the playwright, George Bernard Shaw. Presents lines from Shaw's own writing to evoke the spirit of the playwright from age 38 to just before his death at 93.
Prod-CANTOR Dist-CANTOR

Max Almy - Deadline C 4 MIN
3/4 OR 1/2 INCH VIDEO CASSETTE
Considers corporate demand and personal drive.
Prod-ARTINC Dist-ARTINC

Max Almy - Leaving The 20th Century C 11 MIN
3/4 OR 1/2 INCH VIDEO CASSETTE
Compares social retardation and technical progress.
Prod-ARTINC Dist-ARTINC

Max Almy - Modern Times B 30 MIN
3/4 OR 1/2 INCH VIDEO CASSETTE
Explores personal relationships and women's roles.
Prod-ARTINC Dist-ARTINC

Max Almy - Perfect Leader C 4 MIN
3/4 OR 1/2 INCH VIDEO CASSETTE
Addresses the coding of a politician for an effective television image.
Prod-ARTINC Dist-ARTINC

Max Bill C 16 MIN
16MM FILM OPTICAL SOUND
Introduces painter Max Bill, including views of his exhibits and of the painter at work.
LC NO. 77-700386
Prod-COMSKY Dist-COMSKY 1976

Max Ernst - Journey Into The Subconscious (1891-1976) C 12 MIN
16MM FILM OPTICAL SOUND
Follows Max Ernst into the undersea world of the subconscious where people are confused with birds and forests melt.
Prod-ROLAND Dist-ROLAND

Max Made Mischief - An Approach To Literature C 30 MIN
16MM FILM OPTICAL SOUND C T
Shows a third grade class as two teachers try out a new curriculum which uses Maurice Sendak's children's book Where The Wild Things Are to introduce the children to the study and appreciation of literature. Shows the teachers in a discussion with Sendak.
LC NO. 78-700675
Prod-MASON Dist-DOCUFL 1977

Max Und Moritz C 80 MIN
16MM FILM OPTICAL SOUND
A German language motion picture. Presents the story of two boys who aggravate the townspeople by constantly thinking up new pranks until the furious miller takes justice into his own hands. A musical production of a picture book by Wilhelm Busch.
Prod-WSTGLC Dist-WSTGLC 1956

Maxi Multiplication C 15 MIN
3/4 INCH VIDEO CASSETTE I
Tells how to multiply three-digit numbers by two-digit numbers. Shows how to check by lattice multiplication.
From The Math - No Mystery Series.
Prod-WCETTV Dist-GPITVL 1977

Maxillary Lateral Incisor, Information Phases, The C 11 MIN
1/2 IN VIDEO CASSETTE BETA/VHS PRO
Describes the cosmetic changes occurring after this restoration.
Prod-RMI Dist-RMI

Maxillofacial Prosthetics - Fabrication Of A Nasal Prosthesis C 19 MIN
3/4 OR 1/2 INCH VIDEO CASSETTE PRO
Demonstrates techniques used in fabricating a nasal prosthesis from the material PDM siloxane. Shows preparation of the stone mold, casting, pressing and heating.
Prod-VAMCNY Dist-USNAC

Maxillofacial Prosthetics - Fabrication Of An Ear Prosthesis C 15 MIN
16MM FILM, 3/4 OR 1/2 IN VIDEO PRO
Shows the steps involved in the fabrication of a polydimethylsiloxane ear prosthesis. Emphasizes timely rehabilitation of patients with facial defects.
Prod-USVA Dist-USNAC

Maxillofacial Prosthetics - Fabrication Of An Ear Prosthesis C 15 MIN
3/4 OR 1/2 INCH VIDEO CASSETTE
Describes in detail the clinical and laboratory steps involved in the fabrication of a polydimethylsiloxane ear prothesis. Emphasizes the timely rehabilitation of patients with facial defects.
Prod-VADTC Dist-AMDA 1980

Maxima And Minima In Several Variables B 34 MIN
3/4 OR 1/2 INCH VIDEO CASSETTE
See series title for descriptive statement.
From The Calculus Of Several Variables - Matrix-- Algebra Series.
Prod-MIOT Dist-MIOT

Maximizing Input With Aphasic Patients C 102 MIN
3/4 OR 1/2 INCH VIDEO CASSETTE
Emphasizes maximizing activation of the brain. Gives attention to the role of cues, syntactic and semantic complexity.
Prod-PUAVC Dist-PUAVC 1981

Maximizing Witness Cooperation C 22 MIN
16MM FILM, 3/4 OR 1/2 IN VIDEO PRO
Dramatizes the problem of the uncooperative witness and gives police officers guidelines on how to deal with witnesses and overcome problems.
Prod-HAR Dist-MTI 1977

Maximizing Your Conferences Resources C 18 MIN
3/4 OR 1/2 INCH VIDEO CASSETTE
Outlines some ways for getting a conference off to a positive start. Shows ways to get the group participating and the different 'roles' of conferees.
From The Conference Leading Skills Series.
Prod-RESEM Dist-RESEM

Maximum C 14 MIN
16MM FILM OPTICAL SOUND H-C A
Presents a montage featuring Swedish ballet dancers. Illustrates good work habits and physical conditioning for female office workers and homemakers.
LC NO. FIA66-481
Prod-AETNA Dist-AETNA 1965

Maximum Effort C 28 MIN
16MM FILM, 3/4 OR 1/2 IN VIDEO
Looks at the racing prowess of the Kialoa, an 80-foot modern maxi-boat.
Prod-OFFSHR Dist-OFFSHR 1981

Maxwell-Boltzmann Distribution C 4 MIN
16MM FILM OPTICAL SOUND H-C A
Presents particles in a box which are started off with the same speed in random directions. Shows that as they collide, their speeds change. Develops histograms at different temperatures to illustrate the steady-state distribution of speeds. Includes two-dimensional Maxwell-Boltzmann curves which are superimposed over the histograms.
From The Kinetic Theory By Computer Animation Series.
LC NO. 73-703249
Prod-KALMIA Dist-KALMIA 1973

Maxwellian And Druyvesteyn Distributions C
3/4 OR 1/2 INCH VIDEO CASSETTE IND
Cites Maxwellian and Druyvesteyn distributions as derived from the Boltzmann equation and compares them. Gives their respective dependence on electron energy. Outlines evaluation of the collision integral and Boltzmann equation for these cases. Discusses the importance of 'tail electrons' and how they 'wag.'
From The Plasma Process Technology Fundamentals Series.
Prod-COLOSU Dist-COLOSU

May I Go To The Library C 15 MIN
2 INCH VIDEOTAPE P
See series title for descriptive statement.
From The Avenida De Ingles Series.
Prod-SDITVA Dist-GPITVL

May I Have A C 15 MIN
2 INCH VIDEOTAPE P
See series title for descriptive statement.
From The Avenida De Ingles Series.
Prod-SDITVA Dist-GPITVL

May I Speak To Mr Page C 25 MIN
16MM FILM OPTICAL SOUND C A
Presents firsthand reports of Christian literature work in 19 countries. Shows the travels of Mr Page commitments from the Wheaton office to all parts of the world.
Prod-CBFMS Dist-CBFMS

May I Speak To The Women Of The House? C 28 MIN
3/4 INCH VIDEO CASSETTE
Examines life conditions for single mothers and government inaction regarding these women. Follows a single mother through daily activities as she tries to provide food, clothing and care for her six children on monthly government benefits of $663.
Prod-OTCME Dist-WMENIF

May It Be C 29 MIN
16MM FILM OPTICAL SOUND
Shows Israel after the Yom Kippur War and just before the tragedy at Ma'alot and continues to New York to see Jews in need and the people who help them. Hosted by Herschel Bernardi.
LC NO. 76-700384
Prod-UJA Dist-ALDEN Prodn-NOWAKA 1975

May O'Donnell, Ray Green, Kenneth Rinker And Tim DeBaets C 30 MIN
3/4 OR 1/2 INCH VIDEO CASSETTE
See series title for descriptive statement.
From The Eye On Dance - The Business And Law Of Dance Series.
Prod-ARTRES Dist-ARTRES

May Peace Begin With Me C 29 MIN
16MM FILM OPTICAL SOUND
Shows four young men, including a Pole, an Iraqui and two Israeli-born Jews, as they leave their frontier kibbutz for family holidays in the city. Follows their journey and family experiences to reveal the diversity of their backgrounds and the meaning of the land as it affects new and older generations in Israel.
LC NO. 73-700737
Prod-GUG Dist-GUG 1972

May We Help You? (Spanish) C 1 MIN
3/4 OR 1/2 INCH VIDEO CASSETTE
Illustrates message of answering public questions about cancer with stylized photography of inner workings of telephone. Uses TV spot format.
Prod-AMCS Dist-AMCS 1982

May 1968 C 10 MIN
16MM FILM OPTICAL SOUND
Presents a brief account of the organizing work of the French students in Paris during April and May of 1968. Shows the brutal repression of the state to try and crush the newly formed worker student alliance.
Prod-NEWSR Dist-NEWSR

May's Miracle C 28 MIN
16MM FILM, 3/4 OR 1/2 IN VIDEO H-C A
Presents a documentary about May Lemke who adopted a blind severely retarded and cerebral palsied baby. Tells how the boy at age 16 suddenly began to play the piano. Shows how he performs on the piano with vigorous emotion and imitates singers from the past. Points out that May believes that what happened was a miracle, but certainly her steadfast mothering contributed to the development of his unusual potential.
From The Man Alive Series.
LC NO. 82-707328
Prod-CANBC Dist-FLMLIB 1982

Maya Angelou C 29 MIN
3/4 OR 1/2 INCH VIDEO CASSETTE H-C A
Tells how thirty years after she left it, Maya Angelou, poet, musician and actress returns to Stamps, Arkansas, the rural southern town where she grew up.
From The Creativity With Bill Moyers Series.
LC NO. 83-706228
Prod-CORPEL Dist-PBS 1982

Maya Lords Of The Jungle C 58 MIN
3/4 OR 1/2 INCH VIDEO CASSETTE
Visits ancient sites on the Yucatan Peninsula where new findings are forcing a reappraisal of the past of the Mayans.
From The Odyssey Series.
LC NO. 82-706433
Prod-PBA Dist-PBS

Maya, The - Crocodile City C 30 MIN
3/4 OR 1/2 INCH VIDEO CASSETTE H-C A
Chronicles a dig in Belize, where archeologists and local workers uncovered an ancient Mayan civilization centered at Lamanai. Discusses the culture of the Mayans and the reasons for their demise.
Prod-CANBC Dist-JOU

Mayakovsky - The Poetry Of Action C 22 MIN
16MM FILM, 3/4 OR 1/2 IN VIDEO H-C A
Presents a portrait, in his own words and tells through his own paintings and drawings of the poetic genius, Vladimir Mayakovsky, who cast a hypnotic spell over the artistic and literary life of Russia in the twenties.
Prod-MANTLH Dist-FOTH 1972

Mayaland C 40 MIN
16MM FILM, 3/4 OR 1/2 IN VIDEO
Discusses the Maya civilization, focusing on sites in Mexico, Guatemala and Honduras.
Prod-MACM Dist-FI

Mayaland Safari C 33 MIN
16MM FILM OPTICAL SOUND J-C A
Relates the story of the Mayans, showing five ancient Mayan cities. Describes the advanced Mayan Stone-Age civilization. Presents illustrations of Mayan architecture, sculpture, pottery and textile products.
LC NO. 70-701923
Prod-HENSON Dist-AVED 1964

Mayan Mystery, The C 17 MIN
16MM FILM, 3/4 OR 1/2 IN VIDEO I A
Shows the ruins of the major Mayan cities in Mexico, Guatemala and the Honduras. Lists possible explanations for the decline of the Mayas.
Prod-HP Dist-AIMS 1970

Mayas, The C 11 MIN
16MM FILM, 3/4 OR 1/2 IN VIDEO I-C
Surveys the Mayan civilization, pointing out the history, culture and achievements of the Indians. Pictures the ruins of the ancient city of Tikal in Guatemala, Uxmal and Chichen Itza.
Prod-CORF Dist-CORF 1957

Maybe Next Week Sometime C 30 MIN
16MM FILM OPTICAL SOUND I-C A
Examines black roots music as it exists in the rural South. Includes music ranging from folk and rock to spirituals and the ceremonial music of the Yoruba people of South Carolina.
LC NO. 75-701088
Prod-BOWRTD Dist-RADIM 1975

Maybe Tomorrow C 20 MIN
2 INCH VIDEOTAPE
Emphasizes the implications of interracial romance within the Black community and the influence the community has on them.
Prod-SPRHIL Dist-PUBTEL

Mayday B 15 MIN
16MM FILM OPTICAL SOUND
Presents the events of the MayDay rally at San Francisco's federal building in honor of Huey P Newton, minister of defense of the Black Panther party and political prisoner.
From The Black Liberation Series.
Prod-SFN Dist-SFN 1969

Mayday Realtime B 60 MIN
3/4 OR 1/2 INCH VIDEO CASSETTE
Shows a personal journal shot on May 3, 1971, in Washington, DC, during the attempted takeover of the city's traffic system by dissident groups as a protest against the Vietnam War.
Prod-EAI Dist-EAI

Mayday, Mayday C 50 MIN
16MM FILM, 3/4 OR 1/2 IN VIDEO I
Portrays what happens when a plane crashes and young Mark and Allison set out in the wilderness to seek help for their injured parents. Shows them learning to rely on each other and courageously keeping going despite being threatened by a pack of wild dogs, an angry rattlesnake and the ever-increasing threat of nightfall. Produced for the ABC Weekend Specials.
Prod-ABCLR Dist-MTI 1983

Mayflower Story, The C 25 MIN
16MM FILM - 3/4 IN VIDEO
Presents the Mayflower story and how history was re-enacted through Mayflower II, a faithful replica of the pilgrim ship of 1620. Shows how it was built and siled across the Atlantic in 1957.
Prod-AEROMT Dist-MTP

Mayfly, The - Ecology Of An Aquatic Insect C 15 MIN
16MM FILM, 3/4 OR 1/2 IN VIDEO J-H
Shows a small, delicate mayfly and species called hexagenia bilineata along parts of the Mississippi River. Includes laboratory shots where the natural environment of the mayfly was duplicated to permit a more controlled study of its habits. Shows the lifespan of all mayfly species.
From The Biology Series. Unit 1 - Ecology
Prod-EBEC Dist-EBEC 1973

Mayo Clinic C 22 MIN
16MM FILM OPTICAL SOUND
Discusses the history and philosophy of the Mayo Clinic, emphasizing that the most important ingredient in the success of the clinic is its people.
LC NO. 75-703626
Prod-MAYO Dist-MAYO Prodn-FULLER 1975

Mayor Ed Koch C 60 MIN
3/4 OR 1/2 INCH VIDEO CASSETTE
See series title for descriptive statement.
From The John Callaway Interviews Series.
Prod-WTTWTV Dist-PBS 1981

Maypo Animated Commercial C 1 MIN
3/4 OR 1/2 INCH VIDEO CASSETTE
Shows a classic animated television commercial with the line, 'I Want My Maypo.'
Prod-BROOKC Dist-BROOKC

Mazda Mood C 3 MIN
16MM FILM OPTICAL SOUND
Presents a 'teaser' shown to Mazda automobile dealers to introduce the Mazda RZ-7 car.
LC NO. 78-701313
Prod-DEULAU Dist-DEULAU 1978

Maze, The C 30 MIN
16MM FILM OPTICAL SOUND H-C A
Studies t8e case of William Kurelek, a professional artist who was once a patient in a mental hospital, in order to investigate the cause, nature, and cure of a common mental disorder. Tells how his illness was evident in his paintings, and includes interviews with his psychiatrist, priest and family.
From The Films At The Frontier Of Psychological Inquiry Series.
LC NO. 72-702199
Prod-HMC Dist-HMC 1971

Maze, The B 81 MIN
16MM FILM OPTICAL SOUND
Presents a horror story with frightstricken women, strange monsters and a corridor of hideous winged bats. Stars Richard Carlson and Veronica Hunt. Available In 3-D.
Prod-UNKNWN Dist-KITPAR 1953

Mbira - Matepe Dza Mhondoro, A Healing Party C 20 MIN
16MM FILM, 3/4 OR 1/2 IN VIDEO
Presents a re-enactment of a healing ceremony in order to show the performance of two complete songs on one type of mbira. Features the famous matepe player Saini Murira as he leads a group of four players. Includes traditional healing dances.
From The Mbira Series.
Prod-PSU Dist-PSU

Mbira - Njari, Karanga Songs In Christian Ceremonies With Simon Mashoko C 24 MIN
16MM FILM, 3/4 OR 1/2 IN VIDEO
Shows Magwenyambira Simon Mashoko, a rural Catholic catechist and Mbira Njari player. Demonstrates his adaptation of the mbira for use in the Catholic church. Includes his participation in dance parties, in catechism classes and a Sunday church service held at his home.
From The Mbira Series.
Prod-PSU Dist-PSU

Mbira - The Technique Of The Mbira Dza Vadzimu C 19 MIN
16MM FILM, 3/4 OR 1/2 IN VIDEO
Provides an introduction to the musical technique and sound of the Mbira dza Vadzium as played by Ephat Mujuru. Demonstrates some of the rhythmic and harmonic elements of the music through animation and freeze-frame techniques. Presents various traditional songs to illustrate the use of improvisation, different styles of playing and the combination of two mbiras in duet.
From The Mbira Series.
Prod-PSU Dist-PSU

Mbira Dza Vadzimu - Dambatsoko, An Old Cult Centre With Muchatera And Ephat Mujuri C 51 MIN
16MM FILM OPTICAL SOUND H-C A
Shows traditional South African cult ceremonies performed by Muchatera and Ephat Mujuru, including a spirit possession ceremony, prayers and a blood sacrifice.
From The Mbira Series.
LC NO. 78-700698
Prod-ZANTZA Dist-PSUPCR 1978

Mbira Dza Vadzimu - Dambatsoko, An Old Cult Center With Muchatera And Ephat Mujuru C 51 MIN
3/4 OR 1/2 INCH VIDEO CASSETTE
Focuses on the life of the late Muchatera Mujuru, leader of one of the few remaining traditional cult centers in Shona country in Zimbabwe. Looks at various aspects of his life and the life of his adherents at Dambatsoko. Shows several kinds of ceremonies.
From The Mbira Series.
Prod-PSU Dist-PSU

Mbira Dza Vadzimu - Religion At The Family Level With Gwanzura Gwenzi C 66 MIN
16MM FILM, 3/4 OR 1/2 IN VIDEO
Establishes a religious background for further films in the series by examining the life of Gwanzura Gwenzi, a man in his middle forties. Shows him at work at home on weekends. Demonstrates an all-night bira, or spirit seance.
From The Mbira Series.
Prod-PSU Dist-PSU

Mbira Dza Vadzimu - Urban And Rural Ceremonies With Hakurotwi Mudhe C 45 MIN
16MM FILM, 3/4 OR 1/2 IN VIDEO
Presents a portrait of Hakurotwi Mudhe, singer and leader of a professional group of mbira players. Shows him in various kinds of performances. Includes an informal urban Friday night bira, a sacrifice and a funeral.
From The Mbira Series.
Prod-PSU Dist-PSU

Mbira—A Series

Examines the use of the traditional African mbira in the cultural life of the Shona people of Rhodesia (Zimbabwe). Demonstrates the techniques used to play the mibira. Shows several performances of the Mbira dza Vadzimu in different settings. Looks at how the Mbira Njari is performed in a traditional village setting and then adapted for use in a contemporary Catholic religious meeting.
Prod-PSU Dist-PSU

Mbira - Matepe Dza Mhondoro, A Healing Party 021 MIN
Mbira - Njari, Karanga Songs In Christian 024 MIN
Mbira - The Technique Of The Mbira Dza Vadzimu 019 MIN
Mbira Dza Vadzimu - Dambatsoko, An Old Cult 045 MIN
Mbira Dza Vadzimu - Religion At The Family 066 MIN
Mbira Dza Vadzimu - Urban And Rural 045 MIN

MBO I - What Is MBO C 13 MIN
16MM FILM, 3/4 OR 1/2 IN VIDEO A
Presents skeptical Charlie at a management by objectives training session where he asks pertinent questions about the philosophy and implementation of management by objectives.
From The Management By Objectives Series.
Prod-BOSUST Dist-CRMP 1981

MBO II - Developing Objectives C 14 MIN
16MM FILM, 3/4 OR 1/2 IN VIDEO A
Presents precise guidelines for well-written objectives.
From The Management By Objectives Series.
Prod-BOSUST Dist-CRMP 1981

MBO III - Performance Appraisal C 14 MIN
16MM FILM, 3/4 OR 1/2 IN VIDEO A
Illustrates the process of management by objectives in action through the techniques of a good performance appraisal.
From The Management By Objectives Series.
Prod-BOSUST Dist-CRMP 1981

Mc Carthy Vs Welch B 25 MIN
16MM FILM, 3/4 OR 1/2 IN VIDEO J-C
Features televised hearings of the Senate commitee investigating charges ranging from black mail to treason brought by Sen Mc Carthy against the Army.
From The Men In Crisis Series.
Prod-WOLPER Dist-FI Prodn-METROM

Mc Culloch V Maryland C 36 MIN
16MM FILM, 3/4 OR 1/2 IN VIDEO H-C
Presents a dramatization of the landmark U S Supreme Court case of Mc Culloch v Maryland in which the Court struck down Maryland's attempt to tax a federally chartered bank.
From The Equal Justice Under Law Series.
Prod-USJUDC Dist-USNAC Prodn-WQED 1977

MC Squared - The Prometheus Factor C 10 MIN
16MM FILM OPTICAL SOUND
Traces man's use of non-renewable fuel resources from the invention of the steam engine to mass production and excessive consumption. Explores ways of meeting energy needs through the use of wastes, renewable resources and the forces of nature.
LC NO. 80-701246
Prod-GAPAC Dist-MTP Prodn-MARALF 1980

McAllister's Dream C 30 MIN
3/4 OR 1/2 INCH VIDEO CASSETTE
Centers on 43-year-old Fred McAllister, an actor for almost 25 years, who is still waiting for artistic success between the commercials he does to make ends meet. Reveals that he is torn between the desires of his girlfriend and his agent, but that he finally gets his chance when a friend asks him to audition for a major film.
Prod-MDCPB Dist-MDCPB

McBroom's Zoo / The Finches' Fabulous Furnace C 15 MIN
3/4 OR 1/2 INCH VIDEO CASSETTE P
See series title for descriptive statement.
From The Best Of Cover To Cover 1 Series.
Prod-WETATV Dist-WETATV

McCulloch Vs Maryland C
3/4 OR 1/2 INCH VIDEO CASSETTE H
Describes the national-bank case that established the 'implied powers' of the federal government.
From The Supreme Court Decisions That Changed The Nation Series.
Prod-GA Dist-GA

McGee, James / Dale Bertch C 29 MIN
3/4 INCH VIDEO CASSETTE
Discusses urban planning, including planning for the poor and the problem of urban sprawl.
From The Like It Is Series.
Prod-OHC Dist-HRC

McKonkey's Ferry - Christmas 1776 C 28 MIN
3/4 INCH VIDEO CASSETTE
Re-creates George Washington's victories at the Battle of Trenton.
Prod-NJPBA Dist-PUBTEL

MCRI Medicine Training Tape C 51 MIN
3/4 OR 1/2 INCH VIDEO CASSETTE
Shows step-by-step procedure which each child and family goes through during evaluations at Meyer Children's Rehabilitation Institute of the University of Nebraska Medical Center. Shows the home visit by a nurse, a family social work interview, a psychological testing session, a medical evaluation, a staffing, and the resulting interpretation.
Prod-UNEBO Dist-UNEBO

MC68000 Microprocessor—A Series
IND
Details ten-lecture course that unravels and clarifies complicated and sophisticated instructions of the 68000 chip.
Prod-COLOSU Dist-COLOSU

Advanced Instructions	030 MIN
Arithmetic, Data And Control Instructions	030 MIN
Asynchronous Bus And Function Control Pins	030 MIN
Indirect Addressing Modes	030 MIN
Introduction To The Programming Model	030 MIN
Modern Programming Practices	030 MIN
Processing States And Exception	030 MIN
Program Exercises	030 MIN
Program Manipulation Instructions	030 MIN
Simple Addressing Modes	030 MIN

MDTA Building Towards A Job Future C 5 MIN
16MM FILM, 3/4 OR 1/2 IN VIDEO
Shows how the Manpower Development and Training Act program makes use of experienced instructors and realistic work settings to train people in occupations in which there are known labor shortages. Issued in 1967 as a motion picture.
From The Career Job Opportunity Film Series.
LC NO. 79-707881
Prod-USDLMA Dist-USNAC Prodn-DEROCH 1979

Me C 10 MIN
16MM FILM OPTICAL SOUND
Draws a parallel between the integrity of the guitar craftsman and the pride of workmanship in all the people who are involved in the manufacture of intricate computers.
LC NO. 72-700046
Prod-RCAM Dist-RCAM 1971

Me C 85 MIN
16MM FILM OPTICAL SOUND
Presents the story of a young man whose cluttered personal life prevents him from becoming a writer.
LC NO. 75-704321
Prod-CFDEVC Dist-CFDEVC 1974

Me C 17 MIN
16MM FILM, 3/4 OR 1/2 IN VIDEO P-I
Deals with self image, identity and personal worth. Shows that each person is unique and each individual's identity is worth preserving and nurturing. Concludes with the statement that damage can be caused by trying to change your image to someone or something you are not.
Prod-PHENIX Dist-CORF 1972

Me (Spanish) C 17 MIN
16MM FILM, 3/4 OR 1/2 IN VIDEO P-I
Explores a child's view of himself and his own image of himself. Shows that each person is unique and that each individual's identity is worth preserving and nurturing.
Prod-PHENIX Dist-CORF 1972

Me - A Cop C 29 MIN
16MM FILM OPTICAL SOUND J-C A
Shows some of the incidents which happen to a policeman on his daily duties. Helps encourage young people of high school and college age to consider a career in law enforcement.
LC NO. 74-703252
Prod-WGTV Dist-WGTV 1974

Me - A Self-Awareness Film C 10 MIN
16MM FILM, 3/4 OR 1/2 IN VIDEO P-I
Creates an awareness of personal identity, the five senses, feelings and the Golden rule. Uses a combination of live action, music, animation and mime.
Prod-MCDOCR Dist-MTI 1974

Me Alone, On My Own C 20 MIN
3/4 OR 1/2 INCH VIDEO CASSETTE P-I
Explores literary selections that deal with personal problems and the need to face them.
From The Once Upon A Town Series.
Prod-MDDE Dist-AITECH 1977

Me And Dad's New Wife C 33 MIN
16MM FILM, 3/4 OR 1/2 IN VIDEO
Presents the story of a seventh grade girl who, on her first day back in school, discovers her father's new wife is to be her math teacher. Based on the book A Smart Kid Like You by Stella Pevsner. Originally shown on the television series ABC Afterschool Specials.
From The Teenage Years Series.
LC NO. 79-707365
Prod-WILSND Dist-TIMLIF 1976

Me And Mom - An Autobiography C 23 MIN
3/4 OR 1/2 INCH VIDEO CASSETTE
Presents a one-woman show about a family of four who represent a composite self. Deals with inter-generational conflict and affection.
Prod-KITCHN Dist-KITCHN

Me And My Brother B 91 MIN
16MM FILM OPTICAL SOUND
Studies the alienation of a man who lives and travels with his brother and the poet Allen Ginsberg. Shows that his alientation is severe enough to be labeled schizophrenia.
Prod-NYFLMS Dist-NYFLMS 1968

Me And My Senses C 10 MIN
16MM FILM, 3/4 OR 1/2 IN VIDEO P-I
Helps children discover the world around them by taking them on a sensory trip to the zoo, emphasizing their senses of sight, sound, touch, taste and smell.
Prod-KINGSP Dist-PHENIX 1970

Me And My Song B 30 MIN
16MM FILM OPTICAL SOUND H-C A
A poetic recitative dramatization about the Harlem renaissance using excerpts from the works of the poets of the 1920's, including the works of Langston Hughes, Sterling Brown, Countee Cullen, Claude Mc Kay, and others which depict the mood and direction of the black community at that time. Features Barbara Ann Teer and the National Black Theatre.
From The Black History Series.
LC NO. 77-704084
Prod-WCBSTV Dist-HRAW 1969

Me And Sam Mc Gee C 26 MIN
16MM FILM OPTICAL SOUND
Shows the trail of '98 through the Klondike gold fields in Canada.
LC NO. 76-702089
Prod-PKCYT Dist-CTFL Prodn-CHET 1975

Me And Stella C 24 MIN
16MM FILM, 3/4 OR 1/2 IN VIDEO H-C A
Interviews Elizabeth Cotton, whose success in song-writing proves that age and race need not be impediments to life.
Prod-ASHUR Dist-PHENIX 1977

Me And The Monsters C 9 MIN
16MM FILM OPTICAL SOUND P
Presents six major problems (six monsters) that confront the young. Includes the notorious danger of drug abuse, failure at school, fearsome adults, kids of other skin color, fighting at home and being disliked.
LC NO. 72-702652
Prod-BBF Dist-BBF 1972

Me And We C 17 MIN
16MM FILM, 3/4 OR 1/2 IN VIDEO A
Tells the story of a new supervisor who is responsible for keeping the organization's communication pipeline open. Shows how the supevisor develops a four-point plan to bring the employees together in a cooperative, productive team.
From The Quality, Production And Me Series.
Prod-PORTA Dist-RTBL 1982

Me And We (Dutch) C 17 MIN
16MM FILM, 3/4 OR 1/2 IN VIDEO A
Tells the story of a new supervisor who is responsible for keeping the organization's communication pipeline open. Shows how the supervisor develops a four-point plan to bring employees together in a cooperative, productive team.
From The Quality, Production And Me Series.
Prod-PORTA Dist-RTBL 1982

Me And We (French) C 17 MIN
16MM FILM, 3/4 OR 1/2 IN VIDEO A
Tells the story of a new supervisor who is responsible for keeping the organization's communication pipeline open. Shows how the supervisor develops a four-point plan to bring employees together in a cooperative, productive team.
From The Quality, Production And Me Series.
Prod-PORTA Dist-RTBL 1982

Me And We (Portuguese) C 17 MIN
16MM FILM, 3/4 OR 1/2 IN VIDEO A
Tells the story of a new supervisor who is responsible for keeping the organization's communication pipeline open. Shows how the supervisor develops a four-point plan to bring employees together in a cooperative, productive team.
From The Quality, Production And Me Series.
Prod-PORTA Dist-RTBL 1982

Me And We (Spanish) C 17 MIN
16MM FILM, 3/4 OR 1/2 IN VIDEO A
Tells the story of a new supervisor who is responsible for keeping the organization's communication pipeline open. Shows how the supervisor develops a four-point plan to bring employees together in a cooperative, productive team.
From The Quality, Production And Me Series.
Prod-PORTA Dist-RTBL 1982

Me And We (Swedish) C 17 MIN
16MM FILM, 3/4 OR 1/2 IN VIDEO A
Tells the story of a new supervisor who is responsible for keeping the organization's communication pipeline open. Shows how the supervisor develops a four-point plan to bring employees together in a cooperative, productive team.
From The Quality, Production And Me Series.
Prod-PORTA Dist-RTBL 1982

Me And You C 17 MIN
16MM FILM OPTICAL SOUND
Uses animation to show new supervisors the importance of dealing with new employees on an individual, rather than impersonal, level.
LC NO. 79-701178
Prod-UPJOHN Dist-UPJOHN Prodn-PORTAP 1979

Me And You C 12 MIN
16MM FILM, 3/4 OR 1/2 IN VIDEO A
Explains how supervisors can make sure employees develop to their maximum potential.
From The Quality, Production And Me Series.
Prod-PORTA Dist-RTBL 1982

Me And You (Dutch) C 12 MIN
16MM FILM, 3/4 OR 1/2 IN VIDEO A
Explains how supervisors can make sure employees develop to their maximum potential.
From The Quality, Production And Me Series.
Prod-PORTA Dist-RTBL 1982

Me And You (French) C 12 MIN
16MM FILM, 3/4 OR 1/2 IN VIDEO A
Explains how supervisors can make sure employees develop to their maximum potential.
From The Quality, Production And Me Series.
Prod-PORTA Dist-RTBL 1982

Me And You (Norwegian) C 12 MIN
16MM FILM, 3/4 OR 1/2 IN VIDEO A
Explains how supervisors can make sure employees develop to their maximum potential.
From The Quality, Production And Me Series.
Prod-PORTA Dist-RTBL 1982

Me And You (Portuguese) C 12 MIN
16MM FILM, 3/4 OR 1/2 IN VIDEO A
Explains how supervisors can make sure employees develop to their maximum potential.
From The Quality, Production And Me Series.
Prod-PORTA Dist-RTBL 1982

Me And You (Spanish) C 12 MIN
16MM FILM, 3/4 OR 1/2 IN VIDEO A
Explains how supervisors can make sure employees develop to their maximum potential.
From The Quality, Production And Me Series.
Prod-PORTA Dist-RTBL 1982

Me And You Kangaroo C 19 MIN
16MM FILM, 3/4 OR 1/2 IN VIDEO I-C A

Presents a story about the love of a young Australian boy for the baby kangaroo which he raises after its mother has been accidentally killed by a car.
Prod-LCOA Dist-LCOA 1974

Me And You Kangaroo (Captioned) C 19 MIN
16MM FILM, 3/4 OR 1/2 IN VIDEO P-I
Presents the story of a young Australian boy who raises a kangaroo and then must set it free.
Prod-LCOA Dist-LCOA 1974

Me Of The Moment, The C 20 MIN
3/4 OR 1/2 INCH VIDEO CASSETTE I
Presents dramatizations of literary works that deal with the search for self-knowledge and self-understanding.
From The Readers' Cube Series.
Prod-MDDE Dist-AITECH 1977

Me Tomorrow, The C 15 MIN
3/4 INCH VIDEO CASSETTE P
Reveals the differences between a growing, changing community and the apparent stagnation of a town which has resisted change. Suggests that an open mind facilitates change.
From The Becoming Me, Unit 2 - Social Identity Series.
Prod-KUONTV Dist-GPITVL 1974

Me Too C 3 MIN
16MM FILM, 3/4 OR 1/2 IN VIDEO K-I
Tells of a young boy who destroys a sand castle built by a group of children who excluded him from their play. Discusses feelings of rejection.
From The Magic Moments Series.
Prod-EBEC Dist-EBEC 1969

ME 1 C 6 MIN
3/4 OR 1/2 INCH VIDEO CASSETTE PRO
Covers energy systems, thermal and fluid processes on six 60-minute videotaped lectures.
From The Professional Engineering Review Series.
Prod-NCSU Dist-AMCEE

ME 2 C 7 MIN
3/4 OR 1/2 INCH VIDEO CASSETTE PRO
Covers mechanical analysis and design on seven 60-minute videotaped lectures.
From The Professional Engineering Review Series.
Prod-NCSU Dist-AMCEE

Me, A Teen Father C 13 MIN
16MM FILM, 3/4 OR 1/2 IN VIDEO J-C A
Explores the pressures, the moments of nostalgic tenderness, the guilt, ambivalence, anguish and anger of a teenage boy who has just learned that his girlfriend is pregnant.
LC NO. 80-707322
Prod-GORKER Dist-CORF 1980

Me, An Alcoholic C 24 MIN
16MM FILM, 3/4 OR 1/2 IN VIDEO J-C A
Presents a dramatization about a male teenage alcoholic who refuses to admit he has a problem. Follows him from a drunk-driving apprehension to court and then to sessions with a local Alcoholic Rehabilitation Program worker.
Prod-SRSPRD Dist-MTI

Me, Myself C 12 MIN
16MM FILM, 3/4 OR 1/2 IN VIDEO J-C A
Presents four vignettes leading to discussions on self image and the meaning of maturity.
From The Vignettes Series.
Prod-PAULST Dist-PAULST 1973

Me, Myself And I C 15 MIN
3/4 OR 1/2 INCH VIDEO CASSETTE K-P
Demonstrates happy and sad feelings and stresses treating others in a nice way.
From The Pass It On Series.
Prod-WKNOTV Dist-GPITVL 1983

Me, Myself And Maybe C 15 MIN
16MM FILM, 3/4 OR 1/2 IN VIDEO I
Shows students how to increase their understanding and acceptance of themselves and their evolving abilities and aspirations, through the story of 11-year-old De Anne, who lacks self-confidence.
From The Bread And Butterflies Series.
LC NO. 74-703177
Prod-AITV Dist-AITECH Prodn-KETCTV 1973

Mea Culpa C 29 MIN
2 INCH VIDEOTAPE
See series title for descriptive statement.
From The Making Things Grow III Series.
Prod-WGBHTV Dist-PUBTEL

Meaders Family, The - North Georgia Potters C 31 MIN
16MM FILM - 3/4 IN VIDEO J-C A
Depicts the Meaders family as they work at the family kiln site in Georgia and tell about their traditional approach to making pottery. Shows each step in making the pottery as the Meaders reflect on the attitudes of folk potters.
From The Smithsonian Folklife Studies Series.
LC NO. 81-707609
Prod-SIFP Dist-PCRFV 1981

Meadow, The C 9 MIN
16MM FILM, 3/4 OR 1/2 IN VIDEO K-J
Shows two boys as they explore a meadow. Discusses the beauty in nature and introduces some common plants and insects.
LC NO. 81-706025
Prod-TEXFLM Dist-TEXFLM 1974

Meadow, The - An Ecosystem C 13 MIN
16MM FILM, 3/4 OR 1/2 IN VIDEO I-H
Considers the relationship of plant and animal organisms in the ecological community of a meadow.
Prod-BARR Dist-BARR Prodn-HALBH 1976

Meadow's Green, The C 25 MIN
3/4 OR 1/2 INCH VIDEO CASSETTE
Presents the Bread and Puppet Theatre's two day 'Domestic Fair and Resurrection Circus,' with 118 puppeteers, more than 50 different shows, and exhibits on the meadows that serve as a stage.
Prod-GMPF Dist-GMPF

Meadowcroft Rockshelter B 30 MIN
16MM FILM OPTICAL SOUND
Explores the on-site and laboratory investigations into the archeological dig at the Meadowcraft Rockshelter in Pennsylvania.
LC NO. 77-701816
Prod-UPITTS Dist-UPITTS 1976

Meadowlark Lemon Presents The World C 17 MIN
16MM FILM, 3/4 OR 1/2 IN VIDEO
Presents Meadowlark Lemon, star of the Harlem Globetrotters, using a basketball to demonstrate global latitude and longitude, equator, axis and other map concepts.
LC NO. 79-706820
Prod-PFP Dist-PFP 1979

Meal Planning C 30 MIN
3/4 OR 1/2 INCH VIDEO CASSETTE
See series title for descriptive statement.
From The Food For Life Series.
Prod-MSU Dist-MSU

Meal Planning And Preparation C 16 MIN
16MM FILM, 3/4 OR 1/2 IN VIDEO J-C A
Demonstrates basic procedures in meal planning and preparation, including menu planning, grocery shopping, and precise scheduling for the preparation of each dish.
LC NO. 81-707261
Prod-CENTRO Dist-CORF 1981

Meals For Two C
1/2 IN VIDEO CASSETTE BETA/VHS
Demonstrates the preparation of recipes such as London Broil with Mushroom Sauce, Rice Salad and Ice Cream Crepes.
From The Video Cooking Library Series.
Prod-KARTES Dist-KARTES

Meals In A Half Hour C 12 MIN
16MM FILM - 3/4 IN VIDEO
Demonstrates that with proper utilization of resources, time and skills, it is possible to prepare quick meals that are attractive, delicious, nutritious and also low in saturated fats, cholesterol and calories.
From The Eat Right To Your Heart's Delight Series.
Prod-IPS Dist-IPS 1976

Mean Streets C 112 MIN
16MM FILM OPTICAL SOUND
Dramatizes the struggle of a man climbing the hierarchy of a Mafia family in New York City. Directed by Martin Scorcese.
Prod-WB Dist-SWANK

Meaning C 60 MIN
3/4 OR 1/2 INCH VIDEO CASSETTE
Discusses the growth of technology and the need for better managment tools, the development of dialogues to aid management, the power of graphics dialogues in portraying complex data relationships and new dialogue capabilities supported by distributed processing and intelligence.
From The Computer Dialogue - The Key To Successful Systems Series.
Prod-DELTAK Dist-DELTAK

Meaning In Child Art C 11 MIN
16MM FILM OPTICAL SOUND C T
Shows how art classes can help develop the child's sensitivity to himself and his environment. Illustrates the philosophy that in teaching art to children, the process is more important than the final product. Uses average work, such as all children can produce, to show how much the child can become involved in his own expression.
Prod-PSU Dist-PSUPCR 1955

Meaning In Communication C 19 MIN
3/4 INCH VIDEOTAPE C A
Features a humanistic psychologist who, by analysis and examples, discusses communication and its meaning in interacting with others.
From The Interpersonal Competence, Unit 02 - Communication Series.
Prod-MVNE Dist-TELSTR 1973

Meaning In Modern Painting, Pt 1 C 23 MIN
16MM FILM, 3/4 OR 1/2 IN VIDEO H-C
Portrays works by Picasso, Klee, Mondrian, Cezanne and other modern artists to illustrate their belief that painting and sculpture need not mirror visible reality. Discusses these artists theories of reality in art.
From The Humanities - The Fine Arts Series.
Prod-EBEC Dist-EBEC 1967

Meaning In Modern Painting, Pt 2 C 17 MIN
16MM FILM, 3/4 OR 1/2 IN VIDEO H-C
Includes works by Picasso, Klee, Mondrian, Cezanne and other modern artists to illustrate their belief that painting and sculpture need not mirror visible reality. Discusses these artists theories of reality in art.
From The Humanities - The Fine Arts Series.
Prod-EBEC Dist-EBEC 1967

Meaning Is More Than Words C 14 MIN
16MM FILM, 3/4 OR 1/2 IN VIDEO I
Shows Tina, Jody, Adam And Dave having a series of adventures originating from the meaning-giving signals that surround the words people use, including emphasis, intonation, context, pauses and nonverbal behaviors.
From The Thinkabout Series. Giving And Getting Meaning
LC NO. 81-706108
Prod-SCETV Dist-AITECH

Meaning Of Addition And Subtraction, Dr W G Quast X 20 MIN
16MM FILM OPTICAL SOUND K-I
See series title for descriptive statement.
From The Teaching Modern School Mathematics - Struc- Ture And Use Series.
Prod-HMC Dist-HMC 1971

Meaning Of AEs C 50 MIN
3/4 OR 1/2 INCH VIDEO CASSETTE
Discusses funtionality, development of the normal value algorithm from intuitive notions of meaning and the substitution rule in computer languages.
From The Computer Languages - Pt 1 Series.
Prod-MIOT Dist-MIOT

Meaning Of Communication, The B 30 MIN
16MM FILM OPTICAL SOUND C A
Presents a working definition of communication and describes typical communication gaps.
From The Nursing - R Plus M Equals C, Relationship Plus Meaning Equals Communication Series.
LC NO. 74-700205
Prod-NTCN Dist-NTCN 1971

Meaning Of Democracy, The B 20 MIN
16MM FILM OPTICAL SOUND H-C
Dr E E Schattschneider, Professor of Governement, Wesleyan University, develops the basic premise of democracy, its respect for the individual and for his personal freedoms.
From The Government And Public Affairs Films Series.
Prod-RSC Dist-MLA 1960

Meaning Of Democracy, The - Dr E E Schattschneider B 20 MIN
16MM FILM OPTICAL SOUND H-C
See series title for descriptive statement.
From The Building Political Leadership Series.
Prod-RSC Dist-MLA 1960

Meaning Of Feudalism C 11 MIN
16MM FILM, 3/4 OR 1/2 IN VIDEO I-H
Features of the feudal castle, an explanation of the feudal system, the element of the church and the land organization of the middle ages are covered.
Prod-CORF Dist-CORF 1950

Meaning Of Multiplication, Dr Marilyn J Zweng, The X 19 MIN
16MM FILM OPTICAL SOUND K-I
See series title for descriptive statement.
From The Teaching Modern School Mathematics - Struc- Ture And Use Series.
Prod-HMC Dist-HMC 1971

Meaning Of Our Experience C 37 MIN
16MM FILM OPTICAL SOUND C A
Focuses on adults participating in a life experience workshop based on the conviction that people can learn from each other and that sharing oneself is a key to self development.
Prod-NYU Dist-NYU

Meaning Of Our Experience, The C 38 MIN
16MM FILM, 3/4 OR 1/2 IN VIDEO C A
Presents a group of middle class people who share important and intimate aspects of their lives, not only to learn from each other but in the realization that sharing oneself is a key to self-development.
Prod-ROBERJ Dist-FI 1974

Meaning Of The Pledge, The C 10 MIN
16MM FILM, 3/4 OR 1/2 IN VIDEO P-I
Features Ben Murphy who visits a typical grade class to find out what the students think the pledge means. Provides a springboard for classroom discussion and inquiry.
From The American Values For Elementary Series.
Prod-EVANSA Dist-AIMS 1972

Meaningful Use Of Time C 29 MIN
3/4 OR 1/2 INCH VIDEO CASSETTE
Focuses on making the best use of time. Presented By Bill Oriol, Associate Director, International Center for Social Gerontology.
From The How People Age 50 And Up Can Plan For A More Successful Retirement Series.
Prod-RCOMTV Dist-SYLWAT

Meanings Are In People C 24 MIN
16MM FILM - 3/4 IN VIDEO IND
Dr David K Berlo uses dramatic reenactments to show how misunderstandings occur when managers and subordinates are at cross-purposes. He directs attention to problems of ineffective communication.
From The Effective Communication Series.
Prod-BNA Dist-BNA Prodn-RAY 1965

Means Of Assistance To Ambulation, A - Crutch Walking B 31 MIN
16MM FILM OPTICAL SOUND PRO
Identifies various types of crutches. Demonstrates preparation of patient and four types of gaits, ascending and desending stairs, and sitting in and rising from a chair.
From The Directions For Education In Nursing Via Technology Series. Lesson 68
LC NO. 74-701844
Prod-DENT Dist-WSU 1974

Measles (Rubeola) In Children C 2 MIN
16MM FILM, 3/4 OR 1/2 IN VIDEO C
Shows measles patients 5 to 9 days after exposure displaying the preliminary symptoms of conjunctivitis, upper respiratory tract infection, catarrh, and Koplick spots, and 12 to 19 days after

exposure when the rash appears on the face and spreads to the neck and trunk.
Prod-UCEMC Dist-UCEMC 1961

Measurable Functions B
16MM FILM OPTICAL SOUND
Presents the measurable functions as an extension of the Lebesgue integrable functions.
Prod-OPENU Dist-OPENU

Measure And Set Theory B 47 MIN
16MM FILM OPTICAL SOUND H-C T
Professor Stanislaw Ulam defines measure and lectures on the existence of measures and the uniqueness where they exist. He discusses the Banach-Tarski paradox and the work of Godel and Paul Cohen.
From The MAA Individual Lecturers Series.
Prod-MAA Dist-MLA 1966

Measure For Measure C 23 MIN
3/4 OR 1/2 INCH VIDEO CASSETTE
Takes an off-beat, informative look at the alcohol content of standard drinks and resulting blood alcohol levels.
Prod-ARFO Dist-ARFO 1979

Measure For Measure C 29 MIN
2 INCH VIDEOTAPE
Features Alan Levitan, associate professor of English at Brandeis University discussing Measure For Measure by Shakespeare.
From The Feast Of Language Series.
Prod-WGBHTV Dist-PUBTEL

Measure For Measure C 145 MIN
3/4 OR 1/2 INCH VIDEO CASSETTE H-C A
Presents Shakespeare's comedy about life in Vienna where sexual relationships between unmarried people are punishable by death. Centers on Isabella, who is torn between her attempts to save her brother's condemned life and her vows to God. Stars Kate Nelligan, Tom Piggott-Smith and Christopher Strauli.
From The Shakespeare Plays Series.
LC NO. 79-706934
Prod-BBCTV Dist-TIMLIF 1979

Measure For Measure - 'Judge Not, Lest Ye Be Judged' B 45 MIN
2 INCH VIDEOTAPE C
See series title for descriptive statement.
From The Shakespeare Series.
Prod-CHITVC Dist-GPITVL Prodn-WTTWTV

Measure For Measure - Vienna, That Wide Open Town B 45 MIN
2 INCH VIDEOTAPE C
See series title for descriptive statement.
From The Shakespeare Series.
Prod-CHITVC Dist-GPITVL Prodn-WTTWTV

Measure For Measure—A Series
T
Explains how to teach the metric system. Discusses basic metric principles and shows classroom activities.
Prod-UWISCM Dist-GPITVL 1979

Area 30 MIN
Introduction 30 MIN
Length 30 MIN
Mass (Weight) 30 MIN
Temperature And Review 30 MIN
Volume 30 MIN

Measure Length - Think Metric C 9 MIN
16MM FILM, 3/4 OR 1/2 IN VIDEO P-I
Shows two young boys exploring their neighborhood with a meter stick and a centimeter rule, discovering the comparative size of things around them.
From The Think Metric Series.
Prod-BARR Dist-BARR

Measure Length - Think Metric (Spanish) C 9 MIN
16MM FILM - VIDEO, ALL FORMATS K-I
Defines the standard metric units of length.
Prod-BARR Dist-BARR

Measure Of A Moment C 55 MIN
16MM FILM OPTICAL SOUND
Portrays the stirring pageant presented at the Congregational General Council in Omaha in 1956, with Raymond Massey as narrator.
Prod-YALEDV Dist-YALEDV

Measure Of Air Flow With A Thermal Anemometer C 11 MIN
1/2 IN VIDEO CASSETTE BETA/VHS
Discusses ventilation, air flow and anemometers.
Prod-RMI Dist-RMI

Measure Of Man, The C 9 MIN
16MM FILM OPTICAL SOUND P-I
Uses animation to present a brief history of measurement and common metric units.
LC NO. 77-703378
Prod-EFCR Dist-BESTF Prodn-HALAS 1977

Measure Of Understanding, A C 29 MIN
16MM FILM, 3/4 OR 1/2 IN VIDEO C A
Demonstrates how to clear up conflicting, double messages and determine the real intent of incongruent communication.
LC NO. 79-714888
Prod-RTBL Dist-RTBL 1970

Measure Of Understanding, A (Captioned) C 29 MIN
3/4 OR 1/2 INCH VIDEO CASSETTE A
Discusses effective communication, techniques for clearing up conflicting meanings, how to recognize the 'double level' of a verbal message, and the causes and prevention of communication breakdown. Available captioned for the deaf. Also available in Dutch and Spanish.
Prod-RTBL Dist-RTBL

Measure Of Understanding, A (Dutch) C 29 MIN
16MM FILM, 3/4 OR 1/2 IN VIDEO C A
Demonstrates how to clear up conflicting, double messages and determine the real intent of incongruent communication.
Prod-RTBL Dist-RTBL 1970

Measure Of Understanding, A (Spanish) C 29 MIN
16MM FILM, 3/4 OR 1/2 IN VIDEO C A
Demonstrates how to clear up conflicting, double messages and determine the real intent of incongruent communication.
Prod-RTBL Dist-RTBL 1970

Measure To Measure—A Series
J-C A
Discusses the metric system.
Prod-WCVETV Dist-GPITVL 1975

Birth Of A System, The 15 MIN
Kilo Sounds Greek To Me 15 MIN
Measuring Up To Tomorrow 15 MIN
Metric - Less Hectic 15 MIN
Three Barleycorns Equal An Inch 15 MIN

Measure Up—A Series
P
Presents the concepts of beginning mathematics. Focuses on counting, measurement, equality, addition, subtraction, place value, time, and fractions.
Prod-WCETTV Dist-GPITVL 1977

Addition - Sums To Ten 15 MIN
Addition And Subtraction Of Two-Digit Numbers 15 MIN
Awareness Of Numbers 15 MIN
Conservation Of Discrete Objects 15 MIN
Conservation Of Liquids And Solids 15 MIN
Counting In Order 15 MIN
Equal And Not Equal 15 MIN
Equalizing 15 MIN
Fractions, Pt 1 15 MIN
Fractions, Pt 2 15 MIN
Fun And Games 15 MIN
Geometry 15 MIN
Graphing 15 MIN
Grouping And Partitioning To Twenty 15 MIN
Matching - Greater Than, Less Than 15 MIN
Measurement, Pt 1 15 MIN
Measurement, Pt 2 15 MIN
Mixed Operations - Sums To Six 15 MIN
Mixed Operations To Sums Of Ten 15 MIN
Place Value - The Teens 15 MIN
Place Value, Pt 1 15 MIN
Place Value, Pt 2 15 MIN
Place Value, Pt 3 15 MIN
Readiness For Addition And Subtraction 15 MIN
Story Problems, Pt 1 15 MIN
Story Problems, Pt 2 15 MIN
Subtraction - Sums To Six 15 MIN
Subtraction - Sums To Ten, Pt 1 15 MIN
Subtraction - Sums To Ten, Pt 2 15 MIN
Sums Up To Six 15 MIN
Time, Pt 1 15 MIN
Time, Pt 2 15 MIN

Measure Volume - Think Metric C 9 MIN
16MM FILM, 3/4 OR 1/2 IN VIDEO P-I
Explains the standard metric units for measuring volume.
From The Think Metric Series.
Prod-BARR Dist-BARR

Measure Weight - Think Metric C 9 MIN
16MM FILM, 3/4 OR 1/2 IN VIDEO P-I
Shows two girls visiting a chemist to learn about the standard metric units of weight.
From The Think Metric Series.
Prod-BARR Dist-BARR

Measure Weight - Think Metric (Spanish) C 9 MIN
16MM FILM - VIDEO, ALL FORMATS K-I
Teaches the standard metric units of weight and explains the importance of measuring weight.
Prod-BARR Dist-BARR

Measured Loaf, The C 15 MIN
3/4 OR 1/2 INCH VIDEO CASSETTE K-P
Explains the methods of measuring matter.
From The Dragons, Wagons And Wax, Set 1 Series.
Prod-CTI Dist-CTI

Measurement B 21 MIN
16MM FILM OPTICAL SOUND H-C
Discusses the art of measurement, using the speed of a rifle bullet as an example. Discusses such problems as noise, bias, use of black boxes and the element of decision.
From The PSSC Physics Films Series.
Prod-PSSC Dist-MLA 1959

Measurement C 15 MIN
3/4 OR 1/2 INCH VIDEO CASSETTE P-I
Presents measurement as an important process used constantly in everyday life. Focuses on the different things that need to be measured, the practical reasons for measuring them and the instrument used to measure them.
From The First Films On Science Series.
Prod-MAETEL Dist-AITECH 1975

Measurement B 30 MIN
2 INCH VIDEOTAPE
Suggests methods of introducing children to concepts of measurement. Explains that measurement is the process of comparing an unknown to a known quantity and that all systems of measurement are arbitrary, although not equally useful.
From The Science In Your Classroom Series.
Prod-WENHTV Dist-GPITVL

Measurement - Dividing Regions Into Subregions For Finding Area C 15 MIN
3/4 OR 1/2 INCH VIDEO CASSETTE I
Shows how to divide irregular region into subregions to determine total area.
From The Math Works Series.
Prod-AITECH Dist-AITECH

Measurement - Finding Areas Of Rectangles C 15 MIN
3/4 OR 1/2 INCH VIDEO CASSETTE I
Demonstrates the formula for finding the area of a rectangle.
From The Math Works Series.
Prod-AITECH Dist-AITECH

Measurement - Introduction To Distance, Mass And Volume C 16 MIN
3/4 OR 1/2 INCH VIDEO CASSETTE P
Shows how to measure distance, mass and volume.
From The Math Cycle Series.
Prod-WDCNTV Dist-GPITVL 1983

Measurement - The Difference Between Perimeter And Area C 15 MIN
3/4 OR 1/2 INCH VIDEO CASSETTE I
Illustrates the difference between perimeter and area by showing that the perimeter can surround very different areas.
From The Math Works Series.
Prod-AITECH Dist-AITECH

Measurement - Time And Temperature C 16 MIN
3/4 OR 1/2 INCH VIDEO CASSETTE P
Tells how to read a clock and a thermometer.
From The Math Cycle Series.
Prod-WDCNTV Dist-GPITVL 1983

Measurement - Use Of The Analytical Balance C 24 MIN
16MM FILM OPTICAL SOUND
Introduces the student to the nature and measurement of mass. Shows how to operate automatic analytical balances and the degree of accuracy that can be expected from the different types. Shows proper techniques for weighing different kinds of materials.
From The Experimental General Chemistry Series.
Prod-MLA Dist-MLA

Measurement And Estimation Of Length C 30 MIN
3/4 OR 1/2 INCH VIDEO CASSETTE
See series title for descriptive statement.
From The Infinity Factory Series.
Prod-EDFCEN Dist-MDCPB

Measurement And Estimation Of Volume C 30 MIN
3/4 OR 1/2 INCH VIDEO CASSETTE
See series title for descriptive statement.
From The Infinity Factory Series.
Prod-EDFCEN Dist-MDCPB

Measurement And Estimation Of Weight C 30 MIN
3/4 OR 1/2 INCH VIDEO CASSETTE
See series title for descriptive statement.
From The Infinity Factory Series.
Prod-EDFCEN Dist-MDCPB

Measurement And Man X 16 MIN
16MM FILM, 3/4 OR 1/2 IN VIDEO P-I
Demonstrates the importance of mathematics in measurement, observation, communication and data recording.
Prod-IU Dist-IU 1965

Measurement And Results C 60 MIN
3/4 OR 1/2 INCH VIDEO CASSETTE IND
See series title for descriptive statement.
From The Quality Circle Concepts Series.
Prod-NCSU Dist-AMCEE

Measurement And Statistics C 16 MIN
16MM FILM OPTICAL SOUND H-C A
Examines basic concepts in measurement and statistics in psychology, including scales of measurement, measures of central tendency and dispersion and the normal curve.
From The Basic Psychology Series.
LC NO. 76-702921
Prod-EDMDC Dist-EDMDC Prodn-SOREND 1973

Measurement Of Area And Volume C 23 MIN
3/4 OR 1/2 INCH VIDEO CASSETTE IND
Defines and describes plane surfaces and three dimensional solids. Develops formulas for calculating and how they work. Includes discussion of circular measurement and spherical volume.
From The Mathematics And Physics Series.
Prod-AVIMA Dist-AVIMA 1980

Measurement Of Blood Pressure In Dental Practice C 8 MIN
3/4 INCH VIDEO CASSETTE PRO
Defines blood pressure and related terms and demonstrates a technique for measuring blood pressure in dental practice.
LC NO. 79-706751
Prod-MUSC Dist-USNAC 1978

Measurement Of Blood Pressure, The C 23 MIN
3/4 OR 1/2 INCH VIDEO CASSETTE PRO
Presents examples of blood pressure readings on a standard mercury manometer in order to provide a test on the hearing and recording of blood pressure measurements.
From The Blood Pressure Series.
LC NO. 79-706006
Prod-IU Dist-IU 1978

Measurement Of Capacity - Mathematics, Grade 3 B 20 MIN
2 INCH VIDEOTAPE P
See series title for descriptive statement.
From The Mathematics, Grade 3 Series.
Prod-DENVPS Dist-GPITVL Prodn-KRMATV

Measurement Of Cerebral Blood Flow In Health And Disease C 50 MIN
3/4 INCH VIDEO CASSETTE
Discusses the technique of measuring cerebral blood with external probes. Discusses the measurement of blood flow with CT scan.
Prod-UTAHTI Dist-UTAHTI

Measurement Of Electrical Impedence In Single Cell Suspensions As A Rapid Assay For... C 32 MIN
3/4 INCH VIDEO CASSETTE
Discusses cellular metabolism before and after the induction of electrical current.
Prod-UTAHTI Dist-UTAHTI

Measurement Of Elementary Charge B 18 MIN
16MM FILM OPTICAL SOUND C A
Shows the procedure for setting up, adjusting and using the millikan apparatus for the measurement of elementary charge. Discusses sample data and methods for analyzing it. Includes close-up views of what students should see through the microscope.
From The Harvard Project Physics Teacher Briefings Series. No. 14
LC NO. 74-709137
Prod-HPP Dist-HRAW 1969

Measurement Of Impulse Response B 11 MIN
3/4 OR 1/2 INCH VIDEO CASSETTE PRO
Demonstrates the relative invariance of linear time-invariant system responses to the detailed shape of a pulse input of short duration but fixed area.
From The Probability And Random Processes - Linear Systems Series.
Prod-MIOT Dist-MIOT

Measurement Of Length C 10 MIN
16MM FILM OPTICAL SOUND J-C A
Introduces various aspects of linear measurement and the use of such tools as a decimal inch and metric rule, inside and outside calipers and a metric micrometer.
From The Measurement Series.
LC NO. 76-703207
Prod-PSU Dist-PSU Prodn-MSRL 1972

Measurement Of Length C 30 MIN
3/4 OR 1/2 INCH VIDEO CASSETTE
See series title for descriptive statement.
From The Infinity Factory Series.
Prod-EDFCEN Dist-MDCPB

Measurement Of Solids C 30 MIN
16MM FILM OPTICAL SOUND T
Presents the standard formulas for determining the volume of various solids. Employs physical models to introduce the concept of volume. To be used following 'AREA.'
From The Mathematics For Elementary School Teachers Series. No. 28
Prod-SMSG Dist-MLA 1963

Measurement Of Surface And Interfacial Tensions Of Liquids, Pt 1 C 25 MIN
3/4 OR 1/2 INCH VIDEO CASSETTE
See series title for descriptive statement.
From The Colloid And Surface Chemistry - Surface Chemistry Series.
Prod-KALMIA Dist-KALMIA

Measurement Of Surface And Interfacial Tensions Of Liquids 1 B 25 MIN
3/4 OR 1/2 INCH VIDEO CASSETTE PRO
See series title for descriptive statement.
From The Colloid And Surface Chemistry - Surface Chemistry Series.
Prod-MIOT Dist-MIOT

Measurement Of Surface And Interfacial Tensions Of Liquids, Pt 2 C 37 MIN
3/4 OR 1/2 INCH VIDEO CASSETTE
See series title for descriptive statement.
From The Colloid And Surface Chemistry - Surface Chemistry Series.
Prod-KALMIA Dist-KALMIA

Measurement Of Surface And Interfacial Tensions Of Liquids 2 B 37 MIN
3/4 OR 1/2 INCH VIDEO CASSETTE PRO
See series title for descriptive statement.
From The Colloid And Surface Chemistry - Surface Chemistry Series.
Prod-MIOT Dist-MIOT

Measurement Of The Acceleration Of Gravity With Kater's Pendulum, A B 21 MIN
16MM FILM OPTICAL SOUND C
Uses Kater's pendulum in a gravity experiment.
Prod-PUAVC Dist-PUAVC 1961

Measurement Of The Acceleration Of Gravity, A - Falling Body X 8 MIN
16MM FILM OPTICAL SOUND C
Presents a physics experiment in which two photoelectric cells are arranged for use in measuring the time of transit through a known vertical distance.
Prod-PUAVC Dist-PUAVC 1961

Measurement Of The Corrosion Potential And Corrosion Current C 46 MIN
3/4 OR 1/2 INCH VIDEO CASSETTE PRO
See series title for descriptive statement.
From The Corrosion Engineering Series.
Prod-GPCV Dist-GPCV

Measurement Of The Corrosion Potential And Corrosion Current C 46 MIN
3/4 OR 1/2 INCH VIDEO CASSETTE
Discusses corrosion rate measurements in terms of electrochemical techniques such as Tafel extrapolation and linear polarization as well as more conventional weight loss and penetration rate measurements. Describes three elecrode systems.
From The Corrosion Engineering Series.
Prod-MIOT Dist-MIOT

Measurement Of The Speed Of A Rifle Bullet, A B 5 MIN
16MM FILM OPTICAL SOUND C
A bullet is fired through two discs rotating on a common shaft so that its speed may be measured.
Prod-PUAVC Dist-PUAVC 1961

Measurement Of The Universal Gravitational Constant With The Cavendish Balance, A X 27 MIN
16MM FILM OPTICAL SOUND C
Quantitive determination of the universal gravitational constant is achieved with a sensitive torsion balance with a long vibration time. Time lapse photography is used to reduce observation time.
Prod-PUAVC Dist-PUAVC 1961

Measurement Of Vapor Pressure B 12 MIN
16MM FILM OPTICAL SOUND
Offers the procedure for determining the heat of vaporization of a liquid by studying its vapor pressure at various temperatures.
From The Experimental General Chemistry Series.
Prod-MLA Dist-MLA

Measurement Of Volume C 30 MIN
3/4 OR 1/2 INCH VIDEO CASSETTE
See series title for descriptive statement.
From The Infinity Factory Series.
Prod-EDFCEN Dist-MDCPB

Measurement Of Weight C 12 MIN
16MM FILM OPTICAL SOUND J-C A
Shows how scales work, demonstrating both spring scales and balances. Explains why balance-type scales are used for laboratory work and shows the procedure for weighting with both the triple beam balance and analytical balance.
From The Measurement Series.
LC NO. 76-703208
Prod-PSU Dist-PSU Prodn-MSRL 1972

Measurement Of Weight C 30 MIN
3/4 OR 1/2 INCH VIDEO CASSETTE
See series title for descriptive statement.
From The Infinity Factory Series.
Prod-EDFCEN Dist-MDCPB

Measurement Readiness—A Series
16MM FILM, 3/4 OR 1/2 IN VIDEO P
Prod-CORF Dist-CORF 1976

Big And Small 10 MIN
Fast And Slow 11 MIN
Heavy And Light 13 MIN
Hot And Cold 10 MIN

Measurement With Light Waves B 15 MIN
16MM FILM - 3/4 IN VIDEO
Deals with principles of measurement with light waves, the nature of light waves, the cause of interference bands, and use of these bands in ultra-precision measurement. Examines procedures used in gage block inspection. Issued in 1944 as a motion picture.
From The Engineering Series.
LC NO. 79-706432
Prod-USOE Dist-USNAC Prodn-AUDIO 1979

Measurement—A Series
J-C A
Explains the importance of measurement in science and in everyday life.
Prod-PSU Dist-PSU Prodn-MSRL 1972

Measurement Of Length 10 MIN
Measurement Of Weight 12 MIN
Understanding The Metric System 8 MIN
Why Measure 6 MIN

Measurement, Pt 1 C 15 MIN
3/4 INCH VIDEO CASSETTE P
Discusses how to measure length, area and volume with non-standard units.
From The Measure Up Series.
Prod-WCETTV Dist-GPITVL 1977

Measurement, Pt 2 C 15 MIN
3/4 INCH VIDEO CASSETTE P
Shows how to measure length in meters.
From The Measure Up Series.
Prod-WCETTV Dist-GPITVL 1977

Measurements C 45 MIN
3/4 OR 1/2 INCH VIDEO CASSETTE PRO
Speaks on measuring technical achievements and costs. Describes parallel accounting systems.
From The Advanced Project Management Series.
Prod-AMCEE Dist-AMCEE

Measurements For Custom Orthopedic Shoes, VA Form 10-2908 C 17 MIN
3/4 OR 1/2 INCH VIDEO CASSETTE
Demonstrates the correct technique for measuring feet, as required to complete VA form 10-2908.
LC NO. 80-707595
Prod-USVA Dist-USNAC 1980

Measuremetric—A Series
I-J
Presents an instructional series that uses the metric system in dealing with the process of measurement.
Prod-AITV Dist-AITECH 1977

Area 1 - Barbara Arrives In Arealand 15 MIN
Area 2 - Barbara Searches The Squares 15 MIN
Area 3 - Barbara Finds The Formula 15 MIN
Greatest Measurement Show On Earth, The 15 MIN
Length 1 - Who Measures 15 MIN
Length 2 - A Thousand Clicks 15 MIN
Length 3 - The Final Test 15 MIN
Mass 1 - The Case Of The Disappearing Mass 15 MIN
Mass 2 - The Case Of The Disappearing Mass 15 MIN
Volume 1 - Doc Cranshaw And The Kid - The 15 MIN
Volume 2 - Doc Cranshaw And The Kid - The 15 MIN
Volume 3 - Doc Cranshaw And The Kid - The 15 MIN

Measures And Set Theory B 50 MIN
16MM FILM OPTICAL SOUND H
Outlines the background and principal of measure theory, including both finitely and countably additive measures. Explores the relationship of these measures to set theory, concentrating on recent developments of the continuum hypothesis.
From The Mathematics Today Series.
LC NO. FIA66-1280
Prod-COEMM Dist-MLA Prodn-FLDZMN 1966

Measures For Air Quality C 4 MIN
16MM FILM OPTICAL SOUND H-C A
Describes new air quality measurement techniques and calibration standards being developed by the National Bureau of Standards to help improve the accuracy of measuring air pollution. Includes the use of a laser to measure air pollution levels, the sulphur dioxide fluorescence detector and the permeation tube.
LC NO. 73-702598
Prod-USNBOS Dist-USNBOS 1972

Measures Of Volatility C 6 MIN
3/4 OR 1/2 INCH VIDEO CASSETTE
See series title for descriptive statement.
From The Travels - Five Works By Shalom Gorewitz Series.
Prod-EAI Dist-EAI

Measuring C 13 MIN
16MM FILM, 3/4 OR 1/2 IN VIDEO P
Shows that measuring is an indispensable part of daily life. Illustrates that measurements can be qualitative, larger than or smaller than, but that standard limits are necessary for communicating among people. Presents a brief description and comparison of the English and metric systems of measurement.
From The Science Processes Series.
Prod-MGHT Dist-MGHT Prodn-HANBAR 1970

Measuring C 20 MIN
2 INCH VIDEOTAPE P
See series title for descriptive statement.
From The Mathemagic, Unit VI - Measurement Series.
Prod-WMULTV Dist-GPITVL

Measuring - A Way Of Comparing C 10 MIN
16MM FILM, 3/4 OR 1/2 IN VIDEO P-I
Shows that measuring is a way of comparing. Begins with a boy comparing the length of two trains and a girl comparing the height of two dolls. Explains that we often want to know more about two objects than which is longer or taller. Demonstrates the measuring of length, width and volume.
Prod-BOUNDY Dist-PHENIX 1967

Measuring - Blood Pressure, Body Temperatures, Pulse And Respiratory Rates C 25 MIN
3/4 OR 1/2 INCH VIDEO CASSETTE PRO
See series title for descriptive statement.
From The Basic Nursing Skills Series.
Prod-BRA Dist-BRA

Measuring And Calibration C 60 MIN
3/4 OR 1/2 INCH VIDEO CASSETTE IND
Deals with tolerances, measuring, calibration program and metrication.
From The Quality Assurance Series
Prod-LEIKID Dist-LEIKID

Measuring And Comparing Weights B 15 MIN
2 INCH VIDEOTAPE P
See series title for descriptive statement.
From The Just Inquisitive Series. No. 16
Prod-EOPS Dist-GPITVL Prodn-KOACTV

Measuring And Graphing Temperature And Time B 15 MIN
2 INCH VIDEOTAPE P
See series title for descriptive statement.
From The Just Inquisitive Series. No. 13
Prod-EOPS Dist-GPITVL Prodn-KOACTV

Measuring And Layout Tools C 13 MIN
16MM FILM, 3/4 OR 1/2 IN VIDEO J-H A
Demonstrates the use of measuring tools and layout tools.
From The Hand Tools For Wood Working Series. No. 6
Prod-MORLAT Dist-SF 1967

Measuring And Layout Tools C 30 MIN
3/4 OR 1/2 INCH VIDEO CASSETTE IND

Contains information on precision measuring instruments and tools used for transferring dimensions on paper to the materials of fabrication.
From The Aircraft Hardware, Hand Tools And Measuring Devices Series.
Prod-AVIMA Dist-AVIMA

Measuring Area C 15 MIN
3/4 INCH VIDEO CASSETTE P
Discusses aspects of area measurement.
From The Measuring Show Series.
Prod-MAETEL Dist-GPITVL 1979

Measuring Area C 15 MIN
3/4 OR 1/2 INCH VIDEO CASSETTE P
Gives experience in measuring area.
From The Hands On, Grade 2 - Lollipops, Loops, Etc Series. Unit 2 - Measuring
Prod-WHROTV Dist-AITECH 1975

Measuring Blood Pressure C 10 MIN
16MM FILM OPTICAL SOUND PRO
Reviews basic steps involved in measuring blood pressure and offers advice on techniques that may help assure more accurate reading. Includes a brief overview of the problem of high blood pressure in the United States.
LC NO. 76-700288
Prod-MESHDO Dist-MESHDO Prodn-FORMIL 1976

Measuring Blood Pressure C 20 MIN
3/4 OR 1/2 INCH VIDEO CASSETTE PRO
Presents proper blood pressure measurement techniques with emphasis on selection and care of equipment, selection of the appropriate size cuff and explanation of the ausculatory gap.
From The Blood Pressure Series.
Prod-NICEPR Dist-IU 1980

Measuring Blood Pressure C 25 MIN
3/4 OR 1/2 INCH VIDEO CASSETTE PRO
Includes measuring body temperature. Covers measuring pulse and respiratory rates. Discusses nurse-patient relations.
From The Basic Nursing Skills Series. Tape 8
Prod-MDCC Dist-MDCC

Measuring Bulk Materials C 12 MIN
3/4 OR 1/2 INCH VIDEO CASSETTE
Covers the measuring of bulk solids, their storing and handling, conveyors, measuring area, volume, weight, mass and density.
From The Making Measurements Series.
Prod-TPCTRA Dist-TPCTRA

Measuring Change B 15 MIN
2 INCH VIDEOTAPE P
See series title for descriptive statement.
From The Just Wondering Series.
Prod-EOPS Dist-GPITVL Prodn-KOACTV

Measuring Change C 15 MIN
3/4 OR 1/2 INCH VIDEO CASSETTE P
Gives experience in measuring change.
From The Hands On, Grade 2 - Lollipops, Loops, Etc Series. Unit 2 - Measuring
Prod-WHROTV Dist-AITECH 1975

Measuring Distance C 15 MIN
3/4 OR 1/2 INCH VIDEO CASSETTE P-I
Discusses measuring distance.
From The Why Series.
Prod-WDCNTV Dist-AITECH 1976

Measuring Electrical Flow C 20 MIN
3/4 INCH VIDEO CASSETTE T
Shows a science classroom project in which a nichrome wire resistor is added to a simple bulb and battery circuit and its properties explored. Explains how to build a simple electroscale to measure electrical flow through the various circuits.
From The Science In The Elementary School - Physical Science Series.
Prod-UWKY Dist-GPITVL 1979

Measuring Electricity C 12 MIN
3/4 OR 1/2 INCH VIDEO CASSETTE
Covers the measuring of electrical units, potential difference, resistance, power and AC-DC.
From The Making Measurements Series.
Prod-TPCTRA Dist-TPCTRA

Measuring External And Internal Threads C
3/4 OR 1/2 INCH VIDEO CASSETTE
See series title for descriptive statement.
From The Intermediate Engine Lathe Operation Series.
Prod-VTRI Dist-VTRI

Measuring External And Internal Threads C 15 MIN
3/4 OR 1/2 INCH VIDEO CASSETTE
See series title for descriptive statement.
From The Machine Technology III - Intermediate Engine Lathe Series.
Prod-CAMB Dist-CAMB

Measuring External And Internal Threads C 15 MIN
3/4 OR 1/2 INCH VIDEO CASSETTE IND
See series title for descriptive statement.
From The Machining And The Operation Of Machine Tools, Module 3 - Intermediate Engine Lathe series.
Prod-LEIKID Dist-LEIKID

Measuring External And Internal Threads (Spanish) C
3/4 OR 1/2 INCH VIDEO CASSETTE
See series title for descriptive statement.
From The Intermediate Engine Lathe Operation (Spanish) Series.
Prod-VTRI Dist-VTRI

Measuring Fluids C 12 MIN
3/4 OR 1/2 INCH VIDEO CASSETTE
Covers the states of matter, measuring liquid flow, viscosity, humidity, density, measuring specific gravity and measuring flow rate by pressure.
From The Making Measurements Series.
Prod-TPCTRA Dist-TPCTRA

Measuring Forces C 12 MIN
3/4 OR 1/2 INCH VIDEO CASSETTE
Covers force and motion, torque measuring instrument, the action and analysis of force.
From The Making Measurements Series.
Prod-TPCTRA Dist-TPCTRA

Measuring Hearing C 11 MIN
3/4 OR 1/2 INCH VIDEO CASSETTE
Explains that procedures employed in measuring the learning-impaired child's auditory capacity may vary according to the age of the child, the stimulus presented, and the response anticipated. Presents several evaluation techniques.
LC NO. 80-707423
Prod-USBEH Dist-USNAC 1980

Measuring In Astronomy - How Big, How Far C 12 MIN
16MM FILM, 3/4 OR 1/2 IN VIDEO I-J
Discusses how surveyors use their knowlege of geometry and properties common to triangles to measure the large distances on the curved surface of the earth.
Prod-DSFI Dist-PHENIX 1969

Measuring In Review C 15 MIN
3/4 INCH VIDEO CASSETTE P
Discusses metric measurement of temperature. States that the metric unit is based on tens and that there are other prefixes that can be used with metric units.
From The Measuring Show Series.
Prod-MAETEL Dist-GPITVL 1979

Measuring In Science C 14 MIN
3/4 OR 1/2 INCH VIDEO CASSETTE J
Demonstrates how an archaeologist uses measuring to reconstruct and understand the fossil remains of a mammoth.
From The Whatabout Series.
Prod-AITV Dist-AITECH 1983

Measuring Instructional Effectiveness C 30 MIN
3/4 OR 1/2 INCH VIDEO CASSETTE T
Shows how to measure instructional effectiveness. Covers preparing written and performance tests, scoring tests and using reaction sheets.
From The Training The Trainer Series.
Prod-ITCORP Dist-ITCORP

Measuring Instruments C 14 MIN
16MM FILM, 3/4 OR 1/2 IN VIDEO H
Discusses instruments which measure mileage and speed.
From The Math Wise Series. Module 1 - Measuring
Prod-KOCETV Dist-AITECH 1981

Measuring Instruments C 60 MIN
3/4 OR 1/2 INCH VIDEO CASSETTE IND
Focuses on use and care of measuring instruments including steel rule, vernier calipers, thickness gauge, micrometers.
From The Mechanical Maintenance Basics Series.
Prod-ITCORP Dist-ITCORP

Measuring Instruments (Spanish) C 60 MIN
3/4 OR 1/2 INCH VIDEO CASSETTE IND
Explores measuring instruments including steel rule, vernier calipers, thickness gauge and micrometers.
From The Mechanical Maintenance Basics (Spanish) Series.
Prod-ITCORP Dist-ITCORP

Measuring Is C 15 MIN
3/4 INCH VIDEO CASSETTE P
Defines basic measuring words and explains why there is a standard system of measurement.
From The Measuring Show Series.
Prod-MAETEL Dist-GPITVL 1979

Measuring Is Important C 17 MIN
16MM FILM - VIDEO, ALL FORMATS I
Shows a sixth grade class learning the fundamentals of measuring. Shows how the measurement of length, weight, volume, time and temperature apply in daily life. Introduces the metric system.
Prod-SAIF Dist-BARR

Measuring Large Distances B 29 MIN
16MM FILM OPTICAL SOUND H-C
Describes the place of triangulation, parallax and the inverse square law for light in geophysics and astronomy. Uses models of the earth, moon and stars.
From The PSSC Physics Films Series.
Prod-PSSC Dist-MLA 1959

Measuring Length C 15 MIN
3/4 INCH VIDEO CASSETTE P
Identifies meters and centimeters as major units for measuring length.
From The Measuring Show Series.
Prod-MAETEL Dist-GPITVL 1979

Measuring Molecules C 20 MIN
16MM FILM, 3/4 OR 1/2 IN VIDEO P A
Shows students being taken through tunnels to appreciate the size of molecules.
From The Science Twenty Series.
Prod-PRISM Dist-SF 1970

Measuring Motion C 12 MIN
3/4 OR 1/2 INCH VIDEO CASSETTE
Covers the measure of relative motion, displacement, velocity, acceleration, average and instantaneous values.
From The Making Measurements Series.
Prod-TPCTRA Dist-TPCTRA

Measuring My Success C 30 MIN
3/4 OR 1/2 INCH VIDEO CASSETTE
Shows how the performance of the economy is measured in terms of gross national product, net national product, national income and the consumer price index.
From The Money Puzzle - The World Of Macroeconomics Series. Module 6
Prod-MDCC Dist-MDCC

Measuring Objects - Linear Measurements B 15 MIN
2 INCH VIDEOTAPE P
See series title for descriptive statement.
From The Just Curious Series. No. 9
Prod-EOPS Dist-GPITVL Prodn-KOACTV

Measuring Objects - Surface Area Measurement B 15 MIN
2 INCH VIDEOTAPE P
See series title for descriptive statement.
From The Just Curious Series. No. 11
Prod-EOPS Dist-GPITVL Prodn-KOACTV

Measuring Objects - Volume Measurements B 15 MIN
2 INCH VIDEOTAPE P
See series title for descriptive statement.
From The Just Curious Series. No. 10
Prod-EOPS Dist-GPITVL Prodn-KOACTV

Measuring Objects - Weight B 15 MIN
2 INCH VIDEOTAPE P
See series title for descriptive statement.
From The Just Curious Series. No. 12
Prod-EOPS Dist-GPITVL Prodn-KOACTV

Measuring Pipe, Tubing, And Fittings B 15 MIN
16MM FILM - 3/4 IN VIDEO
Identifies types of pipes, tubing, and fittings and shows how to use basic measuring tools. Explains how to measure pipe for offsets and how to make allowances for fittings and offsets when measuring pipes. Issued in 1944 as a motion picture.
From The Shipbuilding Skills - Pipefitting Series. Number 1
LC NO. 80-707268
Prod-USOE Dist-USNAC Prodn-PHOTOS 1980

Measuring Process Variables C 60 MIN
3/4 OR 1/2 INCH VIDEO CASSETTE IND
See series title for descriptive statement.
From The Instrumentation Basics - Process Concepts Series. Tape 2
Prod-ISA Dist-ISA

Measuring Relative Motion B 15 MIN
2 INCH VIDEOTAPE P
See series title for descriptive statement.
From The Just Curious Series. No. 21
Prod-EOPS Dist-GPITVL Prodn-KOACTV

Measuring Shadows - The Universe Today C 28 MIN
16MM FILM, 3/4 OR 1/2 IN VIDEO
Discusses the structure of the universe and the research that led to man's present understanding of it.
From The Understanding Space And Time Series.
Prod-BBCTV Dist-UCEMC 1980

Measuring Short Distances B 20 MIN
16MM FILM OPTICAL SOUND H
Discusses the ways to measure short distances, including the centimeter scale, microscopic dimensions and atom dimensions. Explains the calibration of instruments.
From The PSSC Physics Films Series.
Prod-PSSC Dist-MLA 1959

Measuring Show–A Series
P
Defines various measuring words and examines metrically-expressed concepts of length, area, volume, weight, temperature, time and money.
Prod-MAETEL Dist-GPITVL 1979

Measuring Area	15 MIN
Measuring In Review	15 MIN
Measuring Is	15 MIN
Measuring Length	15 MIN
Measuring Volume	15 MIN
Measuring Weight (Mass)	15 MIN

Measuring Speed C 14 MIN
3/4 OR 1/2 INCH VIDEO CASSETTE I
Gives experience in measuring speed.
From The Hands On, Grade 4 - Cars, Cartoons, Etc Series. Unit 2 - Measuring
Prod-WHROTV Dist-AITECH 1975

Measuring Surface Area B 15 MIN
2 INCH VIDEOTAPE P
See series title for descriptive statement.
From The Just Inquisitive Series. No. 10
Prod-EOPS Dist-GPITVL Prodn-KOACTV

Measuring Temperature C 12 MIN
3/4 OR 1/2 INCH VIDEO CASSETTE
Covers temperature-sensing materials, temperature and heat.
From The Making Measurements Series.
Prod-TPCTRA Dist-TPCTRA

Measuring Temperature C 15 MIN
3/4 OR 1/2 INCH VIDEO CASSETTE P-I
Discusses measuring temperature.
From The Why Series.
Prod-WDCNTV Dist-AITECH 1976

Measuring The Blood Sugar-Chemstrip bG C 24 MIN
3/4 OR 1/2 INCH VIDEO CASSETTE PRO
Demonstrates Bio-Dynamics products. Provides a basic understanding of how strip products work.
Prod-MEDFAC Dist-MEDFAC 1983

Measuring The Blood Sugar-Dextrostix And Visidex C 18 MIN
3/4 OR 1/2 INCH VIDEO CASSETTE PRO
Demonstrates Ames products and how strip products react to glucose. Describes the Glucometer and its use.
Prod-MEDFAC Dist-MEDFAC 1982

Measuring The Performance Of Textiles - Textile Testing—A Series
C A
Describes the capabilities and instructions for use of the Instron universal testing instrument.
Prod-CUETV Dist-CUNIV 1981

Abrasion, Pt 1 - Introduction,
Abrasion, Pt 2 - Accelerator 011 MIN
Abrasion, Pt 3 - Taber Abraser 009 MIN
Abrasion, Pt 4 - CSI Stoll Tester 013 MIN
Atlas Fadeometer 016 MIN
Color Difference Meter 016 MIN
Flammability, Pt 1 - Introduction 017 MIN
Flammability, Pt 2 - Mushroom Apparel 017 MIN
Flammability, Pt 3 - Home Furnishings 010 MIN
Frazier Air Permeability Instrument 015 MIN
Frazier Compressometer 007 MIN
Guarded Hot Plate 014 MIN
Introduction To The Instron 038 MIN
Textile Testing Using The Instron 022 MIN

Measuring The Temperature Of Petroleum And Petroleum Products C 23 MIN
3/4 OR 1/2 INCH VIDEO CASSETTE IND
Discusses temperature measurement and considers proper procedures, equipment care and safety. Conforms to current API Manual of Petroleum Measurement Standards.
Prod-UTEXPE Dist-UTEXPE

Measuring The Universe C 10 MIN
16MM FILM, 3/4 OR 1/2 IN VIDEO J-H
Explains how astronomers have used geometry, the spectrum and apparent brightness to measure the distance between earth and stars in the universe. Demonstrates how powerful telescopes enable man to determine distances of stars outside the galaxy.
Prod-DSFI Dist-PHENIX 1969

Measuring The Universe (Spanish) C 10 MIN
16MM FILM, 3/4 OR 1/2 IN VIDEO I-H
Explains how astronomers have used geometry, the spectrum and apparent brightness to measure the distance between earth and stars in the universe. Demonstrates how powerful telescopes enable man to determine distances of stars outside the galaxy.
Prod-DSFI Dist-PHENIX 1969

Measuring Things 1 - Distance, Time Temperature C 17 MIN
16MM FILM, 3/4 OR 1/2 IN VIDEO P-I
Introduces methods for simple determination of length, time and temperature. Stresses American ways of measurement, but brief comparisons with the metric system are made. Features simple experiments.
Prod-HANDEL Dist-HANDEL 1984

Measuring Time C 15 MIN
3/4 OR 1/2 INCH VIDEO CASSETTE P-I
Discusses measuring time.
From The Why Series.
Prod-WDCNTV Dist-AITECH 1976

Measuring Time C 15 MIN
3/4 OR 1/2 INCH VIDEO CASSETTE P
Gives experience in measuring time.
From The Hands On, Grade 2 - Lollipops, Loops, Etc Series. Unit 2 - Measuring
Prod-WHROTV Dist-AITECH 1975

Measuring Time - Calendars And Clocks C 14 MIN
16MM FILM, 3/4 OR 1/2 IN VIDEO I-H
Traces man as a timekeeper from his earliest observation of celestial phenomena to atomic timekeeping devices. Demonstrates the need for leap days and the basis of solar and lunar calendars.
LC NO. 84-706126
Prod-IFFB Dist-CF 1984

Measuring Tools C 12 MIN
3/4 OR 1/2 INCH VIDEO CASSETTE
Covers linear and angular measurement, units of linear measurement, rules and measuring tapes, using the micrometer and squares.
From The Using Hand Tools Series.
Prod-TPCTRA Dist-TPCTRA

Measuring Tools C 13 MIN
3/4 OR 1/2 INCH VIDEO CASSETTE IND
Discusses the need for measuring tools. Tells how to identify and use such tools as rules, calipers, micrometers and gauge blocks.
From The Introduction To Machine Technology, Module 1 Series.
Prod-LEIKID Dist-LEIKID

Measuring Tools (Spanish) C 12 MIN
3/4 OR 1/2 INCH VIDEO CASSETTE
Covers linear and angular measurement, units of linear measurement, rules and measuring tapes, using the micrometer and squares.
From The Using Hand Tools Series.
Prod-TPCTRA Dist-TPCTRA

Measuring Units - An Introduction C 14 MIN
16MM FILM, 3/4 OR 1/2 IN VIDEO P-I
Explains all of the basic units of measurement—width, length, height, square and cubic. Begins with the simple method of measurement of a string with a stick then moves to area measurement and finally to cubic space measurement.
Prod-BOUNDY Dist-PHENIX 1967

Measuring Up C 13 MIN
16MM FILM, 3/4 OR 1/2 IN VIDEO J-H
Explains the necessity and importance of physical fitness testing. Gives students instruction on how to monitor their own fitness.
From The Fitness For Living Series.
Prod-WDEMCO Dist-WDEMCO 1982

Measuring Up C 21 MIN
3/4 OR 1/2 INCH VIDEO CASSETTE C
Details applications and types of small computers and their integration into a business.
From The Business Computing - Cut Down To Size Series. Pt 1
Prod-ELDATA Dist-GPITVL 1980

Measuring Up C 30 MIN
3/4 OR 1/2 INCH VIDEO CASSETTE K-P
See series title for descriptive statement.
From The Villa Alegre Series.
Prod-BCTV Dist-MDCPB

Measuring Up To Tomorrow C 15 MIN
3/4 INCH VIDEO CASSETTE J-C A
Features super-heroine Meter Maid, young Dr Kilogram, and the French Gourmet in a look at metric measurement in the near future.
From The Measure To Measure Series.
Prod-WCVETV Dist-GPITVL 1975

Measuring Volume C 15 MIN
3/4 INCH VIDEO CASSETTE P
Explains that the liter is the basic unit of metric volume measurement. Tells how to estimate volumes to the nearest half-liter and the nearest metric cup.
From The Measuring Show Series.
Prod-MAETEL Dist-GPITVL 1979

Measuring Volume C 15 MIN
3/4 OR 1/2 INCH VIDEO CASSETTE P
See series title for descriptive statement.
From The Hands On, Grade 3 Series. Unit 2 - Measuring
Prod-VAOG Dist-AITECH Prodn-WHROTV 1975

Measuring Volumes Of Liquids C 11 MIN
16MM FILM, 3/4 OR 1/2 IN VIDEO H-C
Shows the correct use of graduated cylinders and pipets (volumetric and graduated.) Emphasizes accurate reading of the meniscus and proper handling of the equipment.
From The Basic Laboratory Techniques In Chemistry Series.
Prod-SCHLAT Dist-LUF 1972

Measuring Weight C 15 MIN
3/4 OR 1/2 INCH VIDEO CASSETTE P
See series title for descriptive statement.
From The Hands On, Grade 3 Series. Unit 2- Measuring
Prod-VAOG Dist-AITECH Prodn-WHROTV 1975

Measuring Weight C 15 MIN
3/4 OR 1/2 INCH VIDEO CASSETTE P-I
Discusses measuring weight.
From The Why Series.
Prod-WDCNTV Dist-AITECH 1976

Measuring Weight (Mass) C 15 MIN
3/4 INCH VIDEO CASSETTE P
Discusses the use of the gram and kilogram.
From The Measuring Show Series.
Prod-MAETEL Dist-GPITVL 1979

Measuring Your Blood Pressure Using A Wrap-Around Cuff C 9 MIN
3/4 OR 1/2 INCH VIDEO CASSETTE
Describes the benefits of taking accurate blood pressure readings, the equipment used and the procedure for taking and recording blood pressure readings to the person interested in taking his own blood pressure.
Prod-UMICHM Dist-UMICHM 1980

Measuring Your Clarity C 13 MIN
3/4 OR 1/2 INCH VIDEO CASSETTE
See series title for descriptive statement.
From The Put It In Writing Series.
Prod-DELTAK Dist-DELTAK

Measuring, Marking And Sawing Wood C 14 MIN
16MM FILM, 3/4 OR 1/2 IN VIDEO IND
Demonstrates the correct methods for measuring wood using the rule and tri-square. Deals with the selection of saws and the techniques of sawing. Shows correct tool care procedures.
From The Vocational Skillfilms - Woodworking Skills Series.
Prod-RTBL Dist-RTBL 1982

Measuring, Using Urns, Cups And Spoons C 20 MIN
1/2 IN VIDEO CASSETTE BETA/VHS
Discusses the correct methods of weighing dry and liquid ingredients by using various measuring containers. Demonstrates measuring techniques for both liquid and dry ingredients.
Prod-RMI Dist-RMI

Meat C
3/4 INCH VIDEO CASSETTE H A
Discusses various ways to prepare meat. Demonstrates two main dishes. Shows how to carve one's own steaks and chops from whole cuts of meat.
From The Matter Of Taste Series. Lesson 12
Prod-COAST Dist-CDTEL

Meat C 113 MIN
16MM FILM, 3/4 OR 1/2 IN VIDEO J-H A
Presents a documentary concerning the routine activities at a large meat packing plant and slaughterhouse.
LC NO. 76-703472
Prod-KINEFI Dist-ZIPRAH 1976

Meat C 113 MIN
16MM FILM, 3/4 OR 1/2 IN VIDEO
Traces the process through which cattle and sheep become consumer products. Depicts the processing and transportation of meat products, illustrating important points and problems in the area of production, logistics, equipment design, time-motion study and labor management.
Prod-WISEF Dist-ZIPRAH

Meat / OTC Drugs / Second Homes C
3/4 OR 1/2 INCH VIDEO CASSETTE
Presents tips on the purchase of meat, over-the-counter drugs and second homes.
From The Consumer Survival Series.
Prod-MDCPB Dist-MDCPB

Meat And Poultry - How To Select Them C 19 MIN
16MM FILM, 3/4 OR 1/2 IN VIDEO J-C
Explains how to select the best quality veal, chicken, lamb, beef, pork and hamburger. Illustrates the ways in which some stores take advantage of the customer and offers hints on cooking cheaper cuts that still have flavor and nutrition.
Prod-FLMFR Dist-FLMFR

Meat Buying - A Time Of Decision C 25 MIN
16MM FILM OPTICAL SOUND H-C A
Traces the history of beef procuction and retailing in the United States from its inception to the present day. Covers USDA inspection and grading, nutrition of meat and information on buying, indicating the best beef buys and modern methods of preparation and cooking.
LC NO. 79-705158
Prod-ADOL Dist-ADOL Prodn-PRIVOW 1970

Meat Cookery C 18 MIN
16MM FILM, 3/4 OR 1/2 IN VIDEO J-C A
Demonstrates different methods of cooking various cuts of beef depending upon the tenderness and fat content. Includes instructions on the use of a meat thermometer and proper carving techniques.
LC NO. 81-707258
Prod-CENTRO Dist-CORF 1981

Meat Fight, The C 14 MIN
3/4 INCH VIDEO CASSETTE
Illustrates the role of leaders in Kung society and the ability to settle disputes without violence or political organization. Features bushmen of Namibia arguing over an antelope.
From The San (Bushmen) Series.
Prod-DOCEDR Dist-DOCEDR Prodn-MRSHL

Meat Of The Matter, The, Pt 1 C 29 MIN
3/4 OR 1/2 INCH VIDEO CASSETTE H-C A
Explains meat grading, meat tenderizing and meat labeling. Discusses the relationshop of cut to tenderness in beef, pork and lamb along with the variety of ground meat products.
From The Be A Better Shopper Series. Program 7
LC NO. 81-707307
Prod-CUETV Dist-CUNIV 1978

Meat Of The Matter, The, Pt 2 C 29 MIN
3/4 OR 1/2 INCH VIDEO CASSETTE H-C A
Deals with how to get the best buy on meat. Discusses meat merchandizing, butcher-performed services and buying from bulk-meat dealers.
From The Be A Better Shopper Series. Program 8
LC NO. 81-707308
Prod-CUETV Dist-CUNIV 1978

Meat Of The Matter, The, Pt 3 C 29 MIN
3/4 OR 1/2 INCH VIDEO CASSETTE H-C A
Looks at sources of protein in other than meat, including grains, seeds, nuts and dairy products. Discusses hams and other cured meats and poultry products and fish.
From The Be A Better Shopper Series. Program 9
LC NO. 81-707309
Prod-CUETV Dist-CUNIV 1978

Meat-Cooperative, A B 10 MIN
16MM FILM OPTICAL SOUND H-C A
Tells the story of how a meat-cooperative was formed on the Lower East Side of New York to side step high prices, poor quality and weight cheating by local supermarkets.
Prod-SFN Dist-SFN 1968

Meatless Menus C 11 MIN
16MM FILM - 3/4 IN VIDEO
Demonstrates the preparation of meatless meals that are completely balanced nutritionally. Emphasizes complementary proteins, with descriptive art work to show the essential amino acids and how they are completed by proper combinations of proteins in each meal.
From The Eat Right To Your Heart's Delight Series.
Prod-IPS Dist-IPS 1976

Meats Coming West C 29 MIN
2 INCH VIDEOTAPE
Presents host Sam Arnold, presenting western recipes on cooking meats.
From The Frying Pans West Series.
Prod-KRMATV Dist-PUBTEL

Mechanic's Tool Box, The C 30 MIN
3/4 OR 1/2 INCH VIDEO CASSETTE IND

Describes tools to be included in every mechanic's tool box plus use of special tools for particular jobs.
From The Aircraft Hardware, Hand Tools And Measuring Devices Series.
Prod-AVIMA Dist-AVIMA

Mechanical - Electrical—A Series

Prod-TAT Dist-TAT 1973

Bearings 25 MIN
Brakes And Clutches 29 MIN

Mechanical Aids C 10 MIN
16MM FILM, 3/4 OR 1/2 IN VIDEO
Shows common mistakes associated with using the saw bench, skill saw, concrete mixer, dumper and electrical hand tools. Defines procedures which should become routine for safe work habits.
From The Safety In Construction Series.
Prod-NFBTE Dist-IFB

Mechanical Aids To Breathing And Pulmonary Resuscitation C 56 MIN
3/4 INCH VIDEO CASSETTE
Illustrates and describes the purpose and the use of the various sizes of oropharyngeal airways. Demonstrates the proper technique for inserting the airways and describes the purpose and operation of suction equipment.
From The Medical Legal Component Film Series.
LC NO. 74-706496
Prod-KYDHPS Dist-USNAC Prodn-UKY 1974

Mechanical Capers For Fun And Fitness C 12 MIN
16MM FILM OPTICAL SOUND P-I
Depicts physical activities in which children imitate the motions of earth moving and highway building machinery and equipment.
Prod-MMP Dist-MMP 1967

Mechanical Component Reliability Prediction, Probalistic Design For Reliability...—A Series

Presents Dimitri Kececioglu, Professor of Aerospace and Mechanical Engineering at the University of Arizona, discussing mechanical component reliability prediction, probabilistic design for reliability, and the stress/ strength interference or overlap approach to component reliability prediction with applications.
Prod-UAZMIC Dist-UAZMIC 1980

Applications Of The Methodologies
Component Reliability And Its Confidence 060 MIN
Methodology Overview And Calculation Of 060 MIN
Synthesis Of The Failure Governing Stress 060 MIN

Mechanical Compounds C 8 MIN
16MM FILM, 3/4 OR 1/2 IN VIDEO IND
See series title for descriptive statement.
From The You Need To Know Series.
Prod-UTEXPE Dist-UTEXPE 1981

Mechanical Crabs C 10 MIN
16MM FILM, 3/4 OR 1/2 IN VIDEO J-C A
Uses animation to tell a science fiction story about a military scientist who develops the ultimate weapon, automatic machines shaped like crabs and strong enough to devour metal and crush anything in their path.
Prod-SFSP Dist-PHENIX 1977

Mechanical Design C 180 MIN
3/4 OR 1/2 INCH VIDEO CASSETTE PRO
Covers, in three one-hour lectures, component design including springs, belts, ropes, power screws, shafts and bearings, and system design including clutches, brakes and gear trains.
From The Professional Engineer Review Series.
Prod-UILU Dist-AMCEE

Mechanical Design In Lifts C 24 MIN
16MM FILM OPTICAL SOUND
Demonstrates practical applications of engineering mechanics in the redesign of a traditional mining elevator and a passenger elevator in a multi-story building. Shows engineers designing the member of an elevator sling using concepts of stress analysis for structures, dynamics, kinematics and statics.
Prod-BBCTV Dist-OPENU 1981

Mechanical Drives, Couplings And Alignment C 120 MIN
3/4 OR 1/2 INCH VIDEO CASSETTE IND
Deals with couplings, alignment, belts, chains, speed reducers and vibration.
From The Mechanical Equipment Maintenance Series.
Prod-ITCORP Dist-ITCORP

Mechanical Drives, Couplings And Alignment (Spanish) C 120 MIN
3/4 OR 1/2 INCH VIDEO CASSETTE IND
Deals with couplings, alignment, belts, chains, speed reducers and vibration.
From The Mechanical Equipment Maintenance (Spanish) Series.
Prod-ITCORP Dist-ITCORP

Mechanical Electricity C 15 MIN
3/4 INCH VIDEO CASSETTE I
Surveys two ways of creating electricity and discovers the things which make possible mechanical electricity.
From The Search For Science (2nd Ed.) Unit V - Electricity Series.
Prod-WVIZTV Dist-GPITVL

Mechanical Energy And Thermal Energy B 22 MIN
16MM FILM OPTICAL SOUND H-C
Shows several models to illustrate both the bulk motion and random motion of molecules. Shows their interconnection as the energy of bulk motion. Discusses thermal conduction and absolute temperature scale.
From The PSSC Physics Films Series.
Prod-PSSC Dist-MLA 1959

Mechanical Equipment Maintenance (Spanish)—A Series
IND
Discusses mechanical equipment maintenance. Includes student workbooks, discussion guides and overhead transparencies.
Prod-ITCORP Dist-ITCORP

Advanced Alignment (Spanish) 060 MIN
Advanced Pipefitting (Spanish) 240 MIN
Air Compressors (Spanish) 180 MIN
Bearings And Lubrication (Spanish) 180 MIN
Boilers And Boiler Equipment (Spanish) 120 MIN
Centrifugal Pumps (Spanish) 240 MIN
Coal And Ash Handling Equipment, Conveyors 120 MIN
Diesel Engines (Spanish) 180 MIN
Hydraulic Equipment (Spanish) 120 MIN
Mechanical Drives, Couplings And Alignment 120 MIN
Packing And Seals (Spanish) 120 MIN
Piping (Spanish) 240 MIN
Relief Valves (Spanish) 120 MIN
Rigging And Lifting (Spanish) 240 MIN
Specialized Centrifugal Pumps (Spanish) 060 MIN
Valves (Spanish) 240 MIN
Vibration Analysis (Spanish) 060 MIN

Mechanical Equipment Maintenance—A Series
IND
Encompasses the maintenance of principal components of shop and factory, from rigging and lifting to couplings and alignment, packing and seals, pipes, pumps, valves and pipefitting.
Prod-ITCORP Dist-ITCORP

Advanced Alignment 060 MIN
Advanced Pipefitting 240 MIN
Air Compressors 180 MIN
Bearings And Lubrication 180 MIN
Boilers And Boiler Equipment 120 MIN
Centrifugal Pumps 240 MIN
Coal And Ash Handling Equipment, Conveyors 120 MIN
Diesel Engines 180 MIN
Hydraulic Equipment 120 MIN
Mechanical Drives, Couplings And Alignment 120 MIN
Packing And Seals 120 MIN
Piping 240 MIN
Relief Valves 120 MIN
Rigging And Lifting 240 MIN
Specialized Centrifugal Pumps 060 MIN
Valves 240 MIN
Vibration Analysis 060 MIN

Mechanical Equipment Maintenance, Module 1 Rigging And Lifting—A Series
IND
Focuses on several aspects of rigging and lifting. Forms one of twenty-one modules in mechanical maintenance training.
Prod-LEIKID Dist-LEIKID

Forklifts And Mobile Cranes 060 MIN
Hand Operated Hoists 060 MIN
Ladders And Scaffolds 060 MIN
Power Operated Hoists And Cranes 060 MIN

Mechanical Equipment Maintenance, Module 10 - Boiler And Boiler equipment—A Series
IND
Covers tube and boiler maintenance. Forms one of twenty-one mechanical maintenance training modules.
Prod-LEIKID Dist-LEIKID

Boiler Equipment 060 MIN
Tube Repair 060 MIN

Mechanical Equipment Maintenance, Module 11 - Coal And Ash Handling Equipment—A Series
IND
Focuses on maintenance of coal and ash handling conveyors. Constitutes one of twenty-one mechanical maintenance training modules.
Prod-LEIKID Dist-LEIKID

Ash Handling Equipment 060 MIN
Coal Handling Equipment 060 MIN

Mechanical Equipment Maintenance, Module 12 - Diesel Engines—A Series
IND
Focuses on maintenance of diesel engines. Forms one module of a twenty-one module section on mechanical maintenance training.
Prod-LEIKID Dist-LEIKID

Diesel Systems 060 MIN
Preventive Maintenance, Pt 1 060 MIN
Preventive Maintenance, Pt 2 060 MIN

Mechanical Equipment Maintenance, Module 13 - Vibration Analysis C 60 MIN
3/4 OR 1/2 INCH VIDEO CASSETTE IND
Covers measurements, evaluation and correction. Comprises one of twenty-one mechanical maintenance training modules.
Prod-LEIKID Dist-LEIKID

Mechanical Equipment Maintenance, Module 14 - Relief Valves—A Series
IND
Covers operation and maintenance of safety and relief valves. Forms one of twenty-one mechanical maintenance training modules.
Prod-LEIKID Dist-LEIKID

Electrically Operated Relief Valves 060 MIN
Steam And Gas Safety Valves 060 MIN

Mechanical Equipment Maintenance, Module 15 - Advanced Alignment C 60 MIN
3/4 OR 1/2 INCH VIDEO CASSETTE IND
Examines double dial indicator techniques. Comprises one of twenty-one mechanical maintenance training modules.
Prod-LEIKID Dist-LEIKID

Mechanical Equipment Maintenance, Module 16 - Hydraulic Equipment—A Series
IND
Covers maintenance of hydraulic equipment. Forms one of twenty-one modules in mechanical maintenance training.
Prod-LEIKID Dist-LEIKID

Basic Hydraulics, Cylinder Overhaul 060 MIN
Gear Pumps, Vane Pumps 060 MIN

Mechanical Equipment Maintenance, Module 17 Advanced Pipefitting—A Series
IND
Covers instruction and mainteance of piping. Comprises one of twenty-one modules in mechanical maintenance training.
Prod-LEIKID Dist-LEIKID

Blueprints, Piping Layout 060 MIN
Joint Lubrication 060 MIN
Piping Prepartion And Installation 060 MIN
Plastic Piping 060 MIN

Mechanical Equipment Maintenance, Module 2 - Mechanical Drives, Couplings...—A Series
IND
Covers aspects of couplings and alignment in mechanical drives. Comprises one of twenty-one modules in mechanical maintenance training.
Prod-LEIKID Dist-LEIKID

Chains, Speed Reducers, Vibration 060 MIN
Couplings, Alignment And Belts 060 MIN

Mechanical Equipment Maintenance, Module 3 - Packing And Seals—A Series
IND
Covers maintenance aspects of bearings and lubrication. Comprises one of twenty-one modules in mechanical maintenance training.
Prod-LEIKID Dist-LEIKID

Mechanical Seals 060 MIN
Pump And Valve Packing 060 MIN

Mechanical Equipment Maintenance, Module 4 - Bearings And Lubrication—A Series
IND
Examines types of bearings and how to maintain them. Comprises one of twenty-one modules in mechanical maintenance.
Prod-LEIKID Dist-LEIKID

Anti-Friction Bearings 060 MIN
Plain Journal Bearings 060 MIN
Tilting Pad, Oil Film, Trust Bearings 060 MIN

Mechanical Equipment Maintenance, Module 5 - Centrifugal Pumps—A Series
IND
Focuses on disassembly, repair and assembly of pumps and rotors. Comprises one of twenty-one modules in mechanical maintenance training.
Prod-LEIKID Dist-LEIKID

Pump Assembly 060 MIN
Pump Disassembly 060 MIN
Rotor Assembly 060 MIN
Rotor Repair 060 MIN

Mechanical Equipment Maintenance, Module 6 - Special Centrifugal Pumps C 60 MIN
3/4 OR 1/2 INCH VIDEO CASSETTE IND
Covers standardized end suction and vertical pumps. Comprises one of twenty-one modules in mechanical maintenance.
Prod-LEIKID Dist-LEIKID

Mechanical Equipment Maintenance, Module 7 - Piping—A Series
IND
Focuses on aspects of piping maintenance. Comprises one of twenty-one modules in mechanical maintenance training.
Prod-LEIKID Dist-LEIKID

General Maintenance 060 MIN
Heat Exchangers 060 MIN
Strainers, Filters, And Traps 060 MIN
Tubing And Piping 060 MIN

Mechanical Equipment Maintenance, Module 8 - Vavles—A Series
IND
Covers several aspects of valve maintenance. Comprises one of twenty-one modules in mechanical maintenance training.
Prod-LEIKID Dist-LEIKID

Control Valves 060 MIN
Diaphragm And Butterfly Valves 060 MIN
Gate Valves 060 MIN
Globe Valves 060 MIN

Mechanical Interest And Ability In A Home-Raised Chimpanzee, Pt 1 B 17 MIN
16MM FILM SILENT C T
Briefly demonstrates the structure and function of a chimpanzee's hands, following the development of manual dexterity

from age eight months to six years in such activities as playing with blocks and toys, fastening snap-and-ring sets, attempting to tie knots, filing nails and using carpenter's tools.
Prod-PSUPCR Dist-PSUPCR 1954

Mechanical Interest And Ability In A Home-Raised Chimpanzee, Pt 2 B 18 MIN
16MM FILM SILENT C T
Shows a female chimpanzee's behavior in response to water from ages nine months to six years and behavior in response to fire from ages three to five years. Demonstrates cigarette smoking, sand play, scribbling, use of knife, stringing of beads and use of needle and thread at various ages.
Prod-PSUPCR Dist-PSUPCR 1954

Mechanical Interest And Ability In A Home-Raised Chimpanzee, Pt 3 B 16 MIN
16MM FILM SILENT C T
Shows a female chimpanzee's responses to and usage of such objects as lights and light switches, electric fan, telephone, phonograph, music-box, mirror, iodine applicator, toys and blocks. Covers ages two to five years.
Prod-PSUPCR Dist-PSUPCR 1954

Mechanical Interest And Ability In A Home-Raised Chimpanzee, Pt 4 B 18 MIN
16MM FILM SILENT C T
Presents instances of formal training, including putting on clothes, using a toilet chair, eating with a spoon, opening bottles, cans and jars, pouring coffee, using faucets and solving classical problems.
Prod-PSUPCR Dist-PSUPCR 1954

Mechanical Maintenance Basics (Spanish)—A Series
IND
Provides basic instruction in mechanical maintenance. Includes student workbooks, discussion guides and overhead transparencies.
Prod-ITCORP Dist-ITCORP

General Shop Practices (Spanish) 180 MIN
Hand Tools (Spanish) 120 MIN
Measuring Instruments (Spanish) 060 MIN
Mechanical Print Reading (Spanish) 060 MIN

Mechanical Maintenance Basics—A Series
IND
Covers basics of shop practice, including use and maintenance of hand tools, measuring instruments, general shop practices, including layout and drilling operations, grinding, cutting. Shows mechanical print reading including symbols and layout drawings, and print reading and interpretation.
Prod-ITCORP Dist-ITCORP

General Shop Practices 180 MIN
Hand Tools 120 MIN
Measuring Instruments 060 MIN
Mechanical Print Reading 060 MIN

Mechanical Maintenance Basics, Module A - Hand Tools—A Series
IND
Examines several hand tools used in mechanical maintenance. Comprises one of twenty-one modules on mechanical maintenance training.
Prod-LEIKID Dist-LEIKID

Chisels, Hacksaws, Files, Reamers, Power Drills 060 MIN
Vises, Clamps, Pliers, Screwdrivers, Wrenches 060 MIN

Mechanical Maintenance Basics, Module B - Measuring Instruments C 60 MIN
3/4 OR 1/2 INCH VIDEO CASSETTE IND
Covers steel rule, Vernier calipers, thickness gauges and micrometers. Comprise one of twenty-one modules on modules on mechancal maintenance training.
Prod-LEIKID Dist-LEIKID

Mechanical Maintenance Basics, Module C - General Shop Practices—A Series
IND
Focuses on drilling, grinding and cutting practices. Forms one of twenty-one modules on mechanical maintenance basics.
Prod-LEIKID Dist-LEIKID

Cutting 060 MIN
Grinding 060 MIN
Layout And Drilling Operations 060 MIN

Mechanical Maintenance Basics, Module D - Mechanical Print Reading C 60 MIN
3/4 OR 1/2 INCH VIDEO CASSETTE IND
Covers symbols, layout drawings, print reading and interpretation. Comprises one of twenty-one modules.
Prod-LEIKID Dist-LEIKID

Mechanical Melodies C 5 MIN
16MM FILM OPTICAL SOUND I-H A
Shows the beautifully shaped parts inside the mechanical pianorchestra as they move, beat, tap and turn fantastic patterns while creating gay music.
LC NO. 73-700488
Prod-STONEB Dist-CONNF 1973

Mechanical Needle C 9 MIN
16MM FILM, 3/4 OR 1/2 IN VIDEO P-I
Shows how a woodpecker who uses his beak to help Boy mend a torn sail gives Boy the idea for inventing a sewing machine using a needle with an eye in the point attached to a wheel driven by a foot pedal.
From The Inventive Child Series.
Prod-POLSKI Dist-EBEC 1983

Mechanical Operation Of The Model 28 Teletypewriter - Automatic Typer Selecting... B 11 MIN
16MM FILM OPTICAL SOUND
Shows the chain of action in the automatic typer of the Model 28 teletypewriter from the signal generator to and through the selecting mechanism that operates the code bars.
LC NO. FIE58-29
Prod-USN Dist-USNAC 1954

Mechanical Operation Of The Model 28 Teletypewriter - Function Mechanism B 11 MIN
16MM FILM OPTICAL SOUND
Shows the mechanical chain of action in the function mechanism of the Model 28 teletypewriter. Emphasizes the operation of the function clutch as opposed to the main shaft clutch.
LC NO. FIE58-31
Prod-USN Dist-USNAC 1954

Mechanical Operation Of The Model 28 Teletypewriter - Keyboard Transmitting... B 13 MIN
16MM FILM OPTICAL SOUND
Shows the mechanical operation of the keyboard transmitting mechanism of the Model 28 teletypewriter. Traces the action from the key punched to the signal generator and explains each part in the chain between keyboard and generator.
LC NO. FIE58-28
Prod-USN Dist-USNAC 1954

Mechanical Operation Of The Model 28 Teletypewriter - Type Box Positioning Mechanism B 20 MIN
16MM FILM OPTICAL SOUND
Shows the chain of action of the mechanical levers that position the type box of the Model 28 teletypewriter in the proper position so that the letter or figure key that is punched may be printed.
LC NO. FIE58-30
Prod-USN Dist-USNAC 1954

Mechanical Packing Aboard Ship B 30 MIN
16MM FILM OPTICAL SOUND
Demonstrates how to pack a spiral wound gasket and a steam reciprocating pump rod, repack a centrifugal part, and replace packing around a condenser tube.
LC NO. FIE52-1081
Prod-USN Dist-USNAC Prodn-BEF 1948

Mechanical Paradise, The C 52 MIN
16MM FILM, 3/4 OR 1/2 IN VIDEO C A
Takes a look at Western art between 1870 and 1914. Shows how art adapted to a fragmented world by depicting its subjects in a fragmented manner, specifically through cubism. Describes the work of Delaunay, Duchamp, and Picabia.
From The Shock Of The New Series.
LC NO. 80-706950
Prod-BBCTV Dist-TIMLIF 1980

Mechanical Power Transmission—A Series
16MM FILM, 3/4 OR 1/2 IN VIDEO IND
Describes the mechanical power principles of machines, exploring such operating components as belts, bearings, gears, chains and joining devices. Emphasizes the importance of early machine designs to man and how these early plans still govern modern components.
Prod-LUF Dist-LUF 1977

Bearings 019 MIN
Chain And Chain Drives 017 MIN
From Muscle To Machine 016 MIN
Gears And Gear Drives 018 MIN
Shafting, Couplings And Joining Devices 018 MIN
V-Belts And V-Belt Drives 019 MIN

Mechanical Print Reading C 60 MIN
3/4 OR 1/2 INCH VIDEO CASSETTE IND
Focuses on symbols, layout drawings, print reading and interpretation.
From The Mechanical Maintenance Basics Series.
Prod-ITCORP Dist-ITCORP

Mechanical Print Reading (Spanish) C 60 MIN
3/4 OR 1/2 INCH VIDEO CASSETTE IND
Teaches mechanical print reading. Covers symbols, layout drawings and interpretation.
From The Mechanical Maintenance Basics (Spanish) Series.
Prod-ITCORP Dist-ITCORP

Mechanical Refrigeration - How It Works B 22 MIN
16MM FILM OPTICAL SOUND H A
Explains the function, theory and operation of a refrigeration system.
LC NO. FIE52-77
Prod-USN Dist-USNAC Prodn-HANDY 1947

Mechanical Reliability—A Series
C
Provides an overview of most modern methodology of predicting the reliability of components at the design stage and of designing a specified reliability goal into components at a desired confidence level.
Prod-UAZMIC Dist-AMCEE

Applications Of The Methodologies 060 MIN
Component Reliability And Its Confidence Limit 060 MIN
Methodology Overview And Calculation Of 060 MIN
Synthesis Of The Failure Governing Stress And 060 MIN

Mechanical Seal Installation C 20 MIN
3/4 OR 1/2 INCH VIDEO CASSETTE IND
Demonstrates the function and installation of single inside, double inside and single outside mechanical seals. Shows how to prevent seal wear and keep maintenance expense at a minimum.
From The Marshall Maintenance Training Programs Series. Tape 18
Prod-LEIKID Dist-LEIKID

Mechanical Seal Installation C 20 MIN
16MM FILM, 3/4 OR 1/2 IN VIDEO IND
Demonstrates the function and installation of single inside, double inside and single outside mechanical seals. Deals with ways of preventing seal wear to keep maintenance expense at a minimum.
Prod-MOKIN Dist-MOKIN

Mechanical Seals C 60 MIN
3/4 OR 1/2 INCH VIDEO CASSETTE IND
From The Mechanical Equipment Maintenance, Module 3 - Packing And Seals Series.
Prod-LEIKID Dist-LEIKID

Mechanical Switch, The C
3/4 OR 1/2 INCH VIDEO CASSETTE
See series title for descriptive statement.
From The Basic DC Circuits Series.
Prod-VTRI Dist-VTRI

Mechanical Switch, The C 15 MIN
3/4 OR 1/2 INCH VIDEO CASSETTE
See series title for descriptive statement.
From The Basic Electricity And D.C. Circuits, Laboratory Series.
Prod-TXINLC Dist-TXINLC

Mechanical Testing Of Metals C 35 MIN
3/4 INCH VIDEO CASSETTE C A
See series title for descriptive statement.
From The Elements Of Metallurgy Series.
LC NO. 81-706194
Prod-AMCEE Dist-AMCEE 1980

Mechanical Testing Of Metals C 45 MIN
3/4 OR 1/2 INCH VIDEO CASSETTE PRO
See series title for descriptive statement.
From The Elements Of Metallurgy Series.
Prod-ICSINT Dist-ICSINT

Mechanical Troubleshooting C 60 MIN
3/4 OR 1/2 INCH VIDEO CASSETTE IND
Explores general procedures for troubleshooting, short cycling, high discharge pressure and low suction pressure.
From The Air Conditioning And Refrigeration– Training Series.
Prod-ITCORP Dist-ITCORP

Mechanical Universe—A Series
C A
Teaches the physics course developed by Dr David Goodstein and introduced at the California Institute of Technology in 1979. Features scenes at Newton's home and Galileo's haunts in Italy as well as using intricate sets, demonstration experiments and computer animation.
Prod-ANNCPB Dist-FI

Angular Momentum 030 MIN
Apple And The Moon, The 030 MIN
Conservation Of Energy 030 MIN
Conservation Of Momentum 030 MIN
Derivatives 030 MIN
Energy And Eccentricity 030 MIN
From Kepler To Einstein 030 MIN
Fundamental Forces, The 030 MIN
Gravity, Electricity, Magnetism 030 MIN
Harmonic Motion 030 MIN
Harmony Of The Spheres 030 MIN
Inertia 030 MIN
Integration 030 MIN
Introduction To The Mechanical Universe 030 MIN
Kepler Problem, The 030 MIN
Kepler's Three Laws 030 MIN
Law Of Falling Bodies, The 030 MIN
Millikan Experiment, The 030 MIN
Moving In Circles 030 MIN
Navigating In Space 030 MIN
Newton's Laws 030 MIN
Potential Energy 030 MIN
Resonance 030 MIN
Torques And Gyroscopes 030 MIN
Vectors 030 MIN
Waves 030 MIN

Mechanical Waves C 20 MIN
16MM FILM, 3/4 OR 1/2 IN VIDEO H-C
Uses real-life examples and laboratory experiments to explain the properties of mechanical waves. Explores such concepts as wave amplitude, frequency, wavelength, velocity, pulse, bore, periodic waves, standing waves, the Law of Reflection, diffraction, the Doppler Effect and interference.
From The Energy And Waves Series.
Prod-CASDEN Dist-BARR 1983

Mechanics Of Composite Materials—A Series
C A
Examines the problems involved in fiber reinforced composite materials. Considers micromechanical and macromechanical behavior of fiber reinforced composites. Contains 41 fifty-minute videotape lectures.
Prod-UIDEEO Dist-UIDEEO

Mechanics Of Flight In Flying Foxes C 8 MIN
16MM FILM, 3/4 OR 1/2 IN VIDEO H-C A
Uses ultra-slow-motion photography inside an experimental wind tunnel to analyze the flight of large bats.
From The Aspects Of Animal Behavior Series.
Prod-UCLA Dist-UCEMC 1974

Mechanics Of Life - Blood And Circulation C 8 MIN
16MM FILM, 3/4 OR 1/2 IN VIDEO I
Uses X-ray photography and animation to describe how the human blood system is designed. Shows the composition of blood through microphotography and discusses the role of each blood component.
From The Mechanics Of Life Series.
Prod-EOTHEN Dist-PHENIX 1971

Mechanics Of Life - Bones And Joints C 8 MIN
16MM FILM, 3/4 OR 1/2 IN VIDEO I
Describes the skeletal construction of the human body. Notes that although a unity of pattern exists in the skeletal structures of vertebrates, each organism has developed a skeleton that provides support and allows movements needed for its particular lifestyle.
From The Mechanics Of Life Series.
Prod-EOTHEN Dist-PHENIX 1971

Mechanics Of Life - Breathing And Respiration C 9 MIN
16MM FILM, 3/4 OR 1/2 IN VIDEO I
Points out that organisms with very small volumes, such as amoebae, can get the oxygen they need through the membranes that define their bodies. Shows that larger organisms have developed systems that increase the surface area that can be used for oxygen-carbon dioxide transfer. Notes that the lung system in the human provides a very large surface for gas exchange, but is very delicate.
From The Mechanics Of Life Series.
Prod-EOTHEN Dist-PHENIX 1971

Mechanics Of Life - Digestion And The Food We Eat C 9 MIN
16MM FILM, 3/4 OR 1/2 IN VIDEO
Points out that the body needs a well-balanced diet in order to remain healthy. Explains that a good diet provides the right amounts of proteins, fats, carbohydrates, vitamins and minerals. Describes the process of preparing foods rich in these basic materials for use within the body.
From The Mechanics Of Life Series.
Prod-EOTHEN Dist-PHENIX 1971

Mechanics Of Life - Muscles And Movement C 10 MIN
16MM FILM, 3/4 OR 1/2 IN VIDEO
Explains what muscles are and how they work. Describes the difference between voluntary and involuntary muscles, and stresses that good posture and proper exercise help muscles work efficiently.
From The Mechanics Of Life Series.
Prod-EOTHEN Dist-PHENIX 1971

Mechanics Of Life—A Series
16MM FILM, 3/4 OR 1/2 IN VIDEO I
Explores the various systems of the body, including bone, muscles, digestion, respiration and blood.
Prod-EOTHEN Dist-PHENIX 1971

Mechanics Of Life - Blood And Circulation 8 MIN
Mechanics Of Life - Bones And Joints 8 MIN
Mechanics Of Life - Breathing And Respiration 9 MIN
Mechanics Of Life - Digestion And The Food We 9 MIN
Mechanics Of Life - Muscles And Movement 10 MIN

Mechanics Of Materials B 150 MIN
3/4 OR 1/2 INCH VIDEO CASSETTE PRO
See series title for descriptive statement.
From The Professional Engineer's Exam Refresher Course Series.
Prod-UMICE Dist-AMCEE

Mechanics Of Television, The C
3/4 INCH VIDEO CASSETTE T
Explains the physical principles behind the television picture. Demonstrates the operation of a color television set and videocassette player.
From The Visual Learning Series. Session 4
Prod-NYSED Dist-NYSED

Mechanics Of The Photoelectric Paper Tape Reader B 14 MIN
16MM FILM OPTICAL SOUND H A
Describes the mechanical components of the photoelectric paper tape reader and indicates the proper loading procedure.
LC NO. FI67-2000
Prod-IBUSMA Dist-IBUSMA 1963

Mechanism Of An Organic Reaction C 20 MIN
16MM FILM OPTICAL SOUND H
A study of the hydrolysis of the ester methyl benzoate shows that the discovery of a reaction mechanism includes a determination of the chemical equation, the structures of the reactants and products, the fate of each atom of the reactants and the structures of the intermediate molecules. Discusses bond polarity.
From The CHEM Study Films Series.
Prod-CHEMS Dist-MLA 1962

Mechanism Of Machining B
16MM FILM OPTICAL SOUND
Presents a study from the University of Michigan on the mechanism of machining.
Prod-MASTER Dist-MASTER

Mechanisms - An Introduction To Machine Motions And Kinematics X 21 MIN
16MM FILM OPTICAL SOUND C A
Animated toys are used to demonstrate concepts in the study of mechanisms and kinematics.
Prod-PUAVC Dist-PUAVC 1961

Mechanisms For Voice Frequency Change C 10 MIN
16MM FILM, 3/4 OR 1/2 IN VIDEO
Surveys available information on vocal fold lengthening and thinning, cricoid cartilage rocking and the upward position of the larynx in the neck as voice frequency is increased. Analyzes the interactions of these factors and explains the mechanics responsible for laryngeal alterations.
Prod-UCSF Dist-UCEMC 1977

Mechanisms Of Bacterial Transformation C 56 MIN
3/4 INCH VIDEO CASSETTE
Discusses advances in the research about bacterial transformation and gives attention to DNA cycling.
Prod-UTAHTI Dist-UTAHTI

Mechanisms Of Chip Formation C 22 MIN
3/4 INCH VIDEO CASSETTE
Shows the physical characteristics of various metals during machining, turning, shaping or drilling. Explains behavior of several types of metal under stress of a sharper blade.
Prod-UMITV Dist-UMITV 1967

Mechanisms Of Defense - Accident C 26 MIN
3/4 OR 1/2 INCH VIDEO CASSETTE
Points out that the body is like a self-supporting hospital, able to deal on its own with wounds, bacterial invasions, fractures and obstructions to its various passages. Follows the sequence of events over seconds or weeks when skin or bone are damaged, and shows the defensive reactions of blood clotting, fever and mending bone fracture.
From The Living Body - An Introduction To Human Biology Series.
Prod-FOTH Dist-FOTH 1985

Mechanisms Of Defense - Internal Defenses C 26 MIN
3/4 OR 1/2 INCH VIDEO CASSETTE
Discusses the mechanisms of defense used by the body when bacteria or viruses invade the whole system. Shows the roles of the spleen, the lymphatic system and the white blood cells, and explains the body's production of antibodies. Uses the common cold as an example to follow the sequence from viral attack to recovery.
From The Living Body - An Introduction To Human Biology Series.
Prod-FOTH Dist-FOTH 1985

Mechanisms Of Disease - Host Defenses—A Series
PRO
Offers a basic understanding of human defense mechanisms, how they work and, sometimes, don't work. Explains body's normal functions, then discusses typical abnormalities and how they result.
Prod-BRA Dist-BRA

Dynamics Of Immunocompetence 019 MIN
Hypersensitivity And Autoimmunity 016 MIN
Immunodeficiency Diseases 016 MIN
Nonspecific Defense Mechanisms 015 MIN

Mechanisms Of Evolution C 45 MIN
3/4 OR 1/2 INCH VIDEO CASSETTE C
Discusses the mechanisms of evolution.
From The Biology I Series.
Prod-MDCPB Dist-MDCPB

Mechanisms Of Neurosurgical Football Injuries C 14 MIN
3/4 INCH VIDEO CASSETTE
Consists of actual high school, college and professional football plays which have caused serious and fatal head and spinal injuries.
Prod-UMITV Dist-UMITV 1967

Mechanisms Of Respiratory Clearance C 15 MIN
16MM FILM, 3/4 OR 1/2 IN VIDEO
Shows the mechanisms of cilia beating, the influence of mucus load and the measurement and significance of the viscoelasticity of mucus. Describes how variations on these factors determine the clearance of mucus.
Prod-VAMBNY Dist-USNAC 1982

Mechanisms Of The Intrinsic Muscles Of The Larynx C 25 MIN
16MM FILM - 3/4 IN VIDEO
Demonstrates the cartilaginous and musculature anatomy of the human larynx. Exhibits the functions of the muscles during speech, breathing and other activities. Issued in 1965 as a motion picture.
LC NO. 77-706122
Prod-USPHS Dist-USNAC Prodn-NMAC

Mechanization C 10 MIN
16MM FILM, 3/4 OR 1/2 IN VIDEO
Shows how mechanization contributes to the creation of wealth.
From The Foundations Of Wealth Series.
Prod-FOTH Dist-FOTH

Mechanization In Plant Breeding C 17 MIN
16MM FILM OPTICAL SOUND H-C
Shows how new techniques of mechanized sowing allow a small group of plant breeders to handle an increased breeding program. Follows these techniques through a year's field testing.
LC NO. FIA65-1065
Prod-CSIROA Dist-CSIROA Prodn-CSIRFU 1963

Meconium Ilues And The Meconium Plug Syndrome C 18 MIN
16MM FILM OPTICAL SOUND PRO
Explains that among the strange catastrophes that befall the intestinal tract of the newborn infant, meconium ileus and obstruction due to meconium plug are among the rarest and the most difficult to treat. Illustrates four distinct types of obstruction due to meconium.
Prod-ACYDGD Dist-ACY 1958

Medal Of Honor C 30 MIN
3/4 OR 1/2 INCH VIDEO CASSETTE H-C A
See series title for descriptive statement.
From The World War II - GI Diary Series.
Prod-TIMLIF Dist-TIMLIF 1980

Medal Of Honor - A Team Man B 5 MIN
16MM FILM OPTICAL SOUND
Cites Forrest Vosler for bravery and self-sacrifice while serving as a radio operator-air gunner on a mission over Bremen, Germany, in 1943.
LC NO. 74-705105
Prod-USAF Dist-USNAC 1967

Medal Of Honor - Ace Of Aces B 5 MIN
16MM FILM OPTICAL SOUND
Cites Captain Eddy Rickenbacker for his heroism as a World War I fighter pilot.
LC NO. 74-705106
Prod-USAF Dist-USNAC 1967

Medal Of Honor - America Strikes Back B 7 MIN
16MM FILM OPTICAL SOUND
Cites General James Doolittle for leadership in the first air raid over Tokyo.
LC NO. 74-706138
Prod-USAF Dist-USNAC 1967

Medal Of Honor - Burning Ploesti Oil B 7 MIN
16MM FILM OPTICAL SOUND
Cites Col Leon Johnson and Col John Krane for bravery in Ploesti oil raids.
LC NO. 74-705107
Prod-USAF Dist-USNAC 1967

Medal Of Honor - By Act Of Congress B 5 MIN
16MM FILM OPTICAL SOUND
Cites Charles A Lindbergh for navigational skill and courage in his historic flight from New York to Paris.
LC NO. 75-703725
Prod-USAF Dist-USNAC 1967

Medal Of Honor - Capt Hilliard A Wilbanks C 10 MIN
16MM FILM OPTICAL SOUND
Cites the late Capt Hilliard A Wilbanks, a forward air control pilot, for saving the lives of many Americans by using his small plane to divert enemy fire in Vietnam combat.
LC NO. 75-703749
Prod-USAF Dist-USNAC 1968

Medal Of Honor - Capt Jay Zeamer B 5 MIN
16MM FILM OPTICAL SOUND
Cites Captain Jay Zeamer, bomber pilot for heroism during World War II reconnaissance mission.
LC NO. 74-706139
Prod-USAF Dist-USNAC 1967

Medal Of Honor - Heading Home B 5 MIN
16MM FILM OPTICAL SOUND
Cites Captain William R Lawley for heroism and exceptional flying skill on a heavy bombardmanet mission over enemy occupied Europe.
LC NO. 74-705108
Prod-USAF Dist-USNAC 1967

Medal Of Honor - One For One B 5 MIN
16MM FILM OPTICAL SOUND
Pays tribute to Major Bernard Fisher, the first Vietnam hero to receive the Medal of Honor for saving a fellow pilot's life in the Battle of Ashau.
LC NO. 74-706140
Prod-USAF Dist-USNAC 1967

Medal Of Honor - One Man Air Force B 7 MIN
16MM FILM OPTICAL SOUND
Cites Col James H Howard for his valor as a World War II fighter pilot.
LC NO. 74-705109
Prod-USAF Dist-USNAC 1967

Medal Of Honor - Only A Few Returned B 5 MIN
16MM FILM OPTICAL SOUND
Cites Sgt Maynard Smith for his fearlessness as World War II B-17 gunner.
LC NO. 74-705110
Prod-USAF Dist-USNAC 1967

Medal Of Honor - Pacific Age B 5 MIN
16MM FILM OPTICAL SOUND
Cites Major Richard Bong for bringing down over 40 enemy aircraft.
LC NO. 74-705112
Prod-USAF Dist-USNAC 1969

Medal Of Honor - Seven Down B 5 MIN
16MM FILM OPTICAL SOUND
Cites Major Willaim Shomg for downing seven World War II enemy aircraft.
LC NO. 74-705113
Prod-USAF Dist-USNAC 1969

Medal Of Honor - Trial By Fire B 4 MIN
16MM FILM OPTICAL SOUND
Pays tribute to Sgt Edward Erwin, who ditched an ignited phosphorous bomb from his aircraft during a World War II raid over enemy territory.
LC NO. 74-705114
Prod-USAF Dist-USNAC 1969

Medal Of Honor - With One Hand B 4 MIN
16MM FILM OPTICAL SOUND
Cites Lt John Morgan who single-handedly guided his plane to a target during a World War II raid over Europe.
LC NO. 74-705115
Prod-USAF Dist-USNAC 1967

Medal Of Honor Rag C 54 MIN
3/4 OR 1/2 INCH VIDEO CASSETTE H-C A
Presents the story of a black Vietnam veteran who won the Congressional Medal of Honor and was later shot and killed while holding up a supermarket in Detroit. Offers an imaginary dialogue between the soldier and a psychiatrist in which they come to the conclusion that the medal had a terrible effect on the soldier's life.
Prod-CHOPRA Dist-FI 1983

Medbourne Primary School B 12 MIN
16MM FILM OPTICAL SOUND T

Focuses mainly on the juniors, ages 7-11, and the teacher, in a small rural 3-room school in which the total enrollment is 48. Shot in the spring over a period of five days, the film shows the continual hustle, bustle and activity. Some children are painting with homemade paints and brushes, others are printing a report on their printing press, while others are cooking a chicken outside next to their replica of an Anglo-Saxon hut.
LC NO. 78-710677
Prod-EDS Dist-EDC 1970

Medea C 90 MIN
3/4 OR 1/2 INCH VIDEO CASSETTE
Presents an adaptation of Euripedes' classic play Medea, starring Zoe Caldwell and Judith Anderson.
Prod-WQED Dist-FOTH 1983

Medex - The Person C 25 MIN
3/4 INCH VIDEO CASSETTE
Reviews the Medex program to extend the physician's capacity to provide care through the utilization of paraphysicians.
LC NO. 76-706055
Prod-WARMP Dist-USNAC 1972

Medex - The Program C 28 MIN
3/4 INCH VIDEO CASSETTE
Reviews the Medex program to extend the physician's capacity to provide care through the utilization of paraphysicians.
LC NO. 76-706056
Prod-WARMP Dist-USNAC 1972

Media C 15 MIN
3/4 INCH VIDEO CASSETTE P-I
Shows equipment used at a television station and discusses radio and records as non-visual media. Presents special versions of a quiz show, an entertainment show and a soap opera.
From The Look And A Closer Look Series.
Prod-WCVETV Dist-GPITVL 1976

Media - Massaging The Mind C 19 MIN
16MM FILM, 3/4 OR 1/2 IN VIDEO
Explores developments in communications, showing the possibilities of lasers and holograms. Looks at the future of newspapers and magazines.
Prod-DOCUA Dist-CNEMAG

Media And Campaigning C 30 MIN
3/4 OR 1/2 INCH VIDEO CASSETTE C
Reveals the importance of using the mass media effectively in political campaigns.
From The American Government 1 Series.
Prod-DALCCD Dist-DALCCD

Media And Message C 60 MIN
3/4 OR 1/2 INCH VIDEO CASSETTE H-C A
Discusses the role of media in society.
From The Art Of Being Human Series.
Prod-FI Dist-FI 1978

Media Burn C
3/4 OR 1/2 INCH VIDEO CASSETTE
Is a live performance transformed by TV into a media event. Is a potent mixture of America's love affair with the automobile and its addiction to TV.
Prod-ANTFRM Dist-EAI

Media Center In Action, The C 14 MIN
16MM FILM, 3/4 OR 1/2 IN VIDEO C A
Shows how today's modern media center is working with schools, with a media specialist as coordinator to help teachers make the best use of media.
Prod-CORF Dist-CORF 1972

Media Dreams B 10 MIN
16MM FILM OPTICAL SOUND
Portrays a man who returns from a business trip with a 'BARBIE' doll which he has purchased as a gift for his three-year-old daughter. Explains that his wife and daughter won't be home until the next day and during that evening the 'BARBIE' doll comes to life and seduces him.
Prod-UPENN Dist-UPENN 1964

Media Ecology Ads C 11 MIN
3/4 OR 1/2 INCH VIDEO CASSETTE
Records the artist's reactions to the speed, narration and formats used in television commercials.
Prod-EAI Dist-EAI

Media For Presentations C 20 MIN
16MM FILM, 3/4 OR 1/2 IN VIDEO
Offers an introduction to audiovisual communication by highlighting the benefits obtained through its use. Describes the characteristics of various media.
LC NO. 79-706289
Prod-IU Dist-IU 1978

Media In The Classroom C 48 MIN
3/4 OR 1/2 INCH VIDEO CASSETTE T
Shows how to use various media in the classroom to increase student involvement and to improve the quality of instruction.
From The Strategies In College Teaching Series.
LC NO. 79-706190
Prod-IU Dist-IU 1977

Media Machine—A Series
J-H
Surveys the functions of newspapers, television, radio, film and film production and what is involved in preparing them for public consumption. Discusses how media activities relate to daily life.
Prod-WVIZTV Dist-GPITVL 1975

Film-Editing, Commercials 015 MIN
Film-Making, Featurettes 015 MIN
Image-Making 015 MIN
It Pays To Advertise 015 MIN
Newspapers 015 MIN
Radio Goes After Its Audience 015 MIN
Television 015 MIN
Television News 015 MIN

Media Probes—A Series
16MM FILM, 3/4 OR 1/2 IN VIDEO H-C A
Discusses the ways in which such mass media as photography, industrial design, television journalism, political spots, language and computers affect the public.
Prod-LAYLEM Dist-TIMLIF 1982

Design 030 MIN
Future, The 030 MIN
Language 030 MIN
Photography 030 MIN
Political Spots 030 MIN
Soap Operas 030 MIN
Soundaround 030 MIN
TV News 030 MIN

Media Shuttle - New York/Moscow B 30 MIN
3/4 OR 1/2 INCH VIDEO CASSETTE
Contrasts Dimitri Devyatkin's footage with Nam June Paik's humorous view of New York followed by various scenes of life in New York.
Prod-EAI Dist-EAI

Media Utilization C 29 MIN
3/4 OR 1/2 INCH VIDEO CASSETTE C A
Illustrates the problems a teacher may encounter when not pre-viewing a film before using. Shows several media consultants being interviewed as to the many media resources available. Concludes with look at opaque projector.
From The Instructional Technology Introduction Series.
Prod-MCGILU Dist-BCNFL

Median Patellar Desmotomy B 8 MIN
16MM FILM OPTICAL SOUND PRO
Describes the surgical separation of the medial patellar ligament and anatomic landmarks for infecting the anesthesia and the surgical procedures. (Kinescope)
Prod-AMVMA Dist-AMVMA

Median Sternotomy And Elective Cardiac Arrest In Open Heart Surgery C 36 MIN
16MM FILM OPTICAL SOUND PRO
Shows the operative techniques used in heart-lung surgery at Stanford University hospitals. Demonstrates the repair of intracardiac defects through the median sternotomy incision.
Prod-ACYDGD Dist-ACY 1958

Mediastinoscopy Using Bivalve Speculum C 16 MIN
16MM FILM OPTICAL SOUND
Uses operative scenes, anatomic drawings, and cadaver views to demonstrate the technique of mediastinoscopy using a bivalve speculum. Presents case reports to show the application of mediastinoscopy in evaluating pulmonary disease.
LC NO. 74-715463
Prod-KAISRF Dist-SQUIBB 1971

Mediating C 57 MIN
16MM FILM, 3/4 OR 1/2 IN VIDEO H-C A
Analyzes the breakdown of a Chinese marriage and the pressures that are brought on the couple to reconcile their differences.
From The Heart Of The Dragon Series. Pt 10
Prod-ASH Dist-TIMLIF 1984

Medic 4 C 24 MIN
3/4 OR 1/2 INCH VIDEO CASSETTE
Presents a dramatic story about a typical 24-hour day for a para-medic team of the St Paul Fire Department.
Prod-WCCOTV Dist-WCCOTV 1974

Medical And Institutional Aspects C 40 MIN
3/4 OR 1/2 INCH VIDEO CASSETTE C A
Presents an illustrated classification of disabilities. Includes children and adults who have been suddenly or progressively disabled.
From The Sexuality And Physical Disability Video Tape Series.
Prod-MMRC Dist-MMRC

Medical And Institutional Aspects C 40 MIN
3/4 INCH VIDEO CASSETTE
Presents the issue of sexuality of the physically disabled through the perspectives of the past and current institutional practices. Presents a sampling of devices used to deal with altered sexual performance.
From The Sexuality And Physical Disability Series.
Prod-UMITV Dist-UMITV 1976

Medical And Surgical Management Of Angina Pectoris, The C 58 MIN
3/4 OR 1/2 INCH VIDEO CASSETTE PRO
Discusses the diagnosis of significant coronary disease and the management of stable angina pectoris by medical and surgical therapy.
LC NO. 81-706295
Prod-USVA Dist-USNAC 1980

Medical And Surgical Treatment Of Dizziness C 50 MIN
3/4 OR 1/2 INCH VIDEO CASSETTE
See series title for descriptive statement.
From The Dizziness And Related Balance Disorders Series.
Prod-GSHDME Dist-GSHDME

Medical And Surgical Treatment Of Valvular Heart Disease, The B 92 MIN
16MM FILM OPTICAL SOUND PRO
Discusses various types of acquired valvular cardiac defects including clinical and hemodynamic assessment, indications for and results of surgery.
From The Boston Medical Reports Series.
LC NO. 74-705116
Prod-NMAC Dist-NMAC 1968

Medical Asepsis B 30 MIN
16MM FILM OPTICAL SOUND PRO
Discusses means of transmission of microorganisms and prevention of transmission. Demonstrates hand washing and applies the concepts of medical asepsis to nursing activities in the hospital.
From The Directions For Education In Nursing Via Technology Series. Lesson 1
LC NO. 74-701773
Prod-DENT Dist-WSU 1974

Medical Aspects C 28 MIN
3/4 OR 1/2 INCH VIDEO CASSETTE J A
Features Dr Max A Schneider as he discusses the various parts of the body affected by excessive drinking.
Prod-SUTHRB Dist-SUTHRB

Medical Aspects Of Alcohol, Pt 1 C 30 MIN
3/4 OR 1/2 INCH VIDEO CASSETTE J A
Presents a detailed overview of the signs and symptoms of disease resulting from the use of alcohol and other drugs. Constitutes the first of a two-part series.
Prod-SUTHRB Dist-SUTHRB

Medical Aspects Of Alcohol, Pt 2 C 30 MIN
3/4 OR 1/2 INCH VIDEO CASSETTE J A
Presents the second of a two-part overview of the signs and symptoms of disease resulting from the use of alcohol and other drugs.
Prod-SUTHRB Dist-SUTHRB

Medical Aspects Of Diving, Pt 1 - Mechanical Effects Of Pressure C 28 MIN
16MM FILM - 3/4 IN VIDEO
Provides information on the safety and efficiency of persons concerned with diving and underwater swimming. Describes physiological pressure stresses. Issued in 1962 as a motion picture.
LC NO. 80-706862
Prod-USN Dist-USNAC 1980

Medical Aspects Of Diving, Pt 2 - Effects Of Elevated Partial Pressures Of Gases C 28 MIN
16MM FILM - 3/4 IN VIDEO
Explains how the body is affected by what one breathes. Discusses the physical laws relating to the partial pressure of gases and the problems of deep sea diving and underwater swimming. Looks at the causes and symptoms associated with nitrogen narcosis, decompression sickness, oxygen toxicity, anoxia and carbon dioxide poisoning. Issued in 1962 as a motion picture.
LC NO. 80-706863
Prod-USN Dist-USNAC 1980

Medical Aspects Of High Intensity Noise - General Effects B 21 MIN
16MM FILM OPTICAL SOUND
Explains the increasingly serious hazards of high intensity noise. Describes the nature of noise and some of its physiological and psychological effects.
Prod-USN Dist-USNAC 1955

Medical Aspects Of High Intensity Noise - Ear Defense B 21 MIN
16MM FILM OPTICAL SOUND
Points out the hazards associated with high noise levels produced by jet aircraft and other noisy equipment found ashore and aboard ship.
Prod-USN Dist-USNAC 1955

Medical Aspects Of Nuclear Radiation C 20 MIN
16MM FILM OPTICAL SOUND H A
Explains effects of radiation upon the human body, internal and external radiation hazards, and the relative gravity of the hazards of nuclear radiation, blast and heat.
LC NO. FIE52-2069
Prod-USA Dist-USNAC 1952

Medical Assistant's Transcribing C 6 MIN
1/2 IN VIDEO CASSETTE BETA/VHS
From The Typing - Medical Series.
Prod-RMI Dist-RMI

Medical Audit Process C 14 MIN
3/4 OR 1/2 INCH VIDEO CASSETTE PRO
Presents a way of evaluating the patterns and quality of medical practice.
Prod-UMICHM Dist-UMICHM 1975

Medical Care During Pregnancy C 29 MIN
3/4 OR 1/2 INCH VIDEO CASSETTE H-C A
Explains that medical care and advice during pregnancy are most important to the health of the mother and baby.
From The Tomorrow's Families Series.
LC NO. 81-706898
Prod-MSDOE Dist-AITECH 1980

Medical Care For The McDaniel Family - A Compact Course In Family Medicine C 60 MIN
3/4 OR 1/2 INCH VIDEO CASSETTE PRO
Introduces family medicine in six two-hour workshop sessions. Presents an encounter between members of a family practice group and the McDaniel family.
Prod-HSCIC Dist-HSCIC 1980

Medical Careers - It's Not All Dr Kildare C 26 MIN
16MM FILM, 3/4 OR 1/2 IN VIDEO
Surveys the variety of medical careers and shows how a woman patient comes into contact with different medical professionals during her stay in the hospital.
Prod-DOCUA Dist-CNEMAG

Medical Committee For Human Rights C 15 MIN
16MM FILM OPTICAL SOUND
Shows the medical committee's role during the long strike at San Francisco State College and the need for a tactical knowledge of first aid as the struggles of student demonstrations intensify.
Prod-NEWSR Dist-NEWSR

Medical Crisis Intervention—A Series
PRO
Designed to familiarize the physician with behavioral disorders encountered in the practice of emergency medicine and with various levels of burn treatment.
Prod-LEIKID Dist-LEIKID

Major Burns	020 MIN
Minor Burns	020 MIN
Psychotic Assaultive Patient, The	020 MIN
Suicidal Patient, The	020 MIN

Medical Effects Of Alcohol C 13 MIN
16MM FILM, 3/4 OR 1/2 IN VIDEO A
Shows the effects of alcohol on the human body over a period of years.
Prod-MIFE Dist-EBEC 1984

Medical Effects Of The Atomic Bomb, The, Pt 1 - Physics, Physical Destruction, Casualty... C 32 MIN
16MM FILM OPTICAL SOUND
Explains nuclear physics, fission and general reaction, thermal energy and mechanical force, nuclear radiation and ionizing effects. Portrays the physical destruction and casualty effects of atomic bombing.
LC NO. FIE52-1730
Prod-USA Dist-USNAC 1950

Medical Emergencies C 146 MIN
3/4 INCH VIDEO CASSETTE
Deals with various medical emergencies. Covers snake and insect bites, stings, heart attack, stroke, illnesses that may cause dyspnea, diabetes, acute abdomen, communicable diseases, emotionally disturbed patients, epilepsy, convulsions and unconsciousness.
From The Medical Legal Component Film Series.
LC NO. 74-706497
Prod-KYDHPS Dist-USNAC Prodn-UKY 1974

Medical Emergencies In The Dental Office C 25 MIN
16MM FILM - 3/4 IN VIDEO PRO
Presents a series of simulated emergencies occurring in a dentist's office and explains the recommended management of these emergencies.
LC NO. 79-707990
Prod-NMAC Dist-USNAC 1979

Medical Ethic, The C 30 MIN
3/4 OR 1/2 INCH VIDEO CASSETTE H-C A
Presents Louis Lasagna, professor of medicine, and Robert M Veatch, senior associate at the Institute of Society, Ethics and the Life Sciences, outlining changing attitudes in medical ethics and decisions confronting the profession. Focuses on rights of patients, sustaining life in seemingly hopeless cases, use of placebos and doctor-patient relationships.
From The Ethics In America Series.
Prod-AMHUMA Dist-AMHUMA

Medical Ethics And Aging - Medicine As An Instrument Of Social Control C 30 MIN
3/4 OR 1/2 INCH VIDEO CASSETTE PRO
Shows four physicians in a conversation about medicine as an institution of social control. Raises moral, religious and ethical questions.
Prod-HSCIC Dist-HSCIC 1982

Medical Examination Of Your Eyes, The C 13 MIN
16MM FILM, 3/4 OR 1/2 IN VIDEO H-C A
Discusses the benefits and techniques of regular ophthalmological examinations, explaining diagnostic procedures and possible treatments for several conditions.
Prod-JOU Dist-JOU 1974

Medical Examination Of Your Eyes, The (Spanish) C 13 MIN
16MM FILM, 3/4 OR 1/2 IN VIDEO H-C A
Discusses the benefits and techniques of regular ophthalmological examinations, explaining diagnostic procedures and possible treatments for several conditions.
Prod-PRORE Dist-JOU 1974

Medical Facts For Pilots C 25 MIN
16MM FILM, 3/4 OR 1/2 IN VIDEO
Provides facts concerning some of the fundamental physical, physiological and psychological limitations in flight. Discusses such aeromedical factors as disorientation, the effect of alcohol, oxygen requirements and pilot vision.
LC NO. 80-706840
Prod-USFAA Dist-USNAC 1980

Medical History, The C
3/4 OR 1/2 INCH VIDEO CASSETTE
Prod-MEDMDS Dist-MEDMDS

Medical Hypnosis C 29 MIN
3/4 OR 1/2 INCH VIDEO CASSETTE
Discusses therapeutic hypnosis and its use as a pain reliever in patients whose medical conditions cannot be alleviated by drugs.
From The Daniel Foster, MD Series.
Prod-KERA Dist-PBS

Medical Implications Of Nuclear Energy C 38 MIN
3/4 INCH VIDEO CASSETTE A
Presents Dr Helen Caldicott giving a lecture in which she traces the nuclear fuel cycle, cites the medical perils of each stage, and takes issue with the nuclear establishment.
LC NO. 80-706750
Prod-EAI Dist-EAI 1979

Medical Instrumentation For Nurses—A Series
PRO
Presents basic information on common types of hospital equipment. Uses layman's language. Narrated by William F Betts, Emanuel Furst, Stuart A Hoenig, Edward Lonsdale, Kenneth C Mylrea and Alan Rester.
Prod-UAZMIC Dist-UAZMIC 1976

Blood Pressure Measurements And Cardiac Monitoring Techniques For Nurses	050 MIN
Defibrillators And Pacemakers (Reeter)	050 MIN
Electricity And Electrical Safety In The	050 MIN
Electrosurgery - Principles And Precautions	050 MIN
Introduction To Clinical Apparatus	050 MIN
Neonatal Instrumentation (Furst)	050 MIN

Medical Interview, The C 13 MIN
3/4 INCH VIDEO CASSETTE PRO
Presents a complete medical interview of a new patient by the chief medical resident of the Larue Carter Hospital in Indianapolis.
From The Patient Interview - Science Or Art Series.
Prod-PRIMED Dist-PRIMED

Medical Laboratory Technician C 17 MIN
16MM FILM OPTICAL SOUND
Describes the U S Navy's training program for medical laboratory technicians. Discusses classroom and on-the-job training in various branches, admission requirements, length of the course and career opportunities.
LC NO. 77-703726
Prod-USN Dist-USNAC 1974

Medical Legal Aspects Of Amniocentesis For Prenatal Diagnosis C 13 MIN
16MM FILM, 3/4 OR 1/2 IN VIDEO
Discusses the legal aspects of amniocentesis that physicians need to be aware of.
Prod-USDHEW Dist-USNAC

Medical Legal Component Film—A Series

Gives basic training for emergency medical technicians.
Prod-KYDHPS Dist-USNAC Prodn-UKY 1974

Airway Obstruction And Pulmonary Arrest	46 MIN
Bleeding And Shock	51 MIN
Cardiac Arrest	36 MIN
Childbirth And Problems Of Child Patients	59 MIN
Emergency Medical Technician, The - His Role,	71 MIN
Environmental Emergencies	41 MIN
Fractures Of The Lower Extremity	32 MIN
Fractures Of The Upper Extremity	58 MIN
Injuries To The Eye, Chest, Abdomen, Pelvis,	91 MIN
Injuries To The Head, Face, Neck And Spine	40 MIN
Mechanical Aids To Breathing And Pulmonary	56 MIN
Medical Emergencies	146 MIN
Wounds	20 MIN

Medical Malpractice - The Physician As Witness C 35 MIN
3/4 OR 1/2 INCH VIDEO CASSETTE PRO
Portrays a physician in two roles - the first involving professional negligence, the second involves physician as a witness in a malpractice case.
Prod-HSCIC Dist-HSCIC 1984

Medical Malpractice / Home Repairs / Car Rental C
3/4 OR 1/2 INCH VIDEO CASSETTE
Discusses various aspects of medical malpractice, home repair and car rentals.
From The Consumer Survival Series.
Prod-MDCPB Dist-MDCPB

Medical Management - Role Of The Nurse In Confirming A Diagnosis C 28 MIN
3/4 INCH VIDEO CASSETTE PRO
Discusses the stages of diagnosing coronary artery disease, emphasizing cardiac catheterization.
From The Coronary Artery Disease Series.
LC NO. 79-706228
Prod-AJN Dist-AJN 1978

Medical Management - Role Of The Nurse In Establishing A Diagnosis C 40 MIN
3/4 INCH VIDEO CASSETTE PRO
Illustrates the risk factors associated with coronary artery disease. Demonstrates complete cardiac assessment, including ausculation of heart sounds and evaluation of pulses, EKG'S and chest X-rays. Discusses indication for Swan-Ganz catheter, use of medications and interprofessional relationships between nursing and medical staff.
From The Critical Care Nursing - Acutely Ill Patients With Coronary Artery Disease Series.
LC NO. 79-706224
Prod-AJN Dist-USNAC 1978

Medical Management - Role Of The Nurse In Confirming A Diagnosis C 28 MIN
3/4 OR 1/2 INCH VIDEO CASSETTE
Targets the interpretive and decision-making stages of diagnosis of coronary heart disease, including the preparation of the patient and family and the patient's aftercare. Features a multidisciplinary catherization conference. Explains the cardiac catherization technique.
From The Coronary Artery Disease Series.
Prod-AJN Dist-AJN

Medical Management Of Spinal Spasticity C 22 MIN
16MM FILM OPTICAL SOUND PRO
Shows examinations, case histories, treatment and a discussion on the pathophysiology of spasticity caused by spinal cord lesions.
Prod-GEIGY Dist-GEIGY

Medical Management Of The Hypertensive Patient C 16 MIN
3/4 OR 1/2 INCH VIDEO CASSETTE PRO
Presents two methods of patient management which may be used when antihypertensive therapy is indicated. Covers the elements of both techniques and methods to ensure patient compliance with prescribed therapies.
Prod-UMICHM Dist-UMICHM 1981

Medical Management Of The Sexually Abused Child C 24 MIN
3/4 OR 1/2 INCH VIDEO CASSETTE PRO
Provides medical information to professionals who may be called on to deal with sexually abused children.
Prod-HSCIC Dist-HSCIC 1984

Medical Mystery Tours B 15 MIN
3/4 INCH VIDEO CASSETTE J-H
Discusses careers in health and physical education. Includes nursing, medical stenography, physical therapy and the role of orderlies.
From The Work Is For Real Series.
Prod-STETVC Dist-GPITVL

Medical Mystery Tours, Pt 1 C 15 MIN
2 INCH VIDEOTAPE J-H
Discusses careers in health and physical education, covering nursing, medical stenography, the role of orderlies and physical therapy.
From The Work Is For Real Series.
Prod-STETVC Dist-GPITVL

Medical Mystery Tours, Pt 2 C 15 MIN
2 INCH VIDEOTAPE J-H
Discusses careers in health and physical education, covering nursing, medical stenography, the role of orderlies and physical therapy.
From The Work Is For Real Series.
Prod-STETVC Dist-GPITVL

Medical Mystery Tours, Pt 3 C 15 MIN
2 INCH VIDEOTAPE J-H
Discusses careers in health and physical education, covering nursing, medical stenography, the role of the orderlies and physical therapy.
From The Work Is For Real Series.
Prod-STETVC Dist-GPITVL

Medical Office Instruments C 26 MIN
1/2 IN VIDEO CASSETTE BETA/VHS
Discusses instruments used in a physician's office.
Prod-RMI Dist-RMI

Medical Potential Of Lasers C 21 MIN
16MM FILM OPTICAL SOUND PRO
Explains and demonstrates the potential of lasers in experimental medicine and surgery, in microbiology, and in analytic and diagnostic procedures.
From The Upjohn Vanguard Of Medicine Series.
LC NO. 76-713212
Prod-UPJOHN Dist-UPJOHN 1971

Medical Problems C 30 MIN
3/4 OR 1/2 INCH VIDEO CASSETTE
Features a discussion of the impact of medical problems on the educational performance of special-needs students and chronic problems teachers should be aware of it.
From The Teaching Students With Special Needs Series.
Prod-MSITV Dist-PBS 1981

Medical Problems Of The Addict C 35 MIN
16MM FILM OPTICAL SOUND PRO
Covers a range of medical problems presented by addicts and drug abusers. Discusses the medical techniques for withdrawing an individual from opiates and barbiturates. Includes the drug abuser as a patient, serum hepatitis and other infections, respiratory problems, anemia, abscesses, skin lesions, tetanus and endocarditis.
From The Films And Tapes For Drug Abuse Treatment Personnel Series.
LC NO. 73-702454
Prod-NIMH Dist-NIMH 1973

Medical Records - Written Link To Patient Care C 11 MIN
3/4 INCH VIDEO CASSETTE
Describes the functions of the University of Texas MD Anderson's Dept of Medical Records.
Prod-UTAHTI Dist-UTAHTI

Medical Research Seeks Relief Of Pain C 12 MIN
16MM FILM OPTICAL SOUND
Discusses the scientific search to aid people suffering from chronic pain.
Prod-ALLFP Dist-NSTA

Medical Residency Training At Wilford Hall USAF Hospital C 21 MIN
16MM FILM OPTICAL SOUND
Cites the USAF Hospital, Wilford Hall, for the quality of its professional care, contributions to clinical medicine and support of orbital space flights. Describes 11 residence programs, fellowships and other educational opportunities for physicians and surgeons.
LC NO. 74-706141
Prod-USAF Dist-USNAC 1965

Medical Residency, - Years Of Change C 29 MIN
3/4 OR 1/2 INCH VIDEO CASSETTE PRO

Illustrates the work of two physicians who are residents in a teaching hospital. Presents interviews with them and discussions with faculty members on how medical residency has changed in thirty years.
LC NO. 82-707306
Prod-WAT Dist-KWSU 1982

Medical Risk Management - Plan For Action C 31 MIN
3/4 OR 1/2 INCH VIDEO CASSETTE
Stresses that hospitals that do not learn from their mistakes are destined to repeat them. Describes how a liability control system works and shows a typical system in action.
Prod-TEACHM Dist-TEACHM

Medical School And The Community, The - How Are They Related B 29 MIN
16MM FILM OPTICAL SOUND PRO
Emphasizes that the function of medicine involves community health at all levels and that good medical care depends upon further development of excellence at the medical schools.
From The Concepts And Controversies In Modern Medicine series.
LC NO. 74-705118
Prod-NMAC Dist-NMAC 1969

Medical Self-Help (Spanish)—A Series

Prod-USPHS Dist-USNAC

Artificial Respiration (Spanish) 14 MIN
Bleeding And Bandaging (Spanish) 28 MIN
Burns (Spanish) 14 MIN
Emergency Childbirth (Spanish) 28 MIN
Fractures And Splinting (Spanish) 28 MIN
Healthful Living In Emergencies (Spanish) 28 MIN
Infant And Child Care (Spanish) 14 MIN
Nursing Care Of The Sick And Injured (Spanish) 28 MIN
Radioactive Fallout And Shelter (Spanish) 28 MIN
Shock (Spanish) 14 MIN
Transportation Of The Injured (Spanish) 14 MIN

Medical Self-Help—A Series

Prod-USPHS Dist-USNAC

Emergency Childbirth 28 MIN

Medical Skills Films—A Series
PRO
Presents a concise demonstration of a specific medical technique.
Prod-WFP Dist-WFP

Arterial Puncture 009 MIN
Cardiac Arrest And Defibrillation 009 MIN
Central Venous Pressure Measurement 009 MIN
Emergency Nasal Packing 009 MIN
Endotracheal Intubation 009 MIN
External Cardiac Compression 009 MIN
Gastric Lavage 009 MIN
Intermittent Pressure Breathing 009 MIN
Intravenous Techniques - Infusion 009 MIN
Local Infiltration Anesthesia 009 MIN
Lumbar Puncture 009 MIN
Manual Positive Pressure Ventilation 009 MIN
Nasogastric Intubation 009 MIN
Paracentesis (Abdominal) 009 MIN
Proctosigmoidoscopy 009 MIN
Removal Of A Superficial Foreign Body From 009 MIN
Thoracentesis 009 MIN
Tonometry 009 MIN
Tracheostomy 009 MIN
Urethral Catheterization 009 MIN
Veni-Puncture 009 MIN
Venous Cutdown 009 MIN
Ventricular Defibrillation 009 MIN

Medical Skills Library—A Series

Prod-AMCP Dist-SUTHLA Prodn-MEDEX

Gastric Lavage 14 MIN
Tonometry 9 MIN

Medical Supply System, U S Army, Pt 1 - Organization And Administration B 24 MIN
16MM FILM OPTICAL SOUND
Describes the mission and operational relationship of the major organizations within the Medical Supply System.
LC NO. 74-705120
Prod-USA Dist-USNAC 1967

Medical Supply System, U S Army, Pt 2 - Operations At Conus And Overseas Installations B 22 MIN
16MM FILM OPTICAL SOUND
Demonstrates Medical Supply operations at a typical depot in CONUS (Ft Knox.)
LC NO. 74-705119
Prod-USA Dist-USNAC 1967

Medical Terminology - Adjectival Endings C 16 MIN
1/2 IN VIDEO CASSETTE BETA/VHS
Prod-RMI Dist-RMI

Medical Terminology - Five Basic Rules C 21 MIN
1/2 IN VIDEO CASSETTE BETA/VHS
Reviews the five rules for forming and identifying medical terms.
Prod-RMI Dist-RMI

Medical Terminology - Prefixes C 19 MIN
1/2 IN VIDEO CASSETTE BETA/VHS
Prod-RMI Dist-RMI

Medical Terminology - Suffixes C 7 MIN
1/2 IN VIDEO CASSETTE BETA/VHS
Prod-RMI Dist-RMI

Medical Terminology - Verbal Derivatives C 15 MIN
1/2 IN VIDEO CASSETTE BETA/VHS
Prod-RMI Dist-RMI

Medical Terminology - Word Roots C 17 MIN
1/2 IN VIDEO CASSETTE BETA/VHS
Prod-RMI Dist-RMI

Medical Terminology - Word Roots II C 21 MIN
1/2 IN VIDEO CASSETTE BETA/VHS
Prod-RMI Dist-RMI

Medical Terminology—A Series
PRO
Tells how to analyze, spell and pronounce medical terminology.
Prod-HSCIC Dist-HSCIC

Introduction To Medical Terminology 020 MIN
Pronunciation Of Medical Terminology 015 MIN
Spelling Medical Terminology 018 MIN

Medical Tests C 30 MIN
3/4 OR 1/2 INCH VIDEO CASSETTE C T
Reviews medical testing. Takes away some of the mystique surrounding medical testing. Encourages people to recognize their right to be an active participant during medical testing.
From The Here's To Your Health Series.
Prod-DALCCD Dist-DALCCD

Medical Transcribing C 8 MIN
1/2 IN VIDEO CASSETTE BETA/VHS
From The Typing - Medical Series.
Prod-RMI Dist-RMI

Medical Typing - Consultation Report C 4 MIN
1/2 IN VIDEO CASSETTE BETA/VHS
From The Typing - Medical Series.
Prod-RMI Dist-RMI

Medical Typing - Discharge Summary Or Clinical Resume C 6 MIN
1/2 IN VIDEO CASSETTE BETA/VHS
From The Typing - Medical Series.
Prod-RMI Dist-RMI

Medical Typing - Electroencephalogram C 6 MIN
1/2 IN VIDEO CASSETTE BETA/VHS
From The Typing - Medical Series.
Prod-RMI Dist-RMI

Medical Typing - Filing Rules C 10 MIN
1/2 IN VIDEO CASSETTE BETA/VHS
From The Typing - Medical Series.
Prod-RMI Dist-RMI

Medical Typing - History And Physical C 12 MIN
1/2 IN VIDEO CASSETTE BETA/VHS
From The Typing - Medical Series.
Prod-RMI Dist-RMI

Medical Typing - Introduction C 6 MIN
1/2 IN VIDEO CASSETTE BETA/VHS
From The Typing - Medical Series.
Prod-RMI Dist-RMI

Medical Typing - Laboratory C 17 MIN
1/2 IN VIDEO CASSETTE BETA/VHS
From The Typing - Medical Series.
Prod-RMI Dist-RMI

Medical Typing - Medical Records C 12 MIN
1/2 IN VIDEO CASSETTE BETA/VHS
From The Typing - Medical Series.
Prod-RMI Dist-RMI

Medical Typing - Operative Report C 4 MIN
1/2 IN VIDEO CASSETTE BETA/VHS
From The Typing - Medical Series.
Prod-RMI Dist-RMI

Medical Typing - Radiology C 16 MIN
1/2 IN VIDEO CASSETTE BETA/VHS
From The Typing - Medical Series.
Prod-RMI Dist-RMI

Medical Witness And Juvenile Court, The C 35 MIN
3/4 OR 1/2 INCH VIDEO CASSETTE PRO
Focuses on a mock contested child-dependency hearing to familiarize expert medical witnesses with courtroom formalities.
Prod-UARIZ Dist-UARIZ

Medical Witness, The C 35 MIN
16MM FILM - 3/4 IN VIDEO
Dramatizes a physician's experience in preparing for and testifying in court on a child abuse case.
From The We Can Help Series.
LC NO. 79-706246
Prod-NCCAN Dist-USNAC 1979

Medical-Legal Aspects Of Amniocentesis For Prenatal Diagnosis C 13 MIN
16MM FILM, 3/4 OR 1/2 IN VIDEO PRO
Discusses some of the legal aspects of amniocentesis.
Prod-NMAC Dist-USNAC Prodn-CFDISC 1979

Medical/Technical/Nursing Programs C 30 MIN
3/4 OR 1/2 INCH VIDEO CASSETTE
Reviews basic principles and techniques of ABO testing, then looks at some of the most common serologic discrepancies and ways to resolve them.
Prod-AMRC Dist-AMRC 1976

Medicare Patient Classification - Assigning DRGs C 32 MIN
3/4 OR 1/2 INCH VIDEO CASSETTE
Stresses the need of a basic understanding of the new Medicare payment system. Features in-depth interviews with staff members of a New Jersey hospital where a cost-based reimbursement plan has been instituted. Helps staff understand the structure of DRG's, the importance of the patient's principal diagnosis and recording of secondary diagnoses in assuring proper payment to the hospital as well as the effects of case-mix load on financial viability.
Prod-AHOA Dist-AHOA

Medicare Payment - A Technical Briefing On The Implementing Regulations For...—A Series

Presents four one-hour videotapes of a live four-hour teleconference held October 6, 1983. Offers an in-depth analysis of the regulations covering prospective pricing implementation concerning Medicare payments.
Prod-AHOA Dist-AHOA

Medicated Generation, The - Medication C 56 MIN
3/4 OR 1/2 INCH VIDEO CASSETTE
Addresses the special concerns of the elderly in medication management and the responsibilities of health professionals to support the elderly by communicating information and caring.
Prod-UMDSM Dist-UMDSM

Medicating Children C 23 MIN
3/4 OR 1/2 INCH VIDEO CASSETTE
Presents important information for nursing students and nurses about administering medications to children of various ages. Presents general considerations and details related to all routes of medication administration, safety factors in calculation and administration, and comfort measures.
Prod-UNCN Dist-AJN

Medication History Interview, The (2nd Ed) C 122 MIN
3/4 OR 1/2 INCH VIDEO CASSETTE PRO
Teaches students how to take accurate medication history. Treats drug use, reactions, compliance, open-ended and closed questions, non verbals, anxiety, and reassurance. Includes 15 min audiocassette and 125 page paperback.
Prod-HSCIC Dist-HSCIC 1981

Medications - Avoiding Errors C
3/4 OR 1/2 INCH VIDEO CASSETTE
Illustrates the types of medication errors, the steps in medication administration which reduce opportunity for error and other measures designed to prevent medication error.
Prod-FAIRGH Dist-FAIRGH

Medications And You - A Special Report C 13 MIN
3/4 OR 1/2 INCH VIDEO CASSETTE
Encourages patients to ask questions and accept responsibility for caring for themselves. Answers typical questions regarding prescription medications.
Prod-UARIZ Dist-UARIZ

Medicinal Drug Development At The Walter Reed Army Institute Of Research C 19 MIN
16MM FILM OPTICAL SOUND PRO
Describes the search for new drugs for the prevention and treatment of drug-resistant Plasmodium falciparum malaria. Outlines the drug development program at Walter Reed Army Institute of Research which uses a computerized chemical information system to track over 350,000 medicinal chemicals through selection, testing, approval by the Federal Drug Administration, and clinical trials around the world.
LC NO. 79-710663
Prod-WRAIR Dist-USNAC 1979

Medicinal Drug Development At The Walter Reed Army Institute Of Research C 19 MIN
3/4 OR 1/2 INCH VIDEO CASSETTE PRO
Describes the search for new drugs for the prevention and treatment of drug-resistant Plasmodium falciparum malaria. Outlines the drug development program at Walter Reed Army Institute of Research which uses a computerized chemical information system to track over 350,000 medicinal chemicals through selection, testing, approval by the Federal Drug Administration, and clinical trials around the world.
Prod-WRAIR Dist-USNAC 1979

Medicine - Living To Be 100 C 20 MIN
16MM FILM, 3/4 OR 1/2 IN VIDEO
Looks at areas of medical research aimed at prolonging life. Discusses radiation therapy, preventive medicine, heart transplants, and other topics.
Prod-DOCUA Dist-CNEMAG

Medicine And Money C 48 MIN
16MM FILM, 3/4 OR 1/2 IN VIDEO H-C A
Examines government-funded medical programs, including Medicare and Medicaid. Tells how taxpayer money is spent and discusses alternatives.
LC NO. 79-707398
Prod-ABCTV Dist-CRMP 1977

Medicine And The Physician In Western Civilization - The Seventeenth And... C 23 MIN
16MM FILM OPTICAL SOUND
Details the changing role and image of the physician and other health practitioners in the 17th and 18th centuries. Discusses medical education, approaches to disease, the care of the insane and the poor, and major figures and discoveries of this period.
Prod-USC Dist-USC 1980

Medicine Behind Bars C 29 MIN
3/4 INCH VIDEO CASSETTE
Examines the quality of health care behind bars. Features interviews with inmates at Jackson State Prison.
Prod-UMITV Dist-UMITV 1977

Medicine Flower And Lonewolf C 29 MIN
3/4 OR 1/2 INCH VIDEO CASSETTE
Focuses on American Indian artists Grace Medicine Flower and her brother Joseph Lonewolf, both potters from Santa Clara Pueblo in New Mexico.
From The American Indian Artists Series.
Prod-KAETTV Dist-PBS

Medicine For The Layman—A Series

Presents a lecture series on health and disease to show how the human body works and what can be done to improve or maintain health. Shows the research being done at the National Institutes of Health.
Prod-NIH Dist-USNAC 1980

Arthritis	060 MIN
Biofeedback - Therapeutic Self-Control	060 MIN
Blood Transfusions - Benefits, Risks	060 MIN
Breast Cancer	060 MIN
Cancer - What Is It	060 MIN
Cancer And The Environment	060 MIN
Cancer Treatment	060 MIN
Cholesterol, Diet And Heart Disease	060 MIN
Control And Therapy Of Genetic Disease	045 MIN
Genetics And Recombinant DNA	060 MIN
Heart Attacks	060 MIN
Immunity	060 MIN
Interferon	060 MIN
Obesity And Energy Metabolism	060 MIN
Peptic Ulcer	060 MIN
Stroke	060 MIN

Medicine On The Tube C 30 MIN
3/4 OR 1/2 INCH VIDEO CASSETTE
Discusses medicine on television.
From The Lifelines Series.
Prod-UGATV Dist-MDCPB

Medicine Show, The C 28 MIN
16MM FILM OPTICAL SOUND
Presents conservationist H H Gilman, who lectures on the value of soil and water conservation.
LC NO. 76-700920
Prod-UNEBR Dist-UNEBR 1974

Medicine, Drugs And You - A First Film C 12 MIN
16MM FILM, 3/4 OR 1/2 IN VIDEO P-J
Discusses safe, intelligent use of substances which may help or harm us depending on our attitudes. Tells how drugs are found, how pharmacists do their work, proper usage and the differences between drugs.
LC NO. 84-706797
Prod-BRUNOS Dist-PHENIX 1983

Medicines Used During Pregnancy C 5 MIN
3/4 OR 1/2 INCH VIDEO CASSETTE H-C A
Emphasizes the dangers of using any medicines during pregnancy without a doctor's permission. Covers drugs known to cause serious fetal abnormalities, drugs suspected of causing problems, and those for which there is no conclusive evidence.
LC NO. 84-706397
Prod-USFDA Dist-USNAC 1983

Medieval Crusades, The C 27 MIN
16MM FILM, 3/4 OR 1/2 IN VIDEO I-H
Re-creates events that led to the Crusades, follows the fate of one noble family through the first Crusade, reviews the most important later Crusades and shows their influence on life in Europe. Historical scenes are filmed in several medieval cities in Asia Minor, France and Palestine.
Prod-EBF Dist-EBEC 1956

Medieval Crusades, The (Spanish) C 27 MIN
16MM FILM, 3/4 OR 1/2 IN VIDEO J-H
Follows the fate of one family and their manor through the First Crusade. Reviews the most important later Crusades and the influence of the crusaders on life in Europe.
Prod-EBEC Dist-EBEC

Medieval England - The Peasants' Revolt C 31 MIN
16MM FILM, 3/4 OR 1/2 IN VIDEO J-C
Portrays the men and women of the Middle Ages and discusses the Peasants' Revolt of 1381 which reveals the condition of slavery and the weaknesses of the feudal system such as its oppressive tax structure, its cruelty and its social inequity.
From The Western Civilization - Majesty And Madness Series.
Prod-KING Dist-LCOA 1969

Medieval England - The Peasants' Revolt (Spanish) C 31 MIN
16MM FILM, 3/4 OR 1/2 IN VIDEO H-C A
Signals the beginning of the end of feudalism with the peasants' revolt in England in 1381.
Prod-KING Dist-LCOA 1970

Medieval England - The Peasants' Revolt (French) C 31 MIN
16MM FILM, 3/4 OR 1/2 IN VIDEO H-C A
Signals the beginning of the end of feudalism with the peasants' revolt in England in 1381.
Prod-KING Dist-LCOA 1970

Medieval England - The Peasants' Revolt (Captioned) C 31 MIN
16MM FILM, 3/4 OR 1/2 IN VIDEO H-C A
Signals the beginning of the end of feudalism with the peasants' revolt in England in 1381.
Prod-KING Dist-LCOA 1970

Medieval Gilds, The (Spanish) C 21 MIN
16MM FILM, 3/4 OR 1/2 IN VIDEO J-C
Tells the story of a medieval town from its beginnings as a feudal manor through its evolution into a gild town and later into a commercial center of the late Middle Ages.
Prod-EBEC Dist-EBEC

Medieval Guilds, The C 21 MIN
16MM FILM, 3/4 OR 1/2 IN VIDEO I-C
Traces the development of a medieval town from a feudal manor to a commercial center in the late middle ages. Tells of the emergence and significance of gilds. Photographed in old gild towns of Western Europe.
Prod-EBF Dist-EBEC 1956

Medieval Kings, The C 60 MIN
16MM FILM, 3/4 OR 1/2 IN VIDEO H-C A
Shows the riches contributed by the medieval kings. Visits Westminster, Caernarvon Castle in Wales, and some early tombs in France.
From The Royal Heritage Series.
Prod-BBCTV Dist-FI 1977

Medieval Knights, The X 22 MIN
16MM FILM, 3/4 OR 1/2 IN VIDEO I-H
Describes the development of the social class of knights in the 12th and 13th centuries. Follows one knight through his apprenticeship in arms, first as a page, then as a squire. Ends with a detailed illustration of the knighting ceremony. Photographed in several medieval castles in France.
Prod-EBF Dist-EBEC 1956

Medieval Life - The Monastery C 15 MIN
16MM FILM, 3/4 OR 1/2 IN VIDEO I-C
Depicts the pattern of life in the Spanish monastery during the 15th century.
Prod-ACI Dist-AIMS 1970

Medieval Life - The Monastery (Afrikaans) C 15 MIN
16MM FILM, 3/4 OR 1/2 IN VIDEO I-C
Depicts the pattern of life in the Spanish monastery during the 15th century.
Prod-ACI Dist-AIMS 1970

Medieval Manor, The C 22 MIN
16MM FILM, 3/4 OR 1/2 IN VIDEO I-C
Describes the way of life in the feudal community of Montbref. Includes a look at peasant life, local justice, a noble marriage and the position of the Church.
Prod-EBF Dist-EBEC 1956

Medieval Mind, The C 26 MIN
16MM FILM, 3/4 OR 1/2 IN VIDEO H-C
Points out the tensions and conflicts of the middle ages, and shows how the architecture of the cathedrals reflects the uneasy balance of opposing forces with their soaring columns, arches and flying buttresses. Explains how this left a permanent mark on Western civilization.
From The Humanities - Philosophy And Political Thought Series.
Prod-EBEC Dist-EBEC 1969

Medieval Society - The Nobility C 13 MIN
16MM FILM, 3/4 OR 1/2 IN VIDEO H
Simulates daily life in the thirteenth century, showing the roles performed by nobles and clergy.
From The Medieval Series.
Prod-CORF Dist-CORF 1976

Medieval Society - The Villagers C 11 MIN
16MM FILM, 3/4 OR 1/2 IN VIDEO
Depicts life in the Middle Ages, showing medieval villagers, including a reeve and a serf, explaining something of their life and work.
From The Medieval Series.
Prod-CORF Dist-CORF 1976

Medieval Theater - The Play Of Abraham And Isaac C 26 MIN
16MM FILM, 3/4 OR 1/2 IN VIDEO H-C
Uses a medieval mystery play about Abraham and Isaac to relate medieval drama, as a means of social control, to the attitudes of the aristocracy and the religious doctrines of the church.
From The Humanities - The Drama Series.
Prod-MOVSCO Dist-EBEC 1974

Medieval Times - Guilds And Trade C 14 MIN
16MM FILM, 3/4 OR 1/2 IN VIDEO I-C
Discusses the rise of the Venetian and Genoese merchant princes and the formation and spread of the guilds or hanses. Illustrates the economic role of craft guilds in medieval society and relates the guilds to today's European Common Market. Scenes in Europe visualize medieval trade.
From The Medieval Series.
Prod-CORF Dist-CORF 1965

Medieval Times - Role Of The Church C 14 MIN
16MM FILM, 3/4 OR 1/2 IN VIDEO H-C
Illustrates the influences of the Church on medieval society, and describes the role of the church in shaping European history. Captures the spirit of the times through re-enactments and by studying the cathedrals, churches and art works of the Middle Ages.
From The Medieval Series.
Prod-CORF Dist-CORF 1961

Medieval Times - The Crusades C 14 MIN
16MM FILM, 3/4 OR 1/2 IN VIDEO I-C
Re-evaluates the effects of the crusades, the religious wars which wracked Europe and the Near East for almost two centuries. Pictures some historical sites and examines original sources of information. Characterizes the crusades as a divisive force in history.
From The Medieval Series.
Prod-CORF Dist-CORF 1965

Medieval World, The (2nd Ed) C 14 MIN
16MM FILM, 3/4 OR 1/2 IN VIDEO I-C
Portrays medieval times, discussing knights and feudalism, Chaucer's pilgrims, castles and crusades. Uses the English-walled city of York, the Flemish guildhalls of Ghent and the French cathedral of Chartres to supply the background.
Prod-CORF Dist-CORF 1980

Medieval—A Series
16MM FILM, 3/4 OR 1/2 IN VIDEO
Takes a look at lifestyles, social classes and religion during the medieval period in Europe.
Prod-CORF Dist-CORF

Medieval Society - The Nobility	13 MIN
Medieval Society - The Villagers	11 MIN
Medieval Times - Guilds And Trade	14 MIN
Medieval Times - Role Of The Church	14 MIN
Medieval Times - The Crusades	14 MIN

Medisense C 20 MIN
16MM FILM, 3/4 OR 1/2 IN VIDEO
Points out with facts and figures that employees are paying the nation's health bills through taxes, lost wages and the increased cost of goods and services.
Prod-DRUKRR Dist-JONEST

Meditation B 29 MIN
16MM FILM OPTICAL SOUND
Features Indian spiritual leader Krishnamurti who explains the process of meditation, which he defines not as concentration of self-stimulation but as the acute awareness of a quiet mind. Gives as the philosophy that man can free himself from his troubled image of of himself by finding life beyond daily existence through meditation.
From The Real Revolution - Talks By Krishnamurti Series.
LC NO. 73-703034
Prod-KQEDTV Dist-IU 1968

Meditation C 29 MIN
2 INCH VIDEOTAPE
Explains that more and more people in today's busy world are turning to meditation for relief from their pressures. Features Dr Puryear answering questions in the field of meditation.
From The Who Is Man Series.
Prod-WHROTV Dist-PUBTEL

Meditation - The Inward Journey C 20 MIN
16MM FILM, 3/4 OR 1/2 IN VIDEO
Explores some of the techniques for meditation, 'the journey inward', the importance of posture, the use of mantra, the imageless silence of the Buddhists, the Sufi's use of dance as a meditation and the Christian's use of the Jesus prayer.
Prod-HP Dist-HP

Meditation - Yoga, T'ai Chi, And Other Spiritual Trips C 18 MIN
16MM FILM, 3/4 OR 1/2 IN VIDEO
Describes the benefits and possibilities of meditation techniques.
Prod-DOCUA Dist-CNEMAG

Meditation Crystallized - Lama Govinda On Tibetan Art C 14 MIN
16MM FILM, 3/4 OR 1/2 IN VIDEO
Shows mandalas and paintings as a guide to meditation.
Prod-HP Dist-HP

Meditation On Violence B 12 MIN
16MM FILM OPTICAL SOUND H-C A
Presents a choreography of the movements and rhythms of Wu-Tang and Saolin schools of Chinese boxing filmed by Mayan Deren.
Prod-GROVE Dist-GROVE

Meditation—A Series
I-H A R
Prod-IKONOG Dist-IKONOG

Amen	002 MIN
Faith	002 MIN
Glory Be	002 MIN
Hope	002 MIN
Joy	002 MIN
Love	002 MIN
Peace	002 MIN
Prayer	002 MIN
Present Moment	002 MIN
Self	002 MIN
Trust	002 MIN
Wonder	002 MIN

Mediterranean - Cradle Or Coffin C 21 MIN
16MM FILM, 3/4 OR 1/2 IN VIDEO I-H A
Documents the five-month cruise of Jacques Cousteau and his crew in the Mediterranean, where they took samples of the water and ocean bottom, looked into the impact of industrial and urban waste on the Mediterranean Sea and interviewed scientists regarding the pollution.
From The Cousteau Odyssey, Series 2 Series.
Prod-COUSTS Dist-WDEMCO 1979

Mediterranean Mosaic B 27 MIN
16MM FILM, 3/4 OR 1/2 IN VIDEO J-H
Looks at the importance of Gibraltar and Malta during World War II and the enemy fleets in the Mediterranean.
From The Victory At Sea Series.
Prod-NBCTV Dist-LUF

Mediterranean Prospect, A C 58 MIN
3/4 INCH VIDEO CASSETTE
Discusses the pollution of the Mediterranean Ocean. Tells how the pollution problems facing the 18 countries along the Mediterranean have gotten the nations working together with the exception of Albania. Tells how the number of marine research laboratories contributing to the battle against pollution emergencies has risen from less than a dozen in four countries to 83 in 16 countries.
From The Nova Series.
LC NO. 80-707475
Prod-BBCTV Dist-PBS 1980

Mediterranean World, The X 23 MIN
16MM FILM, 3/4 OR 1/2 IN VIDEO I-H

Explains the significance of the Mediterranean region in the development of Western civilization. Depicts life today in Greece, Italy and the Arab countries, stressing the importance of the region as a focal point of world tension.
Prod-EBF Dist-EBEC 1961

Mediterranean World, The (Spanish) C 23 MIN
16MM FILM, 3/4 OR 1/2 IN VIDEO I-H
Explains the significance of the Mediterranean region in the development of Western civilization. Depicts 20th century life in Greece, Italy and the Arab countries.
Prod-EBEC Dist-EBEC

Medium C 60 MIN
3/4 OR 1/2 INCH VIDEO CASSETTE
Examines the explosive growth of interactive technology and introduces the modes and devices of human-computer conversation.
From The Computer Dialogue - The Key To Successful Systems Series.
Prod-DELTAK Dist-DELTAK

Medium Cool C
1/2 IN VIDEO CASSETTE BETA/VHS
Presents a documentary-style drama about the events inside and outside the Chicago Democratic National Convention of 1968.
Prod-GA Dist-GA

Medium Is The Masseuse, The- A Balinese Massage C 30 MIN
3/4 INCH VIDEO CASSETTE
Presents a Balinese spirit medium who also practices healing massage. Concentrates on a case of seizures and infertility.
Prod-DOCEDR Dist-DOCEDR

Medium Is The Medium, The—A Series

Presents work by independent producers to be aired on TV.
Prod-WGBHTV Dist-EAI

Archetron
Black
Capriccio For TV
Electronic Light Ballet
Electronic Opera No. 1
Hello

Medium- And Large-Scale ICs (Spanish) C 12 MIN
3/4 OR 1/2 INCH VIDEO CASSETTE
Covers binary and binary-coded decimals (BCD), operations of BCD counters, functions of BCD counters, adders, ROM vs RAM, functions, operations and contrasts of ROM and RAM devices.
From The Industrial Electronics - Logic Circuits (Spanish) Series.
Prod-TPCTRA Dist-TPCTRA

Medium-And Large-Scale ICs C 12 MIN
3/4 OR 1/2 INCH VIDEO CASSETTE
Covers binary and binary-coded decimals (BCD), operations of BCD counters, functions of BCD counters, adders, ROM vs RAM, functions, operations and contrasts of ROM and RAM devices.
From The Industrial Electronics - Logic Circuits Series.
Prod-TPCTRA Dist-TPCTRA

Medlars On Line - Medline C 23 MIN
3/4 OR 1/2 INCH VIDEO CASSETTE PRO
Explains the concept of on-line retrieval of bibliographic citations to medical literature by use of communications terminals in medical libraries throughout the United States.
Prod-USDHEW Dist-USNAC

Medley Of Danish—A Series

Prod-CULINA Dist-CULINA

Medley Of Danish, Pt 1
Medley Of Danish, Pt 2

Medley Of Danish, Pt 2 C
3/4 OR 1/2 INCH VIDEO CASSETTE
See series title for descriptive statement.
From The Medley Of Danish Series.
Prod-CULINA Dist-CULINA

Medley Of Dianish, Pt 1 C
3/4 OR 1/2 INCH VIDEO CASSETTE
See series title for descriptive statement.
From The Medley Of Danish Series.
Prod-CULINA Dist-CULINA

Medoonak, The Stormmaker C 13 MIN
16MM FILM, 3/4 OR 1/2 IN VIDEO I-H
Offers a Micmac Indian legend in which a mighty bird is trapped by an Indian brave.
LC NO. 80-707239
Prod-NFBC Dist-IFB 1975

Medulla Oblongata, The C 15 MIN
3/4 OR 1/2 INCH VIDEO CASSETTE PRO
Identifies the macroscopic structures of the medulla oblongata using brain specimens and diagrams. Discusses briefly physiology and pathology of the medulla oblongata where applicable.
From The Neurobiology Series.
Prod-HSCIC Dist-HSCIC

Medullary Nailing C 17 MIN
3/4 OR 1/2 INCH VIDEO CASSETTE
Illustrates the indication, principles and performance of both closed and open medullary nailing.
Prod-SPRVER Dist-SPRVER

Medusa Challenger C 25 MIN
16MM FILM, 3/4 OR 1/2 IN VIDEO I-H A
Tells the story of what happens when a flower vendor and his nephew are separated when a drawbridge is raised to allow the Medusa Challenger, the largest freighter on the Great Lakes, to pass.
Prod-KOCHP Dist-PHENIX 1978

Meecology C 26 MIN
16MM FILM OPTICAL SOUND P-I
Portrays children from rural, suburban, urban and inner-city surrounding and shows how each relates to their environment in an ecologically productive way.
LC NO. 75-700123
Prod-MCDONS Dist-CHRSTP 1974

Meet And Greet C 15 MIN
3/4 OR 1/2 INCH VIDEO CASSETTE
See series title for descriptive statement.
From The Children In Action Series.
Prod-LVN Dist-LVN

Meet Jerry Leavy C 43 MIN
16MM FILM OPTICAL SOUND
Shows that a bilateral upper extremity amputee can be completely independent in the activities of his daily life. Shows Jerry Leavy driving a car and flying a plane.
LC NO. 74-706377
Prod-USOE Dist-USNAC

Meet John Doe B 135 MIN
16MM FILM OPTICAL SOUND
Features Gary Cooper as an unemployed man picked as the 'typical American' by a newspaper publisher. Tells how he discovers that he is being exploited to further the publisher's political ambitions. Stars Barbara Stanwyck, Edward Arnold and Walter Brennen. Directed by Frank Capra.
Prod-WB Dist-REELIM 1941

Meet Lisa C 5 MIN
16MM FILM, 3/4 OR 1/2 IN VIDEO C S
Presents a personal statement reflecting the world as seen through the eyes of a brain injured child and those of her parents.
Prod-AIMS Dist-AIMS 1971

Meet Lisa (Spanish) C 5 MIN
16MM FILM, 3/4 OR 1/2 IN VIDEO P-C A
Presents a statement of the world as seen by a brain damaged child. Involves her parents, friends and attitudes towards her in general.
Prod-LEARN Dist-AIMS 1971

Meet Margie C 10 MIN
16MM FILM, 3/4 OR 1/2 IN VIDEO J-C A
Shows how a student paying for her own education uses energy and imagination to make ends meet. Explains how she travels by bike, belongs to a food co-op, trades chores and appliances with her neighbors, and barters her skills for someone else's. Points out that a great deal of money is not needed for a comfortable lifestyle.
Prod-FLMFR Dist-FLMFR

Meet Marlon Brando B 28 MIN
16MM FILM OPTICAL SOUND
Presents improvisational conversations between Marlon Brando and interviewers of the TV world providing a personal portrait of the major film star.
Prod-MAYSLS Dist-MAYSLS 1965

Meet Me In St Louis B 2 MIN
16MM FILM, 3/4 OR 1/2 IN VIDEO
Offers a sequence done for a 1962 television special.
Prod-EAMES Dist-PFP 1962

Meet Meter Man C 3 MIN
3/4 OR 1/2 INCH VIDEO CASSETTE P-I
Introduces the animated superhero Meter Man, who specializes in converting distances to metric terms by using his magic Metric Measuring Stick.
From The Metric Marvels Series.
Prod-NBCTV Dist-GA 1978

Meet Mr Lincoln B 27 MIN
16MM FILM, 3/4 OR 1/2 IN VIDEO I-C
Old photographs, pictures, newspapers and posters review the life of Lincoln. Portraits of Civil War soldiers, their camps and battles, and scenes of cities and backwoods reconstruct the America Lincoln knew in the 1860's.
Prod-NBCTV Dist-EBEC 1960

Meet Mr Noise C 26 MIN
16MM FILM OPTICAL SOUND
Points out hazards of working in an area of vibration and noise. Shows how noise of heightened intensity can impair hearing and general health. Demonstrates how properly fitted protective devices worn by personnel reduces adverse effects of noise.
LC NO. 74-705121
Prod-USAF Dist-USNAC 1962

Meet Mr O B 15 MIN
2 INCH VIDEOTAPE P
See series title for descriptive statement.
From The Just Curious Series. No. 15
Prod-EOPS Dist-GPITVL Prodn-KOACTV

Meet Mr Stork C 17 MIN
16MM FILM, 3/4 OR 1/2 IN VIDEO
Introduces Artie Elgart, an auto parts distributor who also runs the Golden Cradle adoption agency and spends most of his time finding babies for childless couples. Explains that unlike most adoption agencies, the Golden Cradle provides the birth-mother with the best possible care, paid for by the adopting couple. Originally shown on the CBS program 60 Minutes.
Prod-CBSNEW Dist-CAROUF

Meet The Actors C 11 MIN
16MM FILM OPTICAL SOUND I
Shows that wild animals, born to kill, can be taught to go through their hair-raising routines without so much as missing a cue. Stars Tamba, the humorous chimpanzee, and Humpy, the talking camel.
Prod-AVED Dist-AVED 1961

Meet The Author C 20 MIN
2 INCH VIDEOTAPE P-I
See series title for descriptive statement.
From The Learning Our Language, Unit V - Exploring With Books Series.
Prod-MPATI Dist-GPITVL

Meet The Computer C 18 MIN
3/4 OR 1/2 INCH VIDEO CASSETTE J-C A
Describes basic computer functions and presents information about some of the most familiar small computers such as Apple II, Atari 400 and Texas Instruments' 99/4.
From The Little Computers - See How They Run Series.
LC NO. 81-706563
Prod-ELDATA Dist-GPITVL 1980

Meet The DC-9 C 10 MIN
16MM FILM OPTICAL SOUND C A
Serves as an introduction to the DC-9. It literally 'TAKES APART' its most important features and compoments.
Prod-DAC Dist-MCDO 1966

Meet The Hiraokas X 30 MIN
2 INCH VIDEOTAPE I
Shows members of a Japanese American family and the many activities of their daily lives at school, at work and at play. (Broadcast quality)
From The Cultural Understandings Series. No. 3
Prod-DENVPS Dist-GPITVL Prodn-KRMATV

Meet The Master—A Series

Examines and illustrates the painting methods and techniques as well as the artistic attitudes of various well-known artists. Hosted by Guy Palazzola, artist and professor.
Prod-UMITV Dist-UMITV 1966

El Greco	029 MIN
Michelangelo	029 MIN
Mondrian	029 MIN
Paul Cezanne	029 MIN
Paul Klee	029 MIN
Rembrandt	029 MIN
Seurat	029 MIN
Tintoretto	029 MIN
Toulouse-Lautrec	029 MIN

Meet The Sioux Indian C 11 MIN
16MM FILM, 3/4 OR 1/2 IN VIDEO I-H
Shows how the Sioux Indians adapted to their environment and found food, shelter and clothing on the Western plains.
Prod-DEU Dist-IFB 1956

Meet What You Eat C 18 MIN
16MM FILM OPTICAL SOUND I-H
Offers a lesson in basic nutrition. Includes an introduction to the basic food groups and nutrient interspersed with historical food anecdotes.
Prod-SWIFT Dist-FILAUD Prodn-CREATW 1979

Meet Your Parent, Adult, Child C 9 MIN
16MM FILM, 3/4 OR 1/2 IN VIDEO J-C A
Uses animation to explain why people have difficulty communicating on the same level. Explains the transactional analysis theory that each person develops a parent, child and adult ego state early in childhood upon which later relationships depend. Stresses the importance of effective interpersonal relationships.
From The Transactional Analysis Series.
Prod-CBSTV Dist-PHENIX 1975

Meet Your Parent, Adult, Child (Dutch) C 9 MIN
16MM FILM, 3/4 OR 1/2 IN VIDEO J-C A
Uses animation to explain why people have difficulty communicating on the same level. Explains the transactional analysis theory that each person develops a parent, child and adult ego state early in childhood upon which later relationships depend. Stresses the importance of effective interpersonal relationships.
From The Transactional Analysis Series.
Prod-CBSTV Dist-PHENIX 1975

Meet Your Parent, Adult, Child (Swedish) C 9 MIN
16MM FILM, 3/4 OR 1/2 IN VIDEO J-C A
Uses animation to explain why people have difficulty communicating on the same level. Explains the transactional analysis theory that each person develops a parent, child and adult ego state early in childhood upon which later relationships depend. Stresses the importance of effective interpersonal relationships.
From The Transactional Analysis Series.
Prod-CBSTV Dist-PHENIX 1975

Meet Your VCR C 50 MIN
1/2 IN VIDEO CASSETTE (VHS)
Joan Lunden and animated friends show how to get the most out of a VHS or Beta Videorecorder.
Prod-KARLVI Dist-KARLVI

Meeting A New Friend C 20 MIN
2 INCH VIDEOTAPE P
See series title for descriptive statement.
From The Learning Our Language, Unit 2 - Dictionary Skills Series.
Prod-MPATI Dist-GPITVL

Meeting Artists C 15 MIN
3/4 OR 1/2 INCH VIDEO CASSETTE P
Considers the artist at work through visits to the studios of sculptor Edgar Britton, weaver Kathryn Wertenberger, potter Henry Mead and painter Mina Conant.
From The Primary Art Series.
Prod-WETATV Dist-AITECH

Meeting At Night C 20 MIN
16MM FILM OPTICAL SOUND
Shows five basic meeting situations and the proper night whistle signals on the ocean, in inland waters and in narrow channels. Explains the causes of head-on collisions and shows emergency action signals.
LC NO. FIE52-943
Prod-USN Dist-USNAC 1943

Meeting Emotional Needs In Childhood - Groundwork Of Democracy B 33 MIN
16MM FILM OPTICAL SOUND C T
Suggests ways parents and teachers contribute to the kinds of attitudes toward people and the sense of community responsibility the seven- to ten-year-old child is developing as he grows to adulthood.
From The Studies Of Normal Personality Development Series.
Prod-NYU Dist-NYU 1947

Meeting Ground, The C 15 MIN
16MM FILM OPTICAL SOUND
Tells of the recruitment of prior-service Marines for enlistment in the U S Marine Corps Reserve.
LC NO. 74-705122
Prod-USMC Dist-USNAC 1969

Meeting Gulf People Who Are Meeting The Challenge C 25 MIN
16MM FILM OPTICAL SOUND
Introduces the Gulf Oil Corporation advertising campaign. Features Gulf employees who explain the challenge of their particular jobs and how they contribute to Gulf's overall effort.
LC NO. 77-702486
Prod-GULF Dist-COMCRP Prodn-COMCRP 1976

Meeting In Progress C 43 MIN
16MM FILM, 3/4 OR 1/2 IN VIDEO H-C A
Offers a means of teaching conference leadership through group participation. Asks trainees to decide at 12 critical points in a typical problem-solving conference which group relations or task function they would use if they were the leader.
LC NO. 73-700186
Prod-RTBL Dist-RTBL 1969

Meeting In Progress (Captioned) C 43 MIN
16MM FILM, 3/4 OR 1/2 IN VIDEO H-C A
Offers a means of teaching conference leadership through group participation. Asks trainees to decide at 12 critical points in a typical problem-solving conference which group relations or task function they would use if they were the leader.
Prod-RTBL Dist-RTBL 1969

Meeting In Progress (Danish) C 43 MIN
16MM FILM, 3/4 OR 1/2 IN VIDEO H-C A
Offers a means of teaching conference leadership through group participation. Asks trainees to decide at 12 critical points in a typical problem-solving conference which group relations or task function they would use if they were the leader.
Prod-RTBL Dist-RTBL 1969

Meeting In Progress (Dutch) C 43 MIN
16MM FILM, 3/4 OR 1/2 IN VIDEO H-C A
Offers a means of teaching conference leadership through group participation. Asks trainees to decide at 12 critical points in a typical problem-solving conference which group relations or task function they would use if they were the leader.
Prod-RTBL Dist-RTBL 1969

Meeting In Progress (French) C 43 MIN
16MM FILM, 3/4 OR 1/2 IN VIDEO H-C A
Offers a means of teaching conference leadership through group participation. Asks trainees to decide at 12 critical points in a typical problem-solving conference which group relations or task function they would use if they were the leader.
Prod-RTBL Dist-RTBL 1969

Meeting In Progress (German) C 43 MIN
16MM FILM, 3/4 OR 1/2 IN VIDEO H-C A
Offers a means of teaching conference leadership through group participation. Asks trainees to decide at 12 critical points in a typical problem-solving conference which group relations or task function they would use if they were the leader.
Prod-RTBL Dist-RTBL 1969

Meeting In Progress (Japanese) C 43 MIN
16MM FILM, 3/4 OR 1/2 IN VIDEO H-C A
Offers a means of teaching conference leadership through group participation. Asks trainees to decide at 12 critical points in a typical problem-solving conference which group relations or task function they would use if they were the leader.
Prod-RTBL Dist-RTBL 1969

Meeting In Progress (Norwegian) C 43 MIN
16MM FILM, 3/4 OR 1/2 IN VIDEO H-C A
Offers a means of teaching conference leadership through group participation. Asks trainees to decide at 12 critical points in a typical problem-solving conference which group relations or task function they would use if they were the leader.
Prod-RTBL Dist-RTBL 1969

Meeting In Progress (Portuguese) C 43 MIN
16MM FILM, 3/4 OR 1/2 IN VIDEO H-C A
Offers a means of teaching conference leadership through group participation. Asks trainees to decide at 12 critical points in a typical problem-solving conference which group relations or task function they would use if they were the leader.
Prod-RTBL Dist-RTBL 1969

Meeting In Progress (Spanish) C 43 MIN
16MM FILM, 3/4 OR 1/2 IN VIDEO H-C A
Offers a means of teaching conference leadership through group participation. Asks trainees to decide at 12 critical points in a typical problem-solving conference which group relations or task function they would use if they were the leader.
Prod-RTBL Dist-RTBL 1969

Meeting In Progress (Swedish) C 43 MIN
16MM FILM, 3/4 OR 1/2 IN VIDEO H-C A
Offers a means of teaching conference leadership through group participation. Asks trainees to decide at 12 critical points in a typical problem-solving conference which group relations or task function they would use if they were the leader.
Prod-RTBL Dist-RTBL 1969

Meeting In The Desert C 15 MIN
3/4 OR 1/2 INCH VIDEO CASSETTE I
Introduces a Western family to Bedouin nomads.
From The Encounter In The Desert Series.
Prod-CTI Dist-CTI

Meeting Individual Needs C 30 MIN
3/4 OR 1/2 INCH VIDEO CASSETTE T
Uses interviews and candid classroom scenes to show how innovative teachers are developing strategies to help the student learn to read at a pace suited to his or her individual needs.
From The Reading Is Power Series. No. 2
LC NO. 81-707517
Prod-NYCBED Dist-GPITVL 1981

Meeting Leading—A Series

Covers all aspects of proper meeting leading, including meeting preparation, mechanics, objectives, group dynamics and a resulting action plan. Addresses key topics, including Why Hold A Meeting, Preparing The Leader, Preparing The Participants, Developing The Meeting Guide, Off To A Good Start, Getting Involvement And Commitment, Managing The Meeting, Visual Aids and Closing The Meeting. Includes a participant's guide and a discussion leader's guide.
Prod-PRODEV Dist-DELTAK

Conducting And Managing Meetings 040 MIN
Planning For Impact 040 MIN

Meeting Nature's Challenge C 19 MIN
16MM FILM OPTICAL SOUND
Tells the story of Ohio Medical Products' role in the development of medical life-support technology, showing how interaction between medical practitioners and design engineers contributes to the solution of critical-care and life-support problems.
LC NO. 80-700302
Prod-OHMED Dist-OHMED Prodn-REINAC 1980

Meeting Near Mafeking C 23 MIN
16MM FILM OPTICAL SOUND
Presents the story of six Scouts out on a hiking trip who find themselves going through time and space ending up in the midst of Scouting's origins.
Prod-BSA Dist-BSA Prodn-HEN 1982

Meeting Objections C
3/4 OR 1/2 INCH VIDEO CASSETTE IND
Lists basic objection types like need more information, as to price, doubts value and can't afford, stalls and miscellaneous. Shows how to handle negative reactions, such as is objection clear, probing or paraphrasing until clear, getting prospect's reaction and, if favorable, close, and if negative, offer more information or continue probe but avoid argument. Includes six sales demonstrations and two sets of role plays.
From The Telephone Selling Series.
Prod-COLOSU Dist-COLOSU

Meeting Of Minds, A C 22 MIN
16MM FILM OPTICAL SOUND
Discusses the need for open communication and objectivity in conducting employment rating interviews.
LC NO. 78-701438
Prod-CONED Dist-CONED Prodn-ZAMA 1978

Meeting Of Minds, The C 14 MIN
3/4 OR 1/2 INCH VIDEO CASSETTE
Illustrates the way to identify and remove barriers to create a meeting of the minds and make the sale.
From The Sales Communications Series.
Prod-VISUCP Dist-VISUCP

Meeting Of Minds, The C 15 MIN
3/4 OR 1/2 INCH VIDEO CASSETTE A
Presents techniques for breaking down barriers that prevent sales. Shows how to establish rapport with customers and ease their doubts.
Prod-XICOM Dist-XICOM

Meeting Place C 9 MIN
16MM FILM OPTICAL SOUND
A recuiting film which takes the prospective student on a tour of Temple University. Emphasizes the broad spectrum of educational, intellectual, and recreationAl facilities that are available at this Philadelphia University.
LC NO. 72-700599
Prod-TEMPLU Dist-TEMPLU 1971

Meeting Residents' Needs C 12 MIN
16MM FILM, 3/4 OR 1/2 IN VIDEO
Shows the importance of meaningful work, social relationship and recreation for nursing home residents.
From The It Can't Be Home Series.
Prod-USDHEW Dist-USNAC

Meeting Steam Vessels B 18 MIN
16MM FILM OPTICAL SOUND
Gives examples of steam vessels meeting on the ocean and in inland waters. Demonstrates whistle signals for various situations and shows how to figure the degree of a vessel's turn at various distances.
LC NO. 74-705123
Prod-USN Dist-USNAC 1943

Meeting Strangers - Red Light, Green Light C 20 MIN
16MM FILM, 3/4 OR 1/2 IN VIDEO P-I
Helps the child to understand when the meeting of strangers might be potentially dangerous and provides him with specific suggestions for behavior at such times.
Prod-BFA Dist-PHENIX 1969

Meeting Strangers - Red Light, Green Light (Spanish) C 20 MIN
16MM FILM, 3/4 OR 1/2 IN VIDEO P-I
Helps the child to understand when the meeting of strangers might be potentially dangerous and provides him with specific suggestions for behavior at such times.
Prod-BFA Dist-PHENIX 1969

Meeting The Communication Needs Of The Severely/Profoundly Handicapped 1980—A Series

A series of 15 proceedings from a multidisciplinary institute aimed at providing practitioners with the assessment and intervention techniques necessary for meeting the communication needs of severely and profoundly handicapped individuals.
Prod-PUAVC Dist-PUAVC

Behavioral Analysis And Operant Techniques 144 MIN
Cognitive Assessment 121 MIN
Cognitive Development 145 MIN
Communication Assessment 138 MIN
Communication Intervention 107 MIN
Focusing On Next Environments For 108 MIN
Hearing 060 MIN
Management Of Interfering And Annoying 129 MIN
Nonspeech Communication-Augmentative
Systems 314 MIN
Oral Motor Problems 045 MIN
Parent Training 150 MIN
Phonological Development 130 MIN
Pragmatic Development 112 MIN
Preparing The Sensory And Visual Perceptual 050 MIN
Syntactic And Semantic Development 136 MIN

Meeting The Communication Needs Of The Severely/Profoundly Handicapped 1981—A Series

A series of 10 proceedings from a multidisciplinary institute aimed at providing practitioners with the assessment and intervention techniques necessary for meeting the communication needs of severely and profoundly handicapped individuals.
Prod-PUAVC Dist-PUAVC

Behavioral Analysis And Operant Techniques 144 MIN
Cognitive Assessment 121 MIN
Cognitive Development 145 MIN
Communication Assessment 138 MIN
Communication Intervention 107 MIN
Focusing On Next Environments For 108 MIN
Hearing 060 MIN
Management Of Interfering And Annoying 129 MIN
Nonspeech Communication-Augmentative
Systems 314 MIN
Oral Motor Problems 045 MIN
Parent Training 150 MIN
Phonological Development 130 MIN
Pragmatic Development 130 MIN
Preparing The Sensory And Visual Perceptual 050 MIN
Syntactic And Semantic Development 136 MIN

Meeting The Man C 27 MIN
16MM FILM OPTICAL SOUND
Documents the trials that James Baldwin had to have experienced before he could drop his guard, relax his suspicions and quiet the anger and hostility indigenous to all Black people.
Prod-IMPACT Dist-IMPACT 1971

Meeting The Man - James Baldwin In Paris C 27 MIN
16MM FILM OPTICAL SOUND H-C A
Presents a documentary on James Baldwin as a Black man, a writer and a political figure.
LC NO. 72-702628
Prod-IMPACT Dist-IMPACT 1972

Meeting The Needs Of The Physically Handicapped C 10 MIN
16MM FILM OPTICAL SOUND T S
Shows handicapped children in a regular classroom situation and in a classroom where handicapped students use special facilities and equipment.
From The Exceptional Learners Series.
LC NO. 79-700713
Prod-MERILC Dist-MERILC 1978

Meeting The Union Challenge—A Series
IND
Aims at informing supervisors and other personnel of ways to avoid unionization to the benefit of both the company and the work force.
Prod-GPCV Dist-GPCV

They Never Told Me
Unions - Awareness And Organizing Tactics
Unions - Strategies For Prevention

Meeting, The C 30 MIN
3/4 OR 1/2 INCH VIDEO CASSETTE
Analyzes the activities of the police in dealing with drug abuse. Shows the ramifications of reporting drug use to the police and

the alternative courses to law enforcement agencies. Explains that it is important for teachers to know how police treat young people and how, in turn, students feel about the police. Issued in 1971 as a motion picture.
From The Social Seminar Series.
LC NO. 80-707355
Prod-NIMH Dist-USNAC 1980

Meetings - Isn't There A Better Way? C 32 MIN
3/4 OR 1/2 INCH VIDEO CASSETTE
Places emphasis on teaching leaders and participants collaborative problem-solving techniques in achieving consensus. Identifies four types of meetings presentation, feedback, problem-solving and decision-making, and explains how to run each.
Prod-VISUCP Dist-VISUCP

Meetings, Bloody Meetings C 30 MIN
3/4 OR 1/2 INCH VIDEO CASSETTE A
Portrays a manager brought up before a court on the charge of negligent conduct of meetings. Points out specific ways meetings are often run badly and how they could be improved.
Prod-XICOM Dist-XICOM

Meetings, Bloody Meetings C 31 MIN
3/4 OR 1/2 INCH VIDEO CASSETTE
Points out five most common faults meeting leaders make - failure to plan in advance, failure to communicate the intention, failure to prepare, failure to structure and control the discussion and failure to record the decision.
Prod-VIDART Dist-VISUCP

Mega-Buildings - Giants Cast Long Shadows C 17 MIN
16MM FILM, 3/4 OR 1/2 IN VIDEO
Asks whether skyscrapers are the heralds of the future or symbols of technology run wild.
Prod-DOCUA Dist-CNEMAG

Megalopolis - The Golden Door C 30 MIN
3/4 INCH VIDEO CASSETTE
See series title for descriptive statement.
From The Of Earth And Man Series.
Prod-MDCPB Dist-MDCPB

Megan At 2 C 30 MIN
3/4 OR 1/2 INCH VIDEO CASSETTE H-C A
Presents Lawrence Solow and Sharon Neumann Solow introducing American Sign Language used by the hearing-impaired. Emphasizes signs having to do with a two-year-old named Megan.
From The Say It With Sign Series. Part 33
Prod-KNBCTV Dist-FI 1982

Megapolis C 29 MIN
16MM FILM - 3/4 IN VIDEO
Presents a look at the harshness of the urban environment and its indifference to the mortals who are caught under the wheels.
From The Earthkeeping Series.
Prod-WTTWTV Dist-PUBTEL

Meggido - City Of Destruction C 29 MIN
16MM FILM, 3/4 OR 1/2 IN VIDEO H-C R
Provides a guided view of excavations at Meggido, Israel, conducted by archaeologist Yigael Yadin of Hebrew University. Relates the interpretation of the Old Testament of the architectural and cultural clues which tie together the excavated cities of Meggido, Hazor and Gezer as parts of Solomon's kingdom.
Prod-CAFM Dist-IU Prodn-SHEVAT 1980

Megohmmeters, Voltage Testers, Clamp-on Ammeters C 60 MIN
3/4 OR 1/2 INCH VIDEO CASSETTE IND
See series title for descriptive statement.
From The Electrical Maintenance Training, Module B - Test Instruments Series.
Prod-LEIKID Dist-LEIKID

Meiji Transformation, The C 28 MIN
3/4 OR 1/2 INCH VIDEO CASSETTE A
Uses drawings, period films and sound effects to chronicle the reign of Meiji, Emperor of Japan.
From The Japan - The Changing Tradition Series.
LC NO. 80-706224
Prod-UMA Dist-GPITVL 1979

Meiosis C 7 MIN
16MM FILM, 3/4 OR 1/2 IN VIDEO
Uses the apple tree as a model, as well as time-lapse microphotography and animation, to explain and reinforce the concept of meiosis.
From The Life Cycle Of A Flowering Plant Series. No. 3
Prod-SCHLAT Dist-LUF 1971

Meiosis C 12 MIN
16MM FILM, 3/4 OR 1/2 IN VIDEO H-C
Shows the entire process of meiosis up until the final formation of daughter cells.
Prod-IFB Dist-IFB 1956

Meiosis (Spanish) C 15 MIN
16MM FILM, 3/4 OR 1/2 IN VIDEO J-H
A Spanish language version of the film and videorecording Meiosis.
Prod-EBEC Dist-EBEC Prodn-ACORN 1980

Meiosis (2nd Ed) C 15 MIN
16MM FILM, 3/4 OR 1/2 IN VIDEO J-H
Uses live microscopic footage, animation and artwork to illustrate the process of meiosis. Highlights the role of meiosis in sexual reproduction in plants and animals and discusses the direct implications of meiosis in producing genetic variations.
From The Biology Series. Unit 5 - Genetics
LC NO. 81-706142
Prod-EBEC Dist-EBEC Prodn-ACORN 1980

Mekong (Ed Ver) C 26 MIN
16MM FILM, 3/4 OR 1/2 IN VIDEO J-H
Prod-SIPC Dist-EBEC 1967

Mekong Farmer Of Thailand C 14 MIN
16MM FILM OPTICAL SOUND I-C A
Tells the story of Soi and his family who live in Huei Suem, a village in the northeast of Thailand, far down the Mekong River.
From The Human Family, Pt 1 - South And Southeast Asia Series.
Prod-AVED Dist-AVED 1972

Mel On Wheels C 19 MIN
16MM FILM, 3/4 OR 1/2 IN VIDEO J-C A
Tells about Melvin Manger, who was born with severe cerebral palsy and led a sheltered life until, with the help of friends and an electric wheelchair, he learned to become more independent. Shows how now, in his sixties, he is able to participate in the community.
LC NO. 82-706797
Prod-WRMFZY Dist-CF 1982

Melancholy Maybe C 23 MIN
16MM FILM OPTICAL SOUND
Features excerpts from the screenplay Last Card by John Kuti, depicting a tragic relationship between two lovers.
LC NO. 77-702965
Prod-ONCA Dist-ONCA 1976

Melanesian Nightmare B 27 MIN
16MM FILM, 3/4 OR 1/2 IN VIDEO J-H
Highlights the New Guinea campaign during World War II.
From The Victory At Sea Series.
Prod-NBCTV Dist-LUF

Melanomas - Diagnosis And Treatment C 21 MIN
16MM FILM, 3/4 OR 1/2 IN VIDEO PRO
Describes how the physician can recognize and treat melanomas. Diagnostic interia are detailed and illustrated with many clinical examples. Describes the surgical procedure to remove and minimize recurrence of melanomas.
Prod-WFP Dist-WFP

Melbourne Olympic Games C 22 MIN
16MM FILM OPTICAL SOUND H-C
Records action shots of numerous track and field events of the 16th Olympiad held at Melbourne, Austrailia. Depicts the colorful pageantry and spirit of the age-old Olympic games for the general public as well as sports fans.
LC NO. FIA59-558
Prod-HANDY Dist-COCA 1958

Melbourne, Florida At Its Best C 15 MIN
16MM FILM OPTICAL SOUND
Explores the community of Melbourne, Florida.
Prod-FLADC Dist-FLADC

Meli C 21 MIN
16MM FILM OPTICAL SOUND
Examines the struggles and joys of Meli Davis Kaye, who has managed to raise a family while at the same time continuing her work as a dancer and mime artist.
LC NO. 80-701330
Prod-IDIM Dist-IDIM 1980

Melies - Catalogue C 9 MIN
16MM FILM OPTICAL SOUND
Presents a homage to Georges Melies, 1862-1938, a founder of the cinema.
LC NO. 70-704322
Prod-CANFDC Dist-CANFDC 1973

Melina Mercouri's Athens C 25 MIN
16MM FILM, 3/4 OR 1/2 IN VIDEO H-C A
Presents actress Melina Mercouri as she tours her native Athens and explains the music, poetry and legends of Greece. Includes views of the Acropolis, the Port of Pireaus and the Monasteraki.
From the Cities Series.
Prod-NIELSE Dist-LCOA 1980

Melinda's Blind C 24 MIN
16MM FILM, 3/4 OR 1/2 IN VIDEO
Tells the story of a blinded girl's gradual triumph over her handicap.
From The Young People's Specials Series.
Prod-MULTPP Dist-MULTPP

Melinex - A Product Of Craftsmanship C 14 MIN
16MM FILM OPTICAL SOUND
Discusses the size and scope of ICI Americas and illustrates the care that is taken in manufacturing the polymer Melinex.
LC NO. 80-701180
Prod-ICIA Dist-ICIA Prodn-SECOM 1980

Mellah B 30 MIN
16MM FILM OPTICAL SOUND I-C A
Tells the story of a young boy from the Mellah, the slum quarter of Casablanca, and how his life was changed by going to a vocational school sponsored by the organization for rehabilitation through training.
LC NO. 72-700014
Prod-WAORT Dist-WAORT Prodn-SHARFF 1955

Mellem To Kultutrer (Between Two Cultures) B 54 MIN
16MM FILM OPTICAL SOUND
A Danish language film. Examines and documents the conditions and effects of developmental work in SouthEastern Mexico.
Prod-STATNS Dist-STATNS 1967

Mellow Moods C 29 MIN
2 INCH VIDEOTAPE
Presents the free-form electronic rock sound of the Mellow Moods in Ain't No Sunshine, What's Going On, Who Was He and Slipping Into Darkness.

From The Changing Rhythms Series.
Prod-KRMATV Dist-PUBTEL

Melodic Inversion C 9 MIN
16MM FILM OPTICAL SOUND
Reflects the inner world of man in quest of the ideal, beautiful, desirable and unattainable through a visual melodic study of transposal in which colors with fluid movements reveal the moods embedded in the theme.
Prod-HUGOI Dist-RADIM

Melodies C 14 MIN
3/4 OR 1/2 INCH VIDEO CASSETTE P-I
Discusses musical melodies.
From The Music And Me Series.
Prod-WDCNTV Dist-AITECH 1979

Melody C 8 MIN
16MM FILM, 3/4 OR 1/2 IN VIDEO K-I
Uses animation to follow the story of Melody, a young bird rejected by her family because of her ability to sing rather than to chirp. Shows how Melody meets, sings and plays with the instruments of the different instrument groupings, including the instruments of the brass family, the woodwinds and the string and rhythm families.
Prod-SAIF Dist-AIMS 1972

Melody C 28 MIN
3/4 OR 1/2 INCH VIDEO CASSETTE
Presents portraits of Lesley Frost Ballantine, daughter of poet Robert Frost and herself a poet and author, and of famous black blues singer John Jackson.
From The Old Friends - New Friends Series.
Prod-FAMCOM Dist-PBS 1981

Melody (Spanish) C 8 MIN
16MM FILM, 3/4 OR 1/2 IN VIDEO K-I
Tells the story of Melody, a bird who meets, sings and plays with instruments of the brass, woodwind, string and rhythm families.
Prod-SAIF Dist-AIMS 1972

Melody - Bi-Lingual C 15 MIN
16MM FILM, 3/4 OR 1/2 IN VIDEO K-I
Presents the story of Melody, a bird who sings rather than chirps. Explains how she discovers all the instruments of the orchestra in the process of looking for a friend.
Prod-SAIF Dist-AIMS 1973

Melody And Timbre C 25 MIN
3/4 OR 1/2 INCH VIDEO CASSETTE K-J
See series title for descriptive statement.
From The Arts Express Series.
Prod-KYTV Dist-KYTV 1983

Melody Of Birds And Flowers, A C 20 MIN
3/4 OR 1/2 INCH VIDEO CASSETTE J-C A
Shows the egret, laughing gull, golden eagle and other birds, along with views of flowers in various regions of America.
LC NO. 82-706772
Prod-AWSS Dist-AWSS 1980

Melon Tossing Game, The C 15 MIN
3/4 INCH VIDEO CASSETTE
Documents a dancing game among women of the bushmen in Namibia.
From The San (Bushmen) Series.
Prod-DOCEDR Dist-DOCEDR Prodn-MRSHL

Melting Point Determination C 17 MIN
3/4 OR 1/2 INCH VIDEO CASSETTE
Shows procedures for determining a melting point. Demonstrates various types of apparatus. Illustrates the principles behind phase changes.
From The Organic Chemistry Laboratory Techniques Series.
Prod-UCLA Dist-UCEMC

Melting Pot, The B 24 MIN
16MM FILM OPTICAL SOUND I-J
Pictures California's growth in terms of its varied peoples, from the days of the Indian through the immigration of national groups. Shows the contributions of the various nationalities to modern civilization.
Prod-ABCTV Dist-MLA 1963

Melting Pot, The C 30 MIN
3/4 OR 1/2 INCH VIDEO CASSETTE H-C A
Shows the urban environment in the work of American artists.
From The Art America Series.
Prod-CTI Dist-CTI

Melting Statues/Jazz Dance C 30 MIN
3/4 OR 1/2 INCH VIDEO CASSETTE
Features performances by Kei Takei, Mel Pate and John Parton, and animation with Gay Delanghe.
From The Doris Chase Dance Series.
Prod-CHASED Dist-CHASED

Melvin Arbuckle, Famous Canadian C 5 MIN
16MM FILM, 3/4 OR 1/2 IN VIDEO I-C A
Presents an animated look at a childhood prank perpetrated on the Canadian prairies.
Prod-NFBC Dist-NFBC 1980

Melvin Calvin C 45 MIN
3/4 OR 1/2 INCH VIDEO CASSETTE
Discusses and demonstrates the work of Dr Melvin Calvin on porphyrins and his work on photosynthesis.
From The Eminent Chemists - The Interviews Series.
Prod-AMCHEM Dist-AMCHEM 1982

Member Of Society, A C 10 MIN
16MM FILM, 3/4 OR 1/2 IN VIDEO
Discusses animals as members of their ecological society and the importance of each type to the ecological balance of the environment.

From The BSCS Behavior Film Series.
Prod-BSCS Dist-PHENIX 1974

Members Of The Original Chorus Line Talk About Where They Have Gone Since Then C 30 MIN
3/4 OR 1/2 INCH VIDEO CASSETTE
See series title for descriptive statement.
From The Broadway Series.
Prod-ARCVID Dist-ARCVID

Membrane Filtration Procedure - Fecal Determination In Wastewater And Wastewater... C 22 MIN
1/2 IN VIDEO CASSETTE BETA/VHS
Complete title is Membrane Filtration Procedure Fecal Determination In Wastewater And Wastewater Effluent - Membrane Filtration Technique. Discusses water reuse, sewage purification, water and the membrane filtration technique in wastewater technology.
Prod-RMI Dist-RMI

Membrane Oxygenation In Extracorporeal Life Support C 6 MIN
16MM FILM OPTICAL SOUND
Demonstrates the use of the general electric membrane oxygenator in open heart surgery. Shows how the unit is connected to the human body to provide oxygenated blood.
LC NO. 73-700890
Prod-GE Dist-GE 1972

Membrane Potentials - Incomplete Selectivity, Bi-Ionic Potentials, Filtration Through... B 40 MIN
3/4 OR 1/2 INCH VIDEO CASSETTE
Teaches membrane potentials. Shows incomplete selectivity, hi-ionic potentials and filtration through membrane.
From The Colloids And Surface Chemistry Electrokinetics And Membrane...-Series.
Prod-MIOT Dist-MIOT

Membrane Potentials, Incomplete Selectivity, Bio-Ionic Potentials, Filtration Through... C 40 MIN
3/4 OR 1/2 INCH VIDEO CASSETTE
Discusses membrane potentials, incomplete selectivity, bio-ionic potentials and filtration through membrane.
From The Colloid And Surface Chemistry - Electrokinetics And Membrane...Series.
Prod-KALMIA Dist-KALMIA

Memling - Painter Of Bruges C 27 MIN
16MM FILM, 3/4 OR 1/2 IN VIDEO H-C A
Evokes the civilization of Bruges, Belgium, near the end of the Middle Ages through the paintings of Flemish artist, Memling. Shows how Memling depicts the customs, rich costumes, religious beliefs and economics of his time.
Prod-IFB Dist-IFB 1974

Memo From A Grateful Spy C 10 MIN
16MM FILM, 3/4 OR 1/2 IN VIDEO
Uses vignettes in illustrating that information disclosure in an organization is due to employee negligence and careless security practices. Asks employees to consider how they may be contributing unintentionally to a security problem and urges them to take action to prevent information loss.
Prod-XEROXF Dist-MTI 1981

Memo From A Grateful Spy (Spanish) C 10 MIN
16MM FILM, 3/4 OR 1/2 IN VIDEO
Discusses action to be taken to prevent information loss.
Prod-XEROXF Dist-MTI

Memo Reports B 45 MIN
2 INCH VIDEOTAPE C
See series title for descriptive statement.
From The Business Writing Series. Unit IV - Letters About Employment - Reports
Prod-CHITVC Dist-GPITVL Prodn-WTTWTV

Memoirs Of A Movie Palace C 45 MIN
16MM FILM OPTICAL SOUND
Explores the aura and significance of a grand, pre-Depression movie palace through the recollections of a vaudevillian, patrons, the theater's decorator, and its former manager, projectionist and organist.
LC NO. 80-700326
Prod-BLACKW Dist-BLACKW 1980

Memorable Animal Characters C 30 MIN
1/2 IN VIDEO CASSETTE BETA/VHS K-I
See series title for descriptive statement.
From The Jump Over The Moon - Sharing Literature With Young Children Series.
Prod-HRAW Dist-HRAW

Memorable Moments C 28 MIN
16MM FILM OPTICAL SOUND H-C
Uses a story about a little lost girl to show various floats that participated in the Tournament of Roses Parade at Pasadena, California, in 1963.
LC NO. FIA64-740
Prod-TRA Dist-TRA Prodn-ROCKMP 1963

Memorandum B 58 MIN
16MM FILM, 3/4 OR 1/2 IN VIDEO H-C
Deals with Goering's memorandum of July, 1941, which set in motion Nazi concentration camps and other methods of exterminating the Jews of Germany. Depicts a group of Bergen-Belsen survivors on a visit to the camp. Uses German and British footage to show alternating scenes of the past and of today's Germany.
Prod-NFBC Dist-NFBC 1966

Memorandum On Security C 9 MIN
16MM FILM OPTICAL SOUND
Shows research activity being carried on in various universities, research centers and industrial laboratories for the department of defense and explains the purpose of security regulations and procedures required to enforce them.
LC NO. FIE59-209
Prod-USA Dist-USNAC 1959

Memorandum To Industry C 31 MIN
16MM FILM OPTICAL SOUND
Shows not only what industry should do, but what industry is doing in planning its civil defense preparations. Tells what various industries have accomplished to provide fallout shelter for employees and the public, to assure continuity of company management in the event of an attack on the United States.
LC NO. 74-705125
Prod-USOCD Dist-USNAC 1966

Memorial C
16MM FILM OPTICAL SOUND H-C A
Re-enacts the battle of the Somme. Marches over battlegrounds now covered with grain. Conveys the futility and valor of war.
LC NO. 73-702554
Prod-MMA Dist-MMA 1972

Memorial Day B 21 MIN
16MM FILM OPTICAL SOUND
Tells the story of a small New England town's observance of Memorial Day with special emphasis on the part played in it by a young sailor who has just returned from active duty in Korea.
Prod-USN Dist-USNAC 1952

Memorial Day C 14 MIN
3/4 OR 1/2 INCH VIDEO CASSETTE I-C A
Conveys the meaning of Memorial Day by viewing a traditional parade in East Hampton, New York.
LC NO. 83-706967
Prod-DIRECT Dist-DIRECT 1984

Memorial Day C 14 MIN
3/4 OR 1/2 INCH VIDEO CASSETTE
Shows how a small American town annually commemorates its fallen soldiers and sailors from past wars on Memorial Day.
Prod-ULICKM Dist-ULICKM 1983

Memorial Day C 15 MIN
3/4 INCH VIDEO CASSETTE P
See series title for descriptive statement.
From The Celebrate Series.
Prod-KUONTV Dist-GPITVL 1978

Memories C 26 MIN
3/4 OR 1/2 INCH VIDEO CASSETTE PRO
Deals with anyone who comes in contact with parents after they have experienced a stillbirth, miscarriage, or infant death.
Prod-HSCIC Dist-HSCIC 1982

Memories C 28 MIN
3/4 OR 1/2 INCH VIDEO CASSETTE
Presents host Fred Rogers visiting with Kenneth Koch and his class of octogenarian poets, and the Reverend William Sloane Coffin, Jr, pastor of the Riverside Church in New York.
From The Old Friends - New Friends Series.
Prod-FAMCOM Dist-PBS 1981

Memories Along The Patapsco C 30 MIN
3/4 OR 1/2 INCH VIDEO CASSETTE
Looks at the history and development of the Howard County community of Elkridge, Maryland, once a busy seaport.
Prod-HCPL Dist-LVN

Memories From Eden C 57 MIN
16MM FILM, 3/4 OR 1/2 IN VIDEO H-C A
Explains how zoos are involved in breeding studies and in public education programs that will affect the future of both animal and human life. States that with the world losing 15 million acres of wilderness every year zoos may become the last refuge of wildlife.
From The Nova Series.
LC NO. 79-708137
Prod-WGBHTV Dist-TIMLIF 1978

Memories I - Basic Concepts C 30 MIN
3/4 OR 1/2 INCH VIDEO CASSETTE
Discusses types of memory cells available and develops fundamentals of storage configurations. Develops basic configurations of shift register, random access (RAM's) and read only memories (ROM's).
From The Digital Sub-Systems Series.
Prod-TXINLC Dist-TXINLC

Memories II - Applications C 30 MIN
3/4 OR 1/2 INCH VIDEO CASSETTE
Takes basic theory developed in previous session and shows how to design with RAM's and ROM's through five examples.
From The Digital Sub-Systems Series.
Prod-TXINLC Dist-TXINLC

Memories Of An Old Cowboy C 9 MIN
16MM FILM, 3/4 OR 1/2 IN VIDEO P-I
Uses animation to tell a story about an aging cowboy who recalls the exciting old days of the wild, wild West when he was a sheriff of a small town, defending it against all malefactors. Questions whether his memory of these events is real or if he has just seen too many westerns.
Prod-POLSKI Dist-SF 1980

Memories Of Ancestral Power - The Moro Movement In The Solomon Islands C 36 MIN
3/4 OR 1/2 INCH VIDEO CASSETTE
Records the life concepts and artifacts of a dying culture as related by an elder of the tribe Moro.
Prod-EAI Dist-EAI

Memories Of Family C 24 MIN
16MM FILM, 3/4 OR 1/2 IN VIDEO H-C A
Helps us understand the complex ties that bind us to our families and which we perpetuate in forming our own families.
Prod-POLYMR Dist-POLYMR

Memories Of Mewar B 10 MIN
16MM FILM OPTICAL SOUND I-C A
Explains that Mewar, the cradle of Rajput chivalry, still echoes with the tales of its rulers and the songs of Meerabai, the princess turned saint. Shows the ancient palaces of Udaipur built with granite and marble and embellished with sculpture.
Prod-INDIA Dist-NEDINF

Memories Of Prince Albert Hunt C 30 MIN
3/4 INCH VIDEO CASSETTE
Uses experimental techniques to tell the story of Prince Albert Hunt, a fiddler from East Texas who performed during the 1920's.
Prod-KERA Dist-PUBTEL

Memories Of The Cangaco B 26 MIN
16MM FILM OPTICAL SOUND J-C A
Explains that banditry has long been an important social phenomenon in Latin America, at times serving the peasantry as a vehicle for social protest. Portrays the Brazilian bandit of the 1930's, his motivations and activities.
Prod-NYFLMS Dist-NYFLMS

Memory C 29 MIN
3/4 INCH VIDEO CASSETTE C A
Examines wide variety of information known about short-term and long-term memory. Shows techniques of remembering.
From The Understanding Human Behavior - An Introduction To Psychology Series. Lesson 17
Prod-COAST Dist-CDTEL

Memory C 30 MIN
16MM FILM, 3/4 OR 1/2 IN VIDEO H-C A
Centers on the improvement of long-term memory. Suggests methods for categorizing and referencing of memory to facilitate fast, efficient recall.
LC NO. 81-706742
Prod-CRMP Dist-CRMP 1980

Memory And Intelligence C 45 MIN
16MM FILM OPTICAL SOUND
Features the Swiss psychologist, Jean Piaget, presenting his new work on memory and intelligence at the International Congress of Preschool Educational Specialists in Kyoto, Japan. Includes English subtitles to supplement Piaget's presentation in French.
From The Piaget's Developmental Theory Series.
LC NO. 75-712350
Prod-DAVFMS Dist-DAVFMS 1971

Memory And Pride C 24 MIN
16MM FILM, 3/4 OR 1/2 IN VIDEO H-C
Outlines the Gestalt approach to anxiety as Dr Frederick Perls works with a young woman who is self-conscious about her height.
From The Gestalt Series.
Prod-PMI Dist-FI 1969

Memory Array, The And The Decoding Logic Of A Memory System C 30 MIN
3/4 OR 1/2 INCH VIDEO CASSETTE IND
Shows organization of RAM and ROM devices in an array, and sets out techniques and implementations of address decoding logic-linear selection, fully decoding and decoding using bipolar PROM.
From The Microcomputer Memory Design Series.
Prod-COLOSU Dist-COLOSU

Memory Fixing C 67 MIN
16MM FILM, 3/4 OR 1/2 IN VIDEO C A
Presents business training consultant Dr Ken Cooper introducing techniques that will help business executives develop alertness, save time and improve productivity.
Prod-PROSOR Dist-FI 1983

Memory Functions And Economics C 60 MIN
1 INCH VIDEOTAPE IND
Chracterizes the memory functions of sequentially accessed, random accessed and fixed program memories.
From The Semiconductor Memories Course Series. No. 1
Prod-TXINLC Dist-TXINLC

Memory Improvement B 30 MIN
3/4 OR 1/2 INCH VIDEO CASSETTE
Improves the memory by means of subliminal suggestions.
Prod-ADVCAS Dist-ADVCAS

Memory Improvement—A Series

Enhances ability to achieve professional, social or academic goals. Teaches association to improve one's memory.
Prod-UAZMIC Dist-UAZMIC

How To Improve Concentration, Eliminate	
How To Remember Facts From Reading, Linking	060 MIN
How To Remember Jokes, Anecdotes And	060 MIN
How To Remember Names, Faces And Facts About	060 MIN
How To Remember Numbers, Formulas, Equations,	060 MIN
How To Remember Schematics, Diagrams And	060 MIN
How To Remember Vocabulary, Terms And	060 MIN
Introduction, Digital Alphabet, First Ten	060 MIN
Lecture On Theory Of Memory Association	060 MIN
Master Hook System, Master Exchange System,	060 MIN

Memory Interface Timing C 30 MIN
3/4 OR 1/2 INCH VIDEO CASSETTE IND
Shows how buffered and buffer-free address and data buses are designed. Identifies desirable bus-extender properties and tim-

ing constraints for memory devices and uses them in actual examples.
From The Interface Programming (6809) Series.
Prod-COLOSU Dist-COLOSU

Memory Is Made Of This C 30 MIN
16MM FILM, 3/4 OR 1/2 IN VIDEO I-H
Explains the various types of memory, RAM, ROM and floppy disk, and how information is put into the computer memory. Clarifies the differences between human memory (associative) and the computer's perfect memory.
From The Mr Microchip Series.
Prod-JOU Dist-JOU

Memory Of Christmas C 12 MIN
16MM FILM, 3/4 OR 1/2 IN VIDEO I-C A
Uses photographs to illustrate playwright Moss Hart's reminiscence of his impoverished childhood. Describes two Christmases a generation apart that illustrate the gap that existed between Hart and his father. Explains how that gap was finally bridged. Adapted from Hart's autobiography Act One.
From The Simple Gifts Series.
Prod-WNETTV Dist-TIMLIF

Memory Of The Park C 9 MIN
16MM FILM OPTICAL SOUND
Presents an impression of the movements, color, sound and people in Washington Square Park in New York City.
LC NO. 72-700190
Prod-CRAR Dist-CRAR 1972

Memory Surfaces And Mental Prayers—A Series

Video artists Bill Viola continues his experiments in perception and awareness.
Prod-EAI Dist-EAI

Morning After The Night Of Power, The 010 MIN
Sweet Light 010 MIN
Wheel Of Becoming, The 007 MIN

Memory Technologies, Microcomputer Organization And Operation C 30 MIN
3/4 OR 1/2 INCH VIDEO CASSETTE IND
Covers introduction, memory technologies, semiconductor memories, block diagram of a microcomputer and its operation, and general organization of a memory unit.
From The Microcomputer Memory Design Series.
Prod-COLOSU Dist-COLOSU

Memory, Pt 1 C 15 MIN
3/4 OR 1/2 INCH VIDEO CASSETTE K
See series title for descriptive statement.
From The I-Land Treasures Series.
Prod-UWISC Dist-AITECH 1980

Memory, Pt 2 C 13 MIN
3/4 OR 1/2 INCH VIDEO CASSETTE K
See series title for descriptive statement.
From The I-Land Treasure Series.
Prod-NETCHE Dist-AITECH 1980

Memotion Examples C 20 MIN
16MM FILM OPTICAL SOUND
Explains that memotion photography is one method of analyzing motion and time study work. Features examples of memotion including a street operation performed by a crew from a gas company, operation of a railroad yard with humping operations and a crew operation in a steel foundry.
Prod-MUNDEL Dist-CCNY

Memphis Belle C 42 MIN
16MM FILM - 3/4 IN VIDEO
Shows a bombing mission over Germany during World War II, including preparations for the raid, the takeoff from England, the flight, bombing the submarine base at Wilhelmshaven and the return to base. Issued in 1944 as a motion picture.
LC NO. 79-706473
Prod-USAAF Dist-USNAC 1979

Memphis Belle, The B 43 MIN
3/4 OR 1/2 INCH VIDEO CASSETTE
Documents the final mission of the Flying Fortress 'Memphis Belle' as it led a squadron of bombers in a daring daylight attack on the submarine pens at Wilhelmshaven during World War II.
Prod-IHF Dist-IHF

Men Against Tanks/Engineers To The Front (German) C 48 MIN
3/4 OR 1/2 INCH VIDEO CASSETTE
Presents training drama of an entrenched German infantry platoon, unsupported by aircraft, heavy weapons or reinforcements which must repel an overwhelming attack of Soviet T-34 tanks.
Prod-IHF Dist-IHF

Men And The Sea C 9 MIN
16MM FILM OPTICAL SOUND
Shows the operations of Exxon Corporation as it searches for oil beneath the North Atlantic.
LC NO. 75-701593
Prod-EXXON Dist-EXXON Prodn-JERSW 1975

Men And Women In Management C 29 MIN
16MM FILM OPTICAL SOUND
Interviews male executives who discuss their growing personal and professional awareness of women in management positions.
Prod-STURTM Dist-IMPACT

Men At Bay C 26 MIN
16MM FILM, 3/4 OR 1/2 IN VIDEO J-C
Presents a case history of the imminent destruction of San Francisco Bay, an example of the overwhelming environmental problems facing every major American city. Uses graphic photography and interviews of the angry and confused San Francisco residents.
Prod-KINGSP Dist-PHENIX 1970

Men Bathing C 14 MIN
3/4 INCH VIDEO CASSETTE
Documents bushmen of Namibia exchanging sexual jokes as they bathe.
From The San (Bushmen) Series.
Prod-DOCEDR Dist-DOCEDR Prodn-MRSHL

Men From Boeing, The C 24 MIN
16MM FILM OPTICAL SOUND
Shows the effort and skill required of Boeing's 747 aircraft on-ground crew as they are brought in to fix an airplane which crashed off the runway in Frankfurt, Germany.
LC NO. 80-700212
Prod-BOEING Dist-WELBIT Prodn-WELBIT 1980

Men From The Boys, The C 28 MIN
16MM FILM OPTICAL SOUND
Shows how new recruits are transformed into trained soldiers during the first eight weeks of basic training, focusing on the role of the assigned drill sergeant and the reactions of the young inductees.
From The Big Picture Series.
LC NO. 82-700089
Prod-USA Dist-USNAC 1982

Men In Cages B 52 MIN
16MM FILM, 3/4 OR 1/2 IN VIDEO H-C A
Shows some of the worst penal institutions in America and discusses their problems.
Prod-CBSNEW Dist-CAROUF

Men In Early Childhood Education C 24 MIN
16MM FILM, 3/4 OR 1/2 IN VIDEO
See series title for descriptive statement.
From The Early Childhood Development Series.
Prod-DAVFMS Dist-DAVFMS

Men In The Cockpit, The C 25 MIN
16MM FILM OPTICAL SOUND
Examines the problems and dangers of pilot fatigue and jet lag during long, nonstop domestic flights and on international runs with multiple time zone changes.
LC NO. 77-702516
Prod-CTV Dist-CTV 1976

Men In War B 104 MIN
16MM FILM OPTICAL SOUND
Focuses on a platoon during the Korean War, showing how it must reach a specified destination regardless of the odds.
Prod-UAA Dist-KITPAR 1957

Men O War B 24 MIN
16MM FILM OPTICAL SOUND
Presents a Laurel and Hardy comedy in which Ollie tries to stretch the 15 cents they have between them to cover refreshments for four, Stan gets stuck with the check, plays a one-armed bandit and hits the jackpot.
From The Laurel And Hardy Comedy Series.
LC NO. 71-711884
Prod-ROACH Dist-BHAWK 1929

Men Of Action C 30 MIN
3/4 OR 1/2 INCH VIDEO CASSETTE H-C A
See series title for descriptive statement.
From The Japan - The Changing Tradition Series.
Prod-UMA Dist-GPITVL 1978

Men Of Bronze C 58 MIN
16MM FILM, 3/4 OR 1/2 IN VIDEO H-C A
Focuses on the 369th Combat Regiment, an all-black unit which spent more time under fire during World War I than any other regiment.
Prod-KILLIS Dist-FI 1977

Men Of Courage C 15 MIN
16MM FILM, 3/4 OR 1/2 IN VIDEO
Focuses on the many explorers whose lives are linked with the discovery and exploration of Antarctica. Profiles Captain James Cook, Dumont D'Urville, Charles Wilkes, james Ross and others.
From The Odyssey Series.
Prod-KRMATV Dist-GPITVL

Men Of Dark Tears, The C 40 MIN
16MM FILM OPTICAL SOUND
Presents the story of a young Crete revolutionary and his relationship with a middle aged Greek wanderer during one of the many revolts against the Turkish Empire in 1889. Explains that through their relationship and experiences, the young man learns that humanity transcends national boundaries and ethnic hatreds.
LC NO. 72-702408
Prod-USC Dist-USC 1972

Men Of Iron C 20 MIN
16MM FILM, 3/4 OR 1/2 IN VIDEO IND
Tells how working with iron and steel high in the sky requires training, experience and a concern for safety. Gives safety precautions for workers and also shows the manufacture and installation of laminated wooden beams.
Prod-CSAO Dist-IFB

Men Of Justice C 29 MIN
16MM FILM OPTICAL SOUND
Discusses the human aspects of the Supreme Court, showing how the personalities and prejudices of the justices affect their interpretations of the law.
From The Government Story Series. No. 39
LC NO. 73-707172
Prod-WBCPRO Dist-WBCPRO 1968

Men Of Maintenance - Southeast Asia C 15 MIN
16MM FILM, 3/4 OR 1/2 IN VIDEO
Highlights aircraft maintenance operations in Southeast Asia. Depicts specialized personnel using sophisticated electronic equipment to check out complex aircraft systems.
LC NO. 81-707697
Prod-USAF Dist-USNAC 1968

Men Of Pontiac B 11 MIN
16MM FILM OPTICAL SOUND
A typical salesman discusses techniques of good salesmanship and the advantages of running a Pontiac dealership.
From The Destination - Dotted Line Series. No. 1
LC NO. 70-707695
Prod-GMPD Dist-GM Prodn-SOU 1952

Men Of The Canefields B 20 MIN
16MM FILM OPTICAL SOUND H-C
Explains that time is the crucial factor in getting sugar cane to the sugar mill. Shows how a Cuban volunteer work crew spends long hours in the fields and still attends classes. Views recreational activities enjoyed by the crew.
Prod-ICAIC Dist-SFN 1967

Men Of The Sea C 28 MIN
16MM FILM, 3/4 OR 1/2 IN VIDEO
Portrays the story of Navy combat art.
LC NO. 82-706244
Prod-USN Dist-USNAC 1970

Men Of The Tall Ships C 60 MIN
16MM FILM, 3/4 OR 1/2 IN VIDEO
Presents a story about the men who sailed across the Atlantic to New York City for the Operation Sail '76 competition.
Prod-DREWAS Dist-DIRECT 1978

Men Of The Wilderness X 30 MIN
16MM FILM OPTICAL SOUND J-C A
Portrays the three temptations.
From The Living Christ Series.
Prod-CAFM Dist-ECUFLM

Men Under Siege - Life With The Modern Woman C 33 MIN
16MM FILM, 3/4 OR 1/2 IN VIDEO H-C
Appraises the impact of changing sex roles in American life.
LC NO. 79-706600
Prod-ABCNEW Dist-MTI 1979

Men Who Are Working With Women In Management C 28 MIN
16MM FILM - 3/4 IN VIDEO J-C A
Tells how some male executives have coped with training, advancing, advising, and criticizing their women colleagues. Shows how they have changed their personal and corporate awareness of the status of women.
From The Are You Listening Series.
LC NO. 80-707147
Prod-STURTM Dist-STURTM 1973

Men Who Feed The World C 14 MIN
16MM FILM OPTICAL SOUND
Presents the story of Jimmy and his prize winning Swiss calf, Heida.
Prod-FLADC Dist-FLADC

Men Who Marched Away, The - Poetry From World War I C 30 MIN
3/4 INCH VIDEO CASSETTE H-C A
Features Darren Mc Gavin and the First Poetry Quartet in a tribute to the soldier-poets of World War I.
Prod-NETCHE Dist-GPITVL

Men Who Tread On The Tiger's Tail, The (Japanese) B 60 MIN
3/4 OR 1/2 INCH VIDEO CASSETTE
Tells a story set in 12th Century Japan of a clan lord hunted by his brother, the reigning shogun. Describes his flight with six followers and their disguise as monks and how the border magistrate allows them to pass. Based on the Kubuki drama Kanjincho. Directed by Akira Kurosawa. With English subtitles.
Prod-IHF Dist-IHF

Men With Green Faces C 29 MIN
16MM FILM - 3/4 IN VIDEO
Shows the life and service of the U S Navy's frogmen commandos, the Seals. Issued in 1969 as a motion picture.
LC NO. 79-706666
Prod-USN Dist-USNAC 1979

Men With Wings B 14 MIN
16MM FILM - 3/4 IN VIDEO
Illustrates the courage and achievements of military pilots over the last half century. Describes the rise of airpower and heroism of fighter pilots and bomber crews in World Wars I and II and the Korean conflict.
Prod-USNAC Dist-USNAC 1972

Men, Machines And The Secretary C 24 MIN
16MM FILM, 3/4 OR 1/2 IN VIDEO
Documents how a company reorganized its use of secretaries because of the introduction of a word processor. Studies the replacement of the conventional system of personal secretaries with administrative support centers in the headquarters office of a large multi-national oil company.
Prod-OPENU Dist-MEDIAG Prodn-BBCTV 1981

Men, Women And Children C 20 MIN
3/4 OR 1/2 INCH VIDEO CASSETTE
Tells about fire in the home, their real causes and the resulting injury and destruction.
Prod-FPF Dist-FPF

Men, Women, And Language C 30 MIN
3/4 OR 1/2 INCH VIDEO CASSETTE
See series title for descriptive statement.
From The Language - Thinking, Writing, Communicating Series.
Prod-MDCPB Dist-MDCPB

Men's Basketball Basics C 56 MIN
1/2 IN VIDEO CASSETTE BETA/VHS A
Presents Marv Harshman, who demonstrates the drills he uses to school his teams on sound defensive principles. Begins with individual reaction drills and progresses to team defense, including both man-for-man and zone defensive strategy.
Prod-RMI Dist-RMI

Men's Basketball Basics - Creating An Offense C 57 MIN
1/2 IN VIDEO CASSETTE BETA/VHS A
Explains how to create an offense which takes advantage of what the opposition defense gives them. Discusses offensive strategy for man-for-man and zone defenses. Includes creating a lead, post play, the double stack, using the back door and the passing game. Features Marv Harshman, one of the outstanding coaches in college basketball.
Prod-RMI Dist-RMI

Men's Basketball Basics - Offensive Drills C 59 MIN
1/2 IN VIDEO CASSETTE BETA/VHS A
Demonstrates drills to help build an offense in basketball, including shooting, passing, dribbling, screening, rebounding and movement without the ball. Features Marv Harshman, University of Washington coach.
Prod-RMI Dist-RMI

Men's Basketball Basics—A Series

Demonstrates offensive and defensive strategy and techniques for men's basketball. Includes practice drills. Features University of Washington coach Mary Harshman.
Prod-MOHOMV Dist-MOHOMV

Drills That Get Scoreboard Results 059 MIN
Tough Defense - It'll Keep You In The Game 056 MIN
Winning Offense, A 057 MIN

Men's Championship Basketball—A Series
16MM FILM, 3/4 OR 1/2 IN VIDEO H-C
Stresses Coach Jack Ramsay's total team approach to championship basketball.
Prod-ATHI Dist-ATHI 1976

Jack Ramsay's Championship Defense 015 MIN
Jack Ramsay's Championship Offense 015 MIN

Men's Dance (Pushtu) C 11 MIN
16MM FILM, 3/4 OR 1/2 IN VIDEO
See series title for descriptive statement.
From The Mountain Peoples Of Central Asia (Afghanistan) Series.
Prod-IFF Dist-IFF

Men's Golf With Al Geiberger C 60 MIN
1/2 IN VIDEO CASSETTE BETA/VHS
Presents neuromuscular training using Al Geiberger as the model for an improved golf game. Includes four audiocassettes and personal training guide.
Prod-SYBVIS Dist-SYBVIS

Men's Liberation C 29 MIN
3/4 INCH VIDEO CASSETTE
Features Warren Farrell, author of Beyond Masculinity, explaining that men can be victims of stereotyping.
From The Woman Series.
Prod-WNEDTV Dist-PUBTEL

Men's Lives C 43 MIN
16MM FILM OPTICAL SOUND I-C A
Shows by a series of candid interviews what American boys and men believe about the American concept of masculinity.
LC NO. 75-701564
Prod-NEWDAY Dist-NEWDAY 1974

Menagerie C 22 MIN
16MM FILM OPTICAL SOUND K-H
A collection of eight short animated films created by children, ages 8-16, students at the pilot film workshop of the Lexington School of Modern Dance, 1967. Includes techniques of black and white clay animation, color, cut-outs, tear-outs, collage and flip cards.
LC NO. FIA67-5629
Prod-LSMD Dist-CELLAR 1967

Mendelssohn Concerto, The C 22 MIN
16MM FILM OPTICAL SOUND P-C A
Shows children and teenagers dancing classical ballet to the music of Mendelssohn.
Prod-WSU Dist-WSU 1956

Mendelssohn's Dream C 24 MIN
16MM FILM, 3/4 OR 1/2 IN VIDEO
Discusses the overture and incidental music written by 19th century German composer Felix Mendelssohn for A Midsummer Night's Dream. Establishes the importance of the overture to Mendelssohn's career.
Prod-OPENU Dist-MEDIAG Prodn-BBCTV 1979

Mendelssohn's Midsummer Night's Dream B 20 MIN
16MM FILM OPTICAL SOUND
Franco Ferrara directs the Radio Philharmonic Orchestra of Italy playing 'NOCTURNE,' 'SCHERZO' and 'WEDDING MARCH' from Mendelssohn's 'MIDSUMMER NIGHT'S DREAM.'
From The Musical Masterpieces Series.
Prod-SG Dist-SG

Mending Bodies And Souls C 29 MIN
3/4 INCH VIDEO CASSETTE
Shows how rapid change has affected northern Canadians. Examines the effects of stress, altered eating habits and alcohol on the physical and mental health of the people. Also available in two-inch quad and one-inch videotape.
From The North Of 60 Degrees - Destiny Uncertain Series.
Prod-TVOTAR Dist-NAMPBC

Mending Books C 15 MIN
2 INCH VIDEOTAPE
See series title for descriptive statement.
From The Making Things Work Series.
Prod-WGBHTV Dist-PUBTEL

Mending China And Glass C 15 MIN
2 INCH VIDEOTAPE
See series title for descriptive statement.
From The Making Things Work Series.
Prod-WGBHTV Dist-PUBTEL

Mending Wall C 10 MIN
16MM FILM, 3/4 OR 1/2 IN VIDEO J-H
Presents Leonard Nemoy reading the poem Mending Wall by Robert Frost, as scenes evocative of the poem are pictured. Shows the words of the poem as it is reread to appropriate scenes.
From The Reading Poetry Series.
Prod-EVANSA Dist-AIMS 1972

Meningitis C 20 MIN
3/4 OR 1/2 INCH VIDEO CASSETTE PRO
Focuses on meningitis by covering the basic pathophysiology of the condition, clinical signs and symptoms, and laboratory tests. Includes animated segments.
From The Major Medical Syndromes Series.
LC NO. 80-706595
Prod-NMAC Dist-USNAC 1979

Meningitis C 29 MIN
3/4 OR 1/2 INCH VIDEO CASSETTE
Discusses the different forms of meningitis and the treatments available.
From The Daniel Foster, MD Series.
Prod-KERA Dist-PBS

Menneskets Natur (Man's Nature) C 15 MIN
16MM FILM OPTICAL SOUND
A Danish language film. Portrays pollution of nature by modern man.
Prod-STATNS Dist-STATNS 1970

Mennonites Of Ontario C 16 MIN
3/4 INCH VIDEO CASSETTE J-C A R
Traces the influx of several waves of Mennonites into Ontario, Canada. Describes the community which has resulted from the mixture of traditional Mennonites with more liberal members of that sect. Examines their common values.
Prod-BULLER Dist-BULLER

Menominee C 59 MIN
3/4 INCH VIDEO CASSETTE
Examines the historical development of the many social and political problems faced by the Menominee Indians of northwestern Wisconsin, and their battle to regain tribal status with the U S government. Also available in two-inch quad and one-inch videotape.
Prod-GBCTP Dist-NAMPBC

Menopause C 10 MIN
16MM FILM OPTICAL SOUND H-C A
Examines many of the fears women face when confronted with menopause and suggests how one can look upon this period in life from a realistic perspective.
From The Obstetrics And Gynecology Series.
LC NO. 75-700045
Prod-MIFE Dist-MIFE 1974

Menopause C
3/4 OR 1/2 INCH VIDEO CASSETTE
Details the menopausal experience of an individual woman. Features eight older women discussing their menopause interspersed with the main story line. Discusses mild estrogen therapy.
Prod-MIFE Dist-MIFE

Menopause C 9 MIN
16MM FILM, 3/4 OR 1/2 IN VIDEO A
Explains menopause as a normal physiological change and examines the physiology and effects of the change of life process. Gives benefits and limitations of treatment, including the role of estrogens and psychosocial adjustment.
Prod-PRORE Dist-PRORE

Menopause C 19 MIN
16MM FILM, 3/4 OR 1/2 IN VIDEO H-C A
States that there is no way of determining, in advance, how a particular woman will react to this stage of her life. Explains that the only preparation is to try to thoroughly understand what menopause is and why it can cause certain physical symptoms. Gives a detailed, animated explanation of the menopause process.
From The Woman Talk Series.
Prod-CORF Dist-CORF 1983

Menopause (Spanish) C 9 MIN
16MM FILM, 3/4 OR 1/2 IN VIDEO PRO
Discusses menopause and the benefits and limitations of the various treatments for it.
Prod-PRORE Dist-PRORE

Menopause (2nd Ed) C 7 MIN
3/4 OR 1/2 INCH VIDEO CASSETTE
Defines menopause. Explains physiologic changes responsible for menopause and basic principles of treatment.
Prod-MEDFAC Dist-MEDFAC 1981

Menopause - How To Cope C 29 MIN
3/4 INCH VIDEO CASSETTE
Looks at ways to prevent acute depression during menopause.
From The Woman Series.
Prod-WNEDTV Dist-PUBTEL

Menopause - Myths And Realities C 22 MIN
16MM FILM, 3/4 OR 1/2 IN VIDEO A
Deals with causes and consequences of menopause and shows that the symptoms are not usually as bad as anticipated, they are not painful and not permanent.
Prod-BURN Dist-PEREN

Menopause - Myths And Realities C 22 MIN
3/4 OR 1/2 INCH VIDEO CASSETTE A
Explores symptoms of menopause, both physical and psychological and suggestions are made for helping a woman regain self-esteem and self-pride.
Prod-WFP Dist-WFP

Menopause Story, The C 30 MIN
16MM FILM, 3/4 OR 1/2 IN VIDEO A
Looks at the myths and realities of menopause. Discusses worries about aging, keeping fit and sexuality.
Prod-MOBIUS Dist-CF 1982

Mensch Mutter C 80 MIN
16MM FILM OPTICAL SOUND
A German language film with English subtitles. Presents a study of the survival of Helga Fuchs, who with a minimal home job attempts to support her three children. Portrays Helga's futile fight to be a 'good mother,' although she does not possess the inner strength to succeed and lives in constant fear that her children might capsize her already barely floating boat.
Prod-WSTGLC Dist-WSTGLC 1977

Menschen Untereinander B 90 MIN
16MM FILM SILENT
A silent motion picture without subtitles. Presents a vivid picture of varying human emotions. Explores the lives of people with different fates, with arrogance, despondence, happiness and sorrow.
Prod-WSTGLC Dist-WSTGLC 1926

Menstruation (2nd Ed) C 14 MIN
3/4 OR 1/2 INCH VIDEO CASSETTE
Explains menstruation, ovulation and menstrual flow. Discusses common symptoms related to menstruation and their management.
Prod-MEDFAC Dist-MEDFAC 1981

Menstruation - Hormones In Harmony C 19 MIN
3/4 OR 1/2 INCH VIDEO CASSETTE I-H
Uses graphics and narration to explain the process of menstruation. Includes advice on hygiene and charting the cycle.
Prod-PPPO Dist-PEREN

Menstruation And Premenstrual Tension C 29 MIN
3/4 INCH VIDEO CASSETTE
Examines the problems surrounding menstruation and premenstrual tension. Emphasizes the role of parents in determining how their daughters will react to menstruation.
From The Woman Series.
Prod-WNEDTV Dist-PUBTEL

Menstruation And Sexual Development C 28 MIN
16MM FILM, 3/4 OR 1/2 IN VIDEO
Discusses the bodily changes which occur in young women.
From The Inner Woman Series.
Prod-WXYZTV Dist-CRMP 1977

Mental Computation - Using Mental Computation For Addition C 15 MIN
3/4 OR 1/2 INCH VIDEO CASSETTE I
Demonstrates left-right method and plus-minus method of adding two-digit numbers.
From The Math Works Series.
Prod-AITECH Dist-AITECH

Mental Health C 15 MIN
3/4 OR 1/2 INCH VIDEO CASSETTE P
Shows how to express feelings without losing control by thinking it over and talking to someone, if necessary.
From The Well, Well, Well With Slim Goodbody Series.
Prod-AITECH Dist-AITECH

Mental Health C 20 MIN
3/4 OR 1/2 INCH VIDEO CASSETTE J-C A
Discusses various aspects of mental health.
From The Safety Sense Series. Pt. 14
Prod-WCVETV Dist-GPITVL 1981

Mental Health C 30 MIN
3/4 OR 1/2 INCH VIDEO CASSETTE
See series title for descriptive statement.
From The Health, Safety And Well-Being Series.
Prod-MAETEL Dist-CAMB

Mental Health C 30 MIN
3/4 OR 1/2 INCH VIDEO CASSETTE
Presents tips on maintaining mental health.
From The Consumer Survival Series. Health
Prod-MDCPB Dist-MDCPB

Mental Health - New Frontiers Of Sanity C 18 MIN
16MM FILM, 3/4 OR 1/2 IN VIDEO
Offers an introduction to concepts and treatment methods in the field of mental health.
Prod-DOCUA Dist-CNEMAG

Mental Health Care - One Patient's View C 29 MIN
3/4 OR 1/2 INCH VIDEO CASSETTE
Offers the insights of a woman who was a mental patient for ten years. Focuses on the need for greater respect for patients. Urges formation of patients' rights groups.

From The Woman Series.
Prod-WNEDTV Dist-PBS

Mental Health Care For Women, Pt 1 C 29 MIN
3/4 OR 1/2 INCH VIDEO CASSETTE
Features a psychiatrist and a psychologist discussing different definitions of a normal adult and telling how these stereotypes tend to affect mental health care for men and women.
From The Woman Series.
Prod-WNEDTV Dist-PBS

Mental Health Care For Women, Pt 2 C 29 MIN
3/4 INCH VIDEO CASSETTE
Discusses what qualities to look for in a therapist.
From The Woman Series.
Prod-WNEDTV Dist-PUBTEL

Mental Health Challenges - Past And Future C 16 MIN
16MM FILM OPTICAL SOUND
Uses animation to present a review of the progress in the field of mental health during the last 25 years. Features Drs Robert H Felix, Stanley F Yolles and Bertram S Brown, the first three directors of the U S National Institute of Mental Health.
LC NO. 75-700863
Prod-NIMH Dist-USNAC 1971

Mental Health Concepts For Nursing—A Series
PRO
Demonstrates how mental health principles can be helpful to nursing in any setting.
Prod-SREB Dist-GPITVL 1971

Acceptance Of Others - Assessment Of	
Acceptance Of Others - Introduction To The	30 MIN
Acceptance Of Others - Planning And	30 MIN
Acceptance Of Others - The Patient's Point Of	30 MIN
Acceptance Of Others - The Right To Be	30 MIN
Acceptance Of Others - The Struggle For	30 MIN
Communication In The Nurse-Patient Relationship	30 MIN
Introduction To The Nurse-Patient Relationship	30 MIN
Nurse-Patient Relationhsip - Termination Phase	30 MIN
Nurse-Patient Relationship - Orientation Phase	30 MIN
Nurse-Patient Relationship - The Nursing	30 MIN
Nurse-Patient Relationship - Therapeutic Use	30 MIN
Nurse-Patient Relationship - Understanding	30 MIN
Nurse-Patient Relationship - Working Phase	30 MIN
Self-Acceptance - Role Of The Significant	30 MIN
Self-Acceptance - The Individual	30 MIN
Self-Understanding - Developing A Self-Concept	30 MIN
Self-Understanding - Introduction To Series	30 MIN
Self-Understanding - Perception Of Reality	30 MIN
Self-Understanding - The Autonomous Self	30 MIN
Self-Understanding - The Key To Mastery Of	30 MIN
Self-Understanding - The Process Of Becoming	30 MIN
Self-Understanding - Toward An Integrated	30 MIN

Mental Health Concepts For Nursing, Unit 1 - Self-Understanding—A Series
PRO
Prod-GPITVL Dist-GPITVL 1971

Autonomous Self, The	30 MIN
Developing A Self-Concept	30 MIN
Introduction To Mental Health Concepts	30 MIN
Key To Mastery Of Environment, The	30 MIN
Perception Of Reality	30 MIN
Process Of Becoming, The	30 MIN
Toward An Integrated Personality	30 MIN

Mental Health Concepts For Nursing, Unit 2 - Self-Acceptance—A Series
PRO
Prod-GPITVL Dist-GPITVL 1971

Self-Acceptance - Role Of The Significant	
Self-Acceptance - The Individual	30 MIN

Mental Health Concepts For Nursing, Unit 3 - Acceptance Of Others—A Series
PRO
Prod-GPITVL Dist-GPITVL 1971

Assessment Of Patient's Nursing Needs	30 MIN
Introduction To The Nursing Process	30 MIN
Patient's Point Of View, The	30 MIN
Planning And Evaluating Nursing Care	30 MIN
Right To Be, The	30 MIN
Struggle For Objectivity, The	30 MIN

Mental Health Concepts For Nursing, Unit 4 - The Nurse-Patient Relationship—A Series
PRO
Prod-GPITVL Dist-GPITVL 1971

Communication In The Nurse-Patient Relationship	30 MIN
Introduction To Nurse-Patient Relationship	30 MIN
Nurse-Patient Relationship - Orientation Phase	30 MIN
Nurse-Patient Relationship - Termination Phase	30 MIN
Nurse-Patient Relationship - Working Phase	30 MIN
Nursing Challenge, The	30 MIN
Therapeutic Use Of Self	30 MIN
Understanding The Patient (Cultural Factors)	30 MIN

Mental Health Needs Of Women With Medically High Risk Pregnancy, The C
3/4 INCH VIDEO CASSETTE PRO
Illustrates the emotional needs and reponses of women with medically high-risk pregancies, encouraging health-care professionals to be sensitive to their needs. Describes the role of the mental health nurse in obstetrics.
LC NO. 79-707726
Prod-UMICHM Dist-UMMCML Prodn-UMISU 1978

Mental Health Nursing C 30 MIN
16MM FILM - 3/4 IN VIDEO PRO
Presents course instructor Eugene I Pavalon and guest Patrick Murphy analyzing the concepts of patients' rights to treatment, confidentiality, least restrictive alternative and privacy. Discusses legal implications for nurses involved in mental health care.
From The Nurse And The Law Series.
LC NO. 77-700128
Prod-AJN Dist-AJN Prodn-WGNCP 1977

Mental Health Nursing - Out Of Bounds - The Drug Culture B 30 MIN
16MM FILM OPTICAL SOUND
A nurse, a doctor and a pharmacist discuss with teenaged drug users the reasons for taking drugs and physiology of habituation.
LC NO. 70-712476
Prod-VDONUR Dist-AJN 1971

Mental Health Nursing - Wednesday's Child, Pt 1 B 30 MIN
16MM FILM OPTICAL SOUND
Presents five case studies of children to alert the nurse to some of the common experiences of childhood which can lead to emotional disturbances.
From The Pediatric Nursing Series.
LC NO. 76-712475
Prod-VDONUR Dist-AJN 1971

Mental Health Nursing - Wednesday's Child, Pt 2 B 30 MIN
16MM FILM OPTICAL SOUND
Presents five case studies of children to alert the nurse to some of the common experiences of childhood which can lead to emotional disturbances.
From The Pediatric Nursing Series.
LC NO. 76-712475
Prod-VDONUR Dist-AJN 1971

Mental Illness, Pt 2 - The Search C 25 MIN
16MM FILM OPTICAL SOUND
Shows the research and treatment of the mentally ill conducted at Tulane University.
Prod-MGHT Dist-CCNY

Mental Patients' Association C 29 MIN
16MM FILM, 3/4 OR 1/2 IN VIDEO H-C A
Shows how ex-mental patients and their friends formed the Vancouver Mental Patients' Association, a democratically-organized, self-help group to assist people during the critical post-release period.
Prod-NFBC Dist-NFBC 1977

Mental Processes In Problem Solving C
16MM FILM OPTICAL SOUND
Eavesdrops on a mathematical quiz show in which students are posed some problems by a chairman who invites them to discuss the thinking behind their answers. Explores the psychological states in problem solving.
Prod-OPENU Dist-OPENU 1979

Mental Retardation - The Hopeless C 25 MIN
16MM FILM, 3/4 OR 1/2 IN VIDEO H-C A
Portrays the realistic view of the mentally retarded, in an effort to refute the popular prejudices and misconceptions that surround them. Shows how a vast majority of the retarded have the ability to relate to others and the proven potential for varying degrees of self-care, productivity and independence.
Prod-MONWIL Dist-AIMS 1972

Mental Retardation And Social Work C 18 MIN
3/4 OR 1/2 INCH VIDEO CASSETTE
Designed to increase the social worker's awareness of the needs of the mentally retarded and the facilities available. Discusses the trainable, moderately retarded, severely retarded and profoundly retarded.
Prod-LASSWC Dist-UWISC 1979

Mental Retardation Plus - The Twice Afflicted C 20 MIN
16MM FILM OPTICAL SOUND
Focuses on mobility, sight and communication disorders among the profoundly retarded and on beginning efforts on institutions to assess, educate and train this population.
LC NO. 74-705131
Prod-USDHEW Dist-USNAC 1974

Mental Retardation Special 3 Per Cent, Pt 1 B 30 MIN
16MM FILM OPTICAL SOUND
Discusses the etiology, care, treatment and future of the six million mentally retarded in American society. Shows mental institutions, day care schools and residential treatment centers. Describes how the nurse can assist families in making use of community mental health resources.
From The Pediatric Nursing Series.
LC NO. 70-710013
Prod-VDONUR Dist-AJN 1970

Mental Retardation Special 3 Per Cent, Pt 2 B 30 MIN
16MM FILM OPTICAL SOUND
Discusses the etiology, care, treatment and future of the six million mentally retarded in American society. Shows mental institutions, day care schools and residential treatment centers. Describes how the nurse can assist families in making use of community mental health resources.
From The Pediatric Nursing Series.
LC NO. 70-710013
Prod-VDONUR Dist-AJN 1970

Mental Retardation, Pt 1 C 29 MIN
16MM FILM OPTICAL SOUND
Focuses upon the needs and progress made on behalf of the most severely and profoundly retarded. Emphasis is upon medical aspects, manpower needs, research efforts and activities within training centers.
Prod-UWISC Dist-UWISC 1966

Mental Retardation, Pt 2 C 29 MIN
16MM FILM OPTICAL SOUND
Deals with the needs and most recent breakthroughs in the training, education and habilitation of the moderately, mild and borderline groups of mentally retarded. Special education facilities, sheltered workshop and work adjustment services are featured.
Prod-UWISC Dist-UWISC 1966

Mental Status Exam C
3/4 OR 1/2 INCH VIDEO CASSETTE
See series title for descriptive statement.
From The Physical Assessment - Neurologic System Series.
Prod-CONMED Dist-CONMED

Mental Status Exam, The, Pt I B 60 MIN
3/4 OR 1/2 INCH VIDEO CASSETTE
Features a discussion by Dr Leonard Stein on the mental status exam he uses to judge a client's psychological state. Topics include general or immediate observation, one's capacity to abstract, mood and affect.
Prod-VRL Dist-UWISC

Mental Status Exam, The, Pt II B 15 MIN
3/4 OR 1/2 INCH VIDEO CASSETTE
Concludes discussion with Dr Leonard Stein on his mental status exam. Covers perception, memory and judgement.
Prod-VRL Dist-UWISC

Mental Status Examination, The B 34 MIN
16MM FILM - 3/4 IN VIDEO PRO
Demonstrates techniques of initial or mental status interviews in psychiatric practice. Issued in 1962 as a motion picture.
LC NO. 78-706235
Prod-USPHS Dist-USNAC Prodn-NMAC 1978

Mentally Retarded And Slow Learning Child, The C 30 MIN
3/4 OR 1/2 INCH VIDEO CASSETTE T
Reviews the characteristics of the slow learning and mentally retarded child, how the curriculum should be adapted and how the regular classroom can help this child experience success.
From The Promises To Keep Series. Module 2
Prod-VPISU Dist-LUF 1979

Mentally Retarded Child, The B 44 MIN
16MM FILM OPTICAL SOUND PRO
Describes down's syndrome and discusses the growth and development patterns and associated problems. Presents definition, manifestations and care of the mentally retarded, including diagnosis, educational needs and planning.
From The Pediatric Nursing Series.
LC NO. 79-703417
Prod-VDONUR Dist-AJN Prodn-WTTWTV 1967

Mente C 30 MIN
3/4 OR 1/2 INCH VIDEO CASSETTE K-P
See series title for descriptive statement.
From The Villa Alegre Series.
Prod-BCTV Dist-MDCPB

Menu For An Astronaut C 15 MIN
16MM FILM OPTICAL SOUND
Focuses on the modern processing of food preparation for the astronauts.
Prod-FLADC Dist-FLADC

Menu For Space Flight C 6 MIN
16MM FILM OPTICAL SOUND
Shows the preparation of nutritious and appetizing foods for space flight and demonstrates how foods can be eaten by space travelers.
Prod-NASA Dist-NASA

Menura - The Lyrebird C 22 MIN
16MM FILM OPTICAL SOUND I-C A
Describes the life cycle of the superb lyrebird, the cleverest of all bird mimics. Includes close-ups of the mating dance, nest building, female incubating her single egg and raising her young.
From The Australian Wildlife Series.
Prod-POLLCK Dist-AVEXP

Meow, Meow C 8 MIN
16MM FILM OPTICAL SOUND K-I
Presents a series of animated cut-out designs made by children.
Prod-YELLOW Dist-YELLOW 1969

Mephisto's Little Film Plays C 18 MIN
16MM FILM OPTICAL SOUND K-H
Presents a collection of short film plays by young filmmakers, aged 14 to 21. Includes the film plays Ethereal Voyage, POW, Subway, 27, Read 'Em and Weep, Skyway Drive-in and Cosmic Crystal.
Prod-YELLOW Dist-YELLOW

Mer A Mer C 25 MIN
16MM FILM OPTICAL SOUND
A French language version of the 1975 film Sea To Sea. Views the Canadian fishing industry on both the east and west coasts of Canada and the way of life of those who work in the fishing industry.
LC NO. 76-701478
Prod-WILFGP Dist-WILFGP 1975

Mer Cruiser 470 C 9 MIN
16MM FILM OPTICAL SOUND
Introduces a new stern drive marine engine, the Mer Cruiser 470.
LC NO. 76-702849
Prod-MERMAR Dist-MERMAR Prodn-HANSEN 1976

Mercado Mexicana C 10 MIN
16MM FILM OPTICAL SOUND I-H
A Spanish language Film. Presents scenes of a town market near

Mexico City. Shows native shoppers, animals, fruits and vegetables, textiles and clothing, pottery and flowers.
Prod-ACI Dist-UILL

Merce And Marcel C 15 MIN
3/4 OR 1/2 INCH VIDEO CASSETTE
Shows Nam June Paik and Shigeko Kubota use material including Russell Connor's 1964 interview with Marcel Duchamp.
From The Merce By Merce By Paik Series.
Prod-EAI Dist-EAI

Merce By Merce By Paik C 30 MIN
3/4 INCH VIDEO CASSETTE
Divided into 'Blue Studio' and 'Merce and Marcel.' Presents dance sequences by Merce Cunningham and an interview with Marcel Duchamp.
Prod-WNETTV Dist-CUNDAN

Merce By Merce By Paik—A Series

Shows video artists Merce Cunningham and Nam June Paik in programs divided into two parts.
Prod-EAI Dist-EAI

Blue Studio - Five Segments 015 MIN
Merce And Marcel 015 MIN

Merce Cunningham C 30 MIN
3/4 OR 1/2 INCH VIDEO CASSETTE
Focuses on the development of videodance.
From The Eye On Dance - Dance On TV And Film Series.
Prod-ARTRES Dist-ARTRES

Merce Cunningham C 60 MIN
3/4 INCH VIDEO CASSETTE
Includes interviews with choreographer/dancer Merce Cunningham and performance excebpts from 'Exchange,' 'Squaregame,' and 'Travelogue.'
Prod-LONWTV Dist-CUNDAN

Merce Cunningham C 60 MIN
3/4 OR 1/2 INCH VIDEO CASSETTE H-C A
Presents Merce Cunningham leading his dance company in a group of selections from their own diverse repertoire. Includes such dances as the 1954 Minutiae and the Video Triangle created especially for television.
From The Dance In America Series.
Prod-WNETTV Dist-FI

Merce Cunningham And Company C 55 MIN
3/4 INCH VIDEO CASSETTE
Presents choreographer/dancer Merce Cunningham with his company and in an interview relevant to his work.
Prod-LINLA Dist-CUNDAN

Merce Cunningham, Charles Atlas And Chris Komar C 30 MIN
3/4 OR 1/2 INCH VIDEO CASSETTE
Discusses collaborating on videodance.
From The Eye On Dance - Dance On TV And Film Series.
Prod-ARTRES Dist-ARTRES

Mercenary Game, The C 60 MIN
3/4 OR 1/2 INCH VIDEO CASSETTE I-C A
Analyzes the international political implications of mercenary attempts to subvert foreign governments. Traces an ill-fated 1980 attempt by a group of American mercenaries to take over the small Caribbean island of Dominica. Shows how the plot, which involved members of the Ku Klux Klan, was foiled by the FBI.
LC NO. 84-707171
Prod-IP Dist-CNEMAG 1983

Merchandise Control For Retailers C 14 MIN
16MM FILM, 3/4 OR 1/2 IN VIDEO H-C A
Focuses on four main elements for proper control which are what to sell, getting the right supplier, good procedures for receiving, checking and storing merchandise, and proper control for merchandise in stock.
From The Running A Small Business Series.
Prod-MVM Dist-BCNFL 1983

Merchant Marine Safety C 28 MIN
16MM FILM OPTICAL SOUND PRO
Defines the responsibilities of the coast guard in Merchant Marine safety, such as inspection and approval of blueprints for vessel construction, safety requirements for construction and equipment of vessels, annual or periodic inspection thereafter and licensing and certification of the officers and crews of vessels.
Prod-USGS Dist-USNAC 1962

Merchant Of Four Seasons, The (German) C 88 MIN
16MM FILM OPTICAL SOUND
Tells the story of Hans, a squat, cloddish fruit peddler whose mother despises him and whose sweetheart rejects him because his job is too dirty. Follows him through numerous episodes of almost unbelievable bad luck.
Prod-NYFLMS Dist-NYFLMS 1972

Merchant Of Venice, The C 157 MIN
3/4 OR 1/2 INCH VIDEO CASSETTE H-C A
Dramatizes William Shakespeare's play The Merchant Of Venice which strives to answer the question of whether the moneylender Shylock is an implacable villain, a comic buffoon, a tragic hero or a venomous monster.
From The Shakespeare Plays Series.
LC NO. 81-706561
Prod-BBCTV Dist-TIMLIF 1980

Merchant Of Venice, The - Act I, Scene III, Act IV, Scene I C 26 MIN
16MM FILM, 3/4 OR 1/2 IN VIDEO J-C A
Through a wide range of selection of scenes from Shakespeare, shows the great variety of Shakespeare's art and his understanding of man as an individual and as a member of society.
From The Great Scenes From Shakespeare Series.
Prod-SEABEN Dist-PHENIX 1971

Merchant Of Venice, The - Incredibility Of Plot, Specifically Trial Scene B 45 MIN
2 INCH VIDEOTAPE C
See series title for descriptive statement.
From The Shakespeare Series.
Prod-CHITVC Dist-GPITVL Prodn-WTTWTV

Merchant Of Venice, The - Shylock - Hero Or Villain B 45 MIN
2 INCH VIDEOTAPE C
See series title for descriptive statement.
From The Shakespeare Series.
Prod-CHITVC Dist-GPITVL Prodn-WTTWTV

Merchant's Tale, The B 30 MIN
1 INCH VIDEOTAPE A
See series title for descriptive statement.
From The Canterbury Tales Series.
Prod-UMITV Dist-UMITV 1967

Merchants Of Grain C 57 MIN
3/4 OR 1/2 INCH VIDEO CASSETTE
Uses charts, animation and music to discuss the complexity of the grain trade and the large companies that control it. Presents spokesmen for one of the large companies who describe various aspects of the world's grain traffic. Demonstrates the growing importance of the grain trade as a instrument of foreign policy.
LC NO. 83-707212
Prod-CANBC Dist-FLMLIB 1983

Mercury - Exploration Of A Planet C 28 MIN
16MM FILM, 3/4 OR 1/2 IN VIDEO
Uses animation and photography to illustrate the flight of Mariner X to Mercury and Venus.
LC NO. 81-706421
Prod-NASA Dist-USNAC 1981

Mercury And Venus C 29 MIN
3/4 INCH VIDEO CASSETTE C A
Describes space explorations of Mercury and Venus since 1970. Uses animation to illustrate the unusual backtracking path the sun would appear to take when seen from Mercury's surface. Compares physical characteristics of Venus with the earth.
From The Project Universe - Astronomy Series. Lesson 8
Prod-COAST Dist-CDTEL Prodn-SCCON

Merdeka Joy B 19 MIN
16MM FILM OPTICAL SOUND
Shows the joy felt by Independence and the celebrations which were held throughout the country of Malaysia.
Prod-FILEM Dist-PMFMUN 1967

Meredith Monk B 40 MIN
3/4 OR 1/2 INCH VIDEO CASSETTE
Features an interview with Meredith Monk. Presented by Kate Horsfield and Lyn Blumenthal.
Prod-ARTINC Dist-ARTINC

Meredith Monk And Laura Dean C 30 MIN
3/4 OR 1/2 INCH VIDEO CASSETTE
Discusses the experience of working with television. Shows dancers in excerpts from thier work. Includes a performance of 'Esoterica' with Kenneth Archer.
From The Eye On Dance - Dance On TV Series.
Prod-ARTRES Dist-ARTRES

Merged Latches And The Substrate Injection Of Electrons B 75 MIN
3/4 OR 1/2 INCH VIDEO CASSETTE
See series title for descriptive statement.
From The Analog IC Layout Design Considerations Series. Pt 3
Prod-UAZMIC Dist-UAZMIC

Merging Control Systems C 15 MIN
16MM FILM OPTICAL SOUND
Reports on a research study aimed at assisting the driver in entering the freeway traffic stream as smoothly and easily as possible. Shows how two merging control systems are developed and tested. Explains the racer system and the green band system to avoid rear-end and sidewipe accidents.
LC NO. 74-706145
Prod-USDTFH Dist-USNAC 1971

Merit Pay C 18 MIN
3/4 INCH VIDEO CASSETTE
Discusses merit pay under the system created by the Civil Service Reform Bill. Discusses a timetable for implementation of the system, employees covered by the system, the earning of pay based on performance, and distribution of merit pay funds.
From The Launching Civil Service Reform Series.
LC NO. 79-706268
Prod-USOPMA Dist-USNAC 1978

Merlin The Magician—A Series

Introduces children of all ages to the fascinating world around them through the art of magic. Uses the medieval castle of King Arthur in Camelot as the setting for narrator, Merlin the magician.
Prod-WOUBTV Dist-PUBTEL

Merlin's Magic Of Learning C 15 MIN
16MM FILM, 3/4 OR 1/2 IN VIDEO P-I
Uses a story about a magician named Merlin to demonstrate the relevancy of studying and schoolwork.
Prod-ALTPRO Dist-JOU 1979

Merlin's Magical Message C 6 MIN
16MM FILM, 3/4 OR 1/2 IN VIDEO I
Points out the importance of home dental care, especially brushing.
Prod-AMDA Dist-AMDA 1969

Merlin's Magical Message C 7 MIN
16MM FILM, 3/4 OR 1/2 IN VIDEO
Presents an animated film, with Merlin and King Arthur as the characters, pointing out the importance of home dental care, especially brushing, in preserving good dental health.
Prod-PRORE Dist-PRORE

Merlo B 16 MIN
3/4 OR 1/2 INCH VIDEO CASSETTE
Deals with the perception of image and sound over varying distances.
Prod-KITCHN Dist-KITCHN

Mermaid Princess, The - A Hans Christian Andersen Tale C 14 MIN
16MM FILM, 3/4 OR 1/2 IN VIDEO P-I
Presents an adaptation of Hans Christian Anderson's story about a little mermaid and her love for a shipwrecked prince.
Prod-CORF Dist-CORF 1976

Merrill Ashley, Dr Joseph D'Amico And Dr Tom Novella C 30 MIN
3/4 OR 1/2 INCH VIDEO CASSETTE
Looks at the repair and care of dancers' feet. Includes a performance of 'Esoterica' with Harvey Lichtenstein Hosted by Irene Dowd.
From The Eye On Dance - Dancers' Health Series.
Prod-ARTRES Dist-ARTRES

Merrill Brockway And Kinberg C 30 MIN
3/4 OR 1/2 INCH VIDEO CASSETTE
Tells the story of 'Dance in America.' Looks at a performance of 'Esoterica' with Catrina Neiman. Hosted by Celia Ipiotis.
From The Eye On Dance - Dance On TV And Film Series.
Prod-ARTRES Dist-ARTRES

Merry Chase, A - Debussy's Afternoon Of A Faun C 10 MIN
16MM FILM OPTICAL SOUND C A
Offers an animated story set to the music of Debussy's Afternoon Of A Faun. Tells the story of a squat and aging satyr who lusts for the sexual attention of the young nymphs of the serene woodland. Reveals that when the nymphs ignore him, he takes a forlorn walk through the desert, unaware that the desert is actually the body of a gigantic, beautiful woman.
From The Animations From Allegro Non Troppo Series.
Prod-BOZETO Dist-TEXFLM 1978

Merry Christmas C 14 MIN
3/4 OR 1/2 INCH VIDEO CASSETTE P
Introduces hand bells and heralds the Christmas season with favorite holiday songs.
From The Stepping Into Rhythm Series.
Prod-WVIZTV Dist-AITECH

Merry Wives Of Windsor, The C 167 MIN
3/4 OR 1/2 INCH VIDEO CASSETTE H-C A
Presents William Shakespeare's play The Merry Wives of Windsor which brings together an inept con man, a jealous husband with a mischievous wife, a pair of young lovers, a dose of disguise, considerable slapstick, an elopement and a concluding spectacle.
From The Shakespeare Plays Series.
Prod-BBCTV Dist-TIMLIF 1984

Merry-Go-Round B 24 MIN
16MM FILM OPTICAL SOUND J-C A S
A doctor, talking to patients, doctors and others, asks why tuberculosis has not yet been defeated.
Prod-NTBA Dist-AMLUNG 1961

Merry-Go-Round C 45 MIN
16MM FILM - 3/4 IN VIDEO
Dramatizes three family situations to describe the causes, effects and treatments of child abuse. Notes the cyclical nature of the problem, in that abusive parents were often abused children. Issued in 1977 as a motion picture.
LC NO. 80-706636
Prod-WRAIR Dist-USNAC 1980

Merry-Go-Round Horse, The C 17 MIN
16MM FILM, 3/4 OR 1/2 IN VIDEO P-I
Presents an art film without narration about the love of a little ragamuffin for an old wooden merry-go-round horse which is mistreated by a wealthy child for whom the horse was purchased at the flea market.
Prod-LCOA Dist-LCOA 1969

Mersey Forth C 14 MIN
16MM FILM OPTICAL SOUND
Explores the tourist attractions of the Mersey Forth area of Tasmania.
LC NO. 80-700913
Prod-TASCOR Dist-TASCOR 1979

Merton C 57 MIN
3/4 INCH VIDEO CASSETTE
Examines the life, work and impact of Thomas Merton, Trappist monk. Features all the places around the world important to Merton and interviews those who knew him best.
Prod-FIRS Dist-FIRS

Mesa Verde - Mystery Of The Silent Cities C 14 MIN
16MM FILM, 3/4 OR 1/2 IN VIDEO I
Introduces students to an ancient North American Indian culture that thrived briefly in a plateau in what is now Mesa Verde National Park in Colorado. Shows how archaeologists are able to reach some conclusions about how they lived.
Prod-EBEC Dist-EBEC 1975

Mesencephalon, The C 15 MIN
3/4 OR 1/2 INCH VIDEO CASSETTE PRO
Identifies the macroscopic structures of the midbrain using brain specimens and diagrams. Discusses briefly the physiology and pathology of the midbrain.
From The Neurobiology Series.
Prod-HSCIC Dist-HSCIC

Mesenteric Caval Shunt For Extrahepatic Obstruction C 21 MIN
16MM FILM OPTICAL SOUND PRO
Explains that mesenteric-caval anastomosis has proven to be an effective means of portal decompression in patients with extrahepatic portal obstruction. Illustrates operative technique and discusses patient care.
Prod-ACYDGD Dist-ACY 1966

Mesenteric Thrombosis And Adhesion Band Strangulation C 18 MIN
16MM FILM SILENT PRO
Shows mesenteric thrombosis as seen at surgery and at autopsy, and examples of adhesion band strangulation with and without gangrene. Demonstrates the mechanism of strangulation by an experiment in animal surgery.
Prod-ACYDGD Dist-ACY 1951

Mesentric Vascular Insufficiency C 24 MIN
3/4 INCH VIDEO CASSETTE PRO
Discusses mesenteric vascular insufficiency, showing associated factors, etiology, arteriography and surgical management.
LC NO. 76-706057
Prod-WARMP Dist-USNAC 1969

Meshie B 28 MIN
16MM FILM OPTICAL SOUND C
Studies a chimpanzee raised among humans and subjected to training designed to test the limits of a chimpanzee's ability to acquire human behavior patterns. Records some of Meshie's activities.
LC NO. 75-702185
Prod-AMNH Dist-PSUPCR 1975

Mesolithic Society, The C 18 MIN
16MM FILM, 3/4 OR 1/2 IN VIDEO J-C A
Examines the known facts regarding the inhabitans of Northern Europe at the end of the last great Ice Age. Provides insight into the practical problems faced by people who bridged the period between the Paleolithic and Neolithic cultures.
Prod-LUF Dist-LUF 1980

Mesothelioma And Malignant Effusion C 27 MIN
3/4 INCH VIDEO CASSETTE
Discusses the different types of mesothelioma and their relationship to asbestos.
Prod-UTAHTI Dist-UTAHTI

Mesquakie C 11 MIN
16MM FILM OPTICAL SOUND
Documents the contemporary way of life of the Mesquakie Indians of Iowa. Shows scenes of the annual powwow, squash preservation, weaving and beadwork.
LC NO. 77-702276
Prod-IOWA Dist-IOWA 1976

Mess Management - Conservation Control In The Management Of A Mess C 14 MIN
16MM FILM OPTICAL SOUND
Explains the basic functions of mess management and the importance of meal planning. Discusses on-the-job training of mess personnel and the functions and responsibilities of the mess officer, food adviser and unit commanders.
LC NO. FIE56-92
Prod-USA Dist-USNAC 1956

Message From A Dinosaur X 10 MIN
16MM FILM, 3/4 OR 1/2 IN VIDEO I
Shows how paleontologists reconstruct life of the past from fossil remains and how new forms of life evolved from environmental changes. Explains that organisms unable to adapt to changing conditions do not survive.
Prod-EBF Dist-EBEC 1965

Message From Silence Dogwood, A C 11 MIN
16MM FILM OPTICAL SOUND
Portrays the adage 'Time is money' from Ben Franklin's autobiography, emphasizing the cost effectiveness of the Xerox telecopier.
LC NO. 76-703138
Prod-XEROX Dist-STOKB Prodn-STOKB 1976

Message From Space X 30 MIN
16MM FILM OPTICAL SOUND I-H T R
Tells the story of two young scientists who work at a remote radio astronomy monitoring station, where they are joined by a woman scientist and the father of one of the men. Examines basic issues of Christian faith against a background of new scientific thought.
LC NO. FIA67-5776
Prod-FAMF Dist-FAMF 1967

Message From The Stone Age - The Story Of The Tasaday C 16 MIN
16MM FILM, 3/4 OR 1/2 IN VIDEO I A
Describes how, in 1971, the Tasaday hiked 30 miles from their home in a Philippine rain forest to the forest's edge where they discovered and were discovered by the modern world, a transition of 30,000 years from the Stone Age to the Space Age. Looks at this self-contained social environment and encourages students to look at their own culture and beliefs.
Prod-NWDIMF Dist-NWDIMF

Message From Women In Japan (Japanese) B 25 MIN
1/2 INCH VIDEOTAPE
Introduces women's spaces and events in Japan.
Prod-WMV Dist-WMENIF

Message In The Rocks C 57 MIN
16MM FILM, 3/4 OR 1/2 IN VIDEO H-C A
Demonstrates how studying rock specimens may reveal clues to the age of the earth and how it was formed. Analyzes the geologic significance of the eruption of volcanoes such as Mt St Helens.
From The Nova Series.
LC NO. 83-706024
Prod-WGBHTV Dist-TIMLIF 1982

Message Is The Medium, The C 43 MIN
3/4 INCH VIDEO CASSETTE
Provides detailed information about all aspects of video production as it applies to mental health. Presents basics for using television in medicine and pschiatry.
Prod-UWASHP Dist-UWASHP

Message Is Yours, The - Don't Lose it C 11 MIN
3/4 OR 1/2 INCH VIDEO CASSETTE
Explains how the new supervisor can overcome the barriers to good communication, in writing, in face-to-face conversation and in a conference.
From The New Supervisor Series. Module 2
Prod-RESEM Dist-RESEM

Message Of Life, A C 26 MIN
16MM FILM OPTICAL SOUND
Portrays the impact of the Yom Kippur War on the people of Israel.
Prod-UJA Dist-ALDEN

Message Of Starlight C 24 MIN
3/4 OR 1/2 INCH VIDEO CASSETTE H-C
Explains how astronomers deduce the history of stars using observations of the stars from telescopes and related instruments. Shows how aspects of light are measured by spectrograph. Describes spectral curve and Hertzprung-Russell plot. Filmed at Britain's Royal Greenwich Observatory and Oxford.
From The Discoverning Physics Series.
Prod-BBCTV Dist-MEDIAG Prodn-OPENU 1983

Message Of Starlight, The C 29 MIN
3/4 INCH VIDEO CASSETTE C A
Explains how measurements of magnitudes and spectroscopic analysis yield extensive information about the properties of individual stars. Reviews modern spectroscopic techniques.
From The Project Universe - Astronomy Series. Lesson 17
Prod-COAST Dist-CDTEL Prodn-SCCON

Message, A C 5 MIN
3/4 OR 1/2 INCH VIDEO CASSETTE S
Presents an animated story to motivate hearing impaired children to read.
Prod-GALCO Dist-GALCO 1981

Messages C 6 MIN
16MM FILM OPTICAL SOUND K-I
Features a collection of five one-minute service spots on nutrition and consumerism, made by children, ages 11 to 19.
Prod-YELLOW Dist-YELLOW 1972

Messages C 24 MIN
16MM FILM OPTICAL SOUND I-C
Examines the numerous ways in which animals communicate, including flashes of color, vibrations, odors and touch. Discusses how human language evolved from such primitive forms of expression.
From The Animal Secrets Series.
LC NO. FIA68-1035
Prod-NBC Dist-GRACUR 1967

Messages By Hand C 8 MIN
16MM FILM, 3/4 OR 1/2 IN VIDEO P-I
Features a deaf boy explaining his experiences in a special summer camp.
From The Zoom Series.
Prod-WGBHTV Dist-FI

Messenger From Violet Drive B 30 MIN
16MM FILM OPTICAL SOUND H-C A
Interviews Elijah Muhammed, leader of the Black Muslims, who discusses the philosophy of total separation of Negroes and Whites in America. Discusses Muhammed's beliefs concerning the origins of the Negro and caucasian races, his prophesied destruction of America and his mission as the last messenger from Allah to the American Negro.
From The American In The 70's, Pt 3 Series.
LC NO. FIA68-1580
Prod-NET Dist-IU 1965

Messiah C 90 MIN
3/4 INCH VIDEO CASSETTE
Presents selections from George Handel's Messiah, performed by the combined choirs of the U S Naval Academy and Hood College. Offers background on Handel and the Naval Academy and draws parallels between 18th century London and Annapolis.
Prod-MDCPB Dist-MDCPB

Messiah, The C
1/2 IN VIDEO CASSETTE BETA/VHS
Presents Handel's Messiah performed by the Westminster Abbey Choir.
Prod-GA Dist-GA

Messiah, The C 170 MIN
3/4 OR 1/2 INCH VIDEO CASSETTE A
Recreates George Frederick Handel's 'The Messiah' in its original setting. Utilizes Westminster Abbey's fine acoustics and visual setting.
Prod-EDDIM Dist-EDDIM

Messianic Idea In Jewish History, The C 30 MIN
3/4 INCH VIDEO CASSETTE
Discusses personalities and theology of Messiahs through Jewish history.
From The Indiana University Discussion Series.
Prod-ADL Dist-ADL

Messy Sally C 13 MIN
3/4 OR 1/2 INCH VIDEO CASSETTE P
See series title for descriptive statement.
From The Magic Pages Series.
Prod-KLVXTV Dist-AITECH 1976

Meta Mayan II C 20 MIN
3/4 OR 1/2 INCH VIDEO CASSETTE
Captures the angry mood of the Guatemalan populace. Exposes what is passing in the hearts and minds of the people.
Prod-EAI Dist-EAI

Metabolic Acidosis And Alkalosis C 27 MIN
3/4 OR 1/2 INCH VIDEO CASSETTE PRO
Describes acidosis and alkalosis resulting from problems related to metabolism. Shows signs and symptoms related to metabolic problems plus appropriate health-team actions and treatments.
From The Fluids And Electrolytes Series.
Prod-BRA Dist-BRA

Metabolic Coma - An Overview C 23 MIN
3/4 OR 1/2 INCH VIDEO CASSETTE PRO
Identifies metabolic conditions causing coma, abnormalities, and differentiation from other pathophysiologic categories.
From The Comatose Patient Series.
Prod-BRA Dist-BRA

Metabolic Pathways C 24 MIN
16MM FILM, 3/4 OR 1/2 IN VIDEO
Demonstrates two relatively new technologies used by biochemists to trace metabolic pathways and to yield data about biochemical reactions. Reenacts the development of the Calvin cycle, the experimental procedure used in 1945 to establish the route by which carbon dioxide is incorporated into sugars during the first part of photosynthesis.
Prod-OPENU Dist-MEDIAG Prodn-BBCTV 1982

Metabolism - Background C 45 MIN
3/4 OR 1/2 INCH VIDEO CASSETTE C
Provides information on various aspects of metabolism.
From The Biology I Series.
Prod-MDCPB Dist-MDCPB

Metabolism - The Fire Of Life C 36 MIN
1/2 IN VIDEO CASSETTE (VHS) J-C A
Illustrates the biochemical process of metabolism. Tells how the body burns food, the role of key nutrients, and describes calories and the basal metabolic rate. Details cellular respiration, both aerobic and anaerobic.
LC NO. 85-703880
Prod-HRMC Dist-HRMC

Metabolism And Activity Of Lizards C 12 MIN
16MM FILM, 3/4 OR 1/2 IN VIDEO
Shows patterns of energy metabolism in relation to locomotor activity in diversely adapted lizards. Shows animals running on a treadmill and feeding. Demonstrates methods of measuring gas exchange during activity and the ecology of each type of lizard.
From The Aspects Of Animal Behavior Series.
Prod-UCLA Dist-UCEMC 1981

Metabolism II C 45 MIN
3/4 OR 1/2 INCH VIDEO CASSETTE C
Provides information on various aspects of metabolism.
From The Biology I Series.
Prod-MDCPB Dist-MDCPB

Metabolism III C 45 MIN
3/4 OR 1/2 INCH VIDEO CASSETTE C
Provides information on various aspects of metabolism.
From The Biology I Series.
Prod-MDCPB Dist-MDCPB

Metabolism IV C 45 MIN
3/4 OR 1/2 INCH VIDEO CASSETTE C
Provides information on various aspects of metabolism.
From The Biology I Series.
Prod-MDCPB Dist-MDCPB

Metal C 29 MIN
2 INCH VIDEOTAPE
Provides a glimpse of Hawaiian craftsmen working with metal.
From The Directions In Design Series.
Prod-HETV Dist-PUBTEL

Metal Collectibles C 30 MIN
3/4 INCH VIDEO CASSETTE
See series title for descriptive statement.
From The Antiques Series.
Prod-NHMNET Dist-PUBTEL

Metal Conditioning C 7 MIN
1/2 IN VIDEO CASSETTE BETA/VHS
Deals with auto body repair. Explains the use of metal conditioners.
Prod-RMI Dist-RMI

Metal Cutting Chisels, Pt 6 B 5 MIN
16MM FILM OPTICAL SOUND
Describes the correct uses of the cold chisel, cape advection fog, ground fog and low ceiling clouds. Explains the cutting action of the chisel, diamond point and half-round chisel and how they are sharpened.
LC NO. FIE58-7
Prod-USN Dist-USNAC 1954

Metal Fabrication - Different Types Of Sheet Metal In Common Use Today—A Series
IND

Discusses the different gauging methods used and the characteristics of different types of sheet metal materials.
Prod-RMI Dist-RMI

Aluminum Sheet Metal Theory	005 MIN
Cold Rolled Sheet Metal Theory	009 MIN
Galvanized Sheet Metal Theory	010 MIN
Hot Rolled Sheet Metal Theory	010 MIN
Hot Roller Pickled And Oiled Sheet Metal Theory	011 MIN

Metal Fabrication - Duct End Cap Layout—A Series
IND
Demonstrates two different methods of laying out the patterns for making end caps to seal the end of a duct.
Prod-RMI Dist-RMI

Square And Rectangular Duct End Cap Layout	
Square And Rectangular Duct End Cap Layout I-	010 MIN

Metal Fabrication - Eight-Foot Hydraulic Squaring Shear—A Series
IND
Illustrates the operation and gauging on an eight-foot, ten-gauge capacity squaring shear. Emphasizes the safety aspect of its operation.
Prod-RMI Dist-RMI

Eight-Foot Hydraulic Squaring Shear	
Eight-Foot Hydraulic Squaring Shear I-	010 MIN

Metal Fabrication - Fitup And Assembly—A Series
IND
Explains the fitup and assembly of the component parts for a fabrication and the tacking together prior to final welding.
Prod-RMI Dist-RMI

Fitup And Assembly Tacking Together, Pt I	037 MIN
Fitup And Assembly Tacking Together, Pt II	024 MIN

Metal Fabrication - Hand Tool Identification, Demonstration And Applications—A Series
IND
Deals with the accepted practices used in fabricating light and heavy gauge sheet metal. Teaches duct construction as applied to the building and sheet metal trades. Demonstrates the various hand tools used in the sheet metal trades and their use and application.
Prod-RMI Dist-RMI

General Hand Tools	015 MIN
Hammers Used In Sheet Metal Work	004 MIN
Hand Snips And Shears	020 MIN
Use Of Basic Layout Tools	007 MIN

Metal Fabrication - Lock Former Machine—A Series
IND
Presents the operation of the lock former machine for applying a Pittsburgh seam to the edge of a sheet. Shows the application of the Acme or pipelock seam along the edge of a sheet (No. 108 Pittsburgh seam) (No. 109 Pipelock seam).
Prod-RMI Dist-RMI

Lock Former Machine Acme Or Pipelock Seam	011 MIN
Lock Former Machine Pittsburgh Seam	014 MIN

Metal Fabrication - Parallel Line Development—A Series
IND
Deals with the accepted practices used in fabricating light and heavy gauge sheet metal. Teaches duct construction as applied to the building and sheet metal trades, including shop sketches, blueprints, and pattern layout of the various fittings. Discusses the basic theory of parallel line development and layout fundamentals in its use. Explains the most common type of layout problems, two round elbow layout methods and two shortcut methods of developing tee patterns for round pipes intersecting round tapers at various angles.
Prod-RMI Dist-RMI

Five P C 90 Degree Round Elbow	037 MIN
Introduction To Parallel Line Development	024 MIN
Ninety Degree Round Elbow Using Rise Method	010 MIN
Round Elbow Pattern Layout Using End Gore	017 MIN
Round Pipe Different Diameters 45 Degree	021 MIN
Round Pipe Different Diameters 90 Degree	022 MIN
Round Pipe Intersected By Rectangular Pipe	020 MIN
Round Pipe Intersecting A Round Taper At	018 MIN
Round Pipe Intersecting A Round Taper At	013 MIN
Round Pipe Mitered End	032 MIN
Round Pipe Same Diameter 45 Degree Intersection	024 MIN
Round Pipe Same Diameter 90 Degree Intersection	040 MIN

Metal Fabrication - Round Pipe Fabrication—A Series
IND
Shows two methods of seaming a round pipe, using a hand-formed seam and a machine-formed seam.
Prod-RMI Dist-RMI

Round Pipe Fabrication - Grooved Lock Seam	019 MIN
Round Pipe Fabrication - Machine Formed Seam	009 MIN

Metal Fabrication - Round Tapers—A Series
IND
Deals with the accepted practices used in fabricating light and heavy gauge sheet metal. Teaches duct construction as applied to the building and sheet metal trades. Demonstrates the pattern development of round tapers, showing the application of the process called radial line development for cones, frustrums of cones, and truncated cones. Describes the process of triangulation, demonstrated for round tapers, employing the plan or profile view along with the given elevation. Includes discussion of the side view method, shortcut methods, and the sweep triangulation method.
Prod-RMI Dist-RMI

Centered Round Taper - Triangulation Plan	
China Cup - Weather Cap Dimensioning And	015 MIN
Gradual Taper - Shortcut, Three-Side View	015 MIN
Offset Taper - Side View Method, Openings Not	035 MIN
Offset Taper - Side View Rotational	032 MIN
Offset Taper - Triangulation Plan View	031 MIN
Radial Line - 180 Degree Shortcut Method	012 MIN
Radial Line Theory For Cone Or Frustrum Of	020 MIN
Round Taper Intersecting A Round Pipe At	014 MIN
Round Taper Intersecting A Round Pipe At 45	032 MIN
Round Tapers - Internal Or External Offset	019 MIN
Round Y-Branch Layout	057 MIN
Truncated Cone - Radial Line Method, Openings	019 MIN

Metal Fabrication - Square To Round Layout—A Series
IND
Deals with the accepted practices used in fabricating light and heavy gauge sheet metal. Teaches duct construction as applied to the building and sheet metal trades. Discusses square to round layout, using a variety of methods and shortcut techniques. Introduces pattern development, using a plan or profile view and one or more elevation views, and a side view method, employing a rotational subtractive method for transitions where more than one elevation is required. Demonstrates offset one-way and two-way examples.
Prod-RMI Dist-RMI

Introduction To Square To Rounds	026 MIN
Rectangular To Larger Round Transition -	015 MIN
Rectangular To Round Transition - Double Offset	037 MIN
Rectangular To Round Transition - Offset	034 MIN
Rectangular To Round Transition - Offset	044 MIN
Rectangular To Round Transitioned - Centered	020 MIN
Square To Round - Offset One-Way Openings Not	028 MIN
Square To Round Transition - Offset One-Way	032 MIN

Metal Fabrication - Tap Collar Type Of Fittings—A Series
IND
Demonstrates two methods of attaching a tap collar connection to a fitting.
Prod-RMI Dist-RMI

Tap Collar Closed Corners Fabrication	009 MIN
Tap Collar Open Corners Fabrication	013 MIN

Metal Fabrication - Transitional Elbows—A Series
IND
Demonstrates the development of a transitional elbow of a change cheek or same size cheek, flat on top or on the bottom, or a central taper.
Prod-RMI Dist-RMI

Transitional Elbow - Flat Top Or Bottom,	
Transitional Elbow - Flat Top Or Bottom, Same	037 MIN

Metal Fatigue - Recent Developments In Probabilistic Design—A Series

Summarizes recent developments in fatigue analysis under random stress processes and recent developments in the application of probabilistic design theory to the metal fatigue problem. Focuses on research being conducted at the University of Arizona. Consists of two 50-minute tapes.
Prod-UAZMIC Dist-UAZMIC 1978

Metal Files C 13 MIN
16MM FILM, 3/4 OR 1/2 IN VIDEO J-H A
Presents sizes, shapes and cuts, types of files, care of files, straight filing, draw filing and fine filing.
From The Metalwork - Hand Tools Series.
Prod-MORLAT Dist-SF 1967

Metal Finishing, Large Dent C 31 MIN
1/2 IN VIDEO CASSETTE BETA/VHS
Deals with auto body repair.
Prod-RMI Dist-RMI

Metal Finishing, Tool Identification And Minor Dent C 33 MIN
1/2 IN VIDEO CASSETTE BETA/VHS
Deals with auto body repair.
Prod-RMI Dist-RMI

Metal Forming C 30 MIN
3/4 OR 1/2 INCH VIDEO CASSETTE
Demonstrates non-traditional metal forming techniques, including high energy rate forming that uses high explosives and other forces to create new parts for modern architecture and the space program.
Prod-CONNTV Dist-SME Prodn-SME

Metal Lost In Rolling C 10 MIN
1/2 IN VIDEO CASSETTE BETA/VHS IND
Demonstrates graphically the metal lost in rolling when forming a cylinder and how to maintain an accurate inside or outside diameter. Deals with the bend allowance theory.
Prod-RMI Dist-RMI

Metal Shop - Safety And Operations—A Series
16MM FILM, 3/4 OR 1/2 IN VIDEO J A
Prod-EPRI Dist-AIMS Prodn-EPRI 1971

Arc Welding - Safety And Operations	14 MIN
Facing On The Lathe	11 MIN
Oxyacetylene Welding - Safety And Operations	14 MIN
Safety And Basic Fundamentals On The Engine	11 MIN
Safety And Basic Fundamentals On The Engine	13 MIN
Straight Turning Between Centers On The Lathe	18 MIN

Metal Stretch C 13 MIN
1/2 IN VIDEO CASSETTE BETA/VHS
Deals with auto body repair. Defines metal stretch and demonstrates shrinking.
Prod-RMI Dist-RMI

Metal Working C 10 MIN
16MM FILM, 3/4 OR 1/2 IN VIDEO J-C A
Demonstrates various metalwork techniques including annealing, rolling mill, forging and finishing. Reveals how the pieces are soldered together, finished in an acid bath, sanded and brushed.
From The Jewelry Making Series.
Prod-LUF Dist-LUF 1978

Metals And Non-Metals (2nd Ed) C 13 MIN
16MM FILM, 3/4 OR 1/2 IN VIDEO H-C
Shows the differences in the physical properties of metals and non-metals, explains their chemical properties and their positions in the periodic table, and illustrates closest-packing of atoms in metals.
Prod-CORF Dist-CORF 1963

Metals Frontier C 22 MIN
16MM FILM OPTICAL SOUND C A
Portrays the development, at the Ames laboratory of the USAEC, of a process for the separation of tytrium from the rare earth metals and the production of highpurity tytrium metal.
Prod-IOWA Dist-USERD 1961

Metals Information Center Of Tomorrow C 13 MIN
16MM FILM OPTICAL SOUND
Describes in lay terms the activities of the Western Reserve University in the field of metallurgy. Shows the potentials for mechanical computing machines in library research.
Prod-CWRU Dist-CWRU

Metalwork - Hand Tools—A Series
3/4 OR 1/2 INCH VIDEO CASSETTE
Prod-MORLAT Dist-SF

Forge And Ornamental Iron	13 MIN
Layout Tools For Metal Work	13 MIN
Metal Files	13 MIN
Snips And Shears	13 MIN
Soldering	13 MIN
Welding	13 MIN

Metalwork - Machine Operation—A Series
3/4 OR 1/2 INCH VIDEO CASSETTE
Prod-MORLAT Dist-SF

Drill Press, The	13 MIN
Fastening Metals	13 MIN
Lathe - Chuck Work	13 MIN
Lathe - Work Between Centers	13 MIN
Machine Operations - Sheet Metal	13 MIN

Metalwork Series - Aluminum And Copper Tooling With A Mold C 21 MIN
3/4 OR 1/2 INCH VIDEO CASSETTE
Explains and demonstrates the procedures for tooling a design from a mold into sheet metal, for finishing the sheet, and for matting it for display. First of three-program unit on metalworking.
Prod-HSCIC Dist-HSCIC

Metalwork Series - Copper Enameling C 16 MIN
3/4 OR 1/2 INCH VIDEO CASSETTE
Explains and demonstrates copper enameling.
Prod-HSCIC Dist-HSCIC

Metalwork Series - Freeform Copper Tooling C 20 MIN
3/4 OR 1/2 INCH VIDEO CASSETTE
Teaches procedures for tooling a design into copper foil without the use of a mold, for finishing the piece, and for mounting it for display.
Prod-HSCIC Dist-HSCIC

Metalworking - Precision Measuring—A Series
A
Describes the uses of the vernier caliper and height gage, outside micrometer, combination set, combination square and bevel protractor in metalworking.
Prod-VISIN Dist-VISIN

Bevel Protractor, The	013 MIN
Combination Set, The	013 MIN
Combination Square, The	013 MIN
Outside Micrometer, The	013 MIN
Vernier Caliper	013 MIN
Vernier Height Gage	013 MIN

Metalworking Tools C 12 MIN
3/4 OR 1/2 INCH VIDEO CASSETTE
Covers metalworking tools, such as vises, hacksaws, files, dies, reamers and their uses.
From The Using Hand Tools Series.
Prod-TPCTRA Dist-TPCTRA

Metalworking Tools (Spanish) C 12 MIN
3/4 OR 1/2 INCH VIDEO CASSETTE
Covers metalworking tools, such as vises, hacksaws, files, dies, reamers and their uses.
From The Using Hand Tools Series.
Prod-TPCTRA Dist-TPCTRA

Metamorphic Rock C 15 MIN
3/4 OR 1/2 INCH VIDEO CASSETTE I

See series title for descriptive statement.
From The Discovering Series. Unit 6 - Rocks And Minerals
Prod-WDCNTV Dist-AITECH 1978

Metamorphic Rock - Composition Of The Earth C 20 MIN
2 INCH VIDEOTAPE I
See series title for descriptive statement.
From The Exploring With Science, Unit II - Geology Series.
Prod-MPATI Dist-GPITVL

Metamorphism C 30 MIN
3/4 OR 1/2 INCH VIDEO CASSETTE C
Explains the origin of many rocks and minerals.
From The Earth, Sea And Sky Series.
Prod-DALCCD Dist-DALCCD

Metamorphoses C 3 MIN
16MM FILM, 3/4 OR 1/2 IN VIDEO I-C A
The animation artist, Laurent Coderre, has created a clown so versatile in the art of juggling that, between times, he even juggles himself. One moment the clown stands tossing balls, the next he becomes dismembered, following the balls about on the screen but coming together again all in one piece to finish the act.
Prod-NFBC Dist-NFBC 1969

Metamorphosis C 5 MIN
16MM FILM OPTICAL SOUND
An animated film, which poetically interprets the history of the evolution of man, plants and animals.
LC NO. 78-712036
Prod-ROSSED Dist-RADIM 1970

Metamorphosis C 8 MIN
16MM FILM OPTICAL SOUND
An art film which presents computer-generated everchanging colors edited to the music of Saliere's Symphony in D major.
LC NO. 74-702489
Prod-LILYAN Dist-LILYAN 1974

Metamorphosis B 10 MIN
16MM FILM OPTICAL SOUND
Features a comical look at a man riding an elevator.
LC NO. 76-701344
Prod-CCAAT Dist-CCAAT 1975

Metamorphosis C 10 MIN
16MM FILM, 3/4 OR 1/2 IN VIDEO P-J
Documents the transformation of a caterpillar into a monarch butterfly. Presents a young girl who tracks down the caterpillar, provides it with appropriate food, keeps a record of its progress, devises a simple alarm system that sounds a bell when the butterfly is ready to emerge and finally sets it free.
Prod-MERWAL Dist-TEXFLM 1977

Metamorphosis - Life Story Of The Wasp X 14 MIN
16MM FILM, 3/4 OR 1/2 IN VIDEO I
Uses photomicrography to present the development of the wasp from egg to larva, pupa and adult.
Prod-EBF Dist-EBEC 1963

Metamorphosis Of An Oncology Nurse C 12 MIN
3/4 INCH VIDEO CASSETTE
Discusses the different stages in an oncology nurse's career.
Prod-UTAHTI Dist-UTAHTI

Metamorphosis Of Mr Samsa, The - From A Story By Franz Kafka C 10 MIN
16MM FILM, 3/4 OR 1/2 IN VIDEO H-C A
Offers an interpretation of Franz Kafka's short story Die Verwandlung. Tells how a man awakens one morning to find himself transformed into a beetle.
LC NO. 80-706232
Prod-NFBC Dist-TEXFLM 1979

Metamorphosis Of The Cello, The B 14 MIN
16MM FILM OPTICAL SOUND H-C
Pictures the construction and the performance of the Violoncello. Features the French virtuoso Maurice Gendron playing music by Haydn, Bach, Boccherini and Chopin.
LC NO. FIA65-1037
Prod-DELOUD Dist-RADIM 1965

Metastasizing Basal Cell Carcinoma C 10 MIN
16MM FILM OPTICAL SOUND PRO
Presents a case study of basal cell carcinoma lesions on the skin of a 69-year-old man which had metastasized from a single, ulcerative basal cell carcinoma present on the patient's leg for five years without being diagnosed or adequately treated.
Prod-SQUIBB Dist-SQUIBB

Metathesis C 3 MIN
16MM FILM OPTICAL SOUND
Offers a blending of computer graphics and animation which makes use of exotic, flowing forms, colors and electronic music.
Prod-LILYAN Dist-LILYAN

Metco / Oreo Cookie / Interracial Dating C 29 MIN
3/4 INCH VIDEO CASSETTE
Describes a voluntary busing program in Boston which enriched the lives of city and suburban students. Presents students from Wichita, Kansas, examining pressures resulting from desegregation. Shows Portland, Oregon, students who indicate that attitudes are not as tolerant as many would like.
From The As We See It Series.
Prod-WTTWTV Dist-PUBTEL

Meteor C 104 MIN
16MM FILM OPTICAL SOUND
Asks whether scientists can save the earth from a giant meteor. Stars Sean Connery, Natalie Wood and Karl Malden.
Prod-AIP Dist-SWANK

Meteor C 107 MIN
16MM FILM OPTICAL SOUND H A
Shows the diplomatic efforts of the American President with the Soviets who saves the world from a blazing comet hurtling toward earth. Stars Sean Connery, Natalie Wood and Henry Fonda.
Prod-AIP Dist-TIMLIF 1979

Meteorology - Fog And Low Ceiling Clouds Advection Fog And Ground Fog C 25 MIN
16MM FILM, 3/4 OR 1/2 IN VIDEO A
Discusses in detail the characteristics and conditions conducive to fog with explanation of theory of fog formation.
Prod-FAAFL Dist-AVIMA 1962

Meteorology - Fog And Low Ceiling Clouds - Advection Fog And Ground Fog C 23 MIN
16MM FILM, 3/4 OR 1/2 IN VIDEO
Discusses the theory of fog formation, providing examples of advection fog, ground fog and low ceiling clouds.
Prod-USN Dist-USNAC 1961

Meteorology - Fog And Low Ceiling Clouds - Upslope Fog And Frontal Fog C 10 MIN
16MM FILM OPTICAL SOUND
Illustrates how upslope fog, frontal fog and low straclouds generated. Compares warm front fog and cold front fog, analyzes their formation and discusses their effect on flying.
Prod-FAAFL Dist-USFAA 1962

Meteorology - Fog And Low Ceiling Clouds, Upslope Fog And Frontal Fog C 10 MIN
16MM FILM, 3/4 OR 1/2 IN VIDEO
Shows how upslope fog, frontal fog and low stratus clouds gather. Compares warm front fog and cold front fog and discusses their effect on flying.
Prod-USN Dist-USNAC

Meteorology - Fog, A Terminal Problem C 23 MIN
16MM FILM, 3/4 OR 1/2 IN VIDEO
Explains the theory of fog formation and dissipation. Discusses the effects of fog on aviation.
LC NO. 81-706650
Prod-USN Dist-USNAC 1971

Meteorology - Ice Formation On Aircraft B 20 MIN
16MM FILM OPTICAL SOUND
Shows how structural ice interferes with normal flight procedures and how its hazard can be reduced. Discusses carburetor and pilot tube icing and turbo-jet engine icing problems.
LC NO. 74-705132
Prod-FAAFL Dist-USFAA 1960

Meteorology - The Cold Front C 14 MIN
16MM FILM, 3/4 OR 1/2 IN VIDEO A
Explains formations, characteristics and dangers of cold fronts. Demonstrates how to avoid hazards of cold fronts by either high or low level flight.
Prod-FAAFL Dist-AVIMA

Meteorology - The Cold Front C 14 MIN
16MM FILM, 3/4 OR 1/2 IN VIDEO
Shows formation characteristics and flight hazards of cold fronts. Tells how to fly cold front weather with maximum safety.
Prod-USN Dist-USNAC

Meteorology - The Warm Front C 20 MIN
16MM FILM OPTICAL SOUND
Explains the meeting boundaries of warm and cold air, dangerous stratified layers of clouds formed, how to plan a course around them, types of visibility precipitation and ceiling conditions, their location and cirrus, cirrostratus and altostratus clouds.
LC NO. 74-705134
Prod-FAAFL Dist-USFAA 1962

Meteorology - The Warm Front C 17 MIN
16MM FILM, 3/4 OR 1/2 IN VIDEO
Shows formation characteristics and dangers of warm fronts and how to recognize and deal with the flight problems involved.
Prod-USN Dist-USNAC

Meteorology—A Series
H
Presents the basic concepts of meteorology.
Prod-AMS Dist-MLA 1967

Formation Of Raindrops	26 MIN
Planetary Circulation	22 MIN
Sea Surface Meteorology	24 MIN
Solar Radiation, Sun And Earth	18 MIN

Meter C 15 MIN
3/4 OR 1/2 INCH VIDEO CASSETTE P
Discusses rhythmical structure in music.
From The Music Machine Series.
Prod-INDIPS Dist-GPITVL 1981

Meter Reader C 15 MIN
3/4 OR 1/2 INCH VIDEO CASSETTE P-I
Discusses meter in music.
From The Music And Me Series.
Prod-WDCNTV Dist-AITECH 1979

Meter The Leader - Linear Measure C 14 MIN
3/4 OR 1/2 INCH VIDEO CASSETTE P
Shows how Lionel learns the advantages of a standardized system of measurement.
From The Math Country Series.
Prod-KYTV Dist-AITECH 1979

Meter-Making Arguments C 30 MIN
2 INCH VIDEOTAPE J-H
See series title for descriptive statement.
From The From Franklin To Frost - Ralph Waldo Emerson Series.
Prod-MPATI Dist-GPITVL

Meter, Liter And Gram (2nd Ed) C 13 MIN
16MM FILM, 3/4 OR 1/2 IN VIDEO I-C A
Describes how the metric system uses related units of length, volume and mass - the meter, liter and kilogram and relates these units to real objects. Adds information on how temperature can be measured according to the decimal system.
Prod-EDOGNC Dist-PHENIX 1981

Meter, Liter, And Gram (2nd Ed) C 13 MIN
16MM FILM, 3/4 OR 1/2 IN VIDEO I-H
Relates units in the metric system to real objects. Shows how the system of tens in the metric system names different units through the use of prefixes such as deci-, centi-, milli-, and kilo-.
Prod-EDOGNC Dist-SALENG 1981

Methadone - An American Way Of Dealing B 60 MIN
16MM FILM OPTICAL SOUND H-C A
Examines the social, historical and economic causes of drug dependency. Examines efforts to break drug dependency at a methadone clinic in the Midwest.
LC NO. 74-703706
Prod-METHIC Dist-METHIC 1974

Methadone Treatment Program, A C 25 MIN
16MM FILM OPTICAL SOUND PRO
Presents in detail the organization and operations of a methadone treatment program. Follows the progress of an addict through such a program. Emphasizes strict application of security procedures for urine surveillance and control of methadone dispensing.
From The Films And Tapes For Drug Abuse Treatment Personnel Series.
LC NO. 73-703452
Prod-NIMH Dist-NIMH 1973

Method C 60 MIN
3/4 OR 1/2 INCH VIDEO CASSETTE
Presents a new approach for the development of effective and powerful dialogues, a comprehensive methodology for the analysis, design and development of dialogues that are efficient from the computer perspective and psychologically effective for their end users.
From The Computer Dialogue - The Key To Successful Systems Series.
Prod-DELTAK Dist-DELTAK

Method For Cleaning The Machida Flexible Bronchoscope, A C 29 MIN
3/4 OR 1/2 INCH VIDEO CASSETTE
Demonstrates procedures for cleaning the Machida flexible bronchoscope and explains precautions required to avoid damaging the equipment during cleaning.
LC NO. 80-707207
Prod-USVACE Dist-USNAC 1979

Method For Cleaning The Olympus Flexible Bronchoscope, A C 29 MIN
3/4 OR 1/2 INCH VIDEO CASSETTE
Demonstrates procedures for cleaning the Olympus flexible bronchoscope and explains precautions required to avoid damaging the equipment during cleaning.
LC NO. 80-707208
Prod-USVACE Dist-USNAC 1979

Method For Rapid Electrophoresis C 11 MIN
16MM FILM OPTICAL SOUND
Explains how to set up electrophoretic apparatus and describes the functions of its parts. Demonstrates a typical run, portraying the technique of applying serum samples to the membrane and the step-by-step procedure of clearing and staining the resulting image.
Prod-USPHS Dist-USNAC 1966

Method Of Galerkin B 34 MIN
3/4 OR 1/2 INCH VIDEO CASSETTE
See series title for descriptive statement.
From The Nonlinear Vibrations Series.
Prod-MIOT Dist-MIOT

Method Of Krylov-Bogliubov B 24 MIN
3/4 OR 1/2 INCH VIDEO CASSETTE
See series title for descriptive statement.
From The Nonlinear Vibrations Series.
Prod-MIOT Dist-MIOT

Method Of Multipliers, The C 60 MIN
3/4 OR 1/2 INCH VIDEO CASSETTE
See series title for descriptive statement.
From The Engineering Design Optimization II Series. Pt 23
Prod-UAZMIC Dist-UAZMIC

Method Of Thoracoplasty For Chronic Empyema, A C 20 MIN
16MM FILM OPTICAL SOUND PRO
Explains that when thoracoplasty is necessary in the treatment of a chronic empyema the ideal operation should provide for certain closure of the pleural space, should cause minimal damage to the anatomical components of the chest wall, should permit closure of bronchopleural fistulae, and should result in a stable chest wall.
Prod-ACYDGD Dist-ACY 1955

Method Of Treatment For The Intrabony Pocket C 14 MIN
16MM FILM OPTICAL SOUND
Demonstrates the surgical technique used in subgingival curettage.
Prod-USA Dist-USNAC 1962

Method Of Treatment For The Intrabony Pocket, A C 13 MIN
16MM FILM OPTICAL SOUND
Shows the surgical technique used in subgingival curettage. Em-

phasizes the clinical value of the method to eliminate intrabony pocket and improve dental bone density.
LC NO. 75-701347
Prod-USA Dist-USNAC 1962

Methodist Hospital Psychiatric Patient Care Team, Pt I B 60 MIN
3/4 OR 1/2 INCH VIDEO CASSETTE
Offers a panel presentation from a psychiatric patient care team at a hospital in Madison, Wisconsin, and consists of talks with registered nurses, mental health workers and an occupational therapist, a social worker and a unit clerk. Discusses their philosophies, responsibilities, a typical day in the ward and maintaining a good working relationship with other staff members since many patients look to the team as role models.
Prod-UWISC Dist-UWISC 1979

Methodist Hospital Psychiatric Patient Care Team, Pt II B 25 MIN
3/4 OR 1/2 INCH VIDEO CASSETTE
Continues a panel discussion among personnel at a psychiatric ward in a Wisconsin hospital. Discusses how they take care of themselves and look out for each other in what sometimes can be a dangerous environment.
Prod-UWISC Dist-UWISC 1979

Methodology - The Psychologist And The Experiment C 31 MIN
16MM FILM, 3/4 OR 1/2 IN VIDEO H-C A
Explores the basic rules or methods common to all psychological research by actual documentation of two different experiments. Includes Dr Stanley Schachter's 'fear and affiliation' social psychology experiment using human subjects and Dr Austin Riessen's experiment on the development of visual motor coordination using kittens as subjects.
From The Psychology Today Films Series.
Prod-MGHT Dist-MGHT 1975

Methodology Of Energy Audits For Industrial And Commercial Facilities (Fazzolare) B 60 MIN
3/4 OR 1/2 INCH VIDEO CASSETTE
See series title for descriptive statement.
From The How To Save Energy Dollars In Industrial And Commercial Facilities Series. Pt 2
Prod-UAZMIC Dist-UAZMIC 1978

Methodology Overview And Calculation Of Reliability B 60 MIN
3/4 OR 1/2 INCH VIDEO CASSETTE C
See series title for descriptive statement.
From The Mechanical Component Reliability Prediction, Probabilistic Design For Reliability...Series. Pt 1
Prod-UAZMIC Dist-UAZMIC

Methods And Instruments Of Oceanography C 18 MIN
16MM FILM, 3/4 OR 1/2 IN VIDEO J-H
Defines oceanography, describes the basic instruments used in oceanographic research and shows the methods by which these instruments are employed.
Prod-WILEYJ Dist-MEDIAG 1970

Methods And Techniques C 30 MIN
3/4 OR 1/2 INCH VIDEO CASSETTE T
Explores the methods and techniques used to teach adult basic education students.
From The Basic Education - Teaching The Adult Series.
Prod-MDDE Dist-MDCPB

Methods For Obtaining Anaerobiasis C 12 MIN
16MM FILM - 3/4 IN VIDEO
Demonstrates two methods for culturing organisms which require an oxygen-free environment. Issued in 1965 as a motion picture.
LC NO. 78-706103
Prod-USPHS Dist-USNAC Prodn-NMAC 1978

Methods For Teaching Information C 30 MIN
3/4 OR 1/2 INCH VIDEO CASSETTE T
Explores methods for teaching information, including lectures, question-and-answer sessions and group discussions.
From The Training The Trainer Series.
Prod-ITCORP Dist-ITCORP

Methods For Teaching Skills C 30 MIN
3/4 OR 1/2 INCH VIDEO CASSETTE T
Deals with methods for teaching skills, including demonstrations, simulators and role playing.
From The Training The Trainer Series.
Prod-ITCORP Dist-ITCORP

Methods In Diagnostic Parasitology C 34 MIN
3/4 OR 1/2 INCH VIDEO CASSETTE PRO
Presents an introduction to techniques used in the detection of intestinal and blood parasites. Covers proper method for submitting a stool specimen for parasitological study, performance of the ova-parasite (OP) test and the blood-ova-parasite (BOP) test, the trichrome staining method and the preparation and staining of blood films.
Prod-HSCIC Dist-HSCIC

Methods Of Birth Control C 13 MIN
3/4 OR 1/2 INCH VIDEO CASSETTE
Discusses birth control pills, IUDs, diaphrgam, vasectomy, tubal ligation, condom, contraceptive foam and theoretical and actual effectiveness rates. Describes briefly natural birth controls as well.
LC NO. 78-730127
Prod-TRAINX Dist-TRAINX

Methods Of Birth Control (Spanish) C 13 MIN
3/4 OR 1/2 INCH VIDEO CASSETTE
Discusses birth control pills, IUDs, Diaphragms, vasectomy, tubal ligation, condoms, contraceptive foam and theoretical and actual effectiveness rates. Describes natural birth controls as well, briefly.
LC NO. 78-730127
Prod-TRAINX Dist-TRAINX

Methods Of Birth Control (2nd Ed) C 21 MIN
3/4 OR 1/2 INCH VIDEO CASSETTE
Presents all available systems of birth control through artwork and cartoons. Discusses advantages and disadvantages.
Prod-MEDFAC Dist-MEDFAC 1979

Methods Of Energy Waste Measurement C 45 MIN
3/4 OR 1/2 INCH VIDEO CASSETTE PRO
Describes process accounting of various measurements of reducing energy consumption, and talks about the role of cycling operations, power factors in efficient energy use, and the need for instrumentation.
From The Energy Auditing And Conservation Series.
LC NO. 81-706438
Prod-AMCEE Dist-AMCEE 1979

Methods Of Family Planning C 18 MIN
16MM FILM, 3/4 OR 1/2 IN VIDEO H-C A
Explains all of the presently practiced methods of contraception and illustrates the rhythm method, pills, the diaphragm, intra-uterine devices, vaginal spermicides and condoms, as well as the surgical methods of vasectomy and tubal litigation. Includes moral stipulations to the right or wrong of any or all of these methods. Gives factual medical explanations and shows couples counseling with doctors in order to relate the medical pros and cons to their individual circumstances.
Prod-MORLAT Dist-AIMS 1972

Methods Of Family Planning (Spanish) C 18 MIN
16MM FILM, 3/4 OR 1/2 IN VIDEO H-C A
Explains methods of contraception, including rhythm, pills, diaphragm, intrauterine device and condoms. Includes the surgical methods of vasectomy and tubal ligation.
Prod-MORLAT Dist-AIMS 1972

Methods Of Forming Metals C 35 MIN
3/4 INCH VIDEO CASSETTE C A
See series title for descriptive statement.
From The Elements Of Metallurgy Series.
LC NO. 81-706194
Prod-AMCEE Dist-AMCEE 1980

Methods Of Forming Metals C 45 MIN
3/4 OR 1/2 INCH VIDEO CASSETTE PRO
See series title for descriptive statement.
From The Elements Of Metallurgy Series.
Prod-ICSINT Dist-ICSINT

Methods Of Naso-Enteral Alimentation C 11 MIN
16MM FILM OPTICAL SOUND PRO
Discusses the case of a patient with short-bowel syndrome on whom an ileostomy has been performed. Shows the patient at home as she functions with a nasoenteral tube.
LC NO. 80-701414
Prod-EATONL Dist-EATONL Prodn-AEGIS 1979

Methods Of Processing Plastics Materials B 25 MIN
16MM FILM OPTICAL SOUND
Discusses fundamentals of lamination and of the compression, transfer, extrusion and injection molding methods. Shows how to finish molded parts.
From The Plastics Series. No. 2
LC NO. FIE52-294
Prod-USOE Dist-USNAC Prodn-CARFI 1945

Methods Of Ranking Project Proposals C 30 MIN
3/4 OR 1/2 INCH VIDEO CASSETTE PRO
Describes four alternative methods which can be used to evaluate appropriation requests. Discusses methods of Accounting, Return on Investment, Payback Period, Net Present Value and Internal Rate Of Return.
From The Analysis Of Appropriations Series.
Prod-GMIEMI Dist-AMCEE

Methods To Section A Whole Chicken C 20 MIN
1/2 IN VIDEO CASSETTE BETA/VHS
Explains how to section, portion and cut up a whole chicken, and illustrates an easy method of working with poultry and how to utilize the by-products.
Prod-RMI Dist-RMI

Metis, The C 27 MIN
16MM FILM, 3/4 OR 1/2 IN VIDEO J-H
Deals with the Metis people of North America who trace their ancestry to both Indian and European roots.
Prod-DEVGCF Dist-MGHT 1978

Metrazol Induced Convulsions In Normal And Neurotic Rats B 16 MIN
16MM FILM SILENT C
A neurotic strain of rats and a normal strain are both subjected to metrazol convulsion. In comparison to normal rats the neurotic strain exhibits a lower threshhold to the effect of metrazol, a delayed onset of convulsions, hops and excessive forepaw clonus following initial torsion and a succession of convulsive reactions following a single injection. Neurotic rats often show seizures from the auditory stimulation of the jingling of keys. Rats of the normal strain seldom respond so violently.
Prod-PSUPCR Dist-PSUPCR 1940

Metre And Litre Are Neater C 45 MIN
16MM FILM OPTICAL SOUND T
Covers the history of the metric system, explaining the SI metric system. Studies problems encountered in teaching metrics to elementary school children. Shows a workshop for teachers being conducted by Robert Tardif.
LC NO. 75-704371
Prod-SRSPRD Dist-SRSPRD 1975

Metre, The C 20 MIN
3/4 INCH VIDEO CASSETTE I
Tells how to use the metre stick and outlines the four units of measure commonly used in the metric system.
From The Metric Marmalade Series.
Prod-WCVETV Dist-GPITVL 1979

Metres, Litres And Grams C 11 MIN
16MM FILM OPTICAL SOUND
Uses animation to examine metrics.
Prod-GM Dist-GM

Metric - Less Hectic C 15 MIN
3/4 INCH VIDEO CASSETTE J-C A
Explains the interrelationship between metric units and the comparative ease with which one can move from one metric unit to a smaller or larger unit. Reviews prefixes and their values.
From The Measure To Measure Series.
Prod-WCVETV Dist-GPITVL 1975

Metric America C 32 MIN
3/4 OR 1/2 INCH VIDEO CASSETTE
Discusses the philosophy, rationale and utilization of metric education using SI units. Includes sample activities.
From The Metric Education Video Tapes For Pre And Inservice Teachers (K-8) Series.
Prod-PUAVC Dist-PUAVC

Metric America, A (2nd Ed) C 16 MIN
16MM FILM, 3/4 OR 1/2 IN VIDEO J-C A
Presents a parable about an imaginary people with a cumbersome measuring system. Highlights reasons for metric conversion in the United States and introduces metric units.
Prod-AIMS Dist-AIMS

Metric Day, A C 20 MIN
3/4 INCH VIDEO CASSETTE I
Reviews the metric units of measure for length, mass, volume, temperature and time. Shows how to have a metric field day at school.
From The Metric Marmalade Series.
Prod-WCVETV Dist-GPITVL 1979

Metric Education Video Tapes For Pre And Inservice Teachers (K-8)–A Series

Ten programs on metric education for pre and inservice teachers in grades K-8. Contains ideas for incorporating metrics into all curricular areas including reading, language arts, mathematics, science and social studies.
Prod-PUAVC Dist-PUAVC

Area And Perimeter	025 MIN
Consumer Metrics	026 MIN
History	025 MIN
Length	025 MIN
Mass And Weight	024 MIN
Metric America	032 MIN
Metric Units	026 MIN
Pros And Cons	028 MIN
Temperature	025 MIN
Volume	027 MIN

Metric Film, The C 13 MIN
16MM FILM, 3/4 OR 1/2 IN VIDEO J-C A
Discusses the history of the metric system, conversion to the metric system and how to solve measurement problems.
Prod-HALLL Dist-AMEDFL 1975

Metric Marmalade Teacher In-Service C 20 MIN
3/4 INCH VIDEO CASSETTE A
Demonstrates the metric system and learning aids in teaching metrics. Notes that only length, time, mass and temperature measuring units are necessary for day-to-day consumer use.
From The Metric Marmalade Series.
Prod-WCVETV Dist-GPITVL 1979

Metric Marmalade–A Series
I
Discusses metric units of measure.
Prod-WCVETV Dist-GPITVL 1979

Business And Metrication	20 MIN
Centimetres And Decimetres	20 MIN
History Of Measurement, The	20 MIN
Kilogram, The	20 MIN
Kilometres And Seconds	20 MIN
Legislative Fight For Metrication	20 MIN
Litres And Millilitres	20 MIN
Metre, The	20 MIN
Metric Day, A	20 MIN
Metric Marmalade Teacher In-Service	20 MIN
Metrics In The Kitchen	20 MIN
Millimetres	20 MIN
Science And Metrics	20 MIN
Temperature	20 MIN
Weather Report, A	20 MIN

Metric Marvels–A Series
3/4 OR 1/2 INCH VIDEO CASSETTE P-I
Features four animated superheroes who are out to vanquish metric ignorance.
Prod-NBCTV Dist-GA 1978

Eeny, Meeny, Miney Milliliter	3 MIN
I'm Your Liter Leader	3 MIN
Mara-Mara-Marathon	3 MIN
Meet Meter Man	3 MIN
Super Celsius	3 MIN
Wonder Baby	3 MIN
Wonder Gram	3 MIN

Metric Matter, The C 30 MIN
3/4 INCH VIDEO CASSETTE
Focuses on the debate over converting America to the metric system. Points out that the metric system is accurate and easily learned.
Prod-NETCHE Dist-NETCHE 1975

Metric Measure Made Easy C 13 MIN
16MM FILM, 3/4 OR 1/2 IN VIDEO P-J
Discusses the nature of the metric system.
Prod-AIMS Dist-AIMS

Metric Measurement C 12 MIN
3/4 OR 1/2 INCH VIDEO CASSETTE
Covers the history of measuring terms, length, area, volume, mass, time, frequency, speed, velocity and other metric measurements.
From The Making Measurements Series.
Prod-TPCTRA Dist-TPCTRA

Metric Measurement - Length And Area C 12 MIN
16MM FILM - 3/4 IN VIDEO I-J
Introduces the prefixes used for all measuring operations done with the metric system. Stresses the use of the meter to find length and area.
Prod-SF Dist-SF 1974

Metric Measurement - Mass C 9 MIN
16MM FILM - 3/4 IN VIDEO I-J
Describes how multiples and submultiples of the kilogram are used to determine mass. Explains how the adoption of the metric system can help world-wide communication and trade.
Prod-SF Dist-SF 1974

Metric Measurement - Volume And Capacity C 9 MIN
16MM FILM - 3/4 IN VIDEO I-J
Explains how to measure volume using metric units.
Prod-SF Dist-SF 1974

Metric Measurement, Film 1 C 14 MIN
16MM FILM, 3/4 OR 1/2 IN VIDEO P
Tells how measurement is used in day-to-day life and discusses the metric system of measurement.
From The Beginning Mathematics Series.
Prod-JOU Dist-JOU

Metric Measurement, Film 1 (Spanish) C 14 MIN
16MM FILM, 3/4 OR 1/2 IN VIDEO P
Shows how the metric system is based on the number ten. Uses a variety of examples from everyday life in order to show how metric units are employed to measure weight, distance and temperature.
From The Beginning Mathematics Series.
Prod-JOU Dist-JOU 1974

Metric Measurement, Film 2 C 14 MIN
16MM FILM, 3/4 OR 1/2 IN VIDEO I
Compares each unit of the metric system to familiar objects and situations.
From The Intermediate Mathematics Series.
Prod-JOU Dist-JOU

Metric Measurement, Film 2 (Spanish) C 14 MIN
16MM FILM, 3/4 OR 1/2 IN VIDEO P-I
Compares each unit of the metric system with its multiples and divisions to familiar objects and situations. Examines the relationship of the gram and liter and reviews the Celsius system of temperature measurement.
From The Intermediate Mathematics Series.
Prod-JOU Dist-JOU 1974

Metric Meets The Inchworm C 10 MIN
16MM FILM, 3/4 OR 1/2 IN VIDEO P-C A
Uses a story about Fred Inchworm to explore the basic components of the metric system and show the advantages of converting to this form of measurement.
Prod-BOSUST Dist-CF 1974

Metric Micrometer, The C 9 MIN
3/4 OR 1/2 INCH VIDEO CASSETTE IND
Teaches basics of how to read any micrometer.
From The Marshall Maintenance Training Programs Series. Tape 36
Prod-LEIKID Dist-LEIKID

Metric Micrometer, The C 9 MIN
16MM FILM, 3/4 OR 1/2 IN VIDEO IND
Shows how to use the metric micrometer.
Prod-MOKIN Dist-MOKIN

Metric Movie, The C 15 MIN
16MM FILM OPTICAL SOUND I-H A
Presents a brief, animated history of measurement. Introduces, compares, illustrates and clarifies the fundamental concepts of the SI metric system.
LC NO. 76-703718
Prod-GRAP Dist-BESTF 1975

Metric Properties Of Figures C 30 MIN
16MM FILM OPTICAL SOUND T
Discusses the metric properties of various geometric figures. Shows how to determine a measure by an arbitrary unit. To be used following 'POLYGONS AND ANGLES.'
From The Mathematics For Elementary School Teachers Series. No. 15
Prod-SMSG Dist-MLA 1963

Metric System C 15 MIN
16MM FILM, 3/4 OR 1/2 IN VIDEO I-H
Shows the basic principles of the metric system and explains the interrelationship of metric units. Shows how the metric system can simplify daily life and how it applies to sophisticated 20th-century technology.
Prod-FILCOM Dist-MCFI 1974

Metric System - Linear Measure C 15 MIN
3/4 OR 1/2 INCH VIDEO CASSETTE I-J
Identifies the terms kilometer, meter, centimeter and millimeter as referring to standards of length in the metric system of measurement and compares them as to their relative size.
From The Math Matters Series. Blue Module
Prod-STETVC Dist-AITECH Prodn-KLRNTV 1975

Metric System - Weight And Capacity C 15 MIN
3/4 OR 1/2 INCH VIDEO CASSETTE I-J
Identifies the terms gram and kilogram as standards of weight in the metric system. Considers a liter as a measurement of capacity.
From The Math Matters Series. Blue Module
Prod-STETVC Dist-AITECH Prodn-KLRNTV 1975

Metric System - Weight—A Series
16MM FILM, 3/4 OR 1/2 IN VIDEO IND
Presents the basic concepts of the metric system, describing how long a meter is, how much a kilogram weighs, how much a liter contains and the physical relationships between the measures for length, volume and weight. Treats the kilogram as a unit of weight.
Prod-WFP Dist-PEREN 1974

Kilogram, The - Weight 011 MIN
Liter, The - Weight 006 MIN
Meter, The - Weight 011 MIN
Meters, Liters And Kilograms - Weight 023 MIN

Metric System Of Measurement - SI Base Units C 19 MIN
3/4 OR 1/2 INCH VIDEO CASSETTE
Discusses the conversion of standard scientific units into the Standard International System (Metric System).
From The Metric System Of Measurements Series.
Prod-USDHEW Dist-USNAC

Metric System Of Measurement - SI Radiation Units C 31 MIN
3/4 OR 1/2 INCH VIDEO CASSETTE
Discusses the conversion from special or traditional radiation units to the SI or Metric system.
From The Metric System Of Measurements Series.
Prod-USDHEW Dist-USNAC

Metric System Of Measurements—A Series

Discusses the base units and prefixes of the metric system. Describes the four quantities used in the radiation sciences, using the SI system.
Prod-USDHEW Dist-USNAC

Metric System Of Measurement - SI Base Units 019 MIN
Metric System Of Measurement - SI Radiation 031 MIN

Metric System—A Series
P-I
Prod-SF Dist-SF

Linear Measurement 10 MIN
What Is Measurement 10 MIN

Metric System—A Series
J-C A
Discusses the metric system of measurement.
Prod-MAETEL Dist-GPITVL 1975

Comparing Lengths 20 MIN
Comparing Units Of Volume 20 MIN
Comparing Units Of Weight 20 MIN
Introducing The Metric System 20 MIN
It's All Based On The Meter 20 MIN
Metric Units Of Length 20 MIN
Metric Units Of Volume 20 MIN
Metric Units Of Weight 20 MIN
Prefixes 20 MIN
Science And The Metric System 20 MIN
System Is Based On 10, The 20 MIN
Using The Metric System Every Day 20 MIN
What Do We Know About The Metric System 20 MIN
What Is The Metric System 20 MIN
You Can Use It Now 20 MIN

Metric System, Pt 1 C 13 MIN
3/4 INCH VIDEO CASSETTE I-H A
Presents the history, advantages, decimal calculating and comparison of English and metric systems.
Prod-VISIN Dist-VISIN

Metric System, Pt 2 C 13 MIN
3/4 INCH VIDEO CASSETTE I-H A
Presents weights, volumes and short and long lengths.
Prod-VISIN Dist-VISIN

Metric System, The C 13 MIN
16MM FILM OPTICAL SOUND I-J
Presents an animated film on the metric system.
From The Mathematical Relationships Series.
Prod-OECA Dist-NBC 1972

Metric Systems, Welding Terms And Symbols C
3/4 OR 1/2 INCH VIDEO CASSETTE PRO
Discusses the SI International system of units, as well as basic metric units. Explains welding terms and symbols.
From The Welding Inspection And Quality Control Series.
Prod-AMCEE Dist-AMCEE

Metric Units C 26 MIN
3/4 OR 1/2 INCH VIDEO CASSETTE
Reviews the common metric units of length, volume, mass and temperature. Gives instruction on how to construct metric measuring equipment. Suggests activities to familiarize students with these metric units.
From The Metric Education Video Tapes For Pre And Inservice Teachers (K-8) Series.
Prod-PUAVC Dist-PUAVC

Metric Units Of Length C 20 MIN
3/4 INCH VIDEO CASSETTE J-C A
Emphasizes the common units of metric length. Discusses the millimeter, centimeter, meter and kilometer.
From The Metric System Series.
Prod-MAETEL Dist-GPITVL 1975

Metric Units Of Volume C 20 MIN
3/4 INCH VIDEO CASSETTE J-C A
Introduces the liter as the basic unit of volume.
From The Metric System Series.
Prod-MAETEL Dist-GPITVL 1975

Metric Units Of Weight C 20 MIN
3/4 INCH VIDEO CASSETTE J-C A
Discusses the gram and kilogram and describes the use of the Celsius temperature scale.
From The Metric System Series.
Prod-MAETEL Dist-GPITVL 1975

Metrics - Length And Distance C 10 MIN
16MM FILM, 3/4 OR 1/2 IN VIDEO I
Illustrates the subdivisions and extrapolations of metrication.
From The Metrics For Elementary Series.
Prod-CINEDU Dist-AIMS 1974

Metrics - Length And Distance (Spanish) C 10 MIN
16MM FILM, 3/4 OR 1/2 IN VIDEO I
Illustrates the subdivisions and extrapolations of metrication.
From The Metrics For Elementary (Spanish) Series.
Prod-CINEDU Dist-AIMS 1974

Metrics - Mass C 10 MIN
16MM FILM, 3/4 OR 1/2 IN VIDEO I
Presents units of mass as used in household activities, sports events and amusements. Illustrates the relationship between mass and other measures, such as the litre.
From The Metrics For Elementary Series.
Prod-CINEDU Dist-AIMS 1974

Metrics - Mass (Spanish) C 10 MIN
16MM FILM, 3/4 OR 1/2 IN VIDEO I
Presents units of mass as used in household activities, sports events and amusements. Illustrates the relationship between mass and other measures, such as the litre.
From The Metrics For Elementary (Spanish) Series.
Prod-CINEDU Dist-AIMS 1974

Metrics - Volume And Capacity C 10 MIN
16MM FILM, 3/4 OR 1/2 IN VIDEO I
Provides a basis for judging volume through utilization of everyday situations. Demonstrates the litre and its companion volume measurement, the cubic centimeter.
From The Metrics For Elementary Series.
Prod-CINEDU Dist-AIMS 1974

Metrics - Volume And Capacity (Spanish) C 10 MIN
16MM FILM, 3/4 OR 1/2 IN VIDEO I
Provides a basis for judging volume through utilization of everyday situations. Demonstrates the litre and its companion volume measurement, the cubic centimeter.
From The Metrics For Elementary (Spanish) Series.
Prod-CINEDU Dist-AIMS 1974

Metrics For Elementary (Spanish)—A Series
16MM FILM, 3/4 OR 1/2 IN VIDEO I
Shows how to think and judge in metric terms.
Prod-CINEDU Dist-AIMS 1974

Metrics - Length And Distance (Spanish) 10 MIN
Metrics - Mass (Spanish) 10 MIN
Metrics - Volume And Capacity (Spanish) 10 MIN

Metrics For Elementary—A Series
16MM FILM, 3/4 OR 1/2 IN VIDEO I
Shows how to think and judge in metric terms.
Prod-CINEDU Dist-AIMS 1974

Metrics - Length And Distance 10 MIN
Metrics - Mass 10 MIN
Metrics - Volume And Capacity 10 MIN

Metrics For Measure C 13 MIN
16MM FILM, 3/4 OR 1/2 IN VIDEO P-C A
Uses an animated story about an inchworm in order to introduce the background and characteristics of the metric system.
Prod-PETAW Dist-PHENIX 1975

Metrics For Primary (Spanish)—A Series
16MM FILM, 3/4 OR 1/2 IN VIDEO P
Introduces the metric system.
Prod-CINEDU Dist-AIMS 1976

Metrics For Primary - How Big Is Big (Spanish) 011 MIN
Metrics For Primary - How Heavy Is Heavy 011 MIN
Metrics For Primary - How Hot Is Hot (Spanish) 011 MIN
Metrics For Primary - How Long Is Long 011 MIN

Metrics For Primary - How Big Is Big C 11 MIN
16MM FILM, 3/4 OR 1/2 IN VIDEO P
Explores nonstandard and standard units for measuring liquid and solid materials, illustrating that one cubic decimetre has the capacity of one litre.
From The Metrics For Primary Series.
Prod-CINEDU Dist-AIMS 1976

Metrics For Primary - How Big Is Big (Spanish) C 11 MIN
16MM FILM, 3/4 OR 1/2 IN VIDEO P
Explores nonstandard and standard units for measuring liquid and solid materials, illustrating that one cubic decimetre has the capacity of one litre.
From The Metrics For Primary (Spanish) Series.
Prod-CINEDU Dist-AIMS 1976

Metrics For Primary - How Heavy Is Heavy C 11 MIN
16MM FILM, 3/4 OR 1/2 IN VIDEO P
Introduces metric measures of mass, illustrating concepts of light and heavy and explaining the gram and kilogram as standard metric units.
From The Metrics For Primary Series.
Prod-CINEDU Dist-AIMS 1976

Metrics For Primary - How Heavy Is Heavy (Spanish) C 11 MIN
16MM FILM, 3/4 OR 1/2 IN VIDEO P
Introduces metric measures of mass, illustrating concepts of light and heavy and explaining the gram and kilogram as standard metric units.
From The Metrics For Primary (Spanish) Series.
Prod-CINEDU Dist-AIMS 1976

Metrics For Primary - How Hot Is Hot C 11 MIN
16MM FILM, 3/4 OR 1/2 IN VIDEO P
Discovers that the terms hot, warm and cold are relative and investigates the Celsius scale as a standard metric measure.
From The Metrics For Primary Series.
Prod-CINEDU Dist-AIMS 1976

Metrics For Primary - How Hot Is Hot (Spanish) C 11 MIN
16MM FILM, 3/4 OR 1/2 IN VIDEO P
Discovers that the terms hot, warm and cold are relative and investigates the Celsius scale as a standard metric measure.
From The Metrics For Primary (Spanish) Series.
Prod-CINEDU Dist-AIMS 1976

Metrics For Primary - How Long Is Long C 11 MIN
16MM FILM, 3/4 OR 1/2 IN VIDEO P
Emphasizes units of informal measurement and standard units of length, explores the relationship between the metre, decimetre and centimetre and compares length, height and distance.
From The Metrics For Primary Series.
Prod-CINEDU Dist-AIMS 1976

Metrics For Primary - How Long Is Long (Spanish) C 11 MIN
16MM FILM, 3/4 OR 1/2 IN VIDEO P
Emphasizes units of informal measurement and standard units of length, explores the relationship between the metre, decimetre and centimetre and compares length, height and distance.
From The Metrics For Primary (Spanish) Series.
Prod-CINEDU Dist-AIMS 1976

Metrics For Primary—A Series
16MM FILM, 3/4 OR 1/2 IN VIDEO P
Introduces the metric system.
Prod-CINEDU Dist-AIMS 1976

Metrics For Primary - How Big Is Big 11 MIN
Metrics For Primary - How Heavy Is Heavy 11 MIN
Metrics For Primary - How Hot Is Hot 11 MIN
Metrics For Primary - How Long Is Long 11 MIN

Metrics In The Kitchen C 20 MIN
3/4 INCH VIDEO CASSETTE I
Shows metric measuring instruments being used in the kitchen. Notes the use of estimation and indicates that many grocery items carry metric designations.
From The Metric Marmalade Series.
Prod-WCVETV Dist-GPITVL 1979

Metrics—A Series
3/4 OR 1/2 INCH VIDEO CASSETTE I-C
Looks at the history of the metric system and its use in measuring length, volume, mass and temperature.
Prod-BNCHMK Dist-BNCHMK

Metrics, Pt 1 - History, Length And Decimals 012 MIN
Metrics, Pt 2 - Volume 011 MIN
Metrics, Pt 3 - Mass And Temperature 009 MIN

Metrics, Pt 1 - History, Length And Decimals C 12 MIN
16MM FILM, 3/4 OR 1/2 IN VIDEO I-C
Describes early measurement systems based on body parts. Shows how the meter is the base unit of length which is successively divided or multiplied by ten.
From The Metrics Series.
Prod-BNCHMK Dist-BNCHMK

Metrics, Pt 2 - Volume C 11 MIN
16MM FILM, 3/4 OR 1/2 IN VIDEO I-C
Describes the relationship between meters and grams which measure length and weight, and liters which measure volume.
From The Metrics Series.
Prod-BNCHMK Dist-BNCHMK

Metrics, Pt 3 - Mass And Temperature C 9 MIN
16MM FILM, 3/4 OR 1/2 IN VIDEO I-C
Describes the use of various metric units of mass such as the gram, milligram and kilogram to measure the weights of common objects.
From The Metrics Series.
Prod-BNCHMK Dist-BNCHMK

Metrics, Unit 1, Lesson 1 C 15 MIN
3/4 INCH VIDEO CASSETTE J-C A
Tells how to measure an object to the nearest whole number of units, given an appropriate nonstandard unit of length. Explains how to match metric units with their symbols.
Prod-AALC Dist-NYSED 1977

Metrics, Unit 1, Lesson 2 C 6 MIN
3/4 INCH VIDEO CASSETTE J-C A
Tells how to choose the metric unit of length that will give the most accurate measurement in a particular situation.
Prod-AALC Dist-NYSED 1977

Metrics, Unit 1, Lesson 3 C 11 MIN
3/4 INCH VIDEO CASSETTE J-C A
Presents a picture and a metric unit of length and then shows how to estimate the size of the real-life object.
Prod-AALC Dist-NYSED 1977

Metrics, Unit 1, Lesson 4 C 9 MIN
3/4 INCH VIDEO CASSETTE J-C A
Presents two standard metric units of length and an illustration. Tells how to state the length of that illustration in the larger and smaller units.
Prod-AALC Dist-NYSED 1977

Metrics, Unit 1, Lesson 5 C 12 MIN
3/4 INCH VIDEO CASSETTE J-C A
Explains how to convert linear measurements into measurements in another unit, changing into or from decimal notation.
Prod-AALC Dist-NYSED 1977

Metrics, Unit 2, Lesson 1 C 8 MIN
3/4 INCH VIDEO CASSETTE J-C A
Discusses how to change a metric distance into a measurement in two units.
Prod-AALC Dist-NYSED 1977

Metrics, Unit 2, Lesson 2 C 10 MIN
3/4 INCH VIDEO CASSETTE J-C A
Gives a situation and three measurements in different metric units, showing how to choose the measurement which best fits the situation.
Prod-AALC Dist-NYSED 1977

Metrics, Unit 2, Lesson 3 C 13 MIN
3/4 INCH VIDEO CASSETTE J-C A
Explains how to read a distance in meters and decimal parts of a meter, and then round off to the nearest whole number of meters. Tells how to estimate distance in meters.
Prod-AALC Dist-NYSED 1977

Metrics, Unit 3, Lesson 1 C 13 MIN
3/4 INCH VIDEO CASSETTE J-C A
Shows how to calculate perimeter with metric units.
Prod-AALC Dist-NYSED 1977

Metrics, Unit 3, Lesson 2 C 11 MIN
3/4 INCH VIDEO CASSETTE J-C A
Explains how to estimate a perimeter in metric units.
Prod-AALC Dist-NYSED 1977

Metrics, Unit 3, Lesson 3 C 14 MIN
3/4 INCH VIDEO CASSETTE J-C A
Presents a number of figures and their dimensions and tells how to calculate their perimeters and order them from greatest to least.
Prod-AALC Dist-NYSED 1977

Metrics, Unit 4, Lesson 1 C 11 MIN
3/4 INCH VIDEO CASSETTE J-C A
Shows how to calculate the area of a simple geometric figure in metric area units.
Prod-AALC Dist-NYSED 1977

Metrics, Unit 4, Lesson 2 C 10 MIN
3/4 INCH VIDEO CASSETTE J-C A
Discusses how to do metric problems involving the area of geometric figures.
Prod-AALC Dist-NYSED 1977

Metrics, Unit 5, Lesson 1 C 13 MIN
3/4 INCH VIDEO CASSETTE J-C A
Illustrates how to calculate volume in metric units.
Prod-AALC Dist-NYSED 1977

Metrics, Unit 5, Lesson 2 C 12 MIN
3/4 INCH VIDEO CASSETTE J-C A
Illustrates how to calculate volume in metric units.
Prod-AALC Dist-NYSED 1977

Metrics, Unit 5, Lesson 3 C 12 MIN
3/4 INCH VIDEO CASSETTE J-C A
Explains how to calculate capacity in metric units.
Prod-AALC Dist-NYSED 1977

Metrics, Unit 5, Lesson 4 C 7 MIN
3/4 INCH VIDEO CASSETTE
Points out how to choose the best metric capacity unit for each situation.
Prod-AALC Dist-NYSED 1977

Metrics, Unit 6, Lesson 1 C 11 MIN
3/4 INCH VIDEO CASSETTE J-C A
Gives a measurement in one mass unit and explains how to convert it to a measurement in another mass unit.
Prod-AALC Dist-NYSED 1977

Metrics, Unit 6, Lesson 2 C 12 MIN
3/4 INCH VIDEO CASSETTE J-C A
Tells how to choose the unit of metric mass that best suits each object or situation.
Prod-AALC Dist-NYSED 1977

Metrics, Unit 6, Lesson 3 C 14 MIN
3/4 INCH VIDEO CASSETTE J-C A
Tells how to choose the unit of metric mass that best suits each object or situation.
Prod-AALC Dist-NYSED 1977

Metrics, Unit 7, Lesson 1 C 10 MIN
3/4 INCH VIDEO CASSETTE J-C A
Discusses body temperature, boiling points, and freezing points in Celsius measurement.
Prod-AALC Dist-NYSED 1977

Metrics, Unit 7, Lesson 2 C 7 MIN
3/4 INCH VIDEO CASSETTE J-C A
Explains how to estimate temperature in degrees Celsius.
Prod-AALC Dist-NYSED 1977

Metrics, Unit 7, Lesson 3 C 11 MIN
3/4 INCH VIDEO CASSETTE J-C A
Discusses Celsius temperature measurement.
Prod-AALC Dist-NYSED 1977

Metrics, Unit 8, Lesson 1 And 2 C 24 MIN
3/4 INCH VIDEO CASSETTE J-C A
Reviews linear metric measurement.
Prod-AALC Dist-NYSED 1977

Metrics, Unit 8, Lesson 3 C 14 MIN
3/4 INCH VIDEO CASSETTE J-C A
Reviews linear metric measurement.
Prod-AALC Dist-NYSED 1977

Metrics, Unit 8, Lesson 4 C 11 MIN
3/4 INCH VIDEO CASSETTE J-C A
Reviews the use of metric units to calculate perimeters.
Prod-AALC Dist-NYSED 1977

Metrics, Unit 8, Lesson 5 C 11 MIN
3/4 INCH VIDEO CASSETTE J-C A
Reviews the use of metric units to calculate area.
Prod-AALC Dist-NYSED 1977

Metrics, Unit 8, Lesson 6 C 12 MIN
3/4 INCH VIDEO CASSETTE J-C A
Discusses the metric measurement of volume and capacity.
Prod-AALC Dist-NYSED 1977

Metrics, Unit 8, Lesson 7 C 12 MIN
3/4 INCH VIDEO CASSETTE J-C A
Discusses the metric measurement of mass.
Prod-AALC Dist-NYSED 1977

Metro-Mobility C 22 MIN
16MM FILM OPTICAL SOUND A
Explores the need for the free movement of people and goods in our ever-expanding cities and satellite suburbs.
Prod-GM Dist-GM

Metromatic B 5 MIN
16MM FILM OPTICAL SOUND K-C
Emphasizes dehumanizing aspects of airport technology by showing crowd movements in a large metropolitan air terminal.
LC NO. 72-700044
Prod-PCHENT Dist-PCHENT 1971

Metropolis B 115 MIN
3/4 OR 1/2 INCH VIDEO CASSETTE
Science fiction film which depicts an incredible city of the future. Has an underlying story of love against a background of social conflict.
Prod-IHF Dist-IHF

Metropolis, The C 57 MIN
16MM FILM, 3/4 OR 1/2 IN VIDEO H-C A
Portrays problems of the industrial society as seen in the urban metropolis. Based on the book The Age Of Uncertainty by John Kenneth Galbraith.
From The Age Of Uncertainty Series.
LC NO. 77-701491
Prod-BBCL Dist-FI 1977

Metropolitan Avenue C 60 MIN
16MM FILM - 3/4 IN VIDEO
Introduces seven women from a deteriorating Brooklyn neighborhood who take leadership roles in their community and challenge City Hall. Shows how the growth of racial cooperation and grassroots leadership is essential to the survival of communities.
Prod-NEWDAY Dist-NEWDAY

Metropolitan Cats C 24 MIN
16MM FILM, 3/4 OR 1/2 IN VIDEO J-C A
Presents a tribute to the cat, as seen through 4,000 years of art and sculpture in the Metropolitan Museum Of Art.
Prod-ABCVID Dist-CORF 1984

Metropolitan Museum Seminars In Art—A Series

Analyzes and compares great paintings from different periods and examines composition, styles of painting, techniques and themes.
Prod-GA Dist-GA

Artist As Social Critic-Visionary, The
Composition
Expressionism / Abstraction
Techniques
What Is A Painting / Realism

Metropolitan Police Department C 15 MIN
3/4 OR 1/2 INCH VIDEO CASSETTE I
Explains the qualifications and personal qualities required for a successful career in the metropolitan police department.
From The Career Awareness Series.
Prod-KLVXTV Dist-GPITVL 1973

Metropolitan Washington Heroin Test, The C 46 MIN
16MM FILM OPTICAL SOUND
Helps develop an awareness of the drug problem by presenting a test regarding the key issues surrounding the heroin problem in the Washington, DC, metropolitan area.
LC NO. 74-700621
Prod-FEDCC Dist-FORM 1973

Metropolitanism C 30 MIN
3/4 OR 1/2 INCH VIDEO CASSETTE C
Uses greater Chicago as a focal point for examining the many governmental agencies involved in a major city. Looks at ways the states differ in their ability and willingness to deal with urban programs.
From The American Government 1 Series.
Prod-DALCCD Dist-DALCCD

Mexican Boy - The Story Of Pablo X 22 MIN
16MM FILM, 3/4 OR 1/2 IN VIDEO P-I

Tells of Pablo and his family who live in a small mountain village in Mexico. Pictures a one-room adobe house, school and church, market place and farm.
Prod-EBF Dist-EBEC 1961

Mexican Bus Ride B 73 MIN
16MM FILM OPTICAL SOUND H-C
Presents the misadventures of an innocent young man sent over the mountains to fetch a lawyer. Taking a bus in Mexico, he learns that buses have supernatural and surreal qualities.
Prod-CON Dist-TRANSW 1951

Mexican Dances, Pt 1 C 18 MIN
16MM FILM, 3/4 OR 1/2 IN VIDEO J-H A
Introduces a background of Mexican-American communities and parts of Mexico from where the parents and relatives of these highly skilled youthful dancers have come.
Prod-AIMS Dist-AIMS 1971

Mexican Dances, Pt 1 (Spanish) C 18 MIN
16MM FILM, 3/4 OR 1/2 IN VIDEO I-C A
Features the ballet Folklorico Estudiantil Los Angeles, portraying famous Mexican dances dating back to Aztec times. Introduces Mexican-American students and their cultural contributions.
Prod-ASSOCF Dist-AIMS 1971

Mexican Dances, Pt 2 C 18 MIN
16MM FILM, 3/4 OR 1/2 IN VIDEO J-H A
Begins with a fast moving folk dance, El Carretero (the wagon driver,) then quickly moves on to show parallel background in early American and Mexican history to provide cultural understanding and appreciation of the periods and influences behind the dances.
Prod-AIMS Dist-AIMS 1971

Mexican Dances, Pt 2 (Spanish) C 18 MIN
16MM FILM, 3/4 OR 1/2 IN VIDEO I-C A
Features the ballet Folklorico Estudiantil Los Angeles, portraying Mexican dances and their place in history and culture, paralleling Mexican and American history.
Prod-ASSOCF Dist-AIMS 1971

Mexican Heritage (Spanish)—A Series
16MM FILM, 3/4 OR 1/2 IN VIDEO
Highlights facets of life in Mexico and the rich heritage of the Mexican people.
Prod-STEXMF Dist-FI

Artes Creativos De Mexico 16 MIN
Descubrir Veracruz 16 MIN
Estos Fueron Los Mayas 19 MIN
La Historia De Las Aztecas 19 MIN
La Navidad En Oaxaca 14 MIN
La Primera Ciudad De Las Americas - Teotihuacan 18 MIN
Las Muchas Caras De Mexico 17 MIN
Monumento Del Sol - La Historia De La Piedra 16 MIN

Mexican Heritage—A Series
16MM FILM, 3/4 OR 1/2 IN VIDEO
Highlights facets of life in Mexico and the rich heritage of the Mexican people.
Prod-STEXMF Dist-FI

America's First City - Teotihuacan 18 MIN
Christmas In Oaxaca 14 MIN
Creative Arts And Crafts Of Mexico 16 MIN
Discover Veracruz 16 MIN
Many Faces Of Mexico, The 17 MIN
Monument To The Sun - The Story Of The Aztec 16 MIN
Story Of The Aztecs, The 19 MIN
These Were The Maya 19 MIN

Mexican Indian Legends C 16 MIN
16MM FILM, 3/4 OR 1/2 IN VIDEO I-H
Dramatizes several Indian legends from Toltec, Mayan and Aztec cultures, pointing out different themes such as the explanation of natural phemomena, moral lessons, heroic adventures and stories of the gods.
Prod-BFA Dist-PHENIX Prodn-BRUNOS 1976

Mexican Leaf Frog And Its Reproductive Behavior, The C 14 MIN
16MM FILM, 3/4 OR 1/2 IN VIDEO
Studies the mating behavior of the leaf frog, an inhabitant of the semi-tropical lowlands of Mexico. Shows the entire egg-laying process, male and female coupling behavior, interaction with additional males, hatching of tadpoles, emergence at metamorphosis and other aspects of leaf frog biology.
Prod-UARIZ Dist-UCEMC 1980

Mexican Market C 10 MIN
16MM FILM, 3/4 OR 1/2 IN VIDEO I-H
Presents a marketplace just outside Mexico City. Discusses the day-to-day activities there and the experience of taking part in a public market, a typical aspect of Latin American village life.
Prod-ACI Dist-AIMS 1971

Mexican Market (Spanish) C 10 MIN
16MM FILM, 3/4 OR 1/2 IN VIDEO I-H
Presents a marketplace just outside Mexico City. Discusses the day-to-day activities there and the experience of taking part in a public market, a typical aspect of Latin American village life.
Prod-ACI Dist-AIMS 1971

Mexican Murals - A Revolution On The Walls C 30 MIN
3/4 OR 1/2 INCH VIDEO CASSETTE
Examines the revolutionary mural paintings of Mexico. Looks at the murals, not only for their great aesthetic value, but also as an essential and fascinating part of Mexico's history. Focuses on the murals of the three major artists of the period, Diego Rivera, Jose Clemente Orozco and David Alfaro Siqueiros.
Prod-OHUTC Dist-OHUTC

Mexican Or American C 17 MIN
16MM FILM - 3/4 IN VIDEO J-H A
Faces the fundamental problem of Mexican cultural conflict in the United States. Asks if it is possible to enjoy the freedoms and opportunities of this land without giving up completely the heritage of one's parents.
Prod-ATLAP Dist-ATLAP

Mexican Rebellion B 20 MIN
16MM FILM OPTICAL SOUND C A
Follows the initail stages of the Mexican student rebellion during the summer of 1968. Compiled from stills, films and film clips made by the students.
Prod-UNKNWN Dist-SFN 1968

Mexican Revolution, The C 30 MIN
3/4 OR 1/2 INCH VIDEO CASSETTE
Features experts on Mexico in a symposium examining the history of the Mexican Revolution of 1910 and its significance to Mexico today. Includes historic photographs of the Revolution by Augustin V Casasola who recorded the fighting from both sides.
From The Fronteras Series.
Prod-KPBS Dist-KPBS

Mexican Tapes, The - A Chronicle Of Life Outside The Law - Pt I - El Gringo C 29 MIN
16MM FILM - 3/4 IN VIDEO
Presents a documentary on the lives of three families of illegal Mexican immigrants living covertly in a wealthy Southern Californian community. Reveals how they got there, how they feel about being there and their dreams about making it in the United States, living with the chronic fear of arrest by government authorities. In English and Spanish with English subtitles.
From The Presente Series.
Prod-KCET Dist-KCET

Mexican Tapes, The - A Chronicle Of Life Outside The Law - Pt II - El Rancho Grande C 29 MIN
16MM FILM - 3/4 IN VIDEO
Documents the tension-filled life of undocumented Mexican immigrants who live mostly in cities and follow the American way of life but face the chronic hazards of deportation, unstable employment and a lack of fluency in English. Shows how this has become a major structural element in the socio-economic make-up of the United States. In English and Spanish with English subtitles.
From The Presente Series.
Prod-KCET Dist-KCET

Mexican Tapes, The - A Chronicle Of Life Outside The Law - Pt III - The Winner's... C 29 MIN
16MM FILM - 3/4 IN VIDEO
Complete title is Mexican Tapes, The - A Chronicle Of Life Outside the Law - Pt III - The Winner's Circle. Looks at the women who live with their men and children as undocumented Mexican workers in San Diego. Reveals their ambivalent feelings about being working partners with the men as they are torn between loyalty to them and the new-found independence brought on by wage-earning. In English and Spanish with English subtitles.
From The Presente Series.
Prod-KCET Dist-KCET

Mexican Tapes, The - A Chronicle Of Life Outside The Law - Pt IV - La Migra C 29 MIN
16MM FILM - 3/4 IN VIDEO
Reveals the negative bias towards Latinos of the Immigration and Naturalization Services' arrest procedure and its effects on the children and parents. Shows the difference between life in the United States and Mexico for undocumented immigrants with scenes in the laundromat on both sides of the border. Shows these immigrants driven out of their apartments by redevelopment and immigration authority raids. In English and Spanish with English subtitles.
From The Presente Series.
Prod-KCET Dist-KCET

Mexican Village In Transition - Tepoztlan C 11 MIN
16MM FILM OPTICAL SOUND I-C A
Describes the Mexican village of Tepoztlan, long studied by archaeologists as an isolated folk village of pre-hispanic times. Shows how the old and new exist together as the village is slowly taking its place in the national life of Mexico.
LC NO. FIA66-553
Prod-BOUWM Dist-SF 1965

Mexican War And The Civil War, The C 28 MIN
16MM FILM OPTICAL SOUND
Describes Ohio's participation in and reactions to the Mexican and Civil Wars. Discusses the first military conscription during the Civil War.
From The Glory And The Dream - Ohio's Response To War Series.
Prod-OHC Dist-HRC

Mexican 1000 (Twenty-Seven And One-Half Hours To La Paz) C 26 MIN
16MM FILM OPTICAL SOUND I-C A
Shows the championship car race of 'THE BAJA' from Ensenada to La Paz. Illustrates man's struggle with natural terrain consisting of cliffs, gulches, silt and sand.
LC NO. 72-702087
Prod-SFI Dist-SFI 1970

Mexican-American Children C 27 MIN
16MM FILM OPTICAL SOUND H-C T
Covers the Rio Grand Valley, near Edinburg, Texas, an area where traditional cultural values are maintained and actively passed on to young children. Presents the importance of fiestas, dancing, music seranade and family. Observes children in numerous play episodes in the center and at home. Shows prescribed modes of interaction between boys and girls and emphasizes mutual respect and affection between the very old and the very young and perpetuating their bilingual heritage.
From The Play And Cultural Continuity Series. Part 3
Prod-CFDC Dist-CFDC 1977

Mexican-American Culture - Its Heritage C 18 MIN
16MM FILM OPTICAL SOUND I
Demonstrates visually and musically the origins and history of the Mexican-American culture.
From The Uses Of Music Series.
LC NO. 78-708130
Prod-CGWEST Dist-CGWEST 1970

Mexican-American Family, A C 17 MIN
16MM FILM, 3/4 OR 1/2 IN VIDEO J-H A
Provides an insight into the life of a Mexican-American family.
Prod-ATLAP Dist-ATLAP

Mexican-American Speaks, The - Heritage In Bronze C 20 MIN
16MM FILM, 3/4 OR 1/2 IN VIDEO J-H
Traces the history of the Spanish and the Indians on the American continent, the annexation to the United States and their role as second class citizens in the Southwest. Presents the cultural heritage of these Spanish-Indian descendents and the importance of their unity and pride in becoming full fledged citizens.
Prod-EBEC Dist-EBEC 1972

Mexican-American, The - Heritage And Destiny (2nd Ed) C 29 MIN
16MM FILM, 3/4 OR 1/2 IN VIDEO J-C A
Tells how a Mexican-American who feels culturally deprived and unsure of his identity is shown his cultural heritage. Discusses Mexican history and shows how Spanish words, architecture and music have become part of American culture. Describes contributions of outstanding Mexican-Americans.
From The Americana Series. No. 7
Prod-HANDEL Dist-HANDEL 1977

Mexican-American, The - Heritage And Destiny (2nd Ed) (Spanish) C 29 MIN
16MM FILM, 3/4 OR 1/2 IN VIDEO J-C A
Tells how a Mexican-American who feels culturally deprived and unsure of his identity is shown his cultural heritage. Discusses Mexican history and shows how Spanish words, architecture and music have become part of American culture. Describes contributions of outstanding Mexican-Americans.
From The Americana Series. No. 7
Prod-HANDEL Dist-HANDEL 1977

Mexican-Americans - An Historic Profile B 29 MIN
16MM FILM OPTICAL SOUND
Presents Maclovio Barraza, Chairman of the Board of the southwest council of La Raza, who traces the history of the Mexican-American from the time of the Spanish Conquistadores to the present.
LC NO. 72-700816
Prod-ADL Dist-ADL 1970

Mexican-Americans - Quest For Equality B 29 MIN
16MM FILM OPTICAL SOUND J-C A
Presents Dr Ernesto Galarza, noted author and educator, who defines the cultural and economic patterns in both rural and urban Mexican-American communities in the Southwest.
LC NO. M2-700815
Prod-ADL Dist-ADL 1970

Mexican-Americans - The Invisible Minority C 38 MIN
16MM FILM, 3/4 OR 1/2 IN VIDEO H-C
Describes the struggle of Mexican-Americans for an identity within the protest movement, discussing their economic poverty, their employment as unskilled laborers and their education in a system designed for white English-speaking students.
From The Public Broadcast Laboratory Series.
LC NO. 80-707096
Prod-NET Dist-IU 1969

Mexico C 17 MIN
16MM FILM, 3/4 OR 1/2 IN VIDEO I-H
Illustrates Mexican heritage and customs, giving a contemporary view of Mexico today. Presents views on solutions to social and economic problems and indicates some directions the government is taking.
From The Latin American Series - A Focus On People Series.
Prod-CLAIB Dist-SF 1973

Mexico C 29 MIN
2 INCH VIDEOTAPE
Features home economist Joan Hood presenting a culinary tour of specialty dishes from around the world. Shows the preparation of Mexican dishes ranging from peasant cookery to continental cuisine.
From The International Cookbook Series.
Prod-WMVSTV Dist-PUBTEL

Mexico - A Changing Land (2nd Ed) C 22 MIN
16MM FILM, 3/4 OR 1/2 IN VIDEO I-J
Discusses the history and geography of Mexico. Looks at the development of land, oil and gas resources, the fishing industry, and the tourist trade.
Prod-HIGGIN Dist-HIGGIN 1980

Mexico - A Family-Style Menu C 28 MIN
16MM FILM, 3/4 OR 1/2 IN VIDEO J-C A
Depicts the tasty creations of Mexican master chef Joaquin Guzman.
From The World Of Cooking Series.
Prod-SCRESC Dist-MTI

Mexico - An Introduction C 24 MIN
16MM FILM, 3/4 OR 1/2 IN VIDEO I-J
Presents a view of a rapidly changing nation. Explains that Mexico is emerging as a strong nation because of its oil reserves and it is important for people in the United States to understand Mexico better.
Prod-BFA Dist-PHENIX 1982

Mexico - Four Views C 15 MIN
16MM FILM, 3/4 OR 1/2 IN VIDEO I-H
Revised edition of the 1955 film Mexico - Geography Of The Americas. Takes a look at Mexico through the eyes of four of its people, a farmer, a truck driver, a teacher and a housing contractor.
Prod-CORF Dist-CORF 1975

Mexico - Giant Of Latin America C 23 MIN
16MM FILM, 3/4 OR 1/2 IN VIDEO I-C
Portrays the geography, people, history, agriculture, industry, education and art of Mexico. Discusses the blend of Indian and hispanic culture, the economic boom and the one party democracy in Mexico.
Prod-LEMONT Dist-LUF 1971

Mexico - Land In The Sun C 20 MIN
3/4 OR 1/2 INCH VIDEO CASSETTE J-C A
Visits Mexico, including the beaches and restaurants of Puerto Vallarta, Acapulco, Mazatlan, Guadalajara, Cozumel, Cuernavaca and the coastline of Baja California.
LC NO. 82-706775
Prod-AWSS Dist-AWSS 1980

Mexico - Land Of Contrast C 3 MIN
16MM FILM OPTICAL SOUND P-I
Discusses the country of Mexico.
From The Of All Things Series.
Prod-BAILYL Dist-AVED

Mexico - Quatro Aspectos C 15 MIN
16MM FILM, 3/4 OR 1/2 IN VIDEO I-H
A Spanish language version of Mexico - Four Views. Offers four personal views of Mexico, from the eyes of a farmer, a truck driver, a teacher and a housing contractor. Shows the daily life of a farm family, the movement of farmers to Mexico City, the heritage of historic Mexico and construction for the future.
Prod-CORF Dist-CORF

Mexico - The Frozen Revolution (Captioned) C 5 MIN
16MM FILM, 3/4 OR 1/2 IN VIDEO A
Presents a socio-historical analysis of Mexico in view of continuing poverty and the failed hopes of the 1910 revolution. Spanish dialog with English subtitles.
Prod-TRIFCW Dist-CNEMAG 1971

Mexico - The Land And The People (2nd Ed) X 20 MIN
16MM FILM, 3/4 OR 1/2 IN VIDEO I-H
Illustrates the contrasts of Mexico between aristocrat and farmer, city and village and the old and new methods in industry and agriculture. Traces the cultural, religious and economic heritage of the people.
Prod-EBEC Dist-EBEC

Mexico - The Oil Boom C 25 MIN
3/4 OR 1/2 INCH VIDEO CASSETTE H-C A
States that the oil reserves of Mexico might prove greater than those of Saudi Arabia. Reviews the impact of oil on the Mexican people and charts the potential for the future.
Prod-UPI Dist-JOU

Mexico Before Cortez C 14 MIN
16MM FILM, 3/4 OR 1/2 IN VIDEO I-C A
Uses the art and architecture of the Aztecs, Zapotecs, Mixtecs and Toltecs, combined with the murals of the modern Mexican artist, Diego Rivera, to reconstruct a picture of the life of the original inhabitants of the Americas.
Prod-HP Dist-AIMS 1972

Mexico City C 3 MIN
16MM FILM OPTICAL SOUND P-I
Discusses Mexico City, Mexico.
From The Of All Things Series.
Prod-BAILYL Dist-AVED

Mexico City C 20 MIN
16MM FILM OPTICAL SOUND J-C A
Depicts art objects and architectural interiors and exteriors of Mexico City. Shows the progress that has been made in the city since the turn of the century.
Prod-BARONA Dist-AVED 1957

Mexico City - Ole! C 20 MIN
3/4 OR 1/2 INCH VIDEO CASSETTE J-C A
Takes viewers to Mexico City and shows the bullfights, modern squares, buildings, streets and monuments. Visits the opera house and catches some of the city's old-world traditions.
LC NO. 82-706774
Prod-AWSS Dist-AWSS 1980

Mexico In The 70's - A City Family B 18 MIN
16MM FILM, 3/4 OR 1/2 IN VIDEO I-H
Discusses how the fast growing industrial economy of Mexico is affecting the life style of its people. Takes a look at a family from Mexico City to show the traditional and family culture and the increased economic well-being which has accompanied Mexico's industrialization.
Prod-GARDON Dist-PHENIX 1971

Mexico In The 70's - Heritage And Progress C 12 MIN
16MM FILM, 3/4 OR 1/2 IN VIDEO I-H
Examines Mexico's blend of old and new through the eyes of a farmer, a butcher and an architect. Explains how the National Museum of Anthropology symbolizes the Mexican's unique ability to blend centuries of tradition with modern technology.
Prod-GARDON Dist-PHENIX 1971

Mexico Y Sus Contornos C 20 MIN
16MM FILM, 3/4 OR 1/2 IN VIDEO H-C
A Spanish language film. Revised edition of 'MEXICO CIUDAD ENCANTADORA.' Begins with an illustrated sequence on the origin of Mexico city and continues with views of the city and its environs. Includes a sequence on the bull fight.
Prod-IFB Dist-IFB 1958

Mexico 68 C 20 MIN
16MM FILM OPTICAL SOUND
Shows the student-worker mass actions of hundreds of thousands of people as they down the regime of Diaz Urdaz. Shows how the government answered with the military invasion of the university, the October 2nd Tlateloco Massacre.
Prod-NEWSR Dist-NEWSR 1968

Mexico, England, Utah C 27 MIN
16MM FILM OPTICAL SOUND P-I
Presents the sporting activities of children in Mexico, England and Utah. Retells a Greek folk tale about the gods who live on Mount Olympus.
From The Big Blue Marble - Children Around The World Series. Program S
LC NO. 76-700631
Prod-ALVEN Dist-VITT 1975

Mexico's Folk Artists—A Series

Presents examples of Mexican folk art by showing the work of a papier-mache artist, an embroiderer, a woodcarver and a fireworks maker.
Prod-WORKS Dist-WORKS

Manuel Jimenez - Woodcarver 022 MIN
Marcelo Ramos - The Firework Maker's Art 023 MIN
Pedro Linares - Papier Mache Artist 023 MIN
Sabina Sanchez - The Art Of Embroidery 022 MIN

Mexico's History C 16 MIN
16MM FILM, 3/4 OR 1/2 IN VIDEO I-H
Presents the history of Mexico within the framework of four great events, including the Spanish conquest of the Indians in 1519, the revolt against Spain in 1810, the Juarez revolt of 1857 and the social revolution of 1910.
Prod-CORF Dist-CORF 1969

Mexico's Sea Of Cortes C
16MM FILM OPTICAL SOUND I-C A
Presents a travel-documentary about the Gulf of California and the major ports on or near it. Emphasizes the wonderful fishing found near the gulf.
LC NO. FIA61-807
Prod-CLI Dist-CLI Prodn-CLI 1959

Mezzo The Musical Mouse C 15 MIN
3/4 OR 1/2 INCH VIDEO CASSETTE P
Discusses the concepts of high and low tones.
From The Music Machine Series.
Prod-INDIPS Dist-GPITVL 1981

MGM-TV Syndicating 'Chips' Case History C 30 MIN
3/4 OR 1/2 INCH VIDEO CASSETTE
Explains MGM's use of market research, advertising, sales promotion, personal selling and pricing in marketing syndicated programs, using the popular 'Chips' series as an example.
From The Contemporary Issues In Marketing Series.
Prod-CANTOR Dist-IVCH

Mgodo Wa Mbanguzi, 1973, The C 53 MIN
3/4 OR 1/2 INCH VIDEO CASSETTE
See series title for descriptive statement.
From the Mgodo 1973 Series.
Prod-PSU Dist-PSU

Mgodo Wa Mkandeni, 1973, The C 48 MIN
3/4 OR 1/2 INCH VIDEO CASSETTE
See series title for descriptive statement.
From The Mgodo 1973 Series.
Prod-PSU Dist-PSU

Mgodo 1973—A Series

Documents a music and dance performance, a mgodo, composed for the chiefs of Chopi villages in southern Mozambique. Shows dancers accompanied by large xylophone orchestras. Shows the history, current affairs and local events that are contained in the shouts and songs. Uses subtitles in Chopi and English for words in the film.
Prod-PSU Dist-PSU

Mgodo Wa Mbanguzi, 1973, The 053 MIN
Mgodo Wa Mkandeni, 1973, The 048 MIN

Mi Abuelo C 30 MIN
3/4 OR 1/2 INCH VIDEO CASSETTE
See series title for descriptive statement.
From The Que Pasa, U S A Series.
Prod-WPBTTV Dist-MDCPB

Mi Amor Disperato C 7 MIN
16MM FILM OPTICAL SOUND
Presents a spoof of Italian movies. Shows a protagonist reflecting on his sorrowful past as he mourns his lost and desperate love for a beautiful woman.
LC NO. 78-701561
Prod-KRUNIC Dist-KRUNIC 1978

Miami - A Snowman's Holiday B 14 MIN
16MM FILM OPTICAL SOUND
Portrays the fantasy journey of Mr and Mrs Snowman who succumb to the irresistible lure of a magical Miami vacation and who venture from snow-bound northern New England to a fatal, for snowpeople, sunswept Miami Beach.
Prod-MIMET Dist-MIMET

Miami Is For You C 14 MIN
16MM FILM OPTICAL SOUND
Stresses the variety of events and attractions available to visitors throughout the year in Miami and why the area is an ideal place for a convention.
Prod-MIMET Dist-MIMET

Miami, Si - Cuba, No C 29 MIN
3/4 OR 1/2 INCH VIDEO CASSETTE
Looks at race relations and social problems in Dade County, Florida, where Cuban refugees, native black Americans, and Haitian immigrants interact.
From The Interface Series.
Prod-WETATV Dist-PBS

Miao Year, Pt 1 C 30 MIN
16MM FILM, 3/4 OR 1/2 IN VIDEO C A
Presents the life of the Blue Miao of Northern Thailand. Covers a full year in the life of these people and deals with the subject of poppy cultivation and efforts to eliminate this crop.
Prod-GEDDES Dist-MGHT 1970

Miao Year, Pt 2 C 31 MIN
16MM FILM, 3/4 OR 1/2 IN VIDEO C A
Presents the life of the Blue Miao of Northern Thailand. Covers a full year in the life of these people and deals with the subject of poppy cultivation and efforts to eliminate this crop.
Prod-GEDDES Dist-MGHT 1970

Mica Industry B 11 MIN
16MM FILM OPTICAL SOUND J-C A
Explains that India supplies 80 percent of the world's requirements of mica, which is being increasingly used in the manufacture of industrial appliances. Introduces the various stages of production and testing of Mica.
Prod-INDIA Dist-NEDINF

Micah And Isaiah C 30 MIN
3/4 OR 1/2 INCH VIDEO CASSETTE A
Focuses on the messages of Old Testament prophets Micah and Isaiah. Features theologian Dr James A Sanders.
From The True And False Prophecy Series.
Prod-UMCOM Dist-ECUFLM 1982

Micawber Equation, The C 25 MIN
16MM FILM, 3/4 OR 1/2 IN VIDEO A
Dramatizes how a hi-fi equipment company averts disaster when sales of their best-selling equipment drop. Designed to promote discussion of general financial principles and specific problems related to roles of managers and the development of supporting skills and attitudes.
LC NO. 81-707644
Prod-LOYDSB Dist-IFB Prodn-MILLBK 1980

Mice And How They Live C 11 MIN
16MM FILM, 3/4 OR 1/2 IN VIDEO P-I
Uses extreme close-up photography to reveal basic concepts about mice, including playing, eating, the family, natural enemies and habitat.
Prod-AIMS Dist-AIMS 1969

Mice And How They Live (Spanish) C 11 MIN
16MM FILM, 3/4 OR 1/2 IN VIDEO P-I
Shows mice, their habits and behavior as found in a deserted shack on the desert. Available with or without narration.
Prod-CAHILL Dist-AIMS 1969

Mice Are Nice C 15 MIN
3/4 OR 1/2 INCH VIDEO CASSETTE P
Presents the children's stories Henry The Uncatchable Mouse by Sidney Simon and Frederick by Leon Lionni. Includes the poem The City Mouse And The Country Mouse by Christina Rossetti.
From The Picture Book Park Series. Green Module
Prod-WVIZTV Dist-AITECH 1974

Michael C 9 MIN
16MM FILM OPTICAL SOUND I-H
Introduces Michael, a 12-year-old boy who leaves his secluded farm life to undertake a grueling 3,000-mile bike trip. Tells of the trials and rewards experienced in order to show the conflicts faced by individuals who attempt difficult and unusual undertakings.
From The Rebop Series.
LC NO. 79-700476
Prod-WGBHTV Dist-IU 1979

Michael - A Mongoloid Child B 14 MIN
16MM FILM OPTICAL SOUND C T
An intimate study of a mongoloid teenager living on a farm in England. Shows his acceptance by the community, his ordinary family life and his activities.
Prod-BFI Dist-NYU 1961

Michael And Me C 13 MIN
16MM FILM OPTICAL SOUND H-C A
Illustrates the advances in the treatment of leukemia in children by recounting how Michael Finamore, who at age 12 contracted leukemia, is now living a normal life after experimental treatment with drug combination.
LC NO. 77-701313
Prod-AMCS Dist-AMCS 1975

Michael Caine C 29 MIN
2 INCH VIDEOTAPE
Presents exchanges and arguments between the dean of American theatre critics, Elliot Norton, and Michael Caine.
From The Elliot Norton Reviews II Series.
Prod-WGBHTV Dist-PUBTEL

Michael Cardew C 29 MIN
3/4 OR 1/2 INCH VIDEO CASSETTE H-C A
Portrait of master potter Cardew filmed in Cornwall, England shortly before his death in February 1983.
Prod-VDO Dist-CEPRO

Michael Dunn C 12 MIN
16MM FILM OPTICAL SOUND
Features Michael Dunn, a Vancouver guitar maker.
LC NO. 76-703247
Prod-BCPEMC Dist-BCPEMC 1975

Michael Hall - Sculptor C 10 MIN
16MM FILM, 3/4 OR 1/2 IN VIDEO
Shows Michael Hall, large-scale metal sculptor, as he assembles a massive sculpture. Reveals new ways of seeing the obvious.
From The Working Artist Series.
Prod-MARXHA Dist-MARXS

Michael Hall - Sculptor C 10 MIN
3/4 OR 1/2 INCH VIDEO CASSETTE
Illustrates his work as a metal sculptor.
From The Working Artists Series.
Prod-SWARR Dist-LRF

Michael Lax, Industrial Designer B 29 MIN
2 INCH VIDEOTAPE
See series title for descriptive statement.
From The Design 2000 Series.
Prod-WITFTV Dist-PUBTEL

Michael Smith - Mike Builds A Shelter C 25 MIN
3/4 OR 1/2 INCH VIDEO CASSETTE
Introduces Mike, a present day anti-hero.
Prod-ARTINC Dist-ARTINC

Michael Stewart, Tommy Walsh And Ronald Dennis C 30 MIN
3/4 OR 1/2 INCH VIDEO CASSETTE
Features members of the original Chorus Line cast as they talk about where they've gone since then. Hosted by Celia Ipiotis.
From The Eye On Dance - Broadway Series.
Prod-ARTRES Dist-ARTRES

Michael, A Gay Son C 27 MIN
16MM FILM, 3/4 OR 1/2 IN VIDEO A
Examines the experiences and emotions of homosexuals revealing to their families their chosen life-styles. Follows Michael Collins as he faces this with a peer support group and as he deals with the surfacing issues in a tense family discussion.
LC NO. 82-706302
Prod-FLMLIB Dist-FLMLIB 1981

Michael, My Brother C
16MM FILM OPTICAL SOUND
Tells the story of a 12-year-old boy with Down's Syndrome and the difficulties encountered and progress made when he is tutored by his older brother.
Prod-SMTTPG Dist-SMTTPG

Michael, Row The Boat Ashore C 14 MIN
3/4 OR 1/2 INCH VIDEO CASSETTE P-I
See series title for descriptive statement.
From The Ready, Sing Series.
Prod-ARKETV Dist-AITECH 1979

Michael's First Day C 6 MIN
16MM FILM OPTICAL SOUND J-C A
Explains that it is the first day at school for both four-year-old Michael and his student helper. Follows the student's efforts to understand Michael's feelings when he becomes unhappy. Focuses on the different ways in which children and older people approach and handle unfamiliar situations.
From The Exploring Childhood Series.
LC NO. 76-701889
Prod-EDC Dist-EDC 1975

Michael's Story C 29 MIN
3/4 OR 1/2 INCH VIDEO CASSETTE
Guided by Dr Cottle, a man painfully reveals a history of physical violence against his wife. Shows the man probing his early childhood, his relationship with his parents and his own marriage for clues to his behavior.
From The Tom Cottle Show Series.
Prod-WGBHTV Dist-PBS 1981

Michel Ander - Catastrophe C 3 MIN
3/4 OR 1/2 INCH VIDEO CASSETTE
Deals with captivity.
Prod-ARTINC Dist-ARTINC

Michel Ander - Flying Back From Europe B 4 MIN
3/4 OR 1/2 INCH VIDEO CASSETTE
Deals with captivity.
Prod-ARTINC Dist-ARTINC

Michel Auder - A Coupla White Faggots Sitting Around Talking C 90 MIN
3/4 OR 1/2 INCH VIDEO CASSETTE
Presents a wealthy homosexual who becomes involved in the life of his neighbors, gabby homosexuals and freelance dominatrices.
Prod-ARTINC Dist-ARTINC

Michel Auder - Jesus C 55 MIN
3/4 OR 1/2 INCH VIDEO CASSETTE
Highlights captivity and confession.
Prod-ARTINC Dist-ARTINC

Michel Auder - Made For Denise C 4 MIN
3/4 OR 1/2 INCH VIDEO CASSETTE
Highlights confession of the captive.
Prod-ARTINC Dist-ARTINC

Michel Auder - My Love C 5 MIN
3/4 OR 1/2 INCH VIDEO CASSETTE
Deals with confession of the captire.
Prod-ARTINC Dist-ARTINC

Michel Auder - Portrait Of Hassan, Portrait Of An Island B 28 MIN
3/4 OR 1/2 INCH VIDEO CASSETTE
Deals with confession and captivity.
Prod-ARTINC Dist-ARTINC

Michel Auder - Seduction Of Patrick C 43 MIN
3/4 OR 1/2 INCH VIDEO CASSETTE
Deals with confession of the captive.
Prod-ARTINC Dist-ARTINC

Michel Auder - The Games C 28 MIN
3/4 OR 1/2 INCH VIDEO CASSETTE
Deals with confession of the captive.
Prod-ARTINC Dist-ARTINC

Michel Auder - TV America C 24 MIN
3/4 OR 1/2 INCH VIDEO CASSETTE
Examines confession of the captive.
Prod-ARTINC Dist-ARTINC

Michel Tatu C 29 MIN
3/4 INCH VIDEO CASSETTE
Features an interview with a Washington Correspondent for Le Monde of Paris.
From The Foreign Assignment - U S A Series.
Prod-UMITV Dist-UMITV 1978

Michelangelo B 29 MIN
3/4 INCH VIDEO CASSETTE
Demonstrates Michelangelo's wet plaster painting technique, the same method the master used to paint the Sistine Chapel ceiling.
From The Meet The Masters Series.
Prod-UMITV Dist-UMITV 1966

Michelangelo X 30 MIN
16MM FILM, 3/4 OR 1/2 IN VIDEO J-C
Relates the story of Michelangelo and portrays the art-centered world of his time which demanded his talents in painting, architecture and engineering in spite of his desire to be only a sculptor. Presents such works as Bacchus, David, Victory, Moses, the Pieta, the Dying Captive, and his frescoes in the Sistine Chapel.
Prod-EBF Dist-EBEC 1965

Michelangelo (1475 - 1564) C 65 MIN
16MM FILM OPTICAL SOUND
Presents the work of Michelangelo.
Prod-ROLAND Dist-ROLAND

Michelangelo - The Last Giant C 67 MIN
16MM FILM, 3/4 OR 1/2 IN VIDEO H-C A
Traces the life of Michelangelo through his paintings, sculpture and architecture, as well as through quotations from his biographers and excerpts from his own writings.
Prod-NBC Dist-CRMP 1967

Michelangelo - The Medici Chapel C 22 MIN
16MM FILM OPTICAL SOUND C
Examines the sculpture of Michelangelo in the new sacristy of the Basilica of San Lorenzo in Florence.
From The Treasures Of Tuscany Series.
LC NO. FIA64-741
Prod-WESTCB Dist-RADIM 1964

Michelangelo And His Art C 16 MIN
16MM FILM, 3/4 OR 1/2 IN VIDEO I-H A
Traces the life and career of Michelangelo--sculptor, painter, architect, poet and leading figure of the Italian Renaissance. Among the original works photographed and analyzed are 'DAVID,' 'LA PIETA,' 'MOSES,' THE MEDICI CHAPEL AND 'THE DEPOSITION.'
Prod-NETHIS Dist-CORF Prodn-HA 1963

Michelangelo's Last Judgement C 24 MIN
16MM FILM, 3/4 OR 1/2 IN VIDEO
Considers the meaning of the painting The Last Judgement painted by Michelangelo on the altar walls of the Sistine Chapel in the context of the iconographic scheme for the rest of the chapel. Uses quotations from Dante, the Bible and a variety of 16th century critics to clarify the meaning of the fresco.
Prod-OPENU Dist-MEDIAG Prodn-BBCTV 1980

Michelle At Home (Hi, Daddy) C 10 MIN
16MM FILM OPTICAL SOUND J-C A
Demonstrates different family situations. Follows the family of a four-year-old girl through one afternoon showing her mother, father and her five-year-old brother.
From The Exploring Childhood Series.
LC NO. 76-701890
Prod-EDC Dist-EDC Prodn-FRIEDJ 1975

Michelle Knight And Kim Lemon C 28 MIN
3/4 OR 1/2 INCH VIDEO CASSETTE
Presents Fred Rogers profiling two young thirteen year-old girls who may be on their way to the top in gymnastics. Reveals that the rigors of their lives are emotional as well as physical.
From The Old Friends - New Friends Series.
Prod-FAMCOM Dist-PBS 1981

Michelson Interferometer L-4 C 3 MIN
16MM FILM SILENT H-C
Illustrates the adjustment of mirrors, monochromatic and white-light fringes, and displacement of fringes by insertion of thin film. Shows the Mach-zehnder interferometer.
From The Single-Concept Films In Physics Series.
Prod-OSUMPD Dist-OSUMPD 1963

Michigan State University Jazz Ensemble C 29 MIN
2 INCH VIDEOTAPE
Presents the music of the Michigan State University Jazz Ensemble. Features host Jim Rockwell interviewing band members.
From The People In Jazz Series.
Prod-WTVSTV Dist-PUBTEL

Michigan Year C 28 MIN
16MM FILM OPTICAL SOUND
A fast paced tour of Michigan in which the beauty of the four seasons are shown as well as places of interest like Hollands Tulip Festival, Interlockens Music Camp, Traverse Citys Cherry Festival, and Dunes of the Upper Penninsula. Art fair at Ann Arbor, plus winter and summer sports.
Prod-CONPOW Dist-CONPOW

Mick And The Moon C 20 MIN
16MM FILM OPTICAL SOUND
Shows how the art of the Desert Nomads of Central Australia took the form of elaborate body decorations and sand mosaics painted with ochre on the ground. Tells how this art form evolved into many graphic symbols for various desert motifs and has now been transposed onto hardboard using acrylic and poster paints.
LC NO. 80-700824
Prod-BARDON Dist-TASCOR 1978

Mickey C 61 MIN
2 INCH VIDEOTAPE
See series title for descriptive statement.
From The Toys That Grew Up II Series.
Prod-WTTWTV Dist-PUBTEL

Mickey Mantle C 20 MIN
16MM FILM OPTICAL SOUND I-J
Presents Mickey Mantle talking about his boyhood in Oklahoma, how he signed a contract with the Yankees right out of high school and reviews film footage of many of the great moments in his playing days.
From The Sports Legends Series.
Prod-COUNFI Dist-COUNFI

Mickey Mouse - The Early Years--A Series
16MM FILM, 3/4 OR 1/2 IN VIDEO K-H
Presents a series of Walt Disney cartoons from the 1930's.
Prod-DISNEY Dist-WDEMCO

Band Concert, The 008 MIN
Steamboat Willie 008 MIN
Thru The Mirror 008 MIN

Mickey's Christmas Carol C 26 MIN
16MM FILM, 3/4 OR 1/2 IN VIDEO
Presents an adaptation of Charles Dickens' story A Christmas Carol with Mickey Mouse as overworked, underpaid Bob Cratchit and Scrooge McDuck as Ebenezer Scrooge.
Prod-WDEMCO Dist-WDEMCO 1983

Mickey's Trailer C 8 MIN
16MM FILM, 3/4 OR 1/2 IN VIDEO
Portrays what happens when Goofy leaves a trailer driverless when he is called back to eat breakfast.
From The Gang's All Here Series.
Prod-DISNEY Dist-WDEMCO

Micro Revolution, The C
3/4 OR 1/2 INCH VIDEO CASSETTE
Explains why silicon chips have become so important and why they are used. Provides a non-technical discussion of the new micro chip technology.
From The Audio Visual Library Of Computer Education Series.
Prod-PRISPR Dist-PRISPR

Micro 70 C 23 MIN
16MM FILM OPTICAL SOUND
Shows the role of the microscope in modern technology and provides instruction in its use.
LC NO. 75-700081
Prod-BLSOPD Dist-BLSOPD Prodn-MLC 1974

Micro-Dermagrafting Procedure C 10 MIN
16MM FILM OPTICAL SOUND PRO
Illustrates the use of the meek-wall microdermatome in the treatment of patients with severe, extensive burns where there is a need to cover a large area of burn with a small amount of donor skin. Details the technique and the results.
LC NO. FIA66-55
Prod-EATONL Dist-EATONL Prodn-AVCORP 1963

Micro-Electronics C 25 MIN
3/4 OR 1/2 INCH VIDEO CASSETTE H-C A
Discusses aspects of micro-electronics.
From The Technical Studies Series.
Prod-BBCTV Dist-FI 1981

Micro-Techniques In Serology C 8 MIN
16MM FILM OPTICAL SOUND PRO
Demonstrates the use of micro-equipment for performing serologic titration tests. Explains that the method is economical in the use of reagents and time--it enables one technologist to test 144 Sera against three antigens in an eight hour day.
LC NO. 74-705139
Prod-USPHS Dist-USNAC

Microbial Sampling Of The Operating Room Environment C 20 MIN
16MM FILM OPTICAL SOUND PRO
Counsels all personnel concerned with infection control in hospitals of facts concerning microbial sampling of the operating room environment.
From The AORN Film Series.
LC NO. 75-703021
Prod-AORN Dist-ACY 1975

Microbial Susceptibility C 29 MIN
3/4 OR 1/2 INCH VIDEO CASSETTE PRO
Details the results of a nationwide study of microbial susceptibility.
Prod-WFP Dist-WFP

Microbiology C 48 MIN
3/4 OR 1/2 INCH VIDEO CASSETTE
Includes 48 half-hour videotape lessons on aspects of microbiology.
Prod-TELSTR Dist-TELSTR

Microbiology Teaching--A Series
16MM FILM, 3/4 OR 1/2 IN VIDEO J-C
Prod-UCEMC Dist-UCEMC 1961

Anaphylaxis In Guinea Pigs 8 MIN
Cholera 3 MIN
Clinical Aspects Of Chicken Pox (Varicella) 2 MIN
Clinical Aspects Of Leprosy 4 MIN
Clinical Aspects Of Tetanus 2 MIN
Complement Fixation Test, The 5 MIN
Development Of Bacteriophage Plaques 2 MIN
Effect Of Poliomyelitis Virus On Human 5 MIN
Life Cycle Of A Bacteriophage 1 MIN
Life Cycle Of The Malaria Parasite, The 12 MIN
Measles (Rubeola) In Children 2 MIN
Phagocytosis 4 MIN
Pharmacological Testing Of New Antibiotic 2 MIN
Production Of Poliomyelitis Vaccine 12 MIN
Rabies In A Human Patient 4 MIN
Rumen Ciliate Protozoa 15 MIN
Spread Of Typhus, The 2 MIN
Surgical Removal Of Lesions In Pulmonary 2 MIN

Microbiology—A Series
16MM FILM, 3/4 OR 1/2 IN VIDEO J-H
Demonstrates that technology wedded to scientific research manipulates light and lenses to reveal the amazing complexity of single-celled organisms.
Prod-CORF Dist-CORF 1984

Classifying Microorganisms 015 MIN
Imaging A Hidden World - The Light Microscope 015 MIN

Microcomputer Applications Series, The C 30 MIN
3/4 OR 1/2 INCH VIDEO CASSETTE
See series title for descriptive statement.
From The Promedia - Microcomputer Applications Series.
Prod-DSIM Dist-DSIM

Microcomputer Basic C
3/4 OR 1/2 INCH VIDEO CASSETTE
See series title for descriptive statement.
From The Microprocessor Video Training Course Series.
Prod-VTRI Dist-VTRI

Microcomputer Basics C
3/4 OR 1/2 INCH VIDEO CASSETTE
See series title for descriptive statement.
From The Microprocessor Series.
Prod-HTHZEN Dist-HTHZEN

Microcomputer Bus Structures - Introduction C 60 MIN
3/4 OR 1/2 INCH VIDEO CASSETTE C
Covers 'why use a bus structure,' the make versus buy argument, design to market timeline, bus structure market place and the Basic Computer system utilizing bus structures.
From The Microcomputer Bus Structures Series.
Prod-NEU Dist-AMCEE

Microcomputer Bus Structures - Summary And Conclusion C 60 MIN
3/4 OR 1/2 INCH VIDEO CASSETTE C
Covers review, design considerations, selection criteria, application examples, and the market place on review.
From The Microcomputer Bus Structures Series.
Prod-NEU Dist-AMCEE

Microcomputer Bus Structures—A Series
C
Traces use of microcomputer systems in applications ranging from industrial process control to electronic data processing. Explores evolution of bus structures, why they are increasingly popular and their particular market. Includes history, advantage, description, pinouts and application areas for each bus.
Prod-NEU Dist-AMCEE

DEC Busses - Unibus And Q-Bus, The 060 MIN
Microcomputer Bus Structures - Introduction 060 MIN
Microcomputer Bus Structures - Summary And 060 MIN
Multibus, The 060 MIN
S-100 Bus, The 060 MIN
STD Bus, The 060 MIN
VME Bus, The 060 MIN

Microcomputer Example C 30 MIN
3/4 OR 1/2 INCH VIDEO CASSETTE H-C A
Reviews basics of building parsers by considering a very tiny block-structured programming language for microcomputers. Concludes with demonstration of cross-Pascal compiler for the HP64000 and an example of a recursive function for factorial evaluation.
From The Pascal, Pt 3 - Advanced Pascal Series.
LC NO. 81-706049
Prod-COLOSU Dist-COLOSU 1980

Microcomputer Executive Program, A C 45 MIN
3/4 OR 1/2 INCH VIDEO CASSETTE IND
See series title for descriptive statement.
From The Microprocessors - Fundamental Concepts And Applications Series.
Prod-ICSINT Dist-ICSINT

Microcomputer Hardware, Input/Output Methods B 60 MIN
3/4 OR 1/2 INCH VIDEO CASSETTE
See series title for descriptive statement.
From The Introduction To Microcomputers Series. Pt 5
Prod-UAZMIC Dist-UAZMIC 1978

Microcomputer Manages Information, And Some Do's And Don'ts C 40 MIN
3/4 OR 1/2 INCH VIDEO CASSETTE
Features computer experts John and Barbara McMullen acquainting new user Chip Mann with microcomputer applications such as weather forecasting, inventory management, apartment rental indexing and mailing lists. Offers tips on the proper handling of hardware and software using the Apple II as a representative computer.
Prod-STURTM Dist-STURTM 1982

Microcomputer Memory Design—A Series
IND
Offers ideas for future products and specific knowledge for design of memory circuits. Covers important theoretical and practical design aspects. Discusses problems in detail and says material applicable to any microprocessor.
Prod-COLOSU Dist-COLOSU

Advanced Memory Logic 030 MIN
Design Example Of A Complete Memory System 030 MIN
Direct Memory Access (DMA) 030 MIN
Dynamic RAMS 030 MIN
Hierarchical Memories And Some Physical 030 MIN
Magnetic Bubble Memories(MBM) 030 MIN
Memory Away, The And The Decoding Logic Of A 030 MIN
Memory Technologies, Microcomputer 030 MIN
Microprocessor And Memory Timing 030 MIN
More On Decoding Logic And Data And Address 030 MIN
Semiconductor Memory Devices 030 MIN

Microcomputer Overview B 60 MIN
3/4 OR 1/2 INCH VIDEO CASSETTE
See series title for descriptive statement.
From The Understanding Microprocessors Series. Pt 5
Prod-UAZMIC Dist-UAZMIC 1979

Microcomputer Presents And Gathers Information, The C 38 MIN
3/4 OR 1/2 INCH VIDEO CASSETTE
Features computer experts John and Barbara McMullen demonstrating how the Apple II can present visual comparisons by plotting graphs and by producing charts. Discusses word processing and explains the global search and vocabulary features. Emphasizes that microcomputers competitive with large word processors are available at a reasonable price.
Prod-STURTM Dist-STURTM 1982

Microcomputer Real-Time Executives—A Series
PRO
Covers theory and practice of operating system and use, giving a detailed, implementation-oriented study of OS concepts and principles. Emphasizes multitasking, intertask synchronization/cooperation and real-time applications. Uses classroom format to videotape 42 one-hour cassettes.
Prod-UMAEEE Dist-AMCEE

Microcomputer Software, Advanced Programming B 60 MIN
3/4 OR 1/2 INCH VIDEO CASSETTE
See series title for descriptive statement.
From The Introduction To Microcomputers Series. Pt 4
Prod-UAZMIC Dist-UAZMIC 1978

Microcomputer, The - A Tool And A Challenge C 34 MIN
3/4 OR 1/2 INCH VIDEO CASSETTE
Features computer experts John and Barbara McMullen showing friends a typical microcomputer system, including an Apple II with CRT screen, printer, and Visicalc software. Explains the usefulness to business of employing conventional telephone lines to gain access to databases throughout the country.
Prod-STURTM Dist-STURTM 1982

Microcomputer, What It Can Do And The Power Of Visicalc, The C 23 MIN
3/4 OR 1/2 INCH VIDEO CASSETTE
Features computer experts John And Barbara McMullen demonstrating to economist Chip Mann the graphics and word processing capabilities of the Apple II system using Visicalc. Shows the McMullens communicating with the databases of Dow Jones, Associated Press, and New York Times, as well as university, legal medical and insurance databases.
Prod-STURTM Dist-STURTM 1982

Microcomputers C
3/4 OR 1/2 INCH VIDEO CASSETTE
Explains the structure of microcomputers and includes pictures of the very latest equipment. Demonstrates how the different components of a microcomputer contribute to its operation, and location photographs represent the wide variety of devices available.
From The Audio Visual Library Of Computer
Prod-PRISPR Dist-PRISPR

Microcomputers C 30 MIN
3/4 OR 1/2 INCH VIDEO CASSETTE H-C A
Describes the characteristics and applications of microcomputers starting with a simplified explanation of logic circuits and going on to describe their integration on small silicon chips. Discusses bus architecture in mircrocomputers, several types of memory, and the advantages of microcomputer size, price, speed, and capacity to numerous applications.
From The Making It Count Series.
LC NO. 80-707581
Prod-BCSC Dist-BCSC 1980

Microcomputers - An Introduction C 26 MIN
16MM FILM, 3/4 OR 1/2 IN VIDEO C A
Discusses what a microcomputer is, how it works and how it can be used.
LC NO. 82-707050
Prod-ONEPAS Dist-CRMP 1982

Microcomputers - An Introduction Or The Computer And The Crook C 15 MIN
16MM FILM, 3/4 OR 1/2 IN VIDEO K-I
Shows Jeff learning how a microcomputer helps run his cousin's farm, assists in household matters and provides entertainment. Depicts how it can be used to catch a crook.
From The Simply Scientific Series.
LC NO. 82-707289
Prod-LCOA Dist-LCOA Prodn-MBROS 1982

Microcomputers - An Overview For Managers And Engineers—A Series
C
Illustrates basic elements and components of microcomputers for people with little background and for those who do not work directly with them but are affected by them. Includes software and hardware fundamentals and development and project management. Features Gene H Miller, Professor of Electrical Engineering at GMI Engineering and Management Institute.
Prod-GMIEMI Dist-AMCEE

Hardware Development 050 MIN
Hardware Fundamentals 050 MIN
Project Management 050 MIN
Software Development 050 MIN
Software Fundamentals 050 MIN
What They Are And How They're Used 050 MIN

Microcomputers - The Personal Assistant C
16MM FILM - 3/4 IN VIDEO H-C A
Looks at a computer fair, surveys microprocessor applications, visits Silicon Valley and discusses microcomputer use at home and in the office.
From The Computers At Work - Concepts And Applications Series. Module 12
Prod-BNA Dist-BNA 1983

Microcomputers - The Personal Assistant C
3/4 OR 1/2 INCH VIDEO CASSETTE
Describes a microprocessor, the components of a microcomputer system and illustrates the reasons why microcomputers are commonly used in business.
From The Computers At Work Series.
Prod-COMTEG Dist-COMTEG

Microcomputers At School—A Series

Presents the most recent information on the use of microcomputers in schools. Contains numerous sequences videotaped in actual classrooms.
Prod-EPCO Dist-EDCORP

Computer Literacy - The Fourth R
Planning And Decision Making
Using Microcomputers - An Introduction

Microcomputers For Instruction C 29 MIN
3/4 OR 1/2 INCH VIDEO CASSETTE T
Describes briefly the basics of microcomputer technology and its application in the school.
From The On And About Instruction Series.
Prod-VADE Dist-GPITVL 1983

Microcomputers In Your School C
3/4 OR 1/2 INCH VIDEO CASSETTE T
Includes three videotapes on planning, implementing and using microcomputers in the school. Discusses grade-level increase, budgeting for computers and community support.
From The School Inservice Videotape Series.
Prod-TERRAS Dist-SLOSSF

Microcosms Of The Mouth I - Technique C 14 MIN
3/4 OR 1/2 INCH VIDEO CASSETTE
Describes and demonstrates the development of new methods for study of the microbial masses adhering to the teeth and soft tissues in the mouth. Discusses improvements in photographic equipment, light sources and film.
Prod-AMDA Dist-AMDA 1961

Microcultural Incidents In Ten Zoos C 34 MIN
16MM FILM OPTICAL SOUND H-C A
Shows Professor Ray L Birdwhistell demonstrating the context control method for comparative analysis of cross-cultural situations. Short film excerpts illustrate the interaction of families' members with each other and with animals in zoos in England, France, Italy, Hong Kong, India, Japan and the United States. An epilogue illustrates observer and, particularly, cameraman biases in recording interactional data.
LC NO. 71-711892
Prod-COMPEN Dist-PSUPCR 1971

Microelectrodes In Muscle C 19 MIN
16MM FILM, 3/4 OR 1/2 IN VIDEO PRO
Shows the intracellular microelectrode technique being used to measure transmembrane potential changes. Uses a frog dissection to demonstrate that the electrical responses of an excitable cell depend upon the ionic composition of the external solution.
From The Physiology Series.
Prod-WILEYJ Dist-MEDIAG 1970

Microelectronics Explosion—A Series

Covers the nature and development of microelectronics technology and the direction it is likely to take in the future. Describes changes in products and operations.
Prod-DELTAK Dist-DELTAK

Business Applications 040 MIN
Changing Workforce, The 040 MIN
Microelectronics Technology 040 MIN

Microelectronics Technology C 40 MIN
3/4 OR 1/2 INCH VIDEO CASSETTE
Examines microelectronics technology and the impact it is having on products.
From The Microelectronics Explosion Series.
Prod-DELTAK Dist-DELTAK

Microfiche, Microfilm And Other Minutiae C 9 MIN
16MM FILM, 3/4 OR 1/2 IN VIDEO H-C A
Illustrates the use of micrographics to facilitate storage and handling of printed and graphic material in libraries and other institutions. Compares the cumbersome and wasteful storage of hardcopy with the ease and compactness of microform use. Examines microfiche, ultrafiche, aperture cards, microcopying, and computer-generated micrographics. Includes a discussion of the lack of uniformity in microform indexing.

LC NO. 81-707294
Prod-IU Dist-IU 1981

Microfilariae Of Wuchereria Bancrofti C 4 MIN
16MM FILM SILENT
Uses cinemicrography to show activity of diurnally periodic microfilariae of wuchereria bancrofti from the blood of a soldier infected in the society islands. For professional use.
From The Parasitology Series.
LC NO. FIE52-2238
Prod-USPHS Dist-USNAC 1947

Micrometer C 15 MIN
3/4 OR 1/2 INCH VIDEO CASSETTE IND
Focuses on telescope gages, caliper and hole gages.
From The Machining And The Operation Of Machine Tools, Module 1 - Basic Machine Technology Series.
Prod-LEIKID Dist-LEIKID

Micrometer (Telescope Gages, Caliper, Hole Gages) C
3/4 OR 1/2 INCH VIDEO CASSETTE
See series title for descriptive statement.
From The Basic Machine Technology Series.
Prod-VTRI Dist-VTRI

Micrometer (Telescope Gages, Caliper, Hole Gages) C 15 MIN
3/4 OR 1/2 INCH VIDEO CASSETTE
See series title for descriptive statement.
From The Machine Technology II - Engine Lathe Accessories Series.
Prod-CAMB Dist-CAMB

Micrometer (Telescope Gages, Caliper, Hole Gages) (Spanish) C
3/4 OR 1/2 INCH VIDEO CASSETTE
See series title for descriptive statement.
From The Basic Machine Technology (Spanish) Series.
Prod-VTRI Dist-VTRI

Micrometer, The B 15 MIN
16MM FILM - 3/4 IN VIDEO
Shows various types of micrometers, how to use and care for the instrument, how to read the barrel and thimble scales and how to check the accuracy of readings. Issued in 1941 as a motion picture.
From The Machine Shop Work - Precision Measurement Series. No. 2
LC NO. 79-707076
Prod-USOE Dist-USNAC Prodn-LNS 1979

Micrometer, The (Spanish) B 15 MIN
16MM FILM OPTICAL SOUND
Explains the care, use and maintenance of micrometers.
From The Machine Shop Work Series.
LC NO. FIE62-71
Prod-USOE Dist-USNAC 1941

Micrometer, The (Spanish) B 15 MIN
3/4 OR 1/2 INCH VIDEO CASSETTE
Explains the care, use and maintenance of micrometers.
From The Machine Shop Work - Precision Measurement Series.
Prod-USOE Dist-USNAC 1941

Microorganisms - Beneficial Activities C 15 MIN
16MM FILM, 3/4 OR 1/2 IN VIDEO H-C A
Contrasts various related activities of microorganisms. Indicates by animation that only a small number of all microorganisms are harmful while much greater numbers are beneficial. Shows the means whereby microorganisms produce change in their environment and cause the formation of new substances.
From The Bacteriology Series.
LC NO. 80-707043
Prod-IU Dist-IU 1958

Microorganisms - Beneficial Activities (Arabic) C 15 MIN
16MM FILM, 3/4 OR 1/2 IN VIDEO H-C A
Contrasts various related activities of microorganisms. Indicates by animation that only a small number of all all microorganisms are harmful while much greater numbers are beneficial. Shows the means whereby microorganisms produce change in their environment and cause the formation of new substances.
From The Bacteriology Series.
Prod-IU Dist-IU 1958

Microorganisms - Harmful Activities C 15 MIN
16MM FILM, 3/4 OR 1/2 IN VIDEO H-C A
Presents some of the methods developed for protection against disease and against undesirable decomposition of foods. Through animation explains how bacteria produce enzymes and toxic waste products which may cause disease and decomposition.
From The Bacteriology Series.
LC NO. 80-707044
Prod-IU Dist-IU 1958

Microorganisms In The Health Care Setting C 15 MIN
16MM FILM - 3/4 IN VIDEO H-C A
Presents general concepts of microbiology, including characteristics of microorganisms and ways to control them in a health care facility.
From The Basic Procedures For The Paramedical Employee Series.
LC NO. 80-707005
Prod-COPI Dist-COPI 1969

Microorganisms Of Gas Gangrene C 9 MIN
16MM FILM SILENT
Shows species of clostridium causing gas gangrene, the morphological characteristics of these bacteria, and studies of the bacteria in various cultures.
LC NO. FIE54-115
Prod-USPHS Dist-USNAC 1954

Microorganisms That Cause Disease C 11 MIN
16MM FILM, 3/4 OR 1/2 IN VIDEO J-H
Presents five kinds of pathogenic microorganisms, including fungi, bacteria, viruses, rickettsiae and protozoa. Explains that the organisms cause infectious diseases through destruction of cells.
Prod-CORF Dist-CORF 1960

Micropack C 10 MIN
16MM FILM OPTICAL SOUND
Uses closeups and microscope photography to show various aspects of design, manufacture and packaging of the new breed of integrated circuits. Shows the potential uses of these circuits in computers.
LC NO. 77-702108
Prod-HONEYW Dist-HONIS 1977

Microprocessing Interfacing–A Series
PRO
Introduces the theory and practice of microprocessor interfacing. Covers grounding and shielding techniques, transmission lines, busing, interrupt signaling, serial and parallel I/O, protocols for the IEEE-488 bus, magnetic tape storage techniques and floppy disk controllers.
Prod-AMCEE Dist-AMCEE

Busing, Pt 1	043 MIN
Busing, Pt 2	043 MIN
Grounding And Shielding, Pt 1	043 MIN
Grounding And Shielding, Pt 2	043 MIN
Magnetic Disk Interfacing, Pt 1	043 MIN
Magnetic Disk Interfacing, Pt, 2	043 MIN
Magnetic Tape Interfacing, Pt 1	043 MIN
Magnetic Tape Interfacing, Pt 2	043 MIN
Parallel Interfacing, Pt 1	043 MIN
Parallel Interfacing, Pt 2	043 MIN
Serial Interfacing, Pt 1	043 MIN
Serial Interfacing, Pt 2	043 MIN

Microprocessor - Computer On A Chip C 13 MIN
16MM FILM, 3/4 OR 1/2 IN VIDEO
Traces the development of the microprocessor from early man's attempts to count and keep time. Discusses the key components, which are reviewed and compared to the computer.
Prod-FORDFL Dist-FORDFL

Microprocessor And Memory Timing C 30 MIN
3/4 OR 1/2 INCH VIDEO CASSETTE IND
Discusses read and write cycle timing of memory devices, microprocessor memory cycle timing analysis, and timing examples for 8080 and 6800.
From The Microcomputer Memory Design Series.
Prod-COLOSU Dist-COLOSU

Microprocessor Applications - Communications Design C 30 MIN
3/4 OR 1/2 INCH VIDEO CASSETTE PRO
Discusses problems of digital communications and describes cost-effective hardware solutions using microprocessors. Describes typical system using one of today's better known chip sets.
From The Designing With Microprocessors Series.
Prod-TXINLC Dist-TXINLC

Microprocessor Applications - Other Terminal Functions C 30 MIN
3/4 OR 1/2 INCH VIDEO CASSETTE PRO
Uses general purpose video terminal to illustrate benefits of microprocessors in improving capabilities of interactive terminals.
From The Designing With Microprocessors Series.
Prod-TXINLC Dist-TXINLC

Microprocessor Applications - Point Of Sale Terminals C 30 MIN
3/4 OR 1/2 INCH VIDEO CASSETTE PRO
Defines requirements of POS terminal and discusses advantages of certain chip sets for this application. Analyzes design of a specific terminal using a microprocessor.
From The Designing With Microprocessors Series.
Prod-TXINLC Dist-TXINLC

Microprocessor Architecture I C 45 MIN
3/4 OR 1/2 INCH VIDEO CASSETTE IND
See series title for descriptive statement.
From The Management Of Microprocessor Technology Series.
Prod-ICSINT Dist-ICSINT

Microprocessor Architecture I C 50 MIN
3/4 OR 1/2 INCH VIDEO CASSETTE
Discusses software and hardware, conceptualizing buzz words, computer data structure, memory types, computer operations and system organization.
From The Management Of Microprocessor Technology Series.
Prod-MIOT Dist-MIOT

Microprocessor Architecture II C 45 MIN
3/4 OR 1/2 INCH VIDEO CASSETTE IND
See series title for descriptive statement.
From The Management Of Microprocessor Technology Series.
Prod-ICSINT Dist-ICSINT

Microprocessor Architecture II C 49 MIN
3/4 OR 1/2 INCH VIDEO CASSETTE
Discusses instruction sets, interfacing to the real world input/output, interrupts, direct memory access, peripheral chips and hardware trends in microprocessor architecture.
From The Management Of Microprocessor Technology Series.
Prod-MIOT Dist-MIOT

Microprocessor Background Via Digital Computer System Architecture C 30 MIN
3/4 OR 1/2 INCH VIDEO CASSETTE PRO
Explores digital computer system architecture as a basis for understanding microprocessors. Discusses peripheral controllers, distributed networks, and direct memory access channels.
From The Designing With Microprocessors Series.
Prod-TXINLC Dist-TXINLC

Microprocessor Based Product Opportunities C 45 MIN
3/4 OR 1/2 INCH VIDEO CASSETTE IND
See series title for descriptive statement.
From The Management Of Microprocessor Technology Series.
Prod-ICSINT Dist-ICSINT

Microprocessor Bus Timing C 45 MIN
3/4 OR 1/2 INCH VIDEO CASSETTE IND
See series title for descriptive statement.
From The Microprocessors - Fundamental Concepts And Applications Series.
Prod-ICSINT Dist-ICSINT

Microprocessor Chip Architecture C 30 MIN
3/4 OR 1/2 INCH VIDEO CASSETTE PRO
Surveys chips and chip sets architectural types available. Groups architectural types to simplify selection process. Provides guidelines for selection of proper chip architecture for particular applications.
From The Designing With Microprocessors Series.
Prod-TXINLC Dist-TXINLC

Microprocessor Chip Fabrication C 30 MIN
3/4 OR 1/2 INCH VIDEO CASSETTE PRO
Examines major fabrication technologies in use today, their advantages and disadvantages. Enables designer to acquire insight into selection of right technology for specific applications. Gives background on Schottky TTL, ECL, PMOS, NMOS, CMOS, SOS and revolutionary new I-squared L.
From The Designing With Microprocessors Series.
Prod-TXINLC Dist-TXINLC

Microprocessor CPU Hardware Concepts And Signals C 45 MIN
3/4 OR 1/2 INCH VIDEO CASSETTE IND
See series title for descriptive statement.
From The Microprocessors - Fundamental Concepts And Applications Series.
Prod-ICSINT Dist-ICSINT

Microprocessor Fundamentals For Decision Makers–A Series
IND
Presents microprocessor technology in a manner requiring little or no technical sophistication on part of student. Imparts sufficient microprocessor vocabulary/terminology to enable student to participate intelligently in microprocessor based design discussions. Relates to managers, students, engineers and technicians involved in any way with microprocessor use or application.
Prod-NCSU Dist-AMCEE

Applications	060 MIN
Basic Architecture	060 MIN
History	060 MIN
Input/Output	060 MIN
Management Of Processors	060 MIN
Program Conception/Development	060 MIN
Selection Of Hardware/Software	060 MIN
Why Switch To Computers	060 MIN

Microprocessor In Avionics, The C 30 MIN
3/4 OR 1/2 INCH VIDEO CASSETTE PRO
Develops general problems encountered in avionics and offers improved solutions through use of microprocessors. Studies a specific hardware and software problem using one of today's advanced bit-slice architecture.
From The Designing With Microprocessors Series.
Prod-TXINLC Dist-TXINLC

Microprocessor Instruction Sets C 30 MIN
3/4 OR 1/2 INCH VIDEO CASSETTE PRO
Describes various instruction sets, grouped by categories. Studies examples to provide in-depth understanding of selection process. Enables engineer to develop a software package for his specific application.
From The Designing With Microprocessors Series.
Prod-TXINLC Dist-TXINLC

Microprocessor Interface Design C 30 MIN
3/4 OR 1/2 INCH VIDEO CASSETTE PRO
Studies solutions to interface design problems. Explores problems encountered in interfacing microprocessors with equipments. Describes devices currently available to solve various interface problems.
From The Designing With Microprocessors Series.
Prod-TXINLC Dist-TXINLC

Microprocessor Interfacing B 50 MIN
3/4 OR 1/2 INCH VIDEO CASSETTE
See series title for descriptive statement.
From The Microprocessors And Applications Series. Pt 6
Prod-UAZMIC Dist-UAZMIC 1976

Microprocessor Interfacing–A Series
C
Discusses aspects of microprocessor interfacing.
LC NO. 81-706199
Prod-AMCEE Dist-AMCEE 1980

Busing, Pt 1	035 MIN
Busing, Pt 2	035 MIN
Grounding And Shielding, Pt 1	035 MIN
Grounding And Shielding, Pt 2	035 MIN
Magnetic Disk Interfacing, Pt 1	035 MIN
Magnetic Disk Interfacing, Pt 2	035 MIN
Magnetic Tape Interfacing, Pt 1	035 MIN
Magnetic Tape Interfacing, Pt 2	035 MIN

Parallel Interfacing, Pt 1 035 MIN
Parallel Interfacing, Pt 2 035 MIN
Serial Interfacing, Pt 1 035 MIN
Serial Interfacing, Pt 2 035 MIN

Microprocessor Interfacing—A Series
IND
Deals in hands-on-fashion with busing and interfacing techniques for computer systems. Features Dr Harold S Stone, Professor of Electronic and Computer Engineering at the University of Massachusetts. Emphasizes principles, implementation and demonstration.
Prod-ICSINT Dist-ICSINT

Busing, Part 1 045 MIN
Busing, Part 2 045 MIN
Grounding And Shielding, Part 1 045 MIN
Grounding And Shielding, Part 2 045 MIN
Magnetic Disk Interfacing, Part 1 045 MIN
Magnetic Disk Interfacing, Part 2 045 MIN
Magnetic Tape Interfacing, Part 1 045 MIN
Magnetic Tape Interfacing, Part 2 045 MIN
Parallel Interfacing, Part 1 045 MIN
Parallel Interfacing, Part 2 045 MIN
Serial Interfacing, Part 1 045 MIN
Serial Interfacing, Part 2 045 MIN

Microprocessor Interfacing—A Series

Provides an introduction to the theory and practice of microprocessor interfacing.
Prod-MIOT Dist-MIOT

Busing, Pt 1 043 MIN
Busing, Pt 2 033 MIN
Grounding And Shielding, Pt 1 038 MIN
Grounding And Shielding, Pt 2 046 MIN
Magnetic Disc Interfacing, Pt 1 048 MIN
Magnetic Disc Interfacing, Pt 2 044 MIN
Magnetic Tape Interfacing, Pt 1 045 MIN
Magnetic Tape Interfacing, Pt 2 045 MIN
Parallel Interfacing, Pt 1 042 MIN
Parallel Interfacing, Pt 2 044 MIN
Serial Interfacing, Pt 1 048 MIN
Serial Interfacing, Pt 2 041 MIN

Microprocessor Programming B 50 MIN
3/4 OR 1/2 INCH VIDEO CASSETTE
See series title for descriptive statement.
From The Microprocessors And Applications Series. Pt 4
Prod-UAZMIC Dist-UAZMIC 1976

Microprocessor Programming (Continued) B 50 MIN
3/4 OR 1/2 INCH VIDEO CASSETTE
See series title for descriptive statement.
From The Microprocessors And Applications Series. Pt 5
Prod-UAZMIC Dist-UAZMIC 1976

Microprocessor Video Training Course—A Series

Covers all aspects of microprocessor training, offering the theory and hands-on skill training. Presents microprocessor concepts in plain, easy-to-understand language, reinforced with simple to follow instructions.
Prod-VTRI Dist-VTRI

Computer Math
Interfacing Basics
Interfacing Peripheral Adapters
Interfacing RAMS/Displays
Interfacing Switches
Introduction To Programming/Algorithms
Introduction To Programming/Branching
Microcomputer Basic
Numbers Systems And Codes
Sixty-Eight Hundred I/0
Sixty-Eight Hundred Microprocessor
Sixty-Eight Hundred MPU Stack

Microprocessor—A Series

Covers microprocessor theory and operation, computer arithmetic, programming and interfacing.
Prod-HTHZEN Dist-HTHZEN

Computer Math
Interfacing Basics
Interfacing Peripheral Adaptors
Interfacing RAMS, Displays
Interfacing Switches
Introduction To Programming, Algorithms
Introduction To Programming, Branching
Microcomputer Basics
Number Systems And Codes
Sixty-Eight Hundred I, O Operations, Interrupts
Sixty-Eight Hundred Microprocessor
Sixty-Eight Hundred Stack Operations,

Microprocessor-Based Product Opportunities C 56 MIN
3/4 OR 1/2 INCH VIDEO CASSETTE
Discusses the low, medium and high volume product areas and active industrial and consumer product areas in microprocessor technology.
From The Management Of Microprocessor Technology Series.
Prod-MIOT Dist-MIOT

Microprocessors C
16MM FILM - 3/4 IN VIDEO IND
Teaches digital control techniques, data transfer and direct digital control system maintenance and troubleshooting. Explains diagnostic software and troubleshooting a distributed system.
From The Instrumentation Maintenance Series.
Prod-ISA Dist-ISA

Microprocessors - Fundamental Concepts And Applications—A Series
IND
Deals with both microprocessor hardware and software, with emphasis on programming concepts, and is presented by Christoper E Strangio of MIT Proceeds from concepts in digital electronics through basics programming, systems, interfacing and applications.
Prod-ICSINT Dist-ICSINT

Algorithms, Flowcharts Program Planning 045 MIN
Arithmentic Subroutines 045 MIN
Characteristics Of The INTEL 8080 045 MIN
Comparative Evaluation Of Microprocessor 045 MIN
Debugging And Use Of The MMD-1 045 MIN
Fundamental Computer Concepts I 045 MIN
Fundamental Computer Concepts II 045 MIN
Hardware Configurations Of A Typical 045 MIN
I/O Interfacing I 045 MIN
I/O Interfacing II 045 MIN
Interrupts 045 MIN
Introduction 045 MIN
Microcomputer Executive Program, A 045 MIN
Microprocessor Bus Timing 045 MIN
Microprocessor CPU Hardware Concepts 045 MIN
Real-Time Microcomputer Applications I 045 MIN
Real-Time Microcomputer Applications II 045 MIN
Real-Time Microcomputer Applications III 045 MIN
Simple Programming Example, A 045 MIN
Stack Architecture, Subroutines 045 MIN

Microprocessors And Applications—A Series

Presents a general introduction to microprocessors, including their pros and cons as well as specific laboratory experience with the MOS Technology microprocessor. Emphasizes interfacing microprocessor with low power SCHOTTKY TTL logic and programming microprocessors to meet flexible product specifications. Explains how to make the necessary tradeoffs between hardware and software, how to understand the cost factors in design, and how to implement a small microprocessor- based design, including both the hardware and software.
Prod-UAZMIC Dist-UAZMIC 1976

Microprocessor Interfacing 050 MIN
Microprocessor Programming 050 MIN
Microprocessor Programming (Continued) 050 MIN
Microprocessors In The Marketplace, Number 050 MIN
Number Systems (Continued), Review, 050 MIN
Review, Microprocessor Architecture (Continued) 050 MIN

Microprocessors And Digital-Systems - Introduction C
16MM FILM - 3/4 IN VIDEO IND
Introduces digital basics, memory devices and microprocessor programming. Explains digital logic AND, OR, NOT, NAND, NOR and binary numbering systems. Presents digital test equipment, combinational and sequential logic. Deals with troubleshooting - test programs, single-stepping, timing diagrams, logic analyzers.
From The Instrumentation Maintenance Series.
Prod-ISA Dist-ISA

Microprocessors And Small Digital Computers—A Series

Provides a comprehensive introduction to small digital computer systems, including hardware, software, interfacing and peripherals for microcomputers and minicomputers. Surveys microcomputer and minicomputer families and the effect of different instruction sets on system design, programming, interface logic, hardware/software tradeoffs and prototype development systems. A short course consisting of 24 tapes.
Prod-UAZMIC Dist-UAZMIC 1978

Microprocessors For Monitoring And Control—A Series
IND
Shows engineers and scientists how to use a microprocessor for monitoring and control in a videotaped short course of fourteen lessons on sixteen tapes. Uses an MST-80B Microcomputer training device plus design examples and implementation on the trainer.
Prod-COLOSU Dist-COLOSU

Algorithmic State Machine Chart, The 030 MIN
Class-3 Machines, Class-4 Machines 030 MIN
Development Of Boolean Equations From ASM 030 MIN
Frequency-Counter Design, A - State 000, 030 MIN
Frequency-Counter Design, A - State 000, 030 MIN
Introduction - Binary And Octal Numbers 030 MIN
Introduction To The 8080 - Instructions For 030 MIN
Logic Modules - Task Description Using An 030 MIN
Logical Or Boolean Expressions - Table 030 MIN
More On Agorithms 030 MIN
More On Map Representations - Map-Entered 030 MIN
Program Execution - A Grey Code-Counter 030 MIN
Simple Time-Interval Measurement System, A 030 MIN
Simple Time-Interval Measurement System, A 030 MIN
State Machine, The - Definition Of Input And 030 MIN
Table Representations Of The Next State 030 MIN

Microprocessors In Automotive Applications C 30 MIN
3/4 OR 1/2 INCH VIDEO CASSETTE PRO
Explores unique requirements of automotive field. Describes how a microprocessor can be used in numerous applications requiring a comparatively sophisticated controller. Examines one subsystem in detail and relates the bit-slice architecture solution to four others.
From The Designing With Microprocessors Series.
Prod-TXINLC Dist-TXINLC

Microprocessors In Controllers C 30 MIN
3/4 OR 1/2 INCH VIDEO CASSETTE PRO
Describes various forms of control systems and how microprocessors meet their needs. Shows by examples three types of applications ranging from a simplified controller to a complex programmable sequence, with feedback, that can be controlled by a central computer.
From The Designing With Microprocessors Series.
Prod-TXINLC Dist-TXINLC

Microprocessors In The Marketplace, Number Systems B 50 MIN
3/4 OR 1/2 INCH VIDEO CASSETTE
See series title for descriptive statement.
From The Microprocessors And Applications Series. Pt 1
Prod-UAZMIC Dist-UAZMIC 1976

Micropuncture Of Cells By U V Microbeam B 10 MIN
16MM FILM OPTICAL SOUND PRO
Studies anatomy at the cellular level, using phase-contrast and time-lapse photo-microscopy. Examines the effect of irradiation at the cellular level and points out that the results obtained from controlled irradiation are of considerable help in furthering knowledge of cellular physiology.
Prod-SQUIBB Dist-SQUIBB

Micros And The Arts C 30 MIN
3/4 OR 1/2 INCH VIDEO CASSETTE
Focuses on computer courseware available in the arts, especially music and the visual arts. Shows how computer skills can become an integral part of arts education.
From The Ready Or Not Series.
Prod-NCSDPI Dist-PCATEL

Micros And The Writing Process C 30 MIN
3/4 OR 1/2 INCH VIDEO CASSETTE
Focuses on integrating the use of microcomputers and communications skills. Shows programs that teach writing rather than simple word processing.
From The Ready Or Not Series.
Prod-NCSDPI Dist-PCATEL

Micros For Managers - Software—A Series
IND
Gives detailed analysis of software development life cycle, sample programs and impetus behind BASIC, FORTRAN, Pascal, Ada and LISP. Shows concrete examples of key microcomputer topics and recommends approaches for objectives leading to better management decisions.
Prod-COLOSU Dist-COLOSU

Background And Definitions 030 MIN
Intro Ada 030 MIN
Intro BASIC 030 MIN
Intro FORTRAN And Pascal 030 MIN
Intro LISP 030 MIN
Operating Systems 030 MIN
Structured Programming And Software Maintenance 030 MIN
Trade-Offs And Future Trends 030 MIN

Microscope - Making It Big C 28 MIN
16MM FILM, 3/4 OR 1/2 IN VIDEO H-C A
Traces the development of the microscope from the magnifying glass to the world's most powerful microscope. Shows how microscopes permit surgeons to perform delicate eye operations and neurosurgery, and a seven-ton electron microscope can take pictures of atomic structures.
LC NO. 83-706240
Prod-CANBC Dist-FLMLIB 1982

Microscope And The Prayer Shawl, The B 30 MIN
16MM FILM OPTICAL SOUND
Tells the story of Waldemar Haffkine, a scientist who, because he refused to convert to Christianity, was not permitted to continue his research in his native Russia. Discusses his discovery to a vaccine against cholera when he was invited to France to work with Louis Pasteur. (Kinescope)
Prod-JTS Dist-NAAJS Prodn-NBCTV 1954

Microscope, The C 15 MIN
16MM FILM, 3/4 OR 1/2 IN VIDEO
Describes the theory of darkfield illumination, which involves diffraction of light around the edges of a backlighted object. Deals with the theory and use of special darkfield condensers to show how modern compound microscopes are adapted for darkfield observation of specimens. Shows the preparation of a microscope slide using an oral specimen containing the spirochete and procedures for setting up and focusing the microscope.
From The Darkfield Microscopy Series. Part 1
Prod-USNHET Dist-USNAC 1978

Microscope, The C 15 MIN
3/4 INCH VIDEO CASSETTE I
Demonstrates how a microscope is constructed and how it is used.
From The Search For Science (2nd Ed.) Unit III - The Micro-World Series.
Prod-WVIZTV Dist-GPITVL

Microscope, The - How To Use It B 9 MIN
16MM FILM OPTICAL SOUND J-H A
Describes the basic parts and the correct use of the standard microscope used by students. Illustrates similarities between this basic instrument and highly specialized research microscopes.
LC NO. FIA67-1722
Prod-IOWA Dist-IOWA 1967

Microscope, The - Passport To The Miniworld C 15 MIN
16MM FILM, 3/4 OR 1/2 IN VIDEO I-H
Describes the different types of microscopes and provides a step-by-step demonstration of proper care and use of these instruments. Explains the preparation of a sample and the process of staining.
Prod-HANDEL Dist-HANDEL 1979

Microscopic Look At Digestion C 21 MIN
3/4 OR 1/2 INCH VIDEO CASSETTE
Reveals the processes of digestion using time lapse and macrophotography, models and drawings. Includes examples of enzymes, fat particles, starch granules and protein fibers.
Prod-BANDER Dist-BANDER

Microscopic Plants B 20 MIN
2 INCH VIDEOTAPE I
See series title for descriptive statement.
From The Science Room Series.
Prod-MCETV Dist-GPITVL Prodn-WVIZTV

Microscopic Pond Life C 15 MIN
3/4 OR 1/2 INCH VIDEO CASSETTE I-J
Demonstrates that microscopic life is complex despite its smallness. Shows amoeba, paramecia and volvox.
From The Animals And Such Series. Module Blue - Habitats
Prod-WHROTV Dist-AITECH 1972

Microscopic Vasovasotomy C 30 MIN
16MM FILM OPTICAL SOUND
Presents Dr Sherman J Silber, who shows microsurgery techniques used to reanastomose the vas deferens. Features his answers to questions from a panel of three urologists and a moderator.
LC NO. 76-702602
Prod-EATONL Dist-EATONL Prodn-NWMOTV

Microscopy B 30 MIN
2 INCH VIDEOTAPE J
See series title for descriptive statement.
From The Investigating The World Of Science, Unit 2 - Energy Within Living Systems Series.
Prod-MPATI Dist-GPITVL

Microsecond C 5 MIN
16MM FILM OPTICAL SOUND
Uses a variety of techniques, including the split screen, kinestasis film, time lapse photography and animation, to define the term microsecond.
Prod-SLFP Dist-SLFP

Microstructure Of Steels - Ferrite, Pearlite And Bainite C 50 MIN
3/4 OR 1/2 INCH VIDEO CASSETTE PRO
Describes the microstructure of steels. Recounts the development of the iron-iron carbide diagram.
From The Heat Treatment - Metallurgy And Application Series.
Prod-AMCEE Dist-AMCEE

Microsurgery C 27 MIN
16MM FILM, 3/4 OR 1/2 IN VIDEO C A
Follows step-by-step the design of new microsurgical instruments, the training of surgeons to use them to make minute stitches and the performance of a life-prolonging operation upon a man's brain.
From The Perspective Series.
Prod-LONTVS Dist-STNFLD

Microsurgery For Accidents C 19 MIN
3/4 OR 1/2 INCH VIDEO CASSETTE
Gives a surgeon's eye-view of limb and digit replantations as well as microvascular free tissue transplantation.
Prod-SPRVER Dist-SPRVER

Microteaching C 28 MIN
16MM FILM OPTICAL SOUND T
Presents a preliminary teaching experience. Explores training effects under controlled conditions.
Prod-EDUC Dist-EDUC

Microvascular Surgery - Clinical Case Examples C 30 MIN
3/4 OR 1/2 INCH VIDEO CASSETTE PRO
Demonstrates of microvascular surgery experiences of surgeons throughout the world by Dr Harry J Buncke. Part two of a three part series.
Prod-ASSH Dist-ASSH

Microvascular Surgery - Demonstration Of Technique C 60 MIN
3/4 OR 1/2 INCH VIDEO CASSETTE PRO
Shows the operating field as Dr Harry J Buncke conducts an experimental microvascular surgery. Final part of a three part series.
Prod-ASSH Dist-ASSH

Microvascular Surgery - History And Technique C 35 MIN
3/4 OR 1/2 INCH VIDEO CASSETTE PRO
Reviews the history and techniques of microvascular surgery as presented by Dr Harry J Buncke. Part one of a series.
Prod-ASSH Dist-ASSH

Microwave Landing System C 15 MIN
3/4 OR 1/2 INCH VIDEO CASSETTE C
Explains how a Microwave Landing System (MLS) functions, and highlights advantages over conventional Instrument Landing System (ILS). Provides explanation of MLS techniques known as Time Reference Scanning Beam (TRSB) which will serve all aviation well into the next century.
Prod-FAAFL Dist-AVIMA

Microwave Landing Systems C 16 MIN
16MM FILM, 3/4 OR 1/2 IN VIDEO A
Examines the functions of new microwave landing systems and highlights the advantages of these systems over conventional instrument landing systems.
LC NO. 82-707232
Prod-USFAA Dist-USNAC 1976

Microwave Optics - An Introduction B 13 MIN
16MM FILM OPTICAL SOUND C
Dr James Meyer, using a small tungsten filament lamp as a director, demonstrates the polarity of microwaves, determines the wavelength, and shows the interference pattern of 2-slits and focusing effects of glass and pitch lenses. Describes a crystal detector, and illustrates how it is used to determine the polarization of radiation scattered from the tungsten lamp.
From The College Physics Film Program Series.
LC NO. FIA68-3022
Prod-EDS Dist-MLA 1968

Microwave Oscillators - Reflex Klystrons B 20 MIN
16MM FILM - 3/4 IN VIDEO
Describes the characteristics, components, and operation of reflex klystron tubes used as local oscillators in radar receiving systems. Issued in 1965 as a motion picture.
LC NO. 79-707775
Prod-USA Dist-USNAC 1979

Microwave Oven, The C 11 MIN
16MM FILM, 3/4 OR 1/2 IN VIDEO A
Shows how a wide variety of foods can be heated quickly and efficiently in the microwave oven. Explains the differences between microwave heating and conventional oven heating. Covers all factors affecting microwave oven heating time, including food thickness, density, temperature, quantity, shape and oven power.
From The Professional Food Preparation And Service Programs Series.
Prod-NEM Dist-NEM

Microworld C 50 MIN
16MM FILM, 3/4 OR 1/2 IN VIDEO H-C A
Discusses Britain's attempt to compete with America and Japan in microchip technology.
Prod-BBCTV Dist-FI 1984

Mid-Atlantic States, The C 27 MIN
16MM FILM, 3/4 OR 1/2 IN VIDEO I-J
Explores the states of New York, New Jersey, Pennsylvania, Delaware, Maryland and Washington, DC which contain mountains, valleys, rivers, harbors, bountiful farms and burgeoning metropolitan areas.
From The United States Geography Series.
Prod-NGS Dist-NGS 1983

Mid-Atlantic States, The C 30 MIN
16MM FILM, 3/4 OR 1/2 IN VIDEO I-C
Edited from the motion picture These States. Features the battles, places of reverence and historical figures of New York, New Jersey, Pennsylvania, Delaware and Maryland. Includes scenes of Saratoga, Fort Ticonderoga, Valley Forge and Annapolis.
Prod-BCTOS Dist-FI 1975

Mid-East Power Politics C
16MM FILM OPTICAL SOUND
Features the director general of Israel's ministry of foreign affairs, Ambassador Mordechai Gazit, who evaluates Soviet involvement in the Middle East and America's 25 years of friendship with his country.
From The Dateline Israel, 1973 Series.
Prod-ADL Dist-ADL

Mid-Latitude Climates, The C 20 MIN
3/4 INCH VIDEO CASSETTE H-C
See series title for descriptive statement.
From The Geography For The '70's Series.
Prod-KLRNTV Dist-GPITVL

Mid-Torso Of Inez, The B 26 MIN
3/4 OR 1/2 INCH VIDEO CASSETTE
Portrays in a dreamlike manner mysterious incidents in the early life of Grandfather, as told to his granddaughter, Lois Ann, at a family dinner at which he is apparently an unwelcome guest. An experimental film.
Prod-MEDIPR Dist-MEDIPR 1979

Middle Age Blues, The C 49 MIN
16MM FILM OPTICAL SOUND
Examines the lives, careers and attitudes of two men in middle age, pointing out that middle age can be a time for change and a reconsideration of life's goals.
LC NO. 75-702655
Prod-RKOTV Dist-SSC 1975

Middle Ages, The C 30 MIN
16MM FILM OPTICAL SOUND
Traces the history of the Christian church during the Middle Ages, focusing on its corruption by political power and materialism. Based on the book How Should We Then Live by Francis A Schaeffer.
From The How Should We Then Live Series. No. 2
LC NO. 77-702364
Prod-GF Dist-GF 1977

Middle Ages, The C 31 MIN
16MM FILM, 3/4 OR 1/2 IN VIDEO H-C
Traces the social, economic and cultural development of Western Europe during the Middle Ages.
From The Outline History Of Europe Series.
LC NO. 80-706989
Prod-POLNIS Dist-IFB 1976

Middle Ages, The (Dutch) C 30 MIN
16MM FILM OPTICAL SOUND
Traces the history of the Christian church during the Middle Ages, focusing on its corruption by political power and materialism. Based on the book How Should We Then Live by Francis A Schaeffer.
From The How Should We Then Live (Dutch) Series. No. 2
LC NO. 77-702364
Prod-GF Dist-GF 1977

Middle Ages, The (Swedish) C 31 MIN
16MM FILM, 3/4 OR 1/2 IN VIDEO H-C A
Traces the social, economic and cultural development of western Europe, emphasizing the life of the people during the Middle Ages.
Prod-IFB Dist-IFB 1973

Middle Ages, The - A Wanderer's Guide To Life And Letters C 27 MIN
16MM FILM, 3/4 OR 1/2 IN VIDEO J-C A
Describes the atmosphere of the Middle Ages through enactment of excerpts from the literature of the period.
Prod-SCNDRI Dist-LCOA 1971

Middle Ages, The - A Wanderer's Guide To Life And Letters (Spanish) C 27 MIN
16MM FILM, 3/4 OR 1/2 IN VIDEO J-C A
Features excerpts from such stories as Everyman, Dante's Love Sonnets and The Wife Of Bath.
Prod-SCNDRI Dist-LCOA 1971

Middle Ages, The - Culture Of Medieval Europe (Ed Ver) C 24 MIN
16MM FILM, 3/4 OR 1/2 IN VIDEO J-H
Prod-NBCTV Dist-EBEC 1966

Middle Ages, The - Rise Of Feudalism (Ed Ver) C 20 MIN
16MM FILM, 3/4 OR 1/2 IN VIDEO J-H
Prod-NBCTV Dist-EBEC 1966

Middle And Long Distances C 4 MIN
16MM FILM SILENT
Shows female athletes competing in middle and long distance events, including Tabb, Larrieu, Olizaryenko, Mineyeva and Providokhina.
Prod-TRACKN Dist-TRACKN 1982

Middle Atlantic Region, The C 17 MIN
16MM FILM, 3/4 OR 1/2 IN VIDEO J
Examines the people, industry, economy and landscape of the Middle Atlantic region of the United States.
From The U S Geography Series.
Prod-MGHT Dist-MGHT 1976

Middle Distance Running C 12 MIN
16MM FILM, 3/4 OR 1/2 IN VIDEO H-C A
Presents a 3,000-meter race featuring world class middle distance runners. Shows middle distance training exercises.
From The Athletics Series.
LC NO. 80-706584
Prod-GSAVL Dist-IU 1980

Middle Distance Running C 42 MIN
1/2 IN VIDEO CASSETTE BETA/VHS
See series title for descriptive statement.
From The Women's Track And Field Series.
Prod-MOHOMV Dist-MOHOMV

Middle Distance Running C 42 MIN
1/2 IN VIDEO CASSETTE BETA/VHS A
Presents Dr Ken Foreman's holistic preparation of middle distance runners, which includes time spent in off-track training programs.
Prod-RMI Dist-RMI

Middle Distances C 4 MIN
16MM FILM SILENT
Presents male athletes competing in middle distance events, including Coghlan, Scott, Walker, Flynn, Padilla, Ovett, Maree, Byers and Wessinghage.
Prod-TRACKN Dist-TRACKN 1982

Middle Ear Infection C 8 MIN
3/4 OR 1/2 INCH VIDEO CASSETTE
Explains middle ear infections and counters misconceptions patients may have. Describes treatment and signs that indicate the need to call a doctor.
From The Take Care Of Yourself Series.
Prod-UARIZ Dist-UARIZ

Middle Ear Infections C 11 MIN
16MM FILM, 3/4 OR 1/2 IN VIDEO A
Describes the anatomy and function of the middle ear and eustachian tube. Examines causes and treatment of middle ear infections and fluid in the ear. Includes information on myringotomy, adenoidectomy, drugs, ventilating tubes and home care.
Prod-PRORE Dist-PRORE

Middle East 1967 C 20 MIN
16MM FILM OPTICAL SOUND
Shows various aspects of the emergency relief work of the International Committee of the Red Cross following the outbreak of the 1967 Middle East war.
Prod-ICRCRS Dist-AMRC 1967

Middle East—A Series
16MM FILM, 3/4 OR 1/2 IN VIDEO I-H
Introduces the lifestyles, customs and values of the Middle Eastern peoples.
Prod-BIBICF Dist-CORF

Middle East, The - Building A Dream (Israel) 28 MIN
Middle East, The - Leadership And Identity 28 MIN
Middle East, The - Mosaic Of Peoples (An 28 MIN
Middle East, The - Oil And Sudden Wealth 28 MIN

Middle East, Journey Into The Future C 15 MIN
16MM FILM, 3/4 OR 1/2 IN VIDEO I-H
Tells the story of a Middle Eastern village farmer in order to show the hardships encountered by a culture whose people are forced to move suddenly from the past to the future.
Prod-BARR Dist-BARR Prodn-BIBICF 1978

Middle East, The C 27 MIN
16MM FILM, 3/4 OR 1/2 IN VIDEO J-C A
Explores the Arab/Israeli conflict during the 1970's, focusing on

various efforts to resolve it. Details step-by-step negotiations leading to the Begin-Sadat summits. Covers the civil wars in Jordan and Lebanon.
From The Seventies Series.
Prod-UPI Dist-JOU 1980

Middle East, The - From Mohammed To Sadat C
3/4 OR 1/2 INCH VIDEO CASSETTE H
Explores key events in Middle Eastern history, from the birth of Islam to the modern age. Illustrated with Islamic paintings, artifacts and location photography.
Prod-EAV Dist-GA

Middle East, The - Leadership And Identity (Egypt) C 28 MIN
16MM FILM, 3/4 OR 1/2 IN VIDEO I-H
Presents a study of Egypt during the 1970's. Shows the economic gap between city dwellers and village farmers, the growing population and government programs for improving the future of the country and its people.
From The Middle East Series.
Prod-BIBICF Dist-CORF

Middle East, The - Mosaic Of Peoples (An Overview) C 28 MIN
16MM FILM, 3/4 OR 1/2 IN VIDEO I-H
Surveys the diversified cultures of the Middle East, focusing on the ancient heritages of Sumer, Babylon and Persia, the lifestyles of ethnic minority groups and the coexistence of different religious sects.
From The Middle East Series.
Prod-BIBICF Dist-CORF 1979

Middle East, The - Oil And Sudden Wealth (Gulf Countries) C 28 MIN
16MM FILM, 3/4 OR 1/2 IN VIDEO I-H
Investigates the lives of the people of the Gulf countries of the Middle East as they are changed by the discovery and development of rich oil fields. Presents some long-range thinking of national policy makers concerning future direction and use of oil profits.
From The Middle East Series.
Prod-BIBICF Dist-CORF 1979

Middle Manager As Innovator, The C 30 MIN
3/4 OR 1/2 INCH VIDEO CASSETTE PRO
Teaches the three major phases of the innovation process - how to define a new idea to fit the environment, how to build a coalition of supporters, and how to mobilize the working team that will turn the idea into a reality.
Prod-WGBHTV Dist-GOODMI

Middle Of The World, The (French) C 115 MIN
16MM FILM OPTICAL SOUND
An English subtitle version of the French language film. Describes the love affair of a Swiss engineer and an Italian emigrant over a period of 112 days.
Prod-NYFLMS Dist-NYFLMS 1974

Middle Phase Of Field Instruction, The C 107 MIN
3/4 OR 1/2 INCH VIDEO CASSETTE C T
Shows field instructors how they can deal with student defensiveness and resistance, help the student make more effective use of the field instructor, use effective teaching methods in field instruction conferences and deal with evaluation.
From The Core Skills For Field Instructors Series. Program 3
LC NO. 83-706440
Prod-MCGILU Dist-MCGILU 1983

Middle Protest C 30 MIN
3/4 OR 1/2 INCH VIDEO CASSETTE C
Discusses the black protests for civil rights in America.
From The Afro-American Perspectives Series.
Prod-MDDE Dist-MDCPB

Middle Road Traveler—A Series
J-C A
Presents vignettes focusing on parenting.
Prod-BAYUCM Dist-GPITVL 1979

Child Development, Family Living Styles And Communication, Safety And Nutrition 30 MIN
Discipline, Child Development And Family 30 MIN
Expectations, Economics And Nurturance 30 MIN
Expectations, Nurturance And Interpersonal 30 MIN
Family Living Styles, Legal Rights And 30 MIN
Health, Interpersonal Relationships And 30 MIN
Legal Implications, Communication And Family 30 MIN
Nutrition, Safety And Child Development 30 MIN
Parenting Review 30 MIN
Safety, Health And Discipline 30 MIN
Safety, Nurturance And Expectations 30 MIN

Middle School Interview With Bernard Bragg C 24 MIN
3/4 OR 1/2 INCH VIDEO CASSETTE S
Presents discussion and questions with young elementary students and Bernard Bragg. Signed.
Prod-GALCO Dist-GALCO

Middle School Years, The - Guidance For Transition C 30 MIN
16MM FILM OPTICAL SOUND C T
Depicts guidance activities proven successful with middle school students, such as advisor-advisee programs, parent groups and various classroom guidance projects.
LC NO. 77-703459
Prod-EDMDC Dist-EDMDC 1977

Middle School, The C 30 MIN
3/4 OR 1/2 INCH VIDEO CASSETTE T
Explains the concept of the middle school and explores alternatives.
From The On And About Instruction Series.
Prod-VADE Dist-GPITVL 1983

Middle Years, The C 17 MIN
16MM FILM, 3/4 OR 1/2 IN VIDEO J-C A
Deals with adulthood, the years of parenting and participating in society.
Prod-HUBLEY Dist-PFP

Middle-Stage Collections B 45 MIN
2 INCH VIDEOTAPE C
See series title for descriptive statement.
From The Business Writing Series. Unit III - Persuasive Messages
Prod-CHITVC Dist-GPITVL Prodn-WTTWTV

Middleness Concept In Chimpanzees B 7 MIN
16MM FILM OPTICAL SOUND C T
Illustrates a research project to determine the extent to which a five-and-a-half year-old chimpanzee can perceive the middle object in varying arrays of objects. Uses the Wisconsin general test apparatus containing 25 food wells arranged in an arc. Circular plugs which fit into the wells are used as stimulus objects and food pellets are used as rewards.
Prod-KANSSU Dist-PSUPCR 1966

Middletown—A Series
16MM FILM, 3/4 OR 1/2 IN VIDEO J-C A
Explores both the continuity and change embodied in the people and institutions of one Midwestern community, Muncie, Indiana.
Prod-WQED Dist-FI 1982

Big Game, The 060 MIN
Campaign, The 090 MIN
Community Of Praise 060 MIN
Family Business 090 MIN
Second Time Around 060 MIN
Seventeen 090 MIN

Mideast - Arts, Crafts And Architecture C 18 MIN
16MM FILM, 3/4 OR 1/2 IN VIDEO J-C A
Views craftsmen at work and presents the role of the Islamic religion in shaping artistic activity and expression in the Middle East.
From The Mideast Series.
Prod-VOFI Dist-PHENIX 1977

Mideast - Arts, Crafts And Architecture (French) C 18 MIN
16MM FILM, 3/4 OR 1/2 IN VIDEO J-C A
Veiws craftsmen at work and presents the role of the Islamic religion in shaping artistic activity and expression in the Middle East.
From The Mideast Series.
Prod-VOFI Dist-PHENIX 1977

Mideast - Economic Development C 18 MIN
16MM FILM, 3/4 OR 1/2 IN VIDEO J-C A
Discusses the economic development of the Middle East. Explores the impact of oil on the region and examines the plans of Mideast nations to build a strong economic future.
From The Mideast Series.
Prod-VOFI Dist-PHENIX 1977

Mideast - Economic Devlopment (French) C 18 MIN
16MM FILM, 3/4 OR 1/2 IN VIDEO J-C A
Discusses the economic development of the Middle East. Explores the impact of oil on the region and examines the plans of Mideast nations to build a strong economic future.
From The Mideast Series.
Prod-VOFI Dist-PHENIX 1977

Mideast - Islam, The Unifying Force C 17 MIN
16MM FILM, 3/4 OR 1/2 IN VIDEO J-C A
Discusses the history, beliefs and practices of the Islamic religion and its role in the lives of Muslims all over the world.
From The Mideast Series.
Prod-VOFI Dist-PHENIX 1977

Mideast - Islam, The Unifying Force (French) C 17 MIN
16MM FILM, 3/4 OR 1/2 IN VIDEO J-C A
Discusses the history, beliefs and practices of the Islamic religion and its role in the lives of Muslims all over the world.
From The Mideast Series.
Prod-VOFI Dist-PHENIX 1977

Mideast - Land And People C 20 MIN
16MM FILM, 3/4 OR 1/2 IN VIDEO J-C A
Shows the Middle East, located at the juncture of Asia, Africa and Europe. Illustrates the landscapes which vary from parched deserts to subtropical farming regions, as well as the ruins of ancient civilizations which coexist with traditional bazaars and modern skylines. Discusses the countries of Saudi Arabia, Egypt, Iran, Iraq, Morocco and the Gulf States.
From The Mideast Series.
Prod-VOFI Dist-PHENIX 1977

Mideast - Land And People (French) C 20 MIN
16MM FILM, 3/4 OR 1/2 IN VIDEO J-C A
Shows the Middle East, located at the juncture of Asia, Africa and Europe. Illustrates the landscapes which vary from parched deserts to subtropical farming regions, as well as the ruins of ancient civilizations which coexist with traditional bazaars and modern skylines. Discusses the countries of Saudi Arabia, Egypt, Iran, Iraq, Morocco and the Gulf States.
From The Mideast Series.
Prod-VOFI Dist-PHENIX 1977

Mideast - Land And People (Swedish) C 20 MIN
16MM FILM, 3/4 OR 1/2 IN VIDEO J-C A
Shows the Middle East, located at the juncture of Asia, Africa and Europe. Illustrates the landscapes which vary from parched deserts to subtropical farming regions, as well as the ruins of ancient civilizations which coexist with traditional bazaars and modern skylines. Discusses the countries of Saudi Arabia, Egypt, Iran, Iraq, Morocco and the Gulf States.
From The Mideast Series.
Prod-VOFI Dist-PHENIX 1977

Mideast - Pioneers Of Science C 20 MIN
16MM FILM, 3/4 OR 1/2 IN VIDEO J-C A
Enumerates various contributions to modern civilization originating in the Middle East, including the wheel and axle, writing, the use of the decimal point, anesthetics and the number system.
From The Mideast Series.
Prod-VOFI Dist-PHENIX 1977

Mideast - Pioneers Of Science (French) C 20 MIN
16MM FILM, 3/4 OR 1/2 IN VIDEO J-C A
Enumerates various contributions to modern civilization originating in the Middle East, including the wheel and axle, writing, the use of the decimal point, anesthetics and the number system.
From The Mideast Series.
Prod-VOFI Dist-PHENIX 1977

Mideast—A Series
16MM FILM, 3/4 OR 1/2 IN VIDEO J-C A
Prod-VOFI Dist-PHENIX 1977

Mideast - Arts, Crafts And Architecture 18 MIN
Mideast - Economic Development 18 MIN
Mideast - Islam - The Unifying Force 17 MIN
Mideast - Land And People 20 MIN
Mideast - Pioneers Of Science 20 MIN

Midnight Cowboy C 113 MIN
16MM FILM OPTICAL SOUND
Focuses on a Texan who arrives in New York City hoping to make his fortune by selling himself to lonely rich women. Tells how he meets a seedy, crippled con artist. Stars Dustin Hoffman and Jon Voight. Direct by John Schlesinger.
Prod-UNKNWN Dist-UAE 1969

Midnight Express C 120 MIN
16MM FILM OPTICAL SOUND
Dramatizes an escape from a horrifying Turkish prison.
Prod-CPC Dist-SWANK

Midnight Ride Of Paul Revere, The C 11 MIN
16MM FILM, 3/4 OR 1/2 IN VIDEO I-J
Re-creates the events of Longfellow's famous poem, Paul Revere's Ride. Traces the ride from the belfry steps of the Old North Church to the Battle of Concord.
Prod-CORF Dist-CORF 1957

Midnight Ride Of Paul Revere, The B 11 MIN
16MM FILM, 3/4 OR 1/2 IN VIDEO I-H
Re-creates the episodes that occurred on the night of April 18, 1775. Explains why Paul Revere's ride was a memorable incident in the events leading to the War for Independence and why it has become a symbol of resistance to tyranny.
Prod-EBF Dist-EBEC 1957

Midsummer Mush B 20 MIN
16MM FILM OPTICAL SOUND I-C
Presents the 1933 comedy film, 'MIDSUMMER MUSH,' featuring Charlie Chase as a New York scoutmaster who takes his troop of scouts from Broadway and 42nd street to the side of a lake for summer camping. Also features Betty Mack.
Prod-ROACH Dist-BHAWK 1933

Midsummer Night's Dream, A B 117 MIN
16MM FILM OPTICAL SOUND
Offers a version of Shakespeare's play A Midsummer Night's Dream, starring James Cagney, Dick Powell, Joe E Brown, Mickey Rooney, and Olivia de Havilland.
Prod-UNKNWN Dist-UAE 1935

Midsummer Night's Dream, A C 30 MIN
3/4 OR 1/2 INCH VIDEO CASSETTE J-C A
Presents an adaptation of Shakespeare's A Midsummer Night's Dream, a classic comedy of the trials and errors of four lovers lost in a woods, of Oberon who seeks revenge on his wife Titania, and of a company of rustics rehearsing the story of Pyramus and Thisbe. Includes the plays King Lear, The Tempest and As You Like It on the same tape.
From The Shakespeare In Perspective Series.
LC NO. 84-707155
Prod-FI Dist-FI 1984

Midsummer Night's Dream, A C 110 MIN
3/4 OR 1/2 INCH VIDEO CASSETTE H-C A
Presents A Midsummer Night's Dream, William Shakespeare's play about devilish fairies, bedeviled lovers, and tradesmen-actors.
From The Shakespeare Plays Series.
LC NO. 82-707359
Prod-BBCTV Dist-TIMLIF 1982

Midsummer Night's Dream, A C 165 MIN
3/4 OR 1/2 INCH VIDEO CASSETTE
Presents an American production of the Shakespearean play A Midsummer Night's Dream, directed by Joseph Papp and starring William Hurt.
Prod-FOTH Dist-FOTH 1984

Midsummer Night's Dream, A C 180 MIN
3/4 OR 1/2 INCH VIDEO CASSETTE H-C A
Presents an American Repertory Theatre production which evokes the charm and mystery of Shakespeare's most famous romantic comedy.
LC NO. 81-707480
Prod-KINGFT Dist-KINGFT

Midsummer Night's Dream, A - An Introduction C 26 MIN
16MM FILM, 3/4 OR 1/2 IN VIDEO J-C A
Selects scenes performed by an English company to introduce Shakespeare's comedy A Midsummer Night's Dream.
From The Shakespeare Series.
Prod-SEABEN Dist-PHENIX 1970

Midway C 30 MIN
3/4 OR 1/2 INCH VIDEO CASSETTE H-C A
See series title for descriptive statement.
From The World War II - GI Diary Series.
Prod-TIMLIF Dist-TIMLIF 1980

Midway Is East B 27 MIN
16MM FILM, 3/4 OR 1/2 IN VIDEO J-H
Documents Japanese victories in the Pacific and the Battle of Midway.
From The Victory At Sea Series.
Prod-NBCTV Dist-LUF

Midway Is East - Japanese Victories And The Battle Of Midway B 30 MIN
16MM FILM OPTICAL SOUND I-C
Describes Japanese victories at Hong Kong, Singapore, Bataan, Corregidor and the Philippines. Describes the Japanese supply build up and pictures the battle at the Coral Sea and at Midway. Explains that the allied victory at midway ended Japanese plans of dominating the Eastern Pacific.
From The Victory At Sea Series.
Prod-GRACUR Dist-GRACUR

Midwest - Heartland Of The Nation X 24 MIN
16MM FILM, 3/4 OR 1/2 IN VIDEO I-H
Shows how agriculture and industry have made the midWest a wealthy region vital to the American economy. Examines contributions made by farming, livestock and dairying, mining and shipping, steel mills and the automobile industry.
Prod-EBEC Dist-EBEC 1968

Midwest Holiday C 26 MIN
16MM FILM OPTICAL SOUND J
Presents the Michigan Dunes to the Grand Tetons of Wyoming. Shows Mount Rushmore in South Dakota's Black Hills, Minnesota's Iron Range, Lincoln's home, Tom Sawyer's habitat and many other beautiful scenes in ten midwestern States.
Prod-AMROIL Dist-AMROIL 1953

Midwest Old Threshers C 29 MIN
16MM FILM OPTICAL SOUND
Shows the activities, displays and attractions at the annual reunion of the Midwest Old Settlers and Threshers Association. Depicts the sights and sounds of steam engines, locomotives, trolleys and handicrafts of a bygone era.
LC NO. 80-701321
Prod-MOSAT Dist-UIOWA Prodn-UIOWA 1980

Midwife C 26 MIN
16MM FILM OPTICAL SOUND
Explores the home birth practice of Suellen Miller and Marcia Hansen, who are certified nurse-midwives in Marin County, California. Shows two home births and a discussion among three midwives, as well as scenes of prenatal and post partum care.
LC NO. 79-701236
Prod-ANDMIC Dist-ANDMIC 1979

Midwife - With Woman C 28 MIN
16MM FILM, 3/4 OR 1/2 IN VIDEO
Traces the uneasy history of midwifery in America using archival drawings and photographs. Illustrates modern concept of nurse-midwife and addresses opposing viewpoints of physician-obstetrician and nurse-midwife.
Prod-FANPRO Dist-FANPRO

Midwifery - The Second Oldest Profession C 26 MIN
3/4 OR 1/2 INCH VIDEO CASSETTE
Reveals how renewed interest in home birth has created a demand for lay mid-wives, the ageless art of women attending women in childbirth. Shows actual births.
Prod-WCCOTV Dist-WCCOTV 1978

MIG And TIG Welding (Spanish)—A Series

Presents a series on various phases of MIG and TIG welding.
Prod-VTRI Dist-VTRI

Butt Joint, T-Joint And Lap Joint With Dual
Butt Joint, T-Joint, Lap Joint And Outside
Butt Joint, T-Joint, Lap Joint And Outside
Multi Pass Welding With Dual Shielded (Spanish)
Safety And Equipment For Gas Shielded Arc
Safety In Gas Tungsten Arc Welding (Spanish)
Selection Of Electrode, Gas, Cups And Filler
Setting Up Aluminum Wire Feed And Running
Setting Up And Padding Of The Inert-Gas
Setting Up Flux Cored Wire And Running
Submerged Arc Welding (Spanish)
Welding Aluminum With Inert Gas Tungsten Arc
Welding Mild Steel With Inert Gas Tungsten
Welding Stainless Steel With Inert Gas

Might Of The Pen, The C 28 MIN
16MM FILM OPTICAL SOUND
Describes the work of the combat historians and combat artists who record the actions and faces of an army at war.
LC NO. 75-701349
Prod-USA Dist-USNAC 1965

Mighty Fistful, The C 60 MIN
3/4 OR 1/2 INCH VIDEO CASSETTE J-C A
Presents flutist James Galway discussing the founding of the Russian style of music. Includes a performance of Osipov's Balalaika Orchestra, the Bolshoi Opera's grand production of the coronation scene from Mussorgsky's Boris Godunov and Tchaikovsky's Violin Concerto.
From The James Galway's Music In Time Series.
Prod-POLTEL Dist-FOTH 1982

Mighty Hunters C 15 MIN
3/4 OR 1/2 INCH VIDEO CASSETTE P
Presents the children's story Good Hunting Little Indian by Peggy Parish and The Mighty Hunter by Berta Bader. Includes the poem Indian Children by Annette Wynne from For Days And Days.
From The Picture Book Park Series. Green Module
Prod-WVIZTV Dist-AITECH 1974

Mighty Moose And The Quarterback Kid C 31 MIN
16MM FILM, 3/4 OR 1/2 IN VIDEO I-C A
Shows how 12-year-old Benny plays football only to placate his father, and how the new football coach emphasizes playing the game for fun instead of for competition. Explains how the coach manages to bring Benny and his father closer together.
From The Teenage Years Series.
LC NO. 80-706926
Prod-BERKAR Dist-TIMLIF 1977

Mighty Volga, The C 25 MIN
16MM FILM, 3/4 OR 1/2 IN VIDEO
Follows the flagship Lenin of the Volga fleet on its cruise down the Volga River, the lifeline of European Russia and the longest river in Europe.
LC NO. 80-706322
Prod-NGS Dist-NGS 1977

Mighty Warriors B 30 MIN
16MM FILM OPTICAL SOUND I-C A
Describes the white settlers' hard and costly victory over the plains Indians in the push westward, picturing such battles as the Little Big Horn, the Sand Creek Massacre and the Fetterman Massacre. Stresses knowledge the whites acquired from their contact with indians.
From The Glory Trail Series.
LC NO. FIA66-1239
Prod-NET Dist-IU Prodn-KRMATV 1964

Mignon C 30 MIN
16MM FILM, 3/4 OR 1/2 IN VIDEO J-C A
Presents Joan Sutherland singing the opera Mignon. Features puppets in an opera box acting as a reviewing audience conversing with the performers as they enter or leave front stage.
From The Who's Afraid Of Opera Series.
Prod-PHENIX Dist-PHENIX 1973

Migraine - Diagnosis And Management C 30 MIN
3/4 INCH VIDEO CASSETTE PRO
Focuses on the migraine. Interviews three prominent headache specialists. Includes the most common headache-symptom profiles, organic and nonorganic etiologic factors and patient counseling.
Prod-AYERST Dist-AYERST

Migrant Farmworkers C 20 MIN
3/4 OR 1/2 INCH VIDEO CASSETTE
Portrays the poor quality of life among migrant laborers. Focuses on illegal aliens, Haitians, cardboard housing, a successful Arizona Farmworker's Union strike and the hope for further improvements for migrant workers.
Prod-DCTVC Dist-DCTVC

Migrant Health B 30 MIN
16MM FILM - 3/4 IN VIDEO PRO
Presents certain insights into the phenomenon of migratory agricultural labor providing a general overview of the subject--the characteristics of the migrant laborer and the public health implications regarding the migrant and his way of life. (Broadcast quality)
From The Public Health Science Series. Unit V - Introduction To Bioenvironmental Health
Prod-TEXWU Dist-GPITVL Prodn-KUHTTV

Migrants 1980, The C 52 MIN
16MM FILM, 3/4 OR 1/2 IN VIDEO H-C A
Examines the plight of the migrant farmworkers. Documents the use of child labor, the substandard housing, and the traffic in illegal aliens. Narrated by Chris Wallace.
Prod-NBC Dist-FI 1980

Migration C 7 MIN
3/4 OR 1/2 INCH VIDEO CASSETTE
Presents a majestic exercise in perception.
Prod-EAI Dist-EAI

Migration - Adaptations C 20 MIN
2 INCH VIDEOTAPE I
See series title for descriptive statement.
From The Exploring With Science, Unit III - Animals Series.
Prod-MPATI Dist-GPITVL

Migration And Accumulation C 43 MIN
3/4 OR 1/2 INCH VIDEO CASSETTE IND
See series title for descriptive statement.
From The Basic And Petroleum Geology For Non-Geologists - Hydrocarbons And...-Series.
Prod-PHILLP Dist-GPCV

Migration Of Birds - The Canada Goose C 11 MIN
16MM FILM, 3/4 OR 1/2 IN VIDEO I-H
Maps show the migratory patterns of the Canadian goose. Habits and characteristics shown include nesting, raising the young, teaching them to fly and flocking.
Prod-EBF Dist-EBEC 1959

Migration Of The Primordial Sex Cells Into The Genital Ridge C 18 MIN
16MM FILM OPTICAL SOUND
Demonstrates the development of the female reproductive system with emphasis on migration of the primordial sex cells into the genital ridge.
From The Development Of The Female Reproductive System Series.
LC NO. 74-702456
Prod-EATONL Dist-EATONL Prodn-AVCORP 1974

Migrations Of A Melody, The B 30 MIN
16MM FILM OPTICAL SOUND H-C A
Based on a story by Yitzhak Leib Peretz, 'THE FATHER OF YIDDISH LITERATURE,' and presented in commemoration of the 50th anniversary of his death. Dramatizes the history of a melody which for years remained lost, unsung and presumed dead, but which periodically returned to life in different situations. (Kinescope)
From The Eternal Light Series.
LC NO. 79-700955
Prod-JTS Dist-NAAJS 1966

Miguel B 10 MIN
16MM FILM OPTICAL SOUND
Tells the story of a Puerto Rican boy who rebels against his background in a failed attempt to escape his environment.
Prod-NYU Dist-NYU

Miguel - Up From Puerto Rico C 15 MIN
16MM FILM, 3/4 OR 1/2 IN VIDEO I-J
Portrays some events in the life of a boy born in Puerto Rico who must now cope with life in New York City. Tells of his dejection when he finds he cannot catch a fish in the city river and of his happiness when he discovers he can work as a translator for Spanish speaking customers at a neighborhood store. Shows the close family relationships and gives a lesson in resourcefulness and the advantages of bi-cul turalism.
From The Many Americans Series.
Prod-LCOA Dist-LCOA 1970

Miguel - Up From Puerto Rico (Captioned) C 15 MIN
16MM FILM, 3/4 OR 1/2 IN VIDEO I-J A
Shows a young boy using bilingual abilities to solve a problem.
Prod-LCOA Dist-LCOA 1970

Miguel Angel Asturias - Cadaveres Para La Publicidad (Spanish) C 60 MIN
3/4 OR 1/2 INCH VIDEO CASSETTE
Presents an adaptations of Miguel Angel Asturias' work Cadaveres Para La Publicidad which depicts how the execution and mass burial of a group of labor organizers is hushed up until the government discovers a taste for publicity and decides that people love to read about murder.
Prod-FOTH Dist-FOTH 1984

Miguel De Cervantes - El Licenciado Vidriera (Spanish) C 60 MIN
3/4 OR 1/2 INCH VIDEO CASSETTE
Offers an adaptation of Cervantes' work El Licenciado Vidriera.
Prod-FOTH Dist-FOTH

Miguel de Unamuno - Niebla (Spanish) C 60 MIN
3/4 OR 1/2 INCH VIDEO CASSETTE
Presents a version of Miguel de Unamuno's absurdist work Niebla.
Prod-FOTH Dist-FOTH 1984

Miguel Muligan Y Su Pala De Vapor C 11 MIN
16MM FILM, 3/4 OR 1/2 IN VIDEO
A Spanish version of 'MIKE MULLIGAN AND HIS STEAM SHOVEL.' Explains that in his haste to dig the cellar for a town hall, Miguel Muligan forgets to leave a way out for his steam shovel. Shows how the problem is solved when the steam shovel is converted into a furnace for the new building.
Prod-WWS Dist-WWS 1960

Miguelin X 63 MIN
16MM FILM - 3/4 IN VIDEO I-C
A Spanish-language motion picture which tells of a small boy's effort to cope with poverty by taking the poor box from the church. Shows that when he realizes his mistake, he sells his burro to leave money in the poor box. Recounts that when the villagers discover what he has done, they help him recover his burro for the blessing of the animals.
Prod-IFB Dist-TRANSW 1964

Mike B 11 MIN
16MM FILM OPTICAL SOUND
A story of Mike, a potential drop-out. Shows some of Mike's feelings about school and acceptance of authority. The case worker tries to help Mike understand the importance of school at his age.
LC NO. FIA63-667
Prod-USC Dist-USC 1961

Mike C 22 MIN
3/4 INCH VIDEO CASSETTE H-C A
Depicts a 15-year-old boy who apparently refuses to fit in either at school or at home. Tells how his unconventional behavior finally gets him into trouble with the law and how his interview with a psychologist reveals the dour facts of his lonely life.
From The Handle With Care Series.
Prod-CHERIO Dist-GPITVL

Mike And Kathy C 28 MIN
16MM FILM OPTICAL SOUND
Presents a cinema verite portrait of Mike Burton, a blind Vietnam veteran, and his wife, Kathy, as they struggle to find a new life for themselves.
From The Jason Films Portrait Series.
LC NO. 73-700739
Prod-JASON Dist-JASON 1973

Mike And Lee Moore C 28 MIN
16MM FILM OPTICAL SOUND
Portrays the aspirations, dreams, and frustrations of average Americans by presenting the private lives of a typical young couple who live in Oakland, California. Characterizes the husband, a former Marine and Vietnam veteran, as an automobile mechanic who enjoys the hobbies of drag racing and motorcycle riding while the wife is employed as a waitress.
From The Private Lives Of Americans Series.
LC NO. 72-700470
Prod-KQEDTV Dist-KQEDTV 1972

Mike Fright B 18 MIN
16MM FILM OPTICAL SOUND
Describes what happens when the Little Rascals enter their International Silver String Submarine Band in a radio station contest.
Prod-ROACH Dist-BHAWK 1934

Mike Kolarov C 12 MIN
16MM FILM, 3/4 OR 1/2 IN VIDEO H-C A
Presents Mike Kolarov sharing his traditional Yugoslav Macedonian music and dance with American enthusiasts in the California redwoods. Features Novo Selo playing gajda, kaval, tambura and tupan.
Prod-AGINP Dist-AGINP

Mike Makes His Mark C 29 MIN
16MM FILM OPTICAL SOUND C T
Mike hated the new school. He challenged it by slashing an ugly mark on its front. Then he found that the mark would stay on the wall and on his conscience until he removed it by his own decision. Mike began to change his mark of resentment into the mark of manhood.
Prod-AGRA Dist-NEA 1955

Mike Mulligan And His Steam Shovel C 11 MIN
16MM FILM, 3/4 OR 1/2 IN VIDEO K-P
An iconographic film using the pictures and text of Virginia Lee Burton's story of the steam shovel that defied obsolescence by becoming the furnace in the Popperville Town Hall.
Prod-WWS Dist-WWS 1958

Mike The Bike C 11 MIN
16MM FILM, 3/4 OR 1/2 IN VIDEO P-J
Demonstrates correct ways to ride bikes on the streets and highways. Shows the importance of properly equipping bikes and checking their condition before taking them on the road.
Prod-JRDNJR Dist-AIMS 1975

Mike Wallace C 60 MIN
3/4 OR 1/2 INCH VIDEO CASSETTE
Presents John Callaway interviewing Mike Wallace of the CBS television program 60 Minutes. Discusses journalistic ethics, techniques used by the 60 Minutes team and other journalistic insights and personal anecdotes.
From The John Callaway Interviews Series.
LC NO. 82-706690
Prod-WTTWTV Dist-PBS 1981

Mikey And Nicky C 205 MIN
16MM FILM OPTICAL SOUND
Looks at a friendship between two men that is falling apart. Illustrates the axiom that sometimes even paranoids have real enemies.
Prod-TLECUL Dist-TLECUL

Mikhail Tahl C 29 MIN
2 INCH VIDEOTAPE
See series title for descriptive statement.
From The Koltanowski On Chess Series.
Prod-KQEDTV Dist-PUBTEL

Mil-STD-781C - Examples C 30 MIN
3/4 OR 1/2 INCH VIDEO CASSETTE IND
Describes procedures to select appropriate sampling plans.
From The Reliability Engineering Series.
Prod-COLOSU Dist-COLOSU

Mila 23 - Simion's World C 15 MIN
16MM FILM, 3/4 OR 1/2 IN VIDEO C A
Describes a group of people living at the marshy delta of Europe's River Danube. Tells how they have adapted to this harsh way of life and how they have been strengthened by their traditions and beliefs.
Prod-LESFMA Dist-WOMBAT

Milani Comparetti Motor Development Test C 25 MIN
3/4 OR 1/2 INCH VIDEO CASSETTE PRO
Describes and demonstrates the Milani Comparetti test, a series of simple procedures designed to evaluate a child's motor development from birth to about two years.
Prod-UNEBO Dist-UNEBO

Mild Salt-Restricted Diet C
3/4 OR 1/2 INCH VIDEO CASSETTE
Shows a middle-aged man who is urged to cut back on his use of salt. Recommends examination of food lables, substitute spices and eliminating certain foods.
Prod-MIFE Dist-MIFE

Mildred Dilling - Memoiors Of A Harp Virtuoso C 60 MIN
3/4 OR 1/2 INCH VIDEO CASSETTE
Features Mildred Dilling, an 84-year old harpist, as she combines performance with rembrances of her experiences with her teacher and with her own star pupil, Harpo Marx. Presented in two half-hour programs.
Prod-OHUTC Dist-OHUTC

Miles Of Smiles, Years Of Struggle - The Untold Story Of The Pullman Porter C 59 MIN
16MM FILM, 3/4 OR 1/2 IN VIDEO H-C A
Provides a history of the Black Pullman Porters, who during the 100 years after the Civil War were envied by some Blacks for the good jobs they had and reviled by others for being Uncle Toms. Reveals how they finally succeeded in forming their own Black Trade Union in 1925, which became a prime force behind the Civil Rights movement.
Prod-BNCHMK Dist-BNCHMK 1982

Miles To Go B 30 MIN
16MM FILM OPTICAL SOUND
Tells about an independent Black trucker from rural Texas, who has been driving a truck for 25 years and a million miles. Shows the driver on a long solitary drive as he reminisces about his life, friends and work.
LC NO. 77-702109
Prod-GORDNB Dist-GORDNB 1976

Miles To Go C 80 MIN
3/4 OR 1/2 INCH VIDEO CASSETTE H A
Illustrates the good and bad experiences of eight neophyte female backpackers ranging in age from 27 to 72 who take a guided trek through the mountains of North Carolina and Georgia.
LC NO. 84-707156
Prod-MADDBP Dist-MADDBP 1984

Miles To Go Before We Sleep C 58 MIN
3/4 OR 1/2 INCH VIDEO CASSETTE
Documents the physical, emotional and financial aspects of mandatory retirement. Narrated by Helen Hayes.
LC NO. 80-707182
Prod-WTTWTV Dist-PBS 1979

Milestones C 14 MIN
16MM FILM OPTICAL SOUND
Shows a program in which parents help their pre-school deaf children learn to speak by utilizing their residual hearing.
Prod-FLMLIB Dist-FLMLIB

Milestones In Missilery C 10 MIN
16MM FILM OPTICAL SOUND
Describes outstanding milestones in missile development and testing accomplished at the White firings of the V2 rocket in 1945.
LC NO. FIE63-65
Prod-USA Dist-USNAC 1961

Milestones In Space B 5 MIN
16MM FILM OPTICAL SOUND J-H
Describes Telstar out in orbit as a peaceful servant of mankind, helping nations to communicate through its relay system.
From The Screen News Digest Series. Vol 5, Issue 1
Prod-HEARST Dist-HEARST 1962

Milisen - Articulation Testing B 37 MIN
16MM FILM OPTICAL SOUND C S
Shows Dr Robert L Milisen of Indiana University testing the articulation of several young children. Includes a segment of an interview with the parents of one of the children.
From The Videoclinical Series Series.
LC NO. 73-702603
Prod-WMICHU Dist-WMICHU 1972

Milisen - Articulation Therapy B 30 MIN
16MM FILM OPTICAL SOUND C S
Shows Dr L Milisen of Indiana University working with a 19-year-old student with a lateral lisp. Demonstrates Milisen's analysis of the problem and attempts to modify the behavior in a series of three therapy sessions that took place on three consecutive days.
From The Videoclinical Series Series.
LC NO. 73-702604
Prod-WMICHU Dist-WMICHU 1972

Military C 29 MIN
2 INCH VIDEOTAPE
See series title for descriptive statement.
From The Commonwealth Series.
Prod-WITFTV Dist-PUBTEL

Military C 30 MIN
3/4 OR 1/2 INCH VIDEO CASSETTE C A
Compares a career in the military to working for a large corporation. Discusses how students can gain training or further education while serving in the military. Examines travel opportunities, lifestyles, and benefits.
From The Clues To Career Opportunities For Liberal Arts Graduates Series.
LC NO. 80-706238
Prod-IU Dist-IU 1979

Military Budget - Dollars And Defense C 28 MIN
3/4 OR 1/2 INCH VIDEO CASSETTE J-C
Looks at differing views of military spending by the Reagan Administration. Includes the views of such experts as Admiral Eugene J Carrol, Jr, former Commanding Officer of the USS Midway, Congresswoman Pat Schroeder of Colorado, Admiral Stanley Fine, Pentagon budget analyst for three administrations and General David Jones, former Chairman of the Joint Chiefs of Staff.
From The Issues In The News Series.
LC NO. 84-707122
Prod-FUNPC Dist-CNEMAG 1984

Military Civic Action B 31 MIN
16MM FILM OPTICAL SOUND
Reveals past and present roles of the U S Army in military civic action.
LC NO. 74-706146
Prod-USA Dist-USNAC 1964

Military Eyewear - Measurement, Fit And Adjustment C 30 MIN
16MM FILM, 3/4 OR 1/2 IN VIDEO A
Demonstrates measurement methods and techniques for fitting a patient for eyewear.
Prod-WRAIR Dist-USNAC 1983

Military Immunization - General Procedures B 25 MIN
16MM FILM OPTICAL SOUND
Depicts the procedures which enable a small team of medical personnel to immunize large groups of men safely and speedily. Stresses the proper planning and organization and the use of an individual sterile syringe and needle for each injection.
Prod-USN Dist-USNAC

Military Immunization - Smallpox Vaccination C 10 MIN
16MM FILM OPTICAL SOUND
Depicts the procedures for smallpox vaccination and for observing and recording the effects of vaccination.
LC NO. FIE59-142
Prod-USN Dist-USNAC 1954

Military Instruction--A Series

Prod-USA Dist-USNAC

Principles Of Learning 23 MIN
Speech Techniques 11 MIN
Stages Of Instruction, The - Application 20 MIN
Stages Of Instruction, The - Preparation 12 MIN
Stages Of Instruction, The - Presentation 12 MIN
Training Aids 23 MIN

Military Medicine B 19 MIN
16MM FILM OPTICAL SOUND
Reports on advances made in military medicine. Reviews the benefits to humanity as well as to military personnel. Deals with Major Walter Reed's fight against yellow fever. Covers accomplishments in tissue grafting and nuclear, submarine and aerospace medicine.
LC NO. FIE63-269
Prod-USDD Dist-USNAC 1962

Military Oceanography - Bathythermograph Observations C 16 MIN
16MM FILM OPTICAL SOUND
Explains the features and operation of a bathythermograph and demonstrates its lowering and recovery, removal of the slide and proper care of the bathythermograph.
Prod-USN Dist-USNAC 1950

Military Oceanography - Occupying An Oceanographic Station C 29 MIN
16MM FILM OPTICAL SOUND
Shows the principal design features of nansen bottles as they are used in drawing water samples and in performing other procedures.
Prod-USN Dist-USNAC 1950

Military Pipeline System B 24 MIN
16MM FILM OPTICAL SOUND
Tells the story of a pipeline built by American troops in difficult terrain under hazardous conditions.
LC NO. FIE52-1692
Prod-USA Dist-USNAC 1948

Military Pipeline System - CBI Theater B 24 MIN
3/4 INCH VIDEO CASSETTE
Tells the story of a pipeline built by American troops in difficult terrain under hazardous conditions during World War II. Issued in 1948 as a motion picture.
From The Historical Reports Series.
LC NO. 80-706768
Prod-USA Dist-USNAC 1980

Military Police Operation, Pt 3 - Military Police Patrol Investigations B 28 MIN
16MM FILM OPTICAL SOUND
Outlines the mission of the individual military policeman in patrol investigations - shows a patrol in action investigating an assault.
LC NO. 74-705142
Prod-USA Dist-USNAC 1971

Military Police Story, The B 33 MIN
16MM FILM OPTICAL SOUND
Illustrates the training, duties and responsibilities of the Military Police Corps. Shows MP activities in Germany and Korea today.
LC NO. FIE54-238
Prod-USA Dist-USNAC 1954

Military Police Support In Amphibious Operations B 14 MIN
16MM FILM OPTICAL SOUND
Explains the duties and functions of the U S Military Police in a combined amphibious assault.
LC NO. FIE53-469
Prod-USA Dist-USNAC 1953

Military Police Town Patrol, Pt 2 - Motor Patrols B 16 MIN
16MM FILM OPTICAL SOUND
Explains the responsibilities and techniques involved in motor patrolling, showing how motor patrols are organized and how patrol missions are performed.
Prod-USAF Dist-USNAC

Military Police Traffic Control, Pt 4 - Traffic Control Reconnaissance C 27 MIN
16MM FILM OPTICAL SOUND
Depicts various aspects of traffic control reconnaissance under safe and occasional enemy action conditions.
LC NO. 74-705143
Prod-USA Dist-USNAC 1970

Military Roads And Airfields, Pt 2 - Drainage B 23 MIN
16MM FILM OPTICAL SOUND
Shows the construction, application and maintenance of drainage devices, the crown or grade of road and airfield surfaces and side, intercepting and diversion ditches. Demonstrates how to check dams and culverts.
LC NO. 75-703727
Prod-USA Dist-USNAC 1968

Military Rock Climbing - Technique Of Climbing B 32 MIN
16MM FILM OPTICAL SOUND
Shows the organization of two and three man 'CLIMBING TEAMS,' equipment and its use, climbing technique for various types of formations and types of holds and knots.

LC NO. FIE52-1512
Prod-USA Dist-USNAC 1948

Military Sea Transportation Service, The - Introduction B 19 MIN
16MM FILM OPTICAL SOUND
Explains the functions, organization and operations of the military transportation service of the U S Navy.
LC NO. FIE54-101
Prod-USN Dist-USNAC 1953

Military Sea Transportation Service, The - Troop Transportation B 20 MIN
16MM FILM OPTICAL SOUND
Illustrates the problems and procedures involved in the formation, functions and duties of the advance parties and voyage staffs aboard MSTS transports.
LC NO. FIE55-258
Prod-USN Dist-USNAC 1954

Military Stevedoring, Pt 2 - Slings And Bridles B 20 MIN
16MM FILM OPTICAL SOUND
Shows several types of slings and bridles and their uses. Emphasizes the importance of using the right equipment for the job.
LC NO. 74-705145
Prod-USA Dist-USNAC 1971

Military Stevedoring, Pt 8 - Rigging Expedients For Heavy Lifts C 24 MIN
16MM FILM OPTICAL SOUND
Shows several methods for using standard riggings to create a heavy lift capability for loading and unloading military cargo.
LC NO. 74-706147
Prod-USA Dist-USNAC 1971

Milk - From Farm To You (3rd Ed) C 13 MIN
16MM FILM, 3/4 OR 1/2 IN VIDEO K-P
Follows the production of milk from the milking of the cows to the creamery to the home. Explains the processes of homogenization and pasteurization. Depicts the production of related dairy products, such as cheese and ice cream.
Prod-EBEC Dist-EBEC 1972

Milk And Milk Foods C 14 MIN
16MM FILM, 3/4 OR 1/2 IN VIDEO P
Shows where milk comes from and what it consists of. Visits a modern dairy plant to show how milk is pasteurized, homogenized, how vitamin D is added and the many ways milk is made into a wide variety of nourishing foods.
Prod-CORF Dist-CORF 1969

Milk And Public Health B 12 MIN
16MM FILM OPTICAL SOUND
Points out the dangers of haphazard milk production, the resultant public health problem and the need for regulatory legislation. Reviews steps taken to insure healthy cows and sanitary equipment and supplies. For professional use only.
LC NO. FIE53-208
Prod-USPHS Dist-USNAC 1951

Milk And Republic Health (Spanish) B 11 MIN
16MM FILM OPTICAL SOUND
Points out the dangers of haphazard milk production, the resultant public health problem, and the need for regulatory legislation. Reviews the steps taken to insure healthy cows, sanitary equipment and supplies, and other hygenic methods throughout the production and processing of milk.
LC NO. 74-705147
Prod-NMAC Dist-USNAC 1951

Milk In The Computer Age C 13 MIN
16MM FILM OPTICAL SOUND I-J
Accompanies two sixth grade students as the visit a dairy farm and a milk processing plant. Follows milk production techniques from the time it leaves the cow until it is ready for delivery to consumers.
Prod-NDC Dist-NDC 1983

Milk Products C 5 MIN
16MM FILM, 3/4 OR 1/2 IN VIDEO K-C A
See series title for descriptive statement.
From The How It's Made Series.
Prod-HOLIA Dist-LUF

Milk...In The Computer Age C 13 MIN
16MM FILM OPTICAL SOUND I-J
Shows a sixth-grade class touring a modern dairy farm and a milk-processing plant. Emphasizes the steps taken to protect the quality, safety, and good flavor of milk.
Prod-NDC Dist-NDC

Milk, Milk, Milk C 1 MIN
3/4 OR 1/2 INCH VIDEO CASSETTE
Describes the goodness of milk and where you can find it. Uses two calves and their mother in this singing television spot.
Prod-KIDSCO Dist-KIDSCO

Milking Goats C 15 MIN
3/4 OR 1/2 INCH VIDEO CASSETTE I
Deals with milking goats and making cheese and butter among the Bedouin nomads.
From The Encounter In The Desert Series.
Prod-CTI Dist-CTI

Milky Way Discovered, The C 29 MIN
3/4 INCH VIDEO CASSETTE C A
Discusses effects of dust in space on astronomic observations. Reviews Herschel's method by which he determined possible shape of the galaxy.
From The Project Universe - Astronomy Series. Lesson 19
Prod-COAST Dist-CDTEL Prodn-SCCON

Milky Way Structure, The C 29 MIN
3/4 INCH VIDEO CASSETTE C A
Illustrates problems in obtaining an accurate picture of our galaxy. Recounts development of radio astronomy. Describes operation of radio telescope at Harvard University.
From The Project Universe - Astronomy Series. Lesson 20
Prod-COAST Dist-CDTEL Prodn-SCCON

Milky Way, The B 82 MIN
3/4 OR 1/2 INCH VIDEO CASSETTE
Features a comedy about a shy milkman who accidentally clips the middleweight boxing champ.
Prod-ADVCAS Dist-ADVCAS

Mill-In C 12 MIN
16MM FILM OPTICAL SOUND
Shows anti-war demonstrators as they take to the street in New York, christmas 1967 and last minute Christmas shoppers who are hassled by the police.
Prod-NEWSR Dist-NEWSR

Mill, The C 15 MIN
16MM FILM, 3/4 OR 1/2 IN VIDEO C A
Presents a dramatization of women's lives in Yugoslavia, culminating with an abortion.
Prod-WOMBAT Dist-WOMBAT

Millay At Steepletop C 25 MIN
16MM FILM, 3/4 OR 1/2 IN VIDEO J-C A
LC NO. 84-707079
Prod-BFA Dist-PHENIX 1984

Millenia C 5 MIN
3/4 OR 1/2 INCH VIDEO CASSETTE
Depicts the evolution of five aspects of physical life - geometry,men, animals, moons and the dead. Uses analog and digital imaging techniques.
Prod-KITCHN Dist-KITCHN

Millennia C 6 MIN
3/4 OR 1/2 INCH VIDEO CASSETTE
Uses digital and analog image processing techniques to depict an evolution of geometry, men, animals, moons and the dead over thousands of years.
From The Three Short Tapes By Barbara Buckner Series.
Prod-EAI Dist-EAI

Millennia - Barbara Buckner C 5 MIN
3/4 INCH VIDEO CASSETTE C A
Silent.
Prod-AFA Dist-AFA 1981

Miller A C Transformer 180 Amp Shielded Arc Machine Set-Up C 3 MIN
1/2 IN VIDEO CASSETTE BETA/VHS IND
Shows the set-up for a Miller A C 180 amp shielded arc machine.
Prod-RMI Dist-RMI

Miller Moves Out C 4 MIN
16MM FILM OPTICAL SOUND
Presents, without narration, the story of Miller Brewing Company's expansion program. Shows the company's new facilities under construction.
LC NO. 75-700324
Prod-MBC Dist-MBC Prodn-SMITHJ 1975

Miller's Tale C 45 MIN
3/4 OR 1/2 INCH VIDEO CASSETTE
Analyzes the British literary work Miller's Tale.
From The Survey Of English Literature I Series.
Prod-MDCPB Dist-MDCPB

Millersville State College - Guest Frank Fletcher, Program A C 29 MIN
2 INCH VIDEOTAPE
Features French folk singer Sonia Malkine and her special guest Frank Fletcher visiting Millersville State College in Pennsylvania.
From The Sonia Malkine On Campus Series.
Prod-WITFTV Dist-PUBTEL

Millersville State College - Guest Frank Fletcher, Program B C 29 MIN
2 INCH VIDEOTAPE
Features French folk singer Sonia Malkine and her special guest Frank Fletcher visiting Millersville State College in Pennsylvania.
From The Sonia Malkine On Campus Series.
Prod-WITFTV Dist-PUBTEL

Millhouse - A White Comedy B 93 MIN
16MM FILM OPTICAL SOUND
Questions the American electoral process and chronicles the public career of Richard Nixon. Documents Nixon's image-building through the media.
Prod-NYFLMS Dist-NYFLMS 1971

Millicent B 30 MIN
16MM FILM OPTICAL SOUND
Presents a case study of a four-and-a-half-year-old girl who is mentally retarded, hyperactive, and distractible. Demonstrates the Else Haeussermann techniques for testing children with multiple handicaps.
LC NO. FIA67-5316
Prod-HAEUS Dist-UCPA Prodn-NWSUSA 1965

Millicent Hodson And Annabelle Gamson C 30 MIN
3/4 OR 1/2 INCH VIDEO CASSETTE
Features dancers recreating the earliest modern dance. Hosted by Julinda Lewis.
From The Eye On Dance - Passing On Dance Series.
Prod-ARTRES Dist-ARTRES

Millikan Experiment B 30 MIN
16MM FILM OPTICAL SOUND H
Discusses the use of conservation of energy principles in analyzing the behavior of electrical systems. Shows a simplified Millikan experiment as photographed through a microscope.
From The PSSC Physics Films Series.
Prod-PSSC Dist-MLA 1959

Millikan Experiment, The C 30 MIN
16MM FILM, 3/4 OR 1/2 IN VIDEO C A
Describes how Robert Millikan, understanding the electric force on a charged droplet and viscosity, measured the charge of a single electron.
From The Mechanical Universe Series.
Prod-ANNCPB Dist-FI

Millimetres C 20 MIN
3/4 INCH VIDEO CASSETTE I
Demonstrates the use of the 3-centimeter ruler. Illustrates the preciseness of using the millimeter measurement.
From The Metric Marmalade Series.
Prod-WCVETV Dist-GPITVL 1979

Milling C 9 MIN
3/4 OR 1/2 INCH VIDEO CASSETTE
Covers types of milling machines, major components of a vertical milling machine, types of milling cutters and description of milling process.
From The Manufacturing Materials And Processes Series.
Prod-GE Dist-WFVTAE

Milling A Circular T-Slot B 22 MIN
16MM FILM - 3/4 IN VIDEO
Shows how to mill a circular T-slot in solid metal, how to use a rotary table for continuous circular milling and how to use a two-lip end mill, an end mill and a T-slot cutter. Demonstrates the use of a dial indicator with a test bar in aligning a table. Issued in 1943 as a motion picture.
From The Machine Shop Work - Operations On The Vertical Milling Machine Series. No. 5
LC NO. 79-707066
Prod-USOE Dist-USNAC Prodn-RAYBEL 1979

Milling A Helical Cutter B 18 MIN
16MM FILM, 3/4 OR 1/2 IN VIDEO
Shows how to Mount Arbor, Cutter and Arbor support, mount workpiece between centers, set dividing head for specified number of divisions, position workpiece for first cut, and rough- and finish-mill the workpiece.
From The Machine Shop Work - Operations On The Milling Machine Series. No. 8
Prod-USOE Dist-USNAC Prodn-HP 1945

Milling A Helical Groove B 28 MIN
16MM FILM - 3/4 IN VIDEO
Shows how to mill a helical groove in a cylindrical shaft, how to select and set the machine gears for milling a helical groove with any lead and how to use the dividing head. Explains lead and backlash. Issued in 1943 as a motion picture.
From The Machine Shop Work - Operations On The Vertical Milling Machine Series. No. 4
LC NO. 79-707067
Prod-USOE Dist-USNAC Prodn-RAYBEL 1979

Milling A Template B 17 MIN
16MM FILM, 3/4 OR 1/2 IN VIDEO
Shows how to mount the end mill in the milling machine spindle, position the table and workpiece in relation to the cutter, rough- and finish-mill the piece and check for finished dimensions.
From The Machine Shop Work - Operations On The Milling Machine Series. No. 5
Prod-USOE Dist-USNAC Prodn-HP 1945

Milling And Tool Sharpening (Spanish)—A Series

Presents a series on the operation and use of milling machines and tool sharpeners.
Prod-VTRI Dist-VTRI

Cutters And Machining Operations For The
Gouging Of End Mill 2 And 4 Flute (Spanish)
Identification Of Parts And Operation Of A
Identification Of Parts And Operation Of A
Machine Keyways On The Vertical Milling
Reamer Sharpening Between Centers (Spanish)
Setup For Holding Work To Be Milled (Spanish)
Sharpening Ends Of End Mills (Spanish)
Sharpening Lathe Tools Including N/C Lathe
Sharpening Side Milling Cutters, Slitting
Sharpening The Periphery Of End Mills (Spanish)
Use Of Dividing Head And Rotary Table (Spanish)
Use Of Face Milling Cutters On The Horizontal
Use Of Plain And Side Milling Cutters On The

Milling And Tool Sharpening—A Series

Presents information on the operation and use of the milling machine and tool sharpening.
Prod-VTRI Dist-VTRI

Cutters And Machining Operations For The
Gouging Of End Mill 2 And 4 Flute
Identification Of Parts And Operation Of A
Identification Of Parts And Operation Of A
Machine Keyways On The Vertical Milling
Reamer Sharpening Between Centers
Setup For Holding Work To Be Milled
Sharpening Ends Of End Mills
Sharpening Lathe Tools Including N/C Lathe
Sharpening Side Milling Cutters, Slitting
Sharpening The Periphery Of End Mills
Use Of Dividing Head And Rotary Table
Use Of Face Milling Cutters On The Horizontal
Use Of Plain And Side Milling Cutters On The

Milling Cutters And Accessories C 18 MIN
3/4 OR 1/2 INCH VIDEO CASSETTE IND

Focuses on the types and uses of milling cutters.
From The Introduction To Machine Technology, Module 2 Series
Prod-LEIKID Dist-LEIKID

Milling Machine, The B 8 MIN
16MM FILM, 3/4 OR 1/2 IN VIDEO IND
Shows types of jobs which can be done on the milling machine. Demonstrates how to mount the cutter on the arbor, adjust the overarm bracket and set cutter speeds and table feeds.
From The Machine Shop Work - Operations On The Milling Machine Series.
Prod-USOE Dist-USNAC 1941

Milling Machine, The B 15 MIN
16MM FILM, 3/4 OR 1/2 IN VIDEO
Explains the functions, characteristics and basic operations of the milling machine.
From The Machine Shop Work - Basic Machines Series.
Prod-USOE Dist-USNAC Prodn-LNS 1944

Milling Machine, The (Spanish) B 15 MIN
16MM FILM OPTICAL SOUND
Explains the functions, characteristics and basic operations of the milling machine.
From The Machine Shop Work Series. Basic Machines
LC NO. 74-705148
Prod-USOE Dist-USNAC 1944

Milling Machines C 16 MIN
3/4 OR 1/2 INCH VIDEO CASSETTE IND
Covers verticle and horizontal mills, milling operations and the universal dividing head.
From The Introduction To Machine Technology, Module 2 Series.
Prod-LEIKID Dist-LEIKID

Million Acre Playground C 15 MIN
16MM FILM OPTICAL SOUND
Surveys the one million acres maintained by the Florida Flood Control District for sports and recreation.
Prod-FLADC Dist-FLADC

Million Club, The C 28 MIN
16MM FILM OPTICAL SOUND C A
Dramatizes the threat of cancer and discusses its increasing curability.
LC NO. FIA65-845
Prod-AMCS Dist-AMCS Prodn-REED 1964

Million Dollar Customer, The B 12 MIN
16MM FILM OPTICAL SOUND C A
Shows that an alert and aggressive sales staff is a protection against shoplifting.
LC NO. FI67-93
Prod-LATOUR Dist-FRAF 1960

Million Dollar Dreams C 30 MIN
16MM FILM, 3/4 OR 1/2 IN VIDEO J-C A
Looks at six Americans who started with nothing but an idea and a commitment to hard work. Shows how they became millionaires who make cookies, suntan lotion, computer programs, herbal tea and cosmetics.
LC NO. 84-706143
Prod-GANNET Dist-MTI 1983

Million Dollar Scan, The C 30 MIN
16MM FILM, 3/4 OR 1/2 IN VIDEO H-C A
Tells about the struggle of a company to hold its own in the marketplace after failing to move fast enough in the field of nuclear magnetic resonance scanning.
From The Enterprise Series.
Prod-MTI Dist-MTI

Million Mile Driver Quiz C 22 MIN
16MM FILM OPTICAL SOUND
Provides a review of signs, right-of-way rules and principles of good decision-making which prepare special education students for driver's license examinations. Uses an up-beat TV game show format that holds attention and encourages response. Includes multiple choice quiz questions and answers and a teacher's guide.
Prod-BUMPA Dist-BUMPA

Million Mile Driver Quiz, The C 22 MIN
16MM FILM OPTICAL SOUND
Reviews specific safety concepts and principles of good driving for special education and mentally retarded students.
LC NO. 79-701328
Prod-PARPRO Dist-PARPRO 1979

Million Mile Driver Show C 21 MIN
16MM FILM OPTICAL SOUND
Introduces special education students to the role and responsibilities of the driver and the importance of safe driving. Uses an up-beat TV game show format to hold attention and encourage response. Includes a teacher's guide.
Prod-BUMPA Dist-BUMPA

Million Mile Driver Show, The C 21 MIN
16MM FILM OPTICAL SOUND
Demonstrates the role and responsibilities of the driver and shows safe driving behavior for special education and mentally retarded students.
LC NO. 79-701329
Prod-PARPRO Dist-PARPRO 1979

Million Other Things, A (2) C
3/4 OR 1/2 INCH VIDEO CASSETTE
Changes in light and sound during an eight hour period are composed into rhythmic variations resembling music.
From The Red Tape Series.
Prod-EAI Dist-EAI

Million Teenagers, A (4th Ed) C 23 MIN
16MM FILM, 3/4 OR 1/2 IN VIDEO J-H
Explains the physiology, transmission, symptoms, treatment and dangers of gonorrhea, syphilis, herpes, chlamydia, PID, NGU and AIDS.
Prod-CF Dist-CF

Million To One, A B 5 MIN
16MM FILM OPTICAL SOUND H
Shows a flea pulling a massive dry ice puck, thus demonstrating the small force needed to move a nearly frictionless body. Includes a short excerpt from the film 'INERTIA' which describes the dry ice puck.
From The PSSC Physics Films Series.
LC NO. 75-702719
Prod-EDS Dist-MLA 1961

Million Years Of Man, A C 24 MIN
16MM FILM, 3/4 OR 1/2 IN VIDEO I-J
Presents an introduction to anthropology, explaining how this science of man has contributed to knowledge of the ancestors of modern man.
From The Smithsonian Series.
Prod-NBCTV Dist-MGHT 1967

Millionaires Of Poverty Gulch B 30 MIN
16MM FILM OPTICAL SOUND I-C A
Depicts the gold rush days in Colorado and the problems of a sudden increase in wealth and population. Traces the rise and fall of the small mining town of Cripple Creek.
From The Glory Trail Series.
LC NO. FIA66-1241
Prod-NET Dist-IU Prodn-KRMATV 1964

Millions Of Cats B 10 MIN
16MM FILM, 3/4 OR 1/2 IN VIDEO K-P
An iconographic motion picture based on the children's book of the same title by Wanda Gag.
Prod-WWS Dist-WWS 1958

Millions Of Pies C 15 MIN
16MM FILM, 3/4 OR 1/2 IN VIDEO
Shows machines doing most of the work in making pies, such as cutting, mixing, shaping, rolling and filling. Compares the machines to a mother who does all of these jobs herself.
From The Ripples Series.
LC NO. 73-702145
Prod-NITC Dist-AITECH

Millions Of Years Ago And Now B 15 MIN
2 INCH VIDEOTAPE P
Shows that organisms have changed over the years.
From The Science Is Everywhere Series. No. 30
Prod-DETPS Dist-GPITVL

Millones De Gatos B 10 MIN
16MM FILM, 3/4 OR 1/2 IN VIDEO
A Spanish version of 'MILLIONS OF CATS.' Tells how a homely kitten, the lone survivor of a fight in which millions of cats devour each other, becomes the most beautiful cat in the world because of the loving care of an elderly couple.
Prod-WWS Dist-WWS 1960

Mills Brothers, The C 58 MIN
3/4 OR 1/2 INCH VIDEO CASSETTE
See series title for descriptive statement.
From The Evening At Pops Series.
Prod-WGBHTV Dist-PBS 1978

Millstone Sewing Center, The C 13 MIN
16MM FILM - 3/4 IN VIDEO
Relates how a community center for sewing clothes for needy children was established. Tells how different resources were combined to fund the center.
Prod-APPAL Dist-APPAL 1972

Milo's Journey C 15 MIN
16MM FILM OPTICAL SOUND P-I
An excerpt from the motion picture The Phantom Tollbooth. Tells the story of a boy who discovers the joys of living and the need for learning. Based on the book The Phantom Tollbooth by Norman Juster.
From The Peppermint Stick Selection Series.
LC NO. 77-701719
Prod-FI Dist-FI 1976

Milton And 17th Century Poetry C 35 MIN
3/4 OR 1/2 INCH VIDEO CASSETTE
Focuses on Milton's Paradise Lost and the work of Donne, Herbert and Marvell. Discusses the epic form and the characteristics of metaphysical poetry.
Prod-FOTH Dist-FOTH

Milton Eisenhower C 30 MIN
3/4 OR 1/2 INCH VIDEO CASSETTE
Presents an interview conducted by Dr Frederick Breitenfeld with prominent Marylander Milton Eisenhower.
From The In Person Series.
Prod-MDCPB Dist-MDCPB

Milton Friedman Speaking—A Series
C
Features economist Milton Friedman offering his opinions on American economy, government, education and labor.
Prod-HBJ Dist-HBJ 1980

Economics Of Medical Care, The 045 MIN
Energy Crisis, The - A Human Solution 087 MIN
Equality And Freedom In The Free Enterprise 084 MIN
Free Trade - Producer Versus Consumer 080 MIN
Future Of Our Free Society, The 045 MIN
Is Capitalism Humane 069 MIN
Is Tax Reform Possible 081 MIN
Money And Inflation 081 MIN
Myths That Conceal Reality 082 MIN
Putting Learning Back In The Classroom 045 MIN
Role Of Government In A Free Society, The 076 MIN
What Is America 072 MIN
What Is Wrong With The Welfare State 087 MIN
Who Protects The Consumer 085 MIN
Who Protects The Worker 082 MIN

Mime Control C 9 MIN
16MM FILM OPTICAL SOUND
Presents a mime who performs in real time while an artist uses a computer to accent and control the mime's disciplined choreography.
Prod-LILYAN Dist-LILYAN

Mime Of Marcel Marceau, The C 23 MIN
16MM FILM, 3/4 OR 1/2 IN VIDEO J-C
Views the French pantomimist at work both on stage and behind the scenes.
Prod-LCOA Dist-LCOA 1972

Mime One C 27 MIN
3/4 OR 1/2 INCH VIDEO CASSETTE
Introduces five pieces performed by the Oregon Mime Theater, directed by Francisco Reynders. Includes The Bird.
Prod-MEDIPR Dist-MEDIPR 1980

Mime Over Matter C 15 MIN
16MM FILM OPTICAL SOUND J-C A
Examines the use of pantomine to explore ideas and provoke open-ended discussion of such topics as man's relationships to the material objects that make his life comfortable. Features Ladislav Fialka.
LC NO. 70-711341
Prod-KRATKY Dist-SIM 1970

Mime Technique, Pt 1 C 27 MIN
16MM FILM, 3/4 OR 1/2 IN VIDEO H-C A
Introduces mime Paul Gaulin as he brings to life a story about an ape who is transformed into a man. Shows the new man experimenting with the art of mime when he finds a book on the basic techniques.
Prod-LIPPES Dist-PHENIX 1977

Mime Time C 10 MIN
3/4 OR 1/2 INCH VIDEO CASSETTE K-P
Deals with the ability to interpret actions and expressions of a pantomimist as a storyteller.
From The Book, Look And Listen Series.
Prod-MDDE Dist-AITECH 1977

Mimi B 12 MIN
16MM FILM OPTICAL SOUND J-C A
Presents a young woman paralyzed from birth, talking about herself and her life, relating to 'NORMAL' people and how they relate to her.
LC NO. 73-700891
Prod-BBF Dist-BBF 1972

Mimi And Richard Farina C 52 MIN
3/4 OR 1/2 INCH VIDEO CASSETTE
Features many songs written by Richard Farina as he plays harmonica and dulcimer and Mimi Farina plays guitar.
From The Rainbow Quest Series.
Prod-SEEGER Dist-CWATER

Min Have I Provence (My Garden In Provence) C 18 MIN
16MM FILM OPTICAL SOUND
A Danish language film. Presents the Danish sculptor Ib Schmedes' description of the insect fauna in Provence where he now lives.
Prod-STATNS Dist-STATNS 1963

Minawanamut C 19 MIN
16MM FILM OPTICAL SOUND
Explores the water-wealthy province of Ontario which has one-quarter of the world's fresh water and the greatest sailing surface in North America. 'MINAWANAMUT' Is the Indian word for 'A KIND, FRESH WIND' and to sailors it means a brisk wind for sailing.
LC NO. 74-706955
Prod-ONTPRO Dist-CTFL 1969

Mind And Hand C 24 MIN
16MM FILM OPTICAL SOUND I-C
Considers the dimensions that life had to pass through before the evolutionary mind appeared. Shows how a one-celled animal responds to its environment. Describes the simple nervous system of the coelenterates, the ganglionic system of the invertebrates and the central nervous system of the vertebrates. Explains the evolution of the hand.
From The Animal Secrets 1967 Series.
Prod-NEA Dist-GRACUR 1967

Mind And Hand C 28 MIN
16MM FILM, 3/4 OR 1/2 IN VIDEO
Outlines the different views on the relationship between mind and body as seen by such disparate disciplines as Eastern philosophy and modern cybernetics. Explores psychosomatic illness, hypnosis, biofeedback and meditation and shows how these techniques are applied to such areas as pain control and the self-mastery of involuntary responses.
Prod-CANBC Dist-FLMLIB

Mind And Muscle Power C 20 MIN
3/4 OR 1/2 INCH VIDEO CASSETTE P-I
Explores literary selections that deal with physical health and discipline as crucial to achievements in many fields.
From The Once Upon A Town Series.
Prod-MDDE Dist-AITECH 1977

Mind At Large - Adler On Aristotle C 60 MIN
3/4 OR 1/2 INCH VIDEO CASSETTE A
Presents an interview with Mortimer Adler in which he discusses

philosophical issues, such as the nature of the good life, the role and attainment of virtue, the function of philosophy in modern society, and concepts of the rational and virtuous man.
From The Bill Moyers' Journal Series.
LC NO. 79-708090
Prod-WNETTV Dist-WNETTV 1979

Mind Control C 25 MIN
3/4 OR 1/2 INCH VIDEO CASSETTE J-C A
Considers people's ability to develop additional psychic power. Demonstrates exercises which can enhance awareness of intuition.
Prod-SIRS Dist-SIRS

Mind Machines, The C 59 MIN
16MM FILM, 3/4 OR 1/2 IN VIDEO H-C A
Discusses research being done in Artificial Intelligence, a branch of computer science. Explores possible developments, such as computer controlled robots equipped with vision and the ability to respond flexibly to changing conditions.
From The Nova Series.
LC NO. 79-708147
Prod-WGBHTV Dist-TIMLIF 1978

Mind Of A Murderer, Pt 1 C 60 MIN
3/4 OR 1/2 INCH VIDEO CASSETTE
Focuses on convicted murderer Kenneth Bianchо, known as the Hillside Strangler. Probes the complex area of criminal psychology.
From The Frontline Series.
LC NO. 84-707627
Prod-BARNEM Dist-PBS

Mind Of A Murderer, Pt 2 C 60 MIN
3/4 OR 1/2 INCH VIDEO CASSETTE
Focuses on convicted murderer Kenneth Bianchо, known as the Hillside Strangler. Probes the complex area of criminal psychology.
From The Frontline Series.
LC NO. 84-707627
Prod-BARNEM Dist-PBS

Mind Of Man C 24 MIN
16MM FILM OPTICAL SOUND I-C
Explains that a child is not born with ready-made intelligence, only with intellectual potential and that man's long childhood allows time for brain growth.
From The Animal Secrets 1967 Series.
Prod-GRACUR Dist-GRACUR 1967

Mind Of Man, The C 119 MIN
16MM FILM, 3/4 OR 1/2 IN VIDEO
Presents a survey of modern research on the mind in various countries of the world. Covers areas of mind development in children, effects of drugs, dreams, brain structure, chemical changes within the brain, the brain and sexuality, reasoning and the power of the mind in controlling bodily functions. Includes interviews with Sir John Eccles, Donald Hebb and B F Skinner.
LC NO. 80-707097
Prod-NET Dist-IU 1971

Mind Of Music, The C 29 MIN
16MM FILM OPTICAL SOUND H-C A
Inquires into the link forged between an individual and music. Interviews composers, a musician, a musicologist and a biologist.
LC NO. 81-700106
Prod-LAWFI Dist-LAWFI 1980

Mind Over Body C 49 MIN
16MM FILM, 3/4 OR 1/2 IN VIDEO H-C
Shows recently developed techniques which teach patients to use their minds to produce bodily changes that can ward off or cure illness. Includes bizarre examples of the power of mind over body.
LC NO. 79-707825
Prod-BBCTV Dist-TIMLIF 1973

Mind Over Matter C 10 MIN
16MM FILM OPTICAL SOUND
See series title for descriptive statement.
From The Safety Management Series.
Prod-NSC Dist-NSC

Mind Your Back C 13 MIN
16MM FILM OPTICAL SOUND IND
Shows how proper lifting methods can prevent back injuries to industrial workers and demonstrates the right and wrong way to handle and lift timber, steel rails, oil drums, gas cylinders and other heavy objects.
LC NO. FIA68-1743
Prod-ANAIB Dist-AUIS 1966

Mind Your Back C 17 MIN
16MM FILM, 3/4 OR 1/2 IN VIDEO A
Discusses bad lifting habits developed by men and women at home and at work. Presents experts on lifting and posture who show that with a little care and know-how it is possible for everyone to take care of their back, avoid pain and avoid losing days at work as well.
LC NO. 83-706692
Prod-MILLBK Dist-IFB 1982

Mind Your Manners C 15 MIN
2 INCH VIDEOTAPE P
Provides an enrichment program in the communitive arts area by showing character and respect.
From The Word Magic (2nd Ed) Series.
Prod-CVETVC Dist-GPITVL

Mind-Altering Drugs B 30 MIN
16MM FILM OPTICAL SOUND PRO
Reviews the five major mind-altering drugs, amphetamines, barbiturates, hallucinogenics, heroin and pop drugs.

From The Directions For Education In Nursing Via Technology Series. Lesson 87
LC NO. 74-701866
Prod-DENT Dist-WSU 1974

Mind-Slaughter C 18 MIN
16MM FILM, 3/4 OR 1/2 IN VIDEO J
Presents basic planetary life support principles and man's potential impact on other planets with a tale about an experiment to create an atmosphere for human habitation on another planet which ends in killing an intelligent life form already there.
From The Universe And I Series.
LC NO. 80-706484
Prod-KYTV Dist-AITECH 1977

Mind, Body And Spirit C 28 MIN
16MM FILM, 3/4 OR 1/2 IN VIDEO H-C A
Tells how barefoot doctors, drawn from local communities, are trained to attend to the basic health care needs of the rural people of China. Explains the emphasis of preventive medicine.
From The Human Face Of China Series.
Prod-FLMAUS Dist-LCOA 1979

Mind's Eye C 28 MIN
16MM FILM OPTICAL SOUND
Shows the wide spectrum of job capabilities of rehabilitated blinded war veterans. Presents 12 blinded veterans in various sections of the country living as members of their communities and performing effectively in a wide variety of occupations.
Prod-USVA Dist-USVA 1963

Mind's Eye, The C 29 MIN
2 INCH VIDEOTAPE
See series title for descriptive statement.
From The Museum Open House Series.
Prod-WGBHTV Dist-PUBTEL

Mind's Eye, The C 50 MIN
16MM FILM, 3/4 OR 1/2 IN VIDEO H-C A
Examines the mystery of sight, illustrating the amazing things the brain can do in only a few seconds.
Prod-BBCTV Dist-FI 1981

Mindful Way, The C 24 MIN
16MM FILM, 3/4 OR 1/2 IN VIDEO
Explores the religious life in and around the Buddhist monastery of Wat Ba Pong near Ubol in a forest in northeastern Thailand. Describes how monks live, shows their relationships with lay people and unlocks a number of open secrets about monastic life.
Prod-OPENU Dist-MEDIAG Prodn-BBCTV 1979

Minds And Machines C 25 MIN
3/4 OR 1/2 INCH VIDEO CASSETTE C
See series title for descriptive statement.
From The Introduction To Philosophy Series.
Prod-UDEL Dist-UDEL

Minds Of Men, The C 52 MIN
3/4 OR 1/2 INCH VIDEO CASSETTE
Offers a detailed look at the life and teachings of Socrates and his pupil Plato, and the worlds of the first historians, Herodotus and Thucydides. Exemplifies the vital curiousity of the Greeks about the wellsprings of human behavior, the nature of man and his place in the world around him.
From The Greeks Series.
Prod-FOTH Dist-FOTH 1984

Minds Or Eyeballs C 29 MIN
3/4 INCH VIDEO CASSETTE
Looks at the advertiser's role in determining children's programming. Discusses responses from the broadcast industry to lobbyists' pressures for more diversified programming.
From The Children And Television Series.
Prod-UMITV Dist-UMITV

Mindscape B 5 MIN
16MM FILM OPTICAL SOUND H-C A
Presents a visual interpretation of a youth's 'trip' after taking a drug. Follows him as he imagines he is in a slaughter house and then that he is being dragged underwater.
LC NO. 75-703210
Prod-USC Dist-USC 1967

Mindscape C 8 MIN
16MM FILM, 3/4 OR 1/2 IN VIDEO H-C A
Explores, through the use of pinscreen animation, creative processes of the mind. Shows a painter as he steps into the scene of the landscape that he is painting and travels the regions of the mind. Uses flowing images to show the interior landscape of the mind.
LC NO. 77-701096
Prod-NFBC Dist-PFP 1976

Mine And The Minotaur, The C 59 MIN
16MM FILM OPTICAL SOUND I-J
Tells about four youngsters who discover that local potters have hidden a priceless gold mythological figure in a disused Cornish tin mine. Describes how they prevent the figure from being smuggled out of the country.
Prod-LUF Dist-LUF 1981

Mine Emergency Operations - MEO (Rev) C 17 MIN
16MM FILM, 3/4 OR 1/2 IN VIDEO IND
Shows emergency rescue and recovery procedures for situations in which trapped miners cannot be reached through existing tunnels. Details the MEO system which includes seismic and electromagnetic communication and location equipment, drilling from the surface, and survival instructions for trapped miners.
Prod-USDL Dist-USNAC 1982

Mine Fire Control C 26 MIN
16MM FILM OPTICAL SOUND H-C A
Explains how the bureau of mines, in cooperation with state and local agencies, works to control underground mine fires, thereby saving coal resources and restoring the surface to constructible use.
Prod-USDIBM Dist-USDIBM

Mine For Growth, A C 16 MIN
16MM FILM OPTICAL SOUND H-C A
Presents the story of the development and operation of The Griffith Mine, a modern iron ore mining and pelletizing complex at Bruce Lake in northwestern Ontario.
Prod-PICMAT Dist-PICMAT

Mine For Keeps C 15 MIN
3/4 OR 1/2 INCH VIDEO CASSETTE P
See series title for descriptive statement.
From The Best Of Cover To Cover 1 Series.
Prod-WETATV Dist-WETATV

Mine Forces In Action C 14 MIN
16MM FILM OPTICAL SOUND
Discusses mine laying as a defense system. Focuses on laying mines and mine countermeasures and describes strategic significance.
LC NO. 75-700864
Prod-USN Dist-USNAC 1957

Mine In The Valley, The C 22 MIN
16MM FILM OPTICAL SOUND J-C A
Shows the step-by-step construction of the Hilton Mines in the Ottawa River Valley of Quebec, the first ore pelletizing operation in the province, followed by a tour of the property in operation, including mining the ore, crushing, concentrating and pelletizing.
Prod-PICMAT Dist-PICMAT

Mine In The Valley, The (French) C 22 MIN
16MM FILM OPTICAL SOUND J-C A
A French language film. Shows the step-by-step construction of the Hilton Mines in the Ottawa River Valley of Quebec, the first ore pelletizing operation in the province, followed by a tour of the property in operation, including mining the ore, crushing, concentrating and pelletizing.
Prod-PICMAT Dist-PICMAT

Mine Of El Teniente C 26 MIN
16MM FILM OPTICAL SOUND
Describes cooperative efforts between firms in North and South America to modernize a 200-year-old copper mine in the Chilean Andes and move 13,000 miners from their mountainous isolation to a modern townsite.
LC NO. 72-702198
Prod-BECHTL Dist-BECHTL 1972

Mine Rescue Contest Training C 25 MIN
16MM FILM OPTICAL SOUND
Photographs participants going through a typical rescue-recovery problem, on a field course laid out to stimulate a working section in an underground mine. Shows step-by-step procedures that are taken by each member of a team in an actual mine rescue and gives an explanation for each action.
LC NO. 74-705149
Prod-USBM Dist-USNAC 1962

Miner's Daughter, The C 8 MIN
16MM FILM OPTICAL SOUND
Presents an animated story based on the song My Darling Clementine.
Prod-TIMLIF Dist-TIMLIF 1982

Mineral Challenge, The C 28 MIN
16MM FILM OPTICAL SOUND
Explains the technological advances used to meet needs for fuels, metals and other minerals. Includes conservation of resources to take care of future needs.
Prod-USDIBM Dist-USDIBM 1970

Mineral Curiosities C 29 MIN
2 INCH VIDEOTAPE
See series title for descriptive statement.
From The Observing Eye Series.
Prod-WGBHTV Dist-PUBTEL

Mineral King C 28 MIN
16MM FILM OPTICAL SOUND
Presents the American environment as her early artists envisioned, as her photographers saw it and as it exists today. Investigates the mineral King controversy and values it represents.
LC NO. 72-702411
Prod-USC Dist-USC 1972

Mineral Resources C 30 MIN
3/4 OR 1/2 INCH VIDEO CASSETTE
Describes the minerals found in the oceans of the earth. Includes salt, magnesium, bromine and iodine. Discusses the origin of petroleum.
From The Oceanus - The Marine Environment Series. Lesson 26
Prod-SCCON Dist-CDTEL

Mineral Resources C 43 MIN
3/4 OR 1/2 INCH VIDEO CASSETTE IND
See series title for descriptive statement.
From The Basic And Petroleum Geology For Non-Geologists - Earth's Interior...--Series
Prod-PHILLP Dist-GPCV

Minerals C 15 MIN
3/4 OR 1/2 INCH VIDEO CASSETTE I
See series title for descriptive statement.
From The Discovering Series. Unit 6 - Rocks And Minerals
Prod-WDCNTV Dist-AITECH 1978

Minerals C 30 MIN
3/4 OR 1/2 INCH VIDEO CASSETTE
See series title for descriptive statement.
From The Food For Life Series.
Prod-MSU Dist-MSU

Minerals - Finds For The Future C 24 MIN
3/4 OR 1/2 INCH VIDEO CASSETTE H-C
Explores the use of satellites to create geological surveys of vast areas and the complementary use of computers to analyze surveys and locate mineral deposits. Describe analysis of surface dust to locate buried mineral deposits.
Prod-BBCTV Dist-MEDIAG Prodn-OPENU 1985

Minerals And Man C 30 MIN
3/4 INCH VIDEO CASSETTE J
Explains how minerals form and offers an interview with Jim Irvine, salesman, chemist and rockhound. Provides a biographical sketch of James Dana, the scientist who developed the first systematic classification system for minerals.
From The What On Earth Series.
Prod-NCSDPI Dist-GPITVL 1979

Minerals And Rocks B 45 MIN
2 INCH VIDEOTAPE C
See series title for descriptive statement.
From The Physical Science Series. Unit 1 - Geology
Prod-CHITVC Dist-GPITVL Prodn-WTTWTV

Minerals And Rocks (Spanish) C 15 MIN
16MM FILM, 3/4 OR 1/2 IN VIDEO J A
A Spanish language version of the film and videorecording Minerals And Rocks.
Prod-EBEC Dist-EBEC 1979

Minerals And Rocks (2nd Ed) C 15 MIN
16MM FILM, 3/4 OR 1/2 IN VIDEO I
Investigates the structure and composition of minerals and describes methods and instruments used by mineralogists in analyzing some of the nearly 3,000 identified mineral species.
Prod-EBEC Dist-EBEC 1979

Minerals From Iowa's Beautiful Land C 20 MIN
16MM FILM OPTICAL SOUND H-C A
Documents the joint efforts of state government and industry in achieving effective regulation of surface mining practices in Iowa. Describes how and why Iowa's mined-law reclamation law evolved, as well as the reasons for its success, using comments of governmental officials, mining industry representatives and the general public.
LC NO. 81-701623
Prod-ISOCON Dist-IOWA Prodn-IOWA 1981

Minerals In The Diet - Barbara Harland, PhD C 35 MIN
3/4 INCH VIDEO CASSETTE
Introduces Dr Harland discussing the essential minerals, their functions, and their occurrences in foods. Tells how an excess of one or more minerals may cause an imbalance in the nutritional state.
From The Food And Nutrition Seminars For Health Professionals Series.
LC NO. 78-706162
Prod-USFDA Dist-USNAC 1976

Minerals In The Sea B 20 MIN
2 INCH VIDEOTAPE I
See series title for descriptive statement.
From The Science Room Series.
Prod-MCETV Dist-GPITVL Prodn-WVIZTV

Miners Of Bolivia C 15 MIN
16MM FILM, 3/4 OR 1/2 IN VIDEO P-C
Depicts the sub-marginal living of Indian miners digging for tin ore. Shows their daily life of work, chewing of coca leaf and then return to ghetto like huts.
From The Man And His World Series.
Prod-FI Dist-FI 1969

Ming-Oi The Magician C 25 MIN
16MM FILM, 3/4 OR 1/2 IN VIDEO I-J A
Introduces Ming-Oi, a girl of Hong Kong who is studying the secrets of ancient Chinese magic from one of that style's two remaining practitioners. Shows her practicing diligently to prepare for her opening night.
From The World Cultures And Youth Series.
LC NO. 80-706678
Prod-SUNRIS Dist-CORF 1980

Minga - We Work Together C 14 MIN
16MM FILM, 3/4 OR 1/2 IN VIDEO I-J
Shows the lifestyle of an eight year old Quechuan Indian girl in the mountains of Ecuador. Traces her day spent carrying water and other supplies, sewing, weaving, marketing and farming, but without school since there is little need to learn what is not taught at home.
From The Just One Child Series.
Prod-REYEXP Dist-BCNFL 1983

Mingus B 60 MIN
16MM FILM OPTICAL SOUND
Documents the turbulent night in November, 1966 as the internationally renowned bassist-composer, Mingus, and his five year old daughter, Carolyn, awaited the arrival of the city Marshal and police who were to evict them from their bowery loft for non-payment of rent.
Prod-IMPACT Dist-IMPACT 1966

Mini Movies - Springboard For Learning - Unit 1, Who Are We—A Series
P-I
Prod-MORLAT Dist-MORLAT 1975

Body Talk 4 MIN
Hands And Feet 4 MIN
Summertime - Wintertime 4 MIN
Talking 4 MIN
Touching 4 MIN

Mini Movies - Springboard For Learning - Unit 2, What Do We—A Series
P-I
Prod-MORLAT Dist-MORLAT 1975

Cans 4 MIN
Chocolate 4 MIN
Glass 4 MIN
Toothpicks 4 MIN

Mini Movies - Springboard For Learning - Unit 3, Why Is It—A Series
P-I
Prod-MORLAT Dist-MORLAT 1975

Beans And Seeds 4 MIN
Blow-Ups 4 MIN
Flight 4 MIN
Growth 4 MIN
On-Off 4 MIN

Mini Movies, Unit 1 - Who Are We—A Series
16MM FILM, 3/4 OR 1/2 IN VIDEO K-I
Focuses on a child's awareness of himself and his need to communicate with others.
Prod-CORF Dist-CORF 1977

Who Are We - Body Talk 004 MIN
Who Are We - Hands And Feet 004 MIN
Who Are We - Summertime, Wintertime 004 MIN
Who Are We - Talking 005 MIN
Who Are We - Touching 004 MIN

Mini Movies, Unit 2 - What Do We—A Series
16MM FILM, 3/4 OR 1/2 IN VIDEO K-I
Explores everyday objects and how they're made for a new perspective of a child's environment.
Prod-CORF Dist-CORF 1977

What Do We - Cans 004 MIN
What Do We - Chocolate 004 MIN
What Do We - Glass 004 MIN
What Do We - Shoes 004 MIN
What Do We - Toothpicks 004 MIN

Mini Movies, Unit 3 - Why Is It—A Series
16MM FILM, 3/4 OR 1/2 IN VIDEO K-I
Invites inquiry and discovery about how things grow and how things work in a child's world.
Prod-CORF Dist-CORF 1977

Why Is It - Beans And Seeds 004 MIN
Why Is It - Blow-Ups 004 MIN
Why Is It - Flight 004 MIN
Why Is It - Growth 004 MIN
Why Is It - On-Off 003 MIN

Mini-Laparotomy C 12 MIN
16MM FILM OPTICAL SOUND
Portrays the preparation, equipment and actual technique used in a mini-laparotomy, the most popular type of female interval sterilization.
Prod-RMABDI Dist-PODY 1976

Mini-Lectures To Accompany Black Studies 220 B 60 MIN
3/4 OR 1/2 INCH VIDEO CASSETTE
Uses ROOTS by Alex Haley as its text.
From The Black Studies Series. Pt 1
Prod-UAZMIC Dist-UAZMIC 1979

Mini-Marathon C 25 MIN
16MM FILM, 3/4 OR 1/2 IN VIDEO
Follows the running of the 10,000 meter Bonne Belle mini marathon in New York City's Central Park. Includes interviews with many of the 2,500 women contestants who talk about their motivations, strategies and enthusiasm for running.
LC NO. 79-707851
Prod-HANMNY Dist-WOMBAT 1979

Mini-Stretches C 10 MIN
2 INCH VIDEOTAPE
See series title for descriptive statement.
From The Janaki Series.
Prod-WGBHTV Dist-PUBTEL

Miniature Geometry C 20 MIN
3/4 OR 1/2 INCH VIDEO CASSETTE H
Presents teachers Beth McKenna and David Edmonds encouraging the use of an intuitive approach in developing a geometric system. Shows them presenting the elements of a mathematical system, developing a four-point geometry and demonstrating five postulates by building a model. Urges the proposal of theorems based on observations.
From The Shapes Of Geometry Series. Pt 3
LC NO. 82-707389
Prod-WVIZTV Dist-GPITVL 1982

Miniature Theatre, The - Notes From An Unknown Source - A Science Fiction C 30 MIN
3/4 INCH VIDEO CASSETTE
Deals with the nature of bureaucracy, its technocratic layerings and basic anti-humanism. Presented as a continuous, rolling, character-generated script-over-image.
Prod-WMENIF Dist-WMENIF

Miniature Worlds C 25 MIN
3/4 OR 1/2 INCH VIDEO CASSETTE H-C A
Teaches how to make a doll house.
From The Blizzard's Wonderful Wooden Toys Series.
Prod-BBCTV Dist-FI

Miniatures Magnificent, The C 19 MIN
16MM FILM OPTICAL SOUND J-C A
Presents postage stamps of Papua and New Guinea.
Prod-ANAIB Dist-AUIS 1971

Miniatures, Stylized (Sculptured) And Oriental Designs C 60 MIN
1/2 IN VIDEO CASSETTE BETA/VHS
Deals with sculptured and Oriental designs, utilizing one or two flowers, branches or weeds. Describes how to make miniature arrangements. Features Pat Quigley.
Prod-RMI Dist-RMI

Minigardens C 13 MIN
16MM FILM, 3/4 OR 1/2 IN VIDEO
Shows that Americans are growing minigardens, little vegetable and flower gardens in all sorts of containers such as old shoes, pots, plastic bags and pails. Portrays their attractive effect on cities as they spring up in dark cellars, drab halls, back steps, schoolrooms and fire escapes.
Prod-KLEINW Dist-KLEINW 1971

Minilaparotomy C 16 MIN
16MM FILM, 3/4 OR 1/2 IN VIDEO A
Provides important, comprehensive information to help obtain informed consent, how tubal sterilization prevents pregnancy, alternative methods, facts about how, when and where minilap can be performed, and possible complications.
Prod-PRORE Dist-PRORE

Minilaparotomy Techniques C 27 MIN
16MM FILM, 3/4 OR 1/2 IN VIDEO PRO
Shows clincial examples photographed in Far East, Africa and South America for performing tubal ligation by minilaparotomy. Discusses indications, contra-indications and patient care. (Also available in Spanish and French).
Prod-WFP Dist-WFP

Minimal Brain Dysfunction, Pt 1 C 6 MIN
3/4 OR 1/2 INCH VIDEO CASSETTE PRO
Prod-PRIMED Dist-PRIMED

Minimal Brain Dysfunction, Pt 2 C 6 MIN
3/4 OR 1/2 INCH VIDEO CASSETTE PRO
Prod-PRIMED Dist-PRIMED

Minimal Expectations For Health Supervision Of Sports C 19 MIN
3/4 OR 1/2 INCH VIDEO CASSETTE T
Discusses sports participation as a system in which safety requirements function as a vehicle to protect athletes. Emphasizes a functional plan that meets applicable standards so that when injuries do occur, they are transient. Addresses key components of sports participation including conditioning, skill development, performance, supervision and proper use of facilities.
From The Sports Medicine Series.
Prod-UNIDIM Dist-EBEC 1982

Minimizing Back Injury C 24 MIN
3/4 OR 1/2 INCH VIDEO CASSETTE IND
Examines how back injuries occur. Addresses proper lifting techniques. Focuses on day-to-day strains of lifting, sitting, pushing and bending.
Prod-TAT Dist-TAT

Minimizing Back Strain On The Job C
3/4 OR 1/2 INCH VIDEO CASSETTE
Demonstrates specific techniques to reduce back strain on the job.
Prod-TAT Dist-TAT

Minimizing The Stress Of Surgery C 28 MIN
3/4 OR 1/2 INCH VIDEO CASSETTE
Helps remove some of the mystery and fear about surgery and shows the usual activities and procedures that take place before and after surgery.
Prod-FAIRGH Dist-FAIRGH

Minimum Impact On Wilderness C 15 MIN
3/4 OR 1/2 INCH VIDEO CASSETTE
Shows ways in which people should and should not treat the wilderness in order to preserve it.
LC NO. 81-707148
Prod-WESTWN Dist-WESTWN

Minimum Mean-Square Error Estimation B 18 MIN
3/4 OR 1/2 INCH VIDEO CASSETTE PRO
Reviews the idea of the minimum mean-square error estimation. Presents an example involving the joint Gaussian probability density.
From The Probability And Random Processes - Statistical Averages Series.
Prod-MIOT Dist-MIOT

Minimum Principle Of Pontryagin, The-Continuous Time Case C 49 MIN
3/4 OR 1/2 INCH VIDEO CASSETTE PRO
See series title for descriptive statement.
From The Modern Control Theory - Deterministic Optimal Control Series.
Prod-MIOT Dist-MIOT

Minimum Principle Vs Dynamic Programming C 50 MIN
3/4 OR 1/2 INCH VIDEO CASSETTE PRO
Contrasts from a technical and algorithmic viewpoint the two methods for solving optimal control problems.
From The Modern Control Theory - Deterministic Optimal Control Series.
Prod-MIOT Dist-MIOT

Minimum Principle, The - Discrete Time Case C 43 MIN
3/4 OR 1/2 INCH VIDEO CASSETTE PRO
Discusses discrete optimal control problems and the associated minimum principles for their solutions.

From The Modern Control Theory - Deterministic Optimal Control Series.
Prod-MIOT Dist-MIOT

Mining Community, A - Kimberley C 14 MIN
16MM FILM, 3/4 OR 1/2 IN VIDEO P-I
Introduces one of the world's largest lead-zinc mines in operation since the beginning of the century. Shows how when the ore runs out, inhabitants have to depend on other ways to mabe a living. Describes development of the tourist industry in Kimberley.
From The This Is My Home Series.
Prod-BCNFL Dist-BCNFL 1984

Mining Engineer C 15 MIN
16MM FILM, 3/4 OR 1/2 IN VIDEO I
From The Career Awareness Series.
Prod-KLVXTV Dist-GPITVL

Mining Nickel C 35 MIN
16MM FILM OPTICAL SOUND
Shows modern methods used in the development of nickel mines and the excavation of ore.
Prod-MTP Dist-MTP

Mining Noise Hazards C 21 MIN
16MM FILM OPTICAL SOUND
Promotes a general awareness of noise hazards in the coal mining industry. Defines the sound and its characteristics. Shows the actual underground mining scenes, on-the-job noise surveys, and laboratory tests and analysis. Demonstrates the preventive methods along with various forms of engineering controls and protective devices.
LC NO. 74-705150
Prod-USBM Dist-USNAC 1973

Mining's Challenge C 15 MIN
16MM FILM OPTICAL SOUND
Discusses the challenges and career opportunities that exist in the mining profession today.
Prod-COLOMN Dist-CROMAR

Minister Of Hate (Josef Goebbels) B 27 MIN
16MM FILM, 3/4 OR 1/2 IN VIDEO J-C
Examines the techniques of totalitarian control of communications evolved by the Nazi, Joseph Goebbels. Includes actual scenes of the burning of all books considered hostile to the Nazi regime. Trevor-Roper, author of 'THE LAST DAYS OF HITLER,' comments on Goebbels' career.
From The Twentieth Century Series.
Prod-CBSNEW Dist-CRMP 1959

Minister's Black Veil, The C 30 MIN
2 INCH VIDEOTAPE J-H
Presents the short story The Minister's Black Veil by Nathaniel Hawthorne.
From The From Franklin To Frost - Nathaniel Hawthorne Series.
Prod-MPATI Dist-GPITVL

Ministry Of John The Baptist X 20 MIN
16MM FILM OPTICAL SOUND I-H T R
Jesus comes to John to be baptized. John calls him 'THE LAMB OF GOD.' John continues to preach and to baptize until he is imprisoned by Herod. John sends two disciples to ask Jesus if the Christ has really come.
From The Living Bible Series.
Prod-FAMF Dist-FAMF

Ministry On An Escalator C 30 MIN
16MM FILM OPTICAL SOUND R
Shows the ministry of the Christian church on various college campuses.
Prod-TRAFCO Dist-ECUFLM 1974

Ministry On An Escalator C 27 MIN
3/4 OR 1/2 INCH VIDEO CASSETTE A
Looks at the concept of a 'campus ministry' and how it has changed. Features five campus ministers representing different universities who strive to create a church enviornment which can act as a catalyst in the shaping of the student's lives.
Prod-UMCOM Dist-ECUFLM 1975

Minnesota Soap Series C 21 MIN
3/4 OR 1/2 INCH VIDEO CASSETTE C A
Twelve skits focusing on counseling situations in which questions and concerns about sexuality can arise. Exemplifies good and bad ways of dealing with problems.
Prod-NATSF Dist-MMRC

Minnesota Valley National Wildlife Refuge C 16 MIN
16MM FILM, 3/4 OR 1/2 IN VIDEO
Chronicles the evolution of the valley and floodplain of the Minnesota River in the Twin City metropolitan area from an ignored and abused bottomland to an area recognized for its unique cultural, environmental and recreational values.
Prod-USBSFW Dist-USNAC

Minnesotanos Mexicanos C 61 MIN
16MM FILM OPTICAL SOUND
Examines Mexican Americans in Minnesota, dealing with their pre-Columbian heritage, their years spent in the American Southwest, and their arrival in Minnesota in the late 19th century. Explores 20th century issues, such as bilingual education, migrant workers and the Bakke case.
LC NO. 79-701377
Prod-SPSP Dist-SPSP 1978

Minnie Remembers C 5 MIN
16MM FILM, 3/4 OR 1/2 IN VIDEO J A
Adapted from the Donna Swanson poem of the same name. Focuses on an old woman, sitting alone, who reminisces about the past. Contrasts the warmth and love which has typified her youth and womanhood. Demonstrates the needs and feelings of the elderly which are the same as any other age group.
Prod-UMCOM Dist-ECUFLM 1976

Minnie The Moocher And Many Many More C 55 MIN
3/4 INCH VIDEO CASSETTE
Cab Calloway leads a nostalgic tour through the Harlem jazz clubs of the 30's and 40's. Shows legendary stars that performed in them such as Duke Ellington, Fats Waller and others.
Prod-FIRS Dist-FIRS

Minor Altercation, A C 30 MIN
16MM FILM, 3/4 OR 1/2 IN VIDEO A
Discusses the racial conflict in our public schools.
Prod-CNEMAG Dist-CNEMAG

Minor Burns C
3/4 OR 1/2 INCH VIDEO CASSETTE
Presents a program of discussion and illustration of the effect of burns on the skin, the skin's role in healing and emergency department procedures for treatment.
From The Burns - Emergency Management Series.
Prod-VTRI Dist-VTRI

Minor Burns C 20 MIN
3/4 OR 1/2 INCH VIDEO CASSETTE PRO
Designed to provide the participant with the knowledge to care for minor burn injuries. Demonstrates how to determine when a particular burn should be referred to a specialist. Gives a description of the anatomical structure and normal function of the skin and the psysiological events associated with minor burns. Tells how to inform patient about the procedure for follow-up treatment.
From The Medical Cisis Intervention Series.
Prod-LEIKID Dist-LEIKID

Minor Crafts Series - Decoupage C 10 MIN
3/4 OR 1/2 INCH VIDEO CASSETTE
Explains and demonstrates decoupage (a French term for decorating wood surfaces with pictures).
Prod-HSCIC Dist-HSCIC

Minor Electrical Repairs Of Small Appliances C 13 MIN
16MM FILM, 3/4 OR 1/2 IN VIDEO J-C A
Illustrates the basic tools needed to make simple electrical repairs. Shows several common problems and tells how to solve them.
From The Home Repairs Series.
LC NO. 81-706034
Prod-CENTRO Dist-CORF 1981

Minor Oral Surgery Technics In Dentistry C 135 MIN
3/4 OR 1/2 INCH VIDEO CASSETTE PRO
Presents the surgical procedure for the correction of central incisor diastemas. Shows the removal of a torus palatinus by interrupting the circulation, leading to necrosis and the nontraumatic removal of the torus. Also shows method for uncovering embedded canines.
Prod-CHIDEN Dist-USNAC

Minorities C 15 MIN
16MM FILM, 3/4 OR 1/2 IN VIDEO H-C A
Presents a documentary about a skilled Black worker and his economic problems. Shows that his efforts to find steady work in his craft as a firebrick mason typify many of the problems of Black workers. Examines the status of Blacks today, how far they have come and their prospects for the future.
From The American Condition Series.
Prod-ABCTV Dist-MGHT 1976

Minorities C 30 MIN
3/4 OR 1/2 INCH VIDEO CASSETTE C
Discusses the present status of minorities in socieity.
From The Focus On Society Series.
Prod-DALCCD Dist-DALCCD

Minorities - What's A Minority C 14 MIN
16MM FILM, 3/4 OR 1/2 IN VIDEO J-C
Interviews members of various groups to provide perspectives on the problems of prejudice and of different races, religions and ethnic groups living together.
Prod-CORF Dist-CORF 1972

Minorities In Agriculture - The Winnebago C 29 MIN
3/4 INCH VIDEO CASSETTE
Highlights the economic development programs of the Winnebago tribe of Nebraska, beginning with a brief history of the tribe and moving to a description of their food self-sufficiency program. Also available in two-inch quad and one-inch videotape.
Prod-BRCLFC Dist-NAMPBC

Minorities In Communications C 30 MIN
16MM FILM OPTICAL SOUND J-C A
Discusses career opportunities for minorities, giving direction and supplying answers to questions raised by minority members themselves.
Prod-NWMA Dist-NWMA 1974

Minority Candidates C 35 MIN
3/4 OR 1/2 INCH VIDEO CASSETTE A
Focuses on avoiding illegal questions while conducting job interviews with minority candidates.
From The Interview - EEO Compliance Series. Pt 2
Prod-XICOM Dist-XICOM

Minority Carriers In Semiconductors B 26 MIN
3/4 INCH VIDEOTAPE
Demonstrates the existence and behavior of injected excess minority carriers in semiconductors by repeating in modified form the Haynes-Shockley drift-mobility experiment.
Prod-NCEEF Dist-EDC

Minority Of One C 28 MIN
16MM FILM, 3/4 OR 1/2 IN VIDEO H-C
Discusses the neurological disorder known as autism, the children who suffer from it and the problems faced by their parents.
Prod-NBCTV Dist-FI 1977

Minority Report C 29 MIN
16MM FILM, 3/4 OR 1/2 IN VIDEO T
Presents an in-depth look at two related concerns, the special problems of minorities in what many observers consider an alien educational environment and, secondly, the pros and cons of what has become known as 'RADICAL SCHOOL REFORM.' Discusses free and alternative schools.
From The Human Relations And School Discipline Series.
Prod-MFFD Dist-FI

Minority Youth - Adam C 10 MIN
16MM FILM, 3/4 OR 1/2 IN VIDEO I-H
Describes the problems of Adam, an Indian boy in a predominantly Anglo society. He shows pride in his cultural heritage as he chooses to retain the strengths of his own culture in the face of assimilation into the American way of life.
Prod-ROE Dist-PHENIX 1971

Minority Youth - Akira C 15 MIN
16MM FILM, 3/4 OR 1/2 IN VIDEO I-H
Describes Akira's frustrations and pride in having a different racial background from most of the people in his society. Relates his choice to adhere to the cultural heritage of his Japanese ancestry in the face of assimilation into the American way of life.
Prod-ROE Dist-PHENIX 1971

Minority Youth - Angie C 11 MIN
16MM FILM, 3/4 OR 1/2 IN VIDEO
A girl relates her personal feelings about being Mexican-American.
Prod-ROE Dist-PHENIX 1971

Minority Youth - Felicia B 12 MIN
16MM FILM, 3/4 OR 1/2 IN VIDEO I-H
Presents the problems of young black people and tells the story of a girl who has feelings of alienation from the predominately white American culture.
Prod-ROE Dist-PHENIX 1971

Minority Youth—A Series
16MM FILM, 3/4 OR 1/2 IN VIDEO
Examines the problems facing minority youths in America.
Prod-ROE Dist-PHENIX

Adam - Minority Youth 010 MIN
Akira - Minority Youth 013 MIN
Angie - Minority Youth 011 MIN
Felicia - Minority Youth 012 MIN

Minors C 36 MIN
16MM FILM, 3/4 OR 1/2 IN VIDEO J-H A
Features story of a minor-league baseball player and a young 14-year-old girl who wants to coach him.
Prod-LCOA Dist-LCOA 1985

Minors' Rights C 29 MIN
3/4 INCH VIDEO CASSETTE C A
Concentrates on laws that govern persons prior to age of majority. Discusses major areas where the law applies differently to adults. Examines juvenile deliquency.
From The You And The Law Series. Lesson 11
Prod-COAST Dist-CDTEL Prodn-SADCC

Minotaur, The C 55 MIN
3/4 OR 1/2 INCH VIDEO CASSETTE PRO
Allows students to see how their own responses may affect the course of evaluation and treatment.
Prod-HSCIC Dist-HSCIC 1979

Mint 400, The C 24 MIN
16MM FILM OPTICAL SOUND
Depicts the Mint 400, the richest off-road race in America held in Las Vegas, Nevada. Shows the planning and preparation, support crews, the exotic racing machines and the race itself.
Prod-GC Dist-MTP

Minus One C
16MM FILM OPTICAL SOUND
See series title for descriptive statement.
From The Rats Series.
Prod-MLA Dist-MLA

Minus Three Miles C 7 MIN
16MM FILM OPTICAL SOUND
Shows the movement of assembled rocket to launch pad.
From The Apollo Digest Series.
LC NO. 74-705151
Prod-NASAMS Dist-USNAC 1969

Minus Three Miles C 3 MIN
3/4 INCH VIDEO CASSETTE
Analyzes the mobility concept of assembling a 36-story rocket and moving it to the launch area. Issued in 1969 as a motion picture.
From The Apollo Digest Series.
LC NO. 79-706985
Prod-NASA Dist-USNAC 1979

Minus Tide, The C 12 MIN
3/4 OR 1/2 INCH VIDEO CASSETTE J-H
Details the movements of the waters, both violent and peaceful, that have carved the environment for plants and animals of the tidal regions on California's coast when the lowest of the low tides reveals sponges, starfish, anemones, kelp, algae, and various mollusks.
Prod-CEPRO Dist-CEPRO

Minute And A Half Man C 6 MIN
16MM FILM, 3/4 OR 1/2 IN VIDEO P
Introduces Hector Heathcote, a minute man who is always late. Show how his tardiness is rewarded when the enemy is routed.
Prod-SF Dist-SF 1975

Minute Hand, The C 20 MIN
2 INCH VIDEOTAPE P
See series title for descriptive statement.
From The Mathemagic, Unit VI - Measurement Series.
Prod-WMULTV Dist-GPITVL

Minute Saved, The B 29 MIN
16MM FILM, 3/4 OR 1/2 IN VIDEO
Concerns the element of haste that all too often acts as the catalyst of destruction in aviation.
LC NO. 82-707209
Prod-USA Dist-USNAC 1967

Minute Waltz C 3 MIN
3/4 INCH VIDEO CASSETTE
Speeds up twenty minutes of actual dancing time to produce three minutes of hilarious video to Chopin's Minute Waltz.'
From The Laurie McDonald Series.
Prod-WMENIF Dist-WMENIF

Minuteman - Missile And Mission C 20 MIN
16MM FILM OPTICAL SOUND H
Explains the role of the thiokel chemical corporation in the development and manufacture of the Minuteman Intercontinental Ballistic Missile. Features testing and live firing of the missile.
LC NO. FIA67-2336
Prod-THIOKL Dist-THIOKL 1962

Miracle B 15 MIN
16MM FILM SILENT J-C A
Depicts the images of a city as they shift from dawn to noon.
Prod-UWFKD Dist-UWFKD

Miracle At Point Of Cut C 22 MIN
16MM FILM OPTICAL SOUND
Explores the differences in single point tool removal of various materials through a wide range of rake angles.
Prod-MASTER Dist-MASTER

Miracle At San Rafael C 22 MIN
16MM FILM OPTICAL SOUND
Shows the training of dogs at Guide Dogs for the Blind in San Rafael, California.
LC NO. 80-700429
Prod-GDOGS Dist-STRICR Prodn-STRICR 1979

Miracle At The Time B 18 MIN
16MM FILM OPTICAL SOUND
Shows how a bitter, alienated motel owner in a decadent urban situation discovers that his happiness can be provided by the very people who have been the source of his bitterness. Tells how one such person provides him with a miracle that opens up his small, enclosed world.
Prod-USC Dist-USC

Miracle In Color C 22 MIN
16MM FILM OPTICAL SOUND
Begins with the birth of latex in the Dow labs and carries through to the final application of latex in your home or office building.
Prod-DCC Dist-DCC

Miracle In Java B 25 MIN
16MM FILM OPTICAL SOUND H-C A
Presents the story of how the attempts of one man to help his handicapped fellows became a modern article of international cooperation.
Prod-UN Dist-UN 1957

Miracle In The Desert - The Story Of Hanford C 29 MIN
16MM FILM OPTICAL SOUND
Tells the story of the development of the Hanford Engineer Works in southern Washington during World War II. Shows how the discovery of plutonium and the first successful nuclear chain reaction by Dr Enrico Fermi led to the construction of the billion dollar plant.
LC NO. 74-705155
Prod-USAEC Dist-USNAC 1966

Miracle In Tonga C 16 MIN
16MM FILM OPTICAL SOUND
Records the cooperative efforts of the Tongan Medical Department and the communicable disease center to protect against smallpox in Tonga. Explains and illustrates a new method for smallpox vaccination.
LC NO. FIE67-45
Prod-USPHS Dist-USNAC Prodn-USPHS 1965

Miracle Machine, The C 20 MIN
16MM FILM OPTICAL SOUND J-H
Accompanies a housewife on a world trip as she learns the importance of a modern combine harvester. Teaches how the harvester is vital to the world's supply of food.
Prod-SRCNHD Dist-SRCNHD

Miracle Months, The C
3/4 OR 1/2 INCH VIDEO CASSETTE
Expresses the drama and the wonder of conception, gestation and birth. Covers human ovulation, the instant of penetration of the sperm into the egg, a living 40-day embryo inside its mother's uterus, its two-chambered heart beating vigorously. Documents major medical advances including a hazardous intrauterine transfusion that pumps blood directly into a baby dying in its mother's womb of Rh disease, and a perfectly timed decision, based on sophisticated testing of amniotic fluid, that allows suvival of mother and child, both threatened by a condition called placenta previa.
From The Body Human Series.
Prod-TRAINX Dist-TRAINX

Miracle Of Birth C 30 MIN
16MM FILM OPTICAL SOUND C A
Prepares expectant parents for childbirth. Shows the live birth of three infants. Captures the joy and beauty of the occasion as it is shared by the young couples.
LC NO. 75-700308
Prod-BYU Dist-BYU 1974

Miracle Of Czechoslovakia C 29 MIN
2 INCH VIDEOTAPE
See series title for descriptive statement.
From The Course Of Our Times I Series.
Prod-WGBHTV Dist-PUBTEL

Miracle Of Grass C 22 MIN
16MM FILM OPTICAL SOUND
Gives details of grass seeding, growing, planting and experimentation. Explains good ways to grow and improve grass, and the many uses of grass.
Prod-UPR Dist-UPR 1965

Miracle Of Life (Arabic) C 15 MIN
16MM FILM, 3/4 OR 1/2 IN VIDEO J-C A
Presents a microscopic study of the reproductive process, showing the living processes of fertilization, cell division, and growth and development of the fetus to the moment of the first heartbeat. Describes both human and animal fetus development, from the point at which human development differs.
Prod-CINSCI Dist-PFP

Miracle Of Life, The C 15 MIN
16MM FILM, 3/4 OR 1/2 IN VIDEO J-C A
Explores the processes of fertilization, cell division and growth by means of microscope photography.
Prod-CINSCI Dist-PFP

Miracle Of Life, The C 57 MIN
16MM FILM, 3/4 OR 1/2 IN VIDEO H-C A
Describes the male and female productive organs, showing the formation of sperm and the passage of a fertile egg through the fallopian tubes. Uses a microscope to observe DNA, chromosomes and other minute body details.
From The Nova Series.
LC NO. 83-706634
Prod-SVERTV Dist-TIMLIF 1983

Miracle Of Reproduction, The (2nd Ed) C 15 MIN
16MM FILM, 3/4 OR 1/2 IN VIDEO P-I
Explains how plants, fish, animals and human beings reproduce their species.
Prod-DAVP Dist-AIMS 1974

Miracle Of Taxila C 45 MIN
16MM FILM OPTICAL SOUND
Tells the story of the Christian Hospital Taxila, a small Christian hospital in Islamic Pakistan that restores sight to more than 12,000 blind people yearly.
Prod-WHTLIN Dist-WHTLIN 1983

Miracle Of The Helicopter C 17 MIN
3/4 OR 1/2 INCH VIDEO CASSETTE
Traces the progress of Sikorsky helicopters from the first flight of Igor Sikorsky's VS-300 to the early 1970s. Illustrates the range of military and civilian missions performed by Sikorsky models with worldwide operations including rescues, astronaut retrieval, airline service and timber harvesting.
Prod-IHF Dist-IHF

Miracle Of The Mind C 19 MIN
16MM FILM, 3/4 OR 1/2 IN VIDEO J-C A
Edited version of the 1968 motion picture of the same title. Describes the attempts made by man to understand the nature of the mind and surveys the contribution science has made to this understanding. Evaluates present knowledge of the brain and mental functions in terms of man's future.
From The Twenty-First Century Series.
Prod-CBSNEW Dist-MGHT 1975

Miracle Of The Mind C 26 MIN
16MM FILM, 3/4 OR 1/2 IN VIDEO J-C A
Describes the attempts made by man to understand the nature of the mind and surveys the contribution science has made to this understanding. Evaluates present knowledge of the brain and mental functions in terms of man's future.
From The Twenty-First Century Series.
Prod-CBSNEW Dist-MGHT 1968

Miracle Of The Mind C 30 MIN
1 INCH VIDEOTAPE
Indicates how some day man may be able to control and manipulate his thoughts, memories and emotions.
From The Twenty-First Century Series.
Prod-UCC Dist-MTP

Miracle Of Vision B 15 MIN
16MM FILM OPTICAL SOUND
Covers structure of eye and its function for seeing. Discusses optical illusions, abnormal conditions of the eye which cause poor vision, and corrective measures for vision defects. Presents a brief history of optometry and the work of the optometrist.
Prod-AMOP Dist-FILAUD

Miracle Of Water, The C 20 MIN
16MM FILM, 3/4 OR 1/2 IN VIDEO
Describes water resource development in the West by the Bureau of Reclamation. Shows dams and reservoirs, and tells of the benefits derived from the various projects.
Prod-USBR Dist-USNAC

Miracle On Second Avenue C 22 MIN
16MM FILM OPTICAL SOUND
Presents an account of the way in which the Bell System restored telephone service to a major central office switching center destroyed by the worst fire in its history.
LC NO. 75-703287
Prod-ATAT Dist-MGS Prodn-GLENNG 1975

Miracle Woman, The B 90 MIN
16MM FILM OPTICAL SOUND
Tells how an embittered young woman (Barbara Stanwyck) opens a religious tabernacle in order to fleece the masses. Directed by Frank Capra.
Prod-CPC Dist-KITPAR 1931

Miracles From Agriculture C 14 MIN
3/4 INCH VIDEO CASSETTE
Reports on the farming and ranching, marketing, processing, storing, transporting, and merchandising of food and other agricultural products. Describes the role of research and agricultrual services from farm to market to home.
Prod-USDA Dist-USDA 1972

Miraculous Arabian Steed, The - A Middle East Folk Tale C 7 MIN
16MM FILM OPTICAL SOUND K-I
Presents an animated story about a wily police chief who tries to cheat Djoha out of his horse and is, in the end, outwitted himself.
From The Folk Tales From Around The World Series.
LC NO. 80-700789
Prod-ADPF Dist-SF 1980

Miraculous Arabian Steed, The - A Middle East Folk Tale C 7 MIN
3/4 OR 1/2 INCH VIDEO CASSETTE K-I
Presents an animated story about a wily police chief who tries to cheat Djoha out of his horse and is, in the end, outwitted himself.
From The Folk Tales From Around The World Series.
Prod-ADPF Dist-SF 1980

Miraculous Pool, The C 28 MIN
16MM FILM OPTICAL SOUND
Portrays the story of medical research at the National Institutes of Health, emphasizing the role of the National Institute of Allergy and Infectious Diseases and its efforts to combat viral and other infectious diseases through a collaborative vaccine development program.
LC NO. 70-707509
Prod-BECDIC Dist-NMAC Prodn-IVC 1967

Mirage At The Desert's Edge C 22 MIN
16MM FILM OPTICAL SOUND C A
Shows that Islam, the spiritual mirage of the country of Senegal, can be dispelled only by the reality of Jesus Christ.
Prod-CBFMS Dist-CBFMS

Miranda And The Right To Counsel C 50 MIN
3/4 OR 1/2 INCH VIDEO CASSETTE PRO
Distinguishes between the Miranda warning and the sixth amendment right to counsel. Explores eyewitness identification and its limitations and the subject of prior confessions.
From The Criminal Procedure And The Trial Advocate Series.
Prod-ABACPE Dist-ABACPE

Miranda Interrogation B 20 MIN
16MM FILM OPTICAL SOUND C
Deals with various aspects of a criminal lawsuit involving a liquor store robbery case. Shows policemen questioning the adult suspect in a manner consistent with recent court decisions regarding the rights of criminal suspects.
From The Criminal Law Series. No. 4
LC NO. 70-714036
Prod-RPATLF Dist-RPATLF 1968

Miriam Fried - A Profile C 30 MIN
3/4 OR 1/2 INCH VIDEO CASSETTE H-C A
Features a closeup of Miriam Field, a violinist, as she discusses the balance she seeks between the critical elements of her life - performance and family.
Prod-IU Dist-IU 1982

Mirror Images - Figures And Symmetry B 20 MIN
3/4 INCH VIDEO CASSETTE P
See series title for descriptive statement.
From The Let's Figure It Out Series.
Prod-WNYETV Dist-NYSED 1968

Mirror Of America B 36 MIN
16MM FILM - 3/4 IN VIDEO
Reflects the American way of life from 1914-1921. Gives a cross-sectional illustration of people and progress, the people's daily activities, dress and habits. Includes views of Presidents Wilson and Harding, Thomas Edison and Henry Ford.
LC NO. 79-706460
Prod-USNAC Dist-USNAC 1972

Mirror Of Gesture C 21 MIN
16MM FILM, 3/4 OR 1/2 IN VIDEO
Focuses on the relationship between the sculpture and dance of India using sculpture from the Indian galleries of the Los Angeles County Museum of Art. Intercuts Indian sculpture with dance sequences to emphasize the artistic correspondences between the two media and to demonstrate how effectively the rhythms of the dancer have been translated into sculptural form.
Prod-LACMOA Dist-UCEMC Prodn-DIA 1974

Mirror People C 4 MIN
16MM FILM OPTICAL SOUND
An animated film in which elegant, goon-faced characters cavort with their double images.
LC NO. 75-700149
Prod-ROSEK Dist-CFS 1974

Mirror Road C 7 MIN
3/4 OR 1/2 INCH VIDEO CASSETTE
See series title for descriptive statement.
From The Gary Hill, Pt 1 Series.
Prod-EAI Dist-EAI

Mirror, Mirror C 11 MIN
16MM FILM OPTICAL SOUND

Deals with mystery, mythology and psychology.
LC NO. 77-702967
Prod-ASTIRM Dist-CANFDC 1972

Mirrored Reason C 10 MIN
3/4 OR 1/2 INCH VIDEO CASSETTE
Studies distorted reason or paranoia in a film work derived from a Franz Kafka story.
From The Four Programs By Stan Vanderbeek Series.
Prod-EAI Dist-EAI

Mirrors - Reflections Of A Culture C 16 MIN
16MM FILM, 3/4 OR 1/2 IN VIDEO J-C A
Shows how the murals of three Mexican-Americans present images that help the Chicano see himself as the inheritor of a strong and important tradition.
LC NO. 82-706568
Prod-PAULMI Dist-CF 1980

Mirrors Of Time C 26 MIN
3/4 OR 1/2 INCH VIDEO CASSETTE
Reveals the excitement of finding clues which reveal the secrets of eons of layering and shifting of the earth's structure.
Prod-HBS Dist-IVCH

Mirrors On The Universe - The MMT Story C 29 MIN
16MM FILM OPTICAL SOUND
Uses animated segments to document the construction of the laser- and computer-controlled multiple mirror telescope at the Mt Hopkins Observatory, located atop an 8,500-foot mountain in southern Arizona.
LC NO. 79-701007
Prod-SMITHS Dist-UARIZ 1979

Mirrors To The Sun C 23 MIN
16MM FILM OPTICAL SOUND
Shows the beauty and splendor of British Columbia.
LC NO. 76-702449
Prod-BCDTI Dist-CTFL 1974

Misa Colombiana C 20 MIN
3/4 INCH VIDEO CASSETTE
Focuses on one woman who survives, as do other Tuguriano families, in Medellin, Colombia, by scavenging the municipal dump. Features a dissident priest who ministers to the squatters.
Prod-DOCEDR Dist-DOCEDR 1976

Misadventures Of Merlin Jones, The C 91 MIN
16MM FILM OPTICAL SOUND
Presents Merlin Jones, an oddball college student whose weird mental experiments involve him and his beautiful girlfirend in an unending series of situations.
Prod-DISNEY Dist-UAE 1965

Misbehavior - What You Could Have Done But Didn't C 29 MIN
3/4 OR 1/2 INCH VIDEO CASSETTE T
See series title for descriptive statement.
From The Coping With Kids Series.
Prod-MFFD Dist-FI

Misbehavior - What You Could Have Done But Didn't C 30 MIN
3/4 OR 1/2 INCH VIDEO CASSETTE
Identifies the goals of disruptive behavior and how these relate to discouragement. Discusses the methods used to break the chain of events which contribute to disruptive behavior.
From The Coping With Kids Series.
Prod-OHUTC Dist-OHUTC

Miscellaneous Biochemical Tests/IMViC Reactions C 29 MIN
3/4 OR 1/2 INCH VIDEO CASSETTE
Includes two presentations on tape numbered 6205. Shows ways of performing and reading tests for catalase, oxidase, nitrate reduction, ammonia production and urea hydrolysis and, in addition, explains the biochemical basis for each. Illustrates the usefulness of the LMViC tests in the identification of gram-negative bacilli. Information on the IMViC tests includes the biochemical basis, media and reagents used, method of inoculation and interpretation of results.
Prod-AMSM Dist-AVMM

Miscellaneous Electrical Equipment C 7 MIN
16MM FILM, 3/4 OR 1/2 IN VIDEO H-C A
Deals with such pieces of electrical equipment as the relay, meters, the moving coil, the potentiometer in a circuit and the rheostat.
From The Basic Electricity Series.
Prod-STFD Dist-IFB 1979

Miscellaneous Pointers C 30 MIN
3/4 OR 1/2 INCH VIDEO CASSETTE IND
See series title for descriptive statement.
From The Drafting - Piping Pointers Series.
Prod-GPCV Dist-GPCV

Miscellaneous Taping C 30 MIN
3/4 OR 1/2 INCH VIDEO CASSETTE
Covers the other joints of the body, which do not receive much attention but can cause problems, including the shoulder, elbow, fingers, thumb, feet, toes, arms, thighs and lower legs.
From The Athletic Trainer Series.
Prod-NETCHE Dist-NETCHE 1972

Miscellaneous Test Instruments C 60 MIN
3/4 OR 1/2 INCH VIDEO CASSETTE IND
Covers bridges, phase rotation, phase sequence and variable current tester.
From The Electrical Maintenance Training, Module B - Test Instruments Series.
Prod-LEIKID Dist-LEIKID

Mischief C 8 MIN
16MM FILM, 3/4 OR 1/2 IN VIDEO K-P
Uses felt-cut animation to tell the story of a naughty boy who is finally punished by the animals in his yard for playing dirty tricks on them.
Prod-SFSP Dist-PHENIX 1974

Miscommunications C 5 MIN
16MM FILM OPTICAL SOUND I-C A
Satirizes obstacles to individual communication in four animated vignettes.
LC NO. 74-702118
Prod-MMA Dist-MMA 1972

Misconceptions Regarding Good Health Care C 30 MIN
3/4 OR 1/2 INCH VIDEO CASSETTE
See series title for descriptive statement.
From The Care And Feeding Of Dancers Series.
Prod-ARCVID Dist-ARCVID

Misconduct On And Off The Job C
16MM FILM - 3/4 IN VIDEO
Shows how to handle cases of misconduct on and off the job. Stresses that it is important to investigate, get the facts first, warn employees about off-the-job misconduct, to avoid jumping to conclusions and, where possible, head off potentially explosive situations.
From The Preventive Discipline (2nd Ed) Series. Unit 2
Prod-BNA Dist-BNA

Mise En Place C
3/4 OR 1/2 INCH VIDEO CASSETTE
See series title for descriptive statement.
From The Vegetable Cutting Series.
Prod-CULINA Dist-CULINA

Miserable Merry Christmas, A C 15 MIN
16MM FILM, 3/4 OR 1/2 IN VIDEO I-J
Presents an account of an episode from the life of Lincoln Steffens which helps stimulate thought on the spirit and values of Christmas.
Prod-EDUCBC Dist-EBEC 1974

Miseries Of War, The - Paintings By Felix Labisse C 10 MIN
16MM FILM, 3/4 OR 1/2 IN VIDEO C A
Shows Felix Labisse's surrealistic paintings as a fierce protest against the threat of atomic warfare. Issued as a motion picture in Belgium in 1962.
LC NO. 80-706704
Prod-STORCH Dist-IFB 1978

Misery In The Borinage B 29 MIN
16MM FILM, 3/4 OR 1/2 IN VIDEO H-C A
Presents a revised, English version of the 1933 motion picture Misere Au Borinage. Documents the harsh punishment meted out to the striking coal miners in the Borinage region of Belgium.
LC NO. 80-706555
Prod-STORCH Dist-IFB 1979

Misery Merchants B 29 MIN
16MM FILM OPTICAL SOUND
Exposes the greed of quack remedy merchants who promote 'sitting in an abandoned uranium mine as a treatment for arthritis.' Includes simple explanations of arthritis and its accepted treatment. Features Dennis O'Keefe and Everett Sloan.
Prod-WSTGLC Dist-WSTGLC

Misfit C 63 MIN
16MM FILM OPTICAL SOUND
Exposes the truth about church-school-and home dropouts. Offers a Christian solution to the problem clearly presenting the drop-out's problem, misfit dynamically portrays his real need and the answer to it. A never-to-be-forgotten message that is realistically presented with teen-age appeal. Answers the question, 'IS THERE HOPE FOR THE DROP-OUT.'
Prod-YOUTH Dist-GF 1965

Mislabeled And Unlabeled Deaths C 236 MIN
3/4 INCH VIDEO CASSETTE PRO
Discusses mislabeled deaths.
From The Forensic Medicine Teaching Programs Series. No. 11
LC NO. 78-706054
Prod-NMAC Dist-USNAC Prodn-NYUCM 1978

Misplaced Goals C 30 MIN
3/4 OR 1/2 INCH VIDEO CASSETTE P-I
See series title for descriptive statement.
From The Sonrisas Series.
Prod-KRLNTV Dist-MDCPB

Miss America B 7 MIN
16MM FILM OPTICAL SOUND
Shows how women's liberation groups attempted to disrupt the annual miss America pageant and make boardwalk and contestant spectators more aware of the insidious contest with its image of mindless womanhood.
Prod-SFN Dist-SFN

Miss Clara Let Us Be C 29 MIN
2 INCH VIDEOTAPE
See series title for descriptive statement.
From The Our Street Series.
Prod-MDCPB Dist-PUBTEL

Miss Esta Maude's Secret C 10 MIN
16MM FILM, 3/4 OR 1/2 IN VIDEO K-I
Tells the story of a school teacher's secret adventures in her racing car. An animated film.
From The Storybook Series.
Prod-MGHT Dist-MGHT 1964

Miss Goodall And The Baboons Of Gombe C 52 MIN
16MM FILM, 3/4 OR 1/2 IN VIDEO I-C A
Examines the habits, inter-group relationships and leadership rivalries of the East African baboon.
From The Jane Goodall And The World Of Animal Behavior Series.
Prod-METROM Dist-FI 1974

Miss Goodall And The Hyena Story C 52 MIN
16MM FILM, 3/4 OR 1/2 IN VIDEO J-C A
Describes Jane Goodall's study of the hyenas of East Africa.
Prod-METROM Dist-FI 1975

Miss Goodall And The Lions Of Serengeti C 52 MIN
16MM FILM, 3/4 OR 1/2 IN VIDEO J-H A
Tells how Jane Goodall observed lion behavior in East Africa.
Prod-METROM Dist-FI 1976

Miss Goodall And The Wild Chimpanzees C 52 MIN
16MM FILM OPTICAL SOUND
Describes Jane Goodall and her studies as she observes and records the activities of wild chimpanzees in Africa.
Prod-AETNA Dist-WOLPER Prodn-WOLPER 1965

Miss Goodall And The Wild Chimpanzees C 52 MIN
16MM FILM, 3/4 OR 1/2 IN VIDEO
Documents the experiences of British zoologist Jane Goodall, who spent five years studying chimpanzees in Tanzania's Gombe Stream Preserve. Discusses her belief that through understanding chimpanzee behavior it will lead man toward clearer understanding of himself.
LC NO. 80-706359
Prod-NGS Dist-NGS 1966

Miss Goodall And The Wild Dogs Of Africa C 52 MIN
16MM FILM, 3/4 OR 1/2 IN VIDEO I-C A
Records a study made by animal behaviorist Jane Goodall of a pack of wild dogs on the plains of the Serengeti in Africa. Follows one young pup who gets detached from the pack as he searches for a new family.
From The Jane Goodall And The World Of Animal Behavior Series.
Prod-METROM Dist-FI 1973

Miss Grouse C 5 MIN
3/4 OR 1/2 INCH VIDEO CASSETTE J-H
Deals with avoiding cliches in writing.
From The Write On, Set 1 Series.
Prod-CTI Dist-CTI

Miss Indian America C 59 MIN
3/4 INCH VIDEO CASSETTE
Covers the 20th annual Miss Indian America Pageant in 1973 in Sheridan, Wyoming. The colorful costumes and tribal dances show some of the similarities and differences among modern Indian cultures. Also available in two-inch quad and one-inch videotape.
Prod-KBYU Dist-NAMPBC

Miss Julie C 60 MIN
3/4 OR 1/2 INCH VIDEO CASSETTE H-C A
Conveys an understanding of the role of the director in blending dramatic elements and synthesizing the work of the artists. Uses the play Miss Julie as an example.
From The Drama - Play, Performance, Perception Series. Backstage / Behind The Scenes
Prod-BBCTV Dist-FI 1978

Miss Nelson Is Back C 30 MIN
3/4 OR 1/2 INCH VIDEO CASSETTE P
Presents Ruth Buzzi narrating the book Miss Nelson Is Back which is all about surprises. Shows LeVar Burton finding some surprises of his own as he embarks on a birthday treasure hunt.
From The Reading Rainbow Series. No. 2
Prod-WNEDTV Dist-GPITVL 1982

Miss Nelson Is Missing C 14 MIN
16MM FILM, 3/4 OR 1/2 IN VIDEO P-I
Tells what happens when Miss Nelson, an excellent but ignored teacher, decides to disappear for a day, leaving her class to cope with the poisonous personality of Miss Swamp, the odious substitute.
Prod-LCOA Dist-LCOA 1979

Miss Newton's Trial C 5 MIN
3/4 OR 1/2 INCH VIDEO CASSETTE J-H
Teaches the use of commas in a series.
From The Write On, Set 1 Series.
Prod-CTI Dist-CTI

Miss Twiggley's Tree C 13 MIN
16MM FILM, 3/4 OR 1/2 IN VIDEO K-I
Presents a lovable character living happily in her tree house who faces eviction by the townspeople because they do not understand her strange ways.
Prod-SF Dist-SF 1971

Miss U S A 1965 C 15 MIN
16MM FILM OPTICAL SOUND
Shows the Miss U S A competition held in Miami Beach every year. Winner of the 1965 title is Sue Ann Downey, representing the state of Ohio.
Prod-FDC Dist-FDC

Miss Universe 1965 C 15 MIN
16MM FILM OPTICAL SOUND
Shows the Miss Universe Contest in Miami and Miami Beach. Apasra Hongsakula, Miss Thailand, is selected as Miss Universe 1965.
Prod-FDC Dist-FDC

Miss, Mrs Or Ms - What's It All About C 25 MIN
3/4 OR 1/2 INCH VIDEO CASSETTE I-J

Reports on the progress being made by feminist philosophies, showing that the stereotyping of traditional roles is decreasing in American society.
LC NO. 78-701834
Prod-CBSNEW Dist-CAROUF 1977

Miss, Mrs Or Ms - What's It All About (Interpreted) C 25 MIN
16MM FILM, 3/4 OR 1/2 IN VIDEO I-J
Reports on the progress being made by feminist philosophies, showing that the stereotyping of traditional roles is decreasing in American society.
Prod-CBSNEW Dist-CAROUF 1977

Missile Explosive Device Safety C 14 MIN
16MM FILM OPTICAL SOUND
Demonstrates hazards involved when missile explosive devices are manhandled. Explains the purpose and nature of fuses, squibs, igniters and initiators. Outlines safety procedures for handling, installing and testing such devices.
LC NO. FIE63-318
Prod-USDD Dist-USNAC 1961

Missile Fuels, Propellants And Oxidizers - Liquid Oxygen C 22 MIN
16MM FILM OPTICAL SOUND
Describes receipt, transfer, storage and disposal of liquid oxygen. Shows safety measures for transferring fuel from tank trucks to storage areas and procedures for disposing of contaminated fuel.
LC NO. 74-706148
Prod-USAF Dist-USNAC 1961

Missile Safety At Vandenberg Air Force Base C 23 MIN
16MM FILM OPTICAL SOUND
Describes Vandenberg's physical layout and hazards peculiar to missile operations. Explains the need for rigid enforcement of safety practices. Illustrates safety requirements at missile complexes before, during and after a launching.
LC NO. FIE62-72
Prod-USDD Dist-USNAC 1960

Missiles Of October - A Case Study In Decision Making—A Series

Illustrates decision making in action, using the Cuban missile crisis of 1962 and the problems that President Kennedy and his advisors faced as the basis for an in-depth study of the elements of decision making. Includes a discussion leader's guide.
Prod-LCOA Dist-DELTAK

Data Gathering - Understanding The Problem 015 MIN
Examining The Alternatives 020 MIN
Implementing The Decision 030 MIN
Managing The Decision 060 MIN
Power, Control, And Decision Making 040 MIN
Waiting Game, The - Control Or Confrontation 020 MIN

Missiles Of October, The (Captioned) C 155 MIN
3/4 OR 1/2 INCH VIDEO CASSETTE J-C A
Reenacts the 12 days in October 1962 that followed the U S discovery of Soviet missile bases in Cuba.
Prod-VIACOM Dist-LCOA 1974

Missiles Of October, The (Spanish) C 155 MIN
3/4 OR 1/2 INCH VIDEO CASSETTE J-C A
Reenacts the 12 days in October 1962 that followed the U S discovery of Soviet missile bases in Cuba.
Prod-VIACOM Dist-LCOA 1974

Missing Addends, The C 15 MIN
3/4 OR 1/2 INCH VIDEO CASSETTE P
See series title for descriptive statement.
From The Math Mission 2 Series.
Prod-WCVETV Dist-GPITVL 1980

Missing Person's Bureau C 27 MIN
16MM FILM, 3/4 OR 1/2 IN VIDEO H-C A
Describes a Vietnam veteran's return home to find his son dead and his wife unfaithful. Shows the veteran going to a Missing Person's Bureau where he learns the value of forgiveness instead of hate. Stars Hector Elizondo.
From The Insight Series.
Prod-PAULST Dist-PAULST

Missing Person's Bureau, The C 27 MIN
3/4 OR 1/2 INCH VIDEO CASSETTE J A
Tells the story of a Vietnam veteran who returns home to his son's death and his wife's infidelity and eventually learns forgiveness instead of hatred.
Prod-SUTHRB Dist-SUTHRB

Missing Persons - The Drama Of The Disappeared Political Prisoners In Chile B 26 MIN
16MM FILM OPTICAL SOUND H-C A
Presents three spokeswomen who discuss the inexplicable disappearance of their husbands, their children, even a two-and-one-half-year-old grandchild and other terrorist practices of the post-Allende Chilean regime.
LC NO. 81-701527
Prod-ICARUS Dist-ICARUS 1981

Missing Pieces - Georgia Folk Art, 1770-1976 C 29 MIN
16MM FILM OPTICAL SOUND
Examines the work of five folk artists of Georgia, including potter Lanier Meaders, painter Mattie Lou O'Kelley, carver Ulysses Davis, painter Ed Martin and Rev Howard Finster, who created a paradise garden in his backyard.
LC NO. 77-702278
Prod-GCAH Dist-GACA Prodn-ODYSSP 1976

Missing You In Southern California C 31 MIN
16MM FILM, 3/4 OR 1/2 IN VIDEO
Points out that after almost colliding with a C-141, a couple in a private plane learns more about civilian and military flying rules and procedures.
Prod-USAF Dist-USNAC 1982

Mission - Mind Control C 52 MIN
16MM FILM, 3/4 OR 1/2 IN VIDEO H-C
Describes attempts by the American government to control the human mind. Looks at the experiments done with consciousness-altering drugs and brainwashing techniques. Presents interviews with intelligence officials and with victims of this research.
LC NO. 79-707928
Prod-ABCNEW Dist-MTI 1979

Mission Beyond Healing C 20 MIN
3/4 INCH VIDEO CASSETTE
Gives the history of the University of Texas System Cancer Center and its main goal of fighting cancer. Includes statistics about the average patient load and a description of some of the equipment in use.
Prod-UTAHTI Dist-UTAHTI

Mission Control C 5 MIN
3/4 INCH VIDEO CASSETTE
Shows Mission Control at the U S Manned Spacecraft Center in Houston. Shows how the center monitors and controls Apollo flights after the launching of the Saturn from the pad. Reveals five methods by which a flight is monitored and controlled. Issued in 1969 as a motion picture.
From The Apollo Digest Series.
LC NO. 79-706667
Prod-NASA Dist-USNAC 1979

Mission Dustoff - Helicopter Evacuation C 12 MIN
16MM FILM OPTICAL SOUND
Depicts the role of the helicopter ambulance and its crew in evacuation of battlefield casualities in Vietnam.
LC NO. 74-706149
Prod-USA Dist-USNAC 1969

Mission For Mariner, A C 15 MIN
16MM FILM OPTICAL SOUND I A
Describes the results of the Mariner V mission to Venus and describes the continuing Mariner program for exploration of the other planets. Uses animation to show various theories about the nature of Venus and its capabilities for supporting life, and explains how these theories were affected by the Mariner Fly-by.
LC NO. 71-703344
Prod-NASA Dist-NASA Prodn-JETPL 1969

Mission Houses C 12 MIN
16MM FILM OPTICAL SOUND J-H
Shows the homes and the people that comprised the first protestant missionaries to Hawaii in 1820.
Prod-CINEPC Dist-CINEPC

Mission Oceanography B 29 MIN
16MM FILM - 3/4 IN VIDEO
Presents a documentary history of oceanography. Reexamines the discoveries and research by ocean scientists of the early 1800's, the navy's involvement with the seas and oceanography and the progress of oceanography from early sailing days.
Prod-USNAC Dist-USNAC 1972

Mission Of Apollo-Soyuz, The C 29 MIN
16MM FILM - 3/4 IN VIDEO
Stresses the spirit of cooperation and friendship that helped make the joint Soviet-American Apollo-Soyuz mission a success. Shows the period of development and training and comments on future joint efforts. Issued in 1976 as a motion picture.
LC NO. 79-708021
Prod-NASA Dist-USNAC 1979

Mission Of Apollo/Soyuz, The C 30 MIN
3/4 OR 1/2 INCH VIDEO CASSETTE
Discusses the joint Apollo/Soyuz space mission.
From The History Of Space Travel Series.
Prod-NASAC Dist-MDCPB

Mission Of Discovery B 27 MIN
16MM FILM OPTICAL SOUND
Presents various aspects of the Peace Corps services, including the tedium and hardship, the pleasure and accomplishment. Shows volunteers on the job, at home and socializing with friends in the host countries where they serve.
LC NO. 75-700865
Prod-USPC Dist-USNAC Prodn-WILDNG 1963

Mission Possible - Bike Safety C 15 MIN
16MM FILM OPTICAL SOUND
Examines rules of bike safety, courtesy, maintenance and theft prevention. Explains how to meet federal, state and local guidelines for bicycle safety.
Prod-APS Dist-APS

Mission Support B 420 MIN
3/4 OR 1/2 INCH VIDEO CASSETTE PRO
See series title for descriptive statement.
From The Spacecraft System Design Series.
Prod-USCITV Dist-AMCEE

Mission Third Planet - Creatures Of The Land C 13 MIN
16MM FILM, 3/4 OR 1/2 IN VIDEO
Shows how two voyagers from another galaxy classify the land animals of Earth. Demonstrates basic methods of classification, identifies and compares body structures of vertebrates and invertebrates and examines reproductive, protective and food-getting behaviors.
From The Mission Third Planet Series.
Prod-CORF Dist-CORF

Mission Third Planet - Creatures Of The Seas C 13 MIN
16MM FILM, 3/4 OR 1/2 IN VIDEO I-J
Portrays the deep-sea adventure of two voyagers from another planet, who visit Earth on a scientific mission. Compares the behavior, structure and habitat of some of the vertebrates and invertebrates in the sea.
From The Mission Third Planet Series.
Prod-CORF Dist-CORF

Mission Third Planet - Green Grow The Plants C 13 MIN
16MM FILM, 3/4 OR 1/2 IN VIDEO I-J
Tells how two young scientists and their robot journey to Earth from a distant planet to classify plant life. Shows how they learn the basic methods of plant classification, examine and compare the structures of various plants and relate form to function.
From The Mission Third Planet Series.
Prod-CORF Dist-CORF

Mission Third Planet—A Series
16MM FILM, 3/4 OR 1/2 IN VIDEO I-J
Introduces the classification of plants and animals by telling the story of two young visitors from a distant galaxy who travel to Earth.
Prod-CORF Dist-CORF

Mission Third Planet - Creatures Of The Land 013 MIN
Mission Third Planet - Creatures Of The Seas 013 MIN
Mission Third Planet - Green Grow The Plants 013 MIN

Mission To Earth—A Series
16MM FILM, 3/4 OR 1/2 IN VIDEO I-H
Uses the story of a spaceship from an unknown galaxy on a mission to explore the Earth in discussing the geography, life forms, environment and resources of the Earth.
Prod-BARR Dist-BARR 1977

Mission To Earth, Pt 1 - Physical Geography 15 MIN
Mission To Earth, Pt 2 - Life Forms And 17 MIN
Mission To Earth, Pt 3 - Urban Geography 16 MIN

Mission To Earth, Pt 1 - Physical Geography C 15 MIN
16MM FILM, 3/4 OR 1/2 IN VIDEO I-H
Explains about the Earth's rotation, the composition of the atmosphere, the water cycle, the processes of weathering and erosion, the Earth's temperature and other aspects of the Earth's geography in a story about a spaceship from another galaxy on a mission to gather information about the Earth.
From The Mission To Earth Series.
Prod-BARR Dist-BARR 1977

Mission To Earth, Pt 2 - Life Forms And Resources C 17 MIN
16MM FILM, 3/4 OR 1/2 IN VIDEO I-H
Uses the story of a spaceship from another galaxy exploring the Earth's life forms and natural resources to discuss the Earth's natural and cultivated plant life, animal life that gets its sustenance from plant life, humanoids that utilize and modify the planet's resources and the planet's heavy reliance on energy sources.
From The Mission To Earth Series.
Prod-BARR Dist-BARR 1977

Mission To Earth, Pt 3 - Urban Geography C 16 MIN
16MM FILM, 3/4 OR 1/2 IN VIDEO I-H
Presents a story about aliens from another galaxy who explore the Earth's urban centers. Investigates population densities, the consumption of resources, the division of urban areas into business and residential districts, the planet's highly organized transportation system and the manufacture and distribution of goods.
From The Mission To Earth Series.
Prod-BARR Dist-BARR 1977

Mission To The Moon - Report On Project Apollo B 16 MIN
16MM FILM OPTICAL SOUND J-C A
Presents highlights of the space rendezvous between Geminis 6 and 7. Uses animation to explain how the manned flight to the moon will be carried out by 1970.
From The Screen News Digest Series. Vol 8, Issue 6
LC NO. 76-700504
Prod-HEARST Dist-HEARST 1966

Mission To Yenan C 32 MIN
16MM FILM, 3/4 OR 1/2 IN VIDEO J-H A
Presents an historical reevaluation of America's China policy.
Prod-FI Dist-FI 1972

Mission, The C 33 MIN
16MM FILM OPTICAL SOUND C A
Shows the activites of old missionaries throughout the federation of Nigeria in schools, training colleges, hospitals, maternity wards, a leper colony and an operating theater.
Prod-DKB Dist-DKB 1962

Missions Abroad C 37 MIN
16MM FILM, 3/4 OR 1/2 IN VIDEO H-C A
Discusses one of the most dramatic examples of Christian revival in the 19th century, the spread of missionary activity in the slums of Europe's industrial cities and in the lands of the new colonial empires.
From The Christians Series. Episode 11
Prod-GRATV Dist-MGHT 1978

Mississippi - Ol'Man River And The 20th Century C 21 MIN
16MM FILM, 3/4 OR 1/2 IN VIDEO
Traces the history of the Mississippi River.
Prod-KAWVAL Dist-KAWVAL

Mississippi - Prize And Pawn Of Empires, The C 22 MIN
16MM FILM, 3/4 OR 1/2 IN VIDEO
Deals with the Mississippi River.
Prod-KAWVAL Dist-KAWVAL

Mississippi - Prologue To Statehood C 27 MIN
16MM FILM OPTICAL SOUND
Depicts the struggle of the Mississippi territory for statehood. Uses old pictures, documents and live action to portray the history of the territory up to 1817.
LC NO. 72-705061
Prod-UMISS Dist-UMISS 1967

Mississippi - Steamboat A-Comin', The C 21 MIN
16MM FILM, 3/4 OR 1/2 IN VIDEO J-C A
Recounts the history and romance of the era of the steamboat. Focuses on the Mississippi River, tells how railroads supplanted riverboats.
LC NO. 82-706988
Prod-KAWVAL Dist-KAWVAL 1981

Mississippi Delta Blues B 28 MIN
16MM FILM OPTICAL SOUND
Features the research done by Bill Ferris from 1968 to 1970 as he traveled from farms to books to homes to collect music he felt best expressed the richness of delta blues.
Prod-SOFOLK Dist-SOFOLK

Mississippi Delta Blues B 18 MIN
16MM FILM - 3/4 IN VIDEO C A
Reveals the vanishing world of live music found in juke joints, shops and house parties.
Prod-SOFOLK Dist-SOFOLK

Mississippi River C 17 MIN
16MM FILM, 3/4 OR 1/2 IN VIDEO I-H
Explains how the history of the United States has been influenced by the Mississippi River as it travels its course from Minnesota to the Gulf of Mexico. Examines the early settlements, transportation, farming, urbanization, and the serious problems of pollution and flooding along the Mississippi River.
Prod-LUF Dist-LUF 1979

Mississippi River - Lower River C 14 MIN
16MM FILM OPTICAL SOUND I-J
Pictures scenes of disastrous floods and their effects on cities and farms. Emphasizes the value of such flood control devices as levee construction and sandbagging. Shows the river ports of Memphis and New Orleans.
Prod-ACA Dist-ACA 1948

Mississippi River - Upper River C 14 MIN
16MM FILM OPTICAL SOUND I-J
A study of America's greatest river showing how it affects the agriculture and industry throughout its drainage area.
Prod-ACA Dist-ACA 1948

Mississippi River Festival C 20 MIN
16MM FILM OPTICAL SOUND
Discusses the factors that were necessary to make the Mississippi River Festival, a summer music program, an important cultural experience for the St Louis area. Shows the work of the many volunteers, civic and university leaders.
LC NO. 75-711345
Prod-SILLU Dist-SIUFP 1970

Mississippi River, The (Rev Ed) C 15 MIN
16MM FILM, 3/4 OR 1/2 IN VIDEO I-J
Explores the Mississippi River and the people who have settled along it and used it.
Prod-CORF Dist-CORF

Mississippi Suite C 14 MIN
16MM FILM, 3/4 OR 1/2 IN VIDEO I
Presents the Mississippi Suite, by Ferde Grofe, played by a symphony orchestra and directed by Grofe. Uses animation and live photography to convey basic music concepts.
From The Music Experiences Series.
Prod-STEVNS Dist-AIMS 1969

Mississippi Suite (Spanish) C 14 MIN
16MM FILM, 3/4 OR 1/2 IN VIDEO I
Presents the Mississippi Suite, by Ferde Grofe, played by a symphony orchestra and directed by Grofe. Uses animation and live photography to convey basic music concepts.
From The Music Experiences Series.
Prod-STEVNS Dist-AIMS 1969

Mississippi System, The - Waterway Of Commerce X 17 MIN
16MM FILM, 3/4 OR 1/2 IN VIDEO I-H
Traces the development of river traffic along the Mississippi from 1541 through the beginning of the steamboat era in 1812 and the first railroads, which put the river queens out of business after the Civil War. Continues with the neglect of the river, floods, congressional acts and today's revitalized river system.
Prod-ADMFLM Dist-EBEC 1970

Missouri - Gateway To The West C 15 MIN
16MM FILM OPTICAL SOUND
Depicts Missouri's history from pioneer to modern times. Includes scenes of the Old Cathedral, St Genevieve, the capitol building in Jefferson City, Daniel's judgment Tree at Defiance, Grant's farm, Mark Twain's birthplace, the Old Courthouse in St Louis and Carver National Monument. Presents vignettes from the lives of famous Missourians such as Jesse James, General John J Pershing and Harry S Truman.
Prod-MODT Dist-MODT

Missouri - Seven Ways To Get Away C 13 MIN
16MM FILM OPTICAL SOUND
Features Missouri's seven famous vacationlands, including the Big Springs Region of southeast Missouri, the St Louis Area, the Mark Twain Region centering on Hannibal, the Lake of the Ozarks Region, The Ozark Playground Region of southwest Missouri, the Kansas City area and the Pony Express Region of northwest Missouri.
Prod-MODT Dist-MODT

Mist Of Death C 29 MIN
3/4 INCH VIDEO CASSETTE
Focuses on the fighting and dying on the plains of Troy.
From The Iliad Of Homer Series.
Prod-UMITV Dist-UMITV 1974

Mistake-Proof Wallpapering C 30 MIN
1/2 IN VIDEO CASSETTE BETA/VHS
Gives tips for wallpapering.
From The This Old House, Pt 2 - Suburban '50s Series.
Prod-WGBHTV Dist-MTI

Mistake, The C 15 MIN
3/4 OR 1/2 INCH VIDEO CASSETTE K-P
Deals with French-American children. Focuses on a learning experience.
From The La Bonne Aventure Series.
Prod-MPBN Dist-GPITVL

Mistaken Identity C 20 MIN
16MM FILM OPTICAL SOUND A
Introduces a man and a woman who meet at a party and think in the first flush of their infatuation that they are right for each other. Shows them ending up in a motel and discovering that they are wrong for each other in every way.
LC NO. 81-701272
Prod-PARALX Dist-PARALX 1981

Mister Gimme C 28 MIN
16MM FILM, 3/4 OR 1/2 IN VIDEO I-C A
Tells the story of a youngster who wants a set of drums, but can't afford to buy them. Shows how his determination to get them leads him into a 'get rich quick' scheme.
Prod-LCOA Dist-LCOA 1979

Mister Gimme (Captioned) C 28 MIN
16MM FILM, 3/4 OR 1/2 IN VIDEO P-J A
Tells the story of a boy who wants a set of drums and the trouble it causes him and his family when he tries to make money selling greeting cards.
Prod-LCOA Dist-LCOA 1979

Mister Gimme (Spanish) C 28 MIN
16MM FILM, 3/4 OR 1/2 IN VIDEO P-J A
Tells the story of a boy who wants a set of drums and the trouble it causes him and his family when he tries to make money selling greeting cards.
Prod-LCOA Dist-LCOA 1979

Mister Klein Looks At Geometry C 24 MIN
16MM FILM, 3/4 OR 1/2 IN VIDEO
Examines how different properties can be preserved under transformations of the plane. Focuses on affine geometry.
Prod-OPENU Dist-MEDIAG Prodn-BBCTV 1979

Mister Magoo—A Series
16MM FILM, 3/4 OR 1/2 IN VIDEO
Prod-BOSUST Dist-CF

Grizzly Golfer 007 MIN
Magoo's Puddle Jumper 007 MIN
When Magoo Flew 007 MIN

Mister Magrooter's Marvelous Machine C 8 MIN
16MM FILM OPTICAL SOUND J-C A
Presents an animated fable with the theme of technological overkill. Makes viewers reflect on the value of the many 'MARVELOUS MACHINES' that have made their appearance in the American consumer market in recent years.
LC NO. 73-701425
Prod-BOSUST Dist-HRAW 1972

Mister Midwife C 29 MIN
3/4 INCH VIDEO CASSETTE
Offers an interview with a male midwife.
From The Woman Series.
Prod-WNEDTV Dist-PUBTEL

Mister Rogers - Conceptual Behavior—A Series
P-J
Deals with themes important to all children and conceptual behavior to be expected. Features Mister Rogers.
Prod-BRENTM Dist-BRENTM

Death Of A Goldfish 030 MIN
Dentist And A Tooth Fairy, A 030 MIN
Visit To The Doctor, A 030 MIN
What Is Love 030 MIN

Mister Rogers - Health And Safety (Spanish)—A Series
P-J
Provides basic information and reassurance about hospital experiences in four video programs featuring Mister Rogers.
Prod-BRENTM Dist-BRENTM

Going To The Hospital (Spanish) 030 MIN
Having An Operation (Spanish) 030 MIN
Visit To The Emergency Department, A (Spanish) 030 MIN
Wearing A Cast (Spanish) 030 MIN

Mister Rogers - Health And Safety—A Series
P-J
Provides basic information and reassurance about hospital experiences in four video programs featuring Mister Rogers.
Prod-BRENTM Dist-BRENTM

Going To The Hospital 030 MIN
Having An Operation 030 MIN
Visit To The Emergency Department, A 030 MIN
Wearing A Cast 030 MIN

Mister Rogers Talks With Parents About Competition C 58 MIN
3/4 OR 1/2 INCH VIDEO CASSETTE
Deals with competition, sibling rivalry and children.
From The Mister Rogers Talks With Parents Series.
Prod-FAMCOM Dist-FAMCOM

Mister Rogers Talks With Parents About Make-Believe C 28 MIN
3/4 OR 1/2 INCH VIDEO CASSETTE
Talks with parents about ways to encourage children's capacity for imagination.
From The Mister Rogers Talks With Parents Series.
Prod-FAMCOM Dist-FAMCOM

Mister Rogers Talks With Parents About Discipline C 28 MIN
3/4 OR 1/2 INCH VIDEO CASSETTE
Addresses the problem of determining the limits of discipline.
From The Mister Rogers Talks With Parents Series.
Prod-FAMCOM Dist-FAMCOM

Mister Rogers Talks With Parents About Day Care C 28 MIN
3/4 OR 1/2 INCH VIDEO CASSETTE
Explores some of the rewards, difficulties and ambivalent emotions associated with day care.
From The Mister Rogers Talks With Parents Series.
Prod-FAMCOM Dist-FAMCOM

Mister Rogers Talks With Parents About Divorce C 58 MIN
3/4 OR 1/2 INCH VIDEO CASSETTE
Talks openly about the crisis of divorce.
From The Mister Rogers Talks With Parents Series.
Prod-FAMCOM Dist-FAMCOM

Mister Rogers Talks With Parents About Pets C 28 MIN
3/4 OR 1/2 INCH VIDEO CASSETTE
Explores the problems and joys and complex relationship between children and pets.
From The Mister Rogers Talks With Parents Series.
Prod-FAMCOM Dist-FAMCOM

Mister Rogers Talks With Parents About School C 58 MIN
3/4 OR 1/2 INCH VIDEO CASSETTE K-H A
Discusses children's expectations, attitudes and fears about going to school
From The Mister Rogers Talks With Parents Series.
Prod-FAMCOM Dist-FAMCOM

Mister Rogers Talks With Parents—A Series
A
Discusses various topics of concern to children with Fred Rogers.
Prod-FAMCOM Dist-FAMCOM

Mister Rogers Talks With Parents About
Mister Rogers Talks With Parents About 028 MIN
Mister Rogers Talks With Parents About 028 MIN
Mister Rogers Talks With Parents About Day Care 028 MIN
Mister Rogers Talks With Parents About Divorce 058 MIN
Mister Rogers Talks With Parents About Pets 028 MIN
Mister Rogers Talks With Parents About School 058 MIN

Mister Rogers' Neighborhood—A Series
Features Mister Rogers in dealing with themes important to children, from the Emmy award-winning television series.
Prod-FAMCOM Dist-FAMCOM

Death Of A Goldfish 030 MIN
Dentist And A Toothfairy, A 030 MIN
Visit To The Doctor, A 030 MIN
What Is Love? 030 MIN

Mister, You Made A Big Mistake On My Bill C 17 MIN
16MM FILM OPTICAL SOUND H-C A
Features Don Knotts playing a man who receives his hospital bill and thinks it is too much. Shows a series of different scenes at the hospital in which he is informed about why a hospital charges what it does.
LC NO. 76-703958
Prod-BYU Dist-BYU 1976

Misty Of Chincoteague C 15 MIN
3/4 OR 1/2 INCH VIDEO CASSETTE I
Tells of the colt Misty, from the book by Marguerite Henry.
From The Book Bird Series.
Prod-CTI Dist-CTI

Misty Wizards C 30 MIN
2 INCH VIDEOTAPE
Presents the jazz music of Misty Wizards. Features host Jim Rockwell interviewing the artist.
From The People In Jazz Series.
Prod-WTVSTV Dist-PUBTEL

Misunderstood Monsters C 44 MIN
16MM FILM, 3/4 OR 1/2 IN VIDEO P-I
Tells the story of Stanley, who gets the reputation of being a 'monster' because he has reacted to taunts in anger and frustration. Shows how an understanding animated character, the Mouth, counsels him, producing three animated stories based on the authors' books about misunderstood monsters. Includes Creole by Stephen Cosgrove, The Reluctant Dragon by Kenneth Grahame and Beauty And The Beast retold by Marianna Mayer. Emphasizes self-esteem and individual differences.
LC NO. 81-707560
Prod-BOSUST Dist-CF 1981

Misunderstood Monsters—A Series
16MM FILM, 3/4 OR 1/2 IN VIDEO P-J
Prod-BOSUST Dist-CF 1981

Beauty And The Beast 012 MIN

Creole 008 MIN
Reluctant Dragon, The 012 MIN

Misunderstood Pain, The C 30 MIN
3/4 OR 1/2 INCH VIDEO CASSETTE
Tells how pain in the chest may not be a heart attack, but may be a sign of pulmonary or digestive problems. Gives tips on how to cope with chest pain and how to determine its origin.
From The Here's To Your Health Series.
Prod-KERA Dist-PBS 1979

Misunderstood Pain, The C 30 MIN
3/4 OR 1/2 INCH VIDEO CASSETTE
See series title for descriptive statement.
From The Here's To Your Health Series.
Prod-PBS Dist-DELTAK

Mitchell Kriegman - Always Late C 10 MIN
3/4 OR 1/2 INCH VIDEO CASSETTE
Presented by Mitchell Kriegman.
Prod-ARTINC Dist-ARTINC

Mitchell Kriegman - Bill Irwin, The Dancing Man C 3 MIN
3/4 OR 1/2 INCH VIDEO CASSETTE
Introduces Bill Irwin.
Prod-ARTINC Dist-ARTINC

Mitchell Kriegman - Heart To Heart C 2 MIN
3/4 OR 1/2 INCH VIDEO CASSETTE
Presented by Mitchell Kriegman.
Prod-ARTINC Dist-ARTINC

Mitchell Kriegman - My Neighborhood C 27 MIN
3/4 OR 1/2 INCH VIDEO CASSETTE
Presents a comic story about a guy who loves his neighborhood and claims to know everyone in it and everything about it.
Prod-ARTINC Dist-ARTINC

Mitchell Kriegman - Someone's Hiding In My Apartment C 2 MIN
3/4 OR 1/2 INCH VIDEO CASSETTE
Presented by Mitchell Kriegman.
Prod-ARTINC Dist-ARTINC

Mitchell Kriegman - The Marshall Klugman Show C 29 MIN
3/4 OR 1/2 INCH VIDEO CASSETTE
Mirrors frustrations and anxieties in a comic story.
Prod-ARTINC Dist-ARTINC

Mitchell Vs Military Tradition B 25 MIN
16MM FILM, 3/4 OR 1/2 IN VIDEO J-C
Presents the story of Brig Gen Billy Mitchell, who crusades to prove that the airplane is our most effective combat weapon, runs a crucial bombing test in 1921 and clearly demonstrates the superiority of air attack over surface units.
From The Men In Crisis Series.
Prod-WOLPER Dist-FI Prodn-METROM 1964

Mitchell, Parren C 29 MIN
3/4 INCH VIDEO CASSETTE
Discusses problems faced by black politicians and how blacks are affected by unemployment and urban problems.
From The Like It Is Series.
Prod-OHC Dist-HRC

Mitos N Leyendas Show C 30 MIN
3/4 OR 1/2 INCH VIDEO CASSETTE K-P
See series title for descriptive statement.
From The Villa Alegre Series.
Prod-BCTV Dist-MDCPB

Mitosis C 9 MIN
16MM FILM, 3/4 OR 1/2 IN VIDEO H-C
Illustrates how cells divide and multiply. Describes the cell, cell wall, nucleus, nucleus membrane, chromosomes and centrioles.
Prod-IFB Dist-IFB 1959

Mitosis C 11 MIN
16MM FILM, 3/4 OR 1/2 IN VIDEO
Uses the apple tree to explain the process of mitosis.
From The Life Cycle Of A Flowering Plant Series. No. 2
Prod-SCHLAT Dist-LUF 1971

Mitosis (Spanish) C 14 MIN
16MM FILM, 3/4 OR 1/2 IN VIDEO J-H
A Spanish language version of the film and videorecording Mitosis.
Prod-EBEC Dist-EBEC 1980

Mitosis (2nd Ed) C 15 MIN
16MM FILM, 3/4 OR 1/2 IN VIDEO J-H
Uses microphotography, animation and artwork to show how the basic process of mitosis occurs in plants and animals. Explains the roles of the cell nucleus, DNA, chromosomes, chromatids and the centriole. Examines the issue of cloning.
From The Biology Series. Unit 5 - Genetics
Prod-EBEC Dist-EBEC Prodn-ACORN 1980

Mitosis And Meiosis X 17 MIN
16MM FILM, 3/4 OR 1/2 IN VIDEO J-C
Illustrates the life cycle of common organisms and the two basic types of cell division--mitosis, accounting for growth from the fertilized egg to the adult - and meiosis, essential to the production of sex cells-by examining the life cycle of a starfish.
From The Continuity Of Life Series.
LC NO. 80-707065
Prod-IU Dist-IU 1956

Mitosis And Meiosis - How Cells Divide C
3/4 OR 1/2 INCH VIDEO CASSETTE H
Uses photomicrographs and computer graphics to analyze the different phases of cell division.
Prod-GA Dist-GA

Mitosis Y Miosis C 20 MIN
16MM FILM, 3/4 OR 1/2 IN VIDEO H-C A
A Spanish language version of Cell Division - Mitosis And Meiosis. Presents an inside look at living cells, showing the processes of mitosis and meiosis.
Prod-KATTNS Dist-MGHT 1978

Mitsuye And Nellie, Asian American Poets C 58 MIN
3/4 OR 1/2 INCH VIDEO CASSETTE
Shows how a common heritage as Asian-American women binds poets Mitsuye Yamada and Nellie Wong in this examination of oriental ethnicity in the United States. They recite poetry and discuss the impact of Japanese and Chinese cultures on their upbringing.
LC NO. 82-706954
Prod-SARLGT Dist-SARLGT 1981

Mitt, The C 17 MIN
16MM FILM, 3/4 OR 1/2 IN VIDEO P-I
Tells the story of a 12-year-old boy who dreams of buying a new baseball mitt and who earns enough money to do so. Shows how he passes up the mitt to buy his mother something she has been secretly wanting.
Prod-CEDARF Dist-LCOA 1978

Mitt, The (Captioned) C 17 MIN
16MM FILM, 3/4 OR 1/2 IN VIDEO P-J A
Tells the story of a boy eager for a baseball mitt but who instead buys something for his mother.
Prod-CEDARF Dist-LCOA 1978

Mitzi A Da Si - A Visit To Yellowstone National Park C 20 MIN
3/4 OR 1/2 INCH VIDEO CASSETTE
Shows Yellowstone Park, the wildlife and the thermal features found there.
From The Nature Episodes Series.
Prod-EDIMGE Dist-EDIMGE

Mitzvah To Serve, A C 26 MIN
16MM FILM OPTICAL SOUND
Provides an orientation to the meaning, responsibilities and value of Jewish lay leadership in the U S armed forces.
LC NO. 74-706150
Prod-USA Dist-USNAC 1969

Mix A Material C 25 MIN
16MM FILM, 3/4 OR 1/2 IN VIDEO I-H
Explains why materials bend, stretch and break, demonstrates the behavior of molecular lattices in common substances, from fudge to balloons.
From The Start Here - Adventure Into Science Series.
Prod-LANDMK Dist-LANDMK

Mix And Application C 18 MIN
16MM FILM OPTICAL SOUND
Shows proper methods of mixing and applying polysulfide base sealants and caulking materials to a variety of building materials.
Prod-THIOKL Dist-THIOKL 1970

Mix Yarn With Wheat Paste B 15 MIN
2 INCH VIDEOTAPE P
Deal with manipulating yarn dipped in wheat paste to form designs and shapes.
From The Art Corner Series.
Prod-CVETVC Dist-GPITVL Prodn-WCVETV

Mixed Bag, A C 30 MIN
3/4 OR 1/2 INCH VIDEO CASSETTE
See series title for descriptive statement.
From The Rebop Series.
Prod-WGBHTV Dist-MDCPB

Mixed Double C 5 MIN
16MM FILM OPTICAL SOUND
Presents a Pas De Deux performed by Sorella Englund and Eske Holm of the Royal Danish Ballet.
Prod-RDCG Dist-AUDPLN

Mixed Marriages - Homosexual Husbands C 13 MIN
16MM FILM, 3/4 OR 1/2 IN VIDEO H-C A
Focuses on the lifestyles and problems of two marriages in which the husbands are homosexuals.
LC NO. 78-701770
Prod-CBSNEW Dist-CAROUF 1978

Mixed Numbers And Improper Fractions C 23 MIN
3/4 INCH VIDEO CASSETTE
See series title for descriptive statement.
From The Basic Math Skills Series. Fraction Understanding
Prod-TELSTR Dist-TELSTR

Mixed Operation - Sums To Six C 15 MIN
3/4 INCH VIDEO CASSETTE P
Explains the use of plus, minus and equal signs in doing mathematic operations with sums up to six.
From The Measure Up Series.
Prod-WCETTV Dist-GPITVL 1977

Mixed Operations To Sums Of Ten C 15 MIN
3/4 INCH VIDEO CASSETTE P
Tells how to write two addition facts and two subtraction facts when given three numbers.
From The Measure Up Series.
Prod-WCETTV Dist-GPITVL 1977

Mixed Potentials - Passivity - Corrosion I C 46 MIN
3/4 OR 1/2 INCH VIDEO CASSETTE
See series title for descriptive statement.
From The Electrochemistry, Pt V - Electrokinetics Series.
Prod-MIOT Dist-MIOT

Mixed Potentials, Passivity, Corrosion, Pt 1 C 46 MIN
3/4 OR 1/2 INCH VIDEO CASSETTE
See series title for descriptive statement.
From The Electrochemistry Series.
Prod-KALMIA Dist-KALMIA

Mixed Random Variables B 30 MIN
3/4 OR 1/2 INCH VIDEO CASSETTE PRO
Illustrates mixed random variables.
From The Probability And Random Processes - Random Variables Series.
Prod-MIOT Dist-MIOT

Mixed-In-Place Soil-Cement Construction C 18 MIN
16MM FILM OPTICAL SOUND
Shows how durable, low-cost pavements can be built with soil-cement. Includes scenes from a variety of soil-cement paving projects in the United States and Canada, illustrating the basics of mixed-in-place construction, current equipment and technology and successful practices.
LC NO. 82-700039
Prod-PRTLND Dist-PRTLND 1977

Mixed-Up 'Middles' B 30 MIN
16MM FILM OPTICAL SOUND C
Shows the problems and rewards as well as the responsibilities of middle age. Discusses the need for adjusting to problems of younger and older generations and planning for changes in a future life style.
From The Growth And Development, The Adult Years Series.
LC NO. 74-706817
Prod-VDONUR Dist-AJN Prodn-WTTWTV 1969

Mixing It Up With Colors And Paints C 15 MIN
16MM FILM OPTICAL SOUND K-I
Follows Yoffy and Fingermouse as they mix colors in order to paint a picture.
From The Fingermouse, Yoffy And Friends Series.
LC NO. 73-700444
Prod-BBCTV Dist-VEDO 1972

Mixing The Media C 29 MIN
3/4 INCH VIDEO CASSETTE
Demonstrates drawing the traditional ballerina with chalks, pencils and pastels.
From The Artist At Work Series.
Prod-UMITV Dist-UMITV 1973

Mixing Zinc Phosphate Cement, Final Cementation C 6 MIN
1/2 IN VIDEO CASSETTE BETA/VHS PRO
Discusses dental cements.
Prod-RMI Dist-RMI

Mixtures And Mechanical Separation C 60 MIN
3/4 OR 1/2 INCH VIDEO CASSETTE IND
Covers heterogeneous and homogeneous mixtures, constituents of mixtures in the air, filtration, sedimentation and centrifurging and deep-bed filtration of river water.
From The Chemistry Training Series.
Prod-ITCORP Dist-ITCORP

Mixtures And Solutions, Pt 1 B 15 MIN
2 INCH VIDEOTAPE P
See series title for descriptive statement.
From The Just Curious Series. No. 13
Prod-EOPS Dist-GPITVL Prodn-KOACTV

Mixtures And Solutions, Pt 2 B 15 MIN
2 INCH VIDEOTAPE P
See series title for descriptive statement.
From The Just Curious Series. No. 14
Prod-EOPS Dist-GPITVL Prodn-KOACTV

Miyuke Horibe (Japan), Tape B, No. 23 C
3/4 OR 1/2 INCH VIDEO CASSETTE
Shows adaptations of an oriental theme applied to long hair.
Prod-MPCEDP Dist-MPCEDP 1984

Miyuki Horibe (Japan), Tape A, No. 13 C
3/4 OR 1/2 INCH VIDEO CASSETTE
Shows a blend of wash-and-wear cuts. Gives Japanese techniques for hair decoration.
Prod-MPCEDP Dist-MPCEDP 1984

Mo Simpson C
3/4 OR 1/2 INCH VIDEO CASSETTE
Portrays Mo Simpson, British Columbian filmmaker with interviews and film clips.
From The Filmmakers' Showcase Series.
Prod-CANFDW Dist-CANFDW

Moan And Groan, Inc B 21 MIN
16MM FILM OPTICAL SOUND
Tells how Jackie, Wheezer and Chubby dig for buried treasure in a mansion haunted by a codger intent on keeping intruders out. A Little Rascals film.
Prod-ROACH Dist-BHAWK 1929

Moat Monster, The C 12 MIN
16MM FILM OPTICAL SOUND A
Shows several young boys enacting a child's frightening dream of a sea monster. Shows through the role of the moat monster the children working out their ideas of rescue and escape and facilitates study and discussion for students and practitioners in child development, child psychology and other related disciplines.
From The Training Module On Role Enactment In Children's Play. Three
LC NO. 76-700935
Prod-UPITTS Dist-CFDC Prodn-CFDC 1974

Mobile By Alexander Calder C 24 MIN
16MM FILM, 3/4 OR 1/2 IN VIDEO
Documents the mobile that is the last major work by sculptor Alexander Calder, from idea through completion, and shows the

craftsmanship used in meeting the challenges posed in the fabrication of this complex work of art. Tells how it was the first work of art to be installed in the East Building of the National Gallery Of Art.
LC NO. 81-706307
Prod-USNGA Dist-USNAC 1980

Mobile Home Fire Safety C 15 MIN
16MM FILM, 3/4 OR 1/2 IN VIDEO H-C A
Depicts special fire hazards unique to mobile homes, including windows too small to crawl through, flammable walls and drapes and a lack of fire warning devices. Explains how to correct these problems. Reviews essentials of fire safety, such as escape planning, early detection, prevention and suppression.
Prod-FILCOM Dist-FILCOM Prodn-AVISOF 1977

Mobile Homes C 30 MIN
3/4 OR 1/2 INCH VIDEO CASSETTE
Presents tips on the maintenance of mobile homes.
From The Consumer Survival Series. Homes
Prod-MDCPB Dist-MDCPB

Mobile Lab - Any Questions C 6 MIN
16MM FILM, 3/4 OR 1/2 IN VIDEO I-C A
Describes the curriculum of a mobile science laboratory traveling from high school to high school in Washington, DC. Shows how the program demonstrates that science is relevant to urban living.
Prod-NSF Dist-AMEDFL 1974

Mobile Programs C 30 MIN
3/4 INCH VIDEO CASSETTE
See series title for descriptive statement.
From The Growing Old In Modern America Series.
Prod-UWASHP Dist-UWASHP

Mobile Unit Assistants C 17 MIN
3/4 OR 1/2 INCH VIDEO CASSETTE
Instructs on the use of the new blood collection equipment in various phases of its operation.
From The What's In It For Me? Series.
Prod-AMRC Dist-AMRC 1977

Mobile Videotape Production C 30 MIN
3/4 OR 1/2 INCH VIDEO CASSETTE
Presents a checklist for evaluating remote locations, considering the pysical needs of the production and crew. Illustrates problems encountered, including lighting, sound, power and mobility.
From The Video - A Practical Guide...and More Series.
Prod-VIPUB Dist-VIPUB

Mobile Yoke C 16 MIN
16MM FILM OPTICAL SOUND
Pictures mobile yoke, a goodwill-training exercise in which a tactical air command composite air strike force is deployed to Thailand. Includes briefings, support activities, actual deployment and arrival.
LC NO. FIE62-73
Prod-USDD Dist-USNAC 1960

Mobile, By Alexander Calder C 24 MIN
16MM FILM OPTICAL SOUND
Looks at how artist Alexander Calder, architect I M Pei, artist/engineer Paul Matisse, craftsmen and museum officials faced the challenge of producing Calder's work Mobile for the National Gallery of Art's East Building.
Prod-USNGA Dist-USNGA

Mobiles And Stabiles B 20 MIN
2 INCH VIDEOTAPE I
Explains that balancing and counterbalancing become ideas to challenge young artists in designing and building a mobile, a sculpture using motion as a basic element. (Broadcast quality)
From The For The Love Of Art Series.
Prod-GWTVAI Dist-GPITVL Prodn-WETATV

Mobility B 15 MIN
16MM FILM OPTICAL SOUND
Pictures nato's operational material. Develops the theme that mobility is adaptation to any situation. Includes shots of modern maneuvers and action sequences from World Wars I and II.
LC NO. FIE65-106
Prod-NATO Dist-USDS

Mobility C 19 MIN
3/4 OR 1/2 INCH VIDEO CASSETTE H
Traces the rise to success of a young photographer, pointing out where she made her major career decisions.
From The Jobs - Seeking, Finding, Keeping Series.
Prod-MSDOE Dist-AITECH 1980

Mobility - Life As A Nomad C 14 MIN
16MM FILM, 3/4 OR 1/2 IN VIDEO
Points out that every year one in five North Americans changes his address. Looks at these American nomads, as well as New York City subway commuters, automobile users, mobile homes, and tent cities.
Prod-DOCUA Dist-CNEMAG

Mobilization For Progress - The Story Of International Development Service C 29 MIN
16MM FILM OPTICAL SOUND
Shows international voluntarism in Kenya, Panama, Iran and Malaysia in 1970.
LC NO. 75-700866
Prod-USPC Dist-USNAC Prodn-KENLEE 1970

Mobilization Of The Stroke Patient C 21 MIN
3/4 OR 1/2 INCH VIDEO CASSETTE PRO
Views techniques for the mobilization of the stroke patient from the first post-stroke days.
Prod-UMICHM Dist-UMICHM 1975

Mobin-Uddin Umbrella Filter, The C 17 MIN
3/4 OR 1/2 INCH VIDEO CASSETTE PRO
Shows the implantation of an umbrella filter in the vena cava, below the left kidney. Discusses indications and contra-indications for this procedure.
Prod-WFP Dist-WFP

Moby Dick - The Great American Novel C 25 MIN
16MM FILM, 3/4 OR 1/2 IN VIDEO H-C A
Introduces an awareness of the timelessness of the novel MOBY DICK by Herman Melville and suggests that similar value lies in all great literature.
Prod-CBSTV Dist-PHENIX 1969

Mock Code C 22 MIN
3/4 OR 1/2 INCH VIDEO CASSETTE
Demonstrates initial patient management in cardiopulmonary arrest along with the roles that must be assumed. Portrays events as they normally would occur, and then again with a voice-over narration describing the events and rationale for intervention.
Prod-AHHCC Dist-AJN

Mockingbird, The B 39 MIN
16MM FILM OPTICAL SOUND
Based on the short story of the same title by Ambrose Bierce. Concerns a Union soldier in the Civil War who accidentally kills his Confederate twin brother.
LC NO. FIA68-3284
Prod-BF Dist-FI 1968

Mod's Hair (France), Tape A, No. 9 C
3/4 OR 1/2 INCH VIDEO CASSETTE
Shows the 'Elizabeth' cut, following the three basic steps, in which a full, thick look is achieved. Covers the 'Veronica,' for semi-long hair.
Prod-MPCEDP Dist-MPCEDP 1984

Modal Analysis C 60 MIN
3/4 OR 1/2 INCH VIDEO CASSETTE C
Covers derivation of equations and uncoupling simultaneous differential equations to get modal equations.
From The Fundamentals Of Dynamic Analysis For Structural Design Series.
Prod-USCCE Dist-AMCEE

Mode Of Action Of Tetracyclines, The C 13 MIN
16MM FILM OPTICAL SOUND PRO
Uses animation to present the basic facts on tetracycline in this synthesis, the difference between bacteriostatic and bactericidal action and the development of resistance to tetracycline. Reviews the theory of how minocycline works and its differences from tetracycline as set forth in the approved minocycline circular.
Prod-ACYLLD Dist-LEDR 1974

Mode Superposition Analysis - Time History C 48 MIN
3/4 OR 1/2 INCH VIDEO CASSETTE
Discusses solution of dynamic response by mode superposition and the basic idea of mode superposition.
From The Finite Element Methods In Engineering Mechanics Series.
Prod-MIOT Dist-MIOT

Model C 129 MIN
16MM FILM, 3/4 OR 1/2 IN VIDEO
Shows men and women at work as models for TV commercials, fashion shows, print advertising, posing for magazine covers and ads for a variety of products. Shows them at work with photographers whose techniques illustrate different styles of fashions and product photography.
Prod-WISEF Dist-ZIPRAH

Model City, The C 15 MIN
16MM FILM OPTICAL SOUND P-C A
Presents the problem of polluted air and the ultimate results of the direction of current technology. Explains that the public must pay for the comforts brought about by the increasing technological advances with the ever-increasing problem of air pollution.
Prod-COMICO Dist-COMICO

Model Development B 60 MIN
3/4 OR 1/2 INCH VIDEO CASSETTE
See series title for descriptive statement.
From The Project Management And CPM Series. Pt 1
Prod-UAZMIC Dist-UAZMIC 1977

Model Examination - I With Explanations C 120 MIN
3/4 OR 1/2 INCH VIDEO CASSETTE
See series title for descriptive statement.
From The PSAT And National Merit Scholarship Qualifying Test Preparation Series.
Prod-KRLSOF Dist-KRLSOF

Model Examination - II With Explanations C 120 MIN
3/4 OR 1/2 INCH VIDEO CASSETTE
See series title for descriptive statement.
From The PSAT And National Merit Scholarship Qualifying Test Preparation Series.
Prod-KRLSOF Dist-KRLSOF

Model Examination - III With Explanations C 120 MIN
3/4 OR 1/2 INCH VIDEO CASSETTE
See series title for descriptive statement.
From The PSAT And National Merit Scholarship Qualifying Test Preparation Series.
Prod-KRLSOF Dist-KRLSOF

Model Examination I With Explanations C 120 MIN
3/4 OR 1/2 INCH VIDEO CASSETTE
See series title for descriptive statement.
From The SAT Exam Preparation Series.
Prod-KRLSOF Dist-KRLSOF 1985

Model Examination II With Explanations C 120 MIN
3/4 OR 1/2 INCH VIDEO CASSETTE
See series title for descriptive statement.
From The SAT Exam Preparation Series.
Prod-KRLSOF Dist-KRLSOF 1985

Model Examination III With Explanations C 120 MIN
3/4 OR 1/2 INCH VIDEO CASSETTE
See series title for descriptive statement.
From The SAT Exam Preparation Series.
Prod-KRLSOF Dist-KRLSOF 1985

Model For Community Health Problem Analysis And Intervention, A B 30 MIN
16MM FILM OPTICAL SOUND PRO
Features a discussion among the film instructor and students from different professional schools. Points out that the discussion takes place in a section of a metropolitan city that has inadequate health facilities and services and where the students developed a health project to meet some of the residents' health needs.
From The Public Health Science - Community Organization For Health Services Series.
Prod-KUHTTV Dist-GPITVL

Model For Community Health Problem Analysis And Intervention B 30 MIN
2 INCH VIDEOTAPE PRO
Features a discussion between Mr Livenstein and students from different professional schools. Takes place in a section of a metropolitan city that has inadequate health facilities and services and where the students developed a health project to meet some of the residents' health needs. Uses the student project as a case example to illustrate an intervention model for community organization for health service. (Broadcast quality)
From The Public Health Science Series. Unit IV - Intro To Community Organ For Health Services
Prod-TEXWU Dist-GPITVL Prodn-KUHTTV

Model Houses C 5 MIN
16MM FILM, 3/4 OR 1/2 IN VIDEO P-C A
Shows the steps involved in making cardboard and paper models for a whole town project.
From The Creative Hands Series.
Prod-CRAF Dist-IFB 1949

Model Negotiations C 70 MIN
3/4 OR 1/2 INCH VIDEO CASSETTE PRO
Portrays two sets of lawyers attempting to resolve a dispute between their respective clients. Shows how lawyers employ different approaches and propose different potential solutions.
Prod-ABACPE Dist-ABACPE

Model Oral Argument - Demonstration And Critique C 124 MIN
3/4 OR 1/2 INCH VIDEO CASSETTE PRO
Presents oral arguments in an appeal case. Concludes with a panel discussion of oral arguments focusing on the Griswold-Wright agreement.
From The Appellate Advocacy And The Appellate Process Series.
Prod-ABACPE Dist-ABACPE

Model Railroading Unlimited C 28 MIN
16MM FILM OPTICAL SOUND
Encourages the average individual to get involved with the hobby of model railroading.
LC NO. 75-702752
Prod-MORAIL Dist-MORAIL Prodn-LIBERP 1975

Model Railroading Unlimited (2nd Ed) C 19 MIN
16MM FILM, 3/4 OR 1/2 IN VIDEO J-C A
Presents a brief history of model railroading and a dramatization about a man who enters a hobby shop and comes out as the chief dispatcher of the world's largest model train layout.
LC NO. 78-701044
Prod-LIBERP Dist-PFP 1978

Model Recovery, A - The Story Of Ivy Gunter C 9 MIN
3/4 OR 1/2 INCH VIDEO CASSETTE
Follows model Ivy Gunter from diagnosis of bone cancer and loss of her lower right leg to recovery from surgery and resumption of her modeling career.
Prod-AMCS Dist-AMCS 1984

Model Rocketry - The Last Frontier C 15 MIN
16MM FILM OPTICAL SOUND
Explains the construction and launching of model rockets. Narrated by William Shatner.
Prod-ESTES Dist-MTP

Model 1400 / Model 1500 Golden Combine C 9 MIN
16MM FILM OPTICAL SOUND
Shows some of the features and operation of the new Sperry New Holland combines.
LC NO. 75-700331
Prod-SPRYNH Dist-SRCNHD Prodn-FILMFI 1974

Model, The C 22 MIN
16MM FILM OPTICAL SOUND
Presents a motivation training film for Ford auto salesmen. Uses a dramatization involving a learning lesson between father and son to show the value of setting goals upon which to base actions.
From The Ford Marketing Institute Series.
LC NO. 75-703288
Prod-COMICO Dist-FORDFL 1975

Modeling C 10 MIN
3/4 OR 1/2 INCH VIDEO CASSETTE T
See series title for descriptive statement.
From The Protocol Materials In Teacher Education - The Process Of Teaching, Pt 2 Series.
Prod-MSU Dist-MSU

Modeling C 18 MIN
16MM FILM - 3/4 IN VIDEO I-J
Demonstrates how it is possible to test scientific theories and predictions with the use of a model.
From The Search For Solutions Series.
LC NO. 80-706245
Prod-PLYBCK Dist-KAROL 1979

Modeling And Pottery Making C 20 MIN
2 INCH VIDEOTAPE I
Helps students experiment with a plastic material and construct objects of clay.
From The Creating Art, Pt 2 - Learning To Create Art Forms Series.
Prod-GPITVL Dist-GPITVL

Modeling Atmospheric Conditions C 60 MIN
3/4 OR 1/2 INCH VIDEO CASSETTE
See series title for descriptive statement.
From The Advanced Remote Sensing Techniques Series. Section I, Pt 5
Prod-UAZMIC Dist-UAZMIC

Modeling Clay With Pierrot C 7 MIN
16MM FILM, 3/4 OR 1/2 IN VIDEO P
Shows how Pierrot and his friends make a clay bowl to replace one they have accidentally broken.
From The Pierrot Series.
Prod-CORF Dist-CORF 1978

Modeling Electromagnetic Interaction With The Earth's Surface C 60 MIN
3/4 OR 1/2 INCH VIDEO CASSETTE
See series title for descriptive statement.
From The Advanced Remote Sensing Techniques Series. Section I, Pt 6
Prod-UAZMIC Dist-UAZMIC

Modeling In Science C 14 MIN
3/4 OR 1/2 INCH VIDEO CASSETTE J
Presents a geochemist creating a model of the earth's interior by melting pieces of meteor in a special furnace.
From The Whatabout Series.
Prod-AITV Dist-AITECH 1983

Modeling Photochemical Air Pollution By Computer C 23 MIN
16MM FILM OPTICAL SOUND
Provides an overview of modeling for air pollution. Describes how the photochemical system is simulated and demonstrates the computer output for the particle-in-cell model.
LC NO. 75-701307
Prod-NERC Dist-USNAC 1974

Modeling The Universe C 14 MIN
16MM FILM, 3/4 OR 1/2 IN VIDEO
Features Buckminster Fuller in a discussion of the inherent geometry of nature. States that by comprehending the ways in which nature works, people will be able to design a world that will support all of humanity.
LC NO. 79-706825
Prod-MM Dist-PFP

Modeling With Difference Equations C 30 MIN
3/4 INCH VIDEO CASSETTE C
See series title for descriptive statement.
From The Introduction To Mathematics Series.
Prod-MDCPB Dist-MDCPB

Modeling With Light And Shadow C 30 MIN
3/4 OR 1/2 INCH VIDEO CASSETTE
Discusses modeling with light and shadow, the basic tool of the designer. Explains that by highlighting or dimming certain lines and surfaces, the face can be made to appear fat or thin, young or old, ruddy or callow.
From The Actor's Face As A Canvas Series.
Prod-NETCHE Dist-NETCHE 1973

Modelling Basic Circuits B
16MM FILM OPTICAL SOUND
Discusses the mathematical modelling of simple electric circuits.
Prod-OPENU Dist-OPENU

Modelling Cranes C 24 MIN
16MM FILM, 3/4 OR 1/2 IN VIDEO
Looks at the elementary statics behind crane design. Shows how modelling forces with vectors can predict instability.
Prod-OPENU Dist-MEDIAG Prodn-BBCTV 1979

Modelling Drug Therapy C 24 MIN
16MM FILM, 3/4 OR 1/2 IN VIDEO
Explains how mathematical modelling was used to formulate the best use of the drug Theophylline, used to control asthma.
Prod-OPENU Dist-MEDIAG Prodn-BBCTV 1979

Modelling Pollution C 24 MIN
16MM FILM, 3/4 OR 1/2 IN VIDEO
Shows how the interaction between sewage pollutant and oxygen can be described mathematically, using the polluted Thames as an example.
Prod-OPENU Dist-MEDIAG Prodn-BBCTV 1979

Modelling Stock Control C 24 MIN
16MM FILM, 3/4 OR 1/2 IN VIDEO
Shows how the factors underlying stock control problems can be analyzed in terms of progessively more complicated mathematical models. Concentrates on the simplest model producing the famous square root formula for re-order quantities.
Prod-OPENU Dist-MEDIAG Prodn-BBCTV 1979

Modelling Surveys C 24 MIN
16MM FILM, 3/4 OR 1/2 IN VIDEO
Looks at the idea of sampling and the variability in sampling. Develops the binomial distribution as a simple model of the sampling process.
Prod-OPENU Dist-MEDIAG Prodn-BBCTV 1979

Modelling With Vectors B
16MM FILM OPTICAL SOUND
Shows that forces, moments and angular velocities can be modelled by vectors, but that finite rotations cannot. Solves two physical problems using vectors.
Prod-OPENU Dist-OPENU

Models C 25 MIN
3/4 OR 1/2 INCH VIDEO CASSETTE H-C A
Shows how to build a model of a Scania Truck, a Landrover and a huge forklift truck.
From The Blizzard's Wonderful Wooden Toys Series.
Prod-BBCTV Dist-FI

Models And Audio-Visual Aids B 30 MIN
2 INCH VIDEOTAPE
Illustrates the use of models and audio-visual materials to reinforce and expand the concepts that pupils develop through direct experience. Explains that these materials should not be used as a substitute for direct experience.
From The Science In Your Classroom Series.
Prod-WENHTV Dist-GPITVL

Models For Manpower Development In Education C 28 MIN
16MM FILM OPTICAL SOUND T
Explains how institutional change might be enhanced in the field of education. Suggests the need for new transition strategies to implement alternatives as they are developed.
Prod-EDUC Dist-EDUC

Models For Small Group Instruction C 10 MIN
16MM FILM OPTICAL SOUND H-C A
Utilizes the small group mode of instruction to modify learner behavior in accordance with educational goals.
From The Emerging Educational Patterns Series.
Prod-EDUC Dist-EDUC

Models In the Mind C 29 MIN
16MM FILM, 3/4 OR 1/2 IN VIDEO H-C
Shows how physicists use mathematics to construct elaborate, abstract models of physical events. Includes physical applications of conic sections, the exponential law of growth and decay, and wave research.
From The Dimensions In Science, Series 2 Series.
Prod-OECA Dist-FI 1979

Models Of Development C 30 MIN
3/4 OR 1/2 INCH VIDEO CASSETTE
Deals with the models sometimes used in place of embryonic research in order to make important generalizations about complex subjects.
From The Developmental Biology Series.
Prod-NETCHE Dist-NETCHE 1971

Moderate Retardation In Young Children B 43 MIN
16MM FILM, 3/4 OR 1/2 IN VIDEO
Describes a mentally retarded children's program for ages five through seven and shows how a group of these children react to classroom activities.
Prod-CWRUSM Dist-FEIL 1963

Moderation At All Times C 5 MIN
3/4 OR 1/2 INCH VIDEO CASSETTE
Provides an easy-to-understand presentation of the correlation between total consumption and alcohol-related damage. Characterizes some of the problems related to high levels of alcohol consumption.
Prod-ARFO Dist-ARFO 1977

Modern American Drama - O'Neill, Long Day's Journey Into Night B 47 MIN
3/4 OR 1/2 INCH VIDEO CASSETTE
Presents Eugene O'Neill's play Long Day's Journey Into Night which demonstrates the playwright's method of building a towering structure out of a simple story, without much action and in ordinary language. Stars Katharine Hepburn, Ralph Richardson, Jason Robards, Jr and Dean Stockwell.
From The History Of The Drama Series.
Prod-FOTH Dist-FOTH 1984

Modern And Ancient Climates C 30 MIN
3/4 OR 1/2 INCH VIDEO CASSETTE C
Points out how climate more than anything else determines where people live and work. Compares ancient climates with those of today and considers the future course of climatic changes.
From The Earth, Sea And Sky Series.
Prod-DALCCD Dist-DALCCD

Modern Ballet B 29 MIN
16MM FILM, 3/4 OR 1/2 IN VIDEO C A
Discusses and illustrates trends in ballet which began in the 1940's. Describes the changes in subject and mood which accompany this dance form. Gives reasons for a retention of the traditional steps and positions of classical ballet. Presents excerpts from the ballet Pillar Of Fire.
From The Time To Dance Series.
LC NO. 80-707034
Prod-NET Dist-IU Prodn-WGBHTV 1960

Modern Bankruptcy Practice—A Series
PRO
Provides an overview of the 1978 Bankruptcy Reform Act and comments on the Federal Bankruptcy Code. Provides a general explanation of the effect of the code on commerical loans, real property leases, business contracts and other financial commitments.
Prod-ABACPE Dist-ABACPE

Case Administration - Assets Of The Estate	
Chapter 11 - Reorganization	060 MIN
Court And Administrative Structures	060 MIN
Representing The Individual Debtor	060 MIN

Modern Chemist, The - Diamond Synthesis C 12 MIN
16MM FILM OPTICAL SOUND J-H
Shows how Dr H Tracy Hall discovered diamond synthesis and emphasizes the modern chemist's reliance on discoveries from the past. Points out the chemist's creative thinking and experimental method. Explains how chemistry contributes to the welfare of man.
Prod-SUEF Dist-SUTHLA 1962

Modern Coal Mining B 25 MIN
16MM FILM OPTICAL SOUND
Shows how labor-saving machinery, electrically driven, has replaced the methods used for hundreds of years in coal mines.
Prod-GTARC Dist-GTARC 1946

Modern Control Theory - Deterministic Optimal Control—A Series

Discusses deterministic optimal control in modern control theory.
Prod-MIOT Dist-MIOT

Dynamic Programming Algorithm, The	060 MIN
General Discussion	049 MIN
Minimum Principle Of Pontryagin, The	049 MIN
Minimum Principle Vs Dynamic Programming	050 MIN
Minimum Principle, The - Discrete Time Case	043 MIN
Newton's Method	083 MIN
Numerical Example - Solution Of A Minimum	021 MIN
Steepest Descent Method, The	084 MIN

Modern Control Theory - Deterministic Optimal Linear Feedback—A Series
PRO
Discusses deterministic optimal linear feedback in modern control theory which deals with specific analytical and algorithmic methods which can be used to control complex stochastic dynamic systems so as to optimize their performance.
Prod-MIOT Dist-MIOT

Air Traffic Control In The Near Terminal Area	152 MIN
Asymptotic Behavior Of Steady-State Linear	077 MIN
Control Of Helicopter At Hover	031 MIN
Design Of Proportional-Derivative Integral	044 MIN
Motivation For The Linear-Quadratic Problem	073 MIN
Motivation For The Steady-State Linear	104 MIN
Optimal Control Of A Macroeconomic Model Of	044 MIN
Programs - Helicopter Example	045 MIN
Solution Of The Linear-Quadratic Problem, The	047 MIN
Steady-State Linear Regulator Problem For	070 MIN
Steady-State Linear-Quadratic Problem With	041 MIN
Steady-State Linear-Quadratic Problem, The -	051 MIN
Steady-State Linear-Quadratic Problem, The -	038 MIN

Modern Control Theory - Stochastic Control—A Series
PRO
Teaches stochastic control in modern control theory.
Prod-MIOT Dist-MIOT

Continuous-Time Linear-Quadratic-Gaussian	
Control Of A Nonlinear System About Desired	052 MIN
Control Of A Nonlinear System About Desired	039 MIN
Discrete-Time Linear-Quadratic-Gaussian (LQG)	083 MIN
General Problem, The	089 MIN
Introduction	040 MIN
Numerical Example Of LQG Design For A Third-	027 MIN
Steady State LQR Problem - Continuous-Time	068 MIN
Steady State Theory Computer Programs-	057 MIN
Systematic Procedures And Numerical Example	038 MIN

Modern Control Theory - Stochastic Estimation—A Series
PRO
Discusses stochastic estimation in modern control theory.
Prod-MIOT Dist-MIOT

Bayesian Approach To Parameter Estimation, The	090 MIN
Computer Routines For Linear Stochastic	054 MIN
Continuous-Time Kalman-Bucy Filter, The	048 MIN
Discrete-Time Kalman Filter	086 MIN
Effect Of Changing Covariance Matrix Of	036 MIN
Introduction	047 MIN
Numerical Example - Estimation Of Position,	047 MIN
Numerical Example - Estimation Of Positions	032 MIN
Numerical Example - Sensor Trade-Offs	047 MIN
Response Of Linear Systems To White Noise	046 MIN
Response Of Linear Systems To White Noise	052 MIN
Review Of Probabilistic Concepts	050 MIN
Steady-State Kalman Filter - Discrete-Time Case	043 MIN
Steady-State Kalman-Bucy Filter - Continuous-	048 MIN
Suboptimal Nonlinear Filtering Algorithm-	087 MIN

Modern Control Theory - Systems Analysis—A Series

Discusses system analysis, deterministic optimal control, deterministic optimal linear feedback, stochastic estimation and stochastic control.
Prod-MIOT Dist-MIOT

Computer Routines For Linear System Analysis	038 MIN
Controllability And Observability	050 MIN
Discrete-Time Dynamical Systems	040 MIN
Dynamic Linearization For Continuous Time	027 MIN
From Transfer Functions To State Variables	041 MIN
General Notion Of The State Of A Dynamical	045 MIN
Introduction To Optimal Control And	049 MIN
Introduction To Optimal Control And	036 MIN
Linear Continuous Time Dynamical Systems	042 MIN
Linear Time Invariant Dynamical Systems	052 MIN
Relation Of Transfer Functions And State	053 MIN

Modern Control Theory—A Series
PRO

Teaches specific analytical and algorithmic methods for controlling complex systems in order to optimize their performance. Provides techniques for estimating key variables in a dynamic system with noisy sensors and random disturbances and making on-line feedback corrections so that system response is optimal.
Prod-MIOT Dist-AMCEE

Deterministic Optimal Central	050 MIN
Deterministic Optimal Linear Feedback	050 MIN
Stochastic Control	050 MIN
Stochastic Estimation	050 MIN
System Analsis	050 MIN

Modern Corporation, The X 28 MIN
16MM FILM OPTICAL SOUND H
Deals with the structure and operation of a modern corporation and with the corporation's role in today's economic society.
LC NO. FIA67-1452
Prod-SLOAN Dist-SUTHLA Prodn-SUEF 1967

Modern Counseling Program In North Carolina Elementary Schools C 35 MIN
16MM FILM OPTICAL SOUND A
Presents techniques for promoting class participation in developing an understanding of personal behavior, feelings, sensory awareness, and assertiveness. Discusses the children's need for career awareness and social relations. Recommended for counselors, teachers, and principals.
Prod-AACD Dist-AACD 1982

Modern Design C 29 MIN
3/4 OR 1/2 INCH VIDEO CASSETTE
Features Mrs Ascher using exotic and unusual flowers and plant materials to create flower arrangements in a modern mood.
From The Flower Show Series.
Prod-MDCPB Dist-MDCPB

Modern Diabetic, The (2nd Ed) C 15 MIN
1/2 IN VIDEO CASSETTE (VHS) C A
Deals with diabetes. Relates the story of a woman recently diagnosed as diabetic, who joins a group of other diabetics and learns how she can manage her disease while she maintains her normal activities.
Prod-WSTGLC Dist-WSTGLC

Modern Diagnosis And Control Of The Epileptic Seizure C
3/4 INCH VIDEO CASSETTE PRO
Discusses current approaches to seizure diagnosis and management. Reviews current drug therapy.
Prod-AYERST Dist-AYERST

Modern Egypt C 11 MIN
16MM FILM OPTICAL SOUND J-C A
Pictures Egypt today, commenting on government, EducaTion, industries and agriculture. Scenes include the suez canal, Cairo, Alexandria, the Nile, pyramids, sphinxes, Karnak, Luxor, Abu Simbil and the Aswan Dam.
LC NO. 78-701200
Prod-CBF Dist-AVED 1967

Modern Egyptian Family, A C 17 MIN
16MM FILM, 3/4 OR 1/2 IN VIDEO J-C A
Shows some of the changes that have taken place during the 78-year old life of the family patriarch, a grandfather. Points out the Aswan Dam, a series of wars, re-opening of the Suez Canal, oil exploration in the Red Sea, a movement of the cities and resulting urban problems that make up modern Egypt.
Prod-IFF Dist-IFF

Modern Elementary Mathematics—A Series
16MM FILM, 3/4 OR 1/2 IN VIDEO P-I
Presents elementary math concepts.
Prod-TMP Dist-CRMP

Associativity	012 MIN
Commutativity	012 MIN
Equations	012 MIN
Sets And Numbers	012 MIN

Modern Embalming Techniques C 31 MIN
16MM FILM OPTICAL SOUND C A
Explains modern embalming techniques.
Prod-WSU Dist-WSU 1968

Modern Encryption Techniques C
3/4 OR 1/2 INCH VIDEO CASSETTE A
Discusses modern encryption techniques in computer systems.
From The Techniques For Security And Privacy In Computer Systems Series.
Prod-UCEMC Dist-UCEMC

Modern Engines And Engine Conversion (2nd Ed) C 12 MIN
16MM FILM, 3/4 OR 1/2 IN VIDEO I-J
Compares various types of engines, explaining each in terms of its mechanical operation, heat cycle, and energy efficiency.
Prod-CENTRO Dist-CORF

Modern Europe—A Series
I-H
Shows the way of life in five European Countries.
Prod-JOU Dist-JOU

Belgium	018 MIN
Finland	019 MIN
Norway	017 MIN
Sweden	022 MIN
Switzerland	019 MIN

Modern Falconry C
3/4 OR 1/2 INCH VIDEO CASSETTE
Prod-FO Dist-FO

Modern Fertility Control C 30 MIN
3/4 OR 1/2 INCH VIDEO CASSETTE
Discusses birth control pills, intra-uterine devices, sterilization and other contraceptive methods.
From The Family Planning Series.
Prod-NETCHE Dist-NETCHE 1970

Modern Geodetic Surveying C 18 MIN
16MM FILM OPTICAL SOUND C T
Portrays the need, nature, and means of geodetic surveying as it exists today, with emphasis on the challenge of the future.
LC NO. 72-701471
Prod-USN Dist-USNAC 1967

Modern Golf Instruction In Motion Pictures—A Series
H-C A
Prod-NGF Dist-NGF Prodn-GOLF 1974

Golf - A Special Kind Of Joy	16 MIN
How To Build A Golf Swing, Pt 1	16 MIN
How To Build A Golf Swing, Pt 2	16 MIN
Putting - A Golf's End Game	12 MIN
Short Approach Shots, The	9 MIN
Special Challenge Shots, The	14 MIN

Modern Identity, A C 11 MIN
16MM FILM OPTICAL SOUND
Focuses on the new creativity of American architecture. Explains that in past centuries city architecture in the United States revealed worldwide influences and the diverse cultures of the past. Shows that American architecture eventually broke with tradition and that the wide variety of imaginative Designs which are being created have a modern identity and are of a national origin.
From The Changing Environment USA Series.
LC NO. 79-711346
Prod-ALEF Dist-ALEF 1971

Modern Innkeepers C 20 MIN
16MM FILM OPTICAL SOUND H
Introduces viewers to the many interesting facets of hotel-motel employment. Describes job opportunities at the front desk, in sales, catering, accounting and management. Portrays food preparation, housekeeping, engineering and laundry as other possibilities.
From The Career Guidance Series.
Prod-KRMATV Dist-GPITVL

Modern Israel C 20 MIN
3/4 OR 1/2 INCH VIDEO CASSETTE J-C A
Highlights Israel as an ancient but modern land. Includes visits to Haifa, Tel Aviv, Galilee, Jerusalem and Negev.
LC NO. 82-706776
Prod-AWSS Dist-AWSS 1981

Modern Livestock Systems C 22 MIN
16MM FILM OPTICAL SOUND
Shows new methods for feed-processing and waste-disposal. Describes an artificial environment with climate-controlled steel buildings and easily maintained steel equipment that results in smooth-running, labor-saving systems, thereby increasing productivity.
Prod-USSC Dist-USSC

Modern Logic Design, Pt 1—A Series

Discusses the basics of logic design and explains how to apply it to typical industrial design problems.
Prod-RCAHSS Dist-RCAHSS

Modern Logic Design, Pt 2—A Series

Covers topics in modern logic design, including design failures and failure modes, multiple function design, decoders and encoders, and the design of counters.
Prod-RCAHSS Dist-RCAHSS

Modern Management Of Multiple Births C 20 MIN
16MM FILM OPTICAL SOUND PRO
Discusses the problems of multiple births and their increased risks. Reviews conditions such as prematurity, toxemia, anemia and stress and shows the use of the placentogram and obstetrical procedures involved in breech and transverse presentations. Presents sequences taken during the birth of identical quadruplets.
Prod-ACYLLD Dist-LEDR 1964

Modern Management Of Tuberculosis, The C 60 MIN
16MM FILM OPTICAL SOUND PRO
Explains modern theories regarding the diagnosis, transmission and treatment of tuberculosis.
LC NO. 73-702041
Prod-DCC Dist-AMLUNG 1973

Modern Management—A Series
16MM FILM - 3/4 IN VIDEO IND
Prod-BNA Dist-BNA

Case Of The Missing Magnets, The	10 MIN
Challenge Of Leadership, The	10 MIN
Good Beginning, A	10 MIN
Instructions Or Obstrictions	10 MIN
Listen, Please	10 MIN
Trouble With Archie, The	10 MIN
Winning Combination For Cost Control, The	10 MIN

Modern Manufacturing - Command Performance C 33 MIN
16MM FILM, 3/4 OR 1/2 IN VIDEO
Illustrates the need for using modern methods in the production of aerospace vehicles and depicts many of the latest manufacturing techniques. Explains that the use of automation from programming to finished product can supersede conventional methods in speed, reliability and economy.
LC NO. 81-707321
Prod-USAF Dist-USNAC 1963

Modern Manufacturing Systems C 30 MIN
3/4 OR 1/2 INCH VIDEO CASSETTE
Demonstrates computer integrated manufacturing along with all the computerized products and services available to engineers who are automating their manufacturing operations.
Prod-SME Dist-SME

Modern Mapmakers C 20 MIN
3/4 INCH VIDEO CASSETTE I
Explains the entire process of mapmaking from aerial photography and ground control teams to the final inscribing.
From The Understanding Our World, Unit I - Tools We Use Series.
Prod-KRMATV Dist-GPITVL

Modern Mathematics - Number Line C 13 MIN
16MM FILM, 3/4 OR 1/2 IN VIDEO P-I
Introduces the number line and shows uses for it, such as addition, subtraction, comparison and measurement.
Prod-BAILEY Dist-PHENIX 1966

Modern Mathematics - Number Sentences C 11 MIN
16MM FILM, 3/4 OR 1/2 IN VIDEO P-I
Children playing discover relationships between everyday objects and concepts explained by mathematical sentences or simple equations.
Prod-BFA Dist-PHENIX 1966

Modern Mathematics - Sets C 13 MIN
16MM FILM, 3/4 OR 1/2 IN VIDEO P-I
Uses animation to illustrate concepts of sets, one-toone correspondence, associative and commutative laws, cardinal numbers and numerals used in foreign language. Shows their relation to daily family activity.
Prod-BAILEY Dist-PHENIX 1966

Modern Meaning Of Efficiency, The C 25 MIN
16MM FILM - 3/4 IN VIDEO IND
Explains why it is no longer efficient to break down jobs into components that are 'so simple even a child could do it.' Emphasizes that this is not utilization of talent, but it is an ambulation of talent. Stresses that when the manager complains about the 'poor attitude' of subordinates, chances are that these attitudes are usually a result, not a cause, of their inefficiency.
From The Motivation To Work Series.
Prod-BNA Dist-BNA 1969

Modern Medicine B 30 MIN
2 INCH VIDEOTAPE J
See series title for descriptive statement.
From The Investigating The World Of Science, Unit 2 - Energy Within Living Systems Series.
Prod-MPATI Dist-GPITVL

Modern Methods Of Venous Blood Collection C 25 MIN
16MM FILM OPTICAL SOUND PRO
Discusses proper venipuncture techniques, including preparation of equipment and patient, single and multiple specimen collection, handling of blood specimens and tube additives related to various laboratory tests.
LC NO. 77-700389
Prod-BECDIC Dist-SCITIF Prodn-SCITIF 1976

Modern Mexicans, The C 30 MIN
16MM FILM OPTICAL SOUND
Studies the lives of Mexicans of different social and economic levels. Explores the unique mixture of indian and Spanish cultures plus the modern industrial technology that forms present day Mexico. Examines the revolution taking place in Mexico as a new generation is moving into positions of responsibility in government, business and the professions.
Prod-FILCOM Dist-FILCOM

Modern Mexicans, The (Spanish) C 30 MIN
16MM FILM OPTICAL SOUND
Studies the lives of Mexicans of different social and economic levels. Explores the unique mixture of Indian and Spanish cultures plus the modern industrial technology that forms present day Mexico. Examines the revolution taking place in Mexico as a new generation is moving into positions of responsibility in government, business and the professions.
Prod-FILCOM Dist-FILCOM

Modern Newspaper Plant, A C 15 MIN
3/4 INCH VIDEO CASSETTE I-J
Presents a tour through the Omaha World-Herald. Shows the steps in the production and dissemination of a newspaper.
From The Newspaper - What's In It For Me Series.
Prod-MOEBA Dist-GPITVL 1980

Modern Newspaper Plant, A C 20 MIN
3/4 INCH VIDEO CASSETTE I-H
From The Newspaper In The Classroom Series.
Prod-GPITVL Dist-GPITVL

Modern Newspaper Plant, A B 20 MIN
2 INCH VIDEOTAPE I-H
Tours the facilities of the Omaha World Herald, Nebraska, showing the administrative offices, newsrooms and printing presses and the many workers required to publish a daily newspaper. Shows the entire process which one news story goes through before it is delivered. (Broadcast quality)
From The Newspaper In The Classroom Series. No. 4
Prod-MOEBA Dist-GPITVL Prodn-KYNETV

Modern Nutrition C 45 MIN
16MM FILM OPTICAL SOUND
Discusses vitamin deficiencies.
Prod-SQUIBB Dist-SQUIBB 1952

Modern Obstetrics - Cesarean Section C 21 MIN
3/4 OR 1/2 INCH VIDEO CASSETTE PRO

Details the history of Cesarean section as well as indications and diagnostic tests. Discusses and shows in actual deliveries the classical low cervical and extra-peritoneal types of Cesarean section.
Prod-WFP Dist-WFP

Modern Obstetrics - Fetal Evaluation C 25 MIN
3/4 OR 1/2 INCH VIDEO CASSETTE PRO
Describes the techniques that are available for evaluating gestational age, fetal growth, maturation, well being and malformations. Demonstrates amniocentesis, electronic heart monitoring, fetoscopy and ultrasonography.
Prod-WFP Dist-WFP

Modern Obstetrics - Normal Labor And Delivery C 22 MIN
3/4 OR 1/2 INCH VIDEO CASSETTE PRO
Details all the procedures the medical staff undertakes during the course of labor and safe delivery of the baby by following a mother in labor.
Prod-WFP Dist-WFP

Modern Obstetrics - Postpartum Hemorrhage C 25 MIN
3/4 OR 1/2 INCH VIDEO CASSETTE PRO
Illustrates the causes of postpartum hemorrhage and how to diagnose and manage such hemorrhages.
Prod-WFP Dist-WFP

Modern Obstetrics - Pre-Eclampsia, Eclampsia C 27 MIN
3/4 OR 1/2 INCH VIDEO CASSETTE PRO
Demonstrates by means of clinical cases, the diagnosis and treatment of eclampsia and pre-eclampsia. Animation is used to illustrate the etiology of toxemia and the changes which occur as the condition progresses.
Prod-WFP Dist-WFP

Modern Portable Fire Extinguishers - First Line Of Defense Against Fire C 29 MIN
16MM FILM OPTICAL SOUND I-C A
Demonstrates the use of a variety of fire extinguishers, including the BC and ABC dry chemical types, the carbon dioxide gas type and the pressurized water type.
LC NO. 74-703690
Prod-SUMHIL Dist-SUMHIL 1974

Modern Post Office, The X 13 MIN
16MM FILM, 3/4 OR 1/2 IN VIDEO P-I
The movement of a single piece of mail--a post card-is used to illustrate the work of the modern post office.
Prod-WANDIA Dist-PHENIX 1967

Modern Programming Practices C 30 MIN
3/4 OR 1/2 INCH VIDEO CASSETTE IND
Focuses on position independent programs and coding instructions and program counter relative instructions. Describes LEA and PEA instructions.
From The MC68000 Microprocessor Series.
Prod-COLOSU Dist-COLOSU

Modern Protest C 30 MIN
3/4 OR 1/2 INCH VIDEO CASSETTE C
Discusses the black protests for civil rights in America.
From The Afro-American Perspectives Series.
Prod-MDDE Dist-MDCPB

Modern Steel Making C 23 MIN
16MM FILM OPTICAL SOUND H-C A
Shows basic steelmaking today in the blast, open hearth and electric furnaces. Uses animation and live photography with on-the-scene sound effects to illustrate the steelmaking operations.
Prod-SUTHP Dist-USSC 1960

Modern Techniques In Language Teaching B 32 MIN
16MM FILM OPTICAL SOUND H T
Discusses the procedures involved in forming new language habits. Uses an English class for non-English speakers to show how the sound system, grammatical organization and lexicon of a language is taught.
From The Principles And Methods Of Teaching A Second Language Series.
Prod-MLAA Dist-IU Prodn-RAY 1962

Modern Times C 25 MIN
3/4 OR 1/2 INCH VIDEO CASSETTE
Examines aspects of contemporary life through a series of short unusual narratives that intensify and heighten the meaning of ordinary experiences.
From The Nan Hoover - Selected Works I Series.
Prod-EAI Dist-EAI

Modern Times C 28 MIN
3/4 OR 1/2 INCH VIDEO CASSETTE
Explores a woman's experience in contemporary society. Emphasizes a non-linear narrative.
Prod-KITCHN Dist-KITCHN

Modern Times - Revisited - Alternatives To Assembly Lines C 29 MIN
3/4 OR 1/2 INCH VIDEO CASSETTE C A
Visits assembly plants in Sweden and Italy to reveal worker oriented production plants being used by more firms to stimulate employee creativity. Examines self-paced work teams at the Volvo truck division in Sweden and at the Olivetti factory near Turin. Contains employee interviews.
From The Re-Making Of Work Series.
Prod-BLCKBY Dist-EBEC 1983

Modern U S History - From Cold War To Hostage Crisis--A Series
H
Identifies and discusses the turning points in U S history since World War II.
Prod-GA Dist-GA

Nineteen Forty-Five To 1960
Nineteen Sixty-Nine To 1981
Nineteen Sixty-One To 1968

Modern Women - The Uneasy Life B 60 MIN
16MM FILM, 3/4 OR 1/2 IN VIDEO H-C A
Interviews college-educated women who are housewives, professional career women, and women who combine careers and homemaking about the various roles of educated women. Explores the attitudes of husbands and bachelors toward educated women.
From The N E T Journal Series.
Prod-NET Dist-IU 1967

Modern World Of Industrial Arts, The C 13 MIN
16MM FILM OPTICAL SOUND J-H
Stresses the need for a basic education in industrial arts in a world of modern technical complexities. Shows how industrial arts courses relate to the other subjects in the general education curriculum.
Prod-VADE Dist-VADE 1960

Modern X-Ray Generators--A Series
PRO
Explains modern X-ray generators.
Prod-USVA Dist-USNAC

Modern X-Ray Generators, Pt 1, Three-Phase
Modern X-Ray Generators, Pt 2, Primary And 025 MIN
Modern X-Ray Generators, Pt 3, Film Changers 027 MIN
Modern X-Ray Generators, Pt 4, Photospot And 028 MIN

Modern X-Ray Generators, Pt 1, Three-Phase Rectification C 29 MIN
3/4 OR 1/2 INCH VIDEO CASSETTE PRO
Explains interrogation time, kilowatt rating, conversion from fractional to decimal system, three-phase transformers and rectification.
From The Modern X-Ray Generators Series.
Prod-USVA Dist-USNAC

Modern X-Ray Generators, Pt 2, Primary And Secondary Switching, Synchronous And... C 25 MIN
3/4 OR 1/2 INCH VIDEO CASSETTE PRO
Complete title is Modern X-Ray Generators, Pt 2, Primary And Secondary Switching, Synchronous And Nonsynchronous Timing. Discusses approaches to switching or contacting the high voltage to the X-ray tube.
From The Modern X-Ray Generators Series.
Prod-USVA Dist-USNAC

Modern X-Ray Generators, Pt 3, Film Changers And Maximum Available Exposure Time C 27 MIN
3/4 OR 1/2 INCH VIDEO CASSETTE PRO
Explains why a non-synchronous generator increases the amount of MAS.
From The Modern X-Ray Generators Series.
Prod-USVA Dist-USNAC

Modern X-Ray Generators, Pt 4, Photospot And Cine Cameras, Phototimers C 28 MIN
3/4 OR 1/2 INCH VIDEO CASSETTE PRO
Discusses photospot cine cameras, automatic brightness controls and phototimers.
From The Modern X-Ray Generators Series.
Prod-USVA Dist-USNAC

Modern X-Ray Tubes--A Series
PRO
Discusses all phases of X-ray tubes.
Prod-USVA Dist-USNAC

Modern X-Ray Tubes, Pt 1, Production Of An
Modern X-Ray Tubes, Pt 2, Rotating Anode 025 MIN
Modern X-Ray Tubes, Pt 3, Heating And Cooling 020 MIN
Modern X-Ray Tubes, Pt 4, Use And Abuse Of 020 MIN
Modern X-Ray Tubes, Pt 5, How To Select An 018 MIN
Modern X-Ray Tubes, Pt 6, Focal Spot 017 MIN
Modern X-Ray Tubes, Pt 7, Magnification 017 MIN
Modern X-Ray Tubes, Pt 8, Single-Phase Vs 019 MIN

Modern X-Ray Tubes, Pt 1, Production Of An X-Ray Tube C 50 MIN
3/4 OR 1/2 INCH VIDEO CASSETTE PRO
Describes the process of constructing and testing a rotating anode X-ray tube.
From The Modern X-Ray Tubes Series.
Prod-USVA Dist-USNAC

Modern X-Ray Tubes, Pt 2, Rotating Anode X-Ray Tubes, How They Function C 25 MIN
3/4 OR 1/2 INCH VIDEO CASSETTE PRO
Explains the development of rotating anode X-ray tubes, how they work, and factors that affect tube ratings.
From The Modern X-Ray Tubes Series.
Prod-USVA Dist-USNAC

Modern X-Ray Tubes, Pt 3, Heating And Cooling Of X-Ray Tubes C 20 MIN
3/4 OR 1/2 INCH VIDEO CASSETTE PRO
Explains tube ratings, heat monitoring systems and heat dissipation systems.
From The Modern X-Ray Tubes Series.
Prod-USVA Dist-USNAC

Modern X-Ray Tubes, Pt 4, Use And Abuse Of X-Ray Tubes C 20 MIN
3/4 OR 1/2 INCH VIDEO CASSETTE PRO
Explains how tubes are damaged by equipment malfunction and improper operation. Discusses how to protect the tubes.
From The Modern X-Ray Tubes Series.
Prod-USVA Dist-USNAC

Modern X-Ray Tubes, Pt 5, How To Select An X-Ray Tube C 18 MIN
3/4 OR 1/2 INCH VIDEO CASSETTE PRO
Explains recent development, construction and operation of radiographic equipment, and considerations in X-ray tube selection.
From The Modern X-Ray Tubes Series.
Prod-USVA Dist-USNAC

Modern X-Ray Tubes, Pt 6, Focal Spot Measurements C 17 MIN
3/4 OR 1/2 INCH VIDEO CASSETTE PRO
Discusses the importance of focal spot size in high-resolution photography.
From The Modern X-Ray Tubes Series.
Prod-USVA Dist-USNAC

Modern X-Ray Tubes, Pt 7, Magnification Procedures And Biased Focal Spots C 17 MIN
3/4 OR 1/2 INCH VIDEO CASSETTE PRO
Discusses the principles, techniques and problems of magnification focal spot integrity, including biased focal spots.
From The Modern X-Ray Tubes Series.
Prod-USVA Dist-USNAC

Modern X-Ray Tubes, Pt 8, Single-Phase Vs Three-Phase X-Ray Tube Ratings C 19 MIN
3/4 OR 1/2 INCH VIDEO CASSETTE PRO
Explains how a three-phase apparatus is more efficient than a single-phase apparatus.
From The Modern X-Ray Tubes Series.
Prod-USVA Dist-USNAC

Modes And Music B
16MM FILM OPTICAL SOUND
Illustrates that with the same fingering a flute can produce two distinct notes, eight tones apart, and a clarinet two distinct notes, twelve tones apart. Shows how to explain this difference mathematically.
Prod-OPENU Dist-OPENU

Modest Mussorgski - Pictures At An Exhibition C 37 MIN
3/4 OR 1/2 INCH VIDEO CASSETTE
Focuses on Mussorgski's most popular composition, Pictures At An Exhibition. Includes a performance of the work and an examination of the biographical circumstances surrounding the composition.
Prod-FOTH Dist-FOTH

Modification Of Radiation Injury In Mice C 10 MIN
16MM FILM - 3/4 IN VIDEO
Shows the effects on mice of chemical protection by mercaptoethylguanidine (MEG) before irradiation and bone-marrow transplant after exposure to lethal doses of 900 r as well as possible implications regarding treatment of some human diseases. Issued in 1958 as a motion picture.
LC NO. 77-706123
Prod-USAEC Dist-USNAC Prodn-PH 1977

Modified Davis Intubated Ureterotomy C 15 MIN
16MM FILM OPTICAL SOUND
Depicts a case in which the modified Davis intubated ureterotomy was the only procedure that could successfully correct the obstruction. Shows how the operation results in the almost complete return of normal function in the kidney.
From The Surgical Correction Of Hydronephrosis, Pt 1 - Non-Dismembering Procedures Series.
LC NO. 75-702260
Prod-EATONL Dist-EATONL 1968

Modified Denis-Browne Urethroplasty For Hypospadias C 10 MIN
16MM FILM OPTICAL SOUND
Explains that the second stage modified Denis-Browne urethroplasty is performed after an interval of at least 12 months following the initial chordee correction. Shows how the technique differs from the basic Denis-Browne procedure.
LC NO. 75-702278
Prod-EATONL Dist-EATONL 1971

Modified Diets C 15 MIN
16MM FILM, 3/4 OR 1/2 IN VIDEO J-C
Explains modified diets, showing food groups and exchange lists. Includes restricted calorie, residue, fat, sodium and diabetic diets. Points out the reasons diets are usually prescribed and stresses the necessity of following the doctor's directions and accurately measuring quantities.
Prod-SF Dist-SF 1968

Modified Martienssen Method Subharmonic Resonance B 32 MIN
3/4 OR 1/2 INCH VIDEO CASSETTE
See series title for descriptive statement.
From The Nonlinear Vibrations Series.
Prod-MIOT Dist-MIOT

Modified Neurological Examination C 19 MIN
3/4 OR 1/2 INCH VIDEO CASSETTE PRO
Demonstrates a brief screening exam that covers all seven major categories of neurological function.
Prod-HSCIC Dist-HSCIC 1977

Modified Radical Mastectomy C 27 MIN
16MM FILM OPTICAL SOUND PRO
Demonstrates the technique of complete mastectomy with preservation of both pectoral muscles and sub-total axillary dissection for carcinoma. Explains that its advantages, cosmetic and function, make it more acceptable to patients, and evidence suggests that it is as efficacious as conventional radical mastectomy in the treatment of breast cancer.
Prod-ACYDGD Dist-ACY 1971

Modified Retropubic Prostatectomy C 16 MIN
16MM FILM SILENT
Shows a surgical procedure which has been performed by numerous urologists in this country, but has not been widely adopted. Provides rapid access to the hyperplastic prostate under excellent vision.
Prod-USVA Dist-USVA 1955

Modified Turner-Warwick Urethroplasty For Management Of Deep Urethral Strictures C 18 MIN
16MM FILM OPTICAL SOUND
Points out that management of strictures in the proximal bulbous and membranous urethra in adults and children has always been an enigma to the urologist. Presents a modification of the Turner Warwick urethroplasty which has been used successfully in 20 patients without the use of special instruments by using a routine perineal prostatectomy incision and performing the urethral-scrotal inlay anastomosis under direct vision through this incision.
Prod-EATONL Dist-EATONL 1973

Modified Widman Flap C 14 MIN
3/4 INCH VIDEO CASSETTE PRO
Describes a modified Widman flap procedure for the patient with extensive interproximal pockets. Demonstrates the principles of flap design, access to the involved sites, tissue removal, planing of exposed root surfaces, bone recontouring and flap adaptation.
LC NO. 78-706126
Prod-VADTC Dist-USNAC 1978

Modified Widman Flap (2nd Ed) C 14 MIN
16MM FILM, 3/4 OR 1/2 IN VIDEO PRO
Describes a modifed Widman flap procedure for the patient with extensive interproximal pockets. Demonstrates the principles of flap design, access to the involved sites, tissue removal, planing of exposed root surfaces, bone recontouring and flap adaptation.
Prod-VADTC Dist-USNAC 1977

Modifiers - Adjectives And Adverbs C 8 MIN
16MM FILM, 3/4 OR 1/2 IN VIDEO P-I
Uses an animated circus to illustrate various adjectives and adverbs while the people discuss what modifiers do and how they can be told apart.
From The Basic Grammar Series.
LC NO. 81-706573
Prod-LEVYL Dist-AIMS 1981

Modifying Recipes To Control Saturated Fat And Calories C 14 MIN
16MM FILM - 3/4 IN VIDEO
Shows the principles of recipe modification while maintaining taste and eye appeal. Describes how to reduce saturated fats, calories and cholesterol through elimination or substitution of problem ingredients. Emphasizes dishes such as baked lasagna, pancakes, beef stews and entrees with white sauce.
From The Eat Right To Your Heart's Delight Series.
Prod-IPS Dist-IPS 1976

Modmath C 15 MIN
16MM FILM, 3/4 OR 1/2 IN VIDEO I-J
Introduces the concepts of mathematics, including transivity, associativity and commutativity. Defines reflexive and symmetrical relationships.
LC NO. 80-706997
Prod-RESOBL Dist-IFB 1975

Modmath (French) C 15 MIN
16MM FILM, 3/4 OR 1/2 IN VIDEO I-J
Introduces the concepts of mathematics, including transivity, associativity and commutativity. Defines reflexive and symmetrical relationships.
Prod-RESOBL Dist-IFB 1975

Modular Scheduling And Elementary Schools C 29 MIN
16MM FILM OPTICAL SOUND C T
Shows the experience of students, teachers and principals under the new modular scheduling design, and stresses the theme of the learner as a free inquirer. Portrays ideas and practices such as non-structured time, the open laboratory concept, small group-large group instruction, cross-gradedness, resource centers and departmentalization.
LC NO. 70-710822
Prod-EDUC Dist-EDUC 1970

Modulation C 29 MIN
3/4 INCH VIDEO CASSETTE H A
Explains modulation. Reviews A-flat major scales and chords. Introduces E-flat major scales and chords.
From The Beginning Piano - An Adult Approach Series. Lesson 24
Prod-COAST Dist-CDTEL

Module A - Bipolar Transistor Fundamentals And Basic Amplifier Circuits C 45 MIN
3/4 OR 1/2 INCH VIDEO CASSETTE IND
Presents and discusses characterics of diodes and bipolar transistors. Cites low-frequency, small-signal, input and output transistor models, and measuring methods of models shown. Gives methods of obtaining input- and output-equivalent circuits of transistor amplifiers. Show how common-emitter, common-base and common-collector amplifier large- as well as small-signal characteristics are obtained. Gives expressions showing dependence of gain on operating point.
From The Linear Analog Integrated Circuits Series.
Prod-COLOSU Dist-COLOSU

Module B - Current Sources And Applications C 45 MIN
3/4 OR 1/2 INCH VIDEO CASSETTE IND
Presents ideal and actual current-source characteristics and methods of output-characteristic measurement. Discusses in detail basic, widely used integrated circuit. Develops more accurate and versatile current sources, using modifications on basic circuit. The several current sources are compared. Shows use of current sources for getting large signal gains for the common emitter amplifier.
From The Linear Analog Integrated Circuits Series.
Prod-COLOSU Dist-COLOSU

Module Blue - Body I C 15 MIN
3/4 OR 1/2 INCH VIDEO CASSETTE I
Discusses root words which relate to the body. Includes manu, ped, pod, pus and dent.
From The Wordsmith Series.
Prod-NITC Dist-AITECH Prodn-KLCSTV 1975

Module Blue - Body II C 15 MIN
3/4 OR 1/2 INCH VIDEO CASSETTE I
Discusses root words which relate to the body. Includes opt, ops, derm, ocul, cap, capit and corp.
From The Wordsmith Series.
Prod-NITC Dist-AITECH Prodn-KLCSTV 1975

Module Blue - Fire C 15 MIN
3/4 OR 1/2 INCH VIDEO CASSETTE I
Discusses root words which relate to fire. Includes sol, helio, pyr, torr, therm and ign.
From The Wordsmith Series.
Prod-NITC Dist-AITECH Prodn-KLCSTV 1975

Module Blue - Looking C 15 MIN
3/4 OR 1/2 INCH VIDEO CASSETTE I
Discusses root words which relate to looking. Includes spec, vis, vid and orama.
From The Wordsmith Series.
Prod-NITC Dist-AITECH Prodn-KLCSTV 1975

Module Blue - Sound C 15 MIN
3/4 OR 1/2 INCH VIDEO CASSETTE I
Discusses root words which relate to sound. Includes audi and son.
From The Wordsmith Series.
Prod-NITC Dist-AITECH Prodn-KLCSTV 1975

Module Brown - Leading C 15 MIN
3/4 OR 1/2 INCH VIDEO CASSETTE I
Discusses root words which relate to leading. Includes reg, rect, duc, duct, cracy and agog.
From The Wordsmith Series.
Prod-NITC Dist-AITECH Prodn-KLCSTV 1975

Module Brown - Nature C 15 MIN
3/4 OR 1/2 INCH VIDEO CASSETTE I
Discusses root words which relate to nature. Includes terr, geo, nat and eco.
From The Wordsmith Series.
Prod-NITC Dist-AITECH Prodn-KLCSTV 1975

Module Brown - Position C 15 MIN
3/4 OR 1/2 INCH VIDEO CASSETTE I
Discusses root words which relate to position. Includes pos, sta, sed and sid.
From The Wordsmith Series.
Prod-NITC Dist-AITECH Prodn-KLCSTV 1975

Module Brown - Transportation I C 15 MIN
3/4 OR 1/2 INCH VIDEO CASSETTE I
Discusses root words which relate to transportation. Includes mot, mob, mov and drom.
From The Wordsmith Series.
Prod-NITC Dist-AITECH Prodn-KLCSTV 1975

Module Brown - Transportation II C 15 MIN
3/4 OR 1/2 INCH VIDEO CASSETTE I
Discusses root words which relate to transportation. Includes it, port and fug.
From The Wordsmith Series.
Prod-NITC Dist-AITECH Prodn-KLCSTV 1975

Module C - The Differential Amplifier C 45 MIN
3/4 OR 1/2 INCH VIDEO CASSETTE IND
Presents large and small-signal characteristics of the differential amplifier. Shows methods for obtaining input- and output-equivalent circuits. Give expressions for the common-mode and differential-mode gain. Shows effects of mismatches in saturation currents and resistor values. Defines and calculates offset voltage and offset current. Discusses an integrated-circuit differential amplifier with large signal gain and large common-mode rejection ratio.
From The Linear Analog Integrated Circuits Series.
Prod-COLOSU Dist-COLOSU

Module D - Class A, B, And AB Output Stages And The muA741 Operational Amplifier C 45 MIN
3/4 OR 1/2 INCH VIDEO CASSETTE IND
Gives large- and small-signal characterics of Class-A emitter-follower output stage. Shows power and efficiency relations. Discusses crossover distortion present in the Class-B emitter-follower output stage, and methods for eliminating it by using class-AB operations shown. Uses the muA741 operational amplifier as example to show how the differential, the intermediate, and output stages are put together to design an integrated circuit operational amplifier.
From The Linear Analog Integrated Circuits Series.
Prod-COLOSU Dist-COLOSU

Module Eight - Current And Ammeters C
3/4 OR 1/2 INCH VIDEO CASSETTE
Includes The Ammeter (Theory) and Measuring Current (Lab Job).
From The D C Electronics Series.
Prod-WFVTAE Dist-WFVTAE

Module Eight - R L Circuits C
3/4 OR 1/2 INCH VIDEO CASSETTE
Includes Inductive A C Circuits (Theory), Dual Trace Oscilloscope - Measuring Voltage and Dual Trace Oscilloscope - Measuring Phase Shift (Lab Jobs).
From The A C Electronics Series.
Prod-WFVTAE Dist-WFVTAE

Module Eleven - Circuit Analysis C
3/4 OR 1/2 INCH VIDEO CASSETTE
Includes Kirchhoff's Law and Superposition/Network Theorems (Theory) and Resistance Bridge Circuits (Lab Job).
From The D C Electronics Series.
Prod-WFVTAE Dist-WFVTAE

Module Eleven - R L C Circuits C
3/4 OR 1/2 INCH VIDEO CASSETTE
Includes R L C Circuits and Introduction To Resonance (Theory).
From The A C Electronics Series.
Prod-WFVTAE Dist-WFVTAE

Module Five - Capacitive Circuits C
3/4 OR 1/2 INCH VIDEO CASSETTE
Includes Capacitive A C Circuits (Theory) and Capacitive Reactance and Impedance (Lab Job).
From The A C Electronics Series.
Prod-WFVTAE Dist-WFVTAE

Module Five - Resistance C
3/4 OR 1/2 INCH VIDEO CASSETTE
Includes Resistance, Series Parallel Resistive Circuits and the Ohmmeter (Theory), The Calculator-Prefixes and Resistance Problems (Skill Module), Measuring Resistance, Using the Lab Breadboard, Continuity, Opens and Shorts and Measuring Resistance Characteristics (Lab Jobs). With a diskette on Color Code.
From The D C Electronics Series.
Prod-WFVTAE Dist-WFVTAE

Module Four - Batteries And Voltage Drops C
3/4 OR 1/2 INCH VIDEO CASSETTE
Includes Voltage Rises and Voltage Drops (Theory) and the Calculator - Getting Started (Skill Module).
From The D C Electronics Series.
Prod-WFVTAE Dist-WFVTAE

Module Four - Resistive Circuits And Introduction To Capacitors C
3/4 OR 1/2 INCH VIDEO CASSETTE
Includes A C Resistive Circuits and Introduction to Capacitors (Theory).
From The A C Electronics Series.
Prod-WFVTAE Dist-WFVTAE

Module Fourteen - Capacitive Circuits C
3/4 OR 1/2 INCH VIDEO CASSETTE
Includes R C and L R Time Constants (Theory), R C Time Constants, Capacitors in Series and Parallel, and Using Capacitors (Lab Jobs).
From The D C Electronics Series.
Prod-WFVTAE Dist-WFVTAE

Module Green - Numbers I C 15 MIN
3/4 OR 1/2 INCH VIDEO CASSETTE I
Discusses root words which relate to numbers. Includes uni, bi, tw and mono.
From The Wordsmith Series.
Prod-NITC Dist-AITECH Prodn-KLCSTV 1975

Module Green - Numbers II C 15 MIN
3/4 OR 1/2 INCH VIDEO CASSETTE I
Discusses root words which relate to numbers. Includes hemi, semi, amphi, ambi, pan, panto, multi and poly.
From The Wordsmith Series.
Prod-NITC Dist-AITECH Prodn-KLCSTV 1975

Module Green - Numbers III C 15 MIN
3/4 OR 1/2 INCH VIDEO CASSETTE I
Discusses root words which relate to numbers. Includes tri, quart, quadr, dec and cent.
From The Wordsmith Series.
Prod-NITC Dist-AITECH Prodn-KLCSTV 1975

Module Green - Walk And Run C 15 MIN
3/4 OR 1/2 INCH VIDEO CASSETTE I
Discusses root words which relate to ambulation. Includes ambul, grad, gress and cur.
From The Wordsmith Series.
Prod-NITC Dist-AITECH Prodn-KLCSTV 1975

Module Green - Water C 15 MIN
3/4 OR 1/2 INCH VIDEO CASSETTE I
Discusses root words which relate to water. Includes aqua, mar, hydr and flu.
From The Wordsmith Series.
Prod-NITC Dist-AITECH Prodn-KLCSTV 1975

Module Nine - Transformer Theory C
3/4 OR 1/2 INCH VIDEO CASSETTE
Includes Transformers I (Theory) and Measuring Transformer Characteristics (Lab Job).
From The A C Electronics Series.
Prod-WFVTAE Dist-WFVTAE

Module Nine - Voltmeters And Ohmmeters C
3/4 OR 1/2 INCH VIDEO CASSETTE
Includes The Multimeter (Theory) and Loading Effects of Voltmeters(Lab Job).
From The D C Electronics Series.
Prod-WFVTAE Dist-WFVTAE

Module One - Introduction To Alternating Current C
3/4 OR 1/2 INCH VIDEO CASSETTE
Includes Introduction To Alternating Current (Theory).
From The A C Electronics Series.
Prod-WFVTAE Dist-WFVTAE

Module Orange - Communication C 15 MIN
3/4 OR 1/2 INCH VIDEO CASSETTE I
Discusses root words which relate to communication. Includes tele, graph, gram, scrib, script, her and hes.
From The Wordsmith Series.
Prod-NITC Dist-AITECH Prodn-KLCSTV 1975

Module Orange - Connection C 15 MIN
3/4 OR 1/2 INCH VIDEO CASSETTE I

Discusses root words which relate to connection. Includes con, com, co and syn.
From The Wordsmith Series.
Prod-NITC Dist-AITECH Prodn-KLCSTV 1975

Module Orange - Measure And Metrics C 15 MIN
3/4 OR 1/2 INCH VIDEO CASSETTE I
Discusses root words which relate to measurement and the metric system. Includes meter and metr.
From The Wordsmith Series.
Prod-NITC Dist-AITECH Prodn-KLCSTV 1975

Module Orange - Relatives C 15 MIN
3/4 OR 1/2 INCH VIDEO CASSETTE I
Discusses root words which relate to relatives. Includes mater, matr, pater, patr and ped.
From The Wordsmith Series.
Prod-NITC Dist-AITECH Prodn-KLCSTV 1975

Module Orange - Twist And Turn C 15 MIN
3/4 OR 1/2 INCH VIDEO CASSETTE I
Discusses root words which relate to twisting and turning. Includes tor, trop, vert and vers.
From The Wordsmith Series.
Prod-NITC Dist-AITECH Prodn-KLCSTV 1975

Module Red - Animals I C 15 MIN
3/4 OR 1/2 INCH VIDEO CASSETTE I
Discusses root words which relate to animals. Includes anim, zo, can, cyn and ine.
From The Wordsmith Series.
Prod-NITC Dist-AITECH Prodn-KLCSTV 1975

Module Red - Animals II C 15 MIN
3/4 OR 1/2 INCH VIDEO CASSETTE I
Discusses root words which relate to animals. Includes bio, greg and drom.
From The Wordsmith Series.
Prod-NITC Dist-AITECH Prodn-KLCSTV 1975

Module Red - Cutting C 15 MIN
3/4 OR 1/2 INCH VIDEO CASSETTE I
Discusses root words which relate to cutting. Includes cis, sect, tom and ec.
From The Wordsmith Series.
Prod-NITC Dist-AITECH Prodn-KLCSTV 1975

Module Red - Serendipity C 15 MIN
3/4 OR 1/2 INCH VIDEO CASSETTE I
Presents an anecdotal program which emphasizes various word idioms.
From The Wordsmith Series.
Prod-NITC Dist-AITECH Prodn-KLCSTV 1975

Module Red - Time C 15 MIN
3/4 OR 1/2 INCH VIDEO CASSETTE I
Discusses root words which relate to time. Includes chron, temp, ann, enn, pre and post.
From The Wordsmith Series.
Prod-NITC Dist-AITECH Prodn-KLCSTV 1975

Module Seven - Inductive Circuits C
3/4 OR 1/2 INCH VIDEO CASSETTE
Includes Introduction to Inductors (Theory) and Inductive Reactance and Impedance (Lab Job).
From The A C Electronics Series.
Prod-WFVTAE Dist-WFVTAE

Module Seven - Magnetism C
3/4 OR 1/2 INCH VIDEO CASSETTE
Includes Magnetism and A C And D C Generators (Theory), and Electromagnetism, and Magnetic and Electromagnetic Devices (Lab Jobs).
From The D C Electronics Series.
Prod-WFVTAE Dist-WFVTAE

Module Six - Math Applications In A C Circuits C
3/4 OR 1/2 INCH VIDEO CASSETTE
Includes Math Applications (Theory).
From The A C Electronics Series.
Prod-WFVTAE Dist-WFVTAE

Module Six - Ohm's Law And Power C
3/4 OR 1/2 INCH VIDEO CASSETTE
Includes Ohm's Law and Power (Theory), The Calculator - Prefixes and Ohm's Law Problems (Skill Module), Verifying Ohm's Law and Power (Lab Jobs).
From The D C Electronics Series.
Prod-WFVTAE Dist-WFVTAE

Module Ten - Series, Parallel And Voltage Divider Circuits C
3/4 OR 1/2 INCH VIDEO CASSETTE
Includes Series-Parallel Resistive Circuits (Theory) and Voltage Dividers (Theory).
From The D C Electronics Series.
Prod-WFVTAE Dist-WFVTAE

Module Ten - Transformer Applications C
3/4 OR 1/2 INCH VIDEO CASSETTE
Includes Transformers II (Theory), Transformer Loading Effects and Transformers In-Phase and Out-of-Phase (Lab Jobs).
From The A C Electronics Series.
Prod-WFVTAE Dist-WFVTAE

Module Thirteen - Inductance And Capacitance C
3/4 OR 1/2 INCH VIDEO CASSETTE
Includes Inductors and Capacitors (Theory).
From The D C Electronics Series.
Prod-WFVTAE Dist-WFVTAE

Module Thirteen - Parallel Resonance And Filters C
3/4 OR 1/2 INCH VIDEO CASSETTE
Includes Series Resonance/Parallel Resonance (Theory), Parallel Resonance, Band-Pass Band-Stop Filters and Low-Pass and High-Pass Filters (Lab Jobs).
From The A C Electronics Series.
Prod-WFVTAE Dist-WFVTAE

Module Three - A C Measurements C
3/4 OR 1/2 INCH VIDEO CASSETTE
Includes Oscilloscopes (Theory), The Oscilloscope Basic Operations and The Oscilloscope - Determining Period and Frequency (Skill Modules).
From The A C Electronics Series.
Prod-WFVTAE Dist-WFVTAE

Module Three - Electromotive Force C
3/4 OR 1/2 INCH VIDEO CASSETTE
Includes Electromotive Force (Theory), The Voltmeter (Theory), Meter Scales, The Analog Multimeter and The Digital Multimeter (Skill Modules), and Measuring Voltage (Lab Job).
From The D C Electronics Series.
Prod-WFVTAE Dist-WFVTAE

Module Twelve - Series Resonance C
3/4 OR 1/2 INCH VIDEO CASSETTE
Includes Series Resonance/Parallel Resonance (Theory) and Series Resonance and Bandwidth Measurement (Lab Job).
From The A C Electronics Series.
Prod-WFVTAE Dist-WFVTAE

Module Twelve - Thevenin's And Norton's Theorems C
3/4 OR 1/2 INCH VIDEO CASSETTE
Includes Superposition/Network Theorems (Theory).
From The D C Electronics Series.
Prod-WFVTAE Dist-WFVTAE

Module Two - Current Flow And Circuits C
3/4 OR 1/2 INCH VIDEO CASSETTE
Includes Scientific Notation and Metric Prefixes (Theory), Volts, Amps, Ohms, Watts (Skill Module) and a diskette on Prefixes.
From The D C Electronics Series.
Prod-WFVTAE Dist-WFVTAE

Module Two - The Sine Wave And A C Values C
3/4 OR 1/2 INCH VIDEO CASSETTE
Includes Characteristics of the Sine Wave (Theory), and Measuring A C Voltage (Lab Job).
From The A C Electronics Series.
Prod-WFVTAE Dist-WFVTAE

Module Yellow - Food C 15 MIN
3/4 OR 1/2 INCH VIDEO CASSETTE I
Discusses root words which relate to food. Includes carn, coct, vor and sal.
From The Wordsmith Series.
Prod-NITC Dist-AITECH Prodn-KLCSTV 1975

Module Yellow - Form C 15 MIN
3/4 OR 1/2 INCH VIDEO CASSETTE I
Discusses root words which relate to form. Includes form, lic, ly and morph.
From The Wordsmith Series.
Prod-NITC Dist-AITECH Prodn-KLCSTV 1975

Module Yellow - Potpourri C 15 MIN
3/4 OR 1/2 INCH VIDEO CASSETTE I
Presents an anecdotal program which emphasizes various word idioms and homonyms.
From The Wordsmith Series.
Prod-NITC Dist-AITECH Prodn-KLCSTV 1975

Module Yellow - Size C 15 MIN
3/4 OR 1/2 INCH VIDEO CASSETTE I
Discusses root words which relate to size. Includes magn, mega, megalo, equ and min.
From The Wordsmith Series.
Prod-NITC Dist-AITECH Prodn-KLCSTV 1975

Module Yellow - Talking C 15 MIN
3/4 OR 1/2 INCH VIDEO CASSETTE I
Discusses root words which relate to talking. Includes dict, loqu and log.
From The Wordsmith Series.
Prod-NITC Dist-AITECH Prodn-KLCSTV 1975

MOFSET, OSFETS, And High Power Layouts B 75 MIN
3/4 OR 1/2 INCH VIDEO CASSETTE
See series title for descriptive statement.
From The Analog IC Layout Design Considerations Series. Pt 6
Prod-UAZMIC Dist-UAZMIC

Mogul Mike Presents Ski Sense And Safety C 22 MIN
16MM FILM, 3/4 OR 1/2 IN VIDEO
Outlines the responsibilities of a safe skier, the basic elements of ski courtesy and the major aspects of ski safety. Uses animation and live sequences of ski scenes to entertain and instruct every skier, beginner to advanced.
Prod-ATHI Dist-ATHI

Mohammed Reza Pahlavi - Politics Of Oil C 24 MIN
16MM FILM, 3/4 OR 1/2 IN VIDEO H-C A
Deals with the rise and fall of the Shah of Iran. Tells how he succeeded his father in 1941 and was sent into exile after the return of the Ayatollah in 1979. Originally shown on the Canadian television program Portraits Of Power.
From The Leaders Of The 20th Century - Portraits Of Power Series.
Prod-NIELSE Dist-LCOA 1980

Mohawk C 17 MIN
3/4 INCH VIDEO CASSETTE
Discusses modification and updating of the Grumman Mohawk.
Prod-WSTGLC Dist-WSTGLC

Mohawk X 27 MIN
16MM FILM, 3/4 OR 1/2 IN VIDEO J-C A
Describes how an angry Mohawk Indian sits in front of Saint Patrick's Cathedral, stating that he won't move until his prayer is answered.
From The Insight Series.
Prod-PAULST Dist-PAULST

Mohawk Basketmaking - A Cultural Profile C 28 MIN
3/4 OR 1/2 INCH VIDEO CASSETTE
Focuses on the art of basketmaking as practiced by Mary Adams, a nationally recognized Mohawk artist. Uses close-up photography to highlight the baskets' multi-colored splints, textural beauty and abstract designs. Designed to help in the preservation of unique and disappearing traditions of Native Americans.
Prod-PSU Dist-PSU

Moira - A Vision Of Blindness C 23 MIN
3/4 OR 1/2 INCH VIDEO CASSETTE I-C A
Features Moira Egan, who is blind, doing a back dive from a high board, making apple pie, travelling on her own and typing her own poetry.
Prod-DENONN Dist-MOKIN 1979

Moira - A Vision Of Blindness C 24 MIN
16MM FILM, 3/4 OR 1/2 IN VIDEO J-C A
Follows 11-year-old Moira Egan who, though blind, performs many acts in the same manner as do her sighted friends and family. Shows Moira as she discusses her feelings about her blindness, reflecting her independence and enthusiasm for life.
Prod-DENONN Dist-DIRECT Prodn-WABCTV 1979

Moirage C 8 MIN
16MM FILM OPTICAL SOUND
Presents a study in opticular illusions, pattern superimposition producing other patterns and illusions of three dimensionality.
Prod-VANBKS Dist-VANBKS

Moire C 8 MIN
16MM FILM OPTICAL SOUND H-C A
Shows kinetic works of Venezuelan artist J M Cruxent.
LC NO. 75-700286
Prod-OOAS Dist-MOMALA 1970

Moire C 8 MIN
3/4 OR 1/2 INCH VIDEO CASSETTE
Shows kinetic works of Venezuelan artist JM Cruxent.
LC NO. 82-707023
Prod-MOMALA Dist-MOMALA

Moire (Spanish) C 8 MIN
16MM FILM OPTICAL SOUND J-C
Shows kinetic works of Venezuelan artist J M Cruxent.
LC NO. 75-700286
Prod-OOAS Dist-MOMALA 1970

Moire (Spanish) C 8 MIN
3/4 OR 1/2 INCH VIDEO CASSETTE
Shows kinetic works of Venezuelan artist JM Cruxent.
Prod-MOMALA Dist-MOMALA

Moisture Proofing Electrical And Type Connectors C 20 MIN
16MM FILM OPTICAL SOUND
Tells how to apply synthetic rubber to electrical connections, and how to mix, test and store potting compound.
LC NO. 74-705161
Prod-USN Dist-USNAC 1957

Mojo And The Russians C 15 MIN
3/4 OR 1/2 INCH VIDEO CASSETTE I
Tells a story about a gang of children from Harlem and the Russian consulate. From the book by Walter Dean Myers.
From The Storybound Series.
Prod-CTI Dist-CTI

Molala Harai C 19 MIN
16MM FILM OPTICAL SOUND J-C A
Uses animation to tell the story behind a set of stamps designed by the Reverend Bert Brown, missionary and part-time artist in the territory of papua and New Guinea.
LC NO. 72-702915
Prod-ANAIB Dist-AUIS 1971

Molasses And The American Heritage C 15 MIN
16MM FILM, 3/4 OR 1/2 IN VIDEO
Uses scenes from American history and recipes to tell the story of molasses in the United States and to show how its use has influenced many traditional foods.
Prod-KLEINW Dist-KLEINW 1979

Moldau, The C 15 MIN
16MM FILM, 3/4 OR 1/2 IN VIDEO
Follows the Moldau River. Blends music with the towns, cities and countryside of Czechoslovakia.
Prod-KAWVAL Dist-KAWVAL

Molded Papier Mache C 14 MIN
2 INCH VIDEOTAPE
Shows how to use papier mache to make bowls and vases.
From The Living Better II Series.
Prod-MAETEL Dist-PUBTEL

Molders Of Troy C 90 MIN
3/4 OR 1/2 INCH VIDEO CASSETTE
Centers on Brian Duffy, an Irish immigrant who overcame ethnic pressures to organize Troy's Iron Molders Union into one of the strongest unions in the country.
Prod-WMHTTV Dist-PBS 1980

Molding A Horizontal Cored Part B 22 MIN
16MM FILM OPTICAL SOUND
Shows how to use a horizontal core, a split pattern, chaplets and chaplet supports, how to gate a mold to pour a thin casting and how to clean a casting.

From The Foundry Practice Series. Floor Molding, No, 4
LC NO. FIE52-112
Prod-USOE Dist-USNAC Prodn-ATLAS 1945

Molding A Valve Body B 25 MIN
16MM FILM OPTICAL SOUND
Demonstrates use of a split pattern and multipart dry sand core, how to gate a mold for rapid, uniform distribution of clean metals, and how to locate a core and seal the core prints.
LC NO. FIE52-113
Prod-USOE Dist-USNAC 1945

Molding On A Jolt Roll-Over Pattern Draw Machine B 23 MIN
16MM FILM OPTICAL SOUND
Explains the jolt roll-over pattern draw machine. Shows how To fill the drag and jolt it, draw the Pattern, set the drag and cope pattern plates, fill the cope and jolt it, and finish and close the mold.
From The Foundry Practice Series. Machine Molding
LC NO. FIE52-116
Prod-USOE Dist-USNAC Prodn-FCRAFT 1945

Molding On A Jolt Squeeze Machine B 10 MIN
16MM FILM OPTICAL SOUND
Shows the principles of the jolt squeeze molding machine, how to roll the mold, fill the cope and apply pressboard, squeeze the mold, draw the pattern, and finish and close the mold.
LC NO. FIE52-114
Prod-USOE Dist-USNAC 1945

Molding Part Having A Vertical Core B 19 MIN
16MM FILM OPTICAL SOUND
Demonstrates how to mold a gate and riser, make a pouring basin, vent a mold to permit the escape of core gases and locate a vertical core in a mold.
Prod-USOE Dist-USNAC 1944

Molding Part With Deep Green Sand Core B 25 MIN
16MM FILM OPTICAL SOUND
Explains the use of a follow board with a thin boxlike pattern. Shows how to reinforce a green sand core with nails, locate sprue and watch-up pins, use gaggers and ram and vent a green sand core.
LC NO. FIE52-109
Prod-USOE Dist-USNAC 1945

Molding With A Gated Pattern B 11 MIN
16MM FILM OPTICAL SOUND
Explains what a gated pattern is and why it is used. Shows how a match or follow board may simplify making a parting, how facing sand is prepared, and how and why some patterns are rapped through the cope.
From The Foundry Practice Series. Bench Molding, No. 5
LC NO. FIE52-111
Prod-USOE Dist-USNAC Prodn-ATLAS 1944

Molding With A Loose Pattern B 21 MIN
16MM FILM OPTICAL SOUND
Explains how molding sand is prepared. Demonstrates how to face a pattern, ram and vent a mold, roll a drag, cut a sprue, runner, riser and gates, and swabs, and rap and draw a pattern. Uses animation to show what takes place inside a mold during pouring.
Prod-USOE Dist-USNAC 1944

Molding With A Loose Pattern - Bench B 21 MIN
16MM FILM OPTICAL SOUND
Shows how to use bench molder's tools, prepare molding sand, face a pattern, ram and vent a mold, roll a drag and cut a sprue, runner, riser and gates. Depicts with animation the inside of a mold during pouring.
From The Foundry Practice Series. Bench Molding No. 1
LC NO. FIE52-108
Prod-USOE Dist-USNAC Prodn-ATLAS 1944

Molding With A Loose Pattern - Floor B 24 MIN
16MM FILM OPTICAL SOUND
Shows difference between bench and floor molding, how to face a deep pattern, ram a drag and walk it off, clamp a mold, locate sprues and risers, and tuck the crossbars of a large cope.
From The Foundry Practice Series. Floor Molding No. 1
LC NO. FIE52-110
Prod-USOE Dist-USNAC Prodn-ATLAS 1945

Molding With A Split Pattern B 19 MIN
16MM FILM OPTICAL SOUND
Explains how split patterns aid in the molding of some castings. Shows how ramming affects the permeability of sand in a mold, how to reinforce a mold with nails and how to patch a mold.
From The Foundry Practice Series. Bench Molding, No. 4
LC NO. FIE52-105
Prod-USOE Dist-USNAC Prodn-ATLAS 1944

Molding With A Three Part Flask B 35 MIN
16MM FILM OPTICAL SOUND
Explains the use of a deep follow board and outlines techniques of facing, ramming and venting a deep green sand core. Shows how to use a cheek in a three-part flask. Gives the purpose and method of step-gating.
From The Foundry Practice Series. Floor Molding, No. 5
LC NO. FIE52-115
Prod-USOE Dist-USNAC Prodn-ATLAS 1945

Molds And How They Grow C 11 MIN
16MM FILM, 3/4 OR 1/2 IN VIDEO I-J
Uses laboratory demonstrations, photomicrography, and time-lapse photography to show the conditions under which molds grow, their structure, spore production, colony formation and reproduction.
Prod-CORF Dist-CORF 1969

Molds And Models - How They Are Used C 28 MIN
2 INCH VIDEOTAPE
Features Mrs Peterson describing certain ceramic processes for her classroom at the University of Southern California. Discusses the use of molds and models.
From The Wheels, Kilns And Clay Series.
Prod-USC Dist-PUBTEL

Molds And Models - Start To Finish C 28 MIN
2 INCH VIDEOTAPE
Features Mrs Peterson describing certain ceramic processes for her classroom at the University of Southern California. Discusses the use of molds and models.
From The Wheels, Kilns And Clay Series.
Prod-USC Dist-PUBTEL

Mole And The Bulldozer, The C 7 MIN
16MM FILM, 3/4 OR 1/2 IN VIDEO K-I
Presents an animated film about a mole who decides to prevent the construction of a highway on his territory.
From The Mole Series.
Prod-SFSP Dist-PHENIX 1977

Mole And The Camera, The C 7 MIN
16MM FILM, 3/4 OR 1/2 IN VIDEO K-I
Presents an animated film about a mole whose new camera is broken during a fight with his friend Mouse.
From The Mole Series.
Prod-SFSP Dist-PHENIX 1977

Mole And The Car, The C 16 MIN
16MM FILM, 3/4 OR 1/2 IN VIDEO K-I
Presents an animated film about a mole who becomes so fascinated by the cars whizzing past his molehill that he decides to get one of his own.
From The Mole Series.
Prod-SFSP Dist-PHENIX 1977

Mole And The Chewing Gum, The C 9 MIN
16MM FILM, 3/4 OR 1/2 IN VIDEO K-I
An animated cartoon in which a mole is unable, even with the help of other animals, to get rid of the piece of chewing gum that is stuck on him.
From The Mole Series.
Prod-CFET Dist-PHENIX 1972

Mole And The Christmas Tree, The C 6 MIN
16MM FILM, 3/4 OR 1/2 IN VIDEO K-I
Presents an animated film about a mole who brings a Christmas tree home and invites his friend Mouse to Christmas dinner.
From The Mole Series.
Prod-SFSP Dist-PHENIX 1977

Mole And The Egg, The C 6 MIN
16MM FILM, 3/4 OR 1/2 IN VIDEO K-I
Presents an animated film about a mole who finds a hen's abandoned egg and sets out to find the egg's mother.
From The Mole Series.
Prod-SFSP Dist-PHENIX 1977

Mole And The Flying Carpet, The C 6 MIN
16MM FILM, 3/4 OR 1/2 IN VIDEO K-I
Presents the story about the Mole finding a flying carpet in a dustbin and after cleaning the carpet, the Mole is rewarded by the carpet becoming his friend.
From The Mole Series.
Prod-CFET Dist-PHENIX 1976

Mole And The Green Star C 8 MIN
16MM FILM, 3/4 OR 1/2 IN VIDEO K-I
Follows little Mole as he spring cleans his house and discovers a shining green stone that he is sure must be a star. Tells how Mole and his friends try to put it back into the heavens.
From The Mole Film Series.
Prod-CFET Dist-PHENIX 1970

Mole And The Hedgehog, The C 10 MIN
16MM FILM, 3/4 OR 1/2 IN VIDEO K-I
Presents an animated story about how Mole and his friend Mouse rescue the hedgehog who has been captured and taken to a school laboratory.
From The Mole Series.
Prod-KRATKY Dist-PHENIX 1981

Mole And The Lollipop, The C 9 MIN
16MM FILM, 3/4 OR 1/2 IN VIDEO K-I
Uses animation to tell the story about a mole who finds a lollipop but does not know what to do with it.
From The Mole Film Series.
Prod-SFSP Dist-PHENIX 1971

Mole And The Matchbox, The C 6 MIN
16MM FILM, 3/4 OR 1/2 IN VIDEO P-I
Relates what happens when the Mole and the Mouse discover a matchbox and gradually discover the true purpose of the matches.
Prod-KRATKY Dist-PHENIX 1982

Mole And The Music, The C 6 MIN
16MM FILM, 3/4 OR 1/2 IN VIDEO K-I
Tells the story about the Mole's love for music which helps sustain him when he has to make a new record from scratch after breaking his favorite one.
From The Mole Series.
Prod-CFET Dist-PHENIX 1976

Mole And The Rocket, The C 10 MIN
16MM FILM, 3/4 OR 1/2 IN VIDEO K-I
Tells a story about a little mole who is carried by a rocket to a deserted island in the middle of the ocean. Shows how the sea animals help repair the ruined rocket and go off in it with the mole.
From The Mole Series.
Prod-CFET Dist-PHENIX 1973

Mole And The Telephone, The C 7 MIN
16MM FILM, 3/4 OR 1/2 IN VIDEO K-I
Tells the story about the Mole discovering a telephone receiver and giving it a cold as he tries to get a response from it.
From The Mole Series.
Prod-CFET Dist-PHENIX 1976

Mole And The TV Set, The C 8 MIN
16MM FILM, 3/4 OR 1/2 IN VIDEO K-I
Presents an animated story in which little Mole breaks the television aerial in order to keep the gardener from hearing a television program discussing the necessity of exterminating moles.
From The Mole Series.
Prod-CFET Dist-PHENIX 1972

Mole And The Umbrella, The C 9 MIN
16MM FILM, 3/4 OR 1/2 IN VIDEO K-I
Tells the story of a mole who finds an umbrella on a scrap heap. Explains that the wind carries him, hanging on the umbrella, over the lake and the mole lands on its bank where a melon-dealer has his stand. Tells how the umbrella saves the mole from this precarious situation.
From The Mole Film Series.
Prod-SFSP Dist-PHENIX 1973

Mole As A Chemist, The C 7 MIN
16MM FILM, 3/4 OR 1/2 IN VIDEO K-P
Describes how the Mole, while digging a hole, finds a box containing a chemistry set and begins to play with it. Things get out of control until finally the resourceful Mole restores peace and quiet.
From The Mole Series.
Prod-KRATKY Dist-PHENIX

Mole As A Gardener, The C 8 MIN
16MM FILM, 3/4 OR 1/2 IN VIDEO K-I
An animated cartoon in which a mole and a gardener eventually come to an agreement after they quarrel.
From The Mole Series.
Prod-CFET Dist-PHENIX 1972

Mole As A Painter, The C 11 MIN
16MM FILM, 3/4 OR 1/2 IN VIDEO K-I
Describes how a mole's friends help him frighten away their common enemy, the fox, by dramatizing themselves in colorful paints left by a painter.
From The Mole Series.
Prod-CFET Dist-PHENIX 1974

Mole As A Watchmaker, The C 6 MIN
16MM FILM, 3/4 OR 1/2 IN VIDEO K-I
Tells a story about the Mole who gets mixed up with a game of marbles and a cuckoo clock.
From The Mole Series.
Prod-CFET Dist-PHENIX 1976

Mole At The Carnival, The C 6 MIN
16MM FILM, 3/4 OR 1/2 IN VIDEO K-I
Uses animation to tell the story of a mole who goes to a carnival and encounters a large bulldog.
From The Mole Series.
Prod-SFSP Dist-PHENIX 1977

Mole In The Desert, The C 7 MIN
16MM FILM, 3/4 OR 1/2 IN VIDEO K-I
Presents an animated film about a mole who journeys to the desert and helps the desert animals find water.
From The Mole Series.
Prod-SFSP Dist-PHENIX 1977

Mole In The Town C 30 MIN
16MM FILM, 3/4 OR 1/2 IN VIDEO P-C
From The Mole Series.
LC NO. 84-707080
Prod-KRATKY Dist-PHENIX 1984

Mole In The Zoo, The C 10 MIN
16MM FILM, 3/4 OR 1/2 IN VIDEO K-I
Tells how the mole goes where angels fear to tread. Shows how he seeks to give help to an ailing lion by pulling the lion's throbbing tooth.
From The Mole Series.
Prod-CFET Dist-PHENIX 1973

Mole Poblano Con Pollo C 17 MIN
3/4 OR 1/2 INCH VIDEO CASSETTE PRO
Demonstrates the preparation of chicken in a chocolate-chili sauce.
Prod-CULINA Dist-CULINA

Mole-A Series
16MM FILM, 3/4 OR 1/2 IN VIDEO K-I
Presents the cartoon adventures of little Mole and his friends.
Prod-SFSP Dist-PHENIX 1973

How The Mole Got His Trousers	014 MIN
Mole And The Bulldozer, The	007 MIN
Mole And The Camera, The	007 MIN
Mole And The Car, The	016 MIN
Mole And The Chewing Gum, The	009 MIN
Mole And The Christmas Tree, The	006 MIN
Mole And The Egg, The	006 MIN
Mole And The Flying Carpet, The	006 MIN
Mole And The Green Star, The	008 MIN
Mole And The Hedgehog, The	010 MIN
Mole And The Lollipop, The	009 MIN
Mole And The Matchbox, The	006 MIN
Mole And The Music, The	006 MIN
Mole And The Rocket, The	010 MIN
Mole And The Telephone, The	007 MIN
Mole And The TV Set, The	008 MIN
Mole And The Umbrella, The	009 MIN
Mole As A Chemist, The	007 MIN
Mole As A Gardener, The	008 MIN
Mole As A Painter, The	011 MIN
Mole As A Watchmaker, The	006 MIN

Mole At The Carnival, The 006 MIN
Mole In The Desert, The 007 MIN
Mole In The Town, The 030 MIN
Mole In The Zoo, The 010 MIN

Molecular Biology C 15 MIN
16MM FILM, 3/4 OR 1/2 IN VIDEO J-C
Tells how molecular biologists are trying to understand how the molecules of life first formed and began their control of biological processes using energy-rich molecules of ATP that drive the life functions, and DNA, information molecules that guide the cell to produce the needed materials and then are duplicated and passed on.
From The Biological Sciences Series.
LC NO. 82-706959
Prod-CORF Dist-CORF 1981

Molecular Biology - An Introduction C 15 MIN
16MM FILM - 3/4 IN VIDEO
Discusses molecular biology and reviews technological advances, such as the improved resolution of the electron microscope, the isolation of cell parts by ultracentrifugation, the separation capabilities of chromatography, the localization of autoradiography and the sensitivity of liquid scintillation counting. Issued in 1969 as a motion picture.
LC NO. 77-706124
Prod-ANL Dist-USNAC Prodn-USAECA

Molecular Biology Films—A Series
C
Prod-ERCMIT Dist-EDC 1970

Alpha Helix Formation 3 MIN
Amino Acids And Proteins 6 MIN
Biosynthesis Of Steroids 6 MIN
Catalysis By A Co-Enzyme 5 MIN
Chempak 9 MIN
Small Molecules 4 MIN
Structure Of Proteins 10 MIN

Molecular Motions C 13 MIN
16MM FILM OPTICAL SOUND H
Explores the properties of matter, such as fluidity, vaporization and rates of chemical reactions, which indicate that molecular motion must be occurring. Describes the solid, liquid and gaseous States and presents the concepts of translational, rotational and vibrational molecular motions.
From The CHEM Study Films Series.
Prod-CHEMS Dist-MLA 1962

Molecular Reactivity C 270 MIN
3/4 OR 1/2 INCH VIDEO CASSETTE
Uses an integrated thermodynamic-kinetic approach to the study of molecular processes. Presents the important elements to describe molecular reactivity, techniques used for evaluating kinetic data, factors that govern rates of chemical processes and thermodynamic concepts that apply to molecular reactions.
Prod-AMCHEM Dist-AMCHEM

Molecular Reproduction C 45 MIN
3/4 OR 1/2 INCH VIDEO CASSETTE C
Discusses various aspects of cellular reproduction.
From The Biology I Series.
Prod-MDCPB Dist-MDCPB

Molecular Spectroscopy C 23 MIN
16MM FILM OPTICAL SOUND H-C
Uses laboratory experiments, molecular models and animation to show details of the infrared light absorption process and its relation to molecular properties. Presents the concept of natural vibration frequencies in molecules.
From The CHEM Study Films Series.
LC NO. FIA63-379
Prod-CHEMS Dist-MLA 1962

Molecular Theory Of Matter (2nd Ed) X 11 MIN
16MM FILM, 3/4 OR 1/2 IN VIDEO H-C
Uses animation and demonstrations of diffusion to show properties of matter which have led to the kinetic molecular theory. Includes experiments involving gas under various pressures and changes of phase.
Prod-EBF Dist-EBEC 1965

Molecular Theory Of Matter, The (2nd Ed) (Spanish) C 11 MIN
16MM FILM, 3/4 OR 1/2 IN VIDEO H-C
Demonstrates kinetic molecular theory of matter by showing the diffusion of gases in air, the condensation of steam, the evaporation of liquids and the transformation of liquids into solids. Demonstrates brownian movement.
Prod-EBEC Dist-EBEC

Molecular Weight Distributions/Determination Of Average Molecular Weight By Osmotic...-- B 42 MIN
3/4 OR 1/2 INCH VIDEO CASSETTE
Discusses molecular weight distributions and determination of average molecular weight by osmotic pressure, chemical analysis and viscosity.
From The Colloids And Surface Chemistry - Lyophilic Colloids Series.
Prod-MIOT Dist-MIOT

Molecular Weight Distributions, Determination Of Average Molecular Weight By Osmotic... C 42 MIN
3/4 OR 1/2 INCH VIDEO CASSETTE
Discusses molecular weight distributions, determination of average molecular weight by osmotic pressure, chemical analysis and viscosity.
From The Colloid And Surface Chemistry - Lyophilic Colloids Series.
Prod-KALMIA Dist-KALMIA

Molecule Of Management, The C 22 MIN
3/4 OR 1/2 INCH VIDEO CASSETTE
See series title for descriptive statement.
From The Time Management For Managers And Professionals Series.
Prod-DELTAK Dist-DELTAK Prodn-ONCKEW

Molecules - A First Film C 10 MIN
16MM FILM, 3/4 OR 1/2 IN VIDEO I-J
Suggests that there is a similarity in the structure of solid matter, liquids and gases. Uses a molecular model to help explain why a liquid that has changed to a gas occupies a much larger volume than the original liquid.
Prod-IWANMI Dist-PHENIX 1972

Molecules And Life C 20 MIN
16MM FILM, 3/4 OR 1/2 IN VIDEO H
Outlines achievements in molecular biology which have revolutionized understanding of the chemical and physical basis of life. Discusses the molecules vitamin B12, hemoglobin, myoglobin and proteins in general.
Prod-EFVA Dist-MGHT 1971

Molecules And Matter C 15 MIN
3/4 OR 1/2 INCH VIDEO CASSETTE I
See series title for descriptive statement.
From The Discovering Series. Unit 3 - Chemistry
Prod-WDCNTV Dist-AITECH 1978

Molecules At Work, Pt 1 B 15 MIN
2 INCH VIDEOTAPE P
Explains that heat makes molecules move faster, increased molecular motion causes matter to expand and expansion exerts a force that does work.
From The Science Is Everywhere Series. No. 4
Prod-DETPS Dist-GPITVL

Molecules At Work, Pt 2 B 15 MIN
2 INCH VIDEOTAPE P
Explains that heat makes molecules move faster, increased molecular motion causes matter to expand and expansion exerts a force that does work.
From The Science Is Everywhere Series. No. 5
Prod-DETPS Dist-GPITVL

Molecules At Work, Pt 3 B 15 MIN
2 INCH VIDEOTAPE P
Explains that heat makes molecules move faster, increased molecular motion causes matter to expand and expansion exerts a force that does work.
From The Science Is Everywhere Series. No. 6
Prod-DETPS Dist-GPITVL

Molecules In Motion B 30 MIN
2 INCH VIDEOTAPE J
See series title for descriptive statement.
From The Investigating The World Of Science, Unit 1 - Matter And Energy Series.
Prod-MPATI Dist-GPITVL

Molissa Fenley, Dana Reitz And Marta Renzi C 30 MIN
3/4 OR 1/2 INCH VIDEO CASSETTE
See series title for descriptive statement.
From The Experimentalists Series.
Prod-ARCVID Dist-ARCVID

Molissa Fenley, Dana Reitz And Marta Renzi C 30 MIN
3/4 OR 1/2 INCH VIDEO CASSETTE
See series title for descriptive statement.
From The Eye On Dance - The Experimentalists Series.
Prod-ARTRES Dist-ARTRES

Molluscs C 10 MIN
16MM FILM OPTICAL SOUND J-C
Begins with the most generalized life forms, showing how the basic molluscan body plan has become modified to produce a great diversity of specialized life forms. Examines the basic cephalopod features on a hatching octopus and illustrates the locomotion of a land snail and the circulatory mechanism of a clam through use of a die.
From The Inhabitants Of The Planet Earth Series.
LC NO. 76-701108
Prod-RUSB Dist-MLA 1976

Mollusks C 15 MIN
2 INCH VIDEOTAPE K
Illustrates the life of a mollusk both in the water and on land.
From The Let's Go Sciencing, Unit III - Life Series.
Prod-DETPS Dist-GPITVL

Mollusks - Snails, Mussels, Oysters, Octopuses And Their Relatives C 14 MIN
16MM FILM, 3/4 OR 1/2 IN VIDEO J-C
Discusses the distinguishing characteristics and habitats of the five classes of mollusks showing some of the ways in which they are useful to man.
Prod-EBF Dist-EBEC Prodn-ANDERS 1955

Mollusks - The Mussel C 7 MIN
16MM FILM, 3/4 OR 1/2 IN VIDEO H-C
Observes the living mussel's interior vital processes through the use of live photography and animation.
Prod-BNCHMK Dist-BNCHMK 1983

Molly Rush - Turning Swords Into Plowshares C 28 MIN
3/4 INCH VIDEO CASSETTE
Examines the motives and convictions of Molly Rush who joined with the Plowshare activists in their nonviolent protest of the nuclear arms race when they entered a missile assembly plant in Fall, 1980.
Prod-GMPF Dist-GMPF

Molly's Pilgrim C 24 MIN
16MM FILM, 3/4 OR 1/2 IN VIDEO P-I
Tells the story of a newly arrived Russian immigrant, Molly. Shows her being ostracized at school for being different, but finally gaining acceptance.
Prod-PELZRC Dist-BFA 1985

Molten Salt Reactor Experiment C 20 MIN
16MM FILM OPTICAL SOUND
Uses animation to describe the design, construction and operation of the molten salt reactor experiment. Discusses the possibility of using molten-salt reactors as thermal breeders.
LC NO. FIE68-67
Prod-ORNLAB Dist-USNAC 1968

Mom And Dad Can't Hear Me C 47 MIN
16MM FILM, 3/4 OR 1/2 IN VIDEO I-H A
Presents the story of a 14-year-old girl who has just moved to a new town. Shows how she is afraid that her friends will reject her if they discover that her parents are deaf.
From The Teenage Years Series.
LC NO. 80-706923
Prod-WILSND Dist-TIMLIF 1979

Mom And Pop Split Up C 15 MIN
16MM FILM, 3/4 OR 1/2 IN VIDEO P-J
A shortened version of an episode from the television program Fat Albert And The Cosby Kids entitled Mom Or Pop. Shows how Fat Albert and the gang help a little girl cope with her parents' divorce.
From The Fat Albert And The Cosby Kids, Series 1 Series.
Prod-BARR Dist-BARR Prodn-FLMTON 1978

Mom Deserves Some Thanks C 14 MIN
16MM FILM - VIDEO, ALL FORMATS K-J
Shows Fat Albert discovering how many things mothers do when he takes care of the house while his mother is away.
From The Fat Albert And The Cosby Kids IV Series.
Prod-BARR Dist-BARR Prodn-FLMTON

Mom Tapes, The B 27 MIN
3/4 OR 1/2 INCH VIDEO CASSETTE
Portrays a typical mother-daughter relationship. Spans four years. Includes Mom, I'm Bored, Skin Cancer and Household Questions.
Prod-KITCHN Dist-KITCHN

Mom, The Wolfman And Me C 100 MIN
3/4 OR 1/2 INCH VIDEO CASSETTE H-C A
Explains how a little girl overcomes her mother's hesitancy to marry a man who loves her very much. Stars Patty Duke Astin, David Birney and Danielle Brisebois.
Prod-TIMLIF Dist-TIMLIF 1982

Moment Distribution And Numerical Techiques C 60 MIN
3/4 OR 1/2 INCH VIDEO CASSETTE C
Gives a moment distribution example. Outlines numerical techniques for solving modal equations using Taylor series. Shows constant and linear acceleration methods.
From The Fundamentals Of Dynamic Analysis For Structural Design Series.
Prod-USCCE Dist-AMCEE

Moment For Decision C 8 MIN
3/4 OR 1/2 INCH VIDEO CASSETTE IND
Stresses the importance of accepting personal responsibility for protecting oneself and others from work-related injury.
From The Take Ten For Safety Series.
Prod-OLINC Dist-MTI

Moment In History, A C 14 MIN
16MM FILM OPTICAL SOUND J-C
Shows the events leading to the presentation of honorary U S citizenship to Winston Churchill by President Kennedy on April 6, 1963. Includes the ceremony which was transmitted live by relay satellite from the White House to England.
LC NO. 74-705163
Prod-NASA Dist-NASA 1964

Moment In Time, A C
16MM FILM OPTICAL SOUND
Presents an introduction to St Lawrence University that takes the viewer behind the scenes of a modern liberal arts college.
Prod-CAMPF Dist-CAMPF

Moment In Time, A C 25 MIN
16MM FILM OPTICAL SOUND J-C A
Depicts the scope of Navy photography and the mission of major photographic field activities.
LC NO. 74-705164
Prod-USN Dist-USNAC 1968

Moment In Time, A C 22 MIN
16MM FILM, 3/4 OR 1/2 IN VIDEO J-C A
A shortened version of the motion picture A Moment In Time. Traces the history of America by using old photographs, newsreel film and archival recordings.
From The American Documents (Edited) Series.
Prod-LUF Dist-LUF 1979

Moment In Time, A C 55 MIN
16MM FILM, 3/4 OR 1/2 IN VIDEO J-C A
Traces the history of America by using old photographs, newsreel film and archival recordings.
From The American Documents Series.
Prod-LUF Dist-LUF

Moment Of Decision C 11 MIN
16MM FILM OPTICAL SOUND H-C A
Presents techniques for bringing a sale to a successful close in a minimum amount of time. Shows how salespersons can help the indecisive customer reach an affirmative and satisfying buying decision.
From The Professional Selling Practices Series I Series.
LC NO. 77-702361
Prod-SAUM Dist-SAUM Prodn-CALPRO 1967

Moment Of Decision (2nd Ed) C 12 MIN
16MM FILM, 3/4 OR 1/2 IN VIDEO J-H
Points out that decisions are influenced by life experiences, but that each individual must determine which of the lessons of his past will determine his future behavior. Shows what motivated the actions of four different teenage boys who find a sports car with the keys in the ignition.
LC NO. 81-706568
Prod-CAHILL Dist-AIMS 1979

Moment's Glory, A C 23 MIN
16MM FILM, 3/4 OR 1/2 IN VIDEO
Covers the World Catamaran Championships of the 16-foot Hobie Cat. Touches on the many moods of this week-long contest.
Prod-ALLNRP Dist-ALLNRP

Moment's Life, A C 18 MIN
16MM FILM OPTICAL SOUND
Tells the story of a beggarwoman who pawns her only possession of any value to buy a funeral for an infant that she found in a garbage can.
LC NO. 78-701562
Prod-BRADAV Dist-BRADAV 1978

Moments Of A Random Variable B 18 MIN
3/4 OR 1/2 INCH VIDEO CASSETTE PRO
Defines moments and central moments.
From The Probability And Random Processes - Statistical Averages Series.
Prod-MIOT Dist-MIOT

Moments Of History C 30 MIN
3/4 OR 1/2 INCH VIDEO CASSETTE K-P
See series title for descriptive statement.
From The Villa Alegre Series.
Prod-BCTV Dist-MDCPB

Moments Of Joy C 24 MIN
16MM FILM, 3/4 OR 1/2 IN VIDEO J-C A
Describes an Ohio program that seeks to humanize the treatment of the mentally handicapped.
Prod-DRAKED Dist-WOMBAT

Moments Of The Runner C 28 MIN
16MM FILM OPTICAL SOUND
Examines the popularity of running in the United States and traces the roots of long-distance running from ancient Greece. Shows America's most popular road races.
LC NO. 79-701378
Prod-RUNNER Dist-DARRAH Prodn-DARRAH 1979

Momentum C 10 MIN
16MM FILM OPTICAL SOUND
Uses experimental techniques to offer a glimpse of the world of an auto mechanic.
LC NO. 79-701179
Prod-DAYRAY Dist-DAYRAY 1979

Momma Never Told Me About VD C 25 MIN
3/4 OR 1/2 INCH VIDEO CASSETTE
Shows high school students of the Youth Gives A Dam Health Club staging a health happening to present the facts about the venereal disease epidemic. Features skits, student-on-the-street interviews, a 'talking bus', a tour of a VD clinic and a rap session with health officials.
Prod-TRAINX Dist-TRAINX

Momma Violet's Arrival C 30 MIN
3/4 OR 1/2 INCH VIDEO CASSETTE
See series title for descriptive statement.
From The Gettin' To Know Me Series.
Prod-CTI Dist-MDCPB

Momma Violet's Wish C 30 MIN
3/4 INCH VIDEO CASSETTE I-H
See series title for descriptive statement.
From The Gettin' To Know Me Series.
Prod-CTI Dist-GPITVL 1979

Mommies / Are You My Mother / The Way Mothers Are C 15 MIN
3/4 INCH VIDEO CASSETTE P
Presents the children's stories Mommies by Lonnie Carton, Are You My Mother by P D Eastman, and The Way Mothers Are by Miriam Schlein.
From The Tilson's Book Shop Series.
Prod-WVIZTV Dist-GPITVL 1975

Mommy, Daddy And Me C 30 MIN
3/4 OR 1/2 INCH VIDEO CASSETTE I-C A
Examines changes in the family over the past quarter-century. Looks at single-parent households and homes in which both parents work. Features Dr Benjamin Spock introducing a discussion of these changes.
Prod-WETATV Dist-WETATV

Momokko Taro - The Story Of A Boy Who Was Born From A Peach C 17 MIN
16MM FILM OPTICAL SOUND
Tells a Japanese folk tale.
Prod-UNIJAP Dist-UNIJAP

Mon Bras, Ton Nez C 10 MIN
3/4 OR 1/2 INCH VIDEO CASSETTE
Focuses on parts of the body and possessive adjectives.
From The Salut - French Language Lessons Series.
Prod-BCNFL Dist-BCNFL 1984

Mon Pere Est Electricien C 16 MIN
16MM FILM, 3/4 OR 1/2 IN VIDEO P-H
A French-language version of the motion picture My Pop's A Lineman. Shows a lineman who sees his son trying to retrieve a kite tangled in a high voltage line and takes the boy to work with him. Dramatizes several dangerous situations involving high tension wires. Includes flashbacks to a high-voltage demonstration by H C Potthast.
Prod-STSC Dist-IFB 1957

Mon Ticket S'Il Vous Plait B 13 MIN
16MM FILM OPTICAL SOUND I-H
See series title for descriptive statement.
From The Les Francais Chez Vous Series. Set I, Lesson 04
Prod-PEREN Dist-CHLTN 1967

Monarch C 15 MIN
16MM FILM OPTICAL SOUND I-C A
Traces the life cycle of the monarch butterfly.
LC NO. 79-700962
Prod-MELFIL Dist-CANFDC 1979

Monarch And The Milkweed, The C 11 MIN
16MM FILM, 3/4 OR 1/2 IN VIDEO
Shows the unique life histories of both the monarch butterfly and the milkweed plant and their relationship to each other.
From The Many Worlds Of Nature Series.
Prod-MORALL Dist-MTI 1975

Monarch Butterfly Story, The (2nd Ed) C 11 MIN
16MM FILM, 3/4 OR 1/2 IN VIDEO P-C
Pictures the geographical range of the monarch butterfly and shows close-up detail of its structure during various stages of its life cycle--egg, larva, chrysalis and imago. Shows a larva developing within an egg, the larva hatching and molting several times, the spinning of a cocoon and emergence of the adult. Investigates the migratory Habit.
Prod-EBEC Dist-EBEC 1967

Monarch Magic C 20 MIN
3/4 OR 1/2 INCH VIDEO CASSETTE J-C A
Shows the metamorphosis of a caterpillar into a beautiful Monarch butterfly.
Prod-AWSS Dist-AWSS 1981

Moncada Program, The (Captioned) C 51 MIN
16MM FILM, 3/4 OR 1/2 IN VIDEO A
Discusses the programs and accomplishments of the Cuban Revolution, including agrarian reform, nationalization of foreign-owned businesses, and improvements in housing, education and health care for the Cuban people. Spanish dialog with English subtitles.
Prod-CUBAFI Dist-CNEMAG 1973

Mondale - Presidential Candidate C 17 MIN
3/4 OR 1/2 INCH VIDEO CASSETTE H-C A
Presents an in-depth look at Walter Mondale, former Vice-President and Presidential nominee of the Democratic Party. Examines his past political affiliations, their likely effects and possible challengers.
Prod-JOU Dist-JOU

Monday Morning Absentee, The C 21 MIN
16MM FILM OPTICAL SOUND
Relates the case of an employee with a drinking problem who, after a suspension and a final warning, is again absent without calling in. Shows the case going to arbitration when the employee is able to show that he had a good reason for being absent though not for refraining from calling in.
Prod-AARA Dist-AARA 1979

Mondragon Experiment, The C 50 MIN
16MM FILM, 3/4 OR 1/2 IN VIDEO C A
Focuses on a Spanish industrial town where the businesses are cooperatively owned. Explains that the people also run the banks, the college, and the research laboratories.
Prod-BBCTV Dist-FI 1981

Mondrian B 29 MIN
3/4 INCH VIDEO CASSETTE
Presents the technique and profound influence of contemporary painter Mondrian.
From The Meet The Masters Series.
Prod-UMITV Dist-UMITV 1966

Monet C 4 MIN
16MM FILM OPTICAL SOUND
Employs the comments of artist Claude Monet which underscore the development of his style as seen in paintings dating from the 1870s to the early years of the 20th century.
Prod-USNGA Dist-USNGA

Monetary And Fiscal Policy C 45 MIN
3/4 OR 1/2 INCH VIDEO CASSETTE
Discusses aspects of monetary and fiscal policy.
From The Economic Perspectives Series.
Prod-MDCPB Dist-MDCPB

Monetary Policy - How Well Does It Work C 30 MIN
3/4 OR 1/2 INCH VIDEO CASSETTE C
See series title for descriptive statement.
From The Economics USA Series.
Prod-WEFA Dist-ANNCPB

Monetary Policy I C 45 MIN
3/4 OR 1/2 INCH VIDEO CASSETTE
Discusses aspects of American monetary policy.
From The Economic Perspectives Series.
Prod-MDCPB Dist-MDCPB

Monetary Policy II C 45 MIN
3/4 OR 1/2 INCH VIDEO CASSETTE
Discusses aspects of American monetary policy.
From The Economic Perspectives Series.
Prod-MDCPB Dist-MDCPB

Monex - The Monsoon Experiment C 20 MIN
16MM FILM, 3/4 OR 1/2 IN VIDEO H A
Documents a scientific venture undertaken by the United States andSoutheast Asia. It is an attempt to understand the mechanism of monsoons in hope of improving short-range predictions of monsoon rainfall, cyclones and other related events.
Prod-NSF Dist-USNAC 1981

Money B 15 MIN
2 INCH VIDEOTAPE P
Explains that in exchange for work people are given money which they exchange for goods or services. (Broadcast quality)
From The Around The Corner Series. No. 26
Prod-FWCETV Dist-GPITVL Prodn-WEDUTV

Money C 15 MIN
3/4 OR 1/2 INCH VIDEO CASSETTE P
Uses the format of a television program to explain that money is used in exchange for goods and services. Demonstrates how American society uses money, rather than barter, to trade, measure price and save.
From The Pennywise Series. No. 9
LC NO. 82-706011
Prod-MAETEL Dist-GPITVL 1980

Money C 15 MIN
3/4 INCH VIDEO CASSETTE I-H
Highlights the history of money, from cows and elephant tails to credit cards and computers.
LC NO. 78-700966
Prod-WMD Dist-GA 1978

Money C 16 MIN
3/4 OR 1/2 INCH VIDEO CASSETTE P
Discusses valutes of U S currency.
From The Math Cycle Series.
Prod-WDCNTV Dist-GPITVL 1983

Money C 20 MIN
3/4 OR 1/2 INCH VIDEO CASSETTE J-H
See series title for descriptive statement.
From The Contract Series.
Prod-KYTV Dist-AITECH 1977

Money C 29 MIN
3/4 INCH VIDEO CASSETTE
Discusses the extent of women's economic clout and warns of the need for women to avoid exploitation by marketing specialists.
From The Woman Series.
Prod-WNEDTV Dist-PUBTEL

Money - How Its Value Changes C 14 MIN
16MM FILM, 3/4 OR 1/2 IN VIDEO J-C
Explains how changes in the value of money are related to concepts such as cost of living, recession, depression, supply and demand and inflation.
Prod-CORF Dist-CORF 1971

Money - Prosperity B 30 MIN
3/4 OR 1/2 INCH VIDEO CASSETTE
Helps one to achieve financial prosperity through subliminal suggestions.
Prod-ADVCAS Dist-ADVCAS

Money - Summing It Up C 23 MIN
16MM FILM, 3/4 OR 1/2 IN VIDEO I-C A
Chronicles the use of barter and commodity money, then gold and silver, and finally paper money. Describes the function of the Federal Reserve System in regulating the supply of money and shows new money being printed and old money being destroyed.
LC NO. 83-706183
Prod-NGS Dist-NGS 1982

Money - The Nature Of Money C 10 MIN
16MM FILM, 3/4 OR 1/2 IN VIDEO
Explains how money developed to meet the need for a readily acceptable medium of exchange. Discusses the characteristics of money as a measure of worth.
From The Foundations Of Wealth Series.
Prod-FOTH Dist-FOTH

Money - What It's Worth C 16 MIN
16MM FILM, 3/4 OR 1/2 IN VIDEO I-H
Discusses price, barter, the history of money, supply and demand, the gold standard, inflation, and other topics related to money.
Prod-FLMFR Dist-FLMFR

Money And Banking C 28 MIN
16MM FILM OPTICAL SOUND H-C
Explains the American monetary and fiscal policies. Includes how the Federal Reserve exercises control in expanding and contracting bank credit.
LC NO. 75-702723
Prod-SPI Dist-SUTHLA 1968

Money And Banking C 19 MIN
16MM FILM, 3/4 OR 1/2 IN VIDEO
Illustrates the nature and function of money. Explains the role of the Federal Reserve System in controlling the money supply and examines the role of banks in the creation of money.
Prod-OLINC Dist-EBEC 1982

Money And How It Works C 20 MIN
3/4 INCH VIDEO CASSETTE I
Shows how money is made and discusses its distribution.
From The Exploring Our Nation Series.
Prod-KRMATV Dist-GPITVL 1975

Money And Inflation C 81 MIN
3/4 OR 1/2 INCH VIDEO CASSETTE C
Presents economist Milton Friedman examining the causes and possible cures of inflation.
From The Milton Friedman Speaking Series. Lecture 6
LC NO. 79-708065
Prod-HBJ Dist-HBJ Prodn-WQLN 1980

Money And Motives C 18 MIN
16MM FILM OPTICAL SOUND
Examines what motivates people to buy.
From The Consumer Game Series.
LC NO. 74-701205
Prod-OECA Dist-OECA 1972

Money And Politics C 60 MIN
3/4 OR 1/2 INCH VIDEO CASSETTE
Looks at the rising number and increasing influence of corporate and political action committees, citing the influence their money has on legislation.
From The Bill Moyers' Journal Series.
Prod-WNETTV Dist-WNETTV 1980

Money And The Single Woman C 29 MIN
3/4 OR 1/2 INCH VIDEO CASSETTE
Focuses on the problems facing single women who must manage their own finances.
From The Woman Series.
Prod-WNEDTV Dist-PBS

Money And Work - Living It Your Way C 16 MIN
16MM FILM, 3/4 OR 1/2 IN VIDEO J-C
Depicts a young woman who, having just finished school, has to decide whether or not to opt for dollars in traditional careers, or for small cash but big enjoyment at a career she loves.
Prod-HARDAP Dist-BCNFL 1983

Money Business C 15 MIN
3/4 INCH VIDEO CASSETTE P
Presents money problems that require the use of two-place subtraction with regrouping of tens and ones.
From The Math Factory, Module VI - Money Series.
Prod-MAETEL Dist-GPITVL 1973

Money Business C 22 MIN
16MM FILM - VIDEO, ALL FORMATS K-I
Teaches about money through the story of a little bear who wants to buy a saxophone. Deals with such concepts as earning and saving money.
Prod-SANCIN Dist-BARR

Money Can, The C 10 MIN
16MM FILM OPTICAL SOUND
Points out the benefits of recycling aluminum cans.
LC NO. 76-702319
Prod-REYMC Dist-REYMC 1974

Money For Sale C 13 MIN
16MM FILM, 3/4 OR 1/2 IN VIDEO J-C A
Presents an animated film which uses the character of a kindly pawnbroker to show how to borrow money intelligently. Suggests sources for borrowed money, stressing the importance of shopping for a loan and restraint in borrowing. Explains in detail Federal truth in lending legislation.
Prod-NULSEN Dist-AIMS 1974

Money For Sale (Captioned) C 13 MIN
16MM FILM, 3/4 OR 1/2 IN VIDEO J-C A
Presents an animated film which uses the character of a kindly pawnbroker to show how to borrow money intelligently. Suggests sources for borrowed money, stressing the importance of shopping for a loan and restraint in borrowing. Explains in detail Federal truth in lending legislation.
Prod-NULSEN Dist-AIMS 1974

Money For Sale (Spanish) C 13 MIN
16MM FILM, 3/4 OR 1/2 IN VIDEO J-C A
Presents an animated film which uses the character of a kindly pawnbroker to show how to borrow money intelligently. Suggests sources for borrowed money, stressing the importance of shopping for a loan and restraint in borrowing. Explains in detail Federal truth in lending legislation.
Prod-NULSEN Dist-AIMS 1974

Money Game, The C 16 MIN
3/4 OR 1/2 INCH VIDEO CASSETTE H-C A
Tells the story of a young Canadian golfer who is still seeking his first tour victory. Discusses the intense competition and frustration in golf.
Prod-CANBC Dist-JOU

Money Hunt C
1/2 IN VIDEO CASSETTE (VHS)
Presents the Money Hunt contest. Outlines the rules, eligibility and prizes.
Prod-KARLVI Dist-KARLVI

Money In The Marketplace C 15 MIN
16MM FILM, 3/4 OR 1/2 IN VIDEO P-I
Provides an introduction to economics and basic money concepts. Uses a trip through a flea market to examine the ideas of marketplace, consumer, demand and value. Shows that money must be durable, portable and acceptable.
Prod-EBEC Dist-EBEC

Money Magic C 11 MIN
16MM FILM OPTICAL SOUND P-J
Addresses the basic principles of money management and how to spend wisely. Includes some consumer math and good buying practices. Seeks to improve skills of buying through a variety of educational and cinematic techniques including live action, special effects and simple animation combined in a short, fast-paced presentation.
From The Kids And Cash Series.
Prod-COUNFI Dist-COUNFI

Money Management C 20 MIN
3/4 OR 1/2 INCH VIDEO CASSETTE
Shows how to develop a budget and start a savings account as Squad member Karen helps a friend who is constantly running out of money.
From The Consumer Squad Series.
Prod-MSITV Dist-PBS 1982

Money Management And Family Financial Planning—A Series
H-C A
Relates economic theory to everyday living with information and advice on budgeting, banking, using credit, setting buying priorities, investing and determining insurance needs. Follows a young married couple, Jeff and Judy, as they learn how to make basic financial decisions.
Prod-AETNA Dist-AETNA 1973

Banking	18 MIN
Budgeting	12 MIN
Buying	13 MIN
Credit	18 MIN
Insurance	17 MIN
Planning For The Future	15 MIN
Securities	19 MIN

Money Management In Troubled Times C 25 MIN
3/4 OR 1/2 INCH VIDEO CASSETTE
Gives quiz to determine possible financial pitfalls. Presents hints on better money management.
From The Your Money Matters Series.
Prod-FILMID Dist-FILMID

Money Market, The C 30 MIN
3/4 OR 1/2 INCH VIDEO CASSETTE C A
Introduces money market investments such as savings accounts, certificates of deposit, bonds, mutual funds and individual retirement accounts. Defines several terms.
From The Personal Finance Series. Lesson 16
Prod-SCCON Dist-CDTEL

Money Matters C 15 MIN
3/4 OR 1/2 INCH VIDEO CASSETTE P
Tells how a space robot's puppet assistant learns about money, including the names of U S coins, the value of each in cents, and their values as fractional parts of the dollar. Shows how she finds out that items other that coins were used in colonial times.
From The Math Mission 2 Series.
LC NO. 82-706330
Prod-WCVETV Dist-GPITVL 1980

Money Matters - Introduction C 15 MIN
3/4 OR 1/2 INCH VIDEO CASSETTE I
Presents a cast of three ten-year-old children interacting with adults to demonstrate various economic concepts and business activities.
From The Money Matters Series. Pt 1
LC NO. 83-706012
Prod-KEDTTV Dist-GPITVL 1982

Money Matters—A Series
I
Explores aspects of America's free enterprise system.
Prod-KEDTTV Dist-GPITVL 1982

Banking	015 MIN
Industry	015 MIN
Inflation	015 MIN
Money Matters - Introduction	015 MIN
Small Business	015 MIN
Stock Market	015 MIN

Money On The Land C 52 MIN
16MM FILM, 3/4 OR 1/2 IN VIDEO J-C A
Depicts how the focus of America shifts from the farmlands to the cities. Describes how the early inventors like Edison find methods and resources in industry and then the Rockefellers, Carnegies and Vanderbilts move in.
From The America - A Personal History Of The United States Series. No. 8
LC NO. 79-707147
Prod-BBCTV Dist-TIMLIF 1972

Money On The Land (Spanish) C 52 MIN
16MM FILM OPTICAL SOUND
Deals with the industrialization of the United States at the beginning of the 20th century. Discusses the American inventors whose newly discovered methods and resources were exploited by the Rockefellers, Carnegies and other industrialists for business purposes.
From The America - A Personal History Of The United States Series.
LC NO. 77-701681
Prod-BBCTV Dist-TIMLIF 1973

Money Puzzle - The World Of Macroeconomics—A Series

Presents the ongoing story of the Weldons, a couple in their thirties, both of whom work and struggle to cope with economic problems that face people today. Explores a different concept in macroeconomics theory in each program. Looks at the aggregates which make up a macroeconomic system and the interrelationships among them that affect inflation, unemployment, growth and recession.
Prod-MDCC Dist-MDCC

All Of The People, All Of The Time	030 MIN
All That Glitters Is Gold	030 MIN
Balancing Act	030 MIN
Blowing The Whistle	030 MIN
Choice Is yours, The	030 MIN
Don't Let Them Take My Job Away	030 MIN
Economic Roller Coaster, The	030 MIN
Familiar Fallacies	030 MIN
Fast Food Economics	030 MIN
Free Rider, the	030 MIN
Getting And Spending	030 MIN
Go With The Flow	030 MIN
Income, Go Forth And Multiply	030 MIN
Inspectors, The	030 MIN
Investors, The	030 MIN
Invisible Hand, The	030 MIN
Karen Goes Political	030 MIN
Karen's Magic Flute	030 MIN
Loopholes	030 MIN
Man Who Needed Nobody, The	030 MIN
Measuring My Success	030 MIN
Pieces Of The Puzzle, The	030 MIN
Run For Your Money, A	030 MIN
Shrinking Dollar, The	030 MIN
Slippin' Away	030 MIN
Steep And Thorny Path, A	030 MIN
Thomas And The Fiscal Fighters	030 MIN
Tightrope Walkers, The	030 MIN
Withdrawal Symptoms	030 MIN
You Can't Always Get What You Want	030 MIN

Money Smart - A Guide To Personal Finance—A Series
H-C A
Provides practical course in personal financial planning. Uses visuals and dramatized vignettes.
Prod-SOMFIL Dist-BCNFL

Buying A House	025 MIN
Designing Your Financial Plan	025 MIN
Effective Buying	025 MIN
Insuring Your Life	025 MIN
Investing In Stocks	025 MIN
Planning For Financial Success	025 MIN
Planning For Retirement	025 MIN
Principles Of Investment	025 MIN
Property And Liability Insurance	025 MIN
Putting Your Financial Plan Into Action	025 MIN
Renting Your Money For Profit	025 MIN
Using Credit Wisely	025 MIN
Your Will And Estate	025 MIN

Money Talks C 26 MIN
16MM FILM OPTICAL SOUND
Traces the history of taxation in the United States from its beginning to the present.
LC NO. 74-702873
Prod-PTRHG Dist-PTRHG 1974

Money Talks C 20 MIN
16MM FILM, 3/4 OR 1/2 IN VIDEO H-C A
Discusses how advertising penetrates people's imaginations because advertisers have consciously applied a well-developed symbolic language to their messages in any medium. Shows how this special language is mass produced by the advertising industry to communicate a specific value system.
From The Viewpoint Series.
Prod-THAMES Dist-MEDIAG 1975

Money To Burn C 15 MIN
3/4 OR 1/2 INCH VIDEO CASSETTE
Shows how to conserve fuel and cut the home operating budget. Goes on an attic-to-basement tour.
Prod-IVCH Dist-IVCH

Money Tree, The (2nd Ed) C 21 MIN
16MM FILM, 3/4 OR 1/2 IN VIDEO J-C A
Stresses the importance of good money sense, telling the story of a young married couple who are in deep financial trouble. Shows how they are misled by societal and economic pressures as well as their own lack of sophistication in dealing with those pressures.
LC NO. 83-706315
Prod-AIMS Dist-AIMS 1983

Money X-Change, The C 35 MIN
16MM FILM OPTICAL SOUND
Offers an introduction to the mechanics of the world money market and foreign exchange transactions. Traces the historical development of market concepts and explains how socio-political changes affect the values of foreign and domestic currencies.
LC NO. 78-701437
Prod-AMCOL Dist-COUNFI 1977

Money X-Change, The C 30 MIN
3/4 OR 1/2 INCH VIDEO CASSETTE
Takes an excursion into the history and status of the foreign exchange market. Includes social and political changes and their impact on foreign and domestic currencies.
Prod-IVCH Dist-IVCH

Money, Money, Money C 10 MIN
16MM FILM, 3/4 OR 1/2 IN VIDEO P-J
Takes a child far beyond the mere arithmetic of money into the exciting world of shillings, dinars, rupees, pesetas and back to dollars and cents. Depicts the coin as a medium of exchange, a form of sculpture and a monument to history.
Prod-AFI Dist-TEXFLM 1972

Money, Pt 1 C 15 MIN
3/4 INCH VIDEO CASSETTE P
Tells how to name coins needed for sums less than one dollar and how to name the smallest amount of coins for a given amount.
From The Studio M Series.
Prod-WCETTV Dist-GPITVL 1979

Money, Pt 2 C 15 MIN
3/4 INCH VIDEO CASSETTE P
Explains how to use money to show how to rename ten as ten ones.
From The Studio M Series.
Prod-WCETTV Dist-GPITVL 1979

Money, Taxes And Imagination C 19 MIN
16MM FILM, 3/4 OR 1/2 IN VIDEO I-C A
Describes unusual forms of money and taxes through the ages.
Prod-CENTRO Dist-CORF

Moneylenders C 58 MIN
3/4 OR 1/2 INCH VIDEO CASSETTE
Discusses the stability of the world economy which rests on international banking and monetary policies. Travels from the United States to Mexico and London in search of the people whose decisions shape the world's economy.
From The Frontline Series.
Prod-DOCCON Dist-PBS

Moneywatchers—A Series

Discusses aspects of economics.
Prod-SCIPG Dist-PUBTEL

High Cost Of Healing, The	059 MIN
Inflation - The Money Merry-Go-Round	059 MIN
Quality Of Life, The	058 MIN

Monilial Vaginitis C 7 MIN
3/4 OR 1/2 INCH VIDEO CASSETTE
Explains the symptoms and treatment for monilial vagnitis and encourages patient compliance in treatment.
From The Take Care Of Yourself Series.
Prod-UARIZ Dist-UARIZ

Monique Of Amsterdam C 15 MIN
3/4 OR 1/2 INCH VIDEO CASSETTE P
Visits the Anne Frank home and shows a diamond polisher at work in Holland.
From The Other Families, Other Friends Series. Red Module - Holland
Prod-WVIZTV Dist-AITECH 1971

Monitor And The Merrimac, The C 14 MIN
16MM FILM OPTICAL SOUND I-C A
Shows the first encounter between the Monitor and the Merrimack, Explains how this encounter may have changed the course of the Civil War in the United States.
LC NO. 75-701527
Prod-FRITH Dist-FFORIN 1973

Monitoring C 50 MIN
3/4 OR 1/2 INCH VIDEO CASSETTE PRO
Deals with control tools, reviews, computer cost reports, handling changes and problem solving.
From The Project Management For Engineers Series.
Prod-AMCEE Dist-AMCEE

Monitoring Classroom Behavior—A Series
16MM FILM, 3/4 OR 1/2 IN VIDEO C A
Provides concentrated training in observing and categorizing classroom behavior. Introduces tested techniques to help both pre-service and in-service teachers improve monitoring skills. Presents actual student behavior for observation.
Prod-IU Dist-IU 1982

Monitoring Classroom Behavior, Pt 1	009 MIN
Monitoring Classroom Behavior, Pt 2	012 MIN
Monitoring Classroom Behavior, Pt 3	006 MIN

Monitoring Classroom Behavior, Pt 1 C 9 MIN
16MM FILM, 3/4 OR 1/2 IN VIDEO C A
Explains the concept of monitoring and provides examples of five student behavior categories. Shows these behaviors in both secondary and elementary settings.
From The Monitoring Classroom Behavior Series.
Prod-IU Dist-IU 1982

Monitoring Classroom Behavior, Pt 2 C 12 MIN
16MM FILM, 3/4 OR 1/2 IN VIDEO C A
Monitors two classroom situations identifying scenes in which the differenct categories of behavior occur. Provides material for practicing behavior categorization and presents correct categorizations of student behavior based on experts' judgments.
From The Monitoring Classroom Behavior Series.
Prod-IU Dist-IU 1982

Monitoring Classroom Behavior, Pt 3 C 6 MIN
16MM FILM, 3/4 OR 1/2 IN VIDEO C A
Simulates a situation in which the teacher monitors the behavior of more than one group of students at a time. Develops the ability to identify categories of student behavior while quickly scanning different groups.
From The Monitoring Classroom Behavior Series.
Prod-IU Dist-IU 1982

Monitoring The Anesthetized Patient C 22 MIN
16MM FILM OPTICAL SOUND PRO
Demonstrates and explains to medical students the principles of monitoring the resiratory, cardiovascular, and other body systems. Uses dramatizations during which the viewer is asked to interpret monitoring findings and to decide on remedial measures.
LC NO. 72-700365
Prod-AYERST Dist-AYERST Prodn-SCIMED 1973

Monitoring The Work Environment C 40 MIN
3/4 OR 1/2 INCH VIDEO CASSETTE IND
Shows Newell Bolton, who discusses basic approaches to monitoring the safety of the work environment, and describes the importance of management aspects of an adequate sampling program.
From The Safety, Health, and Loss Control - Managing Effective Programs Series.
LC NO. 81-706520
Prod-AMCEE Dist-AMCEE 1980

Monitoring Your Progress C 35 MIN
3/4 INCH VIDEO CASSETTE C A
See series title for descriptive statement.
From The Software Management For Small Computers Series.
LC NO. 81-706201
Prod-AMCEE Dist-AMCEE 1980

Monitos - Portrait Of An Artisan Family C 11 MIN
16MM FILM, 3/4 OR 1/2 IN VIDEO P-J
Portrays a typical summertime day in the life of the Garcia Aguilar family showing farming and household chores and the making of the Monitos people, small clay figures that have brought the mother fame in the world of popular folk art.
Prod-PEREZ Dist-FLMFR 1974

Monkees Up To Bat, The B 15 MIN
2 INCH VIDEOTAPE P
Explains that many people with special talents earn money by entertaining other people. (Broadcast quality)
From The Around The Corner Series. No. 29
Prod-FWCETV Dist-GPITVL Prodn-WEDUTV

Monkey And The Crocodile, The C 15 MIN
3/4 OR 1/2 INCH VIDEO CASSETTE K-P
Tells the story of a crocodile who persuades a monkey to cross a river on his back. Emphasizes the consonant blend cr.
From The Words And Pictures Series.
Prod-FI Dist-FI

Monkey And The Crocodile, The C 15 MIN
3/4 INCH VIDEO CASSETTE P
Presents a folk tale from India.
From The Magic Carpet Series.
Prod-SDCSS Dist-GPITVL 1977

Monkey And The Crododile, The C 15 MIN
3/4 INCH VIDEO CASSETTE K-P
See series title for descriptive statement.
From The Storytime Series.
Prod-WCETTV Dist-GPITVL 1976

Monkey And The Organ Grinder, The C 11 MIN
16MM FILM, 3/4 OR 1/2 IN VIDEO K-P
Traces a typical day in the life of three monkeys and their organ-grinder master.
Prod-EBEC Dist-EBEC 1971

Monkey Business B 14 MIN
16MM FILM OPTICAL SOUND H-C A
Presents an excerpt from the motion picture Monkey Business, issued in 1952. Tells the story of a research chemist seeking a formula to restore youth. Shows how an experimental chimp gets out of his cage and how the magic formula inadvertently ends up in the lab's water cooler, resulting in a series of wild adventures. Exemplifies the comic film genre.
From The American Film Genre - The Comedy Film Series.
LC NO. 77-701141
Prod-TWCF Dist-FI 1975

Monkey Business B 70 MIN
16MM FILM OPTICAL SOUND
Tells how the Marx Brothers stow away on a transatlantic ocean linter.
Prod-UPCI Dist-SWANK

Monkey See, Monkey Do - Verbs C 10 MIN
16MM FILM, 3/4 OR 1/2 IN VIDEO P-I
Deals with word classification, emphasizing action words from basic vocabulary lists. Shows monkeys illustrating verbs such as play, ride, swing, jump and eat. Enables children to see objects and actions, hear the words, read them in simple sentences and review them in rhyme.
From The Reading Motivation Series
Prod-BEAN Dist-PHENIX 1971

Monkey Taming - Adaptation To Humans B 19 MIN
16MM FILM OPTICAL SOUND PRO
Shows pigtail and rhesus monkeys in a training program designed to adapt them to contact with researchers. Explains that the process involves a series of 11 graduated steps.
LC NO. 74-702784
Prod-AARONL Dist-PSUPCR 1972

Monkey Tricks C 15 MIN
16MM FILM OPTICAL SOUND P-I
Shows what occurs when a thunderstorm scares Alice the chimp out of her usual treehouse home and into Mr Graham's bed.
Prod-LUF Dist-LUF 1977

Monkey Who Would Be King, The X 11 MIN
16MM FILM, 3/4 OR 1/2 IN VIDEO P
Uses wild and domestic animals to tell the fable of a greedy monkey who learns that it takes more than a crown to make a king.
Prod-EBF Dist-EBEC 1957

Monkey Who Would Be King, The (Spanish) C 11 MIN
16MM FILM, 3/4 OR 1/2 IN VIDEO P
Tells how the mighty lion decides he's tired of being king and how a monkey snatches his crown. Explains that the monkey learns it takes more than a crown to make a king.
Prod-EBEC Dist-EBEC

Monkey's Paw, The C 19 MIN
16MM FILM, 3/4 OR 1/2 IN VIDEO J-C A
Adapted from the short story The Monkey's Paw by W W Jacobs. Tells the story of an old couple whose wish to have their dead son returned to them is granted by a mysterious monkey's paw.
Prod-MORANM Dist-PHENIX 1978

Monkey's Paw, The C 27 MIN
16MM FILM, 3/4 OR 1/2 IN VIDEO I-H A
Introduces the White family, who finds itself in possession of a monkey's paw which is purported to give them three wishes. Relates that after using the three wishes, the Whites are in worse shape, having lost their son. Based on the short story The Monkey's Paw by W W Jacobs.
From The LCA Short Story Library Series.
LC NO. 83-707274
Prod-STILPG Dist-LCOA 1983

Monkeys C 5 MIN
16MM FILM, 3/4 OR 1/2 IN VIDEO K-P
Shows various types of monkeys, their habits and the environments in which they live.
From The Zoo Animals In The Wild Series.
Prod-CORF Dist-CORF 1981

Monkeys And Apes - An Introduction To The Primates X 11 MIN
16MM FILM, 3/4 OR 1/2 IN VIDEO P-J
Discusses the group of primates, of which the monkeys, apes and their relatives are all a member. Illustrates the characteristics of the primates and their habits.
Prod-BURN Dist-PHENIX 1965

Monkeys And Apes - An Introduction To The Primates (Spanish) C 11 MIN
16MM FILM, 3/4 OR 1/2 IN VIDEO P-I
Discusses the group of primates, of which the monkeys, apes and their relatives are all a member. Illustrates the characteristics of the primates and their habits.
Prod-BURN Dist-PHENIX 1965

Monkeys Of Mysore C 19 MIN
16MM FILM, 3/4 OR 1/2 IN VIDEO H A
Shows the daily activity and social interaction of a troop of bonnet macaque monkeys in their natural environment, which ranges from the Godavari River in India to Cape Commerin.
Prod-UCEMC Dist-UCEMC 1966

Monkeys, Apes And Man C 52 MIN
16MM FILM, 3/4 OR 1/2 IN VIDEO H-C A
Points out that man is learning that the similarity between monkeys and himself is not superficial and explains that man is a primate, bound in evolution to monkeys and apes.
LC NO. 80-706358
Prod-NGS Dist-NGS 1971

Monocot Plant Anatomy C 15 MIN
3/4 OR 1/2 INCH VIDEO CASSETTE H-C
Presents characteristics of corn, such as scattered vascular bundles, floral parts arranged in threes and parallel venation.
Prod-CBSC Dist-CBSC

Monocular Experiences C 10 MIN
3/4 OR 1/2 INCH VIDEO CASSETTE
Prod-PRIMED Dist-PRIMED

Mononucleosis B 40 MIN
16MM FILM OPTICAL SOUND PRO
Discusses epidemiologic studies needed in mononucleosis, along with its unknown but probable viral etiology. Emphasizes its varied hematologic and immunologic aspects. Covers treatment of the disease.
From The Boston Medical Reports Series.
Prod-NMAC Dist-NMAC 1966

Monopoly - Who's In Control C 30 MIN
3/4 OR 1/2 INCH VIDEO CASSETTE C
See series title for descriptive statement.
From The Economics USA Series.
Prod-WEFA Dist-ANNCPB

Monroe C 6 MIN
16MM FILM, 3/4 OR 1/2 IN VIDEO C A
Presents a comedy in which overworked Monroe meets what he wants copied when it materializes.
Prod-MTI Dist-MTI

Monsieur Pointu C 13 MIN
16MM FILM, 3/4 OR 1/2 IN VIDEO K-I
Features Quebecois country style violinist Paul Cormier as Monsieur Pointu, whose efforts to play his instrument are thwarted when the violin begins to have a mind of its own. Uses trick cinematography and pixillation to show how the violin continually eludes his grasp, shrinks and grows, attacks him and shatters into small pieces which fly menacingly at him.
Prod-NFBC Dist-PFP Prodn-LONLED 1976

Monsieur Vincent C 115 MIN
16MM FILM OPTICAL SOUND
Tells of the humbly born priest who fled from the ease and luxury of a noble household in 17th century Paris to devote himself to an unceasing battle against disease, hunger, cruelty and prejudice, always spreading his teaching of spiritual love, brotherhood and peace. Stars Pierre Fresnay.
Prod-UNKNWN Dist-TWYMAN

Monster Concert, A C 28 MIN
3/4 INCH VIDEO CASSETTE
Presents a concert in which 20 pianists play 10 pianos in unison. Includes works by Gottschalk, Stephen Foster, Sousa, and Joplin.
Prod-NETCHE Dist-PUBTEL

Monster Inside Me, The - Child Abuse C 25 MIN
3/4 OR 1/2 INCH VIDEO CASSETTE
Explores new approaches to the problem of child abuse. Features a discussion among parents who have physically abused their children but have found help. Discusses new trends in clinical aid with Drs Morris Paulson and James Apthorp.
Prod-TRAINX Dist-TRAINX

Monster Of Highgate Pond, The B 59 MIN
16MM FILM OPTICAL SOUND K-I
Tells the story of three children who help their uncle unpack specimens from Malaya. They are rewarded by being given an unidentified egg. When it hatches into a baby monster the adventure begins and when the growing monster takes up residence in the town pond, the results are hilarious.
Prod-CHILDF Dist-LUF 1968

Monster Ox, The C 52 MIN
16MM FILM OPTICAL SOUND

A Japanese language film. Tells the story of poor villagers who were long forced to offer a large quantity of rice to their monster God. Explains that, led by a courageous boy, whose girl was locked in a cave by their evil headman, the villagers finally succeed in exposing the headman's treachery and capture the ox God. Points out that the headman has stored for himself the crop supposedly given to the God, and the God was found to be just a mild field ox disguised as a monster.
Prod-UNIJAP Dist-UNIJAP 1970

Monster, The C 15 MIN
16MM FILM, 3/4 OR 1/2 IN VIDEO J-C A
Reconstructs some of the haunting tales of Loch Ness and its monsters and captures the mood of the area.
Prod-CENTRO Dist-CORF

Monsters And Magic C 19 MIN
3/4 OR 1/2 INCH VIDEO CASSETTE P
Presents folktales from Russia and Appalachia which revolve around monsters and magic.
From The Folk Book Series.
Prod-UWISC Dist-AITECH 1980

Monsters And Other Scary Things C 30 MIN
3/4 OR 1/2 INCH VIDEO CASSETTE
Explores the dark places where monsters lurk and examines the evidence for and against their existence. Describes sightings of the Loch Ness monster, Big Foot, and the Abominable Snow Man.
Prod-CANBC Dist-JOU

Monsters Of The City C 15 MIN
2 INCH VIDEOTAPE
Indicates a few of the problems inherent in a metropolitan society and emphasizes that these problems must be recognized and fought.
From The Let's Build A City Series.
Prod-WVIZTV Dist-GPITVL

Monsters We've Known And Loved B 26 MIN
16MM FILM OPTICAL SOUND
Traces the development of the horror film from its beginning in Germany in the twenties through mad doctors, graveyard monsters, creatures from underworld regions and outer space, to the comic-horror attempts of Vincent Price and Peter Lorre. Presents John Barrymore, Lon Chaney, Bela Lugosi and Boris Karloff in their monster roles.
LC NO. FI68-179
Prod-WOLPER Dist-WOLPER 1964

Montage - What Is It Out There B 20 MIN
16MM FILM OPTICAL SOUND C
Uses elaborate play test instruments to test and record responses of infants to their environment. Shows applications for helping handicapped children enrich their experiences.
Prod-PSUPCR Dist-PSUPCR 1967

Montana C 76 MIN
16MM FILM OPTICAL SOUND
Presents the saga of the battle of the sheepmen against the cattlemen for grazing rights. Stars Errol Flynn.
Prod-WB Dist-TWYMAN 1950

Montana And Its Aircraft C 28 MIN
3/4 OR 1/2 INCH VIDEO CASSETTE I-C A
Portrays various aspects of aviation in Montana including changes which are occurring. Depicts new types of facilities and the increasing demand for air travel.
Prod-FO Dist-FO Prodn-FO

Montana And The Sky C 16 MIN
3/4 OR 1/2 INCH VIDEO CASSETTE I-C A
Provides an overview of Montana, portraying wide open spaces, the natural environment and a brief history.
Prod-FO Dist-FO

Montana Indian Children C 27 MIN
16MM FILM OPTICAL SOUND H-C T
Covers the Flathead Indian Reservation and the surrounding countryside, including the Arlee Pow Wow grounds and Missoula, Montana. Shows children and adult members of numerous Indian tribes, including the Salish speaking people, the Black Foot and the Cherokee. Presents the importance of hunting, story telling and traditional teachings as well as the repeated emphasis on reinstating Indian values and pride.
From The Play And Cultural Continuity Series. Part 4
Prod-CFDC Dist-CFDC 1977

Montana, Pt 1 C 30 MIN
3/4 INCH VIDEO CASSETTE
Describes how black cowboys drove cattle from Texas to Montana.
From The South By Northwest Series.
Prod-KWSU Dist-GPITVL 1977

Montana, Pt 2 C 30 MIN
3/4 INCH VIDEO CASSETTE
Presents the story of Cattle Kate and Mary Fields, two black frontierswomen.
From The South By Northwest Series.
Prod-KWSU Dist-GPITVL 1977

Monterey Historic, The C 28 MIN
16MM FILM OPTICAL SOUND
Looks at the Monterey Historic Race in which some of the classic racing cars of yesteryear are driven in competition by racing luminaries.
Prod-MTP Dist-MTP

Monterey Pop C 82 MIN
16MM FILM OPTICAL SOUND
Features the Monterey International Pop Festival with Jimi Hendrix, Janis Joplin, Big Brother and the Holding Company, Otis Redding, Jefferson Airplane, Ravi Shankar, The Who, Country Joe and the Fish, Scott McKenzie, Mamas and Papas, Hugh Maskela, Canned Heat, Eric Burden and the Animals.
Prod-PENNAS Dist-PENNAS

Montessori C 21 MIN
16MM FILM, 3/4 OR 1/2 IN VIDEO
Illustrates expansion of the Montessori core curriculum through application of principles of learning linguistic theory, child development, educational technology and cybernetic principles. Shows how adaptations have resulted in a highly individualized program for the hearing impaired child with learning disabilities.
LC NO. 80-707424
Prod-USBEH Dist-USNAC

Montessori - A Way To Grow C 32 MIN
16MM FILM OPTICAL SOUND
Overviews the Montessori method of childhood education, revealing how the programs provide for individual differences in learning style and pace, social development and creativity. Shows children from two and a half to six years.
Prod-PROMET Dist-PROMET

Monthly Ancestral Offerings In Hinduism C 8 MIN
16MM FILM OPTICAL SOUND C
Presents a Hindu householder of Madreas City making offerings of seasame-seeds and water onto a special burca-grid of sacred grass.
From The Hindu Religion Series. No. 4
Prod-SMTHHD Dist-SYRCU

Monument Of Chief Rolling Mountain Thunder, The C 29 MIN
3/4 OR 1/2 INCH VIDEO CASSETTE
Shows Chief Thunder, American folk artist, who created the Monument on the Nevada Desert. Captures the tragedy of his life, his painful isolation, the beauty of his work and his creative process.
From The Visions Of Paradise Series.
Prod-SARLGT Dist-SARLGT

Monument To The Dream C 27 MIN
16MM FILM, 3/4 OR 1/2 IN VIDEO H-C A
Shows the building of the Gateway Arch in St Louis from its conception to completion.
Prod-GUGGNC Dist-AIMS 1963

Monument To The Dream C 30 MIN
3/4 OR 1/2 INCH VIDEO CASSETTE
Presents the Gateway Arch of the Jefferson National Expansion Memorial as a testament to modern man's pioneering accomplishments.
Prod-AIAS Dist-MPS

Monument To The Sun - The Story Of The Aztec Calendar Stone C 16 MIN
16MM FILM, 3/4 OR 1/2 IN VIDEO
Explains the meaning and history of the monumental carving known as the Aztec calendar stone. Tells how the ancient calendar of the Mayas was handed down through the centuries and how the Aztec astrologers and mathematicians devised their calendar from their ancient ancestors.
From The Mexican Heritage Series.
Prod-STEXMF Dist-FI 1976

Monument Valley - Land Of The Navajo C 22 MIN
16MM FILM, 3/4 OR 1/2 IN VIDEO
Presents a brief look at the life of a Navajo who lives in the four-corner country of Arizona, Colorado, New Mexico and Utah.
Prod-HOE Dist-MCFI 1959

Monumento Del Sol - La Historia De La Piedra Del Sol C 16 MIN
16MM FILM, 3/4 OR 1/2 IN VIDEO
A Spanish language version of Monument To The Sun - The Story Of The Aztec Calendar Stone. Explains the meaning and history of the monumental carving known as the Aztec calendar stone. Tells how the ancient calendar of the Mayas was handed down through the centuries and how the Aztec astrologers and mathematicians devised their calendar from their ancient ancestors.
From The Mexican Heritage (Spanish) Series.
Prod-STEXMF Dist-FI 1976

Monuments C 28 MIN
16MM FILM - 3/4 IN VIDEO
Pays tribute to builders around the world from ancient times to the present. Emphasizes modern building technology.
Prod-CTRACT Dist-MTP

Monuments C 30 MIN
3/4 OR 1/2 INCH VIDEO CASSETTE
Pays tribute to today's 'monument builders' of energy, mining, recycling plants, hospitals, transportation and others in many nations.
Prod-IVCH Dist-IVCH

Monuments C 30 MIN
3/4 OR 1/2 INCH VIDEO CASSETTE
Questions what a monument really is. Asks why some deeply move us and others seem to be merely pretentious.
From The Eye To Eye Series.
Prod-WGBHTV Dist-EAI Prodn-MOFAB

Monuments To Erosion C 11 MIN
16MM FILM, 3/4 OR 1/2 IN VIDEO I-C
Presents a pictorial study of monuments as unique, colorful and dramatic landforms created over the ages by the eroding action of wind and water.
Prod-EBEC Dist-EBEC 1974

Moo-Shi Pork C 29 MIN
2 INCH VIDEOTAPE
Features Joyce Chen showing how to adapt Chinese recipes so they can be prepared in the American kitchen and still retain the authentic flavor. Demonstrates how to prepare moo-shi pork.
From The Joyce Chen Cooks Series.
Prod-WGBHTV Dist-PUBTEL

Mood In Description B 30 MIN
2 INCH VIDEOTAPE J-H
Develops the concept of mood. (Broadcast quality)
From The English Composition Series. Description
Prod-GRETVC Dist-GPITVL Prodn-KUHTTV

Mood Of Zen C 14 MIN
16MM FILM, 3/4 OR 1/2 IN VIDEO
Explains some of the basic teachings of Zen, including the role and goals of meditation, need to flow with the current of life to release creative energy, not to oppose cosmic forces but to conquer them by going with them, and to wake up from illusions under which we suffer.
Prod-HP Dist-HP

Moods In Safety C 21 MIN
16MM FILM, 3/4 OR 1/2 IN VIDEO
Demonstrates how various types of moods and emotions can be detrimental to personal safety on and off the job. Shows how over-confidence, cockiness, anger, depression and tension cause accidents through distortion of intelligence, logic and sense of reason. Stresses the importance of following safety rules on the flight line, in flight, at the missile site and behind the wheel.
LC NO. 82-706288
Prod-USAF Dist-USNAC 1966

Moods Of Surfing, The B 15 MIN
16MM FILM, 3/4 OR 1/2 IN VIDEO I-H A
A poetic interpretation of the sights, sounds, beauty, rhythm and changing moods of the ocean.
Prod-PFP Dist-PFP 1968

Moods Of The Amazon C 18 MIN
16MM FILM OPTICAL SOUND
Gives impressions of the way of life in the region of the Amazon.
LC NO. 75-706371
Prod-INFORF Dist-PACEF Prodn-PACEF 1969

Moods Of The Arctic C 10 MIN
16MM FILM, 3/4 OR 1/2 IN VIDEO J-C
Explains that one of the last frontiers remaining to man is the vast reaches which lie north of the Arctic Circle. Points out that the popular idea that this area is merely a large area of perpetual ice and snow is a misconception.
Prod-COUKLA Dist-AIMS 1973

Moon And The Sledgehammer, The B 65 MIN
16MM FILM OPTICAL SOUND
Presents a real life portrait of a family, their bizarre habits and estranged attitudes.
Prod-IMPACT Dist-IMPACT 1971

Moon Buggy C 25 MIN
3/4 OR 1/2 INCH VIDEO CASSETTE
Documents the technology theory and experimentation behind a trip to the moon.
Prod-IHF Dist-IHF

Moon Creatures C 14 MIN
3/4 OR 1/2 INCH VIDEO CASSETTE P-I
See series title for descriptive statement.
From The Young At Art Series.
Prod-WSKJTV Dist-AITECH 1980

Moon Eyes C 15 MIN
3/4 OR 1/2 INCH VIDEO CASSETTE I
See series title for descriptive statement.
From The Best Of Cover To Cover 2 Series.
Prod-WETATV Dist-WETATV

Moon Is Coming Out, The C 14 MIN
3/4 OR 1/2 INCH VIDEO CASSETTE P
Features Japanese music and introduces the music staff.
From The Stepping Into Rhythm Series.
Prod-WVIZTV Dist-AITECH

Moon Man C 8 MIN
16MM FILM, 3/4 OR 1/2 IN VIDEO K-P
Tells how the man in the moon becomes bored with his life and rockets down to Earth. Based on the children's story Moon Man by Tomi Ungerer.
Prod-WWS Dist-WWS 1981

Moon Old And New, The C 26 MIN
16MM FILM OPTICAL SOUND
Gives a brief history of lunar studies before the Apollo 11 mission. Covers the major findings and questions that have emerged from studying Apollo 11 and 12 lunar samples and the data returned from scientific instruments left on the surface. Closes with a brief resume of investigations that scientists would like to undertake in the future.
LC NO. 70-710254
Prod-NASA Dist-USNAC

Moon Shadows C 29 MIN
16MM FILM - 3/4 IN VIDEO
Looks at the controversial political maneuverings of Reverend Sun Myung Moon's Unification Church and a coalition of Latin American right-wing 'contra' groups. Focuses on exiles from Latin American countries overthrown by Communism, their attempts to fight against Communism and their link to Moon's church. Includes interviews with an ex-Moonie, ex-Black Panther Eldridge Cleaver, an anti-communist backed by a moonie group, a Latin American newspaper editor in San Francisco and Senator Jim Leach of Iowa.
From The Presente Series.
Prod-KCET Dist-KCET

Moon 1969 C 15 MIN
16MM FILM OPTICAL SOUND J-C A
Uses various film techniques to take the viewer on a trip into the human soul. Says that clues to man's essence lie somewhere between the spiritual and the mathematical, between the incomprehensible magnitude of the universe and the knowledge that one day the frontier will be conquered. Uses footage showing man walking in space and landing on the moon, clouds drifting, ocean waves pounding, sunsets and all else that symbolizes the current joy-fear anxiety of a nation in a state of transformation.
LC NO. 79-709315
Prod-BARTLS Dist-SERIUS

Moon, Mist And Wonder B 15 MIN
2 INCH VIDEOTAPE P
See series title for descriptive statement.
From The Children's Literature Series. No. 25
Prod-NCET Dist-GPITVL Prodn-KUONTV

Moon, Old And New, The C 25 MIN
3/4 OR 1/2 INCH VIDEO CASSETTE
Traces the history of lunar studies before the Apollo 11 mission. Examines the findings and questions that have emerged from studying Apollo 11 and 12 lunar samples and from data returned from scientific instruments left on the Moon's surface. Issued in 1970 as a motion picture.
LC NO. 80-707382
Prod-NASA Dist-USNAC 1980

Moon, The C 15 MIN
2 INCH VIDEOTAPE P
Shows how the moon shines by reflected light.
From The Science Is Searching Series.
Prod-DETPS Dist-GPITVL

Moon, The B 20 MIN
2 INCH VIDEOTAPE I
See series title for descriptive statement.
From The Science Room Series.
Prod-MCETV Dist-GPITVL Prodn-WVIZTV

Moon, The B 45 MIN
2 INCH VIDEOTAPE C
See series title for descriptive statement.
From The Physical Science Series. Unit 3 - Astronomy
Prod-CHITVC Dist-GPITVL Prodn-WTTWTV

Moon, The - A Giant Step In Geology C 24 MIN
16MM FILM, 3/4 OR 1/2 IN VIDEO J-H
Uses scenes of scientists at work in Houston's Lunar Receiving Laboratory and animated segments of the moon's surface to indicate what is being done with the scientific information received from lunar rock samples.
From The Earth Science Program Series.
Prod-EBEC Dist-EBEC 1976

Moon, The - An Emerging Planet C 13 MIN
16MM FILM, 3/4 OR 1/2 IN VIDEO
Discusses early events in the history of the moon. Describes accretion, structural formation, volcanic activity, and bombardment. Compares the geology of the moon with that of Earth and other planets.
LC NO. 81-706422
Prod-NASA Dist-USNAC 1981

Moon, The - Old And New C 25 MIN
16MM FILM OPTICAL SOUND
Gives a brief history of lunar studies before the Apollo 11 mission. Covers the major things we have learned and the major questions that have emerged from studying Apollo 11 and 12 lunar samples and the data returns from scientific instruments left on the surface of the moon.
Prod-NASA Dist-NASA 1970

Moonbeam Princess, The - A Japanese Fairy Tale C 19 MIN
16MM FILM, 3/4 OR 1/2 IN VIDEO P
Tells the story of a princess who is sent to earth on a moonbeam as a baby and raised by a woodcutter and his wife. Although sought by three princes, she returns to the moon leaving magical flowers on earth for her loved ones. An animated film.
Prod-GAKKEN Dist-CORF 1967

Moonbird C 10 MIN
16MM FILM, 3/4 OR 1/2 IN VIDEO H-C A
Uses imaginative art work combined with spontaneous dialogue of very young children to provide a glimpse into the world of children as two small boys venture out to catch the moonbird.
Prod-HUBLEY Dist-TEXFLM 1959

Moonblood C 13 MIN
3/4 OR 1/2 INCH VIDEO CASSETTE
See series title for descriptive statement.
From The Reflecting Pool Series.
Prod-EAI Dist-EAI

Moonblood - A Yanamamo Creation Myth As Told By Dedeheiwa C 14 MIN
3/4 INCH VIDEO CASSETTE
A Yanamamo shaman from South America recounts, in his own language, his tribe's creation story which explains why men fight and kill each other. Filmed by Timothy Asch and Napoleon Chagnon. Includes English subtitles.
Prod-DOCEDR Dist-DOCEDR

Moonchild C 49 MIN
16MM FILM, 3/4 OR 1/2 IN VIDEO H-C A
Shows a young man, Chris Carlson, who became a member of Rev Moon's Unification Church, and how his parents were able to extricate him from that group through legal deprogramming. Includes recollections of other ex-Moonies.
LC NO. 82-707034
Prod-MAKPEC Dist-PFP 1982

Mooney Vs Fowle B 55 MIN
16MM FILM, 3/4 OR 1/2 IN VIDEO C A
Depicts the trials of competition between two high school football coaches in a film style making the film entertaining as well as a biting commentary on contemporary life.
Prod-DREW Dist-DIRECT 1970

Moonflights And Medicine C 26 MIN
16MM FILM - 3/4 IN VIDEO
Shows how many inventions which were originally created for the American space program are now used daily in the medical profession.
Prod-MESHDO Dist-NASA 1973

Moongates/Marnee Morris/Rocking Orange III C 30 MIN
3/4 OR 1/2 INCH VIDEO CASSETTE
Features Staton Dance Ensemble. Shows footwork of Marnee Morris, and Kinetic sculptures.
From The Doris Chase Dance Series.
Prod-CHASED Dist-CHASED

Moonglow C 10 MIN
3/4 OR 1/2 INCH VIDEO CASSETTE K A
Presents an animated fairy tale.
Prod-NISER Dist-SUTHRB

Moonies, The - Why Join, Why Stay C 24 MIN
16MM FILM OPTICAL SOUND
Provides insight into the experiences and feelings of a member of the Unification Church, a religious sect popularly known as the Moonies. Interviews the Rhodesian native who left college and moved to England to join the Moonies because he had been looking for some kind of higher value.
Prod-BBCTV Dist-OPENU 1982

Moonies, The - Why Join, Why Stay C 24 MIN
16MM FILM, 3/4 OR 1/2 IN VIDEO
Provides insight into the experiences and feelings of a member of the Unification Church, a religious sect popularly known as the Moonies. Interviews the Rhodesian native who left college and moved to England to join the Moonies because he had been looking for some kind of higher value.
Prod-OPENU Dist-MEDIAG Prodn-BBCTV 1982

Moonlight In Vermont Show, The C 30 MIN
3/4 OR 1/2 INCH VIDEO CASSETTE
Presents basically crazy cooks Larry Bly and Laban Johnson who offer recipes, cooking and shopping tips.
From The Cookin' Cheap Series.
Prod-WBRATV Dist-MDCPB

Moonplay C 18 MIN
16MM FILM, 3/4 OR 1/2 IN VIDEO P-I
Stimulates imaginative thinking in children with a story about a small girl who wishes for the moon and experiences delightful adventures when it materializes as a bright golden ball on her window ledge and leads her on a fantastic chase.
Prod-SVEK Dist-CF 1977

Moonspell C 25 MIN
16MM FILM OPTICAL SOUND
Examines the experience of space travel and the profound effect that it has had on Apollo astronauts, such as James Irwin and Edwin E Aldrin. Finds these men turning to self-worship, or to self-doubt and depression.
LC NO. 77-702517
Prod-CTV Dist-CTV 1976

Moonstones C 76 MIN
3/4 OR 1/2 INCH VIDEO CASSETTE PRO
Traces progress of a relationship between a male psychiatry resident and his thirteen-year-old patient over a three-month period. Comes on two tapes.
Prod-HSCIC Dist-HSCIC 1985

Moonstruck C 26 MIN
3/4 OR 1/2 INCH VIDEO CASSETTE H-C A
Looks at Sun Myung Moon and his followers.
Prod-CANBC Dist-JOU

Moonwalk C 40 MIN
16MM FILM, 3/4 OR 1/2 IN VIDEO P-C A
Presents a visual record of man's first steps on the Moon. Uses spectacular visuals to celebrate man's exploration of the universe. An edited version of the motion picture Moonwalk.
Prod-NASA Dist-LCOA Prodn-THOMPN 1976

Moonwalk C 95 MIN
16MM FILM, 3/4 OR 1/2 IN VIDEO J-C A
Presents a visual record of man's first steps on the Moon. Uses spectacular visuals to celebrate man's exploration of the universe.
Prod-NASA Dist-LCOA Prodn-THOMPN 1976

Moonwalk (Captioned) C 40 MIN
16MM FILM, 3/4 OR 1/2 IN VIDEO I-C A
Documents almost every aspect of the historic voyage of spaceship Apollo 11 in July 1969. Edited version.
Prod-NASA Dist-LCOA Prodn-THOMPN 1976

Moonwalk (Captioned) C 95 MIN
16MM FILM, 3/4 OR 1/2 IN VIDEO J-C A
Documents almost every aspect of the historic voyage of spaceship Apollo 11 in July 1969. Full version.
Prod-NASA Dist-LCOA Prodn-THOMPN 1976

Moonwalk (Danish) C 46 MIN
16MM FILM, 3/4 OR 1/2 IN VIDEO I-C A
Documents almost every aspect of the historic voyage of spaceship Apollo 11 in July 1969. Edited version.
Prod-NASA Dist-LCOA Prodn-THOMPN 1976

Moonwalk (Danish) C 95 MIN
16MM FILM, 3/4 OR 1/2 IN VIDEO I-C A
Documents almost every aspect of the historic voyage of spaceship Apollo 11 in July 1969. Full version.
Prod-NASA Dist-LCOA Prodn-THOMPN 1976

Moonwalk (Spanish) C 40 MIN
16MM FILM, 3/4 OR 1/2 IN VIDEO I-C A
Documents almost every aspect of the historic voyage of spaceship Apollo 11 in July 1969. Edited version.
Prod-NASA Dist-LCOA Prodn-THOMPN 1976

Moonwalk (Spanish) C 95 MIN
16MM FILM, 3/4 OR 1/2 IN VIDEO I-C A
Documents almost every aspect of the historic voyage of spaceship Apollo 11 in July 1969. Full version.
Prod-NASA Dist-LCOA Prodn-THOMPN 1976

Moonwalk, The - A Look Back C 25 MIN
3/4 OR 1/2 INCH VIDEO CASSETTE
Provides footage of the moon missions flown by the United States between July 1969 and December 1972.
Prod-UPI Dist-JOU

Moore Report—A Series
16MM FILM, 3/4 OR 1/2 IN VIDEO J-C A
Presents documentaries on the water crisis, crime in America, a Laotian refugee and the role of the woman in the U S work force.
Prod-WCCOTV Dist-IU

Farewell To Freedom	060 MIN
Fear And Present Danger	055 MIN
Quiet Crisis, The	055 MIN
You've Come A Long Way, Maybe?	055 MIN

Moose, The - Our Largest Deer (2nd Ed) C 11 MIN
16MM FILM, 3/4 OR 1/2 IN VIDEO P-H
Presents information about the moose, covering animal structure and function, behavior, adaptation and environment.
Prod-AIMS Dist-AIMS 1981

Moowis, Where Are You, Moowis C 26 MIN
16MM FILM, 3/4 OR 1/2 IN VIDEO
Dramatizes an Algonquin Indian legend about a young warrior spurned by the chief's daughter.
Prod-FOTH Dist-FOTH

Mopac Delivers C 25 MIN
16MM FILM OPTICAL SOUND
Shows the kinds of technology and services the Missouri Pacific Railroad can offer its customers.
LC NO. 75-702822
Prod-MOPAC Dist-MOPAC Prodn-GULSCH 1975

Moped Safety C 15 MIN
16MM FILM, 3/4 OR 1/2 IN VIDEO J-C A
Emphasizes the excellent fuel economy of the moped and discusses the special safety precautions to be used when riding this vehicle.
Prod-HANDEL Dist-HANDEL 1979

Moped Safety - The Facts Of Life C 18 MIN
16MM FILM, 3/4 OR 1/2 IN VIDEO J-C A
Presents basic information on applicable traffic laws, required safety equipment, and safe riding techniques for beginning mopedalists. Stresses the unique capabilities as well as the limitations of the moped. Shows teenagers, parents and grandparents operating mopeds.
LC NO. 81-707497
Prod-CENTRO Dist-CORF 1981

Moral Choice B 30 MIN
16MM FILM OPTICAL SOUND J-H A
Examines teenage attitudes towards sex. Describes how after a discussion on dating and sex morality, a young couple journey to a mysterious dream island where they are faced with a difficult moral choice. Formerly titled 'DREAM ISLAND.'
LC NO. FIA66-1261
Prod-CAFM Dist-CAFM 1965

Moral Decision Making—A Series
16MM FILM, 3/4 OR 1/2 IN VIDEO I-J
Presents situations that students can identify with in order to explore the problem of moral decision making.
Prod-MORLAT Dist-AIMS

Aggression-Assertion	008 MIN
Anger	008 MIN
Cheating	009 MIN
Envy	007 MIN
Frustration	008 MIN
Response To Misbehavior	009 MIN
Sharing	009 MIN
Stealing	012 MIN

Moral Development C 28 MIN
16MM FILM, 3/4 OR 1/2 IN VIDEO C A
Presents Dr Lawrence Kohlberg's theory on moral development. States that all people develop morality in consistent and unchanging ways and that behavior is determined by the state of moral development that has been reached. Contrasts Kohlberg's theory with the social learning theory.
From The Developmental Psychology Today Film Series.
Prod-CRMP Dist-CRMP 1973

Moral Development C 30 MIN
3/4 INCH VIDEO CASSETTE
Presents the various theories and the stages of moral development in childhood.
From The Growing Years Series.
Prod-COAST Dist-CDTEL

Moral Development C 30 MIN
3/4 OR 1/2 INCH VIDEO CASSETTE
Focuses on moral reasoning and socialization theory, Kohlberg's

six stages of moral reasoning and experiences that are likely to encourage the development of higher stages of moral reasoning.
From The Psychology Of Human Relations Series.
Prod-MATC Dist-WFVTAE

Moral Dimension B 30 MIN
16MM FILM OPTICAL SOUND H-C A
A memorial program presented on the second anniversary of the death of Herbert H Lehman, former U S Senator and governor of the state of New York. Includes an interview of Vice-President Hubert H Humphrey. (Kinescope)
From The Eternal Light Series.
LC NO. 74-700951
Prod-JTS Dist-NAAJS 1966

Moral Education For Children C 30 MIN
3/4 OR 1/2 INCH VIDEO CASSETTE J-C A
Shows James W Prescott, of the National Institute of Child Health and Human Development at HEW, and Roy Fairfield, of the Union For Experimenting Colleges and Universities, talking about moral education for children.
From The Moral Values In Contemporary Society Series.
Prod-AMHUMA Dist-AMHUMA

Moral Education In Our Schools, Pt 1 - Values Clarification C 30 MIN
3/4 OR 1/2 INCH VIDEO CASSETTE H-C A
Describes aims and techniques of innovative values, clarification methods. Discussion by Louis Raths and Joel Goodman. Graphic film sequences with Dr. Sidney Simon.
From The Ethics In America Series.
Prod-AMHUMA Dist-AMHUMA

Moral Education In Our Schools, Pt 2 - Moral Development C 30 MIN
3/4 OR 1/2 INCH VIDEO CASSETTE H-C A
Presents Dr. Lawrence Kohlberg, Professor of Psychology and Social Education at Harvard, explaining moral development methodology, which he pioneered.
From The Ethics In America Series.
Prod-AMHUMA Dist-AMHUMA

Moral Education In Our Schools, Pt 3 - Moral Development C 30 MIN
3/4 OR 1/2 INCH VIDEO CASSETTE H-C A
Shows Ralph Mosher, Professor Lisa Kuhmerke and Thomas Ladenburg discussing practical application of Dr. Lawrence Kohlberg's theories of moral development methodology. Includes on-location classroom discussions and student, teacher and administrator evaluations.
From The Ethics In America Series.
Prod-AMHUMA Dist-AMHUMA

Moral Judgment And Reasoning C 17 MIN
16MM FILM, 3/4 OR 1/2 IN VIDEO H-C A
Describes the characteristics of moral development from three perspectives.
From The Growing Years (CRMP) Series.
Prod-COAST Dist-CRMP 1978

Moral Responsibility Of Safety B 6 MIN
16MM FILM OPTICAL SOUND
Tells of four people directly and indirectly involved in a traffic accident facing the issue of who was morally responsible for the accident.
LC NO. FIE60-163
Prod-USA Dist-USNAC 1959

Moral Revolution, The C 30 MIN
3/4 OR 1/2 INCH VIDEO CASSETTE J-C A
Shows Charles Frankel of Columbia University talking about the moral revolution.
From The Moral Values In Contemporary Society Series.
Prod-AMHUMA Dist-AMHUMA

Moral Value Of Health, The C 16 MIN
3/4 INCH VIDEO CASSETTE PRO
See series title for descriptive statement.
From The Bioethics In Nursing Practice Series. Module 5
LC NO. 81-707063
Prod-BRA Dist-BRA 1981

Moral Values In Contemporary Society–A Series
J-C A
Presents authorities in their fields discussing different aspects of ethical and moral considerations in the major institutions of American life. Treats controversial topics in a straightforward and balanced fashion. Offers guidelines for the future.
Prod-AMHUMA Dist-AMHUMA

Beneficent Euthanasia	030 MIN
Beyond The Sexual Revolution	030 MIN
Biology And The Future Of Humankind, Pt 1	030 MIN
Biology And The Future Of Humankind, Pt 2	030 MIN
Boredom - It's Epidemic!	030 MIN
Church, The State, And The First Amendment, The	030 MIN
Disillusioned Americans, The	030 MIN
Divorce And Alimony - The American Tragedy	030 MIN
Does God Exist?	030 MIN
Ethics And The Law	030 MIN
Ethics Without Religion	030 MIN
Fear Of Eroticism And Its Human Implications	030 MIN
Free Thought And The Mass Media	030 MIN
Future Of The University, The, Pt 1	030 MIN
Future Of The University, The, Pt 2	030 MIN
Growing Old - The Prospects For Happiness	030 MIN
How To Enjoy Your First One Hundred Years	030 MIN
Humanism And Democracy	030 MIN
Humanism And Feminism - New Directions	030 MIN
Humanism And Its Enemies	030 MIN
Humanism And Science	030 MIN
Humanism And The Frontiers Of Education	030 MIN
Humanism In The Churches	030 MIN
Humanizing The Workplace	030 MIN
Immortality - A Debate	030 MIN
Involuntary Commitment	030 MIN
Is The Family Dead?	030 MIN
Moral Education For Children	030 MIN
Moral Revolution, The	030 MIN
New Concepts In Marriage	030 MIN
New Cults As A Social Phenomenon, The	030 MIN
New Sexual Revolution, The	030 MIN
On Black America	030 MIN
Our Disintegrating Public Schools	030 MIN
Paranormal Phenomena - Reality Or Illusion	030 MIN
Religious Liberty	030 MIN
Science And The Free Mind	030 MIN
Situation Ethics	030 MIN
What Is Humanism?	030 MIN

Morality - The Process Of Moral Development C 28 MIN
16MM FILM, 3/4 OR 1/2 IN VIDEO
See series title for descriptive statement.
From The Piaget's Developmental Theory Series.
Prod-DAVFMS Dist-DAVFMS

Morality Of Collaboration, The C 29 MIN
2 INCH VIDEOTAPE
See series title for descriptive statement.
From The Course Of Our Times I Series.
Prod-WGBHTV Dist-PUBTEL

Morals And The Man C 30 MIN
2 INCH VIDEOTAPE J-H
See series title for descriptive statement.
From The From Franklin To Frost - Benjamin Franklin Series.
Prod-MPATI Dist-GPITVL

Morals, Manners And Varmints C 10 MIN
16MM FILM, 3/4 OR 1/2 IN VIDEO P
Presents a tale about morals, manners and varmints in order to point out several human traits which are considered to be rude or impolite. Emphasizes that rude people are not popular.
Prod-SAIF Dist-BARR 1975

Moratorium C 11 MIN
16MM FILM OPTICAL SOUND
Portrays the nationwide protest regarding the involvement of the United States in the Vietnam War which occurred on October 15, 1969. Shows students, teachers and administrators, in harmony and in conflict, as they participated in the demonstration at Southern Illinois University.
LC NO. 77-706062
Prod-SILLU Dist-SIUFP 1970

More C 4 MIN
16MM FILM OPTICAL SOUND I-C
Uses animation to satirize man's insatiable desire for material things.
LC NO. 73-700741
Prod-DAVFMS Dist-TEXFLM 1973

More About Program Construction C 29 MIN
3/4 OR 1/2 INCH VIDEO CASSETTE J-C A
Checks the program designed in the videocassette Nested Loops And More About Program Design in terms of sequence, repetition, alternation or conditional flow, and logical groups. Uses a planning grid to formalize subroutines, along with a top-down approach to implement block structure and for coding and testing.
From The Programming For Microcomputers Series. Unit 20
LC NO. 83-707138
Prod-IU Dist-IU 1983

More About Quotient Rings B
16MM FILM OPTICAL SOUND
Shows how the isomorphism theorems follow naturally if one ring homomorphism is extended to a second. Demonstrates the one-to-one correspondence between ideals in the quotient ring and ideals which contain the kernel of the original homomorphism. Constructs a chain for the integers and uses this chain to introduce new ideas of integral domain, zero divisors, and field.
Prod-OPENU Dist-OPENU

More About Rhythm, Pt 1 C 15 MIN
3/4 OR 1/2 INCH VIDEO CASSETTE P
Reviews the rhythm symbols ta, ti and toe and shows how to accompany a song with rhythm instruments. Relates how to recognize a familiar song by listening to the rhythm of the melody.
From The Song Sampler Series.
LC NO. 81-707061
Prod-JCITV Dist-GPITVL 1981

More About Rhythm, Pt 2 C 15 MIN
3/4 OR 1/2 INCH VIDEO CASSETTE P
Reviews the rhythm symbols ta, ti and toe and shows how to accompany a song with rhythm instruments. Relates how to recognize a familiar song by listening to the rhythm of the melody.
From The Song Sampler Series.
LC NO. 81-707061
Prod-JCITV Dist-GPITVL 1981

More Abundant Life, The C 52 MIN
16MM FILM, 3/4 OR 1/2 IN VIDEO J-C A
Presents a potpourri of impressions by Alistair Cooke. Discusses what in America's experience has been fulfilled and what betrayed. Views Hoover Dam from the confident '30's. Pictures Hawaii showing racial harmony amid pollution and overdevelopment.
From The America - A Personal History Of The United States Series. No. 13
LC NO. 79-707141
Prod-BBCTV Dist-TIMLIF 1972

More Abundant Life, The (Spanish) C 52 MIN
16MM FILM OPTICAL SOUND J-C A
Presents a potpourri of impressions by Alistair Cooke. Discusses what in America's experience has been fulfilled and what has been betrayed. Includes the Hoover Dam from the confident 30's and Hawaii, showing racial harmony amid pollution and overdevelopment.
From The America - A Personal History Of The United States Series. No. 13
Prod-BBCTV Dist-TIMLIF 1972

More Alike Than Different C 29 MIN
3/4 INCH VIDEO CASSETTE
Looks at a special program for visually impaired infants and pre-school youngsters.
Prod-WKARTV Dist-PUBTEL

More And Less C 10 MIN
16MM FILM, 3/4 OR 1/2 IN VIDEO P-I
Illustrates the meaning of the equality and inequality of numbers by matching objects from two sets. Indicates the symbols used to show these relationships.
Prod-BOUNDY Dist-PHENIX 1966

More And Louder C 11 MIN
16MM FILM OPTICAL SOUND P-H
Combines animation and live action to tell about the new United States Postal Service, what it means and how it will work.
Prod-USNAC Dist-USNAC 1971

More And More C 27 MIN
16MM FILM, 3/4 OR 1/2 IN VIDEO
Examines the concept of economic growth, challenging the conventional wisdom that the constant proliferation of an already considerable flow of goods and services is a desirable goal.
From The Five Billion People Series.
Prod-LEFSP Dist-CNEMAG

More Awkard Customers C 30 MIN
3/4 OR 1/2 INCH VIDEO CASSETTE
Shows the proper and improper ways of handling difficult customers. Emphasizes the importance of professional knowledge when dealing with customers.
Prod-VIDART Dist-VISUCP

More Awkward Customers C 31 MIN
3/4 OR 1/2 INCH VIDEO CASSETTE A
Shows additional types of awkward customers, including the snob, the person who won't say what he wants and the finicky person. Presents techniques for handling these customers.
Prod-XICOM Dist-XICOM

More Basic Tools B 30 MIN
16MM FILM - 3/4 IN VIDEO PRO
Considers the construction and uses of graphic forms for presentation of data as well as the use of attack or incidence rates, prevalence rates and the Q index. (Broadcast quality)
From The Public Health Science Series. Unit II - Introduction To Biostatistics
Prod-TEXWU Dist-GPITVL Prodn-KUHTTV

More Blends And Review C 15 MIN
3/4 INCH VIDEO CASSETTE P
See series title for descriptive statement.
From The I Need To Read Series.
Prod-WCETTV Dist-GPITVL 1975

More Bloody Meetings C
3/4 OR 1/2 INCH VIDEO CASSETTE
Moves from the organizational aspects of a meeting to the human side of actually running a meeting.
Prod-VIDART Dist-VISUCP

More Changes C 20 MIN
2 INCH VIDEOTAPE P
See series title for descriptive statement.
From The Learning Our Language, Unit 2 - Dictionary Skills Series.
Prod-MPATI Dist-GPITVL

More Commands C
3/4 OR 1/2 INCH VIDEO CASSETTE
Explains how to execute the pr, grep, sort, wc, tail and stty commands.
From The UNIX Fundamentals Series.
Prod-COMTEG Dist-COMTEG

More Complicated Weaves C 29 MIN
2 INCH VIDEOTAPE
See series title for descriptive statement.
From The Exploring The Crafts - Weaving Series.
Prod-NHN Dist-PUBTEL

More Control Statements C
3/4 OR 1/2 INCH VIDEO CASSETTE
Describes the syntax and use of the switch control statement, specifying the rules for the switch expression, case constants and switch execution flow. Describes the use of the default case, break control, continue control statement and the goto and return statements.
From The 'C' Language Programming Series.
Prod-COMTEG Dist-COMTEG

More Creativity Behind The Scenes C 30 MIN
3/4 OR 1/2 INCH VIDEO CASSETTE
See series title for descriptive statement.
From The Behind The Scenes Series.
Prod-ARCVID Dist-ARCVID

More Cuttings C 29 MIN
2 INCH VIDEOTAPE
See series title for descriptive statement.
From The Making Things Grow III Series.
Prod-WGBHTV Dist-PUBTEL

More Deadly Than War - The Communist Revolution In America, Pt 1 B 38 MIN
16MM FILM OPTICAL SOUND
Presents a lecture by G Edward Griffin on the communist theory and practice of revolution, particularly as applied to the United States.
LC NO. 73-700813
Prod-AMMED Dist-AMMED 1969

More Deadly Than War - The Communist Revolution In America, Pt 2 B 38 MIN
16MM FILM OPTICAL SOUND
Presents a lecture by G Edward Griffin on the communist theory and practice of revolution, particularly as applied to the United States.
LC NO. 73-700813
Prod-AMMED Dist-AMMED 1969

More Different Than Alike C 35 MIN
16MM FILM OPTICAL SOUND C T
Depicts some unique and creative techniques which provide for individual learning differences. Includes a data processing system, to compare, by computer, the progress each student is making with the progress he should be making--a special school for the slow learner--a learning center in which high school students have access to the latest materials and technology for self-instruction--a program of student-planned work schedules and learning projects and a helpmobile for inservice education.
LC NO. 74-707995
Prod-NEA Dist-NEA 1967

More Difficult Solo, A C 29 MIN
2 INCH VIDEOTAPE
See series title for descriptive statement.
From The Playing The Guitar II Series.
Prod-KCET Dist-PUBTEL

More Duple Rhythm C 29 MIN
3/4 INCH VIDEO CASSETTE H A
Tests student comprehension of, and facility with, intervals up to the fifth, pitch notations and keyboard letter names. Introduces a new piece.
From The Beginning Piano - An Adult Approach Series. Lesson 6
Prod-COAST Dist-CDTEL

More Expressions C
3/4 OR 1/2 INCH VIDEO CASSETTE
Discusses the relationship between bits and bytes for each fundamental storage type and describes the use and application of the four bitwise operators. Illustrates the use and application of the two shift operators, the use of the compound assignment operators and the syntax.
From The 'C' Language Programming Series.
Prod-COMTEG Dist-COMTEG

More For Peace C 45 MIN
16MM FILM OPTICAL SOUND J A
Presents a veteran returning from Korea, disillusioned by the seeming contentedness of his community, who finally discovers what his little church is actually doing and decides to support it wholeheartedly.
Prod-YALEDV Dist-YALEDV

More From Less C 28 MIN
16MM FILM OPTICAL SOUND
Explains the practice of planting a crop without prior conventional tillage. Shows work being done to improve the environment by control of erosion.
Prod-ALLISC Dist-IDEALF

More Fun With Finger Paints B 15 MIN
2 INCH VIDEOTAPE P
Explores the possibilities of monoprints.
From The Art Corner Series.
Prod-CVETVC Dist-GPITVL Prodn-WCVETV

More Gag-Gathering Methods C 15 MIN
2 INCH VIDEOTAPE
See series title for descriptive statement.
From The Charlie's Pad Series.
Prod-WSIU Dist-PUBTEL

More I/O C 30 MIN
3/4 OR 1/2 INCH VIDEO CASSETTE H-C A
Reviews the sequential file aspects of Pascal and introduces file buffers of the GET and PUT procedures. Describes problem of using Pascal as an interactive language, and discusses a file-merge program and other file-utility programs.
From The Pascal, Pt 3 - Advanced Pascal Series.
LC NO. 81-706049
Prod-COLOSU Dist-COLOSU 1980

More Income Per Acre C 30 MIN
16MM FILM OPTICAL SOUND H-C A
Presents face-to-face interviews with actual users of sprinkler irrigation who explain its advantages on the farm.
Prod-REYMC Dist-REYMC 1957

More Interactions B 15 MIN
2 INCH VIDEOTAPE P
See series title for descriptive statement.
From The Just Wondering Series.
Prod-EOPS Dist-GPITVL Prodn-KOACTV

More Meat For Your Money (Captioned) C 25 MIN
3/4 OR 1/2 INCH VIDEO CASSETTE S
Presents Catherine Rhoads showing how to balance budget and nutrition. Demonstrates selection and use of economical cuts of meat.
From The Consumer Education For The Deaf Adult Series.
Prod-GALCO Dist-GALCO 1975

More Multiplication C 20 MIN
2 INCH VIDEOTAPE P
See series title for descriptive statement.
From The Mathemagic, Unit VIII - Multiplication And Division Series.
Prod-WMULTV Dist-GPITVL

More Music From Aspen C 59 MIN
3/4 INCH VIDEO CASSETTE
Covers the annual three-day Aspen, Colorado, Music Festival, which brings together famous musicians and gifted students.
Prod-KQEDTV Dist-PUBTEL

More Non-Fiction C 30 MIN
3/4 OR 1/2 INCH VIDEO CASSETTE C
See series title for descriptive statement.
From The Communicating Through Literature Series.
Prod-DALCCD Dist-DALCCD

More Nuclear Power Stations C 48 MIN
3/4 OR 1/2 INCH VIDEO CASSETTE
Offers a glimpse into the workings of the nuclear power industry.
Prod-GMPF Dist-GMPF 1977

More On Algorithms C 30 MIN
3/4 OR 1/2 INCH VIDEO CASSETTE IND
Develops two algorithms, the first describing a simple decoder for events such as an alarm system and the second for a timer to generate desired time interval. Notes latter has many commercial applications.
From The Microprocessors For Monitoring And Control Series.
Prod-COLOSU Dist-COLOSU

More On Decoding Logic And Data And Address Bus Interfaces C 30 MIN
3/4 OR 1/2 INCH VIDEO CASSETTE IND
Discusses design examples of address decoding logic, dynamic mapping of a memory space, address bus interface and data bus interface.
From The Microcomputer Memory Design Series.
Prod-COLOSU Dist-COLOSU

More On Heat Transfer C 180 MIN
3/4 OR 1/2 INCH VIDEO CASSETTE PRO
Includes flow nets and two-dimensional heat flow.
From The Arctic Engineering Series.
Prod-UAKEN Dist-AMCEE

More On Map Representations - Map-Entered Variables, Don't-Care Map Terms C 30 MIN
3/4 OR 1/2 INCH VIDEO CASSETTE IND
Provides more material on map use to represent logical expressions.
From The Microprocessors For Monitoring And Control Series.
Prod-COLOSU Dist-COLOSU

More On Walls, Windows, Doors And Floors C 180 MIN
3/4 OR 1/2 INCH VIDEO CASSETTE PRO
Covers condensation problems, vapor control, vapor barriers and Fick's law.
From The Arctic Engineering Series.
Prod-UAKEN Dist-AMCEE

More Patterns I C 29 MIN
2 INCH VIDEOTAPE
See series title for descriptive statement.
From The Busy Knitter II Series.
Prod-WMVSTV Dist-PUBTEL

More Patterns II C 29 MIN
2 INCH VIDEOTAPE
See series title for descriptive statement.
From The Busy Knitter II Series.
Prod-WMVSTV Dist-PUBTEL

More Power On The Ground C 13 MIN
16MM FILM OPTICAL SOUND
Presents the 'World Series' of tractor-pulls in Louisville, Kentucky. Describes the rules, weight classes and degrees of competition. Shows how pull power means more power on the ground, less man power and less man hours.
Prod-ALLISC Dist-IDEALF

More Power To You C 10 MIN
16MM FILM OPTICAL SOUND
Describes the use of the Euclid Twin Power Scraper in coal stock-piling.
Prod-GM Dist-GM

More Precious Than Gold C 30 MIN
1/2 IN VIDEO CASSETTE BETA/VHS
Explores investing in gold. Discusses choosing a guardian for children. Describes what to look for in a personal computer.
From The On The Money Series.
Prod-WGBHTV Dist-MTI

More Safely Tomorrow C 10 MIN
16MM FILM OPTICAL SOUND
Depicts the need for accident prevention in the years ahead. Stresses the need for safety to a growing economy and improved social order.
Prod-NSC Dist-NSC

More Signs You Already Know C 30 MIN
3/4 OR 1/2 INCH VIDEO CASSETTE H-C A
Presents Lawrence Solow and Sharon Neumann Solow introducing American Sign Language used by the hearing-impaired. Emphasizes signs that resemble gestures already used by many people in spoken conversation.
From The Say It With Sign Series. Part 2
LC NO. 83-706359
Prod-KNBCTV Dist-FI 1982

More Solutions Of Linear Equations B 30 MIN
16MM FILM OPTICAL SOUND H
Presents four steps to use in solving word problems correctly. Obtains solutions to a problem about the relations in the rational number system, a problem in uniform motion, a mixture problem and a river-boat problem involving combined velocities.
From The Intermediate Algebra Series.
Prod-CALVIN Dist-MLA Prodn-UNIVFI 1959

More Storage Space In The Kitchen C 13 MIN
2 INCH VIDEOTAPE
See series title for descriptive statement.
From The Living Better I Series.
Prod-MAETEL Dist-PUBTEL

More Swing Bass C 29 MIN
3/4 INCH VIDEO CASSETTE H A
Applies swing bass to a familiar melody.
From The Beginning Piano - An Adult Approach Series.
Reviews earlier lessons. Adds chords in B-flat major.
Prod-COAST Dist-CDTEL

More Than A Breakfast Cereal C 10 MIN
16MM FILM OPTICAL SOUND
Shows that it is possible for even the beginning student to prepare a variety of dishes with breakfast cereals. Stresses basic cooking skills as demonstrated by a zany gourmet chef and his class of teenage cooks.
Prod-CHEX Dist-MTP

More Than A Carpenter C 58 MIN
16MM FILM OPTICAL SOUND R
Reveals how Josh McDowell visits an archaeological dig and finds compelling evidence concerning the identity of Jesus of Nazareth which challenges a professor, nearly explodes a romance and drives a young archaeologist to the breaking point.
Prod-OUTRCH Dist-OUTRCH

More Than A Contract C 29 MIN
3/4 INCH VIDEO CASSETTE
Investigates some of the problems that occur in the settlement of divorce and remarriage.
From The Life, Death And Taxes Series.
Prod-UMITV Dist-UMITV 1977

More Than A Gut Feeling C 28 MIN
3/4 OR 1/2 INCH VIDEO CASSETTE A
Describes a selection interviewing process designed to train supervisors, managers and personnel employees. Presents ideas in a story format using two characters.
Prod-AMEDIA Dist-AMEDIA

More Than A Memory C 15 MIN
16MM FILM OPTICAL SOUND
Shows scenes from the 1920's to demonstrate that the experiences of children then are similar to the experiences of children in the 1980's.
From The Growing Up - Growing Older Series
Prod-SEARSF Dist-MTP 1982

More Than A Paycheck C 28 MIN
16MM FILM - 3/4 IN VIDEO
Deals with cancer which is caused by exposure to cancer-causing agents found in work environment. Decribes types of work situations in which exposure can occur and discusses methods of protecting employees. Narrated by John Wayne. Issued in 1978 as a motion picture.
LC NO. 80-706623
Prod-GWASHU Dist-USNAC 1980

More Than A Promise C 14 MIN
16MM FILM OPTICAL SOUND T S
Presents an overview of the spirit and implementation of some of the provisions of P L 94-142 and the promises this law makes to handicapped people.
From The Exceptional Learners Series.
LC NO. 79-700708
Prod-MERILC Dist-MERILC 1978

More Than A School C 56 MIN
16MM FILM OPTICAL SOUND H-C A
Portrays an alternative community high school within the regular school and shows its positive effects on students, parents and the community.
Prod-NYU Dist-NYU

More Than A Snapshot C 10 MIN
16MM FILM, 3/4 OR 1/2 IN VIDEO P-I
Tells about two young people who enjoy photography.
From The Zoom Series.
Prod-WGBHTV Dist-FI

More Than Anger C 27 MIN
16MM FILM OPTICAL SOUND I-H
Presents the animated story of the Christmas Seal.
Prod-NTBA Dist-AMLUNG 1968

More Than Bows And Arrows C 56 MIN
16MM FILM OPTICAL SOUND
Deals with the role of the American Indian in shaping various aspects of American culture, ranging from food and housing to philosophy.
LC NO. 78-701467
Prod-CIASP Dist-CIASP 1978

More Than Coffee And Donuts C 26 MIN
16MM FILM OPTICAL SOUND
Presents Lorne Greene who narrates a look at the other side of the Red Cross story. Depicts the Red Cross programs that have been adapted to the particular needs of the community they serve. Contains frank language which some people may find objectionable.
Prod-AMRC Dist-AMRC 1971

More Than Color C 30 MIN
3/4 OR 1/2 INCH VIDEO CASSETTE

Explores several of the issues and problems confronting the black artist in America today. Examines the relationship between black culture and black aesthetics to contemporary mainstream art. Features several black artists.
Prod-OHUTC Dist-OHUTC

More Than Dance B 15 MIN
16MM FILM OPTICAL SOUND
Presents an impressionistic view of a dance studio.
LC NO. 76-703786
Prod-RYERI Dist-RYERI 1976

More Than Food C 25 MIN
16MM FILM OPTICAL SOUND J-C A
Shows how dire conditions of drought-ridden northeast Brazil are improved by cws-crop projects, including construction of a reservoir which should collect and hold an 18-month supply of water for the village of Alagoinha. Includes scenes of the Febem Children's Center and the orobo manioc and cornmeal processing cooperative which are aided by CWS-crop.
LC NO. 74-700046
Prod-CROP Dist-CROP 1972

More Than Friends C 21 MIN
16MM FILM, 3/4 OR 1/2 IN VIDEO J-C S
A sign language drama that depicts the confusion and anxieties of a deaf teenage couple as they try to communicate their feelings and differing points of view about sex.
From The Setting Limits Series.
LC NO. 83-706855
Prod-ODNP Dist-ODNP

More Than Hugs And Kisses - Affective Education In A Mainstreamed Classroom C 23 MIN
16MM FILM, 3/4 OR 1/2 IN VIDEO T
Demonstrates how teacher Alice Brogan, a victim of spina bifida, teaches her students at Jowonio School in Syracuse, NY, where one-third of the students are developmentally delayed. Illustrates activities and attitudes which further the development of the whole child and an approach to affective education which can be used in more traditional school environments.
Prod-VIDDA Dist-FLMLIB Prodn-TOGGFI 1980

More Than M And M's C 30 MIN
3/4 OR 1/2 INCH VIDEO CASSETTE T
See series title for descriptive statement.
From The Dealing In Discipline Series.
Prod-UKY Dist-GPITVL 1980

More Than Meets The Eye C 30 MIN
16MM FILM, 3/4 OR 1/2 IN VIDEO
Shows how the eye functions and how the brain interprets and judges on past experiences and prejudices.
From The Life Around Us Series.
LC NO. 79-707837
Prod-TIMLIF Dist-TIMLIF 1971

More Than Meets The Eye (Spanish) C 30 MIN
16MM FILM OPTICAL SOUND
Examines the process of seeing and the role light plays in seeing. Discusses the difference between seeing and perception and shows how experience, memory and prejudice influence people's view of their surroundings.
From The Life Around Us (Spanish) Series.
LC NO. 78-700082
Prod-TIMLIF Dist-TIMLIF 1971

More Than Money C 23 MIN
16MM FILM, 3/4 OR 1/2 IN VIDEO A
Discusses motivation and managerial expectations in relation to employee production, 'Theory X' and 'Theory Y' managerial styles, and leadership, supervision and interpersonal skills.
Prod-RTBL Dist-RTBL

More Than One C 20 MIN
2 INCH VIDEOTAPE P
See series title for descriptive statement.
From The Learning Our Language, Unit 2 - Dictionary Skills Series.
Prod-MPATI Dist-GPITVL

More Than Retirement C 15 MIN
16MM FILM, 3/4 OR 1/2 IN VIDEO
Discusses the rights and benefits workers have under Social Security.
Prod-USSSA Dist-USNAC 1981

More Than Skin Deep B 25 MIN
16MM FILM OPTICAL SOUND
Discusses the problems of personal cleanliness for both patients and personnel in nursing homes. Shows how and why such cleanliness is essential.
Prod-UHOSF Dist-HF Prodn-HF 1966

More Than Speed C 12 MIN
16MM FILM OPTICAL SOUND
Illustrates driving safety techniques through interviews with professional race drivers at Indianapolis Motor Speedway and tips from professional driving instructors.
LC NO. 80-700213
Prod-CHSPC Dist-CREATC Prodn-CREATC 1979

More Than You Think C 15 MIN
16MM FILM, 3/4 OR 1/2 IN VIDEO I
Tells why Alex thinks he doesn't have enough information to be a fortune teller at the school carnival or to solve a word problem in math class. Shows his discovery that he knows more that he thought he did.
From the Thinkabout Series. Reshaping Information
LC NO. 81-706109
Prod-SCETV Dist-AITECH 1979

More Thermal Interaction B 15 MIN
2 INCH VIDEOTAPE P
See series title for descriptive statement.
From The Just Curious Series. No. 26
Prod-EOPS Dist-GPITVL Prodn-KOACTV

More Time To Live - Flexible Working Time C 30 MIN
3/4 OR 1/2 INCH VIDEO CASSETTE C A
Exemplifies growing trend among industrialized nations to eliminate conventional work routines. Features the Dutch national postal service and a German department store.
From The Re-Making Of Work Series.
Prod-BLCKBY Dist-EBEC 1983

More Water For A Thirsty World C 14 MIN
16MM FILM OPTICAL SOUND
Deals with research into better methods of water management, improved methods of pollution control, and the desalination of sea water.
Prod-ALLFP Dist-NSTA 1975

More We Are Together, The C 21 MIN
16MM FILM, 3/4 OR 1/2 IN VIDEO C A
Shows how a British company suffers business setbacks which are the result of failure to inform, consult and involve management at all levels. Illustrates the attitudes of senior, middle and junior managers to proposed changes in organizational style and procedures.
From The Practical Participation Series.
Prod-MILLBK Dist-IFB

More We Get Together, The C 15 MIN
3/4 OR 1/2 INCH VIDEO CASSETTE P-I
See series title for descriptive statement.
From The Ready, Sing Series.
Prod-ARKETV Dist-AITECH 1979

Morgenrot (German) B 75 MIN
3/4 OR 1/2 INCH VIDEO CASSETTE
A German language film. Depicts a World War I submarine drama.
Prod-IHF Dist-IHF

Mormon Foods C 28 MIN
2 INCH VIDEOTAPE
Presents host Sam Arnold presenting recipes for preparing Mormon foods.
From The Frying Pans West Series.
Prod-KRMATV Dist-PUBTEL

Morning C 16 MIN
16MM FILM MAGNETIC SOUND K-C A S
See series title for descriptive statement.
From The PANCOM Beginning Total Communication Program For Hearing Parents Of... Series. Level 2
LC NO. 77-700504
Prod-CSDE Dist-JOYCE Prodn-CSFDF 1977

Morning - June To August, 1944 C 60 MIN
16MM FILM OPTICAL SOUND H-C A
From The World At War Series.
LC NO. 76-701778
Prod-THAMES Dist-USCAN 1975

Morning - June-August 1944 C 52 MIN
16MM FILM, 3/4 OR 1/2 IN VIDEO H-C A
Documents D-Day, June 6, 1944, when the Allies under the command of General Dwight D. Eisenhower began an advance on Normandy at Cherbourg, a German fortification that later became a major Allied supply base. Preparations insured an oil supply, harbor facilities and accurate weather predictions.
From The World At War Series.
Prod-THAMES Dist-MEDIAG 1973

Morning After C 17 MIN
16MM FILM, 3/4 OR 1/2 IN VIDEO
Shows the vulnerability of a seemingly cool, sophisticated man to the breakup of a long-standing relationship.
Prod-TRAMNC Dist-FLMLIB 1982

Morning After The Night Of Power, The C 10 MIN
3/4 OR 1/2 INCH VIDEO CASSETTE
See series title for descriptive statement.
From The Memory Surfaces And Mental Prayers Series.
Prod-EAI Dist-EAI

Morning Airport C 11 MIN
16MM FILM, 3/4 OR 1/2 IN VIDEO P-I
Looks at the great variety of tasks and duties that must be done during early morning at a major U S airport, focusing on the servicing and readying of a 747 for morning departure.
Prod-FLMFR Dist-FLMFR

Morning Airport (Spanish) C 11 MIN
16MM FILM, 3/4 OR 1/2 IN VIDEO I
Looks at the great variety of tasks and duties that must be done during early morning at a major U S airport, focusing on the servicing and readying of a 747 for morning departure.
Prod-FLMFR Dist-FLMFR

Morning Care B 27 MIN
16MM FILM OPTICAL SOUND PRO
Discusses and demonstrates activities of daily living related to the hospitalized patient.
From The Directions For Education In Nursing Via Technology Series. Lesson 4
LC NO. 74-701777
Prod-DENT Dist-WSU 1974

Morning During, The C 11 MIN
16MM FILM OPTICAL SOUND
Shows a woman on her wedding night fantasizing about the lovers she will never have. Explains that when morning comes she gains a renewed conviction about the choice she has made.
LC NO. 80-700274
Prod-BATB Dist-BATB 1979

Morning Glory C 20 MIN
16MM FILM OPTICAL SOUND A
Offers a portrait of a summer day as seen through the eyes of a woman.
LC NO. 81-700397
Prod-SMITHD Dist-SMITHD 1980

Morning Harbor C 11 MIN
16MM FILM, 3/4 OR 1/2 IN VIDEO P-I
Shows the harbor as a center of a variety of activities where many types of transportation, machinery and skills are used. Focuses on fish being processed upon arrival, grain being tested and weighed before shipping, the use of containerized cargo and the specialized machinery needed to lift it.
Prod-HEDENC Dist-FLMFR 1973

Morning Harbor (Captioned Version) C 11 MIN
16MM FILM, 3/4 OR 1/2 IN VIDEO P-I
Shows the harbor as a center of a variety of activities where many types of transportation, machinery and skills are used. Focuses on fish being processed upon arrival, grain being tested and weighed before shipping, the use of containerized cargo and the specialized machinery needed to lift it.
Prod-HEDENC Dist-FLMFR 1973

Morning Harbor (Spanish) C 11 MIN
16MM FILM, 3/4 OR 1/2 IN VIDEO P-I
Shows the many people who work to maintain a harbor as a center for the shipping and receiving of goods.
Prod-HEDENC Dist-FLMFR 1973

Morning In The Grass C 5 MIN
16MM FILM OPTICAL SOUND K-I
Portrays an insect community in puppet animation. Shows how human beings appear and cause the community problems and dangers, which the insects cope with.
From The Adventures In The High Grass Series.
LC NO. 74-702123
Prod-MMA Dist-MMA 1972

Morning Light B 15 MIN
16MM FILM OPTICAL SOUND
Shows how a middle-aged woman confronts the unfulfillment in her life and then finds that there is still much life ahead to be lived.
LC NO. 79-700248
Prod-DISTER Dist-DISTER 1979

Morning Line C 18 MIN
16MM FILM OPTICAL SOUND
Examines the world of gamblers and ponies.
LC NO. 74-703425
Prod-BRYNTP Dist-CFDEVC 1973

Morning Prayers - A Celebration Of The Gift Of Life C 15 MIN
3/4 OR 1/2 INCH VIDEO CASSETTE
Discusses the personal and everyday consciousness. Focuses on prayer book.
From The Tradition And Contemporary Judaism - Prayer And The Jewish People Series. Program 4
Prod-ADL Dist-ADL

Morning Scene C 29 MIN
3/4 INCH VIDEO CASSETTE
See series title for descriptive statement.
From The Magic Of Oil Painting Series.
Prod-KOCETV Dist-PUBTEL

Morning Song, A C 23 MIN
16MM FILM OPTICAL SOUND A R
Focuses on a Mennonite farmer and his family living near Lancaster, Pennsylvania. Discusses the history and beliefs of the Mennonites and problems caused by the changing world around them.
LC NO. 79-700940
Prod-MARTC Dist-EMBMC 1978

Morning Spider, The C 22 MIN
16MM FILM, 3/4 OR 1/2 IN VIDEO J-C A
Presents, without narration, a humorous children's tale in mime which depicts the life of a hard-working, but often inept morning spider.
LC NO. 77-701098
Prod-CHGRIN Dist-PFP 1976

Morning Star C 36 MIN
16MM FILM, 3/4 OR 1/2 IN VIDEO I-H
Shows spring migration of a herd of sheep across the wildest, most inaccessible area of the United States-the Tonto Basin near Phoenix, Arizona.
Prod-LINE Dist-EBEC 1951

Morning Star Painter C 30 MIN
16MM FILM OPTICAL SOUND
Introduces Jack Wunuwun, an aboriginal bark painter who lives near Maningrida in Arnhemland.
LC NO. 80-700825
Prod-TASCOR Dist-TASCOR 1979

Morning Zoo C 11 MIN
16MM FILM, 3/4 OR 1/2 IN VIDEO P-J
Looks at the early morning, pre-opening chores at a large zoo seen through the eyes of a young girl zooworker who arrives for her tasks at the children's section. Shows the routines of feeding and cleaning and closeups of various animals.
Prod-FLMFR Dist-FLMFR

Morning, Noon And Evening C 14 MIN
16MM FILM, 3/4 OR 1/2 IN VIDEO P-I
Examines the daily patterns of living in the country and in the city.
Prod-FILMSW Dist-FLMFR

Mornings Of Creation B 20 MIN
16MM FILM, 3/4 OR 1/2 IN VIDEO J-C A

Portrays primordial forces of nature. Contemplates their textures, forms and essential beauty. Captures the mood of Henry David Thoreau's 'MORNINGS OF CREATION.'
Prod-UCB Dist-UCEMC 1973

Morocco C 3 MIN
16MM FILM OPTICAL SOUND P-I
Discusses the country of Morocco in Africa.
From The Of All Things Series.
Prod-BAILYL Dist-AVED

Morocco C 10 MIN
16MM FILM OPTICAL SOUND
Shows the geographic features, life-style, handicrafts, architecture and festive celebrations of Morocco.
LC NO. 73-701117
Prod-PICNIC Dist-PICNIC 1972

Morocco For All Seasons C 26 MIN
16MM FILM OPTICAL SOUND
Shows cultural and tourist attractions in Morocco.
LC NO. 76-702853
Prod-WELBIT Dist-WELBIT 1976

Morocco For All Seasons (Arabic) C 26 MIN
16MM FILM OPTICAL SOUND
Shows cultural and tourist attractions in Morocco.
LC NO. 76-702853
Prod-WELBIT Dist-WELBIT 1976

Morocco For All Seasons (French) C 26 MIN
16MM FILM OPTICAL SOUND
Shows cultural and tourist attractions in Morocco.
LC NO. 76-702853
Prod-WELBIT Dist-WELBIT 1976

Morocco For All Seasons (Portuguese) C 26 MIN
16MM FILM OPTICAL SOUND
Shows cultural and tourist attractions in Morocco.
LC NO. 76-702853
Prod-WELBIT Dist-WELBIT 1976

Morris C 9 MIN
16MM FILM OPTICAL SOUND H-C A
Presents a humorous look at an undersea society.
LC NO. 79-700123
Prod-USC Dist-USC 1979

Morris Dances - Ancient Ritual English Dances C 30 MIN
3/4 OR 1/2 INCH VIDEO CASSETTE
See series title for descriptive statement.
From The Shaping Today With Yesterday Series.
Prod-ARCVID Dist-ARCVID

Morris Family Old Time Music Festival C 30 MIN
3/4 INCH VIDEO CASSETTE
Features the 1972 old time music festival in Ivydale, West Virginia. Includes segments with John Martin, Aunt Minnie Moss and Uncle Homer Walker.
Prod-DOCEDR Dist-DOCEDR

Morris, The Midget Moose C 8 MIN
16MM FILM, 3/4 OR 1/2 IN VIDEO P-I
Explains that Morris, the midget moose with the magnificent antlers, teams up with Brawny Balsam, the possessor of a puny set of horns, to prove that two heads are better than one.
Prod-DISNEY Dist-WDEMCO 1973

Morris's Disappearing Bag C 10 MIN
16MM FILM, 3/4 OR 1/2 IN VIDEO K-P
Relates that on Christmas morning, Morris finds himself too little to play with his brother's hockey outfit and too young to play with his sister's chemistry set. Reveals that he finds one more present under the tree - a disappearing bag. Based on the book Morris's Disappearing Bag by Rosemary Wells.
LC NO. 83-706014
Prod-WWS Dist-WWS Prodn-SPORAN 1982

Mortal Body, The B 12 MIN
16MM FILM OPTICAL SOUND
Projects such images as the birth of a child, a couple making love and an old man contemplating eternity to encapsulize the human life cycle.
Prod-ZAGREB Dist-FLMLIB

Mortgages C 29 MIN
3/4 INCH VIDEO CASSETTE C A
Discusses where mortgages originate, the two major elements of a mortgage and some important clauses found in a mortgage. Defines terms such as amortization, escalation privileges and reserve accounts. Gives examples of types of interest rates.
From The You And The Law Series. Lesson 18
Prod-COAST Dist-CDTEL Prodn-SADCC

Mortice And Tenon-Dados C 56 MIN
1/2 INCH VIDEOTAPE
Shows how to do the important woodworking step of joining with the mortice and tenon joint. Goes on to instruction for making a through dado.
From The Woodworking Series.
Prod-ANVICO Dist-ANVICO

Morton Schindel - From Page To Screen C 27 MIN
16MM FILM, 3/4 OR 1/2 IN VIDEO J-C A
Offers a tour of the Weston Woods studios and explains how children's books are adapted to motion pictures and filmstrips.
Prod-WWS Dist-WWS 1981

Morwen Of The Woodlands C 27 MIN
16MM FILM, 3/4 OR 1/2 IN VIDEO
Tells the Welsh tale of a Prince who grows bored with his wife who was once young and beautiful and falls in love with a beautiful maiden whom he finds in the woods. Reveals that she returns to the castle with him on the condition that once a week she return to the forest and he not follow her. Relates that a monk-magician finally reveals that the girl is really the Prince's wife in disguise.
From The Storybook International Series.
Prod-JOU Dist-JOU 1982

MOS - From Design To Product C 30 MIN
3/4 OR 1/2 INCH VIDEO CASSETTE PRO
Illustrates tour of a MOS production facility, tracing MOS device of alrication from circuit specifications to final product. Shows actual facilities needed to produce MOS.
From The MOS Integrated Circuit Series.
Prod-TXINLC Dist-TXINLC

MOS And Linear Integrated Circuits C 60 MIN
1 INCH VIDEOTAPE IND
Tells how MOS integrated circuits differ from others, enabling them to be more complex. Describes the operation of the key element in MOS integrated circuits, the Field Effect Transistor (FET.) Explains how Field Effect Transistors are used and surveys linear integrated circuits.
From The Understanding Semiconductors Course Outline Series. No. 12
Prod-TXINLC Dist-TXINLC

MOS Device Physics C 30 MIN
3/4 OR 1/2 INCH VIDEO CASSETTE PRO
Examines the MOSFET, emphasizing the solid-state physics of materials used in production of the metal-oxide silicon-field effect transistor.
From The MOS Integrated Circuit Series.
Prod-TXINLC Dist-TXINLC

MOS Integrated Circuits—A Series
PRO
Provides overview of current metal-oxide semiconductor (MOS) technology, analyzes motivations showing recent MOS trends, and shows the electronics engineer how to utilize the application benefits of this expanding technology.
Prod-TXINLC Dist-TXINLC

Basic MOS Shift Registers	030 MIN
Bipolar - MOS Interface	030 MIN
CMOS And SOS Inverter Characteristics	030 MIN
CMOS Capabilities, Advantages And Applications	030 MIN
Four-Phase, CMOS And CCD Shift Registers	030 MIN
High Functional Density Design With PLA - I	030 MIN
High Functional Density Design With PLA - II	030 MIN
MOS - From Design To Product	030 MIN
MOS Device Physics	030 MIN
MOS Random-Access Memory Design	030 MIN
MOS ROMS	030 MIN
MOS Special Devices And Chip Layout	030 MIN
MOS Transistor Characteristics	030 MIN
MOS Transistor Characteristics Related To MOS	030 MIN
MOS/LSI Economics	030 MIN
MOS/LSI Reliability	030 MIN
N-Channel, CMOS, SOS And Ion Implantion	030 MIN
Overview Of MOS, An	030 MIN
P And N-Channel Inverter Characteristics	030 MIN
Random-Access Memory Design	030 MIN

MOS Memory C 55 MIN
3/4 OR 1/2 INCH VIDEO CASSETTE PRO
Covers the topic of flip-flops and shift register memory. Treats, also, logic symbolism, circuit diagrams, detailed timing of clock structures.
From The Introduction To VLSI Design Series.
Prod-MIOT Dist-MIOT

MOS Processing C 55 MIN
3/4 OR 1/2 INCH VIDEO CASSETTE PRO
Covers silicon-gate fabrication sequence, HMOS improvements, bulk CMOS Processing, and IC fabrication yields.
From The Introduction To VLSI Design Series.
Prod-MIOT Dist-MIOT

MOS Random Access Semiconductor Storage Design C 60 MIN
1 INCH VIDEOTAPE IND
Discusses static and dynamic storage cells and their design. Covers 8-, 6-, 4-, 3- and 1- transistor cells.
From The Semiconductor Memories Course Series. No. 5
Prod-TXINLC Dist-TXINLC

MOS Random-Access Memory Applications C 30 MIN
3/4 OR 1/2 INCH VIDEO CASSETTE PRO
Charts performance of available MOS RAMs. Discusses signal interface and shows specific applications of D and N-channel MOS RAMS for use in larger memory systems.
From The MOS Integrated Circuit Series.
Prod-TXINLC Dist-TXINLC

MOS Random-Access Memory Design C 30 MIN
3/4 OR 1/2 INCH VIDEO CASSETTE PRO
Looks at design details of random-access storage elements necessary to achieve cost-effective performance required when using MOS.
From The MOS Integrated Circuit Series.
Prod-TXINLC Dist-TXINLC

MOS ROMS C 30 MIN
3/4 OR 1/2 INCH VIDEO CASSETTE PRO
Analyzes design of MOS read-only storage elements. Outlines the process technology and performance characteristics of these MOS devices.
From The MOS Integrated Circuit Series.
Prod-TXINLC Dist-TXINLC

MOS Special Devices And Chip Layout C 30 MIN
3/4 OR 1/2 INCH VIDEO CASSETTE PRO
Discusses special devices such as floating gate MOS, CCDs, and important factors required for implementing an MOS/LSI chip layout.
From The MOS Integrated Circuit Series.
Prod-TXINLC Dist-TXINLC

MOS Transistor Characteristics C 30 MIN
3/4 OR 1/2 INCH VIDEO CASSETTE PRO
Analyzes basic solid-state action that occurs to produce canier current conduction in a metal-oxide-silicon field effect transistors.
From The MOS Integrated Circuit Series.
Prod-TXINLC Dist-TXINLC

MOS Transistor Characteristics Related To MOS Process C 30 MIN
3/4 OR 1/2 INCH VIDEO CASSETTE PRO
Discusses the interrelationships of MOS transistor V-I characteristics, characteristics that depend on variations of subsrate material, gate material and source and drain diffusions.
From The MOS Integrated Circuit Series.
Prod-TXINLC Dist-TXINLC

MOS Transistor, The C 55 MIN
3/4 OR 1/2 INCH VIDEO CASSETTE PRO
Treats physical structure of the Metal-Oxide-Semiconductor (MOS), doping of semiconductors, PN junction, diffusion and drift, and diodes.
From The Introduction To VLSI Design Series.
Prod-MIOT Dist-MIOT

MOS/I L Logic Circuits C
3/4 OR 1/2 INCH VIDEO CASSETTE
See series title for descriptive statement.
From The Digital Techniques Video Training Course Series.
Prod-VTRI Dist-VTRI

MOS/LSI Economics C 30 MIN
3/4 OR 1/2 INCH VIDEO CASSETTE PRO
Looks at the cost-effective process of MOS in large scale integration of high functional density digital systems designs and traces this effectiveness through time.
From The MOS Integrated Circuit Series.
Prod-TXINLC Dist-TXINLC

MOS/LSI Reliability C 30 MIN
3/4 OR 1/2 INCH VIDEO CASSETTE PRO
Examines reliability of MOS/LSI devices showing their progress with time compared to other IC technologies.
From The MOS Integrated Circuit Series.
Prod-TXINLC Dist-TXINLC

MOS, I2L Logic Circuits C
3/4 OR 1/2 INCH VIDEO CASSETTE
See series title for descriptive statement.
From The Digital Techniques Series.
Prod-HTHZEN Dist-HTHZEN

Mosaic C 6 MIN
16MM FILM, 3/4 OR 1/2 IN VIDEO J-C A
Superimposes films 'LINES VERTICAL' and 'LINES HORIZONTAL' to give a geometric and non-figurative example of cinematographic 'OP' art.
Prod-NFBC Dist-IFB 1965

Mosaic - Hobart Smith B 30 MIN
16MM FILM OPTICAL SOUND
Folksinger Hobart Smith discusses his life and his songs and performs several selections on the banjo, guitar and fiddle.
LC NO. FI67-92
Prod-WTTWTV Dist-WTTWTV 1966

Mosaics C 15 MIN
3/4 OR 1/2 INCH VIDEO CASSETTE P-I
Shows how to design a paper mosaic and a mosaic using seeds, pasta and buttons.
From The Art Cart Series.
Prod-WBRATV Dist-AITECH 1979

Mosaics C 30 MIN
3/4 OR 1/2 INCH VIDEO CASSETTE H A
Shows Dr George Baker decorating objects of aesthetic and utilitarian value through the use of mosaic techniques. Explores ceramic tile, natural materials, and seed mosaic techniques for children.
From The Arts And Crafts Series.
LC NO. 81-706357
Prod-GPITVL Dist-GPITVL 1981

Mosaics - Works Of Jeanne Reynal C 20 MIN
16MM FILM OPTICAL SOUND
Artist Jeanne Reynal explains and demonstrates her process for creating a mosaic mural. Includes scenes of the preparation of the tesserae, the proper use of cement mix, acid baths, tools and other requirements needed to create a mosaic.
LC NO. FIA68-3065
Prod-FALKBG Dist-RADIM 1968

Moscow And Leningrad C 14 MIN
16MM FILM, 3/4 OR 1/2 IN VIDEO H-C
A Russian language film. Views Red Square, the Kremlin, the Pokrovskiy Cathedral and aspects of modern urban life in the USSR.
From The Russian Language Series.
Prod-IFB Dist-IFB 1963

Moscow Does Not Believe In Tears (Russian) C 150 MIN
16MM FILM OPTICAL SOUND H-C A
Presents a romantic comedy about three young, working-class country girls who go to Moscow in 1958 to seek work, men and success. Looks at the results of their expedition in 1978.
LC NO. 82-700456
Prod-MOSFLM Dist-IFEX 1981

Moscow Doesn't Answer C 12 MIN
16MM FILM OPTICAL SOUND
Relates the plight of Soviet Jews wishing to immigrate to Israel.

Traces the case histories of leading Jewish scientists not allowed to leave Russia.
Prod-UJA Dist-ALDEN

Moscow Life C 26 MIN
3/4 OR 1/2 INCH VIDEO CASSETTE
Examines the daily life of the average Soviet citizen. Focuses on housing, transportation, work opportunity and consumer goods.
Prod-UPI Dist-JOU

Moscow, City Of Contrasts C 20 MIN
3/4 OR 1/2 INCH VIDEO CASSETTE J-C A
LC NO. 82-706778
Prod-AWSS Dist-AWSS 1981

Moscow's Red Square C 20 MIN
3/4 OR 1/2 INCH VIDEO CASSETTE
Tells the history of Red Square which has witnessed eight centuries of heroic events in the history of Russia and the Soviet Union.
Prod-IHF Dist-IHF

Moses C 20 MIN
16MM FILM OPTICAL SOUND S R
Shows the Moses story from Genesis told by Mr Louie J Fant in AMESLAN (American Sign Language.)
From The Fant Anthology Of AMESLAN Literature Series.
LC NO. 74-701463
Prod-JOYCE Dist-JOYCE 1973

Moses C 63 MIN
16MM FILM, 3/4 OR 1/2 IN VIDEO I-C A
Presents the story of Moses, who is instructed by God to deliver his people from bondage. Reveals that when the Pharoah resists, Moses calls down a series of plagues on Egypt until the Pharoah agrees to set the Hebrews free. Stars John Marley and Julie Adams.
From The Greatest Heroes Of The Bible Series.
Prod-LUF Dist-LUF 1979

Moses And Aaron C 110 MIN
16MM FILM OPTICAL SOUND
Offers an adaptation of Schonberg's opera Moses and Aaron. Directed by Jean-Marie Straub and Daniele Huillet.
Prod-UNKNWN Dist-NYFLMS

Moses And His People C 15 MIN
16MM FILM OPTICAL SOUND P-J
Presents the story of Moses told using puppets. Covers Moses' return to Egypt to the crossing of the Red Sea.
Prod-YALEDV Dist-YALEDV

Moses And The Lime Kiln C 27 MIN
16MM FILM, 3/4 OR 1/2 IN VIDEO
Tells the Israeli tale of Moses, who is called to a great city to impart knowledge to a Caliph. Reveals that when a courtier plots to murder Moses at a lime-kiln, God saves him for being so righteous.
From The Storybook International Series.
Prod-JOU Dist-JOU 1982

Moses And The Mountain Of Fire C 30 MIN
16MM FILM OPTICAL SOUND R
Portrays leadership qualities exhibited by Moses as he brings the people back to a right relationship with God after finding them worshiping a golden idol. Shows Moses to be a man of strong leadership qualities, qualities which church leaders need today.
Prod-BROADM Dist-BROADM 1964

Moses And The Ten Commandments C 15 MIN
16MM FILM OPTICAL SOUND P-J
Presents the story of Moses told using puppets. Covers the wilderness journeys, the golden calf and the giving of the Ten Commandments.
Prod-YALEDV Dist-YALEDV

Moses Coady C 58 MIN
16MM FILM, 3/4 OR 1/2 IN VIDEO H-C A
Presents the story of Moses Coady, a zealous Cape Breton priest, who was responsible for the foundation of the cooperative education movement in the Maritimes.
Prod-NFBC Dist-BULFRG 1976

Moses In Egypt C 15 MIN
16MM FILM OPTICAL SOUND P-J
Presents the story of Moses told using puppets. Covers Moses' birth to his call to lead his people out of bondage.
Prod-YALEDV Dist-YALEDV

MOSFET And The Inverter, The C 55 MIN
3/4 OR 1/2 INCH VIDEO CASSETTE PRO
Treats the shape of the current-voltage curve and design implications. Deals with the inverter and inverter loads - resistor, linear, saturated, and depletion.
From The Introduction To VLSI Design Series.
Prod-MIOT Dist-MIOT

MOSFET Inverter And Simple Gates, The C 55 MIN
3/4 OR 1/2 INCH VIDEO CASSETTE PRO
Treats the sizings of the generalized inverter structure - pull-up / pull-down ratio for inverter pass transistor in the gate circuit. Considers the NAND and NOR structures.
From The Introduction To VLSI Design Series.
Prod-MIOT Dist-MIOT

Moshav, The - Israel's Middle Way C 25 MIN
16MM FILM OPTICAL SOUND
Shows Israel's successful experiment with agricultural and regional planning. Points out that the Moshav, a cooperative settlement, is a middle way between the closely-knit communal kibbutz and the independent farmer.
Prod-ALDEN Dist-ALDEN

Moskusoksen (The Musk Ox) C 10 MIN
16MM FILM OPTICAL SOUND
Presents the musk ox in its natural surroundings in Greenland, among reindeer and Arctic foxes. Includes sound effects.
Prod-STATNS Dist-STATNS 1967

Moskva I Leningrad (Moscow And Leningrad) C 14 MIN
16MM FILM, 3/4 OR 1/2 IN VIDEO H-C
A Russian language film. Pictures urban life in Moscow and Leningrad, showing traffic patterns and the interior of a large department store. Views Red Square, the Kremlin and Polrovskiy Cathedral. Shows the construction of an apartment house on the outskirts of Moscow.
Prod-IFB Dist-IFB 1963

Moslems In Spain, The C 39 MIN
16MM FILM, 3/4 OR 1/2 IN VIDEO H-C
Recounts the 781 years in which Moslems and Spaniards merged two cultures into a distinctive Hispano-Moorish civilization.
Prod-KIRBY Dist-IFB 1979

Mosque, The - Prayer In Its Setting C 24 MIN
16MM FILM, 3/4 OR 1/2 IN VIDEO
Examines the architecture, ornamentation and function of Islamic mosques, designed specifically for congregational prayer and to induce a reflective state in the worshipper. Shows that all mosques face Mecca and that most include many specific features such as the minaret, an external elevation from which the call to prayer is made.
Prod-OPENU Dist-MEDIAG Prodn-BBCTV 1979

Mosquito Fighters C 21 MIN
16MM FILM OPTICAL SOUND J A
Tells how the citizens of a small rural community in the Bayou country of south Louisiana, despite their original skepticism, cooperate in a modern mosquito control program to fight the mosquito-borne disease, encephalitis.
LC NO. 76-711348
Prod-STOKES Dist-FINLYS 1970

Mosquito Prevention In Irrigated Areas B 7 MIN
16MM FILM OPTICAL SOUND
Shows how to control mosquitoes in irrigated areas by good design and careful maintenance of the irrigation system, accurate preleveling of fields, and adequate provision for run-off drains to avoid standing water.
LC NO. FIE55-234
Prod-USPHS Dist-USNAC 1955

Mosquito Stages Of Plasmodium Falciparum B 11 MIN
16MM FILM - 3/4 IN VIDEO
Shows the mosquito stages of Plasmodium falciparum from the time the female Anopheles quadrimaculatus obtains blood to the time the sporozoites are inoculated into the host. Issued in 1954 as a motion picture
LC NO. 78-706104
Prod-USPHS Dist-USNAC Prodn-NMAC 1978

Mosquito Survey Techniques C 15 MIN
16MM FILM OPTICAL SOUND
Shows mosquito survey methods under a variety of circumstances and for various mosquito species. Explains the proper way to collect larvae and adult mosquitoes, to keep accurate records and to evaluate results.
LC NO. FIE58-83
Prod-USPHS Dist-USNAC 1954

Mosquito, The - A Bite For Survival C 29 MIN
16MM FILM, 3/4 OR 1/2 IN VIDEO P-H
Relates the effects of mosquito bites.
Prod-EBEC Dist-EBEC 1984

Mosquitoes And High Water (Captioned) C 25 MIN
3/4 OR 1/2 INCH VIDEO CASSETTE A
Portrays the history and culture of the Spanish-speaking 'Islenos' of St Bernard Parish, Louisiana. Presents their customs and traditions, and discusses some of their problems. Spanish language with English subtitles.
Prod-CNAM Dist-CNEMAG 1983

Mosquitos - Effect On Cattle C 9 MIN
16MM FILM OPTICAL SOUND IND
Investigates the problems of mosquito-caused irritations, weight loss and damage to cattle herds and shows how good management can help solve some of these problems.
LC NO. 77-701958
Prod-ADAIB Dist-CENTWO 1977

Moss Life Cycle C 15 MIN
3/4 OR 1/2 INCH VIDEO CASSETTE
Offers a general introduction to the mosses with emphasis on gametophytic and sporophytic development. Presents the life cycle of a typical moss.
Prod-CBSC Dist-CBSC

Moss, Reverend Otis C 29 MIN
3/4 INCH VIDEO CASSETTE
Presents Rev Otis Moss, who discusses the church's role in developing black leaders and its relationship to the contemporary black family.
From The Like It Is Series.
Prod-OHC Dist-HRC

Mosses, Liverworts And Ferns C 14 MIN
16MM FILM, 3/4 OR 1/2 IN VIDEO J-C
Uses close-ups, microphotography and animation to show how mosses, liverworts and ferns grow and reproduce and how they are adapted for survival on land.
From The Major Phyla Series.
Prod-CORF Dist-CORF 1969

Most Adult Game, The, Pt 1 C 25 MIN
16MM FILM OPTICAL SOUND
Explores the history of the Synanon game and why it has become popular.
LC NO. 79-707704
Prod-KRONTV Dist-KRONTV 1967

Most Adult Game, The, Pt 2 C 25 MIN
16MM FILM OPTICAL SOUND
Illustrates the Synanon game in action with children, teenagers and adults pointing out the potential of the game.
LC NO. 79-707704
Prod-KRONTV Dist-KRONTV 1967

Most Beautiful Home, The C 15 MIN
16MM FILM, 3/4 OR 1/2 IN VIDEO J-C A
Shows how to clean carpets and how to keep them attractive, fresh and useful for extended numbers of years. Illustrates the rights and wrongs of carpet care, describing how to remove surface dirt, deep dirt and unpleasant odors.
Prod-KLEINW Dist-KLEINW

Most Beautiful Place On Earth, The C 28 MIN
16MM FILM, 3/4 OR 1/2 IN VIDEO J-C A
Discusses several facets of the continent of Antarctica, including its climate, wildlife, topography and geology.
Prod-UN Dist-JOU 1974

Most Brilliant Game Of The Year, The C 28 MIN
2 INCH VIDEOTAPE
See series title for descriptive statement.
From The Grand Master Chess Series.
Prod-KQEDTV Dist-PUBTEL

Most Efficient Instrument C 29 MIN
3/4 INCH VIDEO CASSETTE
Gives examples of special trust devices for reducing taxes.
From The Life, Death And Taxes Series.
Prod-UMITV Dist-UMITV 1977

Most Famous Forgotten Writer In America, The C 60 MIN
3/4 OR 1/2 INCH VIDEO CASSETTE C
Depicts Fitzgerald's turn to alcohol and despair, while everyone else it seemed to him turned to Marxism in this dramatization of a Fitzgerald story.
From The World Of F Scott Fitzgerald Series.
Prod-DALCCD Dist-DALCCD

Most For Your Money, The C 28 MIN
16MM FILM, 3/4 OR 1/2 IN VIDEO S
Explores the concepts of wise consumer shopping, including planning a shopping trip, tips on how to make the best buys and suggested questions for receiving helpful information from salespeople.
From The Learning To Live On Your Own Series.
Prod-LINCS Dist-JOU 1979

Most For Your Money, The (Spanish) C 28 MIN
16MM FILM, 3/4 OR 1/2 IN VIDEO S
Explores the concepts of wise consumer shopping, including planning a shopping trip, tips on how to make the best buys and suggested questions for receiving helpful information from salespeople.
From The Learning To Live On Your Own Series.
Prod-LINCS Dist-JOU 1979

Most Frequently Asked Tennis Questions C 29 MIN
3/4 OR 1/2 INCH VIDEO CASSETTE
See series title for descriptive statement.
From The Vic Braden's Tennis For The Future Series.
Prod-WGBHTV Dist-PBS 1981

Most Important Person - Attitudes (Spanish)—A Series
16MM FILM, 3/4 OR 1/2 IN VIDEO K-P
Suggests positive approaches to coping with discouraging situations.
Prod-EBEC Dist-EBEC

I'm Lonely (Spanish) 4 MIN
It's Not Much Fun Being Angry (Spanish) 4 MIN
Nothing Ever Seems To Work Out For Me (Spanish) 4 MIN
Oops, I Made A Mistake (Spanish) 4 MIN
We Can Do It (Spanish) 4 MIN
Why Not Try (Spanish) 4 MIN

Most Important Person - Attitudes—A Series
16MM FILM, 3/4 OR 1/2 IN VIDEO K-I
Suggests some positive approaches to discouraging situations.
Prod-EBEC Dist-EBEC 1973

I'm Lonely 4 MIN
It's Not Much Fun Being Angry 4 MIN
Nothing Ever Seems To Work Out For Me 4 MIN
Oops, I Made A Mistake 4 MIN
We Can Do It 4 MIN
Why Not Try 4 MIN

Most Important Person - Body Movement—A Series
16MM FILM, 3/4 OR 1/2 IN VIDEO K
Focuses on the young child's motor development, motor skills and coordination.
Prod-EBEC Dist-EBEC 1973

Follow The Leader 4 MIN
How Big Is Big 4 MIN
It Takes Muscles 4 MIN
Joints Let You Bend 4 MIN
Put Your Hands On The Top Of Your Head 4 MIN
Watch Your Balance 4 MIN

Most Important Person - Creative Expression—A Series
16MM FILM, 3/4 OR 1/2 IN VIDEO K-I

Stresses that the most important person is a creative person.
Prod-EBEC Dist-EBEC 1973

Be Curious 4 MIN
Rhythm Around You 4 MIN
This Is Me 4 MIN
Use Your Imagination 4 MIN
When You're Waking Up 4 MIN
Without Saying A Word 4 MIN

Most Important Person - Feelings—A Series
16MM FILM, 3/4 OR 1/2 IN VIDEO K-I
Emphasizes feelings of happiness, love or fear, from the child's point of view.
Prod-EBEC Dist-EBEC 1973

Different Kinds Of Love 4 MIN
Feeling Good, Feeling Happy 4 MIN
I Used To Be Afraid 4 MIN

Most Important Person - Getting Along With Others—A Series
16MM FILM, 3/4 OR 1/2 IN VIDEO K-I
Studies interpersonal relationships, including the qualities of co-operation, understanding and thoughtfulness.
Prod-EBEC Dist-EBEC 1973

Doing Something Nice 4 MIN
Growing Up 4 MIN
Living Things Are All Around Us 4 MIN
Share It With Someone 4 MIN
Thinking Of Others 4 MIN
What Do You Mean 4 MIN
What Is A Friend 4 MIN

Most Important Person - Health And Your Body—A Series
16MM FILM, 3/4 OR 1/2 IN VIDEO K-I
Stresses more awareness of body functions and the need for maintenance of good health.
Prod-EBEC Dist-EBEC 1973

Take Care Of Your Teeth 4 MIN
Tell Us How You Feel 4 MIN
Visiting The Doctor 4 MIN
Voice Box, The 4 MIN
When You Get Hurt 4 MIN
Where Does Food Go 4 MIN

Most Important Person - Identity (Spanish)—A Series
16MM FILM, 3/4 OR 1/2 IN VIDEO K-P
Introduces concepts of self-awareness and individuality.
Prod-EBEC Dist-EBEC

Every Family Is Special (Spanish) 4 MIN
How Do We Look (Spanish) 4 MIN
I'm The Only Me (Spanish) 4 MIN
Most Important Person, The (Spanish) 4 MIN
What Do You Think You Want To Be (Spanish) 4 MIN
Where Are You In Your Family (Spanish) 4 MIN

Most Important Person - Identity—A Series
16MM FILM, 3/4 OR 1/2 IN VIDEO K-I
Develops a strong sense of self-awareness and self-importance in the young child.
Prod-EBEC Dist-EBEC 1973

Every Family Is Special 4 MIN
How Do We Look 4 MIN
I'm The Only Me 4 MIN
Most Important Person, The 4 MIN
What Do You Think You Want To Be 4 MIN
Where Are You In Your Family 4 MIN

Most Important Person - Nutrition—A Series
16MM FILM, 3/4 OR 1/2 IN VIDEO K-I
Emphasizes the importance of maintaining health and energy through proper eating habits. Introduces the great diversity of foods available.
Prod-EBEC Dist-EBEC

Foods Around Us 4 MIN
Have A Snack 4 MIN
Tasting Party 4 MIN
What's For Breakfast 4 MIN

Most Important Person - Senses—A Series
16MM FILM, 3/4 OR 1/2 IN VIDEO K-I
Explores ways to heighten sensory awareness.
Prod-EBEC Dist-EBEC 1973

Five Senses, The 4 MIN
Hearing 4 MIN
Seeing 4 MIN
Smelling 4 MIN
Tasting 4 MIN
Touching 4 MIN

Most Important Person, The C 4 MIN
16MM FILM, 3/4 OR 1/2 IN VIDEO K-I
Presents Fumble, Bird and their friends who realize that each individual is, to himself or herself, the most important person.
From The Most Important Person - Identity Series.
Prod-EBEC Dist-EBEC 1972

Most Important Person, The (Spanish) C 4 MIN
16MM FILM, 3/4 OR 1/2 IN VIDEO K-P
See series title for descriptive statement.
From The Most Important Person - Identity (Spanish) Series.
Prod-EBEC Dist-EBEC

Most Important Thing, The C 15 MIN
16MM FILM, 3/4 OR 1/2 IN VIDEO I-J
Stimulates students to compare careers in relation to their own values of what is important in a lifestyle.
From The Whatcha Gonna Do Series.
Prod-NVETA Dist-EBEC 1974

Most Marvelous Cat, The C 11 MIN
3/4 INCH VIDEO CASSETTE P
Describes the adventures of a cat named Johann Sebastian, as he travels to the city to earn rent money for his poor master.
Prod-BOSUST Dist-GA

Most Precious Resource C 29 MIN
16MM FILM OPTICAL SOUND I-C A
Views the organization for rehabilitation through training Israel network, the largest single ORT operation in 22 countries, and shows its role in building the future of Israel.
LC NO. 76-700015
Prod-WAORT Dist-WAORT Prodn-SHARFF 1968

Most Remarkable Cat, The C 15 MIN
3/4 INCH VIDEO CASSETTE K-P
See series title for descriptive statement.
From The Storytime Series.
Prod-WCETTV Dist-GPITVL 1976

Most Thankless Job On Earth, The C 25 MIN
16MM FILM OPTICAL SOUND
Presents correspondent Michael Maclear examining the work of Kurt Waldheim in his job as secretary general of the United Nations. Notes the problems and difficulties that are involved in the job of holding together this world body.
LC NO. 77-702518
Prod-CTV Dist-CTV 1976

Most, The B 28 MIN
16MM FILM OPTICAL SOUND H-C A
Presents a fascinating documentary of 'PLAYBOY' Hugh Hefner. Takes place at a Bacchanalian party at Hefer's mansion, where the 'PLAYBOY PHILOSOPHY' is candidly and ironically revealed.
LC NO. 78-738824
Prod-BALSHE Dist-VIEWFI 1971

Motel C 18 MIN
16MM FILM OPTICAL SOUND
Presents an adaptation of Jean Claude van Itallie's play Motel. Concerns three characters in oversized puppet heads and a man and a woman who arrive in a motel room, seemingly prepared for an evening of sex, while a grotesque motel keeper delivers a monologue of platitudes about America and the homey quality of her motel. Shows how the monologue changes from nonsense to chaos and the couple proceed to wreck the room.
LC NO. 76-703140
Prod-EQINOX Dist-EQINOX 1976

Mother C 30 MIN
1/2 IN VIDEO CASSETTE BETA/VHS
Describes the life of Ann Sweeney of Greenwich, Connecticut, who is 'Mom' to eighteen children. Seven are by her husband, a music publisher, plus eleven multi-national, multi-racial adopted children, ranging in age from eight to thirty.
From The American Professionals Series.
Prod-WTBS Dist-RMI

Mother B 70 MIN
3/4 OR 1/2 INCH VIDEO CASSETTE
Tells the story of a Russian family during the 1905 uprising.
Prod-IHF Dist-IHF

Mother (Prison Visit) B 6 MIN
16MM FILM OPTICAL SOUND J-C A
Presents an excerpt from the 1926 motion picture Mother. Shows the mother visiting her son in prison, passing him a note which reveals plans made for his escape. Directed by Vsevolod Pudovkin.
From The Film Study Extracts Series.
Prod-UNKNWN Dist-FI

Mother And Child C 15 MIN
16MM FILM, 3/4 OR 1/2 IN VIDEO
Features actresses Susan St James and Natalie Wood and the president of La Leche League International, Marian Tompson, in a discussion about the values and techniques of breast feeding.
Prod-MAJAC Dist-KLEINW Prodn-KLEINW 1975

Mother And Child C 25 MIN
16MM FILM, 3/4 OR 1/2 IN VIDEO H-C A
Examines the importance of the physical and psychological relationship existing between mother and child. Discusses the difficulties that can arise with separation or with the arrival of a new baby.
From The Children Growing Up Series.
Prod-BBCTV Dist-FI 1981

Mother And The Whore, The (French) B 215 MIN
16MM FILM OPTICAL SOUND
Presents Alexandre who reads Proust in cafes and wears long flowing silk scarves. Portrays him as an accomplished mock-philosophical raconteur who has no visible means of support at age 30. Surveys the social and sexual lives of Alexandre and the women he meets.
Prod-NYFLMS Dist-NYFLMS 1973

Mother And Toddlers - Humanizing The Growth Experience B 18 MIN
16MM FILM, 3/4 OR 1/2 IN VIDEO
Documents the experiences of the Dr Martin Luther King Family Center with toddler's lab, a program in which children, from 18 months to three years are accepted for what they are and are engaged individually so that each child's special ways of coping with his world are not threatened. Demonstrates what it means to work with a person's strengths rather than his deficiences.
Prod-JOU Dist-JOU 1971

Mother Cat And Her Baby Skunks C 11 MIN
16MM FILM, 3/4 OR 1/2 IN VIDEO P
The story of a mother cat and three orphaned baby skunks which she rescues and raises with her own kittens.
Prod-EBF Dist-EBEC 1958

Mother Corn C 29 MIN
3/4 INCH VIDEO CASSETTE
Examines the historical significance of corn among the Hopi and Pueblo cultures and traces the symbolism of corn across generations to today's modern uses. Explores the relationship of corn to rain dances, Kivas, and Kachina dolls as agents of the supernatural. Also available in two-inch quad and one-inch videotape.
Prod-KBYU Dist-NAMPBC

Mother Deer And Her Twins C 11 MIN
16MM FILM, 3/4 OR 1/2 IN VIDEO P
The story of twin fawns. Shows how the mother protects them at first but later teaches them to care for themselves.
Prod-EBF Dist-EBEC 1959

Mother Duck And The Big Race C 11 MIN
16MM FILM, 3/4 OR 1/2 IN VIDEO K-P
Presents mother duck who builds a nest in Peter's soap box racer, and helps Peter win the race. Provides a backgound for language arts activities.
Prod-CORF Dist-CORF 1972

Mother Earth, Father Sky C 13 MIN
16MM FILM OPTICAL SOUND
Shows people of various ages and ethnic backgrounds as they participate in a wide variety of outdoor activities in mountain, beach, urban and desert environments.
LC NO. 74-702492
Prod-FMCMP Dist-FORDFL Prodn-FECD 1974

Mother Goose C 4 MIN
16MM FILM OPTICAL SOUND
Examines the lyrics and meanings of three Mother Goose favorites.
LC NO. 79-700124
Prod-USC Dist-USC 1978

Mother Goose C 30 MIN
1/2 IN VIDEO CASSETTE BETA/VHS K-I
See series title for descriptive statement.
From The Jump Over The Moon - Sharing Literature With Young Children Series.
Prod-HRAW Dist-HRAW

Mother Goose Rhymes - Background For Reading And Expression C 11 MIN
16MM FILM, 3/4 OR 1/2 IN VIDEO P
Provides an excursion to Mother Goose Land. Pictures such famous characters and places as Little Bo-Peep, Jack-Be-Nimble, the Old Woman Who Lived in a Shoe, Little Boy Blue, Little Miss Muffet, Mother Goose and the London Bridge.
Prod-CORF Dist-CORF 1957

Mother Goose Stories X 11 MIN
16MM FILM, 3/4 OR 1/2 IN VIDEO P-I A
Mother Goose steps out of the nursery rhyme book and brings some of her favorite characters to life, including Little Miss Muffet and Humpty Dumpty. Portrayed by animated figures.
Prod-HARRY Dist-PHENIX 1961

Mother Goose Stories (Captioned) C 11 MIN
16MM FILM, 3/4 OR 1/2 IN VIDEO P-I A
Mother Goose steps out of the nursery rhyme book and brings some of her favorite characters to life, including Little Miss Muffet and Humpty Dumpty. Portrayed by animal figures.
Prod-HARRY Dist-PHENIX 1961

Mother Gooseland B 15 MIN
2 INCH VIDEOTAPE P
See series title for descriptive statement.
From The Sounds Like Magic Series.
Prod-MOEBA Dist-GPITVL Prodn-KYNETV

Mother Infant Interaction - Feeding And Function Pleasure In The First Year Of Life B 42 MIN
16MM FILM OPTICAL SOUND
Describes relationships between types of maternal behavior and maturity of function pleasure in infants. Shows a mother and infant pair from each of seven maternal types. Includes a record of the psychological test performance of an infant.
LC NO. 70-712696
Prod-BROAXE Dist-NYU 1970

Mother Is A Mother, A C 27 MIN
3/4 INCH VIDEO CASSETTE
Documents the lives of seven black teenage mothers. Features these young women discussing their lives and shows what teenage parenting is like.
Prod-BLKFMF Dist-BLKFMF

Mother Kusters Goes To Heaven (German) C 108 MIN
16MM FILM OPTICAL SOUND
Tells how a murderer's widow tries to make sense out of her husband's seemingly pointless act. Directed by Rainer Werner Fassbinder. With English subtitles.
Prod-UNKNWN Dist-NYFLMS 1975

Mother Love B 20 MIN
16MM FILM SILENT C T
Shows the relationship between Johnny and his mother from his birth. Points out that the absence or presence of mother love influences the child's adjustment.
From The Film Studies Of The Psychoanalytic Research Project On Problems In Infancy Series.
Prod-SPITZ Dist-NYU 1952

Mother Love B 26 MIN
16MM FILM, 3/4 OR 1/2 IN VIDEO J-C A
Shows a colony of newborn rhesus monkeys as they react to unusual and inanimate mother substitutes. Demonstrates the importance of holding and nesting to a baby's well-being.
Prod-CBSNEW Dist-CAROUF

Mother Mallard's Portable Masterpiece Company C 20 MIN
3/4 OR 1/2 INCH VIDEO CASSETTE
Explores electronic music with Vito-Brunetti.
Prod-EAI Dist-EAI

Mother May I C 9 MIN
16MM FILM OPTICAL SOUND
A fantasy which portrays changing attitudes towards love and violence and the lack of communication between generations.
LC NO. 74-702475
Prod-PHOCI Dist-MMM 1968

Mother May I C 28 MIN
16MM FILM, 3/4 OR 1/2 IN VIDEO J-C A
Deals with sexuality and teenage pregnancy as seen through the eyes of an 11-year-old girl and her 16-year-old sister who thinks she is pregnant. Shows how they learn to communicate about sexuality and to act responsibly on sexual issues.
LC NO. 82-706513
Prod-SHRFUT Dist-CF 1982

Mother May I (School Version) C 24 MIN
16MM FILM, 3/4 OR 1/2 IN VIDEO J-C A
Deals with sexuality and teenage pregnancy as seen through the eyes of an 11-year-old girl and her 16-year-old sister who thinks she is pregnant. Shows how they learn to communicate about sexuality and to act responsibly on sexual issues.
Prod-SHRFUT Dist-CF 1982

Mother Necessity C 3 MIN
3/4 OR 1/2 INCH VIDEO CASSETTE P-I
Deals with common, everyday inventions, such as the light bulb, radio and television, and with their inventors.
From The America Rock Series.
Prod-ABCTV Dist-GA Prodn-SCOROC 1978

Mother Of Many Children C 58 MIN
16MM FILM, 3/4 OR 1/2 IN VIDEO H-C A
Presents Agatha Marie Goodine, an 108-year-old member of the Hobbema tribe. Contrasts her memories with the conflicts that most Indian and Inuity women face today. Traces the cycle of their lives from birth to old age in a series of sensitive vignettes.
Prod-NFBC Dist-NFBC 1977

Mother Of The Year C 30 MIN
3/4 OR 1/2 INCH VIDEO CASSETTE
Tells the story of 80-year-old Ruth Youngdahl Nelson who was arrested along with others during the Seattle blockade of the first Trident submarine in Puget Sound. Strikes a course for civil disobedience.
Prod-PLOW Dist-NFPS

Mother Rabbit's Family C 11 MIN
16MM FILM, 3/4 OR 1/2 IN VIDEO P
Draws attention to some of the characteristics of rabbits and their natural environment.
Prod-EBF Dist-EBEC 1957

Mother Teresa Of Calcutta C 51 MIN
16MM FILM, 3/4 OR 1/2 IN VIDEO J-H A
Presents an interview by Malcolm Muggeridge of Mother Teresa, a nun who was awarded the 1979 Nobel Prize. Discusses her life and her dedication to rescuing abandoned babies which exemplifies the power for good in the individual.
LC NO. 79-707430
Prod-BBCTV Dist-FI 1971

Mother Tiger, Mother Tiger C 11 MIN
16MM FILM OPTICAL SOUND
Explores a mother's struggle, despair and eventual acceptance of her multi-handicapped child.
From The Contemporary Family Series.
LC NO. 75-700458
Prod-FRACOC Dist-FRACOC 1975

Mother To Daughter C 18 MIN
16MM FILM, 3/4 OR 1/2 IN VIDEO A
Present's a mother's personal statement of love for her daughter and her hope that the child will grow up in a better world.
Prod-MARRUS Dist-PHENIX 1980

Mother To Daughter (Spanish) C 18 MIN
16MM FILM, 3/4 OR 1/2 IN VIDEO A
Presents a mother's personal statement of love for her daughter and her hope that the child will grow up in a better world.
Prod-MARRUS Dist-PHENIX 1980

Mother-Infant Interaction, Pt 1 - Forms Of Interaction At Six Weeks C 49 MIN
16MM FILM OPTICAL SOUND
Shows variations in mothers' ways of touching, holding, looking at and talking to their babies during feeding and the immediate effects of differences in handling on the infant, based on a longitudinal study of behavioral and emotional interactions during the first year of life.
Prod-BROAXE Dist-NYU

Mother-Infant Interaction, Pt 2 - Forms Of Interaction At Six Months C 42 MIN
16MM FILM OPTICAL SOUND
Shows relationships between infantile experience during feeding at six months and the development of tension tolerance. Illustrates ways in which the infant is helped to wait for food, the ways in which the mother notes his wish to take the initiative and responds to it and the ways he can be satisfied or frustrated by his feeding.
Prod-BROAXE Dist-NYU

Mother-Infant Interaction, Pt 3 - Feeding And Object Relations At One Year C 40 MIN
16MM FILM OPTICAL SOUND
Shows connections between the modes of infants' experiences with their mothers and the infants' relationships to persons and things when he is one year old. Portrays the amount of independence the mothers allow their infants and how the infants strive to enjoy feedings.
Prod-BROAXE Dist-NYU

Mother-Infant Interaction, Pt 4 - Feeding And Function-Pleasure In The First Year Of Life C 42 MIN
16MM FILM OPTICAL SOUND
Presents a small longitudinal study with samples of interaction in the feeding situation taken at six weeks, six months and one year. Illustrates seven types of mother-infant behavior and their relation to function-pleasure through seven mother-infant pairs.
Prod-BROAXE Dist-NYU

Mother-Infant Interaction, Pt 5 - Maternal Behavior And The Infant's Cathexis In The... C 41 MIN
16MM FILM OPTICAL SOUND
Illustrates the relationship between the way an infant is mothered (FED) and the development of his object cathexis - the quality and quantity of investment in the outer world. Shows seven types of mother-infant interaction at six weeks, six months and one year, followed by selections from the infants' test performances.
Prod-BROAXE Dist-NYU

Mother-Infant Interaction, Pt 6 - Resemblances In Expressive Behavior C 41 MIN
16MM FILM OPTICAL SOUND
Shows a variety of examples of mother-infant interaction in which particular modes of maternal behavior have been repeatedly available to the infant's experience during feeding. Suggests that the expressive behavior of the infant is derived largely from the maternal behavior to which he has become accustomed and accommodated himself.
Prod-BROAXE Dist-NYU

Mother, Flag And Apple Pie C 30 MIN
3/4 INCH VIDEO CASSETTE H-C A
Presents Ben Wattenberg discussing what happened to the social revolution of the 1960's. Observes that American society has undergone substantial changes in that decade, but most people still hold to surprisingly traditional values.
From The In Search Of The Real America Series.
Prod-WGBHTV Dist-KINGFT 1977

Mother, This Isn't Your Day B 21 MIN
16MM FILM OPTICAL SOUND T
Emphasizes the importance of children being given a choice of subject matter for their writing.
LC NO. 75-701394
Prod-EDC Dist-EDC 1972

Mother's / Father's Day C 15 MIN
3/4 INCH VIDEO CASSETTE P
See series title for descriptive statement.
From The Celebrate Series.
Prod-KUONTV Dist-GPITVL 1978

Mother's Bumblebees C 4 MIN
16MM FILM SILENT P-H S
Tells in American sign language a tale of farm life in 1930 involving a mother who discovers bumblebees in the family's backhouse. Signed for the deaf by Sharon Tate.
LC NO. 76-701694
Prod-JOYCE Dist-JOYCE 1975

Mother's Day 1977 C 60 MIN
3/4 OR 1/2 INCH VIDEO CASSETTE
Recounts parents' experiences with the children's involvement with Yoga.
Prod-IYOGA Dist-IYOGA

Mother's Day 1979 C 60 MIN
3/4 OR 1/2 INCH VIDEO CASSETTE
Shows the ceremonies at Satchidananda Ashram-Yogaville East on Mother's Day. Shows children and adults and the Ashram guests.
Prod-IYOGA Dist-IYOGA

Mother's Day 1981 C 30 MIN
3/4 OR 1/2 INCH VIDEO CASSETTE
Presents Sri Swami Satchidananda giving a special Mother's Day satsang on the Divine Mother.
Prod-IYOGA Dist-IYOGA

Mother's Day, 1980 C 30 MIN
3/4 INCH VIDEO CASSETTE
Shows the celebration on Mother's Day, 1980 when women gathered under one banner 'every Mother is a working Mother.'
Prod-AMELIA Dist-WMENIF

Mother's Diet And Her Baby's Future C 23 MIN
16MM FILM OPTICAL SOUND
Shows what effect the lack of protein in the diet of pregnant rats has on their offspring. States that favorable and far-reaching results of the experiment have promoted similar research in humans.
LC NO. 74-706499
Prod-USN Dist-USNAC 1969

Mother's Worry, A C 33 MIN
3/4 OR 1/2 INCH VIDEO CASSETTE C A
Presents an account of a mother as she experiences the hospitaliztion of her two-year-old son who undergoes tests with inconclusive results. Shows the emergence of the mother's anxiety and the stress which both parents and physcians feel as they struggle to communicate about the child's illness.
From The Emotional Factors Affecting Children And Parents In The Hospital Series.
LC NO. 81-707455
Prod-LRF Dist-LRF 1979

Mothers - What They Do C 11 MIN
16MM FILM, 3/4 OR 1/2 IN VIDEO P-I
Focuses on the work of three mothers, a fulltime housewife, a full-time working mother, and a part-time working mother. Shows how each mother helps provide for her family in the best way suited to the family's needs.
Prod-FILMSW Dist-FLMFR

Mothers After Divorce C 20 MIN
16MM FILM, 3/4 OR 1/2 IN VIDEO
Shows how four suburban women with high school age children deal with the changes in their lives brought on by divorce.
Prod-POLYMR Dist-POLYMR

Mothers Always Have A Reason To Be C 7 MIN
3/4 INCH VIDEO CASSETTE
Shows a mother reflecting on her children and her work.
Prod-WMEN Dist-WMEN

Mothers And Daughters C 29 MIN
3/4 INCH VIDEO CASSETTE
Looks at mother-daughter relationships.
From The Woman Series.
Prod-WNEDTV Dist-PUBTEL

Mothers Are People C 7 MIN
16MM FILM, 3/4 OR 1/2 IN VIDEO H-C A
Features a research biologist, a widow with two school-age children, expressing her own dilemmas about on-the-job discrimination and the absense of universal day care.
From The Working Mother Series.
Prod-NFBC Dist-NFBC 1974

Mothers Of Acari B 10 MIN
16MM FILM OPTICAL SOUND H-C A
Shows how Acari become one of the 200 places in northeast Brazil with modern maternity-and-child-welfare clinics.
Prod-UN Dist-UN 1954

Mothers Who Are Part Of Supportive Day Care C 29 MIN
3/4 INCH VIDEO CASSETTE J-C
Features mothers from various social, economic and ethnic backgrounds discussing their efforts to combine motherhood and jobs outside the home.
From The Are You Listening Series.
LC NO. 81-706008
Prod-STURTM Dist-STURTM 1980

Mothers Who Leave Home C 29 MIN
3/4 INCH VIDEO CASSETTE
Offers an interview with Judy Sullivan, who walked out on her marriage and wrote about it in her book. Examines the conflicts of having a home, a career, and an ambition to write.
From The Woman Series.
Prod-WNEDTV Dist-PUBTEL

Mothlight C 4 MIN
16MM FILM OPTICAL SOUND
An experimental film which presents a fluttering light collage created by pasting moth wings and bits of plants between strips of Mylar tape and running the tape through an optical printer.
LC NO. 76-712467
Prod-BRAKS Dist-FMCOOP 1971

Motility In Parent-Child Relationships B 40 MIN
16MM FILM SILENT C T
Focuses on the important role of motility in the development of personal relationships in the first year and a half of life. Stresses reciprocity between parent and child as the main theme.
Prod-MITM Dist-NYU 1959

Motility Of Entamoeba Histolytica C 4 MIN
16MM FILM OPTICAL SOUND
Presents a photomicrography of scrapings from rectal lesion of a case of amebiasis showing movement of parasites.
LC NO. 74-705171
Prod-USPHS Dist-USNAC

Motion C 9 MIN
16MM FILM OPTICAL SOUND
Portrays different aspects of the beauty, grace and capabilities of human motion.
LC NO. 76-702032
Prod-SENCOL Dist-SENCOL 1975

Motion B 45 MIN
2 INCH VIDEOTAPE C
See series title for descriptive statement.
From The Physical Science Series. Unit 4 - Motion, Work And Energy
Prod-CHITVC Dist-GPITVL Prodn-WTTWTV

Motion And Emotion - Baroque Sculpture C 29 MIN
2 INCH VIDEOTAPE
See series title for descriptive statement.
From The Museum Open House Series.
Prod-WGBHTV Dist-PUBTEL

Motion And Time - An Introduction To Einstein's Theory Of Relativity X 11 MIN
16MM FILM, 3/4 OR 1/2 IN VIDEO I-C A
Describes how the concepts of time, motion and space have changed from the time of Copernicus to that of Einstein. Explains the principles of the theory of relativity, and demonstrates that measurements of both time and space are not absolute, but are functions of motion.
Prod-SF Dist-SF 1960

Motion And Time Study B 9 MIN
16MM FILM OPTICAL SOUND
Several different motions common to industrial production are presented and analyzed by motion and time study techniques.

LC NO. FIA52-303
Prod-USC Dist-USC 1948

Motion Compensators C 17 MIN
3/4 OR 1/2 INCH VIDEO CASSETTE IND
which heave compensators for floating drilling units operate. Features the Vetco single- and dual-cylinder systems.
Prod-UTEXPE Dist-UTEXPE 1978

Motion For Directed Verdict, The B 10 MIN
16MM FILM OPTICAL SOUND
Deals with various aspects of a civil lawsuit involving an automobile accident case. Presents the motion for a directed verdict and the judgment.
From The Civil Advocates Series. No. 23
LC NO. 71-714031
Prod-ATLA Dist-RPATLF 1967

Motion Geometry C 20 MIN
3/4 INCH VIDEO CASSETTE H-C
Introduces congruence, similarity, motion geometry and symmetry.
From The Mainly Math Series.
Prod-WCVETV Dist-GPITVL 1977

Motion Offense B 11 MIN
16MM FILM OPTICAL SOUND H
Presents the fundamentals of motion offense in basketball, including the development of both individual and team skills.
LC NO. 78-701962
Prod-BKBA Dist-BKBA Prodn-BUNDYD 1975

Motion Painting, No. 1 C 11 MIN
16MM FILM OPTICAL SOUND J-C A
Shows a painting in continuous change as it is being painted, from the first stroke to the fully developed sequence of successive overlying compositions that fulfill the concept of the work.
LC NO. 72-703164
Prod-PFP Dist-CFS 1972

Motion Perception, Pt 1 - Two-Dimensional Motion Perception C 7 MIN
16MM FILM OPTICAL SOUND H-C A
Presents Professor Gunnar Johansson who demonstrates how stimuli moving in two-dimensional space are perceived by the viewer. Uses computer generated stimuli and movements of human subjects to show how motions are seen and analyzed in terms of groups and subgroups.
From The Films At The Frontiers Of Psychological Inquiry Series.
LC NO. 72-702269
Prod-HMC Dist-HMC 1971

Motion Perception, Pt 2 - Three-Dimensional Motion Perception C 11 MIN
16MM FILM OPTICAL SOUND H-C A
Presents Professor Gunnar Johansson who uses computer generated stimuli and movements of human subjects to provide the information necessary to give rise to the perception of three-dimensionality. Illustrates motion patterns, changes of size and length and specifies their resulting effects.
From The Films At The Frontiers Of Psychological Inquiry Series.
LC NO. 72-702270
Prod-HMC Dist-HMC 1971

Motion Picture C 18 MIN
16MM FILM OPTICAL SOUND
Presents Torben Ulrich, the Danish tennis player, who practices his strokes, his serve, his running and his jumps.
Prod-STATNS Dist-STATNS 1970

Motion Picture History Of The Korean War B 58 MIN
16MM FILM, 3/4 OR 1/2 IN VIDEO
Reviews the Korean War, showing the fighting and discussing the problems encountered by American and United Nations forces during the major phases of battle. Traces events, from the initial gunfire on June 25, 1950, to the armistice on July 27, 1953.
LC NO. 81-707696
Prod-USDD Dist-USNAC 1958

Motion Picture History Of The Korean War, The B 58 MIN
3/4 OR 1/2 INCH VIDEO CASSETTE
Shows Korean War fighting and problems encountered by American and U N forces during the major phases of the battle from the initial gunfire on June 25, 1950, to the armistice on July 27, 1953.
Prod-IHF Dist-IHF

Motion Pictures B 45 MIN
2 INCH VIDEOTAPE C
See series title for descriptive statement.
From The General Humanities Series. Unit 5 - Combination And Integration Of The Arts
Prod-CHITVC Dist-GPITVL Prodn-WTTWTV

Motion Pictures And The Navy C 24 MIN
16MM FILM OPTICAL SOUND
Shows the operation and responsibilities of the people concerned with the annual Navy motion picture program.
LC NO. 74-706500
Prod-USN Dist-USNAC 1971

Motion Study Applications (2nd Ed) B 22 MIN
16MM FILM OPTICAL SOUND C
Shows old and improved methods of performing such jobs as filling the pin-board, inserting papers in mailing envelopes, folding paper cartons and assembling refrigerator grids.
Prod-UIOWA Dist-UIOWA 1952

Motion Study In Action B 18 MIN
16MM FILM OPTICAL SOUND C
Shows that principles of motion economy can be applied to almost any kind of manual work.
Prod-UIOWA Dist-UIOWA 1949

Motion Study On The Job B 25 MIN
16MM FILM OPTICAL SOUND C
Examines, in detail, work methods of 12 jobs and shows how production was increased in each case by the application of method-improvement techniques.
Prod-UIOWA Dist-UIOWA 1958

Motion Study Principles (2nd Ed) B 22 MIN
16MM FILM OPTICAL SOUND C
Presents 11 principles of motion economy using three applications to illustrate the principles—bolt and washer assembly, refrigerator doorknob assembly and folding X-ray film packing papers.
Prod-UIOWA Dist-UIOWA 1952

Motions During And After Trial C 120 MIN
3/4 OR 1/2 INCH VIDEO CASSETTE PRO
Covers basic techniques for making and opposing trial motions.
Prod-CCEB Dist-ABACPE

Motions Of Attracting Bodies, The C 8 MIN
16MM FILM OPTICAL SOUND H-C A
Uses computer animation to investigate Newton's laws of motion and universal gravitation. Applies these principles to specific instances of Earth satellites and binary star systems.
From The Explorations In Space And Time Series.
LC NO. 75-703976
Prod-HMC Dist-HMC 1974

Motions Of Stars, The C 8 MIN
16MM FILM OPTICAL SOUND H-C A
Uses computer animation to examine the motions of stars in various constellations, showing the changes that will occur in periods up to 200,000 years.
From The Explorations In Space And Time Series.
LC NO. 75-703978
Prod-HMC Dist-HMC 1974

Motivating Children To Learn - Summary B 30 MIN
2 INCH VIDEOTAPE
Features Dr Dreikurs who summarizes and defines the main points of the motivating children to learn course.
From The Motivating Children To Learn Series.
Prod-VTETV Dist-GPITVL

Motivating Children To Learn—A Series

Prod-VTETV Dist-GPITVL

Changing The Child's Relationships And Goals	30 MIN
Clarification Of Basic Principles	30 MIN
Consequences, No. 2	30 MIN
Douglas	30 MIN
Edward	30 MIN
Encouragement	30 MIN
Group Discussion With Teenagers	30 MIN
Group Discussion, Pt 1	30 MIN
Group Discussion, Pt 2	30 MIN
Group Discussions	30 MIN
Learning Problem, A	30 MIN
Logical Consequences And Punishment	30 MIN
Motivating Children To Learn - Summary	30 MIN
Our Present Educational Dilemma	30 MIN
Reading Difficulties	30 MIN

Motivating Scientists And Engineers C 45 MIN
3/4 OR 1/2 INCH VIDEO CASSETTE
See series title for descriptive statement.
From The Management Of Technological Innovation Series.
Prod-MIOT Dist-MIOT

Motivating The Conservative And The Cautious Personality, Case Examples - Personalities... C 35 MIN
3/4 OR 1/2 INCH VIDEO CASSETTE
Looks at the underlying motivational forces at work in people who are of the 'steadiness' style and the 'complaint' style. Presents two vignettes which demonstrate the interaction of personalities in the four behavioral styles.
From The Personality Styles Series.
Prod-AMA Dist-AMA

Motivating The Disadvantaged C 10 MIN
3/4 OR 1/2 INCH VIDEO CASSETTE
Considers the alternatives of reward and punishment and the use of psychological rewards in motivating disadvantaged workers.
From The Supervising The Disadvantaged Series. Module 2
Prod-RESEM Dist-RESEM

Motivating The Dominant And The 'People-Oriented' Personality C 25 MIN
3/4 OR 1/2 INCH VIDEO CASSETTE
Presents data on how to manage, motivate and direct a personality style that is very dominant or very high on the persuasion-people oriented factor of 'inducement.'
From The Personality Styles Series.
Prod-AMA Dist-AMA

Motivating To Achieve Results C
3/4 OR 1/2 INCH VIDEO CASSETTE
See series title for descriptive statement.
From The Management Training Series.
Prod-THGHT Dist-DELTAK

Motivation C 16 MIN
16MM FILM OPTICAL SOUND H-C A
Considers various topics as they apply to the psychology of motivation, including instincts, motives and the major theories of motivation of Freud, Hull and Maslow.
From The Basic Psychology Series.
LC NO. 76-702922
Prod-EDMDC Dist-EDMDC Prodn-SOREND 1973

Motivation B 30 MIN
16MM FILM OPTICAL SOUND
Discusses an exciting breakthrough by the psychologists - how one set of factors operates to produce interest, enthusiasm, job satisfaction and greater productivity, and how another set of factors operates in an opposite direction to bring about job dissatisfaction, less productivity and resignations. Shows how these factors can be used by the supervisor to help his people increase their productivity and job satisfaction.
From The Success In Supervision Series.
LC NO. 74-706152
Prod-WETATV Dist-USNAC 1965

Motivation C 9 MIN
16MM FILM, 3/4 OR 1/2 IN VIDEO
Shows that there is a reason or motive for all human behavior. Points out that understanding motives can lead to a safer, more rewarding life.
From The Safety And You Series.
Prod-FILCOM Dist-FILCOM

Motivation C 25 MIN
3/4 OR 1/2 INCH VIDEO CASSETTE
See series title for descriptive statement.
From The Effective Manager Series.
Prod-DELTAK Dist-DELTAK

Motivation C 26 MIN
3/4 OR 1/2 INCH VIDEO CASSETTE C A
Features a humanistic psychologist whi, by analysis and examples, discusses motivations involved in interpersonal relationships.
From The Interpersonal Competence, Unit 03 - Motivational Series.
Prod-MVNE Dist-TELSTR 1973

Motivation B 29 MIN
16MM FILM, 3/4 OR 1/2 IN VIDEO
Depicts the driving force behind Sam Steinberg, a supermarket corporation's founder and chief executive officer. Shows how Steinberg's drive affects the more than 20,000 employees who work for the corporation.
From The Corporation Series.
Prod-NFBC Dist-NFBC 1973

Motivation C 30 MIN
3/4 OR 1/2 INCH VIDEO CASSETTE
See series title for descriptive statement.
From The Effective Supervision Series.
Prod-ERF Dist-DELTAK

Motivation B 33 MIN
3/4 INCH VIDEOTAPE
See series title for descriptive statement.
From The One Strong Link Series.
Prod-CUETV Dist-CUNIV 1971

Motivation C 41 MIN
3/4 OR 1/2 INCH VIDEO CASSETTE T
Examines and demonstrates the six cognitive principles of motivation. Includes cognitive dissonance, open communication and meaningfulness.
From The Learning And Liking It Series.
Prod-MSU Dist-MSU

Motivation - A Means To Accident Prevention C 11 MIN
16MM FILM, 3/4 OR 1/2 IN VIDEO
Shows how proper motivation prevents accidents at home and on the job. Presents the reasoning that motivates the workmen in a visually interesting manner.
From The Foremanship Training Series.
LC NO. 82-706280
Prod-USBM Dist-USNAC 1969

Motivation - It's Not Just The Money C 26 MIN
16MM FILM, 3/4 OR 1/2 IN VIDEO
Examines the factors which lead to satisfaction and productivity on the job. Takes a look at the Volvo automobile plant in Sweden.
From The Human Resources And Organizational Behavior Series.
Prod-DOCUA Dist-CNEMAG

Motivation - Making It Happen C 12 MIN
16MM FILM, 3/4 OR 1/2 IN VIDEO H-C A
Tells the story of an employee with no musical background who is assigned the duty of organizing a company band. Shows how he finds that with a positive attitude he can easily convince others to overcome their hesitations and agree to participate. Points out that confidence and self-motivation can help people motivate others to buy products, services and ideas.
Prod-BOSUST Dist-CF 1979

Motivation - Myths And Realities C 18 MIN
3/4 OR 1/2 INCH VIDEO CASSETTE
Illustrates various approaches to motivating people. Explores inspiration, initiative, following orders and cooperation.
From The Motivation And Productivity Series.
Prod-BNA Dist-BNA

Motivation - The Test Of Leadership C 20 MIN
3/4 OR 1/2 INCH VIDEO CASSETTE
Familiarizes supervisors with motivation as a qualification for sound leadership. Reviews current thinking on various theoretical and practical factors relating to motivating employees.
From The Supervisory Management Course, Pt. 1 Series. Unit 7
Prod-AMA Dist-AMA

Motivation - Why Employees Work C
3/4 OR 1/2 INCH VIDEO CASSETTE
Discusses the manager's role in motivation and the creation of an environment in which people can motivate themselves. Shows how a manager must work with employee needs, values and expectations.

From The Principles Of Management Series.
Prod-RMI Dist-RMI

Motivation And Goals C 27 MIN
2 INCH VIDEOTAPE C A
Features a humanistic psychologist who, by analysis and examples, discusses motivations and goals involved in human relationships.
From The Interpersonal Competence, Unit 03 - Motivation Series.
Prod-MVNE Dist-TELSTR 1973

Motivation And Hunger C 29 MIN
3/4 INCH VIDEO CASSETTE C A
Details factors that influence motivation. Defines concept of motivation and discusses uses of the term by psychologists.
From The Understanding Human Behavior - An Introduction To Psychology Series. Lesson 12
Prod-COAST Dist-CDTEL

Motivation And Incentives, Pt 1 C 30 MIN
3/4 OR 1/2 INCH VIDEO CASSETTE
Discusses the use of motivation and incentives as applied to managing professionals.
From The Business Of Managing Professionals Series.
Prod-KYTV Dist-KYTV 1983

Motivation And Incentives, Pt 2 C 30 MIN
3/4 OR 1/2 INCH VIDEO CASSETTE
Discusses motivation and incentives as applied to managing professionals.
From The Business Of Managing Professionals Series.
Prod-KYTV Dist-KYTV 1983

Motivation And Needs C 30 MIN
2 INCH VIDEOTAPE C A
Features a humanistic psychologist who, by analysis and examples, discusses motivations and needs involved in interpersonal relationships.
From The Interpersonal Competence, Unit 03 - Motivation Series.
Prod-MVNE Dist-TELSTR 1973

Motivation And Productivity–A Series
16MM FILM - 3/4 IN VIDEO IND
Explores behavioral science theories on motivating employees to their full potential.
Prod-BNA Dist-BNA

Behavioral Modeling 022 MIN
Effective Leadership 027 MIN
Human Nature And Organizational Realities 000 MIN
Management Of Human Assets 000 MIN
Managing Employee Morale 025 MIN
Motivation - Myths And Realities 018 MIN
Motivation In Perspective 000 MIN
Motivation Through Job Enrichment 000 MIN
Self-Motivated Achiever, The 000 MIN
Strategy For Productive Behavior 000 MIN
Theory X And Theory Y - The Work Of Douglas 000 MIN
Theory X And Theory Y - The Work Of Douglas 000 MIN
Understanding Motivation 000 MIN

Motivation And Reinforcement In Classroom C 30 MIN
16MM FILM, 3/4 OR 1/2 IN VIDEO
Demonstrates the use of the principle of motivation and reinforcement in typical classrooms.
From The Aide-ing In Education Series.
Prod-SPF Dist-SPF

Motivation And Reward In Learning B 15 MIN
16MM FILM OPTICAL SOUND C
A photographic story of experimental demonstration with white rats to illustrate the importance of motivation and reward in the learning process. Trial and error learning behavior is shown.
Prod-PSUPCR Dist-PSU 1948

Motivation And Supervision C 20 MIN
3/4 OR 1/2 INCH VIDEO CASSETTE
Shows mistakes many supervisors make when faced with on-the-job motivational problems and then shows how to avoid making them.
Prod-BBP Dist-BBP

Motivation And Team Building, Susan Pistone C
3/4 OR 1/2 INCH VIDEO CASSETTE PRO
See series title for descriptive statement.
From The Management Skills Series.
Prod-AMCEE Dist-AMCEE

Motivation For Behavior C 30 MIN
3/4 OR 1/2 INCH VIDEO CASSETTE T
Discusses the rationale behind specific behavior.
From The Developing Discipline Series.
Prod-SDPT Dist-GPITVL 1983

Motivation For Living C 29 MIN
16MM FILM OPTICAL SOUND H-C
Presents a speech by Bob Richards, twice Olympic pole vault champion. Uses excerpts and events from the worlds of sports and religion as examples of things that motivation and dedication can accomplish. Delivers a message on the urgency of these qualities in young people.
Prod-GEMILL Dist-NINEFC

Motivation For The Linear-Quadratic Problem C 73 MIN
3/4 OR 1/2 INCH VIDEO CASSETTE PRO
See series title for descriptive statement.
From The Modern Control Theory - Deterministic Optimal Linear Feedback Series.
Prod-MIOT Dist-MIOT

Motivation For The Steady-State Linear Quadratic Problem C 104 MIN
3/4 OR 1/2 INCH VIDEO CASSETTE PRO
See series title for descriptive statement.
From The Modern Control Theory - Deterministic Optimal Linear Feedback Series.
Prod-MIOT Dist-MIOT

Motivation In Perspective C 20 MIN
16MM FILM - 3/4 IN VIDEO PRO
Discusses the successful process of managing men and their jobs, using control and incentive to accomplish top quality work.
From The Motivation And Productivity Series.
Prod-BNA Dist-BNA 1969

Motivation In The Classroom C 27 MIN
3/4 OR 1/2 INCH VIDEO CASSETTE T
Presents Dr Raymond J Wlodkowski sharing specific tips with teachers on how they can maximize the learning in their classroom through motivators.
From The Successful Teaching Practices Series.
Prod-UNIDIM Dist-EBEC 1982

Motivation Theory For Teachers B 28 MIN
16MM FILM OPTICAL SOUND C
Features Dr Madeline Hunter discussing the six variables, subject to control, which influence motivation. Suggests how to apply theory in daily classroom practice.
From The Translating Theory Into Classroom Practices Series.
Prod-SPF Dist-SPF

Motivation Through Job Enrichment C 28 MIN
16MM FILM - 3/4 IN VIDEO IND
Dr Frederick Herzberg presents his motivation-hygiene theory, which calls for the restructuring of dull, routine assignments to make jobs more meaningful and rewarding to employees.
From The Motivation And Productivity Series.
Prod-BNA Dist-BNA Prodn-QUEST 1967

Motivation To Learn, The B 30 MIN
2 INCH VIDEOTAPE T
Demonstrates how to talk to youngsters and how to find out what they think. (Broadcast quality)
From The Dynamics Of Classroom Behavior Series.
Prod-VTETV Dist-GPITVL Prodn-WETKTV

Motivation To Work–A Series
16MM FILM - 3/4 IN VIDEO IND
Prod-BNA Dist-BNA 1969

ABC Man - The Manager In Mid Career 25 MIN
Building A Climate For Individual Growth 25 MIN
Job Enrichment In Action 25 MIN
Kita, Or, What Have You Done For Me Lately 25 MIN
Modern Meaning Of Efficiency, The 25 MIN

Motivation Unit C
3/4 OR 1/2 INCH VIDEO CASSETTE A
Depicts common work incidents in which motivation, or the lack of it, affects employees' behaviors and attitudes. Shows the use of feedback, reward and reinforcement as motivators and illustrates the effects of perception and expectation on behavior.
From The Management Skills For Supervisors Series.
Prod-TIMLIF Dist-TIMLIF 1984

Motivation, Coaching And Team-Building C 60 MIN
3/4 OR 1/2 INCH VIDEO CASSETTE
Demonstrates how managers can influence positive behavior for improved sales results. Includes a spectrum of five motivation types, needs and performance, goals and rewards and community and motivation.
From The Dynamics Of Sales Management Series. Session 5
Prod-PRODEV Dist-PRODEV

Motivational Selling/What Motivates You? C
3/4 OR 1/2 INCH VIDEO CASSETTE
Focuses on motivational selling and maintaining personal motivation in order to be a better salesperson. Includes clues to buyer needs, buyer's group behavior, identifying motivational slumps, personal goal setting and motivational chemistry and processes.
From The Making Of A Salesman Series. Session 6, Parts 1 and 2
Prod-PRODEV Dist-PRODEV

Motivational Sports - Positive Vibes C 10 MIN
16MM FILM, 3/4 OR 1/2 IN VIDEO H-C A
Demonstrates how to keep the momentum in a game going. Presents Coach Bill Foster showing how he does it on and off the basketball court.
From The Motivational Sports Series.
Prod-ATHI Dist-ATHI 1981

Motivational Sports - Program For Victory C 10 MIN
16MM FILM, 3/4 OR 1/2 IN VIDEO H-C A
Presents Coach Tom Osborne discussing the general motivational principles of care, understanding and the sharing of mutual goals when playing sports.
From The Motivational Sports Series.
Prod-ATHI Dist-ATHI 1981

Motivational Sports - The Winning Edge C 10 MIN
16MM FILM, 3/4 OR 1/2 IN VIDEO H-C A
Presents former U S Olympic Hockey Coach Herb Brooks discussing what it takes to lead a team to success, even against great odds.
From The Motivational Sports Series.
Prod-ATHI Dist-ATHI 1981

Motivational Sports–A Series
16MM FILM, 3/4 OR 1/2 IN VIDEO H-C A
Discusses the importance of attitude in succeeding at sports.
Prod-ATHI Dist-ATHI 1981

Motivational Sports - Positive Vibes 010 MIN
Motivational Sports - Program For Victory 010 MIN
Motivational Sports - The Winning Edge 010 MIN

Motivational Techniques For Engineers C 30 MIN
3/4 OR 1/2 INCH VIDEO CASSETTE
See series title for descriptive statement.
From The Management For Engineers Series.
Prod-UKY Dist-SME

Motives In Our Lives, The C 30 MIN
3/4 OR 1/2 INCH VIDEO CASSETTE
Presents Dr David McClelland on his studies of human motives for achievement, power and affiliation. Presents steps for developing certain types of motivation in an individual.
From The Psychology Of Human Relations Series.
Prod-MATC Dist-WFVTAE

Moto-Gaz C 8 MIN
16MM FILM, 3/4 OR 1/2 IN VIDEO
Uses animation and music to comment on air pollution, emphasizing the effect of automobile exhaust.
Prod-RADIM Dist-SF 1964

Moto-X C 29 MIN
2 INCH VIDEOTAPE
Explains that motocross is a sport for both amateurs and professionals and consists of competitive motorcycle trail riding.
From The Bayou City And Thereabouts People Show Series.
Prod-KUHTTV Dist-PUBTEL

Motor Activity Disabilities C 30 MIN
3/4 OR 1/2 INCH VIDEO CASSETTE C A
Discusses motor activity disabilities in children.
From The Characteristics Of Learning Disabilities Series.
Prod-WCVETV Dist-FI 1976

Motor Aptitude Tests And Assembly Work B 22 MIN
16MM FILM SILENT C T
Compares a subject with good motor ability with a subject of average capacity. Pictures performance on dynamoter, whipple steadiness, slot-board steadiness, metal-stylus tapping, peg-board, bolt-block and O'Connor Wiggley-block tests. Pictures the two men, after test series, at an assembly work job in which good motor ability is needed.
Prod-PSUPCR Dist-PSUPCR 1941

Motor Bike Safety Tips C 15 MIN
16MM FILM OPTICAL SOUND J-C A
Presents the basic safety rules for motorcycle riders, correlated with the safety guidelines of the National Safety Council, the National Highway Traffic Safety Administration and the Motorcycle Industry Safety Council and Education Foundation.
LC NO. 74-700623
Prod-PF Dist-PF 1973

Motor Boat Racing C 3 MIN
16MM FILM OPTICAL SOUND P-I
Discusses the sport of motor boat racing.
From The Of All Things Series.
Prod-BAILYL Dist-AVED

Motor Conduction Velocity Studies Of The Median And Ulnar Nerves C 8 MIN
16MM FILM OPTICAL SOUND
Defines the character of neuropathic lesions. Presents a method of determining the velocity in motor fibers of the median nerve in the forearm.
LC NO. 74-705173
Prod-USPHS Dist-USNAC 1966

Motor Control Centers C 8 MIN
3/4 OR 1/2 INCH VIDEO CASSETTE IND
Demonstrates recommended safety procedures for maintaining MCCs. Emphasizes need for communication among all operating and maintenance personnel.
From The Electrical Safety Series.
Prod-GPCV Dist-GPCV

Motor Development - Assessment And Intervention C 159 MIN
3/4 OR 1/2 INCH VIDEO CASSETTE
Presents a basic format by which deviations in primary and secondary motor dimensions can be quantitatively assessed for selecting a motor form of communication for children exhibiting deviant motor patterns.
From The Meeting The Communication Needs Of The Severely/Profoundly Handicapped 1981 Series.
Prod-PUAVC Dist-PUAVC

Motor Disorders Of Speech C 100 MIN
3/4 OR 1/2 INCH VIDEO CASSETTE
Reviews neuroanatomy and the hierarchies of oral communication. Discusses the diagnosis and management of persons with motor disorders.
Prod-PUAVC Dist-PUAVC

Motor Evaluation Of An Adult With Limb-Girdle Muscular Dystrophy B 35 MIN
3/4 OR 1/2 INCH VIDEO CASSETTE
Demonstrates gait, abnormalities and presents discussions of causative factors. Shows a gross motor muscle exam with the patient sitting, side-lying, supine and prone.
Prod-BU Dist-BU

Motor Learning C 11 MIN
16MM FILM OPTICAL SOUND
Teaches basic motor learning and development.
From The Coaching Development Programme Series. No. 4
LC NO. 76-701028
Prod-SARBOO Dist-SARBOO Prodn-SVL 1974

Motor Mania C 8 MIN
16MM FILM, 3/4 OR 1/2 IN VIDEO H-C A
Shows how an individual's personality may change when he gets behind the wheel of an automobile.
Prod-DISNEY Dist-WDEMCO 1953

Motor Mania (Arabic) C 8 MIN
16MM FILM, 3/4 OR 1/2 IN VIDEO H
Examines the tendency to drive aggressively. Encourages driving safely.
Prod-WDEMCO Dist-WDEMCO 1953

Motor Mania (Danish) C 8 MIN
16MM FILM, 3/4 OR 1/2 IN VIDEO H
Examines the tendency to drive aggressively. Encourages driving safely.
Prod-WDEMCO Dist-WDEMCO 1953

Motor Mania (Flemish) C 8 MIN
16MM FILM, 3/4 OR 1/2 IN VIDEO H
Examines the tendency to drive aggressively. Encourages driving safely.
Prod-WDEMCO Dist-WDEMCO 1953

Motor Mania (French) C 8 MIN
16MM FILM, 3/4 OR 1/2 IN VIDEO H
Examines the tendency to drive aggressively. Encourages driving safely.
Prod-WDEMCO Dist-WDEMCO 1953

Motor Mania (German) C 8 MIN
16MM FILM, 3/4 OR 1/2 IN VIDEO H
Examines the tendency to drive aggressively. Encourages driving safely.
Prod-WDEMCO Dist-WDEMCO 1953

Motor Mania (Greek) C 8 MIN
16MM FILM, 3/4 OR 1/2 IN VIDEO H
Examines the tendency to drive aggressively. Encourages driving safely.
Prod-WDEMCO Dist-WDEMCO 1953

Motor Mania (Japanese) C 8 MIN
16MM FILM, 3/4 OR 1/2 IN VIDEO H
Examines the tendency to drive aggressively. Encourages driving safely.
Prod-WDEMCO Dist-WDEMCO 1953

Motor Mania (Portuguese) C 8 MIN
16MM FILM, 3/4 OR 1/2 IN VIDEO H
Examines the tendency to drive aggressively. Encourages driving safely.
Prod-WDEMCO Dist-WDEMCO 1953

Motor Mania (Spanish) C 8 MIN
16MM FILM, 3/4 OR 1/2 IN VIDEO H-C
Shows how an individual's personality may change when he gets behind the wheel of an automobile.
From The Safety (Spanish) Series.
Prod-DISNEY Dist-WDEMCO 1953

Motor Mania (Swedish) C 8 MIN
16MM FILM, 3/4 OR 1/2 IN VIDEO H
Examines the tendency to drive aggressively. Encourages driving safely.
Prod-WDEMCO Dist-WDEMCO 1953

Motor Neuron Biology In Health And Disease C
3/4 INCH VIDEO CASSETTE PRO
Discusses age of onset, symptoms and progression rate of amyotrophic lateral sclerosis. Explains lower and upper motor neuron involvement in ALS, illustrates its pathology, examines muscle fiber to determine what is happening in motor neurons and gives the value of muscle biopsy in ALS. Discusses therapeutic trials of the ALS patient and presents studies describing its possible causes.
LC NO. 79-707394
Prod-NINDIS Dist-USNAC 1978

Motor Oils / Paying For College Education / Small Claims Courts C
3/4 OR 1/2 INCH VIDEO CASSETTE
Discusses various aspects of motor oils, paying for a college education and small claims courts.
From The Consumer Survival Series.
Prod-MDCPB Dist-MDCPB

Motor Patterns Of Polar Bears C 12 MIN
16MM FILM OPTICAL SOUND H-C T
Illustrates the typical motor patterns of polar bears, including swimming, walking, trotting, galloping, diving and waking. Shows the bears in their natural habitat in the Spitzbergen Island group in the Arctic near Norway. Demonstrates, through scenes photographed underwater, that the hind legs act only as a rudder while the forelegs are used for propulsion.
LC NO. 76-703729
Prod-SCHEIN Dist-PSUPCR 1965

Motor Starters (Combination And Reversing) C 60 MIN
3/4 OR 1/2 INCH VIDEO CASSETTE IND
See series title for descriptive statement.
From The Electrical Maintenance Training, Module 1 - Control Equipment Series.
Prod-LEIKID Dist-LEIKID

Motor Systems And Reflexes C 29 MIN
3/4 OR 1/2 INCH VIDEO CASSETTE PRO
Provides a background for diagnosing hyperkinetic and hypokinetic patients. Shows the procedures for examining patients for motor system disorders and lists the clues which can be found during a thorough physical examination.
Prod-PRIMED Dist-PRIMED

Motor Testing C
3/4 OR 1/2 INCH VIDEO CASSETTE
See series title for descriptive statement.
From The Physical Assessment - Neurologic System Series.
Prod-CONMED Dist-CONMED

Motor Training C 11 MIN
16MM FILM, 3/4 OR 1/2 IN VIDEO C T
Shows unique devices and exercises that stimulate the passive child to initiate activities which introduce him to a variety of sensations and experiences through which he may increase motor control.
From The Aids For Teaching The Mentally Retarded Series.
Prod-THORNE Dist-IFB 1964

Motor Training (Phase A) C 11 MIN
16MM FILM, 3/4 OR 1/2 IN VIDEO C T
Uses unique devices and special exercises to stimulate the passive child to initate activity and to help him understand cause and effect relationships.
From The Aids For Teaching The Mentally Retarded Series.
Prod-THORNE Dist-IFB 1964

Motor Vehicle Laws B 30 MIN
16MM FILM - 3/4 IN VIDEO C A
See series title for descriptive statement.
From The Sportsmanlike Driving Series.
Prod-AAAFTS Dist-GPITVL Prodn-SCETV

Motorboat Mavericks C 10 MIN
16MM FILM OPTICAL SOUND
Presents an action-filled boat derby in which five drivers wage a bitter and usually comical battle as their boats roar through swamps and by sportscaster Bill Stern.
Prod-MERMAR Dist-TELEFM

Motorcycle C 4 MIN
16MM FILM OPTICAL SOUND H-C
Presents a subjective documentary cinepoem on the female's sexual attraction to motorcycles.
Prod-CFS Dist-CFS 1968

Motorcycle Challenges - Riding Techniques C
16MM FILM OPTICAL SOUND
Shows basic motorcycle riding techniques.
LC NO. 76-702697
Prod-USAF Dist-USNAC Prodn-MRC 1975

Motorcycle Driving Tactics C 15 MIN
16MM FILM, 3/4 OR 1/2 IN VIDEO
Presents pertinent pointers for motorcylists involving excesss of speed, limitation of the bicycle and conspicuousness to the autoist. Features UCLA engineering footage in staged collisions involving motorcycles and cars.
Prod-AIMS Dist-AIMS 1971

Motorcycle Driving Tactics (Spanish) C 15 MIN
16MM FILM, 3/4 OR 1/2 IN VIDEO J-C A
Features pointers for motorcyclists involving excesses of speed. Includes staged collisions of motorcycles and automobiles.
Prod-CAHILL Dist-AIMS 1971

Motorcycle Experience, The C 15 MIN
16MM FILM OPTICAL SOUND H-C A
Dramatizes the importance of maintaining a constant awareness while riding a motorcycle.
LC NO. 76-700513
Prod-STNLYL Dist-FFORIN 1976

Motorcycle Maintenance - EZ4U C 59 MIN
1/2 IN VIDEO CASSETTE BETA/VHS
Demonstrates servicing a motorcycle and taking care of common minor repairs. Features Steve Kimball, managing editor of Cycle World Magazine.
Prod-MOHOMV Dist-MOHOMV

Motorcycle Rider Course—A Series

Prod-MOSAFE Dist-MIFE Prodn-MIFE 1976

Basic Street Riding 19 MIN
Way To Go, The 11 MIN

Motorcycle Safety C 11 MIN
16MM FILM - 3/4 IN VIDEO H-C A
Uses interviews and simulated crashes to address the issue of motorcycle safety. First shown on the CBS program 30 Minutes.
LC NO. 82-706267
Prod-CBSNEW Dist-MOKIN 1981

Motorcycle Safety C 23 MIN
16MM FILM, 3/4 OR 1/2 IN VIDEO J-C A
Provides information on motorcycles, discussing basic skills, protective clothing, safety rules, and inspection and maintenance of cycle safety equipment.
LC NO. 81-706037
Prod-CENTRO Dist-CORF 1981

Motorcycle Safety - Helmet Effectiveness C 22 MIN
16MM FILM, 3/4 OR 1/2 IN VIDEO
Discusses the role of helmets in reducing the severity of motorcycle injuries. Shows that helmets can prevent a minor accident from turning into a fatality.
LC NO. 80-707612
Prod-NHTSA Dist-USNAC Prodn-AAVS 1980

Motorcycle Safety - Sharing The Road C 14 MIN
16MM FILM, 3/4 OR 1/2 IN VIDEO J-C A
Dramatizes urban and rural traffic scenes and outlines rules for safe operation of motorcycles in traffic. Describes proper clothing and protective gear to wear while riding, reviews procedures for examining a motorcycle before riding and illustrates several potentially hazardous traffic situations.
Prod-EBEC Dist-EBEC Prodn-SMITG 1977

Motorcycle Safety Tips C 14 MIN
16MM FILM, 3/4 OR 1/2 IN VIDEO
Demonstrates a variety of basic safety rules for motorcycle riders using live-action enactments of various traffic situations.
Prod-PFP Dist-PFP 1973

Motorcycles C 29 MIN
3/4 OR 1/2 INCH VIDEO CASSETTE
Describes basic operating procedures and traffic interaction.
From The Right Way Series.
Prod-SCETV Dist-PBS 1982

Motorcycles And Helmets C 30 MIN
1/2 IN VIDEO CASSETTE BETA/VHS
Features motorcycles, helmets and cycles. Shows how to assemble a clutch. Explains the gears and flywheel.
From The Last Chance Garage Series.
Prod-WGBHTV Dist-MTI

Motors And Generators C 7 MIN
16MM FILM, 3/4 OR 1/2 IN VIDEO H-C A
Deals with dart notation and direction of current. Presents an experiment with a free-moving wire in a magnetic field. Provides a diagrammatic explanation of the motor effect. Describes the right-hand rule, the left-hand rule and the commutator.
From The Basic Electricity Series.
Prod-STFD Dist-IFB 1979

Motors And Generators, Pt 1 - DC Motors And Generators B 35 MIN
16MM FILM, 3/4 OR 1/2 IN VIDEO
Describes the construction, uses and principles governing the operation of DC motors and generators.
Prod-USA Dist-USNAC 1961

Motors And Generators, Pt 2 - AC Motors And Generators B 25 MIN
16MM FILM, 3/4 OR 1/2 IN VIDEO
Describes the design, characteristics and operation of AC generators and motors. Issued in 1961 as a motion picture.
LC NO. 79-708126
Prod-USA Dist-USNAC

Motors, Pt 1 C 22 MIN
3/4 OR 1/2 INCH VIDEO CASSETTE IND
Gives a history of motors. Explains the differences between AC and DC currents. Gives nine items required to completely identify a motor.
Prod-TAT Dist-TAT

Motors, Pt 1 (Spanish) C 22 MIN
3/4 OR 1/2 INCH VIDEO CASSETTE IND
Gives a history of motors. Explains the differences between AC and DC currents. Gives nine items required to completely identify a motor.
Prod-TAT Dist-TAT

Motors, Pt 2 C 22 MIN
3/4 OR 1/2 INCH VIDEO CASSETTE IND
Defines NEMA. Covers three phase current and induced current in a rotor. Discusses enclosures, mountings, and insulations.
Prod-TAT Dist-TAT

Motors, Pt 2 (Spanish) C 22 MIN
3/4 OR 1/2 INCH VIDEO CASSETTE IND
Defines NEMA. Covers three phase current and induced current in a rotor. Discusses enclosures, mountings, and insulations.
Prod-TAT Dist-TAT

Motors, Tape 1 - Introduction, Motor Disassembly, Testing Bearings C 60 MIN
3/4 OR 1/2 INCH VIDEO CASSETTE IND
See series title for descriptive statement.
From The Electrical Equipment Maintenance Series.
Prod-ITCORP Dist-ITCORP

Motors, Tape 1 - Introduction, Motor-Disassembly, Testing Bearings (Spanish) C 60 MIN
3/4 OR 1/2 INCH VIDEO CASSETTE IND
See series title for descriptive statement.
From The Electrical Equipment Maintenance (Spanish) Series.
Prod-ITCORP Dist-ITCORP

Motors, Tape 2 - Bearing Replacement, C 60 MIN
3/4 OR 1/2 INCH VIDEO CASSETTE IND
See series title for descriptive statement.
From The Electrical Equipment Maintenance Series.
Prod-ITCORP Dist-ITCORP

Motors, Tape 2 - Bearing Replacement, Cleaning (Spanish) C 60 MIN
3/4 OR 1/2 INCH VIDEO CASSETTE IND
See series title for descriptive statement.
From The Electrical Equipment Maintenance (Spanish) Series.
Prod-ITCORP Dist-ITCORP

Motors, Tape 3 - Slip Rings, Brushes, Single Phase, Centrifugal Switch And Capacitor C 60 MIN
3/4 OR 1/2 INCH VIDEO CASSETTE IND
See series title for descriptive statement.
From The Electrical Equipment Maintenance Series.
Prod-ITCORP Dist-ITCORP

Motors, Tape 3 - Slip Rings, Brushes, Single-Phase, Centrifugal Switch And Capacitor... C 60 MIN
3/4 OR 1/2 INCH VIDEO CASSETTE IND
Complete title reads Motors, Tape 3 - Slip Rings, Brushes, Single Phase, Centrifugal Switch And Capacitor (Spanish). Provides training in electrical equipment maintenance.
From The Electrical Equipment Maintenance (Spanish) Series.
Prod-ITCORP Dist-ITCORP

Motors, Tape 4 - DC Motors Commutator Maintenance, Brushes, Brush Holders C 60 MIN
3/4 OR 1/2 INCH VIDEO CASSETTE IND
See series title for descriptive statement.
From The Electrical Equipment Maintenance Series.
Prod-ITCORP Dist-ITCORP

Motors, Tape 4 - DC Motors Commutator-Maintenance, Brushes, Brush Holders (Spanish) C 60 MIN
3/4 OR 1/2 INCH VIDEO CASSETTE IND

See series title for descriptive statement.
From The Electrical Equipment Maintenance (Spanish) Series.
Prod-ITCORP Dist-ITCORP

Motors, Tape 5 - Troubleshooting C 60 MIN
3/4 OR 1/2 INCH VIDEO CASSETTE IND
See series title for descriptive statement.
From The Electrical Equipment Maintenance Series.
Prod-ITCORP Dist-ITCORP

Motors, Tape 5 - Troubleshooting (Spanish) C 60 MIN
3/4 OR 1/2 INCH VIDEO CASSETTE IND
See series title for descriptive statement.
From The Electrical Equipment Maintenance (Spanish) Series.
Prod-ITCORP Dist-ITCORP

Motorweek-A Series

Features two extensive road tests of new import and domestic cars plus spy photos and artist renderings of future car models. Presents practical auto maintenance segments and reports on interesting new tools and automotive gadgets. Issued weekly.
Prod-MDCPB Dist-MDCPB

Motu, The Sentinel C 11 MIN
16MM FILM OPTICAL SOUND I-H
Tells the story of a young boy who, in trying to defend his land from the hated enemy, comes to realize the strength of friendship.
LC NO. FIA67-501
Prod-TAHARA Dist-CINEPC 1967

Moulay Idriss B 11 MIN
16MM FILM OPTICAL SOUND
Records the journey of the Moslem pilgrims who were unable to travel to Mecca as they converge on this holy meeting place in Morocco where the faithful may come and receive exoneration.
Prod-FILIM Dist-RADIM

Moulds We Live With, The C 22 MIN
16MM FILM, 3/4 OR 1/2 IN VIDEO
Provides examples of common moulds to which people are exposed constantly, such as aspergillus, penicillium and fusarium which can be both benefactor and enemy.
Prod-UTORMC Dist-UTORMC

Mount Desert C 21 MIN
16MM FILM - 3/4 IN VIDEO
Documents activities on Mount Desert, a resort island off the coast of Maine, and shows the reactions and feelings of its residents. Issued in 1969 as a motion picture.
LC NO. 79-706140
Prod-USNPS Dist-USNAC 1979

Mount Mc Kinley - The Land Eternal C 24 MIN
16MM FILM - 3/4 IN VIDEO
Traces the interdependence of life through the seasons in the subarctic region of Alaska.
LC NO. 79-706141
Prod-USNPS Dist-USNAC Prodn-PENDLP 1979

Mount McKinley Hang Glide C 19 MIN
16MM FILM, 3/4 OR 1/2 IN VIDEO J-C
Tells the story of four young Americans who attempted a hang gliding flight from the top of Alaska's Mount McKinley.
LC NO. 79-706597
Prod-ABCSRT Dist-MTI 1978

Mount Parnassus - Raphael, Paintings Of Mythology C 45 MIN
2 INCH VIDEOTAPE
See series title for descriptive statement.
From The Humanities Series. Unit II - The World Of Myth And Legend
Prod-WTTWTV Dist-GPITVL

Mount Rushmore C
3/4 OR 1/2 INCH VIDEO CASSETTE P-J
Introduces children to one of man's artworks on nature. Narrated by Burgess Meredith.
Prod-CNVID Dist-KTVID

Mount Snow Ski Week, The C 19 MIN
3/4 INCH VIDEO CASSETTE
Illustrates a week of skiing and nightlife at Mount Snow, a Vermont winter resort. Shows both skiing lessons and entertainment.
Prod-MSSKI Dist-MTP

Mount St Mary's College C 5 MIN
16MM FILM OPTICAL SOUND J-H A
Depicts Mount St Mary's College in Emmitsburg, Maryland, the second oldest Catholic college in the United States. Explains that the college has a pleasant 1200-acre campus and a co-ed student body of 1200.
Prod-CAMPF Dist-CAMPF

Mount Trashmore C 4 MIN
16MM FILM OPTICAL SOUND
Discusses the solid-waste disposal problem facing many communities. Shows how Virginia Beach, Virginia, solved it by combining its trash with that from neighboring communities to build a large sanitary landfill on top of the ground. Shows how the landfill will be used as a recreational area when completed.
LC NO. 75-700687
Prod-USEPA Dist-USNAC 1974

Mount Vernon Blacks C 30 MIN
3/4 OR 1/2 INCH VIDEO CASSETTE
Prod-RCOMTV Dist-SYLWAT 1983

Mountain And Desert Survival - Desert Survival C 31 MIN
16MM FILM OPTICAL SOUND
Outlines principles of desert survival. Shows procedures for promoting rescue and maintaining personnel health and comfort. Points out sources of food and water, explains shelter construction and discusses use of signal fires and mirrors. Emphasizes the importance of calmness and clear thinking.
LC NO. FIE63-66
Prod-USAF Dist-USNAC 1963

Mountain And Desert Survival - Mountain Survival C 28 MIN
16MM FILM OPTICAL SOUND
Outlines principles of survival in mountainous regions, describing procedures for promoting rescue and maintaining personal health and comfort. Shows how to obtain food and water, construct a shelter and build signal fires. Emphasizes the necessity of calmness and clear thinking.
LC NO. 75-700795
Prod-USAF Dist-USNAC 1963

Mountain Awakens, The C 30 MIN
3/4 OR 1/2 INCH VIDEO CASSETTE
Highlights the sport of down-hill skiing, the selection and use of equipment and apparel. Demonstrates the basics of starting, steering and stopping on skis.
From The Alpine Ski School Series.
Prod-PBS Dist-PBS 1983

Mountain Community Of The Himalayas C 11 MIN
16MM FILM - 3/4 IN VIDEO P-I
Presents the story of a way of life in one of the many villages in the Himalaya Mountains that rise high above India. Explains why people live in the mountains, how and why they trade with the people in the lowlands. Shows a typical community hard at work weaving wool, making clothing, planting and harvesting at household tasks and at play.
Prod-ATLAP Dist-ATLAP 1964

Mountain Dance C 12 MIN
16MM FILM OPTICAL SOUND
Attempts to fuse dancing and nature and fit the choreography and filming to the natural element.
LC NO. 76-703248
Prod-CANFDC Dist-CANFDC 1975

Mountain Dew C 30 MIN
3/4 OR 1/2 INCH VIDEO CASSETTE H-C A
Shows how to master various banjo fingering exercises and presents the song Mountain Dew.
From The Bluegrass Banjo (Level One) Series.
Prod-OWL Dist-GPITVL 1980

Mountain Does It For Me, The C 12 MIN
16MM FILM - 3/4 IN VIDEO J-C A
Describes the skiing program for cerebral palsied children which is sponsored by the Children's Hospital in Denver, Colorado.
LC NO. 81-707255
Prod-OAKCRK Dist-CRYSP 1981

Mountain Driving C 20 MIN
16MM FILM OPTICAL SOUND J-C A
Uses cartoon sequences and scenes of narrow, winding roads to demonstrate problems of mountain driving. Discusses acceleration, passing, turnouts, overheating, parking, high altitude, soft shoulders, deceleration and curves.
LC NO. FIA66-1686
Prod-MCKINY Dist-AVED 1964

Mountain Family In Europe C 9 MIN
16MM FILM, 3/4 OR 1/2 IN VIDEO K-P
Contrasts farming in the United States with the traditional style of farming carried on by an Alpine family. Includes scenes of the family members as they milk, make butter and cheese, bake bread, and reap and dry the hay.
Prod-IFFB Dist-FI 1972

Mountain Farmer B 9 MIN
16MM FILM - 3/4 IN VIDEO
Pays tribute to a strong and independent mountaineer, Lee Banks, on his small mountain farm.
Prod-APPAL Dist-APPAL 1973

Mountain Flowers C 15 MIN
16MM FILM, 3/4 OR 1/2 IN VIDEO
Shows the great variety of flowers found in the Rocky Mountains.
Prod-WESTWN Dist-WESTWN

Mountain Flying C 23 MIN
16MM FILM, 3/4 OR 1/2 IN VIDEO A
Shows expert pilots demonstrating mountain flying, and notes how terrain offers special challenges. Urges pilots to know their aircraft capabilities and special peculiarities of local terrain and weather.
Prod-FAAFL Dist-USNAC

Mountain Forests C 15 MIN
16MM FILM, 3/4 OR 1/2 IN VIDEO I-H
Portrays a variety of mountain forests, from straggling spruce at timberline to dense stands of both coniferous and deciduous trees in the valleys below. Shows how the forests harbor the greatest number of plants and animals to be found in the Rockies.
From The Mountain Habitat Series.
Prod-KARVF Dist-BCNFL 1982

Mountain Fun C 13 MIN
16MM FILM OPTICAL SOUND
Shows the famous Cog railway to the top of Pike's Peak with the Manitou Incline, the Royal Gorge and Garden of the Gods.
From The Travelbug Series.
Prod-SFI Dist-SFI

Mountain Glaciers C 19 MIN
16MM FILM OPTICAL SOUND C A
Shows the formation and composition of mountain glaciers. Discusses movement patterns and glacial effects on land surfaces. Pictures Glacier Bay in Alasska, the Tasman Valley in New Zealand and the Victoria Mountains in America.
LC NO. FIA67-502
Prod-OSUMPD Dist-OSUMPD 1966

Mountain Gorilla C 16 MIN
16MM FILM OPTICAL SOUND C T
An intensive year-long behavior study shows the environment, behavior characteristics and social organizations of the mountain gorilla in his natural habitat in central Africa.
LC NO. 76-701855
Prod-NSF Dist-PSUPCR Prodn-CARPC 1959

Mountain Habitat-A Series
16MM FILM, 3/4 OR 1/2 IN VIDEO I-H
Illustrates mountain habitats in North America, including timber line, glaciers, high mountain country rivers in the Rockies, and mountain forests.
Prod-KARVF Dist-BCNFL 1982

Glacier Country	016 MIN
High Country	016 MIN
Mountain Forests	015 MIN
Rivers Of The Rockies	016 MIN
Timberline	016 MIN

Mountain Heritage - The Appalachians C 29 MIN
16MM FILM, 3/4 OR 1/2 IN VIDEO J-C
Explains that the theory of plate tectonics does not explain some very old mountain belts, notably the Appalachians. Suggests that long before the continents there was a possibility of plate movements.
From The Planet Of Man Series.
Prod-OECA Dist-FI 1976

Mountain In The Mist C 29 MIN
3/4 INCH VIDEO CASSETTE
Demonstrates painting a landscape to teach aerial perspective.
From The Artist At Work Series.
Prod-UMITV Dist-UMITV 1973

Mountain Is Yours, The C 30 MIN
3/4 OR 1/2 INCH VIDEO CASSETTE
Presents instruction in down-hill skiing techniques. Shows the step turn and gives a brief review of the Alpine Ski School series.
From The Alpine Ski School Series.
Prod-PBS Dist-PBS 1983

Mountain Life Zone Communities C 21 MIN
16MM FILM, 3/4 OR 1/2 IN VIDEO I-J
Shows how the rapidly changing elevation of the Rocky Mountains drastically affects living conditions, creating distinct life zones. Examines the grassland, deciduous forest, coniferous forest, and alpine-arctic zones.
LC NO. 81-706473
Prod-BERLET Dist-IFB 1976

Mountain Life Zones C 20 MIN
3/4 OR 1/2 INCH VIDEO CASSETTE J-C A
Demonstrates how a series of distinct life zones are passed in travelling up the side of a tall mountain. Explains that temperatures, soil moisture and rainfall govern the life zones and provide insights into determining the effects of the physical environment.
LC NO. 82-706780
Prod-AWSS Dist-AWSS 1982

Mountain Man C 98 MIN
16MM FILM, 3/4 OR 1/2 IN VIDEO P-J
Documents the story of Palan Clark's successful fight to save a magnificent wilderness and its animals. Reveals that he learns from naturalist John Muir the need to save the land from ruthless destruction and goes to Washington to win President Lincoln's support for his momentous cause.
Prod-LUF Dist-LUF 1979

Mountain Men C 15 MIN
16MM FILM, 3/4 OR 1/2 IN VIDEO I
Studies the people who roamed the wilderness in the mid-1800's. Compares the lives of white trappers and hunters with those of the Indians. Re-creates scenes from the trappers' annual get-together.
From The American Scrapbook Series.
Prod-WVIZTV Dist-GPITVL 1977

Mountain Men, The C 100 MIN
16MM FILM OPTICAL SOUND
Follows two trappers who try to survive natural dangers and the dwindling beaver trade. Stars Charlton Heston.
Prod-CPC Dist-SWANK

Mountain Men, The B 15 MIN
16MM FILM, 3/4 OR 1/2 IN VIDEO I-J
Dramatizes the role of the fur trappers as explorers and trailblazers in the Westward Expansion of the United States. Shows early water routes, winter camp, spring trapping and trading activities. A short version of 'FUR TRAPPERS WESTWARD.'
Prod-BARR Dist-BARR 1964

Mountain Men, The C 16 MIN
16MM FILM, 3/4 OR 1/2 IN VIDEO I-H
Discusses the mountain men as an important force in the growth and development of America's West. Explains how these trappers learned to survive in the wilderness, discovered trails through the Rocky Mountains, trapped beaver and helped pioneers cross over to the farmland of Oregon and California. Examines the circumstances that led to the movement of trappers to the wilderness.
From The Growth Of America's West Series.
Prod-CAPFLM Dist-PHENIX 1979

Mountain Monarchs C 26 MIN
16MM FILM, 3/4 OR 1/2 IN VIDEO

Shows Alpine animals in a severe and unpredictable mountain habitat. Presents the four wild sheep of North America as well as the development of the Golden Eagle chick.
Prod-STOUFP Dist-STOUFP

Mountain Music C 9 MIN
16MM FILM, 3/4 OR 1/2 IN VIDEO
Tells how the serenity of the forest is broken by the arrival of three country/rock musicians, who proceed to transform the environment into a screaming sea of electronics and amplifiers.
Prod-VINTN Dist-PFP

Mountain Music Of Peru C 60 MIN
16MM FILM, 3/4 OR 1/2 IN VIDEO A
Portrays the musical culture of the Andes, its importance to its people, its origin, and its function in preserving Indian cultural identity.
Prod-CNEMAG Dist-CNEMAG 1984

Mountain Of The Goddess C 25 MIN
16MM FILM, 3/4 OR 1/2 IN VIDEO
Features a young Yak herder who has spent his life, as his family did before him, surviving on the high altitude grasslands of the Great Himalaya Mountains, depending entirely on the Yak for milk, meat, clothes and transport.
From The Land Of The Dragon Series.
Prod-NOMDFI Dist-LANDMK

Mountain Park C 14 MIN
16MM FILM OPTICAL SOUND
Considers the history of the area surrounding Banff National Park in Alberta, Canada.
From The Journal Series.
LC NO. 75-704324
Prod-FIARTS Dist-CANFDC 1973

Mountain People C 52 MIN
16MM FILM OPTICAL SOUND
Documents the lifestyle of older mountain farmers in rural West Virginia.
LC NO. 78-701268
Prod-FIRESC Dist-CINEMV 1978

Mountain People C 14 MIN
16MM FILM, 3/4 OR 1/2 IN VIDEO I-H A
Describes the force of tradition in the Swiss village of Guarda. Tells how a hardworking group of people, insulated from the outside world, have shaped and retained their harmonious way of life in the steep mountains. Compares the Gurungs of Nepal, living on the slopes of the Himalaya Mountains, whose culture has endured with little change for centuries.
From The Places People Live Series.
Prod-CLAIB Dist-SF 1970

Mountain People, The C 24 MIN
16MM FILM, 3/4 OR 1/2 IN VIDEO J-C A
Tells how the mountain folk of Appalachia retain their pride and humor as they cling to their own customs. Explains that they are also becoming aware of the causes of their poverty.
Prod-GRANDA Dist-WOMBAT

Mountain Peoples Of Central Asi (Afghanistan)–A Series

Pictures without narration the daily activities of the mountain peoples of Badakhstan, in Northeastern Afghanistan, in a series of 14 single concept films.
Prod-IFF Dist-IFF

Baking Oven Bread (Tajik)	011 MIN
Baking Unleavened Bread (Pushtu)	010 MIN
Boy's Games (Pushtu)	005 MIN
Building A Bridge (Tajik)	010 MIN
Buzkashi (Afghan Tribes)	008 MIN
Casting Iron Plow Shares (Tajik)	011 MIN
Grinding Wheat (Tajik)	007 MIN
Making Felt Rugs (Pushtu)	009 MIN
Making Gunpowder (Tajik)	010 MIN
Men's Dance (Pushtu)	011 MIN
Pottery Making (Tajik)	015 MIN
Shearing Yaks (Tajik)	009 MIN
Threshing Wheat (Tajik)	009 MIN
Weaving Cloth (Pushtu)	009 MIN

Mountain Peoples Of Central Asia–A Series
P-C A
Prod-IFF Dist-IFF 1972

Baking Oven Bread - Tajik	011 MIN
Baking Unleavened Bread - Pushtu	010 MIN
Boy's Games - Pushtu	005 MIN
Building A Bridge - Tajik	010 MIN
Buzkashi - Afghan Tribes	008 MIN
Casting Iron Plow Shares - Tajik	011 MIN
Grinding Wheat - Tajik	007 MIN
Making Felt Rugs - Pushtu	009 MIN
Making Gunpowder - Tajik	010 MIN
Men's Dance - Pushtu	011 MIN
Pottery Making - Tajik	015 MIN
Shearing Yaks - Tajik	009 MIN
Threshing Wheat - Tajik	009 MIN
Weaving Cloth - Pushtu	009 MIN

Mountain Rescue C 14 MIN
16MM FILM, 3/4 OR 1/2 IN VIDEO
Demonstrates basic mountain rescue techniques.
From The Outdoor Education Mountaineering Series.
Prod-MORLAT Dist-SF 1973

Mountain Rescue Workers C 5 MIN
16MM FILM, 3/4 OR 1/2 IN VIDEO
Shows the operation of a typical German rescue effort following an avalanche.
From The European Studies - Germany Series. Part 18
Prod-BAYER Dist-IFB 1973

Mountain Silence C 18 MIN
16MM FILM - 3/4 IN VIDEO P-C A
Shows hearing-impaired young people participating in many outdoor summer and winter activities at Mountain Silence, a camp school for the deaf in the Rocky Mountains.
Prod-FLMRAN Dist-CRYSP

Mountain Songs, Pt 1 C 15 MIN
3/4 OR 1/2 INCH VIDEO CASSETTE P
Reviews the meaning of the terms refrain and ballad. Presents the songs She'll Be Coming Round The Mountain, Springfield Mountain and Down In The Valley.
From The Song Sampler Series.
LC NO. 81-707029
Prod-JCITV Dist-GPITVL 1981

Mountain Songs, Pt 2 C 15 MIN
3/4 OR 1/2 INCH VIDEO CASSETTE P
Reviews the meaning of the terms refrain and ballad. Presents the songs She'll Be Coming Round The Mountain, Springfield Mountain and Down In The Valley.
From The Song Sampler Series.
LC NO. 81-707029
Prod-JCITV Dist-GPITVL 1981

Mountain Springtime C 25 MIN
16MM FILM OPTICAL SOUND
Features the Canadian Rockies, showing the game and flowers of the area.
LC NO. 76-702450
Prod-MACBLO Dist-MACBLO Prodn-TOMWLF 1975

Mountain States, The C 25 MIN
16MM FILM, 3/4 OR 1/2 IN VIDEO I-J
Looks at the characteristics of the mountain states Colorado, Idaho, Montana, Nevada, Utah and Wyoming which make up one-fourth of the continental United States, yet contain less than four percent of the population.
From The United States Geography Series.
Prod-NGS Dist-NGS 1983

Mountain Tops C 27 MIN
16MM FILM, 3/4 OR 1/2 IN VIDEO I-C A
Presents the story of a paraplegic who adapts traditional mountain-climbing gear in order to scale a 13,000-foot peak in the High Sierras.
LC NO. 81-706891
Prod-STNLYL Dist-PFP 1981

Mountain Water - A Key To Survival C 16 MIN
3/4 OR 1/2 INCH VIDEO CASSETTE I
Deals with the management of water in mountain regions, including dams, reservoirs, treatment plants and the process of terracing.
From The Natural Science Specials Series. Module Blue
Prod-UNPRO Dist-AITECH 1973

Mountain Waters C 16 MIN
16MM FILM OPTICAL SOUND I-J
Shows how lakes are formed in the high mountains of the northwestern United States.
Prod-MMP Dist-MMP 1958

Mountain, The C 12 MIN
16MM FILM OPTICAL SOUND
Presents an animated allegory about a town with a problem and the eventual solution to the problem, emphasizing the danger of overreaction and hindsight.
LC NO. 79-700729
Prod-FWP Dist-FMSP 1979

Mountain's Domain, A C 20 MIN
16MM FILM OPTICAL SOUND J-C A
Shows the attractions of the area in Northeastern Australia known as the Gold Coast. Highlights the natural beauty of the coast as well as the inland rain forests. Features interviews with farmers, fishermen and those who serve the needs of the numerous tourists.
LC NO. 78-701232
Prod-FLMAUS Dist-AUIS 1976

Mountaineering C 10 MIN
16MM FILM OPTICAL SOUND J-H
Stresses safety precautions in rock climbing at a Rocky Mountain camp.
LC NO. FIA67-5614
Prod-MANSPR Dist-SCHMUN 1967

Mountainous Land C 20 MIN
3/4 INCH VIDEO CASSETTE I
Presents a study of peaks, timberline, mountain passes and valleys. Looks at a zinc mine deep in the Rockies, a ski resort and climbers on Mt Everest.
From The Understanding Our World, Unit II - Geography We Should Know Series.
Prod-KRMATV Dist-GPITVL

Mountains C 9 MIN
16MM FILM, 3/4 OR 1/2 IN VIDEO P-J
Presents the geography of mountains–differences between mountain peaks, ranges and systems, map symbols for mountains, the effect of mountains on the weather and mountain plant and animal life.
Prod-IU Dist-IU 1967

Mountains C 30 MIN
3/4 OR 1/2 INCH VIDEO CASSETTE
Explores the relationship between what people know, see and do and the mountains around them.
From The Land And The People Series.
Prod-EKC Dist-MDCPB

Mountains - A First Film C 9 MIN
16MM FILM, 3/4 OR 1/2 IN VIDEO P-I
Shows the variety of relationships between altitude, climate and life forms that exists as we descend from desert at the mountain base through forests and meadows to the tops of high mountains covered with snow and ice. Includes an introduction to the basic causes and effects of erosion and shows how mountain snows and streams help provide our water supply.
Prod-BFA Dist-PHENIX 1969

Mountains - A First Film (French) C 9 MIN
16MM FILM, 3/4 OR 1/2 IN VIDEO P-I
Shows the variety of relationships between altitude, climate and life forms that exists as we descend from desert at the mountain base through forests and meadows to the tops of high mountains covered with snow and ice. Includes an introduction to the basic causes and effects of erosion and shows how mountain snows and streams help to provide our water supply.
Prod-BFA Dist-PHENIX 1969

Mountains - Hermit Kingdom, Tourist Paradise C 30 MIN
3/4 INCH VIDEO CASSETTE
See series title for descriptive statement.
From The Of Earth And Man Series.
Prod-MDCPB Dist-MDCPB

Mountains - The Challenge Of The Slope C 30 MIN
3/4 INCH VIDEO CASSETTE
See series title for descriptive statement.
From The Of Earth And Man Series.
Prod-MDCPB Dist-MDCPB

Mountains And Mountain Building C 15 MIN
16MM FILM, 3/4 OR 1/2 IN VIDEO J
Examines the forces that shape mountains.
From The Natural Phenomena Series.
Prod-JOU Dist-JOU Prodn-GLDWER 1981

Mountains And Mountain Building - Nature's High Rise C 19 MIN
3/4 OR 1/2 INCH VIDEO CASSETTE I
Explores various kinds of mountain building and considers the theories of isostasy and continental drift.
From The Natural Science Specials Series. Module Green
Prod-UNPRO Dist-AITECH 1973

Mountains And Volcanoes B 15 MIN
2 INCH VIDEOTAPE P
Acquaints children with the great forces below the earth's surface contributing to the earth's changing features. (Broadcast quality)
From The Land And Sea Series.
Prod-TTOIC Dist-GPITVL Prodn-WGBHTV

Mountains Are For Painting C 29 MIN
3/4 INCH VIDEO CASSETTE
Demonstrates how to draw landscapes by the highlighting of shadows, lights and texture.
From The Artist At Work Series.
Prod-UMITV Dist-UMITV 1973

Mountains Don't Care C 20 MIN
16MM FILM OPTICAL SOUND J A
Two young people go on a mountain climbing expedition with an experienced older couple and learn many rules for safety in the mountains.
Prod-MTRES Dist-RARIG 1958

Mountains, The (3rd Ed) C 14 MIN
16MM FILM, 3/4 OR 1/2 IN VIDEO I-J
Live action photography and graphics show mountain formations and the effects of glacial erosion. Close-up photography pictures cascading streams and flowered meadows, and the plants and animals found in forests, rock slides, slopes and other mountain habitats.
Prod-BARR Dist-BARR 1970

Mounting An Electrocardiogram C 6 MIN
1/2 IN VIDEO CASSETTE BETA/VHS
Explains how to mount EKG strips for reading.
Prod-RMI Dist-RMI

Mounting And Casts In A Semi-Adjustable Articulator And Use Of Bite Planes C 14 MIN
3/4 OR 1/2 INCH VIDEO CASSETTE
Shows a step-by-step procedure for mounting of casts in a Hanau semi-adjustable articulator using a conventional face bow and check bites.
Prod-VADTC Dist-AMDA 1970

Mounting And Dressing Of Grinding Wheels C 14 MIN
16MM FILM, 3/4 OR 1/2 IN VIDEO IND
Demonstrates correct procedures for mounting, truing, balancing and dressing of grinding wheels.
From The Vocational Skillfilms - Machine Shop Skills Series.
Prod-RTBL Dist-RTBL 1982

Mounting And Dressing Of Grinding Wheels (Portuguese) C
16MM FILM, 3/4 OR 1/2 IN VIDEO A
Presents correct procedures for mounting, truing, balancing and dressing of grinding wheels. Available in Spanish, too.
From The Vocational Skillfilms - Machine Shop Skills Series.
Prod-RTBL Dist-RTBL

Mounting And Dressing Of Grinding Wheels (Spanish) C
16MM FILM, 3/4 OR 1/2 IN VIDEO A
Presents correct procedures for mounting, truing, balancing and dressing of grinding wheels. Available in Portuguese as well.
From The Vocational Skillfilms - Machine Shop Skills Series.
Prod-RTBL Dist-RTBL

Mounting And Truing In The 4-Jaw Independent Chuck C 15 MIN
3/4 OR 1/2 INCH VIDEO CASSETTE

See series title for descriptive statement.
From The Machine Technology I - Basic Machine Technology Series.
Prod-CAMB Dist-CAMB

Mounting And Truing Work In The 4-Jaw Independent Chuck C
3/4 OR 1/2 INCH VIDEO CASSETTE
See series title for descriptive statement.
From The Basic Engine Lathe Series.
Prod-VTRI Dist-VTRI

Mounting and Truing Work In The 4-Jaw Independent Chuck C 15 MIN
3/4 OR 1/2 INCH VIDEO CASSETTE IND
See series title for descriptive statement.
From The Machining And The Operation Of Machine Tools, Module 2 - Engine Lathe Series.
Prod-LEIKID Dist-LEIKID

Mounting And Truing Work In The 4-Jaw Independent Chuck (Spanish) C
3/4 OR 1/2 INCH VIDEO CASSETTE
See series title for descriptive statement.
From The Basic Engine Lathe (Spanish) Series.
Prod-VTRI Dist-VTRI

Mounting Of Casts In Semi-Adjustable Articulator And Use Of Bite Planes C 14 MIN
16MM FILM OPTICAL SOUND
Shows a step-by-step procedure for mounting a cast in a hanau semi-adjustable articulator using a conventional face bow and cheek bites. Demonstrates adjustment and function of a maxillary bite plane since the use of such appliances often is indicated prior to determination of optimal jaw relations.
LC NO. 74-705175
Prod-USVA Dist-USNAC 1970

Mounting, Facing, And Turning C 20 MIN
3/4 OR 1/2 INCH VIDEO CASSETTE IND
Discusses the procedure to mount with a universal chuck and collets. Gives the method for straight turning with a universal chuck.
From The Introduction To Machine Technology, Module 2 Series.
Prod-LEIKID Dist-LEIKID

Mourning For Mangatopi C 56 MIN
16MM FILM, 3/4 OR 1/2 IN VIDEO
Details a pukamani mortuary ceremony held by the Tiwi tribe of Melville Island - one of the grandest and most colorful Aboriginal ceremonies.
From The Australian Institute Of Aboriginal Studies Series.
Prod-AUSIAS Dist-UCEMC 1977

Mouse And The Motorcycle, The C 14 MIN
16MM FILM OPTICAL SOUND P-I
Presents an adaptation of Beverly Cleary's children's story The Mouse And The Motorcycle.
Prod-PPIPER Dist-PPIPER 1978

Mouse And The Motorcycle, The C 15 MIN
3/4 OR 1/2 INCH VIDEO CASSETTE I
Tells the story of a mouse who craves adventure and danger. From the story by Beverly Cleary.
From The Book Bird Series.
Prod-CTI Dist-CTI

Mouse Morning C 7 MIN
16MM FILM, 3/4 OR 1/2 IN VIDEO K-P
Presents an animated film featuring mice colored improbable shades of blue, green and red, who have difficulty waking a friend. Tells how it requires a group effort to solve their problems.
Prod-PANOWA Dist-PHENIX

Mouse On The Mayflower, The C 57 MIN
16MM FILM OPTICAL SOUND K-I
Depicts, through animation, how the pilgrims came to America, incorporating the voices of Tennessee Ernie Ford, Eddie Albert, John Gary, Joanie Sommers and Paul Frees.
LC NO. 74-700684
Prod-UPA Dist-TWYMAN 1969

Mouse Takes A Chance, The C 9 MIN
16MM FILM, 3/4 OR 1/2 IN VIDEO K-I
Uses a story about a mouse who leaves her safe home for adventures in the world to show that it is sometimes necessary to take a chance.
From The Primary Language Development Series.
Prod-PEDF Dist-AIMS 1975

Mouse Tales By Rumer Godden C 30 MIN
2 INCH VIDEOTAPE
Presents a reading of two of British novelist Rumer Godden's most appealing works for children, The Mouse House and The Mouse Wife.
Prod-WETATV Dist-PUBTEL

Mouse That Roared, The C 85 MIN
16MM FILM OPTICAL SOUND
Shows a world crisis developing when a small country steals a secret weapon and blackmails the rest of the world. Stars Peter Sellers.
Prod-CPC Dist-TIMLIF 1959

Mouse-Activated Candle Lighter, The C 5 MIN
16MM FILM, 3/4 OR 1/2 IN VIDEO J
Shows an amusing Rube Goldberg device consisting of a mouse trap, fishing pole, alarm clock, ice pack, train motor, rubber band, match and candle which illustrates various forms of potential and kinetic energy.
Prod-SF Dist-SF 1973

Mouse's Tale, The C 25 MIN
16MM FILM, 3/4 OR 1/2 IN VIDEO
Looks at the behavior and habitats of four species of mice - house mice, dormice, wood mice and harvest mice - in and around a country cottage in Wiltshire, England. Narrated by David Attenborough.
Prod-BBCTV Dist-FI

Mouseman, The C 14 MIN
16MM FILM, 3/4 OR 1/2 IN VIDEO P-I
Tells the story of a boy whose only friends are his pet mice. Shows how the other kids think he's weird until he gets an opportunity to make new friends. Explains that he must hurt someone else in order to do so.
From The Bloomin' Human Series.
Prod-PAULST Dist-MEDIAG 1975

Mousie Baby C 25 MIN
16MM FILM, 3/4 OR 1/2 IN VIDEO
Presents an adaptation of Tess Slesinger's short story entitled The Mouse-Trap about a young secretary in an advertising agency. Shows how the employees go on strike, but the secretary's handsome boss manipulates them and the strike is abandoned. Portrays the secretary rejecting his overtures and emerging alone.
Prod-COMCO Dist-PHENIX 1977

Mousie Party C 6 MIN
16MM FILM, 3/4 OR 1/2 IN VIDEO P
Presents a puppet animation look at the efforts of a group of determined young mice to attain a goal of seemingly impossible proportions, both literally and figuratively. They try to reach a set of rings dangling from the ceiling.
LC NO. 83-706008
Prod-FILBUL Dist-PHENIX 1982

Mousse Au Chocolat C 29 MIN
2 INCH VIDEOTAPE
A French language videotape. Features Julia Child of Haute Cuisine au Vin demonstrating how to prepare mousse au chocolate. With captions.
From The French Chef (French) Series.
Prod-WGBHTV Dist-PUBTEL

Moutabel And Hummus Bi Tahini C 19 MIN
3/4 OR 1/2 INCH VIDEO CASSETTE PRO
Demonstrates the preparation of two Arabic appetizers, Moutabel, with eggplant, and Hummus bi Tahini, with chick peas.
Prod-CULINA Dist-CULINA

Mouth Music C 29 MIN
3/4 OR 1/2 INCH VIDEO CASSETTE
Tours some interesting and colorful performers in grassroots America such as Jimmy Riddle. Offers a testimony to the richness of American folk culture.
Prod-EAI Dist-EAI

Mouth Preparation For Removable Partial Dentures C 35 MIN
16MM FILM OPTICAL SOUND
Shows principles and procedures for diagnosing and treating the patient's mouth prior to receiving prosthesis.
LC NO. 74-705176
Prod-USVA Dist-USNAC 1964

Mouth Preparation Procedures C 13 MIN
3/4 INCH VIDEO CASSETTE PRO
Demonstrates the preparation of abutment teeth for three-quarter crowns and splinting, impression procedures and surveying the patterns incident to developing guide planes and positive retentive areas. Issued in 1967 as a motion picture.
From The Removable Partial Dentures, Clasp Type - Clinical And Laboratory Procedures Series.
LC NO. 79-706264
Prod-USVA Dist-USNAC Prodn-VADTC 1978

Mouth That Roared, The C 5 MIN
16MM FILM, 3/4 OR 1/2 IN VIDEO J-C A
Presents an animated, avant-garde interpretation of the coming together of a single, self-sufficient component to make a larger, stronger whole, using the parts of the face to make its point.
LC NO. 84-706798
Prod-PHENIX Dist-PHENIX 1983

Mouth-to-Mouth Breathing C 15 MIN
16MM FILM, 3/4 OR 1/2 IN VIDEO H-C A
See series title for descriptive statement.
From The REACT - Review Of Emergency Aid And CPR Training Series.
Prod-MTI Dist-MTI

Mouth-To-Mouth Resuscitation C 12 MIN
3/4 OR 1/2 INCH VIDEO CASSETTE A
A demonstrator, utilizing a recuscitation training mannequin, illustrates the proper procedure for performing mouth-to-mouth resuscitation. Employs animated special effects while a medical officer narrates and explains the correct techniques.
LC NO. 84-706479
Prod-USA Dist-USNAC 1975

Mouthpiece C 1 MIN
3/4 OR 1/2 INCH VIDEO CASSETTE
See series title for descriptive statement.
From The Gary Hill, Part 2 Series.
Prod-EAI Dist-EAI

Movable Bridges C 29 MIN
16MM FILM OPTICAL SOUND J-C A
Depicts the history and development of the movable bridge and shows how one of the largest of all movable bridges was built at Houghton, Michigan.
Prod-HANDY Dist-USSC 1960

Move - Artist In Schools Program C 28 MIN
16MM FILM OPTICAL SOUND
Shows how dancers are helping open new horizons in education by means of the artists in school program sponsored by the National Endowment for the Arts.
LC NO. 74-700356
Prod-NENDOW Dist-NENDOW 1973

Move Along - Enjoy Golf C 28 MIN
16MM FILM OPTICAL SOUND
Presents Arnold Palmer, Amy Alcott and two average golfers playing golf in Hawaii and reviewing the rules of etiquette and courtesy.
Prod-UAL Dist-MTP

Move And Do C 15 MIN
3/4 OR 1/2 INCH VIDEO CASSETTE
See series title for descriptive statement.
From The Children In Action Series.
Prod-LVN Dist-LVN

Move Em Out C 30 MIN
16MM FILM OPTICAL SOUND
Shows how Dick Sparrow, an Iowa farmer, organized and trained a 40-horse hitch to re-create a spectacle from the great circus parades of the past. Includes the training of the horses and men, the circus parade and the homecoming parade.
LC NO. 73-700378
Prod-WMVSTV Dist-WMVSTV 1973

Move In The Right Direction, A C 14 MIN
16MM FILM OPTICAL SOUND
Shows the employee his individual role in cost reduction through correct material handling. Points out the results of employee carelessness, and gives an example of tangible results of proper motivation.
LC NO. 72-701956
Prod-VOAERO Dist-VOAERO 1971

Move It C 19 MIN
16MM FILM OPTICAL SOUND A
Presents the Ririe-Woodbury Dance Company satirizing everyday life in Salt Lake City, Utah, through modern dance.
LC NO. 79-700918
Prod-FILIM Dist-RADIM 1977

Move Those Muscles C 15 MIN
3/4 OR 1/2 INCH VIDEO CASSETTE P
Emphasizes the importance of exercising every day to develop strong muscles. Illustrates good posture and suggests that it should become a lifetime habit.
From The All About You Series.
Prod-WGBHTV Dist-AITECH Prodn-TTOIC 1975

Move To Intermediate Level C 29 MIN
2 INCH VIDEOTAPE
See series title for descriptive statement.
From The Skiing Series.
Prod-KTCATV Dist-PUBTEL

Moveable Feast, A - A Film About Breastfeeding C 22 MIN
16MM FILM, 3/4 OR 1/2 IN VIDEO H-C A
Looks at many of the most common myths, questions, concerns and problems encountered by parents about breastfeeding using documentary footage, animation and dramatization.
From The Prepared Childbirth And Parenting Series.
Prod-JOU Dist-JOU 1982

Movement B 20 MIN
16MM FILM OPTICAL SOUND C A
See series title for descriptive statement.
From The All That I Am Series.
Prod-MPATI Dist-NWUFLM

Movement C 10 MIN
16MM FILM, 3/4 OR 1/2 IN VIDEO
Illustrates the importance of movement as an element of art by means of a series of striking parallels. Shows how movement in the world of nature has been translated into paintings.
From The Art Of Seeing Series.
Prod-AFA Dist-FI Prodn-ACI 1968

Movement C 14 MIN
3/4 OR 1/2 INCH VIDEO CASSETTE P
See series title for descriptive statement.
From The Hands On, Grade One Series. Unit 1 - Observing
Prod-VAOG Dist-AITECH Prodn-WHROTV 1975

Movement C 15 MIN
16MM FILM, 3/4 OR 1/2 IN VIDEO
Compares children at play, workers on a job, an athlete in training and a dancer in motion. Shows how they use similar movements for different activities.
From The Ripples Series.
LC NO. 73-702146
Prod-NITC Dist-AITECH

Movement Disorders In Children C 18 MIN
3/4 OR 1/2 INCH VIDEO CASSETTE PRO
Demonstrates several central nervous system disorders in children. Emphasizes observation of movements and their description.
Prod-UARIZ Dist-UARIZ

Movement Education C 28 MIN
16MM FILM, 3/4 OR 1/2 IN VIDEO T
Demonstrates movement education activities in a variety of circumstances. Shows children at the Frostig Center of Educational Therapy in specific activities calculated to improve coordination, flexibility, strength, agility, static and dynamic balance and endurance.
Prod-MAFC Dist-AIMS 1976

Movement Education (Spanish) C 28 MIN
16MM FILM, 3/4 OR 1/2 IN VIDEO T

Demonstrates movement education activities in a variety of circumstances. Shows children at the Frostig Center of Educational Therapy in specific activities calculated to improve coordination, flexibility, strength, agility, static and dynamic balance and endurance.
Prod-MAFC Dist-AIMS 1976

Movement Everywhere X 11 MIN
16MM FILM, 3/4 OR 1/2 IN VIDEO P
Presents a study of the various ways in which work is done and shows some of the machines that make work easier. Emphasizes the basic concept that it takes work to move things.
Prod-EBEC Dist-EBEC 1970

Movement Exploration - What Am I X 12 MIN
16MM FILM, 3/4 OR 1/2 IN VIDEO P-I
Presents an exercise in movement exploration in which children learn that they can not only move like themselves, but can mimic the movements of birds, animals and machines. Pictures the children developing perceptual abilities and refining concepts which are gateways to improved coordination and reading ability.
Prod-FA Dist-PHENIX 1968

Movement Exploration - What Am I (Spanish) C 12 MIN
16MM FILM, 3/4 OR 1/2 IN VIDEO P-I
Presents an exercise in movement exploration in which children learn that they can not only move like themselves, but can mimic the movements of birds, animals and machines. Pictures the children developing perceptual abilities and refining concepts which are gateways to improved coordination and reading ability.
Prod-FA Dist-PHENIX 1968

Movement Improvisations C 19 MIN
16MM FILM OPTICAL SOUND C T
Presents four different areas of movement expression in dance--free movement of separate body parts, three duets and a trio, designs in movement, and heads, hands and feet.
LC NO. FIA67-5558
Prod-METT Dist-METT 1957

Movement In Classical Dance - The Pelvic Area C 11 MIN
16MM FILM, 3/4 OR 1/2 IN VIDEO J-C
Explains safe and correct principles of position in classical dance.
Prod-IU Dist-IU 1980

Movement Possibilities C 30 MIN
3/4 OR 1/2 INCH VIDEO CASSETTE C
See series title for descriptive statement.
From The In Our Own Image Series.
Prod-DALCCD Dist-DALCCD

Movement Style And Culture—A Series
16MM FILM, 3/4 OR 1/2 IN VIDEO
Discusses the correlation between dance movement styles and the cultures in which they are used.
Prod-CHORP Dist-UCEMC 1978

Dance And Human History	040 MIN
Palm Play	030 MIN
Step Style	030 MIN

Movement Techniques C 17 MIN
3/4 OR 1/2 INCH VIDEO CASSETTE
Demonstrates field and sand table techniques developed by the Army to respond to enemy action. Shows movement techniques designed to make maximum use of terrain, obscure enemy vision, and assure maximum use of fire power.
LC NO. 81-706251
Prod-USA Dist-USNAC 1981

Movement Techniques - The Rifle Platoon C 15 MIN
16MM FILM OPTICAL SOUND
Presents three standard movement techniques used by squads under direction of the platoon leader. Uses simulated battle action to show the benefit of employing cover and concealment of troops.
LC NO. 80-701837
Prod-USA Dist-USNAC 1980

Movement Within Life C 15 MIN
3/4 OR 1/2 INCH VIDEO CASSETTE I-J
Studies internal movement and how it is accomplished in both plants and animals.
From The Animals And Such Series. Module Red - Life Processes
Prod-WHROTV Dist-AITECH 1972

Movements C 25 MIN
16MM FILM OPTICAL SOUND
Depicts the performing arts in Israel.
Prod-ALDEN Dist-ALDEN

Movements And Migrations C 24 MIN
16MM FILM OPTICAL SOUND I-C
Surveys the range of movement among living things and examines the special abilities of different species, such as turtles who cross entire oceans without obvious guides and bats who navigate accurately in dark caves.
From The Animal Secrets Series.
LC NO. FIA68-1029
Prod-NBC Dist-GRACUR 1967

Movements Of Endamoeba Histolytica C 2 MIN
16MM FILM OPTICAL SOUND
Uses cinemicrography to show typical motility and ingested red cells of trophozoite of endamoeba histolytica from a clinical case of amoebic dysentery.
From The Parasitology Series.
LC NO. FIE52-2235
Prod-USPHS Dist-USNAC 1947

Movements Of Organelles In Living Nerve Fibers C 12 MIN
16MM FILM, 3/4 OR 1/2 IN VIDEO PRO
Illustrates the movements of organelles inside living axons from frog nerves in time-lapse cinematography.
Prod-NMAC Dist-USNAC 1975

Movements Of The Alimentary Tract In Experimental Animals B 16 MIN
16MM FILM OPTICAL SOUND C A
Presents a comprehensive study of peristalsis from the stomach to the rectum in the dog, cat and rabbit.
Prod-UCHI Dist-WYLAB

Movements Of The Eyes And Tongue - Somatic Motor System C 18 MIN
16MM FILM, 3/4 OR 1/2 IN VIDEO PRO
See series title for descriptive statement.
From The Anatomical Basis Of Brain Function Series.
Prod-AVCORP Dist-TEF

Movements Of The Jaw And Throat - Branchial Motor System C 18 MIN
16MM FILM, 3/4 OR 1/2 IN VIDEO PRO
See series title for descriptive statement.
From The Anatomical Basis Of Brain Function Series.
Prod-AVCORP Dist-TEF

Movements Of The Shoulder Girdle B 47 MIN
3/4 OR 1/2 INCH VIDEO CASSETTE
Teaches the interrelationships of the movements of the shoulder girdle during functional activities.
Prod-BU Dist-BU

Movie About Light, A C 8 MIN
16MM FILM OPTICAL SOUND C T
Presents first-grade urban school children and their teacher who study light and make a movie about it. Explains that many children who had barriers against learning became interested and excited when given cameras with which to learn.
LC NO. 72-702796
Prod-AECT Dist-AECT 1972

Movie At The End Of The World, The C 57 MIN
3/4 OR 1/2 INCH VIDEO CASSETTE J-C A
Portrays writer Tom McGrath, told as the writer's dream.
Prod-UCV Dist-UCV

Movie Factory C 15 MIN
3/4 OR 1/2 INCH VIDEO CASSETTE P-I
Tours Universal City Studio to learn about some of the illusions used in making movies.
From The Explorers Unlimited Series.
Prod-WVIZTV Dist-AITECH 1971

Movie Memories C 30 MIN
16MM FILM OPTICAL SOUND
Presents a documentary showing the floats, bands and horses of the Rose Parade held in Pasadena, California, New Years Day, 1973.
LC NO. 73-700801
Prod-TRA Dist-TRA 1973

Movie Milestones No. 1 B 10 MIN
16MM FILM OPTICAL SOUND
Highlights sequences from the feature films of the silent days, including 'Blood And Sand' (1922) with Rudolph Valentino, Nita Naldi and Lilo Lee, 'The Covered Wagon' (1923) with Ernest Torrence, J Warren Kerrigan and Alan Hale, 'The Miracle Man' (1919) with Lon Chaney, Thomas Meighan, Betty Compson and Joseph Dowling and 'Beau Geste' (1926) with Ronald Coleman, Ralph Forbes, Noah Beery and William Powell.
Prod-CFS Dist-CFS

Movie Movie C 105 MIN
16MM FILM OPTICAL SOUND
Offers a spoof of the old Hollywood double feature. Includes a black and white boxing melodrama and a lavish musical story.
Prod-WB Dist-SWANK

Movie Star's Daughter, A C 30 MIN
16MM FILM, 3/4 OR 1/2 IN VIDEO I-H
A shortened version of the motion picture A Movie Star's Daughter. Describes the problems of a young girl who fears that her popularity is based on her father's fame.
Prod-HGATE Dist-LCOA 1979

Movie Star's Daughter, A C 46 MIN
16MM FILM, 3/4 OR 1/2 IN VIDEO I-C A
Describes how Dena has to decide whether her popularity is based on her own worth or on the fact that her father is a famous movie star. Shows how she learns the real meaning of friendship. An ABC Afterschool Special.
Prod-HGATE Dist-LCOA 1979

Movie Star's Daughter, A (Spanish) C 33 MIN
16MM FILM, 3/4 OR 1/2 IN VIDEO P-H A
Tells the story of a young junior high girl, the daughter of a movie idol, who encounters difficult choices upon arriving at a new school. Edited.
Prod-HGATE Dist-LCOA 1979

Movie Star's Daughter, A (Spanish) C 46 MIN
16MM FILM, 3/4 OR 1/2 IN VIDEO P-H A
Tells the story of a young girl whose parent is a movie idol. She has to make difficult choices as she enters a new school. Complete version.
Prod-HGATE Dist-LCOA 1979

Movie Stuntmen C 28 MIN
16MM FILM, 3/4 OR 1/2 IN VIDEO
Reveals the skill and courage demanded of motion picture stuntmen and shows how they can perform such stunts as flaming car crashes and leaps from cliffs.
Prod-TRENCH Dist-LCOA 1975

Movie Trailers C 60 MIN
3/4 OR 1/2 INCH VIDEO CASSETTE
Presents previews of Citizen Kane, Yankee Doodle Dandy, Easter Parade and Diplomanics, among others.
Prod-ADVCAS Dist-ADVCAS

Movies B 29 MIN
16MM FILM, 3/4 OR 1/2 IN VIDEO H-C A
Dr Dodds examines the movies of the 20th century for clues about changes and constancies in American taste.
From The American Memoir Series.
Prod-WTTWTV Dist-IU 1961

Movies - Our Modern Art—A Series

Presents films meant to develop an appreciation and enjoyment of the motion picture as an art form.
Prod-SPCTRA Dist-STRFLS

D'Artangan	28 MIN
Gold Rush, The	60 MIN
His Majesty, The Scarecrow Of Oz	28 MIN
Let Katie Do It	28 MIN
Lost World Revisited, The	28 MIN
Man Called Edison, The	28 MIN
Phantom Of The Opera, The	60 MIN
Svengali	45 MIN

Movies From Computers - An Interim Report B 20 MIN
16MM FILM OPTICAL SOUND C
Presents Ellis King who shows excerpts from existing computer-generated industrial and research films and shows applications of computer animation in mathematics, engineering and physics.
From The National Committee For Electrical Engineering film Series.
LC NO. 77-703367
Prod-EDS Dist-EDC 1967

Movies Go West, The C 14 MIN
16MM FILM, 3/4 OR 1/2 IN VIDEO H-C A
Hal Angus, of the original Essanay Film Manufacturing Company western unit, revisits the studio and location sites and reminisces about the early days between 1909-1916 when Gilbert M Anderson produced and starred in hundreds of westerns. He points out that in the role of Bronco Billy, Gilbert Anderson created the prototype of the movie cowboy hero and established the format of the classic American movie western.
Prod-BELLG Dist-UCEMC 1974

Movies Learn To Talk B 26 MIN
16MM FILM, 3/4 OR 1/2 IN VIDEO J-H A
Offers glimpses of 12 silent and sound movies in order to show the development of sound in motion pictures.
Prod-CBSNEW Dist-CRMP 1960

Movies March On, The B 20 MIN
16MM FILM, 3/4 OR 1/2 IN VIDEO
Consists of film clips documenting the history of movies from silents to swashbucklers.
From The March Of Time Series.
LC NO. 79-707367
Prod-TIMLIF Dist-TIMLIF 1974

Movies Today, The - A New Morality C 37 MIN
16MM FILM, 3/4 OR 1/2 IN VIDEO
Takes a look at the life and career of Marilyn Monroe. Examines the movies of the 1960's which became subjects of controversy because of their language, sexuality and violence.
From The Life Goes To The Movies Series. Pt 5
LC NO. 79-707672
Prod-TIMLIF Dist-TIMLIF 1976

Movies, Movies—A Series
J-H
Shows how movies are made. Interviews actors, directors, writers, technicians and critics.
Prod-CTI Dist-CTI

Cheap It Isn't	015 MIN
G, PG, R And X	015 MIN
Say It Again, Sam	015 MIN
So You Want To Be A Star	015 MIN
There's No Business Like Show Business	015 MIN
Which End Do I Look In	015 MIN

Movies' Story, The B 25 MIN
16MM FILM OPTICAL SOUND J-C
Depicts the pioneering days of the film as seen in the films of Edison, Melies, D W Griffith, Chaplin and others.
Prod-SLFP Dist-SLFP 1970

Movin' Around And Movin' Out C 30 MIN
3/4 OR 1/2 INCH VIDEO CASSETTE
See series title for descriptive statement.
From The Bean Sprouts Series.
Prod-CTPROJ Dist-MDCPB

Movin' Around, Movin' Out C 29 MIN
3/4 OR 1/2 INCH VIDEO CASSETTE P-I
Shows a group of school friends in San Francisco's Italian, Latino and Chinese neighborhood shops. Includes incidents of thoughtless racism.
From The Bean Sprouts Series.
Prod-CTPROJ Dist-GPITVL

Movin' In, Movin' On, Part I C 30 MIN
3/4 OR 1/2 INCH VIDEO CASSETTE
See series title for descriptive statement.
From The Up And Coming Series.
Prod-KQEDTV Dist-MDCPB

Movin' In, Movin' On, Part II C 30 MIN
3/4 OR 1/2 INCH VIDEO CASSETTE

See series title for descriptive statement.
From The Up And Coming Series.
Prod-KQEDTV Dist-MDCPB

Movin' On Up C 30 MIN
3/4 OR 1/2 INCH VIDEO CASSETTE
See series title for descriptive statement.
From The Rebop Series.
Prod-WGBHTV Dist-MDCPB

Moving C 10 MIN
3/4 OR 1/2 INCH VIDEO CASSETTE
Presents Fred Rogers on the subject of moving.
From The You (Parents) Are Special Series.
Prod-FAMCOM Dist-FAMCOM

Moving C 15 MIN
3/4 OR 1/2 INCH VIDEO CASSETTE P-I
Shows how the act of moving affects a family. Explains how to prepare for the move, how to move and how to get settled in your new home. Offers advice on how to make the move safely and with as little stress as possible.
From The Safer You Series.
Prod-WCVETV Dist-GPITVL 1984

Moving / Product Liability / Tots C
3/4 OR 1/2 INCH VIDEO CASSETTE
Presents tips on moving, product liability and child care.
From The Consumer Survival Series.
Prod-MDCPB Dist-MDCPB

Moving A Hippo C 15 MIN
3/4 OR 1/2 INCH VIDEO CASSETTE K-P
Examines uses of the wheel, axle and pulley.
From The Dragons, Wagons And Wax, Set 1 Series.
Prod-CTI Dist-CTI

Moving A Patient In Bed C 16 MIN
16MM FILM - 3/4 IN VIDEO H-C A
Assesses the reasons for moving a patient in bed and demonstrates the procedures.
From The Nurse's Aide, Orderly And Attendant Series.
Prod-COPI Dist-COPI 1969

Moving Air Affects The Weather C 15 MIN
3/4 OR 1/2 INCH VIDEO CASSETTE P-I
Discusses how moving air affects the weather.
From The Why Series.
Prod-WDCNTV Dist-AITECH 1976

Moving And Lifting Patients B 23 MIN
16MM FILM MAGNETIC SOUND PRO
Outlines the principles of good body mechanics and practical application in moving and lifting patients in and out of bed. Demonstrates procedures for moving patients with or without a turning sheet.
LC NO. 72-700644
Prod-KRI Dist-KRI 1969

Moving And The Stuck, The C 20 MIN
3/4 OR 1/2 INCH VIDEO CASSETTE
See series title for descriptive statement.
From The Productivity / Quality Of Work Life Series.
Prod-GOODMI Dist-DELTAK

Moving And Turning The Patient C 7 MIN
3/4 OR 1/2 INCH VIDEO CASSETTE PRO
Provides the rationale for frequently moving and turning the patient and explains the importance of enlisting the patient's co-operation. Demonstrates the steps to follow to safely turn and move the patient. Emphasizes the techniques that the home nurse should employ to avoid straining or injuring herself as she turns and moves the patient.
LC NO. 77-731353
Prod-TRAINX Dist-TRAINX

Moving And Turning The Patient (Spanish) C 7 MIN
3/4 OR 1/2 INCH VIDEO CASSETTE PRO
Provides the rationale for frequently moving and turning the patient and explains the importance of enlisting the patient's co-operation. Demonstrates the steps to follow to safely turn and move the patient. Emphasizes the techniques that the home nurse should employ to avoid straining or injuring herself as she turns and moves the patient.
LC NO. 77-731353
Prod-TRAINX Dist-TRAINX

Moving Day, Moving Away C 15 MIN
3/4 OR 1/2 INCH VIDEO CASSETTE P
Combines looking, listening, talking, writing and reading to help establish the link between oral and written language. Presents the story Best Little House by Aileen Fisher.
From The I Want To Read Series.
Prod-LACOS Dist-GPITVL 1976

Moving Experience, The C
1/2 IN VIDEO CASSETTE BETA/VHS
Deals with moving, an unexpected part of life, and examines one family's move and the reactions of the family members to the adjustments in their lives.
From The Adult Years - Continuity And Change Series.
Prod-OHUTC Dist-OHUTC

Moving Image, The - Super-8 C 27 MIN
16MM FILM, 3/4 OR 1/2 IN VIDEO J-C
Shows steps involved in making super 8 mm films. Focuses on a high school filmmaking class and its experiences in using various filmmaking procedures and processes.
LC NO. 80-706099
Prod-IU Dist-IU 1976

Moving In C 15 MIN
3/4 OR 1/2 INCH VIDEO CASSETTE
See series title for descriptive statement.
From The Consumer Education Series.
Prod-MAETEL Dist-CAMB

Moving In And Out Of Your Wheelchair C 5 MIN
3/4 INCH VIDEO CASSETTE
Presents an over-view of the physical preparation and equipment that is generally needed for wheelchair living.
From The Spinal Cord Injury - Patient Education Series.
Prod-PRIMED Dist-PRIMED

Moving In Circles C 30 MIN
16MM FILM, 3/4 OR 1/2 IN VIDEO C A
Explains Plato's idea that stars are heavenly beings orbiting the earth with uniform perfection - uniform speed and perfect circles.
From The Mechanical Universe Series.
Prod-ANNCPB Dist-FI

Moving Is Learning (Perceptual Motor Training) C 18 MIN
16MM FILM OPTICAL SOUND S
Shows teachers and parents of perceptually handicapped children a new method of assisting the children through physical methods of retraining at a visual learning center. Describes the method of training which was developed by Professor Brian Cleary.
LC NO. FIA68-2431
Prod-BRIANC Dist-CRAF Prodn-CRAF 1967

Moving Mountains C 27 MIN
16MM FILM OPTICAL SOUND A
Shows the successful integration of women into the outdoor crew at the Fording Coal Mine Company's open pit mine in Elkford, British Columbia.
LC NO. 82-700543
Prod-USTLW Dist-MOBIUS 1981

Moving Oil C 21 MIN
16MM FILM, 3/4 OR 1/2 IN VIDEO IND
Documents the operation of a crude oil pipeline company from the wellhead to the products terminal. Shows functions of the gauger, operations coordinator, terminal supervisor and other employees as oil and products are moved through the pipeline.
Prod-UTEXPE Dist-UTEXPE 1981

Moving On C 29 MIN
2 INCH VIDEOTAPE
See series title for descriptive statement.
From The Making Things Grow III Series.
Prod-WGBHTV Dist-PUBTEL

Moving On - The Hunger For Land In Zimbabwe C 52 MIN
16MM FILM, 3/4 OR 1/2 IN VIDEO A
Contrasts a black community barely eking out an existence on subpar land and an affluent white family employing modern farming techniques on lush acres in the African nation of Zimbabwe.
LC NO. 84-707115
Prod-BELZIM Dist-CANWRL 1983

Moving On—A Series
A
Presents instruction in lifting, moving and handling techniques.
Prod-LIVACT Dist-IFB

Awkward Loads 012 MIN
Awkward Places 009 MIN
Helping Hands 009 MIN

Moving Pictures C 25 MIN
16MM FILM, 3/4 OR 1/2 IN VIDEO J-C A
Uses portions of the feature films TRON and The Works to show what can be done by the computer in animation of motion pictures. Demonstrates a Computer Aided Design System that allows experimentation and interior design without moving furniture.
From The Making The Most Of The Micro Series. Episode 9
Prod-BBCTV Dist-FI 1983

Moving Pictures - The Art Of Jan Lenica C 19 MIN
16MM FILM, 3/4 OR 1/2 IN VIDEO J-C A
Explores the relationship between the artist and his real world at the moment he conjures his fantasy visions.
Prod-HUFSC Dist-PHENIX 1975

Moving Right Along—A Series
16MM FILM, 3/4 OR 1/2 IN VIDEO J-H A
Looks at some of the problems that confront teenagers and their parents including sibling rivalry, family responsibilities, peer pressure, drug and alcohol abuse, divorce, sex and death.
Prod-WQED Dist-MTI 1983

Bro 030 MIN
Diana's Big Break 030 MIN
Everybody's Doing It 030 MIN
It's A Family Matter 030 MIN
Jennifer's Choice 030 MIN
Matter Of Life And Death, A 030 MIN
Mr Juanderful 030 MIN
Smotherly Love 030 MIN
Stop The World - Maggie Wants To Get Off 030 MIN
Trust Brenda 030 MIN

Moving Still C 57 MIN
3/4 OR 1/2 INCH VIDEO CASSETTE H-C A
Traces the history of photography from the early camera obscura to cinematic revelations of behavior and processes too slow or too fast for the human eye to perceive.
From The Nova Series.
LC NO. 81-706778
Prod-WGBHTV Dist-TIMLIF 1981

Moving Target C 32 MIN
16MM FILM OPTICAL SOUND
Documents the various uses of electro-motive diesel power. Shows the diesel engine in use in the Far East, Europe, Mexico and the United States. Includes scenes of factory assembly of the diesel engine.
LC NO. 78-701316
Prod-GM Dist-GM 1978

Moving The Earth C 15 MIN
3/4 OR 1/2 INCH VIDEO CASSETTE P-I
Explains that three steps in manufacturing earth-moving equipment are fabricating, machining and assembly.
From The Explorers Unlimited Series.
Prod-WVIZTV Dist-AITECH 1971

Moving Toward Parallel Skiing C 29 MIN
2 INCH VIDEOTAPE
See series title for descriptive statement.
From The Skiing Series.
Prod-KTCATV Dist-PUBTEL

Moving Unseen Energy C 26 MIN
16MM FILM OPTICAL SOUND
Shows farmers the use of anhydrous ammonia and how it is delivered by pipeline. A university professor also explains the function of nitrogen in plant growth.
LC NO. 72-712178
Prod-STAFER Dist-STAFER 1970

Moving Up - Making The Transition To Head Nurse C 31 MIN
3/4 OR 1/2 INCH VIDEO CASSETTE
Presents an overview of a nurse's transition from staff nurse to management. Focuses on specific leadership skills required in first-line nursing managers, such as the ability to communicate, make decisions, solve problems and manage stress.
From The Management Skills For Nurses Series.
Prod-INTGRP Dist-AJN Prodn-ANDRAF

Moving With The Center Of Mass B 26 MIN
16MM FILM OPTICAL SOUND H
Demonstrates the conservation of energy and momentum of several magnetic dry ice puck interactions. Discusses and illustrates the partition of energy into two parts—one associated with the motion of the center of mass and the other associated with the motion of the parts with respect to the center of the mass.
From The PSSC Physics Films Series.
LC NO. FIA67-503
Prod-PSSC Dist-MLA 1966

Moving With The Times C 24 MIN
16MM FILM OPTICAL SOUND
Describes how Sears grew to be the world's largest retailer from a modest beginning selling mail order watches.
Prod-SEARS Dist-MTP

Moving Wool C 17 MIN
16MM FILM OPTICAL SOUND H-C A
Describes new and revolutionary methods of wool handling, from shearing and grading to baling and shipping.
LC NO. 76-701869
Prod-AUSTWB Dist-AUIS Prodn-FLMAUS 1974

Mowgli's Brothers C 26 MIN
3/4 INCH VIDEO CASSETTE E
Explores the life of a boy rescued and raised by wolves in the jungles of Africa. Based on the story Mowgli's Brothers by Rudyard Kipling. Features the voices of Roddy Mc Dowall and June Foray.
Prod-CJE Dist-GA

Mowitch The Blacktail X 7 MIN
16MM FILM OPTICAL SOUND J-C T
Documents the transport of a nucleus herd of blacktail deer from Oregon to Tennessee, in order to determine if the species will adapt to the new environment.
Prod-TGAFC Dist-TGAFC 1966

Moyno Processing Cavity Pumps For Waste Treatment - Guest Lecture By Bill McGraw C 19 MIN
1/2 IN VIDEO CASSETTE BETA/VHS
Discusses sewage disposal plants, needed equipment and supplies, and water and wastewater technology.
Prod-RMI Dist-RMI

Mozart And His Music C 14 MIN
16MM FILM, 3/4 OR 1/2 IN VIDEO I-C
Mozart's life and music are described against a background of the 18th century and of the European cities which influenced his career. Stresses the classic character of his compositions.
Prod-CORF Dist-CORF 1954

Mozart, The Clarinet, And Keith Puddy C 26 MIN
16MM FILM, 3/4 OR 1/2 IN VIDEO J-C A
Presents Wolfgang Amadeus Mozart (1756-1791), who was famous for symphonies, operas, chamber music, sonatas and concertos for piano, violin, flute and horn. Features professional musicians Keith Puddy and the Gabriel Quartet playing Mozart's music on the clarinet.
From The Musical Triangle Series.
Prod-THAMES Dist-MEDIAG 1975

Mozart's Magic Flute - Ingmar Bergman C
3/4 OR 1/2 INCH VIDEO CASSETTE
Prod-MSTVIS Dist-MSTVIS

MPBC And The Roots Of Yoga C 60 MIN
3/4 OR 1/2 INCH VIDEO CASSETTE
Interviews Sri Gurudev at the International Vegetarian Conference in Maine, 1975. Presents several unique schools from India and documents the origins of Yoga.
Prod-TIMLIF Dist-IYOGA

Mr Adler And The Opera C 59 MIN
16MM FILM, 3/4 OR 1/2 IN VIDEO H-C A

Presents appearances by internationally celebrated soloists and excerpts from several opera productions in a probing look at one of opera's most distinguished impresarios.
Prod-EBEC Dist-EBEC 1983

Mr And Mrs Maternity C 22 MIN
16MM FILM OPTICAL SOUND H-C A
Provides pre-natal training and information. Discusses the physiological and psychological events of normal pregnancy, labor and delivery.
LC NO. FIA61-804
Prod-CLI Dist-CLI

Mr And Mrs Robin's Family (2nd Ed) C 10 MIN
16MM FILM, 3/4 OR 1/2 IN VIDEO P-I
Tells about a family of robins who arrive in a young girl's backyard in spring. Explains how the mother robin lays her eggs and how the baby robins eat, learn to fly and leave the nest.
Prod-CORF Dist-CORF 1977

Mr Big X 30 MIN
16MM FILM OPTICAL SOUND
Features a businessman from the city finding himself locked up in a small town jail after an auto accident in which he seriously injured an elderly woman.
Prod-FAMF Dist-FAMF

Mr Blandings Builds His Dream House B 93 MIN
1/2 IN VIDEO CASSETTE (BETA)
Stars Cary Grant and Myrna Loy as a couple who decide to move from their New York City apartment to an old home in the Connecticut countryside. Shows how their attempts to remodel the house result in chaos.
Prod-UNKNWN Dist-BHAWK 1948

Mr Chairman B 17 MIN
16MM FILM OPTICAL SOUND
Features a cartoon presentation of why we have rules for meetings and offers examples of the ways in which the rules work. Focuses on the specific aspect of parliamentary procedure and the priority of motions.
Prod-CINEFC Dist-AFLCIO 1958

Mr Chairman - The Fundamentals Of Parliamentary Law X 13 MIN
16MM FILM, 3/4 OR 1/2 IN VIDEO H-C
Uses animated sequences to show why rules of order are essential to democratic debate and decision-making. Suggests ways parliamentary procedures can be adapted to various groups.
Prod-EBF Dist-EBEC 1959

Mr Chimp Goes To The Circus C 11 MIN
16MM FILM OPTICAL SOUND P-I A
Presents a hilarious role for the jungle compound chimpanzee, Tamba, star of the Bonzo pictures. Dubbed in voices for the chimpanzees add to the comic effect.
Prod-AVED Dist-AVED 1958

Mr CIO B 10 MIN
16MM FILM OPTICAL SOUND
Introduces Allan Haywood, one of the pioneers of CIO.
Prod-TWUA Dist-AFLCIO 1952

Mr Clean C 1 MIN
3/4 OR 1/2 INCH VIDEO CASSETTE
Shows a classic animated television commercial which the original theme song.
Prod-BROOKC Dist-BROOKC

Mr Curry Takes A Bath / Fortune Telling C 11 MIN
16MM FILM, 3/4 OR 1/2 IN VIDEO K-I
Describes Paddington Bear's adventures with a sauna and a fortune teller.
From The Paddington Bear, Series 1 Series.
LC NO. 80-707220
Prod-BONDM Dist-FLMFR Prodn-FILMF 1977

Mr Dead And Mrs Free C 50 MIN
3/4 OR 1/2 INCH VIDEO CASSETTE
Juxtaposes disparate elements of American culture such as sex, soft music, violence and power. Emphasizes the brutal and grotesque.
Prod-KITCHN Dist-KITCHN

Mr Deeds Goes To Town B 118 MIN
16MM FILM OPTICAL SOUND J-C A
Stars Gary Cooper as a small-town greeting-card verse writer who inherits an unwanted 20 million dollars and goes on trial for his sanity when he tries to give it all away.
Prod-CPC Dist-TIMLIF 1936

Mr Edison's Dilemma - The Perplexing Problem Of Keeping Our Lights On C 18 MIN
16MM FILM OPTICAL SOUND J-H
Analyzes the electric power business. Provides basic information about the production of electricity in power plants and the fuels used in the process. Explores its distribution in homes, businesses and industry.
Prod-CENTRO Dist-CONPOW

Mr Edler's Class - Drug Education At The Elementary Level C 30 MIN
3/4 OR 1/2 INCH VIDEO CASSETTE
Shows how innovative approaches to learning in elementary schools can help detect, diagnose and treat drug abuse problems. Issued in 1971 as a motion picture.
From The Social Seminar Series.
LC NO. 80-707356
Prod-USDHEW Dist-USNAC 1980

Mr Egbert Nosh / The Biggest House In The World C 15 MIN
3/4 INCH VIDEO CASSETTE P
Presents the children's stories Mr Egbert nosh by Paul Groves and The Biggest House In The World by Leo Lionni.

From The Tilson's Book Shop Series.
Prod-WVIZTV Dist-GPITVL 1975

Mr Eichhorn's Golfball C 5 MIN
16MM FILM OPTICAL SOUND J-C A
Presents a probing examination of a golfball's most inner self.
Prod-UWFKD Dist-UWFKD

Mr Fixit - My Dad C 9 MIN
16MM FILM OPTICAL SOUND J-C A
Presents a dramatization about the problems confronting a father when his son is arrested on a marijuana charge. Shows how he must decide to let justice take its course or intercede on his son's behalf.
Prod-FLMAUS Dist-AUIS 1976

Mr Flanagan, The Chaplain And Mr Lincoln B 30 MIN
16MM FILM OPTICAL SOUND
Dramatizes a Civil War incident which led to the repeal of discriminatory legislation limiting chaplaincy appointments in the armed services to 'ORDAINED MINISTERS OF THE CHRISTIAN FAITH.' Explains that the ultimate result was the commissioning of a Jewish chaplain in the Union army. (Kinescope)
Prod-JTS Dist-NAAJS Prodn-NBCTV 1962

Mr Freedom C 95 MIN
16MM FILM OPTICAL SOUND C A
Presents a cartoon on American intervention abroad in the name of freedom.
Prod-GROVE Dist-GROVE

Mr Frog Went A-Courting C 5 MIN
16MM FILM, 3/4 OR 1/2 IN VIDEO P-I
Presents an animated version of the ancient Scottish folktale about the frog that courted the mouse.
Prod-NFBC Dist-FI 1976

Mr Goshu, The Cellist C 19 MIN
16MM FILM, 3/4 OR 1/2 IN VIDEO P-I
Tells the story of a young cellist who practices every night and is finally rewarded for his hard work.
Prod-GAKKEN Dist-IFB 1970

Mr Horse C 26 MIN
16MM FILM, 3/4 OR 1/2 IN VIDEO H-C A
Views an old man's life, his displacement in the world and his decision to remain in control of his destiny.
Prod-HARK Dist-PHENIX 1981

Mr Hyde C 5 MIN
16MM FILM OPTICAL SOUND J-C
Presents a cartoon twist to the Jekyll and Hyde story, involving the chicken and the egg question as to who came first - Dr Jekyll or Mr Hyde.
Prod-CFS Dist-CFS

Mr Jefferson's Legacy C 29 MIN
16MM FILM OPTICAL SOUND
Uses 18th-century homes, taverns, meeting places and artifacts, as well as Monticello and the University of Virginia to provide a historical background in documenting the influence of Thomas Jefferson's birthplace, Albemarle County, Virginia, on his life.
LC NO. 77-700557
Prod-CHARLT Dist-GUG Prodn-GUG 1976

Mr Juanderful C 30 MIN
16MM FILM, 3/4 OR 1/2 IN VIDEO J-H A
Reveals that when Juan's dream date for the school dance suddenly turns him down, he doesn't cope well with the rejection, especially because he feels he's letting his father down.
From The Moving Right Along Series.
Prod-WQED Dist-MTI 1983

Mr Justice Douglas C 52 MIN
16MM FILM, 3/4 OR 1/2 IN VIDEO H-C A
Presents an interview with Justice Douglas. Narrated by Eric Sevareid.
Prod-CBSNEW Dist-CAROUF

Mr Kennedy And Mr Krushchev C 20 MIN
16MM FILM, 3/4 OR 1/2 IN VIDEO H-C A
Describes Cold War events betwen 1961 and 1963, focusing on the crisis in Cuba.
From The Twentieth Century History Series.
Prod-BBCTV Dist-FI 1981

Mr Klein (French) C 124 MIN
16MM FILM OPTICAL SOUND
Tells about Robert Klein, a gentile art dealer in Nazi-occupied Paris, whose identity becomes confused with that of a Jew with the same name. Includes English subtitles.
Prod-TLECUL Dist-TLECUL

Mr Koumal Battles His Conscience C 2 MIN
16MM FILM OPTICAL SOUND J-C A
A satirical cartoon featuring Mr Koumal, an idea man who is thwarted at every turn. Designed to stimulate discussion on the realities of life and to help each individual develop acceptable patterns of behavior.
From The Mr Koumal Series.
LC NO. 72-713680
Prod-KRATKY Dist-SIM 1971

Mr Koumal Carries The Torch C 2 MIN
16MM FILM OPTICAL SOUND J-C A
Presents Mr Koumal, an idea man, who is stumped at every turn. Stimulates discussion focused on the realities of life and helps each individual develop acceptable patterns of behavior.
From The Mr Koumal Series.
LC NO. 72-704703
Prod-KRATKY Dist-SIM Prodn-DEITCH 1969

Mr Koumal Crusades For Love C 2 MIN
16MM FILM OPTICAL SOUND J-C A

A satirical cartoon featuring Mr Koumal, an idea man who is stumped at every turn. Designed to stimulate discussion on the realities of life and to help each individual develop acceptable patterns of behavior.
From The Mr Koumal Series.
LC NO. 78-705277
Prod-KRATKY Dist-SIM Prodn-DEITCH 1969

Mr Koumal Discovers Koumalia C 2 MIN
16MM FILM OPTICAL SOUND J-C A
A satirical cartoon featuring Mr Koumal, an idea man who is thwarted at every turn. Designed to stimulate discussion on the realities of life and to help each individual develop acceptable patterns of behavior.
From The Mr Koumal Series.
LC NO. 74-713678
Prod-KRATKY Dist-SIM 1971

Mr Koumal Faces Death C 2 MIN
16MM FILM OPTICAL SOUND J-C A
A satirical cartoon featuring Mr Koumal, an idea man who is stumped at every turn. Designed to stimulate discussion on the realities of life and to help each individual develop acceptable patterns of behavior.
From The Mr Koumal Series.
LC NO. 74-705276
Prod-KRATKY Dist-SIM Prodn-DEITCH 1969

Mr Koumal Flies Like A Bird C 2 MIN
16MM FILM OPTICAL SOUND J-C A
A satirical cartoon featuring Mr Koumal, an idea man, who is stumped at every turn. Stimulates discussion focused on the realities of life and helps each individual develop acceptable patterns of behavior.
From The Mr Koumal Series.
LC NO. 70-705275
Prod-KRATKY Dist-SIM Prodn-DEITCH 1969

Mr Koumal Gets Involved C 2 MIN
16MM FILM OPTICAL SOUND J-C A
A satirical cartoon featuring Mr Koumal, an idea man who is thwarted at every turn. Designed to stimulate discussion on the realities of life and to help each individual develop acceptable patterns of behavior.
From The Mr Koumal Series.
LC NO. 78-713679
Prod-KRATKY Dist-SIM 1971

Mr Koumal Invents A Robot C 1 MIN
16MM FILM OPTICAL SOUND J-C A
A satirical cartoon featuring Mr Koumal, an idea man, who is stumped at every turn. Stimulates discussion focused on the realities of life and helps each individual develop acceptable patterns of behavior.
From The Mr Koumal Series.
LC NO. 77-705274
Prod-KRATKY Dist-SIM Prodn-DEITCH 1969

Mr Koumal Moves To The Country C 2 MIN
16MM FILM OPTICAL SOUND J-H A
A satirical cartoon featuring Mr Koumal, an idea man who is stumped at every turn. Designed to stimulate discussion on the realities of life and to help each individual develop acceptable patterns of behavior.
From The Mr Koumal Series.
LC NO. 71-705278
Prod-KRATKY Dist-SIM Prodn-DEITCH 1969

Mr Koumal—A Series
J-H
Illustrates the ironies of life and universally recognized human foibles. Presents Mr Koumal as everyman at his optimistic best. Shows that in every instance he attacks his problems with gusto and good spirits, yet eventually is overwhelmed by agents beyond his control.
Prod-KRATKY Dist-SIM 1972

Mr Koumal Battles His Conscience 2 MIN
Mr Koumal Carries The Torch 2 MIN
Mr Koumal Crusades For Love 2 MIN
Mr Koumal Discovers Koumali 2 MIN
Mr Koumal Faces Death 2 MIN
Mr Koumal Flies Like A Bird 2 MIN
Mr Koumal Gets Involved 2 MIN
Mr Koumal Invents A Robot 2 MIN
Mr Koumal Moves To The Country 2 MIN

Mr Lincoln And The Bible, Pt 1 B 30 MIN
16MM FILM OPTICAL SOUND R
Maurice Samuel and Mark Van Doren discuss the influence of the Bible on the life and writings of Abraham Lincoln. (Kinescope)
Prod-JTS Dist-NAAJS Prodn-NBCTV 1960

Mr Lincoln And The Bible, Pt 2 B 30 MIN
16MM FILM OPTICAL SOUND R
Maurice Samuel and Mark Van Doren discuss the influence of the Bible on the life and writings of Abraham Lincoln. (Kinescope)
Prod-JTS Dist-NAAJS Prodn-NBCTV 1960

Mr Lincoln's Springfield C 25 MIN
16MM FILM - 3/4 IN VIDEO
Uses dramatized live action as well as old photographs to trace the 20-year career of Abraham Lincoln in Springfield, Illinois.
LC NO. 79-706138
Prod-USNPS Dist-USNAC 1979

Mr Magoo At Sea C 112 MIN
16MM FILM OPTICAL SOUND P-I
Prod-FI Dist-FI

Mr Magoo In Sherwood Forest C 105 MIN
16MM FILM OPTICAL SOUND P-I
Prod-FI Dist-FI

Mr Magoo's Christmas Carol C 28 MIN
16MM FILM, 3/4 OR 1/2 IN VIDEO P-I
A shortened version of the motion picture Mr Magoo's Christmas Carol. Presents an animated adaptation of Charles Dickens' story A Christmas Carol with the cartoon character Mr Magoo in the role of Ebenezer Scrooge.
Prod-UPA Dist-MCFI

Mr Magoo's Christmas Carol C 52 MIN
16MM FILM, 3/4 OR 1/2 IN VIDEO P-I
Presents an animated adaptation of Charles Dickens' story A Christmas Carol with the cartoon character Mr Magoo in the role of Ebenezer Scrooge.
Prod-UPA Dist-MCFI

Mr Magrooter's Marvelous Machine C 8 MIN
16MM FILM, 3/4 OR 1/2 IN VIDEO P-C
Tells the story of a man who proposes to add one more mechanized boon to man's creature comforts - a marvelous machine to remove the seeds from watermelons. Points out some things about the consumer market and our own truly marvelous machines.
Prod-KINGSP Dist-PHENIX 1971

Mr Microchip—A Series
16MM FILM, 3/4 OR 1/2 IN VIDEO I-H
Presents Mr Microchip, also known as Skip Lumley, a computer consultant, and his neighbors, twelve-year old Stevie and his ten-year old sister Dayna. During their visits to Mr Microchip, Stevie and Dayna learn about computers through hands-on demonstrations and clear analogy-filled explanations.
Prod-JOU Dist-JOU

Ask The Teacher 030 MIN
Bits Of Programming 030 MIN
Computer Has A Code, The 030 MIN
Computers Don't Do Windows 030 MIN
Does That Compute 030 MIN
Flights Of Fancy 030 MIN
Games Computers Play 030 MIN
Information Please 030 MIN
Memory Is Made Of This 030 MIN
Music On Key 030 MIN
Pixel Is Worth A Thousand Words, A 030 MIN
Problems, Problems, Problems 030 MIN
You Can Count On Computers 030 MIN

Mr Money C 4 MIN
16MM FILM, 3/4 OR 1/2 IN VIDEO
Presents a humorous tale of a man trying to cope with an automated teller machine that has a personality.
Prod-FLMCOM Dist-MTI

Mr Moto Takes A Walk C 13 MIN
16MM FILM, 3/4 OR 1/2 IN VIDEO K-I
Mr Moto, a macaque monkey, introduces the animals of the zoo in an alphabetical tour from aardvark to zebra.
Prod-NYZS Dist-SF Prodn-CLAIB 1965

Mr Pasteur And The Riddle Of Life C 11 MIN
16MM FILM, 3/4 OR 1/2 IN VIDEO I-J
Uses animated puppets to re-create Pasteur's classic experiments and explore the mystery of where living things come from.
Prod-CORF Dist-CORF 1972

Mr Peanut's Guide To Nutrition C 30 MIN
16MM FILM OPTICAL SOUND P-I
Presents Mr Peanut, a cartoon character who takes the viewer through the ABC'S of vitamins, proteins, carbohydrates, fats and minerals. Illustrates the importance of balanced diet and good eating habits.
Prod-SBRAND Dist-MTP

Mr Potter Takes A Rest Cure C 30 MIN
3/4 OR 1/2 INCH VIDEO CASSETTE C A
Presents an adaptation of the short story Mr Potter Takes A Rest Cure by P G Wodehouse.
From The Wodehouse Playhouse Series.
Prod-BBCTV Dist-TIMLIF 1980

Mr Preble Gets Rid Of His Wife C 17 MIN
16MM FILM, 3/4 OR 1/2 IN VIDEO J-C A
Tells how Mrs Preble thwarts her husband's tactics to murder her in the basement. Based on the short story Mr Preble Gets Rid Of His Wife by James Thurber.
LC NO. 81-706985
Prod-MIDMAR Dist-DIRECT 1981

Mr President, Mr President C 58 MIN
3/4 OR 1/2 INCH VIDEO CASSETTE
Examines press coverage of the Reagan Administration. Shows cameras covering the White House press corps, before, during and after a Presidential press conference and gives the viewer a rare inside look at the problems of access and restrictions which those reporters face every day when covering the most important beat in the country.
From The Inside Story Series.
Prod-PBS Dist-PBS 1981

Mr Randall Jarrell B 30 MIN
16MM FILM OPTICAL SOUND
Randall Jarrell reads and explains some of his poems about World War II.
From The North Carolina Books And Authors Series.
LC NO. FI67-558
Prod-UNC Dist-UNC Prodn-WUNCTV

Mr Robinson Crusoe B 76 MIN
16MM FILM OPTICAL SOUND
Tells the story of a man who argues while on a yacht that he too could survive on a primitive paradise like Robinson Crusoe. Details what happens when he is left on the island and is later joined by a girl. Stars Douglas Fairbanks, Sr and Alfred Newman.
Prod-UNKNWN Dist-KILLIS 1932

Mr Rooney Goes To Work, Pt 1 C 26 MIN
16MM FILM, 3/4 OR 1/2 IN VIDEO H-C A
Shows news commentator Andy Rooney talking to workers, company managers and union officials in an effort to determine if American productivity has declined. Concludes that Americans are far more productive than they believe themselves to be.
Prod-CBSNEW Dist-PHENIX 1978

Mr Rooney Goes To Work, Pt 2 C 25 MIN
16MM FILM, 3/4 OR 1/2 IN VIDEO H-C A
Presents news commentator Andy Rooney who explores alternatives to conventional work patterns.
Prod-CBSNEW Dist-PHENIX 1978

Mr Rossi At The Beach C 11 MIN
16MM FILM OPTICAL SOUND
Traces the misadventures of a man trying to have a good time at the beach.
LC NO. 74-702132
Prod-CONNF Dist-CONNF 1973

Mr Rossi Goes Camping C 11 MIN
16MM FILM OPTICAL SOUND I-C
Shows how a search for a peaceful camping site turns into a series of confrontations with bulldozers, cows and mountain-climbing motorcycles.
LC NO. 74-702133
Prod-CONNF Dist-CONNF 1973

Mr Rossi In Venice C 16 MIN
16MM FILM, 3/4 OR 1/2 IN VIDEO J-C A
Presents the animated adventures of Mr Rossi, telling how he tries to conquer pollution in Venice.
Prod-BOZETO Dist-TEXFLM 1977

Mr Shepard And Mr Milne C 29 MIN
16MM FILM, 3/4 OR 1/2 IN VIDEO H-C A
Tells about the collaboration of Ernest Shepard and A A Milne and the story behind their classic children's books through visits to the actual locales which were the scenes of the Pooh stories and poems.
Prod-WWS Dist-WWS 1972

Mr Sherlock Holmes Of London C 43 MIN
16MM FILM, 3/4 OR 1/2 IN VIDEO C A
Presents Anthony D Howlett, a noted London barrister and founding member of the Sherlock Holmes Society of London, who leads the viewer to the sites that figured prominently in Sir Arthur Conan Doyle's books. Recounts the beginning of the Sherlock Holmes mythology and reviews the publishing and film history of Doyle's works.
Prod-TAYLWF Dist-UCEMC 1976

Mr Simplex Saves The Aspidistra C 32 MIN
16MM FILM OPTICAL SOUND H-C T
Uses stop motion model photography to tell a story about Mr Simplex who introduces various maze problems and suggests possible mathematical solutions.
From The MAA Individual Lecturers Series.
LC NO. FIA65-848
Prod-MAA Dist-MLA Prodn-DAVFMS 1966

Mr Smith And Other Nonsense C 29 MIN
2 INCH VIDEOTAPE
Presents an international performance of mime, poetry, puppetry, dance, art and music.
From The Synergism - Encore Series.
Prod-WETATV Dist-PUBTEL

Mr Smith Goes To Washington B 130 MIN
16MM FILM OPTICAL SOUND I-C A
Stars Jimmy Stewart and Jean Arthur in the story of an idealistic young senator who tangles with a political machine and a cynical Washington-wise young woman.
Prod-CPC Dist-TIMLIF 1939

Mr Speaker C 28 MIN
3/4 INCH VIDEO CASSETTE H-C A
See series title for descriptive statement.
Prod-HERIO Dist-GPITVL 1980

Mr Speaker - Tip O'Neill C 58 MIN
16MM FILM, 3/4 OR 1/2 IN VIDEO H-C A
Looks at the day-to-day life and work of House Speaker Thomas P (Tip) O'Neill as he meets with the congressional elite, glad-hands voters back home, relaxes with his family and confers with President Jimmy Carter in the Oval Office.
Prod-WGBHTV Dist-FI 1978

Mr Story C 28 MIN
16MM FILM, 3/4 OR 1/2 IN VIDEO J-C A
Tells of an older man, Albert Story, whose life has produced no exceptional achievements, but who looks back with pride on a good life.
Prod-BFA Dist-BFA

Mr Story C 28 MIN
16MM FILM, 3/4 OR 1/2 IN VIDEO J-C A
Describes the life and attitudes of Albert Story, who has lived a long life and is still spiritually and physically strong.
Prod-THACHA Dist-PHENIX

Mr Symbol Man C 50 MIN
16MM FILM, 3/4 OR 1/2 IN VIDEO C A
Presents a documentary on Charles K Bliss, an Austrian-australian who invented Blissymbols, a means of communication which enables a person to overcome the barriers to understanding posed by differing languages or physical handicap.
Prod-NFBC Dist-BNCHMK Prodn-MOKING 1976

Mr Tense C
3/4 OR 1/2 INCH VIDEO CASSETTE
Discusses treatment and prevention of cardiovascular problems. Focuses on stress.
Prod-MEDFAC Dist-MEDFAC

Mr Thoreau Takes A Trip - A Week On The Concord And Merrimack C 27 MIN
2 INCH VIDEOTAPE
See series title for descriptive statement.
From The Synergism - Profiles, People Series.
Prod-WENHTV Dist-PUBTEL

Mr Tompkins In Wonderland - An Adventure On The Frontiers Of Physics C 31 MIN
16MM FILM OPTICAL SOUND H-C
Communicates the concepts of relativistic mechanics as they affect space, time and gravitation by altering the numerical value of physical constants. Based on the book Mr Tompkins In Wonderland - An Adventure On The Frontier Of Physics by George Gamow.
LC NO. 76-700515
Prod-NSF Dist-UAKRON Prodn-CNMKP 1972

Mr Vanik Leaves Washington C 28 MIN
3/4 OR 1/2 INCH VIDEO CASSETTE J-C A
Presents a portrait of United States Congressman Charles Vanik leaving office. Discusses the process of writing legislation and getting acts passed. Includes scenes of Vanik at a press conference, at subcommittee hearings and having lunch. Highlights the role of today's Congressman in relation to lobbyists.
LC NO. 81-707017
Prod-STORBC Dist-WJKWTV 1980

Mr Willoughby's Christmas C 15 MIN
3/4 INCH VIDEO CASSETTE K-P
See series title for descriptive statement.
From The Storytime Series.
Prod-WCETTV Dist-GPITVL 1976

Mr Winkle Returns C 8 MIN
16MM FILM OPTICAL SOUND
Presents an animated film of General Mills' 1953-1954 Annual Report, featuring a recently awakened Rip Van Winkle on a tour of General Mills.
Prod-GEMILL Dist-GEMILL

Mr Winlucky C 7 MIN
16MM FILM OPTICAL SOUND
An animated cartoon about James Hound, super agent, who is sent to break the bank of the crooked gambling casino.
LC NO. 77-707173
Prod-TERTON Dist-TWCF 1967

Mr Wizard—A Series

Prod-PRISM Dist-MLA

Breathing 28 MIN
Buoyancy 28 MIN
Communication Theory 28 MIN
Errors In Measurement 28 MIN
Fluids In Motion 28 MIN
Hidden Salts 28 MIN
How To Change A Chemical Reaction 28 MIN
How Your Blood Circulates 28 MIN
Science Of Orbiting 28 MIN
Scientific Noise 28 MIN

MR-1 Launch C 14 MIN
16MM FILM OPTICAL SOUND
Examines the flight of the unmanned MR-1.
Prod-NASA Dist-NASA

MR-2 Launch C 14 MIN
16MM FILM OPTICAL SOUND
Presents the flight of the MR-2 and follows Ham, America's first space chimpanzee.
Prod-NASA Dist-NASA

MR-3 Onboard Pilot Observer C 21 MIN
16MM FILM OPTICAL SOUND
Examines America's first manned journey into space with pre-flight preparations, readying of tracking stations and the launch of Freedom 7.
Prod-NASA Dist-NASA

MRO Inventory Forecasting Techniques C
3/4 OR 1/2 INCH VIDEO CASSETTE IND
Discusses Exponential Smoothing as most popular technique for forecasting as age rates for maintenance, repair and operations inventory. Talks about forecast error and general forecasting considerations as well as general guiding principles.
From The Effective Inventory Control Series.
Prod-GPCV Dist-GPCV

Mrs Amworth C 28 MIN
16MM FILM, 3/4 OR 1/2 IN VIDEO H-C A
Presents an adaptation of the short story 'Mrs Amworth' by E F Benson, about modern vampirism in a small English village.
From The Classics, Dark And Dangerous Series.
Prod-LCOA Dist-LCOA 1977

Mrs Amworth (Captioned) C 29 MIN
16MM FILM, 3/4 OR 1/2 IN VIDEO P-C A
Stars Glynis Johns in this tale of vampires and the occult. Based on a story by E F Benson.
From The Classics Dark And Dangerous (Captioned) Series.
Prod-LCOA Dist-LCOA 1977

Mrs Amworth (Spanish) C 29 MIN
16MM FILM, 3/4 OR 1/2 IN VIDEO P-C A
Stars Glynis Johns in this tale of vampires and the occult. Based on a story by E F Benson.
From The Classics Dark And Dangerous (Spanish) Series.
Prod-LCOA Dist-LCOA 1977

Mrs Baker's House C 10 MIN
16MM FILM OPTICAL SOUND
Presents a fun mystery story without an ending about Mrs Barker,

a sweet old lady who lives alone in a Hansel and Gretel-type house in which all sorts of mysterious things happen. Describes the humorous antics of Mr Crochety, a nosy neighbor, and the mysterious happenings inside the house in order to spark creative thinking and storytelling.
Prod-ECI Dist-ECI

Mrs Breadwinner C 12 MIN
16MM FILM, 3/4 OR 1/2 IN VIDEO J-C A
Explores the growing number of women who earn more than their husbands and the effects this has on families. Narrated by Harry Reasoner and originally show on the CBS program 60 Minutes.
LC NO. 83-706303
Prod-CBSNEW Dist-MTI 1982

Mrs Mary Norton - Socialist Suffragette C 30 MIN
3/4 INCH VIDEO CASSETTE
Features Mary Norton, Vancouver Suffragette, reminiscing about the Canadian Womens' struggle for the vote.
Prod-WMENIF Dist-WMENIF

Mrs Mixon B 59 MIN
16MM FILM OPTICAL SOUND C A
An account of the problems of a middle-aged negro woman from the rural South, her rehabilitation in a midwestern university hospital after diabetes had taken her legs and blinded her and her unresolved conflicts with white therapists.
LC NO. 71-702469
Prod-OHIOSU Dist-OSUMPD Prodn-OSUMPD 1969

Mrs Murphy's Chowder C 28 MIN
2 INCH VIDEOTAPE
Views water pollution not as an aesthetic issue but as a threat to man's survival. Looks at two areas of concern, an increasing demand by an ever-growing population and worsening pollution.
From The Environment - Today And Tomorrow Series.
Prod-KRMATV Dist-PUBTEL

Mrs Peabody's Beach C 24 MIN
16MM FILM, 3/4 OR 1/2 IN VIDEO I-H
Tells the story of a teenager who discovers a beach which is ideal for surfing, only to learn that the owner, Mrs Peabody, will permit surfing, only if he helps her develop it as a profitable business. Covers aspects of the law of supply and demand, capital investment and depreciation, diminishing returns and other aspects of basic economics.
Prod-BELLD Dist-WDEMCO 1971

Mrs Perlberg's Partner In Heaven B 30 MIN
16MM FILM OPTICAL SOUND R
Formerly titled 'MRS STEINBERG'S PARTNER IN HEAVEN.' Presents a fantasy about Mrs Perlbery on New York's East Side who, despite her own modest circumstances, is always doing good deeds--she exemplifies the truly pious person, who practices charity as a partner of God. (Kinescope)
Prod-JTS Dist-NAAJS Prodn-NBCTV 1961

Mrs Ripley's Trip By Hamlin Garland C 15 MIN
16MM FILM, 3/4 OR 1/2 IN VIDEO J-C A
Describes how a poor farm woman realizes a 23-year-old ambition by leaving the farm for a trip to experience the civilized wonders of New York. Shows how the fulfillment of her ambition leaves her reconciled to her life of rural poverty upon her return. Based on the short story Mrs Ripley's Trip by Hamlin Garland.
From The Short Story Series.
LC NO. 83-706130
Prod-IITC Dist-IU 1982

Mrs Ryder Has The Blues C 29 MIN
2 INCH VIDEOTAPE
See series title for descriptive statement.
From The Our Street Series.
Prod-MDCPB Dist-PUBTEL

Mrs Warren's Profession C 115 MIN
16MM FILM, 3/4 OR 1/2 IN VIDEO
Offers a production of George Bernard Shaw's play Mrs Warren's Profession. Explains how Mrs Warren works as a madam so that she can afford to educate her daughter.
From The Classic Theatre Series.
LC NO. 79-706925
Prod-BBCTV Dist-FI 1976

Ms - The Struggle For Women's Rights B 14 MIN
16MM FILM OPTICAL SOUND I-C A
Depicts the people, places and events that have given impetus and leadership to the struggle for women's rights.
From The Screen News Digest Series. Vol 15, Issue 2
LC NO. 73-701268
Prod-HEARST Dist-HEARST 1972

Mt Rainier Wonderland C 20 MIN
16MM FILM OPTICAL SOUND J-C A
Presents views of Mt Rainer and of Mt Rainer National Park. Shows various natural wonders--glaciers, ice caves, streams, waterfalls and volcanic craters. Shows wildlife--bear, marmot, blacktail deer, camprobber and the groundsquirrel.
LC NO. FIA63-970
Prod-PFC Dist-PFC 1963

Mt St Helens - Road To Recovery C 29 MIN
16MM FILM, 3/4 OR 1/2 IN VIDEO J-C A
Focuses on the devastation wrought by the Mount St Helens eruption and the efforts of the USDA, Forest Service and State agencies to bring life back to the area.
Prod-USDA Dist-USNAC 1982

Mt St Helens - Why They Died C 30 MIN
3/4 OR 1/2 INCH VIDEO CASSETTE
Questions the role of government officials in disaster planning. Features Governor Dixie Lee Ray responding to criticism of her safety management, and the opinions of of scientists involved with the disaster which killed fifty seven people in legally open areas when Mount St Helens exploded.
From The Synthesis Series.
Prod-KPBS Dist-KPBS

Mt Zao C 25 MIN
16MM FILM OPTICAL SOUND
Points out that Mt Zao in North Japan is well-known for its juhyo, the frozen snow which makes the trees resemble flowers. Shows Yuichiro Miura, a pro-skier, and his teammates ski-rumming thought the Juhyo, together with scenes of the festivals.
Prod-UNIJAP Dist-UNIJAP 1968

Much Ado About DDD And One-Frog Bands C 12 MIN
16MM FILM OPTICAL SOUND H A
Employs puppets to demonstrate how to use direct distance dialing. Describes the new wide scope of DDD service.
LC NO. 76-705614
Prod-SWBELL Dist-SWBELL Prodn-STOKB 1969

Much Ado About Golf B 9 MIN
16MM FILM SILENT
Tells the story of a hapless golfer who has many problems as he tries to drive the first ball in opening the links at a new country club.
From The W C Fields Comedy Series.
LC NO. 76-700502
Prod-PARTOR Dist-BHAWK Prodn-CASTLE

Much Ado About Nothing C 12 MIN
16MM FILM, 3/4 OR 1/2 IN VIDEO H-C
See series title for descriptive statement.
From The Shakespeare Series.
Prod-IFB Dist-IFB 1974

Much Ado About Nothing C 120 MIN
3/4 OR 1/2 INCH VIDEO CASSETTE H-C A
Presents William Shakespeare's play Much Ado About Nothing which involves Hero, an innocent slandered heroine, who is denounced for unchastity by her intended bridegroom, Claudio, at the wedding itself. Reveals that Hero faints and is presumed dead.
From The Shakespeare Plays Series.
Prod-BBCTV Dist-TIMLIF 1984

Much Ado About Nothing - Beatrice And Benedict, Personification Of Reluctant Witty... B 45 MIN
2 INCH VIDEOTAPE C
See series title for descriptive statement.
From The Shakespeare Series.
Prod-CHITVC Dist-GPITVL Prodn-WTTWTV

Much Ado About Nothing - Dogberry And Verges, Typical Native Elizabethan Humor B 45 MIN
2 INCH VIDEOTAPE C
See series title for descriptive statement.
From The Shakespeare Series.
Prod-CHITVC Dist-GPITVL Prodn-WTTWTV

Much Ado About Nut Things - Problem Solving, Estimation C 13 MIN
16MM FILM, 3/4 OR 1/2 IN VIDEO I
Features Captain Calculator demonstrating how estimation can help solve counting problems. Discusses the use of the calculator in estimation.
Prod-EBEC Dist-EBEC

Muchmore's Marvelous Machine C 8 MIN
16MM FILM OPTICAL SOUND P
See series title for descriptive statement.
From The Mathematics For Elementary School Students - Whole Numbers Series.
LC NO. 73-701840
Prod-DAVFMS Dist-DAVFMS 1974

Mud C 23 MIN
16MM FILM OPTICAL SOUND J-C A
Studies urban erosion and sedimentation. Explains how engineering skills and conservation practices often applied to rural areas can be used in cities to prevent flooding and other drainage difficulties.
LC NO. FIA68-3286
Prod-FINLYS Dist-FINLYS 1968

Mud And Water Man C 50 MIN
16MM FILM, 3/4 OR 1/2 IN VIDEO H-C
Presents the life and work of contemporary English potter, Michael Cardew. Traces his working life as potter, teacher and writer in Africa and Cornwall, England. Features Cardew discussing his personal philosophy and his interest in reviving the craft of pottery-making in England.
Prod-BCACGB Dist-FI 1976

Mud House C 29 MIN
16MM FILM OPTICAL SOUND
Examines the design and construction of an all-concrete house using the latest concrete technology.
LC NO. 75-700904
Prod-ALEXP Dist-STUDO 1975

Mud Pit Volume Recorders C 19 MIN
3/4 OR 1/2 INCH VIDEO CASSETTE IND
Explains installation, maintenance and operation of Dresser Swaco pit-level indicators.
Prod-UTEXPE Dist-UTEXPE 1966

Mud Pumps C 33 MIN
3/4 OR 1/2 INCH VIDEO CASSETTE IND
Shows operation, maintenance and installation of the power and fluid ends of duplex and triplex slush pumps used in drilling.
Prod-UTEXPE Dist-UTEXPE 1980

Mudflat Art C 16 MIN
3/4 INCH VIDEO CASSETTE
Concentrates on the unique driftwood art which is found on the Emeryville mudflat. Explores the meaning of 'junk' sculptures.
Prod-RDR Dist-RDR

Mudhorse B 12 MIN
16MM FILM OPTICAL SOUND
Presents a statement on social conditions in Egypt. Describes Nile River workers and horses who mingle in an open-air brick factory, using a method thousands of years old.
Prod-ICARUS Dist-ICARUS 1971

Muffinland - Holiday Specials--A Series

Presents Muffinland, a place where people explore the objects around them. Features Miss Jo delving into the holiday seasons.
Prod-WGTV Dist-PUBTEL

Christmas	14 MIN
Halloween	14 MIN
Thanksgiving - The Pilgrims	14 MIN
Thanksgiving - The Things I Like Best	14 MIN

Muffinland--A Series

Nurtures and feeds the natural curiosity of children. Shows Muffinland as the place where people explore the objects around them.
Prod-WGTV Dist-PUBTEL

Autumn World, The, Pt 1	14 MIN
Autumn World, The, Pt 2	14 MIN
City, The, Pt 1	14 MIN
City, The, Pt 2	14 MIN
Columbus	14 MIN
Community Helpers, Pt 1	14 MIN
Community Helpers, Pt 2	14 MIN
Farm, The	14 MIN
Jungle, The	14 MIN
Ocean, The	14 MIN
Ranch, The, Pt 1	14 MIN
Ranch, The, Pt 2	14 MIN
Smoky Mountains, Pt 1	14 MIN
Smoky Mountains, Pt 2	14 MIN
Trip To The University, A	14 MIN
Visit To The World Of The Muffins, Pt 1	14 MIN
Visit To The World Of The Muffins, Pt 2	14 MIN
Winter World, Pt 1	14 MIN
Winter World, Pt 2	14 MIN
World Of Muffins	14 MIN
World Of The Forest, Pt 1	14 MIN
World Of The Forest, Pt 2	14 MIN

Mugged C 12 MIN
16MM FILM, 3/4 OR 1/2 IN VIDEO
Examines what people, especially seniors, can do if they are mugged. Shows reformed muggers in New York City explaining to senior citizens in workshops what a mugger looks for in a victim.
Prod-CBSNEW Dist-MTI

Muggers C 15 MIN
16MM FILM, 3/4 OR 1/2 IN VIDEO J-C
Tells the story of Andy, a youth with no arrest record, who promised his mother he would watch over his older brother, a paroled drug addict. Portrays how Charlie, despite Andy's efforts, returns to his old habits. Shows how the police subsequently capture both of them and they are found guilty of robbery and grand theft. Depicts how they are sentenced individually in a manner that reflects the personalities of the offenders.
From The Under The Law, Pt 1 Series.
Prod-USNEI Dist-WDEMCO 1974

Mugging - You Can Protect Yourself C 31 MIN
16MM FILM, 3/4 OR 1/2 IN VIDEO J-C A
Offers guidelines on how to avoid threatening situations. Demonstrates specific methods by which a mugging victim can deal with an assailant, even at the point of a knife or gun.
Prod-JASON Dist-LCOA 1977

Muggins C 11 MIN
16MM FILM OPTICAL SOUND J-C
Presents a semi-surrealistic study of the emotional conflict between a shrewish wife and a romantic husband.
Prod-CFS Dist-CFS 1968

Mughal Glory C 19 MIN
16MM FILM OPTICAL SOUND I-C A
Shows the architectural beauty of the monuments of Agra and Fatehpur Sikri - the Taj, Jumma Masjid and Dewan-i-khas.
Prod-INDIA Dist-NEDINF

Mujeres Colombianas C 20 MIN
3/4 INCH VIDEO CASSETTE J-C
Presents a group of Colombian women giving personal testimony to the advantages of using birth control. Discusses the new economic security, stabilized home life, and release from the fear of pregnancy. Discusses how they have dealt with disapproval from husbands and family members.
From The Are You Listening Series.
LC NO. 80-707404
Prod-STURTM Dist-STURTM 1973

Mule Days C 20 MIN
1/2 IN VIDEO CASSETTE BETA/VHS
Highlights the 1983 Mule Days Celebration in Bishop, California.
Prod-SMIFT Dist-EQVDL

Mules C 25 MIN
16MM FILM, 3/4 OR 1/2 IN VIDEO I-H A
Looks at the history of the mule. Discusses the animal's intelligence and strength.
Prod-KAWVAL Dist-MTI

Mullet Country C 13 MIN
16MM FILM OPTICAL SOUND I-H A
Demonstrates the history, biology, catching, processing, cooking and serving of mullets. Views the scenery of Florida, where more mullet are landed than in any other state.
From The Commercial Fisheries Series. No. 23
LC NO. 70-702833
Prod-USBCF Dist-USNOAA 1968

Mulligan Stew—A Series
I
Presents Mulligan Stew, a five-piece kids' rock music group organized to teach good nutrition practices to the youth of the United States.
Prod-GPITVL Dist-GPITVL

Count Down 4-4-3-2 028 MIN
Flim Flam Man, The 030 MIN
Getting It All Together 030 MIN
Great Nutrition Turn On, The 030 MIN
Look Inside Yourself 030 MIN
Racer That Lost His Edge, The 030 MIN

Mulliner's Buck-U-Uppo C 30 MIN
3/4 OR 1/2 INCH VIDEO CASSETTE C A
Presents an adaptation of the short story Mulliner's Buck-U-Uppo by P G Wodehouse.
From The Wodehouse Playhouse Series.
Prod-BBCTV Dist-TIMLIF 1980

Multi Pass Electric Arc Welding C 15 MIN
3/4 OR 1/2 INCH VIDEO CASSETTE
See series title for descriptive statement.
From The Welding II - Basic Shielded Metal Arc Welding series.
Prod-CAMB Dist-CAMB

Multi Pass Welding With Dual Shielded C 15 MIN
3/4 OR 1/2 INCH VIDEO CASSETTE IND
See series title for descriptive statement.
From The Welding - MIG And TIG Welding Series.
Prod-ICSINT Dist-ICSINT

Multi Pass Welding With Dual Shielded (Spanish) C
3/4 OR 1/2 INCH VIDEO CASSETTE
See series title for descriptive statement.
From The MIG And TIG Welding (Spanish) Series.
Prod-VTRI Dist-VTRI

Multi-Cultural Education - A Teaching Style C 29 MIN
16MM FILM, 3/4 OR 1/2 IN VIDEO T
Looks at the changes from the traditional melting pot theory to an appreciation of cultural pluralism. Demonstrates several classroom approaches which encourage ethnic groups to maintain their identity and pride while developing mutual respect for others.
From The Survival Skills For The Classroom Teacher Series.
Prod-MFFD Dist-FI

Multi-Pass Electric Arc Welding (Spanish) C
3/4 OR 1/2 INCH VIDEO CASSETTE
See series title for descriptive statement.
From The Shielded Metal Arc Welding (Spanish) Series.
Prod-VTRI Dist-VTRI

Multi-Pass Electric-Arc Welding C 15 MIN
3/4 OR 1/2 INCH VIDEO CASSETTE IND
See series title for descriptive statement.
From The Welding - Shielded Metal-Arc Welding Series.
Prod-ICSINT Dist-ICSINT

Multi-Pass Fillet C 4 MIN
1/2 IN VIDEO CASSETTE BETA/VHS IND
See series title for descriptive statement.
From The Welding Training (Comprehensive) - Metal Inert Gas (M I G) Welding Series.
Prod-RMI Dist-RMI

Multi-Pass Fillet Flat (Steel) C 5 MIN
1/2 IN VIDEO CASSETTE BETA/VHS IND
See series title for descriptive statement.
From The Welding Training (Comprehensive) - Metal Inert Gas (M I G) Welding Series.
Prod-RMI Dist-RMI

Multi-Pass Fillet V-Up C 3 MIN
1/2 IN VIDEO CASSETTE BETA/VHS IND
See series title for descriptive statement.
From The Welding Training (Comprehensive) - Metal Inert Gas (M I G) Welding Series.
Prod-RMI Dist-RMI

Multibus, The C 60 MIN
3/4 OR 1/2 INCH VIDEO CASSETTE C
See series title for descriptive statement.
From The Microcomputer Bus Structures Series.
Prod-NEU Dist-AMCEE

Multilevel Teaching For Normal And Handicapped Children C 29 MIN
16MM FILM OPTICAL SOUND C T S
Demonstrates techniques for providing individualized instruction while working with both handicapped and normal children who vary greatly in their skill levels.
LC NO. 78-701601
Prod-UKANS Dist-UKANS 1977

Multimate - An Introduction To Word Processing C 30 MIN
3/4 OR 1/2 INCH VIDEO CASSETTE
Describes fully how MULTIMATE is used in making an IBM PC emulate a Wang word processor. Details step-by-step procedure for booting-up, utilizing and creating hard copy from IBM PC. Includes written text.
Prod-MICROV Dist-BERGL

MultiMate - Introduction To The Word Processor C
3/4 OR 1/2 INCH VIDEO CASSETTE A
Introduces the concepts and applications of work processing. Includes creating, changing, copying and deleting documents; inserting, moving, copying and deleting words, paragraphs and pages; merging documents; and formatting. Explains automatic search and replace, math functions how to print selected pages and creating mailing lists with form letters.
Prod-DSIM Dist-DSIM

Multimedia Standard First Aid (Rev 1980) C 54 MIN
3/4 OR 1/2 INCH VIDEO CASSETTE
Teaches standard first aid when used as part of a multi- media method including a student workbook and instructor material.
Prod-ATAT Dist-AMRC 1980

Multimeter Use C 60 MIN
3/4 OR 1/2 INCH VIDEO CASSETTE IND
See series title for descriptive statement.
From The Electrical Maintenance Training, Module B - Test Instruments Series.
Prod-LEIKID Dist-LEIKID

Multimeters, Basic Circuits, Movements C 60 MIN
3/4 OR 1/2 INCH VIDEO CASSETTE IND
See series title for descriptive statement.
From The Electrical Maintenance Training, Module B - Test Instruments Series.
Prod-LEIKID Dist-LEIKID

Multimodal Behavior Therapy C 48 MIN
3/4 INCH VIDEO CASSETTE
Jpresents Arnold A Lazarus, PhD, Professor, Graduate of Applied and Professional Psychology, Rutgers University, New Brunswick, NJ.
From The Three Approaches To Psychotherapy II Series.
Prod-PSYCHD Dist-PSYCHD

Multimodal Marital Therapy C 22 MIN
3/4 OR 1/2 INCH VIDEO CASSETTE
Illustrates effective ways husband and wife can respond to each other's needs and feelings.
From The Multimodal Therapy Series.
Prod-RESPRC Dist-RESPRC

Multimodal Therapy—A Series

Demonstrates the concepts and techniques of multimodal therapy developed by Dr. Arnold A. Lazarus over the last 25 years. Illustrates each point with simulations of actual case histories.
Prod-RESPRC Dist-RESPRC

Assessment/Therapy Connection 029 MIN
Multimodal Marital Therapy 022 MIN
Use Of Bridging And Tracking To Overcome 017 MIN

Multinational Corporation, The C 32 MIN
16MM FILM - 3/4 IN VIDEO IND
Suggests that one of the most significiant developments of the century, a unique mechanism for producing, distributing and marketing goods and services on a world-wide basis is confronting a world-wide shift toward nationalism and protectionism.
From The Managing Discontinuity Series.
Prod-BNA Dist-BNA 1971

MultiPlan C
3/4 OR 1/2 INCH VIDEO CASSETTE
Illustrates the overall concept of an electronic spreadsheet and the basic model-building tools of MultiPlan. Shows how to build a financial model using basic MultiPlan commands and offers an introduction to the 'what if' game.
Prod-LANSFD Dist-ANDRST

Multiple Access And Resources Sharing Techniques C 55 MIN
3/4 OR 1/2 INCH VIDEO CASSETTE C
Discusses satellite capacity and the ultimate distributed network, structured and unstructured resource sharing, multiplexing and concentrating, broadcasting and narrow casting and capacity comparisons of various sharing techniques.
From The Distributed Telecommunications Networks Series.
Prod-AMCEE Dist-AMCEE

Multiple Aortocoronary Saphenous Vein Bypass Grafts C 28 MIN
3/4 OR 1/2 INCH VIDEO CASSETTE
See series title for descriptive statement.
From The Cardiovascular Series.
Prod-SVL Dist-SVL

Multiple Choice C 20 MIN
16MM FILM OPTICAL SOUND J-C A
Portrays the library trustee as he carries out the duties and responsibilities of his position in board meetings and in the community. Emphasizes certain responsibilities in the areas of policy-making, finance and public relations.
LC NO. 73-701193
Prod-INDSLI Dist-INDSLI 1972

Multiple Diverticula Of The Bladder B 15 MIN
16MM FILM OPTICAL SOUND PRO
Presents a surgical dissection and demonstration of multiple diverticula of the bladder.
Prod-WYETH Dist-WYLAB

Multiple Fractures To The Arm C 8 MIN
3/4 OR 1/2 INCH VIDEO CASSETTE PRO
Shows methods for applying a sling, a wireladder splint, and cravats for fractures of both humerus and radial bones.
From The EMT Video - Group Two Series.
LC NO. 84-706480
Prod-USA Dist-USNAC 1983

Multiple Gastric Polyps C 20 MIN
16MM FILM OPTICAL SOUND PRO
Deals with the diagnosis, pathology and surgical technique of subtotal gastrectomy for multiple gastric polyps. Emphasizes roentgenological diagnosis and pathological characteristics.
Prod-ACYDGD Dist-ACY 1964

Multiple Handicapped, The C 23 MIN
16MM FILM OPTICAL SOUND
Shows mentally retarded, cerebral palsied, dysmelia, deaf-blind and emotionally disturbed deaf children in Sweden, Germany, the Netherlands and England.
LC NO. 74-705179
Prod-USBEH Dist-USNAC 1970

Multiple Integration And The Jacobian B 33 MIN
3/4 OR 1/2 INCH VIDEO CASSETTE
See series title for descriptive statement.
From The Calculus Of Several Variables - Multiple-- Integration Series.
Prod-MIOT Dist-MIOT

Multiple Random Variables - Discrete B 34 MIN
3/4 OR 1/2 INCH VIDEO CASSETTE PRO
Discusses the properties of joint probability distribution functions and marginal probability distribution functions.
From The Probability And Random Processes - Random Variables Series.
Prod-MIOT Dist-MIOT

Multiple Sclerosis C 28 MIN
16MM FILM OPTICAL SOUND
Dramatizes the episodic course of multiple sclerosis, following patients from the very earliest signs through characteristic periods of exacerbation and remission. Reviews muscular incoordination visual difficulties and problems of hearing and speech while illustrating the pathological changes that produced these deficits.
Prod-FLEMRP Dist-NMSS 1966

Multiple Star System, A - Xi Ursae Majoris C 8 MIN
16MM FILM OPTICAL SOUND H-C A
Uses computer animation to examine the multiple star system, Xi Ursae Majoris, a four-star system.
From The Explorations In Space And Time Series.
LC NO. 75-703981
Prod-HMC Dist-HMC 1974

Multiple Visceral Arterial Aneurysms C 6 MIN
16MM FILM OPTICAL SOUND PRO
Shows how the workup of a 51-year-old female with complaint of upper abdominal pain includes an arteriography which reveals an aneurysm of the celiac exis and of the superior mesenteric artery. Discusses the anatomy and pathology of the lesions in the course of the operative resection of the lesions and reconstruction of the visceral arterial tree.
Prod-UCLA Dist-UCLA 1970

Multiple-Pass Fillet Weld - 1-F Position C 15 MIN
3/4 OR 1/2 INCH VIDEO CASSETTE IND
See series title for descriptive statement.
From The Arc Welding Training Series.
Prod-AVIMA Dist-AVIMA

Multiple-Pass Fillet Weld - 2-F Position C 15 MIN
3/4 OR 1/2 INCH VIDEO CASSETTE IND
See series title for descriptive statement.
From The Arc Welding Training Series.
Prod-AVIMA Dist-AVIMA

Multiple-Pass Fillet Weld - 3-F Position C 15 MIN
3/4 OR 1/2 INCH VIDEO CASSETTE IND
See series title for descriptive statement.
From The Arc Welding Training Series.
Prod-AVIMA Dist-AVIMA

Multiple-Pass Fillet Weld - 4-F Position C 15 MIN
3/4 OR 1/2 INCH VIDEO CASSETTE IND
See series title for descriptive statement.
From The Arc Welding Training Series.
Prod-AVIMA Dist-AVIMA

Multiple-System Trauma - A Matter Of Minutes C 70 MIN
3/4 OR 1/2 INCH VIDEO CASSETTE PRO
Presents techniques for treating medical emergencies consisting of multiple-system traumas. Dramatically enacts typical cases. Provides actual documentary footage.
From The Continuing Medical Education Emergency Care Programs Series.
Prod-CONTED Dist-CONTED

Multiple-Systems Trauma - A Matter Of Minutes C 70 MIN
3/4 OR 1/2 INCH VIDEO CASSETTE
Examines vital principles and priorities of emergency nursing care. Discusses critical assessment priorities, the ABC approach, recognition of shock and placement fluids. Offers a comprehensive, head-to-toe approach to examination of the patient.
Prod-CONTED Dist-AJN

Multiplexing C 44 MIN
3/4 OR 1/2 INCH VIDEO CASSETTE
Discusses multiplexing techniques.
From The Telecommunications And The Computer Series.
Prod-MIOT Dist-MIOT

Multiplexing C 45 MIN
3/4 OR 1/2 INCH VIDEO CASSETTE C
Discusses bandwidth and motivation for sharing, multiplexing techniques including frequency division multiplexing (FDM), time division multiplexing (TDM), concentration and Shannon's theorem for channel capacity.
From The Telecommunications And The Computer Series.

LC NO. 81-707502
Prod-AMCEE Dist-AMCEE 1981

Multiplexing C 50 MIN
3/4 OR 1/2 INCH VIDEO CASSETTE PRO
Demonstrates the need for multiplexing. Covers various types of multiplexing.
From The Fundamentals Of Data Communications Series.
Prod-AMCEE Dist-AMCEE

Multiplication C 30 MIN
16MM FILM OPTICAL SOUND T
Uses model sets to point up the properties of multiplication. To be used following 'ADDITION AND SUBTRACTION TECHNIQUES.'
From The Mathematics For Elementary School Teachers Series. No. 8
Prod-SMSG Dist-MLA 1963

Multiplication C 15 MIN
16MM FILM, 3/4 OR 1/2 IN VIDEO P
Introduces the idea of multiplication as repeated addition. Develops the multiplication table up to the tens. Introduces the simplest form of multiplication computation.
From The Beginning Mathematics Series.
Prod-JOU Dist-JOU

Multiplication C 16 MIN
3/4 OR 1/2 INCH VIDEO CASSETTE P
Introduces multiplication facts through 5 X 5.
From The Math Cycle Series.
Prod-WDCNTV Dist-GPITVL 1983

Multiplication C 20 MIN
2 INCH VIDEOTAPE P
See series title for descriptive statement.
From The Mathemagic, Unit VIII - Multiplication And Division Series.
Prod-WMULTV Dist-GPITVL

Multiplication (Spanish) C 14 MIN
16MM FILM, 3/4 OR 1/2 IN VIDEO P
Introduces the idea of multiplication as repeated addition.
From The Beginning Mathematics Series.
Prod-GLDWER Dist-JOU 1973

Multiplication (3rd Ed) C 12 MIN
16MM FILM, 3/4 OR 1/2 IN VIDEO P
Uses animation to teach multiplication.
From The Math For Beginners (3rd Ed) Series.
Prod-CORF Dist-CORF

Multiplication And Division C 7 MIN
16MM FILM OPTICAL SOUND P T
See series title for descriptive statement.
From The MAA Elementary Arithmetic Series.
Prod-MAA Dist-MLA 1967

Multiplication And Division C 15 MIN
3/4 INCH VIDEO CASSETTE I
Discusses multiplication by repeated addition. Names the parts of multiplication and division as factors and products.
From The Math - No Mystery Series.
Prod-WCETTV Dist-GPITVL 1977

Multiplication Of Rational Numbers C 24 MIN
16MM FILM OPTICAL SOUND T
Examines various numeration systems. Explores the properties of closure, commutativity, associativity and distributivity. To be used following 'ADDITION AND SUBTRACTION OF RATIONAL NUMBERS.'
From The Mathematics For Elementary School Teachers Series. No. 21
Prod-GNRLLC Dist-MLA 1963

Multiplication Of Rational Numbers B 31 MIN
16MM FILM OPTICAL SOUND H
Shows properties for the multiplication and division of signed numbers, using the idea that (-1)(a) equals (-a) and (-B)(1/-B) equals 1. Applies these concepts to the addition, subtraction, multiplication and division of multiple-term expressions involving powers.
From The Intermediate Algebra Series.
Prod-CALVIN Dist-MLA Prodn-UNIVFI 1959

Multiplication Rock—A Series
3/4 OR 1/2 INCH VIDEO CASSETTE P-I
Translates the elements of arithmetic into original rock songs illustrated by animated cartoons. Deals with mathematical processes involving an individual number.
Prod-ABCTV Dist-GA

Elementary, My Dear (Two's) 004 MIN
Figure Eight 004 MIN
Four-Legged Zoo, The 004 MIN
Good Eleven, The 004 MIN
I Got Six 004 MIN
Little Twelvetoes 004 MIN
Lucky Seven Sampson 004 MIN
My Hero, Zero 004 MIN
Naughty Number Nine 004 MIN
Ready Or Not, Here I Come 004 MIN
Three Is A Magic Number 004 MIN

Multiplication Techniques C 30 MIN
16MM FILM OPTICAL SOUND T
Shows the existence of a multiplicative inverse, and introduces the distributive property. Develops algorithms consistent with the properties. To be used following division.
From The Mathematics For Elementary School Teachers Series. No. 10
Prod-SMSG Dist-MLA 1963

Multiplication 1, Using The Cuisenaire Rods C 9 MIN
16MM FILM OPTICAL SOUND P-I T
Demonstrates the use of cuisenaire colored rods in teaching multiplication.
From The Using Cuisenaire Rods Series. No. 3
LC NO. FIA67-37
Prod-MMP Dist-MMP 1966

Multiplication, Pt 1 C 15 MIN
3/4 INCH VIDEO CASSETTE P
Shows the meaning of multiplication in adding equal addends.
From The Studio M Series.
Prod-WCETTV Dist-GPITVL 1979

Multiplication, Pt 2 C 15 MIN
3/4 INCH VIDEO CASSETTE P
Tells how to solve multiplication facts through the product of 45. Emphasis is on threes and fours.
From The Studio M Series.
Prod-WCETTV Dist-GPITVL 1979

Multiplier Effect, The C 45 MIN
3/4 OR 1/2 INCH VIDEO CASSETTE
Discusses the multiplier effect in economics.
From The Economic Perspectives Series.
Prod-MDCPB Dist-MDCPB

Multiply And Subdue The Earth, Pt 1 C 34 MIN
16MM FILM, 3/4 OR 1/2 IN VIDEO H-C A
Presents an analysis of man's relationship to his environment with great emphasis on the need to maintain the ecological balance with opening up new areas.
LC NO. 80-707088
Prod-NET Dist-IU 1969

Multiply And Subdue The Earth, Pt 2 C 33 MIN
16MM FILM, 3/4 OR 1/2 IN VIDEO H-C A
Presents an analysis of man's relationship to his environment with great emphasis on the need to maintain the ecological balance with opening up new areas.
LC NO. 80-707088
Prod-NET Dist-IU 1969

Multiply Handicapped, The C 23 MIN
3/4 OR 1/2 INCH VIDEO CASSETTE
Shows mentally retarded, cerebral palsied, deaf-blind, and emotionally disturbed children in Sweden, Germany, the Netherlands, and England.
From The International Education Of The Hearing Impaired Child Series.
LC NO. 80-707438
Prod-USBEH Dist-USNAC 1980

Multiplying Decimals C 10 MIN
3/4 INCH VIDEO CASSETTE
See series title for descriptive statement.
From The Basic Math Skills Series. Adding, Subtracting, Multiplying Decimals
Prod-TELSTR Dist-TELSTR

Multiplying Fractions C 9 MIN
3/4 INCH VIDEO CASSETTE
See series title for descriptive statement.
From The Basic Math Skills Series. Multiplying Fractions And Reducing
Prod-TELSTR Dist-TELSTR

Multiplying Fractions C 19 MIN
3/4 INCH VIDEO CASSETTE
See series title for descriptive statement.
From The Basic Math Skills Series. Multiplying Fractions And Reducing
Prod-TELSTR Dist-TELSTR

Multiplying Mixed Numbers C 11 MIN
3/4 INCH VIDEO CASSETTE
See series title for descriptive statement.
From The Basic Math Skills Series. Multiplying And Dividing Fractions
Prod-TELSTR Dist-TELSTR

Multiprogramming And Multiprocessing C 30 MIN
3/4 OR 1/2 INCH VIDEO CASSETTE H-C A
Introduces advanced computer systems by discussing differences in hardware operating speeds and the problems caused by disparities. Describes multiprogramming and multiprocessing, plus associated techniques such as timesharing, timeslicing and interrupt handling.
From The Making It Count Series.
LC NO. 80-707576
Prod-BCSC Dist-BCSC 1980

Multiprogramming And Time Sharing C 30 MIN
3/4 INCH VIDEO CASSETTE H A
Looks at the techniques of using combinations of hardware and software to permit several programs or users to share a common computer.
From The Computing For Every Man Series.
Prod-NYSED Dist-NYSED 1973

Multistage Amplifiers C 12 MIN
3/4 OR 1/2 INCH VIDEO CASSETTE
Covers multistage amplifiers, power gain, amplifier efficiency, current gain, voltage gain, distortion, maximum power transfer and other types of amplifiers.
From The Industrial Electronics - Amplifiers Series.
Prod-TPCTRA Dist-TPCTRA

Multistage Decision Model, The - Further Considerations C 51 MIN
3/4 OR 1/2 INCH VIDEO CASSETTE
See series title for descriptive statement.
From The Decision Analysis Series.
Prod-MIOT Dist-MIOT

Multistage Model, The - A First Example C 55 MIN
3/4 OR 1/2 INCH VIDEO CASSETTE
Discusses structure of the multistage decision model, decision trees and the sequencing of events within a decision tree representation of a decision problem and AI's problem and its solution to maximize monetary value.
From The Decision Analysis Series.
Prod-MIOT Dist-MIOT

Multivibrators C 12 MIN
3/4 OR 1/2 INCH VIDEO CASSETTE
Defines types of multivibrators, astable multivibrators, bistable multivibrators, monostable multivibrators and other types of multivibrators.
From The Industrial Electronics - Oscillators And Multivibrators Series.
Prod-TPCTRA Dist-TPCTRA

Multiview Drawing B 32 MIN
16MM FILM OPTICAL SOUND C A
Demonstrates with models and drawings how to represent an object by means of three orthographic views.
Prod-PUAVC Dist-PUAVC 1959

Mum Deoderant C 1 MIN
3/4 OR 1/2 INCH VIDEO CASSETTE
Shows a classic television commercial.
Prod-BROOKC Dist-BROOKC

Mummies Made In Egypt C 15 MIN
3/4 OR 1/2 INCH VIDEO CASSETTE P
Introduces librarian Phyllis Syracuse reading from the book Mummies Made In Egypt by Aliki. Shows relics from the ancient Egyptian civilization through visits to two museums.
From The Through The Pages Series. No. 5
LC NO. 82-707373
Prod-WVIZTV Dist-GPITVL 1982

Mummy Mosaic, The B 30 MIN
16MM FILM OPTICAL SOUND
Presents highlights from Mummy features films, including 'The Mummy,' 'The Mummy's Tomb' and 'The Mummy's Ghost'.
Prod-CFS Dist-CFS

Munchen C 15 MIN
16MM FILM, 3/4 OR 1/2 IN VIDEO
A German language videocassette. Discusses the monuments and sections of Munich.
From The German Language Series.
Prod-IFB Dist-IFB 1968

Munchers, The - A Fable C 10 MIN
3/4 OR 1/2 INCH VIDEO CASSETTE K-P
Presents clay animation characters in a musical fable about nutrition and the four basic food groups, as well as information on plaque and its prevention.
Prod-AMDA Dist-AMDA 1973

Munchers, The - A Fable:010mpamda C 10 MIN
16MM FILM OPTICAL SOUND
Uses animation techniques in order to examine the interaction of teeth and tooth decay in the mouth. Shows how different food groups have different effects on tooth decay and tooth growth.
LC NO. 74-700534
Prod-AMDA Dist-MTP 1973

Munchhausen C 100 MIN
16MM FILM OPTICAL SOUND
A German language film with English subtitles, adapted from Erich Kastner's novel, MUNCHHAUSEN. Relates the adventures of Baron Munchhausen, known for his unbelievable stories.
Prod-WSTGLC Dist-WSTGLC 1943

Mundo Real—A Series
P-J
Deals with the minority experience through the eyes of a fictitious Puerto Rican family living on mainland U S. Focuses on problems faced by the children particularly racial prejudice - as well as the opportunities that living in America brings them.
Prod-CPT Dist-MDCPB 1976

Ay Bendito 030 MIN
Brotherly Love 030 MIN
Honesty Is The Best Policy 030 MIN
Hottest Day, The 030 MIN
Matter Of Identity, A 030 MIN
My Father My Friend 030 MIN
Pedrito - Part I 030 MIN
Pedrito - Part II 030 MIN
Remembrance Of Toribio, A 030 MIN
Renovation, The 030 MIN
Teacher For Dona Ines, A 030 MIN

Munich Crisis, The C 58 MIN
16MM FILM MAGNETIC SOUND C
Shows a detailed examination of the assumptions behind British policy which led to a great power settlement at the expense of Czechoslovakia.
From The British Universities Historical Studies In Film Series.
LC NO. 72-701256
Prod-IUHFC Dist-KRAUS 1975

Munich Seasons, The C 28 MIN
16MM FILM OPTICAL SOUND C A
Describes a 'Munich year,' a color-and-sound panorama of the varied lifestyles of the city set to the rhythms of the four seasons.
Prod-WSTGLC Dist-WSTGLC

Municipal Water Resources C 180 MIN
3/4 OR 1/2 INCH VIDEO CASSETTE PRO
Covers in three one-hour lectures, water supply, water treatment, sewer systems and sewage treatments.
From The Professional Engineer Review Series.
Prod-UILU Dist-AMCEE

Munro C 9 MIN
16MM FILM, 3/4 OR 1/2 IN VIDEO A
Portrays the trials of Munro, a four-year-old drafted into the army, when no one will believe he is only four.
Prod-AUDBRF Dist-FI

Muppet Meeting—A Series
A
Employs the Muppet characters in humorous stories which introduce various parts of a business meeting.
Prod-HENASS Dist-HENASS 1978

Breaker-Upper 009 MIN
Coffee Break 006 MIN
Gimme A Break 006 MIN
Picker-Upper 008 MIN

Muppet Movie, The C 98 MIN
16MM FILM OPTICAL SOUND
Shows what happens when the Muppets seek stardom in Hollywood.
Prod-UNKNWN Dist-SWANK

Muppet Picker-Upper Films—A Series

Prod-HENASS Dist-HENASS 1975

Final Speech 2 MIN

Mura Dehn, Sally Sommer And Sule Wilson C 30 MIN
3/4 OR 1/2 INCH VIDEO CASSETTE
Presents a documentary on jazz dance. Hosted by Julinda Lewis.
From The Eye On Dance - Glance At The Past Series.
Prod-ARTRES Dist-ARTRES

Mural C 5 MIN
16MM FILM OPTICAL SOUND
Shows the creation of a mural by sculptor Glen Michaels. Uses animation of tile, stone, wood, wax, bronze and brass to show the growth of segments of a mural piece by piece without the intrusion of hands. Shows the finished mural in its architectural setting.
LC NO. 78-700293
Prod-PAJON Dist-PAJON 1977

Mural In The Making C 15 MIN
16MM FILM OPTICAL SOUND
Presents the story of the mural by artist Fred Conway painted in the lobby of Brown Shoe Company's office in St Louis, Missouri.
Prod-BRNSHO Dist-SWANK 1956

Mural Making C 6 MIN
16MM FILM, 3/4 OR 1/2 IN VIDEO P-I
Explains that the urge to draw and paint can be encouraged along constructive lines in the classroom. Shows the making of a mural as a class project with everyone participating.
From The Creative Hands Series.
Prod-CRAF Dist-IFB 1956

Mural Making B 20 MIN
2 INCH VIDEOTAPE I
Discusses mural making which has been an exciting challenge to children. Their uninhibited use of color has resulted in striking and beautiful compositions.
From The For The Love Of Art Series.
Prod-GWTVAI Dist-GPITVL Prodn-WETATV

Mural, The B 22 MIN
16MM FILM OPTICAL SOUND I-H T
A teacher-training film. Shows students in a sixth grade New York City classroom who, following a study of the Netsilik Eskimos, are making a mural about the winter migration of Eskimos.
From The Classroom As A Learning Community Series.
LC NO. 79-714104
Prod-EDC Dist-EDC 1971

Murals And China Repairs - Wallpaper Murals, Gold Leaf And China Repairs C 30 MIN
1/2 IN VIDEO CASSETTE BETA/VHS
See series title for descriptive statement.
From The Wally's Workshop Series.
Prod-KARTES Dist-KARTES

Murals Of Atzlan, The C 23 MIN
3/4 OR 1/2 INCH VIDEO CASSETTE J A
Looks at an art show by Chicano artists in Los Angeles. Shows artists painting murals as the public watches.
Prod-SUTHRB Dist-SUTHRB

Murals Of East Los Angeles, The - A Museum Without Walls C 46 MIN
16MM FILM OPTICAL SOUND
Deals with the visual and artistic revolution in the Barrio of East Los Angeles. Shows how Chicano artists are changing the environment with a multitude of murals that express Chicano concerns and aspirations.
LC NO. 77-700559
Prod-RKOGEN Dist-RKOGEN Prodn-LALUZ 1977

Muratti Greift Ein C 4 MIN
16MM FILM OPTICAL SOUND
Presents a variation on dancing cigarettes.
Prod-PFP Dist-CFS 1934

Muratti Private C 4 MIN
16MM FILM OPTICAL SOUND
Presents the object-animation of marching cigarettes and packets, as 'PRIVATE MURATTI' steps to Mozart's 'RONDO.'
Prod-PFP Dist-CFS 1934

Murder B 102 MIN
16MM FILM OPTICAL SOUND
Focuses on a jurist who becomes sure that a young woman convicted of murder is really innocent. Directed by Alfred Hitchcock.
Prod-UNKNWN Dist-KITPAR 1930

Murder By Death C 94 MIN
16MM FILM OPTICAL SOUND
Offers a satire of mystery movies, telling how an eccentric millionaire sends for five world-famous detectives and tests their investigative prowess.
Prod-CPC Dist-SWANK

Murder By Television B 55 MIN
1/2 IN VIDEO CASSETTE BETA/VHS
Shows how a master electronics wizard and television inventor is murdered during a demonstration of the new marvel. Stars Bela Lugosi.
Prod-UNKNWN Dist-VIDIM 1935

Murder One C 46 MIN
16MM FILM OPTICAL SOUND J-C A
Examines the crimes of six convicted murderers using interviews with the murderers, witnesses and accomplices and backgrounds of the murders.
LC NO. 77-703379
Prod-WNDTTV Dist-BESTF 1977

Murder, My Sweet B 12 MIN
16MM FILM OPTICAL SOUND H-C A
Presents an excerpt from the motion picture Murder, My Sweet, issued in 1945. Tells the story of a private detective who gets drawn into a complex web of murder, blackmail and double-dealing while searching for a missing jade necklace. Exemplifies the gangster film genre.
From The American Film Genre - The Gangster Film Series.
LC NO. 77-701142
Prod-RKOP Dist-FI 1975

Murderer, The C 28 MIN
16MM FILM, 3/4 OR 1/2 IN VIDEO H-C A
An adaptation of the short story, The Murderer by Ray Bradbury, about an individual who decides to liberate a futuristic society from its communication devices.
Prod-SILVEA Dist-PHENIX 1976

Muria, The C 55 MIN
16MM FILM, 3/4 OR 1/2 IN VIDEO H-C A
Visits the Muria of Central India where children live in a central dormitory apart from the parents and marriages are arranged by the families independent of the child's wishes. Follows a girl who discovers she is pregnant by friend in the dormitory, but must carry out an arranged marriage anyway.
From The Worlds Apart Series.
LC NO. 84-706187
Prod-BBCTV Dist-FI 1982

Muriel Cigars C 1 MIN
3/4 OR 1/2 INCH VIDEO CASSETTE
Shows a classic television commercial with dancing cigars.
Prod-BROOKC Dist-BROOKC

Muriel Rukeyser C 28 MIN
16MM FILM, 3/4 OR 1/2 IN VIDEO
Focuses on the work of poet Muriel Rukeyser.
From The Writer In America Series.
Prod-PERSPF Dist-CORF

Muriel Topaz, Tom Brown And Phoebe Neville C 30 MIN
3/4 OR 1/2 INCH VIDEO CASSETTE
See series title for descriptive statement.
From The Eye On Dance - Passing On Dance Series.
Prod-ARTRES Dist-ARTRES

Murini Window C 28 MIN
16MM FILM OPTICAL SOUND H-C A
Describes how glassblower Dudley Giberson creates a stained glass window for the University of Connecticut.
LC NO. 80-701817
Prod-IMAGER Dist-IMAGER 1980

Murita Cycles C 28 MIN
16MM FILM, 3/4 OR 1/2 IN VIDEO
Presents a portrait of the filmmaker's father, Muray Braverman, a part-time philosopher who runs an unconventional bicycle shop in a New York City suburb.
Prod-BRAVE Dist-DIRECT 1979

Murmuring Heart, The B 15 MIN
16MM FILM OPTICAL SOUND H-C A
Demonstrates corrective surgery for a heart murmur in an infant. Shows closeup views of the exposed heart and major blood vessels during surgery. Includes a discussion on the basic anatomy and physiology of the heart.
From The Doctors At Work Series.
LC NO. FIA65-1352
Prod-CMA Dist-LAWREN Prodn-LAWREN 1961

Murray Louis C 30 MIN
3/4 OR 1/2 INCH VIDEO CASSETTE
See series title for descriptive statement.
From The Dance On Television And Film Series.
Prod-ARCVID Dist-ARCVID

Murray Louis C 30 MIN
3/4 OR 1/2 INCH VIDEO CASSETTE
See series title for descriptive statement.
From The Eye On Dance - Dance On TV And Film Series.
Prod-ARTRES Dist-ARTRES

Murrow-Mc Carthy Debate B 45 MIN
16MM FILM OPTICAL SOUND
Presents Murrow's presentation of arguments against Mc Carthy and then shows Mc Carthy's reply. Includes shots of the congressional hearing on the Annie Lee Moss case to show why Murrow objected to Mc Carthy's tactics during investigations.
Prod-FREHOU Dist-AFLCIO 1954

Murs Et Appareils C 12 MIN
16MM FILM OPTICAL SOUND
A French language version of Walls And Bonds. Demonstrates different kinds of wood bonds.
From The Hand Operations - Woodworking (French) Series.
LC NO. 75-704355
Prod-MORLAT Dist-MORLAT 1974

MURUGA C 25 MIN
3/4 INCH VIDEO CASSETTE C A
Documents the Nallur Temple Festival in the Northern section of Sri Lanka. Covers the events during a 26-night period.
Prod-HANMNY Dist-HANMNY 1973

Muscle C 12 MIN
16MM FILM, 3/4 OR 1/2 IN VIDEO J-C A
Shows Pat Perris lifting weights, training for the Manitoba Women's Provincial Body Building Championship. Contains body building sequences as well as footage from the competition.
Prod-NFBC Dist-LUF

Muscle C 25 MIN
16MM FILM, 3/4 OR 1/2 IN VIDEO H-C A
Shows the dynamics of muscle tissue and the amazing processes involved in muscle contraction. Examines the roles of membrane potential and chemical pumps as well as the sliding filament theory of muscle contraction.
Prod-CRMP Dist-CRMP 1972

Muscle C 38 MIN
3/4 OR 1/2 INCH VIDEO CASSETTE
See series title for descriptive statement.
From The Biological Aspects Of Aging - Rehabilitation Considerations Series.
Prod-UMDSM Dist-UMDSM

Muscle - Chemistry Of Contraction X 15 MIN
16MM FILM, 3/4 OR 1/2 IN VIDEO H-C
Describes the internal structure of muscles, showing that actin and myosin are the contractile elements of muscle. Uses a model to explain muscle contraction.
From The Biology Series. Unit 8 - Human Physiology
Prod-EBEC Dist-EBEC 1969

Muscle - Chemistry Of Contraction (Spanish) C 15 MIN
16MM FILM, 3/4 OR 1/2 IN VIDEO H-C
A Spanish language version of the film and videorecording Muscle - Chemistry Of Contraction.
Prod-EBEC Dist-EBEC 1969

Muscle - Dynamics Of Contraction X 21 MIN
16MM FILM, 3/4 OR 1/2 IN VIDEO J-C
Presents views of people engaged in various activities to show the dynamics of muscle contraction. Includes rare electron micrographs which reveal that the contractile properties of the whole muscle can be explained in terms of the properties of a single muscle cell, the basic unit of contraction.
From The Biology Series. Unit 8 - Human Physiology
Prod-EBEC Dist-EBEC 1969

Muscle - Dynamics Of Contraction (Spanish) C 22 MIN
16MM FILM, 3/4 OR 1/2 IN VIDEO H-C
A Spanish language version of the film and videorecording Muscle - Dynamics Of Contraction.
Prod-EBEC Dist-EBEC 1969

Muscle - Electrical Activity Of Contraction (Spanish) C 9 MIN
16MM FILM, 3/4 OR 1/2 IN VIDEO H-C
A Spanish language version of the film and videorecording Muscle - Electrical Activity Of Contraction.
Prod-EBEC Dist-EBEC 1969

Muscle - Electrical Activity Of Contraction X 9 MIN
16MM FILM, 3/4 OR 1/2 IN VIDEO J-C
Demonstrates that all muscle contractions are initiated by nerve impulses and that electrical stimuli can initiate muscle contraction.
From The Biology Series. Unit 8 - Human Physiology
Prod-EBEC Dist-EBEC 1969

Muscle - Unit 4 C 20 MIN
3/4 OR 1/2 INCH VIDEO CASSETTE PRO
Introduces students to the structure, characteristics, and histological organization of skeletal, cardiac, and smooth muscle.
From The Histology Review Series.
Prod-HSCIC Dist-HSCIC

Muscle And Culture C 7 MIN
16MM FILM OPTICAL SOUND
Uses animated sequences with accompanying text to analyze the evolutionary changes in the culture of man as represented by the Olympic Games.
LC NO. 72-711241
Prod-GENOVE Dist-AMEDFL 1972

Muscle Beach Party C 95 MIN
16MM FILM OPTICAL SOUND J-C A
Stars Frankie Avalon, Annette Funicello and Buddy Hackett. Presents the conflict between the surfers and a group of muscle-bound physical culturists, with further complications resulting with the arrival of a countess and her business manager.
Prod-AIP Dist-TWYMAN 1964

Muscle Breathing Patterns In Poliomyelitis C 19 MIN
16MM FILM OPTICAL SOUND
Describes the physical examination findings in patients when respiratory muscles are weakened by paralyzing diseases.
Prod-RLAH Dist-RLAH

Muscle Evaluation - Common Peroneal Nerve C 30 MIN
16MM FILM OPTICAL SOUND
Demonstrates tendons, muscle bellies, surface anatomy and areas of sensory supply on the human leg. Includes a voluntary

muscle test on a patient with common peroneal nerve injury and substitution patterns used by patients to compensate for the loss of function.
LC NO. 75-703056
Prod-AMFSS Dist-USNAC 1968

Muscle Evaluation - Common Peroneal Nerve (Quiz Version) C 15 MIN
16MM FILM OPTICAL SOUND
Presents review and quiz material on muscle evaluation of the common peroneal nerve of the human leg. Covers physiology, injury and compensation for loss of function.
LC NO. 75-703058
Prod-AMFSS Dist-USNAC 1968

Muscle Evaluation - Hip And Knee, Normal C 10 MIN
16MM FILM OPTICAL SOUND
Demonstrates tendons, muscle bellies, surface anatomy and areas of sensory supply on the human hip and lower limb.
LC NO. 75-703059
Prod-AMFSS Dist-USNAC 1968

Muscle Evaluation - Median Nerve C 40 MIN
16MM FILM OPTICAL SOUND
Discusses tendons, muscle bellies, surface anatomy and areas of sensory supply on the human forearm. Includes a voluntary muscle test on a patient with a median nerve injury and substitution patterns used by patients to compensate for the loss of function.
LC NO. 75-703060
Prod-AMFSS Dist-USNAC 1968

Muscle Evaluation - Median Nerve (Quiz Version) C 20 MIN
16MM FILM OPTICAL SOUND
Presents review and quiz material on muscle evaluation of the human median nerve. Covers physiology, injury and compensation for loss of function.
LC NO. 75-703061
Prod-AMFSS Dist-USNAC 1968

Muscle Evaluation - Neck And Shoulder C 49 MIN
16MM FILM OPTICAL SOUND
Depicts tendons, muscle bellies, surface anatomy and areas of sensory supply on the human neck and shoulder. Includes a voluntary muscle test on a patient with left shoulder and upper left limb injury and substitution patterns used by patients to compensate for the loss of function.
LC NO. 75-703062
Prod-AMFSS Dist-USNAC 1968

Muscle Evaluation - Neck And Shoulder (Quiz Version) C 17 MIN
16MM FILM OPTICAL SOUND
Presents review and quiz material on muscle evaluation of the human neck and shoulder. Covers physiology, injury and compensation for loss of function.
LC NO. 75-703063
Prod-AMFSS Dist-USNAC 1968

Muscle Evaluation - Radial Nerve C 31 MIN
16MM FILM OPTICAL SOUND
Discusses tendons, muscle bellies, surface anatomy and areas of sensory supply on the human forearm. Includes a voluntary muscle test on a patient with a radial nerve injury and substitution patterns used by patients to compensate for the loss of function.
LC NO. 75-703064
Prod-AMFSS Dist-USNAC 1968

Muscle Evaluation - Radial Nerve (Quiz Version) C 16 MIN
16MM FILM OPTICAL SOUND
Presents review and quiz material on muscle evaluation of the human radial nerve. Covers physiology, injury and compensation for loss of function.
LC NO. 75-703066
Prod-AMFSS Dist-USNAC 1968

Muscle Evaluation - Sciatic And Posterior Tibial Nerve (Quiz Version) C 14 MIN
16MM FILM OPTICAL SOUND
Presents review and quiz material on muscle evaluation of the human sciatic and posterior tibial nerve. Covers physiology, injury and compensation for loss of function.
LC NO. 75-703068
Prod-AMFSS Dist-USNAC 1968

Muscle Evaluation - Sciatic And Posterior Tibial Nerve C 35 MIN
16MM FILM OPTICAL SOUND
Demonstrates the normal sciatic and posterior tibial nerves of the human body. Includes a voluntary muscle test on a poliomyelitis patient and substitution patterns used by patients to compensate for the loss of nerve function.
LC NO. 75-703067
Prod-AMFSS Dist-USNAC 1968

Muscle Evaluation - Ulnar Nerve C 49 MIN
16MM FILM OPTICAL SOUND
Discusses tendons, muscle bellies, surface anatomy and areas of sensory supply on the human forearm. Includes a voluntary muscle test on a patient with an ulnar nerve injury and substitutional patterns used by patients to compensate for the loss of function.
LC NO. 75-703069
Prod-AMFSS Dist-USNAC 1968

Muscle Evaluation - Ulnar Nerve (Quiz Version) C 17 MIN
16MM FILM OPTICAL SOUND
Presents review and quiz material on muscle evaluation of the human ulnar nerve. Covers physiology, injury and compensation for loss of function.
LC NO. 75-703070
Prod-AMFSS Dist-USNAC 1968

Muscle Of Imagination C 20 MIN
3/4 INCH VIDEO CASSETTE I
Features a dramatics workshop where students participate in improvisational exercises.
From The Wonderama Of The Arts Series.
Prod-WBRATV Dist-GPITVL 1979

Muscle Spindle, The C 19 MIN
16MM FILM, 3/4 OR 1/2 IN VIDEO PRO
Shows how the electrical impulses produced by movement and tension of a muscle are transmitted to and received from the nervous system. Demonstrates the techniques for isolating a muscle spindle and keeping it alive outside the body.
From The Physiology Series.
Prod-WILEYJ Dist-MEDIAG 1970

Muscles And Bones Of The Body C 11 MIN
16MM FILM, 3/4 OR 1/2 IN VIDEO I
Emphasizes the importance of the muscles and bones to the internal and external functioning of the human body by showing how tendons, joints, muscles and the bones of the skeleton work smoothly together as one unit.
Prod-CORF Dist-CORF 1960

Muscles And Exercise C 29 MIN
3/4 INCH VIDEO CASSETTE C A
Examines the muscles as active partners in movement. Identifies and describes three basic types of muscle tissue. Discusses two basic types of exercise, isometric and isotonic.
From The Introducing Biology Series. Program 13
Prod-COAST Dist-CDTEL

Muscles And Joints - Moving Parts C 26 MIN
3/4 OR 1/2 INCH VIDEO CASSETTE
Shows how muscle activity is coordinated by the cerebellum and how position sensors in the muscles and joints and the balancing mechanism of the inner ear enable people to control their bodies. Follows the activities of a waterskier to demonstrate how muscles, joints and organs link up. Looks at the interior of the human knee to provide a clear view of how lubricating fluid is produced.
From The Living Body - An Introduction To Human Biology Series.
Prod-FOTH Dist-FOTH 1985

Muscles And Joints - Muscle Power C 26 MIN
3/4 OR 1/2 INCH VIDEO CASSETTE
Uses a scene in a movie theater to contrast the on-screen strength of a kung fu master with the audience slumped in its seats. Shows how muscles work, how two types of molecule collapsing against each other like a telescope produce enormous strength as they operate in large numbers. Demonstrates how much muscular activity takes place without our being aware of it, as the heart muscle contracts and the digestive tract is in motion.
From The Living Body - An Introduction To Human Biology Series.
Prod-FOTH Dist-FOTH 1985

Muscles And Movement C 15 MIN
16MM FILM, 3/4 OR 1/2 IN VIDEO I-H
Shows how the skeleton acts as a system of levers and works in conjunction with the muscles to provide movement.
From The Human Body Series.
Prod-LUF Dist-LUF 1980

Muscles Of Facial Expression C 16 MIN
3/4 OR 1/2 INCH VIDEO CASSETTE C A
Presents the anatomy of the facial muscles of expression.
Prod-UWO Dist-TEF

Muscles Of Mastication And The Infratemporal Fossa C 15 MIN
16MM FILM, 3/4 OR 1/2 IN VIDEO PRO
Shows in detail, with a specimen and animation, how the temporal bone and the mandible work together at the temporomandibular joint.
From The Cine-Prosector Series.
Prod-AVCORP Dist-TEF

Muscles Of The Anterior Forearm C 14 MIN
16MM FILM, 3/4 OR 1/2 IN VIDEO PRO
Points out skeletal features of the upper limb and landmarks of the ulna and radius.
From The Cine-Prosector Series.
Prod-AVCORP Dist-TEF

Muscles, The C 8 MIN
16MM FILM OPTICAL SOUND
Features two puppets, Orsen the dog and Webster the owl, who introduce concepts about the muscles of the body. Covers concepts, such as brain impulses to the muscles, admitting one's mistakes, group activities, colors, right and left and numbers.
Prod-ECI Dist-ECI

Muscular Coordination, Pt 1 - Cerebellar Cortex And Topography C 18 MIN
16MM FILM, 3/4 OR 1/2 IN VIDEO PRO
See series title for descriptive statement.
From The Anatomical Basis Of Brain Function Series.
Prod-AVCORP Dist-TEF

Muscular Coordination, Pt 2 - Cerebellar Conducting Systems C 18 MIN
16MM FILM, 3/4 OR 1/2 IN VIDEO PRO
See series title for descriptive statement.
From The Anatomical Basis Of Brain Function Series.
Prod-AVCORP Dist-TEF

Muscular Dystrophy C 29 MIN
3/4 OR 1/2 INCH VIDEO CASSETTE
Examines the symptoms and forms of muscular distrophy.
From The Daniel Foster, MD Series.
Prod-KERA Dist-PBS

Musculo C 25 MIN
16MM FILM, 3/4 OR 1/2 IN VIDEO H-C A
A Spanish language version of Muscle. Discusses the three kinds of muscle in the human body and describes the unique properties of each kind of muscle tissue. Shows how different muscle systems are coordinated, how body activity affects the activity of cardiac muscle and how involuntary muscles work. Examines the role of the nervous system in muscular activity.
Prod-LAZRST Dist-MGHT 1978

Musculoskeletal (2nd Ed) C 17 MIN
16MM FILM - 3/4 IN VIDEO PRO
Demonstrates the physical examination of the musculoskeletal system, showing necessary procedures, manipulations, pacing, positions and patient-examiner interaction.
From The Visual Guide To Physical Examination (2nd Ed) Series.
LC NO. 81-707474
Prod-LIP Dist-LIP Prodn-JACSTO 1981

Museum C 30 MIN
16MM FILM, 3/4 OR 1/2 IN VIDEO I-C A
Reveals what goes on in the workrooms, offices and meeting rooms of a typical museum.
LC NO. 80-707720
Prod-GOODF Dist-CAROUF 1980

Museum C 39 MIN
16MM FILM, 3/4 OR 1/2 IN VIDEO J-C A
Details the operation of a museum and offers a tribute to the men and women who recognize, research, acquire, restore and protect the wonders that are exhibited.
Prod-JANUS Dist-FI 1980

Museum - Behind The Scenes At The Art Institute Of Chicago C 28 MIN
16MM FILM OPTICAL SOUND
Offers a behind-the-scenes look at the Art Institute of Chicago, introducing the curators who organize the exhibitions, the installers who handle the works of art, and the conservators who care for and preserve the paintings and prints.
LC NO. 80-700304
Prod-ARTINC Dist-AFA Prodn-OLINC 1979

Museum - Gateway To Perception C 16 MIN
3/4 INCH VIDEO CASSETTE
Combines the scientific approach to observation with the fascination of a museum.
Prod-ATLAP Dist-ATLAP 1964

Museum At Work, The C 30 MIN
3/4 OR 1/2 INCH VIDEO CASSETTE C
See series title for descriptive statement.
From The In Our Own Image Series.
Prod-DALCCD Dist-DALCCD

Museum Backroom C 29 MIN
3/4 INCH VIDEO CASSETTE
Shows how two children learn what goes on behind the scenes of a natural history museum.
Prod-KAETTV Dist-PUBTEL

Museum Means People B 30 MIN
16MM FILM OPTICAL SOUND R
Presents Jewish ceremonial objects from the Jewish Museum in New York City--a ketubah, otrah curtain, mezuzah, tefillin case, haggadah, kiddush cup, etrog box, spice box and Torah crown. (Kinescope)
Prod-JTS Dist-NAAJS Prodn-NBCTV 1963

Museum Of Clocks, A B 5 MIN
16MM FILM OPTICAL SOUND
Presents an excerpt from a 1952 Screen News Digest film which takes the viewer through a museum of clocks at New York University.
From The News Magazine Of The Screen Series. Vol 4, No. 3
Prod-PATHE Dist-HEARST 1953

Museum Of Modern Art Of Latin America C 14 MIN
16MM FILM, 3/4 OR 1/2 IN VIDEO
Documents the collection of the Museum of Modern Art of Latin America.
Prod-MOMALA Dist-MOMALA

Museum Of Modern Art Of Latin America (Spanish) C 14 MIN
16MM FILM, 3/4 OR 1/2 IN VIDEO
Documents the collection of the Museum of Modern Art of Latin America.
Prod-MOMALA Dist-MOMALA

Museum Of The Solar System C 23 MIN
16MM FILM OPTICAL SOUND J A
Documents the analysis of the moon rocks and soil brought to earth by the Apollo voyagers. Presents insights into the methods of modern science by visiting the laboratories of seven lunar scientists to learn how they sought answers to lunar mysteries such as the age of the moon, the composition of its elements, its origin and history and the nature of its minerals.
LC NO. 78-711351
Prod-FINLYS Dist-FINLYS 1970

Museum Open House--A Series

Uses the art treasures of the museum to illustrate the ways in which the artist expresses his view of the world. Discusses the galleries of Boston's Museum of Fine Arts by host Russell Connor.
Prod-WGBHTV Dist-PUBTEL

African Art	29 MIN
American Primitive Masterpieces	29 MIN
Artist And The City, The	29 MIN
Artist And The Mirror, The	29 MIN
Artists And Atoms	29 MIN
Book Of Tea, The	29 MIN
Contemporary Collection, A	29 MIN
Cooking Of French Art, The	29 MIN
Face Of Rome, The	29 MIN
Figure This	29 MIN
Gift Of India, The	29 MIN
Japanese Temple Sculpture	29 MIN
Lautrec In Paris	29 MIN
Light, Dark And Daumier	29 MIN
Made In Japan - Ukiyo-E Prints	29 MIN
Mind's Eye, The	29 MIN
Motion And Emotion - Baroque Sculpture	29 MIN
My Son The Artist	29 MIN
Of Time And The Artist	29 MIN
Other Side Of The Canvas, The	29 MIN
Painters And Pioneers	29 MIN
Piranesi	29 MIN
Portraits For Eternity	29 MIN
Sight Of Sound, The	29 MIN
Spanish Gallery, A	29 MIN
Surrealism - Inner Space	29 MIN
Surrealism - Seekers Of The Dream	29 MIN
Thousand Words, A	29 MIN
Tribal Carvings From New Guinea	29 MIN
Vocabulary Of Art, The	29 MIN

Museum People C 22 MIN
16MM FILM - 3/4 IN VIDEO
Explores the interaction between people and art in a museum.
Prod-KERA Dist-PUBTEL

Museum, The - Gateway To Perception C 16 MIN
16MM FILM OPTICAL SOUND I-C A
Introduces the museum and indicates how its many materials relate to each other and to the museum visitor. Shows how museums contain the story of history.
LC NO. FIA65-527
Prod-ATLAP Dist-ATLAP Prodn-HAGOPN 1964

Museums, Where Fun Is Learning C 17 MIN
16MM FILM, 3/4 OR 1/2 IN VIDEO T
Shows examples of model programs centering around art, history and science exhibitions. Offers suggestions for class trips, including pre- and post-trip activities.
LC NO. 82-707218
Prod-SMITHS Dist-USNAC Prodn-ADAMSF 1978

Mushroom Carving C 13 MIN
3/4 OR 1/2 INCH VIDEO CASSETTE PRO
Demonstrates the techniques of fluting, reliefing and impression.
Prod-CULINA Dist-CULINA

Mushroom Gathering C 10 MIN
16MM FILM OPTICAL SOUND
Shows thousands of people streaming out into the woods to gather mushrooms in Sweden in September and October.
Prod-ASI Dist-AUDPLN

Music C 15 MIN
3/4 OR 1/2 INCH VIDEO CASSETTE K-J
See series title for descriptive statement.
From The Arts Express Series.
Prod-KYTV Dist-KYTV 1983

Music C 20 MIN
3/4 OR 1/2 INCH VIDEO CASSETTE J-H
See series title for descriptive statement.
From The Contract Series.
Prod-KYTV Dist-AITECH 1977

Music C 30 MIN
3/4 OR 1/2 INCH VIDEO CASSETTE
See series title for descriptive statement.
From The Rebop Series.
Prod-WGBHTV Dist-MDCPB

Music (French) C 16 MIN
3/4 OR 1/2 INCH VIDEO CASSETTE H-C A
Shows a traditional dance in a country town and tours a recording studio at the Office de Radio et Television Francaise.
From The En Francais Series. Part 2 - Temporal Relationships, Logical Relationships
Prod-MOFAFR Dist-AITECH 1970

Music - A Bridge To Reality B 50 MIN
3/4 OR 1/2 INCH VIDEO CASSETTE
See series title for descriptive statement.
From The Social Responses To Aging Care And The Caring For Older People Series. Pt 3
Prod-UAZMIC Dist-UAZMIC 1976

Music - Age-Old Search For Meaning C 30 MIN
3/4 INCH VIDEO CASSETTE C A
Surveys history of music over a six-thousand year period. Offers excerpts from Beethoven's Third Symphony. Traces development of today's varied forms of music.
From The Humanities Through The Arts With Maya Angelou Series. Lesson 10
Prod-COAST Dist-CDTEL Prodn-CICOCH

Music - Emotion And Feeling In Sound C 30 MIN
3/4 INCH VIDEO CASSETTE C A
Illustrates through a Brahms symphony that what is heard as music is a blend of carefully chosen elements. Demonstrates the 'look' of sound by showing waves recorded on an electronic apparatus.
From The Humanities Through The Arts With Maya Angelou Series. Lesson 11
Prod-COAST Dist-CDTEL Prodn-CICOCH

Music - From Popular To Concert Stage C 15 MIN
16MM FILM OPTICAL SOUND I-H
Shows how the concert music of the present began as the popular music of another day, using as examples the minuet, the square dance, and the Blue Danube Waltz. Discusses popular music, including the big bands and jazz, and concludes with concert versions of 'I WANT TO HOLD YOUR HAND,' 'SHE LOVES YOU,' and 'YESTERDAY' by the Beatles.
From The Uses Of Music Series.
LC NO. 77-715019
Prod-CGWEST Dist-CGWEST 1969

Music - Listening For The Unexpected C 30 MIN
3/4 INCH VIDEO CASSETTE C A
Discusses criticism with Maya Angelou and a music critic and a director. Debates the qualifications, responsibilities and importance of the music critic.
From The Humanities Through The Arts With Maya Angelou Series. Lesson 13
Prod-COAST Dist-CDTEL Prodn-CICOCH

Music - Meaning Through Structure C 30 MIN
3/4 INCH VIDEO CASSETTE C A
Probes the life and work of Johann Sebastian Bach. Discusses the importance of form to music and the meaning that the artist imparts in his work.
From The Humanities Through The Arts With Maya Angelou Series. Lesson 12
Prod-COAST Dist-CDTEL Prodn-CICOCH

Music And Art - Germany B 30 MIN
16MM FILM OPTICAL SOUND
Compares German paintings and engravings of the Renaissance with contemporary music of the period.
From The Music And The Renaissance Series.
Prod-NET Dist-WQED 1957

Music And Art - Italy B 30 MIN
16MM FILM OPTICAL SOUND
Compares Italian paintings on musical subjects with music of contemporary composers of Italy during the Renaissance. Includes musical performances provided by the Saturday Consort.
From The Music And The Renaissance Series.
Prod-NET Dist-WQED 1957

Music And Art - The Netherlands B 30 MIN
16MM FILM OPTICAL SOUND
Compares Flemish and Dutch paintings dealing with musical subjects with contemporary music of the Renaissance.
From The Music And The Renaissance Series.
Prod-NET Dist-WQED 1957

Music And Cinema C 29 MIN
3/4 INCH VIDEO CASSETTE
Looks at how music enhances or changes a viewer's perception of a film. Features Professor James Dapogny, pianist and authority on American Jazz of the 20's and 30's, as he plays music from some of the classic films.
Prod-UMITV Dist-UMITV 1978

Music And Dance C 30 MIN
3/4 OR 1/2 INCH VIDEO CASSETTE C
Discusses black trends in music and dance.
From The Afro-American Perspectives Series.
Prod-MDDE Dist-MDCPB

Music And Dance From Mindanao, The Philippines B 23 MIN
16MM FILM, 3/4 OR 1/2 IN VIDEO
Includes performances of three groups who inhabit Mindanao, the largest island of the southern Philippines. Shows several instrumental and dance performances.
Prod-UWASHP Dist-UWASHP

Music And Dance From The Sulu Islands, The Philippines B 17 MIN
16MM FILM, 3/4 OR 1/2 IN VIDEO
Shows dances performed on the Sulu Archipelago which extends about 250 miles from Mindanao in the Philippines to northern Borneo.
Prod-UWASHP Dist-UWASHP

Music And Dance Of The Bagobo And Manobo Peoples Of Mindanao, The Philippines C 12 MIN
16MM FILM, 3/4 OR 1/2 IN VIDEO
Presents music and dance of the Bagobo and Manobo peoples of Mindanao, the Philippines.
Prod-UWASHP Dist-UWASHP

Music And Dance Of The Hill People Of The Northern Philippines, Pt 2 C 12 MIN
16MM FILM, 3/4 OR 1/2 IN VIDEO
Presents the varied dance and musical styles which have been preserved in the central highland area of northern Luzon, the Philippines.
Prod-UWASHP Dist-UWASHP

Music And Dance Of The Hill People Of The Northern Philippines, Pt 1 C 29 MIN
16MM FILM, 3/4 OR 1/2 IN VIDEO
Features eleven performances of the different types of gong playing, singing and dancing which have survived in the central part of the northern island of Luzon, the Philippines.
Prod-UWASHP Dist-UWASHP

Music And Dance Of The Ibaloy Group Of The Northern Philippines. B 12 MIN
16MM FILM, 3/4 OR 1/2 IN VIDEO
Includes a number of different group dances by the people living in the Mountain Province of the island of Luzon in the northern Philippines.
Prod-UWASHP Dist-UWASHP

Music And Dance Of The Maranao People Of Mindanao, the Philippines. C 21 MIN
16MM FILM, 3/4 OR 1/2 IN VIDEO
Features two group dances by young girls to traditional gong orchestra music from one of the two main Muslim groups on the island of Mindanao, the Philippines.
Prod-UWASHP Dist-UWASHP

Music And Dance Of The Yakan People Of Basilian Island, the Philippines C 12 MIN
16MM FILM, 3/4 OR 1/2 IN VIDEO
Depicts a variety of the music of the people living on Basilian, the northernmost island of the Sulu Archipelago, the Philippines.
Prod-UWASHP Dist-UWASHP

Music And Me C 15 MIN
3/4 OR 1/2 INCH VIDEO CASSETTE P-I
Presents contemporary music and introduces musical instruments, concepts and traditions.
From The Music And Me Series.
Prod-WDCNTV Dist-AITECH 1979

Music And Me-A Series
I
Introduces basic concepts in music and describes different musical instruments.
Prod-WDCNTV Dist-AITECH 1979

Ballad, The	015 MIN
Best Of Me, The	015 MIN
Brass Family, The	015 MIN
Folk Song, The	015 MIN
I Got The Beat	015 MIN
Intervals	015 MIN
Keyboard Family, The	015 MIN
Makin' Sweet Harmony	015 MIN
Melodies	015 MIN
Meter Reader	015 MIN
Music And Me	015 MIN
Music Of Afro-America	015 MIN
Music Of Christmas And Hanukkah, Pt 1	015 MIN
Music Of Christmas And Hanukkah, Pt 2	015 MIN
Music Of Inspiration	015 MIN
Music Of South America	015 MIN
Music Of The First Americans	015 MIN
Music Of The USA, Pt 1	015 MIN
Music Of The USA, Pt 2	015 MIN
Music Of The USA, Pt 3	015 MIN
Note Value	015 MIN
Percussion Family, The	015 MIN
Songs Of Halloween	015 MIN
Songs Of Thanksgiving	015 MIN
String Family, The	015 MIN
Tempo And Dynamics	015 MIN
Use Your Voice To Sing	015 MIN
Woodwind Family, The	015 MIN

Music And Performance C 58 MIN
3/4 OR 1/2 INCH VIDEO CASSETTE A
Features a tribute to the late musician Peter Ives, who died at age 36. Includes a compilation of the performance series held at Los Angeles Contemporary Exhibitions.
From The Shared Realities Series.
Prod-LBMART Dist-LBMART 1983

Music And Your Mind - A Key To Creative Potential C 21 MIN
16MM FILM OPTICAL SOUND H-C A
Examines the guided imagery and music technique. Explains the procedure and shows what happens when selected music stimuli are administered to relaxed subjects.
LC NO. 75-702600
Prod-CINEMN Dist-CRTVLC 1975

Music Box C 28 MIN
16MM FILM OPTICAL SOUND R
Presents a parable about the rewards of Christian life. Explores the joy of the believer in a story about an ordinary factory worker, five gospel-singing angels and a special music box.
LC NO. 81-700423
Prod-WHTLIN Dist-WHTLIN 1980

Music Box, The B 30 MIN
16MM FILM OPTICAL SOUND I-C
Features Laurel and Hardy as they deliver a new piano to the house on the top of the hill.
From The Laurel And Hardy Festival Series.
LC NO. 77-713152
Prod-ROACH Dist-BHAWK 1932

Music Boxes C 30 MIN
3/4 INCH VIDEO CASSETTE
See series title for descriptive statement.
From The Antiques Series.
Prod-NHMNET Dist-PUBTEL

Music Child, The B 45 MIN
16MM FILM, 3/4 OR 1/2 IN VIDEO
Discusses the use of music therapy in the treatment of nonverbal handicapped children. Includes a wide variety of disabilities and improvizational music techniques.
Prod-PARRYD Dist-BNCHMK 1976

Music Experiences-A Series
16MM FILM, 3/4 OR 1/2 IN VIDEO I-C A
Prod-AIMS Dist-AIMS

Bach Is Beautiful	015 MIN
Edvard Grieg - The Man And His Music	017 MIN
Grand Canyon Suite	017 MIN
Little Train Of The Caipira, The	014 MIN
Mississippi Suite	014 MIN

Music For Metrics C 29 MIN
3/4 INCH VIDEO CASSETTE

Introduces the metric system through song and animation.
Prod-UMITV Dist-UMITV 1976

Music For Prague 1968 C 28 MIN
16MM FILM, 3/4 OR 1/2 IN VIDEO I-C A
Shows the Baltimore Symphony's performance of Karel Husa's Music For Prague 1968. Includes visual images which weave together the performance and Czech themes.
Prod-MUSICP Dist-PFP 1975

Music For The Eyes C 18 MIN
3/4 INCH VIDEO CASSETTE
Focuses on the work and artistic vision of contemporary American sculptor James Rosati. Documents the creation ofa Rosati sculpture from foundry fabrication to installation in corporate headquarters. Shows the artist discussing the creative process and how he became a a sculptor.
Prod-STEEL Dist-MTP

Music From Africa C 15 MIN
3/4 OR 1/2 INCH VIDEO CASSETTE P
Discusses and gives examples of music from Africa.
From The Music Machine Series.
Prod-INDIPS Dist-GPITVL 1981

Music From Aspen C 59 MIN
3/4 OR 1/2 INCH VIDEO CASSETTE
Covers the annual three-day Aspen, Colorado, Music Festival, which brings together famous musicians and gifted students.
Prod-KQEDTV Dist-PBS

Music From Ghana C 29 MIN
3/4 INCH VIDEO CASSETTE
Features Kwasi Aduonum, musician, drummer and music teacher, as he leads viewers into Ghanian folk music. Analyzes the music and describes the story of the dances performed on the program.
Prod-UMITV Dist-UMITV 1978

Music From Japan C 15 MIN
3/4 OR 1/2 INCH VIDEO CASSETTE P
Discusses and gives examples of music from Japan.
From The Music Machine Series.
Prod-INDIPS Dist-GPITVL 1981

Music From Mexico And The Violin C 20 MIN
16MM FILM OPTICAL SOUND I
Introduces the mariachi music of Mexico, in which elements of Mexican, Indian, Spanish and African music can be found. Describes how Mexican music has influenced the folk music of the United States, both through indirect and direct adoption. Includes highlights of an interview with Itzhak Perlman, internationally noted concert violinist.
From The Music Of America Series.
Prod-KQEDTV Dist-GPITVL

Music Image C 22 MIN
3/4 OR 1/2 INCH VIDEO CASSETTE
Reveals the artist's feelings in experiencing works by Ravel and Katchaturian.
Prod-EAI Dist-EAI

Music In Action C 11 MIN
16MM FILM OPTICAL SOUND P-I
Shows how children are involved as composers, performers and listeners during the performance of musical ensembles.
From The Music With Children Series. No. 4
LC NO. 77-700740
Prod-NASHGC Dist-SWRTWT Prodn-SWRTWT 1967

Music In Early Childhood C 28 MIN
16MM FILM OPTICAL SOUND P-I
Features Bob Smith, a noted music educator, sharing some of his ideas and methods for teaching pre-school and primary children to appreciate music. Shows three different age groups of children enthusiastically enjoying music, through singing and through physical response.
LC NO. 73-703093
Prod-UIME Dist-UILL 1973

Music In The Art Of The Renaissance C 28 MIN
16MM FILM OPTICAL SOUND
Offers a collage of art works which depicts musical activity in a variety of settings, both religious and secular during the Renaissance.
Prod-CCNCC Dist-CCNCC

Music In The Kindergarten B 30 MIN
2 INCH VIDEOTAPE
See series title for descriptive statement.
From The Program Development In The Kindergarten Series.
Prod-GPITVL Dist-GPITVL

Music In Therapy C 30 MIN
3/4 OR 1/2 INCH VIDEO CASSETTE
Offers a comprehensive look at the role of the Registered Music Therapist in the treatment of the mentally retarded and the mentally ill. Uses simulated therapy sessions to demonstrate the effect of music therapy in treating a behaviorally disordered adolescent, in teaching social/academic skills to a trainable mentally retarded girl and in promoting transferable music skills with a community mental health center patient.
From The Sounds They Make Series.
Prod-OHUTC Dist-OHUTC

Music In Two Parts C 29 MIN
2 INCH VIDEOTAPE
See series title for descriptive statement.
From The Playing The Guitar I Series.
Prod-KCET Dist-PUBTEL

Music Is C 28 MIN
16MM FILM - 3/4 IN VIDEO
Examines the way music has been used by man as a means of communicating and of expressing feeling. Points out that there are many different kinds of music and that music plays a significant part in many aspects of life.
From The Music Series. No. 1
LC NO. 78-706211
Prod-WETATV Dist-USNAC 1977

Music Is C 30 MIN
3/4 OR 1/2 INCH VIDEO CASSETTE I
See series title for descriptive statement.
From The Music Is Series.
Prod-WETATV Dist-GPITVL

Music Is Composed C 28 MIN
16MM FILM - 3/4 IN VIDEO
Examines the process of composing music, putting together the elements of rhythm, harmony, tone color and form. Focuses on the stylistically revolutionary nature of several composers, such as Mozart, Berlioz and Beethoven.
From The Music Series. No. 7
LC NO. 78-706210
Prod-WETATV Dist-USNAC 1977

Music Is Composed C 30 MIN
3/4 OR 1/2 INCH VIDEO CASSETTE I
See series title for descriptive statement.
From The Music Is Series.
Prod-WETATV Dist-GPITVL

Music Is Conducted C 28 MIN
16MM FILM - 3/4 IN VIDEO
Explores the art of conducting music, pointing out that it is the conductor's role to keep a group of musicians together as they play and to encourage the musicians to play a piece as the conductor thinks the composer intended it to be played. Examines a musical score.
From The Music Series. No. 8
LC NO. 78-706212
Prod-WETATV Dist-USNAC 1977

Music Is Conducted C 30 MIN
3/4 OR 1/2 INCH VIDEO CASSETTE I
See series title for descriptive statement.
From The Music Is Series.
Prod-WETATV Dist-GPITVL

Music Is Form C 28 MIN
16MM FILM - 3/4 IN VIDEO
Explains that through the use of various themes, melodies and variations music can be organized to make different compositions. Shows how distinguishing form can be accomplished by recognizing musical patterns.
From The Music Series. No. 6
LC NO. 78-706213
Prod-WETATV Dist-USNAC 1977

Music Is Form C 30 MIN
3/4 OR 1/2 INCH VIDEO CASSETTE I
See series title for descriptive statement.
From The Music Is Series.
Prod-WETATV Dist-GPITVL

Music Is Harmony C 28 MIN
16MM FILM, 3/4 OR 1/2 IN VIDEO
Explains that harmony occurs when two or more sounds played together lose their separateness and produce a new sound. Explains the difference in sound between a single melody line and the same melody with harmonic accompaniment.
From The Music Series. No. 4
LC NO. 78-706214
Prod-WETATV Dist-USNAC 1977

Music Is Harmony C 30 MIN
3/4 OR 1/2 INCH VIDEO CASSETTE I
See series title for descriptive statement.
From The Music Is Series.
Prod-WETATV Dist-GPITVL

Music Is Improvised C 28 MIN
16MM FILM - 3/4 IN VIDEO
Employs a jazz band to demonstrate musical improvisation, showing how a performer chooses how to get from one musical place to another.
From The Music Series. No. 9
LC NO. 78-706216
Prod-WETATV Dist-USNAC 1977

Music Is Improvised C 30 MIN
3/4 OR 1/2 INCH VIDEO CASSETTE I
See series title for descriptive statement.
From The Music Is Series.
Prod-WETATV Dist-GPITVL

Music Is Melody C 28 MIN
16MM FILM - 3/4 IN VIDEO
Explains that melody is the basic idea of a song and gives a song its sound and direction. Shows the different musical elements which can be changed to vary a melody.
From The Music Series. No. 3
LC NO. 78-706217
Prod-WETATV Dist-USNAC 1977

Music Is Melody C 30 MIN
3/4 OR 1/2 INCH VIDEO CASSETTE I
See series title for descriptive statement.
From The Music Is Series.
Prod-WETATV Dist-GPITVL

Music Is Rhythm C 28 MIN
16MM FILM - 3/4 IN VIDEO
Deals with different elements of rhythm, including beats, rests, duration, tempo and accent. Points out that rhythm is the most immediately recognizable element in music because it can be felt.
From The Music Series. No. 2
LC NO. 78-706218
Prod-WETATV Dist-USNAC 1977

Music Is Rhythm C 30 MIN
3/4 OR 1/2 INCH VIDEO CASSETTE I
See series title for descriptive statement.
From The Music Is Series.
Prod-WETATV Dist-GPITVL

Music Is Style C 28 MIN
16MM FILM - 3/4 IN VIDEO
Explains that style is the mode of expression or the characteristic mood of music. Examines musical styles after 1600, including baroque, classical, romantic, impressionistic and modern.
From The Music Series. No. 10
LC NO. 78-706219
Prod-WETATV Dist-USNAC 1977

Music Is Style C 30 MIN
3/4 OR 1/2 INCH VIDEO CASSETTE I
See series title for descriptive statement.
From The Music Is Series.
Prod-WETATV Dist-GPITVL

Music Is Tone Color C 28 MIN
16MM FILM - 3/4 IN VIDEO
Explains that tone color is the particular sound characteristic of each musical instrument. Points out that the elements of tone color are register, texture, range and dynamics and shows how proper choice of instrumentation can add to the musical meaning of a piece.
From The Music Series. No. 5
LC NO. 78-706220
Prod-WETATV Dist-USNAC 1977

Music Is Tone Color C 30 MIN
3/4 OR 1/2 INCH VIDEO CASSETTE I
See series title for descriptive statement.
From The Music Is Series.
Prod-WETATV Dist-GPITVL

Music Is–A Series

I
Teaches basic musical concepts and characteristics. Demonstrates a variety of musical styles. Includes performances by the National Symphony Orchestra.
Prod-WETATV Dist-GPITVL

Music Is	030 MIN
Music Is Composed	030 MIN
Music Is Conducted	030 MIN
Music Is Form	030 MIN
Music Is Harmony	030 MIN
Music Is Improvised	030 MIN
Music Is Melody	030 MIN
Music Is Rhythm	030 MIN
Music Is Style	030 MIN
Music Is Tone Color	030 MIN

Music Lesson, The B 30 MIN
16MM FILM OPTICAL SOUND C A
Shows a teacher at the Hoff Barthelson Music School as she leads a group of seven-year-olds through a series of musical games and exercises which enables them to learn how to read rhythm and tone from written notes.
From The World Of Music Series.
Prod-NET Dist-IU 1967

Music Lessons C 40 MIN
16MM FILM OPTICAL SOUND
Describes the Kodaly method of music training for children. Depicts music training in American public elementary schools that leads to extraordinary musical competence in fifth and sixth graders.
LC NO. 82-700228
Prod-FDF Dist-KAROL Prodn-CHOPRA 1982

Music Loving Dog, A C 11 MIN
16MM FILM, 3/4 OR 1/2 IN VIDEO J-C
Presents an animated story about a crazy scientist who invents a highly explosive ultrasonic violin, only to have it stolen by his pet dog who first uses it to make music and later to rebel against his master.
LC NO. 77-701528
Prod-LESFG Dist-TEXFLM 1977

Music Machine–A Series

P
Presents musical concepts through singing, movement and listening.
Prod-INDIPS Dist-GPITVL 1981

Barnyard, The	015 MIN
Beat No Beat	015 MIN
Boo It's Halloween	015 MIN
Brass Family, The	015 MIN
Cadences	015 MIN
Duration	015 MIN
Fluff - An Electronic Music Story	015 MIN
Harmony	015 MIN
How Fast To Go - Tempo	015 MIN
How Loud To Sing - Dynamics	015 MIN
Hurray - We're American	015 MIN
I Live In A City	015 MIN
Intervals	015 MIN
Meter	015 MIN
Mezzo The Musical Mouse	015 MIN
Music From Africa	015 MIN
Music From Japan	015 MIN
Music Machine, The - Introduction	015 MIN
Musical Stories	015 MIN
Percussion Family, The	015 MIN
String Family, The	015 MIN

Styles	015 MIN
Summer Songs	015 MIN
Thanksgiving	015 MIN
Tone Color	015 MIN
Valentine Wishes	015 MIN
Which Way Did The Melody Go	015 MIN
Woodwind Family, The	015 MIN

Music Machine, The - Introduction C 15 MIN
3/4 OR 1/2 INCH VIDEO CASSETTE T
Introduces the Music Machine Series which is designed to teach musical concepts through singing, moving and listening.
From The Music Machine Series.
Prod-INDIPS Dist-GPITVL 1981

Music Machines C 15 MIN
16MM FILM, 3/4 OR 1/2 IN VIDEO P-H
Explores today's musical technology - the oscilloscope, synthesizer, mixing panel and tape recorder. Presents the blending of pitch, tonal quality and duration into various musical shapes.
Prod-THAMES Dist-MEDIAG 1984

Music Makers And Miscellaneous C 15 MIN
2 INCH VIDEOTAPE J-H
Emphasizes music teaching careers and notes the keen sense of dedication one must have to become a professional performing artist in the field of music.
From The Work Is For Real Series.
Prod-STETVC Dist-GPITVL

Music Makers Of The Blue Ridge B 48 MIN
16MM FILM, 3/4 OR 1/2 IN VIDEO J-C A
Studies life in Eastern mountain areas by examining folk music and dance. Includes scenes of isolated areas in western North Carolina. Shows the filmmakers guided to the homes of friends and neighbors of folksinger Bascom Lamar Lunsford.
LC NO. 80-707082
Prod-NET Dist-IU Prodn-HOFMND 1966

Music Man, The C 151 MIN
16MM FILM OPTICAL SOUND
Presents Meredith Wilson's hit musical brought to the screen with all the great music and fun which earned it over 1500 performances on Broadway.
Prod-SWAMD Dist-SWANK

Music Migrates C 20 MIN
16MM FILM OPTICAL SOUND I
Describes the places from which American music came and also the movement of music Westward across our country along with the migration of people. Includes music from England, Germany, Greece and Scotland as it was brought to this country by European immigrants. Features some modern experimental jazz, a creation of an early San Francisco concert of the Gold Rush days and music from the Orient.
From The Music Of America Series.
Prod-KQEDTV Dist-GPITVL

Music Mountain-- A Series C 3 MIN
3/4 OR 1/2 INCH VIDEO CASSETTE
Honors singer Carole (Karuna) King for the land she donated.
Prod-IYOGA Dist-IYOGA

Music Of Africa B 30 MIN
16MM FILM OPTICAL SOUND H-C
Fela Sowande of Nigeria, African musicologist, composer, and organist, explains how contemporary African music has mingled traditional African and Western idioms to create new forms.
LC NO. 77-703288
Prod-NETRC Dist-IU Prodn-WNDTTV 1964

Music Of Afro-America C 15 MIN
3/4 OR 1/2 INCH VIDEO CASSETTE I
Introduces Afro-American music, from traditional African drum calls to Dixieland. Shows a field holler and a spiritual, and concludes with a sing-along.
From The Music And Me Series.
LC NO. 80-706872
Prod-WDCNTV Dist-AITECH 1979

Music Of America—A Series
I
Presents various aspects of American music.
Prod-KQEDTV Dist-GPITVL

American Composers	20 MIN
American Indian Music	20 MIN
Appalachian Music	20 MIN
Blues And Gospel	20 MIN
Dance	20 MIN
Jazz	20 MIN
Joy Of Singing, The	20 MIN
Music From Mexico And The Violin	20 MIN
Music Migrates	20 MIN
Music Of The Rivers	20 MIN
Opera	20 MIN
Overture	20 MIN
What Does Music Do	20 MIN
Work Songs - Sea Chanties	20 MIN
Worship And Ceremony	20 MIN

Music Of Auschwitz, The C 16 MIN
16MM FILM, 3/4 OR 1/2 IN VIDEO J-C A
Tells how Fania Fenelon survived Auschwitz by playing in the camp's orchestra. Originally shown on the CBS television program 60 Minutes.
Prod-CBSNEW Dist-CAROUF

Music Of China - Thirty Years Of Change C 110 MIN
3/4 INCH VIDEO CASSETTE
Studies the music of China since 1949. Describes political setting. Western influences and traditional Chinese instruments.
Prod-OHC Dist-HRC

Music Of Erich Zann, The C 17 MIN
16MM FILM, 3/4 OR 1/2 IN VIDEO J-H
Presents H P Lovecraft's story The Music Of Erich Zann, about a young 19th century American who is fascinated by Erich Zann, a mute violinist who plays wondrous music only at night.
Prod-MCFI Dist-MCFI

Music Of Harry Partch, The C 30 MIN
2 INCH VIDEOTAPE
See series title for descriptive statement.
From The Synergism - Variations In Music Series.
Prod-KPBS Dist-PUBTEL

Music Of India - Classical B 16 MIN
16MM FILM OPTICAL SOUND I-C A
Introduces the two time-honored systems of music in India and explains the traditions associated with them. Features a few of the well-known vocalists who sing some 'RAGAS' according to traditon.
Prod-INDIA Dist-NEDINF

Music Of India - Drums B 12 MIN
16MM FILM OPTICAL SOUND I-C A
Shows the variety of drums used in the music and dance of India. Presents the intricate 'BOLS' played on the pakhawaj, mridang and tabla by renowned artists and shows all the other types of drums used in the villages.
Prod-INDIA Dist-NEDINF

Music Of India - Instrumental B 11 MIN
16MM FILM OPTICAL SOUND I-C A
Introduces the rich variety of instruments used in Indian music. Features the been of North India, the veena of South India, the sarod and the sitar.
Prod-INDIA Dist-NEDINF

Music Of Inspiration C 15 MIN
3/4 OR 1/2 INCH VIDEO CASSETTE P-I
Presents music of inspiration.
From The Music And Me Series.
Prod-WDCNTV Dist-AITECH 1979

Music Of Japan, The - Koto Music C 29 MIN
2 INCH VIDEOTAPE
Presents an international performance of mime, poetry, puppetry, dance, art and music. Includes Koto music of Japan.
From The Synergism - Encore Series.
Prod-WKARTV Dist-PUBTEL

Music Of Man—A Series
16MM FILM, 3/4 OR 1/2 IN VIDEO H-C A
Explores the role of music in Western society, from ancient rhythms to classical compositions, folk songs and punk rock.
Prod-CANBC Dist-TIMLIF 1981

Age Of The Composer, The	057 MIN
Age Of The Individual, The	057 MIN
Flowering Of Harmony, The	057 MIN
Known And The Unknown, The	057 MIN
New Voices For Man	057 MIN
Parting Of The Ways, The	057 MIN
Quiver Of Life, The	057 MIN
Sound Or Unsound	057 MIN

Music Of Shakespeare's Time B 30 MIN
16MM FILM OPTICAL SOUND J-C A
Presents the New York Pro Musica playing music of Shakespeare's time with the original compositions and reproductions of the original instruments. Presents short talks on the nature of a particular selection, or the composer or instrument used, between numbers.
From The World Of Music Series.
Prod-NET Dist-IU 1965

Music Of South America C 15 MIN
3/4 OR 1/2 INCH VIDEO CASSETTE P-I
Discusses the music of South America.
From The Music And Me Series.
Prod-WDCNTV Dist-AITECH 1979

Music Of Speech - Pitch And Poetry, The C 29 MIN
3/4 INCH VIDEO CASSETTE
Shows how one word or sentence may imply several different meanings, just by varying pitch, stress and voice quality.
From The Pike On Language Series.
Prod-UMITV Dist-UMITV 1977

Music Of The First Americans C 15 MIN
3/4 OR 1/2 INCH VIDEO CASSETTE P-I
Discusses the music of the First Americans.
From The Music And Me Series.
Prod-WDCNTV Dist-AITECH 1979

Music Of The Rivers C 20 MIN
16MM FILM OPTICAL SOUND I
Presents a group of songs centered around the theme of the river. Points out that this theme is important in American music as the river has been extremely important both in the history and in the folklore of America.
From The Music Of America Series.
Prod-KQEDTV Dist-GPITVL

Music Of The Spheres C 52 MIN
16MM FILM, 3/4 OR 1/2 IN VIDEO J-C A
Presents the evolution of mathematics and its relationship to musical harmony, early astronomy and perspectives in painting.
From The Ascent Of Man Series. No. 5
LC NO. 79-707222
Prod-BBCTV Dist-TIMLIF 1973

Music Of The Spheres (Spanish) C 52 MIN
16MM FILM OPTICAL SOUND H-C A
Presents the evolution of mathematics and its relationship to musical harmony, early astronomy and perspectives in painting.
From The Ascent Of Man Series. No. 5
Prod-BBCTV Dist-TIMLIF 1973

Music Of The Spoken Word, The C 6 MIN
16MM FILM, 3/4 OR 1/2 IN VIDEO H-C A
Points out the little-realized importance of music in the English language.
From The Communicating From The Lectern Series.
Prod-METAIV Dist-AIMS 1976

Music Of The USA I C 15 MIN
3/4 OR 1/2 INCH VIDEO CASSETTE P-I
Discusses the music of America.
From The Music And Me Series.
Prod-WDCNTV Dist-AITECH 1979

Music Of The USA II C 14 MIN
3/4 OR 1/2 INCH VIDEO CASSETTE P-I
Discusses the music of America.
From The Music And Me Series.
Prod-WDCNTV Dist-AITECH 1979

Music Of The USA III C 14 MIN
3/4 OR 1/2 INCH VIDEO CASSETTE P-I
Discusses the music of America.
From The Music And Me Series.
Prod-WDCNTV Dist-AITECH 1979

Music Of Vietnam C 6 MIN
16MM FILM, 3/4 OR 1/2 IN VIDEO
Presents traditional music of Vietnam played on the sixteen-stringed zither. Shows the traditional techniques used for the subtle ornament and tone changes that are characteristic of this music.
Prod-UWASHP Dist-UWASHP

Music On Key C 30 MIN
16MM FILM, 3/4 OR 1/2 IN VIDEO I-H
Takes an introductory look at the new technology of computer music and how computers can be used to teach or make music. Discusses software programs for teaching and arranging and creating music as well as portable pre-programmed keyboards.
From The Mr Microchip Series.
Prod-JOU Dist-JOU

Music Reading B 20 MIN
16MM FILM OPTICAL SOUND I T
Uses a series of demonstrations to show how music experiences in kindergarten and lower elementary grades can help provide a foundation for music reading. Shows how a fifth grade class learns to read music.
Prod-JHP Dist-MLA 1952

Music Research B 24 MIN
16MM FILM OPTICAL SOUND
Shows the application of educational technology to music. Examines a program which employs a keyboard-oriented teaching machine in order to teach elementary school children the basic skills of music.
From The Communication Theory And The New Educational Media Series.
LC NO. 75-700564
Prod-USOE Dist-USNAC 1966

Music School, The C 30 MIN
16MM FILM, 3/4 OR 1/2 IN VIDEO
Depicts a writer struggling, during a 24-hour period, to find a focus in his life. Based on the short story The Music School by John Updike.
From The American Short Story Series.
Prod-LEARIF Dist-CORF

Music Sequence C 10 MIN
16MM FILM, 3/4 OR 1/2 IN VIDEO
Provides a collection of the popular music hits of the 1950's and uses a quick cut technique to illustrate the music.
Prod-EAMES Dist-PFP 1960

Music Shop, The—A Series

Presents an informal tour of the world of music with composer and arranger, Jerry H Bilik.
Prod-UMITV Dist-UMITV 1974

Back To Bach	029 MIN
Backstage Beethoven	029 MIN
Creating The Commercial	029 MIN
Drums Go Bang, The	029 MIN
Faking It	029 MIN
For The Record	029 MIN
Gilbert And Sullivan	029 MIN
Half-Time	029 MIN
In The Mood	029 MIN
Jazz Is A Personal Thing	029 MIN
Let's Make A Musical	029 MIN
Making Movie Music	029 MIN
Rehearsal	029 MIN
Rock - Tilt With A Lilt	029 MIN
Search For Sounds	029 MIN
Selling A Song	029 MIN
Songs And Symphony	029 MIN
Soul To Soul	029 MIN
Twinkle, Twinkle, Little Star	029 MIN
Writing It Down	029 MIN

Music Student, The B 30 MIN
16MM FILM OPTICAL SOUND
A story of an opera singer who serves as cantor in a small synagogue. Discusses the background of the custom of Yahrzeit and Kaddish.
LC NO. FIA64-1144
Prod-JTS Dist-NAAJS Prodn-NBC 1957

Music Therapy - Preclinical Fieldwork C 30 MIN
3/4 OR 1/2 INCH VIDEO CASSETTE
Presents the process used at the Ohio University School of Music to set up and carry out student field work experience in music therapy. Shows student therapists involved in group and individual sessions, working with a mentally retarded child, a geriatric patient and the pre-school developmentally delayed child.
Prod-OHUTC Dist-OHUTC

Music To Express Ideas C 12 MIN
16MM FILM, 3/4 OR 1/2 IN VIDEO I-J
Encourages students to think creatively and to involve the whole class in finding ways of student ability to write music, and express ideas musically.
Prod-AIMS Dist-AIMS 1970

Music To Express Ideas (Spanish) C 12 MIN
16MM FILM, 3/4 OR 1/2 IN VIDEO I-J
A class which is vitally interested in aviation, creates a full symphony, involving every student in research and individual creative expression.
Prod-BRADLY Dist-AIMS 1970

Music To Learn About People C 11 MIN
16MM FILM, 3/4 OR 1/2 IN VIDEO I
Introduces unfamiliar instruments by name and develops an appreciation for musical skill.
Prod-AIMS Dist-AIMS 1970

Music To Live By C 19 MIN
16MM FILM, 3/4 OR 1/2 IN VIDEO H-C A
Illustrates that man throughout history has organized sounds to please him in a variety of ways and has listened to music. Presents music and visuals from several periods and cultures, rock-calypso, oriental, religious, jazz, folk and opera. Portrays the universal need for musical expression.
From The Humanities Series.
Prod-MGHT Dist-MGHT 1971

Music To Tell A Story C 9 MIN
16MM FILM, 3/4 OR 1/2 IN VIDEO P
Shows children how their own ideas may be used to tell stories in many ways.
Prod-AIMS Dist-AIMS 1970

Music To Tell A Story (Spanish) C 9 MIN
16MM FILM, 3/4 OR 1/2 IN VIDEO K-P
Shows children in a class and how they interpret their own story creatively in music and other expression, utilizing science, langauge arts and rhythms.
Prod-BRADLY Dist-AIMS 1970

Music With Balls C 10 MIN
16MM FILM OPTICAL SOUND H-C A
Presents a new kind of music with moving sculpture gigantic, swinging spheres whose orbits make magical music.
Prod-UWFKD Dist-UWFKD

Music With Children—A Series

Prod-SWRTWT Dist-SWRTWT

Music With Children, Pt 1 11 MIN
Music With Children, Pt 2 11 MIN
Music With Children, Pt 3 11 MIN
Music With Children, Pt 4 11 MIN

Music Word Fire And I Would Do It Again, Coo-Coo - The Lessons C 30 MIN
3/4 OR 1/2 INCH VIDEO CASSETTE
Introduces four principal characters - Isolde, Raoul de Noget, Buddy and Donnie. Features variations on the theme song from Episode Three of the television opera, Perfect Lives.
Prod-KITCHN Dist-KITCHN

Music—A Series

Explains basic components of music.
Prod-WETATV Dist-USNAC 1977

Music Is 028 MIN
Music Is Composed 028 MIN
Music Is Conducted 028 MIN
Music Is Form 028 MIN
Music Is Harmony 028 MIN
Music Is Improvised 028 MIN
Music Is Melody 028 MIN
Music Is Rhythm 028 MIN
Music Is Style 028 MIN
Music Is Tone Color 028 MIN

Music—A Series

Discusses various aspects of music.
Prod-WETATV Dist-USNAC 1977

Music Is 28 MIN
Music Is Composed 28 MIN
Music Is Conducted 28 MIN
Music Is Form 28 MIN
Music Is Harmony 28 MIN
Music Is Improvised 28 MIN
Music Is Melody 28 MIN
Music Is Rhythm 28 MIN
Music Is Style 28 MIN
Music Is Tone Color 28 MIN

Music, The Expressive Language C 11 MIN
16MM FILM OPTICAL SOUND K-P
Demonstrates the musical score as a graphic representation of melody and rhythm.
LC NO. FIA62-1679
Prod-SUEF Dist-SUTHLA 1962

Musica C 60 MIN
3/4 INCH VIDEO CASSETTE
Traces the history and development of Latin American music in the United States. Tells the story through the words and music of artists such as Mario Bauza and Paquito D'Rivera.
Prod-BLKFMF Dist-BLKFMF

Musica En La Noche B 85 MIN
16MM FILM OPTICAL SOUND A
A Spanish language film. Interprets the songs and dances of different countries with typical costumes and appropriate sets.
Prod-TRANSW Dist-TRANSW

Musical Encounter—A Series
P-I
Demonstrates the joy and enthusiasm that the performance of music can generate among young people. Presents the sounds of different musical instruments played by young performers.
Prod-PBS Dist-GPITVL 1983

Bassoon-Piano Show, The 030 MIN
Musical Families 030 MIN
Orchestra, The 030 MIN
Piano Show, The 030 MIN
Record Show, A 030 MIN
Team Show, A 030 MIN

Musical Families C 30 MIN
3/4 OR 1/2 INCH VIDEO CASSETTE P-I
Presents musical families, including the Chiu brothers who keep busy with their fiddles and the Argosino brothers who do likewise with a piano and a penchant for musical composition. Features composer-conductor-pianist Lalo Schifrin. Hosted by Florence Henderson.
From The Musical Encounter Series.
Prod-KLCSTV Dist-GPITVL 1983

Musical Forms - The Canon C 18 MIN
16MM FILM, 3/4 OR 1/2 IN VIDEO I-C
Explores the many variations of the canon.
Prod-CENTRO Dist-CORF

Musical Forms - The Fugue C 19 MIN
16MM FILM, 3/4 OR 1/2 IN VIDEO I-C
Illustrates the structure of the fugue, combining live-action photography of musicians with animation of the score of Bach's Fugue In G Minor.
Prod-CENTRO Dist-CORF

Musical Genes C 7 MIN
16MM FILM, 3/4 OR 1/2 IN VIDEO H-C A
Presents CBS News correspondent Charles Osgood, who interviews a scientist who has put DNA chemistry to music. Shows how he uses this music and the state of the art in computer animation to make the 'melody of man' visible to all. Originally shown on the CBS television program Universe.
Prod-CBSNEW Dist-CAROUF

Musical Holdouts C 47 MIN
16MM FILM, 3/4 OR 1/2 IN VIDEO A
Portrays musicians outside the mainstream American tradition, from blacks of the Carolina Sea Islands, to Appalachian Bluegrass players, to Berkeley Street musicians.
Prod-CNEMAG Dist-CNEMAG 1976

Musical Holdouts C 51 MIN
16MM FILM, 3/4 OR 1/2 IN VIDEO H-C A
Examines the music of Americans who have maintained their ethnic and individual identities in their music.
Prod-COHNJ Dist-PHENIX 1975

Musical Instrument Maker Of Williamsburg, The C 54 MIN
16MM FILM OPTICAL SOUND
Shows George Wilson, master medical instrument maker, and his journeymen construct a spinet and a violin commencing with raw materials and ending with the completed instruments.
LC NO. 76-700385
Prod-CWMS Dist-CWMS 1976

Musical Instruments—A Series

Introduces various musical instruments, demonstrating sound, dynamic range, playing techniques, physical features affecting sound, versatility, and history.
Prod-WWVUTV Dist-GPITVL

Classical Percussion, Pt 1 018 MIN
Classical Percussion, Pt 2 016 MIN
Colorful Woodwinds, Pt 1 018 MIN
Colorful Woodwinds, Pt 2 013 MIN
Early Instruments, Pt 1 019 MIN
Early Instruments, Pt 2 019 MIN
East African Instruments, Pt 1 017 MIN
East African Instruments, Pt 2 016 MIN
Majestic Brass, Pt 1 015 MIN
Majestic Brass, Pt 2 016 MIN
South American Instruments, Pt 1 017 MIN
South American Instruments, Pt 2 019 MIN
Vibrant Strings, Pt 1 016 MIN
Vibrant Strings, Pt 2 019 MIN
West African Instruments 017 MIN

Musical Journey Through Eight Centuries With Carl Dolmetsch And Joseph Saxby, A B 30 MIN
3/4 INCH VIDEO CASSETTE
Comprised of two programs which introduce a variety of instruments, including recorder, viol, rebec and others. Comments on works composed from the 13th to the 20th centuries.
Prod-UWASHP Dist-UWASHP

Musical Masterpieces—A Series

Prod-SG Dist-SG

Master Singers Of Nuremberg, The 20 MIN
Mendelssohn's Midsummer Night's Dream 20 MIN

Musical Mosaic - East Africa B 28 MIN
3/4 OR 1/2 INCH VIDEO CASSETTE
Shows Phil Faini and members of the West Virginia Percussion Ensemble explaining and demonstrating four different East African drums, the baakisimba, engalabi, mpunyi and nankasa and the maracas and box rattle. Presents Father Charles Lwanga singing with the instrumentals.
From The Musical Mosaic Series.
Prod-WWVUTV Dist-PBS

Musical Mosaic - West Africa B 27 MIN
3/4 OR 1/2 INCH VIDEO CASSETTE
Presents Phil Faini explaining and demonstrating the West African instruments and rhythms. Shows that much of the interest and vitality of African music lies in its polyrhythms or combination of rhythms.
From The Musical Mosaic Series.
Prod-WWVUTV Dist-PBS

Musical Mosaic—A Series

Presents Phil Faini, associate professor of music at West Virginia University, explaining and demonstrating African instruments and rhythms.
Prod-WWVUTV Dist-PBS

Musical Mosaic - East Africa 028 MIN
Musical Mosaic - West Africa 027 MIN

Musical Possibilities C 30 MIN
3/4 OR 1/2 INCH VIDEO CASSETTE C
See series title for descriptive statement.
From The In Our Own Image Series.
Prod-DALCCD Dist-DALCCD

Musical Stories C 15 MIN
3/4 OR 1/2 INCH VIDEO CASSETTE P
Discusses program music.
From The Music Machine Series.
Prod-INDIPS Dist-GPITVL 1981

Musical Terms Melodrama, A C 11 MIN
16MM FILM OPTICAL SOUND J-C A
Depicts a presentation by a junior high group of a 'SILLY OPERA' designed to teach musical terminology.
Prod-WSU Dist-WSU 1960

Musical Triangles—A Series
16MM FILM, 3/4 OR 1/2 IN VIDEO J-C A
States that every musical performance depends on a combination of composer, performer and musical instrument - a musical triangle. Presents celebrated musical triangles with musicians playing music from the fifteenth century to the present in settings appropriate to the period.
Prod-THAMES Dist-MEDIAG 1975

Bach, The Organ, And Simon Preston 026 MIN
Beethoven, The Cello, And Paul Tortelier 026 MIN
Britten, The Voice, And Peter Pears 026 MIN
Dowland, The Lute, And Julian Bream 026 MIN
Liszt, The Piano, And Craig Sheppard 026 MIN
Mozart, The Clarinet, And Keith Puddy 026 MIN
Paganini, The Violin, And Desmond Bradley 026 MIN
Purcell, The Trumpet, And John 026 MIN
Rameau, The Harpsichord, And George Malcolm 026 MIN
Schubert, The Piano Trio, And Peter Frankl, 026 MIN
Stockhausen, The Percussion, And 026 MIN
Villa-Lobos, The Guitar, And Julian Byzantine 026 MIN
Vivaldi, The Flute, And James Galway 026 MIN

Musician C 15 MIN
3/4 OR 1/2 INCH VIDEO CASSETTE I
Explains the qualifications and personal qualities required for a successful career as a musician.
From The Career Awareness Series.
Prod-KLVXTV Dist-GPITVL 1973

Musician And The General, The C 29 MIN
2 INCH VIDEOTAPE
See series title for descriptive statement.
From The Koltanowski On Chess Series.
Prod-KQEDTV Dist-PUBTEL

Musician's Tale, A C 11 MIN
16MM FILM, 3/4 OR 1/2 IN VIDEO H-C A
Presents the animated story of an old musician and a whistling beaver. Reveals how they attain fame and fortune, only to lose both as well as their friendship.
Prod-CFET Dist-PHENIX Prodn-KRATKY 1982

Musicians In The Woods, The C 14 MIN
16MM FILM, 3/4 OR 1/2 IN VIDEO P
Puppets re-enact the fairy tale in which the donkey, dog, cat and rooster outwit a band of thieves and gain a fortune.
Prod-GAKKEN Dist-CORF 1962

Musicians Of The Ages C 18 MIN
16MM FILM OPTICAL SOUND
Presents the many outstanding musicians featured at Potter's Wax Museum in St Augustine, Florida.
Prod-FLADC Dist-FLADC

Musicmakers C 26 MIN
16MM FILM, 3/4 OR 1/2 IN VIDEO P-J
Presents famous singers, songwriters and instrumentalists showing how to create music. Encourages looking for musical possibilities in commonplace objects.
Prod-MARKS Dist-PHENIX 1978

Musketeers C 6 MIN
16MM FILM, 3/4 OR 1/2 IN VIDEO H-C A

Uses the framework of the novel THE THREE MUSKETEERS by Alexander Dumas to present a surrealistic adventure with a series of characters whose movements and expressions both imitate and mock their real-life counterparts.
Prod-KRATKY Dist-PHENIX 1982

Muskie C 22 MIN
16MM FILM OPTICAL SOUND
Offers an underwater look at the fighting muskie and his habitat capped by a study of the contrasting techniques used in landing this elusive prey.
Prod-BRNSWK Dist-KAROL

Mussau C 32 MIN
16MM FILM OPTICAL SOUND
A Danish language film. Portrays life on the coral island of Mussau which lies in the Bismarck Sea. Points out that even if there has been a certain outside influence, everyday life goes on as it did a hundred years ago.
Prod-STATNS Dist-STATNS 1963

Mussel Specialist, The C 25 MIN
16MM FILM, 3/4 OR 1/2 IN VIDEO H-C A
Studies the behavior of oystercatchers on the coasts of Britain. Points out that these birds are experts in the complicated technique of opening mussels. Asks the question of what is innate and what has been learned.
From The Behavior And Survival Series.
Prod-MGHT Dist-MGHT 1973

Mussolini Visits Hitler (German) B 31 MIN
3/4 OR 1/2 INCH VIDEO CASSETTE
Shows Adolf Hitler and Benito Mussolini speaking at Berlin's Olympic Stadium in September 1937. Reports on the Italian dictator's state visit to Germany. Includes scenes of the Axis leaders' meeting in Munich.
Prod-IHF Dist-IHF

Mussolini's Italy C 29 MIN
2 INCH VIDEOTAPE
See series title for descriptive statement.
From The Course Of Our Times I Series.
Prod-WGBHTV Dist-PUBTEL

Must I, May I C 15 MIN
16MM FILM, 3/4 OR 1/2 IN VIDEO
Presents parallel episodes which Debbie and Bobby try to deal with in situations that give them too much or not enough responsibility. Shows how to cope with the feelings caused by the tension between freedom and responsibility.
From The Inside-Out Series.
Prod-NITC Dist-AITECH

Must We Fall C 17 MIN
16MM FILM, 3/4 OR 1/2 IN VIDEO
Re-enacts several dramatic accidents. Describes how to avoid slipping, tripping and falling.
From The Slips And Falls Series.
Prod-VISUCP Dist-VISUCP

Must We Have Noise C 11 MIN
16MM FILM, 3/4 OR 1/2 IN VIDEO P-I
Presents sounds, both natural and artificial, that have become part of our daily existence. Focuses attention on noises that are rarely heard consciously. Results in a censure of one of the major pollutants of modern society.
From The Caring About Our Community Series.
Prod-GORKER Dist-AIMS 1972

Must We Have Noise (Spanish) C 11 MIN
16MM FILM, 3/4 OR 1/2 IN VIDEO P-I
Presents sounds, both natural and artificial, that have become part of our daily existence. Focuses attention on noises that are rarely heard consciously. Results in a censure of one of the major pollutants of modern society.
From The Caring About Our Community Series.
Prod-GORKER Dist-AIMS 1972

Mustang - Managing A Misfit C 29 MIN
1/2 IN VIDEO CASSETTE BETA/VHS
Explores the American mustang's history. Pictures wild horses in their natural habitats.
Prod-USFS Dist-EQVDL

Mustard - The Spice Of Nations C 26 MIN
3/4 OR 1/2 INCH VIDEO CASSETTE J A
Identifies how and what kind of mustard is used in various countries.
From The Spice Of Life Series.
Prod-BLCKRD Dist-BCNFL 1985

Musvagen - Buteo Buteo (The Common Buzzard) B 10 MIN
16MM FILM OPTICAL SOUND
A Danish language film. Describes the life of the common buzzard in the nest, in the forest and the fields.
Prod-STATNS Dist-STATNS 1962

Mutations C 8 MIN
16MM FILM OPTICAL SOUND
Presents the changing dots, ectoplasmic shapes and electronic music of L Schwartz's Mutations, which has been shot with the aid of computers and lasers.
Prod-LILYAN Dist-LILYAN

Mute C 3 MIN
3/4 OR 1/2 INCH VIDEO CASSETTE
See series title for descriptive statement.
From The Five Short Works by Janice Tanaka Series.
Prod-EAI Dist-EAI

Mutiny On The Bounty B 40 MIN
16MM FILM OPTICAL SOUND I-H
Presents Charles Laughton and Clark Gable in the leading roles of the classic 'MUTINY ON THE BOUNTY.'
LC NO. FIA52-4973
Prod-PMI Dist-FI 1935

Mutiny On The Western Front - WW I C
3/4 OR 1/2 INCH VIDEO CASSETTE
Prod-MSTVIS Dist-MSTVIS

Mutiple Traumatized Patient, The C
3/4 OR 1/2 INCH VIDEO CASSETTE
Presents an approach to the problems of the multiple traumatized patient. Emphasizes procedures applicable to all forms of trauma.
Prod-AMEDA Dist-AMEDA

Mutter Krausens Fahrt Ins Gluck B 106 MIN
16MM FILM SILENT
A silent motion picture with German subtitles. Tells the story of Mother Krause, who lives poorly in a Berlin backyard, her son Paul who is arrested for burglary, and her daughter Erna, who is friends with a communist worker and who wants to fight for a better future. The first proletarian film in Germany.
Prod-WSTGLC Dist-WSTGLC 1929

Mutual Aid - The 'US' In Industry C 25 MIN
16MM FILM, 3/4 OR 1/2 IN VIDEO
Explains the procedures of organizing and conducting an industrial mutual aid association, and its importance in civil defense.
LC NO. 82-707240
Prod-USOCD Dist-USNAC 1965

Mutual Funds C 51 MIN
1/2 IN VIDEO CASSETTE BETA/VHS
Deals with investing in mutual funds. Discusses such subjects as how a mutual fund works, the types available and the protections the industry provides the investor.
From The Investing Series.
Prod-MOHOMV Dist-MOHOMV

Mutual Funds C 51 MIN
1/2 IN VIDEO CASSETTE BETA/VHS
Explains how a mutual fund works, the types and features available, the vocabulary of funds and the protections the industry provides the investor.
Prod-RMI Dist-RMI

Mutuality–A Series

Features a couple in different aspects of their relationship.
Prod-MMRC Dist-MMRC

Oral Love 010 MIN
Self-Pleasuring 005 MIN
Susan and David 028 MIN

MVS/SP Conversion Considerations–A Series

Provides a knowledge base for those who are considering conversion to MVS/SP. Includes an introduction to the first version of SP and its MVS and JES components.
Prod-DELTAK Dist-DELTAK

Impact Of MVS/SP, The 030 MIN
JES2 In The MVS/SP Environment 030 MIN
JES3 In The MVS/SP Environment 030 MIN

MX Debate C 120 MIN
3/4 OR 1/2 INCH VIDEO CASSETTE
Bill Moyers serves as the moderator of a 'town meeting' on the Pentagon's plans to put 200 mobile intercontinental ballisitic missiles in the deserts of Utah and Nevada. Includes a discussion of the necessity of the MX system, a critical look at the efficiency of the system, an examination of the economic and environmental effects of the MX system, and feedback from the audience.
From The Bill Moyers' Journal Series.
Prod-WNETTV Dist-WNETTV 1980

My Aching Back C 8 MIN
16MM FILM, 3/4 OR 1/2 IN VIDEO J-C A
Uses animation to show causes of injury to the back as well as the kinds of care and corrective measures that a person with back problems needs to take.
LC NO. 82-706514
Prod-CF Dist-CF 1982

My Actions Tell On Me C 20 MIN
3/4 INCH VIDEO CASSETTE I
Illustrates the possibility of different kinds of behavior and responses to show that people act in different ways, depending on their basic natures. Suggests that individual behavior and preferences should be modified in group interaction.
From The People Puzzle Series.
Prod-WHROTV Dist-GPITVL

My Art Is Me C 21 MIN
16MM FILM, 3/4 OR 1/2 IN VIDEO C A
A view of children in an experimental nursery school program. Shows them painting, drawing, sewing, mixing playdough, manipulating clay and constructing wood and scrap sculpture. Explains to teachers the benefits of encouraging creativity rather than providing assignments.
Prod-UCEMC Dist-UCEMC 1969

My Brother David C 25 MIN
16MM FILM, 3/4 OR 1/2 IN VIDEO H-C A
Presents Karen Fairman, aged twelve, who looks at the life of her brother David. David is micro-cephalic and partially spastic and is four years of age. David and Karen live with their parents in London, where this documentary was filmed.
Prod-THAMES Dist-MEDIAG 1971

My Brother Is Sick C 12 MIN
3/4 OR 1/2 INCH VIDEO CASSETTE
Focuses on the emotional response of a well sibling to the hospitalization of her brother. Deals with the disruption of family and relationships when a child is hospitalized. Explores the feelings of the well sibling at home.
Prod-KIDSCO Dist-KIDSCO

My Brother Is Sick C 17 MIN
3/4 OR 1/2 INCH VIDEO CASSETTE
Focuses on the emotional response of a well sibling to the hospitalization of her brother. Deals with the disruption of family life-styles and relationships when a child is hospitalized.
Prod-MIFE Dist-MIFE

My Brother, The Guru C 24 MIN
16MM FILM OPTICAL SOUND J-H
Impresses upon the viewer the kind of pain and suffering which may result from an irresponsible life-style such as that of using drugs. Tells the story of Warren and Marcia who are living together in an apartment near the university and who are both very much involved with the campus drug scene and have adopted a rather casual life-style that requires no long-term promises or commitments to one another.
Prod-FAMF Dist-FAMF 1972

My Brush Is My Bait C 29 MIN
3/4 INCH VIDEO CASSETTE
Demonstrates the use of Japanese brushes. Shows how to create an imaginary fish.
From The Artist At Work Series.
Prod-UMITV Dist-UMITV 1973

My Child Is Blind B 22 MIN
16MM FILM OPTICAL SOUND
Shows how a blind child, given patient treatment and proper training at a special nursery school for the blind, can be taught many things normal children do.
LC NO. FIE52-1942
Prod-USA Dist-USNAC Prodn-UNITY 1951

My Childhood B 51 MIN
16MM FILM, 3/4 OR 1/2 IN VIDEO J-C A
Studies the contrasts in the childhoods of Hubert Humphrey and James Baldwin. Emphasizes the effect of parental influence and environment in the forming of a man.
Prod-METROM Dist-BNCHMK 1967

My Childhood, Pt 1 - Hubert Humphrey's South Dakota B 25 MIN
16MM FILM, 3/4 OR 1/2 IN VIDEO
Reveals Hubert Humphrey's happy memories in Doland, South Dakota, as he recreates a boy's admiration for his father and other constructive elements that influenced him.
Prod-METROM Dist-BNCHMK 1967

My Childhood, Pt 2 - James Baldwin's Harlem B 25 MIN
16MM FILM, 3/4 OR 1/2 IN VIDEO
James Baldwin reminisces about his childhood in Harlem.
Prod-METROM Dist-BNCHMK 1967

My City C 22 MIN
16MM FILM OPTICAL SOUND I-J
Provides insights into the world of urban children. Shows how they interpret and react to their environment.
From The Urban Focus Series.
LC NO. 79-702479
Prod-PEPSI Dist-MLA Prodn-ARTMIS 1969

My Country Right Or Wrong C 15 MIN
16MM FILM, 3/4 OR 1/2 IN VIDEO J-C A
Tells how rejection of the Vietnam war and of parental and societal pressures force a crisis in the life of a college student, impelling him to make crucial decisions about his values and his future.
From The Searching For Values - A Film Anthology Series.
Prod-LCOA Dist-LCOA 1972

My Dad's A Cop (Captioned) C 18 MIN
16MM FILM OPTICAL SOUND P-J
Illustrates how a person's work can affect family relations and attitudes.
From The Urban Crisis Series.
Prod-BROSEB Dist-BROSEB 1975

My Dad's Given Up C 14 MIN
16MM FILM, 3/4 OR 1/2 IN VIDEO I-J
Depicts the life of the twelve-year-old son of earthquake victims living in a crowded Guatemala City ghetto. Shows how his day is spent at school until noon, playing with friends, helping with chores and dreaming of a better future. Illustrates how his unemployed father is ready to leave the family and find a job elsewhere, leaving the son with responsibilities he is unprepared to deal with.
From The Just One Child Series.
Prod-REYEXP Dist-BCNFL 1983

My Darling Clementine B 15 MIN
16MM FILM OPTICAL SOUND J-C A
An excerpt from the 1950 film of the same title. Presents a story based on the life of Wyatt Earp, frontier marshall.
From The American Film Genre - The Western Film Series.
LC NO. 75-702625
Prod-TWCF Dist-FI 1975

My Dear Uncle Sherlock C 24 MIN
16MM FILM, 3/4 OR 1/2 IN VIDEO
Presents a story about a 12-year-old boy who solves a mystery in his community by using the powers of deductive reasoning he developed while playing Sherlock Holmes games with his uncle. Based on the story My Dear Uncle Sherlock by Hugh Pentecost. Originally shown on the television series ABC Weekend Specials.
LC NO. 79-707132
Prod-ABCTV Dist-MTI Prodn-ABCCIR 1978

My Dog, The Teacher C 26 MIN
16MM FILM, 3/4 OR 1/2 IN VIDEO K-I A

Demonstrates how a handicapped child learns to care for his pet dog.
Prod-HSUS Dist-KLEINW Prodn-KLEINW 1968

My Dozen Fathers C 12 MIN
16MM FILM, 3/4 OR 1/2 IN VIDEO P-I
Offers an animated tale about a young girl whose parents are separated and her attempt's to get her mother's attention, while her mother is too busy attracting and discarding men.
Prod-CFET Dist-PHENIX 1981

My Fair Lady C
1/2 IN VIDEO CASSETTE BETA/VHS
Presents Lerner and Lowe's musical adaptation of G B Shaw's play Pygmalion, starring Rex Harrison and Audrey Hepburn.
Prod-GA Dist-GA

My Family Business C 12 MIN
16MM FILM, 3/4 OR 1/2 IN VIDEO P-I
Follows the activities of two people who work in their families' businesses.
From The Zoom Series.
Prod-WGBHTV Dist-FI

My Father Calles Me Son - Racism And Native Americans C 29 MIN
3/4 OR 1/2 INCH VIDEO CASSETTE
Examines the history of white oppression of Native Americans from slavery to stereotyping in the movies. Includes discussion between John Trudell, president of the American Indian Movement and singer/activist Buffy Saint-Marie.
Prod-KOCETV Dist-PBS 1976

My Father My Friend C 30 MIN
3/4 OR 1/2 INCH VIDEO CASSETTE
See series title for descriptive statement.
From The Mundo Real Series.
Prod-CPT Dist-MDCPB

My Father Sun-Sun Johnson C 28 MIN
16MM FILM, 3/4 OR 1/2 IN VIDEO I-J
Presents the story of a young Jamaican boy trying to adjust to his parents' divorce and to his mother's remarriage to his father's business rival.
Prod-BBCTV Dist-LCOA 1977

My Father The President C 23 MIN
16MM FILM, 3/4 OR 1/2 IN VIDEO I-C A
Presents a tour of President Theodore Roosevelt's homes at Sagamore Hill and Oyster Bay. Shows the man in the context of his family and his times.
Prod-KIRKPS Dist-PFP

My Father, My Brother, And Me C 24 MIN
3/4 OR 1/2 INCH VIDEO CASSETTE
Tells a young girl's story of her migrant worker father's devotion to her and her mentally retarded brother.
From The Young People's Specials Series.
Prod-MULTPP Dist-MULTPP

My Father, Sun-Sun Johnson (Captioned) C 28 MIN
16MM FILM, 3/4 OR 1/2 IN VIDEO P-H A
Features story of a boy and his family's marriage problems in Jamaica.
Prod-BBCTV Dist-LCOA 1977

My Father, Sun-Sun Johnson (Spanish) C 28 MIN
16MM FILM, 3/4 OR 1/2 IN VIDEO P-H A
Features the story of a boy, and his family's marriage problems in Jamaica.
Prod-BBCTV Dist-LCOA 1977

My Father, The Doctor C 18 MIN
16MM FILM OPTICAL SOUND I-C
Examines the relationship between two people as the filmmaker, at age 25, shows the relationship she has had with her father during her life.
LC NO. 74-702018
Prod-WEINSM Dist-WEINSM 1972

My Father's Dragon C 15 MIN
3/4 OR 1/2 INCH VIDEO CASSETTE P-I
Introduces the story of a young boy who runs away and outsmarts wild animals to rescue a little dragon. Based on the book My Father's Dragon by Ruth Stiles Gannett.
From The Readit Series.
LC NO. 83-706844
Prod-POSIMP Dist-AITECH 1982

My Father's Dragon And The Hundred Dresses C 15 MIN
3/4 OR 1/2 INCH VIDEO CASSETTE
See series title for descriptive statement.
From The Magic Pages Series.
Prod-KLVXTV Dist-AITECH

My Father's House C 10 MIN
16MM FILM OPTICAL SOUND
Follows a young girl as she explores her parish church as God's house and sees in her mind's eye all that she has been told about the celebration of the liturgy.
LC NO. 79-701331
Prod-FRACOC Dist-FRACOC 1979

My Father's Son C 33 MIN
3/4 OR 1/2 INCH VIDEO CASSETTE
Portrays the legacy of chemical dependency. Follows a 16-year old, son of an alcoholic, trying to lead a normal life amidst the chaos of a dysfunctioning family.
Prod-ROGRSG Dist-ROGRSG

My Favorite Brunette C 88 MIN
16MM FILM OPTICAL SOUND
Presents a comedy about an ex-private eye awaiting execution for murder. Stars Bob Hope and Dorothy Lamour.
Prod-PARACO Dist-KITPAR 1947

My Favorite Brunette B 87 MIN
3/4 OR 1/2 INCH VIDEO CASSETTE
Stars Bob Hope as a photographer who gets mixed up with mobsters.
Prod-ADVCAS Dist-ADVCAS

My Feelings C 15 MIN
3/4 OR 1/2 INCH VIDEO CASSETTE P
Presents stories depicting feelings that most young people experience.
From The Spinning Stories Series.
Prod-MDDE Dist-AITECH 1977

My Financial Career C 7 MIN
16MM FILM, 3/4 OR 1/2 IN VIDEO
Animated version of the essay by Canadian humorist, Stephen Leacock, about a young man who is prospering and decides he should open a bank account, only to become over-awed and withdraw every penny he deposited.
Prod-NFBC Dist-SF 1962

My First Job - Checker-Cashier C 10 MIN
16MM FILM, 3/4 OR 1/2 IN VIDEO H-C
Uses the example of a young girl working as a supermarket checker-cashier to show the activities, job setting and occupational opportunities afforded by a first job as a checker-cashier.
From The My First Job Series.
Prod-CORF Dist-CORF 1975

My First Job - Department Store Clerk C 10 MIN
16MM FILM, 3/4 OR 1/2 IN VIDEO H-C
Uses several examples of clerks working in a variety of department store jobs to show the activities, job settings and occupational opportunities afforded by a first job as a department store clerk.
From The My First Job Series.
Prod-CORF Dist-CORF 1975

My First Job - Drugstore Clerk C 10 MIN
16MM FILM, 3/4 OR 1/2 IN VIDEO H-C
Uses the example of a clerk in a medium-sized drugstore to show the activities, job setting and occupational opportunities afforded by a first job as a drugstore clerk.
From The My First Job Series.
Prod-CORF Dist-CORF 1975

My First Job - Food Services C 9 MIN
16MM FILM, 3/4 OR 1/2 IN VIDEO H-C
Uses the examples of a young waitress and a young salad maker in a restaurant to show the activities, job setting and occupational opportunities afforded by a first job in the food service industry.
From The My First Job Series.
Prod-CORF Dist-CORF 1975

My First Job - Service Station Attendant C 11 MIN
16MM FILM, 3/4 OR 1/2 IN VIDEO H-C
Uses the example of a young man working in a service station to show the activities, job setting and occupational opportunities afforded by a first job as a service station attendant.
From The My First Job Series.
Prod-CORF Dist-CORF 1975

My First Job - Stock Clerk C 11 MIN
16MM FILM, 3/4 OR 1/2 IN VIDEO H-C
Uses the example of a young man working as a stock clerk in a record store to show the activities, job setting and occupational opportunities afforded by a first job as a stock clerk.
From The My First Job Series.
Prod-CORF Dist-CORF 1975

My First Job—A Series
16MM FILM, 3/4 OR 1/2 IN VIDEO H-C
Looks at a series of first jobs.
Prod-CORF Dist-CORF 1975

My First Job - Checker-Cashier 010 MIN
My First Job - Department Store Clerk 010 MIN
My First Job - Drugstore Clerk 010 MIN
My First Job - Food Services 009 MIN
My First Job - Service Station Attendant 011 MIN
My First Job - Stock Clerk 011 MIN

My Four Sons C 5 MIN
16MM FILM OPTICAL SOUND
Presents Ross Allen's sons, of Silver Springs Reptile Land, who have followed in their father's footsteps and find excitement working with reptiles.
Prod-FLADC Dist-FLADC

My Friend (Ethnic-Racial Differences) C 15 MIN
16MM FILM, 3/4 OR 1/2 IN VIDEO J
Shows what happens between two friends, a Navaho and a Caucasian, when they leave their rural elementary school and enter junior high.
From The Self Incorporated Series.
LC NO. 75-703952
Prod-AITV Dist-AITECH Prodn-UTSBE 1975

My Friend And I C 15 MIN
3/4 INCH VIDEO CASSETTE K-P
Features the stories How Joe The Bear And Sam The Mouse Got Together by Beatrice De Regniers, and Tatty Mae And Catty Mae by Bill Martin Jr.
From The I Can Read Series.
Prod-WCETTV Dist-GPITVL 1977

My Friend Edi (Juvenile Diabetes) C
3/4 OR 1/2 INCH VIDEO CASSETTE
Shows a young boy and his mother as they learn he has diabetes and try to cope with it.
Prod-MIFE Dist-MIFE

My Friend Edi (Juvenile Diabetes) (French) C
3/4 OR 1/2 INCH VIDEO CASSETTE
Shows a young boy and his mother as they learn he has diabetes and try to cope with it.
Prod-MIFE Dist-MIFE

My Friend Freddy C 30 MIN
3/4 OR 1/2 INCH VIDEO CASSETTE P-I
See series title for descriptive statement.
From The Sonrisas Series.
Prod-KRLNTV Dist-MDCPB

My Friend Joe C 15 MIN
16MM FILM OPTICAL SOUND J-C T
A study of multiple sclerosis, showing its effects on a young father of two children who is stricken. Describes the physical, emotional and financial problems which affect the entire family. Discusses what is being done to uncover the mystery of the disease, explaining that there is hope that the cause, prevention and cure will be found.
LC NO. FIA65-1753
Prod-FLEMRP Dist-NMSS 1964

My Friend The Robin C 10 MIN
16MM FILM, 3/4 OR 1/2 IN VIDEO P
Presents a young boy who tells in his own words his story of watching a pair of robins build a nest and raise a family.
Prod-JOU Dist-JOU 1972

My Friends Call Me Tony C 12 MIN
16MM FILM, 3/4 OR 1/2 IN VIDEO I-J
Tells a story about a boy learning to cope with his blindness.
Prod-NFBC Dist-MEDIAG 1975

My Friends, The Philodendrons C 29 MIN
3/4 INCH VIDEO CASSETTE
Answers common questions about philodendrons.
From The House Botanist Series.
Prod-UMITV Dist-UMITV 1978

My Girlfriend's Wedding C 60 MIN
16MM FILM OPTICAL SOUND
Uses documentary footage to relate the fictional story of a girl who desperately wants to be modern. Explains how she wants to become involved in radical political causes.
Prod-NYFLMS Dist-NYFLMS 1970

My Government USA C 10 MIN
16MM FILM, 3/4 OR 1/2 IN VIDEO I-J
Discusses the relationship between city, state and federal governments. Reviews the responsibilities of each.
Prod-FINA Dist-SF Prodn-WILSON 1966

My Grandpa Died Today C 8 MIN
3/4 OR 1/2 INCH VIDEO CASSETTE
Deals with a young boy's relationship to his grandfather and how he responds to the death of this beloved family member. Uses the story and illustrations from the book of the same title.
Prod-PRIMED Dist-PRIMED

My Grandson Lew C 13 MIN
16MM FILM, 3/4 OR 1/2 IN VIDEO P-I
An adaptation of the children's story, My Grandson Lew by Charlotte Zolotow, about a young boy who discovers the importance of memories when he learns of his grandfather's death.
Prod-BARR Dist-BARR Prodn-DONMAC 1976

My Hands Are The Tools Of My Soul C 54 MIN
16MM FILM, 3/4 OR 1/2 IN VIDEO
Shows American Indian artists at work and examines their carvings, pottery, song and dance in relation to their society.
Prod-SWANN Dist-TEXFLM 1977

My Happiest Years - Unknown Chaplin C 52 MIN
16MM FILM, 3/4 OR 1/2 IN VIDEO H-C A
Focuses on the comic shorts produced by Charlie Chaplin in 1916 and 1917, highlighting previously unseen outtakes and rushes. Narrated by James Mason.
Prod-THAMES Dist-MEDIAG 1983

My Hawaii C 23 MIN
16MM FILM OPTICAL SOUND A
Showcases the tropical splendor of Hawaii, emphasizing the unspoiled beauty, serenity and adventures that await visitors to the islands.
LC NO. 80-701323
Prod-MILP Dist-MILP 1980

My Heart Attack C 16 MIN
3/4 OR 1/2 INCH VIDEO CASSETTE
Provides helpful information for the patient who is recovering from a myocardial infarction. Recounts story by a patient who had a heart attack over a year ago, and alerts viewers to problems he encountered during his recovery period as well as the practical aspects of adjustments necessary after a heart attack.
LC NO. 72-736647
Prod-TRAINX Dist-TRAINX

My Heart, Your Heart C 60 MIN
3/4 OR 1/2 INCH VIDEO CASSETTE
Offers an informative look at heart attacks and heart disease and focuses on Jim Lehrer's personal heart attack experience, the symptoms, attack, surgery, treatment and continuing rehabilitation.
Prod-PBS Dist-PBS

My Heritage C 27 MIN
16MM FILM OPTICAL SOUND C A
Describes the appreciation and use of natural and created teaching aids in the Head Start program on the Marshall Islands in Micronesia. Explains how the five senses are affected by the aids and how the senses are used creatively in the daily life and culture.
LC NO. 74-702138
Prod-USDHEW Dist-CFOP 1973

My Hero Zero C 4 MIN
3/4 OR 1/2 INCH VIDEO CASSETTE P-I
Uses songs and cartoons to explore the mathematical possibilities of zero.
From The Multiplication Rock Series.
Prod-ABCTV Dist-GA 1974

My Husband Left Out On Us C 23 MIN
16MM FILM OPTICAL SOUND
Presents an interview situation in which an eligibility worker must determine whether desertion has actually occurred in the case of a mid-30's woman with six children and a husband who has left them before for periods of time.
From The Essential Elements Of Interviewing Series.
LC NO. 75-703836
Prod-USSRS Dist-USNAC Prodn-BSIDE 1975

My Husband Stopped Support Payments C 22 MIN
16MM FILM OPTICAL SOUND
Follows an interview by an intake worker of a woman with six children whose husband has deserted his family. Shows the responsibility of the Assistance Payments Administration and its clients in establishing eligibility for child support assistance.
From The Essential Elements Of Interviewing Series.
LC NO. 76-703713
Prod-USSRS Dist-USNAC Prodn-BSIDE 1976

My Jack London - A Daughter Remembers C 25 MIN
3/4 OR 1/2 INCH VIDEO CASSETTE
Presents Jack London's daughter Becky tracing her celebrated father's life through personal remembrance, archival family photos and rare motion picture footage.
Prod-BELLG Dist-FOTH 1984

My Life C 4 MIN
16MM FILM SILENT I-C S
Presents Florian Caliguiri relating to the deaf in American sign language his personal experiences of what it was like to be a sick deaf boy in New York City, moving to the South and growing up in the depression years. He recounts his education at Gallaudet College and his work and career experiences as teacher and newspaperman.
LC NO. 76-701695
Prod-JOYCE Dist-JOYCE 1975

My Little Margie C
3/4 OR 1/2 INCH VIDEO CASSETTE
Features two episodes from the comdey TV series starring Gale Storm, Charles Farrell and Don Hayden.
Prod-IHF Dist-IHF

My Love Has Been Burning (Japanese) B 84 MIN
16MM FILM OPTICAL SOUND
Depicts the struggles of a 19th century feminist. Directed by Kenji Mizoguchi. With English subtitles.
Prod-UNKNWN Dist-NYFLMS 1949

My Love, Flying Back From Europe, Disaster C 11 MIN
3/4 OR 1/2 INCH VIDEO CASSETTE
Combines personal diaries with scripted fragments.
Prod-KITCHN Dist-KITCHN

My Main Man C 14 MIN
16MM FILM, 3/4 OR 1/2 IN VIDEO P-I
Tells the story of a black father and son's struggle to relate to each other. Follows an argument they have and their eventual reconciliation.
From The Bloomin' Human Series.
Prod-PAULST Dist-MEDIAG 1975

My Majorca C 17 MIN
16MM FILM OPTICAL SOUND
Presents a modest history of Majorca, one of the islands of the Balearics. Shows a native girl visiting relatives all over the island to whom she brings fish from the family catch.
Prod-CHISH Dist-RADIM

My Majorca C 17 MIN
16MM FILM OPTICAL SOUND P-C A
Depicts the island of Majorca, its towering cliffs, old palaces, ancient towers built by the Phoenicians, white homes, windmills, shrines, mission houses and fiestas.
Prod-FILIM Dist-RADIM 1956

My Man Godfrey B 95 MIN
1/2 IN VIDEO CASSETTE (BETA)
Tells how an unemployed man is hired from the city dump to become a society butler. Stars William Powell and Carole Lombard.
Prod-UNKNWN Dist-VIDIM 1936

My Mind Was A Chaos Of Delight C 52 MIN
16MM FILM, 3/4 OR 1/2 IN VIDEO H-C A
Presents episodes from the life of Charles Darwin, including a journey into the Brazilian rain forests, Darwin's decision to pursue science and his first quarrel with Robert Fitzroy, the captain of the H M S Beagle.
From The Voyage Of Charles Darwin Series.
LC NO. 80-706462
Prod-BBCTV Dist-TIMLIF 1980

My Mind Was A Chaos Of Delight C 52 MIN
1/2 IN VIDEO CASSETTE (VHS)
Describes how Darwin decided to pursue a career in science after his journey into the Brazilian rain forest.
From The Voyage Of Charles Darwin Series.
Prod-OHC Dist-HRC

My Mix C 30 MIN
3/4 OR 1/2 INCH VIDEO CASSETTE
Consists of a rare interview with Nam June Paik in which he discusses his involvement with video, video's non-gravity and sex in space and his friend John Cage.
Prod-EAI Dist-EAI

My Mom's Having A Baby C 47 MIN
16MM FILM, 3/4 OR 1/2 IN VIDEO I-H A
Presents Dr Lendon Smith explaining the events leading to pregnancy and birth to a nine-year-old boy whose mother is pregnant.
From The Teenage Years Series.
LC NO. 79-707358
Prod-DEPFRE Dist-TIMLIF 1977

My Mother Is The Most Beautiful Woman In The World C 9 MIN
16MM FILM, 3/4 OR 1/2 IN VIDEO P-I
Presents an Ukranian folk tale about Tanya, a lost little girl who cannot find her mother during the hustle and bustle of harvest time. Points out that her mother is the most beautiful woman in the world, if only in the eyes of her small daughter.
Prod-BOSUST Dist-PHENIX 1968

My Mother Was Never A Kid C 30 MIN
16MM FILM, 3/4 OR 1/2 IN VIDEO I-H
A shortened version of the motion picture My Mother Was Never A Kid. Describes 14-year-old Victoria's frustration with her mother's lack of understanding. Tells what happens when Victoria receives a bump on the head and is transported back to 1944, where she meets her mother as a child.
Prod-HGATE Dist-LCOA 1981

My Mother Was Never A Kid C 46 MIN
16MM FILM, 3/4 OR 1/2 IN VIDEO I-H
Describes 14-year-old Victoria's frustration with her mother's lack of understanding. Tells what happens when Victoria receives a bump on the head and is transported back to 1944, where she meets her mother as a child.
Prod-HGATE Dist-LCOA 1981

My Mother Was Never A Kid (Captioned) C 30 MIN
16MM FILM, 3/4 OR 1/2 IN VIDEO J-C A
Tells about a teenage girl at odds with her mother, until she travels back in time to see her mother's adolescence. Edited version.
Prod-HGATE Dist-LCOA 1981

My Mother Was Never A Kid (Captioned) C 46 MIN
16MM FILM, 3/4 OR 1/2 IN VIDEO J-C A
Tells the story of a teenage girl at odds with her mother, until she travels back in time to see her mother's adolescence. Full version.
Prod-HGATE Dist-LCOA 1981

My Mother Was Never A Kid (French) C 30 MIN
16MM FILM, 3/4 OR 1/2 IN VIDEO J-C A
Tells the story of a young girl at odds with her mother until she goes back in time to see her mother's impoverished adolescence. Edited version.
Prod-HGATE Dist-LCOA 1981

My Mother Was Never A Kid (French) C 46 MIN
16MM FILM, 3/4 OR 1/2 IN VIDEO J-C A
Tells the story of a young girl at odds with her mother until she goes back in time to see her mother's impoverished adolescence. Unedited version.
Prod-HGATE Dist-LCOA 1981

My Mother, My Daughter, My Self C
1/2 IN VIDEO CASSETTE BETA/VHS
Presents grandmothers, mothers, and daughters from different ethnic backgrounds, who discuss themselves, each other, and their relationships. Explores the impact of community and ethnicity.
From The Adult Years - Continuity And Change Series.
Prod-OHUTC Dist-OHUTC

My Mother, My Father C
16MM FILM OPTICAL SOUND
Shows four different families, each faced with the need to provide care for a frail parent.
Prod-TNF Dist-TNF

My Motor's Missing C 3 MIN
16MM FILM SILENT I-C S
Tells a humorous anecdote in American sign language of a hearing-impaired woman who misunderstands a gas attendant's message concerning her car. Signed for the deaf by Carolyn Larson.
LC NO. 76-701696
Prod-JOYCE Dist-JOYCE 1975

My Name Is Abbie, Orphan Of America C 28 MIN
3/4 OR 1/2 INCH VIDEO CASSETTE
Presents Abbie Hoffman recounting his involvement in the civil rights movement, how he became a Yippie and an organizer and speaker at many anti-Vietnam War demonstrations, the famous Chicago Seven trial, why the movement fell apart, his drug arrest, his eventual flight and underground life.
Prod-ICARUS Dist-ICARUS 1981

My Name Is David - And I'm An Alcoholic C 24 MIN
16MM FILM, 3/4 OR 1/2 IN VIDEO J-C A
Follows the progress of a middle-aged alcoholic who agrees to counseling and group therapy after being threatened with dismissal from his job. Explains the physiological facts of alcoholism and reasons for excessive drinking.
Prod-GORKER Dist-AIMS 1977

My Name Is Mary Brown B 15 MIN
16MM FILM OPTICAL SOUND
Presents the reasons why Mary Brown and thousands like her joined the International Ladies Garment Worker's Union to gain strength through a union.
Prod-ILGWU Dist-AFLCIO 1955

My Name Is Oona C
16MM FILM OPTICAL SOUND
Presents an experimental film by Gunvor Nelson.
Prod-CANCIN Dist-CANCIN

My Name Is Susan Yee C 12 MIN
16MM FILM, 3/4 OR 1/2 IN VIDEO P-I
Features a young Chinese-Canadian schoolgirl describing her life in Montreal in order to provide a glimpse of the life of someone in another area and in different circumstances.
Prod-NFBC Dist-MEDIAG Prodn-YOSHIY 1977

My Neighbor And Me C 15 MIN
3/4 OR 1/2 INCH VIDEO CASSETTE P
Discusses the characteristics of neighborhoods.
From The Neighborhoods Series.
Prod-NEITV Dist-GPITVL 1981

My Neighborhood C 30 MIN
3/4 OR 1/2 INCH VIDEO CASSETTE
Portrays M, who claims to be friendly with everybody in his neighborhood. Shifts from humor to pathos.
Prod-KITCHN Dist-KITCHN

My New Home C 14 MIN
3/4 OR 1/2 INCH VIDEO CASSETTE P
Shows that while in Greenfield Village, Thomas and Anita see the daily life of long ago.
From The Under The Yellow Balloon Series.
Prod-SCETV Dist-AITECH 1980

My Old Dan C 19 MIN
3/4 OR 1/2 INCH VIDEO CASSETTE P-I
Introduces the quarter note.
From The USS Rhythm Series.
Prod-ARKETV Dist-AITECH 1977

My Old Man By Ernest Hemingway X 27 MIN
16MM FILM, 3/4 OR 1/2 IN VIDEO J-C
Presents Ernest Hemingway's story 'MY OLD MAN' in which the main character Joe Butler has a conflict between accepting reality and preserving his illusions. Produced in Paris using actual race track scenes and backgrounds.
From The Humanities - Short Story Showcase Series.
Prod-EBEC Dist-EBEC 1970

My Parrot, Brewster C 17 MIN
16MM FILM, 3/4 OR 1/2 IN VIDEO P-I
Tells the story of Dennis, who carelessly leaves his parrot Brewster's cage unlocked, allowing the pet to wander off. Describes how Dennis, during his search for Brewster, remembers the special qualities and needs of his pet and his responsibility to the animal.
Prod-HIGGIN Dist-HIGGIN 1980

My Partner, Officer Smokey C 17 MIN
16MM FILM OPTICAL SOUND
Shows how a policeman and his partner, a German shepherd named Smokey, work together in patrolling streets and neighborhoods in Washington, DC.
From The Six To Remember Series.
LC NO. 74-700853
Prod-AMEDFL Dist-AMEDFL 1973

My People Are My Home C 45 MIN
16MM FILM OPTICAL SOUND C A
Deals with the political and poetic odyssey of writer Meridel Le Sueur, spokeswoman for workers, the unemployed, women and American Indians.
LC NO. 79-700919
Prod-SERIUS Dist-SERIUS 1977

My Perfect Child Is Deaf C 30 MIN
16MM FILM, 3/4 OR 1/2 IN VIDEO C A
Explores family reactions to the diagnosis, that lead to eventual acceptance.
From The Children And Deafness Series.
Prod-YASNYP Dist-PFP

My Pet Pelican C 11 MIN
16MM FILM OPTICAL SOUND K-P
Presents the story of Snapper, a lame pelican and his home with a young girl. Explains that Snapper quickly adapts himself to this new life as the two become good friends and that Kelley's interest in her pet leads her to the world books where she finds many stories about pelicans and other interesting birds.
From The Nature Guide Film Series.
Prod-AVEXP Dist-AVEXP

My Pet Pelican C 11 MIN
16MM FILM OPTICAL SOUND K-I
Traces the growth and development of a pelican that is found by a nature photographer and taken home as a pet. Follows his life unitl he matures and is taken to a zoo.
LC NO. FIA67-506
Prod-NATURE Dist-AVEXP 1966

My Pop's A Lineman C 16 MIN
16MM FILM, 3/4 OR 1/2 IN VIDEO P-H
Shows a lineman who sees his son trying to retrieve a kite tangled in a high voltage line and takes the boy to work with him. Dramatizes several dangerous situations involving high tension wires. Includes flashbacks to a high-voltage demonstration by H C Potthast.
Prod-STSC Dist-IFB 1957

My Robot Buddy And My Trip To Alpha I C 14 MIN
3/4 OR 1/2 INCH VIDEO CASSETTE P-I
Presents two stories about a young boy and his robot buddy. Explains in the first story that the boy asks for a robot for his tenth birthday so he will have someone to play with, while in the second story the boy finds that interplanetary travel is not without dangers. Based on the books My Robot Buddy and My Trip To Alpha I by Alfred Slote.
From The Readit Series.
LC NO. 83-706835
Prod-POSIMP Dist-AITECH 1982

My Side Of The Mountain C 38 MIN
16MM FILM, 3/4 OR 1/2 IN VIDEO I-J

Tells the story of a boy's life alone in the wilderness and his Thoreau-like reactions to that experience. Based on the book My Side Of The Mountain by Jean George.
Prod-PARACO Dist-AIMS 1979

My Son The Artist C 29 MIN
2 INCH VIDEOTAPE
See series title for descriptive statement.
From The Museum Open House Series.
Prod-WGBHTV Dist-PUBTEL

My Son, Kevin C 24 MIN
16MM FILM, 3/4 OR 1/2 IN VIDEO C A
Tells how 11-year-old English schoolboy Kevin Donnellon has developed a buoyant personality and an optimistic outlook despite cruel handicaps caused by the drug thalidomide. Explains that for Kevin's mother, the future holds many fears.
Prod-GRANDA Dist-WOMBAT

My Son, The Merchandise Manager C 9 MIN
16MM FILM OPTICAL SOUND
Presents Elaine May and Mike Nichols who illustrate a brand new approach to merchandising a new product.
Prod-TALON Dist-CCNY

My Special World C 24 MIN
3/4 OR 1/2 INCH VIDEO CASSETTE
Features life of child television star Adam Rich. Explores behind the scenes of the television production.
From The Young People's Specials Series.
Prod-MULTPP Dist-MULTPP

My Three Year Old C 3 MIN
16MM FILM SILENT I-C A
Presents Sharon L Tate relating in American sign language for the deaf her personal experiences as a deaf mother traveling across the United States with her 3-year-old child.
LC NO. 76-701697
Prod-JOYCE Dist-JOYCE 1975

My Turtle Died Today C 8 MIN
16MM FILM, 3/4 OR 1/2 IN VIDEO P-I
Tells a story about a boy whose pet turtle died and who later discovered that a pet cat had given birth to a litter of kittens. Designed to stimulate discussion on the inevitability of death and the continuity of life.
Prod-BOSUST Dist-PHENIX 1968

My Twenty Pennies C 14 MIN
3/4 OR 1/2 INCH VIDEO CASSETTE P
Introduces the eighth note as a beat and teaches a song with Spanish words in it.
From The Stepping Into Rhythm Series.
Prod-WVIZTV Dist-AITECH

My Very Own Ears C 20 MIN
2 INCH VIDEOTAPE P
See series title for descriptive statement.
From The Learning Our Language, Unit 1 - Listening Skills Series.
Prod-MPATI Dist-GPITVL

My Wife's Relations B 23 MIN
16MM FILM SILENT J-C A
Stars Buster Keaton.
Prod-MGM Dist-TWYMAN 1922

My Wise Daddy B 4 MIN
16MM FILM OPTICAL SOUND I-C A
Presents a happy family with a couple of children, who are well looked after with love and affection from the parents.
Prod-INDIA Dist-NEDINF

My World C 20 MIN
3/4 OR 1/2 INCH VIDEO CASSETTE I
Presents dramatizations of literary works that deal with the community and how it influences the lives of its people.
From The Readers' Cube Series.
Prod-MDDE Dist-AITECH 1977

My World, My Choice C 20 MIN
16MM FILM, 3/4 OR 1/2 IN VIDEO H-C
Describes the misguided decisions and events that lead a young man to the death sentence and serves as both an example and a warning for today's youth on the edge of trouble.
LC NO. 84-706799
Prod-WECARP Dist-PHENIX 1984

My 5th Super Bowl C 29 MIN
3/4 OR 1/2 INCH VIDEO CASSETTE A
Features former professional football star Carl Eller telling the story of his struggle and eventual triumph over dependency on drugs and alcohol. Details his losses as well as his victory.
Prod-SFTI Dist-SFTI

My, My Brooklyn USA C 20 MIN
3/4 OR 1/2 INCH VIDEO CASSETTE
Offers a tour of Brooklyn with its revived brownstone communities, 17th century Dutch Reformed Church, a neo-Japanese house and a southern colonial home. Demonstrates community togetherness in scenes of a neighborhood party and the borough's annual West Indian Day parade.
Prod-IVCH Dist-IVCH

Myasthenia Gravis C 52 MIN
3/4 INCH VIDEO CASSETTE PRO
Presents a lecture by Dr John R Warmolts on myasthenia gravis.
From The Intensive Course In Neuromuscular Diseases Series.
LC NO. 76-706058
Prod-NINDIS Dist-USNAC 1974

Myasthenia Gravis, Diagnosis And Treatment By Thymectomy C 27 MIN
16MM FILM OPTICAL SOUND PRO
Shows a young woman with the characteristic findings of myasthenia gravis, weakness of the facial, pharyngeal and respiratory muscles. Demonstrates the technique of operation and the course of a specific patient.
Prod-ACYDGD Dist-ACY 1958

Mycological Slide Culture Technique C 7 MIN
16MM FILM - 3/4 IN VIDEO
Demonstrates a method of growing fungi on microscopic cover slips to preserve mycelia and spores intact. Issued in 1965 as a motion picture.
LC NO. 77-706126
Prod-USPHS Dist-USNAC Prodn-NMAC 1977

Myelination Of The Central Nervous System Or Myelogenesis C 60 MIN
3/4 INCH VIDEO CASSETTE PRO
Discusses structures of the spinal cord and brain stem where myelination begins in the fourth to fifth month in utero. Outlines critical periods of myelination of certain nuclei, fiber tracts and nerves during fetal development and postnatal life. Uses parts of the central nervous system as examples.
From The Nonbehavioral Sciences And Rehabilitation Series. Part III
Prod-AOTA Dist-AOTA 1980

Myles Horton - Adventures Of A Radical Hillbilly, Pt 1 C 60 MIN
3/4 OR 1/2 INCH VIDEO CASSETTE
Presents an interview with Myles Horton, lifelong crusader for the rights of the poor and the weak.
Prod-WNETTV Dist-WNETTV 1981

Myles Horton - Adventures Of A Radical Hillbilly, Pt 2 C 60 MIN
3/4 OR 1/2 INCH VIDEO CASSETTE
Presents an interview with Myles Horton, lifelong crusader for the rights of the poor and the weak.
Prod-WNETTV Dist-WNETTV 1981

Myocardial Infarction C 94 MIN
3/4 OR 1/2 INCH VIDEO CASSETTE PRO
Stresses the importance of the ECG diagnosis of myocardial infarction and emphasizes need for sequential and comparison ECGs.
From The Electrocardiogram Series.
Prod-HSCIC Dist-HSCIC 1982

Myocardial Infarction (2nd Ed) C 13 MIN
3/4 OR 1/2 INCH VIDEO CASSETTE PRO
Describes the usual clinical course of a patient with a myocardial infarction. Explains signs, symptoms and how the disease will affect life-style.
Prod-MEDFAC Dist-MEDFAC 1974

Myocardial Infarction Patient, The C 24 MIN
3/4 OR 1/2 INCH VIDEO CASSETTE
Presents a simulated home visit of nurse to a client recovering from a myocardial infarction. Discusses effects of patient's pathology, diet, medications, exercise, stress and other factors.
From The Simulated Home Visits Series.
Prod-UTEXN Dist-AJN

Myocardial Revascularization - Vineberg Procedure C 20 MIN
16MM FILM OPTICAL SOUND
Explains a surgical procedure for rehabilitation of cardiac invalids. Includes highlights of actual surgery and utilizes three-dimensional animation to explain why no hematoma occurs, offers before-and-after cine coronary arteriography to prove it works. Summarizes clinical results achieved, and lists indications and contraindications for this procedure.
From The Upjohn Vanguard Of Medicine Series.
LC NO. FIA67-507
Prod-UPJOHN Dist-UPJOHN Prodn-MEDCA 1966

Myocardial Revascularization For Coronary Artery Disease C 34 MIN
16MM FILM OPTICAL SOUND PRO
Illustrates diagnostic coronary arteriography as developed by Dr Sones at the Cleveland clinic. Illustrates the operative procedures which indicate implantation of the internal mammary artery, direct coronary endarterectomy and implantation of the splenic artery.
Prod-ACYDGD Dist-ACY 1967

Myoglobin C 10 MIN
16MM FILM OPTICAL SOUND
Uses computer animation to show the structure of the protein molecule and to analyze protein myoglobin, which stores oxygen in the muscles. Includes music by moog synthesizer.
From The Protein Primer Series.
LC NO. 75-713591
Prod-SENSES Dist-HAR 1971

Myra C 3 MIN
16MM FILM, 3/4 OR 1/2 IN VIDEO P-I
Uses animation to describe a little girl who disrupts her dancing class by turning into the animals the other children are imitating. Based on the children's story Myra by Barbara Bottner.
LC NO. 82-706521
Prod-BOSUST Dist-CF 1980

Myringoplasty C 15 MIN
16MM FILM OPTICAL SOUND PRO
Shows the repair of a perforated ear drum by the use of ear canal skin.
Prod-EAR Dist-EAR

Myself, Yourself C 30 MIN
16MM FILM OPTICAL SOUND
Presents three adults and two teenagers discussing growing up. Reveals how social attitudes affected their outlook on life.
LC NO. 81-700663
Prod-JENF Dist-MOBIUS 1981

Mysore C 17 MIN
16MM FILM OPTICAL SOUND I-C A
Presents the mysore state with its physical features, natural resources, economic developments and places of historic importance. Highlights the colorful Dasserah Festival.
Prod-INDIA Dist-NEDINF

Mysteries Of Consumer Behavior C 47 MIN
3/4 OR 1/2 INCH VIDEO CASSETTE
Offers one professor's opinion of what is really known about consumers and the ability to predict their behavior.
From The Introduction To Marketing, A Lecture Series.
Prod-IVCH Dist-IVCH

Mysteries Of Natrium And Chlorine C 20 MIN
16MM FILM OPTICAL SOUND
Describes the use of natrium and chlorine which are as powerful as poisons, to help students correctly realize the idea of substance and chemical reaction.
Prod-IWANMI Dist-UNIJAP 1969

Mysteries Of The Deep C 24 MIN
16MM FILM, 3/4 OR 1/2 IN VIDEO I-C A
Shows ways various unusual sea animals eat, move, reproduce and protect themselves. Includes pictures of the sea anemone, manta rays, pectin, and various kinds of sea slugs, sand rays and hermit crabs. Pictures the birth of a dolphin.
From The True Life Adventure Nature Series.
Prod-DISNEY Dist-WDEMCO 1961

Mysteries Of The Deep (Afrikaans) C 24 MIN
16MM FILM, 3/4 OR 1/2 IN VIDEO I-H
Explores the lower depths of the sea. Highlights the evolution of life and the struggle for survival.
Prod-WDEMCO Dist-WDEMCO 1961

Mysteries Of The Deep (Dutch) C 24 MIN
16MM FILM, 3/4 OR 1/2 IN VIDEO I-H
Explores the lower depths of the sea. Highlights the evolution of life and the struggle for survival.
Prod-WDEMCO Dist-WDEMCO 1961

Mysteries Of The Deep (French) C 24 MIN
16MM FILM, 3/4 OR 1/2 IN VIDEO I-H
Explores the lower depths of the sea. Highlights the evolution of life and the struggle for survival.
Prod-WDEMCO Dist-WDEMCO 1961

Mysteries Of The Deep (German) C 24 MIN
16MM FILM, 3/4 OR 1/2 IN VIDEO I-H
Explores the lower depths of the sea. Highlights the evolution of life and the struggle for survival.
Prod-WDEMCO Dist-WDEMCO 1961

Mysteries Of The Deep (Greek) C 24 MIN
16MM FILM, 3/4 OR 1/2 IN VIDEO I-H
Explores the lower depths of the sea. Highlights the evolution of life and the struggle for survival.
Prod-WDEMCO Dist-WDEMCO 1961

Mysteries Of The Deep (Swedish) C 24 MIN
16MM FILM, 3/4 OR 1/2 IN VIDEO I-H
Explores the lower depths of the sea. Highlights the evolution of life and the struggle for survival.
Prod-WDEMCO Dist-WDEMCO 1961

Mysteries Of The Hidden Reefs C 23 MIN
16MM FILM, 3/4 OR 1/2 IN VIDEO I-C A
A shortened version of The Mysteries Of The Hidden Reef. Features Jacques Cousteau as he explores the interdependency, adaptation, protective mechanisms and symbiotic relationships of the multitude of life in a reef both day and night.
From The Undersea World Of Jacques Cousteau Series.
Prod-METROM Dist-CF 1977

Mysteries Of The Hidden Reefs C 52 MIN
16MM FILM, 3/4 OR 1/2 IN VIDEO J-C A
Explores the interdependency, adaptation, protective mechanism and symbiotic relationships of the life forms in a reef during both day and night hours.
From The Undersea World Of Jacques Cousteau Series.
Prod-METROM Dist-CF 1977

Mysteries Of The Mind C 59 MIN
16MM FILM, 3/4 OR 1/2 IN VIDEO
Looks inside the brain to examine its structure and unravel some of its mysteries. Shows the chemical and electrical processes and relates human behavior and blood flow to particular parts of the brain. Documents feats of mind control.
LC NO. 80-706354
Prod-NGS Dist-NGS 1980

Mysterious Bee, The C 50 MIN
16MM FILM, 3/4 OR 1/2 IN VIDEO J-C A
Explores the amazingly complex world of bees and illustrates some aspects of beekeeping.
Prod-PSNF Dist-FI 1981

Mysterious Fact, The - Critical Reading And Thinking C 9 MIN
3/4 INCH VIDEO CASSETTE I-J
Tells how Alexander Hawkshaw utilizes critical reading and thinking skills to solve a school vandalism problem.
From The Alexander Hawkshaw's Language Arts Skills Series.
Prod-LUMIN Dist-GA

Mysterious Island C 18 MIN
16MM FILM OPTICAL SOUND
An abridged version of the motion picture Mysterious Island. Tells the story of the escape of five men from a Confederate prison in an observation balloon and their landing on a strange South Sea island. Stars Michael Craig and Gary Merrill.
Prod-CPC Dist-TIMLIF 1982

Mysterious Island C 101 MIN
16MM FILM OPTICAL SOUND J-C A
Stars Michael Craig and Joan Greenwood in Jules Verne's story of castaways on a Pacific island prowled by the inconceivable terrors of a fierce new animal world.
Prod-CPC Dist-TIMLIF 1961

Mysterious Mascot, The - Using Context Analysis C 8 MIN
3/4 INCH VIDEO CASSETTE I-J
Tells how Alex and his friends put together the parts of a puzzle using context analysis skills.
From The Alexander Hawkshaw's Language Arts Skills Series.
Prod-LUMIN Dist-GA

Mysterious Mechanical Bird, The - Reading For Comprehension C 10 MIN
3/4 INCH VIDEO CASSETTE I-J
Uses Alexander's search for a missing book page to illustrate aspects of reading comprehension.
From The Alexander Hawkshaw's Language Arts Skills Series.
Prod-LUMIN Dist-GA

Mysterious Message, The C 12 MIN
16MM FILM, 3/4 OR 1/2 IN VIDEO P-I
Shows the importance of clear, readable handwriting through a humorous suspense story about a mail carrier and two young children, who deal with mysterious messages that are actually unreadable notes. Shows how to improve one's handwriting and illustrates jobs and professions in which handwriting is important.
LC NO. 81-707592
Prod-FLMFR Dist-FLMFR 1981

Mysterious Message, The - Phonics Analysis C 9 MIN
3/4 INCH VIDEO CASSETTE I-J
Shows Alexander and his news sleuths demonstrating the importance of phonics analysis skills.
From The Alexander Hawkshaw's Language Arts Skills Series.
Prod-LUMIN Dist-GA

Mysterious Monsters, The C 92 MIN
16MM FILM, 3/4 OR 1/2 IN VIDEO I-H A
Investigates the existence of giant creatures such as Bigfoot, the Abominable Snowman and the Loch Ness monster with commentary from scientific experts.
Prod-LUF Dist-LUF 1979

Mysterious Mr Eliot, The C 62 MIN
16MM FILM, 3/4 OR 1/2 IN VIDEO H-C A
Provides a historical framework for the work of T S Eliot. Correlates the complexity of 20th century western society to 20th century poetry. Relates the imagery of Eliot's poetry to his life.
Prod-BBCTV Dist-MGHT 1975

Mysterious Mr Eliot, The, Pt 1 C 30 MIN
16MM FILM, 3/4 OR 1/2 IN VIDEO H-C A
Provides a historical framework for the work of T S Eliot. Correlates the complexity of 20th century western society to 20th century poetry. Relates the imagery of Eliot's poetry to his life.
Prod-BBCTV Dist-MGHT 1975

Mysterious Mr Eliot, The, Pt 2 C 32 MIN
16MM FILM, 3/4 OR 1/2 IN VIDEO H-C A
Provides a historical framework for the work of T S Eliot. Correlates the complexity of 20th century western society to 20th century poetry. Relates the imagery of Eliot's poetry to his life.
Prod-BBCTV Dist-MGHT 1975

Mysterious Note, The - Building Word Power C 9 MIN
3/4 INCH VIDEO CASSETTE I-J
Tells how Alexander Hawkshaw and his friends analyze a mysterious note with 'word power' and help avert the shutdown of the school newspaper.
From The Alexander Hawkshaw's Language Arts Skills Series.
Prod-LUMIN Dist-GA

Mysterious White Land C 27 MIN
16MM FILM OPTICAL SOUND
Presents a documentary about skiing on Mt Cook, the peak of the southern Alps in the south island of New Zealand. Covers the landing at the ski-base, the hermitage, with skiers Yuichiro Miura and Mitsuhiro Tachibana on the slopes of Mt Cook.
Prod-UNIJAP Dist-UNIJAP 1967

Mysterious White Land (French) C 27 MIN
16MM FILM OPTICAL SOUND
Presents a documentary about skiing on Mt Cook, the peak of the southern Alps in the south island of New Zealand. Covers the landing at the ski-base, the hermitage, with skiers Yuichiro Miura and Mitsuhiro Tachibana on the slopes of Mt Cook.
Prod-UNIJAP Dist-UNIJAP 1967

Mystery At Smoky Hollow C 28 MIN
16MM FILM OPTICAL SOUND
Traces the origin of a woods fire by questioning several members of a community about their activities in or near the woods at the time the fire started. Shows how each person is impressed with the need for careful attention whenever fire is used in or near a forested area.
LC NO. 74-705183
Prod-USDA Dist-USNAC 1968

Mystery Books C 15 MIN
3/4 OR 1/2 INCH VIDEO CASSETTE P
See series title for descriptive statement.
From The Word Shop Series.
Prod-WETATV Dist-WETATV

Mystery Crash, The C 8 MIN
16MM FILM OPTICAL SOUND I-H
Deals with the one-vehicle accident, which is called the 'MYSTERY CRASH' because often there is no reason for it.
From The Techniques Of Defensive Driving Film Series.
Prod-NSC Dist-NSC

Mystery Map C 16 MIN
16MM FILM, 3/4 OR 1/2 IN VIDEO P-I
Teaches children to draw logical conclusions, as well as to be imaginative, by telling the story of four children who follow a treasure map. Presents three different endings to the story.
From The What Happens Next Series.
Prod-MORLAT Dist-EBEC 1972

Mystery Murals Of Baja California C 29 MIN
16MM FILM, 3/4 OR 1/2 IN VIDEO
Describes the experiences of an amateur archaeologist in Baja California.
Prod-KPBS Dist-UCEMC 1977

Mystery Of Amelia Earhart, The C 22 MIN
16MM FILM, 3/4 OR 1/2 IN VIDEO I-H
Covers the immediate events surrounding the mysterious disappearance of aviatrix Amelia Earhart and the elements that have contributed to that mystery.
From The You Are There Series.
Prod-CBSNEW Dist-PHENIX 1971

Mystery Of Amelia Earhart, The (Captioned) C 22 MIN
16MM FILM, 3/4 OR 1/2 IN VIDEO I-H
Covers the immediate events surrounding the mysterious disappearance of aviatrix Amelia Earheart and the elements that have contributed to that mystery.
From The You Are There Series.
Prod-CBSNEW Dist-PHENIX 1971

Mystery Of Animal Behavior C 51 MIN
16MM FILM, 3/4 OR 1/2 IN VIDEO I-C A
Examines the world of animals and their interesting behavior. Visits the animal behavior institute in Germany where researchers study imprinting in birds, coloration in fish and ways animals care for their young.
LC NO. 80-706361
Prod-NGS Dist-NGS 1969

Mystery Of Heroism, A B 20 MIN
3/4 OR 1/2 INCH VIDEO CASSETTE
Presents a reconstruction of a Civil War background. Based on a Stephen Crane short story about a young Southern soldier who braves hostile fire to bring a bucket of water to his comrades.
Prod-MEDIPR Dist-MEDIPR 1979

Mystery Of Nefertiti, The C 46 MIN
16MM FILM, 3/4 OR 1/2 IN VIDEO H-C A
Follows the six-year efforts of a team of archeologists to reconstruct on paper the Egyptian temple of Nefertiti. Shows how computer techniques were used to match building blocks with the plan to develop an impression of the temple's appearance.
LC NO. 80-707083
Prod-BBCL Dist-IU 1975

Mystery Of Plant Movement B 11 MIN
16MM FILM OPTICAL SOUND
Shows a four month time-lapse record of the growth of a seed in a 14-foot vine, emphasizing the movement of various parts of the plant. Explains the role of auxin in the movement of the leaves, growing tip, tendrils and flowers.
From The Science Close-Up Series.
LC NO. FIA67-5015
Prod-PRISM Dist-SF 1967

Mystery Of Stonehenge, The X 57 MIN
16MM FILM, 3/4 OR 1/2 IN VIDEO H-C A
Presents an account of Stonehenge, a prehistoric stone monument in England. Tests the theory that it was built as an observatory and computer.
Prod-CBSTV Dist-MGHT 1965

Mystery Of The Anasazi, The C 59 MIN
16MM FILM, 3/4 OR 1/2 IN VIDEO H-C A
Inquires into the mysteries surrounding the Anasazi, the pueblo-builders of America's Southwest. Considers who these people were, why they disappeared and where they went.
From The Nova Series.
LC NO. 79-707242
Prod-WGBHTV Dist-TIMLIF 1976

Mystery Of The Sun B 26 MIN
16MM FILM, 3/4 OR 1/2 IN VIDEO J-C A
Tells how rocket astronomy is used to measure X-rays and the ultraviolet rays of the Sun.
Prod-CBSTV Dist-CAROUF

Mystery Of Time (2nd Ed) C 28 MIN
16MM FILM, 3/4 OR 1/2 IN VIDEO J-C R
Shows how high-speed and time-lapse photography help us escape our 'TIME COMPARTMENT.' Samples some of the elemental concepts of the theory of relativity as yardsticks shorten, clocks and heartbeats slow down as the laboratory is 'ACCELERATED' to almost the speed of light to portray the interdependence of time, space and matter.
Prod-MIS Dist-MIS 1968

Mystery Stories C 15 MIN
3/4 OR 1/2 INCH VIDEO CASSETTE P
See series title for descriptive statement.
From The Word Shop Series.
Prod-WETATV Dist-WETATV

Mystery Story And Review C 15 MIN
3/4 INCH VIDEO CASSETTE P
See series title for descriptive statement.
From The I Need To Read Series.
Prod-WCETTV Dist-GPITVL 1975

Mystery Systems And Mental Models C 20 MIN
3/4 INCH VIDEO CASSETTE T
Presents classroom scenes showing demonstration of mystery systems, in which only a mental model of the interior of the system can be formed.
From The Science In The Elementary School - Physical Science Series.
Prod-UWKY Dist-GPITVL 1979

Mystery That Heals, The C 30 MIN
16MM FILM, 3/4 OR 1/2 IN VIDEO H-C A
Deals with the life and philosophy of Carl Gustav Jung in his later years. Discusses the concept of the 'SHADOW' and his attitudes toward Christianity and death.
From The Story Of Carl Gustav Jung Series. No. 3
Prod-BBCTV Dist-FI 1972

Mysto The Great C 27 MIN
16MM FILM, 3/4 OR 1/2 IN VIDEO
Tells of an aging professional magician's search for meaning in his life and of the struggle he and his son have in reaching understanding and love.
Prod-AMERFI Dist-CORF 1976

Myth As History B 29 MIN
3/4 INCH VIDEO CASSETTE
See series title for descriptive statement.
From The Of Greeks And Gods Series.
Prod-UMITV Dist-UMITV 1971

Myth Of Naro As Told By Dedeheiwa C 22 MIN
16MM FILM - 3/4 IN VIDEO
One version of the Yanamamo story of the origin of harmful magic told in Yanamamo with English voice-over. Filmed by Timothy Asch and Napoleon Chagnon. Companion to the Koabawa version.
Prod-DOCEDR Dist-DOCEDR

Myth Of Naro As Told By Kaobowa C
16MM FILM - 3/4 IN VIDEO
One version of the Yanamamo story of the origin of harmful magic told in Yanamamo with English voice-over. Filmed by Timothy Asch and Napoleon Chagnon. Companion to the Dedeheiwa version.
Prod-DOCEDR Dist-DOCEDR

Myth Of Nationalism, The C 30 MIN
16MM FILM, 3/4 OR 1/2 IN VIDEO H-C
Looks at the period of European history between the Franco-Prussian War and the First World War.
From The Outline History Of Europe Series.
LC NO. 80-706991
Prod-POLNIS Dist-IFB 1976

Myth Of The Happy Child, The C 29 MIN
3/4 OR 1/2 INCH VIDEO CASSETTE
Explains society's misconceptions about childhood, stating that children are totally aware of their inadequacy to handle life on their own and are therefore often afraid. Discusses the children's liberation movement.
From The Woman Series.
Prod-WNEDTV Dist-PBS

Myth Of The Pharaohs C 13 MIN
16MM FILM, 3/4 OR 1/2 IN VIDEO I-C
Recounts the Egyptian myth of creation and follows one typical pharaoh, examining his conception, birth, childhood, crowning, feats in war and peace, death and the final judgment before osiris.
Prod-ACI Dist-AIMS 1971

Myth-Conceptions (A Teenage Sex Quiz) C 18 MIN
3/4 OR 1/2 INCH VIDEO CASSETTE J-C A
Portrays a peer group education program for junior high and high school age youth. Explores traditional questions about sex and parenting.
Prod-MMRC Dist-MMRC

Myth, Superstition And Science C 13 MIN
16MM FILM, 3/4 OR 1/2 IN VIDEO P-I
Uses the story of a superstitious grammar school student and her more scientific brother to provide an introduction to the scientific method.
Prod-IFB Dist-IFB 1960

Mythical Cartoon Beasts C 14 MIN
2 INCH VIDEOTAPE
See series title for descriptive statement.
From The Charlie's Pad Series.
Prod-WSIU Dist-PUBTEL

Mythical Monsters Of The Deep C 25 MIN
16MM FILM, 3/4 OR 1/2 IN VIDEO H-C A
Looks at the legends attached to some underwater creatures. Dispels myths about mermaids, sea snakes, humpback whales and others.
Prod-CTV Dist-MTI

Mythology - Gods And Goddesses C
3/4 OR 1/2 INCH VIDEO CASSETTE H-C
Explores the legends of the gods and goddesses of mythology, and other classic characters such as Medusa, King Midas and Romulus and Remus.
Prod-GA Dist-GA

Mythology Lives - Ancient Stories And Modern Literature C
3/4 OR 1/2 INCH VIDEO CASSETTE H-C
Presents stories from the past, points out their recurring themes and characters, and looks at their modern-day counterparts, such as Orpheus and Eurydice - Romeo and Juliet.
Prod-GA Dist-GA

Mythology Of Greece And Rome C 16 MIN
16MM FILM, 3/4 OR 1/2 IN VIDEO I-H
Examines the myths of Ancient Greece and Rome as stories about gods and man invented in an attempt to explain natural phenomena and man's behavior. Includes stories of Ceres and Proserpina, Apollo and Daphne, Pegasus and Bellerophon.
Prod-FA Dist-PHENIX 1969

Mythology Of Greece And Rome (Captioned) C 16 MIN
16MM FILM, 3/4 OR 1/2 IN VIDEO I-H
Examines the myths of Ancient Greece and Rome as stories about gods and man invented in an attempt to explain natural phenomena and man's behavior. Includes stories of Ceres and Proserpina, Apollo and Daphne, Pegasus and Bellerophon.
Prod-FA Dist-PHENIX 1969

Mythology Of Greece And Rome (Spanish) C 16 MIN
16MM FILM, 3/4 OR 1/2 IN VIDEO I-H
Examines the myths of Ancient Greece and Rome as stories about gods and man invented in an attempt to explain natural phenomena and man's behavior. Includes stories of Ceres and Proserpina, Apollo and Daphne, Pegasus and Bellerophon.
Prod-FA Dist-PHENIX 1969

Myths And Fables C 15 MIN
3/4 OR 1/2 INCH VIDEO CASSETTE I
Considers the role of culture and imagination in the evolution of myths and fables.
From The Zebra Wings Series.
Prod-NITC Dist-AITECH Prodn-MAETEL 1975

Myths And Identity C 60 MIN
3/4 OR 1/2 INCH VIDEO CASSETTE H-C A
See series title for descriptive statement.
From The Art Of Being Human Series.
Prod-FI Dist-FI 1978

Myths And Legends - Mirrors Of Mankind C 46 MIN
3/4 OR 1/2 INCH VIDEO CASSETTE
Uses examples of art, literature and music to discuss the myths and legends man has created to explain the nature of the universe and his place in it.
LC NO. 81-706687
Prod-CHUMAN Dist-GA 1981

Myths And Manifest Destiny B 20 MIN
3/4 INCH VIDEO CASSETTE
See series title for descriptive statement.
From The Silent Heritage - The American Indian Series.
Prod-UMITV Dist-UMITV 1966

Myths And Moundbuilders C 58 MIN
3/4 OR 1/2 INCH VIDEO CASSETTE
Features archaeologists who probe mysterious mounds in the eastern United States uncovering clues about a lost Indian civilization.
From The Odyssey Series.
Prod-PBA Dist-PBS

Myths Of Shoplifting, The C 16 MIN
16MM FILM, 3/4 OR 1/2 IN VIDEO J-C
Presents a series of vignettes which dramatize the serious consequences of shoplifting.
Prod-NRMA Dist-MTI Prodn-JACSTO 1979

Myths Of Technology C 30 MIN
3/4 OR 1/2 INCH VIDEO CASSETTE C
Explores the impact of technology on the biosphere and other aspects of planet earth.
From The Living Environment Series.
Prod-DALCCD Dist-DALCCD

Myths That Conceal Reality C 82 MIN
3/4 OR 1/2 INCH VIDEO CASSETTE C
Presents economist Milton Friedman discussing economic myths in American history which have accompanied a shift away from the belief in individual responsibility to an emphasis on social responsibility.
From The Milton Friedman Speaking Series. Lecture 2
LC NO. 79-708060
Prod-HBJ Dist-HBJ Prodn-WQLN 1980

Myths, Legends And Folktales, No. 1 B 20 MIN
2 INCH VIDEOTAPE I
Increases children's knowledge concerning the history, ideas and customs behind folk literature. (Broadcast quality)
From The Quest For The Best Series.
Prod-DENVPS Dist-GPITVL Prodn-KRMATV

Myths, Legends And Folktales, No. 2 B 20 MIN
2 INCH VIDEOTAPE I
Increases children's knowledge concerning the history, ideas and customs behind folk literature. (Broadcast quality)
From The Quest For The Best Series.
Prod-DENVPS Dist-GPITVL Prodn-KRMATV

Myths, Legends And Folktales, No. 3 B 20 MIN
2 INCH VIDEOTAPE I
Increases children's knowledge concerning the history, ideas and customs behind folk literature. (Broadcast quality)
From The Quest For The Best Series.
Prod-DENVPS Dist-GPITVL Prodn-KRMATV

Myths, The Collective Dreams Of Mankind C 30 MIN
3/4 OR 1/2 INCH VIDEO CASSETTE C
See series title for descriptive statement.
From The Art Of Being Human Series. Module 4
Prod-MDCC Dist-MDCC

Myxoma Of Right Atrium - Surgical Removal During Cardiopulmonary Bypass C 10 MIN
16MM FILM OPTICAL SOUND
Shows step by step the procedures followed in an operation on 48-year-old patient for the surgical removal during cardio-pulmonary bypass of a myxoma of the right atrium.
LC NO. FIA66-56
Prod-EATONL Dist-EATONL Prodn-AVCORP 1961

Myxomas Of The Heart C 13 MIN
3/4 OR 1/2 INCH VIDEO CASSETTE PRO
Shows myxomas of the heart.
Prod-WFP Dist-WFP Prodn-UKANMC

Mzima - Portrait Of A Spring C 30 MIN
16MM FILM, 3/4 OR 1/2 IN VIDEO I-H A
A shortened version of Mzima - Portrait Of A Spring. Shows scenes of big and small wildlife in Kenya, including hippopotami, elephants, crocodiles and snakes.
Prod-ROOTA Dist-BNCHMK 1983

Mzima - Portrait Of A Spring C 53 MIN
16MM FILM, 3/4 OR 1/2 IN VIDEO H
Shows scenes of big and small wildlife in Kenya, including hippopotami, elphants, crocodiles and snakes.
Prod-ROOTA Dist-MGHT 1971

Mzima - Portrait Of A Spring, Pt 1 C 27 MIN
16MM FILM, 3/4 OR 1/2 IN VIDEO H
Shows scenes of big and small wildlife in Kenya, including hippopotami, elephants, crocodiles and snakes.
Prod-ROOTA Dist-MGHT 1971

Mzima - Portrait Of A Spring, Pt 2 C 26 MIN
16MM FILM, 3/4 OR 1/2 IN VIDEO H
Shows scenes of big and small wildlife in Kenya, including hippopotami, elephants, crocodiles and snakes.
Prod-ROOTA Dist-MGHT 1971

N

N (Enn-yay) C 10 MIN
3/4 INCH VIDEO CASSETTE
Presents characters and vignettes that deconstruct the myth of America as the immigrant's refuge, and simultaneously plays on the ways in which information is filtered through the media. By Tony Labat.
Prod-EAI Dist-EAI

N And M C 15 MIN
3/4 INCH VIDEO CASSETTE P
From The Writing Time Series.
Prod-WHROTV Dist-GPITVL

N O W Now C 29 MIN
3/4 INCH VIDEO CASSETTE
Looks at the goals of the National Organization for Women.
From The Woman Series.
Prod-WNEDTV Dist-PUBTEL

N Sound, The - Nobody's Nose C 15 MIN
2 INCH VIDEOTAPE P
Introduces some of the consonant sounds met in early reading. Identifies the written letter with the spoken sound.
From The Listen And Say Series.
Prod-MPATI Dist-GPITVL

N Y, N Y C 16 MIN
16MM FILM, 3/4 OR 1/2 IN VIDEO J-C A
Shows the rhythmic impression of New York City through shifting patterns of semi-abstract images of its people, building and traffic.
Prod-THOMPN Dist-PFP 1958

N-Channel, CMOS, SOS and Ion Implantation Technology C 30 MIN
3/4 OR 1/2 INCH VIDEO CASSETTE PRO
Describes variation in MOS V-I characteristics and basic process steps that result when N-channel, CMOS, SOS, and Ion Implantation structures are used.
From The MOS Integrated Circuit Series.
Prod-TXINLC Dist-TXINLC

N-Dimensional Vector Spaces B 32 MIN
3/4 OR 1/2 INCH VIDEO CASSETTE
See series title for descriptive statement.
From The Calculus Of Several Variables - Partial Derivatives Series.
Prod-MIOT Dist-MIOT

N/um Tchai - The Ceremonial Dance Of The !kung Bushmen B 20 MIN
16MM FILM OPTICAL SOUND
Features the dance of the Bushman medicine man, showing it to be both religiously significant in its purpose of warding off death and culturally significant in the music and dancing employed.
LC NO. 75-702857
Prod-DOCEDR Dist-DOCEDR Prodn-MRSHL 1968

N/um Tchai - The Ceremonial Dance Of The Kung Bushmen B 20 MIN
3/4 INCH VIDEO CASSETTE
Presents a medicine dance of the Kung bushmen of Namibia which includes trance walking on hot coals.
From The San (Bushmen) Series.
Prod-DOCEDR Dist-DOCEDR Prodn-MRSHL

NAACP, Urban League And Early Battles For Rights B 30 MIN
2 INCH VIDEOTAPE H-C A
See series title for descriptive statement.
From The Americans From Africa - A History Series. No. 24
Prod-CVETVC Dist-GPITVL Prodn-WCVETV

Nabisco I-Screams, Test Marketing Case History C 54 MIN
3/4 OR 1/2 INCH VIDEO CASSETTE
Describes the differences between 'direct distribution' and 'warehouse distribution' and shows how new products are created and tested.
Prod-HBS Dist-IVCH

Nabucco C 145 MIN
3/4 OR 1/2 INCH VIDEO CASSETTE A
Portrays the reign of Nabucco (Nebuchadnezzar, King of Babylon) in an opera whose theme of a repressed people's yearning for freedom made Verdi the political voice of his own country.
Prod-EDDIM Dist-EDDIM

Naer Himlen - Naer Jorden (Near The Sky - Near The Earth) X 26 MIN
16MM FILM OPTICAL SOUND
A Danish language film. Presents European and American hippies in Nepal. Observes the way of life these hippies have chosen to live 'OUTSIDE OF SOCIETY' in the light of the everyday rites and ceremonies of the Nepalese. Explains that the hippie movement is not just a caprice of fashion, but a religion.
Prod-STATNS Dist-STATNS 1968

Nagasaki - One Man's Return C 55 MIN
16MM FILM OPTICAL SOUND
Tells the story of Buckner Fanning, a marine who lived in Nagasaki after the atomic bomb, who was invited to return to Nagasaki in order to relate his feelings and to get the reactions of the Japanese people 30 years after the bombing of that city.
LC NO. 76-700388
Prod-MILPRO Dist-MILPRO 1976

Nahal C 10 MIN
16MM FILM OPTICAL SOUND
Shows how Israel's nahal (pioneer fighting youth) combines farming and soldiering.
Prod-ALDEN Dist-ALDEN

Nahanni C 25 MIN
16MM FILM OPTICAL SOUND
Covers an expedition by speleologist Jean Porirel and his crew who parachute near the headwaters of the South Nahanni River in western Canada, travel downstream by inflatable boats, scale the canyon walls above the river and explore Nahanni's caves.
LC NO. 72-701241
Prod-CDIAND Dist-CDIAND Prodn-VIAMC 1972

Nahanni B 19 MIN
16MM FILM, 3/4 OR 1/2 IN VIDEO J A
Follows Albert Faille, an aging prospector from Fort Simpson, on his journey down the Nahanni River, through forbidding wilderness and dark canyons.
Prod-NFBC Dist-NFBC 1962

Nahanni (French) C 25 MIN
16MM FILM OPTICAL SOUND
Covers an expedition by speleologist Jean Porirel and his crew who parachute near the headwaters of the South Nahanni River in western Canada, travel downstream by inflatable boats, scale the canyon walls above the river and explore Nahanni's caves.
LC NO. 72-701241
Prod-CDIAND Dist-CDIAND Prodn-VIAMC 1972

Nai - The Story Of A Kung Woman C 58 MIN
16MM FILM OPTICAL SOUND
Presents a compilation of footage of the Kung people of Namibia from 1951 to 1978. Focuses on the changes in the lives of these people as seen through the reflections of one woman, Nai.
LC NO. 80-701249
Prod-DOCEDR Dist-DOCEDR 1980

Nail C 20 MIN
16MM FILM, 3/4 OR 1/2 IN VIDEO
Tells of a lonely secretary who finds a large shiny nail, which proves to be the catalyst that brings her alienated fellow tenants together in a spontaneous celebration of love and fellowship.
Prod-FAMF Dist-AIMS 1973

Nail Soup C 15 MIN
3/4 INCH VIDEO CASSETTE K-P
See series title for descriptive statement.
From The Storytime Series.
Prod-WCETTV Dist-GPITVL 1976

Nails C 4 MIN
16MM FILM, 3/4 OR 1/2 IN VIDEO H-C A
Uses thousands of multiplying nails to present an abstract statement on the problem of over-population.
Prod-IFB Dist-IFB 1973

Nails C 13 MIN
16MM FILM, 3/4 OR 1/2 IN VIDEO J-C A
Contrasts the blacksmith's slow craftsman's approach with the mass production methods of the 80's, using the ordinary nail as a symbol of industrial growth.
Prod-NFBC Dist-NFBC 1980

Naim And Jabar C 50 MIN
16MM FILM OPTICAL SOUND
Analyzes the friendship of two Afghan boys, emphasizing the hopes, fears and aspirations of adolescence.
From The Faces Of Change - Afghanistan Series.
Prod-AUFS Dist-WHEELK

Naked Civil Servant C 78 MIN
16MM FILM, 3/4 OR 1/2 IN VIDEO C A
Presents the autobiography of flamboyant British homosexual Quentin Crisp. Dramatizes the story of courage in spite of years of intolerance, misunderstanding, ostracism and violence. Discusses his boyhood, ill-fated friendships, encounters with the law and rare moments of real happiness, interpreted masterfully by actor John Hurt.
Prod-THAMES Dist-MEDIAG 1975

Naked Kiss, The B 90 MIN
16MM FILM OPTICAL SOUND C A
Presents a drama starring Constance Towers, Tony Eisley and Michael Dante.
Prod-CINEWO Dist-CINEWO 1964

Naked-Eye Astronomy B 28 MIN
16MM FILM OPTICAL SOUND C A
Features three teachers, who discuss astronomical observations of the sun, moon, stars and planets which can be made with the naked eye, and point out various reference systems for locating astronomical objects. They explain that observed motions of these heavenly objects are the bases for the historically important geocentric and heliocentric systems of the world.
From The Harvard Project Physics Teacher Briefings Series. No. 3
LC NO. 73-709150
Prod-HPP Dist-HRAW 1969

Nal Sarovar B 10 MIN
16MM FILM OPTICAL SOUND I-C A
Shows the bird watchers' paradise at Nal Sarovar in Gujarat in India. Explains that it is a sanctuary for migrating birds from as far away as Europe and Siberia.
Prod-INDIA Dist-NEDINF

Nam June Paik Edited For Television C 29 MIN
3/4 OR 1/2 INCH VIDEO CASSETTE
Nam June Paik discusses his work and artistic philosophy with Russell Connor. Includes cuts from a number of Paik's early works.
Prod-EAI Dist-EAI

Namaqualand - Diary Of A Desert Garden C 50 MIN
3/4 OR 1/2 INCH VIDEO CASSETTE H-C A
Explores the Namaqualand region of South Africa, a vast area of desert, rocks and mountains supporting over 4,000 species of flowers. Explains that the little rain that falls comes in winter and evaporates slowly and how a delicate ecosystem has developed between the plants and animals.
Prod-WNETTV Dist-FI Prodn-BBCTV

Namatjira, The Painter C 18 MIN
16MM FILM OPTICAL SOUND
Studies Albert Namatjira, Australia's best-known Aboriginal artist and master of vivid watercolor landscape scenes.
Prod-FLMAUS Dist-AUIS

Name Designs C 15 MIN
3/4 OR 1/2 INCH VIDEO CASSETTE P-I
Discusses name designs in art.
From The Young At Art Series.
Prod-WSKJTV Dist-AITECH 1980

Name It C 15 MIN
3/4 OR 1/2 INCH VIDEO CASSETTE P
Employs a magician named Amazing Alexander and his assistants to explore the use of nouns.
From The Magic Shop Series. No. 6
LC NO. 83-706151
Prod-CVETVC Dist-GPITVL Prodn-WCVETV 1982

Name It C 15 MIN
3/4 OR 1/2 INCH VIDEO CASSETTE T
Uses the adventures of a pirate and his three friends to explore the many facets of language arts. Focuses on nouns and proper nouns and their use in reading and writing.
From The Hidden Treasures Series. No. 9
LC NO. 82-706549
Prod-WCVETV Dist-GPITVL 1980

Name Of The Age, The - James Boswell And Samuel Johnson C 45 MIN
3/4 OR 1/2 INCH VIDEO CASSETTE
Analyzes the work of James Boswell and Samuel Johnson.
From The Survey Of English Literature I Series.
Prod-MDCPB Dist-MDCPB

Name Of The Game C 30 MIN
3/4 OR 1/2 INCH VIDEO CASSETTE I-J
Discusses competition and drug use through the story of the Powerhouse soccer team's use of a ringer to win a match. Shows how the team is caught in a web of deception.
From The Powerhouse Series.
LC NO. 83-707186
Prod-EFCVA Dist-GA 1982

Name Of The Game Is P and L, The C 4 MIN
3/4 OR 1/2 INCH VIDEO CASSETTE PRO
Uses game show format to highlight possible antitrust liabilities. Contestants answer questions which determine whether they incur antitrust liabilities.
Prod-ABACPE Dist-ABACPE

Name Of The Game Is Soccer, The C 28 MIN
16MM FILM OPTICAL SOUND
Provides information about the basic elements of soccer. Highlights professional players on the field and during interviews.
LC NO. 80-701247
Prod-PICA Dist-MTP Prodn-SEVSEA 1980

Name Of The Game Is, The - Baseball C 29 MIN
1 INCH VIDEOTAPE
Little Leaguers and Big Leaguers - all young players learn the fundamentals of baseball from Big League stars. Includes lots of baseball action. Narrated by Curt Gowdy.
Prod-PICA Dist-MTP

Name Of The Game Is, The - Fun C 28 MIN
1 INCH VIDEOTAPE
Follows the evolution of a baseball season from spring training, coaching of rookies and the Grape Fruit League to regular season with a recap of great moments in American League history. Studies the American League.
Prod-CRYSLR Dist-MTP

Name Of The Game, The C 27 MIN
16MM FILM OPTICAL SOUND J-C A
Highlights the 1966 professional football season, featuring team and individual performances of the Minnesota Vikings.
LC NO. FIA68-1408
Prod-NFL Dist-NFL 1967

Name Of The Game, The B 28 MIN
16MM FILM OPTICAL SOUND
Presents a function of the fellowship of Christian athletes. During the weekend of champions in Dallas, Tom Landry had the prayer, Dallas Cowboy tight end Pettis Norman read scripture and Bart Starr delivered the sermon during a Sunday morning worship service.
Prod-FELLCA Dist-FELLCA

Name Of The Game, The C 20 MIN
16MM FILM, 3/4 OR 1/2 IN VIDEO J-H
States that the need is universal for all scientists to identify things as well as processes and events. Identification serves important purposes, especially for quick and international communication. This communication is often accomplished most effectively through drawings.
From The Biology - It's Life Series.
Prod-THAMES Dist-MEDIAG 1980

Name Of The Game, The B 28 MIN
16MM FILM, 3/4 OR 1/2 IN VIDEO
Describes the massive efforts by government and by private industry to train the hardcore unemployed. Includes on-the-spot interviews with trainees, government workers, and business executives. Issued in 1968 as a motion picture.
From The Career Job Opportunity Series.
LC NO. 79-707882
Prod-USBES Dist-USNAC Prodn-CMC 1979

Name Of The Game, The C 30 MIN
3/4 OR 1/2 INCH VIDEO CASSETTE
Stresses the importance of identifying the managerial process. Covers common roadblocks to planning.
From The Managerial Game Plan - Team Building Through MBO Series.
Prod-PRODEV Dist-PRODEV

Name That Label C 15 MIN
3/4 OR 1/2 INCH VIDEO CASSETTE J-H
Presents members of the Twelfth Night Repertory Company using humor, satire, music, dance and drama to focus attention on attitudes regarding prejudices and stereotypes. Shows that Big Guy finds out that almost as soon as he creates Man and Woman, prejudice and stereotyping are born. Reveals that when groups that form to combat these problems don't communicate, the problems increase. Presents student leaders who use communication skills to mediate differences, to separate gossip from truth, and to make the world a better place for themselves and others.
From The TNRC Presents - Health And Self Series.
Prod-KLCSTV Dist-AITECH 1984

Name That Publication - An Introduction To The VA Publication System C 39 MIN
3/4 INCH VIDEO CASSETTE
Deals with a variety of Veterans Administration publications, such as circulars, information letters, hospital bulletins and Title 38 of the Veterans Adminstration manual, part 1 and interim issues. Focuses on the use of these publications by the employees of the Medical Administration Service.
LC NO. 79-707303
Prod-VAHSL Dist-USNAC 1978

Names C 15 MIN
3/4 OR 1/2 INCH VIDEO CASSETTE K-P
Discusses first and last names and nicknames.
From The Pass It On Series.
Prod-WKNOTV Dist-GPITVL 1983

Names For Numbers C 30 MIN
16MM FILM OPTICAL SOUND T
Describes the concept of set, and introduces the number properties of sets. Discusses the properties of order for numbers as well as for sets. To be used following 'WHOLE NUMBERS.'
From The Mathematics For Elementary School Teachers Series. No. 3
Prod-SMSG Dist-MLA 1963

Names Of The Months, The - January Through December C 15 MIN
3/4 INCH VIDEO CASSETTE P
From The Writing Time Series.
Prod-WHROTV Dist-GPITVL

Names We Never Knew C 27 MIN
16MM FILM OPTICAL SOUND
Documents the quest of Oklahoman artist Charles Banks Wilson in order to portray the history of the common man.
From The Spectrum Series.
LC NO. 75-703111
Prod-WKYTV Dist-WKYTV 1975

Names, Names, Names And Why We Need Them C 10 MIN
16MM FILM, 3/4 OR 1/2 IN VIDEO K-P
Points out to children the importance of names for people, places and things. Shows how people could not communicate without names.
Prod-SAIF Dist-BARR 1975

Namibia C 26 MIN
3/4 OR 1/2 INCH VIDEO CASSETTE H-C A
Examines the culture, ecology and government of Namibia.
Prod-UPI Dist-JOU

Naming Of Kwame, The C 30 MIN
3/4 OR 1/2 INCH VIDEO CASSETTE I-H
See series title for descriptive statement.
From The Gettin' To Know Me Series.
Prod-CTI Dist-MDCPB 1979

Naming The Parts C 60 MIN
3/4 OR 1/2 INCH VIDEO CASSETTE H-C A
Argues that man's ignorance of basic physiology leads to unusual attitudes toward the body. Establishes what happens when a person becomes ill. Based on the book The Body In Question by Jonathan Miller. Narrated by Jonathan Miller.
From The Body In Question Series. Program 1
LC NO. 81-706224
Prod-BBCTV Dist-FI 1979

Nan Hoover - Selected Works 1-A Series

Presents video as a rich color palette and a temporal and sculptural medium.
Prod-EAI Dist-EAI

Color Pieces	012 MIN
Impressions	010 MIN
Light And Object	010 MIN
Primary Colors	007 MIN

Nan Hoover - Selected Works 2-A Series

Presents a formalist approach to the creation of landscape using light, shadow and real time.
Prod-EAI Dist-EAI

Desert	011 MIN
Eye Watching	008 MIN
Halfsleep	017 MIN
Landscape	006 MIN
Returning To Fuji	008 MIN

Nan's Class C 40 MIN
16MM FILM OPTICAL SOUND
Provides information about the Lamaze childbirth method.
LC NO. 78-700205
Prod-ASPPO Dist-NEWDAY Prodn-DURRIN 1977

Nana - Un Portrait C 25 MIN
16MM FILM OPTICAL SOUND
A French language film. Presents a portrait of 80-year-old Nana Zilkha who was born in Bagdad and now lives in an apartment in New York. Tells of her life with her husband and seven children and of the people and places she has known.
LC NO. 74-700102
Prod-SIMONJ Dist-SIMONJ 1973

Nana, Mom And Me C 47 MIN
16MM FILM OPTICAL SOUND H-C A
Features a filmmaker, who is considering having a child. Examines interrelationships between herself, her mother and her grandmother. Raises questions about the nature and substance of family relationships.
LC NO. 74-702495
Prod-ANOMFM Dist-NEWDAY 1974

Nancie C 5 MIN
16MM FILM OPTICAL SOUND
Profiles the life of a handicapped junior high school girl.
LC NO. 78-701317
Prod-LCSDNO Dist-LCSDNO Prodn-VOGELP 1978

Nancy Acosta C 28 MIN
3/4 OR 1/2 INCH VIDEO CASSETTE
Features Nancy Acosta, a 21 year-old teacher in the barrios of La Puente outside of Los Angeles, where crime and violence are common. Tells how she is providing an alternative, a school for dropouts where the atmosphere offers uncompromising love and respect.
From The Old Friends - New Friends Series.
Prod-FAMCOM Dist-PBS 1981

Nancy And Her Friends C 28 MIN
16MM FILM OPTICAL SOUND C A
Presents a study of three divorced women who gave up custody of their children and set out on new paths.
Prod-VIERAD Dist-VIERAD 1977

Nancy Astor-A Series
16MM FILM, 3/4 OR 1/2 IN VIDEO H-C A
Describes the life of Nancy Astor, an American who became the wife of English millionaire Waldorf Astor and later the first woman elected to the British House of Commons.
Prod-BBCTV Dist-TIMLIF 1982

Nancy Holt - Locating No. 2 B 14 MIN
3/4 OR 1/2 INCH VIDEO CASSETTE
Focuses on the native turf of Nancy Holt.
Prod-ARTINC Dist-ARTINC

Nancy Holt - Revolve B 77 MIN
3/4 OR 1/2 INCH VIDEO CASSETTE
Tells about a struggle for life.
Prod-ARTINC Dist-ARTINC

Nancy Holt - Underscan B 8 MIN
3/4 OR 1/2 INCH VIDEO CASSETTE
Features a domestic drama.
Prod-ARTINC Dist-ARTINC

Nancy, Henri And Elizabeth C 16 MIN
16MM FILM OPTICAL SOUND
Demonstates that an attempt to humanize Nancy, Henri and Elizabeth on one level while their actions and words function metaphorically, raises questions and stimulates emotions concerning the development and stability of sexual identity.
LC NO. 74-702874
Prod-AIBELR Dist-ANNSC 1973

Nanduti - A Paraguayan Lace C 18 MIN
16MM FILM OPTICAL SOUND
Introduces the origin of nanduti lace through one of its many legends. Juxtaposes the symbolic and representational patterns

of nanduti with natural and manmade objects and documents the process of making nanduti.
LC NO. 78-701318
Prod-CK Dist-CK 1978

Nanduti - A Paraguayan Lace C 17 MIN
16MM FILM, 3/4 OR 1/2 IN VIDEO J A
Introduces the origin of nanduti, Paraguayan lace, through one of its many legends. Juxtaposes the symbolic and representational patterns of nanduti with natural and man-made objects and documents the process of making nanduti.
Prod-CKPRO Dist-IFB

Nanduti - Encaje Paraguayo C 17 MIN
16MM FILM, 3/4 OR 1/2 IN VIDEO
A Spanish language version of Nanduti - A Paraguayan Lace. Details the origin of nanduti through one of its many legends. Juxtaposes the symbolic and representational patterns of nanduti with natural and man-made objects and documents the process of making nanduti.
Prod-CKPRO Dist-IFB

Nanette - An Aside C 44 MIN
16MM FILM OPTICAL SOUND
Presents an adaptation of a short story by Willa Cather in which a famous ballerina and her young secretary discover that their ideas and modes of living have become radically different.
LC NO. 78-700204
Prod-WHITOM Dist-VANGLE 1977

Nanook Of The North B 64 MIN
16MM FILM OPTICAL SOUND J-C A
Reissue of the 1922 silent motion picture Nanook Of The North. Presents a documentary on the saga of an Eskimo family pitting their strength against a vast and inhospitable Arctic.
Prod-FLAH Dist-TEXFLM Prodn-IFSEM 1977

Nanook Of The North B 60 MIN
3/4 OR 1/2 INCH VIDEO CASSETTE
Presents a documentary about the Eskimo's struggle against the harsh elements. Directed by Robert Flaherty.
Prod-IHF Dist-IHF

Naosaki C 8 MIN
16MM FILM OPTICAL SOUND
Presents an aesthetic study of gymnastic movement, emphasizing its visual and kinesthetic elements.
LC NO. 77-702988
Prod-HUNNL Dist-CANFDC

Nap, The C 13 MIN
16MM FILM OPTICAL SOUND
Tells how a well-deserved afternoon nap turns into a nightmare.
LC NO. 79-700846
Prod-ROSENJ Dist-ROSENJ 1979

Naples To Cassino B 26 MIN
16MM FILM - 3/4 IN VIDEO
Shows scenes of fighting during the drive of Allied forces from Naples to Cassino, Italy, during World War II. Issued in 1948 as a motion picture.
From The Historical Reports Series.
LC NO. 80-706774
Prod-USA Dist-USNAC 1980

Napoleon - The End Of A Dictator C 26 MIN
16MM FILM, 3/4 OR 1/2 IN VIDEO J A
Explores the causes of Napoleon's downfall which includes the weariness of war and tyranny in France and the new nationalism throughout Europe.
From The Western Civilization - Majesty And Madness Series.
Prod-LCOA Dist-LCOA Prodn-IFA 1970

Napoleon - The End Of A Dictator (Spanish) C 26 MIN
16MM FILM, 3/4 OR 1/2 IN VIDEO J-C A
Dramatizes Napoleon's return from Elba and his defeat at Waterloo.
Prod-LCOA Dist-LCOA Prodn-IFA 1970

Napoleon - The Making Of A Dictator C 27 MIN
16MM FILM, 3/4 OR 1/2 IN VIDEO J A
Examines the problem of freedom versus stability through the coup d'etat of 1799. Shows how military victories built Napoleon's popularity and how a corrupt government can be overpowered by a dictator.
From The Western Civilization - Majesty And Madness Series.
Prod-LCOA Dist-LCOA Prodn-IFA 1970

Napoleon - The Making Of A Dictator (Spanish) C 27 MIN
16MM FILM, 3/4 OR 1/2 IN VIDEO J-C A
Explores the first modern coup d'etat, the rise to power of Napoleon Bonaparte.
Prod-LCOA Dist-LCOA Prodn-IFA 1970

Napoleonic Era, The C 14 MIN
16MM FILM, 3/4 OR 1/2 IN VIDEO J-C
Describes the Napoleonic era of 1796-1815 and its effects upon France and Europe. Includes scenes typifying Napoleon's rise to power, his governmental reforms in France, his conquests and the disintegration of the Grand Empire.
Prod-CORF Dist-CORF 1957

Napping House, The C 5 MIN
16MM FILM - 1/2 IN VIDEO, VHS
Presents a simple tale of family members and the snuggling heap they make on a rainy day, until a wakeful flea causes the drowsing pyramid to erupt into wakefulness as the sun suddenly appears. Based on the book by Audrey Wood.
Prod-SCHNDL Dist-WWS

Nara - A Stroll Through History C 20 MIN
16MM FILM OPTICAL SOUND H-C A
Presents a tour of the Japanese city of Nara, visiting its historical sites and showing examples of its eighth-century Buddhist art.
LC NO. 77-702436
Prod-JNTA Dist-JNTA 1973

Narcissistic Personality Disorder - An Interview With A Senior Adult C 30 MIN
3/4 OR 1/2 INCH VIDEO CASSETTE PRO
Illustrates some of the characteristic manifestations of a narcissistic personality disorder in an older adult.
Prod-HSCIC Dist-HSCIC 1985

Narcissus C 22 MIN
3/4 OR 1/2 INCH VIDEO CASSETTE J-C A
Expands upon the beauty of ballet by showing the sensual movements of dancers from a distance and the passionate emotions conveyed by their unique interpretation of the Greek myth of Narcissus.
LC NO. 84-707133
Prod-VERRAD Dist-NFBC 1983

Narcolepsy C 12 MIN
16MM FILM OPTICAL SOUND
Presents Dr William C Dement of Stanford University who describes the symptoms and diagnosis of narcolepsy, a disease of deep sleep. Shows narcoleptic patients having sleep attacks, cataleptic attacks and hypnogogic hallucinations. Describes Dr Dement's research which has provided a definitive method of diagnosing narcolepsy using sleep recordings.
Prod-HOFLAR Dist-AMEDA

Narcosynthesis B 22 MIN
16MM FILM SILENT PRO
Demonstrates the injection of ultra-short-acting barbiturates to the point of very light narcosis in various cases. Case one shows the movements. Case two shows the effect of reassurance and suggestion in hysteria with hemiparesis. Case three shows the production of emotional responsiveness in a schizophrenialike state. Case four shows the result of treatment of major hysteria in an 11-year-old girl. restricted.
Prod-PSUPCR Dist-PSUPCR 1944

Narcotic And Non-Narcotic Analgesics C 30 MIN
16MM FILM OPTICAL SOUND C
See series title for descriptive statement.
From The Pharmacology Series.
LC NO. 73-703335
Prod-MVNE Dist-TELSTR 1971

Narcotic Deaths--A Series
PRO
Analyzes types of narcotic deaths encountered, drugs used, and symptomatic changes found externally and internally in the victim.
Prod-PRIMED Dist-PRIMED

Narcotic Deaths, Pt 1 030 MIN
Narcotic Deaths, Pt 2 030 MIN

Narcotic Deaths, Pt 1 B 27 MIN
16MM FILM OPTICAL SOUND PRO
Describes types of narcotic deaths, types of drugs used and symptomatic changes found externally as well as internally. Discusses and demonstrates the implements used to take narcotic drugs and shows slides of overdose victims and the effects of narcotic intravenous infections on veins and subcutaneous tissue. (Kinescope)
From The Clinical Pathology - Forensic Medicine Outlines Series.
LC NO. 74-705184
Prod-NMAC Dist-USNAC 1970

Narcotic Deaths, Pt 1 C 30 MIN
3/4 OR 1/2 INCH VIDEO CASSETTE PRO
See series title for descriptive statement.
From The Narcotic Deaths Series.
Prod-PRIMED Dist-PRIMED

Narcotic Deaths, Pt 2 B 21 MIN
16MM FILM OPTICAL SOUND PRO
Describes types of narcotic deaths, types of drugs used and symptomatic changes found externally as well as internally. Discusses and demonstrates the implements used to take narcotic drugs and shows slides of overdose victims and the effects of narcotic intravenous infections on veins and subcutaneous tissue. (Kinescope)
From The Clinical Pathology - Forensic Medicine Outlines Series.
LC NO. 74-705185
Prod-NMAC Dist-USNAC 1970

Narcotic Deaths, Pt 2 C 30 MIN
3/4 OR 1/2 INCH VIDEO CASSETTE PRO
See series title for descriptive statement.
From The Narcotic Deaths Series.
Prod-PRIMED Dist-PRIMED

Narcotics C 5 MIN
3/4 OR 1/2 INCH VIDEO CASSETTE
Describes the dangerous effects that narcotics can have on the individual. Discusses reasons why people abuse drugs. Issued in 1971 as a motion picture.
From The Single Concept Drug Film Series.
LC NO. 80-706847
Prod-NIMH Dist-USNAC 1980

Narcotics C 10 MIN
16MM FILM, 3/4 OR 1/2 IN VIDEO H A
Discusses the characteristics of narcotics. Identifies the signs of use and abuse, the pharmacological and behavioral effects, and the shortand long-term dangers.
From The Drug Information Series.
LC NO. 84-706155
Prod-MITCHG Dist-MTI 1983

Narcotics C 32 MIN
3/4 OR 1/2 INCH VIDEO CASSETTE PRO
Discusses pharmacologic properties and effects, cross-tolerance, seizures, acute intoxification, and treatment of narcotics.
From The Assessment And Management Of Acute Substance Abuse Series.
Prod-BRA Dist-BRA

Narcotics - A Challenge To Youth/Teachers C 24 MIN
16MM FILM OPTICAL SOUND H A
Shows a troubled boy with emotional difficulties with which he cannot cope and how he becomes addicted to drugs, which release his frustrations. Explains the teacher's responsibility of preventing this through proper education.
Prod-NEFA Dist-NEFA 1956

Narcotics - The Inside Story C 12 MIN
16MM FILM, 3/4 OR 1/2 IN VIDEO I-J
Acquaints the student with the effects of narcotics on the nervous system.
Prod-AIMS Dist-AIMS 1967

Narcotics - The Inside Story (Arabic) C 12 MIN
16MM FILM, 3/4 OR 1/2 IN VIDEO I-J
Presents postive applications of narcotics and drugs when administeered by doctors for medical purposes. Shows how experimenting with drugs and narcotics can seriously upset the central nervous system.
Prod-CAHILL Dist-AIMS 1967

Narcotics - The Inside Story (Spanish) C 12 MIN
16MM FILM, 3/4 OR 1/2 IN VIDEO I-J
Presents postive applications of narcotics and drugs when administeered by doctors for medical purposes. Shows how experimenting with drugs and narcotics can seriously upset the central nervous system.
Prod-CAHILL Dist-AIMS 1967

Narcotics File - The Challenge C 28 MIN
16MM FILM, 3/4 OR 1/2 IN VIDEO H-C A
Describes the life of the Meo hilltribes of northern Thailand and of their cultivation of the poppy and production of opium. Tells of the attempt being made to have these people change their occupation as a means of checking the source of illicit opium.
From The Narcotics File Series.
Prod-UN Dist-JOU 1976

Narcotics File - The Connection C 28 MIN
16MM FILM, 3/4 OR 1/2 IN VIDEO J-C A
Details efforts being made throughout the world to stem the criminal flow of drugs. Follows the poppy from cultivation, harvesting, smuggling, processing into morphine, processing into heroin and final sale on the streets of New York.
From The Narcotics File Series.
Prod-UN Dist-JOU 1974

Narcotics File - The Source C 28 MIN
16MM FILM, 3/4 OR 1/2 IN VIDEO J-C A
Introduces measures that can be taken to eliminate the illicit opium supply at the point of origin. Tells what the United Nations and the rest of a concerned world are doing about drug abuse. Deals with Thailand's part in the Golden Triangle which originates about half of the world's illicit opium supply.
From The Narcotics File Series.
Prod-UN Dist-JOU 1974

Narcotics File - The Victims C 28 MIN
16MM FILM, 3/4 OR 1/2 IN VIDEO J-C A
Describes various treatment programs aimed at rehabilitating the heroin addict. Includes sequences filmed at Hong Kong, Tokyo, Stockholm, London and New York dealing with drug free communes, methadone maintenance, heroin maintenance, harsh jail sentences, one-to-one psychological treatment and prison-cum-treatment centers.
From The Narcotics File Series.
Prod-UN Dist-JOU 1974

Narcotics File--A Series
16MM FILM, 3/4 OR 1/2 IN VIDEO J-C A
Prod-UN Dist-JOU 1974

Narcotics File - The Challenge 28 MIN
Narcotics File - The Connection 28 MIN
Narcotics File - The Source 28 MIN
Narcotics File - The Victims 28 MIN

Narcotism C 23 MIN
3/4 INCH VIDEO CASSETTE PRO
Gives an overview of narcotism. Describes various drugs and shows examples of drug-associated deaths, explaining signs commonly associated with drug addiction.
From The Forensic Medicine Teaching Programs Series. No. 10
LC NO. 78-706055
Prod-NMAC Dist-USNAC Prodn-NYUCM 1978

Narmada B 17 MIN
16MM FILM OPTICAL SOUND I-C A
Traces the entire course of the Narmada River from its source at Amarkantak in Central India, through the hills and forests to the historic town of Broach, where it ends its long journey by joining the Arabian Sea at the Gulf of Cambay.
Prod-INDIA Dist-NEDINF

Narragansetts, The C 30 MIN
3/4 INCH VIDEO CASSETTE
See series title for descriptive statement.
From The People Of The First Light Series.
Prod-WGBYTV Dist-GPITVL 1977

Narration And Description C
3/4 OR 1/2 INCH VIDEO CASSETTE C
Shows one of four lessons studying traditional rhetorical patterns, using a pragmatic approach. Emphasizes the use of traditional patterns to develop individual writing patterns.

From The Write Course - An Introduction To College Composition Series.
Prod-DALCCD Dist-DALCCD

Narration And Description C 30 MIN
3/4 OR 1/2 INCH VIDEO CASSETTE C A
Discusses the use of traditional patterns to develop individual writing patterns. Studies traditional rhetorical patterns, using a programmatic approach.
From The Write Course - An Introduction To College Composition Series.
LC NO. 85-700980
Prod-FI Dist-FI 1984

Narrative Fiction - Divide And Conquer, The Meaning Of Analysis B 30 MIN
2 INCH VIDEOTAPE J-H
From The Franklin To Frost Series.
Prod-GPITVL Dist-GPITVL

Narrative Fiction - Repetition And Contrast B 30 MIN
2 INCH VIDEOTAPE J-H
From The Franklin To Frost Series.
Prod-GPITVL Dist-GPITVL

Narrative Fiction - The Story As Art, The Thing Made B 30 MIN
2 INCH VIDEOTAPE J-H
From The Franklin To Frost Series.
Prod-GPITVL Dist-GPITVL

Narrow Gauge Train To Silverton B 21 MIN
16MM FILM SILENT
Presents the story of 'THE SILVERTON,' the summer passenger train on the Denver and Rio Grande Western's Durango-Silverton branch.
Prod-BHAWK Dist-BHAWK

Narrowcasting Dance For Cable Television C 30 MIN
3/4 OR 1/2 INCH VIDEO CASSETTE
See series title for descriptive statement.
From The Dance On Television - Lorber Series
Prod-ARCVID Dist-ARCVID

NASA - Journey Into Space C 20 MIN
3/4 OR 1/2 INCH VIDEO CASSETTE J-C A
Highlights America's journey into space, including the lift-off and recovery of Apollo 14, the first step on the moon and exploration of the moon's surface. Shows how NASA astronauts lived in space and tours the NASA Kennedy Space Center from within.
LC NO. 82-706779
Prod-AWSS Dist-AWSS 1980

NASA Biosatellite Program, The - Between The Atom And The Star C 28 MIN
16MM FILM OPTICAL SOUND J-C
Biologists explain experiments concerning gravity that will be conducted in an earth-orbiting satellite, how they will be carried out, and the importance of seeking information about weightless atmospheres on life for scientific research and the manned space program.
Prod-NASA Dist-NASA 1965

Nasa Tapes—A Series
J-C A
Prod-NASA Dist-ASTROV 1979

Conclusion Of Apollo Program 056 MIN
Lunar Landing 1 - The Eagle Has Landed 055 MIN

Nasal Cavities C 12 MIN
3/4 OR 1/2 INCH VIDEO CASSETTE C A
Describes the boundaries, demonstrates the bones and identifies the bony regions of the nasal cavities.
From The Skull Anatomy Series.
Prod-UTXHSA Dist-TEF

Nashville - The View From '82 C 60 MIN
3/4 OR 1/2 INCH VIDEO CASSETTE
Uses interviews on various topics with leaders in Nashville, Tennessee, to forecast trends for the city in 1983 based on events and happenings in 1982.
LC NO. 83-706882
Prod-WNGETV Dist-WNGETV 1983

Nasogastric Intubation C 7 MIN
3/4 OR 1/2 INCH VIDEO CASSETTE PRO
Reviews essential equipment and illustrates the step-by-step analysis of the technique as well as demonstrating the actual procedure on two trauma victims. Shows procedure done for detection of upper GI bleeding and for a patient with head and neck injuries.
Prod-UWASH Dist-UWASH

Nasogastric Intubation C 9 MIN
3/4 OR 1/2 INCH VIDEO CASSETTE PRO
See series title for descriptive statement.
From The Medical Skills Films Series.
Prod-WFP Dist-WFP

Nasogastric Intubation C 27 MIN
3/4 OR 1/2 INCH VIDEO CASSETTE
Demonstrates techniques of nasogastric intubation.
From The Emergency Management - The First 30 Minutes, Vol I Series.
Prod-VTRI Dist-VTRI

Nasser - People's Pharoah C 24 MIN
16MM FILM, 3/4 OR 1/2 IN VIDEO H-C A
Documents President Nasser's role in Egypt from the Suez Canal crisis to the Middle East conflict. Narrated by Henry Fonda.
From The Leaders Of The 20th Century - Portraits Of Power Series.
Prod-NIELSE Dist-LCOA 1980

Nasser And The Resurgence Of Egypt C 29 MIN
2 INCH VIDEOTAPE
See series title for descriptive statement.
From The Course Of Our Times II Series.
Prod-WGBHTV Dist-PUBTEL

NASTAR - Go For Gold C 14 MIN
16MM FILM - 3/4 IN VIDEO P-C A
Presents former olympic coach Bob Beattie explaining basic ski racing techniques as pro racers demonstrate ski preparation, the start, running the gates and the finish.
Prod-CRYSP Dist-CRYSP

Nat Horne And Mabal Robinson C 30 MIN
3/4 OR 1/2 INCH VIDEO CASSETTE
Shows how theatre dance productions are prepared.
From The Eye On Dance - Broadway Dance Series.
Prod-ARTRES Dist-ARTRES

Natalie Wood - Hollywood's Child B 26 MIN
16MM FILM OPTICAL SOUND
Traces the career of Natalie Wood, describing her successful transition from a child star to an adult actress. Includes clips from West Side Story and Love with a Proper Stranger.
From The Hollywood And The Stars Series.
LC NO. FI68-184
Prod-WOLPER Dist-WOLPER 1964

Nate The Great And The Sticky Case C 19 MIN
16MM FILM, 3/4 OR 1/2 IN VIDEO K-P
Reveals how Nate the Great, the sharpest sleuth since Sherlock Holmes, solves the mystery of his friend Claude's missing stegosaurus stamp aided by clear-headed logic, keen memory and strong powers of observation.
LC NO. 83-706926
Prod-EBEC Dist-EBEC 1983

Nate The Great Goes Undercover C 10 MIN
16MM FILM, 3/4 OR 1/2 IN VIDEO K-I
Tells about Nate the Great, a 10-year-old who tries to solve the mystery of the garbage snatcher. Based on the book Nate The Great Goes Undercover by Marjorie Weinman Sharmat.
From The Contemporary Children's Literature Series.
Prod-BOSUST Dist-CF 1978

Nathalie (French) B 32 MIN
16MM FILM, 3/4 OR 1/2 IN VIDEO H-C A
Introduces a girl who is confronting her blossoming maturity. Shows her and a girlfriend engaging in unconscious homosexual caresses, becoming aware of the stares of a man on a subway and fantasizing about being a young woman. Includes English subtitles.
Prod-FI Dist-TEXFLM 1970

Nathalie Krebs C 12 MIN
16MM FILM OPTICAL SOUND
Follows Nathalie Krebs, chemical engineer and creator of unique stoneware glazes, in her workshop where the glazes are mixed according to her own secret formulas.
Prod-RDCG Dist-AUDPLN

Nathan Glazer On Affirmative Action C 30 MIN
3/4 OR 1/2 INCH VIDEO CASSETTE
Features sociologist Nathan Glazer expressing his views of ethnicity, discrimination and affirmative action in America today. Includes discussion of his book Ethnic Dilemmas 1964-1982 in which he examines race and ethnicity in the United States since the passage of the Civil Rights Act of 1964.
From The Fronteras Series.
Prod-KPBS Dist-KPBS

Nathan Hale B 20 MIN
2 INCH VIDEOTAPE I
See series title for descriptive statement.
From The Americans All Series.
Prod-DENVPS Dist-GPITVL Prodn-KRMATV

Nathaniel Hawthorne - Light In The Shadows C 23 MIN
16MM FILM, 3/4 OR 1/2 IN VIDEO H
Presents a biography of writer Nathaniel Hawthorne using words from his novels to re-create the world and society which he knew.
LC NO. 82-706964
Prod-UNIPRO Dist-IFB 1982

Nathaniel Hawthorne - The Ambitious Guest B 30 MIN
2 INCH VIDEOTAPE J-H
From The Franklin To Frost Series.
Prod-GPITVL Dist-GPITVL

Nathaniel Hawthorne - The Minister's Black Veil B 30 MIN
2 INCH VIDEOTAPE J-H
From The Franklin To Frost Series.
Prod-GPITVL Dist-GPITVL

Nathaniel Hawthorne - The Scarlet Letter And The Fortunate Fall B 30 MIN
2 INCH VIDEOTAPE J-H
From The Franklin To Frost Series.
Prod-GPITVL Dist-GPITVL

Nathaniel Hawthorne - The World Of The Scarlet Letter And Its Structure B 30 MIN
2 INCH VIDEOTAPE J-H
From The Franklin To Frost Series.
Prod-GPITVL Dist-GPITVL

Nathaniel Hawthorne And Herman Melville C 20 MIN
3/4 OR 1/2 INCH VIDEO CASSETTE H-C A
Offers a dramatization of a visit from Herman Melville to Nathanel Hawthorne, with introductions by Mrs Hawthorne, while Moby Dick and The House of Seven Gables are in progress.
From The American Literature Series.
LC NO. 83-706254
Prod-AUBU Dist-AITECH 1983

Nation Among Equals, A C 30 MIN
3/4 OR 1/2 INCH VIDEO CASSETTE H-C A
See series title for descriptive statement.
From The Japan - The Changing Tradition Series.
Prod-UMA Dist-GPITVL 1978

Nation Builds Under Fire, A B 9 MIN
16MM FILM OPTICAL SOUND J-H
A look at South Vietnam in the summer of 1966 shows how the government of South Vietnam is attempting to build its power with the support of the United States.
From The Screen News Digest Series. Vol 9, Issue 1
Prod-HEARST Dist-HEARST 1966

Nation Builds Under Fire, A C 40 MIN
3/4 OR 1/2 INCH VIDEO CASSETTE
Tells the story of the struggle of the people of the Republic of Vietnam to build a nation while war rages around them. Documents the role of the American Serviceman in helping these people. Narrated by John Wayne.
Prod-IHF Dist-IHF

Nation Family, The C 51 MIN
16MM FILM, 3/4 OR 1/2 IN VIDEO I-C A
Outlines why the traditional customs of social consensus and loyalty are the backbone of Japan's postwar success. Illustrates the national penchant for long-term business planning by focusing on a shipping manufacturer who met the oil crisis head on.
LC NO. 84-706131
Prod-CANBC Dist-WOMBAT 1983

Nation In Crisis, A C 16 MIN
16MM FILM, 3/4 OR 1/2 IN VIDEO I-J
Explains the problems faced by the new nation as a result of the weakness of the Articles of Confederation and the resulting Constitutional Convention to create a true constitution to provide a strong federal government to save the new nation.
From The American History - Birth Of A Nation Series.
Prod-AIMS Dist-AIMS 1967

Nation In Touch, A C 26 MIN
16MM FILM OPTICAL SOUND
Describes the construction of the world's longest microwave system.
Prod-CFI Dist-CFI

Nation Is Born—A Series
16MM FILM, 3/4 OR 1/2 IN VIDEO P-I
Presents animated stories of famous incidents in the history of the United States.
Prod-PIC Dist-LUF

Boston Tea Party, The 8 MIN
Columbus 8 MIN
How The Colonies Grew 8 MIN
Pilgrims, The 8 MIN
Ragged Ragamuffins Of The Continental Army, The 8 MIN

Nation Of Immigrants C 52 MIN
16MM FILM, 3/4 OR 1/2 IN VIDEO J-C A
Compares and contrasts the immigrant experience in America for older, European-based immigrants with the modern immigrant experience for blacks, Puerto Ricans, Asians and Mexicans. Explains that they may be seen as a threat by descendents of earlier immigrants. Many are rediscovering their heritage.
From The Destination America Series.
Prod-THAMES Dist-MEDIAG 1976

Nation Of Immigrants, A B 52 MIN
16MM FILM OPTICAL SOUND
Traces the successive waves of immigration to the United States and highlights contributions to our democracy made by these immigrants. Based on late President Kennedy's book of the same title.
Prod-ADL Dist-ADL

Nation Of Immigrants, A B 53 MIN
16MM FILM, 3/4 OR 1/2 IN VIDEO I-C A
Presents the history of immigration of America, based on John F Kennedy's book A Nation Of Immigrants. Tells of the difficult adjustments the immigrants have had to make in the new land. Covers individuals who have achieved greatness in the period known as the 'great wave,' between 1880 and 1910, when 23 million people left their homelands to come to America.
Prod-FI Dist-FI 1967

Nation Of Islam, The B 30 MIN
16MM FILM OPTICAL SOUND H-C A
Dr C Eric Lincoln discusses the role of the Black Muslims under the leadership of Elijah Muhammad and Malcolm X in fulfilling the dream of black people.
From The Black History, Section 21 - Protest And Rebellion Series.
LC NO. 74-704114
Prod-WCBSTV Dist-HRAW 1969

Nation Of Painters, A C 7 MIN
16MM FILM, 3/4 OR 1/2 IN VIDEO J-C
Presents various painters and their works.
From The Art Awareness Collection Series.
Prod-USNGA Dist-EBEC 1973

Nation Of Spoilers, A (2nd Ed) C 13 MIN
16MM FILM, 3/4 OR 1/2 IN VIDEO I-H
Explores the growing problem of vandalism and illustrates some of the constructive ways in which young people can improve their communities.
Prod-HIGGIN Dist-HIGGIN 1978

Nation State - Dutch/Russian C 30 MIN
3/4 OR 1/2 INCH VIDEO CASSETTE H
Shows how the Netherlands and Russia struggled to become nation states. Documents the struggles of the Netherlands against Spanish control, the Dutch trading empire, and Russia's unification and attempts to westernize. Looks at the roles of Ivan II, Ivan IV, Peter The Great and Catherine the Great in Russian history.
From The Historically Speaking Series. Part 8
Prod-KRMATV Dist-AITECH 1983

Nation State - England C 30 MIN
3/4 OR 1/2 INCH VIDEO CASSETTE H
Shows the development of nation-state characteristics in England. Discusses William the Conqueror, Henry II, royal courts, common law and the jury system.
From The Historically Speaking Series. Part 7
Prod-KRMATV Dist-AITECH 1983

Nation State - France C 30 MIN
3/4 OR 1/2 INCH VIDEO CASSETTE H
Discusses the growth of absolute monarchy in France, the centralized tax system, the Hundred Years' War, Louis XIII and Richelieu, and Louis XIV and divine right.
From The Historically Speaking Series. Part 6
Prod-KRMATV Dist-AITECH 1983

Nation State - Spain C 30 MIN
3/4 OR 1/2 INCH VIDEO CASSETTE H
Presents the commonly accepted traits of a nation-state and the pattern of national development. Discusses the reconquista movement in Spain, the role of Ferdinand and Isabella, Charles V and Philip II. Gives examples of the art of El Greco and Velasquez.
From The Historically Speaking Series. Part 5
Prod-KRMATV Dist-AITECH 1983

Nation Uprooted, A - Afghan Refugees In Pakistan C 58 MIN
3/4 OR 1/2 INCH VIDEO CASSETTE
Documents the work, education, play and worship of the Afghans in exile in Pakistan. Reveals their situation and determination to maintain their endangered culture and traditions.
Prod-DNKMAN Dist-CPEA

Nation Within A Nation, A B 14 MIN
16MM FILM OPTICAL SOUND I-C A
Examines the winds of change that are sweeping across the lives of 140,000 Navajos on the largest Indian reservation in the world.
From The Screen News Digest Series. Vol 15, Issue 1
LC NO. 73-701267
Prod-HEARST Dist-HEARST 1972

National Aboretum, The C 14 MIN
3/4 INCH VIDEO CASSETTE
Presents a tour of the National Arboretum in Washington, D C, picturing the four seasons of the year. Pictured are the scientists who work there and the many varieties of plants.
Prod-USDA Dist-USDA 1972

National Advertising And Public Policy C 30 MIN
3/4 OR 1/2 INCH VIDEO CASSETTE H
Discusses what is, or should be, shown on free TV, public TV and pay TV with representatives of the Association of National Advertisers.
From The Contemporary Issues In Marketing Series.
Prod-CANTOR Dist-IVCH

National Anthem C 3 MIN
16MM FILM, 3/4 OR 1/2 IN VIDEO I-C A
Uses more that 100 engravings, cartoons, paintings and photographs to present a montage of American history from the early days of exploration to the space age.
Prod-SGA Dist-AIMS 1975

National Bible Quiz, The C 28 MIN
16MM FILM, 3/4 OR 1/2 IN VIDEO
Presents a variety of questions and answers about the Bible.
Prod-KLEINW Dist-KLEINW 1981

National Black History Landmarks B 20 MIN
3/4 OR 1/2 INCH VIDEO CASSETTE
Prod-RCOMTV Dist-SYLWAT 1978

National Cancer Quiz C 60 MIN
3/4 OR 1/2 INCH VIDEO CASSETTE
Shows the 1984 Cable TV Special produced by the American Cancer Society National Cable TV Association and Tumor Broadcasting System. Focuses on three cancer sites - lung, breast, and colorectal, and addresses risk-assessment question posed in quiz-style.
Prod-AMCS Dist-AMCS 1984

National Center For Atmospheric Research C 29 MIN
3/4 OR 1/2 INCH VIDEO CASSETTE H-C A
Presents atmospheric researchers in eastern Montana who are challenged by the fact that natural changes occurring in our climate may be further enhanced by new changes caused through human activity.
From The Creativity With Bill Moyers Series.
LC NO. 83-707213
Prod-CORPEL Dist-PBS 1982

National Committee For Electrical Engineering Films—A Series
C
Prod-EDS Dist-EDC 1970

Basic Electromechanical Instrument Mechanism 29 MIN
Harmonic Phasors 7 MIN
Harmonic Phasors II 18 MIN
Introduction To The General-Purpose 24 MIN

National Crime And Violence Test—A Series
16MM FILM, 3/4 OR 1/2 IN VIDEO
Looks at what people should do when faced with the possibility of robbery or rape.
Prod-MTI Dist-MTI

What Would You Do If A Robber Stuck A Gun In
What Would You Really Do If Accosted By A 040 MIN

National Crime Prevention Test, The, Pt 1 - Before It Happens C 30 MIN
16MM FILM, 3/4 OR 1/2 IN VIDEO J-C A
Discusses methods of preventing crimes in and around the home and neighborhood. Focuses on burglary, child abuse, battered wives, locks and safety devices, and Project Identification and Neighborhood Watch programs.
Prod-HAR Dist-MTI Prodn-CALVIN 1978

National Crime Prevention Test, The, Pt 2 - The Odds Against Yesterday C 30 MIN
16MM FILM, 3/4 OR 1/2 IN VIDEO J-C A
Discusses methods of preventing crime on the street and in businesses. Focuses on juvenile crime, shoplifting, white collar crimes, auto theft, crimes against the elderly and general street safety.
Prod-HAR Dist-MTI Prodn-CALVIN 1978

National Crisis - The Limits Of Politics C 29 MIN
2 INCH VIDEOTAPE
See series title for descriptive statement.
From The Black Experience Series.
Prod-WTTWTV Dist-PUBTEL

National Day 1971 C 20 MIN
16MM FILM OPTICAL SOUND
Shows the National Day celebrations during 1971 in the Malaysian city of Kuala Lumpur with the focus on the youth of the country.
Prod-FILEM Dist-PMFMUN 1971

National Dental Care Quiz, The C 14 MIN
16MM FILM, 3/4 OR 1/2 IN VIDEO P-H
Uses an exchange between a studio audience and television star Don Wescott to raise questions and answers about dental care.
Prod-KLEINW Dist-KLEINW 1981

National Diet Quiz, The C 28 MIN
16MM FILM, 3/4 OR 1/2 IN VIDEO H-C A
Presents a quiz about dieting and obesity.
Prod-KLEINW Dist-KLEINW 1981

National Diffusion Network - An Overview Of Educational Programs That Work C 39 MIN
3/4 OR 1/2 INCH VIDEO CASSETTE
Shows what the National Diffusion Network is, what it does and how, and with what success. Describes its elements and its role and relationship to the NDH and the Joint Dissemination Review Panel.
From The National Diffusion Network Series.
Prod-FWLERD Dist-USNAC 1982

National Diffusion Network - Educational Programs That Work C 28 MIN
3/4 OR 1/2 INCH VIDEO CASSETTE
Shows the needs, problems, resources, false starts and procedures involved in a school's adoption of a program approved by the Joint Dissemination Review Panel.
From The National Diffusion Network Series.
Prod-FWLERD Dist-USNAC 1982

National Diffusion Network—A Series

Describes the National Diffusion Network and its criteria, quality control mechanism and procedures.
Prod-FWLERD Dist-USNAC 1982

Joint Dissemination Review
National Diffusion Network - An Overview Of 039 MIN
National Diffusion Network - Educational 028 MIN

National Disaster Survival Test, The C 45 MIN
16MM FILM, 3/4 OR 1/2 IN VIDEO
Discusses public, home, industry and traffic safety within the context of such disasters as fires, floods, tornadoes, hurricanes, earthquakes and other potentially life-threatening situations.
Prod-MTI Dist-MTI

National Driving Test, The C 29 MIN
16MM FILM, 3/4 OR 1/2 IN VIDEO J-H A
Reconstructs traffic accidents to show who was wrong and how the accidents could have been avoided. Offers true/false questions relating to the reenactments and to other basic driving habits.
Prod-CTV Dist-MTI 1981

National Economy Quiz, The C 28 MIN
16MM FILM OPTICAL SOUND H
Explores key elements of the American economy in the form of a quiz.
Prod-AETNA Dist-AETNA 1976

National Family Planning Programs - Restoring The Balance (Spanish) C 28 MIN
16MM FILM OPTICAL SOUND
Presents family planning program leaders from several countries in Asia, Africa, Latin America and the Middle East discussing their feelings, experiences and hopes for family planning in their regions.
From The International Population Programs (Spanish) Series.
LC NO. 76-700101
Prod-USOPOP Dist-USNAC Prodn-AIRLIE 1974

National Family Planning Programs - Restoring The Balance C 28 MIN
16MM FILM OPTICAL SOUND
Presents family planning program leaders from several countries in Asia, Africa, Latin America and the Middle East as they discuss their feelings, experiences and hopes for family planning in their regions.
From The International Population Programs Series.
LC NO. 75-704431
Prod-USOPOP Dist-USNAC Prodn-AIRLIE 1974

National Federation Sports Films—A Series
T
Explains the rules and correct officiating procedures for various sports.
Prod-NFSHSA Dist-NFSHSA Prodn-TWCF 1975

Basketball At Its Best 028 MIN
Challenge Of Track And Field, The 028 MIN
Goal To Go - The Rules Of Football 027 MIN
Key Goals To Winning Soccer, The 017 MIN
One Step Ahead - A Guide To Better 017 MIN
Volleyball - The Winning Points 017 MIN
Volleyball Today 017 MIN
Winning Edge, The - Wrestling By The Rules 017 MIN

National Fire Drill, The C 29 MIN
16MM FILM, 3/4 OR 1/2 IN VIDEO I-H A
Re-enacts case studies of fire situations to demonstrate the safest course of action.
Prod-CTV Dist-MTI 1981

National Fisheries Center And Aquarium C 11 MIN
16MM FILM, 3/4 OR 1/2 IN VIDEO
Shows the architecture of the National Aquarium, something of what it contains, and the general philosophies and disciplines involved.
Prod-EAMES Dist-PFP 1967

National Folk Festival, Pt 1 B 10 MIN
16MM FILM OPTICAL SOUND
Includes Western German and Philippine dances, a New England barn dance and the Scottish Highland fling.
LC NO. FIE52-2099
Prod-USA Dist-USNAC 1950

National Folk Festival, Pt 2 B 10 MIN
16MM FILM OPTICAL SOUND
Includes Polish, English, Croatian, American Indian, Lithuanian, Ukrainian, Texas and Tennessee dances and Negro and Yugoslav songs.
LC NO. FIE52-2100
Prod-USA Dist-USNAC 1950

National Folk Festival, Pt 3 B 10 MIN
16MM FILM OPTICAL SOUND
Includes Israeli, Russian, Czechoslovakian and American dances, Ozark ballads, songs of Pennsylvania coal miners, Spanish American songs and 'CASEY JONES.'
LC NO. FIE52-2101
Prod-USA Dist-USNAC

National Football League Highlights—A Series

Presents the best of action plays in the National Football League competition.
Prod-NBC Dist-NBC

National Football League Highlights - 1957 30 MIN
National Football League Highlights - 1958 30 MIN
National Football League Highlights - 1959 30 MIN
National Football League Highlights - 1960 30 MIN
National Football League Highlights - 1961 30 MIN
National Football League Highlights - 1962 30 MIN
National Football League Highlights - 1963 30 MIN
National Football League Highlights - 1964 30 MIN
National Football League Highlights - 1965 30 MIN

National Gallery Builds, The C 13 MIN
16MM FILM OPTICAL SOUND
Illustrates highlights of conception and construction of the East Building of the National Gallery, beginning with the challenge initially faced by architect I M Pei. Continues through various phases of construction and includes footage on the special works of art commissioned for the building from artists of international reputation such as Henry Moore and Alexander Calder.
Prod-USNGA Dist-USNGA

National Gas Saver's Quiz, The C 28 MIN
16MM FILM, 3/4 OR 1/2 IN VIDEO J-C A
Features television stars McLean Stevenson and JoAnn Pflug in a quiz show which tells how to save on fuel expenses.
LC NO. 81-707095
Prod-KLEINW Dist-KLEINW 1981

National Health Insurance - Should The Federal Government Provide Comprehensive... C 59 MIN
3/4 INCH VIDEO CASSETTE
Asks whether the federal government should provide comprehensive health insurance for every citizen. Features debaters Patricia Butler and William Rusher.
From The Advocates Series.
Prod-WGBHTV Dist-PUBTEL

National Hearing Quiz, The C 30 MIN
16MM FILM, 3/4 OR 1/2 IN VIDEO J-C A
Discusses hearing loss, covering what noise is, how it threatens health, which noises are the most dangerous, other contributions to hearing loss, and how to protect oneself from excessive noise.
LC NO. 83-706918
Prod-KLEINW Dist-KLEINW

National High Blood Pressure Quiz, The C 30 MIN
16MM FILM, 3/4 OR 1/2 IN VIDEO J-C A

Presents newscaster Peter Hackes asking questions about the disease of hypertension. Discusses how to detect high blood pressure, what causes it, how to treat it, who gets it and why it is called a silent disease.
Prod-KLEINW Dist-KLEINW 1979

National Income Tax Quiz, The C 28 MIN
16MM FILM, 3/4 OR 1/2 IN VIDEO H-C A
Presents a quiz which reveals information about income tax.
Prod-KLEINW Dist-KLEINW 1981

National Kids' Quiz C 30 MIN
3/4 INCH VIDEO CASSETTE I-J
Features Michael Landon in a discussion about the problems that trouble many teenagers. Offers re-created scenes of family and school dilemmas, involving such values as honesty, the right to privacy, and loyalty.
Prod-BANPRO Dist-GA

National LP Gas Energy Quiz, The C 30 MIN
16MM FILM, 3/4 OR 1/2 IN VIDEO
Discusses liquified petroleum gas, comparing LP gas with electricity, natural gas, fuel oil and coal.
Prod-KLEINW Dist-KLEINW

National Meat Quiz, The C 30 MIN
16MM FILM, 3/4 OR 1/2 IN VIDEO J-C A
Answers questions about meat, the costliest of consumer food expenses.
Prod-KLEINW Dist-KLEINW

National Naval Medical Center C 28 MIN
16MM FILM OPTICAL SOUND
Illustrates the nationwide mission of the National Naval Medical Center at Bethesda, Maryland, in personnel training, patient treatment and research projects.
LC NO. 74-706155
Prod-USN Dist-USNAC 1966

National Nuclear Debate, The C 120 MIN
3/4 OR 1/2 INCH VIDEO CASSETTE
Presents journalist Jim Lehrer moderating a debate commemorating the first anniversary of the Three Mile Island nuclear accident. Includes experts from both sides of the controversy.
Prod-WITFTV Dist-PBS 1980

National Nutrition Quiz C 60 MIN
3/4 OR 1/2 INCH VIDEO CASSETTE
Leads viewers through the bewildering maze of foodstuffs, and explores facts and fantasies about nutrition. Provides up-to-date scientific data on the protective and destructive properties of food eaten during a given day and its relationship to obesity, diabetes, heart disease and cancer. Hosted by health advocates Jane Brody and David Watts MD.
Prod-PBS Dist-PBS

National Parks - Our Treasured Lands C 28 MIN
16MM FILM, 3/4 OR 1/2 IN VIDEO
Outlines the geographic scope and diversity of sites within the U S National Park system and explains how use of these areas is people-oriented. Narrated by Wally Schirra.
Prod-USNPS Dist-USNAC 1983

National Parks - Playground Or Paradise C 59 MIN
16MM FILM, 3/4 OR 1/2 IN VIDEO
Presents both sides of the ongoing debate between conservationists and environmentalists over the use of the national parks. Uses views of Yellowstone, Yosemite and the Grand Canyon to point out the dilemma as attorney Eric Julber and professor of history and environmental studies Roderick Nash debate the issue.
LC NO. 80-706332
Prod-WQED Dist-NGS 1981

National Parks 1 C 30 MIN
3/4 OR 1/2 INCH VIDEO CASSETTE C
Shows national parks as outdoor laboratories in which the effects of weathering, erosion, deposition, volcanic activity and metamorphism can be observed and studied firsthand. Uses Yellowstone, the Petrified Forest and Padre Island National Parks as examples.
From The Earth, Sea And Sky Series.
Prod-DALCCD Dist-DALCCD

National Parks 2 C 30 MIN
3/4 OR 1/2 INCH VIDEO CASSETTE C
Examines Mesa Verde, Platt and Big Bend, three unique national parks.
From The Earth, Sea And Sky Series.
Prod-DALCCD Dist-DALCCD

National Parks, Promise And Challenge C 23 MIN
16MM FILM, 3/4 OR 1/2 IN VIDEO J-C A
Examines the dual purposes of U S national parks to preserve natural wonders and to serve as recreation areas for the public. Visits Yosemite, Yellowstone and the Grand Canyon, discussing the conflict between developers and conservationists.
LC NO. 82-706275
Prod-NGS Dist-NGS 1981

National Political Campaigning In Other Countries - A Better Answer? C 30 MIN
3/4 OR 1/2 INCH VIDEO CASSETTE
Compares foreign campaigns in such countries as England, West Germany and Canada to those in the United States. Covers fairness and equal time provided by international media and the differing durations of time allocated for primary elections in the United States and abroad. Includes panelists from several countries.
From The Issues In World Communications, 1980 Series.
Prod-OHUTC Dist-OHUTC

National Remembrance, A C 15 MIN
16MM FILM, 3/4 OR 1/2 IN VIDEO
Shows the placing of the presidential wreath at the Tomb of the Unknown Soldier by Max Cleland, Administrator of Veteran Affairs, personal representative of President Carter.
LC NO. 81-707121
Prod-USVA Dist-USNAC 1979

National Save-A-Life Test, The C 52 MIN
16MM FILM, 3/4 OR 1/2 IN VIDEO J-C A
Offers a TV quiz with multiple choice and true-false questions covering such topics as choking, chemical poisoning, automobile accidents, heart attacks, drowning, mugging, driving while intoxicated and home fires. Hosted by Michael Learned and Bernie Kopell.
LC NO. 84-706734
Prod-DBA Dist-FI 1984

National Schiller Museum In Marbach, The C 5 MIN
16MM FILM, 3/4 OR 1/2 IN VIDEO
Describes Marbach, Germany, and explores the museum erected there to the memory of Friedrich Schiller.
From The European Studies - Germany Series. Part 5
Prod-BAYER Dist-IFB 1973

National Scream, The C 28 MIN
16MM FILM, 3/4 OR 1/2 IN VIDEO J-C A
Offers a tongue-in-cheek look at Canada and Canadians. Explains how and why the beaver became the country's symbol. Uses animation and pseudo-documentary style to depict Canada's search for a national identity.
Prod-NFBC Dist-NFBC 1980

National Security And Freedom Of The Press C 60 MIN
3/4 OR 1/2 INCH VIDEO CASSETTE
Questions whether the Constitution grants the American public a right to know. Explores the federal government's ability to conduct what it deems an effective foreign policy within a constitutional framework that demands a free, unfettered press.
From The Constitution - That Delicate Balance Series.
Prod-WTTWTV Dist-FI 1984

National Student Fire Safety Test, The C 12 MIN
16MM FILM, 3/4 OR 1/2 IN VIDEO P-J S
Introduces questions concerning fire safety, dealing with such issues as the dangers of electrical heating and flammable clothing.
From The National Student Safety Test Series.
Prod-BELCHJ Dist-WDEMCO 1979

National Student First Aid Safety Test, The C 12 MIN
16MM FILM, 3/4 OR 1/2 IN VIDEO P-J S
Introduces questions concerning first aid safety, dealing with such problems as severe bleeding and serious sunburn.
From The National Student Safety Test Series.
Prod-BELCHJ Dist-WDEMCO 1979

National Student Recreational Safety Test, The C 12 MIN
16MM FILM, 3/4 OR 1/2 IN VIDEO P-J S
Introduces questions concerning recreational safety. Describes the appropriate clothing for active sports and discusses injuries received in play activities.
From The National Student Safety Test Series.
Prod-BELCHJ Dist-WDEMCO 1979

National Student Safety Test—A Series
16MM FILM, 3/4 OR 1/2 IN VIDEO P-J S
Provides basic questions and answers on such topics as recreational safety, first aid, school safety, traffic safety and fire safety.
Prod-BELCHJ Dist-WDEMCO 1979

National Student Fire Safety Test, The 012 MIN
National Student First Aid Safety Test, The 012 MIN
National Student Recreational Safety Test, The 012 MIN
National Student School Safety Test, The 012 MIN
National Student Traffic Safety Test, The 012 MIN

National Student School Safety Test, The C 12 MIN
16MM FILM, 3/4 OR 1/2 IN VIDEO P-J S
Introduces questions concerning school safety, including such issues as school accidents and school fights.
From The National Student Safety Test Series.
Prod-BELCHJ Dist-WDEMCO 1979

National Student Traffic Safety Test, The C 12 MIN
16MM FILM, 3/4 OR 1/2 IN VIDEO P-J S
Introduces questions concerning traffic safety. Discusses crossing streets, selecting a route, and being concerned with people's safety.
From The National Student Safety Test Series.
Prod-BELCHJ Dist-WDEMCO 1979

National Theater Of The Deaf C 44 MIN
3/4 OR 1/2 INCH VIDEO CASSETTE I A
Shows the National Theater Of The Deaf from New York as it tours Holland.
Prod-SUTHRB Dist-SUTHRB

National Theatre School C 13 MIN
16MM FILM OPTICAL SOUND
Depicts the day-to-day activities at the National Theatre School of Canada, including voice training, improvisations and fencing, as well as makeup, costume and set design classes.
LC NO. 77-702991
Prod-CBCLS Dist-INCC Prodn-BASSTJ 1975

National Velvet C
1/2 IN VIDEO CASSETTE BETA/VHS
Presents Enid Bagnold's story of a girl striving to win a riding championship, starring Elizabeth Taylor and Mickey Rooney.
Prod-GA Dist-GA

National Water Safety Test C 29 MIN
16MM FILM OPTICAL SOUND P-C A
Features comedian Pat Paulsen in a series of multiple choice vignettes illustrating the correct and incorrect things to do in 12 basic water safety situations.
LC NO. 78-713269
Prod-AMRC Dist-AMRC 1971

National Youth Day B 10 MIN
16MM FILM OPTICAL SOUND
Covers the activities of the 1970 National Youth Day in Malaysia including a parade at the Merdeka Stadium.
Prod-FILEM Dist-PMFMUN 1970

Nationalism C 30 MIN
3/4 OR 1/2 INCH VIDEO CASSETTE C
See series title for descriptive statement.
From The American Story - The Beginning To 1877 Series.
Prod-DALCCD Dist-DALCCD

Nationalism And Revolution C 60 MIN
3/4 OR 1/2 INCH VIDEO CASSETTE J-C A
Presents flutist James Galway discussing the classical composers who sought to express political causes in music. Includes music from Berlioz' Requiem, Liszt's Fantasia on Hungarian Folk Themes and Wagner's Siegfried Idyll.
From The James Galway's Music In Time Series.
Prod-POLTEL Dist-FOTH 1982

Nationalists, The (Captioned) C 28 MIN
16MM FILM, 3/4 OR 1/2 IN VIDEO A
Discusses the Puerto Rican independence movement and the activities of the Puerto Rican Nationalist Party in the 1950's. Discusses the shooting incident by four nationalists in March 1954 which resulted in the wounding of two U S Congressmen, and portrays the movements's leading figure, Don Pedro Albizy Campos. Spanish dialog with English subtitles.
Prod-TORREJ Dist-CNEMAG 1973

Native Aliens, The C 22 MIN
3/4 OR 1/2 INCH VIDEO CASSETTE
Discusses the problems and needs of the Hispanic community relating to federal employment.
Prod-VAMCSL Dist-USNAC

Native American Arts C 20 MIN
16MM FILM, 3/4 OR 1/2 IN VIDEO
Surveys native American art, including that of the Indian, Eskimo and Aleut. Shows how efforts in education, community cultural organizations and governmental encouragement are helping native American artists achieve important economic goals and new concepts of cultural identity. Issued in 1974 as a motion picture.
LC NO. 80-706281
Prod-USIACB Dist-USNAC Prodn-DESCEN 1980

Native American Myths C 24 MIN
16MM FILM, 3/4 OR 1/2 IN VIDEO I-H
Presents five animated myths that tell stories of demons, sorcery and the Indian's love for Mother Earth.
From The Wide World Of Adventure Series.
Prod-AVATLI Dist-EBEC 1977

Native American—A Series
16MM FILM, 3/4 OR 1/2 IN VIDEO I-J
Discusses the origin of the American Indians, their diversity as a people and the ways in which the coming of Europeans affected them.
Prod-JOU Dist-JOU 1976

Indian Cultures - From 2000 BC To 1500 AD 019 MIN
Indian Experience, The - After 1500 AD 019 MIN
Indian Origins - The First 50,000 Years 018 MIN

Native Americans—A Series
16MM FILM, 3/4 OR 1/2 IN VIDEO
Covers the history of the North American Indian, focusing on tribes and groups of tribes that illustrate the culture of key regions.
Prod-BBCTV Dist-CNEMAG

Cherokee 026 MIN
Civilized Tribes 026 MIN
How The West Was Lost 026 MIN
Indian Country 026 MIN
Navajo, Race For Prosperity 026 MIN
Potlatch People 026 MIN
Pueblo Renaissance 026 MIN
Six Nations, The 026 MIN
They Promised To Take Our Land 026 MIN
Trail Of Broken Treaties 026 MIN

Native Hawaiian Plants C 30 MIN
1/2 IN VIDEO CASSETTE BETA/VHS
Explores Waimea Falls Park at Oahu, Hawaii. Shows how to make cucumber soup.
From The Victory Garden Series.
Prod-WGBHTV Dist-MTI

Native Indian Treasures - Adapting Indian Art 20th Century Needlecraft C 30 MIN
3/4 OR 1/2 INCH VIDEO CASSETTE
Demonstrates how to adapt Indian art to needlework in ponchos, and the use of silver thread embroidery in making Indian jewelry.
From The Erica Series.
Prod-WGBHTV Dist-KINGFT

Native Land, The C 17 MIN
16MM FILM, 3/4 OR 1/2 IN VIDEO P-C A
Provides an Indian point of view about land and heritage. Narrated by an Indian mother using Indian chronicles and sayings.
Prod-ATLAP Dist-ATLAP 1977

Native Medicine C 60 MIN
3/4 OR 1/2 INCH VIDEO CASSETTE H-C A
Contrasts the practice of modern medicine in an English town

with the traditional magical system of the Azande tribe. Based on the book The Body In Question by Jonathan Miller. Narrated by Jonathan Miller.
From The Body In Question Series. Program 9
LC NO. 81-706953
Prod-BBCTV Dist-FI 1979

Native Music Of The North-West–A Series

Prod-WASU Dist-WASU Prodn-CHVANP

Sla-Hal, The Bone Game 027 MIN

Native Transplants And Crude Drugs C 18 MIN
16MM FILM OPTICAL SOUND P-I
Illustrates how certain species of native trees and shrubs are identified in the forest, commercially dug and prepared for shipment to commercial nurseries. Shows how raw drug products are identified, and also gathered for sale to pharmaceutical companies.
From The Man And The Forest Series. Part 4
Prod-MMP Dist-MMP 1972

Natives Of East Africa C 11 MIN
16MM FILM OPTICAL SOUND H-C A
Depicts the cultures, customs and activities of the East African natives with emphasis on the Masai, Galla and Secuma tribes. Describes the history and economic importance of Kenya, Tanganyika, Mombasa, Nairobi and Uganda.
Prod-CBF Dist-AVED 1960

NATO - After 25 Years C 13 MIN
3/4 OR 1/2 INCH VIDEO CASSETTE
Analyzes the first quarter century of the North Atlantic Treaty Organization.
Prod-UPI Dist-JOU

NATO - Past, Present, Future B 20 MIN
16MM FILM OPTICAL SOUND
Presents an exclusive report on the fate and future of the North Atlantic Treaty Organization
From The Screen News Digest Series. Volume 9, Issue 2
Prod-HEARST Dist-HEARST 1966

NATO Seapower For Peace B 28 MIN
16MM FILM OPTICAL SOUND
Reviews the activities and functions of SACLANT (Supreme Allied Command Atlantic) and its capabilities for the defense of NATO.
Prod-USN Dist-USNAC 1957

Natsik Hunting C 8 MIN
16MM FILM OPTICAL SOUND
Presents a documentary of a seal hunt on Baffin Island, photographed by an Inuit filmmaker.
LC NO. 76-702091
Prod-CDIAND Dist-CDIAND Prodn-NFBC 1975

Natural Balance, The C 15 MIN
3/4 OR 1/2 INCH VIDEO CASSETTE I-J
Describes the natural balance of plants and animals. Explains how weather, overpopulation, lack of food, and human interference can upset the natural balance.
From The Bioscope Series.
Prod-MAETEL Dist-AITECH 1981

Natural Chanel Hydraulics–A Series
C A
Includes properties of sediments, surface erosion processes, application of the universal soil loss equation to engineering problems and an emphasis on Elinstein's bed lood function. Contains 40 one-hour videotapes.
Prod-UIDEEO Dist-UIDEEO

Natural Childbirth C 10 MIN
16MM FILM, 3/4 OR 1/2 IN VIDEO H-C A
Presents a natural childbirth stressing the participation of both husband and wife. Concludes in the delivery room when they both respond to their newborn.
Prod-MIFE Dist-MIFE 1974

Natural Childbirth (French) C
3/4 OR 1/2 INCH VIDEO CASSETTE
Presents a natural childbirth stressing the participation of both husband and wife. Concludes in the delivery room when they both respond to their newborn.
Prod-MIFE Dist-MIFE

Natural Childbirth (Spanish) C
3/4 OR 1/2 INCH VIDEO CASSETTE
Presents a natural childbirth stressing the participation of both husband and wife. Concludes in the delivery room when they both respond to their newborn.
Prod-MIFE Dist-MIFE

Natural Curriculum, A C 29 MIN
3/4 OR 1/2 INCH VIDEO CASSETTE T
Presents an overview of theoretical alternatives that may be used to teach reading and writing.
From The Authoring Cycle - Read Better, Write Better, Reason Better Series.
Prod-IU Dist-HNEDBK

Natural Domain - Birds And Animals In Japan C 30 MIN
16MM FILM OPTICAL SOUND
Introduces some of the rare and fascinating birds and animals found in Japan, such as the rare serow and the wild monkeys of Kyushu. Shows how the Japanese have taken steps to reverse some of the damage caused by pollution and rapid urbanization.
Prod-MTP Dist-MTP

Natural Enemies Of Insect Pests C 27 MIN
16MM FILM, 3/4 OR 1/2 IN VIDEO
Explains the use of beneficial insects to control harmful insect species. Shows the effects of insecticides on beneficial insects.
Prod-UCEMC Dist-UCEMC

Natural Environment–A Series
16MM FILM, 3/4 OR 1/2 IN VIDEO J-H
Presents information about such natural environments as the Amazon region, the North American desert and Antarctica.
Prod-WILFGP Dist-JOU

Amazon 025 MIN
Antarctica - The Unowned Land 028 MIN
Desert Southwest, The 015 MIN
Florida Everglades, The 015 MIN
Galapagos - The Enchanted Islands 025 MIN
Great Lakes, The 014 MIN
High Plains, The - Caribou Country 018 MIN
Northern Lakes, The 014 MIN
Northwest, The - Mountains To The Sea 023 MIN
Voyage To The Arctic 025 MIN
Yukon Territory, The 015 MIN

Natural Forces And The Motorcycle C 14 MIN
16MM FILM OPTICAL SOUND H A
Demonstrates the forces of gravity, inertia, friction and impact and the fact that a thorough knowledge of these forces is necessary for the safe operation of motorcycles. Shows the correct wearing apparel.
From The American Honda Series.
Prod-AHONDA Dist-AHONDA

Natural Gas - Supply And Demand C 28 MIN
16MM FILM OPTICAL SOUND J-H
Presents the problem facing the natural gas industry of increasing demand and dwindling supplies. Traces the formation of natural gas over millions of years and explores various steps being taken to increase gas reserves.
From The Energy - An Overview Series.
Prod-CENTRO Dist-CONPOW

Natural Gas And Clean Air B 22 MIN
16MM FILM OPTICAL SOUND
Examines the major types and sources of air pollution and shows how pollution is measured. Explains that natural gas can eliminate dangerous pollutants entirely where it replaces other fuels.
LC NO. 70-711357
Prod-UGC Dist-BUGAS 1970

Natural Gas And Clean Air C 25 MIN
3/4 OR 1/2 INCH VIDEO CASSETTE
Examines the major types and sources of air pollution, shows how they are measured and how natural gas can eliminate most dangerous pollutants entirely when it replaces other fuels.
Prod-IVCH Dist-IVCH

Natural Gas Fuel Cell C 18 MIN
16MM FILM OPTICAL SOUND
Discusses the adaptation of space age technology used in the Apollo trips to the moon as a down-to-earth power source which provides a more efficient use of fuel with absolutely no air pollutants.
Prod-BUGAS Dist-BUGAS 1972

Natural Gas Fuel Cell C 20 MIN
3/4 OR 1/2 INCH VIDEO CASSETTE
Traces the development of the natural gas fuel cell from the discovery of its basic concepts to its application as a self-contained power plant for home and industrial use.
Prod-IVCH Dist-IVCH

Natural Gas In The '80s C 13 MIN
16MM FILM OPTICAL SOUND
Discusses the role that natural gas plays in the American economy and looks at future sources of gas energy. Presents the story of natural gas exploration, production, transmission, distribution and use.
Prod-FINLYS Dist-AGA 1980

Natural Gas Industry's The Blue Flame C 5 MIN
16MM FILM OPTICAL SOUND
Shows the world land speed record being broken at Bonneville, Utah by the Blue Flame, a vehicle using liquid natural gas as its fuel.
LC NO. 70-710884
Prod-IGT Dist-PROGRP 1970

Natural Highs And How To Get Them C
3/4 OR 1/2 INCH VIDEO CASSETTE J-H
Recognizes that everyone has the potential for getting high naturally and experiencing jubilant feeling without drugs. Designed as a drug education program. Includes teacher's guide.
Prod-SUNCOM Dist-SUNCOM

Natural History Of A Sunbeam–A Series
J-H
Discusses the sun's energy and its relationship to life on earth with explanations and experiments in chemistry, physics and biology.
Prod-KINGFT Dist-KINGFT

Candles From The Sun, Pt 1 030 MIN
Candles From The Sun, Pt 2 030 MIN
First Light, Pt 1 030 MIN
First Light, Pt 2 030 MIN
Leaf From Nature, A, Pt 1 030 MIN
Leaf From Nature, A, Pt 2 030 MIN
Light And Life, Pt 1 030 MIN
Light And Life, Pt 2 030 MIN
Making Light Work, Pt 1 030 MIN
Making Light Work, Pt 2 030 MIN
Survival Under The Sun, Pt 1 030 MIN
Survival Under The Sun, Pt 2 030 MIN

Natural History Of Hepatocellular Carcinoma, The C 51 MIN
3/4 INCH VIDEO CASSETTE
Discusses research on tumor initiation and promotion in rats by injecting drugs at specified times.
Prod-UTAHTI Dist-UTAHTI

Natural History Of Our World, The - The Time Of Man C 50 MIN
16MM FILM, 3/4 OR 1/2 IN VIDEO J-C A
Traces a series of case studies of animal populations and primitive human cultures that have survived or perished according to their ability to adapt to their environment. Emphasizes that if man is to survive, he must maintain the environment that sustains him. Narrated by Richard Basehart.
Prod-EALING Dist-PHENIX 1970

Natural History Of Psychotic Illness In Childhood B 19 MIN
16MM FILM OPTICAL SOUND C T
Describes the evolution of a psychotic child from infancy to adolescence.
Prod-IPSY Dist-NYU 1960

Natural History Of The Water Closet C 29 MIN
3/4 OR 1/2 INCH VIDEO CASSETTE
Utilizes a creative combination of documentary, animation and original music to survey the evolution of the modern-day toilet, complete with detailed descriptions of its actions.
LC NO. 82-706620
Prod-WITFTV Dist-PBS 1980

Natural Ingredients - Development Of The Preschool And School-Age Child C 22 MIN
3/4 OR 1/2 INCH VIDEO CASSETTE H-C A
Presents journalist Reynelda Muse explaining why play may be the most important of all learning activities. Shows child-care providers summarizing how they handle the questions, doubts and fears of preschool to school-age children and discussing how the needs and behavior of school-age children differ from those of younger ones.
From The Spoonful Of Lovin' Series. No. 3
LC NO. 82-706063
Prod-KRMATV Dist-AITECH 1981

Natural Laws C 29 MIN
3/4 OR 1/2 INCH VIDEO CASSETTE
Tells how to maintain equilibrium between the vehicle and the roadway.
From The Right Way Series.
Prod-SCETV Dist-PBS 1982

Natural Liquified Gas C 14 MIN
16MM FILM OPTICAL SOUND PRO
Describes the storage and handling of methane in its liquified state.
Prod-LAFIRE Dist-LAFIRE

Natural Logarithm, The - Graph Of Y Inx C
3/4 INCH VIDEO CASSETTE
See series title for descriptive statement.
From The Calculus Series.
Prod-MDDE Dist-MDCPB

Natural Mysteries C 60 MIN
3/4 OR 1/2 INCH VIDEO CASSETTE H-C A
Explores medieval superstitions of ancient naturalists. Reveals that Frederick II of Hohenstaufen had a passion of falconry that resulted in the book On The Art Of Hunting With Birds.
From The Discovery Of Animal Behavior Series.
Prod-WNETTV Dist-FI 1982

Natural Numbers, Integers And Rational Numbers B 29 MIN
16MM FILM OPTICAL SOUND H
Reviews properties of natural numbers, discussing the closure, associative, commutative and distributive laws. Shows why zero and negative numbers are essential to the integer system. Introduces the reciprocal as a means of developing the rational number system.
From The Intermediate Algebra Series.
Prod-CALVIN Dist-MLA Prodn-UNIVFI 1959

Natural Outside Cartoon Objects C 15 MIN
2 INCH VIDEOTAPE
See series title for descriptive statement.
From The Charlie's Pad Series.
Prod-WSIU Dist-PUBTEL

Natural Phenomena–A Series
16MM FILM, 3/4 OR 1/2 IN VIDEO J-H
Focuses on various natural phenomena including glaciers, hurricanes and volcanoes.
Prod-JOU Dist-JOU

Geysers, Lava And Hot Spots 016 MIN
Hurricanes, Tornadoes And Other Weather 016 MIN
Lakes, Rivers And Other Water Sources 017 MIN
Land That Came In From The Cold, The 013 MIN
Life Between The Tides 020 MIN
Mountains And Mountain Building 016 MIN
Rocks, Fossils And Earth History 017 MIN
Spectacular Canyons 017 MIN
Trees, The Biggest And The Oldest Living 017 MIN
Volcanoes, Earthquakes And Earth Movements 016 MIN

Natural Resources C 10 MIN
3/4 INCH VIDEO CASSETTE P
Examines the many responsibilities of a park ranger. Shows how foresters do everthing from keeping parks clean to planning new parks.
Prod-MINIP Dist-GA

Natural Science Reading C 120 MIN
3/4 OR 1/2 INCH VIDEO CASSETTE
See series title for descriptive statement.
From The A C T Exam Preparation Series.
Prod-KRLSOF Dist-KRLSOF 1985

Natural Science—A Series
16MM FILM, 3/4 OR 1/2 IN VIDEO J-H
Depicts the flora and fauna of the desert, the prairie and the Rocky Mountains.
Prod-BARR Dist-BARR 1980

Desert, The (3rd Ed) 016 MIN
Prairie, The (3rd Ed) 015 MIN
Rocky Mountains, The (2nd Ed) 017 MIN

Natural Science, Tape 1 C 45 MIN
3/4 OR 1/2 INCH VIDEO CASSETTE H A
Prepares students for the College Level Examination Program (CLEP) tests in Natural Science. Explores astronomy.
From The CLEP General Examinations Series.
Prod-COMEX Dist-COMEX

Natural Science, Tape 2 C 45 MIN
3/4 OR 1/2 INCH VIDEO CASSETTE H A
Prepares students for the College Level Examination Program (CLEP) test in Natural Science. Focuses on aspects of earth science such as plate tectonics and earth's formation.
From The CLEP General Examinations Series.
Prod-COMEX Dist-COMEX

Natural Science, Tape 3 C 45 MIN
3/4 OR 1/2 INCH VIDEO CASSETTE H A
Prepares students for the College Level Examination Program (CLEP) tests in Natural Science. Explores the atmosphere, chemistry, atoms, molecules and radioactivity.
From The CLEP General Examinations Series.
Prod-COMEX Dist-COMEX

Natural Science, Tape 4 C 45 MIN
3/4 OR 1/2 INCH VIDEO CASSETTE H A
Prepares students for the College Level Examination Program (CLEP) tests in Natural Science. Focuses on biology.
From The CLEP General Examinations Series.
Prod-COMEX Dist-COMEX

Natural Science, Tape 5 C 45 MIN
3/4 OR 1/2 INCH VIDEO CASSETTE H A
Prepares students for the College Level Examination Program (CLEP) tests in Natural Science. Focuses on living things. Includes the plant and animal kingdoms.
From The CLEP General Examinations Series.
Prod-COMEX Dist-COMEX

Natural Selection X 16 MIN
16MM FILM, 3/4 OR 1/2 IN VIDEO H
Discusses the impact of the theory of evolution, emphasizing the concept of natural selection. Shows how studies by biologists on moths, mosquitoes and plants provide evidence of natural selection.
From The Biology Series. Unit 10 - Evolution
Prod-EBF Dist-EBEC 1963

Natural Selection C 20 MIN
3/4 OR 1/2 INCH VIDEO CASSETTE
Explains how drifting continents, island populations and genetic variability affect natural selection. Deals with the nature of clines.
From The Evolution Series.
Prod-FOTH Dist-FOTH 1984

Natural Selection (Spanish) C 16 MIN
16MM FILM, 3/4 OR 1/2 IN VIDEO H
Reports on three experiments concerning the role of natural selection in evolution. Describes a study of bird predation, a study of natural selection among plant populations and an investigation of insecticide-resistant mosquitoes.
From The Biology (Spanish) Series. Unit 10 - Evolution
Prod-EBEC Dist-EBEC

Natural Selection - Evolution At Work C 24 MIN
16MM FILM, 3/4 OR 1/2 IN VIDEO H-C
Shows how evolution depends on the availability of genetic variation. Uses as examples rats resistant to Warfarin and a copper-tolerant species of grass.
Prod-BBCTV Dist-MEDIAG 1981

Natural Tan, The C 14 MIN
16MM FILM, 3/4 OR 1/2 IN VIDEO J-C A
Presents pantomimes of a frustrated hero, trying vainly to gain a natural tan, to introduce information about proper exposure to the sun and sunlamps.
Prod-KLEINW Dist-KLEINW 1980

Natural Wonders Of Virginia C 20 MIN
16MM FILM OPTICAL SOUND I-H A
Pictures Virginia's natural wonders, such as the caverns, natural bridge, natural tunnel and natural chimneys. Points out their locations and their geological and historical significance.
Prod-VADE Dist-VADE 1961

Natural World C 29 MIN
3/4 INCH VIDEO CASSETTE
Focuses on different points of view and styles of landscape painting.
From The Creation Of Art Series.
Prod-UMITV Dist-UMITV 1975

Naturalists—A Series
16MM FILM, 3/4 OR 1/2 IN VIDEO J-C A
Profiles four renowned American naturalists of the 19th and early 20th centuries, Henry David Thoreau, Theodore Roosevelt, John Muir and John Burroughs. Includes significant excerpts from their writings, with filming on location where each man lived.
Prod-KRMATV Dist-IU 1977

Captain Of A Huckleberry Party, The - Henry
Earth-Planet, Universe - John Muir 29 MIN
He Who Has Planted Will Preserve - Theodore 28 MIN
How Far Are We From Home - John Burroughs 29 MIN

Naturalists—A Series

Profiles several of America's greatest conservationists and naturalists.
Prod-KRMATV Dist-PBS 1973

Henry David Thoreau - The Captain Of A
John Burroughs - How Far Are We From Home 028 MIN
John Muir - Earth-Planet, Universe 028 MIN
Theodore Roosevelt - He Who Has Planted 028 MIN

Naturally B 10 MIN
16MM FILM OPTICAL SOUND
Presents a documentary about a beauty school. Shows a group of girls learning how to walk, talk, 'DO' their hair and faces, and control their figures. Features the head of the school describing her aims, methods and values in relation to teaching girls how to be 'NATURAL,' and why such teaching is necessary.
Prod-UPENN Dist-UPENN 1970

Naturally Better Way - The Application Of Firefly Bioluminescence In The Microbiology Lab C 10 MIN
3/4 INCH VIDEO CASSETTE PRO
Provides an overview of the bioluminescent assay of adenosine triphosphate (ATP) and discusses its applications in the microbiology laboratory focusing on urine screening.
Prod-MMAMC Dist-MMAMC

Nature And Development Of Affection B 19 MIN
16MM FILM SILENT T
Illustrates observations and experiments which analyze variable underlying primate affection. Depicts rhesus monkeys, separated from mothers at birth, raised with cloth and wire surrogate mothers. Shows infants tested for mother preference under a variety of conditions, concluding that contact comfort is the primary variable determining affection of the rhesus for its mother.
LC NO. FIA68-2418
Prod-PSU Dist-PSUPCR 1959

Nature And Structure Of The Hair, The C
3/4 OR 1/2 INCH VIDEO CASSETTE
Provides an understanding of the nature of human hair for those who will go on to study the chemical and physical processes used in professional hair care. Explains the cuticle, cortex, medulla, macrofibrils, polypeptide chains, amino acids and melanin.
Prod-MPCEDP Dist-MPCEDP 1984

Nature And Theory Of Fire C 60 MIN
3/4 OR 1/2 INCH VIDEO CASSETTE IND
See series title for descriptive statement.
From The Industrial Fire Hazard Recognition And Control Series.
Prod-NCSU Dist-AMCEE

Nature As Impression C 11 MIN
16MM FILM OPTICAL SOUND J-C
Illustrates the impressionistic concept of viewing and painting nature.
From The Inspiration From Nature Series.
LC NO. 78-702484
Prod-ALEF Dist-ALEF 1969

Nature As Reality C 11 MIN
16MM FILM OPTICAL SOUND J-C
Illustrates the realistic concept of viewing and painting nature.
From The Inspiration From Nature Series.
LC NO. 71-702485
Prod-ALEF Dist-ALEF 1969

Nature Boy C 18 MIN
3/4 OR 1/2 INCH VIDEO CASSETTE
Shows a young Japanese boy at the Kwannon festival who is told by a mysterious voice to grasp happiness with his own hands. Depicts how, after first grasping only a straw, and through kindness to others, he receives fine fruit, rich cloth, a horse and, finally, his own land to cultivate.
Prod-GAKKEN Dist-EDMI 1983

Nature Craft - An Introduction C 13 MIN
16MM FILM, 3/4 OR 1/2 IN VIDEO I-C A
Discusses how to create art from natural objects like sea shells, leaves, flowers and stones.
Prod-LUF Dist-LUF 1979

Nature Guide Film—A Series

Prod-AVEXP Dist-AVEXP

Great White Pelican 19 MIN
My Pet Pelican 11 MIN
Pelican Island 28 MIN
Return To Pelican Island 26 MIN

Nature In The City C 13 MIN
16MM FILM, 3/4 OR 1/2 IN VIDEO K-I
Shows how grackles, pigeons, house mice, cockroaches, spiders, ants, bees, butterflies, gray squirrels, robbins and earth worms live, develop and adapt to their environment in the city.
Prod-WER Dist-JOU 1971

Nature Is An Artist C 25 MIN
2 INCH VIDEOTAPE I
Points out the design qualities in nature.
From The Art Has Many Forms Series.
Prod-CVETVC Dist-GPITVL

Nature Is Corrupt, Baby Master C 6 MIN
3/4 OR 1/2 INCH VIDEO CASSETTE
Brings together weather, suprematism, death and swimming, for a soothing effect.
Prod-KITCHN Dist-KITCHN

Nature Of Anthropology, The C 30 MIN
3/4 INCH VIDEO CASSETTE C A
Reviews the interdisciplinary nature of anthropology. Looks briefly at the history of the discipline. Includes comments of anthropologists regarding anthropology as a science.
From The Faces Of Culture - Studies In Cultural Anthropology Series. Lesson 1
Prod-COAST Dist-CDTEL Prodn-HRAW

Nature Of Color, The (2nd Ed) C 10 MIN
16MM FILM, 3/4 OR 1/2 IN VIDEO I-H
Discusses Newton's explanation of the rainbow, the principles of color reflection and absorption, the mixing of colors and the application of color principles to painting, printing and photography.
From The Nature Of Energy Series.
Prod-CORF Dist-CORF 1977

Nature Of Communication, The C 30 MIN
3/4 OR 1/2 INCH VIDEO CASSETTE C
See series title for descriptive statement.
From The Writing For A Reason Series.
Prod-DALCCD Dist-DALCCD

Nature Of Crude Oil And Natural Gas, The C 11 MIN
3/4 OR 1/2 INCH VIDEO CASSETTE IND
Shows how oil and gas are measured, molecular structure of hydrocarbon change, and which contaminants occur naturally in oil and gas deposits.
From The Overview Of The Petroleum Industry Series.
Prod-GPCV Dist-GPCV

Nature Of Culture, The C 30 MIN
3/4 INCH VIDEO CASSETTE C A
Presents basic aspects of the concept of culture. Defines ethnocentrism and cultural relativism. Gives examples of the aspects of culture in a variety of cultures and societies.
From The Faces Of Culture - Studies In Cultural Anthropology Series. Lesson 2
Prod-COAST Dist-CDTEL Prodn-HRAW

Nature Of Digital Computing, The B
16MM FILM OPTICAL SOUND
Deals with the fundamental ideas underlying the computing process.
Prod-OPENU Dist-OPENU

Nature Of Energy—A Series
16MM FILM, 3/4 OR 1/2 IN VIDEO J-C
Describes the characteristics of color, light and sound.
Prod-CORF Dist-CORF

Nature Of Color, The (2nd Ed) 10 MIN
Nature Of Light, The (2nd Ed) 17 MIN
Nature Of Sound, The (2nd Ed) 14 MIN

Nature Of Glass C 38 MIN
16MM FILM OPTICAL SOUND
Discusses the nature and structure of glass, its mechanical, thermal, electrical, chemical and optical properties, their bearing on its applications, graded seals and glass-to-metal and special glasses.
Prod-CORGLW Dist-CORGLW 1958

Nature Of Human Color Change, The - Genetic, Hormonal And Neoplastic B 90 MIN
16MM FILM OPTICAL SOUND PRO
Depicts the importance of melanin pigmentation and its relationship to systemic disease. Uses patients, marine animals, mice, film, charts and slides to demonstrate the basic science aspects.
From The Boston Medical Reports Series.
LC NO. 74-705190
Prod-NMAC Dist-NMAC 1968

Nature Of Language And How It Is Learned, The B 32 MIN
16MM FILM OPTICAL SOUND H T
Discusses the nature of language, how it is learned and the validity of the oral approach to teaching. Presents examples of speech from all over the world.
From The Principles And Methods Of Teaching A Second Language Series.
Prod-MLAA Dist-IU Prodn-RAY 1962

Nature Of Language, The C 28 MIN
16MM FILM OPTICAL SOUND H-C T
Examines current knowledge about language from the viewpoint of the scientific linguist. Features staff members of the Center for Applied Linguistics.
From The Language - The Social Arbiter Series.
LC NO. FIA67-5261
Prod-FINLYS Dist-FINLYS Prodn-CALING 1966

Nature Of Language, The - Brain And Mind C 30 MIN
3/4 OR 1/2 INCH VIDEO CASSETTE C
See series title for descriptive statement.
From The Language And Meaning Series.
Prod-WUSFTV Dist-GPITVL 1983

Nature Of Lanuage, The - The Linguistic Perspective C 30 MIN
3/4 OR 1/2 INCH VIDEO CASSETTE C
See series title for descriptive statement.
From The Language And Meaning Series.
Prod-WUSFTV Dist-GPITVL 1983

Nature Of Leadership, The C 15 MIN
3/4 OR 1/2 INCH VIDEO CASSETTE

Shows that leadership-follower relationships are found everywhere and that a leader is nothing without followers. Reveals that wise leaders understand, appreciate and motivate their followers.
From The Leadership Series. Module 1
Prod-RESEM Dist-RESEM

Nature Of Life—A Series
16MM FILM, 3/4 OR 1/2 IN VIDEO J-H
Prod-CORF Dist-CORF 1970

Nature Of Life, The - Cells, Tissue And Organs 11 MIN
Nature Of Life, The - Energy And Living Things 13 MIN
Nature Of Life, The - Living Things Interact 12 MIN
Nature Of Life, The - Respiration In Animals 11 MIN
Nature Of Life, The - The Living Cell 13 MIN
Nature Of Life, The - The Living Organism 12 MIN

Nature Of Life, The - Cells, Tissue And Organs C 11 MIN
16MM FILM, 3/4 OR 1/2 IN VIDEO J-H
Examines cell differentiation, the process that makes possible countless variations in kinds and species, in microscopic and normal scenes of living organisms.
From The Nature Of Life Series.
Prod-CORF Dist-CORF 1974

Nature Of Life, The - Energy And Living Things C 13 MIN
16MM FILM, 3/4 OR 1/2 IN VIDEO J-H
Demonstrates the importance of sunlight, photosynthesis, enzyme action and ATP in energy conversion.
From The Nature Of Life Series.
Prod-CORF Dist-CORF 1970

Nature Of Life, The - Living Things Interact C 12 MIN
16MM FILM, 3/4 OR 1/2 IN VIDEO J-H
Shows how a stray calf, lost in the desert, introduces interaction among organisms, occurring in the nitrogen cycle, the carbon cycle, the calcium cycle, parasitism and predation.
From The Nature Of Life Series.
Prod-CORF Dist-CORF 1973

Nature Of Life, The - Respiration In Animals C 11 MIN
16MM FILM, 3/4 OR 1/2 IN VIDEO J-H
Illustrates respiration throughout the animal kingdom, demonstrating relationships between respiration, blood circulation and feeding.
From The Nature Of Life Series.
Prod-CORF Dist-CORF 1970

Nature Of Life, The - The Living Cell C 13 MIN
16MM FILM, 3/4 OR 1/2 IN VIDEO J-H
Shows how cells obtain food, convert food to energy, respond to the environments and reproduce.
From The Nature Of Life Series.
Prod-CORF Dist-CORF 1970

Nature Of Life, The - The Living Organism C 12 MIN
16MM FILM, 3/4 OR 1/2 IN VIDEO J-H
Explores how organisms exchange substances with their environment, move materials about within their bodies, direct and coordinate their activities, feed and reproduce.
From The Nature Of Life Series.
Prod-CORF Dist-CORF 1973

Nature Of Light, The X 20 MIN
2 INCH VIDEOTAPE I
See series title for descriptive statement.
From The Process And Proof Series. No. 14
Prod-MCETV Dist-GPITVL Prodn-WVIZTV

Nature Of Light, The (2nd Ed) C 17 MIN
16MM FILM, 3/4 OR 1/2 IN VIDEO I-J
Traces the work of scientists of the past three centuries to aid in an explanation of the properties and characteristics of light.
From The Nature Of Energy Series.
Prod-CORF Dist-CORF 1973

Nature Of Logarithms B 31 MIN
16MM FILM OPTICAL SOUND H
Develops the nature of logarithms on the basis of powers of ten and the properties of exponents. Explains the differences between the mantissa and the characteristic and discusses the logarithm of fractional numbers. Shows the use of logs in computation.
From The Advanced Algebra Series.
Prod-CALVIN Dist-MLA Prodn-UNIVFI 1960

Nature Of Management, The C
3/4 OR 1/2 INCH VIDEO CASSETTE
Defines the management work and the management cycle as well as the relationship between the individual, the team and the organization's objectives. Emphasizes building a team of professionally oriented managers and supervisors.
From The Essentials Of Management Series. Unit I.
Prod-AMA Dist-AMA

Nature Of Management, The C 20 MIN
3/4 OR 1/2 INCH VIDEO CASSETTE
Acquaints supervisors with the basic concepts of management.
From The Supervision Management Course, Pt 1 Series. Unit 1
Prod-AMA Dist-AMA

Nature Of Matter And Living Things, The C
3/4 OR 1/2 INCH VIDEO CASSETTE
Provides an introduction to gaseous, solid and liquid forms of matter. Introduces the atom as the basic building block of all matter. Demonstrates how molecules of various substances are formed. Explains cell division and cell specialization with particular emphasis on the creation of hair and skin.
Prod-MPCEDP Dist-MPCEDP 1984

Nature Of Matter, Pt 2 - Motion—A Series
J
Presents concepts which are fundamental to understanding natural phenomena in all the disciplines of science. Discusses forces that are related to motion.
Prod-MPATI Dist-GPITVL

Balanced And Unbalanced Forces 30 MIN
Fluids In Motion 30 MIN
Motion In Space 30 MIN
Motion On Our Planet 30 MIN
Planetary Motion 30 MIN
Time 30 MIN
Velocity And Acceleration 30 MIN

Nature Of Matter, The - An Atomic View C 24 MIN
16MM FILM, 3/4 OR 1/2 IN VIDEO C A
Visits the Dr Erwin Meuller Laboratory at Pennsylvania State University to demonstrate the field-ion microscope. Discusses wave-particle duality and spectroscopy.
From The Physical Science Film Series.
Prod-CRMP Dist-CRMP 1973

Nature Of Mental Retardation C 25 MIN
16MM FILM OPTICAL SOUND C A
Relates vocational counseling to the various adaptive behavior levels of retarded children. Contains examples of the various causes of mental retardation and defines the rehabilitation potential of the different levels.
Prod-UKANS Dist-UKANS 1968

Nature Of Mental Retardation, The C 40 MIN
16MM FILM OPTICAL SOUND PRO
Includes clinical examples of eight different etiologies of mental retardation and explains the rehabilitation potential of the five different adaptive behavior levels of mental retardation.
From The Counseling The Mentally Retarded, Pt 1 Series.
LC NO. 72-702028
Prod-UKANBC Dist-NMAC 1968

Nature Of Mental Retardation, The C 21 MIN
3/4 OR 1/2 INCH VIDEO CASSETTE PRO
Shows graphically what mental retardation means and that it doesn't mean idiocy. Displays that, depending upon the profundity of the retardation, much can be done to create useful lives.
Prod-PRIMED Dist-PRIMED

Nature Of Reading C 30 MIN
2 INCH VIDEOTAPE T
Presents an investigation of the nature of the reading process and its place in the communicative cycle.
From The Child Reads Series.
Prod-WENHTV Dist-GPITVL

Nature Of Sea Water C 29 MIN
16MM FILM OPTICAL SOUND
Describes physical and chemical properties of sea water. Explains how man's understanding of the sea is basic to making use of ocean resources.
LC NO. 74-705191
Prod-USN Dist-USNAC 1967

Nature Of Signs, The C 30 MIN
3/4 OR 1/2 INCH VIDEO CASSETTE C
See series title for descriptive statement.
From The Language And Meaning Series.
Prod-WUSFTV Dist-GPITVL 1983

Nature Of Sound, The (2nd Ed) C 14 MIN
16MM FILM, 3/4 OR 1/2 IN VIDEO J
Establishes sound as a form of wave energy and illustrates sound waves in terms of amplitude, loudness, frequency, pitch, quality and Doppler effect.
From The Nature Of Energy Series.
Prod-CORF Dist-CORF 1971

Nature Of Symbols, The C 30 MIN
3/4 OR 1/2 INCH VIDEO CASSETTE C
See series title for descriptive statement.
From The Language And Meaning Series.
Prod-WUSFTV Dist-GPITVL 1983

Nature Of Things—A Series

Looks at a variety of topics including the history of the piano, psychological illnesses and physical illnesses.
Prod-CANBC Dist-FLMLIB

Bring Back My Bonnie 051 MIN
Brittle Bones 022 MIN
Piano, The 027 MIN
Tipping The Scales 055 MIN

Nature Of Violent Storms, The C 30 MIN
3/4 INCH VIDEO CASSETTE J
Describes the life cycle of a thunderstorm and the phenomena of lightning. Discusses tornadoes and hurricanes.
From The What On Earth Series.
Prod-NCSDPI Dist-GPITVL 1979

Nature Photography C 30 MIN
3/4 OR 1/2 INCH VIDEO CASSETTE
Discusses nature photography while 'roughing it.'
From The Roughing It Series.
Prod-KYTV Dist-KYTV 1984

Nature Story—A Series
16MM FILM, 3/4 OR 1/2 IN VIDEO K-I
Prod-IU Dist-IU

Chucky Lou - The Story Of A Woodchuck 11 MIN
Fish That Turned Gold, The 16 MIN

Nature Walk B 15 MIN
16MM FILM OPTICAL SOUND
Tells the story of a hospital worker and an autistic boy who go for a walk in the woods. Describes their different perceptions of the world around them and shows how they relate to one another.
LC NO. 79-700250
Prod-CARMAG Dist-CARMAG 1976

Nature Walk At Low Tide C 12 MIN
16MM FILM, 3/4 OR 1/2 IN VIDEO P-I
Guides a small group of children along a Pacific Ocean beach examining rocks and tidal pools, discovering many forms of plant and animal life.
From The Nature's Sights And Sounds Series.
Prod-MASLKS Dist-BCNFL 1984

Nature's Builders C 8 MIN
3/4 OR 1/2 INCH VIDEO CASSETTE K-I
Shows a swallow building its nest with mouthfuls of mud, a spider spinning its web and cocooning captured insects, and a caterpillar building its cocoon, later emerging as a moth.
Prod-AFTS Dist-EDMI 1984

Nature's Camouflage C 13 MIN
16MM FILM, 3/4 OR 1/2 IN VIDEO I-H A
Studies the ways in which form and color adaptation can conceal or distort the shapes of living creatures to protect them from their enemies. Uses close-up photography of insects and reptiles to demonstrate the ways in which they are camouflaged.
Prod-ACI Dist-AIMS 1970

Nature's Engineer, The Beaver C 10 MIN
16MM FILM, 3/4 OR 1/2 IN VIDEO I-J
Offers information on beavers.
Prod-EBER Dist-IFB 1947

Nature's Ever-Changing Communities C 14 MIN
16MM FILM, 3/4 OR 1/2 IN VIDEO I-J
Discovers the concepts of renewal, change and interdependence in the natural world. Shows how the living and non-living elements in an area are really an interdependent natural community.
Prod-GLDWER Dist-JOU 1973

Nature's Food Chain C 14 MIN
16MM FILM, 3/4 OR 1/2 IN VIDEO J-H
Examines the hierarchical ordering of predators and prey in natural environment.
Prod-NFBC Dist-BNCHMK 1978

Nature's Forge C 29 MIN
16MM FILM OPTICAL SOUND
Examines the ecological effects of the release of excess heat from power plants, showing research by Government and commercial operators of nuclear plants on the effects of this heat on fish, plants and animals.
LC NO. 74-703083
Prod-USAEC Dist-USNAC Prodn-BEET 1974

Nature's Half Acre C 33 MIN
16MM FILM, 3/4 OR 1/2 IN VIDEO I-C A
Follows the never-ending cycle of life through the four seasons of the year, concentrating on birds, plants and insects. Portrays nature's plan of providing and caring for all.
Prod-DISNEY Dist-WDEMCO 1955

Nature's Half Acre (Afrikaans) C 33 MIN
16MM FILM, 3/4 OR 1/2 IN VIDEO I-H
Stresses the interdependence of man and animals.
Prod-WDEMCO Dist-WDEMCO 1955

Nature's Half Acre (Danish) C 33 MIN
16MM FILM, 3/4 OR 1/2 IN VIDEO I-H
Stresses the interdependence of man and animals.
Prod-WDEMCO Dist-WDEMCO 1955

Nature's Half Acre (French) C 33 MIN
16MM FILM, 3/4 OR 1/2 IN VIDEO I-H
Stresses the interdependence of man and animals.
Prod-WDEMCO Dist-WDEMCO 1955

Nature's Half Acre (German) C 33 MIN
16MM FILM, 3/4 OR 1/2 IN VIDEO I-H
Stresses the interdependence of man and animals.
Prod-WDEMCO Dist-WDEMCO 1955

Nature's Half Acre (Italian) C 33 MIN
16MM FILM, 3/4 OR 1/2 IN VIDEO I-H
Stresses the interdependence of man and animals.
Prod-WDEMCO Dist-WDEMCO 1955

Nature's Half Acre (Norwegian) C 33 MIN
16MM FILM, 3/4 OR 1/2 IN VIDEO I-H
Stresses the interdependence of man and animals.
Prod-WDEMCO Dist-WDEMCO 1955

Nature's Half Acre (Spanish) C 33 MIN
16MM FILM, 3/4 OR 1/2 IN VIDEO I-H
Stresses the interdependence of man and animals.
Prod-WDEMCO Dist-WDEMCO 1955

Nature's Half Acre (Swedish) C 33 MIN
16MM FILM, 3/4 OR 1/2 IN VIDEO I-H
Stresses the interdependence of man and animals.
Prod-WDEMCO Dist-WDEMCO 1955

Nature's Laws C 60 MIN
3/4 INCH VIDEO CASSETTE PRO
Presents certain trends concerning structure and function which appear to be enhanced as the physlogenetic scale is ascended, such as cephalization, the trend of 'stereomorphophysiology,' the increase in commissural systems, and the importance of multisensory input, multipotential receptors, and polysensory neurons in relation to function and plasticity.
From The Nonbehavioral Sciences And Rehabilitation Series. Part V
Prod-AOTA Dist-AOTA 1980

Nature's Patterns C 15 MIN
16MM FILM, 3/4 OR 1/2 IN VIDEO I
Tell show Susan and her cousin use careful experiments and observations to discover why all the fish in the farm's pond have died.
From The Thinkabout Series. Finding Patterns
LC NO. 81-706110
Prod-SCETV Dist-AITECH 1979

Nature's Rhythms C 30 MIN
3/4 OR 1/2 INCH VIDEO CASSETTE J-H
Demonstrates that adults, as well as young people can experience feelings of threat and insecurity when confronted with a situation that requires new learning. Leads viewers to consider ways of coping successfully in such situations.
From The Y E S Inc Series.
Prod-KCET Dist-GPITVL 1983

Nature's Sights And Sounds—A Series
P-I
Reveals through close-up photography how seasonal changes affect the life cycle of small animals.
Prod-MASLKS Dist-BCNFL

Autumn - Nature's Sights And Sounds	014 MIN
Nature Walk At Low Tide	012 MIN
Spider	003 MIN
Spring - Nature's Sights And Sounds	014 MIN
Summer - Nature's Sights And Sounds	014 MIN
Winter - Nature's Sights And Sounds	014 MIN

Nature's Strangest Creatures C 16 MIN
16MM FILM, 3/4 OR 1/2 IN VIDEO I-C A
Shows some of the world's unique wildlife in their native habitat in Australia and Tasmania. The study includes the duck-billed platypus, flying fox, frilled lizard and spiny anteater.
Prod-DISNEY Dist-WDEMCO 1963

Nature's Strangest Creatures (Afrikaans) C 16 MIN
16MM FILM, 3/4 OR 1/2 IN VIDEO I-H
Studies some of the rarest wildlife from the bush country of Australia and Tasmania.
Prod-WDEMCO Dist-WDEMCO 1963

Nature's Strangest Creatures (French) C 16 MIN
16MM FILM, 3/4 OR 1/2 IN VIDEO I-H
Studies some of the rarest wildlife from the bush country of Australia and Tasmania.
Prod-WDEMCO Dist-WDEMCO 1963

Nature's Strangest Creatures (German) C 16 MIN
16MM FILM, 3/4 OR 1/2 IN VIDEO I-H
Studies some of the rarest wildlife from the bush country of Australia and Tasmania.
Prod-WDEMCO Dist-WDEMCO 1963

Nature's Strangest Creatures (Greek) C 16 MIN
16MM FILM, 3/4 OR 1/2 IN VIDEO I-H
Studies some of the rarest wildlife from the bush country of Australia and Tasmania.
Prod-WDEMCO Dist-WDEMCO 1963

Nature's Strangest Creatures (Norwegian) C 16 MIN
16MM FILM, 3/4 OR 1/2 IN VIDEO I-H
Studies some of the rarest wildlife from the bush country of Australia and Tasmania.
Prod-WDEMCO Dist-WDEMCO 1963

Nature's Superlatives C 29 MIN
2 INCH VIDEOTAPE
See series title for descriptive statement.
From The Observing Eye Series.
Prod-WGBHTV Dist-PUBTEL

Nature's Way C 15 MIN
16MM FILM, 3/4 OR 1/2 IN VIDEO I-J
Explains that overcoming some of the problems faced by the handicapped through the design and manufacture of artificial limbs combines past knowledge and experience with space-age technology. Combines requirements for function, comfort and appearance with considerations of performance, reliability and weight.
From The Craft, Design And Technology Series.
Prod-THAMES Dist-MEDIAG 1983

Nature's Way C 22 MIN
16MM FILM - 3/4 IN VIDEO H-C A
Visits Appalachians who are experts in herbal and home remedies and Indian folklore. Talks to a midwife as she delivers twins.
Prod-APPAL Dist-APPAL 1973

Nature's Ways C 26 MIN
16MM FILM OPTICAL SOUND
A study of birds, insects, fish and other wild creatures living close to suburbia in the state of Connecticut.
From The Audubon Wildlife Theatre Series.
LC NO. 77-710205
Prod-KEGPL Dist-AVEXP 1970

Natwaniwa - A Hopi Philosophical Statement C 27 MIN
3/4 OR 1/2 INCH VIDEO CASSETTE
Hopi with English subtitles. Shows the significance of cultivation of the land to the Hopi. Shows many of the Hopi turning from the old ways.
From The Words And Place Series.
Prod-CWATER Dist-CWATER

Naughty Number Nine C 4 MIN
3/4 OR 1/2 INCH VIDEO CASSETTE P-I
Uses songs and cartoons to explore the mathematical possibilities of the number nine.
From The Multiplication Rock Series.
Prod-ABCTV Dist-GA 1974

Naughty Owlet, The C 7 MIN
16MM FILM, 3/4 OR 1/2 IN VIDEO P-I
Uses animation to tell the story of three baby owls who live in a hollow tree and are instructed by their parents in the art of flying.
Prod-UILL Dist-AIMS 1971

Naughty Things C 25 MIN
16MM FILM OPTICAL SOUND
Presents interviews with four children to illustrate Jean Piaget's methods of clinical investigation and his conclusions about the moral development of children contained in his book Le Jugement Moral Chez L'enfant.
From The Social Psychology Series.
LC NO. 78-700330
Prod-OPENU Dist-OPENU 1977

Naughty Things C 25 MIN
16MM FILM, 3/4 OR 1/2 IN VIDEO
Presents interviews with four children to illustrate Jean Piaget's methods of clinical investigation and his conclusions about the moral development of children contained in his book Le Jugement Moral Chez L'enfant.
From The Social Psychology Series.
Prod-OPENU Dist-MEDIAG Prodn-BBCTV 1977

Nautical Astronomy B 23 MIN
16MM FILM, 3/4 OR 1/2 IN VIDEO
Explains how the celestial coordinates are placed in relation to the earth and how declination, Zenith point, Nadir line and the June and September solstices are used in celestial navigation.
From The Navigation Series.
LC NO. 81-706349
Prod-USN Dist-USNAC Prodn-SPRNGR 1943

Navajo C 21 MIN
16MM FILM, 3/4 OR 1/2 IN VIDEO I-C A
Describes the history, customs and life of the Navajo Indian nation, 15 million acres within the southwestern part of the United States. Explains that while much of Navajo life remains the same, other aspects of life have changed drastically.
LC NO. 80-707084
Prod-PAINF Dist-IU 1972

Navajo C 29 MIN
3/4 INCH VIDEO CASSETTE
Tells the story of two children who leave their modern way of life to learn the ways of their traditional Navajo grandparents. Stresses the importance of teaching the old ways to prevent the loss brought on by educational and technological changes. Also available in two-inch quad and one-inch videotape.
Prod-KBYU Dist-NAMPBC

Navajo - The Last Red Indians C 35 MIN
16MM FILM, 3/4 OR 1/2 IN VIDEO H-C A
Tells about the Navajo Indians' fight to preserve their way of life against the inroads of the white man's culture. Contains exclusive and uncensored scenes of Navajo rituals and ceremonies.
LC NO. 79-707438
Prod-BBCTV Dist-TIMLIF 1972

Navajo Canyon Country C 13 MIN
16MM FILM OPTICAL SOUND I
Shows Navajo people in their native country and gives a brief description of their way of life today.
Prod-DAGP Dist-MLA 1954

Navajo Code Talkers C 27 MIN
16MM FILM, 3/4 OR 1/2 IN VIDEO
Deals with the contributions of Navajo Indians to World War II intelligence activities. Interviews some of the surviving Code Talkers. Utilizes Army films taken at Saipan, Guadalcanal and Iwo Jima and archival footage of Navajo reservation life during the 1940's.
Prod-NMFV Dist-ONEWST

Navajo Country C 10 MIN
16MM FILM, 3/4 OR 1/2 IN VIDEO I-J
Shows the dependence of the nomadic Navajos upon sheep and goats to supply their food as well as the wool for clothing and for marketable rugs and blankets. Depicts carding, spinning, weaving and jewelry making.
Prod-UMINN Dist-IFB Prodn-WEBALB 1951

Navajo Coyote Tales C 18 MIN
16MM FILM OPTICAL SOUND T
Presents animated tales of the Coyote.
From The Navajo Folktales Series.
Prod-BIECC Dist-BIECC 1972

Navajo Girl C 21 MIN
3/4 INCH VIDEO CASSETTE P-I
Describes the life of a 10-year-old Navajo girl living on a reservation.
Prod-SCNDRI Dist-GA

Navajo Health Care Practices C 40 MIN
3/4 OR 1/2 INCH VIDEO CASSETTE PRO
Interviews a Navajo practical nurse about the traditions and healing practices of her family. Describes the ways Navajos choose between modern and traditional healing.
Prod-UARIZ Dist-UARIZ

Navajo Indian, The (2nd Ed) C 10 MIN
16MM FILM, 3/4 OR 1/2 IN VIDEO P-I
Pictures the Navajos adjusting to the changes graduually coming to their homeland and shows their life-styles as herdsmen, skilled weavers and creative silversmiths.
Prod-CORF Dist-CORF 1975

Navajo Land Issue C 12 MIN
3/4 OR 1/2 INCH VIDEO CASSETTE H-C A
Discusses the land issue that exists between the Navajo and the Hopi Indians. Interviews participants in the conflict and projects a potential outcome.
Prod-UPI Dist-JOU

Navajo Moon C 24 MIN
3/4 OR 1/2 INCH VIDEO CASSETTE
Examines the view of changing reservation life through the eyes of three Navajo children.
From The Young People's Specials Series.
Prod-MULTPP Dist-MULTPP

Navajo Rain Chant C 3 MIN
16MM FILM OPTICAL SOUND J-C
An animated collage in which an Arizona mesa is transformed into authentic Indian designs, accompanied by a Navajo rain chant.
Prod-CFS Dist-CFS

Navajo Way, The C 52 MIN
16MM FILM, 3/4 OR 1/2 IN VIDEO H-C A
Tells the story of the Navajo people, showing how they have survived within the white man's society because of their complete involvement with tradition.
Prod-NBC Dist-FI 1975

Navajo, Race For Prosperity C 26 MIN
16MM FILM, 3/4 OR 1/2 IN VIDEO
Looks at life on a Navajo reservation and focuses on the development of industries on the reservations. Investigates the possibility of a prosperous Navajo future dependent upon the Indian's management of the reservation's reserves of coal, uranium and steel.
From The Native Americans Series.
Prod-BBCTV Dist-CNEMAG

Navajo, The C
3/4 OR 1/2 INCH VIDEO CASSETTE
Examines the traditional ways of the Navajo and their blending with the new.
Prod-CEPRO Dist-CEPRO

Navajo, The - A Study In Cultural Contrast C 15 MIN
16MM FILM, 3/4 OR 1/2 IN VIDEO P-H
Views the environment, family structure, traditions, ceremonials and art of the Navajo Indians.
Prod-JOU Dist-JOU 1969

Navajo, The - With Beauty All Around Me C 22 MIN
3/4 OR 1/2 INCH VIDEO CASSETTE J-H
Examines the traditional ways of the Navajos - their art, religion, medicine and deep connection to the land. Also covers the new ways and their blending with the old.
Prod-CEPRO Dist-CEPRO

Naval Aviation - A Personal History - The Weapon Is Tested B 29 MIN
3/4 OR 1/2 INCH VIDEO CASSETTE
Depicts the development of naval aviation during the 1920s. Discusses the experiences of pioneers in naval aviation.
Prod-IHF Dist-IHF

Naval Flight Officer, The - Calling The Signals C 28 MIN
3/4 INCH VIDEO CASSETTE
Emphasizes the importance of the naval flight officer to the team effort of an aviation mission. Issued in 1970 as a motion picture.
LC NO. 79-706668
Prod-USN Dist-USNAC 1979

Naval Research Laboratory Reactor B 21 MIN
16MM FILM OPTICAL SOUND
Explains the construction, operation and uses to which the naval research laboratory reactor is adapted.
LC NO. FIE59-193
Prod-USN Dist-USNAC 1958

Naval Steam Turbines - How Turbines Work B 17 MIN
16MM FILM OPTICAL SOUND
Discusses the basic principles and design of main propulsion and auxiliary steam turbines in navy use. Explains differences between impulse and reaction thrust, how turbines work on steam velocity produced by drops in pressure and complexities of the marine steam turbine.
LC NO. FIE56-124
Prod-USN Dist-USNAC 1951

Naval Steam Turbines - Turbine Casualties B 12 MIN
16MM FILM OPTICAL SOUND
Explains the delicate nature of turbine equipment and the care which should be observed in its oiling, cleaning and maintenance.
LC NO. FIE56-241
Prod-USN Dist-USNAC 1950

Navaratri Festival C 60 MIN
3/4 OR 1/2 INCH VIDEO CASSETTE
Explains Mother Worship and how everything is done by the divine Mother. Talks about suffering, vain beauty, Romalinga Swamigal and more on the Mother.
Prod-IYOGA Dist-IYOGA

Navigating In Space C 30 MIN
16MM FILM, 3/4 OR 1/2 IN VIDEO C A
Explains how the amount of energy expended in voyages to other planets can be minimized by using the same force that drives the planets around the solar system.
From The Mechanical Universe Series.
Prod-ANNCPB Dist-FI

Navigation By Transit Satellite C 28 MIN
16MM FILM, 3/4 OR 1/2 IN VIDEO
Deals with navigation by transit satellite. Describes principles of operation, launch sequence, ground support system and basic user requirements.
LC NO. 82-706274
Prod-USN Dist-USNAC 1969

Navigator, The B 63 MIN
16MM FILM SILENT J-C A

Stars Buster Keaton as a rich boy who has never had to lift a finger, marooned on a huge ocean liner adrift at sea with only one other person aboard, an equally rich and helpless young girl.
Prod-MGM Dist-TWYMAN 1924

Navigators, The C 17 MIN
16MM FILM, 3/4 OR 1/2 IN VIDEO I-J
Tells how Magellan sailed through the straits that bear his name and discovered the Pacific Ocean. Recounts how other explorers, following Magellan's route, sighted Hawaii and Australia.
From The Cultures Of The Southern Seas Series.
Prod-HOE Dist-MCFI 1967

Navigators, The - Pathfinders Of The Pacific C 58 MIN
3/4 OR 1/2 INCH VIDEO CASSETTE J A
Follows archaeologists as they seek clues to the origin and achievements of ancient Polynesian seafarers. Shows the excavation of a powerful voyaging canoe on the Tahitian Island of Huahine, early sailing routes in Fiji and traces of Hawaii's first settlers on Molokai.
LC NO. 83-706970
Prod-WGBHTV Dist-DOCEDR 1983

Navy Advisor In Vietnam - The River Force C
3/4 OR 1/2 INCH VIDEO CASSETTE
Emphasizes the role of the U S Navy advisor working with Vietnamese river forces.
Prod-IHF Dist-IHF

Navy And Science, The B 12 MIN
16MM FILM OPTICAL SOUND
Highlights some of the scientific research programs being conducted by the Navy.
LC NO. FIE52-1304
Prod-USN Dist-USNAC 1951

Navy Bobsled Racing Team C 15 MIN
16MM FILM OPTICAL SOUND
Shows phases of bobsled racing and activities of the navy team in both domestic and international competitions.
LC NO. 74-705194
Prod-USN Dist-USNAC 1969

Navy Meteorology For College Graduates C 15 MIN
16MM FILM OPTICAL SOUND
Shows opportunities for meteorologists as officers in the naval weather service.
LC NO. 74-705195
Prod-USN Dist-USNAC 1967

Navy Officer Orientation C 6 MIN
16MM FILM OPTICAL SOUND
Describes and illustrates the duties of the Civil Engineer Corps officer.
LC NO. 76-702713
Prod-USN Dist-USNAC 1975

Navy Officer Orientation - Aeronautical Maintenance Duty Officer C 12 MIN
16MM FILM OPTICAL SOUND
Describes the demanding, complex and detailed work required of an aeronautical maintenance duty officer in the U S Navy.
LC NO. 76-703872
Prod-USN Dist-USNAC 1975

Navy Officer Orientation - Combat Scholar, Intelligence Officer C 10 MIN
16MM FILM OPTICAL SOUND
Shows the duties of an intelligence officer in the U S Navy by following a young officer on his daily work routine with his squadron aboard an aircraft carrier.
LC NO. 76-703873
Prod-USN Dist-USNAC 1975

Navy Officer Orientation - Cryptological Officer C 7 MIN
16MM FILM OPTICAL SOUND
Provides a generalized description of the skills required for work as a cryptological officer in the U S Navy.
LC NO. 76-703874
Prod-USN Dist-USNAC 1975

Navy Officer Orientation - Helo Flight C 5 MIN
16MM FILM OPTICAL SOUND
Describes the work of helicopter flight officers in the U S Navy.
LC NO. 76-703875
Prod-USN Dist-USNAC 1975

Navy Officer Orientation - Jet Flight C 5 MIN
16MM FILM OPTICAL SOUND
Describes the work of jet flight officers in the U S Navy.
LC NO. 76-703876
Prod-USN Dist-USNAC 1975

Navy Officer Orientation - Medical Corps C 18 MIN
16MM FILM OPTICAL SOUND
Presents the challenges and advantages of a career as a doctor in the U S Navy.
LC NO. 76-703877
Prod-USN Dist-USNAC 1975

Navy Officer Orientation - Medical Service Corps C 14 MIN
16MM FILM OPTICAL SOUND
Presents the work of hospital and other medical administrative personnel of the U S Navy's Medical Service Corps.
LC NO. 76-703878
Prod-USN Dist-USNAC 1975

Navy Officer Orientation - Naval Flight Officer C 4 MIN
16MM FILM OPTICAL SOUND PRO
Shows the duties and responsibilities of a flight officer in the U S Navy.
LC NO. 77-700123
Prod-USN Dist-USNAC 1975

Navy Officer Orientation - Navy Lawyer C 10 MIN
16MM FILM OPTICAL SOUND
Presents career opportunities for a lawyer in the U S Navy.
LC NO. 76-703879
Prod-USN Dist-USNAC 1975

Navy Officer Orientation - Navy Nurse Corps C 14 MIN
16MM FILM OPTICAL SOUND
Presents career opportunities as a nurse in the U S Navy Nurse Corps.
LC NO. 76-703880
Prod-USN Dist-USNAC 1975

Navy Officer Orientation - Nuclear Language C 10 MIN
16MM FILM OPTICAL SOUND
Describes a two-year nuclear training program offered by the U S Naval Reserve Officers' Training Corps for selected qualified college juniors and seniors.
LC NO. 76-703881
Prod-USN Dist-USNAC 1975

Navy Officer Orientation - Nuclear Navy C 14 MIN
16MM FILM OPTICAL SOUND
Describes the provisions for young officers in the U S Navy to be trained under the Nuclear Propulsion Officer Candidate Program.
LC NO. 76-703882
Prod-USN Dist-USNAC 1975

Navy Officer Orientation - Officer Candidate School, To Be An Ensign C 18 MIN
16MM FILM OPTICAL SOUND
Describes the training program for an ensign at the U S Navy's Officer Candidate School, Newport, Rhode Island.
LC NO. 76-703883
Prod-USN Dist-USNAC 1975

Navy Officer Orientation - People-People C 10 MIN
16MM FILM OPTICAL SOUND
Features the humanitarian, compassionate work performed by the U S Navy's Medical Service Corps specialists.
LC NO. 76-703884
Prod-USN Dist-USNAC 1975

Navy Officer Orientation - Prop Flight C 4 MIN
16MM FILM OPTICAL SOUND PRO
Shows the duties of a prop flight officer in the U S Navy.
LC NO. 77-700081
Prod-USN Dist-USNAC 1975

Navy Officer Orientation - Sea Fever, Line Officer C 12 MIN
16MM FILM OPTICAL SOUND
Presents career opportunities for line officers in the U S Navy, emphasizing command at sea as the primary goal.
LC NO. 76-703885
Prod-USN Dist-USNAC 1975

Navy Officer Orientation - The Way To The Line C 7 MIN
16MM FILM OPTICAL SOUND
Shows the U S Naval Reserve Officers' Training Corps as an excellent way of becoming an officer in the U S Navy or U S Marine Corps.
LC NO. 76-703886
Prod-USN Dist-USNAC 1975

Navy Officer Orientation - U S Naval Academy, Not For All To Share C 10 MIN
16MM FILM OPTICAL SOUND
Shows the life of a midshipman at the U S Naval Academy, presenting the strong challenge and high standards that can only be met by men equal to the task.
LC NO. 76-703887
Prod-USN Dist-USNAC 1975

Navy Officer Orientation - Wind And Sea C 13 MIN
16MM FILM OPTICAL SOUND
Depicts the daily life of a meteorologist and an oceanographer in the U S Navy during sea duty.
LC NO. 76-703667
Prod-USN Dist-USNAC 1974

Navy Officer Orientation - Woman C 12 MIN
16MM FILM OPTICAL SOUND
Presents the opportunities for a career as a woman officer in the U S Navy.
LC NO. 76-703889
Prod-USN Dist-USNAC 1975

Navy Participation In Atomic Tests C 14 MIN
16MM FILM, 3/4 OR 1/2 IN VIDEO
Describes the work of the Navy in atomic ordnance experiments.
Prod-USDD Dist-USNAC

Navy Photography In Science C 28 MIN
16MM FILM OPTICAL SOUND
Shows uses of photography in scientific research, including time-lapse, high-speed, slow-motion, stroboscopic, microscopic and under-water techniques.
LC NO. FIE52-1344
Prod-USN Dist-USNAC 1948

Navy Sings It Like It Is C 26 MIN
16MM FILM OPTICAL SOUND
Describes the experiences of underwater demolition team personnel, pilots, submariners, corpsmen, nurses and other Navy personnel through the medium of folk ballads.
LC NO. 74-706544
Prod-USN Dist-USNAC 1970

Navy Standard Swimming Tests And Abandoning Ship Drills B 18 MIN
16MM FILM OPTICAL SOUND
Shows various tests given to navy personnel to determine swimming abilities and illustrates abandoning ship drills.
LC NO. FIE52-1099
Prod-USN Dist-USNAC 1944

Navy, The - Decisions C 19 MIN
16MM FILM OPTICAL SOUND
Presents a story designed to create a favorable impression of Navy life on the general public, expecially high school students.
LC NO. 76-702714
Prod-USN Dist-USNAC 1975

Navy's Big Top, The C 18 MIN
16MM FILM OPTICAL SOUND
Shows the preparation of a Navy vessel for a new method of topside encapsulation, focusing on fabrication of the encapsulating cover and installation of the cover on the vessel.
LC NO. 74-706503
Prod-USN Dist-USNAC 1973

Nawi C 22 MIN
16MM FILM, 3/4 OR 1/2 IN VIDEO I-C
A documentary which depicts the drive of the Jie of Uganda during the dry season when they take their cattle to temporary camps or Nawi, where fresh grass is abundant. Portrays the life of the Jie at the cattle camp. With subtitles.
Prod-MCDGAL Dist-UCEMC 1970

Naye Masterji B 23 MIN
16MM FILM OPTICAL SOUND I-C A
Emphasizes the important role a teacher plays in the life of the student community. Points out how the problem of student discipline can be solved by developing the right type of relationship between the teacher and the student.
Prod-INDIA Dist-NEDINF

Nazi Concentration Camps B 59 MIN
3/4 OR 1/2 INCH VIDEO CASSETTE
Records the Nazi death camps as photographed by Allied forces advancing into Germany.
Prod-IHF Dist-IHF

Nazi Concentration Camps B 59 MIN
16MM FILM - 3/4 IN VIDEO
Presents the official film record of the Nazi death camps as photographed by Allied forces advancing into Germany. Shows surviving prisoners, victims of medical experiments, gas chambers and open mass graves. Issued in 1945 as a motion picture.
LC NO. 79-706580
Prod-USCPAC Dist-USNAC 1945

Nazi Germany - Years Of Triumph B 28 MIN
16MM FILM, 3/4 OR 1/2 IN VIDEO H-C A
Traces the career of Hitler, from Chancellor in 1933, when he leads a shaky coalition in the German government, until his total dictatorship of the country. Describes how his lust for power turns outward and Austria, Czechoslovakia and Poland are swallowed up.
From The Rise And Fall Of The Third Reich Series.
Prod-MGMD Dist-FI 1972

Nazi Strike, The B 41 MIN
16MM FILM, 3/4 OR 1/2 IN VIDEO
Documents Germany's preparation for war, the conquest of Austria and Czechoslovakia and the attack upon Poland. Issued in 1943 as a motion picture.
From The Why We Fight Series.
LC NO. 79-706465
Prod-USOWI Dist-USNAC 1979

Nazis Strike, The B 41 MIN
3/4 OR 1/2 INCH VIDEO CASSETTE
Relates the Nazi rise to power as Hitler imposes full dictatorship on Germany and marches in Austria and Czechoslovakia and invades Poland.
From The Frank Capra's 'Why We Fight' Series.
Prod-IHF Dist-IHF

NBA Basketball Championship B 30 MIN
16MM FILM OPTICAL SOUND
Presents the championship playoff between Boston and Los Angeles.
Prod-SFI Dist-SFI

NBC Proficiency Testing C 17 MIN
16MM FILM OPTICAL SOUND
Illustrates the round robin procedure for testing trainees in their individual ability to survive a nuclear, biological or chemical attack.
LC NO. 81-700598
Prod-USA Dist-USNAC 1981

NBC White Paper - China C 100 MIN
3/4 OR 1/2 INCH VIDEO CASSETTE H-C A
Shows what life in China is like by interviewing people in real-life situations, inside prisons, psychiatric institutions, criminal and divorce courts. Profiles factory towns and villages and offers the voices of workers, artists, teen-agers and victims of the Cultural Revolution.
Prod-NBCTV Dist-TIMLIF 1984

Ndando Yawusiwana (Song Of Sadness) C 18 MIN
3/4 OR 1/2 INCH VIDEO CASSETTE
Records a performance of a ndando by Chopi composer Venancio Mbande. Looks at the ndando, a musical oral history of ancestors and friends which can serve as a release from unhappy past events or as a purely pleasurable experience. Narrated and interpreted by Champ Ramohuebo.
Prod-PSU Dist-PSU

Ne Bougeons Plus C 13 MIN
16MM FILM OPTICAL SOUND J A

From The En Francais, Set 1 Series.
Prod-PEREN Dist-CHLTN 1969

NEA C 1 MIN
16MM FILM OPTICAL SOUND
Presents the opening title for the Independent Filmmakers Showcase, a number of short subject motion pictures. Uses animation to convey the progression and variety of film forms since the conception of the motion picture.
LC NO. 77-700391
Prod-NENDOW Dist-NENDOW Prodn-GLDSH 1976

Near And Far C 14 MIN
3/4 OR 1/2 INCH VIDEO CASSETTE P-I
Discusses depth in art.
From The Young At Art Series.
Prod-WSKJTV Dist-AITECH 1980

Near North, The C 16 MIN
16MM FILM OPTICAL SOUND
Looks at the scenic highlights and recreational activities of the Almaquin Highlands in Ontario. Views such pastimes as canoeing, horseback riding, hiking, camping, fishing and skiing.
Prod-OMITOU Dist-MTP

Near The Big Chakra C 15 MIN
16MM FILM OPTICAL SOUND
Explores a portion of the infinite variability of the human body. Views 36 female genitalia, ranging in age from six months to 56 years.
Prod-MMRC Dist-MMRC

Near The Big Chakra C 5 MIN
3/4 OR 1/2 INCH VIDEO CASSETTE C A
Explores a portion of the infinite variability of the body. An unhurried view of thirty-eight women's genitals.
Prod-MMRC Dist-MMRC

Neat In The Street C 18 MIN
16MM FILM, 3/4 OR 1/2 IN VIDEO S
Uses a TV game show format to demonstrate appropriate appearance of clothes.
From The Good Life Series.
LC NO. 81-706176
Prod-DUDLYN Dist-HUBDSC 1981

Neatos And The Litterbugs, The C 7 MIN
16MM FILM, 3/4 OR 1/2 IN VIDEO P
Presents the concept of keeping the environment clean and free of trash that ultimately becomes pollution. Points out the value of taking care of the home environment before going out into other parts of the community.
Prod-SAIF Dist-BARR 1974

Nebraska - Where The Cornbelt Meets The Range C 29 MIN
16MM FILM OPTICAL SOUND J-C A
Presents Nebraska's agricultural and livestock enterprises as major contributions to the national economy by studying its past, present and future.
Prod-KUONTV Dist-UNL 1967

Nebraska For The People - Executive Branch C 23 MIN
16MM FILM OPTICAL SOUND
Describes the authority and responsibility of the office of the Governor of Nebraska, including its limitations.
LC NO. 76-700923
Prod-NEBSL Dist-NTCN Prodn-NETCHE 1974

Nebraska For The People - Judicial Branch C 20 MIN
16MM FILM OPTICAL SOUND
Explains the organization and services of the State of Nebraska's judicial branch of government, describing types of courts and what they do and the impact of the judiciary on the lives of Nebraskans.
LC NO. 76-700924
Prod-NEBSL Dist-NTCN Prodn-NETCHE 1974

Nebraska For The People - Legislative Branch C 33 MIN
16MM FILM OPTICAL SOUND
Describes the functions and services of the Nebraska State Legislature, showing how a legislative bill is passed and how the use of a computer at the University of Nebraska has improved the legislative process.
LC NO. 76-700921
Prod-NEBSL Dist-NTCN Prodn-NETCHE 1974

Nebraska Territory - Boom And Bust B 30 MIN
16MM FILM OPTICAL SOUND H-C A
Discusses the abandonment of the permanent Indian frontier, the organization of Nebraska Territory, the slave question, the establishment of government, the capital controversy, the economic development, the boom of towns and the panic of 1857. Traces the development of agriculture and schools.
From The Great Plains Trilogy, 3 Series. Explorer And Settler - The White Man Arrives
Prod-KUONTV Dist-UNEBR 1954

Nebraska Water Resources—A Series
H-C A
Prod-UNL Dist-UNEBR 1971

Living With Nebraska's Water	27 MIN
Nebraska's Water - Its Future	29 MIN
Water - Nebraska's Heritage	29 MIN
Working With Nebraska's Water	29 MIN

Nebraska's Water - Its Future C 29 MIN
16MM FILM OPTICAL SOUND H-C A
Outlines possibilities for redistributing water supplies in Nebraska by engineering new systems and by altering management practices. Presents development and management methods within a framework of economics, social structure and ideas that may be applicable throughout the entire state. Stresses individual awareness of the water environment and man's responsibility for its management.
From The Nebraska Water Resources Series.
LC NO. 74-700164
Prod-UNL Dist-UNEBR 1971

Nebula 1 C 6 MIN
16MM FILM OPTICAL SOUND J-C
Presents an abstract film exercise.
Prod-CFS Dist-CFS 1969

Nebula 2 C 7 MIN
16MM FILM OPTICAL SOUND J-C
An experimental film which concentrates on the various pulsations made by concentric circles of dots, while incorporating subliminal effects, radiating lines, glowing coloration, and classical and rock music.
LC NO. 72-701344
Prod-FRERCK Dist-CFS 1971

Nebule C 10 MIN
16MM FILM, 3/4 OR 1/2 IN VIDEO P-J
Presents an animated story about a boy who turns a straight line into a magic cord and fulfills all his fantasies by making the cord turn into an endless array of toys and animals.
LC NO. 80-707374
Prod-NFBC Dist-IFB 1975

Necessity Of Influence, The B 30 MIN
2 INCH VIDEOTAPE T
Features Dr Dreikurs reviewing the trend in education from the strict teacher-student relationships of pre-World War II to the more premissive attitude in the classroom today. Equates the present upheaval situation in the schools to the problems of civil rights. Stresses the workability of influence rather than punishment to develop attitude changes in the student. (Broadcast quality)
From The Dynamics Of Classroom Behavior Series.
Prod-VTETV Dist-GPITVL Prodn-WETKTV

Neck Flex C 10 MIN
2 INCH VIDEOTAPE
See series title for descriptive statement.
From The Janaki Series.
Prod-WGBHTV Dist-PUBTEL

Neck Injuries C 16 MIN
3/4 OR 1/2 INCH VIDEO CASSETTE
Discusses the symptoms, diagnosis and treatment of neck injuries.
From The Emergency Management - The First 30 Minutes, Vol I Series.
Prod-VTRI Dist-VTRI

Neck Pain C
3/4 OR 1/2 INCH VIDEO CASSETTE
Presents a carefully detailed anatomical and biomechanical basis for neck/shoulder/arm pain syndromes with the underlying assumption that an understanding of the mechanism of pain will lead to more accurate diagnosis and management.
Prod-AMEDA Dist-AMEDA

Neck Pain C 18 MIN
16MM FILM, 3/4 OR 1/2 IN VIDEO A
Describes the structure and function of the neck. Explains causes of neck pain as well as treatment methods such as rest, traction, neck collars and exercises. Highlights prevention of future problems.
Prod-PRORE Dist-PRORE

Neck Pain (Spanish) C 18 MIN
16MM FILM, 3/4 OR 1/2 IN VIDEO PRO
Discusses causes, treatment and prevention of neck pain.
Prod-PRORE Dist-PRORE

Neck Shaping And Hems B 29 MIN
2 INCH VIDEOTAPE
See series title for descriptive statement.
From The Busy Knitter I Series.
Prod-WMVSTV Dist-PUBTEL

Neck-Related Pain C
3/4 OR 1/2 INCH VIDEO CASSETTE
Deals with the causes of most neck and upper back pain. Explains how proper diagnosis and treatment can lead to relief and long term recovery. Suggests how to avoid future neck problems.
Prod-MIFE Dist-MIFE

Neck-Related Pain (Arabic) C
3/4 OR 1/2 INCH VIDEO CASSETTE
Deals with the causes of most neck and upper back pain. Explains how proper diagnosis and treatment can lead to relief and long term recovery. Suggests how to avoid future neck problems.
Prod-MIFE Dist-MIFE

Neck-Related Pain (Spanish) C
3/4 OR 1/2 INCH VIDEO CASSETTE
Deals with the causes of most neck and upper back pain. Explains how proper diagnosis and treatment can lead to relief and long term recovery. Suggests how to avoid future neck problems.
Prod-MIFE Dist-MIFE

Neck, Pt 1 - Orientation, Fascia Superficial Structures C 15 MIN
16MM FILM, 3/4 OR 1/2 IN VIDEO PRO
Introduces the anatomy of the neck.
From The Cine-Prosector Series.
Prod-AVCORP Dist-TEF

Neck, Pt 2 - Visceral And Neurovascular Units C 17 MIN
16MM FILM, 3/4 OR 1/2 IN VIDEO PRO
Identifies the structures of the visceral unit, starting with the skeletal elements.
From The Cine-Prosector Series.
Prod-AVCORP Dist-TEF 1968

Neck, Pt 3 - Root And Thoracic Inlet C 18 MIN
16MM FILM, 3/4 OR 1/2 IN VIDEO PRO
Locates the boundaries of the root of the neck and the thoracic inlet using several anatomical models.
From The Cine-Prosector Series.
Prod-AVCORP Dist-TEF 1968

Necklace, The C 20 MIN
16MM FILM SILENT I-H S
Tells a mystery story in American sign language by Ralph White.
LC NO. 76-701096
Prod-JOYCE Dist-JOYCE 1975

Necklace, The C 20 MIN
16MM FILM, 3/4 OR 1/2 IN VIDEO J-H
Tells the story of a woman who borrows a diamond necklace to wear for a formal occasion and describes the consequences to her and her husband when she loses it. Based on the short story The Necklace by Guy de Maupassant.
From The Humanities - Short Story Classics Series.
Prod-EBEC Dist-EBEC 1980

Necklace, The C 21 MIN
16MM FILM, 3/4 OR 1/2 IN VIDEO J-C A
Tells the story of a 19th century Frenchwoman who loses a borrowed necklace and is reduced to menial work to replace it. Based on the short story The Necklace by Guy de Maupassant.
Prod-WILETS Dist-BARR 1981

Necklace, The C 23 MIN
16MM FILM, 3/4 OR 1/2 IN VIDEO J-C A
Tells how a borrowed necklace brings sorrow to a young married couple. Adapted from the story The Diamond Necklace by Guy de Maupassant.
Prod-MDBMOK Dist-FLMFR 1979

Necklace, The (Captioned Version) C 23 MIN
16MM FILM, 3/4 OR 1/2 IN VIDEO J-C A
Tells how a borrowed necklace brings sorrow to a young married couple. Adapted from the story The Diamond Necklace by Guy de Maupassant.
Prod-MDBMOK Dist-FLMFR 1979

Neckline Cut (With Curling Iron Technique) C
3/4 OR 1/2 INCH VIDEO CASSETTE
Involves only hair at the back of the head and nape. Selects hair from the crown as a guideline. Starts behind the ear and using vertical partings, hair is cut so that it becomes progressively shorter towards the nape, ending with approximately 1 inch of hair. Presents a short, finished style at the end. Emphasizes techniques for iron use.
From The Lessons On A Mannequin Series, Lesson VI.
Prod-MPCEDP Dist-MPCEDP 1984

Ned Williams Dance Theatre C 14 MIN
16MM FILM, 3/4 OR 1/2 IN VIDEO I-C A
Features Ned Williams and students from the Ned Williams School of Theatre Dance performing African and Haitian dances at Gateway National Recreation Area, Brooklyn, New York.
Prod-PHENIX Dist-PHENIX 1976

NEED C
3/4 OR 1/2 INCH VIDEO CASSETTE
See series title for descriptive statement.
From The Fragments From Willoughby's Video Performances - Pt II Series.
Prod-EAI Dist-EAI

Need A Paycheck C 30 MIN
3/4 OR 1/2 INCH VIDEO CASSETTE H-C A
Present TV hosts Cathy Brugett and Jim Finerty looking at career options and the changing job market as they introduce some real-life examples of people trying to deal with the situation of finding jobs and changing careers.
From The Come Alive Series. No. 2
LC NO. 82-706310
Prod-UAKRON Dist-GPITVL 1981

Need For Economic Education, The B 16 MIN
16MM FILM OPTICAL SOUND H A
Explains the role of economic systems in world affairs and relates this role to U S national, state and local affairs and to the conflict between East and West. Explains the necessity for profits and the role of economics in personal affairs.
From The Building Economic Understanding Series.
LC NO. FI67-371
Prod-RSC Dist-MLA 1963

Need For Pre-Supervisory Training, The C 12 MIN
3/4 OR 1/2 INCH VIDEO CASSETTE
Points out the many reasons why an employee should be trained in supervision before actually becoming a supervisor.
From The Pre-Supervisory Training Series. Module 1
Prod-RESEM Dist-RESEM

Need For Subroutines And Stacks, The C 50 MIN
3/4 OR 1/2 INCH VIDEO CASSETTE
Discusses Backus-Naur Form (BNF) as a recursive structure definition and use of a stack for implementing recursive programs.
From The Computer Languages - Pt 1 Series.
Prod-MIOT Dist-MIOT

Need For Work, The / Death As A Part Of Living / Intimacy And Distance... C 22 MIN
3/4 OR 1/2 INCH VIDEO CASSETTE
Dramatizes the need for work, feelings of dying, eating arrangements and menus and social activities in nursing homes.

From The It Can't Be Home - Nursing Series.
Prod-IVCH Dist-IVCH

Need It, Make It C 10 MIN
3/4 OR 1/2 INCH VIDEO CASSETTE K-P
Focuses on the ability to create useful items from a wide range of materials.
From The Book, Look And Listen Series.
Prod-MDDE Dist-AITECH 1977

Need To Achieve, The - Motivation And Personality B 29 MIN
16MM FILM, 3/4 OR 1/2 IN VIDEO H-C A
Dr David McClelland of Harvard University explains his psychological theory--that the economic growth or decline of nations is dependent to a large extent upon the entrepreneurs of these nations. He seeks to substantiate his theory through motivational tests.
From The Focus On Behavior Series.
Prod-NET Dist-IU 1963

Need To Be Needed, The C 15 MIN
3/4 INCH VIDEO CASSETTE P-I
Presents a study of responsibility.
From The Can You Imagine Series.
Prod-WVIZTV Dist-GPITVL

Need To Know, The C 27 MIN
16MM FILM OPTICAL SOUND
Illustrates several of the safe waste disposal methods being employed by the chemical industry. Emphasizes that the chemical industry is hard at work to correct past mistakes and prevent future ones.
LC NO. 82-700775
Prod-CHEMMA Dist-MTP Prodn-VISION 1982

Need To Know, The C 27 MIN
16MM FILM, 3/4 OR 1/2 IN VIDEO H-C A
Describes the governmental definition of intelligence as being limited to knowing the status of military and weather conditions around the world, a process rationalized as necessary to national defense. Food and other resources have become key factors in the international power struggle, making spy technology imperative.
Prod-THAMES Dist-MEDIAG 1977

Need to Touch, The C 30 MIN
3/4 OR 1/2 INCH VIDEO CASSETTE P-I
See series title for descriptive statement.
From The Sonrisas Series.
Prod-KRLNTV Dist-MDCPB

Needle Injections - Equipment And Medications B 20 MIN
16MM FILM OPTICAL SOUND
Shows the uses of needle injections and the fully-equipped needle tray. Describes the aseptic procedure for preparation of syringes. Shows how to prepare medications for use when supplied as liquids or as powder in sealed vials in ampules or in tablet form.
LC NO. 74-706504
Prod-USN Dist-USNAC 1957

Needle Injections - Intradermal, Subcutaneous And Intramuscular Injection Techniques B 9 MIN
16MM FILM OPTICAL SOUND
Explains the uses of intradermal, subcutaneous and intramuscular needle injections. Discusses precautions, aseptic procedure and appropriate needle size. Shows angle of penetration and location of tissue for injections.
LC NO. 74-706505
Prod-USN Dist-USNAC 1957

Needle Injections - Intravenous Injection B 5 MIN
16MM FILM OPTICAL SOUND
Describes aseptic procedures to be followed in intravenous injections. Shows injections and chart entries after injection and discusses precautions.
LC NO. 74-706506
Prod-USN Dist-USNAC 1957

Needle Play C
3/4 INCH VIDEO CASSETTE PRO
Concludes a presentation on teaching a child about anesthesia. Deals with giving injections to a dummy, clarifying reasons for an injection and play techniques demonstrating injection.
From The Staff Development Series.
Prod-CFDC Dist-CFDC

Needle's Eye C 27 MIN
3/4 OR 1/2 INCH VIDEO CASSETTE J A
Dramatizes the story of a medical intern on a summer trip to Africa who must decide between service to the poor and a lucrative practice.
Prod-SUTHRB Dist-SUTHRB

Needle's Eye, The C 27 MIN
16MM FILM, 3/4 OR 1/2 IN VIDEO H-C A
Deals with the journey of two medical students who travel to Africa and encounter a clinic run by a woman physician. Explains that one of the students has an urge to stay even though it means giving up a lucrative practice. Stars Ron Howard and Jerry Hauser.
From The Insight Series.
Prod-PAULST Dist-PAULST

Needleplay C 30 MIN
3/4 OR 1/2 INCH VIDEO CASSETTE
Focuses on making unusual game sets in needlework. Shows how to adapt the New York skyline to a backgammon board.
From The Erica Series.
Prod-WGBHTV Dist-KINGFT

Needlepoint - Like This—A Series

A series of six 30-minute programs. Describes how to make ten different needlepoint stitches. Shows seven completed designs, including a Tricky Fish, Smooth Sailor, Chunky Elephant, Pink Puppy and Flower Patch.
Prod-WGTV Dist-MDCPB

Needlepoint Tapestries And Rug Making C 30 MIN
3/4 OR 1/2 INCH VIDEO CASSETTE
Inspired by the French tapestry, The Offering Of The Heart, Erica Wilson shows how to use laid work, backstitching and stem stitching to create a masterpiece. Demonstrates the continental stitch and half-cross stitch in rugmaking.
From The Erica Series.
Prod-WGBHTV Dist-KINGFT

Needles And Bread C 15 MIN
3/4 OR 1/2 INCH VIDEO CASSETTE P
Presents two stories based on Revolutionary War incidents that show how sewing and baking helped the war effort.
From The Stories Of America Series.
Prod-OHSDE Dist-AITECH Prodn-WVIZTV 1976

Needs And Wants C 9 MIN
16MM FILM, 3/4 OR 1/2 IN VIDEO J-C A
Uses a game show format to illustrate how consumers can make decisions based on values, goals and lifestyle.
Prod-FLMFR Dist-FLMFR

Needs Of Defense, The B 15 MIN
2 INCH VIDEOTAPE P-I
See series title for descriptive statement.
From The Our Changing Community Series.
Prod-VITA Dist-GPITVL 1967

NEFA, Pt 1 C 15 MIN
16MM FILM OPTICAL SOUND I-C A
Presents the North Eastern Frontier Agency as a fabulous mosaic consisting of over 30 tribes, of whom the Nagas, Abors, Daflas and Mishmis are the better known ones. Studies the pattern of their lives, which has remained unchanged for centuries but is now slowly changing after independence.
Prod-INDIA Dist-NEDINF

NEFA, Pt 2 C 15 MIN
16MM FILM OPTICAL SOUND I-C A
Presents the North Eastern Frontier Agency as a fabulous mosaic consisting of over 0 Tribes, of whom the Nagas, Abors, Daflas and Mishmis are the better known ones. Studies the pattern of their lives, which has remained unchanged for centuries but is now slowly changing after independence.
Prod-INDIA Dist-NEDINF

Negative Aspects In Teaching African History C 58 MIN
3/4 OR 1/2 INCH VIDEO CASSETTE
See series title for descriptive statement.
From The Blacks, Blues, Black Series.
Prod-KQEDTV Dist-PBS

Negative Cultural Carryover C 54 MIN
3/4 OR 1/2 INCH VIDEO CASSETTE
See series title for descriptive statement.
From The Blacks, Blues, Black Series.
Prod-KQEDTV Dist-PBS

Negative Numbers And Problem-Solving C 30 MIN
3/4 OR 1/2 INCH VIDEO CASSETTE
See series title for descriptive statement.
From The Infinity Factory Series.
Prod-EDFCEN Dist-MDCPB

Negative Rational Numbers C 30 MIN
16MM FILM OPTICAL SOUND T
Discusses positive and negative numbers. Describes the law of signs. To be used following 'MEASUREMENT OF SOLIDS.'
From The Mathematics For Elementary School Teachers Series. No. 29
Prod-SMSG Dist-MLA 1963

Negative Reinforcement C 5 MIN
3/4 OR 1/2 INCH VIDEO CASSETTE T
See series title for descriptive statement.
From The Protocol Materials In Teacher Education - The Process Of Teaching, Pt 2 Series.
Prod-MSU Dist-MSU

Neglected, The B 30 MIN
16MM FILM, 3/4 OR 1/2 IN VIDEO C A S
A portrayal of children from hardcore families who are under the protection of community authorities. Considers techniques of child protective services and the problems of the war on poverty.
Prod-MHFB Dist-IFB 1965

Negligent Operation Of Motor Vehicles C 24 MIN
16MM FILM, 3/4 OR 1/2 IN VIDEO
Presents situations which demonstrate to police officers proper and improper use of their motor vehicles. Emphasizes the importance of determining whether or not an emergency situation exists before driving at high speeds, and points out the equipment that must be used during both emergency and non-emergency runs.
From The Police Civil Liability Series. Part 1
Prod-HAR Dist-MTI Prodn-BAY 1978

Negligent Use Of Firearms C 24 MIN
16MM FILM, 3/4 OR 1/2 IN VIDEO
Presents situations which demonstrate to police officers proper and improper use of their firearms. Outlines the types of actions that courts across the United States have held to be reasonable and unreasonable uses of firearms.
From The Police Civil Liability Series. Part 2
Prod-HAR Dist-MTI Prodn-BAY 1978

Negligent Use Of Motor Vehicles, The C 13 MIN
16MM FILM, 3/4 OR 1/2 IN VIDEO PRO
Discusses claims and lawsuits brought against police officers for vehicular negligence. Looks at vehicles in emergency situations, showing how to exercise due care for the safety of others and provide adequate warning to pedestrians and other motorists.
From The Law Enforcement - Civil Liability Series.
Prod-AIMS Dist-AIMS 1978

Negocios, Comportamiento Y Resultados C 23 MIN
16MM FILM, 3/4 OR 1/2 IN VIDEO H-C A
A Spanish language version of Business, Behaviorism And The Bottom Line. Interprets the theories of B F Skinner and shows how they are applied in an industrial setting in order to modify behavior and increase productivity.
Prod-MGHT Dist-MGHT 1977

Negotiating - Strategies And Tactics C 24 MIN
16MM FILM - VIDEO, ALL FORMATS
Illustrates negotiating strategies, whether for negotiating a purchasing order, an advertising campaign of a labor contract.
Prod-SANCIN Dist-BARR

Negotiating Conceptual Framework, Experience And Process C 26 MIN
3/4 OR 1/2 INCH VIDEO CASSETTE
See series title for descriptive statement.
From The Art Of Negotiating Series.
Prod-DELTAK Dist-DELTAK

Negotiating Philosophies C
16MM FILM - 3/4 IN VIDEO A
Shows how to appraise negotiating philosophy, explains why it should be a cooperative process, not a game, plus different philosophies.
From The Art Of Negotiating Series. Module 12
Prod-BNA Dist-BNA 1983

Negotiating Philosophies C 15 MIN
3/4 OR 1/2 INCH VIDEO CASSETTE
See series title for descriptive statement.
From The Art OF Negotiating Series.
Prod-DELTAK Dist-DELTAK

Negotiating Profitable Sales C 22 MIN
3/4 OR 1/2 INCH VIDEO CASSETTE A
Demonstrates how a salesperson can put theory into practice. Shows a seller at briefing time prior to the first major negotiation. Then presents him following through and actually making the sale.
Prod-XICOM Dist-XICOM

Negotiating Profitable Sales—A Series

Stresses that negotiating is not just another form of selling, but a special skill. Points out that lack of this skill can cost the organization more money in a shorter time than any other.
Prod-VISUCP Dist-VISUCP

Negotiation, The 023 MIN
Preparation, The 021 MIN

Negotiating Skills For Managers C 30 MIN
3/4 OR 1/2 INCH VIDEO CASSETTE
Teaches managers how to sway others with timing and association techniques, identify the other side's real but often hidden needs, use questions to control the thrust of a discussion, make concessions without losing, communicate their position clearly and precisely.
Prod-EFM Dist-EFM

Negotiating Successfully—A Series
16MM FILM, 3/4 OR 1/2 IN VIDEO A
LC NO. 79-707431
Prod-TIMLIF Dist-TIMLIF 1975

Better Deal For Both Sides, A 25 MIN
Dangers In Negotiations 25 MIN
How To Avoid A Deadlock 25 MIN
Tactics Of Pressure 25 MIN
What Makes A Good Negotiation 25 MIN
You Have More Power Than You Think 25 MIN

Negotiating Techniques, Arnold Ruskin C
3/4 OR 1/2 INCH VIDEO CASSETTE PRO
See series title for descriptive statement.
From The Management Skills Series.
Prod-AMCEE Dist-AMCEE

Negotiating With The Government C 72 MIN
3/4 OR 1/2 INCH VIDEO CASSETTE PRO
Discusses practices of Justice Department's antitrust division regarding negotiation of consent decrees and civil investigative demands. Provides a set of rules to follow when negotiating with the antitrust division. Debates questions of the division leniency program.
From The Preventive Antitrust - Corporate Compliance Program Series.
Prod-ABACPE Dist-ABACPE

Negotiation C
3/4 OR 1/2 INCH VIDEO CASSETTE
See series title for descriptive statement.
From The Asset Series
Prod-RESPRC Dist-RESPRC

Negotiation C 8 MIN
3/4 OR 1/2 INCH VIDEO CASSETTE J-H
Presents skills involving negotiation which adolescents can use in their dealings with parents, teachers, peers and others.
From The ASSET - A Social Skills Program For Adolescents Series. Session 6
LC NO. 81-706054
Prod-HAZLJS Dist-RESPRC Prodn-BAXLEN 1981

Negotiation C 35 MIN
3/4 OR 1/2 INCH VIDEO CASSETTE PRO
Portrays an attorney attempting to settle a wrongful death case. Discusses competence, diligence, fairness, misrepresentation and disclosure.
From The Legal Ethics - Applying The Model Rules Series.
Prod-ABACPE Dist-ABACPE

Negotiation C 60 MIN
3/4 OR 1/2 INCH VIDEO CASSETTE PRO
Raises several issues concerning attorney preparation, misrepresentation, attorney-client privilege, attorneys' duty to disclose criminal conduct, extortion, settlement tactics and obligation to represent client diligently.
From The Dilemmas In Legal Ethics Series.
Prod-ABACPE Dist-ABACPE

Negotiation - The Win-Win Process C 24 MIN
16MM FILM, 3/4 OR 1/2 IN VIDEO C A
Portrays a negotiating process where everybody wins.
LC NO. 84-700412
Prod-UNDERR Dist-BARR 1983

Negotiation Lectures—A Series
PRO
Presents techniques and strategies for phone and person-to-person negotiations.
Prod-NITA Dist-ABACPE

Preparing For Negotiations 050 MIN
Psychological Factors And Ethical 050 MIN
Strategy And Tactics In Negotiations 050 MIN

Negotiation Preparations, Strategies, Tactics And Problems C 55 MIN
3/4 OR 1/2 INCH VIDEO CASSETTE PRO
See series title for descriptive statement.
From The Negotiation Series.
Prod-ABACPE Dist-ABACPE

Negotiation Settlements In Personal Injury Cases C 120 MIN
3/4 OR 1/2 INCH VIDEO CASSETTE PRO
Discusses procedures and techniques used to negotiate the best settlement for a client.
Prod-CCEB Dist-ABACPE

Negotiation—A Series
PRO
Presents models of effective techniques and strategies for phone and person-to-person negotiations in a law practice.
Prod-ABACPE Dist-ABACPE

Basic Negotiation Approaches 028 MIN
Complete Negotiations - Comparative Techniques 045 MIN
Negotiation Preparations, Strategies, Tactics 055 MIN

Negotiation, The C 23 MIN
3/4 OR 1/2 INCH VIDEO CASSETTE
Shows a contest which calls for clear thinking and quick footwork as a salesman starts his negotiations with a buyer, who is also a skilled negotiator.
From the Negotiating Sales Series. Pt II
Prod-VISUCP Dist-VISUCP

Negro And The American Promise, The B 60 MIN
16MM FILM OPTICAL SOUND C A
Presents Dr Kenneth Clark interviewing James Baldwin, Martin Luther King Jr and Malcolm X.
Prod-NET Dist-IU

Negro And The South, The B 30 MIN
16MM FILM OPTICAL SOUND H-C A
Explores the meaning of 'the Southern way of life.' Includes interviews with black and white citizens and shows scenes of segregated schools.
From The History Of The Negro People Series.
LC NO. FIA68-1284
Prod-NET Dist-IU 1965

Negro Heroes From American History C 11 MIN
16MM FILM - 3/4 IN VIDEO P-I
Introduces the history of the Negro in America through the biographies of several heroes from the Revolutionary War to present day.
Prod-ATLAP Dist-ATLAP 1966

Negro Kingdoms Of Africa's Golden Age C 17 MIN
16MM FILM OPTICAL SOUND I-H
Shows the changing climate of Africa. Discusses the trans-Saharan transportation and the growth of Islam as a prelude to the emergence of several prosperous and mighty empires in topical Africa. Presents the story of medieval Senegal, Mali and Ghana. Describes the initiation of slave trading and the emergence of new African states.
LC NO. 71-700472
Prod-ATLAP Dist-ATLAP 1968

Negro Slavery C 25 MIN
16MM FILM, 3/4 OR 1/2 IN VIDEO J-C A
Depicts the plight of the black man from the 17th century through Lincoln's election in 1861.
From The American History Series.
Prod-CRMP Dist-CRMP 1969

Negro Soldier, The B 40 MIN
3/4 OR 1/2 INCH VIDEO CASSETTE
Focuses on black participation in World War II. Supervised by Frank Capra.
Prod-IHF Dist-IHF

Negro Soldier, The B 42 MIN
16MM FILM - 3/4 IN VIDEO
Traces the role of the Black soldier in American history from 1776 to 1944. Shows the accomplishments of Black troops. Issued in 1944 as a motion picture.
LC NO. 79-706471
Prod-USWD Dist-USNAC 1979

Nehemiah C 30 MIN
16MM FILM OPTICAL SOUND R
Portrays the leadership qualities exemplified by Nehemiah. Explains that Nehemiah went to Jerusalem to unite the people and helped them rebuild the walls around the city.
Prod-BROADM Dist-BROADM 1964

Nehru B 54 MIN
16MM FILM, 3/4 OR 1/2 IN VIDEO C A
Presents Nehru at age 73, the political leader of 400 million people and president of the world's largest democracy, India. Describes how he is still wrestling with more problems than ever before in the history of his young democracy.
Prod-DREW Dist-DIRECT 1967

Nehru's India C 29 MIN
2 INCH VIDEOTAPE
See series title for descriptive statement.
From The Course Of Our Times II Series.
Prod-WGBHTV Dist-PUBTEL

Neigborhoods—A Series
P
Focuses on concepts of rural and urban communities and the geographical relationships within and between them.
Prod-NEITV Dist-GPITVL 1981

City Neighborhood - A Beautiful Place 015 MIN
City Neighborhood - A General Description I 015 MIN
City Neighborhood - A General Description II 015 MIN
City Neighborhood - Good Neighbors Help Each 015 MIN
Communication In Neighborhoods 015 MIN
Ethnic Neighborhoods - City 015 MIN
Ethnic Neighborhoods - Rural 015 MIN
Ethnic Neighborhoods - Town 015 MIN
My Neighbor And Me 015 MIN
Neighbors And Neighborhoods 015 MIN
Older And Newer Neighborhoods 015 MIN
Protection For Neighborhoods 015 MIN
Religious Neighborhoods - City 015 MIN
Religious Neighborhoods - Rural 015 MIN
Religious Neighborhoods - Town 015 MIN
Rural Neighborhood - A Beautiful Place 015 MIN
Rural Neighborhood - A General Description 015 MIN
Rural Neighborhood - Good Neighbors Help Each 015 MIN
Tale Of Two Neighbors 015 MIN
Town Neighborhood - A General Description 015 MIN
Town Neighborhood - Good Neighbors Help Each 015 MIN
Transportation In Neighborhoods 015 MIN
Welcoming New Neighbors 015 MIN

Neighbor Islands, The C 30 MIN
16MM FILM OPTICAL SOUND J-C
Covers in detail the islands of Kauai, Maui and Hawaii, and shows all the landmarks important in Hawaii's historical past which have become famous in legend.
Prod-CINEPC Dist-CINEPC

Neighbor, The C 15 MIN
16MM FILM, 3/4 OR 1/2 IN VIDEO H A
Details the causes of drinking water contamination and illustrates solutions.
Prod-KLEINW Dist-KLEINW

Neighborhood Drums C 30 MIN
3/4 OR 1/2 INCH VIDEO CASSETTE J-H
Shows that it's tough to resist the old gang and familiar neighborhood ways, but that succeeding at a job means sticking with it, in spite of divided loyalties.
From The Y E S Inc Series.
Prod-KCET Dist-GPITVL 1983

Neighborhood Watch C 20 MIN
16MM FILM OPTICAL SOUND J-C A
Discusses techniques designed to protect residences from burglaries. Describes alarm systems, lighting fixtures, locking hardware and other devices.
LC NO. 75-701608
Prod-MCCRNE Dist-MCCRNE 1974

Neighborhood Youth Corps, The C 26 MIN
16MM FILM, 3/4 OR 1/2 IN VIDEO
Demonstrates how youths can stay in school and continue their education while earning needed money under the U S Department of Labor's Neighborhood Youth Corps program. Issued in 1968 as a motion picture.
From The Career Job Opportunity Series.
LC NO. 79-707883
Prod-USDLMA Dist-USNAC Prodn-DEROCH 1979

Neighborhood, The B 18 MIN
16MM FILM OPTICAL SOUND
Presents an entertaining situation as a misunderstanding between a police officer and a slightly unorthodox citizen sets off a chase in the classic silent-move style.
LC NO. 75-701718
Prod-FMCOOP Dist-FMCOOP 1966

Neighborhoods C 16 MIN
16MM FILM, 3/4 OR 1/2 IN VIDEO P-I
Explores the idea that communities offer different ways to live. Shows how many neighborhoods make up the city and how important they are as parts of the community.
From The Community Series. Part 1
Prod-BARR Dist-BARR 1977

Neighborhoods Are Different X 11 MIN
16MM FILM, 3/4 OR 1/2 IN VIDEO P
Uses the personal-interview approach to compare and contrast different neighborhoods—a farm community, a small town, a big city and a suburb. Shows how the activities of children vary in each area.
Prod-EBF Dist-EBEC 1963

Neighboring - The Old West End, Toledo, Ohio C 30 MIN
16MM FILM OPTICAL SOUND
Looks at a renovated neighborhood in Toledo, Ohio. Discusses the loss of neighborhoods in modern society and the pros and cons of urban neighborhoods.
Prod-OHC Dist-HRC

Neighbors B 17 MIN
16MM FILM SILENT J-C A
Stars Buster Keaton.
Prod-MGM Dist-TWYMAN 1920

Neighbors C 9 MIN
16MM FILM, 3/4 OR 1/2 IN VIDEO I-C A
Employs Norman Mc Laren's pixillation technique for animating live actors in a parable of neighbors who battle so greedily over a flower that they destroy everything they hold dear.
Prod-NFBC Dist-IFB 1952

Neighbors C 28 MIN
16MM FILM - 3/4 IN VIDEO
Shows how neighbors have traditionally offered help in times of trouble. Explains that in 20th century society more than neighborly help is needed, and tells how community services offer help to disadvantaged children and adults.
From The No Place Like Home Series.
LC NO. 79-708106
Prod-USSRS Dist-USNAC 1979

Neighbors - Conservation In A Changing Community C 29 MIN
16MM FILM OPTICAL SOUND
Explores the experiences and attitudes of residents of Boston's South End, a neighborhood in transition. Shows what citizens are doing to protect diverse community culture, while accommodating new interest and investment back into the neighborhood.
Prod-CONSF Dist-CONSF 1977

Neighbors - Conservation In A Changing Community C 29 MIN
16MM FILM, 3/4 OR 1/2 IN VIDEO J-C A
Tells the story of Boston's South End. Discusses whether a neighborhood can accommodate growth, and yet be sensitive to the needs of long-time residents.
Prod-BULFRG Dist-BULFRG 1977

Neighbors And Neighborhoods C 15 MIN
3/4 OR 1/2 INCH VIDEO CASSETTE P
Discusses neighbors and neighborhoods.
From The Neighborhoods Series.
Prod-NEITV Dist-GPITVL 1981

Neihardt On Creative Writing B 29 MIN
16MM FILM OPTICAL SOUND J-C A
Explains that great works of literature have endured for the reason that they deal in some measure with characteristic moods which occur in all races and times and relate man in an unbroken descent.
LC NO. 74-700172
Prod-UNL Dist-UNEBR 1968

Neither Laggard Nor Wearied C 29 MIN
3/4 INCH VIDEO CASSETTE
Looks at the history of the computer.
From The Future Without Shock Series.
Prod-UMITV Dist-UMITV 1976

Nekton - Swimmers C 30 MIN
3/4 OR 1/2 INCH VIDEO CASSETTE
Focuses on the nektonic life-style. Lists the four principal categories of swimming organisms.
From The Oceanus - The Marine Environment Series. Lesson 16
Prod-SCCON Dist-CDTEL

Nell And Fred B 28 MIN
16MM FILM, 3/4 OR 1/2 IN VIDEO H-C
Relates the difficulty of elderly people in remaining independent by focusing on a couple who must decide whether to move into a residence for senior citizens or to maintain their own familiar home.
Prod-NFBC Dist-NFBC 1971

Nelli Kim C 29 MIN
16MM FILM, 3/4 OR 1/2 IN VIDEO I-C A
Relates the true story of Nelli Kim, the Korean gymnast who won two gold medals for the USSR team at the 1976 Montreal Summer Olympics. Offers insights into Nelli's relationship with her paternalistic coach as well as her competition with another member of her team, Nadia Comeneci.
Prod-NFBC Dist-TEXFLM

Nellie's Playhouse C 14 MIN
3/4 OR 1/2 INCH VIDEO CASSETTE
Provides an overview of the folk art of Nellie Mae Rowe, black artist who uses found objects to create objects in her yard.
Prod-SOFOLK Dist-SOFOLK

Nematode C 11 MIN
16MM FILM, 3/4 OR 1/2 IN VIDEO J-C
Introduces the species of roundworms or nematoda, commonly found in plant roots.
From The Biology Series. Unit 7 - Animal Classification And Physiology
Prod-EBEC Dist-EBEC 1973

Nematodes C 5 MIN
3/4 INCH VIDEO CASSETTE

Describes how to recognize nematodes and focuses on the damage they do in a garden.
Prod-TUCPL Dist-GPITVL

Nemesis - Germany, February To May, 1945 C 60 MIN
16MM FILM OPTICAL SOUND H-C A
From The World At War Series.
LC NO. 76-701778
Prod-THAMES Dist-USCAN 1975

Nemesis - Germany, February-May 1945 C 52 MIN
16MM FILM, 3/4 OR 1/2 IN VIDEO H-C A
Describes the period from February to May 1945 which brought Germany's defeat and Russia's capture of Berlin. The end of the Third Reich was announced at Hitler's secret headquarters where he ended his own life.
From The World At War Series.
Prod-THAMES Dist-MEDIAG 1973

Neo-Garvey Thought And Movements, The B 30 MIN
16MM FILM OPTICAL SOUND H-C A
Dr E U Essien-udom discusses the effect of Marcus Garvey on the black freedom movements since the end of World War II, pointing out the activities and philosophy of W E B Dubois, of the Muslim movement led by Elijah Muhammed and the revolutionary changes advocated by Malcolm X.
From The Black History, Section 13 - Marcus Garvey And his Movement Series.
LC NO. 76-704081
Prod-WCBSTV Dist-HRAW 1969

Neon C 5 MIN
16MM FILM OPTICAL SOUND
Explores the wonders of luminous tubes.
Prod-USC Dist-USC 1980

Neon C 5 MIN
16MM FILM, 3/4 OR 1/2 IN VIDEO K-C A
See series title for descriptive statement.
From The How It's Made Series.
Prod-HOLIA Dist-LUF

Neonatal Instrumentation (Furst) B 50 MIN
3/4 OR 1/2 INCH VIDEO CASSETTE PRO
See series title for descriptive statement.
From The Medical Instrumentation For Nurses Series. Pt 2
Prod-UAZMIC Dist-UAZMIC 1976

Neonatal Surgery C 27 MIN
16MM FILM OPTICAL SOUND
A Japanese language film with English subtitles. Describes neonatal surgery, which has developed as a new field in Japanese medicine.
Prod-UNIJAP Dist-UNIJAP 1964

Neonate, The B 44 MIN
16MM FILM OPTICAL SOUND PRO
Demonstrates the characteristics of the neonate appearance, reflexes and variations. Discusses parental concerns and implications for nursing care.
From The Maternity Nursing Series.
LC NO. 71-703387
Prod-VDONUR Dist-AJN Prodn-WTTWTV 1966

Neoplastic Disease C 22 MIN
16MM FILM OPTICAL SOUND PRO
Explains that radical neck dissection is a safe and many times curative procedure for the removal of metastatic cancer arising from the head and neck. Demonstrates the anesthesia and positioning of the patient, the lymph nodes and anatomical structures involved.
Prod-ACYDGD Dist-ACY 1957

Neorealism - The Italian Cinema B 30 MIN
16MM FILM, 3/4 OR 1/2 IN VIDEO H-C A
Presents a study of the neo-realistic film in post-war Italy. Includes interviews with directors and excerpts from films by De Sica, Rossellini, Antonioni and Moravia.
Prod-TEXFLM Dist-TEXFLM 1972

Neosho - April 24 C 14 MIN
16MM FILM, 3/4 OR 1/2 IN VIDEO
Shows how the disaster preparedness planning of the small Missouri city of Neosho was responsible for the survival of people who were caught in the tornado of April 24, 1975. Issued in 1976 as a motion picture.
LC NO. 80-707130
Prod-NOAA Dist-USNAC 1980

Nepal - Land Of The Gods C 17 MIN
16MM FILM OPTICAL SOUND P-C A
Explains the nature of the people of Nepal and describes their religions, their way of life, and their country's geography.
LC NO. 71-701201
Prod-BAILYL Dist-AVED 1968

Nepal - People Of The Mountains C 14 MIN
16MM FILM OPTICAL SOUND P-C A
Describes the Sherpas tribe of the Himalaya Mountains of Nepal.
LC NO. 75-701202
Prod-BAILYL Dist-AVED 1968

Nepal - The People And The Culture C 28 MIN
3/4 OR 1/2 INCH VIDEO CASSETTE H-C A
Presents the people, culture and history of Nepal, a small, landlocked country which has a rich heritage. Explores the problems that face the people and their government.
Prod-JOU Dist-JOU

Nepalese Tea Worker Of The Himalayas C 14 MIN
16MM FILM OPTICAL SOUND I-C A
Tells the story of the family of Dorji Lama, whose father and mother were among the Nepal poor farmers who were indentured and brought to work on the tea estates of India. Explains that Dorji has since lived and worked all of his life on the Phuguri Tea Estate and supports his wife, four sons, three daughters and a grandmother.
From The Human Family, Pt 1 - South And Southeast Asia Series.
Prod-AVED Dist-AVED 1972

Nephew From New Jersey C 30 MIN
3/4 OR 1/2 INCH VIDEO CASSETTE
See series title for descriptive statement.
From The Que Pasa, U S A Series.
Prod-WPBTTV Dist-MDCPB

Nephro-Ureterectomy - Modified Single-Incision Approach C 20 MIN
16MM FILM OPTICAL SOUND
Uses medical art and animation along with photography to illustrate an operative technique in a patient with a transitional cell tumor involving the renal pelvis and upper calyces. Employs diagnostic procedures and post-operative follow-up to emphasize the advantages of this modified approach.
LC NO. 75-702281
Prod-EATONL Dist-EATONL 1965

Nephrosis In Children C 18 MIN
16MM FILM OPTICAL SOUND PRO
Describes the onset of nephrosis in children and some of the complications such as hernias, and shows the typical facies. Points out that progressive kidney failure is a major cause of death in childhood nephrosis.
Prod-PFI Dist-PFI 1954

Neptune's Nonsense C 8 MIN
16MM FILM OPTICAL SOUND
Presents a Felix the Cat cartoon.
Prod-VANBRN Dist-BHAWK 1936

Nerine Barrett - Pianist C 29 MIN
2 INCH VIDEOTAPE
Presents the music of pianist Nerine Barrett.
From The Young Musical Artists Series.
Prod-WKARTV Dist-PUBTEL

Nero Versteht Etwas Von Kunst C 15 MIN
16MM FILM, 3/4 OR 1/2 IN VIDEO
See series title for descriptive statement.
From The Guten Tag Wie Geht's Series. Part 9
Prod-BAYER Dist-IFB 1973

Nerve Deafness C 17 MIN
16MM FILM, 3/4 OR 1/2 IN VIDEO A
Reviews tinnitus, hearing aids, speech reading and learning to cope with hearing loss. Describes the function of the ear and causes of nerve deafness.
Prod-PRORE Dist-PRORE

Nerve Hearing Loss C
3/4 OR 1/2 INCH VIDEO CASSETTE
Film utilizes animation to show normal hearing and how hearing is affected through conductive blockage or nerve hearing loss. Subtitled version available.
Prod-MIFE Dist-MIFE

Nerve Hearing Loss (Arabic) C
3/4 OR 1/2 INCH VIDEO CASSETTE
Film utilizes animation to show normal hearing and how hearing is affected through conductive blockage or nerve hearing loss. Subtitled version available.
Prod-MIFE Dist-MIFE

Nerve Impulse, The C 22 MIN
16MM FILM, 3/4 OR 1/2 IN VIDEO J-H
Contains laboratory demonstrations ranging from fairly simple frog nerve-muscle preparations to a re-creation of the single squid axon preparation made famous by Nobel Prize winners Hodgkin and Huxley.
From The Biology Series. Unit 8 - Human Physiology
Prod-EBEC Dist-EBEC 1971

Nerve Impulse, The (Spanish) C 21 MIN
16MM FILM, 3/4 OR 1/2 IN VIDEO J-H
A Spanish language version of the film and videorecording The Nerve Impulse.
Prod-EBEC Dist-EBEC 1971

Nerves, The C 17 MIN
16MM FILM, 3/4 OR 1/2 IN VIDEO PRO
Presents an explanation of the motor and sensory nerve supply for the globe, extraocular muscles and the anterior adnexa, including the light reflex pathways.
From The Anatomy Of The Human Eye Series.
Prod-BAYCMO Dist-TEF 1972

Nervous Dogs C 30 MIN
3/4 OR 1/2 INCH VIDEO CASSETTE H-C A
Shows Barbara Woodhouse's method of handling nervous dogs.
From The Training Dogs The Woodhouse Way.
Prod-BBCTV Dist-FI 1982

Nervous System - Pt 1 - Central Nervous System C 45 MIN
3/4 OR 1/2 INCH VIDEO CASSETTE PRO
Presents the major characteristics of the nervous system in general as well as the specific histological features of the central nervous system.
From The Histology Review Series.
Prod-HSCIC Dist-HSCIC

Nervous System - Pt 2 - Peripheral Nervous System C 39 MIN
3/4 OR 1/2 INCH VIDEO CASSETTE PRO
Discusses the peripheral nerve and examines the components of the reflex arc, includes collection of information in the periphery and transmission of that information to the CNS. Presents the route of the motor response to the peripheral effector organ and describes the components of the reflex arc of the autonomic nervous system.
From The Histology Review Series.
Prod-HSCIC Dist-HSCIC

Nervous System In Man, The C 18 MIN
16MM FILM, 3/4 OR 1/2 IN VIDEO H-C A
Demonstrates how the human nervous system, with the endocrine system, provides coordination of body movement, integration of body functions and regulation of involuntary body systems. An animated film.
From The Human Physiology Series.
LC NO. 80-707066
Prod-IU Dist-IU 1965

Nervous System, The C 8 MIN
16MM FILM, 3/4 OR 1/2 IN VIDEO J-C
Explains the elements of the nervous system and illustrates them through rat dissection.
Prod-CFDLD Dist-CORF

Nervous System, The C 29 MIN
3/4 INCH VIDEO CASSETTE C A
Explains how nervous system controls and coordinates the movements and functions of an organism. Uses animation to supplement discussion of electro-chemical nature of an impulse.
From The Introducing Biology Series. Program 19
Prod-COAST Dist-CDTEL

Nervous System, The (Spanish) C 17 MIN
16MM FILM, 3/4 OR 1/2 IN VIDEO J-H
A Spanish language version of the film and videorecording The Nervous System.
Prod-EBEC Dist-EBEC 1981

Nervous System, The (3rd Ed) C 17 MIN
16MM FILM, 3/4 OR 1/2 IN VIDEO J-H
Uses animation and micrography of actual nerve cells to show how the nervous system controls and integrates all body activities.
LC NO. 82-706658
Prod-EBEC Dist-EBEC 1981

Nervous System, The - Decision C 26 MIN
3/4 OR 1/2 INCH VIDEO CASSETTE
Shows how the brain organizes input and output to make a simple but life-saving decision. Looks at the cortex, which assesses incoming information and sends outgoing messages to the muscles and stores maps of the world and of the body. Discusses how circuits of nerve cells operate in the brain and how individual nerve cells function.
From The Living Body - An Introduction To Human Biology Series.
Prod-FOTH Dist-FOTH 1985

Nervous System, The - Nerves At Work C 26 MIN
3/4 OR 1/2 INCH VIDEO CASSETTE
Looks at nerve signals and how they are transmitted. Discusses the part played by nerve messages in reflex activities and examines the chemical and electrical activities of networks of nerve cells in contact.
From The Living Body - An Introduction To Human Biology Series.
Prod-FOTH Dist-FOTH 1985

Nervous System, The - Our Talented Brain C 26 MIN
3/4 OR 1/2 INCH VIDEO CASSETTE
Explores human culture, including man's physiological brain capacity, his use of memory, and his use of symbols. Discusses its relationship to the neural structure of the brain.
From The Living Body - An Introduction To Human Biology Series.
Prod-FOTH Dist-FOTH 1985

Nervous System, The, Pt 1 C 60 MIN
3/4 OR 1/2 INCH VIDEO CASSETTE A
Presents biologist Humberto Maturana discussing the human nervous system.
From The Biology Of Cognition And Language Series. Program 9
Prod-UCEMC Dist-UCEMC

Nervous System, The, Pt 2 C 60 MIN
3/4 OR 1/2 INCH VIDEO CASSETTE A
Presents biologist Humberto Maturana discussing the human nervous system.
From The Biology Of Cognition And Language Series. Program 10
Prod-UCEMC Dist-UCEMC

Nervous Systems In Animals C 17 MIN
16MM FILM, 3/4 OR 1/2 IN VIDEO H-C A
Shows the response of different animals to stimuli shows the structure of the nervous systems in a variety of animals.
From The Animal Systems Series.
LC NO. 80-707016
Prod-IU Dist-IU 1971

Nesika - A Specialized Group Home C 15 MIN
3/4 INCH VIDEO CASSETTE
Relates the transfer of eight severely/profoundly handicapped adults to a specialized group home. Cautions that transfer should be based on decisions made by the client, family and professionals.
Prod-UWASHP Dist-UWASHP

Nested FOR-NEXT Loops C 60 MIN
3/4 OR 1/2 INCH VIDEO CASSETTE
See series title for descriptive statement.
From The Introduction To BASIC Series. Lecture 10
Prod-UIDEEO Dist-UIDEEO

Nested Loops And More About Program Design C 30 MIN
3/4 OR 1/2 INCH VIDEO CASSETTE J-C A
Examines programs which illustrate nested loops, crossed loops and three-level nesting. Displays programs with loops correctly and incorrectly nested. Demonstrates a program with three-level nesting and a final program which shows nested loops used with strings. Defines and analyzes a problem, then develops a solution and a solution algorithm. Presents criteria against which these steps are checked. Designs program output using grid sheets and storyboarding techniques and shows the criteria to be considered.
From The Programming For Microcomputers Series. Unit 16 And 17
LC NO. 83-707134
Prod-IU Dist-IU 1983

Nesting Behavior Of The Egyptian Plover C 14 MIN
16MM FILM, 3/4 OR 1/2 IN VIDEO
Shows the remarkable environmental adaptations of the Egyptian plover, a bird that inhabits river banks in tropical Africa. Depicts that it nests on open sandbars, concealing its eggs by covering them completely with sand.
From The Aspects Of Animal Behavior Series.
Prod-UCLA Dist-UCEMC 1979

Nesting Of Patterns C 10 MIN
1/2 IN VIDEO CASSETTE BETA/VHS IND
Explains the application of nesting patterns or parts together to eliminate wasteful cutting or shearing of sheet material.
Prod-RMI Dist-RMI

Nesting Redwinged Blackbirds C 8 MIN
16MM FILM OPTICAL SOUND I-C A
Depicts the mating, nesting and migratory habits of the nesting redwinged blackbird. Shows alfalfa fields as nesting sites and explains a new census technique.
LC NO. FIA66-500
Prod-OSUMPD Dist-OSUMPD 1965

Nestle's Quick With Jimmy Nelson And Danny O'Day And Farfel C 1 MIN
3/4 OR 1/2 INCH VIDEO CASSETTE
Shows a classic television commercial with great nostalgia and the Nestle's jingle.
Prod-BROOKC Dist-BROOKC

Net Harvest C 20 MIN
16MM FILM OPTICAL SOUND
Explains that commercial fishing in large reservoirs controlled by game and fish law enforcement personnel, becomes a valuable fish population management tool. Tells how the controlled harvest of non-game fish can result in better fishing for the sports fisherman. Shows that the commercial fisherman catches fish in his net, which are seldom seen by sports fishermen.
Prod-TGAFC Dist-TGAFC

Net Play C 21 MIN
16MM FILM, 3/4 OR 1/2 IN VIDEO J-C A
Features a clinic approach to teaching group tennis. Shows how to teach net play.
From The Tennis Series.
Prod-ATHI Dist-ATHI 1976

Net Result Is Survival, The C 13 MIN
16MM FILM, 3/4 OR 1/2 IN VIDEO IND
Shows how construction safety nets are manufactured, tested and installed, and how essential it is to use one on the site not only to prevent injury but to instill worker confidence.
Prod-CSAO Dist-IFB

Netherlands, The - A Traditional Menu C 28 MIN
16MM FILM, 3/4 OR 1/2 IN VIDEO J-C A
Shows chef Hans Clemens preparing a traditional Dutch meal.
From The World Of Cooking Series.
Prod-SCRESC Dist-MTI

Netherlands, The - Blueprint For An Urban Society (2nd Ed) C 16 MIN
16MM FILM, 3/4 OR 1/2 IN VIDEO I-H
Explains how the Netherlands is handling its development into an urban society. Shows the reclamation of land from the sea, the mechanized agriculture, and the large housing projects.
Prod-EBEC Dist-EBEC 1971

Netherlands, The - People Against The Sea C 16 MIN
16MM FILM, 3/4 OR 1/2 IN VIDEO H
Shows Dutch people engaged in a variety of agricultural, industrial and leisurely activities which characterize their traditions and outlook for the future.
Prod-CORF Dist-CORF 1972

Netsilik Eskimo Today, The C 18 MIN
16MM FILM OPTICAL SOUND
Shows the settled community life of the Netsilik Eskimos, which was established since 1965 under the auspices of the Canadian government, replacing their traditional migrational pattern of life.
LC NO. 73-702043
Prod-EDC Dist-EDC 1973

Netsilik Eskimo—A Series
I-C
Prod-EDS Dist-EDC Prodn-NFBC 1968

At The Autumn River Camp, Pt 1 030 MIN
At The Autumn River Camp, Pt 2 030 MIN
At The Caribou Crossing Place, Pt 1 030 MIN
At The Caribou Crossing Place, Pt 2 030 MIN
At The Spring Sea Ice Camp, Pt 1 027 MIN
At The Spring Sea Ice Camp, Pt 2 027 MIN
At The Spring Sea Ice Camp, Pt 3 027 MIN
At The Winter Sea Ice Camp, Pt 1 036 MIN
At The Winter Sea Ice Camp, Pt 2 036 MIN
At The Winter Sea Ice Camp, Pt 3 030 MIN
At The Winter Sea Ice Camp, Pt 4 035 MIN
Fishing At The Stone Weir, Pt 1 030 MIN
Fishing At The Stone Weir, Pt 2 027 MIN
Group Hunting On The Spring Ice, Pt 1 031 MIN
Group Hunting On The Spring Ice, Pt 2 032 MIN
Group Hunting On The Spring Ice, Pt 3 032 MIN
Jigging For Lake Trout, Pt 1 032 MIN
Jigging For Lake Trout, Pt 2 032 MIN
Stalking Seal On The Spring Ice, Pt 1 025 MIN
Stalking Seal On The Spring Ice, Pt 2 034 MIN

Network C 121 MIN
16MM FILM OPTICAL SOUND
Tells how a TV newsman with low ratings and suicidal tendencies becomes a folk hero and a media star. Stars Faye Dunaway, William Holden, Peter Finch and Robert Duvall. Directed by Sidney Lumet.
Prod-UAA Dist-UAE 1977

Network Access Protocols C 50 MIN
3/4 OR 1/2 INCH VIDEO CASSETTE PRO
Discusses network layer, transmission facilities, data transfer, multiplexing and flow control.
From The Computer Communications - Protocols And Architectures, Pt 2 Series.
Prod-AMCEE Dist-AMCEE

Network Analysis With Muliple Voltage Sources C 15 MIN
3/4 OR 1/2 INCH VIDEO CASSETTE
See series title for descriptive statement.
From The Basic Electricity And D.C. Circuits, Laboratory Series.
Prod-TXINLC Dist-TXINLC

Network Analysis With Multiple Voltage Sources C
3/4 OR 1/2 INCH VIDEO CASSETTE
See series title for descriptive statement.
From The Basic DC Circuits Series.
Prod-VTRI Dist-VTRI

Network Architecture C 45 MIN
3/4 OR 1/2 INCH VIDEO CASSETTE C
Defines term, gives ISO reference model, including Level 1, physical interface, Level 2, link control, Level 3, system control, Level 4, transport, Level 5, session, Level 6, presentation and Level 7, applications.
From The Telecommunications And The Computer Series.
LC NO. 81-707502
Prod-AMCEE Dist-AMCEE 1981

Network Architecture C 48 MIN
3/4 OR 1/2 INCH VIDEO CASSETTE
Describes network architecture.
From The Telecommunications And The Computer Series.
Prod-MIOT Dist-MIOT

Network Architectures - A Communications Revolution—A Series

Presents an overview of the objectives of communications network architectures and discusses the characteristics that all network architectures have in common. Describes the functions and overall structures of two major communications network architectures, IBM's System Network Architecture (SNA) and the proposed Advanced Communication Service (ACS) of AT&T.
Prod-DELTAK Dist-DELTAK

Public Data Networks 045 MIN
Systems Network Architecture 045 MIN
Trends 045 MIN

Network Computations B 60 MIN
3/4 OR 1/2 INCH VIDEO CASSETTE
See series title for descriptive statement.
From The Project Management And CPM Series. Pt 2
Prod-UAZMIC Dist-UAZMIC 1977

Network Concepts For Users C 20 MIN
3/4 OR 1/2 INCH VIDEO CASSETTE
Develops the concepts of computer networks and communications alternatives and discusses the effects of these techniques on the business environment. Illustrates the user's role in planning and implementing these technologies.
From The User-Directed Information Systems Series.
Prod-DELTAK Dist-DELTAK

Network Control For Operators C 45 MIN
3/4 OR 1/2 INCH VIDEO CASSETTE
Discusses the functions involved in network control and the role of the network control operator. Presents the network control operator's responsibilities in monitoring and controlling the network, problem determination and resolution, and recording and reporting network information.
Prod-DELTAK Dist-DELTAK

Network News - That's The Way It Is C 29 MIN
3/4 OR 1/2 INCH VIDEO CASSETTE
Looks at the changing shape and direction of television's network news. Explores the topics of the stakes involved in the highly competitive race for ratings, the proposed hour-long evening news format and the question of whether the increasing use of high-tech video tools and the anchorman 'star' system put a higher premium on the image than on the essence of the story.
From The Inside Story Series.
Prod-PBS Dist-PBS 1981

Network Structures For Finite Impulse Response (FIR) Digital Filters and... C 51 MIN
3/4 OR 1/2 INCH VIDEO CASSETTE PRO
Covers network structures for finite impulse response (FIR)digital filters and parameter-quantification effects in digital filter structures.
From The Digital Signal Processing Series.
Prod-GPCV Dist-GPCV

Network Structures For Finite Impulse Response (FIR) Digital Filters And Parameter... C 51 MIN
3/4 OR 1/2 INCH VIDEO CASSETTE
Discusses network structures for finite impulse response (FIR) digital filters and parameter-quantitization effects in digital filter structures.
From The Digital Signal Processing - An Introduction Series.
Prod-MIOT Dist-MIOT

Network Structures For Infinite Impulse Response (IIR) Digital Filters C 40 MIN
3/4 OR 1/2 INCH VIDEO CASSETTE PRO
See series title for descriptive statement.
From The Digital Signal Processing Series.
Prod-GPCV Dist-GPCV

Network Structures For Infinite Impulse (IIR) Digital Filters C 40 MIN
3/4 OR 1/2 INCH VIDEO CASSETTE
See series title for descriptive statement.
From The Digital Signal Processing - An Introduction Series.
Prod-MIOT Dist-MIOT

Network Topologies And Routing, Pt I C 50 MIN
3/4 OR 1/2 INCH VIDEO CASSETTE C
Covers centralized and distributed networks, hierarchical compared to non-hierarchical networks, relationship of topology to protocol and throughout, network design example and analysis and design of networks for poorly defined requirements.
From The Packet Switching Networks Series.
Prod-AMCEE Dist-AMCEE

Networking C 30 MIN
3/4 OR 1/2 INCH VIDEO CASSETTE
Deals with networking. Covers topologies and access.
From The Programmable Controllers Series.
Prod-ITCORP Dist-ITCORP

Networking Topologies And Routing, Pt II C 50 MIN
3/4 OR 1/2 INCH VIDEO CASSETTE C
Covers random routing, flooding, directory routing, adaptive directory routing and variations on routing techniques.
From The Packet Switching Networks Series.
Prod-AMCEE Dist-AMCEE

Networking Topologies And Routing, Pt 1 C 40 MIN
3/4 OR 1/2 INCH VIDEO CASSETTE
See series title for descriptive statement.
From The Packet Switching Series.
Prod-MIOT Dist-MIOT

Networking Topologies And Routing, Pt 2 C 43 MIN
3/4 OR 1/2 INCH VIDEO CASSETTE
See series title for descriptive statement.
From The Packet Switching Series.
Prod-MIOT Dist-MIOT

Networks And Distributed Data Processing C 30 MIN
3/4 OR 1/2 INCH VIDEO CASSETTE H-C A
Describes data communication techniques, network switching systems and network configurations. Discusses the different types of terminals and compares the advantages of centralized versus distributed systems.
From The Making It Count Series.
LC NO. 80-707583
Prod-BCSC Dist-BCSC 1980

Networks And Matrices C 14 MIN
16MM FILM, 3/4 OR 1/2 IN VIDEO
Shows how a 'flow' in a network can be represented by a matrix.
Prod-OPENU Dist-MEDIAG Prodn-BBCTV 1979

Networks Of Knowledge C 26 MIN
16MM FILM OPTICAL SOUND H-C A
Depicts work being done in various countries by the United Nations University.
LC NO. 81-700066
Prod-UNUNIV Dist-UNUNIV 1979

Neues Leben Bluht Aus Den Ruinen B 107 MIN
16MM FILM OPTICAL SOUND
A German language film with English subtitles. Combines a documentary and newsfilm from the German post-war era on the Ruhr.
Prod-WSTGLC Dist-WSTGLC 1980

Neun Leben Hat Die Katze C 91 MIN
16MM FILM OPTICAL SOUND
A German language film with English subtitles. Presents a collage about five women in the Federal Republic of Germany during a week's time. Portrays the five women, who are in pursuit of happiness, and who have, in reality, adjusted to the circumstances in which they live.
Prod-WSTGLC Dist-WSTGLC 1968

Neuro-Otologic Evaluation C 58 MIN
3/4 OR 1/2 INCH VIDEO CASSETTE PRO
Reviews the auditory, vestibular and radiographic tests used to evaluate patients suspected of having a tumor when these internal audiometry canal and cerebellopontine angle lesions are producing minimal symptoms, particularly when small.
Prod-HOUSEI Dist-HOUSEI

Neuroanatomy Demonstrations Series—A Series
PRO
Presents neuroanatomy demonstrations.
Prod-USDHEW Dist-USNAC

Neuroanatomy Demonstrations, Pt 01 057 MIN
Neuroanatomy Demonstrations, Pt 02 051 MIN
Neuroanatomy Demonstrations, Pt 03 058 MIN
Neuroanatomy Demonstrations, Pt 04 041 MIN
Neuroanatomy Demonstrations, Pt 05 055 MIN
Neuroanatomy Demonstrations, Pt 06 056 MIN
Neuroanatomy Demonstrations, Pt 07 036 MIN
Neuroanatomy Demonstrations, Pt 08 053 MIN
Neuroanatomy Demonstrations, Pt 09 053 MIN
Neuroanatomy Demonstrations, Pt 10 012 MIN

Neuroanatomy Demonstrations, Pt 01 C 57 MIN
3/4 OR 1/2 INCH VIDEO CASSETTE PRO
Includes topography - brain and spinal cord in situ, major divisions of the brain and their relation to the embryonic brain, and detailed topography of the major divisions of the brain.
From The Neuroanatomy Demonstrations Series.
Prod-USDHEW Dist-USNAC

Neuroanatomy Demonstrations, Pt 02 C 51 MIN
3/4 OR 1/2 INCH VIDEO CASSETTE PRO
Includes topography - cranial nerves, cerebral blood vessels, ventricles and cerebrospinal fluid.
From The Neuroanatomy Demonstrations Series.
Prod-USDHEW Dist-USNAC

Neuroanatomy Demonstrations, Pt 03 C 58 MIN
3/4 OR 1/2 INCH VIDEO CASSETTE PRO
Includes dissection of the brain stem - middle cerebellar peduncle and auditory nerve, inferior and superior cerebellar peduncles and dissection of the hemispheres - long association bundles, and extreme and external capsules and related structures.
From The Neuroanatomy Demonstrations Series.
Prod-USDHEW Dist-USNAC

Neuroanatomy Demonstrations, Pt 04 C 41 MIN
3/4 OR 1/2 INCH VIDEO CASSETTE PRO
Includes dissection of the hemispheres - basal ganglia, anterior commissure and internal capsule, olfactory system and limbic system.
From The Neuroanatomy Demonstrations Series.
Prod-USDHEW Dist-USNAC

Neuroanatomy Demonstrations, Pt 05 C 55 MIN
3/4 OR 1/2 INCH VIDEO CASSETTE PRO
Includes proprioception, vibratory, tactile, pain and temperature pathways and trigeminal pathways.
From The Neuroanatomy Demonstrations Series.
Prod-USDHEW Dist-USNAC

Neuroanatomy Demonstrations, Pt 06 C 56 MIN
3/4 OR 1/2 INCH VIDEO CASSETTE PRO
Includes visceral afferents, vestibular and cochlear systems and visual system.
From The Neuroanatomy Demonstrations Series.
Prod-USDHEW Dist-USNAC

Neuroanatomy Demonstrations, Pt 07 C 36 MIN
3/4 OR 1/2 INCH VIDEO CASSETTE PRO
Includes dorsal thalamus and pyradial system.
From The Neuroanatomy Demonstrations Series.
Prod-USDHEW Dist-USNAC

Neuroanatomy Demonstrations, Pt 08 C 53 MIN
3/4 OR 1/2 INCH VIDEO CASSETTE PRO
Includes cerebellar connections and extrapyramidal system.
From The Neuroanatomy Demonstrations Series.
Prod-USDHEW Dist-USNAC

Neuroanatomy Demonstrations, Pt 09 C 53 MIN
3/4 OR 1/2 INCH VIDEO CASSETTE PRO
Includes the autonomic nervous system and olfactory and limbic systems.
From The Neuroanatomy Demonstrations Series.
Prod-USDHEW Dist-USNAC

Neuroanatomy Demonstrations, Pt 10 C 12 MIN
3/4 OR 1/2 INCH VIDEO CASSETTE PRO
Includes a video synopsis.
From The Neuroanatomy Demonstrations Series.
Prod-USDHEW Dist-USNAC

Neuroanatomy—A Series
C A
Places emphasis on the human brain in dissection. Authored by Drs D G Montemurro, R P Singh, P Haase, Department of Anatomy, University of Western Ontario. Designed for medical students and doctors.
Prod-UWO Dist-TEF

Human Brain In Dissection, Pt I - Embryology
Human Brain In Dissection, Pt II - General 015 MIN
Human Brain In Dissection, Pt III - The 025 MIN
Human Brain In Dissection, Pt III - The 024 MIN
Human Brain In Dissection, Pt IV, The Blood 028 MIN
Human Brain In Dissection, Pt IV, The Blood 024 MIN
Human Brain In Dissection, Pt V 036 MIN
Human Brain In Dissection, Pt V 025 MIN
Human Brain In Dissection, Pt V - Topography 020 MIN
Human Brain In Dissection, Pt V - Topography 025 MIN
Human Brain In Dissection, Pt VI - The White 039 MIN
Human Brain In Dissection, Pt VII (A) - The 018 MIN
Human Brain In Dissection, Pt VII (A) - The 019 MIN
Human Brain In Dissection, Pt X (A) - The 040 MIN
Human Brain In Dissection, Pt X - The Brain 037 MIN
Human Brain In Dissection, Pt X - The Brain 025 MIN
Human Brain In Dissection, Pt XI - The Spinal 051 MIN
Human Brain In Dissection, Pt XI - The Spinal 028 MIN
Human Brain In Section, The 057 MIN
Introduction To The Examination Of The Brain 051 MIN
Lateral Cerebral Ventricle And The Fornix - A 018 MIN
Lateral Cerebral Ventricles And The Fornix 020 MIN
Practical Examination In Neuroanatomy, Pt I 056 MIN
Practical Examination In Neuroanatomy, Pt II 034 MIN

Neurobiology—A Series
PRO
Identifies and diagrams the various structures of the human brain, discussing physiology and pathology.
Prod-HSCIC Dist-HSCIC

Basal Ganglia And Related Nuclei, The 015 MIN
Brainstem And Cranial Nerves, The 013 MIN
Cerebellum, The 015 MIN
Diencephalon, The 020 MIN
External Circulation Of The Brain, The 015 MIN
Internal Structure Of The Brain, The 015 MIN
Major Divisions And Areas Of Function 019 MIN
Medulla Oblongata, The 015 MIN
Mesencephalon, The 015 MIN
Pons, The 015 MIN
Ventricular System, The 015 MIN

Neuroleptic Drugs And Adjunctive Medications C 29 MIN
3/4 INCH VIDEO CASSETTE
Illustrates and discusses neuroleptic or antipsychotic medications. Reviews major mental illnesses.
From The Psychotropic Drugs And The Health Care Professional Series.
Prod-UWASHP Dist-UWASHP

Neurologic - Cranial Nerves And Sensory System (2nd Ed) C 22 MIN
16MM FILM - 3/4 IN VIDEO PRO
Demonstrates the physical examination of the cranial nerves and sensory system, showing necessary procedures, manipulation, pacing, positions and patient-examiner interaction.
From The Visual Guide To Physical Examination (2nd Ed) Series.
LC NO. 81-707475
Prod-LIP Dist-LIP Prodn-JACSTO 1981

Neurologic - Motor System And Reflexes (2nd Ed) C 18 MIN
16MM FILM - 3/4 IN VIDEO PRO
Demonstrates the physical examination of the motor system and reflexes, showing necessary procedures, manipulations, pacing, positions and patient-examiner interaction.
From The Visual Guide To Physical Examination (2nd Ed) Series.
LC NO. 81-707476
Prod-LIP Dist-LIP Prodn-JACSTO 1981

Neurologic Examination C 40 MIN
16MM FILM OPTICAL SOUND PRO
Demonstrates techniques and processes of a neurologic examination of normal children from infancy through school age.
From The Pediatric Examination - Art And Process Series.
LC NO. 78-700681
Prod-TUNNEW Dist-LIP 1977

Neurological Assessment - Cerebellar Function, Motor Function, Reflexes And... C 20 MIN
3/4 OR 1/2 INCH VIDEO CASSETTE
Explains how to test for balance and coordination, motor function, reflex arcs and sensory perception of lights, touch, superficial and deep pain, temperature, position and vibration. Emphasizes those tests which are most commonly used.
From The Physical Assessment Series.
Prod-SUNHSC Dist-AJN

Neurological Assessment - Cranial Nerves C 17 MIN
3/4 OR 1/2 INCH VIDEO CASSETTE
Shows how to perform a systematic examination of the cranial nerves. Demonstrates what equipment to use, how to perform each test and how to interpret the findings.
From The Physical Assessment Series.
Prod-SUNHSC Dist-AJN

Neurological Examination C
3/4 OR 1/2 INCH VIDEO CASSETTE
Reviews the appropriate techniques used to challenge or evaluate problems, or suspected problems in the nervous system. Reviews the neurological examination and demonstrates procedures at the patient's bedside.
Prod-AMEDA Dist-AMEDA

Neurological Examination Of Children C 41 MIN
3/4 OR 1/2 INCH VIDEO CASSETTE PRO
Demonstrates neurological examinations of young children. Includes general appearance, head, cranial nerves, motor system and primitive reflexes in newborn, at six, twelve and eighteen months.
Prod-UARIZ Dist-UARIZ

Neurological Examination Of Infants C 26 MIN
16MM FILM MAGNETIC SOUND C
Demonstrates a practical pediatric neurological examination showing changes in growth and development from birth to one-year-old.
LC NO. 72-700643
Prod-KRI Dist-KRI 1965

Neurological Examination Of The Dog With Spinal Disease B 20 MIN
16MM FILM OPTICAL SOUND PRO
Stresses the importance of determining the type and location of the lesions in the dog with spinal disease. Shows the normal reflexes of the dog and discusses how certain lesions will cause a departure from the normal reflex.
Prod-AMVMA Dist-AMVMA

Neurological Examination Of The Newborn Infant C 30 MIN
3/4 OR 1/2 INCH VIDEO CASSETTE PRO
Establishes standards in neonatal examination. Shows normal and abnormal responses to a series of neurological tests.
Prod-WFP Dist-WFP

Neurological Examination Of The One Year Old C 29 MIN
3/4 OR 1/2 INCH VIDEO CASSETTE PRO
Establishes standards for examination of infants at one year of age. Shows normal and abnormal responses to neurological tests.
Prod-WFP Dist-WFP

Neurological Examination, The C
3/4 OR 1/2 INCH VIDEO CASSETTE
Prod-MEDMDS Dist-MEDMDS

Neurological Health Assessment - Cerebellum C 28 MIN
3/4 OR 1/2 INCH VIDEO CASSETTE PRO
Views a physical assessment by a nurse practitioner of the cerebellum spinal nerves of a live patient.
From The Health Assessment Series.
Prod-BRA Dist-BRA

Neurological Health Assessment - Cerebellum C 35 MIN
3/4 OR 1/2 INCH VIDEO CASSETTE PRO
See series title for descriptive statement.
From The Health Assessment Series. Module 11
Prod-MDCC Dist-MDCC

Neurological Health Assessment - Cerebellum Spinal Nerves C 35 MIN
3/4 OR 1/2 INCH VIDEO CASSETTE PRO
Views a physical assessment by a nurse practitioner of the cerebellum cranial nerves of a live patient.
From The Health Assessment Series.
Prod-BRA Dist-BRA

Neurological Health Assessment - Cerebellum Spinal Nerves C 35 MIN
3/4 OR 1/2 INCH VIDEO CASSETTE PRO
See series title for descriptive statement.
From The Health Assessment Series. Module 12
Prod-MDCC Dist-MDCC

Neurological Instruments C 12 MIN
3/4 INCH VIDEO CASSETTE PRO
Demonstrates various types of hammers and tuning forks used in neurological examinations. Discusses the use of common objects, such as safety pins, keys, and coins, during these examinations.
From The Instruments Of Physical Assessment Series.
LC NO. 80-707629
Prod-SUNYSB Dist-LIP 1980

Neurological Test Film C 30 MIN
16MM FILM OPTICAL SOUND PRO
Consists of a film designed for testing neurology students. Presents five patient examinations--multiple sclerosis, Parkinsonism, amyotropic lateral sclerosis, muscular dystrophy (child) and myasthenia gravis.
Prod-UCLA Dist-UCLA 1970

Neurologically Disabled Patient, Pt 1 - Nursing During The Acute Stage—A Series
PRO
Discusses various aspects of nursing care for neurologically disabled patients.
Prod-AJN Dist-AJN Prodn-TVPC 1977

Catastrophe - The Patient And His Family 26 MIN
Critical Care 21 MIN
Nursing Assessment 24 MIN
Supportive Care 28 MIN

Neurologically Disabled Patient, Pt 2 - Nursing During The Rehabilitative...—A Series
PRO
Discusses various aspects of nursing during the rehabilitative stage for neurologically disabled patients.
Prod-AJN Dist-AJN Prodn-TVPC 1977

Activities Of Daily Living - Hygiene And
Activities Of Daily Living - Mobility 29 MIN
Activities Of Daily Living - Skin And Joint 30 MIN
Bowel And Bladder Retraining 30 MIN
New Life, A 26 MIN
Preparation For Home Care 30 MIN
Working It Out 29 MIN

Neurology C 46 MIN
3/4 OR 1/2 INCH VIDEO CASSETTE PRO
Includes a review of basic terminology and anatomy of the nervous system, a description of typical neurological injuries and an explanation of how neurological problems are diagnosed for the benefit of attorneys.
From The Attorneys' Guide To Medicine Series.
Prod-PBI Dist-ABACPE

Neuromotor Assessment Of Cerebral Palsy Spastic Quadriplegia C 50 MIN
3/4 OR 1/2 INCH VIDEO CASSETTE
See series title for descriptive statement.
From The Pediatric Assessment Series.
Prod-UMDSM Dist-UMDSM

Neuromotor Assessment Of Cerebral Palsy, Pre/Post Test C 23 MIN
3/4 OR 1/2 INCH VIDEO CASSETTE
See series title for descriptive statement.
From The Pediatric Assessment Series.
Prod-UMDSM Dist-UMDSM

Neuromotor Assessment Of Cerebral Palsy, Athetosis C 46 MIN
3/4 OR 1/2 INCH VIDEO CASSETTE
See series title for descriptive statement.
From The Pediatric Assessment Series.
Prod-UMDSM Dist-UMDSM

Neuromotor Assessment Of Cerebral Palsy, Spastic Hemiplegia C 52 MIN
3/4 OR 1/2 INCH VIDEO CASSETTE
See series title for descriptive statement.
From The Pediatric Assessment Series.
Prod-UMDSM Dist-UMDSM

Neuromuscular and Skeletal Systems Involvement C 26 MIN
3/4 OR 1/2 INCH VIDEO CASSETTE
Discusses how to assess the effects of renal failure on the nervous system prior to dialysis when changes in the patient's neuromuscular and skeletal systems are most apparent.
From The Individuals With Dysfunction Series.
Prod-AJN Dist-AJN

Neuromuscular Disorders In Systemic Diseases C 49 MIN
3/4 INCH VIDEO CASSETTE PRO
Presents Dr Bernard M Pattern discussing neuromuscular disorders in systemic diseases.
From The Intensive Course In Neuromuscular Diseases Series.
LC NO. 76-706059
Prod-NINDIS Dist-USNAC 1974

Neuromuscular Disorders Of Infancy C 43 MIN
3/4 INCH VIDEO CASSETTE PRO
Presents Dr Hans U Zellweger giving a lecture on neuromuscular disorders of infancy.
From The Intensive Course In Neuromuscular Diseases Series.
LC NO. 76-706060
Prod-NINDIS Dist-USNAC 1974

Neuromuscular Junction Electron Microscopy C 29 MIN
3/4 INCH VIDEO CASSETTE PRO
Presents Dr Michael Fardeau illustrating neuromuscular junction electron microscopy.
From The Intensive Course In Neuromuscular Diseases Series.
LC NO. 76-706061
Prod-NINDIS Dist-USNAC 1974

Neuron Suite, The C 58 MIN
3/4 OR 1/2 INCH VIDEO CASSETTE
Presents host James Burke exploring research in brain chemistry, using a luxury hotel as a vast analog for the operation of the brain as an information transmitter.
LC NO. 83-706164
Prod-PBS Dist-PBS 1982

Neuron, The C 60 MIN
3/4 INCH VIDEO CASSETTE PRO
Describes the structural and functional unit of the nervous system. Discusses the supporting cells in relation to the neuron, types of neurons and differences of myelination in the central nervous system versus the parasympathetic nervous system, growth and development of neurons, and the importance of synapses.
From The Nonbehavioral Sciences And Rehabilitation Series. Part II
Prod-AOTA Dist-AOTA 1980

Neuropathies, The C 42 MIN
3/4 INCH VIDEO CASSETTE PRO
Presents Dr David E Pleasure lecturing on the neuropathies.
From The Intensive Course In Neuromuscular Diseases Series.
LC NO. 76-706062
Prod-NINDIS Dist-USNAC 1974

Neurophysiology Of Pain C 24 MIN
3/4 INCH VIDEO CASSETTE PRO
See series title for descriptive statement.
From The Management Of Pain Series. Module 1
LC NO. 80-707393
Prod-BRA Dist-BRA 1980

Neurosis And Alcohol - An Experimental Study B 27 MIN
16MM FILM SILENT C
Presents experiments with cats, showing how they are affected by drinking milk containing alcohol. Uses trained cats and cats that have been made 'NEUROTIC' by severe motivation conflict. Suggests principles of dynamics of alcoholism which may apply to humans.
Prod-PSUPCR Dist-PSU 1943

Neurosurgery C
3/4 OR 1/2 INCH VIDEO CASSETTE PRO
Discusses the relief of intracranial pressure, anatomy of the intracranial space, intracranial hemorrhage, cerebral abscesses, skull fractures, spinal cord compression, evaluation of the patient, therapy for intracranial mass lesions and increased cranial pressure, the role of the neurosurgical nurse, herniated discs, hydrocephalus and meningomyelocele, tumors, aneurysm and subarachnoid hemorrhage.
Prod-UMICHM Dist-UMICHM 1978

Neurosurgery - Facial Neuralgia C 13 MIN
16MM FILM OPTICAL SOUND PRO
Demonstrates the surgical treatment of trigeminal and glossopharyngeal neuralgia.
LC NO. FIE52-1175
Prod-USN Dist-USNAC 1946

Neurotic Behavior - A Psychodynamic View C 19 MIN
16MM FILM, 3/4 OR 1/2 IN VIDEO C A
Shows the basic dilemma of the neurotic and how mental defenses serve to reduce the anxiety. Takes a psychodynamic approach to neurotic behavior as it follows an episode in the life of Peter, a troubled college student who attempts to cope with reality.
From The Abnormal Psychology Series.
Prod-CRMP Dist-CRMP 1973

Neurotic Child, The B 28 MIN
16MM FILM OPTICAL SOUND C A
Describes a psychoneurotic seven-year-old boy in a clinical interview. Discusses the defensive mechaisms he has aquired in relating to the world. Illustrates his reactions to reality testing, his attitude toward his father and his inhibited aggressions.
LC NO. FIA68-2697
Prod-PSUPCR Dist-PSU 1968

Neurotransmitters C
1/2 IN VIDEO CASSETTE (VHS)
Deals with neurotransnmitter substances in the brain and their function. Explains the process of electrochemical communication between cells.
From The Brain Triggers - Biochemistry And Human Behavior Series.
Prod-IBIS Dist-IBIS

Neutral Zone In Complete Dentures, The, Pt 1 - Clinical Procedures C 19 MIN
16MM FILM - 3/4 IN VIDEO PRO
Demonstrates the clinical procedures involved in recording the neutral zone for positioning denture teeth and defining the contours of the polished surface of dentures.
LC NO. 78-706205
Prod-VADTC Dist-USNAC 1978

Neutral Zone In Complete Dentures, The, Pt 2 - Laboratory Procedures C 11 MIN
16MM FILM - 3/4 IN VIDEO PRO
Demonstrates technical procedures for developing matrices of the neutral zone record and using them in establishing an occlusal plane and in anterior, posterior and medial lateral positioning of the supplied tooth.
LC NO. 78-706206
Prod-VADTC Dist-USNAC 1978

Neutron Activation C 8 MIN
16MM FILM OPTICAL SOUND
Describes the analytic techniques that are involved in measuring the presence of radioactive elements from a substance irradiated with neutrons.
LC NO. FIE64-135
Prod-USAEC Dist-USNAC 1964

Neutron Activation Analysis C 40 MIN
16MM FILM OPTICAL SOUND C A
Presents analysis by neutron activation. Covers types of source used counting techniques and applications.
Prod-USAEC Dist-USERD 1964

Neutron Diffraction C 9 MIN
16MM FILM OPTICAL SOUND
Describes the principles of neutron diffraction and the new fields of investigation involving diffraction effects. Compares wavelengths of thermal neutrons to X-rays used in the study of crystal structures and contrasts their different scattering processes. Discusses the usefulness of neutron diffraction studies in determining the positions of light atoms in the crystal structure and in providing a technique for the study of magnetic orientation.
LC NO. FIE64-137
Prod-USAEC Dist-USNAC 1964

Neutrons At Work C 29 MIN
2 INCH VIDEOTAPE
See series title for descriptive statement.
From The Interface Series.
Prod-KCET Dist-PUBTEL

Nevada C
3/4 OR 1/2 INCH VIDEO CASSETTE
Presents five segments about the state of Nevada, where the landscape is beautiful but the life can be harsh.
From The Portrait Of America Series.
Prod-TBS Dist-TBS

Nevelson In Process C 30 MIN
16MM FILM, 3/4 OR 1/2 IN VIDEO H-C A
Describes the work of sculptor Louise Nevelson.
From The Originals - Women In Art Series.
LC NO. 80-706120
Prod-WNETTV Dist-FI 1977

Never Alone C 18 MIN
16MM FILM OPTICAL SOUND PRO
Portrays some of the ways in which chaplains in institutions for the mentally retarded work with other disciplines to meet the needs of the patients.
Prod-NATMAC Dist-NMAC

Never Among Strangers C 14 MIN
16MM FILM - 3/4 IN VIDEO
Discusses the training, job opportunities and other benefits available to women recruits of the U S Marine Corps. Issued in 1968 as a motion picture.
LC NO. 79-706669
Prod-USMC Dist-USNAC 1979

Never Ask What Country B 30 MIN
16MM FILM OPTICAL SOUND R
Dramatizes the life of William Green, the son of a coal miner, who went into the mines at the age of 15, and had to give up his hopes of becoming a Baptist minister. Tells how from 1924 until his death he was president of the American Federation of Labor. (Kinescope)
Prod-JTS Dist-NAAJS Prodn-NBCTV 1962

Never Cry Rape C
1/2 IN VIDEO CASSETTE BETA/VHS J-C
Shows how to defend oneself against an attacker and how to protect oneself from rape. Demonstrates physical and psychological strategies for self-defense, and what common reactions should be avoided.
Prod-GA Dist-GA

Never Cry Wolf C 30 MIN
16MM FILM, 3/4 OR 1/2 IN VIDEO I-H
Tells of a young government biologist who travels to the Arctic to gather information about wolves. Shows how he finds them to be tender, courageous animals who live in total harmony with their environment. From the book Never Cry Wolf by Farley Mowat.
From The Film As Literature, Series 5 Series.
Prod-WDEMCO Dist-WDEMCO 1983

Never Forget Names And Faces—A Series

Includes four videotapes ranging from 45 to 59 minutes in length. Tells how to remember the names and faces of new acquaintances as well as old friends. Utilizes memory association, a techniques created centuries ago by Greeks and Romans. Reveals process by active participation in memory exercises.
Prod-CSU Dist-AMCEE

Never Give A Sucker An Even Break B 63 MIN
16MM FILM OPTICAL SOUND
Stars W C Fields as a man who somehow becomes the guardian of a young girl.
Prod-UPCI Dist-SWANK

Never Give Up C 30 MIN
3/4 OR 1/2 INCH VIDEO CASSETTE T
Presents illustration of behaviors and motivations for irresponsible actions, and examples of success under extreme conditions.
From The Developing Discipline Series.
Prod-SDPT Dist-GPITVL 1983

Never Give Up - Imogen Cunningham C 28 MIN
16MM FILM, 3/4 OR 1/2 IN VIDEO J A
Pictures a visit with portrait photographer Imogen Cunningham.
Prod-HERSHA Dist-PHENIX 1975

Never Say Die C
16MM FILM, 3/4 OR 1/2 IN VIDEO IND
Tells the story of a rig hand who is 'on trial' for his life. Takes a deep look at 'attitude' and distinguishes the difference between life and death.
Prod-FLMWST Dist-FLMWST 1982

Never Say Yes To A Stranger C 20 MIN
16MM FILM, 3/4 OR 1/2 IN VIDEO
Examines the many ways that strangers try to trick or lure children into peril. Provides safety tips and tactics to get away from strangers who are potentially harmful.
Prod-MTI Dist-MTI

Never Say You Can't Until You Try C 10 MIN
3/4 INCH VIDEO CASSETTE I-J
Emphasizes the importance of trying, failing and succeeding.
Prod-GA Dist-GA

Never The Easy Way, Version 1 C 14 MIN
16MM FILM OPTICAL SOUND I-C A
Tells the story of a life or death race to save a trapped woman in a forest fire. Emphasizes water conservation and other fire prevention measures for rural residents.
LC NO. 76-701747
Prod-PUBSF Dist-FILCOM 1966

Never The Easy Way, Version 2 C 13 MIN
16MM FILM OPTICAL SOUND
Presents the story of a life-or-death race to save a trapped woman in a forest fire caused by the negligence of her husband and son. Deals with fire prevention methods for both rural residents and city dwellers. Stresses child education on fire dangers.
Prod-PUBSF Dist-FILCOM

Never Trust Anyone Under 60 C 60 MIN
16MM FILM, 3/4 OR 1/2 IN VIDEO
Describes graphically problems of aging, such as those discussed at the White House Conference on Aging - isolation, abandonment, housing and other problems.
LC NO. 81-707211
Prod-USSRS Dist-USNAC 1971

Never Turn Back - The Life Of Fannie Lou Hamer C 60 MIN
16MM FILM OPTICAL SOUND
Presents Fannie Lou Hamer, the great heroine of the bitter struggle for justice in Mississippi, speaking of non-violence and black power. Features a chronicle of a movement and a people in the songs and the words of the Southern Black.
Prod-REPRO Dist-REPRO

Never Weaken / Why Worry B 78 MIN
16MM FILM, 3/4 OR 1/2 IN VIDEO
Presents Harold Lloyd in a comedy in which he hustles customers for his girlfriend who works for an osteopath. Shows how he winds up trying to commit suicide and being lifted out of his office on a girder. Includes a reissue of the 1923 silent Harold Lloyd comedy Why Worry. Tells the story of a rich hypochondriac who visits Latin America to cure his ills and becomes embroiled in a revolution without realizing it.
From The Harold Lloyd Series.
Prod-ROACH Dist-TIMLIF 1976

New Actors For The Classics B 60 MIN
16MM FILM OPTICAL SOUND J-C A
Presents a documentary on acting styles. Features the Juillard-trained City Center Acting Company.
LC NO. 74-701904
Prod-WNETTV Dist-CANTOR 1973

New Advances In Recycling C 13 MIN
16MM FILM OPTICAL SOUND
Shows how technologists are finding better ways to extract clean water, energy and raw materials from trash and other waste.
Prod-ALLFP Dist-NSTA 1977

New Age Communities C 40 MIN
16MM FILM OPTICAL SOUND J-C A
Examines contemporary efforts, both secular and spiritual, at establishing a utopian way of life.
LC NO. 77-700137
Prod-HP Dist-HP 1977

New Age Communities - The Search For Utopia C 40 MIN
3/4 OR 1/2 INCH VIDEO CASSETTE
Shows functioning, practical attempts at the utopian life, both secular and spiritual.
Prod-HP Dist-HP

New Age For The Old, A C 27 MIN
16MM FILM OPTICAL SOUND J-C A
Presents an historical survey of the status of the elderly and examines attitudes toward them from classical times to the 1970's.
LC NO. 80-700135
Prod-KLUGDP Dist-ALTANA 1979

New Age Of Diversity, The C 30 MIN
3/4 OR 1/2 INCH VIDEO CASSETTE
See series title for descriptive statement.
From The Third Wave Series.
Prod-TRIWVE Dist-DELTAK

New Age Of The Train C 14 MIN
3/4 OR 1/2 INCH VIDEO CASSETTE
Features the supertrains of Europe and Japan, which are filled to capacity and running 'in the black.' Shows new trains, future designs and some superflops.
Prod-JOU Dist-JOU

New Alchemists, The C 29 MIN
16MM FILM, 3/4 OR 1/2 IN VIDEO I A
Shows how a group of scientists and their families are successfully working an experimental plant and fish farm near Falmouth, Massachusetts. Explains how they use only organic fertilizers and use solar heat and a windmill for energy.
Prod-NFBC Dist-BNCHMK 1975

New Alchemy - A Rediscovery Of Promise C 29 MIN
16MM FILM, 3/4 OR 1/2 IN VIDEO J-C A
A shortened version of the 1984 videocassette New Alchemy - A Rediscovery Of Promise. Looks at the accomplishments of the New Alchemy Institute which has conducted sophisticated and recognized research in the areas of solar aquaculture, bioshelter, wind power and organic agriculture.
LC NO. 84-706255
Prod-FLCK Dist-BULFRG Prodn-BURKEL 1984

New Alchemy - A Rediscovery Of Promise C 58 MIN
16MM FILM, 3/4 OR 1/2 IN VIDEO J-C A
Looks at the accomplishments of the New Alchemy Institute which has conducted sophisticated and recognized research in the areas of solar aquaculture, bioshelters, wind power and organic agriculture.
LC NO. 84-706254
Prod-FLCK Dist-BULFRG Prodn-BURKEL 1984

New Alchemy, The C 27 MIN
16MM FILM, 3/4 OR 1/2 IN VIDEO J-C A
Discusses the many beneficial uses, including industrial uses, of bacteria and fungi.
From The Perspective Series.
Prod-LONTVS Dist-STNFLD

New American Neighborhood Road Show, The C 60 MIN
3/4 OR 1/2 INCH VIDEO CASSETTE
Travels through six of Baltimore's ethnic communities including Highlandtown, Little Italy, Park Heights, Old West Baltimore, Hampden and South Baltimore through a stage production in which the six-member Voices Company portrays longtime residents of the neighborhoods.
Prod-MDCPB Dist-MDCPB

New Americans C 60 MIN
16MM FILM OPTICAL SOUND I-C A
Focuses on the 25-year period from the end of the Civil War to 1891. Points out that these were the major years of westward migration and traces some early explorations in which the black men were participants.
From The Black Frontier Series.
Prod-KUONTV Dist-GPITVL

New Americans—A Series
P-I
Explores five Indochinese cultures, including Vietnamese, Chinese living in Vietnam, Laotian, the Lao-Hmong of Laos and Cambodian.
Prod-KCET Dist-GPITVL 1980

New Amsterdam C 15 MIN
3/4 OR 1/2 INCH VIDEO CASSETTE P
Relates some of the problems encountered by Peter Stuyvesant and the Indians on the island of Manhattan.
From The Stories Of America Series.
Prod-OHSDE Dist-AITECH Prodn-WVIZTV 1976

New And Novel - The Development Of The Novel In England C 45 MIN
3/4 OR 1/2 INCH VIDEO CASSETTE
Recounts the development of the novel in England.
From The Survey Of English Literature I Series.
Prod-MDCPB Dist-MDCPB

New And Renewable Sources Of Energy C 28 MIN
3/4 INCH VIDEOTAPE
Presents a United Nations conference on new and renewable sources of energy. Includes interviews and film clips on energy sources. Hosted by Marilyn Perry.
From The International Byline Series.
Prod-PERRYM Dist-PERRYM

New And Used Cars C 29 MIN
2 INCH VIDEOTAPE
See series title for descriptive statement.
From The Way It Is Series.
Prod-KUHTTV Dist-PUBTEL

New Answers For The Basic Needs Of Food And Clothing B 15 MIN
2 INCH VIDEOTAPE P-I
See series title for descriptive statement.
From The Our Changing Community Series.
Prod-VITA Dist-GPITVL 1967

New Approach To A Great Old Game, A C 10 MIN
16MM FILM, 3/4 OR 1/2 IN VIDEO J-C A
Introduces the game of bowling, featuring the importance of shoe and ball selection and explaining how to keep score. Concludes with an introduction to the approach and delivery recommended for the beginning bowler.
From The Four Steps To Better Bowling Series.
Prod-ATHI Dist-ATHI 1983

New Approach, The - The Aerospace Officer Of The Future C 14 MIN
16MM FILM OPTICAL SOUND
Shows how the ROTC program develops young men physically and mentally and prepares them to be officers.
LC NO. 74-706158
Prod-USAF Dist-USNAC 1966

New Approaches To Big Problems C 29 MIN
16MM FILM, 3/4 OR 1/2 IN VIDEO T
Presents authorities who offer their ideas on a variety of problem areas including discipline, human relationships, authority, self-concept, truancy and violence. Visits a school where counseling is being used to solve campus violence problems.
From The Dealing With Classroom Problems Series.
Prod-MFFD Dist-FI 1976

New Approaches To Childhood Lymphocytic Leukemia C 50 MIN
3/4 INCH VIDEO CASSETTE
Summarizes pediatric lymphocytic leukemia treatment as it is currently practiced. Describes the principles used in diagnosis and the rationale for treatment selection.
Prod-UTAHTI Dist-UTAHTI

New Art In The American West C 22 MIN
16MM FILM OPTICAL SOUND
Looks at the lives and work of five artists of the American West.
LC NO. 80-700177
Prod-PHILMO Dist-PHILMO Prodn-DYP 1979

New Arts C 16 MIN
16MM FILM OPTICAL SOUND H-C A
Introduces technological art and artists. Includes interpretations by Andy Warhol, Roy Lichtenstein, Claes Oldenburg, Boyd Hefferd, Tony Smith, Newton Harrison and Rockne Krebs.
LC NO. 71-713590
Prod-SAARCH Dist-VIEWFI 1971

New Attitude, A C 11 MIN
3/4 OR 1/2 INCH VIDEO CASSETTE
Examines the need for developing a new attitude based on the change in relationships that occurs on assuming the new job as supervisor.
From The New Supervisor Series. Module 1
Prod-RESEM Dist-RESEM

New Awareness, The C 24 MIN
3/4 OR 1/2 INCH VIDEO CASSETTE
Helps develop an understanding of chemical dependency (including alcholism) as a treatable illness.
From The Caring Community - Alcoholism And Drug Abuse Series.
Prod-VTRI Dist-VTRI

New Baby Care (Rev Ed) C 18 MIN
16MM FILM, 3/4 OR 1/2 IN VIDEO PRO
Discusses the skills and equipment needed to care for the newborn, including breast and bottle feeding, handling and bathing of the infant, infant skin care and warning sings of illness.
Prod-PRORE Dist-PRORE

New Baby Care (Spanish) C 18 MIN
16MM FILM, 3/4 OR 1/2 IN VIDEO PRO
Discusses the skills and equipment needed to care for the newborn, including breast and bottle feeding, handling and bathing of the infant, infant skin care and warning sings of illness.
Prod-PRORE Dist-PRORE

New Baby, The C 20 MIN
16MM FILM OPTICAL SOUND J-C
Points out that the way in which the basic needs of the infant are provided for may make a difference to the well-being of the child and the harmony of the home. Illustrates a sound routine of baby care.
Prod-CDNHW Dist-SF 1961

New Baby, The X 20 MIN
16MM FILM OPTICAL SOUND J-C A
Pictures a family preparing for the arrival of a new baby, with emphasis on the mother's prenatal medical supervision. Discusses the new baby's emotional needs and his daily care. Shows how parents can cope with the reactions of older children to the new arrival.
From The Family Life Education And Human Growth Series.
Prod-NFBC Dist-SF 1963

New Beginning, A C 15 MIN
16MM FILM OPTICAL SOUND
Surveys the new bulk mail system. Discusses the identification and philosophy of the system and shows the New York installation.
LC NO. 74-706378
Prod-USPS Dist-USNAC 1974

New Beginnings - Women, Alcohol And Recovery C 20 MIN
16MM FILM, 3/4 OR 1/2 IN VIDEO J-C A
Presents case studies of three women who have successfully overcome alcoholism. Emphasizes the importance of a total commitment to healing aimed at earlier awareness, identification and effective treatment for women.
Prod-PMASS Dist-AIMS 1977

New Blood For A Baby B 15 MIN
16MM FILM OPTICAL SOUND H-C A
Explains to expectant mothers for whom the Rh-factor may present complications, the safety factors at childbirth. Shows an exchange transfusion performed for a baby soon after birth.
From The Doctors At Work Series.
LC NO. FIA65-1353
Prod-CMA Dist-LAWREN Prodn-LAWREN 1962

New Boys, The C 26 MIN
16MM FILM, 3/4 OR 1/2 IN VIDEO J-C A
Describes a Canadian school where adolescent boys are sent on arduous canoe-and-portage trips in the belief that the experience will turn them into men.
Prod-NFBC Dist-WOMBAT

New Breath Of Life (Rev Ed) C 24 MIN
16MM FILM, 3/4 OR 1/2 IN VIDEO J-C A
Demonstrates the correct resuscitation techniques when breathing stops. Shows how to open the airway when it is blocked by the tongue during unconsciousness, how to save a choking victim by back blows and abdominal thrusts and how to restore breathing by mouth to mouth methods.
Prod-PFP Dist-PFP

New Breath Of Life (Rev Ed) (Dutch) C 24 MIN
16MM FILM, 3/4 OR 1/2 IN VIDEO J-C A
A Dutch language version of the revised edition of the film and video, New Breath Of Life. Demonstrates two of the ABC's of basic life support, A-Airway Opened and B-Breathing restored. Teaches how to open the airway of an unconscious victim, how to administer mouth to mouth breathing, and how to save a choking victim with back blows and abdominal thrusts. Narrated by Nanette Fabray.
Prod-PFP Dist-PFP

New Breed Of Cat, A C 27 MIN
16MM FILM, 3/4 OR 1/2 IN VIDEO
Introduces the concept of human factor engineering and shows its application to Air Force Academy cadets.
Prod-USAF Dist-USNAC 1980

New Breed Of Rocket Power, The C 14 MIN
16MM FILM OPTICAL SOUND
Recounts the basic design philosophy and method of manufacture that produced the Bullpup rocket. Pictures the acceptance test as well as several live firings of the Bullpup and describes the Navy's use of air-to-ground missiles utilizing packaged liquid fuel as an engine propellant.
Prod-THIOKL Dist-THIOKL 1964

New Bronchodilators C 16 MIN
3/4 OR 1/2 INCH VIDEO CASSETTE PRO
Reviews the mechanism of relaxation and dilation of bronchial smooth muscle as it reacts to drug preparations. Details the use, mode of action, duration, onset, dosages, side effects and preparation of the bronchodilators, isoproterenol, metaproterenol and terhutaline.
Prod-UMICHM Dist-UMICHM 1976

New Brunswick Promenade C 14 MIN
16MM FILM OPTICAL SOUND
Shows various scenic tourist delights in New Brunswick, canada.
LC NO. 74-702403
Prod-PONB Dist-CTFL Prodn-FIDLHD 1973

New Building Under The Water C 12 MIN
3/4 OR 1/2 INCH VIDEO CASSETTE
Offers the sensation of perspective. Involves a dream of Beirut, and of China invoking the Western economy, causing a crash in Washington, D C.
Prod-KITCHN Dist-KITCHN

New Building Under The Water - Ken Feingold C 14 MIN
3/4 INCH VIDEO CASSETTE A
Prod-AFA Dist-AFA 1982

New Camp, The C 15 MIN
3/4 OR 1/2 INCH VIDEO CASSETTE I
Shows a Bedouin doctor treating a patient.
From The Encounter In The Desert Series.
Prod-CTI Dist-CTI

New Car, The B 8 MIN
16MM FILM OPTICAL SOUND
Tells how Flip the Frog buys a new car, collides with a trolley, and is swallowed by a tunnel.
Prod-UNKNWN Dist-BHAWK 1930

New Cinema, The C 100 MIN
3/4 OR 1/2 INCH VIDEO CASSETTE A
Presents many of the world's foremost filmmakers who attended the llth Annual Montreal International Festival of New Cinema. Includes interviews with the filmmakers, who discuss their views on art and life.
Prod-CNEMAG Dist-CNEMAG 1983

New Cities Of Macarthur C 15 MIN
16MM FILM - 3/4 IN VIDEO
Describes various aspects of the Macarthur Growth Centre, from industrial development and employment opportunities to education, community activities and housing.

LC NO. 81-706510
Prod-NSWF Dist-TASCOR 1980

New Concept Of Centric Relation And Technique For Occlusal Adjustment—A Series

Offers an unedited presentation by Lawrence A Weinberg, DDS, demonstrating how to examine and evaluate the musculature and the temporomandibular joints.
Prod-AMDA Dist-AMDA 1975

New Concept? In Urinary Infections C 28 MIN
3/4 OR 1/2 INCH VIDEO CASSETTE PRO
Describes the pathogenesis of urinary infections and new concepts in the prophylactic control of recurrent infections.
Prod-WFP Dist-WFP

New Concepts In Housing For Adults—A Series

Looks at the housing needs of the elderly and offers some solutions.
Prod-UMITV Dist-UMITV 1978

Architect's Vision, An 022 MIN
Assisted Residential Living - A Form Of 014 MIN
Design Must Be Human, The 018 MIN
Financing 021 MIN

New Concepts In Housing For Older Adults—A Series

A
Explores the possible construction of facilities which enable older adults to live with dignity, safety and help, if needed.
Prod-UMICH Dist-UMICH

Architect's Vision, An 020 MIN
Art Of Managing, The 022 MIN
Assisted Residential Living - A Form Of 014 MIN
Design Must Be Human, The 018 MIN
Financing 021 MIN

New Concepts In Marriage C 30 MIN
3/4 OR 1/2 INCH VIDEO CASSETTE J-C A
Presents Robert Rimmer, author of The Harrad Experiment, and Della Roy of Penn State University discussing new concepts in marriage.
From The Moral Values In Contemporary Society Series.
Prod-AMHUMA Dist-AMHUMA

New Concepts In Sludge Management C 5 MIN
16MM FILM, 3/4 OR 1/2 IN VIDEO
Shows the progress being made in using sludges from municipal wastewater treatment plants to enrich agricultural land.
Prod-NSF Dist-USNAC

New Constitution For Texas, A C 30 MIN
16MM FILM OPTICAL SOUND J-C A
Documents events leading up to the Texas Constitutional Convention held in 1974, including pertinent historical data as well as excerpts from speeches delivered by Texas citizens to the Constitutional Convention committees.
LC NO. 76-700842
Prod-TRIMRK Dist-TSLAD 1974

New Convent Garden - Europe's Super Market C 20 MIN
16MM FILM, 3/4 OR 1/2 IN VIDEO I-J A
Looks at Britain's largest wholesale market which receives fruit, vegetables and flowers from more than 70 countries and has an annual turnover of $200 million.
Prod-LUF Dist-LUF 1979

New Country Doctors, The - Changing Concepts In Rural Medicine C 22 MIN
16MM FILM OPTICAL SOUND
Examines advantages and disadvantages of solo and group medical practice and the attitudes of young family physicians. Offers guidelines to attract health professionals to rural areas.
LC NO. 76-702858
Prod-UIOWA Dist-UIOWA Prodn-UIOWA 1976

New Cults As A Social Phenomenon, The C 30 MIN
3/4 OR 1/2 INCH VIDEO CASSETTE J-C A
Shows Ernest Van den Haag of the New School for Social Research and Rabbi Sherwin Wine of the Society for Humanistic Judaism discussing the new cults as a social phenomenon.
From The Moral Values In Contemporary Society Series.
Prod-AMHUMA Dist-AMHUMA

New Dance C 30 MIN
16MM FILM OPTICAL SOUND J-C A
Presents Doris Humphrey's 1935 dance of affirmation entitled New Dance, as reconstructed in 1972 by the Repertory Company of the American Dance Festival at Connecticut College.
LC NO. 78-701821
Prod-ADFEST Dist-UR 1978

New Dawn, A C 20 MIN
16MM FILM, 3/4 OR 1/2 IN VIDEO
Uses animation to look at a colony's struggle for political independence.
From The History Book Series. Volume 9
Prod-STATNS Dist-CNEMAG

New Day Dawning, A C 20 MIN
16MM FILM OPTICAL SOUND
Features the innovative growing and packing processes of the Florida tomato.
Prod-FLADC Dist-FLADC

New Day, A C 14 MIN
3/4 OR 1/2 INCH VIDEO CASSETTE P
See series title for descriptive statement.
From The Strawberry Square Series.
Prod-NEITV Dist-AITECH 1982

New Deal And The Afro-Americans, The B 30 MIN
2 INCH VIDEOTAPE H-C A
See series title for descriptive statement.
From The Americans From Africa - A History Series. No. 26
Prod-CVETVC Dist-GPITVL Prodn-WCVETV

New Deal, The C 25 MIN
16MM FILM, 3/4 OR 1/2 IN VIDEO J-C A
Analyzes the New Deal as a response to the massive problems of the Depression.
From The American History Series.
Prod-CRMP Dist-CRMP 1972

New Deal, The C 30 MIN
3/4 OR 1/2 INCH VIDEO CASSETTE C
Illustrates the New Deal, during which governmental programs took on an unprecedented scope and permanency.
America - The Second Century Series.
Prod-DALCCD Dist-DALCCD

New Deal, The C 30 MIN
2 INCH VIDEOTAPE
Analyzes both the critics and supporters of the New Deal. Provides a summary of the New Deal legislation.
From The American History II Series.
Prod-KRMATV Dist-GPITVL

New Delhi C 10 MIN
16MM FILM, 3/4 OR 1/2 IN VIDEO I-H
Shows that New Delhi, the capital of India, is a city of stark contrasts reflecting the diversity of social and economic conditions in the country. Visits the crowded streets of Old Delhi and the offices and growing middle class of New Delhi.
Prod-LUF Dist-LUF 1978

New Design For Education, A C 28 MIN
16MM FILM OPTICAL SOUND
Discusses innovations in flexible scheduling, staff utilization and curriculum. Explains how educational requirements can be formulated more flexibly.
Prod-STNFRD Dist-EDUC 1964

New Developments In Communication B 15 MIN
2 INCH VIDEOTAPE P-I
See series title for descriptive statement.
From The Our Changing Community Series.
Prod-VITA Dist-GPITVL 1967

New Developments In Operational Amplifiers C 30 MIN
3/4 OR 1/2 INCH VIDEO CASSETTE PRO
Covers design, characteristics and applications of chopper stabilized operational amplifiers that contain both bipolar and MOS integrated circuitry. Compares standard op-amps and emphasizes advantage of new type op-amp.
From The Linear And Interface Integrated Circuits, Part I - Linear Integrated Circuits Series.
Prod-TXINLC Dist-TXINLC

New Developments In The Clinical Application Of Hyperalimentation C 60 MIN
3/4 INCH VIDEO CASSETTE
Discusses developments relating nutrition to immunology and cancer management.
Prod-UTAHTI Dist-UTAHTI

New Diagnostic Procedures In The Diagnosis Of Pituitary Disease B 35 MIN
16MM FILM - 3/4 IN VIDEO PRO
Summarizes new developments which have resulted in sensitive and specific methods of radioimmunoassay for the measurement in peripheral plasma of all pituitary hormones except prolactin.
From The Clinical Pathology Series.
LC NO. 76-706063
Prod-NMAC Dist-USNAC 1969

New Dimensions C 19 MIN
16MM FILM OPTICAL SOUND
Follows a manager through a typical day showing the advantages of playing the role of host.
LC NO. 75-711361
Prod-MCDONS Dist-MCDONS 1971

New Dimensions In Concrete - Through The 60's C 16 MIN
16MM FILM OPTICAL SOUND
See series title for descriptive statement.
From The Twelve Decades Of Concrete In American Architecture Series.
Prod-PRTLND Dist-PRTLND 1970

New Dimensions In School Building Flexibility C 28 MIN
16MM FILM OPTICAL SOUND T
Presents a functional definition of space needed in a new school design.
Prod-EDUC Dist-EDUC

New Direction In Dance, A C 58 MIN
16MM FILM OPTICAL SOUND
Presents the Barbara Mettler Dance Company of 17 men and women improvising collectively for an hour. Demonstrates dance as the language of movement and as expression of group feeling.
Prod-METT Dist-METT 1978

New Directions C
3/4 OR 1/2 INCH VIDEO CASSETTE C
Emphasizes future uses of the newly acquired writing skills and their application and development later in many areas.
From The Write Course - An Introduction To College Composition Series.
Prod-DALCCD Dist-DALCCD

New Directions C 30 MIN
3/4 OR 1/2 INCH VIDEO CASSETTE C A
Discusses future uses of newly acquired writing skills.
From The Write Course - An Introduction To College Composition Series.
Prod-FI Dist-FI 1984

New Directions For Nursing Service Administration B 30 MIN
16MM FILM OPTICAL SOUND C
Describes the changing roles of hospitals, the continuing shortages of personnel and the various methods which nurses are using to cope with new tasks.
From The Nursing Perspectives Series.
LC NO. 78-706826
Prod-VDONUR Dist-AJN Prodn-WTTWTV 1968

New Directions In Science Fiction C 25 MIN
16MM FILM OPTICAL SOUND H-C T
Presents a seminar conducted by Harlan Ellison on the new direction of science fiction.
From The Literature Of Science Fiction Series.
LC NO. 72-700536
Prod-UKANBC Dist-UKANS 1971

New Double Helical Model For DNA, A C 55 MIN
3/4 INCH VIDEO CASSETTE
Proposes a new model for DNA and discusses its structure in detail.
Prod-UTAHTI Dist-UTAHTI

New Drugs In Gastroenterology C 30 MIN
3/4 OR 1/2 INCH VIDEO CASSETTE
Discusses the organization and the various divisions of the Food and Drug Administration and the process of approval for new gastrointestinal drugs.
Prod-ROWLAB Dist-ROWLAB

New Ear Drums By Surgery B 50 MIN
16MM FILM OPTICAL SOUND PRO
Details a surgical procedure in which a new ear drum is constructed using a section of vein from the patient's hand.
Prod-CMA Dist-LAWREN

New Earth, A B 30 MIN
16MM FILM OPTICAL SOUND
Portrays the life of Philip Murray, who was President of the United Steelworkers of America and of the Congress of Industrial Organizations. Concludes with a message from the honorable Arthur J Goldberg, associate justice of the Supreme Court. (Kinescope)
Prod-JTS Dist-NAAJS Prodn-NBCTV 1963

New Earth, The B 22 MIN
16MM FILM OPTICAL SOUND J-C
Documents the reclaiming of the Zuider Zee in Holland, a process which took ten thousand men ten years to perform.
Prod-IVEFER Dist-CFS

New Elizabethan Era, The C 29 MIN
2 INCH VIDEOTAPE
See series title for descriptive statement.
From The Course Of Our Times II Series.
Prod-WGBHTV Dist-PUBTEL

New Employees And The New Customers, The C
16MM FILM - 3/4 IN VIDEO
Discusses how the changing composition of the population and the growing expectations of people will affect employment policies, marketing strategies and employee motivation. Shows how demographics can be used as a tool to increase productivity and profitability.
From The Managing For Tomorrow Series. Unit 3
Prod-BNA Dist-BNA

New Employees And The New Customers, The (Dutch) C
16MM FILM, 3/4 OR 1/2 IN VIDEO
Examines demographics as a tool to increase productivity and profitability.
From The Managing For Tomorrow (Dutch) Series.
Prod-BNA Dist-BNA

New Employees And The New Customers, The (German) C
16MM FILM, 3/4 OR 1/2 IN VIDEO
Examines demographics as a tool to increase productivity and profitability.
From The Managing For Tomorrow (German) Series.
Prod-BNA Dist-BNA

New England C 15 MIN
16MM FILM, 3/4 OR 1/2 IN VIDEO J
Examines the people, industry, economy and landscape of the New England region of the United States.
From The U S Geography Series.
Prod-MGHT Dist-MGHT 1976

New England C 23 MIN
16MM FILM, 3/4 OR 1/2 IN VIDEO I-J
Explores the New England states including Maine, New Hampshire, Vermont, Massachusetts, Connecticut and Rhode Island. Visits historic sites like Plymouth, where the Pilgrims first landed and Slater Mill, where the American textile industry was born.
From The United States Geography Series.
Prod-NGS Dist-NGS 1983

New England C 30 MIN
16MM FILM, 3/4 OR 1/2 IN VIDEO I-C
Edited from the motion picture These States. Discusses the roles played by New Hampshire, Rhode Island, Massachusetts and Connecticut during the American Revolution. Focuses on the Boston Tea Party, the early battles at Concord and Lexington, and the monuments of Mystic and Saybrook.
Prod-BCTOS Dist-FI 1975

New England - Background Of Literature (2nd Ed) C 12 MIN
16MM FILM, 3/4 OR 1/2 IN VIDEO J-C
Describes the literature of New England, using selections from Bryant, Longfellow, Whittier, Emerson, Hawthorne, Holmes, Lowell, Dickinson and Frost.
Prod-CORF Dist-CORF 1977

New England Begins C 30 MIN
3/4 OR 1/2 INCH VIDEO CASSETTE
Presents a special program based on the Boston Museum of Fine Art's Landmark exhibition of utilitarian and artistic objects from 17th Century New England. Filmed on location at Plymouth Plantation, an authentic working recreation of a 17th century New England village, as well as at the Saugus Iron Works at Hingham.
Prod-KINGFT Dist-KINGFT

New England Cooking C 20 MIN
16MM FILM OPTICAL SOUND
Examines early American recipes still in use today, such as Boston brown bread and brick oven beans, sea foods and clambakes, Anadama bread, corn pudding and fried apple pies.
From The Cooking Film Series.
Prod-BUGAS Dist-BUGAS

New England Cooking C 23 MIN
16MM FILM OPTICAL SOUND
Demonstrates typical New England cooking by showing the preparation of various recipes. Includes scenes of New England.
LC NO. 72-700362
Prod-AGA Dist-AGA Prodn-BAILYB 1971

New England Cooking C 20 MIN
3/4 OR 1/2 INCH VIDEO CASSETTE
Offers six authentic early American recipes from colonial kitchens.
From The Magical Cook's Tour Series.
Prod-IVCH Dist-IVCH

New England Fall Folio, A C 27 MIN
1/2 IN VIDEO CASSETTE (VHS) A
Illustrates the scenic beauty of New England towns and countryside during the fall. Shows historic landmarks and present-day people.
Prod-MAUPIN Dist-MTP

New England Fishermen (2nd Ed) X 11 MIN
16MM FILM, 3/4 OR 1/2 IN VIDEO I-J A
Outlines the New England fishing industry and its problems. Records the events in the life of fishermen, showing fishing methods and equipment. Visits the Boston fish market.
Prod-EBEC Dist-EBEC 1967

New England In Autumn - The Poetry Of Robert Frost C 30 MIN
3/4 INCH VIDEO CASSETTE H-C A
Gives readings of 17 poems by Robert Frost, filmed in the farmland of Massachusetts.
From The Anyone For Tennyson Series.
Prod-NETCHE Dist-GPITVL

New England Potluck Supper C 29 MIN
3/4 OR 1/2 INCH VIDEO CASSETTE
See series title for descriptive statement.
From The Julia Child And Company Series.
Prod-WGBHTV Dist-PBS

New England Sea Community X 17 MIN
16MM FILM, 3/4 OR 1/2 IN VIDEO I-J
Depicts daily life in a seacoast town in 1845, as it is seen by a 13-year-old boy. Pictures the work of the town tradesmen. Describes seafaring life aboard a fishing boat, coastal trading ship and whaling vessel, as well as the home life of the young boy.
From The Pioneer Life Series.
Prod-IU Dist-IU 1963

New England Town 1660 - Call Of The Frontier X 18 MIN
16MM FILM, 3/4 OR 1/2 IN VIDEO J
Describes life in a New England town in 1660, as exemplified in a dramatization of the problems faced by a blacksmith of independent thought.
From The Social Studies Series.
Prod-EBEC Dist-EBEC 1969

New England, An Independence Of Spirit C 30 MIN
16MM FILM, 3/4 OR 1/2 IN VIDEO H A
Records a traditional Rhode Island Independence Day parade, a Vermont oxen-pulling contest, a fog-enshrouded Maine island, and a cog railway on New Hampshire's highest mountain.
From The See America Series.
Prod-MTOLP Dist-MTOLP 1985

New Environments In Sea And Space B 15 MIN
2 INCH VIDEOTAPE P-I
See series title for descriptive statement.
From The Our Changing Community Series.
Prod-VITA Dist-GPITVL 1967

New Equality, The - How Much And For Whom C 60 MIN
3/4 OR 1/2 INCH VIDEO CASSETTE
Explores the evolving concept of equality through interviews with three scholars.
From The Bill Moyers' Journal Series.
Prod-WNETTV Dist-WNETTV

New Era In Control Of Hypertension C 30 MIN
3/4 INCH VIDEO CASSETTE PRO
Reports on impact of beta-adrenergic blockade in treatment of hypertension. Discusses hemodynamic characteristics of essential hypertension, radionuclide imaging, and patient acceptance of beta-blockade therapy.
Prod-AYERST Dist-AYERST

New Era Of A Champion C 15 MIN
16MM FILM OPTICAL SOUND
Presents the birth of a new era in thoroughbred racing history at Gulfstream Park, Florida.
Prod-FLADC Dist-FLADC

New Era Of Biotechnology, The C
1/2 IN VIDEO CASSETTE (VHS)
Focuses on the importance of DNA. Examines the functioning of genes, chromosomes, cucleotide bases, ribosomes and RNA. Describes how gene splicing creates hybrid forms of life.
From The Genetic Engineering - Prospects Of The Future Series.
Prod-IBIS Dist-IBIS

New Era, A C 55 MIN
16MM FILM, 3/4 OR 1/2 IN VIDEO H-C A
Details the emergence of the species Homo sapiens and explores some of the astonishing art man's ancestors left behind, including the beautiful cave at Lascaux. Narrated by Richard Leakey.
From The Making Of Mankind Series.
Prod-BBCTV Dist-TIMLIF 1982

New Europe, The - A Certain Amount Of Violence C 52 MIN
16MM FILM - 1/2 IN VIDEO
Analyzes the major historical developments in Europe in the mid-1950's. Discusses the Soviet suppression of the Polish and Hungarian revolts, British and French involvement in the Suez and the formation of the European Economic Community.
From The Europe, The Mighty Continent Series. No. 12
LC NO. 79-707428
Prod-BBCTV Dist-TIMLIF 1976

New Expectations C 13 MIN
16MM FILM OPTICAL SOUND
Tells of the hope which exists for the mentally retarded, showing that there are more similarities than dissimilarities between normal and retarded people. Suggests what can be done to help the retarded.
LC NO. 75-703112
Prod-HRCA Dist-FMSP 1975

New Experiences For Mentally Retarded Children B 31 MIN
16MM FILM OPTICAL SOUND C A
Shows a camp experience for severely retarded children. Explains good procedures to use in working with those who are retarded.
Prod-VADE Dist-VADE 1958

New Expressions Of Female Identity In Dance C 30 MIN
3/4 OR 1/2 INCH VIDEO CASSETTE
See series title for descriptive statement.
From The Changing Images Of Men And Women Dancing Series.
Prod-ARCVID Dist-ARCVID

New Eyes And New Ears B 20 MIN
16MM FILM OPTICAL SOUND
Explains the use of audio-visual materials in Japan and shows how Civilian Information and Educational (CIE) Films of the Supreme Commander, Allied Powers were produced for and utilized in Japan.
LC NO. FIE52-1940
Prod-USA Dist-USNAC 1951

New Family Homecoming, The C 29 MIN
3/4 OR 1/2 INCH VIDEO CASSETTE H-C A
Explains that when a couple brings their baby home from the hospital, there are always adjustments to make and problems to solve.
From The Tomorrow's Families Series.
LC NO. 81-706907
Prod-MSDOE Dist-AITECH 1980

New Food Plant Employee, The - The Right Start C 12 MIN
3/4 OR 1/2 INCH VIDEO CASSETTE
Emphasizes personal responsibility in handling and production of clean, safe food. Presents the common sense requirements of food plant employment.
Prod-PLAID Dist-PLAID

New Found Land, The C 52 MIN
16MM FILM, 3/4 OR 1/2 IN VIDEO J-C A
Presents Alistair Cooke who explains how the white man got to North America and what he was seeking. Shows the arrival of the continent's two 'great losers,' the Spanish and the French, with the conquistadores, trappers, traders and missionaries.
From The America - A Personal History Of The United States Series. No. 1
LC NO. 79-707154
Prod-BBCTV Dist-TIMLIF 1972

New Found Land, The (Spanish) C 52 MIN
16MM FILM OPTICAL SOUND J-C A
Presents Alistair Cooke who explains how the white man got to North America and what he was seeking. Shows the arrival of the continent's two 'great losers,' the Spanish and the French, with their conquistadores, trappers, traders and missionaries.
From The America - A Personal History Of The United States Series. No. 1
Prod-BBCTV Dist-TIMLIF 1972

New Framework For Federal Personnel Management, A C 30 MIN
3/4 INCH VIDEO CASSETTE
Highlights the main features of the Civil Service Reform Bill, outlining the functions of various agencies with personnel management responsibilities.
From The Launching Civil Service Reform Series.
LC NO. 79-706270
Prod-USOPMA Dist-USNAC 1978

New Friend, The C
16MM FILM - VIDEO, ALL FORMATS P-I
Tells the story of a girl whose best friend becomes friends with another girl. Deals with her feeling betrayed and angry, but eventually realizing that change can mean new beginnings. Based on the book by Charlotte Zolotow.
Prod-BFA Dist-BFA 1984

New Friend, The C 14 MIN
16MM FILM, 3/4 OR 1/2 IN VIDEO I-J
Tells how a 'new friend' threatens the relationship of two little girls, until sorrow and resentment give way to the recognition of new beginnings and the happy possibilities that come with change.
LC NO. 84-706800
Prod-CHIESR Dist-PHENIX 1983

New Friends C 11 MIN
16MM FILM, 3/4 OR 1/2 IN VIDEO K-I
Tells the adventures of Howard, a mallard duck who misses his south bound flock and is forced to winter in the city. Shows how a fast-talking New York City rat helps the mallard muddle through good times, adversity and sometimes culturally enriching adventures. Based on the book Howard by James Stevenson.
Prod-MTOLP Dist-MTOLP 1983

New Friends C 15 MIN
3/4 OR 1/2 INCH VIDEO CASSETTE K-P
Deals with French-American children. Focuses on the theme of making friends.
From The La Bonne Aventure Series.
Prod-MPBN Dist-GPITVL

New Frontier, The C 15 MIN
3/4 OR 1/2 INCH VIDEO CASSETTE I
See series title for descriptive statement.
From The Discovering Series. Unit 5 - Space
Prod-WDCNTV Dist-AITECH 1978

New Frontiers C 20 MIN
3/4 INCH VIDEO CASSETTE I
Discusses exploration at the South Pole, within the oceans and out in space.
From The Exploring Our Nation Series.
Prod-KRMATV Dist-GPITVL 1975

New GED Examination—A Series
H A
Prepares students for the high school equivalency examination (GED). Reviews basic subjects covered in the GED.
Prod-COMEX Dist-COMEX

English And Reading Comprehension, Tape 1
English And Reading Comprehension, Tape 2
English And Reading Comprehension, Tape 3
English And Reading Comprehension, Tape 4
English And Reading Comprehension, Tape 5
English And Reading Comprehension, Tape 6
Mathematics, Tape 1
Mathematics, Tape 1 (Spanish)
Mathematics, Tape 2
Mathematics, Tape 2 (Spanish)
Mathematics, Tape 3
Mathematics, Tape 3 (Spanish)
Mathematics, Tape 4
Mathematics, Tape 4 (Spanish)
Mathematics, Tape 5
Mathematics, Tape 5 (Spanish)
Mathematics, Tape 6
Mathematics, Tape 6 (Spanish)

New Generation Intensive Care Incubators C 10 MIN
16MM FILM OPTICAL SOUND PRO
Integrates live action and state-of-the-art computer animation to explore the innovative design concepts behind the new generation infant life support system.
LC NO. 82-700202
Prod-OHMED Dist-OHMED 1981

New Generation Intensive Care Incubators (Chinese) C 10 MIN
16MM FILM OPTICAL SOUND PRO
Integrates live action and state-of-the-art computer animation to explore the innovative design concepts behind the new generation infant life support system.
LC NO. 82-700202
Prod-OHMED Dist-OHMED 1981

New Generation Intensive Care Incubators (French) C 10 MIN
16MM FILM OPTICAL SOUND PRO
Integrates live action and state-of-the-art computer animation to explore the innovative design concepts behind the new generation infant life support system.
LC NO. 82-700202
Prod-OHMED Dist-OHMED 1981

New Generation Intensive Care Incubators (Spanish) C 10 MIN
16MM FILM OPTICAL SOUND PRO
Integrates live action and state-of-the-art computer animation to explore the innovative design concepts behind the new generation infant life support system.
LC NO. 82-700202
Prod-OHMED Dist-OHMED 1981

New Germany, A - 1933 To 1939 C 60 MIN
16MM FILM OPTICAL SOUND H-C A
From The World At War Series.
LC NO. 76-701778
Prod-THAMES Dist-USCAN 1975

New Germany, A - 1933-1939 C 52 MIN
16MM FILM, 3/4 OR 1/2 IN VIDEO H-C A
Describes the social and political conditions in Germany from 1933 to 1939 which favored the rise of Adolph Hitler through the public's mystical enthusiasm for a New Germany which often took the form of a mass hysteria.
From The World At War Series.
Prod-THAMES Dist-MEDIAG 1973

New Girl, The C 6 MIN
16MM FILM, 3/4 OR 1/2 IN VIDEO I-J
Describes how to make friends if you are the new girl in school and are different from the others.
From The What Should I Do Series.
Prod-DISNEY Dist-WDEMCO 1970

New Girl, The (French) C 6 MIN
16MM FILM, 3/4 OR 1/2 IN VIDEO P
Shows how Susie and Joanie initially reject Mary, the new girl. Encourages consideration and understanding.
From The What Should I Do (French) Series.
Prod-WDEMCO Dist-WDEMCO 1970

New Gold For Old Glory C 24 MIN
3/4 OR 1/2 INCH VIDEO CASSETTE A
Documents the victories of the US Olympic hockey team in the 1980 winter games. Features Coach Herb Brooks. Narrated by Jack Whitaker.
Prod-SFTI Dist-SFTI

New Government, The C 30 MIN
2 INCH VIDEOTAPE
Covers the Washington Administration. Discusses the major topics such as Hamilton's financial plans, the Western Indian problem, and America's neutrality during the French Revolution.
From The American History I Series.
Prod-DENVPS Dist-GPITVL

New Ground C 9 MIN
16MM FILM OPTICAL SOUND
Presents an introduction to the IBM Canada components plant at Bromont, Quebec and its role in IBM Canada's manufacturing and development organization.
LC NO. 75-703419
Prod-IBM Dist-IBM 1972

New Guinea Coffee And Cocoa C 22 MIN
16MM FILM OPTICAL SOUND J-C A
Presents the thriving coffee and cocoa industry of Papua and New Guinea.
Prod-ANAIB Dist-AUIS 1971

New Hampshire Writers And The Small Town C 18 MIN
16MM FILM OPTICAL SOUND H-C A
Explores the attitudes of New hampshire authors toward the small town as revealed in their literary works. Covers three centuries and reveals significant changes in attitudes toward the land, the people and their communities.
Prod-UNH Dist-UNH 1980

New Harmony - An Example And A Beacon C 29 MIN
16MM FILM, 3/4 OR 1/2 IN VIDEO J-C A
Traces the history and significance of New Harmony, Indiana, from its communal origins to its contemporary renaissance as a historic landmark.
Prod-IU Dist-IU 1971

New Healers, The C 59 MIN
3/4 INCH VIDEO CASSETTE
Examines diseases associated with extreme poverty and shows various paths to health care in Tanzania, Guatemala and Lee County, Arkansas.
From The Nova Series.
Prod-WGBHTV Dist-PBS 1977

New Help For Hearts C 14 MIN
16MM FILM OPTICAL SOUND
Explains how medicine and technology are being used to offer hope to people suffering from heart problems.
Prod-ALLFP Dist-NSTA 1976

New Hip, A - Nursing Care Of The Patient With The Total Hip Arthroplasty C 17 MIN
3/4 OR 1/2 INCH VIDEO CASSETTE PRO
Describes nursing care measures important in preoperative, postoperative and discharge planning care of the total hip arthroplasty patient. Includes prevention of dislocation, occupied bedmaking, patient transfer, positioning and exercises.
Prod-VAMCCI Dist-USNAC

New Hired Hand, The C 27 MIN
16MM FILM OPTICAL SOUND
Shows how a computer can be used in the management of a farm.
Prod-ALLISC Dist-IDEALF

New Home For The London Bridge, A C 14 MIN
3/4 OR 1/2 INCH VIDEO CASSETTE
Documents the sale, disassembly and reconstruction of the London Bridge, which was moved to Lake Havasu City, Arizona.
Prod-UPI Dist-JOU

New Hooked On Books, The C
3/4 OR 1/2 INCH VIDEO CASSETTE T
Addresses teachers' concern for reading and writing competencies of students. Illustrates methods for cooperative student efforts to increase literacy.
From The Increasing Children's Motivation To Read And Write Series.
Prod-EPCO Dist-EDCORP

New Hope For The Handicapped C 14 MIN
16MM FILM, 3/4 OR 1/2 IN VIDEO
Documents changes in attitudes about the handicapped and shows the latest technology designed to free the disabled as never before.
Prod-KLEINW Dist-KLEINW 1981

New Horizons C 12 MIN
3/4 OR 1/2 INCH VIDEO CASSETTE
Shows commentary by Howard K. Smith produced in the news format of TV magazine style. Tells how it can be used in its entirety or in three segments? including research, rehabilitation, and a laryngectomee who, through advances in cancer research, learned to speak again.
Prod-AMCS Dist-AMCS 1980

New Horizons - Brazil C 22 MIN
16MM FILM OPTICAL SOUND
Presents a general view of modern Brazil, including its geography, natural resources, topography and people.
Prod-PANWA Dist-PANWA

New Horizons - Fiji, New Caledonia C 9 MIN
16MM FILM OPTICAL SOUND
Depicts the beauty and serenity of the Fiji and New Caledonia Islands.
Prod-PANWA Dist-PANWA

New Horizons - Hawaiian Islands C 13 MIN
16MM FILM OPTICAL SOUND
Views the people and places of Hawaii.
Prod-PANWA Dist-PANWA

New Horizons - New Zealand C 13 MIN
16MM FILM OPTICAL SOUND
Views the people and places of New Zealand.
Prod-PANWA Dist-PANWA

New Horizons - Portugal C 13 MIN
16MM FILM OPTICAL SOUND
Views the people and places of Portugal.
Prod-PANWA Dist-PANWA

New Horizons - Samoa, Tahiti C 9 MIN
16MM FILM OPTICAL SOUND
Presents a brief but pleasant visit to the historic islands of Samoa and Tahiti.
Prod-PANWA Dist-PANWA

New Horizons - The Low Countries C 30 MIN
16MM FILM OPTICAL SOUND
Presents a tour of Belgium, Holland and Luxembourg.
Prod-PANWA Dist-PANWA

New Horizons Along The Milky Way C 26 MIN
16MM FILM OPTICAL SOUND I-C A
Points out the importance and value of milk and shows the advancements made by the dairy farmer in the production of quality milk. Stresses the importance of clean pens and buildings and modern milking facilities and equipment.
Prod-UPR Dist-UPR 1959

New Horizons In Materials Handling C 16 MIN
16MM FILM OPTICAL SOUND
Surveys the engineering and manufacturing of materials handling systems by the Barrett Cravens Company with emphasis on automated machines. Discusses the application of the automated, Guide-O-Matic tractor to traffic and work flows.
Prod-RAY Dist-CCNY

New Horizons—A Series

Prod-TWCF Dist-PANWA

Australia - New Zealand	13 MIN
Hawaiian Islands	14 MIN
Hong Kong - Singapore	15 MIN
India	12 MIN
Ireland	12 MIN
Japan	13 MIN
Pakistan	13 MIN
Philippines	12 MIN
Ski - New Horizons	24 MIN
Thailand	13 MIN
Turkey	13 MIN

New Horizons, The C 29 MIN
3/4 INCH VIDEO CASSETTE
Focuses on the use of remote sensing, the relaying of cartographic information from aircraft or satellite to the ground in map making.
From The Maps - Horizons To Knowledge Series.
Prod-UMITV Dist-UMITV 1980

New Horizons, The (Spanish) C 29 MIN
3/4 INCH VIDEO CASSETTE
Focuses on the use of remote sensing, the relaying of cartographic information from aircraft or satellite to the ground in map making.
From The Maps - Horizons To Knowledge Series.
Prod-UMITV Dist-UMITV 1980

New Human Life, A C 10 MIN
16MM FILM OPTICAL SOUND K-I
Details the stages of growth of a human baby inside the mother during the final five months of pregnancy. Describes the maternity hospital routine. Shows how a new baby is welcomed into a family. Discusses male and female differences at birth.
From The Family Life And Sex Education Series.
Prod-SF Dist-SF 1968

New Ideas In Psychology C 29 MIN
3/4 INCH VIDEO CASSETTE
Discusses why intelligence tests report higher scores for older children in a family rather than younger children. Covers treatment of migraine headaches and decision making.
Prod-UMITV Dist-UMITV 1977

New Image For Black Women C 29 MIN
3/4 OR 1/2 INCH VIDEO CASSETTE
Presents an interview with the editor-in-chief of Essence magazine. Discusses the directions the magazine has taken, her philosophy of women's magazines in general, and her view of the relationships between blacks and whites in American society.
From The Woman Series.
Prod-WNEDTV Dist-PBS

New Image For Nurses, Pt 1 C 29 MIN
3/4 OR 1/2 INCH VIDEO CASSETTE
Discusses the struggle of nurses to attain professional recognition.
From The Woman Series.
Prod-WNEDTV Dist-PBS

New Image For Nurses, Pt 2 C 29 MIN
3/4 OR 1/2 INCH VIDEO CASSETTE
Examines efforts to provide a political voice for nurses. Describes the work of the Nurses' Coalition for Action in Politics.
From The Woman Series.
Prod-WNEDTV Dist-PBS

New Immigrants - Russian Jews In Philadelphia B 23 MIN
16MM FILM OPTICAL SOUND
Documents the experiences of recent Jewish immigrants from the Soviet Union as they struggle to learn English and find new jobs in Philadelphia. Explores their reasons for immigrating and their reactions to urban America.
LC NO. 79-700450
Prod-JELPEP Dist-TEMPLU 1979

New Indians, The C 59 MIN
16MM FILM, 3/4 OR 1/2 IN VIDEO
Shows how various tribes of North American Indians are taking new pride in their ancient ways. Examines some of the problems they encounter.
LC NO. 80-706400
Prod-NGS Dist-NGS 1977

New Industrial Revolution, The C 12 MIN
16MM FILM - 3/4 IN VIDEO
Demonstrates techniques that are making assembly lines more efficient. Shows systems designed to speed up assembly processes and eliminate routine jobs.
LC NO. 80-706864
Prod-NSF Dist-USNAC Prodn-MEDFO 1979

New Insulins - Implications For Clinical Practice C 21 MIN
3/4 OR 1/2 INCH VIDEO CASSETTE PRO
Explains the benefits, limitations, and appropriate clinical uses of new forms of purified and highly purified insulins, including biosynthetic and semisynthetic forms of manufactured human insulin. Provides a brief historical overview of the development and purification of insulin. Describes the structure of new insulins, relates this to their relative levels of immunogenicity, and describes the kinds of patients most likely to benefit from their use. Outlines some possible future developments in insulin research and applications.
Prod-UMICHM Dist-UMICHM 1983

New Jersey C
3/4 OR 1/2 INCH VIDEO CASSETTE
Presents five segments about the state of New Jersey, the most densely populated state in the Union.
From The Portrait Of America Series.
Prod-TBS Dist-TBS

New Job For U Thant, A B 5 MIN
16MM FILM OPTICAL SOUND
Reviews the election and installation of U Thant of Burma as acting Secretary-General of the United Nations.
From The Screen News Digest Series. Vol 4, Issue 5
Prod-HEARST Dist-HEARST 1961

New Joints For Old B 50 MIN
16MM FILM OPTICAL SOUND PRO
Depicts arthroplasty, a surgical procedure which enables elderly patients to regain use of their joints. Shows a stainless steel joint replacing the defective joint of a patient.
Prod-CMA Dist-LAWREN

New Key, A C 29 MIN
3/4 INCH VIDEO CASSETTE H A
Reviews earlier pieces, scale forms and progression. Demonstrates and explains syncopated pedaling to produce legato connections between chords. Introduces the G-major scale.
From The Beginning Piano - An Adult Approach Series. Lesson 9
Prod-COAST Dist-CDTEL

New Kid On The Block C 30 MIN
16MM FILM - 3/4 IN VIDEO
Explains what social skills are, shows how young children acquire them, and suggests ways in which parents can facilitate this learning process.
From The Footsteps Series.
LC NO. 79-707629
Prod-USOE Dist-USNAC 1978

New Kid, The C 11 MIN
16MM FILM, 3/4 OR 1/2 IN VIDEO P-J
Presents insights into the experience of children who have to endure new, unfamiliar worlds when their families move. Shows how, alone, the new kid has to meet the other kids on the block and make some kind of initial approach to them.
Prod-BFA Dist-PHENIX 1972

New Kind Of Joy, A C 20 MIN
16MM FILM OPTICAL SOUND
Presents scenes from the many events of the Special Olympics.
Prod-SPEOLY Dist-SPEOLY

New Leader - Henry Winkler Of U C C 29 MIN
3/4 INCH VIDEO CASSETTE
Presents Henry Winkler, President of the University of Cincinnati. Describes his vision for higher education. Discusses who is responsible for a child's education.
From The Decision Makers Series.
Prod-OHC Dist-HRC

New Leadership Styles - Towards Human And Economic Development C 26 MIN
16MM FILM, 3/4 OR 1/2 IN VIDEO
Looks at the leadership styles of two successful executives who have humanized their companies' work environments by giving more power to the employees.
From The Human Resources And Organizational Behavior Series.
Prod-DOCUA Dist-CNEMAG

New Lease On Learning C 22 MIN
16MM FILM OPTICAL SOUND
Describes the conversion of a former synagogue into a public school for children aged three to five.
Prod-NYU Dist-NYU

New Life For A Spanish Farmer C 18 MIN
16MM FILM, 3/4 OR 1/2 IN VIDEO P-C
Shows attempts of the Spanish government to improve farming and the life of the farmer.
From The Man And His World Series.
Prod-FI Dist-FI 1969

New Life For Old Hands C 23 MIN
16MM FILM OPTICAL SOUND
Deals with the implantation of manmade joints to replace diseased ones. Features an elderly patient who is examined and interviewed before and after joint replacement surgery on hands severely diseased by rheumatoid arthritis. Describes the actual surgical procedure, with a running commentary by the physician.
Prod-WSTGLC Dist-WSTGLC

New Life For Rose, A C 25 MIN
16MM FILM, 3/4 OR 1/2 IN VIDEO H-C A
Presents the planning program of a senior housing project.
Prod-FEIL Dist-FEIL 1976

New Life For Ruined Land C 14 MIN
16MM FILM, 3/4 OR 1/2 IN VIDEO
Documents a two-year project by the Department of Energy's Land Reclamation Program at Argonne National Laboratory to rehabilitate an abandoned coal mining site in Southern Illinois, turning it into a wildlife refuge and recreation facility.
Prod-USDOE Dist-USNAC 1983

New Life For The Great Plains C 12 MIN
16MM FILM OPTICAL SOUND
Promotes the Great Plains soil conservation program by showing the progress made in soil and water conservation in Baca County, Colorado.
LC NO. 74-705204
Prod-USDA Dist-USNAC 1965

New Life In Christ C 21 MIN
16MM FILM OPTICAL SOUND
Features people of all ages discussing their new life in Christ, telling who he was and is. Sheds light on these issues from a Biblical standpoint, presenting Gospel messages.
LC NO. 79-701336
Prod-FAMF Dist-FAMF 1979

New Life New Ways C 16 MIN
16MM FILM OPTICAL SOUND
Focuses on the special problems of migrant women in adapting to Australian society.
LC NO. 80-701571
Prod-TASCOR Dist-TASCOR 1979

New Life Of Sandra Blain, The C 27 MIN
16MM FILM OPTICAL SOUND
Tells the story of a fictional character, Sandra Blain, who has no job, no job skills, no husband, no family and no home. Shows how she puts her life together as a recovering alcoholic.
LC NO. 77-700176
Prod-SUTHRB Dist-SUTHRB 1977

New Life-Styles C 29 MIN
3/4 OR 1/2 INCH VIDEO CASSETTE
Shows a couple living together, several members of a commune, representatives from women's lib and gay lib and an unmarried mother discussing sexual ramifications of their differing life-styles. Features Milton Diamond, Ph D, a biologist at the University of Hawaii, talking with newspaper columnist Ann Landers and several counselors about the impact of new life-styles on sexual practices.
From The Human Sexuality Series.
Prod-KHETTV Dist-PBS

New Life, A C 26 MIN
16MM FILM - 3/4 IN VIDEO PRO
Presents five former neurologically disabled patients, who discuss the process of their reintegration into society, including changes in vocational goals, reestablishment of social activities, living arrangements, role changes within the family and mobility limitations.
From The Neurologically Disabled Patient, Pt 2 - Nursing During The Rehabilitative... Series.
LC NO. 77-700609
Prod-AJN Dist-AJN Prodn-TVPC 1977

New Life, A C 29 MIN
2 INCH VIDEOTAPE
See series title for descriptive statement.
From The That's Life Series.
Prod-KOAPTV Dist-PUBTEL

New Line Of Sight, A C 16 MIN
16MM FILM OPTICAL SOUND
Reviews the USAF research and development achievements since 1954 in missiles, satellites, re-entry projects, aerospace medicine activities and other vital space efforts.
LC NO. 74-706159
Prod-USAF Dist-USNAC 1962

New Look C 13 MIN
16MM FILM OPTICAL SOUND K-P
Provides an explanation of family relations.
From The Family Relations Series.
LC NO. 76-700140
Prod-MORLAT Dist-MORLAT 1974

New Look At Algae, A C 15 MIN
16MM FILM, 3/4 OR 1/2 IN VIDEO J-C
Describes the importance and diversity of algae in the biosphere and shows examples of structure and adaptation.
From The Inhabitants Of The Planet Earth Series.
Prod-BIOMED Dist-WARDS 1979

New Look At An Old Planet, A C 26 MIN
16MM FILM OPTICAL SOUND I-C A
Shows the practical benefits of weather, communication, navigational, and earth resources satellites, through experiences in the lives of a Texas coastal family. Illustrates future potential uses of satellites in agricultural, oceanographic and natural resources studies.
LC NO. 79-701238
Prod-NASA Dist-NASA Prodn-WGBHTV 1969

New Look At Bacteria, A C 16 MIN
16MM FILM, 3/4 OR 1/2 IN VIDEO J-C A
Begins with Pasteur's experiments on the airborne transport of bacteria and then focuses on theories of bacteriology. Shows the great variety of locomotion patterns and behavioral responses of bacteria.
From The Inhabitants Of The Planet Earth Series.
Prod-BIOMED Dist-WARDS 1979

New Look At Jack Be Nimble, A C 30 MIN
2 INCH VIDEOTAPE T
See series title for descriptive statement.
From The Solutions In Communications Series.
Prod-SCCOE Dist-SCCOE

New Look At Leeuwenhoek's Wee Beasties, A C 12 MIN
16MM FILM OPTICAL SOUND J-C
Examines free-living protists as viewed in natural time by differential interference cinemicrography. Discusses the classification and general characteristics of flagellates, amoebas and ciliates.
From The Inhabitants Of The Planet Earth Series.
LC NO. 75-701959
Prod-RUSB Dist-MLA 1975

New Look At Motivation, A C 32 MIN
16MM FILM, 3/4 OR 1/2 IN VIDEO C A
Examines the basic psychological principles of motivation and shows their application to worker behavior and managerial styles.
LC NO. 80-706456
Prod-CRMP Dist-CRMP 1980

New Look At The Surgery Of The Biliary Tree, A C 34 MIN
16MM FILM OPTICAL SOUND PRO
Presents three cases to support the procedure of providing a by-pass for bile into the bowel in the event of further obstruction occuring at the lower end of the common duct.
Prod-ACYDGD Dist-ACY 1962

New Look In Potatoes C 26 MIN
16MM FILM OPTICAL SOUND
Presents the story of potato production, including sorting, grading and packaging, new developments in processing and the role of refrigerated rail transportation.
Prod-UPR Dist-PCF

New Look, The C 28 MIN
16MM FILM OPTICAL SOUND
Stephen Horn discusses the need for congressional reforms with a panel of congressmen including Senator Karl E Mundt, Senator William Proxmire, Representative Jack Brooks and Representative James C Cleveland.
From The Government Story Series. No. 20
LC NO. 74-707175
Prod-WBCPRO Dist-WBCPRO 1968

New Look, The C 4 MIN
3/4 OR 1/2 INCH VIDEO CASSETTE
Gives an overview of the new blood collection equipment being used by many Red Cross blood regional services.
Prod-AMRC Dist-AMRC 1978

New Lost City Ramblers C 52 MIN
3/4 OR 1/2 INCH VIDEO CASSETTE
Features the New Lost City Ramblers performing on fiddle, guitar, banjo, mandolin and autoharp. Shows films of a Japanese Fiddle Band.
From The Rainbow Quest Series.
Prod-SEEGER Dist-CWATER

New Maid, The C 34 MIN
16MM FILM, 3/4 OR 1/2 IN VIDEO J-C
Tells the story of a Guatemalan woman who comes to work for an upper middle-class family when the mother returns to her job. Relates that the youngest son develops a deep affection for the maid and serious problems ensue.
LC NO. 82-706573
Prod-FCLPTF Dist-LCOA Prodn-AMERFI 1980

New Man At Millersville C 20 MIN
3/4 OR 1/2 INCH VIDEO CASSETTE
Shows new food service employees in correctional facilities some of the problems they might encounter and how to solve them.
Prod-USDJ Dist-USNAC

New Manufacturing Environment, The C 30 MIN
3/4 OR 1/2 INCH VIDEO CASSETTE
Discusses causes and effects behind the creation of the new manufacturing environment. 63:010.
From The Manufacturing Automation - A Key To-- Productivity Series.
Prod-DELTAK Dist-DELTAK

New Me, The - Accepting Body Changes C
3/4 OR 1/2 INCH VIDEO CASSETTE I-J
Helps cope with puberty through matter-of-fact, supportive explanations of male and female body changes. Points out that though timetables vary, every boy and girl undergoes physical change. Promotes self-acceptance. Contains separate sections on male and female physiology.
Prod-SUNCOM Dist-SUNCOM

New Media Bible, The - Genesis 4 - Joseph C 93 MIN
1/2 IN VIDEO CASSETTE BETA/VHS
Retells the Genesis, of Joseph's enslavement to the Egyptian pharoah in a series of four programs.
LC NO. 84-706669
Prod-GNPROJ Dist-GNPROJ 1984

New Media Bible, The - Luke I - Nativity To The Baptism C 51 MIN
1/2 IN VIDEO CASSETTE BETA/VHS
Gives the story of Jesus' birth and early life as told in the book of Luke.
LC NO. 84-706670
Prod-GNPROJ Dist-GNPROJ 1984

New Media, The C 26 MIN
16MM FILM, 3/4 OR 1/2 IN VIDEO J-C A
Discusses the beneficial potential of electronic communication through personal access to data bases, by means of computer networking and as seen in the office of the future.
From The Computer Programme Series. Episode 5
LC NO. 82-707087
Prod-BBCTV Dist-FI 1982

New Method For Hospital Narcotics Control, A C 12 MIN
16MM FILM OPTICAL SOUND PRO
Demonstrates a new system of narcotics control developed at Southeastern General Hospital in Lumberton, North Carolina. Places emphasis in the system on simplified record-keeping and on reduction in personnel hours through use of unit-dose medication such as tubex.
LC NO. 74-703663
Prod-WYETH Dist-WYLAB 1965

New Methods Of Hospital Reimbursement C 32 MIN
3/4 OR 1/2 INCH VIDEO CASSETTE PRO
Explains the newest system for hospital payment, the Diagnostic Related Groupings (DRG) system. Discusses the system's pros and cons, long range, and its effects on nursing.
From The Future Of Nursing Series.
Prod-HSCIC Dist-HSCIC 1985

New Mexico C
3/4 OR 1/2 INCH VIDEO CASSETTE
Presents five segments about the state of New Mexico, The Land of Enchantment, a state where pre-Columbian civilizations thrived.
From The Portrait Of America Series.
Prod-TBS Dist-TBS

New Mexico Passive Solar Buildings C 14 MIN
16MM FILM - 3/4 IN VIDEO
Gives a brief description of major passive solar heating systems and how they work. Provides interior and exterior views of privately-owned buildings in New Mexico which make use of the Sun for winter heat.
LC NO. 79-706733
Prod-USDOE Dist-USNAC Prodn-SANLAB 1979

New Militancy And Black Power B 30 MIN
2 INCH VIDEOTAPE H-C A
See series title for descriptive statement.
From The Americans From Africa - A History Series. No. 30
Prod-CVETVC Dist-GPITVL Prodn-WCVETV

New Miracle Workers, The C 15 MIN
16MM FILM - 3/4 IN VIDEO
Explains work being done around the world to teach survival skills to the blind. Shows how vitamin therapy and education about nutrition can prevent blindness. Narrated by Alexander Scourby.
Prod-HKELNT Dist-MTP

New Misadventures Of Ichabod Crane, The C 25 MIN
16MM FILM, 3/4 OR 1/2 IN VIDEO K-I
Recounts how Ichabod Crane tries to prevent the headless horseman from terrorizing a community by trying to steal a book of magic spells from a witch named Velma Van Dam.
Prod-CORF Dist-CORF 1981

New Missionary To Walker's Garage, A C 30 MIN
16MM FILM OPTICAL SOUND
Features Andy Malloy whose aging car breaks down, and takes a job at Walker's garage. Pictures owner, Ted Hunter, sharing his Christian faith with Andy. Depicts Andy's uninterest. Portrays Andy as a loner except for occasional dates with Jill Dennis whose aunt runs the nearby coffee shop. Shows that, on the same night Andy and Jill mysteriously leave town, the garage and coffee shop are burglarized. Advocates that man can only do so much and must trust God to do the rest.
Prod-FAMF Dist-FAMF

New Mobility, The C 19 MIN
16MM FILM OPTICAL SOUND
Describes a fleet of 200 buses designed to serve all of the people of the Southern California Rapid Transit District, particularly the physically handicapped.
LC NO. 78-701319
Prod-SCRTD Dist-MASCOT Prodn-CORPRO 1978

New Mood B 30 MIN
16MM FILM OPTICAL SOUND H-C A
Reviews highlights of the civil rights struggle from 1954-64. Examines the impact of Negro militancy on Negro and white Americans. Shows film coverage showing Martin Luther King, Malcolm X, Medgar Evers and Presidents Kennedy and Johnson. Features Ossie Davis.
From The History Of The Negro People Series.
LC NO. FIA68-1282
Prod-NET Dist-IU 1965

New Moon Prone C 10 MIN
2 INCH VIDEOTAPE
See series title for descriptive statement.
From The Janaki Series.
Prod-WGBHTV Dist-PUBTEL

New Music, The C 29 MIN
16MM FILM - 1/2 IN VIDEO
Features two duets by cornetist Bobby Bradford and clarinetist John Carter. Shows two musicians who were associated with Ornette Coleman in the 1960's.
Prod-RHPSDY Dist-RHPSDY 1980

New Nation, A - The Struggle To Survive, 1789-1815 C 25 MIN
16MM FILM, 3/4 OR 1/2 IN VIDEO I-H
Looks at the personalities and problems which shaped America during the first 26 years after it gained independence. Contrasts the views of such people as George Washington, Alexander Hamilton and Thomas Jefferson. Recounts how the country survived two attempts at secession and the War of 1812.
Prod-BNCHMK Dist-BNCHMK

New Navy C 3 MIN
16MM FILM OPTICAL SOUND
Tells an ancient sea legend which provides an introduction to life at sea in the U S Navy of today.
LC NO. 75-704047
Prod-USN Dist-USNAC 1974

New Negro I, The - Harlem Renaissance C 29 MIN
2 INCH VIDEOTAPE
See series title for descriptive statement.
From The Black Experience Series.
Prod-WTTWTV Dist-PUBTEL

New Negro II, The - Nationalism And Garveyism C 29 MIN
2 INCH VIDEOTAPE
See series title for descriptive statement.
From The Black Experience Series.
Prod-WTTWTV Dist-PUBTEL

New Nursery School—A Series

Describes the responsive environment educational program in use at the New Nursery School, Greeley, Colorado, operated by Colorado State University. Examines ways to improve language, learn problem-solving techniques, self-concepts, interpersonal relations and self-control.
LC NO. 75-700800
Prod-USDHEW Dist-USNAC 1969

Intellectual Development 18 MIN
Introduction To The New Nursery School 25 MIN
Learning Booths 17 MIN

New Or Innovative Areas C 10 MIN
3/4 OR 1/2 INCH VIDEO CASSETTE
See series title for descriptive statement.
From The Practical M B O Series.
Prod-DELTAK Dist-DELTAK

New Order, The C 27 MIN
16MM FILM, 3/4 OR 1/2 IN VIDEO
Offers a historical perspective on the world trend toward neo-colonialism, using the example of current political affairs in Africa to show that the continuing attempt to impose neo-colonialism has become increasingly difficult and discredited.
From The Five Billion People Series.
Prod-LEFSP Dist-CNEMAG

New Orleans C 3 MIN
16MM FILM OPTICAL SOUND P-I
Discusses the city of New Orleans, Louisiana.
From The Of All Things Series.
Prod-BAILYL Dist-AVED

New Orleans Dishes C 30 MIN
1/2 IN VIDEO CASSETTE BETA/VHS
Presents New Orleans dishes including barbeque shrimp, file gumbo and jambalaya.
From The Frugal Gourmet Series.
Prod-WTTWTV Dist-MTI

New Orleans Profile C 13 MIN
16MM FILM OPTICAL SOUND J-C A
Depicts the industry, history, traditions and economic importance of New Orleans, the South's largest city.
Prod-WSU Dist-WSU 1959

New Orleans Tribune C 9 MIN
3/4 OR 1/2 INCH VIDEO CASSETTE
Tells the story of a newspaper published by free blacks in New Orleans in the 1860's. Combines dramatic scenes in period costumes with connecting graphics and narration.
Prod-NOVID Dist-NOVID

New Orleans, Mardi Gras C 3 MIN
16MM FILM OPTICAL SOUND P-I
Discusses the Mardi Gras held in the city of New Orleans, Louisiana.
From The Of All Things Series.
Prod-BAILYL Dist-AVED

New Orleans, The Big Easy C 27 MIN
16MM FILM, 3/4 OR 1/2 IN VIDEO H A
Features map drawings and comments from local residents. Takes a scenic trip to New Orleans.
From The See America Series.
Prod-MTOLP Dist-MTOLP 1985

New Orleans, The Crescent City C 20 MIN
3/4 OR 1/2 INCH VIDEO CASSETTE J-C A
Takes viewers to New Orleans. Discusses the city's historic events and visits the French Quarter and the Mardi Gras. Shows such architectural highlights as the lace balconies and the cornstalk fence.
LC NO. 82-706782
Prod-AWSS Dist-AWSS 1980

New Orleans' Black Indians - A Case Study In The Arts C 30 MIN
3/4 INCH VIDEO CASSETTE C A
Focuses on the annual Mardi Gras Carnival in New Orleans. Examines the origins of the ceremony in the black 'Indian' tribes and African heritage of the participants.
From The Faces Of Culture - Studies In Cultural Anthropology Series. Lesson 22
Prod-COAST Dist-CDTEL Prodn-HRAW

New Partnerships—A Series
16MM FILM, 3/4 OR 1/2 IN VIDEO J-C A
Analyzes the problems facing young dual-career couples. Explores the ways in which traditional sex roles in marriages impede the career development of women.
Prod-BERKS Dist-UCEMC 1982

Almost Home 027 MIN
Your Move 025 MIN

New Parts For Old C 26 MIN
3/4 OR 1/2 INCH VIDEO CASSETTE
Demonstrates the fascinating beginning of a new generation of biochemical substances which interact with the natural living processes of the body.
From The Breakthroughs Series.
Prod-NOMDFI Dist-LANDMK

New Pastures (Czech) B 92 MIN
3/4 OR 1/2 INCH VIDEO CASSETTE
Presents a comedy about three prisoners released from jail and their experiences returning to a small village. Directed by Vladimir Cech. With English subtitles.
Prod-IHF Dist-IHF

New Patterns On The Land C 13 MIN
16MM FILM OPTICAL SOUND
Tells the story of modern conservation farming and how it has brought new patterns on the land to the American rural landscape.
LC NO. 74-705207
Prod-USDA Dist-USNAC 1967

New Perspective, A C 26 MIN
16MM FILM OPTICAL SOUND
Documents the experiences of four UPS middle management men who spend a month living on New York City's lower East Side.
Prod-HSSETT Dist-TOGGFI 1974

New Perspectives In Normal And Neoplastic Lymphoid Cell Proliferation C 60 MIN
3/4 INCH VIDEO CASSETTE
Presents experiments in human cell proliferation.
Prod-UTAHTI Dist-UTAHTI

New Pilgrims, The C 25 MIN
3/4 OR 1/2 INCH VIDEO CASSETTE J-C A
Examines the nationality and origins of the latest U S immigrants. Features interviews with new families from Central America, Mexico, Vietnam, Korea and the Phillipines talking about their adjustment to life in the U S. Examines their effect on the labor force caused by cheap wages and their desire to succeed.
Prod-NBCNEW Dist-FI

New Points In Needlepoint C 30 MIN
3/4 OR 1/2 INCH VIDEO CASSETTE
Tells how the word needlepoint was invented to distinguish woven tapestries from those created with a needle on a canvas. Shows some new variations on needlepoint.
From The Erica Series.
Prod-WGBHTV Dist-KINGFT

New Position, The C 5 MIN
2 INCH VIDEOTAPE A
Uses a case study in order to show what happens when a manager creates a new position in a department and violates certain organizational principles.
From The How To Improve Managerial Performance - The AMA Performance Standards Program Series.
LC NO. 75-704236
Prod-AMA Dist-AMA 1974

New Prescription For Life C 27 MIN
16MM FILM OPTICAL SOUND PRO
Presents detailed instructions in cardiopulmonary, resuscitation, including artificial respiration, artificial circulation, and airway obstruction.
LC NO. 75-703878
Prod-BANDEL Dist-BANDEL 1975

New Prescription For Life C 48 MIN
16MM FILM OPTICAL SOUND PRO
Presents detailed instructions in cardiopulmonary resuscitation, including artificial respiration, artificial circulation, airway obstruction, and definitive treatment of all forms of cardiac arrest.
LC NO. 75-703876
Prod-BANDEL Dist-BANDEL 1975

New Principal, The C 5 MIN
2 INCH VIDEOTAPE A
Presents a case study which dramatizes a manager's attempt to upgrade performance for a key result area.
From The How To Improve Managerial Performance - The AMA Performance Standards Program Series.
LC NO. 75-704242
Prod-AMA Dist-AMA 1974

New Principles of Training And Supervision, II - Quality And The Consumer C
3/4 OR 1/2 INCH VIDEO CASSETTE
See series title for descriptive statement.
From The Deming Videotapes - Quality, Productivity, And Competitive..Series.
Prod-MIOT Dist-MIOT

New Principles Of Training And Supervision C 50 MIN
3/4 OR 1/2 INCH VIDEO CASSETTE
See series title for descriptive statement.
From The Deming Video Tapes - Quality, Productivity And The Competitive..Series.
Prod-MIOT Dist-SME

New Principles Of Training And Supervision I C
3/4 OR 1/2 INCH VIDEO CASSETTE
Discusses the aim of supervision in industry.
From The Deming Videotapes - Quality, Productivity, And Competitive..Series.
Prod-MIOT Dist-MIOT

New Product Development—A Series
IND
Notes that professional advancement, especially in today's competitive R and D environment, requires a mastery of lay concepts like strategic planning, market analysis, product evaluation, profit planning, probability and uncertainty, and promoting teamwork.
Prod-AMCEE Dist-AMCEE

Introduction And Strategy 045 MIN
Market, The 045 MIN
Probability And Uncertainty 045 MIN
Product, The 045 MIN
Profit Plan 045 MIN
Strategic Framework And Fallacies 045 MIN
Teamwork And Concluding Remarks 045 MIN

New Professionals, The C 20 MIN
16MM FILM OPTICAL SOUND C A
A shorter version of the film The New Professionals. Demonstrates to professionals, consumers and providers the range of abilities of Gerontological Nurse Practitioners in the various levels of long term care. Introduces students to the common acute and chronic problems of the aged, showing the individuality of each person's needs. Focuses on institutional settings.
Prod-MTSHC Dist-NWDIMF

New Professionals, The C 38 MIN
16MM FILM OPTICAL SOUND C A
Demonstrates to professionals, consumers and providers the range of abilities of Gerontological Nurse Practitioners in the various levels of long term care. Introduces students to the common acute and chronic problems of the aged and exposes them to the variety of settings suitable for GNP practice. Shows the individuality of aged persons and their needs.
Prod-MTSHC Dist-NWDIMF

New Programs In Elementary Science B 30 MIN
2 INCH VIDEOTAPE
Examines the philosophies, goals, methods and materials of some representative new program in elementary science.
From The Science In Your Classroom Series.
Prod-WENHTV Dist-GPITVL

New Pulse Of Life (Rev Ed) C 28 MIN
16MM FILM, 3/4 OR 1/2 IN VIDEO J-C A
Presents the principles and techniques of cardiopulmonary resuscitation.
Prod-PFP Dist-PFP 1980

New Pulse Of Life (Rev Ed) (Spanish) C 28 MIN
16MM FILM, 3/4 OR 1/2 IN VIDEO J-C A
A Spanish language version of the revised edition of the film and video, New Pulse Of Life. Presents the principles and techniques of C P R. Includes live subjects, manikins, colorful visuals, and dramatic re-enactments, which are used to demonstrate current standards and guidelines for A-Airway Opened, B-Breathing Restored, and C-Circulation Restored. Narrated by John Houseman.
Prod-PFP Dist-PFP

New RCRA, The C 180 MIN
3/4 OR 1/2 INCH VIDEO CASSETTE A
Disusses a teleconference which explains the major provisions of the New Resources Conservation and Recovery Act which became effective November 8, 1984.
Prod-USEPA Dist-USNAC 1984

New RCRA, The Condensed Version C 56 MIN
3/4 OR 1/2 INCH VIDEO CASSETTE A

Presents a condensed version of the teleconference examining the major provisions of the new Resource Conservation and Recovery Act which became effective November 8, 1984.
Prod-USEPA Dist-USNAC 1984

New Reality, A C 51 MIN
16MM FILM, 3/4 OR 1/2 IN VIDEO C
Traces the discovery of the structure of the atom and emphasizes the work of Neils Bohr. Shows how one element can be converted to another and demonstrates color measurement in terms of energy. Illustrates that the electron components of the atom are both particle and wave energies.
Prod-OECD Dist-IFB 1965

New Relations - A Film About Fathers And Sons C 34 MIN
16MM FILM, 3/4 OR 1/2 IN VIDEO A
Discusses the economic and emotional costs of a man's having decided to become a father in his mid-thirties. Concludes with a positive message about becoming parents.
Prod-ACBERG Dist-FANPRO 1980

New Reno-Tahoe, The - Two Worlds In One C 28 MIN
16MM FILM OPTICAL SOUND
Points out various places of interest in and around Reno, Nevada, and Lake Tahoe in order to encourage travel to this vacation area.
LC NO. 79-701180
Prod-UAL Dist-MTP Prodn-TWI 1978

New Reserves Role 2 C 13 MIN
16MM FILM OPTICAL SOUND
Outlines the activities of Canadian Armed Forces reservists.
LC NO. 77-702993
Prod-CDND Dist-CDND Prodn-NFBC

New Roles For Women In Sports C 29 MIN
3/4 OR 1/2 INCH VIDEO CASSETTE
Explores the changing roles of women in athletics.
From The Woman Series.
Prod-WNEDTV Dist-PBS

New Romance - Aspects Of Sexuality And Sexual Roles C 34 MIN
16MM FILM, 3/4 OR 1/2 IN VIDEO
Explores heterosexual and homosexual relationships and suggests that man possesses the intrinsic right to be what he is.
Prod-NFBC Dist-UCEMC 1977

New School, The (Captioned) C 88 MIN
16MM FILM, 3/4 OR 1/2 IN VIDEO A
Discusses the work-study program initiated during Cuba's 1961 literacy campaign in which students combine academic and agricultural work. Spanish dialog with English subtitles.
Prod-CUBAFI Dist-CNEMAG 1973

New Sexual Revolution, The C 30 MIN
3/4 OR 1/2 INCH VIDEO CASSETTE J-C A
Shows Albert Ellis of the Institute for Advanced Study in Rational Psychotherapy and Lester Kirkendall, Professor Emeritus of Oregon State University, talking about the new sexual revolution.
From The Moral Values In Contemporary Society Series.
Prod-AMHUMA Dist-AMHUMA

New Skills For Managing The Work Force C 240 MIN
3/4 OR 1/2 INCH VIDEO CASSETTE
Presents a seminar for direct people managers.
Prod-GOODMI Dist-GOODMI

New Slick And Old Lace C 50 MIN
16MM FILM OPTICAL SOUND
Explores what people wear, where they buy it and how much they pay.
From The Inquiry Series.
LC NO. 77-702835
Prod-CTV Dist-CTV 1976

New Society, The C 30 MIN
3/4 OR 1/2 INCH VIDEO CASSETTE C
Examines what the future may be and addresses the intellectual and value decisions facing U S society. Identifies trends in areas such as urbanism, family, work and leisure.
From The Focus On Society Series.
Prod-DALCCD Dist-DALCCD

New Solar Dawn, The C 26 MIN
3/4 OR 1/2 INCH VIDEO CASSETTE
Shows how an Israeli scientist captures the imagination of scientists and industrialists with a remarkable method of harnessing the sun's energy which he claims will revolutionize solar energy systems.
From The Breakthroughs Series.
Prod-NOMDFI Dist-LANDMK

New Solar System, The C 15 MIN
16MM FILM OPTICAL SOUND C
Deals with the results of the automated spacecraft which have enabled scientists to probe the planets from close-up. Explains the result has been a virtually new portrait of the planets of the solar system, and their interactions with the sun and space. Examines several of these bodies including Mercury, Venus, Comet Kohoutek, Mars, Jupiter and Saturn.
From The Science In Action Series.
Prod-ALLFP Dist-COUNFI

New Sound In The Education Of The Deaf, A (Captioned) C 26 MIN
16MM FILM OPTICAL SOUND A
Explains the community education and continuing education concept as it applies to schools for the deaf.
Prod-GALCO Dist-GALCO 1975

New South And The New North 1876-1900, The B 30 MIN
16MM FILM OPTICAL SOUND H-C A
Describes the period between 1876 and 1900 when Blacks in America sought to absolve stringent racial prejudices. Tells of the many Black business organizations, legal bureaus and newspapers that were formed. Includes the controversy between Booker T Washington and W E B Du Bois over what kind of education Blacks should seek. Describes how white philanthropy became more prominent and the Blacks remained in a semi-colonial status.
From The Black Heritage Series.
LC NO. 75-704070
Prod-WEBSTR Dist-HRAW 1969

New South And The New North, 1876-1888, The B 30 MIN
16MM FILM OPTICAL SOUND H-C A
Dr Elsie M Lewis discusses the characteristics of the new North and the new South as shown in the attitudes of whites towards blacks, the appearance of new laws, and the rise of black leaders to fight for rights under the 13th, 14th and 15th amendments.
From The Black History, Section 10 - New South And New North Series.
LC NO. 77-704068
Prod-WCBSTV Dist-HRAW 1969

New South And The New North, 1888-1900, The B 30 MIN
16MM FILM OPTICAL SOUND H-C A
Dr Elsie M Lewis discusses the effect of state and federal legislation on the rise of the black man from 1888 to 1900, especially the Plesey vs Ferguson decision which sanctioned separation of public facilities, and Booker T Washington's Atlanta Compromise speech.
From The Black History, Section 10 - New South And New North Series.
LC NO. 70-704069
Prod-WCBSTV Dist-HRAW 1969

New South Wales Images C 17 MIN
16MM FILM OPTICAL SOUND
Offers an overview of the sights and way of life in New South Wales.
LC NO. 80-700827
Prod-NSWF Dist-TASCOR 1979

New South, The C 25 MIN
16MM FILM, 3/4 OR 1/2 IN VIDEO H-C A
Reports on how New Orleans has spent a billion and a half dollars on commercial development, while many of its residents are faced with unemployment and substandard housing.
LC NO. 78-701869
Prod-CBSNEW Dist-CAROUF 1978

New Space Race, The C 30 MIN
3/4 OR 1/2 INCH VIDEO CASSETTE C A
Looks at how the exploration of space is causing entrepeneurs to seek contracts to launch satellites and compete for their share of their lucrative market.
From The Enterprise II Series.
Prod-WGBHTV Dist-LCOA 1983

New Spirit In Painting, A - Six Painters Of The 1980s C
3/4 OR 1/2 INCH VIDEO CASSETTE
Explores international developments in painting with portraits of Georg Baselitz, Marku Lupertz, Sandro Chia, Francesco Clemente, David Salle, and Julian Schnabel.
Prod-BLACKW Dist-BLACKW

New Stages For Dance C 30 MIN
3/4 OR 1/2 INCH VIDEO CASSETTE
See series title for descriptive statement.
From The Dance On Television And Film Series.
Prod-ARCVID Dist-ARCVID

New Start, A C 29 MIN
16MM FILM, 3/4 OR 1/2 IN VIDEO
Describes the life of an ex-prisoner before and after rehabilitation. Shows a counselor talking about his success in working with public offenders. Issued in 1969 as a motion picture.
From The To Live Again Series.
LC NO. 80-706859
Prod-USSRS Dist-USNAC 1980

New Strategies For The Cure Of Large Bowel Cancer C 39 MIN
3/4 INCH VIDEO CASSETTE
Discusses new strategies for treating large bowel cancer, the most important of which is early detection and diagnosis.
Prod-UTAHTI Dist-UTAHTI

New Supervisor Takes A Look At His Job, A B 13 MIN
16MM FILM - 3/4 IN VIDEO
Discusses aspects of being a supervisor. Issued in 1944 as a motion picture.
From The Problems In Supervision Series.
LC NO. 79-706515
Prod-USOE Dist-USNAC Prodn-CARFI 1979

New Supervisor—A Series

Examines the new skills, relationships and attitudes a new supervisor must have to be successful. Covers communications, training of subordinates, job enrichment, motivation and self-development.
Prod-RESEM Dist-RESEM

Getting The Job Done Through Others	011 MIN
Message Is Yours, The - Don't Lose It	011 MIN
New Attitude,A	011 MIN
Self-Development - The Key To Success	011 MIN
Training - A Major Responsibility	010 MIN

New Supervisor, The - Making The Transition C 24 MIN
16MM FILM - VIDEO, ALL FORMATS

Examines skills needed to be a successful manager using re-creations of problems experienced by supervisors.
Prod-SAIF Dist-BARR

New Surgical Absorbable Hemostat, A C 21 MIN
3/4 OR 1/2 INCH VIDEO CASSETTE PRO
Demonstrates the properties of an absorbable hemostat derived from organic cellulose in the laboratory and some of its numerous clinical applications in humans.
Prod-WFP Dist-WFP

New Surgical Procedure For The Treatment Of Gastro-Esophageal Reflux, A C 8 MIN
3/4 OR 1/2 INCH VIDEO CASSETTE PRO
Shows placement around the esophagus below the diaphragm and above the stomach of a ring-like prothetic device made of a silicone gel. No recurrences of hiatal hernia or symptoms have occurred in any of the patients treated with this device.
Prod-WFP Dist-WFP

New Swedish Cinema, The B 40 MIN
16MM FILM OPTICAL SOUND
Presents a survey of the Swedish movie scene featuring lesser known Swedish film from the sixties and seventies.
Prod-SIS Dist-SIS

New Talking Shop—A Series
P
Utilizes stories, riddles, poems and games to focus on speech and language development.
Prod-BSPTV Dist-GPITVL 1978

Blends Of L, The	15 MIN
Blends Of R, The	15 MIN
CH Sound, The	15 MIN
Closing Day Auction	15 MIN
Consonants T And D, The - The Vowels Long	15 MIN
Do You Like To Talk	15 MIN
Do You Listen	15 MIN
F Sound And The Vowels, The - Long And	15 MIN
G Sound, The	15 MIN
Grand Opening Of The New Talking Shop	15 MIN
How Do You Talk	15 MIN
How Does Your Voice Sound	15 MIN
J Sound, The	15 MIN
K Sound, The	15 MIN
L Sound, The	15 MIN
Listening For The Th Sounds	15 MIN
R Sound, The	15 MIN
Review	15 MIN
Review - H, W, HW, S, Z, K, G	15 MIN
Review - L, T, R, H, M, N	15 MIN
Review - R, SH, ZH, CH, J	15 MIN
S Sound, The	15 MIN
Scary Sounds - H, W, HW	15 MIN
See, Hear And Feel Sounds	15 MIN
SH Sound, The	15 MIN
Some Blends Of	15 MIN
Special Sounds	15 MIN
TH Sounds, The	15 MIN
V Sound And The Vowels, The - Long And	15 MIN
Y Consonant Sound, The	15 MIN
Z Sound, The	15 MIN
ZH Sound, The	15 MIN

New Technologies / Problems And Possibilities C 26 MIN
3/4 OR 1/2 INCH VIDEO CASSETTE
See series title for descriptive statement.
From The Focus On Change Series.
Prod-TVOTAR Dist-DELTAK

New Technology In Education—A Series
J-C A
Presents a series of lectures discussing learning about computers, learning from and with computers and expanding student access to computers.
Prod-USDOE Dist-USNAC 1983

Computer Gaming As An Integrated Learning	
Computer Literacy - A New Subject In The	030 MIN
Implementing Technology In The Schools - Issues	042 MIN
Logo - The Computer As An Intellectual Tool	027 MIN
Research And Development - Interactive	041 MIN
School District Experiences In Implementing	065 MIN
Software Development - Key Issues And	030 MIN
Statewide Educational Computing Network,	023 MIN
Teacher Training Experiences And Issues	047 MIN
Using Computer Simulations In Social Science,	021 MIN
Using The Computer To Develop Writing Abilities	027 MIN

New Tenant, The C 31 MIN
16MM FILM, 3/4 OR 1/2 IN VIDEO H-C A
Presents The New Tenant by Eugene Ionesco, a play from the Theater of the Absurd which expresses our sense of the ambiguity and incoherence of much of modern life.
From The Humanities - Short Play Showcase Series.
Prod-EBEC Dist-EBEC 1976

New Thing C 60 MIN
3/4 INCH VIDEO CASSETTE
See series title for descriptive statement.
From The Grass Roots Series.
Prod-MDCPB Dist-MDCPB

New Thunder For The USAF - The A-10, The AV10A Bronco, And The Huey Cobra... C 40 MIN
3/4 OR 1/2 INCH VIDEO CASSETTE
Shows three types of aircraft and awesome scenes of firepower, including historical footage of jet planes from the early '40's and '50's.
Prod-IHF Dist-IHF

New Times C 59 MIN
16MM FILM OPTICAL SOUND H-C A

Presents the stories of three fictional families living in New York City in the 1880's and the 1890's. Shows how, on New Years Eve, 1899, the families look back on their lives and unrealized dreams and confront the approaching new century with speculation and renewed hope.
From The Best Of Families Series.
LC NO. 82-700610
Prod-CTELWO Dist-IU 1977

New Times C 59 MIN
3/4 INCH VIDEO CASSETTE
Depicts the lives of three families on New Years Eve in 1899. Shows how the Spanish-American War and the growth of industry have left their mark on these families.
From The Best Of Families Series.
Prod-CTELWO Dist-PUBTEL

New Tomorrows C 19 MIN
16MM FILM OPTICAL SOUND
Highlights emerging types of occupations in a technologically changing world. Shows the role of vocational, technical and adult education in training people to fill these positions.
LC NO. 77-700560
Prod-WBVTAE Dist-WBVTAE 1977

New Tool For Profit, A - The IBM 1440 C 12 MIN
16MM FILM OPTICAL SOUND
Describes the IBM 1440 data processing system, and its input, processing, storage and output capabilities, as well as possible business applications.
LC NO. FI67-2008
Prod-IBUSMA Dist-IBUSMA 1963

New Tribes Mission C 12 MIN
16MM FILM - 3/4 IN VIDEO H-C A
Features a Christian mission to the Yanamamo tribe, showing the degrees of change in the town of Bisasi-Teri. Filmed by Timothy Asch and Napoleon Chagnon in the 1970's.
Prod-DOCEDR Dist-DOCEDR 1975

New Truck Dilemma, The C 23 MIN
16MM FILM - 3/4 IN VIDEO IND
Gives managers a better understanding of fairness as applied to many everyday management decisions.
Prod-BNA Dist-BNA 1965

New Underground Railroad, The C 30 MIN
3/4 OR 1/2 INCH VIDEO CASSETTE J-C A
Presents the story of a group of church people in Madison, Wisconsin, struggling to decide whether or not to defy U S law by giving sanctuary to Salvadorans fleeing the horrors of military persecution in their country. Looks at the story of a young Salvadoran family and their clandestine journey to the United States.
LC NO. 84-700388
Prod-CLOPRO Dist-IU 1984

New Understanding, The C 27 MIN
3/4 OR 1/2 INCH VIDEO CASSETTE
Explains the typical psychological consequences of breaking down the denial system, as well as methods and modes by which the chemically dependent person can be helped to move from a state of demoralization to an understanding and acceptance of his or her illness.
From The Caring Community - Alcoholism And Drug Abuse Series.
Prod-VTRI Dist-VTRI

New Vehicle Technology—A Series

Covers New Vehicle Technology including Aerodynamics, electric and hybrid vehicles and fuel cell vehicle design.
Prod-UAZMIC Dist-UAZMIC

Aerodynamics, Rolling Resistance, Roll Down	
Comparison Of Computer Simulation Using Data	060 MIN
Economic Analysis Of The Fuel Cell Powered	120 MIN
Electric And Hybrid Vehicles, Lead-Acid	120 MIN
Fuel Cell Vehicle Design, Hydrogen-Air Fuel	120 MIN

New View Of Mars, A C 10 MIN
16MM FILM, 3/4 OR 1/2 IN VIDEO I-H
Delves into scientific thought concerning the planet Mars and discusses the possibility of life existing there.
LC NO. 82-706243
Prod-NASA Dist-USNAC Prodn-GRAF 1975

New View Of Space, A C 28 MIN
16MM FILM - 3/4 IN VIDEO J-C A
Describes how the visual image of photography has contributed to many achievements in research and engineering, in space science and exploration, and in benefits to mankind from space studies. Includes examples of lunar and planetary studies, weather forecasting, and surveys of Earth resources. Issued in 1972 as a motion picture.
LC NO. 79-708025
Prod-NASA Dist-USNAC Prodn-IMAGA 1979

New Voice—A Series
H-C A
Centers around the activities of a multi-racial high school newspaper staff as it tackles stories on pregnancy, drugs, venereal disease, parental alcoholism, gang life and alternative careers.
Prod-WGBHTV Dist-GPITVL 1980

Alcoholism	030 MIN
Audition	030 MIN
Battered Teacher	030 MIN
Epilepsy	030 MIN
Feathers	030 MIN
Gangs	030 MIN
Group Dynamics	030 MIN
Halls Of Montezuma, The	030 MIN
Kiko's Pain	030 MIN
Life Science	030 MIN
Marguerite	030 MIN
Mexican Greaser	030 MIN
Pilot Wrap	030 MIN
Pregnancy, Pt 1	030 MIN
Pregnancy, Pt 2	030 MIN
Prom	030 MIN
Racism	030 MIN
Rags, Pt 1	030 MIN
Rags, Pt 2	030 MIN
Rape	030 MIN
Scripted Drugs	030 MIN
Series Wrap	030 MIN
Suicide	030 MIN
Victor	030 MIN

New Voices For Man C 57 MIN
16MM FILM, 3/4 OR 1/2 IN VIDEO H-C A
Explains how the opera was born during the Renaissance with a presentation by Monteverdi for the Court of Mantua. Probes how Corelli created the sonata form and introduced the concerto, with Venice becoming the musical capital of Europe. Looks at the musical contributions of Stradivari and Handel.
From The Music Of Man Series.
Prod-CANBC Dist-TIMLIF 1981

New Way Of Gravure B 13 MIN
16MM FILM OPTICAL SOUND
Presents Stanley William Hayter, a modern artist who describes the technique for engraving on copper from his first sketches on paper through the final print of his series of 'ANGELS WRESTLING.'
Prod-FILIM Dist-RADIM

New Way Of Gravure, A B 13 MIN
16MM FILM OPTICAL SOUND C
American artist Stanley William Hayter describes his technique of engraving on copper, from his first rough sketches on paper through pulling the final print.
Prod-PALEY Dist-RADIM 1951

New Way To Get More Eggs C 11 MIN
16MM FILM OPTICAL SOUND J-C A
Shows the part antibiotics play in mixed feeds for laying flock and points out how to insure high productivity from the birds in and out of the hen house.
Prod-STARIF Dist-PFI 1954

New Way To Lift, A C 10 MIN
16MM FILM, 3/4 OR 1/2 IN VIDEO J-C
Demonstrates the technique for safe lifting developed by B T Davies and shows the palmar grip, the proper position of back, chin, arms, feet and the correct distribution of body weight.
Prod-NSC Dist-JOU 1971

New Ways For Old Morocco B 23 MIN
16MM FILM OPTICAL SOUND
Details the customs, traditions and culture of the Berbers. Gives an explanation of their experiment in living. Shows the collaboration of the Seghouchen tribe of Mount Tichoukt and the tribe of Sidi Sais, a community of farmers.
Prod-LEEN Dist-RADIM

New Ways Of Knowing C 29 MIN
3/4 INCH VIDEO CASSETTE
Documents the clash between traditional technologies of the north and modern scientific methods imported from the south - can the wisdom of the ancients coexist with guns, snowmobiles and communications satellites. Also available in two-inch quad and one-inch videotape.
From The North Of 60 Degrees - Destiny Uncertain Series.
Prod-TVOTAR Dist-NAMPBC

New Ways To Disseminate Scientific Knowledge C 15 MIN
16MM FILM OPTICAL SOUND C
Explains that to keep researchers around the world informed about new relevant scientific discoveries, organizations such as the Smithsonian Institution's Center for Short-Lived Phenomena and the Institute for Scientific Information have been founded.
From The Science In Action Series.
Prod-ALLFP Dist-COUNFI

New Ways With Chicken C 12 MIN
16MM FILM - 3/4 IN VIDEO J-H
Describes simple approaches to saturated fat reduction when preparing poultry. Deals with cutting the chicken, boning and removing the skin.
From The Eat Right To Your Heart's Delight Series.
Prod-IPS Dist-IPS 1976

New Willamette, The C 26 MIN
16MM FILM OPTICAL SOUND
Shows how the Willamette River in Oregon was cleaned up through the cooperative efforts of citizens, industry and government.
LC NO. 75-700152
Prod-USAE Dist-MTP Prodn-GROENG 1974

New Woman Athlete, The C 9 MIN
3/4 OR 1/2 INCH VIDEO CASSETTE
Reviews many of the traditional myths about women involved in active sports. Emphasizes the unique advantages for and athletic potential of the woman athlete, and addresses some of the medical and health-related concerns encountered by a woman's coach.
From The Sports Medicine For Coaches Series.
Prod-UWASH Dist-UWASH

New Womb, The C 30 MIN
3/4 OR 1/2 INCH VIDEO CASSETTE
Points out that with the development of 'in vitro' fertilization it is now possible to begin monitoring life from the moment of conception. Shows that a new medical specialty, prenatal medicine, has begun to develop.
From The Innovation Series.
Prod-WNETTV Dist-WNETTV 1983

New Work For Greenville C 8 MIN
16MM FILM OPTICAL SOUND
Shows job training for industrial survival in Greenville, Mississippi. Emphasizes the role of private industry in the rehabilitation process.
LC NO. 74-705211
Prod-USSRS Dist-USNAC 1969

New World / Day Without Incident C 29 MIN
3/4 INCH VIDEO CASSETTE
Presents Asian-American students in San Francisco showing the changes achieved by bilingual-bicultural education in Bay area schools. Depicts students in Pontiac, Michigan, recommending that the restrictive school rules adopted after 1971 rioting be changed.
From The As We See It Series.
Prod-WTTWTV Dist-PUBTEL

New World From Old C 25 MIN
16MM FILM OPTICAL SOUND
Explores the investigations of Euclid's parallel postulate in the 18th and 19th centuries, which led to the discovery of non-Euclidean geometries. Concludes with a look at Riemannian geometries and a reference to Einstein's theory of space and time.
Prod-OPENU Dist-GPITVL

New World Visions C 120 MIN
3/4 OR 1/2 INCH VIDEO CASSETTE H-C A
Examines and analyzes the first 250 years of concurrently developing styles of American art, architecture and design and how these forms reflected the emerging American consciousness. Begins with the dawn of American colonization and ends before World War I. Uses natural settings and New York's Metropolitan Museum of Art to illustrate various styles of art by well-known and little-known painters and craftsmen.
Prod-WNETTV Dist-FI

New World, More New Math C 29 MIN
2 INCH VIDEOTAPE
Familiarizes parents and teachers with some of the ideas behind the teaching of new math.
Prod-WNETTV Dist-PUBTEL

New World, The C 27 MIN
16MM FILM OPTICAL SOUND
Shows how the 35 Salesian agricultural schools are dedicated to improving farming among the small farmers and to producing dedicated men who can professionally advise and help others. Features the Salesian Agricultural School of La Vega in Santo Domingo.
Prod-SCC Dist-MTP

New World, The C 59 MIN
16MM FILM OPTICAL SOUND
Surveys sculpture in America, beginning with David Smith and the abstract expressionists in the 1940's. Examines pop and minimal art in the works of Segal, Oldenburg, Andre, Serra, Morris, Judd, Christo and Kienholz. Shows the large-scale earthworks of Heizer and Smithson.
From The Masters Of Modern Sculpture Series. No. 3
LC NO. 78-701409
Prod-BLACKW Dist-BLACKW 1978

New World, The C
3/4 INCH VIDEO CASSETTE
Describes growth and development of a child from four weeks to ten weeks.
From The Growth And Development - A Chronicle Of Four Children Series. Series 1
Prod-JUETHO Dist-LIP

New World, The - Gregory, 3 Weeks C 6 MIN
16MM FILM OPTICAL SOUND
See series title for descriptive statement.
From The Growth And Development - A Chronicle Of Four Children Series. Series 1
LC NO. 78-700682
Prod-JUETHO Dist-LIP Prodn-CONCOM 1976

New World, The - Joseph, 10 Weeks C 6 MIN
16MM FILM OPTICAL SOUND
See series title for descriptive statement.
From The Growth And Development - A Chronicle Of Four Children Series. Series 1
LC NO. 78-700682
Prod-JUETHO Dist-LIP Prodn-CONCOM 1976

New World, The - Melissa, 4 Weeks C 6 MIN
16MM FILM OPTICAL SOUND
See series title for descriptive statement.
From The Growth And Development - A Chronicle Of Four Children Series. Series 1
LC NO. 78-700682
Prod-JUETHO Dist-LIP Prodn-CONCOM 1976

New World, The - Terra, 10 Weeks C 6 MIN
16MM FILM OPTICAL SOUND
See series title for descriptive statement.
From The Growth And Development - A Chronicle Of Four Children Series. Series 1
LC NO. 78-700682
Prod-JUETHO Dist-LIP Prodn-CONCOM 1976

New Worlds C 55 MIN
16MM FILM, 3/4 OR 1/2 IN VIDEO H-C A
Reveals how various species have adapted to manmade changes in their environment. Considers the fortunes of man himself and his impact through his time on the earth.

From The Living Planet Series. Pt 12
Prod-BBCTV Dist-TIMLIF 1984

New Year's C 15 MIN
3/4 INCH VIDEO CASSETTE P
See series title for descriptive statement.
From The Celebrate Series.
Prod-KUONTV Dist-GPITVL 1978

New York City C 3 MIN
16MM FILM OPTICAL SOUND P-I
Discusses New York City in the state of New York.
From The Of All Things Series.
Prod-BAILYL Dist-AVED

New York City - Center Of Megalopolis C 15 MIN
3/4 OR 1/2 INCH VIDEO CASSETTE I
Shows that New York City from 1624 to the 1980's has always been a landing point for immigrants as well as a world center for commerce and culture.
From The American Legacy Series. Program 3
Prod-KRMATV Dist-AITECH 1983

New York City, Too Far From Tampa Blues C 47 MIN
16MM FILM, 3/4 OR 1/2 IN VIDEO
Focuses on the problems encountered by a Puerto Rican youngster and his family when they move from Tampa, Florida, to New York City. Based on the book New York City, Too Far From Tampa Blues by T Ernesto Bethancourt. Originally shown on the television series ABC Afterschool Specials.
From The Teenage Years Series.
LC NO. 79-707199
Prod-WILSND Dist-TIMLIF 1979

New York City's Waterfront Legacy C 27 MIN
16MM FILM, 3/4 OR 1/2 IN VIDEO H-C A
Takes a look at New York City's 578 miles of shoreline, including decaying docks, magnificent beaches and marinas, and riverfront expressways. Points out the conflicting demands of industry, commerce, shipping and recreation.
Prod-CUNIV Dist-CUNIV 1977

New York Deafness Commission C 7 MIN
16MM FILM SILENT J-C S
Presents a reading in American sign language of a speech by John Schrodel of the New York Civic Association of the Deaf regarding undereducation, underemployment and discrimination of the deaf. Talks about the establishment of the New York Deafness Commission to act as watchdog and promoter of legislation for the deaf. Signed for the deaf by Lyle Hinks.
LC NO. 76-701698
Prod-JOYCE Dist-JOYCE 1975

New York Faces The Sea C 13 MIN
3/4 OR 1/2 INCH VIDEO CASSETTE J-H A
Considers the problems of commercial fishing, recreational uses of inland and coastal waters, power plant development, shipping and manipulation of wetlands. Introduces New York State's Sea Grant Program and shows how it assists in the development and use of the coastal areas of Long Island, the Great Lakes and the St Lawrence Seaway.
Prod-CUETV Dist-CUNIV 1972

New York School, The C 55 MIN
3/4 OR 1/2 INCH VIDEO CASSETTE
Shows how New York City in the 1940s and 50s became the art center. Tells how artists who came to be called Abstract Expressionists started a group they called 'The New York School.' Features artists Arshile Gorky, Adolph Gottlieb, Philip Guston, Al Held, Hans Hofmann, Franz Kline, William de Kooning, Lee Krasner, Joan Mitchell, Robert Motherwell, Barnett Newman, Jackson Pollock, Mark Rothko and critics Clement Greenberg and Harold Rosenberg.
Prod-BLACKW Dist-BLACKW

New York Times Index, The C 6 MIN
3/4 OR 1/2 INCH VIDEO CASSETTE
Demonstrates how to find a news item on a given subject published in the New York Times.
From The Library Skills Tapes Series.
Prod-MDCC Dist-MDCC

New York Trio Da Camera C 29 MIN
2 INCH VIDEOTAPE
Presents the music of the New York Trio da Camera.
From The Young Musical Artists Series.
Prod-WKARTV Dist-PUBTEL

New York World's Fair, The - Peace Through Understanding B 9 MIN
16MM FILM OPTICAL SOUND J-C A
Describes the New York World's Fair of 1964.
From The Screen News Digest Series. Vol 7, Issue 10.
LC NO. FIA68-2096
Prod-HEARST Dist-HEARST 1965

New York Yankee Broadcast C 34 MIN
3/4 OR 1/2 INCH VIDEO CASSETTE
Deals with the 1980 Yankee American League championship. Analyzes the history of the baseball broadcast.
Prod-KITCHN Dist-KITCHN

New York, Holland, Spain C 27 MIN
16MM FILM OPTICAL SOUND P-I
Examines the lifestyles of children in New York, Holland and Spain. Presents a Dutch folk tale about a selfish widow who wants a sea captain to find her the most precious item in the world.
From The Big Blue Marble - Children Around The World Series. Program U
LC NO. 76-700633
Prod-ALVEN Dist-VITT 1975

New York's My Town C 14 MIN
3/4 OR 1/2 INCH VIDEO CASSETTE P
Shows Sarah conducting a tour of her family's apartment and her city's buildings, parks, transportation, and other attractions.
From The Under The Blue Umbrella Series.
Prod-SCETV Dist-AITECH 1977

New Zealand C 15 MIN
16MM FILM OPTICAL SOUND
Features a travelog on New Zealand.
LC NO. 77-702994
Prod-FIARTS Dist-FIARTS 1977

New Zealand C 21 MIN
16MM FILM, 3/4 OR 1/2 IN VIDEO I-J A
Offers an overview of New Zealand, a productive land of friendly people who are justly proud of the high quality of life they have produced by imagination, hard work and a belief in the importance of the individual.
Prod-LUF Dist-LUF 1978

New Zealand Lamb Promotional Shorts C 29 MIN
16MM FILM OPTICAL SOUND
Presents short discussions of a variety of subjects, including sheep shearing, geysers, dogs, cattle, the Centerbury Plains and meat cuts.
LC NO. 77-702995
Prod-NZLC Dist-CHET Prodn-CHET 1976

New Zealand, The Kiwi Way Of Life C 30 MIN
3/4 OR 1/2 INCH VIDEO CASSETTE
Depicts New Zealand as a land where life is lived outdoors and where man thrives amidst a scenic beauty and diversity that inspires and refreshes.
Prod-IVCH Dist-IVCH

New Zealand's Day With LBJ B 15 MIN
16MM FILM OPTICAL SOUND
Follows President and Mrs Johnson on their round of activities during a day spent in Wellington, New Zealand, in the third week of October 1966, prior to the Manila Conference.
From The Pictorial Parade Series.
LC NO. FI67-272
Prod-NZNFU Dist-NZNFU 1966

New Zebra In Town (Acceptance) C 12 MIN
16MM FILM, 3/4 OR 1/2 IN VIDEO K-P
Uses a puppet story to examine the idea of discrimination in the subtle form of an individual's characteristics and to trace the change from suspicion of the individual to acceptance. Shows how Oni, Coslo and Butch learn a lesson in acceptance after they refuse to let a fellow-puppet, Zaybar Zebra, help them on their school project because he's so different.
From The Forest Town Fables Series.
Prod-CORF Dist-CORF 1974

New Zimbabwe, The C 28 MIN
3/4 OR 1/2 INCH VIDEO CASSETTE H A
Looks at the progress made in the new nation of Zimbabwe, showing how a policy of reconciliation was pursued so that its minority white population and its native Black people could live together peacefully. Covers the role of new educational, agricultural and vocational programs as well as the role of the church in helping Zimbabwe reach its goal of socialism. Features Prime Minister Mugabe and President Banana.
Prod-FRMA Dist-MAR 1983

New 400B Ethylene Oxide Sterilizer, The C 18 MIN
3/4 OR 1/2 INCH VIDEO CASSETTE PRO
Describes how ethylene oxide kills pathogens. Shows sterilization of a typical group of medical instruments as they are processed in the 3M-400B ethylene oxide sterilizer, a machine which incorporates a unique electronic logic which automatically controls the entire sterilization cycle.
Prod-WFP Dist-WFP

New-Fashioned Halloween, A C 21 MIN
16MM FILM OPTICAL SOUND P-C A
Shows the people of Leoniz, N J, preparing for the show, 'TRICK-OR-TREAT FOR UNICEF' with Danny Kaye. Includes examples of UNICEF at work in many lands.
LC NO. FIA66-499
Prod-AFP Dist-UNICEF 1965

Newborn C 28 MIN
16MM FILM, 3/4 OR 1/2 IN VIDEO H-C A
Shows the abilities, reflexes and degree of sensitivity in a newborn infant.
Prod-CANBC Dist-FLMLIB 1978

Newborn C 28 MIN
16MM FILM - 3/4 IN VIDEO
Shows an infant's world through the eyes of a child and the perseptive of the parents. Covers the first three months of life and the dynamic process by which the baby develops into a unique person.
Prod-JAJ Dist-MTP 1972

Newborn C 28 MIN
3/4 INCH VIDEO CASSETTE C A
Deals with the first few months of life and the process through which a newborn child becomes a separate and unique person.
Prod-WSTGLC Dist-WSTGLC

Newborn Calf, The X 11 MIN
16MM FILM, 3/4 OR 1/2 IN VIDEO P-I
Reveals the birth and early development of a calf by showing the pregnant farm cow in the barn where she will give birth and the involvement of the farm children as they get acquainted with the calf and wean him on the fourth day. Helps students better understand reproduction as part of the life cycle.
Prod-EBEC Dist-EBEC 1970

Newborn Care B 29 MIN
16MM FILM OPTICAL SOUND C A
Explains about care of the newborn, discussing the immediate care, infant examination, infant feeding, infant bathing and child development. Features Dr J Robert Bragonier and Leta Power Drake.
From The Nine To Get Ready Series. No. 8
LC NO. 79-704213
Prod-KUONTV Dist-UNEBR 1965

Newborn Care C 29 MIN
2 INCH VIDEOTAPE
See series title for descriptive statement.
From The Nine To Get Ready Series.
Prod-NETCHE Dist-PUBTEL

Newborn, The C 29 MIN
3/4 OR 1/2 INCH VIDEO CASSETTE H-C A
Describes the medical procedures that assess and support the reflexes and capabilities of the infant. Points out that a newborn may appear strange to new parents.
From The Tomorrow's Families Series.
LC NO. 81-706905
Prod-MSDOE Dist-AITECH 1980

Newborn, The C 30 MIN
3/4 INCH VIDEO CASSETTE
Shows the birth of a baby and discusses what reflexes and sensory capacities the normal infant possesses.
From The Growing Years Series.
Prod-COAST Dist-CDTEL

Newburyport - A Measure Of Change C 28 MIN
16MM FILM OPTICAL SOUND
Deals with urban renewal and historic preservation, focusing on a ten-year effort to rehabilitate the 19th-century commercial district of Newburyport, Massachusetts.
Prod-URBNIM Dist-URBNIM 1975

Newcomer In School - Adventure Or Agony? C
3/4 OR 1/2 INCH VIDEO CASSETTE A
Familiarizes parents and teachers with the resources that can be made available to help children adjust to a new school.
From The Vital Link Series.
Prod-EDCC Dist-EDCC

Newcomer, The C 14 MIN
16MM FILM, 3/4 OR 1/2 IN VIDEO I
Dramatizes two situations about a new student in the class. First shows David, the newcomer, unsure of himself and lonely in his interaction with his classmates. Stops the action and replays the scenes to allow students to see what might have been done instead to make David feel welcome.
Prod-MUR Dist-PHENIX 1969

Newcomers To The City--A Series
16MM FILM, 3/4 OR 1/2 IN VIDEO I-J
Shows how children struggle to adapt to their new homes and neighborhoods after leaving their native states or countries.
Prod-EBEC Dist-EBEC

Chicano From The Southwest 15 MIN
Jesse From Mississippi 15 MIN
Johnny From Fort Apache 15 MIN
Linda And Billy Ray From Appalachia 15 MIN
Manuel From Puerto Rico 14 MIN

Newcomers, The B 25 MIN
16MM FILM OPTICAL SOUND H A
Deals with the migration of people to the cities and their problems of adjustment. Shows how the church is trying to meet their needs by fulfilling its function as religious institution, community center and clinic.
LC NO. FIA65-37
Prod-MCBM Dist-ECUFLM Prodn-STONEY 1963

Newcomers, The - Les Arrivants - Prologue C 55 MIN
16MM FILM OPTICAL SOUND
Uses the songs, dances and rituals of the native peoples of Canada to tell a story about the conflicts faced by a young prospective chief, torn between his love and the call of the spirit.
LC NO. 77-702996
Prod-IMO Dist-IMO Prodn-NIELSE 1977

Newcomers, The - Les Arrivants - Prologue (French) C 55 MIN
16MM FILM OPTICAL SOUND
Uses the songs, dances and rituals of the native peoples of Canada to tell a story about the conflicts faced by a young prospective chief, torn between his love and the call of the spirit.
LC NO. 77-702996
Prod-IMO Dist-IMO Prodn-NIELSE 1977

Newcomers, The - Les Arrivants - Prologue (Gitksan) C 55 MIN
16MM FILM OPTICAL SOUND
Uses the songs, dances and rituals of the native peoples of Canada to tell a story about the conflicts faced by a young prospective chief, torn between his love and the call of the spirit.
LC NO. 77-702996
Prod-IMO Dist-IMO Prodn-NIELSE 1977

Newfoundland Sings C 12 MIN
16MM FILM OPTICAL SOUND
Presents a selection of sailor songs, sung by the Tau-men, an informal foursome. Shows the outports, bays, inlets, and small whales while the men sing songs that reflect the heritage of people who have for generations lived by the sea.
LC NO. 76-705255
Prod-CTFL Dist-CTFL 1968

Newly Fathers C 29 MIN
3/4 OR 1/2 INCH VIDEO CASSETTE C A
Presents a specialist in early childhood education discussing the role of fathers in children's development, emphasizing the effects of fathers on educational motivation and achievement.

From The Focus On Children Series.
LC NO. 81-707443
Prod-IU Dist-IU 1981

Newman's Magnetic Motor C
1/2 IN VIDEO CASSETTE (BETA) IND
Consists of an assembly of nine United States telecasts on the controversial device of Joe Newman.
Prod-PLACE Dist-PLACE

Newport Happening, A C 30 MIN
16MM FILM OPTICAL SOUND
Uses a dramatization about three drivers to show the bridge across Narragansett Bay, R I, and the effect of the bridge on the lives of residents and travellers.
LC NO. 72-706373
Prod-SILVER Dist-SILVER 1969

News C 15 MIN
3/4 INCH VIDEO CASSETTE I-J
Traces the history of newspapers. Discusses what news is, where it comes from, how a news story is covered, and how it is written.
From The Newspaper - What's In It For Me Series.
Prod-MOEBA Dist-GPITVL 1980

News - A Closer Look C 15 MIN
16MM FILM, 3/4 OR 1/2 IN VIDEO
Examines some of the constraints and potential pitfalls of news gathering, discussing such issues as honest news reporting, the objectivity of the news and the limits of television news. Emphasizes the need for quickly identifying important emerging public issues and for detailed, in-depth reporting.
From The News Series.
Prod-IITC Dist-IU 1979

News - A Free Press C 15 MIN
16MM FILM, 3/4 OR 1/2 IN VIDEO J-H
Examines some factors affecting freedom and objectivity in journalism. Considers such issues as whether the press is truly free, whether a reporter can bias a story and how freedom of the press affects other declared rights.
From The News Series.
Prod-IITC Dist-IU 1977

News - Careers C 15 MIN
16MM FILM, 3/4 OR 1/2 IN VIDEO J-H
Examines some of the personal rewards and sacrifices of news work, addressing issues such as necessary qualifications, getting started in the business, the glamour of reporting and the demands of the profession.
From The News Series.
Prod-IITC Dist-IU 1977

News - Communication C 15 MIN
16MM FILM, 3/4 OR 1/2 IN VIDEO
Examines the uses of language and visual materials in journalism, emphasizing the need for precision, accuracy and selectivity appropriate to the medium used. Discusses the role of the intended audience and the influence of news topics in determining the way news is presented.
From The News Series.
Prod-IITC Dist-IU 1979

News - The Business C 15 MIN
16MM FILM, 3/4 OR 1/2 IN VIDEO J-H
Presents Walter Cronkite, Bill Moyers and others discussing keeping news reporting honest and objective while operating within a commercial, profitmaking structure.
From The News Series.
Prod-IITC Dist-IU 1979

News - What Is It C 15 MIN
16MM FILM, 3/4 OR 1/2 IN VIDEO J-H
Examines the roles of news writers, editors, columnists, and producers, and discusses topics such as the definition of news, who decides what is news, and the news needs of the public. Compares print and electronic media in terms of the demands which time and space impose on the selection, organization and treatment of news items.
From The News Series.
Prod-IITC Dist-IU 1977

News Connection, The - Effective Public Relations C 39 MIN
3/4 INCH VIDEO CASSETTE
Discusses the particular needs of television, radio, newspapers and magazines in regards to public relations stories.
Prod-MEDIAW Dist-MEDIAW 1979

News Diary '64 B 30 MIN
16MM FILM OPTICAL SOUND
Shows presidential elections, beatles, Warren Report, Vietnam, Cyprus and space.
Prod-SFI Dist-SFI

News Parade '65 B 30 MIN
16MM FILM OPTICAL SOUND
Shows space walk, Dominican revolt, Churchill, Watts riot and the Pope visiting the United States.
Prod-SFI Dist-SFI

News Stories C 15 MIN
3/4 OR 1/2 INCH VIDEO CASSETTE P
See series title for descriptive statement.
From The Word Shop Series.
Prod-WETATV Dist-WETATV

News Story C 20 MIN
16MM FILM, 3/4 OR 1/2 IN VIDEO H-C A
Points out that news is produced industrially, just as advertising is. Tells how news photographs and news copy are based on a set of specific news values.
From The Viewpoint Series.
Prod-THAMES Dist-MEDIAG 1975

News Story, A C 29 MIN
3/4 OR 1/2 INCH VIDEO CASSETTE
Shows how the objectivity and credibility of a television program about drugs is affected by the filming, researching, editing and presentation of the program. Issued in 1971 as a motion picture.
From The Social Seminar Series.
LC NO. 80-707357
Prod-NIMH Dist-USNAC Prodn-UCEMC 1980

News—A Series
16MM FILM, 3/4 OR 1/2 IN VIDEO J-H
Tells the story of the people who gather and present news on television, in the newspapers, on radio and in magazines. Features Jack Anderson, Ben Bradlee, Walter Cronkite, Bill Moyers, Edwin Newman and George Will. Shows the activity and character of life in the newsroom and the TV studio.
Prod-IITC Dist-IU 1977

News - A Closer Look	015 MIN
News - A Free Press	015 MIN
News - Careers	015 MIN
News - Communication	015 MIN
News - The Business	015 MIN
News - What Is It	015 MIN

Newsfocus/Israel - International Press Perspective B 28 MIN
16MM FILM OPTICAL SOUND H-C
Features news analyst David Schoenbrun interviewing three journalists - Clayton Fritchay, American syndicated columinst, Marine de Medici, American correspondent for Il tempo of Rome, and David Adamson, Washington correspondent for the Sanden Sunday Telegraph. Discusses the political and economic interests which shape Western policy toward Israel.
LC NO. 70-707443
Prod-ADL Dist-ADL 1970

Newsfront X 110 MIN
16MM FILM OPTICAL SOUND
Focuses on a group of newsreel-makers in the crucial years from 1948 to 1956. Directed by Phillip Noyce.
Prod-UNKNWN Dist-NYFLMS 1978

Newspaper C 15 MIN
16MM FILM, 3/4 OR 1/2 IN VIDEO J-H A
Deals with the role of the newspaper in a democratic society and discusses the kinds of information gathered to keep readers accurately informed. Explains the role of advertising and the economics that support a free press.
Prod-LUF Dist-LUF 1979

Newspaper - A Business C 15 MIN
3/4 OR 1/2 INCH VIDEO CASSETTE J-H
Discusses how a newspaper operates as a business.
From The Newspaper - Behind The Lines Series.
Prod-CTI Dist-CTI

Newspaper - A Closer Look C 15 MIN
3/4 OR 1/2 INCH VIDEO CASSETTE J-H
Shows how newspapers provide various kinds of information to meet the needs of readers.
From The Newspaper - Behind The Lines Series.
Prod-CTI Dist-CTI

Newspaper - A Free Press C 15 MIN
3/4 OR 1/2 INCH VIDEO CASSETTE J-H
Discusses the importance of freedom of the press.
From The Newspaper - Behind The Lines Series.
Prod-CTI Dist-CTI

Newspaper - Behind The Lines—A Series
J-H
Deals with newspapers as an essential source of news and information. Shows how newspapers are produced and examines their influence on American life.
Prod-CTI Dist-CTI

Newspaper - A Business	015 MIN
Newspaper - A Closer Look	015 MIN
Newspaper - A Free Press	015 MIN
Newspaper - Careers	015 MIN
Newspaper - Communication	015 MIN
Why A Newspaper	015 MIN

Newspaper - Careers C 15 MIN
3/4 OR 1/2 INCH VIDEO CASSETTE J-H
Examines careers in newspaper work.
From The Newspaper - Behind The Lines Series.
Prod-CTI Dist-CTI

Newspaper - Communication C 15 MIN
3/4 OR 1/2 INCH VIDEO CASSETTE J-H
Shows how newspapers provide information in response to the interests of the public.
From The Newspaper - Behind The Lines Series.
Prod-CTI Dist-CTI

Newspaper - Its Role In A Democratic Society C 15 MIN
16MM FILM OPTICAL SOUND I-C A
Presents hard news, background stories, analysis and prediction by columnists, opinions of both editors and general public. Explains and illustrates each of these elements. Deals with the role advertising plays in promoting free press.
LC NO. 72-703000
Prod-ASPTEF Dist-ASPTEF 1969

Newspaper - What's In It For Me—A Series
I-J
Discusses the importance of newspapers and describes the mechanics of newspaper production.
Prod-MOEBA Dist-GPITVL 1980

Advertising	15 MIN
Features	15 MIN
Modern Newspaper Plant, A	15 MIN
News	15 MIN

Newspaper In The Classroom—A Series
I-H
Prod-MOEBA Dist-GPITVL Prodn-KYNETV

History Of The Newspaper	20 MIN
How Is The Newspaper Produced	20 MIN
Modern Newspaper Plant, A	20 MIN
What's In The Newspaper	20 MIN

Newspaper Layout C 13 MIN
16MM FILM, 3/4 OR 1/2 IN VIDEO H-C A
Presents the fundamental principles of newspaper layout, including balance, effective use of white space, accenting of hot spots and elimination of ornamentation. Compares selected pages of daily newspapers and applies principles of layout and redesign.
Prod-COP Dist-AIMS 1972

Newspaper Production Using Space Age Technology C 16 MIN
16MM FILM, 3/4 OR 1/2 IN VIDEO J-H
Shows modern systems of newspaper production. Gives an overview of various newspaper functions and how they have been affected by technology.
Prod-WHICAF Dist-AIMS 1976

Newspaper Serves Its Community, A C 14 MIN
16MM FILM, 3/4 OR 1/2 IN VIDEO I-H
Shows process of printing a newspaper from reporting an event to final distribution of the paper. Includes views of the city room, the library, linotype machines and printing presses.
Prod-GOLD Dist-PHENIX 1959

Newspaper Story (2nd Ed) C 27 MIN
16MM FILM, 3/4 OR 1/2 IN VIDEO
Depicts the steps in the completion of a newspaper story from recording the incident through the taking and finishing of pictures, writing, editing, setting in type, printing the paper and distributing it.
From The World Of Work Series.
Prod-EBEC Dist-EBEC 1973

Newspaper Story (2nd Ed) (Spanish) C 27 MIN
16MM FILM, 3/4 OR 1/2 IN VIDEO J-C
Traces a 24-hour period in the life of the Los Angeles Times. Shows how news is gathered, written and edited and how newspapers are printed.
Prod-EBEC Dist-EBEC

Newspaper Writing C 15 MIN
3/4 OR 1/2 INCH VIDEO CASSETTE I
Illustrates various forms of newspaper writing and stresses the skills a newswriter must use to deal accurately with the facts.
From The Zebra Wings Series.
Prod-NITC Dist-AITECH Prodn-MAETEL 1975

Newspapers C 15 MIN
3/4 OR 1/2 INCH VIDEO CASSETTE J-H
Traces the development of a newspaper story from the original concept to its printing and distribution.
From The Media Machine Series.
Prod-WVIZTV Dist-GPITVL 1975

Newspapers - A Reading Adventure C 19 MIN
16MM FILM, 3/4 OR 1/2 IN VIDEO I
Uses animation and live action sequences to show how a young boy learns about newspapers. Explains how news articles are selected, researched, and written and how they are then organized and indexed for printing.
Prod-HIGGIN Dist-HIGGIN 1983

Newspapers' New Role B 30 MIN
2 INCH VIDEOTAPE C A
Features a conversation with Alistair Cooke concerning the implications for newspapers as to the public's reliance on TV as a source of news and the importance of newspapers not as a branch of profit-seeking enterprise but as a public servant. (Broadcast quality)
From The Communications And Education Series. No. 8
Prod-NYSED Dist-GPITVL Prodn-WNDTTV

Newsprint, Newspaper And Trees C 11 MIN
16MM FILM, 3/4 OR 1/2 IN VIDEO
Presents the story of newsprint told through the operations of St Regis' Newsprint Division, the nation's second largest newsprint producer.
From The Forest Resources Films Series.
Prod-REGIS Dist-GPITVL

Newsreel Of Dreams, A C 24 MIN
3/4 OR 1/2 INCH VIDEO CASSETTE
Recreates the artist's dreams with a display of lights and colors.
Prod-EAI Dist-EAI

Newsreel Of Dreams, Part 2 C 8 MIN
16MM FILM OPTICAL SOUND
Presents dream matrix, history written in lighting image, memory and the TV syntax and images flowing and fused to other images.
Prod-VANBKS Dist-VANBKS

Newsreel Of Dreams, Part 3 C 9 MIN
16MM FILM OPTICAL SOUND
Presents dream matrix, history written in lighting image, memory and the TV syntax and images flowing and fused to other images.
Prod-VANBKS Dist-VANBKS

Newsreel Of Dreams, Pt. 1 C 8 MIN
16MM FILM OPTICAL SOUND

Presents dream matrix, history written in lighting image, memory and the TV syntax and images flowing and fused to other images.
Prod-VANBKS Dist-VANBKS

Newton - The Mind That Found The Future C 27 MIN
16MM FILM, 3/4 OR 1/2 IN VIDEO J-C A
Looks at Newton both in his own time, as a strange, hermetic genius who discovered the law of gravity twenty years before he told anyone about it, and as an influence upon our own time. Edmund Halley, Newton's friend and colleague, tells about Newton.
Prod-INCC Dist-LCOA 1971

Newton - The Mind That Found The Future (Spanish) C 21 MIN
16MM FILM, 3/4 OR 1/2 IN VIDEO J-C A
Dramatizes the life of Sir Isaac Newton as told by his friend Edmund Halley. Takes viewers from Newton's study to the moon launching pad.
Prod-INCC Dist-LCOA 1971

Newton Convergence And Marquardt C 60 MIN
3/4 OR 1/2 INCH VIDEO CASSETTE
See series title for descriptive statement.
From The Engineering Design Optimization II Series. Pt 13
Prod-UAZMIC Dist-UAZMIC

Newton Mini-Films C 15 MIN
16MM FILM OPTICAL SOUND K-H
A demonstration of the creativity and skill of children, ages 11 to 17, as observed in their work in the planning and production of eight short animated films which they created using cutouts, drawing on film and flip cards.
LC NO. FIA67-5630
Prod-NCAC Dist-YELLOW 1967

Newton's Equal Areas C 8 MIN
16MM FILM, 3/4 OR 1/2 IN VIDEO H-C
Uses animation to explain Newton's laws.
Prod-CORNW Dist-IFB 1968

Newton's Law Of Motion C 31 MIN
3/4 OR 1/2 INCH VIDEO CASSETTE IND
Uses simple, practical examples to illustrate three laws of motion, with animation and graphics for illustrative purposes. Includes study of inertia, gravity, acceleration and action-reaction.
From The Mathematics And Physics Series.
Prod-AVIMA Dist-AVIMA 1980

Newton's Laws C 30 MIN
16MM FILM, 3/4 OR 1/2 IN VIDEO C A
Presents Isaac Newton's laws explaining all the phenomena of the Mechanical Universe.
From The Mechanical Universe Series.
Prod-ANNCPB Dist-FI

Newton's Method C 10 MIN
16MM FILM OPTICAL SOUND H-C
Considers the notion of an iterative procedure. Presents Newton's method as such and illustrates it. An animated film narrated by Herbert Wilf.
From The MAA Calculus Series.
LC NO. FIA68-1460
Prod-MAA Dist-MLA 1966

Newton's Method C 3 MIN
16MM FILM, 3/4 OR 1/2 IN VIDEO H-C A
Uses animation to explain Newton's method.
Prod-EAMES Dist-PFP 1974

Newton's Method C 83 MIN
3/4 OR 1/2 INCH VIDEO CASSETTE PRO
Discusses general philosophy of the Newton or quasilinearization method.
From The Modern Control Theory - Deterministic Optimal Control Series.
Prod-MIOT Dist-MIOT

Newton's Second Law Of Motion X 8 MIN
16MM FILM OPTICAL SOUND C
Demonstrates that motion is a uniform linear acceleration by showing the measurements of the motion of a small trolley on a horizontal track.
Prod-PUAVC Dist-PUAVC 1961

Newtonian I C 4 MIN
16MM FILM OPTICAL SOUND
Offers a musical composition by Jean Claude Risset accompanied by graphics which achieve a harmonious interleaving of changing shapes and patterns that move either asynchronously with the music or in counterpoint.
Prod-LILYAN Dist-LILYAN

Newtonian II C 6 MIN
16MM FILM OPTICAL SOUND
Uses computer techniques to blend music and imagery.
LC NO. 78-701690
Prod-LILYAN Dist-LILYAN 1978

NEWtrition 7 C 11 MIN
3/4 OR 1/2 INCH VIDEO CASSETTE J-H A
Characterizes the seven Dietary Guidelines for Americans recently released by the United States Departments of Agriculture, and Health and Human Services. Explains with a 'computer type' voice why following these guidelines is beneficial to the body and enumerates the hazards of not heeding this advice.
Prod-POAPLE Dist-POAPLE

Next Crisis, The - Death In The Mines C 29 MIN
2 INCH VIDEOTAPE
Examines the circumstances surrounding mining disasters of the past decade and the proposals for improving mining safety. Describes Farmington, West Virginia, the site of five major mining disasters.
From The Turning Points Series.
Prod-WMULTV Dist-PUBTEL

Next Door C 24 MIN
16MM FILM, 3/4 OR 1/2 IN VIDEO I-C A
Presents an adaptation of a short story from Welcome To The Monkey House by Kurt Vonnegut which tells what happens to an eight-year-old boy when his parents leave him at home alone for the first time.
Prod-SILVEA Dist-PHENIX 1975

Next Step, The C 13 MIN
16MM FILM OPTICAL SOUND
Presents male and female Navy nurses discussing Navy nursing careers during a student nurse conference at the U S Naval Hospital in San Diego, California. Describes on- and off-duty activities in the Navy Nurse Corps.
LC NO. 74-706507
Prod-USN Dist-USNAC 1972

Next Step, The B 30 MIN
16MM FILM OPTICAL SOUND
Shows a polio campaign in Harrisburg, Pennsylvania. Gives a brief history of polio vaccine research, production of the live virus vaccine, the large scale clinical trials with live vaccine and laboratory techniques of production of vaccine.
LC NO. FIA67-29
Prod-PFI Dist-PFI

Next Steps With Computers In The Classroom—A Series
T
Discusses using computer and other technology as an effective tool in the educational process, now and in the future. Discusses educational change, including changes in educational delivery systems, a look at teaching styles as they exist today and how they might change due to technology, changes in curriculum and basic skills for an information age.
Prod-PBS Dist-PBS

Alternative Futures	028 MIN
Creating Courseware	028 MIN
Creative Arts, The	028 MIN
Electronic Tools	028 MIN
Information Age, The	028 MIN
Interfacing	028 MIN
Learning Management	028 MIN
Programming Perspectives	028 MIN
Software Evaluation	028 MIN
Software Selection	028 MIN
Telecommunications	028 MIN
Writing Process, The	028 MIN

Next Stop - London, Paris, Rome C 20 MIN
3/4 OR 1/2 INCH VIDEO CASSETTE J-C A
Gives an overview of the cities of London, Paris, and Rome. Visits Buckingham Palace and Trafalgar Square in London, the cafes and artists along the Seine River and near the Eiffel Tower in Paris, and the Borghese gardens, Appian Way and other scenic highlights in Rome.
LC NO. 82-706781
Prod-AWSS Dist-AWSS 1980

Next Time C 12 MIN
16MM FILM OPTICAL SOUND
Stimulates discussion of feelings, values and the stigma of venereal disease.
From The VD - Self-Awareness Project Series. Module 2
LC NO. 75-702843
Prod-AAHPER Dist-FMD 1974

Next Time You Go Camping C 25 MIN
3/4 OR 1/2 INCH VIDEO CASSETTE
Shows forestry rangers and search-and-rescue experts telling Mario Machado how to camp, bike and survive in the wilderness. Adds Dan Row and L.A. Dodgers pitching star Jim Brewer to contribute camping health facts.
Prod-TRAINX Dist-TRAINX

Nez Perce - Bring Us The Black Book C 10 MIN
16MM FILM OPTICAL SOUND I-H
Presents the story of four Nez Perce Indians who travelled to St Louis in 1831 to ask for missionaries.
LC NO. 74-703253
Prod-NWFLMP Dist-NWFLMP 1974

Nez Perce - Portrait Of A People C 23 MIN
16MM FILM, 3/4 OR 1/2 IN VIDEO J A
Discusses the history of the Nez Perce Indians who lived throughout Washington, Oregon and Idaho. Includes traditional chants and music, vintage photos, mini-dramatizations and scenes of contemporary tribal life.
Prod-USNPS Dist-USNAC 1984

NFL Championship Games - New York Vs Chicago Bears - 1956 C 30 MIN
16MM FILM OPTICAL SOUND
Presents highlights of the year.
Prod-NBC Dist-NBC

NFL Pro Football B 30 MIN
16MM FILM OPTICAL SOUND
Shows the Chicago Bears and the New York City Giants in four half hour segments.
Prod-SFI Dist-SFI

Nguba Connection, The C 58 MIN
3/4 INCH VIDEO CASSETTE H-C A
Compares First and Third World agriculture, focusing on the peanut industry.
From The World Series.
LC NO. 80-706115
Prod-WGBHTV Dist-PBS 1978

Ngung Lai C 26 MIN
16MM FILM OPTICAL SOUND
Presents the story of vessel preparation, special personnel training, deployment and patrol operations of the 26 82-foot cutters and their crews assigned to operation market time in South Vietnam.
LC NO. 74-705212
Prod-USGS Dist-USNAC 1967

Ngunglai C 26 MIN
3/4 OR 1/2 INCH VIDEO CASSETTE
Depicts Operation Market Time, the special assignment of the U S Coast Guard to stop the Viet Cong bringing in supplies from the north. Shows vessel preparation, crew training and patrol operations of the 26 82-foot Coast Guard cutters involved.
Prod-IHF Dist-IHF

Nguzo Saba - Folklore For Children—A Series
16MM FILM, 3/4 OR 1/2 IN VIDEO K-I
Demonstrates the universality of the human experience and teaches the Seven Principles (Nguzo Saba)-unity, self-determination, economic cooperation, sharing work and responsibility, purpose, creativity and faith. Animated.
Prod-NGUZO Dist-BCNFL 1982

Imani - Beegie And The Egg	008 MIN
Kujichagulia	006 MIN
Kuumba - Simon's New Sound	008 MIN
Nia	005 MIN
Noel's Lemonade Stand (Ujamaa)	009 MIN
Ujima - Modupe And The Flood	005 MIN
Umoja - Tiger And The Big Wind	008 MIN

Nia C 5 MIN
16MM FILM, 3/4 OR 1/2 IN VIDEO K-I
Tells the story of the young girl who saps the strength of her rural community by lack of cooperation. Shows how, when she asked for help, she learns to help others.
From The Nguzo Saba-Folklore For Children Series.
Prod-NGUZO Dist-BCNFL 1982

Niacin-Nitrate Reduction Test C 6 MIN
16MM FILM OPTICAL SOUND
Demonstrates a rapid test for identifying M tuberculosis based on the ability of M tuberculosis both to produce niacin and to reduce nitrates to nitrites.
LC NO. FIE67-49
Prod-USPHS Dist-USNAC 1965

Niagara C 13 MIN
16MM FILM OPTICAL SOUND
Describes the vacation attractions at Niagara Falls and the peninsula.
LC NO. 77-702998
Prod-ONTPRO Dist-CTFL Prodn-KROOTR 1976

Niagara Falls Parkland C 12 MIN
16MM FILM OPTICAL SOUND
Explores the parks, gardens, flowers beds and other landscaping projects that beautify the approaches to Niagara Falls in Ontario.
LC NO. FIA68-1566
Prod-MORLAT Dist-MORLAT 1967

Niambi - Sweet Melody C 25 MIN
16MM FILM, 3/4 OR 1/2 IN VIDEO P-I
Tells the story of Niambi Robinson, a little black girl who, at the age of five, broke the world's record for her age in the 100 meter dash. Explores the values and constant nurturing of her loving family and shows Niambi at school, at ballet class, on the track and at home.
Prod-FI Dist-FI 1979

Nibelungen B 62 MIN
16MM FILM SILENT
An expressionistic silent motion picture with music and English subtitles. Relates the Nibelungen Saga, showing Siegfried's wooing of Kriemhild and Siegfried's death in flashbacks, and continuing with the descent of the Burgunder at the court of the Huns.
Prod-WSTGLC Dist-WSTGLC

Nibelungen Saga, Die - 'Kriemheld's Revenge' B 100 MIN
3/4 OR 1/2 INCH VIDEO CASSETTE
Presents the saga of the Nibelung in its complete second part.
Prod-IHF Dist-IHF

Nicaragua - After The Revolution C 15 MIN
3/4 OR 1/2 INCH VIDEO CASSETTE J-H
Examines the results of the revolution in Nicaragua. Points out that the Sandinista government has developed new alliances and a different political system, but it must still deal with many problems of the past.
Prod-JOU Dist-JOU

Nicaragua - Healing The Wounds Of War C 18 MIN
16MM FILM OPTICAL SOUND
Shows how the Catholic Relief Services brought the first food to the embattled victims of Nicaragua's civil war. Looks at individual people whose stories are relived daily in Central America.
Prod-CATHRS Dist-MTP

Nicaragua - Healing The Wounds Of War (Spanish) C 18 MIN
16MM FILM OPTICAL SOUND
Shows how the Catholic Relief Services brought the first food to the embattled victims of Nicaragua's civil war. Looks at individual people whose stories are relived daily in Central America.
Prod-CATHRS Dist-MTP

Nicaragua - Our Own Country C 19 MIN
16MM FILM, 3/4 OR 1/2 IN VIDEO J-C A
Portrays Nicaragua today, including its history, its people and its hopes for the future.
Prod-FCP Dist-CF

Nicaragua - Planting The Seeds Of Change C 27 MIN
16MM FILM OPTICAL SOUND H
Depicts problems faced by small farmers in Nicaragua. Explains how the rural development program Invierno, which was designed by the Nicaraguan government and supported by the United States, helps farmers by offering farm credit, technical agricultural assistance and social services. Tells the story of one small farmer and his family and how their prospects are brighter as a result of the program.
LC NO. 77-700643
Prod-USAID Dist-USNAC 1977

Nicaragua - Planting The Seeds Of Change (French) C 27 MIN
16MM FILM OPTICAL SOUND H
Depicts problems faced by small farmers in Nicaragua. Explains how the rural development program Invierno, which was designed by the Nicaraguan government and supported by the United States, helps farmers by offering farm credit, technical agricultural assistance and social services. Tells the story of one small farmer and his family and how their prospects are brighter as a result of the program.
LC NO. 77-700643
Prod-USAID Dist-USNAC 1977

Nicaragua - Planting The Seeds Of Change (Spanish) C 27 MIN
16MM FILM OPTICAL SOUND H
Depicts problems faced by small farmers in Nicaragua. Explains how the rural development program Invierno, which was designed by the Nicaraguan government and Supported by the United States, helps farmers by offering farm credit, technical agricultural assistance and social services. Tells the story of one small farmer and his family and how their prospects are brighter as a result of the program.
LC NO. 77-700643
Prod-USAID Dist-USNAC 1977

Nicaragua - Report From The Front C 32 MIN
3/4 INCH VIDEO CASSETTE
Looks at U S foreign policy toward Nicaragua as it is being played out along the border between Nicaragua and Honduras.
LC NO. 84-706099
Prod-FIRS Dist-FIRS 1983

Nicaragua - Scenes From The Revolution (Captioned) C 30 MIN
16MM FILM, 3/4 OR 1/2 IN VIDEO A
Portrays the forces that shaped the Nicaraguan Revolution, from the inception of Sandinismo in the 1930's to the general strike called by the Sandinistas in June of 1979. Discusses the first 100 days after the Sandinista victory and the problems facing the country. Spanish dialog with English subtitles.
Prod-CNEMAG Dist-CNEMAG 1979

Nicaragua - The Other Invasion C 29 MIN
16MM FILM - 3/4 IN VIDEO
Presents a documentary on the changes in health care in Nicaragua since the revolution. Documents the effects of the CIA-directed 'contra' attacks on health care, including the destruction of clinics and the killings of medical personnel. In Spanish with English subtitles.
From The Presente Series.
Prod-KCET Dist-KCET

Nicaragua September 1978 C 41 MIN
16MM FILM, 3/4 OR 1/2 IN VIDEO
Documents the 1978 revolt against the Somoza dictatorship in Nicaragua.
Prod-NEWTIM Dist-NEWTIM

Nicaragua Was Our Home C 56 MIN
16MM FILM, 3/4 OR 1/2 IN VIDEO A
Looks at the Miskito Indians of Nicaragua as they were terrorized by the Sandinista regime and as they fought for survival and freedom to preserve their way of life. Shows their ravaged villages, refugee camps and secret guerrilla bases and their mass exodus from their homeland.
Prod-FI Dist-FI

Nicaragua 1983 C
3/4 OR 1/2 INCH VIDEO CASSETTE
Covers a five day battle between the Sandinista Army and the counter-revolutionaries trained by the United States Central Intelligence Agency. Explores also the conditions of the Miskito Indians both in jail and in the countryside. Looks at daily life of Nicaraguans and the struggle for land reform.
Prod-DCTVC Dist-DCTVC

Nicaragua 79 - In The Beginning C 30 MIN
3/4 OR 1/2 INCH VIDEO CASSETTE
Documents the battle against the Samoza regime, the Sandinista victory and the first days of the revolution. Presents a personal view of a people in the process of making a revolution, who they are and why they revolted.
Prod-DCTVC Dist-DCTVC

Nicaraguan Countryside C 15 MIN
3/4 OR 1/2 INCH VIDEO CASSETTE P
Pictures lava fields, an indian settlement and a coffee plantation in Nicaragua.
From The Other Families, Other Friends Series. Brown Module - Nicaragua
Prod-WVIZTV Dist-AITECH 1971

Nice Flying Machine, A C 9 MIN
16MM FILM, 3/4 OR 1/2 IN VIDEO I-C A
Documents the Manned Maneuvering Unit, the jet pack that astronauts use to travel in space untethered from the space ship.
Prod-BFA Dist-BFA

Nice Guy, The C 4 MIN
16MM FILM, 3/4 OR 1/2 IN VIDEO PRO
Asks what to do with the old company employee whose lack of performance affects the whole department.
From The This Matter Of Motivation Series.
Prod-CTRACT Dist-DARTNL Prodn-CALVIN 1968

Nice Little Ugly Witch, The C 15 MIN
3/4 INCH VIDEO CASSETTE K-P
See series title for descriptive statement.
From The Storytime Series.
Prod-WCETTV Dist-GPITVL 1976

Nicholas And Alexandra - Prelude To Revolution, 1904-1905 C 29 MIN
16MM FILM, 3/4 OR 1/2 IN VIDEO H-C A
Focuses on the years 1904 to 1905. Shows some of the causes of the Russian Revolution that were clearly visible more than a decade before Lenin arrived at the Finland Station. Reveals the extreme contrasts of Russia, the Czar's autocratic power set against the workers' seething powerless misery, the liberal leanings of some of the Czar's advisors versus the radical demands of the revolutionaries and the peasants mystical faith in their Czar contrasted to the remoteness of Nicholas himself.
Prod-LCOA Dist-LCOA Prodn-CPC 1976

Nicholas And Alexandra - The Bolshevik Victory, 1917 C 26 MIN
16MM FILM, 3/4 OR 1/2 IN VIDEO H-C A
Covers the second stage of the Russian Revolution, the October Revolution. Shows the phase that is common to many revolutions, growing radicalization, counterrevolution and civil war. Explains that Lenin returned to Russia promising peace, a new socialist order and all power to the Soviets. Tells how Kerensky and his party wanted to win the war, but became increasingly powerless. Concludes with the execution of the Czar and his entire family, which began a new era.
Prod-LCOA Dist-LCOA Prodn-CPC 1976

Nicholas And Alexandria - Prelude To Revolution - 1904-1905 (Spanish) C 29 MIN
16MM FILM, 3/4 OR 1/2 IN VIDEO H-C A
Explores causes of the later revolutions, the war with Japan, public discontent and the rise of Marxism in Russia in the years 1904-1905.
Prod-LCOA Dist-LCOA Prodn-CPC 1976

Nicholas And Alexandria - The Bolshevik Victory - 1917 (Spanish) C 26 MIN
16MM FILM, 3/4 OR 1/2 IN VIDEO H-C A
Carries the viewer through Lenin's return, the October Revolution, the Kerensky government, the Bolshevik victory and the execution of the Romanov family.
Prod-LCOA Dist-LCOA Prodn-CPC 1976

Nicholas And Alexandria - War And The Fall Of The Tsar - 1914-1917 C 27 MIN
16MM FILM, 3/4 OR 1/2 IN VIDEO H-C A
Dramatizes the effect Russia's involvement in the war with Germany had on Nicholas and his abdication.
Prod-LCOA Dist-LCOA Prodn-CPC 1976

Nicholas And The Baby C 23 MIN
16MM FILM, 3/4 OR 1/2 IN VIDEO K-I T
Introduces children ages 4-12 to the facts and feelings involved with the birth of a sibling and of introducing parents to the perceptions and questions of children.
Prod-NALNDA Dist-CEPRO 1981

Nicholas Nickleby B 108 MIN
16MM FILM OPTICAL SOUND
Presents the story of the hard and hilarious times of a young man beset by the machinations of his unscrupulous uncle and the irrationality of Victorian society.
Prod-UPCI Dist-LCOA 1947

Nichols And Dimes C 25 MIN
16MM FILM, 3/4 OR 1/2 IN VIDEO I-C A
Looks at the beautiful Arabian horses raised by director Mike Nichols. Views the first minutes of life of a horse worth 50 thousand dollars at birth.
Prod-MIDMAR Dist-DIRECT Prodn-MEYERM 1982

Nicht Fur Geld Und Gute Worte C 15 MIN
16MM FILM, 3/4 OR 1/2 IN VIDEO
See series title for descriptive statement.
From The Guten Tag Wie Geht's Series. Part 22
Prod-BAYER Dist-IFB 1973

Nick And Jon C 20 MIN
3/4 OR 1/2 INCH VIDEO CASSETTE C A
Discusses male sexuality and homosexuality through the relationship of two college age men.
Prod-MMRC Dist-MMRC

Nick Kendall C
3/4 OR 1/2 INCH VIDEO CASSETTE
Portrays Nick Kendall, British Columbian filmmaker with interviews and film clips.
From The Filmmakers' Showcase Series.
Prod-CANFDW Dist-CANFDW

Nick Mazzuco - Biography Of An Atomic Vet C 22 MIN
3/4 INCH VIDEO CASSETTE J-C A
Traces the series of dangers to which young, unquestioning soldiers were exposed during the early stages of atomic weapons testing. Focuses on an individual soldier who was stationed at Camp Desert Rock, Nevada.
Prod-FIRS Dist-FIRS

Nick Mazzuco - Biography Of An Atomic Vet C 22 MIN
16MM FILM, 3/4 OR 1/2 IN VIDEO H-C A
Presents a personal account of 18 atomic explosions attended by Nick Mazzuco as a draftee. Reflects on the health effects of ionizing radiation.
Prod-GMPF Dist-GMPF 1982

Nickel For The Movies, A C 21 MIN
16MM FILM, 3/4 OR 1/2 IN VIDEO H-C A
Presents an introduction to motion picture study which tries to touch briefly on most of the issues of contemporary film making.
Prod-IU Dist-IU 1984

Nickelodeon C 121 MIN
16MM FILM OPTICAL SOUND
Stars Ryan O'Neal as a movie writer/director, Burt Reynolds as his leading man, and Tatum O'Neal as a 12-year-old truck driver who rents anything to the pioneer movie makers.
Prod-CPC Dist-SWANK

Nicky - One Of My Best Friends C 15 MIN
16MM FILM, 3/4 OR 1/2 IN VIDEO I-C A
Provides a sympathetic portrait of a multiply handicapped 12-year-old boy and his successful integration into a suburban public school. Reveals his needs, as seen by his friends, and his similarity to them.
Prod-TOGGFI Dist-MGHT 1976

Nicky And Geoffrey In Japan B 26 MIN
16MM FILM OPTICAL SOUND
Recounts the summer's adventure in Japan of two American children, Geoffrey and his sister, Nicky. Captures the historic grace, life styles and monuments of today's Japan.
Prod-GBFP Dist-RADIM

Nicodemus C 20 MIN
16MM FILM OPTICAL SOUND I-H T R
Joseph of Arimathea and Nicodemus agree to make arrangements for the burial of Jesus. They remove the body of Jesus and take it to Joseph's tomb. Nicodemus reflects on his experience with Jesus the night he questioned him about being born again.
From The Living Bible Series.
Prod-FAMF Dist-FAMF

Nicolai Neilsen - Guitarist C 29 MIN
2 INCH VIDEOTAPE
Presents the music of guitarist Nicolai Neilsen.
From The Young Musical Artists Series.
Prod-WKARTV Dist-PUBTEL

Nicolas A Montmartre B 13 MIN
16MM FILM OPTICAL SOUND J-H
See series title for descriptive statement.
From The En France Avec Nicolas Series. Set I, Lesson 12.
LC NO. 75-704480
Prod-PEREN Dist-CHLTN 1968

Nicolas A Montmartre, Student Exercises C 8 MIN
16MM FILM OPTICAL SOUND J-H
See series title for descriptive statement.
From The En France Avec Nicolas Series. Set II, Lesson 12.
LC NO. 79-704481
Prod-PEREN Dist-CHLTN 1968

Nicolas A Orly B 13 MIN
16MM FILM OPTICAL SOUND J-H
See series title for descriptive statement.
From The En France Avec Nicolas Series. Set I, Lesson 9
LC NO. 72-704482
Prod-PEREN Dist-CHLTN 1968

Nicolas A Orly, Student Exercises B 8 MIN
16MM FILM OPTICAL SOUND J-H
See series title for descriptive statement.
From The En France Avec Nicolas Series. Set II, Lesson 9
LC NO. 76-704483
Prod-PEREN Dist-CHLTN 1968

Nicolas Au Theatre B 13 MIN
16MM FILM OPTICAL SOUND J-H
See series title for descriptive statement.
From The En France Avec Nicolas Series. Set I, Lesson 5
LC NO. 70-704484
Prod-PEREN Dist-CHLTN 1968

Nicolas Au Theatre, Student Exercises B 8 MIN
16MM FILM OPTICAL SOUND J-H
See series title for descriptive statement.
From The En France Avec Nicolas Series. Set II, Lesson 5
LC NO. 73-704485
Prod-PEREN Dist-CHLTN 1968

Nicolas Chez Sa Tante B 13 MIN
16MM FILM OPTICAL SOUND J-H
See series title for descriptive statement.
From The En France Avec Nicolas Series. Set I, Lesson 7
LC NO. 77-704486
Prod-PEREN Dist-CHLTN 1968

Nicolas Chez Sa Tante, Student Exercises B 8 MIN
16MM FILM OPTICAL SOUND J-H
See series title for descriptive statement.
From The En France Avec Nicolas Series. Set II, Lesson 7
LC NO. 70-704487
Prod-PEREN Dist-CHLTN 1968

Nicolas Et La Libraire B 13 MIN
16MM FILM OPTICAL SOUND J-H
See series title for descriptive statement.
From The En France Avec Nicolas Series. Set I, Lesson 1
LC NO. 74-704488
Prod-PEREN Dist-CHLTN 1968

Nicolas Et La Libraire, Student Exercises B 8 MIN
16MM FILM OPTICAL SOUND J-H
See series title for descriptive statement.
From The En France Avec Nicolas Series. Set II, Lesson 1
LC NO. 78-704489
Prod-PEREN Dist-CHLTN 1968

Nicolas Prendra-T-Il Son Train B 13 MIN
16MM FILM OPTICAL SOUND J-H

See series title for descriptive statement.
From The En France Avec Nicolas Series. Set I, Lesson 11
LC NO. 72-704490
Prod-PEREN Dist-CHLTN 1968

Nicolas Prendra-T-Il Son Train, Student Exercises B 8 MIN
16MM FILM OPTICAL SOUND J-H
See series title for descriptive statement.
From The En France Avec Nicolas Series. Set II, Lesson 11
LC NO. 76-704491
Prod-PEREN Dist-CHLTN 1968

Nicolas Protege Les Amoureux B 13 MIN
16MM FILM OPTICAL SOUND J-H
See series title for descriptive statement.
From The En France Avec Nicolas Series. Set I, Lesson 4
LC NO. 70-704492
Prod-PEREN Dist-CHLTN 1968

Nicolas Protege Les Amoureux, Student Exercises B 8 MIN
16MM FILM OPTICAL SOUND J-H
See series title for descriptive statement.
From The En France Avec Nicolas Series. Set II, Lesson 4
LC NO. 73-704493
Prod-PEREN Dist-CHLTN 1968

Nicolas S'Ennuie Le Dimanche B 13 MIN
16MM FILM OPTICAL SOUND J-H
See series title for descriptive statement.
From The En France Avec Nicolas Series. Set I, Lesson 10
LC NO. 77-704494
Prod-PEREN Dist-CHLTN 1968

Nicolas S'Ennuie Le Dimanche, Student Exercises B 8 MIN
16MM FILM OPTICAL SOUND J-H
See series title for descriptive statement.
From The En France Avec Nicolas Series. Set II, Lesson 10
LC NO. 70-704495
Prod-PEREN Dist-CHLTN 1968

Nicolas Sur Les Quais B 13 MIN
16MM FILM OPTICAL SOUND J-H
See series title for descriptive statement.
From The En France Avec Nicolas Series. Set I, Lesson 13
LC NO. 74-704496
Prod-PEREN Dist-CHLTN 1968

Nicolas Sur Les Quais, Student Exercises B 8 MIN
16MM FILM OPTICAL SOUND J-H
See series title for descriptive statement.
From The En France Avec Nicolas Series. Set II, Lesson 13
LC NO. 78-704497
Prod-PEREN Dist-CHLTN 1968

Nicolas Telephone B 13 MIN
16MM FILM OPTICAL SOUND J-H
See series title for descriptive statement.
From The En France Avec Nicolas Series. Set I, Lesson 6
LC NO. 71-704498
Prod-PEREN Dist-CHLTN 1968

Nicolas Telephone, Student Exercises B 8 MIN
16MM FILM OPTICAL SOUND J-H
See series title for descriptive statement.
From The En France Avec Nicolas Series. Set II, Lesson 6
LC NO. 75-704499
Prod-PEREN Dist-CHLTN 1968

Nicolas VA A La Peche B 13 MIN
16MM FILM OPTICAL SOUND J-H
See series title for descriptive statement.
From The En France Avec Nicolas Series. Set I, Lesson 2
LC NO. 75-704500
Prod-PEREN Dist-CHLTN 1968

Nicolas VA A La Peche, Student Exercises B 8 MIN
16MM FILM OPTICAL SOUND J-H
See series title for descriptive statement.
From The En France Avec Nicolas Series. Set II, Lesson 2
LC NO. 79-704501
Prod-PEREN Dist-CHLTN 1968

Niels Stensen Liv Og Dod (Life And Death Of Niels Stensen) B 29 MIN
16MM FILM OPTICAL SOUND
A Danish language film. Draws a picture of the famous Danish medical scientist Niels Stensen as a pioneer in the anatomic science and as the founder of geology as a science with his work 'DE SOLIDO.'
Prod-STATNS Dist-STATNS 1970

Nierenberg's Need Theory Of Negotiation C
16MM FILM - 3/4 IN VIDEO A
Deals with satisfaction of needs, basic needs, recognizing needs, changing win-lose stands, finding common interest and varieties of applications in negotiations.
From The Art Of Negotiating Series. Module 3
Prod-BNA Dist-BNA 1983

Nigel Rolfe - Dance Slap For Africa C 23 MIN
3/4 OR 1/2 INCH VIDEO CASSETTE
Provides two channels which juxtapose modern day experience with a more primitive and ethnic source.
Prod-ARTINC Dist-ARTINC

Nigel Rolfe - The Rope That Binds Us Makes Them Free C 15 MIN
3/4 OR 1/2 INCH VIDEO CASSETTE
Focuses on Leitrim, a northwestern county in Ireland where cottages deserted long ago remain mysteriously intact today.
Prod-ARTINC Dist-ARTINC

Nigel Rolfe - The Rope That Binds Us Makes-Them Free C 21 MIN
3/4 OR 1/2 INCH VIDEO CASSETTE
Focuses on Leitrim, a northwestern county in Ireland where cottages deserted long ago remain mysteriously intact today. Provides three channel installation.
Prod-ARTINC Dist-ARTINC

Nigeria - Africa In Miniature C 16 MIN
16MM FILM, 3/4 OR 1/2 IN VIDEO I-J
Describes location, provinces, topography, cities and rivers in colorful maps and outstanding photography. Portrays Nigeria's ethnic groups, its progress in economics, education, politics, religion, transportation and other important areas.
Prod-AIMS Dist-AIMS 1966

Nigeria - Africa In Miniature (Afrikaans) C 16 MIN
16MM FILM, 3/4 OR 1/2 IN VIDEO I-H
Uses maps and photographs to describe the location, provinces, topography and rivers of Nigeria. Portrays major ethnic groups and discusses progress in economics, education, politics, religion, transportation and other important areas.
Prod-ASSOCF Dist-AIMS 1966

Nigeria - Problems Of Nation Building C 22 MIN
16MM FILM - 3/4 IN VIDEO J-H A
Provides a realistic appraisal of nationalism in Africa, particularly Nigeria. Aids in understanding the underlying forces in tropical Africa. Includes geography and climate of West Africa, development of prosperous, medieval African empires, navigation along the Niger River, economy, education and religion.
Prod-ATLAP Dist-ATLAP 1967

Nigeria Among Friends B 28 MIN
16MM FILM OPTICAL SOUND
Examines the newly independent country of Nigeria, showing the homes and workshops of the people. Provides background information on West Africa and tells the kind of aid which Western nations and trade union movements can supply newly emerging nations.
Prod-GTUF Dist-AFLCIO 1961

Nigeria And Biafra - The Story Behind The Struggle B 14 MIN
16MM FILM OPTICAL SOUND J-H
Portrays the underlying and immediate causes of the Civil War between Nigeria and the breakaway province of Biafra.
From The Screen News Digest Series. Vol 11, Issue 2
LC NO. 72-703469
Prod-HEARST Dist-HEARST 1968

Night 'N Gales B 14 MIN
16MM FILM OPTICAL SOUND
Tells how a storm forces the Little Rascals to spend the night at Darla's.
Prod-UNKNWN Dist-BHAWK

Night And Day C 12 MIN
16MM FILM OPTICAL SOUND
Discusses day and night, the rising and setting of the Sun, the lengthening of days and nights at different latitudes, and the origin of the Arctic and Antarctic Circles.
LC NO. 75-700153
Prod-SHAPEC Dist-SHAPEC 1974

Night And Fog B 30 MIN
3/4 OR 1/2 INCH VIDEO CASSETTE
Documents the Nazi concentrations camps and the Nazi atrocities. Creates the feeling of history's nightmare.
Prod-IHF Dist-IHF

Night And Fog (French) C 31 MIN
16MM FILM, 3/4 OR 1/2 IN VIDEO H-C A
A French language film with English subtitles. Examines the world of concentration camps in World War II.
LC NO. 77-701530
Prod-ARGOS Dist-FI 1977

Night At The Peking Opera, A C 20 MIN
16MM FILM OPTICAL SOUND I-C
Presents four vignettes using authentic traditional music and costumes. Includes 'A FAIRY TALE,' 'LEGEND OF THE MONKEY KING AND THE JADE EMPEROR,' 'A COMEDY BALLET OF ERRORS' and 'A BEAUTEOUS LADY.' An American adaptation, originally produced in France.
Prod-FILIM Dist-RADIM Prodn-FALKBG

Night At The Show, A B 15 MIN
16MM FILM OPTICAL SOUND
Presents a rare print of the early Chaplin classic A Night At The Show in which Chaplin plays a dual role. Explains that the plot is an adaptation of his original Karno music act.
Prod-CHAC Dist-CFS

Night At The Show, A B 19 MIN
16MM FILM SILENT
Shows a vaudeville show and its effect on a drunken gallery spectator and a rowdy in the orchestra. Stars Charlie Chaplin.
Prod-ENY Dist-TWYMAN 1915

Night At The Show, A B 25 MIN
16MM FILM OPTICAL SOUND I-C A
Highlights Chaplin's dual role as a drunken playboy in the orchestra and as an obnoxious workman on a night-out in the balcony.
From The Charlie Chaplin Comedy Theater Series.
Prod-MUFLM Dist-TWYMAN 1915

Night Before Christmas C 7 MIN
16MM FILM OPTICAL SOUND K-P
Presents the traditional Christmas poem, The Night Before Christmas, set to music with live action and animation.
Prod-SHUGA Dist-SHUGA 1970

Night Before Christmas, The C 10 MIN
16MM FILM, 3/4 OR 1/2 IN VIDEO
Tells the famous poem of Clement C Moore. Utilizes original music and a delightful three-dimensional technique.
Prod-AIMS Dist-AIMS 1968

Night Before Christmas, The C 11 MIN
16MM FILM, 3/4 OR 1/2 IN VIDEO P-I
A re-enactment of the classic poem, 'VISIT FROM ST NICHOLAS,' with an original musical score, a 19th century setting and authentic costumes.
Prod-EBF Dist-EBEC 1955

Night Before Christmas, The (Captioned) C 10 MIN
16MM FILM, 3/4 OR 1/2 IN VIDEO K-P A
An imaginative three-dimensional animation of the famous Christmas poem by Clement C Moore.
Prod-CAHILL Dist-AIMS 1968

Night Before Christmas, The (Spanish) C 10 MIN
16MM FILM, 3/4 OR 1/2 IN VIDEO K-P A
An imaginative three-dimensional animation of the famous Christmas poem by Clement C Moore.
Prod-CAHILL Dist-AIMS 1968

Night Before Christmas, The (Spanish) C 27 MIN
16MM FILM, 3/4 OR 1/2 IN VIDEO P-I
Re-enacts Clement Moore's poem A Visit From St Nicholas.
Prod-EBEC Dist-EBEC

Night Before, The C 5 MIN
3/4 OR 1/2 INCH VIDEO CASSETTE J-H
Demonstrates effective subordination in writing.
From The Write On, Set 2 Series.
Prod-CTI Dist-CTI

Night Driving C 20 MIN
3/4 OR 1/2 INCH VIDEO CASSETTE
Presents behind-the-wheel scenes which highlight a neglected area of driver education, night driving. Focuses on headlight glare, highbeam and lowbeam problems, fatigue, eye strain, twilight problems and other areas of concern.
Prod-BUMPA Dist-BUMPA

Night Driving And Seeing B 30 MIN
16MM FILM - 3/4 IN VIDEO C A
See series title for descriptive statement.
From The Sportsmanlike Driving Series. Refresher Course
Prod-AAAFTS Dist-GPITVL Prodn-SCETV

Night Driving Tactics (2nd Ed) C 13 MIN
16MM FILM, 3/4 OR 1/2 IN VIDEO J-H A
Shows how the physiology of vision and reaction time make fast nighttime driving dangerous. Presents emergency procedures.
LC NO. 84-706137
Prod-AIMS Dist-AIMS 1984

Night Ferry C 55 MIN
16MM FILM OPTICAL SOUND P-I
Tells the story of three boys who discover a plot to steal an Egyptian mummy and attempt to foil the thieves.
Prod-CHILDF Dist-LUF 1979

Night Flight B 5 MIN
16MM FILM OPTICAL SOUND C A
Presents a modern interpretation of Psalm 62 using scenes of a man and what he sees of the desert at night from his plane.
From The Song Of The Ages Series.
LC NO. 70-702131
Prod-FAMLYT Dist-FAMLYT 1964

Night Flight C 23 MIN
16MM FILM, 3/4 OR 1/2 IN VIDEO H-C A
Tells the story of a young pilot lost in a storm while flying an airmail route in the 1930's. Based on the novel NIGHT FLIGHT by Antoine de Saint-Exupery.
Prod-SINGER Dist-LCOA 1979

Night Flight (Captioned) C 22 MIN
16MM FILM, 3/4 OR 1/2 IN VIDEO J-C A
Tells of a young pilot lost in a storm. Raises questions about the sacrifice of one's life for a greater good. Based on the novel NIGHT FLIGHT by Antoine Saint Exupery.
Prod-SINGER Dist-LCOA 1979

Night Flight (French) C 22 MIN
16MM FILM, 3/4 OR 1/2 IN VIDEO J-C A
Tells of a young pilot lost in a storm. Raises questions about the sacrifice of one's life for a greater good. Based on the novel by Antoine de Saint Exupery.
Prod-SINGER Dist-LCOA 1979

Night In The Art Gallery, A C 18 MIN
16MM FILM OPTICAL SOUND
Presents an allegorical tale about censorship during China's cultural revolution. Depicts symbols representing the Gang of Four touring an art gallery, finding something offensive in each work and defacing it. Shows the figures in the artworks banding together to repair the damage and finally turning on the villains to chase them away.
Prod-CHFE Dist-FLMLIB 1980

Night Is Sinister, The C 18 MIN
16MM FILM, 3/4 OR 1/2 IN VIDEO
Uses animation to explain that revolutions and social unrest characterize the period after the Second World War. Emphasizes problems in colonies and former colonies.
From The Four Seasons Series.
Prod-STATNS Dist-CNEMAG

Night Journey B 29 MIN
16MM FILM, 3/4 OR 1/2 IN VIDEO
A presentation of Martha Graham's interpretation in dance of the Oedipus legend, depicting the moment of Jocasta's death.
Prod-KROLL Dist-PHENIX 1960

Night Of A Million Years B 30 MIN
16MM FILM OPTICAL SOUND
Traces the history of man's development as seen through the eyes of two ten-year-old boys who tour the American Museum of Natural History in New York City. Shows exhibits which range from models of dinosaurs and savage jungles to forecasts of the future.
From The Eye On New York Series.
LC NO. FIA67-523
Prod-WCBSTV Dist-CBSF 1966

Night Of Counting The Years, The (Arabic) C 100 MIN
16MM FILM OPTICAL SOUND
Re-creates the discovery of a Royal Tomb near Thebes in 1881, and the resulting clash between tribal heritage and art preservation. Directed by Shadi Abdelsalam. With English subtitles.
Prod-UNKNWN Dist-NYFLMS 1969

Night Of Terror, A C 30 MIN
16MM FILM OPTICAL SOUND R
Documents the 1972 earthquake that struck Managua, Nicaragua and the efforts of churches to clear the rubble, feed and house the homeless and minister to their spiritual needs.
Prod-GF Dist-GF

Night Of The Generals C 148 MIN
16MM FILM OPTICAL SOUND H-C A
Stars Peter O'Toole and Omar Sharif. Presents a strange manhunt for a psychopathic killer, with evidence pointing to one of three Nazi generals, against the background of the Nazi occupation in Warsaw and Paris in World War II.
Prod-CPC Dist-TWYMAN 1967

Night Of The Hummingbird C 60 MIN
16MM FILM, 3/4 OR 1/2 IN VIDEO H-C A
Uses eyewitness reports to detail how Adolf Hitler seized power on June 30, 1934 by killing his old comrade Roehm and other leaders of the brown shirt movement.
Prod-BBCTV Dist-FI 1983

Night Of The Intruder, Pt 1 C 29 MIN
2 INCH VIDEOTAPE
See series title for descriptive statement.
From The Our Street Series.
Prod-MDCPB Dist-PUBTEL

Night Of The Intruder, Pt 2 C 29 MIN
2 INCH VIDEOTAPE
See series title for descriptive statement.
From The Our Street Series.
Prod-MDCPB Dist-PUBTEL

Night Of The Squid, The C 22 MIN
16MM FILM, 3/4 OR 1/2 IN VIDEO I-C
A shortened version of The Night Of The Squid. Traces the life cycle of the squid from its wanderings in the deep to mating and spawning. Features Jacques Cousteau's underwater photography.
From The Undersea World Of Jacques Cousteau Series.
Prod-METROM Dist-CF 1970

Night Of The Squid, The C 52 MIN
16MM FILM, 3/4 OR 1/2 IN VIDEO
Presents Jacques Cousteau as he traces the life cycle of the squid from its wanderings in the deep to mating and spawning.
From The Undersea World Of Jacques Cousteau Series.
Prod-METROM Dist-CF 1971

Night Of The Sun C 20 MIN
16MM FILM, 3/4 OR 1/2 IN VIDEO
Views various sites within the Wisconsin Ice Age National Scientific Reserve which show the causes, effects, and terrain features left by the last great ice sheet.
LC NO. 81-707709
Prod-USNPS Dist-USNAC 1981

Night On Bald Mountain B 8 MIN
16MM FILM OPTICAL SOUND
Presents the first film made on the pinboard, an animation classic illustrating the music of Moussorgsky's tone poem, Night On Bald Mountain, and creates a fantasy world of witches, demons and skeletons. By Alexander Alexeieff and Claire Parker.
Prod-STARRC Dist-STARRC 1933

Night On Jackrabbit Mesa, A B 23 MIN
3/4 INCH VIDEO CASSETTE
Shows civil officials what to do in case of off-base military accidents. Includes notifying authorities, barring spectators from area and organizing search parties to find dead or injured crewmen. Stresses cooperation of newspapers in witholding premature information.
Prod-USNAC Dist-USNAC 1972

Night Out, A C 10 MIN
16MM FILM, 3/4 OR 1/2 IN VIDEO J-C S
A dramatization in sign language involving a girl looking for romance and a boy looking for sex, which sets the stage for a violent attack of rape.
From The Setting Limits Series.
LC NO. 81-707274
Prod-ODNP Dist-ODNP 1981

Night Over China B 55 MIN
3/4 OR 1/2 INCH VIDEO CASSETTE
Offers a Soviet documentary which claims to expose Maoism including historical footage.
Prod-IHF Dist-IHF

Night Owls B 22 MIN
16MM FILM OPTICAL SOUND
Tells the story of two tramps who try to help a policeman catch some burglars. Stars Stan Laurel and Oliver Hardy.
Prod-ROACH Dist-BHAWK 1930

Night People's Day C 11 MIN
16MM FILM, 3/4 OR 1/2 IN VIDEO
Explores the city at night with special emphasis on the people and their occupations. Re-creates with human voices all of the sounds of the city and its activities.
Prod-FLMFR Dist-FLMFR 1971

Night People's Day (Captioned Version) C 11 MIN
16MM FILM, 3/4 OR 1/2 IN VIDEO
Explores the city at night with special emphasis on the people and their occupations. Re-creates with human voices all of the sounds of the city and its activities.
Prod-FLMFR Dist-FLMFR 1971

Night Piloting, Surface B 18 MIN
16MM FILM, 3/4 OR 1/2 IN VIDEO
Studies a night piloting problem and shows the procedure of bringing the USS Savannah into a harbor at night.
From The Navigation Series.
LC NO. 81-706350
Prod-USN Dist-USNAC 1959

Night Scene C 3 MIN
16MM FILM OPTICAL SOUND
Uses available light photography, without narration, to depict a town at night.
LC NO. 77-700177
Prod-LANCED Dist-CANCIN 1975

Night Shift C 7 MIN
16MM FILM OPTICAL SOUND
Shows a gas station attendant alone in the quiet hours of the night who is increasingly unnerved by seemingly sourceless sounds and visual distortions.
LC NO. 75-703211
Prod-USC Dist-USC 1967

Night Sky, The C 30 MIN
3/4 OR 1/2 INCH VIDEO CASSETTE K-P
See series title for descriptive statement.
From The Villa Alegre Series.
Prod-BCTV Dist-MDCPB

Night Sky, The (2nd Ed) C 11 MIN
16MM FILM, 3/4 OR 1/2 IN VIDEO P-I
Explores the broad scope of human inquiry into the Sun, moon, planets, stars, constellations and galaxies.
Prod-EBEC Dist-EBEC

Night The Animals Talked, The C 27 MIN
16MM FILM, 3/4 OR 1/2 IN VIDEO P-I
An animated film about the Nativity as seen through the eyes of the animals in the stable. Music by Jule Styne and lyrics by Sammy Cahn.
Prod-ABC Dist-MGHT 1971

Night Visions C 11 MIN
3/4 INCH VIDEO CASSETTE
Portrays a woman confronting past experiences in a dream journey. Explores aspects of the woman's personality through the use of masks.
Prod-WMENIF Dist-WMENIF

Night-Eating C 7 MIN
16MM FILM OPTICAL SOUND
Shows animated drawings that invoke the illusion of endless space, etchings in light and the perfect harmony of geometry and color.
Prod-VANBKS Dist-VANBKS

Night's Nice C 10 MIN
16MM FILM, 3/4 OR 1/2 IN VIDEO K-I
Explains that enchanting sounds and images make night a special time for discovery. Shows the stars, yellowed-eyed cats, city lights and sleeping, all elements that make up night's rich tapestry of wonderful things.
Prod-SF Dist-SF 1970

Nightingale, The C 16 MIN
16MM FILM, 3/4 OR 1/2 IN VIDEO K-I
Features animated puppets who realistically unfold the classic Hans Christian Andersen story of the Emperor who finds a treasure living in his own garden - the nightingale.
Prod-CORF Dist-CORF 1984

Nightingale, The C 35 MIN
16MM FILM, 3/4 OR 1/2 IN VIDEO I-C
Presents an adaptation of the story The Nightingale by Hans Christian Anderson about a Chinese kitchen girl and her relationship with a beautiful bird.
Prod-SANDSA Dist-WOMBAT

Nightlife C 11 MIN
16MM FILM, 3/4 OR 1/2 IN VIDEO
Pictures the fantastic variety of color and forms of life found beneath the Irish Sea.
Prod-OPUS Dist-PHENIX 1976

Nightmare C 10 MIN
16MM FILM, 3/4 OR 1/2 IN VIDEO H-C A
Uses animation to tell a story about a man who climbs into bed, eager for repose, and experiences a series of nightmares that leave him unable to distinguish between dream and reality.
Prod-ZAGREB Dist-IFB 1977

Nightmare - The Immigration Of Joachim And Rachael C 24 MIN
3/4 OR 1/2 INCH VIDEO CASSETTE
Focuses on two Jewish children's escape from the Nazioccupied Warsaw ghetto.
From The Young people's Specials Series.
Prod-MULTPP Dist-MULTPP

Nightmare At San Pietro C 30 MIN
3/4 OR 1/2 INCH VIDEO CASSETTE H-C A
See series title for descriptive statement.
From The World War II - GI Diary Series.
Prod-TIMLIF Dist-TIMLIF 1980

Nightmare For The Bold B
16MM FILM OPTICAL SOUND
Presents the story of a young man who thought he could drive better than most people even when he had had a drink or two. Shows how one careless act on the part of the driver can effect the lives of many others. Depicts civil as well as criminal trials that can result. Emphasizes the importance of auto insurance, sober driving and responsibility behind the wheel.
LC NO. FIE60-41
Prod-USAF Dist-USNAC 1959

Nightmare In Red B 55 MIN
16MM FILM, 3/4 OR 1/2 IN VIDEO J-C A
Discusses the growth of communism inside Russia, covering the old czarist order, the revolutions of 1905 and 1917, the provisional government, the early days of the communist era, the purge trials, World War II and postwar conditions.
From The Project 20 Series.
Prod-NBCTV Dist-MGHT 1958

Nightmare In Red, Pt 1 B 27 MIN
16MM FILM, 3/4 OR 1/2 IN VIDEO J-C
Discusses the growth of communism inside Russia, covering the old czarist order, the revolutions of 1905 and 1917, the provisional government, the early days of the communist era, the purge trials, World War II and postwar conditions.
From The Project 20 Series.
Prod-NBCTV Dist-MGHT 1958

Nightmare In Red, Pt 2 B 27 MIN
16MM FILM, 3/4 OR 1/2 IN VIDEO J-C
Discusses the growth of communism inside Russia, covering the old czarist order, the revolutions of 1905 and 1917, the provisional government, the early days of the communist era, the purge trials, World War II and postwar conditions.
From The Project 20 Series.
Prod-NBCTV Dist-MGHT 1958

Nightmare, The X 5 MIN
16MM FILM OPTICAL SOUND
Combines humor with deadly serious subject matter, genocide in America. Erupts into rhythmic, fast paced photographic collage animation set to a pop music background.
Prod-BLKFMF Dist-BLKFMF

Nikita Khrushchev B 10 MIN
3/4 OR 1/2 INCH VIDEO CASSETTE
Presents an in-depth examination of the rise and fall of Nikita Khrushchev providing an insight into his personality and career, including his historic visit to the United States in 1959.
Prod-KINGFT Dist-KINGFT

Nikko National Park C 26 MIN
16MM FILM OPTICAL SOUND
A Japanese language film. Introduces Nikko National Park as one of the famous sight-seeing places in Japan and describes the geological history of the Nikko volcanic zone. Coves Kegon Fall, Mt Nantai, Lake Chuzenji and other places in the Nikko National Park. Depicts the gorgeous Toshogu Shrine and Daiyuin as well as remains of natural formation originating one million years ago.
Prod-UNIJAP Dist-UNIJAP 1967

Nikkolina C 28 MIN
16MM FILM, 3/4 OR 1/2 IN VIDEO J-C A
Presents a story about a girl who does not share her Greek father's feeling for their old world heritage and resents his insistence that she take part in the traditional ceremonies involved in a family wedding when it means missing a figure skating contest for which she has practiced for months.
Prod-LCOA Dist-LCOA Prodn-CINEFL 1978

Nikkolina (Spanish) C 28 MIN
16MM FILM, 3/4 OR 1/2 IN VIDEO P-J A
Tells the story of a young Greek girl who does not share her father's traditional values.
Prod-LCOA Dist-LCOA Prodn-CINEFL 1978

Niko - Boy Of Greece C 21 MIN
16MM FILM, 3/4 OR 1/2 IN VIDEO P-J
Portrays the pride, hardships and pleasures of a traditional island community and one boy's preparation for manhood.
Prod-ACI Dist-AIMS 1968

Nikorima C 27 MIN
16MM FILM, 3/4 OR 1/2 IN VIDEO
Relates the New Zealand tale of an eccentric warrior who is left behind to guard his village. Shows that when a hostile band arrives, he convinces the invaders of their superiority and they retreat, thus making him a hero.
From The Storybook International Series.
Prod-JOU Dist-JOU 1982

Nikos Kazantzakis - Selected Works C 29 MIN
2 INCH VIDEOTAPE
Presents readings from selected works of Nikos Kazantzakis.
From The One To One Series.
Prod-WETATV Dist-PUBTEL

Nile Crocodile, The C 30 MIN
16MM FILM, 3/4 OR 1/2 IN VIDEO J-C
Reveals that the crocodile is well-adapted for survival but is now threatened by man, who is hunting it relentlessly.
LC NO. 84-706003
Prod-EBEC Dist-EBEC 1982

Nile River Basin And The People Of The Upper River - Uganda And Sudan C 17 MIN
16MM FILM OPTICAL SOUND J-C
Follows the river northward from Lake Victoria to central Sudan.

Living conditions, occupations, transportation and other habits of the people who are dependent upon the Nile and its tributaries are shown.
Prod-ACA Dist-ACA 1951

Nile River Valley And The People Of The Lower River - Sudan And Egypt C 17 MIN
16MM FILM OPTICAL SOUND J-C
Explains the importance of the Nile to the people of Egypt and Sudan, by showing scenes of the Aswan Dam, the annual Nile flood which deposits fertile silt, the irrigated fields and the traffic on the river. Also contrasts the archeological ruins along the Nile with the modern city of Cairo.
LC NO. FIA53-189
Prod-ACA Dist-ACA 1951

Nim And Other Oriented Graph Games B 63 MIN
16MM FILM OPTICAL SOUND H-C T
Professor Andrew M Gleason describes nim and related games and constructs an algebraic theory which gives information about games more complicated than nim.
From The MAA Individual Lecturers Series.
Prod-MAA Dist-MLA 1966

Nimmo In Bangkok C 25 MIN
16MM FILM OPTICAL SOUND
Takes a look around Bangkok through the eyes of English comedian Derek Nimmo. Probes the mystery of the American Thai silk millionaire Jim Thompson who vanished without a trace during an Asian holiday.
LC NO. 80-700880
Prod-VISMED Dist-TASCOR 1973

Nimrod Workman - To Fit My Own Category B 35 MIN
16MM FILM - 3/4 IN VIDEO
Focuses on Nimrod Workman, retired miner and singer who writes and performs songs and traditional ballads.
Prod-APPAL Dist-APPAL 1975

Nina Sobel - Chicken On Foot B 8 MIN
3/4 OR 1/2 INCH VIDEO CASSETTE
Shows Nina Sobel smashing eggs on her knee while rocking a chicken on her foot.
Prod-LBMAV Dist-ARTINC

Nina Sobel - Electro-Encephalographic Video Drawings C 6 MIN
3/4 OR 1/2 INCH VIDEO CASSETTE
Combines absurdity and physicality.
Prod-LBMAV Dist-ARTINC

Nina Sobel - Hey Baby Chickey B 10 MIN
3/4 OR 1/2 INCH VIDEO CASSETTE
Combines absurdity and physicality.
Prod-LBMAV Dist-ARTINC

Nina Sobel - Hobby Horses In Paradise C 14 MIN
3/4 OR 1/2 INCH VIDEO CASSETTE
Combines absurdity and physicality. Pokes fun at the housewife model.
Prod-LBMAV Dist-ARTINC

Nina Sobel - Selected Works 1972-74 B 45 MIN
3/4 OR 1/2 INCH VIDEO CASSETTE
Combines absurdity and physicality.
Prod-LBMAV Dist-ARTINC

Nina Sobel - Six Moving Cameras, Six Converging Views B 6 MIN
3/4 OR 1/2 INCH VIDEO CASSETTE
Combines absurdity and physicality.
Prod-LBMAV Dist-ARTINC

Nine Artists of Puerto Rico C 16 MIN
16MM FILM, 3/4 OR 1/2 IN VIDEO J-C
Visits the studios of Puerto Rico's most important artists.
LC NO. 82-707070
Prod-OOAS Dist-MOMALA 1970

Nine Artists Of Puerto Rico (Spanish) C 16 MIN
3/4 OR 1/2 INCH VIDEO CASSETTE
Visits the studios of Puerto Rico's most important artists.
LC NO. 82-707018
Prod-MOMALA Dist-MOMALA

Nine Dollars Plus One Dollar Equals 20 Dollars Shortchanged C 27 MIN
16MM FILM - 3/4 IN VIDEO IND
Explains that large cash losses are highly possible at every market, bank, department store, hotel, restaurant or filling station without any awareness of the cause. Tells how even the experienced clerk or cashier is likely to lose large sums of money to the smooth-talking, quick-acting, aggressive money manipulator.
From The Loss Prevention Series.
Prod-BNA Dist-BNA 1970

Nine Hundred-Thousandths Fine C 28 MIN
16MM FILM OPTICAL SOUND
Combines 19th-century lithographs with live-action sequences to tell the story of the silver bonanza days, particularly the growth of Carson City, nevada, where the famous dollars were minted. Narrated by Burgess Meredith.
LC NO. 74-706508
Prod-USGSA Dist-USNAC 1972

Nine In A Row C 10 MIN
16MM FILM OPTICAL SOUND
Presents a documentary record of a college rowing team in action, showing the hallucinatory experiences the team encounters during the race through psychedelic visual images.
Prod-CFS Dist-CFS

Nine Lives Of Fritz The Cat C 77 MIN
16MM FILM OPTICAL SOUND C A
Presents Ralph Bakaki's sequel to Fritz The Cat. Animated.
Prod-AIP Dist-TIMLIF 1972

Nine Months (Hungarian) C 93 MIN
16MM FILM OPTICAL SOUND
Describes the love affair between a strong-willed young woman and an impulsive, often arbitrary fellow-worker in a chilly industrial city. Directed by Marta Meszaros. With English subtitles.
Prod-UNKNWN Dist-NYFLMS 1977

Nine Months In Motion C 19 MIN
16MM FILM, 3/4 OR 1/2 IN VIDEO
Illustrates exercises for expectant mothers which can strengthen and keep flexible certain muscles during pregnancy.
Prod-PEREN Dist-PEREN 1977

Nine O'Clock News C 2 MIN
16MM FILM OPTICAL SOUND H-C A
Presents a spoof on the communications media and its irrational comments.
Prod-MCLAOG Dist-SLFP

Nine Out Of Ten C 31 MIN
16MM FILM OPTICAL SOUND
Features service-wide fire prevention problems of debris burning, industrial fires and recreation fires. Presents ten essentials for improving fire prevention and how to apply them.
LC NO. 74-705214
Prod-USDA Dist-USNAC 1971

Nine To Eleven Months C 11 MIN
3/4 OR 1/2 INCH VIDEO CASSETTE H-C A
Shows how infants between the ages of nine to eleven months learn by seeing, hearing, feeling, general imitation, spatial relationships, self-awareness and cause-effect.
From The Teaching Infants And Toddlers Series. Pt 4
Prod-BGSU Dist-GPITVL 1978

Nine To Get Ready—A Series

Deals with maternal and child health care beginning with preconception care, pregnancy, delivery and finally to current research in reproductive physiology and family planning.
Prod-NETCHE Dist-PUBTEL

Caesarian Section	29 MIN
Facilities In Counties And States	29 MIN
Family Planning	29 MIN
Growth Of The Fetus	29 MIN
Hospital Care And Labor	29 MIN
Newborn Care	29 MIN
Obstetric Delivery	29 MIN
Physiology Of Conception	29 MIN
Physiology Of Pregnancy And Labor	29 MIN
Preconception Care And Diagnosis Of Pregnancy	29 MIN
Prenatal Care	29 MIN
Recent Advances In Reproductive Physiology	29 MIN

Nine Variations On A Dance Theme B 13 MIN
16MM FILM OPTICAL SOUND
Shows a dance theme repeated and interpreted in a surprising number of ways using the basic elements of film craft.
Prod-RADIM Dist-RADIM 1966

Nine-Hundred-One/-Nine-Hundred-Four B 65 MIN
3/4 INCH VIDEO CASSETTE
Accompanies patrol cars as they ply the streets of Pittsburgh. Includes scenes from short films in the series. Illustrates that ignorance of, and lack of access to, the law often escalates violence. Shows the causes of violence and rage on both sides of law enforcement.
From The Pittsburgh Police Series.
Prod-DOCEDR Dist-DOCEDR Prodn-MSHLLJ

Nine-Step Writing Process In Class C 37 MIN
3/4 OR 1/2 INCH VIDEO CASSETTE T
Presents a step-by-step writing process and discusses the way it can be used.
From The Process-Centered Composition Series.
LC NO. 79-706297
Prod-IU Dist-IU 1977

Nine-To-Eleven Year Olds C 17 MIN
3/4 OR 1/2 INCH VIDEO CASSETTE I
Illustrates prevention of sexual abuse with examples of children using the safety rules of assertion, trusting their feelings and telling of their experiences. Teaches that sexual assault may involve tricks instead of violence and may happen at home or in familiar places. Encourages children to walk assertively, answer the phone when alone and make a scene.
From The Child Sexual Abuse - An Ounce Of Prevention Series.
Prod-PPCIN Dist-AITECH

Nine-Year Olds Talk About Death B 15 MIN
16MM FILM, 3/4 OR 1/2 IN VIDEO C A
Shows fourth grade students relating their feelings about death.
LC NO. 80-706443
Prod-MHFB Dist-IFB 1978

Nineteen Eighteen C
1/2 IN VIDEO CASSETTE BETA/VHS
Tells the story by Horton Foote of the effects of an epidemic on a Texas town during World War I, starring Matthew Broderick.
Prod-GA Dist-GA

Nineteen Eighty - A New Taste Odyssey C 41 MIN
16MM FILM OPTICAL SOUND A
Uses a space fantasy with multiple special effects to announce a food product created by the Coca-Cola company. Describes the sales incentive program.
LC NO. 80-701326
Prod-COCA Dist-COCA Prodn-RUSMAN 1980

Nineteen Eighty - Year In Review C 28 MIN
16MM FILM, 3/4 OR 1/2 IN VIDEO H-C A
Looks at the key events of 1980.
Prod-UPI Dist-JOU

Nineteen Eighty Physician's Recognition Award C 60 MIN
3/4 INCH VIDEO CASSETTE
Presents case studies that have won recognition from the American Medical Association.
Prod-UTAHTI Dist-UTAHTI

Nineteen Eighty-Five C 18 MIN
16MM FILM OPTICAL SOUND
Examines the construction and functions of the Space Shuttle and Space Station by means of computer animation and space-earth photography.
Prod-NASA Dist-NASA

Nineteen Eighty-Four In 1984 C 60 MIN
3/4 OR 1/2 INCH VIDEO CASSETTE
Presents a two-channel installation of the tapes resulting from the 1984 New Year's Day transmission of Good Morning Mr Orwell in New York and in Paris.
Prod-KITCHN Dist-KITCHN

Nineteen Eighty-Four Revisited C 40 MIN
16MM FILM, 3/4 OR 1/2 IN VIDEO J-C A
Reviews aspects of modern society to show how close it is to the Orwellian world of Big Brother. Discusses how networks of computers keep track of people's travels through the passport office, census bureau, credit card companies, banks, supermarkets, department stores, the Social Security system and the Internal Revenue Service.
LC NO. 84-706148
Prod-CBSNEW Dist-MTI 1983

Nineteen Eighty-One - Year In Review C 50 MIN
3/4 OR 1/2 INCH VIDEO CASSETTE J-H
Reviews the events that comprised international headline news in 1981.
Prod-JOU Dist-JOU

Nineteen Eighty-One Annual Clinical Training Research Project Competition, The C 60 MIN
3/4 INCH VIDEO CASSETTE
Presents essays regarding milk protein synthesis in breast carcinoma, tumor-associated gastroparesis correction metoclopramide, computer optimization combining electron and proton beams and the effects of gastro on colon neoplasms in rats.
Prod-UTAHTI Dist-UTAHTI

Nineteen Eighty-One Kemper Open, The C 28 MIN
16MM FILM OPTICAL SOUND
Depicts the excitement and frustration of the preliminaries and finals of the 1981 Kemper Open Golf Tournament. Shows Craig Stadler emerging victorious on the last day.
Prod-MTP Dist-MTP

Nineteen Eighty-One PGA - Laws Principles And Preferences C 58 MIN
3/4 OR 1/2 INCH VIDEO CASSETTE
Explains the five basic laws and twelve principles which are involved in a golfer's swing and demonstrates how to mold the multitude of individual preferences into a perfect swing.
Prod-FILAUD Dist-FILAUD

Nineteen Eighty-Two Hall Of Fame Regatta, The C 60 MIN
1/2 IN VIDEO CASSETTE BETA/VHS
Shows world class sailors racing in the 1982 Hall Of Fame Regatta.
Prod-NORVID Dist-OFFSHR

Nineteen Eighty-Two J-24 Worlds, The C 50 MIN
1/2 IN VIDEO CASSETTE BETA/VHS
Shows the 1982 J-24 Worlds sailing races.
Prod-OFFSHR Dist-OFFSHR

Nineteen Eighty-Two Masters Tournament C 30 MIN
16MM FILM OPTICAL SOUND
Presents the 46th Masters Tournament at the Augusta National Golf Club in Georgia. Follows the leading players to the final showdown, a sudden death playoff with Craig Stadler emerging as the winner.
Prod-OWENSI Dist-MTP

Nineteen Eighty-Two New York 36 Nationals, The C 40 MIN
1/2 IN VIDEO CASSETTE BETA/VHS
Shows the 1982 regatta consisting of the 14 top boats from around the U S.
Prod-OFFSHR Dist-OFFSHR

Nineteen Fifty-Five Eruption Of Kilauea, The C 11 MIN
16MM FILM, 3/4 OR 1/2 IN VIDEO P-C A
Follows the 1955 eruption of Kilauea, Hawaii, from the first opening of fissures in the ground, to the APpearance of lava. Shows the formation of cone, flows, and fountains. Views clouds of steam caused by lava flowing into the ocean.
LC NO. 80-707639
Prod-USGS Dist-USNAC 1958

Nineteen Fifty-Nine Chevy C 2 MIN
3/4 OR 1/2 INCH VIDEO CASSETTE
Shows a classic television commercial with Pat Boone and Dinah Shore singing.
Prod-BROOKC Dist-BROOKC

Nineteen Fifty-Seven Chevy Trucks C 4 MIN
3/4 OR 1/2 INCH VIDEO CASSETTE
Shows a classic television commercial that demonstrates Chevy trucks conquering the Alcan run.
Prod-BROOKC Dist-BROOKC

Nineteen Forty-Five To 1960 C
3/4 OR 1/2 INCH VIDEO CASSETTE H
Covers the Truman-Eisenhower years, including the Cold War, McCarthyism, Korea, Baby Boomers, Sputnik and Russia's first atomic bomb.
From The Modern U S History - From Cold War To Hostage Crisis Series.
Prod-GA Dist-GA

Nineteen Forty-One C 120 MIN
16MM FILM OPTICAL SOUND
Tells what happens when a community becomes convinced that the Japanese are about to attack. Directed by Steven Spielberg.
Prod-UPCI Dist-SWANK

Nineteen Hundred - Passing Of An Age C 25 MIN
16MM FILM OPTICAL SOUND
Describes how the coming of the automobile brought vast changes to small-town America and how quiet towns were replaced finally by smog-filled cities and crowded freeways. Based on Booth Tarkington's novel THE MAGNIFICENT AMBERSONS.
From The American Challenge Series.
Prod-RKOP Dist-FI 1975

Nineteen Hundred Sixty-Nine U S Open C 28 MIN
16MM FILM OPTICAL SOUND
Shows winner, Orville Moody, as he leads top golfers on a charge across Firestone Country Club in Houston, Texas.
Prod-CMD Dist-GM

Nineteen Hundred-Seventy U S Open C 27 MIN
16MM FILM OPTICAL SOUND
Focuses on Tony Jacklin, the first Englishman in 50 years to win the United States open golf championship.
Prod-CMD Dist-GM

Nineteen Minutes To Earth C 15 MIN
16MM FILM, 3/4 OR 1/2 IN VIDEO
Examines scientific findings from the Viking missions to Mars and some of the difficulties in interpreting the data. Includes information on the soil, atmosphere, and geology of Mars.
LC NO. 81-706423
Prod-NASA Dist-USNAC Prodn-WHROTV 1981

Nineteen Ninety-Nine A D C 26 MIN
16MM FILM, 3/4 OR 1/2 IN VIDEO
Looks to the future and how people relate to the computer- controlled environment of 1999 A D.
Prod-FORDFL Dist-FORDFL

Nineteen Seventy All Star (Baseball) Game C 26 MIN
16MM FILM OPTICAL SOUND I-C A
Highlights the 1970 all star baseball game, showing baseball's unique qualities where every man stands alone, and his heroics and errors are seen by everyone.
LC NO. 74-714273
Prod-MLBPC Dist-SFI 1971

Nineteen Seventy Low Speed Car Crash Costs C 35 MIN
16MM FILM OPTICAL SOUND J-C A
Demonstrates the high cost of low speed crashes by showing crash tests on 1970 model sedans, pony cars and small cars traveling at 5, 10 and 15 miles per hour.
LC NO. 72-700542
Prod-IIHS Dist-HF 1970

Nineteen Seventy National League Highlights C 26 MIN
16MM FILM OPTICAL SOUND
Presents highlights of the 1970 National League Championship Series between the Cincinnati Reds and the Pittsburgh Pirates.
Prod-SFI Dist-SFI 1971

Nineteen Seventy One Rose Parade Film (Through The Eyes Of A Child) C 30 MIN
16MM FILM OPTICAL SOUND K-C A
Reproduces the Rose Parade of the year 1971.
LC NO. 73-700799
Prod-TRA Dist-TRA 1971

Nineteen Seventy Press On Regardless, The C 11 MIN
16MM FILM OPTICAL SOUND
Uses a combination documentary/cinema verite style to show highlights of the 1970 press on regardless sports car rally from opening registration and car inspection through the two days of the rally and to the finish.
LC NO. 72-700186
Prod-CIASP Dist-CIASP 1971

Nineteen Seventy Rose Parade Film (Holidays Around The World) C 30 MIN
16MM FILM OPTICAL SOUND K-C A
Reproduces the Rose Parade of the year 1970.
LC NO. 73-700798
Prod-TRA Dist-TRA 1970

Nineteen Seventy Three Rose Parade Film (Movie Memories) C 30 MIN
16MM FILM OPTICAL SOUND K-C A
Reproduces the Rose Parade of the year 1973.
LC NO. 73-700801
Prod-TRA Dist-TRA 1973

Nineteen Seventy Two Rose Parade Film (The Joy Of Music) C 30 MIN
16MM FILM OPTICAL SOUND K-C A
Reproduces the Rose Parade of the year 1972.
LC NO. 73-700800
Prod-TRA Dist-TRA 1972

Nineteen Seventy World Series C 40 MIN
16MM FILM OPTICAL SOUND
Presents highlights of the 1970 World Series between the Baltimore Orioles and the Cincinnati Reds.
Prod-SFI Dist-SFI 1970

Nineteen Seventy-Eight 7up Marketing Plans C 12 MIN
16MM FILM OPTICAL SOUND
Establishes the 1978 marketing plans for 7up, Sugar Free 7up and Fountain 7up. Outlines the markets for each brand and then shows the importance of the local bottler's efforts in making 1978 a successful sales year.
LC NO. 78-700397
Prod-SEVUP Dist-SEVUP Prodn-FILMA 1977

Nineteen Seventy-Five PGA Championship C 28 MIN
16MM FILM OPTICAL SOUND
Documents the 1975 PGA Championship at the Firestone Country Club in Akron, Ohio.
Prod-FTARC Dist-FTARC

Nineteen Seventy-Nine 7up And Sugar Free 7up Marketing Plans Film (Developer's Version) C 19 MIN
16MM FILM OPTICAL SOUND
Shows the strategy, media plans and promotional activities the Seven-Up Company is employing to position and support their products nationally.
LC NO. 79-700251
Prod-SEVUP Dist-FILMA Prodn-FILMA 1978

Nineteen Seventy-Six - No Goyakusoku C 21 MIN
16MM FILM OPTICAL SOUND
A Japanese language film. Enumerates the Chessie System's various technological improvements which have resulted in better export facilities and greater customer services. Concentrates on the active railroad system.
LC NO. 77-700396
Prod-CSCTD Dist-CSCTD Prodn-CSCTD 1976

Nineteen Seventy-Three Mgodo Wa Mbanguzi, The C 53 MIN
16MM FILM OPTICAL SOUND C A
Documents a performance of the music and dance known as mgodo, composed for a Chopi village in southern Mozambique. Depicts dancers who are accompanied by large xylophone orchestras. Contains history and current affairs in the texts of the suites, along with preoccupations of tribe members about local events. Includes subtitles of songs in Chopi and English.
LC NO. 75-700198
Prod-PSUPCR Dist-PSUPCR 1974

Nineteen Seventy-Three Mgodo Wa Mkandeni, The C 48 MIN
16MM FILM OPTICAL SOUND C A
Presents a traditional music and dance performance known as mgodo, composed by members of a Chopi village in southern Mozambique during the winter of 1973. Features dancers and a xylophone orchestra who present their village's suite. Depicts a large number of instruments tuned in several pitches, highly-developed xylophones and distinctive musical structure.
LC NO. 75-700197
Prod-PSUPCR Dist-PSUPCR 1974

Nineteen Seventy-Two AAU Junior Olympics C 28 MIN
16MM FILM OPTICAL SOUND
Follows the preparation of two athletes for the 1972 Junior Olympics and their participation in the events. Includes action highlights of all the major competitions.
LC NO. 73-701276
Prod-GM Dist-GM 1972

Nineteen Sixty Eight Buick Open C 28 MIN
1 INCH VIDEOTAPE
Recaps the $125,000 golf tournament with Tom Weiskopf winning by one stroke. Features Julius Boros, Lee Trevino and Johnny Pott.
Prod-MGM Dist-MTP

Nineteen Sixty Nine Rose Parade Film (A Time To Remember) C 30 MIN
16MM FILM OPTICAL SOUND K-C A
Reproduces the Rose Parade of the year 1969.
LC NO. 73-700797
Prod-TRA Dist-TRA 1969

Nineteen Sixty-Eight - A Look For New Meanings C 110 MIN
16MM FILM, 3/4 OR 1/2 IN VIDEO J-C A
Reviews major political, cultural and social events of the year 1968. Covers the Vietnam War, the Living Room War, student dissent, the Civil Rights movement, the assassinations of Martin Luther King, Jr, and Robert Kennedy, the Democratic National Convention and the election of Richard Nixon.
LC NO. 79-706336
Prod-CBSNEW Dist-FOTH 1978

Nineteen Sixty-Eight Rose Parade, 'Wonderful World Of Adventure' C 32 MIN
16MM FILM OPTICAL SOUND K-C A
Pictures the floats, bands and horses of the floral festival and parade held in Pasadena, California, on New Years Day, 1968.
LC NO. FIA68-627
Prod-TRA Dist-TRA 1968

Nineteen Sixty-Five Green Bay Packers Highlights, The C 27 MIN
16MM FILM OPTICAL SOUND J-C A
Highlights the 1965 professional football season, featuring team and individual performances of the Green Bay Packers.
LC NO. FIA68-1407
Prod-NFL Dist-NFL 1966

Nineteen Sixty-Five St Louis Cardinals Highligts, The C 27 MIN
16MM FILM OPTICAL SOUND J-C A
Highlights the 1965 playing season featuring the St Louis Cardinals professional football team.
LC NO. FIA68-1406
Prod-NFL Dist-NFL 1966

Nineteen Sixty-Four C 54 MIN
16MM FILM, 3/4 OR 1/2 IN VIDEO H-C A
Explores the great power and the complex problems of the United States. Includes discussion on poverty in the midst of affluence, automation, old age, leisure time, unemployment and equal opportunity.
From The Saga Of Western Man Series.
Prod-ABCTV Dist-MGHT Prodn-SCNDRI 1964

Nineteen Sixty-Four Conventions, The - Goldwater, Johnson Nominated B 20 MIN
16MM FILM OPTICAL SOUND
Shows democracy in action at the 1964 Democratic and Republican National Conventions, where Goldwater and Johnson and their running mates were nominated.
From The Screen News Digest Series. Vol 7, Issue 2
Prod-HEARST Dist-HEARST 1964

Nineteen Sixty-Four Presidential Election - Death Of Herbert Hoover - Downfall Of Krushchev B 20 MIN
16MM FILM OPTICAL SOUND
Pictures activities in the 50 states on election day, 1964. Reviews the life of the late President Herbert Hoover, and shows a nation in mourning. Examines the rise and fall of Nikita Krushchev, emphasizing the shake up in the kremlin where he was succeeded by Leonid Brezhnev and Aleksei Kosygin.
From The Screen News Digest Series. Vol 7, Issue 4
Prod-HEARST Dist-HEARST 1964

Nineteen Sixty-Four, Pt 1 C 27 MIN
16MM FILM, 3/4 OR 1/2 IN VIDEO H-C A
Explores the great power and the complex problems of the United States. Includes discussion on poverty in the midst of affluence, automation, old age, leisure time, unemployment and equal opportunity.
From The Saga Of Western Man Series.
Prod-ABCTV Dist-MGHT Prodn-SCNDRI 1965

Nineteen Sixty-Four, Pt 2 C 27 MIN
16MM FILM, 3/4 OR 1/2 IN VIDEO H-C A
Explores the great power and the complex problems of the United States. Includes discussion on poverty in the midst of affluence, automation, old age, leisure time, unemployment and equal opportunity.
From The Saga Of Western Man Series.
Prod-ABCTV Dist-MGHT Prodn-SCNDRI 1965

Nineteen Sixty-Nine - Seventy Coaches All-American Basketball Team C 25 MIN
16MM FILM OPTICAL SOUND H-C
Features members of the 1969-70 coaches all-American basketball team. Includes Pete Maravich of LSU, Charlie Scott of North Carolina, Bob Lanier of St Bonaventure, Dan Issel of Kentucky and Rick Mount of Purdue.
Prod-GEMILL Dist-NINEFC

Nineteen Sixty-Nine To 1981 C
3/4 OR 1/2 INCH VIDEO CASSETTE H
Examines the Nixon, Ford and Carter years, including withdrawal from Vietnam, reopening relations with China, Watergate, the rise of OPEC and the Iranian hostage crisis.
From The Modern U S History - From Cold War To Hostage Crisis Series.
Prod-GA Dist-GA

Nineteen Sixty-Nine Westchester Classic C 27 MIN
16MM FILM OPTICAL SOUND I-C A
Golf champion Jack Nicklaus demonstrates in competition how to handle uphill, sidehill and downhill unplayable lies. Provides split screen and slow motion analysis of the short iron, sand trap and putting techniques. Original theme music and narration by Jack Nicklaus.
LC NO. 79-713001
Prod-TWA Dist-SFI 1970

Nineteen Sixty-One To 1968 C
3/4 OR 1/2 INCH VIDEO CASSETTE H
Focuses on the Kennedy-Johnson years, including black civil rights, the Cuban missile crisis, Kennedy's assassination and Vietnam.
From The Modern U S History - From Cold War To Hostage Crisis Series.
Prod-GA Dist-GA

Nineteenth Century Nationalism / Liberalism C 30 MIN
3/4 OR 1/2 INCH VIDEO CASSETTE H
Discusses the Congress of Vienna and the liberalism and nationalism in France, England, Italy and Germany.
From The Historically Speaking Series. Part 13
Prod-KRMATV Dist-AITECH 1983

Ninety Degree Machine Cutting C 4 MIN
1/2 IN VIDEO CASSETTE BETA/VHS IND
See series title for descriptive statement.
From The Welding Training (Comprehensive) --- Oxy-Acetylene Welding Series.
Prod-RMI Dist-RMI

Ninety Degree Round Elbow Using Rise Method C 10 MIN
1/2 IN VIDEO CASSETTE BETA/VHS IND
See series title for descriptive statement.
From The Metal Fabrication - Parallel Line Development Series.
Prod-RMI Dist-RMI

Ninety Degrees South C 15 MIN
16MM FILM, 3/4 OR 1/2 IN VIDEO
Describes life at South Pole Station in Antarctica.
From The Odyssey Series.
Prod-KRMATV Dist-GPITVL

Ninety-Nine Bottles Of Beer C 23 MIN
16MM FILM, 3/4 OR 1/2 IN VIDEO
Focuses on alcohol abuse in young people. Relates actual experiences and feelings of young people as they relate to alcohol.
Prod-LAC Dist-AIMS 1974

Ninety-Nine Bottles Of Beer C 23 MIN
3/4 OR 1/2 INCH VIDEO CASSETTE J A
Discusses teenagers and drinking.
Prod-SUTHRB Dist-SUTHRB

Ninety-Nine Bottles Of Beer (Spanish) C 23 MIN
16MM FILM, 3/4 OR 1/2 IN VIDEO J-C
Presents young alcoholics who share their experiences with drinking, with school problems, and with their family and friends.
Prod-LAC Dist-AIMS 1974

Ninety-Nine Bottles Of Beer (Spanish) C 23 MIN
3/4 OR 1/2 INCH VIDEO CASSETTE J A
Discusses teenagers and drinking.
Prod-SUTHRB Dist-SUTHRB

Niok - Orphan Elephant Of Cambodia C 29 MIN
16MM FILM, 3/4 OR 1/2 IN VIDEO I-C A
Niok, a baby elephant, is captured by a boy from a small village in the jungles of Cambodia. He recaptures the elephant when it is sold to a Chinese trader and, finally, sets the elephant free.
Prod-DISNEY Dist-WDEMCO 1960

Nirvana C 30 MIN
3/4 OR 1/2 INCH VIDEO CASSETTE
See series title for descriptive statement.
From The Que Pasa, U S A Series.
Prod-WPBTTV Dist-MDCPB

Nisei Legacy C 30 MIN
3/4 OR 1/2 INCH VIDEO CASSETTE
Explores the reasons for the relatively high rate of heart disease among Nisei, second generation Japanese Americans. Reveals a suspected combination of diet and stress compensation to be the reasons for the difference between heart disease rates for two populations with the same heredity.
From The Synthesis Series.
Prod-KPBS Dist-KPBS

Nitric Acid C 18 MIN
16MM FILM OPTICAL SOUND H
Describes the characteristics of nitric acid and discusses its uses. Demonstrates how nitric acid may act as an acid, a base and as an oxidizing agent. Points out how it is manufactured.
From The CHEM Study Films Series.
LC NO. FIA62-1640
Prod-CHEMS Dist-SUTHLA 1962

Nitric Acid C 18 MIN
16MM FILM OPTICAL SOUND H-C
Presents the fundamentals of nitric acid, applying in descriptive chemistry. Describes how nitric acid may act as an acid, a base and as an oxidizing agent. Provides molecular models, activation energy curves and potential energy diagrams, as graphic illustrations of concepts.
Prod-MCA Dist-MLA

Nixon - 'Toughing It Out' C 26 MIN
3/4 OR 1/2 INCH VIDEO CASSETTE H-C A
Studies the attitudes of President Nixon as he fought to maintain office during the Watergate scandal. Chronicles both the legal and emotional defenses put forward, as well as the continuing list of defections from his camp during the affair.
Prod-UPI Dist-JOU

Nixon - Checkers To Watergate C 20 MIN
16MM FILM, 3/4 OR 1/2 IN VIDEO
Looks at the political life of Richard Milhouse Nixon from the Eisenhower years to his resignation from office. Illustrates the intricacies of the executive branch of our government and the extraordinary demands of responsibility upon the office of President.
Prod-BRAMAN Dist-PFP 1976

Nixon's Checkers Speech B 25 MIN
16MM FILM OPTICAL SOUND J-C A
Presents the famous 'Checkers' speech made by Richard Nixon when he was the 1952 vice presidential nominee. Explains how Nixon's defense in this speech against accusations that he financed his campaign through a slush fund kept him on the ticket.
LC NO. 75-702529
Prod-NYFLMS Dist-NYFLMS 1952

Njangaan C 80 MIN
16MM FILM OPTICAL SOUND
A Wolof language film with English subtitles. Tells the story of a boy enslaved by marabouts purportedly teaching him the Koran. Directed by Mahama Johnson Traore.
Prod-UNKNWN Dist-NYFLMS 1974

No Act Of God C 28 MIN
16MM FILM, 3/4 OR 1/2 IN VIDEO H-C A
Examines the topic of nuclear power, focusing on the problems of disposing of nuclear waste and the increasingly tight security that must be maintained to prevent plutonium from falling into the hands of terrorist groups.
LC NO. 82-707174
Prod-NFBC Dist-BULFRG 1978

No Arriesgue Vidas C 14 MIN
16MM FILM, 3/4 OR 1/2 IN VIDEO A
A Spanish-language version of the motion picture Don't Take Chances. Shows common factory accidents. Illustrates efforts made by management to prevent accidents, but warns they will still occur if workers are thoughtless.
Prod-IAPA Dist-IFB 1964

No Better Gift C 22 MIN
3/4 OR 1/2 INCH VIDEO CASSETTE
Provides guidelines for developing good eating habits and quality nutrition for young children.
Prod-SIMONJ Dist-SNUTRE

No Big Money C 15 MIN
16MM FILM, 3/4 OR 1/2 IN VIDEO C A
Tells how a family leaves big city life and goes to the wilderness. Explains that they are willing to endure unremitting labor and personal discomfort.
Prod-NFBC Dist-WOMBAT

No Brushes Today B 15 MIN
2 INCH VIDEOTAPE P
Explores ways of working with finger paints.
From The Art Corner Series.
Prod-CVETVC Dist-GPITVL Prodn-WCVETV

No Budget, Home Movies, Titles Film B 8 MIN
16MM FILM OPTICAL SOUND
Presents a pseudonarrative documentary comedy made without a budget.
LC NO. 77-703003
Prod-LIVNGN Dist-CANFDC 1975

No Comparison C 30 MIN
16MM FILM - 3/4 IN VIDEO
Explains that human differences are a desirable fact of life. Shows some of the ways in which children differ and tells how different responses can help or hinder a child's growth and development.
From The Footsteps Series.
LC NO. 79-707256
Prod-USOE Dist-USNAC 1976

No Cooperation C 6 MIN
16MM FILM OPTICAL SOUND
A dramatization in which a maintenance supervisor relives several situations in which his orders are countermanded by superiors, a subordinate goes over his head in asking for advancement and his subordinates object to working overtime.
LC NO. 79-706068
Prod-EPPI Dist-PSUPCR 1969

No Cop's A Hero - Until You Need One C 24 MIN
16MM FILM, 3/4 OR 1/2 IN VIDEO H A
Dramatizes a number of everyday situations that are potentially troublesome in police-community relations. Shows the problems from both the police and the civilian point of view.
Prod-CAHILL Dist-AIMS 1974

No Deferments In The Working World C 20 MIN
3/4 INCH VIDEO CASSETTE J-H
Focuses on two counseling sessions.
From The Dollar Data Series.
LC NO. 81-707383
Prod-WHROTV Dist-GPITVL 1974

No Easy Answers C 14 MIN
16MM FILM, 3/4 OR 1/2 IN VIDEO J-C A
Draws examples from agriculture, genetic control, meteorology, computer technology and bio-feedback to illustrate the roles of science in the progress of man and to show how everything in the universe is interrelated.
From The Science - New Frontiers Series.
Prod-CREEDM Dist-PHENIX 1974

No Easy Walk To Freedom C 60 MIN
3/4 OR 1/2 INCH VIDEO CASSETTE
Uses the speeches, writings and trial transcripts of Black South African leader Nelson Mandela to show his political odyssey from protest to violence in opposing apartheid.
From The Bill Moyers' Journal Series.
LC NO. 79-706946
Prod-WNETTV Dist-WNETTV 1979

No Easy Way C 29 MIN
16MM FILM OPTICAL SOUND
Tells the story of a union safety committee's investigation of a serious accident, which results in the discovery of unsafe working conditions. Explains how a safety committee should work.
LC NO. 80-700070
Prod-UWISCA Dist-UWISCA 1979

No Entry B 15 MIN
16MM FILM OPTICAL SOUND
Shows an experimental film which places events in the mundane world against events in a fantasy world.
LC NO. 76-701346
Prod-SFRASU Dist-SFRASU 1975

No Exceptions (A Film About Rape) C 24 MIN
16MM FILM, 3/4 OR 1/2 IN VIDEO J-C A
Deals with three aspects of rape, including how to prevent it from happening, what to do if it happens and what to do afterward.
Prod-FLMFR Dist-FLMFR Prodn-VITASC 1977

No Excuse Sir C 53 MIN
16MM FILM OPTICAL SOUND
Examines the role that the U S Military Academy at West Point plays in America's defense. Traces its history and explores it goals and expectations. Includes interviews with cadets, professors, officers trained at West Point, and critics of the academy.
LC NO. 80-701481
Prod-HUDRIV Dist-HUDRIV 1980

No First Use - Preventing Nuclear War C 30 MIN
16MM FILM, 3/4 OR 1/2 IN VIDEO
Asks and answers some of the most crucial questions in the debate over US and NATO defense policy.
Prod-UCS Dist-UCEMC 1983

No Fishing This Year - Care And Handling Of Drill Pipe, Drill Collars And Tool Joints C 25 MIN
16MM FILM, 3/4 OR 1/2 IN VIDEO IND
Tells what the rig crew can do to increase the life of the drill stem. Shows unloading the pipe at the rig, running it into and out of the hole and laying it down after the hole is finished.
Prod-UTEXPE Dist-UTEXPE 1980

No Fitting Habitat C 30 MIN
16MM FILM, 3/4 OR 1/2 IN VIDEO J-C
Offers a history of the city, discussing its origins, its development and its style. Begins with nomadic life and ends with 20th century cities in Africa, Europe and North America.
LC NO. 81-706029
Prod-NFBC Dist-TEXFLM 1980

No Frames, No Boundaries C 21 MIN
16MM FILM, 3/4 OR 1/2 IN VIDEO J-C A
Traces human civilization from the earliest examples of nomadic people to the point where city-states, their defense and weapons developed. Notes the fact that the world's major religions share a belief in the interdependence of people and urges the earth's inhabitants to admit their interdependence and to unite against the threat of nuclear annihilation.
Prod-CREATI Dist-CREATI 1982

No Fuelin' - We're Poolin' C 8 MIN
16MM FILM, 3/4 OR 1/2 IN VIDEO H-C A
Describes the role of the employer in vanpool programs, including carpool matching, driver selection and determining fares.
Prod-USDT Dist-USNAC 1976

No Game B 17 MIN
16MM FILM OPTICAL SOUND
An essay on the October 21st, 1967 Pentagon demonstration to end the war in Vietnam.
Prod-SFN Dist-SFN 1967

No Greater Challenge C 14 MIN
16MM FILM OPTICAL SOUND
Studies the challenge to man to provide sufficient food and water for the future, and the contribution to be made when nuclear-powered agro-industrial desalting complexes are able to convert arid coastal regions into fertile productive communities.
LC NO. 78-702835
Prod-USAEC Dist-USNAC Prodn-STAG 1969

No Greater Love B 74 MIN
3/4 OR 1/2 INCH VIDEO CASSETTE
Tells the World War II story of a Russian who turns her villagers into partisans for revenge against the Germans, who have killed her husband and infant son. Directed by Frederic Emler and starring Vera Maretskaya.
Prod-IHF Dist-IHF

No Greater Power B 24 MIN
16MM FILM OPTICAL SOUND P-C A
Dramatizes the story of Zacheus as recorded by Luke. Shows him as an impoverished potter who takes advantages of circumstances to eventually gain the exalted position of tax collector of Jericho.
Prod-CAFM Dist-CAFM

No Gun Towers, No Fences C 59 MIN
2 INCH VIDEOTAPE
See series title for descriptive statement.
From The Syngerism - Troubled Humanity Series.
Prod-WMVU Dist-PUBTEL

No Handouts For Mrs Hedgepeth X 27 MIN
16MM FILM, 3/4 OR 1/2 IN VIDEO H-C A
Shows the situation of a domestic worker in Durham, North Carolina, to illustrate why, in the world's richest country, a woman can work all her life and still be trapped in poverty.
Prod-NCFUND Dist-PHENIX 1968

No Handouts For Mrs Hedgepeth C 30 MIN
2 INCH VIDEOTAPE
Studies poverty expressed through the thoughts, opinions and dreams of a domestic worker as she moves back and forth between the shack she lives in and her employer's plush home.
Prod-NCFUND Dist-PUBTEL

No Harm In Logging C 18 MIN
16MM FILM OPTICAL SOUND IND
Demonstrates safety precautions in felling and handling timber, showing mechanzied handling methods in timber producing areas of Australia.
LC NO. 77-709257
Prod-ANAIB Dist-AUIS 1970

No Hold Bard - A Video Introduction To Shakespeare C 38 MIN
3/4 OR 1/2 INCH VIDEO CASSETTE
Offers a varied taste of Shakespeare's works by showing actors briskly changing costumes and characters as they quote the famous poet-dramatist. Presented in the manner of a television variety show.
Prod-WALCHJ Dist-WALCHJ

No In-Between - The Manic Depressive B 23 MIN
16MM FILM OPTICAL SOUND PRO
Presents an interview of a 50-year-old male manic depressive during an acutely manic phase of illness, and presents an interview that occurred six weeks later when the patient's behavior appears markedly different.
LC NO. 72-700629
Prod-UOKLA Dist-UOKLA 1970

No Injury, No Accident C 18 MIN
16MM FILM - 3/4 IN VIDEO
Shows how near misses and little incidents that often go unreported can suddenly trigger a major accident situation and se-

rious injuries. Explains the Heinrich Triangle and Theory, which suggests the number of major and minor injuries one can expect from 330 incidents, as well as the percentage of accidents that will result from unsafe acts and conditions. Presents steps to take when an incident occurs.
Prod-ALLIED Dist-BNA

No Jail Can Change Me B 30 MIN
16MM FILM, 3/4 OR 1/2 IN VIDEO
Interviews a black man who has spent most of his life since age 10 in correctional institutions. Deals with his search for masculine identity and control of his life.
Prod-UCEMC Dist-UCEMC

No Japs At My Funeral C 56 MIN
3/4 OR 1/2 INCH VIDEO CASSETTE
Relates the views of an ex-IRA bomber about war in Northern Ireland, politics and experiences. Intercuts contrasting views.
Prod-KITCHN Dist-KITCHN

No Laws Today C 12 MIN
16MM FILM, 3/4 OR 1/2 IN VIDEO I-J
Tells the story of the chaos which ensues when a day without laws is declared. Shows the importance of laws and rules for traffic, consumer affairs and even sports.
LC NO. 84-707309
Prod-GFILM Dist-JOU 1982

No Less A Woman C 23 MIN
3/4 OR 1/2 INCH VIDEO CASSETTE C A
Takes a long look at the problems of single and married women who are attempting to recover from the far-reaching effects of mastectomy.
Prod-MMRC Dist-MMRC

No Lies C 16 MIN
16MM FILM, 3/4 OR 1/2 IN VIDEO H-C A
Explores the problems of rape through the story of a girl who has been raped but feels increasingly guilty about having dropped the whole affair at the police station. Explains that a detective took an unnatural interest in the details of the rape, paralleling it to his wife's own sexual problems. Features Alec Hirschfeld and Shelby Leverington.
Prod-BLOCK Dist-DIRECT 1973

No Lies But C 15 MIN
2 INCH VIDEOTAPE J
Discusses the use of the hyperbole, understatement, paradox and irony in writing.
From The From Me To You...In Writing, Pt 2 Series.
Prod-DELE Dist-GPITVL

No Man Is An Island C 11 MIN
16MM FILM OPTICAL SOUND J-C A
Presents Orson Welles reciting John Donne's poem, 'NO MAN IS AN ISLAND.' Conveys the message 'BECAUSE I AM INVOLVED IN MANKIND' through scenes showing teenagers shaving bedridden patients and teachers feeding the retarded and handicapped.
LC NO. 73-702198
Prod-DANA Dist-DANA 1973

No Man Is An Island C 28 MIN
16MM FILM OPTICAL SOUND
Examines the work of the Salvation Army in helping solve the physical and spiritual problems of troubled people.
LC NO. 74-700625
Prod-SALVA Dist-SALVA 1973

No Man's Land C 26 MIN
3/4 OR 1/2 INCH VIDEO CASSETTE
Records the plight of a quarter-million Kampucheans who are trapped between their homeland and Thailand. Reveals that they cannot return because the Khmer Rouge regime which slaughtered three million of their countrymen is now part of the government.
Prod-GRATV Dist-FLMLIB 1984

No Maps On My Taps C 59 MIN
16MM FILM, 3/4 OR 1/2 IN VIDEO H-C A
Features veteran jazz tap dancing stars, including Bunny Briggs, Chuck Green and Sandman Sims, as they reminisce about their art and careers. Includes scenes of street corner challenge dancing and stills from the 1930's of legendary figures from tap dancing's heyday.
Prod-NIERNG Dist-DIRECT 1979

No Margin For Error C 25 MIN
16MM FILM OPTICAL SOUND
Describes the courses for training aviation safety officers taught at the University of Southern California. Includes scenes of classes in aeronautical engineering, accident investigation, aviation physiology and aviation psychology.
LC NO. FIA60-617
Prod-USC Dist-USC

No More Hibakusha C 55 MIN
16MM FILM, 3/4 OR 1/2 IN VIDEO
Looks at the experiences of the Hibakusha, survivors of the atomic bomb blast at Hiroshima and Nagasaki who now dedicate their lives to warning humanity about the dangers of nuclear war.
Prod-NFBC Dist-ICARUS 1983

No More Kings C 3 MIN
3/4 OR 1/2 INCH VIDEO CASSETTE P-I
Traces the Pilgrims' flight to the New World, showing American Colonists breaking from King George III and fighting to rule themselves freely.
From The America Rock Series.
Prod-ABCTV Dist-GA Prodn-SCOROC 1976

No More Mountains - The Story Of The Hmong C 58 MIN
3/4 OR 1/2 INCH VIDEO CASSETTE
Tells of a small group of mountain people in Vietnam, who called themselves the Hmong, and were recruited by the CIA. After the war the Americans went home and the Hmong were driven from their homes by the Vietnamese government.
From The World Series.
Prod-WGBHTV Dist-PBS 1981

No More Secrets C 13 MIN
16MM FILM, 3/4 OR 1/2 IN VIDEO P-I
Depicts children in circumstances involving various degrees of abuse. Introduces solutions that enable children to articulate feelings and defend themselves against victimization.
Prod-ODNP Dist-ODNP 1982

No Name Show, The C 30 MIN
3/4 OR 1/2 INCH VIDEO CASSETTE
Presents basically crazy cooks Larry Bly and Laban Johnson who offer recipes, cooking and shopping tips.
From The Cookin' Cheap Series.
Prod-WBRATV Dist-MDCPB

No Need To Hide C 55 MIN
16MM FILM OPTICAL SOUND R
Traces the background of former gang leader, Nicky Cruz from his unhappy childhood to his discovery of Christ.
Prod-GF Dist-GF

No Neutral Ground - Cambodia And Laos C 60 MIN
3/4 OR 1/2 INCH VIDEO CASSETTE H-C A
Reveals that the U S extension of the Vietnam War into Laos and Cambodia to stop attacks and supplies from across those borders hurt those countries more than it hurt the object of the attack. Shows that Prince Sihanouk of Cambodia was overthrown and he joined the Khmers Rouges.
From The Vietnam - A Television History Series. Episode 9
Prod-WGBHTV Dist-FI 1983

No News Is Bad News C 14 MIN
16MM FILM OPTICAL SOUND
Shows the key selling points of a newspaper and portrays what life might be like without the newspapers.
LC NO. 79-700252
Prod-CZC Dist-CZC Prodn-COHENF 1979

No Nos Moveran C 25 MIN
3/4 OR 1/2 INCH VIDEO CASSETTE
Examines the Mexican-American population in the Twin Cities, an urban sub-culture which is the largest minority in Minnesota. Reveals where they have come from and why they have chosen to live in Minnesota.
Prod-WCCOTV Dist-WCCOTV 1976

No One Else Can Do It B 10 MIN
16MM FILM OPTICAL SOUND
A foreman learns that only he can do the basic job of preventing accidents by teaching workers, watching for hazards and anticipating problems.
From The Safety And The Foreman Series.
LC NO. FIA67-155
Prod-NSC Dist-NSC Prodn-SARRA 1957

No One Like Me C 15 MIN
3/4 INCH VIDEO CASSETTE P
Explains how thinking and feeling interact to make up independent action. Encourages investigation and reflection upon the actions of people. Emphasizes that the ability to think and feel makes each person unique.
From The Becoming Me, Unit 3 - Emotional Identity Series.
Prod-KUONTV Dist-GPITVL 1974

No One Stays A Child C 14 MIN
16MM FILM OPTICAL SOUND
Pictures a day at Camp Highfields in Onondaga, Michigan, following some of the boys through a variety of everyday activities. Includes comments by the camp director on the philosophy of the institution.
LC NO. 76-700393
Prod-JRLL Dist-CIASP Prodn-CIASP 1975

No One Told Me C 8 MIN
16MM FILM OPTICAL SOUND H-C A
Points out some of the advantages of suggestion selling as a service which contributes to customer satisfaction. Illustrates opportunities for multiple sales.
From The Professional Selling Practices Series 2 Series.
LC NO. 77-702355
Prod-SAUM Dist-SAUM Prodn-CALPRO 1968

No Other Choice C 60 MIN
16MM FILM OPTICAL SOUND
Shows how three men sabotage a weapons' research center and are forced to hide out in the home of a professor, an old friend. Reveals distances between them and questions the real terms of the revolutionary consciousness.
Prod-MACHOR Dist-NEWSR

No Other Generation - Twelve Voices From The Thirty-Seventh Year Of The Nuclear Age C 35 MIN
3/4 OR 1/2 INCH VIDEO CASSETTE
Presents the personal and political thinking of twelve speakers who call upon us to protect life itself from 'threatened planetary extinction.' Features Ram Dass and Daniel Ellsberg.
From The How Then Shall We Live? Series.
Prod-ORGNLF Dist-ORGNLF

No Other Love C 58 MIN
16MM FILM, 3/4 OR 1/2 IN VIDEO I-C A
Presents the story of two marginally retarded young adults who fall in love and plan to get married, only to have to overcome the objections of their families and friends. Shows that the mentally retarded have emotional needs and a right to achieve their potential and independence. Stars Richard Thomas and Julie Kavner.
From The Teenage Years Series.
Prod-TISAVN Dist-TIMLIF 1979

No Other Source C 16 MIN
3/4 OR 1/2 INCH VIDEO CASSETTE
Tells how a young man was too busy to give blood until he discovered how simple it is to donate. Features a boy who is able to recover from a blood disease, thanks in part to blood transfusions.
Prod-AMRC Dist-AMRC

No Place Like Home C 58 MIN
3/4 OR 1/2 INCH VIDEO CASSETTE H-C A
Reports on nursing homes and on a range of alternative approaches to long-term care for the aged, including home care, day care and congregate living. Hosted by Helen Hayes.
LC NO. 82-706432
Prod-WNETTV Dist-FI 1981

No Place Like Home—A Series

Prod-USSRS Dist-USNAC 1979

Bars On Windows	028 MIN
From The Attic	028 MIN
Front Porch	028 MIN
Homebound, The	028 MIN
Homewrecker	028 MIN
House Of Cards	028 MIN
Neighbors	028 MIN
Nursing Home	028 MIN
Open Door, The	028 MIN
Silent Walls	028 MIN

No Place To Be Me C 15 MIN
16MM FILM, 3/4 OR 1/2 IN VIDEO I-J
Depicts a day in the life of a 12-year old boy who is a son of war refugees living in the Somalian desert. Shows how his day begins with Moslem prayers to Allah, includes two hours of rote learning at school, and the rest of his day consists of helping his mother search for fuel, visiting the market and playing briefly with friends.
From The Just One Child Series.
Prod-REYEXP Dist-BCNFL 1983

No Place To Hide C 30 MIN
16MM FILM, 3/4 OR 1/2 IN VIDEO H-C A
Contrasts actual civil defense films of the 1950s with film clips of the atomic devastation of Japan to show how naive the American of the 1950s were in believing the United States government's claims that protection against an atomic attack was as simple as hiding beneath a school desk. Presents actor Martin Sheen re-creating the feelings of a cold-war child and berates the government for minimizing the American people's awareness of the horrors of atomic warfare.
Prod-MEDSTD Dist-DIRECT 1982

No Points For Second Place C 28 MIN
16MM FILM - 3/4 IN VIDEO
Explores the history of fighter aircraft from World War I to the F-14.
Prod-WSTGLC Dist-WSTGLC

No Prenez Pas De Risques C 14 MIN
16MM FILM, 3/4 OR 1/2 IN VIDEO A
A French-language version of the motion picture Don't Take Chances. Shows common factory accidents. Illustrates efforts made by management to prevent accidents, but warns they will still occur if workers are thoughtless.
Prod-IAPA Dist-IFB 1964

No Questions Asked C 19 MIN
16MM FILM, 3/4 OR 1/2 IN VIDEO
Deals with unsafe trenches in the building industry. Concentrates on one accident and the events leading up to it. Shows procedures for accident investigations.
Prod-NFBTE Dist-IFB

No Real Pathology B 21 MIN
16MM FILM OPTICAL SOUND PRO
Describes the techniques in differential diagnosis to determine whether underlying cause is depression or anxiety in patients without symptom-related pathology.
Prod-UPJOHN Dist-UPJOHN 1962

No Respecter Of Persons X 17 MIN
16MM FILM OPTICAL SOUND J-H T R
Presents the story of Peter who preaches Christ to the house of Cornelius. Shows the universality of the Gospel and its application to all people regardless of race and nationality.
From The Book Of Acts Series.
Prod-BROADM Dist-FAMF 1957

No Room At The Inn C 13 MIN
16MM FILM, 3/4 OR 1/2 IN VIDEO I-C A
Presents an animated retelling of the traditional Nativity story based on the book No Room At The Inn by R O Blechman.
From The Simple Gifts Series.
Prod-WNETTV Dist-TIMLIF

No Room For Error C 18 MIN
16MM FILM, 3/4 OR 1/2 IN VIDEO I-H
Stresses safety awareness for students in school chemistry lab. Former teacher who became a human torch urges proper care.
Prod-BORTF Dist-BCNFL 1983

No Room For Weeds C 24 MIN
16MM FILM OPTICAL SOUND
Describes in detail the modern weed control. Illustrates the development and use of herbicides.
Prod-UPR Dist-UPR 1969

No Rouz C 20 MIN
16MM FILM OPTICAL SOUND

Depicts the most important of Iranian festivals, No Rouz, the Iranian New Year, which derives from the ancient Persian festival of spring. Explains the significance of each ritual of the two week festival. Illustrates the preparation of special foods and portrays the fire jumping of Scharharshanbe Suri.
Prod-FRAF Dist-FRAF

No Sad Songs C 10 MIN
16MM FILM OPTICAL SOUND
Depicts four people whose lives were improved as a result of the Cummins Engine Company charity fund.
LC NO. 80-701450
Prod-RICHMA Dist-RICHMA 1979

No Sad Songs For Me B 88 MIN
16MM FILM OPTICAL SOUND
Stars Margaret Sullivan as a dying woman who cheerfully carries on with her everyday routines, as well as choosing her husband's next wife.
Prod-CPC Dist-KITPAR 1950

No Simple Road C 18 MIN
3/4 INCH VIDEO CASSETTE P-C A
Shows handicapped children participating in outdoor sports and activities. Helps youngsters to accept their disabilities, gain self confidence and react positively to their able-bodied peers.
LC NO. 84-706147
Prod-LENATK Dist-CRYSP

No Smoking B 8 MIN
16MM FILM OPTICAL SOUND
Presents an internal monologue by a commuter riding home on the train. Shows how a headline about smoking causing cancer sets him to thinking about smoking, and leads into some thoughts about making your own decisions, not just about smoking, but in other areas of choice. Suggests that the choice may not be as free as they seem.
Prod-UPENN Dist-UPENN 1964

No Smoking, Please C
3/4 OR 1/2 INCH VIDEO CASSETTE
Uses humor to announce that no smoking is allowed. Presents a boss forbidding smoking in an extreme and explosive manner.
Prod-BBB Dist-MEETS Prodn-CFDC

No Snow B 14 MIN
16MM FILM OPTICAL SOUND
Tells how a young man returns from college to his hometown, reunites with an old buddy, and is forced to confront the values he grew up with.
LC NO. 79-700253
Prod-JEFRES Dist-JEFRES 1978

No Strings On You C 15 MIN
3/4 OR 1/2 INCH VIDEO CASSETTE P
Uses a dancing marionette clown to show the muscles of the human body. Considers muscles as bands that hold the framework of the body together and make movement possible. Explains why exercise is important.
From The All About You Series.
Prod-NITC Dist-AITECH Prodn-TTOIC 1975

No Sugar Coating C 17 MIN
16MM FILM OPTICAL SOUND
Follows a medical social worker, who is diabetic, as he helps young people understand and accept the illness of diabetes.
LC NO. 79-701181
Prod-ADAS Dist-ADAS Prodn-TAPPRD 1979

No Swimming B 16 MIN
16MM FILM OPTICAL SOUND
Explores 'FREEDOM,' made at a beach resort in the dead of winter. Examines freedom from meaningless rules, and freedom to explore and to play.
Prod-UPENN Dist-UPENN 1965

No Talking C 6 MIN
16MM FILM, 3/4 OR 1/2 IN VIDEO P
Introduces Lester, who can't talk but still manages to buy a birthday present for his mother.
From The Golden Book Storytime Series.
Prod-MTI Dist-MTI 1977

No Tears For Kelsey X 28 MIN
16MM FILM, 3/4 OR 1/2 IN VIDEO H-C A
Focuses on the relationship between a 14-year-old chronic runaway and her parents.
Prod-PAULST Dist-MEDIAG

No Tears For Kelsey (Spanish) X 28 MIN
16MM FILM, 3/4 OR 1/2 IN VIDEO H-C A
Focuses on the relationship between a 14-year-old chronic runaway and her parents.
From The Insight Series.
Prod-PAULST Dist-PAULST

No Tears For Rachel C 27 MIN
16MM FILM, 3/4 OR 1/2 IN VIDEO J-C A
Explains and illustrates how the law functions and how friends and family react when a woman has been raped. Portrays one victim who discusses the difficulties she experienced when she told her friends that she had been raped and her psychiatrist who explains the importance of their reactions and the stigma associated with being raped.
LC NO. 80-707089
Prod-EDUCBC Dist-IU 1974

No Tenia Por Que Suceder B 13 MIN
16MM FILM, 3/4 OR 1/2 IN VIDEO H A
A Spanish-language version of the motion picture It Didn't Have To Happen. Illustrates how the careless worker who scorns safety devices on modern machinery endangers not only his life but also the lives of fellow workers.
Prod-CRAF Dist-IFB 1954

No Thanks, I'm Driving C 16 MIN
16MM FILM, 3/4 OR 1/2 IN VIDEO H-C A
Presents pilots and racers who explain their guidelines for use of alcohol. Uses animated sequences to follow the path of alcohol in the bloodstream. Employs mime performers to show how situations regarding alcohol may be met and handled by young drivers.
From The Three For The Road Series.
Prod-OMTC Dist-IFB

No Trespassing (Privacy) C 15 MIN
16MM FILM, 3/4 OR 1/2 IN VIDEO J
Shows what one young man does to try to have privacy. Discusses an individual's need for privacy and what happens when opportunities for privacy are denied.
From The Self Incorporated Series.
LC NO. 75-703953
Prod-AITV Dist-AITECH Prodn-NVETA 1975

No Trump Bidding And Play C 30 MIN
3/4 OR 1/2 INCH VIDEO CASSETTE A
See series title for descriptive statement.
From The Play Bridge Series.
Prod-KYTV Dist-KYTV 1983

No Trump Bids And Responses C 30 MIN
3/4 OR 1/2 INCH VIDEO CASSETTE A
See series title for descriptive statement.
From The Bridge Basics Series.
Prod-KYTV Dist-KYTV 1982

No Two Alike C 15 MIN
3/4 OR 1/2 INCH VIDEO CASSETTE P
Explains that each person is a unique individual.
From The All About You Series.
Prod-WGBHTV Dist-AITECH Prodn-TTOIC 1975

No Two Alike C 19 MIN
16MM FILM, 3/4 OR 1/2 IN VIDEO C A
Examines how to meet the educational needs of visually handicapped students.
Prod-AFB Dist-PHENIX 1981

No Two Alike - Individual Differences And Psychological Testing B 29 MIN
16MM FILM, 3/4 OR 1/2 IN VIDEO H-C A
Explores some of the ways in which psychologists are developing new testing methods for measuring and increasing human capabilities. Demonstrates the development of tests for choosing pilots in World War II.
From The Focus On Behavior Series.
Prod-NET Dist-IU 1963

No Two Of These Kids Are Alike C 28 MIN
16MM FILM OPTICAL SOUND
Observes the day-to-day routine of the League School for seriously disturbed children. Shows how teachers in special education, supported by a staff of full-time clinicians, seek to provide as normal a schooling as possible for these withdrawn and often unmanageable children.
From The League School For Seriously Disturbed Children Series.
LC NO. 75-702412
Prod-USBEH Dist-USNAC 1973

No Unskilled 'I' In Industry C 15 MIN
2 INCH VIDEOTAPE J-H
Points out that as production increases in our growing economy, the need for skilled workers will also increase. Covers the jobs of mechanics, vocational instructors, electricians and machinists.
From The Work Is For Real Series.
Prod-STETVC Dist-GPITVL

No Vietnamese Ever Called Me Nigger C 68 MIN
16MM FILM, 3/4 OR 1/2 IN VIDEO
Interviews Harlem residents and Black Vietnam veterans as they speak out against the war in Vietnam, linking it to domestic racial crisis.
Prod-AMDOC Dist-CNEMAG

No Way C 20 MIN
16MM FILM, 3/4 OR 1/2 IN VIDEO H-C A
Points out that access to mass communication media by most members of the general public is limited. Discusses some alternative means of access, showing that major difficulties involve finding economic support and generating popular understanding.
From The Viewpoint Series.
Prod-THAMES Dist-MEDIAG 1975

No Wreath And No Trumpet B 30 MIN
16MM FILM OPTICAL SOUND
Tells the story of Emma Lazarus, the American Jewish poetess, whose verses are inscribed on the base of the Statue of Liberty. (Kinescope)
Prod-JTS Dist-NAAJS Prodn-NBCTV 1961

No. 1 C 10 MIN
16MM FILM, 3/4 OR 1/2 IN VIDEO I-C A
Offers a cinematic view of the game of soccer and the activities of the soccer goalie who is considered player number one on the team.
Prod-KRECK Dist-TEXFLM 1975

No-Fault Insurance / Panty Hose / Homebuying C
3/4 OR 1/2 INCH VIDEO CASSETTE
Discusses various aspects of no-fault insurance, panty hose and homebuying.
From The Consumer Survival Series.
Prod-MDCPB Dist-MDCPB

No-Nonsense Delegation C 30 MIN
16MM FILM, 3/4 OR 1/2 IN VIDEO
Dramatizes various situations in which managers should delegate authority and responsibility and explains the four keys to effective delegation.
Prod-CREMED Dist-CREMED

No-Wax Floors C 30 MIN
1/2 IN VIDEO CASSETTE BETA/VHS
Gives pointers on laying a no-wax floor.
From The This Old House, Pt 2 - Suburban '50s Series.
Prod-WGBHTV Dist-MTI

No, But I Saw The Movie C 12 MIN
16MM FILM OPTICAL SOUND
Provides a humorous approach to the history of recorded communication from cave paintings and the clay tablet to modern art and microfilm. Explores the resources of the modern library.
LC NO. FIA65-419
Prod-SILLU Dist-SIUFP 1961

Noah C 20 MIN
16MM FILM OPTICAL SOUND S R
Shows the Noah story from Genesis told by Mr Louie J Fant in AMESLAN (American Sign Language.)
From The Fant Anthology Of AMESLAN Literature Series.
LC NO. 74-701458
Prod-JOYCE Dist-JOYCE 1973

Noah And The Rainbow C 7 MIN
16MM FILM, 3/4 OR 1/2 IN VIDEO P-I
Presents the story of Noahs's ark and emphasizes the meaning of the rainbow as a sign of God's love for everyone.
Prod-MANTEL Dist-MCFI 1972

Noah Of The North C 29 MIN
16MM FILM OPTICAL SOUND
Traces Al Oeming's interest in wildlife since the age of six and recaptures the mood and locations of his boyhood.
From The Al Oeming - Man Of The North Series.
LC NO. 77-702871
Prod-NIELSE Dist-NIELSE 1977

Noah's Animals C 27 MIN
16MM FILM, 3/4 OR 1/2 IN VIDEO P
Presents the story of Noah and the flood from the animal's viewpoint.
Prod-LUF Dist-LUF 1979

Noah's Ark C 24 MIN
16MM FILM, 3/4 OR 1/2 IN VIDEO P-J
Presents an animated adaptation of the story of Noah and his ark with cartoon character Mr Magoo in the role of Noah.
Prod-UPAPOA Dist-MCFI 1969

Noah's Ark - L'Arche De Noe C 10 MIN
16MM FILM, 3/4 OR 1/2 IN VIDEO J-C
Presents an animated tale, without narration, about a group of scientists who attempt to climb a high mountain where they hope to find the remains of Noah's ark.
LC NO. 77-701531
Prod-LESFG Dist-TEXFLM 1977

Noah's Ark - Multiplying With Fractions C 9 MIN
3/4 INCH VIDEO CASSETTE P
Tells how Noah's animals figure out how to diagram an area which is 1/4 mile wide and 1/2 mile long.
Prod-DAVFMS Dist-GA

Noah's Park C 27 MIN
16MM FILM, 3/4 OR 1/2 IN VIDEO I-C A
Presents an adventure film about Israel's efforts to save and proliferate the Biblical animals that lived before the flood in Noah's time.
Prod-PHENIX Dist-PHENIX 1976

Nobel Prizewinners—A Series
16MM FILM, 3/4 OR 1/2 IN VIDEO J-C A
Looks at the careers of six Nobel prizewinners.
Prod-CFDLD Dist-CORF

Alfred Nobel - The Merchant Of Death	027 MIN
Ernest Hemingway - Rough Diamond	030 MIN
Marie Curie - A Love Story	032 MIN
Martin Luther King Jr - The Assassin Years	026 MIN
Rudyard Kipling - The Road From Mandalay	030 MIN
Theodore Roosevelt - Cowboy In The White House	029 MIN

Noble Venture, A C 28 MIN
16MM FILM OPTICAL SOUND
Describes the vital area of conservation work, the protection and propagation of exotic game. Shows that as exotic game conservation programs spread throughout the United States, brood stock can then be provided for many such endangered species all over the world.
Prod-CMD Dist-GM

Nobody But Yourself—A Series
J
Prod-WQED Dist-GPITVL

Do Not Staple, Bend Or Fold	20 MIN
It's Your Move	20 MIN
Truth And Consequences	20 MIN
Ups, Downs, Ins, Outs	20 MIN
Who Am I Where Are You	20 MIN
You	20 MIN

Nobody Ever Died Of Old Age C 61 MIN
16MM FILM OPTICAL SOUND H-C A
Uses both serious and humorous character studies to show what it is like to grow old in the United States in the 1970s. Dramatizes the lives of a number of resourcefully independent senior citizens who are struggling to survive in a youth-oriented society.

LC NO. 76-700394
Prod-HSSETT Dist-FI 1977

Nobody Likes A Bully C 15 MIN
16MM FILM, 3/4 OR 1/2 IN VIDEO P-J
Shows how Slappy bullies the other kids until Fat Albert makes him stop and urges the gang to offer him friendship.
From The Fat Albert And The Cosby Kids Series III Series.
Prod-BARR Dist-BARR Prodn-FLMTON 1979

Nobody Lives Here C 27 MIN
3/4 OR 1/2 INCH VIDEO CASSETTE
Presents interviews with inmates at Washington State Penitentiary. Emphasizes the sense of confinement and the desire to escape mentally or physically.
Prod-MEDIPR Dist-MEDIPR 1979

Nobody Took The Time B 26 MIN
16MM FILM, 3/4 OR 1/2 IN VIDEO T
Depicts ghetto children handicapped with learning disabilities and most often labeled mentally retarded. Demonstrates that basic trust in himself and others is their first need. Shows how highly structured classroom and playground techniques result in an understanding of order and development of language.
Prod-AIMS Dist-AIMS 1973

Nobody Treats Me Different C 8 MIN
16MM FILM, 3/4 OR 1/2 IN VIDEO P-I
Tells how a boy with cerebral palsy takes part in many activities.
From The Zoom Series.
Prod-WGBHTV Dist-FI

Nobody's Fault C 19 MIN
16MM FILM, 3/4 OR 1/2 IN VIDEO
Shows a succession of seemingly minor incidents in a manufacturing plant which add up to a major accident and fire.
Prod-MILLBK Dist-IFB

Nobody's Perfect C 24 MIN
16MM FILM, 3/4 OR 1/2 IN VIDEO
Shows a scientist whose careless actions in the laboratory continually jeopardize the work and safety of his colleagues and himself. Stresses conscientious attitudes towards safety.
LC NO. 80-707333
Prod-USNIH Dist-USNAC 1980

Nobody's Useless C 29 MIN
16MM FILM, 3/4 OR 1/2 IN VIDEO I-J
Shows how Tom convinces a young amputee that the challenge of overcoming a handicap can be met with humor and courage. Adapted from a portion of the children's book The Great Brain by John D Fitzgerald.
LC NO. 83-707146
Prod-OSCP Dist-EBEC 1980

Nobody's Victim C 20 MIN
16MM FILM, 3/4 OR 1/2 IN VIDEO J-C A
Offers suggestions on avoiding assault, injury, harrassment and robbery. Demonstrates physical defense skills that women can use against would-be attackers.
Prod-RAMFLM Dist-FLMFR

Nobody's Victim 2 C 24 MIN
16MM FILM, 3/4 OR 1/2 IN VIDEO J A
Presents a positive approach to women's self-protection. Gives the latest advice on personal preparedness.
Prod-RAMFLM Dist-SUTHRB 1978

Nobu Fukui - Contemporary Artist C 29 MIN
3/4 INCH VIDEO CASSETTE
Interviews a leading contemporary artist who refuses to discuss what his paintings mean and explains why.
Prod-UMITV Dist-UMITV 1974

Noche Cubana C 30 MIN
3/4 OR 1/2 INCH VIDEO CASSETTE
See series title for descriptive statement.
From The Que Pasa, U S A Series.
Prod-WPBTTV Dist-MDCPB

Nodder, The C 30 MIN
3/4 OR 1/2 INCH VIDEO CASSETTE C A
Presents an adaptation of the short story The Nodder by P G Wodehouse.
From The Wodehouse Playhouse Series.
Prod-BBCTV Dist-TIMLIF 1980

Noel Nutels C 30 MIN
16MM FILM, 3/4 OR 1/2 IN VIDEO
Presents an account of the life and work of Noel Nutels, a Jewish immigrant who dedicated himself to the problems of health and preventive medicine in the Brazilian jungles, particularly in the areas occupied by the Indians. Deals with the history of the government agency for Indian Affairs, the political processes affecting the Indian territories and the harm created by contact with the whites.
Prod-ALTBEM Dist-CNEMAG

Noel's Lemonade Stand (Ujamaa) C 9 MIN
16MM FILM, 3/4 OR 1/2 IN VIDEO K-I
Shows how a young sidewalk entrepreneur, having slow sales, was helped by a neighbor suggesting he offer homemade cookies with the lemonade. Concludes by relating how he bought bulked goods from many neighbors, thus all benefited from the combined effort.
From The Nguzo Saba-Folklore For Children Series.
Prod-NGUZO Dist-BCNFL 1983

Noh Drama, The - Hagoromo C 43 MIN
16MM FILM OPTICAL SOUND
Presents a transcendent drama about a fisherman and an angel.
Prod-KAJIMA Dist-UNIJAP 1968

Noise C 9 MIN
3/4 OR 1/2 INCH VIDEO CASSETTE
Encourages employees to wear hearing protection devices where necessary to prevent premature deafness.
Prod-FLMAUS Dist-FILCOM

Noise C 10 MIN
16MM FILM, 3/4 OR 1/2 IN VIDEO I
Describes various types of noise familiar to young children and raises the questions, what is the difference between sound and noise, how much does noise affect the quality of our lives and how much noise can we tolerate.
Prod-DICD Dist-PHENIX 1970

Noise C 20 MIN
16MM FILM, 3/4 OR 1/2 IN VIDEO
Explains sound and recommends methods of reducing noise levels. Uses animated diagrams to show the components of the ear and demonstrate how sound waves are transmitted through the ear. Illustrates how sound waves are measured.
Prod-NCBD Dist-IFB

Noise - Polluting The Environment X 15 MIN
16MM FILM, 3/4 OR 1/2 IN VIDEO J-C
Considers some of the ways of alleviating the noise polluters. Shows researchers working to lower the noise level because of its possible psychological effects.
From The Environmental Studies Series.
Prod-OMEGA Dist-EBEC 1971

Noise - Polluting The Environment (Spanish) C 16 MIN
16MM FILM, 3/4 OR 1/2 IN VIDEO I-H
Exposes various noise pollutants and shows how they affect man's life by threatening hearing and psychological stability.
From The Environmental Studies (Spanish) Series.
Prod-EBEC Dist-EBEC

Noise - The New Pollutant B 30 MIN
16MM FILM OPTICAL SOUND H-C A
Presents several research projects into the harmful effect of noise on human beings. Dr Vern O Knudsen demonstrates the nature of sound and explains the sensation of hearing.
From The Spectrum Series.
Prod-NET Dist-IU 1967

Noise Abatement C 45 MIN
3/4 OR 1/2 INCH VIDEO CASSETTE
Presents a step-by-step noise control program that includes planning, measurement, surveys, engineering, implementation and follow up. Includes a description of the program General Motors Corporation has developed in conforming to the noise exposure limits set by the federal government.
Prod-SME Dist-SME Prodn-GMI

Noise Analysis Continued C 50 MIN
3/4 OR 1/2 INCH VIDEO CASSETTE PRO
See series title for descriptive statement.
From The Optical Fiber Communications Series.
Prod-NCSU Dist-AMCEE

Noise And Its Effects On Health C 20 MIN
16MM FILM, 3/4 OR 1/2 IN VIDEO J-C A
Focuses on the adverse affects of noise and explains its effects on human physiology and psychology.
Prod-FLMFR Dist-FLMFR

Noise Control In The Chemical, Petroleum And Plastics Industry C 38 MIN
3/4 OR 1/2 INCH VIDEO CASSETTE IND
Covers state-of-the-art solutions for noise control of valves, piping, vents to atmosphere, furnaces, fans, elevated floors, pumps, electric motors, cooling towers, heaters, airfin coolers, engines, aspirators, sheeter, mills, gear systems and materials handling. Shows engineering approaches to noise problems in the rubber and plastics industry.
From The Industrial Noise Control, Part II - Applications Series.
LC NO. 81-707500
Prod-AMCEE Dist-AMCEE 1981

Noise Control In The Food Industry C 47 MIN
3/4 OR 1/2 INCH VIDEO CASSETTE IND
Assesses special FDA and USDA requirements for noise control in food plants, along with noise control solutions for common noise situations found in the food industry, including meat packing plants, poultry plants, dairies, vegetable and fruit canners, material handling, beverage bottling and canning and nut processing.
From The Industrial Noise Control, Part II - Applications Series.
LC NO. 81-707500
Prod-AMCEE Dist-AMCEE 1981

Noise Control In The Metal Industry C 46 MIN
3/4 OR 1/2 INCH VIDEO CASSETTE IND
Shows state-of-the-art engineering approaches to the general types of noise problems found in metal fabrication plants, steel mills and foundries.
From The Industrial Noise Control, Part II - Applications Series.
LC NO. 81-707500
Prod-AMCEE Dist-AMCEE 1981

Noise Control In The Paper And Wood Products Industry C 33 MIN
3/4 OR 1/2 INCH VIDEO CASSETTE IND
Covers latest technology to reduce noise from most sources in papermills and the wood products industry.
From The Industrial Noise Control, Part II - Applications Series.
LC NO. 81-707500
Prod-AMCEE Dist-AMCEE 1981

Noise Is Pollution Too C 15 MIN
16MM FILM, 3/4 OR 1/2 IN VIDEO I-H
Points out that man-made noise seriously endangers hearing and psychological health. Demonstrates the types of dangerous noise that people are exposed to and illustrates ways in which people can protect themselves against this noise.
Prod-WER Dist-JOU 1971

Noise Is Pollution Too (Spanish) C 15 MIN
16MM FILM, 3/4 OR 1/2 IN VIDEO I-H
Points out that man-made noise seriously endangers hearing and psychological health. Demonstrates the types of dangerous noise that people are exposed to and illustrates ways in which people can protect themselves against this noise.
Prod-WER Dist-JOU 1971

Noise Management C 43 MIN
3/4 OR 1/2 INCH VIDEO CASSETTE IND
Covers legal and economic aspects of an industrial noise control program, establishing priorities, OSHA compliance strategies, how to determine feasibility, cost/benefit analysis, estimating noise control costs, new legal precedents and what to do if cited by OSHA for noise.
From The Industrial Noise Control, Part I - Fundamentals Series.
LC NO. 81-707500
Prod-AMCEE Dist-AMCEE 1981

Noise Not Sound C 11 MIN
16MM FILM, 3/4 OR 1/2 IN VIDEO P-J
Depicts particular nature of sound pollution, traces historical background, scientific experimentation and explores solutions.
Prod-ATLAP Dist-ATLAP 1973

Noise Pollution C 18 MIN
16MM FILM, 3/4 OR 1/2 IN VIDEO J-H
Demonstrates the nature of sound and noise and the difference between them. Sees the effects of noise pollution as damaging to the ear, psychologically damaging to the individual and physically damaging to structures and changes in the ecology. Shows how the atmosphere affects the propagation of sound, including effects of wind velocity and temperature reflection, refraction and absorption.
From The Environmental Sciences Series.
Prod-LCOA Dist-LCOA 1972

Noise Pollution (Captioned) C 18 MIN
16MM FILM, 3/4 OR 1/2 IN VIDEO J-C A
Combines physics, biology and meteorology to study the effects of noise on the human ear and mind. Shows how noise pollution is responsible for changing physical structures and creating ecological imbalances.
Prod-LCOA Dist-LCOA 1972

Noise Presentation C 10 MIN
16MM FILM OPTICAL SOUND
Presents various sources of noise pollution, showing how the noise levels range from quiet sounds to some which are extremely loud.
LC NO. 75-701719
Prod-USNBOS Dist-USNAC 1972

Noise Was Deafening, The C 21 MIN
16MM FILM, 3/4 OR 1/2 IN VIDEO
Emphasizes the irreversible effects of excessive noise on hearing, shows how noise surveys can be conducted and points out some methods for noise reduction.
Prod-MILLBK Dist-IFB

Noise? You're In Control C 11 MIN
3/4 OR 1/2 INCH VIDEO CASSETTE
Teaches the effects of not using hearing protection, different types of hearing protection available and motivation for employees to comply with company's commitment to hearing protection.
Prod-EDRF Dist-EDRF

Noises In The Night C 9 MIN
16MM FILM, 3/4 OR 1/2 IN VIDEO P-I
Presents the story of Sherri who feared noises she heard in the dark and her parents who try to help her understand that night noises are made by familiar things.
Prod-BOSUST Dist-PHENIX 1969

Noisy Landscape, The C 15 MIN
16MM FILM OPTICAL SOUND
Examines the need for a sensible process of sign control to keep back the 'jungle of signs' that obliterate the approaches to most cities and business districts. Shows how signs and well planned graphics can add to the beauty of the community.
Prod-AIA Dist-AIA

Noisy Underwater World Of The Weddell Seal, The C 11 MIN
16MM FILM, 3/4 OR 1/2 IN VIDEO P-H
Shows the weddell seal under Antarctic ice. Reports the strange sounds of the seal as picked up on hydrophones by a team of biologists and bio-acousticians.
Prod-NYZS Dist-SF 1966

Noli Me Tangere C 6 MIN
3/4 OR 1/2 INCH VIDEO CASSETTE
Combines sexual and technological anxieties in a single obsessive image.
Prod-KITCHN Dist-KITCHN

Nomads Of Iran C 13 MIN
16MM FILM, 3/4 OR 1/2 IN VIDEO I-J
Reveals the self-reliant, isolated existance of the Quashagai, a united and colorful tribe of the Zagros Mountains in Iran.
From The Middle East Series.
Prod-WULFFR Dist-AIMS 1976

Nomads Of The Rainforest C 59 MIN
16MM FILM - VIDEO, ALL FORMATS
Presents an anthropological study of the Waorani people of the Amazonian rainforests of eastern Ecuador.
Prod-BBCTV Dist-DOCEDR

Nomads On The Move C 15 MIN
3/4 OR 1/2 INCH VIDEO CASSETTE I
Shows nomadic Bedouins moving to a new home.

From The Encounter In The Desert Series.
Prod-CTI Dist-CTI

Nominating Process, The C 30 MIN
3/4 OR 1/2 INCH VIDEO CASSETTE C
Stresses the tremendous amount of organization required to nominate candidates for political office. Includes an overview of the evolution of our election process over the last 200 years, with several specific examples of political elections.
From The American Government 1 Series.
Prod-DALCCD Dist-DALCCD

Nomination Of Abraham Lincoln, The C 22 MIN
16MM FILM, 3/4 OR 1/2 IN VIDEO I-J
Reveals the men, attitudes and machinery of a historic convention and shows the American political system at work.
From The You Are There Series.
Prod-CBSNEW Dist-PHENIX 1972

Nomination, Election And Succession Of The President C 60 MIN
3/4 OR 1/2 INCH VIDEO CASSETTE
Explores the role of political parties in nominating a president, the flexibility of the Electoral College when no candidate is clearly electable and the governmental mechanisms set into motion when a president becomes disabled.
From The Constitution - That Delicate Balance Series.
Prod-WTTWTV Dist-FI 1984

Non-Arthropod Invertebrates C 15 MIN
3/4 OR 1/2 INCH VIDEO CASSETTE I
See series title for descriptive statement.
From The Discovering Series. Unit 2 - Invertebrate Animals
Prod-WDCNTV Dist-AITECH 1978

Non-Compliance - The Hidden Health Hazard C 26 MIN
16MM FILM OPTICAL SOUND
Outlines the extent of patient non-compliance in various therapeutic settings.
LC NO. 80-701572
Prod-SYDUN Dist-TASCOR 1978

Non-Dairy Creamer, A C
3/4 OR 1/2 INCH VIDEO CASSETTE
Concerns the eradication of the individual by self-consumption.
From The Red Tape Series.
Prod-EAI Dist-EAI

Non-Decimal Numeration Systems B 30 MIN
16MM FILM OPTICAL SOUND
Illustrates, explains and presents problems dealing with non-decimal numeration systems.
From The Introduction To Mathematics Series. No. 2
LC NO. FI67-417
Prod-HRAW Dist-SCETV 1964

Non-Destructive Testing C 16 MIN
3/4 OR 1/2 INCH VIDEO CASSETTE
Shows types of non-destructive testing, advantages and disadvantages.
From The Manufacturing Materials And Processes Series.
Prod-GE Dist-WFVTAE

Non-Dismembering Procedures C 20 MIN
16MM FILM OPTICAL SOUND
Reviews the indications, contraindications and advantages of the non-dismembering surgical procedures for the surgical correction of hydronephrosis. Includes the classical Foley Y-Plasty, the modified Davis intubated ureterotomy and the vertical flap (Scardono technique) non-splinted.
From The Surgical Correction Of Hydronephrosis, Pt 1 - Non-Dismembering Procedures Series.
LC NO. 75-702261
Prod-EATONL Dist-EATONL 1968

Non-Education Universe, A C
16MM FILM OPTICAL SOUND
Looks at the euclidean axioms condensed into a diagrammatic form and asks whether they are independent.
Prod-OPENU Dist-OPENU 1979

Non-Equilibrium Thermodynamics Applied to Electro-Osmosis And Streaming Potential C 38 MIN
3/4 OR 1/2 INCH VIDEO CASSETTE
See series title for descriptive statement.
From The Colloid And Surface Chemistry - Electrokinetics And Membrane...Series.
Prod-KALMIA Dist-KALMIA

Non-Equilibrium Thermodynamics Applied To Elecro-Osmosis And Streaming Potential B 38 MIN
3/4 OR 1/2 INCH VIDEO CASSETTE
See series title for descriptive statement.
From The Colloids And Surface Chemistry Electrokinetics And Membrane...--Series.
Prod-MIOT Dist-MIOT

Non-Euclidean Geometries C 20 MIN
3/4 OR 1/2 INCH VIDEO CASSETTE H
Presents teachers Beth McKenna and David Edmonds exploring two different geometries, Lobatchevskian and Riemannian, and differentiating them from Euclidean geometry. Uses spherical and hyperbolic models to investigate the properties of lines and figures.
From The Shapes Of Geometry Series. Pt 6
LC NO. 82-707392
Prod-WVIZTV Dist-GPITVL 1982

Non-Evaluative Feedback C 28 MIN
2 INCH VIDEOTAPE C A
Features a humanistic psychologist who, by analysis and examples, discusses non-evaluative feedback.
From The Interpersonal Competence, Unit 02 - Communication Series.
Prod-MVNE Dist-TELSTR 1973

Non-Green Plants C 15 MIN
2 INCH VIDEOTAPE P
Shows how non-green plants do not produce their own food.
From The Science Is Searching Series.
Prod-DETPS Dist-GPITVL

Non-Hodgkin's Lymphomas, Pt 1 - Systmes Of Classification And Principles Of Staging C 20 MIN
3/4 OR 1/2 INCH VIDEO CASSETTE PRO
Presents a patient with early findings of lymphoma. Describes the Rappaport method of classification.
Prod-UMICHM Dist-UMICHM 1979

Non-Hodgkin's Lymphomas, Pt 2 - Prognosis And Therapy C 17 MIN
3/4 OR 1/2 INCH VIDEO CASSETTE PRO
Focuses on the results of a lymphoma staging and treatment program. Describes favorable prognoses for given lymphomas and subsequent treatment.
Prod-UMICHM Dist-UMICHM 1979

Non-Linear Systems C 30 MIN
3/4 INCH VIDEO CASSETTE C
See series title for descriptive statement.
From The Introduction To Mathematics Series.
Prod-MDCPB Dist-MDCPB

Non-Marrieds, The C 29 MIN
3/4 OR 1/2 INCH VIDEO CASSETTE
Presents a widower, a divorced man, two divorced women and two individuals over 30 who have been married joining Milton Diamond, Ph D, a biologist at the University of Hawaii, for a discussion of these different non-married situations. Features newspaper columnist Ann Landers adding her views and the manager of a singles-only apartment complex talking about the advantages and disadvantages of this life-style.
From The Human Sexuality Series.
Prod-KHETTV Dist-PBS

Non-Metric Geometry, Pt 1 B 30 MIN
16MM FILM OPTICAL SOUND
Illustrates, explains and presents problems dealing with the fundamentals of non-metric geometry. Includes a brief discussion of geometry and of geometric symbols.
From The Introduction To Mathematics Series. No. 5
LC NO. FI67-413
Prod-HRAW Dist-SCETV 1964

Non-Metric Geometry, Pt 2 B 30 MIN
16MM FILM OPTICAL SOUND
Illustrates, explains and presents problems dealing with the fundamentals of non-metric geometry. Includes a disussion of curves, angles, polygons and the intersection and union of sets.
From The Introduction To Mathematics Series. No. 6
LC NO. FI67-414
Prod-HRAW Dist-SCETV 1964

Non-Negotiable C 20 MIN
16MM FILM, 3/4 OR 1/2 IN VIDEO H-C A
Shows how two union negotiators, the plant manager and an impartial mediator, attempt to resolve the impasse that caused workers to strike. Reveals the conflict between management's and labor's goals and the mounting frustration as the negotiations stalemate.
LC NO. 83-706659
Prod-WORLDR Dist-WORLDR 1982

Non-Objective Art C 8 MIN
16MM FILM, 3/4 OR 1/2 IN VIDEO J-C
Defines non-objective art and shows how it differs from other types of painting. Attention is directed to non-objective things in nature.
From The Understanding Modern Art Series.
Prod-THIEB Dist-PHENIX 1957

Non-Parametric Tests C 30 MIN
3/4 OR 1/2 INCH VIDEO CASSETTE IND
Covers non-parametric tests (the sign, Mann-Whitney U and Kolmogorov Smirnov tests) which prove extremely useful where assumptions for specific distributions may not be met, such as with ranked data.
From The Engineering Statistics Series.
Prod-COLOSU Dist-COLOSU

Non-Renewable Resources C 20 MIN
3/4 OR 1/2 INCH VIDEO CASSETTE I-J
Focuses on non-renewable resources, specifically those used in the manufacture and operation of automobiles. Presents a demonstration of recycling and considers the implications of diminishing resources for individual life-styles.
From The Terra - Our World Series.
Prod-MSDOE Dist-AITECH 1980

Non-Root Feeding Of Plants (Spanish) C 21 MIN
16MM FILM OPTICAL SOUND
Describes the techniques of applying nutrients to the visible, above-ground portion of plants. Discusses the method of tracing the nutrients through the plant's system by means of radioisotopes.
LC NO. 80-700533
Prod-MSU Dist-USNAC Prodn-COLWER 1958

Non-Sexist Early Education Films—A Series

Examines nonsexist methods of rearing and teaching young children.
Prod-WAA Dist-THIRD Prodn-SIMONJ 1977

Sooner The Better, The 27 MIN
Time Has Come, The 22 MIN

Non-Skid Surface Is A Myth, The C 7 MIN
3/4 OR 1/2 INCH VIDEO CASSETTE
Describes the coefficient of friction, explains acceptable levels of friction for skid-resistant surfaces and illustrates the use of simple, practical precautions to make the workplace safer.
Prod-FILCOM Dist-FILCOM

NON-SLIP C 25 MIN
16MM FILM OPTICAL SOUND C T
Demonstrates procedures used in the Non-Speech Language Initiation Program training, in which nonverbal mentally retarded persons learn communication skills through the use of plastic symbols representing words.
LC NO. 78-701603
Prod-UKANS Dist-UKANS 1976

Non-Standard Analysis, Pt 1 B 67 MIN
16MM FILM OPTICAL SOUND
Discusses the non-standard real numbers and the form which the calculus takes when based on this enlarged number system which includes infinitesimals.
From The Maa General Mathematics Series.
Prod-MAA Dist-MLA

Non-Standard Analysis, Pt 2 B 67 MIN
16MM FILM OPTICAL SOUND
Discusses the non-standard real numbers and the form which the calculus takes when based on this enlarged number system which includes infinitesimals.
From The Maa General Mathematics Series.
Prod-MAA Dist-MLA

Non-Swimming Rescues C 7 MIN
16MM FILM - 3/4 IN VIDEO J-C A
Emphasizes that jumping into the water to make a rescue should be a last resort. Points out that non-swimming rescues such as extension, throwing and wading are safer, easier and usually faster.
From The Lifesaving And Water Safety Series.
Prod-AMRC Dist-AMRC 1975

Non-Swimming Rescues (Spanish) C 7 MIN
3/4 INCH VIDEO CASSETTE
Emphasizes that jumping into the water to make a rescue should be a last resort. Points out that non-swimming rescues such as extension, throwing and wading are safer, easier and usually faster.
From The Lifesaving And Water Safety Series.
Prod-AMRC Dist-AMRC

Non-Verbal Communication B 27 MIN
16MM FILM OPTICAL SOUND S
Discusses the recognition of the clues of non-verbal communication and the manner in which these clues can be used in an interview situation to obtain information and to further therapy. Illustrates the various points through picture, with subtitles, of actual unrehearsed interview situations.
From The Psychotherapeutic Interviewing Series.
LC NO. FIE53-98
Prod-USVA Dist-USNAC 1952

Non-Verbal Communication (2nd Ed) C 14 MIN
16MM FILM, 3/4 OR 1/2 IN VIDEO H-C A
Presents Dr Albert Mehrabian explaining non-verbal communication and how it works. Points out that an awareness of one's own nonverbal messages and those of others enhances the ability to communicate.
LC NO. 80-706185
Prod-SALENG Dist-SALENG 1980

Non-Violence - Mahatma Gandhi And Martin Luther King, The Teacher And The Pupil C 15 MIN
16MM FILM OPTICAL SOUND
Interviews Mahatma Gandhi and presents his philosophy on non-violent protest and the necessity for his imprisonment in behalf of his cause. Shows how Martin Luther King Jr carries out Gandhis principle of non-violent protest.
Prod-INTEXT Dist-REAF

Non-Violent Protest B 15 MIN
16MM FILM OPTICAL SOUND
Encourages students to inquire into the concept of protest by examining specific issues in the Black protest movement.
Prod-STEVA Dist-REAF

Non-Western C 30 MIN
16MM FILM OPTICAL SOUND H-C A
Presents an in-depth study of early Oriental art including the Buddha figure, bronze works and the importance of Patina as well as the funerary figures. Explores the African collection at the Art Institute of Chicago.
From The Man And His Art Series.
Prod-WTTWTV Dist-GPITVL

Nonbehavioral Sciences And Rehabilitation—A Series
PRO
Presents lectures by Josephine C Moore, occupational therapist, on the neurobehavioral sciences and their relationship to rehabilitation.
Prod-AOTA Dist-AOTA 1980

Behavioral Patterns In Relation To Genetic CNS Vulnerability 060 MIN
Diagnosing CNS Lesions 060 MIN
Extrapyramidal System, The, Pt I 060 MIN
Extrapyramidal System, The, Pt II 060 MIN
Extrapyramidal System, The, Pt III 060 MIN
General Review Of The Nervous System 060 MIN
Learning And Memory 060 MIN
Limbic System, The, Pt I 060 MIN
Limbic System, The, Pt II 060 MIN
Myelination Of The Central Nervous System On Nature's Laws 060 MIN
Neuron, The 060 MIN

Nondestructive Inspection - A Dollar Saving Diagnostic Tool C 20 MIN
16MM FILM OPTICAL SOUND
Reviews the cost of tearing down various aircraft components in order to ascertain the malfunctioning parts. Examines a number of nondestructive methods which can be used to meet the same end and which produce large cost savings.
LC NO. 75-700565
Prod-USAF Dist-USNAC 1974

None For The Road C 12 MIN
16MM FILM, 3/4 OR 1/2 IN VIDEO H A
Presents an emotional thought-provoking approach to the social-drinking-driver problem.
Prod-AIMS Dist-AIMS 1962

None For The Road (Spanish) C 12 MIN
16MM FILM, 3/4 OR 1/2 IN VIDEO H-C A
Considers what happens to an ordinary social drinker when he climbs behind the wheel. Tells the story of one man who found himself facing a year in jail because his blood was found to contain .15 percent alcohol after an accident.
Prod-CAHILL Dist-AIMS 1962

Nonequivalent Sets - Inequalities C 15 MIN
3/4 INCH VIDEO CASSETTE P
Develops understanding of inequality and equality of numbers and presents the symbols for 'equal,' 'is greater than' and 'is less than.'
From The Math Factory, Module I - Sets Series.
Prod-MAETEL Dist-GPITVL 1973

Nonfat Dry Milk C 14 MIN
2 INCH VIDEOTAPE
See series title for descriptive statement.
From The Living Better I Series.
Prod-MAETEL Dist-PUBTEL

Noni B 30 MIN
2 INCH VIDEOTAPE
Presents an interview with a 16-year-old girl and her mother with a focus on life styles.
From The Counseling The Adolescent Series.
Prod-GPITVL Dist-GPITVL

Nonlinear Centrifugal Pendulum B 24 MIN
3/4 OR 1/2 INCH VIDEO CASSETTE
See series title for descriptive statement.
From The Nonlinear Vibrations Series.
Prod-MIOT Dist-MIOT

Nonlinear Vibrations—A Series

Describes various methods - exact and approximate, numerical and graphical, for dealing with vibrations in systems described by nonlinear differential equations.
Prod-MIOT Dist-MIOT

Aircraft Jet Rotor With Ball Bearings With Application Of The Phase-Plane Method	030 MIN
Applications	034 MIN
Exact Solutions (1)	037 MIN
Exact Solutions (2)	035 MIN
Forced Undamped Vibrator With Nonlinear Spring	033 MIN
Forced Vibrator With Nonlinear Damping	031 MIN
Introduction	036 MIN
Method Of Galerkin	034 MIN
Method Of Krylov-Bogliubov	024 MIN
Modified Martienssen Method Subharmonic	032 MIN
Nonlinear Centrifugal Pendulum	024 MIN
Pendulum In A Rotating Plane	032 MIN
Periodic Reversal Of Rotation Of A DC Motor	034 MIN
Phase-Plane Method, The	037 MIN
Physical Interpretation Of The K And B Formulas	029 MIN
Piece-Wise Linear Systems	033 MIN
Relaxation Oscillations	030 MIN
Solution And Interpretation	033 MIN
Sommerfeld Effect, The	032 MIN
Tuned Centrifugal Pendulum	024 MIN
Van Der Pol Equation, The	031 MIN
Volterra's Fishes	037 MIN

Nonorganic Failure To Thrive C 20 MIN
3/4 OR 1/2 INCH VIDEO CASSETTE PRO
Teaches the diagnosis of failure to thrive and explains the hospital therapy recommended when no organic reasons for it are apparent.
From The Child Abuse Series.
Prod-HSCIC Dist-HSCIC 1978

Nonparametric Tests - Examples C 30 MIN
3/4 OR 1/2 INCH VIDEO CASSETTE IND
Presents examples of the sign and the Wilcoxon sign rank tests.
From The Reliability Engineering Series.
Prod-COLOSU Dist-COLOSU

Nonrecurrent Wavefronts W-3 B 3 MIN
16MM FILM OPTICAL SOUND J-C
Considers tidal waves, shock waves from nuclear bombs, the spreading pulse of light from a nova reflected by a nearby cloud of interstellar gas and a disturbance spreading through a crowd of people.
From The Single-Concept Films In Physics Series.
Prod-OSUMPD Dist-OSUMPD 1963

Nonsense And Made-Up Words In Poetry C 15 MIN
3/4 OR 1/2 INCH VIDEO CASSETTE P
See series title for descriptive statement.
From The Word Shop Series.
Prod-WETATV Dist-WETATV

Nonspecific Defense Mechanisms C 15 MIN
3/4 OR 1/2 INCH VIDEO CASSETTE PRO
Provides general description of nonspecific and specific defense mechanisms, compares physical versus physiologic defenses, explores cellular biotransformation, and the role of inflammation.
From The Mechanisms Of Disease - Host Defenses Series.
Prod-BRA Dist-BRA

Nonspeech Communication - Augmentative Systems C 314 MIN
3/4 OR 1/2 INCH VIDEO CASSETTE
Presents information concerning the use of manual signs and gestures and graphic representations.
From The Meeting The Communications Needs Of The Severely/Profoundly Handicapped 1980 Series.
Prod-PUAVC Dist-PUAVC

Nonspeech Communication - Augmentative Systems C 330 MIN
3/4 OR 1/2 INCH VIDEO CASSETTE
Presents information concerning the use of manual signs and gestures and graphic representations.
From The Meeting The Communication Needs Of The Severely/Profoundly Handicapped 1981 Series.
Prod-PUAVC Dist-PUAVC

Nonsubterranean Termites C
3/4 OR 1/2 INCH VIDEO CASSETTE
See series title for descriptive statement.
From The Pest Control Technology Correspondence Course Series.
Prod-PUAVC Dist-PUAVC

Nonsurgical Biliary Drainage And Lithocenosis C 30 MIN
3/4 OR 1/2 INCH VIDEO CASSETTE
Outlines methods for the correct differential diagnosis of obstructive jaundice.
Prod-ROWLAB Dist-ROWLAB

Nonswimming Rescues C 7 MIN
16MM FILM OPTICAL SOUND I-C A
Demonstrates a variety of extension, throwing and wading assists for rescuing swimmers in trouble, which may be used by those unable to swim themselves.
From The Lifesaving And Water Safety Series.
LC NO. 76-701569
Prod-AMRC Dist-AMRC 1975

Nonsyphiltic Venereal Diseases C 30 MIN
16MM FILM OPTICAL SOUND PRO
Discusses the etiology, pathology, diagnosis and treatment of the four most common venereal diseases which are not of syphilitic origin.
Prod-SQUIBB Dist-SQUIBB 1955

Nonverbal Communication C 22 MIN
3/4 OR 1/2 INCH VIDEO CASSETTE H-C A
Gives a review of nonverbal communication. Defines and explores three categories of nonverbal codes and examines the functions of each. Uses the nonverbal communication animation of white-faced mimes to help illustrate the points of interest.
From The Communication Series.
Prod-MSU Dist-MSU

Nonverbal Communication C 23 MIN
16MM FILM, 3/4 OR 1/2 IN VIDEO
Covers the numerous scientific findings on how people communicate on a nonverbal level. Defines what behavior falls into the category of nonverbal communication, what the functions are of nonverbal communication and the origins of nonverbal communication. Features laboratory experiments on proximity and facial expression.
From The Social Psychology Series.
Prod-MTI Dist-MTI

Nonverbal Communication In The Trial C 50 MIN
3/4 OR 1/2 INCH VIDEO CASSETTE PRO
Covers such topics as lawyer's body language, eye contact, gestures, voice inflection and silence. Explores some of the special programs that face the female advocate and explains how courtroom layout and the exchange of questions and answers affect presentation.
From The Effective Communication In The Courtroom Series.
Prod-ABACPE Dist-ABACPE

Nonverbal Communication—A Series

Helps people understand nonverbal communications and improve nonverbal signals to agree with and reinforce spoken words.
Prod-IVCH Dist-IVCH

Eye Behavior	030 MIN
Introduction And Overview	030 MIN
Mannerisms Displayed By Gestures	030 MIN
Proxemics-Spacing, And Touching-Haptics	030 MIN

Nonwovens And Carpets C
3/4 OR 1/2 INCH VIDEO CASSETTE
See series title for descriptive statement.
From The ITMA 1983 Review Series.
Prod-NCSU Dist-NCSU

Noodles C 29 MIN
2 INCH VIDEOTAPE
Features Joyce Chen showing how to adapt Chinese recipes so they can be prepared in the American kitchen and still retain the authentic flavor. Demonstrates how to prepare noodles.
From The Joyce Chen Cooks Series.
Prod-WGBHTV Dist-PUBTEL

Nooks And Crannies C 30 MIN
2 INCH VIDEOTAPE C A
Suggests ways to customize a home to meet individual storage needs. Show examples of how to organize a kitchen work area.
From The Designing Home Interiors Series. Unit 25
Prod-COAST Dist-CDTEL Prodn-RSCCD

Noontime Nonsense X 13 MIN
16MM FILM OPTICAL SOUND
Shows an open campus and wild noontime driving by a small group of students. Illustrates how the student council solved this problem.
From The Secondary School Safety Series.
Prod-NSC Dist-NSC Prodn-EMERFC 1955

Nor Any Drop To Drink C 30 MIN
16MM FILM - 3/4 IN VIDEO J-C A
Explains that water is the most common substance on earth and falls on all of us, but not equally - some regions are always too dry and others too wet. Looks at the problems of distribution of water by examining working projects and their problems in Africa, India, Israel, South Africa, Washington, DC, Long Island, New York and others.
From The Man Builds - Man Destroys Series.
Prod-UN Dist-GPITVL 1973

Nora Ephron On Everything C 29 MIN
3/4 INCH VIDEO CASSETTE
Features author Nora Ephron commenting on a number of issues surrounding the women's movement.
From The Woman Series.
Prod-WNEDTV Dist-PUBTEL

Nordens Arkaeologi (The Archaeology Of Scandinavia) B 31 MIN
16MM FILM OPTICAL SOUND
A Danish language film. Describes the conditions of life of the Scandinavian people in the Stone Age, the Bronze Age and the Iron Age, based on archaeological find.
Prod-STATNS Dist-STATNS 1958

Nordjamb C 58 MIN
16MM FILM OPTICAL SOUND
Presents a behind-the-scenes report of the 1975 World Boy Scout Jamboree in Lillehammer, Norway. Follows the activities of one south Florida scout during the week-long event.
LC NO. 76-700395
Prod-WPBTTV Dist-WPBTTV 1976

Norie Sato - After Image, TTLS C 5 MIN
3/4 OR 1/2 INCH VIDEO CASSETTE
Presents the inner workings of the television as a metaphor for outer space.
Prod-ARTINC Dist-ARTINC

Norie Sato - Farewell To Triangle 1 C 7 MIN
3/4 OR 1/2 INCH VIDEO CASSETTE
Explores the electronic properties of video. Points to the relationship between inner and outer realities.
Prod-ARTINC Dist-ARTINC

Norie Sato - In Plus, Pulse C 3 MIN
3/4 OR 1/2 INCH VIDEO CASSETTE
Compares the world of electrons to the 'real' world through seeing the output of the cross-pulse signal.
Prod-ARTINC Dist-ARTINC

Norie Sato - On Edge C 4 MIN
3/4 OR 1/2 INCH VIDEO CASSETTE
Explores the electronic properties of video. Makes a statement about inner and outer realities.
Prod-ARTINC Dist-ARTINC

Norie Sato - Phosphor Read Out C 4 MIN
3/4 OR 1/2 INCH VIDEO CASSETTE
Presents an image which exists somewhere between 'snow' and 'dropout'.
Prod-ARTINC Dist-ARTINC

Norie Sato - Read Only Phosphor Memory C 7 MIN
3/4 OR 1/2 INCH VIDEO CASSETTE
Presents an ephemeral image.
Prod-ARTINC Dist-ARTINC

Norien Ten C 10 MIN
16MM FILM, 3/4 OR 1/2 IN VIDEO C A
Explores eroticism through unusual photography of intercourse combined with extreme closeups in sharp focus.
Prod-MMRC Dist-MMRC

Norma Rae C
1/2 IN VIDEO CASSETTE BETA/VHS
Presents Sally Field's Oscar-winning performance as a Southern textile worker struggling to organize a union.
Prod-GA Dist-GA

Normal And Abnormal Neurologic Function In Infancy (Updated) - Part 1 C 29 MIN
3/4 OR 1/2 INCH VIDEO CASSETTE PRO
Presents the important gross and fine motor patterns of healthy forty-week-olds and the continuing normal development over the following year, noting salient adaptive behavior.
From The Developmental - Neurologic Approach To Assessment In Infancy And Early Childhood Series.
Prod-HSCIC Dist-HSCIC 1982

Normal And Abnormal Neurologic Function In Infancy (Updated) - Part 2 C 43 MIN
3/4 OR 1/2 INCH VIDEO CASSETTE PRO
Illustrates more severe disabilities than in Part 1 mental deficiency, borderline development, cerebral palsy with unknown intellectual potential, and cerebral palsy with normal intelligence.
From The Developmental - Neurologic Approach To Assessment In Infancy And Early Childhood Series.
Prod-HSCIC Dist-HSCIC 1982

Normal And Abnormal Neurologic Functions In Infancy B 28 MIN
16MM FILM OPTICAL SOUND

Depicts the neuromotor patterns observed in infants with disabilities ranging from minimal to severe.
Prod-OHIOSU Dist-OSUMPD 1964

Normal And Abnormal Platelets B 20 MIN
16MM FILM OPTICAL SOUND PRO
Shows the activity of platelets through the phase-contrast microscope. Examines hereditary thrombopathy in children, immunologic thrombopathy, lysis of platelets in antiserum, giant platelets in myeloid leukemia, giant platelets in platelet leukemia and autolysis.
Prod-SQUIBB Dist-SQUIBB

Normal And Abnormal Swallowing - Pt 1- Normal Anatomy C 21 MIN
3/4 OR 1/2 INCH VIDEO CASSETTE PRO
Discusses normal anatomy of swallowing and the basic musculoskeletal structures involved in deglutition. Intended for students and medical clinicians.
Prod-VAMSLC Dist-USNAC 1984

Normal And Abnormal Swallowing - Pt 2- Physiology C 7 MIN
3/4 OR 1/2 INCH VIDEO CASSETTE PRO
Discusses physiology involved in swallowing and deglutition.
Prod-VAMSLC Dist-USNAC 1984

Normal And Abnormal Swallowing - Pt 3- Evaluation C 13 MIN
3/4 OR 1/2 INCH VIDEO CASSETTE PRO
Discusses the types of dysphagia and how to evaluate suspected cases. Intended for the clinician familiar with anatomy and physiology of swallowing.
Prod-VAMSLC Dist-USNAC 1984

Normal And Abnormal Swallowing - Pt 4- Treatment And Management C 22 MIN
3/4 OR 1/2 INCH VIDEO CASSETTE PRO
Discusses diagnostic evaluation techniques for the types of dysphagia and the treatment and management of dysphagia patients.
Prod-VAMSLC Dist-USNAC 1984

Normal And Emergency Operation C
3/4 OR 1/2 INCH VIDEO CASSETTE IND
Discusses the effects of normal and abnormal conditions. Focuses on emergency operation and necessary actions for system protection.
From The Distribution System Operation Series. Topic 11
Prod-LEIKID Dist-LEIKID

Normal Baby, A C 40 MIN
3/4 INCH VIDEOTAPE PRO
Traces the growth of a normal baby from birth to one year. Covers gross and fine motor development, stages in development of hand function and eye-hand coordination.
Prod-VALHAL Dist-VALHAL

Normal Child B 25 MIN
16MM FILM OPTICAL SOUND C T
Shows Karl, a six-year-old boy, interacting normally and positively with his environment. Shows how he handles affection. Illustrates his capacity for imagination and play and his constructive use of relationship with the examiner. Showings restricted.
LC NO. FIA68-2698
Prod-EPPI Dist-PSUPCR 1967

Normal Cystourethrogram, The C 14 MIN
16MM FILM OPTICAL SOUND PRO
Uses animation and plastic models, combined with Roentgen spotfilms taken during voiding cystourethrograms, to show how the Roentgen anatomy of the bladder, baseplate and urethra will change radically during the voiding cycle and to show normal anatomical landmarks and dynamic patterns which, in the past, have been mistakenly identified as pathological conditions.
LC NO. 70-711368
Prod-WINLAB Dist-WINLAB 1971

Normal Delivery Of Triplets C 12 MIN
16MM FILM OPTICAL SOUND
Details methods and equipment used in the delivery of triplets in order to reduce neonatal death in multiple births.
LC NO. 73-701950
Prod-SCPMG Dist-SCPMG 1968

Normal Distribution C
3/4 OR 1/2 INCH VIDEO CASSETTE IND
Shows commonly occurring distributions which can describe sales distributions as well as lifetimes of products subject to mechanical wear. Discusses calculations of areas under the normal curve. Covers central limit theorem, and demonstrates setting of means and variances to meet specific goals.
From The Statistics For Managers Series.
Prod-COLOSU Dist-COLOSU

Normal Distribution And Central Limit Theorem , The C 30 MIN
3/4 OR 1/2 INCH VIDEO CASSETTE IND
Describes use of normal distribution used for modelling many practical situations. Includes how to determine value of a particular mean or standard deviation to meet goals.
From The Engineering Statistics Series.
Prod-COLOSU Dist-COLOSU

Normal Eye C 81 MIN
3/4 OR 1/2 INCH VIDEO CASSETTE
Presents the normal eye anatomy. Discusses vision and focusing. Explains myopia and hyperopia.
Prod-MEDFAC Dist-MEDFAC 1974

Normal Face, A - The Wonders Of Plastic Surgery C 57 MIN
16MM FILM, 3/4 OR 1/2 IN VIDEO H-C A
Looks at the history, heroes and miracles of plastic surgery in mending the accidents of war and birth.
From The Nova Series.
Prod-WGBHTV Dist-TIMLIF 1982

Normal Forms B
16MM FILM OPTICAL SOUND
Demonstrates the different normal forms to which a matrix can be reduced by changing the bases relative to which it is defined. Includes the canonical form, Hermite normal form, diagonal form, and Jordan normal form.
Prod-OPENU Dist-OPENU

Normal Heart Sounds And Innocent Heart Murmurs C 41 MIN
16MM FILM - 3/4 IN VIDEO PRO
Provides a foundation for the use of the stethescope in the analysis of heart sounds and murmurs. Discusses normal cardiac auscultation and interprets cardiac events. Issued in 1964 as a motion picture.
LC NO. 79-706508
Prod-USPHS Dist-USNAC 1979

Normal Human Locomotion B 180 MIN
16MM FILM OPTICAL SOUND PRO
Presents a lecture by Dr Cameron B Hall of the UCLA Surgery-Orthotics Department on normal human locomotion. Traces the evolutionary development of bipedal gait from the fish to the human and discusses the role of skeletal, muscular and neurological elements of the human anatomy.
Prod-UCLA Dist-UCLA

Normal Labor And Delivery B 44 MIN
16MM FILM OPTICAL SOUND PRO
Demonstrates and discusses the physiology and mechanisms of labor, with emphasis on basic concepts and implications for nursing.
From The Maternity Nursing Series.
LC NO. 75-703388
Prod-VDONUR Dist-AJN Prodn-WTTWTV 1966

Normal Neonate, The C 22 MIN
16MM FILM OPTICAL SOUND
Shows a pediatrician examining a normal human infant.
LC NO. 80-701573
Prod-SYDUN Dist-TASCOR 1977

Normal Nutrition - Body Composition C 38 MIN
3/4 OR 1/2 INCH VIDEO CASSETTE PRO
Covers caloric composition, fluid composition and mineral composition, and anthropometric measurements.
From The Nutrition And Health Series.
Prod-HSCIC Dist-HSCIC 1984

Normal Operating Hazards And Safety, Tape 17A C
3/4 OR 1/2 INCH VIDEO CASSETTE IND
Covers generation, synchronism, transmission, transformers, surge arrestors, switching operations, supervisory control, protection of personnel and clearance procedures.
From The Electric Power System Operation Series.
Prod-LEIKID Dist-LEIKID

Normal Operating Hazards And Safety, Tape 17B C
3/4 OR 1/2 INCH VIDEO CASSETTE IND
Covers generation, synchronism, transmission, transformers, surge arrestors, switching operations, supervisory control, protection of personnel and clearance procedures.
From The Electric Power System Operation Series.
Prod-LEIKID Dist-LEIKID

Normal Patterns Of Development C 12 MIN
3/4 OR 1/2 INCH VIDEO CASSETTE
Describes the intertwining tracks of a baby's physical, mental and social development and the effect that achievement in one area has on the others. Includes development of thumb and finger opposition, learning to sit unsupported, stranger anxiety and object permanence, plus discussing the development of attachment.
LC NO. 81-730128
Prod-TRAINX Dist-TRAINX

Normal Patterns Of Development (Spanish) C 12 MIN
3/4 OR 1/2 INCH VIDEO CASSETTE
Describes the intertwining tracks of a baby's physical, mental and social development and the effect that achievement in one area has on the others. Includes development of thumb and finger opposition, learning to sit unsupported, stranger anxiety and object permanence, plus discussing the development of attachment.
LC NO. 81-730128
Prod-TRAINX Dist-TRAINX

Normal Physical Assessment - A Tool For The Beginning Practitioner C 25 MIN
3/4 OR 1/2 INCH VIDEO CASSETTE
Demonstrates how a nurse carries out a physical assessment, including inspection, palpation, and auscultation of the heart and abdominal areas.
LC NO. 81-707280
Prod-USA Dist-USNAC 1977

Normal Pregnancy B 44 MIN
16MM FILM OPTICAL SOUND PRO
Discusses pregnancy as a socially significant process affecting individuals, the family and the community. Explains and illustrates the physiologic process, including signs and symptoms of pregnancy and the physical and emotional changes during the prenatal period, with emphasis on nursing implications.
From The Maternity Nursing Series.
LC NO. 79-703389
Prod-VDONUR Dist-AJN Prodn-WTTWTV 1966

Normal Puerperium B 44 MIN
16MM FILM OPTICAL SOUND PRO
Discusses the aims of postpartal care, including physiologic changes and the clinical aspects of care. Emphasizes nursing care, including health guidance and parent teaching.
From The Maternity Nursing Series.
LC NO. 73-703390
Prod-VDONUR Dist-AJN Prodn-WTTWTV 1966

Normal Roentgen Anatomy—A Series PRO
Prod-AMCRAD Dist-AMEDA

Roentgen Anatomy Of The Normal Alimentary Canal 27 MIN
Roentgen Anatomy Of The Normal Heart 27 MIN

Normal Speech Articulation C 25 MIN
16MM FILM OPTICAL SOUND
Demonstrates through extensive use of X-ray motion pictures, some of the characteristics of speech sound articulation in normal speakers.
From The Physiological Aspects Of Speech Series.
LC NO. FIA65-1901
Prod-UIOWA Dist-UIOWA Prodn-UIOWA 1965

Normalcy - What Is It C 29 MIN
3/4 OR 1/2 INCH VIDEO CASSETTE
Presents man-on-the-street interviews to illustrate the dependence of definitions of normalcy on age, sex, attitudes and culture. Features Milton Diamond, Ph D, a biologist at the University of Hawaii, discussing general ideas about social norms applied to partner preferences and sexual practices.
From The Human Sexuality Series.
Prod-KHETTV Dist-PBS

Norman And The Killer B 27 MIN
16MM FILM, 3/4 OR 1/2 IN VIDEO
Relates the story of a young man who recognizes the mugger who killed his brother 16 years after the mugging took place. Reveals what happens when he confronts the killer. Based on a short story by Joyce Carol Oates.
Prod-QUKIGR Dist-CORF 1981

Norman Checks In C 10 MIN
16MM FILM, 3/4 OR 1/2 IN VIDEO C A
Features a comedy about Norman, a silently suffering, slow burning man. Pictures him battling with a shower, noisy neighbors and a relaxing machine.
Prod-MTI Dist-MTI

Norman Conquest Of England, The C 20 MIN
16MM FILM OPTICAL SOUND
Depicts the historic conquest of England by William I, Duke of Normandy. Includes the narration of the Battle of Hastings during which King Harold of England was killed.
Prod-RADIM Dist-RADIM 1971

Norman Conquest Of England, The - 1066 C 20 MIN
16MM FILM OPTICAL SOUND
Presents the famous Bayeux tapestry embroidered by the conquerors' Queen Mathilde, which depicts the historic events of William I, Duke of Normandy.
Prod-LEEN Dist-RADIM

Norman Cousins, Education, Public Service C 29 MIN
3/4 OR 1/2 INCH VIDEO CASSETTE A
See series title for descriptive statement.
From The Quest For Peace Series.
Prod-AACD Dist-AACD 1984

Norman Geske C 28 MIN
2 INCH VIDEOTAPE
See series title for descriptive statement.
From The Art Profile Series.
Prod-KUONTV Dist-PUBTEL

Norman Jacobson B 59 MIN
16MM FILM OPTICAL SOUND H-C T
Presents a study of Norman Jacobson, professor of political science, University of California, Berkeley. Features interviews with him, scenes of him with his students in seminars, and scenes of student involvement in current events.
From The Men Who Teach Series.
LC NO. FIA68-2616
Prod-NETRC Dist-IU 1968

Norman Kennedy - A Man And His Songs B 146 MIN
3/4 INCH VIDEO CASSETTE J-C A
Presents a portrait of Norman Kennedy, singer of Scottish ballads and folksongs and master weaver at Colonial Williamsburg. Includes an interview with Kennedy in which he talks about weaving, the history of song, the nature of the oral tradition and the Scottish antecedents of American culture.
LC NO. 80-706066
Prod-HERTZ Dist-HERTZ 1979

Norman Mc Laren's Opening Speech B 8 MIN
16MM FILM, 3/4 OR 1/2 IN VIDEO H-C A
Portrays Norman Mc Laren and his struggle with an animated microscope.
Prod-IFB Dist-IFB 1963

Norman Normal C 6 MIN
16MM FILM OPTICAL SOUND
A modern morality play, arrayed in wit. Deals with the central dilemma of the time - how does one ethical man handle himself so as to save his private dignity within the seething arenas of today's life.
Prod-PFP Dist-VIEWFI

Norman Paul, MD, Associate Professor Of Psychiatry, Boston Universtiy Medical School C 60 MIN
3/4 OR 1/2 INCH VIDEO CASSETTE PRO

Focuses on intergenerational family therapy and the effects of incompleted grief.
From The Perceptions, Pt B - Dialogues With Family Therapists Series. Vol VII, Pt B14.
Prod-BOSFAM Dist-BOSFAM

Norman Rockwell's World - An American Dream C 25 MIN
16MM FILM OPTICAL SOUND
Presents a tribute to America's best known and most popular artist, Norman Rockwell. Explains that Norman Rockwell has been sensitive to the movement of American history.
LC NO. 73-700605
Prod-ARROW Dist-FI Prodn-CUNLIM 1972

Norman Studer And Grant Rogers C 52 MIN
3/4 OR 1/2 INCH VIDEO CASSETTE
Presents Norman Studer talking about the folklore of upstate New York and introduces composer-fiddler-guitarist- quarry-worker Grant Rogers.
From The Rainbow Quest Series.
Prod-SEEGER Dist-CWATER

Norman The Doorman C 14 MIN
16MM FILM, 3/4 OR 1/2 IN VIDEO
Uses the original pictures and text from the children's book of the same title, written and illustrated by Don Freeman. Tells the story of a mouse who is a doorman at an art museum where he wins a prize and many friends with the tiny mobiles that he fashions from mousetraps.
Prod-WWS Dist-WWS 1971

Norman's New Garden C 13 MIN
16MM FILM, 3/4 OR 1/2 IN VIDEO
Tells how Norman decides to pay some attention to his yard and starts planting trees.
Prod-GFILM Dist-WOMBAT 1981

Normandy - D-Day B 30 MIN
16MM FILM OPTICAL SOUND I-C
Describes Operation Overlord and D-Day. Tells how artificial harbors were constructed and how ships departed from British ports carrying troops and supplies. Describes the defeat of Field Marshall Rommel.
From The Victory At Sea Series.
Prod-GRACUR Dist-GRACUR

Normandy Invasion B 19 MIN
16MM FILM, 3/4 OR 1/2 IN VIDEO
Presents a photographic record of the preparations for an invasion of Europe in 1944.
Prod-USCG Dist-USNAC

Norrkoping - The Spiral C 16 MIN
16MM FILM OPTICAL SOUND
Presents a picture of modern Norrkoping with its industries and recreational areas.
Prod-ASI Dist-AUDPLN

North America - Cenozoic C 28 MIN
3/4 OR 1/2 INCH VIDEO CASSETTE IND
See series title for descriptive statement.
From The Basic And Petroleum Geology For Non-Geologists - Historical...--Series.
Prod-PHILLP Dist-GPCV

North America - Early Paleozoic C 43 MIN
3/4 OR 1/2 INCH VIDEO CASSETTE IND
See series title for descriptive statement.
From The Basic And Petroleum Geology For Non-Geologists - Historical...--Series.
Prod-PHILLP Dist-GPCV

North America - Its Coastlines C 14 MIN
16MM FILM, 3/4 OR 1/2 IN VIDEO I-J
Traces the historic and economic roles of coastlines, and shows the different coastlines, how they form and how they slowly change.
From The North America Series.
Prod-CORF Dist-CORF 1971

North America - Its Mountains C 14 MIN
16MM FILM, 3/4 OR 1/2 IN VIDEO I-J
Describes the mountain ranges of North America, showing how they vary in structure, climate, plant and animal life. Discusses ways in which they have affected man.
From The North America Series.
Prod-CORF Dist-CORF 1971

North America - Its Plains And Plateaus C 16 MIN
16MM FILM, 3/4 OR 1/2 IN VIDEO I-J
Shows the characteristics and location of major plains and plateaus of North America, and discusses some of the ways in which they have affected man's use of the land.
From The North America Series.
Prod-CORF Dist-CORF 1971

North America - Its Rivers C 14 MIN
16MM FILM, 3/4 OR 1/2 IN VIDEO I-J
Explores the distinctive features of the major rivers of the continent, and discusses their contributions to the farming, recreation, transportation and hydroelectric power of North America.
From The North America Series.
Prod-CORF Dist-CORF 1971

North America - Late Paleozoic C 37 MIN
3/4 OR 1/2 INCH VIDEO CASSETTE IND
See series title for descriptive statement.
From The Basic And Petroleum Geology For Non-Geologists - Historical...--Series.
Prod-PHILLP Dist-GPCV

North America - Mesozoic C 32 MIN
3/4 OR 1/2 INCH VIDEO CASSETTE IND
See series title for descriptive statement.
From The Basic And Petroleum Geology For Non-Geologists - Historical...--Series.
Prod-PHILLP Dist-GPCV

North America - The Continent C 17 MIN
16MM FILM, 3/4 OR 1/2 IN VIDEO I-J
Shows the basic land forms and climates of the major regions of North America, including the coastal highlands, Western Cordillera and Appalachian highlands. Indicates the relationship of geography and human use.
From The North America Series.
Prod-CORF Dist-CORF 1966

North America--A Series
16MM FILM, 3/4 OR 1/2 IN VIDEO
Explores the geography of North America.
Prod-CORF Dist-CORF

North America - Its Coastlines 14 MIN
North America - Its Mountains 14 MIN
North America - Its Plains And Plateaus 16 MIN
North America - Its Rivers 14 MIN
North America - The Continent 17 MIN

North American Framework C 51 MIN
3/4 OR 1/2 INCH VIDEO CASSETTE IND
See series title for descriptive statement.
From The Basic Geology Series.
Prod-GPCV Dist-GPCV

North American Indian Legends C 21 MIN
16MM FILM, 3/4 OR 1/2 IN VIDEO I-J
Describes tribal traditions, explains natural events and expresses the values of the North American Indian people. Features legends which represent the original stories of Indians in three different geographical regions of North America.
Prod-BFA Dist-PHENIX 1973

North American Indian--A Series
16MM FILM, 3/4 OR 1/2 IN VIDEO
Discusses the plight of the American Indians, from the opening of the West to the present.
Prod-MGHT Dist-MGHT 1971

How The West Was Won And Honor Lost 25 MIN
Lament Of The Reservation 24 MIN
Treaties Made, Treaties Broken 18 MIN

North American Indians Today C 25 MIN
16MM FILM, 3/4 OR 1/2 IN VIDEO H-C A
Deals with the efforts of North American Indians to learn about their cultural heritage and to protect their lands.
LC NO. 80-706338
Prod-NGS Dist-NGS 1977

North American Neighbors C 24 MIN
16MM FILM OPTICAL SOUND H A
Presents the hopes, despairs and conflicts of life in the North American continent from Alaska to the islands of the Caribbean. Discusses the Christian responsibility of Protestantism to work cooperatively toward their solution.
Prod-YALEDV Dist-YALEDV

North American Scene, The B 30 MIN
16MM FILM OPTICAL SOUND H-C A
Dr Vincent Harding surveys the presence of Afro-Americans in the United States and discusses such subjects as the underground railroad, achievements in public office, education, military service and the current migration to the urban north.
From The Black History, Section 02 - Where Are The Afro-Americans Now Series.
LC NO. 71-704029
Prod-WCBSTV Dist-HRAW 1969

North American Species--A Series
16MM FILM, 3/4 OR 1/2 IN VIDEO
Shows how to identify the sensory structures or organs of several bird and animal species, the purpose of specific behavior patterns of a species, including courtship, migration, defensive behavior, and feeding, and distinguishing among herbivores, omnivores and carnivores. Compares protective features, such as coloration and escape techniques.
Prod-KARVF Dist-BCNFL

Autumn With Grizzlies 015 MIN
Bighorns Of Beauty Creek 025 MIN
Double Life Of The Whooping Crane, The 015 MIN
Wolves And Coyotes Of The Rockies 015 MIN

North Brazil C 18 MIN
16MM FILM, 3/4 OR 1/2 IN VIDEO I-H A
Explores Brazil, a land of extraordinary geography and Indian culture.
From The Latin American Series - A Focus On People Series.
Prod-CLAIB Dist-SF 1973

North Carolina - Golf State, USA C 15 MIN
16MM FILM, 3/4 OR 1/2 IN VIDEO J-C A
Portrays North Carolina, the richest golf state, with its 500,000 dollar World Open, World Golf Hall of Fame and many other great attractions. Views public and private Alpine, Piedmont and Sandhill courses of the Tar Heel state.
Prod-KLEINW Dist-KLEINW 1975

North Carolina - Mineral State, USA C 15 MIN
16MM FILM, 3/4 OR 1/2 IN VIDEO
Presents a study of the mineral resources of North Carolina, showing mining reclamation programs resulting in golf courses, baseball fields, parks and lakes.
Prod-KLEINW Dist-KLEINW

North China Commune C 80 MIN
16MM FILM, 3/4 OR 1/2 IN VIDEO H-C A
Looks at harvesting in a North China commune. Shows that intensive cropping methods and the orchestrated effort at harvest time of all commune members make it possible to support a population of 14,500 on only 3,000 acres of land.
Prod-NFBC Dist-NFBC 1979

North China Factory C 57 MIN
16MM FILM, 3/4 OR 1/2 IN VIDEO H-C A
Shows a factory community in China where over 6,000 workers process, spin and weave raw cotton into eighty million meters of high-quality cloth per year. Visits the workers' residential, social, recreational and educational facilities, all of which are located on factory property. Highlights retirement and wedding ceremonies in which factory management plays a major part.
Prod-NFBC Dist-NFBC 1980

North Dakota - Flickertail Flashbacks B 22 MIN
16MM FILM OPTICAL SOUND
Uses still and moving pictures taken from 1915 to 1920 in order to show the life and times of that period in North Dakota.
LC NO. 75-702974
Prod-SNYDBF Dist-SNYDBF 1974

North Dakota - Roughrider Country C 21 MIN
16MM FILM OPTICAL SOUND
A film trip around the state of North Dakota pointing out places of interest to tourists.
LC NO. 74-711369
Prod-GNDA Dist-GNDA 1970

North Dakota Agriculture - Green And Gold C 30 MIN
16MM FILM OPTICAL SOUND
Comments briefly on the world food problem and illustrates various facets of the agricultural industry in North Dakota. Shows the role of North Dakota State University in agricultural research.
LC NO. 77-701821
Prod-NDASU Dist-NDSFL Prodn-SNYDBF 1977

North Hatley Antique Sale C 14 MIN
16MM FILM OPTICAL SOUND
Highlights an antique sale in a small Quebec town.
From The Journal Series.
LC NO. 74-701981
Prod-FIARTS Dist-CANFDC 1973

North Indian Village C 32 MIN
16MM FILM, 3/4 OR 1/2 IN VIDEO H-C
Describes life and culture in the North Indian village of Khalapur.
Prod-HITCHJ Dist-IFB 1958

North Of Hudson Bay B 55 MIN
16MM FILM SILENT
Presents a melodrama in which a man goes to Canada to investigate the murder of his brother, whose partner is wrongfully being charged with the crime.
LC NO. 75-708944
Prod-TWCF Dist-TWCF 1923

North Of Slavery C 29 MIN
2 INCH VIDEOTAPE
See series title for descriptive statement.
From The Black Experience Series.
Prod-WTTWTV Dist-PUBTEL

North Of The Yukon C 103 MIN
3/4 OR 1/2 INCH VIDEO CASSETTE K A
Features Lorne Greene narrating a story of an Eskimo's courage in a raw domain.
Prod-SUTHRB Dist-SUTHRB

North Of 60 Degrees - Destiny Uncertain--A Series

Explores the far north of Canada's Northwest Territories, the Yukon and Alaska, and the realities of life for the people that live there. Questions the future of this land with its reserves of minerals, oil and natural gas, and spotlights the culture of its original inhabitants. Also available in two-inch quad and one-inch videotape.
Prod-TVOTAR Dist-NAMPBC

Alaska Experience, The 029 MIN
Mending Bodies And Souls 029 MIN
New Ways Of Knowing 029 MIN
Tell Me Who I Am 029 MIN
They Came To Stay 029 MIN

North Sea Islanders C 19 MIN
16MM FILM, 3/4 OR 1/2 IN VIDEO P-C
Contrasts living on an island and living on a continental land mass, showing man against the elements and how he survives.
From The Man And His World Series.
Prod-FI Dist-FI 1969

North To Adventure C 30 MIN
16MM FILM OPTICAL SOUND
Shows some of the most magnificent scenery on our continent while exploring a great variety of game as it is seen and hunted.
Prod-SFI Dist-SFI

North To Freedom C 15 MIN
16MM FILM, 3/4 OR 1/2 IN VIDEO I
Describes the establishment and maintenance of the Underground Railroad, which helped freedom-seeking slaves on the journey north.
From The American Scrapbook Series.
Prod-WVIZTV Dist-GPITVL 1977

North Wind And The Sun, The C 9 MIN
16MM FILM, 3/4 OR 1/2 IN VIDEO P-I
Presents the Greek and African legend of The North Wind And

The Sun about a contest between these two powerful forces of nature to see which one is the stronger.
From The Classic Tales Retold Series.
Prod-BFA Dist-PHENIX 1977

North Wind And The Sun, The - A Fable By Aesop C 3 MIN
16MM FILM, 3/4 OR 1/2 IN VIDEO I
Presents an animated version of the Aesop fable about the duel between the North Wind and the Sun to see which was a better force when it comes to making a man take off his coat.
Prod-NFBC Dist-NFBC 1972

North Wind And The Sun, The - An Aesop Fable C 7 MIN
16MM FILM, 3/4 OR 1/2 IN VIDEO P
Animated story of a contest between the North Wind and the Sun. Teaches the lesson that you can sometimes do more by being gentle than you can by using force.
Prod-GAKKEN Dist-CORF 1962

North With The Spring C 52 MIN
16MM FILM, 3/4 OR 1/2 IN VIDEO
Follows spring on a 17,000-mile journey from the Florida Everglades to the Canadian Arctic. Based on the writings of Edwin Way Teale.
Prod-DOCUA Dist-CNEMAG

Northeast Farm Community X 15 MIN
16MM FILM, 3/4 OR 1/2 IN VIDEO I-J
Portrays the life of a typical northeastern family in the early 1800's. Illustrates the farmer's increasing reliance on community services such as grist mill, blacksmith shop, general store, church and school.
From The Pioneer Life Series.
Prod-IU Dist-IU 1960

Northern Australian Regional Survey, Pt 2 - The Barkly Region C 28 MIN
16MM FILM OPTICAL SOUND H A
Deals with the Barkly region of the Northern Territory and Queensland, which was surveyed during 1948-49 by the CSIRO division of Land Research and Regional Survey. Describes the four main areas into which the region is divided, and discusses their topography, soils, vegetation, industries and potentialities.
LC NO. FIA65-1067
Prod-CSIROA Dist-CSIROA 1950

Northern Coastal Lowlands, The, Pt 1 C 25 MIN
16MM FILM OPTICAL SOUND H-C A
Discusses each German region's lifestyles, economy, problems, and opportunities for the future. Provides some unusual helicopter views of Germany's geography.
Prod-WSTGLC Dist-WSTGLC

Northern Elephant Seal C 16 MIN
16MM FILM, 3/4 OR 1/2 IN VIDEO H-C A
Observes a colony of seals during the breeding season in the Channel Islands near Los Angeles. Studies the biology and reproductive behavior of the seals and of the social cohesiveness and vocal communication of animal colonies. Illustrates the structure and the maintenance of dominance hierarchy and shows the correlation between sexual dimorphism, male aggressiveness and a highly polygamous social structure.
Prod-UCLA Dist-UCEMC Prodn-BARBOO 1962

Northern Forests, The C 55 MIN
16MM FILM, 3/4 OR 1/2 IN VIDEO H-C A
Shows that trees of the coniferous forests have special adaptations that enable them to survive long cold winters. Reveals that many animals that inhabit these vast forests are dependent on the trees for leaves, cones or bark. Demonstrates that in the deciduous woodland, bears, skunks, raccoons, squirrels and opossums put on fat for the winter.
From The Living Planet Series. Pt 3
Prod-BBCTV Dist-TIMLIF 1984

Northern Ireland - A Decade Of Civil Strife C 26 MIN
3/4 OR 1/2 INCH VIDEO CASSETTE H-C A
Focuses on the violent events in Northern Ireland between 1969 and 1979.
Prod-UPI Dist-JOU

Northern Ireland - The Hunger Strikers C 15 MIN
3/4 OR 1/2 INCH VIDEO CASSETTE J-H
Discusses the death of IRA hunger strikers at Maze Prison in Belfast, Northern Ireland. Examines the history of the hostilities and the implications of growing world support for the IRA.
Prod-JOU Dist-JOU

Northern Ireland - The Troubles Continue C 27 MIN
3/4 OR 1/2 INCH VIDEO CASSETTE H-C A
Looks at elections in Northern Ireland which were held in hopes that a new Northern Ireland Assembly would aid in a political solution to the violence that has plagued Northern Ireland since 1967. Explores the conflicts, the factions and the government of this divided nation.
Prod-JOU Dist-JOU

Northern Irish People's Peace Movement, Pt 1 C 29 MIN
3/4 INCH VIDEO CASSETTE
Explains the purpose of the nonsectarian and nonpartisan People's Peace Movement of Northern Ireland, founded after three Belfast children were killed during a gun battle. Tells how the violence affects the everyday lives of people on both sides of the political question.
From The Woman Series.
Prod-WNEDTV Dist-PUBTEL

Northern Irish People's Peace Movement, Pt 2 C 29 MIN
3/4 INCH VIDEO CASSETTE
Presents the founders of the People's Peace Movement of Northern Ireland discussing their goals for peace.
From The Woman Series.
Prod-WNEDTV Dist-PUBTEL

Northern Irish Question, The - Another View C 29 MIN
3/4 INCH VIDEO CASSETTE
Describes the Irish Republican movement's political plans for peace. Explains how funds contributed by Americans to the people of Northern Ireland are being used and assesses President Carter's human rights stand.
From The Woman Series.
Prod-WNEDTV Dist-PUBTEL

Northern Lakes, The C 14 MIN
16MM FILM, 3/4 OR 1/2 IN VIDEO I-H A
Surveys the lake region of the upper midwestern states and central provinces of Canada. Explores the ecosystem, the interrelationship of the water habitat and the forest and the relationship of the animal life to each habitat.
From The Natural Environment Series.
Prod-WILFGP Dist-JOU 1978

Northern Lights C 90 MIN
3/4 OR 1/2 INCH VIDEO CASSETTE H-C A
Focuses on the hardships encountered by first and second generation Scandinavians who emigrated to the U S and scattered over the plains, onto homesteads and into sod shanties. Reveals that poor families were victims of price fixing and foreclosure schemes which gave rise to a farmers' movement called the Nonpartisan League.
Prod-FI Dist-FI 1979

Northern Lights B 95 MIN
16MM FILM - 3/4 IN VIDEO J-C A
Tells of the first and second generation Scandinavians who immigrated to the U S and scattered over the barren plains. Reveals the hostility and fierceness of the North Dakota winter.
Prod-FIRS Dist-FIRS

Northern Lights C 95 MIN
3/4 OR 1/2 INCH VIDEO CASSETTE
Reveals the story of one of the most successful agrarian movements in United States history, of firstand second-generation Scandinavians who immigrated to America and scattered over the plains, onto homesteads and into sod shanties.
Prod-NLP Dist-NFPS

Northern Plains, The B 30 MIN
3/4 INCH VIDEO CASSETTE
Examines the history of legendary plains warriors, the Sioux and Crow tribes, who fought tenaciously against the United States for their land and means of survival. Looks at the present status of their descendents.
From The Silent Heritage - The American Indian Series.
Prod-UMITV Dist-UMITV 1966

Northern Reaction, Pt 1 B 30 MIN
16MM FILM OPTICAL SOUND H-C A
William Strickland discusses the reaction in the North to the storm of protest that occurred in the South, the beginnings of the anti-poverty programs and the influence of Black nationalism.
LC NO. 78-704107
Prod-WCBSTV Dist-HRAW 1969

Northern Reaction, Pt 2 - The Urban Rebellions B 30 MIN
16MM FILM OPTICAL SOUND H-C A
William Strickland defines the nature of the United States as racist and discusses the way in which Blacks in the North have begun to react to this realization. He discusses the historic precedents for acts such as urban rebellions which become the basis for legal action if successful, or heightened oppression if unsuccessful.
From The Black History, Section 20 - Freedom Movement Series.
LC NO. 71-704108
Prod-WCBSTV Dist-HRAW 1969

Northern Spring C 8 MIN
16MM FILM, 3/4 OR 1/2 IN VIDEO P-I
Explores the effects of warmer weather on the flora of the forest.
Prod-JOU Dist-JOU 1980

Northern Yukon Research Program C 10 MIN
16MM FILM, 3/4 OR 1/2 IN VIDEO
Describes a major archaeological research project in the northern Yukon which is producing evidence which suggests the presence of man in that region much earlier than was previously suspected.
From The Discovery Series.
Prod-UTORMC Dist-UTORMC

Northward Migration And Urban Conflict B 30 MIN
2 INCH VIDEOTAPE H-C A
See series title for descriptive statement.
From The Americans From Africa - A History Series. No. 22
Prod-CVETVC Dist-GPITVL Prodn-WCVETV

Northwest Coast Indians C 26 MIN
3/4 OR 1/2 INCH VIDEO CASSETTE
Reconstructs an abandoned village site on the basis of material evidence excavated from the artifacts from the Ozette Indian Village at Cape Alava, Washington.
Prod-UWASHP Dist-UWASHP

Northwest Coast Indians - A Search For The Past C 26 MIN
16MM FILM OPTICAL SOUND
Depicts the reconstruction of the abandoned village site of the Ozette Indians at Cape Alava, Washington by archaeologists and their students from Washington State University. Features material evidence they have excavated a rich variety of artifacts, such as pieces of baskets, bone and stone tools, combs, traces of houses and fire hearths.
Prod-KIRL Dist-UWASHP

Northwest Empire C 30 MIN
16MM FILM OPTICAL SOUND
Shows the beauty of the Pacific Northwest from its mountain lakes and snow capped peaks to its rugged coastline. Features the wildlife in the area and calls attention to natural resources which give the northwest empire an amazing industrial potential.
Prod-UPR Dist-UPR

Northwest Medley C 7 MIN
16MM FILM OPTICAL SOUND
Presents scences of the waters, woods and mountains of the American Northwest coordinated with a musical accompaniment to convey the moods of this region.
LC NO. 78-702492
Prod-LOH Dist-LOH 1968

Northwest Ordinance And The Constitutional Convention B 30 MIN
16MM FILM OPTICAL SOUND H-C A
Professor Staughton Lynd analyzes the Northwest Ordinance and those articles of the Constitution which refer to slavery and the slave trade and explains the sectional conflict that accompanied the addition of five states in which slavery was to be prohibited.
From The Black History, Section 04 - Slave Trade And Slavery Series.
LC NO. 74-704043
Prod-WCBSTV Dist-HRAW 1969

Northwest To Alaska C 26 MIN
16MM FILM OPTICAL SOUND
A study of the life of the animals and man in the Alaskan wilderness, from the unpeopled valleys of Robert Service to Eskimo villages on the Northwest Coast. Includes scenes of goats, grizzlies, wolves, caribou and the gyrfalcon.
From The Audubon Wildlife Theatre Series.
LC NO. 70-710206
Prod-KEGPL Dist-AVEXP 1968

Northwest USA B 22 MIN
3/4 INCH VIDEO CASSETTE
Reviews the resources, industries and people of Oregon and Washington. Issued in 1949 as a motion picture.
From The American Scene Series. No. 10
LC NO. 79-706696
Prod-USOWI Dist-USNAC 1979

Northwest Visionaries C 58 MIN
3/4 OR 1/2 INCH VIDEO CASSETTE
Documents the work of the Northwest American artists Mark Tobey, Kenneth Callahan, Morris Graves, Margaret Tomkins, Guy Anderson, Paul Horiuchi, Helmi Junoven and George Tsutakawa. Features the influence of nature and Indian culture.
Prod-LEVINK Dist-MEDIPR 1979

Northwest, The C 15 MIN
3/4 OR 1/2 INCH VIDEO CASSETTE I
Presents John Rugg reviewing the exploration and settlement of the American Northwest, including the Columbia River, the Lewis and Clark expedition and the Oregon Trail. Emphasizes the region's major industries, namely lumber products and aircraft manufacturing.
From The American Legacy Series. Program 14
LC NO. 83-706671
Prod-KRMATV Dist-AITECH 1983

Northwest, The - Mountains To The Sea C 23 MIN
16MM FILM, 3/4 OR 1/2 IN VIDEO I-H A
Surveys the natural habitats and plant and animal life in the seas, marshlands, rain forests and mountains of Northwest Canada.
From The Natural Environment Series.
Prod-WILFGP Dist-JOU 1977

Northwestern American Indian War Dance Contest C 12 MIN
16MM FILM, 3/4 OR 1/2 IN VIDEO J-C A
Shows various Indian peoples competing in the Northwestern War Dance Contest, held annually in Seattle, Washington. Shows a wide variety of regional and individual styles.
Prod-UWASHP Dist-UWASHP 1971

Norway C 17 MIN
16MM FILM, 3/4 OR 1/2 IN VIDEO J-H
Shows the land, people and industry of Norway.
From The Modern Europe Series.
Prod-JOU Dist-JOU

Norway C 29 MIN
2 INCH VIDEOTAPE
Features home economist Joan Hood presenting a culinary tour of specialty dishes from around the world. Shows the preparation of Norwegian dishes ranging from peasant cookery to continental cuisine.
From The International Cookbook Series.
Prod-WMVSTV Dist-PUBTEL

Norway Of Edvard Grieg, The C 17 MIN
16MM FILM OPTICAL SOUND J-C A
Shows composer Edvard Grieg's home and the Norwegian countryside as seen through the eyes of the Idyllwild Youth Symphony and interpreted through their performance of a Grieg concerto.
From The Idyllwild Youth Symphony In Scandinavia Series.
LC NO. FIA66-494
Prod-IDYLWD Dist-AVED 1970

Norwegian Fjord, A C 13 MIN
16MM FILM, 3/4 OR 1/2 IN VIDEO P-C
Shows fishing, dairy farming, fruit farming and manufacturing of aluminum as well as the lakes and rivers that supply the water for an electric power plant along the fjord.
From The Man And His World Series.
Prod-FI Dist-FI 1969

Nose And Tina C 28 MIN
16MM FILM, 3/4 OR 1/2 IN VIDEO C A
Describes the love between Nose and Tina, a brakeman and a hooker. Captures the domestic details of their life together, and their hassles with the law, work and money.
Prod-NFBC Dist-NFBC 1980

Nose For News, A C 30 MIN
3/4 OR 1/2 INCH VIDEO CASSETTE I-J
Stresses that comparative shopping for fresh food is the economical way to good eating.
From The High Feather Series. Pt 4
LC NO. 83-706050
Prod-NYSED Dist-GPITVL 1982

Nose Job C 11 MIN
16MM FILM, 3/4 OR 1/2 IN VIDEO
Studies the role of physical appearance in self-esteem. Follows a teenager before, during and after surgery, and interviews her, her parents and her surgeon.
LC NO. 82-706146
Prod-CBSNEW Dist-MOKIN

Nose, The B 11 MIN
16MM FILM OPTICAL SOUND
Presents Gogol's celebrated short story, The Nose, animated and without words, in fantastic moving pictures that capture the scene and spirit of 19th century Russia. Produced by Alexander Alexeieff and Claire Parker.
Prod-STARRC Dist-STARRC 1963

Nose, The C 20 MIN
16MM FILM OPTICAL SOUND
Demonstrates physical examination of the nose. Includes normal and abnormal views of the exterior, vestibule, septum, mucosa and lateral wall. Shows conditions of rhinophyma, congenital syphilitic saddle nose, atrophy due to leprosy, tuberculin lupus vulgaris and disfigurement due to trauma. Considers nasal discharges as to cause and meaning.
LC NO. 74-705215
Prod-USGSA Dist-USNAC 1969

Nose, The - Structure And Function X 11 MIN
16MM FILM, 3/4 OR 1/2 IN VIDEO J-C
Uses animation and microphotography to illustrate the breathing and smelling functions of the nose. Explains the ingenious protective system of the breathing organs and shows the reasons for breakdowns in the nasal passages.
Prod-EBF Dist-EBEC 1954

Nosegays, One-Sided And Centerpiece Designs C 60 MIN
1/2 IN VIDEO CASSETTE BETA/VHS
Provides a step-by-step program on how to make nosegays, one-sided and centerpiece designs. Discusses basic design theory, and gives an overview of all the materials used in flower arranging.
Prod-RMI Dist-RMI

Nosey Dobson C 55 MIN
16MM FILM OPTICAL SOUND P-I
Tells the story of Nosey Dobson, a compulsive snooper whose attempts at being a detective irritate everyone, including the town constable. Reveals that when he stumbles onto a genuine plot to steal priceless silver, no one will believe him.
Prod-CHILDF Dist-LUF 1979

Nosferatu B 63 MIN
3/4 OR 1/2 INCH VIDEO CASSETTE
Presents the first version of Dracula, a silent picture with musical score.
Prod-ADVCAS Dist-ADVCAS

Nosferatu (German) B 65 MIN
16MM FILM SILENT
A silent motion picture with German subtitles. Tells the story of the Bremer secretary Hutter, who travels to Count Orlock, known as Nosferatu, in order to sign a bill of sale, and discovers that Nosferatu is a vampire. Continues as Nosferatu follows Hutter to Bremen where the plague breaks out, and ends with Hutter's young wife saving her husband and the city from the monster. Based on the book DRACULA by Bram Stoker.
Prod-WSTGLC Dist-WSTGLC 1921

Nosotros Leemos C 20 MIN
3/4 OR 1/2 INCH VIDEO CASSETTE
Twenty half-hour videos dealing with fundamentals of reading. Stresses basic survival skills.
Prod-CAMB Dist-CAMB

Nosotros Venceremos (We Shall Overcome) B 11 MIN
16MM FILM OPTICAL SOUND
An organizing tool for United Farm Workers organizing committee members and their supporters. Presents still photographs of the Delano grape strike. Shows the march to Sacramento, the fast of Casear Chavez and the first victory, all combined with songs and speeches of the movement.
LC NO. 72-700360
Prod-UFWOC Dist-UFWA Prodn-JLV 1971

Nossa Terra B 40 MIN
16MM FILM OPTICAL SOUND
Discusses how Black people can take control of their destiny after 400 years of colonial oppression. Explains why the people of Portuguese Guinea have chosen armed struggle. Shows that conditions of life are constantly improved in the liberated areas while the struggle continues. Narrated by Julius Lester.
Prod-UNKNWN Dist-SFN 1967

Not A Love Story - A Film About Pornography C 69 MIN
16MM FILM, 3/4 OR 1/2 IN VIDEO C A
Documents the journey of two women who set off to explore the world of peep shows, strip joints and sex supermarkets. Offers insights and perspectives from men and women who earn their living in the porn trade, and with some of pornography's most outspoken critics.
Prod-NFBC Dist-NFBC 1981

Not A Place C 28 MIN
16MM FILM OPTICAL SOUND
Documents the teacher-training program at Appalachian State University in Boone, North Carolina, designed to open lines of communication between the university, the public schools and the community.
From The Dynamics Of Change Series.
LC NO. 73-700895
Prod-EDSD Dist-EDSD 1973

Not A Sparrow Falls C 28 MIN
16MM FILM OPTICAL SOUND
Designed to promote understanding and support for the alcoholics program of the Salvation Army's Harbor Light Center in Chicago.
LC NO. 74-702496
Prod-SALVA Dist-SALVA Prodn-SPAPRO 1974

Not A Weapon Or A Star C 29 MIN
16MM FILM, 3/4 OR 1/2 IN VIDEO
Examines successful crime prevention programs in urban, suburban and rural communities. Emphasizes the need for communication and interaction between the community and the police.
Prod-OLINC Dist-MTI 1977

Not As A Black Person, As A Person C 25 MIN
16MM FILM OPTICAL SOUND
Describes a program initiated by Ford to acquaint Black students and faculty with the workings of the Ford Motor Company. Shows executives from the company as they hold talks and conduct seminars concerning business and education.
LC NO. 79-711370
Prod-FMCMP Dist-FORDFL 1970

Not By Accident - A Logical Look At Accident Investigation C 19 MIN
16MM FILM - 3/4 IN VIDEO
Tells supervisors how to investigate an accident. Presents a supervisor who gets help from the company computer with its safety analysis log. Shows how to interview an accident victim, find out what happened, check the accident scene and look for things to prevent similar accidents in the future.
Prod-ALLIED Dist-BNA

Not By Bread Alone B 25 MIN
16MM FILM OPTICAL SOUND
Discusses the problems of feeding and nutrition of the aged and the nurses aide's key role in geriatric care.
Prod-UHOSF Dist-HF Prodn-HF 1966

Not By Chance C 18 MIN
16MM FILM OPTICAL SOUND
Presents a typical day in the life of a life insurance agent.
LC NO. 76-702660
Prod-MASINS Dist-MMLI Prodn-CORWNR 1976

Not By Jeans Alone C 30 MIN
16MM FILM, 3/4 OR 1/2 IN VIDEO C A
Tells how the Levi Strauss company sought to move beyond jeans to Levi Tailored Classics, a market-opening attempt that encountered problems in a fast-changing marketplace.
From The Enterprise Series.
LC NO. 81-707548
Prod-WGBHTV Dist-LCOA Prodn-DORSOL 1981

Not By Magic B 14 MIN
16MM FILM OPTICAL SOUND
Explains the function of the General Services Administration's federal supply service.
LC NO. 74-705216
Prod-USGSA Dist-USNAC

Not Enough C 30 MIN
16MM FILM OPTICAL SOUND J-H
Questions whether the rich countries are doing enough to help the large and growing populations of Africa, Asia and Latin America, and what are the less developed countries doing themselves to improve their standard of living. Illustrates what is being done to solve these problems.
Prod-OECD Dist-MLA 1967

Not Even One Chance B 10 MIN
16MM FILM OPTICAL SOUND
Shows man who takes chances because he's 'IN A HURRY' and for other 'GOOD' reasons. Suggests that taking chances is always a gamble, and that the wrong attitudes that cause chance taking need changing.
From The Safety Wise Series.
Prod-DUNN Dist-NSC 1960

Not Far From Home C 30 MIN
16MM FILM OPTICAL SOUND
Presents a film journal of living in the country.
LC NO. 75-704327
Prod-CANFDC Dist-CANFDC 1974

Not For Everyone C 11 MIN
3/4 OR 1/2 INCH VIDEO CASSETTE
Uses contemporary film techniques creating a montage of image and sound as a recruitment film for radiation technology aimed at high school students. Shows cancer research advantages with inner as well as material rewards.
Prod-AMCS Dist-AMCS 1984

Not For Ourselves Alone C 29 MIN
16MM FILM, 3/4 OR 1/2 IN VIDEO
Emphasizes the contribution of the Armed Forces of the United States in upholding the ideals of the Founding Fathers. Offers an overview of four major crisis periods and conflicts in American history, including the Revolutionary War, the Civil War, the War of 1812 and the two World Wars.
Prod-USOIAF Dist-PHENIX 1975

Not If - But How C 20 MIN
16MM FILM, 3/4 OR 1/2 IN VIDEO S
Focuses on a regular elementary classroom teacher with a new student who has cerebral palsy. Traces her progress from the student's initial seizure and fall, through her search for advice, to her consultation with the principal, the student's mother, a doctor and a physical therapist.
LC NO. 82-706530
Prod-NMMCHP Dist-HUBDSC 1981

Not In My Family - Mothers Speak Out On Sexual Abuse Of Children C 33 MIN
16MM FILM, 3/4 OR 1/2 IN VIDEO C A
Presents mothers who tell how they learned their husbands were molesting their daughters, their reactions and what they wished they had done to protect their children.
LC NO. 84-706002
Prod-BAKRSR Dist-LAWREN 1983

Not Just A Spectator C 35 MIN
16MM FILM OPTICAL SOUND
Depicts sports and recreational activities open to the handicapped person if proper facilities are provided.
Prod-IREFL Dist-IREFL 1974

Not Me Alone C 31 MIN
3/4 OR 1/2 INCH VIDEO CASSETTE A
Shows one couple's labor and delivery, presenting an unromanticized picture which will make childbirth more real and manageable and provide men a better understanding of the role they can play during pregnancy.
Prod-POLYMR Dist-POLYMR

Not Me Alone - Preparation For Childbirth C 31 MIN
16MM FILM OPTICAL SOUND H-C A
Follows a couple at natural childbirth training classes, practicing breathing exercises at home, sharing labor and delivery and caring for the baby in the hospital.
LC NO. 76-703278
Prod-POLYMR Dist-POLYMR Prodn-WEINSM 1970

Not My Problem C 18 MIN
16MM FILM, 3/4 OR 1/2 IN VIDEO
Focuses on a 16-year-old boy's reactions when he learns that his girlfriend is pregnant.
Prod-BARR Dist-BARR 1979

Not My Problem (Captioned) C 18 MIN
16MM FILM - VIDEO, ALL FORMATS J-H
Deals with teenage pregnancy, focusing on the experiences and responsibilities of sexually active teenage boys.
Prod-BARR Dist-BARR

Not Only Spectators B 15 MIN
16MM FILM OPTICAL SOUND
Presents a Swedish view of responsible journalism.
Prod-ASI Dist-AUDPLN

Not Only Strangers C 23 MIN
16MM FILM, 3/4 OR 1/2 IN VIDEO H-C A
Tells the story of a college coed who is brutally raped by a classmate. Describes her shock, revulsion, guilt and anger and shows the painful but necessary process leading up to the filing of criminal charges.
LC NO. 80-706823
Prod-NOTOS Dist-CORF 1980

Not Reconciled (German) B 51 MIN
16MM FILM OPTICAL SOUND
Features the explanations offered by one German generation to another of the losses it suffered and mistakes it committed over a period of 70 years. Based on a novel by Heinrich Boll. Directed by Jean Marie Straub.
Prod-NYFLMS Dist-NYFLMS 1965

Not Sick Enough C 11 MIN
16MM FILM OPTICAL SOUND
Depicts the special problem of mental illness in the unnoticed neurotic.
LC NO. 74-705218
Prod-USSRS Dist-USNAC 1969

Not Since The Pyramids C 29 MIN
16MM FILM OPTICAL SOUND
Shows the characteristics of the construction projects managed by the U S Naval Facilities Engineering Command in Vietnam.
LC NO. 75-700801
Prod-USN Dist-USNAC

Not So Easy - Motorcycle Safety C 17 MIN
16MM FILM, 3/4 OR 1/2 IN VIDEO J-C A
Demonstrates the essential safety rules of motorcycle riding. Emphasizes that if done properly, motorcycle riding is above average in safety and pleasure. Narrated by Peter Fonda.
Prod-FLMFR Dist-FLMFR

Not So Long Ago - 1945-1950 B 54 MIN
16MM FILM, 3/4 OR 1/2 IN VIDEO H-C A
Looks at aspects of American life in the 1940's. Highlights the advent of rockets and television and discusses developments on the political and social scene.
From The Project 20 Series.
Prod-NBC Dist-CRMP 1965

Not So Young As Then C 60 MIN
3/4 OR 1/2 INCH VIDEO CASSETTE
Looks at the life of teenagers today through profiles of five young people of different ages and backgrounds. Examines their views on adults, peers, sexuality, school, drugs, work, values, social concerns and rights.
Prod-WCCOTV Dist-WCCOTV 1979

Not So Young Now As Then C 18 MIN
16MM FILM OPTICAL SOUND
Uses the occasion of a fifteenth anniversary high school reunion in order to explore the feelings of the participants and to reveal the reunion's importance as a cultural event.
LC NO. 74-701398
Prod-BRNDNL Dist-NEWDAY 1974

Not The Same Old Story C 58 MIN
16MM FILM, 3/4 OR 1/2 IN VIDEO H-C A
Offers a positive look at aging in America. Uncovers some extraordinary ways that older people are not only adding years to their lives, but also life to their years. Shatters many of the stereotypes commonly associated with the aged.
LC NO. 84-706100
Prod-DBA Dist-FI 1983

Not The Triumph, But The Struggle C 28 MIN
16MM FILM - 3/4 IN VIDEO
Features the young athletes competing in the AAU Sears National Junior Olympics Championships. Shows more than 1500 boys and girls from all parts of the country.
Prod-SRCCPD Dist-MTP Prodn-UNIVE 1978

Not Together Now C 25 MIN
3/4 OR 1/2 INCH VIDEO CASSETTE
Shows a separated couple and a discussion of why they were first attracted to each other, why they chose to marry and what happened during the course of their lives together.
Prod-POLYMR Dist-POLYMR

Not Together Now - End Of A Marriage C 25 MIN
16MM FILM OPTICAL SOUND H-C A
Features Sheldon and Barbara Renan in separate, informal interviews talking about the breakup of their marriage. Emphasizes one woman's experience of marriage and divorce.
LC NO. 75-700652
Prod-POLYMR Dist-POLYMR 1975

Not With A Bang But With Multiplication - Multiplication, Two Digits Times Two Digits C 15 MIN
3/4 OR 1/2 INCH VIDEO CASSETTE I
Tells how Mac is saved from a kidnapping by Alice's ability to estimate and find the answer to multiplication problems in which regrouping is required.
From The Figure Out Series.
Prod-MAETEL Dist-AITECH 1982

Not With An Empty Quiver C 29 MIN
16MM FILM OPTICAL SOUND H-C A
Features four young Indian men who have either succeeded or failed by society's standards. Combines in-depth interviews and the story of a young Indian boy fighting to overcome obstacles. Stresses the importance of making preparations to adjust to a modern world rather than going forth with 'AN EMPTY QUIVER.'
LC NO. 73-700002
Prod-BYU Dist-BYU 1971

Not Without Sight C 20 MIN
16MM FILM OPTICAL SOUND I-C A
Uses the example of four people with different kinds of eye trouble in order to show the main causes of visual impairment and to show how these impairments affect sight.
LC NO. 74-702922
Prod-AFB Dist-AFB 1974

Not Without Sight C 19 MIN
16MM FILM, 3/4 OR 1/2 IN VIDEO H-C A
Defines the major types of severe visual impairment. Illustrates, using animation, their causes and shows how those with severe impairments can and do function.
Prod-AFB Dist-PHENIX

Not Worth A Continental C 25 MIN
16MM FILM, 3/4 OR 1/2 IN VIDEO
Presents a fictionalized account of the experiences of a colonial American family faced with the conflict between a desire to help the revolutionary forces and a need to keep food for themselves for the winter.
From The Decades Of Decision - The American Revolution Series.
LC NO. 80-706344
Prod-NGS Dist-NGS 1975

Not Yours To Give C 15 MIN
16MM FILM OPTICAL SOUND I-C A
Debate's the government's role as an issuer of charity using an account of an incident from the life of Congressman Davy Crockett.
Prod-WORLDR Dist-WORLDR 1982

Not-So-Private Eyes, The C 26 MIN
16MM FILM, 3/4 OR 1/2 IN VIDEO P-J
Reveals that a young boy decides to play private detective when he becomes convinced that an elderly man is a foreign spy. Tells of the hilarious situations that ensue when the whole gang joins in.
From The Backstreet Six Series.
Prod-LPROP Dist-PHENIX 1980

Not-So-Solid Earth, The C 30 MIN
16MM FILM, 3/4 OR 1/2 IN VIDEO
Traces the discovery of powerful forces deep within the earth that move continents and shift oceans. Shows how geologists, oceanographers, paleontologists and mineralogists gather and analyze supporting data for the theory of continental drift. Illustrates erupting volcanoes and earthquake destruction.
From The Life Around Us Series.
Prod-TIMLIF Dist-TIMLIF

Not-So-Solid Earth, The (Spanish) C 30 MIN
16MM FILM OPTICAL SOUND
Traces the discovery of forces deep within the Earth that move continents and shift oceans.
From The Life Around Us (Spanish) Series.
Prod-TIMLIF Dist-TIMLIF 1971

Notable Contributors To The Psychology Of Personality--A Series

Discusses the emphasis and theories of various psychologists, psychiatrists and other noted authorities in the field of personality psychology.
Prod-EVNSRI Dist-PSUPCR 1966

Dr B F Skinner, Pt 1	50 MIN
Dr B F Skinner, Pt 2	50 MIN
Dr Carl Rogers, Pt 1	
Dr Carl Rogers, Pt 2	
Dr Erich Fromm, Pt 1	50 MIN
Dr Erich Fromm, Pt 2	50 MIN
Dr Erick Erickson, Pt 1	50 MIN
Dr Erick Erickson, Pt 2	50 MIN
Dr Gardner Murphy, Pt 1	50 MIN
Dr Gardner Murphy, Pt 2	50 MIN
Dr Gordon Allport, Pt 1	50 MIN
Dr Gordon Allport, Pt 2	50 MIN
Dr Henry Murray, Pt 1	50 MIN
Dr Henry Murray, Pt 2	27 MIN
Dr J B Rhine, Pt 1	
Dr J B Rhine, Pt 2	
Dr Jean Piaget, Pt 1	
Dr Jean Piaget, Pt 2	
Dr Raymond Cattell, Pt 1	27 MIN
Dr Raymond Cattell, Pt 2	27 MIN

Notating Pitch C 29 MIN
3/4 INCH VIDEO CASSETTE H A
Reviews materials from earlier programs. Introduces one-octave parallel motion scale. Identifies treble and bass clefs, clef signs, leger lines and other symbols.
From The Beginning Piano - An Adult Approach Series. Lesson 3
Prod-COAST Dist-CDTEL

Note From Above, A C 2 MIN
16MM FILM OPTICAL SOUND J-C A
Tells the story of an incorrect issuance of one of the Ten Commandments as 'THOU SHALT KILL.' Shows how people, often too eager to accept and obey laws, followed the commandment before the error could be corrected.
LC NO. 72-700415
Prod-PHID Dist-MMA 1970

Note Machine, The C 14 MIN
3/4 OR 1/2 INCH VIDEO CASSETTE P
Invites students to make up their own quarter and half note sounds and to 'play' them with the note machine.
From The Stepping Into Rhythm Series.
Prod-WVIZTV Dist-AITECH

Note Of Uncertainty, A - The Universe Tomorrow C 28 MIN
16MM FILM, 3/4 OR 1/2 IN VIDEO
Discusses the expansion of the universe and whether it will stop someday and contract upon itself.
From The Understanding Space And Time Series.
Prod-BBCTV Dist-UCEMC 1980

Note Value C 15 MIN
3/4 OR 1/2 INCH VIDEO CASSETTE P-I
Discusses note value in music.
From The Music And Me Series.
Prod-WDCNTV Dist-AITECH 1979

Notes For An African Orestes B 75 MIN
16MM FILM, 3/4 OR 1/2 IN VIDEO A
Documents Pier Paolo Pasolini's plans to make a modern day version of Aeschylus' 'Orestes' in Africa. English language version.
Prod-CNEMAG Dist-CNEMAG 1970

Notes Of A Biology Watcher - A Film With Lewis Thomas C 57 MIN
16MM FILM, 3/4 OR 1/2 IN VIDEO H-C A
Introduces award-winning biologist Lewis Thomas, who explains that all human cells are inhabited by remnants of ancient organisms that took up residence millions of years ago. Offers an intimate portrait of individuality and interconnectedness in nature, examining the courtship of blue crabs, ferocious fights between sea anemones and tiny worms with even tinier plants thriving inside them.
From The Nova Series.
LC NO. 82-707358
Prod-WGBHTV Dist-TIMLIF 1982

Notes Of The Fifth Position C 29 MIN
2 INCH VIDEOTAPE
See series title for descriptive statement.
From The Playing The Guitar II Series.
Prod-KCET Dist-PUBTEL

Notes On A Community Hospital - The Administrator B 29 MIN
16MM FILM OPTICAL SOUND H-C A
Shows the administrator's role as the manager of a formal link between the community and the hospital. Reviews administrative problems and management methods and the hospital board's role and activities.
LC NO. 76-703209
Prod-WPSXTV Dist-PSU Prodn-OCONEL 1976

Notes On A Community Hospital - The Doctor C 28 MIN
16MM FILM OPTICAL SOUND H-C A
Follows an orthopedic surgeon who is vice-president of a hospital's medical staff on his daily routine at the hospital. Includes operating room, emergency room rounds and office scenes and meetings with staff.
LC NO. 76-703210
Prod-WPSXTV Dist-PSU Prodn-OCONEL 1974

Notes On A Community Hospital - The Home-Care Coordinator C 28 MIN
16MM FILM OPTICAL SOUND H-C A
Shows the role of the community hospital home care coordinator, a member of the nursing team who arranges transfer of a patient to a nursing home, deals with a family reluctant to approve transfer and deals with a patient anxious about leaving the hospital.
LC NO. 76-703211
Prod-WPSXTV Dist-PSU Prodn-OCONEL 1974

Notes On A Community Hospital - The Patient C 29 MIN
16MM FILM OPTICAL SOUND H-C A
Follows a young woman admitted to a hospital for surgery as she goes through admission, surgical preparation, surgery and recovery.
LC NO. 76-703212
Prod-WPSXTV Dist-PSU Prodn-OCONEL 1974

Notes On A Community Hospital - The Patient Care Team C 28 MIN
16MM FILM OPTICAL SOUND H-C A
Shows the daily routine of patient care in a hospital focusing on individuals who do the work, primarily the nursing staff, but including medical technologists, dietary and housekeeping staffs.
LC NO. 76-703213
Prod-WPSXTV Dist-PSU Prodn-OCONEL 1974

Notes On A Triangle C 5 MIN
16MM FILM, 3/4 OR 1/2 IN VIDEO J-C A
Uses animation to explore the shape of a triangle.
Prod-NFBC Dist-IFB 1967

Notes On An Appalachia County - Visiting With Darlene B 45 MIN
16MM FILM OPTICAL SOUND C A
Presents a documentary about a 28-year-old married woman with four children who is living on welfare in a 14-dollar-a-month house in Central Pennsylvania. Records her comments and observations as she goes about her household routine.
LC NO. 76-703214
Prod-WPSXTV Dist-PSU Prodn-OCONEL 1974

Notes On Community Hospital B 58 MIN
16MM FILM OPTICAL SOUND
Presents an overview of hospital life as experienced by people involved in the daily operation of a Pennsylvania hospital.
LC NO. 76-703300
Prod-WPSXTV Dist-PSU Prodn-OCONEL 1976

Notes On Nuclear War C 60 MIN
16MM FILM, 3/4 OR 1/2 IN VIDEO C A
Follows the development of the arms race and attempts to unravel some of the political doctrines and military strategies devised by the superpowers to 'govern' their nuclear weapons systems. Looks at the concepts of 'deterrence', 'mutual assured destruction' and 'limited nuclear war.'
From The War Series.
Prod-NFBC Dist-FI

Notes On Seeing - A Film With Dorothy Medhurst C 30 MIN
16MM FILM, 3/4 OR 1/2 IN VIDEO
Presents Canadian art teacher Dorothy Medhurst who has taught children to perceive the excitement and beauty of life around them. Shows how, at the Art Gallery of Ontario, she involves the children in both art and nature and reinforces their explorations in both areas. Explains why she is a critic of early reading, which she feels inhibits creativity in the child.
Prod-FLMLIB Dist-FLMLIB 1982

Notes On The Fifth String C 29 MIN
2 INCH VIDEOTAPE
See series title for descriptive statement.
From The Playing The Guitar I Series.
Prod-KCET Dist-PUBTEL

Notes On The Fifth String, The Eighth Note C 20 MIN
3/4 OR 1/2 INCH VIDEO CASSETTE J-H
See series title for descriptive statement.
From The Guitar, Guitar Series.
Prod-SCITV Dist-GPITVL 1981

Notes On The First Two Strings C 29 MIN
2 INCH VIDEOTAPE
See series title for descriptive statement.
From The Playing The Guitar I Series.
Prod-KCET Dist-PUBTEL

Notes On The Fourth String C 29 MIN
2 INCH VIDEOTAPE
See series title for descriptive statement.
From The Playing The Guitar I Series.
Prod-KCET Dist-PUBTEL

Notes On The Fourth String, Tom Dooley C 20 MIN
3/4 OR 1/2 INCH VIDEO CASSETTE J-H
See series title for descriptive statement.
From The Guitar, Guitar Series.
Prod-SCITV Dist-GPITVL 1981

Notes On The Popular Arts C 20 MIN
16MM FILM, 3/4 OR 1/2 IN VIDEO
Discusses the popular arts in America, telling how they serve as vehicles for self-projection, experience expansion and fantasy fulfillment. Looks at television, pop music, comics, publications and motion pictures.
LC NO. 78-700366
Prod-BASSS Dist-PFP 1978

Notes On The Port Of St Francis B 22 MIN
16MM FILM OPTICAL SOUND H-C
A cinematic poem designed to portray the atmosphere of the city of San Francisco. Narration by Vincent Price is based on a descriptive essay by Robert L Stevenson.
Prod-STAHER Dist-RADIM 1952

Notes On The Second String, Using The Left Hand, Playing A Duet C 20 MIN
3/4 OR 1/2 INCH VIDEO CASSETTE J-H
See series title for descriptive statement.
From The Guitar, Guitar Series.
Prod-SCITV Dist-GPITVL 1981

Notes On The Sixth String C 29 MIN
2 INCH VIDEOTAPE
See series title for descriptive statement.
From The Playing The Guitar I Series.
Prod-KCET Dist-PUBTEL

Notes On The Sixth String, Octaves, The C Scale, The G Scale, On The Bridge To Avignon C 20 MIN
3/4 OR 1/2 INCH VIDEO CASSETTE J-H
See series title for descriptive statement.
From The Guitar, Guitar Series.
Prod-SCITV Dist-GPITVL 1981

Notes On The Third String C 29 MIN
2 INCH VIDEOTAPE
See series title for descriptive statement.
From The Playing The Guitar I Series.
Prod-KCET Dist-PUBTEL

Notes On The Third String, Playing A Trio C 20 MIN
3/4 OR 1/2 INCH VIDEO CASSETTE J-H
See series title for descriptive statement.
From The Guitar, Guitar Series.
Prod-SCITV Dist-GPITVL 1981

Notes, Reports, And Communications C 14 MIN
3/4 OR 1/2 INCH VIDEO CASSETTE
Stresses careful observation and accurate, detailed note-taking as the critical factors in preparing good reports. Shows how to organize information to answer the who, what, where, why, when and how of a situation.
From The Professional Security Training Series. Module 3
Prod-MTI Dist-MTI

Nothin' C 14 MIN
16MM FILM OPTICAL SOUND P-I
Follows a boy and a girl through the environment of San Francisco. Designed to develop and sharpen art, language and social studies skills through observation and awareness of the environment. Based on curriculum developed by Marion Roth.
LC NO. 71-713322
Prod-FILMSM Dist-FILMSM 1971

Nothin' But A Winner C 30 MIN
3/4 OR 1/2 INCH VIDEO CASSETTE A
Presents University of Alabama football coach Bear Bryant illustrating and explaining his techniques for motivating his players toward athletic excellence. Interviewed by behavioral scientist Dr John Geier.
Prod-SFTI Dist-SFTI

Nothing B 3 MIN
16MM FILM OPTICAL SOUND
Images of Chicago and sad young love in summer, set to Petula Clark's recording of 'I WHO HAVE NOTHING.'
Prod-ACDRBR Dist-NWUFLM 1966

Nothing But Lookers C 8 MIN
16MM FILM OPTICAL SOUND H A
Explores the first condition of a successful sale--the customer buys. Emphasizes the positive effects of a co-operative person-to-person relationship with the customer and shows how to satisfy customer requests with available stock.
From The People Sell People Series.
Prod-SAUM Dist-MLA 1965

Nothing But Sing C 15 MIN
3/4 OR 1/2 INCH VIDEO CASSETTE P
Features a classical guitar and an electric guitar as solo instruments and as accompanying instruments.
From The Stepping Into Rhythm Series.
Prod-WVIZTV Dist-AITECH

Nothing But The Best C 37 MIN
16MM FILM OPTICAL SOUND
Deals with the origins of the Jewish community in Latin America and traces the immigration of Jews to that continent. Gives a picture of Jewish life in South America and describes the operations of ORT in many Latin American countries.
Prod-WAORT Dist-WAORT 1982

Nothing Ever Seems To Work Out For Me C 4 MIN
16MM FILM, 3/4 OR 1/2 IN VIDEO K-I
Introduces Hairy, who feels that nothing ever works out for him. Features his friends telling him that everyone is disappointed at some time, but there may be ways to make the best of things.
From The Most Important Person - Attitudes Series.
Prod-EBEC Dist-EBEC 1972

Nothing Ever Seems To Work Out For Me (Spanish) C 4 MIN
16MM FILM, 3/4 OR 1/2 IN VIDEO K-P
See series title for descriptive statement.
From The Most Important Person - Attitudes (Spanish) Series.
Prod-EBEC Dist-EBEC

Nothing For Granted C 14 MIN
16MM FILM, 3/4 OR 1/2 IN VIDEO
Describes the Navy Operational Test and Evaluation Force and procedures for testing and evaluating systems and equipment programmed for future Navy use.
LC NO. 82-706245
Prod-USN Dist-USNAC 1970

Nothing Hurt But My Pride B 15 MIN
3/4 INCH VIDEO CASSETTE
Examines several arrests after street fights involving policemen. Includes discussions of the incidents by the police in cars and at the station.
From The Pittsburgh Police Series.
Prod-DOCEDR Dist-DOCEDR

Nothing To Do - Four Summertime Episodes C 10 MIN
16MM FILM, 3/4 OR 1/2 IN VIDEO P-I
Suggests ways children can enjoy leisure time. Includes activities at home, nature and outdoor fun, day camp and visits to the library, park and zoo.
Prod-JOU Dist-JOU 1961

Nothing To Fear - The Legacy Of FDR C 52 MIN
16MM FILM, 3/4 OR 1/2 IN VIDEO H-C A
Explores the legacy of Franklin Delano Roosevelt by combining interviews from the 1980s with extensive historical material. Examines his response to the Great Depression and the radical changes in the role of the Federal government under his leadership. Lists the Roosevelt legacy including Social Security, collective bargaining, unemployment compensation and control of financial institutions.
LC NO. 83-707114
Prod-NBCNEW Dist-FI 1982

Nothing To Write About C 15 MIN
2 INCH VIDEOTAPE J
Explores the availability to topics for compositions.
From The From Me To You...In Writing, Pt 1 Series
Prod-DELE Dist-GPITVL

Nothing's Stopping You C 7 MIN
3/4 INCH VIDEO CASSETTE
Presents an adventure guide who also happens to be a diabetic teaching mountain climbing skills to teenage diabetics. Explains how chemstrip, a new method of monitoring blood sugar levels, helps diabetics overcome many of the limitations imposed by their condition.
Prod-BIODYN Dist-MTP

Notice To The Public (French) C 15 MIN
3/4 OR 1/2 INCH VIDEO CASSETTE H-C A
Discusses the celebration which occurs on Bastille Day.
From The En Francais Series. Part 2 - Temporal Relationships, Logical Relationships
Prod-MOFAFR Dist-AITECH 1970

Notorious (The Key) B 13 MIN
16MM FILM OPTICAL SOUND J-C A
Presents an excerpt from the 1946 motion picture Notorious. Tells how Alicia steals the key to her Nazi husband's wine cellar and how she and an American agent search it to discover the husband's plot. Directed by Alfred Hitchcock.
From The Film Study Extracts Series.
Prod-UNKNWN Dist-FI

Notorious Jumping Frog Of Calaveras County, The C 25 MIN
16MM FILM, 3/4 OR 1/2 IN VIDEO
Presents an adaptation of Mark Twain's story The Notorious Jumping Frog Of Calaveras County.
Prod-LEARN Dist-BARR 1980

Noun Is A Person, Place Or Thing, A C 3 MIN
3/4 OR 1/2 INCH VIDEO CASSETTE P
Follows a little girl through a series of adventures that teach her all the things nouns can be.
From The Grammar Rock Series.
Prod-ABCTV Dist-GA Prodn-SCOROC 1974

Nouns C 8 MIN
16MM FILM, 3/4 OR 1/2 IN VIDEO P-I
Uses a pixillated robot to introduce persons, places and things and develop the concept of what nouns are and how they work.
From The Basic Grammar Series.
LC NO. 81-706574
Prod-LEVYL Dist-AIMS 1981

Nouns And Adjectives C 9 MIN
16MM FILM, 3/4 OR 1/2 IN VIDEO P-I
Discusses the grammar elements of nouns and adjectives and their relationship to one another.
From The Wizard Of Words Series.
Prod-MGHT Dist-MGHT 1976

Nouns In Sentences C 14 MIN
16MM FILM, 3/4 OR 1/2 IN VIDEO P-I
Defines a noun and shows how to identify nouns in sentences.
From The Grammar Skills Series.
Prod-GLDWER Dist-JOU 1981

Nouns, Pronouns And Adjectives C 8 MIN
16MM FILM, 3/4 OR 1/2 IN VIDEO I
Defines the noun and the difference between common and proper nouns. Explains how the pronoun takes the place of a noun and how adjectives describe a noun. An animated film.
Prod-ROE Dist-PHENIX 1961

Nouns, Pronouns, Adjectives / Root Words C 20 MIN
1/2 IN VIDEO CASSETTE BETA/VHS
Teaches basic vocabulary skills. Uses simple visuals and a story about a visitor from another planet trying to figure out English.
Prod-BFA Dist-BFA

Nous Avons Faim B 13 MIN
16MM FILM OPTICAL SOUND I-H
See series title for descriptive statement.
From The Les Francais Chez Vous Series. Set I, Lesson 7
LC NO. 72-704474
Prod-PEREN Dist-CHLTN 1967

Nous Irons Peut-Etre En Chine B 13 MIN
16MM FILM OPTICAL SOUND I-H
See series title for descriptive statement.
From The Les Francais Chez Vous Series. Set II, Lesson 18
LC NO. 76-704475
Prod-PEREN Dist-CHLTN 1967

Nous Jouons C 10 MIN
3/4 OR 1/2 INCH VIDEO CASSETTE
Focuses on pastimes, the verb etre, and review of the 'Er' verbs-ie, tu, il, elle.
From The Salut - French Language Lessons Series.
Prod-BCNFL Dist-BCNFL 1984

Nous Sommes Seuls B 13 MIN
16MM FILM OPTICAL SOUND I-H
See series title for descriptive statement.
From The Les Francais Chez Vous Series. Set I, Lesson 5
LC NO. 70-704476
Prod-PEREN Dist-CHLTN 1967

Nous Voila—A Series
J-C A
Prod-JOSHUA Dist-HRAW 1969

A La Campagne	16 MIN
A La Plage	15 MIN
A Paris, Un Jour De Fete	14 MIN
En Promenade	13 MIN
En Vacances	13 MIN

Nova Scotia By-Ways C 14 MIN
16MM FILM OPTICAL SOUND
Shows the character of Nova Scotia by vagabonding through the natural beauty of sea and shore. Depicts a ceremonial gathering of Micmac Indians, mysterious happenings in a haunted house and a quiet lily pond.
Prod-CTFL Dist-CTFL 1963

Nova—A Series
H-C A
Explores science and the human quest for knowledge.
Prod-WGBHTV Dist-DISTS

A Is For Atom, B Is For Bomb	058 MIN
Across The Silence Barrier	057 MIN
Adventures Of Teenage Scientists	057 MIN
Aging - The Methuselah Syndrome	057 MIN
Alaska - The Closing Frontier	059 MIN
Alcoholism - Life Under The Influence	057 MIN
Anatomy Of A Volcano	057 MIN
Animal Imposters	057 MIN
Animal Olympians	050 MIN
Antarctica - Earth's Last Frontier	057 MIN
Antarctica - 90 Degrees Below	057 MIN
Anthropology On Trial	057 MIN
Are You Doing This For Me, Doctor, Or Am I	052 MIN
Artificial Heart	057 MIN
Artists In The Lab	057 MIN
Asbestos - A Lethal Legacy	057 MIN
Asteroid And The Dinosaur, The	057 MIN
Beyond The Milky Way	057 MIN
Big If, The - Interferon	050 MIN
Bird Brain - The Mystery Of Bird Navigation	027 MIN
Black Tide	058 MIN
Blindness - Five Points Of View	057 MIN
Blueprints In The Bloodstream	057 MIN
Bridge That Spanned The World, The	058 MIN
Business Of Extinction, The	059 MIN
Cancer Detectives Of Lin Xian	057 MIN
Case Of ESP, The	057 MIN
Case Of The Ancient Astronauts, The	057 MIN
Case Of The Bermuda Triangle, The	052 MIN
Case Of The UFO's	057 MIN
Cashing In On The Ocean	059 MIN
City Of Coral	057 MIN
Cobalt Blues	057 MIN
Computers, Spies And Private Lives	057 MIN
Crab Nebula, The	056 MIN
Dawn Of The Solar Age - Solar Energy	029 MIN
Dawn Of The Solar Age - Wind And Water Energy	025 MIN
Dawn With No Tomorrow	057 MIN
Dead Sea Lives, The	057 MIN
Death Of A Disease	058 MIN
Desert Place, A	030 MIN
Desert's Edge, The	059 MIN
Did Darwin Get It Wrong	057 MIN
Do We Really Need The Rockies	057 MIN
Doctors Of Nigeria, The	057 MIN
Einstein	058 MIN
Elusive Illness, The	057 MIN
End Of The Rainbow, The	059 MIN
Eyes Over China	057 MIN
Fat Chance In A Thin World	057 MIN
Final Frontier, The	057 MIN
Finding A Voice	057 MIN
First Signs Of Washoe, The	059 MIN
Following The Tundra Wolf	044 MIN
Fusion - The Energy Promise	056 MIN
Gene Engineers, The	057 MIN
Genetic Chance, The	057 MIN
Goodbye Louisiana	057 MIN
Great Violin Mystery, The	057 MIN
Great Wine Revolution, The	057 MIN
Green Machine, The	049 MIN
Hawaii - Crucible Of Life	057 MIN
Here's Looking At You, Kid	057 MIN
Hitler's Secret Weapon	059 MIN
Hot-Blooded Dinosaurs	052 MIN

Hunt For The Legion Killer, The	057 MIN
Hunters For The Seal	030 MIN
Icarus' Children	059 MIN
In The Event Of Catastrophe	059 MIN
Incident At Brown's Ferry	058 MIN
India - Machinery Of Hope	058 MIN
Insect Alternative, The	057 MIN
Inside The Golden Gate	059 MIN
Inside The Shark	050 MIN
Invisible Flame, The	057 MIN
Keys Of Paradise, The	057 MIN
Lassa Fever	057 MIN
Life - Patent Pending	057 MIN
Life On A Silken Thread	058 MIN
Light Of The 21st Century	057 MIN
Living Machines	058 MIN
Locusts - War Without End	057 MIN
Long Walk Of Fred Young, The	049 MIN
Lost World Of The Maya, The	036 MIN
Making A Natural History Film, The	052 MIN
Mediterranean Prospect, A	058 MIN
Memories From Eden	057 MIN
Message In The Rocks	057 MIN
Mind Machines, The	059 MIN
Miracle Of Life, The	057 MIN
Moving Still	057 MIN
Mystery Of The Anasazi, The	059 MIN
New Healers, The	059 MIN
Normal Face, A - The Wonders Of Plastic Surgery	057 MIN
Notes Of A Biology Watcher - A Film With	057 MIN
Nuclear Strategy For Beginners	057 MIN
One Small Step	057 MIN
Other Way, The	050 MIN
Palace Of Delights	058 MIN
Pill For The People, The	059 MIN
Pinks And Blues, The	057 MIN
Plague On Our Children, A, Pt 1 - Dioxins	057 MIN
Plague On Our Children, A, Pt 2 - PCBS	057 MIN
Planets, The	052 MIN
Plastic Prison, The	058 MIN
Pleasure Of Finding Things Out	057 MIN
Plutonium Connection, The	059 MIN
Portrait Of A Killer	058 MIN
Predictable Disaster, A	032 MIN
Race For Gold	057 MIN
Red Planet	052 MIN
Renewable Tree, The	059 MIN
Resolution On Saturn	057 MIN
Road To Happiness	059 MIN
Safety Factor, The	058 MIN
Salmon On The Run	057 MIN
Science Of Murder, The	057 MIN
Sea Behind The Dunes, The	057 MIN
Search For Life, The	030 MIN
Secrets Of Sleep	052 MIN
Signs Of The Apes, Songs Of The Whales	057 MIN
Sixty Minutes To Meltdown	084 MIN
Sociobiology - The Human Animal	057 MIN
Still Waters	059 MIN
Strange Sleep	059 MIN
Sunspot Mystery, The - Sun-Weather Connection	030 MIN
Sunspot Mystery, The - Sunspots Explained	031 MIN
Sweet Solutions	042 MIN
Talking Turtle	057 MIN
Television Explosion, The	057 MIN
Termites And Telescopes	058 MIN
Test-Tube Babies - A Daughter For Judy	057 MIN
To Live Until You Die	057 MIN
Tongues Of Men, Pt 1 - Disaster At Babel	058 MIN
Tongues Of Men, Pt 2 - A World Language	058 MIN
Touch Of Sensitivity	050 MIN
Tracking The Supertrains	057 MIN
Transplant Experience, The	050 MIN
Trial Of Denton Cooley, The	059 MIN
Tsetse Trap, The	059 MIN
Umealit - The Whale Hunters	058 MIN
War From The Air	057 MIN
Water Crisis, The	057 MIN
Whale Watch	057 MIN
Whales, Dolphins And Men	052 MIN
What Price Coal	060 MIN
What Time Is Your Body	023 MIN
Where Did The Colorado Go	059 MIN
Whisper From Space, A	058 MIN
Why America Burns	057 MIN
Why Do Birds Sing	027 MIN
Will The Fishing Have To Stop	031 MIN
Williamsburg File, The	045 MIN
Wizard Who Spat On The Floor, The - Thomas	041 MIN
Woman Rebel, The	059 MIN
World Of Difference, A	058 MIN

Novel—A Series
16MM FILM, 3/4 OR 1/2 IN VIDEO J-C A
Presents dramatizations of selected portions of three novels to stimulate interest in the novel as a major literary medium for 'reporting news of the human condition.'
Prod-IITC Dist-IU 1982

Awakening, The - A Novel By Kate Chopin	015 MIN
Maggie, A Girl Of The Streets - A Novel By	015 MIN
Time Machine, The - A Novel By H G Wells	015 MIN

Novel, The - Ralph Ellison On Work In Progress B 30 MIN
16MM FILM OPTICAL SOUND J-C A
Ralph Ellison explains the genesis of his first novel, 'THE INVISIBLE MAN,' and discusses his philosophy as to writers, American novels and the unity of the American spirit.
From The USA Series.
Prod-NET Dist-IU Prodn-KQEDTV 1966

Novel, The - Saul Bellow - The World Of The Dangling Man B 29 MIN
16MM FILM, 3/4 OR 1/2 IN VIDEO J-C A
Norman Podhoretz of 'CONTEMPORARY' magazine discusses the works of Saul Bellow. Quotations and annotations from Bellow's novels are included.
LC NO. 80-707090
Prod-NET Dist-IU Prodn-KQEDTV 1966

Novel, The - The Nonfiction Novel - A Visit With Truman Capote B 30 MIN
16MM FILM OPTICAL SOUND J-C A
Truman Capote describes his latest book 'IN COLD BLOOD' as a new art form, and explains how and why he wrote it.
From The USA Series.
Prod-NET Dist-IU Prodn-KQEDTV 1966

Novel, The - Vladimir Nabokov B 30 MIN
16MM FILM OPTICAL SOUND H-C A
Interviews Vladimir Nabokov about his life and work, illustrating his discussion of his past with scenes of that era. Nabokov demonstrates how he jots notes on index cards for later combination to form a novel.
From The USA Series.
Prod-NET Dist-IU Prodn-KQEDTV 1966

Novel, The - What It Is, What It's About, What It Does C 35 MIN
16MM FILM, 3/4 OR 1/2 IN VIDEO H-C
Presents Clifton Fadiman explaining motivation, characterization, style and the establishment of mood through description. Features the actors from the Old Vic Company.
From The Humanities - Narrative Series.
Prod-EBF Dist-EBEC 1962

Novel, The - 1914-1942 - The Loss Of Innocence B 30 MIN
16MM FILM, 3/4 OR 1/2 IN VIDEO J-C A
Discusses the themes of the major works of prominent American authors--Hemingway, Dos Passos, Anderson, Steinbeck, Wolfe, Fitzgerald, Farrell, faulkner and West--and the relationship of each theme to certain geographical parts of America.
From The USA Series.
Prod-NET Dist-IU Prodn-KQEDTV 1966

November 3 C 24 MIN
16MM FILM OPTICAL SOUND
Presents a drama about four escapees from a penitentiary who terrorize a young couple.
LC NO. 76-703791
Prod-CONCRU Dist-CONCRU 1975

Novi B 30 MIN
16MM FILM OPTICAL SOUND
A race fan's love affair.
Prod-SFI Dist-SFI

Novice Dog Obedience C 15 MIN
16MM FILM, 3/4 OR 1/2 IN VIDEO
Illustrates some basic techniques of novice dog training.
From The Dog Obedience Training Series.
Prod-KLEINW Dist-KLEINW 1973

Noviciat B 19 MIN
16MM FILM OPTICAL SOUND H-C
Presents a Freudian psychodrama about a masochistic voyeur.
Prod-CFS Dist-CFS 1960

Now B 5 MIN
16MM FILM OPTICAL SOUND
Presents a montage which captures the spirit and tempo of the civil rights movements, assembled from news footage and stills. Lena Horne sings the song 'NOW.'
Prod-ICAIC Dist-SFN Prodn-ALV 1964

Now C 14 MIN
16MM FILM OPTICAL SOUND
Examines the heritage of Marion County, Florida.
Prod-FLADC Dist-FLADC

Now - After All These Years C 60 MIN
16MM FILM OPTICAL SOUND J-C A
Analyzes life in the Prussian village of Rhina where, before 1939, Christians and Jews lived in close harmony until a wave of anti-semitism swept the village. Interviews both Jews who left the village and residents who blame the Jews' troubles on the Nazis.
LC NO. 83-700627
Prod-CANTOR Dist-CANTOR 1982

Now - West Africa C 17 MIN
16MM FILM OPTICAL SOUND
Promotes interest in West Africa as a market for business and as a center for industrial development.
LC NO. 73-702047
Prod-MCDO Dist-MCDO 1973

Now About Lamb C 14 MIN
16MM FILM OPTICAL SOUND J-H A
Includes basic lamb cookery showing easy, versatile lamb dishes as prepared in the family kitchen and on the outdoor grill.
LC NO. 75-701972
Prod-ASPC Dist-AUDPLN 1965

Now And Forever C 77 MIN
16MM FILM OPTICAL SOUND J-C A
Presents an historical survey of life in Oregon during the first half of the 20th century.
LC NO. 79-700543
Prod-OREGHS Dist-OREGHS 1979

Now And Forever C 30 MIN
3/4 OR 1/2 INCH VIDEO CASSETTE P-I
See series title for descriptive statement.
From The Sonrisas Series.
Prod-KRLNTV Dist-MDCPB

Now And Here My Hand - A Genesis Of Christian Unity C 27 MIN
3/4 OR 1/2 INCH VIDEO CASSETTE A
Uses an historical docu-drama to retell the story of the first grass-root ecumenical initiative in the United States, one which led to the founding of the Christian Church (Disciples of Christ). Notes some reasons for the success of the unlikely unity venture. Concludes with an affirmation of the Disciples' ecumenical heritage and a plea for continued unity of all Christians.
Prod-DCCMS Dist-ECUFLM 1982

Now Can I Tell You My Secret C 15 MIN
16MM FILM, 3/4 OR 1/2 IN VIDEO P
Shows that children have the right to protect themselves against sexual advances by any adults. Tells the story of a young boy who is keeping the secret that he was molested by a neighbor. Points out the difference between a 'good touch' and a 'bad touch' and shows children how to say no to situations that are uncomfortable to them.
Prod-WDEMCO Dist-WDEMCO

Now Crowd, The C 30 MIN
16MM FILM OPTICAL SOUND H A
Dramatizes the pressures placed on a college student and his girl friend to conform to the sexual attitudes of their peers. Shows that Christian principles should be able to withstand the pressure of conformity.
LC NO. 77-715496
Prod-CONCOR Dist-CPH 1968

Now For A Change C 15 MIN
3/4 OR 1/2 INCH VIDEO CASSETTE K-P
Discusses natural changes that can affect an ecosystem.
From The Dragons, Wagons And Wax, Set 2 Series.
Prod-CTI Dist-CTI

Now Hear This C 15 MIN
16MM FILM OPTICAL SOUND
Presents the Sanford Naval Academy in Florida, a boys' preparatory school which offers a liberal arts education for 350 students.
Prod-FLADC Dist-FLADC

Now Hear This C 23 MIN
3/4 OR 1/2 INCH VIDEO CASSETTE H-C A
Presents a quiz on hearing.
Prod-WNBCTV Dist-CAROUF

Now I Am Bigger C 10 MIN
16MM FILM, 3/4 OR 1/2 IN VIDEO K-P
Builds self-esteem and self-awareness in young children.
Prod-BARR Dist-BARR Prodn-HALBH 1975

Now I Am Bigger (Captioned) C 10 MIN
16MM FILM - VIDEO, ALL FORMATS K-P
Deals with children getting bigger and learning to do many new things, and having much to learn before they are grown up.
Prod-BARR Dist-BARR Prodn-HALBH

Now I Can Speak C 20 MIN
3/4 INCH VIDEO CASSETTE
Illustrates the usage of pictographic language by the disabled.
Prod-LAURON Dist-LAURON

Now I Can Talk - A Fluency-Shaping Program For Stutterers C 21 MIN
16MM FILM, 3/4 OR 1/2 IN VIDEO H-C A
Takes a look at a three-week speech reconstruction program being carried out at Hollins College. Considers various aspects of the program, including its administration, its use of computer aids and the ways in which speech fluency is maintained after the program.
Prod-HANOVC Dist-MTI 1975

Now Is The Time B 32 MIN
3/4 INCH VIDEO CASSETTE
Shows the struggle of blacks from slavery to equal rights through the words of poets and writers. Stars Ruby Dee and Ossie Davis.
Prod-ADL Dist-ADL

Now Scene, The C 14 MIN
16MM FILM OPTICAL SOUND
Shows U S Air Force facilities and demonstrations, such as the building of the North American Air Defense Command (NORAD,) suspended on coils inside mountains. Features the Thunderbirds and their spectacular F4 E Phantom demonstrations and life at Oxnard Air Force Base where fighter-interceptor squadrons are trained.
LC NO. 74-705221
Prod-USAF Dist-USNAC 1969

Now That My World Is Small C 27 MIN
3/4 INCH VIDEO CASSETTE
Shows a nursing home resident as she compares her past and present life and shares her feelings regarding the lack of understanding of perceptual problems that have led to her being labeled 'confused.'
Prod-SUCBUF Dist-SUCBUF

Now That The Buffalo's Gone C 7 MIN
16MM FILM OPTICAL SOUND I-J
Uses group and individual still-photograph portraits of American Indians, combined with footage from old films treated in psychedelic techniques, to point up the silent dignity of the Indian in the face of his oppressors.
LC NO. 74-709232
Prod-GERSHB Dist-CFS 1969

Now That The Buffalo's Gone C 75 MIN
16MM FILM, 3/4 OR 1/2 IN VIDEO H-C A
Examines the fact that American Indians have endured a terrible past and suffer a hopeless present. Their history is one of mas-

sacres, broken promises, worthless treaties and land-grabbing. Most of the Indians in the United States live in barren reservations and infant mortality, suicide and alcoholism are common problems.
Prod-THAMES Dist-MEDIAG 1969

Now That The Dinosaurs Are Gone C 25 MIN
16MM FILM OPTICAL SOUND
Examines the current state of nuclear energy development in the United States and shows the role it will play in the future energy requirements of America.
LC NO. 74-703228
Prod-AIF Dist-AIF Prodn-STOKB 1974

Now That The Dinosaurs Are Gone C 25 MIN
16MM FILM OPTICAL SOUND J-H
Probes the reasons for the accelerated development of nuclear power plants. Discusses the issues surrounding the use of nuclear fission in power production.
From The Energy - An Overview Series.
Prod-CENTRO Dist-CONPOW

Now That The Dinosaurs Are Gone (French) C 25 MIN
16MM FILM OPTICAL SOUND
Examines the current state of nuclear energy development in the United States and shows the role it will play in the future energy requirements of America.
LC NO. 74-703228
Prod-AIF Dist-AIF Prodn-STOKB 1974

Now That You Have A New Baby C 12 MIN
3/4 OR 1/2 INCH VIDEO CASSETTE
Helps new parents recognize the importance of childhood immunization and encourages them to complete their babies' vaccinations at an early age.
Prod-AHOA Dist-AHOA

Now That You're Postpartum C 21 MIN
16MM FILM, 3/4 OR 1/2 IN VIDEO A
Deals with the physical and emotional changes experienced by new mothers. Uses scenes from a postpartum class to convey information regarding the body's healing process after delivery, hormonal changes, sexual activity and the need to plan activity at home.
LC NO. 81-707014
Prod-POLYMR Dist-POLYMR 1980

Now The Chips Are Down C 52 MIN
16MM FILM, 3/4 OR 1/2 IN VIDEO H-C A
Discusses silicon chips called microprocessors, showing how they are made, the different kinds of applications in use and research for future use.
From The Silicon Factor Series.
LC NO. 80-706909
Prod-BBCTV Dist-FI

Now We Are Free B 26 MIN
16MM FILM OPTICAL SOUND
Follows a Hungarian family from Budapest, first to Austria, then to Camp Kilmer in New Jersey and finally to resettlement in a midwest city in the United States.
LC NO. FIE57-147
Prod-USIA Dist-USOE 1957

Now We Are Parents X 30 MIN
16MM FILM OPTICAL SOUND J-H T R
Presents a story about a young couple whose first baby suddenly becomes a third personality in the home. Shows how the solutions to their problems include spiritual insights into the meaning of the new life God has given them, their responsibilities to each other and the implications of Christian faith for their home.
Prod-FAMF Dist-FAMF

Now What C 20 MIN
2 INCH VIDEOTAPE P
See series title for descriptive statement.
From The Learning Our Language, Unit 1 - Listening Skills Series.
Prod-MPATI Dist-GPITVL

Now You See Me, Now You Don't C 20 MIN
16MM FILM, 3/4 OR 1/2 IN VIDEO J-C A
Examines the various defense mechanisms employed by insects to avoid predators.
Prod-MANTIS Dist-MOKIN Prodn-FRAZIJ 1977

Now You're An Artist C 29 MIN
2 INCH VIDEOTAPE
See series title for descriptive statement.
From The Tin Lady Series.
Prod-NJPBA Dist-PUBTEL

Now, That's A Report C 28 MIN
16MM FILM, 3/4 OR 1/2 IN VIDEO C A
Presents the four steps of report writing through the story of a young executive who is asked to write a report on report preparation. Discusses investigation, planning, writing and revision and points out that a report has to be clear, concise, complete and correct.
Prod-RANKAV Dist-RTBL 1977

Now, Voyager B 117 MIN
16MM FILM OPTICAL SOUND
Stars Bette Davis as an obsessively aloof spinster who is transformed into a vibrant young woman. Tells how she falls in love with a married man. Stars Paul Heinreid and Claude Rains.
Prod-UNKNWN Dist-UAE 1942

Nowhere To Hide C 26 MIN
3/4 OR 1/2 INCH VIDEO CASSETTE
Reveals startling statistics that show that radiation can't be avoided.
Prod-WCCOTV Dist-WCCOTV 1980

Nowhere To Run C 20 MIN
16MM FILM, 3/4 OR 1/2 IN VIDEO
Uses the capture of wild horses of the western range as an example of the problem of preserving the natural heritage of the West.
Prod-JMAX Dist-PHENIX 1976

Nozzleman, The C 25 MIN
16MM FILM OPTICAL SOUND PRO
Demonstrates the application of water on fire, using straight stream and fog nozzle.
Prod-LAFIRE Dist-LAFIRE

Nozzleman, The C 11 MIN
16MM FILM, 3/4 OR 1/2 IN VIDEO H-C A
Uses animation, an isolated situation and a complex situation to show the use of the direct, indirect and combination approach to fire situations in wooden structures. Explains thermal balance, nozzle operation, effects of steam and final overhaul.
Prod-ABMC Dist-FILCOM Prodn-IOWA 1961

NPI Video CLE–A Series
PRO
Discusses various legal issues, such as negotiations, trial techniques, mergers, and the tax aspects of divorce.
Prod-NPRI Dist-NPRI

Acquisitions, Mergers, And Business Purchases	060 MIN
Acquisitions, Mergers, And Business Purchases	060 MIN
Acquisitions, Mergers, And Business Purchases	060 MIN
Acquisitions, Mergers, And Business Purchases	060 MIN
Acquisitions, Mergers, And Business Purchases	060 MIN
Acquisitions, Mergers, And Business Purchases	060 MIN
Acquisitions, Mergers, And Business Purchases	060 MIN
Acquisitions, Mergers, And Business Purchases	060 MIN
Art Of Legal Negotiations With Professor	070 MIN
Art Of Legal Negotiations With Professor	070 MIN
Art Of Legal Negotiations With Professor	070 MIN
Art Of Legal Negotiations With Professor	070 MIN
Art Of Legal Negotiations With Professor	070 MIN
Art Of Legal Negotiations With Professor	070 MIN
Art Of Legal Negotiations With Professor	070 MIN
Buying And Selling The Small Business With	072 MIN
Buying And Selling The Small Business With	072 MIN
Buying And Selling The Small Business With	072 MIN
Buying And Selling The Small Business With	072 MIN
Buying And Selling The Small Business With	072 MIN
Tax Aspects Of Divorce With Professor Frank	052 MIN
Tax Aspects Of Divorce With Professor Frank	052 MIN
Tax Aspects Of Divorce With Professor Frank	053 MIN
Tax Aspects Of Divorce With Professor Frank	053 MIN
Trial Techniques With Professor Irving	052 MIN
Trial Techniques With Professor Irving	052 MIN
Trial Techniques With Professor Irving	053 MIN
Trial Techniques With Professor Irving	052 MIN
Trial Techniques With Professor Irving	052 MIN
Trial Techniques With Professor Irving	053 MIN
Trial Techniques With Professor Irving	053 MIN
Trial Techniques With Professor Irving	053 MIN

NRC Respiratory Protection–A Series
A
Discusses the types of respirators available for use by workers in nuclear power plants and the reasons for using them.
Prod-USNRC Dist-USNAC Prodn-LASL

Acceptable Practices For Fitting Respirator	020 MIN
Acceptable Practices For The Use Of	014 MIN
Acceptable Practices For The Use Of	015 MIN

NRL - The Naval Research Laboratory C 29 MIN
16MM FILM OPTICAL SOUND
Describes the variety of research conducted at the U S Naval Research Laboratory.
LC NO. 75-701309
Prod-USN Dist-USNAC 1974

NSBA Reports - The Global Connection C 30 MIN
16MM FILM, 3/4 OR 1/2 IN VIDEO J-C A
Demonstrates how to prepare children for citizenship in the 21st century. Gives a presentation on how world events affect daily lives.
Prod-NSBA Dist-SWRLFF

NSBA Reports - The Partnership In Career Education C 34 MIN
16MM FILM, 3/4 OR 1/2 IN VIDEO
Tells the story of what a tough network reporter discovered about career education in the National School Board Association's 'model' community in Springfield. Reports on how the Springfield Board of Education entered into a 'partnership relationship' with its surrounding community in order to provide students with a more complete educational experience.
Prod-NSBA Dist-SWRLFF

Nubia 64 - Saving The Temples Of Ancient Egypt (3500 BC - 1000 A D) C 40 MIN
16MM FILM OPTICAL SOUND
Discusses saving the temples of Ancient Egypt dating from 3500 BC to 1000 A D.
Prod-ROLAND Dist-ROLAND

Nuclear Beach Party B 15 MIN
16MM FILM OPTICAL SOUND
Offers a beach movie satire in which a group of teenagers enact the boy-meets-girl, boy-loses-girl, boy-gets-girl plot in a bomb shelter after World War III.
LC NO. 81-700424
Prod-HOWTAL Dist-HOWTAL 1980

Nuclear Countdown C 28 MIN
16MM FILM, 3/4 OR 1/2 IN VIDEO
Focuses on the threat to human survival posed by nuclear weaponry and stresses that a lasting world peace cannot be achieved without disarmament.
From The Disarmament Series.
Prod-UN Dist-JOU 1978

Nuclear Defense At Sea C 45 MIN
3/4 OR 1/2 INCH VIDEO CASSETTE
Illustrates evasive and survival techniques that US surface ships would have to employ in order to survive a nuclear war.
Prod-IHF Dist-IHF

Nuclear Energy - A Perspective C 28 MIN
3/4 INCH VIDEO CASSETTE
Presents the many steps in the uranium fuel process, from the search for ore-bearing uranium to the shipping containers carrying the final fuel assemblies to the reactors. Highlights the future of the breeder reactor.
Prod-EXXON Dist-MTP

Nuclear Energy - Peril Or Promise C
3/4 OR 1/2 INCH VIDEO CASSETTE H
Describes how atomic power works and explains its potential for producing low-cost electricity. Discusses the benefits and hazards of this energy resource.
Prod-SCIMAN Dist-GA

Nuclear Energy - The Great Controversy C 29 MIN
16MM FILM OPTICAL SOUND
Questions the possibility of changing the image of nuclear power from weapon to energy producer. Discusses fission processes versus fusion technology and reactors and their possible dangers.
From The Energy Sources - A New Beginning Series.
Prod-UCOLO Dist-UCOLO

Nuclear Energy - The Question Before Us C 25 MIN
16MM FILM, 3/4 OR 1/2 IN VIDEO J-C A
Concentrates on the decisions about nuclear energy made and being made in the state of Wisconsin. Polls several professors, an engineer and a state representative about the short- and long-term effects of this controversial fuel.
LC NO. 82-706427
Prod-NGS Dist-NGS 1981

Nuclear Energy / Home Filing Systems / Supermarket Alternatives C
3/4 OR 1/2 INCH VIDEO CASSETTE
Discusses aspects of nuclear energy, home filing systems and supermarket alternatives.
From The Consumer Survival Series.
Prod-MDCPB Dist-MDCPB

Nuclear Energy And Living Things C 30 MIN
2 INCH VIDEOTAPE I-J
Discusses sources and uses of radiation with living things, individual radioisotopes, natural radiation, useful and damaging aspects of radiation, somatic and genetic effects and applications in agriculture and medicine.
From The Living In A Nuclear Age Series.
Prod-GPITVL Dist-GPITVL

Nuclear Energy Fundamentals And Issues C 50 MIN
3/4 OR 1/2 INCH VIDEO CASSETTE
Examines the fundamental principles of conventional nuclear fission along with breeder technology and fusion energy. Explains the operation of both pressurized and boiling water reactors.
From The Energy Issues And Alternatives Series.
Prod-UIDEEO Dist-UIDEEO

Nuclear Fallout - Fiction And Fact B 10 MIN
16MM FILM OPTICAL SOUND J-H
Discusses the hazards and shows the basic difference between local and world-wide nuclear fallout. Based on research by the Defense Atomic Support Agency.
From The Screen News Digest Series. Vol 5, Issue 2
Prod-HEARST Dist-HEARST 1962

Nuclear Gas Stimulation - Tapping Our National Heritage C 29 MIN
16MM FILM OPTICAL SOUND
Traces the historical use of natural gas. Explains that some reserves are only accessible through nuclear fracturing. Considers the potential dangers of this process to society and the environment.
From The Energy Sources - A New Beginning Series.
Prod-UCOLO Dist-UCOLO

Nuclear Innovations In Process Control C 17 MIN
16MM FILM OPTICAL SOUND PRO
Depicts the versatility and sophistication of nuclear methods that are now available for control of industrial processes and for nondestructive testing.
LC NO. 72-714172
Prod-BATELL Dist-USERD 1971

Nuclear Know-How C 26 MIN
16MM FILM OPTICAL SOUND
Presents an up-to-date report on United Kingdom Atomic Energy Authority experimental facilities and services for reactor and fuel development.
Prod-UKAEA Dist-UKAEA 1971

Nuclear Magnetic Resonance C 28 MIN
16MM FILM, 3/4 OR 1/2 IN VIDEO
Uses animation, sound, and color to demonstrate the basic working principles of nuclear magnetic resonance, the operation of the analytical instrument, and the interpretation of the data obtained.
Prod-UCLA Dist-MEDIAG 1968

Nuclear Medicine C 26 MIN
3/4 OR 1/2 INCH VIDEO CASSETTE
Describes the six most widely used tests, the brain scan, bone scan, thyroid scan, liver scan, lung scan and cardiac imaging. Illustrates how these scans provide information that assists in diagnosis.

From The X-Ray Procedures In Layman's Terms Series.
Prod-FAIRGH Dist-FAIRGH

Nuclear Medicine C 62 MIN
3/4 INCH VIDEO CASSETTE PRO
Reviews the basic physics involved in the use of isotopes for medical applications. Discusses brain scanning, the diagnosis of pulmonary emboli through lung scanning and the diagnostic application of liver and spleen scanning. Describes the diagnosis and management of hyperthyroidism and hypothyroidism and the mechanism and diagnostic use of bone scanning.
LC NO. 76-706064
Prod-WARMP Dist-USNAC 1971

Nuclear Navy, The C 28 MIN
16MM FILM, 3/4 OR 1/2 IN VIDEO
Frank Blair narrates the story of the Navy's development of nuclear power and its application in longrange submarines and the growing nuclear surface force.
LC NO. 81-707720
Prod-USN Dist-USNAC 1967

Nuclear Newsreel - Reports On International Protest C 28 MIN
3/4 OR 1/2 INCH VIDEO CASSETTE
Presents both sides of the nuclear debate with footage of the International Day of Nuclear Disarmment.
Prod-FINLIN Dist-FINLIN

Nuclear Nightmare, The B 50 MIN
16MM FILM, 3/4 OR 1/2 IN VIDEO
Portrays how a nuclear bomb dropped on New York City would affect a family living 50 miles away. A dramatization.
Prod-USOCD Dist-USNAC 1950

Nuclear Nightmares - Wars That Must Never Happen C 90 MIN
3/4 OR 1/2 INCH VIDEO CASSETTE
Presents four 'nightmares' acted out by Peter Ustinov that imagine circumstances leading to nuclear conflict. Includes footage of the U S, Russian and NATO defense systems.
Prod-WNETTV Dist-WNETTV

Nuclear Power C 28 MIN
16MM FILM OPTICAL SOUND H-C A
Examines the positive and negative aspects of replacing older methods of energy production with nuclear energy. Considers the dangers inherent in the disposal of nuclear waste and safety precautions taken to ensure the security of neighboring communities.
Prod-CANBC Dist-FI

Nuclear Power - Pro And Con C 50 MIN
16MM FILM, 3/4 OR 1/2 IN VIDEO H-C A
Investigates the advantages and disadvantages of utilizing nuclear energy power sources.
Prod-ABCF Dist-MGHT 1977

Nuclear Power - Pro And Con, Pt 1 - Against C 25 MIN
16MM FILM, 3/4 OR 1/2 IN VIDEO H-C A
Presents arguments against nuclear power.
Prod-ABCF Dist-MGHT 1977

Nuclear Power - Pro And Con, Pt 2 - For C 25 MIN
16MM FILM, 3/4 OR 1/2 IN VIDEO H-C A
Presents arguments in favor of nuclear power.
Prod-ABCF Dist-MGHT 1977

Nuclear Power - Time, Space, And Spirit - 12 Keys To Scientific Literacy—A Series
J-H
Examines history of nuclear energy, including noted scientists, politicans, historical events, power plant facilities and anti-nuclear protests. Explains scientific principles and current controversies.
LC NO. 84-730272
Prod-HAWHIL Dist-HAWHIL 1984

History Of Nuclear Power, The 030 MIN
Nuclear Power - Today And Tomorrow 017 MIN

Nuclear Power - Today And Tomorrow C 80 MIN
16MM FILM OPTICAL SOUND
Presents the 88th Faraday lecture of the Institution of Electrical Engineers, which was delivered by Mr R V Moore, managing director, reactor group of the United Kingdom Atomic Energy Authority. Explains how the UKAEA demonstrated that nuclear power was practicable, how they made it economic and how they plan to make it abundant for centuries.
Prod-UKAEA Dist-UKAEA 1967

Nuclear Power - Today And Tomorrow C 17 MIN
3/4 OR 1/2 INCH VIDEO CASSETTE J-H
See series title for descriptive statement.
From The Nuclear Power - Time, Space, And Spirit - 12 Keys To Scientific Literacy Series.
LC NO. 84-730272
Prod-HAWHIL Dist-HAWHIL 1984

Nuclear Power - Today And Tomorrow, Pt 1 C 40 MIN
16MM FILM OPTICAL SOUND
Presents the 88th Faraday lecture of the Institution of Electrical Engineers, which was delivered by Mr R V Moore, managing director, reactor group of the United Kingdom Atomic Energy Authority. Explains how the UKAEA demonstrated that nuclear power was practicable, how they made it economic and how they plan to make it abundant for centuries.
Prod-UKAEA Dist-UKAEA 1967

Nuclear Power - Today And Tomorrow, Pt 2 C 40 MIN
16MM FILM OPTICAL SOUND
Presents the 88th Faraday lecture of the Institution of Electrical Engineers, which was delivered by Mr R V Moore, managing director, reactor group of the United Kingdom Atomic Energy Authority. Explains how the UKAEA demonstrated that nuclear power was practicable, how they made it economic and how they plan to make it abundant for centuries.
Prod-UKAEA Dist-UKAEA 1967

Nuclear Power And The Environment C 14 MIN
16MM FILM OPTICAL SOUND
Explores the problems that stem from the growing demands for electrcity in the U S and discusses the great care taken in studying and controlling effects of nuclear power plants on the environment.
LC NO. 76-706559
Prod-STAG Dist-USNAC 1970

Nuclear Power And You—A Series

Examines nuclear energy as a power source. Looks at its controversial status, how it works, the risks and benefits involved.
Prod-UMITV Dist-UMITV 1979

Fear And The Fact, The 029 MIN
Future, The 029 MIN
Radioactivity 029 MIN
Reactor, The 029 MIN
Risk 029 MIN

Nuclear Power For Space - Snap - 9A C 12 MIN
3/4 INCH VIDEO CASSETTE
Shows the launching of a new satellite powered by a nuclear generator. Uses animation to explain the use of an isotopic generator to create power in operating electronic equipment, recording equipment and transmitting data back to earth for analysis. Discusses the advantages of nuclear energy over the use of chemical or solar energy.
Prod-USNAC Dist-USNAC 1972

Nuclear Power In Air Defense Command C 7 MIN
16MM FILM OPTICAL SOUND
Tells the story of the first nuclear power plant for remote radar sites. Reviews component shipment, assembly and radiological monitoring of the reactor. Explains safety features, economy and self-sufficiency of nuclear power.
LC NO. FIE64-96
Prod-USAF Dist-USNAC 1963

Nuclear Power In The United States C 28 MIN
16MM FILM OPTICAL SOUND PRO
Portrays the energy philosophy of the U S Atomic Energy Commission, examines the implementation of plutoniumrecycle programs, and describes the thrust of the liquid metal fast breeder.
LC NO. 76-714173
Prod-ANL Dist-USERD 1971

Nuclear Power Plant Fire Fighting C 30 MIN
3/4 INCH VIDEO CASSETTE IND
Examines fire safety procedures for nuclear power plants, covering topics such as fixed extinguisher systems, personnel and housekeeping safety, fire strategies, foam selection and fire suppression.
From The Fire Protection Training Series. Tape 3
Prod-ITCORP Dist-ITCORP

Nuclear Power Plant Fire Fighting C 60 MIN
3/4 OR 1/2 INCH VIDEO CASSETTE IND
Includes a regulatory guide and information on coordinating with outside agencies, contamination and radiation.
From The Fire Fighting Training Series.
Prod-LEIKID Dist-LEIKID

Nuclear Propulsion In Space C 24 MIN
16MM FILM OPTICAL SOUND J-C A
Describes principles of nuclear rocket propulsion, indicating the possible use of such a system as the third stage of the Saturn Five rocket. Compares nuclear propulsion to chemical propulsion and electrical propulsion and describes a rocket which would use all three systems in future space travel.
LC NO. FIE68-92
Prod-NASA Dist-NASA 1968

Nuclear Reactions C 28 MIN
2 INCH VIDEOTAPE
Looks at a Michigan community's debates over the construction of a nuclear reactor in their town.
From The Turning Points Series.
Prod-WUCM Dist-PUBTEL

Nuclear Reactor Space Power Systems C 8 MIN
16MM FILM OPTICAL SOUND
Summarizes the program aimed at developing nuclear reactor power supplies for large space vehicles. Reviews the reliability, high power levels, long unattended operating life and safety characteristics of space nuclear power systems.
LC NO. FIE64-133
Prod-USAEC Dist-USNAC 1964

Nuclear Reactors For Space C 18 MIN
16MM FILM OPTICAL SOUND
Tells of the construction, testing and use of compact, low-powered nuclear reactors developed for use in the systems for nuclear auxiliary power program.
LC NO. 74-705224
Prod-USAEC Dist-USNAC Prodn-AUTICS 1961

Nuclear Safety Debate C 26 MIN
3/4 OR 1/2 INCH VIDEO CASSETTE H-C A
Documents the debates between pro- and anti-nuclear spokespeople.
Prod-UPI Dist-JOU

Nuclear Ship 'Savannah,' The C 29 MIN
16MM FILM OPTICAL SOUND
Discusses the basic principle of steam generation by nuclear reactor. Shows the world's first nuclear merchant ship Savannah, the design and construction of its pressurized water reactor and associated machinery.
LC NO. 74-705226
Prod-USIA Dist-USNAC 1960

Nuclear Spectrum C 28 MIN
16MM FILM OPTICAL SOUND
Documents some of the current research underway in the fields of physics, biology, radiation and anthropology conducted under the aegis of the Atomic Energy Commission and other organizations.
LC NO. 74-700710
Prod-ANL Dist-USNAC 1973

Nuclear Strategy For Beginners C 57 MIN
16MM FILM, 3/4 OR 1/2 IN VIDEO H-C A
Looks back over the four decades of the atomic age to try to understand how the modern world has acquired an arsenal of over 50,000 nuclear weapons ready to be fired at a moment's notice. Explores whether nuclear weapons deter such a war or only make it more likely.
From The Nova Series.
Prod-WGBHTV Dist-TIMLIF 1982

Nuclear Sunset C 25 MIN
3/4 OR 1/2 INCH VIDEO CASSETTE
Examines nuclear energy as a source of electrical power. Considers the questions of plant safety, waste, storage and costs.
Prod-WCCOTV Dist-WCCOTV 1978

Nuclear Theory And Energy C 24 MIN
16MM FILM, 3/4 OR 1/2 IN VIDEO T
Discusses basic nuclear theory relating to fission and fusion. Shows applications of both and points out the potential dangers of both.
Prod-EBEC Dist-EBEC 1985

Nuclear Transplantation C 12 MIN
16MM FILM, 3/4 OR 1/2 IN VIDEO H-C A
Uses photomicrography and time-lapse sequences to reveal the research technique of nuclear transplantation. Shows how nuclei are transplanted from donor body cells into activated eggs.
LC NO. 80-706100
Prod-IU Dist-IU 1976

Nuclear War - A Guide To Armageddon C 25 MIN
16MM FILM, 3/4 OR 1/2 IN VIDEO
Dramatizes the projected outcome of a one-megaton nuclear bomb exploding a mile above the dome of St Paul's Cathedral in the heart of London. Assesses the effectiveness of measures governments have proposed to protect their populations.
Prod-BBCTV Dist-FI 1983

Nuclear War - The Incurable Disease C 60 MIN
3/4 OR 1/2 INCH VIDEO CASSETTE J-C A
Presents three American and three Soviet physicians who meet to discuss the medical consequences of nuclear war. Considers subjects including the effects of a one megaton bomb on a city, medical care for nuclear victims, long-term effects and the insanity of civil defense systems.
Prod-FI Dist-FI 1982

Nuclear Warning C 23 MIN
3/4 OR 1/2 INCH VIDEO CASSETTE
Examines the nuclear debate. Discusses nuclear strategy, the civil defense system and the growing grassroots movement trying to end the arms race.
Prod-WCCOTV Dist-WCCOTV 1982

Nuclear Waste - Political And Social Decisions C 17 MIN
16MM FILM OPTICAL SOUND H-C A
Looks at the social and political issues inherent in the debate over what to do with nuclear waste.
From The Battelle Science Education Series.
LC NO. 83-706570
Prod-CIASP Dist-CIASP 1982

Nuclear Waste - What Is It C 26 MIN
16MM FILM OPTICAL SOUND H-C A
Defines the terms which apply to the problem of nuclear waste disposal using diagrams, animation and visual analogies to illustrate the elements of nuclear structure, fission and radiation.
From The Battelle Science Education Series.
LC NO. 83-706568
Prod-CIASP Dist-CIASP 1982

Nuclear Waste - What To Do With It C 22 MIN
16MM FILM OPTICAL SOUND H-C A
Emphasizes the technology available to cope with the problem of nuclear waste. Shows nuclear fuel in temporary storage and debates the merits of reprocessing versus permanent disposal.
From The Battelle Science Education Series.
LC NO. 83-706569
Prod-CIASP Dist-CIASP 1982

Nuclear Waste Isolation - A Progress Report C 25 MIN
16MM FILM OPTICAL SOUND
Reports on what has been accomplished and what is being done to find a safe disposal system for highly radioactive waste. Emphasizes the concept of totally isolating high-level nuclear waste from the environment.
Prod-USDOE Dist-MTP

Nuclear Waste, Political And Social Decisions C 17 MIN
3/4 INCH VIDEO CASSETTE H A
Points out that it is the political process and public opinion that ultimately will choose between the viewpoints of engineers and environmentalists and will shape the future of the nuclear industry.
LC NO. 83-706570
Prod-CINAS Dist-CINAS 1982

Nuclear Waste, What Is It? C 26 MIN
3/4 INCH VIDEO CASSETTE H A

Introduces the concepts and concerns of nuclear waste disposal. Defines terms using diagrams, animation and visual analogies to illustrate the elements of nuclear structure, fission and radiation.
LC NO. 83-706568
Prod-CINAS Dist-CINAS 1982

Nuclear Waste, What To Do With It! C 22 MIN
3/4 INCH VIDEO CASSETTE H A
Discusses what can be done with nuclear waste, focusing on the technology and looking at the debate between reprocessing and permanent disposal. Surveys proprosed methods and visits a trial burial site.
LC NO. 83-706569
Prod-CINAS Dist-CINAS 1982

Nuclear Watchdogs, The C 13 MIN
16MM FILM, 3/4 OR 1/2 IN VIDEO H-C A
Describes safety inspections at the South Texas Nuclear Project. Points out that the Nuclear Regulatory Commission relies on written reports from employees of the project's construction company. Originally shown on the CBS television series Magazine.
LC NO. 80-707741
Prod-CBSNEW Dist-CAROUF 1980

Nuclear Weapons - Can Man Survive C 24 MIN
3/4 OR 1/2 INCH VIDEO CASSETTE
Examines the challenges and dangers of living in the nuclear age. Traces what has happened since 1945, explains where we are today, and suggests America's options for the future. Includes interviews with Senator Mark Hatfield and Dr Edward Teller.
Prod-HEARST Dist-HEARST 1982

Nucleation C 30 MIN
3/4 INCH VIDEO CASSETTE PRO
Examines the energetics of the phase change, with due attention to surface energy.
From The Elements Of Physical Metallurgy Series.
Prod-AMCEE Dist-AMCEE

Nucleus And Its Parts, The C 17 MIN
16MM FILM OPTICAL SOUND H-C
Focuses attention on atomic nuclei. Discusses transformation, anti-matter, fission, fusion and cosmic ray informational concepts as they are related to nuclear structure. Explains particle accelerators and detection devices.
LC NO. FIA66-1169
Prod-CLI Dist-CLI 1966

Nude, The C 29 MIN
3/4 INCH VIDEO CASSETTE
Discusses the human form as a source of interest and inspiration to artists throughout the ages.
From The Creation Of Art Series.
Prod-UMITV Dist-UMITV 1975

Nuer, The C 75 MIN
16MM FILM, 3/4 OR 1/2 IN VIDEO C A
Presents the important relationships and events in the lives of the nuer, nilotic people in Sudan and on the Ethiopian border.
Prod-GARDNR Dist-MGHT 1971

Nuer, The, Pt 1 C 39 MIN
16MM FILM, 3/4 OR 1/2 IN VIDEO C A
Presents the important relationships and events in the lives of of the Nuer, nilotic people in Sudan and on the Ethiopian border.
Prod-GARDNR Dist-MGHT 1971

Nuer, The, Pt 2 C 36 MIN
16MM FILM, 3/4 OR 1/2 IN VIDEO C A
Presents the important relationships and events in the lives of of the Nuer, nilotic people in Sudan and on the Ethiopian border.
Prod-GARDNR Dist-MGHT 1971

Nuestras Familias C 30 MIN
3/4 OR 1/2 INCH VIDEO CASSETTE K-P
See series title for descriptive statement.
From The Villa Alegre Series.
Prod-BCTV Dist-MDCPB

Nuestro Milwaukee - Breakin' C 28 MIN
16MM FILM - 3/4 IN VIDEO
Presents a musical adventure into the world of break dancing, developed in part by the Latino population of New York's South Bronx. Shows clips from videos by Gladys Knight and Chaka Khan inter-cut with scenes of sidewalk jam sessions which include Milwaukee's Lady Breakers. Includes interviews with instructors who explain the dance, gymnastic and martial art aspects of break dancing.
Prod-WMVSTV Dist-KCET

Nueva - An Alternative C 18 MIN
16MM FILM, 3/4 OR 1/2 IN VIDEO
Shows and explains the approach of Nueva Day School and Learning Center, an alternative elementary school in Hillsborough, California. Describes class activities at various age levels, involvement of parents in school activities and faculty educational research and development work.
Prod-NUEVA Dist-UCEMC 1974

Nueva Artistas De Puerto Rico C 16 MIN
16MM FILM OPTICAL SOUND J-C
Visits the studios of Puerto Rico's most important artists.
LC NO. 75-700622
Prod-OOAS Dist-PAN 1970

Nukumanu - En Atoll I Stillehavet (Nukumanu - An Atoll In The Pacific C 28 MIN
16MM FILM OPTICAL SOUND
A Danish language film. Presents Nukumanu Atoll, an island in a coral reef inhabited by a small community whose culture is still undisturbed by the white man. Points out that living conditions in general are extremely bad.
Prod-STATNS Dist-STATNS 1967

Num-Ti-Jah Lodge C 32 MIN
16MM FILM OPTICAL SOUND
Presents a study of nature and geography.
From The Journal Series.
LC NO. 74-701637
Prod-FIARTS Dist-CANFDC 1973

Numbat, The C 14 MIN
16MM FILM OPTICAL SOUND J-C A
Uses close-up photography, including feeding scenes and shots of young numbats, to show this little-known Australian animal in its natural habitat.
LC NO. 71-709549
Prod-ANAIB Dist-AUIS 1970

Number One Sun C 15 MIN
3/4 OR 1/2 INCH VIDEO CASSETTE K-P
Shows how the earth is affected by the sun.
From The Dragons, Wagons And Wax, Set 2 Series.
Prod-CTI Dist-CTI

Number Our Days C 29 MIN
16MM FILM OPTICAL SOUND
Documents the lives of Jewish senior citizens who make the Israel Levin Senior Adult Center in Venice, California, the focal point of their existence. Offers views of the center, which serves to bring the spirited citizens together in a common bond of unity. Based on field research from the book Number Our Days by Barbara Myerhoff.
LC NO. 79-700437
Prod-LITMAN Dist-LITMAN 1978

Number Patterns C 20 MIN
3/4 INCH VIDEO CASSETTE H-C
Studies three areas involving numerical patterns, focusing on factoring, number divisibility and numerical sequences.
From The Mainly Math Series.
Prod-WCVETV Dist-GPITVL 1977

Number Sentences, Dr Ernest Duncan X 20 MIN
16MM FILM OPTICAL SOUND K-I T
See series title for descriptive statement.
From The Teaching Modern School Mathematics - Struc- Ture And Use Series.
Prod-HMC Dist-HMC 1971

Number Systems B 60 MIN
3/4 OR 1/2 INCH VIDEO CASSETTE
See series title for descriptive statement.
From The Understanding Microprocessors Series. Pt 3
Prod-UAZMIC Dist-UAZMIC 1979

Number Systems (Continued), Review, Microprocessor Architecture B 50 MIN
3/4 OR 1/2 INCH VIDEO CASSETTE
See series title for descriptive statement.
From The Microprocessors And Applications Series. Pt 2
Prod-UAZMIC Dist-UAZMIC 1976

Number Systems And Codes C
3/4 OR 1/2 INCH VIDEO CASSETTE
See series title for descriptive statement.
From The Microprocessor Series.
Prod-HTHZEN Dist-HTHZEN

Number 23 C 10 MIN
16MM FILM OPTICAL SOUND
Shows the experiences involved in treatment of venereal disease at a typical public health facility.
From The VD - Self-Awareness Project Series. Module 3
LC NO. 75-702844
Prod-AAHPER Dist-FMD 1974

Numbering Systems, Numbering Codes, And Logic Concepts C 30 MIN
3/4 OR 1/2 INCH VIDEO CASSETTE
Discusses numbering systems and codes including decimal, binary Octal and hexadecimal. Explores logic concepts.
From The Programmable Controllers Series.
Prod-ITCORP Dist-ITCORP

Numbers B
16MM FILM OPTICAL SOUND
Discusses the peculiar flavor of infinite processes intimately associated with this branch of mathematics. Examines an approximation to the irrational number root 2 by rational numbers.
Prod-OPENU Dist-OPENU

Numbers C 15 MIN
3/4 OR 1/2 INCH VIDEO CASSETTE P
Presents techniques of handwriting, focusing on numbers.
From The Cursive Writing Series.
Prod-WHROTV Dist-GPITVL 1984

Numbers C 30 MIN
3/4 OR 1/2 INCH VIDEO CASSETTE H-C A
Presents Lawrence Solow and Sharon Neumann Solow introducing American Sign Language used by the hearing-impaired. Emphasizes signs that have to do with numbers.
From The Say It With Sign Series. Part 14
Prod-KNBCTV Dist-FI 1982

Numbers - O Through 9 C 15 MIN
3/4 INCH VIDEO CASSETTE P
From The Writing Time Series.
Prod-WHROTV Dist-GPITVL

Numbers All Around Us C 13 MIN
16MM FILM, 3/4 OR 1/2 IN VIDEO P
Shows how numbers help people in different ways. Discusses zip codes, telephone numbers, room numbers, and measurements.
From The Beginning Mathematics Series.
Prod-JOU Dist-JOU

Numbers All Around Us (Spanish) C 11 MIN
16MM FILM, 3/4 OR 1/2 IN VIDEO P-I
Points out the uses of numbers in identifying and coding such things as room numbers, addresses, telephone numbers and zip codes.
From The Beginning Mathematics Series.
Prod-GLDWER Dist-JOU 1974

Numbers And Order C 9 MIN
16MM FILM, 3/4 OR 1/2 IN VIDEO P
Reviews vocabulary associated with comparison, such as same, different, more and less. Shows that arranging numbers in the order of a number line helps solve problems involving how many or how much.
From The Basic Math Series.
Prod-BFA Dist-PHENIX 1979

Numbers For Beginners X 11 MIN
16MM FILM OPTICAL SOUND P
Through animation of familiar objects, visualizes the numbers from one through six to assist in separating the idea of number from the counting of objects. Emphasizes group recognition and number relationships.
Prod-JHP Dist-MLA 1954

Numbers Game, Pt 1-A Series P-I

Introduces primary mathematical concepts.
Prod-MDDE Dist-MDDE

Backward Times	015 MIN
Coming Back To Meet Yourself	015 MIN
Five Sides And More	015 MIN
Follow The Yellow Brick Path	015 MIN
Going 'Round In Circles	015 MIN
Ins And Outs Of Simple, Closed Paths	015 MIN
Meet Me At The Square Corner	015 MIN
Points About A Point	015 MIN
Score - 1 To 0	015 MIN
Times, They Are A'Changing, The	015 MIN
Tips On Triangles	015 MIN
Trading Post, The	015 MIN
What Are The Odds It's Even	015 MIN
What's In A Name	015 MIN
When Line Segments Get Together	015 MIN

Numbers Game, The C 30 MIN
16MM FILM - 3/4 IN VIDEO J-C A
Discusses cancer and other diseases associated with man's environment. Questions the connection between the benefits of technology and the potential hazards they impose.
From The Man Builds - Man Destroys Series.
LC NO. 75-704151
Prod-UN Dist-GPITVL 1975

Numbers In Our Lives C 9 MIN
16MM FILM, 3/4 OR 1/2 IN VIDEO K-P
Focuses attention on some of the ways in which numbers and number names are used by almost everyone from the children to people working in the community. Shows that we use numbers to count, to measure and to play games.
Prod-BOUNDY Dist-PHENIX 1970

Numbers In Sign Language C 15 MIN
16MM FILM OPTICAL SOUND I-C A S
Shows the American sign language numbering system. Includes practice sentences which demonstrate how to form the numbers with the hands and how to read the numbers from another person's hands.
From The Quick Flicks Series.
LC NO. 75-700657
Prod-JOYCE Dist-JOYCE 1975

Numbers Now And Then C 25 MIN
16MM FILM OPTICAL SOUND
Explains the Hindu-Arabic origins of the Western number system. Illustrates different features of the number systems of the ancient Babylonians, Egyptians and Greeks.
Prod-OPENU Dist-GPITVL

Numbers Racket, The C 29 MIN
2 INCH VIDEOTAPE
See series title for descriptive statement.
From The Koltanowski On Chess Series.
Prod-KQEDTV Dist-PUBTEL

Numbers Start With The River, The C 15 MIN
16MM FILM - 3/4 IN VIDEO A
Depicts the quality of life in a small town in Iowa, which is representative of thousands of such towns across the United States. Illustrates an old farm couple's memories of play, work, family life, courtship and marriage.
LC NO. 77-706001
Prod-USIA Dist-USNAC Prodn-WHP 1971

Numbers Systems And Codes C
3/4 OR 1/2 INCH VIDEO CASSETTE
See series title for descriptive statement.
From The Microprocessor Video Training Course Series.
Prod-VTRI Dist-VTRI

Numerals Everywhere C 9 MIN
16MM FILM, 3/4 OR 1/2 IN VIDEO P-I
Depicts an ordinary shopping trip that illustrates the use of numerals everywhere.
Prod-EBEC Dist-EBEC

Numeration Systems C 30 MIN
16MM FILM OPTICAL SOUND T
Examines the various numeration systems. Studies the behavioral pattern of whole numbers under addition and subtraction. To be used following 'NAMES FOR NUMBERS.'
From The Mathematics For Elementary School Teachers Series. No. 4

LC NO. FI67-435
Prod-SMSG Dist-MLA 1963

Numeration To 999 C 15 MIN
3/4 INCH VIDEO CASSETTE P
Explains how to read and write the numbers 1 through 999.
From The Studio M Series.
Prod-WCETTV Dist-GPITVL 1979

Numeric Display Applications C 30 MIN
3/4 OR 1/2 INCH VIDEO CASSETTE PRO
Illustrates use of visible light-emitting diodes in numeric display applications with specific circuit examples and device operation.
From The Optoelectronics, Part II - Optoelectronic Displays Series.
Prod-TXINLC Dist-TXINLC

Numerical Abnormalities Of Human Chromosomes B 28 MIN
16MM FILM OPTICAL SOUND PRO
Points out that errors in cell division can result in embryos and occasionally live-born individuals with an abnormal number of chromosomes (aneuploidy.) Gives a brief description of monomy (45,X) trisomy 13, trisomy 18, trisomy 21 and polysomy for the X and Y sex chromosomes.
From The Clinical Pathology Series.
Prod-NMAC Dist-USNAC 1969

Numerical Comparisons C 14 MIN
16MM FILM, 3/4 OR 1/2 IN VIDEO H
Presents examples of people making numerical comparisons, including a stereo salesperson comparing frequencies and a restaurant manager explaining his ratio of waiters to customers.
From The Math Wise Series. Module 2 - Comparing
Prod-KOCETV Dist-AITECH 1981

Numerical Control C 30 MIN
3/4 OR 1/2 INCH VIDEO CASSETTE
Deals with the conversion to and setup of a numerically controlled machine shop. Points out problem areas.
Prod-CONNTV Dist-SME Prodn-SME

Numerical Control No. 1 - Introduction To A Two Axis Vertical Mill C 8 MIN
1/2 IN VIDEO CASSETTE BETA/VHS IND
Provides an overview of a two axis vertical mill for the operation of both drilling and straightline milling through the point-to-point control system.
From The Machine Shop - C N C Machine Operations Series.
Prod-RMI Dist-RMI

Numerical Control No. 2 - Setup Of Machine And Indexed Controls C 19 MIN
1/2 IN VIDEO CASSETTE BETA/VHS IND
Continues Numerical Control No. 1. Demonstrates the adjustment of spindle stops, insertion of tape in the Slo-Syn indexer and the settling of machine controls.
From The Machine Shop - C N C Machine Operations Series.
Prod-RMI Dist-RMI

Numerical Control No. 3 - Tape Controlled Drilling Operations C 5 MIN
1/2 IN VIDEO CASSETTE BETA/VHS IND
Demonstrates a drilling setup, incorporating Numerical Control No. 1 and Numerical Control No. 2 as prerequisites.
From The Machine Shop - C N C Machine Operations Series.
Prod-RMI Dist-RMI

Numerical Control/Computer Numerical Control, Pt 1 - Fundamentals—A Series
PRO
Stresses Numerical Control/Computer Numerical Control (NC/CNC) concepts and programming fundamentals and aims at helping the operator to learn how to speed production.
Prod-ICSINT Dist-ICSINT

Basic Drilling 015 MIN
Circular Milling 015 MIN
Complete Milling Programs 015 MIN
Coordinate Measurement Systems 015 MIN
Drilling, Boring And Spot Facing 015 MIN
Introduction To NC/CNC 015 MIN
Machinery Set-Up And Safety 015 MIN
Manual Data Input 015 MIN
One And Two Axis Linear Milling 015 MIN
Program Preparation 015 MIN
Punching And Editing 015 MIN
Three Axis Linear Milling 015 MIN

Numerical Control/Computer Numerical Control, Pt 2 - Advanced Programming—A Series
PRO
Develops advanced programming techniques to help speed programming. Emphasizes practical application of this information and role of machine operator.
Prod-ICSINT Dist-ICSINT

Cutter Radius Compensation 015 MIN
Looping 015 MIN
Polar Coordinate Program 015 MIN
Rotation 015 MIN
Scaling 015 MIN
Special Cycles 015 MIN
Subroutines 015 MIN
Translations 015 MIN

Numerical Control/Computerized Numerical Control, Module 1 - Fundamentals—A Series
IND
Provides an introduction to the basic principles, capabilities and applications of numerical and numerical computerized control. Emphasizes practical application and role of the machine operator. Can be used as both an introduction and review.
Prod-LEIKID Dist-LEIKID

Basic Drilling 016 MIN
Circular Millin g- 019 MIN
Completed Milling Programs 016 MIN
Coordinate Measurement Systems 017 MIN
Drilling, Boring And Spot Facing 019 MIN
Introduction To NC And CNC 015 MIN
Machine Setup And Safety 014 MIN
Manual Data Input 017 MIN
One-And Two-Axis Linear Milling 018 MIN
Program Preparation 016 MIN
Punching And Editing 016 MIN
Three-Axis Linear Milling 018 MIN

Numerical Control/Computerized Numerical Control, Module 2 - Advanced...—A Series
IND
Comprises the second module of a two-part series on numerical control. Emphasizes practical application and role of the machine operator. Designed as both an introduction and a review.
Prod-LEIKID Dist-LEIKID

Cutter Radius Compensation 018 MIN
Loopings 016 MIN
Polar Coordinate Program 019 MIN
Rotation 018 MIN
Scaling 016 MIN
Special Cycles 017 MIN
Sub-Routines 018 MIN
Translations 018 MIN

Numerical Eigenvalues B
16MM FILM OPTICAL SOUND
Explains the significance of the eigenvalue problem and discusses how the problem could be solved using determinants.
Prod-OPENU Dist-OPENU

Numerical Example - Estimation Of Position, Velocity, And Ballistic Parameter For A... C 47 MIN
3/4 OR 1/2 INCH VIDEO CASSETTE PRO
Gives numerical example illustrating how bias estimation errors associated with the use of an extended Kalman filter can he removed through the use of a second-order filter.
From The Modern Control Theory - Stochastic Estimation Series.
Prod-MIOT Dist-MIOT

Numerical Example - Estimation Of Positions Velocities, And Accelerations C 32 MIN
3/4 OR 1/2 INCH VIDEO CASSETTE PRO
See series title for descriptive statement.
From The Modern Control Theory - Stochastic Estimation Series.
Prod-MIOT Dist-MIOT

Numerical Example - Sensor Trade-Offs C 47 MIN
3/4 OR 1/2 INCH VIDEO CASSETTE PRO
See series title for descriptive statement.
From The Modern Control Theory - Stochastic Estimation Series.
Prod-MIOT Dist-MIOT

Numerical Example - Solution Of A Minimum Fuel Problem In The Apollo Project C 21 MIN
3/4 OR 1/2 INCH VIDEO CASSETTE PRO
See series title for descriptive statement.
From The Modern Control Theory - Deterministic Optimal Control Series.
Prod-MIOT Dist-MIOT

Numerical Example And Miscellaneous C 60 MIN
3/4 OR 1/2 INCH VIDEO CASSETTE C
Shows wind load analysis with a FORTRAN program for numerical technique and its application to earthquake codes.
From The Fundamentals Of Dynamic Analysis For Structural Design Series.
Prod-USCCE Dist-AMCEE

Numerical Example Of LQG Design For A Third- Order Continuous Time System C 27 MIN
3/4 OR 1/2 INCH VIDEO CASSETTE PRO
See series title for descriptive statement.
From The Modern Control Theory - Stochastic Control Series.
Prod-MIOT Dist-MIOT

Numerical Integration And Isoparametric Mapping B 60 MIN
3/4 OR 1/2 INCH VIDEO CASSETTE
See series title for descriptive statement.
From The Finite Element Method And Some Of Its-Developments Series. Pt 3
Prod-UAZMIC Dist-UAZMIC 1980

Numerical Integrations C 46 MIN
3/4 OR 1/2 INCH VIDEO CASSETTE
See series title for descriptive statement.
From The Finite Element Methods In Engineering Mechanics Series.
Prod-MIOT Dist-MIOT

Numerical Mathematics B
16MM FILM OPTICAL SOUND
Shows an example of a simple problem for which a numerical method is useful. Points out the increasing importance of numerical mathematics and digital computers in engineering.
Prod-OPENU Dist-OPENU

Numerical Solutions Of Differential Equations B
16MM FILM OPTICAL SOUND
Discusses three numerical methods of solutions of a first-order differential equation.
Prod-OPENU Dist-OPENU

Nun And Deviant B 20 MIN
3/4 OR 1/2 INCH VIDEO CASSETTE
Explores identity issues of both woman and artist. Dispels stereotypes. Presented by Nancy Angelo and Candace Compton.
Prod-ARTINC Dist-ARTINC

Nun's Priest's Tale And The Manciple's Tale, The B 30 MIN
1 INCH VIDEOTAPE A
See series title for descriptive statement.
From The Canterbury Tales Series.
Prod-UMITV Dist-UMITV 1967

Nunu And The Zebra C 27 MIN
16MM FILM, 3/4 OR 1/2 IN VIDEO P-I
Tells a story about a boy in East Africa who goes on an expedition with his father. Tells how they encounter a lion and how the boy becomes lost, makes friends with a zebra who protects him from a leopard and is found by his father and a park ranger.
Prod-ROBROL Dist-AIMS 1973

Nuremberg B 76 MIN
16MM FILM, 3/4 OR 1/2 IN VIDEO
Records the trials of the Nazi leaders at Nuremberg, Germany. Includes scenes from films made by the Nazis which were presented as the documentary evidence of the atrocities committed at concentration camps. Issued in 1949 as a motion picture.
LC NO. 79-706509
Prod-USDD Dist-USNAC 1976

Nuremberg Chronicle, The B 22 MIN
16MM FILM OPTICAL SOUND H-C
Explores the woodcuts of the book, 'THE NUREMBERG CHRONICLE,' published in 1943, recounting world history as it was conceived in that period of turmoil and change.
Prod-CONNF Dist-CONNF

Nuremberg Trial B 31 MIN
16MM FILM, 3/4 OR 1/2 IN VIDEO H-C
Tells that on October 18, 1945, the most sweeping indictment in history was filed against 24 Nazi leaders. Evaluates the evidence which showed the involvement of the defendents and gives the verdict of the special international tribunal. Concludes that some legalists continue to debate the validity of the trials.
Prod-METROM Dist-FI 1974

Nuremberg Trials, The B 76 MIN
16MM FILM OPTICAL SOUND
Presents a film record of the trials of the Nazi leaders at Nuremberg, Germany. Includes scenes from films made by the Nazis, which were presented as the documentary evidence of the atrocities committed at concentration camps.
Prod-USDD Dist-USNAC 1949

Nurse C 30 MIN
1/2 IN VIDEO CASSETTE BETA/VHS
Describes the life of Barbara Subczyk, head emergency nurse at the Jersey City Medical Center, who suggests that her job is a test of the idea of 'survival of the fittest'.
From The American Professionals Series.
Prod-WTBS Dist-RMI

Nurse And Her Employer, The B 44 MIN
16MM FILM OPTICAL SOUND
Discusses the doctrine of respondeat superior, federal and state labor relations laws, and the way in which they affect nurses.
From The Nursing And The Law Series.
LC NO. 76-703372
Prod-VDONUR Dist-AJN Prodn-WTTWTV 1968

Nurse And The Critically Ill, The - A Personal Approach To Helping, Pt I C 14 MIN
3/4 OR 1/2 INCH VIDEO CASSETTE C A
Deals with the emotional needs of the patient and the common feelings of the nurse.
Prod-RALPRO Dist-TEF

Nurse And The Critically Ill, The - A Personal Approach To Helping, Pt II C 14 MIN
3/4 OR 1/2 INCH VIDEO CASSETTE C A
Discusses interpersonal communication skills and the rewards of working with the critically ill and dying patient.
Prod-RALPRO Dist-TEF

Nurse And The Employer, The C 30 MIN
16MM FILM OPTICAL SOUND PRO
Presents a roundtable discussion in which four nursing experts explore the responsibilities of both nurses and employers to one another and to clients. Covers the effect of the 1974 amendment to the Taft-Hartley Act and the collective bargaining process.
From The Nurse And The Law Series.
LC NO. 76-701550
Prod-AJN Dist-AJN Prodn-WGNCP 1974

Nurse And The Law—A Series
PRO
Presents the common legal problems nurses should know.
Prod-AJN Dist-AJN Prodn-WGNCP 1974

Ethical-Legal Aspects Of Nursing Practice 30 MIN
Malpractice 30 MIN
Mental Health Nursing 30 MIN
Nurse And The Employer, The 30 MIN
Nurse Practice Acts 30 MIN
Nursing Torts 30 MIN
Parents And Children 30 MIN
Rights Of Patients, No. 1 30 MIN
Rights Of Patients, No. 2 30 MIN
Scope Of Practice And Standards Of Care 30 MIN

Nurse Combats Disease, The C 12 MIN
16MM FILM OPTICAL SOUND

Shows how nurses safeguard the public by understanding the transmission of disease and the measures necessary to prevent disease and promote recovery from illness.
LC NO. FIE63-112
Prod-USPHS Dist-USNAC 1962

Nurse Edith Cavell B 108 MIN
16MM FILM OPTICAL SOUND
Tells how Nurse Cavell and two other women hide and nurse injured soldiers in Brussels after the Kaiser has seized Belgium. Describes their trial after they are caught. Stars Anna Neagle, Edna May Oliver and George Sanders.
Prod-RKOP Dist-KITPAR 1939

Nurse In Child Abuse Prevention, The C 30 MIN
16MM FILM - 3/4 IN VIDEO PRO
Examines antecedents and manifestations of the child abuse syndrome. Discusses the nurse's role in detecting, treating and preventing this serious disorder of parenthood, considering the history taking, physical examination and community involvement required.
LC NO. 76-701620
Prod-AJN Dist-AJN Prodn-WGNCP 1976

Nurse In Community Psychiatry, The B 44 MIN
16MM FILM OPTICAL SOUND
Presents current trends in preventive, therapeutic and rehabilitative mental health programs at the community level.
From The Nursing In Psychiatry Series.
LC NO. 73-703429
Prod-VDONUR Dist-AJN Prodn-WTTWTV 1968

Nurse In Family Therapy, The B 44 MIN
16MM FILM OPTICAL SOUND PRO
Discusses the role of the nurse as co-therapist in working with families and as therapeutic agent in working with patients whose primary therapy is in the area of family relationships.
From The Nursing In Psychiatry Series.
LC NO. 78-703430
Prod-VDONUR Dist-AJN Prodn-WTTWTV 1968

Nurse In Group Work, The B 44 MIN
16MM FILM OPTICAL SOUND PRO
Describes the evolving role of the nurse in group work, both formally and informally structured.
From The Nursing In Psychiatry Series.
LC NO. 71-703431
Prod-VDONUR Dist-AJN Prodn-WTTWTV 1968

Nurse In The Community, The B 44 MIN
16MM FILM OPTICAL SOUND
Discusses the problems of the nurse who gives care outside the hospital situation, the responsibilities and special problems of the industrial nurse, and the liability of the nurse as a citizen in emergency situations.
From The Nursing And The Law Series.
LC NO. 70-703376
Prod-VDONUR Dist-AJN Prodn-WTTWTV 1968

Nurse Maid B 7 MIN
16MM FILM OPTICAL SOUND
Explains how Flip the Frog, who is short of pocket money, agrees to watch an innocent-looking baby carriage for a mother.
Prod-UNKNWN Dist-BHAWK 1930

Nurse Midwifery B 44 MIN
16MM FILM OPTICAL SOUND PRO
Illustrates the historical development of obstetrics and midwifery, using old film clips to show the role of early nurse midwives of the frontier nursing service. Explains current standards and preparation for nurse midwifery in the U S and future prospects for service.
From The Maternity Nursing Series.
LC NO. 77-703391
Prod-VDONUR Dist-AJN Prodn-WTTWTV 1966

Nurse Practice Acts C 30 MIN
16MM FILM - 3/4 IN VIDEO PRO
Describes common provisions of all states' nurse practice acts. Emphasizes the necessity for disciplinary action as a protection to the public and mandatory continuing education for licensure.
From The Nurse And The Law Series.
LC NO. 76-701551
Prod-AJN Dist-AJN Prodn-WGNCP 1974

Nurse Practitioner C 14 MIN
3/4 OR 1/2 INCH VIDEO CASSETTE J A
Depicts how many patients are now being treated by nurse practitioners.
Prod-SUTHRB Dist-SUTHRB

Nurse Practitioner, The C 14 MIN
16MM FILM, 3/4 OR 1/2 IN VIDEO J-C A
Deomonstrates the complex and diverse duties performed by the nurse practitioner by following several of them at work in hospitals and clinics. Reveals educational requirements for on-the-job training needed to achieve certification.
Prod-LACFU Dist-IA 1978

Nurse-Patient Communication C 19 MIN
16MM FILM OPTICAL SOUND
Defines communication, lists some of the problems in nurse-patient communication and provides methods which lead to effective communication between nurse and patient.
From The Developing Skills In Communications Series.
LC NO. 78-712978
Prod-TRNAID Dist-TRNAID 1969

Nurse-Patient Relationship - Orientation Phase B 30 MIN
16MM FILM - 3/4 IN VIDEO PRO
Acquaints nursing students with the introductory phases of the nurse-patient relationship.
From The Mental Health Concepts For Nursing, Unit 4 - The Nurse - Patient Relationship Series.
LC NO. 73-702653
Prod-SREB Dist-GPITVL 1971

Nurse-Patient Relationship - Termination Phase B 30 MIN
16MM FILM - 3/4 IN VIDEO PRO
Helps nursing students understand the termination phase of the nurse-patient relationship.
From The Mental Health Concepts For Nursing, Unit 4 - The Nurse - Patient Relationship Series.
LC NO. 73-702655
Prod-SREB Dist-GPITVL 1971

Nurse-Patient Relationship - The Nursing Challenge B 30 MIN
16MM FILM OPTICAL SOUND PRO
Helps nursing students understand the challenge posed by nurse-patient relationships.
From The Mental Health Concepts For Nursing Series.
LC NO. 73-702656
Prod-SREB Dist-GPITVL 1971

Nurse-Patient Relationship - Therapeutic Use Of Self B 30 MIN
16MM FILM OPTICAL SOUND PRO
Helps nursing students understand how a therapeutic use of the self can improve their abilities in treating patients.
From The Mental Health Concepts For Nursing Series.
LC NO. 73-702651
Prod-SREB Dist-GPITVL 1971

Nurse-Patient Relationship - Understanding The Patient (Cultural Factors) B 30 MIN
16MM FILM OPTICAL SOUND PRO
Helps nursing students develop an understanding of the variety of cultural factors which may impede acceptance and understanding of the patient.
From The Mental Health Concepts For Nursing Series.
LC NO. 73-702650
Prod-SREB Dist-GPITVL 1971

Nurse-Patient Relationship - Working Phase B 30 MIN
16MM FILM - 3/4 IN VIDEO PRO
From The Mental Health Concepts For Nursing, Unit 4 - The Nurse - Patient Relationship Series.
LC NO. 73-702654
Prod-SREB Dist-GPITVL 1971

Nurse-Patient Relationship, The C 240 MIN
3/4 OR 1/2 INCH VIDEO CASSETTE PRO
Shows eight scenes from an eleven-week relationship between a psychiatric nurse and her psychiatric patient. Contains eight videocassettes, a student work book of exercises, and instructor's guide.
Prod-HSCIC Dist-HSCIC 1981

Nurse-Patient Relationships C 17 MIN
16MM FILM OPTICAL SOUND
Explains how terminally ill patients cope with death and shows the nurse how to care for the dying patient.
From The Care Of The Dying Patient Series.
LC NO. 71-712979
Prod-TRNAID Dist-TRNAID 1970

Nurse/Physician Interaction C 10 MIN
3/4 INCH VIDEO CASSETTE PRO
Presents three approaches to nurse/physician interactions, including the nurse who fails to communicate important patient information to the attending physician, the nurse who communicates ineffectively, and the nurse who communicates effectively.
LC NO. 79-707732
Prod-UMICHM Dist-UMMCML Prodn-UMISU 1977

Nurse, Please B 28 MIN
16MM FILM OPTICAL SOUND PRO
Presents the practical nursing field as a challenging one for those who can qualify. Demonstrates the requirements for education and the responsibilities of the job.
Prod-ANANLN Dist-AJN 1954

Nurse, The Physician, The Hospital And The Law, The B 31 MIN
16MM FILM OPTICAL SOUND
Illustrates the responsibility of the hospital for negligence or malpractice on the part of its employees by enacting a preliminary meeting between the attorney and the participants in a suit.
Prod-HOFLAR Dist-AMEDA

Nurse, Where Are You C 49 MIN
3/4 OR 1/2 INCH VIDEO CASSETTE H-C A
Documents the critical shortage of hospital nurses, explaining that they are overworked, underpaid and disillusioned. Shows an effort to unionize nurses.
Prod-CBSNEW Dist-CAROUF

Nurse, Where Are You? C 49 MIN
3/4 OR 1/2 INCH VIDEO CASSETTE
Portrays nurses in the acute care hospital setting, their responsibilities and frustrations. Portrays nurses feelings of being overworked, underpaid and disillusioned.
Prod-CBSNEW Dist-AJN

Nurse's Aide, Orderly And Attendant—A Series
IND
Discusses methods, procedures and techniques used by the paramedical employee to carry out various functions.
Prod-COPI Dist-COPI 1971

Ambulating A Patient To A Chair Or Wheelchair	018 MIN
Answering The Patient's Call Signal	016 MIN
Bedbath, The - Preparation And Emotional	013 MIN
Bedbath, The - Procedure	015 MIN
First Time Ambulation Of The Patient	020 MIN
Giving A Bedpan Or Urinal	018 MIN
Hospital Beds - Variable Heights	022 MIN
Making The Surgical (Postoperative) Bed	019 MIN
Making The Unoccupied (Closed) Bed	019 MIN
Moving A Patient In Bed	016 MIN
Observation Of Feces And Urine	019 MIN
Prevention And Care Of Decubiti	018 MIN
Skin, The - Its Function And Care	016 MIN
Stretcher Transport	016 MIN
Use Of Side Rails	022 MIN
Vital Signs - Blood Pressure	020 MIN
Vital Signs - Pulse And Respiration	017 MIN
Vital Signs - Temperature	020 MIN
Wheelchair Transport	020 MIN

Nurse's Day With The Mentally Ill X 22 MIN
16MM FILM OPTICAL SOUND C T
Shows the activities of a student nurse in a psychiatric hospital. Explains and demonstrates reassuring and supporting roles and illustrates nursing care in connection with schock therapies and a lobotomy operation. Includes many examples of the behavior of the mentally ill.
Prod-PSUPCR Dist-PSUPCR 1954

Nurse's Role And Resources In Providing Therapeutic Care To Psychiatric Patients, The B 44 MIN
16MM FILM OPTICAL SOUND PRO
Discusses the nurse's responsibility in defining her role and functions in the areas of patient care and interdisciplinary relationships, and the resources available to her.
From The Nursing In Psychiatry Series.
LC NO. 75-703432
Prod-VDONUR Dist-AJN Prodn-WTTWTV 1968

Nurse's Role In Acute Psychiatric Emergencies, The C 120 MIN
3/4 OR 1/2 INCH VIDEO CASSETTE PRO
Discusses several types of psychiatric patients and presents examples of aggressive behavior and problem-solving techniques.
LC NO. 81-706296
Prod-USVA Dist-USNAC 1980

Nurse's Role In Changing Mental Health Programs, The B 44 MIN
16MM FILM OPTICAL SOUND PRO
Presents specific community mental health programs and the nurse's role.
From The Nursing In Psychiatry Series.
LC NO. 79-703433
Prod-VDONUR Dist-AJN Prodn-WTTWTV 1968

Nursery Rhymes C 15 MIN
3/4 INCH VIDEO CASSETTE K-P
Presents Mother Goose nursery rhymes.
From The I Can Read Series.
Prod-WCETTV Dist-GPITVL 1977

Nursery School Child-Mother Interaction - Three Head Start Children And Their Mothers C 41 MIN
16MM FILM OPTICAL SOUND
Depicts three Negro mothers alone with their four-year-old boys, two of the children being 'DIFFICULT' and the third well-adjusted. Emphasizes the mother's influence and child's attachment to her. Shows the three children in their Head Start school, emphasizing social attitudes with scenes of mealtime behavior, preferred activities and goal pursuit. Points out differences in interaction patterns and maternal attitudes.
Prod-VASSAR Dist-NYU

Nursery School For The Blind C 20 MIN
16MM FILM OPTICAL SOUND
Explains that because the problems of the blind child are usually greater than parents can cope with unaided, they are often sent away from home into residential nurseries. Depicts a nursery school that enables blind children to stay at home by supplementing the care given by their parents - by helping to make up for missed stages of development, by encouraging curiousity and by keeping up continual verbal communication to facilitate orientation and compensate for missing visual contact.
Prod-VASSAR Dist-NYU

Nursery Sepsis C 29 MIN
16MM FILM, 3/4 OR 1/2 IN VIDEO PRO
Illustrates how staphylococcus infection is spread in hospital nurseries and what can be done to control cross-infection. (Also available in French, Spanish and Portuguese).
Prod-WFP Dist-WFP 1961

Nursery Worker C 15 MIN
3/4 OR 1/2 INCH VIDEO CASSETTE I
Explains the qualifications and personal qualities required for a successful career as a nursery worker.
From The Career Awareness Series.
Prod-KLVXTV Dist-GPITVL 1973

Nurses C 23 MIN
3/4 OR 1/2 INCH VIDEO CASSETTE
Concludes instruction on the use of the new blood collection equipment in various phases of its operation.
From The What's In It For Me? Series.
Prod-AMRC Dist-AMRC 1977

Nurses Caps And Bakers Hats B 15 MIN
2 INCH VIDEOTAPE P
Discusses the clothing associated with different occupations. (Broadcast quality)
From The Around The Corner Series. No. 25
Prod-FWCETV Dist-GPITVL Prodn-WEDUTV

Nurses Talk About Epilepsy C 13 MIN
16MM FILM OPTICAL SOUND

Covers drug therapy for epilepsy, the nurse's role in observing and reporting seizure patterns, fears and concerns of epileptics and the nurse's role in handling these concerns.
LC NO. 76-700533
Prod-EFA Dist-GEIGY 1975

Nurses's Aide, Orderly And Attendant—A Series
H-C A
Discusses methods, procedures and techniques used by the paramedical employee to carry out various functions.
Prod-COPI Dist-COPI 1969

Ambulating A Patient To A Chair Or Wheelchair 016 MIN
Answering The Patient's Call Signal 009 MIN
Bedbath, The - Preparation And Emotional 013 MIN
Bedbath, The - Procedure 019 MIN
Care And Prevention Of Decubiti 018 MIN
First Time Ambulation Of The Patient 013 MIN
Giving A Bedpan Or Urinal 014 MIN
Hospital Beds - Variable Heights 014 MIN
Making The Surgical (Postoperative) Bed 019 MIN
Making The Unoccupied (Closed) Bed 013 MIN
Moving A Patient In Bed 016 MIN
Observation Of Feces And Urine 017 MIN
Skin, The - Its Function And Care 016 MIN
Stretcher Transport 016 MIN
Use Of Side Rails 009 MIN
Vital Signs - Blood Pressure 020 MIN
Vital Signs - Pulse And Respiration 017 MIN
Vital Signs - Temperature 020 MIN
Wheelchair Transport 014 MIN

Nursing - A Family Affair C 28 MIN
16MM FILM, 3/4 OR 1/2 IN VIDEO A
Covers complete information about breastfeeding information for new mothers. Demonstrates techniques which will make breastfeeding more comfortable and successful. Includes information on how breastfeeding works, prenatal preparation of nipples, preventing cracking and sore nipples, breast engorgement, when and how to begin nursing, inverted nipples and frequency of feedings.
LC NO. 83-707197
Prod-CWRU Dist-PEREN 1983

Nursing - A Professional Career B 15 MIN
16MM FILM OPTICAL SOUND H-C A
Explains the advantages of a nursing career. Stresses the need for both a cultural and technical education.
Prod-WSU Dist-WSU 1958

Nursing - Effective Evaluation—A Series
C A
Illustrates how nursing instructors can utilize effective evaluation techniques in the classroom and clinical laboratory.
Prod-NTCN Dist-NTCN 1971

Analyzing Classroom Tests 28 MIN
Analyzing The Clinical Lab Experience 28 MIN
Classroom Tools Of Evaluation 28 MIN
Clinical Tools Of Evaluation 28 MIN
Evaluation - A Form Of Communication 28 MIN
Evaluation - Its Meaning 28 MIN
Grades - Nemesis Or Recompense 28 MIN
Individual Differences 28 MIN
Planning Classroom Tests 28 MIN
Principles Of Evaluation 28 MIN

Nursing - Patient Teaching—A Series
C A
Introduces and analyzes the key issues of patient teaching.
Prod-NTCN Dist-NTCN 1971

Implementing Patient Teaching 30 MIN
Philosophy Of Patient Teaching 30 MIN
Planning Patient Teaching 30 MIN
Principles Of Learning 30 MIN
Readiness For Learning 30 MIN

Nursing - R Plus M Equals C, Relationship Plus Meaning Equals Communication—A Series
C A
Develops a basic theory of communication around the formula R plus M equals C. Explains that this formula stands for relationship plus meaning equals communication. Applies this theory to classroom activities as well as the specific processes of nursing utilized in the clinical laboratory.
Prod-NTCN Dist-NTCN 1971

Barriers To Communication 30 MIN
Basic Principles Of Communication 30 MIN
Communicating With Colleagues 30 MIN
Communication Processes In Nursing 30 MIN
Communication Skills 30 MIN
Giving Instructions, Charting, Reporting 30 MIN
Interviews And Process Recordings 30 MIN
Meaning Of Communication, The 30 MIN
Team Conferences 30 MIN
Utilizing Effective Communication 30 MIN

Nursing - The Politics Of Caring C 22 MIN
16MM FILM, 3/4 OR 1/2 IN VIDEO PRO
Explores the evolution of nurses' attitudes towards their work, their relationship with the medical profession, and their right to take an active role in the shaping of health care in the U S.
Prod-ILEXFI Dist-FANPRO 1977

Nursing - Where Are You Going, How Will You Get There—A Series
C A
Prod-NTCN Dist-NTCN 1971

Care Plan, The 30 MIN
Combining Teaching Strategies 30 MIN
Developing Behavioral Objectives 30 MIN
Evaluation As A Teaching Strategy 30 MIN
Implementing A Curriculum 30 MIN
Lecture And Role-Playing Strategy, The 30 MIN
Perspective On Teaching, A 30 MIN
Planning Clinical Experiences 30 MIN
Pre And Post Conferences 30 MIN
Seminar And Role-Playing Strategy, The 30 MIN

Nursing Aids For Normal Elimination B 29 MIN
16MM FILM OPTICAL SOUND PRO
Discusses the functions of the bowel and bladder. Discusses and demonstrates selected nursing measures that may be used to assist the process of elimination.
From The Directions For Education In Nursing Via Technology Series. Lesson 14
LC NO. 74-701788
Prod-DENT Dist-WSU 1974

Nursing And The Law—A Series

Prod-VDONUR Dist-AJN Prodn-WTTWTV 1968

Health Team Relationships 44 MIN
Malpractice 44 MIN
Medical-Moral-Legal Issues 44 MIN
Nurse And Her Employer, The 44 MIN
Nurse In The Community, The 44 MIN
Nurse Practice Acts 44 MIN
Nursing Torts 44 MIN
Rights Of Patients 44 MIN
Standard Of Care, The 44 MIN
Wills, Insurance, Witness 44 MIN

Nursing Appraisal Of Infant Neurological Development B 44 MIN
16MM FILM OPTICAL SOUND PRO
Discusses normal neuro-motor-sensory system of the infant in the first year of life. Demonstrates normal reflexes of one-, three, and nine-month old babies, with emphasis on the methods which nurses should employ in observing infants for normal growth and development.
From The Pediatric Nursing Series.
LC NO. 72-703418
Prod-VDONUR Dist-AJN Prodn-WTTWTV 1967

Nursing As A Profession C 30 MIN
3/4 OR 1/2 INCH VIDEO CASSETTE
Discusses nursing as a profession.
From The Lifelines Series.
Prod-UGATV Dist-MDCPB

Nursing Assessment C 24 MIN
16MM FILM - 3/4 IN VIDEO PRO
Discusses nursing assessment of neurologically disabled patients in terms of their general appearance, level of consciousness, changes in mental status, vital signs, motor and sensory function, autonomic dysfunction and nursing history.
From The Neurologically Disabled Patient, Pt 1 - Nursing During The Acute Stage Series.
LC NO. 77-700603
Prod-AJN Dist-AJN Prodn-TVPC 1977

Nursing Audit, The C 12 MIN
3/4 OR 1/2 INCH VIDEO CASSETTE PRO
Provides a step-by-step approach to the nursing audit. Discusses the use of the audit process in evaluating the quality of health services, selection of criteria measurements numerical rating scales and recording sheets.
Prod-UMICHM Dist-UMICHM 1977

Nursing Care - The Diabetic Patient C 29 MIN
16MM FILM OPTICAL SOUND
Illustrates five points in the care of the diabetic patient, such as urine tests, insulin administration, proper diet, regulated physical activity and proper personal hygiene.
LC NO. 75-700802
Prod-USVA Dist-USNAC 1966

Nursing Care For The Oral Surgery Patient C 17 MIN
3/4 OR 1/2 INCH VIDEO CASSETTE
Depicts the special nursing care required for oral surgery patients.
Prod-VADTC Dist-AMDA 1975

Nursing Care For The Patient In Traction C 30 MIN
3/4 OR 1/2 INCH VIDEO CASSETTE
Points out common complications of traction. Discusses potential nursing care problems related to the various types of traction and suggests specific nursing measures to solve these problems.
From The Traction Series.
Prod-FAIRGH Dist-FAIRGH

Nursing Care Of Burn Patients - The Intermediate Phase C 45 MIN
3/4 INCH VIDEO CASSETTE PRO
Shows continued wound care, including hydrotherapy, debridement, and selection and application of topical medications. Stresses the importance of active patient participation and the vital role of nutrition in patient recovery. Discusses skin grafting and the psychological problems of the patient.
From The Critical Care Nursing - Patients With Burns Series.
LC NO. 79-706232
Prod-AJN Dist-AJN 1978

Nursing Care Of Burn Patients - The Acute Phase C 45 MIN
3/4 INCH VIDEO CASSETTE PRO
Presents an overview of care required by major burn patients during the first 72 hours following injury. Discusses crucial problems in maintaining adequate oxygenation and fluid and electrolyte balance. Includes demonstrations of the care of the burn site and a review of major, life-threatening complications.
LC NO. 79-706231
Prod-AJN Dist-AJN 1978

Nursing Care Of Children With Cardiovascular Problems C 36 MIN
3/4 INCH VIDEO CASSETTE PRO
Teaches the elements of Pediatric Cardiovascular Assessment and its application.
Prod-UMITV Dist-UMITV 1981

Nursing Care Of Children With Respiratory Problems C 30 MIN
3/4 INCH VIDEO CASSETTE PRO
Teaches the elements of Pediatric Respiratory Physical Assessment and its application.
Prod-UMITV Dist-UMITV 1980

Nursing Care Of Patients In Acute Ventilatory Failure C 30 MIN
3/4 INCH VIDEO CASSETTE PRO
Deals with the care of a young patient who develops pulmonary edema as a result of an overdose of heroin. Evaluates assessment parameters and demonstrates the implementation of findings.
From The Critical Care Nursing - Patients In Acute Respiratory Distress Series.
LC NO. 79-706230
Prod-AJN Dist-USNAC Prodn-JOHLD 1977

Nursing Care Of Patients In Chronic Ventilatory Failure C 30 MIN
3/4 INCH VIDEO CASSETTE PRO
Deals with the care of a patient with chronic obstructive pulmonary disease who develops acute respiratory distress due to an infection. Explores case history, arterial blood gas studies, chest X-rays, respiratory pattern, ausculation and spirometry.
From The Critical Care Nursing - Patients In Acute Respiratory Distress Series.
LC NO. 79-706229
Prod-AJN Dist-USNAC Prodn-JOHLD 1977

Nursing Care Of The Adult With Coronary Artery Surgery C 21 MIN
16MM FILM OPTICAL SOUND PRO
Comments on the nature of coronary artery surgery, mortality rates and advancements in techniques. Covers the course of treatment of a patient, beginning with admission to the hospital.
Prod-UKY Dist-NMAC 1972

Nursing Care Of The Aged B 30 MIN
16MM FILM OPTICAL SOUND
Uses scenes of a gerontological nursing care conference to illustrate the kind of information that should be shared with all nursing staff members. Summarizes the more important problems discussed by the staff.
From The Gerontological Nursing Series. No. 6
LC NO. 70-710010
Prod-VDONUR Dist-AJN Prodn-WTTWTV 1970

Nursing Care Of The Confused Patient - An Update C 30 MIN
3/4 OR 1/2 INCH VIDEO CASSETTE PRO
Helps viewers recognize, evaluate and use the behavioral skills necessary to care successfully for the confused patient.
Prod-HSCIC Dist-HSCIC 1984

Nursing Care Of The Oral Surgery Patient C 17 MIN
16MM FILM - 3/4 IN VIDEO PRO
Demonstrates the special nursing care needed by oral surgery patients.
LC NO. 78-706004
Prod-USVA Dist-USNAC 1977

Nursing Care Of The Sick And Injured C 28 MIN
16MM FILM OPTICAL SOUND
Discusses general care of illness and long-term care of injuries. Stresses the treatment of symptoms using medications found in the public shelter medical kit and the type kit usually found in the home. To be used with the course 'MEDICAL SELF-HELP TRAINING.'
From The Medical Self-Help Series.
LC NO. 74-705227
Prod-USDHEW Dist-USNAC Prodn-USOCD 1965

Nursing Care Of The Sick And Injured (Spanish) C 28 MIN
16MM FILM OPTICAL SOUND
Teaches the individual how to take care of his medical and health needs in time of disaster when medical assistance might not be readily available. Presents instructions on nursing care of the sick and injured.
From The Medical Self-Help Series.
LC NO. 75-702547
Prod-USPHS Dist-USNAC 1965

Nursing Care Plan, The B 30 MIN
2 INCH VIDEOTAPE PRO
Explains why the nursing care plan is needed and shows how to formulate and use it.
Prod-SUNY Dist-AJN

Nursing Care Plans B 27 MIN
16MM FILM OPTICAL SOUND PRO
Uses dramatization to identify the purposes of nursing care plans. Discusses types and steps involved in the development of plans and the role of the nurse in these processes.
From The Directions For Education In Nursing Via Technology Series. Lesson 93
LC NO. 74-701872
Prod-DENT Dist-WSU 1974

Nursing Care Plans B 16 MIN
2 INCH VIDEOTAPE PRO
Shows the initiation and implementation of a nursing care plan.
Prod-TVWORK Dist-AJN 1969

Nursing Career Development—A Series
PRO
Deals with methods that nurses can use to advance their careers.
Prod-USVA Dist-USNAC 1981

Career Entry Transition And Early Years Of 023 MIN
Leadership Roles - First Line To Executive 045 MIN
Nursing Career Strategies And A Program Model 033 MIN

Nursing Career Strategies And A Program Model C 33 MIN
3/4 OR 1/2 INCH VIDEO CASSETTE PRO
Focuses on the options open to those in nursing to deal with a locked in feeling problematic to many staff members on long-term assignments, fear of change, or lack of information channeled to those able to facilitate lateral moves. Discusses the rationale for career planning and career revitalization.
From The Nursing Career Development Series. Pt 2
LC NO. 81-707108
Prod-USVA Dist-USNAC 1981

Nursing Challenge, The B 30 MIN
2 INCH VIDEOTAPE PRO
Helps nursing students understand the challenge posed by the nurse-patient relationship.
From The Mental Health Concepts For Nursing, Unit 4 - The Nurse - Patient Relationship Series.
LC NO. 73-702656
Prod-GPITVL Dist-GPITVL 1971

Nursing History Interview With A Recently Sober Alcoholic Woman C 50 MIN
3/4 INCH VIDEO CASSETTE
Demonstrates a nurse's assessment by interview with a recently sober alcoholic woman for the purpose of obtaining a history and screening physical examination.
Prod-UWASHP Dist-UWASHP

Nursing History Interview With A Recently Sober Alcoholic Man C 59 MIN
3/4 INCH VIDEO CASSETTE
Demonstrates a nurse's assessment by interview with a recently sober alcoholic man for the purpose of obtaining a history and screening physical examination.
Prod-UWASHP Dist-UWASHP

Nursing Home C 28 MIN
16MM FILM - 3/4 IN VIDEO
Shows a nursing home in Connecticut, pointing out the expert care a good nursing home can provide and explaining what to look for in a nursing home.
From The No Place Like Home Series.
LC NO. 79-708108
Prod-USSRS Dist-USNAC 1979

Nursing Home Volunteer, The C 15 MIN
3/4 OR 1/2 INCH VIDEO CASSETTE C A
Presents cancer specialist Dr Ernest H Rosenbaum along with numerous volunteers, sharing experiences in working with critically ill and geriatric patients.
Prod-RALPRO Dist-TEF

Nursing Homes C 30 MIN
3/4 OR 1/2 INCH VIDEO CASSETTE
Presents tips on picking a nursing home.
From The Consumer Survival Series. Health
Prod-MDCPB Dist-MDCPB

Nursing Implications In The Administration Of Chemotherapy C 47 MIN
3/4 INCH VIDEO CASSETTE
Discusses several aspects of chemotherapy, including side effects, management, patient education and administration.
Prod-UTAHTI Dist-UTAHTI

Nursing In A Multi-Cultural Society C 30 MIN
16MM FILM - 3/4 IN VIDEO PRO
Discusses how socio-cultural differences between nurse and patient influence mutual expectations and participation in care, showing the need for a health care system designed to accommodate diverse groups which form a pluralistic society. Examines particular needs and problems of racial and ethnic minorities.
LC NO. 76-701621
Prod-AJN Dist-AJN Prodn-WGNCP 1976

Nursing In Psychiatry—A Series
PRO
Prod-VDONUR Dist-AJN Prodn-WTTWTV 1968

Acting-Out Patient, The 44 MIN
Anxious Patient And Common Defensive Patterns 44 MIN
Behavioral Change And Learning 44 MIN
Communication - The Concept And The Skill 44 MIN
Communication In The Nurse-Patient Relationship 44 MIN
Concept Of Anxiety, The 44 MIN
Depressed Patient, The 44 MIN
Directions For The Future In Psychiatric 44 MIN
Elements Of The Nurse-Patient Relationship, The 44 MIN
Environmental Aspects Of Therapeutic Care 44 MIN
Nurse In Community Psychiatry, The 44 MIN
Nurse In Family Therapy, The 44 MIN
Nurse In Group Work, The 44 MIN
Nurse's Role And Resources In Providing 44 MIN
Nurse's Role In Changing Mental Health 44 MIN
One To One Nurse-Patient Relationship, The 44 MIN
Patient With Addictive Behavior, The 44 MIN
Patients With Manipulative And Acting-Out 44 MIN
Psychiatric Nursing - Past And Present 44 MIN
Ritualistic Patient, The 44 MIN
Suspicious Patient, The 44 MIN
Symptom As Expression Of Anxiety, The 44 MIN
Withdrawn Patient - Implications For The 44 MIN
Withdrawn Patient, The 44 MIN

Nursing Intervention - One Facet Of Dementia C 20 MIN
3/4 INCH VIDEO CASSETTE PRO
Features a simulated interview between a patient and a nurse which illustrates various senile reactions. Shows appropriate nursing intervention skills.
From The Communicating With The Psychiatric Patient Series.
LC NO. 79-707283
Prod-VAHSL Dist-USNAC 1977

Nursing Intervention - The Admission Interview, The Depressed Patient C 29 MIN
3/4 INCH VIDEO CASSETTE PRO
Demonstrates nursing personnel's verbal and nonverbal communication skills with a newly admitted depressed patient.
From The Communicating With The Psychiatric Patient Series.
LC NO. 79-707280
Prod-VAHSL Dist-USNAC 1976

Nursing Intervention - The Delusional Patient C 23 MIN
3/4 INCH VIDEO CASSETTE PRO
Offers a simulated interview depicting nursing intervention involving a patient who is delusional. Highlights various aspects of the patient's reactions.
From The Communicating With The Psychiatric Patient Series.
LC NO. 79-707281
Prod-VAHSL Dist-USNAC 1975

Nursing Intervention - The Patient Who Is Experiencing Hallucinations C 23 MIN
3/4 INCH VIDEO CASSETTE PRO
Shows a simulated interview between a nurse and a hallucinating patient. Demonstrates the hallucinating process and appropriate nursing intervention skills.
From The Communicating With The Psychiatric Patient Series.
LC NO. 79-707284
Prod-VAHSL Dist-USNAC 1975

Nursing Intervention - The Patient With Aggressive Behavior C 21 MIN
3/4 INCH VIDEO CASSETTE PRO
Presents a simulated interview between a patient and a nurse, demonstrating the dynamics of anger and the value of prompt and appropriate nursing intervention.
From The Communicating With The Psychiatric Patient Series.
LC NO. 79-707285
Prod-VAHSL Dist-USNAC

Nursing Intervention - The Patient With Manipulative Behavior C 21 MIN
3/4 INCH VIDEO CASSETTE PRO
Presents a simulated interview between a nurse and a manipulative patient.
From The Communicating With The Psychiatric Patient Series.
LC NO. 79-707286
Prod-VAHSL Dist-USNAC 1975

Nursing Intervention - The Patient With Suspicious Behavior C 37 MIN
3/4 INCH VIDEO CASSETTE PRO
Presents a simulated interview between a nurse and a patient which demonstrates the dynamics of suspicious behavior and the appropriate intervention skills.
From The Communicating With The Psychiatric Patient Series.
LC NO. 79-707287
Prod-VAHSL Dist-USNAC 1976

Nursing Management Of Children With Cancer C 22 MIN
16MM FILM OPTICAL SOUND PRO
Demonstrates the skills, commitment and rewards involved in pediatric cancer nursing. Shows nursing procedures, such as infusions, mouth care, control of infections and fevers, ostomy care, play therapy and emotional support of patients and their families. Emphasizes the detection of side effects of therapy and examines methods for managing side effects.
LC NO. 77-701314
Prod-AMCS Dist-AMCS 1974

Nursing Management Of The Patient Receiving Radiation Therapy C 22 MIN
16MM FILM OPTICAL SOUND PRO
Depicts the role of the nurse with patients being treated by radiation for cancer. Shows the nurse and physician explaining procedures to patients and giving them instructions in matters of diet, rest and skin care as well as providing emotional support.
Prod-AMCS Dist-AMCS 1973

Nursing Management Of The Patient With Cancer C 29 MIN
16MM FILM OPTICAL SOUND PRO
Illustrates in detail nursing procedures used after laryngectomy, tracheotomy, colostomy, or cystectomy.
LC NO. FI68-87
Prod-AMCS Dist-AMCS Prodn-CFDC 1966

Nursing Management Of The Patient With Head And Neck Cancer C 31 MIN
16MM FILM OPTICAL SOUND PRO
Discusses special nursing procedures for patients who have had an orbital exenteration or combined jaw resection and radial neck dissection. Shows tracheostomy care and nasal feeding tube techniques.
Prod-AMCS Dist-AMCS 1970

Nursing Measures To Restore Postoperative Ventilation C 30 MIN
3/4 OR 1/2 INCH VIDEO CASSETTE
Shows a nurse ausculating the patient's chest, providing examples of normal breathing, inaudible vs audible rales and cleared rales. Reviews natural breathing mechanisms and the effects of anesthesia.
Prod-UKYN Dist-AJN

Nursing Problems In The Implanting Of The Internal Cardiac Pacemaker C 18 MIN
16MM FILM OPTICAL SOUND PRO
Demonstrates a technique in repairing and implanting the internal cardiac pacemaker, and stresses the need for nursing and medical cooperation in preventing possible foreign body reaction.
Prod-ACYDGD Dist-ACY 1965

Nursing Process In Action—A Series
PRO
Covers nursing procedures.
Prod-WRAIR Dist-USNAC

Nursing Process In Action, The, Pt 1, The Use
Nursing Process In Action, The, Pt 2, 023 MIN
Nursing Process, The 008 MIN

Nursing Process In Action, The, Pt 1, The Use Of Nursing Process To Plan, Implement,... C 32 MIN
16MM FILM, 3/4 OR 1/2 IN VIDEO PRO
Complete title is Nursing Process In Action, The, Pt 1, The Use Of Nursing Process To Plan, Implement, Evaluate Nursing Care. Reviews four phases of the nursing process as it applies to a diabetic patient and explains the nursing care plan and clinical nursing record.
From The Nursing Process In Action Series.
Prod-WRAIR Dist-USNAC

Nursing Process In Action, The, Pt 2, Discharge Planning - The Key To Continuing Care C 23 MIN
16MM FILM, 3/4 OR 1/2 IN VIDEO PRO
Covers nursing care by emergency room, ward and recovery room nurses as they assess, plan, implement and evaluate the patient's nursing care.
From The Nursing Process In Action Series.
Prod-WRAIR Dist-USNAC

Nursing Process, Pt 1 - Assessment B 25 MIN
16MM FILM OPTICAL SOUND PRO
Describes assessment, the first step in the nursing process. Demonstrates assessment in a patient situation.
From The Directions For Education In Nursing Via Technology Series. Lesson 23
LC NO. 74-701796
Prod-DENT Dist-WSU 1974

Nursing Process, Pt 2 - Planning And Implementation Of Plan B 28 MIN
16MM FILM OPTICAL SOUND PRO
Uses a dramatization to show planning and implementation in patient care.
From The Directions For Education In Nursing Via Technology Series. Lesson 24
LC NO. 74-701797
Prod-DENT Dist-WSU 1974

Nursing Process, Pt 3 - Evaluating Effectiveness Of Implementation B 24 MIN
16MM FILM OPTICAL SOUND PRO
Deals with evaluating effectiveness of implementation.
From The Directions For Education In Nursing Via Technology Series. Lesson 25
LC NO. 74-701798
Prod-DENT Dist-WSU 1974

Nursing Process, The C 8 MIN
16MM FILM, 3/4 OR 1/2 IN VIDEO PRO
Explains the four phases of the nursing process and the nursing care plan which helps nurses and staff members to function more effectively and give patients better care.
From The Nursing Process In Action Series.
Prod-WRAIR Dist-USNAC

Nursing Process, The C 55 MIN
3/4 OR 1/2 INCH VIDEO CASSETTE
Presents the implementation and evaluation phases of the nursing process. Emphasizes the barriers to implementation that can exist when the patient, nurse, family and the health care team are not working together.
Prod-FAIRGH Dist-FAIRGH

Nursing Responsibilities - Nasal Suctioning, Oral Suctioning And Mouth Care B 29 MIN
16MM FILM OPTICAL SOUND PRO
Identifies the need for, and demonstrates the process of nasal and oral suctioning. Discusses and demonstrates means of providing mouth care for helpless patients.
From The Directions For Education In Nursing Via Technology Series. Lesson 67
LC NO. 74-701843
Prod-DENT Dist-WSU 1974

Nursing Responsibilities - Sterile Dressings B 31 MIN
16MM FILM OPTICAL SOUND PRO
Identifies various types of dressings and demonstrates application of a simple dressing, dressing to a wound with drainage and a pressure dressing.
From The Directions For Education In Nursing Via Technology Series. Lesson 69
LC NO. 74-701846
Prod-DENT Dist-WSU 1974

Nursing Responsibilities In Care Of Patient Having Gastric Or Intestinal Decompression... B 30 MIN
16MM FILM OPTICAL SOUND PRO
Demonstrates appropriate nursing action for discomforts of patients having gastric or intestinal decompression therapy. Demonstrates procedures to be followed prior to, during and following ambulation of a patient.
From The Directions For Education In Nursing Via Technology Series. Lesson 42
LC NO. 74-701816
Prod-DENT Dist-WSU 1974

Nursing Responsibilities In Care Of Patients Receiving Various Methods Of Gavage B 33 MIN
16MM FILM OPTICAL SOUND PRO
Identifies indications for gavage feeding and discusses types of feedings. Demonstrates methods, gravity and nursing responsibilities.
From The Directions For Education In Nursing Via Technology Series. Lesson 43
LC NO. 74-701817
Prod-DENT Dist-WSU 1974

Nursing Responsibilities In Radiotherapy, Pt 1 B 31 MIN
16MM FILM OPTICAL SOUND PRO
Identifies sources of radiation. Compares and contrasts alpha, beta and gamma emanations. Discusses biologic effects of radiation on the cell and the concepts of time, distance and shielding.
From The Directions For Education In Nursing Via Technology Series. Lesson 72
LC NO. 74-701849
Prod-DENT Dist-WSU 1974

Nursing Responsibilities In Radiotherapy, Pt 2 B 30 MIN
16MM FILM OPTICAL SOUND PRO
Compares external and internal radiotherapy and sealed and unsealed therapy. Describes nursing responsibilities for patients receiving each type of therapy.
From The Directions For Education In Nursing Via Technology Series. Lesson 73
LC NO. 74-701850
Prod-DENT Dist-WSU 1974

Nursing Responsibilities In Screening And Detection Of Breast Cancer C 33 MIN
3/4 OR 1/2 INCH VIDEO CASSETTE PRO
Teaches nurses, in a four-module package, the current information on screening and detection of breast cancer. On two tapes.
Prod-HSCIC Dist-HSCIC 1984

Nursing Responsibilities In The Care Of Patients With Arterial Peripheral Vascular... B 31 MIN
16MM FILM OPTICAL SOUND PRO
Reviews anatomy, pathophysiology and the scientific basis for nursing care for patients with arterial peripheral vascular diseases.
From The Directions For Education In Nursing Via Technology Series. Lesson 44
LC NO. 74-701818
Prod-DENT Dist-WSU 1974

Nursing Responsibilities In The Care Of The Patient In A Cast, Pt 1 B 30 MIN
16MM FILM OPTICAL SOUND PRO
Identifies reasons for a cast and discusses materials used. Demonstrates application of a cast and care of a patient in a new cast.
From The Directions For Education In Nursing Via Technology Series. Lesson 48
LC NO. 74-701822
Prod-DENT Dist-WSU 1974

Nursing Responsibilities In The Care Of The Patient In A Cast, Pt 2 B 29 MIN
16MM FILM OPTICAL SOUND PRO
Demonstrates the nurse's responsibility in the care of the patient in a cast.
From The Directions For Education In Nursing Via Technology Series. Lesson 49
LC NO. 74-701823
Prod-DENT Dist-WSU 1974

Nursing Responsibilities In The Care Of The Patient In Traction, Pt 1 B 35 MIN
16MM FILM OPTICAL SOUND PRO
Lists major methods used to provide traction. Demonstrates parts, types and operational principles of equipment used in straight, suspension and fixed traction.
From The Directions For Education In Nursing Via Technology Series. Lesson 50
LC NO. 74-701824
Prod-DENT Dist-WSU 1974

Nursing Responsibilities In The Care Of The Patient In Traction, Pt 2 B 29 MIN
16MM FILM OPTICAL SOUND PRO
Demonstrates the nurse's responsibility in the care of the patient in traction.
From The Directions For Education In Nursing Via Technology Series. Lesson 51
LC NO. 74-701825
Prod-DENT Dist-WSU 1974

Nursing Responsibilities In The Care Of The Patient On A Circ-Olectric Bed B 27 MIN
16MM FILM OPTICAL SOUND PRO
Identifies the parts and operational principles of the Circ-Olectric bed. Demonstrates the use of the bed, turning patient and meeting the needs for intake and elimination.
From The Directions For Education In Nursing Via Technology Series. Lesson 52
LC NO. 74-701826
Prod-DENT Dist-WSU 1974

Nursing Responsibilities In The Evaluation Of Central Venous Pressure B 29 MIN
16MM FILM OPTICAL SOUND PRO
Identifies indications for measuring central venous pressure and displays equipment that is used. Demonstrates the nurse's responsibilities when taking central venous pressure.
From The Directions For Education In Nursing Via Technology Series. Lesson 63
LC NO. 74-701839
Prod-DENT Dist-WSU 1974

Nursing Responsibilities In The Use Of Rotating Tourniquets B 28 MIN
16MM FILM OPTICAL SOUND PRO
Identifies the physiologic basis for the use of rotating tourniquets. Demonstrates the use of manual- and machine-type rotating tourniquets.
From The Directions For Education In Nursing Via Technology Series. Lesson 62
LC NO. 74-701838
Prod-DENT Dist-WSU 1974

Nursing Responsibilities In The Use Of A Mechanical Device In The Transfer Of Patients B 29 MIN
16MM FILM OPTICAL SOUND PRO
Identifies and demonstrates parts and operational principles of the Hoyer lift. Demonstrates transfer of the patient from bed to chair and return to bed, and the use of scale attachment for weighing the patient.
From The Directions For Education In Nursing Via Technology Series. Lesson 53
LC NO. 74-701827
Prod-DENT Dist-WSU 1974

Nursing Scene, The C 12 MIN
16MM FILM OPTICAL SOUND
Describes the nursing profession, what nurses do, their specialties, the kind of training they need and the courses they should take in high school.
LC NO. 74-705228
Prod-NIMH Dist-USNAC 1972

Nursing Service Orientation - Beyond Medicine C 28 MIN
16MM FILM, 3/4 OR 1/2 IN VIDEO
Describes the role of the naval chaplain and discusses spiritual beliefs as they relate to illness. Examines the nurse officer's role in identifying the patient who needs spiritual support in dealing with illness.
Prod-USN Dist-USNAC 1977

Nursing Situations C 31 MIN
3/4 INCH VIDEO CASSETTE PRO
Presents nine commonly encountered nurse-patient situations to analyze verbal and nonverbal communication and to evaluate the effectiveness of various interventive techniques in dealing with patients.
LC NO. 76-706162
Prod-NHWSN Dist-USNAC 1975

Nursing Skills - Intra-Arterial Balloon Pump - An Introduction To Counterpulsation C 17 MIN
3/4 OR 1/2 INCH VIDEO CASSETTE PRO
Introduces the counterpulsation and the intra-aortic balloon pump. Illustrates the therapeutic effects of counterpulsation in the presence of myocardial depression. Shows a balloon pump system and control console.
LC NO. 80-730879
Prod-TRAINX Dist-TRAINX

Nursing Skills - Intra-Arterial Balloon Pump - Elements In Nursing Care C 14 MIN
3/4 OR 1/2 INCH VIDEO CASSETTE PRO
Introduces important elements in the nursing care of patients receiving intra-aortic balloon pump therapy. Reviews counterpulsation and discusses implications to nursing care. Demonstrates techniques for changing the dressing over the catheter insertion site.
LC NO. 80-730880
Prod-TRAINX Dist-TRAINX

Nursing Skills - Intra-Arterial Pressure Monitoring - System Operation C 14 MIN
3/4 OR 1/2 INCH VIDEO CASSETTE PRO
Explains the major components of systems used for intra-arterial pressure monitoring. Explains the specific criteria for evaluating the operation of the system.
LC NO. 80-730877
Prod-TRAINX Dist-TRAINX

Nursing Skills - Intra-Arterial Pressure Monitoring - System Assessment C 14 MIN
3/4 OR 1/2 INCH VIDEO CASSETTE PRO
Identifies nursing skills used during intra-arterial pressure monitoring. Illustrates common waveform abnormalities, such as damped waveform and specific steps in assessment.
LC NO. 80-730878
Prod-TRAINX Dist-TRAINX

Nursing Skills - The 12-Lead Electrocardiogram C 21 MIN
3/4 OR 1/2 INCH VIDEO CASSETTE PRO
Demonstrates nursing skills in 12-lead electrocardiography. Illustrates the formation of 12 leads using five electrodes and the difference in the way bipolar and unipolar leads monitor the heart's electrical activity.
LC NO. 80-730881
Prod-TRAINX Dist-TRAINX

Nursing Skills - Transfusion Therapy - Red Blood Cells C 23 MIN
3/4 OR 1/2 INCH VIDEO CASSETTE PRO
Demonstrates the transfusion of red blood cells. Reviews the function of red cells and the use of this blood component in transfusion therapy. Gives a step-by-step procedure used for the transfusion of red blood cells.
LC NO. 80-730882
Prod-TRAINX Dist-TRAINX

Nursing Skills - Transfusion Therapy, Platelets, Plasma, Cryoprecipitate C 18 MIN
3/4 OR 1/2 INCH VIDEO CASSETTE PRO
Reviews the composition of whole blood and methods for obtaining specific blood components. Demonstrates transfusions of platelets, plasma and cryoprecipitate in clinical setting and explains specific precautions in the transfusion of these products.
LC NO. 80-730883
Prod-TRAINX Dist-TRAINX

Nursing Support During Dialysis Therapy C 12 MIN
3/4 OR 1/2 INCH VIDEO CASSETTE PRO
Illustrates the nurse's role in long-term dialysis therapy. Emphasizes interventions when explaining the nurse's role as a member of the dialysis team.
LC NO. 80-730457
Prod-TRAINX Dist-TRAINX

Nursing The Cancer Patient - Diagnosis - Cancer Of The Rectum B 20 MIN
16MM FILM OPTICAL SOUND PRO
Increases the understanding of the total impact of cancer to the patient and the family. Depicts problems of a patient undergoing surgery and the role of the nurse in comforting and assisting him and his family through the ordeal.
Prod-AMCS Dist-AMCS 1962

Nursing The Psychiatric Patient C 28 MIN
16MM FILM, 3/4 OR 1/2 IN VIDEO
Trains corpsmen as technicians in the care of disturbed patients. Tells how to observe and report behavior patterns and emphasizes the importance of paramedical personnel in psychiatric service.
LC NO. 81-706380
Prod-USN Dist-USNAC 1972

Nursing Torts B 44 MIN
16MM FILM OPTICAL SOUND
Defines nursing torts and presents examples of various situations in which nurses could be liable for defamation, assault and battery, and false imprisonment.
From The Nursing And The Law Series.
LC NO. 70-703373
Prod-VDONUR Dist-AJN Prodn-WTTWTV 1968

Nursing Torts C 30 MIN
16MM FILM - 3/4 IN VIDEO PRO
Discusses the major civil wrongs which a nurse may commit, often unknowingly. Shows four vignettes demonstrating assault and battery, unlawful restraint, defamation and invasion of privacy.
From The Nurse And The Law Series.
LC NO. 76-701553
Prod-AJN Dist-AJN Prodn-WGNCP 1974

Nursing Worldwide C 17 MIN
16MM FILM OPTICAL SOUND H-C A
Nursing leaders, who are educators, executives and world travelers, discuss their work and their ambitions. They show nursing to be a career offering opportunity for more than bedside care.
LC NO. FIA65-126
Prod-WSU Dist-WSU 1960

Nursing—A Series

Prod-USOE Dist-USNAC

Bathing The Patient - Home Care	24 MIN
Care Of The Patient With Diabetes Mellitus -	23 MIN
Care Of The Patient With Diabetes Mellitus -	29 MIN
Fundamentals Of Massage	12 MIN
Hydrotherapy	22 MIN
Radiotherapy - High Dosage Treatment	17 MIN
Therapeutic Uses Of Heat And Cold, Pt 1,	21 MIN
Therapeutic Uses Of Heat And Cold, Pt 2,	22 MIN
Vital Signs And Their Interrelation - Body	32 MIN

Nursing-Cues Behavior Consequences—A Series

Demonstrates the application of behavior modification techniques in caring for patients.
Prod-NTCN Dist-UNEBR 1973

Behavioral Approach To Nursing Care, A	30 MIN
Pinpointing And Recording Patient Behavior	30 MIN
Using Reinforcement Techniques To Manage	30 MIN

Nurturing C 17 MIN
16MM FILM, 3/4 OR 1/2 IN VIDEO J-C A
Offers practcal suggestions of what caregivers can do to optimize infant development.
From The Infant Development Series.
Prod-DAVFMS Dist-DAVFMS Prodn-ECLIF 1978

Nurturing Creativity C 10 MIN
3/4 OR 1/2 INCH VIDEO CASSETTE
Explains the importance of nurturing creativity in children, with Fred Rogers.
From The You (Parents) Are Special Series.
Prod-FAMCOM Dist-FAMCOM

Nutcracker, The C
1/2 IN VIDEO CASSETTE BETA/VHS
Presents The Nutcracker, performed by Mikhail Baryshnikov and the American Ballet Theater.
Prod-GA Dist-GA

Nutcracker, The C 26 MIN
16MM FILM, 3/4 OR 1/2 IN VIDEO K-J
Presents an adaptation of the tale The Nutcracker by E T A Hoffman in which a servant girl and a prince defeat the evil Mouse King and Queen and live happily ever after in their magical kingdom.
Prod-BARR Dist-BARR 1979

Nutmeg - Nature's Perfect Package C 26 MIN
3/4 OR 1/2 INCH VIDEO CASSETTE J A
Describes the uses of nutmeg and mace.
From The Spice Of Life Series.
Prod-BLCKRD Dist-BCNFL 1985

Nutrician, Belajacion E Informacion - La Clave Para Amamantar Con Exito C 19 MIN
3/4 OR 1/2 INCH VIDEO CASSETTE
Spanish language version of the program, Nutrition, Relaxation and Information – Your Keys To Successful Breastfeeding Reviews the nutrients important to breastfeeding, food sources and substitutes that provide protein and calcium. Includes the importance of fluid intake and the baby's sucking action.
Prod-UARIZ Dist-UARIZ

Nutrient Express, The C 11 MIN
3/4 OR 1/2 INCH VIDEO CASSETTE K-P
Tells the story of a little girl who ate the most improper foods, and how she changed after a train trip to the Land of Nutrients.
From The Nutrition For Children Series. Pt II
Prod-POAPLE Dist-POAPLE

Nutrient Needs - Basic Metabolic Processes C 38 MIN
3/4 OR 1/2 INCH VIDEO CASSETTE PRO
Covers food and nutrients, the digestive process and metabolism.
From The Nutrition And Health Series.
Prod-HSCIC Dist-HSCIC 1984

Nutrient Needs - Fatty Acids And Vitamins C 64 MIN
3/4 OR 1/2 INCH VIDEO CASSETTE PRO
Covers minimum daily requirement, recommended dietary allowance, essential fatty acids and vitamins.
From The Nutrition And Health Series.
Prod-HSCIC Dist-HSCIC 1984

Nutrient Needs - Protein And Calories C 17 MIN
3/4 OR 1/2 INCH VIDEO CASSETTE PRO
Covers minimum daily requirement, recommended dietary allowance, protein needs, caloric needs.
From The Nutrition And Health Series.
Prod-HSCIC Dist-HSCIC 1984

Nutrient Needs - Water And Minerals C 50 MIN
3/4 OR 1/2 INCH VIDEO CASSETTE PRO
Covers minimum and recommended daily requirements, water needs and mineral needs.
From The Nutrition And Health Series.
Prod-HSCIC Dist-HSCIC 1984

Nutrition C 30 MIN
3/4 INCH VIDEO CASSETTE
Discusses the importance of nutrition for the three-to six-year-old child.
From The Growing Years Series.
Prod-COAST Dist-CDTEL

Nutrition C 30 MIN
3/4 OR 1/2 INCH VIDEO CASSETTE
Presents tips on nutrition.
From The Consumer Survival Series. Health
Prod-MDCPB Dist-MDCPB

Nutrition - A Lifetime Of Good Eating C 8 MIN
3/4 OR 1/2 INCH VIDEO CASSETTE
Stresses the importance of good eating habits as people age. Presents basic information on nutrition with suggestions for maintaining interest in buying and preparing nutritious meals for people living alone.
Prod-UMICHM Dist-UMICHM 1976

Nutrition - Comment Savez-Vous Quels Aliments Sont Bons C 11 MIN
16MM FILM OPTICAL SOUND
A French language version of the motion picture Nutrition - How Do You Know What Foods Are Good. Explains that both the human body and a car need a source of energy to run, but that the human body needs nourishment even when at rest.
From The Health (French) Series.
LC NO. 76-700142
Prod-MORLAT Dist-MORLAT 1974

Nutrition - Diet Therapy B 30 MIN
16MM FILM OPTICAL SOUND PRO
Discusses modification of the normal diet in relation to consistency, caloric value and nutrients. Deals with variations of the bland diet.
From The Directions For Education In Nursing Via Technology Series. Lesson 78
LC NO. 74-701856
Prod-DENT Dist-WSU 1974

Nutrition - Energy, Carbohydrates, Fats And Proteins, Pt 1 B 29 MIN
16MM FILM OPTICAL SOUND PRO
Discusses the purposes of energy and factors which determine caloric content of food. Identifies factors affecting weight maintenance, gain or loss. Shows the merits of various types of reduction diets.
From The Directions For Education In Nursing Via Technology Series. Lesson 75
LC NO. 74-701852
Prod-DENT Dist-WSU 1974

Nutrition - Energy, Carbohydrates, Fats And Proteins, Pt 2 B 26 MIN
16MM FILM OPTICAL SOUND PRO
Identifies the three energy-producing nutrients. Discusses the function of each nutrient in detail and identifies major food sources for each nutrient.
From The Directions For Education In Nursing Via Technology Series. Lesson 76
LC NO. 74-701854
Prod-DENT Dist-WSU 1974

Nutrition - Foods, Fads, Frauds, Facts C
3/4 OR 1/2 INCH VIDEO CASSETTE
Describes the physiology of hunger and appetite. Explains how eating habits develop early in life and are affected by stress. Discusses nutrition and gives guidelines for an intelligently planned diet.
Prod-GA Dist-GA

Nutrition - Fueling The Human Machine C 18 MIN
16MM FILM, 3/4 OR 1/2 IN VIDEO J-C
Demonstrates how nutrition affects the condition of the human body. Emphasizes the importance of nutritional balance and variety and the need for exercise, and points out the possible dangers of food additives and sugar.
Prod-WINTNC Dist-PHENIX 1978

Nutrition - How Do You Know What Foods Are Good C 11 MIN
16MM FILM OPTICAL SOUND
Explains that both the human body and a car need a source of energy to run, but that the human body needs nourishment even when at rest.
From The Health Series.
LC NO. 76-700142
Prod-MORLAT Dist-MORLAT 1974

Nutrition - Inner Environment (Spanish) C 15 MIN
16MM FILM, 3/4 OR 1/2 IN VIDEO J-C
Provides insights into the why and what of sensible eating, showing how it influences the way we look, act and feel, how the digestive process works and what constitutes a balanced diet. Explains the elements of good nutrition that occur in the foods favored by the Black, Mexican and Asian cultures.
Prod-AMEDFL Dist-AMEDFL

Nutrition - Minerals And Vitamins B 31 MIN
16MM FILM OPTICAL SOUND PRO
Discusses major minerals and vitamins, their functions and food sources. Identifies recommended daily allowance for selected minerals and vitamins.
From The Directions For Education In Nursing Via Technology Series. Lesson 77
LC NO. 74-701855
Prod-DENT Dist-WSU 1974

Nutrition - Psychosocial And Physiologic Basis B 30 MIN
16MM FILM OPTICAL SOUND PRO
Discusses psychosocial factors which influence an individual's pattern of eating. Identifies nutrients of an adequate diet and food sources of the essential nutrients.
From The Directions For Education In Nursing Via Technology Series. Lesson 74
LC NO. 74-701851
Prod-DENT Dist-WSU 1974

Nutrition - Some Food For Thought C 16 MIN
16MM FILM, 3/4 OR 1/2 IN VIDEO I-J
Deals with proper nutrition by examining the various categories of nutrients, offering examples of types of food which supply them and explaining the importance of each. Stresses the need for a balanced diet.
LC NO. 81-707325
Prod-CENTRO Dist-CORF 1981

Nutrition - The All American Meal C 11 MIN
16MM FILM, 3/4 OR 1/2 IN VIDEO I-H
Points out that there is more to food than just eating. Combines interviews on the street and sequences at a fast food emporium with an analysis of the nutritional and sociological implications of the hamburger, fries and soft drink American diet. Offers suggestions for improving the nutritional value of meals.
From The Nutrition Series.
Prod-BARR Dist-BARR 1976

Nutrition - The Consumer And The Supermarket C 15 MIN
16MM FILM, 3/4 OR 1/2 IN VIDEO H-C A
Combines consumer interviews and an analysis of the products and merchandising techniques used in supermarkets to show shoppers how to select the best nutritional value for their food dollar. Explains the basic food groups available and explores the role of advertising, store layout, packaging and labeling in consumer decision making.
From The Nutrition Series.
Prod-BARR Dist-BARR 1976

Nutrition - The First Year C 30 MIN
3/4 INCH VIDEO CASSETTE H-C A
Investigates the problems and satisfactions of infant feeding. Discusses birth weight as an index of the infant's nutritional status and indicates changing nutritional needs as weight and height increase. Compares advantages of breast and bottle feeding.
From The Changing Nutritional Needs Series.
Prod-UWISCA Dist-GPITVL 1976

Nutrition - The First Years C 16 MIN
16MM FILM, 3/4 OR 1/2 IN VIDEO A
Discusses basic information for mothers on child care and nutrition.
Prod-USNAC Dist-USNAC 1980

Nutrition - The Inner Environment C 15 MIN
16MM FILM, 3/4 OR 1/2 IN VIDEO P-J
Explores from the earliest time to the present what men have eaten, why and what it has done to their bodies. Shows what we must eat and how we can improve our health by eating properly.
From The Aef Health Film Library Series.
Prod-AMEDFL Dist-AMEDFL 1972

Nutrition - The Spice Of Life C 8 MIN
16MM FILM, 3/4 OR 1/2 IN VIDEO
Offers an overview of nutritional research studies in a university environment. Discusses the effect of diet on human behavior, improving intravenous feeding and the development of new foods from existing Canadian crops.
From The Discovery Series.
Prod-UTORMC Dist-UTORMC

Nutrition - Try It, You'll Like It C 11 MIN
16MM FILM, 3/4 OR 1/2 IN VIDEO P-I
Points out that there really is a difference between good, nutritious food and junk food. Introduces the concept of the four food groups.
Prod-AIMS Dist-AIMS 1981

Nutrition - Try It, You'll Like It (Spanish) C 11 MIN
16MM FILM, 3/4 OR 1/2 IN VIDEO P-I
Points out that there really is a difference between good, nutritious food and junk food. Introduces the concept of the four food groups.
Prod-AIMS Dist-AIMS 1981

Nutrition - Two Differing Perspectives C 30 MIN
3/4 OR 1/2 INCH VIDEO CASSETTE
See series title for descriptive statement.
From The Dancer's Health Series.
Prod-ARCVID Dist-ARCVID

Nutrition - Vitamin Wise C 19 MIN
16MM FILM, 3/4 OR 1/2 IN VIDEO H-C A
Explains what vitamins are, how the body uses them, and which foods have which vitamins. Provides tips on choosing a balanced diet and preserving the vitamins in preparing and cooking food. Emphasizes the importance of vitamins and points out that supplements probably aren't necessary for people who follow the guidelines presented.
Prod-AIMS Dist-AIMS 1981

Nutrition - What's In It For Me C 26 MIN
16MM FILM, 3/4 OR 1/2 IN VIDEO
Offers information on food and nutrition and points out that the way people buy, cook, serve and eat food actually influences who and what they are.
Prod-DOCUA Dist-CNEMAG

Nutrition - You Are What You Eat C 10 MIN
16MM FILM, 3/4 OR 1/2 IN VIDEO P-I
Explores the basic concepts of nutrition in a series of animated sequences. Shows sequences on diet, digestion, nutrients and exercise and discusses the importance of these for strong, healthy bodies.
From The Nutrition Series.
Prod-BARR Dist-BARR 1976

Nutrition And Body Composition C 30 MIN
3/4 OR 1/2 INCH VIDEO CASSETTE
Discusses nutrition and body composition as it pertains to physical fitness.
From The Bodyworks Series.
Prod-KTXTTV Dist-MDCPB

Nutrition And Dental Health C 12 MIN
16MM FILM, 3/4 OR 1/2 IN VIDEO J-C A
Shows how proper dental care and good nutrition aids in preventing the formation of plaque which attacks teeth and causes cavities.
Prod-PRORE Dist-PRORE 1981

Nutrition And Fad Diets C 29 MIN
3/4 OR 1/2 INCH VIDEO CASSETTE
Explores questions surrounding nutrition and fad diets. Discusses concern over cancer-causing foods and emphasizes adequate vitamin supplies.
From The Daniel Foster, MD Series.
Prod-KERA Dist-PBS

Nutrition And Fitness In Pregnancy C
3/4 OR 1/2 INCH VIDEO CASSETTE
Stresses the necessity of good nutrition for mother and baby alike. Discusses the need for sensible, physical activity.
Prod-MIFE Dist-MIFE

Nutrition And Fitness In Pregnancy (Arabic) C
3/4 OR 1/2 INCH VIDEO CASSETTE
Stresses the necessity of good nutrition for mother and baby alike. Discusses the need for sensible, physical activity.
Prod-MIFE Dist-MIFE

Nutrition And Fitness In Pregnancy (French) C
3/4 OR 1/2 INCH VIDEO CASSETTE
Stresses the necessity of good nutrition for mother and baby alike. Discusses the need for sensible, physical activity.
Prod-MIFE Dist-MIFE

Nutrition And Fitness In Pregnancy (Spanish) C
3/4 OR 1/2 INCH VIDEO CASSETTE
Stresses the necessity of good nutrition for mother and baby alike. Discusses the need for sensible, physical activity.
Prod-MIFE Dist-MIFE

Nutrition And Health–A Series
PRO
Treats seven different aspects of nutrition, and more especially malnutrition in hospital patients.
Prod-HSCIC Dist-HSCIC 1984

Introduction To Nutritional Assessment	019 MIN
Malnutrition - Diagnosis And Therapeutic	040 MIN
Normal Nutrition - Body Composition	038 MIN
Nutrient Needs - Basic Metabolic Processes	038 MIN
Nutrient Needs - Fatty Acids And Vitamins	064 MIN
Nutrient Needs - Protein And Calories	017 MIN
Nutrient Needs - Water And Minerals	050 MIN

Nutrition And Its Place In The Wellness Program C 29 MIN
3/4 OR 1/2 INCH VIDEO CASSETTE
Prod-RCOMTV Dist-SYLWAT 1982

Nutrition Education–A Series
16MM FILM, 3/4 OR 1/2 IN VIDEO P A
Prod-PEREN Dist-PEREN 1973

Big Dinner Table, The 11 MIN

Food For A Modern World	22 MIN
Food For Life	22 MIN
Food, Energy And You	20 MIN
How A Hamburger Turns Into You	19 MIN
Vitamins From Food	20 MIN
What's Good To Eat	18 MIN

Nutrition for Better Health C 15 MIN
16MM FILM, 3/4 OR 1/2 IN VIDEO H A
Shows how many Americans are beset by problems of overindulgence. Points out benefits of good nutrition.
Prod-NIFE Dist-EBEC 1984

Nutrition For Children—A Series
K-P
Shows a three part series on nutrition for children including the importance of breakfast, proper foods, and eating habits.
Prod-POAPLE Dist-POAPLE

Break The Fast	007 MIN
George Gorge And Nicky Persnicky	012 MIN
Nutrient Express, The	011 MIN

Nutrition For Sports - Facts And Fallacies C 20 MIN
16MM FILM, 3/4 OR 1/2 IN VIDEO J-C A
Offers a nutritional program for athletes, discussing protein, fats, carbohydrates and calories.
Prod-HIGGIN Dist-HIGGIN 1982

Nutrition For The Low Birth Weight Infant (2nd Ed) C 13 MIN
3/4 OR 1/2 INCH VIDEO CASSETTE PRO
Discusses nutritional considerations for non-stressed infants of more than 30 weeks' gestation weighing 1500 to 2500 grams at birth. Considers fluid, caloric, electrolyte and vitamin requirements as well as feeding schedules.
Prod-UMICHM Dist-UMICHM 1983

Nutrition For The Newborn—A Series
J-H A
Presents a three-part series on the joys and tribulations of feeding a baby during the first twelve months.
Prod-POAPLE Dist-POAPLE

Breast Feeding	015 MIN
Formula Feeding	015 MIN
Supplemental Foods	013 MIN

Nutrition For The Overweight C
3/4 OR 1/2 INCH VIDEO CASSETTE
Cautions the overweight dieter to be nutrition conscious in adapting a reducing diet. Stresses maximum nutrition with minimum calories.
Prod-MIFE Dist-MIFE

Nutrition For The Overweight (Spanish) C
3/4 OR 1/2 INCH VIDEO CASSETTE
Cautions the overweight dieter to be nutrition conscious in adapting a reducing diet. Stresses maximum nutrition with minimum calories.
Prod-MIFE Dist-MIFE

Nutrition For Young People - You Are What You Eat C
3/4 OR 1/2 INCH VIDEO CASSETTE J-H
Provides a full range of information about foods and nutrition and gives a basic understanding of the relationship of food to health. Graphics trace the steps in digestion and the process of cell building in the human body.
Prod-GA Dist-GA

Nutrition Gap, The C 30 MIN
3/4 OR 1/2 INCH VIDEO CASSETTE C A
Focuses on the food we eat. Depicts a 'typical' family eating 'typical' foods throughout the day. Examines the impact of these poor nutritional habits on one's health.
From The Contemporary Health Issues Series. Lesson 12
Prod-SCCON Dist-CDTEL

Nutrition In Black Americans C 28 MIN
16MM FILM OPTICAL SOUND P-C A
Points out the necessity of a well-balanced diet for Black Americans.
LC NO. 74-702348
Prod-LEECC Dist-LEECC 1974

Nutrition In Pregnancy C
3/4 OR 1/2 INCH VIDEO CASSETTE PRO
See series title for descriptive statement.
From The Care Of The Pregnant Patient Series.
Prod-OMNIED Dist-OMNIED

Nutrition In The Injured Patient C 15 MIN
16MM FILM OPTICAL SOUND
Discusses nutrition in the injured and post-operative patient. Compares the nutritional status of the starved individual and that of the post-operative patient. Shows that the surgical patient loses more protein than in simple starvation and that this protein loss cannot be prevented by calories alone.
Prod-EATONL Dist-EATONL 1973

Nutrition In The Later Years C 24 MIN
16MM FILM, 3/4 OR 1/2 IN VIDEO C A
Discusses the special nutritional requirements of older people, as well as the dangers and discomforts of too much or too little. Presents tips on how to change.
From The Be Well - The Later Years Series.
LC NO. 83-706446
Prod-CF Dist-CF 1983

Nutrition Is C 26 MIN
16MM FILM OPTICAL SOUND
Summarizes the basic principles of nutrition and their relationship to good health.
LC NO. 76-702861
Prod-SUGARI Dist-WSTGLC Prodn-WSTGLF 1976

Nutrition Labeling - Marilyn Stephenson, RD, MS C 27 MIN
3/4 INCH VIDEO CASSETTE PRO
Explores the background of nutrition labeling and its use on food products. Discusses how to use the labels of products to save money and provide a good diet.
From The Food And Nutrition Seminars For Health Professionals Series.
LC NO. 78-706163
Prod-USFDA Dist-USNAC 1976

Nutrition News C 29 MIN
3/4 INCH VIDEO CASSETTE
Shows nutrition editor Carol Williams and nutrition educator Ronald Deutsch commenting on current nutritional information. Explains how food consumers can be better informed. Demonstrates techniques used at Kroger stores to put nutritional knowledge to work.
Prod-KROGER Dist-MTP

Nutrition Puppets C 10 MIN
3/4 INCH VIDEO CASSETTE P-I
Presents nineteen thirty-second public service announcements concerning food, nutrition and eating habits. Features Grandma and Puddles, Super Broccoli and Junk Food Monster.
LC NO. 81-707091
Prod-CUETV Dist-CUNIV 1979

Nutrition Resource Centers - The Information Connection C
3/4 INCH VIDEO CASSETTE
Examines the operations of five nutrition resource centers, comparing their similarities and differences while emphasizing the need for reliable sources of information.
Prod-RYERI Dist-RYERI

Nutrition Resources C 30 MIN
3/4 OR 1/2 INCH VIDEO CASSETTE
See series title for descriptive statement.
From The Food For Life Series.
Prod-MSU Dist-MSU

Nutrition Survey - Kingdom Of Thailand C 36 MIN
16MM FILM OPTICAL SOUND
Depicts the work of scientists in a nutritional survey of Thailand and relates their findings. Represents the daily activities of clinicians, dentists, biochemists, nutritionists and food technologists. Presents important findings about anemia, endemic goiter, riboflavin and thiamaine malnutrition, and dental disease.
LC NO. FIE65-65
Prod-WRAIR Dist-USNAC 1962

Nutrition Survey - Republic Of Lebanon C 15 MIN
16MM FILM OPTICAL SOUND
Presents a nationwide survey of nutrition conducted in Lebanon. Shows exactly how the survey was conducted. Explains that goiter and mouth lesions were widely prevalent due to lack of iodine and B vitamins.
Prod-USPHS Dist-NMAC 1963

Nutrition—A Series
16MM FILM, 3/4 OR 1/2 IN VIDEO
Discusses shopping in the supermarket for nutritious foods, the value of a hamburger meal and choosing foods for maximum nutritional value.
Prod-CRAINW Dist-BARR 1976

Nutrition - The All American Meal	011 MIN
Nutrition - The Consumer And The Supermarket	015 MIN
Nutrition - You Are What You Eat	010 MIN

Nutrition—A Series
16MM FILM, 3/4 OR 1/2 IN VIDEO
Presents basic nutrition information and dispels old myths.
Prod-JOU Dist-JOU

Basic Nutrition - Let's Make A Meal	017 MIN
Food Preparation (2nd Ed)	015 MIN
Options For Life	012 MIN
Weight Control	013 MIN

Nutrition, Food, Growth, And Development C 29 MIN
3/4 OR 1/2 INCH VIDEO CASSETTE C A
Presents a consultant to a state board of health discussing and illustrating the variable nutritional needs of children from the prenatal period to the teenage years.
From The Focus On Children Series.
LC NO. 81-707444
Prod-IU Dist-IU 1981

Nutrition, Relaxation And Information - Your Keys To Successful Breastfeeding C 19 MIN
3/4 OR 1/2 INCH VIDEO CASSETTE
Reviews the nutrients important to breastfeeding, food sources and substitutes that provide protein and calcium. Includes the importance of fluid intake and the baby's sucking action.
Prod-UARIZ Dist-UARIZ

Nutrition, Safety And Child Development C 30 MIN
16MM FILM, 3/4 OR 1/2 IN VIDEO J
Reveals that responsible parenting requires an awareness of good nutrition and that order and routine help assure physical safety. Explains that children grow and mature at different rates.
From The Middle Road Traveler Series.
LC NO. 80-707467
Prod-BAYUCM Dist-GPITVL 1979

Nutritional Anemia, Pt 2 - Megaloblastic Anemia C 32 MIN
16MM FILM OPTICAL SOUND PRO
Uses clinical samples and case studies in order to show the effects of anemia due to vitamin B12 and folic acid deficiencies. Presented by Dr William B Castle.
Prod-FLEMRP Dist-WSU 1975

Nutritional Assessment And Therapy In Cancer C 30 MIN
3/4 OR 1/2 INCH VIDEO CASSETTE
Brings out the recent developments in nutritional assessment and the role of nutrition in the cancer patient.
Prod-ROWLAB Dist-ROWLAB

Nutritional Consideration For The Athlete C 24 MIN
3/4 OR 1/2 INCH VIDEO CASSETTE T
Discusses athletes' vulnerability to food fads and nutritional misinformation. Provides guidelines for a good athletic diet, with emphasis on the four basic food groups and the importance of caloric intake and fluids. Gives recommendations for weight loss and glycogen loading.
From The Sports Medicine Series.
Prod-UNIDIM Dist-EBEC 1982

Nutritional Management Of High-Risk Pregnancy C 22 MIN
3/4 OR 1/2 INCH VIDEO CASSETTE
Demonstrates the effectiveness of a team approach to counseling in which doctor, nurse, nutritionist, and the pregnant patient herself are all actively involved.
Prod-SNUTRE Dist-SNUTRE

Nutritional Needs In Growing Up C 30 MIN
3/4 OR 1/2 INCH VIDEO CASSETTE
See series title for descriptive statement.
From The Food For Life Series.
Prod-MSU Dist-MSU

Nutritional Needs Of Older Folks C 30 MIN
3/4 OR 1/2 INCH VIDEO CASSETTE
See series title for descriptive statement.
From The Food For Life Series.
Prod-MSU Dist-MSU

Nutritional Needs Of Our Bodies C 11 MIN
16MM FILM, 3/4 OR 1/2 IN VIDEO I-J
Covers the four general groups of foods, the six nutrients which they contain and what the nutrients supply to the body.
Prod-CORF Dist-CORF 1961

Nutritional Quackery C 20 MIN
16MM FILM, 3/4 OR 1/2 IN VIDEO H A
Explains the four diet-disease favorite myths of nutritional quackery, including the diet-disease myth (all diseases are due to faulty diets), the soil-depletion myth (soil depletion causes malnutrition), the over-processing myth (present processing practices rob us of most nutritional food value) and the subclinical-deficiency myth (that tired feeling or almost any ache or pain is due to an undetectable vitamin deficiency).
Prod-AIMS Dist-AIMS 1967

Nutritional Therapy - Some New Perspectives C 43 MIN
16MM FILM OPTICAL SOUND PRO
Reports on current aspects in four different areas of nutritional therapy—malnutrition due to chronic illness, obesity, conditions requiring surgical treatment and alcoholism. Follows patients through therapy and shows the results of diets geared to their nutritional needs.
LC NO. 72-707713
Prod-SQUIBB Dist-SQUIBB Prodn-STGT 1967

Nutritional Therapy Of The Lung Cancer Patient C 24 MIN
3/4 INCH VIDEO CASSETTE
Describes how to recognize nutritional depletion in patients with lung cancer and suggests ways of improving nutrition.
Prod-UTAHTI Dist-UTAHTI

Nutritious Snacks And Fast Foods C 15 MIN
16MM FILM, 3/4 OR 1/2 IN VIDEO P-I
Shows that snacks don't have to be junk food. Demonstrates how to create healthy snacks that fulfill all the nutritional needs of the four food groups.
Prod-BFA Dist-PHENIX 1981

Nuts And Bolts Of Health Care Management Communication C 30 MIN
16MM FILM, 3/4 OR 1/2 IN VIDEO A
Deals specifically with health care problems, demonstrating how effective communication is essential to successful job performance and a smooth-running health care facility. Provides the tools for effective communication and shows how these tools can improve an organization.
Prod-CREMED Dist-CREMED

Nuts And Bolts Of Performance Appraisal, The C 32 MIN
16MM FILM, 3/4 OR 1/2 IN VIDEO
Provides techniques for improving performance appraisal programs. Includes guidelines on checklists and tools to use and rules to follow in devising a performance appraisal program.
LC NO. 74-703314
Prod-CREMED Dist-CREMED 1973

Nuts And Bolts Of Performance Appraisals, The C 32 MIN
3/4 OR 1/2 INCH VIDEO CASSETTE
Deals with a specific function of supervisory management, and teaches skills in identifying the four tools and seven rules of a good performance appraisal, planning a performance appraisal, and improving communication. Includes a training leader's guide.
Prod-CREMED Dist-DELTAK

Nuts To You C 8 MIN
16MM FILM OPTICAL SOUND P
See series title for descriptive statement.
From The Mathematics For Elementary School Students - Whole Numbers Series.

LC NO. 73-701846
Prod-DAVFMS Dist-DAVFMS 1974

NY-NJ USA C 17 MIN
3/4 INCH VIDEO CASSETTE A
Presents the wide variety of unusual tourist attractions in New York and New Jersey. Narrated by actor Eli Wallach.
Prod-PANYNJ Dist-MTP Prodn-THOMPN 1983

Nyangatom - Yellow Rifles C 90 MIN
3/4 INCH VIDEO CASSETTE
Documents the daily lives of the Nyangatom people of Ethiopia who suffered disasters in the 1970's. Filmed by Jean Arland and Philippi Senechal between 1975 and 1977.
Prod-DOCEDR Dist-DOCEDR

Nyaya Panchayat B 16 MIN
16MM FILM OPTICAL SOUND I-C A
Shows how under the new dispensation of the Panchayati Raj, people in the rural areas of India are able to get justice at a quicker pace and lower cost. Explains that judicial wings attached to village panchayats are welcome substitutes to law courts in remote areas.
Prod-INDIA Dist-NEDINF

Nzuri - East Africa C 32 MIN
16MM FILM, 3/4 OR 1/2 IN VIDEO J-C
Visualizes the Biblical creation of the earth and follows man from ancient times to the modern city of Nairobi, Kenya. Shows the people, animals, rivers and cities to convey the mood of East Africa.
Prod-TWA Dist-PFP Prodn-SUMMIT 1970

O

O And C C 15 MIN
3/4 INCH VIDEO CASSETTE P
From The Writing Time Series.
Prod-WHROTV Dist-GPITVL

O And D C 15 MIN
3/4 INCH VIDEO CASSETTE P
From The Writing Time Series.
Prod-WHROTV Dist-GPITVL

O Canada C 4 MIN
16MM FILM OPTICAL SOUND
Presents a kinestatic history of Canada from the arrival of the French to the present. Without narration.
LC NO. 72-712458
Prod-SWGMNM Dist-VIEWFI 1971

O Captain, My Captain C 12 MIN
16MM FILM, 3/4 OR 1/2 IN VIDEO I-H
Presents a reading of Walt Whitman's poem O Captain, My Captain in three sections that lend mood, feeling and tempo to the work. Shows a sailing ship in the first section, the words of the poem superimposed over visuals of Lincoln and Civil War scenes in the second section and scenes superimposed over pictures of national heroes in the third section.
From The Reading Poetry Series.
Prod-EVANSA Dist-AIMS 1971

O Dear - A History Of Woman Suffrage In Ohio C 39 MIN
16MM FILM - 3/4 IN VIDEO
Describes the personalities, places and politics of women's suffrage in Ohio.
Prod-OHC Dist-HRC

O Dreamland B 14 MIN
16MM FILM OPTICAL SOUND H-C A
Lindsay Anderson comments on modern popular culture as seen at a British amusement park.
Prod-GROVE Dist-GROVE

O Henry's Jimmy Valentine C 30 MIN
16MM FILM, 3/4 OR 1/2 IN VIDEO J-C A
Features story of a former safecracker turned straight, who must reveal his background as a result of rescuing a young boy locked in a vault. Edited version.
Prod-LCOA Dist-LCOA 1985

O Henry's Jimmy Valentine C 55 MIN
16MM FILM, 3/4 OR 1/2 IN VIDEO J-C A
Features story of a former safecracker turned straight, who must reveal his background as a result of rescuing a young boy locked in a vault. Full version.
Prod-LCOA Dist-LCOA 1985

O Is For Old People C 6 MIN
3/4 OR 1/2 INCH VIDEO CASSETTE H-C
Asks why so many Canadian old people are confined to institutions, why mental disorders are the main reason for their hospital stays, why two out of three widows live in poverty and how the younger population can be more responsive to the needs of old people.
From The ABC's Of Canadian Family Life Series.
Prod-UTORMC Dist-UTORMC 1978

O Is For Our Old People C 6 MIN
16MM FILM, 3/4 OR 1/2 IN VIDEO
Asks why so many elderly Canadians are confined to institutions, why mental disorders are the main reason for their hospital stays, why two out of three widows live in poverty and how Canadians can be more responsive to the needs of their elderly.
From The ABC's Of Canadian Life Series.
Prod-UTORMC Dist-UTORMC

O J Simpson - Juice On The Loose C 47 MIN
16MM FILM OPTICAL SOUND
Offers insight into the career of football player O J Simpson. Includes interviews with Howard Cosell, Lou Saban and John McKay.
Prod-COUNFI Dist-COUNFI 1974

O Say Can You Sing C 60 MIN
2 INCH VIDEOTAPE
Explores the allegations that the Star Spangled Banner is unsingable. Offers suggested substitutes played by the Marine Corps Band, contrasted with anthems from other countries.
From The Synergism - Command Performance Series.
Prod-WETATV Dist-PUBTEL

O T O - A Classroom Community C 29 MIN
16MM FILM, 3/4 OR 1/2 IN VIDEO T
Introduces the Opportunities To Teach Ourselves program, which is an integrated learning experience at Andrew Warde High School in Fairchild, Connecticut. Visits with OTO teachers and students, whose real-life experiences are an integral part of their learning climate.
From The Dealing With Classroom Problems Series.
Prod-MFFD Dist-FI 1976

O That We Were There C 26 MIN
16MM FILM, 3/4 OR 1/2 IN VIDEO J-C A
Shows the Madrigal Singers of Saint Louis and their unusual performances of Renaissance music which include songs in English, Italian, Spanish and French. Offers an integrated study of the fine arts during the Renaissance through performances featuring authentic songs, dances, musical instruments and period costumes.
Prod-PHENIX Dist-PHENIX 1979

O Youth And Beauty C 60 MIN
16MM FILM, 3/4 OR 1/2 IN VIDEO H-C A
Tells how a frustrated, middle-aged executive tries to recapture the glories of his years in college athletics by hurdling the living room furniture. Based on the short story O Youth And Beauty by John Cheever.
From The Cheever Short Stories Series.
LC NO. 81-707482
Prod-WNETTV Dist-FI 1979

O'er Upland And Lowland C 29 MIN
3/4 INCH VIDEO CASSETTE
Demonstrates how to identify plant foliage in the spring for use in autumn harvesting.
From The Edible Wild Plants Series.
Prod-UMITV Dist-UMITV 1978

O'Mara's Chain Miracle B 10 MIN
16MM FILM OPTICAL SOUND
Deals with personal experiences in getting along with other people.
Prod-GM Dist-GM

Oak Ridge National Laboratory And Its Scientific Activities C 17 MIN
16MM FILM OPTICAL SOUND
Surveys the numerous and varied activities and facilities at the Atomic Energy Commission's Oak Ridge National Laboratory, including activities involving nuclear research, fundamental and applied research in all fields of science and research on the central technical problems of society.
LC NO. FIE67-92
Prod-ORNLAB Dist-USNAC 1967

Oak Ridge Research Reactor C 20 MIN
16MM FILM OPTICAL SOUND
Describes the components, facilities, uses and operation of the Oak Ridge research reactor, a tank-type, heterogenous reactor, immersed in a pool, designed to operate at 20 to 30 MW.
LC NO. FIE63-172
Prod-USAEC Dist-USNAC 1958

Oak, The C 12 MIN
16MM FILM, 3/4 OR 1/2 IN VIDEO I-H A
Studies the characteristics of the oak, which provides shelter and food for more wild animals than any other wild plant in North America.
From The Many Worlds Of Nature Series.
Prod-SCRESC Dist-MTI

Oakleaf Project B 28 MIN
16MM FILM OPTICAL SOUND C T S
Documents individual-centered instruction at Baldwin school district's Oakleaf Elementary School. Follows one child in the project.
LC NO. FIA68-2315
Prod-UPITTS Dist-MATHWW 1968

Oaksie C 22 MIN
16MM FILM - 3/4 IN VIDEO H A
Portrays basketmaker, fiddler and harp player Oaksie Caudill. Captures his spirit and the beauty of his life as he created baskets and music.
Prod-APPAL Dist-APPAL 1979

Oars And Paddles B 24 MIN
16MM FILM OPTICAL SOUND J-C A
Teaches the skills necessary to prevent accidents in small boats and canoes, including proper methods of launching, techniques of handling small craft and rescues.
Prod-GANZ Dist-AMRC 1943

Oasis B 15 MIN
16MM FILM OPTICAL SOUND
Presents a humorous look at student life, showing a 'TYPICAL' student reviewing his experiences. Portrays a 'SURE FIRE' study system that was more system than study, how a friend helped him register for classes, and how he fell in love when his car broke down in a snowstorm.
Prod-UPENN Dist-UPENN 1963

Oasis X 11 MIN
16MM FILM, 3/4 OR 1/2 IN VIDEO I
Explains how an oasis is an island community separated from the rest of the world by sand. Shows how North African desert dwellers make use of their limited resources, especially the date palm.
Prod-EBF Dist-EBEC 1965

Oasis In Space—A Series

Prod-COSTU Dist-EDMDC

Population Time-Bomb 28 MIN

Oasis In The Desert B 5 MIN
16MM FILM OPTICAL SOUND
Takes a look at the work of Sister Malinda Thorne and her efforts to relieve some of the loneliness and despair experienced by those living in Vancouver's Skid Row.
LC NO. 76-701347
Prod-SFRASU Dist-SFRASU 1973

Oasis In The Sahara C 16 MIN
16MM FILM, 3/4 OR 1/2 IN VIDEO P-C
Shows the variety of geography and the varying natural forces in the Sahara which produce the Saharan climate and weather. Describes the way of life of the inhabitants of this region.
From The Man And His World Series.
Prod-FI Dist-FI 1969

Oath Is Taken, The B 8 MIN
16MM FILM OPTICAL SOUND
Follows the events of President Johnson's inauguration day in 1965, emphasizing the inauguration's significance as a symbol of continuing U S democracy. Shows the actual ceremony, the inaugural address, the parade and the ball.
From The Screen News Digest Series. Vol 7, Issue 7
Prod-HEARST Dist-HEARST 1965

OAU C 28 MIN
3/4 INCH VIDEOTAPE
Interviews Ambassador Omarou Youssoufou of the Organization of African United on the goals and main objectives of the international organization. Includes a film clip. Hosted by Marilyn Perry.
From The International Byline Series.
Prod-PERRYM Dist-PERRYM

Obedience B 45 MIN
16MM FILM OPTICAL SOUND C T
Presents an experiment conducted during 1962 at Yale University on obedience to authority. Describes both obedient and defiant reactions of subjects who are instructed to administer electric shock of increasing severity to another person.
LC NO. 71-702990
Prod-MILS Dist-NYU 1965

Oberammergau - The Passion Story And The Jews C 20 MIN
3/4 INCH VIDEO CASSETTE
Documents the Anti-Defamation League delegation trip to Germany to attend a new production of a passion play that partially elemented some anti-semitic distortions. Narrated by Leonard Swidler, professer at Temple University.
Prod-ADL Dist-ADL

Obesity B 40 MIN
16MM FILM OPTICAL SOUND PRO
Compares the function of caloric input and expenditures in normal man and in obesity.
From The Boston Medical Reports Series.
LC NO. 74-705229
Prod-NMAC Dist-NMAC 1966

Obesity C 29 MIN
3/4 OR 1/2 INCH VIDEO CASSETTE
Explains why a person becomes obese and what he can do about it. Interviews a formerly obese patient who describes how she lost 160 pounds.
From The Daniel Foster, MD Series.
Prod-KERA Dist-PBS

Obesity C 58 MIN
3/4 INCH VIDEO CASSETTE
Features Dr Lester B Salans, Associate Director of the National Institute of Arthritis, Metabolism and Digestive Disease, explaining energy metabolism. Discusses the effects of too much food and too little exercise on waistline and health.
Prod-NIH Dist-MTP

Obesity - Effective Management C 27 MIN
3/4 OR 1/2 INCH VIDEO CASSETTE PRO
Provides an overview of how a multidisciplinary approach can be used to effectively manage the obese patient. Discusses caloric restriction, physical exercise and training, psychosocial support and vocational rehabilitation.
From The University Of Michigan Media Library - Clinical Commentary Series.
LC NO. 81-707080
Prod-UMICH Dist-UMICH 1981

Obesity And Energy Metabolism C 60 MIN
3/4 OR 1/2 INCH VIDEO CASSETTE
Present Dr Lester Salans defining obesity from a biochemical point of view. Explains how the human body uses food as fuel and suggests that good eating habits from birth may prevent obesity.
From The Medicine For The Layman Series.
LC NO. 81-707589
Prod-NIH Dist-USNAC 1980

Obesity And Overweight C
3/4 OR 1/2 INCH VIDEO CASSETTE
Follows the progress of actual patients who have undertaken weight reduction programs. Examines the multiple causes of excess weight. Distinguishes between overweight and obesity. Describes fat metabolism and evaluates methods of quantitative measurement.
Prod-AMEDA Dist-AMEDA

Object Lesson In Fire Prevention, An B 21 MIN
16MM FILM OPTICAL SOUND

Explains the fire hazards in aviation overhaul and repair shops and the importance of protective measures.
LC NO. FIE52-1283
Prod-USN Dist-USNAC 1950

Object Permanence C 23 MIN
16MM FILM OPTICAL SOUND
Depicts stages in early cognitive development in accordance with Piaget's definition. Shows the developmental sequences involved, beginning when infants behave as though an object has ceased to exist when it disappears from view to the point when behavior indicates the presence of an internalized 'MENTAL REPRESENTATION.'
From The Aecom Scales Of Motorsensori Development Series.
Prod-VASSAR Dist-NYU

Object Permanence C 40 MIN
16MM FILM OPTICAL SOUND C A
Presents a demonstration of a scale on the development of visual pursuit and the permanence of objects. Shows 12 different infants ranging in age from three weeks to two years as their psychological development is tested.
From The Ordinal Scales Of Infant Psychological Development Series.
LC NO. 73-703095
Prod-UILLVA Dist-UILL 1968

Object Relations In Space C 28 MIN
16MM FILM OPTICAL SOUND C A
Presents a demonstration of the scale for the construction of object relations in space. Shows evidences of perceiving and of anticipating the loci of concrete things with 12 infants ranging in age from three to 23 months.
From The Ordinal Scales Of Infant Psychological Development Series.
LC NO. 73-703095
Prod-UILLVA Dist-UILL 1968

Objective - Acculturation C 30 MIN
2 INCH VIDEOTAPE
See series title for descriptive statement.
From The Unconscious Cultural Clashes Series.
Prod-SCCOE Dist-SCCOE

Objective - Healthy Babies C 25 MIN
3/4 OR 1/2 INCH VIDEO CASSETTE
Illustrates a few of the new techniques developed by March of Dime research scientists to combat birth defects, along with health tips for prospective mothers.
Prod-TRAINX Dist-TRAINX

Objective Hemodynamic Measurement Of The Impact Of Lifestyle, Behavior And Stress On... C 52 MIN
3/4 OR 1/2 INCH VIDEO CASSETTE PRO
Relates the investigation into the alarming rate of sudden death among aerospace workers during the 1960's at Kennedy Space Center and shows that the classical risk factors of smoking, hypertension, etc could not account for the high incidence of sudden death. Places coronary artery disease, myocardial disease, and electrical instability against a biobehavioral background.
Prod-AMCARD Dist-AMCARD

Objective Slip Preparation C 11 MIN
16MM FILM OPTICAL SOUND J-C A
Demonstrates a new method of woolclassing.
LC NO. 76-700569
Prod-FLMAUS Dist-AUIS 1975

Objectives C 60 MIN
3/4 OR 1/2 INCH VIDEO CASSETTE IND
See series title for descriptive statement.
From The Quality Circle Concepts Series.
Prod-NCSU Dist-AMCEE

Objectives In The Affective Domain B 30 MIN
16MM FILM OPTICAL SOUND T
Presents Dr Madeline Hunter teaching the Krathwohl Taxonomy Of Educational Objectives, Handbrook II - Affective Domain. Discusses levels of internalization of feelings, attitudes and apreciations in classroom terms. Develops examples of behavioral objectives for each level of this domain using the taxonomy to teach appreciation of poetry and to develop desirable self-concept. Shows how values and attitudes can become teachable objectives.
From The Making Behavioral Objectives Meaningful Series.
Prod-SPF Dist-SPF

Objectives In The Cognitive Domain B 30 MIN
16MM FILM OPTICAL SOUND T
Presents Dr Madeline Hunter teaching the six levels of Bloom's Taxonomy Of Educational Objectives, Handbook I - Cognitive Domain. Cites classroom examples for each level in several subject areas. Describes the relationship of behavioral objectives to problem solving, critical thinking and the higher cognitive processes. Demonstrates the importance of the taxonomy to individualization of instruction with examples of use in daily teaching.
From The Making Behavioral Objectives Meaningful Series.
Prod-SPF Dist-SPF

Objectives, Strategy, Behaviors C 30 MIN
3/4 OR 1/2 INCH VIDEO CASSETTE T
See series title for descriptive statement.
From The Eager To Learn Series.
Prod-KTEHTV Dist-KTEHTV

Objects With Destinations C 4 MIN
3/4 OR 1/2 INCH VIDEO CASSETTE
See series title for descriptive statement.
From The Gary Hill, Part 1 Series.
Prod-EAI Dist-EAI

Oblique Strategist Too C 12 MIN
3/4 OR 1/2 INCH VIDEO CASSETTE
Prod-EAI Dist-EAI

Oblomov (Russian) C 145 MIN
16MM FILM OPTICAL SOUND H-C A
Presents a comedic drama about a landowner in 19th-century Russia whose idolence destroys his life. Based on the novel Oblomov by Ivan Goncharov.
LC NO. 82-700457
Prod-MOSFLM Dist-IFEX 1981

Obmaru C 4 MIN
16MM FILM OPTICAL SOUND H-C
Captures the moods of stylized voodoo ritual music.
Prod-MARX Dist-CFS

Oboe Reed, The C 21 MIN
16MM FILM, 3/4 OR 1/2 IN VIDEO
Shows the process of making an oboe reed.
Prod-UTORMC Dist-UTORMC 1973

Oboe, The C 18 MIN
16MM FILM, 3/4 OR 1/2 IN VIDEO
Studies the oboe using a combination of live performances, examinations of related instruments and verbal explanations. Explores the history of the instrument and its musical characteristics.
Prod-UTORMC Dist-UTORMC

Oboe, The - Advanced Seminar C 62 MIN
1/2 IN VIDEO CASSETTE BETA/VHS
Demonstrates techniques for the advanced oboe player. Features John Mack, principal oboist of the Cleveland Orchestra.
Prod-MOHOMV Dist-MOHOMV

Oboe, The - Beginning C 59 MIN
1/2 IN VIDEO CASSETTE BETA/VHS
Provides instruction in learning to play the oboe.
Prod-MOHOMV Dist-MOHOMV

Observation C 15 MIN
2 INCH VIDEOTAPE PRO
Explains to management assessors the pitfalls of objective observation in evaluating management potential.
From The AMA Assessment Center Program For Identifying Supervisory Potential Series.
LC NO. 75-704222
Prod-AMA Dist-AMA 1974

Observation B 30 MIN
2 INCH VIDEOTAPE
Explains to the science teacher the necessity of giving children every chance to utilize and develop their information-collecting powers of observation.
From The Science In Your Classroom Series.
Prod-WENHTV Dist-GPITVL

Observation And Conversation B 15 MIN
2 INCH VIDEOTAPE P
See series title for descriptive statement.
From The Language Corner Series.
Prod-CVETVC Dist-GPITVL Prodn-WCVETV

Observation And Inferences B 15 MIN
2 INCH VIDEOTAPE P
See series title for descriptive statement.
From The Just Inquisitive Series. No. 8
Prod-EOPS Dist-GPITVL Prodn-KOACTV

Observation And Memory C 13 MIN
16MM FILM OPTICAL SOUND I-C A
Presents a series of flash tests to improve observation and memory. Includes 'BALLOONS ARE FLYING,' 'JACK-O-LANTERN HAS LOST HIS HAT,' 'BIRTHDAY FLASH,' 'FUN THINGS FLASH, PART 1,' 'FUN THINGS FLASH, PART 2' AND 'LOLLIPOP GARDEN.'
Prod-SF Dist-SF 1968

Observation And Perception C 22 MIN
16MM FILM, 3/4 OR 1/2 IN VIDEO PRO
Explains how police officers can improve their powers of observation, perception and decision-making.
From The Law Enforcement - Patrol Procedures Series.
Prod-MTROLA Dist-MTI Prodn-WORON 1973

Observation Of Behavior C 30 MIN
3/4 OR 1/2 INCH VIDEO CASSETTE T
Deals with the observation of behavior when dealing with children with special needs.
From The Teaching Children With Special Needs Series.
Prod-MDDE Dist-MDCPB

Observation Of Centipede C 20 MIN
16MM FILM OPTICAL SOUND
Shows the relation between mode of life and environment of the centipede and the difference from other arthropods.
Prod-TOEI Dist-UNIJAP 1971

Observation Of Feces And Urine C 17 MIN
16MM FILM - 3/4 IN VIDEO H-C A
Illustrates the observation of the characteristics of normal and abnormal urine and feces as an indicator of the patient's condition.
From The Nurse's Aide, Orderly And Attendant Series.
Prod-COPI Dist-COPI 1971

Observation Of Ferns C 14 MIN
16MM FILM OPTICAL SOUND
A Japanese language film. Shows in detail the native environment and life-history of the fern, the representative of the sporophyte generation. Depicts various types of ferns and their respective habitats, their structure, bearing of spores and fertilization and formation of a new fern plant. Points out important areas of differences from other plants.
Prod-GAKKEN Dist-UNIJAP 1969

Observation Of Mushrooms C 21 MIN
16MM FILM OPTICAL SOUND
Points out that there are several thousand kinds of mushrooms in Japan and that therefore sunshine is not requisite for the living and growth of mushrooms. Stresses this unique feature of the mushroom. Uses microscopic and slow-motion photography. Explains its interrelation with other plants in the natural world.
Prod-TOEI Dist-UNIJAP 1970

Observational Learning C 23 MIN
16MM FILM, 3/4 OR 1/2 IN VIDEO C
Gives a detailed overview of the workings of observational learning, the role of the model and the role of the observer. Uses experiments, findings of research and practical applications of the observational learning model to demonstrate that observational learning is a complex and powerful method of learning in both children and adults.
Prod-HAR Dist-MTI Prodn-MAMMEN 1978

Observations In The Aquarium C 20 MIN
3/4 INCH VIDEO CASSETTE T
Shows how an aquarium can be used to teach science students the concepts of birth, growth and death.
From The Science In The Elementary School - Life Science Series.
Prod-UWKY Dist-GPITVL 1980

Observations Of Living Primordial Germ Cells In The Mouse B 10 MIN
16MM FILM, 3/4 OR 1/2 IN VIDEO A
Shows the appearance of the living primordial germ cells in the mouse embryo. Demonstrates the ability of the germ cells to undergo ameboid movement at a number of different stages of development.
Prod-BLDHAY Dist-UWASHP

Observatories, The C 27 MIN
16MM FILM, 3/4 OR 1/2 IN VIDEO
Visits six new astronomy centers in North and South America. Describes the functions of different telescopes, newly-developed equipment and explains many space phenomena.
Prod-NSF Dist-USNAC 1982

Observed Variability In Design Factors B 50 MIN
3/4 OR 1/2 INCH VIDEO CASSETTE
See series title for descriptive statement.
From The Probabilistic Design Series. Pt 1
Prod-UAZMIC Dist-UAZMIC 1976

Observing C 15 MIN
3/4 OR 1/2 INCH VIDEO CASSETTE P
Shows that while in the grocery store and in the library, Molly and her friends learn to use all their senses to observe the characteristics of an object.
From The Out And About Series.
Prod-STSU Dist-AITECH Prodn-WETN 1984

Observing And Classifying C 15 MIN
3/4 OR 1/2 INCH VIDEO CASSETTE P
See series title for descriptive statement.
From The Hands On, Grade One Series. Unit 1 - Observing
Prod-VAOG Dist-AITECH Prodn-WHROTV 1975

Observing And Describing C 10 MIN
16MM FILM, 3/4 OR 1/2 IN VIDEO I
Discusses the importance of observing and describing to the scientist, and shows that people use their senses to collect information and need only to describe their observations in a clear and accurate way.
From The Science Processes Series.
Prod-MGHT Dist-MGHT Prodn-HANBAR 1969

Observing And Documenting In A Mental Health Setting, Pt III C 27 MIN
3/4 OR 1/2 INCH VIDEO CASSETTE
Continues a presentation concerning observing and documenting in a mental health setting. Emphasizes the documentation of the familiar as well as the unusual actions of the patient.
Prod-SCDMH Dist-UWISC 1979

Observing And Documenting In A Mental Health Setting, Pt I C 60 MIN
3/4 OR 1/2 INCH VIDEO CASSETTE
Discusses the important principles of observation and documentation of clients in a mental health setting. Shows a number of principles to be essential, such as objectivity in observation and documentation, being descriptive and precise and meeting the needs of the facility.
Prod-MORVMC Dist-UWISC 1979

Observing Animal Camouflage C 15 MIN
3/4 OR 1/2 INCH VIDEO CASSETTE I
Gives experience in observing animal camouflage.
From The Hands On, Grade 4 - Cars, Cartoons, Etc Series. Unit 1 - Observing
Prod-WHROTV Dist-AITECH 1975

Observing Animal Feeding Behavior C 14 MIN
3/4 OR 1/2 INCH VIDEO CASSETTE I
Gives experience in observing animal feeding behavior.
From The Hands On, Grade 4 - Cars, Cartoons, Etc Series. Unit 1 - Observing
Prod-WHROTV Dist-AITECH 1975

Observing Behavior C 15 MIN
16MM FILM, 3/4 OR 1/2 IN VIDEO
Follows two high school students as they observe the nesting behavior of some geese.
From The BSCS Behavior Film Series.
Prod-BSCS Dist-PHENIX 1974

Observing Change C 15 MIN
3/4 OR 1/2 INCH VIDEO CASSETTE P

See series title for descriptive statement.
From The Hands On, Grade 3 Series. Unit 1 - Observing
Prod-VAOG Dist-AITECH Prodn-WHROTV 1975

Observing Changes B 15 MIN
2 INCH VIDEOTAPE P
See series title for descriptive statement.
From The Just Wondering Series.
Prod-EOPS Dist-GPITVL Prodn-KOACTV

Observing Drips And Drops C 14 MIN
3/4 OR 1/2 INCH VIDEO CASSETTE I
Gives experience in observing drips and drops.
From The Hands On, Grade 4 - Cars, Cartoons, Etc Series. Unit 1 - Observing
Prod-WHROTV Dist-AITECH 1975

Observing Eye—A Series

Looks close-up at the natural and physical wonders in our world. Presents family entertainment by the educational department of Boston's Museum of Science.
Prod-WGBHTV Dist-PUBTEL

American Lobster, The	29 MIN
Animal Tails	29 MIN
Animal Weapons	29 MIN
Animals From A To Z	29 MIN
Animals That Lay Eggs	29 MIN
Chisel Tooth Tribe	29 MIN
Dangerous To Man	29 MIN
Eight-Legged Pets	29 MIN
Eye And Sight, The	29 MIN
Fossils Are Fun	29 MIN
How Do Animals Eat	29 MIN
Insects	29 MIN
Laws Of Motion, The	29 MIN
Mineral Curiosities	29 MIN
Nature's Electricity	29 MIN
Nature's Superlatives	29 MIN
Old Flame, The	29 MIN
Our Ocean Of Air	29 MIN
Physics Of Diving	29 MIN
Records In The Rocks	29 MIN
Reptiles	29 MIN
Science On The Light Side	29 MIN
Seashore Life	29 MIN
Seeing Is Deceiving	29 MIN
Sense Of Balance	29 MIN
Sound Around	29 MIN
Sound Of Music	29 MIN
Swing Of Things, The	29 MIN
Unfried Clams	29 MIN
Up In The Air	29 MIN
Wild Pets	29 MIN

Observing For Safety C 20 MIN
3/4 OR 1/2 INCH VIDEO CASSETTE IND
Deals with the psychology of observation and perception as they relate to the supervisors' accident prevention responsibilities.
From The Foreman's Accident Prevention Series.
Prod-GPCV Dist-GPCV

Observing In Science C 14 MIN
3/4 OR 1/2 INCH VIDEO CASSETTE J
Shows a biologist using special night-vision equipment to observe how bats pollinate tropical plants.
From The Whatabout Series.
Prod-AITV Dist-AITECH 1983

Observing Motion C 15 MIN
3/4 OR 1/2 INCH VIDEO CASSETTE P
See series title for descriptive statement.
From The Hands On, Grade 3 Series. Unit 1- Observing
Prod-VAOG Dist-AITECH Prodn-WHROTV 1975

Observing Ourselves B 29 MIN
16MM FILM OPTICAL SOUND
Features Indian spiritual leader Krishnamurti who discusses man's need to change himself and his society by removing the network of escapes that prevent him from knowing himself and his problems. Teaches that man must free his mind of all beliefs and experiences in gaining the truth.
From The Real Revolution - Talks By Krishnamurti Series.
LC NO. 73-703038
Prod-KQEDTV Dist-IU 1968

Observing Relative Motion B 15 MIN
2 INCH VIDEOTAPE P
See series title for descriptive statement.
From The Just Curious Series. No. 20
Prod-EOPS Dist-GPITVL Prodn-KOACTV

Observing Role Play B 15 MIN
3/4 OR 1/2 INCH VIDEO CASSETTE PRO
Illustrates role play experiences teachers can recognize and encourage in children, such as pretending to be someone else, sharing a 'pretend' situation with another person and imitating actions or sounds.
Prod-HSERF Dist-HSERF

Observing Sounds C 15 MIN
3/4 OR 1/2 INCH VIDEO CASSETTE P
See series title for descriptive statement.
From The Hands On, Grade 3 Series. Unit 1 - Observing
Prod-VAOG Dist-AITECH Prodn-WHROTV 1975

Observing Spatial Arrangements C 14 MIN
3/4 OR 1/2 INCH VIDEO CASSETTE P
Gives experience in observing spatial arrangements.
From The Hands On, Grade 2 - Lollipops, Loops, Etc Series. Unit 1 - Observing
Prod-WHROTV Dist-AITECH 1975

Observing Teaching C 50 MIN
3/4 OR 1/2 INCH VIDEO CASSETTE T
Shows how to conduct a preobservation interview, what to look for in observing a class and how to conduct a followup session with the instructor.
From The Strategies In College Teaching Series.
LC NO. 79-706290
Prod-IU Dist-IU 1977

Obsidian Point-Making C 13 MIN
16MM FILM, 3/4 OR 1/2 IN VIDEO J-C A
A Tolowe Indian of Northern California demonstrates pressure flaking as a method of making obsidian arrow points. Other types of projectile points and the uses and significance of many obsidian artifacts in aboriginal cultures are described.
From The American Indian Series.
Prod-UCEMC Dist-UCEMC Prodn-UCEMC 1964

Obsolescence And Burnout C 30 MIN
3/4 OR 1/2 INCH VIDEO CASSETTE
Discusses obsolescence and burnout as it pertains to managing professionals.
From The Business Of Managing Professionals Series.
Prod-KYTV Dist-KYTV 1983

Obsolete Menopause, The C 18 MIN
16MM FILM OPTICAL SOUND
Six medical authorities explain why and how millions of suffering women can be spared physical and mental deterioration through the easy and inexpensive replacement of their former levels of female sex hormones.
From The Upjohn Vanguard Of Medicine Series.
LC NO. FIA67-530
Prod-UPJOHN Dist-UPJOHN Prodn-SHNKRN 1966

Obstacles To Success C 50 MIN
3/4 OR 1/2 INCH VIDEO CASSETTE
See series title for descriptive statement.
From The Deming Video Tapes - Quality, Productivity And The Competitive...Series.
Prod-MIOT Dist-SME

Obstacles To Success, II C
3/4 OR 1/2 INCH VIDEO CASSETTE
See series title for descriptive statement.
From The Deming Videotapes - Quality, Productivity, And Competitive...Series.
Prod-MIOT Dist-MIOT

Obstetric Delivery B 29 MIN
16MM FILM OPTICAL SOUND C A
Explains about obstetric delivery, discussing labor, hospital versus home delivery, analgesia and anesthesia and normal delivery. Includes views of the delivery room. Features Dr J Robert Bragonier and Leta Powell Drake.
From The Nine To Get Ready Series. No. 7
LC NO. 72-704214
Prod-KUONTV Dist-UNEBR 1965

Obstetric Delivery C 29 MIN
2 INCH VIDEOTAPE
See series title for descriptive statement.
From The Nine To Get Ready Series.
Prod-NETCHE Dist-PUBTEL

Obstetric Hemorrhage C 27 MIN
16MM FILM OPTICAL SOUND
Points out that obstetric hemorrhage is one of the chief causes of maternal death in many countries. Shows the mechanism of the obstetric hemorrhage, mainly cases of hypofibrinogenemia, the methods of hematrogic and blood chemical examinations, the emergency treatments at delivery and after parturition and periodic management and guidance for the pregnant. Emphasizes that in Japan today, an acute shortage of blood for transfusion is posing a grave social problem.
Prod-UNIJAP Dist-UNIJAP 1970

Obstetrical Anesthesia - Cesarean Section (2nd Ed) C 27 MIN
3/4 OR 1/2 INCH VIDEO CASSETTE PRO
Describes the preparation for cesarean section and the choice of anesthesia. Indicates regional block as a preferred method. Discusses technical aspects of the administration of spinal or epidural anesthesia in this group of patients. Considers the use of general anesthesia for cesarian section.
From The Anesthesiology Clerkship Series.
Prod-UMICHM Dist-UMICHM 1982

Obstetrical Anesthesia - Evaluation And Preparation (2nd Ed) C 20 MIN
3/4 OR 1/2 INCH VIDEO CASSETTE PRO
Discusses the preoperative evaluation of the patient requiring obstetrical anesthesia. Emphasizes potentially serious problems such as dehydration, the full stomach and caval compression. Describes patient education in the goals of obstetrical anesthesia. Considers analgesia and sedation during labor.
From The Anesthesiology Clerkship Series.
Prod-UMICHM Dist-UMICHM 1982

Obstetrical Anesthesia - Normal Vaginal Delivery (2nd Ed) C 20 MIN
3/4 OR 1/2 INCH VIDEO CASSETTE PRO
Discusses the provision of anesthesia and analgesia for normal vaginal delivery. Reviews parturition pain pathways which must be understood for the use of regional anesthesia, and discusses commonly used regional blocks. Considers inhalation analgesia for spontaneous delivery. Covers management of problems which may arise during and after labor and delivery.
From The Anesthesiology Clerkship Series.
Prod-UMICHM Dist-UMICHM

Obstetrical Anesthesia And Analgesia C
3/4 OR 1/2 INCH VIDEO CASSETTE
Presents various types of anesthesia and analgesia available to obstetrical patients annd explains the risks and benefits of using each as they relate to the patient and her unborn child.
Prod-MIFE Dist-MIFE

Obstetrical Ultrasound C
3/4 OR 1/2 INCH VIDEO CASSETTE
Describes how an ultrasound examination provides important information about the well being of the fetus without the risk of x-rays.
Prod-MIFE Dist-MIFE

Obstetrical Ultrasound (Spanish) C
3/4 OR 1/2 INCH VIDEO CASSETTE
Describes how an ultrasound examination provides important information about the well being of the fetus without the risk of x-rays.
Prod-MIFE Dist-MIFE

Obstetrics And Gynecology In A West African Community C 40 MIN
16MM FILM OPTICAL SOUND PRO
Deals with the problems of gynecology and obstetrics in West African cultures.
Prod-UCLA Dist-UCLA

Obstetrics And Gynecology—A Series
H-C A
Prod-MIFE Dist-MIFE 1974

Birth	10 MIN
Breast Self-Examination	10 MIN
Caesarean Birth	10 MIN
Contraceptive Methods, Pt 1	10 MIN
Contraceptive Methods, Pt 2	10 MIN
Diaphragm, The	10 MIN
Genetic Counseling I - Heredity And Birth	10 MIN
Genetic Counseling II - Amniocentesis	10 MIN
Genetic Counseling III - The Rh Negative	10 MIN
Hysterectomy	10 MIN
IUD, The	10 MIN
Menopause	10 MIN
Natural Childbirth	10 MIN
Pill, The	10 MIN
Pre-Natal Care	10 MIN
Routine Health Examination	10 MIN

Obstructed Airway Management C 17 MIN
3/4 OR 1/2 INCH VIDEO CASSETTE PRO
Shows how to manage obstructed airways for adult or infant victims who are conscious, become unconscious or are found unconscious.
From The Basic Life Support Series. Module 3
Prod-NICEPR Dist-IU

Obstructing Carcinoma Of The Transverse Colon C 25 MIN
3/4 OR 1/2 INCH VIDEO CASSETTE
See series title for descriptive statement.
From The Gastrointestinal Series.
Prod-SVL Dist-SVL

Obstructive Jaundice Complicated By Diaphragmatic Hiatal Hernia C 27 MIN
16MM FILM OPTICAL SOUND PRO
Presents Harry H Mc Carthy, MD, who points out that it is often necessary to make the operative procedure flexible enough to fit the individual problem, and instead use compromising techniques. Stresses a method of approach to a complicated problem, whereas, the technique of the operation assumes a relatively minor role.
Prod-ACYDGD Dist-ACY 1955

Obstructive Lung Disease (Rev Ed) C 18 MIN
16MM FILM, 3/4 OR 1/2 IN VIDEO PRO
Discusses illnesses which cause chronic lung obstruction, including emphysema, chronic bronchitis and asthma, and their treatment.
Prod-PRORE Dist-PRORE

Obstructive Lung Disease (Spanish) C 18 MIN
16MM FILM, 3/4 OR 1/2 IN VIDEO PRO
Discusses illnesses which cause chronic lung obstruction, including emphysema, chronic bronchitis and asthma, and their treatment.
Prod-PRORE Dist-PRORE

Obtaining Agreement On Objectives C 10 MIN
3/4 OR 1/2 INCH VIDEO CASSETTE
See series title for descriptive statement.
From The Practical M B O Series.
Prod-DELTAK Dist-DELTAK

Obturator Construction For A Surgical Soft Palate Defect, Pt 1 - Impression And... C 14 MIN
16MM FILM - 3/4 IN VIDEO PRO
Describes an impression procedure for construction of an obturator in an edentulous patient. Shows insertion of the complete hollow obturator.
LC NO. 79-708079
Prod-VADTC Dist-USNAC 1979

Obturator Construction For A Surgical Soft Palate Defect, Pt 2 - Laboratory Impressions C 9 MIN
16MM FILM - 3/4 IN VIDEO PRO
Describes laboratory procedures for developing a hollow acrylic resin obturator which is attached to an existing maxillary complete denture. Demonstrates flasking, waxing, boil-out, packing and processing.
LC NO. 79-708028
Prod-VADTC Dist-USNAC 1979

Ocamo Is My Town C 22 MIN
16MM FILM OPTICAL SOUND H-C A

Describes the work of one Roman Catholic priest who has tried for 14 years to soften the impact of outside civilization on a Yanomama Indian village in Venezuela.
From The Yanomama Series.
LC NO. 75-702186
Prod-DOCEDR Dist-PSUPCR 1975

Ocamo Is My Town C 25 MIN
3/4 INCH VIDEO CASSETTE
Features a Salesian priest ministering to the Yanamamo tribe on the Ocamo River in South America. Explains the priest's role as a mediator between Western encroachment and native customs. Raises questions as to the ramifications of change.
Prod-DOCEDR Dist-DOCEDR

Occasional Invaders C
3/4 OR 1/2 INCH VIDEO CASSETTE
See series title for descriptive statement.
From The Pest Control Technology Correspondence Course Series.
Prod-PUAVC Dist-PUAVC

Occlusal Adjustment, Pt I C 17 MIN
3/4 OR 1/2 INCH VIDEO CASSETTE
Entails indications, principles and methods for adjustment of occlusion to optimal freedom and stability, both in centric relation and centric occlusion.
Prod-VADTC Dist-AMDA 1970

Occlusal Adjustment, Pt II - Lateral And Protrusive Excursions C 12 MIN
3/4 OR 1/2 INCH VIDEO CASSETTE
Illustrates adjustment of occlusal interferences in various eccentric contact relations on mounted casts and by intraoral recording. Explains to what extent eccentric movement patterns should be adjusted.
Prod-VADTC Dist-AMDA 1970

Occlusal Adjustment, Pt 1 - Centric C 17 MIN
16MM FILM OPTICAL SOUND
Shows indications, principles and methods for adjustment of occlusion to optimal freedom and stability, both in centric relation and centric occlusion.
LC NO. 74-705231
Prod-USVA Dist-USNAC 1970

Occlusal Adjustment, Pt 2 - Lateral And Protrusive Excursions C 12 MIN
16MM FILM OPTICAL SOUND
Illustrates adjustment of occlusal interferences in various eccentric contact relations by means of mounted casts and intra-oral recording. Explains to what extent eccentric movement patterns should be adjusted.
LC NO. 74-705232
Prod-USVA Dist-USNAC 1970

Occlusal Path Record, The C 15 MIN
16MM FILM, 3/4 OR 1/2 IN VIDEO PRO
Discusses how the generated path or occlusal path records make it possible to record jaw relations under actual mastication conditions, resulting in a harmonious occlusion. Presents the technical procedures incident to registering the occlusal path. Issued in 1967 as a motion picture.
From The Removable Partial Dentures, Clasp Type - Clinical And Laboratory Procedures Series.
LC NO. 78-706181
Prod-USVA Dist-USNAC Prodn-VADTC 1978

Occlusal Path Record, The C 15 MIN
3/4 OR 1/2 INCH VIDEO CASSETTE
Reveals a method which makes it possible to record jaw relations under actual mastication conditions. Demonstrates technical procedures incident to registering the occlusal path.
From The Removable Partial Dentures, Clasp Type Clinical And Laboratory Procedures Series.
Prod-VADTC Dist-AMDA 1969

Occlusal Radiography, Pt 1 - Introduction And Maxillary Projections C 13 MIN
16MM FILM - 3/4 IN VIDEO PRO
Presents five types of occlusal radiographic examination of the maxilla. Explains common errors in positioning and demonstrates corrections for them. Issued in 1972 as a motion picture.
LC NO. 78-706191
Prod-USVA Dist-USNAC Prodn-VADTC 1978

Occlusal Radiography, Pt 2 - Mandibular Projections C 8 MIN
16MM FILM - 3/4 IN VIDEO PRO
Demonstrates a technique for obtaining a mandibular anterior occlusal radiograph. Describes errors in positioning and suggests corrections.
LC NO. 78-706192
Prod-USVA Dist-USNAC Prodn-VADTC 1978

Occlusal Reconstruction And Restoration With Fixed Prosthesis, Pt I - Occlusal... C 8 MIN
3/4 OR 1/2 INCH VIDEO CASSETTE
Demonstrates the restoration of the occlusal curve by tooth reduction and tooth preparation for fixed prosthesis.
Prod-VADTC Dist-AMDA 1974

Occlusal Reconstruction And Restoration With Fixed Prosthesis, Pt 2 - Construction And... C 9 MIN
16MM FILM - 3/4 IN VIDEO PRO
Shows construction of a temporary bridge using a hand-formed rectangular block of activated acrylic placed directly on the prepared teeth. Issued in 1974 as a motion picture.
LC NO. 79-707557
Prod-USVA Dist-USNAC 1979

Occlusal Reconstruction And Restoration With Fixed Prosthesis, Pt 1 - Occlusal... C 14 MIN
16MM FILM - 3/4 IN VIDEO PRO
Demonstrates restoration of the occlusal curve by tooth reduction and tooth preparation for fixed prosthesis. Issued in 1974 as a motion picture.
LC NO. 79-707556
Prod-USVA Dist-USNAC 1979

Occlusal Reconstruction And Restoration With Fixed Prosthesis, Pt II - Construction And... C 9 MIN
3/4 OR 1/2 INCH VIDEO CASSETTE
Demonstrates the construction of a temporary bridge using a hand-formed rectangular block of activated acrylic placed directly on the prepared teeth.
Prod-VADTC Dist-AMDA 1974

Occlusal Reconstruction And Restoration With Fixed Prosthesis, Pt 3 - Waxing Of Dies And... C 12 MIN
16MM FILM - 3/4 IN VIDEO PRO
Shows the waxing procedure for full dental crowns. Emphasizes the proper anatomical considerations in the formation of contact areas, marginal ridges and alignment of the central grooves and buccal and lingual cusps. Issued in 1974 as a motion picture.
LC NO. 79-707558
Prod-USVA Dist-USNAC 1979

Occlusal Reconstruction And Restoration With Fixed Prosthesis, Pt 4 - Bridge Completion,... C 14 MIN
16MM FILM - 3/4 IN VIDEO
Demonstrates bridge assembly and methods for maintaining proper oral hygiene after bridge cementation. Issued in 1974 as a motion picture.
LC NO. 79-707559
Prod-USVA Dist-USNAC 1979

Occlusal Reconstruction And Restoration With Fixed Prosthesis, Pt III - Waxing Of Dies... C 12 MIN
3/4 OR 1/2 INCH VIDEO CASSETTE
Shows the waxing procedure for the full crowns, demonstrating the investing, casting and methodology for evaluation of the finished castings.
Prod-VADTC Dist-AMDA 1974

Occlusal Reconstruction And Restoration With Fixed Prosthesis, Pt IV - Bridge Completion... C 14 MIN
3/4 OR 1/2 INCH VIDEO CASSETTE
Uses autopolymerizing acrylic to demonstrate a bridge assembly to join the units prior to investing for soldering. Shows soldering operation.
Prod-VADTC Dist-AMDA 1974

Occult, The - Mysteries Of The Supernatural C 24 MIN
16MM FILM, 3/4 OR 1/2 IN VIDEO J-H
Explores the occult through interviews with a witch, an astrologer and an ESP expert.
From The Wide World Of Adventure Series.
Prod-AVATLI Dist-EBEC 1977

Occupant Restraint C 8 MIN
16MM FILM, 3/4 OR 1/2 IN VIDEO H-C A
Portrays the importance of wearing seat belts and shoulder harnesses.
Prod-NHTSA Dist-USNAC 1981

Occupant USA C 29 MIN
3/4 OR 1/2 INCH VIDEO CASSETTE
See series title for descriptive statement.
From The All About Welfare Series.
Prod-WITFTV Dist-PBS

Occupation - Auto Mechanic C 13 MIN
1 INCH VIDEOTAPE
Shows potential young job seekers how to get started and what opportunities exist for a boy beginning a career in the automotive field. Portrays realistically the experiences of a youth as he interviews for and begins his new job as an auto mechanic.
Prod-GMSS Dist-MTP

Occupation - Holland, 1940 To 1944 C 60 MIN
16MM FILM OPTICAL SOUND H-C A
From The World At War Series.
LC NO. 76-701778
Prod-THAMES Dist-USCAN 1975

Occupation - Holland, 1940-1944 C 52 MIN
16MM FILM, 3/4 OR 1/2 IN VIDEO H-C A
Describes how the Gestapo, the German secret police commanded by Himmler, carried out Germany's crimes and atrocities during its occupation of Holland from 1940 to 1944, creating a nightmare for its citizens. Jews were victims of genocide and 105,000 of Holland's 140,000 Jews were killed during the Nazi occupation.
From The World At War Series.
Prod-THAMES Dist-MEDIAG 1973

Occupation - Mother C 29 MIN
3/4 INCH VIDEO CASSETTE
Explores the conflict between women's needs for individual fulfillment and the demands made on them as mothers of young children.
From The Woman Series.
Prod-WNEDTV Dist-PUBTEL

Occupational Behavior - Application And Justification C 24 MIN
3/4 INCH VIDEO CASSETTE PRO
Shows transfer of training skills used by a former drug addict to apply cultivated relaxation to stress in order to maintain a drug-free lifestyle. Discusses how these stress-control principles can be applied to numerous physical or psychological stress-related dysfunctions.
From The Biofeedback Strategies Series. Pt VI
Prod-AOTA Dist-AOTA 1981

Occupational Behavior Expectations C 15 MIN
3/4 INCH VIDEO CASSETTE PRO
Presents a view of the future of the occupational therapy profession and suggests steps to prevent failure. Narrated by Mary Reilly.
Prod-AOTA Dist-AOTA 1977

Occupational Communication C 15 MIN
2 INCH VIDEOTAPE P
Provides an enrichment program in the communitive arts area through job communication.
From The Word Magic (2nd Ed) Series.
Prod-CVETVC Dist-GPITVL

Occupational Health B 30 MIN
16MM FILM - 3/4 IN VIDEO PRO
See series title for descriptive statement.
From The Public Health Science Series. Unit V - Introduction To Bioenvironmental Health
Prod-TEXWU Dist-GPITVL Prodn-KUHTTV

Occupational Profiles - Careers In Computer Services C 30 MIN
16MM FILM, 3/4 OR 1/2 IN VIDEO J A
Introduces the full range of computer service occupations, from programmers and analysts to technicians and sales personnel. Examines training requirements.
Prod-EDUDYN Dist-EBEC Prodn-KIROF 1983

Occupational Profiles - Careers In Food Services C 30 MIN
16MM FILM, 3/4 OR 1/2 IN VIDEO H-C
Looks at careers in food services, emphasizing the job requirements and duties of waiters and waitresses, cooks, restaurant managers, cocktail waitresses, bartenders and executive chefs.
Prod-EDUDYN Dist-EBEC 1983

Occupational Profiles - Careers In Food Services - Bartender C 5 MIN
16MM FILM, 3/4 OR 1/2 IN VIDEO J-C A
Relates the duties and qualifications of a bartender.
Prod-EBEC Dist-EBEC 1983

Occupational Profiles - Careers In Food Services - Cocktail Waitress C 5 MIN
16MM FILM, 3/4 OR 1/2 IN VIDEO J-C A
Relates the duties and qualifications of a cocktail waitress.
Prod-EBEC Dist-EBEC 1983

Occupational Profiles - Careers In Food Services - Cook C 5 MIN
16MM FILM, 3/4 OR 1/2 IN VIDEO J-C A
Relates the duties and qualifications of a cook.
Prod-EBEC Dist-EBEC 1983

Occupational Profiles - Careers In Food Services - Executive Chef C 5 MIN
16MM FILM, 3/4 OR 1/2 IN VIDEO J-C A
Relates the duties and qualifications of an executive chef.
Prod-EBEC Dist-EBEC 1983

Occupational Profiles - Careers In Food Services - Restaurant Manager C 5 MIN
16MM FILM, 3/4 OR 1/2 IN VIDEO J-C A
Relates the duties and qualifications of a restaurant manager.
Prod-EBEC Dist-EBEC 1983

Occupational Profiles - Careers In Food Services - Waiter/Waitress C 5 MIN
16MM FILM, 3/4 OR 1/2 IN VIDEO J-C A
Relates the duties and qualifications of a waiter or waitress.
Prod-EBEC Dist-EBEC 1983

Occupational Profiles - Careers In Health C 37 MIN
16MM FILM, 3/4 OR 1/2 IN VIDEO J-C A
Delineates the kinds of training, responsibilities, physical and mental traits and qualifying examinations required to launch a career in health care. Gives information about salaries and opportunities for advancement as it explores the demanding daily routines of paramedics, physical therapists, respiratory therapists, lab technicians, nursing aids and orderlies, medical secretaries and accredited record technicians.
Prod-EDUDYN Dist-EBEC 1983

Occupational Profiles - Careers In Health - Accredited Records Technician C 5 MIN
16MM FILM, 3/4 OR 1/2 IN VIDEO J-C A
Relates the duties and qualifications of an accredited records technician.
Prod-EBEC Dist-EBEC 1982

Occupational Profiles - Careers In Health - Lab Technician C 5 MIN
16MM FILM, 3/4 OR 1/2 IN VIDEO J-C A
Relates the duties and qualifications of a lab technician.
Prod-EBEC Dist-EBEC 1982

Occupational Profiles - Careers In Health - Medical Secretary C 5 MIN
16MM FILM, 3/4 OR 1/2 IN VIDEO J-C A
Relates the duties and qualifications of a medical secretary.
Prod-EBEC Dist-EBEC 1982

Occupational Profiles - Careers In Health - Nursing Aide/Orderly C 5 MIN
16MM FILM, 3/4 OR 1/2 IN VIDEO J-C A
Relates the duties and qualifications of a nursing aide or orderly.
Prod-EBEC Dist-EBEC 1982

Occupational Profiles - Careers In Health - Paramedic C 5 MIN
16MM FILM, 3/4 OR 1/2 IN VIDEO J-C A
Relates the duties and qualifications of a paramedic.
Prod-EBEC Dist-EBEC 1982

Occupational Profiles - Careers In Health - Physical Therapist C 5 MIN
16MM FILM, 3/4 OR 1/2 IN VIDEO J-C A
Relates the duties and qualifications of a physical therapist.
Prod-EBEC Dist-EBEC 1982

Occupational Profiles - Careers In Health - Respiratory Therapist C 5 MIN
16MM FILM, 3/4 OR 1/2 IN VIDEO J-C A
Relates the duties and qualifications of a respiratory therapist.
Prod-EBEC Dist-EBEC 1982

Occupational Research C 30 MIN
3/4 OR 1/2 INCH VIDEO CASSETTE C A
Centers around the 'What, Where, How' approach to job hunting. Emphasizes the need for high self esteem and relaxation during the job hunt. Gives tips on maintaining self esteem.
From The Making A Living Work Series. Program 107
Prod-OHUTC Dist-OHUTC

Occupational Safety, Impact 1980 C 40 MIN
3/4 OR 1/2 INCH VIDEO CASSETTE IND
Depicts Jerry Purswell and James Hoag responding to questions from the audience concerning US Occupational Safety and Health Administration regulations and industry's views on these regulations and occupational safety in general.
From The Safety, Health, and Loss Control - Managing Effective Programs Series.
LC NO. 81-706517
Prod-AMCEE Dist-AMCEE 1980

Occupational Therapist Evaluating Functional Living Skills In Psychiatry, An C
3/4 OR 1/2 INCH VIDEO CASSETTE
Presents the philosophy of assessing basic living skills, as well as the utilization of results in treatment planning. Discusses the Kohlman Evaluation of Living Skills, an assessment tool developed by an occupational therapist working in a University of Washington affiliated hospital, which evaluates a person's ability to function in the areas of self-care, safety and health, money management, transportation and telephone, and work and leisure.
Prod-UWASH Dist-UWASH

Occupational Therapist Teaching Functional Living Skills In Psychiatry, An C
3/4 OR 1/2 INCH VIDEO CASSETTE
Shows an occupational therapist utilizing an educational approach in working with patients on functional living skills. Presents the rationale and philosophy of the treatment. Demonstrates individual work with patients in the areas of self-care and transportation, and group work with patients in the area of communication skills.
Prod-UWASH Dist-UWASH

Occupational Therapist Using A Screening Test, An C
3/4 OR 1/2 INCH VIDEO CASSETTE
Reviews the utilization and guidelines for administration of the Denver Developmental Screening Tests. Illustrates actual scenes with therapists giving the test to two four-year-old children. Discusses test scores and interpretations.
Prod-UWASH Dist-UWASH

Occupational Therapy Evaluation - Klein-Bell Activities C 29 MIN
3/4 OR 1/2 INCH VIDEO CASSETTE
Describes and presents guidelines for utilizing the Klein-Bell ADL scale. Illustrates the administration of this scale with a woman who has left hemiplegia. Shows procedure for marking the form as well as transferring this information to the score sheet. Reviews advantages of this scale.
Prod-UWASH Dist-UWASH

Occupational Therapy Evaluation Of The Hemiplegic Patient C 11 MIN
16MM FILM OPTICAL SOUND
Demonstrates techniques and methods for the occupational evaluation of hemiplegic patients prior to initiating therapy.
LC NO. 74-705234
Prod-USPHS Dist-USNAC 1966

Occupational Therapy Patient On The Nursing Unit, The C 14 MIN
16MM FILM, 3/4 OR 1/2 IN VIDEO
Points out how important it is for nursing unit personnel to let occupational therapy patients help themselves with dressing, personal hygiene and meals.
Prod-USA Dist-USNAC

Occupational Therapy Skills - Handicrafts—A Series

Designed to acquaint occupational therapy students with art activities.
Prod-HSCIC Dist-HSCIC

Art Series - Block Printing 013 MIN
Art Series - Silk Screening 027 MIN
Art Series - Stenciling 009 MIN

Occupational Therapy Using A Screening-Sensory-Motor Evaluation Of Hemiplegia C 3 MIN
3/4 OR 1/2 INCH VIDEO CASSETTE
Illustrates portions of a sensory motor evaluation with a 30-year-old man who has left hemiplegia. Includes a study guide that provides an extensive list of references and reviews the major theoretical bases for evaluation and treatment of hemiplegia.
Prod-UWASH Dist-UWASH

Occupations C 15 MIN
16MM FILM OPTICAL SOUND P-J
See series title for descriptive statement.
From The Off To Adventure Series.
Prod-YALEDV Dist-YALEDV

Occupied Bed Making C 15 MIN
16MM FILM, 3/4 OR 1/2 IN VIDEO J-C A
Describes the various articles of bedding, their purpose and preferred type of material for hospital use. Demonstrates the changing of linen when the bed is occupied by a patient and shows the techniques of stripping and making the bed.
Prod-SF Dist-SF 1968

Occurrence At Owl Creek Bridge, An C 17 MIN
16MM FILM OPTICAL SOUND
A dramatic adaptation of Ambrose Bierce's famous Civil War story, told in flash back during the hanging of a Southern planter being executed for sabotage. (A USC Cinema Graduate Workshop Production.)
LC NO. FIA60-618
Prod-USC Dist-USC 1956

Occurrence At Owl Creek Bridge, An B 27 MIN
16MM FILM, 3/4 OR 1/2 IN VIDEO H-C A
Offers an adaptation of Ambrose Bierce's short story An Occurrence At Owl Creek Bridge.
Prod-ICHAC Dist-FI 1962

Ocean C 10 MIN
16MM FILM, 3/4 OR 1/2 IN VIDEO I-C
Presents a poetic interpretation of the sea in all its moods. Includes The Sea by John Keats and selections from Byron's Childe Harolde. Features specially composed music.
Prod-PFP Dist-PHENIX 1969

Ocean Animals C 15 MIN
3/4 OR 1/2 INCH VIDEO CASSETTE I-J
Considers characteristics of a host of marine creatures, including starfish, sea slugs and octopi.
From The Animals And Such Series. Module Blue - Habitats
Prod-WHROTV Dist-AITECH 1972

Ocean Corridors To World Trade C 15 MIN
16MM FILM OPTICAL SOUND I-H
Shows how maritime trade has made people interdependent and has encouraged the growth of large population centers and harbors. Features harbor operations and various modes of cargo handling.
LC NO. 79-700033
Prod-INMATI Dist-INMATI 1979

Ocean Currents C 30 MIN
3/4 OR 1/2 INCH VIDEO CASSETTE
Lists the physical factors that cause ocean currents. Explains some of the effects of currents on surface productivity and localized weather conditions.
From The Oceanus - The Marine Environment Series. Lesson 12
Prod-SCCON Dist-CDTEL

Ocean Dynamics - The Work Of The Sea C 23 MIN
16MM FILM, 3/4 OR 1/2 IN VIDEO J-H
Presents an investigation of ocean movement. Describes the movement and direction of waves and longshore currents, the appearance and formation of the sea floor, the creation of surface currents, and the tracking of deep-sea storm systems.
LC NO. 82-706465
Prod-BORKBV Dist-EBEC 1981

Ocean Environment, The B 30 MIN
2 INCH VIDEOTAPE J
See series title for descriptive statement.
From The Investigating The World Of Science, Unit 2 - Energy Within Living Systems Series.
Prod-MPATI Dist-GPITVL

Ocean Heritage C 28 MIN
16MM FILM OPTICAL SOUND
Presents a poetic view of Newfoundland.
LC NO. 75-701047
Prod-NEWSTJ Dist-CTFL Prodn-NACOM 1974

Ocean Instruments For Deep Submergence Vehicles C 29 MIN
16MM FILM OPTICAL SOUND
Describes the special instrumentation requirements for deep submergence vehicles and highlights developments in this field.
LC NO. 74-706546
Prod-USN Dist-USNAC 1969

Ocean Life C 30 MIN
3/4 OR 1/2 INCH VIDEO CASSETTE C
Explores the phenomena of upwelling and its influence on ocean life. Demonstrates methods of studying the ocean. Explains the requirements, joys and dangers of scuba and snorkel diving.
From The Earth, Sea And Sky Series.
Prod-DALCCD Dist-DALCCD

Ocean Phenomenon - The Deep Scattering Layer C 29 MIN
16MM FILM - 3/4 IN VIDEO
Describes the search for the cause of sound-reflecting layers of marine life in the oceans. Issued in 1970 as a motion picture.
LC NO. 79-706717
Prod-USN Dist-USNAC 1979

Ocean Racing C 100 MIN
1/2 IN VIDEO CASSETTE BETA/VHS
Features ocean racing. Combines the short films 'Maximum Effort,' 'Kialoa To Jamaica,' 'Reckon With The Wind' And 'Rapid Transit.' Includes footage of the 1979 Transpac, the 1976 Victoria to Maui race and the voyage of Kialola III from Miami to Montego Bay.
Prod-OFFSHR Dist-OFFSHR

Ocean Shore, The C 18 MIN
16MM FILM OPTICAL SOUND I-H
Examines some of the different kinds of ocean shorelines and shows the variety of plants and animals that live in a shoreline environment.
LC NO. 74-703484
Prod-JHP Dist-MLA 1974

Ocean Tides - Bay Of Fundy X 14 MIN
16MM FILM, 3/4 OR 1/2 IN VIDEO I-H
Explains that the constant rhythmic motion of ocean tides is caused by the gravitational pull of the moon and the sun, how the tidal range varies in different localities, and how the tides affect the activities of people who live near the ocean.
Prod-EBF Dist-EBEC 1957

Ocean Treasures C 30 MIN
3/4 OR 1/2 INCH VIDEO CASSETTE K-P
See series title for descriptive statement.
From The Villa Alegre Series.
Prod-BCTV Dist-MDCPB

Ocean World C 29 MIN
16MM FILM, 3/4 OR 1/2 IN VIDEO
Highlights resources of the sea and coastal zone, shows commercial fishery management, aquaculture research, seafloor mineral mining, and scientific measurements along the sea-air boundary to improve weather forecasting.
Prod-USNOAA Dist-USNAC

Ocean, Desert And Thin Air C 60 MIN
3/4 OR 1/2 INCH VIDEO CASSETTE H-C A
Shows a condor flying over the Pacific Coast of South America where the cold waters are among the richest in the world while the shore is the driest desert in the world. Views the condor searching the beach for carrion while vampire bats feed on the blood of sleeping sea lions.
From The Flight Of The Condor Series.
Prod-BBCTV Dist-FI 1982

Ocean, The C 14 MIN
2 INCH VIDEOTAPE
Features nature photographer Jim Bones celebrating the beauty of the ocean.
From The Images And Memories Series.
Prod-KERA Dist-PUBTEL

Ocean, The C 14 MIN
2 INCH VIDEOTAPE
See series title for descriptive statement.
From The Muffinland Series.
Prod-WGTV Dist-PUBTEL

Ocean, The - A First Film C 11 MIN
16MM FILM, 3/4 OR 1/2 IN VIDEO P-I
Explains that the ocean, which is the home of most of the world's life, influences all living things, including man.
Prod-FA Dist-PHENIX 1968

Ocean, The - A First Film (Spanish) C 11 MIN
16MM FILM, 3/4 OR 1/2 IN VIDEO P-I
Discusses the marine life in the ocean, shows the ocean as a source of food and a great influence on all living things, including man. Explains that without the waters of the ocean, life as we know it could not exist.
Prod-BAILEY Dist-PHENIX 1968

Ocean, The - Always The Weak And The Strong C 15 MIN
3/4 INCH VIDEO CASSETTE I
Establishes the relationship between symbiosis and predation.
From The Search For Science (2nd Ed.) Unit IV - Life In The Ocean Series.
Prod-WVIZTV Dist-GPITVL

Ocean, The - Animal Relationships C 15 MIN
3/4 INCH VIDEO CASSETTE I
Shows that unique relationships occur among and between the simplest animals.
From The Search For Science (2nd Ed.) Unit IV - Life In The Ocean Series.
Prod-WVIZTV Dist-GPITVL

Ocean, The - Animals Of A Different Kind C 15 MIN
3/4 INCH VIDEO CASSETTE I
Looks at the unusual animals which live in the tidepools and shows their unique adaptive qualities.
From The Search For Science (2nd Ed.) Unit IV - Life In The Ocean Series.
Prod-WVIZTV Dist-GPITVL

Ocean, The - Microscopic Plants And Animals B 20 MIN
2 INCH VIDEOTAPE I
See series title for descriptive statement.
From The Science Room Series.
Prod-MCETV Dist-GPITVL Prodn-WVIZTV

Ocean, The - Resource For The World C 15 MIN
16MM FILM, 3/4 OR 1/2 IN VIDEO I-C A
Examines the nature and diversity of the ocean's resources and emphasizes the need for conservation.
Prod-HANDEL Dist-HANDEL 1980

Ocean, The - Resource For The World (Captioned) C 15 MIN
16MM FILM, 3/4 OR 1/2 IN VIDEO I-C A
Examines the nature and diversity of the ocean's resources and emphasizes the need for conservation.
Prod-HANDEL Dist-HANDEL 1980

Ocean's Edge C 30 MIN
3/4 OR 1/2 INCH VIDEO CASSETTE
Discusses the seashore as a changing, dynamic environment. Looks at the various kinds of coastlines of the world. Explores the minerals found in both continental and island beach sands.

From The Oceanus - The Marine Environment Series. Lesson 5
Prod-SCCON Dist-CDTEL

Oceanic Environment C 22 MIN
3/4 OR 1/2 INCH VIDEO CASSETTE IND
See series title for descriptive statement.
From The Basic Geology Series.
Prod-GPCV Dist-GPCV

Oceanic Processes C 46 MIN
3/4 OR 1/2 INCH VIDEO CASSETTE IND
See series title for descriptive statement.
From The Basic And Petroleum Geology For Non-Geologists - Landforms II Series.
Prod-PHILLP Dist-GPCV

Oceanic Topography C 38 MIN
3/4 OR 1/2 INCH VIDEO CASSETTE IND
See series title for descriptive statement.
From The Basic And Petroleum Geology For Non-Geologists - Landforms II Series.
Prod-PHILLP Dist-GPCV

Oceanographer In The Polar Regions C 29 MIN
16MM FILM OPTICAL SOUND
Explains how oceanographers study the polar regions.
LC NO. 77-705625
Prod-USNO Dist-USNPC Prodn-AUDIO 1969

Oceanographic Prediction System C 30 MIN
16MM FILM OPTICAL SOUND
Discusses oceanographic prediction systems and programs and their relationship to defense and economic needs. Tells how predictions increase the use of oceanographic data for a fuller understanding and exploration of the seas.
LC NO. 73-701248
Prod-USN Dist-USNAC 1966

Oceanographic Research With The Cousteau Diving Saucer C 27 MIN
16MM FILM OPTICAL SOUND
Describes how U S Naval Electronics Laborabory scientists made use of the souscoupe and sous-marine of Jacques Cousteau over a period of six months.
LC NO. 74-705236
Prod-USN Dist-USNAC 1966

Oceanography C 30 MIN
3/4 OR 1/2 INCH VIDEO CASSETTE C
Explores the Gulf Stream.
From The Earth, Sea And Sky Series.
Prod-DALCCD Dist-DALCCD

Oceanography - Science For Survival C 27 MIN
16MM FILM OPTICAL SOUND
Shows the role of the navy within the framework of the inter-agency committee on numerous projects in oceanography.
LC NO. 74-705237
Prod-USN Dist-USNAC 1964

Oceanography - Science Of The Sea X 11 MIN
16MM FILM, 3/4 OR 1/2 IN VIDEO I-H
Describes how oceanographers explore the ocean waters, the sea floor and the earth's interior beneath the floor. Explains how sediments from the ocean floor provide clues to past history. Discusses the moho-the boundary between the earth's crust and mantle.
Prod-FA Dist-PHENIX 1962

Oceanography - The Role Of People In Ocean Sciences C 19 MIN
16MM FILM, 3/4 OR 1/2 IN VIDEO I-H
Demonstrates the importance of personal investigation in the science of oceanography using simple tools, such as a snorkle, metric square and bags of dye.
Prod-LIVDC Dist-PHENIX Prodn-COUSJM 1966

Oceanography - The Study Of Oceans C 15 MIN
16MM FILM, 3/4 OR 1/2 IN VIDEO
Describes the scientific disciples involved in oceanography, including meteorology, physics, chemistry, biology and geology.
Prod-WER Dist-JOU 1970

Oceanography - The Study Of Oceans (Captioned) C 15 MIN
16MM FILM, 3/4 OR 1/2 IN VIDEO
Describes the scientific disciples involved in oceanography, including meteorology, physics, chemistry, biology and geology.
Prod-WER Dist-JOU 1970

Oceanography In The Polar Regions C 29 MIN
16MM FILM OPTICAL SOUND
Discusses oceanographic research in the Arctic and the Antarctic. Shows how men master the oceans for defense and for the economic betterment of the world.
LC NO. 74-706511
Prod-USN Dist-USNAC 1969

Oceans C 16 MIN
3/4 OR 1/2 INCH VIDEO CASSETTE
Employs irony in an investigation of the conflicts between the personal and the political, the meditative and the active in a political mystery. An experimental film.
Prod-MEDIPR Dist-MEDIPR 1980

Oceans C 55 MIN
16MM FILM, 3/4 OR 1/2 IN VIDEO H-C A
Looks at oceans in their broadest aspects, from drowned plants and hidden mountains to minute drifting plankton and forests of kelp. Features the food webs of the oceans and the evolution of fish and mammals that live there.
From The Living Planet Series. Pt 11
Prod-BBCTV Dist-TIMLIF 1984

Oceans And Continents B 45 MIN
2 INCH VIDEOTAPE C
See series title for descriptive statement.
From The Physical Science Series. Unit 1 - Geology
Prod-CHITVC Dist-GPITVL Prodn-WTTWTV

Oceans Of Water, But - None To Spare (Spanish) C 22 MIN
16MM FILM, 3/4 OR 1/2 IN VIDEO I-H A
Shows what is happening to the sea and its life, and explores the problems involved in conserving its resources. Features C Leroy French.
Prod-TFW Dist-AIMS 1971

Oceans Of Water, But None To Spare C 22 MIN
16MM FILM, 3/4 OR 1/2 IN VIDEO I-C A
Features C Leroy French, Underwater Photographer of the Year.
Prod-AIMS Dist-AIMS 1971

Oceans Surround Us C 20 MIN
3/4 INCH VIDEO CASSETTE I
Shows hidden plant and animal worlds in the depths of the oceans.
From The Understanding Our World, Unit II - Geography We Should Know Series.
Prod-KRMATV Dist-GPITVL

Oceans, The - Living In Liquid Air C 19 MIN
16MM FILM, 3/4 OR 1/2 IN VIDEO
Interviews marine researchers who believe that man will one day live in underwater habitats and breath through artificial gills.
Prod-DOCUA Dist-CNEMAG

Oceanus - The Marine Environment - Epilogue C 30 MIN
3/4 OR 1/2 INCH VIDEO CASSETTE
Comprises final lecture in series. Focuses on future aspects of the world's oceans.
From The Oceanus - The Marine Environment Series. Lesson 30
Prod-SCCON Dist-CDTEL

Oceanus - The Marine Environment–A Series
C A
Presents information in areas of scientific interest and public concerns. Includes ocean pollutants plate tectonics and earthquake predictions. Emphasizes the interaction of the living world and the physical environment.
Prod-SCCON Dist-CDTEL

Beyond Land's End	030 MIN
Biological Resources	030 MIN
Continental Margins	030 MIN
Cosmic Origins	030 MIN
Ebb And Flow, The	030 MIN
Hawaii - A Case Study	030 MIN
Historical Perspectives	030 MIN
Intertidal Zone, The	030 MIN
Islands	030 MIN
Life Under Pressure	030 MIN
Light In The Sea	030 MIN
Living Together	030 MIN
Mammals - Seals And Otters	030 MIN
Mammals - Whales	030 MIN
Marine Meteorology	030 MIN
Marine Pollution	030 MIN
Mineral Resources	030 MIN
Nekton - Swimmers	030 MIN
Ocean Currents	030 MIN
Ocean's Edge	030 MIN
Oceanus - The Marine Environment - Epilogue	030 MIN
Plankton - Floaters And Drifters	030 MIN
Plate Tectonics	030 MIN
Polar Seas, The	030 MIN
Reptiles And Birds	030 MIN
Sound In The Sea	030 MIN
Tropic Seas, The	030 MIN
Water Planet, The	030 MIN
Waters Of The Earth, The	030 MIN
Wind Waves And Water Dynamics	030 MIN

OCS - Officer Candidate School C 28 MIN
16MM FILM OPTICAL SOUND
Shows a dynamic and intimate personal profile of men enrolled in the training program of the U S Naval Officer Candidate School, which prepares them to be naval officers.
LC NO. 74-705238
Prod-USN Dist-USNAC 1972

OCS Story, The C 29 MIN
16MM FILM OPTICAL SOUND
Describes the special training which officer candidates receive in the U S Army Officer Candidate Schools.
From The Big Picture Series.
LC NO. 74-706162
Prod-USA Dist-USNAC 1967

Octavio Paz - An Uncommon Poet C 29 MIN
16MM FILM, 3/4 OR 1/2 IN VIDEO H-C A
Presents Mexican poet Octavio Paz talking about his childhood, his activities as a political activist, and his views on poets, poetry and language.
LC NO. 79-706407
Prod-WNETTV Dist-FOTH 1979

October - Ten Days That Shook The World B 106 MIN
16MM FILM, 3/4 OR 1/2 IN VIDEO H-C A
Depicts events of the Russian Revolution of October, 1917. Describes the Kerensky regime and the European War, and discusses the conflicting plans and ambitions of various participants.
Prod-SOVKNO Dist-PHENIX 1981

Octopuff In Kumquat C 9 MIN
16MM FILM OPTICAL SOUND P-I
Presents an anti-smoking message in the form of a cartoon adventure story.
Prod-NTBA Dist-AMLUNG 1975

Octopus, Octopus C 22 MIN
16MM FILM, 3/4 OR 1/2 IN VIDEO J-C
A shortened version of the 1971 motion picture Octopus, Octopus. Uses the undersea photography of Jacques Cousteau and his team to reveal little-known facts about the life of the octopus.
From The Undersea World Of Jacques Cousteau Series.
Prod-METROM Dist-CF 1977

Octopus, Octopus C 52 MIN
16MM FILM, 3/4 OR 1/2 IN VIDEO
Jacques Cousteau and his divers show the octopus to be a shy and gentle marine creature.
From The Undersea World Of Jacques Cousteau Series.
Prod-METROM Dist-CF 1971

Octopus, The C 12 MIN
16MM FILM, 3/4 OR 1/2 IN VIDEO
Studies the eating habits, survival techniques, and mating behavior of the octopus. Edited from the television program Wild, Wild World Of Animals.
From The Wild, Wild World Of Animals Series.
LC NO. 79-707918
Prod-TIMLIF Dist-TIMLIF 1976

Octopus, The Unique Mollusk C 14 MIN
16MM FILM OPTICAL SOUND
Studies the octopus and it's characteristics such as very good eyesight and a brain larger than that of any other invertebrate animal. Views its method of reproduction.
Prod-RARIG Dist-RARIG

Ocular Examination, Pt 1 C 14 MIN
3/4 OR 1/2 INCH VIDEO CASSETTE PRO
Discusses such topics as taking a pertinent history for ocular patients, evaluating visual acuity and visual fields, giving an external examination and the appropriate methods for examination.
Prod-UMICHM Dist-UMICHM 1976

Ocular Examination, Pt 2 C 14 MIN
3/4 OR 1/2 INCH VIDEO CASSETTE PRO
Presents a detailed evaluation of the external eye and intraocular structures. Provides a comprehensive description of the examination procedures, and discussion of an opthalmic examination.
Prod-UMICHM Dist-UMICHM 1976

Ocular Injuries, Pt 1 C 16 MIN
3/4 OR 1/2 INCH VIDEO CASSETTE PRO
Discusses the evaluation process for ocular injuries commonly seen by primary care physicians, including how to avert the eyelids. Describes treatment of foreign bodies, corneal abrasions, chemical burns and radiant burns.
Prod-UMICHM Dist-UMICHM 1976

Ocular Injuries, Pt 2 C 16 MIN
3/4 OR 1/2 INCH VIDEO CASSETTE PRO
Discusses initial evaluation and treatment of ocular trauma and indications for referral to an opthalmologist.
Prod-UMICHM Dist-UMICHM 1976

Oculomotor Disorders, The C 30 MIN
16MM FILM OPTICAL SOUND
Shows the recent advance of electrophysiology in the field of neuro-ophthalmology. Points out that the extraocular muscle is one of the most important parts for diagnosing the diseases occurring in the brain if we employ modern electronics for analysis. Explains clinical and basic problems of neuro-ophthalmology in the past several years, including possible sympathetic innervation and parasympathetic innervation onto the extrocaular muscle.
Prod-UNIJAP Dist-UNIJAP 1967

Odd And Even C 15 MIN
3/4 INCH VIDEO CASSETTE P
Tells how to distinguish between odd and even digits.
From The Studio M Series.
Prod-WCETTV Dist-GPITVL 1979

Oddball, The C 30 MIN
16MM FILM OPTICAL SOUND R
Shows the importance of maintaining keenly felt Christian convictions in the face of any pressure. Points out that the oddball in this story is Christian young person who is on trial for being a misfit in his peer group.
Prod-BROADM Dist-BROADM 1971

Odds And Ends C 5 MIN
16MM FILM OPTICAL SOUND H-C
Presents a collage film comedy.
Prod-CFS Dist-CFS 1959

Odds And Ends C 15 MIN
3/4 OR 1/2 INCH VIDEO CASSETTE P
Shows how old scraps of wood, plastic, cardboard and other materials can be used to make art. Examines the assemblage works of Pablo Picasso, Kurt Schwitter and Abe Vigil.
From The Primary Art Series.
Prod-WETATV Dist-AITECH

Odds And Ends Playground, The C 6 MIN
16MM FILM, 3/4 OR 1/2 IN VIDEO P
Shows how Danny and his neighbors turn a littered vacant lot into a playground.
From The Golden Book Storytime Series.
Prod-MTI Dist-MTI 1977

Ode To Joy C 28 MIN
16MM FILM OPTICAL SOUND

Shows that the development of rhythm and appreciation for music is natural and progressive. Shows children playing percussion instruments, attending live concerts, opera and ballet. Alternates between scenes of children participating in project activities, and scenes relating the music to their total environment.
LC NO. 74-705239
Prod-USOE Dist-USNAC 1968

Ode To Nature C 5 MIN
16MM FILM OPTICAL SOUND I-C A
Presents a series of short vignettes on recycling and anti-litter scenes relevant to today's environmental problems.
LC NO. 74-700075
Prod-MARALF Dist-MARALF 1973

Odessa Steps Sequence B 10 MIN
16MM FILM SILENT
Features the Odessa Steps sequence from Sergei Eisenstein's film Potemkin.
Prod-ESNSTN Dist-REELIM 1925

Odors C 15 MIN
2 INCH VIDEOTAPE K
Identifies many kinds of matter by their distinctive odors.
From The Let's Go Sciencing, Unit I - Matter Series.
Prod-DETPS Dist-GPITVL

Odyssey C 4 MIN
16MM FILM OPTICAL SOUND
Presents a graphic journey through a world of apparent horrors where the main character strives to return to its womb, but learns that one can never return to the past.
Prod-USC Dist-USC 1980

Odyssey In Black--A Series
J-H
Takes the viewer from the African origins of the Black race through the American Civil War to today's Black revolution.
Prod-KLVXTV Dist-GPITVL

African Origins 30 MIN
Aftermath Of War, The 30 MIN
Black Revolution, The 30 MIN
Black's Role In The Civil War, The 30 MIN
Coming Of War, The 30 MIN
Decades Of Disappointment 30 MIN
Depression And The New Deal 30 MIN
Education Issue, The 30 MIN
Harlem Renaissance 30 MIN
Post-Reconstruction Era, The 30 MIN
Slavery 30 MIN
War Years And Beyond, The 30 MIN
World War I 30 MIN
Years Of Crisis, The 30 MIN

Odyssey Of Dr Pap, The C 30 MIN
16MM FILM OPTICAL SOUND C A
Traces the career of Dr Papanicolaou from the early days in Greece to his emergence as one of the world's outstanding scientists. Points out that Dr Pap's discovery of cancer cells in the vaginal discharges of women, before there were symptoms of the disease, was a landmark in medicine.
LC NO. 72-700665
Prod-OLSKRH Dist-AMCS 1969

Odyssey Of Rita Hayworth B 26 MIN
16MM FILM OPTICAL SOUND
Presents a study of the career of Rita Hayworth, using clips from her films. Includes scenes of her personal life and her comments on her life and career.
From The Hollywood And The Stars Series.
LC NO. 74-701940
Prod-WOLPER Dist-WOLPER 1964

Odyssey Tapes, The C 30 MIN
3/4 OR 1/2 INCH VIDEO CASSETTE
Presents spoken form of Homer's ancient poem The Odyssey by concert artist Richard Dyer-Bennet.
Prod-SULANI Dist-SULANI

Odyssey--A Series

Depicts the wonders and excitement found in various regions of the world, focusing on Antarctica, the Arctic, and the Equator.
Prod-KRMATV Dist-GPITVL 1978

Arctic Conquest, The 15 MIN
Arctic Ice, The 15 MIN
Arctic People, The 15 MIN
Arctic Resources, The 15 MIN
Arctic Tundra, The 15 MIN
Creatures Of The Continent 15 MIN
Equatorial Conquest 15 MIN
Equatorial Contrast 15 MIN
Equatorial Jungle 15 MIN
Equatorial Products 15 MIN
Equatorial Young People 15 MIN
Ice Over Land 15 MIN
Men Of Courage 15 MIN
Ninety Degrees South 15 MIN
Operation Deep Freeze 15 MIN

Odyssey--A Series

Presents archaeologists and anthropologists in the study of man.
Prod-PBA Dist-PBS 1980

Ancient Mariners 058 MIN
Ben's Mill 058 MIN
Chaco Legacy, The 059 MIN
Dadi's Family 058 MIN
Incas, The 058 MIN
Little Injustices - Laura Nader Looks 058 MIN
Margaret Mead - Taking Note 058 MIN
Maya Lords Of The Jungle 058 MIN
Myths And Moundbuilders 058 MIN
On The Cowboy Trail 058 MIN
Other People's Garbage 058 MIN
Seeking The First Americans 060 MIN
Three Worlds Of Bali, The 059 MIN

Odyssey, The, Pt 1 - The Structure Of The Epic C 27 MIN
16MM FILM, 3/4 OR 1/2 IN VIDEO H-C
Presents Gilbert Highet discussing the basic framework of the Odyssey and tracing the background of the Trojan War and events in Odysseus' home while he was away. Dramatizes highlights of Odysseus' travels.
From The Humanities - Narrative Series.
Prod-EBF Dist-EBEC 1966

Odyssey, The, Pt 2 - The Return Of Odysseus C 26 MIN
16MM FILM, 3/4 OR 1/2 IN VIDEO H-C
Focuses upon Odysseus' activities after his return to Ithaca and the manner in which these actions slowly reveal his true character.
From The Humanities - Narrative Series.
Prod-EBF Dist-EBEC 1965

Odyssey, The, Pt 3 - The Central Themes C 28 MIN
16MM FILM, 3/4 OR 1/2 IN VIDEO H-C
Presents Gilbert Highet discussing the central themes of the Odyssey, including Odysseus' wanderings among giants and monsters, Odysseus' return home and Telemachus' growing to manhood.
From The Humanities - Narrative Series.
Prod-EBF Dist-EBEC 1965

Oedipus Rex (Oedipus The King) C 20 MIN
3/4 OR 1/2 INCH VIDEO CASSETTE S
Presents the classic Greek Play Oedipus Rex. Signed.
Prod-GALCO Dist-GALCO 1957

Oedipus Rex, Pt 3 - Man And God C 30 MIN
16MM FILM, 3/4 OR 1/2 IN VIDEO H-C
Explains that one philosophical message of Oedipus is that man, no matter how great his ability, is subordinate to God. Shows how this theme is reinforced when Oedipus, representing the worldly liberal thought infusing Greek civilization, is beaten by the gods.
From The Humanities - The Drama Series.
Prod-EBEC Dist-EBEC 1959

Oedipus Rex, Pt 3 - Man And God (Spanish) C 30 MIN
16MM FILM, 3/4 OR 1/2 IN VIDEO H-C
Explains that one philosophical message of Oedipus is that man, no matter how great his ability, is subordinate to God. Shows how this theme is reinforced when Oedipus, representing the worldly liberal thought infusing Greek civilization, is beaten by the gods.
From The Humanities - The Drama Series.
Prod-EBEC Dist-EBEC 1959

Oedipus Rex, Pt 4 - The Recovery Of Oedipus C 30 MIN
16MM FILM, 3/4 OR 1/2 IN VIDEO H-C
Considers how the Greek tragedy shows man as somewhere between God and beast, always looking for his rightful place.
From The Humanities - The Drama Series.
Prod-EBEC Dist-EBEC 1959

Oedipus Rex, Pt 4 - The Recovery Of Oedipus (Spanish) C 30 MIN
16MM FILM, 3/4 OR 1/2 IN VIDEO H-C
Considers how the Greek tragedy shows man as somewhere between God and beast, always looking for his rightful place.
From The Humanities - The Drama Series.
Prod-EBEC Dist-EBEC 1959

Oedipus The King C 30 MIN
3/4 OR 1/2 INCH VIDEO CASSETTE C
See series title for descriptive statement.
From The Communicating Through Literature Series.
Prod-DALCCD Dist-DALCCD

Oedipus The King C 58 MIN
2 INCH VIDEOTAPE
Features Dean Robert A Goldwin of St John's College of Annapolis and three of his students discussing Oedipus the King with a special guest.
From The Dialogue Of The Western World Series.
Prod-MDCPB Dist-PUBTEL

Oedipus Tyrannus C 60 MIN
3/4 OR 1/2 INCH VIDEO CASSETTE H-C A
Explores methods of character development. Uses the play Oedipus Tyrannus as an example.
From The Drama - Play, Performance, Perception Series. Dramatis Personae
Prod-BBCTV Dist-FI 1978

Of All Places To Meet A Monster C 14 MIN
16MM FILM, 3/4 OR 1/2 IN VIDEO
Presents The Old Country section of Busch Gardens in Williamsburg, Virginia. Features scenes reminiscent of 17th and 18th century and also a replica of the Loch Ness monster.
Prod-ANHBUS Dist-MTP Prodn-EUESG 1979

Of All The Nerves C 22 MIN
3/4 OR 1/2 INCH VIDEO CASSETTE J-H
See series title for descriptive statement.
From The Phenomenal World Series.
Prod-EBEC Dist-EBEC 1983

Of All Things--A Series
P-C A
Prod-BAILYL Dist-AVED

Acapulco (Water Sports) 3 MIN
Alaska Fur Seals 3 MIN
Alaskan Salmon Industry 3 MIN
Amusement Park, An 3 MIN
Animals Of Africa 3 MIN
Animals Under The Sea 3 MIN
Argentina 3 MIN
Avocets 3 MIN
Banana Industry (Ecuador) 3 MIN
Birds Of Prey 3 MIN
Black-Crowned Night Heron, The 3 MIN
Boats Of The Mississippi 3 MIN
Brazil 3 MIN
Brussels' World's Fair 3 MIN
Bullfight 3 MIN
Butterflies - Life Cycle 3 MIN
Capri 3 MIN
Carlsbad Caverns 3 MIN
Castles On The Rhine 3 MIN
Cedar Waxwing 3 MIN
Chile 3 MIN
Circus, The 3 MIN
Commercial Fishing - Tuna 3 MIN
Copenhagen 3 MIN
County Fair 3 MIN
Cypress Gardens 3 MIN
Dairy Industry 3 MIN
Dog Show 3 MIN
Dogs - Field Trials 3 MIN
Down The Mississippi 3 MIN
Duck Families 3 MIN
Ducks Of North America 3 MIN
Ecuador 3 MIN
Egret, The 3 MIN
Egypt 3 MIN
Endless Caverns Of Virginia 3 MIN
Face Of The Land 3 MIN
Finches, The 3 MIN
Fireworks (Mexico) 3 MIN
Flamingoes 3 MIN
Food Processing 3 MIN
Frankfurt 3 MIN
Fruit Harvest 3 MIN
Grape Industry 3 MIN
Great Blue Heron, The 3 MIN
Grosbeak, The 3 MIN
Hamlet's Castle 3 MIN
Handicrafts (Mexico) 3 MIN
Harness Horses 3 MIN
Helpful Insects 3 MIN
Historic Virginia 3 MIN
Honeybees 3 MIN
Horse Farm 3 MIN
Horse Show 3 MIN
Hummingbird, The 3 MIN
Indians Of New Mexico 3 MIN
Insect Enemies 3 MIN
Irrigation 3 MIN
London 3 MIN
London, Historic City 3 MIN
Los Angeles 3 MIN
Mammals 3 MIN
Mexico - Land Of Contrast 3 MIN
Mexico City 3 MIN
Morocco 3 MIN
Motor Boat Racing 3 MIN
New Orleans 3 MIN
New Orleans, Mardi Gras 3 MIN
New York City 3 MIN
Orange Industry 3 MIN
Panama Canal 3 MIN
Panama Hats (Ecuador) 3 MIN
Paris, Left Bank 3 MIN
Paris, Tourist Town 3 MIN
Peru 3 MIN
Petroleum Industry 3 MIN
Phalaropes 3 MIN
Polo 3 MIN
Pompeii 3 MIN
Quarter Horses 3 MIN
Red-Winged Blackbirds 3 MIN
Rio De Janeiro 3 MIN
River Logging 3 MIN
Rocks And Gems 3 MIN
Rodeo 3 MIN
Rome 3 MIN
Rome, City Of Fountains 3 MIN
Rose Parade (Pasadena) 3 MIN
Sailing 3 MIN
Salmon - Life Cycle 3 MIN
San Francisco - City Of Bridges 3 MIN
San Francisco - City Of Hills 3 MIN
Sandpipers, Pt 1 3 MIN
Sandpipers, Pt 2 3 MIN
Sea Gulls 3 MIN
Sea Otter, The 3 MIN
Skiing 3 MIN
Snakes 3 MIN
Sparrow Family, The 3 MIN
Sports Car Racing 3 MIN
Sports Fishing 3 MIN
St Peters, Rome 3 MIN
Steel Industry 3 MIN
Story Of Power 3 MIN
Summer Sports (Summer Fun) 3 MIN
Swallows 3 MIN
Textile Industry 3 MIN
Tobacco 3 MIN
University Of Mexico 3 MIN
Vegetable Industry 3 MIN
Vintage Cars 3 MIN
Warsaw, Poland 3 MIN
Washington, DC 3 MIN
Water Skiing, Acapulco 3 MIN

Winter Fun 3 MIN
Wonders Of Florida 3 MIN
Woodpeckers 3 MIN
Work Of Rivers, The 3 MIN
Yellow-Headed Blackbird 3 MIN
Yellowstone 3 MIN
Yosemite 3 MIN
Zurich 3 MIN

Of Birds, Beaks And Behavior C 11 MIN
16MM FILM, 3/4 OR 1/2 IN VIDEO
Shows the wide variety of physical features, nesting habits, songs and displays of birds. Tells how these relate to a bird's food and habitat preferences.
From The Many Worlds Of Nature Series.
Prod-MORALL Dist-MTI 1975

Of Broccoli And Pelicans And Celery And Seals C 30 MIN
16MM FILM, 3/4 OR 1/2 IN VIDEO H-C A
Traces the deterioration of environment in California. Points out how pesticides sprayed on the Oxnard Plain are being washed to sea where they are contaminating fishes which are in turn, eaten by birds, seals and man. Stresses the dangers of DDT to man and nature.
From The Our Vanishing Wilderness Series. No. 1
LC NO. 80-707020
Prod-IU Dist-IU 1971

Of Course You Can C 19 MIN
16MM FILM OPTICAL SOUND
Watches a mother teach her teenage son and daughter how to can fresh fruits and vegetables safely and then follows the teenagers as they attempt to handle the task themselves.
LC NO. 79-701443
Prod-BALCOR Dist-MTP Prodn-KEATL 1979

Of Course You Can C 20 MIN
3/4 OR 1/2 INCH VIDEO CASSETTE
Offers a practical program showing beginners and gourmets how to can and preserve vegetables and fruits.
From The Magical Cook's Tour Series.
Prod-IVCH Dist-IVCH

Of Dances, Dreams And Musical Themes C 12 MIN
16MM FILM OPTICAL SOUND
Shows a dance company's performance in a school gymnasium. Describes how this experience is carried into the classroom, where teachers and young people explore the theater through art and creative writing.
LC NO. 75-701904
Prod-PROPER Dist-VIP Prodn-INST 1974

Of Earth And Man - A Telecourse In Geography—A Series

Examines the different geographical regions of Earth. Includes elements of anthropology, economics, political science, history, biology, geology and climatology.
Prod-MDCPB Dist-MDCPB

Amazonia - Balancing Man And Nature 030 MIN
Amazonia - Greenhouse Or Green Hell 030 MIN
America's Heartland - The Unconditional 030 MIN
American City, The - Growth To Metropolis 030 MIN
China - The Good Earth And The Middle 030 MIN
China - The People's Republic And The New 030 MIN
Cities - The Man-Made World 030 MIN
Deserts - Saharan Coins Of Gold 030 MIN
Deserts - The Dry World 030 MIN
Earth, The - Child Of The Sun 030 MIN
Earth, The - Movement, Fire, Renewal 030 MIN
Eskimos - Life At The Top Of The World 030 MIN
Geography - A World Of Possibilities 030 MIN
Great Plains, The - World Of The Cowboy 030 MIN
India - A Glorious Harmony of Opposites 030 MIN
India - Working For New Tomorrows 030 MIN
Japan - A Costly Miracle 030 MIN
Japan - From The Sword To The Bomb 030 MIN
Mapping - Exploring The Globe 030 MIN
Mapping - Round World, Flat Maps 030 MIN
Megalopolis - The Golden Door 030 MIN
Mountains - Hermit Kingdom, Tourist 030 MIN
Mountains - The Challenge Of The Slope 030 MIN
Soviet Union, The - A Riddle Wrapped In A 030 MIN
Soviet Union, The - Land Of The Peasant 030 MIN
Soviet Union, The - Temples Of Industry 030 MIN
Trobriand Islands - Kula And Cricket 030 MIN
United States, The - One Out Of Many 030 MIN
World Today, The - Listening To The Earth 030 MIN
World Tomorrow, The - Possibilities And 030 MIN

Of Forest Soil C 10 MIN
16MM FILM, 3/4 OR 1/2 IN VIDEO
Describes the Weyerhaeuser Company's soil survey process. Explains the benefits that Weyerhaeuser has received from its own surveys and other possible benefits to forest management.
LC NO. 82-706095
Prod-WEYCO Dist-AMMPCO 1981

Of Greeks And Gods—A Series

Reviews the days when Greek gods wooed earth women and moral men were heroes. Looks at the relevance of the myth to the ancient Greeks and to modern man.
Prod-UMITV Dist-UMITV 1971

Adventurers 030 MIN
Myth As History 029 MIN

Of Holes And Corks C 10 MIN
16MM FILM, 3/4 OR 1/2 IN VIDEO J-C A
An animated allegory which explores man's problems with reality, illusion and self-deception.
Prod-ZAGREB Dist-IFB 1970

Of Human Bondage B 83 MIN
16MM FILM OPTICAL SOUND
Presents Somerset Maugham's study of a club-foot young doctor and the Cockney prostitute who obsesses and almost destroys him. Stars Bette Davis and Leslie Howard.
Prod-NYFLMS Dist-NYFLMS 1934

Of Masks And Men C 30 MIN
3/4 OR 1/2 INCH VIDEO CASSETTE C
See series title for descriptive statement.
From The In Our Own Image Series.
Prod-DALCCD Dist-DALCCD

Of Men And Demons C 10 MIN
16MM FILM, 3/4 OR 1/2 IN VIDEO
An animated parable showing man in his constant quest to better his environment. Emphasizes the growing threat of pollution of air, water and natural resources.
Prod-IBMWTC Dist-TEXFLM Prodn-HUBLEY 1969

Of Men And Machines - Engineering Psychology B 29 MIN
16MM FILM, 3/4 OR 1/2 IN VIDEO H-C A
Studies the man-machine relationship by examining the ways in which man handles and processes information, the dynamics of information feedback between man and machines, the human being's behavior in complex man-machine systems and the redesigning of machines.
From The Focus On Behavior Series.
Prod-NET Dist-IU 1963

Of Men And Women C 1 MIN
16MM FILM OPTICAL SOUND
Presents a prolog for a series of Warner Brothers specials for television showing the volatile and humorous relations between men and women.
LC NO. 73-702344
Prod-WB Dist-WB 1972

Of Mice And Men C
1/2 IN VIDEO CASSETTE BETA/VHS
Presents a 1981 TV adaptation of Steinbeck's story, OF MICE AND MEN, starring Robert Blake and Randy Quaid.
Prod-GA Dist-GA

Of Monkeys And Men B 30 MIN
16MM FILM OPTICAL SOUND H-C A
Reports on the issues surrounding the repeal by the Tennessee Legislature of the so-called 'MONKEY LAW' which prohibited teaching of the principle of evolution in the state. Presents speeches by legislators and interviews John T Scopes and citizens of Tennessee.
LC NO. FIA68-1776
Prod-NET Dist-IU Prodn-WDCNTV 1968

Of Pawns And Powers C 29 MIN
3/4 INCH VIDEO CASSETTE
Looks at power politics in Southeast Asia. Reflects on small countries caught up in big events and dominated by big powers.
From The Conversations With Allen Whiting Series.
Prod-UMITV Dist-UMITV 1979

Of Picks, Shovels And Words C 30 MIN
16MM FILM OPTICAL SOUND H-C A
Shows how the archeologists use picks, shovels and words to reveal the ancient cities of Babylon and Persepolis, the walls of Jericho and the Dead Sea scrolls.
From The Human Dimension Series.
LC NO. 77-711375
Prod-GRACUR Dist-GRACUR 1971

Of Preemies And Pills C 25 MIN
3/4 OR 1/2 INCH VIDEO CASSETTE
Tells of the latest progress in reducing infant mortality. Shows how infants, born prematurely, are nurtured until their fragile little bodies can support life. Discusses, in second portion of program, a new distribution system that helps prevent drug accidents, and the role of the pharmacist as part of the health team.
Prod-TRAINX Dist-TRAINX

Of Progress And Plenty C 17 MIN
16MM FILM OPTICAL SOUND
Shows world-wide aspects of agriculture, from the most primitive farming methods used in both the Near and Far East to the modern methods used in the United States. Explains how agriculture affects the economy and lives of the people.
LC NO. FIA65-540
Prod-GTARC Dist-GTARC Prodn-WILDNG 1964

Of Race And Blood C 89 MIN
3/4 OR 1/2 INCH VIDEO CASSETTE
Presents a documentary on the art and artists of the Third Reich and Adolf Hitler's use of art as an important part of the Nazi movement.
Prod-KRMATV Dist-PBS

Of Rockets, Ships And Sealing Wax C 17 MIN
16MM FILM OPTICAL SOUND
Relates the growth of the Thiokol Chemical Corporation and the expansion of the locale around the Wasatch Division, Brigham City, Utah.
Prod-THIOKL Dist-THIOKL 1959

Of Stars And Men C 53 MIN
16MM FILM, 3/4 OR 1/2 IN VIDEO I-H
Presents Dr Harlow Shapley's views on man's place in the universe, and his relation to space, time, matter and energy. An animated film.
Prod-HUBLEY Dist-TEXFLM 1964

Of Stars And Men (2nd Ed)—A Series
J-C A
Uses animation in presenting an adaptation of Dr Harlow Shapley's book OF STARS AND MEN. Discusses man's place in the universe through an examination of life's four basic elements, space, time, matter and energy.
LC NO. 76-701274
Prod-HUBLEY Dist-RADIM 1976

Journey Through Space, A 8 MIN
Journey Through Time, A 9 MIN
Life On Other Planets 18 MIN
Matter And Energy 11 MIN
Prologue - The Lion And The Crown 7 MIN

Of Sugar Cane And Syrup C 15 MIN
16MM FILM, 3/4 OR 1/2 IN VIDEO
Documents the traditional techniques of making syrup from sugar cane. Centers on a Southern man and his wife who have been making syrup since the days when this was a necessary part of rural life.
Prod-KSPRO Dist-CORF 1977

Of That Time C 17 MIN
16MM FILM OPTICAL SOUND
Tells the story of a young girl whose family moves to a new neighborhood. Shows how she gives up a special doll because of peer and family pressures, and makes friends with the boy next door.
LC NO. 81-701142
Prod-USC Dist-USC 1981

Of The People C 28 MIN
16MM FILM OPTICAL SOUND
A profile of the United States Congress, its history and present functions. Includes interviews with Carl Albert, Melvin Laird, Bourke B Hickenlooper, Charles Vanik and James H Scheuer.
From The Government Story Series. No. 1
LC NO. 71-707177
Prod-WBCPRO Dist-WBCPRO 1968

Of The People C 30 MIN
3/4 OR 1/2 INCH VIDEO CASSETTE H-C A
See series title for descriptive statement.
From The Japan - The Changing Tradition Series.
Prod-UMA Dist-GPITVL 1978

Of Thee I Sing C 15 MIN
3/4 OR 1/2 INCH VIDEO CASSETTE P
Teaches patriotic songs and introduces a brass ensemble.
From The Stepping Into Rhythm Series.
Prod-WVIZTV Dist-AITECH

Of Time And A River C 27 MIN
16MM FILM, 3/4 OR 1/2 IN VIDEO
Tells the story of the Columbia River and the Grand Coulee Dam, covering the geological forces that formed the river basin.
Prod-USBR Dist-USNAC 1982

Of Time And Consequence C 29 MIN
3/4 INCH VIDEO CASSETTE
Illustrates the role and milieu of the engineer from ancient to modern times. Analyzes the changing environment in which the engineer works today.
From The Future Without Shock Series.
Prod-UMITV Dist-UMITV 1976

Of Time And The Artist C 29 MIN
2 INCH VIDEOTAPE
See series title for descriptive statement.
From The Museum Open House Series.
Prod-WGBHTV Dist-PUBTEL

Of Time, Tombs And Treasure C 27 MIN
3/4 INCH VIDEO CASSETTE
Presents a journey through the resplendent 3000-year-old tomb of King Tutankhamen. Examines the treasures found in the tomb. Tells the story of the tomb's discovery.
Prod-EXXON Dist-MTP

Of Time, Tombs And Treasures - The Treasures Of Tutankhamun C 27 MIN
16MM FILM OPTICAL SOUND
Takes a look at artifacts in the exhibit entitled The Treasures of Tutankhamun, shown in various cities in the United States beginning in 1976.
LC NO. 77-702119
Prod-EXXON Dist-USNGA Prodn-CHAPA 1977

Of Wings And Women C 15 MIN
16MM FILM - 3/4 IN VIDEO
Includes the history, contributions and traditions of the Women's Air Force. Focuses on career opportunities available to eligible women, as well as the educational, occupational and social aspects of life as a WAF.
Prod-USNAC Dist-USNAC 1972

Off On A Magic Carpet B 15 MIN
2 INCH VIDEOTAPE P
See series title for descriptive statement.
From The Sounds Like Magic Series.
Prod-MOEBA Dist-GPITVL Prodn-KYNETV

Off Stage—A Series

Looks at some of the contemporary activities in the Professional Theatre Program at the University of Michigan.
Prod-UMITV Dist-UMITV 1975

Alternative Theatre 029 MIN
Artist In Residence 029 MIN
Body Language And The Art Of Mime 030 MIN
Bread And Roses - A New Play 029 MIN
Dance Theatre 029 MIN
Experimental Theatre Festival 029 MIN
Marionette Theatre 029 MIN
Theatre - Why Criticize? 029 MIN

Theatre Of China 029 MIN

Off The Pig B 15 MIN
16MM FILM OPTICAL SOUND
Presents a dialogue between Black Panthers Huey P Newton and Eldridge Cleaver. Includes illustrative pictures of Panthers.
Prod-SFN Dist-SFN 1968

Off The Wall C 15 MIN
16MM FILM, 3/4 OR 1/2 IN VIDEO
Uses live action footage to capture the game of racquetball as it is played by professionals and amateurs.
Prod-PFP Dist-PFP Prodn-MORSTF 1979

Off To Adventure—A Series
P-J
Presents an insight into life and customs in Japan.
Prod-YALEDV Dist-YALEDV

Arts	15 MIN
Buddhism	15 MIN
City Life Of A Small Boy	15 MIN
Farm Life	15 MIN
Going To Church	15 MIN
Home Life	15 MIN
Occupations	15 MIN
School	15 MIN
Shintoism	15 MIN

Off To See The Dentist C 15 MIN
2 INCH VIDEOTAPE P
Provides an enrichment program in the communitive arts area by building a paragraph.
From The Word Magic (2nd Ed) Series.
Prod-CVETVC Dist-GPITVL

Off We Go C 15 MIN
3/4 INCH VIDEO CASSETTE P-I
Discusses families who are in the process of moving.
From The Can You Imagine Series.
Prod-WVIZTV Dist-GPITVL

Off Your Duff C 30 MIN
16MM FILM, 3/4 OR 1/2 IN VIDEO H-C A
Presents experts, amateurs and beginners engaged in various physical activities. Offers advice and suggestions for finding the right kind of exercise.
Prod-WGBHTV Dist-LCOA 1979

Off-Air Australia X 30 MIN
3/4 OR 1/2 INCH VIDEO CASSETTE
Documents Ant Farm's 1976 tour of Australia with an unusual performance at the Sydney Opera House and unlikely TV talk-show appearances.
Prod-ANTFRM Dist-EAI

Off-Target Interview, The C 15 MIN
3/4 INCH VIDEO CASSETTE H-C A
Explains what not to do during a job interview.
From The Job Seeking Series.
Prod-WCETTV Dist-GPITVL 1979

Offense C 30 MIN
3/4 OR 1/2 INCH VIDEO CASSETTE
Discusses offense, which requires patience while the team works the ball around the floor and finds the defensive mistake. Illustrates methods of drilling the team to learn the multiple possibilities of the offense.
From The Basketball Fundamentals Series.
Prod-NETCHE Dist-NETCHE 1972

Offensive Backfield, The C 15 MIN
16MM FILM, 3/4 OR 1/2 IN VIDEO J-C
Football players and coaches discuss the offensive backfield. Illustrates the center exchange, hand-off, stance, cutting, guarding against fumbles, play-calling, passing and receiving. Joe Namath and Mike Taliaferro demonstrate quarterback moves in the passing and running game.
Prod-MOKIN Dist-MOKIN 1967

Offensive Basketball C 11 MIN
16MM FILM OPTICAL SOUND J
Presents the fundamentals of offensive basketball, including both individual and team skills.
LC NO. 78-701961
Prod-BKBA Dist-BKBA Prodn-NDYD 1973

Offensive Line, The C 15 MIN
16MM FILM, 3/4 OR 1/2 IN VIDEO J-C
Football players and coaches discuss the offensive line. Pictures the option trap, cut-off, and pass protection blocks and shows the function of the center in the kicking game.
Prod-MOKIN Dist-MOKIN 1967

Offensive Play C 61 MIN
1/2 IN VIDEO CASSETTE BETA/VHS
Demonstrates and discusses offensive play in women's basketball.
From The Fundamentals Of Women's Basketball Series.
Prod-MOHOMV Dist-MOHOMV

Office Automation Concepts—A Series

Focuses on three objectives of the automated or future office..to help managers reduce paperwork, to help managers make better decisions and to improve human communications. Explores various services that can help realize these objectives.
Prod-DELTAK Dist-DELTAK

Office Automation Game Plan C 45 MIN
3/4 OR 1/2 INCH VIDEO CASSETTE
Outlines a generic blueprint for managing office automation evolution. Covers such topics as managing expectations, states of office automation growth, staffing, management awareness, user involvement and continuing evolution.
From The Management Strategies For Office Automation Series.
Prod-DELTAK Dist-DELTAK

Office Automation Technologies—A Series

Provides a fairly technical overview of the components and technologies involved in the executive automated office.
Prod-DELTAK Dist-DELTAK

Office Evaluation Of Urinary Incontinence C 18 MIN
3/4 OR 1/2 INCH VIDEO CASSETTE PRO
Discusses office evaluation of urinary incontinence.
Prod-WFP Dist-WFP

Office Machines - Amount And Percent Of Increase Or Decrease C 10 MIN
1/2 IN VIDEO CASSETTE BETA/VHS
Discusses percentage problems.
From The Office Machines - Calculations Series.
Prod-RMI Dist-RMI

Office Machines - Bank Reconciliation C 11 MIN
1/2 IN VIDEO CASSETTE BETA/VHS
From The Office Machines - Calculations Series.
Prod-RMI Dist-RMI

Office Machines - Calculations—A Series

Prod-RMI Dist-RMI

Office Machines - Amount And Percent Of	
Office Machines - Bank Reconciliation	011 MIN
Office Machines - Cash Discount And Net Amount	008 MIN
Office Machines - Compound Annual Interest	014 MIN
Office Machines - Compound Semi-Annual Interest	014 MIN
Office Machines - Determining The Real Estate	006 MIN
Office Machines - Discounting Notes	006 MIN
Office Machines - Markup Based On Cost And On	013 MIN
Office Machines - Payroll, Gross Earnings	009 MIN
Office Machines - Payroll, Net Earnings	012 MIN
Office Machines - Percent Of Markup Based On	009 MIN
Office Machines - Proration, Direct Method	008 MIN
Office Machines - Proration, Indirect Method	012 MIN
Office Machines - Simple Interest, Exact Days	012 MIN
Office Machines - Simple Interest, Finding	012 MIN
Office Machines - Simple Interest, Finding	013 MIN
Office Machines - Simple Interest, Finding	012 MIN
Office Machines - Simple Interest, 360 Day	012 MIN
Office Machines - Taxes, Determining Amount	010 MIN
Office Machines - Taxes, Determining Total	006 MIN
Office Machines - Trade Discount, Single And	013 MIN

Office Machines - Cash Discount And Net Amount C 8 MIN
1/2 IN VIDEO CASSETTE BETA/VHS
From The Office Machines - Calculations Series.
Prod-RMI Dist-RMI

Office Machines - Compound Annual Interest C 14 MIN
1/2 IN VIDEO CASSETTE BETA/VHS
From The Office Machines - Calculations Series.
Prod-RMI Dist-RMI

Office Machines - Compound Semi-Annual Interest C 14 MIN
1/2 IN VIDEO CASSETTE BETA/VHS
From The Office Machines - Calculations Series.
Prod-RMI Dist-RMI

Office Machines - Determining The Real Estate Tax Rate C 6 MIN
1/2 IN VIDEO CASSETTE BETA/VHS
From The Office Machines - Calculations Series.
Prod-RMI Dist-RMI

Office Machines - Discounting Notes C 6 MIN
1/2 IN VIDEO CASSETTE BETA/VHS
From The Office Machines - Calculations Series.
Prod-RMI Dist-RMI

Office Machines - Markup Based On Cost And On Selling Price C 13 MIN
1/2 IN VIDEO CASSETTE BETA/VHS
From The Office Machines - Calculations Series.
Prod-RMI Dist-RMI

Office Machines - Payroll, Gross Earnings C 9 MIN
1/2 IN VIDEO CASSETTE BETA/VHS
From The Office Machines - Calculations Series.
Prod-RMI Dist-RMI

Office Machines - Payroll, Net Earnings C 12 MIN
1/2 IN VIDEO CASSETTE BETA/VHS
From The Office Machines - Calculations Series.
Prod-RMI Dist-RMI

Office Machines - Percent Of Markup Based On Cost Or On Selling Price C 9 MIN
1/2 IN VIDEO CASSETTE BETA/VHS
From The Office Machines - Calculations Series.
Prod-RMI Dist-RMI

Office Machines - Proration, Direct Method C 8 MIN
1/2 IN VIDEO CASSETTE BETA/VHS
From The Office Machines - Calculations Series.
Prod-RMI Dist-RMI

Office Machines - Proration, Indirect Method C 12 MIN
1/2 IN VIDEO CASSETTE BETA/VHS
From The Office Machines - Calculations Series.
Prod-RMI Dist-RMI

Office Machines - Simple Interest, Exact Days And Exact Interest C 12 MIN
1/2 IN VIDEO CASSETTE BETA/VHS
From The Office Machines - Calculations Series.
Prod-RMI Dist-RMI

Office Machines - Simple Interest, Finding The Principal C 12 MIN
1/2 IN VIDEO CASSETTE BETA/VHS
From The Office Machines - Calculations Series.
Prod-RMI Dist-RMI

Office Machines - Simple Interest, Finding The Time C 13 MIN
1/2 IN VIDEO CASSETTE BETA/VHS
From The Office Machines - Calculations Series.
Prod-RMI Dist-RMI

Office Machines - Simple Interest, Finding The Rate C 12 MIN
1/2 IN VIDEO CASSETTE BETA/VHS
From The Office Machines - Calculations Series.
Prod-RMI Dist-RMI

Office Machines - Simple Interest, 360 Day Method C 12 MIN
1/2 IN VIDEO CASSETTE BETA/VHS
From The Office Machines - Calculations Series.
Prod-RMI Dist-RMI

Office Machines - Taxes, Determining Amount Of Real Estate Taxes C 10 MIN
1/2 IN VIDEO CASSETTE BETA/VHS
From The Office Machines - Calculations Series.
Prod-RMI Dist-RMI

Office Machines - Taxes, Determining Total Assessed Valuation C 6 MIN
1/2 IN VIDEO CASSETTE BETA/VHS
From The Office Machines - Calculations Series.
Prod-RMI Dist-RMI

Office Machines - Trade Discount, Single And Chain C 13 MIN
1/2 IN VIDEO CASSETTE BETA/VHS
From The Office Machines - Calculations Series.
Prod-RMI Dist-RMI

Office Management Of Chronic Emphysema C 22 MIN
3/4 INCH VIDEO CASSETTE PRO
Discusses office treatment of chronic emphysema. Describes prophylactic treatment, methods of monitoring treatment progress, and tests and equipment useful in office treatment.
LC NO. 76-706065
Prod-WARMP Dist-USNAC 1970

Office Management Of Vascular Tension Headache C 23 MIN
3/4 INCH VIDEO CASSETTE PRO
Discusses approaches to the treatment of vascular tension headache. Emphasizes the establishment of rapport and confidence with the patient. Explains drug therapy.
LC NO. 76-706066
Prod-WARMP Dist-USNAC 1970

Office Manual, The - Need And Preparation B 60 MIN
3/4 OR 1/2 INCH VIDEO CASSETTE
Discusses the need for office manuals, various types of manuals, sources of information for manuals, their format, their contents, their preferred language and sentence forms, and their readability.
Prod-UAZMIC Dist-UAZMIC 1977

Office On The Move C 25 MIN
3/4 OR 1/2 INCH VIDEO CASSETTE H-C A
Examines the broad principles of what technology can do to make the tasks of those who work in offices easier. Shows how a typical chain of administrative tasks can be tackled on a computer system and explores the extent which text, voice, image and data can be handled by office systems. Includes a look at a mature system in use in an American company.
From The Electronic Office Series.
Prod-BBCTV Dist-FI 1984

Office Practice - Manners And Customs C 14 MIN
16MM FILM, 3/4 OR 1/2 IN VIDEO H-C A
Provides an introduction to the manners and customs of office work, including reception of visitors, telephone courtesy and forms of address for co-workers.
From The Office Practice Series.
Prod-CORF Dist-CORF 1972

Office Practice - Working With Others C 14 MIN
16MM FILM, 3/4 OR 1/2 IN VIDEO H-C A
Fosters an awareness of the importance of human relations in office work through use of appropriate behavior and language.
From The Office Practice Series.
Prod-CORF Dist-CORF 1972

Office Practice - Your Attitude C 11 MIN
16MM FILM, 3/4 OR 1/2 IN VIDEO H-C A
Shows how personal attitudes are reflected by the way in which people talk and listen and through their grooming, posture and dress.
From The Office Practice Series.
Prod-CORF Dist-CORF 1972

Office Practice—A Series
16MM FILM, 3/4 OR 1/2 IN VIDEO H-C A
Emphasizes the importance of having good manners and a good attitude when working in an office
Prod-CORF Dist-CORF 1972

Office Practice - Manners And Customs 14 MIN

Office Practice - Working With Others 14 MIN
Office Practice - Your Attitude 11 MIN

Office Safety C 12 MIN
16MM FILM OPTICAL SOUND A
Points out that it takes just a bit of caution and common sense to avoid most office accidents.
Prod-XEROXF Dist-GA 1978

Office Safety C 17 MIN
3/4 OR 1/2 INCH VIDEO CASSETTE A
Shows how seemingly innocent actions can result in serious accidents involving open file drawers and swinging doors.
Prod-OLINC Dist-MTI 1980

Office Safety - The Thrill Seekers C 12 MIN
16MM FILM, 3/4 OR 1/2 IN VIDEO A
Points out safety hazards that seem to attract a breed of office workers termed 'thrill seekers.' Shows how they consider themselves too adventurous to heed prudent safety rules. Discusses the remedy for this situation.
Prod-CENTRO Dist-CORF 1983

Office Surgery C 58 MIN
16MM FILM OPTICAL SOUND PRO
Demonstrates many of the minor diagnostic and therapeutic surgical procedures that could be done in the office by general practitioners and industrial physicians.
Prod-ACYDGD Dist-ACY 1961

Office Visit - Sexual Review Of Systems C 30 MIN
3/4 OR 1/2 INCH VIDEO CASSETTE PRO
Provides examples of how the primary care physician can incorporate questions about sexual functioning and sex-related concerns of patients into the office visit.
Prod-HSCIC Dist-HSCIC

Officer As A Source Of Change B
16MM FILM OPTICAL SOUND PRO
Explores the officer's role in inmate security and rehabilitation.
From The View And Do Series.
LC NO. 73-700191
Prod-SCETV Dist-SCETV 1971

Officer Down, Code 3 C 25 MIN
16MM FILM, 3/4 OR 1/2 IN VIDEO
Explains and explores ten errors that are often the cause of the deaths of policemen.
From The Police Training Films Series.
Prod-MTROLA Dist-MTI Prodn-WORON 1975

Officer Stress Awareness C 20 MIN
16MM FILM, 3/4 OR 1/2 IN VIDEO PRO
Uses a number of different physical, emotional and interpersonal stresses encountered by patrol officers in surveying the mental and physical stress of law enforcement.
Prod-HAR Dist-MTI Prodn-BAY 1976

Officer Stress Awareness - Externalizing Problems C 20 MIN
16MM FILM, 3/4 OR 1/2 IN VIDEO PRO
Examines conditions of physical, emotional and interpersonal stress presented by the aggressive, tough policeman. Shows how he may become careless, callous and create bad will toward the entire police force by his actions.
Prod-HAR Dist-MTI Prodn-BAY 1976

Officer Stress Awareness - Internalizing Problems C 20 MIN
16MM FILM, 3/4 OR 1/2 IN VIDEO PRO
Examines conditions of physical, emotional and interpersonal stress presented by the police officer who internalized problems. Shows how to recognize these internalizations of stress before they affect the officer, his partner or the department.
Prod-HAR Dist-MTI Prodn-BAY 1976

Officer Survival - An Approach To Conflict Management—A Series
16MM FILM, 3/4 OR 1/2 IN VIDEO PRO
Discusses methods for controlling conflict in various situations.
Prod-HAR Dist-MTI 1976

Approaching Potentially Explosive Conflicts 22 MIN
Conflict Resolution - Mediating Disputes 22 MIN
Conflict Resolution - Utilizing Community 22 MIN
Day Everything Went Wrong, The 22 MIN
Defusing Hostile Individuals 22 MIN
Problem Identification - Determining The 22 MIN

Officer Survival - Night Vs Day Patrol C 20 MIN
16MM FILM, 3/4 OR 1/2 IN VIDEO
Presents reenactments of various situations which may occur during day and night patrols and discusses issues and questions which may arise as a result.
Prod-HAR Dist-MTI Prodn-SALMIN 1979

Officer Survival III C 10 MIN
16MM FILM OPTICAL SOUND
Presents a re-enactment of a shooting incident resulting in the death of four California Highway Patrol officers. Shows the correct procedures to be followed in similar situations.
LC NO. 77-701822
Prod-LACSD Dist-LACSD 1977

Officer Survival—A Series
16MM FILM, 3/4 OR 1/2 IN VIDEO
Describes how police officers can deal with assaults made upon them. Recreates actual incidents to introduce the practical realities of life and death situations.
Prod-LACSD Dist-MTI

Armed Suspect 006 MIN
Barricaded Suspect 006 MIN
Felony Stop 012 MIN

Officer-Inmate Relationship B
16MM FILM OPTICAL SOUND PRO
Explores the background and reasons behind the importance of the correctional officer.
From The View And Do Series.
LC NO. 73-700190
Prod-SCETV Dist-SCETV 1971

Official Rules Of Golf Explained, The C 35 MIN
1/2 IN VIDEO CASSETTE BETA/VHS
Explains the rules of golf, including unplayable lies, water hazards, lifting and dropping and movable and immovable obstructions. Gives tips on golf etiquette and shows highlights from championship events. With Tom Watson and Peter Alliss.
Prod-CARAVT Dist-CARAVT

Official Sports Films—A Series
J-C A
Prod-OSFS Dist-OSFS 1970

Basketball By The Rules 28 MIN

Official War Films B 30 MIN
3/4 OR 1/2 INCH VIDEO CASSETTE
Offers official War Films from the U S, 1934-44 including U S Marines at New Britain and Advance on Burma.
Prod-IHF Dist-IHF

Offset Taper - Side View Method, Openings Not Parallel C 35 MIN
1/2 IN VIDEO CASSETTE BETA/VHS IND
See series title for descriptive statement.
From The Metal Fabrication - Round Tapers Series.
Prod-RMI Dist-RMI

Offset Taper - Side View Rotational Subtraction Method, Openings Not Parallel C 32 MIN
1/2 IN VIDEO CASSETTE BETA/VHS IND
See series title for descriptive statement.
From The Metal Fabrication - Round Tapers Series.
Prod-RMI Dist-RMI

Offset Taper - Triangulation Plan View Method, Openings Parallel C 31 MIN
1/2 IN VIDEO CASSETTE BETA/VHS IND
See series title for descriptive statement.
From The Metal Fabrication - Round Tapers Series.
Prod-RMI Dist-RMI

Offshore C 18 MIN
3/4 INCH VIDEO CASSETTE
Narrates the story of the extensive search for offshore petroleum, which will become increasingly important to the world's energy supply. Describes the efforts being taken to preserve the environment while the search goes on.
Prod-EXXON Dist-MTP

Offshore - The Search For Oil And Gas C 18 MIN
16MM FILM OPTICAL SOUND
Describes the intensive search for petroleum supplies from the ocean. Describes the big equipment, big investment and big risks involved and discusses the efforts to preserve the ocean environment.
Prod-EXXON Dist-MTP

Offshore Crane Operation, Pt 1 C 34 MIN
3/4 OR 1/2 INCH VIDEO CASSETTE IND
Describes how offshore pedestal cranes work, how the operator determines load capacity and how the crane must be checked out prior to use. Comprises the first of a two-part section on offshore crane operation.
Prod-UTEXPE Dist-UTEXPE 1972

Offshore Crane Operation, Pt 2 C 21 MIN
3/4 OR 1/2 INCH VIDEO CASSETTE IND
Covers hoisting techniques, safety devices, rough-water techniques and proper handling of personnel nets. Comprises the second of a two-part section on offshore crane operation.
Prod-UTEXPE Dist-UTEXPE 1972

Offshore Oil - Are We Ready C 37 MIN
16MM FILM, 3/4 OR 1/2 IN VIDEO H-C A
Explores the impact that offshore oil discoveries have had on Stavanger, Norway and on Aberdeen and the Shetland Islands in Scotland, especially on fisheries.
Prod-NFBC Dist-NFBC 1981

Offshore Operations—A Series
IND
Covers main elements of offshore exploration and produc- tion of petroleum, usually from giant platforms set in deep water. Discusses working with offshore cranes, do's and don'ts of first tour offshore, terms and equipment, drill floor terms and equipment and Whittacker 50-man Escape Capsule.
Prod-GPCV Dist-GPCV

Drill Floor Terms And Equipment
Going Offshore For The First Time
Offshore Terms And Equipment
Whittacker 50-Man Escape Capsule
Working With Offshore Cranes

Offshore Rescue C 23 MIN
3/4 OR 1/2 INCH VIDEO CASSETTE
Follows the abandonment of an offshore oil installation by enclosed lifeboat and the successful evacuation of the lifeboat. Emphasizes how to get out of an enclosed lifeboat safely.
From The Offshore Safety Series.
Prod-FLMWST Dist-FLMWST

Offshore Rig Abandonment C 25 MIN
3/4 OR 1/2 INCH VIDEO CASSETTE IND
Provides an overview of the safety procedures, equipment and possible hazards involved in a rig abandonment.
Prod-UTEXPE Dist-UTEXPE 1970

Offshore Safety—A Series
Presents a series on offshore safety.
Prod-FLMWST Dist-FLMWST

Helicopter Operations 021 MIN
Offshore Rescue 023 MIN
Safe Diving 022 MIN

Offshore Terms And Equipment C
3/4 OR 1/2 INCH VIDEO CASSETTE IND
Presents a visual glossary of terms for offshore tasks and equipment. Details major rig work areas, job titles and general duties, basic drilling activities and equipment, basic crane activities, mud mixing and circulation terms and equipment, personal safety gear and basic hand tools in use offshore.
From The Offshore Operations Series.
Prod-GPCV Dist-GPCV

Ogden And Dorothy, Phyllis And Yip C 30 MIN
3/4 INCH VIDEO CASSETTE H-C A
Offers humorous poetry from the razor-sharp pens of Ogden Nash, Dorothy Parker, Phyllis Mc Ginley and lyricist Yip Harburg. Features Jack Lemmon and the First Poetry Quartet.
From The Anyone For Tennyson Series.
Prod-NETCHE Dist-GPITVL

Oh C 12 MIN
16MM FILM OPTICAL SOUND
Presents a haunting view of man through animation and graphics. Depicts mankind as falling down.
Prod-VANBKS Dist-VANBKS

Oh Brother, My Brother C 14 MIN
16MM FILM, 3/4 OR 1/2 IN VIDEO
Focuses on the love and affection of two young brothers, following the boys through a day of ordinary activity.
LC NO. 79-706878
Prod-LOWCAR Dist-PFP 1979

Oh Come, All Ye Faithful - Christmas C 14 MIN
3/4 OR 1/2 INCH VIDEO CASSETTE P-I
See series title for descriptive statement.
From The Ready, Sing Series.
Prod-ARKETV Dist-AITECH 1979

Oh Freedom C 26 MIN
16MM FILM, 3/4 OR 1/2 IN VIDEO
Traces the Black Civil Rights Movement from 1955 when a Black woman refused to give up her seat on a bus to a White man, to the cry for Black Power nearly a decade later. Explores the movement and its impact through the words of the people involved and through examination of the concept of Black Power.
From The New York Times - Arno Press Films On Black Americans Series.
Prod-NYT Dist-SF Prodn-REPRO 1970

Oh Happy Day C 23 MIN
16MM FILM OPTICAL SOUND
Features Ray Hildebrand and John Westbrook of the Fellowship of Christian Athletes displaying their comedy and musical repertoire in a high school assembly. John sings 'I BELIEVE' and Ray adds songs he has written, including the national pop hit 'MR BALLOON MAN.'
Prod-FELLCA Dist-FELLCA

Oh My Aching Back C 21 MIN
16MM FILM, 3/4 OR 1/2 IN VIDEO
Shows workmen the correct method of lifting, including good posture, position and smooth application of lifting power. Illustrates how strains occur and how discs are pinched. Emphasizes the need for proper lifting and handling of working tools and materials.
LC NO. 81-707201
Prod-USBM Dist-USNAC 1965

Oh My Aching Back C 30 MIN
3/4 OR 1/2 INCH VIDEO CASSETTE
Presents orthopedic specialist Dr Vert Mooney explaining ways to prevent back pains, and demonstrates exercises to strengthen the back. Offers tips on good posture.
From The Here's To Your Health Series.
Prod-KERA Dist-PBS 1979

Oh My Darling C 8 MIN
3/4 OR 1/2 INCH VIDEO CASSETTE H-C A
Tells the story of a girl growing up to womanhood and of the growing her family has to do to keep up with her. Animation and no narration.
Prod-CRAMAN Dist-MOKIN 1980

Oh No...Not Another Lab Test C 25 MIN
3/4 OR 1/2 INCH VIDEO CASSETTE A
Describes the reasons for and the processes involved in conducting hospital lab tests. Shows how blood tests are performed and analyzed, and observes medical technologists doing various tests to analyze body chemistry.
LC NO. 81-706191
Prod-CONTED Dist-CONTED 1980

Oh Shoelaces C 7 MIN
16MM FILM OPTICAL SOUND K-P
Provides the stimulus for learning the basic skill of typing shoelaces. Shows many and various types of shoes in the process of being tied by children and adults.
LC NO. 72-701244
Prod-FILMSM Dist-FILMSM 1971

Oh Susannah C 19 MIN
3/4 OR 1/2 INCH VIDEO CASSETTE P-I
Considers the elements of a folk song.
From The USS Rhythm Series.
Prod-ARKETV Dist-AITECH 1977

Oh Theatre, Pt 1 C 29 MIN
2 INCH VIDEOTAPE
See series title for descriptive statement.
From The University Of Chicago Round Table Series.
Prod-WTTWTV Dist-PUBTEL

Oh Theatre, Pt 2 C 29 MIN
2 INCH VIDEOTAPE
See series title for descriptive statement.
From The University Of Chicago Round Table Series.
Prod-WTTWTV Dist-PUBTEL

Oh What A Beautiful Morning B 7 MIN
16MM FILM OPTICAL SOUND
Contrasts the fantasies of luxury dreamed of by three wandering youths with the realities of unemployment and hunger which they face.
LC NO. 75-703212
Prod-USC Dist-USC 1967

Oh Yes, These Are Very Special Children C 20 MIN
16MM FILM OPTICAL SOUND J-C A
Uses an example of retarded children and their dancing teacher to show how much retarded children can learn if given the chance.
LC NO. 72-702321
Prod-CAMPF Dist-CAMPF 1971

Oh, For A Life Of Sensations C 22 MIN
16MM FILM, 3/4 OR 1/2 IN VIDEO C A
Shows educators using innovative techniques to involve students. Highlights a visiting poet and construction of a dome by students under an architect's supervision.
LC NO. 81-707279
Prod-KANLEW Dist-KANLEW 1981

Oh, Freedom - The Story Of The Civil Rights Movement C 28 MIN
16MM FILM OPTICAL SOUND J-H
Traces the Black Civil Rights Movement from 1955 when a Black woman refused to give up her seat on a bus to a White man, to the cry for Black Power nearly a decade later. Explores the movement and its impact through the words of the people involved, and through examination of the concept of Black Power.
LC NO. 76-701620
Prod-REPRO Dist-REPRO

Oh, I Saw A Fox C 14 MIN
3/4 OR 1/2 INCH VIDEO CASSETTE P
Demonstrates playing tone bells and singing with various accompaniments.
From The Stepping Into Rhythm Series.
Prod-WVIZTV Dist-AITECH

Oh, My Aching Back B 25 MIN
3/4 OR 1/2 INCH VIDEO CASSETTE
Discusses low back pain caused by faulty posture, arthritis and stress. Demonstrates body mechanics to relieve low back pain.
Prod-BU Dist-BU

Oh, My Aching Back C 30 MIN
3/4 OR 1/2 INCH VIDEO CASSETTE
See series title for descriptive statement.
From The Here's To Your Health Series.
Prod-PBS Dist-DELTAK

Oh, What A Knight C 4 MIN
16MM FILM, 3/4 OR 1/2 IN VIDEO A
Features the drawings of Dutch animator Paul Driessen.
Prod-CRAMAN Dist-MTOLP 1984

Oh, What A Zany Zoo C 10 MIN
3/4 OR 1/2 INCH VIDEO CASSETTE K-P
Presents a collection of fanciful animals.
From The Book, Look And Listen Series.
Prod-MDDE Dist-AITECH 1977

Ohio Heritage Film—A Series

Prod-CINE Dist-CINE

Agriculture In The Ohio Heritage, Pt 2	15 MIN
Ancient Man In The Ohio Heritage	15 MIN
Automobile In The Ohio Heritage, The	15 MIN
Heritage Of Agriculture	15 MIN
Heritage Of Architecture	15 MIN
Heritage Of Flight	15 MIN
Heritage Of The Lakes	15 MIN
Heritage Of The River, Pt 1	15 MIN
Heritage Of The River, Pt 2	15 MIN
Newspapers In The Ohio Heritage	15 MIN
Water Resources In The Ohio Heritage	15 MIN

Ohio River - Industry And Transportation C 16 MIN
16MM FILM, 3/4 OR 1/2 IN VIDEO J
Follows the Ohio River from Pittsburgh to Cairo, Illinois, showing the locks and dams that make the river navigable. Shows the many factories that have been built along the Ohio and discusses how they have contributed to the pollution of the river.
Prod-EVANSA Dist-PHENIX 1970

Ohm's Law C 9 MIN
16MM FILM, 3/4 OR 1/2 IN VIDEO H-C A
Discusses amperes, volts, ohms, the effect of resistance and resistors in a circuit.
From The Basic Electricity Series.
Prod-STFD Dist-IFB 1979

Ohm's Law B 21 MIN
16MM FILM - 3/4 IN VIDEO H-C
Explains current and voltage in relation to time, the relationship of current and voltage curves, the measurement of voltage at source, the addition of phase components and the effect of impedance on resonance.
LC NO. 78-706319
Prod-USA Dist-USNAC 1978

Ohm's Law And Power C
3/4 OR 1/2 INCH VIDEO CASSETTE
See series title for descriptive statement.
From The Basic Electricity - DC Series.
Prod-VTRI Dist-VTRI

Ohm's Law And Power C 30 MIN
3/4 OR 1/2 INCH VIDEO CASSETTE
Applies Ohm's law to predict voltage, current and resistance behavior in simple circuits. Allows calculation of resistive power loss through concept of power dissipation, plus mathematics of squares and square roots.
From The Basic Electricity And D.C. Circuits Series.
Prod-TXINLC Dist-TXINLC

Ohm's Law And Series Circuits C
3/4 OR 1/2 INCH VIDEO CASSETTE
See series title for descriptive statement.
From The Basic DC Circuits Series.
Prod-VTRI Dist-VTRI

Ohm's Law And Series Circuits (Including Building Circuits From Schematic Diagrams) C 15 MIN
3/4 OR 1/2 INCH VIDEO CASSETTE
See series title for descriptive statement.
From The Basic Electricity And D.C. Circuits, Laboratory Series.
Prod-TXINLC Dist-TXINLC

Ohmeter And Its Use, The C
3/4 OR 1/2 INCH VIDEO CASSETTE
See series title for descriptive statement.
From The Basic DC Circuits Series.
Prod-VTRI Dist-VTRI

Ohmeter And Its Use, The C 15 MIN
3/4 OR 1/2 INCH VIDEO CASSETTE
See series title for descriptive statement.
From The Basic Electricity And D.C. Circuits, Laboratory Series.
Prod-TXINLC Dist-TXINLC

Ohoyo - Indian Women Speak C 33 MIN
3/4 OR 1/2 INCH VIDEO CASSETTE
Features a panel of Indian women speaking to an assembly on the issue of sovereignty and the struggles to maintain and retain Indian life and traditions. Discusses such topics as equality, the non-Indian court system, adoption and activism.
Prod-VRL Dist-UWISC 1983

Oil - Finds For The Future C 25 MIN
3/4 OR 1/2 INCH VIDEO CASSETTE H-C
Shows the location of liquid crude oil reserves by digital seismic recording. Examines efforts to discover alternate fuel sources and increase yields from know wells. Describes method used to extract oil from shale. Looks at experiments to convert coal to methane.
Prod-BBCTV Dist-MEDIAG Prodn-OPENU 1985

Oil - From Fossil To Flame C 13 MIN
16MM FILM, 3/4 OR 1/2 IN VIDEO I-J
Provides a general description of the oil industry, including its geographic distribution, production and drilling, transportation, uses and economic importance.
Prod-CENTEF Dist-CORF 1976

Oil - From Fossil To Flame (Captioned) C 13 MIN
16MM FILM, 3/4 OR 1/2 IN VIDEO I-J
Provides a general description of the oil industry, including its geographic distribution, production and drilling, transportation, uses and economic importance.
Prod-CENTEF Dist-CORF 1976

Oil - The OPEC Case C 17 MIN
3/4 OR 1/2 INCH VIDEO CASSETTE H-C A
Focuses on the pledge of oil-consuming nations to reduce their oil imports, as well as the changes and modernization occurring within the exporting countries.
Prod-UPI Dist-JOU

Oil Age, The C 26 MIN
16MM FILM, 3/4 OR 1/2 IN VIDEO H-C
Tells how later twentieth century history is inextricably entwined with the history of oil. Examines oil, and its parallels with coal, from Kuwait in the 1920's through the crisis of 1974 to oil's shaky future.
From The Today's History Series.
Prod-JOU Dist-JOU 1984

Oil And American Power—A Series
16MM FILM, 3/4 OR 1/2 IN VIDEO H-C A
Details the history, geography and internal politics of the Middle Eastern countries. Emphasizes the importance of these countries to American security. Extracted from the NBC News White Paper entitled No More Vietnams, But.
Prod-NBC Dist-FI 1979

Egypt	016 MIN
Iran	022 MIN
Israel	013 MIN
Pressure Points - Oman, South	021 MIN
Saudi Arabia	018 MIN

Oil And Gas Production C 24 MIN
3/4 OR 1/2 INCH VIDEO CASSETTE IND
Covers the nature of oil and gas reservoirs and gives the sequence of events involved in producing and processing oil, gas and water from the reservoir to the pipeline.
Prod-UTEXPE Dist-UTEXPE 1974

Oil And Its Products C 14 MIN
16MM FILM, 3/4 OR 1/2 IN VIDEO I-C A
Tells how oil is formed, located, mined and refined into fuels and made into petrochemicals. Surveys the impact of petroleum in the 20th century and probes into the possible effects it may have on the future.
Prod-BAYERW Dist-PHENIX 1979

Oil And Its Products (Swedish) C 14 MIN
16MM FILM, 3/4 OR 1/2 IN VIDEO I-C A
Tells how oil is formed, located, mined and refined into fuels and made into petrochemicals. Surveys the impact of petroleum in the 20th century and probes into the possible effects it may have on the future.
Prod-BAYERW Dist-PHENIX 1979

Oil And The Overlive Society C 15 MIN
16MM FILM OPTICAL SOUND
Examines the ethical dilemma many scientists confront when accepting jobs in research from government and industry.
LC NO. 74-703745
Prod-UTORMC Dist-HRAW 1973

Oil But For One Day B 30 MIN
16MM FILM OPTICAL SOUND R
Theodore Bikel celebrates Hanukkah with drama and songs. (Kinescope)
Prod-JTS Dist-NAAJS Prodn-NBCTV 1959

Oil Country Tubular Goods - An Introduction C 25 MIN
16MM FILM, 3/4 OR 1/2 IN VIDEO IND
Explains in basic terms the need for casing and tubing in oil and gas wells. Discusses some of the factors necessary for the planning of good tubular strings.
Prod-HYDRIL Dist-UTEXPE 1980

Oil Driller C 30 MIN
1/2 IN VIDEO CASSETTE BETA/VHS
Describes the life of Steve Joiner, an oil driller who works on an oil rig 15 miles off the coast of Louisiana, in the Gulf of Mexico. Discusses the effects his work has on family relationships, as he works two weeks of every month, from noon to midnight.
From The American Professionals Series.
Prod-WTBS Dist-RMI

Oil Field Corrosion—A Series
IND
Discusses the principles of corrosion and its control.
Prod-UTEXPE Dist-UTEXPE

Consequences Of Change	025 MIN
Corrosion Measuring And Monitoring	025 MIN
Inspection Techniques	025 MIN
What Is Corrosion	025 MIN

Oil Field Electricity, Pt 1 C 22 MIN
3/4 OR 1/2 INCH VIDEO CASSETTE IND
Outlines the basic principles of electricity. Points out safe procedures that should be followed when working with electrical components on the lease.
Prod-UTEXPE Dist-UTEXPE 1983

Oil Films In Action C 18 MIN
16MM FILM OPTICAL SOUND H-C T
Shows how oil film pressures vary at different points around the circumference of a journal and proportionally with the load. Demonstrates that viscosity and journal speeds have no effect on oil film pressures. Illustrates the action of converging oil films.
Prod-GM Dist-GM 1951

Oil Films In Action C 20 MIN
3/4 OR 1/2 INCH VIDEO CASSETTE
Shows how oil films behave in bearings.
Prod-HBS Dist-IVCH

Oil Filter Story C 26 MIN
16MM FILM OPTICAL SOUND
Shows how oil filters are made and tested. Illustrates their significance to the operation of an automobile engine.
Prod-GM Dist-GM

Oil From The Great Land C 28 MIN
16MM FILM OPTICAL SOUND
Presents a progress report on the historic trans-Alaskan oil pipeline, the largest project ever undertaken by private enterprise.
LC NO. 76-703325
Prod-GUNNR Dist-STOILC 1975

Oil Gear Hydraulic Traversing Mechanism, Principles Of Operation, The B 22 MIN
16MM FILM OPTICAL SOUND
Shows how the oil gear traverse mechanism operates and the path and functioning of oil through an elevated mechanism.
LC NO. FIE52-1336
Prod-USA Dist-USNAC 1944

Oil In Libya C 15 MIN
16MM FILM, 3/4 OR 1/2 IN VIDEO P-C
A study of the oil industry and market in Tripoli, Libya. Includes the process of oil-drilling to the final loading of oil on tankers for transportation to foriegn markets.
From The Man And His World Series.
Prod-FI Dist-FI 1969

Oil On The River C 23 MIN
16MM FILM OPTICAL SOUND P-H
Documents problems of oil pollution on the Ohio River from 1865 to the present, describing various examples of pollution, their causes, and ways to prevent future occurrences. Explains that most manufacturers and oil handlers are assuming their responsibilities and that the careless general public is becoming the largest contributor to pollution.
Prod-ORVWSC Dist-FINLYS 1961

Oil Over The Andes C 27 MIN
16MM FILM OPTICAL SOUND

Focuses on oil exploration and discovery in the rain forests of Peru.
LC NO. 80-701250
Prod-OCCPC Dist-MTP Prodn-SAIF 1980

Oil Pollution Prevention Regulations C 18 MIN
3/4 OR 1/2 INCH VIDEO CASSETTE IND
Gives a general orientation to the scope of the Federal Water Pollution Control Act of 1972 and the Spill Prevention Control and Countermeasure (SPCC) plans required to comply with the act.
Prod-UTEXPE Dist-UTEXPE 1975

Oil Shale - The Rock That Burns C 29 MIN
16MM FILM OPTICAL SOUND
Asks if today's technology and pre-planning can prevent the feared consequences of strip mining. Considers the economic and environmental problems which would remain unsolved.
From The Energy Sources - A New Beginning Series.
Prod-UCOLO Dist-UCOLO

Oil Shales And Tar Sands C 36 MIN
3/4 OR 1/2 INCH VIDEO CASSETTE IND
See series title for descriptive statement.
From The Basic And Petroleum Geology For Non-Geologists - Hydrocarbons And...--Series.
Prod-PHILLP Dist-GPCV

Oil Strike B 15 MIN
16MM FILM OPTICAL SOUND
Presents oil workers in Northern California who strike Standard and Shell Oil Companies. Shows the companies response with goon squads. Includes scenes of students at San Francisco State College and U C Berkeley coming out and supporting the strike.
Prod-SFN Dist-SFN

Oil The Hard Way - An Introduction To Enhanced Recovery C 25 MIN
16MM FILM, 3/4 OR 1/2 IN VIDEO IND
Provides a nontechnical description of the reasons for and the basic mechanics of various secondary and tertiary recovery techniques.
Prod-UTEXPE Dist-UTEXPE 1979

Oil Well Drilling C
3/4 OR 1/2 INCH VIDEO CASSETTE
Visits a number of oil well drill sites showing the sequence of events from land acquisition and drilling to site reclamation and product transportation. Stresses the geologic aspects of a producing well and the uncertainty of exploration and production.
From The Field Trips in Environmental Geology - Technical And Mechanical Concerns Series.
Prod-KENTSU Dist-KENTSU

Oil-In-Water Emulsions - Formation And Stability, Pt 1 C 3 MIN
16MM FILM SILENT J-C A
Illustrates factors which influence structures in food. Demonstrates the preparation of typical temporary, semi-permanent and permanent emulsions and compares the stability of each type at specified intervals after emulsification.
From The Food And Nutrition Series.
LC NO. 70-710175
Prod-IOWA Dist-IOWA 1971

Oil-In-Water Emulsions - Formation And Stability, Pt 2 C 3 MIN
16MM FILM SILENT J-C A
Illustrates factors which influence structures in food. Demonstrates the preparation of typical temporary, semi-permanent and permanent emulsions and compares the stability of each type at specified intervals after emulsification.
From The Food And Nutrition Series.
LC NO. 70-710175
Prod-IOWA Dist-IOWA 1971

Oilwell C 11 MIN
16MM FILM OPTICAL SOUND
Presents a timely satire about man's self-destructive urge, using oilwells to portray pollution, mechanization and self-interest.
LC NO. 75-703213
Prod-USC Dist-USC 1960

Oilwell Blowouts - An Introduction C 25 MIN
16MM FILM, 3/4 OR 1/2 IN VIDEO IND
Covers the principles of kick detection and well control techniques in a basic manner.
Prod-HYDRIL Dist-UTEXPE 1976

Oisin C 17 MIN
16MM FILM, 3/4 OR 1/2 IN VIDEO I-C A
Records the images of trees, mountains, lakes, flowers and animals of Ireland.
Prod-AENGUS Dist-IFB 1973

Ojiisan B 9 MIN
16MM FILM OPTICAL SOUND H-C A
Shows how a young man comes to grips with his feelings as he stands a vigil over his grandfather who is dying in a hospital.
LC NO. 79-700125
Prod-USC Dist-USC 1979

Ojo Alerta C 15 MIN
16MM FILM, 3/4 OR 1/2 IN VIDEO K-P
A Spanish-language version of the motion picture One Little Indian. Portrays Magic Bow, a young boy on his first visit to the city who is mystified by the whirl of traffic until he learns some basic safety precautions.
Prod-NFBC Dist-IFB 1973

OK Classroom, The C 29 MIN
16MM FILM, 3/4 OR 1/2 IN VIDEO C
Introduces the techniques and terminology of transactional (TA) analysis explicated by Dr Thomas Harris, author of 'I'M OK, YOU'RE OK.' Discusses ta concepts with teachers and explains the special meaning of the terms 'PARENT,' 'CHILD,' 'ADULT,' 'TRANSACTION,' 'STROKES,' 'LIFE POSITIONS' and 'GAMES.'
From The Human Relations And School Discipline Series.
Prod-MFFD Dist-FI

Okies, The - Uprooted Farmers B 24 MIN
16MM FILM OPTICAL SOUND J A
Examines the plight of American farmers who were forced off their farms by drought and foreclosure during the 1930's. Based on the motion picture entitled The Grapes Of Wrath.
From The American Challenge Series.
LC NO. 75-703356
Prod-TWCF Dist-FI 1975

Okinawa C 22 MIN
16MM FILM OPTICAL SOUND
No descriptive material available.
Prod-NAMP Dist-NAMP 1972

Okinawa - At The Emperor's Doorstep C 30 MIN
3/4 OR 1/2 INCH VIDEO CASSETTE H-C A
See series title for descriptive statement.
From The World War II - GI Diary Series.
Prod-TIMLIF Dist-TIMLIF 1980

Oklahoma C 148 MIN
16MM FILM OPTICAL SOUND H-C A
Stars Gordon Mac Rae, Gloria Grahame and Shirley Jones in the Rodgers and Hammerstein musical classic Oklahoma. Includes the musical numbers Oh, What A Beautiful Morning, All Er Nuthin, People Will Say We're In Love and Oklahoma.
Prod-UNKNWN Dist-TWYMAN 1955

Oklahoma Forestry C 19 MIN
16MM FILM OPTICAL SOUND
Depicts sequences of Oklahoma's woodland areas and forest products industries. Stresses the importance of forestry in soil conservation, with particular emphasis on the value and technique of farm reforestration projects. Concludes with a discussion of the forest fire menace, spotlighting the work of the state division of forestry in combatting wood blazes.
Prod-UOKLA Dist-UOKLA 1950

Oklahoma Oasis C 15 MIN
16MM FILM - 3/4 IN VIDEO
Presents Chief Dan George, who talks about the natural beauty and history of Platt National Park in Oklahoma. Issued in 1974 as a motion picture.
LC NO. 79-706142
Prod-USNPS Dist-USNAC Prodn-MYERK 1979

Old Acquaintance B 110 MIN
16MM FILM OPTICAL SOUND
Stars Bette Davis and Miriam Hopkins as competing novelists who are also old friends.
Prod-UNKNWN Dist-UAE 1943

Old African Blasphemer, The C 55 MIN
16MM FILM, 3/4 OR 1/2 IN VIDEO
Depicts the horrors of a typical slave ship which crossed the Atlantic during the late 18th century.
From The Fight Against Slavery Series. No. 1
LC NO. 79-707648
Prod-BBCTV Dist-TIMLIF 1977

Old Age - Do Not Go Gentle, Pt 1 - Problems Of The Aged C 52 MIN
16MM FILM, 3/4 OR 1/2 IN VIDEO H-C
Looks at the daily lives of American senior citizens. Explores the effects of poverty, isolation, violent crime, and discrimination.
LC NO. 80-707523
Prod-KGOTV Dist-MTI 1978

Old Age - Do Not Go Gentle, Pt 2 - Alternate Solutions C 52 MIN
16MM FILM, 3/4 OR 1/2 IN VIDEO H-C
Investigates a variety of programs for old people in Europe. Points out that Americans should reconsider attitudes toward old age, reassess obligations to the elderly, and think more critically about how American serves their needs.
LC NO. 80-707489
Prod-KGOTV Dist-MTI 1978

Old Age - Out Of Sight Out Of Mind B 60 MIN
16MM FILM, 3/4 OR 1/2 IN VIDEO C A
Provides a documentary on the institutions and rehabilitation programs for the aged. Includes segments of the U S Senate subcommittee investigation of nursing homes. Shows Goldwater and Middletown hospitals in New York and an 'OLD-FOLKS' farm in Kentucky.
From The America's Crises Series.
Prod-NET Dist-IU 1968

Old Age - The Wasted Years B 60 MIN
16MM FILM OPTICAL SOUND C A
Discusses the problem of reduced income for the aged caused by retirement or unemployment. Contrasts living in the slums with that of luxury retirement. Provides interviews with senior citizens, government officials and social workers.
From The America's Crises Series.
LC NO. 72-709123
Prod-NET Dist-IU 1966

Old And New Investments C 25 MIN
3/4 OR 1/2 INCH VIDEO CASSETTE
Teaches how and why municipal bonds are good tax shelters.
From The Your Money Matters Series.
Prod-FILMID Dist-FILMID

Old Art For A New Science C 28 MIN
16MM FILM - 3/4 IN VIDEO
Demonstrates the process of designing and building a glass dewar or cryostat for Raman studies of crystals.
Prod-UTORMC Dist-UTORMC 1974

Old Astronomical Clock, The C 13 MIN
16MM FILM, 3/4 OR 1/2 IN VIDEO J-C A
Uses animation of the wood carvings of Jan Tippmann to dramatize the legendary creation of the astronomical clock on Prague's old town hall. Tells how upon completion of the clock, the town and its council were consumed with pride and selfish greed and set out to make certain that there would never be another clock like theirs.
Prod-KRATKY Dist-PHENIX 1978

Old Believers C 28 MIN
3/4 OR 1/2 INCH VIDEO CASSETTE
Explores the traditions and beliefs of 5000 members of an Old Believer community in Woodburn, Oregon. Focuses on the preparations for a wedding ceremony, the roles of men and women, the richness of the rituals and traditions and the beautiful costumes.
Prod-MEDIPR Dist-MEDIPR 1981

Old Box, An C 9 MIN
16MM FILM, 3/4 OR 1/2 IN VIDEO J-C A
Uses experimental animation to tell how an elderly man finds an old box in the trash. Reveals that when he paints it and pretends it is a music box, the box becomes a rainbow of colors and Christmas scenes.
Prod-NFBC Dist-NFBC 1976

Old Chief's Dance C 9 MIN
16MM FILM OPTICAL SOUND I-C
Depicts a Sioux Indian chief's own life story, especially his deeds of valor, told in dance form. Danced by Reginald and Gladys Laubin.
From The Plains Indian Culture Series.
Prod-UOKLA Dist-UOKLA 1951

Old Clothing And Textiles C 30 MIN
3/4 OR 1/2 INCH VIDEO CASSETTE
Presents guests who are experts in their respective fields who share tips on collecting and caring for old clothing and textiles.
From The Antique Shop Series.
Prod-WVPTTV Dist-MDCPB

Old Confederacy - New Direction C 28 MIN
3/4 INCH VIDEO CASSETTE
Looks at the 1973 elections in Atlanta, Georgia.
From The Interface Series.
Prod-WETATV Dist-PUBTEL

Old Corner Store Will Be Knocked Down By The Wreckers, The B 22 MIN
16MM FILM OPTICAL SOUND
Shows the destruction of a neighborhood area in Montreal, including a 70-year-old corner store, in order to make way for a new high rise complex.
LC NO. 74-703605
Prod-BRUCKJ Dist-CFDEVC

Old Delhi - New Delhi C 16 MIN
16MM FILM, 3/4 OR 1/2 IN VIDEO J-C
Contrasts the twin cities of Old Delhi, an ancient city, and New Delhi, a modern city constructed by the British.
Prod-COLSON Dist-MCFI 1975

Old Dog - New Tricks - The Coyote C 23 MIN
3/4 OR 1/2 INCH VIDEO CASSETTE K-C A
Focuses on the coyote, the one animal in North America which can adapt to anything man throws at him. Celebrates the wily coyote, an old dog who knows all the new tricks.
Prod-NWLDPR Dist-NWLDPR 1982

Old Economy Kunstfest C 57 MIN
2 INCH VIDEOTAPE
Presents a visit to the annual festival of the Harmony Society, a two-day crafts festival which goes through the village of Old Economy, Pennsylvania, for a review of history.
From The Festivals Of Pennsylvania Series.
Prod-WQED Dist-PUBTEL

Old English C 8 MIN
16MM FILM OPTICAL SOUND
Depicts the period of the Viking raids on Anglo-Saxon England. Shows a peasant, whose house has been destroyed by Vikings, being interviewed by the captain of a troop of Anglo-Saxon militiamen who have come to the rescue.
LC NO. 74-702754
Prod-QFB Dist-QFB Prodn-SDAPRO 1973

Old Enough To Care--A Series
H A
Portrays four characters and how they relate in a continuing story - a 75-year-old widow, an injured high school athlete, a poor, lonely retiree afraid of dying and a high school junior working for the first time outside her home. Seeks to eliminate stereotypes and myths about age groups, to encourage students to communicate with older people and sensitize them to the problems of aging by drawing parallels with their lives.
Prod-ETVCON Dist-AITECH

Alterations	015 MIN
Buried Treasures	015 MIN
Hello/Goodbye	015 MIN
Paper Slippers	015 MIN
Taking Stock	015 MIN
Third Wind	015 MIN

Old Enough To Do Time C 60 MIN
3/4 OR 1/2 INCH VIDEO CASSETTE
Examines the impact of 'get tough' juvenile justice policies across America. Explores the methods that different states employ to crack down on juvenile crime and looks at four alternative correctional programs.
Prod-WNETTV Dist-WNETTV

Old Fashioned Bread Baking In Rural Pennsylvannia B 13 MIN
16MM FILM SILENT J-C T
Mrs Yoder of Mifflin County, Pennsylvania, demonstrates essential steps and equipment in old-fashioned bread baking.
LC NO. 76-703215
Prod-PSU Dist-PSUPCR Prodn-MOOKMA 1966

Old Fashioned Deer Camp C 15 MIN
16MM FILM OPTICAL SOUND
Shows deer hunting in Michigan's Upper Peninsula, when hunters thought nothing of camping out among the hemlocks in zero weather.
Prod-SFI Dist-SFI

Old Flame, The C 29 MIN
2 INCH VIDEOTAPE
See series title for descriptive statement.
From The Observing Eye Series.
Prod-WGBHTV Dist-PUBTEL

Old Folks Are A-Okay C 15 MIN
16MM FILM, 3/4 OR 1/2 IN VIDEO P-J
Shows how Fat Albert and the gang learn that old people aren't weird and mean when they visit the house of old Mrs Bakewell on Halloween night and get treated to soda and cookies.
From The Fat Albert And The Cosby Kids Series III Series.
Prod-BARR Dist-BARR Prodn-FLMTON 1979

Old Friends - New Friends–A Series

Presents Fred Rogers, also known as MISTER ROGERS, hosting a series which spotlights people who have made a difference by being important to other people.
Prod-FAMCOM Dist-PBS 1981

Carradines, The	028 MIN
Edgar Tolson	028 MIN
Gerald Jampolsky	028 MIN
Helen Hayes And Millie Jewett	028 MIN
Henry John Heinz III	028 MIN
Hoagy	028 MIN
Interviewers, The	058 MIN
Lee Strasberg	028 MIN
Lorin Hollander	028 MIN
Melody	028 MIN
Memories	028 MIN
Michelle Knight And Kim Lemon	028 MIN
Nancy Acosta	028 MIN
Orville Harrison/Chris Chirdon	028 MIN
Padre	028 MIN
Ruth Ellen Patton Totten/Helen Ross	028 MIN
Uncle Miltie And The Whiz	028 MIN
Welcome	028 MIN
Willie Stargell	028 MIN

Old Globe, The - A Theatre Reborn C 30 MIN
3/4 OR 1/2 INCH VIDEO CASSETTE
Traces the Globe Theatre's history from its roots in Elizabethan England to its rebirth at the San Diego Exposition of 1935, through the fire of 1978 and gala reopening in 1982. Includes the World War II years when the Globe hosted Bob Hope, Bing Crosby and other entertainers of the troops stationed in Balboa Park and the post-war era when Craig Noel became artistic director and the first Shakespeare Festival was held.
Prod-KPBS Dist-KPBS

Old Glory B 28 MIN
16MM FILM - 3/4 IN VIDEO
Presents an historical account of the U S flag from the Jamestown English flag of 1607 to the 50-star flag of 1960.
Prod-USNAC Dist-USNAC 1960

Old Gold With Dennis James C 1 MIN
3/4 OR 1/2 INCH VIDEO CASSETTE
Shows a classic television commercial with a dancing cigarette pack.
Prod-BROOKC Dist-BROOKC

Old House, New House C 27 MIN
16MM FILM, 3/4 OR 1/2 IN VIDEO H-C A
Documents the renovation of Canada's Ecology House, a Victorian-era mansion, which now houses literature on energy conservation and natural resources and where lectures and tours are held. Includes animated sequences of various retrofitting procedures.
Prod-OMENGY Dist-FLMLIB 1981

Old Houseworks–A Series

Shows how the owner of an old house can plan and carry out the rehabilitation and preservation of a home. Demonstrates how to tackle such do-it-yourself projects as replacing a defective floor joist, glazing a sash, hanging a door and removing a partition.
Prod-MDCPB Dist-MDCPB

Old Is C 13 MIN
16MM FILM, 3/4 OR 1/2 IN VIDEO
Reveals the challenges, frustrations, pleasures and satisfactions of aging through the portraits of four vigorously active women and men in their seventies, eighties and nineties.
From The Aging In Our Times Series.
Prod-SF Dist-SF Prodn-REPRO 1978

Old King Log C 60 MIN
16MM FILM, 3/4 OR 1/2 IN VIDEO C A
Tells how Claudius dies knowing that Nero will end family rule violently, but certain that his epic history will make him immortal.
From The I, Claudius Series. Number 13
Prod-BBCTV Dist-FI 1977

Old Ladies Lost C 29 MIN
2 INCH VIDEOTAPE
See series title for descriptive statement.
From The Our Street Series.
Prod-MDCPB Dist-PUBTEL

Old Lady's Camping Trip C 10 MIN
3/4 OR 1/2 INCH VIDEO CASSETTE H-C A
Features an animated cartoon which stresses fire prevention and safety on camping trips, barbeques and simple outings.
Prod-NFBC Dist-FILCOM

Old Man C 8 MIN
16MM FILM OPTICAL SOUND
Portrays the last moments of an old man's life as he remembers his most beautiful dream, which is only to be fulfilled in his death.
LC NO. 76-703144
Prod-JANOWJ Dist-JANOWJ 1976

Old Man And Outdoor Cooking C 15 MIN
16MM FILM, 3/4 OR 1/2 IN VIDEO J-C A
Uses a humorous story to tell viewers about outdoor cooking grills and outdoor cookery.
Prod-KLEINW Dist-KLEINW 1978

Old Man And The Gun, The C 58 MIN
1/2 IN VIDEO CASSETTE BETA/VHS
Examines the conflict in Ireland through the eyes of Irish-Americans who support the Irish Republican Army and its strategy of violence. Follows Michael Flannery through his day as the Grand Marshal of New York City's Saint Patrick's Day Parade, then travels back to Ireland to the spot where Flannery participated in an ambush on British troops some 50 years ago.
From The Frontline Series.
Prod-DOCCON Dist-PBS

Old Man And The Lake, The C 19 MIN
16MM FILM OPTICAL SOUND
Tells how an old man takes his grandson fishing at a lake on Ottawa Silica Company property and explains how, many years ago, he actually mined silica sand at the bottom of the lake.
LC NO. 79-701444
Prod-OTTASC Dist-IPHC Prodn-IPHC 1979

Old Man And The Paragraph, The C 5 MIN
3/4 OR 1/2 INCH VIDEO CASSETTE J-H
Shows how to develop paragraphs through the use of comparison.
From The Write On, Set 2 Series.
Prod-CTI Dist-CTI

Old Man And The Rose, The C 5 MIN
16MM FILM OPTICAL SOUND J-C A
Portrays an old man's admiration for a rose, based on Donald Bisset's poem 'THE ROSE AND THE MAN.'
LC NO. 73-702555
Prod-LONWTV Dist-MMA 1973

Old Man And The Sea, The, Pt 1 C 30 MIN
2 INCH VIDEOTAPE J-H
Presents the novel THE OLD MAN AND THE SEA by Ernest Hemingway.
From The From Franklin To Frost - Ernest Hemingway Series.
Prod-MPATI Dist-GPITVL

Old Man And The Sea, The, Pt 2 - The Tragic Affirmation C 30 MIN
2 INCH VIDEOTAPE J-H
Presents the novel THE OLD MAN AND THE SEA by Ernest Hemingway.
From The From Franklin To Frost - Ernest Hemingway Series.
Prod-MPATI Dist-GPITVL

Old Man In A Hurry B 25 MIN
1/2 IN VIDEO CASSETTE BETA/VHS
Tells the life story of Bion Shively, the oldest man to win the Hambletonian Trotting Classic.
Prod-USTROT Dist-EQVDL

Old Man Stone B 30 MIN
16MM FILM OPTICAL SOUND
Tells the story of old man stone, an immigrant druggist in a Detroit slum, who fought juvenile delinquency by having faith in individual boys and girls. (Kinescope)
Prod-JTS Dist-NAAJS Prodn-NBCTV 1956

Old Man Tucker C 30 MIN
3/4 OR 1/2 INCH VIDEO CASSETTE H-C A
Shows how to master various banjo fingering exercises and presents the song Old Man Tucker.
From The Bluegrass Banjo (Level One) Series.
Prod-OWL Dist-GPITVL 1980

Old Man's Story, The (Junior Version) C 25 MIN
16MM FILM, 3/4 OR 1/2 IN VIDEO P-I
Describes how a boy's idyllic life on a New Zealand farm is disrupted by a tragic chain of events. Based on the short story The Old Man's Story by Frank Sargeson.
Prod-GFILM Dist-MTI 1979

Old Man's Story, The (Senior Version) C 25 MIN
16MM FILM, 3/4 OR 1/2 IN VIDEO J-C
Describes how a boy's idyllic life on a New Zealand farm is disrupted by a tragic chain of events. Based on the short story The Old Man's Story by Frank Sargeson.
LC NO. 80-707501
Prod-GFILM Dist-MTI 1979

Old Mill, The C 9 MIN
16MM FILM, 3/4 OR 1/2 IN VIDEO I-H A
Pictures a night in the life of an old mill during a storm, showing how the moods created by the storm frighten the animals who occupy the mill.
Prod-DISNEY Dist-WDEMCO 1971

Old Oregon Trail, The - 1928 Classic B 39 MIN
16MM FILM SILENT I A
Offers a 'classic Western' made in the John Day River country in 1928. Shown only at a preview and never circulated, a print was discovered in 1978 and given to the Oregon Historical Society. Stars Art Mix, brother of Tom Mix, and assorted local folks.
Prod-OREGHS Dist-OREGHS

Old People B 32 MIN
16MM FILM OPTICAL SOUND
Presents a debate on the problems of senior citizens in Denmark.
Prod-RDCG Dist-AUDPLN

Old People And The New Politics C 30 MIN
3/4 INCH VIDEO CASSETTE
See series title for descriptive statement.
From The Growing Old In Modern America Series.
Prod-UWASHP Dist-UWASHP

Old San Francisco B 26 MIN
16MM FILM OPTICAL SOUND I T
Presents Delores Costello and Warner Oland in the motion picture production Old San Francisco. Tells the story of the boss of San Francisco's Chinatown underworld plots whose dastardly efforts are foiled by the 1906 earthquake.
From The History Of The Motion Picture Series.
Prod-SF Dist-KILLIS 1970

Old Sheepdog, The C 10 MIN
16MM FILM, 3/4 OR 1/2 IN VIDEO P-I
Tells the story of an old sheepdog who is supplanted by a new, young dog in his duties of guarding his master's sheep, but who proves his worth and trust when the wolf comes.
Prod-UILL Dist-AIMS 1973

Old Skills Alive C 17 MIN
3/4 OR 1/2 INCH VIDEO CASSETTE
Reports on the many ancient skills and crafts kept alive by a handful of skilled artisans. Includes demonstrations of lace-making, hand bookbinding, glass blowing and silversmithing.
Prod-UPI Dist-JOU

Old Soldier, The - A Biography Of Douglas Mac Arthur B 15 MIN
16MM FILM OPTICAL SOUND
Presents the life and times of Douglas Mac Arthur.
From The Screen News Digest Series. Vol 6, Issue 10
LC NO. FIA68-2084
Prod-HEARST Dist-HEARST 1964

Old Speak For Themselves, The B 30 MIN
16MM FILM OPTICAL SOUND C
Shows people of widely different life styles as they discuss their children, money, sex, health, living with infirmities and death, in order to illustrate the rewards and problems of growing old.
From The Growth And Development, The Adult Years Series.
LC NO. 78-706818
Prod-VDONUR Dist-AJN Prodn-WTTWTV 1969

Old Testament Scriptures–A Series
P A
Prod-CONCOR Dist-CPH 1959

Abraham, Man Of Faith	17 MIN
David, A Young Hero	17 MIN
David, King Of Israel	17 MIN
Elijah, A Fearless Prophet	17 MIN
Gideon, The Liberator	17 MIN
Jacob, Bearer Of The Promise	17 MIN
Joseph, Ruler Of Egypt	17 MIN
Joseph, The Young Man	17 MIN
Joshua, The Conqueror	17 MIN
Moses, Called By God	17 MIN
Moses, Leader Of God's People	17 MIN
Ruth, A Faithful Woman	17 MIN
Samuel, A Dedicated Man	17 MIN
Solomon, A Man Of Wisdom	17 MIN

Old Time Music C 60 MIN
3/4 INCH VIDEO CASSETTE
See series title for descriptive statement.
From The Grass Roots Series.
Prod-MDCPB Dist-MDCPB

Old Treasures From New China C 55 MIN
16MM FILM, 3/4 OR 1/2 IN VIDEO H-C A
Portrays China's evolution from primitive society through the Yuan dynasty by telling the story of its technological and artistic achievements and its contributions to world civilization. Shows selections from the 1975 archaeological exhibit from the People's Republic of China.
Prod-UCEMC Dist-UCEMC 1977

Old Woman In A Shoe - Beginning Number Concepts (2nd Ed) C 9 MIN
16MM FILM, 3/4 OR 1/2 IN VIDEO K-P
Uses the nursery rhyme about the old lady in the shoe to introduce primary number concepts.
Prod-CORF Dist-CORF 1980

Old Woman, The C 2 MIN
16MM FILM, 3/4 OR 1/2 IN VIDEO J-C A
Presents a confrontation between an old woman and Death, in the form of a skeleton. Shows, in animated style, how the unwelcome visitor leaves when he sees how much work the woman still has to do.
Prod-ACI Dist-AIMS 1973

Old World, New World C 52 MIN
16MM FILM, 3/4 OR 1/2 IN VIDEO J-C A
Describes how sixteen million immigrants arrived through Ellis Island after enduring the incredible hardships of transatlantic voyages and meeting the conditions necessary to leave their

countries and enter America. Historical film footage and interviews describe the promise of freedom and opportunity in a new world.
From The Destination America Series.
Prod-THAMES Dist-MEDIAG 1976

Old Yeller C 28 MIN
16MM FILM, 3/4 OR 1/2 IN VIDEO P-J
Edited from the Disney film Old Yeller, based on the book of the same title by Fred Gipson. Tells the story of two young brothers and a stray dog, Old Yeller, who risks his life to save the boys.
From The Film As Literature, Series 2 Series.
Prod-DISNEY Dist-WDEMCO Prodn-WDEMCO 1979

Old-Fashioned Christmas, An B 20 MIN
2 INCH VIDEOTAPE P-I
Deals with appreciation of hand-crafted toys and decorations of long ago.
From The Art Adventures Series.
Prod-CVETVC Dist-GPITVL Prodn-WCVETV

Old, Black And Alive - Some Contrasts In Aging C 27 MIN
16MM FILM OPTICAL SOUND J-C A
Uses a variety of interviews with aging blacks in order to show the different ways in which blacks adapt to the aging process.
LC NO. 74-702146
Prod-NEWFLM Dist-NEWFLM 1974

Old, Old Tales B 15 MIN
2 INCH VIDEOTAPE P
See series title for descriptive statement.
From The Children's Literature Series. No. 15
Prod-NCET Dist-GPITVL Prodn-KUONTV

Olde English C 19 MIN
3/4 OR 1/2 INCH VIDEO CASSETTE
Shows the different perspectives students, teachers and administrators have about common experiences and situations in an urban New England high school. Explains how each of these groups has developed defenses, values and strategies. Issued in 1974 as a motion picture.
From The Social Seminar Series.
LC NO. 80-707360
Prod-NIMH Dist-USNAC 1980

Olden Days Coat, The C 30 MIN
16MM FILM, 3/4 OR 1/2 IN VIDEO I-J A
Tells the story of Sal who anticipates being bored when she must spend Christmas with her grandmother. Shows her discovering an old blue coat in a trunk which magically transports her back in time. Based on the book The Olden Days Coat by Margaret Laurence.
LC NO. 81-707526
Prod-ATLAP Dist-LCOA

Olden Days Coat, The (Captioned) C 30 MIN
16MM FILM, 3/4 OR 1/2 IN VIDEO P-H A
Tells how a little girl's Christmas holiday is disrupted when her parents decide to spend Christmas at Grandmother's house.
Prod-ATLAP Dist-LCOA 1981

Older And Bolder C 14 MIN
3/4 INCH VIDEO CASSETTE
Examines the experience of aging. Shows a group of older women who meet weekly to talk, laugh and share problems.
Prod-WGBHTV Dist-EDC

Older And Newer Neighborhoods C 15 MIN
3/4 OR 1/2 INCH VIDEO CASSETTE P
Compares older and newer neighborhoods.
From The Neighborhoods Series.
Prod-NEITV Dist-GPITVL 1981

Older But Wiser - The Case Of The Disputed Promotion C 23 MIN
16MM FILM, 3/4 OR 1/2 IN VIDEO
Tells the story of an employee at a tire manufacturing plant who lost out on a promotion to a junior employee. Asks whether a company can use different standards in evaluating the qualifications of job applicants and whether a company will be subject to criticism when it allows a supervisor to provide informal training to an ambitious worker.
Prod-AARA Dist-AARA 1982

Older People C 28 MIN
3/4 INCH VIDEO CASSETTE J-C A
Presents a group of senior citizens talking about ways to keep on living and growing in a country that worships youth. Discusses the need to be in contact with younger people, social security problems, senior citizen centers as political power bases, and mandatory retirement.
From The Are You Listening Series.
LC NO. 80-707148
Prod-STURTM Dist-STURTM 1976

Older Person In The Family, The C 30 MIN
3/4 INCH VIDEO CASSETTE
See series title for descriptive statement.
From The Growing Old In Modern America Series.
Prod-UWASHP Dist-UWASHP

Oldest Game, The C 28 MIN
16MM FILM OPTICAL SOUND
Concerns the pursuit of America's most common and most sought after big game animal–the whitetail deer.
Prod-SFI Dist-SFI

Oldies - 1962 C
16MM FILM OPTICAL SOUND
Presents the 1962 America's Cup races.
Prod-OFFSHR Dist-OFFSHR

Oldies - 1964 C
16MM FILM OPTICAL SOUND
Consists of footage of the 1964 America's Cup races.
Prod-OFFSHR Dist-OFFSHR

Oldies - 1967 C
16MM FILM OPTICAL SOUND
Consists of footage of the 1967 America's Cup races.
Prod-OFFSHR Dist-OFFSHR

Oldies - 1970 C
16MM FILM OPTICAL SOUND
Consists of footage from the 1970 America's Cup races.
Prod-OFFSHR Dist-OFFSHR

Ole Eyemo Sees The Truth C 13 MIN
16MM FILM, 3/4 OR 1/2 IN VIDEO I-J
Explores the real world that lies behind outward appearances, telling the story of a boy with a painted third eye which comes magically alive and allows him unusual insights into himself and others.
Prod-CALLFM Dist-BARR 1976

Ole Eyemo Sees The Truth (Spanish) C 13 MIN
16MM FILM - VIDEO, ALL FORMATS K-I
Tells the story of a boy who paints a third eye on his forehead, and it magically becomes alive and sees the truth.
Prod-CALLFM Dist-BARR

Oleo Strut Servicing - (ITP Practical Project Series) C 15 MIN
3/4 OR 1/2 INCH VIDEO CASSETTE IND
Gives complete rundown of servicing procedures for oleo struts. Includes complete breakdown of strut components and a description of general operating theory of the air-oil shock strut.
From The Aviation Technician Training Program Series.
Prod-AVIMA Dist-AVIMA 1980

Olga - A Film Portrait B 47 MIN
16MM FILM, 3/4 OR 1/2 IN VIDEO J-C A
Presents a biographical study of Russian gymnast Olga Korbut. Illustrates the special training received by Russian gymnasts.
Prod-GRATV Dist-CAROUF

Oligopolies - Whatever Happened To Price Competition C 30 MIN
3/4 OR 1/2 INCH VIDEO CASSETTE C
See series title for descriptive statement.
From The Economics USA Series.
Prod-WEFA Dist-ANNCPB

Oliver C 145 MIN
16MM FILM OPTICAL SOUND
Presents a musical adaptation of Charles Dickens' novel OLIVER TWIST.
Prod-CPC Dist-TIMLIF 1968

Oliver Twist B 77 MIN
16MM FILM SILENT
Presents the story of Oliver Twist and the nefarious Fagin. Based on the novel OLIVER TWIST by Charles Dickens. Stars Jackie Coogan and Lon Chaney.
Prod-COOGAN Dist-BHAWK 1922

Oliver Wendell Holmes Jr B 20 MIN
2 INCH VIDEOTAPE I
See series title for descriptive statement.
From The Americans All Series.
Prod-DENVPS Dist-GPITVL Prodn-KRMATV

Ollero Yucateco (Yucatan Potter) C 25 MIN
16MM FILM OPTICAL SOUND
Demonstrates the technique of Mayan pottery making, traces the evolution of this ceramic tradition and illustrates an experimental design by which archeologists and ethnographers hope to increase their knowledge.
LC NO. FIA66-503
Prod-UIMPPC Dist-UILL 1965

Olly Olly Oxen Free C 89 MIN
3/4 OR 1/2 INCH VIDEO CASSETTE
Describes how Miss Pudd, an eccentric junkyard owner helps young Alby celebrate his late grandfather's birthday by flying the circus balloon his grandfather used to fly. Stars Katherine Hepburn and Dennis Dimster.
Prod-TIMLIF Dist-TIMLIF 1982

Olympia - Diving Sequence B 4 MIN
16MM FILM, 3/4 OR 1/2 IN VIDEO H-C A
Features the diving sequence in the classic film documentary, Olympia by Leni Riefenstahl of the 1936 Olympic Games in Berlin.
Prod-RIEFSL Dist-PHENIX

Olympia - Marathon Sequence B 13 MIN
16MM FILM, 3/4 OR 1/2 IN VIDEO H-C A
Features the marathon sequence in the classic film documentary, Olympia by Leni Riefenstahl of the 1936 Olympic Games in Berlin.
Prod-RIEFSL Dist-PHENIX

Olympia I And II B 212 MIN
16MM FILM, 3/4 OR 1/2 IN VIDEO H-C A
Presents the classic film documentary by Leni Riefenstahl of the 1936 Olympic Games in Berlin.
Prod-RIEFSL Dist-PHENIX

Olympia, Part 1 (Festival Of The People) B 112 MIN
3/4 OR 1/2 INCH VIDEO CASSETTE
Presents the 1936 Olympics held in Berlin, the capital of the third Reich, Berlin. Directed by Leni Riefenstahl, with music by Herbert Windt.
Prod-IHF Dist-IHF

Olympia, Part 2 (Festival Of Beauty) B 91 MIN
3/4 OR 1/2 INCH VIDEO CASSETTE
Presents the 1936 Olympics held in Berlin, the capital of the third Reich. Directed by Leni Riefenstahl, with music by Herbert Windt.
Prod-IHF Dist-IHF

Olympia, Pt 1 B 115 MIN
16MM FILM, 3/4 OR 1/2 IN VIDEO H-C A
Presents part one of Leni Riefenstahl's original filming of the 1936 Olympic Games in Berlin.
Prod-RIEFSL Dist-PHENIX

Olympia, Pt 2 B 97 MIN
16MM FILM, 3/4 OR 1/2 IN VIDEO H-C A
Presents part two of Leni Riefenstahl's original filming of the 1936 Olympic Games in Berlin.
Prod-RIEFSL Dist-PHENIX

Olympiad C 3 MIN
16MM FILM OPTICAL SOUND
Presents figures of computer-stylized athletes in brilliant hues chasing each other across the screen.
Prod-LILYAN Dist-LILYAN

Olympic Cavalcade C 15 MIN
3/4 OR 1/2 INCH VIDEO CASSETTE
Highlights the history of the Olympic games from their beginnings in 776 BC.
From The Screen News Digest Series.
Prod-HEARST Dist-HEARST

Olympic Champ C 8 MIN
16MM FILM, 3/4 OR 1/2 IN VIDEO
Presents an animated cartoon in which Goofy leads a comical history of the Olympics.
Prod-DISNEY Dist-WDEMCO 1979

Olympic Coins C 8 MIN
16MM FILM OPTICAL SOUND
Presents Canada's designers and makers of coins as they practice the skills that produce valuable and lasting mementos of events in history.
LC NO. 76-702457
Prod-CEAEAO Dist-CEAEAO Prodn-CRAF 1975

Olympic Elk C 26 MIN
16MM FILM, 3/4 OR 1/2 IN VIDEO I-C A
Follows the spring migration of elk into the high mountains where they mate and stay until the autumn snows come.
Prod-DISNEY Dist-WDEMCO 1956

Olympic Elk, The (French) C 26 MIN
16MM FILM, 3/4 OR 1/2 IN VIDEO I-H
Documents the Olympic elk's annual trek through Washington wilderness areas.
Prod-WDEMCO Dist-WDEMCO 1956

Olympic Elk, The (Spanish) C 26 MIN
16MM FILM, 3/4 OR 1/2 IN VIDEO I-H
Documents the Olympic elk's annual trek through Washington wilderness areas.
Prod-WDEMCO Dist-WDEMCO 1956

Olympic Elk, The (Swedish) C 26 MIN
16MM FILM, 3/4 OR 1/2 IN VIDEO I-H
Documents the Olympic elk's annual trek through Washington wilderness areas.
Prod-WDEMCO Dist-WDEMCO 1956

Olympic Fragments C 10 MIN
3/4 OR 1/2 INCH VIDEO CASSETTE
Records performances of athletes at the Olympics held at Lake Placid, New York.
Prod-EAI Dist-EAI

Olympic Fragments C 12 MIN
3/4 OR 1/2 INCH VIDEO CASSETTE
Comments on the normal media appraisal of sport. Emphasizes the skill, beauty and joy of kineticism.
Prod-KITCHN Dist-KITCHN

Olympic Rain Forest C 11 MIN
16MM FILM OPTICAL SOUND I-C A
Locates and explains the rain forest of Olympic National Park. Explains the role of rotting logs, lichens, mosses and animals in the life cycle of the forest.
Prod-PFC Dist-PFC 1956

Olympic Sailing C 54 MIN
1/2 IN VIDEO CASSETTE BETA/VHS
Features Olympic sailing. Combines the shorter titles Kingston Olympiad and Kiel Olympiad.
Prod-OFFSHR Dist-OFFSHR

Olympic Skates And Skis C 14 MIN
1 INCH VIDEOTAPE
Reviews the Tenth Winter Olympic Games at Grenoble, France, highlighting skiing and skating events and medal winner Peggy Fleming. Shows scenery, opening and closing ceremonies.
Prod-AMDAS Dist-MTP

Olympic Sports C 3 MIN
16MM FILM OPTICAL SOUND
Uses the kinestasis technique to present photographs of Olympic athletes.
LC NO. 80-701251
Prod-GUSD Dist-GUSD 1980

Olympic Wilderness Encounters C 23 MIN
16MM FILM, 3/4 OR 1/2 IN VIDEO
Features backpackers and area residents commenting on their feelings towards the Olympic National Park in northwestern Washington.

LC NO. 81-706314
Prod-USNPS Dist-USNAC Prodn-HAYPRO 1981

Olympics - The Eternal Torch C 27 MIN
16MM FILM, 3/4 OR 1/2 IN VIDEO H-C A
Traces the history of modern Olympic Games with footage dating back to their revival in 1896. Discusses the ideals of sportsmanship in the quadrennial Games.
Prod-ASPRSS Dist-AIMS 1973

Olympics Of Racing, The C 14 MIN
16MM FILM OPTICAL SOUND
Presents thoroughbred racing at Gulfstream Park, Florida.
Prod-FLADC Dist-FLADC

Olympics Of The Mind C 29 MIN
3/4 OR 1/2 INCH VIDEO CASSETTE H-C A
Presents host Bill Moyers examining an extracurricular school program called Olympics of the mind. Shows how a competition of mental games can illustrate that creative thought can be taught in schools.
From The Creativity With Bill Moyers Series.
LC NO. 83-706165
Prod-CORPEL Dist-PBS 1982

Olympics, The - Images Of Gold C 24 MIN
3/4 OR 1/2 INCH VIDEO CASSETTE
Focuses on track and field, swimming and gymnastics as well as the dedication young athletes exhibit necessary to compete in the most prestigious amateur sporting events.
Prod-KAROL Dist-KAROL

Om Ma Ni Pad Me Hum - Filling Space To Benefit Things C 28 MIN
16MM FILM OPTICAL SOUND
Shows a Bhutanese monk preaching the teachings of Buddha, offering prayers and repeating the mantra of Chenrezi, patron saint of Tibet.
LC NO. 77-700303
Prod-INFIN Dist-CANCIN 1976

Om Ma Ni Pad Me Hum - Filling Space To Benefit Things (Tibetan) C 28 MIN
16MM FILM OPTICAL SOUND
Shows a Bhutanese monk preaching the teachings of Buddha, offering prayers and repeating the mantra of Chenrezi, patron saint of Tibet.
LC NO. 77-700303
Prod-INFIN Dist-CANCIN 1976

Oman C 28 MIN
3/4 INCH VIDEOTAPE
Interviews Sheikh Farid Mbarak Ali Al-Hinai, Ambassador of Oman to the United States. Hosted by Marilyn Perry.
From The International Byline Series.
Prod-PERRYM Dist-PERRYM

Omega C 13 MIN
16MM FILM, 3/4 OR 1/2 IN VIDEO P-C A
Deals with the end of mankind on earth, emphasizing rebirth rather than death. Uses special effects to prophesy man's liberation from his earthly bounds in order to roam the universe at will, implying man's faith and idealism. Renders into visual imagery the complex philosophical concept of the filmmaker. Stimulates thought and discussion.
Prod-FOXD Dist-PFP 1970

Omega Long-Range Navigation System - AN/SRN-12 Receiver Operation C 17 MIN
16MM FILM OPTICAL SOUND
Shows the use of the AN/SRN-12 receiver in the Omega long-range navigation program.
LC NO. 74-706547
Prod-USN Dist-USNAC 1970

Omega Long-Range Navigation System, The C 18 MIN
16MM FILM OPTICAL SOUND
Shows a worldwide long-range navigation system that is simple and dependable under all weather conditions. Shows how to use the AN/SRN-2 receiver.
LC NO. 74-706512
Prod-USN Dist-USNAC 1970

Omelette Show C 30 MIN
3/4 OR 1/2 INCH VIDEO CASSETTE H-C
Julia Child shows how make an omelette in 30 seconds, and how to serve it for breakfast, lunch, supper or as a flaming desert.
From The French Chef Series.
Prod-WGBH Dist-KINGFT

Omelette Show, The (French) C 29 MIN
2 INCH VIDEOTAPE
Features Julia Child of Haute Cuisine au Vin demonstrating how to prepare an omelette. With captions.
From The French Chef (French) Series.
Prod-WGBHTV Dist-PUBTEL

Omnivac's Troubles Add Up - Addition Of Hundreds C 15 MIN
3/4 OR 1/2 INCH VIDEO CASSETTE I
Tells how Mac and Alice attempt to repair the world computer. Explains addition with and without regrouping of digits.
From The Figure Out Series.
Prod-MAETEL Dist-AITECH 1982

Omowale - The Child Returns Home B 30 MIN
16MM FILM OPTICAL SOUND H-C A
Discusses negro novelist John William's trip to Africa to explore his ancestral roots. Studies the relationship of the American Negro to the African. Presents an interview with James Meredith. Discusses the 'BACK TO AFRICA' movement. Features Ossie Davis.
From The History Of The Negro People Series.
LC NO. FIA66-825
Prod-NET Dist-IU 1965

On A Clear Day You Could See Boston C 52 MIN
16MM FILM, 3/4 OR 1/2 IN VIDEO J-C A
Relates that by 1900 one-third of the population of Ireland, which lost more of its people to the United States than any other single country, had emigrated to America. They were fleeing the famine and became the first immigrant group who achieved a political foothold, especially in Boston.
From The Destination America Series.
Prod-THAMES Dist-MEDIAG 1976

On A Perdu Nicolas B 13 MIN
16MM FILM OPTICAL SOUND J-H
See series title for descriptive statement.
From The En France Avec Nicolas Series. Set I, Lesson 3
Prod-PEREN Dist-CHLTN 1968

On A Perdu Nicolas, Student Exercises C 8 MIN
16MM FILM OPTICAL SOUND J-H
See series title for descriptive statement.
From The En France Avec Nicolas Series. Set II, Lesson 3
Prod-PEREN Dist-CHLTN 1968

On A String C 8 MIN
16MM FILM, 3/4 OR 1/2 IN VIDEO K-I
Presents a story about a father, mother and son. Tells how the father and son get the idea of using a clothes line as a springboard for flying.
Prod-CZECFM Dist-PHENIX 1974

On American Soil C 28 MIN
16MM FILM OPTICAL SOUND J-C A
Looks at why farmers are ignoring methods for preventing soil erosion even though they have been known since the 1930s and threaten America's status as the world's most agriculturally-productive nation in the world.
LC NO. 83-700321
Prod-CONSF Dist-CONSF 1983

On American Soil C 28 MIN
16MM FILM, 3/4 OR 1/2 IN VIDEO J-C A
Discusses the nature and extent of the soil erosion problem in America today.
Prod-BULFRG Dist-BULFRG

On And About Instruction—A Series
T
Deals with aspects of classroom instruction. Incorporates on-site visits to classrooms, interviews with prominent educators, classroom parodies, excerpts from workshops and skits.
Prod-VADE Dist-GPITVL 1983

Buying Hardware	030 MIN
Buying Software	030 MIN
Classroom Management Skills	030 MIN
Microcomputers For Instruction	030 MIN
Middle School, The	030 MIN
Role Of Department Chairpersons	030 MIN
Shaping Curriculum	030 MIN
Shaping Instruction	030 MIN
Shaping The Classroom	030 MIN
Teacher Stress, Pt 1	030 MIN
Teacher Stress, Pt 2	030 MIN
Teaching And Testing For Results	030 MIN
Teaching Styles	030 MIN
Teaching To Objectives, Pt 1	030 MIN
Teaching To Objectives, Pt 2	030 MIN
Videotape-Disc-Or...?	030 MIN
Volunteerism	030 MIN

On Any Street C 30 MIN
16MM FILM, 3/4 OR 1/2 IN VIDEO H-C A
Looks at the complex life of police work. Documents the fears, frustrations, pressures and rewards experienced by actual officers on the job while illustrating the difficulties in a constantly changing environment.
LC NO. 84-706162
Prod-LAPD Dist-MTI 1983

On Becoming A Nurse-Psychotherapist C 42 MIN
16MM FILM, 3/4 OR 1/2 IN VIDEO J-C A
A dramatized case study of the experience of a young nursing student as she learns to assume the role of nurse-psychotherapist. Follows her first case and shows the development of two parallel relationships, nurse with patient and nurse with instructor.
Prod-UCSNUR Dist-UCEMC 1970

On Being An Effective Parent - Thomas Gordon C 45 MIN
16MM FILM OPTICAL SOUND C A
Explains the basics of the parent effectiveness training movement. Shows that such things as discussion and role playing help to explain the technique of 'ACTIVE LISTENING.' Deals with the 'NO LOSE' method of conflict resolution, the core of P E T.
LC NO. 73-703071
Prod-KETCTV Dist-AACD 1973

On Being Human C 30 MIN
3/4 OR 1/2 INCH VIDEO CASSETTE C
See series title for descriptive statement.
From The In Our Own Image Series.
Prod-DALCCD Dist-DALCCD

On Being Sexual C 22 MIN
16MM FILM, 3/4 OR 1/2 IN VIDEO C A
Features a discussion between parents and professionals about sexuality and the mentally retarded. Emphasizes that the mentally retarded are sexual beings.
Prod-SLARC Dist-STNFLD Prodn-MEDAWR 1975

On Black America C 30 MIN
3/4 OR 1/2 INCH VIDEO CASSETTE J-C A
Presents James Farmer, founder of the Congress of Racial Equality and Director of Public Policy Training Institute, talking about Black America.
From The Moral Values In Contemporary Society Series.
Prod-AMHUMA Dist-AMHUMA

On Borrowed Time - Living With Heart Disease C 50 MIN
16MM FILM, 3/4 OR 1/2 IN VIDEO H-C
Discusses the role of diet, smoking, exercise and other factors implicated in coronary illness. Describes diagnostic techniques which allow doctors to find out what is happening inside the heart and arteries.
LC NO. 80-707524
Prod-BBINC Dist-MTI 1980

On Camera 1960-61—A Series

Prod-GSUSA Dist-GSUSA

Close Ups	13 MIN
Men In Her Life, The	14 MIN
Simply Exhibiting	13 MIN

On Camera—A Series
H-C A
Presents instruction on the use of film and video, from the same training material used by the BBC. Intended for those involved in program production for the first time, and for professionals involved in training program makers. Includes an accompanying set of notes for each title in the series.
Prod-BBCTV Dist-FI 1984

Camera, The	035 MIN
Editing	059 MIN
Interviews	022 MIN
Planning A Program	018 MIN

On Death And Dying C 58 MIN
16MM FILM, 3/4 OR 1/2 IN VIDEO H-C A
Presents Dr Elizabeth Kubler-Ross discussing her experiences in helping the terminally ill face death.
Prod-NBCNEW Dist-FI 1974

On Every Hand C 10 MIN
16MM FILM, 3/4 OR 1/2 IN VIDEO J-H
Informs students how to escape serious hand injury from commonly used but potentially dangerous equipment such as shearing devices, fans, drills and presses. Concludes with a poignant reminder of the importance of our hands. Produced in conjunction with the National Safety Council.
Prod-NSC Dist-JOU Prodn-ALTSUL 1970

On Every Hand (Captioned) C 10 MIN
16MM FILM, 3/4 OR 1/2 IN VIDEO J-H
Informs students how to escape serious hand injury from commonly used but potentially dangerous equipment such as shearing devices, fans, grills and presses. Concludes with a poignant remainder of the importance of our hands. Produced in conjunction with the National Safety Council.
Prod-NSC Dist-JOU Prodn-ALTSUL 1970

On Giant's Shoulders C 92 MIN
3/4 OR 1/2 INCH VIDEO CASSETTE J-C A
Presents Terry Wiles, a thalidomide-damaged child who was adopted by Leonard and Hazel Wiles after they overcame their initial fears. Shows how Leonard's considerable talents at invention resulted in devices that made Terry's life much more pleasant and mobile while Hazel spent her time teaching Terry to fend for himself.
Prod-BBCTV Dist-FI 1982

On Golden Pond C
1/2 IN VIDEO CASSETTE BETA/VHS
Features Henry Fonda and Katharine Hepburn in Academy Award-winning performances as an older couple grappling with their own mortality and their family's emotional distance.
Prod-GA Dist-GA

On Guard C 14 MIN
16MM FILM OPTICAL SOUND
Outlines the benefits of Thiokol polysulfide base sealants and caulking materials.
Prod-THIOKL Dist-THIOKL 1971

On Guard C 28 MIN
3/4 OR 1/2 INCH VIDEO CASSETTE J A
Illustrates schemes that are used to defraud the public.
Prod-SUTHRB Dist-SUTHRB

On Guard C 51 MIN
3/4 INCH VIDEOTAPE
Depicts four women conspiring to sabotage the research program of a multinational firm engaged in reproductive engineering. Raises the issue of the ethical debate over biotechnology as a potential threat to women and their rights to self-determination.
Prod-REDHP Dist-WMEN

On Guard - Bunco C 26 MIN
16MM FILM, 3/4 OR 1/2 IN VIDEO H A
Informs the audience about those subtle criminals who prey upon the unwary through fraudulent schemes.
Prod-AIMS Dist-AIMS 1970

On Guard - Bunco C 26 MIN
3/4 OR 1/2 INCH VIDEO CASSETTE
Alerts and informs the public about the various methods and the con games criminals use to prey upon the unwary.
Prod-LACFU Dist-IA

On Guard - Bunco (Spanish) C 26 MIN
16MM FILM, 3/4 OR 1/2 IN VIDEO J-C A
Dramatizes various schemes used by criminals and con men to defraud the public.
Prod-CAHILL Dist-AIMS Prodn-LAC 1971

On Halloween C 20 MIN
3/4 OR 1/2 INCH VIDEO CASSETTE P-I
Contrasts major and minor tonalities.
From The USS Rhythm Series.
Prod-ARKETV Dist-AITECH 1977

On Key C 30 MIN
16MM FILM, 3/4 OR 1/2 IN VIDEO H-C A
Explores the possibility of becoming too successful in business.
From The Enterprise Series.
Prod-MTI Dist-MTI

On Key C 30 MIN
3/4 OR 1/2 INCH VIDEO CASSETTE H-C A
Features the small business of Ned Steinberger, which has a single product - an innovative electric bass guitar. Tells how the business is perhaps too successful.
From The Enterprise III Series.
Prod-WGBHTV Dist-KINGFT

On Loan From Russia - Forty-One French Masterpieces C 30 MIN
16MM FILM OPTICAL SOUND J-C A
Documents the exhibition entitled 'IMPRESSIONIST AND POST-IMPRESSIONIST PAINTING FROM THE USSR' which was held at the national gallery of art in 1973. Shows behind-the-scenes preparations for the exhibit and provides historical background on the paintings, which were selected from the Hermitage and Pushkin Museums.
LC NO. 73-702241
Prod-WNETTV Dist-USNGA 1973

On Location C 30 MIN
3/4 OR 1/2 INCH VIDEO CASSETTE C
See series title for descriptive statement.
From The In Our Own Image Series.
Prod-DALCCD Dist-DALCCD

On Location - Night Of The Iguana B 26 MIN
16MM FILM OPTICAL SOUND
Features Director John Huston describing on-location filming of the motion picture 'NIGHT OF THE IGUANA,' near the Mexican village of Puerto Vallarta. Shows the building of the set and demonstrates how day and night scenes are shot.
From The Hollywood And The Stars Series.
LC NO. FI68-193
Prod-WOLPER Dist-WOLPER 1964

On Location With Rolf Harris C 28 MIN
16MM FILM OPTICAL SOUND
Highlights the making of the film Rolf Harris In Tasmania.
LC NO. 80-700914
Prod-TASCOR Dist-TASCOR 1976

On Making A Thumb - One Hundred Years Of Surgical Effort C 45 MIN
3/4 OR 1/2 INCH VIDEO CASSETTE PRO
Discusses the principles and methods for providing a prime thumb-like digit.
Prod-ASSH Dist-ASSH

On Merit C 23 MIN
16MM FILM, 3/4 OR 1/2 IN VIDEO J-C A
Investigates the Federal Government's commitment to the merit system and its effect on the employment and promotion of women and minorities.
Prod-USCSC Dist-GREAVW Prodn-GREAVW 1975

On Metals And Men C 24 MIN
16MM FILM, 3/4 OR 1/2 IN VIDEO
Develops and evaluates an inorganic chemistry classification based on such characteristics of metals as compound forming tendencies, difficulty of extraction and ability to be oxidized.
Prod-OPENU Dist-MEDIAG Prodn-BBCTV 1982

On My Own, Feeling Proud C 15 MIN
16MM FILM OPTICAL SOUND
Shows the process of preparing handicapped people, especially young people, for vocations. Includes a three part process of appraisal, education and placement accompanied by a musical theme.
Prod-MILPRO Dist-MILPRO

On Our Own C 29 MIN
16MM FILM, 3/4 OR 1/2 IN VIDEO A
Explores the development of responsibility in children through the dramatization of a situation in the fictional Tristan family, in which young Paul learns that he must give as well as receive. Includes a brief introduction and commentary by real-life families and child development experts.
From The Footsteps Series.
LC NO. 80-707200
Prod-USDED Dist-USNAC Prodn-EDFCEN 1980

On Our Way C 60 MIN
16MM FILM OPTICAL SOUND H-C A
From The World At War Series.
LC NO. 76-701778
Prod-THAMES Dist-USCAN 1975

On Our Way - U S A, 1939-1942 C 52 MIN
16MM FILM, 3/4 OR 1/2 IN VIDEO H-C A
States that when Roosevelt declared war on Japan, Hitler declared war on the United States, relieving the President of many of the domestic political difficulties he faced, such as rationing, blackouts and the internment of Japanese-Americans as security risks.
From The World At War Series.
Prod-THAMES Dist-MEDIAG 1973

On Parade (2nd Ed) C 18 MIN
16MM FILM OPTICAL SOUND
Describes the reflections of a young WAC on her growth as a result of her military training and experiences since joining the Women's Army Corps.
LC NO. 74-706164
Prod-USA Dist-USNAC 1969

On Post Safety B 22 MIN
16MM FILM OPTICAL SOUND
Analyzes the causes of common accidents in the armed forces, re-creating typical accidents in which carelessness of the individual soldier was the cause.
LC NO. FIE52-2200
Prod-USA Dist-USNAC 1952

On Responsibility C 40 MIN
3/4 OR 1/2 INCH VIDEO CASSETTE IND
Shows Sheldon Samuels of the AFL-CIO talking about ethical considerations in the management of an industrial society, including the responsibilities of individuals and organizations.
From The Safety, Health, and Loss Control - Managing Effective Programs Series.
LC NO. 81-706521
Prod-AMCEE Dist-AMCEE 1980

On Seeing Film - Film And Literature B 17 MIN
16MM FILM OPTICAL SOUND
Made from footage filmed behind the scenes in Ceylon during production of the academy-winning film, The Bridge on the River Kwai.
LC NO. FIA60-619
Prod-USC Dist-USC 1957

On Seven Hills They Built A City (Rome) C 26 MIN
16MM FILM, 3/4 OR 1/2 IN VIDEO H-C A
Presents the diversity of the people and places of Rome.
From The Village Life Series.
Prod-JOU Dist-JOU 1978

On Silent Wings C 16 MIN
16MM FILM, 3/4 OR 1/2 IN VIDEO P-H
Depicts the appearance, feeding habits and adaptability of the owl. Discloses the predatory skills of this commonly unobserved species.
From The North American Species Series.
Prod-KARVF Dist-BCNFL 1984

On Snow White C 51 MIN
16MM FILM, 3/4 OR 1/2 IN VIDEO I-J
Presents the story of Katka, who spins girlish fantasies about being carried off by a prince on a white horse. Tells how she must drop out of a school play of Snow White when she falls and breaks her leg while riding with Jerry, a handsome horseman. Shows that, while she can no longer prepare for the play, she has finally caught Jerry's attention and enjoys a visit by the entire cast in costume.
From The Featurettes For Children Series.
Prod-AUDBRF Dist-FI

On Special B 14 MIN
16MM FILM OPTICAL SOUND
Presents a comedy of errors made on almost no money at all.
LC NO. 74-702404
Prod-QUAF Dist-QUEENU 1973

On Stage C 15 MIN
3/4 OR 1/2 INCH VIDEO CASSETTE P
See series title for descriptive statement.
From The Strawberry Square Series.
Prod-NEITV Dist-AITECH 1982

On Stage B 20 MIN
2 INCH VIDEOTAPE P
Deals with writing a play and presenting it. (Broadcast quality)
From The Language Lane Series. Lesson 27
Prod-CVETVC Dist-GPITVL Prodn-WCVETV

On Stage And Screen C 10 MIN
16MM FILM, 3/4 OR 1/2 IN VIDEO P-I
Shows one boy acting in The Wizard Of Oz and another who creates his own films.
From The Zoom Series.
Prod-WGBHTV Dist-FI

On Strike C 30 MIN
16MM FILM OPTICAL SOUND
Presents an in-depth study on the people and the issues behind the country's longest student strike and how it relates nationally.
Prod-NEWSR Dist-NEWSR

On Strike - San Francisco State B 23 MIN
16MM FILM OPTICAL SOUND
Studies the people and issues behind the nation's longest student strike. Examines the real nature of the BSU and Third World demands.
Prod-SFN Dist-SFN

On Target B 22 MIN
16MM FILM OPTICAL SOUND
Portrays the exciting story of the Strategic Air Command's annual bombing, navigational and reconnaisance competition from the viewpoint of a B-47 crew member.
LC NO. FIE58-325
Prod-USDD Dist-USNAC 1958

On Target C 66 MIN
16MM FILM OPTICAL SOUND
Depicts Columbus aircraft division products and activities.
Prod-NAA Dist-RCKWL

On Target C 21 MIN
3/4 OR 1/2 INCH VIDEO CASSETTE
Documents the USMC F-4s flying mission out of Danang, South Vietnam.
Prod-IHF Dist-IHF

On Television - The Violence Factor C 58 MIN
3/4 OR 1/2 INCH VIDEO CASSETTE H-C A
Examines television as a powerful tool of commerce, reviews the findings of numerous scientific studies and Congressional hearings from the last 30 years and compares gratuitous violence to violence used in appropriate context. Explores the possible relationship between TV violence and an increase in real-life crime and the influence of TV violence on children. Shows both positive and negative impacts of TV.
Prod-SCETV Dist-FI

On The Air B 22 MIN
16MM FILM OPTICAL SOUND
Tells how radio DJ Barry Roberts tires of his 'on the air' persona and seeks to reveal his real self in a nightclub act. Shows how Barry and some of his most devoted fans find out who they are.
Prod-USC Dist-USC 1980

On The Beach B
3/4 OR 1/2 INCH VIDEO CASSETTE
Deals with the devastating effects of nuclear war. Stars Gregory Peck, Ava Gardner, Fred Astaire and Anthony Perkins.
Prod-IHF Dist-IHF

On The Border Of Life B 20 MIN
16MM FILM OPTICAL SOUND
Presents glimpses of French biological research on the embryonic cell. Reviews the structure and function of the cell, ovum, spermatozoon, chromosome and gene. Uses experiments in the use of sexual hormones to raise the question of whether man's dream for immortality will be realized.
Prod-VEDROS Dist-RADIM

On The Boulevard C 28 MIN
16MM FILM, 3/4 OR 1/2 IN VIDEO A
Examines the relationship between romance and economics. Portrays a fictional couple seeking artistic success in Hollywood. Filmed in Hollywood by Gregory Andracke, with Lawrence Hilton-Jacobs and Gloria Charles in the title roles. Written by Pamela Douglas and Martin Yarbuongh, who adapted it from an article in a Los Angeles newspaper. Encourages an examination of male-female relationships in a success-oriented society.
Prod-BRNSTC Dist-CHAMBA

On The Boulevard C 29 MIN
3/4 OR 1/2 INCH VIDEO CASSETTE
Documents the Independent Owner-Operator Trucker, the modern successor to the Cowboy of the wild west as symbol of fierce American individualism.
Prod-OPTIC Dist-EAI

On The Brink C 29 MIN
16MM FILM, 3/4 OR 1/2 IN VIDEO A
Examines child abuse through the dramatization of a situation in the fictional Tristero family, in which Ann Marie helps a friend who is an abusing parent. Points out that both the parent and the child are victims in child abuse. Includes a brief introduction and commentary by real-life families and child development experts.
From The Footsteps Series.
LC NO. 80-707201
Prod-USDED Dist-USNAC Prodn-EDFCEN 1980

On The Brink - Child Abuse C 23 MIN
16MM FILM - VIDEO, ALL FORMATS
Tells about sources of help for abusing parents. Shows how abusing parents are usually reacting to stress in their own lives.
From The Footsteps Series.
Prod-PEREN Dist-PEREN

On The Bus C 30 MIN
3/4 OR 1/2 INCH VIDEO CASSETTE C
See series title for descriptive statement.
From The Art Of Being Human Series. Module 14
Prod-MDCC Dist-MDCC

On The Cowboy Trail C 58 MIN
3/4 OR 1/2 INCH VIDEO CASSETTE
Shows a visit to a ranch in Montana to examine how modern technology and ranching methods are changing the role of the American cowboy.
From The Odyssey Series.
Prod-PBA Dist-PBS

On The Downbeat C 29 MIN
3/4 OR 1/2 INCH VIDEO CASSETTE J-C A
Reviews the history of jazz in Indiana from the beginnings of ragtime at the turn of the century, through the big-band era of the thirties to the flourishing bebop following World War II and to current forms.
LC NO. 84-706389
Prod-DERKDA Dist-IU 1983

On The Edge C 90 MIN
3/4 OR 1/2 INCH VIDEO CASSETTE
Follows a foursome of black, inner-city teenagers who, after minor brushes with the law, are trying to make decisions about jobs, careers, school, family, street life and themselves.
Prod-WCCOTV Dist-WCCOTV 1982

On The Edge Of Paradise C 60 MIN
3/4 OR 1/2 INCH VIDEO CASSETTE H-C A
Looks at how the future of the Caribbean is being threatened by such factors as hurricanes and volcanoes, while man hacks out banana farms, denuding the jungles, mangrove swamps become marinas and coral reefs fall victim to pollution.
Prod-WNETTV Dist-FI 1982

On The Edge Of The Forest C 32 MIN
16MM FILM, 3/4 OR 1/2 IN VIDEO
Presents author, lecturer and economist E F Schumacher's views on forests, fuel, mankind and all of Earth's resources.
LC NO. 82-707175
Prod-OLDMB Dist-BULFRG 1979

On The Eighth Day C 60 MIN
3/4 OR 1/2 INCH VIDEO CASSETTE J-C A
Considers the effects of global nuclear war beyond radioactivity. Shows how scientists tested a model of the earth's atmosphere to discover that the temperatures would fall to below freezing for months. Discusses the possible destruction caused by this nuclear winter.
Prod-BBCTV Dist-FI

On The Fifth Day C 30 MIN
16MM FILM OPTICAL SOUND
Traces horses from pre-historic times to the beginning of the quarter horse breed in the new world.
Prod-AQHORS Dist-AQHORS

On The Floor C 10 MIN
2 INCH VIDEOTAPE
See series title for descriptive statement.
From The Janaki Series.
Prod-WGBHTV Dist-PUBTEL

On The Ground C 15 MIN
16MM FILM, 3/4 OR 1/2 IN VIDEO I-H
Looks at small invertebrates, such as slugs and woodlice, which live under stones, dead wood or litter. Includes other life forms which live at ground level, such as toadstools and ground beetles.
From The Place To Live Series.
Prod-GRATV Dist-JOU

On The Island Of Taveuni C 17 MIN
16MM FILM OPTICAL SOUND I-C
Provides a visit to a copra plantation, located on Taveuni, one of the Fiji Islands. Shows the production and processing of copra and coconuts. Depicts the life of the planters and native and East Indian workers on the prosperous plantation.
From The South Pacific Series.
Prod-MMP Dist-MMP 1958

On The Job C 19 MIN
3/4 OR 1/2 INCH VIDEO CASSETTE H
Tells how Sandy has a hard time at her first job on a dockyard welding crew and how another employee helps her out.
From The Jobs - Seeking, Funding, Keeping Series.
Prod-MSDOE Dist-AITECH 1980

On The Level–A Series
J-H
Dramatizes common concerns of teenagers and encourages active participation in growing toward a more mature understanding of the whole self.
Prod-AITV Dist-AITECH 1980

Alternate Route - Thinking	015 MIN
Behind The Scenes - Accepting Feelings	015 MIN
Daddy's Girl - Changing Family Relationships	015 MIN
Face To Face - Dealing With Conflict	015 MIN
Getting Together - Love	015 MIN
Journey Through Stress - Coping With Stress	015 MIN
Little Help From My Friends, A - Friendship	015 MIN
Side By Side - Prejudice	015 MIN
Solo - Alone Versus Lonely	015 MIN
Surrounded - Peer Group Membership	015 MIN
What Next - Career Aspirations	015 MIN
Who Am I - Developing Self-Concept	015 MIN

On The Line C 13 MIN
16MM FILM OPTICAL SOUND A
Tells the story of a factory worker who resists going for a health checkup because of a great fear that he might have cancer. Shows that his gradual turnabout is climaxed when a representative of the American Cancer Society speaks to the plant's employees urging them to have regular checkups. Features James Broderick and all-pro football star, Jack Pardee.
Prod-AMCS Dist-AMCS

On The Line C 37 MIN
3/4 OR 1/2 INCH VIDEO CASSETTE
Follows the actual experiences of four American workers who visited a Japanese factory, immersed themselves in its day-to-day life, and intensively examined its methods and operations. Portrays their reactions and discoveries, showing why they returned to their jobs in the States determined to work smarter and with greater pride.
Prod-KINGA Dist-KINGA

On The Line C 50 MIN
16MM FILM, 3/4 OR 1/2 IN VIDEO A
Examines contemporary problems of the American economy. Discusses how these problems affect the lives of people and their communities.
Prod-CNEMAG Dist-CNEMAG 1977

On The Mines B 13 MIN
16MM FILM OPTICAL SOUND H-C A
Explores the world of the South African mines in order to bring an understanding and appreciation of what it means to labor in the mines of South Africa.
LC NO. 76-703920
Prod-BFPS Dist-BFPS 1976

On The Money–A Series

Explores personal and family money management and provides common-sense insights into the world of finance and economics.
Prod-WGBHTV Dist-MTI

All Things Beautiful	030 MIN
Baby Makes Three	030 MIN
Bills, Bills, Bills	030 MIN
Give And Take	030 MIN
Home Sweet Home	030 MIN
Investments - They're Debatable	030 MIN
Just In Case	030 MIN
More Precious Than Gold	030 MIN
On Your Own	030 MIN
Risky Business	030 MIN
Smart Money	030 MIN
Starting Small	030 MIN
Taking Stock	030 MIN

On The Move C 19 MIN
16MM FILM OPTICAL SOUND
Presents a profile of the 4-H movement, depicting various 4-H projects, communications programs, camp and special activities, and support services.
LC NO. 79-701472
Prod-ADAIB Dist-CENTWO Prodn-CENTWO 1979

On The Move C 28 MIN
16MM FILM, 3/4 OR 1/2 IN VIDEO
Explains many aspects of packaging and shipping radioactive materials, including the extreme concern for safety in normal and accident environments. Emphasizes the package testing program for highly radioactive materials and shows the accident environment that accident-resistant packages are designed to protect against.
Prod-USAEC Dist-USNAC Prodn-SANDIA 1974

On The Move - Careers In Transportation C 13 MIN
16MM FILM OPTICAL SOUND I-H
Explores the variety of careers available in transportation.
From The Working Worlds Series.
LC NO. 75-701537
Prod-OLYMPS Dist-FFORIN 1974

On The Night Stage B 100 MIN
16MM FILM SILENT
Stars William S Hart as a soft-hearted bandit who is tamed by a dance-hall girl.
Prod-UNKNWN Dist-KITPAR 1915

On The Nose C 13 MIN
16MM FILM, 3/4 OR 1/2 IN VIDEO P-I
Employs animation to show how odor molecules released into the air enter the nose and are picked up by smell receptors that carry the information to the brain.
From The Human Senses Series.
LC NO. 82-706608
Prod-NGS Dist-NGS 1982

On The Open Sea C 30 MIN
1/2 IN VIDEO CASSETTE BETA/VHS
Explains how to use weight and balance to control boat direction and speed. Focuses upon navigation.
From The Under Sail Series.
Prod-WGBHTV Dist-MTI

On The Path To Self-Reliance C 45 MIN
3/4 INCH VIDEO CASSETTE
Presents an overview of Seminole tribal history and current economic development. Through their cattle operation, agriculture and aguaculture programs and bingo enterprises, the Seminoles are becoming self-sufficient as well as maintaining their cultural identity. Also available in two-inch quad and one-inch videotape.
Prod-SEMNL Dist-NAMPBC

On The Right Course C 21 MIN
16MM FILM, 3/4 OR 1/2 IN VIDEO C A
Shows how a British company attempts to rectify management problems by identifying participation skills needed by their managers and providing training in those skills. Examines the changes that managers may need to make in their ways of managing in order to develop a different approach toward working together.
From The Practical Participation Series.
Prod-MILLBK Dist-IFB

On The Road C 15 MIN
3/4 OR 1/2 INCH VIDEO CASSETTE P
Depicts a young boy selecting a bicycle and practicing stops, signals and turns before he drives in street traffic.
From The It's Your Move Series.
Prod-WETN Dist-AITECH 1977

On The Road - In The City C 25 MIN
16MM FILM OPTICAL SOUND H A
Shows city driving situations and discusses proper turning procedures, parking, route alterations, accidents, driver illness, and night driving.
Prod-VISUCP Dist-VISUCP

On The Road - In The Country C 26 MIN
16MM FILM OPTICAL SOUND H A
Discusses rural driving, focusing on blocked roads, passenger illness, bus breakdown, railroad hazards, convoy driving and freeway driving.
Prod-VISUCP Dist-VISUCP

On The Road To Find Out C 70 MIN
16MM FILM OPTICAL SOUND
Explores the day-to-day experiences of five Boston teenagers to help reveal their attitudes about their lives, their futures and the people around them.
From The Time Of Youth Series.
LC NO. 73-700898
Prod-WCVBTV Dist-WCVBTV 1973

On The Road With Duke Ellington C 55 MIN
16MM FILM, 3/4 OR 1/2 IN VIDEO
An informal study of American composer-conductormusician Duke Ellington. Follows him during a performance, on tour and in moments of relaxation as he reminisces about his family and background.
From The Bell Telephone Hour Series.
Prod-NBCTV Dist-DIRECT 1967

On The Rocks C 29 MIN
16MM FILM, 3/4 OR 1/2 IN VIDEO J-C A
Offers a lighthearted perspective on rock gymnastics, the sport which applies the natural grace and rhythm of gymnastics to the art of rock climbing. Reveals the motivation and climbing methods of some of the world's best climbers. Filmed during climbs in California, Colorado and Wyoming.
Prod-PFP Dist-PFP

On The Roof (French) C 15 MIN
3/4 OR 1/2 INCH VIDEO CASSETTE H-C A
Involves a chief electrician and a chimney repairman.
From The En Francais Series. Part 2 - Temporal Relationships, Logical Relationships
Prod-MOFAFR Dist-AITECH 1970

On The Run C 22 MIN
16MM FILM, 3/4 OR 1/2 IN VIDEO J-C A
Presents running trainer Arthur Lydiard and the world competition runners who use his program as they comment about long-distance mountain running and its resulting increase in their stamina and the pleasures of roaming over the varied terrain. Features scenes of New Zealand.
Prod-EVRARD Dist-PFP Prodn-TITANF 1980

On The Run C 27 MIN
16MM FILM, 3/4 OR 1/2 IN VIDEO
Examines the reasons why kids run away. Presents actual runaways who provide insights into the situations that caused them to leave home and what they expected to find elsewhere. Shows youth facilities designed to help young people cope with life on the run.
Prod-MCBRID Dist-MTI

On The Run C 55 MIN
3/4 OR 1/2 INCH VIDEO CASSETTE H-C A
Looks at the issue of runaway children in our society. Features encounters with more than a dozen runaways, who are usually female, trying to escape an abusive home situation. From the Moore Report Series.
Prod-WCCOTV Dist-IU 1983

On The Safe Side C 20 MIN
16MM FILM OPTICAL SOUND
Outlines the necessary precautions and uses the message as an easily remembered word to cover the sequences that must be followed to make apparatus safe in a high voltage research environment.
Prod-UKAEA Dist-UKAEA 1967

On The Scent C 24 MIN
16MM FILM, 3/4 OR 1/2 IN VIDEO
Discusses the biosynthesis of terpenes, proposing the route by which they are thought by organic chemists to be incorporated into living systems, and testing that hypothesis.
Prod-OPENU Dist-MEDIAG Prodn-BBCTV 1982

On The Seven Seas C 22 MIN
16MM FILM OPTICAL SOUND
Describes the world-wide exchange of goods which make shipping an all-important factor in international trade and commerce. Shows the importance of Danish shipping for the economy of the country.
Prod-RDCG Dist-AUDPLN

On The Seventh Day B 20 MIN
16MM FILM OPTICAL SOUND I-C T
Shows a Jewish family preparing for and celebrating their Sabbath.
Prod-NYU Dist-NYU 1962

On The Seventh Day She Wore It C 15 MIN
2 INCH VIDEOTAPE
See series title for descriptive statement.
From The Umbrella Series.
Prod-KETCTV Dist-PUBTEL

On The Shoals C 15 MIN
1/2 IN VIDEO CASSETTE BETA/VHS I-J
Focuses on an electrical failure, which leaves the Mimi in danger of running aground in the shallow waters of George's Shoals, calling upon the crew to save the voyage from an early end. Includes a visit to Lamont-Doherty Geological Observatory, where scientists map the ocean floor using data collected by ship and by satellite.
From The Voyage Of The Mimi Series.
Prod-HRAW Dist-HRAW

On The Shoulders Of Giants C 60 MIN
3/4 OR 1/2 INCH VIDEO CASSETTE J-C A
Journeys to the Galapagos and Cook Islands with naturalist David Steadman. Shows exotic creatures and cultures. Sheds new light on the work of Charles Darwin and the mysteries of evolution.
From The Smithsonian World Series.
Prod-WETATV Dist-WETATV

On The Side Of Life C 9 MIN
16MM FILM OPTICAL SOUND
Features a folk music background and fast-changing scenes of nursing activities that emphasize the challenge and involvement of the profession.
Prod-JAJ Dist-JAJ 1970

On The Spring Ice C 45 MIN
16MM FILM - 3/4 IN VIDEO J-C A
Shows a walrus hunt by the Eskimos of Gambell on St Lawrence Island. Notes the rescue of a drifting hunting party by Coast Guard helicopter.
Prod-AKNATH Dist-DOCEDR 1976

On The Surface B
16MM FILM OPTICAL SOUND
Discusses the geometry of surfaces. Examines the problem of finding local maxima and minima of a function of two variables.
Prod-OPENU Dist-OPENU

On The Surface Of Things C 8 MIN
16MM FILM, 3/4 OR 1/2 IN VIDEO
Explores a facet of chemical research being conducted to gain a better understanding of the way atoms and molecules act at the interface of two materials.
From The Discovery Series.
Prod-UTORMC Dist-UTORMC

On The Threshold Of The Future C 30 MIN
3/4 INCH VIDEO CASSETTE
See series title for descriptive statement.
From The Changing Music Series.
Prod-WGBHTV Dist-PUBTEL

On The Tiles C 16 MIN
16MM FILM OPTICAL SOUND P-I
Details what occurs when Alice the chimp escapes from the children's grandmother's house and climbs on to the roof of the house next door. Reveals what happens when she climbs down the chimney.
Prod-LUF Dist-LUF 1977

On The Totem Trail C 30 MIN
3/4 OR 1/2 INCH VIDEO CASSETTE I-H
Tells how a school assignment helps two students discover the rich heritage of the Pacific Northwest Indian tribes. Visits an Indian museum, a working artist, and an Indian village.
Prod-CANBC Dist-JOU

On The Track Of The Bog People C 35 MIN
16MM FILM OPTICAL SOUND
Shows the method Danish archeologists employ in tracing the habits and patterns of daily life of the people of the Iron Age.
Prod-RDCG Dist-AUDPLN

On The Track To The Midnight Sun C 34 MIN
16MM FILM OPTICAL SOUND
Depicts a train ride through the northern part of Sweden where the summer sun shines twenty-four hours a day. Pictures the age-old customs and folk dances of the Lapps.
LC NO. FIA66-1392
Prod-SSRR Dist-SWNTO 1955

On The Twelfth Day C 21 MIN
16MM FILM OPTICAL SOUND J-H
Dramatizes the traditional English folksong 'The Twelve Days Of Christmas,' in which a lover brings his lady an unusual assortment of gifts.
LC NO. FIA67-1871
Prod-ARTHUR Dist-FI 1964

On The Wallaby Track C 10 MIN
16MM FILM OPTICAL SOUND
Presents a painting by Frederick Mc Cubbin. Illustrates the artist's adaptations of the French Impressionists' techniques of brushwork to make his figures meld naturally into their atmospheric space.
From The Australian Eye Series.
LC NO. 80-700786
Prod-FLMAUS Dist-TASCOR 1978

On The Waterfront B 18 MIN
16MM FILM OPTICAL SOUND
An abridged version of the motion picture On The Waterfront. Portrays what happens when a member of New York's longshoreman's union defies its leaders by testifying against them after his brother is killed. Stars Marlon Brando, Eva-Marie Saint and Karl Malden.
Prod-CPC Dist-TIMLIF 1982

On The Waterfront B 108 MIN
16MM FILM OPTICAL SOUND
Portrays a broken-down ex-prizefighter who must decide whether to testify against his fellow longshoremen. Stars Marlon Brando, Rod Steiger, Eva Marie Saint, Karl Malden and Lee J Cobb.
Prod-CPC Dist-TIMLIF 1957

On The Way C 31 MIN
16MM FILM OPTICAL SOUND
Documents development problems in general and transport facilities in particular in Malawi, Lebanon, Iran and Afghanistan.
Prod-RDCG Dist-AUDPLN

On Their Way - The Courage Story C 18 MIN
16MM FILM OPTICAL SOUND
Shows how the rehabilitative services at the Courage Center in Golden Valley, Minnesota, affect the lives of people with disabilities, helping them on their way to more active and productive lives.
LC NO. 81-700340
Prod-COURGE Dist-COURGE Prodn-MEDLFT 1980

On This Day C 27 MIN
16MM FILM OPTICAL SOUND
Presents the advantages of complete prepaid medical service programs by showing how a family in New York City comes to realize that good medical care can be within the financial reach of most people. Explains how this health insurance plan works to meet family health problems.
Prod-HINPNY Dist-AFLCIO 1953

On Time, Tombs And Treasure C 29 MIN
3/4 OR 1/2 INCH VIDEO CASSETTE
Takes a journey through the 3000-year-old final resting place of King Tutankhamen. Tells the story of the tomb's discovery and observes the fabulous artifacts found in the tomb.
Prod-IVCH Dist-IVCH

On To The Bay C 25 MIN
16MM FILM OPTICAL SOUND
Presents the story of the building of the Hudson's Bay Railway across the northern Manitoba tundra of Canada.
LC NO. 77-702597
Prod-CNRM Dist-CANFDC Prodn-QUEENU 1977

On To Tomorrow—A Series

Examines technology assessment - the systematic analysis of the social, economic, environmental and societal impacts of new technology.
Prod-UMITV Dist-UMITV 1976

Beyond Earth	029 MIN
Do No Harm	029 MIN
Energy Systems	030 MIN
In Control Or In Fear	029 MIN
Time To Live, A	029 MIN
World Society	029 MIN

On Trial - Criminal Justice C 75 MIN
16MM FILM OPTICAL SOUND J-H
Depicts the Maryland workshop on crime and correction, convened with the goal of promoting needed reform in the penal system. Explains that the eight-day conference, designed to bring confrontation, communication and revelation, brought together more than 100 judges, prison officials, correctional officers, parole supervisors, policemen, lawyers, private citizens, ex-convicts and prison inmates.
Prod-WBCPRO Dist-WBCPRO 1970

On We Go C
16MM FILM, 3/4 OR 1/2 IN VIDEO
Demonstrates a selection of teaching points about English as a second language through scenes in the daily life of four young teenagers who are away from home for the first time.
Prod-NORTNJ Dist-NORTNJ

On Wings Of Love C 36 MIN
16MM FILM OPTICAL SOUND
Looks at the personal lives of a couple preparing for overseas service with Mission Aviation Fellowship.
LC NO. 77-701449
Prod-ECRF Dist-ECRF 1977

On With Your Life C 13 MIN
16MM FILM OPTICAL SOUND C A
Takes the viewer behind the scenes during the production of the television show 'MISSION IMPOSSIBLE' where the cast discusses the importance of an annual health checkup, including the procto. Features Peter Graves, Greg Morris, Peter Lupus and others from the 'MISSION - IMPOSSIBLE' cast.
Prod-AMCS Dist-AMCS

On Working C 30 MIN
3/4 OR 1/2 INCH VIDEO CASSETTE
Documents the nature of work in America. Offers insight into the lives of working men and women and the emotional, psychological and social factors which influence career decisions and self image. Features commentary by Studs Terkel.
Prod-OHUTC Dist-OHUTC

On Your Marks, Pt 1 C 7 MIN
16MM FILM OPTICAL SOUND J-H
Examines punctuation marks and gives examples of their use. Identifies the eight most common punctuation marks - the period, comma, question mark, colon, quotation marks, apostrofphe, exclamation point and hyphen. Shows each punctuation mark taking on a persoality that shows its proper use.
LC NO. 70-714193
Prod-CGWEST Dist-CGWEST 1971

On Your Marks, Pt 2 C 7 MIN
16MM FILM OPTICAL SOUND J-H
Provides an imaginative look at punctuation marks. Identifies eight less common marks - the semicolon, underlining, parentheses, dash, asterisk, caret, brackets and ellipses.
LC NO. 70-714193
Prod-CGWEST Dist-CGWEST 1971

On Your Own C 21 MIN
16MM FILM, 3/4 OR 1/2 IN VIDEO H-C
Features interviews with four young people to focus on skills needed to live on one's own.
From The Making It On Your Own Series.
Prod-BARR Dist-BARR 1979

On Your Own C 23 MIN
16MM FILM, 3/4 OR 1/2 IN VIDEO J-C A
Presents students describing what consumer and homemaking education means to them. Explores a wide range of instruction and offers an overview of consumer and homemaking education curriculum.
Prod-FLMFR Dist-FLMFR

On Your Own C 30 MIN
1/2 IN VIDEO CASSETTE BETA/VHS
Discusses financing a college education. Gives advice on avoiding having a tax shelter roof fall in. Examines being self-employed.
From The On The Money Series.
Prod-WGBHTV Dist-MTI

On Your Own - Being Your Own Best Motivator C 7 MIN
16MM FILM, 3/4 OR 1/2 IN VIDEO
Deals with self-motivation, and contrasts the training a racehorse receives with educational opportunities provided throughout life. Narrated by Dennis Weaver.
Prod-CCCD Dist-CCCD

On Your Own - Preparing For A Standardized Test C 26 MIN
16MM FILM, 3/4 OR 1/2 IN VIDEO J-C A
Covers basic concepts of test preparation. Develops such topics as use of test bulletins, types of tests, understanding content of the test and knowing item formats.
LC NO. 83-776738
Prod-ETS Dist-CORF Prodn-SEVSEA 1983

On Your Own—A Series

Presents former members of major dance companies relating how they made it on their own. Each tape is a program from the New York City Cable TV series Eye On Dance.
Prod-ARCVID Dist-ARCVID

David Anderson And Elizabeth Gottlieb	030 MIN
Jennifer Muller And Marjorie Mussman	030 MIN
Phyllis Lamhut And Dan Wagoner	030 MIN

On Your Way To School C 8 MIN
16MM FILM, 3/4 OR 1/2 IN VIDEO P
Shows a girl winding her way to school through a bright collage of images, colors and textures.
From The Learning To Look Series.
Prod-MGHT Dist-MGHT 1973

On Your Way To School C 10 MIN
16MM FILM, 3/4 OR 1/2 IN VIDEO P-I
Follows two school children to school pointing out the safety rules.
Prod-DAVP Dist-AIMS 1971

On-Line Systems Concepts For Users—A Series

Describes the functional characteristics of on-line systems, the difference between them and traditional batch type systems and demonstrates what on-line systems can do for the end users.
Prod-DELTAK Dist-DELTAK

Communications Facilities	020 MIN
Understanding On-Line Systems	020 MIN
Using On-Line Systems	020 MIN

On-Off C 4 MIN
16MM FILM OPTICAL SOUND P-I
Presents an introduction to electricity during a day of a child.
From The Mini Movies - Springboard For Learning - Unit 3, Why Is It Series.
LC NO. 76-703326
Prod-MORLAT Dist-MORLAT 1975

On-Target Interview, The C 15 MIN
3/4 INCH VIDEO CASSETTE H-C A
Explains how to prepare for an interview, telling what to bring, discussing the most frequently asked questions, and emphasizing appearance and attitude. Demystifies the interview, encouraging the job seeker to have some control over the situation.
From The Job Seeking Series.
LC NO. 80-706573
Prod-WCETTV Dist-GPITVL 1979

On-The-Job Assessment C 13 MIN
3/4 OR 1/2 INCH VIDEO CASSETTE
Shows how to consider all requirements of a job to be filled and make maximum use of on-the-job observations to determine suitability for promotion.
From The Assessing Employee Potential Series.
Prod-RESEM Dist-RESEM

On-The-Job Training C 30 MIN
3/4 OR 1/2 INCH VIDEO CASSETTE T
Points out the difference between classroom and on-the-job training, highlighting the use of job aids.
From The Training The Trainer Series.
Prod-ITCORP Dist-ITCORP

Ona People - Life And Death In Tierra Del Fuego C 55 MIN
3/4 INCH VIDEO CASSETTE
Documents the history of the Ona people of Tierra del Fuego at the tip of South America from the 1880's to the death of the last survivor in 1974. Uses old photographs and interviews to reconstruct a story of genocide committed against the people called Selk'nam.
Prod-DOCEDR Dist-DOCEDR 1977

Onandarka Fire C 18 MIN
16MM FILM OPTICAL SOUND
Presents footage of coverage of the fire at Newhall, Olive View Sanitarium and Gene Autry's Melody Ranch in August, 1962.
Prod-LAFIRE Dist-LAFIRE

Once In A Million Years C 50 MIN
16MM FILM, 3/4 OR 1/2 IN VIDEO H-C A
Discusses the safety factors which engineers have been designing into nuclear reactors since 1950 in order to contain certain explosive reactions which could pump lethal quantities of radioactivity into the environment.
Prod-BBCTV Dist-FI 1982

Once Insane, Twice Forgotten C 25 MIN
3/4 OR 1/2 INCH VIDEO CASSETTE
Presents a report on the lack of help for the criminally insane who have been released from state mental hospitals. Traces experiences of a man who six years ago shot and killed another man, but has been released to a life with no job, few friends, and an income of welfare money.
Prod-TRAINX Dist-TRAINX

Once The Ferns C 9 MIN
16MM FILM OPTICAL SOUND K-C
Presents a film-poem fantasy about the human condition as revealed in a fantasy acted out by ferns and ladybugs.
LC NO. 72-703329
Prod-ALBM Dist-MARALF 1973

Once The Fire Is Out - What Next C 16 MIN
16MM FILM, 3/4 OR 1/2 IN VIDEO
Describes the Forest Service role in managing and protecting Na-

tional Forest watersheds in the aftermath of wildfire. Describes how vulnerable burned-over soil is to erosion.
Prod-USFS Dist-USNAC

Once There Was C 15 MIN
3/4 OR 1/2 INCH VIDEO CASSETTE P
Introduces examples of folklore from various cultures.
From The Spinning Stories Series.
Prod-MDDE Dist-AITECH 1977

Once There Was A Last Call C 8 MIN
16MM FILM OPTICAL SOUND
Looks at various forms of wildlife found in Ontario, Canada. Draws attention to the common loon and its status as an endangered species.
LC NO. 77-702598
Prod-BOGNER Dist-VIK 1976

Once There Was A Strike In Levittown C 60 MIN
3/4 OR 1/2 INCH VIDEO CASSETTE
Explores the underlying issues and consequences of a prolonged teachers' strike in Levittown, Long Island.
From The Bill Moyers' Journal Series.
Prod-WNETTV Dist-WNETTV 1979

Once There Were Bluebirds C 5 MIN
16MM FILM, 3/4 OR 1/2 IN VIDEO P-I
Uses animation to show how technology has usurped nature. Ends with a view of Earth from space and the sound of coughing. Based on the book Once There Were Bluebirds by Bill Martin, Jr.
Prod-FLMFR Dist-FLMFR

Once To Every Man C 30 MIN
3/4 OR 1/2 INCH VIDEO CASSETTE
Offers a fictional account of an encounter between a typical colonial farmer and a foraging party of British soldiers.
Prod-MDCPB Dist-MDCPB

Once To Make Ready C 8 MIN
16MM FILM OPTICAL SOUND
Explains to the average citizen what it can mean to him personally when his local government undertakes a Community Shelter Program (CSP) to provide the best available protection for all its citizens.
LC NO. 75-700566
Prod-USOCD Dist-USNAC 1967

Once Upon A Boa C 28 MIN
16MM FILM, 3/4 OR 1/2 IN VIDEO K-J
Features a boy describing his adventures with his pet snake, trying to help his neighbor decide whether or not to buy a snake for his family.
LC NO. 81-706772
Prod-HAYS Dist-PHENIX 1978

Once Upon A Choice C 15 MIN
3/4 OR 1/2 INCH VIDEO CASSETTE
Raises issues of conventional sex roles, marriage, independence and responsibility. Shows that there are real, desirable and attainable alternatives to 'waiting for Prince Charming.'
Prod-NEWDAY Dist-NEWDAY

Once Upon A Climb B 7 MIN
16MM FILM OPTICAL SOUND
Illustrates old and new mountain climbing techniques.
LC NO. 76-702038
Prod-SFRASU Dist-SFRASU 1975

Once Upon A Couch - Gretel C 120 MIN
3/4 OR 1/2 INCH VIDEO CASSETTE PRO
Uses the fairy tale character Gretel to introduce the ten crucial steps in the psychotherapeutic session.
Prod-HSCIC Dist-HSCIC 1981

Once Upon A Dime C 11 MIN
16MM FILM OPTICAL SOUND P-J
Addresses the subject of savings. Encourages direct money savings by students and promotes the saving of money through conservation of resources, such as electric lights, water and fuel.
From The Kids And Cash Series.
Prod-COUNFI Dist-COUNFI

Once Upon A Dinosaur C 15 MIN
3/4 OR 1/2 INCH VIDEO CASSETTE K-P
Explores evidence of life that existed in the past.
From The Dragons, Wagons And Wax, Set 1 Series.
Prod-CTI Dist-CTI

Once Upon A Morning C 5 MIN
16MM FILM OPTICAL SOUND P-J
Presents a modern interpretation of Psalm 138 using scenes of a little boy and girl on a deserted beach.
From The Song Of The Ages Series.
LC NO. 70-702140
Prod-FAMLYT Dist-FAMLYT 1964

Once Upon A Mouse C 26 MIN
16MM FILM, 3/4 OR 1/2 IN VIDEO
Offers segments from various Walt Disney cartoons which show a variety of Disney themes including music, love, villains and happy endings.
Prod-DISNEY Dist-WDEMCO 1982

Once Upon a Time C 5 MIN
16MM FILM OPTICAL SOUND
Shows how Dr Einstein's theory of relativity goes berserk when a college student takes an overdose of time-release tablets to calm his nerves.
LC NO. 79-700254
Prod-CINESO Dist-CINESO 1978

Once Upon A Time C 25 MIN
16MM FILM OPTICAL SOUND J-C T
Emphasizes the importance of protecting economic and political freedom from excessive government controls.
Prod-CCUS Dist-CCUS

Once Upon A Time C 11 MIN
16MM FILM, 3/4 OR 1/2 IN VIDEO P-J
Explores time as a practical force, as an abstract concept and as a measure of life. Captures the art and wizardry man has used over the centuries to tell time.
Prod-AFI Dist-TEXFLM 1972

Once Upon A Time C 15 MIN
3/4 INCH VIDEO CASSETTE K-P
Presents a reading of the story The Great Big Enormous Turnip by Alexei Tolstoy.
From The I Can Read Series.
Prod-WCETTV Dist-GPITVL 1977

Once Upon A Time There Was A Point C 8 MIN
16MM FILM, 3/4 OR 1/2 IN VIDEO
Shows a point that transforms itself into a myriad of different shapes and forms. Previously released as Once Upon A Time There Was A Dot.
Prod-ZAGREB Dist-IFB 1977

Once Upon A Town—A Series
P-I
Explores literary selections that deal with universal themes, including self-discovery, social issues, the relationship between the human world and the animal world, and fantasy versus reality.
Prod-MDDE Dist-AITECH 1977

All Kinds Of Animals 20 MIN
Because I Am Different 20 MIN
Beyond Words 20 MIN
Caring And Sharing 20 MIN
Earth Care 20 MIN
Hobbies Happening 20 MIN
How Do I Do It 20 MIN
Is My Way Better 20 MIN
It Makes Me Laugh 20 MIN
Matter Of Time, A 20 MIN
Me Alone, On My Own 20 MIN
Mind And Muscle Power 20 MIN
Scare Me 20 MIN
Where Do I Live 20 MIN
Who Am I 20 MIN

Onchocerciasis In Ghana C 31 MIN
16MM FILM - 3/4 IN VIDEO
Traces the life cycle of the African vector of onchocerciasis, Simulium damnosum theobald. Describes the development of the parasite Onchocerca volvulus in the fly and human host and explains its relationship to blindness in Ghana. Issued in 1967 as a motion picture.
LC NO. 79-706026
Prod-NMAC Dist-USNAC Prodn-USPHS 1978

Ondra And The Snow Dragon C 7 MIN
3/4 OR 1/2 INCH VIDEO CASSETTE K-P
Presents Ondra, a lonely young boy who is transported to a faraway land by the Snow Dragon, a friendly winged creature. Shows how Ondra finds a ballroom full of dancers frozen by a strange spell, and a princess whose heart is frozen in sadness. Tells how Ondra, by his kindness, frees the dancers and the princess.
Prod-KRATKY Dist-MOKIN 1983

One B 10 MIN
16MM FILM OPTICAL SOUND J-C A
Presents a drama set at a railroad station where a young woman awaits the arrival of the man she loves.
Prod-UWFKD Dist-UWFKD

One C 10 MIN
16MM FILM OPTICAL SOUND
Presents a fusion of electric-collage-graphics and the painted image.
Prod-VANBKS Dist-VANBKS 1969

One C 14 MIN
16MM FILM, 3/4 OR 1/2 IN VIDEO K-I
Depicts an encounter between a little boy and a street mime. Describes the boy's adventures with an invisible balloon.
Prod-LRF Dist-LRF 1980

One A Day C 15 MIN
2 INCH VIDEOTAPE J
Offers practical suggestions for developing a good vocabulary.
From The From Me To You...In Writing, Pt 2 Series.
Prod-DELE Dist-GPITVL

One And A Half Dreams C 21 MIN
16MM FILM OPTICAL SOUND
Presents an account of what is being done through the United Nations and its development program to make poverty a thing of the past within the foreseeable future.
LC NO. 73-702048
Prod-UN Dist-UN 1973

One And More Than One - Birthday On A Farm C 8 MIN
16MM FILM, 3/4 OR 1/2 IN VIDEO P
Describes ways of making plural words through a story about three children who go shopping for birthday presents for a friend. Gives examples of single and plural forms of words.
From The Read On Series.
Prod-ACI Dist-AIMS 1971

One And Only Bing, The B 26 MIN
16MM FILM OPTICAL SOUND
Presents the biography of Bing Crosby, the nonchalant crooner who became a star in radio, recording, and television, as well as in films. Includes clips from his early pictures and scenes of his home life and children.
From The Hollywood And The Stars Series.
LC NO. 75-701943
Prod-WOLPER Dist-WOLPER 1963

One And Only, The C 15 MIN
3/4 OR 1/2 INCH VIDEO CASSETTE K-P
Illustrates the characteristics which make humans different from other creatures.
From The Dragons, Wagons And Wax, Set 2 Series.
Prod-CTI Dist-CTI

One And Two Axis Linear Milling C 15 MIN
3/4 OR 1/2 INCH VIDEO CASSETTE PRO
See series title for descriptive statement.
From The Numerical Control/Computer Numerical Control, Pt 1 - Fundamentals Series.
Prod-ICSINT Dist-ICSINT

One Armed Man, The X 27 MIN
16MM FILM, 3/4 OR 1/2 IN VIDEO J-C A
Explores the life of a one-armed travelling salesman who tries to hide his loneliness with lies and jokes. Tells how his encounter with a deaf woman shatters his self-absorption and gives him confidence. Stars John and Patty Duke Astin.
From The Insight Series.
Prod-PAULST Dist-PAULST

One At A Time C 20 MIN
16MM FILM OPTICAL SOUND
Shows the manufacturing of equipment at the Allis-Chalmers plant.
Prod-ALLISC Dist-IDEALF

One Beautiful Experience C 14 MIN
16MM FILM, 3/4 OR 1/2 IN VIDEO
Uses a comedy about a junior executive's first venture into cigar smoking to illustrate the qualities of a well-made cigar, different types of cigars and how to smoke a cigar.
Prod-AMCIG Dist-KLEINW Prodn-KLEINW 1978

One Big Ocean C 13 MIN
16MM FILM, 3/4 OR 1/2 IN VIDEO K-P
Illustrates basic concepts about the ocean, includes scenes of men at work on the ocean floor and of creatures that inhabit the ocean. Explains what causes the ocean waves, why the ocean tastes salty and the ways in which the ocean is important to man.
Prod-WER Dist-JOU 1970

One Big Ocean (Captioned) C 13 MIN
16MM FILM, 3/4 OR 1/2 IN VIDEO K-P
Illustrates basic concepts about the ocean, includes scenes of men at work on the ocean floor and of creatures that inhabit the ocean. Explains what causes the ocean waves, why the ocean tastes salty and the ways in which the ocean is important to man.
Prod-WER Dist-JOU 1970

One Bite At The Apple C 38 MIN
16MM FILM OPTICAL SOUND
Stresses familiarization with procurement procedures relative to contracting by formal advertising. Shows a discussion between a disappointed bidder and a procurement agent setting the scene for procedural review, focusing on the role of the Federal Supply Service.
LC NO. 74-705248
Prod-USGSA Dist-USNAC 1970

One By One C 28 MIN
16MM FILM, 3/4 OR 1/2 IN VIDEO IND
Presents the minority person as an individual. Defines and exposes unconscious prejudice and examines why it still exists. Focuses on the dangers of grouping people, of oversensitivity, of racial backlash and of special treatment of minorities.
Prod-DRUKRR Dist-JONEST

One Can Be A Lonely Number C 20 MIN
3/4 OR 1/2 INCH VIDEO CASSETTE I
Presents dramatizations of literary works that deal with people who are alone, by choice or circumstance.
From The Readers' Cube Series.
Prod-MDDE Dist-AITECH 1977

One Day B 18 MIN
16MM FILM OPTICAL SOUND I-C A
Gives an impressionistic view of an average Indian town, poona. Shows glimpses of the lives of people in different strata of society.
Prod-INDIA Dist-NEDINF

One Day At A Time C
1/2 IN VIDEO CASSETTE (VHS)
Shows the day-to-day realities of running a single-parent household.
From The Daddy Doesn't Live Here Anymore - The Single-Parent Family Series.
Prod-IBIS Dist-IBIS

One Day At Teton Marsh C 47 MIN
16MM FILM, 3/4 OR 1/2 IN VIDEO I-C A
Describes the wild life in a swamp where animals and birds are free and nature reigns supreme. Based on a book by Sally Carrighar.
Prod-DISNEY Dist-WDEMCO 1966

One Day In The Life Of Ivan Denisovich C 105 MIN
16MM FILM OPTICAL SOUND H A
Tells the harrowing story of life in a Siberian labor camp. Adapted from the book. Stars Tom Courtenay.
Prod-GROUPW Dist-TIMLIF 1971

One Day With Shiva C 8 MIN
16MM FILM OPTICAL SOUND

Presents an impressionistic documentary of south India.
LC NO. 76-701348
Prod-CONCRU Dist-CONCRU 1974

One Dimension, Two Dimension, Three Dimension Four B 15 MIN
3/4 INCH VIDEO CASSETTE
Illustrates the plight of urban centers in the United States, the problems of pollution, transportation, education and housing. Describes how these problems affect its inhabitants and how some urban areas have tried to solve these problems. Stresses planning for the future as essential to the survival of the cities.
Prod-USNAC Dist-USNAC 1972

One Dish Meals C
1/2 IN VIDEO CASSETTE BETA/VHS
Demonstrates recipes for one-dish meals such as Veal au Gratin and Lemon Garlic Salmon.
From The Video Cooking Library Series.
Prod-KARTES Dist-KARTES

One Door C 28 MIN
16MM FILM OPTICAL SOUND
Explains that today, with 35 specialties in medicine, one doctor cannot be expected to know all there is to know about medicine. Shows that the average doctor is associated with 10 or 12 medical specialists. Describes the advantages of a team approach to medical care.
Prod-USDHEW Dist-AFLCIO 1969

One Film / Three Scripts C 21 MIN
16MM FILM, 3/4 OR 1/2 IN VIDEO H-C
Presents the same footage of Puerto Rico three times with different narratives to show how different communication techniques can be used in film.
Prod-IFFB Dist-FI 1974

One Five Six C 19 MIN
16MM FILM OPTICAL SOUND
Touches briefly on the background of the 'big solids' (solid propellant rockets) now being considered for the space shuttle and progresses to the 156-inch motor program. Concludes with a static test of the motor which generates more than 1.4 million pounds of thrust.
Prod-THIOKL Dist-THIOKL 1965

One Flew Over The Cuckoo's Nest C 129 MIN
16MM FILM OPTICAL SOUND
Focuses on a free-spirited man (Jack Nicholson) who tries to explain to the other mental hospital patients that the difference between sanity and insanity is just society's attempt to stifle individualism. Based on the novel ONE FLEW OVER THE CUCKOO'S NEST by Ken Kesey. Directed by Milos Forman.
Prod-UAA Dist-UAE 1976

One For My Baby C 28 MIN
16MM FILM, 3/4 OR 1/2 IN VIDEO H-C A
Presents the potential dangers of alcohol use by pregnant women.
LC NO. 82-706800
Prod-WHATV Dist-AIMS 1983

One For The Money C 30 MIN
16MM FILM OPTICAL SOUND
Shows the hard work, planning, preparation and teamwork involved in entering a car in the Indianapolis 500.
LC NO. FIA66-750
Prod-TI Dist-SFI Prodn-SFI 1966

One For The Road C 29 MIN
16MM FILM, 3/4 OR 1/2 IN VIDEO J-H A
Looks at what happens to a driver's vision and judgment while under the influence of alcohol. Shows volunteers at a party taking part in a series of games which require alertness, information processing and split attention, first while sober, then while drunk.
Prod-CTV Dist-MTI 1981

One Force B 20 MIN
16MM FILM OPTICAL SOUND
Points out heroic deeds from 1776 to the Korean conflict, which provide evidence that Americans, although of many racial and national origins, join in one military force dedicated to peace and freedom.
LC NO. 74-706165
Prod-USDD Dist-USNAC 1964

One Fourth Of Humanity C 74 MIN
16MM FILM OPTICAL SOUND
Documents China in 1935 when Edgar Snow first met Mao-Tse Tung at the beginning of Mao's historic rise to power and contrasts that with what happened to China in the wake of the 'PROLETARIAN CULTURAL REVOLUTION.'
Prod-IMPACT Dist-IMPACT 1968

One Friday C 10 MIN
16MM FILM OPTICAL SOUND
Follows a tiny boy who is unaware of the death and destruction around him as he chases his dog into the open and by his innocence wins over an armed combatant.
LC NO. 73-702346
Prod-COUNTR Dist-COUNTR 1973

One Generation Is Not Enough C 23 MIN
16MM FILM, 3/4 OR 1/2 IN VIDEO
Describes a family which has been in the violin-making business for 200 years. Shows a 19-year-old being taught to carve a viola.
Prod-DENONN Dist-DIRECT 1979

One Giant Leap C 60 MIN
3/4 OR 1/2 INCH VIDEO CASSETTE
Explores the history of the Apollo program, including the death of three astronauts in a launch pad fire, Wally Schirra's manning of the successful flight of Apollo 7, powered by Wehrner Von Braun's Saturn 5 rockets, and the climatic flight of Apollo 11 and Neil Armstrong's walk on the moon. Discusses Soviet achievements and setbacks, the first space station and the last Apollo mission's historic handshake in space with the Soviets.
From The Spaceflight Series.
Prod-PBS Dist-PBS

One God C 1 MIN
16MM FILM OPTICAL SOUND
Features a presentation of many things that have gained importance along side of God.
LC NO. 77-702501
Prod-USC Dist-USC 1968

One Good Turn C 20 MIN
16MM FILM OPTICAL SOUND J-C A
Examines the principles behind the Social Security program.
Prod-WORLDR Dist-WORLDR 1982

One Good Turn/Social Security C 20 MIN
3/4 OR 1/2 INCH VIDEO CASSETTE
Examines the principles behind Social Security. Promotes discussion on the philosophical and sociological implications of welfare systems.
Prod-WORLDR Dist-WORLDR

One Hoe For Kalabo C 27 MIN
16MM FILM OPTICAL SOUND J-C A
The story of how machine tools have given dignity and power to human labor and world civilization.
Prod-NATMTB Dist-MTP

One Hour A Week C 18 MIN
16MM FILM OPTICAL SOUND
Describes the home training program of the League School for seriously disturbed children, showing how it helps parents cope with their child's emotional handicap by demonstrating techniques in behavior modification that they can practice at home.
From The League School For Seriously Disturbed Children Series.
LC NO. 75-702417
Prod-USBEH Dist-USNAC 1973

One Hour To Zero C 56 MIN
16MM FILM OPTICAL SOUND P-I
Portrays what happens when two children set off to find a runaway boy and return to their village, not knowing it has been abandoned because of the imminent danger of explosion at a nearby nuclear research station.
Prod-LUF Dist-LUF 1980

One Hundred And Fifteen Volts - Deadly Shipmate C 19 MIN
16MM FILM - 3/4 IN VIDEO
Dramatizes actual incidents to point out the disastrous effects of low voltage electrical shock when the basic rules of electrical safety are violated or ignored. Issued in 1960 as a motion picture.
LC NO. 79-707973
Prod-USN Dist-USNAC 1979

One Hundred And One Critical Days C 6 MIN
16MM FILM OPTICAL SOUND
Cites the interval from Memorial Day through Labor Day as a critical period for accidents, urging strict observance of safety rules by swimmers, boaters and motorists.
LC NO. 74-706166
Prod-USAF Dist-USNAC 1968

One Hundred And One Dalmatians - A Lesson In Self-Assertion C 8 MIN
16MM FILM, 3/4 OR 1/2 IN VIDEO K-I
Uses a sequence from 101 Dalmatians to show two children and two dogs standing up to a villainess. Shows that it is important to defend one's own rights and the rights of others.
From The Disney's Animated Classics - Lessons In Living, Series 2 Series.
Prod-DISNEY Dist-WDEMCO 1982

One Hundred And One Dalmations C 79 MIN
16MM FILM OPTICAL SOUND
Shows how the hateful Cruella De Vil dognaps 15 dalmation puppies so that she can use their pelts for a fur coat.
Prod-DISNEY Dist-UAE 1961

One Hundred Entertainments C 28 MIN
16MM FILM, 3/4 OR 1/2 IN VIDEO H-C A
Focuses on the Shensi Provincial Acrobatic Troupe of China.
From The Human Face Of China Series.
Prod-FLMAUS Dist-LCOA 1979

One Hundred Sixty-Seven St, Bronx '83 C 29 MIN
3/4 OR 1/2 INCH VIDEO CASSETTE
Provides an impressionistic view of a street jam. Presented by Bob Harris and Rii Kanzaki.
Prod-ARTINC Dist-ARTINC

One Hundred Thousand Piece Jigsaw Puzzle C 26 MIN
16MM FILM OPTICAL SOUND
Describes the work and care involved in restoring and preserving the remnants of old Viking ships found in Roskilde Fjord in Denmark.
Prod-RDCG Dist-AUDPLN

One Hundred Twenty-Five Rooms Of Comfort C 80 MIN
16MM FILM OPTICAL SOUND
Tells how the owner of a hotel in St Thomas, Ontario, returns from a mental hospital where he went to recover after the death of his father.
LC NO. 75-701906
Prod-CFDEVC Dist-CFDEVC 1974

One Hundred Twenty-Nine Close-Up C 7 MIN
16MM FILM OPTICAL SOUND
Examines the manufacture of the IBM 129 Data Recorder at IBM Canada.
LC NO. 75-701907
Prod-IBM Dist-IBM 1972

One Hundred Watts, 120 Volts C 6 MIN
16MM FILM, 3/4 OR 1/2 IN VIDEO
Shows a machine producing light bulbs to musical accompaniment.
Prod-DAVC Dist-TEXFLM 1977

One Hundred Year Voyage C 28 MIN
3/4 INCH VIDEO CASSETTE
Traces the changes over the past hundred years in the ways oil has been transported in ships to the world's ports of call. Treats sailing ships, World War II tankers and the supertankers of today.
Prod-EXXON Dist-MTP

One Hundred Years To Live C 30 MIN
16MM FILM - 1/2 IN VIDEO, VHS
Shows how a 99-year-old mother and her daughter react to being placed in a nursing home. Looks at various attitudes toward old age.
Prod-OHC Dist-HRC

One Hundred-Thirty-Nine B 25 MIN
16MM FILM OPTICAL SOUND
Shows the student take-over of Sproul and Moses Halls on the Berkeley campus to protest the regents' refusal to grant credit for Social Analysis 139x, a course for which Eldridge Cleaver was to be a guest lecturer.
Prod-SFN Dist-SFN 1968

One In Eleven C 14 MIN
16MM FILM, 3/4 OR 1/2 IN VIDEO
Informs women that there is a viable alternative to mastectomy. Presents evidence that early detection of breast cancer can make it possible to avoid surgical removal of a breast. Notes that this knowledge tends to produce more breast self-examination and early treatment.
LC NO. 82-706611
Prod-STANDC Dist-PFP 1982

One In Five C 17 MIN
16MM FILM, 3/4 OR 1/2 IN VIDEO A
Presents the basic facts of heart disease and explains that the manual laborer is just as susceptible as the executive.
LC NO. 83-706812
Prod-MILLBK Dist-IFB 1982

One In The Lord C 30 MIN
3/4 OR 1/2 INCH VIDEO CASSETTE A
Studies the people and ministry of the ethnic minority local Methodist churches. Focuses on a Black church, an Hispanic congregation, an Asian church and a Native American congregation. Looks at their cultural heritage and current needs and the challenges they face in the future.
Prod-UMCOM Dist-ECUFLM 1978

One In The Spirit C 20 MIN
16MM FILM OPTICAL SOUND
Shows the activities of a group of teen-aged White boys and girls from a reformed church who participate in a work-camp project on a Black school campus in Brewton, Alabama, working with the Black students for one week.
LC NO. 78-705628
Prod-RECA Dist-RECA Prodn-MIRABC 1969

One Kitten For Kim C 16 MIN
16MM FILM, 3/4 OR 1/2 IN VIDEO P-I
Presents the story of a little boy who owns seven kittens and is told by his parents that he may only keep one and must give the other six away. Encourages discussion of Kim's adventures, the reactions of his parents and the students own experiences with finding homes for animals in the lower grades.
From The Reading Short Stories Series.
Prod-MORLAT Dist-AIMS 1973

One Lap Around The World C 28 MIN
16MM FILM OPTICAL SOUND
Shows professional drivers travelling around the world in two cars owned by National Car Rental System.
LC NO. 78-701563
Prod-NCRENT Dist-MTP Prodn-BADFRE 1977

One Last Shock C 21 MIN
16MM FILM, 3/4 OR 1/2 IN VIDEO IND
Dramatizes the events leading to an electrical accident. Outlines the misuses of electrical equipment in the factory and office.
LC NO. 81-706565
Prod-MILLBK Dist-IFB 1980

One Length Bob-Cut C
3/4 OR 1/2 INCH VIDEO CASSETTE
Shows how the mannequin is sectioned using a special technique, and how to establish length. Explains many haircutting terms as work progresses. Emphasizes scissor control. Demonstrates how hair is held low during cutting with special emphasis to the sectioning and cutting of the nang area.
From The Lessons On A Mannequin Series, Lesson I.
Prod-MPCEDP Dist-MPCEDP 1984

One Little Girl Alone C 6 MIN
3/4 OR 1/2 INCH VIDEO CASSETTE
Portrays the successful efforts of a somewhat retarded child discovering pride and self-respect in learning to do interesting things within the scope of her learning power. Uses the story and illustrations from the book of the same title.
Prod-PRIMED Dist-PRIMED

One Little Indian X 15 MIN
16MM FILM, 3/4 OR 1/2 IN VIDEO K-J T

A story told with puppets of an Indian boy who learns basic rules of pedestrian safety on his first visit to the big city.
Prod-NFBC Dist-IFB 1954

One Little Kitten And Where Is It C 6 MIN
16MM FILM, 3/4 OR 1/2 IN VIDEO K-I
Presents the story One Little Kitten, which follows the adventures of a small kitten on a typical summer afternoon. Includes the story Where Is It about a white rabbit who searches through a lush garden and finds a very satisfying prize.
Prod-HOBAN Dist-TEXFLM

One Loaf Of Bread C 15 MIN
16MM FILM OPTICAL SOUND H-C
Symbolizes man's age-old struggle against hunger and want in a never-ending search for a better life for all. Traces thousands of years of human history, highlighting the evolution of wheat growing, milling and baking from prehistoric times to the automated electronically controlled triumphs of the present.
Prod-GEMILL Dist-NINEFC

One Man B 30 MIN
16MM FILM OPTICAL SOUND
Reconstructs the mysterious case of Raoul Wallenberg, a Swedish diplomat, who disappeared behind the Iron Curtain in 1945, while attempting to save the Jewish community of Budapest.
LC NO. FIA64-1163
Prod-JTS Dist-NAAJS Prodn-NBC 1958

One Man Show B 14 MIN
16MM FILM OPTICAL SOUND
Depicts the struggles of a contemporary sculptor in a satire aimed at pop art.
Prod-NYU Dist-NYU

One Man's Alaska C 27 MIN
16MM FILM, 3/4 OR 1/2 IN VIDEO
Profiles conservationist and wildlife cinematographer Dick Proenneke at his wilderness home in the Lake Clark area of Alaska. Includes scenes of Alaskan wildlife and clips of Proenneke carving his log cabin home out of the wilderness.
LC NO. 79-706143
Prod-USNPS Dist-USNAC 1979

One Man's Family C 27 MIN
16MM FILM OPTICAL SOUND
A shortened version of the motion picture Thirty-Nine Hundred Million And One. Takes a look at India's population problem with special emphasis on women's roles and problems.
LC NO. 76-703251
Prod-OXFAM Dist-ASTRSK 1975

One Man's Fight For Life C 56 MIN
3/4 OR 1/2 INCH VIDEO CASSETTE A
Records Saif Ullah's lung cancer and its treatment. Looks at the emotional toll cancer takes on its victims and their families.
LC NO. 84-706265
Prod-BELLDA Dist-FI 1983

One Man's Multinational C 30 MIN
16MM FILM, 3/4 OR 1/2 IN VIDEO C A
Tells about Thomas Bata's shoe-manufacturing empire and how, as he moves into Third World countries, he willingly does business with democracies and dictatorships alike.
From The Enterprise Series.
LC NO. 81-707546
Prod-WGBHTV Dist-LCOA Prodn-DORSOL 1981

One Man's Property C 56 MIN
16MM FILM, 3/4 OR 1/2 IN VIDEO
Traces the events leading up to the Somerset Case in 1772, in which the judge declared that it was unlawful for one man to be the property of another on the soil of England.
From The Fight Against Slavery Series. No. 2
LC NO. 79-707813
Prod-BBCTV Dist-TIMLIF 1977

One Man's Revolution - Mao Tse-tung C 20 MIN
16MM FILM, 3/4 OR 1/2 IN VIDEO H-C A
Focuses on the life and career of Mao Tse-tung, who led the Chinese Communist Party for 42 years.
From The Twentieth Century History Series.
Prod-BBCTV Dist-FI 1981

One Man's Sewage Is Another Man's Drinking Water C 20 MIN
16MM FILM, 3/4 OR 1/2 IN VIDEO J-H
States that safe, clean available water is necessary for all life, but water is often contaminated to some degree. Sewage can be recycled and water can be cleaned up using modern techniques.
From The Biology - It's Life Series.
Prod-THAMES Dist-MEDIAG 1980

One Million Hiroshimas C 28 MIN
16MM FILM, 3/4 OR 1/2 IN VIDEO
Captures the workings and the spirit of the Second Congress of the International Physicians for the Prevention of Nuclear War. Addresses the greatest single threat to health that the world has ever known, nuclear war. Features many prominent scientists, physicians and military experts.
Prod-ANDMIC Dist-ANDMIC 1982

One Million Hours C 21 MIN
16MM FILM, 3/4 OR 1/2 IN VIDEO
Deals with an accident investigation in an engineering plant in England where an employee has been struck and injured by a truck. Shows how the work force and management can work together in accident investigation in order to prevent recurring incidents and future accidents.
Prod-MILLBK Dist-IFB

One Minute Cook, The - Microwave Made Easy With Best Selling Author, B Harris C 61 MIN
1/2 IN VIDEO CASSETTE BETA/VHS
Provides instruction in microwave cooking. Features Barbara Harris, author of Let's Cook Microwave.
Prod-MOHOMV Dist-MOHOMV

One Minute Manager, The C 50 MIN
3/4 OR 1/2 INCH VIDEO CASSETTE A
Presents Dr Ken Blanchard offering advice about how to manage one's time and one's employees more efficiently. Focuses on goals, praises and reprimands.
Prod-CBSFOX Dist-CBSFOX

One Minute Please C 8 MIN
16MM FILM OPTICAL SOUND H A
Presents attitudes, behavior and techniques which enable the salesperson to give individual attention and service to more than one customer at a time, thus multiplying sales without sacrificing goodwill.
From The Professional Selling Practices Series 1 Series.
LC NO. 77-702358
Prod-SAUM Dist-SAUM Prodn-CALPRO 1967

One Monday Morning C 10 MIN
16MM FILM, 3/4 OR 1/2 IN VIDEO P
Presents the children's story 'ONE MONDAY MORNING' by Ura Shulevitz.
Prod-WWS Dist-WWS 1972

One More Commandment C 15 MIN
16MM FILM OPTICAL SOUND J-C A
Dramatizes the Emma Lent poem 'THE MASTER IS COMING,' based on Jesus' words 'ONE NEW COMMANDMENT I GIVE UNTO YOU, THAT YE LOVE ONE ANOTHER.'
Prod-CAFM Dist-CAFM

One More Smoke C
3/4 OR 1/2 INCH VIDEO CASSETTE
Details the effect of nicotine on the lungs and heart as well as the lethal dangers of carbon monoxide.
Prod-MIFE Dist-MIFE

One More Smoke (Spanish) C
3/4 OR 1/2 INCH VIDEO CASSETTE
Details the effect of nicotine on the lungs and heart as well as the lethal dangers of carbon monoxide.
Prod-MIFE Dist-MIFE

One More Winter C 15 MIN
16MM FILM OPTICAL SOUND H-C
Shows how an old couple's romance generates envy in a young man who is still untouched by love. Written and directed by Francoise Sagan.
Prod-PROBEL Dist-FI 1976

One More Year On The Family Farm C 22 MIN
16MM FILM, 3/4 OR 1/2 IN VIDEO J-C A
Analyzes alternatives in the farming profession in the 1970's. Expresses the opinions and values of two families which exemplify the changes occurring in farming.
Prod-CORF Dist-CORF 1977

One Nation Under God C 60 MIN
3/4 OR 1/2 INCH VIDEO CASSETTE
Tours the so-called 'New Right' and 'Moral Majority.' Features interviews with James Robison, Rev Jerry Falwell and Sen George McGovern.
Prod-WCCOTV Dist-WCCOTV 1981

One Of A Kind C 58 MIN
16MM FILM, 3/4 OR 1/2 IN VIDEO
Deals with the love between a mother and daughter and the problem of child abuse.
Prod-BAKERD Dist-PHENIX 1978

One Of A Million B 22 MIN
16MM FILM OPTICAL SOUND H-C A
A few startling events cause a young executive to recognize his impending state of alcholism and to seek rehabilitation.
From The Doctors At Work Series.
LC NO. FIA65-1354
Prod-CMA Dist-LAWREN Prodn-LAWREN 1963

One Of Many - Dr Nhan C 16 MIN
16MM FILM, 3/4 OR 1/2 IN VIDEO J-C A
Highlights the problems faced by the displaced 'boat people' of Vietnam who emigrated to the West.
Prod-LUF Dist-LUF

One Of Our Own C 55 MIN
16MM FILM, 3/4 OR 1/2 IN VIDEO H-C A
Presents the story of the close-knit family of a mentally retarded boy that moves to a new community and must re-evaluate the wisdom of keeping him at home. Shows the retarded boy adjusting to his new home and learning skills that will help him become independent.
LC NO. 82-706506
Prod-CANBC Dist-FLMLIB 1981

One Of The Family C 27 MIN
16MM FILM, 3/4 OR 1/2 IN VIDEO A
Shows the difficulties and rewards associated with the adoption of an older child through the actual experience of one adoptive family. Explores every aspect of the adoption process.
Prod-LACFU Dist-IA 1974

One Of The Family C 27 MIN
3/4 OR 1/2 INCH VIDEO CASSETTE J A
Explores the moods and behavior of adopted children of varying ages and races.
Prod-SUTHRB Dist-SUTHRB

One Of The Gang C 30 MIN
3/4 OR 1/2 INCH VIDEO CASSETTE I-J
Reveals that despite a physical handicap, Mike holds his own and prevents a diamond theft at the Powerhouse.
From The Powerhouse Series.
LC NO. 83-707185
Prod-EFCVA Dist-GA 1982

One Of The Missing B 6 MIN
16MM FILM OPTICAL SOUND
Deals with the bizarre fate of a sharpshooter in the Civil War. Based on the story One Of The Missing by Ambrose Bierce.
LC NO. 78-701621
Prod-USC Dist-USC

One Of Thirty-Five Million C 18 MIN
3/4 OR 1/2 INCH VIDEO CASSETTE
Presents the story of one arthritic sufferer, George Brown, and a critical year in his life, the year in which his arthritis is diagnosed, treated and controlled, and the year when his sense of humor, determination, and medical regimen help him to learn how to live with his disease.
Prod-WSTGLC Dist-WSTGLC

One Of Those Days C
16MM FILM - 3/4 IN VIDEO A
Uses humor to motivate workers to analyze their materials handling procedures and make them safer.
Prod-BNA Dist-BNA 1983

One Of Those People C 29 MIN
16MM FILM OPTICAL SOUND A
Looks at corporate/industrial alcoholism and the possibilities for effectiveness of a well-developed Employee Assistance Program. Stresses on-the-job performance, personal interaction, intervention and company-union cooperation.
Prod-UPR Dist-FMSP 1975

One Out Of Five B 6 MIN
16MM FILM OPTICAL SOUND
Describes a situation in which a new truck has arrived to replace one of the five used in a telephone company's installation and repair operation. Discusses how to select the driver to whom this new truck should be assigned, and how a formula can be worked out to settle this kind of problem.
LC NO. FIA66-1146
Prod-UGA Dist-GCCED Prodn-GCCED 1959

One Out Of Ten C 28 MIN
3/4 OR 1/2 INCH VIDEO CASSETTE
Reveals that medical authorities agree that at least ten per cent of the people who drink are alcoholics. Presents the latest medical information and demonstrates therapy and treatment.
Prod-LACFU Dist-IA

One People C 12 MIN
16MM FILM OPTICAL SOUND I-C A
Shows how the United States was settled by groups of every nationality. Points out the various contributions of each group. An animated film, narrated by Ralph Bellamy.
Prod-ADL Dist-ADL 1946

One Person Too Late C 28 MIN
3/4 INCH VIDEO CASSETTE
Carries the Red Cross home safety message to the public.
Prod-GALSD Dist-AMRC

One Picture, 100 Words C 15 MIN
2 INCH VIDEOTAPE J
Discusses methods of adding concreteness as well as clarity and compactness to a composition.
From The From Me To You...In Writing, Pt 1 Series
Prod-DELE Dist-GPITVL

One Plus One C 25 MIN
16MM FILM OPTICAL SOUND R
Takes a humorous look at problems that plague the home, exposing conflicts that trouble marriages whether they be good or bad. Shows how God's plan for happy marriages is summed up in a simple equation.
Prod-GF Dist-GF

One Plus One Equals New C 15 MIN
3/4 OR 1/2 INCH VIDEO CASSETTE P
Employs a magician named Amazing Alexander and his assistants to explore compound words.
From The Magic Shop Series. No. 4
LC NO. 83-706149
Prod-CVETVC Dist-GPITVL Prodn-WCVETV 1982

One Plus One Equals Three C 10 MIN
16MM FILM OPTICAL SOUND K-I
A satire on the power struggle at every level of life, and the distortion of truth which ensues. Tells the story of a midget who fails in his attempt to persuade a giant that one plus one equals two.
LC NO. 72-700414
Prod-VIBAF Dist-MMA 1970

One PM C 95 MIN
16MM FILM OPTICAL SOUND
Features Jean-Luc Godard's never completed One American Movie (One AM). With Rip Torn, Jefferson Airplane, Leroi Jones, Tom Hayden, and Eldridge Cleaver. By D A Pennebaker with Jean-Luc Godard and Richard Leacock.
Prod-PENNAS Dist-PENNAS

One Rescuer CPR C 15 MIN
16MM FILM, 3/4 OR 1/2 IN VIDEO H-C A
See series title for descriptive statement.
From The REACT - Review Of Emergency Aid And CPR Training Series.
Prod-MTI Dist-MTI

One Room Schoolhouse C
16MM FILM, 3/4 OR 1/2 IN VIDEO
Shows one teacher coping with fifteen children in eight grades in one room.
Prod-DREWAS Dist-DIRECT 1979

One Sky C 13 MIN
16MM FILM OPTICAL SOUND A
Describes the aviation training program for foreign nationals at the Federal Aviation Administration Academy in Oklahoma City, Oklahoma.
LC NO. 77-702204
Prod-USFAA Dist-USNAC 1977

One Small Step C 17 MIN
16MM FILM OPTICAL SOUND I-C A
Captures the momentous events of President Nixon's visit to the people's Republic of China.
From The Screen News Digest Series. Vol 14, Issue 8
LC NO. 72-702749
Prod-HEARST Dist-HEARST 1972

One Small Step C 28 MIN
16MM FILM, 3/4 OR 1/2 IN VIDEO
Advises people to think about the world in which they live, and to reevaluate the era of self and remember there are other selfs in the world. Points out the contagious quality of good and bad behavior and provides some ideas on how managers and employees can improve their work environments through cooperation. Features James Whitmore and Dr Roderic Gorney.
Prod-CCCD Dist-CCCD

One Small Step C 55 MIN
3/4 OR 1/2 INCH VIDEO CASSETTE H-C A
Presents the discovery of the oldest human footprints near Olduvai Gorge in Tanzania by Dr Richard Leakey's mother Mary who is also an anthropologist. Declares that this discovery is the earliest evidence of man's shift from four legs to two. Narrated by Richard Leakey.
From The Making Of Mankind Series.
Prod-BBCTV Dist-TIMLIF 1982

One Small Step C 57 MIN
16MM FILM, 3/4 OR 1/2 IN VIDEO H-C A
Examines the history of space exploration up to July, 1975, when the Soviet Soyuz and the American Apollo met and docked in space. Explores the vistas that remain ahead.
From The Nova Series.
LC NO. 79-708144
Prod-WGBHTV Dist-TIMLIF 1979

One Special Dog C 17 MIN
16MM FILM, 3/4 OR 1/2 IN VIDEO P-I
Presents the story of a Southwest Indian family and their special dog. Portrays the universal qualities of family life, concern for another, warmth and understanding.
Prod-BOSUST Dist-PHENIX 1968

One Special Dog / A Boy And A Boa C 30 MIN
1/2 IN VIDEO CASSETTE BETA/VHS
Tells the story of an American Indian boy who befriends a stray dog. Presents an adaptation of the book by Abby Israel about a boy and his pet boa.
Prod-BFA Dist-BFA

One Species Among Many C 18 MIN
16MM FILM, 3/4 OR 1/2 IN VIDEO I-J
Explains how humans differ from animals.
Prod-CENTRO Dist-CORF

One Stage Pan-Colectomy For Ulcerative Colitis C 21 MIN
16MM FILM OPTICAL SOUND PRO
Points out that one stage pan-colectomy and abdominal ileostomy is the procedure of choice in patients with irretrievable damage to the colon from chronic ulcerative colitis or in patients with fulminating attacks of ulcerative colitis or massive hemorrhage.
Prod-ACYDGD Dist-ACY 1969

One Step Ahead - A Guide To Better Football Officiating C 17 MIN
16MM FILM OPTICAL SOUND I-C A
Covers the complex strategies and formations of football. Shows the official's responsibility for controlling the game flow without dominating it.
From The National Federation Sports Films Series.
LC NO. 80-701096
Prod-NFSHSA Dist-NFSHSA Prodn-CALVIN 1980

One Step Ahead I C 28 MIN
16MM FILM, 3/4 OR 1/2 IN VIDEO H-C A
Explores the various types of emotional crisis situations and presents viable solutions based on the degree of violence involved. Presents three main goals of crisis control in mental health patient care facilities.
Prod-AMERIM Dist-MTI 1975

One Step Ahead II - The Seclusion Room C 24 MIN
16MM FILM, 3/4 OR 1/2 IN VIDEO
Provides in-depth information on the use of the seclusion room in hospital crisis control. Observes its therapeutic use for patients who are dangerous to themselves or others. Illustrates the requirements for the physical set-up of the room, as well as the procedures involved in entrance, exit, observation and patient transport.
Prod-MTI Dist-MTI

One Step Ahead III - Verbal Techniques C 20 MIN
16MM FILM, 3/4 OR 1/2 IN VIDEO
Focuses on proper intervention techniques which can deescalate a volatile situation and calm a potentially aggressive patient. Shows several verbal techniques in action and stresses their use in responding to the patient's needs while avoiding physical confrontation.
Prod-MTI Dist-MTI

One Step At A Time C 15 MIN
16MM FILM, 3/4 OR 1/2 IN VIDEO I
Shows how Rudy makes a movie by breaking the complex project into an ordered sequence of steps. Tells how this results in a successful product.
From The Thinkabout Series. Sequencing And Scheduling
LC NO. 81-706111
Prod-OECA Dist-AITECH 1979

One Step At A Time C 25 MIN
16MM FILM, 3/4 OR 1/2 IN VIDEO H-C A
Tells how a child gradually develops control over its body as muscles and bones develop. Explains that doctors can assess the physical development of a child in relation to its age.
From The Children Growing Up Series.
Prod-BBCTV Dist-FI 1981

One Step At A Time - An Introduction To Behavior Modification C 32 MIN
16MM FILM, 3/4 OR 1/2 IN VIDEO C
Reveals that behavioral characteristics are much more effectively shaped by rewarding for desirable traits rather than by punishing for undesirable ones. Points out that positive reinforcement can take many forms.
From The Abnormal Psychology Series.
Prod-CRMP Dist-CRMP 1973

One Step At A Time - Deinstitutionalizing The Mentally Retarded X 28 MIN
16MM FILM, 3/4 OR 1/2 IN VIDEO
Discusses the deinstitutionalizing of the mentally retarded.
LC NO. 84-706191
Prod-UWISC Dist-LAWREN 1983

One Step Closer C 13 MIN
3/4 INCH VIDEO CASSETTE PRO
Presents the theory behind surgical skin asepsis and use of plastic surgical drapes.
Prod-MMAMC Dist-MMAMC

One Strong Link—A Series

Presents a program for training of paraprofessionals selected to work as nutrition aides. Presents concepts that are adaptable for education in other areas as well.
Prod-CUETV Dist-CUNIV 1971

Definition Of The Aide's Job	30 MIN
Evaluation	26 MIN
Home Visit, The, I	25 MIN
Home Visit, The, II	29 MIN
Learning	29 MIN
Motivation	33 MIN
Values And Attitudes	27 MIN
Working With Groups	30 MIN

One Teacher's Dreams And Harvests C 58 MIN
16MM FILM OPTICAL SOUND C A
Presents a visit to retired superintendent of schools for Blair County, Pennsylvania, Paul Kurtz, during which he discusses his educational and administrative philosophies, techniques and strategies and relates them to his long-time interest in gardening.
LC NO. 76-703301
Prod-WPSXTV Dist-PSU 1976

One Thing After Another C 25 MIN
16MM FILM, 3/4 OR 1/2 IN VIDEO J-C A
Defines a computer program as a series of instructions that a computer must follow.
From The Computer Programme Series. Episode 2
LC NO. 82-707086
Prod-BBCTV Dist-FI 1982

One Thing Leads To Another C 15 MIN
16MM FILM OPTICAL SOUND I
Describes the business problems faced by the Rocket Babysitting Service.
From The Thinkabout Series.
LC NO. 81-700138
Prod-EDFCEN Dist-AITECH 1980

One Thing Leads To Another C 14 MIN
3/4 OR 1/2 INCH VIDEO CASSETTE I
Describes how a babysitting service learns about the price of success as one new business problem leads to another.
From The Thinkabout Series. Solving Problems
LC NO. 81-706112
Prod-EDFCEN Dist-AITECH 1979

One Thousand And One Launches C 26 MIN
16MM FILM OPTICAL SOUND
Traces the development of the American space program from early rocket experiments to the exploration of the Moon's surface by men in 1969.
LC NO. 74-702498
Prod-RCKWL Dist-RCKWL 1973

One Thousand Dollar Bill, The C 24 MIN
16MM FILM, 3/4 OR 1/2 IN VIDEO
Presents a story about a young man who tells off his employer, makes plans to wed his sweetheart, and takes on the local establishment when a huge sum of money temporarily changes his life. Illustrates that what a person believes about himself can be worth more than any sum of money. Originally shown on the television series ABC Weekend Specials.
LC NO. 79-707134
Prod-ABCTV Dist-MTI Prodn-ABCCIR 1979

One Thousand Dozen, The C 55 MIN
16MM FILM, 3/4 OR 1/2 IN VIDEO H-C A
Tells how David Rasmussen anticipates making a fortune with the 1,500 pounds of eggs which he intends to sell to miners at exorbitant prices. Shows that after a torturous journey to get the eggs to the miners intact, his dream of riches falls apart when some of the eggs are cracked into a frying pan. Based on the short story The One Thousand Dozen by Jack London.
From The Jack London's Tales Of The Klondike Series.
LC NO. 84-706230
Prod-NORWK Dist-EBEC 1982

One Thousand Years Of Muscogee (Creek) Art C 28 MIN
3/4 INCH VIDEO CASSETTE
Traces the development of Creek Indian art forms from the prehistoric to the present. Views objects from museums all over the world and includes prints, photographs and rare footage of Creek ceremonies showing some of the objects in actual use. Also available in two-inch quad and one-inch videotape.
Prod-CREEK Dist-NAMPBC

One To Grow On - Prologue X 10 MIN
16MM FILM, 3/4 OR 1/2 IN VIDEO T
Outlines the methods used and goals aimed at in reaching an understanding of the mental health aspects of student-teacher relationships.
From The One To Grow On Series.
LC NO. 80-706193
Prod-NIMH Dist-USNAC Prodn-UCLA 1979

One To Grow On—A Series
T
Discusses various aspects of teaching.
Prod-NIMH Dist-USNAC 1979

Act II - Lindsey	017 MIN
He Comes From Another Room	028 MIN
Individuals	018 MIN
Learning Strategies	011 MIN
One To Grow On - Prologue	010 MIN
Pretty Good Class For A Monday, A	025 MIN
Sarah	010 MIN
Teacher In Reflection, A	011 MIN
What Is Teaching - What Is Learning	023 MIN

One To One Nurse-Patient Relationship, The B 44 MIN
16MM FILM OPTICAL SOUND PRO
Discusses the role of the nurse as a patient counselor.
From The Nursing In Psychiatry Series.
LC NO. 72-703434
Prod-VDONUR Dist-AJN Prodn-WTTWTV 1968

One To One—A Series

Prod-WETATV Dist-PUBTEL

Adlai Stevenson - Campaign Speeches	29 MIN
Children's Books	29 MIN
Dramatic Literature - THE Skin OF OUR TEETH	29 MIN
E B White - Essays And A Short Story	29 MIN
Emily Dickinson - Selected Poems	28 MIN
F Scott Fitzgerald - THE GREAT GATSBY	29 MIN
Graham Greene - THE HEART OF THE MATTER	29 MIN
Henry David Thoreau - WALDEN	29 MIN
Henry James - THE BEAST IN THE JUNGLE	29 MIN
James Agee - A DEATH IN THE FAMILY	29 MIN
Literature Of Sports, The	29 MIN
Mark Twain - HUCKLEBERRY FINN	29 MIN
Mark Van Doren - Poems And Criticism	29 MIN
Nikos Kazantzakis - Selected Works	29 MIN
Sampler Of Selections From Favorite Authors, A	29 MIN
Short Stories By John Cheever And Eudora Welty	29 MIN
T H White - THE ONCE AND FUTURE KING	26 MIN
T S Eliot - Selected Poetry	29 MIN
Vladimir Nabokov - LOLITA	29 MIN
William Shakespeare - ANTONY AND CLEOPATRA	29 MIN

One To Speak, One To Hear C 15 MIN
16MM FILM, 3/4 OR 1/2 IN VIDEO
Portrays the life of a hearing impaired woman. Shows that many of the difficulties and obstacles confronting the impaired are self-imposed while others are presented by a verbally oriented society. Stresses communication between the hearing and the nonhearing.
Prod-BOURKR Dist-STNFLD 1977

One To Three Months C 9 MIN
3/4 OR 1/2 INCH VIDEO CASSETTE H-C A
Discusses seeing, hearing and feeling in infants from one to three months.
From The Teaching Infants And Toddlers Series. Pt 1
Prod-BGSU Dist-GPITVL 1978

One Too Many C 30 MIN
16MM FILM, 3/4 OR 1/2 IN VIDEO J-C A
Centers around four high school students affected by drinking and driving. Edited version.
Prod-ABCTV Dist-LCOA 1985

One Too Many C 46 MIN
16MM FILM, 3/4 OR 1/2 IN VIDEO J-C A
Centers around four high school students affected by drinking and driving. Full version.
Prod-ABCTV Dist-LCOA 1985

One Tough Texan C 21 MIN
16MM FILM OPTICAL SOUND
Features A J Foyt, five times USAC National Driving Champion and three times winner of the Indianapolis 500. Shows his shop in Houston, Texas and his crew telling what it is like to work for him.
Prod-GTARC Dist-GTARC

One Tough Texan C 30 MIN
3/4 OR 1/2 INCH VIDEO CASSETTE
Reveals the motivation and team work behind auto racer A J Foyt, who doesn't win every race he runs, but is always the man to beat when the green flag falls.
Prod-HBS Dist-IVCH

One Trillion Dollars For Defense C 60 MIN
16MM FILM, 3/4 OR 1/2 IN VIDEO J-C A

Shows why the United States requires such a large defense budget. Looks at sophisticated weapons as Bill Moyers talks with military personnel, representatives from weapons manufacturers, a government defense expert and others about the issue of where all the high technology will lead.
LC NO. 83-706385
Prod-WNETTV Dist-FI 1982

One Turkey, Two Turkey C 6 MIN
16MM FILM, 3/4 OR 1/2 IN VIDEO K-P
Introduces the youngest readers and pre-readers to words and concepts, including pictures and songs.
From The Starting To Read Series.
Prod-GME Dist-AIMS 1971

One Turn Of Earth C 30 MIN
3/4 OR 1/2 INCH VIDEO CASSETTE
Captures the dust and rubble of men shaping a better tomorrow on seven continents. Shows a dam complex rising in Brazil, giant logs being harvested in North Borneo and legions of machines at work on the mighty Indus River project.
Prod-IVCH Dist-IVCH

One Voice In The Cosmic Fugue C 60 MIN
16MM FILM, 3/4 OR 1/2 IN VIDEO J-C A
Addresses the topic of life and its origins. Speculates on life in other worlds and examines molecular biology, the Miller-Urey experiment, and DNA. Based on the book Cosmos by Carl Sagan. Narrated by Carl Sagan.
From The Cosmos Series. Program 2
LC NO. 81-707176
Prod-KCET Dist-FI 1980

One Was Johnny C 3 MIN
16MM FILM, 3/4 OR 1/2 IN VIDEO P
Uses verses by Maurice Sendak to teach the fundamentals of counting.
Prod-WWS Dist-WWS 1978

One Way B 8 MIN
3/4 INCH VIDEO CASSETTE
Features a video in which the artist physically confronts objects with his camera, scraping and pushing, so the objects' materiality and textures can be felt.
From The James Byrne - Five Works 1974-79 Series.
Prod-EAI Dist-EAI

One Way To Better Cities C 29 MIN
16MM FILM OPTICAL SOUND C A
Shows influence of property tax on urban decay, suburban sprawl and land speculation. Explains how private industry can be provided with better incentives to help meet renewal and development needs of the country.
Prod-SCHALK Dist-MTP 1970

One Way To Build A Flat B 15 MIN
16MM FILM OPTICAL SOUND
Demonstrates a method of building a stage flat from reference to the blueprint through the covering of the flat with cloth.
Prod-UCLA Dist-UCLA 1950

One Week C
16MM FILM OPTICAL SOUND J-H
Shows the working methods and psychological realities of a journalist's life.
LC NO. 74-707447
Prod-NEWSWK Dist-MLA Prodn-STEEGP 1969

One Week B 20 MIN
16MM FILM SILENT J-C A
Stars Buster Keaton.
Prod-MGM Dist-TWYMAN 1920

One Week In October B 29 MIN
16MM FILM OPTICAL SOUND
Tells the story of the cuban crisis, describing the civil and military buildup during this critical period.
LC NO. 74-705254
Prod-USOCD Dist-USNAC 1964

One Week In October B 29 MIN
3/4 OR 1/2 INCH VIDEO CASSETTE
Tells the story of the 1962 Cuban missile crisis with original American reconnaissance-plane footage. Features extensive scenes of the faces and voices of the key figures involved - President Kennedy, Robert McNamara, Dean Rusk and Adlai Stevenson.
Prod-IHF Dist-IHF

One Week In October B 29 MIN
3/4 INCH VIDEO CASSETTE
Tells the story of the Cuban Missile Crisis and the U S civil and military build-up which followed. Begins with aerial reconnaissance photographs of Cuba taken from U S jets. Includes coverage filmed during these crucial weeks by camera crews of the U S military services, newsreels and television stations.
Prod-USNAC Dist-USNAC 1972

One Who Was There C 36 MIN
3/4 OR 1/2 INCH VIDEO CASSETTE J A
Dramatizes the journey home of sixty-year-old Mary Magdalene who is saddened by the lonely years of waiting for Jesus' return. Shows how the journey becomes spiritual as well as physical as she discovers that the strong faith of the disciples has been passed to a new generation of believers. Uses flashbacks to show the events of the Passion, Passover and the healing of Mary Magdalene.
Prod-UMCOM Dist-ECUFLM Prodn-UCHC 1979

One Within, The C 16 MIN
3/4 INCH VIDEO CASSETTE H-C A
Shows a young woman's quest for a satisfying philosophy, a sense of unity and participation in life. Tells how she explores T'ai Chi, Zen, Sufi dancing and the teachings of Pir Vilayat Khan.
Prod-LAWREN Dist-LAWREN

One Within, The - A Journey Of Self-Discovery C 20 MIN
16MM FILM OPTICAL SOUND H-C A
Shows how a young American working woman finds a greater sense of unity and participation through self-discipline and self-mastery. Offers an alternative to drug-induced experiences.
LC NO. 75-701609
Prod-PERLE Dist-LAWREN 1975

One Woman's Divorce C 29 MIN
3/4 OR 1/2 INCH VIDEO CASSETTE
Features Susan Braudy discussing her book, which is a personal account of her divorce.
From The Woman Series.
Prod-WNEDTV Dist-PBS

One World - A Series
16MM FILM, 3/4 OR 1/2 IN VIDEO J-H
Looks at the economic and social interrelationship between Great Britain and its former Caribbean colonies.
Prod-BBCTV Dist-FI 1982

From The Caribbean 020 MIN
Made In Barbados 020 MIN
People On The Move 020 MIN
Trading The Sun 020 MIN

One Your With, The C 29 MIN
2 INCH VIDEOTAPE
See series title for descriptive statement.
From The Our Street Series.
Prod-MDCPB Dist-PUBTEL

One 2 3 4 5 6 7 8 9 0 Keys B 30 MIN
2 INCH VIDEOTAPE
From The Typewriting, Unit 3 - Number Key Control Series.
Prod-GPITVL Dist-GPITVL

One-Alpha C 13 MIN
3/4 OR 1/2 INCH VIDEO CASSETTE PRO
Simulates the crash of a 70-passenger jet plane to describe to potential rescuers what they might expect to deal with in such an emergency.
Prod-FILCOM Dist-FILCOM

One-And Two-Axis Linear Milling C 18 MIN
3/4 OR 1/2 INCH VIDEO CASSETTE IND
Discusses climb and conventional milling, programming rapid position movement and several aspects of programming.
From The Numerical Control/Computerized Numerical Control, Module 1 - Fundamentals Series.
Prod-LEIKID Dist-LEIKID

One-Color Spectrum C 30 MIN
3/4 OR 1/2 INCH VIDEO CASSETTE
Tells how one-color needlework concentrates on fine pattern details and texture. Shows how varying stitches can alter color intensity and produce special effects.
From The Erica Series.
Prod-WGBHTV Dist-KINGFT

One-Eyed Men Are Kings C 15 MIN
16MM FILM, 3/4 OR 1/2 IN VIDEO J-C A
Tells the story of a man's quest for friendship, told with humor and pathos. Describes how he masquerades as a blind man, acquires new respect and becomes the center of attention. Depicts how his ruse is detected and he resumes his lonely existence.
Prod-CAPAC Dist-MGHT 1974

One-Half, One-Fourth, 5 6 Keys, Centering Review B 30 MIN
2 INCH VIDEOTAPE
From The Typewriting, Unit 3 - Number Key Control Series.
Prod-GPITVL Dist-GPITVL

One-Rescuer CPR C 18 MIN
3/4 OR 1/2 INCH VIDEO CASSETTE PRO
Teaches how to tell whether a person is unconscious, how to administer rescue breathing and how to perform external chest compressions.
From The Cardiopulmonary Resuscitation Series.
Prod-HSCIC Dist-HSCIC 1984

One-Sample Testing - Product Evaluation C
3/4 OR 1/2 INCH VIDEO CASSETTE IND
Cites one-sample testing as a formal way to determine if goals are being met, as defined by mean and variance. Discusses hypothesis testing and confidence intervals in the one-sample case for the mean with variance known or unknown. Tells about testing for variance as well.
From The Statistics For Managers Series.
Prod-COLOSU Dist-COLOSU

One-Sample Tests For Qualitative Data C 30 MIN
3/4 OR 1/2 INCH VIDEO CASSETTE IND
Incorporates hypothesis testing and confidence intervals for the normal and student's distributions. Shows a useful and practical discussion for those with sample means. Reviews question, 'Do we have an unusual sample mean value or has our process shifted?'
From The Engineering Statistics Series.
Prod-COLOSU Dist-COLOSU

One-Shot Stapler, The C 9 MIN
3/4 INCH VIDEO CASSETTE PRO
Illustrates use of skin stapling closure by a stapler dispensing a single staple. Shows Emergency Room (ER) and office treatment of minor wounds and lacerations.
Prod-MMAMC Dist-MMAMC

One-Sided Triangle, The C 24 MIN
16MM FILM - 3/4 IN VIDEO

Tells how trouble ensues when people within a group can't communicate. Points out that once the communication barrier is broken, the situation changes from one of discord to one of trust and team work.
From The Communicating Series.
Prod-BNA Dist-BNA

One-Stage Hypospadias Repair, A - A Combined Urological And Plastic Procedure C 20 MIN
16MM FILM OPTICAL SOUND
Points out that hypospadias, a congenital defect in which there is incomplete development of the urethra, occurs about three to four times in each 1000 live male births. Emphasizes the execution and technique of handling tissue in several types of hypospadias. Demonstrates a complete repair procedure and shows post-operative results in several cases.
LC NO. 75-702279
Prod-EATONL Dist-EATONL 1960

One-Stage Total Colectomy For Ulcerative Colitis C 22 MIN
16MM FILM OPTICAL SOUND PRO
Points out that experience has demonstrated that a one-stage total colectomy for ulcerative colitis has great advantages over the multistage procedures which include a permanent ileostomy, a right hemicolectomy and a left hemicolectomy.
Prod-ACYDGD Dist-ACY 1950

One-To-One C 13 MIN
16MM FILM OPTICAL SOUND IND
Documents the importance of establishing a person-to-person relationship between customer and salesperson.
From The People Sell People Series.
LC NO. 77-702362
Prod-SAUM Dist-MLA Prodn-CALVIN 1975

One-To-One Correspondence C 20 MIN
2 INCH VIDEOTAPE P
See series title for descriptive statement.
From The Mathemagic, Unit I - Place Value Series.
Prod-WMULTV Dist-GPITVL

One-To-One Correspondence C 45 MIN
2 INCH VIDEOTAPE
See series title for descriptive statement.
From The Fundamentals Of Mathematics (2nd Ed,) Unit I - Number Theory Series.
Prod-CHITVC Dist-GPITVL

One-Two-Three - Advanced Features C
3/4 OR 1/2 INCH VIDEO CASSETTE A
Covers the use of keyboard macros, advanced graphics, multiple spreadsheet consolidation and data management for the experienced Lotus 1-2-3 user.
Prod-DSIM Dist-DSIM

One-Two-Three - Advanced Features C 30 MIN
3/4 OR 1/2 INCH VIDEO CASSETTE
Continues the presentation of Lotus 1-2-3. Fully describes various features such as consolidation, keyboard macros, graphic generation and data management. Includes written text.
Prod-MICROV Dist-BERGL

One-Two-Three - An Introduction C 35 MIN
3/4 OR 1/2 INCH VIDEO CASSETTE
Introduces Lotus 1-2-3. Presents the concept of integrated programs. Explains loading and spreadsheet construction. Details range creation and copy command. Includes written text.
Prod-MICROV Dist-BERGL

One-Two-Three - Introduction To The Integrated Spreadsheet C
3/4 OR 1/2 INCH VIDEO CASSETTE A
Shows how to create a Lotus 1-2-3 spreadsheet. Covers the basics including the Lotus 1-2-3 control panel, menu selection and entering labels, numbers and formulas. Moves to the command structures such as changing column widths, using the anchor cell and the free cell in range commands, moving and centering labels, and formatting the display. Explains naming, storing on disk, and printing the worksheet.
Prod-DSIM Dist-DSIM

One, Going On Two C 25 MIN
3/4 OR 1/2 INCH VIDEO CASSETTE
Shows how pediatricians chart the physical and psychological developments during a child's second year. Has a group of mothers with their children enjoying a picnic in the park and a chance to question the doctors about discipline, potty training, thumb sucking and other early childhood problems.
Prod-TRAINX Dist-TRAINX

One, Two, Many - Dealing With Multiple Objects C 15 MIN
16MM FILM, 3/4 OR 1/2 IN VIDEO
Studies the child's mastery of dealing with multiple objects.
From The Cognitive Development Series.
Prod-WILEYJ Dist-MEDIAG 1972

One, Two, Plop C 11 MIN
16MM FILM, 3/4 OR 1/2 IN VIDEO P-J
Presents a schizophrenic witch who manages to make all the 3's in the kingdom disappear to point up the value of being able to regard matters from another person's unique point of view.
From The Kingdom Of Kite Series.
Prod-KINGSP Dist-PHENIX 1971

One, Two, Three - Clean C 13 MIN
16MM FILM OPTICAL SOUND J-C A
Describes today's modern sewage treatment process and how a sewage treatment plant works.
Prod-FINLYS Dist-FINLYS

One, Two, Three - Un, Deux, Trois C 5 MIN
16MM FILM, 3/4 OR 1/2 IN VIDEO J-C

Presents an animated story, without narration, about the life of an imaginary Mr X, for whom the slightest variation of daily routines creates insolvable problems.
LC NO. 77-701532
Prod-LESFG Dist-FI 1977

One, Two, Three, Zero - Infertility C 28 MIN
16MM FILM, 3/4 OR 1/2 IN VIDEO A
Discusses infertility, focusing on several couples who have sought help for their inability to have children. Deals with the couples' feelings of failure, anxiety and hopelessness and shows one couple being questioned, tested and treated. Notes the common causes and methods for treating and circumventing the medical difficulties posed by these health problems.
Prod-CANBC Dist-FLMLIB 1980

One's A Heifer C 26 MIN
16MM FILM, 3/4 OR 1/2 IN VIDEO I-J
Describes how conscientious Peter loses two calves and must travel to a remote area of his uncle's ranch to find them. Reveals what can happen when a situation is approached by a preconceived point of view. Based on the story by Sinclair Ross.
Prod-ATLAF Dist-BCNFL Prodn-CANBC 1985

One's A Heifer (French) C 26 MIN
16MM FILM, 3/4 OR 1/2 IN VIDEO I-J
A French language version of the film and videorecording One's A Heifer.
Prod-ATLAF Dist-BCNFL Prodn-CANBC 1985

Oneida C 28 MIN
3/4 OR 1/2 INCH VIDEO CASSETTE
Takes a look at the past and present lives of the Oneida people in northern Wisconsin. Includes interviews with a few of the older members of the tribe who talk about their personal past experiences and their feelings about the younger generation.
Prod-UWISC Dist-UWISC 1975

Ones And Tens C 20 MIN
2 INCH VIDEOTAPE P
See series title for descriptive statement.
From The Mathemagic, Unit I - Place Value Series.
Prod-WMULTV Dist-GPITVL

Ongoing Prenatal Assessment, The C 18 MIN
16MM FILM, 3/4 OR 1/2 IN VIDEO
See series title for descriptive statement.
From The Family-Oriented Maternity Care By The Nurse Clinician Series.
Prod-EMORYU Dist-USNAC

Onion Celebration, An C 30 MIN
1/2 IN VIDEO CASSETTE BETA/VHS
Demonstrates cooking stuffed onion leaves and onions sauteed with peppers Italian style. Discusses the Walla Walla Sweet and the Georgia Vandalia onions.
From The Frugal Gourmet Series.
Prod-WTTWTV Dist-MTI

Onion Farming C 7 MIN
16MM FILM OPTICAL SOUND K-C
Shows the growing of onions and explains that it is a highly developed skill among the natives of the Dogon tribe who live along the Niger River.
From The African Village Life In Mali Series.
LC NO. 73-707531
Prod-BRYAN Dist-IFF

Onion Farming (Dogon People) C 7 MIN
3/4 OR 1/2 INCH VIDEO CASSETTE
See series title for descriptive statement.
From The African Village Life (Mali) Series.
Prod-IFF Dist-IFF

Onions - Rings, Halving, Slicing And Mincing C 20 MIN
3/4 OR 1/2 INCH VIDEO CASSETTE PRO
Explains how to prepare green, Spanish and Bermuda onions, and tells what tools and techniques to use.
Prod-CULINA Dist-CULINA

Online Processing C 30 MIN
3/4 OR 1/2 INCH VIDEO CASSETTE H-C A
Introduces and compares online with batch processing. Studies characteristics of online systems such as I/O functions, data transmissions, file access and response time.
From The Making It Count Series.
LC NO. 80-707575
Prod-BCSC Dist-BCSC 1980

Online, Or How Do You Spell Relief C 9 MIN
3/4 OR 1/2 INCH VIDEO CASSETTE
Describes some of the advantages of an automated library circulation system.
Prod-LVN Dist-LVN

Only About Woman B 45 MIN
3/4 OR 1/2 INCH VIDEO CASSETTE
Documents the different occupations open to women in the USSR.
Prod-IHF Dist-IHF

Only Angels Have Wings B 121 MIN
16MM FILM OPTICAL SOUND H-C A
Describes the deterioration of the friendship of two South American cargo fliers who both fall for the same girl. Stars Cary Grant and Jean Arthur.
Prod-CPC Dist-TIMLIF 1939

Only Benjy Knows - Should He Tell X 4 MIN
16MM FILM, 3/4 OR 1/2 IN VIDEO K-P
Provides a situation in which a child sees other children stealing toys as a basis for a discussion about tattling.
Prod-EBEC Dist-EBEC 1970

Only Child, The C 7 MIN
16MM FILM, 3/4 OR 1/2 IN VIDEO J-C A
Presents an animated satirical statement about a father whose misguided love leads him to direct his son's life from pampering infancy through school, romance and finally medical school. Reveals that while he is unprepared for his role as a doctor, the son is shocked to discover that his first patient on the operating table is his father.
LC NO. 81-706971
Prod-SFTB Dist-PHENIX 1981

Only Fools Break The Rules C 15 MIN
16MM FILM, 3/4 OR 1/2 IN VIDEO P-J
Tells how Fat Albert and the gang come to realize the importance of following rules after a near-disaster in an abandoned amusement park.
From The Fat Albert And The Cosby Kids Series II Series.
Prod-BARR Dist-BARR Prodn-FLMTON 1979

Only Good Indian..., The C 24 MIN
16MM FILM OPTICAL SOUND J-H
Shatters myths regarding American Indians by recounting how unfairly they were treated by the white man. Tells how a cavalry scout named Tom Jeffords discovers the humanity of the Indian when he arranges a deal with the great chief Cochise to allow mail riders to pass through Indian land. Uses excerpts from the motion picture Blood Brother starring James Stewart and Jeff Chandler.
From The American Challenge Series.
Prod-TWCF Dist-FI 1975

Only Hooked A Little C 29 MIN
16MM FILM OPTICAL SOUND
Features a hospital chaplain discussing the helplessness felt by addicts in the drug rehabilitation program he runs. Describes how he speaks from first-hand knowledge because he was an addict himself.
From The This Is The Life Series.
Prod-LUTTEL Dist-LUTTEL 1981

Only In America C 20 MIN
16MM FILM OPTICAL SOUND J-H
Underscores the importance of innovation, invention and enterprise in the growth of the United States. Presents the history of Michigan as well and explains how the state's natural resources helped produce an industrial economy.
Prod-CENTRO Dist-CONPOW

Only Losers Play C 10 MIN
16MM FILM, 3/4 OR 1/2 IN VIDEO P-J
Shows the seriousness of the shoplifting crime and warns young people about the consequences, including guilt, embarrassment, the shame of disappointing one's parents, and a criminal record.
Prod-KLEINW Dist-KLEINW

Only One Earth C 30 MIN
3/4 INCH VIDEO CASSETTE J-C A
Focuses on the United Nations Conference on the Human Environment held in Stockholm, Sweden, in 1972. Features participants who are taking to heart the concept that the earth is one world with interdependent nations and people and that pollution causes everyone to suffer.
From The Man Builds - Man Destroys Series.
LC NO. 75-704137
Prod-UN Dist-GPITVL 1972

Only One Earth (The Stockholm Conference) C 30 MIN
16MM FILM OPTICAL SOUND J-C A
Focuses on the theme of the United Nations Conference on the Human Environment held in Stockholm. Suggests that pollution of the oceans or the air affects everyone in the world.
From The Man Builds - Man Destroys Series.
LC NO. 75-704137
Prod-UN Dist-GPITVL 1972

Only One Road - The Bike / Car Traffic Mix C 26 MIN
16MM FILM OPTICAL SOUND H-C A
Shows ways for motorists and bicyclists to share the road safely.
LC NO. 75-702825
Prod-AAA Dist-AAA Prodn-AVSFP 1975

Only One Road - Three Families Coping With Childhood Cancer C 53 MIN
3/4 OR 1/2 INCH VIDEO CASSETTE PRO
Presents interviews of three children, ages 5-9, and their families who are past the initial stages of diagnosis and treatment of cancer. Reveals through interviews with and actual footage of these families interacting in the home, public school and hospital settings, concerns regarding remission of cancer, school problems, long-term side effects, survival of the marriage and handling 'left out' siblings.
Prod-UMICHM Dist-UMICHM 1983

Only The Ball Was White C 30 MIN
16MM FILM, 3/4 OR 1/2 IN VIDEO J-C A
Explores the gruelling, gritty life in the Negro baseball leagues and tells how the color line was finally broken when the Dodgers signed Jackie Robinson.
LC NO. 81-706797
Prod-WTTWTV Dist-FI 1980

Only The Beginning C 10 MIN
16MM FILM OPTICAL SOUND
Deals with the confrontation which took place in the streets of Paris in May 1968 between students and the police.
Prod-NEWSR Dist-NEWSR

Only The Strong C 27 MIN
16MM FILM OPTICAL SOUND
Documents and compares the various weapons systems of the United States and the Soviet Union. Includes portions filmed inside the USSR.
Prod-THIOKL Dist-THIOKL 1972

Only Thing I Can't Do Is Hear, The C 27 MIN
16MM FILM, 3/4 OR 1/2 IN VIDEO
Describes the pre-college programs available for deaf high school students at Gallaudet College. Presents classroom situations and comments by students and faculty. Uses sign language.
Prod-GALCO Dist-GALCO Prodn-COMCRP 1977

Only Thing You Know, The C 85 MIN
16MM FILM OPTICAL SOUND
Presents the story of an 18-year-old girl from a middle class family who is searching for substance and meaning in her life.
LC NO. 74-701211
Prod-CFDEVC Dist-CANFDC 1971

Only Yesterday (Award Series 1965) B 29 MIN
2 INCH VIDEOTAPE
Points out the ever-changing environment of man. Focuses on the sights and sounds of yesterday's 'gaslight America.'
From The Synergism - Gallimaufry Series.
Prod-WMVSTV Dist-PUBTEL

Only You Can Put Your Best Foot Forward C 51 MIN
3/4 OR 1/2 INCH VIDEO CASSETTE
Discusses standard procedures for job announcements and interviews for civil service positions. Portrays interviews with not-so-typical applicants.
LC NO. 80-706508
Prod-VAHSL Dist-USNAC 1978

Onset Of Labor C
3/4 OR 1/2 INCH VIDEO CASSETTE
Deals with the real concerns women have about labor. Discusses contractions, thinning, dilation and other stages until birth.
Prod-MIFE Dist-MIFE

Onset Of Labor (Arabic) C
3/4 OR 1/2 INCH VIDEO CASSETTE
Deals with the real concerns women have about labor. Discusses contractions, thinning, dilation and other stages during birth.
Prod-MIFE Dist-MIFE

Onset Of Labor (Spanish) C
3/4 OR 1/2 INCH VIDEO CASSETTE
Deals with the real concerns women have about labor. Discusses contractions, thinning, dilation and other stages during birth.
Prod-MIFE Dist-MIFE

Onshore Planning For Offshore Oil - Voices From Scotland C 21 MIN
16MM FILM OPTICAL SOUND J-C A
Examines the social, physical and economic impact of offshore oil development on the residents of Scotland's coastal communities.
LC NO. 77-700209
Prod-CONSF Dist-CONSF Prodn-MENDEJ 1976

Onshore Planning For Offshore Oil - Voices From Scotland C 21 MIN
16MM FILM, 3/4 OR 1/2 IN VIDEO J-C A
Dramatizes the onshore buildup that accompanies offshore oil development and its effect on those who live and work along Scotland's coast.
Prod-BULFRG Dist-BULFRG

Onstage At Quartz Mountain C 21 MIN
16MM FILM OPTICAL SOUND
Documents the 1978 Oklahoma Summer Arts Program, a camp offering Oklahoma high school students a chance to study their particular arts discipline under working professionals.
LC NO. 79-701182
Prod-OKSAI Dist-TULSAS Prodn-TULSAS 1979

Onstage At Quartz Mountains C 20 MIN
16MM FILM OPTICAL SOUND
Focuses on high school students who attended the Oklahoma summer arts camp in 1978. Tells of their experiences studying ballet, modern dance, acting, mime, painting, printmaking, poetry and music.
Prod-OKSAI Dist-MTP 1978

Onstage With Judith Somogi C 29 MIN
16MM FILM OPTICAL SOUND
Focuses on Judith Somogi, a young conductor. Demonstrates the dedication and hard work needed to build a music career.
LC NO. 80-701457
Prod-OKSAI Dist-MTP Prodn-TULSAS 1980

Ontario A La Carte C 21 MIN
16MM FILM OPTICAL SOUND J-C A
Presents many attractions in this province including Toronto, upper Canada Village, Niagara Falls and changing of the guard at Ottawa.
LC NO. 71-714303
Prod-ONTPRO Dist-CTFL 1971

Ontario Land B 7 MIN
16MM FILM OPTICAL SOUND
Features experiments with color, time intervals and sound by painting and scratching clear film and black leader.
LC NO. 77-702599
Prod-CANFDC Dist-CANFDC 1972

Ontario Place C 16 MIN
16MM FILM OPTICAL SOUND
Explores the commemorative showcase of the Province of Ontario.
LC NO. 74-702405
Prod-ONTPRO Dist-CTFL 1973

Onto The Page And Into The World C 13 MIN
16MM FILM OPTICAL SOUND
Follows the project of the production of a book of poems by mentally retarded students at the Dr Franklin Perkins School in

Lancaster, Massachusetts. Shows the work on the book as the students compose the poems, carve woodcuts for illustrations, set the type, print, bind and mail copies to customers.
Prod-CAMPF Dist-CAMPF 1973

Ontogenesis C 6 MIN
3/4 OR 1/2 INCH VIDEO CASSETTE
See series title for descriptive statement.
From The Five Short Works by Janice Tanaka Series.
Prod-EAI Dist-EAI

Ontogeny C 60 MIN
3/4 OR 1/2 INCH VIDEO CASSETTE A
Presents biologist Humberto Maturana discussing ontogeny.
From The Biology Of Cognition And Language Series. Program 7
Prod-UCEMC Dist-UCEMC

Ontological Argument, The C 25 MIN
3/4 OR 1/2 INCH VIDEO CASSETTE C
See series title for descriptive statement.
From The Introduction To Philosophy Series.
Prod-UDEL Dist-UDEL

Oom-Pah-Pah B 15 MIN
2 INCH VIDEOTAPE P
See series title for descriptive statement.
From The Children's Literature Series. No. 27
Prod-NCET Dist-GPITVL Prodn-KUONTV

Oompahs, The C 8 MIN
16MM FILM OPTICAL SOUND
Presents an animated story about a family of musical instruments.
Prod-TIMLIF Dist-TIMLIF 1982

Oopa C 14 MIN
16MM FILM OPTICAL SOUND
Presents a day in the life of a cabaret belly dancer, filmed in the cinema verite style.
Prod-NYU Dist-NYU

Oops C 20 MIN
16MM FILM OPTICAL SOUND C A
Shows how careless actions within an industrial plant can result in stream pollution. Points out ways to guard against such situations, emphasizing the individual's control of potential pollution sources within a plant.
LC NO. 70-714052
Prod-ORVWSC Dist-FINLYS 1965

Oops, I Made A Mistake C 4 MIN
16MM FILM, 3/4 OR 1/2 IN VIDEO K-I
Explains that a disappointing mistake can be solved by figuring out what went wrong and trying again.
From The Most Important Person - Attitudes Series.
Prod-EBEC Dist-EBEC

Oops, I Made A Mistake (Spanish) C 4 MIN
16MM FILM, 3/4 OR 1/2 IN VIDEO K-P
See series title for descriptive statement.
From The Most Important Person - Attitudes (Spanish) Series.
Prod-EBEC Dist-EBEC

Op Art C 15 MIN
3/4 OR 1/2 INCH VIDEO CASSETTE P-I
Discusses op art.
From The Young At Art Series.
Prod-WSKJTV Dist-AITECH 1980

Op Odyssey/Dance Ten C 30 MIN
3/4 OR 1/2 INCH VIDEO CASSETTE
Presents dance performance based on Doris Chase Kinetic sculpture.
From The Doris Chase Dance Series.
Prod-CHASED Dist-CHASED

Opaque Watercolor C 12 MIN
16MM FILM, 3/4 OR 1/2 IN VIDEO J-C A
Shows the basic techniques used to apply opaque watercolors.
From The Introduction To Commercial Art Series.
Prod-SF Dist-SF Prodn-ACORN 1979

OPEC - End Of An Era C 12 MIN
3/4 OR 1/2 INCH VIDEO CASSETTE H-C A
Describes OPEC, once a powerful, united group, forced to lower its prices in the face of an international oil surplus. Looks at the OPEC ministers, their countries and their policies.
Prod-JOU Dist-JOU

Open Alveolus, The C 20 MIN
16MM FILM OPTICAL SOUND
Describes respiratory rehabilitation of postoperative patients.
LC NO. 79-701051
Prod-CHEPON Dist-CHEPON Prodn-COM 1979

Open And Closed Wounds (Rev Ed) C 11 MIN
3/4 OR 1/2 INCH VIDEO CASSETTE
Highlights practical application of first aid techniques showing different types of open and closed wounds, and the proper methods of first aid treatment. Demonstrates control of bleeding, application of sterile dressings, cravat and triangular cover bandages, and care of the injured for physical shock. Stresses the importance of obtaining competent medical assistance.
From The First Aid (Rev Ed) Series.
Prod-USMESA Dist-USNAC 1981

Open And Shut C 15 MIN
2 INCH VIDEOTAPE
See series title for descriptive statement.
From The Umbrella Series.
Prod-KETCTV Dist-PUBTEL

Open And Shut Case C 15 MIN
16MM FILM, 3/4 OR 1/2 IN VIDEO J-C A
Discusses garage door openers, covering garage door cost, installation, power, security, fire protection, carbon monoxide protection and safety.
Prod-KLEINW Dist-KLEINW

Open Cathedral, The C 13 MIN
16MM FILM OPTICAL SOUND R
Explains that when members in the congregation of a typical church are confronted by non-members they are made aware of the role of people in the church.
LC NO. 72-702194
Prod-FAMF Dist-FAMF 1972

Open Channel And River Engineering-A Series
PRO
Uses classroom format to cover subject in series of 14 three hour lectures on 42 videotapes. Discusses theory and practice in essential features of open channel flows and river engineering. Reviews basic fluid mechanical principles, theory and applications for a variety of engineering problems.
Prod-UAKEN Dist-AMCEE

Open Classroom, The C 29 MIN
16MM FILM, 3/4 OR 1/2 IN VIDEO C
Studies the various forms of open education in operation in several public schools in New York, Washington and California, featuring Professor Lillian Weber, a leading proponent of the open-class-roon concept and director of ccny's workshop center for open education.
From The Human Relations And School Discipline Series.
Prod-MFFD Dist-FI

Open Corner Joint C 5 MIN
1/2 IN VIDEO CASSETTE BETA/VHS IND
See series title for descriptive statement.
From The Welding Training (Comprehensive) — Oxy-Acetylene Welding Series.
Prod-RMI Dist-RMI

Open Corner Ten-Gauge Weld Joint Demonstration C 5 MIN
1/2 IN VIDEO CASSETTE BETA/VHS IND
Demonstrates the proper technique for applying the weld on an open corner join in ten-gauge steel.
Prod-RMI Dist-RMI

Open Corner 16-Gauge Steel Horizontal Or Flat Demonstration C 4 MIN
1/2 IN VIDEO CASSETTE BETA/VHS IND
Illustrates the proper technique for welding an open corner joint in 16-gauge steel in the horizontal or flat position.
Prod-RMI Dist-RMI

Open Corner 16-Gauge Steel Vertical Down Demonstration C 3 MIN
1/2 IN VIDEO CASSETTE BETA/VHS IND
Points out the proper technique for welding an open corner joint in 16-gauge steel in the vertical down position.
Prod-RMI Dist-RMI

Open Cuff Technique In Vaginal Hysterectomy, The C 10 MIN
3/4 OR 1/2 INCH VIDEO CASSETTE PRO
Shows the Open Cuff Technique in which the patient required abdominal surgery for a hernia as well as for a vaginal hysterectomy. Includes drawings of the procedure.
Prod-WFP Dist-WFP

Open Dog Obedience C 15 MIN
16MM FILM, 3/4 OR 1/2 IN VIDEO
Illustrates a variety of techniques for developing open dog obedience.
From The Dog Obedience Training Series.
Prod-KLEINW Dist-KLEINW 1974

Open Door, The C 28 MIN
16MM FILM - 3/4 IN VIDEO
Shows the activities and training of recovered mental patients in the friendly, supportive atmosphere of a halfway house.
From The No Place Like Home Series.
LC NO. 79-708105
Prod-USSRS Dist-USNAC 1979

Open Doors - The Marion Story C 13 MIN
16MM FILM OPTICAL SOUND C A
Presents a report of the activities of the people of Marion, Indiana, who initiated the first locally financed community education within the state of Indiana. Local leaders explain their procedure in starting the program and includes scenes of classes in action.
LC NO. FIA67-5753
Prod-PUCES Dist-PUAVC 1967

Open Fender Straightening C 31 MIN
1/2 IN VIDEO CASSETTE BETA/VHS
Deals with auto body repair. Provides a step-by-step description of the rough-out through metal finishing, using a Ford Pinto as an example.
Prod-RMI Dist-RMI

Open Fractures C 20 MIN
3/4 OR 1/2 INCH VIDEO CASSETTE PRO
See series title for descriptive statement.
From The Fracture Management Series.
Prod-WFP Dist-WFP

Open Hearing C 51 MIN
3/4 OR 1/2 INCH VIDEO CASSETTE
Offers a response to the 'Fair Game Faggot' program about gays. Offers wide range of opinions on such issues as gay teachers, civil rights legislation for gays and the Bible's stand on homosexuality.
Prod-WCCOTV Dist-WCCOTV 1977

Open Heart Surgery C
16MM FILM OPTICAL SOUND
Features Dr Joseph Berman, an Hadassah Hospital heart surgeon trained in London and Los Angeles, who reports on Israel's open heart surgery program, available to Jews and Arabs on either side of the border.
From The Dateline Israel, 1973 Series.
Prod-ADL Dist-ADL

Open Heart Surgery C 27 MIN
16MM FILM OPTICAL SOUND PRO
Portrays the physiologic hemodynamics related to defects in the interventricular septum and demonstrates methods of closure utilizing extracorporeal bypass with a pump-oxygenator.
Prod-ACYDGD Dist-ACY 1958

Open Heart Surgery - An Overview (Parts 1 And 2) C 64 MIN
3/4 OR 1/2 INCH VIDEO CASSETTE PRO
Provides, on two tapes, information about all aspects of bypass surgery. Covers anatomy of chest and heart (tape 1), surgery preparation (tape 1), skin grafts (tape 1) and the operation itself (tape 2).
Prod-HSCIC Dist-HSCIC 1984

Open Hearth Furnace, The C 7 MIN
16MM FILM OPTICAL SOUND J-H
See series title for descriptive statement.
From The Making, Shaping And Treating Steel Series.
Prod-USSC Dist-USSC

Open Laboratory, The C 28 MIN
16MM FILM OPTICAL SOUND
Dr Dwight Allen, Professor of Education at Stanford University, describes laboratories which provide for individualization and an expanded range of instructional alternatives based on performance criteria.
From The Innovations In Education Series.
Prod-STNFRD Dist-EDUC 1966

Open Mind, An C 20 MIN
3/4 OR 1/2 INCH VIDEO CASSETTE J-H
Contrasts student comments about police and law in general with the thoughts of three police officers as they act out their rights and responsibilities in daily routines.
From The Rights And Responsibilities Series.
Prod-VAOG Dist-AITECH Prodn-WHROTV 1975

Open Mind, The - A Talk With Margaret Mead B 29 MIN
3/4 INCH VIDEO CASSETTE
Features anthropologist Margaret Mead as she offers her views on a variety of topics, including women's liberation and the Vietnam War.
Prod-UMITV Dist-UMITV 1972

Open Plan Concept/Nongraded School B 19 MIN
16MM FILM OPTICAL SOUND C T
Describes the open plan concept and the nongraded school, and shows how these programs are used to individualize learning for elementary grade students.
From The Individualizing Elementary Education Series.
LC NO. 72-701999
Prod-EDUC Dist-EDUC 1971

Open Reduction And Fixation Of A Fracture Of Mandible At The Angle - The Submandibular... C 14 MIN
3/4 OR 1/2 INCH VIDEO CASSETTE
Shows the soft tissue dissection required to expose the angle of the mandible. Demonstrates direct wiring procedures for an open reduction and immobilization of a fracture at this site.
Prod-VADTC Dist-AMDA 1969

Open Reduction And Fixation, Fracture Of Mandible At The Angle - The Submandibular... C 16 MIN
16MM FILM OPTICAL SOUND
Demonstrates the open reduction and fixation of a mandibular fracture at the angle by the submandibular approach.
LC NO. 74-705255
Prod-USVA Dist-USNAC 1968

Open Reduction And Internal Fixation Of Forearm Fractures C 35 MIN
16MM FILM OPTICAL SOUND PRO
Deals with the technique for the two standard procedures for operative reduction and internal fixation of forearm fractures, namely, fixation by intramedullary device and by plates and screws.
Prod-ACYDGD Dist-ACY 1952

Open Reduction Of 'T' And 'Y' Fractures Of The Humerus C 15 MIN
16MM FILM OPTICAL SOUND PRO
Shows the operative treatment of 'T' and 'Y' fractures of the lower end of the humerus. Uses the transolecranon approach and the fragments fixed with screws.
Prod-ACYDGD Dist-ACY 1962

Open Road, The C 27 MIN
16MM FILM OPTICAL SOUND
Presents a handicapped war veteran who starts his personal rehabilitation during a fishing trip to Alaska.
Prod-MERMAR Dist-TELEFM

Open Season B 30 MIN
16MM FILM OPTICAL SOUND
Relates the true experiences of a Wisconsin game warden in 1928 who refused to be intimidated by a vacationing mobster and who risked his life to uphold the game laws.
LC NO. FI67-107
Prod-GE Dist-WB Prodn-WB 1963

Open Season C 10 MIN
16MM FILM, 3/4 OR 1/2 IN VIDEO

Tells how a young boy tries unsuccessfully to make two deer hunters leave the woods on his family's land.
LC NO. 81-706889
Prod-SUGERA Dist-PHENIX 1979

Open Secrets C 25 MIN
16MM FILM, 3/4 OR 1/2 IN VIDEO J-C A
Encourages communication within the family and between teenagers and their peers to avert the possibly tragic consequences of substance abuse.
Prod-MTI Dist-MTI

Open Secrets C 30 MIN
3/4 OR 1/2 INCH VIDEO CASSETTE
Explores examples of the paradox of artists dealing with issues which are basic to our lives which somehow often run afoul of public sensibilities.
From The Eye To Eye Series.
Prod-WGBHTV Dist-EAI Prodn-MOFAB

Open Space B 28 MIN
3/4 INCH VIDEO CASSETTE
Emphasizes the need for acquiring open spaces in rapidly growing urban areas and the importance of correctly using present urban spaces. Urges community groups to create new recreational areas in inner cities and suburbia.
Prod-USNAC Dist-USNAC 1972

Open Surgical Prostatectomy Techniques C 34 MIN
16MM FILM OPTICAL SOUND PRO
Explains that no single method of prostatectomy can be used for the relief of bladder neck and prostatic obstruction if best results are to be obtained. Depicts methods of open prostatectomy, perineal, suprapubic, retropubic and trans-vesico-capsular used at the Massachusetts General Hospital.
Prod-ACYDGD Dist-ACY 1963

Open Talk About Sex C 20 MIN
3/4 INCH VIDEOTAPE H
Presented in American sign language with voice interpretation. Explains sexual anatomy by a deaf peer counselor using anatomical models and charts to teach male and female differences.
Prod-PPASED Dist-PPASED

Open The Door C 28 MIN
16MM FILM, 3/4 OR 1/2 IN VIDEO
Features communications expert Bill Welp who presents his system OPEN Communication. Stars Ron Masak.
Prod-CCCD Dist-CCCD

Open The Door To Advanced Skiing C 29 MIN
2 INCH VIDEOTAPE
See series title for descriptive statement.
From The Skiing Series.
Prod-KTCATV Dist-PUBTEL

Open Theatre Presents The Serpent, The B 80 MIN
16MM FILM OPTICAL SOUND
Features a performance of The Serpent, concerning the creation and fall of man as interpreted by playwright Jean-Claude Van Italie and as presented by the Open Theatre.
Prod-CANTOR Dist-CANTOR

Open Treatment Of Aortic Stenosis With Pump Oxygenator C 19 MIN
16MM FILM OPTICAL SOUND PRO
Shows the surgical relief of congenital valvular and subvalvular and acquired valvular aortic stenosis. Combines cardiopulmonary bypass with hypothermia to allow work on the aortic valve and adjacent heart.
Prod-ACYDGD Dist-ACY 1960

Open Up My Eyes C 10 MIN
16MM FILM, 3/4 OR 1/2 IN VIDEO
Focuses on the color, texture, rhythm, melody, harmony, dynamics and majesty of nature.
Prod-FLMFR Dist-FLMFR

Open Waters C 20 MIN
16MM FILM, 3/4 OR 1/2 IN VIDEO
Describes the role of the Army Corps of Engineers in the development, maintenance and operation of the nation's waterway system.
Prod-USAE Dist-USNAC

Open Window C 18 MIN
16MM FILM, 3/4 OR 1/2 IN VIDEO H-C
Covers various approaches to landscape painting from the 15th century to the French Impressionists.
Prod-IFB Dist-IFB 1957

Open Window, The C 12 MIN
16MM FILM, 3/4 OR 1/2 IN VIDEO
Presents an adaptation of the short story The Open Window by Saki. Concerns a young girl who alarms a visitor by telling him that they are expecting the return of her long lost uncle and cousin, killed three years earlier in a hunting accident.
Prod-AMERFI Dist-PFP

Open Wire Transposition Systems B 17 MIN
16MM FILM OPTICAL SOUND
Illustrates and explains the need for transpositions, how they improve communication and the construction of various types of physical or single-point transpositions.
LC NO. FIE55-75
Prod-USA Dist-USNAC 1954

Open Your Eyes C 29 MIN
16MM FILM OPTICAL SOUND J-C A
Describes the service Senior Girl Scouts can give to their communities in small towns and in big cities. Explains the projects with which these teen-age girls are related.
LC NO. FIA65-444
Prod-GSUSA Dist-GSUSA 1965

Open-Heart Surgery C 17 MIN
3/4 OR 1/2 INCH VIDEO CASSETTE
Explains to the patient what will take place before and after open-heart surgery, equipment used and operation procedures. Describes recovery room, intensive care unit and discusses need for postoperative deep-breathing and coughing. Emphasizes caution and graduality in recovery.
LC NO. 77-730600
Prod-TRAINX Dist-TRAINX

Open-Heart Surgery Using The Kay-Anderson Heart-Lung Machine C 22 MIN
16MM FILM OPTICAL SOUND PRO
Presents Dr Jerome H Kay and his surgical team as they correct a narrowing at the origin of the pulmonary artery and also repair a ventricular septal defect, assisted by Dr Robert M Anderson and his heart-lung machine.
Prod-UPJOHN Dist-UPJOHN 1958

Open-Pit Mining Hazards C 17 MIN
16MM FILM OPTICAL SOUND
Re-enacts mining accidents involving dump trucks, power shovels, front-end loaders, rail haulage and highwall blasting to show what happens from workers' carelessness, when safety precautions are overlooked, or where unsafe machinery and mining methods are used. Explains why the accidents happened and then stresses the correct and safe way of performing various mining jobs to prevent future accidents.
LC NO. 74-705257
Prod-USBM Dist-USNAC 1967

Openers C 7 MIN
16MM FILM, 3/4 OR 1/2 IN VIDEO
Teaches how to open a sales call. Demonstrates how to use a prospect's interests to make a sale.
Prod-BNA Dist-BNA

Opening A Telemarketing Call C 14 MIN
3/4 OR 1/2 INCH VIDEO CASSETTE
See series title for descriptive statement.
From The Telemarketing For Better Business Results Series.
Prod-COMTEL Dist-DELTAK

Opening Day At The Fair B 29 MIN
2 INCH VIDEOTAPE K-P
See series title for descriptive statement.
From The Children's Fair Series.
Prod-WMVSTV Dist-PUBTEL

Opening Doors C 13 MIN
3/4 OR 1/2 INCH VIDEO CASSETTE H A
Explains that job seeking is easier if the seeker is prepared with a job history, a letter of application, and references or recommendations. Shows how Pete learns from a personnel director how to gather these materials and send them.
From The Making It Work Series.
Prod-ERF Dist-AITECH 1983

Opening Doors To Creative Expression C 28 MIN
16MM FILM, 3/4 OR 1/2 IN VIDEO
Shows how to increase productivity through awareness of personal decision, style, promoting better interpersonal relations and building cooperative team skills.
Prod-HP Dist-HP

Opening Doors To The Future C 25 MIN
3/4 OR 1/2 INCH VIDEO CASSETTE
Discussion and demonstration of career possibilities and educational requirements for fields of physical therapy, occupational therapy, special education, speech pathology, and psychology.
Prod-UNEBO Dist-UNEBO

Opening In Moscow C 45 MIN
16MM FILM OPTICAL SOUND
Discloses impressions of Moscow and its citizens under the Krushchev regime. Centered around the opening of the 1959 American Exhibition. By D A Pennebaker.
Prod-PENNAS Dist-PENNAS

Opening Leads And Play Of The Hand C 30 MIN
3/4 OR 1/2 INCH VIDEO CASSETTE A
See series title for descriptive statement.
From The Bridge Basics Series.
Prod-KYTV Dist-KYTV 1982

Opening Night C 30 MIN
3/4 OR 1/2 INCH VIDEO CASSETTE C
See series title for descriptive statement.
From The In Our Own Image Series.
Prod-DALCCD Dist-DALCCD

Opening Of The Controlled Environment Research Laboratory C 29 MIN
16MM FILM OPTICAL SOUND H A
A record of the opening on August 29, 1962, of Ceres, a new laboratory of the division of plant industry designed for growing plants in a wide range of closely controlled climatic conditions. Includes portions of addresses given by Sir Robert Menzies, Sir Frederick White and Dr O H Frankel.
LC NO. FIA65-1068
Prod-CSIROA Dist-CSIROA Prodn-CSIROA 1963

Opening Statements C 59 MIN
3/4 OR 1/2 INCH VIDEO CASSETTE PRO
Gives opening statement demonstrations. Gives suggestions on what juries need to see and hear during opening statements.
From The Training The Advocate Series.
Prod-AMBAR Dist-ABACPE

Opening Statements - Civil And Criminal C 28 MIN
3/4 OR 1/2 INCH VIDEO CASSETTE PRO
Demonstrates several techniques common to effective opening statements in a trial, including introductory remarks, presentation of the story, its theme, characters and evidence, use of exhibits and varied pace, voice and gestures.
Prod-ABACPE Dist-ABACPE

Opening Statements - Criminal And Complex Civil C 50 MIN
3/4 OR 1/2 INCH VIDEO CASSETTE PRO
Presents model opening statements in two cases - State vs Diamond, a murder case, and Spotts vs General Construction Manufacturer, Inc, a tort action.
Prod-ABACPE Dist-ABACPE Prodn-NITA

Opening Statements And First Witness C 43 MIN
3/4 OR 1/2 INCH VIDEO CASSETTE PRO
Shows opening statements that cover burdens of proof and the kinds of exhibits to be presented. Demonstrates the examination and cross-examination of the first claimant.
From The Remedies Phase Of An EEO Case - Individual Determinations Series. Pt 2
Prod-ALIABA Dist-ABACPE

Opening Statements In A Federal Narcotics Case C 27 MIN
3/4 OR 1/2 INCH VIDEO CASSETTE PRO
Demonstrates techniques and styles for an effective opening statement in a federal narcotics case.
From The Trial Of a Criminal (Federal Narcotics) Case Series.
Prod-ABACPE Dist-ABACPE

Opening Statements In A Products Liability Case C 60 MIN
3/4 OR 1/2 INCH VIDEO CASSETTE PRO
Presents opening statements for plaintiff and defense in a products liability case. Offers critiques of the presentations by skilled litigators.
From The Trial Techniques - A Products Liability Case Series.
Prod-ABACPE Dist-ABACPE

Opening Suit Bids Of One And Responses C 30 MIN
3/4 OR 1/2 INCH VIDEO CASSETTE A
See series title for descriptive statement.
From The Bridge Basics Series.
Prod-KYTV Dist-KYTV 1982

Opening The Door C 19 MIN
3/4 OR 1/2 INCH VIDEO CASSETTE
Examines preparation and procedures for first sales calls and shows how to handle this crucial first step successfully.
From The Basic Sales Series.
Prod-RESEM Dist-RESEM

Opening The Era Of Outer Space B 6 MIN
16MM FILM OPTICAL SOUND
Paresents a 1957 Screen News Digest excerpt showing the race between USSR and United States in the space race beginning with Sputnik and underscores the importance of scientific research. Depicts various early missle attempts in preparation for the trip to the moon.
From The News Magazine Of The Screen Series. Vol 8, No. 4
Prod-PATHE Dist-HEARST 1957

Opening The West C
3/4 OR 1/2 INCH VIDEO CASSETTE
Prod-MSTVIS Dist-MSTVIS

Opening To Grief - The Task / Purification By Fire - The Passage Through Pain C 54 MIN
3/4 OR 1/2 INCH VIDEO CASSETTE
Examines the healing nature of grief and the process of coping with loss. Features author and thanatologist Stephen Levine.
From The How Then Shall We Live? Series.
Prod-ORGNLF Dist-ORGNLF

Opening To Grief - The Threshold Task C 23 MIN
3/4 OR 1/2 INCH VIDEO CASSETTE
Reveals several participants deepest feelings about their own deaths and the deaths of those close to them. Observes that if confronting death is postponed, life is postponed.
From The Conscious Living/Conscious Dying - The Work Of A Lifetime Series.
Prod-ORGNLF Dist-PELICN

Opening Your House To Solar Energy C 28 MIN
16MM FILM, 3/4 OR 1/2 IN VIDEO A
Describes how to retrofit homes with passive solar devices, such as greenhouses, solar-heated water tanks and thermal chimneys.
From The Home Energy Conservation Series.
LC NO. 81-706763
Prod-RPFD Dist-BULFRG 1980

Opening, The C 15 MIN
16MM FILM OPTICAL SOUND
Studies the life and work of Canadian artist Gerald Humen. Shows him working to meet a deadline for an exhibition of 70 of his paintings.
From The Journal Series.
LC NO. 77-702862
Prod-FIARTS Dist-CANFDC 1976

Opera C 20 MIN
16MM FILM OPTICAL SOUND I
Points out that opera combines the vocal and instrumental aspects of music with the stagecraft of the theater. Explains that grand opera is normally tragic drama, and comic opera is humorous or non-tragic. Features excerpts from various famous operas.
From The Music Of America Series.
Prod-KQEDTV Dist-GPITVL

Opera C 15 MIN
3/4 OR 1/2 INCH VIDEO CASSETTE K-P
Focuses on plays, music and operas.
From The Pass It On Series.
Prod-WKNOTV Dist-GPITVL 1983

Opera B 45 MIN
2 INCH VIDEOTAPE C

See series title for descriptive statement.
From The General Humanities Series. Unit 5 - Combination And Integration Of The Arts
Prod-CHITVC Dist-GPITVL Prodn-WTTWTV

Opera - Man, Music And Drama C 18 MIN
16MM FILM, 3/4 OR 1/2 IN VIDEO H-C
Introduces the study of the opera.
From The Humanities Series.
Prod-MGHT Dist-MGHT Prodn-CINEMK 1971

Opera - One Hundred Years Of Bayreuth C 17 MIN
3/4 OR 1/2 INCH VIDEO CASSETTE H-C A
Discusses the Bayreuth Festival, which celebrates the musical genius of Richard Wagner.
Prod-UPI Dist-JOU

Opera With Henry Butler C 26 MIN
16MM FILM, 3/4 OR 1/2 IN VIDEO H-C A
Illuminates the nature of traditional and modern opera in top professional performances from Pagliacci and La Traviata. Henry Butler, stage director for the Metropolitan Opera Company, comments on the emotional inspiration for opera, famous opera houses and trends in opera today. Includes interviews with the performers.
Prod-IQFILM Dist-LCOA Prodn-SAUDEK 1970

Opera With Henry Butler (Spanish) C 26 MIN
16MM FILM, 3/4 OR 1/2 IN VIDEO J-C A
Explains the lure of opera. Uses scenes from Pagliacci to demonstrate how music and plot are interwoven to portray the full range of emotions.
Prod-IQFILM Dist-LCOA Prodn-SAUDEK 1970

Operando Su Grua Con Confianza C 17 MIN
16MM FILM, 3/4 OR 1/2 IN VIDEO IND
A Spanish-language version of the motion picture Craning With Confidence. Explains how to ensure safe crane operation and reviews how to set up a crane for a job, how to read and use the load chart and how to tell when a crane might tip or break.
Prod-IFB Dist-IFB 1975

Operant Audiometry With Severely Retarded Children C 15 MIN
16MM FILM OPTICAL SOUND PRO
Demonstrates the use of positive reinforcement to test the hearing of a severely retarded subject. Traces the progress of a 13-year-old retarded boy through several clinical sessions designed to detect and diagnose impairments. Demonstrates how the child is conditioned to wear a headset and how reinforcement techniques are employed to train the child to respond to auditory stimuli.
LC NO. 72-702026
Prod-UKANBC Dist-UKANS 1968

Operant Conditioning C 16 MIN
16MM FILM OPTICAL SOUND H-C A
Considers various aspects of operant conditioning in psychology, including punishment, discrimination, escape and avoidance and schedules of reinforcement.
From The Basic Psychology Series.
LC NO. 76-702924
Prod-EDMDC Dist-EDMDC Prodn-SOREND 1973

Operant Conditioning C 29 MIN
3/4 INCH VIDEO CASSETTE C A
Examines B F Skinner's theory of operant conditioning. Discusses examples of the wide applications of operant conditioning in advertising, classrooms and therapy.
From The Understanding Human Behavior - An Introduction To Psychology Series. Lesson 16
Prod-COAST Dist-CDTEL

Operant Learning C 10 MIN
3/4 OR 1/2 INCH VIDEO CASSETTE T
See series title for descriptive statement.
From The Protocol Materials In Teacher Education - The Process Of Teaching, Pt 2 Series.
Prod-MSU Dist-MSU

Operating A Calder Hall Reactor—A Series
PRO
Prod-UKAEA Dist-UKAEA 1959

Full Power 20 MIN
Refuelling 32 MIN

Operating A Self-Service Meat Department X 35 MIN
16MM FILM OPTICAL SOUND C A
Pictures techniques of receiving, blocking on the rail, storage, cutting, packaging, weighing and marking of prices at a self-service meat department.
Prod-PUAVC Dist-PUAVC 1959

Operating An Incubator Or Radiant Warmer (2nd Ed) C 14 MIN
3/4 OR 1/2 INCH VIDEO CASSETTE PRO
Describes the main features of both incubators and radiant warmer, operation of each in both manual and serva mode, monitoring infant and incubator temperatures and daily equipment maintenance.
Prod-UMICHM Dist-UMICHM 1983

Operating And Financial Leverage C 34 MIN
3/4 OR 1/2 INCH VIDEO CASSETTE
Provides an in-depth analysis of the positive impact on profits that could result from utilization of financial and operating leverages.
Prod-IVCH Dist-IVCH

Operating Drill Presses C 13 MIN
3/4 OR 1/2 INCH VIDEO CASSETTE IND
1 Series. Gives basic safety procedures for operating drill presses. Discusses setup and operation of a sensitive drill and a radial drill.
From The Introduction To Machine Technology, Module
Prod-LEIKID Dist-LEIKID

Operating Experience - Dresden C 10 MIN
16MM FILM OPTICAL SOUND
Reports on the routine-day operation of the Dresden Nuclear Power Station, reviewing the success of the operating experience of the boiling water nuclear electric power station in terms of dependability, safety and ease of operation and maintenance.
LC NO. FIE64-138
Prod-USAEC Dist-USNAC 1964

Operating Experience - Hallam C 10 MIN
16MM FILM OPTICAL SOUND
Describes the operation of the 79-megawatt electric Hallam Nuclear Power Station, which is powered by a 252-megawatt sodium-graphite reactor. Demonstrates Hallam's heat transfer cycle and plant-operation features, including fuel transfer and sodium handling.
LC NO. FIE64-139
Prod-USAEC Dist-USNAC 1964

Operating Experience - Yankee C 10 MIN
16MM FILM OPTICAL SOUND
Examines the various plant features and performance data of the nuclear power station that is operated by the Yankee Atomic Electric Company.
LC NO. FIE64-141
Prod-USAEC Dist-USNAC 1964

Operating Room C 30 MIN
3/4 OR 1/2 INCH VIDEO CASSETTE A
Shows how to multiply and divide fractions and solve some of the real-life problems of adult math students.
From The Adult Math Series.
Prod-KYTV Dist-KYTV 1984

Operating Room Deaths B 28 MIN
16MM FILM, 3/4 OR 1/2 IN VIDEO
Discusses operating room deaths due to improperly controlled diagnostic or therapeutic procedures, such as perforation of the bowel with a barium enema, perforation of the trachea during an attempt to remove an obstruction, transfixation of the trachea during an attempt to remove an obstruction and traumatic death due to explosion of anesthetic gases. (Kinescope)
From The Clinical Pathology - Forensic Medicine Outlines Series.
Prod-NMAC Dist-USNAC 1970

Operating Room Kaleidoscope - Oral Endoscopy C 20 MIN
16MM FILM OPTICAL SOUND PRO
Shows the nursing and surgical management of a pediatric patient having general anesthesia for a laryngoscopy and an adult patient having a local anesthetic for bronchoscopy. Shows the nurse teaching and assisting a patient in rehabilitation.
Prod-ACYDGD Dist-ACY 1968

Operating Room Nursing Care Of The Burn Patient C 26 MIN
16MM FILM OPTICAL SOUND PRO
Illustrates operating room nursing care of the severely burned patient. Emphasizes the importance of preplanning to save anesthesia time during the many procedures involved in cleansing, debridement, dressings and skin grafting.
Prod-ACYDGD Dist-ACY 1962

Operating Room Nursing Care Plan For The Separation Of Conjoined Twins C 29 MIN
3/4 OR 1/2 INCH VIDEO CASSETTE PRO
Acquaints nurses, anesthesiologists, pediatricians, and surgical residents with a complex nursing care plan for the separation of conjoined twins.
Prod-HSCIC Dist-HSCIC 1984

Operating Room Orientation - Attire, Scrubbing, Gowning, And Gloving C 25 MIN
3/4 OR 1/2 INCH VIDEO CASSETTE PRO
Reviews basic principles of asepsis to be observed while preparing to serve as a scrubbed surgical team member. Demonstrates step-by-step procedures to follow in donning proper attire, performing a timed scrub, and maintaining asepsis while gowning and gloving. Presents techniques for maintaining asepsis of both sterile areas of clothing and sterile fields in the operating room during surgery.
Prod-UMICHM Dist-UMICHM 1982

Operating Room Table Set-Up C 18 MIN
1/2 IN VIDEO CASSETTE BETA/VHS
Demonstrates the tasks and procedures an operating room technician follows to set up the operating room for surgery.
Prod-RMI Dist-RMI

Operating Room Techniques C 15 MIN
3/4 OR 1/2 INCH VIDEO CASSETTE PRO
Illustrates proper techniques for opening and maintaining sterile fields, anesthesia induction, skin prepping, draping and instrument handling.
From The Basic Clinical Skills Series.
Prod-HSCIC Dist-HSCIC 1984

Operating Systems C 30 MIN
3/4 OR 1/2 INCH VIDEO CASSETTE IND
Describes general operating-system concepts, and discusses the popular UNIX operating system as an example. Pros and cons of using UNIX are explored.
From The Micros For Managers - Software Series.
Prod-COLOSU Dist-COLOSU

Operating The Commercial Meat Slicer C 20 MIN
1/2 IN VIDEO CASSETTE BETA/VHS
Explains the basic parts of the commercial meat slicer which must be operated with special care. Features Chef Paul, who explains how to set up, clean and operate a slicer.
Prod-RMI Dist-RMI

Operating The Food Grinder C 20 MIN
1/2 IN VIDEO CASSETTE BETA/VHS
Shows the basic parts of the grinder, and how to assemble, operate and clean it.
Prod-RMI Dist-RMI

Operating The Pendant Crane C 7 MIN
3/4 OR 1/2 INCH VIDEO CASSETTE IND
Discusses the accuracy and good judgement required of the person operating the pendant crane.
From The Steel Making Series.
Prod-LEIKID Dist-LEIKID

Operating Tractors And Equipment C 21 MIN
3/4 OR 1/2 INCH VIDEO CASSETTE
Focuses on safely starting and stopping tractors powered by different fuels. Explains the safe handling of the tractor's hydraulic system. Shows how to release hydraulic pressure in an emergency.
From The Agricultural Accidents And Rescue Series.
Prod-PSU Dist-PSU

Operation Affirmative C 14 MIN
16MM FILM OPTICAL SOUND
Emphasizes the importance of the Ready Reserve when a Naval Reserve destroyer crew is called to duty to track a Russian fishing trawler off the coast of Seattle, Washington.
LC NO. 74-705259
Prod-USN Dist-USNAC 1970

Operation Amigo B 15 MIN
16MM FILM OPTICAL SOUND
Travels with President Eisenhower on his goodwill trip to South America. Tells students how they can help the old suspicions about the U S that still exist in South America.
From The Screen News Digest Series. Vol 2, Issue 8
Prod-HEARST Dist-HEARST 1960

Operation Amigo - A New Look At Latin America B 20 MIN
16MM FILM OPTICAL SOUND
Presents a report on the history of Latin America and traces the development of and new emphasis on the 'GOOD NEIGHBOR POLICY.'
From The Screen News Digest Series. Vol 9, Issue 9
Prod-HEARST Dist-HEARST 1967

Operation And Maintenance Of a Video System C 30 MIN
3/4 OR 1/2 INCH VIDEO CASSETTE
Outlines a step-by-step procedure for setting up, checking and maintaining a video system.
From The Video - A Practical Guide...and More Series.
Prod-VIPUB Dist-VIPUB

Operation And Process Control C
3/4 OR 1/2 INCH VIDEO CASSETTE IND
Reviews safety and operating parameters. Examines various control systems and protection devices.
From The Pulp And Paper Training - Thermo-Mechanical Pulping Series.
Prod-LEIKID Dist-LEIKID

Operation At The Suction Side Of A Pump C 17 MIN
16MM FILM, 3/4 OR 1/2 IN VIDEO IND
Discusses pump location, measuring atmospheric pressure, cavitation, and terms and idioms associated with the suction side of a pump.
From The Industrial Hydraulic Technology Series. Chapter 3
Prod-TAT Dist-TAT

Operation Banyarwanda B 18 MIN
16MM FILM OPTICAL SOUND
Depicts the League Of Red Cross Societies' resettlement operation for Watusi refugees from Rwanda in the Kivu Province of the Congo.
Prod-LRCSF Dist-AMRC 1964

Operation Behavior Modification B 40 MIN
16MM FILM OPTICAL SOUND PRO
Traces the progress of an institutionalized retarded girl through a program of behavior modification designed to give her a better chance at integration with girls her own age and train her for employment as a nurse's aid.
LC NO. 72-702025
Prod-UKANBC Dist-NMAC 1967

Operation Biberon B 13 MIN
16MM FILM OPTICAL SOUND I-H
See series title for descriptive statement.
From The Les Francais Chez Vous Series. Set I, Lesson 02
Prod-PEREN Dist-CHLTN 1967

Operation Big Lift B 6 MIN
16MM FILM OPTICAL SOUND J-C A
Studies 'OPERATION BIG LIFT,' showing the military airlift from Bergstron Air Force Base in Texas to Rhein Main in Germany. Discusses the lift's implications throughout the world.
From The Screen News Digest Series. Vol 6, Issue 4
LC NO. FIA68-2073
Prod-HEARST Dist-HEARST 1963

Operation Bluenose C 27 MIN
16MM FILM OPTICAL SOUND
Discusses the mission over the North Pole by a B-52.
Prod-NAA Dist-RCKWL

Operation Breakthrough C 28 MIN
16MM FILM OPTICAL SOUND
Describes the research and development program which result-

ed in the Navy's Polaris missle system. Explains how military and private industry worked together to develop the project.
Prod-USN Dist-CCNY

Operation Brotherhood - The Ibew Story B 27 MIN
16MM FILM OPTICAL SOUND
Deals with the history of the International Brotherhood of Electrical Workers Union. Recounts the history of the coming of electricity and the organization of the electrical workers into a union through the life story of Oley Munsen, one of the early members.
Prod-IBEW Dist-AFLCIO 1958

Operation Cool-It C 26 MIN
16MM FILM OPTICAL SOUND
Shows scenes of a weekend of snowmobiling in northern Wisconsin, including views of trail rides, dances, games and competition.
LC NO. 79-706076
Prod-OMCJM Dist-SS Prodn-MATTCO 1970

Operation Crossroads C 26 MIN
16MM FILM, 3/4 OR 1/2 IN VIDEO
Documents the Able Day and Baker Day blasts of the atomic bomb tests at Bikini Island in the Pacific.
Prod-USN Dist-USNAC 1949

Operation Cue (2nd Ed) B 14 MIN
16MM FILM OPTICAL SOUND
Points out the contrast between the Nevada test in 1955 and present nuclear devices, continues as a documentary report on the operation cue exercise of 1955 as told from the viewpoint of a newspaper woman who was invited as an observer.
LC NO. 74-705998
Prod-USOCD Dist-USNAC 1964

Operation Cue (2nd Ed) C 14 MIN
3/4 INCH VIDEO CASSETTE
Points out the contrast between the Nevada testing in 1955 and nuclear devices of 1964. Continues as a documentary report on the operation cue exercise of 1955. Features slow motion photography of the effects of the blast on houses and radio towers.
Prod-USNAC Dist-USNAC 1972

Operation Deep Freeze C 15 MIN
16MM FILM, 3/4 OR 1/2 IN VIDEO
Describes Operation Deep Freeze, the U S Navy's scientific research program in Antarctica.
From The Odyssey Series.
Prod-KRMATV Dist-GPITVL

Operation Firestop C 25 MIN
16MM FILM OPTICAL SOUND PRO
Documents fire research conducted at Camp Pendleton, pertaining mainly to watershed fires.
Prod-LAFIRE Dist-LAFIRE

Operation For Vaginal Agenesis C 20 MIN
16MM FILM OPTICAL SOUND
Presents the most up-to-date information on the development of the female genital tract. Illustrates the construction of an artificial vagina using the embryologic development of the vagina as the basis for the operative approach.
LC NO. 75-702327
Prod-EATONL Dist-EATONL 1969

Operation Greenhouse C 25 MIN
16MM FILM, 3/4 OR 1/2 IN VIDEO
Describes the scientific and technical operations during the proof-testing of atomic weapons at Eniwetok in the spring of 1951. Illustrates the blast and thermal effects on structures, aircraft, and various other items.
Prod-USAEC Dist-USNAC 1951

Operation Head Start B 27 MIN
16MM FILM OPTICAL SOUND
Describes the objectives of Operation Head Start and shows how these objectives are carried into action in a pre-school classroom.
LC NO. FIA66-131
Prod-CHIBED Dist-GOLDSH Prodn-GOLDSH 1965

Operation Ivy X 28 MIN
16MM FILM OPTICAL SOUND
Presents a documentary record of a thermonuclear test at the Atomic Energy Commission's Pacific proving grounds in 1952. Includes introductory remarks by President Dwight D Eisenhower and a closing statement by FCDA administrator Val Peterson.
LC NO. FIE54-454
Prod-USAF Dist-USNAC 1954

Operation Last Patrol C 54 MIN
16MM FILM OPTICAL SOUND
Examines the cross-country march to the Republican National Convention, staged by the Vietnam Veterans against the War in 1972.
Prod-IMPACT Dist-IMPACT

Operation Long Shot C 13 MIN
16MM FILM OPTICAL SOUND
Reports on an underground nuclear test in the fall of 1965 in the Aleutian Islands that was part of the Vela uniform series of experiments to increase U S capability to detect, identify and locate underground nuclear detonations at intercontinental ranges. Follows the steps involved in Operation Long Shot to investigate the possible travel-time anomalies associated with seismic events occurring in island-arc structures.
LC NO. FIE66-10
Prod-USAEC Dist-USNAC 1966

Operation Nightwatch C 30 MIN
16MM FILM OPTICAL SOUND I-H
Provides a you-are-there look at an inspiring ministry being carried on in the skidrow section of Seattle, Washington. Follows Bud, a suburban minister, as he walks the downtown streets from midnight until dawn, visiting the bars and cafes and bringing the presence of Christ to the lonely and dispossessed.
Prod-FAMF Dist-FAMF

Operation Of An Oxy-Fuel Gas Heating Torch C 14 MIN
3/4 OR 1/2 INCH VIDEO CASSETTE IND
Looks at the operation and safety requirements of the heating torch.
From The Steel Making Series.
Prod-LEIKID Dist-LEIKID

Operation Of Jet Aircraft Engines B 18 MIN
16MM FILM OPTICAL SOUND
Illustrates principles of jet propulsion by Newton's law of action and shows its application to a jet engine to produce horsepower and thrust power.
LC NO. FIE58-290
Prod-USN Dist-USNAC 1949

Operation Of Quality Circle Programs C 60 MIN
3/4 OR 1/2 INCH VIDEO CASSETTE IND
See series title for descriptive statement.
From The Quality Circle Concepts Series.
Prod-NCSU Dist-AMCEE

Operation Of The GM Unit Injectors B 4 MIN
16MM FILM - 3/4 IN VIDEO
Shows construction, function and operation of the GM unit, including location and operations of the components and the flow of fuel through the unit to the engine. Emphasizes the importance of proper maintenance. Issued in 1958 as a motion picture.
LC NO. 79-707542
Prod-USA Dist-USNAC 1979

Operation Of The Hypodermic Jet Injection Apparatus C 43 MIN
16MM FILM OPTICAL SOUND
Demonstrates the functioning and operation of the hypodermic jet injector, showing cocking, firing, dosage adjustment, disassembly, sterilization, assembly and safety precautions.
LC NO. 74-706168
Prod-USA Dist-USNAC 1972

Operation Of The Laminar Flow Biological Safety Cabinet C 23 MIN
3/4 INCH VIDEO CASSETTE
Compares the various safety cabinets available to the clinical laboratory technician. Focuses on the safe, effective use of the class III laminar flow cabinet, stressing the role and responsibilities of the researcher.
LC NO. 80-706596
Prod-CFDISC Dist-USNAC 1979

Operation Of The Motorcycle C 14 MIN
16MM FILM OPTICAL SOUND H A
Stresses the safe operation of the motorcycle with emphasis on defensive driving tactics.
From The American Honda Series.
Prod-AHONDA Dist-AHONDA

Operation Of The Shredder-Grater Attachment C 20 MIN
1/2 IN VIDEO CASSETTE BETA/VHS
Explains the correct method of assembling the grater and shredder attachment to the standard 20-quart table mixer.
Prod-RMI Dist-RMI

Operation Of The Varian A60A NMR Spectrometer C 28 MIN
3/4 OR 1/2 INCH VIDEO CASSETTE C A
Demonstrates the operation of the Varian Associates A60A NMR spectrometer for ambient temperature work. Illustrates tuning the instrument, running a spectrum of a sample, integrating the peak, and expanding the scale.
From The Chemistry - Master/Apprentice Series. Program 500
LC NO. 82-706060
Prod-CUETV Dist-CUNIV 1981

Operation One Plus Two C 15 MIN
16MM FILM OPTICAL SOUND
Shows the U S Marine Corps naval flight officer's program for college students.
LC NO. 75-702459
Prod-USMC Dist-USNAC 1973

Operation Orchid C 16 MIN
16MM FILM OPTICAL SOUND
Presents a tour of the Orchid Isle, the Big Island of Hawaii and features the sun, sand, surf and spectacular sights of Hawaii's largest island.
Prod-UAL Dist-MTP

Operation Paradise C 7 MIN
16MM FILM, 3/4 OR 1/2 IN VIDEO I
Presents an animated story about two enterprising Italian cats named Don Porfirio and Pepe who endeavor to bring together a young woman and her shy suitor.
From The Don Porfirio Series.
LC NO. 81-706618
Prod-ITCART Dist-PHENIX 1980

Operation Reentry B 30 MIN
16MM FILM OPTICAL SOUND H-C A
Demonstrates successful rehabilitation of patients through first giving them tokens for rewards, then making a transition from token use to sheltered workshop training and finally to work outside of the hospital.
From The To Save Tomorrow Series.
Prod-NET Dist-IU

Operation Responsible, Safe Refuse Collection C 20 MIN
16MM FILM - 3/4 IN VIDEO
Describes safety techniques in refuse collection. Shows how supervisors can train the men who collect solid waste. Issued in 1972 as a motion picture.
LC NO. 80-707128
Prod-USEPA Dist-USNAC 1980

Operation Responsible, Safe Refuse Collection (Spanish) C 20 MIN
16MM FILM - 3/4 IN VIDEO
Describes safety techniques in refuse collection. Shows how supervisors can train the men who collect solid waste. Issued in 1972 as a motion picture.
LC NO. 80-707128
Prod-USEPA Dist-USNAC 1980

Operation Sandstone C 21 MIN
16MM FILM, 3/4 OR 1/2 IN VIDEO
Explains the extensive preparations for the first USAEC development and test at the Pacific proving grounds in spring 1948. Shows the three test detonations at Eniwetok Atoll.
Prod-USAF Dist-USNAC

Operation Under Fallout C 28 MIN
16MM FILM OPTICAL SOUND
Portrays the preplanning, organization, training and rehearsals required to insure proper performance of base personnel and their dependents in event of attack.
LC NO. 75-700568
Prod-USAF Dist-USNAC 1963

Operation Undersea C 20 MIN
16MM FILM OPTICAL SOUND
Revised edition of 'WINFRITH PIPELINE.' Discusses the Winfrith Pipeline, showing underwater sequences.
Prod-UKAEA Dist-UKAEA 1960

Operation Up-Lift C 30 MIN
16MM FILM OPTICAL SOUND
Documents the success story of 'The Young Saints,' an Academy for the Performing Arts based in Los Angeles. Shows the group performing before Ed Sullivan, Jonathan Winters and in many television and community shows.
Prod-CARNA Dist-MTP

Operation Usak B 20 MIN
16MM FILM OPTICAL SOUND
Examines how a nation shows grief, and how a film can and should convey grief. Presents homage to the great, and a study of a nation's attitude toward greatness and mourning.
Prod-UPENN Dist-UPENN 1964

Operation Van Pool C 16 MIN
16MM FILM OPTICAL SOUND
Presents the story of corporate-sponsored commuter service programs. Shows how these programs provide the answer to reducing traffic congestion and conserving precious energy while cutting commuter costs by 25 percent.
Prod-GM Dist-MTP

Operation X-70 C 10 MIN
16MM FILM, 3/4 OR 1/2 IN VIDEO J-C A
Uses animation to satirize scientific warfare. Deals with the unexpected effects of a gas that has been accidently dropped on a friendly Western nation.
LC NO. 80-707240
Prod-PENFIL Dist-IFB 1975

Operation You C 15 MIN
16MM FILM OPTICAL SOUND
Provides information which suggests that patients might need to more fully participate in decisions about their surgical care.
Prod-AMCSUR Dist-MTP

Operation Zero-Zero - Project Narrow Gauge B 19 MIN
16MM FILM OPTICAL SOUND
Shows the extensive testing of an integrated visual approach and landing aids system (IVALA) to prove that this improvement can provide aviation with greater and safer aircraft landing capability.
LC NO. FIE60-44
Prod-USDD Dist-USNAC 1959

Operation, The - Coronary Artery Bypass, Pt 2 - The Nursing Care C 30 MIN
3/4 OR 1/2 INCH VIDEO CASSETTE
Shows the ICU nurse and physician planning and beginning immediate postoperative care and monitoring of the patient's cardiovascular, respiratory and neurological status following coronary artery bypass surgery.
Prod-ARIZHI Dist-AJN

Operation, The - Coronary Artery Bypass, Pt 1 - The Surgery C 60 MIN
3/4 OR 1/2 INCH VIDEO CASSETTE
Gives close-ups of the coronary artery bypass surgery, clear graphics and detailed explanations of the responsibilities procedures and equipment in the OR and ICU.
Prod-ARIZHI Dist-AJN

Operational Amplifier Applications - I C 30 MIN
3/4 OR 1/2 INCH VIDEO CASSETTE PRO
Discusses general items important to the application of operational amplifiers, first, followed by specific examples and actual studio demonstration of a sample and hold circuit.
From The Linear And Interface Integrated Circuits, Part I - Linear Integrated Circuits Series.
Prod-TXINLC Dist-TXINLC

Operational Amplifier Applications - II C 30 MIN
3/4 OR 1/2 INCH VIDEO CASSETTE PRO
Covers more specific applications including design of active filters, differential amplifiers, servo motor devices, clamping circuits and a low-noise audio pre-amplifier.
From The Linear And Interface Integrated Circuits, Part I - Linear Integrated Circuits Series.
Prod-TXINLC Dist-TXINLC

Operational Amplifier Circuits—A Series
IND
Covers in three parts and 32 lectures how to improve effectiveness of circuit design engineers. Shows practical limitations of operational amplifier circuits, a catalog of proven circuits used successfully in a multitude of instruments.
Prod-COLOSU Dist-COLOSU

Part One - Frequency Domain 040 MIN
Part Three - Active Filters 040 MIN
Part Two - Operational Amplifiers 040 MIN

Operational Amplifier Design - I C 30 MIN
3/4 OR 1/2 INCH VIDEO CASSETTE PRO
Deals with low frequency characteristics. Goes into past and present of linear integrated circuit design of operational amplifiers; from ideal characteristics to that of present day. Includes discussion of synthesized circuit components, active load devices, super beta transistors, split-collector fixed beta transistors and pinch resistors.
From The Linear And Interface Integrated Circuits, Part I - Linear Integrated Circuits Series.
Prod-TXINLC Dist-TXINLC

Operational Amplifier Design - II C 30 MIN
3/4 OR 1/2 INCH VIDEO CASSETTE PRO
Discusses operational amplifier frequency response and techniques used to compensate those amplifiers and assure stability. Discusses large signal operation as well to define terms such as sleu-rate settling time, and transient response.
From The Linear And Interface Integrated Circuits, Part I - Linear Integrated Circuits Series.
Prod-TXINLC Dist-TXINLC

Operational Amplifiers C 12 MIN
3/4 OR 1/2 INCH VIDEO CASSETTE
Covers differential amplifiers, virtual ground and summing functions, operational summers, noninverting amplifiers and special op amp circuits.
From The Industrial Electronics - Amplifiers Series
Prod-TPCTRA Dist-TPCTRA

Operational Causality C 21 MIN
16MM FILM OPTICAL SOUND C A
Demonstrates the scale for the construction of operational causality. Includes concepts of causality, space and time. Shows infants ranging in age from 12 weeks to 23 months.
From The Ordinal Scales Of Infant Psychological Development Series.
LC NO. 73-703095
Prod-UILLVA Dist-UILL 1968

Operational Definitions, Conformance, And Performance C
3/4 OR 1/2 INCH VIDEO CASSETTE
Discusses the operational definitions of quality needed for understanding between vendor and purchaser.
From The Deming Videotapes - Quality, Productivity, And Competitive...Series.
Prod-MIOT Dist-MIOT

Operational Definitions, Conformation, And Performance C 50 MIN
3/4 OR 1/2 INCH VIDEO CASSETTE
See series title for descriptive statement.
From The Deming Video Tapes - Quality, Productivity And The Competitive...Series.
Prod-MIOT Dist-SME

Operational Readiness C 19 MIN
16MM FILM OPTICAL SOUND
Explains logistics by following the logistic results of a battle in Vietnam and showing how aircraft engines are ordered and repaired. Describes various activities of the Air Force Logistics Command and its methods of supplying forces.
LC NO. 74-706169
Prod-USAF Dist-USNAC 1969

Operational Tests, Checking For Short And Grounds C 60 MIN
3/4 OR 1/2 INCH VIDEO CASSETTE IND
See series title for descriptive statement.
From The Electrical Maintenance Training, Module 1 - Control Equipment Series.
Prod-LEIKID Dist-LEIKID

Operations For Correction Of Congenital Biliary Atresia C 30 MIN
16MM FILM OPTICAL SOUND PRO
Presents the operative treatment of biliary obstruction in infancy. Includes cases of congenital atresia and post hepatitis ductal obliseration.
Prod-ACYDGD Dist-ACY 1954

Operations Frequently Performed On The Drill Press C
3/4 OR 1/2 INCH VIDEO CASSETTE
See series title for descriptive statement.
From The Basic Machine Technology Series.
Prod-VTRI Dist-VTRI

Operations Frequently Performed On The Drill Press C 15 MIN
3/4 OR 1/2 INCH VIDEO CASSETTE
See series title for descriptive statement.
From The Machine Technology II - Engine Lathe Accessories Series.
Prod-CAMB Dist-CAMB

Operations Frequently Performed On The Drill Press C 15 MIN
3/4 OR 1/2 INCH VIDEO CASSETTE IND
See series title for descriptive statement.
From The Machining And The Operation Of Machine Tools, Module 1 - Basic Machine Technology Series.
Prod-LEIKID Dist-LEIKID

Operations Frequently Performed On The Drill Press (Spanish) C
3/4 OR 1/2 INCH VIDEO CASSETTE
See series title for descriptive statement.
From The Basic Machine Technology (Spanish) Series.
Prod-VTRI Dist-VTRI

Operations Research—A Series
PRO
Covers mathematical techniques for aiding managerial decision-making. Discusses waiting line theory, inventory models, linear programming, transportation problem, dynamic programming, PERT/CPM, machine scheduling and simulation.
Prod-UAKEN Dist-AMCEE

Operations With Fractions C 15 MIN
3/4 INCH VIDEO CASSETTE I
Discusses adding and subtracting unlike fractions and shows how to state the order of two fractions.
From The Math - No Mystery Series.
Prod-WCETTV Dist-GPITVL 1977

Operations With Whole Numbers C 22 MIN
16MM FILM OPTICAL SOUND
Explores procedures for interrelating addition and substraction. Shows materials, methods and strategies that are particularly effective. Focuses on the use of multiple techniques for misproving instruction in multiplication. Emphasizes algorithms, which have been found to be particularly effective.
From The Interpreting Machematics Education Research Series.
LC NO. 74-705263
Prod-USOE Dist-USNAC 1970

Operative Cholangiography And Its Indications C 18 MIN
16MM FILM OPTICAL SOUND PRO
Describes the advantages of operative cholangiography in locating stones that may be overlooked by palpation and inspection. Illustrates the technic of positioning the patient, and injecting the contrast medium.
Prod-ACYDGD Dist-ACY 1960

Operative Dentistry - Advanced Concepts C 28 MIN
16MM FILM OPTICAL SOUND
Demonstrates how to introduce and prepare dental patients. Shows the preparation of cavity, matrix, removal of dam, checking of occulusion and reappointment. Describes the techniques of finishing and polishing.
LC NO. 74-706548
Prod-USN Dist-USNAC 1966

Operative Drainage For Empyema C 9 MIN
3/4 OR 1/2 INCH VIDEO CASSETTE
See series title for descriptive statement.
From The Pediatric Series.
Prod-SVL Dist-SVL

Operative Laparoscopy - Tubal Sterilization C 16 MIN
16MM FILM OPTICAL SOUND PRO
Demonstrates the techniques of electrocauterization and division of the uterine tubes on an extripated specimen.
Prod-SCITIF Dist-SCITIF 1969

Operative Procedures C 17 MIN
16MM FILM, 3/4 OR 1/2 IN VIDEO H-C A
Considers a woman's fears when she is faced with surgery involving her reproductive system. Dismisses old wives' tales and the patient is given a better understanding of procedures and results so that she gains a positive attitude.
From The Woman Talk Series.
Prod-CORF Dist-CORF 1983

Operative Repair Of Single Cleft Lips, The C 34 MIN
16MM FILM OPTICAL SOUND PRO
Includes simple standard design and marking to uniformly obtain the best possible result with the least sacrifice of tissue and the operation to repair a single cleft lip, step-by-step.
Prod-ACYDGD Dist-ACY 1957

Operative Treatment Of Chronic Stasis Ulcer, The C 26 MIN
16MM FILM OPTICAL SOUND PRO
Demonstrates the technique of excision of chronic stasis ulcers and the covering of the cutaneous defect with grafts. Shows a method of delimiting the requisite area of excision by lymphatic injections.
Prod-ACYDGD Dist-ACY 1955

Operative Treatment Of Hirschsprung's Disease C 16 MIN
16MM FILM OPTICAL SOUND PRO
Demonstrates Dr Swenson's technique for Hirschsprung's disease. Explains that he found that by removing a region in the upper rectum lacking proper nerve cells and then re-establishing the continuity of the colon, it was possible to cure this disease.
Prod-ACYDGD Dist-ACY 1950

Operator And His Job, The B 12 MIN
16MM FILM OPTICAL SOUND
Illustrates the three responsibilities of the bus operator--safety and comfort of his passengers, maintenance of schedules and a courteous attitude toward passengers.
LC NO. FIE52-331
Prod-USOE Dist-USNAC 1945

Operator And His Passengers, The B 18 MIN
16MM FILM OPTICAL SOUND
Discusses the importance of good customer relations and shows ways of handling such problems as expired transfers, people who miss their stops and persuading passengers to move to the rear of the bus.
LC NO. FIE52-332
Prod-USOE Dist-USNAC 1945

Operator-Patient And Light Positions C 9 MIN
3/4 INCH VIDEO CASSETTE PRO
Demonstrates operator, patient and light positioning for maximum vision and comfort while working on upper and lower arches.
From The Scaling Techniques Series. No. 2
LC NO. 77-706008
Prod-UTENN Dist-USNAC 1976

Operator's Role, The C
3/4 OR 1/2 INCH VIDEO CASSETTE IND
Focuses on operator's role and how it fits into other associated areas such as maintenance and power system operation. Covers press and public communication.
From The Distribution System Operation Series. Topic 13
Prod-LEIKID Dist-LEIKID

Ophthalmic Optics - Refraction By The Eye C 10 MIN
16MM FILM, 3/4 OR 1/2 IN VIDEO H-C A
From The Optics Of The Human Eye Series.
Prod-BAYCMO Dist-TEF

Ophthalmic Optics - Refractive Errors And Optical Aberrations C 10 MIN
16MM FILM, 3/4 OR 1/2 IN VIDEO H-C A
From The Optics Of The Human Eye Series.
Prod-BAYCMO Dist-TEF

Ophthalmic Surgery System At The Jules Stein Eye Institute C 13 MIN
16MM FILM OPTICAL SOUND PRO
Describes the unique features of the Jules Stein Eye Institute such as the operating room facilities, which includes a patient transport system, hydraulic columns, a remote control operating pedestal, closed circuit television, surgical microscopes, and facilities for filming and television recording.
Prod-UCLA Dist-UCLA

Ophthalmoscope C 11 MIN
3/4 INCH VIDEO CASSETTE PRO
Demonstrates how to use and care for an ophthalmoscope. Describes the anatomical features the examiner should be able to see when the instrument is used correctly.
From The Instruments Of Physical Assessment Series.
LC NO. 80-707625
Prod-SUNYSB Dist-LIP 1980

Opinion Of The Publics C 37 MIN
16MM FILM OPTICAL SOUND
Presents a composite of mini-case histories showing public relations programs in action. Features people meeting challenges with documented solutions.
Prod-PRSAIC Dist-MTP 1973

Opium Poppies Bloom Again, The - Turkey C 13 MIN
3/4 OR 1/2 INCH VIDEO CASSETTE H-C A
Describes the cultivation and distribution of opium in Turkey.
Prod-UPI Dist-JOU

Opportunities C 19 MIN
3/4 OR 1/2 INCH VIDEO CASSETTE H
Shows Andy and Brenda learning about job-opportunity resources.
From The Jobs - Seeking, Finding, Keeping Series.
Prod-MSDOE Dist-AITECH 1980

Opportunities For Learning B 27 MIN
3/4 OR 1/2 INCH VIDEO CASSETTE PRO
Illustrates how most one- and two-year-olds learn the process of exploration and discovery through play situations. Suggests how parents can provide opportunites for learning in the home.
Prod-HSERF Dist-HSERF

Opportunities For Productive Roles C 30 MIN
3/4 INCH VIDEO CASSETTE
See series title for descriptive statement.
From The Growing Old In Modern America Series.
Prod-UWASHP Dist-UWASHP

Opportunities For The Disadvantaged C 16 MIN
16MM FILM, 3/4 OR 1/2 IN VIDEO J-H
Discusses the development of special strategies for the minority group individual or economically deprived. Describes agencies and programs designed for the disadvantaged along with dramatic examples of success by people from minority backgrounds.
From The Future Street - New Directions In Career Education Series.
Prod-AMEDFL Dist-AMEDFL 1972

Opportunities In Clerical Work C 10 MIN
16MM FILM, 3/4 OR 1/2 IN VIDEO J A
Explores the many opportunities for today's clerical worker and stresses the necessity for every applicant to acqure the basic skill of typing as well as the ability to transcribe rapidly.
Prod-SF Dist-SF 1970

Opportunities In Clerical Work C 10 MIN
16MM FILM, 3/4 OR 1/2 IN VIDEO
Describes a variety of clerical jobs, covering career entry jobs and company-sponsored training programs. Emphasizes opportunities in computer data processing areas and stresses the possibilities for steady advancement. Issued in 1970 as a motion picture.
From The Career Job Opportunity Series.
LC NO. 79-707884
Prod-USDLMA Dist-USNAC Prodn-DEROCH 1979

Opportunities In Logging C 28 MIN
16MM FILM OPTICAL SOUND
Shows the opportunities available to young men who like the outdoors and the challenge of physical work including the operation of heavy equipment. Covers the many facets of the logging industry.
Prod-RARIG Dist-RARIG 1967

Opportunities In Sales And Merchandising C 11 MIN
16MM FILM, 3/4 OR 1/2 IN VIDEO J A
Portrays the career opportunities in sales and merchandising occupations, including work settings, levels of occupations and information about preparatory work experience available through part-time work or a summer job in the retailing industry. Shows actual work settings and the occupational skills to be found in sales and merchandising.
Prod-SF Dist-SF 1970

Opportunities In Sales And Merchandising C 11 MIN
16MM FILM, 3/4 OR 1/2 IN VIDEO
Discusses career opportunities in sales and merchandising in department stores. Explains how entry-level jobs fit into career ladders. Issued in 1967 as a motion picture.
From The Career Job Opportunity Series.
LC NO. 79-707886
Prod-USDLMA Dist-USNAC 1979

Opportunities In The Machine Trades C 7 MIN
16MM FILM, 3/4 OR 1/2 IN VIDEO J A
Presents many job opportunities for beginners in the machine trades. Stresses good pay for entry workers and points out avenues for career advancement, including shop ownership for those who have mastered their trade.
Prod-SF Dist-SF 1970

Opportunities In The Retail Automobile Business C 20 MIN
16MM FILM OPTICAL SOUND
Presents the story of two high school seniors who visit an automotive dealership and learn about the opportunities in the retail automotive business.
Prod-GM Dist-GM

Opportunities In Welding C 7 MIN
16MM FILM, 3/4 OR 1/2 IN VIDEO J A
Describes job sites and opportunities in welding. Shows welding in shops, shipyards, airports and on a construction site 20 stories high.
Prod-SF Dist-SF 1970

Opportunities Presented By Television, The C 30 MIN
3/4 OR 1/2 INCH VIDEO CASSETTE
See series title for descriptive statement.
From The Dance On Television - Ipiotis Series.
Prod-ARCVID Dist-ARCVID

Opportunities Unlimited C 20 MIN
16MM FILM OPTICAL SOUND J-H A
Describes the advantages for students in enrolling in a vocational education program.
LC NO. 72-700615
Prod-VADE Dist-VADE 1970

Opportunity Acres C 15 MIN
16MM FILM OPTICAL SOUND
Demonstrates to dairymen and cattle feeders the profitable use of farmland in the high rainfall area of the Southern Gulf Coast.
LC NO. 77-713589
Prod-VENARD Dist-VENARD 1971

Opportunity Class, The C 22 MIN
16MM FILM OPTICAL SOUND
Documents the origin, development and activities of a special nursery class for both handicapped and normal children under seven years of age. Shows how the opportunity class plays a useful role in preparing the physically or mentally handicapped child for entrance into a formal classroom setting. Points out that mothers also benefit from social contact with other parents.
Prod-VASSAR Dist-NYU

Opportunity For All - Making A Go Of EEO C
16MM FILM, 3/4 OR 1/2 IN VIDEO A
Explains how managers and supervisors can avoid discrimination complaints when hiring. Discusses the Equal Employment Opportunity law and specific guidelines for performance, documentation, career development planning, defining minimum qualifications, recognizing and correcting equal pay problems and identifying nonprofessional behavior which results in discriminatory practices.
Prod-RTBL Dist-RTBL

Opportunity For Leadership, The C 30 MIN
3/4 OR 1/2 INCH VIDEO CASSETTE
Establishes the achievements and satisfactions available to both the organization and individual at all levels. Focuses on a positive idea of leadership. Uses the idea of a three person personality of human behavior, the 'parent, adult and child.'
From The Organizational Transactions Series.
Prod-PRODEV Dist-PRODEV

Opportunity To Become, An C 20 MIN
16MM FILM OPTICAL SOUND
Documents the ten areas of athletics sponsored by the Department of Women's Intercollegiate Athletics at the University of Minnesota. Explores the emotions experienced by people involved in athletics and how these experiences help women in their lives after college.
LC NO. 79-700397
Prod-UMNAD Dist-FILMA Prodn-FILMA 1978

Opportunity Unlimited - Friendly Atoms In Industry C 29 MIN
16MM FILM OPTICAL SOUND
Presents the nature and method of use of radioisotopes. Covers their application to thickness control, density measurement, quality control and industrial radiography and their use as tracers in chemical reactions.
Prod-USAEC Dist-USERD 1962

Opposite / Same Machine, The C 15 MIN
3/4 OR 1/2 INCH VIDEO CASSETTE P
Employs a magician named Amazing Alexander and his assistants to explore word meanings.
From The Magic Shop Series. No. 9
LC NO. 83-706154
Prod-CVETVC Dist-GPITVL Prodn-WCVETV 1982

Opposite Of Love, The C 30 MIN
3/4 INCH VIDEO CASSETTE
See series title for descriptive statement.
From The Ounce Of Prevention Series.
Prod-CFDC Dist-CFDC

Opposites In Harmony C 17 MIN
16MM FILM - 3/4 IN VIDEO
Describes the development of the executive branch of the American government. Depicts a meeting between George Washington and his small Cabinet, showing the human element involved in the growth of the government.
LC NO. 79-706144
Prod-USNPS Dist-USNAC 1979

Optical Alignment C 34 MIN
3/4 OR 1/2 INCH VIDEO CASSETTE IND
Shows the application of optical alignment to production lines where straightness is important. Shows the optical instrument as the 'third eye.'
From The Marshall Maintenance Training Programs Series. Tape 12
Prod-LEIKID Dist-LEIKID

Optical Alignment C 34 MIN
16MM FILM, 3/4 OR 1/2 IN VIDEO IND
Shows the application of optical alignment equipment to production lines where straightness is of utmost importance.
Prod-MOKIN Dist-MOKIN

Optical Character Reader C 11 MIN
16MM FILM OPTICAL SOUND
Shows the use of control data's OCR page reader in a variety of applications for translation of ASA-font typewriting into digital terms recorded on magnetic tape.
Prod-CONTR Dist-CONTR

Optical Couplers C 50 MIN
3/4 OR 1/2 INCH VIDEO CASSETTE PRO
Shows types, properties, examples, design principles and WDM grating demultiplexer design principle.
From The Optical Fiber Communications Series.
Prod-NCSU Dist-AMCEE

Optical Detectors, Pt 1 C 50 MIN
3/4 OR 1/2 INCH VIDEO CASSETTE PRO
Covers available types of optical detectors, physics of photovoltaic and photoconductive junctions and PIN photodiodes.
From The Optical Fiber Communications Series.
Prod-NCSU Dist-AMCEE

Optical Detectors, Pt 2 C 50 MIN
3/4 OR 1/2 INCH VIDEO CASSETTE PRO
Covers avalanche photodiodes.
From The Optical Fiber Communications Series.
Prod-NCSU Dist-AMCEE

Optical Fiber Communications—A Series
PRO
Uses classroom format to videotape 28 50-minute lectures on 28 cassettes. Provides understanding of components, subsystems and system design techniques used in application of optical fiber communications systems. Emphasizes practical analysis and design approaches for both system and subsystem levels.
Prod-NCSU Dist-AMCEE

Advanced Systems, Pt 1 050 MIN
Advanced Systems, Pt 2 050 MIN
Analog System Design Examples 050 MIN
Applications - Data Communications Systems 050 MIN
Applications - Local Area Networks 050 MIN
Applications - Telephone Systems - Subscriber 050 MIN
Applications - Telephone Transmission Systems 050 MIN
Cabling Techniques And Installation Examples 050 MIN
Cabling Technologies 050 MIN
Comparison Of Fiber Optics With Conventional 050 MIN
Digital Transmission Design Examples 050 MIN
Fiber Optic System Design 050 MIN
Fiber Testing Techniques, Mode Transmission 050 MIN
Interconnection And Jointing 050 MIN
Introduction To Fiber Optic System Design 050 MIN
Noise Analysis Continued 050 MIN
Optical Couplers 050 MIN
Optical Detectors, Pt 1 050 MIN
Optical Detectors, Pt 2 050 MIN
Optical Fibers, Pt 1 050 MIN
Optical Fibers, Pt 2 050 MIN
Optical Receiver Design Examples 050 MIN
Optical Receivers 050 MIN
Optical Sources, Pt 1 050 MIN
Optical Sources, Pt 2 050 MIN
Optical Transmitter Design 050 MIN
Overview Of Optical Fiber Communications 050 MIN
Trade-Offs Between Optical Source Types 050 MIN

Optical Fibers, Pt 1 C 50 MIN
3/4 OR 1/2 INCH VIDEO CASSETTE PRO
Covers guiding properties and total internal reflection, fiber type, introduction to transmission properties, fiber compositions and material technologies, manufacturing techniques, strength properties and coating technology.
From The Optical Fiber Communications Series.
Prod-NCSU Dist-AMCEE

Optical Fibers, Pt 2 C 50 MIN
3/4 OR 1/2 INCH VIDEO CASSETTE PRO
Covers multimode fiber transmission properties, loss, dispersion, Keck/Olshansky theories, zero dispersion wavelength, single mode fiber transmission properties and dispersion-shifted fibers.
From The Optical Fiber Communications Series.
Prod-NCSU Dist-AMCEE

Optical Fibre Communications C 2 MIN
16MM FILM OPTICAL SOUND
Shows how advances in optical fibre research can hasten the advent of community wide communications.
Prod-ALLFP Dist-NSTA 1973

Optical Fibres and Telecommunication C 44 MIN
3/4 OR 1/2 INCH VIDEO CASSETTE
Shows how optical fibres can be used to handle large amounts of information and transmit the information up to a thousand kilometers at very high speeds.
Prod-FLMWST Dist-FLMWST

Optical Inspection Methods, Pt 1 B 26 MIN
16MM FILM OPTICAL SOUND
Explains visual methods of inspection, the use of gages, the necessity for checking the gages and the theory and use of Newton's rings as an inspection method.
Prod-USN Dist-USNAC 1944

Optical Motions And Transformations As Stimuli For Visual Perception B 25 MIN
16MM FILM SILENT C T
Describes the dimensions of movement of geometric forms in terms of simple mathematical transformations. Presents examples showing how such dimensions of movement arouse the perception of moving objects in tridimensional space. The film is an exposition of some of the recent research of J J Gibson.
LC NO. 76-703730
Prod-GIBSOJ Dist-PSUPCR 1957

Optical Poem C 7 MIN
16MM FILM, 3/4 OR 1/2 IN VIDEO H-C
Sets Oskar Fischinger's abstractions to the music of The Hungarian Rhapsody.
Prod-MGM Dist-FI 1939

Optical Receiver Design Examples C 50 MIN
3/4 OR 1/2 INCH VIDEO CASSETTE PRO
Shows 'RC' type preamp, integrating preamp and transimpedance preamp.
From The Optical Fiber Communications Series.
Prod-NCSU Dist-AMCEE

Optical Receivers C 50 MIN
3/4 OR 1/2 INCH VIDEO CASSETTE PRO
Takes into account design considerations and noise analysis of bipolar and Field Effect Transistor (FET) preamps.
From The Optical Fiber Communications Series.
Prod-NCSU Dist-AMCEE

Optical Sources, Pt 1 C 50 MIN
3/4 OR 1/2 INCH VIDEO CASSETTE PRO
Gives an overview and focuses on light-emitting diodes.
From The Optical Fiber Communications Series.
Prod-NCSU Dist-AMCEE

Optical Sources, Pt 2 C 50 MIN
3/4 OR 1/2 INCH VIDEO CASSETTE PRO
Discusses injection laser diodes and peculiarities of laser/fiber systems.
From The Optical Fiber Communications Series.
Prod-NCSU Dist-AMCEE

Optical Spectroscopy For Diagnostics And Process Control C
3/4 OR 1/2 INCH VIDEO CASSETTE IND
Covers uses of optical emission or absorption spectroscopy as well as mass spectroscopy in plasma etching and deposition reactors. Describes commercial optical monitors for end-point detection in a plasma-etch reactor.
From The Plasma Process Technology Fundamentals Series.
Prod-COLOSU Dist-COLOSU

Optical Transmitter Design C 50 MIN
3/4 OR 1/2 INCH VIDEO CASSETTE PRO
Discusses design considerations, and Light-Emitting Diode-(LED)-based and laser-based transmitter designs.
From The Optical Fiber Communications Series.
Prod-NCSU Dist-AMCEE

Optical Waveguide Modes C 34 MIN
3/4 OR 1/2 INCH VIDEO CASSETTE C
Describes optical wave propagation in various types of waveguides illustrated with photographs and experimentally measured mode profiles.
From The Integrated Optics Series.
Prod-UDEL Dist-UDEL

Optics Of The Human Eye—A Series
H-C A
Explains the optics of the human eye. Directed toward medical students and contact lens technicians.
Prod-BAYCMO Dist-TEF

Ophthalmic Optics - Refraction By The Eye 010 MIN
Ophthalmic Optics - Refractive Errors And 010 MIN
Refraction Of Light By Spherical Lenses 010 MIN
Refraction Of Light By Spherocylindrical Lenses 010 MIN

Optics—A Series
H
Covers basic requirements in the study of light and discusses the wave theory of light. Includes practical demonstration of each point discussed, reinforced by diagrams or film animation.
Prod-CETO Dist-GPITVL

Curved Mirrors, Pt 1 22 MIN
Curved Mirrors, Pt 2 22 MIN
Lenses, Pt 1 22 MIN
Lenses, Pt 2 22 MIN
Light And Shadow 22 MIN
Light And Sight 22 MIN
Light Waves 22 MIN
Reflection 22 MIN
Refraction, Pt 1 22 MIN
Refraction, Pt 2 22 MIN

Optimal Column And The Circuit Breaker, The B 60 MIN
3/4 OR 1/2 INCH VIDEO CASSETTE
See series title for descriptive statement.
From The Engineering Design Optimization I Series. Pt 5
Prod-UAZMIC Dist-UAZMIC

Optimal Control Of A Macroeconomic Model Of The US Economy (1957-1962) C 44 MIN
3/4 OR 1/2 INCH VIDEO CASSETTE PRO
See series title for descriptive statement.
From The Modern Control Theory - Deterministic Optimal Linear Feedback Series.
Prod-MIOT Dist-MIOT

Optimal Sampling And Penalty Methods B 60 MIN
3/4 OR 1/2 INCH VIDEO CASSETTE
See series title for descriptive statement.
From The Finite Element Method And Some Of Its-Developments Series. Pt 4
Prod-UAZMIC Dist-UAZMIC 1980

Optimality Criteria I C 60 MIN
3/4 OR 1/2 INCH VIDEO CASSETTE
See series title for descriptive statement.
From The Engineering Design Optimization II Series. Pt 16
Prod-UAZMIC Dist-UAZMIC

Optimality Criteria Methods B 60 MIN
3/4 OR 1/2 INCH VIDEO CASSETTE
See series title for descriptive statement.
From The Engineering Design Optimization I Series. Pt 14
Prod-UAZMIC Dist-UAZMIC

Optimist And Pessimist C 8 MIN
16MM FILM, 3/4 OR 1/2 IN VIDEO C A
Uses animation to tell the story of an optimist who tries to get a chuckle from a pessimist who is dissatisfied with everything. Satirizes major social mores as they are portrayed by the film industry.
LC NO. 80-707375
Prod-ZAGREB Dist-IFB 1975

Optimum Burn-In C 30 MIN
3/4 OR 1/2 INCH VIDEO CASSETTE IND
Uses plot of data on Weibull Probability Paper to locate transition from early to chance failure. Says transition point is maximum burn-in. Uses published Xerox data to illustrate procedures to define optimum burn-in less than maximum.
From The Reliability Engineering Series.
Prod-COLOSU Dist-COLOSU

Option For Excellence C 13 MIN
16MM FILM OPTICAL SOUND
Shows how advanced placement functions in South Carolina as a system of educational articulation and improvement. Interviews film students, teachers, principals and college professors about advanced placement courses, examinations and benefits from their personal perspectives.
Prod-SCETV Dist-CEEB 1979

Option For The Future C 16 MIN
16MM FILM OPTICAL SOUND
Justifies the Bell System's switch from flat-rate pricing to measured-rate pricing. Shows how telephone usage has evolved and how disparities in individual usage have led to inequities with flat-rate pricing and to measured service as a response to change.
LC NO. 80-700432
Prod-MTBAVC Dist-MTBAVC Prodn-CNSER 1979

Option To See, An C 17 MIN
16MM FILM OPTICAL SOUND
Shows how a student learns about the importance of eye safety from his teacher and his employer.
LC NO. 78-700119
Prod-NSPB Dist-NSPB Prodn-NOWAKA 1977

Option, An C 19 MIN
16MM FILM - 3/4 IN VIDEO
Focuses on Washington, DC'S Summer In The Parks program by highlighting the reactions of inner-city neighborhood leaders. Issued in 1971 as a motion picture.
LC NO. 79-706145
Prod-USNPS Dist-USNAC 1979

Optional Dives, Pt 1 C 20 MIN
16MM FILM, 3/4 OR 1/2 IN VIDEO
Demonstrates the most commonly performed optional dives.
From The Diving Series. No 3
Prod-ATHI Dist-ATHI 1977

Optional Dives, Pt 2 C 20 MIN
16MM FILM, 3/4 OR 1/2 IN VIDEO
Demonstrates the most commonly performed optional dives.
From The Diving Series. No 3
Prod-ATHI Dist-ATHI 1977

Options - Dental Health In The Later Years C 16 MIN
16MM FILM, 3/4 OR 1/2 IN VIDEO A
Emphasizes that dental disease is not an inevitable result of aging to be passively accepted along with its depressing consequences. Focuses on the prevention of periodontal disease through daily personal care, diet and proper nutrition.
Prod-AMDA Dist-AMDA 1979

Options For Life C 12 MIN
16MM FILM, 3/4 OR 1/2 IN VIDEO J-C A
Shows how a person can facilitate the making of informed decisions regarding eating habits, exercise, smoking and drugs.
From The Nutrition Series.
Prod-ALTSUL Dist-JOU 1979

Optische Glaser - Brillenglasfertigung C 5 MIN
16MM FILM, 3/4 OR 1/2 IN VIDEO H-C A
A German-language version of the motion picture Making Eye Glass Lenses. Describes the modern German eye glass manufacturing industry as well as the historical development of the process.
From The European Studies - Germany (German) Series.
Prod-MFAFRG Dist-IFB Prodn-BAYER 1973

Optoelectronic Device Reliability (Optoelectronics, Part I) C 30 MIN
3/4 OR 1/2 INCH VIDEO CASSETTE PRO
Reviews basic fabrications to help establish similarities and differences of reliability of optoelectronic devices compared to silicon. Cites actual data to establish data base, and covers all types of optoelectronic devices.
From The Optoelectronics, Part I - Optoelectronic Emitters, Sensors And Couplers Series.
Prod-TXINLC Dist-TXINLC

Optoelectronic Device Reliability (Optoelectronics, Part II) C 30 MIN
3/4 OR 1/2 INCH VIDEO CASSETTE PRO
Repeats from Part I the comparison of optoelectronic devices compared to silicon. Completes working engineer's knowledge of displays in cases where section on emitters, sensors and couplers has not been viewed.
From The Optoelectronics, Part II - Optoelectronic Displays Series.
Prod-TXINLC Dist-TXINLC

Optoelectronics, Part I - Optoelectronic Emitters, Sensor, And Couplers—A Series
PRO
Provides information needed to evaluate the contribution optoelectronics can make in electronics equipment. Allows designer to determine his device options and relate them to specific equipment requirements and applications. Covers, in Part I, optoelectronic emitters, sensors and couplers.
Prod-TXINLC Dist-TXINLC

Emitter And Its Characteristics, The 030 MIN
General Emitter, Sensor, Coupler Applications 030 MIN
Infrared Emitter Applications 030 MIN
Introduction To Optoelectronics 030 MIN
Optoelectronic Device Reliability 030 MIN
Photocoupler Applications 030 MIN
Photocouplers And Their Characteristics 030 MIN
Sensor And Its Characteristics, The 030 MIN
Sensor Applications 030 MIN

Optoelectronics, Part II - Optoelectronic Displays—A Series
PRO
Provides information needed to evaluate the contribution optoelectronics can make in electronic equipment. Allows designer to determine his device options and relate them to specific equipment requirements and applications. Covers in Part II, optoelectronic displays.
Prod-TXINLC Dist-TXINLC

Alphanumeric Display Applications 030 MIN
Applications Of Visible Displays Integrated 030 MIN
Critical Emitter Parameters And Their 030 MIN
Human Factors Associated With Displays 030 MIN
Introduction To Displays 030 MIN
Introduction To Optoelectronics 030 MIN
Numeric Display Applications 030 MIN
Optoelectronic Device Reliability 030 MIN
VLED Device - Process And Fabrication 030 MIN

Opus I C 5 MIN
16MM FILM SILENT
Presents a long-lost film by Walter Ruttmann, the first abstract film to be shown publicly anywhere in the world and which was recently discovered in a European film archive in its original hand-colored version.
Prod-STARRC Dist-STARRC 1921

Opus II, III, IV B 10 MIN
16MM FILM SILENT
Presents 'a series of moving patterns' in a film by Walter Ruttman, one of the world's great abstract artists. Produced 1922-25.
Prod-STARRC Dist-STARRC

Opus 1 C 4 MIN
16MM FILM OPTICAL SOUND
Explores the primary techniques of film painting.
Prod-SPINLB Dist-FMCOOP 1967

Opus 44, Jerry West's Own Story C 24 MIN
16MM FILM OPTICAL SOUND
Examines the private and public life of basketball player Jerry West.
LC NO. 74-700360
Prod-JANTZN Dist-JANTZN 1973

Or-Or-War C 6 MIN
16MM FILM OPTICAL SOUND
Presents man's symmetrical hate-love, love-hate duel.
Prod-VANBKS Dist-VANBKS

Oracle Of The Branch C 12 MIN
16MM FILM, 3/4 OR 1/2 IN VIDEO A
Presents a dance composed by Marks and performed by soloist James Croshaw.
Prod-SFCT Dist-CNEMAG 1965

Oral Administration Of Medications B 14 MIN
16MM FILM OPTICAL SOUND
Presents the duties of hospital corpsmen in administering medications by mouth to patients in wards of naval hospitals. Demonstrates in detail the preparation of medication and treatment cards in accordance with the orders of medical officers.
LC NO. FIE60-84
Prod-USN Dist-USNAC 1959

Oral Biopsy Procedure C 15 MIN
16MM FILM - 3/4 IN VIDEO PRO
Presents examples of some of the most common oral lesions and suggests biopsy procedures for each lesion, including excisional, incisional and aspirational techniques. Shows suturing techniques.
LC NO. 79-707997
Prod-VADTC Dist-USNAC 1978

Oral Cancer C 22 MIN
16MM FILM OPTICAL SOUND
Demonstrates a five-minute visual and digital examination for oral cancer. Shows various oral lesions, discusses the necessity for a biopsy in diagnosis, and describes several successfully treated cases, stressing early detection as the key to cure.
LC NO. FI68-88
Prod-AMCS Dist-AMCS Prodn-AEGIS 1966

Oral Cancer - Intra-Oral Examination C 6 MIN
16MM FILM OPTICAL SOUND
Demonstrates a methodical procedure for examining the intra-oral soft tissues. Presents six cases of early cancer in this area, pointing out their clinical signs.
LC NO. 75-702034
Prod-VADTC Dist-USNAC 1968

Oral Cancer - Intra-Oral Examination C 6 MIN
3/4 INCH VIDEO CASSETTE PRO
Demonstrates a methodical procedure for examining the intraoral soft tissues. Presents six cases of early cancer in this area, pointing out their clinical signs. Issued in 1968 as a motion picture.
LC NO. 78-706193
Prod-USVA Dist-USNAC Prodn-VADTC 1978

Oral Cancer Screening C 24 MIN
3/4 OR 1/2 INCH VIDEO CASSETTE PRO
Consists of videotape and teaching guide designed to help health professionals to perform a thorough cancer screening.
Prod-HSCIC Dist-HSCIC 1984

Oral Care C 7 MIN
3/4 OR 1/2 INCH VIDEO CASSETTE PRO
See series title for descriptive statement.
From The Basic Nursing Skills Series.
Prod-BRA Dist-BRA

Oral Care C 8 MIN
3/4 OR 1/2 INCH VIDEO CASSETTE PRO
See series title for descriptive statement.
From The Basic Nursing Skills Series. Tape 4
Prod-MDCC Dist-MDCC

Oral Cavity, The C 11 MIN
3/4 OR 1/2 INCH VIDEO CASSETTE C A
Describes the boundaries, demonstrates the bones and identifies the bony regions of the oral cavity.
From The Skull Anatomy Series.
Prod-UTXHSA Dist-TEF

Oral Communication C 28 MIN
16MM FILM OPTICAL SOUND A
Defines what things are most important in oral communication and applies them to person-to-person communication, informal interviews and group discussions.
From The You In Public Service Series.
LC NO. 77-700965
Prod-USOE Dist-USNAC 1977

Oral Contraception - The 21 Day Pill (3rd Ed) C 15 MIN
3/4 OR 1/2 INCH VIDEO CASSETTE
Explains how to use the birth control pill. Focuses on the use of the 21 day package.
Prod-MEDFAC Dist-MEDFAC 1979

Oral Contraception - The 28 Day Pill (3rd Ed) C 16 MIN
3/4 OR 1/2 INCH VIDEO CASSETTE
Explains how to use the birth control pill. Focuses on the use of the 28 day package.
Prod-MEDFAC Dist-MEDFAC 1979

Oral Contraceptives, Current Thinking On Metabolic Effects And Clinical Concerns C 28 MIN
16MM FILM OPTICAL SOUND
Provides findings by five international research laboratories on the metabolic effects of oral contraceptives. Discusses how this information influences management of patients.
LC NO. 79-701380
Prod-WYLAB Dist-AMCOG Prodn-EFFCOM 1979

Oral Contraceptives, The B 29 MIN
16MM FILM OPTICAL SOUND PRO
Debates the efficacy of oral contraceptives versus their adverse consequences.
From The Concepts And Controversies In Modern Medicine series.
LC NO. 74-705265
Prod-NMAC Dist-NMAC 1969

Oral Endoscopy C 20 MIN
16MM FILM OPTICAL SOUND
Shows the nursing and surgical management of a pediatric patient having general anesthesia for a laryngoscopy and an adult patient having a local anesthetic for bronchoscopy. Includes scenes showing the care and handling of oral endoscopic instruments and equipment.

LC NO. 79-702507
Prod-ACYDGD Dist-ACY 1968

Oral Exam C 10 MIN
3/4 OR 1/2 INCH VIDEO CASSETTE
Describes a three-part oral examination for the detection of cancer in dental patients. Consists of visual inspection, palpatory examination and lymph adenopathy examination.
Prod-UWASH Dist-UWASH

Oral Exfoliative Cytology C 17 MIN
16MM FILM OPTICAL SOUND
Depicts how oral exfoliative cytology can disclose early and unsuspected cancer of the mouth. Demonstrates the technique for obtaining a cytology specimen and presents the variation of the microscopic appearance of normal cells and cancer cells.
LC NO. 74-705266
Prod-USVA Dist-NMAC 1963

Oral Exfoliative Cytology - A Diagnostic Tool For Detection Of Early Mouth Cancer C 18 MIN
3/4 INCH VIDEO CASSETTE
Describes how oral exfoliative cytology can disclose early and unsuspected cancer of the mouth. Shows several clinical examples of unsuspected mouth cancers andd illustrates the technique for obtaining a cytology specimen. Issued in 1963 as a motion picture.
LC NO. 78-706105
Prod-USVA Dist-USNAC Prodn-NMAC 1978

Oral Expressive Language C 30 MIN
3/4 OR 1/2 INCH VIDEO CASSETTE T
Deals with oral expressive language in children with special needs.
From The Teaching Children With Special Needs Series.
Prod-MDDE Dist-MDCPB

Oral Facial Examination In Speech Pathology C 107 MIN
3/4 OR 1/2 INCH VIDEO CASSETTE
See series title for descriptive statement.
Prod-PUAVC Dist-PUAVC

Oral History C 20 MIN
3/4 INCH VIDEO CASSETTE T
Gives an overview of what is involved in undertaking an oral history project, including estimates of the staff, equipment and time necessary.
From The Access Series.
LC NO. 76-706249
Prod-UDEN Dist-USNAC 1976

Oral History C 60 MIN
16MM FILM - 1/2 IN VIDEO, VHS
Relates how a black village chief learns that members of his village are hiding guerrilla infiltrators and takes that information to the police - with tragic results.
Prod-TLECUL Dist-TLECUL

Oral Hygiene C 17 MIN
16MM FILM - 3/4 IN VIDEO
Explains that proper oral care at home, proper eating habits, and periodic visits to the dental office are prime weapons against dental disease. Shows techniques of proper brushing on a model and in a live mouth. Issued in 1961 as a motion picture.
LC NO. 80-706124
Prod-USN Dist-USNAC Prodn-AMFMP 1979

Oral Hygiene For Hospitalized Patients C 14 MIN
16MM FILM OPTICAL SOUND
Presents a hygienist demonstrating how to clean teeth on a model, on herself, on a sitting patient and on a bed patient.
Prod-USVA Dist-USVA 1957

Oral Hygiene For The Orthodontic Patient C 8 MIN
16MM FILM, 3/4 OR 1/2 IN VIDEO
Demonstrates the importance of personal care of teeth and removing harmful bacteria from hard-to-reach places using the toothbrush and pick, dental floss, water irrigator and disclosing wafers.
Prod-PRORE Dist-PRORE

Oral Hygiene For The Total-Care Patient C 14 MIN
16MM FILM - 3/4 IN VIDEO PRO
Points out that oral hygiene is a problem for the hospitalized patient who is physically or mentally incapacitated. Shows the value of ingestible toothpaste, completely-stable stannous fluoride jel and the electric toothbrush in the oral hygiene care of these patients. Issued in 1970 as a motion picture.
LC NO. 79-706059
Prod-USVA Dist-USNAC Prodn-VADTC 1979

Oral Intubation In The Adult, Using The MacIntosh Laryngoscope C 19 MIN
3/4 OR 1/2 INCH VIDEO CASSETTE PRO
Demonstrates the proper technique for tracheal intubation using the MacIntosh blade. Reviews the rationale for intubation, the equipment needed for successful intubation, and the correct procedures for positioning and intubating the patient.
Prod-HSCIC Dist-HSCIC

Oral Language C 30 MIN
3/4 OR 1/2 INCH VIDEO CASSETTE A
Shows how parents can help their children develop oral or spoken language through riddles, games and wordless books, and by talking with them and listening to their children.
From The Rainbow Road Series. Pt 2
LC NO. 82-707394
Prod-KAIDTV Dist-GPITVL 1982

Oral Language - A Breakthrough To Reading C 24 MIN
16MM FILM OPTICAL SOUND
Describes a six-week language development project conducted by the Columbus City School District. Shows how an art teacher, a music teacher, a physical education teacher and a language teacher cooperate to develop the language abilities of a group of inner-city children.
LC NO. FIA68-782
Prod-COLPS Dist-OSUMPD Prodn-OSUMPD 1967

Oral Language Development - Views Of Five Teachers C 30 MIN
16MM FILM, 3/4 OR 1/2 IN VIDEO T
Stresses oral language as the foundation of reading and writing skills. Presents five teachers showing how they create environments that promote oral expression, the integration of oral language into the total curriculum, and the development of respect for the spoken word.
From The Child's Right To Read Series.
LC NO. 80-706436
Prod-CSDE Dist-AITECH 1977

Oral Language Proficiency Test, The C 23 MIN
3/4 INCH VIDEO CASSETTE T
Illustrates a technique for testing foreign language speaking and comprehension skills. Describes the test, the interview techniques commonly employed, the government's civil service proficiency definitions, the rating standards and their general application.
LC NO. 77-706160
Prod-USILR Dist-USNAC 1977

Oral Language Teaching Techniques C 20 MIN
16MM FILM OPTICAL SOUND T
Explores reasons why many urban youngsters are not totally familiar with standard English, and discusses the theory behind language materials prepared by the Michigan Department of Education. Covers special problem areas for teachers, including large classes, boredom, non-talkers and mixed ability groups.
LC NO. 72-700184
Prod-CIASP Dist-CIASP 1971

Oral Love C 10 MIN
3/4 OR 1/2 INCH VIDEO CASSETTE
Provides a sustained look at fellatio and cunnilingus. Documents the emotional bond in which two adults responsively give of themselves to each other.
From The Mutuality Series.
Prod-MMRC Dist-MMRC

Oral Motor Problems C 45 MIN
3/4 OR 1/2 INCH VIDEO CASSETTE
Discusses congenital pathologies of the central nervous system, primitive and pathological oral motor reflexes and the minimum motor prerequisites for speech.
From The Meeting The Communications Needs Of The Severely/Profoundly Handicapped 1980 Series.
Prod-PUAVC Dist-PUAVC

Oral Receptive Language C 30 MIN
3/4 OR 1/2 INCH VIDEO CASSETTE T
Deals with oral receptive language in children with special needs.
From The Teaching Children With Special Needs Series.
Prod-MDDE Dist-MDCPB

Oral Rehabilitation C 29 MIN
16MM FILM OPTICAL SOUND
Deals with the surgical treatment of gingival hyperplasia in a patient in whom the condition has developed as a result of the administration of diphenyl hydantoin sodium for the control of epilepsy. and demonstrates curettage, postoperative treatment, insertion of the acrylic splint and the instruction of the patient in oral hygiene.
Prod-USVA Dist-USVA 1954

Oral Sex C 11 MIN
3/4 OR 1/2 INCH VIDEO CASSETTE
Demonstrates a variety of oral sex techiques. A couple discusses their religiously-based concerns about engaging in this behavior.
From The EDCOA Sexual Counseling Series.
Prod-MMRC Dist-MMRC

Oral Surgery Clinic Routine—A Series

Prod-MUSC Dist-USNAC 1978

Establishing An Uninterrupted Intra-Oral
Hand Scrub And Basic Protocol For Clinical 7 MIN
Patient Positioning And Preparation Of The 7 MIN
Sterilizing Oral Surgery Instruments 9 MIN

Oral Surgery Clinic Routine, Pt 1, Sterilizing Oral Surgery Instruments C 9 MIN
3/4 OR 1/2 INCH VIDEO CASSETTE
Demonstrates the process of sterilizing oral surgery instruments and explains the importance of each step.
Prod-MUSC Dist-USNAC

Oral Surgery Clinic Routine, Pt 2, Patient Positioning And Preparation Of The... C 7 MIN
3/4 OR 1/2 INCH VIDEO CASSETTE
Complete title is Oral Surgery Clinic Routine, Pt 2, Patient Positioning And Preparation of The Instrument Tray For Clinical Oral Surgery.
Prod-MUSC Dist-USNAC

Oral Surgery Clinic Routine, Pt 3, Hand Scrub And Basic Protocol For Clinical Oral Surgery C 7 MIN
3/4 OR 1/2 INCH VIDEO CASSETTE
Demonstrates proper scrubbing and gloving techniques to be used in an oral surgery clinic.
Prod-MUSC Dist-USNAC

Oral Surgery Clinic Routine, Pt 4, Establishing An Uninterrupted Intraoral... C 7 MIN
3/4 OR 1/2 INCH VIDEO CASSETTE
Complete title is Oral Surgery Clinic Routine, Pt 4, Establishing An Uninterrupted Intraoral Surgical Field. Shows the step-by-step process with explanations of each step in establishing an uninterrupted intraoral surgical field.
Prod-MUSC Dist-USNAC

Oral Surgery For The General Practitioner C 180 MIN
3/4 OR 1/2 INCH VIDEO CASSETTE
Offers a presentation by James R Hayward, DDS, Ann Arbor, Michigan, which provides the general practitioner with procedures and knowledge which he can apply to the surgical treatment of his patients. Demonstrates surgical manipulation of soft tissue flaps, reflections and retraction of tissues, bone relief and contouring, removal of pathology and tissue orientation for uneventful healing.
Prod-AMDA Dist-AMDA

Orange C 2 MIN
16MM FILM, 3/4 OR 1/2 IN VIDEO C A
Offers a sensuous macro-study of the hidden universe within a fruit usually taken for granted.
Prod-MMRC Dist-MMRC

Orange And Blue C 15 MIN
16MM FILM, 3/4 OR 1/2 IN VIDEO P A
Provides a visual perspective of the world as seen by two child-like personalities, orange and blue. Juxtaposes visual images with a musical score.
Prod-CHE Dist-EBEC 1962

Orange And Blue C 15 MIN
16MM FILM, 3/4 OR 1/2 IN VIDEO P-I
Pictures the adventures of two bouncing balls, one orange and one blue, in a junk and surplus yard. Describes their childlike play and shows them expressing curiosity, adventurousness, timidity, coyness and pure joy.
Prod-CHERPC Dist-MGHT 1962

Orange Bowl Festival C 27 MIN
16MM FILM OPTICAL SOUND
Presents colorful Orange bowl Festival activities including the famed nighttime parade and football classic.
Prod-MIMET Dist-MIMET

Orange Bowl 1972-1973 C 28 MIN
16MM FILM OPTICAL SOUND
Highlights the King Orange Jamboree Parade in downtown Miami and the annual gridiron classic Orange Bowl 1972-1973.
Prod-FLADC Dist-FLADC

Orange Grower, The (2nd Ed) C 16 MIN
16MM FILM, 3/4 OR 1/2 IN VIDEO I
Depicts all phases of orange growing from planting to shipping and emphasizes the work and care required to produce quality fruit. Portrays a typical orange grower and his family at work, budding, pruning, planting, fertilizing, irrigating and controlling insects and frost.
Prod-EBEC Dist-EBEC 1967

Orange Grower, The (2nd Ed) (Spanish) C 16 MIN
16MM FILM, 3/4 OR 1/2 IN VIDEO I
Depicts all phases of orange growing from planting to shipping and emphasizes the work and care required to produce quality fruit. Portrays a typical orange grower and his family at work, budding, pruning, planting, fertilizing, irrigating and controlling insects and frost.
Prod-EBEC Dist-EBEC 1967

Orange Industry C 3 MIN
16MM FILM OPTICAL SOUND P-I
Discusses the orange industry.
From The Of All Things Series.
Prod-BAILYL Dist-AVED

Orbit From Above, The C 11 MIN
16MM FILM, 3/4 OR 1/2 IN VIDEO C A
Focuses on the head and neck. Demonstrates the orbit.
From The Guides To Dissection Series.
Prod-UCLA Dist-TEF

Orbit Plotting B 29 MIN
16MM FILM OPTICAL SOUND A
Features two teachers and a professor discussing the purposes and techniques of several laboratory experiments in which students plot astronomical orbits.
From The Harvard Project Physics Teacher Briefings Series. No. 6
LC NO. 71-709147
Prod-HPP Dist-HRAW 1969

Orbit, The C 10 MIN
3/4 OR 1/2 INCH VIDEO CASSETTE C A
Describes the boundaries, demonstrates the bones and identifies the bony regions of the orbit.
From The Skull Anatomy Series.
Prod-UTXHSA Dist-TEF

Orbit, The C 13 MIN
16MM FILM, 3/4 OR 1/2 IN VIDEO C A
From The Anatomy Of The Eye Series.
Prod-BAYCMO Dist-TEF

Orbital Recession Operation For Malignant Exophthalmos C 37 MIN
16MM FILM OPTICAL SOUND PRO
Presents a number of patients suitable for operation for progressive exophthalmos. Demonstrates measurements of the degree of proptosis and shows the operative technique in detail.
Prod-ACYDGD Dist-ACY 1951

Orbital Repair With Methlethacrylate C 11 MIN
16MM FILM OPTICAL SOUND PRO
Demonstrates the method of using methylmethacrylate in its rapidly polymerizing form for the repair of orbital floor fractures.

Shows the skin approach, the method of elevating the periosteum and the use of retractors for inspection of the floor.
Prod-ACYDGD Dist-ACY 1971

Orbital Shapes And Paths C 11 MIN
16MM FILM, 3/4 OR 1/2 IN VIDEO I-H
Illustrates how a stellite's shape, path and period may be modified. Demonstrates the establishing of weather and communications satellites.
From The Space Science Series.
Prod-ALTPRO Dist-JOU 1984

Orbiter Assembly And Operation B 420 MIN
3/4 OR 1/2 INCH VIDEO CASSETTE PRO
See series title for descriptive statement.
From The Spacecraft System Design Series.
Prod-USCITV Dist-AMCEE

Orbiter Configuration And Design B 420 MIN
3/4 OR 1/2 INCH VIDEO CASSETTE PRO
See series title for descriptive statement.
From The Spacecraft System Design Series.
Prod-USCITV Dist-AMCEE

Orbiter Thermal Protection System C 6 MIN
16MM FILM, 3/4 OR 1/2 IN VIDEO
Describes how the thermal protection system shields the space craft from high temperatures during re-entry and ascent, the types of insulation used on the orbiter and the advantages of silica fiber tiles.
From The Space Shuttle Profile Series.
Prod-NASA Dist-USNAC

Orbiting Solar Observatory C 26 MIN
3/4 OR 1/2 INCH VIDEO CASSETTE
Discusses the functioning of the orbiting solar observatory in gathering data about the effects of the Sun on the Earth and its inhabitants, pointing out that the solar observatory was launched March 7, 1962, to study the Sun from above the Earth's atmosphere.
LC NO. 81-706391
Prod-USGSFC Dist-USNAC 1981

Orchestra Rehearsal (Italian) C 72 MIN
16MM FILM OPTICAL SOUND
Uses the spectacle of the orchestra rehearsal as a metaphor for the chaos of 20th century Western civilization. Directed by Federico Fellini. With English subtitles.
Prod-UNKNWN Dist-NYFLMS 1979

Orchestra, The C 30 MIN
3/4 OR 1/2 INCH VIDEO CASSETTE P-I
Presents the Cleveland Instiutue Of Music Youth Orchestra and its conductor Christopher Wilkins. Demonstrates the great variety of sounds capable of being produced by the orchestra, 'the world's largest musical instrument.'
From The Musical Encounter Series.
Prod-WVIZTV Dist-GPITVL 1983

Orchid Fancier C 29 MIN
3/4 INCH VIDEO CASSETTE
Explores the world of exotic orchids. Includes simple and wild varieties.
From The House Botanist Series.
Prod-UMITV Dist-UMITV 1978

Ordeal Of A President C 22 MIN
16MM FILM, 3/4 OR 1/2 IN VIDEO I-J
Covers President Woodrow Wilson's decision to enter America into World War I and discusses the influence of the publication of the Zimmermann telegram on the opinion of the American people.
From The You Are There Series.
Prod-CBSNEW Dist-PHENIX 1971

Ordeal Of Greece And Cyprus, The C 29 MIN
2 INCH VIDEOTAPE
See series title for descriptive statement.
From The Course Of Our Times II Series.
Prod-WGBHTV Dist-PUBTEL

Ordeal Of Jacobo Timerman, The C 60 MIN
3/4 OR 1/2 INCH VIDEO CASSETTE
Presents an interview with Argentine newspaper editor Jacobo Timerman, who discusses imprisonment and torture, resurgent Nazism and the politics of hate in Argentina.
From The Bill Moyers' Journal Series.
Prod-WNETTV Dist-WNETTV 1981

Ordeal Of Power - The President And The Presidency C 56 MIN
3/4 OR 1/2 INCH VIDEO CASSETTE
Explains how the powers of the presidency are defined by the Constitution and shows how these powers have changed, grown and been curbed through history. Illustrates the decision-making process of the presidency through examples from recent history. Asks how a fictional president might solve a typical policy problem.
LC NO. 81-706674
Prod-GA Dist-GA 1981

Order C 30 MIN
3/4 OR 1/2 INCH VIDEO CASSETTE C
See series title for descriptive statement.
From The Writing For A Reason Series.
Prod-DALCCD Dist-DALCCD

Order Of Nature, The C 15 MIN
3/4 OR 1/2 INCH VIDEO CASSETTE I
Looks at the observable patterns in nature.
From The L-Four Series.
Prod-CTI Dist-CTI

Order Of The Silver Platter, The C 30 MIN
3/4 OR 1/2 INCH VIDEO CASSETTE A
Teaches basic sales skills. Demonstrates how to turn seven sins of selling into strengths. Narrated by Ed McMahon.
Prod-AMEDIA Dist-AMEDIA

Order Of The Silver Platter, The (Portuguese) C 30 MIN
3/4 OR 1/2 INCH VIDEO CASSETTE A
Teaches basic sales skills. Demonstrates how to turn seven sins of selling into strengths. Narrated by Ed McMahon.
Prod-AMEDIA Dist-AMEDIA

Order Of The Silver Platter, The (Spanish) C 30 MIN
3/4 OR 1/2 INCH VIDEO CASSETTE A
Teaches basic sales skills. Demonstrates how to turn seven sins of selling into strengths. Narrated by Ed McMahon.
Prod-AMEDIA Dist-AMEDIA

Ordered Pairs And The Cartesian Product C 6 MIN
16MM FILM OPTICAL SOUND T
Introduces the concept of an ordered pair and defines the cartesian product using examples from navigation and rectangular grids.
From The Maa Arithmetic Series.
LC NO. 73-703198
Prod-MLA Dist-MLA 1966

Ordering By Volume And Capacity B 15 MIN
2 INCH VIDEOTAPE P
See series title for descriptive statement.
From The Just Inquisitive Series. No. 6
Prod-EOPS Dist-GPITVL Prodn-KOACTV

Orderly Development Of A Partial Denture Design, Pt 2 - The Maxillary Cast C 14 MIN
16MM FILM OPTICAL SOUND
Presents Dr J Demer stating that the requirements of partial denture design include rigidity, support, retention, reciprocation, guidance and mesh for resin bases. Demonstrates the fulfillment of these requirements in designing a maxillary partial denture using a stone cast mounted on a dental surveyor.
LC NO. 75-701353
Prod-USVA Dist-USNAC 1970

Orderly Development Of Removable Partial Design, Pt 1 - The Mandibular Cast C 14 MIN
16MM FILM OPTICAL SOUND
Presents Dr J Demer stating that the requirements of partial denture design include rigidity, support, retention, reciprocation, guidance and mesh for resin bases. Demonstrates the fulfillment of these requirements in designing a manibular partial denture using a stone cast mounted on a dental surveyor.
LC NO. 75-701352
Prod-USVA Dist-USNAC 1970

Orderly Development Of Removable Partial Denture Design, Pt 1 - The Mandibular Cast C 15 MIN
3/4 INCH VIDEO CASSETTE PRO
Describes requirements for partial denture design, including rigidity, support, retention, reciprocation, guidance and mesh for resin bases. Demonstrates the fulfillment of these requirements in designing a partial denture using a stone case mounted on a dental surveyor. Issued in 1970 as a motion picture.
LC NO. 78-706194
Prod-USVA Dist-USNAC Prodn-VADTC 1978

Orderly Development Of Removable Partial Denture Design, Pt I - The Mandibular Cast C 15 MIN
3/4 OR 1/2 INCH VIDEO CASSETTE
Illustrates a logical step-by-step procedure to help simplify the development of removable partial denture design.
Prod-VADTC Dist-AMDA 1971

Orderly Development Of Removable Partial Denture Design, Pt 2 - The Maxillary Cast C 15 MIN
3/4 INCH VIDEO CASSETTE PRO
Describes requirements for partial denture design, including rigidity, support, retention, reciprocation, guidance and mesh for resin bases. Demonstrates the fulfillment of these requirements in designing a partial denture using a stone case mounted on a dental surveyor. Issued in 1970 as a motion picture.
LC NO. 78-706196
Prod-USVA Dist-USNAC Prodn-VADTC 1978

Orderly Development Of Removable Partial Denture Design, Pt II - The Maxillary Cast C 15 MIN
3/4 OR 1/2 INCH VIDEO CASSETTE
Continues the illustration of a logical step-by-step procedure to help simplify the development of removable partial denture design.
Prod-VADTC Dist-AMDA 1971

Orders C 13 MIN
16MM FILM, 3/4 OR 1/2 IN VIDEO
Explains the various categories of common insects.
From The Discovering Insects Series.
Prod-MORALL Dist-MTI 1979

Orders And Acknowledgements - Credit Approvals C 45 MIN
2 INCH VIDEOTAPE C
From The Business Writing Series. Unit I - Neutral Good-News Messages.
Prod-CHITVC Dist-GPITVL Prodn-WTTWTV

Ordinal Numbers C 20 MIN
2 INCH VIDEOTAPE P
See series title for descriptive statement.
From The Mathemagic, Unit I - Place Value Series.
Prod-WMULTV Dist-GPITVL

Ordinal Scales Of Infant Psychological Development—A Series
C A
Concerns the sensori-motor development of infants as six separate processes.
LC NO. 73-703095
Prod-UILLVA Dist-UILL 1968

Development Of Means	34 MIN
Development Of Schemas	36 MIN
Imitation - Gestural And Vocal	35 MIN
Object Permanence	40 MIN
Object Relations In Space	28 MIN
Operational Causality	21 MIN

Ordinary Can Be Extraordinary, The C 15 MIN
3/4 OR 1/2 INCH VIDEO CASSETTE I
Deals with developing new perceptions about ordinary situations.
From The Tyger, Tyger Burning Bright Series.
Prod-CTI Dist-CTI

Ordinary Days B 24 MIN
16MM FILM OPTICAL SOUND
Depicts the struggles of a woman as she seeks to identify her needs in and apart from her situation with the man with whom she lives.
LC NO. 74-702659
Prod-HECKS Dist-NLC 1974

Ordinary Differential Equations C 43 MIN
3/4 OR 1/2 INCH VIDEO CASSETTE C
Covers classification, initial and boundary value problems of one variable, exact equations, methods of solving higher-order linear equations, second-order equations with constant coefficients, series solutions, systems of linear equations, Laplace transforms and existence theorems.
Prod-UIDEEO Dist-AMCEE

Ordinary Life, An C 27 MIN
16MM FILM, 3/4 OR 1/2 IN VIDEO C A
Takes a look at some of the many advances which are helping the disabled to find a voice and a place in our society.
Prod-LONTVS Dist-STNFLD

Ordinary People C 28 MIN
16MM FILM OPTICAL SOUND PRO
Presents a dramatization about a family under stress. Tells the story of a woman living in a new town and finding it difficult to handle her problems. Shows how she looks for help when she begins abusing her child.
LC NO. 77-701823
Prod-UPITTS Dist-UPITTS 1977

Ordinary People C
1/2 IN VIDEO CASSETTE BETA/VHS
Presents the story of a middle class family's emotional disintegration, directed by Robert Redford and starring Mary Tyler Moore and Donald Sutherland.
Prod-GA Dist-GA

Ordinary People C 25 MIN
16MM FILM, 3/4 OR 1/2 IN VIDEO C A
Investigates the family dynamics of child abuse and the indications that point to it.
Prod-UPITTS Dist-MTI 1977

Ordinary Work C 19 MIN
16MM FILM OPTICAL SOUND
Shows the successful rehabilitation of mentally retarded subjects in the field of agricultural work. Shows the detailed use of sports activities in teaching coordination, self-confidence, learning to work in a group and independence.
From The Audiovisual Research Brief Series.
LC NO. 74-705269
Prod-USSRS Dist-USNAC 1972

Orefus And Julie C 7 MIN
16MM FILM OPTICAL SOUND
Expresses feelings of danger and happiness through modern ballet and animation. Performed by Sorella Englund and Eske Holm of the Royal Danish Ballet.
Prod-RDCG Dist-AUDPLN

Oregon C
3/4 OR 1/2 INCH VIDEO CASSETTE
Presents five segments about the state of Oregon, a state of beautand majesty where the power of nature is always present and the people live with a respect for the land.
From The Portrait of America Series.
Prod-TBS Dist-TBS

Oregon Industry - Logging Douglas Fir B 10 MIN
16MM FILM OPTICAL SOUND I-J A
Pictures the logging operations in Oregon's Coast Range Mountains. Describes the equipment, the conservation practices and the process of balloon logging.
Prod-OSSHE Dist-OSSHE 1966

Oregon Message, An C 24 MIN
3/4 OR 1/2 INCH VIDEO CASSETTE
Features Oregon poet William Stafford. Uses actors, documentary footage, old historical stills, animation and a sound track of poetry music and interviews.
Prod-MEDIPR Dist-MEDIPR 1977

Oregon Scenics C 13 MIN
16MM FILM OPTICAL SOUND
Shows the Columbia River Highway, trip up Mt Hood to Timberline Lodge and Crater Lake National Park.
From The Travelbug Series.
Prod-SFI Dist-SFI

Oregon Trail C 15 MIN
3/4 OR 1/2 INCH VIDEO CASSETTE P
Spins a couple of adventures of Moses the cat who traveled the Oregon Trail by wagon train.
From The Stories Of America Series.
Prod-OHSDE Dist-AITECH Prodn-WVIZTV 1976

Oregon Trail, The B 25 MIN
16MM FILM, 3/4 OR 1/2 IN VIDEO I-H
Re-creates the saga of the westward movement. Dramatizes the experiences of a pioneer family migrating to Oregon in a wagon train. Shows how they are involved not only in the forces of history but also with their own very human family problems.
Prod-EBF Dist-EBEC 1956

Oregon Trail, The C 31 MIN
16MM FILM, 3/4 OR 1/2 IN VIDEO I A
Recounts the period of migration westward on the Oregon Trail and the experiences of the pioneers who made the journey.
Prod-WHITEJ Dist-PHENIX 1975

Oregon Trail, The C 32 MIN
16MM FILM, 3/4 OR 1/2 IN VIDEO
Describes the travels of 19th century pioneers over the Oregon Trail.
Prod-KAWVAL Dist-KAWVAL

Oregon Trail, The (Spanish) B 25 MIN
16MM FILM, 3/4 OR 1/2 IN VIDEO I-H
Dramatizes the experiences of a family migrating to Oregon in a wagon train. Stresses the hardships of the journey, the long treks under the prairie sun, the dangerous river crossing, the threat of Indian attack and the punishing climb into the mountains.
Prod-EBEC Dist-EBEC

Oregon Woodcarvers C 24 MIN
3/4 OR 1/2 INCH VIDEO CASSETTE
Explores the works, lives and philosophies of four very different Oregon wood artists. Portrays Ed Quigley, Douglas MacGregor, Gary Hauser and Roy Setzoil.
Prod-MEDIPR Dist-MEDIPR 1980

Oregon Work C 30 MIN
3/4 OR 1/2 INCH VIDEO CASSETTE
Features Dave Vincent, owner of a small mill in Philomath, Oregon, discussing how he made a profit while fulfilling his responsibility to the community. Examines the practice and attitudes of corporate responsibility in general.
Prod-MEDIPR Dist-MEDIPR 1982

Oregon's State Capitol C 15 MIN
16MM FILM OPTICAL SOUND I-C A
Tours Oregon's state capitol with Jim Gilchrist, exguide of the capitol.
Prod-OSSHE Dist-OSSHE

Oresteia, The C
3/4 OR 1/2 INCH VIDEO CASSETTE
Presents a performance of The Oresteia trilogy, classical Greek tragedy by Aeschylus.
Prod-FOTH Dist-FOTH

Organelles In Living Plant Cells (2nd Ed) C 26 MIN
16MM FILM, 3/4 OR 1/2 IN VIDEO H-C
Shows the appearance and behavior of all organelles that can be resolved by the phase and dark-field microscope, such as nuclei, chloroplasts, golgi bodies and kinoplasm. Discloses the interactions between the organelles and cytoplasmic network.
Prod-KAHANA Dist-UCEMC 1965

Organic Chemistry Laboratory Techniques—A Series

Covers theory and procedures for one particular organic chemistry laboratory techniques. Stresses equipment care and safety.
Prod-UCLA Dist-UCEMC

Column Chromatography	015 MIN
Extraction	013 MIN
Fractional Distillation	020 MIN
Gas Chromatography	017 MIN
Infrared Spectroscopy	016 MIN
Melting Point Determination	017 MIN
Recrystallization	021 MIN
Simple Distillation	012 MIN
Thin Layer Chromatography	013 MIN

Organic Farming - Can It Feed The Multitudes C 20 MIN
16MM FILM, 3/4 OR 1/2 IN VIDEO
Explains how organic gardening techniques will not only allow the small farmer with a little capital the chance to get into agriculture but it will also provide Americans with a safer, more nutritious diet.
Prod-DOCUA Dist-CNEMAG

Organic Gardening - Composting C 11 MIN
16MM FILM, 3/4 OR 1/2 IN VIDEO
Explains the role compost plays in natural life processes. Includes demonstrations of how to build a compost heap, samples of different types of composts piles and bins, what materials can go into the heap and how compost can be used as a natural fertilizer.
LC NO. 82-707176
Prod-RPFD Dist-BULFRG 1972

Organic Mental Disorders C 30 MIN
3/4 OR 1/2 INCH VIDEO CASSETTE PRO
Deals with organic brain syndromes (section one). Covers all other organic mental disorders, related to aging and drug consumption.
From The Psychiatry Learning System, Pt 2 - Disorders Series.
Prod-HSCIC Dist-HSCIC 1982

Organism C 20 MIN
16MM FILM, 3/4 OR 1/2 IN VIDEO J A
Studies urbanization, in which the structure of cities is compared to living tissus. Shows traffic arteries as the bloodstream circulating through the urban body and skyscrapers as the skeletal structure.
Prod-HARH Dist-PHENIX 1975

Organismic Reproduction C 45 MIN
3/4 OR 1/2 INCH VIDEO CASSETTE C
Discusses various aspects of organismic reproduction.
From The Biology I Series.
Prod-MDCPB Dist-MDCPB

Organiverse C 8 MIN
16MM FILM OPTICAL SOUND
Presents a visual interpretation of the miracle called life, embracing art, science, religion and philosophy.
LC NO. 76-703252
Prod-CANFDC Dist-CANFDC 1975

Organization B 30 MIN
16MM FILM OPTICAL SOUND
Explains the difference between good organizations and poor ones and suggests some ideas for development of a smooth-running organization.
From The Success In Supervision Series.
LC NO. 74-706170
Prod-WETATV Dist-USNAC 1965

Organization C 30 MIN
3/4 OR 1/2 INCH VIDEO CASSETTE P-I
See series title for descriptive statement.
From The Sonrisas Series.
Prod-KRLNTV Dist-MDCPB

Organization C 31 MIN
3/4 OR 1/2 INCH VIDEO CASSETTE
Discusses typical organizational arrangements and responsibilities for a quality-control function.
From The Quality Planning Series.
Prod-MIOT Dist-MIOT

Organization - Key To Air Power C 17 MIN
16MM FILM OPTICAL SOUND
Shows the basic principles of organization and their application to various types of Air Force activities. Stresses the need for organizational methods that will insure a quick-striking air force.
LC NO. FIE58-266
Prod-USDD Dist-USNAC 1957

Organization - Stations, Everyone C 30 MIN
3/4 OR 1/2 INCH VIDEO CASSETTE T
Uses interviews and candid classroom scenes to show how innovative teachers are designing and organizing their classrooms in order to enhance learning and reading comprehension.
From The Reading Is Power Series. No. 3
LC NO. 81-707518
Prod-NYCBED Dist-GPITVL 1981

Organization And Mechanics Of Writing B 35 MIN
16MM FILM OPTICAL SOUND
Explains techniques used to develop good paragraphs and ideas. Shows how to organize a paper, arrange the words in proper order and punctuate.
LC NO. FIE60-115
Prod-USAF Dist-USNAC 1959

Organization And Mechanics Of Writing B 35 MIN
3/4 INCH VIDEO CASSETTE
Introduces the techniques used to develop good paragraphs and ideas, to arrange words in proper order, to punctuate and to organize a paper.
Prod-USNAC Dist-USNAC 1972

Organization And Planning C 12 MIN
3/4 OR 1/2 INCH VIDEO CASSETTE
Shows how to plan a day's work by preparing a list of tasks to be done, establishing priorities, and keeping the work area neat.
LC NO. 84-706399
Prod-USSS Dist-USNAC 1983

Organization And The Service Technician C
3/4 OR 1/2 INCH VIDEO CASSETTE
See series title for descriptive statement.
From The Pest Control Technology Correspondence Course Series.
Prod-PUAVC Dist-PUAVC

Organization At The Top C 29 MIN
16MM FILM OPTICAL SOUND
Traces the history of the changing roles of the Vice President and the President's Cabinet, and discusses the role of the Cabinet as an administrative tool. Examines the creation and growth in importance of the White House office.
From The Government Story Series. No. 24
LC NO. 79-707179
Prod-WBCPRO Dist-WBCPRO 1968

Organization Development—A Series

Provides a quick look at the concepts of organization development (OD) and how it complements the many alternatives to management development. Gives an overview of OD for human resource developers and information for middle and lower management of what OD is and how it works.
Prod-RESEM Dist-RESEM

Approaches To Organization Development	017 MIN
Getting Started In OD	016 MIN
Well Being Of The Organization, The	013 MIN
What Is Organization Development?	017 MIN

Organization In Transition, The C 45 MIN
3/4 OR 1/2 INCH VIDEO CASSETTE
Discusses the forces that are affecting organizations and the information explosion they must deal with. 60-010.
From The Information Resource Management - Challenge For The 1980s Series.
Prod-DELTAK Dist-DELTAK

Organization Of A Microcomputer, Logic Operations B 60 MIN
3/4 OR 1/2 INCH VIDEO CASSETTE
See series title for descriptive statement.
From The Introduction To Microcomputers Series. Pt 2
Prod-UAZMIC Dist-UAZMIC 1978

Organization Of African Unity C 28 MIN
3/4 INCH VIDEOTAPE
Presents an up-date on the present situation in Africa. Includes an interview with Ambassador Dramane Ouattara, Executive Secretary of the Organization of African Unity.
From The International Byline Series.
Prod-PERRYM Dist-PERRYM

Organization Of Language, The B 33 MIN
16MM FILM OPTICAL SOUND H T
Discusses pre-school children's use of form and arrangements of words. Explains that these forms and arrangements constitute the organization or grammar of language. Uses a German class for English speakers to show how to teach grammatical patterns and variations.
From The Principles And Methods Of Teaching A Second Language Series.
Prod-MLAA Dist-IU Prodn-RAY 1961

Organization Of The Living, The C 60 MIN
3/4 OR 1/2 INCH VIDEO CASSETTE A
Presents biologist Humberto Maturana discussing how living things are organized.
From The Biology Of Cognition And Language Series. Program 3
Prod-UCEMC Dist-UCEMC

Organization Renewal—A Series
16MM FILM - 3/4 IN VIDEO IND
Prod-BNA Dist-BNA 1969

Confrontation, Search And Coping	025 MIN
Coping With Change	025 MIN
Growth Stages Of Organizations	025 MIN
How Organization Renewal Works	025 MIN
Individuality And Teamwork	027 MIN

Organization-Precision-Efficiency - The Three Keys To Successful Restorative...—A Series

Offers an unedited tape presentation by Alvin J Fillastre, DDS, Lakeland, Florida which emphasizes that successful restorative dentistry depends on a thorough diagnosis and treatment plan, laid out in logical sequence from early periodontal treatment through adjustment and sealing.
Prod-AMDA Dist-AMDA 1978

Organizational Communication C 30 MIN
3/4 OR 1/2 INCH VIDEO CASSETTE C A
Looks at the kinds of information passed through organization channels, and barriers that can occur along the way. Features leaders from various companies discussing techniques used by their organizations.
From The Business Of Management Series. Lesson 12
Prod-SCCON Dist-SCCON

Organizational Conflict C 30 MIN
3/4 OR 1/2 INCH VIDEO CASSETTE C A
Indicates that dealing with conifict is never an easy task. Explores ways to effectively manage organization conflict so that the results can be beneficial, both for the individuals or groups involved, and for the organization as a whole.
From The Business Of Management Series. Lesson 17
Prod-SCCON Dist-SCCON

Organizational Development C 30 MIN
16MM FILM, 3/4 OR 1/2 IN VIDEO
Discusses approaches used in TRW, Inc to create lasting cultural changes within organizations.
From The Management Development Series.
Prod-UCLA Dist-UCEMC

Organizational Goal-Planning B 29 MIN
16MM FILM OPTICAL SOUND IND
See series title for descriptive statement.
From The Management By Objectives Series.
LC NO. 70-703325
Prod-EDSD Dist-EDSD

Organizational Patterns C 30 MIN
3/4 OR 1/2 INCH VIDEO CASSETTE
Shows how to recognize structure and organize while listening.
From The Effective Listening Series. Tape 6
Prod-TELSTR Dist-TELSTR

Organizational Quality Improvement—A Series

Shows how to implement a system of quality improvement in every area, from product development through sales and service.
Prod-BNA Dist-BNA

Charting Activities And Processes
Comparing Costs And Benefits
Getting Started
Improving Processes
Introduction To Organizational Quality
Looking At Processes
Problem Solving
Putting It All Together
Quality Circles
Using Industrial Statistics

Organizational Transactions—A Series

Designed to increase individual and group interpersonal and communication skills awareness. Gives ideas on how to deal constructively with conflict situations. Shows how to analyze your own style for managing conflict.
Prod-PRODEV Dist-PRODEV

Competition And Conflict 030 MIN
Customer Transactions 030 MIN
Opportunity For Leadership, The 030 MIN
Planning And Control 030 MIN
Problem-Solving And Decision Making 030 MIN
Time, The Most Precious Resource 030 MIN

Organizations, The C 27 MIN
16MM FILM, 3/4 OR 1/2 IN VIDEO
Examines the rules which govern the operation of all contemporary financial institutions, including local, national or international, and considers some of the implications of their growing power.
From The Five Billion People Series.
Prod-LEFSP Dist-CNEMAG

Organize B 15 MIN
16MM FILM OPTICAL SOUND
Shows an organizing project in Appalachia that is helping the people fight the destructive effects of strip mining.
Prod-SFN Dist-SFN

Organized Brain C 5 MIN
16MM FILM OPTICAL SOUND
Accompanies a man on a journey through his mind as he describes the memories and images he has filed away there.
LC NO. FIA68-783
Prod-HENASS Dist-HENASS 1968

Organized Mosquito Control C 16 MIN
16MM FILM OPTICAL SOUND
Shows a sampling to determine the species of mosquitoes, their relative abundance and types of breeding places. Demonstrates dipping for larvae to determine major problem areas. Discusses breeding sites as determinants of flight ranges. Shows three common methods of mosquito abatement and five big problem areas.
LC NO. FIE55-328
Prod-USPHS Dist-USNAC 1955

Organizers, The - Careers In Business Office C 13 MIN
16MM FILM OPTICAL SOUND I-H
Explores the variety of careers available in businesss and office services.
From The Working Worlds Series.
LC NO. 75-701548
Prod-OLYMPS Dist-FFORIN 1974

Organizing C
3/4 OR 1/2 INCH VIDEO CASSETTE
Concentrates on the vital technique of organizing through delegation. Teaches managers to use their own talents and the talents of others for maximum effectiveness.
From The Essentials Of Management Series. Unit III.
Prod-AMA Dist-AMA

Organizing C 12 MIN
3/4 OR 1/2 INCH VIDEO CASSETTE
Examines the structural and social aspects of organizing and some of the problems and decisions associated with them.
From The Management of Work Series. Module 3
Prod-RESEM Dist-RESEM

Organizing C 50 MIN
3/4 OR 1/2 INCH VIDEO CASSETTE
See series title for descriptive statement.
From The Effective Writing Series.
Prod-TWAIN Dist-DELTAK

Organizing - Making It All Happen C 28 MIN
3/4 OR 1/2 INCH VIDEO CASSETTE
Examines the uses and misuses of authority, and emphasizes a clear chain of command.
From The Management Skills For Nurses Series.
Prod-INTGRP Dist-AJN Prodn-ANDRAF

Organizing - Structuring The Work Of The Plan C 14 MIN
3/4 OR 1/2 INCH VIDEO CASSETTE
Shows first-line supervisors what the problems of organization are likely to be and how they can be solved effectively.
Prod-AMA Dist-AMA

Organizing - Structuring The Work Of The Plan C 20 MIN
3/4 OR 1/2 INCH VIDEO CASSETTE
Defines organization, reviews its purposes and outlines ways to organize subordinates for maximum productivity.
From The Supervisory Management Course, Pt 1 Series. Unit 3
Prod-AMA Dist-AMA

Organizing - The Structuring Function C
3/4 OR 1/2 INCH VIDEO CASSETTE
Differentiates between the various types of organizational structures. Describes the delegation process and the relationship of authority, responsibility and accountability.
From The Principles Of Management Series.
Prod-RMI Dist-RMI

Organizing A Group C 15 MIN
3/4 OR 1/2 INCH VIDEO CASSETTE H
Discusses various individual roles which can help or hinder the group process.
From The By The People Series.
Prod-CTI Dist-CTI

Organizing A Year's Program C 29 MIN
3/4 OR 1/2 INCH VIDEO CASSETTE
Presents guidelines to make a long-range plan and goals and identifies characteristics of a successful writing assignment.
From The Teaching Writing - A Process Approach Series.
Prod-MSITV Dist-PBS 1982

Organizing And Planning For Results C 12 MIN
3/4 OR 1/2 INCH VIDEO CASSETTE
Offers some practical steps for organizing and planning and shows some examples for typical job situations. Examines difference between procrastination and simply deciding not to decide.
From The Improving Managerial Skills Series.
Prod-RESEM Dist-RESEM

Organizing Business Writing C 16 MIN
3/4 OR 1/2 INCH VIDEO CASSETTE
Presents seven basic rules of organization and offers examples of proper and improper application in organizing business writing.
From The Business Writing Skills Series.
Prod-RESEM Dist-RESEM

Organizing For Productivity C 20 MIN
3/4 OR 1/2 INCH VIDEO CASSETTE
See series title for descriptive statement.
From The Productivity / Quality Of Work Life Series.
Prod-GOODMI Dist-DELTAK

Organizing For Successful Project Management C 30 MIN
3/4 OR 1/2 INCH VIDEO CASSETTE
Describes the process of project management. Discusses a systems approach. Identifies major organizational structures.
From The Project Management Series.
Prod-ITCORP Dist-ITCORP

Organizing Free Play B 20 MIN
16MM FILM OPTICAL SOUND J-C T
Shows that free play in nursery school is neither helter-skelter chaos nor regimented uniformity, but a crucially important segment of the day when children may choose among a variety of carefully prepared activities. Presents scenes from a dozen Head Start and other pre-school centers to show how a teacher organizes and supervises such a program and what it means to children as a curriculum of discovery.
From The Head Start Training Series.
LC NO. FIE-101
Prod-VASSAR Dist-NYU

Organizing Free Play B 22 MIN
16MM FILM OPTICAL SOUND T S R
Focuses on the facet of early childhood education called free play.
LC NO. FIE67-101
Prod-USOEO Dist-USNAC 1967

Organizing Ideas C 30 MIN
3/4 OR 1/2 INCH VIDEO CASSETTE A
Presents basic writing skills for office workers, emphasizing the importance of organizing ideas. Describes various ways of organizing ideas, such as chronological, inductive and deductive. Hosted by Cicely Tyson.
From The Writing For Work Series. Pt 5
LC NO. 81-706738
Prod-TIMLIF Dist-TIMLIF 1981

Organizing Information C
16MM FILM, 3/4 OR 1/2 IN VIDEO H
Explains how public health workers and the members of a rock band gather and organize information.
From The Math Wise Series. Module 3 - Locating/Interpreting
Prod-KOCETV Dist-AITECH 1981

Organizing Information C 20 MIN
3/4 INCH VIDEO CASSETTE I
Focuses on organizing, outlining, writing and preparing presentations.
From The Study Skills Series.
Prod-WCVETV Dist-GPITVL 1979

Organizing Pointers C 30 MIN
3/4 OR 1/2 INCH VIDEO CASSETTE IND
See series title for descriptive statement.
From The Drafting - Piping Pointers Series.
Prod-GPCV Dist-GPCV

Organizing Skills C 45 MIN
3/4 OR 1/2 INCH VIDEO CASSETTE IND
Discusses forms of organization, line versus staff, the informal organization, impact of overtime and illness, 'theory X and theory Y,' use of an issue census to help the organization, organizational conflict and harmony and improving creativity and productivity.
From The Basic Management Skills For Engineers And Scientists Series.
Prod-USCITV Dist-AMCEE

Organizing Technical Activities C 30 MIN
3/4 OR 1/2 INCH VIDEO CASSETTE
See series title for descriptive statement.
From The Management For Engineers Series.
Prod-UKY Dist-SME

Organizing The Fire Ground C
3/4 OR 1/2 INCH VIDEO CASSETTE
Urges fire ground commanders to make advanced preparations for problems, and to train and organize fire fighters for fire ground operations.
From The Safety Series.
Prod-NFPA Dist-NFPA 1980

Organizing The Reading Environment C 29 MIN
16MM FILM, 3/4 OR 1/2 IN VIDEO
Examines the premise that experiences which encourage language growth can and should be so organized that they can happen any time a student wants or needs them, not only during a daily reading period. Includes numerous documentary tips for the teacher.
From The Teaching Children To Read Series.
Prod-MFFD Dist-FI 1975

Organizing Your Message C 15 MIN
3/4 OR 1/2 INCH VIDEO CASSETTE J
Presents the story of the staff of the Weekly Bull Dog who can't decide on the best way to organize its upcoming issue. Presents Dr Robert Cockrell emphasizing that communicating information to patients and to other hospital staff members requires him to think and speak in a clear, organized way.
From The In Other Words Series. Organizing Ideas, Pt 4
LC NO. 83-707210
Prod-AITV Dist-AITECH Prodn-KOCETV 1983

Organizing Your Time C 31 MIN
3/4 OR 1/2 INCH VIDEO CASSETTE
See series title for descriptive statement.
From The Personal Time Management Series.
Prod-TELSTR Dist-DELTAK

Organizing Your Work And Others' Work C 30 MIN
3/4 OR 1/2 INCH VIDEO CASSETTE
Discusses short and long range details of time organization. Covers bi-weekly agenda and 12 month calendar.
From The Personal Time Management Series.
Prod-TELSTR Dist-TELSTR

Organizing Your Writing Course C 31 MIN
3/4 OR 1/2 INCH VIDEO CASSETTE T
Shows how to organize a composition course around a nine-step writing process, including the editing process, the use of journals and specifics on structuring a syllabus.
From The Process-Centered Composition Series.
LC NO. 79-706296
Prod-IU Dist-IU 1977

Organophosphate Pesticide Poisonings - Diagnosis And Treatment C 20 MIN
16MM FILM, 3/4 OR 1/2 IN VIDEO
Shows that a correct diagnosis of organophosphate poisoning and proper treatment can save lives.
LC NO. 82-706398
Prod-NMAC Dist-USNAC 1969

Organs Of Special Sense - Pt 1 - Eye C 45 MIN
3/4 OR 1/2 INCH VIDEO CASSETTE PRO
Reviews the major histological and functional features of the eye, as well as its accessory structures (including eyelids, conjunctiva, and lacrimal, sebaceous, and Meibomian glands).
From The Histology Review Series.
Prod-HSCIC Dist-HSCIC

Organs Of Special Sense - Pt 2 - The Ear C 25 MIN
3/4 OR 1/2 INCH VIDEO CASSETTE PRO
Covers the structure and histology of the external, middle, and inner ear.
From The Histology Review Series.
Prod-HSCIC Dist-HSCIC

Orgasmic Expulsions Of Fluid In The Sexually Stimulated Female C 9 MIN
3/4 OR 1/2 INCH VIDEO CASSETTE C A
Depicts the event of orgasmic expulsions of fluid in the sexually stimulated female. Examines examples of beginning evidence of the existence of a yet to be fully explained sexual function and/or anatomical feature.
Prod-MMRC Dist-MMRC

Orient / Occident C 30 MIN
3/4 OR 1/2 INCH VIDEO CASSETTE
Shows the influence that Islam has had on the Western world by causing the crusades, strongly influencing the cultures of Spain, Sicily and Southern France, and providing concepts of chivalry and courtly love.
From The World Of Islam Series.
Prod-FOTH Dist-FOTH 1984

Oriental Art C 30 MIN
3/4 OR 1/2 INCH VIDEO CASSETTE
Presents guests who are experts in their respective fields who share tips on collecting and caring for antique Oriental art.
From The Antique Shop Series.
Prod-WVPTTV Dist-MDCPB

Oriental Odyssey C 27 MIN
16MM FILM OPTICAL SOUND
Shows two young couples cruising and sightseeing on the Inland Sea of Japan and presents the legends and customs of the Far East.
Prod-MERMAR Dist-TELEFM

Oriental Rugs C 30 MIN
3/4 OR 1/2 INCH VIDEO CASSETTE
Presents guests who are experts in their respective fields who share tips on collecting and caring for antique Oriental rugs.
From The Antique Shop Series.
Prod-WVPTTV Dist-MDCPB

Oriental Vegetables C 30 MIN
1/2 IN VIDEO CASSETTE BETA/VHS
Explores the Protea Gardens in Hawaii. Features bok choy and chinese greens. Shows how to plant pumpkins, beans and lettuce.
From The Victory Garden Series.
Prod-WGBHTV Dist-MTI

Orientation C 29 MIN
2 INCH VIDEOTAPE
See series title for descriptive statement.
From The Discover Flying - Just Like A Bird Series.
Prod-WKYCTV Dist-PUBTEL

Orientation - Attitude, Appearance, Approach C 13 MIN
16MM FILM, 3/4 OR 1/2 IN VIDEO H-C
Explains how a positive attitude, likable appearance, effective approach and active listening skills can help people deal more successfully with other people, particularly in the area of salesmanship.
Prod-BOSUST Dist-CF 1979

Orientation And Indoctrination Of Safe Workmen C 27 MIN
16MM FILM OPTICAL SOUND
Follows a group of new employees through pre-employment testing, hiring and actual working situations. Highlights job safety and the value of accident prevention training for all employees.
LC NO. 74-705272
Prod-USBM Dist-USNAC 1961

Orientation And Training C 30 MIN
3/4 OR 1/2 INCH VIDEO CASSETTE PRO
Explores the task of orientating a new employee into the company and training him to do the job. Introduces the principles of learning, which must be observed in the industrial setting.
From The You - The Supervisor Series.
Prod-PRODEV Dist-DELTAK

Orientation Of New Workers, Pt I Of Styles Of Supervision B 45 MIN
3/4 OR 1/2 INCH VIDEO CASSETTE
Demonstrates two contrasting types of supervision in role plays depicting a new worker meeting with his/her super- visor for the first time. Deals with some of the employees' initial fears.
Prod-UWISC Dist-UWISC 1977

Orientation To ABE C 30 MIN
3/4 OR 1/2 INCH VIDEO CASSETTE T
Gives an overview of adult basic education.
From The Basic Education - Teaching The Adult Series.
Prod-MDDE Dist-MDCPB

Orientation To Civil Service Reform - A Discussion Of The Highlights C 31 MIN
3/4 INCH VIDEO CASSETTE
Outlines the development of the Civil Service Reform Act and highlights its major provisions.
From The Launching Civil Service Reform Series.
LC NO. 79-706275
Prod-USOPMA Dist-USNAC 1978

Orientation To Communication Methods In The Metal Fabricating Industries C 20 MIN
1/2 IN VIDEO CASSETTE BETA/VHS IND
Discusses the importance of proper communications in the various metal fabricating industries and the different methods used.
Prod-RMI Dist-RMI

Orientation To Communication Skills I C 14 MIN
1/2 IN VIDEO CASSETTE BETA/VHS
See series title for descriptive statement.
From The English And Speech Series.
Prod-RMI Dist-RMI

Orientation To Course - Misconceptions About Shakespeare - Elizabethan Life, No. 1 B 45 MIN
2 INCH VIDEOTAPE C
See series title for descriptive statement.
From The Shakespeare Series.
Prod-CHITVC Dist-GPITVL Prodn-WTTWTV

Orientation To Sexuality Of The Physically Disabled C 39 MIN
3/4 INCH VIDEO CASSETTE
Introduces the seven-part series. Discusses several assumptions and objectives basic to the sexuality and disability sex education and treatment program at the University of Michigan.
From The Sexuality And Physical Disability Series.
Prod-UMITV Dist-UMITV 1976

Orientation To The Audit Process, An C 29 MIN
3/4 INCH VIDEO CASSETTE PRO
Suggests ways of formulating guidelines for setting up an audit committee and explains why an orientation is essential for all audit committee members. Emphasizes the importance of encouraging peer discussion during the audit process.
LC NO. 79-707717
Prod-UMICHM Dist-UMMCML Prodn-UMISU 1977

Orientation To The Sexuality Of Physical Disability C 40 MIN
3/4 OR 1/2 INCH VIDEO CASSETTE C A
Discusses assumptions and objectives basic to disability sex education and treatment programs.
From The Sexuality And Physical Diability Video Tape Series.
Prod-MMRC Dist-MMRC

Orientation To The Use Of Crutches C 6 MIN
16MM FILM - 3/4 IN VIDEO
Demonstrates the fitting of underarm crutches, the tripod principle and walking with crutches. Shows disadvantages of ill-fitting crutches and how to manipulate crutches on stairs. Issued in 1965 as a motion picture.
LC NO. 79-706493
Prod-USPHS Dist-USNAC Prodn-NMAC 1979

Orientation To Volunteerism C 27 MIN
3/4 OR 1/2 INCH VIDEO CASSETTE
Presents an overview of volunteerism. Includes the historical context of volunteers, the motivation for volunteering, society's need for volunteers, various types of volunteer activities and the management of volunteers. Shows the problems and potential of working with volunteers.
Prod-PSU Dist-PSU 1984

Orientation/Test Taking Skills C 30 MIN
3/4 OR 1/2 INCH VIDEO CASSETTE
See series title for descriptive statement.
From The Reading Series.
Prod-KYTV Dist-CAMB

Orienteering C 10 MIN
16MM FILM, 3/4 OR 1/2 IN VIDEO J-H A
Explains the sport of orienteering in which contestants must travel a course as quickly as possible, choosing the routes by map and compass. Pictures scenes from the first Canadian orienteering championship in Guelph, Ontario.
Prod-CRAF Dist-IFB Prodn-CRAF 1969

Orienteering C 30 MIN
1/2 IN VIDEO CASSETTE BETA/VHS
Describes the Scandinavian sport of orienteering. Features the wilderness of Minnesota's Boundary Waters and the temples of Katmandu.
From The Great Outdoors Series.
Prod-WGBHTV Dist-MTI

Orifice Plates And Orifice Fittings C 24 MIN
3/4 OR 1/2 INCH VIDEO CASSETTE IND
Describes the types of plates and fittings most commonly used and gives instructions for proper installation.
Prod-UTEXPE Dist-UTEXPE

Origami C 9 MIN
16MM FILM, 3/4 OR 1/2 IN VIDEO I-J A
Demonstrates the ancient art of paper folding. Suggests many shapes and figures that can be conjured out of colored paper.
Prod-NFBC Dist-NFBC 1970

Origami - Free Form C 12 MIN
16MM FILM OPTICAL SOUND I-J
Describes the simple basics of free-form origami and demonstrates the variety of forms and animals which can be made using the diamond base and kite base.
LC NO. 74-702299
Prod-DANREE Dist-DANREE 1974

Origami - Geometrical Form C 10 MIN
16MM FILM OPTICAL SOUND J-H
Presents origami expert Wendy Mukai demonstrating the construction of a variety of three-dimensional figures, flowers and designs using the geometrical blintz base.
LC NO. 74-702300
Prod-DANREE Dist-DANREE 1974

Origami - The Folding Paper Of Japan C 16 MIN
16MM FILM OPTICAL SOUND
Looks at origami, the ancient art of Japanese paper folding.
Prod-MTP Dist-MTP

Origin And Accumulation Of Oil And Gas C 15 MIN
3/4 OR 1/2 INCH VIDEO CASSETTE IND
Presents a comprehensive introductory lesson on the natural process of how oil and gas form and become trapped in rock layers.
Prod-UTEXPE Dist-UTEXPE 1983

Origin And History Of Program Budgeting, The B 25 MIN
16MM FILM OPTICAL SOUND
Traces the history of planning-programming-budgeting (PPB) and describes the fundamentals of the system.
LC NO. 74-705273
Prod-USCSC Dist-USNAC 1970

Origin And Synthesis Of Plastics Materials B 16 MIN
16MM FILM OPTICAL SOUND
Explores the organic origin of plastics and the resemblance of synthetic compounds to natural substances. Shows how plastics are made and typical uses for them.
From The Plastics Series. No. 1
Prod-USOE Dist-USNAC Prodn-CARFI 1945

Origin Of Land Plants - Liverworts And Mosses C 14 MIN
16MM FILM, 3/4 OR 1/2 IN VIDEO H
Traces the evolution of land plants and illustrates the structural characteristics, reproductive processes and adaptive mechanisms of liverworts and mosses. Shows their relationship to the development of higher land plants.
From The Biology Series.
Prod-EBEC Dist-EBEC 1963

Origin Of Land Plants - Liverworts And Mosses (Spanish) C 14 MIN
16MM FILM, 3/4 OR 1/2 IN VIDEO H
Traces the evolution of land plants and illustrates the structural characteristics, reproductive processes and adaptive mechanisms of liverworts and mosses. Shows their relationship to the development of higher land plants.
From The Biology (Spanish) Series.
Prod-EBEC Dist-EBEC 1963

Origin Of Life C
3/4 OR 1/2 INCH VIDEO CASSETTE
Prod-MSTVIS Dist-MSTVIS

Origin Of Life C 25 MIN
16MM FILM, 3/4 OR 1/2 IN VIDEO
Uses animated diagrams, cinemicrography and narration to illustrate the organization and development of the living cell. Examines the structure, atomic components and characteristics of the four major categories of organic compounds. Shows the growth of organic compounds from the primitive elements of methane, ammonia and water, and pictures the development of the more complex and efficient cell that utilized oxygen and evolved into more intricate and varied forms of life.
Prod-WILEYJ Dist-MEDIAG 1971

Origin Of Life B 30 MIN
2 INCH VIDEOTAPE J
See series title for descriptive statement.
From The Investigating The World Of Science, Unit 5 - Life In The Universe Series.
Prod-MPATI Dist-GPITVL

Origin Of Life C 45 MIN
3/4 OR 1/2 INCH VIDEO CASSETTE C
Discusses the biological origin of life.
From The Biology I Series.
Prod-MDCPB Dist-MDCPB

Origin Of Life Theories C 45 MIN
3/4 OR 1/2 INCH VIDEO CASSETTE C
Presents various origin of life theories.
From The Biology I Series.
Prod-MDCPB Dist-MDCPB

Origin Of Life, The C 21 MIN
16MM FILM, 3/4 OR 1/2 IN VIDEO J-H
Describes human cells, DNA replication, and genetic code. Re-creates the famous experiment of Miller and Urey in which the environment of the primitive Earth is reproduced in a laboratory flask. Edited from an episode of the Cosmos series.
From The Cosmos (Edited Version) Series.
Prod-SAGANC Dist-FI Prodn-KCET 1980

Origin Of Life, The - Chemical Evolution X 12 MIN
16MM FILM, 3/4 OR 1/2 IN VIDEO
Describes evidence supporting the evolution of life in the Primordial Sea and traces the evolution of life from the molecular level to the present.
From The Biology Series. Unit 10 - Evolution
Prod-EBEC Dist-EBEC 1969

Origin Of Life, The - Chemical Evolution (Spanish) C 11 MIN
16MM FILM, 3/4 OR 1/2 IN VIDEO H
Offers evidence supporting the evolution of life in the primordial sea.
From The Biology (Spanish) Series. Unit 10 - Evolution
Prod-EBEC Dist-EBEC

Origin Of The Crown Dance - An Apache Narrative And Ba'ts'oosee - An Apache Trickster C 40 MIN
3/4 OR 1/2 INCH VIDEO CASSETTE
Apache with English subtitles. Shows an Apache elder telling a story of a boy who became a gaan, a supernatural being with curative powers.
From The Words And Place Series.
Prod-CWATER Dist-CWATER

Origin Of The Elements, The C 18 MIN
16MM FILM, 3/4 OR 1/2 IN VIDEO C A
Explores the five major processes instrumental in the formation of all the elements in the universe. Explains the evolution of the universe and the birth, life and death of stars.
From The Physical Science Film Series.
Prod-CRMP Dist-CRMP 1973

Origin Of The Moon C 5 MIN
16MM FILM, 3/4 OR 1/2 IN VIDEO I-J
Discusses the how the earth and its moon may have begun about five billion years ago in a cloud of cold gases.
Prod-CBSTV Dist-PHENIX 1970

Origin Of The Solar System B 45 MIN
2 INCH VIDEOTAPE C
See series title for descriptive statement.
From The Physical Science Series. Unit 3 - Astronomy
Prod-CHITVC Dist-GPITVL Prodn-WTTWTV

Originals - Women In Art—A Series
16MM FILM, 3/4 OR 1/2 IN VIDEO H-C A
Looks at the lives and work of women artists.
Prod-WNETTV Dist-FI 1977

Anonymous Was A Woman	030 MIN
Frankenthaler - Toward A New Climate	030 MIN
Georgia O'Keeffe	060 MIN
Mary Cassatt - Impressionist From	030 MIN
Nevelson In Process	030 MIN
Spirit Catcher - The Art Of Betye Saar	030 MIN

Originals, The C 15 MIN
16MM FILM OPTICAL SOUND
Presents the 1976 Dr Pepper radio advertising campaign. Shows six musicians singing and performing their own arrangements of the Dr Pepper song in recording sessions.
LC NO. 77-702488
Prod-DRPEP Dist-COMCRP Prodn-COMCRP 1976

Origins C 7 MIN
16MM FILM OPTICAL SOUND H-C A
Presents a tongue-in-cheek look at the origins of life on a distant planet.
LC NO. 79-700126
Prod-USC Dist-USC 1978

Origins And Evidence C 58 MIN
16MM FILM, 3/4 OR 1/2 IN VIDEO A
Discusses the sudden emergence of the Persian Empire under the leadership of Cyrus the Great. Portrays Darius's founding of the Achaemenian dynasty in which mankind moved from primitive to civilized society.
From The Crossroads Of Civilization Series.
Prod-CNEMAG Dist-CNEMAG 1978

Origins And Influences Of Ethnic Dance C 30 MIN
3/4 OR 1/2 INCH VIDEO CASSETTE
See series title for descriptive statement.
From The Third World Dance - Tracing Roots Series.
Prod-ARCVID Dist-ARCVID

Origins Of Art In France, The (Neolithic 400 A D) B 40 MIN
16MM FILM OPTICAL SOUND
Discusses the origins of art in France from the Neolothic period to 400 A D.
Prod-ROLAND Dist-ROLAND

Origins Of Change, The C 20 MIN
3/4 OR 1/2 INCH VIDEO CASSETTE

Discusses the functions of DNA and recapitulates the evidence for evolution.
From The Evolution Series.
Prod-FOTH Dist-FOTH 1984

Origins Of Courses In Business C 45 MIN
3/4 OR 1/2 INCH VIDEO CASSETTE
Describes economics as the 'parent one study' and shows how it relates to courses in management and marketing.
From The Introduction To Marketing, A Lecture Series.
Prod-IVCH Dist-IVCH

Origins Of Man B 30 MIN
16MM FILM OPTICAL SOUND H-C A
Dr William White Howells, Professor of Anthropology at Harvard University, presents the latest findings and theories on the origins of man. Visits Harvard's Peabody Museum, showing its large collection of fossils. Points out that many of the most important discoveries about the early forerunners of man have been made in the last twenty years.
Prod-NET Dist-IU 1967

Origins Of Spread Spectrum Communications—A Series
C
Uses classroom format to videotape five 60-minute lectures on five cassettes. Covers events, circa 1920-1960, leading to development of the spread-spectrum communication systems. Discusses the WHYN, hush-up, BLADES, F9C-A/Rake, CODORAC and ARC-50 systems. Describes, also, prior art in secure communications and introductions to other early spread-spectrum efforts.
Prod-USCITV Dist-AMCEE

Origins Of The Motion Picture B 21 MIN
16MM FILM - 3/4 IN VIDEO
Presents an historical record of the development of machinery and the art of the motion picture, dating from the earliest suggestions of Leonardo da Vinci to the sound motion picture of Edison. Includes the work of Plateu and Daguerre as well as historical naval pictures.
LC NO. 79-706459
Prod-USN Dist-USNAC 1979

Orion C 15 MIN
3/4 OR 1/2 INCH VIDEO CASSETTE P
See series title for descriptive statement.
From The Strawberry Square II - Take Time Series.
Prod-NEITV Dist-AITECH 1984

Orison C 18 MIN
16MM FILM OPTICAL SOUND
Portrays the spirit of Nova Scotia as reflected in historic and modern churches. Accompanied by choir and organ music.
LC NO. FIA67-5679
Prod-CTFL Dist-CTFL 1967

Orissa - The Land And The People B 19 MIN
16MM FILM OPTICAL SOUND I-C A
Shows the rich tradition in temple architecture which can be seen in Bhubaneshwar, Puri and Konarak. Explains how Orissa takes pride in its Rourkella steel complex and Hirakud Dam. Documents the old and new Orissa.
Prod-INDIA Dist-NEDINF

Orlando Story, The C 22 MIN
16MM FILM OPTICAL SOUND
Shows construction of the Navy's newest training facility, a campus-like school where recruits learn to become sailors.
LC NO. 74-706550
Prod-USN Dist-USNAC 1972

Oroville Kaleidoscope C 11 MIN
16MM FILM - 3/4 IN VIDEO
Presents the Oroville Dam, keystone of the California State Water Project and one of the largest earthfill dams in the world. Shows the kaleidoscope of activities that built the dam and describes the benefits the facilities provide today.
Prod-CSDWR Dist-CALDWR 1973

Orphan Boy Of Vienna, An (German) B 85 MIN
3/4 OR 1/2 INCH VIDEO CASSETTE
Tells the story of an orphan boy who meets a street singer who gets him accepted by the Vienna Boys Choir. Features songs by the Vienna Boys Choir. Directed by Max Neufeld. With English subtitles.
Prod-IHF Dist-IHF

Orphan Lions, The C 18 MIN
16MM FILM, 3/4 OR 1/2 IN VIDEO I-C A
Presents an edited version of the film Living Free, which documents the concern of Joy and George Adamson with the survival of the lion Elsa's cubs after her death.
Prod-LCOA Dist-LCOA 1973

Orphans Of The Storm B 126 MIN
16MM FILM SILENT
Tells the story of two orphans, marooned in Paris, who become separated by the turbulent maelstrom that preceded the French Revolution. Reveals that one orphan is released from the Bastille and seeks to find her sister in the chaos that is the new Paris. Shows that after terrifying adventures, the orphans are finally reunited at the tribunal of Robespierre's Reign of Terror. Stars Lillian and Dorothy Gish. Directed by D W Griffith.
Prod-GFITH Dist-KILLIS 1921

Orphans, The C 21 MIN
16MM FILM, 3/4 OR 1/2 IN VIDEO P-I
Presents a tale of four orphans who find love and a sense of belonging in their new life with a solitary farmer.
Prod-SINCIN Dist-LCOA 1975

Orphans, The (Russian) C 100 MIN
16MM FILM OPTICAL SOUND H-C A
A Russian-language film with English subtitles. Tells about a successful novelist who searches for his two brothers whom he hasn't seen since adulthood in an effort to reconstruct his own identity. Shows him discovering the value of human sympathy, passion, love and care.
LC NO. 83-700201
Prod-MOSFLM Dist-IFEX Prodn-SOVEXP 1980

Orphans, The (Spanish) C 21 MIN
16MM FILM, 3/4 OR 1/2 IN VIDEO P-H A
Describes life on a farm for a man and four city orphans he takes in.
Prod-SINCIN Dist-LCOA 1975

Orpheus B 96 MIN
16MM FILM OPTICAL SOUND
A French language motion picture. Retells the Greek legend of Orpheus, the poet whose wife Euridice was kidnapped and carried off to the underworld. Tells how he followed and rescued her, beguiling her guardians with his songs. Includes English subtitles.
Prod-UNKNWN Dist-KITPAR 1949

Orpheus And Eurydice C 10 MIN
16MM FILM, 3/4 OR 1/2 IN VIDEO P-C A
Puppet version of the classic Greek legend of the Minstrel Orpheus and his descent into Hades in quest of his lost bride, Eurydice.
Prod-VIKING Dist-SF 1963

Orpheus, With A Difference - Offenbach C 45 MIN
2 INCH VIDEOTAPE
See series title for descriptive statement.
From The Humanities Series. Unit II - The World Of Myth And Legend
Prod-WTTWTV Dist-GPITVL

Orson Welles Great Mysteries—A Series
16MM FILM, 3/4 OR 1/2 IN VIDEO I-C
Prod-ANGLIA Dist-EBEC 1973

Ice Storm 25 MIN
Ingenious Reporter, The 25 MIN
Inspiration Of Mr Budd, The 25 MIN
La Grande Breteche 25 MIN
Terribly Strange Bed, A 24 MIN

Orthodontic Correction Of The Mesially Inclined Molar—A Series

Offers an unedited presentation by Robert L Vanarsdall, Jr, DDS, on orthodontic correction of the mesially inclined molar. Illustrates a predictable and efficient appliance design to upright a molar for prosthetic replacement, and for the favorable periodontal changes that can occur with proper tooth repositioning.
Prod-AMDA Dist-AMDA 1977

Orthodontics - A Special Kind Of Dentistry C 14 MIN
16MM FILM OPTICAL SOUND
Emphasizes the importance of orthodontic treatment as a means of conserving dental health by showing the analogous relationship between ancient engineer and architects who built cities to last forever and the orthodontist who plans the functions of the teeth to last a lifetime.
LC NO. 73-702199
Prod-AAORTH Dist-AAORTH 1973

Orthodontics - A Special Kind Of Dentistry (Spanish) C 14 MIN
16MM FILM OPTICAL SOUND
Emphasizes the importance of orthodontic treatment as a means of conserving dental health by showing the analogous relationship between ancient engineers and architects who built cities to last forever and the orthodontist who plans the functions of the teeth to last a lifetime.
LC NO. 73-702199
Prod-AAORTH Dist-AAORTH 1973

Orthodontics And You C 25 MIN
16MM FILM OPTICAL SOUND
Explores the orthodontic experience as seen by doctors, patients, parents and educators.
LC NO. 79-700398
Prod-AAORTH Dist-MTP Prodn-MANGO 1979

Orthodontics And You (Spanish) C 25 MIN
16MM FILM OPTICAL SOUND
Explores the orthodontic experience as seen by doctors, patients, parents and educators.
LC NO. 79-700398
Prod-AAORTH Dist-MTP Prodn-MANGO 1979

Orthodox Christianity - The Rumanian Solution C 52 MIN
16MM FILM, 3/4 OR 1/2 IN VIDEO H-C A
Examines the relationship between the Eastern Orthodox Church and the communist state in Rumania. Visits a number of Rumanian churches and shows how the Orthodox liturgy is conducted.
From The Long Search Series. No. 6
LC NO. 79-707786
Prod-BBCTV Dist-TIMLIF 1978

Orthognathic Surgery C 10 MIN
3/4 OR 1/2 INCH VIDEO CASSETTE
Explains what orthognathic surgery is and why it is recommended. Discusses relationship between patient, orthodontist and oral surgeon to make certain best results are obtained. Covers what to expect upon entering the hospital, surgery procedure and recovery.
Prod-TRAINX Dist-TRAINX

Orthogonal Functions B 34 MIN
3/4 OR 1/2 INCH VIDEO CASSETTE
See series title for descriptive statement.
From The Calculus Of Linear Algebra Series.
Prod-MIOT Dist-MIOT

Orthogonal Projection C 13 MIN
16MM FILM, 3/4 OR 1/2 IN VIDEO H-C
Introduces an elementary transformation involving triangles transformed into a problem involving conics.
From The Geometry Series.
Prod-UMINN Dist-IFB 1971

Orthographic Projection - Three-View Working Drawings, Blueprints C 7 MIN
1/2 IN VIDEO CASSETTE BETA/VHS IND
Explains the application of the positioning of a part for illustration on a blueprint by using a clear glass box visual aid.
Prod-RMI Dist-RMI

Orthographic Projections C
3/4 OR 1/2 INCH VIDEO CASSETTE IND
See series title for descriptive statement.
From The Drafting - Process Piping Drafting Series.
Prod-GPCV Dist-GPCV

Orthographic Projections (Drafting - Piping Familiarization) C
3/4 OR 1/2 INCH VIDEO CASSETTE IND
See series title for descriptive statement.
From The Drafting - Piping Familiarization Series.
Prod-GPCV Dist-GPCV

Orthopaedic Examination Of The Lower Extremities, Pt 1 - Pelvis To Knee C 16 MIN
1/2 IN VIDEO CASSETTE BETA/VHS PRO
Prod-RMI Dist-RMI

Orthopaedic Examination Of The Lower Extremities, Pt 2 - Knee To Foot C 22 MIN
1/2 IN VIDEO CASSETTE BETA/VHS PRO
Prod-RMI Dist-RMI

Orthopedic Procedures C 15 MIN
3/4 OR 1/2 INCH VIDEO CASSETTE PRO
Presents various orthopedic procedures.
Prod-WFP Dist-WFP Prodn-UKANMC

Orthopedics C 50 MIN
3/4 OR 1/2 INCH VIDEO CASSETTE PRO
Includes a brief review of basic terminology and anatomy of the skeletal system and an explanation of the considerations in selecting treatment for the benefit of attorneys.
From The Attorneys' Guide To Medicine Series.
Prod-PBI Dist-ABACPE

Orthoplast Resting Splint C 11 MIN
3/4 OR 1/2 INCH VIDEO CASSETTE PRO
Shows how to construct an orthoplast resting splint. Presents procedure for making a pattern, forming the splint, and adding support straps, includes tips on a preparatory procedure that makes the orthoplast easier to cut.
Prod-HSCIC Dist-HSCIC

Orville Harrison/Chris Chirdon C 28 MIN
3/4 OR 1/2 INCH VIDEO CASSETTE
Portrays Orville Harrison, a musician and ex-convict who now counsels prisoners at Sing-Sing as well as leading his own jazz group. Fred Rogers explores the world of five-year-old Chris Chirdon who uses creativity in his play and his painting to explore and learn about the new world of kindergarten and growing up.
From The Old Friends - New Friends Series.
Prod-FAMCOM Dist-PBS 1981

Os Fuzis B 109 MIN
16MM FILM OPTICAL SOUND
An English subtitle version of the Portuguese language film. Tells a story of suffering experienced by Brazilians during a drought. Considers the problems of maintaining law and order among starving, desperate people.
Prod-NYFLMS Dist-NYFLMS 1963

Oscar C 8 MIN
3/4 OR 1/2 INCH VIDEO CASSETTE J A
Focuses on alcohol abuse problems in Black America. Filmed in the Bedford Stuyvesant area of New York City.
Prod-SUTHRB Dist-SUTHRB

Oscar At Home B 10 MIN
16MM FILM OPTICAL SOUND J-C A
Shows Oscar, a four-year-old, and his family at mealtime. Shows he is a member of a working-class Mexican-American family living in Texas.
From The Exploring Childhood Series.
LC NO. 76-701892
Prod-EDC Dist-EDC Prodn-FRIEDJ 1975

Oscar At School B 6 MIN
16MM FILM OPTICAL SOUND J-C A
Shows Oscar on the playground and in class where his teacher takes a strong, directive role and alternates between speaking Spanish and English.
From The Exploring Childhood Series.
LC NO. 76-701893
Prod-EDC Dist-EDC Prodn-FRIEDJ 1975

Oscar Howe - The Sioux Painter C 29 MIN
3/4 OR 1/2 INCH VIDEO CASSETTE
Features Oscar Howe, a full-blooded Sioux Indian. Explains that he specializes in the art and culture of the Sioux Indian nation. Narrated by Vincent Price.
Prod-KUSD Dist-PUBTEL

Oscar Howe - The Sioux Painter C 29 MIN
16MM FILM, 3/4 OR 1/2 IN VIDEO

Features artist Oscar Howe who describes his early life and tells how much the lines he drew meant to him. Shows Howe in his studio starting a painting and as the painting develops he talks of his theories about art. Examines seven of the artist's paintings.
Prod-SDAC Dist-CORF 1973

Oscar Micheaux, Film Pioneer C 29 MIN
16MM FILM, 3/4 OR 1/2 IN VIDEO I-C A
Oscar Micheaux, remembered for his work as a pioneer producer-director whose films offered a positive image and an alternative for black people in the 1920s and 1930s. Displays the on-camera reminiscences of two performers who appeared in Micheaux films - Bee Freeman, dubbed the 'Sepia Mae West' and Lorenzo Tucker, the 'Black Valentino.
From The Were You There? Series.
LC NO. 83-706596
Prod-NGUZO Dist-BCNFL 1982

Oscar Peterson C 58 MIN
3/4 OR 1/2 INCH VIDEO CASSETTE
See series title for descriptive statement.
From The Evening At Pops Series.
Prod-WGBHTV Dist-PBS 1978

Oscar W Underwood B 51 MIN
3/4 OR 1/2 INCH VIDEO CASSETTE I-H
Dramatizes Alabama Senator Oscar Underwood's opposition to the Ku Klux Klan during his campaign for the 1924 Democratic presidential nomination. Based on book Profiles In Courage by John F Kennedy. Stars Sidney Blackmer and Victor Jory.
From The Profiles In Courage Series.
LC NO. 83-706541
Prod-SAUDEK Dist-SSSSV 1964

Oscar, Aunt Lorrie And The Top Hat C 15 MIN
16MM FILM, 3/4 OR 1/2 IN VIDEO I-J
Shows that many different stories may be written using the same basic ingredients. Helps develop critical skills and the ability to evaluate style and content.
From The Creative Writing Series.
Prod-MORLAT Dist-AIMS 1973

Oscars, The - Moments Of Greatness, Pt 1 B 26 MIN
16MM FILM OPTICAL SOUND
Traces the history of the academy of Motion Picture Arts and Sciences. Includes excerpts of award-winning films and some presentations of Oscars.
From The Hollywood And The Stars Series.
LC NO. FI68-198
Prod-WOLPER Dist-WOLPER 1964

Oscars, The - Moments Of Greatness, Pt 2 B 26 MIN
16MM FILM OPTICAL SOUND
Discusses the activities behind the Oscar headlines, the scramble for nominations, and the top secret security of the ballot. Shows various ways in which movie stars accept awards.
From The Hollywood And The Stars Series.
LC NO. FI68-199
Prod-WOLPER Dist-WOLPER 1964

Oscillations Along A Heavy Spring B
16MM FILM OPTICAL SOUND
Analyzes oscillations along a spring.
Prod-OPENU Dist-OPENU

Oscillators C 12 MIN
3/4 OR 1/2 INCH VIDEO CASSETTE
Covers oscillation, oscillators and amplifiers, oscillation frequency, crystal-controlled and a variety of other oscillators.
From The Industrial Electronics - Oscillators And Multivibrators Series.
Prod-TPCTRA Dist-TPCTRA

Oscillators B 13 MIN
16MM FILM, 3/4 OR 1/2 IN VIDEO
Explains basic principles of electronic oscillation. Issued in 1945 as a motion picture.
From The Radio Technician Training Series.
LC NO. 78-706296
Prod-USN Dist-USNAC Prodn-LNS 1978

Oscillators, Modulators, Demodulators C 16 MIN
16MM FILM OPTICAL SOUND IND
Defines and discusses oscillators, modulators and demodulators.
From The Solid State Electronics Series. Chapter 6
LC NO. 80-701540
Prod-TAT Dist-TAT 1980

Oscillators, Modulators, Demodulators C 17 MIN
3/4 OR 1/2 INCH VIDEO CASSETTE IND
Discusses method by which oscillator develops an AC signal with only DC applied. Explains use of positive and negative feedback. Covers different types of circuits.
From The Introduction To Solid State Electronics Series. Chapter 6
LC NO. 80-707264
Prod-TAT Dist-TAT

Oscillators, Modulators, Demodulators (Spanish) C 17 MIN
3/4 OR 1/2 INCH VIDEO CASSETTE IND
Discusses method by which oscillator develops an AC signal with only DC applied. Explains use of positive and negative feedback. Covers different types of circuits.
From The Introduction To Solid State Electronics (Spanish) Series. Chapter 6
Prod-TAT Dist-TAT

Oscilloscope - Calibration And Use C 20 MIN
3/4 OR 1/2 INCH VIDEO CASSETTE
See series title for descriptive statement.
From The Basic AC Circuits, Laboratory--Sessions--A Series.
Prod-TXINLC Dist-TXINLC

Oscilloscope - Input Coupling And Waveform Analysis C 20 MIN
3/4 OR 1/2 INCH VIDEO CASSETTE
See series title for descriptive statement.
From The Basic AC Circuits, Laboratory--Sessions--A Series.
Prod-TXINLC Dist-TXINLC

Oscilloscope - Triggering C 20 MIN
3/4 OR 1/2 INCH VIDEO CASSETTE
See series title for descriptive statement.
From The Basic AC Circuits, Laboratory--Sessions--A Series.
Prod-TXINLC Dist-TXINLC

Oscilloscope And Its Use, The C
3/4 OR 1/2 INCH VIDEO CASSETTE
See series title for descriptive statement.
From The Basic Electricity - AC Series.
Prod-VTRI Dist-VTRI

Oscilloscope Calibration And Use C
3/4 OR 1/2 INCH VIDEO CASSETTE
See series title for descriptive statement.
From The Basic AC Circuits Series.
Prod-VTRI Dist-VTRI

Oscilloscope Input Coupling And Waveform Analysis C
3/4 OR 1/2 INCH VIDEO CASSETTE
See series title for descriptive statement.
From The Basic AC Circuits Series.
Prod-VTRI Dist-VTRI

Oscilloscope Operation, Soldering And Troubleshooting Solid-State Devices C 60 MIN
3/4 OR 1/2 INCH VIDEO CASSETTE IND
See series title for descriptive statement.
From The Electrical Maintenance Training, Module 7 - Solid-State Devices Series.
Prod-LEIKID Dist-LEIKID

Oscilloscope Triggering C
3/4 OR 1/2 INCH VIDEO CASSETTE
See series title for descriptive statement.
From The Basic AC Circuits Series.
Prod-VTRI Dist-VTRI

Oscilloscopes - Frequency And Measurement B 21 MIN
16MM FILM - 3/4 IN VIDEO
Shows various waveshapes of different frequencies, amplitudes and phase relationships on an oscilloscope screen. Demonstrates operation of the oscilloscope, showing how to find frequency and voltage amplitude.
LC NO. 78-706318
Prod-USAF Dist-USNAC 1978

OSHA - Life At Work II C 15 MIN
16MM FILM, 3/4 OR 1/2 IN VIDEO H-C A
Discusses occupational diseases, covering techniques of prevention. Deals with personal cleanliness, proper ventilation, reduction of noise pollution and job accidents. Examines the tenets of the government's occupational health and safety regulations.
Prod-KLEINW Dist-KLEINW 1977

OSHA And Us C 17 MIN
3/4 INCH VIDEO CASSETTE
Discusses the Occupational Safety And Health Act and the impact of the regulations. Filmed on location in research and teaching laboratories. Illustrates potentially dangerous health and safety situations.
Prod-UMITV Dist-UMITV 1977

OSHA File - Cases And Compliances, The C 20 MIN
3/4 OR 1/2 INCH VIDEO CASSETTE
Shows supervisors, through court cases drawn from actual OCcupational Safety and Health Administration (OSHA) files, the steps they must take to live up to the law.
Prod-BBP Dist-BBP

Osmosis And Fluid Compartments B 31 MIN
16MM FILM OPTICAL SOUND PRO
Defines and demonstrates the concepts of diffusion, osmosis and osmotic pressure. Describes and demonstrates the effects of hypotonic, hypertonic and isotonic solutions on living cells. Identifies the major fluid compartments of the body, the major electrolytes and the factors involved in maintenance of a constant volume in each compartment.
From The Directions For Education In Nursing Via Technology Series. Lesson 35
LC NO. 74-701808
Prod-DENT Dist-WSU 1974

Osprey C 35 MIN
16MM FILM, 3/4 OR 1/2 IN VIDEO I-C A
Explores the breeding behavior and fishing adaptations of osprey, or sea eagle, in Scotland. Depicts how the osprey had been hunted to extinction in the early 1900s, but revived with the return to the lock of a single breeding pair. Shows complete breeding cycle, from pair formation, nest construction, incubation and feeding habits.
From The RSPB Collection Series.
Prod-RSFPB Dist-BCNFL 1980

Osprey's Domain C 15 MIN
16MM FILM, 3/4 OR 1/2 IN VIDEO J-C A
Examines the life cycle of the osprey, a fish-eating hawk.
From The Animals And Plants Of North America Series.
Prod-KARVF Dist-LCOA 1980

Oss, 'Oss, Wee 'Oss ('Oss, 'Oss, Wee 'Oss) C 17 MIN
16MM FILM OPTICAL SOUND
Shows spring-time rites in Padstow, Cornwall, featuring a strange dance which is a modern remnant of ancient practices celebrating the revived fertility of the land.
Prod-CRAF Dist-CFI

Osseous Graft Techniques - Induction And Replacement C 180 MIN
3/4 OR 1/2 INCH VIDEO CASSETTE
Offers a presentation by Anthony W Gargiulo, DDS, Chicago, exploring intraoral donor sites in osseous graft techniques and shows the areas of osseous coagulum, trephined grafts and bone scrapings.
Prod-AMDA Dist-AMDA 1975

Osseous Surgery In The Maxilla, Pt II C 11 MIN
3/4 OR 1/2 INCH VIDEO CASSETTE
Shows a suturing technique which was selected after the periodontal osseous surgery had been completed, permitting suturing of the buccal flap, independently of the lingual or palatal flap.
Prod-VADTC Dist-AMDA 1969

Osseous Surgery In The Maxilla, Pt 1 C 18 MIN
16MM FILM, 3/4 OR 1/2 IN VIDEO
Demonstrates the surgical elimination of supra and infra periodontal bony defects in the maxilla. Shows the osseous contouring to establish physiologic architecture of the soft tissues in detail.
LC NO. 82-707225
Prod-USVA Dist-USNAC 1968

Osseous Surgery In The Maxilla, Pt 2 C 11 MIN
16MM FILM OPTICAL SOUND
Describes techniques which permit suturing of the buccal flap, independently of the lingual or palatal flap, showing how it is performed with a continuous how it assures close adaptation of the tissue to the teeth and bone.
LC NO. 74-705274
Prod-USVA Dist-NMAC 1968

Ossicular Problems In Middle Ear Surgery C 32 MIN
16MM FILM OPTICAL SOUND PRO
Illustrates the various types of ossicular discontinuity and demonstrates their surgical correction.
Prod-EAR Dist-EAR

Osteology Of The Skull - A Self-Evaluation Exercise C 22 MIN
3/4 OR 1/2 INCH VIDEO CASSETTE C A
From The Osteology Of The Skull Series.
Prod-UWO Dist-TEF

Osteology Of The Skull - An Introduction C 26 MIN
3/4 OR 1/2 INCH VIDEO CASSETTE C A
From The Osteology Of The Skull Series.
Prod-UWO Dist-TEF

Osteology Of The Skull - Inferior Surface Of The Cranium C 26 MIN
3/4 OR 1/2 INCH VIDEO CASSETTE C A
From The Osteology Of The Skull Series.
Prod-UWO Dist-TEF

Osteology Of The Skull - The Cranial Cavity C 28 MIN
3/4 OR 1/2 INCH VIDEO CASSETTE C A
From The Osteology Of The Skull Series.
Prod-UWO Dist-TEF

Osteology Of The Skull - The Mandible C 23 MIN
3/4 OR 1/2 INCH VIDEO CASSETTE C A
From The Osteology Of The Skull Series.
Prod-UWO Dist-TEF

Osteology Of The Skull - The Mandible - A Self-Evaluation Exercise C 16 MIN
3/4 OR 1/2 INCH VIDEO CASSETTE C A
From The Osteology Of The Skull Series.
Prod-UWO Dist-TEF

Osteology Of The Skull - The Temporal Bone - A Self-Evaluation Exercise C 25 MIN
3/4 OR 1/2 INCH VIDEO CASSETTE C A
From The Osteology Of The Skull Series.
Prod-UWO Dist-TEF

Osteology Of The Skull - The Temporal Bone C 30 MIN
3/4 OR 1/2 INCH VIDEO CASSETTE C A
From The Osteology Of The Skull Series.
Prod-UWO Dist-TEF

Osteology Of The Skull--A Series
C A
Provides an overview of the osteology of the skull. Features self-evaluation programs for individual use and study. By Drs D G Montemurro, R P Singh, and P Haase, Department of Anatomy, University of Western Ontario.
Prod-UWO Dist-TEF

Osteology Of The Skull - A Self-Evaluation	
Osteology Of The Skull - An Introduction	026 MIN
Osteology Of The Skull - Inferior Surface Of	026 MIN
Osteology Of The Skull - The Cranial Cavity	028 MIN
Osteology Of The Skull - The Mandible	023 MIN
Osteology Of The Skull - The Mandible - A	016 MIN
Osteology Of The Skull - The Temporal	025 MIN
Osteology Of The Skull - The Temporal Bone	030 MIN

Osteology Of The Upper Limb, Pt I - The Upper Limb Girdle C 23 MIN
3/4 OR 1/2 INCH VIDEO CASSETTE C A
Presents the anatomy of the upper limb.
Prod-UWO Dist-TEF

Osteopathic Examination And Manipulation--A Series
PRO
Presents an overview of osteopathic examination and manipulation in several areas of the body. Includes demonstrations and graphics.
Prod-MSU Dist-MSU

Articulatory Procedures I 014 MIN
Cervical Region Pt 1 013 MIN
Cervical Region, Pt 2 - Occipitaotlantal 015 MIN
Introduction To Soft Tissue Techniques, Pt 1 013 MIN
Lower Extremity, Pt 1 000 MIN
Lumbar Region, Pt 1 017 MIN
Lumbar Region, Pt 2 010 MIN
Manipulative Techniques To Assist Fluid Flow 014 MIN
Pelvic Region, Pt 1 - Iliosacral 017 MIN
Pelvic Region, Pt 2 - Sacroiliac 013 MIN
Pelvic Region, Pt 3 - Alternative Direct 012 MIN
Structural Examination - Gross Motion Testing 014 MIN
Structural Examination - Initial Screen 014 MIN
Structural Examination - Local Scan 018 MIN
Structural Examination - Spinal Segment 000 MIN
Thoracic Cage, Pt 1 - True Ribs 014 MIN
Thoracic Region, Pt 1 014 MIN
Thoracic Region, Pt 2 012 MIN
Upper Extremity - Clavicle 020 MIN

Ostomy - A New Beginning C
3/4 OR 1/2 INCH VIDEO CASSETTE
Deals primarily with the psychological aspects of having an Ostomy as experienced by actual Ostomates. Demonstrates how the normal digestive system works and how a colostomy or ileastomy changes things.
Prod-MIFE Dist-MIFE

Ostomy - A New Beginning (Spanish) C
3/4 OR 1/2 INCH VIDEO CASSETTE
Deals primarily with the psychological aspects of having an Ostomy as experienced by actual Ostomates. Demonstrates how the normal digestive system works and how a colostomy or ileastomy changes things.
Prod-MIFE Dist-MIFE

Ostomy Visitor, The C 12 MIN
16MM FILM OPTICAL SOUND PRO
Shows how rehabilitated ostomates can help newly operated ostomy patients by visiting the hospital and giving general facts about diet, appearance, day-to-day care and activity.
LC NO. 77-701316
Prod-AMCS Dist-AMCS 1974

Ostrich C 12 MIN
16MM FILM, 3/4 OR 1/2 IN VIDEO P A
Records the mating, nesting and everyday rituals of the ostrich.
From The Silent Safari Series.
Prod-CHE Dist-EBEC 1984

Ostriches C 5 MIN
16MM FILM, 3/4 OR 1/2 IN VIDEO K-P
Describes the lifestyle of the ostrich, the tallest, heaviest bird on the planet which can run as fast as a horse and lay eggs 20 times heavier than chicken eggs.
From The Zoo Animals In The Wild Series.
Prod-CORF Dist-CORF 1981

OT Story, The B 17 MIN
16MM FILM OPTICAL SOUND C A
Describes a career of occupational therapy, work with the handicapped and information on preparation of an OT career.
Prod-AOTA Dist-AOTA 1957

Otello C 145 MIN
3/4 OR 1/2 INCH VIDEO CASSETTE A
Presents Vladimir Atlantov as Otello from the Arena di Verona in the classic Verdi opera.
Prod-EDDIM Dist-EDDIM

Othello B 44 MIN
16MM FILM OPTICAL SOUND
A condensed version of 'OTHELLO' presented by an English cast including John Slater, Sebastian Cabot and Luanne Shaw.
Prod-HALST Dist-BHAWK 1947

Othello C 10 MIN
16MM FILM, 3/4 OR 1/2 IN VIDEO H-C
See series title for descriptive statement.
From The Shakespeare Series.
Prod-IFB Dist-IFB 1974

Othello B 29 MIN
3/4 INCH VIDEO CASSETTE
Discusses the themes of faith and treachery and love and hatred. Tells the story of the fall of a man who is destroyed by jealousy.
From The Plays Of Shakespeare Series.
Prod-UMITV Dist-UMITV 1961

Othello C 202 MIN
3/4 OR 1/2 INCH VIDEO CASSETTE H-C A
Presents Othello, William Shakespeare's play about a man whose jealousy of his wife leads to tragic consequences.
From The Shakespeare Plays Series.
LC NO. 82-707355
Prod-BBCTV Dist-TIMLIF 1982

Othello - Iago - Incarnation Of Evil For Its Own Sake B 45 MIN
2 INCH VIDEOTAPE C
See series title for descriptive statement.
From The Shakespeare Series.
Prod-CHITVC Dist-GPITVL Prodn-WTTWTV

Othello - Shakespeare's Only Domestic Tragedy B 45 MIN
2 INCH VIDEOTAPE C
See series title for descriptive statement.
From The Shakespeare Series.
Prod-CHITVC Dist-GPITVL Prodn-WTTWTV

Other Child, The - Burns In Children C 50 MIN
3/4 OR 1/2 INCH VIDEO CASSETTE
Presents poignant and revealing conversations with several children with severe burns as well as informative interviews with nurses, physicians, psychiatrists and physio- therapists. Examines the physical and emotional suffering of the young victims, emphasizing the critical importance of helping parents deal with their child's injury.
Prod-CANBC Dist-AJN

Other City, The C 11 MIN
16MM FILM OPTICAL SOUND H-C A
Explains that 75,000 Americans could be saved each year through health checkups and learning to recognize the Seven Danger Signals of cancer.
Prod-AMCS Dist-AMCS

Other Clawed Animals C 15 MIN
3/4 INCH VIDEO CASSETTE P
Explains how other animals, such as oppossums, raccoons and skunks are adapted for living in a wild state.
From The Tell Me What You See Series.
Prod-WVIZTV Dist-GPITVL

Other Data Structures C 30 MIN
3/4 OR 1/2 INCH VIDEO CASSETTE H-C A
Describes structure of variant RECORDS and shows examples. Introduces the stack data structure and an example of execution of a Pascal arithmetic expression using a stack.
From The Pascal, Pt 2 - Intermediate Pascal Series.
LC NO. 81-706049
Prod-COLOSU Dist-COLOSU 1980

Other Diabetes, The C 24 MIN
16MM FILM OPTICAL SOUND P-C A
Addresses persons with Type II diabetes, covering all aspects of this disease from diagnosis and treatment to emotional issues.
Prod-ADAS Dist-ADAS

Other Diabetes, The C 22 MIN
3/4 OR 1/2 INCH VIDEO CASSETTE
Explains risk factors which can lead to Type II diabetes and the lifestyle measures which can be taken to control it, such as exercise, nutrition and weight control.
Prod-PELICN Dist-PELICN

Other Families, Other Friends—A Series
P
Shows families in various lands. Emphasizes the influence of culture, climate and terrain on the lives of families at home, at school, at work and at play.
Prod-WVIZTV Dist-AITECH 1971

Aloha 15 MIN
Amanda 15 MIN
Amanda's Adventures In London 15 MIN
At Home On San Blas Island 15 MIN
Bon Bini 15 MIN
City Of The Smoky Bay 15 MIN
City Of 500 Mosques 15 MIN
Crossroads Of The World 15 MIN
Gift Of The Nile, The 15 MIN
Island In The Sun 15 MIN
Jane And Suzanne 15 MIN
Jerusalem The Golden 15 MIN
Land Of Frost And Fire 15 MIN
Land Of The Kapriska Purara 15 MIN
Land Of The Pineapple 15 MIN
Little Bit Of Paris, A 15 MIN
Little Dutch Island 15 MIN
Lobsterman 15 MIN
Long Way From Home, A 15 MIN
Maria And The Coconuts 15 MIN
Monique Of Amsterdam 15 MIN
Nicaraguan Countryside 15 MIN
Out Of Many, One People 15 MIN
Said The Whiting To The Snail 15 MIN
School Days 15 MIN
Shalom Aleichem 15 MIN
Steve And Kathy And Al 15 MIN
Vasillis Of Athens 15 MIN
Visit To Aruba 15 MIN
Watchia 15 MIN
Weather Is Out, The 15 MIN
Windmills And The Wooden Shoes 15 MIN

Other Features, Pt 1 C 30 MIN
3/4 OR 1/2 INCH VIDEO CASSETTE H-C A
Introduces the unconditional branch and the GOTO statement. Shows block, statement and type syntax diagrams completed for Pascal. Presents packed data structures as well.
From The Pascal, Pt 2 - Intermediate Pascal Series.
LC NO. 81-706049
Prod-COLOSU Dist-COLOSU 1980

Other Features, Pt 2 C 30 MIN
3/4 OR 1/2 INCH VIDEO CASSETTE H-C A
Concludes discussion of Pascal programming features and describes commenting, forward references, function and procedure names as argument parameters and formatting within the WRITE and WRITELN output procedures.
From The Pascal, Pt 2 - Intermediate Pascal Series.
LC NO. 81-706049
Prod-COLOSU Dist-COLOSU 1980

Other Finger Weaves C 29 MIN
2 INCH VIDEOTAPE
See series title for descriptive statement.
From The Exploring The Crafts - Weaving Series.
Prod-NHN Dist-PUBTEL

Other Guy, The C 60 MIN
16MM FILM OPTICAL SOUND J-C A
Examines the problem of alcoholism from the perspective of several experts in the field and from the experiences of alcoholics themselves.
LC NO. 76-701822
Prod-NABSP Dist-NABSP 1971

Other Guy, The, Pt 1 C 30 MIN
3/4 OR 1/2 INCH VIDEO CASSETTE J A
Focuses on the subject of troubled employees.
Prod-BCBSA Dist-SUTHRB

Other Guy, The, Pt 2 C 30 MIN
3/4 OR 1/2 INCH VIDEO CASSETTE J A
Focuses on the subject of troubled employees.
Prod-BCBSA Dist-SUTHRB

Other Half Of The Safety Team C 12 MIN
3/4 OR 1/2 INCH VIDEO CASSETTE
Promotes a positive safety attitude. Emphasizes need for positive state of mind, cooperation with supervisors, awareness of safety hazards and importance of reporting even the slightest accident.
Prod-EDRF Dist-EDRF

Other Half Of The Safety Team, The C 10 MIN
16MM FILM, 3/4 OR 1/2 IN VIDEO
Points out that good safety attitudes can prevent most job-related accidents. Discusses OSHA, protective equipment and proper handling of materials.
Prod-ERF Dist-MTI

Other Half Of The Sky, The - A China Memoir C 74 MIN
16MM FILM OPTICAL SOUND J-C A
Depicts life in the People's Republic of China as seen by a delegation of eight American women who visited in 1973. Includes glimpses of a Peking family's apartment, visits to schools, nurseries and recreational centers and interviews with Chinese citizens who discuss their own and American lifestyles.
LC NO. 77-700785
Prod-SMLCW Dist-NEWDAY 1976

Other Half Of The Sky, The - A China Memoir, Pt 1 C 25 MIN
16MM FILM OPTICAL SOUND J-C A
Depicts life in the People's Republic of China as seen by a delegation of eight American women who visted in 1973. Includes glimpses of a Peking family's apartment, visits to schools, nurseries and recreational centers and interviews with Chinese citizens who discuss their own and American lifestyles.
LC NO. 77-700785
Prod-SMLCW Dist-NEWDAY 1976

Other Half Of The Sky, The - A China Memoir, Pt 2 C 25 MIN
16MM FILM OPTICAL SOUND J-C A
Depicts life in the People's Republic of China as seen by a delegation of eight American women who visited in 1973. Includes glimpses of a Peking family's apartment, visits to schools, nurseries and recreational centers and interviews with Chinese citizens who discuss their own and American lifestyles.
LC NO. 77-700785
Prod-SMLCW Dist-NEWDAY 1976

Other Half Of The Sky, The - A China Memoir, Pt 3 C 24 MIN
16MM FILM OPTICAL SOUND J-C A
Depicts life in the People's Republic of China as seen by a delegation of eight American women who visited in 1973. Includes glimpses of a Peking family's apartment, visits to schools, nurseries and recreational centers and interviews with Chinese citizens who discuss their own and American lifestyles.
LC NO. 77-700785
Prod-SMLCW Dist-NEWDAY 1976

Other Hazards C 12 MIN
3/4 OR 1/2 INCH VIDEO CASSETTE
Covers other hazards such as knives, dangerous materials, liquids, solvents and welding hazards and safety.
From The Protecting Your Safety And Health In the Plant Series.
Prod-TPCTRA Dist-TPCTRA

Other Hazards (Spanish) C 12 MIN
3/4 OR 1/2 INCH VIDEO CASSETTE
Covers other hazards such as knives, dangerous materials, liquids, solvents and welding hazards and safety.
From The Protecting Your Safety And Health In The Plant Series.
Prod-TPCTRA Dist-TPCTRA

Other Hearts In Other Lands C 15 MIN
16MM FILM OPTICAL SOUND I-C A
Depicts two American farm youngsters on an Israeli kibbutz, as part of a United States-Israel exchange program. Shows them learning their neighbors' way of life by living it and in turn, imparting American farm know-how on this two-way road to peace and democracy.
Prod-BRWNB Dist-ADL 1959

Other Implementations C 30 MIN
3/4 OR 1/2 INCH VIDEO CASSETTE IND
Covers problems created by new, low-cost, nonstandard devices and other ways to implement the IEEE 488 Bus but with their associated limitations.
From The IEEE 488 Bus Series.
Prod-COLOSU Dist-COLOSU

Other Investment Opportunities C 30 MIN
3/4 OR 1/2 INCH VIDEO CASSETTE C A
Focuses on speculative investments including the commodity market, the foreign exchange money market, precious and strategic metals, collectible items and equipment leasing. Discusses alternative opportunities such as investing in either an existing or a new business.
From The Personal Finance Series. Lesson 19
Prod-SCCON Dist-CDTEL

Other Lands And People B 20 MIN
2 INCH VIDEOTAPE I
Stresses the necessity of knowing about the customs and ideas of people in other countries. (Broadcast quality)

From The Quest For The Best Series.
Prod-DENVPS Dist-GPITVL Prodn-KRMATV

Other People At School C 7 MIN
16MM FILM OPTICAL SOUND
Introduces beginning school children to the mysterious grown-ups they meet at school, including the principal, the office and custodial staff and the cafeteria personnel.
From The Project Bilingual Series.
LC NO. 75-703524
Prod-SANISD Dist-SUTHLA 1975

Other People's Garbage C 59 MIN
16MM FILM OPTICAL SOUND
Reviews the findings of archaeologists working at three sites in the United States and explains what their findings reveal about day-to-day life in America's recent past.
From The Odyssey Series.
LC NO. 81-700371
Prod-PBA Dist-DOCEDR 1980

Other People's Garbage C 59 MIN
3/4 OR 1/2 INCH VIDEO CASSETTE
Reviews the findings of archaeologists working at three sites in the United States and explains what their findings reveal about day-to-day life in America's recent past.
From The Odyssey Series.
LC NO. 81-707484
Prod-PBA Dist-PBS 1980

Other Pieces Of The Puzzle C 30 MIN
2 INCH VIDEOTAPE T
See series title for descriptive statement.
From The Solutions In Communications Series.
Prod-SCCOE Dist-SCCOE

Other Planets - No Place Like Earth C 30 MIN
16MM FILM, 3/4 OR 1/2 IN VIDEO
Points out the similarities and differences between Earth and other planets. Takes a simulated 'grand tour' of the solar system.
From The Life Around Us Series.
LC NO. 79-707840
Prod-TIMLIF Dist-TIMLIF

Other Planets - No Place Like Earth (Spanish) C 30 MIN
16MM FILM OPTICAL SOUND
Summarizes the knowledge that scientists have gathered about the planets. Covers topics such as the seasonal changes on Mars, the atmosphere of Venus, the motion of Jupiter, the rings of Saturn and the discoveries of Neptune and Pluto.
From The Life Around Us (Spanish) Series.
LC NO. 78-700062
Prod-TIMLIF Dist-TIMLIF 1971

Other Poland, The C 40 MIN
16MM FILM, 3/4 OR 1/2 IN VIDEO J-C A
Portrays the steam engines called 'chukchas', which are still the main means of transport in Poland from one village to another. Shows old soldiers on a train north of Warsaw and a wedding in a 500 year old church.
Prod-BBCTV Dist-FI 1983

Other Realities Tested C
3/4 INCH VIDEO CASSETTE
Describes growth and development of a child from 40 to 41 months.
From The Growth And Development - A Chronicle Of Four Children Series. Series 9
Prod-JUETHO Dist-LIP

Other Realities Tested - Gregory, 40 Months C 6 MIN
16MM FILM OPTICAL SOUND
See series title for descriptive statement.
From The Growth And Development - A Chronicle Of Four Children Series. Series 9
LC NO. 78-700690
Prod-JUETHO Dist-LIP Prodn-CONCOM 1976

Other Realities Tested - Joseph, 41 Months C 6 MIN
16MM FILM OPTICAL SOUND
See series title for descriptive statement.
From The Growth And Development - A Chronicle Of Four Children Series. Series 9
LC NO. 78-700690
Prod-JUETHO Dist-LIP Prodn-CONCOM 1976

Other Realities Tested - Melissa, 40 Months C 6 MIN
16MM FILM OPTICAL SOUND
See series title for descriptive statement.
From The Growth And Development - A Chronicle Of Four Children Series. Series 9
LC NO. 78-700690
Prod-JUETHO Dist-LIP Prodn-CONCOM 1976

Other Realities Tested - Terra, 41 Months C 6 MIN
16MM FILM OPTICAL SOUND
See series title for descriptive statement.
From The Growth And Development - A Chronicle Of Four Children Series. Series 9
LC NO. 78-700690
Prod-JUETHO Dist-LIP Prodn-CONCOM 1976

Other Side Of Rape, The C 30 MIN
3/4 OR 1/2 INCH VIDEO CASSETTE PRO
Increases awareness of the many difficulties faced by the victims of rape.
Prod-HSCIC Dist-HSCIC 1982

Other Side Of The Canvas, The C 29 MIN
2 INCH VIDEOTAPE
See series title for descriptive statement.
From The Museum Open House Series.
Prod-WGBHTV Dist-PUBTEL

Other Side Of The Desk, The C 25 MIN
3/4 OR 1/2 INCH VIDEO CASSETTE
See series title for descriptive statement.
From The Desk Set II Series.
Prod-ERF Dist-DELTAK

Other Side Of The Desk, The C 30 MIN
3/4 OR 1/2 INCH VIDEO CASSETTE H A
Features a secretary promoted to supervisor, who knows her subordinates and communicates constructively with them, suggests to unsuccessful job applicants how to improve their prospects through promptness, organization and discretion and asks her staff for suggestions while delegating responsibilities appropriately. Emphasizes importance of clear communication.
From The Desk Set II Series.
Prod-ERESI Dist-AITECH

Other Side Of The Mountain, The B 30 MIN
16MM FILM OPTICAL SOUND I-C A
Relays the spirit of adventure in the exploration and conquest of the American West.
From The Glory Trail Series.
LC NO. FIA66-1237
Prod-NET Dist-IU 1965

Other Side Of The Mountain, The - A Story Of Plant Zonation C 15 MIN
3/4 OR 1/2 INCH VIDEO CASSETTE
Illustrates the changes in climate and plant communities that occur with changes in altitude. Discusses six general zones, from desert to alpine tundra.
Prod-CBSC Dist-CBSC

Other Side Of The Mountains, The C 16 MIN
3/4 OR 1/2 INCH VIDEO CASSETTE
Describes the study for base-line information on the wildlife and environment of the north slope in Alaska.
Prod-HBS Dist-IVCH

Other Side Of The River, The C 29 MIN
16MM FILM, 3/4 OR 1/2 IN VIDEO J-C A
Discusses floods, showing the causes, the terrors of a flood in action, and the emotional, social and economic impact associated with such a disaster.
Prod-COUKLA Dist-MCFI 1975

Other Side Of The River, The (Captioned) C 29 MIN
16MM FILM, 3/4 OR 1/2 IN VIDEO J-C A
Discusses floods, showing the causes and terrors of a flood in action, and the emotional, social and economic impact associated with such a disaster.
Prod-COUKLA Dist-MCFI 1975

Other Side, The B 10 MIN
16MM FILM OPTICAL SOUND H
Presents a commentary without words on the tragedy of conformity in which men and women ruled by a hidden fascist dictatorship are forced to sidestep down the sidewalk in a single, shoulder-to-shoulder line, bodies facing the buildings, hands sliding along the walls.
LC NO. 72-701714
Prod-WUYTS Dist-VIEWFI 1972

Other Side, The C 30 MIN
3/4 OR 1/2 INCH VIDEO CASSETTE
Reports on some of the contrasts and complexities of the Soviet Union.
Prod-WCCOTV Dist-WCCOTV 1982

Other Six Days, The C 30 MIN
16MM FILM OPTICAL SOUND J-H T R
Compares the values of the Church with the values of the business world, discussing whether or not a Christian can be both a good churchman and businessman wiouout conflict.
LC NO. FIA66-1140
Prod-FAMF Dist-FAMF 1965

Other Treatment Modalities C 18 MIN
3/4 OR 1/2 INCH VIDEO CASSETTE PRO
Explains somatic therapies and hypnotherapy.
From The Psychiatry Learning System, Pt 2 - Disorders Series.
Prod-HSCIC Dist-HSCIC 1982

Other Uses For Ceramics C 28 MIN
2 INCH VIDEOTAPE
Features Mrs Peterson describing certain ceramic processes for her classroom at the University of Southern California. Demonstrates various uses for ceramics.
From The Wheels, Kilns And Clay Series.
Prod-USC Dist-PUBTEL

Other Voices B 90 MIN
16MM FILM OPTICAL SOUND
Explores the lives of five young mental patients. Follows their lives together in a family setting in the homes of married staff therapists and as they undergo treatment called reality confrontation.
Prod-NATTAL Dist-NATTAL

Other Way, The C 50 MIN
16MM FILM, 3/4 OR 1/2 IN VIDEO C A
Suggests that a more appropriate use of technology could make people self-sufficient and make work an enjoyable experience. Gives examples from tractors to home-made bread.
Prod-BBCTV Dist-FI 1975

Other World, The C 19 MIN
16MM FILM, 3/4 OR 1/2 IN VIDEO I-C A
Demonstrates that in a balanced ecology the materials of life and death are constantly recycled by showing the biological ladder from microscopic plants and animals to the otter.
Prod-NFBC Dist-MOKIN 1976

Other World, The (Captioned) C 19 MIN
3/4 OR 1/2 INCH VIDEO CASSETTE I-C A
Demonstrates that in a balanced ecology the materials of life and death are constantly recycled by showing the biological ladder from microscopic plants and animals to the otter.
Prod-NFBC Dist-MOKIN 1976

Other 23 Hours, The B 15 MIN
16MM FILM OPTICAL SOUND
Documents a workshop held for non-medical personnel who work with mental patients. Shows them discussing problems and receiving advice on how to serve the patients better.
LC NO. 74-705059
Prod-UMISMC Dist-UMISS Prodn-UMISS 1967

Others C 13 MIN
16MM FILM, 3/4 OR 1/2 IN VIDEO I-J
Presents a story about an act of vandalism.
Prod-WOMBAT Dist-WOMBAT

Othon (English) C 88 MIN
16MM FILM OPTICAL SOUND
An English subtitle version of the German language film. Bases its story on the drama by Corneille. juxtaposes the requirements of a man's drive for power with those of his love affair with a woman. Takes place in ancient settings with modern noises in the background.
Prod-NYFLMS Dist-NYFLMS 1969

Othon (French) C 88 MIN
16MM FILM OPTICAL SOUND
A French subtitle version of the German language film. Bases its story on the drama by Corneille. Juxtaposes the requirements of a man's drive for power with those of his love affair with a woman. Takes place in ancient settings with modern noises in the background.
Prod-NYFLMS Dist-NYFLMS 1969

Otoneurological Examination For Vestibular Cerebellar Function, The C 25 MIN
3/4 OR 1/2 INCH VIDEO CASSETTE PRO
Illustrates various office procedures for establishing a patient's degree of vestibular-cerebellar function.
Prod-WFP Dist-WFP

Otoplasty - A Tribute To Dr Becker C 24 MIN
16MM FILM OPTICAL SOUND PRO
Illustrates the dissecting techniques used by Dr Oscar J Becker and outlines the mattress suture technique.
Prod-SCITIF Dist-SCITIF 1971

Otorhinolaryngological Hemorrhage C 28 MIN
16MM FILM OPTICAL SOUND
Points out nosebleeding is a symptom very commonly encountered in daily clinical activities. Shows the capillary structures and function at the nasal area, the mechanism of nosebleeding, especially cases of epistaxis, the methods of the hematrogic and blook chemical examinations, the effects of local hemostatic agents by microscopy and treatment of bleeding in surgical operation.
Prod-UNIJAP Dist-UNIJAP 1971

Otosclerosis - The Fenestration And Stapes Eras C 58 MIN
3/4 OR 1/2 INCH VIDEO CASSETTE PRO
Presents recollections of the historical aspects and early days of otosclerosis surgery.
Prod-HOUSEI Dist-HOUSEI

Otosclerosis Surgery C 50 MIN
3/4 OR 1/2 INCH VIDEO CASSETTE PRO
Presents a review of all aspects of otosclerotic surgery, including the early history of stapes surgery, a step-by- step presentation of technique, various footplate problems, causes of sensorineural hearing impairment following stapes surgery, the incus replacement prosthesis procedure, fistula problems, and dizziness.
Prod-HOUSEI Dist-HOUSEI

Otosclerosis Surgery - The Early Years C 55 MIN
3/4 OR 1/2 INCH VIDEO CASSETTE PRO
Presents the recollections of Drs House and Shambaugh about their early experience in otosclerosis surgery.
Prod-HOUSEI Dist-HOUSEI

Otosclerosis Surgery - The Stapes Era C 79 MIN
3/4 OR 1/2 INCH VIDEO CASSETTE PRO
Presents recollections about the Lempert era and the early years of stapes surgery.
Prod-HOUSEI Dist-HOUSEI

Otoscope C 15 MIN
3/4 INCH VIDEO CASSETTE PRO
Discusses various types of otoscopes and tells how to use and maintain each piece of equipment.
From The Instruments Of Physical Assessment Series.
LC NO. 80-707626
Prod-SUNYSB Dist-LIP 1980

Ottawa - Canada's Capital C 11 MIN
16MM FILM OPTICAL SOUND
Pictures different parts of Ottawa. Views the Parliament and describes ceremonies associated with the Parliament building.
LC NO. FIA68-1222
Prod-MORLAT Dist-MORLAT 1967

Ottawa Parklands C 10 MIN
16MM FILM OPTICAL SOUND
Presents a portrait of the city of Ottawa in the splendor of springtime finery. Depicts the tulips, the city parks and their brilliant flower beds, the scenic waterways and an open-air concert by the Royal Canadian Mounted Police Band.
Prod-CTFL Dist-CTFL

Ottawa 76 C 5 MIN
16MM FILM OPTICAL SOUND
Presents computer animation of the owl logo of the first international animated film festival held in North America, Ottawa 76.
LC NO. 77-700233
Prod-CFI Dist-CFI 1976

Otters, Clowns Of The Sea C 14 MIN
16MM FILM, 3/4 OR 1/2 IN VIDEO J-H
Presents the Southern sea otter in a variety of moods. Shows the mothers' devoted care and feeding of the pups and their playful antics as they are growing up and begin their own constant search for food. Explains that as a protected species, it is now flourishing in colonies along the California coast.
Prod-CHANGW Dist-AIMS 1973

Otto - A Study In Abnormal Psychology C 27 MIN
16MM FILM, 3/4 OR 1/2 IN VIDEO C
Presents Otto as a middle-aged man suffering from real and imagined pressures at home and at work. Shows how he feels overburdened and insecure in his job as senior book editor. Observes him struggling to relate calmly to his secretary, his assistant and his boss. Shows also how, at home, his wife complains that he never listens to her and never tells her about his feelings. Watches Otto suffering from insomnia and becoming increasingly withdrawn and anxious.
From The Otto Series.
LC NO. 80-706081
Prod-IU Dist-IU 1976

Otto - The Behavioral Perspective C 26 MIN
16MM FILM, 3/4 OR 1/2 IN VIDEO C
Presents Dr John Gottman of Indiana University interpreting the Otto case study film from the behavioral perspective. Tells how he sees Otto coping with catastrophic expectations by trying to be all things to all people and how he does not see people as resources to help him cope with stress. Discusses how, in terms of treatment, Dr Gottman would align himself with Otto's goals and Otto's perception of things and how he believes Otto would benefit from social skills training both in terms of his work and his marriage.
From The Otto Series.
LC NO. 80-706083
Prod-IU Dist-IU 1976

Otto - The Phenomenological Perspective C 25 MIN
16MM FILM, 3/4 OR 1/2 IN VIDEO C
Presents Dr Gary Stollak of Michigan State University interpreting the Otto case study film from the phenomenological perspective. Tells how he does not believe that Otto necessarily has a problem and how he feels that Otto is very lonely because neither his wife nor his co-workers share his particular sense of values. Discusses how Dr Stollak would not consider Otto as a patient but rather as a fellow human being and how his encounters with Otto would not focus on producing changes but on giving him a sense of togetherness.
From The Otto Series.
LC NO. 80-706084
Prod-IU Dist-IU 1976

Otto - The Psychoanalytic Perspective C 28 MIN
16MM FILM, 3/4 OR 1/2 IN VIDEO C
Presents Dr Bruce Denner of Governors State University, Illinois, interpreting the Otto case study film from the psychoanalytic perspective. Tells how he believes that Otto is not coping with getting old and how he sees Otto moving away from mature reactions, over-reacting and using defense mechanisms. Discusses how, according to Dr Denner, the reality principle has broken down for Otto and how, as Otto's analyst, Dr Denner would act as a transfer figure, taking on properties of early figures in Otto's life so Otto could work out his early conflicts.
From The Otto Series.
LC NO. 80-706082
Prod-IU Dist-IU 1976

Otto - The Social Perspective C 26 MIN
16MM FILM, 3/4 OR 1/2 IN VIDEO C
Presents Dr Richard Price of the University of Michigan interpreting the Otto case study film from the social perspective. States that the world is making unreasonable demands on Otto and that he does not believe that anything inside of Otto is causing his breakdown. Tells that, according to Dr Price, Otto is being cast in the role of mental patient by the people around him. Discusses how Dr Price would try to help Otto by teaching him to appreciate the nature of the external events around him.
From The Otto Series.
LC NO. 80-706085
Prod-IU Dist-IU 1976

Otto - Zoo Gorilla C 58 MIN
16MM FILM, 3/4 OR 1/2 IN VIDEO I A
Portrays Otto, a 400 pound gorilla resident of Chicago's Lincoln Park Zoo. Discusses the period when the apes were moved from the cramped cages of the past into a new habitat that simulates the jungle.
Prod-LINCPK Dist-FI 1978

Otto Asks A Riddle C 5 MIN
16MM FILM OPTICAL SOUND K-P
Otto the auto wants everyone to obey school safety patrols. He figures out an unusual method to accomplish this.
From The Otto The Auto Series.
Prod-AAAFTS Dist-AAAFTS 1958

Otto Goes Ice Skating C 4 MIN
16MM FILM OPTICAL SOUND K-I
Points out why a driver might not see a child pedestrian even though the child would appear to be in plain sight.
From The Otto The Auto Series.
Prod-AAAFTS Dist-AAAFTS 1971

Otto Meets A Puppet C 5 MIN
16MM FILM OPTICAL SOUND K-P
Otto the auto is concerned that everyone 'LOOK ALL WAYS BEFORE CROSSING.' He effectively uses a puppet show to get across the message.
From The Otto The Auto Series.
Prod-AAAFTS Dist-AAAFTS 1958

Otto Messmer And Felix The Cat C 25 MIN
16MM FILM, 3/4 OR 1/2 IN VIDEO J-C T
Creates a portrait of the first cartoon star, Felix the Cat, and his shy, unknown creator, Otto Messmer. Includes excerpts from five vintage Felix the Cat shorts.
LC NO. 81-706791
Prod-CANEJ Dist-PHENIX 1978

Otto The Auto–A Series
P-I
Prod-AAAFTS Dist-AAAFTS

Billy's New Tricycle	5 MIN
Bright Yellow Raincoat, The	5 MIN
Horseplay	4 MIN
Inky And Blinky	5 MIN
Little White Line That Cried	5 MIN
Otto Asks A Riddle	5 MIN
Otto Goes Ice Skating	4 MIN
Otto Meets A Puppet	5 MIN
Peter The Pigeon	5 MIN
Secret Of The Push Buttons, The	6 MIN
Squeaky And His Playmates	5 MIN
Surprise For Otto, A	4 MIN
Timothy The Turtle	5 MIN
Tommy Tricycle	5 MIN
Two Sleeping Lions	5 MIN

Otto The Auto, Series A C 14 MIN
16MM FILM OPTICAL SOUND K-P
Presents three films entitled Two Sleeping Lions, Inky And Blinky and The Little White Line That Cried. Uses animation to illustrate traffic safety rules for pedestrians, including crossing streets at the corner instead of between parked cars, and the importance of wearing white at night.
LC NO. 72-701492
Prod-AAAFTS Dist-AAAFTS 1957

Otto The Auto, Series B C 14 MIN
16MM FILM OPTICAL SOUND K-I
Presents three films entitled The Bright Yellow Raincoat, Otto Meets A Puppet and Otto Asks A Riddle. Uses animation to illustrate pedestrian traffic safety rules for school areas, bad weather and crossing streets.
LC NO. 72-701493
Prod-AAAFTS Dist-AAAFTS 1958

Otto The Auto, Series C C 18 MIN
16MM FILM OPTICAL SOUND K-I
Presents four films entitled Squeaky And His Playmates, Billy's New Tricycle, Peter The Pigeon and Timothy The Turtle. Uses animation to illustrate safety rules for walking, playing and bike riding near traffic.
LC NO. 72-701494
Prod-AAAFTS Dist-AAAFTS 1959

Otto The Auto, Series D C 22 MIN
16MM FILM OPTICAL SOUND K-I
Presents four films entitled A Surprise For Otto, Otto Goes Ice Skating, Horseplay and The Secret Of Push Buttons. Uses animation to illustrate traffic safety rules for pedestrians.
LC NO. 78-711386
Prod-AAAFTS Dist-AAAFTS 1971

Otto–A Series
16MM FILM, 3/4 OR 1/2 IN VIDEO C
Presents the case study of Otto.
Prod-IU Dist-IU 1976

Otto - A Study In Abnormal Psychology	27 MIN
Otto - The Behavioral Perspective	26 MIN
Otto - The Phenomenological Perspective	25 MIN
Otto - The Psychoanalytic Perspective	28 MIN
Otto - The Social Perspective	26 MIN

Otto, Zoo Gorilla C 58 MIN
16MM FILM, 3/4 OR 1/2 IN VIDEO I-H
Takes a behind-the-scenes look at the Lincoln Park Zoo in Chicago. Focuses on the transfer of the great apes to new quarters, telling how the process afforded scientists an opportunity to gather data on the apes.
LC NO. 79-706039
Prod-LINCPK Dist-FI 1978

Ottorino Respighi - A Dream Of Italy C 75 MIN
3/4 OR 1/2 INCH VIDEO CASSETTE
Presents the work of composer Ottorino Respighi. Examines the influence of Italy on his musical vision.
Prod-FOTH Dist-FOTH

Ou Va-t-il, D'ou Vient-Il B 13 MIN
16MM FILM OPTICAL SOUND I-H
See series title for descriptive statement.
From The Les Francaise Chez Vous Series.
Prod-PEREN Dist-CHLTN 1967

Ounce Of Cure, An C 26 MIN
16MM FILM, 3/4 OR 1/2 IN VIDEO H-C A
Tells the story of a woman who looks back with humor and irony as she recalls her first experience with love and heartbreak in the 1950's. Her steadfast friend sees her through an impulsive experiment with alcohol from which she emerges with a new appreciation for life's absurdities. From the story by Alice Munro.
Prod-ATLAF Dist-BCNFL Prodn-CANBC 1984

Ounce Of Prevention C 25 MIN
16MM FILM OPTICAL SOUND H-C A
Demonstrates ways and means of preventing loss from improper care and handling of livestock.
LC NO. FIE52-2021
Prod-SEARSF Dist-VENARD 1946

Ounce Of Prevention C 30 MIN
3/4 OR 1/2 INCH VIDEO CASSETTE T
See series title for descriptive statement.
From The Dealing In Discipline Series.
Prod-UKY Dist-GPITVL 1980

Ounce Of Prevention–A Series

Presents information on child health and parenting.
Prod-CFDC Dist-CFDC

Accidents And Emergencies	030 MIN
Allergies - Nothing To Sneeze At	030 MIN
Building Love	030 MIN
Building More Love	030 MIN
Catch As Catch Can - I	030 MIN
Catch As Catch Can - II	030 MIN
Decisions! Decisions! Before Your Baby Is Born	030 MIN
Eyes Have It, The	030 MIN
First Line Of Defense - The Parent	030 MIN
Opposite Of Love, The	030 MIN
Thinking Ahead	030 MIN
Your Skin Problem - Let's Face It	030 MIN

Ounce Of Prevention, An C 27 MIN
16MM FILM OPTICAL SOUND
Presents interviews with authorities on alcoholism in order to highlight the problem. Details methods of rehabilitation tried in Saskatchewan in the mid-1970's.
LC NO. 77-702602
Prod-SASKDH Dist-SASKDH Prodn-HARVP 1976

Ounce Of Prevention, An C
3/4 OR 1/2 INCH VIDEO CASSETTE
Features Bugs Bunny and Daffy Duck who demonstrate practical ways to prevent burn injuries at home.
Prod-NFPA Dist-NFPA

Ounce Of Prevention, An C 14 MIN
16MM FILM, 3/4 OR 1/2 IN VIDEO P-I
Tells how the kids help their friend Lucius with his drinking problem.
From The Learning Values With Fat Albert Series.
Prod-FLMTON Dist-CRMP 1977

Ounce Of Prevention, An C 26 MIN
16MM FILM, 3/4 OR 1/2 IN VIDEO J-C A
Sheds light on such problems as why people drink alcohol, what does excessive drinking do to the body and the cost of alcohol abuse to alcoholics, their families, industry and government.
Prod-HARVP Dist-MTI

Ounce Of Prevention, An C 30 MIN
3/4 OR 1/2 INCH VIDEO CASSETTE C A
See series title for descriptive statement.
From The Loosening The Grip Series.
Prod-UMA Dist-GPITVL 1980

Ounces Of Prevention C 16 MIN
16MM FILM OPTICAL SOUND H A
Shows the effectiveness of new fuel cell systems, which reduce the possibility of fire, and are used in race cars and military aircraft.
LC NO. 74-701723
Prod-FTARC Dist-FTARC 1968

Our Aching Backs C 14 MIN
16MM FILM OPTICAL SOUND H-C A
Combines limited animation, live action, artwork, and still photography to present information on back safety, with major emphasis on home hazards.
LC NO. 76-706078
Prod-SANDIA Dist-SANDIA 1969

Our Aching Backs C 18 MIN
16MM FILM, 3/4 OR 1/2 IN VIDEO
Presents information on back safety in animation, with emphasis on home hazards. Includes humor, stylized sets and mod dress.
Prod-USAEC Dist-USNAC

Our American Crossroads C 15 MIN
16MM FILM OPTICAL SOUND J-H A
Shows what the typical little crossroads community was like back at the turn of the century and how it was changed by the increasing popularity of the automobile.
Prod-GM Dist-GM 1968

Our American Flag C 8 MIN
16MM FILM, 3/4 OR 1/2 IN VIDEO P-I
John Forsythe narrates what the American flag represents and the role of each person as a citizen of his community and his country.
From The American Values For Elementary Series.
Prod-EVANSA Dist-AIMS 1971

Our Animal Neighbors (2nd Ed Rev) C 11 MIN
16MM FILM, 3/4 OR 1/2 IN VIDEO P-I
Presents a remarkable rabbit that takes Sherry and Jason on a delightful tour. Shows squirrels, chipmunks, an opossum with babies on her back, a rabbit and her babies, a raccoon, mice, a shrew that has trouble catching a meal, a mole and some bats.
Prod-CORF Dist-CORF 1977

Our Art Class Makes A Film - We Travel With Marco Polo C 14 MIN
16MM FILM, 3/4 OR 1/2 IN VIDEO
Follows each step in the production of a 16mm film on the travels of Marco Polo made by seventh graders. Shows the motion picture the students made.
Prod-SIGMA Dist-FLMFR

Our Birth Film - Prepared Childbirth - The Human Drama Of A Woman And Man In A Delivery... C 26 MIN
16MM FILM OPTICAL SOUND H-C A
Shows the emotional interactions of a woman and a man sharing the experience of natural childbirth in the delivery room.
LC NO. 75-700011
Prod-MIFE Dist-MIFE 1973

Our Bodies, Ourselves C 29 MIN
3/4 INCH VIDEO CASSETTE
Interviews the authors of the women's health book Our Bodies, Ourselves.
From The Woman Series.
Prod-WNEDTV Dist-PUBTEL

Our Bread Basket C 15 MIN
3/4 OR 1/2 INCH VIDEO CASSETTE I
Provides an insight into modern-day wheat farming on both irrigated and dry land in the Great Plains. Shows cultivating the soil, planting seed, harvesting the kernels and marketing the crop. Highlights the history of the area by showing a sod house and shed, prairie grass, a one-room school, a windmill and other aspects of prairie life.
From The American Legacy Series. Program 6
LC NO. 83-706663
Prod-KRMATV Dist-AITECH 1983

Our Challenging Future C 24 MIN
16MM FILM OPTICAL SOUND
Points out General Mills' accomplishments and contributions toward a better world and emphasizes the need for all Americans to meet aggressively today the challenge of the future.
Prod-GEMILL Dist-GEMILL

Our Changing Cities - Can They Be Saved C 16 MIN
16MM FILM, 3/4 OR 1/2 IN VIDEO I-J
Presents a short history of the development of cities in the U S. Examines the social forces and movements which have shaped modern cities. Describes life in the city, past and present and the problems which have developed.
Prod-EBEC Dist-EBEC 1972

Our Changing Community—A Series
P-I
Compares the present with the past and examines the concept of change from many viewpoints. Suggests a variety of related activities designed to enrich the experiences of children.
Prod-VITA Dist-GPITVL

Availability Of Natural Resources 15 MIN
Demands Of Industry, The 15 MIN
Freeways 15 MIN
Housing 15 MIN
In Community Government 15 MIN
In Community Service 15 MIN
In The Family 15 MIN
In The School 15 MIN
Influence Of Land Forms, The 15 MIN
Manufacturing And Industry 15 MIN
Needs Of Defense, The 15 MIN
New Answers For Basic Needs Of Food And 15 MIN
New Developments In Communication 15 MIN
New Environments Of Sea And Space 15 MIN
New Meanings For Conservation 15 MIN
New Ways To Use The Land 15 MIN
Power 15 MIN
Problems Communities Face 15 MIN
Problems People Face 15 MIN
Redevelopment 15 MIN
Trains And Planes 15 MIN
Water 15 MIN
Web Of Transportation, The 15 MIN
What Is A Community 15 MIN
What Is Change 15 MIN
What's Next 15 MIN
When People Move 15 MIN
Where Have We Been 15 MIN

Our Changing Earth C 14 MIN
16MM FILM, 3/4 OR 1/2 IN VIDEO I-C
Points out changes in land masses through maps depicting different geologic periods. Shows geologists unearthing fossils and working in laboratories to determine the ages of rocks and fossils.
Prod-FA Dist-PHENIX 1961

Our Changing Earth (Spanish) C 14 MIN
16MM FILM, 3/4 OR 1/2 IN VIDEO I-C
Points out changes in land masses through maps depicting different geologic periods. Shows geologists unearthing fossils and working in laboratories to determine the ages of rocks and fossils.
Prod-FA Dist-PHENIX 1961

Our Changing Shores C 21 MIN
16MM FILM OPTICAL SOUND J-C
Pictures how wind, water, ice and other natural phenomena affect the shore line of the Great Lakes area.
Prod-OSUMPD Dist-OSUMPD 1958

Our Changing Skylines - Mirror Of The World C 22 MIN
16MM FILM OPTICAL SOUND H-C A
Shows the transition in America from traditional designs in architecture and art to a unique, modern style.
LC NO. 73-705632
Prod-ALEF Dist-ALEF 1970

Our Changing Way Of Life - Cattleman - A Rancher's Story (2nd Ed) C 22 MIN
16MM FILM, 3/4 OR 1/2 IN VIDEO I-J
Shows activities on a cattle ranch during the four seasons, leading to the annual shipment of livestock to market. Compares old and new methods of operation, showing how technology is affecting cattle industries.
Prod-EBF Dist-EBEC 1964

Our Changing Way Of Life - Cattleman - A Rancher's Story (2nd Ed) (Spanish) C 22 MIN
16MM FILM, 3/4 OR 1/2 IN VIDEO I-J
Shows activities on a cattle ranch during the four seasons, leading to the annual shipment of livestock to market. Compares old and new methods of operation, showing how technology is affecting cattle industries.
Prod-EBF Dist-EBEC 1964

Our Changing Way Of Life - The Cotton Farmer C 14 MIN
16MM FILM, 3/4 OR 1/2 IN VIDEO I-J
Reveals evidence of increasing mechanization in the cotton industry and its effects on the people and the economy. Illustrates cotton production, from the seed to the processing of cotton into finished cloth.
Prod-EBEC Dist-EBEC

Our Changing Way Of Life - The Dairy Farmer C 17 MIN
16MM FILM, 3/4 OR 1/2 IN VIDEO I-J
Presents the contrasting views of two dairy farmers on problems associated with rising farm labor costs. Examines the changing way of life in the Midwest dairy region and discusses the role of automation in the modern dairy community.
Prod-EBF Dist-EBEC 1965

Our Changing Way Of Life - The Dairy Farmer (Spanish) C 17 MIN
16MM FILM, 3/4 OR 1/2 IN VIDEO I-J
Presents the contrasting views of two dairy farmers on problems associated with rising farm labor costs. Examines the changing way of life in the Midwest dairy region and discusses the role of automation in the modern dairy community.
Prod-EBF Dist-EBEC 1965

Our Choice, Our Challenge C 26 MIN
16MM FILM OPTICAL SOUND
Shows enlisted Navy women as they participate in some of the nontraditional jobs open to women.
LC NO. 80-700515
Prod-USN Dist-USNAC Prodn-USNPC 1979

Our Cities - Our Right C 26 MIN
16MM FILM OPTICAL SOUND H-C A
Uses the example of Paris in order to show how high-rise buildings and other structures are making life and the urban environment unlivable for the average citizen.
LC NO. 76-702149
Prod-BERTUC Dist-NYFLMS 1975

Our City Government X 10 MIN
16MM FILM, 3/4 OR 1/2 IN VIDEO A
Views the urban community and its government. Considers how a city government provides services and makes and enforces laws. A city councilman cites the functions of a city council, mayor or city manager and courts, and he reviews the citizen's role.
Prod-WAT Dist-PHENIX 1965

Our Class Explores The Moon C 11 MIN
16MM FILM, 3/4 OR 1/2 IN VIDEO P
Provides some basic imformation about the moon's surface and about travelling to the moon, in the context of a classroom project.
Prod-CORF Dist-CORF 1968

Our Clothes C 17 MIN
16MM FILM, 3/4 OR 1/2 IN VIDEO P-I
Examines the raw materials and the manufacturing process used to make clothes.
LC NO. 83-706707
Prod-BHA Dist-IFB 1978

Our Clothes (Captioned) C 17 MIN
16MM FILM, 3/4 OR 1/2 IN VIDEO P-I
Examines the raw materials and the manufacturing process used to make clothes. Shows the sources of leather, wool, cotton, rubber and synthetic fiber.
Prod-BHA Dist-IFB 1978

Our Community Services X 12 MIN
16MM FILM, 3/4 OR 1/2 IN VIDEO P
Uses a story about a boy who is hit by a motorcycle to demonstrate many public services, such as police and fire departments. Discusses how these services are paid for by everyone through taxes.
Prod-EBEC Dist-EBEC 1969

Our Community USA C 48 MIN
16MM FILM OPTICAL SOUND
Illustrates the wide range of programs in which labor groups are now engaged.
Prod-AFLCIO Dist-AFLCIO

Our Constitution B 13 MIN
16MM FILM OPTICAL SOUND I-C A
Explains the Indian constitution and how liberty, equality and justice are ensured for all Indians.
Prod-INDIA Dist-NEDINF

Our Country, Too B 30 MIN
16MM FILM OPTICAL SOUND H-C A
Examines the values and attitudes of the American Negro. Shows such things as an African rite in Harlem, a Negro debutante ball, a Negro radio station, a Negro newspaper and the New York experimental social welfare group, Haryou-act. Features Ossie Davis.
From The History Of The Negro People Series.
LC NO. FIA68-1584
Prod-NET Dist-IU 1965

Our Country's Birthday C 15 MIN
3/4 OR 1/2 INCH VIDEO CASSETTE P
Presents an overview of the events that preceded the signing of the Declaration of Independence.
From The Stories Of America Series.
Prod-OHSDE Dist-AITECH Prodn-WVIZTV 1976

Our Country's Flag C 10 MIN
16MM FILM, 3/4 OR 1/2 IN VIDEO P-H
Presents the story of the American flag, its origin and development. Illustrates this story by using prints, paintings, manuscripts and animated maps plus the actual flags themselves.
Prod-WALLAL Dist-LUF 1971

Our Country's Flag (2nd Ed) C 11 MIN
16MM FILM, 3/4 OR 1/2 IN VIDEO P-J
Describes the new American flag of fifty stars and thirteen stripes and explains its symbolism. Discusses why the flag should be respected and reviews the rules of respect to the flag. Explains the meaning of the 'PLEDGE OF ALLEGIANCE' in terms of everyday activities.
Prod-CORF Dist-CORF 1960

Our Credo C 15 MIN
16MM FILM OPTICAL SOUND
Shows how a large corporation re-evaluates its moral responsibilities towards its employees and the community at large through a series of top-level meetings.
LC NO. 76-702863
Prod-JAJ Dist-JAJ Prodn-WSTGLF 1976

Our Crucial Deterrent C 28 MIN
16MM FILM, 3/4 OR 1/2 IN VIDEO
Gives a historical review of the fleet ballistic missile weapon system.
LC NO. 81-707721
Prod-USN Dist-USNAC 1973

Our Cultural Heritage C 10 MIN
16MM FILM OPTICAL SOUND J-H
Raises essential questions about the value of national cultural heritages in relation to current problems of population growth and poverty. Looks at the international problems of preserving cultural monuments. Shows a variety of cultural landmarks and the threat to them from tourism, industrial pollution and other modern developments as they become more familiar and more accessible.
From The Problems Of World Order Series.
LC NO. 73-703428
Prod-VISNEW Dist-AGAPR 1972

Our Daily Bread B 71 MIN
16MM FILM OPTICAL SOUND
Looks at life on a subsistence farm during the Depression. Tells how the men and women attempt to defeat the drought by digging a two-mile irrigation ditch. Directed by King Vidor.
Prod-UNKNWN Dist-REELIM 1934

Our Disintegrating Public Schools C 30 MIN
3/4 OR 1/2 INCH VIDEO CASSETTE J-C A
Shows Albert Shanker, President of the American Federation of Teachers, and Maxine Greene of Columbia Teachers College discussing the plight of American public schools.
From The Moral Values In Contemporary Society Series.
Prod-AMHUMA Dist-AMHUMA

Our Dog Show C 15 MIN
16MM FILM OPTICAL SOUND P
A family attends a large dog show and the children decide to have a dog show of their own. Good sportsmanship and desirable social attitudes are illustrated.
Prod-JHP Dist-MLA 1958

Our Dynamic Earth C 23 MIN
16MM FILM, 3/4 OR 1/2 IN VIDEO H-C A
Examines information about continental drift gathered from deep sea research.
LC NO. 80-706268
Prod-NGS Dist-NGS 1979

Our Economic World C 20 MIN
2 INCH VIDEOTAPE J-H
Discusses the concept of scarcity and shows that scarcity stems from the conflict between the unlimited wants of men and the scarce resources of our world.
From The Our World Of Economics Series.
Prod-MPATI Dist-GPITVL

Our Endangered Wildlife C 51 MIN
16MM FILM, 3/4 OR 1/2 IN VIDEO J A
Describes those species of wildlife which are becoming extinct. Discusses the present-day conservation methods applied by various agencies in the United States.
Prod-NBC Dist-MGHT 1968

Our Endangered Wildlife, Pt 1 C 25 MIN
16MM FILM, 3/4 OR 1/2 IN VIDEO J A
Describes those species of wildlife which are becoming extinct. Discusses the present-day conservation methods applied by various agencies in the United States.
Prod-NBC Dist-MGHT 1968

Our Endangered Wildlife, Pt 2 C 26 MIN
16MM FILM, 3/4 OR 1/2 IN VIDEO J A
Describes those species of wildlife which are becoming extinct. Discusses the present-day conservation methods applied by various agencies in the United States.
Prod-NBC Dist-MGHT 1968

Our Environment - Everybody's Business C 14 MIN
16MM FILM, 3/4 OR 1/2 IN VIDEO J-C A
Shows how citizen concern about the environment has changed to citizen action.
Prod-NYSTAL Dist-CUNIV 1972

Our Fair Lady C 12 MIN
16MM FILM OPTICAL SOUND
Describes the different uses of a new home appliance, the kitch-

en center. Shows Judy making new friends and amazing her neighbors with her skill at preparing foods, the climax of the fun being a food contest.
Prod-OSTER Dist-MTP

Our Family Album - Nuestro Album De La Familia C 7 MIN
16MM FILM, 3/4 OR 1/2 IN VIDEO P-I
Discusses family introduction via photographs the children take.
From The Bilingual Film Series, Module 1 - Let's Get Ready Series.
Prod-BRNTNO Dist-CAROUF 1973

Our Family Works Together (2nd Ed) C 11 MIN
16MM FILM, 3/4 OR 1/2 IN VIDEO P
Tells the story of two children whose mother returns to school. Shows how they discover that there's more time left for play when everyone pitches in to do chores.
Prod-CORF Dist-CORF 1978

Our Father C 10 MIN
16MM FILM OPTICAL SOUND
Uses three vignettes to pose the fundamental question of having acknowledged God as our Father, do we have the right to choose our brothers.
LC NO. 73-713273
Prod-MARTC Dist-MARTC 1970

Our Federal Constitutional System B 20 MIN
16MM FILM OPTICAL SOUND H A
Dr Ivan Hinderaker, Professor of Political Science, UCLA, shows that the Federal government is the result of compromise and fear of centralized political power.
From The Government And Public Affairs Films Series.
Prod-RSC Dist-MLA 1960

Our Federal Constitutional System - Dr Ivan Hinderaker B 20 MIN
16MM FILM OPTICAL SOUND H-C
See series title for descriptive statement.
From The Building Political Leadership Series.
Prod-RSC Dist-MLA 1960

Our Federal District C 15 MIN
3/4 OR 1/2 INCH VIDEO CASSETTE I
Presents John E Rugg visiting significant locations in and around Washington, DC, to show its important role in the country's history and contemporary times. Uses archival photographs and a historical reenactment to help tell the story.
From The American Legacy Series. Program 1
LC NO. 83-706638
Prod-KRMATV Dist-AITECH 1983

Our Feelings Affect Each Other C 13 MIN
16MM FILM, 3/4 OR 1/2 IN VIDEO P
Shows how understanding our own feelings and how we show them helps us to understand and respect the feelings of others. Includes appropriate ways to show strong feelings, including anger, as well as suggestions for healthy expression of other feelings.
LC NO. 83-707215
Prod-HIGGIN Dist-HIGGIN 1984

Our First Plane Ride - Nuestro Primer Viaje En Avion C 10 MIN
16MM FILM, 3/4 OR 1/2 IN VIDEO P-I
Presents an airport tour and inspection of the Boeing 747. Explains a plane ride and airline careers.
From The Bilingual Film Series, Module 4 - Transportation And Community Workers Series.
Prod-BRNTNO Dist-CAROUF 1973

Our Food C 19 MIN
16MM FILM, 3/4 OR 1/2 IN VIDEO P-I
Traces the sources and processing of many familiar foods. Shows both the old-fashioned and modern ways of raising wheat, making bread, milking cows and separating cream.
LC NO. 83-706708
Prod-ALMBRG Dist-IFB

Our Friend Angela B 25 MIN
3/4 OR 1/2 INCH VIDEO CASSETTE
Highlights the controversial visit to the USSR of Angela Davis with friends Kendra and Franklin Alexander.
Prod-IHF Dist-IHF

Our Friend The Policeman C 11 MIN
16MM FILM, 3/4 OR 1/2 IN VIDEO P-I
Explains the daily work of a policeman, with emphasis on ways he helps people. Uses simple narration and a song superimposing words on appropriate scenes to build reading vocabulary.
Prod-ACI Dist-AIMS 1972

Our Friends In Historic Cities - Philadelphia, Pennsylvania, Washington, DC C 7 MIN
16MM FILM, 3/4 OR 1/2 IN VIDEO P-I
Describes the life of two people who live in the historic cities of Philadelphia and Washington, DC.
From The Friends In The City Series.
Prod-BOBC Dist-EBEC

Our Friends The Germans C 50 MIN
3/4 OR 1/2 INCH VIDEO CASSETTE H-C A
Presents correspondent Bill Moyers reporting on the people and government of West Germany. Focuses on topics that directly involve the United States, such as the rapidly growing German peace movement, relations with the Soviet bloc, the plight of Berlin and America's military presence in West Germany.
LC NO. 83-707216
Prod-CBSNEW Dist-MOKIN 1983

Our Future With The Third World B 30 MIN
16MM FILM OPTICAL SOUND H-C A
Dr Vincent Harding serves as moderator as James Foreman and Le Roi Jones discuss the relationship between Afro-Americans and other non-white oppressed people in the world. They surmise that the non-white people of the world are moving toward unity of purpose in the struggle against racist oppression and that Black Americans since they are really Africans, have a humanitarian outlook even toward Europeans.
From The Black History, Section 26 - What Is The Future Of Black America Series.
LC NO. 71-704132
Prod-WCBSTV Dist-HRAW 1969

Our Gang Follies Of 1936 B 18 MIN
16MM FILM OPTICAL SOUND
Shows that the neighborhood musical is going great until the boys are forced to don the girls' costumes for the finale. A Little Rascals film.
Prod-ROACH Dist-BHAWK 1936

Our Gang Follies Of 1938 B 21 MIN
16MM FILM OPTICAL SOUND
Features the Little Rascals in a take-off of the swing musicals of the 1930's.
Prod-ROACH Dist-BHAWK 1938

Our Glittering Playmates B 15 MIN
2 INCH VIDEOTAPE P
See series title for descriptive statement.
From The Sounds Like Magic Series.
Prod-MOEBA Dist-GPITVL Prodn-KYNETV

Our Goal Is Giving...Our Task Is Asking C 60 MIN
3/4 OR 1/2 INCH VIDEO CASSETTE
Discusses the financial dilemma of the American Red Cross. Puts forth a program which can be used to help provide staff and fund-raising teams with a realistic assessment of the problems they face and how they can succeed in their fund-raising efforts.
Prod-AMRC Dist-AMRC

Our Hidden National Product C 25 MIN
16MM FILM OPTICAL SOUND H-C A
Examines the problem of hazardous waste disposal. Offers possible solutions to the problem and shows various technologies available for treatment and disposal of hazardous materials. Discusses the social problems of siting waste treatment facilities.
LC NO. 80-700434
Prod-WMEAC Dist-DURRIN Prodn-DURRIN 1979

Our Hidden National Product C 25 MIN
16MM FILM, 3/4 OR 1/2 IN VIDEO
Shows hazardous waste facilities around the country where wastes are recycled, treated and disposed of in monitored landfills. Discusses regulations and the conflict between public demand for action vs public opposition to local sites.
Prod-USEPA Dist-USNAC

Our Hidden Wealth B 11 MIN
16MM FILM OPTICAL SOUND I-C A
Gives a detailed description of the discovery, examination and mining of minerals such as gold, bauxite, manganese, mica, coal and oil.
Prod-INDIA Dist-NEDINF

Our Hispano-American Friends C 10 MIN
16MM FILM, 3/4 OR 1/2 IN VIDEO P-I
Profiles three children who have Hispano-American ethnic heritages. Describes their lives in Miami, Florida, East Los Angeles and New York City.
Prod-BOBC Dist-EBEC

Our Hospitality B 72 MIN
16MM FILM SILENT J-C A
Stars Buster Keaton in a satire on the famed Hatfield-Mc Coy feud ending with a chase sequence involving a rescue at a waterfall.
Prod-MGM Dist-TWYMAN 1923

Our House Is Safe C 15 MIN
16MM FILM, 3/4 OR 1/2 IN VIDEO J-C A
Shows how to make a home safe. Tells which common plants are poisonous. Suggests how to avoid appliance shocks and slippery surfaces.
Prod-KLEINW Dist-KLEINW

Our Job In Japan B 18 MIN
16MM FILM, 3/4 OR 1/2 IN VIDEO
Focuses on the Japanese mind as perceived by the United States after World War II. Suggests there must be changes in the Japanese psyche before Japan can hope to rejoin the community of peaceful nations.
Prod-USAPS Dist-USNAC 1982

Our Korean Children C 29 MIN
16MM FILM OPTICAL SOUND A
Discusses the different life-style and cultural background from which the Korean child comes. Shows and describes the various aspects of a Korean child's life in a family environment and in a children's center. Explains that the child's adjustment to his new environment can be eased by helping understand the cultural differences.
LC NO. 74-702015
Prod-CHSM Dist-VCI 1974

Our Land - It's Many Faces C 14 MIN
3/4 INCH VIDEO CASSETTE
Illustrates the ways in which man has preserved the land as a source of food, fiber and water.
Prod-USDA Dist-USDA 1972

Our Land Australia C 12 MIN
16MM FILM OPTICAL SOUND J-C A
Presents a collage of Australian scenes, giving a brief overall view of the country and its people.
LC NO. 73-702483
Prod-FLMAUS Dist-AUIS 1973

Our Land, Its Many Faces C 14 MIN
16MM FILM OPTICAL SOUND
Features the story of the conservation movement since the time of Jefferson. Shows many kinds of land we have in America and the conservation work of our farmers and ranchers.
LC NO. FIE63-212
Prod-USSCS Dist-USNAC 1961

Our Largest Minority - The Disabled C 60 MIN
16MM FILM OPTICAL SOUND
Looks at the wide variety of persons who are supposedly disabled including Roy Campanella, violinist Itzhak Perlman and Ray Charles. Demonstrates the creative approaches of such groups as the Quad Squad and the Center for Independent Living. Introduces disabled theologians Howard Rice and Harold Wilke who put the church's attitudes and efforts toward positive goals in perspective.
Prod-NBCTV Dist-CCNCC

Our Last Full-Rigger B 6 MIN
16MM FILM OPTICAL SOUND
Presents a 1958 Screen News Digest excerpt and tells of the sailing days of the M0 year old 'BALCLUTHA' and the reconstruction done by volunteer citizens of San Francisco to restore the ship as a symbol of the link between sailing ships and today's liners.
From The News Magazine Of The Screen Series. Vol 8, No. 9
Prod-PATHE Dist-HEARST 1958

Our Legal System C 19 MIN
3/4 OR 1/2 INCH VIDEO CASSETTE H
Presents interviews with prominent attorneys from around the country.
From The Ways Of The Law Series.
Prod-SCITV Dist-GPITVL 1980

Our Life - The Journey C 27 MIN
3/4 OR 1/2 INCH VIDEO CASSETTE A
Focuses on the 1982 Assembly of United Methodist Women which was held in Philadelphia and attended by 10,000. Shows women discussing their journey of faith. Discusses the Christian response to issues such as nuclear disarmament, racism and sexism.
Prod-WDBGM Dist-ECUFLM 1982

Our Living Bill Of Rights—A Series
16MM FILM, 3/4 OR 1/2 IN VIDEO
Prod-EBEC Dist-EBEC

Equality And The Law - California Fair	
Equality Under Law - Lost Generation Of	25 MIN
Free Press Vs Trial By Jury - Sheppard Case	27 MIN
Freedom To Speak - People Of New York Vs	23 MIN
Justice Under Law - The Gideon Case	23 MIN
Schempp Case - Bible Reading In Public Schools	35 MIN

Our Living Heritage C 28 MIN
16MM FILM - 3/4 IN VIDEO
Explores various parks and national shrines in order to promote an understanding of people and events in American history. Explains that much of America's natural and historic heritage is preserved in the National Park system. Issued in 1966 as a motion picture.
LC NO. 79-706146
Prod-USNPS Dist-USNAC 1979

Our Magic Brew B 15 MIN
2 INCH VIDEOTAPE P
See series title for descriptive statement.
From The Sounds Like Magic Series.
Prod-MOEBA Dist-GPITVL Prodn-KYNETV

Our Magic Bubble Pop B 15 MIN
2 INCH VIDEOTAPE P
See series title for descriptive statement.
From The Sounds Like Magic Series.
Prod-MOEBA Dist-GPITVL Prodn-KYNETV

Our Magic Land C 17 MIN
16MM FILM OPTICAL SOUND
Introduces a magician performing in a carnival setting to point up the magic of man and nature working together to maintain and improve land through conservation.
LC NO. FIE58-158
Prod-USSCS Dist-USNAC 1961

Our March C 21 MIN
3/4 OR 1/2 INCH VIDEO CASSETTE
Celebrates the Russian Revolution and the communistic doctrine it spawned, affecting the whole world. Features speeches by Lenin, the massacre of peasant marchers in city streets and the final storming of government buildings. Highlights other events of that period culminating in World War II and the victory that followed. Uses a wide-screen triptych technique and includes clips from Soviet feature films.
Prod-IHF Dist-IHF

Our Middle Life C 30 MIN
3/4 OR 1/2 INCH VIDEO CASSETTE
Looks at the physiological and psychological changes that may occur in middle life. Covers the role of estrogens in the menopause and bone changes in this period. Discusses whether or not there is a male menopause. Examines the idea of the re-evaluation of one's life that can occur in middle life.
Prod-UILCCC Dist-AL

Our Mineral Heritage C 27 MIN
16MM FILM, 3/4 OR 1/2 IN VIDEO J-H A
Surveys the Geological mechanisms that create minerals.
From The Of Energy, Minerals, And Man Series.
Prod-GAZEL Dist-JOU

Our Mineral World C 28 MIN
3/4 OR 1/2 INCH VIDEO CASSETTE H-C A
Surveys the world's mineral deposits and mankind's dependence on such resources. Shows world's outstanding natural features in North America, Africa, New Zealand, Europe and Britain, and gives clear explanation of continental drift and formation of minerals over millions of years.
Prod-GAZEL Dist-EDMI 1978

Our Mr Sun C 60 MIN
16MM FILM - 3/4 IN VIDEO P-H
Discusses the Sun and its effect on life on Earth. Shows the Sun in eclipse, its corona, sun spots and explosions on its surface. Discusses solar energy.
From The Bell System Science Series.
Prod-ATAT Dist-WAVE Prodn-CAPRA 1956

Our Mutual Friend C 29 MIN
3/4 INCH VIDEO CASSETTE
Examines Dickens' rebuke to the status quo and the shallow people it can create.
From The Dickens World Series.
Prod-UMITV Dist-UMITV 1973

Our National Parks C 15 MIN
3/4 OR 1/2 INCH VIDEO CASSETTE I
Presents John Rugg introducing the national park system, focusing on Yellowstone, Grand Canyon and Mesa Verde. Shows historical reenactments portraying Theodore Roosevelt, John Burroughs and John Wesley Powell. Examines the Anasazi Indian culture.
From The American Legacy Series. Program 12
LC NO. 83-706669
Prod-KRMATV Dist-AITECH 1983

Our Native American Friends C 10 MIN
16MM FILM, 3/4 OR 1/2 IN VIDEO P-I
Introduces three American Indian youngsters, who give a tour of their communities and a look at their ways of life.
Prod-BOBC Dist-EBEC

Our Nearest Star C 12 MIN
16MM FILM OPTICAL SOUND
Depicts the first application of nuclear power in space--the snap isotopic power system used in transit4A navigation satellite. Gives a semi-technical explanation of development and testing of the radioisotope fuel capsule and thermoelectric generator.
LC NO. FIE63-174
Prod-USAEC Dist-USERD Prodn-MARTC 1961

Our Obligation C 26 MIN
16MM FILM, 3/4 OR 1/2 IN VIDEO H-C A
The story of a school fire, the panic that developed and the loss of life that occurred. Discusses the obligation of teachers, school administrators and parents to provide fireproof buildings and all other safety devices necessary to prevent fires.
Prod-LACFD Dist-FILCOM 1960

Our Ocean Of Air C 26 MIN
3/4 INCH VIDEO CASSETTE J
Discusses the relationship of the atmosphere to living organisms. Explores the structure of the atmosphere and some of the phenomena occurring at various altitudes. Takes a look at air pollution and shows how radiosondes are used to measure conditions in the upper atmosphere.
From The What On Earth Series.
Prod-NCSDPI Dist-GPITVL 1979

Our Ocean Of Air C 29 MIN
2 INCH VIDEOTAPE
See series title for descriptive statement.
From The Observing Eye Series.
Prod-WGBHTV Dist-PUBTEL

Our Original Inhabitants B 10 MIN
16MM FILM OPTICAL SOUND I-C A
Discusses the tribal population of India. Explains that, numbering over 25 million, the tribals belong to 172 distinctive groups each with its own culture pattern, dress, decorations and dances. Highlights the lives of some of the tribes, such as the Gonds, Bhils, Santhals, Nagas and Todas.
Prod-INDIA Dist-NEDINF

Our Own Two Hands C 15 MIN
16MM FILM, 3/4 OR 1/2 IN VIDEO I
Makes the point that dignity resides in man, not in the job, and that everyone who works honestly contributes to society, regardless of the type of work performed.
From The Bread And Butterflies Series.
LC NO. 74-703188
Prod-AITV Dist-AITECH Prodn-WHROTV 1973

Our Place C 15 MIN
3/4 OR 1/2 INCH VIDEO CASSETTE K-P
Deals with French-American children. Focuses on the theme of needing to be alone sometimes.
From The La Bonne Aventure Series.
Prod-MPBN Dist-GPITVL

Our Planet Earth C 9 MIN
16MM FILM, 3/4 OR 1/2 IN VIDEO K-I
Discusses the concept of the earth as a planet, its physical properties and man's relationship to it.
From The Basic Facts About The Earth, Sun, Moon And Stars Series.
Prod-MORLAT Dist-SF 1967

Our Political Future B 30 MIN
16MM FILM OPTICAL SOUND H-C A
Dr Vincent Harding serves as moderator as Rev Andrew Young and William Strickland discuss the role of black people in the structuring of a new kind of America, built upon institutions which reflect the true dictates of the masses of the people.
LC NO. 78-704131
Prod-WCBSTV Dist-HRAW 1969

Our Polluted Waters C 15 MIN
3/4 OR 1/2 INCH VIDEO CASSETTE I
Introduces plants, plant-like organisms and sea animals that thrive in polluted water.
From The Matter And Motion Series. Module Blue
Prod-WHROTV Dist-AITECH 1973

Our Present Educational Dilemma B 30 MIN
2 INCH VIDEOTAPE
Presents an examination of the educational environment today where traditional methods of raising children no longer bring results. Presents Dr Dreikurs who introduces the teloanalytic approach which deals with the purposes and holistic perception of the total child in his total environment.
From The Motivating Children To Learn Series.
Prod-VTETV Dist-GPITVL

Our Priceless Gift X 34 MIN
3/4 OR 1/2 INCH VIDEO CASSETTE S
Presents various selections from deaf culture and sign language from 1910 to 1980's. Signed.
Prod-GALCO Dist-GALCO 1982

Our Priceless Heritage C 15 MIN
16MM FILM OPTICAL SOUND
Depicts several before and after pollution scenes, including both air and water scenes, at eight company plant locations. Demonstrates the complexity of many pollution problems and shows that they can be solved by the same technology that created them.
Prod-HERC Dist-HERC

Our Responsibilities - Theresa Demus, MS C 27 MIN
3/4 INCH VIDEO CASSETTE PRO
Discusses the responsibility of the consumer in making the Food and Drug Administration (FDA) a responsible government agency. Focuses on the FDA'S function, how to communicate with the FDA and the limits of the FDA'S responsibilities.
From The Food And Nutrition Seminars For Health Professionals Series.
LC NO. 78-706165
Prod-USFDA Dist-USNAC 1976

Our Round Earth - How It Changes C 11 MIN
16MM FILM, 3/4 OR 1/2 IN VIDEO P-I
Shows forces that change the land, and uses demonstrations with clay models to compare views of molten lava, earthquakes and giant cracks in the earth's surface.
From The Our Round Earth Series.
Prod-CORF Dist-CORF 1971

Our Round Earth - Its Atmosphere C 11 MIN
16MM FILM, 3/4 OR 1/2 IN VIDEO P-I
Describes visible clues to the nature of the invisible atmosphere that protects the earth. Uses special breathing equipment to reveal the importance of the atmosphere for living things.
From The Our Round Earth Series.
Prod-CORF Dist-CORF 1971

Our Round Earth - Its Land C 11 MIN
16MM FILM, 3/4 OR 1/2 IN VIDEO P-I
Views land masses and land forms from the air, states the importance of the land for farming and mining and emphasizes the problems of conservation.
From The Our Round Earth Series.
Prod-CORF Dist-CORF 1971

Our Round Earth - Its Waters C 11 MIN
16MM FILM, 3/4 OR 1/2 IN VIDEO P-I
Shows what the oceans are like from above, as well as below the water and gives sources of fresh water and ways in which it can be controlled.
From The Our Round Earth Series.
Prod-CORF Dist-CORF 1971

Our Round Earth - What It's Like C 11 MIN
16MM FILM, 3/4 OR 1/2 IN VIDEO P-I
Views of the earth from the ground, from a plane and from a space ship show major features of the land, the oceans and the atmosphere.
From The Our Round Earth Series.
Prod-CORF Dist-CORF 1971

Our Round Earth--A Series
16MM FILM, 3/4 OR 1/2 IN VIDEO P-I
Presents views of the Earth and emphasizes man's involvement with his planet.
Prod-CORF Dist-CORF 1971

Our Round Earth - How It Changes 11 MIN
Our Round Earth - Its Atmosphere 11 MIN
Our Round Earth - Its Land 11 MIN
Our Round Earth - Its Waters 11 MIN
Our Round Earth - What It's Like 11 MIN

Our Russian Front B 43 MIN
3/4 OR 1/2 INCH VIDEO CASSETTE
Deals with the Russian people's determination and preparation for war against the advancing German Army. Includes many scenes of civilian life and abrupt changes incurred by war.
Prod-IHF Dist-IHF

Our School C 12 MIN
16MM FILM, 3/4 OR 1/2 IN VIDEO H-C A
Covers a day's activities in the kindergarten of the San Francisco Waldort School, including painting, singing, puppet show, circle time and more.
Prod-AGINP Dist-AGINP

Our Schools Have Kept Us Free X 30 MIN
16MM FILM OPTICAL SOUND J-C A
Based on an article of the same title by Henry Steele Commager. Discusses the role of education in helping to shape and preserve democracy in the United States.
LC NO. FIA64-1324
Prod-NEA Dist-NEA Prodn-CALVIN 1964

Our Senior Years B 30 MIN
16MM FILM OPTICAL SOUND J-H T R
Presents the story of a retired man who becomes bored and bewildered. Describes how he is helped by his wife, grandson and Christian friends to find a new adventure in living by serving God.
Prod-FAMF Dist-FAMF

Our Senses C 15 MIN
2 INCH VIDEOTAPE K
Perceives the world around us through our five senses.
From The Let's Go Sciencing, Unit I - Matter Series.
Prod-DETPS Dist-GPITVL

Our Small World C 6 MIN
16MM FILM OPTICAL SOUND
Discusses the involvement of people in the United States in helping people in the developing countries around the world work their way out of poverty and despair. Shows how CARE'S International Partnership Programs help bring a better life to needy people who are still without the basic necessities of life.
Prod-CARE Dist-CARE

Our Small World - Business And Industry Volunteers C 9 MIN
16MM FILM OPTICAL SOUND
Provides suggestions from volunteers on how people from business and industry can participate in helping to improve the plight of needy people.
Prod-CARE Dist-CARE

Our Small World - Student Volunteers C 10 MIN
16MM FILM OPTICAL SOUND
Presents suggestions from volunteers on how students can help to improve the plight of needy people.
Prod-CARE Dist-CARE

Our Small World - Women Volunteers C 9 MIN
16MM FILM OPTICAL SOUND
Provides suggestions from volunteers on how women volunteers can participate in helping to improve the plight of needy people.
Prod-CARE Dist-CARE

Our Solar System C 5 MIN
16MM FILM, 3/4 OR 1/2 IN VIDEO
Uses animation to teach the names, placement and characteristics of the planets in the solar system.
LC NO. 83-706100
Prod-NASA Dist-USNAC 1973

Our Son John C 25 MIN
16MM FILM OPTICAL SOUND
Deals with the value systems in interpersonal relations. Shows the parents of a handicapped child, pointing out how they consider themselves fortunate.
LC NO. 74-700106
Prod-SCHMNJ Dist-CMHOSP 1973

Our Songs Will Never Die C 35 MIN
16MM FILM, 3/4 OR 1/2 IN VIDEO
Visits the Yurok, Karuk and Tolowa cultural sites which were established for the purpose of reconstructing early village dance sites. Shows young visitors working with tribal elders and experiencing surf-fishing, fish drying, sand-breadmaking, Indian card games, songs, stick-games, net making, and the history of their grandfathers and great-grandfathers.
Prod-SHENFP Dist-SHENFP

Our Special Way Of Life C 22 MIN
16MM FILM OPTICAL SOUND
Shows the lifestyles of a farmer, a rancher and their families in the United States.
LC NO. 79-700063
Prod-FARMI Dist-FARMI Prodn-FILMMA 1978

Our Speech Rainbow B 15 MIN
2 INCH VIDEOTAPE P
See series title for descriptive statement.
From The Sounds Like Magic Series.
Prod-MOEBA Dist-GPITVL Prodn-KYNETV

Our Spiritual And Cultural Future B 30 MIN
16MM FILM OPTICAL SOUND H-C A
Dr Vincent Harding serves as moderator as Rev Albert Cleage and John Henrik Clarke discuss the meaning of cultural and religious life as it will affect the future of black Americans, and describe the various efforts of black artists and religious leaders to give cultural substance to the Black Liberation movement.
From The Black History, Section 26 - What Is The Future Series.
LC NO. 74-704130
Prod-WCBSTV Dist-HRAW 1969

Our Story In Stamps C 12 MIN
16MM FILM OPTICAL SOUND
Shows how new Malaysian stamps are printed from designs drawn by Malaysian artists.
Prod-FILEM Dist-PMFMUN 1957

Our Street--A Series

Presents the problems and solutions of a fictional black family, the Robinsons, consisting of Mae, Bull, Slick, Jet, Tony and Grandma. Explains that the difficulties of inner-city living are often resolved through the use of available city, state and federal services and programs.
Prod-MDCPB Dist-PUBTEL

Audition	29 MIN
Before You Walk	29 MIN
Books And Covers	29 MIN
Cathy's Turn	29 MIN
Caught	29 MIN
Dark Darkness	29 MIN
Departure	29 MIN
Doomsday	29 MIN
Family Affair	29 MIN
From Whence He Came	29 MIN
Fronts	29 MIN
Glory Bag, The	29 MIN
Happy Birthday, Brother	29 MIN
Have You Seen My Little Boy	29 MIN
Home Again, Home Again	29 MIN
I'm Staying	29 MIN
It's A Small World	29 MIN
Keep Track	29 MIN
Let Me Count The Ways, Baby	29 MIN
Lineage, The	29 MIN
Lost Days Of Glory, The, Pt 1	29 MIN
Lost Days Of Glory, The, Pt 2	29 MIN
Love's Sweet Song	29 MIN
Making Friends	29 MIN
Man Of The House, The	29 MIN
Miss Clara Let Us Be	29 MIN
Mrs Ryder Has The Blues	29 MIN
Night Of The Intruder, Pt 1	29 MIN
Night Of The Intruder, Pt 2	29 MIN
Old Ladies Lost	29 MIN
One Your With, The	29 MIN
Political Candidate, The	29 MIN
Pride	29 MIN
Reverence Day	29 MIN
Struck	29 MIN
There Goes The Bride	29 MIN
Too Proud To Beg	29 MIN
Ultimates, The	29 MIN

Our Sun And Its Planets C 11 MIN
16MM FILM, 3/4 OR 1/2 IN VIDEO P
Explains how young astronomers learn about a planet, the sun and solor systems, how our solar system is formed and why planets shine. Explores their physical features and moons.
Prod-CORF Dist-CORF 1970

Our Sweet Heritage C 29 MIN
16MM FILM OPTICAL SOUND
Examines the love affair between Americans and the cookie. Presents a journey through history to explore the background behind some of the cookies that have served as tasty footnotes to America's past.
Prod-ARCHCO Dist-MTP

Our Time Is Our Time C 13 MIN
3/4 OR 1/2 INCH VIDEO CASSETTE
Shows how to save time by conducting efficient meetings and how to treat all meetings and contacts with others with a view toward saving time.
From The Management of Time Series. Module 4
Prod-RESEM Dist-RESEM

Our Times C 58 MIN
3/4 OR 1/2 INCH VIDEO CASSETTE H-C A
Uses historic footage to recall the events of the 1960's and 1970's.
From The Bill Moyers' Journal Series.
LC NO. 80-706744
Prod-WNETTV Dist-WNETTV 1980

Our Totem Is The Raven C 21 MIN
16MM FILM, 3/4 OR 1/2 IN VIDEO I-H
Dramatizes the ordeal of an Indian boy in his endurance and ritual ascent to manhood. Shows how Indians clash with twentieth-century values by giving some background into the Indian cultural heritage.
Prod-KINGSP Dist-PHENIX 1972

Our Town C 28 MIN
16MM FILM OPTICAL SOUND
Compares a contemporary industrial city to a mythical American turn-of-the-century city. Analyzes a contemporary city with respect to one of its most vicious problems - drugs.
LC NO. 73-702347
Prod-PATRSN Dist-PATRSN 1973

Our Town B 90 MIN
16MM FILM, 3/4 OR 1/2 IN VIDEO
Presents an adaptation of Thornton Wilder's play Our Town.
Prod-UAE Dist-PHENIX 1940

Our Town, Pt 1 - Our Town And Our Universe C 30 MIN
16MM FILM, 3/4 OR 1/2 IN VIDEO H-C
Introduces the play Our Town. Presents an evaluation of the play by Clifton Fadiman who comments on the contrast between each tiny moment of our lives and the vast stretches of time and place in which each individual plays his role.
From The Humanities - The Drama Series.
Prod-EBF Dist-EBEC 1959

Our Town, Pt 2 - Our Town And Ourselves C 30 MIN
16MM FILM, 3/4 OR 1/2 IN VIDEO H-C
Discusses the conventions and techniques used in Our Town, such as the playwright's use of music, of light motif and variations, and of the condensed line or word. Considers the significance of the play for each member of the audience.
From The Humanities - The Drama Series.
Prod-EBF Dist-EBEC 1959

Our Union B 22 MIN
16MM FILM, 3/4 OR 1/2 IN VIDEO
Portrays the history of the UE from the Depression, showing concrete gains in wages and working conditions.
Prod-CNEMAG Dist-CNEMAG 1949

Our Vanishing Lands C 24 MIN
16MM FILM, 3/4 OR 1/2 IN VIDEO I-H
Discusses the problem of conservation of America's resources, including its land, wildlife and natural beauty.
From The Smithsonian Series.
Prod-NBCTV Dist-MGHT 1967

Our Vanishing Wilderness—A Series
16MM FILM, 3/4 OR 1/2 IN VIDEO
Prod-NET Dist-IU

Chain Of Life, The	30 MIN
Of Broccoli And Pelicans And Celery And Seals	30 MIN
Prairie Killers	30 MIN
Prudhoe Bay - Or Bust	30 MIN
Santa Barbara - Everybody's Mistake	30 MIN
Slow Death Of Desert Water	30 MIN
Water Is So Clear That A Blind Man Could See	30 MIN
Will The Gator Glades Survive	30 MIN

Our Violent Heritage C 28 MIN
16MM FILM, 3/4 OR 1/2 IN VIDEO H-C A
Studies the harm being done to American political candidates and citizens. Discusses political assassinations and shows how ordinary citizens are trying to protect their lives. Originally shown on the CBS television program Sunday Morning.
Prod-CBSNEW Dist-CAROUF

Our Way C 14 MIN
16MM FILM OPTICAL SOUND
Shows how the United Way of Metropolitan Tarrant County has improved the quality of life in this area of Texas.
LC NO. 78-700206
Prod-UWTC Dist-UWTC Prodn-SBRTC 1977

Our Wealth Of Waters C 27 MIN
16MM FILM OPTICAL SOUND I-C A
Shows both the value of water and the problem resulting from misuse. Includes the water cycle and emphasizes man's role in altering the abundance of water given us by nature.
Prod-TGAFC Dist-TGAFC 1960

Our Winning Season C 92 MIN
16MM FILM OPTICAL SOUND
Follows a group of teenagers through their senior year in high school.
Prod-AIP Dist-SWANK

Our Wonderful Body - How It Grows C 11 MIN
16MM FILM, 3/4 OR 1/2 IN VIDEO P
Illustrates that people grow at different rates and to different sizes. Explains that different parts of the body grow at different rates and shows the physical reasons for growth. Introduces the concepts of cell multiplication and growth. Explains that growth brings increased body control.
From The Our Wonderful Body Series. No. 5
Prod-CORF Dist-CORF 1968

Our Wonderful Body - How It Moves C 11 MIN
16MM FILM, 3/4 OR 1/2 IN VIDEO P
Uses a skeleton to demonstrate body movements. Illustrates the co-ordinated movement of muscles, bones and joints. Teaches ways of keeping the body healthy.
From The Our Wonderful Body Series. No. 3
Prod-CORF Dist-CORF 1968

Our Wonderful Body - How Its Parts Work Together C 11 MIN
16MM FILM, 3/4 OR 1/2 IN VIDEO P
Uses life size models to demonstrate how parts of the body work together in different situations. Indicates that the brain signals muscles to move.
From The Our Wonderful Body Series. No. 4
Prod-CORF Dist-CORF 1968

Our Wonderful Body - How We Breathe C 11 MIN
16MM FILM, 3/4 OR 1/2 IN VIDEO P
Uses an operating model of a lung to illustrate breathing. Shows the movement of the diaphragm and carbon dioxide.
From The Our Wonderful Body Series. No. 2
Prod-CORF Dist-CORF 1968

Our Wonderful Body - How We Keep Fit C 10 MIN
16MM FILM, 3/4 OR 1/2 IN VIDEO P
Shows how exercise, food and rest, dressing for the weather, proper treatment of injuries and sickness and getting regular check-ups are important in keeping fit.
From The Our Wonderful Body Series. No. 6
Prod-CORF Dist-CORF 1973

Our Wonderful Body - Medicines, Drugs And Poisons C 10 MIN
16MM FILM, 3/4 OR 1/2 IN VIDEO P
Offers such safety guidelines as the importance of reading labels, following a doctor's recommendation and the storage of drugs, medicines and household chemicals away from children.
From The Our Wonderful Body Series. No. 7
Prod-CORF Dist-CORF 1973

Our Wonderful Body - The Heart And Its Work C 11 MIN
16MM FILM, 3/4 OR 1/2 IN VIDEO P
Constructs a model of the circulatory system which indicates functions of the heart, blood and blood vessels.
From The Our Wonderful Body Series. No. 1
Prod-CORF Dist-CORF 1968

Our Wonderful Body—A Series
16MM FILM, 3/4 OR 1/2 IN VIDEO P
Presents a series about our wonderful body. Includes life-size models to visualize and simplify human body functions for beginners.
Prod-CORF Dist-CORF

Our Wonderful Body - How It Grows	11 MIN
Our Wonderful Body - How It Moves	11 MIN
Our Wonderful Body - How Its Parts Work	11 MIN
Our Wonderful Body - How We Breathe	11 MIN
Our Wonderful Body - How We Keep Fit	10 MIN
Our Wonderful Body - Medicines, Drugs And	10 MIN
Our Wonderful Body - The Heart And Its Work	11 MIN

Our Wonderful Senses C 13 MIN
16MM FILM, 3/4 OR 1/2 IN VIDEO K-P
Describes the five senses, their functions, and how to take care of them.
Prod-HIGGIN Dist-HIGGIN 1980

Our World Is An Island C 17 MIN
16MM FILM OPTICAL SOUND J-H
Interprets the relationship of life found on an island, focusing on the ecology of living things. Traces the history of the island as a land formation from its volcanic origins through the geo-physical changes that have occurred before and after the arrival of man.
LC NO. 76-700460
Prod-INMATI Dist-INMATI 1976

Our World Of Economics—A Series
J-H
Presents the main principles of economics including scarcity, specialization, interdependence and exchange. Introduces the concepts of stocks and flows and the coordinated decisions that control these flows. Explores the various economics which affect the everyday lives of the students.
Prod-MPATI Dist-GPITVL

All Systems Go - For Analyzing Problems	20 MIN
All Systems Go - Models	20 MIN
All Systems Go - Systems Analysis	20 MIN
American Economic System, The - Economic Growth	20 MIN
American Economic System, The - Input, Output	20 MIN
American Economic System, The - Measuring The	20 MIN
American Economic System, The - The American	20 MIN
Focus On The Consumer Market - Markets, Where	20 MIN
Focus On The Consumer Market - Supply And	20 MIN
Focus On The Consumer Market - The Market	20 MIN
Job Market, The - The American Labor Force	20 MIN
Keeping Our Economy Healthy, Pt 1	20 MIN
Keeping Our Economy Healthy, Pt 2	20 MIN
Making Producing And Trading Easier	20 MIN
Making Producing And Trading Easier - Capital	20 MIN
Making Producing And Trading Easier - Money	20 MIN
Making Producing And Trading Easier - Savings	20 MIN
Managing Production - Automotive Industry,	20 MIN
Managing Production - How To Bake A Cake,	20 MIN
Managing Production - Junior Achievement,	20 MIN
Our Economic World	20 MIN
People, People, People - Bane Or Blessing	20 MIN
Profile Of A Dropout, The	20 MIN
Trading And Sharing With The World	20 MIN
Where Do Jobs Come From	20 MIN
Where To - The City And The Future	20 MIN
Working For And With Others - Economic	20 MIN
Working For And With Others - Taxes	20 MIN
Working Together - Government As A Producer	20 MIN
Working Together - Government As A Rulemaker	20 MIN
Working Together - Protecting The Consumer	20 MIN

Our Youth Culture C 30 MIN
16MM FILM OPTICAL SOUND J-H T R
Investigates the struggle of youth for maturity and identity in an adult world. Points out that the church must make its message relevant to the needs of youth.
LC NO. FIA67-5773
Prod-FAMF Dist-FAMF 1966

Our 49th State C 15 MIN
3/4 OR 1/2 INCH VIDEO CASSETTE I
Presents John Rugg discussing Alaska, covering geographical features, wildlife and the Eskimo. Covers such topics as climate changes, the importance of the floatplane, comparisons between the modern Eskimo and their ancestors, and the significance of Prudhoe oil and the trans-Alaska pipeline to the American economy. Uses a dramatic vignette portraying William Seward's determination to purchase Alaska from Russia.
From The American Legacy Series. Program 15
LC NO. 83-706672
Prod-KRMATV Dist-AITECH 1983

Ours Is A Word-Order Language B 15 MIN
2 INCH VIDEOTAPE I
Explains that words must be arranged in a certain order in language if they are to create the sound of sense. Features selections Little Orphan Annie by James Whitcomb Riley and Comparisons, written anonymously. (Broadcast quality)
From The Bill Martin Series. No. 2
Prod-BRITED Dist-GPITVL Prodn-KQEDTV

Ourselves C 30 MIN
3/4 INCH VIDEO CASSETTE H-C A
Presents five women sharing what it is like to grow up Asian and female in America.
From The Pearls Series.
Prod-EDFCEN Dist-GPITVL 1979

Ourselves And That Promise C 27 MIN
16MM FILM - 3/4 IN VIDEO
Presents Kentucky poets, James Still, Robert Penn Warren, and Ronnie Criswell and photographer Billy Davis, as they discuss their work and their relationship to the environment in which they live.
Prod-APPAL Dist-APPAL 1977

Ourselves To Know - Alexander Pope's Essay On Man - What Oft Was Thought But Ne'er So Well... C 45 MIN
3/4 OR 1/2 INCH VIDEO CASSETTE

Analyzes Alexander Pope's Essay On Man.
From The Survey Of English Literature I Series.
Prod-MDCPB Dist-MDCPB

Out B 25 MIN
16MM FILM OPTICAL SOUND
Shows the plight of the Hungarian refugee. Contains scenes of actual escapes across the border and tells the story of one family, a mother and two children, who, after they reach Austria are faced with finding a nation that will give them a home.
Prod-UN Dist-AFLCIO 1956

Out And About–A Series
P
Presents five-year-old Molly with her parents and her friends learning about some important social skills.
Prod-STSU Dist-AITECH Prodn-WETN 1984

Describing 015 MIN
Detecting 015 MIN
Keeping Friends 015 MIN
Making Friends 015 MIN
Observing 015 MIN
Think Ahead 015 MIN
Ways To Solve A Problem 015 MIN
Why Did It Happen 015 MIN

Out Art C 29 MIN
3/4 OR 1/2 INCH VIDEO CASSETTE H-C A
Describes how artists break with tradition to shape new messages that are unique, outrageous, unconventional, delightful and even absurd.
From The Creativity With Bill Moyers Series.
Prod-CORPEL Dist-PBS 1982

Out Of Body Travel B 42 MIN
3/4 OR 1/2 INCH VIDEO CASSETTE
Examines the fluctuating borders between opposites such as mind versus body and male versus female. Emphasizes the distance between things.
Prod-KITCHN Dist-KITCHN

Out Of Bondage C 25 MIN
16MM FILM OPTICAL SOUND
Traces the roots of Russian Jewry and the events which led to the recent exodus to Israel.
Prod-UJA Dist-ALDEN

Out Of Conflict - Accord–A Series

Discusses aspects of collective bargaining and techniques of mediating between labor and management.
Prod-USDL Dist-USNAC Prodn-RUDWIT 1978

Dimensions Of Bargaining 029 MIN
Harmonics Of Conflict, The 025 MIN
Waldenville I 038 MIN
Waldenville II 031 MIN
Waldenville III 036 MIN
Waldenville Jogger 039 MIN

Out Of Hands C 8 MIN
16MM FILM OPTICAL SOUND P-I
Considers the many ways in which humans need and use their hands. Observes a musician, a technician, kindergartners finger-painting, a potter, a glass cutter, a silversmith and a draftsman.
LC NO. 73-701256
Prod-KINGSP Dist-HRAW 1972

Out Of Left Field C 7 MIN
16MM FILM, 3/4 OR 1/2 IN VIDEO J-H
LC NO. 84-707081
Prod-AFB Dist-PHENIX 1984

Out Of Many, One People C 15 MIN
3/4 OR 1/2 INCH VIDEO CASSETTE P
Shows preparations for Christmas, a fair and a concert in Jamaica.
From The Other Families, Other Friends Series. Brown Module - Jamaica
Prod-WVIZTV Dist-AITECH 1971

Out Of Michigan's Past C 9 MIN
16MM FILM OPTICAL SOUND P-C A
Visits Michigan's historical and geographical landmarks, such as Greenfield Village, Mackinaw Island and the Sleeping Bear Sand Dunes.
Prod-WSU Dist-WSU 1958

Out Of Rock C 30 MIN
16MM FILM, 3/4 OR 1/2 IN VIDEO H-C A
Looks at the work of sculptor Boz Vaadia.
Prod-KEYBER Dist-FI 1980

Out Of Step C 30 MIN
16MM FILM, 3/4 OR 1/2 IN VIDEO J-H
Features story of a teenage girl who chooses dance as her life career. Presents excellent dance sequences. Edited version.
Prod-HGATE Dist-LCOA 1985

Out Of Step C 45 MIN
16MM FILM, 3/4 OR 1/2 IN VIDEO J-H
Features story of a teenage girl who chooses dance as her life career. Presents excellent dance sequences. Full version.
Prod-HGATE Dist-LCOA 1985

Out Of The Blue C 15 MIN
3/4 OR 1/2 INCH VIDEO CASSETTE J-H
Presents members of the Twelfth Night Repertory Company using humor, satire, music, dance and drama to focus attention on attitudes regarding pollution. Recounts that when J J Biggley's Progress Products plans to build a factory on the last virgin forest in the state, Rodney Redwood organizes a boycott. Shows that Morganna Doomsday thinks it's hopeless until a close encounter with a spaceship captain and Mr Smock convinces her that she can make a difference in the fight against pollution.
From The TNRC Presents - Health And Self Series.
Prod-KLCSTV Dist-AITECH 1984

Out Of The Body Travel B 43 MIN
3/4 OR 1/2 INCH VIDEO CASSETTE
Juxtaposes visual metaphors with fragmented statements. Examines the layers of interaction that involve time, space, language and self-image.
Prod-EAI Dist-EAI

Out Of The Cradle C 24 MIN
16MM FILM OPTICAL SOUND I-C
Describes the abundant variety of life in the sea and discusses the possibility of farming the ocean floor.
From The Animal Secrets Series.
LC NO. FIA68-1031
Prod-NBC Dist-GRACUR 1967

Out Of The Depths - The Miners' Story C 55 MIN
3/4 OR 1/2 INCH VIDEO CASSETTE
Deals with the struggle of miners and laborers in the American West, with miners recalling working conditions in the mines of the early 1900s. Describes the events which led to the famous 1913 United Mine Workers' strike and the 1914 Ludlow Massacre.
From The Walk Through The 20th Century With Bill Moyers Series.
Prod-CORPEL Dist-PBS

Out Of The Dust C 40 MIN
16MM FILM OPTICAL SOUND J A
Features an American engineer who has become a missionary in Latin America, telling his story to an amazed salesman.
Prod-YALEDV Dist-YALEDV

Out Of The East B 26 MIN
16MM FILM OPTICAL SOUND
Uses documentary footage to describe a series of successful Japanese military victories in 1941-42, including the sinking of the British Navy's ships Prince of Walse and repulse. Shows Churchill and Roosevelt meeting in a series of talks in Washington, and describes the American sea victory at Midway.
From The Winston Churchill - The Valiant Years Series. No. 10
LC NO. FI67-2110
Prod-ABCTV Dist-SG 1961

Out Of The Limelight, Home In The Rain C 52 MIN
16MM FILM, 3/4 OR 1/2 IN VIDEO J-C A
Explores the life of the dancer, including the rigors of ballet class, the rehearsals and preparation, and the moment of performance.
From The Magic Of Dance Series.
Prod-BBCTV Dist-TIMLIF 1980

Out Of The Mouths Of Babes C 28 MIN
16MM FILM, 3/4 OR 1/2 IN VIDEO C A
Presents the chronology of normal language development, including random babbling, jargon, one-word sentences, complicated structures and linguistic concepts.
From The Nature Of Things Series.
Prod-CANBC Dist-FLMLIB 1978

Out Of The Mouths Of Babes And Other People Too C 29 MIN
3/4 OR 1/2 INCH VIDEO CASSETTE T
See series title for descriptive statement.
From The Coping With Kids Series.
Prod-MFFD Dist-FI

Out Of The Mouths Of Babes And Other People, Too C 30 MIN
3/4 OR 1/2 INCH VIDEO CASSETTE
Provides an overview to conducting classroom meetings, what they are and how they can be helpful. Features Dr Brenda Dew as guest expert.
From The Coping With Kids Series.
Prod-OHUTC Dist-OHUTC

Out Of The Sea C
16MM FILM OPTICAL SOUND I-C
Records one of the many incidents that took place along the North Pacific coast during a violent October storm. Shows how a shipwrecked seaman managed to obtain his needs. Illustrates numerous survival techniques, including shelter construction, fire building, setting a fishing line and obtaining drinking water on the ocean beach.
LC NO. 72-701039
Prod-LSTI Dist-LSTI

Out Of The Shadows C 17 MIN
16MM FILM OPTICAL SOUND C A
Demonstrates an intensive care program for severely retarded children instituted at Parsons State Hospital and Training Center at Parsons, Kansas.
LC NO. 72-702024
Prod-UKANBC Dist-UKANS 1969

Out Of The Wilderness C 28 MIN
16MM FILM OPTICAL SOUND
Features General Avraham Joffee speaking on ecology in Israel.
Prod-ALDEN Dist-ALDEN

Out Of This World C 13 MIN
16MM FILM OPTICAL SOUND
Examines five futuristic kitchens from the General Motors Futurama exhibit at the New York World's Fair.
Prod-GM Dist-GM

Out Of This World C 21 MIN
16MM FILM OPTICAL SOUND
Shows the early stages of the Mercury program with particular emphasis on Minuteman and Polaris rocket motors.
Prod-HERC Dist-HERC

Out Of This World C 20 MIN
2 INCH VIDEOTAPE P
See series title for descriptive statement.
From The Learning Our Language, Unit III - Creative Writing Series.
Prod-MPATI Dist-GPITVL

Out On The Edge C 25 MIN
3/4 INCH VIDEO CASSETTE
Illustrates that the edge to a downhill racer is years of training, split-second decision and sometimes, the luck of the draw.
Prod-LAURON Dist-LAURON

Out There, A Lone Island B 67 MIN
16MM FILM, 3/4 OR 1/2 IN VIDEO
Portrays life on a remote Korean Island where the Eastern philosophy of subordination of self to oneness with nature is lived daily. Presented without narration or subtitles and with only incidental Korean dialogue.
Prod-UCEMC Dist-UCEMC

Out They Go C 20 MIN
16MM FILM OPTICAL SOUND
Pays tribute to the people who are the heart and soul of the old fruit and vegetable markets in Sydney, Australia. Questions whether progress is always for the best.
LC NO. 79-700527
Prod-FLMAUS Dist-AUIS 1975

Out To The Moon C 15 MIN
16MM FILM, 3/4 OR 1/2 IN VIDEO
Shows a real space suit and rocket model in a classroom setting. Explains in simple terms such things as rocket stages, weightlessness and moon landings.
From The Ripples Series.
LC NO. 73-702147
Prod-NITC Dist-AITECH

Out With The Girls C 5 MIN
3/4 OR 1/2 INCH VIDEO CASSETTE
Documents screaming women in the audience of male dancers. Deals with sexual politics. Presented by Carol Porter and Joan Merrill.
Prod-ARTINC Dist-ARTINC

Outback C 24 MIN
16MM FILM OPTICAL SOUND
Presents an overview of the Peace River area of Canada.
From The Heading Out Series.
LC NO. 76-703071
Prod-CENTWO Dist-CENTWO 1975

Outboard Fiesta C 27 MIN
16MM FILM OPTICAL SOUND
Presents the adventures and misadventures of an American family on a boating holiday in Mexico. Concentrates on little-known areas of the country, including little-used recreational boating areas.
Prod-MERMAR Dist-TELEFM

Outboard Fisherman USA C 27 MIN
3/4 OR 1/2 INCH VIDEO CASSETTE
Shows how independent commercial fishermen, using outboard motors, contribute to the national economy. Issued as a motion picture in 1956.
LC NO. 80-707613
Prod-USBSFW Dist-USNAC 1980

Outboard Fisherman, USA C 27 MIN
16MM FILM OPTICAL SOUND P-C
Shows how small, independent commercial fishermen, using outboard motors, contribute to the national economy. Reveals various fishing techniques showing the catch of 10 different species of fish and shellfish from many areas of the United States.
Prod-USBCF Dist-USNOAA 1956

Outbreak Of Salmonella Infection, An C 14 MIN
16MM FILM, 3/4 OR 1/2 IN VIDEO
Studies a simulated outbreak of food-borne illness caused by organisms of the salmonella group. Examines source and means of contamination, factors aiding the survival and transfer of the organism, conditions of environment and general food handling practices, and effects of the outbreak.
From The Food Handling Series.
Prod-USPHS Dist-USNAC 1954

Outbreak Of Salmonella Infection, An (Spanish) C 14 MIN
16MM FILM OPTICAL SOUND
Presents a stimulated typical outbreak of food-borne illness caused by organisms of the salmonella group. Discusses source and means of contamination, factors contributing to the survival and transfer of the organism, important conditions of environment and general good handling practices and effects of the outbreak.
LC NO. 74-705280
Prod-USPHCD Dist-USNAC 1954

Outbreak Of Staphylococcus Intoxication, An C 12 MIN
16MM FILM OPTICAL SOUND
Studies a typical outbreak of food-borne illness due to staphylococcus organisms. Examines the symptoms of the victims and traces the source of the organisms to Staphylococcus aureus in pastry filling. Gives reasons for the incidence of the organisms in the food.
From The Food Handling Series.
LC NO. FIE55-36
Prod-USPHS Dist-USNAC 1954

Outbreak Of Staphylococcus Intoxication, An (Spanish) C 12 MIN
16MM FILM OPTICAL SOUND
Presents a case study of a typical outbreak of food-borne illness caused by staphylococcus organisms, including symptoms of the victims, tracing the source of the organisms as staphylococcus aureus in pastry filling and the reasons for the incidence of the organisms in the food.
LC NO. 74-705281
Prod-USPHCD Dist-USNAC 1954

Outcomes Of Child Abuse And Neglect C 30 MIN
3/4 OR 1/2 INCH VIDEO CASSETTE H-C A
See series title for descriptive statement.
From The Child Abuse And Neglect Series.
Prod-UMINN Dist-GPITVL 1983

Outdoor Activities B 30 MIN
2 INCH VIDEOTAPE
See series title for descriptive statement.
From The Program Development In The Kindergarten Series.
Prod-GPITVL Dist-GPITVL

Outdoor Cooking C 15 MIN
16MM FILM OPTICAL SOUND
Features outdoor dishes demonstrations on a city terrace by sportscaster Bud Palmer, on a golf course by Whitey Ford and by teenagers at a party by the swimming pool.
From The Cooking Film Series.
Prod-BUGAS Dist-BUGAS

Outdoor Cooking C 10 MIN
16MM FILM, 3/4 OR 1/2 IN VIDEO I-C A
Describes how to prepare a kitchen area in a winter wilderness camp. Explains that subsistence diets are not an automatic part of roughing it outdoors. Shows ways of using nature's natural resources to aid in personal comfort.
From The Outdoor Recreation - Winter Series.
Prod-MORLAT Dist-SF 1967

Outdoor Cooking C 15 MIN
3/4 OR 1/2 INCH VIDEO CASSETTE
Demonstrates the tricks of outdoor cooking on a gas grill. Features favorites of Sportscaster Bud Palmer and ex-baseball great Whitey Ford.
From The Magical Cook's Tour Series.
Prod-IVCH Dist-IVCH

Outdoor Cooking C 30 MIN
3/4 OR 1/2 INCH VIDEO CASSETTE
Discusses outdoor cooking as part of 'roughing it' during camping.
From The Roughing It Series.
Prod-KYTV Dist-KYTV 1984

Outdoor Education C 29 MIN
16MM FILM OPTICAL SOUND T
Shows how outdoor experiences may be provided for today's children through the use of the school site and other outdoor settings as learning laboratories, outdoor schools, outdoor interests, skills and teacher education.
Prod-AAHPER Dist-AAHPER Prodn-CAPFS

Outdoor Education Mountaineering–A Series

Views the thrills and hazards of outdoor mountaineering.
Prod-MORLAT Dist-MORLAT 1973

Advanced Rock Climbing 17 MIN
Basic Rock Climbing 14 MIN
Mountain Rescue 14 MIN
Solo Survival 11 MIN

Outdoor Education White Water Paddling–A Series

Prod-MORLAT Dist-MORLAT 1973

Lake And River Kayaking 14 MIN

Outdoor Fish Cookery C 28 MIN
16MM FILM OPTICAL SOUND P-C
Links the past with today by showing fishing and some methods of cooking fish outdoors. Includes mention of chowders, stews, fish fries and oyster and clam bakes.
LC NO. FIE67-201
Prod-USBSFW Dist-USNOAA 1959

Outdoor Gear C 30 MIN
3/4 OR 1/2 INCH VIDEO CASSETTE
Discusses outdoor gear needed for various outdoor activities when 'roughing it.'
From The Roughing It Series.
Prod-KYTV Dist-KYTV 1984

Outdoor Laboratory, The B 30 MIN
2 INCH VIDEOTAPE
Demonstrates some of the advantages that experience in an outdoor laboratory has over classroom activities designed to meet the same objectives.
From The Science In Your Classroom Series.
Prod-WENHTV Dist-GPITVL

Outdoor Play - A Motivating Force For Learning C 17 MIN
16MM FILM OPTICAL SOUND
Presents the unique physical and intellectual development provided by outdoor play activities and shows the extensive use of improvised materials. Highlights children's exploration of space, experimentation with balance, development of muscular coordination and body awareness. Illustrates developmental differences, self-determined activities and goals and the role of the teacher.
Prod-QC Dist-CFDC 1973

Outdoor Recreation - Winter–A Series
3/4 OR 1/2 INCH VIDEO CASSETTE I-C A
Prod-MORLAT Dist-SF

Ice Fishing, Pt 1 12 MIN
Ice Fishing, Pt 2 12 MIN
Ice Safety 11 MIN
Outdoor Cooking 10 MIN
Proper Winter Clothing 13 MIN

Outdoor Skills C 30 MIN
3/4 OR 1/2 INCH VIDEO CASSETTE J A
Covers creative teaching activities for outdoor ministry. Includes movement and values education, communication games and the flow hike. Features Clifford Knapp and Joseph Cornell.
From The Sow Seeds/Trust The Promise Series.
Prod-UMCOM Dist-ECUFLM

Outdoor Toys C 25 MIN
3/4 OR 1/2 INCH VIDEO CASSETTE H-C A
Shows how to build a see-saw and other yard toys like a wheelbarrow, stilts and rope ladders.
From The Blizzard's Wonderful Wooden Toys Series.
Prod-BBCTV Dist-FI

Outer Banks Fisherman C 25 MIN
16MM FILM OPTICAL SOUND
Presents a pair of fisherman chasing trophy stripers from surf and boat.
Prod-BRNSWK Dist-KAROL

Outer Circle, The C 30 MIN
3/4 OR 1/2 INCH VIDEO CASSETTE C
See series title for descriptive statement.
From The Art Of Being Human Series. Module 6
Prod-MDCC Dist-MDCC

Outer Door Panel Replacement C 40 MIN
1/2 IN VIDEO CASSETTE BETA/VHS
Deals with auto body repair.
Prod-RMI Dist-RMI

Outer Space C 15 MIN
3/4 OR 1/2 INCH VIDEO CASSETTE P
See series title for descriptive statement.
From The Let's Draw Series.
Prod-OCPS Dist-AITECH Prodn-KOKHTV 1976

Outfitting A Welder With A Personal Sample Collector C 8 MIN
1/2 IN VIDEO CASSETTE BETA/VHS
Discusses dust measurement, air filters and air sampling apparatus.
Prod-RMI Dist-RMI

Outfitting A Worker With A Personal Sample Collector C 8 MIN
1/2 IN VIDEO CASSETTE BETA/VHS
Discusses dust measurement and environmental health.
Prod-RMI Dist-RMI

Outing In The Park, An / Trouble In The Bargain Basement / Paddington Takes The Stage C 15 MIN
16MM FILM, 3/4 OR 1/2 IN VIDEO K-I
Describes Paddington Bear's adventures at a park concert and in a bargain basement. Based on chapters two and six of the book Paddington At Large by Michael Bond.
From The Paddington Bear, Series 2 Series.
LC NO. 80-707215
Prod-BONDM Dist-FLMFR Prodn-FILMF 1980

Outlasting The Quakes C 4 MIN
16MM FILM, 3/4 OR 1/2 IN VIDEO I-H
Points out areas of the United States that are vulnerable to earthquakes. Describes the tragedies that earthquakes cause. Shows the largest earthquake simulator and the research efforts in earthquake engineering.
Prod-NSF Dist-AMEDFL 1974

Outline History Of Europe–A Series
16MM FILM, 3/4 OR 1/2 IN VIDEO H-C
Traces the development of Western civilization.
Prod-POLNIS Dist-IFB

Age Of Revolutions, An 026 MIN
Greeks, The 029 MIN
Middle Ages, The 031 MIN
Myth Of Nationalism, The 030 MIN
Romans, The 024 MIN
Towards A Modern Europe 030 MIN

Outloading Of Diesel Locomotives B 13 MIN
16MM FILM OPTICAL SOUND
Presents the problems and proper techniques for loading diesel locomotives aboard a cargo ship. Emphasizes the importance of teamwork and of stevedoring know-how.
LC NO. FIE52-2051
Prod-USA Dist-USNAC 1952

Outlook C 30 MIN
2 INCH VIDEOTAPE
See series title for descriptive statement.
From The Unconscious Cultural Clashes Series.
Prod-SCCOE Dist-SCCOE

Outlook Southeast Asia C 17 MIN
16MM FILM OPTICAL SOUND
Depicts the political, social and economic progress of Indonesia, Malaysia, Philippines, Singapore, Republic of Vietnam, Laos, Cambodia, Thailand and Burma. Describes the rich agricultural and industrial resources of Southeast Asia.
LC NO. 75-700569
Prod-USDD Dist-USNAC 1968

Outpatient Chemotherapy - Patient-Teaching Session C 25 MIN
3/4 INCH VIDEO CASSETTE
Shows staff how to deal with patients involved in chemotherapy.
Prod-UTAHTI Dist-UTAHTI

Outpatient Hemorrhoidectomy - Ligation Technique C 11 MIN
16MM FILM OPTICAL SOUND PRO
Demonstrates an effective painless treatment of internal hemorrhoids by the rubber-band ligation technique. Points out that the technique has been performed on over 700 patients within a period of five years and is a time-saving procedure performed in the clinic.
LC NO. 73-701951
Prod-SCPMG Dist-SQUIBB 1969

Outpatient Treatment of Minor Burn Injuries C 18 MIN
3/4 OR 1/2 INCH VIDEO CASSETTE PRO
Identifies the nurse's role in the care of the patient with a minor burn injury. Discusses the causes of minor burn injuries and gives a definition of a minor burn wound. Discusses promotion of patient comfort, wound care, infection control, patient teaching and follow-up care.
LC NO. 81-730384
Prod-TRAINX Dist-TRAINX

Outpost Berlin B 35 MIN
16MM FILM OPTICAL SOUND
Shows Berlin from May 1945 to the September 1960 Billy Graham Crusade conducted before the Reichstag.
Prod-GRAHAM Dist-WWPI 1960

Outside C 28 MIN
3/4 INCH VIDEO CASSETTE H-C A
Presents filmmaker and narrator Barry Corbet showing how survivors of spinal cord injuries have integrated themselves into the able bodied world and offers encouragement for other victims.
LC NO. 83-706820
Prod-NRAMRC Dist-CRYSP

Outside - Spinal Cord Injury And The Future C 28 MIN
16MM FILM OPTICAL SOUND J-C A
Presents people with spinal cord injuries who feel they are not deprived of choice because of a physically disabling accident and talk about the diverse and challenging opportunities that were open to them in their new life outside the rehabilitation center.
LC NO. 83-700673
Prod-NRAMRC Dist-CRYSP 1983

Outside Corner V Groove C 15 MIN
3/4 OR 1/2 INCH VIDEO CASSETTE IND
See series title for descriptive statement.
From The Arc Welding Training Series.
Prod-AVIMA Dist-AVIMA

Outside Leg Sweep (O-Soto-Gari) B 4 MIN
16MM FILM OPTICAL SOUND
Demonstrates the outside leg sweep in judo and explains its effectiveness.
From The Combative Measures - Judo Series.
LC NO. 75-700836
Prod-USAF Dist-USNAC 1955

Outside Micrometer, The C 13 MIN
3/4 OR 1/2 INCH VIDEO CASSETTE A
Tells types of micrometers, their main parts, how to handle, read and care for them.
From The Metalworking - Precision Measuring Series.
Prod-VISIN Dist-VISIN

Outside Safety C 15 MIN
3/4 OR 1/2 INCH VIDEO CASSETTE P
Demonstrates how to be safe on a bike, walking, swimming, on the playground and in a car. Teaches children safe places to play andhow to deal with people who try to touch private parts of their bodies. Tells how to act around wild or stray animals.
From The Well, Well, Well With Slim Goodbody Series.
Prod-AITECH Dist-AITECH

Outside The Golden Ring C 22 MIN
16MM FILM OPTICAL SOUND H-C A
Examines various kinds of nontraditional marriages today. Shows the lifestyles of several different couples along with comments by psychologists and a marriage counselor.
LC NO. 75-702603
Prod-WRCTV Dist-CRTVLC 1975

Outside The Law B 78 MIN
16MM FILM SILENT
Tells a story of crime, Oriental philosophy, and social reform, set in San Francisco's Chinatown. Stars Lon Chaney in a duel role as a ruthless gangster and a soft-spoken servant.
Prod-UPCI Dist-KITPAR 1921

Outsiders, The C 20 MIN
3/4 OR 1/2 INCH VIDEO CASSETTE J-H
Presents THE OUTSIDERS by Susan E H Hinton. Focuses on warring gangs in a Midwestern city whose conflicts result in the death of a boy. (Broadcast quality)
From The Matter Of Fiction Series. No. 10
Prod-WETATV Dist-AITECH

Outsmarting Crime - An Older Person's Guide To Safer Living C 16 MIN
16MM FILM, 3/4 OR 1/2 IN VIDEO
Discusses the vulnerability of senior citizens to robbery, burglary and fraud. Demonstrates measures that can be taken by older citizens to avoid being victimized.
Prod-HAR Dist-MTI 1984

Outtakes C 14 MIN
16MM FILM, 3/4 OR 1/2 IN VIDEO J-C A

Tells the story of an incompetent actor who is given the opportunity to make a film.
Prod-MIP Dist-WOMBAT

Outtakes - Paysage De Guerre C 26 MIN
16MM FILM OPTICAL SOUND
Uses experimental techniques to reveal the horror and tragedy of war by creating a contrast between detachment and objective reality.
LC NO. 79-700258
Prod-BREKEP Dist-BREKEP 1979

Outtakes-Paysage De Guerre C 26 MIN
3/4 OR 1/2 INCH VIDEO CASSETTE
Reveals a series of events in a bombing mission and the resulting effect upon the landscape by means of many shifts in time and space. An experimental film.
Prod-BREKEP Dist-MEDIPR 1979

Outward Bound C 28 MIN
16MM FILM - 3/4 IN VIDEO J-C A
Explores the challenges of the Outward Bound Schools with beauty and sensitivity. Depicts the lives of young men from all backgrounds as they experience the demands of the outdoor world.
Prod-OUTB Dist-CRYSP Prodn-SUMMIT

Outwitting The Purse Snatcher C 9 MIN
16MM FILM, 3/4 OR 1/2 IN VIDEO A
Opens with brief scenes of a purse snatcher at work and then re-enacts each scene to show how the thief could have been outwitted.
Prod-RTBL Dist-RTBL

OV-10A Multi-Mission C 8 MIN
16MM FILM OPTICAL SOUND
Presents early development footage of the ov-10a.
Prod-NAA Dist-RCKWL

Ovals C 15 MIN
3/4 OR 1/2 INCH VIDEO CASSETTE P
See series title for descriptive statement.
From The Let's Draw Series.
Prod-OCPS Dist-AITECH Prodn-KOKHTV 1976

Ovarian Tumor Resection And Abdominal Hysterectomy C 19 MIN
3/4 OR 1/2 INCH VIDEO CASSETTE
See series title for descriptive statement.
From The Gynecologic Series.
Prod-SVL Dist-SVL

Ovarian Tumors C 24 MIN
16MM FILM OPTICAL SOUND PRO
Illustrates the gross diagnosis of ovarian tumors with a series of cases at the operating table ranging from the simple retention cysts through complicated carcinomas. Discusses implications for treatment.
Prod-ACYDGD Dist-ACY 1965

Over A Barrel C 15 MIN
3/4 INCH VIDEO CASSETTE H-C A
Examines the power of oil companies in controlling supply and setting prices. Explores the ramifications in terms of human suffering, especially as it affects the elderly and those on fixed incomes.
Prod-USERI Dist-USERI 1979

Over A Barrel - Energy In The 80's C 90 MIN
3/4 INCH VIDEO CASSETTE J-C A
Presents a panel discussion between a labor leader, a consumer advocate and an oil company spokesman on the power of oil companies.
Prod-USERI Dist-USERI 1979

Over And Under C 25 MIN
2 INCH VIDEOTAPE I
Demonstrates weaving techniques.
From The Art For Every Day Series.
Prod-CVETVC Dist-GPITVL

Over Hill, Over Dale C 15 MIN
3/4 OR 1/2 INCH VIDEO CASSETTE K-P
Looks at the things around us when traveling to a park or taking a hike.
From The Pass It On Series.
Prod-WKNOTV Dist-GPITVL 1983

Over In The Meadow C 10 MIN
16MM FILM, 3/4 OR 1/2 IN VIDEO K-P
Features a sing-along film. Presents an old counting song for children.
Prod-WWS Dist-WWS 1969

Over The Andes In Ecuador C 18 MIN
16MM FILM, 3/4 OR 1/2 IN VIDEO P-C
Presents transportation, industry, dress and customs of the people of Ecuador.
From The Man And His World Series.
Prod-FI Dist-FI 1969

Over The Counter Drugs - Smooth Talk And Small Print C 22 MIN
16MM FILM, 3/4 OR 1/2 IN VIDEO J-C
Discusses advertising claims for non-prescription drugs and explodes many of these claims.
LC NO. 83-706801
Prod-VISF Dist-BARR 1980

Over The Hill To The Moon C 8 MIN
16MM FILM, 3/4 OR 1/2 IN VIDEO I-H
Explains how a spacecraft overcomes conflicting gravity pulls when traveling to the moon. Dramatizes an entire lunar flight, with animation and live footage. Clarifies the process of moving a spacecraft through the gravity fields of earth and moon.
From The Space Science Series.
Prod-ALTPRO Dist-JOU 1984

Over There C 24 MIN
16MM FILM OPTICAL SOUND J-H
Follows American expeditionary forces from 1914 until the day of armistice as seen in Paris, London, New York and the White House.
Prod-INTEXT Dist-REAF

Over-The-Counter Drugs And Valium C
1/2 IN VIDEO CASSETTE (VHS)
Provides a framework for choosing and using over-the-counter drugs, including aspirin. Deals with Valium.
From The Surviving Lifestyle Drugs Series.
Prod-IBIS Dist-IBIS

Over-The-Counter Pills And Promises C 17 MIN
16MM FILM, 3/4 OR 1/2 IN VIDEO J-C A
Describes how millions of dollars are spent each year on over-the-counter medication as a result of misleading advertising. Shows alternative remedies for many health problems.
Prod-HIGGIN Dist-HIGGIN 1977

Overall Organization C 30 MIN
3/4 OR 1/2 INCH VIDEO CASSETTE
Focuses on the main idea in a letter. Shows where to put the main idea in a sales letter and a collection letter.
From The Better Business Letters Series. Lesson 2
Prod-TELSTR Dist-TELSTR

Overall Organization Of The Letter C 26 MIN
3/4 OR 1/2 INCH VIDEO CASSETTE
See series title for descriptive statement.
From The Better Business Letters Series.
Prod-TELSTR Dist-DELTAK

Overall Skiing C 30 MIN
3/4 OR 1/2 INCH VIDEO CASSETTE
Covers several aspects of waterskiing. Includes competition, training, tournament strategy and the future. Stars Sammy Duvall.
From The Superstar Sports Tapes Series.
Prod-TRASS Dist-TRASS

Overanxious Patient And The Overactive Patient, The C 19 MIN
3/4 OR 1/2 INCH VIDEO CASSETTE
Presents issues concerned with the anxious patient and includes documentation, nursing care plans, associated hypochondria, preoccupation with his/her body, planned rest times and prescribed sedatives.
From The Basic Therapeutic Approaches To Abnormal Behaviors Series.
Prod-SCDMH Dist-UWISC 1979

Overarm Sweep And Shoulder Shrug / Trunk Stretcher / Forward And Backward Leg Lifts C 15 MIN
3/4 OR 1/2 INCH VIDEO CASSETTE P
Presents several exercises which can be performed in a classroom setting.
From The Roomnastics Series.
Prod-WVIZTV Dist-GPITVL 1979

Overcalls C 30 MIN
3/4 OR 1/2 INCH VIDEO CASSETTE A
See series title for descriptive statement.
From The Bridge Basics Series.
Prod-KYTV Dist-KYTV

Overcoming C 30 MIN
16MM FILM OPTICAL SOUND
Documents different types of unique and unusual educational processes for deaf and blind children from preschool to secondary school. Concentrates on the adjustment and education of one such student, Donald Lenhartz.
LC NO. 79-700259
Prod-DIETEL Dist-DIETEL 1978

Overcoming Barriers In Negotiations C 24 MIN
3/4 OR 1/2 INCH VIDEO CASSETTE
See series title for descriptive statement.
From The Art Of Negotiating Series.
Prod-DELTAK Dist-DELTAK

Overcoming Direct Mail Pitfalls C 30 MIN
3/4 OR 1/2 INCH VIDEO CASSETTE
Explains how to overcome direct mail pitfalls.
From The Business Of Direct Mail Series.
Prod-KYTV Dist-KYTV 1983

Overcoming Erection Problems, Pt 1 C 11 MIN
3/4 OR 1/2 INCH VIDEO CASSETTE
Demonstrates interrupted stimulation exercises designed to reduce and extinguish anxieties related to the male's ability to attain an erection and/or regain a 'lost' erection.
From The EDCOA Sexual Counseling Series.
Prod-MMRC Dist-MMRC

Overcoming Erection Problems, Pt 2 C 10 MIN
3/4 OR 1/2 INCH VIDEO CASSETTE
Shows how to combine interrupted penile stimulation with successive vaginal approximation until couple is assured of the male's erectile competence.
From The EDCOA Sexual Counseling Series.
Prod-MMRC Dist-MMRC

Overcoming Objections C 17 MIN
16MM FILM, 3/4 OR 1/2 IN VIDEO C A
Explains and demonstrates how to anticipate customers' objections, listen for their expressed needs, define problem areas and then overcome specific objections.
LC NO. 82-707108
Prod-CRMP Dist-CRMP 1982

Overcoming Resistance C 60 MIN
3/4 OR 1/2 INCH VIDEO CASSETTE A
Shows how to make each of the buyer's objections in a selling situation the basis for a joint problem-solving situation that can lead to a close.
From The Strategic Selling - A Thinking Person's Guide Series. Pt 3
Prod-TIMLIF Dist-TIMLIF 1984

Overcoming Resistance To Change C 30 MIN
16MM FILM, 3/4 OR 1/2 IN VIDEO H-C
Shows how supervisors can overcome and prevent serious morale conditions and losses in efficiency during periods of change in an organization.
LC NO. FIA66-1085
Prod-RTBL Dist-RTBL 1962

Overcoming Resistance To Change (Danish) C 30 MIN
16MM FILM, 3/4 OR 1/2 IN VIDEO H-C
Shows how supervisors can overcome and prevent serious morale conditions and losses in efficiency during periods of change in an organization.
Prod-RTBL Dist-RTBL 1962

Overcoming Resistance To Change (Dutch) C 30 MIN
16MM FILM, 3/4 OR 1/2 IN VIDEO H-C
Shows how supervisors can overcome and prevent serious morale conditions and losses in efficiency during periods of change in an organization.
Prod-RTBL Dist-RTBL 1962

Overcoming Resistance To Change (German) C 30 MIN
16MM FILM, 3/4 OR 1/2 IN VIDEO H-C
Shows how supervisors can overcome and prevent serious morale conditions and losses in efficiency during periods of change in an organization.
Prod-RTBL Dist-RTBL 1962

Overcoming Resistance To Change (Portuguese) C 30 MIN
16MM FILM, 3/4 OR 1/2 IN VIDEO H-C
Shows how supervisors can overcome and prevent serious morale conditions and losses in efficiency during periods of change in an organization.
Prod-RTBL Dist-RTBL 1962

Overcoming Resistance To Change (Spanish) C 30 MIN
16MM FILM, 3/4 OR 1/2 IN VIDEO H-C
Shows how supervisors can overcome and prevent serious morale conditions and losses in efficiency during periods of change in an organization.
LC NO. FIA66-1085
Prod-RTBL Dist-RTBL 1962

Overcoming Resistance To Change (Swedish) C 30 MIN
16MM FILM, 3/4 OR 1/2 IN VIDEO H-C
Shows how supervisors can overcome and prevent serious morale conditions and losses in efficiency during periods of change in an organization.
Prod-RTBL Dist-RTBL 1962

Overdenture Technique - Diagnosis C 9 MIN
16MM FILM, 3/4 OR 1/2 IN VIDEO
Shows how the overdenture procedure provides a practical and simple alternative to conventional complete dentures. Emphasizes selection of roots to be retained and demonstrates the advantages of the overdenture technique.
From The Overdenture Technique Series.
Prod-USVA Dist-USNAC Prodn-VADTC 1975

Overdenture Technique - Laboratory Procedures, Denture Insertion And Oral Hygiene C 7 MIN
16MM FILM, 3/4 OR 1/2 IN VIDEO
Demonstrates technical variations which are utilized in adapting the usual laboratory procedures to the fabrication of an overdenture. Shows the use of pressure indicator paste to obtain equalized contacts at the time of delivery and explains oral hygiene procedures.
From The Overdenture Technique Series.
Prod-USVA Dist-USNAC Prodn-VADTC 1975

Overdenture Technique - Treatment Procedures C 10 MIN
16MM FILM, 3/4 OR 1/2 IN VIDEO
Shows how some teeth can frequently be selected to be retained beneath an overdenture. Shows how the retained teeth are modified by endodontics, periodontal treatment, crown reduction and an amalgam restoration. Shows how to make the final impression.
From The Overdenture Technique Series.
Prod-USVA Dist-USNAC Prodn-VADTC 1975

Overdenture Technique—A Series
3/4 OR 1/2 INCH VIDEO CASSETTE
Prod-USVA Dist-USNAC Prodn-VADTC 1975

Overdenture Technique - Diagnosis 9 MIN
Overdenture Technique - Laboratory 7 MIN
Overdenture Technique - Treatment Procedures 10 MIN

Overdentures - Step-By-Step, From Start To Finish C 120 MIN
3/4 INCH VIDEO CASSETTE
Offers an unedited presentation by Joseph C Morganelli, DDS, Chicago, showing steps from diagnosis through delivery of the methodology used to stabilize full prosthetic appliances.
Prod-AMDA Dist-AMDA 1977

Overdose C 17 MIN
3/4 OR 1/2 INCH VIDEO CASSETTE IND
Discusses not only what to do, but what not to do, for victims of chemical overdose.
From The Emergency Medical Training Series. Lesson 2
Prod-LEIKID Dist-LEIKID

Overdose C 17 MIN
3/4 OR 1/2 INCH VIDEO CASSETTE
Shows how to understand major life threatening dangers to overdose victims, identify suspected overdose victims, administer appropriate emergency treatment and follow the five steps outlined in the program.
From The Emergency Medical Training Series.
Prod-VTRI Dist-VTRI

Overdose - The Crucial Minutes C 28 MIN
3/4 OR 1/2 INCH VIDEO CASSETTE
Deals with the management of an acute poisoning victim involving medicinal drugs. Follows a victim from initial unconsciousness in his home to the emergency room at the hospital.
LC NO. 81-706268
Prod-USFDA Dist-USNAC 1979

Overhand Throw And Ball Dodging C 15 MIN
3/4 OR 1/2 INCH VIDEO CASSETTE T
Explains how to teach primary students the overhand throw for the pattern, distance, force or accuracy, and how to dodge a rolled or thrown ball.
From The Leaps And Bounds Series. No. 13
Prod-HSDE Dist-AITECH 1984

Overhaul Procedures C 21 MIN
3/4 OR 1/2 INCH VIDEO CASSETTE PRO
Describes techniques for securing the fire scene and procedures for total extinguishment. Shows how the importance of fire cause is tied in to overhaul procedures.
Prod-LACFD Dist-FILCOM

Overhauling Camshaft Assembly And Crankcase Section B 19 MIN
16MM FILM OPTICAL SOUND
Explains how to inspect the camshaft and gear case cover assembly, inspect and recondition the crankcase section, measure crankcase bearings and inspect and recondition the remaining parts.
From The Aircraft Work Series. Power Plant Maintenance
LC NO. FIE52-149
Prod-USOE Dist-USNAC Prodn-AUDIO 1945

Overhauling Crankshaft Assembly B 19 MIN
16MM FILM OPTICAL SOUND
Explains how to clean the parts of a disassembled engine, inspect and recondition crankshaft assembly parts, determine clearances and check for out-ofround and inspect clearances against specifications.
From The Aircraft Work Series. Power Plant Maintenance
LC NO. FIE52-150
Prod-USOE Dist-USNAC Prodn-AUDIO 1945

Overhauling The Carburetor B 23 MIN
16MM FILM OPTICAL SOUND
Shows how to remove the carburetor assembly from the engine, disassemble, clean, inspect and reassemble the carburetor, check the fuel level and reinstall the carburetor assembly.
From The Aircraft Work Series. Power Plant Maintenance
LC NO. FIE52-251
Prod-USOE Dist-USNAC Prodn-AUDIO 1945

Overhead Fillet Weld C 8 MIN
1/2 IN VIDEO CASSETTE BETA/VHS IND
See series title for descriptive statement.
From The Welding Training (Comprehensive) - Advanced Shielded Metal Arc Welding Series.
Prod-RMI Dist-RMI

Overhead Router, The C 37 MIN
3/4 OR 1/2 INCH VIDEO CASSETTE IND
Reviews ordinal skills of shaping stock edge and routing vein lines or decorative designs into the face of the stock. Shows rabbit cuts, grooves and dovetail joints.
From The Furniture Manufacturing Series.
Prod-LEIKID Dist-LEIKID

Overhead V-Butt Weld C 9 MIN
1/2 IN VIDEO CASSETTE BETA/VHS IND
See series title for descriptive statement.
From The Welding Training (Comprehensive) - Advanced Shielded Metal Arc Welding Series.
Prod-RMI Dist-RMI

Overhead, The C 29 MIN
3/4 OR 1/2 INCH VIDEO CASSETTE
See series title for descriptive statement.
From The Vic Braden's Tennis For The Future Series.
Prod-WGBHTV Dist-PBS 1981

Overload Relays, Controllers, Coils C 60 MIN
3/4 OR 1/2 INCH VIDEO CASSETTE IND
See series title for descriptive statement.
From The Electrical Maintenance Training, Module 1 - Control Equipment Series.
Prod-LEIKID Dist-LEIKID

Overly Suspicious Patient, The C 27 MIN
3/4 OR 1/2 INCH VIDEO CASSETTE
Presents an in-depth definition of the overly suspicious patient and methods used to effectively deal with this type of patient in a hospital setting. Illustrates identifying characteristics such as insecurity, delusions of persecution and grandeur, hypochondria and hallucinations.
Prod-SCDMH Dist-UWISC 1979

Overmanagement Or How An Exciting Idea Can Be Transferred Into A Dull Project C 13 MIN
16MM FILM, 3/4 OR 1/2 IN VIDEO C A
Illustrates the effect a complicated, bureaucratic, decisionmaking process has on a simple idea. Promotes discussion on overmanagement of corporations.
Prod-SYKES Dist-SALENG 1976

Overnight At The Hospital C 15 MIN
16MM FILM, 3/4 OR 1/2 IN VIDEO
Follows a boy as he meets other hospitalized children, learns to swallow a pill and enjoys a visit from his dad. Shows him lying alone, wide awake in the middle of the night, figuring out a way to get company that will help him fall asleep.
From The Ripples Series.
LC NO. 73-702148
Prod-NITC Dist-AITECH

Overnight Camping C 30 MIN
3/4 OR 1/2 INCH VIDEO CASSETTE
Discusses overnight camping as outdoor activity that requires 'roughing it.'
From The Roughing It Series.
Prod-KYTV Dist-KYTV 1984

Overnight Sensation C 30 MIN
16MM FILM, 3/4 OR 1/2 IN VIDEO H-C A
Presents a contemporary film adaptation of Somerset Maugham's short story, The Colonel's Lady. Focuses on a couple whose marriage is tested when the wife's first novel is an unexpected success, and the husband must deal with a new perspective on a traditional relationship. Features actors, Louise Fletcher, Robert Loggia, and Shari Belafonte.
Prod-PFP Dist-PFP 1984

Overtaking At Night C 15 MIN
16MM FILM OPTICAL SOUND
Illustrates the correct use of whistle signals in overtaking situations on the ocean and in inland waters.
LC NO. FIE52-947
Prod-USN Dist-USNAC 1943

Overtaking Situation B 15 MIN
16MM FILM OPTICAL SOUND
Gives whistle signals to be used when overtaking on the ocean, in inland waters and in narrow channels. Demonstrates examples of their use.
LC NO. FIE52-944
Prod-USN Dist-USNAC 1943

Overton Park Zoo C 15 MIN
16MM FILM OPTICAL SOUND I-C A
Presents an interview with Mr Robert Mattlin, director of the Overton Park Zoo, who discourages the keeping of exotic animals as house pets. Points out that animals in the Overton Park Zoo are well cared for and live a comfortable and reasonably tranquil life. Explains that this type of care and special feeding cannot be satisfactorily maintained in the home.
Prod-TGAFC Dist-TGAFC

Overture C 20 MIN
16MM FILM OPTICAL SOUND I
Points out that American music is a melting pot of sounds - some started here in our country like the American Indian chant and dance, some was imported and then developed here like jazz and our folk music, some from other countries that was not Americanized like classical symphonies and opera and others that came with the immigrants from their native lands.
From The Music Of America Series.
Prod-KQEDTV Dist-GPITVL

Overture - Linh From Vietnam C 26 MIN
16MM FILM, 3/4 OR 1/2 IN VIDEO J-C A
Introduces Linh Tran, a Vietnamese girl who has settled with her family into the first real home they have had since immigrating from Vietnam to America. Shows the hardships they endure and the adjustments they must make in a country where they are neither accepted or wanted.
Prod-LCOA Dist-LCOA Prodn-SPRBRE 1981

Overture 2012 C 6 MIN
16MM FILM, 3/4 OR 1/2 IN VIDEO H-C A
Presents an animated interpretation of the future of man's discordant world.
Prod-ZAGREB Dist-IFB 1977

Overuse Injuries - Too Much, Too Fast, Too Soon C 10 MIN
3/4 OR 1/2 INCH VIDEO CASSETTE
Presents information on recognizing and managing overuse injuries. Presents definitions of the injury, how they develop and the mechanism of injury, particularly in the lower extremity. Describes treatment techniques as well as steps coaches and athletes can take to help prevent overuse injuries.
From The Sports Medicine For Coaches Series.
Prod-UWASH Dist-UWASH

Overuse Syndromes Of The Lower Extremity C 27 MIN
3/4 OR 1/2 INCH VIDEO CASSETTE T
Discusses the prevalence of disabilities caused by overuse syndromes, their syndromes, their symptoms and effect on athletic performance. Demonstrates the causes, diagnosis and treatments of such disorders as shin splints, runner's knee, jumper's knee, Osgood Schlatter's disease, ankle pronation, Cavas' foot and Morton's foot.
From The Sports Medicine Series.
Prod-UNIDIM Dist-EBEC 1982

Overview C 14 MIN
2 INCH VIDEOTAPE PRO
Explains the purpose of the AMA Assessment Center and the manner in which it functions.
From The AMA Assessment Center Program For Identifying Supervisory Potential Series.
LC NO. 75-704221
Prod-AMA Dist-AMA 1974

Overview C 18 MIN
3/4 OR 1/2 INCH VIDEO CASSETTE A
Discusses Executive Order 12356, signed by President Reagan in April, 1982. Defines National Security Information, information security personnel and their responsibilities, and methods used in classification and declassification of materials.
From The Information Security Briefing Series.
Prod-USISOO Dist-USNAC 1983

Overview C 50 MIN
3/4 OR 1/2 INCH VIDEO CASSETTE PRO
Discusses fully connected topology, circuit switching, datagrams and the Local Area Network, among other things.
From The Communication Networks Series.
Prod-AMCEE Dist-AMCEE

Overview - Ideas, Things And People C 45 MIN
3/4 OR 1/2 INCH VIDEO CASSETTE IND
Focuses on the five functions of management, the crucial importance of people, strengths and weaknesses of technically trained people, what management is all about and management pitfalls.
From The Basic Management Skills For Engineers And Scientists Series.
Prod-USCITV Dist-AMCEE

Overview - Job Analysis And Manning Table B 29 MIN
16MM FILM OPTICAL SOUND IND
See series title for descriptive statement.
From The Job Instructor Training Series.
LC NO. 77-703324
Prod-EDSD Dist-EDSD

Overview - Teaching Operations And Associated Strategies C 29 MIN
3/4 OR 1/2 INCH VIDEO CASSETTE T
Provides an introduction to the Strategies Of Effective Teaching series.
From The Strategies Of Effective Teaching Series.
Prod-PCSB Dist-AITECH 1980

Overview And Disease-Specific Isolation C
3/4 OR 1/2 INCH VIDEO CASSETTE
Discusses the basic principles of disease transmission, the initiation of isolation precautions, the psychologic impact of isolation and the importance of patient teaching.
From The Infection Control III Series.
Prod-CONMED Dist-CONMED

Overview And Natural History Of Lung Cancer C 32 MIN
3/4 INCH VIDEO CASSETTE
Presents a statistical study of lung cancer and identifies the major predisposing factors, including environmental, personal habits, occupational and date of birth.
Prod-UTAHTI Dist-UTAHTI

Overview Of Decision Analysis, An C 55 MIN
3/4 OR 1/2 INCH VIDEO CASSETTE
Discusses the objectives, structure and central issues of decision analysis.
From The Decision Analysis Series.
Prod-MIOT Dist-MIOT

Overview Of Laryngectomy - Pre-Op And Post-Op Care C 9 MIN
3/4 OR 1/2 INCH VIDEO CASSETTE PRO
Decribes the voicebox and surrounding structures, the surgical procedure and the postoperative period relating to larynx cancer.
Prod-HSCIC Dist-HSCIC 1984

Overview Of Mainstreaming C 29 MIN
3/4 OR 1/2 INCH VIDEO CASSETTE T
Provides an overview of mainstreaming.
From The Mainstreaming The Exceptional Child Series.
Prod-MFFD Dist-FI

Overview Of Management And Treatment Issues In Acute Intervention In Emergency Room... C 30 MIN
3/4 OR 1/2 INCH VIDEO CASSETTE
Discusses control of staff, patients and their families and dystonic and dysphoric qualities of violence as a symptom of the violent patient.
From The Management And Treatment Of The Violent Patient Series.
Prod-HEMUL Dist-HEMUL

Overview Of MOS, An C 30 MIN
3/4 OR 1/2 INCH VIDEO CASSETTE PRO
Looks at past, present and future of MOS, outlining history and citing motivations behind the rapid growth of MOS technology.
From The MOS Integrated Circuit Series.
Prod-TXINLC Dist-TXINLC

Overview Of Optical Fiber Communications C 50 MIN
3/4 OR 1/2 INCH VIDEO CASSETTE PRO
Includes a description of optical fiber communications systems, historical aspects, benefits of fiber optics, applications, the exploitation of each benefit and evalution of components and systems.
From The Optical Fiber Communications Series.
Prod-NCSU Dist-AMCEE

Overview Of Preventive Antitrust Activities C 89 MIN
3/4 OR 1/2 INCH VIDEO CASSETTE PRO
Offers a panel discussion touching on major issues involved in antitrust compliance programs.
From The Preventive Antitrust - Corporate Compliance Program Series.
Prod-ABACPE Dist-ABACPE

Overview Of School Mathematics In The 80's, An C
3/4 OR 1/2 INCH VIDEO CASSETTE T
Provides an overview of the Third R - Teaching Basic Mathematics Skills series and of Ten Basic Skill areas. Suggests how skills can be imcorporated into total math curriculum. Includes a brief segment from five programs in the series.
From The Third R - Teaching Basic Mathematics Skills Series.
Prod-EPCO Dist-EDCORP

Overview Of The Petroleum Industry–A Series IND

Provides a non-technical review of all major aspects of the petroleum industry and beneficial to lawyers, accountants, banking and financial personnel, clerical and secretarial staff and any others not directly involved in exploration or production.
Prod-GPCV Dist-GPCV

Completing A Well 017 MIN
Crust Of The Earth, The 018 MIN
Drilling A Well 015 MIN
Exploration For Oil And Gas 012 MIN
Formation Of Oil And Gas Deposits 015 MIN
Nature Of Crude Oil And Natural Gas, The 011 MIN
Transporting And Defining 012 MIN

Overview, An C 30 MIN
3/4 OR 1/2 INCH VIDEO CASSETTE
Covers rationale of course and describes the current on-going revolution in digital design techniques. Gives insight of how digital systems are designed.
From The Digital Sub-Systems Series.
Prod-TXINLC Dist-TXINLC

Overwater Flying C 25 MIN
16MM FILM OPTICAL SOUND PRO
Demonstrates equipment and procedures for aviation pilots flying over water in light aircraft. Shows emergency survival gear, optical illusions over water and navigational and radio equipment. Covers proper ditching procedures and water survival techniques.
LC NO. 76-704008
Prod-USFAA Dist-USNAC 1976

Overwater Flying C 25 MIN
3/4 OR 1/2 INCH VIDEO CASSETTE A
Shows skilled pilots experienced in overwater flying explaining hazards and precautions necessary. Covers emergency survival gear, optical illusions overwater, minimal navigation and radio equipment, ditching procedures and survival techniques.
Prod-FAAFL Dist-AVIMA

Overweight C 30 MIN
3/4 OR 1/2 INCH VIDEO CASSETTE C T
Discusses poor eating habits and ways to break them. Describes the many health risks of being fat.
From The Here's To Your Health Series.
Prod-DALCCD Dist-DALCCD

Overweight - How Did I Get This Way? C
3/4 OR 1/2 INCH VIDEO CASSETTE
Presents the psychological inputs that seduce one into eating more than one needs. Explains the signals that trigger improper eating and offers ways to combat their influence.
Prod-MIFE Dist-MIFE

Overweight - What Can I Do About It? C
3/4 OR 1/2 INCH VIDEO CASSETTE
Gives the overweight person guidelines for losing weight and keeping it off. Covers setting a daily calorie limit and substituting low for high calorie foods.
Prod-MIFE Dist-MIFE

Overweight - What Can I Do About It? (Arabic) C
3/4 OR 1/2 INCH VIDEO CASSETTE
Gives the overweight person guidelines for losing weight and keeping it off. Covers setting a daily calorie limit and substituting low for high calorie foods.
Prod-MIFE Dist-MIFE

Overweight - What Can I Do About It? (Spanish) C
3/4 OR 1/2 INCH VIDEO CASSETTE
Gives the overweight person guidelines for losing weight and keeping it off. Covers setting a daily calorie limit and substituting low for high calorie foods.
Prod-MIFE Dist-MIFE

Overweight Americans C 30 MIN
3/4 OR 1/2 INCH VIDEO CASSETTE
Focuses on overweight Americans citing the evidence of the problem and noting the medical and social difficulties it entails. Uses animation to explore the psychology of food and the emotional/societal problem of weight.
From The Here's To Your Health Series.
LC NO. 82-706498
Prod-KERA Dist-PBS 1979

Overweight Americans C 30 MIN
3/4 OR 1/2 INCH VIDEO CASSETTE
See series title for descriptive statement.
From The Here's To Your Health Series.
Prod-PBS Dist-DELTAK

Ovicide Called Lannate, An C 7 MIN
16MM FILM OPTICAL SOUND
Introduces an insecticide which controls cotton pests before they hatch.
LC NO. 78-701321
Prod-DUPONT Dist-DUPONT 1978

Ovulation And Egg Transport In Mammals C 15 MIN
16MM FILM, 3/4 OR 1/2 IN VIDEO
Illustrates the phenomena of ovulation and egg transport in the mammal using the rabbit and cat as subjects.
Prod-UWASHP Dist-UWASHP

Owl - Master Hunter Of The Night C 23 MIN
3/4 OR 1/2 INCH VIDEO CASSETTE K-C A
Explores the true nature of the fabled night predator, the great horned owl. Shows a new breed of conservationist, one who intervenes on the owl's behalf.
Prod-NWLDPR Dist-NWLDPR

Owl And The Lemming, The C 6 MIN
16MM FILM, 3/4 OR 1/2 IN VIDEO P-I
Presents an animated story in which two puppets act out an Eskimo legend in which an owl hunts a lemming because his family needs food. Shows how he is outsmarted by the lemming.
Prod-CDIAND Dist-NFBC 1971

Owl And The Pussycat, The C 3 MIN
16MM FILM, 3/4 OR 1/2 IN VIDEO
Uses the pictures and text of the poem by Edward Lear to tell the story about the owl and the pussycat who take an amorous voyage.
Prod-WWS Dist-WWS 1971

Owl And The Pussycat, The C 6 MIN
16MM FILM, 3/4 OR 1/2 IN VIDEO P
Uses animation to portray the children's poem, 'THE OWL AND THE PUSSYCAT,' by Edward Lear, in which the owl and the pussycat jump into their pea-green boat and sail out to sea.
Prod-NBCTV Dist-MGHT Prodn-KORTY 1962

Owl And The Pussycat, The C 7 MIN
16MM FILM, 3/4 OR 1/2 IN VIDEO
Offers an animated version of the romance and marriage of an owl and a pussycat.
Prod-HALAS Dist-PHENIX 1981

Owl And The Pussycat, The / Little Birds C 8 MIN
16MM FILM, 3/4 OR 1/2 IN VIDEO P
Offers an animated version of nonsense poems by Edward Lear and Lewis Carroll.
LC NO. 81-706172
Prod-TEXFLM Dist-TEXFLM 1980

Owl And The Raven, The C 8 MIN
16MM FILM, 3/4 OR 1/2 IN VIDEO P-I
Presents an Eskimo legend which explains why the raven is black.
Prod-CDIAND Dist-NFBC Prodn-NFBC 1974

Owl Who Gave A Hoot, The B 14 MIN
16MM FILM OPTICAL SOUND
Discusses the exploitation, connivance and fraud in the consumer world of the ghetto and what to do about it.
LC NO. 74-705282
Prod-USOEO Dist-USNAC 1967

Owl Who Gave A Hoot, The B 14 MIN
3/4 INCH VIDEO CASSETTE
Presents an animated cartoon depicting the exploitation, connivance and fraud in the consumer world of the ghetto.
Prod-USNAC Dist-USNAC 1972

Owl Who Gave A Hoot, The (Spanish) C 14 MIN
16MM FILM, 3/4 OR 1/2 IN VIDEO
An animated cartoon film that tells it like it is exploitation, connivance and fraud in the consumer world of the ghettos and what to do about it.
Prod-USOEO Dist-USNAC 1967

Owl Who Married A Goose, The C 8 MIN
16MM FILM, 3/4 OR 1/2 IN VIDEO P-C A
Based on an Eskimo legend on a theme of nature, this imaginary tale done in animated style unfolds with subtle humor the interaction between an owl and a goose and the owl's attempts to follow the goose's lifestyle. Uses actual Eskimo voices imitating the geese and owl noises.
Prod-CDIAND Dist-CF Prodn-NFBC 1974

Owlfie's Whooing School C 15 MIN
3/4 OR 1/2 INCH VIDEO CASSETTE P
Presents Dr Allhart and her friend Patience discussing the similarities between animal and human needs.
From The Dr Allhart And Patience Series.
LC NO. 81-707536
Prod-JCITV Dist-GPITVL 1979

Owls - Lords Of Darkness C 26 MIN
16MM FILM, 3/4 OR 1/2 IN VIDEO
Shows the primary species of owls which are found in North America.
LC NO. 84-700165
Prod-STOUFP Dist-STOUFP 1983

Owls In The Family C 15 MIN
3/4 OR 1/2 INCH VIDEO CASSETTE P
See series title for descriptive statement.
From The Best Of Cover To Cover 1 Series.
Prod-WETATV Dist-WETATV

Owning A Car C 29 MIN
3/4 INCH VIDEO CASSETTE C A
Examines rights and responsibilities of owning and operating a car. Focuses on buying a car, registration and driver's responsibilities.
From The You And The Law Series. Lesson 21
Prod-COAST Dist-CDTEL Prodn-SADCC

Ox Cell Hemolysin Test For Diagnosis Of Infectious Mononucleosis C 10 MIN
16MM FILM OPTICAL SOUND
Demonstrates a rapid test based on the presence of a hemolysin in the sera in I M patients that will cause lysis of ox cells in the presence of complements.
LC NO. FI67-52
Prod-USPHS Dist-USNAC 1965

Ox Tail Soup C 7 MIN
16MM FILM SILENT I-C A
Tells in American sign language a true life adventure of a large family growing up on a sharecrop farm in the depression years and what happened one day when they were making oxtail soup. Signed for the deaf by Herb Larson.
LC NO. 76-701699
Prod-JOYCE Dist-JOYCE 1975

Oxcart, The (Spanish) C 20 MIN
16MM FILM, 3/4 OR 1/2 IN VIDEO
Portrays the migration of a Puerto Rican family from the countryside, to a San Juan ghetto, to Spanish Harlem in New York City. Examines the issue of modern technology as opposed to a return to the land. Based on the three-act play by Puerto Rican playwright Rene Marques. English subtitles.
Prod-CNEMAG Dist-CNEMAG

Oxford Philosophy, Pt 1 - Logic Lane C 60 MIN
16MM FILM OPTICAL SOUND
Presents a retrospective of philosophy at Oxford over the past 40 years as explained by Professor Sir Alfred Ayer. Discusses the social and historical background of the university and its importance in the training of British politicians.
Prod-NYFLMS Dist-NYFLMS 1972

Oxford Philosophy, Pt 2 - I'm Going To Tamper With Your Beliefs A Little C 60 MIN
16MM FILM OPTICAL SOUND
Discusses the philosophy of J L Austin, who lectured at Harvard before he died in 1960. Includes an excerpt from the only surviving recording of his lectures, made one year before his death and never before heard publicly.
Prod-NYFLMS Dist-NYFLMS 1972

Oxford Philosophy, Pt 3 - The Idea Of Freedom C 60 MIN
16MM FILM OPTICAL SOUND
Presents a conversation between Iris Murdoch, novelist and philosopher, and Oxford professor, David Pears on the subject of Murdoch's book, THE SOVEREIGNTY OF GOOD. Focuses on individual freedom, determinism and self-knowledge.
Prod-NYFLMS Dist-NYFLMS 1972

Oxford Philosophy, Pt 4 - Appearance And Reality C 60 MIN
16MM FILM OPTICAL SOUND
Presents a conversation between Sir Alfred Ayer and Professor Bernard Williams of Cambridge University on science and its relation to philosophy.
Prod-NYFLMS Dist-NYFLMS 1972

Oxford Philosophy, Pt 5 - You Might Just As Well Say That I See What I Eat The Same... C 60 MIN
16MM FILM OPTICAL SOUND
Focuses on linguistic philosophy and the work of one of its chief exponents, Gilbert Ryle. Questions whether linguistic philosophy has somehow missed certain issues which have always been believed to be central to traditional philosophy.
Prod-NYFLMS Dist-NYFLMS 1972

Oxford Philosophy, Pt 6 - Language And Creativity C 60 MIN
16MM FILM OPTICAL SOUND
Discusses linguistic and semantic theory as viewed by P F Strawson and Gareth Evans. Asks if language is something organic and constantly changing.
Prod-NYFLMS Dist-NYFLMS 1972

Oxidase Test, The C 5 MIN
3/4 INCH VIDEO CASSETTE
Demonstrates a method of differentiating oxidase positive from oxidase negative organisms.
LC NO. 77-706127
Prod-NMAC Dist-USNAC 1977

Oxidation And Reduction C 8 MIN
3/4 INCH VIDEO CASSETTE
Demonstrates several redox reactions. Introduces electrochemical cell as a source of information about redox strengths.
From The Chemistry Videotape Series.
Prod-UMITV Dist-UMITV

Oxidation And Reduction C 35 MIN
3/4 INCH VIDEO CASSETTE C A
See series title for descriptive statement.
From The Elements Of Metallurgy Series.
LC NO. 81-706194
Prod-AMCEE Dist-AMCEE 1980

Oxidation And Reduction (Extractive Metallurgy) C 45 MIN
3/4 OR 1/2 INCH VIDEO CASSETTE PRO
See series title for descriptive statement.
From The Elements Of Metallurgy Series.
Prod-ICSINT Dist-ICSINT

Oxidative Phosphorylation I C 24 MIN
16MM FILM, 3/4 OR 1/2 IN VIDEO
Introduces the concept of respiratory electron transport in the microenvironment of the mitochondrial membrane. Shows the structure of mitochondria, the general nature of oxidation reactions and the energy-requiring phosphorylation reactions. Considers the nature of the string which couples energy-releasing and energy-requiring processes in the pulley model.
Prod-OPENU Dist-MEDIAG Prodn-BBCTV 1978

Oxidative Phosphorylation II C 25 MIN
16MM FILM, 3/4 OR 1/2 IN VIDEO
Demonstrates that proton pumping is produced by an oxidation reaction known as electron transport. Describes the four main tenets of Mitchell's chemiosmotic hypothesis and explores some of the current ideas about how ATP is synthesized by an enzyme.
Prod-OPENU Dist-MEDIAG Prodn-BBCTV 1978

Oxidizers C
3/4 OR 1/2 INCH VIDEO CASSETTE
Focuses upon safety and health measures to take where oxidizers are concerned.
From The Chemsafe Series.
Prod-BNA Dist-BNA

Oxo-Omo-Ono C 2 MIN
16MM FILM OPTICAL SOUND
Presents an animated pop-art battle between eye-creatures and Mickey Mouse.
LC NO. 75-703217
Prod-USC Dist-USC 1970

Oxy-Acetylene Equipment Set-Up And Safety C 33 MIN
1/2 IN VIDEO CASSETTE BETA/VHS IND
See series title for descriptive statement.
From The Welding Training (Comprehensive) — Oxy-Acetylene Welding Series.
Prod-RMI Dist-RMI

Oxy-Acetylene Flame, The Master Of Metals C 19 MIN
16MM FILM OPTICAL SOUND
Shows how oxygen and acetylene are blended to form a flame to cut, weld, solder, braze and harden metal. Depicts uses, such as forming teeth on tractor gears, molding grey cast iron and hardening edges of plows.
Prod-USDIBM Dist-USDIBM 1950

Oxy-Acetylene Welding - Light Metal B 21 MIN
16MM FILM OPTICAL SOUND
Shows how to assemble a gas welding outfit, adjust gas pressures, adjust the flame, and make a butt weld and a 'T' weld in light tubing.
From The Welding Procedures Series. Oxyacetylene Welding, No. 1
LC NO. FIE52-293
Prod-USOE Dist-USNAC Prodn-DEFREN 1944

Oxy-Acetylene Welding And Cutting - Braze Welding C 13 MIN
16MM FILM, 3/4 OR 1/2 IN VIDEO
Demonstrates techniques for braze welding of sheet steel, plate and castings. Shows how to set up welding equipment, adjust oxygen and acetylene pressures, light the welding torch and adjust the flame for braze welding.
From The Welding Series.
Prod-UCC Dist-FI 1972

Oxy-Acetylene Welding Series C 120 MIN
3/4 OR 1/2 INCH VIDEO CASSETTE IND
Contains 12 separate programs encompassing two hours on Basic Oxy-Acetylene Welding. Includes equipment setup, flame adjustment, and chemistry, puddle control, edge welding, running beads with filler, butt-joint welding, lap-joint welding, beads on tubing, butt-joint on tubing, T-joint on tubing and cluster welding techniques.
From The Aviation Technician Training Program Series.
Prod-AVIMA Dist-AVIMA 1979

Oxy-Acetylene Welding T-Joints, Lap Joints, Corner Joints And Edge Joints (Spanish) C
3/4 OR 1/2 INCH VIDEO CASSETTE
See series title for descriptive statement.
From The Oxy-Acetylene Welding (Spanish) Series.
Prod-VTRI Dist-VTRI

Oxy-Acetylene Welding T-Joints, Lap Joints, Corner Joints And Edge Joints C 15 MIN
3/4 OR 1/2 INCH VIDEO CASSETTE IND
See series title for descriptive statement.
From The Welding - Oxy-Acetylene Welding Series.
Prod-ICSINT Dist-ICSINT

Oxy-Acetylene Welding, (Spanish)—A Series

Presents a series on oxy-acetylene welding, covering such subjects as equipment, safety, types of flames, welding terms and various welding procedures.
Prod-VTRI Dist-VTRI

Automatic Flame Cutting With Oxy-Acetylene
Brazing And Fusion Welding On Gray Cast Iron
Bronze Welding In Flat And Horizontal
Cutting Metal With The Combination Torch
Flat And Horizontal Butt Welds With Filler
Joint Design And Welding Terms (Spanish)
Oxy-Acetylene Welding T-Joints, Lap Joints,
Piercing, Cutting Holes And Cutting 45-Degree
Puddling And Running Beads With Oxy-Acetylene
Set-Up And Shut Down Of Oxy-Acetylene Welding
Silver Braxing And Soft Soldering (Spanish)
Three Types Of Oxy-Acetylene Flames, The -
Vertical And Overhead Butt Welds With Filler
Welding Equipment, Accessories And Shop

Oxyacetylene Cutting C 12 MIN
3/4 OR 1/2 INCH VIDEO CASSETTE IND
Shows how to safely set up the oxyacetylene outfit, how to put it away and proper safety practices.
From The Marshall Maintenance Training Programs Series. Tape 5
Prod-LEIKID Dist-LEIKID

Oxyacetylene Cutting C 12 MIN
16MM FILM, 3/4 OR 1/2 IN VIDEO IND
Demonstrates how to set up an oxyacetylene outfit in a safe fashion, how to pull it away, the proper safety practices and how to always make a clean cut with little practice.
Prod-MOKIN Dist-MOKIN

Oxyacetylene Safety C 24 MIN
16MM FILM, 3/4 OR 1/2 IN VIDEO IND
Introduces safe practices in handling and using oxyacetylene welding and burning equipment.
LC NO. 80-707267
Prod-TAT Dist-TAT 1980

Oxyacetylene Welding - Equipment C 16 MIN
16MM FILM, 3/4 OR 1/2 IN VIDEO H A
Describes the equipment used in bench-type gas welding and brazing. Shows the correct procedures for assembling the equipment, lighting the torch and adjusting the flame.
From The Industrial Education Series.
Prod-BROSEB Dist-PHENIX 1971

Oxyacetylene Welding - Equipment (Spanish) C 16 MIN
16MM FILM, 3/4 OR 1/2 IN VIDEO H A
Describes the equipment used in bench-type gas welding and brazing. Shows the correct procedures for assembling the equipment, lighting the torch and adjusting the flame.
From The Industrial Education Series.
Prod-BROSEB Dist-PHENIX 1971

Oxyacetylene Welding - Joining Steel C 14 MIN
16MM FILM, 3/4 OR 1/2 IN VIDEO
Shows advanced techniques of gas welding, including multiple pass (thick plate) joining, structural section fabrication and forming horizontal, vertical and overhead welds.
From The Industrial Education Series.
Prod-BROSEB Dist-PHENIX 1971

Oxyacetylene Welding - Joining Steel (Spanish) C 14 MIN
16MM FILM, 3/4 OR 1/2 IN VIDEO H A
Shows advanced techniques of gas welding, including multiple pass (thick plate) joining, structural section fabrication and forming horizontal, vertical and overhead welds.
From The Industrial Education Series.
Prod-BROSEB Dist-PHENIX 1971

Oxyacetylene Welding - Safety And Operations C 14 MIN
16MM FILM, 3/4 OR 1/2 IN VIDEO J-C A
Discusses the safety points and basic techniques in oxyacetylene welding.
From The Metal Shop - Safety And Operations Series.
Prod-EPRI Dist-AIMS 1970

Oxyacetylene Welding - Safety And Operations (Arabic) C 14 MIN
16MM FILM, 3/4 OR 1/2 IN VIDEO J-C A
Discusses the safety points and basic techniques in oxyacetylene welding.
From The Metal Shop - Safety And Operations Series.
Prod-EPRI Dist-AIMS 1970

Oxyacetylene Welding - Safety And Operations (Spanish) C 14 MIN
16MM FILM, 3/4 OR 1/2 IN VIDEO J-C A
Discusses the safety points and basic techniques in oxyacetylene welding.
From The Metal Shop - Safety And Operations Series.
Prod-EPRI Dist-AIMS 1970

Oxyacetylene Welding - Torch Techniques C 19 MIN
16MM FILM, 3/4 OR 1/2 IN VIDEO H A
Explains the correct techniques for running a bead, welding without a rod, adding a rod to a butt weld and blazing.
From The Industrial Education Series.
Prod-BROSEB Dist-PHENIX 1971

Oxyacetylene Welding - Torch Techniques (Spanish) C 19 MIN
16MM FILM, 3/4 OR 1/2 IN VIDEO H A
Explains the correct techniques for running a bead, welding without a rod, adding a rod to a butt weld and blazing.
From The Industrial Education Series.
Prod-BROSEB Dist-PHENIX 1971

Oxygen - An Introduction To Chemistry C 15 MIN
16MM FILM, 3/4 OR 1/2 IN VIDEO I-J
Explores the nature of oxygen. Explains the structure of atoms and molecules, oxidation and the production of oxygen through the process of photosynthesis.
From The Elementary Physical Science Series.
Prod-HALDAR Dist-BARR Prodn-BARR 1979

Oxygen Equipment C 27 MIN
16MM FILM OPTICAL SOUND PRO
Depicts various types of aircrew oxygen equipment, including constant flow, demand and pressure demand masks and emergency and seat kits. Demonstrates use of each type of equipment and defines advantages and limitations of each.
LC NO. 77-701152
Prod-USAF Dist-USNAC 1964

Oxygen Therapy (2nd Ed) C 13 MIN
3/4 OR 1/2 INCH VIDEO CASSETTE PRO
Discusses guidelines for safe use of oxygen therapy in newborn infants. Stresses monitoring of arterial or arterialized capillary oxygen tension and inspired oxygen concentration. Outlines consequences of inadequate and excessive oxygenation.
Prod-UMICHM Dist-UMICHM 1983

Oxygen-Fuel Gas Cutting C 60 MIN
3/4 OR 1/2 INCH VIDEO CASSETTE IND
Covers safety, equipment setup and use and cutting procedures.
From The Welding Training Series.
Prod-ITCORP Dist-ITCORP

Oxygen-Nitrogen Generating Plant Distillation Column Control C 24 MIN
16MM FILM OPTICAL SOUND
Shows the progressive flow and treatment of atmospheric air through a typical oxygen-nitrogen generating plant to produce either liquid or gaseous oxygen or nitrogen.
LC NO. FIE62-75
Prod-USAF Dist-USNAC 1960

Oxygenation Assessment Of The Critically Ill Patient C 30 MIN
3/4 OR 1/2 INCH VIDEO CASSETTE PRO
Explains that the assessment of oxygenation in the critically ill patient requires more than the usual patient assessment and measurement of arterial blood gases. Discusses variables which must be considered and how they interrelate and stresses the importance of oxygen delivery. Covers the measurement of oxyhemoglobin-dissocation curves, wedge pressure cardiac output and the mixed venous pO2.
From The University Of Michigan Media Library - Clinical Commentary Series.
LC NO. 81-707081
Prod-UMICH Dist-UMICH 1981

Oye Depiertate C 30 MIN
3/4 OR 1/2 INCH VIDEO CASSETTE P-I
See series title for descriptive statement.
From The Sonrisas Series.
Prod-KRLNTV Dist-MDCPB

Oyster Development And Survival C 26 MIN
16MM FILM OPTICAL SOUND
Looks at the life of oysters in the waters of the Pacific Northwest, from the fertilization of the egg to full growth.
Prod-RARIG Dist-RARIG

Oysters Are In Season B 17 MIN
16MM FILM OPTICAL SOUND
Features the improvised humor of Swede Sorenson, Dean Preece and Molly Parkin as they play out sharply satiric situations, in three skits.
Prod-IMPACT Dist-IMPACT 1966

Ozone Stories C 30 MIN
3/4 OR 1/2 INCH VIDEO CASSETTE
Prod-EAI Dist-EAI

P

P A G E S, Case Of The Missing Stock Certificate C 20 MIN
3/4 OR 1/2 INCH VIDEO CASSETTE
Pictures police officers trying to track down a stock certificate left in a book. Highlights all aspects of a library circulation assistant's job, including shelving, straightening shelves and possessing a courteous attitude.
Prod-HRFDCL Dist-LVN

P A T C H - Positive Approach To Changing Humans C 16 MIN
16MM FILM, 3/4 OR 1/2 IN VIDEO C A
Illustrates the process teachers go through to acquire the skills for improving students' academic skills, controlling their inappropriate behavior and motivating them in a positive way.
Prod-CORF Dist-CORF 1973

P C Friend, Railroad Agent C 19 MIN
16MM FILM OPTICAL SOUND P-C A
Introduces the history of railroads and their role in current and future transportation.
Prod-COMICO Dist-COMICO

P E - Lever To Learning C 20 MIN
16MM FILM OPTICAL SOUND C T
Discusses how specially organized physical education programs can be most productive both physically and mentally.
LC NO. 70-702249
Prod-FINLYS Dist-FINLYS 1969

P J And The President's Son C 47 MIN
16MM FILM, 3/4 OR 1/2 IN VIDEO
Tells how an ordinary teenager and the President's son decide to change places for a few days. Originally shown on the television series ABC Afterschool Specials.
From The Teenage Years Series.
LC NO. 79-707351
Prod-WILSND Dist-TIMLIF 1976

P S A T And N M S Q T Overview And Test Taking Strategy C 2 MIN
3/4 OR 1/2 INCH VIDEO CASSETTE
See series title for descriptive statement.
From The PSAT And National Merit Scholarship Qualifying Test Preparation Series.
Prod-KRLSOF Dist-KRLSOF

P S My Sister Sends Her Love C 20 MIN
16MM FILM OPTICAL SOUND
Demonstrates the vital importance of overseas mail movement in keeping the postal link unbroken between servicemen and families. Includes quotations from letters and flashbacks which connect hometown scenes with overseas servicemen.
LC NO. 78-702843
Prod-USPOST Dist-USPOST Prodn-VISION 1968

P Sound C 14 MIN
3/4 OR 1/2 INCH VIDEO CASSETTE K
See series title for descriptive statement.
From The I-Land Treasure Series.
Prod-UWISC Dist-AITECH 1980

P-N-P Transistor And Transistor Specifications C 60 MIN
1 INCH VIDEOTAPE IND
Describes how P-N-P transistors are used in circuits and how they work.
From The Understanding Semiconductors Course Outline Series. No. 08
Prod-TXINLC Dist-TXINLC

P-47 Thunderbolt High-Altitude Flight And Aerobatics B 22 MIN
3/4 OR 1/2 INCH VIDEO CASSETTE
Depicts the P-47 aircraft in various power-driving and aerobatic maneuvers.
Prod-IHF Dist-IHF

P, B, M, F, V C
3/4 OR 1/2 INCH VIDEO CASSETTE
See series title for descriptive statement.
From The Educational Video Concepts For Early Childhood Language Development Series.
Prod-ECCOAZ Dist-ECCOAZ

P, J C 15 MIN
3/4 OR 1/2 INCH VIDEO CASSETTE P
Presents techniques of handwriting, focusing on the lower case letters p and j.
From The Cursive Writing Series.
Prod-WHROTV Dist-GPITVL 1984

P, R And B C 15 MIN
3/4 INCH VIDEO CASSETTE P
From The Writing Time Series.
Prod-WHROTV Dist-GPITVL

P'tit Jean S'en Va Aux Chantiers C 16 MIN
16MM FILM, 3/4 OR 1/2 IN VIDEO P-I
A French language version of Ti-Jean Goes Lumbering. Presents a French-Canadian folk tale about a mysterious stranger who behaves like a young Paul Bunyan.
Prod-NFBC Dist-IFB 1953

Pa-Hay-Okee - Grassy Waters C 18 MIN
16MM FILM, 3/4 OR 1/2 IN VIDEO
Explores the natural features, wildlife and relationship between man and nature in the Everglades of south Florida.
LC NO. 81-706315
Prod-USNPS Dist-USNAC 1981

Pablita Velarde - An Artist And Her People C 20 MIN
16MM FILM, 3/4 OR 1/2 IN VIDEO J A
Portrays the work of Pablita Velarde, a native American Indian and noted painter who paints to preserve Indian heritage and provide a bridge for Anglo and Indian culture.
Prod-USNPS Dist-USNAC 1984

Pablo Neruda - Fulgor Y Muerte De Joaquin Murrieta (Spanish) C 60 MIN
3/4 OR 1/2 INCH VIDEO CASSETTE
Offers an adaptation of Pablo Neruda's play Fulgor Y Muerte De Joaquin Murrieta which takes place during the California gold rush.
Prod-FOTH Dist-FOTH 1984

Pablo Neruda - Poet B 30 MIN
16MM FILM, 3/4 OR 1/2 IN VIDEO
Offers a testament to the life and work of Nobel Prize-winning poet Pablo Neruda. Presents the poet giving his views on love, hate, life and death, and explains his work methods. Intercuts the discussion with poems and commentary tracing the development of Neruda's poetic vision.
Prod-CNEMAG Dist-CNEMAG

Pablo Neruda - Poet (Spanish) B 30 MIN
16MM FILM, 3/4 OR 1/2 IN VIDEO
Offers a testament to the life and work of Nobel Prize-winning poet Pablo Neruda. Presents the poet giving his views on love, hate, life and death, and explains his work methods. Intercuts the discussion with poems and commentary tracing the development of Neruda's poetic vision.
Prod-CNEMAG Dist-CNEMAG

Pablo Picasso - The Legacy Of A Genius C 44 MIN
16MM FILM OPTICAL SOUND J-C A
Traces the life of Pablo Picasso. Presents experts who comment on and compare the content and styles of representative pieces of the master's works. Shows how the regions in which Picasso resided and the women with whom he lived influenced his paintings and sculpture.
LC NO. 82-701119
Prod-BLACKW Dist-BLACKW 1982

Pablo Picasso - The Legacy Of A Genius C 88 MIN
3/4 OR 1/2 INCH VIDEO CASSETTE
Traces the life and art of Pablo Picasso. Focuses on the content and style of representative pieces of his work, as well as showing the people and places that influenced his painting and sculpture.
Prod-BLACKW Dist-BLACKW 1982

Pablo, Un Nino De Mexico X 22 MIN
16MM FILM, 3/4 OR 1/2 IN VIDEO J-H
A Spanish language film. Presents a view of daily life in a Mexican village through the story of a young Mexican boy. Provides insights into the educational programs and religious beliefs. To be used after lesson 42 of 'LA FAMILIA FERNANDEZ.'
From The Viajando Por Mexico Y Espana Series.
Prod-EBEC Dist-EBEC 1966

PACA - Parents As Change Agents C 27 MIN
16MM FILM OPTICAL SOUND C A
Describes the function and purpose of PACA, a community base behavior management program in which paraprofessionals teach parents how to measure and change specific problem behaviors in children.
LC NO. 78-701604
Prod-UKANS Dist-UKANS 1976

Pace C 22 MIN
16MM FILM OPTICAL SOUND H-C A
Takes a look at the sport of trotting in Australia, including a view behind the scenes.
LC NO. 79-700528
Prod-FLMAUS Dist-AUIS 1976

Pace Of The Seasons C 15 MIN
16MM FILM - 3/4 IN VIDEO
Captures seasonal changes in the Lake Superior area. Focuses on Voyageurs National Park and the wilderness area of the peninsula between Lake Kabetogam and Rainy Lake, telling how travel is still done on foot or by canoe.
LC NO. 79-706148
Prod-USNPS Dist-USNAC 1979

Pacemaker, The - Clinical Evaluation Elective Replacement C 14 MIN
16MM FILM OPTICAL SOUND PRO
Explains that impending pacemaker failure can be detected by external electronic testing in a pacemaker clinic. Points out that the rate of change of various aspects of the amplified electrical stimulus is determined and the impulse, repetition rate, pulse width, amplitude and configuration are measured.
Prod-ACYDGD Dist-ACY 1969

Pacemakers C 15 MIN
16MM FILM, 3/4 OR 1/2 IN VIDEO A
Explains what pacemakers are and how they benefit patients with heart problems. Reviews pathophysiology of the heart, pacemaker components, how they work and various procedures of implantation. Teaches postoperative monitoring techniques, warning signs and precautionary measures.
Prod-PRORE Dist-PRORE

Pacemakers - Technology's Gift Of Life C 10 MIN
16MM FILM OPTICAL SOUND
Looks at the effect pacemakers have on heart patients' lives. Explains the workings of the heart's electrical system and how pacemakers can correct malfunctions in the system. Discusses the history and future technology of heart pacing.
Prod-MTP Dist-MTP

Pacer C 22 MIN
16MM FILM OPTICAL SOUND
Presents a documentary on trotters, horses trained by men which represent man's exploitation of nature for his own selfish interests.
LC NO. 76-703148
Prod-KOSALB Dist-TEMPLU 1976

Pacesetter In Aisle Number Three, The C 16 MIN
16MM FILM OPTICAL SOUND H-C
Presents a training film for store clerks in food industry. Portrays a young man eagerly starting on the job in a supermarket. Shows the store manager training him in proper shelf stocking and product space allocation, highlighting the importance of this job.
Prod-GEMILL Dist-NINEFC

Pacesetter, The C 6 MIN
16MM FILM, 3/4 OR 1/2 IN VIDEO PRO
Asks what to do with a good man of genuine promise who isn't giving his best effort to the job.
From The This Matter Of Motivation Series.
Prod-CTRACT Dist-DARTNL Prodn-CALVIN 1968

Pachanga / Camp Out C 30 MIN
3/4 OR 1/2 INCH VIDEO CASSETTE P-I
See series title for descriptive statement.
From The Sonrisas Series.
Prod-KRLNTV Dist-MDCPB

Pacific C 60 MIN
16MM FILM OPTICAL SOUND H-C A
From The World At War Series.
LC NO. 76-701778
Prod-THAMES Dist-USCAN 1975

Pacific Boils Over, The B 27 MIN
16MM FILM, 3/4 OR 1/2 IN VIDEO J-H
Shows the background to the attack on Pearl Harbor on December 7, 1941.
From The Victory At Sea Series.
Prod-NBCTV Dist-LUF

Pacific Boils Over, The - Pearl Harbor, December 7, 1941 B 30 MIN
16MM FILM OPTICAL SOUND I-C
Pictures Hawaii and Japan in 1941. Tells how the Japanese sought ways to secure the oil of Southeast Asia. Describes the rendezvous of the Japanese in a hidden harbor in the Kurile Islands, assembling the Pearl Harbor striking force. Pictures the attack on Pearl Harbor.
From The Victory At Sea Series.
Prod-GRACUR Dist-GRACUR

Pacific Bridges—A Series
I-J
Focuses on the role of Asian-Americans in the growth and development of the United States.
Prod-EDFCEN Dist-GPITVL 1978

By Our Hands	30 MIN
Do Our Best	30 MIN
Stand Tall	30 MIN
Staying Here	30 MIN
Then And Now	30 MIN
To A New Land	30 MIN

Pacific Coast Of Mexico - Baja California X 11 MIN
16MM FILM OPTICAL SOUND I-J
Shows the people and their mode of living on the peninsula of Baja California. Scenes include Ensenada, Turtle Bay, Magdalena Bay, Cape San Lucal, vineyards at Santo Tomas, lobster fishing and abalone fishing.
Prod-JHP Dist-MLA 1949

Pacific Coast Of Mexico - The Mainland X 11 MIN
16MM FILM OPTICAL SOUND I-J
Deals with the coast from Mazatlan to Acapulco. Shows the towns, the people and the modes of living.
Prod-JHP Dist-MLA 1949

Pacific Coast States, The C 25 MIN
16MM FILM, 3/4 OR 1/2 IN VIDEO I-J
Looks at the characteristics of California, Oregon and Washington where original tiny settlements have grown into major cities. Shows the effect of nature in the area such as the Mount St Helens volcano.
From The United States Geography Series.
Prod-NGS Dist-NGS 1983

Pacific Frontier C 29 MIN
16MM FILM OPTICAL SOUND
Surveys the operations of the Pacific and Seventh Fleets of the U S Navy. Shows how they perform everything from antisubmarine warfare to goodwill activities ashore. Includes some of the Navy activities in Vietnam.
LC NO. 75-700871
Prod-USN Dist-USNAC 1965

Pacific Island B 18 MIN
16MM FILM OPTICAL SOUND P-I
Shows life on Likiep, one of the Marshall Islands-practicing navigation, building a boat, basket weaving, repairing thatched homes and village activities.
Prod-IFF Dist-IFF 1949

Pacific Island Life—A Series

Shows every aspect of family life on the Atoll, Nuguria, Melanesia in the South Pacific. All Unnarrated.
Prod-IFF Dist-IFF

Coconut Tree, The	015 MIN
Family Life	016 MIN
Fishing	014 MIN
Food From The Sea	013 MIN
Village Life	015 MIN

Pacific Missile Range, The C 15 MIN
16MM FILM OPTICAL SOUND
Shows the operation and mission of the navy-operated Pacific Missile Range at Point Mugu, California.
Prod-USN Dist-USNAC 1960

Pacific Northwest, The C 18 MIN
16MM FILM, 3/4 OR 1/2 IN VIDEO J
Examines the people, industry, economy and landscape of the Pacific Northwest region of the United States.
From The U S Geography Series.
Prod-MGHT Dist-MGHT 1976

Pacific West, The X 24 MIN
16MM FILM, 3/4 OR 1/2 IN VIDEO I-J
Presents an overview of the Pacific west, its people, resources, industries, cities, opportunities and history, emphasizing the people as the primary resource.
Prod-EBEC Dist-EBEC 1969

Pacific, February 1942-1945 C 52 MIN
16MM FILM, 3/4 OR 1/2 IN VIDEO H-C A
Describes an island-hopping strategy that captured islands one at a time across the Pacific, finally ending the war there, winning back the Philippines and bringing a striking force to Japan's doorstep at Iwo Jima and Okinawa.
From The World At War Series.
Prod-THAMES Dist-MEDIAG 1973

Pacing Road, The C 20 MIN
3/4 OR 1/2 INCH VIDEO CASSETTE
Demonstrates how to develop reading skills that overcome bad reading habits by the pacing technique.
From The Efficient Reading - Instructional Tapes Series. Tape 5
Prod-TELSTR Dist-TELSTR

Pack Up Your Troubles B 75 MIN
16MM FILM OPTICAL SOUND H-C A
Stars Laurel and Hardy in a story about two misfit army privates who upset Uncle Sam's routine.
Prod-ROACH Dist-KITPAR

Package Bees C 30 MIN
3/4 OR 1/2 INCH VIDEO CASSETTE
Shows how to select an apiary site, dressing properly, installing and feeding, package building and the 21-day cycle.
From The Bees And Honey Series.
Prod-WGTV Dist-MDCPB

Packaged To Sell C 13 MIN
16MM FILM OPTICAL SOUND
Shows packaging line operations, demonstrating quality control steps throughout the packaging line.
LC NO. 81-701363
Prod-MBC Dist-MBC Prodn-MARITZ 1981

Packaging B 10 MIN
16MM FILM SILENT C
Presents old methods of packaging versus new ones.
Prod-NYUIME Dist-NYU 1940

Packaging And Labeling C 30 MIN
3/4 OR 1/2 INCH VIDEO CASSETTE
Covers the role of packaging in the marketing mix, role of shape and function in packaging design, use of packaging as a communications tool and types of labelling.
From The Marketing Perspectives Series.
Prod-MATC Dist-WFVTAE

Packaging Food For You C 17 MIN
16MM FILM OPTICAL SOUND
Tells that by improved packaging of foods, made possible through research by the USDA and private industry, there are improvements in economy, quality, freshness and convenience of packaged foods.
LC NO. 74-705286
Prod-USDA Dist-USNAC 1966

Packaging Rocket Power C 27 MIN
16MM FILM OPTICAL SOUND

Summarizes the liquid and solid fuel propellant rocket manufacturing capability of the Thiokol Chemical Corporation. Stresses systems used by the Armed Services and NASA.
Prod-THIOKL Dist-THIOKL 1960

Packaging The Product C 15 MIN
3/4 INCH VIDEO CASSETTE H-C A
Tells how to make the best appearance for an interview and emphasizes that dress is crucial in selling oneself on a job interview.
From The Job Seeking Series.
LC NO. 80-706689
Prod-WCETTV Dist-GPITVL 1979

Packet - Switched Networks - Operation And Routing C 50 MIN
3/4 OR 1/2 INCH VIDEO CASSETTE PRO
Describes the principles of packet-switching. Deals with datagrams, flooding and short-comings.
From The Communication Networks Series.
Prod-AMCEE Dist-AMCEE

Packet - Switched Networks - Traffic Control And Error Control C 50 MIN
3/4 OR 1/2 INCH VIDEO CASSETTE PRO
Describes types of traffic and error controls.
From The Communication Networks Series.
Prod-AMCEE Dist-AMCEE

Packet Of An Uncertain Gaussian, The C 10 MIN
16MM FILM, 3/4 OR 1/2 IN VIDEO C
Combines computer animation with conventional artwork to display properties of wave function in introductory quantum mechanics. Among the topics covered are plane waves, the Fourier composition of the Gaussian wave packet and its transform, Heisenberg's uncertainty principle, and the spreading of the time dependent Gaussian wave packet.
LC NO. 83-706689
Prod-POLYIB Dist-IFB 1968

Packet Radio Networks C 50 MIN
3/4 OR 1/2 INCH VIDEO CASSETTE PRO
Deals with centralized and distributed architecture, repeaters, throughput, and persistence and delay.
From The Communication Networks Series.
Prod-AMCEE Dist-AMCEE

Packet Switching Networks—A Series
C
Provides a comprehensive foundation in the most modern, up-to-date techniques including multiplexing, switching techniques, error control, computer networks, database distribution systems, security in data communications and the management of computer networks. Features Roy Daniel Rosner, Director of Advanced Planning for the Automated Data and Telecommunications Service, US General Services Administration.
Prod-AMCEE Dist-AMCEE

Analysis And Comparison Of Switched Networks,	
Analysis And Comparison Of Switched Networks,	050 MIN
Common Carrier Services, Pt I	050 MIN
Common Carrier Services, Pt II	050 MIN
Elements Of Packet Day Networks	050 MIN
Integrated Services Digital Networks, Pt I	050 MIN
Integrated Services Digital Networks, Pt II	050 MIN
Introduction To Packet Networks	050 MIN
Networking Topologies And Routing, Part I	050 MIN
Networking Topologies And Routing, Part II	050 MIN
Packet Switching Operation And Protocols,	050 MIN
Packet Switching Operation And Protocols,	050 MIN
Packet Switching Operation And Protocols,	050 MIN
Packet Switching Operation And Protocols,	050 MIN
Satellite Applications And Demand Assignment	050 MIN
Satellite Applications And Demand Assignment	050 MIN

Packet Switching Operation And Protocols, Pt 2 C 49 MIN
3/4 OR 1/2 INCH VIDEO CASSETTE
See series title for descriptive statement.
From The Packet Switching Series.
Prod-MIOT Dist-MIOT

Packet Switching Operation And Protocols, Pt 4 C 53 MIN
3/4 OR 1/2 INCH VIDEO CASSETTE
See series title for descriptive statement.
From The Packet Switching Series.
Prod-MIOT Dist-MIOT

Packet Switching Operation And Protocols, Pt 1 C 54 MIN
3/4 OR 1/2 INCH VIDEO CASSETTE
See series title for descriptive statement.
From The Packet Switching Series.
Prod-MIOT Dist-MIOT

Packet Switching Operation And Protocols, Pt 3 C 57 MIN
3/4 OR 1/2 INCH VIDEO CASSETTE
See series title for descriptive statement.
From The Packet Switching Series.
Prod-MIOT Dist-MIOT

Packet Switching Operation And Protocols, Pt II C 50 MIN
3/4 OR 1/2 INCH VIDEO CASSETTE C
Covers multiple packet per segment protocols, single packet per segment protocols, internal protocol timing, delay and flow management.
From The Packet Switching Networks Series.
Prod-AMCEE Dist-AMCEE

Packet Switching Operation And Protocols, Pt III C 50 MIN
3/4 OR 1/2 INCH VIDEO CASSETTE C
Covers subscriber interface protocols, CCITT x.25, Physical interface, x.21, RS 232, RS 449, Link level interface, error correction, bit independence, x.25 packet structure and field functions, packet ordering, flow control and virtual circuit control.
From The Packet Switching Networks Series.
Prod-AMCEE Dist-AMCEE

Packet Switching Operation And Protocols, Pt IV C 50 MIN
3/4 OR 1/2 INCH VIDEO CASSETTE C
Covers optional packet network facilities, packet assembly-disassembly (PAD) and X.28/X.29, network gateways X.75/X.121, control and management of packet networks and network control center (NCC).
From The Packet Switching Networks Series.
Prod-AMCEE Dist-AMCEE

Packet Switching Operations And Protocols, Part I C 50 MIN
3/4 OR 1/2 INCH VIDEO CASSETTE C
Shows International Standards (ISO) Protocol Hierarchy, Protocol functional requirements in packet networks, concept of virtual circuits and link multiplexing, virtual circuit/datagram comparison.
From The Packet Switching Networks Series.
Prod-AMCEE Dist-AMCEE

Packet Switching—A Series

Provides a foundation in how packet switching works, how it compares to alternative techniques and how to utilize packet switching to your own best advantage.
Prod-MIOT Dist-MIOT

Analysis And Comparison Of Switched Networks	
Analysis And Comparison Of Switched Networks	056 MIN
Common Carrier Services, Pt 1	058 MIN
Common Carrier Services, Pt 2	054 MIN
Elements Of Packet Data Networks	055 MIN
Integrated Services Digital Networks, Pt 1	055 MIN
Integrated Services Digital Networks, Pt 2	052 MIN
Introduction To Packet Networks	055 MIN
Networking Topologies And Routing, Pt 1	040 MIN
Networking Topologies And Routing, Pt 2	043 MIN
Packet Switching Operation And Protocols,	049 MIN
Packet Switching Operation And Protocols,	053 MIN
Packet Switching Operation And Protocols,	057 MIN
Packet Switching Operation And Protocols,	054 MIN
Satellite Applications And Demand Assignment	053 MIN
Satellite Applications And Demand Assignment	055 MIN

Packet Switching, Pt 1 C 29 MIN
3/4 OR 1/2 INCH VIDEO CASSETTE
Introduces definitions applicable to packet-switched networks, traffic types, hierarchy of design concepts in a network and design issues in a network.
From The Distributed Processor Communication Architecture Series.
Prod-MIOT Dist-MIOT

Packet Switching, Pt 1 C 36 MIN
3/4 OR 1/2 INCH VIDEO CASSETTE PRO
Gives definitions applicable to packet switched networks. Focuses upon design concepts and issues.
From The Introduction To Distributed Processor Communication Series.
Prod-AMCEE Dist-AMCEE

Packet Switching, Pt 2 C 27 MIN
3/4 OR 1/2 INCH VIDEO CASSETTE
Discusses protocols, layered structure of protocols, routing taxonomy and routing algorithms, distributed routing techniques and centralized routing techniques.
From The Distributed Processor Communication Architecture Series.
Prod-MIOT Dist-MIOT

Packet Switching, Pt 2 C 36 MIN
3/4 OR 1/2 INCH VIDEO CASSETTE PRO
Describes protocols, including ARPANET, ETHERNET and PTT. Examines distributed and centralized routing techniques.
From The Introduction To Distributed Processor Communication Architecture Series.
Prod-AMCEE Dist-AMCEE

Packet Switching, Pt 3 C 36 MIN
3/4 OR 1/2 INCH VIDEO CASSETTE PRO
Discusses flow control. Provides error control strategies.
From The Introduction To Distributed Processor Communication Architecture Series.
Prod-AMCEE Dist-AMCEE

Packet Switching, Pt 3 C 36 MIN
3/4 OR 1/2 INCH VIDEO CASSETTE
Discusses flow control, segmentation and addressing in a network, error control strategies, name management and name space hierarchies.
From The Distributed Processor Communication Architecture Series.
Prod-MIOT Dist-MIOT

Packets In A Perfect Crystal B 4 MIN
16MM FILM SILENT C
Shows a wave packet composed of crystal momenta near to a band edge, one composed of crystal momenta in the band and one composed of crystal momenta far from the band edge, all moving in a perfect periodic potential.
From The College Physics - Quantum Physics Series. No. 6
LC NO. 77-709336
Prod-ERCMIT Dist-EDC 1970

Packets Incident On A Crystal B 4 MIN
16MM FILM SILENT C
Shows packets with suitable chosen energies either penetrating a periodic potential from free space or being reflected from the periodic potential. Computer generated.
From The College Physics - Quantum Physics Series. No. 7
LC NO. 70-709337
Prod-ERCMIT Dist-EDC 1970

Packing And Seals C 120 MIN
3/4 OR 1/2 INCH VIDEO CASSETTE IND
Discusses pump and valve packing. Examines mechanical seals.
From The Mechanical Equipment Maintenance Series.
Prod-ITCORP Dist-ITCORP

Packing And Seals (Spanish) C 120 MIN
3/4 OR 1/2 INCH VIDEO CASSETTE IND
Discusses pump and valve packing. Examines mechanical seals.
From The Mechanical Equipment Maintenance (Spanish) Series.
Prod-ITCORP Dist-ITCORP

Packing Front Wheel Bearings C 4 MIN
16MM FILM OPTICAL SOUND
Illustrates how to remove a front wheel, remove the bearing from the wheel, inspect, clean and grease the bearing and replace the bearing and the wheel on the car.
LC NO. FI68-212
Prod-RAYBAR Dist-RAYBAR 1966

Packingtown, USA C 32 MIN
16MM FILM OPTICAL SOUND C A
Presents the story of the meat strike of 1904. Includes the efforts of the Meatcutters Union, the Teamsters, Jane Addams and Mary Mc Dowell to help the immigrant workers in their fight for human liberties.
LC NO. 73-703096
Prod-UILLVA Dist-UILL 1968

Packy C 25 MIN
16MM FILM, 3/4 OR 1/2 IN VIDEO J-C A
Revolves around the encounter in heaven between God and a flamboyant theatrical agent, who has always thought of himself as a failure. Shows that God does not think of him as a failure because of his many acts of kindness. Stars Bob Newhart and Jack Klugman.
From The Insight Series.
Prod-PAULST Dist-PAULST

Pad Your Pad C 20 MIN
3/4 INCH VIDEO CASSETTE J-H
Presents examples of how old inexpensive furniture can be remodeled to meet furnishing needs. Gives helpful hints on buying furniture.
From The Dollar Data Series.
LC NO. 81-707363
Prod-WHROTV Dist-GPITVL 1974

Paddington And The 'Cold Snap' / Paddington Makes A Clean Sweep / Mr Gruber's Mystery... C 22 MIN
16MM FILM, 3/4 OR 1/2 IN VIDEO K-I
Discusses Paddington Bear's efforts as a plumber and a chimney sweep. Tells how he visits a wax museum and makes preparations to attend his aunt's birthday party. Based on chapters one, three, four and seven of the book Paddington Marches On by Michael Bond.
From The Paddington Bear, Series 1 Series.
LC NO. 80-707221
Prod-BONDM Dist-FLMFR Prodn-FILMF 1977

Paddington And The 'Finishing Touch' / Paddington And The Mystery Box C 11 MIN
16MM FILM, 3/4 OR 1/2 IN VIDEO K-I
Tells how Paddington bear tries to spruce up Mr Gruber's patio. Explains how he solves the mystery of a buried treasure. Based on the books Paddington Goes To Town and The Great Big Paddington Book by Michael Bond.
From The Paddington Bear, Series 2 Series.
LC NO. 80-707217
Prod-BONDM Dist-FLMFR Prodn-FILMF 1980

Paddington Bakes A Cake / Paddington Clears The Coach / Paddington Weighs In C 16 MIN
16MM FILM, 3/4 OR 1/2 IN VIDEO K-I
Tells how Paddington Bear bakes a birthday cake and misinterprets a chef's instructions in a train dining car. Explains what happens when he steps onto a weighing machine. Based on chapters one, three and six of the book Paddington Takes To TV by Michael Bond.
From The Paddington Bear, Series 2 Series.
LC NO. 80-707210
Prod-BONDM Dist-FLMFR Prodn-FILMF 1980

Paddington Bear Program Number Eight C 23 MIN
3/4 OR 1/2 INCH VIDEO CASSETTE K-I
See series title for descriptive statement.
From The Paddington Bear Programs Series.
Prod-BONDM Dist-FLMFR

Paddington Bear Program Number Eleven C 28 MIN
3/4 OR 1/2 INCH VIDEO CASSETTE K-I
See series title for descriptive statement.
From The Paddington Bear Programs Series.
Prod-BONDM Dist-FLMFR

Paddington Bear Program Number Five C 24 MIN
3/4 OR 1/2 INCH VIDEO CASSETTE K-I
See series title for descriptive statement.
From The Paddington Bear Programs Series.
Prod-BONDM Dist-FLMFR

Paddington Bear Program Number Four C 24 MIN
3/4 OR 1/2 INCH VIDEO CASSETTE K-I
See series title for descriptive statement.
From The Paddington Bear Programs Series.
Prod-BONDM Dist-FLMFR

Paddington Bear Program Number Nine C 23 MIN
3/4 OR 1/2 INCH VIDEO CASSETTE K-I
See series title for descriptive statement.
From The Paddington Bear Programs Series.
Prod-BONDM Dist-FLMFR

Paddington Bear Program Number One C 24 MIN
3/4 OR 1/2 INCH VIDEO CASSETTE K-I
See series title for descriptive statement.
From The Paddington Bear Programs Series.
Prod-BONDM Dist-FLMFR

Paddington Bear Program Number Seven C 23 MIN
3/4 OR 1/2 INCH VIDEO CASSETTE K-I
See series title for descriptive statement.
From The Paddington Bear Programs Series.
Prod-BONDM Dist-FLMFR

Paddington Bear Program Number Six C 24 MIN
3/4 OR 1/2 INCH VIDEO CASSETTE K-I
See series title for descriptive statement.
From The Paddington Bear Programs Series.
Prod-BONDM Dist-FLMFR

Paddington Bear Program Number Ten C 23 MIN
3/4 OR 1/2 INCH VIDEO CASSETTE K-I
See series title for descriptive statement.
From The Paddington Bear Programs Series.
Prod-BONDM Dist-FLMFR

Paddington Bear Program Number Three C 24 MIN
3/4 OR 1/2 INCH VIDEO CASSETTE K-I
See series title for descriptive statement.
From The Paddington Bear Programs Series.
Prod-BONDM Dist-FLMFR

Paddington Bear Program Number Two C 24 MIN
3/4 OR 1/2 INCH VIDEO CASSETTE K-I
See series title for descriptive statement.
From The Paddington Bear Programs Series.
Prod-BONDM Dist-FLMFR

Paddington Bear Programs—A Series
K-I
Presents Paddington Bear, a Peruvian bear found on a railway platform in England and adopted by the Browns, and his adventures in the world of human beings, as related in over a dozen children's books since his creation in 1958.
Prod-BONDM Dist-FLMFR

Paddington Bear, Series 1—A Series
16MM FILM, 3/4 OR 1/2 IN VIDEO K-I
Presents an adaptation of the Paddington Bear books by Michael Bond.
Prod-BONDM Dist-FLMFR Prodn-FILMF 1977

Unexpected Party 022 MIN

Paddington Bear, Series 2—A Series
16MM FILM, 3/4 OR 1/2 IN VIDEO K-I
Depicts the adventures of Paddington Bear, adapted from the books by Michael Bond.
Prod-BONDM Dist-FLMFR Prodn-FILMF 1980

Paddington Comes To Virginia Beach 028 MIN

Paddington Buys A Share / Paddington In A Hole C 11 MIN
16MM FILM, 3/4 OR 1/2 IN VIDEO K-I
Tells how Paddington buys oil stocks from a shady character. Describes his foray into home construction. Based on chapters three and five of the book Paddington At Work by Michael Bond.
From The Paddington Bear, Series 2 Series.
LC NO. 80-707214
Prod-BONDM Dist-FLMFR Prodn-FILMF 1980

Paddington Cleans Up C 6 MIN
16MM FILM, 3/4 OR 1/2 IN VIDEO K-I
Tells how Paddington Bear becomes a salesbear for a vacuum cleaner company. Based on chapter two of the book Paddington On Top by Michael Bond.
From The Paddington Bear, Series 1 Series.
LC NO. 80-707222
Prod-BONDM Dist-FLMFR Prodn-FILMF 1977

Paddington Comes To Virginia Beach C 28 MIN
16MM FILM, 3/4 OR 1/2 IN VIDEO K-I
Shows the creative teaching possibilities that exist for the utilization of the Paddington Bear films. Shows a wide variety of locally-made learning materials which were created for the project and which are circulated from the media center.
Prod-VBCSB Dist-FLMFR 1982

Paddington Goes To The Movies C 20 MIN
16MM FILM, 3/4 OR 1/2 IN VIDEO K-I
Tells what hilarious things happen when Paddington Bear is introduced to the world of motion pictures through a peek in a theater playing Singing In The Rain.
From The Paddington Bear, Series 2 Series.
LC NO. 83-706517
Prod-FILMF Dist-FLMFR 1983

Paddington Hits Out / A Visit To The Hospital C 11 MIN
16MM FILM, 3/4 OR 1/2 IN VIDEO K-I
Describes Paddington Bear's work as a golf caddy and his accidental visit to a psychiatrist. Based on chapters two and three of the book Paddington Goes To Town by Michael Bond.
From The Paddington Bear, Series 1 Series.
LC NO. 80-707223
Prod-BONDM Dist-FLMFR Prodn-FILMF 1980

Paddington Hits The Jackpot / A Sticky Time C 11 MIN
16MM FILM, 3/4 OR 1/2 IN VIDEO K-I
Tells how Paddington Bear goes on a television quiz show and how he makes toffee. Based on chapters four and five of the book Paddington Hits The Jackpot by Michael Bond.
From The Paddington Bear, Series 1 Series.
LC NO. 80-707224
Prod-BONDM Dist-FLMFR Prodn-FILMF 1977

Paddington In Court / Keeping Fit / Paddington In Touch / Comings And Goings At... C 22 MIN
16MM FILM, 3/4 OR 1/2 IN VIDEO K-I
Describes Paddington's adventures in court and in a rugby match. Tells how he builds a body building set and pulls part of the fence down. Based on chapters three, five, six and seven of the book Paddington On Top by Michael Bond.
From The Paddington Bear, Series 2 Series.
LC NO. 80-707209
Prod-BONDM Dist-FLMFR Prodn-FILMF 1980

Paddington In The Hot Seat / Paddington's Puzzle / Paddington Takes A Snip C 17 MIN
16MM FILM, 3/4 OR 1/2 IN VIDEO K-I
Describes Paddington's adventures on a quiz show and tells how he tries to create a jig-saw puzzle. Explains how he tries his hand at topiary.
From The Paddington Bear, Series 2 Series.
LC NO. 80-707211
Prod-BONDM Dist-FLMFR Prodn-FILMF 1980

Paddington Lace C 24 MIN
16MM FILM OPTICAL SOUND A
Portrays the Bohemian life-style of the Australian artists' colony Paddington, a suburb of Sydney, by presenting a dramatization about two young people who live there.
LC NO. 78-713557
Prod-ANAIB Dist-AUIS 1971

Paddington Makes A Bid / Do-It-Yourself / Something Nasty In The Kitchen / Trouble At... C 22 MIN
16MM FILM, 3/4 OR 1/2 IN VIDEO K-I
Describes Paddington Bear's visit to an auction and his attempts to make a do-it-yourself magazine rack. Tells how he creates a beef stew and goes to the launderette. Based on chapters two, three, five and six of the book Paddington Helps Out by Michael Bond.
From The Paddington Bear, Series 1 Series.
LC NO. 80-707225
Prod-BONDM Dist-FLMFR Prodn-FILMF 1977

Paddle And Portage - The Art Of Canoeing C 12 MIN
16MM FILM OPTICAL SOUND
Demonstrates basic strokes and advanced techniques of canoeing. Demonstrates canoe rescue and water safety.
LC NO. FIA67-2245
Prod-GIB Dist-CTFL 1966

Paddle Or Ski C 15 MIN
3/4 INCH VIDEO CASSETTE J-C A
Tells how to spot trouble when canoeing and water skiing.
From The Afloat And Aboat Series.
Prod-MDDE Dist-GPITVL 1979

Paddle-To-The-Sea C 8 MIN
16MM FILM OPTICAL SOUND K-I
An animated cartoon. Tells the story of a carved figure on a toy canoe that is sent on a journey from Canada through the Great Lakes to the sea.
From The Language Arts Series.
LC NO. FIA68-1047
Prod-NBC Dist-GRACUR 1968

Paddle-To-The-Sea C 28 MIN
16MM FILM OPTICAL SOUND I
Tells about the journey of a hand-carved toy canoeman from Canada's northern forest downstream to the sea. Adapted from story of same title by Holling C Holling.
LC NO. FIA67-1617
Prod-NFBC Dist-NFBC 1967

Paddle-To-The-Sea C 28 MIN
3/4 OR 1/2 INCH VIDEO CASSETTE I
Tells about the journey of a hand-carved toy canoeman from Canada's northern forest downstream to the sea. Adapted from story of same title by Holling C Holling.
Prod-NFBC Dist-NFBC 1967

Paddy Chayefsky C 29 MIN
2 INCH VIDEOTAPE
Presents exchanges and arguments between the dean of American theatre critics, Elliot Norton, and Paddy Chayefsky.
From The Elliot Norton Reviews II Series.
Prod-WGBHTV Dist-PUBTEL

Padre C 28 MIN
3/4 OR 1/2 INCH VIDEO CASSETTE
Presents a portrait of American priest, William Wasson and some of the 4,000 Mexican children whom he has adopted in the past 25 years.
From The Old Friends - New Friends Series.
Prod-FAMCOM Dist-PBS 1981

Paella Valenciana C 23 MIN
3/4 OR 1/2 INCH VIDEO CASSETTE PRO
Demonstrates the preparation of Paella with chicken, clams, mussels, scallops, shrimp and chorizo.
Prod-CULINA Dist-CULINA

Paganini, The Violin, And Desmond Bradley C 26 MIN
16MM FILM, 3/4 OR 1/2 IN VIDEO J-C A
Presents Italian violinist and composer Niccolo Paganini (1782-1840), who is considered a legendary virtuoso. Features professional violinist Desmond Bradley discussing Paganini's music and life and playing some of Paganini's music. Includes several of his 24 caprices for solo violin.

From The Musical Triangles Series.
Prod-THAMES Dist-MEDIAG 1975

Page 169 C 30 MIN
3/4 OR 1/2 INCH VIDEO CASSETTE T
See series title for descriptive statement.
From The Eager To Learn Series.
Prod-KTEHTV Dist-KTEHTV

Page, Dr Joyce C 29 MIN
3/4 INCH VIDEO CASSETTE
Describes the Children's Defense Fund. Discusses the needs of poor and minority children.
From The Like It Is Series.
Prod-OHC Dist-HRC

Pageants, Parades And Festivals C 20 MIN
16MM FILM, 3/4 OR 1/2 IN VIDEO
Focuses on the special occasions, festivals and significant events at which people come together to celebrate. Looks at the contributions of artists to the design of and creation of objects for these celebrations.
From The Images And Things Series.
LC NO. 73-702104
Prod-NITC Dist-AITECH

Pages From The Talmud B 30 MIN
16MM FILM OPTICAL SOUND
Presents readings and dramatizations from the Aggadic portions of Talmud, with many excerpts from the Ethics of the Fathers (pirke Avot.)
LC NO. FIA64-1142
Prod-JTS Dist-NAAJS Prodn-NBC 1954

Paige C 10 MIN
16MM FILM, 3/4 OR 1/2 IN VIDEO I-H
Focuses on an 11-year-old girl with Down's syndrome, a form of mental retardation. Shows how she copes with her condition and adjusts to her surroundings.
From The People You'd Like To Know Series.
Prod-WGBHTV Dist-EBEC 1978

Pain C 17 MIN
16MM FILM OPTICAL SOUND PRO
Traces the subjectivity and treatment of pain from its aboriginal beginnings to modern psychiatry.
LC NO. FIA66-529
Prod-HOFLAR Dist-AMEDA Prodn-MLSWID

Pain X 30 MIN
16MM FILM, 3/4 OR 1/2 IN VIDEO C A
Shows approaches to coping with both pain and fear of pain. Explains the effect of suffering on the personality, the differences between types of pain and methods available in treating pain. Hosted by Meryl Streep.
From The Coping With Serious Illness Series. No. 1
LC NO. 80-707394
Prod-TIMLIF Dist-TIMLIF 1980

Pain - Examples Of Frequent Types Of Pain And How To Examine For Pain C 58 MIN
3/4 OR 1/2 INCH VIDEO CASSETTE PRO
See series title for descriptive statement.
From The Pain And Soft Tissue Injury Series.
Prod-PBI Dist-ABACPE

Pain - Mechanisms And Management C
3/4 OR 1/2 INCH VIDEO CASSETTE
Focuses on clinical applicability of major pain research developments. Reviews progress in the individualized management of chronic pain due to benign or malignant disease and considers patients' psychological experiences.
Prod-AMEDA Dist-AMEDA

Pain And Hypnosis C 29 MIN
3/4 INCH VIDEO CASSETTE C A
Shows that many factors influence pain. Discusses pain-treating strategies. Compares differing interpretations of hypnosis.
From The Understanding Human Behavior - An Introduction To Psychology Series. Lesson 18
Prod-COAST Dist-CDTEL

Pain And Its Alleviation C 24 MIN
16MM FILM, 3/4 OR 1/2 IN VIDEO PRO
Stresses the complexity of the pain phenomenon, and discusses the role of nursing in providing help and comfort on a professional level. Indicates variations in response to pain and explores the causes of pain.
Prod-SIGNTR Dist-UCEMC 1961

Pain And Soft Tissue Injury—A Series
PRO
Explores causes and treatment of pain to help attorneys prove or disprove the validity of pain in a claimant.
Prod-PBI Dist-ABACPE

Approaches To Treatment 057 MIN
Interplay Of Psychology And Physiology 055 MIN
Pain - Examples Of Frequent Types Of Pain And 058 MIN

Pain Control Through Behavior Modification C 23 MIN
3/4 INCH VIDEO CASSETTE PRO
See series title for descriptive statement.
From The Management Of Pain Series. Module 5
LC NO. 80-707393
Prod-BRA Dist-BRA 1980

Pain Factor, The C
3/4 OR 1/2 INCH VIDEO CASSETTE
See series title for descriptive statement.
From The Fragments from Willoughby's Video Performances - Pt I Series.
Prod-EAI Dist-EAI

Pain Management B 37 MIN
3/4 INCH VIDEO CASSETTE
See series title for descriptive statement.
From The Terminal Illness Series.
Prod-UWASHP Dist-UWASHP

Pain Of Silence, The C 13 MIN
16MM FILM OPTICAL SOUND J
Focuses on the personal concern of a teenage girl who suspects that she has contracted a venereal disease.
Prod-MLA Dist-MLA 1971

Pain Relief Through Depth Brain Stimulation System C 35 MIN
3/4 INCH VIDEO CASSETTE PRO
Provides details on one method of pain relief. Focuses on several aspects, including patient selection, lead implantation, care of transmitter, skin care and follow-up.
Prod-KRI Dist-KRI

Pain Relief Through PISCES System C 42 MIN
3/4 INCH VIDEO CASSETTE PRO
Provides specific information about the percutaneously inserted spinal cord epidural stimulation system. Details one method used for pain relief.
Prod-KRI Dist-KRI

Painful Confession C 30 MIN
16MM FILM OPTICAL SOUND H-C R
A dramatization about a hit-and-run accident and the ensuing guilt of the person who committed it to show the importance of God's forgiveness.
LC NO. 70-715497
Prod-CONCOR Dist-CPH 1968

Painful Step, The B 19 MIN
16MM FILM OPTICAL SOUND H-C A
Uses drawings of the foot's anatomy and X-rays to explain the cause of bunions. Shows the corrective surgery for a bunion condition. Demonstrates procedures for correction of the foot from the initial binding of the foot to the final excision of bone and closing sutures.
From The Doctors At Work Series.
LC NO. FIA65-1356
Prod-CMA Dist-LAWREN Prodn-LAWREN 1961

Paint C 14 MIN
16MM FILM, 3/4 OR 1/2 IN VIDEO
Deals with paint and painting, both artistic and commercial.
Prod-KAWVAL Dist-KAWVAL

Paint C 15 MIN
3/4 OR 1/2 INCH VIDEO CASSETTE P
Demonstrates various painting techniques and the uses of a variety of painting tools. Shows a group of primary level children at a painting party.
From The Primary Art Series.
Prod-WETATV Dist-AITECH

Paint An Exciting Picture Without A Brush C 59 MIN
1/2 IN VIDEO CASSETTE BETA/VHS K-P
Shows how to paint with materials such as string, cotton swabs and rollers.
From The Children's Crafts Series.
Prod-MOHOMV Dist-MOHOMV

Paint Engravings C 15 MIN
3/4 OR 1/2 INCH VIDEO CASSETTE P-I
Discusses paint engravings.
From The Young At Art Series.
Prod-WSKJTV Dist-AITECH 1980

Paint Gun Operation C 18 MIN
1/2 IN VIDEO CASSETTE BETA/VHS
Deals with auto body repair. Covers the usual paint gun problems and adjustment.
Prod-RMI Dist-RMI

Paint Me A Mood C 10 MIN
3/4 OR 1/2 INCH VIDEO CASSETTE K-P
Points out that moods can be created or induced by external forces.
From The Book, Look And Listen Series.
Prod-MDDE Dist-AITECH 1977

Paint Plus Imagination B 20 MIN
2 INCH VIDEOTAPE P-I
Deals with experimenting with blotting and blowing paint and using imagination to create stories or poems about paintings.
From The Art Adventures Series.
Prod-CVETVC Dist-GPITVL Prodn-WCVETV

Paint Safety C 10 MIN
1/2 IN VIDEO CASSETTE BETA/VHS
Deals with auto body repair. Explains the hazards involved in painting and what precautions should be practiced. Shows the proper use of paint respirators.
Prod-RMI Dist-RMI

Paint Stripping Hints C 30 MIN
1/2 IN VIDEO CASSETTE BETA/VHS
Shows work on the deck of an old house underway, and offers hints paint stripping. Introduces an alternative to ceramic wall tile around a bathtub.
From The This Old House, Pt 1 - The Dorchester Series.
Prod-WGBHTV Dist-MTI

Paint The Rain C 10 MIN
16MM FILM OPTICAL SOUND
Presents a dramatization about a young mental patient's brief escape from the bleakness of his surroundings. Shows how the palette and canvas of an old artist become the vehicles which carry him momentarily into a world of life and color.
LC NO. 74-702880
Prod-PANHAL Dist-BROSEB 1974

Paint To Music C 15 MIN
3/4 OR 1/2 INCH VIDEO CASSETTE P
Compares art and music explaining that the rhythm, movement, mood and pattern of music can be expressed in art by line, color, shape and texture.
From The Primary Art Series.
Prod-WETATV Dist-AITECH

Paint Your World C 25 MIN
2 INCH VIDEOTAPE I
Uses tempera paints and various perspectives.
From The Art For Every Day Series.
Prod-CVETVC Dist-GPITVL

Paint-A Series
H-C A
Shows some of the basic techniques and materials used by a painter and the problems faced by a painter in translating reality onto canvas.
Prod-BBCTV Dist-FI

Abstract Painting	025 MIN
Beginning A Still Life	025 MIN
Completing A Still Life	025 MIN
Completing An Interior View	025 MIN
Flower Painting	025 MIN
How To Tackle An Interior View	025 MIN
Painting From Photographs	025 MIN
Painting Outdoors	025 MIN
Perspective And Painting With A	025 MIN
Wash Techniques Of Painting	025 MIN

Painted Day-Glo Smile C 4 MIN
16MM FILM OPTICAL SOUND H-C
Presents a visual interpretation of the Chad and Jeremy recording 'PAINTED DAY-GLO SMILE.'
Prod-CFS Dist-CFS 1958

Painted Poor; The C 26 MIN
16MM FILM, 3/4 OR 1/2 IN VIDEO
Tells the story of love, regret and death. Describes how the marriage of John and Anne disintegrates when their farm becomes the dominant factor in John's life and Anne's existence is only lightened by the friendship of their neighbor, Stephen. During a blizzard Anne betrays her husband with Stephen only to quickly realize the horrifying implications of her betrayal. From the Sinclair Ross story.
Prod-BCNFL Dist-BCNFL 1985

Painted Truck, The C 28 MIN
16MM FILM OPTICAL SOUND J-C A
Features an Afghanistani, multi-colored truck loaded with rice, soap, wheat, wood, melons and seasoned truck travelers making a rugged journey across the 12,700 foot Hajigak Pass from Kabul to Bamian. Views the unusual twists modernity creates in Afghanistan's culture and the inequity of the master-servant relationship.
LC NO. 73-702756
Prod-RADIM Dist-RADIM 1973

Painter Of The American West C 55 MIN
16MM FILM - 3/4 IN VIDEO
Focuses on the life and work of artist Olaf Wieghorst.
LC NO. 79-706307
Prod-NOSMER Dist-NOSMER 1978

Painter/Sculptor/Welder, Gerald Scheck C 29 MIN
3/4 OR 1/2 INCH VIDEO CASSETTE H-C A
Explores the painter's sense of purpose and his unconscious drives and feelings.
From The Creativity With Bill Moyers Series.
Prod-CORPEL Dist-PBS 1982

Painter, The C 8 MIN
16MM FILM, 3/4 OR 1/2 IN VIDEO J-C
Presents an interpretation of The Painter In Central Park by Marcel Marceau.
From The Humanities - The Performing Arts, Art Of Silence, Pantomimes With Marcel Marceau Series.
Prod-EBEC Dist-EBEC 1975

Painter's Eye, The C 45 MIN
16MM FILM OPTICAL SOUND H A
Gives an insight into the contemporary artists such as Kandinsky and Klee. Describes their techniques in line and color composition and compares them to older, more traditional artists.
From The Man And His Art Series.
Prod-WTTWTV Dist-GPITVL

Painters And Pioneers C 29 MIN
2 INCH VIDEOTAPE
See series title for descriptive statement.
From The Museum Open House Series.
Prod-WGBHTV Dist-PUBTEL

Painters In The Modern World C 20 MIN
16MM FILM, 3/4 OR 1/2 IN VIDEO H-C
Presents three part-time artists and the ways in which they deal with the problems of painting in the context of today's world. Points out that they are typical of the artists of today who are free to choose their own subject and style, and who stand alone economically.
Prod-WONASO Dist-IFB Prodn-CHICA 1970

Painters Painting C 116 MIN
16MM FILM OPTICAL SOUND
Illustrates and examines the work and ideas of several modern, abstract, expressionist painters, including Willem De Kooning, Jasper Johns, Robert Motherwell and Andy Warhol.
LC NO. 74-701038
Prod-NYFLMS Dist-NYFLMS 1973

Painting C 15 MIN
3/4 OR 1/2 INCH VIDEO CASSETTE P-I
Shows how to use flat and round brushes and tempura paint. Demonstrates color mixing and shading.
From The Art Cart Series.
LC NO. 79-708039
Prod-WBRATV Dist-AITECH 1979

Painting C 20 MIN
2 INCH VIDEOTAPE I
Helps students learn about using paint and other media for painting.
From The Creating Art, Pt 2 - Learning To Create Art Forms Series.
Prod-GPITVL Dist-GPITVL

Painting C 29 MIN
3/4 INCH VIDEO CASSETTE
Discusses historical and contemporary Native American art. Also available in two-inch quad and one-inch videotape.
From The Indian Arts At The Phoenix Heard Museum Series.
Prod-KAETTV Dist-NAMPBC

Painting C 30 MIN
16MM FILM, 3/4 OR 1/2 IN VIDEO
Provides basic information on painting.
From The Do It Yourself Home Repairs Series.
Prod-ODECA Dist-BULFRG

Painting - A Visual Record C 18 MIN
16MM FILM, 3/4 OR 1/2 IN VIDEO J-C
Presents an introduction to painting.
From The Humanities Series.
Prod-MGHT Dist-MGHT 1971

Painting - Creating A Point Of View C 30 MIN
3/4 INCH VIDEO CASSETTE C A
Explores major elements of painting. Shows how color can have sensory impact. Illustrates specific points about elements of painting by looking at the work of such artists as Monet, Delacroix and El Greco.
From The Humanities Through The Arts With Maya Angelou Series. Lesson 19
Prod-COAST Dist-CDTEL Prodn-CICOCH

Painting - Drawing - Stasack C 11 MIN
16MM FILM OPTICAL SOUND H-C
Features artist Stasack revealing his personal approach to art which brought him acclaim in his field.
Prod-CINEPC Dist-CINEPC

Painting - Group Figure Compositions, I B 45 MIN
2 INCH VIDEOTAPE C
See series title for descriptive statement.
From The General Humanities Series. Unit 2 - The Visual Arts
Prod-CHITVC Dist-GPITVL Prodn-WTTWTV

Painting - Group Figure Compositions, II B 45 MIN
2 INCH VIDEOTAPE C
See series title for descriptive statement.
From The General Humanities Series. Unit 2 - The Visual Arts
Prod-CHITVC Dist-GPITVL Prodn-WTTWTV

Painting - Light, Space And Atmosphere B 45 MIN
2 INCH VIDEOTAPE C
See series title for descriptive statement.
From The General Humanities Series. Unit 2 - The Visual Arts
Prod-CHITVC Dist-GPITVL Prodn-WTTWTV

Painting - Portraits And Single Figure Compositions B 45 MIN
2 INCH VIDEOTAPE C
See series title for descriptive statement.
From The General Humanities Series. Unit 2 - The Visual Arts
Prod-CHITVC Dist-GPITVL Prodn-WTTWTV

Painting - Rousseau - The Lovely Dream C 30 MIN
3/4 INCH VIDEO CASSETTE C A
Examines what are known as the innocent and poetic works of Henri Rousseau. Offers a biography of Rousseau as a framework within which the artist and his works can be understood.
From The Humanities Through The Arts With Maya Angelou Series. Lesson 20
Prod-COAST Dist-CDTEL Prodn-CICOCH

Painting - Still Life B 45 MIN
2 INCH VIDEOTAPE C
See series title for descriptive statement.
From The General Humanities Series. Unit 2 - The Visual Arts
Prod-CHITVC Dist-GPITVL Prodn-WTTWTV

Painting - The Creative Process C 15 MIN
16MM FILM, 3/4 OR 1/2 IN VIDEO J-C A
Features artist Reginald Pollack and shows a painting from conception to completion. Conveys the idea that a work of art comes from the artist's mastery of tools and materials, his factual and visual information, his emotions and moods, and his knowledge of all past art.
Prod-KAHANA Dist-PHENIX 1967

Painting - Things We Have Passed C 30 MIN
3/4 INCH VIDEO CASSETTE C A
Discusses criticism in painting. Focuses on abstract painting and reactions to it. Includes painter Glen White and Maya Angelou.
From The Humanities Through The Arts With Maya Angelou Series. Lesson 21
Prod-COAST Dist-CDTEL Prodn-CICOCH

Painting - Visions Through The Ages C 30 MIN
3/4 INCH VIDEO CASSETTE C A
Demonstrates how humans from diverse cultures and different times have expressed in two-dimensional forms their unique perceptions of the world around them. Shows several artists' work.
From The Humanities Through The Arts With Maya Angelou Series. Lesson 18
Prod-COAST Dist-CDTEL Prodn-CICOCH

Painting A Panelled Door C 14 MIN
3/4 OR 1/2 INCH VIDEO CASSETTE H-C A
Shows dusting, cleaning and knotting, preparation of the primer, application of the primer, stopping and filling, the undercoat and the final coat.
Prod-SF Dist-SF

Painting And Decorating - Paperhanging Application C 14 MIN
16MM FILM OPTICAL SOUND H-C A
Shows paste preparation, commercial and individual mixes, paper fitting, pattern and paper matching, applying paste, pasting the wall, lapping and butt joints. Starting and finishing points in a room, plumb line and chalk marks. Fitting around doors and windows, smoothing out bubbles, achieving a professional finish.
Prod-SF Dist-SF

Painting And Decorating - Paperhanging Preparation C 14 MIN
16MM FILM OPTICAL SOUND H-C A
Shows the various methods of cutting wallpaper. Depicts the needed equipment, such as shears, rollers, smoothing utensils, and the various types of knives. Describes the paster process, preparation of the wall, filling cracks, removing old paint or calcimine, stripping old paper and wall sizing.
Prod-SF Dist-SF

Painting And Decorating - The Art Of Painting A Door C 14 MIN
16MM FILM OPTICAL SOUND H-C A
Shows dusting, cleaning and knotting, preparation of the primer, application of the primer, stopping and filling, the undercoat and the final coat.
Prod-SF Dist-SF

Painting And Possessions C 25 MIN
16MM FILM, 3/4 OR 1/2 IN VIDEO H-C A
Presents art critic John Berger, who discusses paintings as material possessions and how paintings and advertising present objects in a way which makes people want to possess them.
From The Ways Of Seeing Series.
Prod-BBCTV Dist-FI 1974

Painting And Staining - Spray And Roller Painting, Staining Wood C 30 MIN
1/2 IN VIDEO CASSETTE BETA/VHS
See series title for descriptive statement.
From The Wally's Workshop Series.
Prod-KARTES Dist-KARTES

Painting By Numbers C 60 MIN
16MM FILM, 3/4 OR 1/2 IN VIDEO H-C A
Introduces the world of computer graphics, demonstrating how computers can be programmed to produce sophisticated Disney-like animated images. Interviews the engineer who invented the very first video game and the inventor of the first coin-operated arcade games.
LC NO. 83-706616
Prod-BBCTV Dist-FI 1982

Painting From Photographs C 25 MIN
3/4 OR 1/2 INCH VIDEO CASSETTE H-C A
See series title for descriptive statement.
From The Paint Series. Program 7
Prod-BBCTV Dist-FI

Painting In America - Copley To Audubon C 21 MIN
16MM FILM OPTICAL SOUND J-C A
A survey of 18th century art in America from Copley to Audubon.
Prod-DETRIA Dist-RADIM 1957

Painting Marge Ann C 29 MIN
3/4 INCH VIDEO CASSETTE
Gives a lesson in the flexibility of oil paint.
From The Artist At Work Series.
Prod-UMITV Dist-UMITV 1973

Painting On Copper B 5 MIN
16MM FILM OPTICAL SOUND J-H
Shows the thousand-year-old relics of the Maya civilization in the jungles of Honduras. Presents the works of artist Arturo Lopez-Rodezno, who finds the inspiration for his copper enamellings in the Mayan stone sculptures. Shows his copper enamelling technique.
From The Screen News Digest Series. Vol 4, Issue 10
Prod-HEARST Dist-HEARST 1962

Painting Outdoors C 25 MIN
3/4 OR 1/2 INCH VIDEO CASSETTE H-C A
See series title for descriptive statement.
From The Paint Series. Program 5
Prod-BBCTV Dist-FI

Painting People C 28 MIN
16MM FILM OPTICAL SOUND H-C A
Several contempory Australian portrait painters discuss their styles of painting and the problems involved in their work.
LC NO. FIA67-5960
Prod-ANAIB Dist-AUIS 1966

Painting Potential C 24 MIN
3/4 OR 1/2 INCH VIDEO CASSETTE H-C
Introduces the physical science concepts of field and potential by demonstrating the relationships between those concepts as well as their application. Shows computer assisted mapping of gradiant and distance, relationships between force and energy, and electrostatic spray painting to explain how charged terminals form a pattern in chemical powder.
From The Discovering Physics Series.
Prod-BBCTV Dist-MEDIAG Prodn-OPENU 1983

Painting The Town C 30 MIN
3/4 OR 1/2 INCH VIDEO CASSETTE
Looks at the art that is all around us, such as, graffiti, skywriting, city wall murals, street sculpture and others.
From The Eye To Eye Series.
Prod-WGBHTV Dist-EAI Prodn-MOFAB

Painting Time C 8 MIN
16MM FILM OPTICAL SOUND J-C A
Shows a four-year-old using his already developed abilities in making lines and shapes. Provides strong data for exploring ways in which children continually teach themselves.
From The Exploring Childhood Series.
LC NO. 76-701894
Prod-EDC Dist-EDC Prodn-FRIEDJ 1974

Painting With Words C 10 MIN
16MM FILM, 3/4 OR 1/2 IN VIDEO I-J
Focuses on the expansion of a 'kernal' sentence. Emphasizes the correct placing of the added words in the sentence.
Prod-AIMS Dist-AIMS 1970

Painting With Words (Spanish) C 10 MIN
16MM FILM, 3/4 OR 1/2 IN VIDEO P-J
Illustrates the expansion of a 'kernel' sentence, with emphasis on the correct placing of added words in a sentence.
Prod-ASSOCF Dist-AIMS Prodn-SADLO 1970

Paintings - Rx For Survival C 40 MIN
16MM FILM OPTICAL SOUND H
Covers the conservation basics relative to the care and handling of oil paintings. Describes the delicate physical makeup of an oil painting, the harm that may come to a painting while hanging or being hung, how a layman can check for signs of deterioration and decay, how to physically carry a painting, how a professional conservator cleans the surface and describes first-aid procedures in case of major or minor damage.
Prod-HAMPRO Dist-HAMPRO 1980

Paintings And Plastics C 12 MIN
16MM FILM OPTICAL SOUND
Presents James Davis, an American painter and sculptor in transparent plastics, opening new fields of art and design. Records his art in the collections of the Museum of Modern Art, other museums and private collections.
Prod-DAVISJ Dist-RADIM

Paintings In The White House - A Close-Up C 28 MIN
16MM FILM OPTICAL SOUND J-C A
Surveys 47 paintings in the White House, picturing events of the last 150 years. Includes works by Stuart, Peale, Whistler and Sargent. Presents an introduction by Mrs Lyndon B Johnson.
LC NO. FIA68-1773
Prod-WEC Dist-MLA Prodn-JENSEN 1965

Paints And Coatings C 12 MIN
3/4 OR 1/2 INCH VIDEO CASSETTE
Covers protective materials such as paints and other coatings.
From The Working With Nonmetals In The Plant Series.
Prod-TPCTRA Dist-TPCTRA

Pair Of Red Clogs, A C 15 MIN
3/4 OR 1/2 INCH VIDEO CASSETTE P
See series title for descriptive statement.
From The Magic Pages Series.
Prod-KLVXTV Dist-AITECH 1976

Pak Menggung - A Javanese Aristocrat C 21 MIN
16MM FILM OPTICAL SOUND H-C A
Examines the life of a Javanese aristocrat who devotes his life to recording the disappearing traditions and ceremonies of his culture.
From The Asian Neighbors - Indonesia Series.
LC NO. 75-703585
Prod-FLMAUS Dist-AVIS 1975

Pakistan - Children Of The Road C 26 MIN
3/4 OR 1/2 INCH VIDEO CASSETTE
Documents the lives of children in Pakistan.
From The Growing Up Young Series.
Prod-FOTH Dist-FOTH

Pakistan - Land Of Promise C 15 MIN
16MM FILM OPTICAL SOUND
Surveys the relief effort of the U S government and other international sources in helping Pakistan increase food production and improve health conditions, emphasizing the role of the U S Agency for International Development. Recounts Pakistan's efforts to reduce its birthrate by at least 20 percent by 1978.
LC NO. 76-703714
Prod-USAID Dist-USNAC 1976

Pakistan - Mound Of The Dead C 27 MIN
16MM FILM, 3/4 OR 1/2 IN VIDEO I-C A
Tells the story of Mohenjo Daro (Mound of the Dead), a meticulously planned city thousands of years old, discovered in the Indus Valley by archeologists in the 1920's.
From The People And Places Of Antiquity Series.
Prod-CFDLD Dist-CORF

Pakistani Chapli Kebabs And Pearl Barley And Nuts C 28 MIN
3/4 OR 1/2 INCH VIDEO CASSETTE PRO
Shows how to saute pine nuts and cook them with ground lamb and serve in pita bread with barley.
Prod-CULINA Dist-CULINA

Pal Joey C 109 MIN
16MM FILM OPTICAL SOUND C A
Stars Rita Hayworth, Frank Sinatra and Kim Novak in the story of a night-club entertainer, a heel with a heart of gold, and two women, a beautiful socialite who responds to his rowdy appeal and a beautiful chorine who teaches him that he has a heart after all. Presents a score by Rogers and Hart, including songs 'BEWITCHED, BOTHERED AND BEWILDERED,' 'I DIDN'T KNOW WHAT TIME IT WAS' and 'THE LADY IS A TRAMP.'
Prod-CPC Dist-TIMLIF 1957

Palace Cars And Paradise C 28 MIN
16MM FILM OPTICAL SOUND
Presents the story of the Pullman model town, created in the 1880s by George Pullman as the ideal industrial community.
Prod-ILHS Dist-ILHS

Palace Of Delights C 58 MIN
16MM FILM, 3/4 OR 1/2 IN VIDEO
Visits San Francisco's Exploratorium, a hands-on science museum dedicated to the joys of curiosity and understanding.
From The Nova Series.
LC NO. 83-706191
Prod-WGBHTV Dist-TIMLIF 1982

Palace Of The Sun King - Louis XIV And Versailles C 45 MIN
2 INCH VIDEOTAPE
See series title for descriptive statement.
From The Humanities Series. Unit I - Persons, Places And Events
Prod-WTTWTV Dist-GPITVL

Palatal Flap In Periodontics, The C 13 MIN
16MM FILM, 3/4 OR 1/2 IN VIDEO
Demonstrates the surgical management of osseous deformities involving the palatal and proximal periodontal areas. Shows how a palatal flap is created using an internal beveled incision, thus preserving the remaining attached gingiva and permitting access to the underlying alveolar process.
LC NO. 81-706823
Prod-USVA Dist-USNAC 1968

Palawan C 15 MIN
16MM FILM OPTICAL SOUND
A Danish language film. Portrays daily life in a small community on the philippine Island Palawan. Shows housebuilding, primitive farming and preparation of a meal.
Prod-STATNS Dist-STATNS 1963

Palazzo Giustiniani, Venice C 26 MIN
16MM FILM, 3/4 OR 1/2 IN VIDEO H-C A
Describes how this last of the palazzos, which was originally financed by merchants of Venice, is now maintained by receipts from a section that has been turned into flats by the only living descendant of the family. Descendants of original merchant families meet weekly for coffee.
From The Place In Europe Series.
Prod-THAMES Dist-MEDIAG 1975

Paleface, The B 22 MIN
16MM FILM SILENT J-C A
Stars Buster Keaton.
Prod-MGM Dist-TWYMAN 1921

Paleolithic Society, The C 21 MIN
16MM FILM, 3/4 OR 1/2 IN VIDEO J-C A
Appraises the lives of the people of the lower, middle and upper Paleolithic eras by traditional archaeology, examination of artifacts and habitation sites, and the study of primitive societies in Africa and Australia from which possible parallels may be deduced.
Prod-LUF Dist-LUF 1980

Palestine - Abdication C 86 MIN
16MM FILM, 3/4 OR 1/2 IN VIDEO H-C A
Tells how the United Nations partitioned Palestine but could not enforce its policy. Shows how Jews and Arabs resorted to terrorism and massacre, resulting in the siege of Jerusalem.
From The Palestine Series.
Prod-THAMES Dist-MEDIAG 1978

Palestine - Promises C 72 MIN
16MM FILM, 3/4 OR 1/2 IN VIDEO H-C A
Points out that Palestine, primarily populated by Arabs and placed under British supervision in 1914, is the location of Jerusalem, Holy City of Christians, Jews and followers of Islam. Shows how the decades of the 1920s and 1930s brought violence and social upheaval because of resettlement and rebellion.
From The Palestine Series.
Prod-THAMES Dist-MEDIAG 1978

Palestine - Rebellion C 86 MIN
16MM FILM, 3/4 OR 1/2 IN VIDEO H-C A
Shows that the 1940s era in Palestine witnessed political and employment discrimination against Arabs and the emergence of Zionist forces demanding a homeland for Jews fleeing Hitler and looking to America for support. Points out that the resulting violence depleted Britain's patience and resources, culminating in Britain's withdrawal.
From The Palestine Series.
Prod-THAMES Dist-MEDIAG 1978

Palestine Liberation Organization C 28 MIN
3/4 INCH VIDEOTAPE
Interviews Mr Zehdi Terzi, permanent observer to the United Nations, about the position and objectives of the Palestinians. Hosted by Marilyn Perry and John Law, former Middle East editor of U S News And World Report.
From The International Byline Series.
Prod-PERRYM Dist-PERRYM

Palestine—A Series
16MM FILM, 3/4 OR 1/2 IN VIDEO H-C A
Focuses on the history of the mid-east conflict. Presents Palestine's story as told by Jews and Arabs who struggled for a homeland.
Prod-THAMES Dist-MEDIAG 1978

Palestine - Abdication 086 MIN
Palestine - Promises 072 MIN
Palestine - Rebellion 086 MIN

Palestinian People Do Have Rights, The C 48 MIN
16MM FILM, 3/4 OR 1/2 IN VIDEO H-C A

Traces events in Palestine from 1947, when the United Nations recommended a partition of the region. Includes archival footage, maps, shots of refugee camps, and interviews with Palestinians.
Prod-UN Dist-ICARUS 1979

Palestinian Question, The, Pt 1 C 30 MIN
3/4 OR 1/2 INCH VIDEO CASSETTE
See series title for descriptive statement.
From The Arabs And Israelis Series.
Prod-WGBHTV Dist-PBS

Palestinian Question, The, Pt 2 C 30 MIN
3/4 OR 1/2 INCH VIDEO CASSETTE
See series title for descriptive statement.
From The Arabs And Israelis Series.
Prod-WGBHTV Dist-PBS

Palestinians C 29 MIN
3/4 OR 1/2 INCH VIDEO CASSETTE H-C A
Dwells upon a number of Palestinians dispersed throughout the world as refugees. Describes their anguish in trying to keep their culture alive, and how they say they want to resolve the Israeli problem without destroying the Jewish nation, but offer no concrete formulas to accomplish this.
From The Are You Listening Series.
LC NO. 84-706134
Prod-STURTM Dist-STURTM 1983

Palette Knife Painting C 28 MIN
16MM FILM OPTICAL SOUND
Presents a step-by-step demonstration of all the conventional aspects of rendering a landscape, from preparation of the white ground to mixing the basic color wheel and filling the overlapping planes of depth.
Prod-NILLU Dist-NILLU 1973

Palette Knife Painting C 29 MIN
16MM FILM, 3/4 OR 1/2 IN VIDEO J-C A
Shows an artist performing palette knife painting, showing step-by-step aspects of rendering a landscape from preparation of the white ground to mixing the basic color wheel and filling the overlapping planes of depth.
Prod-NILLU Dist-MCFI

Palette Of Glass, A C 25 MIN
16MM FILM, 3/4 OR 1/2 IN VIDEO J-C A
Documents the creation of Marc Chagalls' American windows, located in the Chagall Gallery of Chicago's Art Institute. Shows how appropriate glass is chosen and blown into colored sheets and how Chagall applies the grisaille, the painted decorations that give unity and dimension to the glass fragments.
Prod-ARTINC Dist-PHENIX 1978

Palio C 29 MIN
16MM FILM, 3/4 OR 1/2 IN VIDEO H-C A
Shows an 18th-century political horse race still held in Siena, Italy, between 17 city districts.
Prod-PHENIX Dist-PHENIX 1976

Pall Corporation Marketing Case History B 50 MIN
3/4 OR 1/2 INCH VIDEO CASSETTE
Discusses problems of a manufacturer of highly technical filter products for the space industry switching to serve the automotive industry.
Prod-HBS Dist-IVCH

Palladio - Three Villas C 24 MIN
16MM FILM OPTICAL SOUND
Studies three Italian residential architectural reconstructions designed by Palladio in the 16th century.
Prod-BBCTV Dist-OPENU 1981

Palladio - Three Villas C 24 MIN
16MM FILM, 3/4 OR 1/2 IN VIDEO
Studies three Italian residential architectural reconstructions designed by Palladio in the 16th century.
Prod-OPENU Dist-MEDIAG Prodn-BBCTV 1981

Palm Beach Arts Festival C 12 MIN
16MM FILM OPTICAL SOUND I-C
Highlights the annual Creative Arts Pageant in Palm Beach, Florida. Features ballerina Claudi Cravi.
LC NO. FIA66-511
Prod-FDC Dist-FDC 1965

Palm Play C 30 MIN
16MM FILM, 3/4 OR 1/2 IN VIDEO
Demonstrates palm presentation patterns used by dancers throughout the world and discusses the distribution of these patterns in various geographic regions as well as the correlation with subsistence cultures.
From The Movement Style And Culture Series.
Prod-CHORP Dist-UCEMC 1978

Palm Sunday C 15 MIN
3/4 OR 1/2 INCH VIDEO CASSETTE
Mixes documentary footage with extravagant subtitles to create an experimental film.
Prod-KROGST Dist-MEDIPR 1980

Palm Sunday With The Disciples Of Christ C 58 MIN
3/4 OR 1/2 INCH VIDEO CASSETTE A
Presents a Palm Sunday worship at National City Christian Church in Washington, D C as it is presided over by Dr William C Howard, minister. Looks at the Disciples' emphasis on communion as well as National City's music program and the architectural grandeur of the church in the nation's capital.
Prod-NBCNEW Dist-ECUFLM 1982

Palm Trees And Icebergs C 24 MIN
3/4 OR 1/2 INCH VIDEO CASSETTE
Shows reports by the youth of Alaska and Hawaii.
From The Young People's Specials Series.
Prod-MULTPP Dist-MULTPP

Palm Trees On The Moon C 22 MIN
3/4 OR 1/2 INCH VIDEO CASSETTE
Collects images from visits to several of the islands of the Solomon chain. Centers around a festival of traditional music and dance.
Prod-EAI Dist-EAI

Palmar Hand, The, Pt 1 C 14 MIN
16MM FILM, 3/4 OR 1/2 IN VIDEO
Presents a demonstration of the anatomy of the palmar hand, its muscles, blood supply and nerves.
From The Cine-Prosector Series.
Prod-TEF Dist-TEF 1968

Palmar Hand, The, Pt 2 Intrinsic Muscles C 14 MIN
16MM FILM, 3/4 OR 1/2 IN VIDEO
Presents a demonstration of the anatomy of the intrinsic muscles of the palmar hand and their function.
From The Cine-Prosector Series.
Prod-TEF Dist-TEF 1968

Palmetto, The C 14 MIN
2 INCH VIDEOTAPE
Features nature photographer Jim Bones celebrating the beauty of the palmetto.
From The Images And Memories Series.
Prod-KERA Dist-PUBTEL

Palpable Osler, The C 33 MIN
3/4 OR 1/2 INCH VIDEO CASSETTE
Reviews Sir William Osler's life and contributions to clinical medicine, medical literature and the practice of humanistic medicine.
Prod-USDHEW Dist-USNAC

Pals C 15 MIN
16MM FILM OPTICAL SOUND
Offers a look at day care programs for preschool children. Discusses the advantages for working parents and suggests how to evaluate existing programs.
LC NO. 79-701184
Prod-VICTFL Dist-VICTFL 1979

Pals C 29 MIN
16MM FILM, 3/4 OR 1/2 IN VIDEO A
Focuses on peer groups and pressures through the dramatization of a situation in the fictional Riley family, in which young Ned questions the price he must pay for friendship. Includes a brief introduction and commentary by real-life families and child development experts.
From The Footsteps Series.
LC NO. 80-707202
Prod-USDED Dist-USNAC Prodn-EDFCEN 1980

Pals C 60 MIN
3/4 OR 1/2 INCH VIDEO CASSETTE J A
Tells of four high school friends of various backgrounds who produce a local teen program via a public access channel and struggle to keep the show afloat after one of the group suddenly becomes ego-maniacal.
From The Rainbow Movie Of The Week Series.
Prod-RAINTV Dist-GPITVL 1981

Pals, Pouches, And Pockets C 15 MIN
3/4 OR 1/2 INCH VIDEO CASSETTE P
Presents Dr Allhart using puppets and live animals to discuss the characteristics of marsupials.
From The Dr Allhart And Patience Series.
LC NO. 81-707533
Prod-JCITV Dist-GPITVL 1979

Pamela Wong's Birthday For Grandma C 8 MIN
16MM FILM, 3/4 OR 1/2 IN VIDEO P-I
Depicts a special event in the life of a Chinese-American family while showing various aspects of life in Chicago's Chinatown.
Prod-LIFSTY Dist-EBEC 1977

Pamela Wong's Birthday For Grandma (Captioned) C 8 MIN
16MM FILM, 3/4 OR 1/2 IN VIDEO P-I
Depicts a special event in the life of a Chinese-American family while showing various aspects of life in Chicago's Chinatown.
Prod-LIFSTY Dist-EBEC 1977

Pamela's Tree C 14 MIN
16MM FILM OPTICAL SOUND
Tells what help both large and small timber owners can obtain from their state forester to save their trees, through the story of Pamela, a tree farmer's daughter. Shows how her favorite tree becomes infested with bark beetles and how it is saved.
LC NO. 74-705288
Prod-USDA Dist-USNAC 1965

Pamplona - The Running Of The Bulls C 10 MIN
3/4 OR 1/2 INCH VIDEO CASSETTE
Documents the running of the bulls in Pamplona, Spain.
Prod-UPI Dist-JOU

Pan Am's World C 24 MIN
16MM FILM OPTICAL SOUND
Tells how Pan American Airways travels to most of the places people want to go, and that their employees work to make the trip a success when they get there. Shows activities that make running an international airline a full-time job.
LC NO. 72-702324
Prod-PANWA Dist-PANWA 1972

Pan Am's World - Czechoslovakia C 14 MIN
16MM FILM OPTICAL SOUND
A travel documentary that includes glimpses of the culture and history of Czechoslovakia.
Prod-PANWA Dist-PANWA

Pan Am's World - Romania C 14 MIN
16MM FILM OPTICAL SOUND
Shows the routes of Pan Am Airways and the activities of the airline on a trip to Romania.
Prod-PANWA Dist-PANWA

Pan Pacific C 22 MIN
16MM FILM OPTICAL SOUND
Traces the history of the Pan Pacific Auditorium in Hollywood, an example of streamline modern architecture. Raises the issue of whether the auditorium should be preserved or demolished.
LC NO. 80-700217
Prod-ASLA Dist-PELICN Prodn-PELICN 1979

Panama C 11 MIN
16MM FILM, 3/4 OR 1/2 IN VIDEO K-P
Tells the story of Little Bear and Little Tiger, who leave their comfortable home to go in search of Panama, the land of their dreams and end up in the most beautiful place in the world.
Prod-WWS Dist-WWS 1982

Panama - The Fifth Frontier (Captioned) B 78 MIN
16MM FILM, 3/4 OR 1/2 IN VIDEO A
Discusses the Panama Canal, its construction, the role of the U S, its operation and its social, political and economic impact. Spanish dialog with English subtitles.
Prod-CUBAFI Dist-CNEMAG 1975

Panama Canal C 3 MIN
16MM FILM OPTICAL SOUND P-I
Discusses the Panama Canal.
From The Of All Things Series.
Prod-BAILYL Dist-AVED

Panama Canal B 16 MIN
3/4 OR 1/2 INCH VIDEO CASSETTE
Covers the construction and history of the Panama Canal. Interspersed with rare footage from the early 1900's.
Prod-KINGFT Dist-KINGFT

Panama Canal - The Longest Shortcut C 28 MIN
16MM FILM, 3/4 OR 1/2 IN VIDEO I-C A
Employs archival photographs, color maps, live footage and animation to recall the digging of the Panama Canal, one of man's greatest engineering achievements.
Prod-SWAIN Dist-MCFI

Panama Canal, The C 32 MIN
16MM FILM, 3/4 OR 1/2 IN VIDEO
Recounts the history of the Isthmus and the task of digging a canal through Panama.
Prod-KAWVAL Dist-KAWVAL

Panama Canal, The (2nd Ed) C 11 MIN
16MM FILM, 3/4 OR 1/2 IN VIDEO
Traces the history of the Panama Canal from its construction to the 1978 treaty. Explains how the canal operates and its significance to world tranportation.
Prod-CORF Dist-CORF 1978

Panama Canal, The - Gateway To The World X 14 MIN
16MM FILM, 3/4 OR 1/2 IN VIDEO I-H
Shows the mighty locks in action. Includes a review of the history of the building of the canal, using copies of the original photographs and news clippings describing the construction.
Prod-EBF Dist-EBEC 1961

Panama Hats (Ecuador) C 3 MIN
16MM FILM OPTICAL SOUND P-I
Discusses the industry for Panama hats in the country of Ecuador.
From The Of All Things Series.
Prod-BAILYL Dist-AVED

Panare, The - Scenes From The Frontier C 60 MIN
16MM FILM, 3/4 OR 1/2 IN VIDEO J-C A
Argues that unless the Panare tribe of Venezuela are protected by legal title to their traditional hunting and fishing grounds, one more group of America's original inhabitants will fall victim to the process of national development. Explains that roads are being driven through their land, a huge mine is planned, and there are more and more cattle.
From The Worlds Apart Series.
Prod-BBCTV Dist-FI 1982

Pancake Party C 15 MIN
3/4 OR 1/2 INCH VIDEO CASSETTE P
Combines looking, listening, talking, writing and reading to help establish the link between oral and written language. Presents the folk tale The Pancake.
From The I Want To Read Series.
Prod-LACOS Dist-GPITVL 1976

Pancakes With Surprises C 9 MIN
16MM FILM, 3/4 OR 1/2 IN VIDEO K-P
Shows how a little dog makes pancakes only to have them stolen by a lazy cat.
From The Little Dog Series.
Prod-ROMAF Dist-PHENIX 1977

Pancho B 25 MIN
3/4 INCH VIDEO CASSETTE
Illustrates the development of a young boy of Mexican descent. Features his physical and mental change from cretin to normal child through the aid of the Head Start program.
Prod-USNAC Dist-USNAC 1972

Pancho Villa B 27 MIN
16MM FILM OPTICAL SOUND H-C A
Recalls the life and career of the Mexican revolutionary, Pancho Villa, with period photographs and a narrative taken from his biography.
Prod-NYU Dist-NYU

Pancho Villa's Columbus Raid C 26 MIN
16MM FILM, 3/4 OR 1/2 IN VIDEO J-C A

Discusses the raid of Columbus, New Mexico, by Pancho Villa in 1916 and the subsequent 11 month expedition led by General John Pershing into Northern Mexico to capture Villa and his men.
LC NO. 84-707123
Prod-NMNR Dist-CNEMAG 1983

PANCOM - Beginning Total Communication Program For Hearing Parents Of...—A Series
K-C A S
Presents Level One of a beginning total communication program for hearing parents of deaf children and staff development. Shows beginners how to use sign language and treats common problems that new parents of deaf children experience.
LC NO. 77-700504
Prod-CSDE Dist-JOYCE Prodn-CSFDF 1977

Action Words 16 MIN
Asking Questions And Making Statements 16 MIN
Basic Question Pattern 16 MIN
Being Specific About People And Objects 16 MIN
Descriptive Language Pattern 16 MIN
People Signs 16 MIN
Places Pattern 16 MIN
Relating Facts 15 MIN
Signs For Time 15 MIN
Where Action Happens 16 MIN

PANCOM - Beginning Total Communication Program For Hearing Parents Of...—A Series
K-C A S
Presents Level Two of a beginning total communication program for hearing parents of deaf children and staff development. Teaches expanded sign language skills wchich include making complete English sentences and questions.
LC NO. 77-700504
Prod-CSDE Dist-JOYCE Prodn-CSFDF 1977

Backyard Activity 16 MIN
Backyard Discovery 15 MIN
Coming Home From School 16 MIN
Dinner 16 MIN
Leaving For School 16 MIN
Manual Alphabet 16 MIN
Morning 16 MIN
Playing In The Park 16 MIN
Preparing For Bed 16 MIN
Preparing For Dinner 16 MIN
Some Problems 15 MIN

Pancreatic Cysts C 28 MIN
16MM FILM OPTICAL SOUND PRO
Includes retention cysts and pseudocysts of the pancreas. Shows roentgenograms which aid in the diagnosis of pancreatic cysts. Demonstrates the various types of surgical therapy.
Prod-ACYDGD Dist-ACY 1953

Pancreatic Disease C 30 MIN
3/4 OR 1/2 INCH VIDEO CASSETTE
Discusses and updates some of the newer modalities of diagnosis and certain aspects of treatment of diseases of the pancreas.
Prod-ROWLAB Dist-ROWLAB

Pancreatitis Update C 30 MIN
3/4 OR 1/2 INCH VIDEO CASSETTE
Reveals the conceptual changes which the treatment of pancreatitis has undergone in the past decade. Relates that toxic metabolic processes rather than mechanical factors induce pancreatic inflammation especially as regards the alcoholic variety.
Prod-ROWLAB Dist-ROWLAB

Pandas C 23 MIN
16MM FILM, 3/4 OR 1/2 IN VIDEO J-H A
Joins American and Chinese researchers as they work to save the panda, one of the world's most engaging and elusive animals.
Prod-NGS Dist-NGS 1984

Pandas - A Gift From China C 14 MIN
16MM FILM, 3/4 OR 1/2 IN VIDEO P-I
Portrays giant pandas whose natural home is in the bamboo forest of the high mountain country of southern China where today about 2,000 of these furry, rotund animals live.
Prod-EBEC Dist-EBEC 1974

Pandas And Applesauce C 10 MIN
3/4 OR 1/2 INCH VIDEO CASSETTE K-P
Focuses on the ability to differentiate between fantasy and reality, and an appreciation of the need in life for fantasy and imagination.
From The Book, Look And Listen Series.
Prod-MDDE Dist-AITECH 1977

Pandora's Bottle - The Drinking Woman C 41 MIN
16MM FILM, 3/4 OR 1/2 IN VIDEO
Explores the social background and behavior of the female alcoholic for causes, preventions and solutions. With Mariette Hartley.
Prod-AVANTI Dist-MTVTM

Pandora's Box C 12 MIN
16MM FILM, 3/4 OR 1/2 IN VIDEO K-I
Relates the ancient story first written by the Greek poet and story teller, Hesiod, and retold often by such as Milton, Voltaire, Goethe and Longfellow. Justifies the myth's perpetuation as an entertaining story because it portrays the human condition in a way that gives insights into important problems of our lives.
Prod-BROKEV Dist-BCNFL 1983

Pandora's Easy Open Pop-Top Box B 16 MIN
3/4 INCH VIDEO CASSETTE
Compares Pandora's Box of misery and evil to the onrush of urbanization opening of a Pandora's Box. Symbolizing the contrasts the sound and fury of the city with the unspoiled countryside.
Prod-USNAC Dist-USNAC 1972

Pandramic Impression Of Old New York (1903 - 05) B 14 MIN
16MM FILM OPTICAL SOUND
Explains that as 1899 faded into the twentieth century, New York City was growing by leaps and bounds. Points out that all over the city the landscape was changing, old buildings were demolished to make way for the new and giant skyscrapers and the growing city was captured by early motion picture cameras erected from the top of the New York Times Building which overlooked Times Square.
LC NO. 72-701847
Prod-BHAWK Dist-BHAWK

Panel Cartoons C 15 MIN
2 INCH VIDEOTAPE
See series title for descriptive statement.
From The Charlie's Pad Series.
Prod-WSIU Dist-PUBTEL

Panel Discussion C 37 MIN
3/4 OR 1/2 INCH VIDEO CASSETTE PRO
Presents the trial attorneys and judge as they are joined in a panel discussion with law faculty. Focuses on the utility of case-by-case determinations rather than a formula approach in both liability and remedy phases.
From The Remedies Phase Of An EEO Case - Individual Determinations Series. Pt 2
Prod-ALIABA Dist-ABACPE

Panel Discussion Of The Problems Of The Artist As A Creator B 45 MIN
2 INCH VIDEOTAPE C
See series title for descriptive statement.
From The General Humanities Series. Unit 1 - Introduction
Prod-CHITVC Dist-GPITVL Prodn-WTTWTV

Panel Discussion On Loxapine Succinate Lederle - A Clinical Review Of A New... C 25 MIN
16MM FILM OPTICAL SOUND PRO
Presents a panel discussion on Loxapine Succinate Lederle, a new chemical entity for the manifestations of schizophrenia. Features the participants reviewing their own experiences with the new drug in treating acute and chronic schizophrenia. Touches on symptoms of schizophrenia encountered, the dosages used, the side effects encountered and the relative effectiveness of the new entity.
Prod-ACYLLD Dist-LEDR 1975

Panel Discussion On Surgery Of The Colon C 46 MIN
16MM FILM OPTICAL SOUND PRO
Recreates the panel discussion on colon surgery held at the 1955 Cine Clinic Program of the A C S.
Prod-ACYDGD Dist-ACY 1956

Panel Discussion On The Management Of Incurable Breast Cancer, A C 46 MIN
16MM FILM OPTICAL SOUND PRO
Presents a panel discussion on the management of incurable breast cancer with Dr Joseph H Farrow, Chief of the Breast Service at Memorial Hospital in New York, bringing eleven typical composite cases of breast cancer before the panelists. Features Dr H Gilbert discussing radiological treatment, Dr Samuel G Taylor III speaking on the use of hormonal therapy, Dr Jeanne C Batemen speaking for the use of chemical agents and Dr Henry T Randall reporting on the surgical approach.
Prod-ACYLLD Dist-LEDR 1962

Panel Discussions C 49 MIN
3/4 OR 1/2 INCH VIDEO CASSETTE PRO
Features a panel discussion concerning the back pay conference. Includes participants in the conference speaking candidly about their strategies and objectives.
From The Remedies Phase Of An EEO Case - Class Back Pay And Proof Of Claims Series. Pt 1
Prod-ALIABA Dist-ABACPE

Panel Feedback Session, A - Midway In Course B 29 MIN
16MM FILM OPTICAL SOUND T
CHEM study staff members and high school teachers discuss questions raised by teachers using the CHEM study materials and participating in the in-service training program. The topics include difficulties in teaching certain concepts, teacher preparation and institutes, further applications of the concept of randomness, the use of models, specific laboratory techniques and evaluations.
From The CHEM Study Teacher Training Series.
LC NO. 76-701169
Prod-CHEMS Dist-MLA 1966

Paneling - Wood Paneling, Wood Paneling Over Masonry C 30 MIN
1/2 IN VIDEO CASSETTE BETA/VHS
See series title for descriptive statement.
From The Wally's Workshop Series.
Prod-KARTES Dist-KARTES

Panels For The Walls Of The World C 8 MIN
16MM FILM OPTICAL SOUND
Presents an experiment in video tape control, an electric collage that mixes the images by way of electronic mats, superimpositions and other electronic means of integration.
Prod-VANBKS Dist-VANBKS 1966

Panographic Diagnostic Pathology Radiolucencies, Pt 1 C 11 MIN
16MM FILM OPTICAL SOUND
Deals with panographic diagnostic pathology radiolucencies. Illustrates radiographic findings, pointing out the importance of recognizing the abnormal, providing differential diagnosis and establishing a definitive diagnosis.
LC NO. 74-705290
Prod-USVA Dist-USNAC 1968

Panographic Diagnostic Pathology Radiolucencies, Pt 2 C 19 MIN
16MM FILM OPTICAL SOUND
Shows abnormal radiolucencies in a series of panographic radiographs, discussing etiology and treatment.
LC NO. 74-705291
Prod-USVA Dist-USNAC 1968

Panographic Diagnostic Pathology Radiolucencies C 30 MIN
3/4 INCH VIDEO CASSETTE PRO
Deals with panographic diagnostic pathology radiolucencies, showing abnormal radiolucencies. Discusses etiology and treatment. Issued in 1968 as a motion picture.
LC NO. 78-706198
Prod-USVA Dist-USNAC Prodn-VADTC 1978

Panographic Diagnostic Pathology Radiopacities C 9 MIN
16MM FILM - 3/4 IN VIDEO PRO
Deals with panographic diagnostic pathology radiopacities. Illustrates radiographic findings, pointing out the importance of recognizing the abnormal, providing differential diagnosis and establishing a definitive diagnosis. Issued in 1968 as a motion picture.
LC NO. 78-706197
Prod-USVA Dist-USNAC Prodn-VADTC 1978

Panorama Of Smokers' Attitudes, A C 6 MIN
16MM FILM OPTICAL SOUND I-J
Presents a variety of opinions from ordinary people about smoking.
LC NO. 74-703691
Prod-SUMHIL Dist-SUMHIL 1974

Panoramic Radiography - Operating Procedure For Panorex C 14 MIN
16MM FILM - 3/4 IN VIDEO PRO
Shows the function of each component part of the Panorex machine and focuses on its complete cycle of operation, the method of skull measurement for obtaining optimum exposure factors, the results of incorrect technique and common technical errors and their correction. Issued in 1967 as a motion picture.
LC NO. 78-706242
Prod-USVA Dist-USNAC Prodn-VADTC 1978

Pantomime - Large And Small Action C 20 MIN
3/4 OR 1/2 INCH VIDEO CASSETTE I
Shows some things that pantomime can do and presents beginning pantomime activities.
From The Creative Dramatics Series.
Prod-NEWITV Dist-AITECH 1977

Pantomime - Large And Small Action (Teacher) C 30 MIN
3/4 OR 1/2 INCH VIDEO CASSETTE T
Demonstrates various pantomime areas and activities, some that would be useful in language arts and social studies.
From The Creative Dramatics (Teacher) Series.
Prod-NEWITV Dist-AITECH 1977

Pantomime - The Language Of The Heart C 10 MIN
16MM FILM, 3/4 OR 1/2 IN VIDEO J-C
Presents Marcel Marceau talking about mime and how body movement and gestures communicate attitudes and emotions. Includes brief clips from many pantomimes to illustrate his words.
From The Humanities - The Performing Arts, Art Of Silence, Pantomimes With Marcel Marceau Series.
Prod-EBEC Dist-EBEC 1975

Pantomime Dame, The C 50 MIN
16MM FILM, 3/4 OR 1/2 IN VIDEO J-C A
Explores the British Christmas custom of portraying in pantomime a mother caricature called the dame. Presents leading comedic actors who explain how the figure is portrayed by a man and give the reasons for the annual tradition. Includes archival stills and film footage.
LC NO. 84-706013
Prod-BCACGB Dist-WOMBAT 1983

Pantomime For The Actor C 20 MIN
16MM FILM OPTICAL SOUND J-C
Earl Lewin, pantomime artist, demonstrates the importance of pantomime to the beginning actor. He shows how pantomime can be used to convey emotion, action, character, setting and plot.
LC NO. FIA65-1587
Prod-SLFP Dist-SLFP 1965

Pantone - The Language Of Color C 17 MIN
3/4 INCH VIDEO CASSETTE
Describes the workings of the Pantone Matching System, which is used for matching colors. Explains its use in all phases of graphic arts, from the creative end to production and printing.
Prod-PANTN Dist-MTP

Paolo Carbonara C 5 MIN
3/4 OR 1/2 INCH VIDEO CASSETTE J-H
Teaches subject-verb agreement.
From The Write On, Set 1 Series.
Prod-CTI Dist-CTI

PAP Test And Self-Breast Examination (2nd Ed) C 9 MIN
3/4 OR 1/2 INCH VIDEO CASSETTE
Explains what a pelvic exam and PAP test are. Presents step-by-step method for self-breast examination.
Prod-MEDFAC Dist-MEDFAC 1981

PAPA - Participant Action Plan Approach - Or How Do I Know Training Is Worth All That Money C 20 MIN
3/4 OR 1/2 INCH VIDEO CASSETTE
Describes a five-step process by which trainers-managers can assess the usefulness of their training programs. Tells how to use the Participant Action Plan Approach (PAPA) and how to adapt it to a particular organization's needs.
Prod-USOPMA Dist-USNAC

PAPA - Participant Action Plan Approach - The Follow-Up Interview C 20 MIN
3/4 OR 1/2 INCH VIDEO CASSETTE
Tells how to conduct the follow-up interview and stresses the importance of gathering meaningful data on the impact of training from the participant.
Prod-USOPMA Dist-USNAC

Papa Penguin's Home Movies C 8 MIN
16MM FILM, 3/4 OR 1/2 IN VIDEO P
Presents Papa Penguin showing home movies of his penguin friends from the Falkland Islands nesting ground. Describes the penguins' daily activities, feeding habits, nesting process and life cycle.
Prod-CORF Dist-CORF 1978

Papa What's It C 13 MIN
16MM FILM OPTICAL SOUND I-C A
Depicts the feeding habits, nesting area and hatching of the Great Blue Heron in its natural habitat. Uses macro and time lapse photography to show the development of the embryo.
Prod-SHUGA Dist-SHUGA

Papageno B 10 MIN
16MM FILM, 3/4 OR 1/2 IN VIDEO A
Presents a silhouette animated fantasy based on the Bird Catcher's Theme from Mozart's Magic Flute.
Prod-PRIMP Dist-TEXFLM

Papanicolaou Stain - Materials And Methods C 21 MIN
3/4 OR 1/2 INCH VIDEO CASSETTE PRO
See series title for descriptive statement.
From The Cytotechnology Techniques Series.
Prod-WFP Dist-WFP

Papanicolaou Stain - Principles C 15 MIN
3/4 OR 1/2 INCH VIDEO CASSETTE PRO
See series title for descriptive statement.
From The Cytotechnology Techniques Series.
Prod-WFP Dist-WFP

Paper C 15 MIN
3/4 OR 1/2 INCH VIDEO CASSETTE P
Examines paper as a versatile medium for the artist and child. Discusses contemporary paper sculpture of American and Japanese artists and the use of paper in the folk art of Mexico, Japan and Poland.
From The Primary Art Series.
Prod-WETATV Dist-AITECH

Paper Animals C 29 MIN
3/4 INCH VIDEO CASSETTE
Uses live animals to show how to paint animals on canvas.
From The Drawing With Guy Palazzola Series.
Prod-UMITV Dist-UMITV 1970

Paper Bag Puppets B 15 MIN
2 INCH VIDEOTAPE P
Utilizes experimenting with paper bags and crayons and cut paper to create puppets resulting in individual, spontaneous creative dramatics.
From The Art Corner Series.
Prod-CVETVC Dist-GPITVL Prodn-WCVETV

Paper Blizzard C 30 MIN
16MM FILM OPTICAL SOUND
Introduces the array of information sources within the federal government and identifies the use of these resources with professionalism. Surveys the range of services that may be expected from a representative information source from the viewpoint of the librarian.
LC NO. 73-700515
Prod-USOE Dist-USNAC 1970

Paper Construction C 15 MIN
16MM FILM, 3/4 OR 1/2 IN VIDEO I-C A
Introduces the use of paper as a sculptural medium. Shows how the techniques of cutting, scoring, bending and folding may be used to create three-dimensional forms which lend themselves to an unlimited range of variations and combinations.
From The Rediscovery - Art Media Film Series.
Prod-ACI Dist-AIMS 1967

Paper Construction (French) C 14 MIN
16MM FILM, 3/4 OR 1/2 IN VIDEO I-C A
Presents a variety of possibilities for working with the material of paper. Stresses the importance of using the imagination and demonstrates the basic techniques of folding, cutting and scoring.
From The Rediscovery - Art Media (French) Series.
Prod-ACI Dist-AIMS 1967

Paper Construction (Spanish) C 14 MIN
16MM FILM, 3/4 OR 1/2 IN VIDEO I-C A
Presents a variety of possibilities for working with the material of paper. Stresses the importance of using the imagination and demonstrates the basic techniques of folding, cutting and scoring.
From The Rediscovery - Art Media (Spanish) Series.
Prod-ACI Dist-AIMS 1967

Paper Makers, The C 22 MIN
16MM FILM OPTICAL SOUND
Shows the activities of the Australian newsprint mills in Southern Tasmania through the eyes of five men.
LC NO. 80-700916
Prod-TASCOR Dist-TASCOR 1980

Paper Of Analysis, The C 30 MIN
3/4 OR 1/2 INCH VIDEO CASSETTE C
See series title for descriptive statement.
From The Writing For A Reason Series.
Prod-DALCCD Dist-DALCCD

Paper Of Classification, The C 30 MIN
3/4 OR 1/2 INCH VIDEO CASSETTE C
See series title for descriptive statement.
From The Writing For A Reason Series.
Prod-DALCCD Dist-DALCCD

Paper Of Comparison, The C 30 MIN
3/4 OR 1/2 INCH VIDEO CASSETTE C
See series title for descriptive statement.
From The Writing For A Reason Series.
Prod-DALCCD Dist-DALCCD

Paper Of Definition, The C 30 MIN
3/4 OR 1/2 INCH VIDEO CASSETTE C
See series title for descriptive statement.
From The Writing For A Reason Series.
Prod-DALCCD Dist-DALCCD

Paper Play C 60 MIN
1/2 IN VIDEO CASSETTE BETA/VHS K-P
Demonstrates paper crafts such as collage and greeting cards.
From The Children's Crafts Series.
Prod-MOHOMV Dist-MOHOMV

Paper Route C 13 MIN
16MM FILM OPTICAL SOUND
Shows an 18-year-old retarded boy's budding relationship with a woman he meets on his newspaper route.
LC NO. 80-701369
Prod-RAINY Dist-RAINY 1980

Paper Sculpture X 10 MIN
16MM FILM OPTICAL SOUND I-H A
Techniques of paper sculpturing are demonstrated and varied uses of this medium from party favors to lifesize figures for drapery displays are illustrated. (Also known as 'TECHNIQUES OF PAPER SCULPTURE')
Prod-ALLMOR Dist-AVED 1958

Paper Sculpture C 5 MIN
16MM FILM, 3/4 OR 1/2 IN VIDEO P-J
Illustrates the variety of three-dimensional objects that can be made out of paper and cardboard.
From The Creative Hands Series.
Prod-IFB Dist-IFB 1949

Paper Sculpture B 20 MIN
2 INCH VIDEOTAPE I
Demonstrates how flat, ordinary construction paper can be magically turned into a variety of three-dimensional forms by scoring, cutting, bending, rolling and folding.
From The For Love Of Art Series.
Prod-GWTVAI Dist-GPITVL Prodn-WETATV

Paper Sculpture And Masks C 15 MIN
3/4 OR 1/2 INCH VIDEO CASSETTE P-I
Explains how to make paper sculptures and paper monster masks.
From The Art Cart Series.
Prod-WBRATV Dist-AITECH 1979

Paper Sculpture Animals C 14 MIN
3/4 OR 1/2 INCH VIDEO CASSETTE P-I
Discusses paper sculpture animals.
From The Young At Art Series.
Prod-WSKJTV Dist-AITECH 1980

Paper Slippers C 15 MIN
3/4 OR 1/2 INCH VIDEO CASSETTE H A
Shows the retiree in the hospital with the other characters providing support.
From The Old Enough To Care Series.
Prod-ETVCON Dist-AITECH

Paper Stencils C 29 MIN
2 INCH VIDEOTAPE
See series title for descriptive statement.
From The Exploring The Crafts - Silk Screen Printing Series.
Prod-NHN Dist-PUBTEL

Paper Takes Shape B 15 MIN
2 INCH VIDEOTAPE P
Presents a demonstration of paper sculpture. (Broadcast quality)
From The Art Discoveries Series. Lesson 18
Prod-CVETVC Dist-GPITVL Prodn-WCVETV

Paper Wasp (Polistes Exclamans) Behavior C 17 MIN
16MM FILM OPTICAL SOUND C A
Documents the behavior of paper wasps, Polistes exclamans, at the wasp nest. Looks at feeding, cell construction, egg laying, defense and social grooming.
LC NO. 80-701579
Prod-MAHERG Dist-PSUPCR 1979

Paper Weaving C 15 MIN
3/4 INCH VIDEO CASSETTE P
See series title for descriptive statement.
From The Is The Sky Always Blue Series.
Prod-WDCNTV Dist-GPITVL 1979

Paper Wings C 13 MIN
16MM FILM, 3/4 OR 1/2 IN VIDEO P
Portrays a young girl and a woman who share an interest in an unusual paper airplane.
Prod-CF Dist-CF

Paperhanging Application C 14 MIN
3/4 OR 1/2 INCH VIDEO CASSETTE H-C A
Shows paste preparation, commercial and individual mixes, paper fitting, pattern and paper matching, applying paste, pasting the wall, lapping and butt joints.
Prod-SF Dist-SF

Paperhanging Preparation C 14 MIN
3/4 OR 1/2 INCH VIDEO CASSETTE H-C A
Shows the various methods of cutting wallpaper. Depicts the needed equipment, such as shears, rollers, smoothing utensils, and the various types of knives. Describes the paster process, preparation of the wall, filling cracks, removing old paint or calcimine, stripping old paper and wall sizing.
Prod-SF Dist-SF

Papermaking, Pt 1 C
3/4 OR 1/2 INCH VIDEO CASSETTE IND
Covers the basic process in papermaking and Fourdrinier and cylinder machines.
From The Pulp And Paper Training, Module 3 - Papermaking Series.
Prod-LEIKID Dist-LEIKID

Papermaking, Pt 2 C
3/4 OR 1/2 INCH VIDEO CASSETTE IND
Discusses grades, qualities and chemical additives used in papermaking. Covers definition of types.
From The Pulp And Paper Training, Module 3 - Papermaking Series.
Prod-LEIKID Dist-LEIKID

Papermaking, Pt 3 C
3/4 OR 1/2 INCH VIDEO CASSETTE IND
Includes several aspects of papermaking such as color, deposits, fibre structure and stock process.
From The Pulp And Paper Training, Module 3 - Papermaking Series.
Prod-LEIKID Dist-LEIKID

Papermill C 15 MIN
3/4 OR 1/2 INCH VIDEO CASSETTE P-I
Journeys to the Hammermill Company to learn how paper is made from pulpwood.
From The Explorers Unlimited Series.
Prod-WVIZTV Dist-AITECH 1971

Paperweights C 30 MIN
3/4 INCH VIDEO CASSETTE
See series title for descriptive statement.
From The Antiques Series.
Prod-NHMNET Dist-PUBTEL

Papier Mache C 15 MIN
16MM FILM, 3/4 OR 1/2 IN VIDEO I-C A
Demonstrates the wide expressive range achieved with this easily available material. Presents the basic processes in fashioning three-dimensional forms, from making the core to finishing and painting the surface.
From The Rediscovery - Art Media Series.
Prod-ACI Dist-AIMS 1967

Papier Mache C 30 MIN
3/4 OR 1/2 INCH VIDEO CASSETTE H A
Demonstrates techniques and materials used in making papier-mache objects.
From The Arts And Crafts Series.
LC NO. 81-706996
Prod-GPITVL Dist-GPITVL 1981

Papier Mache (French) C 15 MIN
16MM FILM, 3/4 OR 1/2 IN VIDEO I-C A
Demonstrates the wide expressive range achieved with this easily available material. Presents the basic processes in fashioning three-dimensional forms, from making the core to finishing and painting the surface.
From The Rediscovery - Art Media (French) Series.
Prod-ACI Dist-AIMS 1967

Papier Mache (Spanish) C 15 MIN
16MM FILM, 3/4 OR 1/2 IN VIDEO I-C A
Demonstrates the wide expressive range achieved with this easily available material. Presents the basic processes in fashioning three-dimensional forms, from making the core to finishing and painting the surface.
From The Rediscovery - Art Media (Spanish) Series.
Prod-ACI Dist-AIMS 1967

Papier-Mache B 20 MIN
2 INCH VIDEOTAPE
Describes papier mache which can be used in dozens of ways to create objects that are among the most beautiful in three-dimensional art.
From The For The Love Of Art Series.
Prod-GWTVAI Dist-GPITVL Prodn-WETATV

Papier-Mache Birds C 14 MIN
3/4 OR 1/2 INCH VIDEO CASSETTE P-I
Discusses the construction of papier-mache birds.
From The Young At Art Series.
Prod-WSKJTV Dist-AITECH 1980

Papillon C 150 MIN
16MM FILM OPTICAL SOUND
Recounts the attempts of one man to escape from Devil's Island. Stars Steve McQueen. Based on the novel PAPILLON by Henri Charriere.
Prod-AA Dist-CINEWO 1973

Papo C 20 MIN
16MM FILM OPTICAL SOUND
Chronicles a day in the life of a teenager who seeks revenge against a street gang as a test of his own code of honor.
Prod-BLKFMF Dist-BLKFMF

Papua And New Guinea Development C 13 MIN
16MM FILM OPTICAL SOUND H-C A
Describes the part to be played by private enterprise in the industrial and economic development of Papua and New Guinea.
LC NO. FIA68-3059
Prod-ANAIB Dist-AUIS 1968

Papua New Guinea Report C 42 MIN
16MM FILM OPTICAL SOUND H-C A
Examines a wide range of social and economic conditions in Papua New Guinea and reviews the changing political climate as the territory comes closer to self-government.
LC NO. 72-701525
Prod-AUSCOF Dist-AUIS 1971

Paquita Y Su Conejo C 11 MIN
16MM FILM, 3/4 OR 1/2 IN VIDEO P
A Spanish language version of Frances And Her Rabbit. Tells how Frances and her pet rabbit draw a crayon picture.
Prod-IFB Dist-IFB 1955

Para Diddle C 14 MIN
3/4 OR 1/2 INCH VIDEO CASSETTE P
Associates high with small and low with large in a story about two drums.
From The Stepping Into Rhythm Series.
Prod-WVIZTV Dist-AITECH

Para El Hombre - Esterilizacion Como Un Metodo Anticonceptivo C 27 MIN
16MM FILM, 3/4 OR 1/2 IN VIDEO A
A Spanish language film. Provides basic information about surgical contraception for men.
From The Consentimiento Informado Por Modelos De Instruccion Series.
Prod-USOFP Dist-USNAC Prodn-PATERP 1977

Para La Mujer - La Esterilizacion Voluntaria C 42 MIN
16MM FILM, 3/4 OR 1/2 IN VIDEO A
A Spanish language film. Provides basic information about surgical contraception for women.
From The Consentimiento Informado Por Modelos De Instruccion Series.
Prod-USOFP Dist-USNAC Prodn-PATERP 1977

Para 1000 C 17 MIN
16MM FILM OPTICAL SOUND I-C A
An art film which uses psychedelic lighting and colors, set against sounds of folk-rock and electronic music, to show pop culture and the mod generation.
LC NO. 78-708662
Prod-BACONB Dist-GROVE 1970

Paracelsus B 105 MIN
16MM FILM OPTICAL SOUND C A
A German language motion picture which tells the story of the unconventional Swiss doctor and sometime professor whose life and personality are considered as a basis for the Faust legend. Shows Paracelsus' attempt to save the city from the plague, despite the suspicions and stubbornness of the people. Includes English subtitles.
Prod-TRANSW Dist-TRANSW 1943

Paracentesis (Abdominal) C 9 MIN
3/4 OR 1/2 INCH VIDEO CASSETTE PRO
See series title for descriptive statement.
From The Medical Skills Films Series.
Prod-WFP Dist-WFP

Parachute Development At Sandia C 11 MIN
16MM FILM OPTICAL SOUND H-C
Describes the special uses for parachutes being developed at the Sandia Corporation, New Mexico. Uses live action and animation to illustrate the problems of and solutions to the deployment of large parachutes at supersonic speeds. Includes test footage.
LC NO. FIA67-546
Prod-SANDIA Dist-SANDIA 1966

Parade C 18 MIN
16MM FILM OPTICAL SOUND
Offers an overview of the goals and spirit of a school marching band program.
LC NO. 73-701618
Prod-LEE Dist-FAIRFX 1973

Parade C 26 MIN
16MM FILM OPTICAL SOUND
Features industrial sites of Nova Scotia, interspersed with marching bands and rural and country scenes. Designed to promote industrial growth in Nova Scotia.
LC NO. 71-707553
Prod-NOSIS Dist-CRAF Prodn-CRAF 1970

Parade Of The Tall Ships C 20 MIN
16MM FILM OPTICAL SOUND
Presents sailboat crews and captains as they prepare for a transatlantic race. Follows the ships as they parade into New York Harbor on July 4, 1976.
LC NO. 77-701450
Prod-IBM Dist-MTP Prodn-DREWAS 1977

Paradice C 17 MIN
16MM FILM OPTICAL SOUND
Examines the history of Atlantic City as a background for the changes accompanying casino development there.
LC NO. 80-701217
Prod-SMIRUS Dist-ANNSC 1979

Paradise Lost C 4 MIN
3/4 OR 1/2 INCH VIDEO CASSETTE I-H A
Depicts the threat to all living creatures posed by the great despoiler, man, because of his use of pesticides.
Prod-NFBC Dist-NFBC 1970

Paradise Lost - The Firebird By Igor Stravinsky C 9 MIN
16MM FILM OPTICAL SOUND J-C A
Retells the story of Adam and Eve, using the music of Stravinsky's Firebird Suite as background.
From The Animations From Allegro Non Troppo Series.
LC NO. 80-700528
Prod-BOZETO Dist-TEXFLM 1979

Paradise Polluted C 15 MIN
16MM FILM OPTICAL SOUND
Prod-FENWCK Dist-FENWCK

Paradise Principle, The C 15 MIN
16MM FILM OPTICAL SOUND J-C A
Portrays and assesses Washington State's coastal land and water resources. Examines the effects of management decisions on the preservation, conservation and restoration of natural resources.
LC NO. 77-701864
Prod-MARALF Dist-MARALF 1977

Paradox C 10 MIN
16MM FILM OPTICAL SOUND
Shows three volunteers at a soup kitchen as they are arrested for salvaging food from a produce warehouse. Tells how they must decide if they will continue their actions with the hope of changing the law.
LC NO. 78-701506
Prod-FRACOC Dist-FRACOC Prodn-TKF 1977

Paradox Of Plenty, The C 22 MIN
16MM FILM OPTICAL SOUND
Studies electricity and its role in the energy problem. Uses live action and animation to show where electricity comes from and possible choices for the future.
LC NO. 77-702120
Prod-DUQLC Dist-DUQLC 1977

Paradox On 72nd Street C 60 MIN
16MM FILM, 3/4 OR 1/2 IN VIDEO H-C A
Looks at how the goings-on at the intersection of 72nd Street and Broadway in New York can reflect the larger society. Includes voiceovers by Philip Slater and Lewis Thomas who discuss the American conflict between individual freedom/expression and social harmony/equality.
Prod-WNETTV Dist-FI 1982

Paradoxical Puzzle C 3 MIN
3/4 INCH VIDEO CASSETTE
Explains how an artist discovered more about herself through the experiences of other women documented in her work.
Prod-WMENIF Dist-WMENIF

Paragraph Patterns C
3/4 OR 1/2 INCH VIDEO CASSETTE C
Examines the paragraph's flexibility and realistic use in writing. Avoids traditional misconceptions about its role as a unit writing.
From The Write Course - An Introduction To College Composition Series.
Prod-DALCCD Dist-DALCCD

Paragraph Patterns C 30 MIN
3/4 OR 1/2 INCH VIDEO CASSETTE C A
Discusses the flexibility of the paragraph and its use in expository writing. Avoids traditional misconceptions about its role as a unit.
From The Write Course - An Introduction To College Composition Series.
LC NO. 85-700984
Prod-FI Dist-FI 1984

Paragraph Reading Road C 20 MIN
3/4 OR 1/2 INCH VIDEO CASSETTE
Discusses reading paragraphs to structure the main idea and improve comprehension.
From The Efficient Reading - Instructional Tapes Series. Tape 10
Prod-TELSTR Dist-TELSTR

Paragraph Review - Order Of Details B 30 MIN
2 INCH VIDEOTAPE J-H
Emphasizes the importance of arranging supportive details in the most effective order. (Broadcast quality)
From The English Composition Series. Exposition
Prod-GRETVC Dist-GPITVL Prodn-KUHTTV

Paragraph, The C 30 MIN
3/4 OR 1/2 INCH VIDEO CASSETTE C
See series title for descriptive statement.
From The Writing For A Reason Series.
Prod-DALCCD Dist-DALCCD

Paragraphs - Like Scenes In A Film C 15 MIN
16MM FILM, 3/4 OR 1/2 IN VIDEO I-H
Illustrates the usefulness of paragraphs by comparing them to scene changes in a motion picture. Demonstrates the value of a topic sentence and shows ways to create supporting sentences.
From The Sentences And Paragraphs Series.
LC NO. 81-706040
Prod-CENTRO Dist-CORF 1981

Paragraphs With Ralph And Stanley C 14 MIN
16MM FILM, 3/4 OR 1/2 IN VIDEO P
Tells how two boys learn the basic skills involved in organizing a paragraph when they embark upon an adventurous escapade.
From The Writing Skills Series.
Prod-BEANMN Dist-PHENIX 1979

Parallel Bars - Beginning Exercises C 12 MIN
16MM FILM, 3/4 OR 1/2 IN VIDEO J-C A
Demonstrates proper width adjustment of the bars, how to mount and such elementary stunts as - support positions, basic swinging movements, straddle seat travels, upper arm stands and rolls, front and rear swing rises, simple turns and dismounts. Emphasizes proper composition of routines.
Prod-AIMS Dist-AIMS 1965

Parallel Circuits Analysis C
3/4 OR 1/2 INCH VIDEO CASSETTE
See series title for descriptive statement.
From The Basic Electricity - DC Series.
Prod-VTRI Dist-VTRI

Parallel Circuits Analysis C 30 MIN
3/4 OR 1/2 INCH VIDEO CASSETTE
Outlines circuit analysis of parallel circuits including procedures for calculating unknown voltages, current and resistances in any part of a simple parallel circuit. Covers differences between series and parallel circuits for predicting circuit behavior.
From The Basic Electricity And D.C. Circuits Series.
Prod-TXINLC Dist-TXINLC

Parallel Circuits And Their Analysis C
3/4 OR 1/2 INCH VIDEO CASSETTE
See series title for descriptive statement.
From The Basic DC Circuits Series.
Prod-VTRI Dist-VTRI

Parallel Circuits And Their Analysis C 15 MIN
3/4 OR 1/2 INCH VIDEO CASSETTE
See series title for descriptive statement.
From The Basic Electricity And D.C. Circuits, Laboratory Series.
Prod-TXINLC Dist-TXINLC

Parallel For Variety C 29 MIN
2 INCH VIDEOTAPE
See series title for descriptive statement.
From The Skiing Series.
Prod-KTCATV Dist-PUBTEL

Parallel Interfacing, Part 1 C 45 MIN
3/4 OR 1/2 INCH VIDEO CASSETTE IND
See series title for descriptive statement.
From The Microprocessor Interfacing Series.
Prod-ICSINT Dist-ICSINT

Parallel Interfacing, Part 2 C 45 MIN
3/4 OR 1/2 INCH VIDEO CASSETTE IND
See series title for descriptive statement.
From The Microprocessor Interfacing Series.
Prod-ICSINT Dist-ICSINT

Parallel Interfacing, Pt 1 C 35 MIN
3/4 INCH VIDEO CASSETTE C
See series title for descriptive statement.
From The Microprocessor Interfacing Series. Part 7
LC NO. 81-706199
Prod-AMCEE Dist-AMCEE 1980

Parallel Interfacing, Pt 1 C 42 MIN
3/4 OR 1/2 INCH VIDEO CASSETTE
See series title for descriptive statement.
From The Microprocessor Interfacing Series.
Prod-MIOT Dist-MIOT

Parallel Interfacing, Pt 1 C 43 MIN
3/4 OR 1/2 INCH VIDEO CASSETTE PRO
Describes types of I/O connections. Introduces the IEEE-488 bus.
From The Microprocessing Interfacing Series.
Prod-AMCEE Dist-AMCEE

Parallel Interfacing, Pt 2 C 35 MIN
3/4 INCH VIDEO CASSETTE C
See series title for descriptive statement.
From The Microprocessor Interfacing Series. Part 8
LC NO. 81-706199
Prod-AMCEE Dist-AMCEE 1980

Parallel Interfacing, Pt 2 C 43 MIN
3/4 OR 1/2 INCH VIDEO CASSETTE PRO
Describes protocols and implementation techniques for the IEEE-488 bus. Covers control, talker and listener functions.
From The Microprocessing Interfacing Series.
Prod-AMCEE Dist-AMCEE

Parallel Interfacing, Pt 2 C 44 MIN
3/4 OR 1/2 INCH VIDEO CASSETTE
See series title for descriptive statement.
From The Microprocessor Interfacing Series.
Prod-MIOT Dist-MIOT

Parallel Lines X 10 MIN
16MM FILM OPTICAL SOUND I-J
Explains the concept of parallel lines, illustrates the prevalence of parallel lines in industry and architecture and gives specific instances of the application of the laws of parallel lines.
Prod-JHP Dist-MLA 1951

Parallel Needle Internal Jugular Catheterization Technique C 4 MIN
3/4 OR 1/2 INCH VIDEO CASSETTE PRO
Illustrates the combination of a small gauge needle to locate the vein and a larger bore over-the-needle catheter to enter the vein.
Prod-UARIZ Dist-UARIZ

Parallel RC Circuits C
3/4 OR 1/2 INCH VIDEO CASSETTE
See series title for descriptive statement.
From The Basic AC Circuits Series.
Prod-VTRI Dist-VTRI

Parallel RC Circuits C 20 MIN
3/4 OR 1/2 INCH VIDEO CASSETTE

See series title for descriptive statement.
From The Basic AC Circuits, Laboratory--Sessions--A Series.
Prod-TXINLC Dist-TXINLC

Parallel RC Circuits B 20 MIN
16MM FILM, 3/4 OR 1/2 IN VIDEO
Reviews the operation of parallel RC circuits and shows how to solve for branch currents and total impedance using Ohm's Law. Discusses vector representations and the approximation of total current and phase angle by vector measurement. Introduces trig functions and reviews power.
Prod-USAF Dist-USNAC 1983

Parallel RC, RL And RCL Circuits (Trigonometric Solutions) B 39 MIN
16MM FILM OPTICAL SOUND
Shows how parallel RC, RL and RCL circuit values are computed by trigonemetric functions.
LC NO. 74-705294
Prod-USAF Dist-USNAC 1972

Parallel RC, RL And RCL Circuits (Graphic Solutions) B 34 MIN
16MM FILM OPTICAL SOUND
Uses Ohm's law and vectors to show how to solve for branch current, total current, total impedance and phase angle in parallel RC, RL and RCL circuits.
LC NO. 74-705295
Prod-USAF Dist-USNAC 1972

Parallel RC, RL, And RCL Circuits - Trigonometric Solutions B 39 MIN
3/4 INCH VIDEO CASSETTE
Shows how parallel RC, RL and RCL circuit values are computed in trigonometric functions by first determining the phase angle and then computing theta. Presents the procedure for solving for total impedance by Ohm's law.
LC NO. 79-707513
Prod-USAF Dist-USNAC 1979

Parallel RC, RL, And RCL Circuits - Graphic Solutions B 32 MIN
3/4 INCH VIDEO CASSETTE
Shows how to solve for branch current, total current, total impedance, and phase angle in parallel RC, RL and RCL circuits using Ohm's law and vectors.
LC NO. 79-707512
Prod-USAF Dist-USNAC 1979

Parallel RCL Circuits B 17 MIN
16MM FILM, 3/4 OR 1/2 IN VIDEO
Shows the formula for determining the resonant frequency of a parallel tank circuit. Compares the Z, live current and tank current below, above and at resonance. Compares series and parallel resonant circuits and discusses Q. Uses vectors to show phase angles.
Prod-USAF Dist-USNAC 1983

Parallel Resistances C
3/4 OR 1/2 INCH VIDEO CASSETTE
See series title for descriptive statement.
From The Basic DC Circuits Series.
Prod-VTRI Dist-VTRI

Parallel Resistances C 15 MIN
3/4 OR 1/2 INCH VIDEO CASSETTE
See series title for descriptive statement.
From The Basic Electricity And D.C. Circuits, Laboratory Series.
Prod-TXINLC Dist-TXINLC

Parallel Resistive And Reactive Circuits C
3/4 OR 1/2 INCH VIDEO CASSETTE
See series title for descriptive statement.
From The Basic AC Circuits Series.
Prod-VTRI Dist-VTRI

Parallel Resistive And Reactive Circuits C 20 MIN
3/4 OR 1/2 INCH VIDEO CASSETTE
See series title for descriptive statement.
From The Basic AC Circuits, Laboratory--Sessions--A Series.
Prod-TXINLC Dist-TXINLC

Parallel Resistive Circuit - Power Troubleshooting B 17 MIN
16MM FILM, 3/4 OR 1/2 IN VIDEO
Tells what determines power in a parallel circuit. Uses a voltmeter, ammeter and ohmmeter to show symptoms of open and shorted components.
Prod-USAF Dist-USNAC 1983

Parallel Resistive Circuits B 33 MIN
16MM FILM - 3/4 IN VIDEO
Explains the requirements for a parallel circuit. Shows how to measure the voltage across each branch and compute the total voltage. Demonstrates how to measure current and resistance in a parallel circuit.
LC NO. 79-707514
Prod-USAF Dist-USNAC 1979

Parallel Resistive Circuits - Analysis B 17 MIN
16MM FILM, 3/4 OR 1/2 IN VIDEO
Discusses how current, voltage and resistance are related in a parallel circuit.
Prod-USAF Dist-USNAC 1983

Parallel Resistive Circuits - Bridges B 14 MIN
16MM FILM, 3/4 OR 1/2 IN VIDEO
Explains the principles of the Wheat Stone Bridge and demonstrates its use in measuring resistance and as part of a control system.
Prod-USAF Dist-USNAC 1983

Parallel Resistive Circuits - Circuit Analysis B 22 MIN
16MM FILM - 3/4 IN VIDEO
Defines the principles of Ohm's and Kirchoff's laws as they apply to solving problems related to branch currents, resistances, and applied voltage.
LC NO. 79-707515
Prod-USAF Dist-USNAC 1979

Parallel Resistive Circuits - DC Power B 14 MIN
16MM FILM - 3/4 IN VIDEO
Demonstrates the distribution of power in a parallel circuit. Shows how to determine the power dissipated in the individual branches as well as the total power.
LC NO. 79-707516
Prod-USAF Dist-USNAC 1979

Parallel Resistive Circuits - Troubleshooting B 21 MIN
16MM FILM - 3/4 IN VIDEO
Discusses symptoms produced by open and shorted parallel resistors. Shows how an ammeter and voltmeter are used to detect such troubles.
LC NO. 79-707517
Prod-USAF Dist-USNAC 1979

Parallel Resonant Circuits B 24 MIN
16MM FILM OPTICAL SOUND
Shows how to compare the impedance and current curves of parallel and series RCL circuits. Compares the line current of a parallel resonant circuit to that of a series resonant circuit.
LC NO. 74-705302
Prod-USAF Dist-USNAC 1971

Parallel Resonant Circuits B 53 MIN
3/4 INCH VIDEO CASSETTE IND
Shows how to calculate resonant frequency and compare the magnitude of current at and off resonance. Shows how to compare the impedance and current curves of parallel and series RCL circuits.
LC NO. 79-707518
Prod-USAF Dist-USNAC 1979

Parallel RL Circuits C
3/4 OR 1/2 INCH VIDEO CASSETTE
See series title for descriptive statement.
From The Basic AC Circuits Series.
Prod-VTRI Dist-VTRI

Parallel RL Circuits B 11 MIN
16MM FILM, 3/4 OR 1/2 IN VIDEO
Reviews several methods of solving parallel RL circuits when frequency and applied voltage are known. Shows how to find total current and phase angle vectorially and trigonometrically and discusses true and apparent power.
Prod-USAF Dist-USNAC 1983

Parallel RL Circuits C 20 MIN
3/4 OR 1/2 INCH VIDEO CASSETTE
See series title for descriptive statement.
From The Basic AC Circuits, Laboratory--Sessions--A Series.
Prod-TXINLC Dist-TXINLC

Parallel Structure C 8 MIN
1/2 IN VIDEO CASSETTE BETA/VHS
See series title for descriptive statement.
From The English And Speech Series.
Prod-RMI Dist-RMI

Parallel-Pin Retention For A Full Crown C 14 MIN
16MM FILM, 3/4 OR 1/2 IN VIDEO PRO
Demonstrates the use of a parallel-pin technique to retain a full crown for a tooth with insufficient coronal tooth structure remaining for adequate retention by means of conventional preparation.
LC NO. 81-706362
Prod-VADTC Dist-USNAC 1977

Parallel-Series Circuits C
3/4 OR 1/2 INCH VIDEO CASSETTE
See series title for descriptive statement.
From The Basic Electricity - DC Series.
Prod-VTRI Dist-VTRI

Parallel-Series Circuits C 30 MIN
3/4 OR 1/2 INCH VIDEO CASSETTE
Reviews behavior rules for series and parallel circuits. Introduces series-parallel and parallel-series circuits with an in-depth parallel-series circuit analysis. Includes explanation of process of circuit reduction.
From The Basic Electricity And D.C. Circuits Series.
Prod-TXINLC Dist-TXINLC

Parallels - The President And The Dictator, Pt 1 C 24 MIN
16MM FILM OPTICAL SOUND
Traces parallel developments in the United States and Germany in the years between world wars.
Prod-INTEXT Dist-REAF

Parallels - The President And The Dictator, Pt 2 C 24 MIN
16MM FILM OPTICAL SOUND
Examines two wartime leaders - Franklin Delano Roosevelt and Adolf Hitler.
Prod-INTEXT Dist-REAF

Paralyzed Face, The C 60 MIN
3/4 OR 1/2 INCH VIDEO CASSETTE PRO
Discusses various degrees of facial paralysis and includes a presentation of facial anatomy and neurology.
LC NO. 81-706297
Prod-USVA Dist-USNAC 1980

Paramagnetism Of Liquid Oxygen E-2 C 3 MIN
16MM FILM OPTICAL SOUND J-C
Shows a comparison between liquid oxygen, which adheres to pole pieces of magnet, and liquid nitrogen, which is not paramagnetic.
From The Single-Concept Films In Physics Series.
Prod-OSUMPD Dist-OSUMPD 1963

Paramecium, Euglena And Amoeba C 15 MIN
16MM FILM OPTICAL SOUND P-I
An illustrated lecture in which William H Weston discusses and answers questions about three species of protozoa--paramecium, euglena and amoeba.
From The Small Things Series.
LC NO. FIA67-2428
Prod-EDS Dist-EDC 1963

Paramecium, The C 12 MIN
16MM FILM, 3/4 OR 1/2 IN VIDEO H-C
Describes the appearance, external structures and internal structures of paramecium. Relates that the macronucleus regulates all vital processes and that two contractile vacuoles are very efficient in pumping out excess water.
Prod-BNCHMK Dist-BNCHMK 1983

Paramecium, The C 30 MIN
3/4 OR 1/2 INCH VIDEO CASSETTE
Illustrates the complexities of the paramecium. Includes fourteen follow-up questions at end of program.
Prod-EDMEC Dist-EDMEC

Paramedic C 15 MIN
3/4 OR 1/2 INCH VIDEO CASSETTE I
Explains the qualifications and personal qualities required for a successful career as a paramedic.
From The Career Awareness Series.
Prod-KLVXTV Dist-GPITVL 1973

Paramedic C 30 MIN
1/2 IN VIDEO CASSETTE BETA/VHS
Presents Bill Olsen, who brings the emergency room to the patient, and who describes his work as a 'no second chance' profession.
From The American Professionals Series.
Prod-WTBS Dist-RMI

Paramedic, The C 16 MIN
16MM FILM, 3/4 OR 1/2 IN VIDEO I-C A
Presents on-the-scene footage of various medical emergencies being handled by paramedics from the Santa Ana Fire Department. Provides narration by the men describing the function of their jobs. Describes the paramedics' training, duty hours and relations with other fire department employees, police, physicians and nurses.
Prod-BRAVC Dist-PFP 1977

Paranoid State And Deterioration Following Head Injury B 11 MIN
16MM FILM OPTICAL SOUND C
Paranoid delusions, violent rages and serious neglect of person led to the commitment of a patient two years after a skull fracture. The film illustrates the rambling, circumstantial flow of talk which conveys disjointed, inconsistent, but dominant notions of persecution.
Prod-PSUPCR Dist-PSUPCR 1939

Paranormal Phenomena - Reality Or Illusion? C 30 MIN
3/4 OR 1/2 INCH VIDEO CASSETTE J-C A
Features Lawrence LeShan, author of the Medium, The Mystic And The Physicist, and Khoren Arisian, Leader of the New York Society for Ethical Culture, discussing paranormal phenomena.
From The Moral Values In Contemporary Society Series.
Prod-AMHUMA Dist-AMHUMA

Paranormal, The - Science Or Pseudoscience? C 30 MIN
3/4 OR 1/2 INCH VIDEO CASSETTE H-C A
Presents professional conjurer James Randi, professor of psychology Ray Hayman, author Ethel Grodzins and psycho-physicist Wilbur Franklin discussing the mushrooming interest in the paranormal and psychic phenomena.
From The Ethics In America Series.
Prod-AMHUMA Dist-AMHUMA

Paraplegic Ambulation, Initial Parallel Bar Exercises C 8 MIN
16MM FILM OPTICAL SOUND
Describes how the ambulation of the paraplegic patient wearing bilateral long leg braces with a pelvic band is preceded by exercises in the parallel bars to develop initial balance during stance and trunk movements, and initial weight shifting with accompanying anterior pelvic tilt and head positon. Outlines the therapists spotting carefully and portrays push-ups in the bars and jackknifing which are the last of the initial parallel bar exercises taught.
LC NO. 74-705305
Prod-USPHS Dist-USNAC

Paraplegic Patient Education - Activities In Your New Life C 7 MIN
16MM FILM OPTICAL SOUND
Examines some of the problems of adjusting to a new life following a crippling disease or accident. Suggests ways to solve these problems, build self-confidence and achieve physical and financial independence.
LC NO. 74-705306
Prod-NMAC Dist-USNAC 1969

Paraplegic Patient Education - Activities In Your New Life C 7 MIN
3/4 INCH VIDEO CASSETTE
Examines problems of adjusting to a new life following a crippling disease or accident. Suggests ways to solve these problems, build self-confidence and achieve physical and financial independence. Issued in 1969 as a motion picture.
LC NO. 79-706722
Prod-AMRF Dist-USNAC Prodn-BRUCER 1979

Paraplegic Patient Education - An Active Future C 5 MIN
16MM FILM OPTICAL SOUND

Stresses the importance of setting realistic goals during the rehabilitation program of a paraplegic in order to achieve success later. Emphasizes the necessity of maintaining good health, activity and interest.
LC NO. 74-705307
Prod-NMAC Dist-USNAC 1969

Paraplegic Patient Education - An Active Future C 5 MIN
3/4 INCH VIDEO CASSETTE
Stresses the importance of setting realistic goals during the rehabilitation program of a paraplegic. Emphasizes the necessity of maintaining good health, activity and interest. Issued in 1969 as a motion picture.
LC NO. 79-706724
Prod-AMRF Dist-USNAC Prodn-BRUCER 1979

Paraplegic Patient Education - Joint Motion C 5 MIN
16MM FILM OPTICAL SOUND
Explains methods of maintaining joint motion for the paraplegic including range of motion exercises, positioning and activity.
LC NO. 74-705308
Prod-NMAC Dist-USNAC 1969

Paraplegic Patient Education - Joint Motion C 5 MIN
3/4 INCH VIDEO CASSETTE
Explains methods which the paraplegic can use to maintain joint motion, including range of motion exercises, positioning and activity. Issued in 1969 as a motion picture.
LC NO. 80-706282
Prod-AMRF Dist-USNAC Prodn-BRUCER 1980

Paraplegic Patient Education - Moving In And Out Of Your Wheelchair C 5 MIN
16MM FILM OPTICAL SOUND
Explains the steps involved in the independent transfer of a paraplegic to and from a wheelchair.
LC NO. 74-705309
Prod-NMAC Dist-USNAC 1969

Paraplegic Patient Education - Moving In And Out Of Your Wheelchair C 5 MIN
3/4 INCH VIDEO CASSETTE
Explains the steps involved in the independent transfer of a paraplegic to and from a wheelchair. Issued in 1969 as a motion picture.
LC NO. 80-706283
Prod-AMRF Dist-USNAC Prodn-BRUCER 1980

Paraplegic Patient Education - Planning Your Bowel Program C 6 MIN
16MM FILM OPTICAL SOUND
Stresses the importance for the paraplegic of a well-planned bowel program based on scheduling, diet and stimulation.
LC NO. 74-705310
Prod-NMAC Dist-USNAC 1969

Paraplegic Patient Education - Planning Your Bowel Program C 5 MIN
3/4 INCH VIDEO CASSETTE
Stresses the importance of a paraplegic establishing a well-planned bowel program based on scheduling, diet and stimulation. Issued in 1969 as a motion picture.
LC NO. 80-706284
Prod-AMRF Dist-USNAC Prodn-BRUCER 1980

Paraplegic Patient Education - Prevention Of Bladder Problems C 8 MIN
3/4 INCH VIDEO CASSETTE
Explains bladder dysfunction related to spinal cord injury. Stresses the importance of catheter irrigation, good drainage and fluid intake in the prevention of calcium deposits in the bladder or kidneys. Issued in 1969 as a motion picture.
LC NO. 77-706159
Prod-AMRF Dist-USNAC Prodn-BRUCER 1979

Paraplegic Patient Education - Prevention Of Skin Problems C 8 MIN
16MM FILM OPTICAL SOUND
Cites causes of decubitus ulcers resulting from pressure sores. Warns of the dangers involved and outlines a simple deterring program.
LC NO. 74-705311
Prod-NMAC Dist-USNAC 1970

Paraplegic Patient Education - Prevention Of Skin Problems C 8 MIN
3/4 INCH VIDEO CASSETTE
Cites causes of decubitus ulcers among paraplegics resulting from pressure sores. Warns of dangers involved and outlines a deterring program. Issued in 1969 as a motion picture.
LC NO. 79-706725
Prod-AMRF Dist-USNAC Prodn-BRUCER 1979

Paraplegic Patient Education - Prevention Of Bladder Problems C 8 MIN
16MM FILM OPTICAL SOUND
Explains bladder dysfunction related to spinal cord injury. Stresses the importance of catheter irrigation, good drainage and fluid intake in the prevention of calcium deposits in the bladder or kidneys.
LC NO. 74-705313
Prod-NMAC Dist-USNAC 1970

Paraplegic Patient Education - The Effects Of Spinal Cord Injury C 8 MIN
16MM FILM OPTICAL SOUND
Cites causes of spinal injuries, discusses the effect these injuries may have on the individual and points out how best to become as independent as possible.
LC NO. 74-705314
Prod-NMAC Dist-USNAC 1970

Paraplegic Patient Education - The Effects Of Spinal Cord Injury C 8 MIN
3/4 INCH VIDEO CASSETTE
Cites causes of spinal injuries, discusses the effects these injuries may have on the individual and points out how the individual can best become as independent as possible. Issued in 1969 as a motion picture.
LC NO. 77-706143
Prod-AMRF Dist-USNAC Prodn-BRUCER

Paraplegic Patient Education - Walking With Braces And Crutches C 5 MIN
16MM FILM - 3/4 IN VIDEO
Stress the physical limitations of paraplegics as well as the need for preparation for ambulation training, balance drills, and mobility exercises.
LC NO. 80-706285
Prod-AMRF Dist-USNAC Prodn-BRUCER 1980

Paraplegic Patient, The - In And Out Of Car - Patient Using Crutches And Wearing Braces C 5 MIN
16MM FILM OPTICAL SOUND
Demonstrates the use of crutches and braces in moving in and out of a car.
LC NO. 74-705316
Prod-NMAC Dist-USNAC 1970

Paraplegic Patient, The - Putting On A Full Body Brace In Wheelchair C 11 MIN
16MM FILM OPTICAL SOUND
Depicts the most effective methods for the paraplegic patient to put on full body braces in a wheelchair.
LC NO. 74-705317
Prod-USPHS Dist-USNAC 1968

Paraplegic Patient, The - Taking Off A Full Body Brace In Bed C 8 MIN
16MM FILM OPTICAL SOUND
Depicts the method used by a paraplegic to remove a full body brace in bed.
LC NO. 74-705318
Prod-USPHS Dist-USNAC 1968

Paraplegic Patient, The - Transfer From Wheelchair To Car And Reverse C 4 MIN
16MM FILM OPTICAL SOUND
Demonstrates the transfer between wheel chair and car.
LC NO. 74-705319
Prod-NMAC Dist-USNAC 1970

Paraplegic Patient, The - Transfer From Wheelchair To Car And Reverse C 4 MIN
3/4 INCH VIDEO CASSETTE
Demonstrates the transfer of a paraplegic between wheelchair and car. Issued in 1970 as a motion picture.
LC NO. 78-706138
Prod-NYUMC Dist-USNAC 1978

Paraprofessionals And Volunteers C 30 MIN
3/4 OR 1/2 INCH VIDEO CASSETTE T
Discusses the uses of paraprofessionals and volunteers when teaching adult basic education students.
From The Basic Education - Teaching The Adult Series.
Prod-MDDE Dist-MDCPB

Pararescue - Its Role In The Space Age C 24 MIN
16MM FILM OPTICAL SOUND
Portrays the role of the air rescue service pararescue teams. Presents rigorous physical and mental training that prepares airmen for pararescue service in any environment.
LC NO. 76-700483
Prod-USAF Dist-USNAC 1976

Parasacral Approach To Lesions Of The Rectum C 18 MIN
3/4 OR 1/2 INCH VIDEO CASSETTE PRO
Illustrates parasacral approach to removal of lesions of the rectum.
Prod-HSCIC Dist-HSCIC 1984

Parasites C 11 MIN
16MM FILM, 3/4 OR 1/2 IN VIDEO J-H
Describes the relationships between some common parasites and their hosts, and shows that both plants and animals may be parasites.
Prod-BFA Dist-PHENIX 1970

Parasites (French) C 11 MIN
16MM FILM, 3/4 OR 1/2 IN VIDEO J-H
Describes the relationships between some common parasites and their hosts, and shows that both plants and animals may be parasites.
Prod-BFA Dist-PHENIX 1970

Parasites (Swedish) C 11 MIN
16MM FILM, 3/4 OR 1/2 IN VIDEO J-H
Describes the relationships between some common parasites and their hosts, and shows that both plants and animals may be parasites.
Prod-BFA Dist-PHENIX 1970

Parasitism - Parasitic Flatworms X 17 MIN
16MM FILM, 3/4 OR 1/2 IN VIDEO H
Traces the development of parasitic flatworms, showing several life-cycle stages. Shows blood, lung and liver flukes and tapeworms. Defines predation, mutualism, internal parasitism and external parasitism and illustrates each of these animal relationships.
From The Biology Series. Unit 7 - Animal Classification And Physiology
Prod-EBF Dist-EBEC 1963

Parasitism - Parasitic Flatworms (Spanish) C 17 MIN
16MM FILM, 3/4 OR 1/2 IN VIDEO H
Traces the development of parasitic flatworms. Illustrates predation, mutualism, and internal and external parasitism.
From The Biology (Spanish) Series. Unit 7 - Animal Classification And Physiology
Prod-EBEC Dist-EBEC

Parasympathetic System, The C 11 MIN
16MM FILM OPTICAL SOUND
Presents, in schematic form, the basic features of the parasympathetic system in humans.
LC NO. 80-700436
Prod-UTXHSA Dist-UTXHSA Prodn-TEXAL 1980

Parasympathomimetic Blocking Agents, Anticholinergics And Antispasmodics B 30 MIN
16MM FILM OPTICAL SOUND C
Shows the effect produced by parasympathetic blocking agents and describes their clinical uses and side effects.
From The Pharmacology Series.
LC NO. 73-703342
Prod-MVNE Dist-TELSTR 1971

Parasympathomimetics B 30 MIN
16MM FILM OPTICAL SOUND C
See series title for descriptive statement.
From The Pharmacology Series.
LC NO. 73-703341
Prod-MVNE Dist-TELSTR 1971

Parathyroidectomy C 12 MIN
3/4 OR 1/2 INCH VIDEO CASSETTE
See series title for descriptive statement.
From The Head And Neck Series.
Prod-SVL Dist-SVL

Parathyroidectomy C 27 MIN
3/4 OR 1/2 INCH VIDEO CASSETTE
See series title for descriptive statement.
From The Head And Neck Series.
Prod-SVL Dist-SVL

Parathyroidectomy C 40 MIN
3/4 OR 1/2 INCH VIDEO CASSETTE
See series title for descriptive statement.
From The Head And Neck Series.
Prod-SVL Dist-SVL

Paratransits C 6 MIN
16MM FILM OPTICAL SOUND A
Demonstrates two prototype taxicabs operating in both city and suburban settings. Highlights innovations, such as ramps for the elderly and handicapped, increased luggage space and protection for the driver.
LC NO. 78-700813
Prod-USDT Dist-USNAC 1977

Paratroopers C 95 MIN
16MM FILM OPTICAL SOUND
Calls for a reassessment of life in contemporary Israel. Tells th- story of a misfit in an army boot camp, who commits suicide during training maneuvers. Portrays the army as a microcosm of Israeli society, regimented and disciplined, with little leeway for dissidence.
Prod-ICARUS Dist-ICARUS

Pardon And Peace - Sacrament Of Reconciliation C 11 MIN
3/4 OR 1/2 INCH VIDEO CASSETTE J-C A
Presents the story of a young teenage runaway whose experience of pain and brokenness make him long for home. Discusses the human stories of separation and reconciliation.
Prod-FRACOC Dist-FRACOC

Pardon Me For Living C 30 MIN
16MM FILM, 3/4 OR 1/2 IN VIDEO I-H
Deals with the value of true friendship when a girl named Emily is tricked into presenting a petition against geography homework to her stern teacher Miss Holderness. Based on the short story The Scarlet Letter by Jean Stafford.
From The LCA Short Story Library Series.
Prod-LCOA Dist-LCOA Prodn-SPRBRE 1982

Pardon Us B 56 MIN
16MM FILM OPTICAL SOUND
Tells the story of two men who decide to market their own home brew during Prohibition. Shows what happens when they make their first sale to a policeman and land in jail. Stars Stan Laurel and Oliver Hardy.
Prod-ROACH Dist-BHAWK 1931

Pardoner's Secret C 45 MIN
3/4 OR 1/2 INCH VIDEO CASSETTE C
Features a close reading of the crucial passages of Pardoner's Secret, as part of a sophomore literature course.
From The Survey Of English Literature I Series.
Prod-MDCPB Dist-MDCPB

Parent - Adult - Child C 27 MIN
2 INCH VIDEOTAPE C A
Features a humanistic psychologist who, by analysis and examples, discusses that helping relationships are an important aspect of interpersonal relationships. Describes the helping relationships involved between parents and their children.
From The Interpersonal Competence, Unit 04 - Helping Series.
Prod-MVNE Dist-TELSTR 1973

Parent / Child Relationships - It's My Decision As Long As It's What You Want C 14 MIN
16MM FILM, 3/4 OR 1/2 IN VIDEO J-H
Tells how Jane and her mother disagree about a Saturday night outing. Opens discussions of responsibilities, insecurities, guilt feelings, and fears of both parents and children.
From The Conflict And Awareness Series.
Prod-CRMP Dist-CRMP 1974

Parent Conferencing C 30 MIN
3/4 OR 1/2 INCH VIDEO CASSETTE
Features consultants who discuss parent and teacher attitudes reflected in conferencing. Recommendations are made for productive parent-professional interactions that provide support, while avoiding adversarial situations.

From The Teaching Students With Special Needs Series.
Prod-MSITV Dist-PBS 1981

Parent Consumers Speak Out! B 40 MIN
3/4 OR 1/2 INCH VIDEO CASSETTE
Presents three different conceptual models of looking at family stress within families who have developmentally disabled children.
Prod-VRL Dist-UWISC 1983

Parent Counseling C 30 MIN
3/4 OR 1/2 INCH VIDEO CASSETTE T
Presents methods for effective counseling of parents of handicapped children.
From The Stretch Strategies For Teaching Handicapped Children Series.
Prod-HUBDSC Dist-HUBDSC

Parent Crunch, The C 14 MIN
16MM FILM, 3/4 OR 1/2 IN VIDEO C T
Uses a dramatization involving a teacher and a parent who is angry over his child's achievement in school to present problems teachers must meet in communicating with parents and others.
From The Heart Of Teaching Series.
LC NO. 80-706426
Prod-AITV Dist-AITECH Prodn-KETCTV 1976

Parent Education C 24 MIN
16MM FILM, 3/4 OR 1/2 IN VIDEO
Shows home and clinic instruction for parents of hearing impaired children in Sweden, Germany, England, and the Netherlands.
From The International Education Of The Hearing Impaired Child Series.
LC NO. 80-707442
Prod-USBEH Dist-USNAC Prodn-GWASHU 1980

Parent Education - Attitude Films—A Series

Shows several days in the lives of Dick and Ann Johnson, parents of a deaf child. Focuses on the family at a time when certain incidents have highlighted some of their problems and frustrations. Deals specifically with individual possible problem areas.
Prod-TC Dist-TC

Anger And Fear 10 MIN
Creative Play 10 MIN
Discipline 10 MIN
Feelings 10 MIN
Fundamental Needs Of People 10 MIN
Learning 10 MIN
Learning To Live Together 10 MIN
Parental Aspirations 10 MIN
Problem Solving 10 MIN

Parent Education - Information Films—A Series
S
Illustrates the techniques used to develop communication skills in very young deaf children.
Prod-TC Dist-TC

Beginnings Of Speech, The 10 MIN
Check And Double Check 10 MIN
Eyes, Ears And Hands 10 MIN
Getting The Idea 10 MIN
Hearing And Not Hearing 10 MIN
Holding The Reins 10 MIN
Making A Choice 10 MIN
Stepping Stones 10 MIN
Talk, Talk, Talk 10 MIN

Parent Education At Heidelberg C 11 MIN
16MM FILM OPTICAL SOUND
Presents Professor Arman Lowe's home teaching and parent education program at the Paedo-Audiological Guidance Center.
From The International Education Of The Hearing Impaired Child Series.
LC NO. 74-705322
Prod-USBEH Dist-USNAC 1970

Parent Education At Heidelberg, Germany C 11 MIN
3/4 OR 1/2 INCH VIDEO CASSETTE
Presents Arman Lowe's home teaching and parent education program at the Paedo-audiological Guidance Center in Germany.
From The International Education Of The Hearing Impaired Child Series.
LC NO. 80-707443
Prod-USBEH Dist-USNAC Prodn-GWASHU 1980

Parent Education Film—A Series

Prod-TC Dist-TC

Fundamental Needs Of People 10 MIN
Getting The Idea 8 MIN

Parent For Tonight C 15 MIN
16MM FILM, 3/4 OR 1/2 IN VIDEO I-C A
Tells the story of today's baby-sitter. Demonstrates safe and proper baby-sitting conduct.
Prod-KLEINW Dist-KLEINW 1975

Parent Involvement C 29 MIN
3/4 OR 1/2 INCH VIDEO CASSETTE T
Discusses the role of the parents in helping their handicapped child be successfully mainstreamed into a regular school.
From The Mainstreaming The Exceptional Child Series.
Prod-MFFD Dist-FI

Parent To Child About Sex C 31 MIN
16MM FILM, 3/4 OR 1/2 IN VIDEO
Emphasizes the positive approach to communication about sex. Allows the parent to present his own ethical and religious concepts within the framework of 'the truth.'
LC NO. FIA67-2007
Prod-PEREN Dist-PEREN

Parent Training C 150 MIN
3/4 OR 1/2 INCH VIDEO CASSETTE
Focuses on training parents to take an active role in intervention. Discusses traditional roles for parents, approaches to parent training, as well as critical issues in implementing a program.
From The Meeting The Communications Needs Of The Severely/Profoundly Handicapped 1980 Series.
Prod-PUAVC Dist-PUAVC

Parent Training Group - A Behavioral Perspective B 14 MIN
3/4 OR 1/2 INCH VIDEO CASSETTE
Features a discussion by a parents group talking about what has occurred in the week since the last meeting. Focuses on one couple whose daughter dallies at bedtime.
Prod-VRL Dist-UWISC

Parent-Child Relations In The Early Years—A Series

Discusses the relationships between parents and their young children.
Prod-NYU Dist-NYU

Getting Ready For The Dentist 011 MIN
Let Your Child Help You 011 MIN

Parent-Child Value Conflicts About Drugs C 7 MIN
3/4 INCH VIDEO CASSETTE
Dramatized situations of parent-child conflicts about drugs. Shows typical situations in our modern world regarding drug use.
Prod-UWASHP Dist-UWASHP

Parent-Teacher Conference C
3/4 OR 1/2 INCH VIDEO CASSETTE A
Demonstrates the way an informative working relationship can be established in a parent-teacher conference.
From The Vital Link Series.
Prod-EDCC Dist-EDCC

Parent-Teenager Communications C 20 MIN
16MM FILM, 3/4 OR 1/2 IN VIDEO A
Presents 13 vignettes explaining how a parent can handle discussions with a teenager dealing with independence and responsibility, drugs and alcohol, honesty and openness, interpersonal relationships, sex, schoolwork and sibling rivalry.
Prod-MTI Dist-MTI

Parent's Group, The C 19 MIN
3/4 OR 1/2 INCH VIDEO CASSETTE J A
Explores the unique challenges of integrating an older child into an adoptive family.
Prod-SUTHRB Dist-SUTHRB

Parent's Responses To Their Children's Illnesses C 27 MIN
3/4 OR 1/2 INCH VIDEO CASSETTE PRO
Presents a discussion between a hospital social worker and four parents of cronically ill children. Illustrates parent's responses to their children's illnesses which parallel those of dying patients outlined by Elisabeth Kubler-Ross. Shows denial, anger, bargaining, depression and acceptance.
Prod-UMICHM Dist-UMICHM 1977

Parent's Underground Guide To Understanding Teenagers, A C 25 MIN
16MM FILM, 3/4 OR 1/2 IN VIDEO J-C A
Provides answers, direction and hope for parents who find themselves confronting the problem of teenage drug and alcohol abuse. Offers specific approaches, attitudes and actions that open lines of communication between parents and teenagers.
Prod-WQED Dist-MTI

Parental Aspirations B 10 MIN
16MM FILM OPTICAL SOUND
See series title for descriptive statement.
From The Parent Education - Attitude Films Series.
Prod-TC Dist-TC

Parental Imperative, The C 29 MIN
3/4 INCH VIDEO CASSETTE
Details results of an aging study in Kansas City.
From The Country Of Old Men Series.
Prod-UMITV Dist-UMITV 1974

Parental Scripts C 16 MIN
16MM FILM, 3/4 OR 1/2 IN VIDEO H-C A
Enacts five scripts, showing the roles parents may assume and how they affect the child.
From The Giving Birth And Independence Series.
Prod-JRLLL Dist-LAWREN 1981

Parenteral Therapy—A Series
PRO
Treats three different aspects of parenteral therapy.
Prod-HSCIC Dist-HSCIC 1981

Blood Drawing Procedures - Part 1 010 MIN
Special Procedures In IV Therapy - Part 3 019 MIN
Starting Intravenous Infusions - Part 2 017 MIN

Parenthood - Bringing New Life Into The World—A Series

Uses a highly dramatic approach to cover the subject of parenthood, from parent readiness to actual birth of a child.
Prod-GA Dist-GA

Active Parenting
Birth
Caring For Your Newborn With Dr Spock
Pregnancy
Preparing For Parenthood
Preparing To Give Birth

Parenthood - Training Before Trouble C 20 MIN
16MM FILM OPTICAL SOUND J-C A
Dramatizes everyday conflicts between parents and children, showing how these problems can be solved through better understanding and effective communication techniques.
LC NO. 76-700264
Prod-TECKLA Dist-TECKLA 1976

Parenting C 30 MIN
3/4 INCH VIDEO CASSETTE
Explores the parental problems that can occur during mid-life.
From The Transitions - Caught At Midlife Series.
Prod-UMITV Dist-UMITV 1980

Parenting - Discipline As Teaching, Pt 2 C 9 MIN
3/4 OR 1/2 INCH VIDEO CASSETTE
Concludes a course in parenting, for parents of children from birth to two years of age.
Prod-AMRC Dist-AMRC 1978

Parenting - Emotional Development, Pt 1 C 10 MIN
3/4 OR 1/2 INCH VIDEO CASSETTE
Presents a course in parenting, for parents of children from birth to two years of age.
Prod-AMRC Dist-AMRC 1978

Parenting - Growing With Children C 22 MIN
16MM FILM, 3/4 OR 1/2 IN VIDEO J-C A
Looks at the realities, responsibilities and rewards of parenting as seen in the lives of four families.
Prod-FLMFR Dist-FLMFR

Parenting Concerns - Preparing For Kindergarten C 21 MIN
16MM FILM, 3/4 OR 1/2 IN VIDEO A
Shows methods of handling the various normal problems that arise during a child's second to fifth years of age. Deals with such problems as possessiveness, aggression, interaction with others, self-control, self-esteem, sex roles and independence.
Prod-CINIMA Dist-PEREN

Parenting Concerns - The First Two Years C 21 MIN
16MM FILM, 3/4 OR 1/2 IN VIDEO H-C A
Explores common child-rearing problems encountered during the child's first two years. Includes information on discipline, a child's independence, toilet training and sibling rivalry.
Prod-PEREN Dist-PEREN 1978

Parenting Experience—A Series
H-C A
Discusses various aspects of parenthood.
Prod-PARPIC Dist-PARPIC Prodn-COURTR 1978

Breastfeeding Experience, The 024 MIN
Teenage Pregnancy Experience, The 026 MIN

Parenting In Today's Society C 30 MIN
3/4 OR 1/2 INCH VIDEO CASSETTE C A
Examines the many aspects of parenting, beginning with the decision to have or not to have children. Discusses advantages and disadvantages of having children. Emphasizes the parent's role in the child's emotional, social and intellectual development.
From The Contemporary Health Issues Series. Lesson 9
Prod-SCCON Dist-CDTEL

Parenting Review C 30 MIN
16MM FILM OPTICAL SOUND J-H
Outlines the responsibilities and decisions involved in parenting.
From The Middle Road Traveler Series.
LC NO. 80-701708
Prod-GRETVO Dist-GPITVL 1978

Parenting Review C 30 MIN
3/4 OR 1/2 INCH VIDEO CASSETTE J
Reviews concepts relating to parenting, including nurturance, discipline, child development, family lifestyles, health, safety and interpersonal skills.
From The Middle Road Traveler Series.
LC NO. 80-707468
Prod-BAYUCM Dist-GPITVL 1979

Parenting The Special Needs Child C 25 MIN
16MM FILM, 3/4 OR 1/2 IN VIDEO A
Presents 16 vignettes showing situations which the parent of a special needs child is likely to encounter including teachers and coaches who stereotype children and exaggerate their vulnerabilities, relatives who offer well-meaning but unacceptable advice, babysitters and neighbors who are afraid to accept any responsibility for the child and parents themselves whose relationship is strained by guilt and anger.
Prod-MTI Dist-MTI

Parenting/Adolescence C 15 MIN
3/4 OR 1/2 INCH VIDEO CASSETTE
See series title for descriptive statement.
From The Health, Safety And Well-Being Series.
Prod-MAETEL Dist-CAMB

Parents C 14 MIN
16MM FILM, 3/4 OR 1/2 IN VIDEO
Discusses the need for parents. Shows dogs, cats and monkeys nurturing, protecting and teaching their young. Includes human parent-child interactions.
From The BSCS Behavior Film Series.
Prod-BSCS Dist-PHENIX 1974

Parents / Learning Disabilities C 30 MIN
3/4 OR 1/2 INCH VIDEO CASSETTE C A

Discusses the parent's role in caring for and educating the learning disabled child.
From The Characteristics Of Learning Disabilities Series.
Prod-WCVETV Dist-FI 1976

Parents / Teens - Bridging The Communication Gap C 23 MIN
16MM FILM OPTICAL SOUND H-C A
Shows parents and teens from a peer facilitator class meeting to discuss their feelings and expectations.
LC NO. 81-700048
Prod-EMCORP Dist-EMCORP 1980

Parents And Children C 24 MIN
16MM FILM, 3/4 OR 1/2 IN VIDEO
Deals exclusively with teaching children through proper use of behavioral methods, provides an overview of reinforcement principles.
Prod-RESPRC Dist-RESPRC

Parents And Children C 30 MIN
16MM FILM - 3/4 IN VIDEO PRO
Presents course instructor Eugene I Pavalon discussing the legal problems arising from the abortion issue, artificial insemination, consent for treatment of minors, use of restraints for minors and nursing responsibilities in the care of abused wives and children.
From The Nurse And The Law Series.
LC NO. 77-700129
Prod-AJN Dist-AJN Prodn-WGNCP 1977

Parents And Children - A Positive Approach To Child Management C 24 MIN
16MM FILM OPTICAL SOUND
Discusses the teaching of children by parents using behavioral techniques. Features an overview of reinforcement principles in nontechnical language and offers common examples of this approach.
LC NO. 80-701254
Prod-RESPRC Dist-RESPRC 1979

Parents And Children Who Have Adopted Each Other C 29 MIN
3/4 OR 1/2 INCH VIDEO CASSETTE H-C A
Shows adoptive parents discusssing the risks, fears, and rewards they have encountered, and some of the children describe their early relationships with their parents and tell why they asked to be adopted. Shows some parents telling of obstacles they faced, such as in the adoption of of a child of a different race.
From The Are You Listening Series.
LC NO. 82-706878
Prod-STURTM Dist-STURTM 1982

Parents And Staff In A Children's Ward B 45 MIN
16MM FILM OPTICAL SOUND PRO
Deals with the sick child's need for emotional support when in the hospital. Gives both parents' and staff's views of the other's roles, difficulties and concerns with the ideas of improving mutual relations.
LC NO. 72-700824
Prod-PSUPCR Dist-PSUPCR 1972

Parents And The Young Teen - A Delicate Balance C
3/4 OR 1/2 INCH VIDEO CASSETTE A
Explores areas in which teenagers and parents can work towards a better understanding of each other.
From The Vital Link Series.
Prod-EDCC Dist-EDCC

Parents Are Teachers Too B 22 MIN
16MM FILM OPTICAL SOUND
Discusses the role of parents as the child's first and continuing teachers. Points out that learning comes easier with a flow of understanding between school and home.
From The Head Start Starts At Home Series.
LC NO. FIE67-137
Prod-USOEO Dist-USNAC 1967

Parents Are Teachers, Too B 18 MIN
3/4 INCH VIDEO CASSETTE
Stresses the role of parents as the child's first and continuing teachers. Shows how learning comes easier with a flow of understanding between school and home.
Prod-USNAC Dist-USNAC 1972

Parents Education Programs C 30 MIN
16MM FILM, 3/4 OR 1/2 IN VIDEO
Illustrates both formal and informal programs for parents of young hearing impaired children. Presents issues in family dynamics and parent-child communication and language development.
LC NO. 80-707425
Prod-USDHEW Dist-USNAC

Parents Look At Genetic Counseling C 27 MIN
3/4 OR 1/2 INCH VIDEO CASSETTE PRO
Presents comments from parents of handicapped or impaired children who are involved in genetic counseling at The University of Michigan Medical Center. Discusses topics such as how they were informed of the condition, their reactions, positive and negative aspects, their opinion of genetic couseling and their plans for future children.
Prod-UMICHM Dist-UMICHM 1981

Parents Of Disturbed Children C 28 MIN
16MM FILM - 3/4 IN VIDEO
Presents a group of parents exploring the problems and challenges of dealing with disturbed children.
From The Are You Listening Series.
LC NO. 80-707172
Prod-STURTM Dist-STURTM 1975

Parents Weekend 1978 C 60 MIN
3/4 OR 1/2 INCH VIDEO CASSETTE
Shows Sri Gurudev speaking on the purpose of life and spiritual meaning of Mother and Father.
Prod-IYOGA Dist-IYOGA

Parents Who Have Lost Children C 29 MIN
3/4 OR 1/2 INCH VIDEO CASSETTE PRO
Presents a couple talking about their efforts to cope with the loss of their thirteen-month-old daughter. Illustrates the importance of a local support group. Discusses their feelings of grief, depression, isolation and panic.
Prod-UARIZ Dist-UARIZ

Parents, The B 60 MIN
16MM FILM OPTICAL SOUND H-C A
A documentary report of today's American parents and their attempts to find identity, meaning and purpose in their lives.
From The America's Crises Series.
LC NO. FIA65-551
Prod-NET Dist-IU 1965

Parents' Group, The C 19 MIN
3/4 OR 1/2 INCH VIDEO CASSETTE
Discusses the common frustrations and victories experienced when integrating an older child into an adoptive family.
Prod-LACFU Dist-IA

Parents' Group, The - Working With The Adoptive Family C 19 MIN
16MM FILM OPTICAL SOUND PRO
Shows how a parents' group can be a useful device for dealing with some of the frustrations experienced when integrating a child into an adoptive family.
LC NO. 79-700699
Prod-LAC Dist-IA 1975

Parents' Hospital Experience, The C 29 MIN
3/4 OR 1/2 INCH VIDEO CASSETTE H-C A
Discusses the experiences of the parents during the period after the birth of their child. Tells how the mother begins her physical recovery and both parents begin their emotional adjustment to parenting.
From The Tomorrow's Families Series.
LC NO. 81-706906
Prod-MSDOE Dist-AITECH 1980

Parents' Responses To Their Children's Illness C 27 MIN
3/4 INCH VIDEO CASSETTE
Presents a discussion between a social worker and four parents of chronically ill children. Illustrates parents' responses, including denial, anger, bargaining, depression and acceptance.
LC NO. 79-707894
Prod-UMICH Dist-UMMCML Prodn-UMISU 1977

Parents' Voices C 12 MIN
16MM FILM, 3/4 OR 1/2 IN VIDEO
Features two young people who enact their reactions to sexual intercourse, while others act as parents' voices. Shows how parental influence affects sexual behavior. Challenges parents' use of drugs and alcohol.
From The Sex, Feelings And Values Series.
Prod-DF Dist-LRF 1976

Parergastic Reaction (Schizophrenia) In A Person Of Low Intelligence B 15 MIN
16MM FILM OPTICAL SOUND C T
Shows stereotypic grimaces and speech, vagueness, concrete use of abstract expressions and neologism in a schizophrenic with probable mental retardation.
Prod-PSUPCR Dist-PSUPCR 1939

Pareto Diagram C
3/4 OR 1/2 INCH VIDEO CASSETTE
Introduces the Pareto diagram, a graph used to help set priorities.
From The Implementing Quality Circles Series.
Prod-BNA Dist-BNA

Paricutin B 23 MIN
16MM FILM OPTICAL SOUND
A documentary of the 1946 research expedition to Paricutin Volcano in Mexico.
Prod-USAF Dist-USNAC 1949

Paris C 25 MIN
16MM FILM OPTICAL SOUND J-H
Shows how the fashion industry operates in Paris, Describing the changing nature of the industry and discussing designing and marketing.
LC NO. 75-703871
Prod-BASIST Dist-BASIST 1975

Paris (Metro) C 5 MIN
3/4 OR 1/2 INCH VIDEO CASSETTE
Reveals the ambiguity and confusion felt by a Paris Metro passenger with a linguistic parallel to the visual image.
Prod-EAI Dist-EAI

Paris - Imperial City C 24 MIN
16MM FILM, 3/4 OR 1/2 IN VIDEO
Delineates conditions and policies encouraged by Napoleon in the beginning of the 19th century to sustain and control societal instability and to encourage the urban growth of Paris as an administrative and cultural center.
Prod-OPENU Dist-MEDIAG Prodn-BBCTV 1981

Paris - La Belle Epoque C 24 MIN
16MM FILM, 3/4 OR 1/2 IN VIDEO A
Looks at Paris at the beginning of the 20th century and the milieu in which Claude Debussy and his contemporaries composed their revolutionary music. Provides examples of the cultural influences that shaped his music and includes performances of some of his works and those of his contemporaries.
From The Rise Of Modernism In Music Series.
Prod-BBCTV Dist-MEDIAG 1982

Paris - Living Space C 27 MIN
16MM FILM, 3/4 OR 1/2 IN VIDEO H-C A
Traces the history of Paris' design through the work of five individuals whose efforts shaped the city. Shows that their work set in motion a self-perpetuating system of linked thoroughfares, boulevards and axes that created a vision of life of its own which transcended individual projects to form the modern city.
From The Understanding Cities Series.
Prod-FI Dist-FI 1983

Paris A La Carte C 30 MIN
3/4 OR 1/2 INCH VIDEO CASSETTE
Offers a portrait of Paris today which, thanks to a large infusion of American culture, is quite different from the image of the City of Light that most Americans have in their minds.
Prod-EAI Dist-EAI

Paris A Mon Coeur C 10 MIN
16MM FILM OPTICAL SOUND H-C
A French language film. Describes famous landmarks of Paris and gives their historical significance.
From The Aspects De France Series.
Prod-WSU Dist-MLA Prodn-BORGLM 1955

Paris Commune B 20 MIN
16MM FILM OPTICAL SOUND C A
Jan pere documents the struggle of Paris against the Prussians during the Franco-German War of 1870-1871. Emphasizes the conditions of the poor and working class and draws an analogy to oppression in the U S.
Prod-GROVE Dist-GROVE

Paris Commune, The C 30 MIN
3/4 INCH VIDEO CASSETTE
Talks about the worker's revolution of Paris, 1871, and women's contributions to the revolution. Raises questions about women's strategies within other social movements.
Prod-WMENIF Dist-WMENIF

Paris Hier C 19 MIN
16MM FILM, 3/4 OR 1/2 IN VIDEO H-C
Features ordering food and something to drink in a Paris cafe, visiting traditional Parisian sights such as the Seine, the Madeleine, Sacre-Coeur, Notre-Dame, the Eiffel Tower, the Metro and the boulevards.
From The La France Telle Qu'Elle Est Series.
Prod-THAMES Dist-MEDIAG 1977

Paris In The Month Of May C 35 MIN
16MM FILM OPTICAL SOUND
Outlines the demands of French students as they take to the streets to breathe the air of revolution and almost succeed in toppling the De Gaulle government. Shows workers and students united behind the closed doors of the factories fighting pitched battles with the police.
Prod-NEWSR Dist-NEWSR

Paris Mai 68 B 9 MIN
16MM FILM OPTICAL SOUND H-C A
A French language film. Documents the student revolution which seized the Sorbonne and rocked the French government. Includes English subtitles.
Prod-UWFKD Dist-UWFKD

Paris Of Robert Doisneau, The C 20 MIN
16MM FILM OPTICAL SOUND H-C A
Presents photographer Robert Doisneau's famous black-and-white photographs taken over a period of 30 years juxtaposed with filmed color sequences from similar vantage points in the city of Paris.
LC NO. 76-702384
Prod-PORCIL Dist-RADIM 1976

Paris On The Seine C 20 MIN
16MM FILM OPTICAL SOUND
Presents a camera study of Paris. Photographed by Jack Cardiff.
Prod-RFL Dist-RFL Prodn-BERNRD 1955

Paris Uprising - May 1968 B 30 MIN
16MM FILM OPTICAL SOUND A
Focuses on the violent reaction against the Paris police during the social protests of May, 1968. Sketches the upheaval taking place in French society at that time.
Prod-NYFLMS Dist-NYFLMS

Paris, Aujourd' Hui C 19 MIN
16MM FILM, 3/4 OR 1/2 IN VIDEO H-C
Highlights buying tickets and requesting information in Paris, a modern city with a new airport and cultural center. Shows La Defense, a new suburb and a new deep-level suburban metro system.
From The La France Telle Qu'Elle Est Series.
Prod-THAMES Dist-MEDIAG 1977

Paris, Left Bank C 3 MIN
16MM FILM OPTICAL SOUND P-I
Discusses the Left Bank of the city of Paris in France.
From The Of All Things Series.
Prod-BAILYL Dist-AVED

Paris, Tourist Town C 3 MIN
16MM FILM OPTICAL SOUND P-I
Discusses the city of Paris in France.
From The Of All Things Series.
Prod-BAILYL Dist-AVED

Parisian Sights And Shops C 20 MIN
16MM FILM, 3/4 OR 1/2 IN VIDEO H-C A
Presents a visit to Sacre Coeur, a boatride on the Seine, buying souvenirs and exploring the stores in a modern shopping complex. Shows how to ask questions of sales people.
From The Touring Paris Series.
Prod-THAMES Dist-MEDIAG 1985

Park Community, A C 10 MIN
16MM FILM, 3/4 OR 1/2 IN VIDEO I-J
Shows how a community park forms an ecosystem of plants and animals which are mutually dependent on one another. Examines the interrelationships of these different forms of life.
Prod-BARR Dist-BARR 1974

Park Police Driver Training C 22 MIN
16MM FILM - 3/4 IN VIDEO
Shows how the National Park Service trains its uniform patrol drivers. Stresses the importance of the driver's attitude toward safety and offers tips for handling the automobile in skids, in sharp turns and at high speeds. Issued in 1970 as a motion picture.
LC NO. 79-706149
Prod-USNPS Dist-USNAC 1979

Park That Kids Built, The C 19 MIN
16MM FILM, 3/4 OR 1/2 IN VIDEO I-J
Follows a group of children who, in their efforts to get a neighborhood park, learn how to work with each other and within their community. Shows how the children circulate petitions, lobby, and, with the help of some business people, succeed in raising enough money to purchase some vacant lots and turn them into a park.
LC NO. 82-706814
Prod-CF Dist-CF 1982

Park That Went To Sea, The C 14 MIN
16MM FILM OPTICAL SOUND
A view of Pennekamp, an underwater state park in the Florida Keys, the only living coral reef in the United States. Uses underwater photography to reveal the beauty of the coral formations, the richness of the marine life, and the pleasures of skin diving.
LC NO. 75-702514
Prod-FDC Dist-FDC Prodn-GOODWY 1968

Park, The C 28 MIN
16MM FILM OPTICAL SOUND J
Analyzes the effect of the nuclear materials industry on the National Environmental Research Park in South Carolina. Explores the effects of nuclear industry on natural resources and the living species around it.
LC NO. 76-702700
Prod-USERD Dist-USNAC 1975

Park, The C 7 MIN
16MM FILM, 3/4 OR 1/2 IN VIDEO P-I
Uses mood music, a narration which includes Thoreau's 'WALDEN,' and color photography to portray a park as it blends one season into the next.
Prod-COMICO Dist-AIMS 1970

Park, The C 11 MIN
16MM FILM, 3/4 OR 1/2 IN VIDEO P
Shows how a boy discovers things in the park he has not noticed before.
Prod-AIMS Dist-AIMS 1970

Parker Adderson, Philosopher C 39 MIN
16MM FILM, 3/4 OR 1/2 IN VIDEO
Depicts a confrontation between a captured Rebel spy and a Confederate general. Based on the short story Parker Adderson, Philosopher by Ambrose Bierce.
From The American Short Story Series.
Prod-LEARIF Dist-CORF

Parking C 24 MIN
3/4 OR 1/2 INCH VIDEO CASSETTE
Tells how to make parking, often a stressful situation, easier.
From The Right Way Series.
Prod-SCETV Dist-PBS 1982

Parking On Hills C 8 MIN
16MM FILM, 3/4 OR 1/2 IN VIDEO H
Presents two methods of parking on hills, with the use of the foot brake or the parking brake. Covers the method of parking up anddown hills and how to leave the curb when parked on a hill.
Prod-SF Dist-SF 1974

Parking Tactics C 16 MIN
16MM FILM, 3/4 OR 1/2 IN VIDEO H-C A
Details parallel, diagonal and hill parking, as well as parking lots and the backing of an automobile.
Prod-AIMS Dist-AIMS 1968

Parking Tactics (Spanish) C 16 MIN
16MM FILM, 3/4 OR 1/2 IN VIDEO H A
Presents the importance of parking skills to overall driving ability, and techniques for parallel parking, diagonal parking, hill parking, backing and parking in parking lots.
Prod-CAHILL Dist-AIMS 1968

Parkinson's Disease - Natural And Drug-Induced Causes C 59 MIN
3/4 OR 1/2 INCH VIDEO CASSETTE A
Describes the symptoms of Parkinson's disease that have developed in young people as a result of experimentation with an illicit drug contaminated with a toxic substance. Discusses the parts of the brain affected, the chemical abnormalities that occur, the successes and limitations of current treatments and the search for better therapies.
Prod-USPHS Dist-USNAC 1985

Parkinson's Law B 7 MIN
16MM FILM OPTICAL SOUND H A
Tells a story about a man at a lathe making metal parts who fades out of the picture completely as the machinery of organization becomes both the end and the means of production. Uses miniaturization, multiple image and other special effects to show how bureaucracy often defeats its purpose.
LC NO. 72-700413
Prod-ZAGREB Dist-MMA 1970

Parkinsonism And Convulsive Disorders C 30 MIN
16MM FILM OPTICAL SOUND C
See series title for descriptive statement.
From The Pharmacology Series.
LC NO. 73-703338
Prod-MVNE Dist-TELSTR 1971

Parks And Plazas C 25 MIN
3/4 INCH VIDEOTAPE A
Discusses typology of urban parks based on source, size and demographics with examples drawn from New York City. Shows utility of parks, variety of users and their contribution to the urban environment.
LC NO. 80-707697
Prod-SLDTRS Dist-SLDTRS 1980

Parks, Pleasant Occasions And Happiness C 17 MIN
16MM FILM OPTICAL SOUND P-C
Dramatizes, without narrations, occasions of pleasure and happiness that city parks provide throughout the seasonal calendar. Depicts the companionship that an elderly man finds with an elderly woman in the course of visiting a city's various parks in different seasons over a two-year period. Emphasizes the importance of public parks for leisure and recreation.
LC NO. 77-700993
Prod-MARALF Dist-MARALF 1977

Parkside - A Neighborhood Comes Back C 28 MIN
16MM FILM, 3/4 OR 1/2 IN VIDEO H-C A
Demonstrates how Parkside, a Chicago neighborhood of deteriorated and abandoned buildings with a high tenant turnover, is transformed to a place where the buildings have been dramatically improved and the residents really care about their neighborhood.
LC NO. 83-706916
Prod-OLINC Dist-MTI 1983

Parliamentary Procedures In Action (2nd Ed) C 16 MIN
16MM FILM, 3/4 OR 1/2 IN VIDEO J-H
Describes parliamentary procedure, explaining the duties of officers, proper order of the agenda, activities of committees and several types of motions. Shows how the procedure is used at an actual meeting to insure the right of each individual to speak.
Prod-CORF Dist-CORF 1965

Parole C 59 MIN
3/4 OR 1/2 INCH VIDEO CASSETTE
Presents actor E G Marshall narrating this study of the nations' parole system. Raises questions about the rationale of the parole system and whether the rate of recidivism indicates a need for change.
Prod-NPACT Dist-PBS 1976

Parole Agent C 30 MIN
1/2 IN VIDEO CASSETTE BETA/VHS
Describes the life of G A Patrick, who has been a parole agent for the California Department of Corrections for 26 years, and who began his career as a correctional officer at San Quentin.
From The American Professionals Series.
Prod-WTBS Dist-RMI

Parole Game, The C 48 MIN
16MM FILM, 3/4 OR 1/2 IN VIDEO H-C A
Looks at the parole system in America. Traces the course of the parole process, beginning with the convict's initial parole board hearing through his/her attempts at adjusting to life on the outside with the aid of the parole officer.
LC NO. 83-706821
Prod-CBSNEW Dist-MTI 1983

Parotid And Submandibular Regions, The C 14 MIN
16MM FILM, 3/4 OR 1/2 IN VIDEO C A
Focuses on the head and neck. Demonstrates the dissection of the parotid and submandibular regions.
From The Guides To Dissection Series.
Prod-UCLA Dist-TEF

Parotid Gland And Facial Nerve, The C 14 MIN
3/4 INCH VIDEO CASSETTE PRO
Examines the structures surrounding, contained in and related to the parotid gland.
From The Anatomy Of The Head And Neck Series.
LC NO. 78-706250
Prod-USVA Dist-USNAC Prodn-VADTC 1978

Parotidectomy C 18 MIN
16MM FILM OPTICAL SOUND
Demonstrates an effective technique of parotidectomy, showing how to successfully remove the tumor mass and to preserve the facial nerve that runs through the gland.
LC NO. 73-700745
Prod-EATONL Dist-EATONL 1972

Parotidectomy C 25 MIN
16MM FILM OPTICAL SOUND PRO
Presents surgical removal of the superficial lobe of the parotid gland. Shows the method of identifying the facial nerve prior to its entrance and demonstrates the use of a nerve stimulator to aid in the identification.
Prod-ACYDGD Dist-ACY 1951

Parquet And Tile Floors C 30 MIN
1/2 IN VIDEO CASSETTE BETA/VHS
Demonstrates how to lay a parquet kitchen floor. Considers a home security system. Shows how to install a tile floor in the bathroom.
From The This Old House, Pt 1 - The Dorchester Series.
Prod-WGBHTV Dist-MTI

Parquet Floors And Carpet Installations C 30 MIN
1/2 IN VIDEO CASSETTE BETA/VHS
See series title for descriptive statement.
From The Wally's Workshop Series.
Prod-KARTES Dist-KARTES

Parrish Blue C 26 MIN
16MM FILM, 3/4 OR 1/2 IN VIDEO H-C
Explores the life and work of the American artist-illustrator, Maxfield Parrish, whose imaginative book illustrations, advertisements, magazine covers and prints are a landmark in American history. Interviews Norman Rockwell, who evaluates the role and status of the commercial artist. Explains the stylistic qualities which may have accounted for Parrish's popularity, and shows a wide sampling of Parrish's work.
Prod-IFB Dist-IFB Prodn-MARQRS 1971

Parrot Jungle C 29 MIN
16MM FILM OPTICAL SOUND
Tours Miami's parrot jungle with a look at its birds and plant life and features a segment on performing birds.
Prod-MIMET Dist-MIMET

Parrying And Striking B 8 MIN
16MM FILM OPTICAL SOUND
Demonstrates parries, blocks and counters in judo. Shows fist, hand and elbow blows, finger thrusts, knuckle blows and kicking.
From The Combative Measures - Judo Series.
LC NO. 75-700843
Prod-USAF Dist-USNAC 1955

Part Of Something C 15 MIN
3/4 OR 1/2 INCH VIDEO CASSETTE P
Shows how a space robot helps two second-graders divide up their purchase of candy equitably and then brings them back to his spaceship for a lesson on fractions. By dividing candy bars in different ways, the children find out that all parts of a fraction must be the same size.
From The Math Mission 2 Series.
LC NO. 82-706331
Prod-WCVETV Dist-GPITVL 1980

Part Of This World C 28 MIN
3/4 INCH VIDEO CASSETTE
Features psychologist Ken Moses in a parent counseling situation and shows how two parents learned to cope with, understand and ultimately accept their child's deafness. Depicts pre-service and in-service teacher preparation programs and supplements group parental counseling.
Prod-SHANDA Dist-BELLAG 1981

Part Of Your Loving C 9 MIN
16MM FILM, 3/4 OR 1/2 IN VIDEO J-C A
Observes Brooklyn baker Ben Togati at his early morning task of making bread. Includes Togati's own commentary on the personal, professional and spiritual satisfaction of his work.
Prod-DENONN Dist-DIRECT 1977

Part Of Your Loving C 10 MIN
3/4 OR 1/2 INCH VIDEO CASSETTE
Focuses on baker Ben Togati, who brings the breadmaking process to life.
Prod-DENONN Dist-DENOPX

Part One - Frequency Domain C 40 MIN
3/4 OR 1/2 INCH VIDEO CASSETTE IND
Covers techniques of circuit theory which are widely used in solution of practical problems. Shows how to apply theory to practice in order to calculate and interpret the step and sinusoidal steady-state response of networks and relate changes in frequency response to circuit elements.
From The Operational Analysis Circuits Series.
Prod-COLOSU Dist-COLOSU

Part One - Taking Charge C 30 MIN
3/4 OR 1/2 INCH VIDEO CASSETTE
See series title for descriptive statement.
From The Sky's The Limit Series.
Prod-LCOA Dist-DELTAK

Part Positioning For Shear Layout Using Architect's Scale C 14 MIN
1/2 IN VIDEO CASSETTE BETA/VHS IND
Shows the common sense approach to planning the arrangement of parts for economical shearing, eliminating as much waste as possible. Demonstrates use of an architect's scale to position parts 'to scale' on a simulated shear layout.
Prod-RMI Dist-RMI

Part Three - Active Filters C 40 MIN
3/4 OR 1/2 INCH VIDEO CASSETTE IND
Covers pole-zero control schemes using feedback and feedforward amplifiers, second order filter functions and their active realizations, characteristics of bandpass, lowpass, highpass, bandstop and allpass functions, all with special emphasis on practical considerations.
From The Operational Analysis Circuits Series.
Prod-COLOSU Dist-COLOSU

Part Two - Operational Amplifiers C 40 MIN
3/4 OR 1/2 INCH VIDEO CASSETTE IND
Covers techniques of solving circuit problems using operational amplifiers. Examines many practical circuits with reagard to frquency response, bandwidth, step response, ouput impedance and other features. Discusses, in addition to frequency-dependent gain characteristics, other operational amplifier limitations such as offset, slewing, and dynamic range.
From The Operational Amplifiers Circuits Series.
Prod-COLOSU Dist-COLOSU

Part Two - Winning All The Time C 30 MIN
3/4 OR 1/2 INCH VIDEO CASSETTE
See series title for descriptive statement.
From The Sky's The Limit Series.
Prod-LCOA Dist-DELTAK

Part 1 - Career Planning And Goal Setting C
3/4 OR 1/2 INCH VIDEO CASSETTE A
Looks at how the a Administrative woman of the eighties must

learn new skills and accept new responsibilities and how the computer can enhance work life. Tells how to put together a clear cut path for planning and implementing career goals.
From The Administrative Woman Series.
Prod-GPCV Dist-GPCV

Part 1 - Introduction C 26 MIN
3/4 OR 1/2 INCH VIDEO CASSETTE IND
Explains the uses of diving, diving terms, responsibilities and the physiological and psychological changes that occur to the underwater diver.
From The Diving Orientation For Offshore Personnel Series.
Prod-UTEXPE Dist-UTEXPE 1980

Part 2 - Air Diving C 13 MIN
3/4 OR 1/2 INCH VIDEO CASSETTE IND
Presents information on depth limits to air diving, Coast Guard regulations, equipment techniques and operations involved in a typical air-diving job.
From The Diving Orientation For Offshore Personnel Series
Prod-UTEXPE Dist-UTEXPE 1980

Part 3 - Mixed-Gas Diving C 13 MIN
3/4 OR 1/2 INCH VIDEO CASSETTE IND
Explains the need for mixed-gas diving. Lists Coast Guard requirements. Discusses a pipe tie-in operation using mixed gas.
From The Diving Orientation For Offshore Personnel Series.
Prod-UTEXPE Dist-UTEXPE 1980

Part 4 - Mixed-Gas Saturation Diving C 19 MIN
3/4 OR 1/2 INCH VIDEO CASSETTE IND
Discusses the theory of saturation, equipment used and a hyperbaric welding job in 500 feet of water.
From The Diving Orientation For Offshore Personnel Series.
Prod-UTEXPE Dist-UTEXPE 1980

Partial Dentures - Biomechanics C 15 MIN
16MM FILM OPTICAL SOUND
Demonstrates the influence of forces of mastication on the design of partial dentures by dividing parts of partial dentures into bracing, supporting and retaining elements. Emphasizes important construction details.
LC NO. FIE52-1488
Prod-USN Dist-USNAC 1951

Partial Differential Equations—A Series
C A
Presents the first part of an elementary introduction to the Fourier series and integrals. Emphasizes those properties needed in solving partial differential equations by separation of variables. Contains 45 one-hour videotape lectures.
Prod-UIDEEO Dist-UIDEEO

Partial Glossectomy And Osteotomy To Improve Function C 24 MIN
16MM FILM OPTICAL SOUND
Presents the case history of a teenage girl who has an osteotomy and a partial glossectomy. Follows her from the preoperative interview, through surgery, to one-week and one-year postoperative interviews.
LC NO. 72-700356
Prod-OSUMPD Dist-OSUMPD 1972

Partial Ileal By-Pass Operation For Hypercholesterolemia C 34 MIN
16MM FILM OPTICAL SOUND PRO
Explains that the partial ileal bypass operation is a direct surgical approach to treatment of the hyperlipidemias and atherosclerosis. Reviews patient data and shows the operative procedure.
Prod-ACYDGD Dist-ACY 1969

Partial Nephrectomy C 22 MIN
16MM FILM OPTICAL SOUND
Illustrates a technique for the conservation of renal tissue. Stresses the principles of partial nephrectomy, including accurate diagnosis of focal disease, good exposure of vessels, ligate vessels of the diseased segment, saving capsule for closure, suturing small vessels and calyx drain.
LC NO. 75-702297
Prod-EATONL Dist-EATONL 1966

Partially Hearing, The C 15 MIN
16MM FILM OPTICAL SOUND
Shows classes at the newly constructed school for people with partial hearing in Stockholm, in the Alviksskolan.
From The International Education Of The Hearing Impaired Child Series.
LC NO. 74-705326
Prod-USBEH Dist-USNAC 1971

Participant's Overview C 5 MIN
2 INCH VIDEOTAPE PRO
Familiarizes management assessors with the training course objectives and management simulation workshop activities.
From The AMA Assessment Center Program For Identifying Supervisory Potential Series.
LC NO. 75-704228
Prod-AMA Dist-AMA 1974

Participating In Implementation C 45 MIN
3/4 OR 1/2 INCH VIDEO CASSETTE
Illustrates the challenges which the information system user will face in the implementation process and presents feasible alternatives for project management.
From The User Responsibilities In Information Management Series.
Prod-DELTAK Dist-DELTAK

Participation B 30 MIN
16MM FILM OPTICAL SOUND
Shows how a supervisor can get his people to work with him to solve problems, set goals and get results.
From The Success In Supervision Series.
LC NO. 74-706171
Prod-WETATV Dist-USNAC 1965

Participation The CBI Way C 24 MIN
16MM FILM, 3/4 OR 1/2 IN VIDEO H-C A
Discusses the consultative system of the Confederation of British Industries (CBI), in which worker participation starts on the shop floor to avoid disputes before they arise. Shows how problems arise when shop stewards act as management personnel.
From The What About The Workers Series.
Prod-THAMES Dist-MEDIAG 1978

Participative Management C 30 MIN
3/4 OR 1/2 INCH VIDEO CASSETTE
See series title for descriptive statement.
From The Management For Engineers Series.
Prod-UKY Dist-SME

Participative Management - We Learn From The Japanese C 28 MIN
16MM FILM, 3/4 OR 1/2 IN VIDEO C A
Presents a case study of participative management at Nissan's Smyrna plant. Examines some of the key ideas from Japanese business philosophy and how these ideas help improve productivity and employee relations. Includes comments from leaders in business, industry, unions and education.
Prod-EBEC Dist-EBEC 1984

Participative Management Skills C
3/4 OR 1/2 INCH VIDEO CASSETTE
Teaches the skills needed to implement participative decision making, and allows participants to examine the characteristics of a participative environment, explore ways to enhance power through participation, improve team communication and achieve consensus decisions. Includes a student text and a set of diskettes.
Prod-CONCO Dist-DELTAK

Particle Model Of Matter, The C 60 MIN
3/4 OR 1/2 INCH VIDEO CASSETTE IND
Covers states of aggregation and energy content, states of aggregation and thermal motion, density of matter in the three states of aggregation, diffusion, osmosis, attractive forces between particles and the nature of the atttractive forces between particles.
From The Chemistry Training Series.
Prod-ITCORP Dist-ITCORP

Particle Size Determination, Optics C 56 MIN
3/4 OR 1/2 INCH VIDEO CASSETTE
See series title for descriptive statement.
From The Colloid And Surface Chemistry - Lyophobic Colloids Series.
Prod-KALMIA Dist-KALMIA

Particle Size Determination, Optics B 56 MIN
3/4 OR 1/2 INCH VIDEO CASSETTE
See series title for descriptive statement.
From The Colloid And Surface Chemistry - Lyophobic Colloids Series.
Prod-MIOT Dist-MIOT

Particles In Space B 4 MIN
16MM FILM OPTICAL SOUND
Deals with the energy of movement, of shaping light in darkness, by scratching on the film surface. By Len Lye.
Prod-STARRC Dist-STARRC Prodn-LYEL 1979

Particular Solutions B
16MM FILM OPTICAL SOUND
Illustrates the algebraic ideas of vector spaces and linear transformations behind the method of 'undetermined coefficients.' Shows how this method works for a simple case study equation.
Prod-OPENU Dist-OPENU

Particularly Poor Albert C 17 MIN
16MM FILM, 3/4 OR 1/2 IN VIDEO
Presents the various events which culminate in a fatal accident while operating a forklift. Reviews loading, driving and parking procedures.
Prod-WALGRV Dist-IFB

Parting Of The Ways, The C 57 MIN
16MM FILM, 3/4 OR 1/2 IN VIDEO
Points out that in America, the synthesis of cultures and musical forms created new music, such as the songs of Stephen Foster, the rags of Scott Joplin and the marches of John Philip Sousa. Shows how the Victorian Age ushered in concert hall melodramas and parlor pianos. Discusses how in Europe the old conventions were fragmented under the impact of the impressionism of Debussy, and the splendors of Strauss and Mahler. Tells how Stravinsky advanced the revolution with The Rite Of Spring.
From The Music Of Man Series.
Prod-CANBC Dist-TIMLIF 1981

Parting, The C 16 MIN
16MM FILM, 3/4 OR 1/2 IN VIDEO H-C A
Documents life and death in a remote European village.
Prod-WOMBAT Dist-WOMBAT

Partitioning Sets, Pt I C 20 MIN
2 INCH VIDEOTAPE P
See series title for descriptive statement.
From The Mathemagic, Unit II - Addition And Subtraction Series.
Prod-WMULTV Dist-GPITVL

Partitioning Sets, Pt 2 C 20 MIN
2 INCH VIDEOTAPE P
See series title for descriptive statement.
From The Mathemagic, Unit II - Addition And Subtraction Series.
Prod-WMULTV Dist-GPITVL

Partner (Italian) C 112 MIN
16MM FILM OPTICAL SOUND
Presents a Dostoyevksy-inspired story of a man who meets his own double. Directed by Bernardo Bertolucci. With English subtitles.
Prod-UNKNWN Dist-NYFLMS 1968

Partner Genital Exam, The C 13 MIN
3/4 OR 1/2 INCH VIDEO CASSETTE
Demonstrates the systematic exploration of each partner's genitals and examines erotic responses to a variety of forms of tactile stimulation.
From The EDCOA Sexual Counseling Series.
Prod-MMRC Dist-MMRC

Partner Stunts For Cheerleading C 25 MIN
3/4 OR 1/2 INCH VIDEO CASSETTE
See series title for descriptive statement.
From The Video For Cheerleading Series.
Prod-ATHI Dist-ATHI

Partner Video Sequences - German - Advanced German C 100 MIN
3/4 OR 1/2 INCH VIDEO CASSETTE H-C A
Provides conversational practice for advanced German classes and for those who plan to travel abroad. Follows a family through their daily life and a trip to Austria. Increases gradually in sophistication and complexity.
Prod-THAMES Dist-MEDIAG 1985

Partners C 13 MIN
16MM FILM, 3/4 OR 1/2 IN VIDEO I-J
Examines a number of interrelationships occurring within nature. Looks at such host specific insects as the monarch, viceroy and Baltimore butterflies contrasted with the more mutually beneficial partnerships occurring among fungus and algae, aphids and ants, yucca and the yucca moth, and bees and flowers.
From The Many Worlds Of Nature Series.
LC NO. 84-707054
Prod-MORALL Dist-MTI 1984

Partners C 15 MIN
16MM FILM, 3/4 OR 1/2 IN VIDEO I-J
Encourages students to visualize themselves as future independent business owners and to evaluate the aptitudes, temperament and skills needed to run an independent business and the advantages inherent in the operation.
From The Whatcha Gonna Do Series.
Prod-NVETA Dist-EBEC 1974

Partners In Crime C 60 MIN
16MM FILM OPTICAL SOUND
Uses a series of crimes staged in the Miami area to illustrate the apathy and fear of bystanders and to point out their responsibility as citizens in apprehending criminals.
LC NO. 71-702844
Prod-WCKTTV Dist-WCKTTV 1968

Partners In Dance—A Series

Presents shows from the New York City Cable TV series Eye On Dance. Profiles dancers who work together as a team.
Prod-ARCVID Dist-ARCVID

Eiko And Koma, Sara And Jerry Pearson 030 MIN
Kathy Bernson And Stormy Mullis 030 MIN
Loretta Abbott And Al Perryman 030 MIN
Sean Lavery And Merrill Ashley 030 MIN

Partners In Health C 22 MIN
16MM FILM OPTICAL SOUND
Uses an animated cartoon character to inform Department of the Army employees about the scope of on-the-job health protection services offered by the Army's occupational health clinics. Emphasizes worker responsibility in following safety procedures, wearing safety equipment and reporting injuries.
LC NO. 79-700002
Prod-USAEHA Dist-USNAC Prodn-WRAIR 1977

Partners In Mission C 16 MIN
16MM FILM OPTICAL SOUND H-C T
Mortimer Arias, a Bolivian pastor, and Dick Chartier, a missionary to Argentina, speak on the social revolution now occurring in Latin America and how the church and the American people participate in this liberating change.
LC NO. FIA67-5571
Prod-MCBM Dist-UMCBM 1967

Partners In Safety C 13 MIN
16MM FILM, 3/4 OR 1/2 IN VIDEO
Illustrates safety techniques used in the handling of traffic that has been disrupted because of construction or maintenance. Demonstrates the use of signs, barricades and flagmen. Issued in 1975 as a motion picture.
LC NO. 80-707118
Prod-USDTFH Dist-USNAC 1980

Partners With Industry C 13 MIN
16MM FILM OPTICAL SOUND J-H A
Tells how America's industry can benefit from NASA technology now and in the future. Touches almost every branch of science in almost every discipline of technology.
LC NO. 76-701538
Prod-NASA Dist-USNAC 1975

Partnership For Progress B
16MM FILM OPTICAL SOUND C A
Traces federal involvement in the control of infectious diseases, the origins of the national institutes of health and the work of the vaccine development program of the National Institute of Allergy and Infectious Diseases.
Prod-CAPFL Dist-NMAC 1967

Partnership Into Space - Mission Helios C 27 MIN
16MM FILM OPTICAL SOUND
Documents the United States-German joint space venture which culminated in the launching of the spacecraft Helios, a capsule which orbits the sun more closely than any other manmade object. Discusses the significance of the sun and its influence on the Earth.
LC NO. 75-704048
Prod-GERINF Dist-USNAC 1975

Partnership Into Space - Mission Helios C 27 MIN
16MM FILM OPTICAL SOUND H-C A
Deals with the spaceship Helios, the product of an American-German partnership, with an orbit closer to the sun than any other spacecraft.
Prod-WSTGLC Dist-WSTGLC

Partnerships C 30 MIN
3/4 OR 1/2 INCH VIDEO CASSETTE PRO
Presents questions on partnerships as affected by the Tax Reform Act of 1984 with answers by the individuals from government who developed the legislation.
From The Tax Reform Act Of 1984 Series.
Prod-ALIABA Dist-ALIABA

Partons En Vacances C 6 MIN
16MM FILM OPTICAL SOUND I-C A
A French language film. Provides a tour of French scenic and historic landmarks. Pictures several winter and summer sports.
From The Voix Et Images De France Series.
LC NO. 70-710640
Prod-PEREN Dist-CHLTN Prodn-CRDDF 1962

Parts And Materials C 30 MIN
3/4 OR 1/2 INCH VIDEO CASSETTE
Describes the parts and materials control process. Illustrates inventory control. Stresses making procurement decisions.
From The Maintenance Management Series.
Prod-ITCORP Dist-ITCORP

Parts And Wholes C 16 MIN
3/4 OR 1/2 INCH VIDEO CASSETTE P
Discusses parts and wholes in arithmetic.
From The Math Cycle Series.
Prod-WDCNTV Dist-GPITVL 1983

Parts Of A Plant B 30 MIN
2 INCH VIDEOTAPE J
See series title for descriptive statement.
From The Investigating The World Of Science, Unit 4 - Plants And Their Adaptations Series.
Prod-MPATI Dist-GPITVL

Parts Of Speech, The C 13 MIN
16MM FILM, 3/4 OR 1/2 IN VIDEO I-J
Uses the experiences of children at the beach to provide an opportunity to use the parts of speech in building the pictures shown. Names the eight parts of speech and explains that they may name things, modify other words or tell about actions.
Prod-CORF Dist-CORF 1962

Parts Of The Guitar, Types Of Guitars Holding The Guitar, Striking The String,... C 20 MIN
3/4 OR 1/2 INCH VIDEO CASSETTE J-H
Provides instruction on how to play the guitar, discussing parts of the guitar, types of guitars, holding the guitar, striking the string and notes on the first string.
From The Guitar, Guitar Series.
Prod-SCITV Dist-GPITVL 1981

Parturition In The Cow C
16MM FILM OPTICAL SOUND PRO
Documents the labor, birth and afterbirth of two cows. Discusses some of the dangers, the veterinary procedures and the progressive stages of parturition.
LC NO. 73-703090
Prod-UILLCA Dist-UILL 1973

Party Fare C 4 MIN
16MM FILM OPTICAL SOUND
See series title for descriptive statement.
From The Beatrice Trum Hunter's Natural Foods Series.
Prod-PUBTEL Dist-PBS 1974

Party Fare C 3 MIN
2 INCH VIDEOTAPE
Shows how to make a crustless cheese and onion pie, assembling most of the ingredients in a blender. Demonstrates how to make a pizza using a whole wheat dough layered with cheese and tomatoes and sprinkled with spices.
From The Beatrice Trum Hunter's Natural Foods Series.
Prod-WGBH Dist-PUBTEL

Party Game, The C 8 MIN
16MM FILM, 3/4 OR 1/2 IN VIDEO
Presents the story of a teenage girl whose dancing partner sexually assaults her. Emphasizes the need for young people to understand their own sexual values and those of others.
From The Acquaintance Rape Prevention Series.
LC NO. 82-706074
Prod-ODNP Dist-ODNP 1980

Party Game, The C 30 MIN
3/4 OR 1/2 INCH VIDEO CASSETTE H
Focuses on an interview with a young woman who tells what it is like to be the victim of an acquaintance rape.
From The Acquaintance Rape Prevention Series.
Prod-GPITVL Dist-GPITVL

Party Line C 25 MIN
3/4 OR 1/2 INCH VIDEO CASSETTE
Tells a story about an outlandish conflict between two telephone companies. Uses black humor in an experimental film.
Prod-KROGST Dist-MEDIPR 1977

Party Pajamas And Evening Skirts C 29 MIN
2 INCH VIDEOTAPE
See series title for descriptive statement.
From The Designing Women Series.
Prod-WKYCTV Dist-PUBTEL

Party, The X 28 MIN
16MM FILM, 3/4 OR 1/2 IN VIDEO J-C A
Describes six teenagers at a beach party who display differing attitudes toward the sexual act.
Prod-PAULST Dist-MEDIAG

Party, The (Spanish) X 28 MIN
16MM FILM, 3/4 OR 1/2 IN VIDEO J-C A
Describes six teenagers at a beach party who display differing attitudes toward the sexual act.
From The Insight Series.
Prod-PAULST Dist-PAULST

Party's Over, The C 15 MIN
3/4 OR 1/2 INCH VIDEO CASSETTE I-J
Deals with boys who crash a slumber party, bringing along wine and beer.
From The Jackson Junior High Series.
Prod-EFLMC Dist-GPITVL

Party's Over, The C 15 MIN
16MM FILM, 3/4 OR 1/2 IN VIDEO J
Introduces problems of alcohol and peer pressure. Depicts a girl's quiet slumber party, which becomes raucous when a group of high school boys arrive with liquor. Shows how the girl's parents step in and control the situation.
From The Jackson Junior High Series.
Prod-USOLLR Dist-USNAC Prodn-NVETA 1976

Party's Over, The C 18 MIN
3/4 OR 1/2 INCH VIDEO CASSETTE
Offers a new approach to the drinking driver problem.
Prod-PARPRO Dist-PARPRO

Pas De Deux B 14 MIN
16MM FILM, 3/4 OR 1/2 IN VIDEO K-C A
Illuminates the grace and movement of classical ballet form through the use of strobe-like or multi-image patterns. Features Margaret Mercier and Vincent Warren of Les Grands Ballets Canadiens.
Prod-NFBC Dist-LCOA Prodn-MCLN 1969

Pas De Moutarde C 10 MIN
3/4 OR 1/2 INCH VIDEO CASSETTE
Focuses on food and expressions of equality.
From The Salut - French Language Lessons Series.
Prod-BCNFL Dist-BCNFL 1984

Pasadena Tournament Of Roses Story, The - Tradition On Parade C 31 MIN
16MM FILM OPTICAL SOUND
Takes a look at the history and traditions of the Tournament of Roses Parade in Pasadena, California.
LC NO. 76-702207
Prod-TRA Dist-INMATI Prodn-SOLTYS 1976

PASCAL - A Modern Programming Language--A Series

Teaches PASCAL programming language through developmental method. Knowledge of BASIC suggested.
Prod-EDUACT Dist-EDUACT

Decision Making
Introduction To PASCAL
Loops
Procedures
Variables And Keyboard Input

Pascal, Pt 1 - Beginning Pascal--A Series
H-C A
Teaches Pascal, a computer language for educators, engineers and managers who wish to progress from a program language to a modern, structured language.
LC NO. 81-706049
Prod-COLOSU Dist-COLOSU 1980

Array Structure Data Types 030 MIN
Control Structures - Loops 030 MIN
Control Structures - Selectors 030 MIN
Declarations - Data Types 030 MIN
Example Program 030 MIN
Expressions 030 MIN
Functions 030 MIN
Introduction 030 MIN
Procedures 030 MIN
User-Defined Data Types 030 MIN

Pascal, Pt 2 - Intermediate Pascal--A Series
H-C A
Tells about structured data type facilities offered within Pascal and capability of building data items of increasing complexity and readability. Teaches additional complexities one can write in Pascal.
LC NO. 81-706049
Prod-COLOSU Dist-COLOSU

File Structures 030 MIN
Limitations 030 MIN
Other Data Structures 030 MIN
Other Features, Pt 1 030 MIN
Other Features, Pt 2 030 MIN
Pointers 030 MIN
Record Structures 030 MIN
Sets 030 MIN

Pascal, Pt 3 - Advanced Pascal--A Series
H-C A
Goes into advanced usage of the Pascal programming language, including concepts such as recursion, how the compiler works, what it looks like, how to do I/O, how to link Pascal to real-time applications, extensions, use with small computers, and new developments and languages based on Pascal.
Prod-COLOSU Dist-COLOSU 1980

Beyond Pascal 030 MIN
Compiler, The 030 MIN
Microcomputer Example 030 MIN
More I/O 030 MIN
Recursion 030 MIN
Writing Compilers 030 MIN

Pasciak Family, The C 52 MIN
3/4 OR 1/2 INCH VIDEO CASSETTE A
Features the daily routine of a second-generation Polish-American family who speak their native tongue and belong to ethnic organizations and generally cling to the 'old ways'. Shows how the younger children seem to be moving away. Looks at a traditional Christmas celebration where the family is reunited, perhaps for the last time.
From The Six American Families Series.
Prod-GROUPW Dist-ECUFLM Prodn-UCHC 1976

Pasciaks Of Chicago, The C 59 MIN
16MM FILM, 3/4 OR 1/2 IN VIDEO H-C A
Describes a blue collar Polish-American family whose traditions and ethnic roots are challenged by the lifestyles of their children.
From The Six American Families Series.
Prod-GROUPW Dist-CAROUF

Pass It On C 11 MIN
16MM FILM, 3/4 OR 1/2 IN VIDEO
Points out that unclear or misunderstood messages or instructions or meanings are costly in loss of time and energy and in frustration. Presents the verify and clariy technique to prevent communication problems.
Prod-CCCD Dist-CCCD 1982

Pass It On--A Series
K-P
Integrates a study of the arts with basic skills and topics in the area of social studies.
Prod-WKNOTV Dist-GPITVL 1983

Acting Is Pretending 015 MIN
Architecture 015 MIN
Ballet 015 MIN
Black History And Art 015 MIN
Body Parts 015 MIN
Communicating 015 MIN
Computer Magic 015 MIN
Fire, Fire 015 MIN
Hobbies 015 MIN
Holiday A - Halloween 015 MIN
Holiday B - An International Holiday Feast 015 MIN
Holiday C - An International Holiday Season 015 MIN
Holiday D - Be My Valentine 015 MIN
Junior Art Exhibit, A 015 MIN
Listening And Singing 015 MIN
Literature 015 MIN
Man's Best Friend 015 MIN
Me, Myself, And I 015 MIN
Names 015 MIN
Opera 015 MIN
Over Hill, Over Dale 015 MIN
Recycling 015 MIN
Ring, Ring 015 MIN
River Museum, A 015 MIN
Round Shapes 015 MIN
Safe Summer Fun 015 MIN
Spring Is Here 015 MIN
Trip To The Hospital, A 015 MIN
TV Is For Learning 015 MIN
Winter - A Museum Experience 015 MIN

Pass Transistor Networks For Gating C 55 MIN
3/4 OR 1/2 INCH VIDEO CASSETTE PRO
Discusses pull-down structures of inverters. Gates and good or bad forms are reviewed, plus the selector as a network of pass transistors. Includes use of enhancement and depletion mode transistors in networks, and switches, counting circuits and gate comparisons.
From The Introduction To VLSI Design Series.
Prod-MIOT Dist-MIOT

Pass, Dribble, Shoot C 10 MIN
16MM FILM OPTICAL SOUND H
Shows three ways of moving the ball in soccer, passing with the side of the foot, dribbling with the inside and outside of the foot and kicking with the instep. Isolates the techniques and shows them in practice sessions and in actual game situations.
Prod-SOCCER Dist-SOCCER 1970

Passage C 4 MIN
16MM FILM OPTICAL SOUND
Presents a mood piece which uses stills to reveal the lonely aspects of the airport and its transitory inhabitants.
LC NO. 73-702349
Prod-ROCOM Dist-SUTHLA 1973

Passage Of Time, The B 26 MIN
16MM FILM OPTICAL SOUND C A
Illustrates superposition and the process of transfer. Explains that transfer is composed of the elements of erosion, which removes rock--transportation, which moves rock and deposition, which produces rock. Points out that faults, intrusions and fossils are other indications of the passage of time. Discusses the principle that like fossil assemblages at two points indicate like geologic ages of the rocks sur rounding them.
Prod-UTEX Dist-UTEX 1960

Passage, A Life Drawing C 12 MIN
3/4 OR 1/2 INCH VIDEO CASSETTE
Explores the human figure as a compositional material.
Prod-EAI Dist-EAI

Passages From Finnegans Wake B 97 MIN
16MM FILM, 3/4 OR 1/2 IN VIDEO
Recreates James Joyce's novel, FINNEGANS WAKE, in a film based on a play by Mary Manning. Produced and directed by Mary Ellen Bute.
Prod-STARRC Dist-STARRC

Passages In Fathering - Sharing My Work And Myself B 28 MIN
3/4 OR 1/2 INCH VIDEO CASSETTE
Features five panelists discussing their childhood experiences and the relationships they had with their fathers. Presents ideas on bettering the father/child relationship.
Prod-SWWGFP Dist-UWISC 1981

Passe Compose Et Imparfait (French) C
3/4 OR 1/2 INCH VIDEO CASSETTE
See series title for descriptive statement.
From The French Language Videotapes (French) Series.
Prod-UCEMC Dist-UCEMC

Passengers - Driving Hazards, Safety B 14 MIN
16MM FILM OPTICAL SOUND
Points out the driver's responsibility for the safety of child passengers. Discusses safe driving habits and safety in handling children getting on and off the bus.
LC NO. FIE52-330
Prod-USOE Dist-USNAC 1945

Passer, The B 11 MIN
16MM FILM OPTICAL SOUND
Illustrates with slow-motion photography, the correct techniques of grip, position, and balance in passing a football. Narrated by Eddie Erdalatz of Annapolis.
Prod-BORDEN Dist-COCA

Passing By B 2 MIN
16MM FILM OPTICAL SOUND
Presents Alexander Alexeieff and Claire Parker's film set to a French-Canadian folk song, En Passant. Made for the National Film Board of Canada during Alexeieff and Parker's stay in the U S during World War II.
Prod-STARRC Dist-STARRC 1942

Passing Hours, The B 13 MIN
16MM FILM OPTICAL SOUND
Explains the history of clocks from the days of the Egyptians and shows how their style always reflected fashion. Depicts how life is governed by clocks and the difficulties encountered in keeping up with various timepieces.
Prod-RAYMIL Dist-RADIM

Passing Lane C 15 MIN
16MM FILM OPTICAL SOUND
Presents a satire on urbanization which has created many problems for society, not the least of which is the impersonal nature of the megalopolis.
LC NO. 75-703218
Prod-USC Dist-USC 1969

Passing Of Peron - The End Of An Era C 24 MIN
3/4 OR 1/2 INCH VIDEO CASSETTE H-C A
Examines the life of Juan Peron, the best-known leader of Argentina. Studies his personal and political life, his career, his famous wives and Argentinian culture.
Prod-JOU Dist-JOU

Passing On Dance—A Series

Presents programs from the New York City Cable TV series Eye On Dance. Recreates early dance forms and traditions.
Prod-ARCVID Dist-ARCVID

Carrying On Tradition In A Company Dedicated
Doris Humphrey Dance Reconstruction 030 MIN
Reconstruction Of Early Ballet Repertory 030 MIN
Recreating The Earliest Modern Dance 030 MIN

Passing On Tradition C 15 MIN
3/4 OR 1/2 INCH VIDEO CASSETTE I
Explains that when a group passes on traditions, it provides for cultural continuity and identity. Recounts how the Indians of West Africa pass on woodcarving, weaving and ceramics, the Japanese pass on gardening, flower arranging and the tea ceremony and the Tarahumara pass on musical instrument making, costumes and dance.
From The Across Cultures Series.
Prod-POSIMP Dist-AITECH Prodn-WETN 1983

Passing Phase, A C 7 MIN
16MM FILM OPTICAL SOUND J A
Shows how the evolution of man is related to the evolution of war weaponry and human power struggles.
LC NO. 72-700412
Prod-PHID Dist-MMA 1970

Passing Quietly Through B 28 MIN
16MM FILM OPTICAL SOUND
Presents a story about an old man, dying, alone and bereft, who tries to understand his dying and to establish his eternity through a relationship with his only contact, a practical nurse assigned to him by the city.
LC NO. 77-711391
Prod-NYU Dist-GROVE 1970

Passing The Message C 47 MIN
16MM FILM, 3/4 OR 1/2 IN VIDEO
Views the struggle to organize trade unions for the black majority in South Africa in the face of a vast entanglement of repressive government policies.
Prod-BSTGAV Dist-ICARUS 1983

Passing The Word B 24 MIN
16MM FILM OPTICAL SOUND I-J
Portrays the development of communication lines in California. Includes pony express, stage coach operations, telegraph, railroad and mail systems.
Prod-ABCTV Dist-MLA 1963

Passion C 8 MIN
16MM FILM OPTICAL SOUND
Tells Jozsef Nepp's amusing tale about a compulsive smoker who is ordered by his doctor to cut it out. Shows how the passion for the weed obsesses him and nearly makes him a murderer. Concludes with his death by a falling flowerpot on his head instead of smoking.
Prod-PANNOF Dist-FI 1961

Passion And Coolness C 52 MIN
3/4 OR 1/2 INCH VIDEO CASSETTE
Explains that Shakespearean drama demands a balancing of heightened language, naturalistic performance, emotion and intellect. Reveals how Hamlet's advice to the players expresses Shakespeare's direction that actors be natural and not false or grotesque. Shows how Shakespeare's language can be made to work on the audience. Uses examples from King Lear, Hamlet, Julius Caesar and King John.
From The Royal Shakespeare Company Series.
Prod-FOTH Dist-FOTH 1984

Passion Of Christ, The C 28 MIN
16MM FILM, 3/4 OR 1/2 IN VIDEO J-C A
Presents an interpretation of the Easter story from the Gospel according to St. Matthew, chapters 26-27, as depicted through a series of 160 paintings by the late artist, William Kurelek.
LC NO. 83-706717
Prod-BCNFL Dist-BCNFL 1982

Passion Of Joan Of Arc, The B 82 MIN
16MM FILM SILENT H-C A
Presents the story of the trial of Joan of Arc.
LC NO. 73-701738
Prod-UNKNWN Dist-KITPAR 1929

Passion Of Spain, The C 25 MIN
16MM FILM OPTICAL SOUND
Examines the sport of bullfighting in Spain, pointing out that the viewing audience participates in the sport.
From The Eye Of The Beholder Series.
LC NO. 75-701910
Prod-RCPDF Dist-VIACOM 1972

Passion Vine Butterfly - Gulf Fritillary C 10 MIN
16MM FILM, 3/4 OR 1/2 IN VIDEO I-C A
Presents the life cycle of the butterfly. Covers the larva to fully developed caterpillar to chrysalis, through metamorphosis to butterfly.
Prod-AIMS Dist-AIMS 1973

Passion Vine Butterfly - Gulf Fritillary (Captioned) C 10 MIN
16MM FILM, 3/4 OR 1/2 IN VIDEO I-C A
Presents the life cycle of the butterfly. Covers the larva to fully developed caterpillar to chrysalis, through metamorphosis to butterfly.
Prod-AIMS Dist-AIMS 1973

Passion Vine Butterfly - Gulf Fritillary (Spanish) C 10 MIN
16MM FILM, 3/4 OR 1/2 IN VIDEO I-C A
Presents the life cycle of the butterfly. Covers the larva to fully developed caterpillar to chrysalis, through metamorphosis to butterfly.
Prod-AIMS Dist-AIMS 1973

Passione D'Amore (Captioned) C 117 MIN
16MM FILM, 3/4 OR 1/2 IN VIDEO A
Portrays an unusual love affair in 19th century Italy, during the period of the Risorgimento and at the height of the Romantic movement. Italian dialog with English subtitles.
Prod-CNEMAG Dist-CNEMAG 1981

Passivation C 60 MIN
3/4 OR 1/2 INCH VIDEO CASSETTE PRO
See series title for descriptive statement.
From The Corrosion Engineering Series.
Prod-GPCV Dist-GPCV

Passivation C 60 MIN
3/4 OR 1/2 INCH VIDEO CASSETTE
Discusses the phenomenology and theories of passivation and describes polarization diagrams involving passive metals.
From The Corrosion Engineering Series.
Prod-MIOT Dist-MIOT

Passive Range Of Motion Exercises C 15 MIN
16MM FILM - 3/4 IN VIDEO A
Demonstrates motion exercises for patients with upper and lower extremity involvement. Shows procedures for exercising in supine or prone positions.
Prod-KRI Dist-KRI

Passive Solar Heating And Insulation—A Series

H-C A
Prod-NCDCC Dist-MOKIN

Choosing And Modifying A House Site 011 MIN
Home Insulation 027 MIN
How To Control Air Leaks 016 MIN
Passive Solar Space Heating 024 MIN

Passive Solar Space Heating C 24 MIN
3/4 OR 1/2 INCH VIDEO CASSETTE H-C A
Explains the theory and advantages of passive solar space heating and shows various methods, including double-glazed, south-facing windows, moveable nighttime insulation and thermal mass.
From The Passive Solar Heating And Insulation Series.
Prod-NCDCC Dist-MOKIN

Passover C 15 MIN
16MM FILM OPTICAL SOUND
Shows how the Festival of Passover is celebrated in Israel.
Prod-ALDEN Dist-ALDEN

Passover C 15 MIN
3/4 OR 1/2 INCH VIDEO CASSETTE P
See series title for descriptive statement.
From The Celebrate Series.
Prod-KUONTV Dist-GPITVL 1978

Passover C 30 MIN
16MM FILM, 3/4 OR 1/2 IN VIDEO J-C A
Describes the history, practice and significance of Passover, one of the oldest religious customs in existence. Narrated by Ed Asner.
LC NO. 83-706399
Prod-FI Dist-FI 1981

Passover Of Rembrandt Van Rijn, The B 30 MIN
16MM FILM OPTICAL SOUND
Relates the story of Rembrandt's search for a model of Moses in the streets of Amsterdam. Tells how the face of a poor bread-seller inspires him and he becomes imbued with the spirit of Judaism while taking part in a Passover Seder.
Prod-JTS Dist-NAAJS Prodn-NBCTV 1953

Passover With Jan Pierce B 30 MIN
16MM FILM OPTICAL SOUND H-C A
Jan Pierce, Metropolitan Opera Star, sings traditional and modern melodies associated with the Passover holiday and the seder service. He explains some of the Passover customs and comments on the answers to the traditional four questions. (Kinescope)
From The Eternal Light Series.
LC NO. 76-700973
Prod-JTS Dist-NAAJS 1968

Passover, The C 30 MIN
16MM FILM OPTICAL SOUND R
Introduces Christians to the festival meal of the first night of the Jewish Passover. Presents three generations of one family gathered together in a Dallas, Texas home.
Prod-GF Dist-GF

Past And Future C 10 MIN
16MM FILM OPTICAL SOUND
Uses live action and graphics in showing how the Earth's natural resources and synthetic laboratory chemicals are researched and developed to produce a variety of drugs and medicines.
From The Drugs And Medicine Series.
LC NO. 76-702553
Prod-MORLAT Dist-MORLAT 1975

Past In Our Words, The C 30 MIN
3/4 OR 1/2 INCH VIDEO CASSETTE C
See series title for descriptive statement.
From The Language And Meaning Series.
Prod-WUSFTV Dist-GPITVL 1983

Past Is Prologue, The C 30 MIN
3/4 OR 1/2 INCH VIDEO CASSETTE
Discusses the factors that may influence high school graduates in their career choices.
From The Career Alternatives Series.
Prod-NETCHE Dist-NETCHE 1974

Past, The C 15 MIN
3/4 OR 1/2 INCH VIDEO CASSETTE K-J
See series title for descriptive statement.
From The Arts Express Series.
Prod-KYTV Dist-KYTV 1983

Pasta C
3/4 INCH VIDEO CASSETTE H A
Shows how even inexperienced cooks can make basic pasta. Demonstrates several types of pasta dishes.
From The Matter Of Taste Series. Lesson 7
Prod-COAST Dist-CDTEL

Pasta, Pasta, Pasta C
1/2 IN VIDEO CASSETTE BETA/VHS
Demonstrates the preparation of pasta recipes such as fettuccine Alfredo and cannelloni with veal and spinach.
From The Video Cooking Library Series.
Prod-KARTES Dist-KARTES

Pasteur's Experiments C 14 MIN
16MM FILM OPTICAL SOUND
Describes the view of spontaneous generation using a puppet scholar in classic attire performing various experiments to test its validity. Proves Pasteur's position that micro-organisms are not generated spontaneously.
Prod-GAKKEN Dist-UNIJAP 1970

Pastoral B 21 MIN
16MM FILM OPTICAL SOUND
Depicts a world in which sub-human creatures create a disturbing symbolism. Produces different interpretations and ideas with each individual.
Prod-FILIM Dist-RADIM

Pastoral Balance, The C 20 MIN
16MM FILM OPTICAL SOUND J-C A
Describes some of the features of the Australian beef cattle industry, concentrating on recent advances in breeding and pasture improvement and on how the modern livestock rancher has to preserve the balance of nature while making a living.
LC NO. 74-703288
Prod-ANAIB Dist-AUIS Prodn-FLMAUS 1974

Pastorale C 8 MIN
16MM FILM OPTICAL SOUND
Deals with a choreography of trees, sky and sun.
Prod-VANBKS Dist-VANBKS

Pastorale C 14 MIN
16MM FILM OPTICAL SOUND
Demonstrates traditional dances and songs of the people living in the regions of the Carpathian Mountains in Rumania.
From The Journal Series.
LC NO. 75-703422
Prod-FIARTS Dist-CANFDC 1973

Pastries And Pies C 33 MIN
16MM FILM, 3/4 OR 1/2 IN VIDEO
Gives procedures for baking attractive and tasty pastries and pies. Issued as a motion picture in 1968.
LC NO. 80-707636
Prod-USN Dist-USNAC 1980

Pastry C
3/4 INCH VIDEO CASSETTE H A
Demonstrates how to make pie dough. Emphasizes the importance of freshness in ingredients. Hosted by Michel Richard, a master patisserie from Beverly Hills.
From The Matter Of Taste Series. Lesson 8
Prod-COAST Dist-CDTEL

Pastures Of The Sea C 6 MIN
16MM FILM, 3/4 OR 1/2 IN VIDEO I-H
Examines the various approaches and techniques used by scientists in the study of marine food chains.
Prod-NSF Dist-AMEDFL 1975

Pat Boone And The Kids C 28 MIN
16MM FILM OPTICAL SOUND
Tells about the only home in America caring exclusively for the children of prisoners.
Prod-BBS Dist-MTP

Pat Explores His City C 14 MIN
16MM FILM, 3/4 OR 1/2 IN VIDEO P
Examines the experiences of a young boy and his family to point out the many factors which must be considered by a family when looking for a new home in a representative American city.
Prod-EBEC Dist-EBEC 1971

Pat Sky And The Pennywhistlers C 52 MIN
3/4 OR 1/2 INCH VIDEO CASSETTE
Presents a combination of recent and traditional songs. Features the Pennywhistler performing songs from Bulgaria, Russia and South Africa.
From The Rainbow Quest Series.
Prod-SEEGER Dist-CWATER

Patagonia Force 10 C 52 MIN
16MM FILM - 1/2 IN VIDEO
Shows French adventurers sailing for the tip of South America. Dubbed into English.
Prod-RIVFIL Dist-OFFSHR

Patagonian Playground C 10 MIN
16MM FILM OPTICAL SOUND
Pictures the national park of Nahuel Huapi on the eastern slope of the Andes in Argentina and the recreational activities in the park.
Prod-UWF Dist-USOIAA 1942

Patch Pockets And Fitting C 29 MIN
2 INCH VIDEOTAPE
Features Mrs Ruth Hickman demonstrating how to make patch pockets and fit the coat.
From The Sewing Skills - Tailoring Series.
Prod-KRMATV Dist-PUBTEL

Patching Fabric B 22 MIN
16MM FILM - 3/4 IN VIDEO IND
Shows how to cut out and prepare the damaged area on an airplane. Discusses how to prepare, dope, rib-stitch and finish a patch. Issued in 1945 as a motion picture.
From The Aircraft Work - Aircraft Maintenance Series.
LC NO. 79-706788
Prod-USOE Dist-USNAC Prodn-HANDY 1979

Patching Plywood B 26 MIN
16MM FILM - 3/4 IN VIDEO IND
Illustrates how to splay the edges of a hole in the plywood part of an airplane. Explains how to prepare and apply a splay patch, how to make a flush or plug-type patch, how to make a frame or doubler and how to apply a flush patch. Issued in 1945 as a motion picture.
From The Aircraft Work - Aircraft Maintenance Series.
LC NO. 79-706789
Prod-USOE Dist-USNAC Prodn-HANDY 1979

Patching Walls C 30 MIN
16MM FILM, 3/4 OR 1/2 IN VIDEO
Provides basic information on patching walls.
From The Do It Yourself Home Repairs Series.
Prod-ODECA Dist-BULFRG

Patchwork C 30 MIN
3/4 OR 1/2 INCH VIDEO CASSETTE
Demonstrates classical patterns of patchwork quilts, such as Grandma's Dream and Cathedral Window.
From The Erica Series.
Prod-WGBHTV Dist-KINGFT

Patchwork Cover And Pillows C 14 MIN
2 INCH VIDEOTAPE
See series title for descriptive statement.
From The Living Better I Series.
Prod-MAETEL Dist-PUBTEL

Patchwork In Time C 30 MIN
3/4 OR 1/2 INCH VIDEO CASSETTE
Discusses the differences between quilting as a domestic craft and as a contemporary art form. Features a visit to Quilt National '83 held in Athens, Ohio. Shows the resulting taped interviews with the participating quilters as they talk about their wares and the differences between traditional and contemporary quilting.
Prod-OHUTC Dist-OHUTC

Pate En Croute C 8 MIN
3/4 OR 1/2 INCH VIDEO CASSETTE PRO
Presents a follow-up to Pate Maison, showing how to make a crust for the pate. Describes the tools needed, the making of the dough with a decoration of dough roses, and the baking process before filling.
Prod-CULINA Dist-CULINA

Pate Maison C 6 MIN
3/4 OR 1/2 INCH VIDEO CASSETTE PRO
Displays the utensils needed and the preparation and serving of pate maison, a blend of liver, meat and spices.
Prod-CULINA Dist-CULINA

Patent Ductus Arteriosus C 25 MIN
16MM FILM OPTICAL SOUND PRO
Designed to give a basic understanding of patient ductus arteriosus and the general principles of surgical treatment. Follows the case study of a child with a typical patent ductus arteriosus from examination, diagnosis and corrective surgery, to two different, postoperative stages.
Prod-SQUIBB Dist-SQUIBB

Patent Leather Kid B 27 MIN
16MM FILM OPTICAL SOUND
Presents Rupert Hughes' story about the conversion of an anti-military young boxer to a flag-saluting hero. Stars Richard Barthemless.
from The History Of The Motion Picture Series.
Prod-SF Dist-KILLIS

Patent Pending C 22 MIN
16MM FILM, 3/4 OR 1/2 IN VIDEO J-H
A shortened version of the motion picture Patent Pending. Shows models of inventions originally left with the U S Patent Office during the first 100 years of its existence when a working model of each invention had to be submitted in order to obtain a patent. Views examples from some of the remaining 200,000 models scattered between the Smithsonian Institute and private collectors.
From The American Documents (Edited) Series.
Prod-LUF Dist-LUF 1974

Patent Pending C 53 MIN
16MM FILM, 3/4 OR 1/2 IN VIDEO J-H
Shows models of inventions originally left with the U S Patent Office during the first 100 years of its existence when a working model of each invention had to be submitted in order to obtain a patent. Views examples from some of the remaining 200,000 models scattered between the Smithsonian Institute and private collectors.
From The American Documents Series.
Prod-LUF Dist-LUF 1974

Patent-Antitrust Considerations - Developing And Licensing A Product C 40 MIN
3/4 OR 1/2 INCH VIDEO CASSETTE PRO
Discusses various terms to be included in the licensing agreements for a new electronic chip.
From The Antitrust Counseling And The Marketing Process Series.
Prod-ABACPE Dist-ABACPE

Path Of Least Resistance, The C 15 MIN
3/4 OR 1/2 INCH VIDEO CASSETTE
Makes the point that electricity is a potential hazard that everyone should be reminded of at work and at home.
From The Safety Management Course Series.
Prod-EDRF Dist-EDRF

Path Of Life, The C 26 MIN
16MM FILM, 3/4 OR 1/2 IN VIDEO
Dramatizes the third part of an Ojibway Indian legend telling of a man's journey to the spirit world to find his dead wife. Begins in The Path Of Souls and The World Between.
Prod-FOTH Dist-FOTH

Path Of Souls, The C 26 MIN
16MM FILM, 3/4 OR 1/2 IN VIDEO
Dramatizes the first part of an Ojibway Indian legend telling how a young man entered on the Path of Souls to find his dead wife. Continues in The World Between and The Path Of Life.
Prod-FOTH Dist-FOTH

Path Of The Paddle—A Series
3/4 OR 1/2 INCH VIDEO CASSETTE J-C A
Introduces paddling techniques used in canoeing and shows the type of wildlife a canoeist can see.
Prod-NFBC Dist-NFBC 1978

Doubles Basic 028 MIN
Doubles Whitewater 028 MIN
Solo Basic 028 MIN
Solo Whitewater 028 MIN

Path Taken, The C 15 MIN
2 INCH VIDEOTAPE J
Reviews the past 15 lessons.
From The From Me To You...In Writing, Pt 2 Series.
Prod-DELE Dist-GPITVL

Path To Adulthood B 44 MIN
16MM FILM OPTICAL SOUND
Discusses the effects of parental and cultural attitudes upon the young adult and his resultant behavior.
From The Man - His Growth And Development, Birth Through Adolescence Series.
LC NO. 75-703684
Prod-VDONUR Dist-AJN Prodn-WTTWTV 1967

Path To Fulfillment C 38 MIN
16MM FILM OPTICAL SOUND
Presents an overview of the facilities and techniques of the care of the mentally retarded in Europe. Features Scandinavian and English facilities in particular.
Prod-GWASHU Dist-USOE

Path To Fulfillment C 38 MIN
16MM FILM OPTICAL SOUND
Gives an overview of the philosophy, facilities and techniques used in the care of the mentally retarded, principally in Scandinavia and England.
LC NO. 74-705327
Prod-USBEH Dist-USNAC 1970

Path To Peace, The C
16MM FILM OPTICAL SOUND
Features political-military analyst and former Chief of Intelligence of the Israeli defense forces, General Haim Herzog, who outlines what he considers a realistic path to a Middle East peace.
From The Dateline Israel, 1973 Series.
Prod-ADL Dist-ADL

Path To Prosperity, The C 10 MIN
16MM FILM, 3/4 OR 1/2 IN VIDEO
Compares primitive subsistence economies and complicated modern industrial economies. Summarizes the stages of the change from subsistence to surplus.
From The Foundations Of Wealth Series.
Prod-FOTH Dist-FOTH

Path To Rome, The C 54 MIN
16MM FILM OPTICAL SOUND
Retraces the path taken in 1902 by Hilaire Belloc on a pilgrimage from Toul to Rome. Compares the path as it is today to the path of the 1902 journey.
LC NO. 73-700489
Prod-MEYERF Dist-MEYERF 1972

Path To Safety C 20 MIN
16MM FILM OPTICAL SOUND
Points out that more accidents are caused by human eRror than by any other factor. Stars Cliff Robertson as a flight instructor briefing a class of student pilots on dramatic incidents occurring as a result of misjudgment.
LC NO. FIE67-104
Prod-FAAFL Dist-USFAA 1967

Path To Success In Changing Times C 15 MIN
3/4 OR 1/2 INCH VIDEO CASSETTE IND
Provides a comprehensive list of pork cuts that can help in matching the pork product mix with the customer mix. Covers importance of packaging, piece and demand.
Prod-NLSAMB Dist-NLSAMB

Path To Wings, A - The Air Force ROTC Flight Instruction Program C 15 MIN
16MM FILM OPTICAL SOUND
Encourages Air Force ROTC cadets to pursue a career as Air Force pilots through the flight instruction program. Shows how the program determines the cadet's potential for formal Air Force training. Cites the benefits of learning to fly and of possessing a pilot's license regardless of future plans.
LC NO. 74-705328
Prod-USAF Dist-USNAC 1968

Path, The C 21 MIN
16MM FILM OPTICAL SOUND
Describes the Buddhist religion, with shots of Rangoon.
Prod-STATNS Dist-STATNS 1969

Pathfinders From The Stars C 48 MIN
16MM FILM, 3/4 OR 1/2 IN VIDEO
Describes the progress made through the centuries in determining geographic position and direction using the stars.
LC NO. 80-707614
Prod-NOAA Dist-USNAC 1980

Pathfinders To Progress C 25 MIN
16MM FILM OPTICAL SOUND
Tells the story of the 1370th Photo-Mapping Wing and its worldwide photographic and charting responsibilities. Shows the Wing's contributions to the global geodetic puzzle and the tools and techniques used to carry out this mission.
LC NO. 74-706172
Prod-USAF Dist-USNAC 1963

Pathnames C
3/4 OR 1/2 INCH VIDEO CASSETTE
Describes how the UNIX file system is organized as a hierarchical inverted tree and identifies the levels of a UNIX file system. Describes the common administrative directories and full pathname and how to reference a file by a full pathname.
From The UNIX Fundamentals Series.
Prod-COMTEG Dist-COMTEG

Pathogenesis And Management Of Hemochromatosis B 29 MIN
3/4 INCH VIDEO CASSETTE PRO
Presents therapeutic approaches and diagnostic tests for the metabolic hereditary disease involving the liver and pancreas - hemochromatosis.
From The Clinical Pathology Series.
LC NO. 76-706068
Prod-NMAC Dist-USNAC 1969

Pathogenesis Of Anemia B 31 MIN
16MM FILM, 3/4 OR 1/2 IN VIDEO PRO
Discusses the major types of anemias, their differentiation, tests to establish specific types, and basis for therapy.

From The Clinical Pathology Series.
Prod-NMAC Dist-USNAC 1969

Pathogenesis Of Burn Trauma, Part 1 C 22 MIN
3/4 OR 1/2 INCH VIDEO CASSETTE PRO
Presents specific responses of three key organ systems of burn trauma, discusses normal functions of skin and its vulnerability. Describes each class of burn trauma as they relate to destruction of skin layers and functions. Highlights major cardiovascular and hemodynamic responses to burn trauma.
From The Burn Trauma Series.
Prod-BRA Dist-BRA

Pathogenesis Of Burn Trauma, Part 2 C 23 MIN
3/4 OR 1/2 INCH VIDEO CASSETTE PRO
Covers more specific responses of major organ systems to burn trauma. Emphasizes multi-system assault of burn trauma. Describes pulmonary system with causes of inhalation injury/pulmonary edema in burn trauma highlighted. Features renal, cerebral, gastro-intestinal and metabolic responses.
From The Burn Trauma Series.
Prod-BRA Dist-BRA

Pathogenesis Of Spinal Cord Damage In Decompression Sickness, The C 33 MIN
16MM FILM, 3/4 OR 1/2 IN VIDEO
Documents research conducted at the Naval Medical Research Institute in Bethesda, Maryland, showing that the fundamental pathogenetic underlying spinal cord damage in decompression sickness is not arterial embolization of bubbles, but rather venous obstruction at the level of the epidural vertebral venous system.
Prod-USN Dist-USNAC 1977

Pathologic Conference Case Presentation C 60 MIN
3/4 INCH VIDEO CASSETTE
Presents the case study of a 59-year-old woman with epigastric pain.
Prod-UTAHTI Dist-UTAHTI

Pathology Of Intramuscular Nerve Endings And The Neuromuscular Junction C 48 MIN
3/4 INCH VIDEO CASSETTE PRO
Presents Dr Christian Coers lecturing on the pathology of intramuscular nerve endings and the neuromuscular junction.
From The Intensive Course In Neuromuscular Diseases Series.
LC NO. 76-706070
Prod-NINDIS Dist-USNAC 1974

Pathology Of Screening And Detection Of Breast Cancer C
3/4 INCH VIDEO CASSETTE
Discusses breast cancer, including incidence, prognostic factors, screening methods, and pathological and psychological factors. Includes multimedia kit.
Prod-OHIOSU Dist-USNAC

Pathophysiological Approach To Calcium Stones, A C 21 MIN
3/4 OR 1/2 INCH VIDEO CASSETTE PRO
Provides a review of the etiological bases for hypercalcemia, hypercalciuria, hyperoxaluria, hyperuricosuria and decreased inhibitors which are considered to be metalbolic risk factors for calcium nephrolithiasis. Shows how the identification of these disorders would allow specific and more rational therapy.
Prod-UMICHM Dist-UMICHM 1981

Pathophysiological Approach To Calcium Stones C 21 MIN
3/4 OR 1/2 INCH VIDEO CASSETTE PRO
Provides a review of the etiological bases for hypercalcemia, hypercalciuria, hyperoxaluria, hyperuricosuria and decreased inhibitors which are considered to be metabolic risk factors for calcium nephrolithiasis. Cites examples showing how the identification of these disorders would allow specific and more rational therapy.
LC NO. 81-707082
Prod-UMICH Dist-UMICH 1981

Pathophysiology C 20 MIN
3/4 INCH VIDEO CASSETTE PRO
Describes and explains underlying pathophysiological changes occuring in patients with acute myocardial infarction in terms of changes in ventricular force generation and compliance.
From The Acute Myocardial Infarction Series. Unit 1
LC NO. 77-706059
Prod-NMAC Dist-USNAC 1977

Pathophysiology And Surgical Management Of Achalasia Of The Esophagus C 27 MIN
16MM FILM OPTICAL SOUND PRO
Presents a classification of achalasia of the esophagus, followed by a description of the physiological derangement demonstrated by motility and cineroentgenographic studies. Discusses the indications for surgical treatment and preoperative preparation.
Prod-ACYDGD Dist-ACY 1961

Pathophysiology Of Alcohol Abuse C 24 MIN
3/4 OR 1/2 INCH VIDEO CASSETTE
See series title for descriptive statement.
Alcohol - A Critical Illness Series.
Prod-BRA Dist-BRA

Pathophysiology Of Diarrhea C 18 MIN
16MM FILM OPTICAL SOUND
Describes the three pathophysiology diarrheal conditions - celiac sprue, cholera and lactase deficiency.
LC NO. 73-701619
Prod-EATONL Dist-EATONL 1973

Pathophysiology Of Opthalmology C
3/4 OR 1/2 INCH VIDEO CASSETTE PRO
Reviews anatomy and normal physiology, trauma, inflammation, degenerations of the eye and systemic diseases of the eye.
Prod-UMICHM Dist-UMICHM 1977

Pathophysiology Of Otorhinolaryngology C
3/4 OR 1/2 INCH VIDEO CASSETTE PRO
Reviews ear anatomy, hearing loss and hearing tests, diseases of the external, middle and inner ear, anatomy of the nose and throat, conditions of the nose and conditions of the mouth and throat.
Prod-UMICHM Dist-UMICHM 1977

Paths In The Wilderness C 28 MIN
16MM FILM OPTICAL SOUND
Portrays the humanistic and explorative achievements of Padre Eusebio Kino, a Jesuit who helped settle the Southwest. Features the Sonora Desert of Northern Mexico and Southern Arizona.
LC NO. 76-702662
Prod-UARIZ Dist-UARIZ 1976

Paths Of Steel C 26 MIN
16MM FILM OPTICAL SOUND J-C A
A description of the engineering and technical aspects of men and machines illustrating the use of various scientific instruments.
Prod-USSC Dist-USSC

Pathway From Within, A C 18 MIN
16MM FILM, 3/4 OR 1/2 IN VIDEO H-C A
Discusses the works and philosophy of Elizabeth Fraser Williamson, a prominent Canadian sculptor.
Prod-HAMILB Dist-JOU 1975

Pathway To A Winning Season C 8 MIN
3/4 OR 1/2 INCH VIDEO CASSETTE
Addresses the many problems encountered in the weight control program of the high school wrestler, such as the common dehydration problem and starvation practices. Provides information on how to determine the best competitive weight for each athlete and then how to maintain that weight through a sensible diet and exercise program.
From The Sports Medicine For Coaches Series.
Prod-UWASH Dist-UWASH

Pathway To Craftsmanship C 20 MIN
16MM FILM OPTICAL SOUND H
Describes apprenticeship training within the building trades. Takes the viewer to many construction sites to see journeymen and apprentices at work. Reviews basic qualifications to enter the apprenticeship program, along with the advantages and opportunities within the building trades themselves.
From The Career Guidance Series.
Prod-KRMATV Dist-GPITVL

Pathway To The Stars C 20 MIN
16MM FILM OPTICAL SOUND
Presents a typical flight of the X-15 research airplane from pre-flight arrangements to touch-down.
Prod-THIOKL Dist-THIOKL 1961

Pathways To Reading–A Series
I-J
Prod-CBF Dist-AVED

How To Read 13 MIN
Was It Worth Reading 14 MIN
What's In A Book 9 MIN
Why Did You Read 15 MIN
Why Read 15 MIN

Pathways To Success C 30 MIN
3/4 OR 1/2 INCH VIDEO CASSETTE T
Discusses the importance of people taking control of their lives and building personal strengths.
From The Developing Discipline Series.
Prod-SDPT Dist-GPITVL 1983

Patient Admission To And Discharge From A Hospital B 34 MIN
16MM FILM OPTICAL SOUND PRO
Dramatizes a patient's reaction to admission and discharge from a hospital. Demonstrates the nurse's responsibility to patients and emergency admission procedures.
From The Directions For Education In Nursing Via Technology Series. Lesson 27
LC NO. 74-701799
Prod-DENT Dist-WSU 1974

Patient Advocacy In Nursing Practice C 17 MIN
3/4 INCH VIDEO CASSETTE PRO
See series title for descriptive statement.
From The Bioethics In Nursing Practice Series. Module 2
LC NO. 81-707063
Prod-BRA Dist-BRA 1981

Patient Care Appraisal C 30 MIN
3/4 INCH VIDEO CASSETTE PRO
Discusses methods of appraising patient care in hospitals, clinics or offices.
LC NO. 76-706071
Prod-WARMP Dist-USNAC 1972

Patient Care Appraisal - Establishing Criteria, Setting Standards C 26 MIN
3/4 INCH VIDEO CASSETTE PRO
Discusses how to establish criteria and standards for patient care.
LC NO. 76-706072
Prod-WARMP Dist-USNAC 1972

Patient Counseling Films–A Series
PRO
Introduces patients to the nature and treatment of diabetes in adults, ear surgery and hysterectomy.
Prod-WFP Dist-WFP

Diabetes In Adults
Ear Surgery
Hysterectomy

Patient Counseling Library–A Series

Prod-ROCOM Dist-SUTHLA Prodn-MEDEX 1975

Controlling Heartburn 10 MIN
Controlling High Blood Pressure 10 MIN

Patient Education Programs - Clinical Diet–A Series

Discusses the coronary care diet, the ulcer diet, the cancer diet, the renal diet, and a weight reduction diet.
Prod-POAPLE Dist-POAPLE

Your Cancer Diet 013 MIN
Your Coronary Care Diet 011 MIN
Your Renal Diet 009 MIN
Your Ulcer Diet 009 MIN
Your Weight Reduction Diet 012 MIN

Patient History C 26 MIN
3/4 OR 1/2 INCH VIDEO CASSETTE
Reviews the medication history and laboratory reports of a patient who is admitted to the medical center's renal unit where he and his wife give the nurse details of their family history.
From The Individuals With Renal Dysfunction Series.
Prod-AJN Dist-AJN

Patient Not In Acute Distress, The - Admission, Care And Discharge C 25 MIN
16MM FILM OPTICAL SOUND PRO
Discusses the team approach to coronary care. Compares treatment of the patient not in acute distress and the patient suffering acute distress.
From The Intensive Coronary Care Multimedia Learning System (ICC/MMLS) Series.
LC NO. 73-701770
Prod-SUTHLA Dist-SUTHLA 1969

Patient Positioning And Preparation Of The Instrument Tray For Clinical Oral Surgery C 7 MIN
3/4 INCH VIDEO CASSETTE
Depicts proper positioning of a patient during oral surgery and demonstrates the handling of sterile forceps in arranging surgical instruments on a tray.
From The Oral Surgery Clinic Routine Series.
LC NO. 79-706763
Prod-MUSC Dist-USNAC

Patient Problems In Emergency Psychiatry C 60 MIN
3/4 OR 1/2 INCH VIDEO CASSETTE PRO
Illustrates common psychiatric disorders seen in emergency settings. Features patients who are: inaccessible, violent, anxious, depressed, and or psychotic. Identifies important symptoms.
Prod-UARIZ Dist-UARIZ

Patient Rights C 30 MIN
3/4 OR 1/2 INCH VIDEO CASSETTE
Presents tips on how a medical patient can protect his rights.
From The Consumer Survival Series. Health
Prod-MDCPB Dist-MDCPB

Patient Rights / Air Fare / OTC Drugs C
3/4 OR 1/2 INCH VIDEO CASSETTE
Presents tips on patient rights, air fare and over-the-counter drugs.
From The Consumer Survival Series.
Prod-MDCPB Dist-MDCPB

Patient Room Cleaning C 17 MIN
16MM FILM - 3/4 IN VIDEO IND
Presents the techniques and equipment used in cleaning the patient's room. Stresses consideration of the patient while working in the room.
From The Housekeeping Personnel Series.
Prod-COPI Dist-COPI 1973

Patient Safety I C 22 MIN
3/4 OR 1/2 INCH VIDEO CASSETTE
Points out hazards and illustrates how to prevent accidental injuries to patients in and around patients' rooms.
Prod-FPF Dist-FPF

Patient Safety II C 14 MIN
3/4 OR 1/2 INCH VIDEO CASSETTE
Teaches nursing staff orderlies and others how to prevent accidental injuries to patients while they are ambulatory, on crutches, using walker and other situations.
Prod-FPF Dist-FPF

Patient With Addictive Behavior, The B 44 MIN
16MM FILM OPTICAL SOUND PRO
Illustrates characteristic behavior of patients who are overdependent on alcohol and drugs. Discusses attendant nursing problems in therapeutic management of these patients.
From The Nursing In Psychiatry Series.
LC NO. 76-703435
Prod-VDONUR Dist-AJN Prodn-WTTWTV 1968

Patient With Malignancy And Hypercalcemia C 60 MIN
3/4 INCH VIDEO CASSETTE
Presents case studies of patients with malignant tumors and hypercalcemia. Discusses diagnosis and treatment of both problems.
Prod-UTAHTI Dist-UTAHTI

Patient With Rheumatoid Arthritis, The C 23 MIN
3/4 OR 1/2 INCH VIDEO CASSETTE PRO
Describes a comprehensive management plan for the patient with rheumatoid arthiritis which includes differential diagnosis and patient education.
Prod-UMICHM Dist-UMICHM 1975

Patient-Operator Positioning In Dental Hygiene C 9 MIN
3/4 INCH VIDEO CASSETTE
Demonstrates positioning for the dental hygienist and patient during dental hygiene procedures.
LC NO. 79-706752
Prod-MUSC Dist-USNAC 1978

Patient, The - Preanesthetic Evaluation (2nd Ed) C 25 MIN
3/4 OR 1/2 INCH VIDEO CASSETTE PRO
Explains the medical and legal importance of conducting a preanesthetic evaluation. Outlines steps for evaluating the patient's preanesthetic condition. Shows how to elicit both individual and family anesthetic history, reviews current medications (especially cardiovascular, corticosteroid and neurologic drugs) for expected interaction with various anesthetic agents and altered physiologic responses. Assesses the patient's physical status (especially cardiovascular, respiratory, airway airway and renal systems). Determines patient's ASA risk classification.
From The Anesthesiology Clerkship Series.
Prod-UMICHM Dist-UMICHM 1982

Patient, The - Preoperative Preparation Choice Of Anesthesia And Premedication (2nd Ed) C 22 MIN
3/4 OR 1/2 INCH VIDEO CASSETTE PRO
Discusses the preoperative cardiovascular and respiratory preparation of the patient for anesthesia. Indentifies factors to be considered in choosing the anesthetic agent and technique. Describes rationale for premedication selection.
From The Anesthesiology Clerkship Series.
Prod-UMICHM Dist-UMICHM 1982

Patient's Guide To CT Scanning, A C
3/4 OR 1/2 INCH VIDEO CASSETTE
Addresses the fears of patients facing their first CT scan and explains the value of this complex technology in lay terms.
Prod-GRANVW Dist-GRANVW

Patient's Point Of View, The B 30 MIN
2 INCH VIDEOTAPE PRO
Helps nursing students understand the importance of the patient's point of view in developing an acceptance of others and in improving their abilities to treat patients.
From The Mental Health Concepts For Nursing, Unit 3 - Acceptance Of Others Series.
LC NO. 73-702643
Prod-GPITVL Dist-GPITVL 1971

Patient's Right To Know The Truth, The C 59 MIN
3/4 INCH VIDEO CASSETTE
Deals with the consent to therapy and access to records of hospitalized competent adult patients.
From The Ethics And Medicine Series.
Prod-OHC Dist-HRC

Patient's With Rheumatic Disorders—A Series

Expands the scope of nursing care through assessment and intervention that will result in greater comfort, self-care and mobility of patients with rheumatic disorders.
Prod-AJN Dist-AJN

Common Patient Problems - Alterations In 046 MIN
An Overview
Common Patient Problems - Alterations In 030 MIN

Patients Are People—A Series
H A
Presents hospital and nursing home procedures, emphasizing the patient's care and comfort.
Prod-DEFREN Dist-MLA 1967

Bathing The Patient 18 MIN
Bed And The Bedside Unit, The 18 MIN
Patient Feeding And Mouth Care 18 MIN
Patient's Excretory Needs, The 18 MIN
To Care Enough 18 MIN
Tpr - Temperature, Pulse And Respiration 18 MIN

Patients At Risk Of Delivering Low Birth Weight Infants (2nd Ed) C 10 MIN
3/4 OR 1/2 INCH VIDEO CASSETTE PRO
Describes how socioeconomic deprivation, obstetric history, maternal age and medical conditions affect the risk of delivering a low birth weight infant. Presents the management measures which minimize this risk.
Prod-UMICHM Dist-UMICHM 1983

Patients With Manipulative And Acting-Out Behaviors B 44 MIN
16MM FILM OPTICAL SOUND PRO
Describes behaviors that charactierize the acting-out patient and discusses some social and theoretical issues surrounding his treatment.
From The Nursing In Psychiatry Series.
LC NO. 70-703436
Prod-VDONUR Dist-AJN Prodn-WTTWTV 1968

Patients Without Doctors C 29 MIN
2 INCH VIDEOTAPE
Examines the grass-roots beginning of a revolution in health care delivery. Includes the townspeople throughout Tennessee banding together to create a new form of medical care for themselves.
From The Turning Points Series.
Prod-WDCNTV Dist-PUBTEL

Patients' Rights And Physician Accountability - Problems With PSRO's C 59 MIN
3/4 INCH VIDEO CASSETTE
Dicusses professional standards review organizations.
From The Ethics And Medicine Series.
Prod-OHC Dist-HRC

Patio Gardening C 30 MIN
1/2 IN VIDEO CASSETTE BETA/VHS
Gives pointers on starting a deck or brick walkway garden in containers.
From The Victory Garden Series.
Prod-WGBHTV Dist-MTI

Patria And Company C 30 MIN
3/4 OR 1/2 INCH VIDEO CASSETTE
See series title for descriptive statement.
From The Que Pasa, U S A Series.
Prod-WPBTTV Dist-MDCPB

Patricia's Moving Picture C 26 MIN
16MM FILM, 3/4 OR 1/2 IN VIDEO A
Focuses on a woman who experienced deep depression when her children began to grow up and her duties as a wife and mother began to shrink. Explains how her husband, her psychiatrist, and a woman's center helped her come to grips with her new life role.
Prod-NFBC Dist-MEDIAG 1980

Patrick C 7 MIN
16MM FILM, 3/4 OR 1/2 IN VIDEO P-I
Presents an animated feature in which Patrick sets out for the town marketplace, searching for a fiddle which he buys from a junkman.
Prod-WWS Dist-WWS 1973

Patrick Henry Of Virginia X 16 MIN
16MM FILM OPTICAL SOUND I-H A
Depicts the life of Patrick Henry from his early struggles, through Williamsburg and the 'GIVE ME LIBERTY OR DEATH' speech, to his days at Red Hill. Narrated in first person.
Prod-VADE Dist-VADE 1948

Patrick Henry's Liberty Or Death C 15 MIN
16MM FILM, 3/4 OR 1/2 IN VIDEO J-C
Features Barry Sullivan.
From The Great American Patriotic Speeches Series.
Prod-EVANSA Dist-AIMS 1973

Patrick Hogan C 28 MIN
3/4 OR 1/2 INCH VIDEO CASSETTE
Presents unusual and evocative wall constructions by California Artist Patrick Hogan.
Prod-NEWHAM Dist-EAI

Patriotic Music - Its Influence On United States History, 1775-1900 C 21 MIN
16MM FILM OPTICAL SOUND I-C A
Tells the story behind the seven most popular patriotic anthems and how they affected the history of the United States.
Prod-DANA Dist-DANA 1974

Patriotism C 10 MIN
16MM FILM, 3/4 OR 1/2 IN VIDEO P-I
Illustrates the meaning of the word patriotism. Features actor Bob Crane, who narrates an exploration of the place of a person in relation to the community.
From The American Values For Elementary Series.
Prod-EVANSA Dist-AIMS 1972

Patriots And Western Pioneers X 30 MIN
2 INCH VIDEOTAPE I
Presents a recounting of the important contributions made by American Negro patriots and pioneers in history, in wartime as soldiers and in the early American West as cattlemen and other important personalities. (Broadcast quality)
From The Cultural Understandings Series. No. 11
Prod-DENVPS Dist-GPITVL Prodn-KRMATV

Patriots, The (German and Russian) B 82 MIN
3/4 OR 1/2 INCH VIDEO CASSETTE
Tells the story of a German prisoner of war who gets a job as a shoemaker in a Russian provincial town in World War I. Directed by B Barnett. Stars Elena Kuzmina and Hans Klering. With English subtitles.
Prod-IHF Dist-IHF

Patrolling Your Health Care Facility C 15 MIN
3/4 OR 1/2 INCH VIDEO CASSETTE
Teaches essential patrol skills and stresses communicating with other hospital employees.
From The Health Care Security Training Series.
Prod-GREESM Dist-MTI

Patron - Piaget In New Perspective C 18 MIN
16MM FILM OPTICAL SOUND
Presents a personal view of child psychologist and educator, Jean Piaget, as seen by friends and colleagues. Shows Piaget lecturing and in private moments.
LC NO. 78-700207
Prod-PARENT Dist-PARENT 1977

Pattern Alteration C 29 MIN
2 INCH VIDEOTAPE
Features Mrs Ruth Hickman demonstrating how to alter a pattern.
From The Sewing Skills - Tailoring Series.
Prod-KRMATV Dist-PUBTEL

Pattern Fixer, The - Word Problems And Repeating Patterns C 14 MIN
3/4 OR 1/2 INCH VIDEO CASSETTE P
Shows that discovering missing elements helps in verbalizing math problems and solution strategies.
From The Math Country Series.
Prod-KYTV Dist-AITECH 1979

Pattern For Change C 32 MIN
16MM FILM OPTICAL SOUND
Illustrates how the institution provides for its permanent members today and how it acts as a catalytic agent to involve community services for the more able retarded.
LC NO. 74-705332
Prod-USBEH Dist-USNAC

Pattern For Change C 33 MIN
16MM FILM OPTICAL SOUND
Presents an overview of the care of the mentally retarded in the United States. Emphasizes historical and institutional out reach programs.
Prod-GWASHU Dist-USOE

Pattern For Instruction (2nd Ed) C 21 MIN
16MM FILM, 3/4 OR 1/2 IN VIDEO IND
Uses actual basketball sequences to illustrate each step of proper job instruction. Shows how a four-step method can be used to teach anything.
Prod-RTBL Dist-RTBL 1982

Pattern For Instruction (2nd Ed) (Danish) C 21 MIN
16MM FILM, 3/4 OR 1/2 IN VIDEO IND
Uses actual basketball sequences to illustrate each step of proper job instruction. Shows how a four-step method can be used to teach anything.
Prod-RTBL Dist-RTBL 1982

Pattern For Instruction (2nd Ed) (Dutch) C 21 MIN
16MM FILM, 3/4 OR 1/2 IN VIDEO IND
Uses actual basketball sequences to illustrate each step of proper job instruction. Shows how a four-step method can be used to teach anything.
Prod-RTBL Dist-RTBL 1982

Pattern For Instruction (2nd Ed) (French) C 21 MIN
16MM FILM, 3/4 OR 1/2 IN VIDEO IND
Uses actual basketball sequences to illustrate each step of proper job instruction. Shows how a four-step method can be used to teach anything.
Prod-RTBL Dist-RTBL 1982

Pattern For Instruction (2nd Ed) (Norwegian) C 21 MIN
16MM FILM, 3/4 OR 1/2 IN VIDEO IND
Uses actual basketball sequences to illustrate each step of proper job instruction. Shows how a four-step method can be used to teach anything.
Prod-RTBL Dist-RTBL 1982

Pattern For Instruction (2nd Ed) (Portuguese) C 21 MIN
16MM FILM, 3/4 OR 1/2 IN VIDEO IND
Uses actual basketball sequences to illustrate each step of proper job instruction. Shows how a four-step method can be used to teach anything.
Prod-RTBL Dist-RTBL 1982

Pattern For Instruction (2nd Ed) (Spanish) C 21 MIN
16MM FILM, 3/4 OR 1/2 IN VIDEO IND
Uses actual basketball sequences to illustrate each step of proper job instruction. Shows how a four-step method can be used to teach anything.
Prod-RTBL Dist-RTBL 1982

Pattern For Instruction (2nd Ed) (Swedish) C 21 MIN
16MM FILM, 3/4 OR 1/2 IN VIDEO IND
Uses actual basketball sequences to illustrate each step of proper job instruction. Shows how a four-step method can be used to teach anything.
Prod-RTBL Dist-RTBL 1982

Pattern Layouts For Plaids C 29 MIN
2 INCH VIDEOTAPE
Features Mrs Ruth Hickman demonstrating how to layout a pattern for plaids.
From The Sewing Skills - Tailoring Series.
Prod-KRMATV Dist-PUBTEL

Pattern Measurements And Alterations C 20 MIN
3/4 OR 1/2 INCH VIDEO CASSETTE C A
Covers taking body measurements, altering bust size, altering pattern hip size, altering pattern sleeve length and circumference, and fitting pants patterns.
From The Clothing Construction Techniques Series.
Prod-IOWASP Dist-IOWASP

Patterned Films - Dry-Plasma Etching, I C 35 MIN
3/4 OR 1/2 INCH VIDEO CASSETTE IND
Outlines dry-plasma etching mechanisms in terms of physical and chemical mechanisms that occur at the surface. Notes how this process allows for tailored etch profiles from the vertical to gently sloped. Includes overview of wet versus dry processes.
From The Plasma Etching And Pattern - For VLSI Fabrication Series.
Prod-COLOSU Dist-COLOSU

Patterned Films - Dry-Plasma Etching, II C 35 MIN
3/4 OR 1/2 INCH VIDEO CASSETTE IND
Describes some commercial plasma equipment used for dry etching, from gas-phased chemical etch of photoresist and parts of a living cell, which are in constant motion as compared silicon nitride in barrel reactors, to the physical etching of silicon dioxide in rare-gas ion beams, and to the chemical plus ion-assisted etching of polysilicon in plasma diode reactors.
From The Plasma Etching And Pattern - For VLSI Fabrication Series.
Prod-COLOSU Dist-COLOSU

Patterned Films - Wet Chemical Etching, I C 35 MIN
3/4 OR 1/2 INCH VIDEO CASSETTE IND
Discusses patterned microelectronic films produced by wet chemical etching and photoresist masking. Talks in terms of selectivity to contiguous films, device damage, etch profiles and minimum feature size.
From The Plasma Etching And Pattern Transfer - For VSLI Fabrication Series.
Prod-COLOSU Dist-COLOSU

Patterned Films - Wet Chemical Etching, II C 35 MIN
3/4 OR 1/2 INCH VIDEO CASSETTE IND
Discusses wet chemical etching in five conceptual stages, including parent reactants in liquid phase, absorption of reactants on the surface, chemical breakdown of reactants at the surface, formation of new soluble products, and the desorption and release of products from the surface into solution.
From The Plasma Etching And Pattern - For VLSI Fabrication Series.
Prod-COLOSU Dist-COLOSU

Patterns C 12 MIN
16MM FILM, 3/4 OR 1/2 IN VIDEO
Illustrates the premise that the infinite variety of forms in nature are based on only a few basic patterns.
From The Many Worlds Of Nature Series.
Prod-MORALL Dist-MTI 1979

Patterns C 15 MIN
3/4 INCH VIDEO CASSETTE P-I
Discusses a variety of methods of creating patterns. Looks at common objects that create patterns and at natural patterns formed by roads, buildings and rivers.
From The Look And A Closer Look Series.
Prod-WCVETV Dist-GPITVL 1976

Patterns C 18 MIN
16MM FILM - 3/4 IN VIDEO I-J
Demonstrates how identifying patterns helps to facilitate the problem solving process in scientific investigation.
From The Search For Solutions Series.
Prod-PLYBCK Dist-KAROL 1979

Patterns - Aids In Generalization B 20 MIN
3/4 INCH VIDEO CASSETTE P
See series title for descriptive statement.
From The Let's Figure It Out Series.
Prod-WNYETV Dist-NYSED 1968

Patterns And Fabrics C 29 MIN
2 INCH VIDEOTAPE
Features Mrs Ruth Hickman demonstrating various patterns and fabrics.
From The Sewing Skills - Tailoring Series.
Prod-KRMATV Dist-PUBTEL

Patterns For Health B 14 MIN
16MM FILM OPTICAL SOUND
Discusses the establishment of early health habits for the pre-school child, and shows how this early training develops patterns found in the well-adjusted adult. Covers general as well as specific health needs of the four-to-five-year-old child.
LC NO. FIE68-138
Prod-USOEO Dist-USNAC Prodn-ACI 1967

Patterns For Survival - A Study Of Mimicry And Protective Coloration In Tropical Insects C 27 MIN
16MM FILM OPTICAL SOUND I-C A
Presents an over-all view of protective coloration in insects. Interprets how the various adaptations have evolved in the context of predators' feeding behavior.
LC NO. 77-709100
Prod-AMHRST Dist-AMHRST 1968

Patterns In Development C 24 MIN
16MM FILM, 3/4 OR 1/2 IN VIDEO
Presents three systems of pattern specification by which cells receive differential spatial signals during development. Shows three different methods for studying the development of pattern specification direct observation, genetic tricks and surgical transplantations.
Prod-OPENU Dist-MEDIAG Prodn-BBCTV 1982

Patterns In Development - Cell Movement C 24 MIN
16MM FILM, 3/4 OR 1/2 IN VIDEO
Describes two aspects of cell movements during morphogenesis - one where cells cooperate to organize themselves to rebuild an organ and another where cells interact during cellular reaggregation. Demonstrates such characteristics of cell development as contact guidance, the recognition of and alignment of cells along underlying patterns of collagen bundles.
Prod-OPENU Dist-MEDIAG Prodn-BBCTV 1982

Patterns In Language C 20 MIN
16MM FILM, 3/4 OR 1/2 IN VIDEO T
Focuses on literacy instruction techniques involving the development of patterning skills to improve reading comprehension. Shows a tutor and a student demonstrating patterns of words, phrases, sentences, and larger units, and their usefulness in improving comprehension.
From The Literacy Instructor Training Series.
LC NO. 80-706061
Prod-IU Dist-IU 1978

Patterns In Multiplication C 15 MIN
3/4 INCH VIDEO CASSETTE I
Explains how to find a multiplication product without using a model or counting.
From The Math - No Mystery Series.
Prod-WCETTV Dist-GPITVL 1977

Patterns In Teacher-Pupil Interaction - Bacteria C 11 MIN
16MM FILM, 3/4 OR 1/2 IN VIDEO T
Shows a high school science class reviewing the forms and uses of bacteria and applying this information to a demonstration of bacterial action.
From The Concepts And Patterns In Teacher-Pupil Interaction Series.
LC NO. 80-706076
Prod-IU Dist-IU 1975

Patterns In Teacher-Pupil Interaction - Ecology C 11 MIN
16MM FILM, 3/4 OR 1/2 IN VIDEO T
Shows a field trip in which a seventh-grade teacher analyzes the problem of environmental pollution with her students. Exemplifies the conceptss of probing and informing and approving and disapproving.
From The Concepts And Patterns In Teacher-Pupil Interaction Series.
LC NO. 80-706073
Prod-IU Dist-IU 1975

Patterns In Teacher-Pupil Interaction - Esentials For Life C 10 MIN
16MM FILM, 3/4 OR 1/2 IN VIDEO T
Shows a seventh-grade class recitation on the basic essentials of life and the discussion that follows. Shows the teacher's behavior in this situation and emphasizes the concepts of reproductive and productive questioning and approving and disapproving.
From The Concepts And Patterns In Teacher-Pupil Interaction Series.
LC NO. 80-706074
Prod-IU Dist-IU 1975

Patterns In Teacher-Pupil Interaction - People Who Help Us C 11 MIN
16MM FILM, 3/4 OR 1/2 IN VIDEO T
Presents a second-grade teacher and her class exploring the topic of community helpers. Shows the teacher's behavior in this situation.
From The Concepts And Patterns In Teacher-Pupil Interaction Series.
LC NO. 80-706071
Prod-IU Dist-IU 1975

Patterns In Teacher-Pupil Interaction - Population Control C 10 MIN
16MM FILM, 3/4 OR 1/2 IN VIDEO T
Shows a high school social studies class as they discuss the problem of population growth and control. Shows the teacher's behavior in this situation and exemplifies probing and informing techniques.
From The Concepts And Patterns In Teacher-Pupil Interaction Series.
LC NO. 80-706075
Prod-IU Dist-IU 1975

Patterns In Teacher-Pupil Interaction - The Five Senses C 12 MIN
16MM FILM, 3/4 OR 1/2 IN VIDEO T
Shows a second-grade teacher as she explores with her class the concept of the five senses. Shows the teacher's behavior in this situation and exemplifies learning concepts.
From The Concepts And Patterns In Teacher-Pupil Interaction Series.
LC NO. 80-706072
Prod-IU Dist-IU 1975

Patterns Of Change C 14 MIN
16MM FILM OPTICAL SOUND
Offers an impressionistic view of the interaction between man and his environment. Depicts seasonal change, elemental forces, growth of life forms and man's modification of the land.
LC NO. 75-700469
Prod-NYSM Dist-NYSM Prodn-THOMPN 1975

Patterns Of Eating Behavior In Infants C 80 MIN
16MM FILM OPTICAL SOUND PRO
Directs attention to the postural adjustments in healthy infants that adapt the mouth for sucking, chewing and biting, and the arms and hands for grasping and lifting. Demonstrates mother-infant interaction showing examples of reinforcement of sensitivity and consistency in social behavior.
Prod-UCLA Dist-UCLA

Patterns Of Pain C 28 MIN
16MM FILM, 3/4 OR 1/2 IN VIDEO
Presents a professor of psychology, a zoologist and a doctor discussing the perception of pain in the nervous system. Deals with such phenomena as the absence of pain perception by the wounded in battle, pain control through hypnosis, acupuncture and yoga, thresholds of pain, the body's ability to produce its own analgesic, and surgical techniques for implanting electrodes in the brain to block the perception of chronic pain.
Prod-CANBC Dist-FLMLIB

Patterns Of Play C 14 MIN
16MM FILM OPTICAL SOUND
Describes the history of tennis, squash, table tennis and badminton.
Prod-GNRLPO Dist-MTP

Patterns Of Slave Resistance C 29 MIN
2 INCH VIDEOTAPE
See series title for descriptive statement.
From The Black Experience Series.
Prod-WTTWTV Dist-PUBTEL

Patterns Of Sound C 13 MIN
16MM FILM OPTICAL SOUND H
Points out that Shakespeare used not only the meaning of words, but also their sounds to express ideas.
Prod-SINGER Dist-SVE 1969

Patterns Of Subcultures C 20 MIN
3/4 INCH VIDEO CASSETTE I
Discusses the different groups of people practicing various cultural traditions in the United States.
From The Exploring Our Nation Series.
Prod-KRMATV Dist-GPITVL 1975

Patterns Of Subsistence - Food-Producers And The Rise Of Civilization C 30 MIN
3/4 INCH VIDEO CASSETTE C A
Covers transition from a hunting-gathering way of life to a food-producing way of life. Suggests some of the factors which lead to this change. Shows examples of cultures following subsistence patterns.
From The Faces Of Culture - Studies In Cultural Anthropology Series. Lesson 5
Prod-COAST Dist-CDTEL Prodn-HRAW

Patterns Of Subsistence - Hunter-Gatherers And Pastoralists C 30 MIN
3/4 INCH VIDEO CASSETTE C A
Reviews the characteristics and environmental setting for two types of subsistence. Presents concepts of adaptation, cultural ecology and culture area.
From The Faces Of Culture - Studies In Cultural Anthropology Series. Lesson 4
Prod-COAST Dist-CDTEL Prodn-HRAW

Patterns Of The Wild C 26 MIN
16MM FILM, 3/4 OR 1/2 IN VIDEO
Shows, through the eyes of a wild fox, that the wildlife of a forest is a part of its structure. Shows what proper wildlife management is doing to make the National Forests more livable for animals and more enjoyable for people.
Prod-USDA Dist-USNAC

Patterns Of Time And Distance C 19 MIN
16MM FILM OPTICAL SOUND J-C A
Shows how time has changed the southern continent of Australia as it sets out the overall pattern of Australia's development from primitive isolation to modern urbanized society. Explains that although once isolated by distance, Australia is today linked by communications and transport into the global society.
LC NO. 73-702484
Prod-FLMAUS Dist-AUIS 1973

Patterns—A Series
3/4 OR 1/2 INCH VIDEO CASSETTE J-C
Uses segments of feature motion pictures to examine issues of individualism, attitude and personal values.
Prod-SF Dist-SF 1977

Anti-Hero, The 020 MIN
Hunters, The 020 MIN
Loser, The 020 MIN
Woman's Touch, A 020 MIN

Patti Page Video Songbook, The B 60 MIN
1/2 IN VIDEO CASSETTE BETA/VHS
Features songs by vocalist Patti Page.
Prod-KARTES Dist-KARTES

Patty Berg - Fairway To Fame B 15 MIN
1/2 IN VIDEO CASSETTE BETA/VHS
Features Patty Berg, one of the all-time great golf players.
Prod-STAR Dist-STAR

Patty Goes To Washington C 30 MIN
16MM FILM OPTICAL SOUND
Shows how Patty and her classmates organize a study of the amount of energy used by home appliances and how energy can be used more efficiently.
Prod-GRAVAR Dist-SUNCO

Patty's Dark Christmas C 40 MIN
16MM FILM OPTICAL SOUND
Relates how a power failure on Christmas Eve forces Santa Claus to make an unexpected personal visit to a family, explain why the lights went out and show the family how to avoid blackouts in the future.
Prod-GRAVAR Dist-SUNCO

Patuxent Wildlife Research Center, The C 20 MIN
16MM FILM, 3/4 OR 1/2 IN VIDEO
Explains the research being conducted at the Patuxent Wildlife Research Center near Laurel, Md, into modern society's impact on wildlife. Reviews their studies on the effects of organic phosphates and the DDT-derivative DDE on life cycles and environment, breeding patterns of endangered species and birds' migratory behavior.
LC NO. 81-707281
Prod-USBSFW Dist-USNAC Prodn-VANINO 1981

Patzcuaro X 11 MIN
16MM FILM OPTICAL SOUND J-C A
Displays architectural highlights of Patzcuaro. Shows the House of the Giant, the Cross of Humility and other famous landmarks. The Dance of Old Men is presented with a background of native music.
Prod-BARONA Dist-AVED 1957

Pauce Droit, Pouce Gauche C 9 MIN
16MM FILM OPTICAL SOUND
A French language version of the motion picture Right Thumb. Tells the story of a young boy who is sent to the store on his own for the first time. Shows how he learns the value of being attentive and following directions. Based on the book Right Thumb - Left Thumb by Osmond Molarsky.
LC NO. 74-703751
Prod-MORLAT Dist-MORLAT 1973

Paul Adams - In The Trenches C 31 MIN
16MM FILM OPTICAL SOUND H-C
Uses some actual newsreel footage to tell the story of the life of Paul Adams, who was killed on Armistice Day, while leading his company in a raid on a German stronghold, unaware of the truce, during World War I.
Prod-WOLPER Dist-FI 1974

Paul Adams - Soldier For Democracy C 22 MIN
16MM FILM OPTICAL SOUND H-C
Tells of a world plunging from peace into catastrophic war and of the political and military leaders who forged the events that would become the destiny of millions including Paul Adams during World War I.
Prod-WOLPER Dist-FI 1974

Paul Bunyan C 11 MIN
16MM FILM, 3/4 OR 1/2 IN VIDEO I-J
Tells the legend of Paul Bunyan through the use of artwork and music.
From The American Folklore Series.
Prod-HRAW Dist-PHENIX Prodn-LUMIN 1970

Paul Bunyan C 17 MIN
16MM FILM, 3/4 OR 1/2 IN VIDEO I-J
Presents the legend of larger-than-life Paul Bunyan and his partner, Babe, an ox, as they cut a wide swath through the woods from Maine to the West.
Prod-DISNEY Dist-WDEMCO 1970

Paul Bunyan - Lumber Camp Tales C 11 MIN
16MM FILM, 3/4 OR 1/2 IN VIDEO P-I
Recounts some of the most famous tall tales of the American folk-hero, Paul Bunyan, such as the bunkhouse beds stacked 137 feet high, the gigantic flapjack riddle, the popcorn blizzard and the straightening of the Big Onion River.
Prod-CORF Dist-CORF 1962

Paul Bunyan And The Blue Ox C 6 MIN
16MM FILM, 3/4 OR 1/2 IN VIDEO K-P
Puppets re-create the story of Paul Bunyan and Babe, the Blue Ox.
Prod-CORF Dist-CORF 1952

Paul Cadmus - Enfant Terrible C 64 MIN
16MM FILM, 3/4 OR 1/2 IN VIDEO
Presents a film portrait of WPA painter Paul Cadmus, in which the artist is both host and subject and in which Cadmus, now eighty, draws from the nude, demonstrates his mastery of ancient painting techniques and recounts his past as a prominent American scene painter and controversial social satirist. Produced by David Sutherland.
Prod-STHLND Dist-STHLND

Paul Cadwell, Mississippi John Hurt C 52 MIN
3/4 OR 1/2 INCH VIDEO CASSETTE
Presents Paul Cadwell playing several banjo solos including a cakewalk. Features Mississippi John Hurt, a singer who faded from public view and was rediscovered in his eighties and began a whole new career.
From The Rainbow Quest Series.
Prod-SEEGER Dist-CWATER

Paul Carlson Story, The C 53 MIN
16MM FILM OPTICAL SOUND
Tells the story of Paul Carlson, a missionary who was slain in the Congo, November 24, 1964.
LC NO. FIA66-515
Prod-ECCA Dist-GF Prodn-JONY

Paul Cezanne B 29 MIN
3/4 INCH VIDEO CASSETTE
Illustrates Cezanne's geometric techniques that led to analytical cubism and earned him the title Father of Modern Art.
From The Meet The Masters Series.
Prod-UMITV Dist-UMITV 1966

Paul Delvaux Dans Son Atelier C 8 MIN
16MM FILM, 3/4 OR 1/2 IN VIDEO
A French language videocassette. Features the painter Paul Delvaux explaining his view of sketches as related to a painting. Comments on the objects he uses in his paintings and tells how these objects are related to his own childhood and memories.
Prod-STORCH Dist-IFB 1978

Paul Delvaux In His Studio C 8 MIN
16MM FILM, 3/4 OR 1/2 IN VIDEO
Shows surrealist painter Paul Delvaux at work while he explains his views on art.
LC NO. 80-706698
Prod-STORCH Dist-IFB 1978

Paul Draper C 52 MIN
3/4 OR 1/2 INCH VIDEO CASSETTE
Features dancer Paul Draper improvising to music played by accompanist Coleridge Perkinson and to several songs and rhythms played by Pete Seeger.
From The Rainbow Quest Series.
Prod-SEEGER Dist-CWATER

Paul Hodge C 30 MIN
3/4 OR 1/2 INCH VIDEO CASSETTE A
Presents bridge master Paul Hodge discussing bidding, dummy play and defensive problems.
From The Play Bridge With The Experts Series. Pt 5
Prod-KUHTTV Dist-GPITVL 1980

Paul Hornung C 20 MIN
16MM FILM OPTICAL SOUND I-J
Interviews Paul Hornung. Presents some action-filled segments of Paul's career at Notre Dame and with the champion Green Bay Packers. Discusses the difficulties and pleasures of being a recognizable athlete and sports commentator.
From The Sports Legends Series.
Prod-COUNFI Dist-COUNFI

Paul J Flory C 40 MIN
3/4 OR 1/2 INCH VIDEO CASSETTE
Reviews the experiences of Dr Paul J Flory in polymer research and his perspectives on research gained from his industrial experiences.
From The Eminent Chemists - The Interviews Series.
Prod-AMCHEM Dist-AMCHEM 1982

Paul Jacobs And The Nuclear Gang C 60 MIN
16MM FILM OPTICAL SOUND
Documents the effects on health of atomic testing in Utah and Nevada.
Prod-PSR Dist-PSR

Paul Jacobs And The Nuclear Gang C 58 MIN
16MM FILM, 3/4 OR 1/2 IN VIDEO
Tells how reporter Paul Jacobs began investigating the health effects of exposure to low-level radiation on soldiers and civilians present at the atomic bomb tests in Nevada.
Prod-CNDOC Dist-NEWTIM 1979

Paul Jacobs And The Nuclear Gang (German) C 58 MIN
16MM FILM, 3/4 OR 1/2 IN VIDEO
Tells how reporter Paul Jacobs began investigating the health effects of exposure to low-level radiation on soldiers and civilians present at the atomic bomb tests in Nevada.
Prod-CNDOC Dist-NEWTIM 1979

Paul Kane Goes West C 16 MIN
16MM FILM, 3/4 OR 1/2 IN VIDEO I-H
Follows 19th century Canadian artist Paul Kane as he creates visual impressions of the Indian life and customs of the North American continent.
Prod-NFBC Dist-EBEC 1974

Paul Klee B 29 MIN
3/4 INCH VIDEO CASSETTE
Shows how Paul Klee's ideas have been copied by commercial artists and discusses his unique use of line, light and humor. Explores his contribution to the modern art world.
From The Meet The Masters Series.
Prod-UMITV Dist-UMITV 1966

Paul Klee - Child Of Creation C 8 MIN
16MM FILM, 3/4 OR 1/2 IN VIDEO P-H
Presents an introduction to Paul Klee. Points out the message which Paul Klee conveys to the student of the arts of any age—having the courage to be simple. Includes quotations of Paul Klee, candid commentary by children and contrasts the works of the artist with those of the children.
Prod-KINGSP Dist-PHENIX 1970

Paul Klee Or The Act Of Creation 1879-1940 C 25 MIN
16MM FILM OPTICAL SOUND
Examines the representative works of the artist Paul Klee which illustrate the general theme of creation of forms.
Prod-FILIM Dist-RADIM

Paul Kos - Battle Mountain B 24 MIN
3/4 OR 1/2 INCH VIDEO CASSETTE
Blurs fact and fiction.
Prod-ARTINC Dist-ARTINC

Paul Kos - Deposit C 6 MIN
3/4 OR 1/2 INCH VIDEO CASSETTE
Features Marlene Kos.
Prod-ARTINC Dist-ARTINC

Paul Kos - Search Olga-Gold B 19 MIN
3/4 OR 1/2 INCH VIDEO CASSETTE
Transforms Olga' into gold,' repeating the fact-fiction of Olga's disappearance.
Prod-ARTINC Dist-ARTINC

Paul Laurence Dunbar C 22 MIN
16MM FILM, 3/4 OR 1/2 IN VIDEO J-C A
Presents a visit to the home of America's first black poet, Paul Laurence Dunbar. Portrays his childhood as one of the first generation of blacks to be born free in the U S. Includes close-ups of first editions, a pen, spectacles and a ride in the elevator in which he first worked.
Prod-PFP Dist-PFP 1973

Paul Laurence Dunbar - American Poet C 14 MIN
16MM FILM, 3/4 OR 1/2 IN VIDEO A
Portrays the life of American poet Paul Dunbar, a Negro whose poems reflect pride in his race and heritage. Relates his struggles from age 13, when his father, an escaped slave who fought in the Civil War, died, to his time of world-wide fame.
Prod-VIGNET Dist-PHENIX 1966

Paul Masson C 12 MIN
16MM FILM OPTICAL SOUND
Shows the winemaking process at the Paul Masson vineyards in California. Touches on the life of Paul Masson, who brought the winemaking tradition to America over 100 years ago.
LC NO. 76-703151
Prod-FURMAN Dist-FURMAN 1976

Paul Newman - Actor In A Hurry B 26 MIN
16MM FILM OPTICAL SOUND
Describes the personality and the acting career of Paul Newman. Includes scenes from some of his films.
From The Hollywood And The Stars Series.
LC NO. FI68-216
Prod-WOLPER Dist-WOLPER 1964

Paul R Ehrlich, Biology C 29 MIN
3/4 OR 1/2 INCH VIDEO CASSETTE A
See series title for descriptive statement.
From The Quest For Peace Series.
Prod-AACD Dist-AACD 1984

Paul Revere C 24 MIN
16MM FILM, 3/4 OR 1/2 IN VIDEO P-J
Presents an animated reconstruction of the life of Paul Revere with Mr Magoo in the role of the American patriot.
Prod-UPAPOA Dist-MCFI 1976

Paul Revere's Ride B 11 MIN
16MM FILM OPTICAL SOUND I-C A
The story of Paul Revere's famous ride is told with sketches by Bernard Garbutt, and narration which includes the vocabulary of colonial New England.
Prod-JHP Dist-MLA 1955

Paul Revere's Ride C 10 MIN
16MM FILM, 3/4 OR 1/2 IN VIDEO I-H
Gives a reading and visualization of Henry Wadsworth Longfellow's poem Paul Revere's Ride. Describes the circumstances surrounding the British march and Revere's ride to clarify the action in the poem.
Prod-FA Dist-PHENIX 1964

Paul Revere's Ride C 15 MIN
16MM FILM, 3/4 OR 1/2 IN VIDEO P
Describes the ride of Paul Revere.
From The Magic Carpet Series.
Prod-SDCSS Dist-GPITVL 1977

Paul Revere's Ride C 22 MIN
16MM FILM, 3/4 OR 1/2 IN VIDEO I-H
Simulates on-the-spot interviews by CBS correspondents with Patriot and Tory leaders that reveal the conflicts and immediate events leading to the American Revolution. Discusses the role of Paul Revere and his ride to warn the Patriots of the arrival of the British soldiers.
From The You Are There Series.
Prod-CBSNEW Dist-PHENIX 1971

Paul Robeson - The Tallest Tree In Our Forest C 90 MIN
16MM FILM, 3/4 OR 1/2 IN VIDEO H-C A
Features the contributions of Paul Robeson, scholar, actor, singer and humanitarian. Includes footage on Mr Robeson's career gathered from the Paul Robeson archives and other sources throughout the world.
Prod-NOBLEG Dist-PHENIX

Paul Robeson - Tribute To An Artist C 29 MIN
16MM FILM, 3/4 OR 1/2 IN VIDEO H-C A
Offers a tribute to Paul Robeson, describing his accomplishments in the theater, the concert stage, and the movie studio.
Prod-JANUS Dist-FI 1980

Paul Taylor C 60 MIN
3/4 OR 1/2 INCH VIDEO CASSETTE H-C A
Presents the Paul Taylor Dance Company performing Esplanade, set to the music of Bach's E Major and D Minor Violin Concertos and Runes, a Druidic-inspired dance of mystery and imagination.
From The Dance In America Series.
Prod-WNETTV Dist-FI

Paul Taylor And Company - An Artist And His Work C 32 MIN
16MM FILM, 3/4 OR 1/2 IN VIDEO
Documents the Paul Taylor modern dance company.
Prod-HARCOM Dist-PFP 1968

Paul Tillich B 30 MIN
16MM FILM OPTICAL SOUND H-C A
Presents Paul Tillich, Protestant theologian and authority on religious philosophy, explaining his concept of Ultimate Concern, or concern about the meaning of one's life. Develops his distinction between faith and belief.
From The Sum And Substance Series.
LC NO. FIA67-5104
Prod-USC Dist-MLA 1964

Paul Tomkowicz, Street-Railway Switchman B 10 MIN
16MM FILM, 3/4 OR 1/2 IN VIDEO H-C A
Presents a Polish-born Canadian in the streets of Winnipeg as he sweeps the tracks of mud and snow. Talks about his work and the retirement he is looking forward to after 23 years on the job.
Prod-NFBC Dist-NFBC 1953

Paul's Case C 55 MIN
16MM FILM, 3/4 OR 1/2 IN VIDEO J-C A
Tells the story of a romantic young man who drops out of high school in turn-of-the-century Pittsburgh and journeys to New York City. Based on the short story Paul's Case by Willa Cather.
From The American Short Story Series.
LC NO. 80-706661
Prod-LEARIF Dist-CORF 1979

Paul's Case (Spanish) C 55 MIN
16MM FILM, 3/4 OR 1/2 IN VIDEO J-C
Presents an adaptation of Willa Cather's short story Paul's Case. Tells about a romantic young man who drops out of high school in turn-of-the-century Pittsburgh and journeys to New York City.
From The American Short Story Series.
Prod-LEARIF Dist-CORF 1980

Paula Modersohn-Becker (1876 - 1907) C 15 MIN
16MM FILM OPTICAL SOUND
Presents the work of Paula Modersohn-Becker who spent much of her life painting the black canals, brown fields and crisp fir trees of her native North Germany.
Prod-ROLAND Dist-ROLAND

Pauline - Water - Cracker C 5 MIN
16MM FILM OPTICAL SOUND
Uses experimental techniques to show a phone ringing, a woman standing naked in a hallway and a whistling kettle on a stove.
LC NO. 77-702605
Prod-LOCKK Dist-CANFDC 1976

Pause B 7 MIN
16MM FILM OPTICAL SOUND
Presents a fable-documentary on street people.
LC NO. 76-703851
Prod-SFRASU Dist-SFRASU 1976

Pavarotti At Juilliard C 28 MIN
16MM FILM OPTICAL SOUND
Shows operatic tenor Luciano Pavarotti working in a class at Juilliard School with a group of gifted young singers, sharing his musical expertise in a critique and demonstration of Italian operatic arias.

LC NO. 80-700439
Prod-KROLL Dist-KROLL 1980

Pavarotti At Juilliard C 168 MIN
16MM FILM, 3/4 OR 1/2 IN VIDEO J-C A
Presents famed master of operatic repertory, Luciano Pavarotti as he shares his expertise with a group of talented young singers at the Juilliard School in New York.
Prod-KROLL Dist-PHENIX 1980

Pavarotti At Juilliard, Pt 1 C 30 MIN
16MM FILM, 3/4 OR 1/2 IN VIDEO
Shows Luciano Pavarotti, the world's leading operatic tenor, working in a class situation at the Juilliard School with a group of gifted young singers, sharing his musical expertise in a critique and demonstration of Italian operatic arias and responding to questions from the audience.
Prod-KROLL Dist-PHENIX 1980

Pavarotti At Juilliard, Pt 2 C 30 MIN
16MM FILM, 3/4 OR 1/2 IN VIDEO
Shows Luciano Pavarotti, the world's leading operatic tenor, working in a class situation at the Juilliard School with a group of gifted young singers, sharing his musical expertise in a critique and demonstration of Italian operatic arias and responding to questions from the audience.
Prod-KROLL Dist-PHENIX 1980

Pavarotti At Juilliard, Pt 3 C 30 MIN
16MM FILM, 3/4 OR 1/2 IN VIDEO
Shows Luciano Pavarotti, the world's leading operatic tenor, working in a class situation at the Juilliard School with a group of gifted young singers, sharing his musical expertise in a critique and demonstration of Italian operatic arias and responding to questions from the audience.
Prod-KROLL Dist-PHENIX 1980

Pavarotti At Juilliard, Pt 4 C 30 MIN
16MM FILM, 3/4 OR 1/2 IN VIDEO
Shows Luciano Pavarotti, the world's leading operatic tenor, working in a class situation at the Juilliard School with a group of gifted young singers, sharing his musical expertise in a critique and demonstration of Italian operatic arias and responding to questions from the audience.
Prod-KROLL Dist-PHENIX 1980

Pavarotti At Juilliard, Pt 5 C 30 MIN
16MM FILM, 3/4 OR 1/2 IN VIDEO
Shows Luciano Pavarotti, the world's leading operatic tenor, working in a class situation at the Juilliard School with a group of gifted young singers, sharing his musical expertise in a critique and demonstration of Italian operatic arias and responding to questions from the audience.
Prod-KROLL Dist-PHENIX 1980

Pavarotti At Juilliard, Pt 6 C 30 MIN
16MM FILM, 3/4 OR 1/2 IN VIDEO
Shows Luciano Pavarotti, the world's leading operatic tenor, working in a class situation at the Juilliard School with a group of gifted young singers, sharing his musical expertise in a critique and demonstration of Italian operatic arias and responding to questions from the audience.
Prod-KROLL Dist-PHENIX 1980

Pave It And Paint It Green X 27 MIN
16MM FILM, 3/4 OR 1/2 IN VIDEO H-C A
A documentary film without narration which shows the effect of tourist overpopulation at Yosemite National Park and portrays how society's insistence on physical comfort, convenience and luxury deprives the people of real enjoyment of natural surroundings.
Prod-PARTDG Dist-UCEMC 1970

Pavement C 9 MIN
16MM FILM, 3/4 OR 1/2 IN VIDEO A
Describes, without narration, the characteristics, textures, patterns and use of pavement. Includes scenes of rain glistening on pavement, children rollerskating on it, pennies stuck in it and flowers growing through it.
Prod-GOLLIN Dist-PHENIX 1972

Pavement Analysis And Design—A Series
C A
Covers methods and comparative analyses of structural and other performance capabilities of flexible and rigid pavements. Contains 40 one-hour videotape lectures.
Prod-UIDEEO Dist-UIDEEO

Pavement Design—A Series
PRO
Covers in classroom format a series of one-hour and one 1 1/2-hour lectures each week for 13 weeks on 39 video- tapes. Discusses properties of pavement components, earthwork, design of flexible pavements and rigid pavements, pavement evaluation and strengthening, and testing of materials.
Prod-USCCE Dist-AMCEE

Pavement Systems Definitions B 60 MIN
3/4 OR 1/2 INCH VIDEO CASSETTE
See series title for descriptive statement.
From The Bases For Several Pavement Design Methods Series. Pt 1
Prod-UAZMIC Dist-UAZMIC 1977

Pavlov - The Conditioned Reflex B 25 MIN
16MM FILM, 3/4 OR 1/2 IN VIDEO H-C A
English version of the Russian film Academician Pavlov. Depicts Ivan Pavlov in his Leningrad research center. Uses documentary footage to recreate the salivating dog experiment which led the physiologist to the concept of the conditioned reflex. Features Pavlov who speaks about the need for objectivity in scientific experimentation and the application of conditioned reflex methods to the problems of neurology and psychiatry.
Prod-MANTLH Dist-FOTH 1975

Pavlov's Experiment - The Conditioned Reflex C 9 MIN
16MM FILM, 3/4 OR 1/2 IN VIDEO H-C
Uses a live dog in a laboratory in a re-creation of the famous experiment of Ivan Pavlov which shows the relationship between a particular stimulus and response.
Prod-CORF Dist-CORF 1976

Pawnee - Men Of Men B 30 MIN
16MM FILM OPTICAL SOUND H-C A
Tells the story of the oldest of Nebraska tribes, the Pawnee, friend of the white man and his scout against hostile Indians. Describes how the Pawnees lived, hunted and farmed.
From The Great Plains Trilogy, 2 Series. Nomad And Indians - Early Man On The Plains
Prod-UNL Dist-UNEBR 1954

Pawnee Pronghorn C 15 MIN
16MM FILM OPTICAL SOUND
Discusses the research conducted on pronghorn antelope as a component of the grassland ecosystem studies. Shows how the pronghorn were captured and studied and discusses various aspects of the study and some of the findings.
LC NO. 74-702682
Prod-NREL Dist-OPCOMM 1974

Pay As You Go - Social Security C 20 MIN
3/4 INCH VIDEO CASSETTE J-H
Gives a brief history of the Social Security Act to show why social security is compulsory.
From The Dollar Data Series.
LC NO. 81-707385
Prod-WHROTV Dist-GPITVL 1974

Pay Attention - Problems Of Hard Of Hearing Children B 29 MIN
16MM FILM OPTICAL SOUND C T
Shows the problems of the child who is hard of hearing but not deaf and tells how parents and teachers help. Stresses understanding the problem, early treatment, and use of 'CONTEXT' methods of speech reading.
From The Studies Of Normal Personality Development Series.
Prod-NYU Dist-NYU 1949

Pay For Performance C 30 MIN
16MM FILM - 3/4 IN VIDEO IND
Answers the question, how do you avoid negative effects of poorly understood pay policies. Describes the method of goal-setting, which is rapidly replacing traditional performance appraisal programs as one of improving performance.
From The Effective Organization Series.
Prod-BNA Dist-BNA 1971

Pay Or Die B 111 MIN
16MM FILM OPTICAL SOUND C A
Presents a drama based on the chilling, factual incidents in the life of a New York detective who has uncovered the roots of the Mafia of 1908. Shows that he risks everything he holds dear in his relentless pursuit of the vicious brotherhood who prey on their fellow Italians.
Prod-CINEWO Dist-CINEWO 1960

Pay To The Order Of... C 20 MIN
3/4 INCH VIDEO CASSETTE J-H
Considers the vital role commercial banks play in an individual's or a community's life.
From The Dollar Data Series.
LC NO. 81-707388
Prod-WHROTV Dist-GPITVL 1974

Pay-Off, The C 27 MIN
3/4 OR 1/2 INCH VIDEO CASSETTE J-H
Reveals a reading pattern which can be applied to any type of reading.
From The Speed Learning Series.
Prod-LEARNI Dist-AITECH 1982

Pay-Off, The C 30 MIN
3/4 OR 1/2 INCH VIDEO CASSETTE
Demonstrates the combination of all seven skills needed in reading. Presents a complete review of reading skills presented in the eight preceding programs.
From The Speed Learning Video Series. Show 9
Prod-LEARNI Dist-LEARNI

Paycheck Power C 16 MIN
16MM FILM, 3/4 OR 1/2 IN VIDEO J-C A
Defines Paycheck Power as the ability to control your money in a precise, controlled manner, thus establishing the basis for a successful and secure life. Details a step-by-step approach to building paycheck power from an understanding of the use of money, to constructing budgets, to avoiding credit traps, to preparing for the future, as well as providing a whole new series of tips on how to spend wisely and enhance income.
Prod-JOU Dist-JOU 1981

Payday C 19 MIN
16MM FILM OPTICAL SOUND
Describes the computerized payroll system. Follows payroll through Chemical Bank's processing cycles, showing typical clients at critical points for testimonials.
LC NO. 80-701482
Prod-CHMBNK Dist-CHMBNK Prodn-SGWRKS 1979

Paying For Programs C 15 MIN
3/4 OR 1/2 INCH VIDEO CASSETTE J-H
Examines some of the decisions advertisers make when scheduling an advertisement on a broadcast station.
From The Broadcasting Series.
Prod-CTI Dist-CTI

Paying It Back C 15 MIN
3/4 OR 1/2 INCH VIDEO CASSETTE
Portrays the plight of a recent college graduate faced with the upcoming need to begin repaying his student loans. Provides loan repayment information.
Prod-UCEMC Dist-UCEMC

Payoff In The Pacific, Pt 1 B 30 MIN
16MM FILM, 3/4 OR 1/2 IN VIDEO
Surveys World War II from Pearl Harbor and the loss of the Philippines to the early victories in the South Pacific. Describes the B-29 bases constructed on Saipan.
From The Big Pictures Series.
Prod-USA Dist-USNAC 1960

Payoff In The Pacific, Pt 2 B 29 MIN
16MM FILM, 3/4 OR 1/2 IN VIDEO
Documents the war in the Pacific. Covers the island hopping victories of the Allies to the Japanese surrender aboard the battleship Missouri.
From The Big Pictures Series.
Prod-USA Dist-USNAC 1960

Payoff, The C 26 MIN
3/4 OR 1/2 INCH VIDEO CASSETTE
See series title for descriptive statement.
From The Art Of Reading/Speed Learning Series.
Prod-LEARNI Dist-DELTAK

Pays Francophones—A Series
16MM FILM, 3/4 OR 1/2 IN VIDEO H-C
A French language motion picture series. Provides an introduction to the countries, people and customs of France and four other French-speaking countries.
Prod-EBEC Dist-EBEC

Aux Quatre Coins De France	11 MIN
Quebec, La Belle Province	11 MIN
Une Lettre De Suisse	10 MIN
Une Recette D'Abidjan	11 MIN
Visitons La Belgique	11 MIN

PCP C 20 MIN
16MM FILM, 3/4 OR 1/2 IN VIDEO J-C A
Explains the chemical makeup of PCP and follows the activities of a PCP pusher.
Prod-NEWDON Dist-PHENIX 1981

PCP - You Never Know C 15 MIN
16MM FILM, 3/4 OR 1/2 IN VIDEO I-C
Presents information on PCP, known as 'angel dust', 'Sherman' and 'crystal' and reveals the unique dangers of this drug.
LC NO. 82-706544
Prod-CF Dist-CF 1979

PCP Labs, FS-64 C 60 MIN
3/4 OR 1/2 INCH VIDEO CASSETTE PRO
Shows how to recognize a PCP lab and become alert to chemical hazards of ethers and other noxious chemicals. Includes a look at victims of chemical explosions.
Prod-LACFD Dist-FILCOM

PCP Story, The C 25 MIN
16MM FILM OPTICAL SOUND
Presents an overview of the physiological and psychological effects of the drug phencyclidine and its dangers.
Prod-ARTCOP Dist-ARTCOP 1976

PDQ Bach C 58 MIN
3/4 OR 1/2 INCH VIDEO CASSETTE
See series title for descriptive statement.
From The Evening At Pops Series.
Prod-WGBHTV Dist-PBS 1978

Peace C 2 MIN
16MM FILM OPTICAL SOUND I-H A R
Creates a mood for discussion, thought, prayer or meditation on the subject of peace.
From The Meditation Series.
LC NO. 80-700745
Prod-IKONOG Dist-IKONOG 1975

Peace - A Conscious Choice C 4 MIN
16MM FILM, 3/4 OR 1/2 IN VIDEO I-C A
Presents a Russian and an American verbalizing their fear of war between their two nations.
LC NO. 82-707100
Prod-FADMND Dist-BULFRG 1982

Peace Child C 30 MIN
16MM FILM OPTICAL SOUND R
Documents the reaction of today's Stone Age people to the message of the Gospel.
Prod-GF Dist-GF

Peace Corps C 28 MIN
16MM FILM OPTICAL SOUND
Gives a broad picture of Peace Corps activities in Asia, Africa and Latin America.
Prod-USPC Dist-AFLCIO 1962

Peace Corps In Tanganyika, The C 55 MIN
16MM FILM OPTICAL SOUND
Follows the first group of 35 volunteers through their training period in Texas and Puerto Rico to their assignment in East Africa where they were to build roads in the newly independent country of Tanganyika.
Prod-NBCTV Dist-AFLCIO 1961

Peace Corps Partnership Program C 18 MIN
16MM FILM OPTICAL SOUND
Demonstrates how the Peace Corp combines financial assistance and cultural exchange to enable people in foreign countries to meet basic needs with limited resources.
Prod-ACTON Dist-MTP

Peace Corps To Go C 68 MIN
16MM FILM OPTICAL SOUND
Depicts different situations which involve Peace Corps staff and volunteers, including a staff meeting, individual staff-volunteer confrontations, staff site visits, volunteers on the job, meetings

with host country officials and the wedding ceremony of a Peace Corps couple.
LC NO. 75-700872
Prod-USPC Dist-USNAC 1968

Peace Fund B 30 MIN
3/4 OR 1/2 INCH VIDEO CASSETTE
Documents Soviet workers contributing to the fund which helps victims of earthquakes, floods and U S bombing raids in North Vietnam.
Prod-IHF Dist-IHF

Peace Is At Hand C 60 MIN
3/4 OR 1/2 INCH VIDEO CASSETTE H-C A
Recalls that from 1968 to 1973, Richard Nixon and Henry Kissinger worked to end the war, preferably with a victory through increased bombing, but end it any way necessary. Shows that Vietnamization continued, prisoners of war exchanged and the spirit of detente with Russia and China helped lead to a sort of peace.
From The Vietnam - A Television History Series. Episode 10
Prod-WGBHTV Dist-FI 1983

Peace Is Our Profession C 20 MIN
16MM FILM, 3/4 OR 1/2 IN VIDEO J-H A
Presents the daily life of Officer Bryan--his home, his family, his involvement in different cases and situations.
Prod-DAVP Dist-AIMS

Peace Of Mind A Green Place Gives Me C 28 MIN
16MM FILM OPTICAL SOUND H-C A
Presents Mike Ondik, deer pen supervisor at a whitetail deer research farm at the Pennsylvania State University, explaining the facets of deer research. Made in 1972.
LC NO. 76-703302
Prod-WPSXTV Dist-PSU 1976

Peaceful Ones C 12 MIN
16MM FILM OPTICAL SOUND I-J
Shows life and customs of the Hopi in the Painted Desert. Includes cultivating the land, harvesting crops, weaving, kachinas and snake dance.
Prod-DAGP Dist-MLA 1953

Peacemaker C 7 MIN
16MM FILM OPTICAL SOUND
Presents the subject of fear and mistrust of peace and nonviolence with an allegory about a medieval knight who spares the life of a young challenger, an act of peace the young man cannot understand.
LC NO. 75-703526
Prod-FRACOC Dist-FRACOC 1974

Peacock, The - A Sculpture In Watermelon C 7 MIN
3/4 OR 1/2 INCH VIDEO CASSETTE PRO
Shows how to make a peacock from a watermelon and how to prepare the strawberries, melon balls and pineapple fans which decorate the body of the centerpiece.
Prod-CULINA Dist-CULINA

Peak Harvest C 30 MIN
1/2 IN VIDEO CASSETTE BETA/VHS
Introduces two semi-finalists in The Fifth Annual Victory Garden Contest. Presents a Greek tomato salad. Features a vegetable harvest at its peak.
From The Victory Garden Series.
Prod-WGBHTV Dist-MTI

Peak Performance C
1/2 IN VIDEO CASSETTE BETA/VHS
Presents Dr Charles A Garfield's instruction in the skills necessary to become a high achiever.
Prod-KARTES Dist-KARTES

Peano Axioms - The Natural Numbers C 45 MIN
2 INCH VIDEOTAPE
See series title for descriptive statement.
From The Fundamentals Of Mathematics (2nd Ed,) Unit I - Number Theory Series.
Prod-CHITVC Dist-GPITVL

Peanut Butter C 5 MIN
16MM FILM, 3/4 OR 1/2 IN VIDEO K-C A
See series title for descriptive statement.
From The How It's Made Series.
Prod-HOLIA Dist-LUF

Peanut News And Views C 15 MIN
16MM FILM OPTICAL SOUND
Shows where and how peanuts are grown and harvested, lists their varied uses and discusses their nutritional value.
Prod-ELANCO Dist-MTP

Peanut The Pinto Horse C 15 MIN
16MM FILM, 3/4 OR 1/2 IN VIDEO P-J
Documents the first five months of the life of a show horse and shows her emerging victorious in her first competition.
LC NO. 83-706709
Prod-BERLET Dist-IFB 1983

Peanuts - And The Peanut Butter Plant C 10 MIN
16MM FILM, 3/4 OR 1/2 IN VIDEO I-J
Describes the economic importance of the peanut plant and illustrates non-food uses of peanuts.
Prod-CENTRO Dist-CORF

Peanuts To The Presidency C 30 MIN
3/4 OR 1/2 INCH VIDEO CASSETTE J-C A
A shortened version of the motion picture Peanuts To The Presidency. Follows Jimmy Carter's campaign for the Presidency from its inception through the cross-country campaigning, the primaries, the Democratic Convention and the election itself.
Prod-BRAMAN Dist-PFP

Peanuts To The Presidency C 75 MIN
16MM FILM, 3/4 OR 1/2 IN VIDEO J-C A
Follows Jimmy Carter's campaign for the Presidency from its inception through the cross-country campaigning, the primaries, the Democratic Convention and the election itself.
Prod-BRAMAN Dist-PFP 1978

Pearl Bailey C 58 MIN
3/4 OR 1/2 INCH VIDEO CASSETTE
See series title for descriptive statement.
From The Evening At Pops Series.
Prod-WGBHTV Dist-PBS 1978

Pearl Buck - The Woman, The Word And Two Good Earths C 25 MIN
16MM FILM OPTICAL SOUND
Discusses the life and works of novelist Pearl Buck. Features a tour of her farm in Bucks County, Pennsylvania.
From The American Lifestyle - Cultural Leaders Series.
LC NO. 78-700208
Prod-COMCO Dist-COMCO 1978

Pearl Buck - The Woman, The Words And Two Good Earths C 23 MIN
16MM FILM, 3/4 OR 1/2 IN VIDEO J-C A
Provides a tour of Green Hills, home of Nobel Prize winner Pearl Buck.
From The American Lifestyle - Cultural Leaders Series.
LC NO. 84-706110
Prod-COMCO Dist-AIMS 1984

Pearl Harbor To Hiroshima C 20 MIN
16MM FILM, 3/4 OR 1/2 IN VIDEO H-C A
Traces the economic, political, and military background of Japan from the 1930's to the attack on Pearl Harbor.
From The Twentieth Century History Series.
Prod-BBCTV Dist-FI 1981

Pearl Of The Orient C 20 MIN
16MM FILM OPTICAL SOUND
Presents Penang as home to a medley of cultures primarily based on Asia's three great civilizations, Chinese, Indian and Malay. Shows the unique Snake Temple, the third largest statue in the world of a reclining Buddha, the Kek Lok Si Pagoda, the rice fields and rubber estates and how batik making is done.
Prod-FILEM Dist-PMFMUN 1973

Pearls In The Alphabet Soup C 30 MIN
16MM FILM, 3/4 OR 1/2 IN VIDEO C A
Presents a variety of program models which can be adapted to the educational needs of gifted students at primary and secondary levels. Shows alternatives such as gifted students in a congregated class, or in the framework of the regular classroom, or partial-withdrawal classes, and at high school level, enriched classes and mentor programs.
Prod-PLAYTM Dist-BCNFL

Pearls In The North C 14 MIN
16MM FILM OPTICAL SOUND J-C A
Shows the revival of the pearling industry and the operation of a cultured pearl farm on Australia's north-west coast.
LC NO. 73-702258
Prod-ANAIB Dist-AUIS 1972

Pearls--A Series
H-C A
Explores the history and culture of Americans of Asian descent.
Prod-EDFCEN Dist-GPITVL 1979

Emi	30 MIN
Fujikawa	30 MIN
Gin And Don	30 MIN
Mako	30 MIN
Ourselves	30 MIN
Pinoy	30 MIN

Peary's Race For The North Pole C 53 MIN
16MM FILM OPTICAL SOUND J-C A
Describes Commander Robert Peary's discovery of the North Pole. Narrated by Lorne Greene.
Prod-WOLPER Dist-FI 1974

Peas And Spinach C 29 MIN
3/4 OR 1/2 INCH VIDEO CASSETTE
See series title for descriptive statement.
From The Crockett's Victory Garden Series.
Prod-WGBHTV Dist-KINGFT

Peasant Ecology In The Rural Phillippines C 26 MIN
16MM FILM OPTICAL SOUND C
Illustrates the complexity of relationships between culture patterns, physical environment and limited technology in the rural Philippines.
LC NO. 74-702799
Prod-PSUPCR Dist-PSUPCR 1971

Peasant's Pea Patch, The C 8 MIN
3/4 INCH VIDEO CASSETTE P
Tells of the misadventures of a Russian peasant trying in vain to protect his pea patch from a flock of hungry cranes.
From The Desire To Read Series.
Prod-BOSUST Dist-GA

Peck's Bad Boy B 51 MIN
16MM FILM SILENT
Introduces a young boy who is the nemesis of grocers, parsons, dogcatchers and, most especially, his own parents. Stars Jackie Coogan and Raymond Hatton. Directed by Sam Wood.
Prod-UNKNWN Dist-KILLIS 1921

Pecos C 12 MIN
16MM FILM, 3/4 OR 1/2 IN VIDEO J A
Portrays the history of the Pecos National Monument in New Mexico from the first nomadic peoples, to the building of Indian pueblos, to the Spanish Conquistadors. Includes vintage photos, original illustrations and costumed reenactments. Available in Spanish language version narrated by Ricardo Montalban.
Prod-USNPS Dist-USNAC 1984

Pecos (Spanish) C 12 MIN
16MM FILM, 3/4 OR 1/2 IN VIDEO J A
Portrays the history of the Pecos National Monument in New Mexico from the first nomadic peoples to the building of Indian pueblos and the coming of the Spanish Conquistadors. Includes vintage photos, original illustrations and costumed reenactments. Available in Spanish language version narrated by Ricardo Montalb
Prod-USNPS Dist-USNAC 1984

Pecos - Una Promesa C 16 MIN
16MM FILM - 3/4 IN VIDEO
Explains how an annual festival Mass has been held for 350 years at the ruin of a Spanish mission church at Pecos National Monument in New Mexico. Tells how Indians, Spanish-Americans and visitors to the Southwest United States still meet to celebrate this special Catholic Mass. Issued in 1973 as a motion picture.
LC NO. 79-706150
Prod-USNPS Dist-USNAC 1979

Pecos Bill C 11 MIN
16MM FILM, 3/4 OR 1/2 IN VIDEO I-J
Tells the story of Pecos Bill, an American folk character, through the use of artwork and original music.
From The American Folklore Series.
Prod-HRAW Dist-PHENIX Prodn-LUMIN 1970

Pecos Bill C 15 MIN
3/4 OR 1/2 INCH VIDEO CASSETTE P
Spins a few yarns about Pecos Bill and early cowpunching days in the Southwest.
From The Stories Of America Series.
Prod-OHSDE Dist-AITECH Prodn-WVIZTV 1976

Pectoral Region And Axilla - Unit 10 C 20 MIN
3/4 OR 1/2 INCH VIDEO CASSETTE PRO
Discusses the muscles and thoracoacromial trunk of the pectoral region, locates the boundaries of the axilla and describes the brachial plexus and the axillary artery.
From The Gross Anatomy Prosection Demonstration Series.
Prod-HSCIC Dist-HSCIC

Pectoral Region, The C 9 MIN
16MM FILM, 3/4 OR 1/2 IN VIDEO C A
Demonstrates the dissection of the pectoral region.
From The Guides To Dissection Series.
Prod-UCLA Dist-TEF

Pectoralis Major Transplant For Serratus Anterior Paralysis C 14 MIN
16MM FILM OPTICAL SOUND PRO
Shows the manner in which the pectoralis major transplant was performed to alleviate serratus anterior paralysis.
Prod-UCLA Dist-UCLA

Pectus Excavatum C 29 MIN
3/4 OR 1/2 INCH VIDEO CASSETTE
See series title for descriptive statement.
From The Thoracic Series.
Prod-SVL Dist-SVL

Pectus Excavatum - Indications For Surgery And Operative Management C 23 MIN
16MM FILM OPTICAL SOUND PRO
Explains that severe pectus excavatum (funnel chest) is a serious cosmetic and postural deformity which can be corrected with a modified ravitch-type repair. Shows the indications, technique and management.
From The Cine Clinic Series.
Prod-ACYDGD Dist-NMAC 1970

Peculiar People, A C 39 MIN
16MM FILM, 3/4 OR 1/2 IN VIDEO H A
Traces the first centuries of Christianity from the days when the religion was only practiced by a few bewildered men to the time of Constantine's conversion in the year 312.
From The Christians Series.
Prod-GRATV Dist-MGHT 1978

Pedal Power C 19 MIN
16MM FILM, 3/4 OR 1/2 IN VIDEO I-C
Uses animated still photographs, drawings and early motion picture footage to trace the history of pedal-powered machines from Leonardo da Vinci to the 1970's. Based on the book Pedal Power In Work, Leisure And Transportation by James C Mc Cullagh.
LC NO. 82-707177
Prod-RPFD Dist-BULFRG Prodn-BULFRG 1978

Peddlin' Safety C 14 MIN
16MM FILM OPTICAL SOUND P-J
Discusses bicycle safety practices, including hand signals, observance of traffic laws and riding defensively.
Prod-VADE Dist-VADE 1975

Pedestal Grinder, The C
3/4 OR 1/2 INCH VIDEO CASSETTE
See series title for descriptive statement.
From The Basic Machine Technology Series.
Prod-VTRI Dist-VTRI

Pedestal Grinder, The C 15 MIN
3/4 OR 1/2 INCH VIDEO CASSETTE
See series title for descriptive statement.
From The Machine Technology II - Engine Lathe Accessories Series.
Prod-CAMB Dist-CAMB

Pedestal Grinder, The C 15 MIN
3/4 OR 1/2 INCH VIDEO CASSETTE IND
See series title for descriptive statement.
From The Machining And The Operation Of Machine Tools, Module 1 - Basic Machine Technology Series.
Prod-LEIKID Dist-LEIKID

Pedestal Grinder, The (Spanish) C
3/4 OR 1/2 INCH VIDEO CASSETTE
See series title for descriptive statement.
From The Basic Machine Technology (Spanish) Series.
Prod-VTRI Dist-VTRI

Pedestrian Safety C 15 MIN
3/4 OR 1/2 INCH VIDEO CASSETTE P-I
Demonstrates the proper attire to wear when walking at night. Explains the meanings of stop and yield signs, walk/don't walk signals, traffic lights and the proper ways to cross at each.
From The Safer You Series.
Prod-WCVETV Dist-GPITVL 1984

Pedestrian Signs And Signals C 11 MIN
16MM FILM, 3/4 OR 1/2 IN VIDEO P-I
Points out that streets are made for cars, not pedestrians. Describes the variety of signs, signals and markings to help people cross streets safely. Features the new international signs.
Prod-AIMS Dist-AIMS 1972

Pedestrian Signs And Signals (Spanish) C 11 MIN
16MM FILM, 3/4 OR 1/2 IN VIDEO P-I
Point out that streets are made for cars, not pedestrians. Describes the variety of signs, signals and markings to help people cross streets safely. Features the new international signs.
Prod-AIMS Dist-AIMS 1972

Pedestrians - Watch Out C 10 MIN
16MM FILM, 3/4 OR 1/2 IN VIDEO K-I
Shows various traffic situations and how pedestrians should deal with them. Uses animation to emphasize situations which could be dangerous for the pedestrian.
Prod-GOLDCF Dist-AIMS 1978

Pedestrians - Watch Out (Spanish) C 10 MIN
16MM FILM, 3/4 OR 1/2 IN VIDEO K-I
Shows various traffic situations and how pedestrians should deal with them. Uses animation to emphasize situations which could be dangerous for the pedestrian.
Prod-GOLDCF Dist-AIMS 1978

Pediatric Anesthesia (2nd Ed) C 27 MIN
3/4 OR 1/2 INCH VIDEO CASSETTE PRO
Describes the differences in anatomy and physiology of the pediatric patient, with special attention to the child's airway. Identifies specific problems of pediatric gas exchange. Discusses cardiovascular monitoring, pediatric fluid/blood replacement and problems related to thermal regulation. Covers unique problems of drug administration in children.
From The Anesthesiology Clerkship Series.
Prod-UMICHM Dist-UMICHM 1982

Pediatric Assessment—A Series

Presents pediatric assessment of cerebral palsy patients by Certified Neuro-Development Treatment Instructor Coordinator.
Prod-UMDSM Dist-UMDSM

Neuromotor Assessment Of Cerebral Palsy,	
Neuromotor Assessment of Cerebral Palsy,	023 MIN
Neuromotor Assessment Of Cerebral Palsy,	046 MIN
Neuromotor Assessment Of Cerebral Palsy,	050 MIN
Principles Of Neuromuscular Assessment	019 MIN

Pediatric Emergency Management—A Series

Presents a series which focuses on a wide variety of acute illnesses and injuries to children. Stresses the essential elements of initial patient assessment, diagnosis, and therapeutic intervention needed for effective stabilization, correlating basic pathophysiology with practical aspects of management.
Prod-VTRI Dist-VTRI

Accidental Ingestions In Children	020 MIN
Cardiopulmonary Resuscitation	028 MIN
Foreign Bodies	025 MIN
Head Trauma	022 MIN
Status Epilepticus	020 MIN
Upper Airway Infections	019 MIN

Pediatric Examination - Art And Process—A Series
PRO
Discusses techniques and processes of a thorough physical examination of normal children from infancy through school age. Shows various methods of gaining the child's cooperation during the exam.
Prod-TUNNEW Dist-LIP 1977

Examination Of The Infant	50 MIN
Examination Of The Pre-School Age Child	45 MIN
Examination Of The School Age Child	45 MIN
Examination Of The Toddler	35 MIN
Neurologic Examination	40 MIN

Pediatric Growth Measurements - Height, Weight, And Head Circumference C 6 MIN
3/4 OR 1/2 INCH VIDEO CASSETTE PRO
Illustrates basic procedures involved in measuring and charting a child's height, weight and head circumference.
Prod-HSCIC Dist-HSCIC 1982

Pediatric Mist Tent C 20 MIN
3/4 OR 1/2 INCH VIDEO CASSETTE
Designed to identify nursing responsibilities related to the care of a child in a mist tent. Discusses potential problems and solutions.
Prod-FAIRGH Dist-FAIRGH

Pediatric Neurologic Examination C 40 MIN
3/4 INCH VIDEO CASSETTE PRO
Demonstrates techniques and processes of a neurologic examination of normal children from infancy through school age.
From The Pediatric Examination - Art And Process Series.
Prod-TUNNEW Dist-LIP 1977

Pediatric Nursing—A Series
PRO
Prod-VDONUR Dist-AJN Prodn-WTTWTV 1967

Abused Child, The	44 MIN
Accidents In Children	44 MIN
Adolescent Patient, The	44 MIN
Burned Child, The	44 MIN
Child Guidance Clinic, The	44 MIN
Child Who Undergoes Open-Heart Surgery, The	44 MIN
Child With A Heart Defect, The	44 MIN
Child With A Nephrotic Syndrome, The	44 MIN
Child With A Neurological Condition, The	44 MIN
Child With An Orthopedic Anomaly, A	44 MIN
Child With Cerebral Palsy, The	44 MIN
Child With Cystic Fibrosis, The	44 MIN
Child With Hemophilia, The	44 MIN
Child With Muscular Dystrophy, The	44 MIN
Child With Rheumatic Fever, The	44 MIN
Child With Severe Emotional Problems, The	44 MIN
Cleft Lip And Palate	44 MIN
Conference On The Dying Child, The	44 MIN
Hospitalized Child, The	44 MIN
Kidney Transplants And Hemodialysis	44 MIN
Mentally Retarded Child, The	44 MIN
Nursing Appraisal Of Infant Neurological	44 MIN

Pediatric Office Bacteriology - Obtaining And Culturing Urine C 14 MIN
3/4 OR 1/2 INCH VIDEO CASSETTE PRO
Details three means of obtaining urine - clean catch, catheterization, and superpubic bladder aspiration.
Prod-HSCIC Dist-HSCIC 1981

Pediatric Physiotherapy C 14 MIN
16MM FILM, 3/4 OR 1/2 IN VIDEO C A
Discusses the application of respiratory physiotherapy to neonates and children, including patient psychology, proper techniques and infant physiology.
From The Physical Respiratory Therapy Series.
Prod-VISCI Dist-TEF

Pediatric Ultrasonography C 21 MIN
3/4 INCH VIDEO CASSETTE
Discusses areas in which ultrasound is being used as a diagnosis tool in pediatric medicine. Describes the use of ultrasound in determining midline shifts in the head, congenital and acquired abnormalities in the heart and in outlining effusions on the chest.
From The Ultrasound In Diagnostic Medicine Series.
LC NO. 79-707579
Prod-NSF Dist-USNAC 1976

Pediatric—A Series

Presents a series on pediatric surgery.
Prod-SVL Dist-SVL

Abdomino-Perineal Pull Through For	
Ambulatory Surgery Clinic And Myriogotomy	012 MIN
Circumcision By Dissection/Circumcision With	010 MIN
Excision Of Thyroglossal Duct Cyst	028 MIN
Gastroschsis	027 MIN
Hepato-Enterostomy For Biliary Atresia	018 MIN
Indirect Hernia	020 MIN
Operative Drainage For Empyema	009 MIN
Pyloric Stenosis	009 MIN
Resection Of An Adrenal Tumor	010 MIN
Scrotal Hydrocele	015 MIN
Three Appendectomies	030 MIN
Undescended Testis	015 MIN

Pedicle Flap From Edentulous Area In Periodontal Therapy, The C 13 MIN
3/4 OR 1/2 INCH VIDEO CASSETTE
Demonstrates the use of a pedicle flap to correct a periodontal lesion.
Prod-VADTC Dist-AMDA 1969

Pedicle Flaps For Wound Closure C 23 MIN
16MM FILM OPTICAL SOUND PRO
Explains that when important muscle structures, nerves, tendons, bones, joints or major blood vessels are exposed in a wound, they must be covered and protected with skin and its attached subcutaneous fat. Points out that if this covering is not available because of the magnitude of the defect, one may use some type of pedicle to supply this deficiency.
Prod-ACYDGD Dist-ACY 1960

Pediculosis And Scabies - Questions Of Concern C 24 MIN
16MM FILM OPTICAL SOUND
Summarizes current data on the human louse insect and scabies mite and samples common patient concerns. Provides information on the accepted diagnostic procedures and preferred course of therapy for each of these frequently encountered infestations.
Prod-REDCRN Dist-MTP

Pedigree Patterns C 17 MIN
16MM FILM OPTICAL SOUND PRO
Describes pedigree patterns in genetics, sex-linked inheritance, distribution of traits, allelism and non-allelism.
From The General Genetics Series.
Prod-MIFE Dist-MIFE 1972

Pedigree Patterns C 17 MIN
16MM FILM OPTICAL SOUND
Presents symbols used in construction of the human pedigree. Uses pedigrees of brachydactyly and achondroplastic dwarfism in order to illustrate dominal inheritance and pedigrees of albinism, Crigler-Najjar syndrome, and Morquio syndrome in order to illustrate autosomal recessive inheritance.
From The Human Genetics Series. No. 4
LC NO. 75-700019
Prod-NFMD Dist-MIFE Prodn-MIFE 1968

Pedigree Patterns (Spanish) C 17 MIN
16MM FILM OPTICAL SOUND
Presents symbols used in construction of the human pedigree. Uses pedigrees of brachydactyly and achondroplastic dwarfism in order to illustrate dominal inheritance and pedigrees of albinism, Crigler-Najjar syndrome, and Morquio syndrome in order to illustrate autosomal recessive inheritance.
From The Human Genetics (Spanish) Series. No. 4
LC NO. 75-700019
Prod-NFMD Dist-MIFE Prodn-MIFE 1968

Pedlar's Dream, The C 27 MIN
16MM FILM, 3/4 OR 1/2 IN VIDEO
Relates the English tale of a pedlar who dreams of finding his fortune in a faraway market. Reveals that once he gets there, he finds that his fortune is really back at his own house and that his generousity to his friends is appreciated.
From The Storybook International Series.
Prod-JOU Dist-JOU 1982

Pedodontics For The General Practitioner—A Series

Offers an unedited tape presentation by Roy M Wolff, DDS, Creve Coeur, Missouri, on the first visit, patient and parent education, disclosing solution, x-ray technique, case presentation with one patient, vital pulpotomy chrome crown on another patient, restoration of fractured anterior with bonded filling material on a third patient, and interceptive and preventive orthodontics on patients ages eight to ten.
Prod-AMDA Dist-AMDA 1975

Pedophile (Child Molester) C 20 MIN
16MM FILM, 3/4 OR 1/2 IN VIDEO H-C A
Presents an in-depth study of the child molester, showing the many different types of child molesters, the tricks of how they operate and the underlying causes of their deviation.
Prod-DAVP Dist-AIMS 1972

Pedrito - Part I C 30 MIN
3/4 OR 1/2 INCH VIDEO CASSETTE
See series title for descriptive statement.
From The Mundo Real Series.
Prod-CPT Dist-MDCPB

Pedrito - Part II C 30 MIN
3/4 OR 1/2 INCH VIDEO CASSETTE
See series title for descriptive statement.
From The Mundo Real Series.
Prod-CPT Dist-MDCPB

Pedro Linares - Artesano Cartonero C 23 MIN
16MM FILM OPTICAL SOUND
A Spanish version of Pedro Linares - Papier Mache Artist. Examines the work of Mexican folk artist Pedro Linares as he creates fiesta figures using papier-mache.
From The Artesanos Mexicanos Series.
LC NO. 75-704283
Prod-WORKS Dist-WORKS 1975

Pedro Linares - Papier Mache Artist C 23 MIN
16MM FILM OPTICAL SOUND
Shows the beauty and skill of the work of Mexican papier-mache artist Pedro Linares. Describes his life and his work, how he began with papier-mache and his deep feelings about the traditions which his art serves.
From The Mexico's Folk Artists Series.
Prod-WORKS Dist-WORKS 1975

Pee Wee Reese For Gillete C 1 MIN
3/4 OR 1/2 INCH VIDEO CASSETTE
Shows a classic television commercial with a Brooklyn Dodgers ball player.
Prod-BROOKC Dist-BROOKC

Peege C 28 MIN
16MM FILM, 3/4 OR 1/2 IN VIDEO
Shows how a young man who comes home from college for the Christmas holidays is able to break through communication barriers and reach his grandmother who has become isolated by age and failing mental and physical capacities.
Prod-KLEKNP Dist-PHENIX 1973

Peege C 30 MIN
3/4 OR 1/2 INCH VIDEO CASSETTE
Shows how a fairly typical middle class family deals with an aging mother and grandmother during the annual Christmas visit to the nursing home where the grandmother resides.
Prod-PHOEFS Dist-AJN

Peege (Captioned) C 28 MIN
16MM FILM, 3/4 OR 1/2 IN VIDEO
Shows how a young man who comes home from college for the Christmas holidays is able to break through communication barriers and reach his grandmother who has become isolated by age and failing mental and physical capacities.
Prod-KLEKNP Dist-PHENIX 1973

Peel's Beer With Bert And Harry Peel C 1 MIN
3/4 OR 1/2 INCH VIDEO CASSETTE
Shows a classic television commercial with live and animated action.
Prod-BROOKC Dist-BROOKC

Peelings C 7 MIN
16MM FILM, 3/4 OR 1/2 IN VIDEO H-C A

Introduces the viewer to latex sculpture by following the process required to produce this type of art.
Prod-FEINSP Dist-PHENIX 1976

Peep Show, The C 30 MIN
3/4 INCH VIDEO CASSETTE
See series title for descriptive statement.
From The Antiques Series.
Prod-NHMNET Dist-PUBTEL

Peer Conducted Behavior Modification C 24 MIN
16MM FILM, 3/4 OR 1/2 IN VIDEO C A
Illustrates the way in which a child's schoolmates and their parents are mobilized in a neighborhood to modify some behavior problems.
Prod-MEDIAG Dist-MEDIAG 1976

Peer Facilitators - Youth Helping Youth C 27 MIN
16MM FILM OPTICAL SOUND J-C A
Presents a model for training high school students in helping skills. Features counselor Tom Erney in a demonstration of the peer facilitator program that he developed for high school students in Gainesville, Florida.
LC NO. 76-703659
Prod-EDMDC Dist-EDMDC 1976

Peer Group Interactions C 30 MIN
3/4 OR 1/2 INCH VIDEO CASSETTE T
Looks at peer group interactions in an educational setting.
From The Interaction - Human Concerns In The Schools Series.
Prod-MDDE Dist-MDCPB

Peer Groups - Ages 3-13 B 44 MIN
16MM FILM OPTICAL SOUND
Presents examples of the rise of the group as a sign of increasing independence from parents.
From The Man - His Growth And Development, Birth Through Adolescence Series.
LC NO. 79-703685
Prod-VDONUR Dist-AJN Prodn-WTTWTV 1967

Peer Gynt C 60 MIN
3/4 OR 1/2 INCH VIDEO CASSETTE H-C A
Provides a framework for understanding drama and the basic skills needed to view a play critically. Uses the play Peer Gynt as an example.
From The Drama - Play, Performance, Perception Series. Introduction To Critical Appreciation
Prod-BBCTV Dist-FI 1978

Peer Pressure C 25 MIN
3/4 OR 1/2 INCH VIDEO CASSETTE J-C A
Looks at groups of teens from three high schools in the Boston area to reveal their differences in dress, speech and attitudes.
Prod-SIRS Dist-SIRS

Peer Pressure - Learning To Be Yourself C 21 MIN
16MM FILM, 3/4 OR 1/2 IN VIDEO J-H
Emphasizes the importance of teenagers making decisions themselves.
LC NO. 84-706386
Prod-SAIF Dist-BARR 1983

Peer Pressure - Nobody Tells Me What To Do C 24 MIN
16MM FILM, 3/4 OR 1/2 IN VIDEO J-H
Presents vignettes dealing with the importance of teenagers making decisions themselves.
LC NO. 84-706387
Prod-SAIF Dist-BARR 1983

Peer Tutoring C 30 MIN
3/4 OR 1/2 INCH VIDEO CASSETTE T
Explores reasons and techniques for implementing peer tutoring for special students within regular classrooms.
From The Stretch Concepts For Teaching Handicapped Children Series.
Prod-HUBDSC Dist-HUBDSC

Peer Tutoring C 30 MIN
3/4 OR 1/2 INCH VIDEO CASSETTE T S
Shows a teacher interacting with a group of high school students as they implement a peer tutoring program for elementary level children.
From The Project STRETCH (Strategies To Train Regular Educators To Teach Children With...) Series. Module 8
LC NO. 80-706644
Prod-METCO Dist-HUBDSC 1980

Peermanship C 10 MIN
3/4 OR 1/2 INCH VIDEO CASSETTE
See series title for descriptive statement.
From The Leadership Link - Fundamentals Of Effective Supervision Series.
Prod-CHSH Dist-DELTAK

Peers In Middle Childhood C 24 MIN
16MM FILM, 3/4 OR 1/2 IN VIDEO C
Shows the importance of the peer group to the nine-year-old child and examines the child's growing social identity, his/her desire to master learning skills and the development of new methods of building self-esteem.
LC NO. 80-707376
Prod-MHFB Dist-IFB 1975

Peewee Had A Little Ape C 20 MIN
16MM FILM OPTICAL SOUND K-I
Tells how the Magnificent Six And 1/2 mistake one of their members for an ape after he dons a gorilla suit. Concludes with a chase involving the police, a clown and a keeper from the circus.
From The Magnificent 6 And 1/2 Series.
Prod-CHILDF Dist-LUF 1970

Peewee's Pianola C 16 MIN
16MM FILM OPTICAL SOUND K-I
Shows how the Magnificent Six And 1/2 gang stumbles upon a player piano in the country and attempts to get it back to the city.
From The Magnificent 6 And 1/2 Series.
Prod-SF Dist-LUF 1970

Pegasus C 9 MIN
16MM FILM, 3/4 OR 1/2 IN VIDEO H-C
Presents an animated story about the world's last blacksmith who creates a horse's head in remembrance of a bygone age. Shows the head developing a life of its own as it grows in size and reproduces itself with great abandon.
LC NO. 80-707336
Prod-PENFIL Dist-IFB Prodn-SERVA 1975

Peggy And Pierre B 13 MIN
16MM FILM OPTICAL SOUND K-J T
A light-hearted vignette about a small girl and a large dog.
Prod-NYU Dist-NYU 1962

Peggy Collins C 9 MIN
16MM FILM, 3/4 OR 1/2 IN VIDEO H-C A
Focuses on a single mother trying to work as a waitress and raise her 14-year-old daughter.
From The American Family - An Endangered Species Series.
Prod-NBC Dist-FI 1979

Peggy's Final Victory C 28 MIN
16MM FILM OPTICAL SOUND H-C A
Features the husband of a world class runner who died of cancer at age 28. Shows how they dealt with each other, family, friends and health care professionals during the illness and his thoughts at the time of her death.
LC NO. 83-700620
Prod-IOWA Dist-IOWA 1983

Peindre Sans Pinceaux C 5 MIN
16MM FILM, 3/4 OR 1/2 IN VIDEO I-H
Discusses directions for making finger paint, techniques in terms of age and experience and shows a beginner experimenting by using the palm, the side of the hand, the fist, the thumb and the finger tips.
Prod-CRAF Dist-IFB

Peiping Family B 21 MIN
16MM FILM, 3/4 OR 1/2 IN VIDEO
Prod-IFF Dist-IFF

Peking Duck, Pt 1 C 29 MIN
2 INCH VIDEOTAPE
Features Joyce Chen showing how to adapt Chinese recipes so they can be prepared in the American kitchen and still retain the authentic flavor. Demonstrates how to prepare Peking duck.
From The Joyce Chen Cooks Series.
Prod-WGBHTV Dist-PUBTEL

Peking Duck, Pt 2 C 29 MIN
2 INCH VIDEOTAPE
Features Joyce Chen showing how to adapt Chinese recipes so they can be prepared in the American kitchen and still retain the authentic flavor. Demonstrates how to prepare Peking duck.
From The Joyce Chen Cooks Series.
Prod-WGBHTV Dist-PUBTEL

Peking Ravioli C 29 MIN
2 INCH VIDEOTAPE
Features Joyce Chen showing how to adapt Chinese recipes so they can be prepared in the American kitchen and still retain the authentic flavor. Demonstrates how to prepare Peking ravioli.
From The Joyce Chen Cooks Series.
Prod-WGBHTV Dist-PUBTEL

Pele - The Master And His Method C 32 MIN
16MM FILM OPTICAL SOUND
Presents Argentine soccer player, Edson Arantes Do Nascimento, known as Pele, demonstrating his techniques.
LC NO. 73-701865
Prod-PEPSI Dist-PEPSI 1973

Pele - The Master And His Method (Dutch) C 32 MIN
16MM FILM OPTICAL SOUND
Presents Argentine soccer player, Edson Arantes Do Nascimento, known as Pele, demonstrating his techniques.
LC NO. 73-701865
Prod-PEPSI Dist-PEPSI 1973

Pele - The Master And His Method (French) C 32 MIN
16MM FILM OPTICAL SOUND
Presents Argentine soccer player, Edson Arantes Do Nascimento, known as Pele, demonstrating his techniques.
LC NO. 73-701865
Prod-PEPSI Dist-PEPSI 1973

Pele - The Master And His Method (German) C 32 MIN
16MM FILM OPTICAL SOUND
Presents Argentine soccer player, Edson Arantes Do Nascimento, known as Pele, demonstrating his techniques.
LC NO. 73-701865
Prod-PEPSI Dist-PEPSI 1973

Pele - The Master And His Method (Portuguese) C 32 MIN
16MM FILM OPTICAL SOUND
Presents Argentine soccer player, Edson Arantes Do Nascimento, known as Pele, demonstrating his techniques.
LC NO. 73-701865
Prod-PEPSI Dist-PEPSI 1973

Pele - The Master And His Method (Spanish) C 32 MIN
16MM FILM OPTICAL SOUND
Presents Argentine soccer player, Edson Arantes Do Nascimento, known as Pele, demonstrating his techniques.
LC NO. 73-701865
Prod-PEPSI Dist-PEPSI 1973

Pelecaniform Birds C 16 MIN
16MM FILM OPTICAL SOUND
Explains mating behavior, nesting and feeding habits and physiognomy of the sea birds of the order pelecaniformes that breed on the Galapogos.
From The Galapagos - Laboratory For Evolution Series.
LC NO. 73-702573
Prod-UCEMC Dist-HAR 1971

Peleliu - The Killing Ground C 30 MIN
3/4 OR 1/2 INCH VIDEO CASSETTE H-C A
See series title for descriptive statement.
From The World War II - GI Diary Series.
Prod-TIMLIF Dist-TIMLIF 1980

Pelican C 22 MIN
16MM FILM, 3/4 OR 1/2 IN VIDEO P-I
Presents Edward Lear's tale The Pelican Chorus told through animation and takes a whimsical at the pelican's sociable nature. Describes how an ornithologist studies this bird's life style, migration and feeding, and shows how a Floridian couple care for wounded birds at their sanctuary. Hosted by Hal Linden.
From The Animals, Animals, Animals Series.
Prod-ABCNEW Dist-MEDIAG 1977

Pelican Island C 28 MIN
16MM FILM OPTICAL SOUND H A
Presents the fascinating story of the white pelican, member of the species pelecanus erthrorhynchos, who, year after year, travel thousands of miles to a small island in the Great Salt Lake of Utah to build nests and hatch their eggs.
From The Nature Guide Film Series.
Prod-AVEXP Dist-AVEXP

Pelican Island C 28 MIN
16MM FILM OPTICAL SOUND J-C A
Explains that the white pelican returns each year from the southern part of the United States, Mexico and Central America to nest on Gunnison Island in Great Salt Lake in Utah. Uses close-up views to picture the life cycle of the pelican, showing the hatching and protection of the eggs, the feeding of the young and the young pelicans learning to fly. Points out the importance of wildlife conservation with particular emphasis on the white pelican.
LC NO. FIA64-1377
Prod-NATURE Dist-AVEXP 1964

Pelicans C 6 MIN
16MM FILM, 3/4 OR 1/2 IN VIDEO K-P
Depicts the habits of pelicans as they gracefully fly, build nests, catch fish and feed their young.
From The Zoo Animals In The Wild Series.
Prod-CORF Dist-CORF 1981

Pelicula A Las Once, Sandinista TV News C 28 MIN
3/4 OR 1/2 INCH VIDEO CASSETTE
Attacks the ideology and economics of mass media. Presented by Paper Tiger Television.
Prod-ARTINC Dist-ARTINC

Pelvic And Balanced Suspension Traction C 13 MIN
1/2 IN VIDEO CASSETTE BETA/VHS
Demonstrates how to apply and adjust pelvic and balanced suspension traction.
Prod-RMI Dist-RMI

Pelvic Area - Female C 30 MIN
3/4 OR 1/2 INCH VIDEO CASSETTE PRO
Views a physical assessment by a nurse practitioner of the pelvic area of a live female patient.
From The Health Assessment Series.
Prod-BRA Dist-BRA

Pelvic Area - Female C 30 MIN
3/4 OR 1/2 INCH VIDEO CASSETTE PRO
See series title for descriptive statement.
From The Health Assessment Series. Module 9
Prod-MDCC Dist-MDCC

Pelvic Area - Male C 25 MIN
3/4 OR 1/2 INCH VIDEO CASSETTE PRO
Views a physical assessment by a nurse practitioner of the pelvic area of a live male patient.
From The Health Assessment Series.
Prod-BRA Dist-BRA

Pelvic Area - Male C 25 MIN
3/4 OR 1/2 INCH VIDEO CASSETTE PRO
See series title for descriptive statement.
From The Health Assessment Series. Module 10
Prod-MDCC Dist-MDCC

Pelvic Examination For Contraception C 25 MIN
16MM FILM OPTICAL SOUND
Uses animation to demonstrate the key elements of pelvic anatomy and shows bimanual examination through both live and animated footage. Teaches proper techniques for insertion of intrauterine devices (both push-in and withdrawal methods) and diaphragm fitting.
Prod-PATHFU Dist-PATHFU 1981

Pelvic Examination For Contraception C 23 MIN
3/4 OR 1/2 INCH VIDEO CASSETTE PRO
Describes how to do a thorough pelvic examination in preparation for IUD insertion or fitting a diaphragm. (Available in Spanish, Portuguese and Bengali.)
Prod-WFP Dist-WFP

Pelvic Examination For Contraception (Portuguese) C 25 MIN
16MM FILM OPTICAL SOUND

Uses animation to demonstrate the key elements of pelvic anatomy and shows bimanual examination through both live and animated footage. Teaches proper techniques for insertion of intrauterine devices (both push-in and withdrawal methods) and diaphragm fitting.
Prod-PATHFU Dist-PATHFU 1981

Pelvic Examination For Contraception (Bengali) C 25 MIN
16MM FILM OPTICAL SOUND
Uses animation to demonstrate the key elements of pelvic anatomy and shows bimanual examination through both live and animated footage. Teaches proper techniques for insertion of intrauterine devices (both push-in and withdrawal methods) and diaphragm fitting.
Prod-PATHFU Dist-PATHFU 1981

Pelvic Examination For Contraception (Spanish) C 25 MIN
16MM FILM OPTICAL SOUND
Uses animation to demonstrate the key elements of pelvic anatomy and shows bimanual examination through both live and animated footage. Teaches proper techniques for insertion of intrauterine devices (both push-in and withdrawal methods) and diaphragm fitting.
Prod-PATHFU Dist-PATHFU 1981

Pelvic Examination-A Series
PRO
Designed to give students a clear understanding of the speculum in relation to pelvic structures. Portrays the inner pelvic structure with three-dimensional models.
Prod-OMNIED Dist-OMNIED

Anatomy For Abdominal And Pelvic Examination
Exam Findings - Description And Classification
Examination Procedures

Pelvic Exenteration For Cervical Cancer C 31 MIN
16MM FILM OPTICAL SOUND PRO
Illustrates the technique employed in total excision of the pelvic organs for cancer of the uterine cervix. Shows excision of pelvic viscera, pelvic lymphadenectomy, terminal sigmoid colostomy and ileal conduit procedures.
LC NO. FIA68-788
Prod-UMIAMI Dist-EATONL 1968

Pelvic Inflammatory Disease C
3/4 OR 1/2 INCH VIDEO CASSETTE
Explains how pelvic inflammatory disease (PID) is an infection problem caused in most ABS cases by contracting a veneral disease. Describes the symptoms, treatment and what the long term effects may be if allowed to go untreated.
Prod-MIFE Dist-MIFE

Pelvic Lymph Node Dissection And I-125 Implantation For Prostatic Cancer C 20 MIN
16MM FILM OPTICAL SOUND PRO
Demonstrates the procedure for implanting needles into the prostate for application of I-125 therapy. Describes how to calculate correct dosage and shows how to administer the medication.
LC NO. 79-700260
Prod-EATONL Dist-EATONL Prodn-AEGIS 1978

Pelvic Mass In An Amenorrheic Woman C 45 MIN
3/4 INCH VIDEO CASSETTE
Presents a case study of a 27-year-old amenorrheic woman who has secondary symptoms of ovarian neoplasm.
Prod-UTAHTI Dist-UTAHTI

Pelvic Region, Pt 1 - Iliosacral C 17 MIN
3/4 OR 1/2 INCH VIDEO CASSETTE PRO
Focuses on diagnostic and manipulative procedures for iliosacral aspects of pelvic motion. Shows a test for pelvic mobility by introduction of motion from below. Demonstrates direct manipulative techniques for iliosacral dysfunction.
From The Osteopathic Examination And Manipulation Series.
Prod-MSU Dist-MSU

Pelvic Region, Pt 2 - Sacroiliac C 13 MIN
3/4 OR 1/2 INCH VIDEO CASSETTE PRO
Presents examples of postural stresses in the sagittal plane and gives manipulative techniques to relieve such stress. Identifies more complex minor motion properties. Applies the principles of both direct and indirect manipulation for sacroiliac dysfunction in the seated position.
From The Osteopathic Examination And Manipulation Series.
Prod-MSU Dist-MSU

Pelvic Ultrasound C
3/4 OR 1/2 INCH VIDEO CASSETTE
See series title for descriptive statement.
From The X-Ray Procedures In Layman's Terms Series.
Prod-FAIRGH Dist-FAIRGH

Pelvis Region, Pt 3 - Alternative Direct Techniques C 12 MIN
3/4 OR 1/2 INCH VIDEO CASSETTE PRO
Continues discussion of the development of concepts of sacroiliac dysfunction. Demonstrates direct sacroiliac manipulative procedures in sidelying and supine positions.
From The Osteopathic Examination And Manipulation Series.
Prod-MSU Dist-MSU

Pen And Ink C 12 MIN
16MM FILM, 3/4 OR 1/2 IN VIDEO J-C A
Shows common tools used to produce black and white illustrations and techniques to create texture and shading in the rendering of an animal.
From The Introduction To Commercial Art Series.
Prod-SF Dist-SF Prodn-ACORN 1979

Pen Is Mightier Than The Sword, The C 28 MIN
16MM FILM OPTICAL SOUND
Discusses the language of the Western World, the fall of the Roman empire, Celtic scripts in the Dark Ages, the Carolingian script, the making of a quill pen and the techniques of illumination.
From The Alphabet - The Story Of Writing Series.
Prod-CFDLD Dist-FILAUD 1982

Pen Is Mightier Than The Sword, The C 30 MIN
3/4 OR 1/2 INCH VIDEO CASSETTE
Deals with Celtic scripts in the Dark Ages, the Carolingian script, the impact of the new quill pen and the medieval scribes and illuminators.
From The Alphabet - The Story Of Writing Series.
Prod-WSTGLC Dist-WSTGLC

Pen Point Percussion With Loops C 10 MIN
16MM FILM, 3/4 OR 1/2 IN VIDEO C A
Presents an explanation of the principles and production of synthetic sound, showing Norman Mc Laren's experimentation with hand-drawn sounds on film. Closes with 'LOOPS,' an example of this technique.
Prod-NFBC Dist-IFB 1951

Pen Register, The C 14 MIN
3/4 INCH VIDEO CASSETTE J-C
Describes the Texas wiretap law, including the legal rulings on use of the pen register and civil liberties concerns.
LC NO. 82-707073
Prod-SWINS Dist-SWINS 1982

Penance - Sacrament Of Peace C 11 MIN
16MM FILM OPTICAL SOUND J-C A
Uses a dramatization about the emotional response of a young architect who seriously injures a ten-year-old girl while driving home from a cocktail party to suggest various aspects and effects of the Sacrament of Penance.
From The Sacrament Series.
LC NO. 72-700509
Prod-FRACOC Dist-FRACOC 1969

Pencil, The C 5 MIN
16MM FILM, 3/4 OR 1/2 IN VIDEO K-C A
See series title for descriptive statement.
From The How It's Made Series.
Prod-HOLIA Dist-LUF

Pencil, The C 8 MIN
16MM FILM, 3/4 OR 1/2 IN VIDEO P-I
Presents a visual description without narration to show how pencils are made and the variety of ordinary and unusual ways in which they can be used.
Prod-INCC Dist-JOU 1977

Pendulum C 26 MIN
16MM FILM, 3/4 OR 1/2 IN VIDEO H-C A
Examines the events and emotions which threaten to tear apart a school and a community when a school principal resigns.
Prod-FIELDA Dist-CORF 1978

Pendulum In A Rotating Plane B 32 MIN
3/4 OR 1/2 INCH VIDEO CASSETTE
Discusses application of phase-plane method to a simple pendulum rotating about a vertical center line in a vertical plane. Teaches effect of centrifugal force on the oscillation.
From The Nonlinear Vibrations Series.
Prod-MIOT Dist-MIOT

Pendulums C 15 MIN
3/4 OR 1/2 INCH VIDEO CASSETTE P
Uses clocks and swings to introduce the concept of a pendulum. Presents Hocus and Myrtle investigating pendulums at home and a magician demonstrating how they work.
From The Let Me See Series. No. 1
Prod-WETN Dist-AITECH Prodn-STSU 1982

Penetrating Eye, The C 22 MIN
3/4 OR 1/2 INCH VIDEO CASSETTE PRO
Demonstrates the functioning of a scanning electron microscope and shows how an electron beam, instead of light waves, is used to produce revealing images of microscopically-sized specimens. Shows and interprets scanning electron microscope photographs of numerous specimens from the biological world.
Prod-WFP Dist-WFP

Penetrating Wounds Of The Abdomen C 14 MIN
16MM FILM OPTICAL SOUND
Demonstrates five steps for handling penetrating wounds of the abdomen, including make a speedy and accurate diagnosis, keep the patient on his back, apply a sterile dressing, treat for shock and prepare for speedy evacuation.
LC NO. FIE54-448
Prod-USN Dist-USNAC 1953

Penetrating Wounds Of The Large Intestine C 21 MIN
16MM FILM OPTICAL SOUND PRO
Points out that mortality and morbidity from penetrating wounds of the colon have been reduced progressively during the twentieth century through aggressive surgery. Presents various types of colon wounds to illustrate these principles in two cases.
Prod-ACYDGD Dist-ACY 1962

Penguins C 8 MIN
16MM FILM, 3/4 OR 1/2 IN VIDEO
Shows thousands of penguins to illustrate the parallels between penguins and people.
Prod-PERSPF Dist-CORF

Penguins Of The Antarctic C 13 MIN
16MM FILM, 3/4 OR 1/2 IN VIDEO I-C A
Presents emperor and adelie penguins exhibiting their eccentric habits in the comfort of their Antarctic homeland. Supplies information emphasizing man's positive role in assisting the penguin in its formidable environment.
Prod-BOSMS Dist-AIMS 1972

Penguins Of The Antarctic (Captioned) C 13 MIN
16MM FILM, 3/4 OR 1/2 IN VIDEO I-C A
Presents emperor and adelie penguins exhibiting their eccentric habits in the comfort of their Antarctic homeland. Supplies information emphasizing man's positive role in assisting the penguin in its formidable environment.
Prod-BOSMS Dist-AIMS 1972

Penile Curvature - Lateral And Ventral C 20 MIN
3/4 OR 1/2 INCH VIDEO CASSETTE PRO
Describes a unique surgical procedure to correct penile curvature.
Prod-WFP Dist-WFP

Penile Implant C 9 MIN
3/4 OR 1/2 INCH VIDEO CASSETTE
Provides a basic review of anatomy and physiology of the penis and discusses the two most commonly used prosthetic devices, the rod-shaped silicone and the inflatable version.
Prod-TRAINX Dist-TRAINX

Penman, Printer And Engraver C 28 MIN
16MM FILM OPTICAL SOUND
Deals with the making of books and the chair libraries, how the scribe corrected his errors, the Gothic and Italic script, the development of printing, copperplate engraving, copperplate handwriting and the birth of the steel nib.
From The Alphabet - The Story Of Writing Series.
Prod-CFDLD Dist-FILAUD 1982

Penman, Printer And Engraver C 30 MIN
3/4 OR 1/2 INCH VIDEO CASSETTE
Deals with the making of books, the Gothic and Italic scripts, the development of printing and metal engraving, and the steel nib pen that made everyone a writer.
From The Alphabet - The Story Of Writing Series.
Prod-WSTGLC Dist-WSTGLC

Pennies From Heaven B 81 MIN
16MM FILM OPTICAL SOUND H-C A
Relates the story of a drifter who befriends an orphaned girl and her grandfather. Stars Bing Crosby, Edith Fellows and Madge Evans.
Prod-CPC Dist-TIMLIF 1936

Pennsylvania Country Cooking C 20 MIN
3/4 OR 1/2 INCH VIDEO CASSETTE
Features five Pennsylvania country recipes which are representative of the every day foods served on the bountiful tables of the Pennsylvania Dutch.
From The Magical Cook's Tour Series.
Prod-IVCH Dist-IVCH

Pennsylvania Journey C 27 MIN
3/4 OR 1/2 INCH VIDEO CASSETTE
Focuses on the geographic space and history of Pennsylvania. Features professor of geography, Peirce Lewis, as he travels through the state. Includes historical sites, farm country, mining areas, mountains, business and industry and the major city of Pittsburgh.
Prod-PSU Dist-PSU 1984

Penny And Sonya Cohen C 52 MIN
3/4 OR 1/2 INCH VIDEO CASSETTE
Covers work songs and lullabyes. Shows men singing as they work. Pete Seeger welcomes his sister Penny and her infant daughter Sonya Cohen to the show.
From The Rainbow Quest Series.
Prod-SEEGER Dist-CWATER

Penny Serenade B 125 MIN
16MM FILM OPTICAL SOUND
Features Irene Dunne as a woman about to break up with her husband, played by Cary Grant. Directed by George Stevens.
Prod-UNKNWN Dist-REELIM 1940

Penny Suite, A C 5 MIN
16MM FILM, 3/4 OR 1/2 IN VIDEO
Presents an animated story about a carousel whose animals come to life and play like children.
Prod-AFI Dist-PHENIX Prodn-SILVRJ 1977

Penny Wise C 30 MIN
2 INCH VIDEOTAPE C A
Discusses how to create interesting effects in interior design with a limited budget. Demonstrates one room with three different designs and three budgets.
From The Designing Home Interiors Series. Unit 29
Prod-COAST Dist-CDTEL Prodn-RSCCD

Pennywise - Review C 15 MIN
3/4 OR 1/2 INCH VIDEO CASSETTE P
Uses the format of a television program to review the economic concepts presented in the first 11 recordings of the Pennywise Series. Summarizes how wants and needs, consumption of goods and services, production, income, money and credit are important to understanding how the American economy works.
From The Pennywise Series. No. 12
LC NO. 82-706014
Prod-MAETEL Dist-GPITVL 1980

Pennywise-A Series
P
Uses puppets and real-life characters to create an understanding of essential economic fundamentals.
Prod-MAETEL Dist-GPITVL 1980

Banking	015 MIN
Consumption	015 MIN
Credit	015 MIN
Exchange	015 MIN
Income	015 MIN
Interdependence	015 MIN
Making Decisions	015 MIN

Money 015 MIN
Pennywise - Review 015 MIN
Production 015 MIN
Specialization 015 MIN
Wants And Needs 015 MIN

Pennzoil Day, A C 34 MIN
16MM FILM OPTICAL SOUND
Describes the scope of the Pennzoil Company with views of its employees making the most of natural resources in different parts of the United States.
LC NO. 75-703527
Prod-PENNZ Dist-PENNZ Prodn-SANDLR 1975

Penology - The Keeper Of The Keys C 20 MIN
16MM FILM, 3/4 OR 1/2 IN VIDEO
Explores the philosophy, difficulties, and future possibilities of penology.
Prod-DOCUA Dist-CNEMAG

Pensacola Panorama C 15 MIN
16MM FILM OPTICAL SOUND
Presents Pensacola, one of Florida's oldest cities and the home of the Naval Air Training Command.
Prod-FLADC Dist-FLADC

Pensions - The Broken Promise C 39 MIN
16MM FILM OPTICAL SOUND C A
Looks at the fiction of pensions for many American employees who work long hard years for a company, spurred on by the idea that their retirement years will be carefree, only to find this dream of security has faded along with their pension funds.
Prod-ACI Dist-UILL

Pentagon Papers, The B 30 MIN
16MM FILM OPTICAL SOUND
Examines our government's shocking record of public deception, the right of the public to receive full information on government policy, the rights of free speech and the need to support a government which is truly responsible to the people. Depicts the dramatic change in Ellsberg's social conscience, from that of a dedicated defense department worker to a public citizen understanding that our first trust must be in the Constitution and in the Bill of Rights.
Prod-STOLLJ Dist-IMPACT 1973

Pentagon Papers, The C 14 MIN
3/4 OR 1/2 INCH VIDEO CASSETTE H-C A
Tells how the secret history of America's conduct in Vietnam was revealed through the nation's press. Documents the controversy between the government's need for secrecy and the people's right to know.
Prod-UPI Dist-JOU

Pentagon, Inc C 58 MIN
3/4 OR 1/2 INCH VIDEO CASSETTE
Examines military procurement, raising questions concerning how well and how effectively the defense budget is being spent.
From The Frontline Series.
LC NO. 83-706519
Prod-DOCCON Dist-PBS

Pentode Crystal Oscillator B 30 MIN
16MM FILM OPTICAL SOUND
Explains the importance of stability in the pentode crystal oscillator and discusses the importance of each component. Tells how the correct amount and phase of feedback voltage is obtained and demonstrates the correct tuning procedure for the most stable operation.
LC NO. 74-705337
Prod-USAF Dist-USNAC 1970

Pentodes And Pentagrids B 28 MIN
16MM FILM OPTICAL SOUND
Illustrates the schematic of a pentode tube and identifies the elements. Explains the purpose of the suppressor grid. Shows the schematic of a pentagrid grid and the additional screen grid. Discusses multiknit tubes, explaining what they are and how they work. (Kinescope)
LC NO. 74-705338
Prod-USAF Dist-USNAC 1972

People C 22 MIN
16MM FILM OPTICAL SOUND
Looks at the men and women of the U S Army Corps of Engineers who perform a variety of jobs in the U S and overseas. Describes the wide range of Corps missions that support the Army and the nation, and portrays the spectrum of surprising jobs performed.
Prod-USAE Dist-MTP

People C 11 MIN
16MM FILM, 3/4 OR 1/2 IN VIDEO P-I
Provides a vivid gallery of different kinds of human beings.
Prod-FILMSW Dist-FLMFR

People C 15 MIN
3/4 OR 1/2 INCH VIDEO CASSETTE P
See series title for descriptive statement.
From The Let's Draw Series.
Prod-OCPS Dist-AITECH Prodn-KOKHTV 1976

People - Bringing Life To The City C 13 MIN
16MM FILM, 3/4 OR 1/2 IN VIDEO
Examines the ethnic neighborhood and earlier immigrant neighborhoods and shows a variety of activities in which people act out parts of their own particular traditions. Includes scenes of the Chinese New Year celebration, an ice hockey game, the smashing of the pinata at a Mexican party and a Black choir singing gospel music.
Prod-JOU Dist-JOU 1971

People - Different But Alike C 10 MIN
16MM FILM, 3/4 OR 1/2 IN VIDEO P-I
Uses pantomime, music and rhyme to show the effects of making fun of people who are superficially different. Emphasizes that it is what is inside a person that counts. Formerly entitled Little Bigots.
Prod-CAHILL Dist-AIMS 1975

People - Different But Alike (Spanish) C 10 MIN
16MM FILM, 3/4 OR 1/2 IN VIDEO P-I
Uses pantomime, music and rhyme to show the effects of making fun of people who are superficially different. Emphasizes that it is what is inside a person that counts Formerly entitled Little Bigots.
Prod-CAHILL Dist-AIMS 1975

People - Figures In Action C 15 MIN
3/4 OR 1/2 INCH VIDEO CASSETTE P
See series title for descriptive statement.
From The Let's Draw Series.
Prod-OCPS Dist-AITECH Prodn-KOKHTV 1976

People Afloat C 12 MIN
16MM FILM OPTICAL SOUND H A
Shows a variety of boats and how they should be handled. Stresses basic elements of safety in boating and recreation.
Prod-AREDC Dist-AMRC

People Afloat X 15 MIN
16MM FILM OPTICAL SOUND I A
Teaches safety measures to be taken by owners of inboard and outboard boats when the family takes to the waterways. Discusses the need for craft safety and skills in swimming and lifesaving, first aid and water safety.
Prod-AMRC Dist-AMRC 1962

People And Apollo, The C 19 MIN
16MM FILM OPTICAL SOUND
Tells a unique story of civil preparedness at the local level in connection with the Apollo 16 moon shot from Cape Kennedy. Shows how the Civil Defense Office organized a task force for traffic control, crowd handling and a variety of emergency services.
LC NO. 74-705340
Prod-USDCPA Dist-USNAC 1973

People And Events - Major Powell B 20 MIN
2 INCH VIDEOTAPE I
Aids children in identifying with the great men and deeds of the past. (Broadcast quality)
From The Quest For The Best Series.
Prod-DENVPS Dist-GPITVL Prodn-KRMATV

People And Particles B 28 MIN
16MM FILM OPTICAL SOUND
Follows physicists at the Cambridge electron accelerator as they design, construct and assemble equipment for an experiment in high energy physics.
LC NO. FIA68-544
Prod-HPP Dist-MLA Prodn-CCVISA 1967

People And Places Of Antiquity—A Series
16MM FILM, 3/4 OR 1/2 IN VIDEO I-C A
Examines six civilizations of pre-history. Narrated by Anthony Quayle.
Prod-CFDLD Dist-CORF

Egypt - Gift Of The Nile 029 MIN
Iran - Landmarks In The Desert 027 MIN
Iraq - Stairway To The Gods 027 MIN
Pakistan - Mound Of The Dead 027 MIN
Peru - People Of The Sun 025 MIN
Turkey - Crossroads Of The Ancient World 027 MIN

People And Productivity - We Learn From The Japanese C 28 MIN
16MM FILM, 3/4 OR 1/2 IN VIDEO H-C A
Presents a former U S ambassador to Japan and a professor from the Harvard business school who analyze the values of the respectful and industrious Japanese people that have made them world leaders in manufacturing. Includes views of assembly lines in Japan and the Honda plant in Ohio which applies proven Japanese practices to its U S operation.
LC NO. 82-706710
Prod-OLINC Dist-EBEC 1982

People And Statistics B 30 MIN
16MM FILM OPTICAL SOUND PRO
Explains the 'HOW AND WHY' of statistics and discusses the appropriateness of sample, design, collection, tabulation, analysis and interpretation of data.
From The Public Health Science - Biostatistics Series.
Prod-KUHTTV Dist-GPITVL

People And Statistics B 30 MIN
2 INCH VIDEOTAPE PRO
Presents Dr Glasser explaining the 'how and why' of statistics and discusses the appropriateness of sample design, collection, tabulation, analysis and interpretation of data. (Broadcast quality)
From The Public Health Science Series. Unit II - Introduction To Biostatistics
Prod-TEXWU Dist-GPITVL Prodn-KUHTTV

People And Their Guns, The B 97 MIN
16MM FILM OPTICAL SOUND
Provides an understanding of the way in which the Laotian people relate to each other and their struggle to develop the new patterns of socialist life which are being forged in the very process of struggle.
Prod-IMPACT Dist-IMPACT 1970

People And Things - Careers In Manufacturing C 13 MIN
16MM FILM OPTICAL SOUND I-H
Deals with the broad range of career opportunities within the manufacturing industry. Looks at these careers in terms of the design function, capital goods manufacturing and consumer goods manufacturing. Examines assembly line occupations as both a source of career opportunity and as an area of the working world which has been a source of worker dissatisfaction.
From The Working Worlds Series.
LC NO. 75-701543
Prod-OLYMPS Dist-FFORIN 1974

People Are All Alike C 10 MIN
16MM FILM OPTICAL SOUND
Uses case histories of five completely different workers to demonstrate to supervisors that people all have the same basic motivations and needs, which must be recognized in an efficiently run operation.
From The Human Factors In Safety Series.
LC NO. FIA66-518
Prod-NSC Dist-NSC Prodn-ALTSUL 1965

People Are Different And Alike C 11 MIN
16MM FILM, 3/4 OR 1/2 IN VIDEO P-I
Points out that it is easy to see differences in people but that people are more alike in the important ways. Shows that all people need friendship and love, food and a place to live and that they want an education, fun and happiness.
Prod-CORF Dist-CORF 1967

People Are Just People C 18 MIN
16MM FILM OPTICAL SOUND H-C
Discusses human frailties and the costly effects of the frailties when they are allowed to affect one's performance on the job. Shows human weaknesses, indifference, laziness, carelessness, forgetfulness and temptation.
LC NO. 74-700471
Prod-NCR Dist-NCR 1966

People Are Many, Fields Are Small C 32 MIN
16MM FILM OPTICAL SOUND
Presents three farm families who are engaged in Taiwan's long two-crop summer rice cycle and compares their lives to those of industrial laborers. Shows them expressing both pride and anger concerning conditions of farm life.
From The Faces Of Change - Taiwan Series.
Prod-AUFS Dist-WHEELK

People Are People C 8 MIN
16MM FILM, 3/4 OR 1/2 IN VIDEO
Introduces Ginny, who is an 11-year-old dwarf. Shows her daily activities such as helping her mother, riding her bike, and playing with her brother and other children. Reveals some of the problems with which she is faced.
From The Zoom Series.
Prod-WGBHTV Dist-FI 1978

People Are The Puzzle C 10 MIN
16MM FILM OPTICAL SOUND
Shows that the relation of the foreman to his men is a key ingredient in safety.
From The Key Man Series.
Prod-NSC Dist-NSC

People Ask About Cancer C 25 MIN
3/4 OR 1/2 INCH VIDEO CASSETTE
Presents five top cancer researchers who take questions on cancer from an in-studio audience. Includes topics on current theories on the diagnosis and cure of cancer, cancer quacks and promising areas of research that may lead to a cure of this dreaded disease.
Prod-TRAINX Dist-TRAINX

People Ask About Heart Disease C 25 MIN
3/4 OR 1/2 INCH VIDEO CASSETTE
Shows a heart surgeon, cardiologists and heart attack victims answering questions from a studio audience. Includes as topics the effects of smoking and cholesterol on the circulatory system, the vein-graft bypass operation and what life is like after a heart attack.
Prod-TRAINX Dist-TRAINX

People At Work C 20 MIN
3/4 INCH VIDEO CASSETTE I
Shows people who make goods and provide services. Tells how they get to work and discusses labor and management.
From The Exploring Our Nation Series.
Prod-KRMATV Dist-GPITVL 1975

People At Work - A Right To Refuse C 13 MIN
16MM FILM, 3/4 OR 1/2 IN VIDEO H-C A
Shows workers in an industrial boiler room who begin to question the safety of their working conditions. Shows the workers' foreman who has a deadline to meet for management, but what can he do when the workers walk off the job.
LC NO. 82-706512
Prod-NFBC Dist-CRMP 1982

People At Work - How Jobs Change C 12 MIN
16MM FILM, 3/4 OR 1/2 IN VIDEO I-J
Shows how the world of work is constantly changing and how these changes affect job opportunities.
From The People At Work Series.
Prod-CORF Dist-CORF 1976

People At Work - How People Choose Jobs C 14 MIN
16MM FILM, 3/4 OR 1/2 IN VIDEO I-J
Shows how aptitude, interest, training, pay, availability, fringe benefits and company size influence the jobs that workers choose.
From The People At Work Series.
Prod-CORF Dist-CORF 1976

People At Work - Many Kinds Of Jobs C 10 MIN
16MM FILM, 3/4 OR 1/2 IN VIDEO I-J
Shows how people use what they know of themselves and the work itself in choosing a job that is satisfying to them.
From The People At Work Series.
Prod-CORF Dist-CORF 1976

People At Work–A Series
16MM FILM, 3/4 OR 1/2 IN VIDEO I-J
Observes and discusses different workers.
Prod-CORF Dist-CORF 1976

People At Work - How Jobs Change 12 MIN
People At Work - How People Choose Jobs 14 MIN
People At Work - Many Kinds Of Jobs 10 MIN

People Business C 17 MIN
16MM FILM OPTICAL SOUND
Traces the history of the London Life Insurance Company in celebration of its 100th anniversary.
LC NO. 74-702501
Prod-LONLIF Dist-LONLIF Prodn-CUNLIM 1974

People Called Methodist, The C 28 MIN
16MM FILM OPTICAL SOUND
Shows the variety of ministries among Methodists in five representative locations, including Australia, Singapore, Bolivia, Sierra Leone and Jerusalem.
LC NO. 76-700401
Prod-UMCOM Dist-ECUFLM 1975

People Called Methodist, The (Spanish) C 28 MIN
16MM FILM OPTICAL SOUND
Shows the variety of ministries among Methodists in five representative locations, including Australia, Singapore, Bolivia, Sierra Leone and Jerusalem.
LC NO. 76-700401
Prod-UMCOM Dist-ECUFLM 1975

People Chosen, A - Who Is A Jew C 57 MIN
16MM FILM, 3/4 OR 1/2 IN VIDEO J-C A
Centers on the intensive, continuing debate by governments and their private sectors, inside and outside of Israel, over the role that religion plays in identity. Questions Jews from different walks of life about their identity.
Prod-KROSNY Dist-PHENIX 1976

People Don't Dance To Jazz C 30 MIN
16MM FILM, 3/4 OR 1/2 IN VIDEO J-C A
Deals with the day in a teenager's life when he must decide about his life's ambitions despite changes in his family and pressures from his friends.
Prod-PREMI Dist-MOKIN 1979

People Don't Resist Change C 24 MIN
16MM FILM - 3/4 IN VIDEO IND
Examines the different approaches to motivating people to accept change.
Prod-BNA Dist-BNA 1967

People Factor In Our Productivity Improvement, The C 35 MIN
3/4 OR 1/2 INCH VIDEO CASSETTE
Explains why the people factor in productivity improvement for one company focuses on specific projects instead of psychological generalities, enabling employees to make substantial productivity improvements.
Prod-SME Dist-SME

People Factor, The - The Hawthorne Studies For Today's Managers C 11 MIN
16MM FILM, 3/4 OR 1/2 IN VIDEO C A
Considers research associated with the Hawthorne studies and its implications in personnel management. Shows that informal social organizations among employees can have important effects on employee morale and productivity.
Prod-ROBINH Dist-SALENG 1976

People Helping People - Nursing Home C 9 MIN
16MM FILM OPTICAL SOUND
Depicts the modern facilities of well-built, well-managed and well-equipped nursing homes.
LC NO. 75-700806
Prod-USDHUD Dist-USNAC 1970

People In Action C 25 MIN
2 INCH VIDEOTAPE I
Demonstrates figure drawing.
From The Art For Every Day Series.
Prod-CVETVC Dist-GPITVL

People In Crisis C 30 MIN
3/4 OR 1/2 INCH VIDEO CASSETTE
Deals with the importance of coordinating a hospital's efforts to assure timely and efficient patient discharges. Illustrates hospital and patient benefits through interaction among medical, nursing, social work and community services.
Prod-AHOA Dist-AHOA

People In Jazz–A Series

Portrays jazz musicians as individuals with wide ranges of experience, interests and expertise. Mixes informal conversation with musical performance. Includes famous and lesser-known jazz musicians, featuring jazz disc jockey Jim Rockwell as host.
Prod-WTVSTV Dist-PUBTEL

Dorothy Ashby 29 MIN
George Benson 29 MIN
H P Barmun 29 MIN
Joe Williams 29 MIN
Lou Rawls 29 MIN
Michigan State University Jazz Ensemble 29 MIN
Misty Wizards 29 MIN
Roland Kirk 29 MIN
Ron Brooks And Group 29 MIN
Trudy Pitts 29 MIN
Wes Montgomery 29 MIN

People In Management C 18 MIN
16MM FILM, 3/4 OR 1/2 IN VIDEO J-C A
Takes a look at jobs in the management field through the experiences of several people with jobs covering all levels of management experience, from management trainee to company president.
Prod-BFA Dist-PHENIX Prodn-SILSHA 1976

People In Progress, A - Ecuador C 28 MIN
16MM FILM OPTICAL SOUND
Explains how the Salesian Missions are helping small farmers in Ecuador achieve independence and a measure of prosperity through cooperatives and low interest loans. Shows how poverty can be overcome by personal effort, organization and cooperation.
Prod-SCC Dist-MTP

People In The North C 180 MIN
3/4 OR 1/2 INCH VIDEO CASSETTE PRO
Tells about the historical and anthropological aspects of people in the North, and logistics, including frostbite, hypothermia and productivity.
From The Arctic Engineering Series.
Prod-UAKEN Dist-AMCEE

People Left Behind, The B 31 MIN
16MM FILM OPTICAL SOUND H-C A
Depicts the plight of Mississippi's ex-plantation laborers whose jobs have been eliminated by the cotton picking machine, minimum-wage laws and legislation, which pays farmers for not cultivating land. Former plantation workers describe their situation and show scenes of their impoverished environment.
From The Public Broadcast Laboratory Series.
LC NO. FIA68-1503
Prod-NET Dist-IU 1968

People Make It Happen C 23 MIN
16MM FILM OPTICAL SOUND
Emphasizes the importance of consumer behavior in product safety. Shows how selection, use, maintenance, storage and disposal of consumer products affects the safety of those products.
LC NO. 76-703437
Prod-CPSAFC Dist-USNAC 1976

People Make It Happen C 24 MIN
16MM FILM OPTICAL SOUND T
Discusses the need for creating effective adult education courses.
From The Further Education Series.
LC NO. 77-702845
Prod-ADEAV Dist-CENTWO Prodn-CENTWO 1976

People Make Music C 15 MIN
16MM FILM, 3/4 OR 1/2 IN VIDEO
Presents a young folksinger singing and talking about the songs that his great grandfather sang on a mountain farm in North Carolina.
From The Ripples Series.
LC NO. 73-702149
Prod-NITC Dist-AITECH

People Make Programs C 12 MIN
16MM FILM, 3/4 OR 1/2 IN VIDEO I-J
Uses narration, dramatizations and tours of a TV studio to help show how television programs are developed from the original idea to the finished show.
From The Getting The Most Out Of TV Series.
LC NO. 81-706058
Prod-TAPPRO Dist-MTI 1981

People Management C 45 MIN
3/4 OR 1/2 INCH VIDEO CASSETTE PRO
Highlights motivation. Sets forth the expectancy theory and project goals. Explores dual reporting.
From The Advanced Project Management Series.
Prod-AMCEE Dist-AMCEE

People March, The - Mass Demonstration B 30 MIN
16MM FILM OPTICAL SOUND H-C A
Joanne Grant discusses the use of mass demonstrations in the struggle for civil rights, the rise of civil rights organizations, the achievements of demonstrations and the violent responses from whites.
From The Black History, Section 20 - Freedom Movement Series.
LC NO. 73-704111
Prod-WCBSTV Dist-HRAW 1969

People Movers, The C 10 MIN
16MM FILM OPTICAL SOUND
Describes a twin hull ferry designed and built by a Hobart, Australia firm.
LC NO. 80-700917
Prod-TASCOR Dist-TASCOR 1977

People Need People C 15 MIN
16MM FILM, 3/4 OR 1/2 IN VIDEO I
Shows the importance of working together and the effectiveness of interdependent relationships. Presents examples of positive dependent and interdependent relationships in work and leisure activities.
From The Bread And Butterflies Series.
LC NO. 74-703187
Prod-AITV Dist-AITECH Prodn-WHROTV 1973

People Of Brazil, The C 23 MIN
16MM FILM OPTICAL SOUND
Looks at the life of Brazilians in the cities, on the waterways and the plantations, in the marketplaces, including views of the people at work, at prayer and at play.
LC NO. 74-702660
Prod-MMAMC Dist-MMAMC Prodn-FILMA 1974

People Of Hungary, The C 18 MIN
16MM FILM OPTICAL SOUND I-H A
Portrays an eastern European country under the dominance of Russian communism. The land, people and culture are depicted through a variety of scenes emphasizing the history and the current political implications faced by the people of Hungary.
Prod-WIANCK Dist-AVED 1962

People Of Influence C 30 MIN
16MM FILM, 3/4 OR 1/2 IN VIDEO H-C A
Examines the human 'troika' which governs the lives of all Russians at the local level and which includes the Director, the Trade Union Chairman and the Communist Party Secretary.
From The Russians Series.
Prod-FLMAUS Dist-LCOA 1979

People Of Nes Ammin, The C 60 MIN
16MM FILM, 3/4 OR 1/2 IN VIDEO
Focuses on a farming community of ecumenical Christians in northern Israel, whose inhabitants seek to build a bridge of understanding and mutual respect between Jews and Christians. Shows how their participation in the State of Israel serves as an act of atonement for crimes perpetrated against the Jews by avowedly Christian nations.
From The Bill Moyers' Journal Series.
LC NO. 79-706331
Prod-WNETTV Dist-WNETTV 1979

People Of People's China, The C 52 MIN
3/4 INCH VIDEO CASSETTE H-C
Probes the myths and realities of life in China. Discusses the lifestyles and values of typical working people and focuses on the struggle between educational traditionalists and revolutionaries since the Cultural Revolution.
Prod-ABCTV Dist-GA

People Of People's Temple C 24 MIN
16MM FILM, 3/4 OR 1/2 IN VIDEO H-C A
Asks what caused the mass suicide at Jonestown, Guyana.
Prod-NBC Dist-FI 1979

People Of The Book, The B 30 MIN
16MM FILM OPTICAL SOUND
Portrays the diversity of Israel's inhabitants. Includes scenes of Premier David Ben-gurion, engineers and technicians at Israel's Institute of Technology at Haifa, Druse children taught by a Christain Arab woman, Jewish orphans studying and learning trades at a children's village as well as scribes, soldiers, clerics, curators, archeologists, farmers, shepherds, stone-masons and merchants.
LC NO. FIA64-1122
Prod-JTS Dist-NAAJS Prodn-NBC 1962

People Of The Book, The C 41 MIN
16MM FILM, 3/4 OR 1/2 IN VIDEO H A
Discusses the effects which Christian, Islamic and Jewish people have had on each other throughout the centuries. Describes the Crusades, the Inquisition and the expulsion of Jews from Spain.
From The Christians Series.
Prod-GRATV Dist-MGHT 1978

People Of The Buffalo (Rev Ed) C 15 MIN
16MM FILM, 3/4 OR 1/2 IN VIDEO I-H
Portrays the relationship between Indians and buffalo through contemporary painting of life on the Western Plains. Explains the westward advance of the white settlers and Plains Indians for possession of the Western Plains.
Prod-NFBC Dist-EBEC 1969

People Of The Chad, B 13 MIN
16MM FILM OPTICAL SOUND
Records native life in the interior of French Equatorial Africa. Shows how the inhabitants work the natural resources of the region in the most primitive ways.
Prod-VICASV Dist-RADIM 1945

People Of The Cities C 30 MIN
16MM FILM, 3/4 OR 1/2 IN VIDEO H-C A
Shows a bus driver, a dockworker and a doctor in Russia. Examines the urban structure of Russian cities.
From The Russians Series.
Prod-FLMAUS Dist-LCOA 1979

People Of The Country C 30 MIN
16MM FILM, 3/4 OR 1/2 IN VIDEO H-C A
Explores the collective farms of Russia.
From The Russians Series.
Prod-FLMAUS Dist-LCOA 1979

People Of The Cumberland B 18 MIN
16MM FILM OPTICAL SOUND J-C A
Details the community function of the Highlander Folk School in Monteagle, Tennessee, and its early work in training union organizers and providing guidance to the miners and textile workers of the Cumberland Mountains.
Prod-HILSTE Dist-AFLCIO 1938

People Of The First Light–A Series

Discusses the Native American Indian tribes populating the states of Rhode Island, Massachusetts and Connecticut. Focuses on the Narragansetts, Pequots, Wampanoags, Mohegans, Nipmucs and Paugausetts.
Prod-WGBYTV Dist-GPITVL 1977

Boston Indian Community, The 30 MIN
Indian Experience, The 303 MIN
Indians Of Connecticut, The 30 MIN
Indians Of Southern New England 30 MIN
Mashpee Wampanogs, The 30 MIN
Narragansetts, The 30 MIN
Wampanoags Of Gay Head, The 30 MIN

People Of The Free Train C 15 MIN
16MM FILM OPTICAL SOUND I-J

Depicts the life of the East Indian farmers of Fiji who work for the sugar company and use the free train ride to visit friends or the market. Shows sugar cane planting, rice harvesting, villages and the market.
From The Pacific Islands Series.
Prod-MMP Dist-MMP 1961

People Of The Seal--A Series

Summarizes the migratory cycle of the Netsilik Eskimo. Comprises a condensed version of an 11-hour ethnographic film made in 1963 to 1965.
Prod-EDC Dist-EDC

Eskimo Summer 052 MIN
Eskimo Winter 052 MIN

People Of The Seal, Pt 1 C 52 MIN
16MM FILM OPTICAL SOUND J-C A
Presents an examination of the lives of the Netsilik Eskimos of the Canadian Arctic, their work and play and the ways in which they cope with the frigid climate of the North.
LC NO. 73-700245
Prod-BBCL Dist-EDC 1971

People Of The Seal, Pt 2 C 52 MIN
16MM FILM OPTICAL SOUND J-C A
Presents an examination of the lives of the Netsilik Eskimos of the Canadian Arctic, their work and play and the ways in which they cope with the frigid climate of the North.
LC NO. 73-700245
Prod-BBCL Dist-EDC 1971

People On Market Street--A Series
16MM FILM, 3/4 OR 1/2 IN VIDEO H A
Explains the basic principles of economics that affect events in everyone's life.
Prod-FNDREE Dist-WDEMCO Prodn-KAHNT 1977

Cost 19 MIN
Demand 21 MIN
Market Clearing Price 23 MIN
Property Rights And Pollution 19 MIN
Scarcity And Planning 16 MIN
Supply 19 MIN
Wages And Production 18 MIN

People On The Macon Plateau C 12 MIN
16MM FILM, 3/4 OR 1/2 IN VIDEO
Introduces the history of Indian cultures of the Macon Plateau in Georgia and the area around the Ocmulgee National Monument. Emphasizes the Mississippian Indian culture.
LC NO. 81-707122
Prod-USNPS Dist-USNAC 1981

People On The Move C 20 MIN
16MM FILM, 3/4 OR 1/2 IN VIDEO J-H
Portrays a Jamaican family whose roots are in a relatively poor rural mountain part of the island. Reveals that part of the family still lives in the country while the rest have migrated to Kingston and beyond.
From The One World Series.
Prod-BBCTV Dist-FI 1982

People Patterns C 15 MIN
16MM FILM, 3/4 OR 1/2 IN VIDEO I
Explains how Richie's class studies the way people act or behave. Describes what happens when Richie notices that an elderly neighbor hasn't left his apartment as usual.
From The Thinkabout Series. Finding Patterns
LC NO. 81-706113
Prod-KOCETV Dist-AITECH 1979

People People In Social Services C 13 MIN
16MM FILM, 3/4 OR 1/2 IN VIDEO H
Introduces the various aspects of the social service field to students.
Prod-SCLARA Dist-AIMS 1975

People Places, The C 22 MIN
3/4 OR 1/2 INCH VIDEO CASSETTE J-H
See series title for descriptive statement.
From The Phenomenal World Series.
Prod-EBEC Dist-EBEC 1983

People Project, The C 13 MIN
16MM FILM OPTICAL SOUND
Presents an overview of the Salt River Project in Arizona.
LC NO. 79-700399
Prod-SARIV Dist-SARIV Prodn-LINMAN 1978

People Puzzle--A Series
I
Prod-WHROTV Dist-GPITVL

Anger 20 MIN
Copy Cats 20 MIN
Feelings 20 MIN
I Want To Be Wanted 20 MIN
My Actions Tell On Me 20 MIN
Ways I Am Me, The 20 MIN

People Sampler, A C 29 MIN
3/4 INCH VIDEO CASSETTE
Looks at the ordinary citizens of China, Russia and the United States.
From The Conversations With Allen Whiting Series.
Prod-UMITV Dist-UMITV 1979

People Sell People--A Series

Prod-SAUM Dist-MLA

Goodwill Ambassadors 7 MIN
Nothing But Lookers 8 MIN
One-To-One 13 MIN
Sales Building Role, The 7 MIN
You've Sold Me, Mrs Marlowe 9 MIN

People Shop, The - The Hospital In Your Community C 18 MIN
16MM FILM, 3/4 OR 1/2 IN VIDEO K-I
Presents a typical community hospital and the services it offers. Surveys the job of the hospital in the community. Confronts a child's concern when he has to enter.
Prod-ASPTEF Dist-LUF 1972

People Side Of Cancer, The C 14 MIN
16MM FILM OPTICAL SOUND PRO
Acquaints doctors and medical personnel and others with the human anguish of those experiencing cancer. Probes aspects including cancer in children, the effects of cancer on the family and the acceptance of death and the realities of terminal cancer.
LC NO. 73-700746
Prod-AMCS Dist-AMCS 1972

People Signs C 16 MIN
16MM FILM MAGNETIC SOUND K-C A S
See series title for descriptive statement.
From The PANCOM Beginning Total Communication Program For Hearing Parents Of... Series. Level 1
LC NO. 77-700504
Prod-CSDE Dist-JOYCE Prodn-CSFDF 1977

People Sing All Over The World B 15 MIN
2 INCH VIDEOTAPE P
Explains that the fun of singing together is universal wherever there are children. (Broadcast quality)
From The Around The Corner Series. No. 34
Prod-FWCETV Dist-GPITVL Prodn-WEDUTV

People Soup C 13 MIN
16MM FILM, 3/4 OR 1/2 IN VIDEO K-C A
Tells of the knack two brothers have for mixing magic potions from household ingredients. Enhances the inter-relationship of the two boys by one turning into a chicken and the other becoming a sheepdog. Produced by Alan Arkin and features his two sons.
Prod-PNGLOS Dist-LCOA 1970

People Talking B 27 MIN
16MM FILM OPTICAL SOUND
Deals with the problems of camera direction and composition during an interview-type presentation. Points out the diverse factors involved.
From The CETO Television Training Films Series.
Prod-CETO Dist-GPITVL

People That Time Forgot C 90 MIN
16MM FILM OPTICAL SOUND I A
Describes the rescue by major McBride of his old friend from a prehistoric island. Sequel to Land That Time Forgot. Stars Patrick Wayne and Doug McClure.
Prod-AIP Dist-TIMLIF 1977

People To People - Careers In Communications And Media C 13 MIN
16MM FILM OPTICAL SOUND I-H
Explores the variety of careers available in communications and media.
From The Working Worlds Series.
LC NO. 75-701542
Prod-OLYMPS Dist-FFORIN 1974

People Vs Inez Garcia, The C 88 MIN
3/4 OR 1/2 INCH VIDEO CASSETTE
Presents a dramatization of the explosive rape and murder trial of Inez Garcia, based on an adaptation of the actual court transcription of the 1974 trial in Monterey, California.
Prod-KQEDTV Dist-PBS 1975

People Vs Job Shattuck, The C 31 MIN
16MM FILM, 3/4 OR 1/2 IN VIDEO
Tells how Revolutionary War veteran Job Shattuck led a group of debt-ridden farmers to the courthouse in Concord, Massachusetts, to prevent the court from sitting, thereby forestalling foreclosures. Relates that Shattuck was later arrested and tried for treason.
From The Decades Of Decision - The American Revolution Series.
LC NO. 80-706343
Prod-NGS Dist-NGS 1975

People who Are Fighting Blindness C 29 MIN
3/4 OR 1/2 INCH VIDEO CASSETTE H-C A
Victims of genetic diseases which cause blindness and, in some cases, loss of hearing talk about the adjustments that they and their family members have made.
From The Are You Listening Series.
LC NO. 83-706226
Prod-STURTM Dist-STURTM 1982

People Who Have Epilepsy C 28 MIN
16MM FILM - 3/4 IN VIDEO I-C
Introduces several epileptics who discuss such topics as recognition of a seizure, the importance of feeling independent, and ways of coping with marriage, jobs and travel.
From The Are You Listening Series.
LC NO. 80-707173
Prod-STURTM Dist-STURTM 1979

People Who Help - Careers In Aviation C 16 MIN
16MM FILM, 3/4 OR 1/2 IN VIDEO J-C A
Discusses commercial aviation, general aviation and aerospace, focusing on career opportunities in these areas.
Prod-LIEBJH Dist-PHENIX 1975

People Who Help - Health Careers C 18 MIN
16MM FILM, 3/4 OR 1/2 IN VIDEO H-C A
Examines some of the career opportunities available in the field of health.
Prod-SMITG Dist-PHENIX 1975

People Who Sell Things C 18 MIN
16MM FILM, 3/4 OR 1/2 IN VIDEO H A
Describes the different kinds of sales careers and the kinds of people suited to them with examples of the daily activities of an insurance agent, a real estate broker, a telephone systems salesman and an automobile salesman.
Prod-SMITG Dist-PHENIX 1975

People Who Work In Factories C 11 MIN
16MM FILM, 3/4 OR 1/2 IN VIDEO P-I
Explains what a factory is, and shows the various kinds of jobs performed in factories. Follows factory workers through a typical day to show how people work together, combining their skills to produce a bicycle.
Prod-CORF Dist-CORF 1971

People Who Work In Manufacturing C 17 MIN
16MM FILM, 3/4 OR 1/2 IN VIDEO H-C A
Presents a vocational education film which shows key personnel in an electronics factory as they work, give their reasons for entering electronics and tell of the rewards and problems they meet each day.
Prod-SMITG Dist-PHENIX 1975

People Who Work With People C 14 MIN
16MM FILM, 3/4 OR 1/2 IN VIDEO J-C A
Explores the importance and rewards of working to help others. Follows the daily routine of several service workers as they discuss why they chose service work, what they get out of their jobs and what they offer in return.
Prod-BARR Dist-BARR Prodn-HALBH 1976

People Will Talk C 4 MIN
16MM FILM, 3/4 OR 1/2 IN VIDEO IND
Shows the effect which rumors and gossip can have on both the employees and employer.
From The This Matter Of Motivation Series.
Prod-CTRACT Dist-DARTNL Prodn-CALVIN 1966

People Working C 20 MIN
16MM FILM, 3/4 OR 1/2 IN VIDEO
Shows six artists of various kinds at work. Demonstrates the discipline and dedication demanded by art and considers the personal rewards of creating.
From The Images And Things Series.
LC NO. 73-702105
Prod-NITC Dist-AITECH

People Working - Behavior Modification As A Management Tool C 30 MIN
3/4 INCH VIDEO CASSETTE C A
Presents the key concepts of behavior modification and their application to industry. Gives examples of how behavior modification was used to motivate employees in three organizational situations.
LC NO. 79-706003
Prod-CSUF Dist-CSUF 1978

People Working - George Allen On Motivation And Leadership C 20 MIN
3/4 INCH VIDEO CASSETTE C
Presents football coach George Allen giving his views on motivation and leadership.
LC NO. 80-706790
Prod-CSUF Dist-CSUF 1979

People Working - Management Behavior, What Does A Manager Do All Day C 20 MIN
3/4 INCH VIDEO CASSETTE C
Presents Robert Clifford, president of Air California, discussing his activities as an executive, the roles he performs, and his views on being a manager.
LC NO. 80-706788
Prod-CSUF Dist-CSUF 1980

People Working - Pat Haden On Career And Life Planning C 20 MIN
3/4 INCH VIDEO CASSETTE C
Presents professional football player Pat Haden discussing his views on career and life planning.
LC NO. 80-706789
Prod-CSUF Dist-CSUF 1979

People Working With Data C 7 MIN
16MM FILM, 3/4 OR 1/2 IN VIDEO P
Explores careers that involve collecting, organizing and communicating data.
From The Career Awareness Series.
Prod-MGHT Dist-CRMP 1975

People Working With People C 7 MIN
16MM FILM, 3/4 OR 1/2 IN VIDEO P
Explores careers that focus on teaching, serving and caring for others.
From The Career Awareness Series.
Prod-MGHT Dist-CRMP 1975

People Working With Things C 7 MIN
16MM FILM, 3/4 OR 1/2 IN VIDEO P
Discovers the career possibilities open to those who like to make, operate or fix things.
From The Career Awareness Series.
Prod-MGHT Dist-CRMP 1975

People You Meet C
16MM FILM, 3/4 OR 1/2 IN VIDEO
Presents different episodes to demonstrate an important language item in English, at the intermediate level.
Prod-NORTNJ Dist-NORTNJ

People You Never See, The C 28 MIN
16MM FILM, 3/4 OR 1/2 IN VIDEO
Depicts a 12-year-old girl with severe cerebral palsy eagerly participating in class activities through the use of Bliss symbols and a typewriter. Shows six handicapped adults who have left the protection of institutions and live as an extended family despite the architectural barriers they encounter.
Prod-CANBC Dist-FLMLIB

People You'd Like To Know - An Introduction C 20 MIN
16MM FILM, 3/4 OR 1/2 IN VIDEO C A
Concerns the need for a change of attitudes toward handicapped children as they increasingly participate in school and the community.
From The People You'd Like To Know Series.
Prod-EBEC Dist-EBEC 1977

People You'd Like To Know—A Series
16MM FILM, 3/4 OR 1/2 IN VIDEO I-H
Introduces young people with various physical and emotional disabilities, and shows how they are working to deal with these problems.
Prod-WGBHTV Dist-EBEC 1978

C J 010 MIN
Dee 010 MIN
Diana 010 MIN
Elizabeth 010 MIN
Harold 010 MIN
John 010 MIN
Kai 010 MIN
Mark 010 MIN
Mary 010 MIN
Paige 010 MIN
People You'd Like To Know - An Introduction 020 MIN

People, Communication And Negotiation C 13 MIN
3/4 OR 1/2 INCH VIDEO CASSETTE A
Reveals that instead of the traditional clash method of negotiation, an exploratory process called exlectics can be used in which the 'logic bubbles' of other people are looked at and all sides of a situation can be examined.
From The Thinking In Action Series. Module 3
Prod-BBCTV Dist-FI 1983

People, Not Paper C 18 MIN
16MM FILM, 3/4 OR 1/2 IN VIDEO A
Documents the problem caused by bureaucratic paperwork. Includes illustrations and examples drawn from the work of the two-year Commission on Federal Paperwork. Demonstrates steps which can be taken to alleviate the situation.
Prod-USCFP Dist-USNAC Prodn-ADMONE 1977

People, People, People C 5 MIN
16MM FILM, 3/4 OR 1/2 IN VIDEO I-C A
Gives an animated overview of America's many-peopled heritage. Shows the peopling of America from the first Mongolian crossing the Bering land bridge on through the many explorers, settlers and immigrants.
Prod-HUBLEY Dist-PFP 1976

People, People, People C 5 MIN
3/4 INCH VIDEO CASSETTE I-C A
Gives an animated overview of America's many-peopled heritage. Shows the peopling of America from the first Mongolian crossing the Bering land bridge on through the many explorers, settlers and immigrants.
LC NO. 76-706223
Prod-USARBA Dist-USNAC Prodn-HUBLEY 1976

People, People, People - Bane Or Blessing C 20 MIN
2 INCH VIDEOTAPE J-H
Poses the problem of population explosion and examines whether it is possible to have too many people and if there is a balance between human and other resources.
From The Our World Of Economics Series.
Prod-MPATI Dist-GPITVL

People, Places, Things, Now—A Series

Prod-WPSXTV Dist-PSUPCR 1973

Who Is Tracy Williams 28 MIN

People, Product And Performance C 29 MIN
16MM FILM OPTICAL SOUND
Shows 23 different General Motors Corporation plants in different countries as well as the people, customs and lifestyles in these nations.
LC NO. 78-700209
Prod-GM Dist-GM Prodn-PETSON 1978

People, Products And Prices (A Film On Hedging And Speculating) C 26 MIN
16MM FILM OPTICAL SOUND
Discusses both hedging and speculating in the futures market from the vantage point of a farmer, exporter, processor, the brokerage house and traders on the floor. Explains the complexities of the futures market in operation and how it can benefit all levels of the marketing chain as well as public speculators.
Prod-CBT Dist-MTP

People, The C 20 MIN
3/4 OR 1/2 INCH VIDEO CASSETTE I-J
Explains that the Middle East is a region of paradoxes, where boys and girls in rural villages chant their Koranic verses and men and women operate television stations and computerized newspaper plants.
From The Project Middle East Series.
Prod-UNICEF Dist-GPITVL

People, The B 22 MIN
16MM FILM, 3/4 OR 1/2 IN VIDEO I-H
Uses newsreel footage to focus on important people of the 20th century.
From The Eyewitness To History Series.
Prod-WDEMCO Dist-WDEMCO 1978

People, The C 28 MIN
3/4 OR 1/2 INCH VIDEO CASSETTE
Documents the struggle of the Siletz Indian tribe in Oregon to regain federal recognition of their tribe. Interweaves a history of federal Indian policies with personal remembrances from tribal members.
Prod-DAWSH Dist-MEDIPR 1976

People's Charter B 17 MIN
16MM FILM OPTICAL SOUND
Discusses how the idea of the United Nations was born. Shows how the United Nations was organized in San Francisco and pictures the first meeting of the U N Assembly in London.
Prod-UN Dist-UN 1947

People's Court C 28 MIN
3/4 OR 1/2 INCH VIDEO CASSETTE PRO
Describes the operation of the People's Court in Chicago. Explains the purpose and procedures. Offers suggestions for out-of-court settlements and preparations for court appearances.
Prod-ABACPE Dist-ABACPE

People's Music, A - Soviet Style C 23 MIN
16MM FILM, 3/4 OR 1/2 IN VIDEO J-C A
Examines Soviet culture, from highly regarded professional troupes to the work of amateurs who've achieved remarkably high standards. Shows how traditional songs and dances are kept alive by all the people.
From The Soviet Style Series.
LC NO. 84-707066
Prod-JOU Dist-JOU 1982

People's Park B 20 MIN
16MM FILM OPTICAL SOUND
Shows the giant university using brutal repression as the students and community of Berkeley transform a vacant university-owned lot into a people's park. Explains that private property is valued over human life and that the police and National Guard will protect the interests of the giant corporations while new weapons of counter-insurgency are tested on the citizens.
Prod-SFN Dist-SFN

People's Temple C 24 MIN
16MM FILM OPTICAL SOUND
Documents the origins of the People's Temple Community in California. Includes interviews with Pastor Jim Jones, providing insight into his charismatic character, and presents case histories.
LC NO. 73-702353
Prod-USC Dist-USC 1973

People's Wall C 25 MIN
16MM FILM OPTICAL SOUND J-C A
Shows the progress of a 200-foot-long mural in San Francisco which depicts the unofficial labor history of the city. Includes footage of the events shown on the mural.
LC NO. 81-701583
Prod-FINLIN Dist-CANCIN 1978

People's War B 45 MIN
16MM FILM OPTICAL SOUND
Presents the trip to North Vietnam in the summer of 1969 and shows the daily struggle of the Vietnamese people.
Prod-SFN Dist-SFN

Peoples Like Us C 15 MIN
16MM FILM, 3/4 OR 1/2 IN VIDEO I-H A
Shows how diversity is reflected in the equally vast variety of social structures that different people have developed over many hundreds of years.
Prod-LUF Dist-LUF 1982

Peoples Of The Island World C 17 MIN
16MM FILM, 3/4 OR 1/2 IN VIDEO I-J
Describes how the islands of the South and Central Pacific were originally populated by three major groups of native people—the Melanesians, the Micronesians and the Polynesians. Shows their movement to Australia from Asia, then migrating by fragile canoes to the islands to the north, east and south.
From The Cultures Of Southern Seas Series.
Prod-HOE Dist-MCFI 1967

Peoples Of The Soviet Union B 38 MIN
3/4 OR 1/2 INCH VIDEO CASSETTE J-C A
Prod-IFF Dist-IFF

Peoples Of The Soviet Union (2nd Ed) B 33 MIN
16MM FILM OPTICAL SOUND I-C
Surveys the different nationalities that make up the people of the USSR, from the city dwellers of Moscow and Leningrad to the primitive tribes of the Caucasus and Siberia. Photographed in the 30's.
Prod-IFF Dist-IFF Prodn-BRYAN 1952

Peoples Theatre, The C 30 MIN
3/4 OR 1/2 INCH VIDEO CASSETTE
See series title for descriptive statement.
From The Kaleidoscope Series.
Prod-KTEHTV Dist-SCCOE

Pepe C 157 MIN
16MM FILM OPTICAL SOUND I-C
Stars Cantinflas as Pepe, a simple-hearted peon ranch hand, who, through his devotion to a horse he has raised from a colt, finds himself flung into the never-never land of the entertainment world to have amusing encounters with many famous stars.
Prod-CPC Dist-TWYMAN 1960

Pepe Teaches Us - Pepe Nos Ensena C 7 MIN
16MM FILM, 3/4 OR 1/2 IN VIDEO P-I
Introduces words for parts of the body.
From The Bilingual Film Series, Module 1 - Let's Get Ready Series.
Prod-BRNTNO Dist-CAROUF 1973

Pepe's Family B 45 MIN
16MM FILM, 3/4 OR 1/2 IN VIDEO H-C A
Concerns the rural exodus from Andalusia, Spain, and its effect on the family life of a migrant laborer who works in Germany. Depicts the family relationships while the father is absent and focuses on his concerns during holiday visits.
LC NO. 79-706044
Prod-MINTZJ Dist-IU 1978

Pepper - The Master Spice C 26 MIN
3/4 OR 1/2 INCH VIDEO CASSETTE J A
Documents the importance of pepper in medieval times and how it motivated the voyages of early European explorers. Describes the various uses of pepper today.
From The Spice Of Life Series.
Prod-BLCKRD Dist-BCNFL 1985

Peppercorns - Fresh Ground Flavor C 26 MIN
3/4 OR 1/2 INCH VIDEO CASSETTE J A
Describes the uses of peppercorn around the world.
From The Spice Of Life Series.
Prod-BLCKRD Dist-BCNFL 1985

Peppermint Soda (French) C 97 MIN
16MM FILM OPTICAL SOUND
Centers on the friends, family, classes, vacations, sulks, sexual misconceptions, pop records, bad grades, adventures, and misadventures of a French-Jewish schoolgirl in 1963. Directed by Diane Kurys. With English subtitles.
Prod-UNKNWN Dist-NYFLMS 1978

Peppermint Stick Selection—A Series
16MM FILM, 3/4 OR 1/2 IN VIDEO P-I
Presents a series of children's stories.
Prod-FI Dist-FI 1976

Dancing Princess, The 015 MIN
Delicious Inventions 015 MIN
Milo's Journey 015 MIN
Pushmi-Pullyu 011 MIN
Runt Of The Litter 013 MIN
Singing Bone, The 013 MIN
Talk To The Animals 010 MIN
Wilbur's Story 015 MIN

Pepsodent Commercial C 1 MIN
3/4 OR 1/2 INCH VIDEO CASSETTE
Shows a classic television commercial with the line 'You'll wonder where the yellow went.'
Prod-BROOKC Dist-BROOKC

Peptic Ulcer C
3/4 OR 1/2 INCH VIDEO CASSETTE
Examines the inter-relationships of anatomical and physiologic factors in the genesis of peptic ulcer. Assesses indications, advantages and limitation of modern methods of diagnosis. Summarizes the role of H-2 blocking agents.
Prod-AMEDA Dist-AMEDA

Peptic Ulcer C
3/4 OR 1/2 INCH VIDEO CASSETTE
Covers the classic symptoms of peptic ulcer happening to ordinary people. Stresses the importance of accurate diagnosis and explains appropriate therapy to relieve pain, promote healing, prevent recurrence and avoid compications.
Prod-MIFE Dist-MIFE

Peptic Ulcer C 60 MIN
3/4 OR 1/2 INCH VIDEO CASSETTE
Presents Dr Denis McCarthy explaining the difference between gastric and peptic ulcers. Discusses warning signals indicating the onset of ulcers, types of jobs associated with increased risk of ulcers and factors that aggravate ulcers.
From The Medicine For The Layman Series.
LC NO. 81-707590
Prod-NIH Dist-USNAC 1980

Peptic Ulcer (Rev Ed) C 16 MIN
16MM FILM, 3/4 OR 1/2 IN VIDEO PRO
Discusses peptic ulcer disease and the patient's role in therapy.
Prod-PRORE Dist-PRORE

Peptic Ulcer (Spanish) C
3/4 OR 1/2 INCH VIDEO CASSETTE
Covers the classic symptoms of peptic ulcer happening to ordinary people. Stresses the importance of accurate diagnosis and explains appropriate therapy to relieve pain, promote healing, prevent recurrence and avoid compications.
Prod-MIFE Dist-MIFE

Peptic Ulcer (Spanish) C 16 MIN
16MM FILM, 3/4 OR 1/2 IN VIDEO PRO
Discusses peptic ulcer disease and the patient's role in therapy.
Prod-PRORE Dist-PRORE

Peptic Ulcer Disease C 30 MIN
3/4 OR 1/2 INCH VIDEO CASSETTE
Discusses the latest aspects of the diagnosis, treatment and Pathophysiology of peptic ulcer, a disorder in which advances have been startling.
Prod-ROWLAB Dist-ROWLAB

Peptic Ulcers C 28 MIN
3/4 OR 1/2 INCH VIDEO CASSETTE
Discusses the causes, symptoms and treatment of peptic ulcers. Shows patients undergoing the two common examinations for ulcers.

From The Daniel Foster, MD Series.
Prod-KERA Dist-PBS

Peptic Ulcers C 58 MIN
3/4 INCH VIDEO CASSETTE
Shows Dr Denis McCarthy, senior investigator for the National Institute of Arthritis, Metabolism and Digestive Diseases, talking about kinds of ulcers, who gets them, why and various treatments.
Prod-NIH Dist-MTP

Per Cent Problems C 12 MIN
3/4 INCH VIDEO CASSETTE
See series title for descriptive statement.
From The Basic Math Skills Series. Converting To Per Cent
Prod-TELSTR Dist-TELSTR

Perc, Pop, Sprinkle C 11 MIN
16MM FILM OPTICAL SOUND K-I
Presents a series of visual experiences for children after which they are asked to interpret the experience physically.
LC NO. 76-702954
Prod-MMP Dist-MMP 1969

Perceiving And Believing C 28 MIN
3/4 OR 1/2 INCH VIDEO CASSETTE
Develops the essential ground work for effective Affirmative Action. Shows that the act of pre-judging others based on stereotyped preconceptions is an act of prejudice. With Ed Asner.
Prod-MTVTM Dist-MTVTM

Percent C 14 MIN
3/4 OR 1/2 INCH VIDEO CASSETTE I-J
Illustrates the meaning of percent in the context of commercials, newscasts, a quiz show and a consumer tips feature.
From The Math Matters Series. Green Module
Prod-KRLNTV Dist-AITECH 1975

Percent C 15 MIN
16MM FILM, 3/4 OR 1/2 IN VIDEO H
Shows how percentages make laboratory analyses clear. Tells how Hollis uses percentages to decide to buy or rent a tractor.
From The Math Wise Series. Module 2 - Comparing
Prod-KOCETV Dist-AITECH 1981

Percent C 15 MIN
3/4 OR 1/2 INCH VIDEO CASSETTE I-J
Explains the meaning of percent and presents some practical applications of dividing by percent. Examines the relationship of fractions to percent and demonstrates how decimals are the easiest method of working problems involving percent.
From The Mathways Series.
LC NO. 80-706230
Prod-STSU Dist-AITECH 1980

Percent - Why And How C 11 MIN
16MM FILM, 3/4 OR 1/2 IN VIDEO I-J
Shows the value of percent in making comparisons. Presents several percent problems.
Prod-CORF Dist-CORF

Percent Defectives For Small Samples C 20 MIN
3/4 OR 1/2 INCH VIDEO CASSETTE IND
Presents necessary distributions for acceptance sampling. Shows where sample sizes are small the Poisson and binomial distributions are often appropriate. Discusses when and how to use these distributions for calculating the probabilities of occurrence of a number of defectives.
From The Statistics For Technicians Series.
Prod-COLOSU Dist-COLOSU

Percentage X 10 MIN
16MM FILM OPTICAL SOUND I
Gives in animation the definition of percentage. Treats percentage as a special form of fractions and emphasizes its relationship to decimal fractions. Gives examples of two different types of problems.
LC NO. 77-701208
Prod-JHP Dist-MLA 1968

Percentage Of Modulation B 29 MIN
16MM FILM - 3/4 IN VIDEO
Explains over, under, and complete modulation and gives the advantages and disadvantages of each. Tells how to determine the percentage of modulation.
LC NO. 79-707776
Prod-USAF Dist-USNAC 1979

Percentage Revolution, The C 30 MIN
3/4 OR 1/2 INCH VIDEO CASSETTE A
Shows adult math students the importance of percentages when paying property tax, borrowing money and checking prices on marked-down sale items in stores.
From The Adult Math Series.
Prod-KYTV Dist-KYTV 1984

Percentages C 20 MIN
3/4 INCH VIDEO CASSETTE H-C
Discusses the use of percentages, focusing on practical math problems dealing with discounts, sales taxes and interest.
From The Mainly Math Series.
Prod-WCVETV Dist-GPITVL 1977

Percentages C 30 MIN
3/4 OR 1/2 INCH VIDEO CASSETTE
See series title for descriptive statement.
From The Infinity Factory Series.
Prod-EDFCEN Dist-MDCPB

Perception C 15 MIN
16MM FILM OPTICAL SOUND PRO
Provides insight into how man perceives the world around him, which influences how he behaves. Includes demonstrations of figure-ground relationships, Bruner's experiment, phi phenomenon, color satiation and others.
Prod-APPLE Dist-PHM 1970

Perception C 16 MIN
16MM FILM OPTICAL SOUND H-C A
Considers concepts associated with perception in psychology, including Gestalt psychology, figure-ground relationship, perceptual satiation and depth perception.
From The Basic Psychology Series.
LC NO. 76-702925
Prod-EDMDC Dist-EDMDC Prodn-SOREND 1973

Perception C 27 MIN
16MM FILM, 3/4 OR 1/2 IN VIDEO H-C A
Explores the physiological, psychological and cultural forces that influence human perception. Explains the necessity of a balance between subjective perceptions and objective truths.
LC NO. 79-706736
Prod-CRMP Dist-CRMP 1979

Perception C 30 MIN
3/4 OR 1/2 INCH VIDEO CASSETTE
Examines the effects of perceptual processes on sensory information, the effects of expectation of perception, the figure-ground principle of perception and other aspects of perception.
From The Psychology Of Human Relations Series.
Prod-MATC Dist-WFVTAE

Perception - Key To Effective Management Communication C 52 MIN
16MM FILM, 3/4 OR 1/2 IN VIDEO C A
Presents a training program on perception designed to help correct communication problems in management. Makes participants aware of their unconscious misperceptions about themselves, their co-workers and their work environment.
LC NO. 81-706599
Prod-MGHT Dist-CRMP 1981

Perception - The Effect Of Past Experience On What We See B 29 MIN
16MM FILM OPTICAL SOUND IND
See series title for descriptive statement.
From The Developing Communication Skills Series.
LC NO. 70-703322
Prod-EDSD Dist-EDSD

Perception - The Eye Within C 12 MIN
16MM FILM, 3/4 OR 1/2 IN VIDEO J-C A
Shows how people interpret what they see.
Prod-BARR Dist-BARR 1975

Perception - Tragedy Of The Friendly Breakfast C 6 MIN
16MM FILM, 3/4 OR 1/2 IN VIDEO
Tells how a fatal shot ruins a friendly breakfast and how three eyewitnesses offer different versions of the tragedy. Edited from the motion picture Communications Roadblocks.
LC NO. 79-707402
Prod-JOHR Dist-SALENG 1977

Perception And Communication B 32 MIN
16MM FILM OPTICAL SOUND P-C
Gives concrete examples of how human perceptions affect the communication process and the individual's concept of reality, introduces two major theories of perception--the cognitive and the transactional.
From The Communication Theory And The New Educational Media Series.
LC NO. 74-705342
Prod-USOE Dist-USNAC 1967

Perception Of Danger C 20 MIN
16MM FILM OPTICAL SOUND
Presents a police training film which explains normal behavioral responses to danger. Discusses relative and distorted perceptions and encourages police personnel to discuss fear openly and to assist each other in overcoming it.
LC NO. 75-700471
Prod-UNCMID Dist-UNCMID Prodn-IACP 1974

Perception Of Reality B 30 MIN
2 INCH VIDEOTAPE PRO
Helps nursing students understand the role an accurate perception of reality plays in their abilities in treating patients.
From The Mental Health Concepts For Nursing, Unit 1 - Self-Understanding Series.
LC NO. 73-702637
Prod-GPITVL Dist-GPITVL 1971

Perception Of Words B 12 MIN
16MM FILM SILENT C T
Presents a test to demonstrate influence of word usage frequency on perception. Uses group data computed to show whether frequency of usage influences perceptual accuracy.
LC NO. 70-713859
Prod-SF Dist-PSUPCR 1971

Perceptions, Pt A - Interventions In Family Therapy--A Series
PRO
Shows family therapy sessions in which real families are interviewed. Demonstrates intervention techniques. Focuses on the therapist's process.
Prod-BOSFAM Dist-BOSFAM

Alberto Serrano, MD - A Nice Family	060 MIN
Carl Whitaker, MD - An Isolated Father In The	060 MIN
Charles Kramer, MD, Jan Kramer, RN	060 MIN
David Rubinstein, MD - The Past In Your Eyes	060 MIN
Frederick J Duhl, MD, Bunny S Duhl,	060 MIN
Frederick J Duhl, MD, Bunny S Duhl,	060 MIN
James Framo, PhD - A Couple's Group	060 MIN
John Howells, MD - Assessment Of The Family	060 MIN
Leonard Unterberger, MA - Just Making It - On	060 MIN
Lois Jaffe, MSW - A Need To Know - A Family	060 MIN
Robert MacGregor, PhD, Mary MacGregor,	060 MIN
Salvador Minuchin, MD - Anorexia Is A Greek	060 MIN
Vincent Sweeney, MD And Jane Donner,	060 MIN
Virginia Satir, MDE - The Light And The Dark	060 MIN
Virginia Satir, MSW -Sisters And Parents - A	060 MIN
Yetta Bernhard, MA - Conflict Resolution With	060 MIN

Perceptions, Pt B - Dialogues With Family Therapists--A Series
PRO
Shows discussions between individual therapists and Frederick J Duhl, Director of the Boston Family Institute. Features also Bunny S Duhl and Carl Whitaker as interviewers.
Prod-BOSFAM Dist-BOSFAM

Alberto Serrano, MD, Professor Of Psychiatry,	
Carl Whitaker, MD - Professor Of Psychiatry,	060 MIN
Carolyn Attneave, PhD, Professor Of Indian	060 MIN
Charles Kramer, MD, Director, Jan Kramer, RN,	060 MIN
David Rubenstein, MD, Professor Of Psychiatry	060 MIN
Edgar Auerswald, MD, Interview With Frederick	060 MIN
Frederick J Duhl, MD - Bunny S Duhl, Med,	060 MIN
James Frams, PhD, Professor Of Psychology	060 MIN
John Howells, MD, Director, Institute Of	060 MIN
Leonard Unterberger, MA, Director, Family	060 MIN
Lois Jaffe, MSW, Associate Professor,	060 MIN
Norman Paul, MD, Associate Professor Of	060 MIN
Robert MacGregor, PhD, Mary MacGregor,	060 MIN
Salvador Minuchin, MD, Director, Philadelphia	060 MIN
Vincent Sweeney, MD, Jane Donner, PhD, Center	060 MIN
Virginia Satir, MSW - Private Practice,	060 MIN
Yetta Bernhard, MA, Private Practice Los	060 MIN

Perceptrons And Hill Climbing C 26 MIN
3/4 OR 1/2 INCH VIDEO CASSETTE C
See series title for descriptive statement.
From The Artificial Intelligence, Pt 1 - Fundamental Concepts Series.
Prod-MIOT Dist-AMCEE

Perceptrons And Hill Climbing C 45 MIN
3/4 OR 1/2 INCH VIDEO CASSETTE PRO
Features such topics as seduction of neural imitations, perceptrons, the limits of learning, and a search alternative - hill climbing.
From The Artificial Intelligence - Pt 1, Fundamental Concepts Series.
Prod-MIOT Dist-MIOT

Perceptual Disabilities C 30 MIN
3/4 OR 1/2 INCH VIDEO CASSETTE C A
Defines perception in terms of learning disabilities and describes types of perceptual disorders.
From The Characteristics Of Learning Disabilities Series.
Prod-WCVETV Dist-FI 1976

Perceptual Motor Evaluation Of A Child With Dysfunction B 33 MIN
16MM FILM OPTICAL SOUND PRO
Uses standard and non-standard tests in evaluating the degree and type of perceptual-motor dysfunction in a seven-year-old girl with a neurological deficit. Assesses visual, tactile, and kinesthetic perception and motor planning.
Prod-UCLA Dist-UCLA

Perceptual Motor Evaluation Of A Perceptually Normal Child B 33 MIN
16MM FILM OPTICAL SOUND PRO
Presents a method of assessing visual, tactile, and kinesthetic perception and related motor functions using standardized tests and some non-standardized procedures.
Prod-UCLA Dist-UCLA

Perceptual Movements And Activities C 17 MIN
16MM FILM OPTICAL SOUND P-I
Presents children who demonstrate many exceptional movements that should help develop body awareness, balance, posture, flexibility, gross motor coordination and other perceptual motor skills.
Prod-MMP Dist-UILL

Perceptual-Motor Skills/System Approach To Instruction C
3/4 OR 1/2 INCH VIDEO CASSETTE T
See series title for descriptive statement.
From The Learning System Design Series. Unit 6
Prod-MSU Dist-MSU

Perceptual-Motor Specialist In The Arlington School System, The B 26 MIN
3/4 OR 1/2 INCH VIDEO CASSETTE
Shows how the perceptual-motor specialist assesses learning disabilities in five-year-old students and plans remediation in conjunction with a tutor, physical education specialist and classroom teacher.
Prod-BU Dist-BU

Perceval C 140 MIN
16MM FILM OPTICAL SOUND
A French language film with English subtitles. Presents a 12th century courtly romance spoken in verse. Directed by Eric Rohmer.
Prod-UNKNWN Dist-NYFLMS 1978

Perch Anatomy C 17 MIN
16MM FILM, 3/4 OR 1/2 IN VIDEO H-C A
Shows dissection techniques and internal structures of a perch. Examines the circulatory, respiratory, digestive, excretory and reproductive systems, the olfactory tract and the brain.
From The Anatomy Series.
LC NO. 80-707138
Prod-IU Dist-IU 1963

Perchance To Dream C 5 MIN
3/4 OR 1/2 INCH VIDEO CASSETTE J-H

Reviews lessons in the Write On, Set 1 Series. See also the title The Dreamer.
From The Write On, Set 2 Series.
Prod-CTI Dist-CTI

Perchance To Dream C 30 MIN
3/4 OR 1/2 INCH VIDEO CASSETTE
Explores sleep, pointing out that people spend a third of their lives sleeping and yet for some this is not a peaceful sleep.
From The Innovation Series.
Prod-WNETTV Dist-WNETTV 1983

Percussion C 25 MIN
3/4 INCH VIDEO CASSETTE
See series title for descriptive statement.
From The Instruments Of The Orchestra And Their Techniques Series.
Prod-UWASHP Dist-UWASHP

Percussion And Auscultation Of The Lungs And Thorax, Pt 1 C 20 MIN
3/4 INCH VIDEO CASSETTE PRO
Presents the nature and characteristics of sound as they relate to percussion and auscultation. Discusses various percussion tones and where they might be encountered, demonstrates techniques of indirect percussion and delineates the procedure for percussion of the thorax.
From The Physical Assessment - Heart And Lungs Series. Program 2
Prod-CONMED Dist-CONMED 1976

Percussion And Auscultation Of The Lungs And Thorax, Pt 2 C 30 MIN
3/4 INCH VIDEO CASSETTE PRO
Focuses on aspects of auscultation of lungs, covering breath, adventitious, voice and whispered sounds and the procedure for auscultation.
From The Physical Assessment - Heart And Lungs Series. Program 3
Prod-CONMED Dist-CONMED 1976

Percussion And Vibration Techniques B 37 MIN
3/4 OR 1/2 INCH VIDEO CASSETTE
Demonstrates techniques of postural drainage, and twelve positions for patient to assume during treatment.
Prod-BU Dist-BU

Percussion Family C 14 MIN
3/4 OR 1/2 INCH VIDEO CASSETTE P
Demonstrates a number of percussion instruments.
From The Stepping Into Rhythm Series.
Prod-WVIZTV Dist-AITECH

Percussion Family, The C 15 MIN
3/4 OR 1/2 INCH VIDEO CASSETTE P
Teaches recognition of percussion musical instruments.
From The Music Machine Series.
Prod-GPITVL Dist-GPITVL

Percussion Family, The C 15 MIN
3/4 OR 1/2 INCH VIDEO CASSETTE I
Introduces the concept of rhythmic beats, defines percussion instruments, identifies several groups, and demonstrates the versatility of these instruments.
From The Music And Me Series.
LC NO. 80-706749
Prod-WDCNTV Dist-AITECH 1979

Percutaneous Nephrostomy C 15 MIN
16MM FILM OPTICAL SOUND
Discusses the rationale and advantages of percutaneous nephrostomy. Shows required armamentarium and demonstrates the procedure on a patient who required emergency nephrostomy drainage.
Prod-EATONL Dist-EATONL 1971

Percutaneous Nephrostomy With Needle And Guide Wire C 12 MIN
16MM FILM OPTICAL SOUND
Shows to members of the medical profession the procedures followed in performing a nephrostomy with the use of a needle and guide wire rather than a trocar needle.
LC NO. 72-700183
Prod-EATONL Dist-EATONL 1971

Percutaneous Transluminal Coronary Angioplasty C 7 MIN
3/4 OR 1/2 INCH VIDEO CASSETTE PRO
Introduces techniques involved in percutaneous transluminal coronary angioplasty.
Prod-HSCIC Dist-HSCIC 1984

Perfect Balance, The C 8 MIN
3/4 OR 1/2 INCH VIDEO CASSETTE A
Presents Olympic standout basketball player Ann Meyers telling of the challenges she faced as a woman athlete. Shows the heights reached by her and her team.
From The Winner's Circle Series.
Prod-SFTI Dist-SFTI

Perfect Competition And Inelastic Demand - Can The Farmer Make A Profit C 30 MIN
3/4 OR 1/2 INCH VIDEO CASSETTE C
See series title for descriptive statement.
From The Economics USA Series.
Prod-WEFA Dist-ANNCPB

Perfect Drug Film, The C 32 MIN
16MM FILM OPTICAL SOUND J-C A
Presents a historical examination of mankind's quest for relaxation and enjoyment through narcotics. Concludes that drugs are not needed for these purposes.
LC NO. 72-701573
Prod-AVANTI Dist-FI 1971

Perfect Gift, The C 22 MIN
16MM FILM, 3/4 OR 1/2 IN VIDEO
Demonstrates what could happen to an unprotected infant in a crash, encourages proper choice and usage of infant car safety belts, presents ridiculous excuses for not protecting infants and tells why parents should use a crash-tested safety seat on every ride.
Prod-VISUCP Dist-VISUCP

Perfect Job For Jim, The C 4 MIN
16MM FILM, 3/4 OR 1/2 IN VIDEO PRO
Asks how to handle the situation with an employee who is very capable in his present job, but is unhappy and would rather resign, if he is unable to attain a transfer with the company.
From The This Matter Of Motivation Series.
Prod-CTRACT Dist-DARTNL Prodn-CALVIN

Perfect Leader C 4 MIN
3/4 OR 1/2 INCH VIDEO CASSETTE
Features a satire about an omnipotent computer.
Prod-KITCHN Dist-KITCHN

Perfect Leader C 5 MIN
3/4 OR 1/2 INCH VIDEO CASSETTE
Prod-EAI Dist-EAI

Perfect Lives C 182 MIN
3/4 OR 1/2 INCH VIDEO CASSETTE
Features the keyboard inventions of 'Blue' Gene Tyranny and the singing of Jill Kroesen and David Van Tieghem. Produced for Channel Four Television, Great Britain.
Prod-KITCHN Dist-KITCHN

Perfect Moment, The C 11 MIN
16MM FILM, 3/4 OR 1/2 IN VIDEO
Focuses on that moment in sports when technique, opportunity, training, drive and environmental conditions produce a super-charged moment of excitement. Shows a hang-glider, a skier and a surfer experiencing this moment of perfection.
LC NO. 79-707037
Prod-MCGIF Dist-PFP 1979

Perfect Mother, The - Paradox Or Possibility C 29 MIN
3/4 INCH VIDEO CASSETTE
Shows how society pressures women to have children and to meet impossibly high standards in raising them.
From The Woman Series.
Prod-WNEDTV Dist-PUBTEL

Perfect President, The - A Man For His Time C 52 MIN
16MM FILM, 3/4 OR 1/2 IN VIDEO J-C A
Discusses the 12 successive presidents from Teddy Roosevelt to Gerald Ford in order to examine presidential personalities.
From The Presidency Series.
Prod-CORPEL Dist-LUF 1976

Perfect Sale, The C 20 MIN
16MM FILM, 3/4 OR 1/2 IN VIDEO H-C
Demonstrates the steps involved in making a sale successfully.
LC NO. 84-706413
Prod-HALBH Dist-BARR 1983

Perfecting Parallel C 29 MIN
3/4 OR 1/2 INCH VIDEO CASSETTE
See series title for descriptive statement.
From The Skiing Series.
Prod-KTCATV Dist-PBS

Perfectly Frank C 30 MIN
16MM FILM, 3/4 OR 1/2 IN VIDEO H-C A
Deals with a new product, the chicken frankfurter.
From The Enterprise Series.
Prod-MTI Dist-MTI

Perfectly Frank C 30 MIN
3/4 OR 1/2 INCH VIDEO CASSETTE H-C A
Tells the story of Frank Perdue, the man who turned chicken into a brand name item. Shows how he is using his merchandising talents to launch a new product, chicken franks.
From The Enterprise III Series.
Prod-WGBHTV Dist-KINGFT

Perfectly Normal Day, A C 27 MIN
16MM FILM, 3/4 OR 1/2 IN VIDEO C A
Shows how to reduce and manage crises and interruptions, presenting a typical day as a jigsaw puzzle.
Prod-CCCD Dist-CCCD 1978

Perform Minor Maintenance Of Welding Equipment C 15 MIN
3/4 OR 1/2 INCH VIDEO CASSETTE
See series title for descriptive statement.
From The Welding II - Basic Shielded Metal Arc Welding series.
Prod-CAMB Dist-CAMB

Performance C 41 MIN
3/4 OR 1/2 INCH VIDEO CASSETTE
Provides a general systematic approach for analyzing system performance. Illustrates the procedure for performing a system error analysis.
From The Systems Engineering And Systems Management Series.
Prod-MIOT Dist-MIOT

Performance And Dance Theatre C 30 MIN
3/4 OR 1/2 INCH VIDEO CASSETTE
See series title for descriptive statement.
From The Political And Social Comment In Dance Series.
Prod-ARCVID Dist-ARCVID

Performance And Evaluation C 30 MIN
3/4 OR 1/2 INCH VIDEO CASSETTE
Discusses performance and evaluation as part of managing professionals.
From The Business Of Managing Professionals Series.
Prod-KYTV Dist-KYTV 1983

Performance And Potential Review C 21 MIN
16MM FILM - 3/4 IN VIDEO IND
Shows how the measurable targets set jointly by a manager and his superiors are then used to discuss and appraise his results and later, as an aid in reviewing his potential for new responsibilities.
From The Management By Objectives Series.
Prod-BNA Dist-BNA 1970

Performance Appraisal C
3/4 OR 1/2 INCH VIDEO CASSETTE
Outlines an approach to effective performance appraisal.
Prod-DBMI Dist-DBMI

Performance Appraisal C
3/4 OR 1/2 INCH VIDEO CASSETTE
See series title for descriptive statement.
From The Management Training Series.
Prod-THGHT Dist-DELTAK

Performance Appraisal C 120 MIN
3/4 OR 1/2 INCH VIDEO CASSETTE
Explains how the appraisal process relates to the overall management function and presents a concise four-step process for effectively planning and conducting a performance appraisal within an organization.
From The AMA's Program For Performance Appraisal Series.
Prod-AMA Dist-AMA

Performance Appraisal - The Human Dynamics C 25 MIN
16MM FILM, 3/4 OR 1/2 IN VIDEO H-C A
Explains how performance appraisals can motivate employees to work with more enthusiasm toward organizational goals.
Prod-CRMP Dist-CRMP 1978

Performance Appraisal - The Human Dynamics (Spanish) C 25 MIN
16MM FILM, 3/4 OR 1/2 IN VIDEO C A
Explains a different approach to performance appraisal, emphasizing the open exchange of ideas to motivate employees to work with more enthusiasm toward organizational goals.
Prod-MGHT Dist-MGHT Prodn-CRMP 1978

Performance Appraisal And Workforce Discipline C 22 MIN
3/4 INCH VIDEO CASSETTE
Outlines the major changes brought about by the Civil Service Reform Bill affecting actions involving unacceptable performance and conduct problems.
From The Launching Civil Service Reform Series.
LC NO. 79-706271
Prod-USOPMA Dist-USNAC 1978

Performance Appraisal For Managers—A Series
16MM FILM, 3/4 OR 1/2 IN VIDEO A
Offers an on-going, systematic appraisal process that gives managers the structure and guidelines they need to evaluate performance objectively.
Prod-TIMLIF Dist-TIMLIF 1982

Performance Appraisal Training—A Series

Deals with performance appraisals, and includes concepts and techniques based on research and experience, videotaped 'live' appraisal situations, interactive exercises, and skill practice activities. Presents dramatizations depicting good and bad interaction between supervisor and subordinate during the appraisal. Includes a participant's workbook and leader's guide.
Prod-DELTAK Dist-DELTAK

Communicating The Performance Appraisal 033 MIN
Doing The Performance Appraisal 025 MIN
Giving Negative Feedback (A Model) 020 MIN
Planning For Improvement (A Model) 020 MIN

Performance Appraisal—A Series

Provides a course in performance appraisal for the supervisor. Covers the reasons for appraisal, the means for evaluating important job facts and techniques for effective appraisals.
Prod-RESEM Dist-RESEM

How And When To Appraise 010 MIN
What To Appraise 008 MIN
Why Appraise? 008 MIN

Performance Appraisals C 28 MIN
2 INCH VIDEOTAPE A
Features James L Hayes, president of the American Management Associations, explaining how the performance appraisal process relates to the overall management function and presents a four-step process for planning and conducting a performance appraisal.
From The How To Improve Managerial Performance - The AMA Performance Standards Program Series.
LC NO. 75-704235
Prod-AMA Dist-AMA 1974

Performance Bounds - The Cramer Rao Inequality B 28 MIN
3/4 OR 1/2 INCH VIDEO CASSETTE PRO
See series title for descriptive statement.
From The Probability And Random Processes - Limit Theorems And Statistics Series.
Prod-MIOT Dist-MIOT

Performance Counseling B 21 MIN
16MM FILM OPTICAL SOUND
Presents guidelines for effective performance and non-directive methods of counseling.

LC NO. FIE64-19
Prod-USA Dist-USNAC 1963

Performance Curriculum I - Issues In Innovation C 28 MIN
16MM FILM OPTICAL SOUND
Dr Dwight Allen, Professor of Education at Stanford University, discusses the problems and issues of innovation, emphasizing curriculum and educational change.
From The Innovations In Education Series.
Prod-STNFRD Dist-EDUC 1966

Performance Curriculum II - Issues In Organization C 28 MIN
16MM FILM OPTICAL SOUND
Dr Dwight Allen, Professor of Education at Stanford University, considers a flexible model for organizational innovation.
From The Innovations In Education Series.
Prod-STNFRD Dist-EDUC 1966

Performance Evaluation C 10 MIN
16MM FILM OPTICAL SOUND
Presents a review of the philosophy, objectives and techniques of performance evaluations. Emphasizes the need for accurate and objective record-keeping and portrays the value of anecdotal records and self-evaluation.
From The Supervison And Management Series.
LC NO. 74-712977
Prod-TRNAID Dist-TRNAID 1969

Performance Evaluation B 26 MIN
16MM FILM OPTICAL SOUND
Explains to Air Force supervisors the importance of discussing frequently with their employees their performance of duties.
LC NO. 74-705343
Prod-USDD Dist-USNAC 1960

Performance Evaluation Of Computing Systems—A Series
PRO
Uses classroom format to videotape two 75-minute lectures weekly for 14 weeks and 56 cassettes. Covers performance modeling, measurement and evaluation techniques, Central Processing Unit (CPU) scheduling disciplines, queueing network models of computing systems, aggregation and decomposition, approximately queueing network models, memory hierarchies and interference and reliability models.
Prod-USCITV Dist-AMCEE

Performance Feeding For Your Horse C 61 MIN
1/2 IN VIDEO CASSETTE BETA/VHS
Deals with proper feeding of horses, from colts to mature adults.
From The Horse Care And Training Series.
Prod-MOHOMV Dist-MOHOMV

Performance Improvement Program—A Series
A
focused on problem solving rather than fault finding to improve employee performance.
Presents an ongoing process emphasizing two way communications,
Prod-PRODEV Dist-PRODEV

Developing Job Accountabilities And Writing
Identifying Developmental Needs And Actions 045 MIN
Introducing The Performance Appraisal Process 045 MIN
Preparing For And Conducting Effective 040 MIN

Performance Of Skills - The Pyramidal System C 18 MIN
16MM FILM, 3/4 OR 1/2 IN VIDEO PRO
See series title for descriptive statement.
From The Anatomical Basis Of Brain Function Series.
Prod-AVCORP Dist-TEF

Performance Of The Minuet C 30 MIN
3/4 OR 1/2 INCH VIDEO CASSETTE
See series title for descriptive statement.
From The Glances At The Past Series.
Prod-ARCVID Dist-ARCVID

Performance Review C 11 MIN
3/4 OR 1/2 INCH VIDEO CASSETTE
See series title for descriptive statement.
From The Applied Management Series.
Prod-ORGDYN Dist-DELTAK

Performance Reviews B 50 MIN
3/4 OR 1/2 INCH VIDEO CASSETTE
Features Psychologist Joyce Vesper discussing various kinds of employee performance reviews, including the interview review, the essay review, the rating on 'check box' review and the MBO (management by objective) review. Gives step-by-step guidelines on how to conduct a performance interview and requirements for reviews that comply with equal rights or fair employment programs.
Prod-UAZMIC Dist-UAZMIC 1979

Performance Reviews That Build Commitment—A Series

Provides the student with the ability to conduct performance reviews that are work-oriented and meaningful, including understanding how goals, specific objectives and performance standards are all interrelated, identifying the necessary steps in evolving sound performance standards, writing meaningful performance standards, differentiating job descriptions, distinguishing between boss and manager, recognizing and practicing the different types of listening, and understanding how the performance review serves other organizational purposes.
Prod-PRODEV Dist-DELTAK

Critical Role Of Performance Review, The 030 MIN
Developing Performance Standards 030 MIN
Review That Builds Commitment, The 030 MIN
Supportive Coaching 030 MIN
Why The Traditional Approach Fails 030 MIN
Writing Challenging Specific Objectives 030 MIN

Performance Reviews That Get Results C 30 MIN
3/4 OR 1/2 INCH VIDEO CASSETTE PRO
Deals with the concept of performance reviews and introduces an approach to performance standards that can be useful to the new supervisor.
From The You - The Supervisor Series.
Prod-PRODEV Dist-DELTAK

Performed Word, The C 58 MIN
3/4 OR 1/2 INCH VIDEO CASSETTE
Views black religion in its cultural context. Examines a variety of performance situations. Captures the power of the performed word and the congregation's strong response to it.
Prod-SOFOLK Dist-SOFOLK

Performer, The C 30 MIN
3/4 OR 1/2 INCH VIDEO CASSETTE
Presents Grant Johannesen, who performs Faure's Ballade and Prokofieff's Seventh Sonata, and comments that performers shouldn't 'rely on someone else's success with a selection, but go into a recital and play what you feel with the greatest naturalness'.
From The Grant Johannesen - Pianist Series.
Prod-NETCHE Dist-NETCHE 1973

Performing After A Serious Injury C 30 MIN
3/4 OR 1/2 INCH VIDEO CASSETTE
See series title for descriptive statement.
From The Dancers' Bodies Series.
Prod-ARCVID Dist-ARCVID

Performing Arts, The C 19 MIN
16MM FILM, 3/4 OR 1/2 IN VIDEO H-C A
Illustrates how man expresses his attitudes toward himself and his world through the performing arts. Shows performing artists in the process of mastering techniques in order to convey them to the audience. Includes scenes of Phillip Burton directing student actors in Shakespeare's 'AS YOU LIKE IT.'
From The Humanities Series.
Prod-MGHT Dist-MGHT 1971

Performing Arts, The, Pt 1 C 30 MIN
3/4 OR 1/2 INCH VIDEO CASSETTE H-C A
Examines the performing arts in Japan.
From The Japan - The Living Tradition Series.
Prod-UMA Dist-GPITVL 1976

Performing Arts, The, Pt 2 C 30 MIN
3/4 OR 1/2 INCH VIDEO CASSETTE H-C A
Examines the performing arts in Japan.
From The Japan - The Living Tradition Series.
Prod-UMA Dist-GPITVL 1976

Perfumed Nightmare C 91 MIN
3/4 OR 1/2 INCH VIDEO CASSETTE
Presents a semi-autobiographical fable about a young Filipino and his awakening to and reaction against American cultural colonialism.
Prod-FLOWER Dist-FLOWER

Perfumes (French) C 14 MIN
3/4 OR 1/2 INCH VIDEO CASSETTE H-C A
Leads a young couple to the altar and provides an anniversary present.
From The En Francais Series. Part 2 - Temporal Relationships, Logical Relationships
Prod-MOFAFR Dist-AITECH 1970

Perfusion Failure C 19 MIN
3/4 INCH VIDEO CASSETTE PRO
Explains the basic defect underlying shock, describing clinical and physiologic signs, hemodynamic effects, and the different classifications of shock.
From The Shock Series. Module 2
LC NO. 80-707733
Prod-BRA Dist-BRA 1980

Periaortic Approach To The Renal Pedicle, The C 22 MIN
16MM FILM OPTICAL SOUND
Shows two procedures illustrating the periaortic approach to the renal pedicle in patients with renal neoplasm or renal trauma. Explains that the occlusion of the renal artery and vein early in the operation is made possible, thus preventing tumor embolization or hemorrhage while dissecting the kidney.
LC NO. FIA66-57
Prod-EATONL Dist-EATONL Prodn-AVCORP 1965

Pericardiectomy C 25 MIN
16MM FILM OPTICAL SOUND PRO
Illustrates the operative technique for the cure of chronic constrictive pericarditis. Emphasizes completeness of the resection.
Prod-ACYDGD Dist-ACY 1958

Pericles C 177 MIN
3/4 OR 1/2 INCH VIDEO CASSETTE H-C A
Presents William Shakespeare's play Pericles which tells the story of the Prince of Tyre, who is pursued by the vengeance of the King Antiochus because he discovered the monarch's incestuous relationship with his daughter. Reveals the adventures which befall Pericles and his family as he tries to elude the king.
From The Shakespeare Plays Series.
Prod-BBCTV Dist-TIMLIF 1984

Perilous Voyage, The C 23 MIN
3/4 OR 1/2 INCH VIDEO CASSETTE K-C A
Shows a young seal, vulnerable and stranded on the California beach, rescued by a man.
Prod-NWLDPR Dist-NWLDPR

Perils Of Barley, The C 15 MIN
16MM FILM OPTICAL SOUND
Dramatizes the advantage of using high moisture barley rather than dry barley for feeding cattle.
LC NO. 76-713586
Prod-VENARD Dist-VENARD 1971

Perils Of Priscilla, The C 14 MIN
16MM FILM, 3/4 OR 1/2 IN VIDEO P
A shortened version of the film The Perils Of Priscilla. Points out the needs of a pet cat by presenting the adventures of a cat who endures the indignation of a busy family and the dangers of being lost in a big city. Contains no narration.
LC NO. 82-706590
Prod-DF Dist-CF 1980

Perils Of Priscills, The C 17 MIN
16MM FILM, 3/4 OR 1/2 IN VIDEO P-J
Shows that through the eyes of a cat, an ordinary household and neighborhood looks quiet different. Follows Priscilla the cat as she meets such needs as food, warmth and a place to rest.
Prod-DF Dist-CF 1969

Perinatal And Child Development C 30 MIN
3/4 OR 1/2 INCH VIDEO CASSETTE
Describes the process through which the child first identifies its gender. Reviews some of the major findings concerning the extent to which this process is influenced by heredity (in the form of the endocrine system) and the environment (both social and physical).
From The Endocrine Gland Function Series.
Prod-NETCHE Dist-NETCHE 1975

Perineal External Urethrotomy C 10 MIN
16MM FILM OPTICAL SOUND
Explains that perineal external urethrotomy is of value to the transurethral resectionist in cases of anterior urethral strictures and large prostate glands. Demonstrates Dr Michael K O'Heeron's technique and discusses its advantages.
LC NO. 75-702311
Prod-EATONL Dist-EATONL 1965

Perineal Hernia - Surgical Repair C 28 MIN
16MM FILM OPTICAL SOUND PRO
Describes the preparation of the patient (dog) and usual precautions prior to surgery. Gives a detailed explanation of the entire surgical procedure with schematic drawings used to illustrate the logical approach to be considered.
Prod-CIBA Dist-AMVMA

Perineal Prostatectomy C 15 MIN
16MM FILM OPTICAL SOUND
Demonstrates a modified Huson-belt (simple) perineal prostatectomy, stressing surgical detail. Emphasizes the technique and importance of post-prostatectomy perineal exercises and their relationship to urinary continence.
LC NO. 75-702247
Prod-EATONL Dist-EATONL 1972

Perineal Repair Of Urethral Strictures With Skin Graft Patch C 14 MIN
16MM FILM OPTICAL SOUND PRO
Demonstrates the surgical repair of a urethral stricture by approaching the stricture through a perineal incision, incising the strictured area and replacing the deficient tissue with a patch graft of full thickness skin removed from the penis.
LC NO. 75-702236
Prod-EATONL Dist-EATONL 1975

Perineal Rib Graft For Male Incontinence C 15 MIN
16MM FILM OPTICAL SOUND
Illustrates an operation devised to correct post-prostatectomy incontinence using a segment of the seventh rib, which is screwed to permanently bridge the ischial tuberosities and raise the urogenital diaphragm into the -nonvoiding- position.
LC NO. 75-702291
Prod-EATONL Dist-EATONL 1969

Periodic Check-Up, The B 18 MIN
16MM FILM OPTICAL SOUND
Shows how to tune up the engine, check and adjust the brake system and inspect the steering system, chassis and body.
From The Automotive Operation And Maintenance Series. Automobile Operation, No. 4
LC NO. FIE52-343
Prod-USOE Dist-USNAC Prodn-HANDY 1945

Periodic Functions B 17 MIN
16MM FILM, 3/4 OR 1/2 IN VIDEO
Defines periodic functions, illustrates the graphing of sine angles and relates sine waves to the amount of voltage produced by a generator. Issued in 1945 as a motion picture.
From The Radio Technician Training Series.
LC NO. 78-706297
Prod-USN Dist-USNAC Prodn-LNS 1978

Periodic Inputs And Fourier Series B 28 MIN
3/4 OR 1/2 INCH VIDEO CASSETTE PRO
Continues the frequency domain analysis of LTI systems by developing the Fourier series representation for periodic signals and considering the response of such systems to periodic inputs.
From The Probability And Random Processes - Linear Systems Series.
Prod-MIOT Dist-MIOT

Periodic Inspection - Engine B 22 MIN
16MM FILM OPTICAL SOUND
Shows how to inspect the general condition of an engine, examine internal parts, check ignition and fuel system, examine the propeller and prepare an engine for run-up.
LC NO. FIE52-257
Prod-USOE Dist-USNAC 1945

Periodic Motion B 33 MIN
16MM FILM OPTICAL SOUND H-C
Uses a simple harmonic motion as an example of periodic motion. Shows how a pen moving in SHM plots its own displacement time graph and how graphs of velocity and acceleration versus time are derived from it.
From The PSSC Physics Films Series.
Prod-PSSC Dist-MLA 1961

Periodic Paralysis, The C 48 MIN
3/4 INCH VIDEO CASSETTE PRO
Presents Dr Robert C Griggs lecturing on periodic paralysis.
From The Intensive Course In Neuromuscular Diseases Series.
LC NO. 76-706073
Prod-NINDIS Dist-USNAC 1974

Periodic Preventive Medical Examinations, Pt 1, Principles And Plan C 16 MIN
3/4 OR 1/2 INCH VIDEO CASSETTE PRO
Presents a plan for doing preventive medical exams. Identifies desirable characteristics of screening tests. Presents the principles of screening and follow-up.
Prod-UMICHM Dist-UMICHM 1979

Periodic Reversal Of Rotation Of A DC Motor B 34 MIN
3/4 OR 1/2 INCH VIDEO CASSETTE
See series title for descriptive statement.
From The Nonlinear Vibrations Series.
Prod-MIOT Dist-MIOT

Periodic Table And Periodicity, The C 23 MIN
16MM FILM, 3/4 OR 1/2 IN VIDEO J-C
Uses animation to show the development of the relationship between an atom's electronic structure and its properties, demonstrating why there are families of elements and why properties are periodic when elements are arranged by atomic number across the table.
From The Chemistry Series.
Prod-CORF Dist-CORF

Periodicals And Anthologies, Indexes And Abstracts C
3/4 OR 1/2 INCH VIDEO CASSETTE
See series title for descriptive statement.
From The College Library Series.
Prod-NETCHE Dist-NETCHE 1973

Periodicity - The Logical And Systematic Arrangement Of Symbols C 30 MIN
3/4 OR 1/2 INCH VIDEO CASSETTE PRO
See series title for descriptive statement.
From The HTM - Hazardous Toxic Materials Series. Unit I
Prod-FILCOM Dist-FILCOM

Periodontal Disease (Rev Ed) C 7 MIN
16MM FILM, 3/4 OR 1/2 IN VIDEO PRO
Describes the nature of periodontal disease, its causes, progression and prevention.
Prod-PRORE Dist-PRORE

Periodontal Disease - Prevention And Early Treatment C 22 MIN
3/4 INCH VIDEO CASSETTE PRO
Stresses the importance of early diagnosis and treatment of periodontal disease. Issued in 1963 as a motion picture.
LC NO. 79-707566
Prod-USN Dist-USNAC 1979

Periodontal Examination, Pt 1 - Examination Procedures C 17 MIN
16MM FILM - 3/4 IN VIDEO PRO
Illustrates clinical examination of the periodontium, emphasizing gingival color, density, relation of the gingival margin to the cemento-enamel junction, pocket depth and bleeding tendency. Includes roentgenological examination.
LC NO. 77-706186
Prod-USVA Dist-USNAC 1970

Periodontal Examination, Pt 2 - Charting C 18 MIN
16MM FILM, 3/4 OR 1/2 IN VIDEO PRO
Illustrates periodontal examination of single teeth and recording of the findings on a chart. Presented by Drs Sigurd P Ramfjord and Edward Green.
LC NO. 81-706825
Prod-USVA Dist-USNAC 1970

Periodontal Packs C 11 MIN
3/4 INCH VIDEO CASSETTE
Demonstrates procedures for mixing and applying two types of periodontal packs and discusses the advantages and disadvantages of each.
LC NO. 79-706753
Prod-MUSC Dist-USNAC 1978

Periodontal Prosthesis, Pt 2a, Abutment Tooth Preparation And Provisional Restoration B 39 MIN
16MM FILM OPTICAL SOUND PRO
Deals with the surgical and dental techniques employed in periodontal prosthesis. Shows gingival surgery to prepare arch for application of prosthetic device. (Kinescope.)
Prod-WYETH Dist-WYLAB 1962

Periodontal Prosthesis, Pt 2b, Continuation, Tooth Hemisection And Provisional Restroation B 31 MIN
16MM FILM OPTICAL SOUND PRO
Demonstrates hemisectioning of tooth and installations of provisional restoration.
Prod-WYETH Dist-WYLAB 1962

Periodontal Surgery C 180 MIN
3/4 OR 1/2 INCH VIDEO CASSETTE PRO
Shows a maxillary quadrant of surgery which involves five mm and six mm deep pockets in premolar and molar areas. Diagrams the differences between buccal and palatal internal bevelled incisions, discusses tuberosity management and presents a new technique.
Prod-USDHEW Dist-USNAC

Periodontal Surgery For The General Practitioner—A Series

Offers an unedited presentation by Zigmund C Porter, DDS, Oak Brook, Illinois, demonstrating such periodontal surgery as the general practitioner might find necessary to perform in the overall complete dental care of his patients. Shows such procedures as frenectomy, gingivectomy, laterally sliding flap to cover a denuded root, caries subgingivally, anterior curtain procedures and the Widman flap for difficult procedures where there is an esthetic problem.
Prod-AMDA Dist-AMDA 1977

Periodontal Suturing C 10 MIN
3/4 INCH VIDEO CASSETTE
Describes the instruments and materials used in suturing and presents procedures for placing interrupted and sling sutures.
LC NO. 79-706754
Prod-MUSC Dist-USNAC 1978

Periodontal Suturing C 15 MIN
16MM FILM - 3/4 IN VIDEO
Demonstrates four methods of periodontal suturing, using patients and a typodent. Shows techniques for making an interrupted suture, sling ligation, continuous sling ligation, and anchor suture.
LC NO. 80-707111
Prod-VADTC Dist-USNAC 1979

Periodontal Therapy For Patients—A Series

Offers an unedited presentation by Claude L Nabers, San Antonio, Texas, of his clinical techniques for examination, diagnosis and treatment planning for patients with periodontal pathosis. Demonstrates scaling, root planing, subgingival curettage and minor surgical procedures for pocket elimination.
Prod-AMDA Dist-AMDA 1978

Periodontics C 6 MIN
16MM FILM, 3/4 OR 1/2 IN VIDEO A
Presents the course of professional care and treatment. Includes the anatomy of teeth and gums, cementum ligaments, bone opposing teeth, effects of periodontal disease, gingivitis, plaque, calculus, periodontitis, systemic disorders, home care and professional care.
Prod-PRORE Dist-PRORE

Periodontics - Some Realistic And Practical Approaches—A Series

Offers an unedited presentation by Edward P Barrington, DDS, Chicago, providing dental practitioners with a means for rapid periodontal evaluation. Demonstrates examination and charting, prognosis of individual teeth and of the entire cases, consultation with the patient and instructions in oral hygiene procedures.
Prod-AMDA Dist-AMDA 1979

Peripheral Nerve Grafting - Demonstraion Of Technique C 60 MIN
3/4 OR 1/2 INCH VIDEO CASSETTE PRO
Demonstrates Dr Hanno Millesi's technique of nerve grafting as done under the microscope. Accompanies film 'Peripheral Nerve Grafting And Results.'
Prod-ASSH Dist-ASSH

Peripheral Nerve Grafting And Results C 60 MIN
3/4 OR 1/2 INCH VIDEO CASSETTE PRO
Demonstrates various points in peripheral nerve grafting and its results. Narrated by Dr Hanno Millesi. Accompanies film 'Peripheral Nerve Grafting-Demonstration of Technique.'
Prod-ASSH Dist-ASSH

Peripheral Nerve Surgery - Repair Of The Radial Nerve In The Distal One-Third Of The Arm C 12 MIN
16MM FILM OPTICAL SOUND
Demonstrates a complete lesion of the radial nerve in the lower one-third of the arm, the surgical exploration and suture and the clinical resuet.
Prod-USVA Dist-USVA 1962

Peripheral Nerve Surgery - Result Following Repair Of The Radial Nerve In Mid-Third Arm C 6 MIN
16MM FILM OPTICAL SOUND
Demonstrates complete lesion of radial nerve in the mid-one-third of the arm, the surgical exploration and suture and the result following suture two and one-half years postoperatively.
Prod-USVA Dist-USVA 1961

Peripheral Nervous System, The C 19 MIN
16MM FILM, 3/4 OR 1/2 IN VIDEO H-C
Deals with reflex action and the components of the spinal reflex arc. Covers the nature of the nerve impulse and the transmission of the nerve impulse from neuron to neuron. Relates reflex action to the spinal cord and its connection to and from the brain.
LC NO. 80-706719
Prod-BFL Dist-IFB 1977

Peripheral Neuropathies - Clinical And Investigative Aspects C 51 MIN
3/4 INCH VIDEO CASSETTE PRO
Reviews the pathology of peripheral nerve disease, enumerates the mechanisms producing pathology and outlines a clinical approach to diagnosis.
LC NO. 79-707688
Prod-NINDIS Dist-USNAC 1976

Peripheral Vascular C 20 MIN
3/4 OR 1/2 INCH VIDEO CASSETTE PRO
Views a physical assessment by a nurse practitioner of the peripheral vascular of a live patient.
From The Health Assessment Series.
Prod-BRA Dist-BRA

Peripheral Vascular C 20 MIN
3/4 OR 1/2 INCH VIDEO CASSETTE PRO
See series title for descriptive statement.
From The Health Assessment Series. Module 5
Prod-MDCC Dist-MDCC

Periquin C 9 MIN
16MM FILM, 3/4 OR 1/2 IN VIDEO
A Spanish version of 'LENTIL.' Tells of a boy whose harmonica playing contributes to the success of his town's homecoming celebration for its leading citizen.
Prod-WWS Dist-WWS 1960

Perishable Goods C 60 MIN
3/4 OR 1/2 INCH VIDEO CASSETTE H-C A
Shows how the detective work of the post mortem reveals the secrets of bodily function. Confronts the inevitability of death and celebrates the renewal of life by presenting an extract from a production of Monteverdi's Orfeo. Based on the book The Body In Question by Jonathan Miller. Narrated by Jonathan Miller.
From The Body In Question Series. Program 13
LC NO. 81-706956
Prod-BBCTV Dist-FI 1979

Peritoneal Dialysis C 8 MIN
16MM FILM OPTICAL SOUND PRO
Demonstrates the use of peritoneal dialysis in cases of acute or chronic renal failure, severe electrolyte imbalance, refractory heart failure or poisoning.
LC NO. 72-706452
Prod-UWISC Dist-UWISC 1969

Peritoneal Dialysis C 18 MIN
3/4 OR 1/2 INCH VIDEO CASSETTE PRO
Demonstrates the nurse's role in the delivery of peritoneal dialysis. Gives a brief review of selected highlights of principles and techniques of peritoneal dialysis and presents and explains step-by-step procedures for manual peritoneal dialysis. Demonstrates nurse's responsibilities.
LC NO. 80-730456
Prod-TRAINX Dist-TRAINX

Peritoneal Dialysis - A Bedside Procedure C 24 MIN
3/4 OR 1/2 INCH VIDEO CASSETTE PRO
Shows use of peritoneal dialysis in great detail on several patients with renal failure. Animated drawings develop the theoretical aspects of the procedure.
Prod-WFP Dist-WFP

Peritoneal Lavage C 10 MIN
3/4 OR 1/2 INCH VIDEO CASSETTE PRO
Outlines the diagnostic value of peritoneal lavage in blunt abdominal trauma, reviews essential equipment and provides an illustrated step-by-step analysis of demonstration of the procedure as carried out on two trauma victims.
Prod-UWASH Dist-UWASH

Peritoneal Lavage In Blunt Abdominal Trauma C 25 MIN
3/4 OR 1/2 INCH VIDEO CASSETTE PRO
Gives clinical examples which determine when peritoneal lavage should be performed and the proper technique to be used. Discusses the advantages of lavage versus paracentesis. Presents methods of evaluating the results.
Prod-UMICHM Dist-UMICHM 1972

Peritonitis - Some Causes And Management C 22 MIN
16MM FILM OPTICAL SOUND PRO
Presents three pathologic conditions which illustrate common mechanisms by which peritonitis and its complications are produced—perforated peptic ulcer, small bowel obstruction and the mechanism by which left colon obstruction results in perforation of the cecum.
Prod-ACYDGD Dist-ACY 1960

Periyar, The B 13 MIN
16MM FILM OPTICAL SOUND
Shows dams, hydroelectric stations, irrigation systems industries and the life of the people along the 140 mile length of the Periyar River, Kerala, India.
LC NO. FI67-2303
Prod-INDIA Dist-NEDINF 1959

Perk Up The Salad C 4 MIN
16MM FILM OPTICAL SOUND
See series title for descriptive statement.
From The Beatrice Trum Hunter's Natural Foods Series.
Prod-PUBTEL Dist-PBS 1974

Perk Up The Salad C 3 MIN
2 INCH VIDEOTAPE
Suggests perking up the salad bowl by adding such ingredients as grated raw turnip, onion rings soaked in beet juice, sunflower or pumpkin seeds and bits of onions that have begun to sprout, as well as a modification of the basic oil and vinegar dressing with the additions of herbs, yogurt or a favorite cheese.
From The Beatrice Trum Hunter's Natural Foods Series.
Prod-WGBH Dist-PUBTEL

Perkins Story, The C 40 MIN
16MM FILM OPTICAL SOUND I-C A
Presents a documentary film about the Perkins School for the Blind, located in Watertown, Massachusetts. Deals primarily with the children and their daily life at the school—their classes, sports and fun, including roller skating, a square dance party and other activities which the average person would think impossible for a blind child.
Prod-CAMPF Dist-CAMPF 1959

Permafrost Frontier, The C 28 MIN
16MM FILM OPTICAL SOUND
Illustrates the properties of permafrost and explains the engineering methods used to design and build the trans-Alaskan pipeline
LC NO. 77-702121
Prod-ALYSKA Dist-MTP Prodn-CORPOR 1977

Permafrost, The C 14 MIN
16MM FILM OPTICAL SOUND I-H
Shows the problems of piping oil from Alaska to an ice-free port through permanently frozen ground.
Prod-ALLFP Dist-NSTA 1978

Permanency Planning - Use Of The Task-Centered Model With An Adolescent...Pt I C 43 MIN
3/4 OR 1/2 INCH VIDEO CASSETTE
Presents scenes from a task-centered contracting session between an actual social practitioner and her teenage client, showing the practitioner helping an involuntary client target a problem which she wishes to reduce voluntarily.
Prod-UWISC Dist-UWISC 1981

Permanency Planning - Use Of The Task-Centered Model With An Adolescent...Pt II C 46 MIN
3/4 OR 1/2 INCH VIDEO CASSETTE
Includes scenes from a task-centered review session in which obstacles are identified and new tasks are mutually developed. Provides guidance for the middle phase of task-centered casework.
Prod-UWISC Dist-UWISC 1981

Permanency Planning - Work With The Child C 40 MIN
3/4 OR 1/2 INCH VIDEO CASSETTE
Explains the causes of child placement in a foster home, explores expectations and develops plans with a nine-year-old client.
Prod-UWISC Dist-UWISC 1981

Permanency Planning - Work With The Family Of An Adolescent C 50 MIN
3/4 OR 1/2 INCH VIDEO CASSETTE
Shows a session contract in which target problems have included return home of a teenager and compliance with curfew and chores. Reveals problems which can arise between parents and social practitioner.
Prod-UWISC Dist-UWISC 1981

Permanency Planning At Intake C 40 MIN
3/4 OR 1/2 INCH VIDEO CASSETTE
Carries out a non-emergency child welfare investigation of neglect in which potential danger exists though actual harm does not warrant removal of the foster child.
Prod-UWISC Dist-UWISC 1981

Permanency Planning With Natural Parents B 60 MIN
3/4 OR 1/2 INCH VIDEO CASSETTE
Presents a role play between a social worker and a parent of a child presently in foster care. Illustrates stable relationships for foster children.
Prod-UWISC Dist-UWISC 1979

Permanent Magnets - Characteristics C 20 MIN
2 INCH VIDEOTAPE I
See series title for descriptive statement.
From The Exploring With Science, Unit VII - Magnetism Series.
Prod-MPATI Dist-GPITVL

Permanent Planning Casework - The Initial Interview B 18 MIN
3/4 OR 1/2 INCH VIDEO CASSETTE
Features the initial interview between a young mother with a child in foster care and a permanency planning caseworker for the purpose of developing a permanent plan. Demonstrates the skills and techniques necessary to obtain the three goals of this first contact.
Prod-PSC Dist-UWISC

Permanent Teeth C 14 MIN
3/4 OR 1/2 INCH VIDEO CASSETTE I
Discusses dental health.
From The Conrad Series.
Prod-SCETV Dist-AITECH 1977

Permanent Wave Blocking Patterns C
3/4 OR 1/2 INCH VIDEO CASSETTE
Illustrates and demonstrates the single halo, double halo and the straight back wrap. Demonstrates special wraps for bangs, drop crown and piggyback for long hair. Includes body waves and permanent waving for men, the partial perm and the stack perm techniques.
Prod-MPCEDP Dist-MPCEDP 1984

Permeability Of Plant Cell Membranes, The C 2 MIN
16MM FILM SILENT
Shows the rehydration of dried apple sections with water and the cooking of hydrated dried and fresh apples in a sugar solution to demonstrate applications of osmosis and dialysis. Compares the cellular structure of prepared apples with fresh samples.
From The Food And Nutrition Series.
LC NO. 79-710172
Prod-IOWA Dist-IOWA 1971

Permit To Work C 23 MIN
16MM FILM, 3/4 OR 1/2 IN VIDEO
Dramatizes an accident in the confined space of a chemical storage tank and shows safety procedures for those who work in potentially hazardous, confined spaces.
LC NO. 83-706693
Prod-MILLBK Dist-IFB

Permutation Group, The B
16MM FILM OPTICAL SOUND
Demonstrates the general principle that permutations are compounded of cycles. Develops a relationship between permutations and group cards.
Prod-OPENU Dist-OPENU

Permutations C 8 MIN
16MM FILM OPTICAL SOUND
A computer-made art film which demonstrates the graphic art potential of the computer. Presents a set of permutations of an equation in geometry.
LC NO. 72-702516
Prod-IBM Dist-MOMA Prodn-WHIT 1968

Permutations C 27 MIN
16MM FILM, 3/4 OR 1/2 IN VIDEO
Demonstrates the newest computer production in the field of 'motion graphics' and an explanation of how it was done.
Prod-WHIT Dist-PFP 1968

Permutations And Combinations C 8 MIN
16MM FILM OPTICAL SOUND
Creates movements by using experimental techniques coupled with still images.
LC NO. 77-702609
Prod-LITWKS Dist-CANFDC 1976

Permutations And Combinations B 31 MIN
16MM FILM OPTICAL SOUND H
States the fundamental principle of permutations and combinations and uses it to solve several problems. Uses three formulas to solve the problem of designing license plates under various restrictive conditions.
From The Advanced Algebra Series.
Prod-CALVIN Dist-MLA Prodn-UNIVFI 1960

Pernicious Anemia C 29 MIN
3/4 OR 1/2 INCH VIDEO CASSETTE
Outlines the causes and treatment of pernicious anemia.
From The Daniel Foster, MD Series.
Prod-KERA Dist-PBS

Perpetual Motion C 11 MIN
16MM FILM, 3/4 OR 1/2 IN VIDEO I-H
Uses several models of man's attempts to create a perpetual motion machine to explore the laws of thermodynamics. Points out that energy must be continually added to any system to maintain orderly operation.
Prod-BFA Dist-PHENIX 1969

Perpetum And Mobile C 5 MIN
16MM FILM OPTICAL SOUND J-C A
Portrays the technological crisis and the power of industrialism over man by telling the story of a man who runs an assembly-line machine which makes metal bolts. Shows how he is magnetized by the beeping call of the machine, fed into a cylinder and shaped into a metal nut to be mated to a bolt.
LC NO. 72-700411
Prod-ZAGREB Dist-MMA 1971

Pershing Story, The/The American Siberian Expeditionary Force B 58 MIN
3/4 OR 1/2 INCH VIDEO CASSETTE
Offers a biography of General John Pershing which emphasizes his exploits during World War I.
Prod-IHF Dist-IHF

Persia C 29 MIN
2 INCH VIDEOTAPE
Features home economist Joan Hood presenting a culinary tour of specialty dishes from around the world. Shows the preparation of Persian dishes ranging from peasant cookery to continental cuisine.
From The International Cookbook Series.
Prod-WMVSTV Dist-PUBTEL

Persimmon - A Nuclear Physics Experiment C 16 MIN
16MM FILM OPTICAL SOUND
Explains that for several years the Los Alamos Scientific Laboratory has used intense bursts of neutrons produced by underground detonations of nuclear explosives to perform a variety of nuclear physics experiments. Discusses the experiments and describes the nuclear detonations and the collapse and cratering of the ground above it.
LC NO. FIE68-26
Prod-LASL Dist-LASL 1968

Persistence Of Memory, The C 60 MIN
16MM FILM, 3/4 OR 1/2 IN VIDEO J-C A
Explores the study of genetic information, the functions of the human brain, the relationship of brain and environment, and the physiologic synaptic response. Based on the book Cosmos by Carl Sagan. Narrated by Carl Sagan.
From The Cosmos Series. Program 11
LC NO. 81-707181
Prod-KCET Dist-FI 1980

Persistent Ones, The C 50 MIN
16MM FILM OPTICAL SOUND
Presents a television special from the CTV program Olympiad, which focuses on athletes who have overcome physical or emotional handicaps to become Olympic gold medal winners.
LC NO. 77-702542
Prod-CTV Dist-CTV 1976

Persistent Stapedial Artery C 7 MIN
16MM FILM OPTICAL SOUND PRO
Shows two cases of persistent stapedial artery accidentially found during stapes surgery. Explains that the stapedial artery in man normally disappears early in embryonic development and very rarely persists into adult life.
Prod-EAR Dist-EAR

Person To Person - Learning To Communicate C
3/4 OR 1/2 INCH VIDEO CASSETTE J-C
Teaches interpersonal communication skills. Examines typical problems in speaking and listening. Includes teacher's guide.
Prod-SUNCOM Dist-SUNCOM

Person To Person - Making Communications Work For You C 10 MIN
16MM FILM, 3/4 OR 1/2 IN VIDEO H-C A
Explores four areas of office communication, including facial expression, body language, eye contact and vocal enthusiasm. Presents examples of both positive and negative communication in each area.
Prod-SAIF Dist-BARR 1973

Person To Person Communication C 14 MIN
16MM FILM, 3/4 OR 1/2 IN VIDEO H-C
Emphasizes listening with understanding. Shows that false assumptions, preconceived viewpoints and exaggerated personal feelings can lead to misunderstandings in normal conversation.
Prod-MCMGP Dist-RTBL 1956

Person To Person Communication (Danish) C 14 MIN
16MM FILM, 3/4 OR 1/2 IN VIDEO H-C
Emphasizes listening with understanding. Shows that false assumptions, preconceived viewpoints and exaggerated personal feelings can lead to misunderstandings in normal conversation.
Prod-MCMGP Dist-RTBL 1956

Person To Person Communication (Dutch) C 14 MIN
16MM FILM, 3/4 OR 1/2 IN VIDEO H-C
Emphasizes listening with understanding. Shows that false assumptions, preconceived viewpoints and exaggerated personal feelings can lead to misunderstandings in normal conversation.
Prod-MCMGP Dist-RTBL 1956

Person To Person Communication (German) C 14 MIN
16MM FILM, 3/4 OR 1/2 IN VIDEO H-C
Emphasizes listening with understanding. Shows that false assumptions, preconceived viewpoints and exaggerated personal feelings can lead to misunderstandings in normal conversation.
Prod-MCMGP Dist-RTBL 1956

Person To Person Communication (Japanese) C 14 MIN
16MM FILM, 3/4 OR 1/2 IN VIDEO H-C
Emphasizes listening with understanding. Shows that false assumptions, preconceived viewpoints and exaggerated personal feelings can lead to misunderstandings in normal conversation.
Prod-MCMGP Dist-RTBL 1956

Person To Person Communication (Norwegian) C 14 MIN
16MM FILM, 3/4 OR 1/2 IN VIDEO H-C
Emphasizes listening with understanding. Shows that false assumptions, preconceived viewpoints and exaggerated personal feelings can lead to misunderstandings in normal conversation.
Prod-MCMGP Dist-RTBL 1956

Person To Person Communication (Swedish) C 14 MIN
16MM FILM, 3/4 OR 1/2 IN VIDEO H-C
Emphasizes listening with understanding. Shows that false assumptions, preconceived viewpoints and exaggerated personal feelings can lead to misunderstandings in normal conversation.
Prod-MCMGP Dist-RTBL 1956

Person To Person In Infancy C 22 MIN
16MM FILM OPTICAL SOUND
Stresses the importance of the human relationships between infant and adult, and shows that in group care as well as at home there can be a considerable range of warmth and adequacy of relationship. Suggests the impact of this relationship of the infant's readiness and eagerness for new experience.
LC NO. 73-700106
Prod-USDHEW Dist-USNAC 1970

Person-To-Person Relationships C 28 MIN
16MM FILM OPTICAL SOUND A
Explores skills and attitudes that aid people in public service in getting along well with others in one-to-one situations.
From The You In Public Service Series.
LC NO. 77-700966
Prod-USOE Dist-USNAC 1977

Personal Accounts Of Near-Death Experiences C 24 MIN
3/4 OR 1/2 INCH VIDEO CASSETTE
Details four people's accounts of their near-death experiences, men and women who have been clinically dead for minutes.
Prod-SILVEA Dist-AJN

Personal And Family Security C 25 MIN
16MM FILM, 3/4 OR 1/2 IN VIDEO
Provides security information which can be followed by executives and their families to counteract the threat of terrorist violence. Covers security procedures for the home, the office and while driving.
Prod-WORON Dist-MTI

Personal And Family Security (Spanish) C 22 MIN
16MM FILM, 3/4 OR 1/2 IN VIDEO
Covers protection for executives and their families. Deals with maintaining a low profile, driving tips, office security and communications procedures.
Prod-WORON Dist-MCI

Personal Care Considerations Of The Diabetic C 22 MIN
3/4 OR 1/2 INCH VIDEO CASSETTE
Outlines daily care routines and the diabetic's personal responsibility. Explains techniques, evaluation and equipment for self-administered urine tests, recognizing an insulin reaction

and what to do about it, importance of personal hygiene and precautions during non-diabetic illness.
From The Understanding Diabetes Series.
Prod-FAIRGH Dist-FAIRGH

Personal Computer Applications In Business C 30 MIN
3/4 OR 1/2 INCH VIDEO CASSETTE
Defines the nature of personal computers and explores the impact they are having on the business community.
From The Personal Computers In Business Series.
Prod-DELTAK Dist-DELTAK

Personal Computer Hardware C 30 MIN
3/4 OR 1/2 INCH VIDEO CASSETTE
Examines the terminology and functions of different hardware components and discusses some of the purchasing and service issues involved in using a personal computer.
From The Personal Computers In Business Series.
Prod-DELTAK Dist-DELTAK

Personal Computer Software C 30 MIN
3/4 OR 1/2 INCH VIDEO CASSETTE
Examines the 'buy vs create' software question and looks at some of the advantages and disadvantages on both sides. Discusses the various programming languages and operating systems available for personal computers and what they mean to the user.
From The Personal Computers In Business Series.
Prod-DELTAK Dist-DELTAK

Personal Computers - Basic Concepts C
3/4 OR 1/2 INCH VIDEO CASSETTE
Presents an overview of home computers, describing how they operate. Defines basic computer terminology.
From The Computer Concepts Series.
Prod-LIBFSC Dist-LIBFSC

Personal Computers In Business—A Series

Presents some of the current uses of personal computers in business and discusses how business professionals determine their need for a personal computer. Explores the growing impact of personal computers on the business community and provides a guide to determining which business needs can be met by a personal computer.
Prod-DELTAK Dist-DELTAK

Determining Your Needs 030 MIN
Personal Computer Applications In Business 030 MIN
Personal Computer Hardware 030 MIN
Personal Computer Software 030 MIN

Personal Construct Theory As Applied To Nutrition Education C 42 MIN
3/4 INCH VIDEO CASSETTE
Reveals how psychologists use personal construct theory to predict behavior. Reveals that this theory makes it possible to understand and change eating patterns by recording and analyzing a person's beliefs about food.
Prod-SNUTRE Dist-SNUTRE

Personal Development And Professional Growth- Mike McCaffrey's Focus Seminar—A Series

Presents Mike McCaffrey's focus seminar, which helps individuals define personal and professional goals, and suggests ways to develop more positive attitudes, exhibit greater goal orientation, comunicate more effectively, build better teamwork and increase personal productivity. Includes a facilitator's guide and a participant's progress guide.
Prod-DELTAK Dist-DELTAK

Affirmations 030 MIN
Building Your Self-Esteem 030 MIN
Conclusions 030 MIN
Conditioning 030 MIN
Dealing With Pressure 030 MIN
Goal Achievement 030 MIN
How To Commuicate - Receiving 030 MIN
How To Communicate - Sending 030 MIN
How To Use Affirmations 030 MIN
Image Impressions 030 MIN
Responsibility - The Key To Freedom 030 MIN
Thought Processes - Conscious And Subconscious 030 MIN
Your Self-Images 030 MIN

Personal Development Objectives / Appraisal By Results C 12 MIN
3/4 OR 1/2 INCH VIDEO CASSETTE
See series title for descriptive statement.
From The Practical M B O Series.
Prod-DELTAK Dist-DELTAK

Personal Encounter B 60 MIN
3/4 INCH VIDEO CASSETTE
Features hand-to-hand fighting principles of judo, including the technique of falling correctly, throwing, following through, defense against body holds, defense against choke holds, taking prisoners, defense against wrestling holds, defense against knife or club and offensive use of the police riot club.
Prod-USNAC Dist-USNAC 1972

Personal Finance—A Series
C A
Discusses the complex world of personal finance. Presents an in-depth study of personal financial decisions the average person can expect to confront. Includes the basics of budgeting, home ownership, income taxes and the wise use of insurance, wills and trusts.
Prod-SCCON Dist-CDTEL

Buying A Home 030 MIN
Creating A Workable Financial Plan 030 MIN
Credit And Borrowing 030 MIN
Economy, The 030 MIN
Estate Planning - Achieving Your Objectives 030 MIN
Estate Planning - The Tools You'll Use 030 MIN
Financial Institutions 030 MIN
Financial Planning For Later Years 030 MIN
Financing A Home 030 MIN
Frauds And Swindles 030 MIN
Health And Income Insurance 030 MIN
Housing Costs And Regulations 030 MIN
How Income Taxes Work 030 MIN
Leisure And Recreation 030 MIN
Life Insurance 030 MIN
Making Your Money Grow 030 MIN
Money Market, The 030 MIN
Other Investment Opportunities 030 MIN
Real Estate Investments 030 MIN
Renting 030 MIN
Selling Your Home 030 MIN
Smart Shopper, The 030 MIN
Stock Market, The 030 MIN
Tax-Saving Strategies 030 MIN
Transportation 030 MIN
Work, Income, And Your Career 030 MIN

Personal Finances C 19 MIN
3/4 OR 1/2 INCH VIDEO CASSETTE H
Describes a stock boy who finally learns to budget his income realistically.
From The Jobs - Seeking, Finding, Keeping Series.
Prod-MSDOE Dist-AITECH 1980

Personal Financial Planning X 11 MIN
16MM FILM OPTICAL SOUND J-H
Discusses the relationship between financial planning and the attainment of goals, showing how to handle personal income wisely to guarantee personal security and to perpetuate our free economic system.
LC NO. FIA62-1677
Prod-SUEF Dist-SUTHLA 1960

Personal Financial Planning—A Series
C
Illustrates how to control one's financial future. Shows how to calculate net worth, how to budget as an aid to achieving financial goals, how to establish savings and investment goals, and how to maintain an accurate account of progress toward goals.
Prod-USCITV Dist-AMCEE

Personal Flotation Devices - Your Friends For Life C 7 MIN
3/4 OR 1/2 INCH VIDEO CASSETTE A
Discusses personal flotation devices and care requirements, types, and activities relating to them. Comments on drowning as the second leading cause of accidental death below age 75.
Prod-USCG Dist-USNAC 1983

Personal Gear And Food C 30 MIN
3/4 OR 1/2 INCH VIDEO CASSETTE
Discusses the personal gear and food needed for safe camping.
From The Camping Series.
Prod-UGATV Dist-MDCPB

Personal Grooming And Hygiene C 11 MIN
16MM FILM, 3/4 OR 1/2 IN VIDEO A
Illustrates the importance of proper personal hygiene in a business environment. Offers detailed information on bathing, care of teeth, and use of deodorants, perfumes and cosmetics. Stresses the role played by well-groomed hair, beard and fingernails in non-verbal communication.
From The Communications And Selling Programs Series.
Prod-NEM Dist-NEM

Personal Grooming And Hygiene (Spanish) C 11 MIN
16MM FILM, 3/4 OR 1/2 IN VIDEO
Shows the importance of personal grooming and hygiene in business.
From The Customer Service, Courtesy And Selling Programs (Spanish) Series.
Prod-NEM Dist-NEM

Personal Growth C 30 MIN
3/4 OR 1/2 INCH VIDEO CASSETTE T
Discusses personal growth in a school setting.
From The Interaction - Human Concerns In The Schools Series.
Prod-MDDE Dist-MDCPB

Personal Growth For The Supervisor C 30 MIN
2 INCH VIDEOTAPE PRO
Deals with some of the steps that a supervisor can take to continue to grow on his job.
From The You - The Supervisor Series.
Prod-PRODEV Dist-PRODEV

Personal Health C 16 MIN
16MM FILM, 3/4 OR 1/2 IN VIDEO
Outlines the basics of preventive medicine for promoting physical health. Illustrates personal hygiene techniques which should be used to prevent the spread of germs and infection.
LC NO. 82-706662
Prod-USA Dist-USNAC 1976

Personal Health For Girls (2nd Ed) C 14 MIN
16MM FILM, 3/4 OR 1/2 IN VIDEO J-H
Presents principles of hygiene for girls and shows the importance of observing good habits of eating and cleanliness for health and social reasons.
Prod-CORF Dist-CORF 1972

Personal History, A C 30 MIN
3/4 INCH VIDEO CASSETTE J-C A
Features Dr Jacob Bronowski recalling his life and work. Examines the moral implications of the atomic bomb.
From The Jacob Bronowski - 20th Century Man Series.
Prod-KPBS Dist-GPITVL 1976

Personal Hygiene - Basic Sanitation For Food Handlers C 10 MIN
3/4 OR 1/2 INCH VIDEO CASSETTE PRO
Shows how food can become contaminated by poor hygiene and states the basic rules for cleanliness.
Prod-CULINA Dist-CULINA

Personal Hygiene For Boys (2nd Ed) C 11 MIN
16MM FILM, 3/4 OR 1/2 IN VIDEO I-J
Shows five boys, Bill, Steve, Jeff, Larry and Rick, who all have special problems regarding personal hygiene and the changes taking place in their maturing bodies. Offers guidance on the common standards of of good body care including shaving, showering and skin and hair care.
Prod-CORF Dist-CORF 1971

Personal Identity C 24 MIN
16MM FILM OPTICAL SOUND
Explores how philosophers define personal identity in terms of either a person's body or a person's memory or both simultaneously. Critiques the conclusion that bodily identity is not sufficient for personal identity.
Prod-BBCTV Dist-OPENU 1982

Personal Identity C 24 MIN
16MM FILM, 3/4 OR 1/2 IN VIDEO
Explores how philosophers define personal identity in terms of either a person's body or a person's memory or both simultaneously. Critiques the conclusion that bodily identity is not sufficient for personal identity.
Prod-OPENU Dist-MEDIAG Prodn-BBCTV 1982

Personal Inventory C 25 MIN
3/4 OR 1/2 INCH VIDEO CASSETTE
Discusses the nature of an important component of effective recovery from drug dependency, such as systematic self-assessment.
From The Caring Community - Alcoholism And Drug Abuse Series.
Prod-VTRI Dist-VTRI

Personal Perspectives C 53 MIN
3/4 OR 1/2 INCH VIDEO CASSETTE A
Presents a selection of videotapes produced at LBMA Video.
From The Shared Realities Series.
Prod-LBMART Dist-LBMART 1983

Personal Plan For Wellness, A C 30 MIN
3/4 OR 1/2 INCH VIDEO CASSETTE
Introduces a system designed to initiate and maintain healthy lifestyle changes. Shows how bad habits are replaced by a series of steps and goals.
From The Planning For Wellness System Series.
Prod-MTI Dist-MTI

Personal Protective Equipment C
3/4 OR 1/2 INCH VIDEO CASSETTE IND
Details various personal protective equipment available to workers in industry and visually demonstrates how each is used.
From The Safety Action For Employees Series.
Prod-GPCV Dist-GPCV

Personal Protective Equipment C 12 MIN
3/4 OR 1/2 INCH VIDEO CASSETTE
Discusses work clothes and personal protective equipment in the plant. Covers special work clothing, eye protection, safety harnesses and lifelines.
From The Protecting Your Safety And Health In the Plant Series.
Prod-TPCTRA Dist-TPCTRA

Personal Protective Equipment (Spanish) C 12 MIN
3/4 OR 1/2 INCH VIDEO CASSETTE
Discusses work clothes and personal protective equipment in the plant. Covers special work clothing, eye protection, safety harnesses and lifelines.
From The Protecting Your Safety And Health In The Plant Series.
Prod-TPCTRA Dist-TPCTRA

Personal Safety C 3 MIN
16MM FILM OPTICAL SOUND H-C A
Discusses safety rules including wearing eye protection, tieing back long hair, wearing loose, inexpensive clothing, wearing a lab coat or apron and wearing protective shoes. Shows techniques for smothering a clothing fire with a fire blanket and a lab apron.
From The Safety In The Laboratory Series.
LC NO. 72-702620
Prod-KALMIA Dist-KALMIA 1972

Personal Safety C 12 MIN
16MM FILM, 3/4 OR 1/2 IN VIDEO A
Shows that although personal assault is on the rise, prevention and defense techniques can be employed by the average person to minimize loss and injury. Emphasizes the psychological posture of being prepared.
Prod-RTBL Dist-RTBL

Personal Safety - The Voices Of Victims C 19 MIN
16MM FILM, 3/4 OR 1/2 IN VIDEO J-C A
Suggests how to protect oneself from burglary, robbery, vandalism, and personal assault.
LC NO. 80-706464
Prod-CENTRO Dist-CORF 1979

Personal Safety, Pt 1 C 15 MIN
3/4 OR 1/2 INCH VIDEO CASSETTE IND
Discusses the importance of safety for personal protection. Covers the role of OSHA, use of safety clothes, eye protection and safe lifting practices.

From The Industrial Safety Series.
Prod-LEIKID Dist-LEIKID

Personal Safety, Pt 2 C 20 MIN
3/4 OR 1/2 INCH VIDEO CASSETTE IND
Discusses the need for and types of hearing protection, skin protection, protection of lungs from dangerous particles and types of respirators and which to use.
From The Industrial Safety Series.
Prod-LEIKID Dist-LEIKID

Personal Service C 6 MIN
16MM FILM, 3/4 OR 1/2 IN VIDEO K-I
See series title for descriptive statement.
From The Kingdom Of Could Be You Series.
Prod-EBEC Dist-EBEC 1974

Personal Service Cluster C 20 MIN
3/4 OR 1/2 INCH VIDEO CASSETTE
Discusses the requirements and duties for such jobs as cosmetologists, food service worker, educational assistant and law enforcement worker.
From The Vocational Visions Series.
Prod-GA Dist-GA

Personal Services C 10 MIN
3/4 INCH VIDEO CASSETTE P
Profiles self-employed people in the business of service. Explains how they arrange and maintain the daily undertakings of other people.
Prod-MINIP Dist-GA

Personal Side Of Safety–A Series

Provides a personal formula and approach to keeping safe on the job. Shows how each person must regard safety as a personal concern and personal problem requiring careful thought and analysis.
Prod-NSC Dist-NSC

Decide To Be Safe 10 MIN
Get A Grip On Yourself 10 MIN
Let Habit Help 10 MIN
Safety Record 10 MIN
Two Steps To Safety 10 MIN

Personal Stamp, The C 30 MIN
2 INCH VIDEOTAPE C A
Explores the special qualities imparted by room accessories. Demonstrates how to construct a picture wall.
From The Designing Home Interior Series. Unit 27
Prod-COAST Dist-CDTEL Prodn-RSCCD

Personal Story, The C 10 MIN
16MM FILM OPTICAL SOUND
Presents football great Roger Staubach and other players from the National Football League who discuss personal experiences with the agencies and services supported by the United Way.
LC NO. 82-700809
Prod-UWAMER Dist-UWAMER 1982

Personal Stress Management C
1/2 IN VIDEO CASSETTE BETA/VHS
See series title for descriptive statement.
From The R M I Stress Management Series Series.
Prod-RMI Dist-RMI

Personal Tax And Financial Planning For Professionals C 160 MIN
3/4 OR 1/2 INCH VIDEO CASSETTE PRO
Discusses the options to be considered in structuring a professional business and minimizing taxes on earned and unearned income for a law practice and its professional clients.
Prod-CCEB Dist-ABACPE

Personal Time Management–A Series

Deals with the effective use of time, and presents an organized set of proven, helpful ideas. Includes a student manual and a Student Study Guide.
Prod-DELTAK Dist-DELTAK

Doing The Distasteful And Difficult 022 MIN
Filing Systems That Work For You 025 MIN
How Good Is Your Time Management 025 MIN
Organizing Your Time 031 MIN
Scheduling Your Time 029 MIN
Staff Meetings That Work For You 019 MIN

Personal Time Management–A Series

Presents a course to help viewers organize and make better use of their time.
Prod-TELSTR Dist-TELSTR

Doing The Distasteful And Difficult 030 MIN
Filing For Your Own Needs 030 MIN
Getting Staff Meetings To Work For You 030 MIN
How To Distribute Your Time Effectively 030 MIN
Organizing Your Work And Others' Work 030 MIN
Scheduling Your Time And Others' Time 030 MIN

Personal Touch C 30 MIN
3/4 OR 1/2 INCH VIDEO CASSETTE
Covers how to convey a personal touch in business letters. Includes methods of persuasion and how to get results.
From The Better Business Letters Series. Lesson 6
Prod-TELSTR Dist-TELSTR

Personal Touch C 31 MIN
3/4 OR 1/2 INCH VIDEO CASSETTE
See series title for descriptive statement.
From The Better Business Letters Series.
Prod-TELSTR Dist-DELTAK

Personal Touch, The C 15 MIN
16MM FILM, 3/4 OR 1/2 IN VIDEO H-C A
Aims to dispel the idea that computers are impersonal robots or functionaries useful only in business and industry. Looks at the many ways computers can serve personal interests by expanding the individual's mental capabilities.
From The Adventure Of The Mind Series.
Prod-IITC Dist-IU 1980

Personal Transformation - The Way Through C 44 MIN
3/4 OR 1/2 INCH VIDEO CASSETTE
Presents transformer therapy as a direction-finding experience for those recovering from chemical dependency.
Prod-WHITEG Dist-WHITEG

Personal Values C 11 MIN
16MM FILM, 3/4 OR 1/2 IN VIDEO J-H A
Questions whether the honesty taught in school is better forgotten if it helps one to get ahead in the outside world.
From The Family Life Education And Human Growth Series.
Prod-SF Dist-SF 1970

Personality C 30 MIN
16MM FILM, 3/4 OR 1/2 IN VIDEO H-C A
Shows personality evaluation methods such as self report, multiple input, ink blots and personality tests.
From The Psychology Today Films Series.
Prod-CRMP Dist-CRMP 1971

Personality C 30 MIN
3/4 OR 1/2 INCH VIDEO CASSETTE
Deals with trait theory of personality, Freudian or psychoanalytic approach, social learning theory, humanism, client-centered therapy and self-actualization.
From The Psychology Of Human Relations Series.
Prod-MATC Dist-WFVTAE

Personality (Interviews)–A Series

Presents interviews with experts working in fields of social and economic importance.
Prod-WORLDR Dist-WORLDR

Dr Bernard Siegan 026 MIN
Dr Dom Armentano And Dr Randy Haydon 028 MIN
Dr Walter Williams 026 MIN
Edwin Meese III 026 MIN
Friedrich Von Hayek 030 MIN
John Pugsley 022 MIN

Personality - Adolescence C 21 MIN
16MM FILM, 3/4 OR 1/2 IN VIDEO H-C A
Explores the development of the adolescent personality. Points out that conflict with authority and reliance on peers becomes the norm.
From The Growing Years (CRMP) Series.
Prod-COAST Dist-CRMP 1978

Personality - Early Childhood C 20 MIN
16MM FILM, 3/4 OR 1/2 IN VIDEO H-C A
Describes dependency, identification, aggression and anxiety in the preschool personality.
From The Growing Years (CRMP) Series.
Prod-COAST Dist-CRMP 1978

Personality - Middle Childhood C 19 MIN
16MM FILM, 3/4 OR 1/2 IN VIDEO H-C A
Discusses the child's personality between the ages of six and twelve. Explains the importance of peer groups, parents and teachers.
From The Growing Years (CRMP) Series.
Prod-COAST Dist-CRMP 1978

Personality And Its Effect On Communication B 50 MIN
3/4 OR 1/2 INCH VIDEO CASSETTE
Highlights the importance of personality and its effects on communication. Focuses on the office environment.
Prod-UAZMIC Dist-UAZMIC 1976

Personality Disorders C 66 MIN
3/4 OR 1/2 INCH VIDEO CASSETTE PRO
Identifies theories of the etiology of personality disorders. Discusses paranoia, schizophrenia, narcissism, compulsive and passive aggressivity.
From The Psychiatry Learning System, Pt 2 - Disorders Series.
Prod-HSCIC Dist-HSCIC 1982

Personality Disorders - Failures Of Adjustment C 57 MIN
1/2 IN VIDEO CASSETTE (VHS) J-C A
Dramatizes sociopathic, paranoid, schizoid, avoidant, narcissistic, histrionic, passive-aggressive and compulsive disorder types. Shows causes of these disorders and recent breakthroughs in treatment.
LC NO. 85-703979
Prod-HRMC Dist-HRMC

Personality Disorganization In A 12-Year-Old Negro Boy B 23 MIN
16MM FILM OPTICAL SOUND PRO
Presents Povl Toussieng who interviews a Negro boy who is undergoing an acute psychotic break and thinks that he has two distinct halves, a Negro half and an Indian half. Toussieng and L J West discuss the role of socio-cultural factors in the onset and course of a psychotic episode.
LC NO. 72-700628
Prod-UOKLA Dist-UOKLA 1969

Personality Of A Market C 16 MIN
16MM FILM OPTICAL SOUND
Portrays the Houston, Texas, radio market in order to encourage business concerns to purchase commercial time on the radio.
LC NO. 70-712180
Prod-KXYZ Dist-KXYZ 1970

Personality Styles–A Series

Helps managers understand their own behavioral style, recognize behavioral patterns in others, work with and motivate people with personalities different from their own and develop a communications language.
Prod-AMA Dist-AMA

Describing Nine Classic Personality Styles 036 MIN
Interpreting Your Own Self-Perception Profile 024 MIN
Motivating The Conservative And The Cautious 035 MIN
Motivating The Dominant And The 025 MIN
Practical Approach To Understanding 020 MIN

Personality Tests C 29 MIN
3/4 INCH VIDEO CASSETTE C A
Discusses great number and variety of psychological tests in current use. Makes distinction between IQ and intelligence. Emphasizes many factors that influence intelligence scores.
From The Understanding Human Behavior - An Introduction To Psychology Series. Lesson 23
Prod-COAST Dist-CDTEL

Personality Theory C 29 MIN
3/4 INCH VIDEO CASSETTE C A
Surveys and compares approaches and contributions of the major theories of personality. Defines personality and theory. Looks at work of Freud, Erikson, Rogers and Maslow.
From The Understanding Human Behavior - An Introduction To Psychology Series. Lesson 22
Prod-COAST Dist-CDTEL

Personalize Your Presentation C 9 MIN
16MM FILM OPTICAL SOUND H A
See series title for descriptive statement.
From The Professional Selling Practices Series 1 Series.
LC NO. 77-702360
Prod-SAUM Dist-SAUM Prodn-CALPRO 1967

Personalized Academic Services C 30 MIN
16MM FILM OPTICAL SOUND C A
Uses Navajo Indian children in order to show the techniques and methods used in special education for second language acquisition, for teching language arts, reading and for the development of prescriptive learning.
LC NO. 75-702926
Prod-USBIA Dist-AVED Prodn-BAILYL 1975

Personalizing Reading For Children C 22 MIN
16MM FILM, 3/4 OR 1/2 IN VIDEO T
Shows how one school organized its resources to more fully meet individual reading needs. Urges the development of an appropriate management system and the involvement of teachers in decisions about the use of time, space and materials.
From The Child's Right To Read Series.
LC NO. 80-706434
Prod-CSDE Dist-AITECH 1977

Personnel Basket Safety C 7 MIN
3/4 OR 1/2 INCH VIDEO CASSETTE IND
Shows how to ride the personnel basket when getting on or off offshore rigs and platforms. Gives safety tips and common sense advice for experienced personnel and visitors.
Prod-UTEXPE Dist-UTEXPE

Personnel For Engineering And Science Management–A Series
PRO
Focuses on the human element in management, including labor relations, human relations, personnel administration, industrial psychology, employee relations and labor economics from a manager's viewpoint.
Prod-UAKEN Dist-AMCEE

Personnel Loading Capabilities Of The C-130 Aircraft B 11 MIN
16MM FILM OPTICAL SOUND
Demonstrates the conversion of the C-130 from cargo to personnel carrier. Depicts its capabilities to carry paratroops, personnel and medical station equipment.
LC NO. FIE56-172
Prod-USDD Dist-USNAC 1954

Personnel Parachute Malfunctions And Activation Of Reserve Parachute B 14 MIN
16MM FILM OPTICAL SOUND
Discusses the causes, prevention and appropriate responses to partial or complete parachute malfunction. Stresses timely use of the reserve parachute.
LC NO. 80-701838
Prod-USA Dist-USNAC 1980

Perspective And Painting With A Knife C 25 MIN
3/4 OR 1/2 INCH VIDEO CASSETTE H-C A
See series title for descriptive statement.
From The Paint Series. Program 4
Prod-BBCTV Dist-FI

Perspective Drawing B 8 MIN
16MM FILM, 3/4 OR 1/2 IN VIDEO J-C A
Presents an introduction to mechanical perspective. Useful in teaching free hand sketching.
Prod-UCLAT Dist-UCEMC 1952

Perspective On Pesticides C 15 MIN
16MM FILM OPTICAL SOUND
Describes the various pesticides, their benefits to mankind, the hazards associated with their use - in the home and on the farm and the proper method of application and storage.
LC NO. 74-705348
Prod-USPHS Dist-USNAC 1967

Perspective On Teaching, A B 30 MIN
16MM FILM OPTICAL SOUND C A

Defines teaching, analyzes elements in a philosophy of education and examines related implications.
From The Nursing - Where Are You Going, How Will You Get There Series.
LC NO. 74-700177
Prod-NTCN Dist-NTCN 1971

Perspective—A Series

Prod-WRCTV Dist-WRCTV 1972

Community Priest, A 26 MIN
Families On The Road...To Somewhere 58 MIN
Gospel Singers, The 14 MIN
Let No Man Put Asunder 25 MIN
Lonely Crime, The 48 MIN
Sylvan Sewer, A 25 MIN

Perspective—A Series
J-C A
Discusses a wide variety of scientific research and innovation in Great Britain.
Prod-LONTVS Dist-STNFLD

Computer Aided Design 027 MIN
Consulting Cambridge 027 MIN
Electronic Music 027 MIN
Fifth Generation Computers 027 MIN
Forensic Science 027 MIN
Magic Bullet, The 027 MIN
Microsurgery 027 MIN
New Alchemy, The 027 MIN
Pictures In A Patient 027 MIN
Rampaging Carbons 027 MIN
Science At Kew Gardens 027 MIN
Science In Museums 027 MIN
Uses Of Blood 027 MIN

Perspectives C 30 MIN
2 INCH VIDEOTAPE J-H
See series title for descriptive statement.
From The From Franklin To Frost - Emily Dickinson Series.
Prod-MPATI Dist-GPITVL

Perspectives - Historical, Anthropological, Political, Economic And Social C 30 MIN
3/4 OR 1/2 INCH VIDEO CASSETTE T
Discusses historical, anthropological, political, economic and social perspectives in the field of education.
From The Interaction - Human Concerns In The Schools Series.
Prod-MDDE Dist-MDCPB

Perspectives Of Space C 30 MIN
3/4 OR 1/2 INCH VIDEO CASSETTE H-C A
Demonstrates architectural photography at chateaux in Normandy and the canyons of New York City. Explains the problems of perspective and scale and ways to introduce comment and humor into a photograph. Looks at the relationship of people and their environments, fashion designer Zandra Rhodes, the Pearly King and Queen of Westminster and sculptor Henry Moore.
From The What A Picture - The Complete Photography Course By John Hedgecoe Series. Program 6
Prod-THREMI Dist-FI

Perspectives On Insulin Pump Therapy C 29 MIN
3/4 OR 1/2 INCH VIDEO CASSETTE PRO
Examines the principles involved in the use of continuous subcutaneous insulin infusion (CSII) for patients with Type 1 diabetes. Covers the basis for the use of the insulin pump, the principles of how it works, the identification of patients suitable for pump therapy, hazards of CSII therapy, and the patient and professional responsibilities involved in this therapy. Discusses patient training and education program for pump patients on the MDRTC's inpatient unit at The University of Michigan Hospitals.
Prod-UMICHM Dist-UMICHM 1984

Perspectives On Language Training C 30 MIN
16MM FILM OPTICAL SOUND PRO
Discusses and demonstrates four general perspectives concerning language training, including the assessment of the language-delayed child, the structure of a language training session, procedures utilized in a language training session and the extension of training from the clinical to the natural environment.
LC NO. 78-701605
Prod-UKANS Dist-UKANS 1975

Perspectre C 7 MIN
16MM FILM, 3/4 OR 1/2 IN VIDEO H-C
A French language film. Presents an animated film in which a simple geometric form is duplicated, arranged and rearranged into a flow of patterns and perspectives.
LC NO. 77-700203
Prod-NFBC Dist-IFB 1976

Perspectrum C 7 MIN
16MM FILM, 3/4 OR 1/2 IN VIDEO H-C
Presents an animated film in which a simple geometric form is duplicated, arranged and rearranged into a flow of patterns and perspectives.
LC NO. 77-700203
Prod-NFBC Dist-IFB 1976

Persuading The Jury C 35 MIN
3/4 INCH VIDEO CASSETTE PRO
Explains some techniques used to persuade a jury. Describes four fundamental principles of advocacy.
From The Picking And Persuading A Jury Series. Program 6
LC NO. 81-706171
Prod-ABACPE Dist-ABACPE 1980

Persuading The Public C 14 MIN
16MM FILM, 3/4 OR 1/2 IN VIDEO J-C A
Dramatizes humorous episodes illustrating the persuasion techniques of intensifying the positive attributes and downplaying the negative qualities of an idea or product that is to be sold to the public.
Prod-JOHR Dist-PHENIX 1978

Persuasion C 29 MIN
3/4 INCH VIDEO CASSETTE C A
Discusses power and limits of persuasion in spreading ideas and changing attitudes. Uses examples from advertising and political campaigns.
From The Understanding Human Behavior - An Introduction To Psychology Series. Lesson 29
Prod-COAST Dist-CDTEL

Persuasion - Or, The Spoken Heart C 13 MIN
16MM FILM OPTICAL SOUND
Presents a monolog spoken by a girl who is trying to understand her own difficulties in loving.
LC NO. 80-700273
Prod-GIANVJ Dist-GIANVJ 1978

Persuasive Negotiating C 60 MIN
3/4 OR 1/2 INCH VIDEO CASSETTE
Shows Herb Cohen, professional negotiator, demonstrating a collaborative or win-win approach to negotiation. A sequel to Everyone's A Negotiator.
Prod-CBSFOX Dist-CBSFOX

Persuasive Negotiating C 60 MIN
16MM FILM, 3/4 OR 1/2 IN VIDEO C A
Compares competitive and collaborative styles of negotiating.
Prod-MAGVID Dist-FI

Persuasive Paper, The C 30 MIN
3/4 OR 1/2 INCH VIDEO CASSETTE C
See series title for descriptive statement.
From The Writing For A Reason Series.
Prod-DALCCD Dist-DALCCD

Persuasive Speaking C
1/2 IN VIDEO CASSETTE BETA/VHS
Gives pointers from communications experts and shows clips of master speakers in action to explain the keys to speech and presentation-making.
Prod-GA Dist-GA

Persuasive Techniques C 14 MIN
16MM FILM, 3/4 OR 1/2 IN VIDEO I
Describes how Wesley realizes that his friends have been using persuasive techniques to persuade him to reject another boy's friendship.
From The Thinkabout Series. Judging Information
LC NO. 81-706114
Prod-EDFCEN Dist-AITECH 1979

Persuasive Writing C 15 MIN
3/4 OR 1/2 INCH VIDEO CASSETTE I
Considers persuasion and defines propaganda. Analyzes letters to the editor, public service announcements and political persuasive writing.
From The Zebra Wings Series.
Prod-NITC Dist-AITECH Prodn-MAETEL 1975

Persuasive Writing C 40 MIN
3/4 OR 1/2 INCH VIDEO CASSETTE
See series title for descriptive statement.
From The Effective Writing Series.
Prod-TWAIN Dist-DELTAK

PERT - Milestone System - PERT Introduction C 27 MIN
16MM FILM OPTICAL SOUND
Brings management and operating levels together for the planning and execution of complex research and development projects.
LC NO. 74-705349
Prod-USN Dist-USNAC 1962

PERT Computations And Analysis B 60 MIN
3/4 OR 1/2 INCH VIDEO CASSETTE
See series title for descriptive statement.
From The Project Management And CPM Series. Pt 7
Prod-UAZMIC Dist-UAZMIC 1977

Pertaining To Chicago C 15 MIN
16MM FILM OPTICAL SOUND J-C
Presents a series of personal impressions of certain aspects of Chicago, featuring architectural masterpieces of Sullivan, Frank Lloyd Wright and Mies Van der Rohe. Includes the fire escapes of the Loop and the electrical signs which express the American obsession with motion.
LC NO. FIA58-931
Prod-DAVISJ Dist-RADIM 1958

Pertaining To Marin C 10 MIN
16MM FILM OPTICAL SOUND
Presents the water-colorist John Marin and studies his oils and water-colors.
Prod-FILIM Dist-RADIM

Peru C 3 MIN
16MM FILM OPTICAL SOUND P-I
Discusses the country of Peru.
From The Of All Things Series.
Prod-BAILYL Dist-AVED

Peru - Inca Heritage C 17 MIN
16MM FILM, 3/4 OR 1/2 IN VIDEO J-C A
Compares the culture of the Indians of Peru with that of their ancestors, the Incas. Discusses such points as the similarities between religious festivals of the two groups. Concludes with an exploration of the Inca citadel of Machu Pichu, which remains a fitting monument to the stone architecture of the Incas.
Prod-HP Dist-AIMS 1970

Peru - People Of The Sun C 25 MIN
16MM FILM, 3/4 OR 1/2 IN VIDEO I-C A
Describes the Nazca, Mochica, Huari, Chimu and Inca cultures that flourished in ancient Peru.
From The People And Places Of Antiquity Series.
Prod-CFDLD Dist-CORF

Peru - The Revolution That Never Was C 27 MIN
16MM FILM, 3/4 OR 1/2 IN VIDEO J-H
Tells how creating cooperatives from farms formerly run by 15,000 rich landowners forced Peruvian peasants into poverty, even though they now own the land. States that lack of both capitol for financing and cash for provisions produce the irony of revolution that brought a decade of despair.
From The South America - A Trilogy Series.
Prod-THAMES Dist-MEDIAG 1979

Peru - The Vanishing Animals C 27 MIN
16MM FILM OPTICAL SOUND P-C A
As a result of the irresponsible slaughter of wildlife, Felipe Benavide attempts to instill an awareness that the extinction of any species is an irreparable tragedy.
Prod-FISC Dist-AVED

Peruvian Paso, The - For Those With Champagne Taste C 25 MIN
1/2 IN VIDEO CASSETTE BETA/VHS
Gives a history of the Peruvian Paso horse. Demonstrates the smoothness of the gait. Talks about buying and showing.
Prod-MHRSMP Dist-EQVDL

Peruvian Weaving - A Continuous Warp For 5,000 Years C 25 MIN
16MM FILM, 3/4 OR 1/2 IN VIDEO A
Discusses warp pattern weaving in Peru, an Andean Indian tradition. Interviews Dr Junius Bird of the American Museum of Natural History, who traced this weaving tradition in Peru back to a pre-ceramic period. Includes archival footage of his 1946 archaeological excavation in Huaca Prieta.
Prod-CNEMAG Dist-CNEMAG 1980

Pest Control - Fumigating With Aluminum Phosphide C 25 MIN
16MM FILM OPTICAL SOUND
Presents step-by-step procedures for fumigating stock and a railroad car of foodstuff. Shows how to handle aluminum phosphide safely and gives defumigation instructions.
LC NO. 78-701081
Prod-USA Dist-USNAC 1977

Pest Control Technology Correspondence Course—A Series

Provides an opportunity for service technicians, managers and owners in the pest control industry, food processing and handling industry and public health to improve their ability to cope with insect and rodent problems as they are encountered day by day.
Prod-PUAVC Dist-PUAVC

Ants
Bedbugs
Birds
Cockroaches
Equipment
Fabric Insects
Flies
Insect Development
Introduction
Nonsubterranean Termites
Occasional Invaders
Organization And The Service Technician
Pesticides
Public Health
Rats
Safety, Health and Environmental Concerns
Sanitation
Stored Product Pests
Subterranean Termites

Pest Management C 30 MIN
3/4 OR 1/2 INCH VIDEO CASSETTE
Discusses a concept called integrated pest management, a program that integrates the control techniques for weeds, diseases, insects and mites into the total cropping program which is a business approach to protecting the crop against economic loss. Discusses four basic pest management tools, choosing a hybrid variety of seed that has a resistance to disease and a tolerance to insects, planting crops on a planned rotation basis, early planting to give the corn a head start on pests, and pesticides. Shows many of the common pests and ways to determine their presence.
From The Corn - Planning To Harvest Series.
Prod-NETCHE Dist-NETCHE 1981

Pest Management And Programs C 14 MIN
3/4 OR 1/2 INCH VIDEO CASSETTE
Discusses rodents and their control in the food distribution center, including control measures and recommended practices either for an in-house or contracted control program.
From The Supervisor's Role In Food Distribution Series.
Prod-PLAID Dist-PLAID

Pesta Pilau Pinang C 25 MIN
16MM FILM OPTICAL SOUND
Shows a festival on the island of Penang, Malaysia.
Prod-FILEM Dist-PMFMUN 1968

Pesticide And Wildlife C 27 MIN
16MM FILM OPTICAL SOUND
Explains why military and civilian pesticide operators should exercise caution in the use of pesticides. Gives specific recommendations for protecting wildlife from the hazards of pesticide use.

LC NO. 74-706514
Prod-USN Dist-USNAC 1973

Pesticide Politics B 23 MIN
3/4 OR 1/2 INCH VIDEO CASSETTE J-C A
Focuses on the residents of Pritt, Minnesota, who took legal action against the spraying of '245 T,' the chemical brush-killer used in Vietnam that created health problems for animals, people and vegetation overseas and at home.
Prod-UCV Dist-UCV

Pesticides C
3/4 OR 1/2 INCH VIDEO CASSETTE
See series title for descriptive statement.
From The Pest Control Technology Correspondence Course Series.
Prod-PUAVC Dist-PUAVC

Pesticides C 30 MIN
3/4 OR 1/2 INCH VIDEO CASSETTE C A
See series title for descriptive statement.
From The Pests, Pesticides And Safety Series.
Prod-UMA Dist-GPITVL 1976

Pesticides And Pest Management C 26 MIN
3/4 OR 1/2 INCH VIDEO CASSETTE
Presents pest management problems, pesticides and regulations controlling their use as applicable to supervisory monitoring of in-house pest activity and control.
From The Supervisor's Role In Food Distribution Series.
Prod-PLAID Dist-PLAID

Pests C 30 MIN
3/4 OR 1/2 INCH VIDEO CASSETTE C A
Focuses on insects that hurt the garden and insects that help. Discusses use of biological control.
From The Home Gardener With John Lenanton Series. Lesson 20
Prod-COAST Dist-CDTEL

Pests C 30 MIN
3/4 OR 1/2 INCH VIDEO CASSETTE C A
See series title for descriptive statement.
From The Pests, Pesticides And Safety Series.
Prod-UMA Dist-GPITVL 1976

Pests, Pesticides And Safety—A Series
C A
Deals with the proper handling and use of pesticides.
Prod-UMA Dist-GPITVL 1976

Environment And Pesticides, The	030 MIN
Laws And Labels	030 MIN
Pesticides	030 MIN
Pests	030 MIN
Safety	030 MIN

Pet Care C 10 MIN
16MM FILM OPTICAL SOUND P-I
Emphasizes the 'why' of pet care. Explains the basics of 'how' to care for the family pet. Discusses the elements of food, water, sleep, exercise and general care.
LC NO. 75-701529
Prod-FFORIN Dist-FFORIN 1974

Pet Evaporated Milk C 2 MIN
3/4 OR 1/2 INCH VIDEO CASSETTE
Shows a classic television commercial featuring a lullaby with mother and baby.
Prod-BROOKC Dist-BROOKC

Pet Shop, The C 15 MIN
3/4 OR 1/2 INCH VIDEO CASSETTE P
See series title for descriptive statement.
From The Strawberry Square Series.
Prod-NEITV Dist-AITECH 1982

Pete Seeger - Solo C 52 MIN
3/4 OR 1/2 INCH VIDEO CASSETTE
Features Pete Seeger, tracing the history of political satire from the early days of the U S.
From The Rainbow Quest Series.
Prod-SEEGER Dist-CWATER

Pete Takes A Chance C 26 MIN
16MM FILM, 3/4 OR 1/2 IN VIDEO I-J
Deals with a youngster who borrows money from a girl for joke and novelty items then buys raffle tickets instead. Shows that when one of the boy's dissatisfied customers threatens violence for a refund, the lad sells off his tickets, repays his disgruntled customer and creditor, and surprieses all with the raffle's outcome.
Prod-PLAYTM Dist-BCNFL 1983

Peter And Elba - Travel Training Of A Retardate C 15 MIN
16MM FILM OPTICAL SOUND
Features Elba Becknam, a travel training instructor, teaching Peter Panos, a retardate, how to travel through the streets of New York.
LC NO. 76-700403
Prod-NYCDT Dist-HF Prodn-HF 1976

Peter And The Magic Egg C 24 MIN
16MM FILM, 3/4 OR 1/2 IN VIDEO K-I
Presents an animated film, narrated by Ray Bolger, about Mama and Papa Doppler who needed a miracle to save their farm from arch-villain Tobias Tinwhistle. The miracle arrives in the form of Peter, a baby who grew to be as big as a twelve-year-old in one year.
Prod-PERSPF Dist-CORF 1984

Peter And The Wolf C 12 MIN
16MM FILM OPTICAL SOUND
Tells the story of Peter, a little boy who wanders into the forest after his grandfather warned him not to leave the yard. Shows how Peter meets a wolf in the forest and captures him.
From The Animatoons Series.
LC NO. FIA67-5507
Prod-ANTONS Dist-RADTV 1968

Peter And The Wolf C 14 MIN
16MM FILM, 3/4 OR 1/2 IN VIDEO P-H A
An excerpt from the feature length film 'MAKE MINE MUSIC,' which is an adaptation of Serge Prokofieff's famous composition in which the characters in the tale are represented by different musical instruments.
Prod-DISNEY Dist-WDEMCO 1964

Peter And The Wolf C 28 MIN
3/4 OR 1/2 INCH VIDEO CASSETTE
Features actress Karen Gilfoy narrating the traditional story of Peter And The Wolf. Includes Prokofiev's music performed by the Jackson Symphony Orchestra conducted by Lewis Dalvit.
Prod-MAETEL Dist-PBS

Peter And The Wolf C 28 MIN
16MM FILM, 3/4 OR 1/2 IN VIDEO
Re-creates Prokofiev's orchestral fairy tale about a boy who, ignoring his grandfather's warnings, proceeds to capture a wolf.
LC NO. 82-706296
Prod-SHIRE Dist-PFP 1981

Peter And The Wolf (Swedish) C 28 MIN
16MM FILM, 3/4 OR 1/2 IN VIDEO P-I
A Swedish language version of the film of Peter And The Wolf, Prokofiev's musical introduction to the orchestra. Features real people and real animals in a turn-of-the-century American setting. Narrated by Ray Bolger, with music performed by the Santa Cruz Chamber Orchestra.
Prod-SHIRE Dist-PFP

Peter Berton C 5 MIN
3/4 OR 1/2 INCH VIDEO CASSETTE J-H
Teaches the use of commas with dates and addresses.
From The Write On, Set 1 Series.
Prod-CTI Dist-CTI

Peter Bryant C
3/4 OR 1/2 INCH VIDEO CASSETTE
Portrays Peter Bryant, British Columbian filmmaker with interviews and film clips.
From The Filmmakers' Showcase Series.
Prod-CANFDW Dist-CANFDW

Peter Caranicas And Bobby Mariano C 30 MIN
3/4 OR 1/2 INCH VIDEO CASSETTE
Discusses narrowcasting dance for cable television.
From The Eye On Dance - Dance On Television Series.
Prod-ARTRES Dist-ARTRES

Peter D'Agostino - A Selection Of Works C 20 MIN
3/4 INCH VIDEO CASSETTE
Presents video art by Peter D'Agostino.
Prod-EAI Dist-EAI

Peter Hill Puzzle, The C 31 MIN
16MM FILM, 3/4 OR 1/2 IN VIDEO
Tells a story about an organization with serious low-cost problems that threaten its existence and the search for the reasons why. Identifies the causes of mismanagement to be lack of communication, poor leadership, isolation and strong-willed, uncontrollable subordinates.
From The Professional Management Program Series.
Prod-NEM Dist-NEM 1975

Peter Hill Puzzle, The (French) C 31 MIN
16MM FILM, 3/4 OR 1/2 IN VIDEO
Tells a story about an organization with serious low-cost problems that threaten its existence and the search for the reasons why. Identifies the causes of mismanagement to be lack of communication, poor leadership, isolation and strong-willed, uncontrollable subordinates.
From The Professional Management Program Series.
Prod-NEM Dist-NEM 1975

Peter Hill Puzzle, The (Spanish) C 31 MIN
16MM FILM, 3/4 OR 1/2 IN VIDEO
Tells a story about an organization with serious low-cost problems that threaten its existence and the search for the reasons why. Identifies the causes of mismanagement to be lack of communication, poor leadership, isolation and strong-willed, uncontrollable subordinates.
From The Professional Management Program Series.
Prod-NEM Dist-NEM 1975

Peter Keenan - Why Me B 5 MIN
3/4 OR 1/2 INCH VIDEO CASSETTE
Pokes fun at everything.
Prod-ARTINC Dist-ARTINC

Peter Lipskis C
3/4 OR 1/2 INCH VIDEO CASSETTE
Portrays Peter Lipskis, British Columbian filmmaker with interviews and film clips.
From The Filmmakers' Showcase Series.
Prod-CANFDW Dist-CANFDW

Peter Principle, The C 25 MIN
16MM FILM, 3/4 OR 1/2 IN VIDEO
Features Dr Laurence J Peter as he discusses the Peter principle and its implications for individual employees and the organizations in which they work.
Prod-BBCTV Dist-FI 1975

Peter Principle, The - Why Things Go Wrong C 31 MIN
16MM FILM, 3/4 OR 1/2 IN VIDEO H-C A
Presents Dr Laurence Peter explaining in a satire of management theory, why things always go wrong.
Prod-SALENG Dist-SALENG 1975

Peter Sichel's Complete Guide To Wine C 92 MIN
16MM FILM OPTICAL SOUND
Features Peter Sichel of the French and German wine-producing family, as he discusses domestic and imported vintages. Explains every aspect of wine-making, blending, tasting and storing.
Prod-NYFLMS Dist-NYFLMS 1973

Peter Tchaikovsky Story, The C 30 MIN
16MM FILM, 3/4 OR 1/2 IN VIDEO I-C A
Tells the story of the struggles, loves, failures and successes of Peter Tchaikovsky.
Prod-DISNEY Dist-WDEMCO 1964

Peter The Pigeon X 5 MIN
16MM FILM OPTICAL SOUND K-P
On roads without sidewalks, Otto the Auto and Peter the Pigeon, with his big sombrero, impress children about walking single file on the left side, facing oncoming vehicles.
From The Otto The Auto Series.
Prod-AAAFTS Dist-AAAFTS

Peter Ustinov's Leningrad C 25 MIN
16MM FILM, 3/4 OR 1/2 IN VIDEO H-C A
A shortened version of the motion picture Peter Ustinov's Leningrad. Presents actor Peter Ustinov on a tour of the city of Leningrad.
From The Cities Series.
Prod-NIELSE Dist-LCOA Prodn-MCGREE 1980

Peter Ustinov's Leningrad C 51 MIN
16MM FILM, 3/4 OR 1/2 IN VIDEO I-C A
Presents actor Peter Ustinov as he tours the Russian city of Leningrad.
From The Cities Series.
Prod-NIELSE Dist-LCOA Prodn-MCGREE 1978

Peter Ustinov's Leningrad (Spanish) C 25 MIN
16MM FILM, 3/4 OR 1/2 IN VIDEO H-C A
Investigates the culture and history of Leningrad, the birthplace of the Russian Revolution. Edited version.
Prod-NIELSE Dist-LCOA Prodn-MCGREE 1980

Peter Ustinov's Leningrad (Spanish) C 50 MIN
16MM FILM, 3/4 OR 1/2 IN VIDEO H-C A
Investigates the culture and history of Leningrad, the birthplace of the Russian Revolution. Full version.
Prod-NIELSE Dist-LCOA Prodn-MCGREE

Peter's Chair C 6 MIN
16MM FILM, 3/4 OR 1/2 IN VIDEO K-P T
Illustrates the skill of Ezra Jack Keats in capturing the small but important events that fill a youngster's life.
Prod-WWS Dist-WWS Prodn-SCHNDL 1971

Petersburg - Cannon Firing C 6 MIN
16MM FILM - 3/4 IN VIDEO
Demonstrates how a mounted artillery unit moved, set up and fired its artillery piece. Explains the use of horsedrawn limbers and depicts the uniforms and guns of the period. Issued in 1973 as a motion picture.
LC NO. 79-706151
Prod-USNPS Dist-USNAC 1978

Petey And Johnny C
3/4 OR 1/2 INCH VIDEO CASSETTE
Describes the experiences of a former teen gang leader who returns as a social worker.
Prod-DREWAS Dist-DIRECT

Petey The Pelican C 10 MIN
16MM FILM, 3/4 OR 1/2 IN VIDEO P
Tells how Petey grows from an ugly, featherless weakling into a beautiful white pelican.
LC NO. 80-706578
Prod-BERLET Dist-IFB 1978

Petey The Pelican (Danish) C 10 MIN
16MM FILM, 3/4 OR 1/2 IN VIDEO P
Introduces Petey the Pelican, who tells about the growth of his new feathers, his fear of gulls, his eating habits, his parents' fishing tactics and his struggle to learn how to fly.
Prod-BERLET Dist-IFB 1978

Petrified Forest, The B 83 MIN
16MM FILM OPTICAL SOUND
Presents an adaptation of Robert Sherwood's play about a group of travelers trapped by a fleeing gangster.
Prod-UAA Dist-UAE 1936

Petroleum Exploration C 31 MIN
3/4 OR 1/2 INCH VIDEO CASSETTE IND
See series title for descriptive statement.
From The Petroleum Geology Series.
Prod-GPCV Dist-GPCV

Petroleum Exploration Methods C 53 MIN
3/4 OR 1/2 INCH VIDEO CASSETTE IND
See series title for descriptive statement.
From The Basic And Petroleum Geology For Non-Geologists - Reservoirs And...-Series.
Prod-PHILLP Dist-GPCV

Petroleum Geology - Eastern United States C 49 MIN
3/4 OR 1/2 INCH VIDEO CASSETTE IND
See series title for descriptive statement.
From The Basic And Petroleum Geology For Non-Geologists - Petroleum Geology Series.
Prod-PHILLP Dist-GPCV

Petroleum Geology - Western United States C 56 MIN
3/4 OR 1/2 INCH VIDEO CASSETTE IND
See series title for descriptive statement.
From The Basic And Petroleum Geology For Non-Geologists - Petroleum Geology Series.
Prod-PHILLP Dist-GPCV

Petroleum Geology - World C 39 MIN
3/4 OR 1/2 INCH VIDEO CASSETTE IND
See series title for descriptive statement.
From The Basic And Petroleum Geology For Non-Geologists - Petroleum Geology Series.
Prod-PHILLP Dist-GPCV

Petroleum Geology - World Exploration C 27 MIN
3/4 OR 1/2 INCH VIDEO CASSETTE IND
See series title for descriptive statement.
From The Basic And Petroleum Geology For Non-Geologists - Petroleum Geology Series.
Prod-PHILLP Dist-GPCV

Petroleum Geology Case Histories C 58 MIN
3/4 OR 1/2 INCH VIDEO CASSETTE IND
See series title for descriptive statement.
From The Petroleum Geology Series.
Prod-GPCV Dist-GPCV

Petroleum Geology—A Series
IND
Explains physical and chemical properties of hydrocarbons, source rocks, reservoir, traps and the mechanisms by which oil are gas and found and exploited.
Prod-GPCV Dist-GPCV

Drilling And Completing A Well 045 MIN
Hydrocarbons 033 MIN
Petroleum Exploration 031 MIN
Petroleum Geology Case Histories 058 MIN
Reservoir Mechanics And Secondary And 027 MIN
Reservoir Rocks 037 MIN
Source Rocks, Generation, Migration, And 033 MIN
Traps 043 MIN
Well Logging 040 MIN

Petroleum Industry C 3 MIN
16MM FILM OPTICAL SOUND P-I
Discusses the petroleum industry.
From The Of All Things Series.
Prod-BAILYL Dist-AVED

Petroleum Safety Hazard Precautions At Unit And Organizational Level B 26 MIN
16MM FILM, 3/4 OR 1/2 IN VIDEO A
Illustrates safe handling practices at military field fuel supply points, explains the health hazards posed by fuel and shows how fire may occur.
Prod-USA Dist-USNAC 1984

Petroleum Stock Footage C 12 MIN
16MM FILM SILENT IND
Presents footage from PETEX movies cut together and printed as a B-wind roll. Also available as a CRI, can be used in movie or video productions without copyright infringement.
Prod-UTEXPE Dist-UTEXPE

Petroleum's Progress C 6 MIN
16MM FILM, 3/4 OR 1/2 IN VIDEO J-C
Offers a brief history of oil, oil by-products, and the petrochemical industry.
LC NO. 81-706036
Prod-NFBC Dist-TEXFLM 1980

Petronella C 12 MIN
16MM FILM, 3/4 OR 1/2 IN VIDEO P-I
Presents an animated fairytale about a princess who, because she is an only child, must perform the traditionally princely duty of rescuing a princess. Shows how she rescues a prince instead. Based on the book Petronella by Jay Williams.
Prod-FLMFR Dist-FLMFR Prodn-DOURB 1977

Petronella (Captioned Version) C 12 MIN
16MM FILM, 3/4 OR 1/2 IN VIDEO P-I
Presents an animated fairytale about a princess who, because she is an only child, must perform the traditionally princely duty of rescuing a princess. Shows how she rescues a prince instead. Based on the book Petronella by Jay Williams.
Prod-FLMFR Dist-FLMFR Prodn-DOURB 1977

Petronella (Swedish) C 12 MIN
16MM FILM, 3/4 OR 1/2 IN VIDEO P-I
Presents an animated fairytale about a princess who, because she is an only child, must perform the traditionally princely duty of rescuing a princess. Shows how she rescues a prince instead. Based on the book Petronella by Jay Williams.
Prod-FLMFR Dist-FLMFR Prodn-DOURB 1977

Petrosian Vs Fischer C 13 MIN
16MM FILM OPTICAL SOUND
Presents a chess match in which Tigran Petrosian defeats Bobby Fischer.
From The Check And Mate Series.
LC NO. 74-703435
Prod-OECA Dist-OECA 1972

Pets - A Boy And His Dog C 11 MIN
16MM FILM, 3/4 OR 1/2 IN VIDEO K-I
Shows the companionship and affection between a boy in the inner city and his pet. No narration.
Prod-GABOR Dist-PHENIX 1969

Pets - A First Film C 14 MIN
16MM FILM, 3/4 OR 1/2 IN VIDEO K-I
Presents the story of a little boy who searches for the owner of a beautiful dog and in the process learns about animal shelters, veterinarians, pet stores and the responsibilities that accompany the fun of having a pet.
Prod-BEAN Dist-PHENIX 1979

Pets - A Girl And Her Lamb C 11 MIN
16MM FILM, 3/4 OR 1/2 IN VIDEO P-I
Presents the story of Linda, who learns that even though she loves her pet lamb and tries to take good care of him, he is just not the right kind of pet for her home setting.
Prod-GABOR Dist-PHENIX 1969

Pets - Responsibility For Care C 20 MIN
2 INCH VIDEOTAPE I
See series title for descriptive statement.
From The Exploring With Science, Unit XI - Vertebrates series.
Prod-MPATI Dist-GPITVL

Pets And People C 14 MIN
16MM FILM OPTICAL SOUND
Presents a primer for pet owners, including choosing the right pet for the owner's lifestyle and rules for the proper care and feeding of a dog or cat. Hosted by Ed Asner.
Prod-PURINA Dist-MTP 1982

Petunia C 10 MIN
16MM FILM, 3/4 OR 1/2 IN VIDEO K-P
Features Petunia, the silly goose, who goes about giving advice to all the farm animals with a book under her wing which she can't read. Concludes with naive Petunia learning a bit of philosophy and the definition of wisdom.
Prod-AVANZ Dist-WWS 1971

Petunia C 15 MIN
3/4 INCH VIDEO CASSETTE P
Presents the children's story Petunia by Roger Duvoisin.
From The Tilson's Book Shop Series.
Prod-WVIZTV Dist-GPITVL 1975

Peutz-Jeghers Syndrome C 30 MIN
16MM FILM OPTICAL SOUND PRO
Presents two interesting patients with Peutz-Jeghers syndrome and illustrates the essential diagnostic components, complications and surgical treatment of this disease.
Prod-ACYDGD Dist-ACY 1964

Pewter C 15 MIN
2 INCH VIDEOTAPE
See series title for descriptive statement.
From The Making Things Work Series.
Prod-WGBHTV Dist-PUBTEL

Peyronie's Disease C 11 MIN
3/4 OR 1/2 INCH VIDEO CASSETTE PRO
Describes a surgical technique to correct the effects of Peyronie's disease.
Prod-WFP Dist-WFP

PFR C 27 MIN
16MM FILM OPTICAL SOUND IND
Records the construction of the Prototype Fast Reactor.
Prod-UKAEA Dist-UKAEA 1975

PH C 21 MIN
3/4 OR 1/2 INCH VIDEO CASSETTE PRO
Discusses normal maintenance of acid-base balance and the body's buffering systems. Explains the chemistry of hydrogen in movements.
From The Fluids And Electrolytes Series.
Prod-BRA Dist-BRA

PH Meter C 11 MIN
3/4 OR 1/2 INCH VIDEO CASSETTE C A
Uses a Fisher Scientific Company model 230 pH/ion meter and a combination electrode to titrate an acid sample with standard base.
From The Chemistry - Master/Apprentice Series. Program 5
Prod-CUETV Dist-CUNIV 1981

Phacoemulsification C 11 MIN
16MM FILM, 3/4 OR 1/2 IN VIDEO A
Describes cataract formation, anatomy of the eye and the Phacoemulsification procedure. Details possible complications and benefits of this technique.
Prod-PRORE Dist-PRORE

Phaethon C 7 MIN
16MM FILM OPTICAL SOUND
Presents an experimental film directed to sensory stimulation. Features expanding and contracting superimposed concentric circles, kaleidoscopic images of geometrically patterned female torsos and exploding colors accompanied by electronic music.
LC NO. 73-700689
Prod-FRERCK Dist-CFS 1972

Phagocytes - The Body's Defenders C 10 MIN
16MM FILM, 3/4 OR 1/2 IN VIDEO I-C A
Presents microphotographs of the circulatory system and the processes of mitosis and phagocytosis. Shows in detail how the body is protected from disease by white blood corpuscles, or phagocytes.
Prod-SF Dist-SF 1965

Phagocytosis B 4 MIN
16MM FILM, 3/4 OR 1/2 IN VIDEO H-C A
Uses phase contrast photography at three times actual speed to show the process of phagocytosis of dead and living streptococci. Points out the nuclear lobes, vacuoles and neutrophilic granules in the leucocyte. Pictures cytoplasmic streaming, positive chemotaxis and ingestion of streptococci.
From The Microbiology Teaching Series.
Prod-UCEMC Dist-UCEMC 1960

Phalarope Feeding Behavior C 10 MIN
16MM FILM, 3/4 OR 1/2 IN VIDEO
Illustrates the feeding behavior and morphological specializations of Wilson's and red necked phalaropes.
From The Aspects Of Animal Behavior Series.
Prod-UCEMC Dist-UCEMC

Phalaropes C 3 MIN
16MM FILM OPTICAL SOUND P-I
Discusses the birds known as phalaropes.
From The Of All Things Series.
Prod-BAILYL Dist-AVED

Phans Of Jersey City, The C 49 MIN
16MM FILM, 3/4 OR 1/2 IN VIDEO H-C A
Focuses on a 20-member refugee family from Vietnam, describing their efforts to cope with American society.
LC NO. 81-707222
Prod-HSP Dist-FI 1979

Phantasmagoria B 8 MIN
16MM FILM OPTICAL SOUND C
Illustrates an abstract expression of conflict, using ball bearings in weird, surrealistic settings. Evokes subjective responses.
Prod-OPLIN Dist-CFS

Phantastron B 26 MIN
16MM FILM OPTICAL SOUND
Identifies phantastron circuit and states the purpose of each component. Constructs a time amplitude graph during explanation of circuit operation. (Kinescope)
LC NO. 74-705352
Prod-USAF Dist-USNAC

Phantasy X 5 MIN
16MM FILM OPTICAL SOUND I-C A
Depicts the feeling of loneliness by using various objects and media found in a cellar in order to express a young girl's longing.
LC NO. 74-701547
Prod-CELLAR Dist-CELLAR 1970

Phantasy, A C 8 MIN
16MM FILM, 3/4 OR 1/2 IN VIDEO H-C
A surrealist abstract art film with pastel drawings and 'CUT-OUT' animation by Norman Mc Laren, saxophone music and synthetic sound by Maurice Blackburn.
Prod-NFBC Dist-IFB Prodn-MCLN 1952

Phantom India, Pt 1 - The Impossible Camera C 52 MIN
16MM FILM OPTICAL SOUND
Captures the daily life of the section of India south of Calcutta. Shows women handshaping bricks for the construction of a large tourist hotel.
Prod-NYFLMS Dist-NYFLMS 1967

Phantom India, Pt 2 - Things Seen In Madras C 52 MIN
16MM FILM OPTICAL SOUND
Presents a religious festival, movie studios, man-drawn carts, a dancing school where girls learn the sacred dances of India and other aspects of the Madras area's culture.
Prod-NYFLMS Dist-NYFLMS 1967

Phantom India, Pt 3 - The Indians And The Sacred C 52 MIN
16MM FILM OPTICAL SOUND
Explores the religions of India, including aspects of esoterism, the Hindu philosophy of wordly negation and the transcendence of reality in quest of immortality.
Prod-NYFLMS Dist-NYFLMS 1967

Phantom India, Pt 4 - Dream And Reality C 52 MIN
16MM FILM OPTICAL SOUND
Looks at the palm-fringed beaches, tea plantations, game preserves, primitive fishermen and beautiful women of Kerala. Explains that Kerala is the only Indian state where a local government has a Communist majority as well as the largest Christian minority.
Prod-NYFLMS Dist-NYFLMS 1967

Phantom India, Pt 5 - A Look At The Castes C 52 MIN
16MM FILM OPTICAL SOUND
Focuses on the castes in a village in Rajastan and shows how the social heirarchy established from birth acts as a rigid force in maintaining traditional Indian society.
Prod-NYFLMS Dist-NYFLMS 1967

Phantom India, Pt 6 - On The Fringes Of Indian Society C 52 MIN
16MM FILM OPTICAL SOUND
Views groups living in India for centuries, yet who are either excluded from Indian society or who refuse to become a part of it. Includes glimpses at the Bonda, an aboriginal tribe, the Ashran in Pondicherry, the Jews in Cochin, the Catholics and the Pharsees in Bombay.
Prod-NYFLMS Dist-NYFLMS 1967

Phantom India, Pt 7 - Bombay - The Future India C 52 MIN
16MM FILM OPTICAL SOUND
Presents Bombay as a city of five million with the same slums as Calcutta, but enjoying an economic boom. Explains that Bombay is a city where the values of Hindu civilization are likely to disappear first.
Prod-NYFLMS Dist-NYFLMS 1967

Phantom Of Liberty (French) C 104 MIN
16MM FILM OPTICAL SOUND
Presents a comedy that contemplates man's survival in spite of his idiocies. Comprised of dozens of stories that lead from one to another with a dreamlike logic. Includes English subtitles.
Prod-TLECUL Dist-TLECUL

Phantom Of The Opera B 61 MIN
16MM FILM, 3/4 OR 1/2 IN VIDEO
Presents a melodrama about a phantom who lives in the catacombs below the Paris opera house and tutors a young singer. Shows that, driven by hatred, the phantom kills a workman and is pursued to his lair.
Prod-UPCI Dist-SF 1925

Phantom Of The Opera, The B 57 MIN
16MM FILM SILENT
Presents the melodramatic horror tale of the embittered, disfig-

ured composer who haunts the sewers beneath the Paris Opera House and takes a pretty young singer as his protege. Stars Lon Chaney, Mary Philbin and Norman Kerry.
Prod-BHAWK Dist-BHAWK 1925

Phantom Of The Opera, The B 79 MIN
16MM FILM OPTICAL SOUND
Stars Lon Chaney as a scarred genius methodically plotting revenge in the Paris Opera House.
Prod-UNKNWN Dist-KILLIS 1925

Phantom Of The Rue Morgue, The C 84 MIN
16MM FILM OPTICAL SOUND
Based on Edgar Allan Poe's 'MURDERS IN THE RUE MORGUE.' Recreates the story of young girls being murdered in the 19th century streets of Paris.
Prod-WB Dist-TWYMAN 1954

Phantoms Of The Mind C 26 MIN
3/4 OR 1/2 INCH VIDEO CASSETTE
Reveals how such everyday pursuits as flying, driving, swimming, eating or even walking are unattainable for thousands of people whose lifestyles are crippled by phobias. Gives case histories from the world's first phobic clinic.
From The Breakthroughs Series.
Prod-NOMDFI Dist-LANDMK

Pharaoh's Daughter, The C 5 MIN
3/4 OR 1/2 INCH VIDEO CASSETTE J-H
Demonstrates how to make an outline.
From The Write On, Set 2 Series.
Prod-CTI Dist-CTI

Phares O'Daffer C
3/4 OR 1/2 INCH VIDEO CASSETTE
Discusses the importance of providing children with extensive experience in inductive discovery of geometric relationships that occur naturally.
From The Third R - Teaching Basic Mathematics Skills Series.
Prod-EDCPUB Dist-EDCPUB

Pharmaceutical Research For Health B 22 MIN
16MM FILM OPTICAL SOUND PRO
Describes the complicated processes and procedures of modern pharmaceutical research and development. Uses charts, film clips, slides and live animal demonstrations to follow the progress of a drug–a new psychotropic compound–from its birth in a chemical laboratory to its final preparation for human use. (Kinescope.)
LC NO. 74-703664
Prod-WYETH Dist-WYLAB 1960

Pharmacist And Cancer, The C 22 MIN
16MM FILM OPTICAL SOUND PRO
Shows the pharmacist's role in cancer control as a link between the public and physicians. Relates symptoms to actual cancers, which are shown, and demonstrates modern medical diagnostic and therapeutic procedures.
LC NO. 75-706083
Prod-AMCS Dist-AMCS Prodn-CFDC 1969

Pharmacological Testing Of New Antibiotic Agents C 2 MIN
16MM FILM, 3/4 OR 1/2 IN VIDEO C
Demonstrates the therapeutic effect of streptomycin as observed in the treatment of guinea pigs which were infected with tubercle bacilli. Demonstrates the toxicity of an antibiotic agent by showing the differing reactions of cats.
From The Microbiology Teaching Series.
Prod-UCEMC Dist-UCEMC 1961

Pharmacology C 26 MIN
3/4 OR 1/2 INCH VIDEO CASSETTE
Contains 26 half-hour videotape on aspects of pharmacology.
Prod-TELSTR Dist-TELSTR

Pharmacology - Administration Of Drugs C 12 MIN
1/2 IN VIDEO CASSETTE BETA/VHS
Discusses pharmacology and how drugs are administered.
Prod-RMI Dist-RMI

Pharmacology - Drug Legislation And Standardization C 15 MIN
1/2 IN VIDEO CASSETTE BETA/VHS
Prod-RMI Dist-RMI

Pharmacology - General Principles B 30 MIN
16MM FILM OPTICAL SOUND C
See series title for descriptive statement.
From The Pharmacology Series.
LC NO. 73-703330
Prod-MVNE Dist-TELSTR 1971

Pharmacology - Parenteral Administration C 15 MIN
1/2 IN VIDEO CASSETTE BETA/VHS
Describes the administration of drugs by injection.
Prod-RMI Dist-RMI

Pharmacology - Prescription C 5 MIN
1/2 IN VIDEO CASSETTE BETA/VHS
Explains the abbreviations used and how to make out and phone in prescriptions.
Prod-RMI Dist-RMI

Pharmacology And Clinical Use Of Local Anesthetics (2nd Ed) C 26 MIN
3/4 OR 1/2 INCH VIDEO CASSETTE PRO
Describes the physiology and pharmacology of nerve conduction. Classifies the anatomy of individual neurons, and identifies the relationship between nerve fiber size and local anesthetics. Discusses the chemical structure of both the ester and amide local anesthetics. Covers complications associated with local anesthesia and their treatment.
From The Anesthesiology Clerkship Series.
Prod-UMICHM Dist-UMICHM 1982

Pharmacology Of Antiarrhythmic Drugs, Pt 1 - Electrophysiology And Quinidine C 22 MIN
3/4 OR 1/2 INCH VIDEO CASSETTE PRO
Develops an understanding of quinidine's pharmacological and electrophysiological effects upon the cardiovascular system.
Prod-UMICHM Dist-UMICHM 1975

Pharmacology Of Antiarrhythmic Drugs, Pt 2 - Procainamide, Lidocaine And DPH C 30 MIN
3/4 OR 1/2 INCH VIDEO CASSETTE PRO
Discusses procainamides, lidocaine and diphenylhydantoin in terms of drug action, clinical use, administration, contraindications and the possibility of adverse effects. Compares the agents in this program with guinidine in both structure and action.
Prod-UMICHM Dist-UMICHM 1975

Pharmacology Of Antiarrhythmic Drugs, Pt 3 - Propranolol And Bretylium C 25 MIN
3/4 OR 1/2 INCH VIDEO CASSETTE PRO
Concentrates on the clinical pharmacology of propranolol and hretylium in their antiarrhythmic applications and contraindications.
Prod-UMICHM Dist-UMICHM 1976

Pharmacology Of Drug Abuse, The C 48 MIN
16MM FILM OPTICAL SOUND PRO
Presents Dr Sidney Cohen, associate professor of psychiatry at the University of Southern California in Los Angeles, who discusses the pharmacology of various drugs of abuse. Includes definitions and explanations of how drug abuse affects the body, the psychopharmacology of the treatment of drug abuse and other related issues. Covers the nervous system in relation to drug abuse.
From The Films And Tapes For Drug Abuse Treatment Personnel Series.
LC NO. 73-703450
Prod-NIMH Dist-NIMH 1973

Pharmacology Of Neuromuscular Transmissions In Normal And Diseased States C 52 MIN
3/4 INCH VIDEO CASSETTE PRO
Presents Dr David Grob lecturing on the pharmacology of neuromuscular transmissions in normal and diseased states.
From The Intensive Course In Neuromuscular Diseases Series.
LC NO. 76-706074
Prod-NINDIS Dist-USNAC 1974

Pharmacology Of Oncologic Agents, Pt 1 C 24 MIN
3/4 OR 1/2 INCH VIDEO CASSETTE PRO
Details the general therapeutic principles which must be understood when administering oncologic agents, the chemotherapy program using cyclophosphamide, methotrexate, 5-fluorouracil and Adriamycin, the acute and chronic toxicities of these agents and the way to minimize the occurrance of excessive toxicity of these agents by appropriate dose modification.
Prod-UMICHM Dist-UMICHM 1977

Pharmacology Of Oncologic Agents, Pt 2 C 21 MIN
3/4 OR 1/2 INCH VIDEO CASSETTE PRO
Details the general therapeutic principles which must be understood when administering oncologic agents, the chemotherapy programs using bleomycin, vincristine, vinblastine, CCNU, BCNU and dacarbazine, the acute and chronic toxicities of these agents and the way to minimize the occurrence of excessive toxicity by appropriate dose modifications.
Prod-UMICHM Dist-UMICHM 1978

Pharmacology Of Oncologic Agents, Pt 3 C 14 MIN
3/4 OR 1/2 INCH VIDEO CASSETTE PRO
Discusses types of bone marrow toxicity due to various chemotherapeutic agents, the appropriate management of bone marrow toxicity in the neutropenic cancer patient, and newer approaches to the management of the bone marrow toxicity such as platelet and granulocyte transfusion therapy.
Prod-UMICHM Dist-UMICHM 1980

Pharmacology–A Series
C
Identifies major classifications of drugs and discusses the chemical and physiological principles governing their use.
Prod-MVNE Dist-TELSTR 1971

Adrenocorticorsteroids	30 MIN
Anticoagulants And Hematinics	30 MIN
Antitubercular Drugs And Broad Spectrum	30 MIN
Cardiac Depressants And Vasodilators	30 MIN
Cardiac Stimulants	30 MIN
Diuretics	30 MIN
General Anesthetics	30 MIN
Hematinics	30 MIN
Histamine, Antihistamine And Drugs Used For	30 MIN
Insulin And Oral Hypoglycemics	30 MIN
Local Anesthetics	30 MIN
Narcotic And Non-Narcotic Analgesics	30 MIN
Parasympathomimetic Blocking Agents,	30 MIN
Parasympathomimetics	30 MIN
Parkinsonism And Convulsive Disorders	30 MIN
Pharmacology - General Principles	30 MIN
Pituitary Hormones	30 MIN
Psychopharmacological Drugs, Pt 1	30 MIN
Psychopharmacological Drugs, Pt 2	30 MIN
Sedatives, Hypnotics And Alcohol	30 MIN
Sex Hormones, Oxytocics	30 MIN
Skeletal Muscle Relaxants, Their Antagonists	30 MIN
Sulfonamides And Penicillins	30 MIN
Sympathomimetic Blocking Agents, Ganglionic	30 MIN
Sympathomimetics	30 MIN
Thyroid And Antithyroid Drugs	30 MIN

Pharmacy Communication Skills–A Series
PRO
Features three videocassette programs that address the pharmacist-patient relationship.
Prod-HSCIC Dist-HSCIC 1982

Barriers To Communication	016 MIN
Factors Affecting Pharmacist-Patient	062 MIN
Interviewing Techniques And Communication	021 MIN

Pharynx And Nasal Cavities - Unit 5 C 16 MIN
3/4 OR 1/2 INCH VIDEO CASSETTE PRO
Describes the pharynx as it relates to the superior and middle constrictors, as well as its internal aspects, shows parts of the nasal cavity, including the nasal septum, the lateral wall, and structures related to meatuses and conchae.
From The Gross Anatomy Prosection Demonstration Series.
Prod-HSCIC Dist-HSCIC

Pharynx Topographical Anatomy, The C 9 MIN
16MM FILM - 3/4 IN VIDEO
Shows the topography of the pharynx as viewed through the posterior neck. Illustrates the extent and volume that edema may assume in these areas.
From The Anatomy Of The Head And Neck Series.
LC NO. 78-706251
Prod-USVA Dist-USNAC Prodn-VADTC 1978

Pharynxtopographical Anatomy, The C 9 MIN
3/4 INCH VIDEO CASSETTE PRO
Shows the topography of the pharynx as viewed through the posterior neck. Illustrates the extent and volume that edema may assume in these areas.
From The Anatomy Of The Head And Neck Series.
LC NO. 78-706251
Prod-USVA Dist-USNAC Prodn-VADTC 1978

Phascolarctos Cinereus - The Koala C 18 MIN
16MM FILM, 3/4 OR 1/2 IN VIDEO H-C
Looks at the history, habitat, physical characteristics, and habits of the koala.
Prod-FLMFR Dist-FLMFR

Phase Diagrams C 30 MIN
3/4 OR 1/2 INCH VIDEO CASSETTE PRO
Presents the uses of the binary phase diagram.
From The Elements Of Physical Metallurgy Series.
Prod-AMCEE Dist-AMCEE

Phase Equilibria–A Series
C
Prod-NSF Dist-PSU Prodn-MSRL

Free Energy Curves And Binary Phase Diagrams	
Gibbs Free Energy - Enthalpy And Entropy	11 MIN
Isothermal Sections With Simple Ternary	8 MIN
Isothermal Sections With Solid Solution	8 MIN
Reading Ternary Phase Diagrams	8 MIN
Ternary Diagrams Derived From Binaries	6 MIN

Phase One - Prince Charles Mountains C 22 MIN
16MM FILM OPTICAL SOUND H-C A
Shows a party of men from the Australian National Antarctic Research Expedition conducting a topographical and geological survey of the Prince Charles Mountains in Antarctica. Includes the scientists evaluation of the material collected and the construction of maps of the surveyed area.
LC NO. 73-709256
Prod-ANAIB Dist-AUIS 1969

Phase Shift Oscillator - VT B 34 MIN
16MM FILM OPTICAL SOUND
Describes the principle characteristics of the phase shift oscillator, with emphasis on its frequency range, stability and economy. Explains the effect of varying feedback as well as the frequency characteristics of the phase shift oscillator. (Kinescope)
LC NO. 74-705354
Prod-USAF Dist-USNAC 1963

Phase-Plane Method, The B 37 MIN
3/4 OR 1/2 INCH VIDEO CASSETTE
Illustrates the phase-plane method for simple linear systems.
From The Nonlinear Vibrations Series.
Prod-MIOT Dist-MIOT

Phasemicroscopy Of Normal Living Blood C 28 MIN
16MM FILM, 3/4 OR 1/2 IN VIDEO
Compares the various circulating blood cells as they appear in a Wright's stained preparation and in the living state when examined with dark medium contrast phase objectives.
Prod-UWASHP Dist-UWASHP

Phasor Algebra C
3/4 OR 1/2 INCH VIDEO CASSETTE
See series title for descriptive statement.
From The Basic Electricity - AC Series.
Prod-VTRI Dist-VTRI

Phenelzine Sulfate C 15 MIN
16MM FILM OPTICAL SOUND
Deals with the issue of taking drugs to cure psychological ills. Tells how a woman who relies on phenelzine sulfate to relieve depression, stops taking the drug and ends up in the hospital faced with the choice of resuming drug usage or facing reality.
Prod-TWOCH Dist-TWOCH 1979

Phenix City Story, The B 100 MIN
16MM FILM OPTICAL SOUND H-C A
Dramatizes the history of a small Alabama town.
Prod-CINEWO Dist-CINEWO 1955

Phenomena 1 C 30 MIN
3/4 INCH VIDEO CASSETTE
Looks at a unique trigger film used by teachers of English to encourage writing skills.

From The Phenomena Series.
Prod-UMITV Dist-UMITV 1981

Phenomena 10 C 29 MIN
3/4 INCH VIDEO CASSETTE
Reports on toxic pollutants in the Great Lakes, basket weaving, bone playing and horticulture therapy for the aged.
From The Phenomena Series.
Prod-UMITV Dist-UMITV 1981

Phenomena 11 C 29 MIN
3/4 INCH VIDEO CASSETTE
Covers a variety of topics including a new library addition, a glass blower who makes scientific instruments for libraries, and a visiting pet program for geriatric patients.
From The Phenomena Series.
Prod-UMITV Dist-UMITV 1981

Phenomena 2 C 30 MIN
3/4 INCH VIDEO CASSETTE
Features Ken Yoshida using songs and games to teach English to foreign-born three- to five-year-old children. Includes discussions on mushrooms and the construction of the hologram.
From The Phenomena Series.
Prod-UMITV Dist-UMITV 1981

Phenomena 3 C 29 MIN
3/4 INCH VIDEO CASSETTE
Reports on a university 'fitness lab' which helps people determine their own levels of fitness. Looks at the spherocentric artificial knee. Discusses the sinking of the Edmund Fitzgerald.
From The Phenomena Series.
Prod-UMITV Dist-UMITV 1981

Phenomena 4 C 29 MIN
3/4 INCH VIDEO CASSETTE
Examines a hospital school and a school for firefighters. Looks at the cobalt camera.
From The Phenomena Series.
Prod-UMITV Dist-UMITV 1981

Phenomena 5 C 29 MIN
3/4 INCH VIDEO CASSETTE
Includes segments on the car shredder, Pointe Mouillee, Michigan, and sickle cell anemia.
From The Phenomena Series.
Prod-UMITV Dist-UMITV 1981

Phenomena 6 C 29 MIN
3/4 INCH VIDEO CASSETTE
Reports on student industrial design projects, the study of one of the martial arts, and a child care center where children play games that have been highly structured to provide useful learning experiences.
From The Phenomena Series.
Prod-UMITV Dist-UMITV 1981

Phenomena 7 C 29 MIN
3/4 INCH VIDEO CASSETTE
Includes segments on the restoration of harpsicords, a camp for children with hemophilia, laboratory animal care and competitive rowing.
From The Phenomena Series.
Prod-UMITV Dist-UMITV 1981

Phenomena 8 C 29 MIN
3/4 INCH VIDEO CASSETTE
Looks at The world of miniatures, hot air ballooning, a radio telescope, the value of exercise in slowing the aging process and a computer operated 'reading machine.'
From The Phenomena Series.
Prod-UMITV Dist-UMITV 1981

Phenomena 9 C 29 MIN
3/4 INCH VIDEO CASSETTE
Contains segments on a variety of sports and games which teach many topics.
From The Phenomena Series.
Prod-UMITV Dist-UMITV 1981

Phenomenal World—A Series
J-H
Explores the world of science, with special emphasis on science as related to ecology. Emphasizes such areas as earth science, life science and ecological science. Teacher's guide provided.
Prod-EBEC Dist-EBEC 1983

Circle Of Life, The 021 MIN
Flowers Are Forever 021 MIN
Furnace In The Sky 021 MIN
Of All The Nerves 022 MIN
People Places, The 022 MIN
River Of Life, The 022 MIN
Sea Beneath The Earth 022 MIN
Seasons Of Survival 021 MIN
This Trembling Earth 022 MIN
When The Earth Explodes 022 MIN
Winds Of Change, The 022 MIN

Phenomenological Analysis Of Catatonic Expression, A B 35 MIN
16MM FILM OPTICAL SOUND
Demonstrates the strange and rigid postures, and the fixed stance and stare of the catatonic patient. Shows the discrete shifts in this rigidity and demonstrates the effects of barbiturates on catatonic stupor.
Prod-USVA Dist-USVA 1960

Phenomenon No. One C 7 MIN
16MM FILM OPTICAL SOUND
Illustrates an opticular experiment in animation, making use of graphics that, when moved, produce optical illusions of color and form from black and white material.
Prod-VANBKS Dist-VANBKS 1965

Phenomenon Of Thermoelastic Instability C 14 MIN
16MM FILM OPTICAL SOUND C
Reports on oscillation frequency by thermal radiation and thermoelastic instability of boons.
Prod-NASA Dist-NASA

Phenomenon Of World, The C 120 MIN
3/4 OR 1/2 INCH VIDEO CASSETTE A
See series title for descriptive statement.
From The Beyond Philosophy - The Thought Of Martin Heidegger Series. Program 3
Prod-UCEMC Dist-UCEMC

Phenylketonuria, A Preventable Cause Of Mental Retardation C 16 MIN
16MM FILM OPTICAL SOUND
Illustrates the manifestation of phenylketonuria. Discusses its detection and treatment.
Prod-CRAF Dist-CFI 1962

Pheochromocytoma C 18 MIN
16MM FILM OPTICAL SOUND PRO
Illustrates the management of a patient with pheochromocytoma. Shows diagnostic measures, preoperative preparation and methods to control fluctuation in the blood pressure.
Prod-ACYDGD Dist-ACY 1955

Pheochromocytoma - Diagnosis, Localization, Preoperative Preparation And Anterior... C 18 MIN
16MM FILM OPTICAL SOUND PRO
Discusses diagnosis, tumor location and preoperative preparation of a patient with pheochromocytoma and shows surgery performed for transabdominal excision of the tumor.
LC NO. 75-702238
Prod-EATONL Dist-EATONL 1974

Pheresis - Using The Haemonetics Model 30 C 13 MIN
3/4 OR 1/2 INCH VIDEO CASSETTE
Demonstrates setup, priming and operation of Haemonetics Model 30 blood processor for plateletpheresis and leukapheresis.
Prod-AMRC Dist-AMRC 1977

Phil Black, Robin Black, Wade Goss And Alvin McDuffie C 30 MIN
3/4 OR 1/2 INCH VIDEO CASSETTE
Shows how the dancer prepares for Broadway.
From The Eye On Dance - Broadway Dance Series.
Prod-ARTRES Dist-ARTRES

Phil Borsos C
3/4 OR 1/2 INCH VIDEO CASSETTE
Portrays Phil Borsos, British Columbian filmmaker with interviews and film clips.
From The Filmmakers' Showcase Series.
Prod-CANFDW Dist-CANFDW

Phil Saunders On Trade-Offs C 25 MIN
3/4 OR 1/2 INCH VIDEO CASSETTE T
Presents Phil Saunders, chief consultant for the economic education series entitled Trade-Offs, discussing the background of the series, the rationale of the program clusters and the nature of economics as a field of study.
From The Trade-Offs Series.
LC NO. 80-706419
Prod-AITV Dist-AITECH 1978

Phil's Friends C 15 MIN
3/4 OR 1/2 INCH VIDEO CASSETTE J-C A
Presents young television stars who discuss the value of friendship.
From The Chemical People Educational Modules Series.
Prod-MTI Dist-MTI

Philadelphia Woodwind Quintet, The B 30 MIN
16MM FILM, 3/4 OR 1/2 IN VIDEO J-C A
Discusses the evolution of woodwind music from exclusive use outdoors to performances for the concert hall and illustrates this with examples of compositions from various periods played by the Philadelphia Woodwind Quintet.
Prod-NET Dist-IU 1965

Philadelphia 76 C 25 MIN
16MM FILM OPTICAL SOUND A
Presents highlights of the 26th annual meeting of the Mental Health Association, held in cooperation with the National Institute of Mental Health in Philadelphia, Pennsylvania.
LC NO. 77-700695
Prod-NIMH Dist-USNAC Prodn-USTSB 1977

Philip Morris In 1976 C 14 MIN
16MM FILM OPTICAL SOUND H-C A
Shows the world's largest and most modern cigarette manufacturing complex, the Philip Morris plant in Richmond, Va. Shows Philip Morris activities in beer brewing, housing and paper manufacture.
LC NO. 76-703153
Prod-PHILMO Dist-LYNCHV Prodn-LYNCHV 1976

Philip Morris Way, The C 16 MIN
16MM FILM OPTICAL SOUND
Surveys the history of tobacco. Shows the manufacturing process of cigarettes from leaf to finished product. Includes a tour of the Philip Morris Operations Center in Richmond, Virginia.
LC NO. 75-703024
Prod-PHILMO Dist-PHILMO Prodn-MPO 1975

Philippians - Rejoice In The Lord C 22 MIN
16MM FILM OPTICAL SOUND
Presents Harold Songer, professor of New Testament interpretation at Southern Baptist Theological. Seminary, Louisville, Kentucky, outlining the book of Philippians.
Prod-BROADM Dist-BROADM 1981

Philippines C 28 MIN
3/4 INCH VIDEOTAPE
Presents an interview with Amabassador Alejandro Yango of the Philippines. Includes a film clip on the Philippines and the Manila Conference Center. Hosted by Marilyn Perry.
From The Marilyn's Manhatten Series.
Prod-PERRYM Dist-PERRYM

Philippines C 29 MIN
2 INCH VIDEOTAPE
Features home economist Joan Hood presenting a culinary tour of specialty dishes from around the world. Shows the preparation of Philippine dishes ranging from peasant cookery to continental cuisine.
From The International Cookbook Series.
Prod-WMVSTV Dist-PUBTEL

Philippines - Blackboard Newspaper C 15 MIN
3/4 OR 1/2 INCH VIDEO CASSETTE H-C A
Studies the people, their lives and their culture on a remote island in the Philippines where there is no TV and few radios. Tells how they keep informed by using a blackboard newspaper.
Prod-JOU Dist-JOU

Philippines - Economic Progress B 14 MIN
16MM FILM OPTICAL SOUND
Shows the aid given to the Philippine Islands' government by the United Nations Technical Assistance Program. Includes progress in the paper pulp industry and Philippine Air Lines.
Prod-UN Dist-UN 1953

Philippines, The - Martial Law Ends C 27 MIN
3/4 OR 1/2 INCH VIDEO CASSETTE H-C A
Examines the effects of martial law on the Philippines. Discusses Philippine culture, politics and economy.
Prod-UPI Dist-JOU

Philippines, The - Ricardo The Jeepney Driver C 22 MIN
16MM FILM, 3/4 OR 1/2 IN VIDEO J-C A
Follows the activities of Ricardo and his family during their day-to-day lives in the Philippines. Describes a jeepney, developed from the battle-scarred jeeps of World War II, and now the main form of transportation in the Philippines.
Prod-HANDEL Dist-HANDEL 1984

Phillip And The White Colt C 23 MIN
16MM FILM, 3/4 OR 1/2 IN VIDEO I-J A
Focuses on a young boy's love for a white colt and the effect of that love on the boy himself. Explains that ten-year-old Phillip developed a stammer and then stopped talking entirely at the age of five, but that when Phillip's colt is stuck in the mud he speaks again.
Prod-LCOA Dist-LCOA 1973

Phillip And The White Colt (Captioned) C 23 MIN
16MM FILM, 3/4 OR 1/2 IN VIDEO P-H
Starts with a lonely, mute boy, age 5 who falls in love with a wild colt. Restores his power of speech through working with the colt.
Prod-LCOA Dist-LCOA 1973

Phillip And The White Colt (Spanish) C 23 MIN
16MM FILM, 3/4 OR 1/2 IN VIDEO P-H
Starts with a lonely boy, mute since age five, who falls in love with a wild colt. His power of speech is restored through working with the colt.
Prod-LCOA Dist-LCOA 1973

Philobolus And Joan C 58 MIN
3/4 OR 1/2 INCH VIDEO CASSETTE
Relates the love story about a cockroach which becomes a man who falls in love with a woman named Joan.
Prod-EAI Dist-EAI

Philosophies Of Representation C 30 MIN
3/4 OR 1/2 INCH VIDEO CASSETTE C
Answers questions about congressional and senatorial representation.
From The American Government 2 Series.
Prod-DALCCD Dist-DALCCD

Philosophy - Eastern/Western Consciousness C 60 MIN
3/4 OR 1/2 INCH VIDEO CASSETTE H-C A
Compares and contrasts Eastern and Western consciousness.
From The Art Of Being Human Series.
Prod-FI Dist-FI 1978

Philosophy - The Question Of Man C 18 MIN
16MM FILM, 3/4 OR 1/2 IN VIDEO H-C
Presents an introduction to the study of philosophy.
From The Humanities Series.
Prod-MGHT Dist-MGHT Prodn-CLAIB 1971

Philosophy And Concepts Of Newborn Assessment With t Berry, MD B 50 MIN
3/4 INCH VIDEOTAPE
Shows Dr T Berry Brazelton conducting a detailed examination of a neonate. Explains each step in using the scale and the scoring and its meaning. Provides an introduction to the scale and its uses.
From The Brazelton Neonatal Behavioral Assessment Scale Films Series.
Prod-EDC Dist-EDC

Philosophy And Faith C 60 MIN
3/4 OR 1/2 INCH VIDEO CASSETTE H-C A
Discusses the connection between philosophy and faith.
From The Art Of Being Human Series.
Prod-FI Dist-FI 1978

Philosophy And Moral Values C 60 MIN
3/4 OR 1/2 INCH VIDEO CASSETTE H-C A
Discusses the connection between philosophy and moral values.
From The Art Of Being Human Series.
Prod-FI Dist-FI 1978

Philosophy Of Communications And The Arts, The B 120 MIN
16MM FILM OPTICAL SOUND
Presents Professor Richard Mc Keon of the University of Chicago in 'PHILOSOPHY OF COMMUNICATIONS AND THE ARTS' with response by Dr Kenneth Burke, visiting professor at Harvard University.
From The Philosophy Year Addresses And Responses Series.
Prod-SUNY Dist-SUNY 1968

Philosophy Of Community C 15 MIN
3/4 OR 1/2 INCH VIDEO CASSETTE
Explains differences between philosopher's and prophet's view of the world. Shows how Maimonides fused both concepts to define an introspective community.
From The Tradition And Contemporary Judaism - Maimonides - Torah And Philosophic... Series.
Prod-ADL Dist-ADL

Philosophy Of Ethics, The B 120 MIN
16MM FILM OPTICAL SOUND
Presents the address by visiting professor Milton Munitz, State University College at Brockport, with the response by Anthony Quinton, University lecturer, Oxford University.
From The Philosophy Year Addresses And Responses Series.
Prod-SUNY Dist-SUNY

Philosophy Of Human Rights, The B 120 MIN
16MM FILM OPTICAL SOUND
Features the address by Professor Sidney Hook of New York University, 'REFLECTIONS ON HUMAN RIGHTS.'
From The Philosophy Year Addresses And Responses Series.
Prod-SUNY Dist-SUNY

Philosophy Of Logic And Language, The B 120 MIN
16MM FILM OPTICAL SOUND
Presents 'PHILOSOPHICAL PROGRESS IN LANGUAGE THEORY' by Professor W O Quine, Harvard University, with response by Professor Max Black, Cornell University.
From The Philosophy Year Addresses And Responses Series.
Prod-SUNY Dist-SUNY 1968

Philosophy Of Love, The C 29 MIN
3/4 INCH VIDEO CASSETTE
Traces Dickens' idea that love was the answer to the chaos he saw in the world.
From The Dickens World Series.
Prod-UMITV Dist-UMITV 1973

Philosophy Of Mind, The B 120 MIN
16MM FILM OPTICAL SOUND
Features the address 'SOME PROBLEMS ABOUT THINKING' by Professor Gilbert Ryle, Oxford University, with response by Professor Stuart Hampshire, Princeton University.
From The Philosophy Year Addresses And Responses Series.
Prod-SUNY Dist-SUNY 1968

Philosophy Of Patient Teaching B 30 MIN
16MM FILM OPTICAL SOUND C A
Analyzes philosophical issues in developing a comprehensive patient teaching program.
From The Nursing - Patient Teaching, Pt 1 Series.
LC NO. 74-700199
Prod-NTCN Dist-NTCN 1971

Philosophy Of Practice, The C 120 MIN
16MM FILM OPTICAL SOUND
Records the address by Professor Charles Frankel, of Columbia University with a response by Professor Walter Kaufman, Princeton University.
From The Philosophy Year Addresses And Response Series.
Prod-SUNY Dist-SUNY

Philosophy Of Rehabilitation And Its Application, Pt 1 B 27 MIN
16MM FILM OPTICAL SOUND PRO
Identifies and discusses the physical and psychosocial effects of prolonged bed rest and immobilization. Discusses the nurse's role in the prevention of adverse effects.
From The Directions For Education In Nursing Via Technology Series. Lesson 79
LC NO. 74-701857
Prod-DENT Dist-WSU 1974

Philosophy Of Rehabilitation And Its Application, Pt 2 B 31 MIN
16MM FILM OPTICAL SOUND PRO
Presents the philosophy of rehabilitation as it relates to physical and physiological effects of immobility. Identifies the use of items within the patient's environment that promote patient safety.
From The Directions For Education In Nursing Via Technology Series. Lesson 80
LC NO. 74-701858
Prod-DENT Dist-WSU 1974

Philosophy Of Science, The C 120 MIN
16MM FILM OPTICAL SOUND
Presents Professor Ernest Nagel, Columbia University speaking on 'ISSUES IN THE LOGIC OF REDUCTIVE EXPLANATIONS.' Features the response given by Professor Richard Schlegel of Michigan State University.
From The Philosophy Year Addresses And Response Series.
Prod-SUNY Dist-SUNY 1968

Philosophy Of Science, The, Pt 1 C 24 MIN
16MM FILM OPTICAL SOUND
Uses excerpts from Microbes And Men to demonstrate the development of a scientific theory as the result of observations, inductive methods, analysis and inspiration. Explains how Ignaz Semmelweis of the Great General Hospital in Vienna discovered the cause of puerperal fever by creating a paradigm for thinking and by breaking out of the old theory.
Prod-BBCTV Dist-OPENU 1982

Philosophy Of Science, The, Pt 1 C 24 MIN
16MM FILM, 3/4 OR 1/2 IN VIDEO
Uses excerpts from Microbes And Men to demonstrate the development of a scientific theory as the result of observations, inductive methods, analysis and inspiration. Explains how Ignaz Semmelweis of the Great General Hospital in Vienna discovered the cause of puerperal fever by creating a paradigm for thinking and by breaking out of the old theory.
Prod-OPENU Dist-MEDIAG Prodn-BBCTV 1982

Philosophy Of Science, The, Pt 2 C 24 MIN
16MM FILM OPTICAL SOUND
Demonstrates how a scientific theory is developed to become more sophisticated and is modified. Presents the theoretical insights and detailed research of 19th century French chemist and biologist Louis Pasteur and German bacteriologist Robert Koch.
Prod-BBCTV Dist-OPENU 1982

Philosophy Of Science, The, Pt 2 C 24 MIN
16MM FILM, 3/4 OR 1/2 IN VIDEO
Demonstrates how a scientific theory is developed to become more sophisticated and is modified. Presents the theoretical insights and detailed research of 19th century French chemist and biologist Louis Pasteur and German bacteriologist Robert Koch.
Prod-OPENU Dist-MEDIAG Prodn-BBCTV 1982

Philosophy Of Social Science, The B 120 MIN
16MM FILM OPTICAL SOUND
Records Professor H L A Hart, Oxford University, in his address, 'KELSEN'S DOCTRINE OF THE UNITY OF LAW' with response given by Professor R M Dworkin, Yale University.
From The Philosophy Year Addresses And Responses Series.
Prod-SUNY Dist-SUNY 1968

Philosophy Of Supervision C 17 MIN
16MM FILM OPTICAL SOUND
Presents a basic introduction to the principles of effective leadership. Explains the general philosophy of supervision and practical application in a nursing situation.
From The Supervision And Management Series.
LC NO. 70-712976
Prod-TRNAID Dist-TRNAID 1969

Philosophy Of The Cartoonist, The C 15 MIN
2 INCH VIDEOTAPE
See series title for descriptive statement.
From The Charlie's Pad Series.
Prod-WSIU Dist-PUBTEL

Philosophy Of The Obvious, The C 25 MIN
16MM FILM, 3/4 OR 1/2 IN VIDEO H-C
Introduces the use of dreams in Gestalt therapy, examines our two levels of existence, the inner world and the outer world, and connects the Gestalt in our fantasy with the gestalt in the real world.
From The Gestalt Series.
Prod-AQUARP Dist-FI 1969

Philosophy Year Addresses And Responses—A Series
16MM FILM OPTICAL SOUND
Presents a series of presentations by prominent scholars who participated in the International Philosophy Year Conference held at the State University College at Brockport, New York 1967-68.
Prod-SUNY Dist-SUNY 1968

Philosophy Of Communications And The Arts, The	120 MIN
Philosophy Of Ethics, The	120 MIN
Philosophy Of Human Rights, The	120 MIN
Philosophy Of Logic And Language, The	120 MIN
Philosophy Of Mind, The	120 MIN
Philosophy Of Practice, The	120 MIN
Philosophy Of Science, The	120 MIN
Philosophy Of Social Science, The	120 MIN

Phlebotomy C 11 MIN
3/4 OR 1/2 INCH VIDEO CASSETTE
Shows phlebotomy technique used by the American Red Cross for blood donations.
Prod-AMRC Dist-AMRC 1979

Phloem C 24 MIN
16MM FILM OPTICAL SOUND
Reports on the partially understood relationship between the function of phloem and the structure of sieve tubes. Scans prepared views of organisms using both an electron microscope to illustrate the position, appearance and differentiation of sieve tubes to determine their internal resistance to flow.
Prod-BBCTV Dist-OPENU 1982

Phloem C 24 MIN
16MM FILM, 3/4 OR 1/2 IN VIDEO
Reports on the partially understood relationship between the function of phloem and the structure of sieve tubes. Scans prepared views of organisms using both an electron microscope to illustrate the position, appearance and differentiation of sieve tubes to determine their internal resistance to flow.
Prod-OPENU Dist-MEDIAG Prodn-BBCTV 1982

PHN (Public Health Nurse) B 25 MIN
16MM FILM OPTICAL SOUND
Follows a public health nurse as she performs her duties in a clinic setting and in the patient's home. Illustrates that the variety and the personal nature of her work contribute to its appeal as a profession.
LC NO. FIA67-2147
Prod-VIRDH Dist-VADE Prodn-VADE 1967

Phoebe - Story Of A Premarital Pregnancy B 28 MIN
16MM FILM, 3/4 OR 1/2 IN VIDEO
Studies the emotional impact of premarital pregnancy on a sensitive high school girl. Reveals her relationships with the boy and her parents and stresses her need for outside counseling.
Prod-NFBC Dist-CRMP 1965

Phoebe - Story Of A Premarital Pregnancy (Spanish) B 28 MIN
16MM FILM, 3/4 OR 1/2 IN VIDEO H-C A
Examines the emotional impact of a sensitive high school girl's premarital pregnancy. Reveals her relationship with the boy and her need for outside counseling.
Prod-NFBC Dist-MGHT 1975

Phoenix B 55 MIN
3/4 OR 1/2 INCH VIDEO CASSETTE
Highlights rejection and reinterpretation of roles. Protrays a Southern family.
Prod-KITCHN Dist-KITCHN

Phoenix And Finnegan C 30 MIN
3/4 OR 1/2 INCH VIDEO CASSETTE C
See series title for descriptive statement.
From The Art Of Being Human Series. Module 12
Prod-MDCC Dist-MDCC

Phoenix Country II C 28 MIN
16MM FILM OPTICAL SOUND
Shows hang gliding in many countries, including the United States, Canada, Brazil, Chile, Argentina, Japan and Italy.
LC NO. 79-701022
Prod-BENARN Dist-BENARN 1979

Phoenix Rises, A C 15 MIN
3/4 OR 1/2 INCH VIDEO CASSETTE P-I
Demonstrates the value of the scrap metal industry as it conserves and reclaims waste material.
From The Explorers Unlimited Series.
Prod-WVIZTV Dist-AITECH 1971

Phoenix, The C 22 MIN
16MM FILM OPTICAL SOUND
Explores the materials use cycle and its role in solid waste. Traces the collection, transportation and disposal of waste in Kansas and analyzes current attempts to recover materials and energy from the solid waste stream. Shows the roles consumers can play in solid waste disposal programs.
LC NO. 75-702477
Prod-KLWV Dist-USNAC 1975

Phone Call, The C 24 MIN
16MM FILM OPTICAL SOUND J-H A
Tells the story of courtship and the difficulty of reaching out to touch someone.
LC NO. 78-700210
Prod-BYU Dist-EBEC 1977

Phone Freak, The C 6 MIN
16MM FILM OPTICAL SOUND
Presents a satire of the Bell Telephone Company.
LC NO. 76-701353
Prod-CONCRU Dist-CONCRU 1975

Phone Isn't Working, The C 14 MIN
3/4 OR 1/2 INCH VIDEO CASSETTE P
Explains that when Jeff tries to talk to Steve, he can't. Presents a service technician explaining the machinery of the telephone and how people are needed to keep the phone system in order.
From The Under The Yellow Balloon Series.
Prod-SCETV Dist-AITECH 1980

Phonetic Level Speech Evaluation C 28 MIN
3/4 INCH VIDEO CASSETTE PRO
Evaluates a 12-year-old boy's hearing impairment to show procedures used to assess phonologic competence and to plan a remedial program.
LC NO. 82-706187
Prod-MCGILL Dist-SYRFRC 1981

Phonetic Level Speech Teaching C 55 MIN
3/4 INCH VIDEO CASSETTE PRO
Presents the principles and practice of evoking and rehearsing speech patterns. Discusses strategies for evoking suprasegmental patterns, vowels and diphthongs, consonants and blends and alternative strategies.
LC NO. 82-706188
Prod-MCGILL Dist-SYRFRC 1981

Phonics And Augmented Alphabets C 30 MIN
2 INCH VIDEOTAPE T
Focuses on three specific phonic approaches—the analytical-gradual, intensive and augmented alphabets, designed to facilitate the mastery of sound-symbol relationships.
From The Child Reads Series.
Prod-WENHTV Dist-GPITVL

Phonics And Word Structure C 15 MIN
16MM FILM, 3/4 OR 1/2 IN VIDEO P-I
Uses animated sequences of a 'WORD FACTORY' to put together the meaningful parts of words.
From The Reading Skills, Set 2 Series.
Prod-GLDWER Dist-JOU 1972

Phonograph, The B 30 MIN
16MM FILM OPTICAL SOUND
Dramatizes how the communist revolution in Russia affected the life of a cobbler by making him realize the importance of freedom of worship on the sabbath and the menace of communism to individual liberties.
LC NO. FIA64-1141
Prod-JTS Dist-NAAJS Prodn-NBC 1956

Phonologic Level Speech Development C 40 MIN
3/4 INCH VIDEO CASSETTE PRO
Examines problems of generalizing phonetic level speech skills into meaningful spoken language.

LC NO. 82-706189
Prod-MCGILL Dist-SYRFRC 1981

Phonologic Level Speech Evaluation C 20 MIN
3/4 INCH VIDEO CASSETTE PRO
Describes sampling techniques, analysis of the spoken language sample and specifies phonologic and linguistic goals for a 12-year-old boy with profound hearing impairment.
LC NO. 82-706190
Prod-MCGILL Dist-SYRFRC 1981

Phonological Approach To Children's Speech And Sound Disorders C 104 MIN
3/4 OR 1/2 INCH VIDEO CASSETTE
Discusses the diagnostic and remedial approaches for speech sound disorders in children.
Prod-PUAVC Dist-PUAVC

Phonological Development C 130 MIN
3/4 OR 1/2 INCH VIDEO CASSETTE
Discusses the different perspectives from which children's sound systems can be examined and the major stages of phonological development.
From The Meeting The Communications Needs Of The Severely/Profoundly Handicapped 1980 Series.
Prod-PUAVC Dist-PUAVC

Phonovisual In Action C 29 MIN
16MM FILM OPTICAL SOUND K-I T
Describes the phonovisual method of teaching children to read. Shows use with every age and type, with the procedure needing only slight modification because of the common goal, skill in reading.
LC NO. FIA65-840
Prod-POTMAC Dist-PHNVSL 1961

Phony Issue, The Real Issue And You, The C 15 MIN
16MM FILM OPTICAL SOUND A
Outlines issues involved in the 1976 election campaign, labeling 'big government' as the phony issue and taxes, inflation, unemployment and national health insurance as the real issues.
LC NO. 76-702987
Prod-AFLCIO Dist-AFLCIO 1976

Phony War, The C 26 MIN
16MM FILM, 3/4 OR 1/2 IN VIDEO H-C
Shows how Hitler's invasion of Poland triggered the Second World War. Explains that the 1930's ended with America still unconvinced that its destiny was intertwined with the rest of the world.
From The Between The Wars Series.
Prod-LNDBRG Dist-FI 1978

Photgraphic Vision, The - All About Photography—A Series

Contains 20 half-hour lectures on various aspects of photography, from history to processing. Instructors include many famous photographers. A Coast Community Colleges Telecourse.
Prod-COAST Dist-CDTEL

Artistic Expression 030 MIN
Camera, The 030 MIN
Color 030 MIN
Controlling Exposure 030 MIN
Darkroom, The 030 MIN
Film, The 030 MIN
Image And Impact 030 MIN
Landscape And Cityscape 030 MIN
Lifetime In Photography, A 030 MIN
Marketplace, The 030 MIN
Photojournalism 030 MIN
Portrait, The 030 MIN
Reading Photographs 030 MIN
Responding To Light 030 MIN
Seeing With The Camera 030 MIN
Structure Within The Image 030 MIN
Studio, The 030 MIN
Time And Motion 030 MIN
Visual Documents 030 MIN
Visual Heritage 030 MIN

Photo Fun Club—A Series
I
Prod-WMVSTV Dist-GPITVL

Photo Fun Club, Pt 1 30 MIN
Photo Fun Club, Pt 2 30 MIN
Photo Fun Club, Pt 3 30 MIN
Photo Fun Club, Pt 4 30 MIN
Photo Fun Club, Pt 5 30 MIN
Photo Fun Club, Pt 6 30 MIN

Photo Fun Club, Pt 1 C 30 MIN
3/4 INCH VIDEO CASSETTE I
Shows how to take care of a camera and how to load it to take a picture.
From The Photo Fun Club Series.
Prod-WMVSTV Dist-GPITVL

Photo Fun Club, Pt 2 C 30 MIN
3/4 INCH VIDEO CASSETTE I
Shows how to hold a camera, how to achieve proper exposure, how to file for negatives and how to mount a photo.
From The Photo Fun Club Series.
Prod-WMVSTV Dist-GPITVL

Photo Fun Club, Pt 3 C 30 MIN
3/4 INCH VIDEO CASSETTE I
Presents a critique session in photography and shows how to make a picture story.
From The Photo Fun Club Series.
Prod-WMVSTV Dist-GPITVL

Photo Fun Club, Pt 4 C 30 MIN
3/4 INCH VIDEO CASSETTE I
Shows errors in picture taking and how they could have been corrected. Features a 4-H agent visiting a group and asking them to take photographs in order to make posters for store windows to participate in community conservation week.
From The Photo Fun Club Series.
Prod-WMVSTV Dist-GPITVL

Photo Fun Club, Pt 5 C 30 MIN
3/4 INCH VIDEO CASSETTE I
Features Frank Pallo of Eastman Kodak Company discussing different parts of a camera. Shows movies of the conservation photo field trip.
From The Photo Fun Club Series.
Prod-WMVSTV Dist-GPITVL

Photo Fun Club, Pt 6 C 30 MIN
3/4 INCH VIDEO CASSETTE I
Shows picture stories created for a community conservation week.
From The Photo Fun Club Series.
Prod-WMVSTV Dist-GPITVL

Photo Opportunity C 29 MIN
3/4 OR 1/2 INCH VIDEO CASSETTE
Explores the question of whether reporters have a moral or a professional obligation to intervene in stories they cover.
From The Inside Story Series.
LC NO. 83-706852
Prod-PBS Dist-PBS 1981

Photo Show—A Series

Presents Jonathan Goell showing the basic skills and the finer points of photography. Offers tips and advice on camera selection, operation and darkroom techniques.
Prod-WGBHTV Dist-PBS 1981

Accentuate The Negative 029 MIN
Change Of Lens, A 029 MIN
Filters, Dodging And Burning 029 MIN
Hue And Eye 029 MIN
It's About Time 029 MIN
Let There Be Light 029 MIN
Making Contacts 029 MIN
Right Exposure, The 029 MIN
Starting To Print 029 MIN
Three Key Controls 029 MIN
To Choose A Camera 029 MIN
Tough Shots 029 MIN
What's In A Frame 029 MIN

Photo Started It All, A C 15 MIN
16MM FILM OPTICAL SOUND
Uses a yearbook staff photograph to help four junior high school students become acquainted with the basics of good grooming and dress.
Prod-SEARS Dist-MTP

Photo-Electric Effect C 28 MIN
16MM FILM OPTICAL SOUND H-C
Presents qualitative demonstrations of the photoelectric effect, employing the sun and a carbon arc as sources. Also shows an experiment measuring the kinetic energy of the photoelectrons emitted from a potassium surface.
From The PSSC Physics Films Series.
Prod-PSSC Dist-MLA 1962

Photo-Electric Effect (Spanish) B 28 MIN
16MM FILM OPTICAL SOUND
Shows qualitative demonstrations of photo-electric effect. Shows a quantitive experiment which measures kinetic energy of photo-electrons emitted from a potassium surface.
From The PSSC Physics Series.
Prod-PSSC Dist-MLA

Photocoupler Applications C 30 MIN
3/4 OR 1/2 INCH VIDEO CASSETTE PRO
Uses the equivalent circuit to introduce photocoupler applications. Points out device capabilities in specific applications, including the important optical isolator application.
From The Optoelectronics, Part I - Optoelectronic Emitters, Sensors And Couplers Series.
Prod-TXINLC Dist-TXINLC

Photocouplers And Their Characteristics C 30 MIN
3/4 OR 1/2 INCH VIDEO CASSETTE PRO
Tells how photo couplers are emitters and sensors in the same package. Discusses effects of different fabrication types as well as the electrical characteristics with the sensor as a phototransistor or photodiode.
From The Optoelectronics, Part I - Optoelectronic Emitters, Sensors And Couplers Series.
Prod-TXINLC Dist-TXINLC

Photoelectric Effect B 25 MIN
16MM FILM OPTICAL SOUND C A
Shows a teacher using a zinc plate, an electroscope and ultraviolet light to demonstrate the photoelectric effect and how it can readily be shown to a class. He then emphasizes the many pitfalls in gathering and interpreting data and demonstrates how quantitative data can be obtained and analyzed to yield a value for Planck's constant.
From The Harvard Project Physics Teacher Briefings Series. No. 2
LC NO. 75-709148
Prod-HPP Dist-HRAW 1969

Photofinishing Story, The C 22 MIN
16MM FILM OPTICAL SOUND
Describes what happens to film that is sent for processing in a modern photofinishing plant. Shows the modern equipment and quality control procedures that produce beautiful prints and slides.
Prod-EKC Dist-EKC 1983

Photographer, The B 30 MIN
16MM FILM OPTICAL SOUND H-C A
Shows the personality, philosophy, techniques and artistry of Edward Weston through scenes of the artist at home, on location and at work with his students.
LC NO. FIE52-154
Prod-USDS Dist-USNAC 1948

Photographer's Eye, The C 29 MIN
3/4 OR 1/2 INCH VIDEO CASSETTE H-C A
Looks at the creative impulse in the art and practice of photography. Features the work of photographers Emmet Gowin and Garry Winogrand.
From The Creativity With Bill Moyers Series.
Prod-CORPEL Dist-PBS 1982

Photographers Of The American Frontier-1860-1880 C 58 MIN
3/4 OR 1/2 INCH VIDEO CASSETTE
Shows how an inspired group of artists in the new medium of photography captured the American frontier. Features the work of Carleton Watkins, Eadweard Muybridge, A J Russell, William Henry Jackson and T H O'Sullivan.
Prod-BLACKW Dist-BLACKW

Photographic Arts Centre C 1 MIN
16MM FILM OPTICAL SOUND
Looks at the Photographic Arts Centre, one of Ryerson Polytechnical Institute's most popular buildings.
LC NO. 76-702042
Prod-RYERC Dist-RYERC 1975

Photographic Memory C 5 MIN
3/4 INCH VIDEO CASSETTE
Features an ethereal study of the colors and the textures of the landscape of the Southwest.
From The South-Western Landscape Series.
Prod-EAI Dist-EAI

Photographic Study Of Gold Flow C 14 MIN
16MM FILM OPTICAL SOUND
Presents research on the character of gold flow. Demonstrates to dentists how gold actually fills a void and shows the function of the sprue.
LC NO. 72-700476
Prod-LOMA Dist-LOMA 1967

Photographics C 30 MIN
3/4 OR 1/2 INCH VIDEO CASSETTE
Presents guests who are experts in their respective fields who share tips on collecting and caring for antique photographics.
From The Antique Shop Series.
Prod-WVPTTV Dist-MDCPB

Photographing The Nude C 30 MIN
3/4 OR 1/2 INCH VIDEO CASSETTE
Deals comprehensively with photographing the nude. Emphasizes the importance of being ready at all times to catch a potential shot.
Prod-SHERVP Dist-SHERVP

Photography B 12 MIN
16MM FILM OPTICAL SOUND J-C A
Shows the growth of flowers in a tour through the greenhouses of John Ott, using stop-motion photography. Shows the ivied walls of Eastman House in Rochester, telling the story of how the science of motion pictures was born and developed from the magic lantern slides to the film pageants of today.
Prod-HEARST Dist-HEARST

Photography C 30 MIN
16MM FILM, 3/4 OR 1/2 IN VIDEO H-C A
Profiles five photographers including photo-essayist Bruce Davidson, Pulitzer Prize winner David Kennerly, New York Daily News photojournalist Mary DiBiase, commercial photographer Michael O'Neill and wedding photographer Gil Amaral. Explains how a photographic image can take on a reality all its own. Narrated by Cheryl Tiegs.
From The Media Probes Series.
Prod-LAYLEM Dist-TIMLIF 1982

Photography - Black And White Outdoors B 18 MIN
16MM FILM OPTICAL SOUND J-C A
Presents techniques for improving outdoor photography. Describes black and white film characteristics and explains how to use filters. Covers composition, exposure, lighting, close-ups, depth-of-field, natural posing, panning and basic shutter speed.
LC NO. 71-715406
Prod-PFC Dist-PFC 1972

Photography - Dorothea Lange - The Closer For Me B 30 MIN
16MM FILM, 3/4 OR 1/2 IN VIDEO J-C A
Mrs Dorothea Lange discusses a new photographic project for the present generation of photographers. Many of her photographs of American cities from various periods are presented.
From The USA - Photography Series.
LC NO. 80-707042
Prod-NET Dist-IU Prodn-KQEDTV 1966

Photography - Dorothea Lange - Under The Trees B 30 MIN
16MM FILM, 3/4 OR 1/2 IN VIDEO J-C A
Shows Dorothea Lange at home making preparation for an exhibition of her work covering the past 50 years. Presents many of her photographs while she comments on the reasons and emotions that have moved her to photograph particular scenes.
From The USA Series.
Prod-NET Dist-IU Prodn-KQEDTV 1966

Photography - How It Works C 11 MIN
16MM FILM OPTICAL SOUND I-C

Introduces the camera user to the basics of photography. Looks at the camera and its basic parts. Clarifies the interrelationship between lens opening and shutter speed in an explanation of how an automatic or adjustable camera compensates for various lighting conditions.
Prod-EKC Dist-EKC 1979

Photography - Stop-Motion Miracles B 12 MIN
16MM FILM OPTICAL SOUND I A
Explains the techniques of stop-motion or 'time-lapse' photography through a visit to the greenhouse studio of John Ott, one of the foremost authorities on this technique. Tells how stop-motion photography is used in cancer research and agricultural experiments as well as to enable the viewer to watch the growth of flowers and plants ten thousand times faster than normal speed.
Prod-PATHE Dist-HEARST

Photography - The Daybooks Of Edward Weston - How Young I Was B 30 MIN
16MM FILM, 3/4 OR 1/2 IN VIDEO H-C A
Quotes from 'THE DAYBOOKS OF EDWARD WESTON' accompany photographs from his soft-focus portrait period, his abstract motifs and his work done in Mexico. Two of Weston's sons, his second wife and one of his former students discuss and evaluate the artist.
From The USA - Photography Series.
LC NO. 80-707040
Prod-NET Dist-IU Prodn-KQEDTV 1966

Photography - The Daybooks Of Edward Weston - The Strongest Way Of Seeing B 30 MIN
16MM FILM, 3/4 OR 1/2 IN VIDEO H-C A
Depicts various photographs by Edward Weston, such as his work on Point Lobos, California, his record of California and the Western United States, portraits of his cats, and samples from his satirical series and his civil defense series.
From The USA - Photography Series.
LC NO. 80-707041
Prod-NET Dist-IU Prodn-KQEDTV 1966

Photography - The Incisive Art—A Series
16MM FILM, 3/4 OR 1/2 IN VIDEO H-C A
Prod-NET Dist-IU Prodn-KQEDTV 1960

Language Of The Camera Eye, The 029 MIN
Photography As An Art 029 MIN
Points of View 029 MIN
Professional Photography 029 MIN
Technique 029 MIN

Photography As An Art B 29 MIN
16MM FILM, 3/4 OR 1/2 IN VIDEO H-C A
Presents Ansel Adams as he photographs Yosemite National Park. Explains how a sense of discovery and re-discovery is conveyed through his photography. Discusses his methods of teaching.
From The Photography - The Incisive Art Series.
LC NO. 80-707010
Prod-NET Dist-IU Prodn-KQEDTV 1960

Photography In Action C 7 MIN
16MM FILM OPTICAL SOUND
Shows how slow motion, time-lapse and split-frame photography are used in obtaining engineering data at the Waterways Experiment Station.
LC NO. 74-706381
Prod-USAE Dist-USNAC 1969

Photography In The USAF - Optical Instrumentation At Vandenberg Air Force Base C 17 MIN
16MM FILM OPTICAL SOUND
Depicts how optical instrumentation during missile launchings is achieved through engineering sequential photography. Pictures the cameras used and explains their characteristics and capabilities.
LC NO. 74-706174
Prod-USDD Dist-USNAC 1961

Photojournalism C 30 MIN
3/4 OR 1/2 INCH VIDEO CASSETTE
See series title for descriptive statement.
From The Photographic Vision - All About Photography Series.
Prod-COAST Dist-CDTEL

Photojournalist C 30 MIN
1/2 IN VIDEO CASSETTE BETA/VHS
Describes the life of photojournalist Vanessa Barns Hillian, who tries to create a dynamic image that sums up a whole story, as she records a piece of history for The Washington Post.
From The American Professionals Series.
Prod-WTBS Dist-RMI

Photons B 19 MIN
16MM FILM OPTICAL SOUND H-C
Uses the photomultiplier and oscilloscope to demonstrate that light shows particle behavior.
From The PSSC Physics Films Series.
Prod-PSSC Dist-MLA 1960

Photos C 5 MIN
16MM FILM, 3/4 OR 1/2 IN VIDEO K-C A
See series title for descriptive statement.
From The How It's Made Series.
Prod-HOLIA Dist-LUF

Photosynthesis (Spanish) C 20 MIN
16MM FILM, 3/4 OR 1/2 IN VIDEO J-C
A Spanish language version of the film and videorecording Photosynthesis.
Prod-EBEC Dist-EBEC 1982

Photosynthesis (3rd Ed) C 20 MIN
16MM FILM, 3/4 OR 1/2 IN VIDEO J-H
Explains how green plants transform light energy into food by the process of photosynthesis. Discusses light and dark reactions and the importance of ATP and NADPH in chloroplasts.
LC NO. 82-706523
Prod-EBEC Dist-EBEC Prodn-BORKBV 1982

Photosynthesis - A Demonstration—A Series
16MM FILM, 3/4 OR 1/2 IN VIDEO J-H
Discusses the effect of light, chlorophyll and carbon dioxide on plants.
Prod-IWIF Dist-IFB

Effect Of Chlorophyll And Carbon Dioxide On
Effect Of Chlorophyll And Carbon Dioxide On 005 MIN
Effect Of Light On Oxygen Production 004 MIN
Effect Of Light On Starch Formation 006 MIN

Photosynthesis - Chemistry Of Food Making (2nd Ed) C 18 MIN
16MM FILM, 3/4 OR 1/2 IN VIDEO J-C
Shows that through the process of photosynthesis, food is manufactured within the cells of green plants. Examines the chain of events that is responsible for the oxygen we breathe and the food we eat.
Prod-CORF Dist-CORF 1985

Photosynthesis - Energy From Light C 52 MIN
3/4 OR 1/2 INCH VIDEO CASSETTE
Analyzes the process of photosynthesis with an explanation of the basic chemistry underlying the process.
LC NO. 81-706670
Prod-SCIMAN Dist-GA 1981

Photosynthesis - Life Energy C 18 MIN
16MM FILM, 3/4 OR 1/2 IN VIDEO J-H A
Explains the basic process of photosynthesis and describes its importance in the food pyramid. Looks at newly discovered photosynthetic organisms which may provide fuel for the future.
LC NO. 83-706730
Prod-NGS Dist-NGS 1983

Photosynthesis - The Flow Of Energy From Sun To Man C 15 MIN
3/4 OR 1/2 INCH VIDEO CASSETTE
Tells the story of how photosynthesis works in plants.
Prod-CBSC Dist-CBSC

Photosynthesis And Respiration C 29 MIN
3/4 INCH VIDEO CASSETTE C A
Discusses the sun as the place where photosynthesis begins. Gives detailed explanation of the photosynthesis equation. Covers cellular respiration.
From The Introducing Biology Series. Program 5
Prod-COAST Dist-CDTEL

Photosynthesis In Purple Bacteria—A Series
16MM FILM, 3/4 OR 1/2 IN VIDEO H-C
Discusses various aspects of photosynthesis in purple bacteria.
Prod-IWIF Dist-IFB

Comparison With Higher Plants - Van Niel's
Isolating Pure Cultures - Van Niel's Technique 005 MIN
Photosynthesis Without Oxygen - Moslich's 007 MIN

Photosynthesis Without Oxygen - Moslich's Assertion C 7 MIN
16MM FILM, 3/4 OR 1/2 IN VIDEO H-C
Shows the charateristics of purple bacteria, living where oxygen is deficient and hydrogen sulfide is present. Records how they move away from a solution's surface where oxygen is present and retreat from algae's photosynthetic oxygen. Reveals how anoxygenic photosynthesis was proven by Hans Moslich for the first time.
From The Photosynthesis In Purple Bacteria Series.
Prod-IWIF Dist-IFB

Photosynthesis, Pt 1 C 8 MIN
3/4 OR 1/2 INCH VIDEO CASSETTE I
Explains that the green plant is the only organism on earth which produces its own food and describes how it does so.
From The Search For Science (2nd Ed), Unit VIII - Plants Series.
Prod-WVIZTV Dist-GPITVL

Photosynthesis, Pt 2 C 7 MIN
3/4 OR 1/2 INCH VIDEO CASSETTE I
Explains that the green plant is the only organism on earth which produces its own food and describes how it does so.
From The Search For Science (2nd Ed), Unit VIII - Plants Series.
Prod-WVIZTV Dist-GPITVL

Photosynthetic Fixation Of Carbon Dioxide, Pt 1 C 6 MIN
16MM FILM OPTICAL SOUND H
Demonstrates measurement of the rate of photosynthesis using a radio-tracer technique. Uses green and white portions of verigated coleus leaves for a chlorophyl-non-chlorophyl variable and a light and dark chamber.
From The Plant Science Series.
LC NO. FIA66-170
Prod-IOWA Dist-MLA 1964

Photosynthetic Fixation Of Carbon Dioxide, Pt 2 C 6 MIN
16MM FILM OPTICAL SOUND H
Demonstrates measurement of the rate of photosynthesis using a radio-tracer technique. Uses green and white portions of verigated coleus leaves for a chlorophyl-non-chlorophyl variable and a light and dark chamber.
From The Plant Science Series.
Prod-IOWA Dist-MLA 1964

Phrase Reading—A Series
J-C A
This complete series consists of an introductory film, and three beginning, six intermediate and six advanced level reading films. Reading rates range from 100 to 240 words-per-minute in the beginning set, from 180 to 360 words-per-minute in the intermediate set and as high as 536 words-per-minute in the advanced set.
Prod-CBF Dist-AVED 1960

Introduction To Phrase Reading, An - It's In
Beginning Phrase Reading, Pt 1, Alaska 7 MIN
Beginning Phrase Reading, Pt 2, Blue Whale 7 MIN
Beginning Phrase Reading, Pt 3, San Francisco 7 MIN
Intermediate Phrase Reading, Pt 1 7 MIN
Intermediate Phrase Reading, Pt 2 7 MIN
Intermediate Phrase Reading, Pt 3 7 MIN
Intermediate Phrase Reading, Pt 4 7 MIN
Intermediate Phrase Reading, Pt 5 6 MIN
Intermediate Phrase Reading, Pt 6 6 MIN
Advanced Phrase Reading, Pt 1 6 MIN
Advanced Phrase Reading, Pt 2 6 MIN
Advanced Phrase Reading, Pt 3 6 MIN
Advanced Phrase Reading, Pt 4 6 MIN
Advanced Phrase Reading, Pt 5 7 MIN
Advanced Phrase Reading, Pt 6 6 MIN

Phrases C 18 MIN
1/2 IN VIDEO CASSETTE BETA/VHS
See series title for descriptive statement.
From The English And Speech Series.
Prod-RMI Dist-RMI

Phyla, The C 12 MIN
16MM FILM OPTICAL SOUND J-C A
Deals with sea life from the protozoa to chordates, tracing the development of animals from the simplest forms to the most advanced. Shows unusual specimens appearing along the trail from sea creatures to man.
Prod-REELA Dist-MIAMIS 1970

Phyllis Lamhut And Dan Wagoner C 30 MIN
3/4 OR 1/2 INCH VIDEO CASSETTE
See series title for descriptive statement.
From The On Your Own Series.
Prod-ARCVID Dist-ARCVID

Phyllis Lamhut And Dan Wagoner C 30 MIN
3/4 OR 1/2 INCH VIDEO CASSETTE
See series title for descriptive statement.
From The Eye On Dance - On Your Own Series.
Prod-ARTRES Dist-ARTRES

Phylogeny Of Cellular Recognition C 35 MIN
3/4 INCH VIDEO CASSETTE
Presents a study of specific and nonspecific surveillance cells in protozoans and man.
Prod-UTAHTI Dist-UTAHTI

Physiatry - A Physician's Perspective C 26 MIN
16MM FILM OPTICAL SOUND
Encourages a career in rehabilitative medicine.
Prod-TOGGFI Dist-RIFL 1981

Physical Abuse C 34 MIN
3/4 OR 1/2 INCH VIDEO CASSETTE PRO
Provides in-depth information on physical abuse of children - its incidence, identification, and treatment. Teaches identification by physical examination and interviewing the child.
From The Child Abuse Series.
Prod-HSCIC Dist-HSCIC 1978

Physical Abuse Of Children C 30 MIN
3/4 OR 1/2 INCH VIDEO CASSETTE H-C A
See series title for descriptive statement.
From The Child Abuse And Neglect Series.
Prod-UMINN Dist-GPITVL 1983

Physical Adjustment To Dizziness C 55 MIN
3/4 OR 1/2 INCH VIDEO CASSETTE
See series title for descriptive statement.
From The Dizziness And Related Balance Disorders Series.
Prod-GSHDME Dist-GSHDME

Physical And Biological Principles Of Hyperthermia C 50 MIN
3/4 INCH VIDEO CASSETTE
Discusses the use of heat in treating cancer.
Prod-UTAHTI Dist-UTAHTI

Physical And Chemical Changes C 15 MIN
3/4 OR 1/2 INCH VIDEO CASSETTE I
See series title for descriptive statement.
From The Discovering Series. Unit 3 - Chemistry
Prod-WDCNTV Dist-AITECH 1978

Physical And Chemical Properties Of The Elements—A Series
H-C A
Prod-KALMIA Dist-KALMIA 1972

Group Viia Elements - Chemical Properties 4 MIN
Group Viia Elements - Physical Properties, Pt 1 4 MIN
Group Viia Elements - Physical Properties, Pt 2 4 MIN
Group Viib Elements - Manganese 4 MIN

Physical And Emotional Change As The Dance Artist Matures C 30 MIN
3/4 OR 1/2 INCH VIDEO CASSETTE
See series title for descriptive statement.
From The Dancers' Bodies Series.
Prod-ARCVID Dist-ARCVID

Physical And Occupational Therapy Of The Burn Patient C 13 MIN
16MM FILM OPTICAL SOUND

Deals with the physical and occupational therapy of the patient suffering from burns.
LC NO. 74-706175
Prod-USA Dist-USNAC 1973

Physical And Sexual Aspects Of Relating, The C 30 MIN
3/4 OR 1/2 INCH VIDEO CASSETTE C A
Discusses attitudes toward sex. Compares research into human sexual behavior. Establishes patterns between social attitudes and sexual behavior.
From The Family Portrait - A Study Of Contemporary Lifestyles Series. Lesson 4
Prod-SCCON Dist-CDTEL

Physical Assessment - Heart And Lungs—A Series
PRO
Describes characteristics and functions of the heart and lung. Covers procedures of examination.
Prod-CONMED Dist-CONMED 1976

Assessing Respirations	20 MIN
Auscultation Of Heart Sounds	28 MIN
Initial Assessment Of The Heart	27 MIN
Inspection And Palpation Of The Anterior Chest	25 MIN
Inspection And Palpation Of The Lungs And	26 MIN
Percussion And Auscultation Of The Lungs And	20 MIN
Percussion And Auscultation Of The Lungs And	30 MIN

Physical Assessment - Neurologic System—A Series

Focuses on the underlying principles as well as specific procedures for assessing the neurologic system. Shows how the neurologic system, in spite of its complexity, lends itself well to clinical evaluation.
Prod-CONMED Dist-CONMED

Cranial Nerves, Pt 1
Cranial Nerves, Pt 2
Mental Status Exam
Motor Testing
Reflexes
Sensory Testing
Station Gait And Cerebellar Function

Physical Assessment Of A Child C 33 MIN
3/4 OR 1/2 INCH VIDEO CASSETTE
Demonstrates a head-to-toe approach to performing a physical exam on a young child. Covers four basic techniques of inspection, palpation, percussion and auscultation. Shows how to establish trust and positive rapport with child through a skillful and understanding nurse.
Prod-UCALGN Dist-AJN

Physical Assessment Of The Abdomen C 9 MIN
3/4 OR 1/2 INCH VIDEO CASSETTE
Demonstrates the nurse making an assessment of the patient's abdominal status as she prepares him for discharge from the hospital.
From The Physical Assessment Series.
Prod-SUNHSC Dist-AJN

Physical Assessment Of The Comatose Patient C 27 MIN
3/4 OR 1/2 INCH VIDEO CASSETTE PRO
Identifies general physical and neurologic assessment of the comatose patient, relates metabolic causes of coma to abnormal physiologic states, separates etiology of coma into five categories and five critical signs during assessment.
From The Comatose Patient Series.
Prod-BRA Dist-BRA

Physical Assessment Of The Newborn C 32 MIN
3/4 OR 1/2 INCH VIDEO CASSETTE PRO
Shows how to perform a head-to-toe physical assessment of a newborn and to discriminate between normal and abnormal conditions. Demonstrates how to measure head circumference and length of an infant.
Prod-UARIZ Dist-UARIZ

Physical Assessment—A Series

Provides a generalized study of the clinical skills of physical assessment. Discusses how the specific examination is performed, illustrates major points of emphasis and shows a practitioner performing the assessment.
Prod-SUNHSC Dist-AJN

Assessment Of The Ears And Auditory System	011 MIN
Assessment Of The Musculoskeletal System	021 MIN
Breast Exam, The	013 MIN
Cardiac Examination	013 MIN
Examination Of The Eyes And Visual System	020 MIN
Examination Of The Head And Neck	019 MIN
Examination Of The Male Genitalia	013 MIN
Examination Of The Peripheral Pulses	008 MIN
Examination Of The Pregnant Abdomen	008 MIN
Examination Of The Thorax And Lungs	015 MIN
Gynecological Examination, The	019 MIN
Neurological Assessment - Cerebellar	020 MIN
Neurological Assessment - Cranial Nerves	017 MIN
Physical Assessment Of The Abdomen	009 MIN

Physical Changes C 30 MIN
3/4 INCH VIDEO CASSETTE
Discusses the increased awareness of physical changes that occurs during mid-life.
From The Transitions - Caught At Midlife Series.
Prod-UMITV Dist-UMITV 1980

Physical Changes All About Us (2nd Ed) C 14 MIN
16MM FILM, 3/4 OR 1/2 IN VIDEO I-J
Demonstrates and explains physical changes in size, shape and appearance by such means as combination, separation, heating and cooling.
Prod-CORF Dist-CORF

Physical Changes In Matter C 15 MIN
3/4 OR 1/2 INCH VIDEO CASSETTE P-I
Shows that matter changes form according to the forces acting on it. Traces water as its molecules are changed by the action of heat from ice, a solid, to drinking water, a liquid, and then to water vapor, a gas. Points out that matter may undergo physical changes but that amount will always remain the same.
From The First Films On Science Series.
Prod-MAETEL Dist-AITECH 1975

Physical Chemistry Of Immunohematology B 30 MIN
16MM FILM OPTICAL SOUND PRO
Shows how immunological and immunochemical principles are reflected in the performance of routine immunochematologic tests performed in the clinical laboratory.
From The Clinical Pathology Series.
LC NO. 74-705356
Prod-NMAC Dist-NMAC 1968

Physical Conditions C 26 MIN
3/4 OR 1/2 INCH VIDEO CASSETTE
Tells how to deal effectively with handicapped and aged drivers.
From The Right Way Series.
Prod-SCETV Dist-PBS 1982

Physical Controls C 30 MIN
3/4 OR 1/2 INCH VIDEO CASSETTE
Provides basic measures and techniques for the physical protection of data processing resources.
From The Computer Security Techniques Series.
Prod-DELTAK Dist-DELTAK

Physical Development C 21 MIN
16MM FILM, 3/4 OR 1/2 IN VIDEO H-C A
Provides an overview of normal physical growth and development from infancy to adolescence.
From The Growing Years (CRMP) Series.
Prod-COAST Dist-CRMP 1978

Physical Development Of The Infant C 29 MIN
3/4 OR 1/2 INCH VIDEO CASSETTE H-C A
Explains that physical development of the infant is supported by appropriate nutrition, activity and medical care.
From The Tomorrow's Families Series.
LC NO. 81-706916
Prod-MSDOE Dist-AITECH 1980

Physical Diagnosis - Examination Of The Musculosketletal System C 27 MIN
16MM FILM, 3/4 OR 1/2 IN VIDEO PRO
Examines principles of physical diagnosis relating to the musculoskeletal system.
Prod-FEIL Dist-FEIL

Physical Diagnosis - The Examination Of The Neurological System C 36 MIN
16MM FILM, 3/4 OR 1/2 IN VIDEO PRO
Shows details of the technical aspects of the examination of the neurological system and interprets the meaning of the signs elicited. Uses brain slices and anatomical specimens of the nervous system, along with slides, to illustrate the changes or pathological conditions giving rise to the altered signs. Shows patients to illustrate alterations in gait, position sense and tremor.
Prod-CWRUSM Dist-FEIL 1964

Physical Diagnosis Of The Ear, Nose And Throat C 28 MIN
16MM FILM OPTICAL SOUND H-C
Demonstrates the proper use of instruments in the examinations of the ear, nose and throat areas.
Prod-OSUMPD Dist-OSUMPD 1960

Physical Diagnosis—A Series
PRO
Prod-NMAC Dist-USNAC 1970

Ears, The	18 MIN

Physical Distribution C 30 MIN
3/4 OR 1/2 INCH VIDEO CASSETTE
Compares the advantages of shipping by air, rail and trucks. Shows means to differentiate a common carrier's transportation services from those of competitors.
From The Marketing Perspectives Series.
Prod-MATC Dist-WFVTAE

Physical Education - Basic Skills C 16 MIN
16MM FILM, 3/4 OR 1/2 IN VIDEO
Presents basic skills in six sports activities, including apparatus, basketball, football, soccer, softball and tumbling.
Prod-AIMS Dist-AIMS

Physical Education Activities In The Classroom C 16 MIN
16MM FILM OPTICAL SOUND C A
Illustrates warm-ups, relays, self-testing activities, games and rhythms.
Prod-OSSHE Dist-OSSHE

Physical Education At Packwood School B 15 MIN
16MM FILM OPTICAL SOUND
Presents a record of the activities used with mentally subnormal adolescent boys. Illustrates use of the gymnastic table, strengthening activities, log exercises, road-work remedial gymnastics, partner work, special fitness activities and games.
Prod-NYSED Dist-NYSED

Physical Education In Elementary Schools C 20 MIN
16MM FILM OPTICAL SOUND C T
A training film for teachers of physical education in elementary schools. Shows teachers and students during physical education classes and an interview with a school principal.
LC NO. FIA66-788
Prod-FINLYS Dist-FINLYS 1964

Physical Environment, The X 11 MIN
16MM FILM, 3/4 OR 1/2 IN VIDEO J-C A
Describes how organisms adapt to the varied physical and climatic conditions on the earth.
From The Biology Series. Unit 1 - Ecology
Prod-EBF Dist-EBEC 1964

Physical Environment, The (Spanish) C 11 MIN
16MM FILM, 3/4 OR 1/2 IN VIDEO H
Illustrates ways in which organisms adapt to their environment.
From The Biology (Spanish) Series. Unit 1 - Ecology
Prod-EBEC Dist-EBEC

Physical Evidence—A Series
16MM FILM, 3/4 OR 1/2 IN VIDEO
Discusses the various aspects of searching for, identifying, gathering and analyzing evidence for police officers.
Prod-WORON Dist-MTI

Gathering And Analysis	021 MIN
Search And Identification	015 MIN

Physical Examination Of The Chest C 20 MIN
16MM FILM, 3/4 OR 1/2 IN VIDEO C A
Covers the basic elements of a physical examination of the chest, including observation, palpation, percussion and auscultation. Emphasizes the recognition and interpretation of different breathing sounds.
From The Physical Respiratory Therapy Series.
Prod-VISCI Dist-TEF

Physical Examination Of The Elderly C 16 MIN
3/4 OR 1/2 INCH VIDEO CASSETTE PRO
Discusses and illustrates the unique aspects of examining the elderly patient.
Prod-HSCIC Dist-HSCIC 1984

Physical Examination Of The Eye C 12 MIN
3/4 OR 1/2 INCH VIDEO CASSETTE PRO
Shows how to test visual acuity using the Snellen Eye Chart.
Prod-HSCIC Dist-HSCIC 1977

Physical Examination of The Injured Athlete C
3/4 OR 1/2 INCH VIDEO CASSETTE
Shows how to evaluate the severity of an athlete's injury and how to stabilize it until the injury can be properly treated off the field. Includes assessment of vital signs and how to minimize the risk of further injury in transportation of the injured athlete.
From The Sports Medicine Series.
Prod-VTRI Dist-VTRI

Physical Examination Of The Musculoskeletal System C 41 MIN
3/4 OR 1/2 INCH VIDEO CASSETTE PRO
Demonstrates the technique of performing a thorough and systematic examination of the joints. Shows a method to differentiate causes of joint pain and to diagnose specific pathologies of various joints.
Prod-UARIZ Dist-UARIZ

Physical Examination Of The Newborn C 33 MIN
16MM FILM OPTICAL SOUND
Discusses physical examination of the neonate, demonstrating the techniques for routine physical examinations and the techniques for the recognition of abnormalities which may be present. Shows a number of normal conditions which are often mistaken for defects.
Prod-PFI Dist-PFI 1959

Physical Examination Of The Newborn C 25 MIN
3/4 INCH VIDEO CASSETTE PRO
Explains the importance of the initial clinical inspection of the newborn. Discusses how the examination should be carried out and what observations and findings should be made and recorded. Demonstrates a method for determining gestational age.
LC NO. 79-706518
Prod-UMICH Dist-UMMCML 1978

Physical Examination, The C 15 MIN
16MM FILM, 3/4 OR 1/2 IN VIDEO K A
Explains a physical examination to children by taking them through the process.
Prod-BROFLM Dist-SUTHRB

Physical Examination, The (Spanish) C 15 MIN
3/4 OR 1/2 INCH VIDEO CASSETTE K A
Explains a physical examination to children by taking them through the process.
Prod-SUTHRB Dist-SUTHRB

Physical Factors In The Parenthood Decision C 29 MIN
3/4 OR 1/2 INCH VIDEO CASSETTE H-C A
Tells how a mother's physical condition and the parents' genetic makeup affect the pregnancy and the child.
From The Tomorrow's Families Series.
LC NO. 81-706893
Prod-MSDOE Dist-AITECH 1980

Physical Features Of India B 26 MIN
16MM FILM OPTICAL SOUND I-C A
Gives a comprehensive picture of all three regions of India - the Himalayas, the Indo-gangetic plains and the Peninsular India.
Prod-INDIA Dist-NEDINF

Physical Fitness C 29 MIN
16MM FILM OPTICAL SOUND
Shows how the U S Army places much emphasis on physical fitness training in developing the soldier.
From The Big Picture Series.
LC NO. 75-701193
Prod-USA Dist-USNAC 1967

Physical Fitness C 13 MIN
16MM FILM, 3/4 OR 1/2 IN VIDEO I

Defines physical fitness and the need for developing fitness in the areas of cardio-pulmonary endurance, muscle strength, muscle endurance, flexibility and body composition.
From The Fun To Be Fit Series. Film 2
Prod-WDEMCO Dist-WDEMCO 1983

Physical Fitness C 19 MIN
16MM FILM, 3/4 OR 1/2 IN VIDEO H-C A
Discusses the importance of keeping physically fit and shows that through proper diet and exercise a person can lose weight, reduce the risk of heart and blood vessel diseases, and achieve greater endurance and stamina.
From The Physical Fitness Series.
Prod-PRORE Dist-JOU 1980

Physical Fitness C 30 MIN
3/4 OR 1/2 INCH VIDEO CASSETTE C T
Explains that each individual must set his or her own goals to become physically fit. Discusses how planned programs succeed.
From The Here's To Your Health Series.
Prod-DALCCD Dist-DALCCD

Physical Fitness C 30 MIN
3/4 OR 1/2 INCH VIDEO CASSETTE
Presents tips on getting physically fit.
From The Consumer Survival Series. Health
Prod-MDCPB Dist-MDCPB

Physical Fitness - It Can Save Your Life C 24 MIN
16MM FILM, 3/4 OR 1/2 IN VIDEO I-H
Suggests a program of daily exercise and diet to overcome poor physical health, due to inactivity and overeating.
From The Wide World Of Adventure Series.
Prod-AVATLI Dist-EBEC 1977

Physical Fitness - The New Perspective C 10 MIN
16MM FILM, 3/4 OR 1/2 IN VIDEO J-C A
Stresses the positive aspects of being physically fit and tells simple ways to increase everyday activity without disrupting one's normal daily routine.
From The World Of Health Series.
Prod-INFORP Dist-SF 1975

Physical Fitness - The New Perspective C 10 MIN
16MM FILM, 3/4 OR 1/2 IN VIDEO A
Describes the adverse effects that sedentary lifestyles can have on physical fitness. Shows the positive aspects of being physically fit, and describes the simple ways to increase daily activity. Presented in animated cartoon format.
Prod-PRORE Dist-PRORE

Physical Fitness And Exercise C 30 MIN
3/4 OR 1/2 INCH VIDEO CASSETTE
Features aerobics expert Dr Kenneth Cooper and members of the Dallas Cowboys football team in a close-up look at exercise and fitness. Narrated by Ossie Davis.
From The Here's To Your Health Series.
LC NO. 82-706499
Prod-KERA Dist-PBS 1979

Physical Fitness And Exercise C 30 MIN
3/4 OR 1/2 INCH VIDEO CASSETTE
See series title for descriptive statement.
From The Here's To Your Health Series.
Prod-PBS Dist-DELTAK

Physical Fitness And Good Health C 10 MIN
16MM FILM, 3/4 OR 1/2 IN VIDEO P-H
Discusses the importance of keeping the body physically fit and stresses the value of exercise to keep the heart and other muscles and organs functioning properly.
From The Triangle Of Health Series.
Prod-UPJOHN Dist-WDEMCO 1969

Physical Fitness And Good Health (Arabic) C 10 MIN
16MM FILM, 3/4 OR 1/2 IN VIDEO I-H
Stresses the effect of physical fitness on social and mental health. Speaks on exercise, rest and proper diet.
From The Triangle Of Health (Arabic) Series.
Prod-WDEMCO Dist-WDEMCO 1969

Physical Fitness And Good Health (French) C 10 MIN
16MM FILM, 3/4 OR 1/2 IN VIDEO I-H
Stresses the effect of physical fitness on social and mental health. Speaks on exercise, rest and proper diet.
From The Triangle Of Health (French) Series.
Prod-WDEMCO Dist-WDEMCO 1969

Physical Fitness And Good Health (German) C 10 MIN
16MM FILM, 3/4 OR 1/2 IN VIDEO I-H
Stresses the effect of physical fitness on social and mental health. Speaks on exercise, rest and proper diet.
From The Triangle Of Health (German) Series.
Prod-WDEMCO Dist-WDEMCO 1969

Physical Fitness And Good Health (Hungarian) C 10 MIN
16MM FILM, 3/4 OR 1/2 IN VIDEO I-H
Stresses the effect of physical fitness on social and mental health. Speaks on exercise, rest and proper dict.
From The Triangle Of Health (Hungarian) Series.
Prod-WDEMCO Dist-WDEMCO 1969

Physical Fitness And Good Health (Spanish) C 10 MIN
16MM FILM, 3/4 OR 1/2 IN VIDEO I-H
Stresses the effect of physical fitness on social and mental health. Speaks on exercise, rest and proper diet.
From The Triangle Of Health (Spanish) Series.
Prod-WDEMCO Dist-WDEMCO 1969

Physical Fitness And Good Health (Swedish) C 10 MIN
16MM FILM, 3/4 OR 1/2 IN VIDEO I-H
Stresses the effect of physical fitness on social and mental health. Speaks on exercise, rest and proper diet.
From The Triangle Of Health (Swedish) Series.
Prod-WDEMCO Dist-WDEMCO 1969

Physical Fitness And Good Health (Thai) C 10 MIN
16MM FILM, 3/4 OR 1/2 IN VIDEO I-H
Stresses the effect of physical fitness on social and mental health. Speaks on exercise, rest and proper diet.
Prod-WDEMCO Dist-WDEMCO 1969

Physical Fitness And Traffic Safety B 30 MIN
16MM FILM - 3/4 IN VIDEO C A
See series title for descriptive statement.
From The Sportsmanlike Driving Series.
Prod-AAAFTS Dist-GPITVL Prodn-SCETV

Physical Fitness For WAVES - Make-Up From The Neck Down B 20 MIN
16MM FILM OPTICAL SOUND
Presents a physical fitness program designed to persuade waves to exercise. Points out the value of sports but stresses the greater value of planned exercises and illustrates some of these exercises.
LC NO. FIE52-1092
Prod-USN Dist-USNAC 1944

Physical Fitness In The Later Years C 23 MIN
16MM FILM, 3/4 OR 1/2 IN VIDEO C A
Explains how exercise can help keep the body parts functioning, lessen pain and provide a feeling of well being. Describes different kinds of exercise programs, offers cautions, and suggests ways to motivate oneself.
From The Be Well - The Later Years Series.
LC NO. 83-706447
Prod-CF Dist-CF 1983

Physical Fitness Program For The United States Navy B 25 MIN
3/4 INCH VIDEO CASSETTE
Shows exercises given the naval trainee and correlates their value with varied duties he will be called upon to perform afloat.
Prod-USNAC Dist-USNAC 1972

Physical Fitness Training - Navy Standard Physical Fitness Test B 20 MIN
3/4 INCH VIDEO CASSETTE
Presents tests of strength, endurance, stamina and degree of agility, such as squat thrusts, sit-ups, push-ups, squat-jumps and pull-ups.
Prod-USNAC Dist-USNAC 1972

Physical Fitness—A Series
16MM FILM, 3/4 OR 1/2 IN VIDEO
Emphasizes the need for physical fitness, the pitfalls of contemporary living and how to overcome them.
Prod-JOU Dist-JOU

Physical Fitness 019 MIN
Superjock 016 MIN
Superjock Scales Down 015 MIN

Physical Form C 30 MIN
3/4 OR 1/2 INCH VIDEO CASSETTE
Discusses what letters should look like. Examines how letters show the corporate image.
From The Better Business Letters Series. Lesson I
Prod-TELSTR Dist-TELSTR

Physical Interpretation Of The K And B Formulas B 29 MIN
3/4 OR 1/2 INCH VIDEO CASSETTE
See series title for descriptive statement.
From The Nonlinear Vibrations Series.
Prod-MIOT Dist-MIOT

Physical Limitations C 10 MIN
16MM FILM, 3/4 OR 1/2 IN VIDEO
Shows how awareness of physical limitations helps prevent accidents and errors in judgment.
From The Safety And You Series.
Prod-FILCOM Dist-FILCOM

Physical Management Of Psychiatric Patients C 27 MIN
16MM FILM, 3/4 OR 1/2 IN VIDEO
Shows how to manage the disturbed patient when psychological techniques fail. Emphasizes the need for practice to assure the safety of both patient and staff.
Prod-USVA Dist-USNAC

Physical Metallurgy - Structure And Properties C 50 MIN
3/4 OR 1/2 INCH VIDEO CASSETTE PRO
Describes the structure and properties of physical metallurgy. Demonstrates tensile, hardness, impact and fatigue tests.
From The Heat Treatment - Metallurgy And Application Series.
Prod-AMCEE Dist-AMCEE

Physical Properties And Molecular Structure C 10 MIN
3/4 INCH VIDEO CASSETTE
Introduces hydrogen bonding and its effects on solubility, melting point and boiling point. Demonstrates measurement techniques to determine melting and boiling points.
From The Chemistry Videotape Series.
Prod-UMITV Dist-UMITV

Physical Rehabilitation C 28 MIN
3/4 OR 1/2 INCH VIDEO CASSETTE H-C A
Describes how individuals handicapped by disease or accident are taught to perform the activities of daily living. Describes techniques of physical therapy and occupational therapy. Shows methods of ambulation for severely disabled paraplegics.
Prod-FO Dist-FO

Physical Respiratory Therapy—A Series C A
Provides professional training in the fundamentals of chest physiotherapy.
Prod-VISCI Dist-TEF

Breathing Exercises - How And Why 013 MIN
Introduction To Chest Physiotherapy 020 MIN
Pediatric Physiotherapy 014 MIN
Physical Examination Of The Chest 020 MIN
Postural Drainage And Percussion 016 MIN

Physical Science (Spanish)—A Series
16MM FILM, 3/4 OR 1/2 IN VIDEO H-C A
Explores the nature of fundamental scientific laws and describes their effect on the universe. Introduces stellar and nuclear evolution, the composition of matter and atomic and molecular movement.
Prod-MGHT Dist-MGHT

El Origen De Los Elementos 18 MIN
La Energia 27 MIN
La Naturalez De La Materia 24 MIN
Los Estados De La Materia 18 MIN

Physical Science - Chemical Energy C 17 MIN
16MM FILM, 3/4 OR 1/2 IN VIDEO I-J
Considers the combining and separation of atoms in molecules that constitute chemical change and discusses how this differs from physical change. Shows means of causing chemical change, particularly by heat energy. Explains the importance of oxidation, providing examples ranging from explosive energy release to slow change in the human body.
Prod-CF Dist-CF 1984

Physical Science - Electrical Energy C 14 MIN
16MM FILM, 3/4 OR 1/2 IN VIDEO I-J
Describes electrons and protons, discusses how an imbalance creates an electric charge, and shows how this can create static electricity or a flow of electrons in a battery. Demonstrates induction of a current with coil and how an electro-magnet spinning between two magnets causes the current to alternate.
Prod-CF Dist-CF 1985

Physical Science - Energy At Work C 13 MIN
16MM FILM, 3/4 OR 1/2 IN VIDEO J-H
Introduces different kinds of energy, including mechanical, heat, light, chemical, electrical and nuclear. Explains concepts of input and output of energy.
LC NO. 83-707021
Prod-CF Dist-CF 1983

Physical Science - Heat Energy C 16 MIN
16MM FILM, 3/4 OR 1/2 IN VIDEO J-H
Introduces heat energy and the way it is used. Describes changes in molecular motion when heat is added and demonstrates expansion in solids, liquids and gases when heated. Explains the difference between heat and temperature and ways of measuring temperature. Gives examples of the way heat energy is used.
LC NO. 83-707022
Prod-CF Dist-CF 1983

Physical Science - Light Energy C 14 MIN
16MM FILM, 3/4 OR 1/2 IN VIDEO I-J
Explains that light sources occur by the transfers of other forms of energy into light energy. Discusses the theory of photons. Considers the wavelengths of light, their place in the electromagnetic spectrum, and various examples of the wave-particle characteristics of light.
Prod-CF Dist-CF 1985

Physical Science - Mechanical Energy C 15 MIN
16MM FILM, 3/4 OR 1/2 IN VIDEO I-J
Describes how mechanical energy exerts a force in solid, liquid and gas states. Explains potential and kinetic energy and how machines provide mechanical energy.
LC NO. 84-706129
Prod-CF Dist-CF 1984

Physical Science Film—A Series
16MM FILM, 3/4 OR 1/2 IN VIDEO C A
Prod-CRMP Dist-CRMP 1973

Energy - A Conversation 27 MIN
Nature Of Matter, The - An Atomic View 23 MIN
Origin Of The Elements, The 18 MIN
States Of Matter, The 18 MIN

Physical Science Learning Lab—A Series
16MM FILM, 3/4 OR 1/2 IN VIDEO P-I
Offers basic information on physical science.
Prod-BARR Dist-BARR 1981

Energy Does Work 014 MIN
Magnetism And Fields Of Force 014 MIN
Matter Changes 014 MIN
Matter Is Everything 012 MIN

Physical Science—A Series C
Features Forest D Etheredge, vice president of Rock Valley College in Rockford, Illinois, discussing the nonliving portion of the universe. Emphasizes orderly change as characteristic of the universe, the antiquity of the earth, the vast size of the universe and the relativity of motion. Draws from Allen and Ordway's PHYSICAL SCIENCE to distinguish between observed or experimental fact and opinion. (Broadcast quality)
Prod-CHITVC Dist-GPITVL Prodn-WTTWTV

Age Of The Earth And The Principles Of
Air Masses And Fronts 45 MIN
Atmospheric Pressure And Circulation 45 MIN
Celestial Sphere 45 MIN
Diastrophism 45 MIN
Earth's Atmosphere, The 45 MIN

Free-Falling Objects And Projectiles 45 MIN
Geologic History Of North America 45 MIN
Geologic Work Of Glaciers 45 MIN
Geologic Work Of Ground Water 45 MIN
Geologic Work Of Streams 45 MIN
Gravitation 45 MIN
Heliocentric And Geocentric Concepts 45 MIN
Highs, Lows And Weather Prediction 45 MIN
Introduction And Scientific Method 45 MIN
Laws Of Motion 45 MIN
Minerals And Rocks 45 MIN
Moon, The 45 MIN
Motion 45 MIN
Oceans And Continents 45 MIN
Origin Of The Solar System 45 MIN
Rock Cycle 45 MIN
Seasons - Latitude And Longitude 45 MIN
Size, Shape And Motions Of The Earth 45 MIN
Space Travel 45 MIN
Sun, Stars And Planets, The 45 MIN
Time And The Calendar 45 MIN
Volcanism 45 MIN
Weathering And Mass-Wasting 45 MIN
Work And Energy 45 MIN

Physical Science—A Series
16MM FILM, 3/4 OR 1/2 IN VIDEO I-H
Shows how science has created our technological world and how the same kinds of transfers and transformations of energy are at work in the biology of living things.
Prod-CORF Dist-CORF 1985

Electric Currents And Circuits 017 MIN
Electricity And Magnetism 017 MIN
Heat And Energy Transfer 013 MIN
Heat, Temperature And The Properties Of Matter 017 MIN
Static And Current Electricity 016 MIN

Physical Security Surveys B 30 MIN
16MM FILM, 3/4 OR 1/2 IN VIDEO
Describes the purpose, fundamentals and procedures for a physical security survey of a military installation to uncover and correct security weakness.
LC NO. 82-707243
Prod-USA Dist-USNAC 1964

Physical Security, Pt 10 - Identification And Control C 22 MIN
16MM FILM, 3/4 OR 1/2 IN VIDEO
Discusses purpose and techniques of ID and control procedures. Includes badges, access lists, duress codes and new equipment.
LC NO. 82-707242
Prod-USA Dist-USNAC 1971

Physical Set-Up Of The Letter C 35 MIN
3/4 OR 1/2 INCH VIDEO CASSETTE
See series title for descriptive statement.
From The Better Business Letters Series.
Prod-TELSTR Dist-DELTAK

Physical Shock - The Third Fundamental C 9 MIN
3/4 INCH VIDEO CASSETTE
Describes characteristics of shock and the shock cycle. Discusses the causes, symptoms and changes associated with shock. Focuses on the treatment of shock and points out that it is a reaction that follows almost all serious injuries. Issued in 1974 as a motion picture.
From The First Aid Series.
LC NO. 79-707958
Prod-USMESA Dist-USNAC 1979

Physical Signs And Effects OF Venereal Diseases C 28 MIN
16MM FILM, 3/4 OR 1/2 IN VIDEO
Discusses several types of venereal diseases and emphasizes the importance of immediate medical attention.
From The Inner Woman Series.
Prod-WXYZTV Dist-CRMP 1977

Physical Therapy For Suppurative Lung Disease Patients C 42 MIN
3/4 INCH VIDEO CASSETTE PRO
Explains the physical therapist's role in the treatment of suppurative pulmonary problems. Discusses therapeutic techniques.
LC NO. 80-706785
Prod-VAHSL Dist-USNAC 1980

Physical Therapy In The Treatment Of Parkinsonism C 15 MIN
16MM FILM OPTICAL SOUND
Presents a group physical therapy approach to the treatment of Parkinsonism which stresses alternating reciprocal movements of the limbs and trunk. Shows that the result of therapy is the re-establishment and retention of normal patterns by these patients.
LC NO. 75-702335
Prod-EATONL Dist-EATONL 1971

Physical Therapy In The Treatment Of The Adult Hemiplegic Patient C 26 MIN
16MM FILM OPTICAL SOUND
Demonstrates physical therapy in the treatment of the adult hemiplegic patient, showing Bobath treatmenttechniques applied to a patient in the following positions--supine, prone, sitting, kneeling, standing and walking.
LC NO. FIE67-84
Prod-USA Dist-USNAC 1962

Physical Therapy Management Of A Bilateral Amputee C 33 MIN
16MM FILM OPTICAL SOUND
Discusses the early management of above-knee and below-knee unilateral amputees, as well as rehabilitation of the bilateral amputee. Shows fitting of and training with protheses.
LC NO. 74-706176
Prod-USA Dist-USNAC 1964

Physical Therapy Management Of Above-Knee And Below-Knee Amputees C 23 MIN
16MM FILM, 3/4 OR 1/2 IN VIDEO
Highlights the major goals that the physical therapist wants the patient to achieve before being discharged from physical therapy care, including stump hygiene, bandaging, crutch walking, adequate range of motion, applying the prosthesis, functional strength, and correct gait ambulation. Details the steps involved in preprosthetic and prosthetic treatment.
Prod-WRAIR Dist-USNAC 1978

Physical Therapy Management Of The Patient With Quadriplegia, Pt 1 C 30 MIN
3/4 INCH VIDEO CASSETTE PRO
Presents therapeutic exercise programs for treating quadriplegia. Discusses treatment goals and demonstrates exercise regimes. Designed for therapists, students, patients and their families.
Prod-RICHGO Dist-RICHGO

Physical Therapy Management Of The Pre- And Postoperative Open Heart Patient C 14 MIN
16MM FILM - 3/4 IN VIDEO PRO
Shows breathing exercises given to patients before and after heart operations.
Prod-USPHS Dist-USNAC 1978

Physical Therapy Techniques For Bulbar Involvement C 26 MIN
16MM FILM OPTICAL SOUND
Discusses the anatomy of the jaw and bulbar region and points out malfunction caused by paralysis of the muscles involved. Offers techniques for the functional training of the muscles of the jaw, tongue, pharynx and larynx.
Prod-RLAH Dist-RLAH

Physical Training In Sweden B 10 MIN
16MM FILM OPTICAL SOUND
Shows how the Swedes take an interest in every aspect of physical education.
Prod-ASI Dist-AUDPLN

Physical World Of A Machine, The C 13 MIN
16MM FILM, 3/4 OR 1/2 IN VIDEO IND
Examines physics of machinery. Includes force, pound, resistance, transmission of energy and inefficiency.
From The Industrial Hydraulic Technology Series. Chapter 1
Prod-TAT Dist-TAT

Physical, The C 25 MIN
3/4 OR 1/2 INCH VIDEO CASSETTE
Shows host Mario Machado undergoing a complete physical examination, during which viewers learn exactly what the doctor is looking for during the exam. Discusses symptoms of major diseases and preventive medicine 'tips' during the workup.
Prod-TRAINX Dist-TRAINX

Physically Handicapped And Health Impaired Child In The Regular Classroom, The C 30 MIN
3/4 OR 1/2 INCH VIDEO CASSETTE T
Considers selected physical conditions which may require special attention in the regular classroom. Discusses possible environmental and material accommodations along with guidelines for promoting acceptance in the classroom.
From The Promises To Keep Series. Module 5
Prod-VPISU Dist-LUF 1979

Physically Handicapped Child In Foster Care C 30 MIN
3/4 OR 1/2 INCH VIDEO CASSETTE
Looks at how one family has met the challenge of caring for three physically handicapped foster children.
Prod-MTI Dist-MTI 1984

Physician As A Community Consultant, The C 30 MIN
3/4 OR 1/2 INCH VIDEO CASSETTE PRO
Stimulates discussion among doctors and medical students on the subject of community consultation.
Prod-HSCIC Dist-HSCIC 1980

Physician Assistant, The - A Rural Profile C 8 MIN
3/4 OR 1/2 INCH VIDEO CASSETTE
Focuses on a physician assistant working in the sparsely populated community of Hardin, Illinois.
LC NO. 80-706786
Prod-VAHSL Dist-USNAC 1980

Physician Assistant, The - An Urban Profile C 9 MIN
3/4 OR 1/2 INCH VIDEO CASSETTE
Offers a profile of a physician assistant in an urban, inner-city environment. Excerpted from the videorecording issued in 1977 under the title The Physician Assistant, New Member Of The Health Care Team.
LC NO. 80-707112
Prod-VAHSL Dist-USNAC 1980

Physician Assistant, The - New Member Of The Health Care Team C 21 MIN
3/4 INCH VIDEO CASSETTE
Describes the historical background, role, education and utilization of the physician's assistant.
LC NO. 79-707300
Prod-VAHSL Dist-USNAC 1977

Physician Surplus C 22 MIN
3/4 OR 1/2 INCH VIDEO CASSETTE PRO
Considers the consequences on health care and nursing with regard to an impending surplus of doctors.
From The Future Of Nursing Series.
Prod-HSCIC Dist-HSCIC 1985

Physician-Administrator Pressure Points C 25 MIN
3/4 OR 1/2 INCH VIDEO CASSETTE
Examines sensitive and important aspects of hospital administration. Answers hard-hitting questions by a sequence of vignettes.
Prod-TEACHM Dist-TEACHM

Physicists, The - Playing Dice With The Universe C 22 MIN
16MM FILM, 3/4 OR 1/2 IN VIDEO
Shows how physicists have changed man's concepts of time, matter and space. Focuses attention on research in deep space and inquiries into the atom.
Prod-DOCUA Dist-CNEMAG

Physics And Chemistry Of Water C 21 MIN
16MM FILM, 3/4 OR 1/2 IN VIDEO H-C A
Shows how the nature of the water molecule determines the physical properties of water. Demonstrates that life is dependent on some of the unusual properties of water--its slow rate of evaporation, its high surface tension, its powers of solution and its high fluid density.
Prod-LEVER Dist-PHENIX Prodn-WWP 1967

Physics In Action—A Series
J-C
Illustrates the basic principles of physics.
Prod-LUF Dist-LUF

Electromagnetic Spectrum, The 018 MIN
Electrostatics, Pt 1 018 MIN
Electrostatics, Pt 2 018 MIN
Expansion Of Metals, The 018 MIN
Generation Of Electricity, Pt 1, The 018 MIN
Generation Of Electricity, Pt 2, The 018 MIN
Laws Of Motion, Pt 1, The 018 MIN
Laws Of Motion, Pt 2, The 018 MIN
Radioactivity 018 MIN

Physics Of Diving C 29 MIN
2 INCH VIDEOTAPE
See series title for descriptive statement.
From The Observing Eye Series.
Prod-WGBHTV Dist-PUBTEL

Physics Of GaAs And Heterojunction Electronic Devices, Part I—A Series
PRO
Focuses on GaAs and heterojunction device physics and additional design freedom for optimization of semiconductor devices. Covers application of design principles to conventional device structures and ballistic transport devices for ultra-high-speed electronics.
Prod-STITV Dist-AMCEE

Physics Of GaAs And Heterojunction Electronic Devices, Part II—A Series
PRO
Focuses on quantum wells where dimensions approach the wavelenth of an electron in the solid. Notes under such conditions that quantum size effects tunneling and hot electron phenomena. Examines lasers, photodetectors, CCDs and entirely new types of solid state devices.
Prod-STITV Dist-AMCEE

Physiologic Changes In Pregnancy C
3/4 OR 1/2 INCH VIDEO CASSETTE PRO
See series title for descriptive statement.
From The Care Of The Pregnant Patient Series.
Prod-OMNIED Dist-OMNIED

Physiologic Manifestations Of Stress C 24 MIN
3/4 INCH VIDEO CASSETTE PRO
Discusses the body's reaction to stressful situations. Describes nursing interventions designed to assist the patient's efforts to resist or adapt to stress.
From The Stress In Critical Illness Series. Module 1
LC NO. 80-707621
Prod-BRA Dist-BRA 1980

Physiologic Modulation Of Pain C 28 MIN
3/4 INCH VIDEO CASSETTE PRO
See series title for descriptive statement.
From The Management Of Pain Series. Module 4
LC NO. 80-707393
Prod-BRA Dist-BRA 1980

Physiological And Behavioral Effects Of Noise C 8 MIN
16MM FILM OPTICAL SOUND H-C A
Observes the behavior and cortisol levels of 12 rhesus monkeys who were exposed to loud, man-made noises for periods of one, three and five hours. Shows the aftereffects of noise on the monkeys.
LC NO. 75-700199
Prod-WIRPRC Dist-PSUPCR 1974

Physiological And Clinical Aspects Of Cardiac Auscultation—A Series
PRO
Discusses the physiological and clinical aspects of cardiac auscultation.
Prod-MEDIC Dist-LIP 1976

Idiopathic Hypertrophic Sub-Aortic Stenosis 007 MIN
Subvalvular Aortic Stenosis 006 MIN
Supravalvular Aortic Stenosis 007 MIN

Physiological And Emotional Aspects Of Pain C 16 MIN
16MM FILM OPTICAL SOUND
Portrays the characteristics of pain and shows the different reactions of individuals to its discomfort. Defines the four types of pain, the causes and physiological basis. Emphasizes the role of the nurse in responding to the patient in pain.
From The Patient As A Person Series.
LC NO. 73-712974
Prod-TRNAID Dist-TRNAID 1970

Physiological Aspects Of Sex C 30 MIN
3/4 OR 1/2 INCH VIDEO CASSETTE C A
Investigates the biological process of sex. Describes functions of the male and female reproductive organs. Discusses causes and treatment of infertility in men and women.
From The Family Portrait - A Study Of Contemporary Lifestyles Series. Lesson 5
Prod-SCCON Dist-CDTEL

Physiological Limitations C 11 MIN
16MM FILM, 3/4 OR 1/2 IN VIDEO
Examines the delicate balance human beings must maintain between their physical, biochemical and emotional make-up. Demonstrates how external and internal factors can affect this balance.
From The Safety And You Series.
Prod-FILCOM Dist-FILCOM

Physiological Responses Of The Sexually Stimulated Female In The Laboratory C 16 MIN
3/4 OR 1/2 INCH VIDEO CASSETTE
Provides observations of the physiological responses of the sexually stimulated female in the laboratory. Illustrates the vagina and external genitalia in orgasmic stages.
Prod-MMRC Dist-MMRC

Physiological Responses Of The Sexually Stimulated Male In The Laboratory C 16 MIN
3/4 OR 1/2 INCH VIDEO CASSETTE
Features x-ray cinematography of physiological responses of the sexually stimulated male in the laboratory. Presented in a non-threatening, intellectual and clinical manner. Allows sex to be discussed in a comfortable nonjudgmental way.
Prod-MMRC Dist-MMRC

Physiology Of Conception B 29 MIN
16MM FILM OPTICAL SOUND C A
Discusses physiology of conception, diagnosis and timing of ovulation, sperm migration, fertilization, early development of the fertilitzed ovum, infertility and female physiology and anatomy. Features Dr J Robert Bragonier and Leta Powell Drake.
From The Nine To Get Ready Series. No. 2
LC NO. 76-704215
Prod-KUONTV Dist-UNEBR 1965

Physiology Of Conception C 29 MIN
2 INCH VIDEOTAPE
See series title for descriptive statement.
From The Nine To Get Ready Series.
Prod-NETCHE Dist-PUBTEL

Physiology Of Food C 15 MIN
16MM FILM OPTICAL SOUND
Explains human food requirements and how these requirements can be met by natural sources.
LC NO. 74-706515
Prod-USN Dist-USNAC 1973

Physiology Of Myocardial Ischemia - Angina Pectoris C 51 MIN
3/4 OR 1/2 INCH VIDEO CASSETTE PRO
Shows how to apply knowledge of basic cardiovascular physiology in the diagnosis and treatment of ischemic heart disease.
Prod-HSCIC Dist-HSCIC 1982

Physiology Of Neuromuscular Blocking Agents The (2nd Ed) C 18 MIN
3/4 OR 1/2 INCH VIDEO CASSETTE PRO
Describes the physiology of the transmission of motor nerve impulses to skeletal muscle. Discusses the types of neuromuscular blockade and their electrophysiologic characteristics, as well as the pharmacology of drugs used to reverse neuromuscular blockade.
From The Anesthesiology Clerkship Series.
Prod-UMICHM Dist-UMICHM 1982

Physiology Of Occlusion, The C 30 MIN
16MM FILM OPTICAL SOUND C
Shows physiology examination techniques, including cineflouroscopy of speech and swallowing, gross dissection of the temporomandibular joint, palpation of muscles for kiagnostic purposes and examinations of occlusion (clinically and pantographyically) before and after equilibration.
LC NO. 72-700940
Prod-UIOWA Dist-UIOWA 1972

Physiology Of Pregnancy And Labor B 29 MIN
16MM FILM OPTICAL SOUND C A
Explains the physiology of pregnancy and labor, discussing the vital placenta, cardiovascular physiology, respiratory physiology, causes of onset of labor and physiology of labor and effects on the fetus. Features Dr J Robert Bragonier and Leta Powell Drake.
From The Nine To Get Ready Series. No. 5
LC NO. 70-704216
Prod-KUONTV Dist-UNEBR 1965

Physiology Of Pregnancy And Labor C 29 MIN
2 INCH VIDEOTAPE
See series title for descriptive statement.
From The Nine To Get Ready Series.
Prod-NETCHE Dist-PUBTEL

Physiology Of The Ear C 49 MIN
3/4 OR 1/2 INCH VIDEO CASSETTE PRO
Presents the physiology of the ear. Discusses early experiments and correlation of physiology to clinical conditions.
Prod-HOUSEI Dist-HOUSEI

Physiology Of The Larynx Under Daily Stress C 23 MIN
16MM FILM OPTICAL SOUND
Explores complexity of laryngeal function in everyday life. Relates physiological changes to clinical reality, vibratory function, biphasic pattern of laryngeal vibrations, effect of intensity, air pressure on components of vibratory cycle and the significance of secondary waves.
From The Larnyx And Voice Series.
Prod-ILAVD Dist-ILAVD 1958

Physiology—A Series
16MM FILM, 3/4 OR 1/2 IN VIDEO C A
Looks at various aspects of animal and human physiology, including muscles, blood pressure and nerves.
Prod-WILEYJ Dist-MEDIAG 1972

Arterial Blood Pressure Regulation	019 MIN
Cochlear Nerve, The - Recording With	021 MIN
Microelectrodes In Muscle	019 MIN
Milk Ejection Reflex, The	021 MIN
Muscle Spindle, The	019 MIN
What Makes Muscles Pull - The Structural	009 MIN

Ph7-68 C Catalase Test For Mycobacterium Tuberculosis C 5 MIN
3/4 INCH VIDEO CASSETTE
Presents step-by-step procedures for performing a 68 degree C catalase test for mycobacterium tuberculosis, pointing out necessary precautions.
LC NO. 80-706132
Prod-CFDISC Dist-USNAC 1978

Piaget On Piaget C 42 MIN
16MM FILM OPTICAL SOUND
Presents Jean Piaget, who discusses his theories on child development and his interpretations of experiments involving Swiss children.
LC NO. 78-701564
Prod-YUMDS Dist-YUMDS 1978

Piaget On Piaget (French) C 42 MIN
16MM FILM OPTICAL SOUND
Presents Jean Piaget, who discusses his theories on child development and his interpretations of experiments involving Swiss children.
LC NO. 78-701564
Prod-YUMDS Dist-YUMDS 1978

Piaget's Development Theory—A Series

Clarifies and illustrates the theories of Developmental Psychologist, Jean Piaget, by presenting children and adults responding to tasks he designed.
Prod-DAVFMS Dist-DAVFMS

Classification	016 MIN
Conservation	029 MIN
Formal Reasoning Patterns	032 MIN
Growth Of Intelligence In The Preschool Years	031 MIN
Jean Piaget - Memory And Intelligence	044 MIN
Morality - The Process Of Moral Development	028 MIN

Pianissimo C 8 MIN
16MM FILM OPTICAL SOUND H-C A
Demonstrates abstractions of color and patterns of sounds, with a piano and an old phonograph.
Prod-GROVE Dist-GROVE 1963

Piano Movers, The C 7 MIN
16MM FILM OPTICAL SOUND
Presents a musical joke in which a young girl begins to play a Mozart exercise and in the course of a few minutes her piano is moved out of the house and replaced by a new one. Contrasts the beauty of the music with the muscle and sweat that accompany the work that goes into moving a heavy piano.
Prod-NFBC Dist-VIEWFI

Piano Show, The C 30 MIN
3/4 OR 1/2 INCH VIDEO CASSETTE P-I
Features three young pianists of different ages who are in different stages of musical proficiency and who excel in different musical styles. Presents a fourth pianist, Tony Barone, who provides an example of what discipline and hard work can accomplish. Hosted by Rheda Becker.
From The Musical Encounter Series.
Prod-MDCPB Dist-GPITVL 1983

Piano, The C 27 MIN
16MM FILM, 3/4 OR 1/2 IN VIDEO
Looks into the music created by and the history of the piano, including its evolution since the 18th century. Discusses how it is constructed and the physics of its sound patterns.
From The Nature Of Things Series.
LC NO. 84-706188
Prod-CANBC Dist-FLMLIB 1982

Picasso - A Painter's Diary, Pt 1 - The Formative Years C 35 MIN
16MM FILM, 3/4 OR 1/2 IN VIDEO H-C A
Re-creates the times, places, experiences and personalities that shaped Pablo Picasso's early years.
LC NO. 81-706798
Prod-WNETTV Dist-CORF 1981

Picasso - A Painter's Diary, Pt 2 - From Cubism To Guernica C 35 MIN
16MM FILM, 3/4 OR 1/2 IN VIDEO H-C A
Examines Pablo Picasso's life and work during his cubist phase, including the creation of the painting entitled Guernica. Uses rare film sequences, unpublished photographs and interviews with friends and art historians to capture the artist's outlook during this period.
LC NO. 81-706799
Prod-WNETTV Dist-CORF 1981

Picasso - A Painter's Diary, Pt 3 - A Unity Of Variety C 21 MIN
16MM FILM, 3/4 OR 1/2 IN VIDEO H-C A
Examines the variety and significance of works produced by Pablo Picasso, using the artist's own words and those of his family and friends. Includes period photographs and archival footage.
LC NO. 81-706800
Prod-WNETTV Dist-CORF 1981

Picasso - An Exhibition At Walker Art Center C 29 MIN
3/4 OR 1/2 INCH VIDEO CASSETTE
Features an exhibition at Minneapolis' Walker Art Center which contains over 160 works from the estate of artist and painter Pablo Picasso.
Prod-KTCATV Dist-PBS 1980

Picasso - Joie De Vivre (1881-1976) C 13 MIN
16MM FILM OPTICAL SOUND
Shows how the town of Antibes, on France's Riviera, offered the aging Picasso their ancient castle for a museum and he responded by filling the rooms with vibrant murals and bright pottery.
Prod-ROLAND Dist-ROLAND

Picasso - Romancero Du Picador (1881-1976) C 13 MIN
16MM FILM OPTICAL SOUND
Shows how Picasso, in swift sketches, makes the despised picador on his padded horse into a true knight, faithful to his duty and alone in his pleasures as he weakens the bull with his harsh lance.
Prod-ROLAND Dist-ROLAND

Picasso - The Saltimbanques C 30 MIN
16MM FILM OPTICAL SOUND
Presents paintings of circus people painted by Pablo Picasso during his Rose Period. Traces the process through which E A Carmean Jr, curator of twentieth century art at the National Art Gallery and Ann Hoenigswald of the Gallery's conservation laboratory, discovered earlier compositions beneath the surface of Picasso's major painting Family Of Saltimbanques.
Prod-USNGA Dist-USNGA

Picasso And The Circus C 7 MIN
16MM FILM OPTICAL SOUND
Shows a young girl visiting an exhibit of Picasso's paintings of jugglers, bareback riders, harlequins and clowns. Reveals the exhibit as it gradually gives way to scenes of a Parisian circus the kind Picasso attended.
Prod-USNGA Dist-USNGA

Picasso Is 90 C 51 MIN
16MM FILM, 3/4 OR 1/2 IN VIDEO H-C A
Traces the life of Picasso from childhood to old age, with a retrospective of his paintings and sculptures.
Prod-CBSNEW Dist-CAROUF

Picasso Is 90 (Captioned) C 51 MIN
16MM FILM, 3/4 OR 1/2 IN VIDEO
Traces the highlights of the life and work of Picasso, and presents comments of personal friends, one of Picasso's sons and one of his ex-wives. Includes film clips showing scenes of Gertrude Stein, Georges Braque, the Spanish Civil War, the bombing of Guernica and Russian communists applauding the political sympathies of Picasso.
Prod-CBSNEW Dist-CAROUF 1971

Picasso, Artist Of The Century C 54 MIN
16MM FILM OPTICAL SOUND H-C A
Examines the artwork of Pablo Picasso through study and analysis of color reproductions of his paintings. Covers a full range of his paintings, places where he lived while producing them and some photographs of the artist at work and recreation. Made in France.
LC NO. 76-701259
Prod-BBCTV Dist-FI Prodn-FLMMAR 1976

Picasso, Artist Of The Century, Pt 1 - Picasso, 1900 To Cubism C 12 MIN
16MM FILM OPTICAL SOUND H-C A
Examines the artwork of Pablo Picasso through study and analysis of color reproductions of his paintings. Covers a full range of his paintings, places where he lived while producing them and some photographs of the artist at work and recreation. Made in France.
LC NO. 76-701259
Prod-MACM Dist-FI Prodn-FLMMAR 1976

Picasso, Artist Of The Century, Pt 2 - Picasso, Volcanic Thirties C 17 MIN
16MM FILM OPTICAL SOUND H-C A
Examines the artwork of Pablo Picasso through study and analysis of color reproductions of his paintings. Covers a full range of his paintings, places where he lived while producing them and some photographs of the artist at work and recreation. Made in France.
LC NO. 76-701259
Prod-MACM Dist-FI Prodn-FLMMAR 1976

Picasso, Artist Of The Century, Pt 3 - Picasso, 1940's And After C 25 MIN
16MM FILM OPTICAL SOUND H-C A
Examines the artwork of Pablo Picasso through study and analysis of color reproductions of his paintings. Covers a full range of his paintings, places where he lived while producing them and some photographs of the artist at work and recreation. Made in France.
LC NO. 76-701259
Prod-MACM Dist-FI Prodn-FLMMAR 1976

Piccolo Saxo And Company C 10 MIN
16MM FILM OPTICAL SOUND K-I
Uses animation to describe each instrument of a symphony orchestra as a member of a family. Each gives a solo so that the listener can identify the sound with the instrument. Concludes with live symphony orchestra music, with each instrumental group contributing to the music being played.
LC NO. 71-701331
Prod-MLA Dist-MLA 1967

Pick A Pumpkin C 19 MIN
3/4 OR 1/2 INCH VIDEO CASSETTE P-I
Discusses the concept of loud and soft in music. Introduces simple percussion instruments.
From The USS Rhythm Series.
Prod-ARKETV Dist-AITECH 1977

Pick And Choose, Pt 1 C 15 MIN
3/4 OR 1/2 INCH VIDEO CASSETTE I-H A
Shows that good nutrition can be fun as well as necessary. Animated characters and live people tell the audience that they should pick and choose what they eat to help make their daily lives better.
Prod-CUETV Dist-CUNIV 1978

Pick And Choose, Pt 2 C 15 MIN
3/4 OR 1/2 INCH VIDEO CASSETTE I-H A
Points out shopper strategy that results in getting the most food value for your money.
Prod-CUETV Dist-CUNIV 1978

Pick Me Up At Peggy Cove (French) C 26 MIN
16MM FILM, 3/4 OR 1/2 IN VIDEO I-J
A French language version of the film and videorecording Pick Me Up At Peggy Cove.
Prod-ATLAF Dist-BCNFL 1982

Pick Me Up At Peggy's Cove C 26 MIN
16MM FILM, 3/4 OR 1/2 IN VIDEO I-J
Dramatizes a young boy trying to cope with his father's desertion, and learning through a series of crises that he has a caring family and good friends who want to help him.
LC NO. 83-706714
Prod-ATLAF Dist-BCNFL 1982

Pick Of The Crop C 30 MIN
1/2 IN VIDEO CASSETTE BETA/VHS
Gives tips on making the most of the fall harvest. Presents the winner of The Fifth Annual Victory Garden Contest.
From The Victory Garden Series.
Prod-WGBHTV Dist-MTI

Pick The Winner C 30 MIN
1/2 IN VIDEO CASSETTE BETA/VHS
Reviews the choices for winner of The Victory Garden Contest.
From The Victory Garden Series.
Prod-WGBHTV Dist-MTI

Pick Up Your Feet - 'The Double Dutch Show' C 30 MIN
3/4 OR 1/2 INCH VIDEO CASSETTE
Covers the 'Double Dutch Champeenship Day' and the many groups of four as they compete for the championship in New York City's Lincoln Center. Depicts their skill at rope skipping and their enthusiasm.
Prod-EAI Dist-EAI

Pick Your Pad C 20 MIN
3/4 INCH VIDEO CASSETTE J-H
Explains how to select living quarters according to needs, desires and ability to pay.
From The Dollar Data Series.
LC NO. 81-707362
Prod-WHROTV Dist-GPITVL 1974

Pick Your Safety Target B
16MM FILM OPTICAL SOUND
Shows foremen how to use accident statistics for accident prevention.
Prod-NSC Dist-NSC

Pick-In By The River B 59 MIN
2 INCH VIDEOTAPE
Captures roving troubadours and provides glimpses of history. Features John Rippey, president of the Brownville Historical Society, recounting the early days of the riverfront town when 13 saloons were supported by the brisk river trade. Includes musicians Ferlin Puny and the Blue Grass Boys, picker John Walker and fiddler Gene Wells.
Prod-NETCHE Dist-PUBTEL

Pick-Up Notes, Michael Row The Boat Ashore, On Top Of Old Smokey C 20 MIN
3/4 OR 1/2 INCH VIDEO CASSETTE J-H
See series title for descriptive statement.
From The Guitar, Guitar Series.
Prod-SCITV Dist-GPITVL 1981

Picker-Upper C 8 MIN
16MM FILM OPTICAL SOUND A
Presents Muppet characters in humorous vignettes which deal with the most trying parts of a business meeting. Includes stories dealing with introductions, announcements and the final speech.
From The Muppet Meeting Series.
Prod-HENASS Dist-HENASS 1981

Picking And Persuading A Jury—A Series
PRO
Features trial lawyers demonstrating voir dire and explaining their strategy and tactics. Includes communications experts, social scientists and linguists critiquing the demonstrations and advising viewers on alternative techniques.
Prod-ABACPE Dist-ABACPE 1980

Case And Community Analysis	045 MIN
Juror's Perspective, The	040 MIN
Language And Communication	030 MIN
Persuading The Jury	035 MIN
Selecting A Jury - A Critique	060 MIN
Selecting A Jury - A Demonstration	150 MIN

Picking It Up C 24 MIN
3/4 INCH VIDEO CASSETTE
See series title for descriptive statement.
From The Homemade American Music Series.
LC NO. 80-707483
Prod-AGINP Dist-LAWREN 1980

Picking The Blue Crab C 8 MIN
16MM FILM OPTICAL SOUND
Presents a description and demonstration of the correct procedures for removing the flake, lump (backfin) and claw meat of the blue crab. Explains that one of the reasons this delicacy is ignored is because of inadequate consumer instructional information on the correct procedures for picking crabs.
Prod-VIRGPI Dist-VIRGPI 1982

Picking The Next Move C 39 MIN
3/4 OR 1/2 INCH VIDEO CASSETTE C
See series title for descriptive statement.
From The Artificial Intelligence, Pt 1 - Fundamental Concepts Series.
Prod-MIOT Dist-AMCEE

Picking The Next Move C 45 MIN
3/4 OR 1/2 INCH VIDEO CASSETTE PRO
Features mini-max, combinatorial explosion, alpha-beta algorithm, heuristic pruning, look-ahead horizon.
From The Artificial Intelligence - Pt 1, Fundamental Concepts Series.
Prod-MIOT Dist-MIOT

Picking The Winner C 22 MIN
16MM FILM OPTICAL SOUND
Explains the development of corn hybrids by the world's largest corn breeding organization using the science of genetics.
Prod-MTP Dist-MTP

Picking Up The Pieces C 27 MIN
16MM FILM OPTICAL SOUND
Shows the contrasts inherent in the clash of North American Indian traditions and white culture.
LC NO. 76-700146
Prod-CCAAT Dist-CCAAT 1974

Picking Up The Pieces - One Woman Speaks C 29 MIN
3/4 OR 1/2 INCH VIDEO CASSETTE
Presents author Lynn Caine describing the slow and painful process she was forced to undergo after her husband's death.
From The Woman Series.
Prod-WNEDTV Dist-PBS

Picking Up The Tab C 30 MIN
3/4 OR 1/2 INCH VIDEO CASSETTE C A
See series title for descriptive statement.
From The Loosening The Grip Series.
Prod-UMA Dist-GPITVL 1980

Picking-Up And Edges B 29 MIN
2 INCH VIDEOTAPE
See series title for descriptive statement.
From The Busy Knitter I Series.
Prod-WMVSTV Dist-PUBTEL

Pickle For A Nickel, A C 6 MIN
16MM FILM, 3/4 OR 1/2 IN VIDEO P
Relates that a quiet man with a quiet parrot is dismayed when a boy teaches the bird to talk.
From The Golden Book Storytime Series.
Prod-MTI Dist-MTI 1977

Pickles And Relishes C 30 MIN
3/4 OR 1/2 INCH VIDEO CASSETTE
Explains how to can pickles and relishes.
From The Food Preservation Series.
Prod-UGATV Dist-MDCPB

Pickpocket (French) B 75 MIN
16MM FILM OPTICAL SOUND
Presents an analysis of a criminal's compulsions and conscience, showing the agitation and transformation of a pickpocket. Includes English subtitles.
LC NO. 77-701046
Prod-NYFLMS Dist-NYFLMS 1963

Picnic C 115 MIN
16MM FILM OPTICAL SOUND C A
Stars William Holden, Kim Novak and Rosalind Russell in the earthy story of a stranger in town and the havoc he creates in the lives of its people, especially its women, in one 24-hour visit.
Prod-CPC Dist-TIMLIF 1956

Picnic C 8 MIN
16MM FILM, 3/4 OR 1/2 IN VIDEO K-P
Introduces words and concepts to the youngest readers and pre-readers. Includes lively pictures and songs.
From The Starting To Read Series.
Prod-BURGHS Dist-AIMS 1972

Picnic On The River, A / Paddington Dines Out C 11 MIN
16MM FILM, 3/4 OR 1/2 IN VIDEO K-I
Discusses Paddington's adventures on the family picnic and at a fancy restaurant. Based on chapters one and seven of the book Paddington Helps Out by Michael Bond.
From The Paddington Bear, Series 2 Series.
LC NO. 80-707212
Prod-BONDM Dist-FLMFR Prodn-FILMF 1980

Picnic, The B 30 MIN
16MM FILM - 3/4 IN VIDEO
Documents the life of a Latin prisoner at Rahway State Prison in New Jersey. Explores prison life and life outside prison for the Latin population. Focuses on an hour-long picnic behind bars with family and friends.
Prod-BLKFMF Dist-BLKFMF

Pico-Union - Urban Community Development C 30 MIN
16MM FILM OPTICAL SOUND
Highlights citizen involvement activities in the Pico-union community in downtown Los Angeles.
LC NO. 72-702860
Prod-UCLA Dist-UCLA 1971

Pictorial Geography, A X 14 MIN
16MM FILM OPTICAL SOUND I-H T R
Shows the geographical importance of the land of Palestine in world history, and particularly in Biblical history. Depicts the natural geographical environment of our Bible.
From The Land Of The Bible Series.
Prod-FAMF Dist-FAMF 1960

Pictorial Views - Sketches C 10 MIN
1/2 IN VIDEO CASSETTE BETA/VHS IND
Demonstrates the two basic types of pictorial views used by a draftsman or person making a freehand sketch for illustrating an object for more clarification. Illustrates isometric and oblique views.
Prod-RMI Dist-RMI

Picture Book Park—A Series
P
Features storyteller Ann Mc Gregor, aided by resident poet Wise Willie the Owl reading various children's stories.
Prod-WVIZTV Dist-AITECH 1974

Alfred	15 MIN
Bedtime For Frances	15 MIN
Benjie	15 MIN
Folktales	15 MIN
Friends	15 MIN
From Japan	15 MIN
Happy Birthday	15 MIN
Lovable Lyle	15 MIN
Mice Are Nice	15 MIN
Mighty Hunters	15 MIN
Presents	15 MIN
Spotty	15 MIN
Sylvester And The Magic Pebble	15 MIN
That's Right, Edie	15 MIN
What Mary Jo Shared	15 MIN
Zoo	15 MIN

Picture Canada C 27 MIN
16MM FILM OPTICAL SOUND
Presents a look at the character and mood of Canada in the work of 15 photographers.
LC NO. 74-701641
Prod-KODAKC Dist-CTFL Prodn-CRAF 1973

Picture For Harold's Room, A C 7 MIN
16MM FILM, 3/4 OR 1/2 IN VIDEO K-P
A story about a boy who draws a picture on his wall, steps into his picture to draw the moon and begins to travel as a giant.
Prod-WWS Dist-WWS

Picture Gallery, The B 9 MIN
16MM FILM OPTICAL SOUND I-C A
Uses animation techniques in a fanciful exploration of the characteristics of ten famous paintings.
LC NO. 74-701510
Prod-CONNF Dist-CONNF 1973

Picture In Your Mind C 17 MIN
3/4 OR 1/2 INCH VIDEO CASSETTE J-C A
Explores the roots of prejudice in animation and delves into the anthropological and psychological origins of man's misconceptions of other men.
Prod-IFF Dist-IFF

Picture It With Words C 15 MIN
3/4 OR 1/2 INCH VIDEO CASSETTE I
Introduces the concept of imagery.
From The Tyger, Tyger Burning Bright Series.
Prod-CTI Dist-CTI

Picture Of Health, A C 20 MIN
16MM FILM, 3/4 OR 1/2 IN VIDEO
Emphasizes the need for people to take responsibility for their own health through behavior patterns which reduce risk of disease and increase self-esteem. Examines the health regimens of Dr Kenneth Cooper's aerobics program, Dr Nathan Pritikin's Longevity Center and Dr Bill Connors family nutrition project.
LC NO. 83-706792
Prod-MITCHG Dist-MTI 1983

Picture Of Health, The - Genetic Platforms C 13 MIN
16MM FILM, 3/4 OR 1/2 IN VIDEO J-C A
Discusses the role heredity plays in determining individual health.
From The Physical Fitness Series.
Prod-ALTSUL Dist-JOU 1979

Picture Story C 7 MIN
3/4 OR 1/2 INCH VIDEO CASSETTE
See series title for descriptive statement.
From The Gary Hill, Part 3 Series.
Prod-EAI Dist-EAI

Picture Trouble / Trouble On The Beach / A Visit To The Theatre C 16 MIN
16MM FILM, 3/4 OR 1/2 IN VIDEO K-I
Focuses on Paddington's encounter with a seaside photographer and his adventures at the beach. Describes his evening at the theater. Based on chapters six and seven of the book A Bear Called Paddington by Michael Bond.
From The Paddington Bear, Series 2 Series.
LC NO. 80-707213
Prod-BONDM Dist-FLMFR Prodn-FILMF 1980

Picture Wings Of Hawaii, The C 24 MIN
16MM FILM OPTICAL SOUND

Documents methods used by a research team to answer questions about the Picture Wing, a species of large Drosophila flies. Looks at the major factors contributing to the rapid increase in the number of species of the flies.
Prod-BBCTV Dist-OPENU 1982

Picture Wings Of Hawaii, The C 24 MIN
16MM FILM, 3/4 OR 1/2 IN VIDEO
Documents methods used by a research team to answer questions about the Picture Wing, a species of large Drosophila flies. Looks at the major factors contributing to the rapid increase in the number of species of the flies.
Prod-OPENU Dist-MEDIAG Prodn-BBCTV 1982

Picture Words C 20 MIN
2 INCH VIDEOTAPE P
See series title for descriptive statement.
From The Learning Our Language, Unit 1 - Listening Skills Series.
Prod-MPATI Dist-GPITVL

Picture Yourself A Marine C 12 MIN
16MM FILM OPTICAL SOUND H-C
Shows the many activities, opportunities and responsibilities of today's woman Marine. Compares these aspects of military life with civilian life.
LC NO. 76-702715
Prod-USMC Dist-USNAC 1975

Picture Yourself In St Petersburg C 22 MIN
16MM FILM OPTICAL SOUND
Features St Petersburg, Florida, an entertainment and cultural center which looks to the future without abandoning its past.
Prod-FLADC Dist-FLADC

Picture, The C 58 MIN
16MM FILM OPTICAL SOUND H-C A
Presents a story in which the relentless pursuit of the buck demeans the artist and degrades art to a species of confection and erotic pastry.
Prod-GROVE Dist-GROVE

Picturephone In Education C 10 MIN
16MM FILM OPTICAL SOUND
Presents a short, spontaneous report on the use of a televised telephone hookup as an aid in teaching. Shows a child working on the famous 'TALKING TYPEWRITER' assisted by a paraprofessional and monitored vai picturephone. Treats the problem of how paraprofessionals in education can be trained and supervised using the advanced technology of picturephone.
Prod-MATHWW Dist-MATHWW 1971

Pictures B 20 MIN
16MM FILM OPTICAL SOUND C A
See series title for descriptive statement.
From The All That I Am Series.
Prod-MPATI Dist-NWUFLM

Pictures At An Exhibition B 10 MIN
16MM FILM OPTICAL SOUND
Illustrates a Moussorgsky tone poem with episodes from the composer's childhood in Russia and Alexander Alexeieff's memories of his own childhood there, using two pinboards, a small one that revolves and a stable one behind it. Introduced in English by Alexeieff.
Prod-STARRC Dist-STARRC 1972

Pictures From A Story C 6 MIN
16MM FILM OPTICAL SOUND
Shows faces which are abstracted in a divisionistic manner.
LC NO. 76-700405
Prod-LILYAN Dist-LILYAN 1976

Pictures In A Patient C 27 MIN
16MM FILM, 3/4 OR 1/2 IN VIDEO C A
Discusses the medical uses of ultrasonic scanning, nuclear magnetic resonance and radioactive isotopes. Describes the ways in which these methods enable health professionals to 'see' inside people.
From The Perspective Series.
Prod-LONTVS Dist-STNFLD

Pictures Of Horyuji Born Again C 45 MIN
16MM FILM OPTICAL SOUND
A Japanese language film. Points out that Horyuji Temple is Japan's oldest and largest wooden structure. Explains that this national property was destroyed by fire in 1952 including the pictures decorating the walls. Shows how Japan's topranking artists used their utmost efforts to restore these valuable pictures to their original state.
Prod-UNIJAP Dist-UNIJAP 1969

Pictures That Moved, The B 45 MIN
16MM FILM OPTICAL SOUND H-C A
Traces the history of Australian film-making from 1896 to 1920. Uses excerpts from early films, stills and interviews to trace the growth of the silent film in Australia.
From The History Of The Australian Cinema Series.
LC NO. 71-709226
Prod-FLMAUS Dist-AUIS 1968

Pictures To Serve The People C 22 MIN
16MM FILM, 3/4 OR 1/2 IN VIDEO J-C A
Traces the American art of lithography, emphasizing the art's inexpensiveness and accessibility.
Prod-AAS Dist-AIMS Prodn-GALENT 1975

Pictures With Words C 20 MIN
2 INCH VIDEOTAPE P
See series title for descriptive statement.
From The Learning Our Language, Unit III - Creative Writing Series.
Prod-MPATI Dist-GPITVL

Piece Of Cake C 26 MIN
16MM FILM, 3/4 OR 1/2 IN VIDEO J-C A
Tells of two retired friends who arrange to catch a goose for Christmas dinner. Reveals that although the dinner is ostensibly for one of the men's daughter, she has really been dead for several years.
LC NO. 82-706851
Prod-AUSFLM Dist-LCOA 1982

Piece Of Sunshine, A C 18 MIN
16MM FILM, 3/4 OR 1/2 IN VIDEO P-I
Shows how, with the aid of a magical time machine, two youngsters are able to travel back through time to learn about man's sources of energy in history. Animated.
LC NO. 84-706801
Prod-EEPOH Dist-PHENIX 1983

Piece Of The Cake, A B 58 MIN
16MM FILM OPTICAL SOUND H-C A
Describes the successful hiring, training and retaining of the hard-core unemployed by the Westinghouse Electric Corporation plant in east Pittsburgh, PA. Explains that the company is hiring 23 men each month and that 90 per cent of these people remain on the job beyond an initial six-month period.
LC NO. 70-704653
Prod-NETRC Dist-IU 1969

Piece Of The Pie, A C 19 MIN
16MM FILM OPTICAL SOUND
Tells the story of four minority group members who are in business for themselves. Provides insights into what the minority business owner must do to succeed in today's business world.
Prod-EXXON Dist-MTP

Piece That Wouldn't Fit C 15 MIN
3/4 INCH VIDEO CASSETTE P
Features Frank and Joy who work to help Benny feel better, showing ways to cope with feelings without using medicine.
From The Think Fine - Feel Fine Series.
Prod-KTCATV Dist-GPITVL

Piece-Wise Linear Systems B 33 MIN
3/4 OR 1/2 INCH VIDEO CASSETTE
See series title for descriptive statement.
From The Nonlinear Vibrations Series.
Prod-MIOT Dist-MIOT

Pieces Of Numbers - Fractions C 14 MIN
3/4 OR 1/2 INCH VIDEO CASSETTE P
Tells how someone steals pieces of things and Martha and Jerry become fraction detectives.
From The Math Country Series.
Prod-KYTV Dist-AITECH 1979

Pieces Of The Puzzle C 28 MIN
16MM FILM, 3/4 OR 1/2 IN VIDEO H
Explores the way a newspaper columnist gathers material for an article.
Prod-EDUCBC Dist-EBEC 1985

Pieces Of The Puzzle, The C 30 MIN
3/4 OR 1/2 INCH VIDEO CASSETTE
Introduces the viewer to the subject of economics. Emphasizes macroeconomics and what it covers.
From The Money Puzzle - The World Of Macroeconomics Series. Module 1
Prod-MDCC Dist-MDCC

Pied Piper Of Hamelin, The C 18 MIN
16MM FILM OPTICAL SOUND I-C A
Relates what happens when the Council of Hamelin fails to pay the Pied Piper for ridding their town of rats and finds their children disappearing into an enchanted mountain.
LC NO. 83-700126
Prod-PPIPER Dist-PPIPER 1982

Pied Piper Of Hamelin, The C 15 MIN
3/4 OR 1/2 INCH VIDEO CASSETTE K-P
See series title for descriptive statement.
From The Gather Round Series.
Prod-CTI Dist-CTI

Pied Piper Of Hamelin, The C 17 MIN
16MM FILM, 3/4 OR 1/2 IN VIDEO I-J
An animated film of Robert Browning's narrative poem of the legend of the Pied Piper. Symbolizes the conflict between greed and honor.
Prod-ARGO Dist-PHENIX 1970

Pied Piper Of Hamelin, The C 18 MIN
16MM FILM, 3/4 OR 1/2 IN VIDEO I-J
Tells the story of the piper who makes Hamelin's children disappear to an enchanted mountain when the council refuses to pay him for ridding the town of rats. Presents the original Browning poem recited by Orson Welles.
Prod-PPIPER Dist-CF 1983

Pied Piper Of Hamelin, The C 29 MIN
16MM FILM, 3/4 OR 1/2 IN VIDEO I-C A
Uses poetry, music, dance film and puppet animation to produce a sophisticated, mystical rendition of the medieval legend of the Pied Piper of Hamelin. After the piper of Hamelin rid the town of rats, its citizens refused to pay him. His revenge was to lead their children away forever.
Prod-THAMES Dist-MEDIAG 1983

Pied Piper Of Hamelin, The - A German Tale C 11 MIN
16MM FILM, 3/4 OR 1/2 IN VIDEO K-P
Presents the German tale The Pied Piper Of Hamelin. Shows how the Pied Piper uses his enchanting music to lure the rats away from Hamelin. Tells how he plays one more tune to take away the children when the town refuses to pay.
From The Favorite Fairy Tales And Fables Series.
Prod-CORF Dist-CORF 1980

Pier Alexandre (England), Tape A, No. 15 C
3/4 OR 1/2 INCH VIDEO CASSETTE
Features the 'L-Shaped Bob' and a slightly asymmetric cut.
Prod-MPCEDP Dist-MPCEDP 1984

Pier Alexandre (England), Tape B, No. 16 C
3/4 OR 1/2 INCH VIDEO CASSETTE
Features the 'Lion's Mane' for long, counter permed hair.
Prod-MPCEDP Dist-MPCEDP 1984

Pier Marton - Happy Medium C 2 MIN
3/4 OR 1/2 INCH VIDEO CASSETTE
Presented by Pier Marton.
Prod-ARTINC Dist-ARTINC

Pier Marton - Heaven Is What I've Done, For My Fellow Beings C 3 MIN
3/4 OR 1/2 INCH VIDEO CASSETTE
Features a public service announcement dealing with distractions and dilemmas.
Prod-ARTINC Dist-ARTINC

Pier Marton - Hope You Croak Before Me C 3 MIN
3/4 OR 1/2 INCH VIDEO CASSETTE
Presented by Pier Marton.
Prod-ARTINC Dist-ARTINC

Pier Marton - Say I'm A Jew C 28 MIN
3/4 OR 1/2 INCH VIDEO CASSETTE
Features interviews with Jews who grew up in post-war Europe. Presents a manifesto-like affirmation of Jewish identity.
Prod-ARTINC Dist-ARTINC

Pier Marton - Tapes C 15 MIN
3/4 OR 1/2 INCH VIDEO CASSETTE
Explores images of excessive anguish. Presents the horrible with humor.
Prod-ARTINC Dist-ARTINC

Pier Marton - Telepathos C 3 MIN
3/4 OR 1/2 INCH VIDEO CASSETTE
Presented by Pier Marton.
Prod-ARTINC Dist-ARTINC

Pier Marton - Unity Through Strength C 7 MIN
3/4 OR 1/2 INCH VIDEO CASSETTE
Deals with unity through strength.
Prod-ARTINC Dist-ARTINC

Piercing, Cutting Holes And Cutting 45 Degree Bevels With The Cutting Torch C 15 MIN
3/4 OR 1/2 INCH VIDEO CASSETTE IND
See series title for descriptive statement.
From The Welding - Oxy-Acetylene Welding Series.
Prod-ICSINT Dist-ICSINT

Piercing, Cutting Holes And Cutting 45-Degree Bevels With The Cutting Torch (Spanish) C
3/4 OR 1/2 INCH VIDEO CASSETTE
See series title for descriptive statement.
From The Oxy-Acetylene Welding (Spanish) Series.
Prod-VTRI Dist-VTRI

Piero Della Francesca (1416 - 1498) C 10 MIN
16MM FILM OPTICAL SOUND
Shows how Piero Della Francesca of the High Renaissance had a sublime contemplation of a harmonious universe that seemed like a world of pure space.
Prod-ROLAND Dist-ROLAND

Pierre C 6 MIN
16MM FILM, 3/4 OR 1/2 IN VIDEO
Tells of Pierre, a boy who is very indifferent until an encounter with a lion helps him to change his mind. Based on the book Pierre by Maurice Sendak.
Prod-WWS Dist-WWS

Pierrot—A Series
16MM FILM, 3/4 OR 1/2 IN VIDEO P
Introduces crafts for children, including puppetry, collages, clay crafts and shadow-making.
Prod-CORF Dist-CORF 1978

Building Puppets With Pierrot 7 MIN
Creating Collages With Pierrot 6 MIN
Making Shadows With Pierrot 6 MIN
Modeling Clay With Pierrot 7 MIN

Piet Mondriaan C 18 MIN
16MM FILM, 3/4 OR 1/2 IN VIDEO H-C A
Explores the work of Piet Mondriaan, an important painter in the history of abstract art. Shows the Dutch painter's development from naturalism through cubism to pure abstraction.
LC NO. 81-706542
Prod-CRAMAN Dist-IFB 1980

Pig Of The World, The C 30 MIN
3/4 INCH VIDEO CASSETTE H-C A
Presents Ben J Wattenberg, author of The Real America, arguing that America's use of world resources is helping, rather than exploiting, the underdeveloped world and that it is not a question of exploitation but of trade.
From The In Search Of The Real America Series.
Prod-WGBHTV Dist-KINGFT 1977

Pig Power C 6 MIN
16MM FILM OPTICAL SOUND
Shows how the forces of order illustrate Mayor Daley's thesis that the police are there to 'PRESERVE DISORDER,' as the students take to the streets in New York and Berkeley.
Prod-NEWSR Dist-NEWSR

Pig Projects Make Profits C 29 MIN
16MM FILM OPTICAL SOUND

Illustrates practices essential to successful hog raising. Covers purchase, record keeping, health factors, and the training and showing of pigs.
Prod-UDUROC Dist-UDUROC

Pigbird C 6 MIN
16MM FILM, 3/4 OR 1/2 IN VIDEO
Relates how a cagey citizen's success at getting a forbidden animal through customs has disastrous consequences for him and the rest of the population.
Prod-NFBC Dist-NFBC 1982

Pigeon That Came Home, The - A Story Of The Fjord Country C 20 MIN
16MM FILM, 3/4 OR 1/2 IN VIDEO P-I
The story of how a pigeon aids in the rescue of a young Norwegian boy. Through the story some geographic concepts are explored and the need to follow safety rules in all outdoor activities is stressed.
Prod-SVEK Dist-PHENIX 1964

Pigeon That Worked A Miracle, The C 47 MIN
16MM FILM, 3/4 OR 1/2 IN VIDEO I-C A
Tells the story of a boy whose love for his pigeon works a miraculous cure and forces him from the confinement of his wheelchair.
Prod-DISNEY Dist-WDEMCO 1964

Pigeons, Pigeons X 9 MIN
16MM FILM, 3/4 OR 1/2 IN VIDEO P-I
A study of pigeons set against the background of city life.
Prod-EBEC Dist-EBEC 1969

Pigs C 11 MIN
16MM FILM, 3/4 OR 1/2 IN VIDEO P-I
Follows a farmer on his rounds as he feeds the pigs. Shows the faces, personalities and the varied textures of the pigs. Discusses their habits and their behavior.
From The Animals Series.
Prod-DF Dist-CF 1967

Pigs And Hippos C 13 MIN
16MM FILM, 3/4 OR 1/2 IN VIDEO P-I
Examines wild and domestic pigs and examines the physiology and behavior of the hippopotamus.
From The Looking At Animals Series.
Prod-IFB Dist-IFB 1973

Pigs No More C 29 MIN
2 INCH VIDEOTAPE
Reports on the progress of a Fort Smith, Arkansas youth center created specifically to improve communications between the city's youth and the local police force.
From The Turning Points Series.
Prod-KETSTV Dist-PUBTEL

Pigs Of The Past B 30 MIN
16MM FILM OPTICAL SOUND H-C A
Presents the geologic story of pig-like mammals. Describes world's largest hog from Siou County, Nebraska. Shows how fossil remains demonstrate evolution in mammals.
From The Great Plains Trilogy, 1 Series. In The Beginning - The Primitive Man
Prod-KUONTV Dist-UNEBR 1954

Pigs Vs The Freaks, The C 15 MIN
16MM FILM, 3/4 OR 1/2 IN VIDEO J-C A
Features a football game between campus longhair students at Michigan State University and the local town police. Presents an event in which two conflicting lifestyles meet.
Prod-EPPSJ Dist-PFP 1975

Pigskin Palooka, The B 11 MIN
16MM FILM OPTICAL SOUND
Tells how Alfalfa's boasts about his prowess as a gridiron star get him into trouble. A Little Rascals film.
Prod-UNKNWN Dist-BHAWK 1937

Pike On Lanaguage—A Series

Features Kenneth L Pike, Chairman of the Department of Linguistics at the University of Michigan, as he presents his personal approach to the relationship between living language and behavior.
Prod-UMITV Dist-UMITV 1977

Into The Unknown	029 MIN
Music Of Speech - Pitch And Poetry, The	029 MIN
Voices At Work	029 MIN
Waves Of Change	029 MIN
Way We Know - The Value Of Theory In	029 MIN

Pikes Paradise C 25 MIN
16MM FILM OPTICAL SOUND
Shows fisherman Ed Ebbinger fishing for Northern pike using the Cardinal 4 and 808 reels in the wilderness of northern Ontario. Includes information on the feeding and breeding habits of pike and information about local wildlife and history.
Prod-BRNSWK Dist-KAROL

Pilafs, Pilavs And Perloos C 5 MIN
16MM FILM OPTICAL SOUND
Shows easy and elegant pilaf dishes from around the world ranging from the traditional Middle Eastern pilaf to a Spanish arroz con pollo.
Prod-MTP Dist-MTP 1982

Pilferage, Cargo Theft And Shoplifting C 13 MIN
16MM FILM, 3/4 OR 1/2 IN VIDEO PRO
Discusses techniques to stop pilferage, cargo theft and shoplifting.
From The Security Officer Series.
Prod-AIMS Dist-AIMS 1976

Pilgrim Adventure, The C 54 MIN
16MM FILM, 3/4 OR 1/2 IN VIDEO J-C A
Describes the Pilgrims' flight from Europe to America. Cites reasons for the emigration, hazards of the journey and difficulties of settlement.
From The Saga Of Western Man Series.
Prod-ABCTV Dist-MGHT Prodn-SCNDRI 1968

Pilgrim Farewell C 110 MIN
3/4 OR 1/2 INCH VIDEO CASSETTE H-C A
Introduces Kate, who is dying of cancer and is concerned about the estrangement between her and her daughter, whom she walked out on years before.
Prod-FI Dist-FI 1982

Pilgrim Journey C 24 MIN
3/4 OR 1/2 INCH VIDEO CASSETTE
Looks at the voyage of the Mayflower as seen through the eyes of a young girl.
From The Young People's Specials Series.
Prod-MULTPP Dist-MULTPP

Pilgrim's Progress C 40 MIN
16MM FILM OPTICAL SOUND
Presents a remake in color animation of John Bunyan's classic story of Pilgrim's Progress. Shows his epic journey from the City of Destruction to the Celestial City, a story that has had major effect on thousands of lives throughout the world. Notes that the immortal classic has given Christians a new vision of the Lord in the story that has as powerful an impact today as when it was written 300 years ago.
Prod-OMEGA Dist-OMEGA

Pilgrimage In The Hindu Tradition C 24 MIN
16MM FILM OPTICAL SOUND
Illustrates the practice and meaning of the two types of pilgrimages used in the Hindu religion. Defines a pilgrimage as one of a variety of meritorious acts which incorporates both a joyous outing and a transforming spiritual experience for the devotee.
Prod-BBCTV Dist-OPENU 1979

Pilgrimage In The Hindu Tradition C 24 MIN
16MM FILM, 3/4 OR 1/2 IN VIDEO
Illustrates the practice and meaning of the two types of pilgrimages used in the Hindu religion. Defines a pilgrimage as one of a variety of meritorious acts which incorporates both a joyous outing and a transforming spiritual experience for the devotee.
Prod-OPENU Dist-MEDIAG Prodn-BBCTV 1979

Pilgrimage To A Hindu Temple C 14 MIN
16MM FILM OPTICAL SOUND
Shows a middle-aged Tengalai Sri-vaisnava Brahmin getting off the bus in the village of Sriperumbudur. Features the pilgrim moving to the temple tank where he bathes and changes into garbs appropriate for worship, going into the temple and circumambulating the precincts, making his way through the shadowy passages and pillared courts to the innermost shrine in the sanctum. Concludes with the man completing his visit to the temple and is shown returning to the bus-stop for his trip back home from the pilgrimage.
From The Hindu Religion Series. No. 6
LC NO. 70-712495
Prod-SMTHHD Dist-SYRCU

Pilgrimage To A Mountain Peak B 4 MIN
16MM FILM OPTICAL SOUND J-C A
Chronicles the conquest of Mt Kennedy, the highest unclimbed peak in North America, by an expedition which included Robert F Kennedy, brother of the late President.
From The Screen News Digest Series. Vol 7, Issue 10
LC NO. FIA68-2097
Prod-HEARST Dist-HEARST 1965

Pilgrimage To Freedom B 21 MIN
16MM FILM OPTICAL SOUND I-C A
Recounts the inspiring story of India's struggle for independence from 1857, when the first banner of revolt was raised, to 1947, when independence was realized.
Prod-INDIA Dist-NEDINF

Pilgrimage To Mecca C 28 MIN
3/4 INCH VIDEOTAPE
Presents a short interview with the Minister of Information of Saudi Arabia, Dr Mohammad Abdo Yamani, as he discusses the role played by his government in assisting the visit of the pilgrims. Includes a film clip of Mecca and the Hajj ceremonies.
From The International Byline Series.
Prod-PERRYM Dist-PERRYM

Pilgrims And Puritans C 30 MIN
3/4 OR 1/2 INCH VIDEO CASSETTE C
See series title for descriptive statement.
From The American Story - The Beginning To 1877 Series.
Prod-DALCCD Dist-DALCCD

Pilgrims, The C 8 MIN
16MM FILM, 3/4 OR 1/2 IN VIDEO P-I
Shows the explorers who followed Columbus, coming from Spain, Portugal, France, Holland and England in search of glory, wealth and adventure. Explains that, after a long struggle, the colonists came to settle and build a better life for themselves. Presents the story of the Pilgrims, who came from England in a small ship called 'THE MAYFLOWER,' and who landed on Plymouth Rock in Massachusetts.
From The A Nation Is Born Series.
Prod-PIC Dist-LUF 1973

Pilgrims, The B 22 MIN
16MM FILM, 3/4 OR 1/2 IN VIDEO I-H
Follows the Pilgrims from England to Holland and to New England. Discusses the Mayflower compact and the hardships in the New World.
Prod-EBF Dist-EBEC 1955

Pill For The People, The C 59 MIN
16MM FILM OPTICAL SOUND H-C A
Tells the story of chemist Russell Marker, who found a cheap and abundant source for the production of estrogen and progesterone, two chemical horomones needed for the production of contraceptive pills which, until his discovery, had been prohibitively expensive to produce.
From The Nova Series.
Prod-WGBHTV Dist-KINGFT 1977

Pill For The People, The C 59 MIN
3/4 INCH VIDEO CASSETTE H-C A
Tells the story of chemist Russell Marker, who found a cheap and abundant source for the production of estrogen and progesterone, two chemical hormones needed for the production of contraceptive pills which, until his discovery, had been prohibitively expensive to produce.
From The Nova Series.
Prod-WGBHTV Dist-PBS 1977

Pill Poppers, The C 20 MIN
16MM FILM, 3/4 OR 1/2 IN VIDEO J-C
Develops an important and thought-provoking tool in communicating the unadulterated facts about 'DROPPING PILLS.' Tells the audience the true, straight-forward stories of three tennagers caught up in 'DROPPING PILLS.'
Prod-DAVP Dist-AIMS 1971

Pill, Population And Family Planning, The C 29 MIN
2 INCH VIDEOTAPE
See series title for descriptive statement.
From The University Of Chicago Round Table Series.
Prod-WTTWTV Dist-PUBTEL

Pill, The C 10 MIN
16MM FILM OPTICAL SOUND H-C A
Presents a patient counseling film on birth control pills.
From The Obstetrics And Gynecology Series.
LC NO. 75-700054
Prod-MIFE Dist-MIFE 1974

Pill, The C
3/4 OR 1/2 INCH VIDEO CASSETTE
Details the normal monthly cycle without and with use of the pill. Explains how to use the pill properly.
Prod-MIFE Dist-MIFE

Pill, The C 7 MIN
3/4 OR 1/2 INCH VIDEO CASSETTE
Describes in detail the way in which the pill prevents pregnancy and the manner in which it is obtained and used.
LC NO. 78-730127
Prod-TRAINX Dist-TRAINX

Pill, The (Spanish C 7 MIN
3/4 OR 1/2 INCH VIDEO CASSETTE
Describes in detail the way in which the pill prevents pregnancy and the manner in which it is obtained and used.
LC NO. 78-730127
Prod-TRAINX Dist-TRAINX

Pilobolus C 60 MIN
3/4 OR 1/2 INCH VIDEO CASSETTE H-C A
Presents members of the Pilobolus Dance Theatre performing Walklyndon, Momix, Alraune and Molly's Not Dead. Questions whether the group's dance style is slapstick, mime, gymnastics, theatrics or tableau vivant.
From The Dance In America Series.
Prod-WNETTV Dist-FI

Pilot C 30 MIN
1/2 IN VIDEO CASSETTE BETA/VHS
Describes the life of Cliff Flood, 54, who has been flying for well over half of his life. He has accumulated hundreds of flight stories from the thirty years he has flown as a commercial pilot for Eastern Airlines.
From The American Professionals Series.
Prod-WTBS Dist-RMI

Pilot Down, Presumed Dead C 15 MIN
3/4 OR 1/2 INCH VIDEO CASSETTE I
Tells of a young man's struggle to survive after his plane crashes. From the book by Marjorie Phleger.
From The Storybound Series.
Prod-CTI Dist-CTI

Pilot For Glacier Skiers C 25 MIN
16MM FILM OPTICAL SOUND
Presents Mr Mike Buckland, chief pilot of the Mount Cook Air Service and describes his job, carrying tourists and skiers to the glaciers by ski-plane. Portrays the difficult landings on the glaciers and the very beautiful scenery from the air. Tells the history of ski-plane.
Prod-UNIJAP Dist-UNIJAP 1967

Pilot Operated Pressure Control Valves C 15 MIN
16MM FILM OPTICAL SOUND IND
Illustrates the override characteristics, construction and operation of direct and pilot-operated pressure valves. Covers pump unloading in accumulator circuits and the differential unloading relief valve.
From The Industrial Hydraulic Technology Series.
LC NO. 77-703436
Prod-TAT Dist-TAT 1976

Pilot Traverse C 15 MIN
3/4 OR 1/2 INCH VIDEO CASSETTE A
Demonstrates the standard pilot tube method for determining average linear velocity and the volume of air flow through ducts. Describes the equipment used, how to find a sample point in the duct, measurement technique and data collection and calculation procedures.
LC NO. 84-706451
Prod-USNAC Dist-USNAC 1978

Pilot Watershed C 22 MIN
16MM FILM OPTICAL SOUND H-C A
Considers the conservation land treatment, flood water retarding structures, and the cost and financial responsibilities.
Prod-UNL Dist-UNEBR 1955

Pilot, The - Value Of Honesty C 25 MIN
16MM FILM, 3/4 OR 1/2 IN VIDEO J-H
Tells the story of a teenage girl who overcomes shyness by breakdancing. Explores development of self-esteem and the value of honesty.
Prod-PAULST Dist-MEDIAG 1985

Piloted Operated Pressure Control Valves C 15 MIN
3/4 OR 1/2 INCH VIDEO CASSETTE IND
Examines valve characteristics, pump unloading and terms associated with pilot operated pressure control valves.
From The Industrial Hydraulic Technology Series. Chapter 10
Prod-TAT Dist-TAT

Piloting, Surface B 33 MIN
16MM FILM, 3/4 OR 1/2 IN VIDEO
Stresses the importance of accurate piloting and discusses briefly the use of the bearing circle, compass repeater and alidade in securing bearings.
From The Navigation Series.
LC NO. 81-706351
Prod-USN Dist-USNAC 1943

Pimentel Discusses Chemical Bonding B 27 MIN
16MM FILM OPTICAL SOUND
Professor George C Pimentel explains the virial theorem and uses it to show that the lowering of the electron's total energy in bond formation can only occur through a lowering of its potential energy by being simultaneously near two or more nuclei. Applies this principle to covalent, ionic and other types of bounding.
LC NO. FIA67-5
Prod-CHEMED Dist-MLA Prodn-DAVFMS 1964

Pimentel Discusses Chemical Bonding B 27 MIN
16MM FILM OPTICAL SOUND
Amplifies the idea that attraction of one or more electrons for two or more nuclei accounts for bond formation. Presents the virial theorem.
From The CHEM Study Teacher Training Series.
Prod-MLA Dist-MLA

Pimentel Discusses The Hydrogen Atom B 32 MIN
16MM FILM OPTICAL SOUND
Professor George C Pimentel discusses the shortcomings of the planetary model in terms of its inconsistency with experiment and with quantum mechanics. Provides a basis for understanding the significance of the Schroedinger equation.
LC NO. FIA67-4
Prod-CHEMED Dist-MLA Prodn-DAVFMS 1964

Pin Retained Foundation For An Amalgam Restoration C 14 MIN
16MM FILM OPTICAL SOUND PRO
Illustrates various items of armamentarium which are utilized with the technique of amalgam restoration. Emphasizes the preparation of the pin-channels by means of a limited depth twist-drill and proper placement of the two-in-one, self-shearing threaded pins.
LC NO. 78-700755
Prod-VADTC Dist-USNAC 1978

Pin Retention For A Class V Restoration C 7 MIN
16MM FILM, 3/4 OR 1/2 IN VIDEO PRO
Demonstrates the use of special superminiature threaded pins as retention for a Class V restoration.
LC NO. 81-706365
Prod-VADTC Dist-USNAC 1976

Pin Retention For An Amalgam Restoration C 14 MIN
3/4 OR 1/2 INCH VIDEO CASSETTE
Shows how the use of threaded pins to provide additional retention for an amalgam restoration allows maximum preservation of the existing tooth structure.
Prod-VADTC Dist-AMDA 1976

Pin-Retained Foundation For A Full Crown C 11 MIN
16MM FILM, 3/4 OR 1/2 IN VIDEO PRO
Demonstrates how a pin-retained foundation is added to a tooth so badly broken that insufficient tooth structure remains for preparation for a full crown restoration.
LC NO. 81-706363
Prod-VADTC Dist-USNAC 1977

Pin-Retained Foundation For An Amalgam Restoration C 14 MIN
3/4 OR 1/2 INCH VIDEO CASSETTE PRO
Illustrates various items of armamentarium which are utilized with the technique of amalgam restoration. Emphasizes the preparation of the pin-channels by means of a limited depth twist-drill and proper placement of the two-in-one, self-shearing threaded pins.
LC NO. 81-706364
Prod-VADTC Dist-USNAC 1978

Pinata C 24 MIN
16MM FILM, 3/4 OR 1/2 IN VIDEO
Tells the story of a small Mexican boy who strives to attain a beautiful pinata. Shows how he is able to reconstruct the pinata after it has been destroyed and how his efforts are rewarded.
Prod-SWAIN Dist-MCFI 1977

Pinball C 9 MIN
16MM FILM OPTICAL SOUND I-H A
Presents an imaginative and expressionistic treatment of the experiences of pinball.
LC NO. 76-701712
Prod-UKANS Dist-UKANS Prodn-KERRW 1975

Pinball Parlour C 4 MIN
16MM FILM OPTICAL SOUND
Presents a look inside a pinball parlour.
LC NO. 74-703004
Prod-INSCA Dist-CANFDC 1973

Pinballs, The C 15 MIN
3/4 OR 1/2 INCH VIDEO CASSETTE I
Presents passages from the story by Betsy Byars about three children in a foster home.
From The Storybound Series.
Prod-CTI Dist-CTI

Pinballs, The C 31 MIN
16MM FILM, 3/4 OR 1/2 IN VIDEO I-H
Adapted from the novel THE PINBALLS by Betsy Byars, about three lonely foster children who learn to care about themselves and each other.
From The Afterschool Specials, Series 1 Series.
Prod-TAHSEM Dist-WDEMCO 1977

Pincers - August 1944-March 1945 C 52 MIN
16MM FILM, 3/4 OR 1/2 IN VIDEO H-C A
Describes how the Allies invaded southern France from the west between August 1944 and March 1945. Russia invaded from the east and this tandem movement, known as Operation Anvil, drove Hitler's armies back across German borders and beyond.
From The World At War Series.
Prod-THAMES Dist-MEDIAG 1973

Pincers - August, 1944 To March, 1945 C 60 MIN
16MM FILM OPTICAL SOUND H-C A
From The World At War Series.
LC NO. 76-701778
Prod-THAMES Dist-USCAN 1975

Pinch C 15 MIN
3/4 OR 1/2 INCH VIDEO CASSETTE I
Presents passages from the book by Larry Callen about a clever boy and his champion pig.
From The Storybound Series.
Prod-CTI Dist-CTI

Pinch Singer, The B 17 MIN
16MM FILM OPTICAL SOUND
Shows Spanky holding tryouts for someone to represent the Gang on a radio station's talent contest. A Little Rascals film.
Prod-ROACH Dist-BHAWK 1936

Pinch, The C 12 MIN
16MM FILM OPTICAL SOUND P
Discusses the concept of role playing in terms of young children. Asks children to talk about something which made them angry.
From The Magic Circle Series.
Prod-TRAFCO Dist-ECUFLM 1975

Pinch, The C 12 MIN
3/4 OR 1/2 INCH VIDEO CASSETTE K A
Shows children how to discuss and act out situations when something made them very angry.
From The Magic Circle Series.
Prod-HDI Dist-UMCOM Prodn-UMCOM

Pine Life Cycle C 15 MIN
3/4 OR 1/2 INCH VIDEO CASSETTE
Presents the life cycle of pine by means of photographs of the plant in its natural environment with emphasis on roots, stems, leaves and cones. Places emphasis on gametophytic and sporophytic development.
Prod-CBSC Dist-CBSC

Pine Nuts - A Food Of The Paiute And Washo Indians C 13 MIN
16MM FILM, 3/4 OR 1/2 IN VIDEO H-C A
Demonstrates how Indians processed pine nuts, a nutritious food obtained from the pinon tree of the Great Basin area. Shows how the nuts were extracted from cones, parched with hot coals, cracked on grinding stones, ground and eaten dry or drunk in a thin gruel.
From The American Indian Series.
Prod-UCEMC Dist-UCEMC 1961

Pine Tree Camp C 13 MIN
16MM FILM OPTICAL SOUND
Shows everyday life at Pine Tree Camp, emphasizing the rapport between campers and staff and the happiness that the camp can bring to a handicapped child.
LC NO. 70-713208
Prod-ENVIC Dist-ENVIC 1970

Ping Chong And Douglas Dunn C 30 MIN
3/4 OR 1/2 INCH VIDEO CASSETTE
See series title for descriptive statement.
From The Experimentalists Series.
Prod-ARCVID Dist-ARCVID

Ping Chong And Douglas Dunn C 30 MIN
3/4 OR 1/2 INCH VIDEO CASSETTE
See series title for descriptive statement.
From The Eye On Dance - The Experimentalists Series.
Prod-ARTRES Dist-ARTRES

Pink Porpoise C 27 MIN
16MM FILM OPTICAL SOUND
Follows an expedition into the Amazon wilds of Peru to collect fresh water porpoise for Marineland of St Augustine.
Prod-FLADC Dist-FLADC

Pink Rink C 7 MIN
16MM FILM OPTICAL SOUND
Presents the Pink Panther in a story designed to show that productivity can be improved with capital investments and innovation. Shows that higher productivity comes from working smarter not harder.
Prod-EXXON Dist-MTP 1982

Pink Triangles C 35 MIN
3/4 INCH VIDEO CASSETTE
Studies prejudice against lesbians and gay men and challenges some of our most deeply rooted feelings, people's people's attitudes toward homosexuality. Synthesizes many disparate ideas and elements.
Prod-CMBRD Dist-CMBRD

Pink Triangles - A Study Of Prejudice Against Lesbians And Gay Men C 34 MIN
16MM FILM OPTICAL SOUND H-C
Takes a look at the nature of discrimination against lesbians and gay men and challenges some of society's attitudes toward homosexuality. Examines historical and contemporary patterns of racial, religious, political and sexual persecution.
LC NO. 81-701655
Prod-CMBRD Dist-CMBRD 1982

Pinkfoot C 19 MIN
16MM FILM, 3/4 OR 1/2 IN VIDEO I-H
Shows how pink-footed geese fly north to their breeding grounds in Iceland and Greenland each spring. Follows their hazardous journey, then focuses on one pair's stuggle to hatch and raise their young before winter drives them south again.
From The RSPB Collection Series.
Prod-RSFPB Dist-BCNFL 1983

Pinks And The Blues, The C 57 MIN
16MM FILM, 3/4 OR 1/2 IN VIDEO A
Probes the subtle ways in which parents and teachers condition babies and young children to accept traditional sex roles.
From The Nova Series.
LC NO. 81-706766
Prod-WGBHTV Dist-TIMLIF 1980

Pinlay Abutments C 26 MIN
16MM FILM OPTICAL SOUND
Demonstrates clinically, the pinlay abutment technique used in restoration of interior teeth.
LC NO. 74-705361
Prod-USA Dist-USNAC 1964

Pinlays Using The Loma Linda Parallelometer C 17 MIN
16MM FILM OPTICAL SOUND
Describes the techniques involved in the preparation, impression and fabrication of pinlays for anterior teeth using the Loma Linda parallelometer. Illustrates the technical, clinical and laboratory procedures.
LC NO. 75-700807
Prod-USVA Dist-USNAC .1965

Pinning Combinations C 20 MIN
16MM FILM, 3/4 OR 1/2 IN VIDEO
Demonstrates pinning combinations in the sport of wrestling.
From The Wrestling Series. No. 4
Prod-ATHI Dist-ATHI 1976

Pinocchio C 72 MIN
16MM FILM OPTICAL SOUND P-I
Presents Pinocchio in a live-action and animated puppet version.
Prod-FI Dist-FI

Pinocchio - A Lesson In Honesty C 8 MIN
16MM FILM, 3/4 OR 1/2 IN VIDEO P-I
Tells how seven-year-old Bobby learns that lying is wrong, with the help of his friend and neighbor, Uncle Phil and a scene from the animated film Pinocchio.
From The Disney's Animated Classics - Lessons In Living, Series 1 Series.
Prod-DISNEY Dist-WDEMCO Prodn-WDEMCO 1978

Pinocchio's Birthday Party C 76 MIN
16MM FILM OPTICAL SOUND
Combines live action and animation to tell the story of Pinocchio's birthday party.
LC NO. 76-701354
Prod-KTEL Dist-KTEL Prodn-INTCOM 1974

Pinoy C 30 MIN
3/4 INCH VIDEO CASSETTE H-C A
Features a 74-year-old Filipino housing activist recalling the early days of Filipino immigration to America.
From The Pearls Series.
Prod-EDFCEN Dist-GPITVL 1979

Pinpointing And Recording Patient Behavior B 30 MIN
16MM FILM OPTICAL SOUND
Describes the application of behavior modification techniques in caring for patients. Features the selection of significant behaviors, defining them and recording their frequency.
From The Nursing-Cues Behavior Consequences Series. No. 2
LC NO. 76-700927
Prod-NTCN Dist-UNEBR 1973

Pins And Needles C 37 MIN
16MM FILM, 3/4 OR 1/2 IN VIDEO A
Explores the effects of multiple sclerosis through the account of Genni Batterham, an Australian communications student who contracted the disease. Presents an unveiled look at Batterham's changed life, her visits to the hospital and the multiple aspects of her relationship with her husband.
Prod-FLMLIB Dist-FLMLIB Prodn-BTRHAM 1980

Pinscreen C 40 MIN
16MM FILM, 3/4 OR 1/2 IN VIDEO H-C A
Features animator Alexandre Alexieff demonstrating and discussing the technique of pinscreen animation to a group of the world's leading animators. Shows how the pinscreen animation screen can create an intimate range of visual images and perspectives.
LC NO. 77-701103
Prod-NFBC Dist-PFP 1977

Pinter People C 58 MIN
16MM FILM OPTICAL SOUND H-C A

Features an interview with Harold Pinter and five early Pinter 'REVIEW SKETCHES' in animated form, with the voices of Vivien Merchant, Donald Pleasence and Harold Pinter.
LC NO. 72-707492
Prod-POTPRO Dist-GROVE Prodn-POTPRO 1969

Pints, Quarts And Pottles C 15 MIN
3/4 OR 1/2 INCH VIDEO CASSETTE P
Presents a math teacher who explains liquid measurements, including such old-fashioned units of liquid measure as pottles. Features a space robot demonstrating different quantities of liquid to his puppet assistant by using different measuring containers.
From The Math Mission 2 Series.
LC NO. 82-706354
Prod-WCVETV Dist-GPITVL 1980

Pioneer Blacksmith, The X 11 MIN
16MM FILM, 3/4 OR 1/2 IN VIDEO I-C A
Shows an authentic blacksmith shop at old Sturbridge Village, Massachusetts. Illustrates how the blacksmith contributed to life in a small community in the early 1800's.
From The Pioneer Life Series.
Prod-IU Dist-IU 1962

Pioneer Home, A C 11 MIN
16MM FILM, 3/4 OR 1/2 IN VIDEO P-I
Shows the physical surroundings and home furnishings, the hard work, the simple pleasures and other characteristics of pioneer family life.
Prod-CORF Dist-CORF 1948

Pioneer Journey Across The Appalachians (Rev Ed) C 14 MIN
16MM FILM, 3/4 OR 1/2 IN VIDEO
Follows a North Carolina fammily on a journey across the Appalachians before the Revolutionary War. Considers why the early settlers moved West and how they travelled. Shows that mountains were a barrier.
Prod-CORF Dist-CORF 1982

Pioneer Life—A Series
16MM FILM, 3/4 OR 1/2 IN VIDEO I-C A
Prod-IU Dist-IU 1960

Canals - Towpaths West 010 MIN
Long Journey West - 1820 017 MIN
New England Sea Community 015 MIN
Northeast Farm Community 015 MIN
Pioneer Blacksmith 011 MIN
Pioneer Mill 012 MIN
Pioneer Spinning And Weaving 009 MIN

Pioneer Living - Education And Recreation C 11 MIN
16MM FILM, 3/4 OR 1/2 IN VIDEO I-H
Shows how pioneer communities in the early 1800's conducted school and enjoyed recreational activities including quilting bees, box socials and hay rides.
From The Pioneer Living Series.
Prod-CORF Dist-CORF 1970

Pioneer Living - Home Crafts C 11 MIN
16MM FILM, 3/4 OR 1/2 IN VIDEO I-H
Shows how a pioneer family had to know such crafts and skills as sheep shearing, cloth making, hooking and braiding, woodworking and others.
From The Pioneer Living Series.
Prod-CORF Dist-CORF 1970

Pioneer Living - Preparing Foods C 11 MIN
16MM FILM, 3/4 OR 1/2 IN VIDEO I-H
Shows pioneer preparations for the winter, including smoking meat, peeling and preserving apples, churning butter, making maple sugar and baking bread
From The Pioneer Living Series.
Prod-CORF Dist-CORF 1970

Pioneer Living - The Farm C 11 MIN
16MM FILM, 3/4 OR 1/2 IN VIDEO I-H
Shows pioneers clearing and plowing the fields, planting crops, harvesting, threshing and grinding grain into flour, working at the flour mill and processing flax.
From The Pioneer Living Series.
Prod-CORF Dist-CORF 1970

Pioneer Living - The Home C 11 MIN
16MM FILM, 3/4 OR 1/2 IN VIDEO I-H
Shows how a pioneer family of the early 1800's selected a site, built a log cabin, cooked, made soap and candles and did other household tasks.
From The Pioneer Living Series.
Prod-CORF Dist-CORF 1970

Pioneer Living - The Village C 11 MIN
16MM FILM, 3/4 OR 1/2 IN VIDEO I-H
Observes women buying and bartering at the general store, and the blacksmith, cobbler, newspaperman and broommaker at work.
From The Pioneer Living Series.
Prod-CORF Dist-CORF 1970

Pioneer Living—A Series
16MM FILM, 3/4 OR 1/2 IN VIDEO I-H
Prod-CORF Dist-CORF 1970

Pioneer Living - Education And Recreation 11 MIN
Pioneer Living - Home Crafts 11 MIN
Pioneer Living - Preparing Foods 11 MIN
Pioneer Living - The Farm 11 MIN
Pioneer Living - The Home 11 MIN
Pioneer Living - The Village 11 MIN

Pioneer Mill C 12 MIN
16MM FILM, 3/4 OR 1/2 IN VIDEO P-I
Points out that corn meal was an important food to early settlers and describes how they ground corn in their home. Shows the operation and activities connected with larger water-powered mills used by early farmers in the Midwest. Explains the miller's importance and function as he goes through each step of the grinding process.
From The Pioneer Life Series.
LC NO. 80-707067
Prod-IU Dist-IU 1972

Pioneer Of Labor C 20 MIN
3/4 INCH VIDEO CASSETTE I
Discusses the life of labor leader Samuel Gompers.
From The Truly American Series.
Prod-WVIZTV Dist-GPITVL 1979

Pioneer Spinning And Weaving X 9 MIN
16MM FILM, 3/4 OR 1/2 IN VIDEO I-C A
Shows how flax was processed into linen thread through retting, drying, braking, switcheling, hatcheling and spinning. Shows how fleece was changed into wool yarn after shearing, cleaning, carding and spinning.
From The Pioneer Life Series.
Prod-IU Dist-IU 1960

Pioneer Trails, Indian Lore And Bird Life Of The Plains C 14 MIN
16MM FILM, 3/4 OR 1/2 IN VIDEO I-C A
Describes the vanishing American prairie, the area between the Mississippi River and the Rocky Mountains. Explains origins of Indian dance forms and describes types of bird life on the prairie.
From The Vanishing Prairie Series.
Prod-DISNEY Dist-WDEMCO 1963

Pioneer Trails, Indian Lore And Bird Life Of The Plains (Norwegian) C 14 MIN
16MM FILM, 3/4 OR 1/2 IN VIDEO I-H
Explains the origins of Indian dance forms. Shows pioneer wagon trails. Describes bird life on the prairie.
From The Vanishing Prairie (Norwegian) Series.
Prod-WDEMCO Dist-WDEMCO 1963

Pioneer Trails, Indian Lore And Bird Life Of The Plains (Portuguese) C 14 MIN
16MM FILM, 3/4 OR 1/2 IN VIDEO I-H
Explains the origins of Indian dance forms. Shows pioneer wagon trails. Describes bird life on the prairie.
From The Vanishing Prairie (Portuguese) Series.
Prod-WDEMCO Dist-WDEMCO 1963

Pioneer Village (2nd Ed) C 20 MIN
16MM FILM, 3/4 OR 1/2 IN VIDEO I-J
Depicts the growth and development of a northeastern pioneer village, covering the years 1790 to 1840. Shows the activities of a typical pioneer family.
Prod-MORLAT Dist-SF 1966

Pioneer Women Of Today C 29 MIN
3/4 INCH VIDEO CASSETTE
Shows interviews with four contemporary women who discuss solving problems, dealing with self-doubt and stress, and sexual discrimination.
From The American Women - Echoes And Dreams Series.
Prod-OHC Dist-HRC

Pioneering Research In Hypertension C 24 MIN
3/4 OR 1/2 INCH VIDEO CASSETTE PRO
Discusses the treatment of hypertension disease and the current concepts in the etiology of this disease, with emphasis on the role of the sympathetic nervous system activity and how this can be modulated by the use of the centrally acting sympatholytic agent, clonidine. Features four specialists. (Also available in French, German, Italian, Japanese and Spanish).
Prod-WFP Dist-WFP

Pioneering, No. 1 B 20 MIN
2 INCH VIDEOTAPE I
Discusses the continuing exploration of pioneers from the past to the present. (Broadcast quality)
From The Quest For The Best Series.
Prod-DENVPS Dist-GPITVL Prodn-KRMATV

Pioneering, No. 2 B 20 MIN
2 INCH VIDEOTAPE I
Discusses the continuing exploration of pioneers from the past to the present. (Broadcast quality)
From The Quest For The Best Series.
Prod-DENVPS Dist-GPITVL Prodn-KRMATV

Pioneers And Modern Rockets C 24 MIN
16MM FILM, 3/4 OR 1/2 IN VIDEO I-C A
Presents an account of the technological advances in rocketry during the first half of the 20th century, with particular emphasis on the efforts of engineering technology to reach the levels of scientific knowledge. Describes the establishment of rocket research and interplanetary societies in europe and the U S during the 1920's.
From The Man Into Space - The Story Of Rockets And Space Science Series.
Prod-ACI Dist-AIMS 1970

Pioneers Of Modern Architecture In Chicago C 20 MIN
16MM FILM, 3/4 OR 1/2 IN VIDEO H-C A
Focuses on the work of Henry Hobson Richardson and Louis H Sullivan that can be seen in the Chicago area. Also shows works by Frank Lloyd Wright and other Prairie School architects and includes both commercial and residential buildings.
Prod-IFB Dist-IFB

Pioneers Of The Southwest C 15 MIN
16MM FILM, 3/4 OR 1/2 IN VIDEO I
Depicts a reconstructed pioneer village in the Southwest, showing the Indian and Spanish influences on its architecture. Discusses early life in a pioneer town.
From The American Scrapbook Series.
Prod-WVIZTV Dist-GPITVL 1977

Pioneers Of The Vertical C 24 MIN
16MM FILM OPTICAL SOUND
Shows the training and care of primates, pointing out their vital use in decompression and radiation studies, blood analysis and experimental medicine.
LC NO. 74-706179
Prod-USAF Dist-USNAC 1967

Pioneers, The C 59 MIN
16MM FILM OPTICAL SOUND
Examines sculpture from the late 19th century to the beginning of World War I, illustrating the breakdown of the classical view of art. Shows works by Rodin, Maillol, Lehmbruck, Matisse, Picasso, Lipschitz and Brancusi.
From The Masters Of Modern Sculpture Series. No. 1
LC NO. 78-701407
Prod-BLACKW Dist-BLACKW 1978

Pipe And Tubing—A Series

Shows the largest and most modern mills in the world in the variety of operations necessary to produce tubular products up to pipe-line diameters.
Prod-USSC Dist-USSC

Seamless Modern (General Pipe Making) 13 MIN
USS Line Pipe 9 MIN
USS Mechanical And Pressure Tubing 10 MIN
USS Oil Country Goods 11 MIN
USS Standard Pipe 9 MIN
USS Structural Tubing 11 MIN

Pipe Dream To Pipeline C 12 MIN
16MM FILM OPTICAL SOUND
Covers the entire route of the Alaska pipeline from the oil fields of Prudhoe Bay on the Arctic Ocean to the terminal of Valdez on Alaska's southern coast. Focuses on what it takes to keep men and machines going on the biggest project ever undertaken by private enterprise.
Prod-GTARC Dist-GTARC

Pipe Dreams C 15 MIN
16MM FILM, 3/4 OR 1/2 IN VIDEO
Traces one man's purchase of a pipe by showing what he looks for in a quality pipe, the various tobaccos offered and how he starts a collection.
Prod-KLEINW Dist-KLEINW 1979

Pipe Fabrication C
3/4 OR 1/2 INCH VIDEO CASSETTE IND
See series title for descriptive statement.
From The Drafting - Piping Familiarization Series.
Prod-GPCV Dist-GPCV

Pipe Fabrication Drawings C
3/4 OR 1/2 INCH VIDEO CASSETTE IND
See series title for descriptive statement.
From The Drafting - Blueprint Reading Basics Series.
Prod-GPCV Dist-GPCV

Pipe Fabrication With Jigs B 22 MIN
16MM FILM - 3/4 IN VIDEO
Describes the purpose of a jig and shows how to lay out and assemble targets for a jig. Tells how to set targets and hangers using a pipe section as a template and how to fabricate pipe on a jig. Issued in 1944 as a motion picture.
From The Shipbuilding Skills - Pipefitting Series. Number 7
LC NO. 80-707276
Prod-USOE Dist-USNAC Prodn-WALKER 1980

Pipe Spring C 15 MIN
16MM FILM OPTICAL SOUND A
Offers a glimpse of the Old West. Shows how typical ranch chores are performed in a corral adjacent to the Pipe Spring National Monument.
LC NO. 77-703234
Prod-USNAC Dist-USNAC 1973

Pipe Spring C 15 MIN
3/4 INCH VIDEO CASSETTE
Offers a glimpse of the Old West. Shows how typical ranch chores are performed in a corral adjacent to the Pipe Spring National Monument. Issued in 1973 as a motion picture.
LC NO. 79-706152
Prod-USNPS Dist-USNAC 1979

Pipe Trades C 15 MIN
3/4 OR 1/2 INCH VIDEO CASSETTE I
Explains the qualifications and personal qualities required for a successful career in the pipe trades.
From The Career Awareness Series.
Prod-KLVXTV Dist-GPITVL 1973

Pipefitting / Cutting / Reaming / Threading C 18 MIN
16MM FILM, 3/4 OR 1/2 IN VIDEO IND
Shows how to correctly cut, ream and thread pipe. Stresses the correct thread length for good tight screwed connections, removing the burr after the pipe is cut, the use of sharp dies and proper cutting oil.
Prod-MOKIN Dist-MOKIN

Pipefitting Tools C 12 MIN
3/4 OR 1/2 INCH VIDEO CASSETTE
Covers various pipefitting tools such as pipe wrenches, vises, reaming pipe, flaring metal tubing and the care of pipe tools.
From The Using Hand Tools Series.
Prod-TPCTRA Dist-TPCTRA

Pipefitting Tools (Spanish) C 12 MIN
3/4 OR 1/2 INCH VIDEO CASSETTE
Covers various pipefitting tools such as pipe wrenches, vises, reaming pipe, flaring metal tubing and the care of pipe tools.

From The Using Hand Tools Series.
Prod-TPCTRA Dist-TPCTRA

Pipefitting/Cutting/Reaming/Threading C 18 MIN
3/4 OR 1/2 INCH VIDEO CASSETTE IND
Shows how to correctly cut, ream and thread pipe. Stresses correct length for good tight screw connection, use of sharp dies and proper cutting oil.
From The Marshall Maintenance Training Programs Series. Tape 9
Prod-LEIKID Dist-LEIKID

Pipefitting, Bell And Spigot C 19 MIN
3/4 OR 1/2 INCH VIDEO CASSETTE IND
Teaches how to measure cast iron soil pipe, to make good cuts and to use all the various yarning irons for good yarning with the oakum. Demonstrates procedures for making vertical and horizontal joints, including proper safety practices and caulking.
From The Marshall Maintenance Training Programs Series. Tape 11
Prod-LEIKID Dist-LEIKID

Pipefitting, Bell And Spigot C 19 MIN
16MM FILM, 3/4 OR 1/2 IN VIDEO
Shows how to measure cast iron soil pipe, how to make cuts, and to use all the various yarning irons for good yarning with the oakum. Views the procedures for making vertical and horizontal joints, including proper safety practices and caulking.
Prod-MOKIN Dist-MOKIN

Pipeline C 28 MIN
16MM FILM OPTICAL SOUND
Tells the story of the Trans-Alaskan pipeline from the initial legal and environmental concerns, through construction problems, to successful completion of the project.
LC NO. 78-701441
Prod-ALYSKA Dist-MTP Prodn-PENDLP 1978

Pipeline C 28 MIN
3/4 INCH VIDEO CASSETTE
Tells the story of the huge pipeline built to transport the crude oil from the North Slope of Alaska near Prudhoe Bay down to the port of Valdez 800 miles away.
Prod-EXXON Dist-MTP

Pipeline - Oil From The Arctic C 29 MIN
16MM FILM OPTICAL SOUND
Presents an overview of the construction of the Alaskan pipeline, emphasizing the management and logistical controls applied by the sponsor company.
LC NO. 77-700021
Prod-PERINI Dist-SILVER Prodn-SILVER 1976

Pipeline, A - And Animals C 28 MIN
16MM FILM OPTICAL SOUND
Shows how well animals are living along the route of the Trans Alaska pipeline.
Prod-MTP Dist-MTP

Pipeline, Alaska, A Lifeline C
3/4 OR 1/2 INCH VIDEO CASSETTE
Profiles the pipeline and the people who work on the edge of the Arctic Sea, one of the most unusual and chilling environments in the world.
From The Alaska Series.
Prod-WCCOTV Dist-WCCOTV 1982

Pipetting I C 8 MIN
3/4 OR 1/2 INCH VIDEO CASSETTE C A
Illustrates steps required to deliver accurate, reproducible volumes with a volumetric transfer pipet.
From The Chemistry - Master/Apprentice Series. Program 2
LC NO. 82-706036
Prod-CUETV Dist-CUNIV 1981

Pipetting II C 9 MIN
3/4 OR 1/2 INCH VIDEO CASSETTE C A
Illustrates the proper steps required to deliver accurate, reprodicible volumes with a volumetric transfer pipet. Inspects the pipet for cleanliness, rinses it, and fills it with a solution using a Mallinckrodt pipet aid (vinyl bulb, polyethylene tip.) Demonstrates errors that result from parallax and shows the proper filling and emptying procedures.
From The Chemistry - Master/Apprentice Series. Program 104
LC NO. 82-706035
Prod-CUETV Dist-CUNIV 1981

Pipetting III C 8 MIN
3/4 OR 1/2 INCH VIDEO CASSETTE C A
Illustrates the proper steps required to deliver accurate, reproducible volumes with a volumetric transfer pipet. Uses a Fisher brand pipet filler to draw liquid into the pipet.
From The Chemistry - Master/Apprentice Series. Program 100
LC NO. 82-706046
Prod-CUETV Dist-CUNIV 1981

Piping C 240 MIN
3/4 OR 1/2 INCH VIDEO CASSETTE IND
Features tubing and piping. Covers strainers, filters, traps and heat exchangers.
From The Mechanical Equipment Maintenance Series.
Prod-ITCORP Dist-ITCORP

Piping (Spanish) C 240 MIN
3/4 OR 1/2 INCH VIDEO CASSETTE IND
Features tubing and piping. Covers strainers, filters, traps and heat exchangers.
From The Mechanical Equipment Maintenance (Spanish) Series.
Prod-ITCORP Dist-ITCORP

Piping And Plumbing Drawings C 12 MIN
3/4 OR 1/2 INCH VIDEO CASSETTE
Covers piping and plumbing materials, kinds of joints, drawings and joining metal pipes.
From The Reading Blueprints Series.
Prod-TPCTRA Dist-TPCTRA

Piping And Plumbing Drawings (Spanish) C 12 MIN
3/4 OR 1/2 INCH VIDEO CASSETTE
Covers piping and plumbing materials, kinds of joints, drawings and joining metal pipes.
From The Reading Blueprints Series.
Prod-TPCTRA Dist-TPCTRA

Piping Diagrams C 12 MIN
3/4 OR 1/2 INCH VIDEO CASSETTE
Covers piping systems, valves, reading of a simple schematic and a piping schematic.
From The Reading Schematics And Symbols Series.
Prod-TPCTRA Dist-TPCTRA

Piping Diagrams (Spanish) C 12 MIN
3/4 OR 1/2 INCH VIDEO CASSETTE
Covers piping systems, valves, reading of a single schematic and a piping schematic.
From The Reading Schematics And Symbols Series.
Prod-TPCTRA Dist-TPCTRA

Piping Drawings - Detail Dimensioning And Symbology C
3/4 OR 1/2 INCH VIDEO CASSETTE IND
See series title for descriptive statement.
From The Drafting - Blueprint Reading Basics Series.
Prod-GPCV Dist-GPCV

Piping Drawings - Fittings And Orthographic Projections C
3/4 OR 1/2 INCH VIDEO CASSETTE IND
From The Drafting - Blueprint Reading Basics Series.
Prod-GPCV Dist-GPCV

Piping Drawings - Terms And Equipment C
3/4 OR 1/2 INCH VIDEO CASSETTE IND
See series title for descriptive statement.
From The Drafting - Blueprint Reading Basics Series.
Prod-GPCV Dist-GPCV

Piping Drawings - Valves, Flanges And Pipe C
3/4 OR 1/2 INCH VIDEO CASSETTE IND
See series title for descriptive statement.
From The Drafting - Blueprint Reading Basics Series.
Prod-GPCV Dist-GPCV

Piping Fabrication For Shipboard High Temperature Steam Systems - Bending And... B 10 MIN
3/4 INCH VIDEO CASSETTE
Emphasizes the care and skills required in the bending and stalling phases of working with chrome-molybdenum piping. Issued in 1958 as a motion picture.
LC NO. 79-707969
Prod-USN Dist-USNAC Prodn-KAYF 1979

Piping Fabrication For Shipboard High Temperature Steam Systems - Introduction B 13 MIN
3/4 INCH VIDEO CASSETTE
Emphasizes the care and skill required for the handling, fabrication and installation of chrome-molybdenum piping in shipboard high temperature, high-pressure steam systems. Issued in 1958 as a motion picture.
LC NO. 79-707968
Prod-USN Dist-USNAC Prodn-KAYF 1979

Piping Fabrication For Shipboard High Temperature Steam Systems - Welding B 13 MIN
3/4 INCH VIDEO CASSETTE
Emphasizes the care and skills required in the welding phases of working with chrome-molybdenum piping. Issued in 1958 as a motion picture.
LC NO. 79-707965
Prod-USN Dist-USNAC Prodn-KAYF 1979

Piping Isometrics C
3/4 OR 1/2 INCH VIDEO CASSETTE IND
See series title for descriptive statement.
From The Drafting - Piping Familiarization Series.
Prod-GPCV Dist-GPCV

Piping Preparation And Installation C 60 MIN
3/4 OR 1/2 INCH VIDEO CASSETTE IND
See series title for descriptive statement.
From The Mechanical Equipment Maintenance, Module 17 - Advanced Pipefitting Series.
Prod-LEIKID Dist-LEIKID

Piping Symbols C 12 MIN
3/4 OR 1/2 INCH VIDEO CASSETTE
Covers piping systems, kinds of diagrams, joints fittings and symbols.
From The Reading Schematics And Symbols Series.
Prod-TPCTRA Dist-TPCTRA

Piping Symbols (Spanish) C 12 MIN
3/4 OR 1/2 INCH VIDEO CASSETTE
Covers Piping Systems, kinds of diagrams, joints, fittings, and symbols.
From The Reading Schematics And Symbols Series.
Prod-TPCTRA Dist-TPCTRA

Pippi Goes On Board C 84 MIN
16MM FILM OPTICAL SOUND P-I
Presents robbers who are out to get Pippi's survival money.
Prod-FI Dist-FI

Pippi In The South Seas C 85 MIN
16MM FILM OPTICAL SOUND P-I
Presents Pippi as she rescues her sea captain father.
Prod-FI Dist-FI

Pippi Longstocking C 99 MIN
16MM FILM OPTICAL SOUND P-I
Presents the story from the book by Astrid Lindgrer.
Prod-FI Dist-FI

Pippi On The Run C 97 MIN
16MM FILM OPTICAL SOUND P-I
Presents Pippi and friends as they run away and have many fanciful adventures.
Prod-FI Dist-FI

Pirandello's Six Characters In Search Of An Author C 60 MIN
3/4 OR 1/2 INCH VIDEO CASSETTE C
See series title for descriptive statement.
From The Drama - Play, Performance, Perception Series. Module 4
Prod-MDCC Dist-MDCC

Piranesi C 29 MIN
2 INCH VIDEOTAPE
See series title for descriptive statement.
From The Museum Open House Series.
Prod-WGBHTV Dist-PUBTEL

Pirate's Treasure, The B 23 MIN
16MM FILM SILENT
Presents an episode of the serial The Perils Of Pauline. Shows what happens when Pauline is trapped on a ship with a time-bomb about to explode. Stars Pearl White.
Prod-UNKNWN Dist-KILLIS 1914

Pirro C 11 MIN
16MM FILM, 3/4 OR 1/2 IN VIDEO K-P
Presents the adventures of Pirro, a marionette. Narrated verbally and in sign language.
Prod-PASPRO Dist-TEXFLM 1978

Pisa - Story Of A Cathedral Square (1000 - 1300 A D) C 10 MIN
16MM FILM OPTICAL SOUND
Presents the story of the Pisa Cathedral Square from 1000 to 1300 A D.
Prod-ROLAND Dist-ROLAND

Pista - The Many Faces Of Stephen Deutch C 28 MIN
16MM FILM OPTICAL SOUND
Traces the life of Hungarian photographer-sculptor Stephen Deutch. Reveals his attitudes toward art, music and family.
LC NO. 80-700272
Prod-TATLOC Dist-TATLOC 1979

Pistol Shooting Fundamentals C 15 MIN
16MM FILM, 3/4 OR 1/2 IN VIDEO J-C A
Presents World Pistol Champion Bill Blankenship and Women's World Air Pistol Champion Ruby E Fox demonstrating the fundamentals of pistol marksmanship. Covers sight alignment, breath control, hold control, trigger control and follow through with a strong emphasis on safety.
From The Rifle Shooting Fundamentals Series.
Prod-ATHI Dist-ATHI 1982

Pistol, The C 10 MIN
16MM FILM OPTICAL SOUND H-C A
A wry commentary on man's tendency to solve problems with a gun.
LC NO. 70-710167
Prod-URCHS Dist-VIEWFI 1970

Piston And Liner Removal B 12 MIN
16MM FILM OPTICAL SOUND
Tells how to remove connecting rod bearings, fork rod piston assembly, blade rod piston assembly and opposite liners.
LC NO. FIE52-1367
Prod-USN Dist-USNAC 1945

Pit And Smoke, The C 20 MIN
3/4 OR 1/2 INCH VIDEO CASSETTE J-H
Presents THE PIT by Reginald Maddock, set in the English industrial midlands. Centers on a boy who finally strikes back after enduring the beatings of his drunkard father. Narrates from SMOKE by William Corbin, set in Oregon. Describes how a boy who cannot accept his stepfather finds a lost dog and then begins to cooperate with his stepfather. (Broadcast quality)
From The Matter Of Fiction Series. No. 1
Prod-WETATV Dist-AITECH

Pit And The Pendulum, The C 8 MIN
16MM FILM OPTICAL SOUND
Presents an adaption of Edgar Allan Poe's short story The Pit And The Pendulum.
LC NO. 76-701474
Prod-CCAAT Dist-CCAAT 1975

Pit And The Pendulum, The C 80 MIN
16MM FILM OPTICAL SOUND H A
Presents the gothic horror tale of lovers who plan to drive her brother mad. The brother responds by locking them in his torture chamber. Based on the Edgar Allan Poe story. Stars Vincent Price.
Prod-AIP Dist-TIMLIF 1961

Pit-Stop C 28 MIN
16MM FILM OPTICAL SOUND
A driver-education film for high school students. Uses scenes of races and race-car drivers to explain that safe practices on the track are similar to safe practices on the highway.
LC NO. 76-702848
Prod-COCA Dist-CMI Prodn-CMI 1968

Pitch Buttoning And Blocking B 30 MIN
16MM FILM OPTICAL SOUND

Demonstrates the blocking of large convex lenses, blocking with pagoda tool, the use of the ring button, buttoning and blocking with pitch points and the pitch buttoning and blocking of very small lenses.
LC NO. FIE52-383
Prod-USOE Dist-USNAC 1944

Pitchers, Spouts And Handles C 12 MIN
16MM FILM, 3/4 OR 1/2 IN VIDEO A
Deals with thrown pitcher forms, including addition of suitable spouts and handles. Stresses the value of practice in achieving hand coordination. Explains how to handle the fushly thrown pitcher so as to form a spout that is both pleasing and functional.
From The Art And The Artist Series.
Prod-CINCPR Dist-PHENIX 1968

Pitching C 29 MIN
3/4 OR 1/2 INCH VIDEO CASSETTE
Presents George Bamberger, Oriole pitching coach and players Dave Mc Nally, Jim Palmer, Grant Jackson and Eddie Watt, teaching stance and foot position, wind-up, concealing pitches, 3/4 delivery, overhand, side-arm, follow-through/balance fast-ball-curve ball, change-up/slider/knuckler, sinker/screw ball, covering first and bunt coverage/backing bases.
From The Basically Baseball Series.
Prod-MDCPB Dist-MDCPB

Pitching For The Yankees C 15 MIN
16MM FILM, 3/4 OR 1/2 IN VIDEO J-C
New York Yankee players, such as Whitey Ford and Al Downing, talk about their approach to various aspects of pitching in baseball.
Prod-SBRAND Dist-MOKIN 1965

Pitchpipe, The B 13 MIN
16MM FILM OPTICAL SOUND T
Illustrates the purpose and use of the pitch pipe. Introduces major key signatures and their key tones.
Prod-JHP Dist-MLA 1955

Pitfalls In Biliary Tract Surgery C 38 MIN
16MM FILM OPTICAL SOUND
Reviews the anatomy of the biliary tract, demonstrates the common mechanisms of vascular and ductile injury occurring during cholecystectomy and illustrates the techniques of safe cholocystectomy.
LC NO. FIA65-851
Prod-ACYDGD Dist-ACY 1964

Pitfalls In Stapes Surgery C 19 MIN
16MM FILM OPTICAL SOUND PRO
Illustrates the difficult problems that may confront the surgeon in performing the stapes operation to correct hearing loss due to otosclerosis.
Prod-EAR Dist-EAR

Pitfalls In Stapes Surgery C 18 MIN
3/4 OR 1/2 INCH VIDEO CASSETTE PRO
Presents the pitfalls in stapes surgery.
Prod-HOUSEI Dist-HOUSEI

Pithole, USA B 14 MIN
16MM FILM OPTICAL SOUND H-C A
Documents the first roistering days of the oil industry in the 1800's.
Prod-USSC Dist-USSC

Pits, Peaks And Passes, A Lecture On Critical Point Theory, Pt 1 C 48 MIN
16MM FILM OPTICAL SOUND H-C T
Professor Marston Morse, with models and animation, derives the simple formula relating the number of pits, peaks and passes on an island with a single shoreline. An account of the professor's career and a discussion on the relationship between mathematics, physics and the arts are included.
From The MAA Individual Lecturers Series.
LC NO. FIA66-1272
Prod-MAA Dist-MLA 1966

Pits, Peaks And Passes, A Lecture On Critical Point Theory, Pt 2 C 26 MIN
16MM FILM OPTICAL SOUND H-C T
Presents a lecture by Professor Marston Morse in which he analyzes the critical points of continuous functions over compact, orientable 3-manifolds. He defines the degree of stability in N-dimensions and presents applications to electrodynamics.
From The MAA Individual Lecturers Series.
LC NO. FIA66-1265
Prod-MAA Dist-MLA 1966

Pittsburgh - An American Industrial City C 43 MIN
16MM FILM OPTICAL SOUND
Reviews the history of the Pittsburgh, Pennsylvania, area and examines the people, places and industries that have contributed to the development of this region. Includes archival lithographs, photographs and film footage.
LC NO. 80-701370
Prod-MAGIC Dist-MAGIC 1980

Pittsburgh Police—A Series

Documents the performance of the Pittsburgh, Pennsylvania, police force in 1969 and 1970. Focuses on the issues of privacy and civil liberties versus police intervention, interrogation, and search and seizure. Filmed by anthropological documentarian John Marshall.
Prod-DOCEDR Dist-DOCEDR Prodn-MSHLLJ

After The Game 009 MIN
Forty Dollar Misunderstanding, A 008 MIN
Fourth And Fifth Exclusionary Rule, The 080 MIN
Henry Is Drunk 007 MIN
Informant, The 024 MIN
Inside/Outside Station Nine 090 MIN
Investigation Of A Hit And Run 035 MIN
Legal Discussion Of A Hit And Run, A 028 MIN
Manifold Controversy 003 MIN
Nine-Hundred-One/Nine-Hundred-Four 065 MIN
Nothing Hurt But My Pride 015 MIN
Three Domestics 036 MIN
Twenty-One Dollars Or Twenty-One Days 008 MIN
Two Brothers 004 MIN
Vagrant Woman 008 MIN
Wrong Kid 004 MIN
You Wasn't Loitering 015 MIN
Youth And The Man Of Property 007 MIN

Pituitary Hormones B 30 MIN
16MM FILM OPTICAL SOUND C
Reviews pituitary anatomy and physiology and shows the mechanism of action, classification and clinical uses of pituitary hormones. Classifies oxytoxic agents.
From The Pharmacology Series.
LC NO. 73-703350
Prod-MVNE Dist-TELSTR 1971

Pixel Is Worth A Thousand Words, A C 30 MIN
16MM FILM, 3/4 OR 1/2 IN VIDEO I-H
Demonstrates how a computer reads and forms pictures, how pictures are stored in the computer and how animation is done. Discusses resolution (image quality) and computer monitors.
From The Mr Microchip Series.
Prod-JOU Dist-JOU

Pizza Pizza Daddy-O B 18 MIN
16MM FILM, 3/4 OR 1/2 IN VIDEO C A
An anthropological and folkloric record of singing games played by Afro-American girls in the fourth grade of a school in Los Angeles.
Prod-HAWESB Dist-UCEMC 1969

Pizza Variations C 30 MIN
3/4 OR 1/2 INCH VIDEO CASSETTE H-C
Using simple devices, shows how to make in your own oven, the kind of pizza you always hope for but seldom get.
From The French Chef Series.
Prod-WGBH Dist-KINGFT

PKU - Preventable Mental Retardation (2nd Ed) C 16 MIN
16MM FILM, 3/4 OR 1/2 IN VIDEO PRO
Reports on the effectiveness of present procedures used in diagnosing PKU. Includes information on new blood tests and new techniques for testing urine that can be used at home.
Prod-IFB Dist-IFB 1967

PKU - Retardo Mental Evitable C 15 MIN
16MM FILM, 3/4 OR 1/2 IN VIDEO H-C
Spanish version uses a series of actual case histories to emphasize the need for the universal examination of all children for phenylketonuria. Illustrates a simple test for PKU which can be made at home.
Prod-IFB Dist-IFB 1962

Place Between Our Bodies, The C 33 MIN
3/4 OR 1/2 INCH VIDEO CASSETTE C A
Comes to grips with the issues involved in one gay man's sexuality. Progresses from sexual observation, cruising, fantasy and pornography films to a lover relationship.
Prod-MMRC Dist-MMRC

Place Called Ardoyne, A C 40 MIN
16MM FILM OPTICAL SOUND
Depicts a Catholic community in Belfast, Northern Ireland. Portrays the traumatic changes in the people's lives since Ardoyne came under Protestant attack in 1968.
Prod-THMPSN Dist-IMPACT

Place For Everything, A C 15 MIN
3/4 OR 1/2 INCH VIDEO CASSETTE P
Uses a space robot and his puppet assistant in a visit to a math class to explain the concepts of place value and zero. Tells how the robot and his assistant show the development of a system to write numbers down and then teach a game which explores number relationships using place value pieces.
From The Math Mission 2 Series.
LC NO. 82-706320
Prod-WCVETV Dist-GPITVL 1980

Place For Growing, A X 15 MIN
16MM FILM OPTICAL SOUND
Highlights the conversion of an anti-social youngster through membership in a boy's club. Illustrates how unsupervised activity may get youth into trouble. Presents an entertaining review of the national youth organization's activities in story form.
Prod-BCLA Dist-BCLA

Place For No Story, The C 59 MIN
16MM FILM OPTICAL SOUND
Presents an ecologically-aware, aerial portrait of California, which captures the panoramic beauty of the varied coastline and countryside as well as the man-made wounds and scars of the State.
LC NO. 74-702882
Prod-KQEDTV Dist-KQEDTV 1974

Place In Europe—A Series
16MM FILM, 3/4 OR 1/2 IN VIDEO H-C A
Features Europe's most historic homes. Includes a seventeenth century Scottish castle, Sweden's Royal Place and houses in Austria, Denmark and France.
Prod-THAMES Dist-MEDIAG 1975

Braemar Castle, Scotland 026 MIN
Burg Clam, Austria 026 MIN
Egeskov, Denmark 026 MIN
Goodwood House, England 026 MIN
Island Of Hydara, Greece, The 026 MIN
Jerez De La Fontera - The House Of 026 MIN
Le Chateau De Jehay, Belgium 026 MIN
Palazzo Giustiniani, Venice 026 MIN
Plas Newydd - Anglesey, Wales 026 MIN
Royal Palace, Stockholm, The 026 MIN
Schloss Johannisberg, Germany 026 MIN
Schloss Vaduz - Liechtenstein 026 MIN
Vaux-Le-Vicomte, France 026 MIN

Place In History, A C 28 MIN
16MM FILM, 3/4 OR 1/2 IN VIDEO
Depicts the life of Dwight Eisenhower, emphasizing his role in World War II and his White House years. Narrated by Lorne Greene.
Prod-NA Dist-USNAC

Place In Our World, A C 14 MIN
16MM FILM OPTICAL SOUND
Shows how the acoupedic approach teaches deaf children to hear. Demonstrates techniques with children in different phases of the program.
LC NO. 76-702665
Prod-TPA Dist-TPA Prodn-MTBAVC 1976

Place In The Sun, A C 52 MIN
16MM FILM, 3/4 OR 1/2 IN VIDEO J-C A
Describes how the first Italians in America were stigmatized for their colored skin, their unfamiliar language and the mafiosa label that lingers today. Four million Italians and Sicilians entered America in a twenty-year period, the most concentrated migration of all European countries and originally the least welcomed.
From The Destination America Series.
Prod-THAMES Dist-MEDIAG 1976

Place In Time B 34 MIN
16MM FILM SILENT
Presents a comedy satire in the silent film tradition of Charlie Chaplin and Buster Keaton. Tells the story of a young street portrait painter. Touches on themes of crime, apathy and alienation in urban society, and the struggles of the artist.
Prod-BLKFMF Dist-BLKFMF

Place Just Right, A C 30 MIN
16MM FILM OPTICAL SOUND
Presents the story of city people moving to the country and their realization that they cannot carry city life with them and that they must learn to adapt to the ways of the backwoods if they are to survive.
LC NO. 80-701483
Prod-GUTKND Dist-PSU 1980

Place Of Being, A C 12 MIN
16MM FILM - 3/4 IN VIDEO
Describes recreational activities available in the Lake Mead National Recreation Area in Nevada. Issued in 1967 as a motion picture.
LC NO. 79-706153
Prod-USNPS Dist-USNAC 1979

Place Of Belonging C 26 MIN
16MM FILM OPTICAL SOUND
Creates an awareness of the different forms of beauty found in cities. Explains that art, not luxury, is necessary and that nature enriches cities.
From The Changing Environment USA Series.
LC NO. 72-702327
Prod-ALEF Dist-ALEF 1972

Place Of Dreams, A - The National Air And Space Museum C 35 MIN
16MM FILM, 3/4 OR 1/2 IN VIDEO J-C A
A shortened version of the motion picture A Place Of Dreams - The National Air And Space Museum. Presents a tour through the National Air And Space Museum in Washington, D C, which is dedicated to the men and women who made air and space flight possible.
Prod-PAPPVA Dist-LCOA 1980

Place Of Dreams, A - The National Air And Space Museum C 59 MIN
16MM FILM, 3/4 OR 1/2 IN VIDEO J-C A
Presents a tour through the National Air and Space Museum in Washington, D C, which is dedicated to the men and women who made air and space flight possible.
Prod-PAPPVA Dist-LCOA 1980

Place Of Refuge, A C 26 MIN
16MM FILM OPTICAL SOUND
Describes the historical Kootenay Valley, located between the Selkirk and the Canadian Rockies, and discusses the year-round recreational activities available there.
LC NO. 78-705967
Prod-BCDTI Dist-CTFL 1969

Place That Comma C 19 MIN
16MM FILM, 3/4 OR 1/2 IN VIDEO J-C A
Uses the format of a television game show to introduce, repeat and reinforce the rules of comma placement.
Prod-PFP Dist-PFP 1979

Place To Be All You Can Be, A C 10 MIN
16MM FILM OPTICAL SOUND
Shows many of the career opportunities available to young people in today's Army including dental technician, a tugboat crewperson, a Military Policewoman, a newscaster, a vehicle driver and a pilot.
Prod-USA Dist-MTP

Place To Be Me, A C 13 MIN
16MM FILM OPTICAL SOUND
Presents the many opportunities available to women in the U S

Army. Includes such widely diverse jobs as dental technician, aviation crew chief and truck driver with emphasis on future opportunities. Stresses recreation, economical living conditions and the camaraderies that exist in the service.
Prod-USA Dist-MTP

Place To Be Yourself, A C 30 MIN
3/4 OR 1/2 INCH VIDEO CASSETTE P-I
See series title for descriptive statement.
From The Sonrisas Series.
Prod-KRLNTV Dist-MDCPB

Place To Be, A C 13 MIN
16MM FILM OPTICAL SOUND J-C A
Tours Vancouver, including panoramic views from Grouse Mountain, as well as, scenes of shopping areas, parks and indoor and outdoor recreational areas.
LC NO. 70-700890
Prod-WILFGP Dist-CTFL 1968

Place To Be, A C 59 MIN
3/4 OR 1/2 INCH VIDEO CASSETTE A
Recounts the construction of a new addition to the National Gallery of Art in Washington, DC. Discusses the problems of scale, design and materials and shows how these were resolved in the attainment of a harmonious trapezoidal building, which houses a museum and study center.
LC NO. 80-707285
Prod-WETATV Dist-PBS 1979

Place To Be, A - The Construction Of The East Building Of The National Gallery Of Art C 60 MIN
16MM FILM OPTICAL SOUND
Follows the creation of the East Building of the National Gallery of Art in Washington, DC, from the time it was designed by architect I M Pei to the final placement of artworks. Includes views of construction workers pouring concrete and shows meetings between artists, the architect, and museum staff.
LC NO. 80-700188
Prod-GUG Dist-USNGA 1979

Place To Belong, A B 9 MIN
16MM FILM OPTICAL SOUND
Tells how a community organization in a depressed neighborhood sets up a boxing association to help keep teenagers off the streets. Shows how their plans are hampered after the group loses its building to an urban renewal project.
LC NO. 73-700609
Prod-TEMPLU Dist-TEMPLU 1972

Place To Call Home, A C 13 MIN
16MM FILM OPTICAL SOUND C A
Shows the kinds of programs and activities offered in nursing homes which care for both the young mentally retarded and elderly residents.
LC NO. 72-702023
Prod-UKANBC Dist-UKANS 1972

Place To Eat And Be Safe, A B 15 MIN
2 INCH VIDEOTAPE P
Describes home as a place where a family eats, sleeps and is protected. Explains that homes are designed to take care of as many needs as possible. (Broadcast quality)
From The Around The Corner Series. No. 15
Prod-FWCETV Dist-GPITVL Prodn-WEDUTV

Place To Get Well, A C 20 MIN
16MM FILM OPTICAL SOUND P-I
Portrays the hospital and its routines through the eyes of a child in an effort to show children that hospitals are not to be feared. Includes doctors, nurses, the admissions procedure, the separation of child from parent, the children's ward, play therapy, meals, the operating room and other features.
Prod-MESHDO Dist-MESHDO 1970

Place To Go, A B 10 MIN
16MM FILM OPTICAL SOUND
A free cinema essay on an espresso coffee house, the patrons and the proprietors, the way they look and what they do.
Prod-KAJMRD Dist-NWUFLM 1960

Place To Go, A B 25 MIN
16MM FILM OPTICAL SOUND
Discusses the adjustment of the aged to nursing homes and the role of the nurses aide in helping make that sometimes difficult adjustment possible.
Prod-UHOSF Dist-HF Prodn-HF 1966

Place To Go, A C 15 MIN
16MM FILM, 3/4 OR 1/2 IN VIDEO A
Reveals the often ignored problem of wifebeating, a crime to which nearly two million American females annually fall victim. Observes women sharing their experiences and show ways communities can aid battered women. Hosted by Dan Rather and originally shown on the program 60 Minutes.
LC NO. 82-706462
Prod-MTI Dist-MTI 1981

Place To Land, A C 20 MIN
3/4 INCH VIDEO CASSETTE
Describes operation metro air support, a two-day exercise sponsored by FAA and state and municipal agencies in November, 1966, demonstrating the ability of V-STOL aircraft and helicopters to provide air access and logistic support to a metropolitan center-city area in time of emergency.
Prod-USNAC Dist-USNAC 1972

Place To Learn, A C 19 MIN
16MM FILM OPTICAL SOUND A
Deals with the multipurpose services of a vital, growing community college learning resource center.
LC NO. 73-700692
Prod-DUPAGE Dist-DUPAGE 1972

Place To Live—A Series
I-H
Looks at the environment of common types of plants and animals. Describes the formation of valleys and the formation of the Grand Canyon.
Prod-GRATV Dist-JOU

Life In The Past	015 MIN
Life In The Valley	015 MIN
On The Ground	015 MIN
Spring In The Woods	015 MIN

Place To Live, A C 27 MIN
16MM FILM OPTICAL SOUND
Tells the story of the rebirth of an American city and what the citizens accomplished between World War II and today.
Prod-SLOUIS Dist-GUG 1960

Place To Live, A C 30 MIN
16MM FILM - 3/4 IN VIDEO J-C A
Examines the dilemmas of rapid urbanization, focusing on Auckland, New Zealand and Jakarta, Indonesia.
From The Man Builds - Man Destroys Series.
LC NO. 75-704155
Prod-UN Dist-GPITVL 1975

Place To Meet, A - A Way To Understand C 35 MIN
16MM FILM OPTICAL SOUND
Documents a unique experiment in American life. Presents the idea that children and the occupational world of most adults do not need to remain apart.
LC NO. 74-705372
Prod-USSRS Dist-USNAC 1971

Place To Meet, A - A Way To Understand C 27 MIN
16MM FILM, 3/4 OR 1/2 IN VIDEO
Explains an experiment in which two groups of children, one from the slums and another from middle income families, went into the plant of the Detroit Free Press and observed and participated in all stages of the production of the newspaper. Shows how this brought children and adults back into each other's lives.
Prod-CUETV Dist-CUNIV 1972

Place To Place C 12 MIN
3/4 INCH VIDEO CASSETTE P
Tells how two competing villages try to outdo one another in making a new mileage counter for an automobile executive. Introduces the concept of place value.
Prod-DAVFMS Dist-GA

Place To Work, A B 25 MIN
16MM FILM OPTICAL SOUND
Discusses the challenges, opportunities and rewards of a career as a nurses aide.
Prod-UHOSF Dist-HF Prodn-HF 1966

Place Value C 15 MIN
3/4 OR 1/2 INCH VIDEO CASSETTE P
Discusses place value in the base ten system.
From The Math Cycle Series.
Prod-WDCNTV Dist-GPITVL 1983

Place Value - Know Your Place C 20 MIN
16MM FILM, 3/4 OR 1/2 IN VIDEO I-J
Discussses aspects of place value.
From The Mathscore One Series.
Prod-BBCTV Dist-FI

Place Value - Ones, Tens, Hundreds (2nd Ed) C 10 MIN
16MM FILM, 3/4 OR 1/2 IN VIDEO P
Uses animation to introduce the concept of place value and explain the function of the one-place, the ten-place and the hundred-place.
Prod-CORF Dist-CORF

Place Value - Place Value Of Large Numbers C 15 MIN
3/4 OR 1/2 INCH VIDEO CASSETTE I
Uses visuals to reinforce a sense of large numbers up to and including one million.
From The Math Works Series.
Prod-AITECH Dist-AITECH

Place Value - Take It Away C 20 MIN
16MM FILM, 3/4 OR 1/2 IN VIDEO I
Discusses aspects of place value.
From The Mathscore Two Series.
Prod-BBCTV Dist-FI

Place Value - The Teens C 15 MIN
3/4 INCH VIDEO CASSETTE P
Explains how to read and write numbers to 20, when given sets of objects.
From The Measure Up Series.
Prod-WCETTV Dist-GPITVL 1977

Place Value And Addition C 30 MIN
16MM FILM OPTICAL SOUND T
Discusses the properties of closure, commutativity and associativity under addition. Describes the additive identity. To be used following 'NUMERATION SYSTEMS.'
From The Mathematics For Elementary School Teachers Series. No. 5
Prod-SMSG Dist-MLA 1963

Place Value And Decimals C 30 MIN
3/4 OR 1/2 INCH VIDEO CASSETTE
See series title for descriptive statement.
From The Infinity Factory Series.
Prod-EDFCEN Dist-MDCPB

Place Value And Fractions C 29 MIN
3/4 INCH VIDEO CASSETTE I
See series title for descriptive statement.
From The Infinity Factory Series.
Prod-EDC Dist-PUBTEL 1976

Place Value, Face Value C 15 MIN
3/4 INCH VIDEO CASSETTE P
Explains the concept of place value and the meaning of two and three digit numbers.
From The Math Factory, Module III - Number Patterns Series.
Prod-MAETEL Dist-GPITVL 1973

Place Value, Pt 1 C 15 MIN
3/4 INCH VIDEO CASSETTE P
Explains how to read and write numbers up to 99.
From The Measure Up Series.
Prod-WCETTV Dist-GPITVL 1977

Place Value, Pt 2 C 15 MIN
3/4 INCH VIDEO CASSETTE P
Tells how to state the order of two two-digit numbers. Explains how to complete a sequence counting by ones, twos, fives and tens.
From The Measure Up Series.
Prod-WCETTV Dist-GPITVL 1977

Place Value, Pt 3 C 15 MIN
3/4 INCH VIDEO CASSETTE P
Tells how many tens there are in sets of hundreds and how to read and write three-digit numbers.
From The Measure Up Series.
Prod-WCETTV Dist-GPITVL 1977

Place, The C 20 MIN
3/4 INCH VIDEO CASSETTE I-J
Introduces the Arab world, focusing on Jordan, Egypt, Syria and Yemen. Examines the geography and culture of this region and emphasizes the impact of Islam.
From The Project Middle East Series.
Prod-UNICEF Dist-GPITVL

Placement Service, The X 27 MIN
16MM FILM, 3/4 OR 1/2 IN VIDEO J-C A
Tells how two men arrive for final placement in eternity.
From The Insight Series.
Prod-PAULST Dist-PAULST

Placement Service, The C 27 MIN
3/4 OR 1/2 INCH VIDEO CASSETTE J A
Dramatizes the story of two men who arrive for final placement Shows one who chooses to make other people happy.
Prod-SUTHRB Dist-SUTHRB

Placental And Foetal Membranes, The C 24 MIN
3/4 OR 1/2 INCH VIDEO CASSETTE C A
Demonstrates the early development of the embryo and its associated membranes. Describes how the placenta develops. Discusses placental circulation. Shows specimen fetuses in development. Illustrates fresh single and twin placentas following birth.
Prod-UTORMC Dist-TEF

Placental Circulation C 18 MIN
16MM FILM OPTICAL SOUND PRO
Studies the pattern of placental vasculature and the dynamics of placental circulation, based on the results of radioangiographic studies in rhesus monkeys. Examines serial and cine radiograms after injection of a radiopaque medium into the maternal and fetal circulation.
Prod-SQUIBB Dist-SQUIBB

Placental Circulation C 20 MIN
3/4 OR 1/2 INCH VIDEO CASSETTE
Demonstrates the growth of endometrial sporal arteries, implantation of the blastocyst, trophoblastic penetration of the endometrium, tapping of maternal blood bessels and establishment of circulation in the intervillous space. Shows serial and cine radiograms made after injection of a radiopaque medium into the maternal or the fetal circulation or both simultaneously.
Prod-AMCOG Dist-AMCOG

Places In The News—A Series
2 INCH VIDEOTAPE I-H
Includes weekly 20-minute lessons which highlight current world events that have major political, economic, scientific or cultural significance. (Broadcast quality)
Prod-NYCPS Dist-GPITVL Prodn-WNYETV

Places Pattern C 16 MIN
16MM FILM MAGNETIC SOUND K-C A S
See series title for descriptive statement.
From The PANCOM Beginning Total Communication Program For Hearing Parents Of... Series. Level 1
LC NO. 77-700504
Prod-CSDE Dist-JOYCE Prodn-CSFDF 1977

Places To Visit B 29 MIN
2 INCH VIDEOTAPE K-P
See series title for descriptive statement.
From The Children's Fair Series.
Prod-WMVSTV Dist-PUBTEL

Places We Eat In C 29 MIN
3/4 OR 1/2 INCH VIDEO CASSETTE J-H A
See series title for descriptive statement.
From The Food For Youth Series.
Prod-CUETV Dist-CUNIV 1975

Places We Eat In C 29 MIN
16MM FILM, 3/4 OR 1/2 IN VIDEO
Takes a look at how children feel about their mealtime environment and discusses why they feel this way. Applies this information to school lunchrooms and discusses portion sizes for children of different ages and management of school dining rooms.
From The Food For Youth Series.
Prod-USFNS Dist-USNAC Prodn-WGBHTV 1974

Places Where People Live C 20 MIN
3/4 OR 1/2 INCH VIDEO CASSETTE I-J
Considers the advantages and disadvantages of rural, urban and suburban living and discusses planned communities.
From The Terra - Our World Series.
Prod-MSDOE Dist-AITECH 1980

Places, Places, Special Places C 10 MIN
3/4 OR 1/2 INCH VIDEO CASSETTE K-P
Focuses on the realization that children, as well as adults, often need a special place where they can be alone.
From The Book, Look And Listen Series.
Prod-MDDE Dist-AITECH 1977

Placing The Right Man On The Job B 13 MIN
16MM FILM - 3/4 IN VIDEO
Dramatizes the cases of five workers who are reassigned to other jobs more suitable to their abilities. Issued in 1944 as a motion picture.
From The Problems In Supervision Series.
LC NO. 79-706449
Prod-USOE Dist-USNAC Prodn-CARFI 1979

Placing The Right Man On The Job (Spanish) B 13 MIN
16MM FILM - 3/4 IN VIDEO
Dramatizes the cases of five workers who are reassigned to other jobs more suitable to their abilities and capacities. Issued in 1944 as a motion picture.
From The Problems In Supervision (Spanish) Series.
LC NO. 79-706670
Prod-USOE Dist-USNAC 1979

Plague Control C 21 MIN
16MM FILM OPTICAL SOUND
Explains the chief clinical types of plague, the type of environment in which plague tends to flourish, the role of the rat and rat flea and rat control measures.
LC NO. FIE52-1338
Prod-USN Dist-USNAC

Plague In Sylvatic Areas C 26 MIN
16MM FILM OPTICAL SOUND
Traces the world history of plague and its introduction into the United States. Explains the importance of the control of transmission agents, including the rodent-borne fleas. Discusses methods of rapid diagnosis and treatment.
LC NO. FIE61-17
Prod-USPHS Dist-USNAC 1961

Plague On Our Children, A, Pt 1 - Dioxins C 57 MIN
16MM FILM, 3/4 OR 1/2 IN VIDEO H-C A
Discusses Dioxin defoliants, like Sylvex sprayed on Oregon forests or Agent Orange dropped on Vietnam, which have caused miscarriages, cancers and disease. Looks at studies which show these herbicides cause serious health problems and theorizes that the Dioxin molecules fit into the basic DNA structure, altering it and causing mutations.
From The Nova Series.
LC NO. 79-708006
Prod-WGBHTV Dist-TIMLIF 1980

Plague On Our Children, A, Pt 2 - PCBS C 57 MIN
16MM FILM, 3/4 OR 1/2 IN VIDEO H-C A
Discusses how banning toxic chemicals has not solved their problem because no solution has been found to clean up chemical dumps or to break down their non-biodegradable structure. Points out that over 90 per cent of all toxic wastes are dumped unsafely, illegally and secretly. Discusses the Hooker Chemical and Plastic Company in Love Canal, New York, which knew toxic chemicals were leaking out of drums they had buried on land they had sold for a school playground.
From The Nova Series.
LC NO. 79-708006
Prod-WGBHTV Dist-TIMLIF 1980

Plain And Fill-In Postal Cards B 30 MIN
2 INCH VIDEOTAPE
From The Typewriting, Unit 7 - Postal Cards, Forms, Manuscripts Series.
Prod-GPITVL Dist-GPITVL

Plain Indexing And Cutting A Spur Gear B 26 MIN
16MM FILM, 3/4 OR 1/2 IN VIDEO
Explains diametral pitch and the parts of a gear tooth, the use of the dividing head for spacing teeth and the operations of a milling machine in the cutting of a spur gear.
From The Machine Shop Work - Operations On The Milling Machine Series. No. 4
Prod-USOE Dist-USNAC 1941

Plain Journal Bearings C 60 MIN
3/4 OR 1/2 INCH VIDEO CASSETTE IND
See series title for descriptive statement.
From The Mechanical Equipment Maintenance, Module 4 - Bearings And Lubrication Series.
Prod-LEIKID Dist-LEIKID

Plain White Envelope, A X 20 MIN
16MM FILM, 3/4 OR 1/2 IN VIDEO I-J
Tells the story of a boy who, wanting very badly to win a spelling contest, accidentally finds a white envelope with the contest words inside and faces the problem of cheating.
Prod-TRAFCO Dist-PHENIX 1965

Plain Wrap Exercise - Men C 43 MIN
1/2 IN VIDEO CASSETTE BETA/VHS
Presents a series of exercises for men which can be done in the home.
Prod-MOHOMV Dist-MOHOMV

Plain Wrap Exercise - Women C 50 MIN
1/2 IN VIDEO CASSETTE BETA/VHS
Presents a home fitness program for women. Includes exercises such as wall stretches, indoor running, leg raises, push-ups and sit-ups.
Prod-MOHOMV Dist-MOHOMV

Plains And Plateaus X 10 MIN
16MM FILM, 3/4 OR 1/2 IN VIDEO P-I
Uses maps of several areas of the United States to depict the physical features which distinguish plains and plateaus. Illustrates the effects which the physical features have on land uses for each landform.
Prod-IU Dist-IU 1968

Plains Indian Culture—A Series

Prod-UOKLA Dist-UOKLA

Indian Musical Instruments 13 MIN
Old Chief's Dance 9 MIN

Plains Indian Girl C 13 MIN
16MM FILM OPTICAL SOUND P-H
Presents an Indian girl who hears stories of her ancestors, sees dances and imagines herself living in olden times, but decides it is more fun to be an Indian today.
Prod-YALEDV Dist-YALEDV

Plains People C 14 MIN
16MM FILM, 3/4 OR 1/2 IN VIDEO I-C A
Describes the life of the Masai, a proud tribe of semi-nomadic herdsmen who live along the great Rift Valley of Kenya and Tanganyika and subsist on the milk, meat and blood of their livestock. Compares the way of life of the Cheyenne and Crow Indians living on the North Cheyenne Reservation in southeastern Montana for whom the ranch is a family enterprise and everyone works for it.
From The Places People Live Series.
Prod-SF Dist-SF

Plains, The C 28 MIN
16MM FILM OPTICAL SOUND C A
Tells of the problems involved in the excavation by the Smithsonian Institution of a fortified earth-lodge village of prehistoric Indians on the Missouri River in South Dakota in the Oahe Reservoir area. Shows at first hand how the archeologist decides where and how to dig in order to gain maximum amount of information from an archeological site.
From The Spadework For History Series.
Prod-UTEX Dist-UTEX 1963

Plains, The C 30 MIN
3/4 OR 1/2 INCH VIDEO CASSETTE
Explores the relationship between what people know, see and do and the plains around them.
From The Land And The People Series.
Prod-EKC Dist-MDCPB

Plainsmen Of The Past B 30 MIN
16MM FILM OPTICAL SOUND H-C A
Traces the prehistory of the Great Plains, from the entrance of man to the arrival of the Europeans. Shows how archaeologists work, presenting photographs, diagrams, specimens and interpretations of finds.
From The Great Plains Trilogy, 2 Series. Nomad And Indians - Early Man On The Plains
Prod-KUONTV Dist-UNEBR 1954

Plaintiff And Defendant Opening Statements C 37 MIN
3/4 OR 1/2 INCH VIDEO CASSETTE PRO
See series title for descriptive statement.
From The Trial Of A Civil Lawsuit Series.
Prod-SBWI Dist-ABACPE

Plan A City Of The Future C 15 MIN
16MM FILM, 3/4 OR 1/2 IN VIDEO I
Presents young people discussing ideas for future cities.
From The Thinkabout Series. Solving Problems
LC NO. 81-706115
Prod-EDFCEN Dist-AITECH 1979

Plan Ahead C 15 MIN
16MM FILM OPTICAL SOUND I
Shows how four children use a schedule to build a secret project at camp.
From The Thinkabout Series.
LC NO. 81-700142
Prod-OECA Dist-AITECH 1980

Plan Ahead C 14 MIN
3/4 OR 1/2 INCH VIDEO CASSETTE I
Tells how a group of young people use careful planning to create a surprise for their summer campmates.
From The Thinkabout Series. Sequencing And Scheduling
LC NO. 81-706116
Prod-OECA Dist-AITECH 1979

Plan For Living, A C 17 MIN
16MM FILM OPTICAL SOUND
Presents a parody dealing with the transformation of a man from a failure to a success.
LC NO. 78-701631
Prod-MORBRA Dist-MORBRA 1978

Plan For Living, A C 29 MIN
16MM FILM, 3/4 OR 1/2 IN VIDEO H-C A
Dramatizes the problems of parents with handicapped children, focusing on parental guilt and the negative effects that these can have on marriage and family life. Concludes showing the parents seeking genetic counseling.
From The Giving Birth And Independence Series.
LC NO. 81-707022
Prod-JRLLL Dist-LAWREN 1981

Plan For Prevention C 10 MIN
16MM FILM OPTICAL SOUND
See series title for descriptive statement.
From The Safety Management Series.
Prod-NSC Dist-NSC

Plan For Security C 12 MIN
3/4 OR 1/2 INCH VIDEO CASSETTE
Presents security as an organized approach to preventing loss of assets. Observes how security works, how the tools of security are used and how the security officer is the vital link in the total protection plan.
From The Professional Security Training Series. Module 1B
Prod-MTI Dist-MTI

Plan For Tomorrow C 29 MIN
2 INCH VIDEOTAPE
See series title for descriptive statement.
From The Environment - Today And Tomorrow Series.
Prod-KRMATV Dist-PUBTEL

Plan, The C 54 MIN
16MM FILM, 3/4 OR 1/2 IN VIDEO
Documents the everyday life story of Utah's 'Young Mother Of The Year' for 1978, Michele Meservy. Follows this young Mormon mother's attempts to organize and control the chaos created by five young children aged five, four, three, two and ten months.
Prod-CNEMAG Dist-CNEMAG 1980

Plan, Till And Plant C 30 MIN
3/4 OR 1/2 INCH VIDEO CASSETTE
Details a series of management decisions which need to be made before the corn is planted. Demonstrates the best compromise of weed, moisture and erosion control, and discusses selection of the proper variety of seed and planting procedures.
From The Corn - Planning To Harvest Series.
Prod-NETCHE Dist-NETCHE 1981

Planar Double Pendulum, The C 28 MIN
16MM FILM, 3/4 OR 1/2 IN VIDEO C A
Uses the planar double pendulum to illustrate the principles of chaotic behavior in three demonstrations. First, computer graphics show periodic, quasiperiodic and chaotic motion. The other two computer demonstrations show how these motions evolve, and how small variations in initial conditions have major consequences.
Prod-IWIF Dist-IFB

Plane Crash B 8 MIN
16MM FILM OPTICAL SOUND
A Spanish language film. Shows the Polaris missile launching from the USS Ethan Allen, John Glenn's address to Congress and the American Airlines astrojet crossing.
From The Spanish Newsreel Series. Vol 45, No. 54
Prod-TWCF Dist-TWCF

Plane Geometry C 20 MIN
3/4 INCH VIDEO CASSETTE H-C
Explains and identifies basic geometric elements and relationships.
From The Mainly Math Series.
Prod-WCVETV Dist-GPITVL 1977

Plane Sense C 20 MIN
16MM FILM OPTICAL SOUND
Acquaints the prospective pilot and airplane owner with the fundamentals of owning and operating an airplane. Offers hints about buying a used aircraft, outlines responsibilities in maintaining and recording the maintenance of the aircraft and engine and shows how to keep abreast of current FAA regulations concerning the operation and maintenance of an airplane.
LC NO. 74-705376
Prod-FAAFL Dist-USNAC 1968

Planes C 14 MIN
16MM FILM, 3/4 OR 1/2 IN VIDEO J-H A
Planes for wood work--construction of common planes, jack plane, smoothing plane, jointer planes, block plane, rabbet plane and router plane.
From The Hand Tools For Wood Working Series.
Prod-MORLAT Dist-SF 1967

Planes In The Sky, Ships In The Sea C 28 MIN
16MM FILM, 3/4 OR 1/2 IN VIDEO
Portrays the role of the Naval Ships Research and Development Center and affiliated laboratories in developing modern Naval ships and equipment.
LC NO. 82-706246
Prod-USN Dist-USNAC 1970

Planet Earth—A Series
C A
Examines the fundamentals of geophysics. Features international scientists sharing their theories about the formation of the earth - its oceans and climate and the universe. Focuses on geologic time, oceanography, climatology, mineral and energy resources, the sun, comparative planetology and the earth's future, using computer graphics, special effects and footage shot on seven continents, in the oceans and outer space.
Prod-ANNCPB Dist-FI

Blue Planet, The 060 MIN
Climate Puzzle, The 060 MIN
Fate Of The Earth 060 MIN
Gifts From The Earth 060 MIN
Living Machine, The 060 MIN
Solar Sea, The 060 MIN
Tales From Other Worlds 060 MIN

Planet Earth, The - A Scientific Model C 24 MIN
16MM FILM, 3/4 OR 1/2 IN VIDEO H-C A
Uses a three-dimensional model of the earth-moon system and animation to give a truer picture of the earth's place and movements in the solar system. Reconstructs the classic Foucault pendulum experiment by hanging a pendulum from the dome of St Paul's Cathedral in London.
Prod-MEDIAG Dist-MEDIAG 1981

Planet Mars C 29 MIN
16MM FILM, 3/4 OR 1/2 IN VIDEO
Discusses what has been learned about the planet Mars from Earth-based telescopes, observations from the fly-by Mariner spacecraft, and the Viking landing.
LC NO. 81-706425
Prod-NASA Dist-USNAC 1979

Planet Ocean C 15 MIN
16MM FILM OPTICAL SOUND
Shows how oceans of liquid water make the Earth a unique life sustaining environment.
LC NO. 75-703530
Prod-GRAF Dist-GRAF 1975

Planet Of Man--A Series
16MM FILM, 3/4 OR 1/2 IN VIDEO J-C
Describes the processes of geology.
Prod-OECA Dist-FI 1976

Animal, Vegetable, Mineral	029 MIN
Cosmic Connection, The	029 MIN
Jigsaw Fit	029 MIN
Mountain Heritage - The Appalachians	029 MIN
Shield Of Plenty	029 MIN
Trail Of The Ice Age Blues	029 MIN
Uneventful Day	029 MIN

Planetary Circulation Of The Atmosphere B 28 MIN
16MM FILM OPTICAL SOUND
Uses simple laboratory experiments to illustrate planetary circulation of heat, the ultimate source of heat, the action of gravity on latitudinal density and the relationship of the rotation of the earth to planetary circulation.
LC NO. 75-702522
Prod-EDS Dist-MLA 1968

Planetary Gears, Principles Of Operation, Pt 1, Single Sets B 18 MIN
16MM FILM OPTICAL SOUND
Describes the use and operation of planetary gears, covering the basic components, the laws of mechanical operation and the results. Uses a scale model to show the mechanics of planetary gears.
Prod-USA Dist-USNAC Prodn-UWF 1953

Planetary Gears, Principles Of Operation, Pt 2, Multiple Sets B 15 MIN
16MM FILM OPTICAL SOUND
Uses a scale model to show the principles of operation governing multiple sets of planetary gears.
LC NO. FIE53-629
Prod-USA Dist-USNAC Prodn-UWF 1953

Planetary Motion And Kepler's Laws C 8 MIN
16MM FILM OPTICAL SOUND H-C A
Uses computer animation to examine the dynamic properties of the solar system. Relates these dynamics to Kepler's laws of planetary motion.
From The Explorations In Space And Time Series.
LC NO. 75-703979
Prod-HMC Dist-HMC 1974

Planetary Motions And Space Travel C 10 MIN
16MM FILM, 3/4 OR 1/2 IN VIDEO I-J
Consists of an animated film that explains and shows the effect of the planets' orbits upon the projected routes toward them. Uses diagrams to describe these routes.
Prod-DOUGDR Dist-PHENIX 1971

Planets In Orbit - The Laws Of Kepler B 10 MIN
16MM FILM, 3/4 OR 1/2 IN VIDEO J-H
Explains some of the ancient beliefs regarding the movements of the planets. Shows how Tycho Brahe made the first accurate measurements of the position of the stars. Explains Kepler's work and his laws.
Prod-EBF Dist-EBEC 1960

Planets Of The Sun C 9 MIN
16MM FILM, 3/4 OR 1/2 IN VIDEO I-J
Uses special effects to simulate a trip through the solar system. Examines the characteristics of the sun and its planets. Narated by Leonard Nimoy.
Prod-DEADYK Dist-AIMS 1974

Planets, The C 52 MIN
16MM FILM, 3/4 OR 1/2 IN VIDEO H-C A
Looks at America's space program. Discusses the objectives of NASA, the results of its space flights and techniques used, such as space photography, communication and radiometric dating. Includes accounts of the geologic history of the moon and the planning of the U S Viking mission.
Prod-BBCTV Dist-FI 1976

Planing A Dovetail Slide B 28 MIN
16MM FILM - 3/4 IN VIDEO
Shows how to set up the workpiece, cutting tools and machine when working with a planer. Explains how to make rough and finish cuts in the clearance slot and how to make angle cuts. Issued in 1945 as a motion picture.
From The Machine Shop Work - Operations On The Planer Series. No. 2
LC NO. 79-707070
Prod-USOE Dist-USNAC Prodn-RAYBEL 1979

Planing A Flat Surface B 22 MIN
16MM FILM - 3/4 IN VIDEO
Discusses the function of a planer and shows how to mount the workpiece and set the tool and table for the cut. Tells how to make a first and second roughing cut and a first and second finishing cut. Issued in 1945 as a motion picture.
From The Machine Shop Work - Operations On The Planer Series. No. 1
LC NO. 79-707069
Prod-USOE Dist-USNAC Prodn-HARFLM 1979

Planing A Flat Surface (Spanish) B 22 MIN
16MM FILM, 3/4 OR 1/2 IN VIDEO
Explains the function of a planer. Shows how to mount the workpiece, set the tool and table for the cut and make a first and second roughing cut and a first and second finishing cut.
From The Machine Shop Work - Operations On The Planer Series.
Prod-USOE Dist-USNAC

Planing Machines C 15 MIN
1/2 IN VIDEO CASSETTE BETA/VHS IND
See series title for descriptive statement.
From The Woodworking Power Tools Series.
Prod-RMI Dist-RMI

Planing Rough Surfaces To Dimensions B 17 MIN
16MM FILM OPTICAL SOUND
Describes how to prepare wood for planing and how to plane stock to uniform thickness, determine the amount of cut to be made, regulate the speed of feeding and adjust the surfacer to cut straight surfaces.
LC NO. FIE52-53
Prod-USOE Dist-USNAC 1945

Plankton C 12 MIN
16MM FILM, 3/4 OR 1/2 IN VIDEO
Surveys the variety of plants and animals comprising the ocean's plankton community. Explains their complex food webs.
From The Bio-Science Series.
LC NO. 80-706311
Prod-NGS Dist-NGS 1976

Plankton - Floaters And Drifters C 30 MIN
3/4 OR 1/2 INCH VIDEO CASSETTE
Contrasts planktonic and nektonic lifestyles. Discusses the places on earth where plankton is most successful and abundant.
From The Oceanus - The Marine Environment Series. Lesson 15
Prod-SCCON Dist-CDTEL

Plankton - Life Of The Sea C 25 MIN
16MM FILM - 3/4 IN VIDEO
Shows how the study of plankton contributes to an understanding of the ocean environment. Issued in 1972 as a motion picture.
LC NO. 79-706711
Prod-USN Dist-USNAC 1979

Plankton - Pastures Of The Ocean C 10 MIN
16MM FILM, 3/4 OR 1/2 IN VIDEO I
Introduces plankton as a vast source of food for all marine life and to the microscopic animals and larvae which feed on planktonic plants. Suggests the increasing importance plankton may hold for man.
Prod-EBEC Dist-EBEC 1965

Plankton And The Open Sea X 19 MIN
16MM FILM, 3/4 OR 1/2 IN VIDEO H
Pictures typical forms of plankton and demonstrates the importance of minute plankton organisms to marine food chains. Photomicrography and laboratory experiments show how plankton is studied.
From The Biology Series. Unit 2 - Ecosystems
Prod-EBF Dist-EBEC 1962

Plankton And The Open Sea (Spanish) C 19 MIN
16MM FILM, 3/4 OR 1/2 IN VIDEO H
Explains the importance of the minute plankton organisms in marine food chains. Shows typical forms of plankton and demonstrates how plankton is studied by scientists.
From The Biology (Spanish) Series. Unit 2 - Ecosystems
Prod-EBEC Dist-EBEC

Plankton To Fish - A Food Cycle C 11 MIN
16MM FILM, 3/4 OR 1/2 IN VIDEO I
Features experiments in an aquarium, illustrating the food chain as a continuous cycle. Shows how each type of living thing depends on the other, when the cycle is properly balanced.
Prod-CORF Dist-CORF 1973

Planned Approach, The C 19 MIN
3/4 OR 1/2 INCH VIDEO CASSETTE
Demonstrates the proper sales techniques for blood donor recruiters to use in arranging with business executives for bloodmobile visits to their organizations.
Prod-AMRC Dist-AMRC

Planned Maintenance C 12 MIN
3/4 OR 1/2 INCH VIDEO CASSETTE
Points out the importance and definition of planned maintenance. Covers the frequency of planned maintenance and unscheduled maintenance.
From The Developing Troubleshooting Skills Series.
Prod-TPCTRA Dist-TPCTRA

Planned Parenthood B 9 MIN
16MM FILM OPTICAL SOUND I-C A
Contrasts the unhappy life of a large family with the happiness of a small one that has chosen to limit its size voluntarily. Emphasizes the need for planned parenthood.
Prod-INDIA Dist-NEDINF

Planned Pethood C 5 MIN
16MM FILM OPTICAL SOUND
Describes problems of pet parenthood and shows how to help prevent the birth of unwanted cats and dogs that will probably have to be destroyed.
Prod-AMVMA Dist-MTP

Planned Re-Entry C 25 MIN
3/4 OR 1/2 INCH VIDEO CASSETTE
Explains the on-going nature of the recovery process of the chemically dependent and the need to plan for its long-term implementation.
From The Caring Community - Alcoholism And Drug Abuse Series.
Prod-VTRI Dist-VTRI

Planning C
3/4 OR 1/2 INCH VIDEO CASSETTE
Teaches managers and supervisors how they can apply planning procedures to their daily work and job and how they can participate in planning the work of their own management team.
From The Essentials Of Management Series. Unit II.
Prod-AMA Dist-AMA

Planning C 9 MIN
3/4 OR 1/2 INCH VIDEO CASSETTE
Shows what planning is, why it's so important and discusses both short-range and long-range planning.
From The Management of Work Series. Module 2
Prod-RESEM Dist-RESEM

Planning C 20 MIN
3/4 OR 1/2 INCH VIDEO CASSETTE
See series title for descriptive statement.
From The Effective Manager Series.
Prod-DELTAK Dist-DELTAK

Planning C 30 MIN
3/4 OR 1/2 INCH VIDEO CASSETTE
Reveals the purpose of maintenance planning. Investigates goals and methods of planning.
From The Maintenance Management Series.
Prod-ITCORP Dist-ITCORP

Planning C 30 MIN
2 INCH VIDEOTAPE IND
Illustrates the vital role of planning work sheets in manufacturing.
From The Basic Machine Shop Practices Series.
Prod-VTETV Dist-GPITVL

Planning - Preparing For Action C 26 MIN
3/4 OR 1/2 INCH VIDEO CASSETTE
Focuses on planning, such as the scheduling of staff time, nurse assignments and coverage when and emergency occurs.
From The Management Skills For Nurses Series.
Prod-INTGRP Dist-AJN Prodn-ANDRAF

Planning - Pt 1 C 43 MIN
3/4 OR 1/2 INCH VIDEO CASSETTE PRO
Discusses the nature of planning, necessity for three plans and the relationship between planning and control.
From The Project Management Series.
Prod-MIOT Dist-MIOT

Planning - Pt 2 C 45 MIN
3/4 OR 1/2 INCH VIDEO CASSETTE PRO
Discusses earliest and latest start and finish, PERT time estimating, bar chart formats for network diagrams, cost estimating, project cost accounting, resource allocation, cost versus time trade-offs and contingency.
From The Project Management Series.
Prod-MIOT Dist-MIOT

Planning - The Future's First Step C 18 MIN
3/4 OR 1/2 INCH VIDEO CASSETTE
Provides managers with a step-by-step analysis of the elements that make up a successful plan.
Prod-AMA Dist-AMA

Planning - The Future's First Step C 20 MIN
3/4 OR 1/2 INCH VIDEO CASSETTE
Provides an introduction to the concept of planning and outlines the basic steps in making and implementing a plan.
From The Supervisory Management Course, Pt 1 Series. Unit 2
Prod-AMA Dist-AMA

Planning - The Primary Function C
3/4 OR 1/2 INCH VIDEO CASSETTE
Defines and explains the importance of planning. Describes the manager's role in the development and application of different types of plans.
From The Principles Of Management Series.
Prod-RMI Dist-RMI

Planning - The Process C
3/4 OR 1/2 INCH VIDEO CASSETTE
Highlights the basic steps in the planning process. Includes an explanation of the process for implementing a plan.
From The Principles Of Management Series.
Prod-RMI Dist-RMI

Planning A New Business C 30 MIN
16MM FILM, 3/4 OR 1/2 IN VIDEO C A
Explores the kinds of planning and the various sources of assistance and advice necessary to start a new business or take over an existing business.
Prod-NETCHE Dist-GPITVL

Planning A Presentation C 15 MIN
16MM FILM, 3/4 OR 1/2 IN VIDEO I
Describes how good planning results in a successful anti-rabies campaign.
From The Thinkabout Series. Communicating Effectively
LC NO. 81-706117
Prod-SCETV Dist-AITECH 1979

Planning A Program C 18 MIN
3/4 OR 1/2 INCH VIDEO CASSETTE H-C A
Employs a television news report riddled with technical problems to illuminate errors and their avoidance. Presents a better planned version of the same report to further emphasize the value of proper planning.
From The On Camera Series.
LC NO. 84-708013
Prod-BBCTV Dist-FI 1984

Planning A Project And Building Your Project Team C 30 MIN
3/4 OR 1/2 INCH VIDEO CASSETTE
Identifies elements of the planning process. Covers project phases, selection of a project team and communication formats.
From The Project Management Series.
Prod-ITCORP Dist-ITCORP

Planning A Technical Presentation C 15 MIN
3/4 OR 1/2 INCH VIDEO CASSETTE
See series title for descriptive statement.
From The Effective Technical Presentations Series.
Prod-DELTAK Dist-DELTAK Prodn-TRESA

Planning Ahead - The Racer C 15 MIN
16MM FILM, 3/4 OR 1/2 IN VIDEO I
Emphasizes that it is often possible to realize one's aspirations, with careful planning and the willingness to invest energy.
From The Bread And Butterflies Series.
LC NO. 74-703185
Prod-AITV Dist-AITECH Prodn-WNVT 1973

Planning Ahead—A Series
16MM FILM, 3/4 OR 1/2 IN VIDEO J-C A
Presents the stories of three women - an Anglo, a Black and a Chicana - who have made important decisions about their educational and career goals and are engaged in a struggle for independence, purpose and identity.
Prod-BERKS Dist-UCEMC 1982

Black Girl 029 MIN
Chile Pequin 030 MIN
Sister Of The Bride 030 MIN

Planning And Building A Retrieval Chart B 20 MIN
16MM FILM OPTICAL SOUND P-H
Illustrates steps to take in assisting children to develop conceptual ideas for a retrieval chart.
Prod-AWPC Dist-AWPC 1968

Planning And Control C 30 MIN
3/4 OR 1/2 INCH VIDEO CASSETTE
Shows control as the ultimate organizational glue. Demonstrates the birth, development and use of policy. Looks at how to improve control.
From The Organizational Transactions Series.
Prod-PRODEV Dist-PRODEV

Planning And Decision Making C 3 MIN
3/4 OR 1/2 INCH VIDEO CASSETTE
Provides many practical, classroom-tested ideas related to issues which face education.
From The Microcomputer At School Series. Program Three.
Prod-EPCO Dist-EDCORP

Planning And Evaluating Nursing Care B 30 MIN
2 INCH VIDEOTAPE PRO
Helps nursing students understand the importance of planning and evaluating nursing care in gaining an acceptance of others and in developing their skills in treating patients.
From The Mental Health Concepts For Nursing, Unit 3 - Acceptance Of Others Series.
LC NO. 73-702647
Prod-GPITVL Dist-GPITVL 1971

Planning And Goal Setting, Time-Waste Or Management Tool (French) C
16MM FILM, 3/4 OR 1/2 IN VIDEO
Highlights the importance of planning. Describes how to establish priorities.
From The Manager And The Organization (French) Series.
Prod-BNA Dist-BNA

Planning And Goal Setting, Time-Waste Or Management Tool C 22 MIN
16MM FILM - 3/4 IN VIDEO IND
Presents Peter F Drucker discussing the importance of planning and goal setting for small and large organizations.
From The Manager And The Organization Series.
Prod-BNA Dist-BNA

Planning And Goal Setting, Time-Waste Or Management Tool (German) C
16MM FILM, 3/4 OR 1/2 IN VIDEO
Highlights the importance of planning. Describes how to establish priorities.
From The Manager And The Organization (German) Series.
Prod-BNA Dist-BNA

Planning And Goal Setting, Time-Waste Or Management Tool (Portuguese) C
16MM FILM, 3/4 OR 1/2 IN VIDEO
Highlights the importance of planning. Describes how to establish priorities.
From The Manager And The Organization (Portuguese) Series.
Prod-BNA Dist-BNA

Planning And Goal Setting, Time-Waste Or Management Tool (Spanish) C
16MM FILM, 3/4 OR 1/2 IN VIDEO
Highlights the importance of planning. Describes how to establish priorities.
From The Manager And The Organization (Spanish) Series.
Prod-BNA Dist-BNA

Planning And Laying Out Work B 10 MIN
16MM FILM - 3/4 IN VIDEO
Illustrates the importance of planning a job in advance. Issued in 1944 as a motion picture.
From The Problems In Supervision Series.
LC NO. 79-706516
Prod-USOE Dist-USNAC Prodn-MODART 1979

Planning And Resourcing C 30 MIN
3/4 OR 1/2 INCH VIDEO CASSETTE J A
Covers the planning process, community resources, early American handtools, no-trace campfires, folklore interview and group development. Features Robert Cagle and Marina Herman.
From The Sow Seeds/Trust The Promise Series.
Prod-UMCOM Dist-ECUFLM

Planning And Scheduling Of Maintenance C 13 MIN
3/4 OR 1/2 INCH VIDEO CASSETTE IND
Focuses on the concept of KAHADA, how a good maintenance foreman 'Keeps a Half A Day Ahead' of his crew.
From The Marshall Maintenance Training Programs Series. Tape 7
Prod-LEIKID Dist-LEIKID

Planning And Scheduling Of Maintenance C 13 MIN
16MM FILM, 3/4 OR 1/2 IN VIDEO IND
Discusses how a good maintenance crew must keep half a day ahead of pressing maintenance matters.
Prod-MOKIN Dist-MOKIN 1966

Planning And Selecting High Payoff Applications C 45 MIN
3/4 OR 1/2 INCH VIDEO CASSETTE
Explores the steps in planning the groundwork in information system development and the environmental factors which affect that process.
From The User Responsibilities In Information Management Series.
Prod-DELTAK Dist-DELTAK

Planning And The Management Process C 30 MIN
3/4 OR 1/2 INCH VIDEO CASSETTE C A
Focuses on the need for organizations to plan. Studies planning as it relates to organizations and to a manager's position in the organizational hierarchy.
From The Business Management Series. Lesson 5
Prod-SCCON Dist-SCCON

Planning Babysitting C 13 MIN
16MM FILM, 3/4 OR 1/2 IN VIDEO J-C A
Demonstrates how to perform some of the basic babysitting tasks, such as bathing, changing, and feeding infants and small children.
From The Babysitter Series. Unit 2
Prod-SOCOM Dist-FILCOM

Planning Better Behavior C 30 MIN
3/4 OR 1/2 INCH VIDEO CASSETTE T
Emphasizes the correct response to inappropriate behavior, a response that leads to responsible, productive behavior.
From The Developing Discipline Series.
Prod-SDPT Dist-GPITVL 1983

Planning Care For The Aged B 30 MIN
16MM FILM OPTICAL SOUND
Demonstrates how to take a nursing history from an old person and shows how to use the history to develop a meaningful nursing care plan.
From The Gerontological Nursing Series. No. 3
LC NO. 78-710007
Prod-VDONUR Dist-AJN Prodn-WTTWTV 1970

Planning Classroom Tests B 28 MIN
16MM FILM OPTICAL SOUND C A
Identifies strengths and weaknesses in objective tests and offers practice in creating different types of objective test questions. Explains elements to be used in planning a test.
From The Nursing - Effective Evaluation Series.
LC NO. 74-700192
Prod-NTCN Dist-NTCN 1971

Planning Clinical Experiences B 30 MIN
16MM FILM OPTICAL SOUND C A
Defines concept teaching and shows examples of how it may be implemented in a nursing curriculum.
From The Nursing - Where Are You Going, How Will You Get There Series.
LC NO. 74-700181
Prod-NTCN Dist-NTCN 1971

Planning Environment, The C 30 MIN
3/4 OR 1/2 INCH VIDEO CASSETTE C A
Compares centralized and participatory approaches to planning. Discusses how successful planning demands an environment in which information flows smoothly and quickly to the right people.
From The Business Management Series. Lesson 7
Prod-SCCON Dist-SCCON

Planning For A Place C 20 MIN
16MM FILM OPTICAL SOUND C A
Offers a dramatized case study of a severely handicapped student's mother as she explores the possibilities of vocational training for her daughter with a special educator, a special education vocational counselor and an employer of handicapped workers.
LC NO. 83-700102
Prod-PEABC Dist-HUBDSC 1983

Planning For A Place C 20 MIN
3/4 OR 1/2 INCH VIDEO CASSETTE T
Shows teachers and prospective teachers how to prepare handicapped students for the job market. Focuses on team effort.
Prod-METCO Dist-HUBDSC

Planning For Bomb Threats C 16 MIN
3/4 OR 1/2 INCH VIDEO CASSETTE T
Covers the nature of bomb threats, search and evacuation procedures, communications and recognition.
Prod-WORON Dist-MTI 1984

Planning For Change C 29 MIN
16MM FILM, 3/4 OR 1/2 IN VIDEO T
Presents reading authorities William Glasser, Vivian Windley and Madeline Hunter discussing ways of implementing new reading instruction techniques.
From The Teaching Children To Read Series.
Prod-MFFD Dist-FI 1975

Planning For Discharge From The Hospital C 14 MIN
3/4 INCH VIDEO CASSETTE
Provides information that a hospitalized patient needs to know prior to the patient's discharge from the hospital in order to have a satisfactory continuity of care.
Prod-UWISN Dist-UWISN

Planning For Effective Training C 30 MIN
3/4 OR 1/2 INCH VIDEO CASSETTE T
Deals with conducting needs, job and task analysis.
From The Training The Trainer Series.
Prod-ITCORP Dist-ITCORP

Planning For Financial Success C 25 MIN
3/4 OR 1/2 INCH VIDEO CASSETTE H-C A
Explains how changes in society motivate individuals to begin planning financial strategies linked to life plans.
From The Money Smart - A Guide To Personal Finance Series.
Prod-SOMFIL Dist-BCNFL 1984

Planning For Floods C 28 MIN
16MM FILM OPTICAL SOUND
Compares the 1973 Mississippi River flood with the 1972 Rapid City, South Dakota flood. Suggests that structural flood control violates intelligent land use policy and may result in an increase in the loss of life and property.
Prod-AMHRST Dist-AMHRST Prodn-STONEY 1974

Planning For Impact C 40 MIN
3/4 OR 1/2 INCH VIDEO CASSETTE
See series title for descriptive statement.
From The Meeting Leading Series.
Prod-PRODEV Dist-DELTAK

Planning For Impact And Control C 30 MIN
3/4 OR 1/2 INCH VIDEO CASSETTE
Discusses why a meeting should be held. Includes making a participant profile which helps anticipate support, attitudes and perhaps hidden agendas.
From The Meeting Leading Series.
Prod-PRODEV Dist-PRODEV

Planning For Improvement (A Model) C 20 MIN
3/4 OR 1/2 INCH VIDEO CASSETTE
See series title for descriptive statement.
From The Performance Appraisal Training Series.
Prod-DELTAK Dist-DELTAK

Planning For Microcomputers C 30 MIN
3/4 OR 1/2 INCH VIDEO CASSETTE
Discusses involving the right people in the planning process, finding out what computers can do, knowing sources of good information, learning from others' successes and failures, and setting goals.
From The Ready Or Not Series.
Prod-NCSDPI Dist-PCATEL

Planning For Personal Goals C
3/4 OR 1/2 INCH VIDEO CASSETTE
Shows how to select and describe realistic non-vocational goals, to specify and develop the steps necessary to accomplish these goals and how to apply time management and planning skills in order to achieve them.
From The Employability Skills Series.
Prod-ILCS Dist-CAMB

Planning For Profit C 11 MIN
16MM FILM OPTICAL SOUND
Demonstrates how to manipulate variable and fixed costs and adjust the break even point when sales begin to falter. Offers insights into the retirement of the principal of businesses loans, and the effect different courses can have on the balance sheet.
From The Running Your Own Business Series.
Prod-EFD Dist-EFD

Planning For Profit C 21 MIN
16MM FILM, 3/4 OR 1/2 IN VIDEO C A
Shows how a management team at a British company plan for future profits in the face of increases in raw material prices and loss of sales to competitors. Deals with such business factors as reducing direct costs, looking at product mix, increasing volume of sales, adjusting prices and controlling overhead.
LC NO. 83-706694
Prod-MILLBK Dist-IFB

Planning For Retirement C 25 MIN
3/4 OR 1/2 INCH VIDEO CASSETTE H-C A
Shows how to assess financial needs for retirement and invest money.
From The Money Smart - A Guide To Personal Finance Series.
Prod-SOMFIL Dist-BCNFL

Planning For The Future - New Microprocessor Trends C 45 MIN
3/4 OR 1/2 INCH VIDEO CASSETTE IND
See series title for descriptive statement.
From The Management Of Microprocessor Technology Series.
Prod-ICSINT Dist-ICSINT

Planning For The Patient's Discharge C 30 MIN
16MM FILM OPTICAL SOUND
Stresses the importance of returning as many patients as possible to their homes and communities.
Prod-USVA Dist-USVA 1956

Planning For Tomorrow C 30 MIN
3/4 OR 1/2 INCH VIDEO CASSETTE C
See series title for descriptive statement.
From The Time's Harvest - Exploring The Future Series.
Prod-MDCPB Dist-MDCPB

Planning For Wellness System—A Series
16MM FILM, 3/4 OR 1/2 IN VIDEO H-C A
Encourages individuals to attain their maximum health potential at home, work and play. Emphasizes behavior modification of individuals to improve productivity and quality of life.
Prod-MTI Dist-MTI 1983

Personal Plan For Wellness, A 030 MIN
Wellness Lifestyle, The 030 MIN

Planning Highway Access C 32 MIN
16MM FILM, 3/4 OR 1/2 IN VIDEO A
Shows how Wisconsin counties, towns, villages and cities can preserve their highways as travel corridors without sacrificing safety or restricting business development or access to properties along them.
Prod-USDA Dist-USNAC 1981

Planning Layout And Graphics B 55 MIN
3/4 OR 1/2 INCH VIDEO CASSETTE IND
See series title for descriptive statement.
From The Technical And Professional Writing For Industry, Government And Business Series.
Prod-UMICE Dist-AMCEE

Planning Lessons C 30 MIN
3/4 OR 1/2 INCH VIDEO CASSETTE
Takes the objectives set down and organizes them into hierarchies and units.
From The Educational Objectives Series.
Prod-NETCHE Dist-NETCHE 1972

Planning Patient Teaching B 30 MIN
16MM FILM OPTICAL SOUND C A
Illustrates specific elements in teaching patients. Concentrates on details of planning for patient teaching.
From The Nursing - Patient Teaching, Pt 1 Series.
LC NO. 74-700203
Prod-NTCN Dist-NTCN 1971

Planning Phase, The C 60 MIN
3/4 OR 1/2 INCH VIDEO CASSETTE IND
See series title for descriptive statement.
From The Value Engineering Series.
Prod-NCSU Dist-AMCEE

Planning Science Activities B 30 MIN
2 INCH VIDEOTAPE
Explains how to develop a procedure for planning the kinds of science activities that are most appropriate to general educational goals.
From The Science In Your Classroom Series.
Prod-WENHTV Dist-GPITVL

Planning Skills C 45 MIN
3/4 OR 1/2 INCH VIDEO CASSETTE IND
Covers basics of plans, annual and project plans, workload forecasting, budget plans, how to plan and time management.
From The Basic Management Skills For Engineers And Scientists Series.
Prod-USCITV Dist-AMCEE

Planning Technical Activities C 30 MIN
3/4 OR 1/2 INCH VIDEO CASSETTE
See series title for descriptive statement.
From The Management For Engineers Series.
Prod-UKY Dist-SME

Planning Techniques C 30 MIN
3/4 OR 1/2 INCH VIDEO CASSETTE C A
Looks at various quantitative and qualitative approaches to planning, and at tools designed to increase a manager's understanding of the future environment. Uses real world examples to illustrate master schedules, break-even analyses, Delphi and scientific management techniques.
From The Business Management Series. Lesson 6
Prod-SCCON Dist-SCCON

Planning The Land C 24 MIN
16MM FILM, 3/4 OR 1/2 IN VIDEO J-C A
Shows how citizens can influence local governments to plan successful land-use policies in their communities. Outlines several legal methods for preserving open space, such as purchase of land by private nonprofit groups, leaseback agreements installment buying and other methods.
Prod-CIASP Dist-AIMS 1975

Planning The Story B 30 MIN
16MM FILM OPTICAL SOUND T
Presents ideas on developing creative writing in children in elementary grades.
From The Starting Tomorrow Series. Unit 1 - New Ways In Composition
Prod-EALING Dist-WALKED

Planning The Use Of Money C 9 MIN
16MM FILM, 3/4 OR 1/2 IN VIDEO I-J
Discusses the relationship between money and time and explains that young people as well as families must plan the use of their money.
Prod-MORLAT Dist-SF 1970

Planning Your Estate C 25 MIN
3/4 OR 1/2 INCH VIDEO CASSETTE
Outlines the basics of setting up an estate. Discusses wills, executors, probate and common mistakes.
From The Your Money Matters Series.
Prod-FILMID Dist-FILMID

Planning Your Speech C 13 MIN
16MM FILM, 3/4 OR 1/2 IN VIDEO H-C A
Takes a look at the process of planning a speech by showing how a speaker prepares to address a group.
From The Art Of Communication Series.
LC NO. 79-701658
Prod-CENTRO Dist-CORF 1979

Planning Your Time C
3/4 OR 1/2 INCH VIDEO CASSETTE
See series title for descriptive statement.
From The Time Management - A Practical Approach Series.
Prod-PACPL Dist-DELTAK Prodn-ONCKEW

Planning, Organizing And Controlling, Pt 1 C 21 MIN
16MM FILM - 3/4 IN VIDEO IND
Points out common sources of contingencies in business planning and tells how to identify them before they happen, what patterns to look for and how to distinguish between general and specific contingencies. Gives tips on budgeting time, including the scheduling of dull, uninteresting work.
From The Practice Of Supervision Series.
Prod-BNA Dist-BNA Prodn-GELLES 1975

Planning, Organizing And Controlling, Pt 2 C 21 MIN
16MM FILM - 3/4 IN VIDEO IND
Looks at the actions supervisors must take to prepare employees to handle all sorts of contingencies. Shows how to reinforce fundamentals, prevent the erosion of training and discusses ways to motivate employees to perform dull, tedious jobs correctly.
From The Practice Of Supervision Series.
Prod-BNA Dist-BNA Prodn-GELLES 1975

Planning, Organizing And Controlling, Pt 3 C 20 MIN
16MM FILM - 3/4 IN VIDEO IND
Centers on the critical decision of whether or not a supervisor should intervene in a contingency and, if so, when. Outlines active steps a supervisor can take to prevent a contingency from getting out of hand.
From The Practice Of Supervision Series.
Prod-BNA Dist-BNA Prodn-GELLES 1975

Planning, Pt 1 C 50 MIN
3/4 OR 1/2 INCH VIDEO CASSETTE PRO
Discusses plans, uncertainty and the Triple Constraint. Comments on maintaining the network diagram.
From The Project Management For Engineers Series.
Prod-AMCEE Dist-AMCEE

Planning, Pt 2 C 50 MIN
3/4 OR 1/2 INCH VIDEO CASSETTE PRO
Surveys time estimating, project cost accounting, and contingency and risk.
From The Project Management For Engineers Series.
Prod-AMCEE Dist-AMCEE

Planning, Scheduling, Organizing Work And Work Improvement B 30 MIN
16MM FILM OPTICAL SOUND
Discusses how supervisors can plan and organize work and tells about a simple approach to simplifying many jobs.
From The Success In Supervision Series.
LC NO. 74-706180
Prod-WETATV Dist-USNAC 1965

Plans, The C 15 MIN
3/4 OR 1/2 INCH VIDEO CASSETTE K-P
Deals with French-Americans. Shows that the unforeseen can be rewarding.
From The La Bonne Aventure Series.
Prod-MPBN Dist-GPITVL

Plant A Seed C 3 MIN
16MM FILM, 3/4 OR 1/2 IN VIDEO P-I
Shows, through the use of music and lyrics, the positive effect that window boxes can create in a city.
Prod-ROSENJ Dist-PHENIX 1977

Plant And Animal Interaction B 15 MIN
2 INCH VIDEOTAPE P
See series title for descriptive statement.
From The Just Wondering Series.
Prod-EOPS Dist-GPITVL Prodn-KOACTV

Plant And Animal Life Distribution - The Natural World C 18 MIN
3/4 OR 1/2 INCH VIDEO CASSETTE I
Examines factors that influence plant and animal growth and distribution. Visits different geological regions where various forms of life flourish.
From The Natural Science Specials Series. Module Green
Prod-UNPRO Dist-AITECH 1973

Plant Care C 29 MIN
2 INCH VIDEOTAPE
Features Tom Lied discussing different types of ground cover and how they can be used. Offers tips on caring for these plants and how to use ornamental materials, such as bark and gravel.
From The Dig It Series.
Prod-WMVSTV Dist-PUBTEL

Plant Care Quiz, The C 15 MIN
16MM FILM, 3/4 OR 1/2 IN VIDEO
Presents horticulture expert Ralph Snodsmith who answers consumer questions about plant care.
Prod-KLEINW Dist-KLEINW

Plant Cell And Male And Female Flower Parts C 11 MIN
16MM FILM, 3/4 OR 1/2 IN VIDEO
Uses the apple tree as a model to explain the characteristics of the plant cell, the male and female flower parts, genes, DNA and sexual and asexual reproduction.
From The Life Cycle Of A Flowering Plant Series. No. 1
Prod-SCHLAT Dist-LUF 1971

Plant Coordinate Systems C
3/4 OR 1/2 INCH VIDEO CASSETTE IND
See series title for descriptive statement.
From The Drafting - Blueprint Reading Basics Series.
Prod-GPCV Dist-GPCV

Plant Eaters And Animal Eaters C 20 MIN
3/4 INCH VIDEO CASSETTE T
Examines ways certain plant and animal interactions can be studied in the classroom. Shows a terrarium with a variety of 'crops' and a resident cricket.
From The Science In The Elementary School - Life Science Series.
Prod-UWKY Dist-GPITVL 1980

Plant Flowering B 30 MIN
2 INCH VIDEOTAPE J
See series title for descriptive statement.
From The Investigating The World Of Science, Unit 4 - Plants And Their Adaptations Series.
Prod-MPATI Dist-GPITVL

Plant Foods C 30 MIN
3/4 OR 1/2 INCH VIDEO CASSETTE C A
Identifies 16 elements essential for plant growth. Explains how to tell what nutrients a gardener might need for his or her particular soil. Teaches how to apply fertilizer.
From The Home Gardener With John Lenanton Series. Lesson 5
Prod-COAST Dist-CDTEL

Plant Growth - Hormones B 20 MIN
2 INCH VIDEOTAPE I
See series title for descriptive statement.
From The Science Room Series.
Prod-MCETV Dist-GPITVL Prodn-WVIZTV

Plant Growth In Compensated Fields C 7 MIN
16MM FILM OPTICAL SOUND
Points out that plant growth is controlled by a sensitive mechanism which responds to brief and minute stimulation. Describes the operation and use of the mechanical servo-system which neutralizes stimuli on plants for experimental purposes.
LC NO. FIE67-132
Prod-ANL Dist-USNAC 1967

Plant Growth Regulators C 12 MIN
3/4 OR 1/2 INCH VIDEO CASSETTE
Describes the principles behind the physiology of plant growth hormones.
Prod-CBSC Dist-CBSC

Plant Kingdom, The - A World Of Green C
3/4 OR 1/2 INCH VIDEO CASSETTE H
Discusses organisms that were once aquatic and have adapted to life on land. Details all types of plant forms, describing size, form, nature and reproductive systems, and relating them to their various aquatic or land environments.
Prod-GA Dist-GA

Plant Life At Work (2nd Ed) C 13 MIN
16MM FILM, 3/4 OR 1/2 IN VIDEO I-H
Uses time-lapse photography to show the processes of plant life. Reveals the impressive energy of plants as they move, grow, reproduce and manufacture food through photosynthesis.
Prod-MIS Dist-MIS 1976

Plant Motions - Roots, Stems, Leaves X 11 MIN
16MM FILM, 3/4 OR 1/2 IN VIDEO I-H
Examines tendency of growing roots, stems and leaves to describe irregular circles or ellipses, and shows how gravity and light affect plant growth. Timelapse photography is used.
Prod-EBF Dist-EBEC 1962

Plant Movement And Transport C 29 MIN
3/4 INCH VIDEO CASSETTE C A
Describes intricacies of external and internal plant movement. Uses time-lapse photography.
From The Introducing Biology Series. Program 8
Prod-COAST Dist-CDTEL

Plant Nutrition C 29 MIN
3/4 INCH VIDEO CASSETTE C A
Identifies structures that enable a plant to make its own food. Discusses water, gas exchange and soil. Includes plants with unusual adaptations for obtaining nutrients.
From The Introducing Biology Series. Program 7
Prod-COAST Dist-CDTEL

Plant Populations C 14 MIN
3/4 OR 1/2 INCH VIDEO CASSETTE I
Studies various plant populations.
From The Hands On, Grade 5 - Our Environment Series.
Prod-WHROTV Dist-AITECH 1975

Plant Propagation - From Seed To Tissue Culture C 27 MIN
16MM FILM OPTICAL SOUND
Shows various means of propagating plants in order to demonstrate the scientific priniciples involved. Introduces the technique of tissue culture by which tissue sections of a single plant, under controlled circumstances, can reproduce the parent plant hundreds of times.
LC NO. 78-700299
Prod-HUAA Dist-FI Prodn-CHVANP 1977

Plant Propogation C 12 MIN
3/4 INCH VIDEO CASSETTE
Demonstrates various ways to propagate house plants from cuttings.
Prod-TUCPL Dist-GPITVL

Plant Pruning (Captioned) C 30 MIN
3/4 OR 1/2 INCH VIDEO CASSETTE S
Discusses the reason for pruning trees, plants and shrubs. Demonstrates pruning techniques and tools.
From The Consumer Education For The Deaf Adult Series.
Prod-GALCO Dist-GALCO Prodn-MCES 1975

Plant Reproduction C 29 MIN
3/4 INCH VIDEO CASSETTE C A
Presents basic features and processes involved in plant reproduction. Details various methods of pollination.
From The Introducing Biology Series. Program 27
Prod-COAST Dist-CDTEL

Plant Safety C 12 MIN
3/4 INCH VIDEO CASSETTE H-C A
Explains how Charlie's thoughtless actions around the plant get him battered, bashed and bruised. Illustrates the need for proper attention and care when working in a plant.
Prod-LUMIN Dist-GA

Plant Science—A Series

Prod-IOWA Dist-MLA

Algal Syngamy - Isogamy In Chlamydomonas 3 MIN
Algal Syngamy - Oogamy In Oedogonium 3 MIN
Algal Syngamy - Zygote Formation In Pandorina 3 MIN
Early Development Of The Shoot In 'QUERCUS' 3 MIN
Effect Of Red And Far-Red Light On Internode 3 MIN
Effects Of Red And Far-Red Light On Seedling 3 MIN
Gamete Transfer In The Bryophytes - The 4 MIN
Gamete Transfer In The Bryophytes - The 4 MIN
Isolation Of Phytochrome 3 MIN
Liberation Of Zoospores In The Alga Basicladia 4 MIN
Liberation Of Zoospores In The Alga Oedogonium 4 MIN
Oxygen Liberation By Isolated Chloroplasts - 10 MIN
Pathways Of Water In Herbaceous Plants 3 MIN
Pathways Of Water In Woody Plants 3 MIN
Photochemical Properties Of Phytochrome 3 MIN
Photosynthetic Fixation Of Carbon Dioxide 8 MIN
Regulation Of Plant Development - Coleoptile 4 MIN
Spore Dispersal In Equisetum 3 MIN
Spore Dispersal In The Fungi - Coprinus 3 MIN

Plant Shutdown C 34 MIN
16MM FILM - 3/4 IN VIDEO
Shows a manager conducting interviews when a pharmaceutical plant is needlessly shut down because of personal conflict between two supervisors. Tells how to use techniques such as probing and reflecting back, how to get to the root of the problem and how to move people of different age, education, experience and outlook to work together and develop further as managers.
From The Interviewing Series.
Prod-MTLTD Dist-BNA

Plant Structure - Leaves, Stems And Roots C 20 MIN
2 INCH VIDEOTAPE I
See series title for descriptive statement.
From The Exploring With Science, Unit X - Plants Series.
Prod-MPATI Dist-GPITVL

Plant Systems C
3/4 OR 1/2 INCH VIDEO CASSETTE IND
Includes circulating water systems, the condenser and condensate system.
From The Industrial Training, Module 4 - Power Production Series.
Prod-LEIKID Dist-LEIKID

Plant Through The Seasons, A - Apple Tree X 11 MIN
16MM FILM, 3/4 OR 1/2 IN VIDEO P
Uses animated artwork and live photography to show the yearly life cycle of an apple tree. Investigates adaptations for growth in temperate climates, flower, seed and fruit formation, and dormancy.
From The Basic Life Science Series. World Of Plants
Prod-EBF Dist-EBEC 1966

Plant Traps - Insect Catchers Of The Bog Jungle (2nd Ed) X 11 MIN
16MM FILM, 3/4 OR 1/2 IN VIDEO J-C
Reveals the behavior of carnivorous plants, such as pitcher plant, sundew and Venus flytrap. Formerly titled 'INSECT CATCHERS OF THE BOG JUNGLE.'
Prod-HARL Dist-EBEC 1955

Plant Tropisms B 30 MIN
2 INCH VIDEOTAPE J
See series title for descriptive statement.
From The Investigating The World Of Science, Unit 4 - Plants And Their Adaptations Series.
Prod-MPATI Dist-GPITVL

Plant Tropisms And Other Movements C 11 MIN
16MM FILM, 3/4 OR 1/2 IN VIDEO J-C
Illustrates the essential movements of several common plants in response to internal and external stimuli. Differentiates the three basic types of movement-tropistic, nastic and nutational. Time-lapse photography and laboratory demonstrations are used.
Prod-CORF Dist-CORF 1965

Plant-Animal Communities - Ecological Succession C 14 MIN
16MM FILM, 3/4 OR 1/2 IN VIDEO J-H
Ecological succession - the long-term replacement of one biome by another - follows a predictable pattern that can be traced from either a bare rock stage or a water environment to the appearance of a climax forest. Tracing both patterns shows that succession is controlled by climate and landform but may also be accelerated, interrupted and retarded by man.
From The Plant-Animal Communities Series.
Prod-CORF Dist-CORF 1968

Plant-Animal Communities - Interrelationships C 14 MIN
16MM FILM, 3/4 OR 1/2 IN VIDEO H
Discusses two major kinds of ecological interrelationships--symbiosis and antagonism. Also provides examples of mutualism, commensalism, antibiosis, exploitation, parasitism, competition and predation.
From The Plant-Animal Communities Series.
Prod-CORF Dist-CORF 1965

Plant-Animal Communities - Physical Environment C 11 MIN
16MM FILM, 3/4 OR 1/2 IN VIDEO J-H
Cites the natural factors which influence any plantanimal community--altitude, atmosphere, heat, light, water and soil conditions. Shows the relationships of these factors in a particular biome found in deciduous and coniferous forests, a grassland and a desert.
From The Plant-Animal Communities Series.
Prod-CORF Dist-CORF 1964

Plant-Animal Communities - The Changing Balance Of Nature C 11 MIN
16MM FILM, 3/4 OR 1/2 IN VIDEO J-H
Illustrates how factors, such as the rate of reproduction of a species, its available food supply and the number of its natural enemies, largely determine the survival of a species within a biome.
From The Plant-Animal Communities Series.
Prod-CORF Dist-CORF 1963

Plant-Animal Communities—A Series
16MM FILM, 3/4 OR 1/2 IN VIDEO J-H
Presents the concepts of communities, ecological succession, plant-animal interrelationships and the effect of environment on the community.
Prod-CORF Dist-CORF

Plant-Animal Communities - Ecological 14 MIN
Plant-Animal Communities - Interrelationships 14 MIN
Plant-Animal Communities - Physical Environment 11 MIN
Plant-Animal Communities - The Changing 11 MIN

Plant, The C 13 MIN
16MM FILM, 3/4 OR 1/2 IN VIDEO I-H A
Presents the story of an extraordinary plant which demands attention and delights in music.
Prod-LUF Dist-LUF

Plant, The C 13 MIN
16MM FILM, 3/4 OR 1/2 IN VIDEO
Presents a light-hearted fantasy about a gentle soul who falls victim to his own kindness.
LC NO. 84-706000
Prod-NFBC Dist-NFBC 1983

Plantanos C 23 MIN
3/4 OR 1/2 INCH VIDEO CASSETTE PRO
Shows four ways of cooking plantains - boiled, baked, sauteed and fried as patties.
Prod-CULINA Dist-CULINA

Plantar Aspect Of The Foot C 15 MIN
16MM FILM, 3/4 OR 1/2 IN VIDEO C A
Demonstrates the dissection of the plantar aspect of the foot.
From The Guides To Dissection Series.
Prod-UCLA Dist-TEF

Plantation Boy (Portuguese) B 85 MIN
16MM FILM OPTICAL SOUND
An English subtitle version of the Portuguese language film. Relates the story of young Carlinho who is sent to live on his grandfather's sugar plantation after his mother's violent death. Depicts the Brazil of 1920 and shows the country and society in a state of transition.
Prod-NYFLMS Dist-NYFLMS 1965

Plantation Economy - The Island Case B 30 MIN
16MM FILM OPTICAL SOUND H-C
Professor Lloyd Best analyzes the plantation society of the Caribbean, traces its evolution over a three hundred year period and explains the changes in the economic, social and political conditions.
From The Black History Series.
LC NO. 79-704039
Prod-WCBSTV Dist-HRAW 1969

Plantation Slavery And Urban Negroes B 30 MIN
2 INCH VIDEOTAPE H-C A
See series title for descriptive statement.
From The Americans From Africa - A History Series. No. 10
Prod-CVETVC Dist-GPITVL Prodn-WCVETV

Plantation South, The X 17 MIN
16MM FILM, 3/4 OR 1/2 IN VIDEO J-C
Traces the development of the plantation system in the southern United States from its beginning in Virginia to its firm establishment in the deep South of the Antebellum Period. Stress is placed upon the plantation as an agricultural and social unit.
Prod-EBF Dist-EBEC 1960

Planting A Bare Root Tree C 26 MIN
3/4 INCH VIDEO CASSETTE
Demonstrates the entire procedure of planting a bare root tree from the size of the hole to the first pruning.
Prod-TUCPL Dist-GPITVL

Planting A New Lawn C 29 MIN
3/4 OR 1/2 INCH VIDEO CASSETTE
See series title for descriptive statement.
From The Crockett's Victory Garden Series.
Prod-WGBHTV Dist-KINGFT

Planting And Artificial Light C 29 MIN
3/4 OR 1/2 INCH VIDEO CASSETTE
See series title for descriptive statement.
From The Crockett's Victory Garden Series.
Prod-WGBHTV Dist-KINGFT

Planting Cactus C 8 MIN
3/4 INCH VIDEO CASSETTE
Demonstrates how to plant cactus, including a discussion of the plant protection act of Arizona.
Prod-TUCPL Dist-GPITVL

Planting With Cuttings C 29 MIN
3/4 OR 1/2 INCH VIDEO CASSETTE
See series title for descriptive statement.
From The Crockett's Victory Garden Series.
Prod-WGBHTV Dist-KINGFT

Plants C 15 MIN
2 INCH VIDEOTAPE K
Characterizes plants, as living things, by their life activities.
From The Let's Go Sciencing, Unit III - Life Series.
Prod-DETPS Dist-GPITVL

Plants C 15 MIN
3/4 OR 1/2 INCH VIDEO CASSETTE P
Presents Pocus explaining that plants make their own food while Hocus learns how dying and changing plants contribute to the plant cycle.
From The Let Me See Series. No. 9
Prod-WETN Dist-AITECH Prodn-STSU 1982

Plants - Reproduction-Pollination B 20 MIN
2 INCH VIDEOTAPE I
See series title for descriptive statement.
From The Science Room Series.
Prod-MCETV Dist-GPITVL Prodn-WVIZTV

Plants And Animals Depend On Each Other C 12 MIN
16MM FILM, 3/4 OR 1/2 IN VIDEO P
Uses the example of the relationship of plants and animals in an aquarium in order to explore plant and animal relationships in other environments, including ponds, grasslands and woodlands.
Prod-CORF Dist-CORF 1974

Plants And Animals Depend On Each Other (Captioned) C 12 MIN
16MM FILM, 3/4 OR 1/2 IN VIDEO P
Uses the example of the relationship of plants and animals in an aquarium in order to explore plant and animal relationships in other environments, including ponds, grasslands and woodlands.
Prod-CORF Dist-CORF 1974

Plants And Animals Share Space And Food C 10 MIN
16MM FILM, 3/4 OR 1/2 IN VIDEO I
Describes how many plants and animals manage to live together in the same environments. Discovers how they share nonliving things, such as sunlight, water and soil. Portrays a rabbit eating grass and a spider's web on a plant as an example of direct animal-plant dependence.
Prod-CORF Dist-CORF 1976

Plants And Animals Share Space And Food (Captioned) C 10 MIN
16MM FILM, 3/4 OR 1/2 IN VIDEO I
Describe how many plants and animals manage to live together in the same environments. Discovers how they share nonliving things, such as sunlight, water and soil. Portrays a rabbit eating grass and a spider's web as an example of direct animal-plant dependence.
Prod-CORF Dist-CORF 1976

Plants And Their Importance C 11 MIN
16MM FILM, 3/4 OR 1/2 IN VIDEO P-I
Gives an introduction to the nature and uses of plants, identifying the parts of the plant and common growth patterns.
Prod-FILMSW Dist-FLMFR

Plants Are Different And Alike C 11 MIN
16MM FILM, 3/4 OR 1/2 IN VIDEO P
Two children in a nursery learn that plants have similar needs, but differ in physical appearance and characteristics, in usefulness to man and in the ways in which they obtain food.
Prod-CORF Dist-CORF 1967

Plants As A Food Source C 20 MIN
16MM FILM, 3/4 OR 1/2 IN VIDEO
Shows how plant life can be utilized for all body food requirements.
LC NO. 81-707494
Prod-USN Dist-USNAC 1973

Plants As Food Makers - Photosynthesis B 20 MIN
2 INCH VIDEOTAPE
See series title for descriptive statement.
From The Science Room Series.
Prod-MCETV Dist-GPITVL Prodn-WVIZTV

Plants As Living Objects B 15 MIN
2 INCH VIDEOTAPE P
See series title for descriptive statement.
From The Just Wondering Series.
Prod-EOPS Dist-GPITVL Prodn-KOACTV

Plants For Dim Places C 30 MIN
2 INCH VIDEOTAPE
Features Thalassa Cruso discussing different aspects of gardening. Names the types of plants that grow well in dim places.
From The Making Things Grow I Series.
LC NO. 80-706144
Prod-WGBHTV Dist-PBS 1979

Plants From Pits And Stones C 29 MIN
3/4 OR 1/2 INCH VIDEO CASSETTE

See series title for descriptive statement.
From The Crockett's Victory Garden Series.
Prod-WGBHTV Dist-KINGFT

Plants In Action C 10 MIN
3/4 OR 1/2 INCH VIDEO CASSETTE J-H
Uses time-lapse photography to reveal that plants, although mostly rooted, do move, act and react. Shows leaves opening by day and closing at night, flowers and clover opening to or pursuing sunlight climbing tendrils looking for support.
Prod-EDMI Dist-EDMI 1983

Plants In Action C 30 MIN
3/4 OR 1/2 INCH VIDEO CASSETTE C A
Uses time-lapse photography to show plants growing. Demonstrates the function of the plants 'plumbing system,' the roots, trunk, leaves and buds. Describes photosynthesis.
From The Home Gardener With John Lenanton Series. Lesson 22
Prod-COAST Dist-CDTEL

Plants Live And Grow, Pt 1 B 15 MIN
2 INCH VIDEOTAPE P
Shows that plants of the same family have common characteristics. Explains that most plants need proper amounts of heat, moisture and air. Describes flowering plants as having four parts which include roots, stem, leaves and flowers.
From The Science Is Everywhere Series. No. 22
Prod-DETPS Dist-GPITVL

Plants Live And Grow, Pt 2 B 15 MIN
2 INCH VIDEOTAPE P
Shows that plants of the same family have common characteristics. Explains that most plants need proper amounts of heat, moisture and air. Describes flowering plants as having four parts which include roots, stem, leaves and flowers.
From The Science Is Everywhere Series. No. 23
Prod-DETPS Dist-GPITVL

Plants Live And Grow, Pt 3 B 15 MIN
2 INCH VIDEOTAPE P
Shows that plants of the same family have common characteristics. Explains that most plants need proper amounts of heat, moisture and air. Describes flowering plants as having four parts which include roots, stem, leaves and flowers.
From The Science Is Everywhere Series. No. 24
Prod-DETPS Dist-GPITVL

Plants Live And Grow, Pt 4 B 15 MIN
2 INCH VIDEOTAPE P
Shows that plants of the same family have common characteristics. Explains that most plants need proper amounts of heat, moisture and air. Describes flowering plants as having four parts which include roots, stem, leaves and flowers.
From The Science Is Everywhere Series. No. 25
Prod-DETPS Dist-GPITVL

Plants Make Food (2nd Ed) C 13 MIN
16MM FILM, 3/4 OR 1/2 IN VIDEO I-J
Shows how plants make food through the process of photosynthesis. Examines the functioning of roots, stems and leaves, and explains the transforming of water, minerals, and carbon dioxide into foods.
LC NO. 82-706539
Prod-CF Dist-CF 1981

Plants Need Energy C 15 MIN
2 INCH VIDEOTAPE P
Illustrates green plants needing light and heat energy in order to grow.
From The Science Is Searching Series.
Prod-DETPS Dist-GPITVL

Plants Need Water C 15 MIN
2 INCH VIDEOTAPE P
Shows how water is very essential in the survival of living plants.
From The Science Is Searching Series.
Prod-DETPS Dist-GPITVL

Plants Of The Galapagos C 15 MIN
3/4 OR 1/2 INCH VIDEO CASSETTE
Documents the many plants of the Galapagos, as well as the geology, of the islands.
Prod-CBSC Dist-CBSC

Plants Of The Saltmarsh, The C 14 MIN
3/4 OR 1/2 INCH VIDEO CASSETTE
Presents the natural history of saltmarsh plants through photographs taken in the Spartina marshes of the Atlantic coast of North America. Emphasizes cordgrass, its ecological importance and its adaptation to life in salt water.
Prod-CBSC Dist-CBSC

Plants Of The Sea C 13 MIN
16MM FILM, 3/4 OR 1/2 IN VIDEO I-H
Examines plant life in the ocean, including plankton, kelp, red algae and grasses. Describes their importance to other living things. Tells how much of the energy that is trapped from the Sun is converted to forms useful to people by the algae of the sea.
Prod-BEANMN Dist-PHENIX 1980

Plants Or Animals C 15 MIN
3/4 OR 1/2 INCH VIDEO CASSETTE I-J
Considers the similarities of and differences between animals and plants, pointing out that some creatures have features of both.
From The Animals And Such Series. Module Green - Animals And Plants
Prod-WHROTV Dist-AITECH 1972

Plants That Grow From Leaves, Stems And Roots (2nd Ed) C 15 MIN
16MM FILM, 3/4 OR 1/2 IN VIDEO I-H
Describes how from the simple act of planting a bulb, to new methods of cloning, new plants can be grown from a single parent, passing along the same favorable characteristics from one generation to the next. Features experiments which show how entire plants can be grown from a single cell, also known as cloning.
Prod-CORF Dist-CORF 1983

Plants That Have No Flowers Or Seeds C 11 MIN
16MM FILM, 3/4 OR 1/2 IN VIDEO I-J
Features microscopic and time-lapse photography and artwork in a study of plants that have neither flowers nor seeds. Investigates how such plants as algae, mosses, ferns and fungi reproduce and obtain food.
Prod-CORF Dist-CORF 1967

Plants That Have No Flowers Or Seeds (Captioned) C 11 MIN
16MM FILM, 3/4 OR 1/2 IN VIDEO I-J
Features microscopic and time-lapse photography and artwork in a study of plants that have neither flowers nor seeds. Investigates how such plants as algae, mosses, ferns and fungi reproduce and obtain food.
Prod-CORF Dist-CORF 1967

Plaque And Prevention C 9 MIN
16MM FILM, 3/4 OR 1/2 IN VIDEO I-C A
Explains and demonstrates the various methods recommended for the prevention of plaque build-up.
From The Dental Health Series.
Prod-JOU Dist-JOU 1972

Plaque And Prevention (Rev Ed) C 9 MIN
16MM FILM, 3/4 OR 1/2 IN VIDEO PRO
Discusses the causes and prevention of tooth loss and decay.
Prod-PRORE Dist-PRORE

Plas Newydd - Anglesey, Wales C 26 MIN
16MM FILM, 3/4 OR 1/2 IN VIDEO H-C A
Presents the beautiful and useful eighteenth-century country home, which is located on Anglesey, the island where the Roman legions ended their conquest of Europe and the merchant navy located a school. A nearby oil refinery provides income but detracts from the naturalness of the grounds.
From The Place In Europe Series.
Prod-THAMES Dist-MEDIAG 1975

Plasma - The Fourth State Of Matter C 10 MIN
16MM FILM, 3/4 OR 1/2 IN VIDEO I-C A
Shows that as temperature increases, matter changes from one to another of the three familiar states-solid, liquid and gas. Explores the properties and potential uses of plasma, the fourth state of matter, in which energy causes the atoms themselves to break down into free electrons and protons or ions.
Prod-MACK Dist-PHENIX 1968

Plasma Deposition Of Other Microelectronic Films C 35 MIN
3/4 OR 1/2 INCH VIDEO CASSETTE IND
Extends plasma deposition from oxide and nitride films into other electronic films such as oxynitride, aluminum oxide, aluminum nitride, zinc oxide and indium tinoxide.
From The Plasma Sputtering, Deposition And Growth Of Microelectronic Films For VLSI Series.
Prod-COLOSU Dist-COLOSU

Plasma Deposition Of Silicon Oxide And Silicon Nitride, I C 35 MIN
3/4 OR 1/2 INCH VIDEO CASSETTE IND
Looks at low temperature plasma deposition of both silicon nitride and silicon oxide films on both Si and III-V substrates for use as an interlayer dielectric, doping mask and encapsulation layer. Gives advantages and disadvantages of plasma deposition of both silicon compounds.
From The Plasma Sputtering, Deposition And Growth Of Microelectronic Films For VLSI Series.
Prod-COLOSU Dist-COLOSU

Plasma Deposition Of Silicon Oxide And Silicon Nitride, II C 35 MIN
3/4 OR 1/2 INCH VIDEO CASSETTE IND
Discusses plasma deposited oxides in terms of their breakdown voltage, index of refraction, pinhole density, deposition rate and physical film qualities such as adhesion, stress and step coverage.
From The Plasma Sputtering, Deposition And Growth Of Microelectronic Films For VLSI Series.
Prod-COLOSU Dist-COLOSU

Plasma Etching And Pattern Transfer - For VLSI Fabrication—A Series
IND
Outlines conventional approaches to the problem of transfer of the pattern printed in the photoresist to the electronic film underneath. Presents plasma etching as solution, and outlines capabilities as well as disadvantages.
Prod-COLOSU Dist-COLOSU

Al-Si-Cu Dry-Plasma Etching	035 MIN
Dry-Plasma Etching - Physical And Chemical	035 MIN
Patterned Films - Dry-Plasma Etching, I	035 MIN
Patterned Films - Dry-Plasma Etching, II	035 MIN
Patterned Films - Wet Chemical Etching, I	035 MIN
Patterned Films - Wet Chemical Etching, II	035 MIN

Plasma Frequency, Mobility, Conductivity And Dielectric Constant C
3/4 OR 1/2 INCH VIDEO CASSETTE IND
Presents concepts of mobility and conductivity to describe charged-particle motion in plasma. Describes concept of electron motion in gas with collisions as mobility-limited motion. Gives sample calculations for accelerated electron motion in helium gas of low pressure, and develops conductivity of the plasma and its relation to electron mobility.
From The Plasma Process Technology Fundamentals Series.
Prod-COLOSU Dist-COLOSU

Plasma Probes For Electron-Distribution Properties And Optical Emissions For Atomic... C
3/4 OR 1/2 INCH VIDEO CASSETTE IND
Describes plasma probes, optical spectroscopy and mass spectroscopy techniques for measuring quantitative atomic species concentrations in the plasma. Outlines electrical characteristics of a metal probe inserted into the plasma. Measures plasma electron temperature, plasma-electron density and plasma potential itself.
From The Plasma Process Technology Fundamentals Series.
Prod-COLOSU Dist-COLOSU

Plasma Process Technology Fundamentals—A Series
IND
Provides an understanding of gas-phase mechanisms, plasma physics and their use in plasma reactor technology. Brings together plasma and solid state device disciplines in the context of plasma processing for VLSI.
Prod-COLOSU Dist-COLOSU

Basic Collision Process And Cross Section
Cathode Emission Of Beam Electrons And
Cathode Sheaths
Debye Shielding And Plasma Oscillation For
Derivation Of The Boltzman Equation
Distribution Functions And Detailed Balance
Electron Density Decay Processes
Electron Density Steady-State Solutions
Floating Sheaths
Free Radicals
Gas Discharge Collision Processes,I
Gas Discharge Collision Processes,II
Gases, Free Radicals And Charged Particles
Langevin Equation, Distribution Function And
Maxwellian And Druyvesteyn Distributions
Optical Spectroscopy For Diagnostics And
Plasma Frequency, Mobility, Conductivity And
Plasma Probes For Electron-Distribution
Plasmas As Fluids, I
Transport Coefficients - Conductivity
Transport Coefficients - Mobility And Diffusion

Plasma Sputtering, Deposition And Growth Of Microelectronic Films For VLSI—A Series
IND
Presents plasma sputtering, plasma-assisted chemical vapor deposition (CVD) and plasma growth of thin films, and compares them to the traditional thermal CVD method of film growth.
Prod-COLOSU Dist-COLOSU

Aluminum Film Deposition Via Sputtering	035 MIN
Chemical Vapor Deposition-Basics	035 MIN
Chemical Vapor Deposition-Practical Aspects	035 MIN
Dry Plasma Development Of Photoresist And	035 MIN
Evaporation And Ion-Beam Deposition	035 MIN
Gas Discharge Sputtering, I	035 MIN
Gas Discharge Sputtering, II	035 MIN
Glow Discharges	035 MIN
Ions Impacting Surfaces	035 MIN
Magnetron Sputtering	035 MIN
Plasma Deposition Of Other Microelectronic	035 MIN
Plasma Deposition Of Silicon Oxide And	035 MIN
Plasma Deposition Of Silicon Oxide And	025 MIN
Plasma-Surface Interactions	035 MIN
RF Glow Discharges	035 MIN
Secondary Particle Emissions From Surfaces, I	035 MIN
Secondary Particle Emissions From Surfaces, II	035 MIN
Sputter Deposition - An Overview	035 MIN

Plasma-Surface Interactings C 23 MIN
3/4 OR 1/2 INCH VIDEO CASSETTE IND
Presents beginning of interaction of plasmas with substrate surfaces. Describes surface topology in terms of macroscopic and microscopic defects, with special emphasis on crystalline silicon surfaces.
From The Plasma Sputtering, Depostion And Growth Of Microelectronic Films For VLSI Series.
Prod-COLOSU Dist-COLOSU

Plasmas As Fluids, I C
3/4 OR 1/2 INCH VIDEO CASSETTE IND
Views plasmas as multicomponent fluids in order to derive a macroscopic equation that includes density, temperature and pressure as variables rather than atomic cross sections. Shows how a fluid equation for plasmas is derived and compares to the classical Navier-Stokes equation.
From The Plasma Process Technology Fundamentals Series.
Prod-COLOSU Dist-COLOSU

Plasmas As Fluids, II C
3/4 OR 1/2 INCH VIDEO CASSETTE IND
Relates how moments of the Boltzmann equation yield three macroscopic equations - particle continuity, momentum conservation and energy conservation. Covers production and loss of electrons through excitation, ionization and recombination.
From The Plasma Process Technology Fundamentals Series.
Prod-COLOSU Dist-COLOSU

Plasmasis C 14 MIN
16MM FILM, 3/4 OR 1/2 IN VIDEO A
Portrays the evolution of the species in this modern ballet from Cuba.
Prod-CUBAFI Dist-CNEMAG 1974

Plaster Casting B 25 MIN
16MM FILM OPTICAL SOUND H-C
Features Tylden W Streett, sculpture instructor and director of graduate schools of the Maryland Institute College of Art, who

demonstrates the process of translating a clay portrait head into a plaster cast through the use of a one-time waste mold. Describes the techniques used, their underlying principles and the use of all of the necessary materials.
Prod-HALLFM Dist-HALLFM

Plaster Dorsal Wrist Cockup Splint With Outrigger C 23 MIN
3/4 OR 1/2 INCH VIDEO CASSETTE PRO
Demonstrates the construction of a plaster dorsal wrist cockup splint with outrigger. Procedures for making a pattern, forming the splint and outrigger, and making and attaching finger loops and a support strap are covered in detail.
Prod-HSCIC Dist-HSCIC

Plasterers, Roofers, Carpenters C 30 MIN
1/2 IN VIDEO CASSETTE BETA/VHS
Shows the renovation of kitchen walls, the chimney and the front porch of an old house.
From The This Old House, Pt 1 - The Dorchester Series.
Prod-WGBHTV Dist-MTI

Plastic And Reconstruction Surgery Of The Hand C 34 MIN
16MM FILM OPTICAL SOUND PRO
Illustrates cases of early traumatic wounds of the hands, methods of elective surgery of the hands and late reconstructive surgery.
LC NO. FIE52-1350
Prod-USN Dist-USNAC 1976

Plastic Filler C 13 MIN
1/2 IN VIDEO CASSETTE BETA/VHS
Deals with auto body repair. Discusses how, where and when to use plastic body filler.
Prod-RMI Dist-RMI

Plastic Isolators - New Tools For Medical Research C 14 MIN
16MM FILM OPTICAL SOUND
Demonstrates how inexpensive plastic isolators protect laboratory animals from contamination during research studies and safeguard personnel from virulent organisms, noxious fumes and radioactive dusts.
LC NO. FIE64-108
Prod-USPHS Dist-USNAC 1964

Plastic Journey C 19 MIN
3/4 INCH VIDEO CASSETTE
Explains how plastic materials were discovered. Demonstrates the manufacture of plastic auto parts at a Michigan Ford plant.
From The Pike On Language Series.
Prod-UMITV Dist-UMITV 1973

Plastic Piping C 60 MIN
3/4 OR 1/2 INCH VIDEO CASSETTE IND
See series title for descriptive statement.
From The Mechanical Equipment Maintenance, Module 17 - Advanced Pipefitting Series.
Prod-LEIKID Dist-LEIKID

Plastic Prison, The C 58 MIN
3/4 INCH VIDEO CASSETTE
Explores the world of children who have no natural defense against disease or infection because they were born with immune deficiencies. Tells the story of David, who has spent the five years of his life in a plastic isolator because he must live in a sterile environment.
From The Nova Series.
Prod-WGBHTV Dist-PBS 1977

Plastic Surgery B 18 MIN
16MM FILM OPTICAL SOUND H-C A
A plastic surgeon explores the motives and emotional stability of a teen-age girl with a high-bridged nose before concluding that surgery is warranted. Shows the operation in progress and the reconstructed nose following surgery.
From The Doctors At Work Series.
LC NO. FIA65-1357
Prod-CMA Dist-LAWREN Prodn-LAWREN 1961

Plastic Surgery C 10 MIN
3/4 OR 1/2 INCH VIDEO CASSETTE P-I
Explores the question of self-image and children's concerns about becoming a new person after plastic surgery, as well as fears they may have about the operation itself.
From The Children's Medical Series.
Prod-HFDT Dist-MTI 1982

Plastic Surgery C 25 MIN
3/4 OR 1/2 INCH VIDEO CASSETTE
Shows that reconstructive surgery is an area in medicine encompassing more than just face-lifts and nose jobs.
Prod-TRAINX Dist-TRAINX

Plastic Surgery / Auto Accesories / Dog-Cat Food C
3/4 OR 1/2 INCH VIDEO CASSETTE
Discusses various aspects of plastic surgery, auto accesories, and dog and cat food.
From The Consumer Survival Series.
Prod-MDCPB Dist-MDCPB

Plasticity - Experimental Observation And Theory, Pt 1 B 60 MIN
3/4 OR 1/2 INCH VIDEO CASSETTE
See series title for descriptive statement.
From The Concepts And Practice In Finite Element Inelastic Analysis Series. Pt 1
Prod-UAZMIC Dist-UAZMIC 1979

Plasticity - Experimental Observation And Theory, Pt 2 B 60 MIN
3/4 OR 1/2 INCH VIDEO CASSETTE
See series title for descriptive statement.
From The Concepts And Practice In Finite Element Inelastic Analysis Series. Pt 2
Prod-UAZMIC Dist-UAZMIC 1979

Plasticity - Experimental Observation And Theory, Pt 3 B 60 MIN
3/4 OR 1/2 INCH VIDEO CASSETTE
See series title for descriptive statement.
From The Concepts And Practice In Finite Element Inelastic Analysis Series. Pt 3
Prod-UAZMIC Dist-UAZMIC 1979

Plasticity - Numerical Implementation Of The Theory, Pt 1 B 60 MIN
3/4 OR 1/2 INCH VIDEO CASSETTE
See series title for descriptive statement.
From The Concepts And Practice In Finite Element Inelastic Analysis Series. Pt 4
Prod-UAZMIC Dist-UAZMIC 1979

Plasticity - Numerical Implementation Of The Theory, Pt 2 B 60 MIN
3/4 OR 1/2 INCH VIDEO CASSETTE
See series title for descriptive statement.
From The Concepts And Practice In Finite Element Inelastic Analysis Series. Pt 5
Prod-UAZMIC Dist-UAZMIC 1979

Plastics C 11 MIN
16MM FILM, 3/4 OR 1/2 IN VIDEO I-H
Describes the versatility that has made plastics such an important part of our lives.
Prod-SANTER Dist-PHENIX 1973

Plastics C 12 MIN
3/4 OR 1/2 INCH VIDEO CASSETTE
Covers the characteristics of plastics, its processing, molding, casting, foaming, extruding and reinforcing.
From The Working With Nonmetals In The Plant Series.
Prod-TPCTRA Dist-TPCTRA

Plastics - Industrial Processes And Products C 24 MIN
16MM FILM OPTICAL SOUND J-C
Uses animation and actual scenes of production to explain the principles of basic manufacturing processes of the plastics industry and their applications to the production of consumer goods.
Prod-STSU Dist-STSU Prodn-BARNRD 1963

Plastics And Fiber Glass—A Series
3/4 OR 1/2 INCH VIDEO CASSETTE H-C
Prod-MORLAT Dist-SF

Fiber Glass 13 MIN
Thermoplastics 13 MIN

Plastics I - Layout, Cutting, Finishing, And Assembly C 30 MIN
3/4 OR 1/2 INCH VIDEO CASSETTE H A
Demonstrates layouts, cutting, finishing, and assembly techniques to be used with acrylic plastics.
From The Arts And Crafts Series.
LC NO. 81-706993
Prod-GPITVL Dist-GPITVL 1981

Plastics Identification And Repair C 29 MIN
1/2 IN VIDEO CASSETTE BETA/VHS
Deals with auto body repair.
Prod-RMI Dist-RMI

Plastics II - Heat Forming and Assembly C 30 MIN
3/4 OR 1/2 INCH VIDEO CASSETTE H A
Demonstrates how to create objects from plastics using cohesive solvents and heat-forming techniques.
From The Arts And Crafts Series.
LC NO. 81-706995
Prod-GPITVL Dist-GPITVL 1981

Plastics III - Casting Polyester And Cutting Plastic Foam C 30 MIN
3/4 OR 1/2 INCH VIDEO CASSETTE H A
Demonstrates how to use liquid polyester resin to encapsulate objects for display. Describes the technique of cutting polystyrene and styrofoam with a hot wire cutter.
From The Arts And Crafts Series.
LC NO. 81-706997
Prod-GPITVL Dist-GPITVL 1981

Plastics, The World Of Imagination C 27 MIN
3/4 OR 1/2 INCH VIDEO CASSETTE
Emphasizes the important role of plastics in the modern world. Explores uses of the material in such diverse fields as flight, architecture, textiles, packaging, transportation, energy conservation and medicine.
Prod-SPLENG Dist-MTP

Plastiphobia C 10 MIN
16MM FILM, 3/4 OR 1/2 IN VIDEO
Shows how modelling clay takes many forms when animation creates crazy characters, objects change shape and become other things in rapid succession. Demonstrates how, with no narration and wide open plot, the climax is reached in a fantastic circus where performers unexpectedly change.
Prod-IFF Dist-IFF

Plate Cutting Manual C 8 MIN
1/2 IN VIDEO CASSETTE BETA/VHS IND
See series title for descriptive statement.
From The Welding Training (Comprehensive) — Oxy-Acetylene Welding Series.
Prod-RMI Dist-RMI

Plate Detector B 30 MIN
16MM FILM, 3/4 OR 1/2 IN VIDEO
Discusses the purpose of each component in the plate detector circuit and explains how the circuit recovers ultrastructure of the megakaryocyte as well as the advantages and limitations of the plate detector with a reference to selectivity, sensitivity and signal handling ability. (Kinescope)
Prod-USAF Dist-USNAC

Plate Tectonics C 8 MIN
3/4 OR 1/2 INCH VIDEO CASSETTE
Shows puppets being used to explain the theory of plate tectonics to children visiting Rock Creek Park.
LC NO. 80-706469
Prod-USNPS Dist-USNAC 1979

Plate Tectonics C 30 MIN
3/4 OR 1/2 INCH VIDEO CASSETTE C
Explores continental drift and sea floor spreading. Follows a scientifically outfitted deep sea drilling ship as it travels the world's oceans collecting data.
From The Earth, Sea And Sky Series.
Prod-DALCCD Dist-DALCCD

Plate Tectonics C 30 MIN
3/4 OR 1/2 INCH VIDEO CASSETTE
Focuses on plate tectonics, the theory that the earth's crust consists of large plates that rub together, collide and move apart thereby causing geologic phenomena such as earthquakes.
From The Oceanus - The Marine Environment Series. Lesson 9
Prod-SCCON Dist-CDTEL

Plate Tectonics C 52 MIN
3/4 OR 1/2 INCH VIDEO CASSETTE IND
See series title for descriptive statement.
From The Basic And Petroleum Geology For Non-Geologists - Earth's Interior...--Series
Prod-PHILLP Dist-GPCV

Plate Tectonics C 55 MIN
3/4 OR 1/2 INCH VIDEO CASSETTE IND
See series title for descriptive statement.
From The Basic Geology Series.
Prod-GPCV Dist-GPCV

Plate Tectonics - A Revolution In The Earth Sciences C 28 MIN
3/4 OR 1/2 INCH VIDEO CASSETTE
Illustrates how mountain building occurs and how animals migrate, Uses animation and visits to the Alps and active volcanic areas.
From The Earth Explored Series.
Prod-BBCTV Dist-PBS

Plate-Coupled Multivibrator - VT B 40 MIN
16MM FILM, 3/4 OR 1/2 IN VIDEO
Discusses the purpose of each component in the plate coupled multivibrator circuit, the construction of a waveform graph and how to maintain stability. (Kinescope)
Prod-USAF Dist-USNAC

Plateau And Pacific C 28 MIN
16MM FILM OPTICAL SOUND C A
Tells that in the lower Monumental Reservoir on the Snake River in southeastern Washington, a field school of archeological students worked in two different sites. By combining the information from the two sites, a history of the reservoir area stretching over more than 8,000 years is being developed.
Prod-UTEX Dist-UTEX 1963

Plateau Farmers In France C 15 MIN
16MM FILM, 3/4 OR 1/2 IN VIDEO P-C
Shows the contrast between traditional and modern farming techniques and mechanization in France.
From The Man And His World Series.
Prod-FI Dist-FI 1969

Platelet Aggregation / Clot Retraction / Platelet Factor 3 C 18 MIN
3/4 OR 1/2 INCH VIDEO CASSETTE
Demonstrates the instrumentation and procedure for assessment of platelet aggregation, a quantitative clot retraction method using platelet-rich plasma and a platelet factor 3 assay in which platelets are stimulated with epinephrine and kaolin to induce platelet factor 3 release and the recalcification time of the plasma is measured.
From The Blood Coagulation Laboratory Techniques Series.
LC NO. 79-707605
Prod-UMICH Dist-UMICH 1977

Platelets And Leukocytes B 20 MIN
16MM FILM OPTICAL SOUND
Dr Julian Schorr discusses the preparation of platelet packs from whole fresh blood and the use of leukocyte concentrates, serum albumin, coagulation concentrates and hyperimmune globulin.
From The Clinical Pathology Series.
LC NO. 74-706181
Prod-NMAC Dist-USNAC 1970

Platform Safety And Emergency Shutdown Procedures C 24 MIN
3/4 OR 1/2 INCH VIDEO CASSETTE IND
Covers the steps to take to abandon a platform and what to do if an employee goes overboard. Describes firefighting equipment, shutdown systems and general safety rules and procedures.
Prod-UTEXPE Dist-UTEXPE

Platinum C 21 MIN
3/4 OR 1/2 INCH VIDEO CASSETTE J-C A
Tells about the mining and use of platinum, an important metal widely used today in medicine, industry and fine jewelry construction. Commences with platinum's discovery and use as the standard metric measure in the 19th century, and shows how it is formed, mined, refined and used.
Prod-GAZEL Dist-EDMI 1981

Platinum Blonde B 91 MIN
16MM FILM OPTICAL SOUND
Tells how a man must choose between his aristocratic wife and a fellow newspaper reporter, played by Loretta Young. Stars Robert Williams and Jean Harlow. Directed by Frank Capra.
Prod-CPC Dist-TWYMAN 1931

Plato In Amerika B 20 MIN
16MM FILM OPTICAL SOUND C A
The escapades of a first generation Greek caught between two cultures.
LC NO. FIA66-517
Prod-NYU Dist-NYU Prodn-NYUTMR 1965

Plato, Pt 1 - The Death Of Socrates C 30 MIN
3/4 INCH VIDEO CASSETTE
Deals with the death of Socrates.
From The From Socrates To Sartre Series.
Prod-MDCPB Dist-MDCPB

Plato, Pt 2 - The Republic, The Socratic Method, The Allegory Of The Cave C 30 MIN
3/4 INCH VIDEO CASSETTE
Looks at The Republic, the Socratic Method, and the Allegory of the Cave.
From The From Socrates To Sartre Series.
Prod-MDCPB Dist-MDCPB

Plato, Pt 3 - Theory Of Knowledge C 30 MIN
3/4 INCH VIDEO CASSETTE
Discusses the theory of knowledge in Plato's works.
From The From Socrates To Sartre Series.
Prod-MDCPB Dist-MDCPB

Plato, Pt 4 - Tripartite Soul And Contemporary Psychology C 30 MIN
3/4 INCH VIDEO CASSETTE
Describes Plato's theory of a tripartite soul and its relation to 20th century psychology.
From The From Socrates To Sartre Series.
Prod-MDCPB Dist-MDCPB

Plato, Pt 5 - Dualism C 30 MIN
3/4 INCH VIDEO CASSETTE
Discusses the concept of dualism in the work of Plato.
From The From Socrates To Sartre Series.
Prod-MDCPB Dist-MDCPB

Plato's Apology C 58 MIN
2 INCH VIDEOTAPE
Features Dean Robert A Goldwin of St John's College of Annapolis and three of his students discussing Plato's Apology with a special guest.
From The Dialogue Of The Western World Series.
Prod-MDCPB Dist-PUBTEL

Plato's Apology - The Life And Teachings Of Socrates C 30 MIN
16MM FILM, 3/4 OR 1/2 IN VIDEO H-C
A study of Socrates, a man whose influence on the minds of men still endures.
From The Humanities - Philosophy And Political Thought Series.
Prod-EBF Dist-EBEC 1962

Plato's Cave C 20 MIN
16MM FILM, 3/4 OR 1/2 IN VIDEO J-C A
Presents an adaptation of Plato's allegory of the cave from the seventh book of the Republic. With dialog in classical Greek.
Prod-GOULDA Dist-PFP 1974

Plato's Crito C 58 MIN
2 INCH VIDEOTAPE
Features Dean Robert A Goldwin of St John's College of Annapolis and three of his students discussing Plato's Crito with a special guest.
From The Dialogue Of The Western World Series.
Prod-MDCPB Dist-PUBTEL

Plato's Meno C 58 MIN
2 INCH VIDEOTAPE
Features Dean Robert A Goldwin of St John's College of Annapolis and three of his students discussing Plato's Meno with a special guest.
From The Dialogue Of The Western World Series.
Prod-MDCPB Dist-PUBTEL

Platte Valley, The - America's Great Road West B 30 MIN
16MM FILM OPTICAL SOUND J-C A
Portrays the Platte Valley as a natural highway to the West, and as a fur trade route. Discusses national expansion. Describes the Oregon Trail through Nebraska, the Mormon emigration, the California Gold Rush and the rugged life along the trail.
From The Great Plains Trilogy, 3 Series. Explorer And Settler - The White Man Arrives
Prod-KUONTV Dist-UNEBR 1954

Platypus - Ornithorhynchus Anatinus C 22 MIN
16MM FILM OPTICAL SOUND J-C A
Gives a comprehensive account of the platypus, the rare animal which is found only in Australia.
LC NO. 74-703289
Prod-ANAIB Dist-AUIS Prodn-FLMAUS 1973

Play - Ibsen's Peer Gynt C 60 MIN
3/4 OR 1/2 INCH VIDEO CASSETTE C
See series title for descriptive statement.
From The Drama - Play, Performance, Perception Series. Module 1
Prod-MDCC Dist-MDCC

Play - Is Trying Out C 25 MIN
16MM FILM, 3/4 OR 1/2 IN VIDEO C A
Shows two children at play, trying out new skills and new ways of combining means and ends to develop a rich repertory of actions and a more flexible approach to achieving goals.
From The Cognitive Development Series.
Prod-WILEYJ Dist-MEDIAG 1973

Play Activities - Ages 6-13 B 44 MIN
16MM FILM OPTICAL SOUND
Discusses the influence of values, culture, seasonal patterns and mass media upon children from the ages of 6 to 13.
From The Man - His Growth And Development, Birth Through Adolescence Series.
LC NO. 72-703686
Prod-VDONUR Dist-AJN Prodn-WTTWTV 1967

Play And Cultural Continuity—A Series
H-C T
Discusses the lives and cultures of children of different races and from different areas.
Prod-CFDC Dist-CFDC 1977

Appalachian Children 25 MIN
Mexican-American Children 27 MIN
Montana Indian Children 27 MIN
Southern Black Children 27 MIN

Play And Personality B 45 MIN
16MM FILM OPTICAL SOUND C T
An actual record of a group of preschool children whose mothers have severe neuroses. Demonstrates that children's anxieties are revealed in play, that the anxieties are related to their mothers', and that a child tries to master his fears in play.
Prod-CASH Dist-NYU 1964

Play Ball C 15 MIN
3/4 OR 1/2 INCH VIDEO CASSETTE P-I
Observes preparations for a major league baseball game at Cleveland Stadium.
From The Explorers Unlimited Series.
Prod-WVIZTV Dist-AITECH 1971

Play Ball, Play Safe C 14 MIN
16MM FILM OPTICAL SOUND
Emphasizes the importance of safety precautions in sports. Features a young baseball team that loses a championship because of injuries, and experienced players who demonstrate techniques used to avoid injuries on the field.
LC NO. FIA66-520
Prod-AETNA Dist-AETNA 1965

Play Better Hockey B 19 MIN
16MM FILM OPTICAL SOUND I-C A
Shows the basic skills and the strategy of attack and defense in hockey, as demonstrated by some of the Indian Olympic team players.
Prod-INDIA Dist-NEDINF

Play Bridge With The Experts—A Series
A
Presents master bridge players giving tips on bidding, dummy play or defensive problems in actual plays.
Prod-KUHTTV Dist-GPITVL 1980

Alfred Sheinwold, Pt 1 030 MIN
Alfred Sheinwold, Pt 2 030 MIN
Betty Ann Kennedy, Pt 1 030 MIN
Betty Ann Kennedy, Pt 2 030 MIN
Bob Hamman, Pt 1 030 MIN
Bob Hamman, Pt 2 030 MIN
Bobby Goldman, Pt 1 030 MIN
Bobby Goldman, Pt 2 030 MIN
Bobby Goldman, Pt 3 030 MIN
Bobby Nail 030 MIN
Bobby Wolff, Pt 1 030 MIN
Bobby Wolff, Pt 2 030 MIN
Carol Sanders, Pt 1 030 MIN
Carol Sanders, Pt 2 030 MIN
Dan Morse 030 MIN
Dr Frank Hoadley, Pt 1 030 MIN
Dr Frank Hoadley, Pt 2 030 MIN
Dr George S Dawkins 030 MIN
Emma Jean Hawes, Pt 1 030 MIN
Emma Jean Hawes, Pt 2 030 MIN
Jim Jacoby, Pt 1 030 MIN
Jim Jacoby, Pt 2 030 MIN
Julius Rosenblum, Pt 1 030 MIN
Julius Rosenblum, Pt 2 030 MIN
Lew Mathe 030 MIN
Paul Hodge 030 MIN

Play Bridge—A Series
A
Designed for the bridge player on the intermediate level. Hosted by Mary McVey.
Prod-KYTV Dist-KYTV 1983

Bidding Problem Hands 030 MIN
Clear Signals 030 MIN
Defensive Strategy 030 MIN
Double Talk 030 MIN
Fooling The Opponents 030 MIN
Judgement In Bidding 030 MIN
No Trump Bidding And Play 030 MIN
Playing The Hand 030 MIN
Safety Plays And End Plays 030 MIN
Simple Overcall, The 030 MIN
Slams - Bidding And Play 030 MIN
Take-Out Doubles 030 MIN
Using The Clues 030 MIN
When They Interfere 030 MIN

Play Experiences During Hospitalization C 15 MIN
3/4 INCH VIDEO CASSETTE PRO
Demonstrates a variety of play sessions which health professionals can utilize in caring for hospitalized children. Depicts diagnostic play, therapeutic play, and school activity sessions, emphasizing that play sessions allow children to express and master fears, release tension and learn.
LC NO. 79-707731
Prod-UMICHM Dist-UMMCML Prodn-UMISU 1976

Play Fair - Voluntary Compliance (Political Science) C 15 MIN
3/4 OR 1/2 INCH VIDEO CASSETTE P
Shows that when Johnny and his sister Dionne accidentally break a window playing baseball, their first impulse is to run.
From The Two Cents' Worth Series.
Prod-WHATV Dist-AITECH Prodn-WIEC 1976

Play For Television, A B 15 MIN
2 INCH VIDEOTAPE K-P
Presents a play created by elementary school children for the television studio. (Broadcast quality)
From The Magic Of Words Series.
Prod-GWTVAI Dist-GPITVL Prodn-WETATV

Play Half Written, A - The Energy Adventure C 26 MIN
16MM FILM OPTICAL SOUND
Explores the relationship between energy and human achievement in the arts and technology. Examines energy sources in use during the 1970's and shows sources being developed for the future.
LC NO. 79-701445
Prod-AIF Dist-MTP Prodn-STOKB 1979

Play Half Written, A - The Energy Adventure C 26 MIN
3/4 INCH VIDEO CASSETTE J-C A
Investigates the relationship of energy to the inventive human spirit. Shows that such things as Buster Keaton's comedic talent, Beethoven's musical genius, and video artistry have all been brought before the public because of technological development supplied by energy. Emphasizes nuclear power as a bridge between the depletable power sources of the past and the energy sources of the future.
LC NO. 79-701445
Prod-STOKB Dist-AIF 1979

Play In The Hospital C 50 MIN
16MM FILM OPTICAL SOUND PRO
Focuses on the fears and anxieties that confront the hospitalized child and demonstrates how a professionally supervised play program helps to provide outlets for these feelings.
LC NO. 73-702921
Prod-CFDC Dist-CFDC 1972

Play Is The Work Of Young Children C 14 MIN
16MM FILM, 3/4 OR 1/2 IN VIDEO
Illustrates the educational philosophy of Lenore Wilson, a specialist in early childhood education. Discusses her belief that young children learn to play with one another in a manner simulating the adult world. Talks about ways to bring out the uniqueness of each child.
Prod-CROMIE Dist-UCEMC 1974

Play It Safe C 12 MIN
16MM FILM - 3/4 IN VIDEO
Reviews safety tips for using power lawnmowers and hedge trimmers.
LC NO. 80-707116
Prod-CPSAFC Dist-USNAC Prodn-NOWAKA 1980

Play It Safe C 15 MIN
3/4 OR 1/2 INCH VIDEO CASSETTE I
Shows how Casey ignores advice to get a license and lock for his new bike and how he returns from a ball game to find the bike stolen.
From The It's Your Move Series.
Prod-WETN Dist-AITECH 1977

Play It Safe - Electrically C 14 MIN
16MM FILM, 3/4 OR 1/2 IN VIDEO K-J
Teaches children safety awareness when playing outdoors. Explains warning signs and gives safety advice.
Prod-BORTF Dist-BCNFL 1983

Play On Belgium, A C 26 MIN
16MM FILM OPTICAL SOUND
Highlights cities and sights of Belgium, including visits to Brussels, Bruges, Liege, Ghent, Antwerp, Dinant, and the war memorial at Bastogne.
LC NO. 78-700666
Prod-BNTO Dist-MCDO Prodn-MCDO 1978

Play Read, The C 30 MIN
2 INCH VIDEOTAPE J-H
See series title for descriptive statement.
From The From Franklin To Frost - Drama Series.
Prod-MPATI Dist-GPITVL

Play Safe C 10 MIN
16MM FILM, 3/4 OR 1/2 IN VIDEO P-I
Explains that most playground safety rules make perfect sense by showing dangerous behavior and allowing the children to correct the behavior. Points out that safe play can be fun.
Prod-FILMSW Dist-FLMFR

Play Seen, The C 30 MIN
2 INCH VIDEOTAPE J-H
See series title for descriptive statement.
From The From Franklin To Frost - Drama Series.
Prod-MPATI Dist-GPITVL

Play The Shopping Game C 20 MIN
16MM FILM, 3/4 OR 1/2 IN VIDEO J-C A
Demonstrates good shopping techniques, using a television game show format to point out the knowledge a consumer needs in the marketplace.
From The Consumers In A Changing World Series.
Prod-EBEC Dist-EBEC 1977

Play Therapy With Mentally Handicapped Children C 20 MIN
3/4 OR 1/2 INCH VIDEO CASSETTE
Utilizes play therapy to convey the handicapped child's natural medium of self-expression by providing an opportunity to express his/her feelings or frustrations.
Prod-LASSWC Dist-UWISC 1979

Play With The Fire C 13 MIN
16MM FILM, 3/4 OR 1/2 IN VIDEO J-C A
Uses the technique of cut-out silhouette animation to create the story of a girl and a boy who chance to meet a friendly imp and discover his lair where he makes diamonds, rubies and emeralds.
Prod-TRICFD Dist-PHENIX

Play Your Best Tennis, Volume One C 82 MIN
1/2 IN VIDEO CASSETTE BETA/VHS
Presents mini-lessons in various levels of tennis. Discusses rackets, personal playing improvement and other topics.
LC NO. 84-706141
Prod-CARAVT Dist-CARAVT

Play Your Best Tennis, Volume Two C 67 MIN
3/4 OR 1/2 INCH VIDEO CASSETTE
Provides instruction on how to play tennis. Focuses on strokes and strategies.
Prod-CARAVT Dist-CARAVT

Play's The Thing C 20 MIN
16MM FILM, 3/4 OR 1/2 IN VIDEO
Examines a variety of playthings and play equipment, focusing particularly on objects that reveal the custom, skill and whimsy of their makers. Considers the emotional responses to toys and the effect of toys upon the user.
From The Images And Things Series.
LC NO. 73-702106
Prod-NITC Dist-AITECH

Play's The Thing, The C 10 MIN
3/4 OR 1/2 INCH VIDEO CASSETTE K-P
Focuses on the skill to interpret story dramatizations and to follow the story line of a play.
From The Book, Look And Listen Series.
Prod-MDDE Dist-AITECH 1977

Play's The Thing, The C 15 MIN
3/4 OR 1/2 INCH VIDEO CASSETTE T
Uses the adventures of a pirate and his three friends to explore the many facets of language arts. Focuses on creative imagination and encourages its use in writing.
From The Hidden Treasures Series. No. 12
LC NO. 82-706552
Prod-WCVETV Dist-GPITVL 1980

Playful Pandas, The C 10 MIN
16MM FILM, 3/4 OR 1/2 IN VIDEO K-P
Shows some of the characteristics and behavior of pandas.
Prod-CORF Dist-CORF 1975

Playful Relaxers C 10 MIN
2 INCH VIDEOTAPE
See series title for descriptive statement.
From The Janaki Series.
Prod-WGBHTV Dist-PUBTEL

Playground C 7 MIN
16MM FILM, 3/4 OR 1/2 IN VIDEO K-P
Introduces the youngest readers and pre-readers to words and concepts, including pictures and songs.
From The Starting To Read Series.
Prod-BURGHS Dist-AIMS 1971

Playground C 11 MIN
16MM FILM, 3/4 OR 1/2 IN VIDEO
Uses the example of three creative playgrounds in Denmark and England to show how children, under the guidance of a leader, enjoy building houses, bridges, towers, windmills and other structures, from junk materials donated by industries, junk collectors, parents and others. Includes descriptions of legal and practical considerations in founding a creative playground.
Prod-GRISTR Dist-UCEMC 1974

Playground Discipline - A Positive Approach C 20 MIN
16MM FILM, 3/4 OR 1/2 IN VIDEO T
Demonstrates how to select and train older students to handle most of the conflicts that occur daily on the playground.
Prod-MFFD Dist-FI

Playground In Six Acts C 22 MIN
16MM FILM OPTICAL SOUND
Presents an experimental film which depicts man as a child in a playground, still in the infancy of development.
LC NO. 74-702757
Prod-YORKU Dist-CANFDC 1973

Playground Safety C 15 MIN
3/4 OR 1/2 INCH VIDEO CASSETTE P-I
Demonstrates playground safety with the help of two mimes. Shows the proper ways to play on swings, slides, seesaws and climbing bars.
From The Safer You Series.
Prod-WCVETV Dist-GPITVL 1984

Playground Safety (2nd Ed) C 11 MIN
16MM FILM, 3/4 OR 1/2 IN VIDEO P-I
Shows how to be safe on a playground by following three rules--be sure the play area is safe, keep out of the way of others, and learn how to play correctly. Demonstrates the violent force of moving objects.
Prod-CORF Dist-CORF 1966

Playground Safety - As Simple As A, B, C C 14 MIN
16MM FILM, 3/4 OR 1/2 IN VIDEO P-I
Offers information on playground safety, discussing roughhousing, climbing, equipment, ball games, races and stray dogs.
Prod-CENTRO Dist-CORF

Playground Safety - The Peeperkorns C 10 MIN
16MM FILM, 3/4 OR 1/2 IN VIDEO P
Presents a family of animated characters demonstrating correct behavior on the playground.
Prod-CROCUS Dist-CRMP 1975

Playhouse, The B 20 MIN
16MM FILM SILENT J-C A
Stars Buster Keaton.
Prod-MGM Dist-TWYMAN 1921

Playing C 15 MIN
16MM FILM, 3/4 OR 1/2 IN VIDEO K-P S
Presents Mr Rogers showing examples of play in sand and a 7-year-old boy playing with him. Encourages the use of pretending, fantasy and creative play.
From The I Am, I Can, I Will, Level I Series.
LC NO. 80-706540
Prod-FAMCOM Dist-HUBDSC 1979

Playing Basketball C 13 MIN
16MM FILM, 3/4 OR 1/2 IN VIDEO P-I
Demonstrates the skills and techniques necessary for playing basketball. Covers passing, catching, dribbling, pivoting and shooting.
From The Sports For Elementary Series.
Prod-CINEDU Dist-AIMS 1975

Playing Basketball (Spanish) C 13 MIN
16MM FILM, 3/4 OR 1/2 IN VIDEO I-J
Demonstrates techniques and skills necessary for developing and improving playing skills in the game of basketball. Explains methods for passing, catching, dribbling, pivoting and shooting.
From The Sports For Elementary (Spanish) Series.
Prod-CINEDU Dist-AIMS 1975

Playing By Ear C 29 MIN
3/4 INCH VIDEO CASSETTE H A
Reviews A-major scales and chords. Introduces E-major scale. Demonstrates circle of fifths. Reviews earlier pieces. Begins discussion of playing by ear.
From The Beginning Piano - An Adult Approach Series. Lesson 15
Prod-COAST Dist-CDTEL

Playing Communication Games C 30 MIN
3/4 OR 1/2 INCH VIDEO CASSETTE H-C A
Focuses on how people can influence whether communication with another person will be positive or negative in style and outcome. Shows how an individual can influence the direction and tone of communication.
From The Principles of Human Communication Series.
Prod-UMINN Dist-GPITVL 1983

Playing Doubles C 29 MIN
3/4 OR 1/2 INCH VIDEO CASSETTE
See series title for descriptive statement.
From The Vic Braden's Tennis For The Future Series.
Prod-WGBHTV Dist-PBS 1981

Playing Folk Guitar C 60 MIN
1/2 IN VIDEO CASSETTE BETA/VHS J-C A
Assumes familiarity with the rudiments of guitar playing and emphasizes techniques, advancing from the basic folk chord progression into blues, flatpicking, country and western, bending tones, and barre chords. Each of the numerous, focused lessons is demonstrated by a professional guitar teacher.
LC NO. 83-706331
Prod-VIPRO Dist-VIPRO

Playing For Keeps C 89 MIN
2 INCH VIDEOTAPE
Features 125 people playing reverse roles as citizens of Penn City, an imaginary middle-sized American city torn by racial conflict and created by the Presbyterian Synod of Pennsylvania as an experiment in human behavior.
Prod-WITFTV Dist-PUBTEL

Playing For Time C
1/2 IN VIDEO CASSETTE BETA/VHS
Tells the story of a group of women prisoners in Auschwitz who save their lives by playing in the camp orchestra. Stars Jane Alexander and Vanessa Redgrave.
Prod-GA Dist-GA

Playing In The Park C 16 MIN
16MM FILM MAGNETIC SOUND K-C A S
See series title for descriptive statement.
From The PANCOM Beginning Total Communication Program For Hearing Parents Of... Series. Level 2
LC NO. 77-700504
Prod-CSDE Dist-JOYCE Prodn-CSFDF 1977

Playing It Safe C 15 MIN
16MM FILM, 3/4 OR 1/2 IN VIDEO K-I
Features the Healthwise puppets, who learn that playing it safe around the house means being on the lookout for common carelessness. Shows how to play it safe outside by driving with seatbelts buckled, crossing the street at the corner, and staying out of culverts and refrigerators.
From The Healthwise Series.
Prod-CORF Dist-CORF 1982

Playing Large Intervals C 29 MIN
3/4 INCH VIDEO CASSETTE H A
Reviews the odd-even technique of reading large intervals. Introduces a new piece in the key of D major that uses broken intervals.
From The Beginning Piano - An Adult Approach Series. Lesson 12
Prod-COAST Dist-CDTEL

Playing Safe In Animal Town C 14 MIN
16MM FILM, 3/4 OR 1/2 IN VIDEO P
Uses a story about animals to demonstrate and motivate safe behavior walking, playing and bike riding, with special attention to the unpredictability of automobiles,trains, and pedestrians.
Prod-CORF Dist-CORF 1976

Playing Softball C 11 MIN
16MM FILM, 3/4 OR 1/2 IN VIDEO P-I
Demonstrates basic techniques for playing softball. Covers pitching, catching, batting, running, throwing and stopping around hits.
From The Sports For Elementary Series.
Prod-CINEDU Dist-AIMS 1975

Playing Softball (Spanish) C 11 MIN
16MM FILM, 3/4 OR 1/2 IN VIDEO I-J
Demonstrates softball techniques for pitching, catching, battling, running, stopping ground hits and throwing.
From The Sports For Elementary (Spanish) Series.
Prod-CINEDU Dist-AIMS 1975

Playing Soul Music To My Freckles C
3/4 OR 1/2 INCH VIDEO CASSETTE
See series title for descriptive statement.
From The Red Tape Series.
Prod-EAI Dist-EAI

Playing Tennis And Going Swimming C 8 MIN
16MM FILM OPTICAL SOUND K-P
Follows Crystal and Alistair as they play a few rounds of tennis. Explains that they are so hot from their exertions that they invite Flutter and Fancy to join them at a swimming pool.
From The Crystal Tipps And Alistair Series.
LC NO. 73-700459
Prod-BBCTV Dist-VEDO 1972

Playing The Cello C 23 MIN
16MM FILM OPTICAL SOUND J-C A
Begins with the fundamentals of playing the cello, such as holding the bow, body position, bowing, fingering exercises and vibrato control. Demonstrates through more advanced techniques shown by Peter Faroll as he teaches cellists. Deals with four students of varying ability.
LC NO. 73-701742
Prod-UIMPPC Dist-UILL 1970

Playing The Guitar I - Course Review C 29 MIN
2 INCH VIDEOTAPE
See series title for descriptive statement.
From The Playing The Guitar I Series.
Prod-KCET Dist-PUBTEL

Playing The Guitar I - Lesson Review C 29 MIN
2 INCH VIDEOTAPE
See series title for descriptive statement.
From The Playing The Guitar I Series.
Prod-KCET Dist-PUBTEL

Playing The Guitar I - The Final Lesson C 29 MIN
2 INCH VIDEOTAPE
See series title for descriptive statement.
From The Playing The Guitar I Series.
Prod-KCET Dist-PUBTEL

Playing The Guitar I--A Series

Presents an introduction to the techniques of guitar. Includes the basics of a music-notation system known as tablature.
Prod-KCET Dist-PUBTEL

Arpeggio Practice In A Piece 29 MIN
Arpeggio Techniques 29 MIN
Beginning To Play 29 MIN
Buying A Guitar 29 MIN
Early History Of The Guitar 29 MIN
Flamenco Forms 29 MIN
Greensleeves, Pt 1 29 MIN
Greensleeves, Pt 2 29 MIN
Half-Bar And Second Position, The 29 MIN
Learning To Read Music 29 MIN
Ligado Technique 29 MIN
Music In Two Parts 29 MIN
Notes On The Fifth String 29 MIN
Notes On The First Two Strings 29 MIN
Notes On The Fourth String 29 MIN
Notes On The Sixth String 29 MIN
Notes On The Third String 29 MIN
Playing The Guitar I - Course Review 29 MIN
Playing The Guitar I - Lesson Review 29 MIN
Playing The Guitar I - The Final Lesson 29 MIN
Position And Tuning 29 MIN
Sharps, Flats, Keys And Scales 29 MIN
Sight Reading And Playing 29 MIN
Simple Chords 29 MIN
Styles In Song Accompaniment 29 MIN
Tone Production, Vibrato And Dynamics 29 MIN

Playing The Guitar II - Course Review C 29 MIN
2 INCH VIDEOTAPE
See series title for descriptive statement.
From The Playing The Guitar II Series.
Prod-KCET Dist-PUBTEL

Playing The Guitar II--A Series

Presents an introduction to the techniques of guitar. Includes the basics of a music-notation system known as tablature.
Prod-KCET Dist-PUBTEL

Complete Sevillana, A 29 MIN
Completion Of The Fifth Position 29 MIN
Correction Of Common Faults 29 MIN
Guitar Makers 29 MIN

Increasing Speed 29 MIN
Introduction To Flamenco Techniques 29 MIN
More Difficult Solo, A 29 MIN
Notes Of The Fifth Position 29 MIN
Playing The Guitar II - Course Review 29 MIN
Sight Reading In Two Parts 29 MIN
Song Accompaniment, Pt 1 29 MIN
Song Accompaniment, Pt 2 29 MIN
Song Recital 29 MIN
Study In A And Vibrato Technique 29 MIN

Playing The Hand C 30 MIN
3/4 OR 1/2 INCH VIDEO CASSETTE A
See series title for descriptive statement.
From The Play Bridge Series.
Prod-KYTV Dist-KYTV 1983

Playing The Percentages C 30 MIN
3/4 OR 1/2 INCH VIDEO CASSETTE A
See series title for descriptive statement.
From The Adult Math Series.
Prod-KYTV Dist-KYTV 1984

Playing The Selective College Admissions Game C 47 MIN
16MM FILM, 3/4 OR 1/2 IN VIDEO H-C A
Pinpoints the specific qualities selective colleges seek in prospective freshmen, considerations college applicants should ponder when choosing a school and ways candidates should present themselves to make a favorable impression in admissions officials.
Prod-AYDA Dist-AUTUMN 1983

Playing The Thing C 16 MIN
16MM FILM OPTICAL SOUND I-C A
Presents an informative musical experience with an accent on the history and development of the harmonica as a means of personal expression.
LC NO. 73-702806
Prod-MORC Dist-SCREEI 1973

Playing The Viol C 29 MIN
3/4 INCH VIDEO CASSETTE
Provides a clear demonstration of the basic principles of playing the viol. Shows many of the older viols and manuscripts.
Prod-UWASHP Dist-UWASHP

Playing to Win For Widebacks And Receivers C 59 MIN
1/2 IN VIDEO CASSETTE BETA/VHS
Demonstrates proper techniques for the tailback and fullback and for a pass receiver.
From The Football Fundamentals Series.
Prod-MOHOMV Dist-MOHOMV

Playing Touch Football C 12 MIN
16MM FILM, 3/4 OR 1/2 IN VIDEO P-I
Demonstrates basic techniques for playing touch football. Covers passing, receiving, punting, place kicking and running skills.
From The Sports For Elementary Series.
Prod-CINEDU Dist-AIMS 1975

Playing Touch Football (Spanish) C 12 MIN
16MM FILM, 3/4 OR 1/2 IN VIDEO I-J
Highlights actions important to playing the game of touch football, such as passing, receiving, punting, place kicking and running skills.
From The Sports For Elementary (Spanish) Series.
Prod-CINEDU Dist-AIMS 1975

Playing Where You Are C 15 MIN
16MM FILM, 3/4 OR 1/2 IN VIDEO
Shows children playing during the winter time at different locations in the United States and Canada. Correlates children's play to the places in which they live.
From The Ripples Series.
LC NO. 73-702150
Prod-NITC Dist-AITECH

Playing With Fire C 17 MIN
16MM FILM, 3/4 OR 1/2 IN VIDEO I-C A
Uses the example of a young boy burned when playing with matches and gasoline in order to show how accidents and burns involving fire can be avoided.
Prod-NFPA Dist-NFPA 1975

Playing With Numbers B
16MM FILM OPTICAL SOUND
Examines the types of numbers possible. Illustrates rational, algebraic, and irrational numbers.
Prod-OPENU Dist-OPENU

Playing With Patterns - Geometric Patterns C 14 MIN
3/4 OR 1/2 INCH VIDEO CASSETTE P
Describes how Uncle Estil teaches Martha and Jerry to see patterns in their environment.
From The Math Country Series.
Prod-KYTV Dist-AITECH 1979

Playing With Scorpions C 4 MIN
3/4 INCH VIDEO CASSETTE
Features children of bushmen of Namibia playing with scorpions.
From The San (Bushmen) Series.
Prod-DOCEDR Dist-DOCEDR Prodn-MRSHL

Playmates C 12 MIN
3/4 OR 1/2 INCH VIDEO CASSETTE C A
Shows how sexual playfulness and communication enliven the relationship of a couple obviously sensitive to each other's desires.
Prod-NATSF Dist-MMRC

Plays C 15 MIN
3/4 OR 1/2 INCH VIDEO CASSETTE I
Presents the elements of playwriting and shows children critiquing three original plays.
From The Zebra Wings Series.
Prod-NITC Dist-AITECH Prodn-MAETEL 1975

Plays Of Shakespeare—A Series

Relives some of the classic works of Shakespeare. Includes dramatic segments.
Prod-UMITV Dist-UMITV 1961

Othello 029 MIN

Playspace C 27 MIN
3/4 OR 1/2 INCH VIDEO CASSETTE C
Examines indoor and outdoor play surroundings for children, focusing on the benefits of a stimulating, flexible environment. Shows how ordinary living space can be made into an enjoyable play area for children.
From The Learning Through Play - Programs Series. Program 4
Prod-UTORMC Dist-UTORMC 1976

Playwrights C 15 MIN
3/4 OR 1/2 INCH VIDEO CASSETTE P
See series title for descriptive statement.
From The Word Shop Series.
Prod-WETATV Dist-WETATV

Plaza C 15 MIN
16MM FILM OPTICAL SOUND
Uses experimental techniques to explore narrative forms in uncovering the facts surrounding a murder.
LC NO. 79-701237
Prod-VANOSD Dist-VANOSD 1977

Plaza, The - Since 1907 C 13 MIN
16MM FILM OPTICAL SOUND
Follows the activities of an out-of-town couple staying at the Plaza Hotel in New York City to attend a convention.
LC NO. 75-703607
Prod-PLAZAH Dist-PLAZAH Prodn-TURTLE 1975

Plazas, Malls And Squares C 20 MIN
16MM FILM, 3/4 OR 1/2 IN VIDEO
Explores man-made outdoor environments and studies the relationship between the design of plazas, malls and squares and their function or purpose.
From The Images And Things Series.
LC NO. 73-702107
Prod-NITC Dist-AITECH

PLC, The - Campus And Corps C 14 MIN
16MM FILM OPTICAL SOUND H-C A
Discusses the advantages of joining the Marine Corps platoon leaders class program.
LC NO. 77-700083
Prod-USMC Dist-USNAC 1974

Plea Bargaining - An American Way Of Justice B 60 MIN
16MM FILM OPTICAL SOUND H-C A
Documents the plea bargaining process, a hidden but persuasive aspect of the American criminal justice system. Shows plea bargaining as it takes place in courtrooms, in judges' chambers, in jails and in backrooms.
LC NO. 80-701459
Prod-THURBR Dist-THURFL 1980

Plea, The C 15 MIN
16MM FILM, 3/4 OR 1/2 IN VIDEO J-C
Presents the story of a young woman who, when upset at hearing news of her husband's death, becomes a hit-and-run driver. Points out the special circumstances surrounding the case as they relate to her treatment in the criminal justice system.
From The Under The Law, Pt 1 Series.
Prod-USNEI Dist-WDEMCO 1974

Please At Least Leave Me The Sun C 10 MIN
16MM FILM, 3/4 OR 1/2 IN VIDEO
Shows children's drawings from the exposition called The City of Tomorrow.
Prod-CAROUF Dist-CAROUF

Please Believe Me - Rheumatoid Arthritis And Young Adults C 29 MIN
3/4 INCH VIDEO CASSETTE
Focuses on four rheumatoid arthritis patients who share their experiences and problems with the disease at different stages of their lives.
Prod-UMITV Dist-UMITV 1978

Please Bring Me Two Cars, Candy Bars, Flowers C 15 MIN
2 INCH VIDEOTAPE P
See series title for descriptive statement.
From The Avenida De Ingles Series.
Prod-SDITVA Dist-GPITVL

Please Construct C 27 MIN
16MM FILM OPTICAL SOUND IND
Describes the building of commercial aviation's newest jet aircraft, the Airbus-A300B, which was built by several companies in West Germany, France, the Netherlands and Spain. The wings were manufactured in Britain and the engines in the United States, with the final assembly in Toulouse, France.
Prod-WSTGLC Dist-WSTGLC

Please Don't Hit Me, Mom C 46 MIN
3/4 OR 1/2 INCH VIDEO CASSETTE
Reveals the story of an eight-year-old boy who is physically beaten by his mother. Features Patty Duke Astin and Sean Astin.
Prod-EMBASY Dist-EMBASY

Please Hurry C 14 MIN
16MM FILM OPTICAL SOUND
Describes the service of the 911 emergency communications system in cutting the response time between the report of an emergency and the arrival of police help. Includes scenes of the New York Police Department communications room where emergency calls are received and answered.
LC NO. 77-705641
Prod-NYTELE Dist-NYTELE Prodn-GORGLY 1969

Please Let Us Help C 18 MIN
16MM FILM, 3/4 OR 1/2 IN VIDEO
Describes a Veterans Administration Drug Dependence Treatment Program. Demonstrates the program's practice of comprehensive assessment and focuses on vocational reskilling as a new client moves through the process.
LC NO. 80-707615
Prod-USVA Dist-USNAC 1980

Please Look After This Bear / A Bear In Hot Water / Paddington Goes Underground C 17 MIN
16MM FILM, 3/4 OR 1/2 IN VIDEO K-I
Presents the adventures of Paddington Bear, telling how he is adopted by the Browns. Describes his first bath and his first trip on the underground. Based on chapters one, two and three of the book A Bear Called Paddington by Michael Bond.
From The Paddington Bear, Series 1 Series.
LC NO. 80-707226
Prod-BONDM Dist-FLMFR Prodn-FILMF 1977

Please Stand By C
3/4 OR 1/2 INCH VIDEO CASSETTE
Uses humor in a presentation of a film projector that goes berserk.
Prod-BBB Dist-MEETS Prodn-CFDC

Please Take Care Of Your Teeth C 10 MIN
16MM FILM, 3/4 OR 1/2 IN VIDEO
Uses a lighthearted approach to oral hygiene which encourages eating nutritiously, brushing and flossing daily and visiting the dentist regularly. Tells who develops cavities, demonstrates proper brushing and flossing techniques and assures that the dentist is a friendly person dedicated to the health of their patients' gums and teeth.
Prod-WHITS Dist-PFP 1982

Pleasure Driving C 10 MIN
16MM FILM, 3/4 OR 1/2 IN VIDEO
Discusses the nature of pleasure driving on horseback and the correct tack and class procedure used.
Prod-AQHORS Dist-AQHORS

Pleasure Drugs - The Great American High C 52 MIN
16MM FILM, 3/4 OR 1/2 IN VIDEO J-C A
Examines the pervasiveness and implications of the use of cocaine, marijuana, quaaludes and alcohol in the United States. Includes personal stories and testimonies of a medical examiner, a researcher and legal officials. Shows police-produced tapes of automobile accidents in which the drivers were under the influence of these substances.
LC NO. 82-707110
Prod-NBCNEW Dist-FI 1982

Pleasure Of Chinese Cooking C 20 MIN
3/4 OR 1/2 INCH VIDEO CASSETTE
Shares the pleasure of cooking as developed over thousands of years. Reveals the methods of preparing Chinese meals in the family kitchen.
From The Magical Cook's Tour Series.
Prod-IVCH Dist-IVCH

Pleasure Of Finding Things Out, The C 57 MIN
3/4 OR 1/2 INCH VIDEO CASSETTE H-C A
Presents physicist Richard Feynman talking about his childhood and the influence of his father, his feelings about having participated in the development of the atomic bomb, the influence of scientific logic on his perceptions and philosophies, and his seemingly unorthodox teaching methods.
From The Nova Series.
LC NO. 83-706602
Prod-BBCTV Dist-TIMLIF 1982

Pleasure Of Play, The C 39 MIN
3/4 OR 1/2 INCH VIDEO CASSETTE
Demonstrates the use of expressive language, creative dramatic play and play therapy activities in developing learning skills and the expression of feelings in special-needs children. Guides the viewer through a number of actual play sessions with therapists and groups of children.
Prod-PITTSG Dist-PSU

Pleasure Of Poetry, The C 30 MIN
3/4 INCH VIDEO CASSETTE H-C A
Features James Whitmore portraying a New England country doctor sharing his pleasure in poetry. Includes the poetry of Robert Bridges, Robert Frost, Matthew Arnold, Arthur O'Shaughnessy and Edwin Markham.
From The Anyone For Tennyson Series.
Prod-NETCHE Dist-GPITVL

Pleasure Of Your Company, The C 15 MIN
16MM FILM, 3/4 OR 1/2 IN VIDEO
Tells of the services of hotels and motels and how the public can get the most from them.
Prod-KLEINW Dist-KLEINW 1977

Pleasure Profits C 29 MIN
3/4 OR 1/2 INCH VIDEO CASSETTE
Intercuts an interview with the woman president of a sexual aids company with footage from a women's home sales party. Presented by John Orentlicher and Carol Porter.
Prod-ARTINC Dist-ARTINC

Pleasure Seekers, The - A Surf Odyssey C 20 MIN
16MM FILM OPTICAL SOUND
Shows two Malibu surfers setting out around the world to find the perfect beach. Illustrates that during their search they pass

hungry children, people living in sickness and squaler, and human beings destined to live their lives in hopelessness. Portrays their apathy, and confronts the viewer with Jesus' statement, 'THEY HAVE EYES TO SEE, BUT DO NOT SEE.'
Prod-FAMF Dist-FAMF

Pleasures Of Chinese Cooking, The C 18 MIN
16MM FILM OPTICAL SOUND
Madame Grace Chu discusses Chinese cooking and presents recipes and menus.
LC NO. FIA65-298
Prod-NORGE Dist-AGA Prodn-BAILYB 1964

Pleasuring C 12 MIN
3/4 OR 1/2 INCH VIDEO CASSETTE
Describes a couple's feelings about behaviors in which they engage and discuss pleasuring as an end in itself.
From The EDCOA Sexual Counseling Series.
Prod-MMRC Dist-MMRC

Pleasuring C 16 MIN
3/4 OR 1/2 INCH VIDEO CASSETTE
Continues to explore ways women can pleasure themselves by experimenting with techniques including erotic body movements.
From The Becoming Orgasmic - A Sexual Growth Program Series.
Prod-MMRC Dist-MMRC

Pledge And The Anthem, The - Behind The Words C
16MM FILM, 3/4 OR 1/2 IN VIDEO
Shows how the U S National Anthem was written and the reasons for its words. Focuses on the meaning behind the Pledge of Allegiance and the National Anthem.
Prod-HIGGIN Dist-HIGGIN

Pledge Of Allegiance C 5 MIN
16MM FILM, 3/4 OR 1/2 IN VIDEO P-J
Takes the Pledge of Allegiance and explains the words used in the verse, their individual meanings, the overall importance of the pledge and the reason for its use.
Prod-GOULDA Dist-PHENIX 1980

Pledge Of Allegiance, The C 8 MIN
16MM FILM, 3/4 OR 1/2 IN VIDEO P-I
Defines the Pledge of Allegiance as a commitment of individual responsibility to uphold the laws and principles of America.
From The American Values For Elementary Series.
Prod-EVANSA Dist-AIMS 1971

Plessy Vs Ferguson C
3/4 OR 1/2 INCH VIDEO CASSETTE H
Explains the decision that gave legal justification to segregation, invoking the concept of 'separate but equal'.
From The Supreme Court Decisions That Changed The Nation Series.
Prod-GA Dist-GA

Pliable Materials C 27 MIN
3/4 OR 1/2 INCH VIDEO CASSETTE C
Shows two- and three-year-olds at a daycare sandtable and ten-year-olds constructing a fort out of junk in a back alley.
From The Learning Through Play - Modules Series. Module 2
Prod-UTORMC Dist-UTORMC 1976

Pliable Materials C 30 MIN
3/4 OR 1/2 INCH VIDEO CASSETTE H-C A
Discusses pliable materials. Presents five illustrations, including two and three year-olds at a daycare sandtable and ten year-olds constructing a fort out of junk in a back alley.
From The Learning Through Play Series.
Prod-UTORMC Dist-UTORMC 1980

Pliers C 12 MIN
16MM FILM, 3/4 OR 1/2 IN VIDEO
Describes common types of pliers.
From The Hand Operations - Woodworking Series.
Prod-MORLAT Dist-SF 1974

Pliers And Screw Drivers B 15 MIN
16MM FILM, 3/4 OR 1/2 IN VIDEO
Demonstrates usage of pliers and screwdrivers and points out safety precautions. Issued in 1943 as a motion picture.
From The Care And Use Of Hand Tools Series. Number 2
LC NO. 80-706600
Prod-USWD Dist-USNAC 1980

Plight Of Soviet Jewry, The - Let My People Go B 28 MIN
16MM FILM OPTICAL SOUND
Points out that there are three million Jews living in Soviet Russia today, but Jewish religious and cultural life is non-existent. Explains that somehow Jewish identity is very much alive and the longing for Israel is stronger than ever, but only a few are allowed to emigrate.
Prod-ALDEN Dist-ALDEN

Plight Of The Afternoon Newspapers, The C 29 MIN
3/4 OR 1/2 INCH VIDEO CASSETTE
Profiles the efforts of the Minneapolis Star to reverse the trend of declining readership for afternoon newspapers in America.
From The Inside Story Series.
Prod-PBS Dist-PBS 1981

Plimpton - Shootout At Rio Lobo C 52 MIN
16MM FILM OPTICAL SOUND H-C A
Describes the experiences of George Plimpton as he joins the cast of the John Wayne movie Rio Lobo. Includes interviews with director Howard Hawks.
Prod-WOLPER Dist-TEXFLM 1974

Plimpton - The Man On The Flying Trapeze C 52 MIN
16MM FILM OPTICAL SOUND
George Plimpton enters the secret, back-stage world of the circus and attempts, in ten days, to become a death-defying, high flying aerialist. Provides unprecedented insights into the personalities of circus performers.
LC NO. 71-712183
Prod-DUPONT Dist-WOLPER 1971

Plot In Science Fiction C 25 MIN
16MM FILM OPTICAL SOUND H-C T
Paul Anderson discusses the role of plot in science fiction with James Gunn, president of the Science Fiction Writers of America.
From The Literature Of Science Fiction Series.
LC NO. 72-700535
Prod-UKANBC Dist-UKANS 1970

Plotting Your Course C 15 MIN
3/4 INCH VIDEO CASSETTE J-C A
Tells how to recognize aids and hazards to boat navigation.
From The Afloat And Aboat Series.
Prod-MDDE Dist-GPITVL 1979

Plov Og Plojning (Plough And Ploughing) B 17 MIN
16MM FILM OPTICAL SOUND
A Danish language film. Describes the development of the plough from the first primitive digging stick to the most modern farm implements. Demonstrates various ploughing methods, and shows a big moorland plough.
Prod-STATNS Dist-STATNS 1951

Plow That Broke The Plains, The B 25 MIN
16MM FILM, 3/4 OR 1/2 IN VIDEO
Traces the social and economic history of the Great Plains from the settlement of the prairies to the years of depression and drought. Issued in 1936 as a motion picture.
LC NO. 79-706027
Prod-USRA Dist-USNAC 1978

Plowshare C 28 MIN
16MM FILM OPTICAL SOUND
Uses motion pictures and animation to explain the development and aims of the Plowshare Program, the Atomic Energy Commission's program for the safe use of nuclear explosives for civilian applications. Discusses the potential uses of nuclear explosives for mining, earth-moving and excavation projects and scientific investigations.
LC NO. FIE66-11
Prod-USAESF Dist-USNAC 1965

Plucked Instruments C 30 MIN
3/4 OR 1/2 INCH VIDEO CASSETTE
Presents the history and development of several musical instruments related to the guitar.
From The Early Musical Instruments Series.
Prod-GRATV Dist-FOTH

Plug Us In C 16 MIN
16MM FILM OPTICAL SOUND
Explains how older job seekers can project a positive image during interviews.
LC NO. 81-700457
Prod-AFAEME Dist-AFAEME 1980

Plug-Back Cementing C 33 MIN
3/4 OR 1/2 INCH VIDEO CASSETTE IND
Looks at the techniques and equipment used to plug back oil or gas wells. Emphasizes plugging wells which will be abandoned.
Prod-UTEXPE Dist-UTEXPE 1978

Plugging Into Meanings B 15 MIN
2 INCH VIDEOTAPE I
Explains that the author talks to the reader through the printed page and the reader must decide whether or not he agrees with the writer by thinking about what he has read. Features selections such as Little Balser And The Big Bear by Charles Major, The Blind Men And The Elephant by John G Saxe and The Burning Rice Fields by Sara Cone Bryant. (Broadcast quality)
From The Bill Martin Series. No. 9
Prod-BRITED Dist-GPITVL Prodn-KQEDTV

Plum Island - Animal Disease Laboratory C 23 MIN
16MM FILM OPTICAL SOUND C A
Describes geographical location and detailed description of the physical plant of the Plum Island Animal Disease Research Facilities. Emphasizes the precautionary procedures in handling employees, animals and supplies to prevent the spread of any disease from the island.
LC NO. FIE58-161
Prod-USDA Dist-AMVMA

Plum Island Afternoon B 13 MIN
16MM FILM OPTICAL SOUND
Tells how a woman goes to the beach with her daughters on a cold, blustery day and experiences a series of flashbacks concerning significant moments in her life.
LC NO. 78-701442
Prod-TATLOC Dist-TATLOC 1977

Plum Pudding C 22 MIN
16MM FILM OPTICAL SOUND K-I
Presents a series of animated designs made by children, including pixillation, clay, flip cards and mache.
Prod-YELLOW Dist-YELLOW 1969

Plumbing C 30 MIN
16MM FILM, 3/4 OR 1/2 IN VIDEO
Provides basic information on plumbing repairs.
From The Do It Yourself Home Repairs Series.
Prod-ODECA Dist-BULFRG

Plumbing - Joints C 13 MIN
16MM FILM, 3/4 OR 1/2 IN VIDEO H-C A
Uses close-ups to take the student 'INSIDE' various joints, stressing aspects which make for a sound, water-tight fixture. Explains terms and measurements and how to calculate thread and fitting allowances. Shows copper soldered joints, methods of checking for a good joint, techniques of soldering, mechanical joints, use of inside and outside irons threaded joints and plastic pipe joints.
Prod-SF Dist-SF 1969

Plumbing - Traps And Vents C 14 MIN
3/4 OR 1/2 INCH VIDEO CASSETTE H-C A
Shows the trap, parts of the trap, types, functions, stack vent, vents and terminals.
Prod-SF Dist-SF 1970

Plumbing Tools C 12 MIN
3/4 OR 1/2 INCH VIDEO CASSETTE
Covers plumbing codes, systems, tube bending, cutting pipe, joining and assembling pipe.
From The Using Hand Tools Series.
Prod-TPCTRA Dist-TPCTRA

Plumbing Tools (Spanish) C 12 MIN
3/4 OR 1/2 INCH VIDEO CASSETTE
Covers plumbing codes, systems, tube bending, cutting pipe, joining and assembling pipe.
From The Using Hand Tools Series.
Prod-TPCTRA Dist-TPCTRA

Plump Jack - Shakespeare's Henry IV - Prince Hal's Rejection Of Falstaff C 45 MIN
3/4 OR 1/2 INCH VIDEO CASSETTE
Analyzes Prince Hal's rejection of Falstaff in Shakespeare's Henry IV.
From The Survey Of English Literature I Series.
Prod-MDCPB Dist-MDCPB

Plunge Cut Grinding B 15 MIN
16MM FILM, 3/4 OR 1/2 IN VIDEO
Shows how to mount a bushing on a mandrel, dress the side of the grinding wheel, set a dial snap gage for the production grinding of bushings, and rough- and finish-grind a bushing. Stresses rhythm in grinding.
From The Machine Shop Work Series. Operations On The Center-Type Grinder, No. 4
Prod-USOE Dist-USNAC Prodn-YORKES 1944

Plus And Minus C 15 MIN
3/4 OR 1/2 INCH VIDEO CASSETTE P
Shows how a space robot's puppet assistant learns how to count money when she wants to buy some candy. Tells how the space robot helps her count it with a review of naming numbers and counting by tens, followed by an introduction to arithmetic drills on 'higher decade' addition facts.
From The Math Mission 2 Series.
LC NO. 82-706316
Prod-WCVETV Dist-GPITVL 1980

Plus Time Served C
16MM FILM, 3/4 OR 1/2 IN VIDEO H-C A
Describes how an arrogant newscaster becomes the mediator for a group of prisoners after a riot. Tells how he grows beyond his ego-centered existence. Stars Jim Farentino, Don Stroud and Gregory Sierra.
From The Insight Series.
Prod-PAULST Dist-PAULST

Pluto's Christmas Tree C 7 MIN
16MM FILM, 3/4 OR 1/2 IN VIDEO K-J
An animated cartoon picturing the antics of the chipmunks, Chip and Dale, who live in the fir tree which Mickey Mouse and Pluto chop down and decorate for Christmas.
Prod-DISNEY Dist-WDEMCO 1971

Pluto's Surprise Package C 8 MIN
16MM FILM, 3/4 OR 1/2 IN VIDEO
Describes Pluto's trip to pick up some mail which becomes a harrowing experience when a turtle emerges from one of the packages and runs off with some letters.
From The Tales Of Pluto Series.
Prod-DISNEY Dist-WDEMCO

Plutonium Connection, The C 59 MIN
16MM FILM, 3/4 OR 1/2 IN VIDEO H-C A
Explains that plutonium is the processed waste product of nuclear reactors and that it is becoming increasingly difficult to control the growing plutonium supply. Examines the complex problems resulting from the general availability of both the technical information and the plutonium needed for constructing an atomic bomb.
From The Nova Series.
LC NO. 79-707246
Prod-WGBHTV Dist-TIMLIF 1976

Plutonium Incident, The C 90 MIN
3/4 OR 1/2 INCH VIDEO CASSETTE H-C A
Offers the story of a woman who works as a technician at the Northern Oregon Nuclear facility and discovers that the safety procedures are woefully negligent. Stars Janet Margolin and Powers Boothe.
Prod-TIMLIF Dist-TIMLIF 1983

Plymouth Colony - The First Year (2nd Ed) C 16 MIN
16MM FILM, 3/4 OR 1/2 IN VIDEO I
Portrays the events which forced the Pilgrims to leave Europe on the Mayflower. Describes the difficulties of the trip and the establishment of a settlement in America.
LC NO. 80-707367
Prod-CORF Dist-CORF 1980

PM Magazine/Acid Rock C 5 MIN
3/4 OR 1/2 INCH VIDEO CASSETTE
Features iconographic images from American broadcast television transformed by high technology, pop music and the artist's vision.
Prod-EAI Dist-EAI

PM Of Hydraulic Systems C 13 MIN
3/4 OR 1/2 INCH VIDEO CASSETTE IND
Demonstrates that preventive maintenance on hydraulic systems pays off. Teaches the proper handling and usage of hydraulic fluids and vital importance of maintaining cleanliness throughout.
From The Marshall Maintenance Training Programs Series. Tape 38
Prod-LEIKID Dist-LEIKID

PM Of Hydraulic Systems C 13 MIN
16MM FILM, 3/4 OR 1/2 IN VIDEO
Discusses the proper handling, storage and usage of hydraulic fluids and the vital importance of maintaining cleanliness throughout.
Prod-MOKIN Dist-MOKIN

PM Of Mobile Equipment C 10 MIN
3/4 OR 1/2 INCH VIDEO CASSETTE IND
Demonstrates preventive maintenance of any over-the-road vehicle that should be inspected before being driven. Shows items that should be checked. Includes check list sample.
From The Marshall Maintenance Training Programs Series. Tape 35
Prod-LEIKID Dist-LEIKID

PM Of Mobile Equipment C 10 MIN
16MM FILM, 3/4 OR 1/2 IN VIDEO IND
Shows the vital components of any over-the-road vehicle that should be inspected before being driven and the items that should be checked while on the road.
Prod-MOKIN Dist-MOKIN

PM-3A Nuclear Power Plant - Antarctica C 20 MIN
16MM FILM OPTICAL SOUND C A
Shows the construction of the first nuclear power station in the Antarctic, a 1500 kilowatt station at Mc Murdo Sound.
LC NO. FIE64-159
Prod-USAEC Dist-USERD 1963

Pneumatic Air Supplies And Regulators C
16MM FILM - 3/4 IN VIDEO IND
Covers filters, air dryers and dew point measurement. Explains troubleshooting of regulators.
From The Instrumentation Maintenance Series.
Prod-ISA Dist-ISA

Pneumatic Controllers C
16MM FILM - 3/4 IN VIDEO IND
Deals with the Ziegler-Nichols method of tuning, tuning cascade control loop and troubleshooting control problems.
From The Instrumentation Maintenance Series.
Prod-ISA Dist-ISA

Pneumatic Drills And Hammers C 12 MIN
3/4 OR 1/2 INCH VIDEO CASSETTE
Covers pneumatic drills and hammers, the different types available, their uses, operation, maintenance and safety.
From The Using Portable Power Tool Series.
Prod-TPCTRA Dist-TPCTRA

Pneumatic Instruments - Sensors, Indicators, Transmitters C
16MM FILM - 3/4 IN VIDEO IND
Teaches calibration of pressure gages and maintenance and calibration of differential pressure transmitters. Explains temperature transmitters.
From The Instrumentation Maintenance Series.
Prod-ISA Dist-ISA

Pneumatic Systems And Controls C 27 MIN
3/4 OR 1/2 INCH VIDEO CASSETTE IND
Discusses equipment, operation and circuitry used to pneumatically control drilling rig equipment.
Prod-UTEXPE Dist-UTEXPE 1968

Pneumatic Transducers, Computing Relays C
16MM FILM - 3/4 IN VIDEO IND
Explains amplifying and computer relays and maintenance and calibration of square root extractors.
From The Instrumentation Maintenance Series.
Prod-ISA Dist-ISA

Pneumonectomy For Carcinoma C 35 MIN
16MM FILM OPTICAL SOUND PRO
Deals with the diagnosis, pathology and surgical technique of total pneumonectomy for primary carcinoma of the lung. Emphasizes roentgenological diagnosis and pathological characteristics through the use of X-ray studies and studies of the surgical specimens of five patients with this disease.
Prod-ACYDGD Dist-ACY 1953

Pneumothorax And Hemothorax C 20 MIN
3/4 OR 1/2 INCH VIDEO CASSETTE
Discusses pneumothorax and hemothorax, giving definitions and classifications, symptoms and techniques for posterior drainage.
From The Emergency Management - The First 30 Minutes, Vol I Series.
Prod-VTRI Dist-VTRI

PNF - Assisting To Postures And Application In Occupational Therapy Activities C 60 MIN
3/4 INCH VIDEO CASSETTE PRO
Demonstrates the PNF procedure for assisting patients to various postures. Suggests occupational therapy activities that may be used in each posture.
From The Proprioceptive Neuromuscular Faciliation Series.
Prod-RICHGO Dist-RICHGO

PNF - Diagonal Patterns And Their Application To Functional Activities C 45 MIN
3/4 INCH VIDEO CASSETTE PRO
Demonstrates the diagonal patterns of the head, neck, trunk and extremities. Gives examples of how each pattern occurs in functional activities.
From The Proprioceptive Neuromuscular Facilitation Series.
Prod-RICHGO Dist-RICHGO

PNF - Patterns And Application In Occupational Therapy C 45 MIN
3/4 INCH VIDEO CASSETTE PRO
Demonstrates how diagonal patterns may be used in occupational therapy for evaluation, range of motion, and as a basis for designing goal directed treatment activities.
From The Proprioceptive Neuromuscular Faciliation Series.
Prod-RICHGO Dist-RICHGO

Pocahontas C 15 MIN
3/4 OR 1/2 INCH VIDEO CASSETTE P
Traces the childhood of Pocahontas, her contributions to Colonial Virginia and later life in England.
From The Stories Of America Series.
Prod-OHSDE Dist-AITECH Prodn-WVIZTV 1976

Pocket Billiards B 30 MIN
16MM FILM OPTICAL SOUND
Shows a green velvet jungle.
Prod-SFI Dist-SFI

Pocket Billiards—A Series
16MM FILM, 3/4 OR 1/2 IN VIDEO J-C A
Discusses both the fundamentals and advanced skills of billiards.
Prod-ATHI Dist-ATHI 1983

Advanced Skills Of Billiards 011 MIN
Fundamentals Of Billiards 011 MIN

Pocket Gopher, The - Adaptations For Living Underground C 13 MIN
16MM FILM, 3/4 OR 1/2 IN VIDEO I-C A
Uses the pocket gopher as a model for analyzing fossorial life in rodents. Follows pocket gophers underground to show movement through the burrow and use of the feet and teeth in digging.
From The Aspects Of Animal Behavior Series.
Prod-UCLA Dist-UCEMC 1977

Pocket Watches C 30 MIN
3/4 OR 1/2 INCH VIDEO CASSETTE
Presents guests who are experts in their respective fields who share tips on collecting and caring for antique pocket watches.
From The Antique Shop Series.
Prod-WVPTTV Dist-MDCPB

Poe's Poetic Theory And Practice C 30 MIN
2 INCH VIDEOTAPE J-H
Discusses the poetic style and works of Edgar Allan Poe.
From The From Franklin To Frost - Edgar Allan Poe Series.
Prod-MPATI Dist-GPITVL

Poem Of Rodia B 4 MIN
16MM FILM OPTICAL SOUND
Presents a poetic interpretation of Watts Towers in Los Angeles. Explores the visual poetry of a handmade monument created out of the refuse of four gererations into an architectual work of art by Simon Rodia, an Italian immigrant.
LC NO. FIA67-558
Prod-USC Dist-USC 1966

Poem Of Rodia B 4 MIN
16MM FILM SILENT I-C A
Presents an exploration of visual poetry inherent in the primitive handmade monument, Watts Towers, constructed by Simon Rodia from four generations of discarded junk.
Prod-UWFKD Dist-UWFKD

Poemfield No. 2 C 5 MIN
16MM FILM OPTICAL SOUND
Combines modern music with brightly colored computer art.
From The Poemfield Series.
Prod-VANBKS Dist-VANBKS 1965

Poemfield No. 3 C 8 MIN
16MM FILM OPTICAL SOUND
See series title for descriptive statement.
From The Poemfield Series.
Prod-VANBKS Dist-VANBKS

Poemfield No. 4 C 10 MIN
16MM FILM OPTICAL SOUND
See series title for descriptive statement.
From The Poemfield Series.
Prod-VANBKS Dist-VANBKS

Poemfield No. 5 C 8 MIN
16MM FILM OPTICAL SOUND
See series title for descriptive statement.
From The Poemfield Series.
Prod-VANBKS Dist-VANBKS

Poemfield No. 7 C 9 MIN
16MM FILM OPTICAL SOUND
See series title for descriptive statement.
From The Poemfield Series.
Prod-VANBKS Dist-VANBKS

Poemfield No.1 C 6 MIN
16MM FILM OPTICAL SOUND J-C A
Presents a visual experiment with language.
LC NO. 73-701191
Prod-VANBKS Dist-VANBKS 1972

Poemfield—A Series

Presents animated computer graphic films which explore variations of poems, computer graphics and in some cases combine live action images and animation collage.
Prod-VANBKS Dist-VANBKS

Poemfield No. 1 5 MIN
Poemfield No. 2 6 MIN
Poemfield No. 3 10 MIN
Poemfield No. 4 10 MIN
Poemfield No. 5 7 MIN
Poemfield No. 7 50 MIN

Poems As Descriptions C 15 MIN
3/4 OR 1/2 INCH VIDEO CASSETTE P
See series title for descriptive statement.
From The Word Shop Series.
Prod-WETATV Dist-WETATV

Poems As Rhythm C 15 MIN
3/4 OR 1/2 INCH VIDEO CASSETTE P
See series title for descriptive statement.
From The Word Shop Series.
Prod-WETATV Dist-WETATV

Poems As Sounds C 15 MIN
3/4 OR 1/2 INCH VIDEO CASSETTE P
See series title for descriptive statement.
From The Word Shop Series.
Prod-WETATV Dist-WETATV

Poems As Stories C 15 MIN
3/4 OR 1/2 INCH VIDEO CASSETTE P
See series title for descriptive statement.
From The Word Shop Series.
Prod-WETATV Dist-WETATV

Poems Of The Sea C 30 MIN
3/4 INCH VIDEO CASSETTE H-C A
Offers readings of 16 poems about the sea.
From The Anyone For Tennyson Series.
Prod-NETCHE Dist-GPITVL

Poet And Hero - Milton's Paradise Lost - The Triumph Of Human Love C 45 MIN
2 INCH VIDEOTAPE
Features Dr Thomas Sheye of Loyola College discussing the significance, conflicts, themes and characters of Milton's PARADISE LOST as well as its place in Renaissance literature. Explains how Milton continued and brought to a conclusion the Renaissance search for a hero.
From The Survey Of English Literature I Series.
Prod-MDCPB Dist-MDCPB

Poet Of His People, Pablo Neruda C 13 MIN
16MM FILM OPTICAL SOUND
Offers a symbolic representation of the life of Chilean poet Pablo Neruda as portrayed in his poem La Barcarola.
LC NO. 78-701691
Prod-LILYAN Dist-LILYAN 1978

Poet Speaks, The B 20 MIN
2 INCH VIDEOTAPE P
Introduces children to some of our famous children's poets. (Broadcast quality)
From The Language Lane Series. Lesson 22
Prod-CVETVC Dist-GPITVL Prodn-WCVETV

Poet, Racer, Dragon Chaser C 10 MIN
3/4 OR 1/2 INCH VIDEO CASSETTE K-P
Discusses the various occupations in which people are engaged.
From The Book, Look And Listen Series.
Prod-MDDE Dist-AITECH 1977

Poet's Eye, The - Shakespeare's Imagery C 16 MIN
16MM FILM, 3/4 OR 1/2 IN VIDEO J-C A
Illustrates Shakespeare's unique imagery, presenting graphic examples of his method. Shows how all human activity appealed to Shakespeare as a source of imagery, using his plays as examples.
Prod-BIGRF Dist-FOTH Prodn-SMITHB 1976

Poet's Journal C 25 MIN
3/4 OR 1/2 INCH VIDEO CASSETTE T
Presents a poet who talks about the relationship of his journal to his writing.
From The Process-Centered Composition Series.
LC NO. 79-706303
Prod-IU Dist-IU 1977

Poet's Testament, The - Santayana, Six Sonnets C 45 MIN
2 INCH VIDEOTAPE
See series title for descriptive statement.
From The Humanities Series. Unit III - The Realm Of Idea And Speculation
Prod-WTTWTV Dist-GPITVL

Poet's World, A C 14 MIN
16MM FILM OPTICAL SOUND
Helps foster sensitivity to the poetic possibilities of familiar objects, such as clouds, trees, wind and water.
LC NO. 73-701620
Prod-CWRU Dist-CWRU 1973

Poet's World, The B 15 MIN
2 INCH VIDEOTAPE K-P
Explores the world of the poet, the ideas and subjects he finds to write about and the light of individuality he casts upon these ideas. (Broadcast quality)
From The Magic Of Words Series.
Prod-GWTVAI Dist-GPITVL Prodn-WETATV

Poetic Feast, A C 30 MIN
3/4 INCH VIDEO CASSETTE H-C A
Presents Vincent Price and the First Poetry Quartet reading poetry that celebrates the joys of wining and dining.
From The Anyone For Tennyson Series.
Prod-NETCHE Dist-GPITVL

Poetical Art Of William Blake, The C 30 MIN
3/4 INCH VIDEO CASSETTE H-C A
Examines the genius of William Blake and includes readings of his poetry.
From The Anyone For Tennyson Series.
Prod-NETCHE Dist-GPITVL

Poetry C 15 MIN
3/4 OR 1/2 INCH VIDEO CASSETTE P
Introduces Grace Butcher and Leonard Trawick reading their poetry and discussing their work with librarian Phyllis Syracuse who seeks to inspire children to read, and especially to write, poetry.
From The Through The Pages Series. No. 4
LC NO. 82-707367
Prod-WVIZTV Dist-GPITVL 1982

Poetry B 20 MIN
2 INCH VIDEOTAPE I
Emphasizes the pleasure in sharing poetry vocally. (Broadcast quality)
From The Quest For The Best Series.
Prod-DENVPS Dist-GPITVL Prodn-KRMATV

Poetry C 30 MIN
1/2 IN VIDEO CASSETTE BETA/VHS K-I
See series title for descriptive statement.
From The Jump Over The Moon - Sharing Literature With Young Children Series.
Prod-HRAW Dist-HRAW

Poetry - Brother Antonius And Michael Mc Clure B 30 MIN
16MM FILM, 3/4 OR 1/2 IN VIDEO J-C A
Describes the poetry of Michael Mc Clure. Discusses his use of hallucinogenic drugs to achieve poetry directly from the emotions. Introduces Brother Antonius, a Dominican lay brother known for his combination of poetry reading and dramatic encounters with audiences.
From The USA Series.
Prod-NET Dist-IU Prodn-KQEDTV 1966

Poetry - Denise Levertov And Charles Olson B 30 MIN
16MM FILM, 3/4 OR 1/2 IN VIDEO J-C A
Denise Levertov discusses her reasons for being a poet and her methods of work and reads some of her poetry. Charles Olson describes his concept of open verse composition and recites several of his poems.
From The USA Series.
Prod-NET Dist-IU Prodn-KQEDTV 1966

Poetry - Diction B 30 MIN
2 INCH VIDEOTAPE J-H
From The Franklin To Frost Series.
Prod-GPITVL Dist-GPITVL

Poetry - Frank O'Hara And Ed Sanders B 30 MIN
16MM FILM, 3/4 OR 1/2 IN VIDEO J-C A
Poet Frank O'Hara reads from his poems and works on a poetical script for a movie. Poet Ed Sanders discusses his pacifism, describes 'LITERARY ROCK-ANDROLL,' and explains why the content of his poetry often creates a scandal.
From The USA Series.
Prod-NET Dist-IU Prodn-KQEDTV 1966

Poetry - Imagery B 30 MIN
2 INCH VIDEOTAPE J-H
From The Franklin To Frost Series.
Prod-GPITVL Dist-GPITVL

Poetry - Louis Zukofsky B 30 MIN
16MM FILM, 3/4 OR 1/2 IN VIDEO J-C A
Objectivist poet Louis Zukofsky describes the circumstances under which his first poem was published, explains the form and philosophy underlying his poetry, and reads from several of his works.
From The USA Series.
Prod-NET Dist-IU Prodn-KQEDTV 1966

Poetry - Philip Whalen And Gary Snyder B 30 MIN
16MM FILM, 3/4 OR 1/2 IN VIDEO J-C A
Provides an introduction to the poetry of Gary Snyder and Philip Whalen and the reasons behind their work. Each poet comments on his poetry and reads selections.
From The USA Series.
Prod-NET Dist-IU Prodn-KQEDTV 1966

Poetry - Rhyme B 30 MIN
2 INCH VIDEOTAPE J-H
From The Franklin To Frost Series.
Prod-GPITVL Dist-GPITVL

Poetry - Rhythm B 30 MIN
2 INCH VIDEOTAPE J-H
From The Franklin To Frost Series.
Prod-GPITVL Dist-GPITVL

Poetry - Richard Wilbur And Robert Lowell B 30 MIN
16MM FILM, 3/4 OR 1/2 IN VIDEO J-C A
Poet Richard Wilbur explains his interest in the formal means of poetic expression and reads several of his poems. Poet Robert Lowell reads some of his poems and describes the origin of the ideas behind them.
From The USA Series.
Prod-NET Dist-IU Prodn-KQEDTV 1966

Poetry - Robert Creeley B 30 MIN
16MM FILM, 3/4 OR 1/2 IN VIDEO J-C A
Robert Creeley tells how other literary figures influenced his works, explains his own method of working, reminisces about his youth and reads several of his poems-'LA NOCHE,' 'THE FIRST TIME,' 'THE PLACE' and 'SOMEPLACE.'
From The USA Series.
Prod-NET Dist-IU Prodn-KQEDTV 1966

Poetry - Robert Duncan And John Wieners B 30 MIN
16MM FILM, 3/4 OR 1/2 IN VIDEO J-C A
Studies the return of the spirit of romance to contemporary poetry, as exemplified by Robert Duncan and John Wieners. Both poets discuss and read examples of their works.
From The USA Series.
Prod-NET Dist-IU Prodn-KQEDTV 1966

Poetry - So Many Kinds C 14 MIN
16MM FILM, 3/4 OR 1/2 IN VIDEO J-H
presents selections of lyric, narrative and dramatic poetry by several famous poets which reveal the wide variations of forms and informal poetic structure used by various poets.
Prod-CORF Dist-CORF 1972

Poetry - The Art Of Words C 18 MIN
16MM FILM OPTICAL SOUND J-C
Presents an introduction to the study of poetry.
From The Humanities Series.
LC NO. 70-714098
Prod-MGHT Dist-JOSHUA 1971

Poetry - The Essence Of Being Human C 18 MIN
16MM FILM, 3/4 OR 1/2 IN VIDEO J-H
Shows how the poet fuses words, images and rhythms to startle the viewer into sharing his vision. Includes narration only to introduce the poetry. Presents poems which discuss man's most basic emotions and his most lofty strivings. Includes poems of love, hate, joy, despair, hope, ecstasy and the mysteries of God, nature and life.
From The Humanities Series.
Prod-MGHT Dist-MGHT 1972

Poetry - William Carlos Williams B 30 MIN
16MM FILM OPTICAL SOUND J-C A
Presents an essay on the life and work of Dr William Carlos Williams, poet and Pulitzer Prize winner.
From The USA Series.
Prod-NET Dist-IU Prodn-KQEDTV 1966

Poetry Alive--A Series
J-C A
Presents the poetry of Ellen Johnston, illustrating the power of poetry for positive communication between students and teachers.
Prod-CMSS Dist-AITECH 1978

From The Fantasies Of A Not-So-Young-Anymore 015 MIN
So - What Happened To You 014 MIN
They Worry About Me 014 MIN
We Don't Do Nothin' In Here 014 MIN
Who Said Today's Kids Don't Have Feelings 015 MIN

Poetry And Hidden Poetry C 53 MIN
3/4 OR 1/2 INCH VIDEO CASSETTE
Reveals the hidden poetry in seemingly unpoetic lines and demonstrates how polysyllables trip easily off the tongue while monosyllabic lines and words are packed with thoughts and feelings in Shakespeare. Uses examples from King Lear, All's Well That Ends Well, King John and Othello.
From The Royal Shakespeare Company Series.
Prod-FOTH Dist-FOTH 1984

Poetry By Americans--A Series
16MM FILM, 3/4 OR 1/2 IN VIDEO J-C
Emphasizes the effect the life of the poet can have upon his works.
Prod-EVANSA Dist-AIMS

Edgar Allan Poe 9 MIN
James Weldon Johnson 12 MIN
Robert Frost 10 MIN
Walt Whitman 10 MIN

Poetry For Beginners C 11 MIN
16MM FILM, 3/4 OR 1/2 IN VIDEO P
Tells the story of Bill, a second-grader who makes up poems about things he thinks, sees and feels. Shows how all of his poems call forth word pictures and explains that all children can make up poems.
Prod-CORF Dist-CORF 1967

Poetry For Fun - Dares And Dreams C 13 MIN
16MM FILM, 3/4 OR 1/2 IN VIDEO P-J
Consists of six poems chosen by children.
Prod-CENTRO Dist-CORF

Poetry For Fun - Poetry About Animals C 13 MIN
16MM FILM, 3/4 OR 1/2 IN VIDEO P-J
Features eight poems written just for fun.
Prod-CENTRO Dist-CORF

Poetry For Fun - Trulier Coolier C 11 MIN
16MM FILM, 3/4 OR 1/2 IN VIDEO P-J
Presents eight humorous poems dealing with children.
Prod-CENTRO Dist-CORF

Poetry For People Who Hate Poetry--A Series
16MM FILM, 3/4 OR 1/2 IN VIDEO J-C A
Features actor/poet Roger Steffens reading and discussing poetry.
Prod-STESHE Dist-CF 1980

About Words 016 MIN
E E Cummings 017 MIN
Shakespeare 012 MIN

Poetry For You C 15 MIN
2 INCH VIDEOTAPE P
Discusses poems for every month of the year.
From The Word Magic (2nd Ed) Series.
Prod-CVETVC Dist-GPITVL

Poetry I C 15 MIN
3/4 OR 1/2 INCH VIDEO CASSETTE I
Presents poetry as a pleasurable way to express feelings and describe experiences.
From The Zebra Wings Series.
Prod-NITC Dist-AITECH Prodn-MAETEL 1975

Poetry II C 15 MIN
3/4 OR 1/2 INCH VIDEO CASSETTE I
Introduces figurative language and discusses the haiku form of poetry.
From The Zebra Wings Series.
Prod-NITC Dist-AITECH Prodn-MAETEL 1975

Poetry In Translation, Pt 1 - Classical And Mediterranean C 30 MIN
3/4 INCH VIDEO CASSETTE H-C A
Offers performances of English translations of Greek and Roman poetry.
From The Anyone For Tennyson Series.
Prod-NETCHE Dist-GPITVL

Poetry In Translation, Pt 2 - Oriental And Russian C 30 MIN
3/4 INCH VIDEO CASSETTE H-C A
Presents English translations of poems from the Orient and Russia.
From The Anyone For Tennyson Series.
Prod-NETCHE Dist-GPITVL

Poetry Is Made By People C 15 MIN
3/4 OR 1/2 INCH VIDEO CASSETTE I
Consists of dramatic presentations showing the relationships among poetry, people and music.
From The Tyger, Tyger Burning Bright Series.
Prod-CTI Dist-CTI

Poetry Of Edward Field, The C 10 MIN
16MM FILM OPTICAL SOUND I-C
A visualization of two poems read by Edward Field. Shows the poet in his environment discussing his work.
From The Poetry Is Alive And Well And Living In America Series.
LC NO. 76-706086
Prod-MPI Dist-MPI 1969

Poetry Of G C Oden, The C 10 MIN
16MM FILM OPTICAL SOUND I-C
A visualization of two poems read by the poet, G C Oden. Shows the poet in his environment discussing his work.
From The Poetry Is Alive And Well And Living In America Series.
LC NO. 70-706087
Prod-MPI Dist-MPI 1969

Poetry Of May Swenson, The C 10 MIN
16MM FILM OPTICAL SOUND I-C
A visualization of two poems read by the poet, May Swenson. Shows the poet in her environment discussing her work.
From The Poetry Is Alive And Well And Living In America Series.
LC NO. 73-706088
Prod-MPI Dist-MPI 1969

Poetry Of Robert Frost, The C 45 MIN
16MM FILM OPTICAL SOUND
Presents dramatizations of 12 of Robert Frost's poems. Explores Frost's view of man and nature.
LC NO. 77-700022
Prod-CWRU Dist-CWRU 1977

Poetry Of Rock, The - A Reflection Of Human Values C
3/4 OR 1/2 INCH VIDEO CASSETTE H-C
Examines the emotional content and poetic techniques found in rock lyrics. Uses hit songs from the 1950's to the 1970's to illustrate poetic tools such as simile, metaphor, hyperbole, symbolism and allegory, and lyric, dramatic and narrative poetic forms.
Prod-GA Dist-GA

Poetry Of The Occult C 30 MIN
3/4 INCH VIDEO CASSETTE H-C A
Features the First Poetry Quartet exorcising an evil spirit through the power of poetry. Offers selections by J R R Tolkien, Kingsley Amis, Stanley Mc Neil, Robert Ervin Howard and Robert Siegel.
From The Anyone For Tennyson Series.
Prod-NETCHE Dist-GPITVL

Poetry Of Youth, The C 30 MIN
3/4 INCH VIDEO CASSETTE H-C A
Features Le Var Burton and members of the First Poetry Quartet reading poems by young poets of the 1970's.
From The Anyone For Tennyson Series.
Prod-NETCHE Dist-GPITVL

Poetry Out Loud B 15 MIN
2 INCH VIDEOTAPE P
See series title for descriptive statement.
From The Language Corner Series.
Prod-CVETVC Dist-GPITVL Prodn-WCVETV

Poetry Playhouse C 24 MIN
16MM FILM OPTICAL SOUND
Dramatizes poems about love.
LC NO. 78-701492
Prod-BERKS Dist-BERKS Prodn-SCRESC 1978

Poetry Today C 30 MIN
3/4 OR 1/2 INCH VIDEO CASSETTE
Describes contemporary poetry as being in a period of extremes in form, technique and intent, but which, at the root, is still the experience of the real world transformed into art.
From The Engle And Poetry Series.
Prod-NETCHE Dist-NETCHE 1971

Poetry—A Series
I-C
Prod-PFP Dist-HRAW Prodn-PFP 1969

Ocean 10 MIN

Poetry, I B 45 MIN
2 INCH VIDEOTAPE C
See series title for descriptive statement.
From The General Humanities Series. Unit 4 - The Literary Arts
Prod-CHITVC Dist-GPITVL Prodn-WTTWTV

Poetry, II B 45 MIN
2 INCH VIDEOTAPE C
See series title for descriptive statement.
From The General Humanities Series. Unit 4 - The Literary Arts
Prod-CHITVC Dist-GPITVL Prodn-WTTWTV

Poetry, The C 30 MIN
3/4 OR 1/2 INCH VIDEO CASSETTE
Presents the works of poets David Rice, Inua Fuller and Benjamin Franklin Gardner.
From The Black Poetry Of The Midwest Series.
Prod-NETCHE Dist-NETCHE 1977

Poets C 15 MIN
3/4 OR 1/2 INCH VIDEO CASSETTE P
See series title for descriptive statement.
From The Word Shop Series.
Prod-WETATV Dist-WETATV

Poets On Campus C 30 MIN
3/4 INCH VIDEO CASSETTE H-C A
Offers poems by people who have combined the careers of writing and teaching. Includes works by A R Ammons, Carolyn Kizer, Theodore Roethke, W D Snodgrass and Ezra Pound.
From The Anyone For Tennyson Series.
Prod-NETCHE Dist-GPITVL

Poets Talking—A Series

Features fifteen American poets who read their works and discuss the process of poetry and such things as the effect of translations on their poems. Hosted by Donald Hall, poet and professor of English.
Prod-UMITV Dist-UMITV 1975

Carolyn Kizer 029 MIN
Donald Hall 029 MIN
Galway Kinnell 029 MIN
Gregory Orr 029 MIN
Howard Norman 029 MIN
Jerome Rothenberg 029 MIN
Joyce Peseroff 029 MIN
Larry Fagin 029 MIN
Lawrence Raab 029 MIN
Louis Simpson 029 MIN
Marvin Bell 029 MIN
Robert Bly 029 MIN
Robert Hayden 029 MIN
W S Merwin 029 MIN
Wendell Berry 029 MIN

Poets, The C 30 MIN
3/4 OR 1/2 INCH VIDEO CASSETTE
Discusses the poetry and other works of black midwestern writers. Features poets Inua Fuller and Estrella Sales, poet-critic Fr Joseph Brown, critic Dr Lillian Anthony and moderator Chester Fontenot.
From The Black Poetry Of The Midwest Series.
Prod-NETCHE Dist-NETCHE 1977

Point Conditioning B 17 MIN
3/4 OR 1/2 INCH VIDEO CASSETTE PRO
Teaches that conditioning is extended to point-conditioning which leads to the definition of conditional distribution functions of random variables.
From The Probability And Random Processes - Random Variables Series.
Prod-MIOT Dist-MIOT

Point Control Of Traffic B 32 MIN
16MM FILM OPTICAL SOUND
Explains that point control of traffic is essential for the smooth and rapid movement of troops and supplies. Demonstrates various procedures in effective point control of traffic.
LC NO. FIE60-376
Prod-USA Dist-USNAC 1955

Point Coordinates - Quadrant One C 13 MIN
16MM FILM OPTICAL SOUND
Shows the need for a method to locate the position of a point on a plane and follows the step-by-step construction of the elements of the cartesian coordinate system in quadrant one. Gives definitions of abcissa and ordinate and the point coordinate notation.
From The Mathematics - Graphing Series.
LC NO. 72-703443
Prod-UNISYS Dist-PHM 1972

Point Ellice Bridge Disaster, May 26, 1896, The C 10 MIN
16MM FILM OPTICAL SOUND
Uses old stills to re-create the Point Ellice Bridge disaster of May 26, 1896, in Victoria, British Columbia, where 55 people drowned when a streetcar overloaded the bridge's center span and fell into the harbor during the Queen's birthday celebrations.
LC NO. 76-703328
Prod-BCPM Dist-BCPM 1974

Point Lobos State Reserve C 23 MIN
3/4 OR 1/2 INCH VIDEO CASSETTE
Presents commissioned work by video artist William Gwin.
Prod-EAI Dist-EAI

Point Of Convergence C 15 MIN
16MM FILM OPTICAL SOUND J-C
Examines the cultures and artifacts of three early pre-Columbian cultures of Costa Rica.
LC NO. 73-702050
Prod-PAN Dist-PAN 1973

Point Of Convergence (Spanish) C 15 MIN
16MM FILM OPTICAL SOUND J-C
Examines the cultures and artifacts of three early pre-Columbian cultures of Costa Rica.
LC NO. 73-702050
Prod-PAN Dist-PAN 1973

Point Of Decimals, The C 30 MIN
3/4 OR 1/2 INCH VIDEO CASSETTE A
Shows adult math students learning the rules about decimals.
From The Adult Math Series.
Prod-KYTV Dist-KYTV 1984

Point Of Departure B 28 MIN
16MM FILM OPTICAL SOUND
Presents the story of a young man's realization that running away from difficulties will not solve or change them.
LC NO. 76-703794
Prod-SFRASU Dist-SFRASU 1976

Point Of Entry C 19 MIN
16MM FILM OPTICAL SOUND J-C A
Discusses quarantine procedures and research facilities at arrival points in Australia.
LC NO. 79-700530
Prod-FLMAUS Dist-AUIS 1975

Point Of No Return B 10 MIN
16MM FILM OPTICAL SOUND
Analyzes an accident step-by-step and discusses how good supervision could prevent it.
From The Key Man Series.
Prod-NSC Dist-NSC

Point Of Order B 97 MIN
16MM FILM OPTICAL SOUND
A documentary composed of the most dramatic and memorable events of the Army-Mc Carthy hearings of 1954.
Prod-SMUSA Dist-NYFLMS 1961

Point Of Pines C 22 MIN
16MM FILM OPTICAL SOUND H-C
Deals with the excavation of prehistoric Indian sites. Shows in detail the techniques of archaeology.
Prod-ARCHIA Dist-NYU 1957

Point Of Return B 24 MIN
16MM FILM, 3/4 OR 1/2 IN VIDEO C A
Recounts events culminating in a suicide attempt. A panel comments on the incidents of suicide, the effect on survivors and the need for preventive programs.
Prod-UOKLA Dist-IFB 1965

Point Of View B 5 MIN
16MM FILM OPTICAL SOUND H-C A
Presents a modern interpretation of Psalm 54 using a dramatization about the divorce of a couple.
From The Song Of The Ages Series.
LC NO. 78-702129
Prod-FAMLYT Dist-FAMLYT 1964

Point Of View B 19 MIN
16MM FILM OPTICAL SOUND
Satirizes cigarette smoking and ridicules the smoking habit, pointing out its deleterious effects.
LC NO. FIA65-1708
Prod-NTBA Dist-AMLUNG Prodn-VISION 1965

Point Of View C 23 MIN
16MM FILM OPTICAL SOUND
Dramatizes how routine hospital procedures such as blood withdrawal, X-ray and surgery can have residual psychological impact on young children.
LC NO. FIA67-1093
Prod-CMHOSP Dist-CMHOSP 1967

Point Of View B 41 MIN
16MM FILM OPTICAL SOUND
Demonstrates the discovery method as applied to the teaching of English. Shows Louis C Zahner leading a class of seventh graders to see the implications of point of view in writing and speaking.
LC NO. FIE63-94
Prod-USOE Dist-USNAC 1962

Point Of View C 15 MIN
3/4 INCH VIDEO CASSETTE K-P
Presents a mime finding new ways to see, exploring a building, and looking at a television studio.
From The Adventures Of Milo And Maisie Series.
Prod-KRLNTV Dist-GPITVL 1977

Point Of View C 15 MIN
16MM FILM, 3/4 OR 1/2 IN VIDEO I
Explains that Joey loves the new park but that Michael hates it because his house was torn down to make room for it. Shows how each boy begins to understand the other's point of view.
From The Thinkabout Series. Judging Information
LC NO. 81-706118
Prod-OECA Dist-AITECH 1979

Point Of View B 41 MIN
3/4 INCH VIDEO CASSETTE
Demonstrates the discovery method as applied to the teaching of English. Features Louis C Zahner instructing a class of seventh graders.
Prod-USNAC Dist-USNAC 1972

Point Of View - A Conversation On The Middle East B 29 MIN
16MM FILM OPTICAL SOUND H-C
Novelist James Michener and producer-playwright Dore Schary discuss the Middle East, and bring greater understanding of the tensions which have led to three armed conflicts in twenty years. James Michener traces the cultural roots of the Jewish people to Israel and analyzes the political forces which led to statehood, the reasons for continued tension and the prospects for peace.
Prod-ADL Dist-ADL

Point Of View Dog B 5 MIN
16MM FILM OPTICAL SOUND
Shows the world as perceived through the eyes and ears of a dog.
LC NO. 74-701989
Prod-CANBC Dist-CANFDC Prodn-FRMDR 1973

Point Of View—A Series

Prod-ADL Dist-ADL

Anti-Semitism In America 25 MIN
Challenge To America 25 MIN

Point Pelee C 30 MIN
3/4 OR 1/2 INCH VIDEO CASSETTE
Demonstrates the variety and complexity of relationships on the wildlife sanctuary of Point Pelee in Canada.
Prod-CANBC Dist-JOU

Point Two Percent Solution, The C 6 MIN
16MM FILM, 3/4 OR 1/2 IN VIDEO
Shows students taking part in a self-applied fluoride program. Uses a weekly rinse method and can be conducted in school.
Prod-USDHEW Dist-USNAC

Pointers C 30 MIN
3/4 OR 1/2 INCH VIDEO CASSETTE H-C A
Reviews structured data types and introduces the pointer concept. Gives examples of tables and linked lists. Shows procedures for list initialization, list search and list insertion.
From The Pascal, Pt 2 - Intermediate Pascal Series.
LC NO. 81-706049
Prod-COLOSU Dist-COLOSU 1980

Pointers And Addresses C
3/4 OR 1/2 INCH VIDEO CASSETTE
Defines the use of the terms, pointer and address, in 'C' language and identifies the type of value contained in a pointer variable. Describes a string constant in terms of pointers and addresses.
From The 'C' Language Programming Series.
Prod-COMTEG Dist-COMTEG

Points And Line C 20 MIN
3/4 OR 1/2 INCH VIDEO CASSETTE J-C
See series title for descriptive statement.
From The Math Topics - Geometry Series.
Prod-BBCTV Dist-FI

Points And Line Segments C 15 MIN
3/4 INCH VIDEO CASSETTE P
Introduces the geometric ideas of point, line, line segment and curve.
From The Math Factory, Module II - Geometry Series.
Prod-MAETEL Dist-GPITVL 1973

Points And Line Segments C 20 MIN
2 INCH VIDEOTAPE P
See series title for descriptive statement.
From The Mathemagic, Unit III - Geometry Series.
Prod-WMULTV Dist-GPITVL

Points In The News C 15 MIN
3/4 INCH VIDEO CASSETTE I
Discusses reading and writing decimal fractions and adding and subtracting decimals.
From The Math - No Mystery Series.
Prod-WCETTV Dist-GPITVL 1977

Points Of Convergence C 15 MIN
16MM FILM, 3/4 OR 1/2 IN VIDEO
Shows an extensive panorama of pre-Colombian culture of Costa Rica.
Prod-MOMALA Dist-MOMALA

Points Of Convergence (Spanish) C 15 MIN
16MM FILM, 3/4 OR 1/2 IN VIDEO
Shows an extensive panorama of pre-Colombian culture of Costa Rica.
Prod-MOMALA Dist-MOMALA

Points Of View B 29 MIN
16MM FILM, 3/4 OR 1/2 IN VIDEO H-C A
Shows Ansel Adams as he photographs an old house and its inhabitants. Explains his point of view as he photographs from many different perspectives to suit many purposes.
From The Photography - The Incisive Art Series.
LC NO. 80-707011
Prod-NET Dist-IU Prodn-KQEDTV 1960

Points Of View - Perspective And Projection C 25 MIN
16MM FILM OPTICAL SOUND
Covers the development of the system of focused perspective in art. Explores the work of Desargues and Pascal in the mathematics of projection and section in the 17th century.
Prod-OPENU Dist-GPITVL

Points, Lines, Planes C 30 MIN
16MM FILM OPTICAL SOUND T

Points out the geometric elements of points, lines and planes. To be used following 'SENTENCES, NUMBER LINE.'
From The Mathematics For Elementary School Teachers Series. No. 13
Prod-SMSG Dist-MLA 1963

Poised For Action C 30 MIN
1 INCH VIDEOTAPE
Duffy Daugherty of Michigan State, narrates and demonstrates the four basic aspects of football. Features essential exercises and finer points of the game by NFL stars including slow-motion sequences and fast game action. Encourages students to start their own physical conditioning program. Award winner.
Prod-PICA Dist-MTP

Poison C 14 MIN
16MM FILM, 3/4 OR 1/2 IN VIDEO A
Demonstrates that the natural curiosity of children sometimes leads to poisoning and that such an event can be avoided only by the care and diligence of parents. Shows measures to prevent and counteract poisoning of small children.
Prod-ALDPH Dist-IFB Prodn-FALCON 1968

Poison C 25 MIN
3/4 OR 1/2 INCH VIDEO CASSETTE
Covers various sources of poisoning from snakebites, plants, spiders and fish through poisons that are swallowed. Includes tips on prevention.
Prod-TRAINX Dist-TRAINX

Poison Animals Of The United States C 15 MIN
16MM FILM, 3/4 OR 1/2 IN VIDEO I-H
Deals with the myths and realities concerning the dangers of bees and wasps as well as other venemous animals in the United States. Includes a brief description of treatments and preventive measures.
Prod-BAYERW Dist-PHENIX 1978

Poison Is Queen C 60 MIN
16MM FILM, 3/4 OR 1/2 IN VIDEO C A
Tells how Claudius' revelation of Livia's plots not only fails to save the succession, but brings him under his grandmother's deadly scrutiny.
From The I, Claudius Series. Number 5
Prod-BBCTV Dist-FI 1977

Poison Ivy C 13 MIN
16MM FILM, 3/4 OR 1/2 IN VIDEO J-C A
Tells about Ivy Granstrom, nicknamed Poison Ivy, who has only two and one half percent vision yet manages to lead an energetic life. Shows her now at sixty-six years of age, jogging, gardening and skiing. Emphasizes how she expresses her approach to life, as she says, the best way she knows how.
Prod-NFBC Dist-PHENIX 1980

Poison Plants C 11 MIN
16MM FILM, 3/4 OR 1/2 IN VIDEO P-I
Describes for children various poisonous plants and explains what action should be taken if poisoning occurs. Displays such plants as poison ivy, poison oak, poison sumac, leaves of the oleander and tomato plant and others.
Prod-EBEC Dist-EBEC 1971

Poison Prevention For Primary C 12 MIN
16MM FILM, 3/4 OR 1/2 IN VIDEO P-I
Points out potential poison hazards in the home. Shows how to make the home poison-proof.
Prod-HALPRM Dist-AIMS 1977

Poison Problem, The C 10 MIN
16MM FILM, 3/4 OR 1/2 IN VIDEO K-I
Points out the many potentially dangerous substances found around the home. Explains the danger warnings that appear on labels and the directions for correct and safe use.
Prod-ASSOCF Dist-AIMS 1978

Poisoned Room, The B 22 MIN
16MM FILM SILENT
Presents an episode from the serial The Exploits of Elaine. Shows Pearl Buck fighting the dreaded Clutching Hand.
Prod-UNKNWN Dist-KILLIS 1914

Poisoning C 5 MIN
16MM FILM, 3/4 OR 1/2 IN VIDEO A
Discusses various types of poisoning and provides first aid techniques for dealing with poison victims.
From The Emergency First Aid Training Series.
LC NO. 81-706708
Prod-CRAF Dist-IFB 1980

Poisoning By Accident C 15 MIN
16MM FILM, 3/4 OR 1/2 IN VIDEO J-C A
Shows the causes of accidental poisoning and demonstrates techniques the layman can perform in an emergency.
Prod-NORMBP Dist-AIMS 1977

Poisoning Of Michigan, The C 65 MIN
16MM FILM, 3/4 OR 1/2 IN VIDEO H-C A
Relates how during the summer of 1973, thousands of Michigan farm animals were poisoned by a chemical substance they ate. Tells how it spread throughout the Michigan food chain into the human population. The chemical was PBB, which can cause cancer, birth defects and genetic changes in humans.
Prod-THAMES Dist-MEDIAG 1977

Poisons C
3/4 OR 1/2 INCH VIDEO CASSETTE
Discusses the different forms of poisons, safe handling procedures and proper storage. Emphasizes personal protection, emergency methods and first-aid.
From The Chemsafe Series.
Prod-BNA Dist-BNA

Poisons - Emergency Procedures C 15 MIN
16MM FILM, 3/4 OR 1/2 IN VIDEO J-H
Describes the signs of poisoning and the steps involved in helping a poisoning victim get treatment. Deals with the essential facts about poisoning including poisonous substances, identifying symptoms and initial treatment before professional help arrives.
From The To Save A Life Series.
LC NO. 83-707262
Prod-EBEC Dist-EBEC 1981

Poisons All Around Us C 11 MIN
16MM FILM, 3/4 OR 1/2 IN VIDEO
Reviews common poisonous substances found in nature and in the average home. Provides instructions on how to handle accidental poisoning.
Prod-HIGGIN Dist-HIGGIN 1977

Poisons That Paralyze - Drug Design C 24 MIN
16MM FILM OPTICAL SOUND
Shows how short-term, reversible muscle relaxant drugs for use in surgery are developed from a knowledge of the structure and action of curare, a natural compound. Uses a piece of live muscle and nerve suspended in a life support liquid to measure the effects of drugs on muscle action recorded as a line trace.
Prod-BBCTV Dist-OPENU 1982

Poisons That Paralyze - Drug Design C 24 MIN
16MM FILM, 3/4 OR 1/2 IN VIDEO
Shows how short-term, reversible muscle relaxant drugs for use in surgery are developed from a knowledge of the structure and action of curare, a natural compound. Uses a piece of live muscle and nerve suspended in a life support liquid to measure the effects of drugs on muscle action recorded as a line trace.
Prod-OPENU Dist-MEDIAG Prodn-BBCTV 1982

Poker Game X 28 MIN
16MM FILM, 3/4 OR 1/2 IN VIDEO H-C A
Tells how a Christ-like hippie comedian invites himself to a regular poker game, treating the poker players with so much interest and concern that they soon begin to reveal their true personalities. Stars Beau Bridges, Bill Bixby and Jeffrey Hunter.
From The Insight Series.
Prod-PAULST Dist-PAULST

Poker Game (Spanish) X 28 MIN
16MM FILM, 3/4 OR 1/2 IN VIDEO H-C A
Tells how a Christ-like hippie comedian invites himself to a regular poker game, treating the poker players with so much interest and concern that they soon begin to reveal their true personalities. Stars Beau Bridges, Bill Bixby and Jeffrey Hunter.
From The Insight Series.
Prod-PAULST Dist-PAULST

Pokey, The Snail C 14 MIN
16MM FILM, 3/4 OR 1/2 IN VIDEO K-P
Explains that Pokey is a sad little snail until he discovers that by using his eyes to view nature, the world can be a big surprise.
Prod-CORF Dist-CORF 1973

Poky Little Puppy, The C 8 MIN
16MM FILM, 3/4 OR 1/2 IN VIDEO K-P
Tells the story of the poky little puppy who outwits the four other puppies in the family and eats all of the dessert each night. Explains that the four puppies decide to do as their mother would have them do and are given their dessert before they go to bed. Shows that the poky little puppy is very surprised when he gets home and must go to bed without any dessert. Develops an awareness of numbers and the use of printed symbols to represent spoken language.
Prod-WPES Dist-BARR 1974

Poland C 26 MIN
16MM FILM, 3/4 OR 1/2 IN VIDEO H-C
Examines how the Poles see themselves, and what their role in history has been. Notes how the Polish state has changed many times during the past thousand years, how Poland's leaders have had a common style, and how Poland has struggled alone for freedom after having fought in other countries' battles.
From The Today's History Series.
Prod-JOU Dist-JOU 1984

Poland C 27 MIN
16MM FILM, 3/4 OR 1/2 IN VIDEO J-C A
Prod-IFF Dist-IFF

Poland C 29 MIN
2 INCH VIDEOTAPE
Features home economist Joan Hood presenting a culinary tour of specialty dishes from around the world. Shows the preparation of Polish dishes ranging from peasant cookery to continental cuisine.
From The International Cookbook Series.
Prod-WMVSTV Dist-PUBTEL

Poland - A New Nightmare C 14 MIN
3/4 OR 1/2 INCH VIDEO CASSETTE
Presents a 200 year chronology of the heroic struggles of the Polish people that culminates with the internal crisis of 1981. Portrays a nation in pain.
Prod-KINGFT Dist-KINGFT

Poland - A Year Of Solidarity C 25 MIN
3/4 OR 1/2 INCH VIDEO CASSETTE J-H
Charts the history of the Solidarity movement in Poland and discusses the concessions it has obtained. Views the pressures, both internal and external, facing the Polish government.
Prod-JOU Dist-JOU

Poland - Martial Law And Solidarity C 19 MIN
3/4 OR 1/2 INCH VIDEO CASSETTE H-C A
Presents a report on the Solidarity Movement in Poland, the people, the government and the leaders of the Polish people. Produced just prior to Lech Walesa's release from prison.
Prod-JOU Dist-JOU

Poland - The News In Uniform C 29 MIN
3/4 OR 1/2 INCH VIDEO CASSETTE
Examines the situation in which Polish journalists now find themselves compared with the relative freedom they enjoyed for 16 months under Solidarity.
From The Inside Story Series.
Prod-PBS Dist-PBS 1981

Poland - The Will To Be C 26 MIN
16MM FILM, 3/4 OR 1/2 IN VIDEO
A shortened version of the videorecording Poland - The Will To Be. Features author James Michener taking a trip through Poland, where he examines the nation's history, heritage and people.
From The James Michener's World Series.
LC NO. 79-700966
Prod-EMLEN Dist-PFP 1979

Poland - The Will To Be C 58 MIN
16MM FILM, 3/4 OR 1/2 IN VIDEO
Features author James Michener taking a trip through Poland, where he examines the nation's history, heritage and people.
From The James Michener's World Series.
LC NO. 79-706859
Prod-EMLEN Dist-PFP 1979

Poland Report C 28 MIN
3/4 OR 1/2 INCH VIDEO CASSETTE H-C A
Examines Poland's economy, politics, religion, social development, and history since World War II. Analyzes the dramatic changes which occurred after the Polish workers' strike.
Prod-UPI Dist-JOU

Polar Bear Alert C 59 MIN
16MM FILM, 3/4 OR 1/2 IN VIDEO I-C A
Shows the annual migration of polar bears through Churchill, Manitoba. Shows the scientists who study them and the town that copes with them.
LC NO. 83-706175
Prod-NGS Dist-NGS 1982

Polar Bears - Soft, White And Deadly C
3/4 OR 1/2 INCH VIDEO CASSETTE
Focuses on a small port town trying to solve a problem with polar bears which congregate near their town every fall waiting to feed on seal.
Prod-NWLDPR Dist-NWLDPR

Polar Coordinate Program C 15 MIN
3/4 OR 1/2 INCH VIDEO CASSETTE PRO
See series title for descriptive statement.
From The Numeical Control/Computer Numerical Control, Part 2 - Advanced Programming Series.
Prod-ICSINT Dist-ICSINT

Polar Coordinate Program C 19 MIN
3/4 OR 1/2 INCH VIDEO CASSETTE IND
Covers polar coordinates, programming drilling on a radius and programming milling using polar coordinates.
From The Numerical Control/Computerized Numerical Control - Advanced Programming Series. Module 2
Prod-LEIKID Dist-LEIKID

Polar Coordinates C 15 MIN
16MM FILM, 3/4 OR 1/2 IN VIDEO H
Describes a system for using polar coordinates for graphing functions such as the equations for circles and rose curves. An angle measured from a base line and a distance from a pole (point) from an ordered pair which lables a point in the same way that an ordered pair (X, Y) label a point in the Cartesian coordinate system. Shows how the two systems are related.
Prod-BOSUST Dist-PHENIX 1970

Polar Coordinates B 30 MIN
3/4 OR 1/2 INCH VIDEO CASSETTE
See series title for descriptive statement.
From The Calculus Of Several Variables - Vector--Calculus Series.
Prod-MIOT Dist-MIOT

Polar Ecology - Predator And Prey C 22 MIN
16MM FILM, 3/4 OR 1/2 IN VIDEO H-C T
Illustrates the interaction of animals in the Arctic and Antartic regions. Documents principles of ecology governing predator-prey relationships, food chains, territories and breeding success of selected animal species.
Prod-UCEMC Dist-UCEMC 1963

Polar Regions - Hunters And Herders C 17 MIN
16MM FILM, 3/4 OR 1/2 IN VIDEO P-I
Describes the location and unique features of the polar regions and explains how the Eskimos and Lapps have learned to live in these frigid lands. Discusses ways in which technology has affected these ancient cultures.
Prod-BAYERW Dist-PHENIX 1978

Polar Seas, The C 30 MIN
3/4 OR 1/2 INCH VIDEO CASSETTE
Looks at the arctic and Antarctic regions. Outlines a brief history of the exploration of the polar regions. Discusses several oceanographic aspects of the regions.
From The Oceanus - The Marine Environment Series. Lesson 24
Prod-SCCON Dist-CDTEL

Polaris To Poseidon C 15 MIN
16MM FILM, 3/4 OR 1/2 IN VIDEO
Presents one of the Navy's major contributions to world peace, the Polaris missile and the men who operate her. Depicts the

men training to be polaris submariners and shows a practice launch.
LC NO. 81-707722
Prod-USN Dist-USNAC 1966

Polaris, Blue And Gold C 10 MIN
16MM FILM OPTICAL SOUND
Depicts a typical Polaris submarine and shows the vital role each man plays in its operation.
LC NO. FIE63-10
Prod-USN Dist-USNAC 1962

Polarization Of Light X 11 MIN
16MM FILM, 3/4 OR 1/2 IN VIDEO J-H
Uses glass sheets and doubly refracting materials to illustrate the properties of polarized light. Demonstrates common polarizing techniques.
Prod-EBEC Dist-EBEC 1969

Polarization Of Light (Spanish) C 11 MIN
16MM FILM, 3/4 OR 1/2 IN VIDEO J-H
Illustrates the properties of polarized light and introduces common polarization techniques. Shows how this type of light is used by engineers, manufacturers and geologists.
Prod-EBEC Dist-EBEC

Polarization Of Single Photons B 15 MIN
16MM FILM OPTICAL SOUND C
Investigates the quantum behavior of polarized photons. Demonstrates that single polarized photons follow the statistical prediction of the cosine squared law.
LC NO. 73-702778
Prod-MIOT Dist-EDC 1972

Polarization Of Single Photons C 15 MIN
3/4 INCH VIDEOTAPE
Investigates the quantum behavior of polarized photon. Demonstrates that single polarized photons follow the statistical prediction of the cosine squared law.
Prod-EDC Dist-EDC

Polaroid-Land Photography, 1 B 16 MIN
16MM FILM OPTICAL SOUND C A
Features one teacher demonstrating to another how a Polaroid photograph of a moving object helps students to understand the concepts of velocity and uniform motion, and how a photograph of the Balmer spectrum of hydrogen can be used to make accurate wavelength determinations.
From The Harvard Project Physics Teacher Briefings Series. No. 1
LC NO. 76-709140
Prod-HPP Dist-HRAW 1969

Polaroid-Land Photography, 2 B 31 MIN
16MM FILM OPTICAL SOUND C A
Features a teacher showing how the camera can be used in experiments to determine acceleration due to gravity, to plot the path of a projectile and to detect ionizing radiation, as well as in other experiments which involve momentum and energy transfer, diffraction patterns, traces on an oscilloscope screen and the nuclear scattering analogue.
From The Harvard Project Physics Teacher Briefings Series. No. 2
LC NO. 70-709141
Prod-HPP Dist-HRAW 1969

Pole Line Construction, Pt 3 - Erecting Poles And Attaching Crossarms B 26 MIN
16MM FILM OPTICAL SOUND
Demonstrates the use of the earth borer and the manual method of installing telephone poles and attaching double crossarms, sidearms and 'H' fixtures. Stresses the selection of the most suitable type of crossarm installation to safely support communication circuits.
LC NO. FIE60-169
Prod-USA Dist-USNAC

Pole Replacement, Pt 1 C
3/4 OR 1/2 INCH VIDEO CASSETTE IND
Shows how to lift and secure conductors to a new pole using rubber gloves and an aerial device.
From The Live Line Maintenance Series.
Prod-LEIKID Dist-LEIKID

Pole Replacement, Pt 2 C
3/4 OR 1/2 INCH VIDEO CASSETTE IND
Shows one method of installing a new electric pole, placing it beside one that is to be replaced.
From The Live Line Maintenance Series.
Prod-LEIKID Dist-LEIKID

Pole To Pole C 20 MIN
3/4 INCH VIDEO CASSETTE I-J
Defines a polar projection as a view directly over either pole. Explains that meridians of longitude run from north to south to measure distance from east to west in degrees. Locates the prime meridian (0 degrees longitude) in Greenwich, England.
From The Project Survival Series.
Prod-MAETEL Dist-GPITVL

Pole Vault C 4 MIN
16MM FILM SILENT
Shows male athletes competing in the pole vault, including Olson, Ripley, Bell, Volz, Vigneron, Pursley, Volkov, Kozakiewicz, Spasov and Bellot.
Prod-TRACKN Dist-TRACKN 1982

Poleo And Poetic Figuration C 28 MIN
16MM FILM, 3/4 OR 1/2 IN VIDEO
Shows life and works of the renowned Venezuelan painter Poleo.
Prod-MOMALA Dist-MOMALA

Poleo And Poetic Figuration (French) C 28 MIN
16MM FILM, 3/4 OR 1/2 IN VIDEO
Shows life and works of the renowned Venezuelan painter Poleo.
Prod-MOMALA Dist-MOMALA

Poleo And Poetic Figuration (Spanish) C 28 MIN
16MM FILM, 3/4 OR 1/2 IN VIDEO
Shows life and works of the renowned Venezuelan painter Poleo.
Prod-MOMALA Dist-MOMALA

Poletop Rescue Breathing With Closed Chest Heart Massage C 28 MIN
16MM FILM OPTICAL SOUND IND
Describes procedures to be followed when a lineman is electrocuted at working location on a 40-foot power pole. Explains safety procedures, shows rescue and resuscitation techniques to be followed, and describes emergencies which can occur pole-top and on the ground, such as suffocation, convulsive seizures and heart stoppage.
LC NO. FIA63-1231
Prod-HERMAN Dist-RBFA Prodn-RBFA 1962

Police B 28 MIN
16MM FILM SILENT I A
Features Charlie Chaplin in the 1916 film, 'POLICE,' a slapstick comedy in which a prisoner just released from the pen meets a former cell-mate and once again strays from the straight and narrow.
Prod-MSENP Dist-BHAWK 1916

Police - The Human Dimension - Authority, Pt A C 23 MIN
16MM FILM, 3/4 OR 1/2 IN VIDEO C
Focuses on the exercise of authority. Shows policemen acting out situations.
From The Police - The Human Dimension Series.
Prod-FLORSU Dist-MTI 1975

Police - The Human Dimension - Authority, Pt B C 20 MIN
16MM FILM, 3/4 OR 1/2 IN VIDEO C
Explains the importance of correct ethical behavior by police officers in applying the law. Offers five vignettes of police behavior.
From The Police - The Human Dimension Series.
Prod-FLORSU Dist-MTI 1975

Police - The Human Dimension - Community, Pt A C 20 MIN
16MM FILM, 3/4 OR 1/2 IN VIDEO C
Explains the importance of proper police behavior.
From The Police - The Human Dimension Series.
Prod-FLORSU Dist-MTI 1975

Police - The Human Dimension - Community, Pt B C 20 MIN
16MM FILM, 3/4 OR 1/2 IN VIDEO C
Examines the professional responsibility and the possibility of strains on a policeman's relations with his community.
From The Police - The Human Dimension Series.
Prod-FLORSU Dist-MTI 1975

Police - The Human Dimension - Ethics, Pt A C 23 MIN
16MM FILM, 3/4 OR 1/2 IN VIDEO C
Focuses on ethical problems a policeman may face. Shows policemen acting out situations.
From The Police - The Human Dimension Series.
Prod-FLORSU Dist-MTI 1975

Police - The Human Dimension - Ethics, Pt B C 20 MIN
16MM FILM, 3/4 OR 1/2 IN VIDEO C
Explains the importance of correct ethical behavior by police officers.
From The Police - The Human Dimension Series.
Prod-FLORSU Dist-MTI 1975

Police - The Human Dimension - Minorities C 23 MIN
16MM FILM, 3/4 OR 1/2 IN VIDEO C
Focuses on problems involving minority groups in law enforcement situations. Shows policemen acting out situations.
From The Police - The Human Dimension Series.
Prod-FLORSU Dist-MTI 1975

Police - The Human Dimension - Stress C 23 MIN
16MM FILM, 3/4 OR 1/2 IN VIDEO C
Focuses on problems causing stress in law enforcement situations. Shows policemen acting out situations.
From The Police - The Human Dimension Series.
Prod-FLORSU Dist-MTI 1975

Police - The Human Dimension—A Series
16MM FILM, 3/4 OR 1/2 IN VIDEO C
Focuses on problems in law enforcement situations. Shows policemen acting out situations.
Prod-FLORSU Dist-MTI 1975

Police - The Human Dimension - Authority, Pt A	023 MIN
Police - The Human Dimension - Authority, Pt B	020 MIN
Police - The Human Dimension - Community, Pt A	020 MIN
Police - The Human Dimension - Community, Pt B	020 MIN
Police - The Human Dimension - Ethics, Pt A	023 MIN
Police - The Human Dimension - Ethics, Pt B	020 MIN
Police - The Human Dimension - Minorities	023 MIN
Police - The Human Dimension - Stress	023 MIN

Police - The Legal Dimension, Pt 1 - Search And Seizure Without A Warrant C 22 MIN
16MM FILM, 3/4 OR 1/2 IN VIDEO
Illustrates the areas in which an officer's actions could jeopardize a case. Deals with situations involving search during temporary detention, search incidental to lawful arrest, search without consent and vehicle searches.
Prod-HAR Dist-MTI

Police - The Legal Dimension, Pt 2 - Admissions And Confessions C 22 MIN
16MM FILM, 3/4 OR 1/2 IN VIDEO
Demonstrates how the admissability of statements made by suspects during and after arrest frequently hinges on the behavior of officers and the conditions under which the statements were obtained.
Prod-HAR Dist-MTI

Police Chief Speaks Out C 30 MIN
3/4 INCH VIDEO CASSETTE
Features an interview with Richard G Hostuick, police chief of Reading, Ohio. Discusses leadership style, career development and problems.
From The Decision Makers Series.
Prod-OHC Dist-HRC

Police Civil Liability—A Series
16MM FILM, 3/4 OR 1/2 IN VIDEO
Presents examples of types of police behavior which could result in police officers being held civilly liable.
Prod-HAR Dist-MTI Prodn-BAY 1980

Civil Rights Violations	023 MIN
Intentional Use Of Deadly Force	022 MIN
Limits Of Physical Force	019 MIN
Negligent Operation Of Motor Vehicles	024 MIN
Negligent Use Of Firearms	024 MIN
Supervisory Liability, Management	024 MIN

Police Dog, Pt 1 C 25 MIN
16MM FILM, 3/4 OR 1/2 IN VIDEO I-C A
Describes the training of police dog 'DUKE' and tells the story of the day he saved his master's life.
Prod-HANDEL Dist-HANDEL 1972

Police Dog, Pt 2 C 25 MIN
16MM FILM, 3/4 OR 1/2 IN VIDEO I-C A
Presents reenactments of true stories of police dogs at work, including searching for a lost child, narcotics, explosives, evidence of a crime, apprehending criminals and preventing an attack on an officer.
Prod-HANDEL Dist-HANDEL 1972

Police Estimate / The Two Worlds Of Max Roach C 29 MIN
3/4 INCH VIDEO CASSETTE
Presents a two-part program dealing with police relations in the ghetto and with a jazz drummer named Max Roach.
From The Interface Series.
Prod-WETATV Dist-PUBTEL

Police Experience Film Modules—A Series

Assists police in gaining street experience and emotional control through stress training.
Prod-IACP Dist-IACP

Fear And Anxiety	9 MIN
Feeling Good	9 MIN
Humiliation And Anger	10 MIN

Police Marriage - Social Issues C 20 MIN
16MM FILM, 3/4 OR 1/2 IN VIDEO A
Considers the social and psychological problems the police officer, his wife and children may have in relating to friends, relatives and the public. Examines sources of conflict in informal settings and off-duty demands and expectations arising from the officer's role.
Prod-HAR Dist-MTI Prodn-BAY 1976

Police Marriage, The - Family Issues C 20 MIN
16MM FILM, 3/4 OR 1/2 IN VIDEO A
Examines the special problems the police officer and his children encounter because of his work. Discusses absence because of odd hours, potential emotional barriers, problems of authoritarianism and unrealistic expectations placed on children of police officers.
Prod-HAR Dist-MTI Prodn-BAY 1976

Police Marriage, The - Husband, Wife Personal Issues C 20 MIN
16MM FILM, 3/4 OR 1/2 IN VIDEO A
Focuses on the kinds of marital problems posed by the police officer's work. Considers the wife's need to adapt to this work and its usual pressures while forming her own identity.
Prod-HAR Dist-MTI Prodn-BAY 1976

Police Officer C 20 MIN
3/4 OR 1/2 INCH VIDEO CASSETTE J-H
Shows two truant officers encountering juveniles involved in burglary, truancy, marijuana violations and driving without a license.
From The Rights And Responsibilities Series.
Prod-VAOG Dist-AITECH Prodn-WHROTV 1975

Police Officer, The (4th Ed) C 14 MIN
16MM FILM, 3/4 OR 1/2 IN VIDEO P-I
Introduces the services performed by the police in a community. Explains how the policeman's major responsibility is law enforcement and how they function as community helpers. Highlights the importance of teamwork in police operations, and the special skills and equipment used by the police department.
Prod-EBEC Dist-EBEC 1981

Police Officers - Day And Night (2nd Ed) C 12 MIN
16MM FILM, 3/4 OR 1/2 IN VIDEO P-I
Follows a police officer through a typical day, discussing the routine of police work and the training. Shows the police officer as a well-trained, intelligent and competent family man who cares about his family and community, and who wants to protect and serve the people.
LC NO. 83-706134
Prod-CAHILL Dist-AIMS 1981

Police On Campus I C 18 MIN
16MM FILM, 3/4 OR 1/2 IN VIDEO

Presents vignettes which explore such topics as racial conflict, dormitory theft, communication problems with foreign students, an arrest during a class session and a rape response. Designed to increase communication skills for campus security officers.
Prod-BARPJ Dist-MTI 1976

Police On Campus II C 10 MIN
16MM FILM, 3/4 OR 1/2 IN VIDEO
Presents six vignettes which explore security officer discretion, parking problems, a supervisor conflict, an off-campus arrest, city police/campus police conflict and a surprise situation. Shows how these situations are handled by campus police officers.
Prod-BARPJ Dist-MTI 1976

Police Pursuit C 19 MIN
16MM FILM, 3/4 OR 1/2 IN VIDEO
Demonstrates techniques and procedures for the safe driving of pursuit vehicles, focusing on police pursuit.
Prod-FILCOM Dist-FILCOM 1974

Police Story C 12 MIN
3/4 OR 1/2 INCH VIDEO CASSETTE
Depicts the administrative organization and functions of hospital police officers at the Veterans Administration Hospital in Memphis, Tennessee.
LC NO. 81-707113
Prod-VAHMT Dist-USNAC 1981

Police Tapes B 49 MIN
16MM FILM, 3/4 OR 1/2 IN VIDEO
Offers a cinema verite look at urban police work and ghetto crime by portraying life at New York City's 44th Precinct. Details the pressures, stress, frustration, violence and brutality that must be faced and how the officers learn to cope.
Prod-MTI Dist-MTI

Police Tapes, The B 90 MIN
3/4 OR 1/2 INCH VIDEO CASSETTE
Reports on a police precinct in the South Bronx and its officers' daily confrontations with crime. Surveys urban crime, violence, brutality and cynical despair.
Prod-KITCHN Dist-KITCHN

Police Tattoo B 14 MIN
16MM FILM OPTICAL SOUND
Presents a pageant staged by the Malaysian police held once every five years to raise funds for police welfare.
Prod-FILEM Dist-PMFMUN 1961

Police Technology C 30 MIN
3/4 OR 1/2 INCH VIDEO CASSETTE
Discusses innovations in law enforcement, pointing out that it take a whole new type of detective to investigate computer crimes.
From The Innovation Series.
Prod-WNETTV Dist-WNETTV 1983

Police Training Films—A Series
16MM FILM, 3/4 OR 1/2 IN VIDEO
Prod-MTROLA Dist-MTI Prodn-WORON 1975

Officer Down, Code 3 25 MIN

Police Unit 2a26 C 18 MIN
16MM FILM OPTICAL SOUND I-C A
Follows two policemen through the activities of a typical day. Includes scenes of their families, and shows one of the men as he competes in the Police Olympics.
LC NO. 78-701243
Prod-DUNLF Dist-AMEDFL 1968

Police/School Relations C 28 MIN
16MM FILM, 3/4 OR 1/2 IN VIDEO T
Discusses how inappropriate police involvement in school campus incidents can lead to more, rather than less, tension. Examines a model memorandum of agreement between local law enforcement agencies and a school system.
Prod-BFA Dist-PHENIX 1984

Police, The C 58 MIN
16MM FILM OPTICAL SOUND H-C A
Presents a satire about a country where every citizen loves the government except one. Points out the necessity of the secret police to turn up revolutionaries even when there aren't any or find itself out of business.
Prod-GROVE Dist-GROVE

Policeman C 11 MIN
16MM FILM OPTICAL SOUND P-I
Depicts both urban and rural officers performing daily duties from protecting property to locating lost children and soothing distraught parents.
Prod-IACP Dist-IACP

Policeman C 12 MIN
16MM FILM, 3/4 OR 1/2 IN VIDEO P-I
Demonstrates how safeguarding lives is the policeman's major responsibility and his most important tool is his knowledge of people. Includes vignettes depicting the law officer as a human being who cares about others.
Prod-LUF Dist-LUF 1979

Policeman - He Is There To Help C 11 MIN
16MM FILM OPTICAL SOUND K-I
Presents the police officer as a man whose job is helping people in a great variety of ways. Depicts officers at street crossings, checking shop doors at night, helping stranded motorists, answering calls and comforting lost children. Tells of the training necessary for policemen.
LC NO. 72-702928
Prod-ASPTEF Dist-ASPTEF 1970

Policeman And His Job, The X 13 MIN
16MM FILM, 3/4 OR 1/2 IN VIDEO I-J
Presents the work of a police officer in the communications division as he tries to assist people with various needs.
Prod-BRAVC Dist-PHENIX 1968

Policeman Is Many Things, A C 24 MIN
2 INCH VIDEOTAPE J-H
Presents the working structure of a police bureau, showing how the various departments interrelate. Traces the routine of an average police officer on his patrol.
From The American System Series.
Prod-WCVETV Dist-GPITVL

Policemen C 28 MIN
3/4 INCH VIDEO CASSETTE J-C
Presents Chicago policemen discussing their life and work.
From The Are You Listening Series.
LC NO. 80-707149
Prod-STURTM Dist-STURTM 1972

Policies And Programs Of Other Governments C 34 MIN
3/4 OR 1/2 INCH VIDEO CASSETTE
See series title for descriptive statement.
From The Technology, Innovation, And Industrial Development Series.
Prod-MIOT Dist-MIOT

Polish Kitchen, The C 30 MIN
1/2 IN VIDEO CASSETTE BETA/VHS
Features traditional Polish dishes including Polish sausage and Pierogi.
From The Frugal Gourmet Series.
Prod-WTTWTV Dist-MTI

Polishing B 28 MIN
16MM FILM OPTICAL SOUND
Explains how to make a concave or convex polishing shell, trim the polishing shell to size and cut breathers.
LC NO. FIE52-381
Prod-USOE Dist-USNAC 1944

Polishing C 15 MIN
3/4 INCH VIDEO CASSETTE PRO
Instructs in the mixing of abrasive agents used for polishing teeth. Discusses instrument speed and pressure used when applying the agent to tooth surfaces.
From The Scaling Techniques Series. No. 10
LC NO. 77-706009
Prod-UTENN Dist-USNAC 1976

Polishing C 30 MIN
3/4 OR 1/2 INCH VIDEO CASSETTE H-C A
See series title for descriptive statement.
From The Introduction To Technical And Business Communication Series.
Prod-UMINN Dist-GPITVL 1983

Polishing, Soldering, Applying The Handle C 30 MIN
3/4 OR 1/2 INCH VIDEO CASSETTE
Shows how to polish, solder and apply the handle when building a knife.
From The How To Build A Knife Series.
Prod-UGATV Dist-MDCPB

Politeness And Enthusiasm C 38 MIN
16MM FILM, 3/4 OR 1/2 IN VIDEO H A
Discusses the two major trends in Christian worship in the 18th century, a staid, complacent worship exemplified by the Church of England and a revivalist enthusiasm exhibited in Midwestern America and elsewhere.
From The Christians Series.
Prod-GRATV Dist-MGHT 1978

Political Advertisement - 1954-1984 X 35 MIN
3/4 INCH VIDEO CASSETTE
Chronicles the development of political advertising from the 1950's to the media campaign phenomenon of the 1980's. Reveals advertising tactics such as retaliatory spots, negative advertising, soft-sell techniques and emotionalism. By Antonio Muntadas.
Prod-EAI Dist-EAI

Political Advertisement - 1956-84 C 35 MIN
3/4 OR 1/2 INCH VIDEO CASSETTE
Examines media landscape. Presented by Antonio Muntadas and Marshall Reese.
Prod-ARTINC Dist-ARTINC

Political And Social Comment In Dance—A Series

Presents programs from the New York City Cable TV series Eye On Dance.
Prod-ARCVID Dist-ARCVID

Black Choreographers' Social Comment In Their
Contemporary Dancers' Social And Political 030 MIN
Dance And Social Consciousness In The 1930's 030 MIN
Performance And Dance Theatre 030 MIN

Political Candidate, The C 29 MIN
2 INCH VIDEOTAPE
See series title for descriptive statement.
From The Our Street Series.
Prod-MDCPB Dist-PUBTEL

Political Cartoon, The C 15 MIN
2 INCH VIDEOTAPE
See series title for descriptive statement.
From The Charlie's Pad Series.
Prod-WSIU Dist-PUBTEL

Political Corruption C 30 MIN
3/4 OR 1/2 INCH VIDEO CASSETTE C
Uses the Grant, Harding and Nixon administrations as case studies of political corruption in America.
America - The Second Century Series.
Prod-DALCCD Dist-DALCCD

Political Executives, The C 29 MIN
16MM FILM OPTICAL SOUND H-C
Explains why the President's top advisers are political appointees, and discusses their problems in representing the President in his dealings with Congress and the federal departments.
From The Government Story Series. No. 29
LC NO. 78-707184
Prod-WBCPRO Dist-WBCPRO 1968

Political Leadership And Stability C 30 MIN
3/4 INCH VIDEO CASSETTE
Focuses on fluctuations within Chinese politics.
From The China After Mao Series.
Prod-UMITV Dist-UMITV 1980

Political Morality In America C 29 MIN
3/4 INCH VIDEO CASSETTE
Explores the civil rights movement and asks how it has been affected by the assassinations of black leaders and by the Watergate scandals.
From The Interface Series.
Prod-WETATV Dist-PUBTEL

Political Organization C 30 MIN
3/4 INCH VIDEO CASSETTE C A
Describes major types of political organizations in the world. Includes decentralized and centralized systems and looks at the cultures in which these systems are usually found.
From The Faces Of Culture - Studies In Cultural Anthropology Series. Lesson 17
Prod-COAST Dist-CDTEL Prodn-HRAW

Political Participation C 30 MIN
3/4 OR 1/2 INCH VIDEO CASSETTE C
Analyzes voting behavior and political participation.
From The American Government 1 Series.
Prod-DALCCD Dist-DALCCD

Political Participation Of The Handicapped C 30 MIN
3/4 OR 1/2 INCH VIDEO CASSETTE C
Provides a case study of the handicapped with a focus on 'socialization' and 'political socialization.'
From The American Government 1 Series.
Prod-DALCCD Dist-DALCCD

Political Parties C 30 MIN
3/4 OR 1/2 INCH VIDEO CASSETTE C
Accounts for the development of today's political parties with their basic philosophical differences. Explores the historical stereotypes of the 'typical Republican' and the 'typical Democrat.'
From The American Government 1 Series.
Prod-DALCCD Dist-DALCCD

Political Parties - Women's Clout C 29 MIN
3/4 INCH VIDEO CASSETTE
Suggests that the national political conventions of 1972 created a new awareness of political power by women.
From The Woman Series.
Prod-WNEDTV Dist-PUBTEL

Political Parties In America - Getting The People Together C 20 MIN
16MM FILM, 3/4 OR 1/2 IN VIDEO J-H
Presents candid interviews which probe the structure, workings and effects of American political parties. Includes interviews of workers in the street, political observers, social commentators, and elected representatives.
Prod-EBEC Dist-EBEC 1976

Political Parties In The United States C 17 MIN
16MM FILM, 3/4 OR 1/2 IN VIDEO J-C A
Answers questions about the two-party political system in the United States, pointing out its advantages and disadvantages. Includes a discussion of the importance of third parties and splinter groups within the two parties.
Prod-MEDFO Dist-PHENIX 1976

Political Posture C 2 MIN
3/4 OR 1/2 INCH VIDEO CASSETTE H-C A
Offers a satire of political advertisements.
Prod-IFEX Dist-IFEX

Political Protest - The Splinter Groups C 15 MIN
16MM FILM OPTICAL SOUND H
Dissent takes many forms, beginning with the founding fathers, themselves violent dissenters. The evolution of the American two-party political system has been anything but immune from protest, to the extent that, often as not, we have had in reality three or more party systems in the 20th Century alone.
Prod-INTEXT Dist-REAF

Political Setting, The B 30 MIN
16MM FILM OPTICAL SOUND H-C A
Dr Charles Hamilton discusses the reaction of blacks to white American political concepts and the relation of the black revolt to the socio-political values of modern society as well as the varying political attitudes among black people ranging from the moral crusader to the alienated revolutionary.
From The Black History, Section 15 - Blacks And White Politics Series.
LC NO. 74-704086
Prod-WCBSTV Dist-HRAW 1969

Political Socialization C 30 MIN
3/4 OR 1/2 INCH VIDEO CASSETTE C
Displays different political options citizens have in their daily lives and shows how political attitudes and behavior may be influ-

enced by families, social class, peer groups, schools and churches.
From The American Government 1 Series.
Prod-DALCCD Dist-DALCCD

Political Spots C 30 MIN
16MM FILM, 3/4 OR 1/2 IN VIDEO H-C A
Offers a primer on the techniques used by political media makers. Shows media spots from across the country, representing several parties and many levels of government. Accompanies two media consultants into their editing rooms as they explain the process in making vote-winning TV commercials.
From The Media Probes Series.
LC NO. 83-706188
Prod-LAYLEM Dist-TIMLIF 1982

Politics B 30 MIN
16MM FILM OPTICAL SOUND H-C
Presents Arthur A Fletcher and Ralph Abernathy who outline the significance of political education for black people. Discusses the elected black official, the Supreme Court 'ONE-MAN, ONE VOTE' decision and its effect on urban politics.
From The Conversations In Black Series.
Prod-HRAW Dist-HRAW

Politics C 30 MIN
3/4 OR 1/2 INCH VIDEO CASSETTE C
Discusses aspects of black politics in America.
From The Afro-American Perspectives Series.
Prod-MDDE Dist-MDCPB

Politics - Electoral Vs Pressure B 30 MIN
16MM FILM OPTICAL SOUND H-C A
Dr Charles Hamilton discusses American political concepts, the application of these concepts to anti-lynch laws, and the role of black community in electoral and pressure-group politics.
From The Black History, Section 15 - Blacks And White Politics Series.
LC NO. 78-704087
Prod-WCBSTV Dist-HRAW 1969

Politics - Soviet Style C 27 MIN
16MM FILM, 3/4 OR 1/2 IN VIDEO J-C A
Provides a brief background on the Russian Revolution and examines the tumultuous history of politics in post-Czarist Russia. Looks at the role of Lenin in the establishment of the Soviet State, Stalin's role in World War II and after, and the function of Party members in contemporary Soviet politics.
From The Soviet Style Series.
LC NO. 84-707067
Prod-JOU Dist-JOU 1982

Politics - The High Cost Of Conviction C 5 MIN
16MM FILM, 3/4 OR 1/2 IN VIDEO J-H
Tells the story of a man who is asked to publicly endorse a senatorial candidate. Explains that he is afraid an endorsement might alienate some of his customers and hurt his business.
Prod-IFB Dist-IFB 1964

Politics And Conflict C 15 MIN
3/4 OR 1/2 INCH VIDEO CASSETTE H
Examines causes and effects of political conflict. Shows how conflict is managed through the political process.
From The By The People Series.
Prod-CTI Dist-CTI

Politics And The Arts C 30 MIN
3/4 OR 1/2 INCH VIDEO CASSETTE
See series title for descriptive statement.
From The Update - Topics Of Current Concern Series.
Prod-ARCVID Dist-ARCVID

Politics And The Individual C 15 MIN
3/4 OR 1/2 INCH VIDEO CASSETTE H
Illustrates how the political process in a democracy provides ways to protect the individual.
From The By The People Series.
Prod-CTI Dist-CTI

Politics And The Prince - Machiavelli C 45 MIN
2 INCH VIDEOTAPE
See series title for descriptive statement.
From The Humanities Series. Unit III - The Realm Of Idea And Speculation
Prod-WTTWTV Dist-GPITVL

Politics And The State - Machiavelli C 45 MIN
2 INCH VIDEOTAPE
See series title for descriptive statement.
From The Humanities Series. Unit III - The Realm Of Idea And Speculation
Prod-WTTWTV Dist-GPITVL

Politics And Youth C 15 MIN
16MM FILM, 3/4 OR 1/2 IN VIDEO J-H
Presents interviews with young people from all across the country, all races, walks of life and political persuasions, talking about politics.
Prod-COP Dist-AIMS 1973

Politics In The Gilded Age C 30 MIN
2 INCH VIDEOTAPE
Covers the presidents from Andrew Jackson to William Mc Kinley. Illustrated with pictures.
From The American History II Series.
Prod-KRMATV Dist-GPITVL

Politics Of Age C
16MM FILM OPTICAL SOUND
Urges legislators, professionals in the aging field and older people to consider the political interests and activities of older persons. Looks at the roles of organizations of older people and the prospects of an older people's political party.
From The Aging In The Future Series.
Prod-UMICH Dist-UMICH

Politics Of Aging C 15 MIN
3/4 INCH VIDEO CASSETTE
Shows older people taking an active role in the politics of age. Focuses on older legislators and those politicians who advise older citizens to help their own interests by being active politically.
From The Aging In The Future Series.
Prod-UMITV Dist-UMITV 1981

Politics Of Genetics, The C 29 MIN
3/4 INCH VIDEO CASSETTE
Features a discussion between a science critic and a research scientist on the wisdom of genetic research. Focuses on recombinant DNA.
From The Issue At Hand Series.
Prod-UMITV Dist-UMITV 1976

Politics Of Hunger In America, The C 29 MIN
2 INCH VIDEOTAPE
See series title for descriptive statement.
From The University Of Chicago Round Table Series.
Prod-WTTWTV Dist-PUBTEL

Politics Of Peacemaking, The (2nd Ed) C 14 MIN
16MM FILM, 3/4 OR 1/2 IN VIDEO J-C
Shows the signing of the armistice after World War I and the failure of the treaty of Versailles.
From The World War I (2nd Ed) Series.
Prod-CORF Dist-CORF

Politics Of Poison C 53 MIN
16MM FILM OPTICAL SOUND
Focuses on herbicide spraying in the United States and shows how the Environmental Protection Agency is dealing with this problem.
LC NO. 79-701011
Prod-KRONTV Dist-KRONTV 1979

Politics Of Regulation, The C 60 MIN
3/4 OR 1/2 INCH VIDEO CASSETTE
Reports on the Federal Trade Commission and the battle in Congress over the power of the regulatory agencies.
From The Bill Moyers' Journal Series.
Prod-WNETTV Dist-WNETTV 1980

Politics Of Unreason, The - Right-Wing Extremism In America, 1790-1970 C 28 MIN
16MM FILM OPTICAL SOUND
Traces the efforts of the right-wing extremists to preserve their status by advocating the denial of rights to minority groups. Discusses movements including the anti-Masonic party of the 1820's and 1830's, the Know-Nothings, the anti-Catholic American Protective Association of the 1890's, the emergence of anti-Semitism in the 1890's, the Ku Klux Klan and the John Birch Society. Analyzes the impact of these movements on the mainstream of American two-party politics.
Prod-ADL Dist-ADL

Politics Of Violence C 27 MIN
16MM FILM, 3/4 OR 1/2 IN VIDEO J-C A
Studies the emergence of international terrorism during the 1970's. Looks at the far-reaching effects of several terrorist organizations.
From The Seventies Series.
Prod-UPI Dist-JOU 1980

Politics Of Working Together In A Gifted And Talented Program, The C 28 MIN
3/4 OR 1/2 INCH VIDEO CASSETTE T
Presents parents, other teachers, the principal and the superintendent talking about how teacher Sally Reis has involved them in the planning and implementing of a successful and satisfying Talented and Gifted program.
From The Successful Teaching Practices Series.
Prod-UNIDIM Dist-EBEC 1982

Politics, Power And The Public Good B 20 MIN
16MM FILM, 3/4 OR 1/2 IN VIDEO J-C A
Tells how a long-term popular politician, proud of 'GETTING THINGS DONE FOR THE PEOPLE,' fights to retain his office with a panoply of unethical tactics.
From The Searching For Values - A Film Anthology Series.
Prod-LCOA Dist-LCOA 1972

Polka Dot Leaves On A Purple Tree C 27 MIN
16MM FILM OPTICAL SOUND
Pictures a studio workshop where children are stimulated by color, design, texture and sound to create their own works of art by using ordinary household materials.
LC NO. 78-713400
Prod-HALMRK Dist-HALMRK 1971

Pollination C 23 MIN
16MM FILM, 3/4 OR 1/2 IN VIDEO I-J
Shows the process of pollination and the various creatures involved in it. Reveals the reproductive parts of a flower and differentiates between self-pollination and cross-pollination. Discusses wind pollination, water pollination and co-evolution of insects and flowering plants.
LC NO. 83-706729
Prod-NGS Dist-NGS 1983

Pollination Mechanisms C 12 MIN
16MM FILM, 3/4 OR 1/2 IN VIDEO I-H A
Discusses various pollination mechanisms, such as cross-pollination and self-pollination.
From The Many Worlds Of Nature Series.
Prod-SCRESC Dist-MTI

Pollution C 3 MIN
16MM FILM OPTICAL SOUND
Uses music and cartoon satire to show the growing hazards of air and water pollution in American cities. An animated film.
LC NO. 76-702525
Prod-USC Dist-USC 1967

Pollution C 14 MIN
16MM FILM, 3/4 OR 1/2 IN VIDEO J-H T
Shows the effects of all types of pollution. Presents the neccessity of positive action to insure the future of mankind.
From The Your Chance To Live Series.
Prod-USDCPA Dist-MTI 1972

Pollution - How Much Is A Clean Environment Worth C 30 MIN
3/4 OR 1/2 INCH VIDEO CASSETTE C
See series title for descriptive statement.
From The Economics USA Series.
Prod-WEFA Dist-ANNCPB

Pollution - Land-Air-Water-Noise C 17 MIN
16MM FILM OPTICAL SOUND P-C
Examines the causes and conditions of four types of pollution--air, land, water and noise.
LC NO. 78-713041
Prod-ACA Dist-ACA 1971

Pollution Below C 14 MIN
16MM FILM - 3/4 IN VIDEO
Presents stories about people in dangerous situations caused by unexpected pollution.
From The Rediscovery Series.
LC NO. 77-706144
Prod-NASA Dist-USNAC 1977

Pollution Control - The Hard Decisions C 28 MIN
16MM FILM - 3/4 IN VIDEO IND
Points out the responsibilities of business to problems of the environment.
From The Managing Discontinuity Series.
Prod-BNA Dist-BNA 1971

Pollution Is Personal C 14 MIN
16MM FILM OPTICAL SOUND
Takes a look at industrial and human pollution.
Prod-TASCOR Dist-TASCOR 1975

Pollution Of The Upper And Lower Atmosphere C 17 MIN
16MM FILM, 3/4 OR 1/2 IN VIDEO J-C A
Shows how auto emissions are changing the physical and chemical composition of the atmosphere. Examines the effects these changes might have on the Earth's climate and on man's health.
From The Environmental Sciences Series.
Prod-DAVFMS Dist-LCOA 1975

Pollution Solution C 15 MIN
16MM FILM OPTICAL SOUND J-H A
Discusses how Landsat's remote sensing capabilities can aid in resolving environmental quality problems. Shows that the satellite can locate and monitor strip-mining operations to facilitate land reclamation programs, help solve meteorological mysteries by tracking the path of airborne pollution and monitor the course of industrial wastes and garbage dumped in lakes, rivers and coastal areas.
From The Environmental Series - Landsat - Satellite For All Seasons Series.
LC NO. 77-700805
Prod-NASA Dist-USNAC Prodn-EDFCEN 1977

Pollution Solution C 15 MIN
3/4 OR 1/2 INCH VIDEO CASSETTE
Illustrates how the LANDSAT satellite monitors strip-mining and land reclamation, path and sources of airborne pollution and industrial waste and contamination of lakes, rivers and coastal waters.
From The LANDSAT Series.
Prod-IVCH Dist-IVCH

Pollution Solution, The C 15 MIN
3/4 INCH VIDEO CASSETTE
Shows how the Landsat satellite's remote sensing capabilities can help in resolving environmental quality problems by monitoring strip mining operations and tracking the paths of air and water pollution.
From The Environmental Series - Landsat - Satellite For All Seasons Series.
LC NO. 78-706005
Prod-NASA Dist-USNAC Prodn-NVETA 1977

Polly Wolly Doodle C 14 MIN
3/4 OR 1/2 INCH VIDEO CASSETTE P-I
See series title for descriptive statement.
From The Ready, Sing Series.
Prod-ARKETV Dist-AITECH 1979

Polo C 3 MIN
16MM FILM OPTICAL SOUND P-I
Discusses the sport of polo.
From The Of All Things Series.
Prod-BAILYL Dist-AVED

Polyelectrolytes (Cont'd), Viscosity, Light Scattering, Osmotic Pressure, Sedimentation C 49 MIN
3/4 OR 1/2 INCH VIDEO CASSETTE
See series title for descriptive statement.
From The Colloid And Surface Chemistry - Lyophilic Colloids Series.
Prod-KALMIA Dist-KALMIA

Polyelectrolytes/Viscosity/Light Scattering, Osmotic Pressure, Sedimentation B 49 MIN
3/4 OR 1/2 INCH VIDEO CASSETTE
See series title for descriptive statement.
From The Colloids And Surface Chemistry - Lyophilic Colloids Series.
Prod-MIOT Dist-MIOT

Polyelectrolytes, Examples, Titration Curves, Electrophoresis B 38 MIN
3/4 OR 1/2 INCH VIDEO CASSETTE
See series title for descriptive statement.
From The Colloids And Surface Chemistry - Lyophilic Colloids Series.
Prod-MIOT Dist-MIOT

Polyester Fiberglass Fracture Repair C 28 MIN
1/2 IN VIDEO CASSETTE BETA/VHS
Deals with auto body repair. Shows damage preparation and complete repair on a small fracture in a Corvette door.
Prod-RMI Dist-RMI

Polyester Yarn C 15 MIN
3/4 OR 1/2 INCH VIDEO CASSETTE P-I
Visits an American Cyanamid plant to learn how polyester yarn is made.
From The Explorers Unlimited Series.
Prod-WVIZTV Dist-AITECH 1971

Polygons (Geometric Figures) C 20 MIN
2 INCH VIDEOTAPE P
See series title for descriptive statement.
From The Mathemagic, Unit III - Geometry Series.
Prod-WMULTV Dist-GPITVL

Polygons And Angles C 30 MIN
16MM FILM OPTICAL SOUND T
Describes the geometric elements of angles and polygons. To be used following 'POINTS, LINES AND PLANES.'
From The Mathematics For Elementary School Teachers Series. No. 14
Prod-SMSG Dist-MLA 1963

Polygraph, The - Demonstration And Discussion C 43 MIN
3/4 OR 1/2 INCH VIDEO CASSETTE PRO
Explains the polygraph and how it works. Discusses the theory behind its development, its use in various tests, and how the test results are interpreted.
From The Scientific Evidence - The Polygraph Series.
LC NO. 80-707190
Prod-ABACPE Dist-ABACPE 1977

Polygraph, The - Useful Tool Or Dangerous Weapon C 58 MIN
3/4 OR 1/2 INCH VIDEO CASSETTE PRO
Presents a panel discussion on the legal and scientific issues involved in using the polygraph. Covers the scientific reliability of the polygraph, competency of polygraph examiners, admitting polygraph results in court, and other related topics.
From The Scientific Evidence - The Polygraph Series.
LC NO. 80-707191
Prod-ABACPE Dist-ABACPE 1977

Polymer Synthesis - The Importance Of Polymers - Their Specific Role B 55 MIN
3/4 OR 1/2 INCH VIDEO CASSETTE
See series title for descriptive statement.
From The Colloids And Surface Chemistry - Lyophilic Colloids Series.
Prod-MIOT Dist-MIOT

Polymer Synthesis, The Role And Importance Of Polymers C 55 MIN
3/4 OR 1/2 INCH VIDEO CASSETTE
See series title for descriptive statement.
From The Colloid And Surface Chemistry - Lyophilic Colloids Series.
Prod-KALMIA Dist-KALMIA

Polymyositis And Related Disorders C 50 MIN
3/4 INCH VIDEO CASSETTE PRO
Reviews Dr Darryl C Devino's discussion on polymyositis and related disorders.
From The Intensive Course In Neuromuscular Diseases Series.
LC NO. 76-706075
Prod-NINDIS Dist-USNAC 1974

Polynesia C 22 MIN
16MM FILM, 3/4 OR 1/2 IN VIDEO I-C A
Presents a glimpse of Polynesia taken from the TV special 'POLYNESIAN ADVENTURE.'
LC NO. 80-706337
Prod-NGS Dist-NGS 1973

Polynesian Adventure C 54 MIN
16MM FILM, 3/4 OR 1/2 IN VIDEO J-H
Describes marine life and the life of the people in the Polynesian islands as exemplified by the life of the diver Stan Waterman and his family.
LC NO. 80-706390
Prod-NGS Dist-NGS 1969

Polynesian—A Series

Looks at various aspects of life in American Samoa.
Prod-IFF Dist-IFF

Best Kept Secret, The	016 MIN
Samoa I Sisifo	026 MIN
Tonga Royal	020 MIN

Polyneuropathies And Nerve Conduction Studies In Neuromuscular Diseases C 42 MIN
3/4 INCH VIDEO CASSETTE PRO
Presents Dr Peter J Dyck lecturing on polyneuropathies and nerve conduction studies in neuromuscular diseases.
From The Intensive Course In Neuromuscular Diseases Series.
LC NO. 76-706076
Prod-NINDIS Dist-USNAC 1974

Polyps Of Colon And Rectum C 29 MIN
16MM FILM OPTICAL SOUND PRO
Discusses the incidence and transproctoscopic management of polyps in the rectum and lower sigmoid. Demonstrates the surgical technique of transabdominal management of patients with familial polyposis, adenomas, adenovillous and villous tumors.
Prod-ACYDGD Dist-ACY 1969

Polyps Of The Large Intestine C 18 MIN
16MM FILM OPTICAL SOUND PRO
Shows four cases, including solitary benign adenomatous polyp, familial polyposis, multiple polyps with double primary carcinoma and inflammatory polyposis due to ulcerative colitis.
Prod-ACYDGD Dist-ACY 1951

Polysulfide Base Industrial Sealants C 14 MIN
16MM FILM OPTICAL SOUND
Describes industrial use of Thiokol Polysulfides for sealing trailers, buildings, aircraft and tanks.
Prod-THIOKL Dist-THIOKL 1963

Polysulfide For Industry C 18 MIN
16MM FILM OPTICAL SOUND
Shows the properties of Thiokol Polysulfide Liquid Polymer and uses of compounds based on this synthetic rubber, including sealants for windows, buildings, tanks, aircraft and truck trailers.
Prod-THIOKL Dist-THIOKL 1961

Polytome Pantopaque Study C 13 MIN
16MM FILM OPTICAL SOUND PRO
Describes the indications of acoustic neuroma and the technique for performing the polytome pantopaque study of the posterior fossa in patients suspected of having this condition.
LC NO. 74-705643
Prod-EAR Dist-EAR

Polytome Pantopaque Study C 20 MIN
16MM FILM, 3/4 OR 1/2 IN VIDEO PRO
Demonstrates the use of the pantopaque dye solution to outline tumors hidden within the internal auditory canal by the temporal bone by way of polytome x-ray.
Prod-HOUSEI Dist-HOUSEI

Polytrauma - A Team Protocol For Basic And Advanced EMTs C 26 MIN
16MM FILM, 3/4 OR 1/2 IN VIDEO H A
Dramatizes a town's procedures for emergency response to a single-victim car accident. Presents a trauma management plan to provide for treatment of additional patients, prolonged extrications and other types of trauma, whatever the situation. Shows coordinated efforts of citizens, police, hospital, fire and ambulance personnel. Introduces viewers to a range of health care careers.
Prod-DOWNPR Dist-FANPRO

Pomeroy Takes A Sex History C 35 MIN
3/4 OR 1/2 INCH VIDEO CASSETTE C A
Demonstrates the sex history-taking procedure integral to therapy and research. Demonstrates the importance of ordering questions properly.
Prod-NATSF Dist-MMRC

Pomo Shaman B 20 MIN
16MM FILM OPTICAL SOUND H-C A
Pictures an ancient healing ceremony performed by a southwestern Pomo doctor. Considers the Indian belief that disease is caused by hostile objects in the body, which must be sucked out.
LC NO. FIA65-565
Prod-HEICK Dist-UCEMC 1964

Pompeii C 3 MIN
16MM FILM OPTICAL SOUND P-I
Discusses the city of Pompeii in Italy.
From The Of All Things Series.
Prod-BAILYL Dist-AVED

Pompeii - City Of Painting (200 BC - 79 A D) C 11 MIN
16MM FILM OPTICAL SOUND
Shows how the fact that the prosperous Roman city of Pompeii was buried in the volcanic lava of Vesuvius was their tragedy but our good fortune, for we are left with a perfect record of the life and art of their time dating from 200 BC to 79 A D.
Prod-ROLAND Dist-ROLAND

Pompeii - Frozen In Fire C 29 MIN
3/4 OR 1/2 INCH VIDEO CASSETTE
Features actor Alexander Scourby leading a tour through the spectacular Pompeii AD 79 exhibition, which presents some 300 artifacts from the ancient Roman city.
Prod-WGBHTV Dist-PBS 1978

Pompeii - Once There Was A City C 25 MIN
16MM FILM, 3/4 OR 1/2 IN VIDEO J-C A
Explores the ruins of the ancient city of Pompeii which was buried by volcanic lava in 79 AD. Recreates the everyday lives of its citizens and gradually intersperses shots of modern day living to suggest that Pompeii's doom, which followed an era of unprecedented material prosperity, may have contemporary parallels.
Prod-LCOA Dist-LCOA 1970

Pompeii - Once There Was A City (Spanish) C 25 MIN
16MM FILM, 3/4 OR 1/2 IN VIDEO H-C A
Juxtaposes life in ancient Pompeii with the quality of life in contemporary America. Poses the timeless question of whether man has learned anything from the past.
Prod-LCOA Dist-LCOA 1970

Pompeii And Vesuvius C 11 MIN
16MM FILM, 3/4 OR 1/2 IN VIDEO I-H
Pictures an actual eruption of Mt Vesuvius and the ruins of the city of Pompeii destroyed in 79 A D. Shows life in present-day Naples.
Prod-EBF Dist-EBEC 1951

Pompeii, AD 79 C 23 MIN
16MM FILM, 3/4 OR 1/2 IN VIDEO
Shows how the ruins of Pompeii reveal information about the lives of its townspeople. Includes footage of the travelling exhibit from Italy which made the rounds of major U S museums.
Prod-DOCUA Dist-CNEMAG

Ponce Project, The - Petrochemicals In Puerto Rico C 25 MIN
16MM FILM OPTICAL SOUND
Shows the problems encountered by Bechtel Corporation in constructing a petrochemical complex in Puerto Rico and the management and engineering techniques used in overcoming these problems.
LC NO. 73-700611
Prod-BECHTL Dist-BECHTL 1972

Pond Succession - A Circle Of Life C 17 MIN
3/4 OR 1/2 INCH VIDEO CASSETTE I
Traces the history of a pond, from the creation of a basin to its disappearance as sediment. Explains that this process causes the pond to become more and more shallow.
From The Natural Science Specials Series. Module Blue
Prod-UNPRO Dist-AITECH 1973

Pond Water, Pt 1 C 20 MIN
16MM FILM OPTICAL SOUND T
Shows a sixth grade class in Long Island, New York, on a field trip to a nearby pond. Shows the children's study, experimentation, classification and discussion of the pond life they collect.
From The Elementary Science Study Series.
LC NO. 74-702016
Prod-EDC Dist-EDC 1971

Pond Water, Pt 2 C 19 MIN
16MM FILM OPTICAL SOUND T
Shows a sixth grade class in Long Island, New York, on a field trip to a nearby pond. Shows the children's study, experimentation, classification and discussion of the pond life they collect.
From The Elementary Science Study Series.
LC NO. 74-702016
Prod-EDC Dist-EDC 1971

Pond-Life Food Web C 10 MIN
16MM FILM, 3/4 OR 1/2 IN VIDEO
Examines the microscopic world of a pond, identifying its inhabitants and their interrelationships, including the complex pattern of food chains within the pond.
From The Bio-Science Series.
LC NO. 80-706310
Prod-NGS Dist-NGS 1976

Pond, The B 15 MIN
2 INCH VIDEOTAPE P
Uses a microscope to explore a small natural habitat. (Broadcast quality)
From The Land And Sea Series.
Prod-TTOIC Dist-GPITVL Prodn-WGBHTV

Pond, The C 15 MIN
3/4 OR 1/2 INCH VIDEO CASSETTE P
Draws together concepts introduced in the Let Me See series and establishes their interrelatedness. Shows Myrtle, who is trying to catch a frog for a jumping contest, using her magic animation to show Hocus changes that take place in a pond during the year.
From The Let Me See Series. No. 12
Prod-WETN Dist-AITECH Prodn-STSU 1982

Pond, The C 20 MIN
16MM FILM, 3/4 OR 1/2 IN VIDEO I-H
Examines the interdependent members of the community in a pond, pointing out that the pond provides an environment containing sunlight, minerals and permanent water of relatively constant temperature.
From The Living Science Series.
Prod-IFB Dist-IFB 1961

Pond, The - A First Film C 11 MIN
16MM FILM, 3/4 OR 1/2 IN VIDEO P-I
Examines the community of living things that grows in a pond. Shows that the community changes as the pool changes with the seasons. Points out that over a long period of time, the pool takes on a different form, and life in the pool community is altered to fit the new conditions.
Prod-BFA Dist-PHENIX 1972

Pondicherry Ashram B 8 MIN
16MM FILM OPTICAL SOUND I-C A
Provides glimpses of the Aurobindo Ashram at Pondicherry, where the one-time revolutionary, Aurobindo set up an Ashram and became a 20th century saint and yogi. Discusses various activities of institutions like the Aurobindo International Centre of Education.
Prod-INDIA Dist-NEDINF

Pong San T'al Chum C 32 MIN
3/4 OR 1/2 INCH VIDEO CASSETTE
Shows performances of traditional masked drama of Northern Korea.
Prod-UWASHP Dist-UWASHP

Pong San T'al Chum - Northern Korean Masked Drama C 32 MIN
16MM FILM OPTICAL SOUND I-C A
Describes T'al Chum, a form of masked drama originating around Ping San in North Korea. Explains that the plays are performed outdoors, without a stage, and tells that they consist of short satires on the monks or the ruling class.
From The Ethnic Music And Dance Series.
LC NO. 72-700243
Prod-UWASH Dist-UWASHP 1971

Ponies C 15 MIN
16MM FILM, 3/4 OR 1/2 IN VIDEO I-J A

Shows, without narration, the birth of a foal, ponies frolicking, horses eating, drinking and sleeping and a pony being groomed and winning a ribbon in the show ring.
Prod-MORLAT Dist-AIMS 1972

Ponies Of Miklaengi C 25 MIN
16MM FILM, 3/4 OR 1/2 IN VIDEO K-I
Tells the story of two children in Iceland who, while searching for lost sheep, wander far from home with their horses and witness the birth of a foal during an earthquake. Based on the book Ponies Of Mykillengi by John Lonzo Anderson.
Prod-EVRGRN Dist-PHENIX 1979

Ponies Of Miklaengi (Captioned) C 25 MIN
16MM FILM, 3/4 OR 1/2 IN VIDEO K-I
Tells the story of two children in Iceland who, while searching for lost sheep, wander far from home with their horses and witness the birth of a foal during an earthquake. Based on the book Ponies Of Mykillengi by John lonzo Anderson.
Prod-EVRGRN Dist-PHENIX 1979

Pons, The C 15 MIN
3/4 OR 1/2 INCH VIDEO CASSETTE PRO
Identifies the macroscopic structures of the pons using brain specimens and diagrams. Discusses briefly its physiology and pathology.
From The Neurobiology Series.
Prod-HSCIC Dist-HSCIC

Pontiac Pours It On C 28 MIN
16MM FILM OPTICAL SOUND J-C A
Presents a dramatic 'TOUR' of an auto assembly plant. Shows all phases of auto manufacture - from casting the engine block to final assembly of the completed car along with the many inspections and tests made to assure quality and reliability.
Prod-GM Dist-GM 1971

Pontic Preparation - Labial Contour Gingival Adaptation C 11 MIN
16MM FILM OPTICAL SOUND
Describes steps required for the proper esthetic and functional preparation of pontics for fixed partial dentures.
LC NO. 75-700873
Prod-USVA Dist-USNAC 1969

Pony Express (3rd Ed) C 10 MIN
16MM FILM, 3/4 OR 1/2 IN VIDEO I
Presents the story of the Pony Express, and discusses its role in the development of the nation. Shows how a letter was carried from Missouri to California. Examines the Pony Express relay system of riders and horses, and describes the duties of station agents.
Prod-BARR Dist-BARR 1965

Pony Express, The C 15 MIN
16MM FILM, 3/4 OR 1/2 IN VIDEO I-H
Deals with the history of the Pony Express and conditions in the United States which demanded fast, efficient mail service to the West.
Prod-CALVIN Dist-PHENIX 1977

Pony Express, The C 15 MIN
3/4 OR 1/2 INCH VIDEO CASSETTE P
Relates the unexpected adventures of one boy on a Pony Express ride.
From The Stories Of America Series.
Prod-OHSDE Dist-AITECH Prodn-WVIZTV 1976

Pony Penning On Chincoteague X 24 MIN
16MM FILM OPTICAL SOUND I-H A
Shows a community custom dating from Colonial times-the round-up, penning and sale of the Chincoteague wild ponies.
Prod-VADE Dist-VADE 1955

Pool C 26 MIN
16MM FILM OPTICAL SOUND I-C A
Presents a series of 12 motion pictures made by children ages seven to 16, using animation and live action techniques.
LC NO. 74-701558
Prod-CELLAR Dist-CELLAR 1968

Pool Sharks B 13 MIN
16MM FILM, 3/4 OR 1/2 IN VIDEO I-C A
Shows the art and technique of one of the major screen comedians, W C Fields.
Prod-JANUS Dist-TEXFLM 1915

Poon-Tang Trilogy B 8 MIN
16MM FILM OPTICAL SOUND C
Presents a dadaistic new American film exercise.
Prod-CFS Dist-CFS 1967

Poor Glassblower, The C 24 MIN
16MM FILM, 3/4 OR 1/2 IN VIDEO
Tells a story about a poor man who finds a genie who grants his every wish. Explains how the man becomes greedy and asks for power over nature. Based on the story The Fisherman And His Wife by the Brothers Grimm.
LC NO. 79-707208
Prod-LONNEM Dist-CAROUF 1979

Poor Pay More, The B 60 MIN
16MM FILM OPTICAL SOUND H-C A
Examines the special hardships of the poor in consumer purchasing. Explores pricing practices of supermarket chains, techniques of food freezer salesmen and methods of furniture and appliance stores and finance companies. Presents officials from various private and governmental programs outlining problems and show how they are being confronted.
From The Net Journal Series.
LC NO. FIA67-5070
Prod-NET Dist-IU 1967

Poor Richard And The Maxim - The Style Of Wit C 30 MIN
2 INCH VIDEOTAPE J-H
See series title for descriptive statement.
From The From Franklin To Frost - Benjamin Franklin Series.
Prod-MPATI Dist-GPITVL

Pop Art C 14 MIN
3/4 OR 1/2 INCH VIDEO CASSETTE P-I
Discusses pop art.
From The Young At Art Series.
Prod-WSKJTV Dist-AITECH 1980

Pop Art C 29 MIN
3/4 INCH VIDEO CASSETTE
Discusses effects of advertising and packaging materials on modern day art.
From The Artist At Work Series.
Prod-UMITV Dist-UMITV 1973

Pop Goes The Revolution C 25 MIN
16MM FILM OPTICAL SOUND
Presents correspondent Michael Maclear interviewing pop star Dean Reed, who discusses his music and politics.
LC NO. 77-702519
Prod-CTV Dist-CTV 1976

Pop Show C 8 MIN
16MM FILM OPTICAL SOUND J-C A
Presents a fast-paced barrage of animated comic strips, campy film clips, pop art constructions and live action sequences letting us know what's 'IN' and what's 'OUT.'
Prod-PFP Dist-VIEWFI

Pop-Pop Video - General Hospital, Olympic Women Speed Skating C 6 MIN
3/4 OR 1/2 INCH VIDEO CASSETTE
Juxtaposes the cross-over in Olympic Women Speed Skating and 'whites' in General Hospital. Combines exertion and frustration.
Prod-KITCHN Dist-KITCHN

Pop-Pop Video - Kojak, Wang C 4 MIN
3/4 OR 1/2 INCH VIDEO CASSETTE
Brings the violence of corporate America to life with shots from the television show Kojak and from the television commercial about the Wang Corporation.
Prod-KITCHN Dist-KITCHN

Pop-Pop-Video - General Hospital/Olympic Women Speed Skaters C 6 MIN
3/4 OR 1/2 INCH VIDEO CASSETTE
See series title for descriptive statement.
From The Five Short Works By Dana Birnbaum Series.
Prod-EAI Dist-EAI

Pop-Pop-Video - Kojak Wang C 4 MIN
3/4 OR 1/2 INCH VIDEO CASSETTE
See series title for descriptive statement.
From The Five Short Works By Dana Birnbaum Series.
Prod-EAI Dist-EAI

Popcorn Lady C 11 MIN
16MM FILM, 3/4 OR 1/2 IN VIDEO I-C A
Visits a small town in upstate New York to which change has come slowly. Portrays one of the town's most famous residents, the popcorn lady and shows her steam popcorn machine of 1925 vintage.
Prod-SCHLAT Dist-LUF 1973

Pope - New Cardinals B 8 MIN
16MM FILM OPTICAL SOUND
A Spanish language film. Shows Pope John XII cresting 10 new cardinals, De Gaulle appealing for support of his France-Algerian truce, Buddhist fire rites in Northern Japan and the Israeli-Syrian border dispute.
From The Spanish Newsreel Series. Vol 45, No. 57
Prod-TWCF Dist-TWCF

Pope In America, The - With Liberty And Justice For All C 24 MIN
16MM FILM, 3/4 OR 1/2 IN VIDEO J-C
Records Pope John Paul II's visit to America in October, 1979.
LC NO. 80-707525
Prod-ABCTV Dist-MTI 1980

Pope John Paul II At The United Nations C 28 MIN
3/4 INCH VIDEOTAPE
Interviews Mr Robert Muller, co-ordinator of the Pope's visit to the United Nations. Includes film clips of the Pope's address to the General Assembly, his walk in the U N Gardens and his visit to the office of Secretary-General Kurt Waldheim.
From The International Byline Series.
Prod-PERRYM Dist-PERRYM

Pope John XXIII, 1881-1963 B 16 MIN
16MM FILM OPTICAL SOUND
Highlights the life of Pope John XXIII. Includes his election, the meeting of the Vatican Ecumenical Council in 1962 and his audiences with world leaders.
LC NO. FI67-1005
Prod-MOVIET Dist-TWCF 1963

Pope Paul VI - Pilgrimage To The Holy Land X 10 MIN
16MM FILM OPTICAL SOUND
Pictures the pilgrimage of Pope Paul VI from Rome to the Holy Land. Shows him as he visits Christendom's most sacred shrines in Jordan, Jerusalem, Israel, Nazareth and Bethlehem. Includes views of the meeting of Pope Paul with patriarch Athenagoras.
LC NO. FIA65-1598
Prod-HEARST Dist-HEARST Prodn-CAPFL 1964

Pope Pius XII B 26 MIN
16MM FILM, 3/4 OR 1/2 IN VIDEO J-C A
Presents the life story and deeds of Pope Pius XII.
From The History Makers Of The 20th Century Series.
Prod-WOLPER Dist-SF 1965

Pope, The - Pilgrim Of Peace C 38 MIN
3/4 OR 1/2 INCH VIDEO CASSETTE
Questions whether religion and revolution can co-exist by reviewing Pope John Paul II's controversial visit to Nicaragua in 1983. Interviews Ernesto Cardenal, a priest and Minister of Culture of the Sandinista government and Miguel Concha, a Mexican theologian and member of the Dominican order.
Prod-REITIR Dist-ICARUS 1983

Popes And Their Art, The - The Vatican Collections C 52 MIN
16MM FILM, 3/4 OR 1/2 IN VIDEO J-C A
Views a great portion of the Vatican art collection which includes works by such masters as Michelangelo, da Vinci, Raphael, Bernini and Caravaggio. Shows the work necessary to maintain it against the effects of modern pollution and age.
LC NO. 84-707375
Prod-NBCNEW Dist-FI 1983

Popliteal Region And Leg - Unit 24 C 29 MIN
3/4 OR 1/2 INCH VIDEO CASSETTE PRO
Covers the popliteal fossa, the anterior and posterior compartments of the leg, including the muscles of the superficial and deep layers and the neurovascular bundles, the lateral compartment and the knee.
From The Gross Anatomy Prosection Demonstration Series.
Prod-HSCIC Dist-HSCIC

Poppa's Legacy C 3 MIN
16MM FILM OPTICAL SOUND
Combines live action and animation in telling the story of a father who wills his three sons a claim check. Tells how after a lengthy search the sons discover their reward from their father's estate.
LC NO. 78-701323
Prod-RODGR Dist-RODGR 1978

Poppe Project, The - Behavior Shaping With The Severely Retarded B 23 MIN
16MM FILM OPTICAL SOUND PRO
Documents a project studying a group of severely retarded children using operant conditioning techniques to shape their behavior in areas of eating, dressing, structured and unstructured play, group interaction and socialization on a beginning level.
LC NO. FIA67-2090
Prod-DARDNM Dist-UCEMC 1967

Popsicle C 10 MIN
16MM FILM, 3/4 OR 1/2 IN VIDEO
Points out that motorcycling is one of the fastest growing sports in America. Includes scenes of motorcycles on racetracks, climbing hills and on pleasure outings.
Prod-GRENWL Dist-AMEDFL 1969

Popular Culture In Dance—A Series

Presents programs from the New York City Cable TV series Eye On Dance.
Prod-ARCVID Dist-ARCVID

Black Dancers And Choreography In Films	030 MIN
How Popular Dance Came To The Stage	030 MIN
World Of 'Hip Hop,' The - Rapping, Break	030 MIN

Popular Dickens, The C 29 MIN
3/4 INCH VIDEO CASSETTE
Explores the life, success and philosophy of Charles Dickens.
From The Dickens World Series.
Prod-UMITV Dist-UMITV 1973

Popularity Storage - Planning The Storage Layout C 20 MIN
16MM FILM OPTICAL SOUND
Discusses planning the storage layout in popularity storage. Shows storage space, layout, control of space, material positioning and the design of a stock location system.
LC NO. 75-700874
Prod-USN Dist-USNAC 1958

Popularity Storage - Principles Of Stock Positioning C 18 MIN
16MM FILM OPTICAL SOUND
Shows basic principles of popularity storage, including similarity, size, characteristics and the advantage of stock positioning at all levels of the supply system.
LC NO. 75-700572
Prod-USN Dist-USNAC 1958

Population C 29 MIN
3/4 OR 1/2 INCH VIDEO CASSETTE
Investigates the effects of population pressures on sex through a look at how sex and sexuality change according to population density and neighborhood structure. Includes descriptions of clinical experiments. Features Milton Diamond, Ph D, a biologist at the University of Hawaii, talking with Walter B Quisenberry, MD, Hawaii Department of Health, about population legislation and control.
From The Human Sexuality Series.
Prod-KHETTV Dist-PBS

Population C 29 MIN
3/4 INCH VIDEO CASSETTE
Looks at the effects of birth and death rates in the East and West.
From The Social Animal Series.
Prod-UMITV Dist-UMITV 1974

Population - Whose Problem Is It? C 29 MIN
3/4 INCH VIDEO CASSETTE
Examines birth control, economics, food production, resource consumption and attitudes of third world countries.
From The Issue At Hand Series.
Prod-UMITV Dist-UMITV 1976

Population And Pollution C 17 MIN
16MM FILM, 3/4 OR 1/2 IN VIDEO I-H

Portrays the environmental crisis in North America caused both by misuse of the environment and by the great demands of a constantly growing population. Emphasizes the need for changes in attitude and for a commitment to finding both short-range and long-range solutions to the problems of air, water and land pollution.
Prod-IFB Dist-IFB Prodn-BERLET 1971

Population And The American Future, Pt 1 C 30 MIN
16MM FILM OPTICAL SOUND H-C
Reports the President's Commission on Population Growth and the American Future's findings on the economic, social, political, environmental and ethical aspects of past and present population trends and future population growth in the United States. Examines the consequences of unlimited population increase on various facets of U S society and shows why the population should become stabilized.
LC NO. 73-701825
Prod-FFG Dist-FFG 1973

Population And The American Future, Pt 2 C 30 MIN
16MM FILM OPTICAL SOUND H-C
Reports the President's Commission on Population Growth and the American Future's findings on the economic, social, political, environmental and ethical aspects of past and present population trends and future population growth in the United States. Emphasizes the need for education of the population regarding consequences of unlimited growth and stresses the ideal of family planning.
LC NO. 73-701825
Prod-FFG Dist-FFG 1973

Population Crisis - India C 16 MIN
3/4 OR 1/2 INCH VIDEO CASSETTE H-C A
Points out that if India is to solve her economic and social problems, the population growth must be sharply reduced. Interviews India's Health Minister.
Prod-UPI Dist-JOU

Population Ecology X 19 MIN
16MM FILM, 3/4 OR 1/2 IN VIDEO H
Shows how environmental conditions, such as natural enemies and food factors, can help increase or reduce births and deaths. Discusses how man, with his ability to change environment, has created the birth surplus over death called the population explosion.
From The Biology Series. Unit 1 - Ecology
Prod-EBF Dist-EBEC 1964

Population Ecology (Spanish) C 19 MIN
16MM FILM, 3/4 OR 1/2 IN VIDEO H
Analyzes the effects of environment as they relate to birth rates, showing the influence of natural enemies, food and other environmental factors on population.
From The Biology (Spanish) Series. Unit 1 - Ecology
Prod-EBEC Dist-EBEC

Population Et Pollution C 17 MIN
16MM FILM, 3/4 OR 1/2 IN VIDEO I-H
A French language version of Population And Pollution. Portrays the environmental crisis in North America caused both by misuse of the environment and by the great demands of a constantly growing population. Emphasizes the need for changes in attitude and for a commitment to finding both short-range and long-range solutions to the problems of air, water and land pollution.
Prod-IFB Dist-IFB Prodn-BERLET 1971

Population Explosion, The C 20 MIN
3/4 INCH VIDEO CASSETTE H-C
See series title for descriptive statement.
From The Geography For The '70's Series.
Prod-KLRNTV Dist-GPITVL

Population Growth C 30 MIN
3/4 OR 1/2 INCH VIDEO CASSETTE C
Discusses the ability of humankind to control the earth's population and to increase the earth's capacity to carry more people.
From The Living Environment Series.
Prod-DALCCD Dist-DALCCD

Population Problem--A Series
16MM FILM, 3/4 OR 1/2 IN VIDEO H-C A
Prod-NET Dist-IU Prodn-INSGHT 1965

Brazil - The Gathering Millions	30 MIN
European Experience, The	30 MIN
Gift Of Choice, The	30 MIN
India - Writing On The Sand	30 MIN
Japan - Answer In The Orient	30 MIN
U S A - Seeds Of Change	30 MIN

Population Story, A - Collision With The Future C 24 MIN
16MM FILM, 3/4 OR 1/2 IN VIDEO J-C
Reveals startling facts about population growth.
LC NO. 83-707266
Prod-EBEC Dist-EBEC 1984

Population Time-Bomb C 28 MIN
16MM FILM OPTICAL SOUND
Compares and contrasts the responses of El Salvador and Costa Rica to their overpopulation problems.
From The Oasis In Space Series.
LC NO. 77-702407
Prod-COSTU Dist-EDMDC 1976

Populations C 16 MIN
16MM FILM, 3/4 OR 1/2 IN VIDEO
Defines populations, investigates the social structure of various populations, illustrates the speed of unchecked population growth, and considers the factors that cause a given population to grow or decline.
Prod-CENTRO Dist-CORF

Por Primera Vez (English) B 10 MIN
16MM FILM OPTICAL SOUND
Explains how the Cuban Film Institute sends mobile film units into the rural provinces and how villagers delight in seeing movies for the first time.
Prod-SFN Dist-SFN

Por Que Juanito (English) C 20 MIN
16MM FILM OPTICAL SOUND
Presents the problem of protein hunger among children of Latin America. Designed primarily for heads of state and policy making specialists in nutrition, economics and agriculture.
Prod-USAID Dist-USNAC Prodn-HF 1966

Porcelain Jacket Crown, Pt 1 - The Matrix C 9 MIN
16MM FILM, 3/4 OR 1/2 IN VIDEO PRO
Depicts the laboratory steps involved in the fabrication of a porcelain jacket crown.
LC NO. 81-706366
Prod-VADTC Dist-USNAC 1977

Porcelain Jacket Crown, Pt 2 - Porcelain Build-Up C 17 MIN
16MM FILM, 3/4 OR 1/2 IN VIDEO PRO
Describes the proper manipulation of the materials used in building up a porcelain jacket crown.
LC NO. 81-706367
Prod-VADTC Dist-USNAC 1977

Porcelain Protected Surface Wiring B 19 MIN
16MM FILM, 3/4 OR 1/2 IN VIDEO IND
Explains how to make an electrical entrance to a building, install wiring and porcelain fittings, support and insulate wires, and prepare and connect wires for service. Issued in 1944 as a motion picture.
From The Electrical Work - Wiring Series. No. 9
LC NO. 79-707486
Prod-USOE Dist-USNAC Prodn-RAYBEL 1979

Porcelain-Fused-To-Gold Crowns And Bridges, Pt 1 - Tooth Preparation C 13 MIN
16MM FILM, 3/4 OR 1/2 IN VIDEO
Demonstrates the correct tooth preparation for porcelain-fused-to-gold crowns, emphasizing adherence to basic principles and techniques. Presents results in the production of an accurate fitting and esthetically pleasing fixed partial denture.
Prod-USVA Dist-USNAC 1972

Porcelain-Fused-To-Gold Crowns And Bridges, Pt I - Tooth Preparation C 13 MIN
3/4 OR 1/2 INCH VIDEO CASSETTE
Presents the basic principles of tooth preparations for porcelain-fused-to-gold restorations.
Prod-VADTC Dist-AMDA 1972

Porcelain-Fused-To-Gold Crowns And Bridges, Pt 2 - Gingival Retraction And Die Preparation C 9 MIN
16MM FILM, 3/4 OR 1/2 IN VIDEO
Shows that accurately fitting gingival margins can be achieved by carefully adhering to the principles and details of gingival retraction. Demonstrates the impression technique and die preparation.
Prod-USVA Dist-USNAC 1972

Porcelain-Fused-To-Gold Crowns And Bridges, Pt II - Gingival Retraction And Die Preparation C 9 MIN
3/4 OR 1/2 INCH VIDEO CASSETTE
Demonstrates the use of gingival retraction cord to create adequate space for rubber base impression material, the impression technique and the die preparation procedures.
Prod-VADTC Dist-AMDA 1972

Porcelain-Fused-To-Gold Fixed Partial Denture - Esthetics Control System, Pt 1... C 17 MIN
16MM FILM, 3/4 OR 1/2 IN VIDEO
Discusses the examination of the patient and tooth preparation. Demonstrates an extraoral method for constructing a temporary restoration that protects the involved teeth.
Prod-USVA Dist-USNAC 1974

Porcelain-Fused-To-Gold Fixed Partial Denture - Esthetics Control System, Pt 2 -... C 8 MIN
16MM FILM, 3/4 OR 1/2 IN VIDEO
Discusses the preparation of a fixed partial denture. Describes the laboratory procedures for developing wax patterns whose dimensions and contours are controlled by preoperative stents.
Prod-USVA Dist-USNAC 1974

Porcelain-Fused-To-Gold Fixed Partial Denture - Esthetics Control System, Pt 3 - Veneering... C 8 MIN
16MM FILM OPTICAL SOUND
Discusses the preparation of a fixed partial denture. Shows procedures for preparing and veneering the casting for an anterior bridge. Demonstrates the use of the polypropylene stents in the laboratory phase and the final cementation of the bridge.
LC NO. 75-701321
Prod-USVA Dist-USNAC 1974

Porcelain-Fused-To-Gold, Fixed Partial Denture, An Esthetic Control System, Pt I... C 17 MIN
3/4 OR 1/2 INCH VIDEO CASSETTE
Begins a presentation on the esthetic control system for fixed partial dentures. Deals with the examination of the patient, tooth preparation and extraoral method for constructing a temporary restoration that will provide protection to the involved teeth.
Prod-VADTC Dist-AMDA 1974

Porcelain-Fused-To-Gold, Fixed Partial Denture, An Esthetic Control System, Pt II... C 8 MIN
3/4 OR 1/2 INCH VIDEO CASSETTE
Describes the laboratory procedures for developing wax patterns whose dimensions and contours are controlled by preoperative stents.
Prod-VADTC Dist-AMDA 1974

Porcelain-Fused-To-Gold, Fixed Partial Denture, An Esthetic Control System, Pt III C 8 MIN
3/4 OR 1/2 INCH VIDEO CASSETTE
Details the procedures for preparing and veneering the casting of an anterior bridge. Shows the use of polypropylene stents in the laboratory phase.
Prod-VADTC Dist-AMDA 1974

Porcelain-Fused-To-Metal, Vita System, Pt 1 - A Single Crown C 17 MIN
16MM FILM - 3/4 IN VIDEO PRO
Demonstrates procedures for making porcelain-fused-to-metal crowns, from application and condensation to firing and cooling. Considers esthetic factors such as color, translucency and labial contour age.
LC NO. 78-706283
Prod-USVA Dist-USNAC Prodn-VADTC 1978

Porcelain-Fused-To-Metal, Vita System, Pt 2 - Multiple Unit Restoration C 17 MIN
16MM FILM - 3/4 IN VIDEO PRO
Demonstrates techniques of multiple-unit porcelain-veneer restoration.
LC NO. 78-706284
Prod-USVA Dist-USNAC Prodn-VADTC 1978

Pork - The Meal With A Squeal C 12 MIN
16MM FILM, 3/4 OR 1/2 IN VIDEO I-J
Surveys the highly mechanized pork industry.
Prod-CENTRO Dist-CORF

Pork Purchasing Guidelines - Training Program C
3/4 OR 1/2 INCH VIDEO CASSETTE
Consists of a pork purchasing training program. Shows foodservices staff how to make better pork purchases through proper use of specifications. Covers the versatility and usefulness of pork.
Prod-NLSAMB Dist-NLSAMB

Porklips Now C 22 MIN
16MM FILM, 3/4 OR 1/2 IN VIDEO H-C A
Offers a satire of the film Apocalypse Now.
Prod-PFP Dist-PFP 1980

Pornography C 29 MIN
3/4 INCH VIDEO CASSETTE
Presents a discussion of the effects of pornography on children, crime rates and morality.
From The Woman Series.
Prod-WNEDTV Dist-PUBTEL

Pornography And Fantasy C 29 MIN
3/4 OR 1/2 INCH VIDEO CASSETTE
Features Milton Diamond, Ph D, a biologist at the University of Hawaii, leading a field trip through a neighborhood noted for its pornographic shops and theatres. Includes movie clips chosen by a church society to represent good and bad sex and illustrates the relationship of pornography to sexual expression through a dance sequence.
From The Human Sexuality Series.
Prod-KHETTV Dist-PBS

Porosity And Permeability B 26 MIN
16MM FILM OPTICAL SOUND C A
Defines porosity and permeability and distinguishes between the two. Discusses and categorizes origin and kinds of voids and describes the sequence of development that rock history will have on the development of porosity and permeability in sandstone, limestone and lime mud.
Prod-UTEX Dist-UTEX 1960

Porpoise With A Purpose, A B 5 MIN
16MM FILM OPTICAL SOUND J-H
Tells how Navy scientists are studying, training and testing a porpoise to discover characteristics that can be adapted to submarines, torpedoes and the development of a sonar system as accurate as that of a porpoise.
From The Screen News Digest Series. Vol 4, Issue 9
Prod-HEARST Dist-HEARST 1962

Port Moresby C 9 MIN
16MM FILM OPTICAL SOUND J-C A
Presents a day in the life of Port Moresby, New Guinea.
Prod-ANAIB Dist-AUIS 1971

Port Noarlunga Reef C 10 MIN
16MM FILM OPTICAL SOUND I-C A
Shows the only marine sanctuary on the southern Australian coast, 22 miles from Adelaid, the capital of South Australia, which is visited by three skin divers.
From The Ecology Of The Ocean Series.
LC NO. 78-709355
Prod-STEEND Dist-AMEDFL 1970

Port Of Call C 15 MIN
3/4 OR 1/2 INCH VIDEO CASSETTE P-I
Summarizes the role of the Great Lakes as a transportation link.
From The Explorers Unlimited Series.
Prod-WVIZTV Dist-AITECH 1971

Port Of Preparedness C 23 MIN
16MM FILM OPTICAL SOUND
Shows how port managements from coast to coast and from the Great Lakes to the Gulf are now making preparations to meet emergencies.
LC NO. 74-705385
Prod-USOCD Dist-USNAC 1967

Port Safety - Vessel Inspection C 23 MIN
16MM FILM OPTICAL SOUND A
Shows inspection procedures for vessels and explains the legal responsibilities of the U S Coast Guard's captain of the port for the inspection of cargo and tank vessels.
LC NO. 77-702237
Prod-USCG Dist-USNAC 1977

Port Safety - Waterfront Facilities Inspection C 15 MIN
16MM FILM OPTICAL SOUND A
Discusses duties and legal responsibilities of the Coast Guard's captain of the port. Shows how the Coast Guard inspects waterfront facilities and informs owners of violations.
LC NO. 77-702206
Prod-USCG Dist-USNAC 1972

Portable Electric Sander C 13 MIN
16MM FILM, 3/4 OR 1/2 IN VIDEO J-C A
Presents six concepts dealing with the portable electric sander--types of sanders, abrasive belts, parts of the belt sander, coarse sanding - belt sander, fine sanding - belt sander, and orbital sander. The projector may be stopped after each concept.
From The Woodwork - Machine Tools Series.
Prod-SF Dist-SF 1967

Portable Electric Saws C 22 MIN
16MM FILM, 3/4 OR 1/2 IN VIDEO A
Demonstrates the metal frame and plastic frame saw and discusses the advantages of each. Covers ripping, cross-cutting, bevelcutting of wood, and use of saw in cutting metals and masonry.
Prod-BFA Dist-PHENIX 1969

Portable Electric Saws (Spanish) C 22 MIN
16MM FILM, 3/4 OR 1/2 IN VIDEO A
Demonstrates the metal frame and plastic frame saw and discusses the advantages of each. Covers ripping, cross-cutting, bevelcutting of wood, and use of saw in cutting metals and masonry.
Prod-BFA Dist-PHENIX 1969

Portable Extinguisers (Korean) C
3/4 OR 1/2 INCH VIDEO CASSETTE IND
Opens with explanation of how extinguishers are rated and expected delivery rate. Looks at different types available, their use, importance of technique and how to use most effectively.
From The Marine Firefighting Series. Pt 2
Prod-GPCV Dist-GPCV

Portable Extinguishers C
3/4 OR 1/2 INCH VIDEO CASSETTE IND
Opens with explanation of how extinguishers are rated and expected delivery rate. Looks at different types available, their use, importance of technique and how to use most effectively.
From The Marine Firefighting Series. Pt 2
Prod-GPCV Dist-GPCV

Portable Extinguishers (Italian) C
3/4 OR 1/2 INCH VIDEO CASSETTE IND
Opens with explanation of how extinguishers are rated and expected delivery rate. Looks at different types available, their use, importance of techniques and how to use most effectively.
From The Marine Firefighting Series. Pt 2
Prod-GPCV Dist-GPCV

Portable Fire Extinguishers C 20 MIN
16MM FILM, 3/4 OR 1/2 IN VIDEO J-C A
Examines different kinds of fire extinguishers, giving their classifications and providing instruction on their use.
Prod-IOWA Dist-FILCOM 1966

Portable Fire Protection Methods C 60 MIN
3/4 OR 1/2 INCH VIDEO CASSETTE IND
See series title for descriptive statement.
From The Industrial Fire Hazard Recognition And Control Series.
Prod-NCSU Dist-AMCEE

Portable Garden, The C 29 MIN
2 INCH VIDEOTAPE
See series title for descriptive statement.
From The Making Things Grow III Series.
Prod-WGBHTV Dist-PUBTEL

Portable Ladders C 6 MIN
3/4 OR 1/2 INCH VIDEO CASSETTE IND
Depicts the variety of hazards involved in using unsafe ladders or work habits.
From The Take Ten For Safety Series.
Prod-OLINC Dist-MTI

Portable Life, A C 30 MIN
3/4 OR 1/2 INCH VIDEO CASSETTE PRO
Introduces the executive and spouse to the realities of living overseas and problems of adjusting to different cultures and conditions. Describes the experiences of four wives who have lived on four continents.
LC NO. 83-706167
Prod-MCGILL Dist-SYRFRC 1982

Portable Phonograph By Walter Van Tilburg Clark, The X 24 MIN
16MM FILM, 3/4 OR 1/2 IN VIDEO J-C A
Presents The Portable Phonograph by Walter Van Tilburg Clark in which four survivors of a devastating war gather in a dugout built by soldiers to hear the portable phonograph one of them has saved.
From The Humanities - Short Story Showcase Series.
Prod-EBEC Dist-EBEC 1977

Portable Phonograph, The C 29 MIN
2 INCH VIDEOTAPE H-C A
Presents Walter Van Tilburg Clark's story about survivors of the world's final holocaust, adapted into an original drama.
From The Just Generation Series.
Prod-WITFTV Dist-PUBTEL 1972

Portable Power Tools C 17 MIN
16MM FILM, 3/4 OR 1/2 IN VIDEO
Demonstrates the electric drill belt sander, orbital sander and saber saw and emphasizes safety. Shows each in detailed working operation.
Prod-BFA Dist-PHENIX 1968

Portable Power Tools (Spanish) C 17 MIN
16MM FILM, 3/4 OR 1/2 IN VIDEO
Demonstrates the electric drill belt sander, orbital sander and saber saw and emphasizes safety. Shows each in detailed working operation.
Prod-BFA Dist-PHENIX 1968

Portable Sander-Grinder Operation C 23 MIN
1/2 IN VIDEO CASSETTE BETA/VHS IND
Demonstrates the operation of a sander-grinder, with different types of grinding wheel attachments.
Prod-RMI Dist-RMI

Portal Decompression C 30 MIN
16MM FILM OPTICAL SOUND PRO
Uses animation to depict the anatomy and physiology of hepatic circulation and to explain the etiologic factors responsible for portal hypertension. Presents a case study of a patient for whom portal decompression is indicated and shows the surgical procedure.
Prod-SQUIBB Dist-SQUIBB

Portal Hypertension C 30 MIN
3/4 OR 1/2 INCH VIDEO CASSETTE
Discusses the diagnosis and management of bleeding varices and the selection of the proper type of shunt to prevent recurrent hemorrhage without impairment of liver function.
Prod-ROWLAB Dist-ROWLAB

Portals Of Vision C 3 MIN
16MM FILM OPTICAL SOUND
Combines abstract sound and images to form reality in one continuous take.
LC NO. 81-700398
Prod-MARGAR Dist-MARGAR 1980

Portion Control - A Team Effort C 12 MIN
16MM FILM, 3/4 OR 1/2 IN VIDEO
Introduces the basic economics of restaurant portion control as it affects jobs and careers. Demonstrates proper techniques of measuring, weighing, preparing and serving food.
From The Professional Food Preparation And Service Programs Series.
Prod-NEM Dist-NEM 1983

Portion Control - Using Scoops and Ladles C 20 MIN
1/2 IN VIDEO CASSETTE BETA/VHS
Describes various scoops, ladles and institutionally packed cans which aid the food service worker in portion control. Demonstrates portioning and ladling products.
Prod-RMI Dist-RMI

Portland Cement Concrete Field Sampling And Testing C 26 MIN
3/4 OR 1/2 INCH VIDEO CASSETTE
Illustrates techniques for the sampling and testing of Portland cement concrete. Includes tests for air, slump, and yield.
LC NO. 81-706786
Prod-USFHAD Dist-USNAC 1981

Portland Cement Concrete Field Sampling And Testing C 26 MIN
16MM FILM OPTICAL SOUND
Illustrates techniques for the sampling and testing of Portland cement concrete. Includes tests for air, slump, yield, casting of cylinders for compressive strength, making of beams for flexural strength, and the ball and chase indicator for entrained air.
LC NO. 81-700880
Prod-USDTFH Dist-USNAC 1981

Portland Glass C 30 MIN
3/4 INCH VIDEO CASSETTE
See series title for descriptive statement.
From The Antiques Series.
Prod-NHMNET Dist-PUBTEL

Portrait C 7 MIN
16MM FILM OPTICAL SOUND H-C
Shows men, machinery and laboratory techniques in a research and development laboratory concerned with materials, processes and testing.
LC NO. 70-711401
Prod-SANDIA Dist-SANDIA 1970

Portrait C 20 MIN
16MM FILM OPTICAL SOUND
Portrays the rejection of an artist.
LC NO. 75-703531
Prod-WILLMD Dist-WILLMD 1975

Portrait - Angus Wilson C 30 MIN
3/4 INCH VIDEO CASSETTE
Features novelist and professor Angus Wilson as he discusses preparation for writing.
Prod-UMITV Dist-UMITV 1979

Portrait - Joseph Heller C 30 MIN
3/4 INCH VIDEO CASSETTE
Interviews Joseph Heller, author of CATCH 22 and SOMETHING HAPPENED, as he discusses his novels, the thirteen-year interim between them and the creative pressures that resulted in his second novel.
Prod-UMITV Dist-UMITV 1975

Portrait - Maggie Kuhn C 30 MIN
3/4 INCH VIDEO CASSETTE
Features Maggie Kuhn, leader of the Gray Panther Network, as she discusses projects, issues, achievements and aspirations of the Gray Panthers.
Prod-UMITV Dist-UMITV 1979

Portrait De Moliere C 62 MIN
16MM FILM OPTICAL SOUND H-C A
A French language motion picture which evokes the life and character of the great French playwright, Moliere. Presents in chronological order the events of Moliere's life and the process of artistic creation by which Moliere transformed his contemporaries into stereotyped characters of segments of society.
Prod-TRANSW Dist-TRANSW 1972

Portrait De Moliere C 62 MIN
16MM FILM, 3/4 OR 1/2 IN VIDEO
A French language videocassette with English subtitles. Offers a series of scenes from the plays of Moliere.
Prod-IFB Dist-IFB 1972

Portrait In Black - A Philip Randolph C 10 MIN
16MM FILM OPTICAL SOUND J-C A
Presents A Philip Randolph, the man whose vision has shaped the Black Labor Movement for half a century, recalling confrontations with Roosevelt and Kennedy and speaking of the continuing struggle for dignity and job equality for Black Americans.
LC NO. 72-702845
Prod-REPRO Dist-REPRO

Portrait In Black - Fannie Lou Hamer C 10 MIN
16MM FILM OPTICAL SOUND
Presents a memorable chronicle of a movement and a people in the words and songs of the Southern black. Portrays Fannie Lou Hamer, the great heroine of the bitter struggle for justice in Mississippi speaking of non-violence and Black-Power.
LC NO. 73-701085
Prod-REPRO Dist-REPRO

Portrait In Painting, The C 21 MIN
16MM FILM, 3/4 OR 1/2 IN VIDEO J-C A
Depicts the transformation of the art of portraiture over many centuries.
Prod-CFDLD Dist-CORF

Portrait In Pastel C 29 MIN
3/4 INCH VIDEO CASSETTE
Focuses on facial bone structure. Demonstrates how to create a convincing face with pastels.
From The Artist At Work Series.
Prod-UMITV Dist-UMITV 1973

Portrait Of A Blind Man B 5 MIN
16MM FILM OPTICAL SOUND
Depicts the everyday life of a blind man living in Montreal.
LC NO. 76-702043
Prod-CONCRU Dist-CONCRU 1975

Portrait Of A Champion Featuring Alysa Gould C 12 MIN
16MM FILM OPTICAL SOUND
Presents Alysa Gould, the high school All-American world class diver, who has won two first places on the one and three meter springboard at the European Diving Games in Zandvoort, Holland. Describes the physical fitness program she has followed to become and stay physically fit.
Prod-GEMILL Dist-GEMILL

Portrait Of A Champion Featuring Mark Wheaton C 12 MIN
16MM FILM OPTICAL SOUND
Presents Mark Wheaton, the 1975 Minnesota State High School Tennis Champion. Describes and illustrates some of the methods he uses to become and stay physically fit.
Prod-GEMILL Dist-GEMILL

Portrait Of A Champion Featuring Tom Ross C 12 MIN
16MM FILM OPTICAL SOUND
Presents Tom Ross,the All-American hockey player at Michigan State University, who was the top scoring hockey player in the nation as a junior. Describes his physical fitness program and shows how it paid off at the Michigan State-Minnesota hockey game.
Prod-GEMILL Dist-GEMILL

Portrait Of A City B 21 MIN
16MM FILM OPTICAL SOUND I-C A
Presents views of the people in the city of Calcutta.
Prod-INDIA Dist-NEDINF

Portrait Of A City - Washington, DC C 28 MIN
16MM FILM OPTICAL SOUND
Familiarizes the viewer with the nation's capital and the meaning behind the historic monuments and buildings.
Prod-EKC Dist-EKC 1976

Portrait Of A Coal Miner C 15 MIN
16MM FILM, 3/4 OR 1/2 IN VIDEO P-I
Presents a portrait of a West Virginia coal miner and his family.
From The Community Life In America Series.
LC NO. 80-706259
Prod-NGS Dist-NGS 1980

Portrait Of A Coast C 29 MIN
16MM FILM OPTICAL SOUND C A
Details the natural and human-exacerbated causes of the erosion which is making the east coast of United States sink at the rate of one foot every 100 years.
LC NO. 82-700934
Prod-COPRO Dist-COPRO 1982

Portrait Of A Conductor C 43 MIN
16MM FILM OPTICAL SOUND

Focuses on conductor David Zinman.
LC NO. 81-700420
Prod-SHWFI Dist-SHWFI 1981

Portrait Of A Deaf City C 15 MIN
16MM FILM, 3/4 OR 1/2 IN VIDEO J-C A
Presents the powerful and the powerless who view their city. Features eight adult insights from the deputy mayor, the black militant, the police, the poverty lawyer, the community organizer and suburbanite and the businessman.
Prod-REPRO Dist-SF

Portrait Of A Disciplinarian C 30 MIN
3/4 OR 1/2 INCH VIDEO CASSETTE C A
Presents an adaptation of the short story Portrait Of A Disciplinarian by P G Wodehouse.
From The Wodehouse Playhouse Series.
Prod-BBCTV Dist-TIMLIF 1980

Portrait Of A Fisherman C 15 MIN
16MM FILM, 3/4 OR 1/2 IN VIDEO K-I
Follows New England fisherman John Sanfilippo and his crew as they go fishing. Shows how his wife is involved in his business and looks at life in a fishing town.
From The Community Life In America Series.
LC NO. 81-707375
Prod-NGS Dist-NGS 1981

Portrait Of A Horse C 8 MIN
16MM FILM OPTICAL SOUND
Presents the story of a proud, freedom-loving horse that a man tries to subdue.
LC NO. 71-712463
Prod-GIERSZ Dist-VIEWFI 1970

Portrait Of A Killer C 18 MIN
16MM FILM OPTICAL SOUND
Details symptoms and signs of Reye's Syndrome, a fatal disease in children.
Prod-MTP Dist-MTP

Portrait Of A Killer C 58 MIN
16MM FILM OPTICAL SOUND
Uses special photographic techniques to go through the cardiovascular system while discussing the causes of heart attacks and strokes. Shows a heart attack and stroke in progress.
From The Nova Series.
Prod-WGBHTV Dist-KINGFT

Portrait Of A Killer C 58 MIN
3/4 INCH VIDEO CASSETTE
Shows the process and progress of cardiovascular disease filmed inside the human body by a lens with a focal length of half a millimeter. Includes footage of a stroke and heart attack in progress. Photographed by Swedish photographer Lennart Nilsson.
From The Nova Series.
Prod-WGBHTV Dist-PBS 1980

Portrait Of A Mime B 11 MIN
16MM FILM OPTICAL SOUND
Takes a look at the work of a mime artist.
LC NO. 76-701355
Prod-YORKU Dist-YORKU 1975

Portrait Of A Minority Group - Americans Of Hispanic Heritage In The United States C 37 MIN
16MM FILM - 3/4 IN VIDEO
Portrays Spanish-speaking Americans in the United States, focusing on Puerto Ricans, Mexican Americans and Latin Americans. Describes the similarities and differences of each group.
LC NO. 79-707954
Prod-USCSC Dist-USNAC 1979

Portrait Of A Nurse C 28 MIN
16MM FILM OPTICAL SOUND
Depicts the role of the nurse as the profession moves toward assuming greater responsibility in the delivery of health care.
LC NO. 77-702123
Prod-BFF Dist-BFF 1976

Portrait Of A President - Lyndon Baines Johnson B 17 MIN
16MM FILM OPTICAL SOUND J A
Traces the life of Lyndon Baines Johnson from his birth in 1908 to his presidency in 1963.
From The Screen News Digest Series. Vol 6, Issue 6.
LC NO. FIA68-2077
Prod-HEARST Dist-HEARST 1964

Portrait Of A Profession C 28 MIN
3/4 OR 1/2 INCH VIDEO CASSETTE H-C A
Shows the many facets of a dental practice and stresses the importance of dentist-patient relationships.
Prod-AMDA Dist-AMDA 1978

Portrait Of A Profession C 30 MIN
3/4 OR 1/2 INCH VIDEO CASSETTE C
Gives an overview of the accounting profession.
From The Accounting Series. Pt 1
Prod-UMA Dist-GPITVL 1980

Portrait Of A Railroad C 26 MIN
16MM FILM OPTICAL SOUND
Offers a look at the people and operations of the nation's longest railroad, the Burlington Northern.
LC NO. 73-701621
Prod-THOMPN Dist-THOMPN 1973

Portrait Of A Rebel - Margaret Sanger C 96 MIN
3/4 OR 1/2 INCH VIDEO CASSETTE H-C A
Details the efforts of Margaret Sanger to repeal the Comstock Act which forbade the dissemination of birth control information. Details her relationship with psychologist Havelock Ellis. Stars Bonnie Franklin and David Dukes.
Prod-TIMLIF Dist-TIMLIF 1982

Portrait Of A Sensei C 30 MIN
16MM FILM OPTICAL SOUND
Presents a portrait of the art of Amanji Inoue, a Japanese Sensei and master porcelain potter.
LC NO. 73-700903
Prod-TOURTE Dist-TOURTE 1973

Portrait Of A Small Hydro, A C 28 MIN
16MM FILM, 3/4 OR 1/2 IN VIDEO J-C A
Looks at the experiences of three hydroelectric entrepreneurs who have bought up old dam sites and are rebuilding them for the production of power.
Prod-LIVNGN Dist-BULFRG 1984

Portrait Of A Steelworker C 15 MIN
16MM FILM, 3/4 OR 1/2 IN VIDEO I-J
Looks at one of the steel mills in southwestern Pennsylvania and introduces a steelworker and his family.
From The Community Life In America Series.
Prod-NGS Dist-NGS 1981

Portrait Of A Teenage Shoplifter C 47 MIN
16MM FILM, 3/4 OR 1/2 IN VIDEO I-H
Tells the story of Karen, a teenage shoplifter, who steals clothes and makeup she can't afford to attract her boyfriend, the school basketball star. Reveals that when she is finally caught, she must face the consequences.
From The Teenage Years Series.
Prod-ALAMAR Dist-TIMLIF 1984

Portrait Of A University C 20 MIN
16MM FILM OPTICAL SOUND
Presents a guided tour through the campus of West Virginia University. Describes the university's functions of education, research and service to the state.
LC NO. 74-701397
Prod-WVAU Dist-WVAU

Portrait Of A Vandal C 13 MIN
16MM FILM, 3/4 OR 1/2 IN VIDEO
Reenacts a true story about a group of boys who vandalize a classmate's house. Deals with the apprehension they experience and the effects on their parents when their identity becomes known.
LC NO. 79-707585
Prod-CENTRO Dist-CORF 1979

Portrait Of A Whale C 12 MIN
16MM FILM, 3/4 OR 1/2 IN VIDEO P-I
Presents a lyrical look at the right whale, perhaps the rarest of the great whales. Takes a close look at the whale's eye, tail, mouth and blowhole.
LC NO. 80-706255
Prod-NGS Dist-NGS 1979

Portrait Of A Wheat Farmer C 15 MIN
16MM FILM, 3/4 OR 1/2 IN VIDEO P-I
Presents a portrait of a family living on a farm in the Midwestern United States.
From The Community Life In America Series.
LC NO. 80-706258
Prod-NGS Dist-NGS 1980

Portrait Of America—A Series

Presents a state by state search for the essential truths and ideas that form the basis of American life. A tribute to the American spirit.
Prod-TBS Dist-TBS

Connecticut
Florida
Georgia
Idaho
Indiana
Iowa
Nevada
New Jersey
New Mexico
Oregon
Texas
Virginia

Portrait Of An American Town C 30 MIN
3/4 OR 1/2 INCH VIDEO CASSETTE
Provides a brief history of the city of Upper Arlington, Ohio, a deliberately-planned suburban community.
Prod-OHC Dist-HRC

Portrait Of An Early American Village C 10 MIN
16MM FILM OPTICAL SOUND I-H A
Depicts life in an early American village. Shows villagers going to church, working on the farm and doing the household chores. Pictures a town meeting.
LC NO. FIA66-1688
Prod-VILF Dist-AVED 1964

Portrait Of An Election C 60 MIN
16MM FILM OPTICAL SOUND
Depicts the 1972 primary elections, the Democratic and Republican Conventions and the campaigns to election day. Features paintings from CBS convention coverage.
From The Artist As A Reporter Series.
Prod-ROCSS Dist-ROCSS 1973

Portrait Of Antarctica C 23 MIN
16MM FILM OPTICAL SOUND
Discusses the Navy's support of scientific efforts being conducted in the Antarctic during Operation Deepfreeze. Shows logistic support operations, scientific surveys and activities of the traverse and winteringover parties on the icebound continent.
LC NO. FIE63-9
Prod-USN Dist-USNAC 1962

Portrait Of Bermuda C 29 MIN
16MM FILM OPTICAL SOUND I-J
Visits the island of Bermuda showing its many attractions.
Prod-BTDB Dist-MTP

Portrait Of Cape Cod C 17 MIN
16MM FILM OPTICAL SOUND
Offers a portrait of Cape Cod including Heritage Plantation, Hyannisport, Provincetown, and the many golf courses, beaches, candle factories and artist colonies.
Prod-CCCOC Dist-MTP

Portrait Of Christine C 26 MIN
16MM FILM, 3/4 OR 1/2 IN VIDEO C A
Tells how an orthopedically handicapped 28-year-old has become a fully involved member of society.
Prod-FILMRT Dist-WOMBAT

Portrait Of Dame Mary Gilmore C 9 MIN
16MM FILM OPTICAL SOUND
Evokes the way a portrait painter approaches his subject, using the voice-overs of William Dobell, artist, Dame Mary Gilmore, subject and James Gleeson, the artist's friend and biographer.
From The Australian Eye Series.
LC NO. 80-700787
Prod-FLMAUS Dist-TASCOR 1978

Portrait Of Earth C 27 MIN
3/4 OR 1/2 INCH VIDEO CASSETTE H A
Explores the history of the artificial satellite, discussing the key roles played by satellites in communication, meteorology, and other scientific and environmental disciplines.
LC NO. 84-706407
Prod-NASA Dist-USNAC 1981

Portrait Of Giselle, A C 97 MIN
16MM FILM, 3/4 OR 1/2 IN VIDEO J-C A
Presents choreographer Sir Anton Dolin interviewing ballerinas on their interpretations of the role of Giselle. Includes the comments of Natalia Makarova, Yvette Chauvire, Alicia Alonso, Galina Ulanova, Alicia Markova, Carla Fracci, Olga Spessivtzeva and Tamara Karasavina.
LC NO. 82-707301
Prod-ABCVID Dist-WOMBAT 1982

Portrait Of Grandpa Doc C 28 MIN
16MM FILM, 3/4 OR 1/2 IN VIDEO J-C A
Presents a young artist painting a portrait of his grandfather who died several years earlier and reflecting on his childhood and the times he spent with his grandfather, who encouraged him to express himself through art.
Prod-PHENIX Dist-PHENIX 1977

Portrait Of Haiti C 14 MIN
16MM FILM, 3/4 OR 1/2 IN VIDEO I-C A
Presents the history, culture and religion of Haiti as viewed through the eyes of a painter of primitive art.
Prod-SWAIN Dist-MCFI 1977

Portrait Of Holland C 12 MIN
16MM FILM OPTICAL SOUND J-C A
Shows Dutch paintings of the 17th century which have been photographed from the originals in full color with shape and scale indicated. Studies one of Jan Steen's country fairs, landscapes by Jan van der Heyden and Jacob Ruisdael, Frans Hals' portrait of Swalmius, still-lifes by Pieter Claesz and Nicholas Van Heussen. Emphasizes Rembrandt and examines the visitation, a Biblical scene in which in which he introduced Dutch types and details of life.
Prod-DETRIA Dist-RADIM 1955

Portrait Of Jason B 105 MIN
16MM FILM OPTICAL SOUND
Tells the story of Jason Holliday, a black male prostitute and sometime nightclub performer. Features people behind the camera who provoke him to reveal hidden aspects of his personality.
Prod-NYFLMS Dist-NYFLMS 1967

Portrait Of Mexico, A C 34 MIN
16MM FILM, 3/4 OR 1/2 IN VIDEO H-C
Introduces the history and tradition of Mexico.
Prod-UARIZ Dist-IFB 1934

Portrait Of Moliere (French) C 62 MIN
16MM FILM OPTICAL SOUND J-C A
An English subtitle version of the French language film. Presents a series of scenes from Moliere's plays which evoke the life and character of the French playwright. Includes scenes from Le Tartuffe, Le Misanthrope, Le Medecin Malgre Lui, Le Malade Imaginaire, L'Avare, Dom Juan, L'Ecole Des Femmes and Le Borugeois Gentihomme.
Prod-IFB Dist-TRANSW 1972

Portrait Of Nelson Mandela C 20 MIN
16MM FILM, 3/4 OR 1/2 IN VIDEO
Documents Nelson Mandela and his leadership of the African National Congress of South Africa. Includes an interview with Mandela filmed in 1961 before his sentence to life imprisonment.
Prod-NEWTIM Dist-NEWTIM

Portrait Of Power, A C 14 MIN
16MM FILM OPTICAL SOUND
Concentrates on mining techniques used to extract coal from the earth.
Prod-AMAX Dist-MTP

Portrait Of The Artist As A Young Man, A C 93 MIN
16MM FILM, 3/4 OR 1/2 IN VIDEO H-C
Traces the childhood, schooldays, adolescence and early adulthood of an Irish poet-scholar. Based on the novel A PORTRAIT OF THE ARTIST AS A YOUNG MAN by James Joyce.
LC NO. 81-706027
Prod-TEXFLM Dist-TEXFLM 1978

Portrait Of The Artist As An Old Lady C 27 MIN
16MM FILM, 3/4 OR 1/2 IN VIDEO
Presents a portrait of Russian born 81 year old artist Paraskeva Clark. Narrated by Germaine Greer.
Prod-NFBC Dist-NFBC 1982

Portrait Of The Enemy C 12 MIN
16MM FILM OPTICAL SOUND
Discusses the treatment of periodontal disease using the analogy of a basketball game strategy.
Prod-AMDA Dist-MTP

Portrait Of The Enemy C 12 MIN
3/4 OR 1/2 INCH VIDEO CASSETTE H-C A
Uses an analogy of basketball game strategy in dealing with gum problems. Recognizes the opponent (gum disease) and his style of play (plaque), effective defense (proper home oral hygiene and regular professional care), and the cost of losing (loss of teeth).
Prod-AMDA Dist-AMDA 1979

Portrait Of The Orient C 27 MIN
16MM FILM OPTICAL SOUND I-C A
Portrays nine countries of the Orient, showing the trend to modernization as well as ancient temples, customs and dances.
LC NO. 77-706089
Prod-JAPAL Dist-MCDO Prodn-MCDO 1969

Portrait Of The Press, Warts And All, By John Chancellor C 50 MIN
3/4 OR 1/2 INCH VIDEO CASSETTE H-C A
Explores journalism in terms of the American standard of fairness, accuracy and objectivity and how the American public views journalists. Examines charges that the press is arrogant, negative, biased, overly ambitious and even venal. Shows how decisions are made and stories covered in the newsroom.
Prod-NBCNEW Dist-FI

Portrait Of The Sculptor, A C 30 MIN
3/4 INCH VIDEO CASSETTE
Interviews sculptor and artist John Mills who discusses his work and the factors which influence his art while he sculpts a portrait of the host, Andrew Watson.
Prod-UMITV Dist-UMITV 1979

Portrait Of The Sun C 18 MIN
16MM FILM OPTICAL SOUND I-H
Uses time-lapse photography and animation to explain the important characteristics of the sun and its relation to the earth. Includes views of the sun's corona, sunspots and spectacular solar prominences photographed with a special sun telescope.
From The Science In Our Space Age Series.
LC NO. FIA60-684
Prod-ACA Dist-ACA 1960

Portrait Of Two Artists C 29 MIN
16MM FILM, 3/4 OR 1/2 IN VIDEO I-C A
Features Black American artists Hughie Lee-Smith and Jacob Lawrence. Shows their work and looks in on a class taught by Mr. Lee-Smith. Visits the artists in their studios and includes animated sequences of the illustrations of Mr. Lawrence's children's book Harriet And The Promised Land.
From The Were You There? Series.
LC NO. 83-706600
Prod-NGUZO Dist-BCNFL 1982

Portrait, The C 30 MIN
3/4 OR 1/2 INCH VIDEO CASSETTE
See series title for descriptive statement.
From The Photographic Vision - All About Photography Series.
Prod-COAST Dist-CDTEL

Portrait, The Blue Angels C 14 MIN
16MM FILM OPTICAL SOUND
Presents the U S Naval Flight Demonstration Squadron displaying aerobatic maneuvers in high-powered Skyhawks.
LC NO. 79-700262
Prod-MCDO Dist-MCDO 1979

Portraits C 28 MIN
16MM FILM OPTICAL SOUND
Shows Exxon employees from the 1930's to the 1970's and how the company's benefit program has improved their lives.
LC NO. 78-701443
Prod-EXXON Dist-EXXON Prodn-CORPOR 1978

Portraits C 15 MIN
3/4 OR 1/2 INCH VIDEO CASSETTE P
Examines portraits from different eras, styles and media. Shows children painting portraits of their teacher. Points out that the individual artist works in his own way and that each artist may see the same subject differently.
From The Primary Art Series.
Prod-WETATV Dist-AITECH

Portraits From Spoon River C 15 MIN
3/4 INCH VIDEO CASSETTE H-C A
Features William Shatner and members of the First Poetry Quartet performing readings from Edgar Lee Master's Spoon River Anthology.
From The Anyone For Tennyson Series.
Prod-NETCHE Dist-GPITVL

Portraits Of Aging C 28 MIN
16MM FILM, 3/4 OR 1/2 IN VIDEO
Deals with aging as a positive process, presenting profiles of older people who have found that the later years can be most enriching and satisfying.
LC NO. 79-707584
Prod-MILPRO Dist-CORF 1979

Portraits Of Eternity C 29 MIN
2 INCH VIDEOTAPE
See series title for descriptive statement.
From The Museum Open House Series.
Prod-WGBHTV Dist-PUBTEL

Portraits Of Goodbye—A Series
A
Presents documentary profiles excerpted from the Begin With Goodbye Series. Depicts individuals struggling to cope with and adjust to fundamental changes in their life situation. Includes divorce, homesickness, death of a spouse, terminal and serious illness.
Prod-UMCOM Dist-ECUFLM 1980

Deborah
Harriet
Island
Marilyn And Orrin
Spencers, The

Portsmouth Story, The B 23 MIN
16MM FILM OPTICAL SOUND
Describes the construction of the Commission's gaseous diffusion plant at Portsmouth, Ohio.
LC NO. FIE58-45
Prod-USAEC Dist-USNAC 1958

Position And Tuning C 29 MIN
2 INCH VIDEOTAPE
See series title for descriptive statement.
From The Playing The Guitar I Series.
Prod-KCET Dist-PUBTEL

Position Classification C 16 MIN
16MM FILM OPTICAL SOUND
Uses the filmograph style to explain fundamental concepts of position classification in the U S Federal Government and how it affects both supervisors and employees.
LC NO. 75-703071
Prod-NASA Dist-USNAC 1968

Position Management Or Position Madness C 23 MIN
3/4 OR 1/2 INCH VIDEO CASSETTE A
Discusses how individual employees and staff advisors solve problems. Emphasizes good position management.
From The Position Management Series.
Prod-USOPMA Dist-USNAC 1984

Position Management—A Series
A
Discusses writing position descriptions, position management, and the process of classifying positions. Intended for new personnel administrators, supervisors and managers.
Prod-USOPMA Dist-USNAC 1984

Classification Process, The 027 MIN
Position Management Or Position Madness 023 MIN
Writing Position Descriptions - A Helping Hand 022 MIN

Position Of Faith, A C 17 MIN
16MM FILM, 3/4 OR 1/2 IN VIDEO C A
Tells the story of William Johnson, a student for the United Church of Christ Ministry, who declared himself to be a homosexual only a short time before ordination. Documents the events that followed, including the seminary's refusal to ordain, the debate within the congregation and the final vote to approve his ordination or not.
Prod-RHODES Dist-MGHT 1972

Position Of The Moon, The C 8 MIN
16MM FILM, 3/4 OR 1/2 IN VIDEO K-P
Discusses the Moon, its rotation and revolution, its light source, its location and the relative size of the sun, moon and earth.
From The Basic Facts About The Earth, Sun, Moon And Stars Series.
Prod-MORLAT Dist-SF 1967

Positional Injuries In Surgery C 13 MIN
3/4 OR 1/2 INCH VIDEO CASSETTE PRO
Describes the most common causes of muscle and nerve damage occurring from malpositioning. Stresses prevention and recognition.
From The Anesthesiology Clerkship Series.
Prod-UMICHM Dist-UMICHM 1976

Positioning A Patient Confined To Bed B 30 MIN
16MM FILM OPTICAL SOUND PRO
Demonstrates positioning a patient in the dorsal, lateral and prone positions. Reviews and makes application of the principles of body mechanics to correct body alignment of the patient and the activities of the nurse. Includes demonstrations on the use of footboard, hand roll and trochanter roll.
From The Directions For Education In Nursing Via Technology Series. Lesson 12
LC NO. 74-701786
Prod-DENT Dist-WSU 1974

Positioning Patient For Comfort And Safety C 7 MIN
3/4 OR 1/2 INCH VIDEO CASSETTE PRO
Emphasizes the exact correlation between correct standing-up posture and lying-down posture. Explains the development, causes and common locations of body deformities and contractures in a bedridden patient and describes the positioning and exercising of the patient that will prevent contractures. Provides instructions for the home nurse so that she will be able to avoid straining or injuring herself as she cares for the patient.
LC NO. 77-731353
Prod-TRAINX Dist-TRAINX

Positioning Patient For Comfort And Safety (Spanish) C 7 MIN
3/4 OR 1/2 INCH VIDEO CASSETTE PRO
Emphasizes the exact conditions between correct standing-up posture and lying-down posture. Explains the development, causes and common locations of body deformities and contractures in a bedridden patient and describes the positioning and exercising of the patient that will prevent contractures. Provides instructions for the home nurse so that she will be able to avoid straining or injuring herself as she cares for the patient.
LC NO. 77-731353
Prod-TRAINX Dist-TRAINX

Positioning The Patient For Surgery C 27 MIN
16MM FILM OPTICAL SOUND PRO
Stresses the basic principles involved in positioning the patient for surgery and demonstrates how the nurse practitioner fulfills her responsibility for proper body posture of the patient. Shows dorsal recumbent, trendelburg, lithotomy, lateral and prone positions.
Prod-ACYDGD Dist-ACY 1957

Positioning The Player And His Cello - The Fusion Of The Right Hand And The Bow C 30 MIN
3/4 OR 1/2 INCH VIDEO CASSETTE J-H A
See series title for descriptive statement.
From The Cello Sounds Of Today Series.
Prod-IU Dist-IU 1984

Positioning, Turning, And Transferring C 60 MIN
3/4 OR 1/2 INCH VIDEO CASSETTE PRO
Provides basic training in the proper positioning and safe turning and transferring of persons with physical disabilities. Instruction in recognizing a client's needs, describing these needs to a clinical specialist, and following a specialist's directions for client care are included.
Prod-UNEBO Dist-UNEBO

Positions And Draping Of Patients For Physical Exams C 14 MIN
1/2 IN VIDEO CASSETTE BETA/VHS
Describes the positions and draping of patients for physical exams.
Prod-RMI Dist-RMI

Positive Approach To The Psychiatric Patient, A B 30 MIN
16MM FILM OPTICAL SOUND
Shows the treatment in Veterans Administration Hospitals for psychiatric patients emerging from acute episodes of mental illness. Stresses the roles of the nurse, aide and physician.
Prod-USVA Dist-USNAC Prodn-USDA 1955

Positive Aspects In Teaching African History C 50 MIN
3/4 OR 1/2 INCH VIDEO CASSETTE
See series title for descriptive statement.
From The Blacks, Blues, Black Series.
Prod-KQEDTV Dist-PBS

Positive Discipline In The Classroom C 28 MIN
3/4 OR 1/2 INCH VIDEO CASSETTE T
Introduces teacher Bill Rose who emphasizes and demonstrates a caring and continuing attitude toward positive discipline which contributes to students' positive self-image. Includes students' comments on how Rose's attitude has had a measurable influence on their learning.
From The Successful Teaching Practices Series.
Prod-UNIDIM Dist-EBEC 1982

Positive Look At Negative Numbers, A C 10 MIN
16MM FILM, 3/4 OR 1/2 IN VIDEO I-J
Uses animation to construct a number line with points marked to represent positive and negative numbers and zero. Analogies from bookkeeping and from reading a thermometer help clarify the negative number concept.
Prod-SIGMA Dist-FILCOM 1964

Positive Patient Safety Through Simplified Operating Room Nursing Techniques C 33 MIN
16MM FILM OPTICAL SOUND PRO
Illustrates simplified, uncomplicated operating room nursing techniques used to limit, confine and destroy bacteria in the operating room and surrounding environment. Emphasizes the relationship of the nurse to the patient and other team members.
Prod-ACYDGD Dist-ACY 1961

Positive Philosophy Of Life—A Series

Prod-DANA Dist-DANA 1975

Joy Of Communication, The 18 MIN

Positive Planning For Defensive Practice Sessions C 27 MIN
3/4 OR 1/2 INCH VIDEO CASSETTE T
Presents Coach Joe Paterno explaining his personal philosophy on practice organization, making the best possible use of available resources and a simple practice schedule.
From The Joe Paterno - Coaching Winning Football Series.
Prod-UNIDIM Dist-EBEC 1982

Positive Reconditioning Of Neurological Injuries C 21 MIN
3/4 INCH VIDEO CASSETTE PRO
Shows how dual-channel EMG training is integrated with other neurodevelopmental techniques for muscle re-education.
From The Biofeedback Strategies Series. Pt III
Prod-AOTA Dist-AOTA 1981

Positive Reinforcement C 10 MIN
3/4 OR 1/2 INCH VIDEO CASSETTE T
See series title for descriptive statement.
From The Protocol Materials In Teacher Education - The Process Of Teaching, Pt 2 Series.
Prod-MSU Dist-MSU

Positive Reinforcement C 40 MIN
3/4 OR 1/2 INCH VIDEO CASSETTE T
Describes the strategies for use and selection of reinforcers to encourage children.

From The Learning And Liking It Series.
Prod-MSU Dist-MSU

Positive Shortage Prevention–A Series
IND
Discusses the inventory shortage problem and dramatizes actual cases and their impact on the store and its employees. Focuses on the roles of the supervisor and the employees in solving this problem.
Prod-SAUM Dist-SAUM Prodn-CALVIN 1972

Dollar Drain, The 16 MIN
First Line Of Defense 14 MIN
Losers, The 19 MIN
Who, Me 14 MIN

Positive Show, The C 28 MIN
16MM FILM - 3/4 IN VIDEO P-I
Illustrates the things that handicapped people can do which others might not expect them to be able to accomplish.
From The Special Delivery Series.
LC NO. 79-706881
Prod-WNVT Dist-LAWREN 1979

Positive Versus Negative Action B 30 MIN
2 INCH VIDEOTAPE T
Features Dr Dreikurs discussing the theory that in order to help a child, the adult must first remove himself from the child's provocations. Presents examples of misbehavior with a description of responses. (Broadcast quality)
From The Dynamics Of Classroom Behavior Series.
Prod-VTETV Dist-GPITVL Prodn-WETKTV

Positive Vibes C 10 MIN
3/4 OR 1/2 INCH VIDEO CASSETTE A
Shows University of South Carolina head basketball coach Bill Foster focusing on the importance of creating a winning attitude, both on the court and off.
Prod-SFTI Dist-SFTI

Positive-Displacement Downhole Mud Motors C 20 MIN
3/4 OR 1/2 INCH VIDEO CASSETTE IND
Discusses the advantage of the Dyna-Drill downhill motor. Shows how it operates and how it is used for drilling both straight and directional holes.
Prod-UTEXPE Dist-UTEXPE 1970

Possessive Nouns And Pronouns C 10 MIN
1/2 IN VIDEO CASSETTE BETA/VHS
See series title for descriptive statement.
From The English And Speech Series.
Prod-RMI Dist-RMI

Possessives, The (Los Posesivos) C 30 MIN
3/4 INCH VIDEO CASSETTE H-C
See series title for descriptive statement.
From The Telespanol Uno Series.
Prod-WUSFTV Dist-GPITVL 1979

Possibilities C 12 MIN
3/4 OR 1/2 INCH VIDEO CASSETTE C A
Portrays a male quadraplegic's sexual relationship with emphasis on the couple's warm feelings for each other and pleasuring techniques. Talks about the injury's impact on his sex life.
Prod-NATSF Dist-MMRC

Possibilities In Clay C 25 MIN
16MM FILM, 3/4 OR 1/2 IN VIDEO H-C A
Examines four different approaches to working with clay and ceramics.
LC NO. 80-706102
Prod-IU Dist-IU 1976

Possible Cures For FUNARG Problems C 50 MIN
3/4 OR 1/2 INCH VIDEO CASSETTE
See series title for descriptive statement.
From The Computer Languages - Pt 1 Series.
Prod-MIOT Dist-MIOT

Possible Human, The C 30 MIN
3/4 OR 1/2 INCH VIDEO CASSETTE
Explores the vast potential in each of us for more fulfilling lives. Presented by Dr Jean Houston.
From The Creating Possible Futures Series.
Prod-BULFRG Dist-BULFRG

Possible Presidents, The - Vice Presidents And Third Parties C 52 MIN
16MM FILM, 3/4 OR 1/2 IN VIDEO J-C A
Looks at five men who have served as Vice President and then as President. Examines how they achieved this position.
From The Presidency Series.
Prod-CORPEL Dist-LUF 1976

Possible Programs And Policies Of The U S C 27 MIN
3/4 OR 1/2 INCH VIDEO CASSETTE
See series title for descriptive statement.
From The Technology, Innovation, And Industrial Development Series.
Prod-MIOT Dist-MIOT

Possible Role Of Sex Hormones In Gynecological Cancer, The C 55 MIN
3/4 INCH VIDEO CASSETTE
Describes a research development concerning steroid hormones and their relationship to gynecologic cancer.
Prod-UTAHTI Dist-UTAHTI

Possible Society, The C 30 MIN
3/4 OR 1/2 INCH VIDEO CASSETTE
Visualizes a society which invests in people and knowledge as its ultimate resource. Presented by Dr Jean Houston.
From The Creating Alternative Futures Series.
Prod-BULFRG Dist-BULFRG

Possible Solution C 30 MIN
3/4 OR 1/2 INCH VIDEO CASSETTE
Discusses solutions to environmental problems, which must include education and awareness.
From The Ecology - Our Road To Survival Series.
Prod-NETCHE Dist-NETCHE 1971

Possibly In Michigan C 12 MIN
3/4 OR 1/2 INCH VIDEO CASSETTE
Prod-EAI Dist-EAI

Possibly So, Pythagoras C 14 MIN
16MM FILM, 3/4 OR 1/2 IN VIDEO J-H
Investigates the Pythagorean theorem through induction as well as through formal deductive proof.
Prod-IFB Dist-IFB 1963

Possibly So, Pythagoras (Arabic) C 14 MIN
16MM FILM, 3/4 OR 1/2 IN VIDEO J-H
Investigates the Pythagorean theorem through inductive experimentation and formal deductive proof.
Prod-IFB Dist-IFB 1963

Possibly So, Pythagoras (Captioned) C 14 MIN
16MM FILM, 3/4 OR 1/2 IN VIDEO J-H
Investigates the Pythagorean theorem through induction as well as through formal deductive proof. Captioned for the hearing impaired.
Prod-IFB Dist-IFB 1963

Possum Living C 29 MIN
16MM FILM OPTICAL SOUND H-C A
Looks at a father and daughter who pursue an independent existence by living off the land. Shows how they subsist on their rabbits, chickens' eggs, garden vegetables, and fish from the river.
LC NO. 81-700009
Prod-SCHNA Dist-NEWDAY 1980

Possum Living C 29 MIN
3/4 INCH VIDEO CASSETTE
Shows 20-year old Dolly Freed and her father, who have maintained a middle-class standard of living on less than 2000 dollars a year.
Prod-FIRS Dist-FIRS

Possum Opossum C 28 MIN
3/4 OR 1/2 INCH VIDEO CASSETTE
Takes a witty and affectionate look at the town and the people who dispense stories about the mythological possum.
Prod-KILLMR Dist-SOFOLK

Possum That Didn't, The X 11 MIN
16MM FILM, 3/4 OR 1/2 IN VIDEO K-J
Deals with superficial values, insensitivity and self-aggrandizement disguised as concern for others.
Prod-BFA Dist-PHENIX 1972

Possum Trot, The Life And Work Of Calvin Black C 29 MIN
3/4 OR 1/2 INCH VIDEO CASSETTE
Presents Calvin Black, folk artist of the Mojave Desert, who created over 80 wooden, nearly life-size dolls and a theater where they perform.
From The Visions Of Paradise Series.
Prod-SARLGT Dist-SARLGT

Possum, The C 13 MIN
16MM FILM OPTICAL SOUND C A
Documents the feeling of a segment of time, a moment on a highway after a storm.
Prod-VIERAD Dist-CANCIN 1975

Post Coronary Care (Rev Ed) C 16 MIN
16MM FILM, 3/4 OR 1/2 IN VIDEO PRO
Reviews causes of myocardial infarction and explains how the heart heals.
Prod-PRORE Dist-PRORE

Post Coronary Care (Spanish) C 16 MIN
16MM FILM, 3/4 OR 1/2 IN VIDEO PRO
Reviews causes of myocardial infarction and explains how the heart heals.
Prod-PRORE Dist-PRORE

Post Coronary Patient, The C
3/4 OR 1/2 INCH VIDEO CASSETTE
Describes a heart attack patient who resumes living with a few modifications in his lifestyle. Describes his rehabilitation from hospital to home to work. Covers eating, exercise and regular check-ups. Stresses resuming an active, healthier life.
Prod-MIFE Dist-MIFE

Post Coronary Patient, The (Spanish) C
3/4 OR 1/2 INCH VIDEO CASSETTE
Describes a heart attack patient who resumes living with a few modifications in his lifestyle. Describes his rehabilitation from hospital to home to work. Covers eating, exercise and regular check-ups. Stresses resuming an active, healthier life.
Prod-MIFE Dist-MIFE

Post Industrial Fiddle C 23 MIN
16MM FILM, 3/4 OR 1/2 IN VIDEO A
Discusses the relationship between work and music for Down East Style Fiddle player Gerry Morrell.
Prod-CNEMAG Dist-CNEMAG 1982

Post Landing Recovery Qualification - Gemini Static Article No. 5 C 15 MIN
3/4 INCH VIDEO CASSETTE
Evaluates the suitability, stability, seaworthiness and structure of the Gemini spacecraft by testing the static article no. 5. Demonstrates how corrective action is taken on tests which result in equipment failure.
Prod-NASA Dist-NASA 1972

Post Mortem C 15 MIN
16MM FILM, 3/4 OR 1/2 IN VIDEO H A
Shows the increasing problem of driving after taking seemingly harmless anti-histamines and related common drugs.
Prod-CINEA Dist-AIMS 1974

Post Mortem C 18 MIN
3/4 OR 1/2 INCH VIDEO CASSETTE H-C A
Presents scientific evidence that Napoleon did not die of natural causes but was poisoned intentionally. Features a Canadian businessman and Napoleon buff, Ben Weider, discussing the evidence and the reasons he believes this information to be true.
Prod-JOU Dist-JOU

Post Mortem Inspection - Cattle Heads C 18 MIN
16MM FILM OPTICAL SOUND IND
Shows post mortem inspection procedures for examining the heads of cattle as a means of assuring their health quality.
LC NO. 77-700954
Prod-USDA Dist-USNAC 1968

Post Mortem Inspection - Cattle Viscera And Carcass C 17 MIN
16MM FILM OPTICAL SOUND IND
Shows post mortem health check and quality control inspection of cattle viscera.
LC NO. 77-700955
Prod-USDA Dist-USNAC 1968

Post Mortem Inspection - Sheep And Calves C 13 MIN
16MM FILM OPTICAL SOUND IND
Shows health check and quality control techniques recommended for post mortem inspection of sheep and calves.
LC NO. 77-700956
Prod-USDA Dist-USNAC 1968

Post Mortem Inspection - Swine C 11 MIN
16MM FILM OPTICAL SOUND IND
Shows health check and quality control techniques recommended for post mortem inspection of swine.
LC NO. 77-700957
Prod-USDA Dist-USNAC 1968

Post No Bills C 9 MIN
16MM FILM OPTICAL SOUND J-H A
A satire on the subject of commitment as revealed in an account about a man who destroys billboards as an act of civil disobedience, becomes a hero and is exploited in an advertisement which is ironically put on a billboard.
LC NO. 72-700410
Prod-AISONE Dist-MMA 1970

Post Office Clerk C 15 MIN
16MM FILM, 3/4 OR 1/2 IN VIDEO I
From The Career Awareness Series.
Prod-KLVXTV Dist-GPITVL

Post Partum C 36 MIN
16MM FILM - 3/4 IN VIDEO PRO
Illustrates the role of the nurse clinician in caring for the post partum patient and her family, using the problem oriented approach as a method of analyzing, categorizing, synthesizing, and utilizing data from medical records. Desmonstrates use of a paper chart in conjunction with centralized computer storage.
LC NO. 79-708031
Prod-NMAC Dist-USNAC 1979

Post Partum Depression C 28 MIN
16MM FILM, 3/4 OR 1/2 IN VIDEO A
Presents two couples who worked their way through post partum depression with the help of a psychiatrist. Looks at the symptoms and causes of the illness.
Prod-NFBC Dist-PEREN 1978

Post Reinforcement - Principles And Armamentarium C 14 MIN
16MM FILM OPTICAL SOUND PRO
Explains how to use post reinforcement, improved techniques of root-canal therapy and other methods of periodontal surgery to contribute to preventive dentistry procedures. Describes the different sizes of color-coded drills and the variety of mated accessories, and lists their indications and use.
LC NO. 79-701428
Prod-VADTC Dist-USNAC 1978

Post Reinforcement For Anterior Teeth, Pt 1 - Composite Core C 13 MIN
16MM FILM - 3/4 IN VIDEO PRO
Shows preparation of the post channel and auxiliary pin channels and cementation of a stainless-steel post and two cemented-type pins. Demonstrates placement and preparation of the composite filling material to create a post-reinforced composite core to serve as the foundation for the full crown.
LC NO. 79-706832
Prod-USVA Dist-USNAC Prodn-VADTC 1978

Post Reinforcement For Anterior Teeth, Pt 2 - Direct Cast Core C 13 MIN
16MM FILM - 3/4 IN VIDEO PRO
Demonstrates a direct technique for fabricating a one-piece, post-reinforced cast core for an anterior tooth. Shows how a precious-metal post and two precious-metal pins are fitted to the prepared post channel and pin channels.
LC NO. 79-706833
Prod-USVA Dist-USNAC Prodn-VADTC 1978

Post Reinforcement For Anterior Teeth, Pt 3 - Indirect Cast Core C 14 MIN
16MM FILM - 3/4 IN VIDEO PRO
Shows steps in making a one-piece, post-reinforced cast core for an anterior tooth using an indirect technique. Demonstrates preparation of the post and pin channels, fitting a smooth plastic post and pins to the channels, impressionmaking, pouring

the cast and use of a resin pattern material to fabricate a pattern indirectly on the cast.
LC NO. 79-706834
Prod-USVA Dist-USNAC Prodn-VADTC 1978

Post Reinforcement For Anterior Teeth, Pt II,- Direct Cast Core C 13 MIN
3/4 OR 1/2 INCH VIDEO CASSETTE
Demonstrates a direct technique for fabricating a one-piece post-reinforced cast core for an anterior tooth.
Prod-VADTC Dist-AMDA 1978

Post Reinforcement For Anterior Teeth, Pt III - Indirect Cast Core C 14 MIN
3/4 OR 1/2 INCH VIDEO CASSETTE
Shows the various steps involved in making a one-piece post-reinforced cast core for an anterior tooth by means of an indirect technique.
Prod-VADTC Dist-AMDA 1978

Post Reinforcement For Anterior Teeth, Pt I - Composite Core C 13 MIN
3/4 OR 1/2 INCH VIDEO CASSETTE
Shows preparation of the post channel and the auxillary pin channels and cementation of a stainless steel post and two cemented-type pins. Demonstrates placement and preparation of the composite filling material to create a post-reinforced composite core, to serve as the foundation of the subsequent full crown.
Prod-VADTC Dist-AMDA 1978

Post Reinforcement For Bicuspid Teeth C 13 MIN
16MM FILM - 3/4 IN VIDEO PRO
Demonstrates three methods of achieving a post-reinforced amalgam core for bicuspid teeth using root canals and stainless steel post and/or pins. Shows how amalgam is packed around the post and/or pins and later prepared for a full-crown foundation.
LC NO. 79-707259
Prod-USVA Dist-USNAC Prodn-VADTC 1978

Post Reinforcement For Molar Teeth C 13 MIN
16MM FILM - 3/4 IN VIDEO PRO
Shows how to accomplish a post-reinforced amalgam core for mandibular and maxillary molars using stainless-steel posts and auxiliary pins. Demonstrates a copper-band matrix with interproximal wedging, packing amalgam material around posts and pins and preparation of the amalgam core to provide a full-crown foundation.
LC NO. 79-706840
Prod-USVA Dist-USNAC Prodn-VADTC 1978

Post Reinforcement For Repair Of Fixed Prosthesis C 14 MIN
16MM FILM - 3/4 IN VIDEO PRO
Explains procedures for making a one-piece, post-reinforced cast inlay which fits the lingual opening of a crown and serves as a dowel-like extension to a depth of approximately two-thirds the length of the root.
LC NO. 79-706835
Prod-USVA Dist-USNAC Prodn-VADTC 1978

Post Reinforcement For Repair Of Fixed Prosthesis C 14 MIN
3/4 OR 1/2 INCH VIDEO CASSETTE
Explains the step-by-step procedures employed in making a one-piece post-reinforced cast inlay which fits the lingual opening of the crown and serves as a dowel-like extension to a depth of approximately two-thirds the length of the root.
Prod-VADTC Dist-AMDA 1978

Post Reinforcement Of Tooth With Endodontics And Full Crown Preparation C 9 MIN
3/4 OR 1/2 INCH VIDEO CASSETTE
Describes a method of reinforcing an endodontically treated tooth requiring a full crown restoration.
Prod-VADTC Dist-AMDA 1978

Post Reinforcement Of Tooth With Endodontics And Full Crown Preparation C 13 MIN
16MM FILM - 3/4 IN VIDEO PRO
Demonstrates how the root canal is prepared to create a post channel with parallel sides, which extends one-half to two-thirds the length of the root. Shows cementation of a cylindrical, stainless-steel, serrated, vented post within the channel to reinforce the tooth.
LC NO. 79-706841
Prod-USVA Dist-USNAC Prodn-VADTC 1978

Post Vaginal Colpotomy C 10 MIN
3/4 OR 1/2 INCH VIDEO CASSETTE PRO
Discussion and illustration of his approach to post vaginal colpotomy by Dr Johnnie Betson.
Prod-WFP Dist-WFP

Post War Russia Under Stalin C 29 MIN
2 INCH VIDEOTAPE
See series title for descriptive statement.
From The Course Of Our Times II Series.
Prod-WGBHTV Dist-PUBTEL

Post-Impressionists, The C 25 MIN
16MM FILM, 3/4 OR 1/2 IN VIDEO
Explores the aims, influences and techniques of Cezanne, Gauguin, Von Gogh, Seurat and Toulouse-Lautrec. Tells how the work of these five artists led to different movements in painting.
Prod-IFB Dist-IFB

Post-Industrial Futures C 30 MIN
3/4 OR 1/2 INCH VIDEO CASSETTE
Explores current social trends, which are seen as effects of the decline of industrialism. Presented by James Robertson and Marvin Harris.
From The Creating Alternative Futures Series.
Prod-BULFRG Dist-BULFRG

Post-Mortem C 15 MIN
16MM FILM OPTICAL SOUND
Uses dramatized incidents to portray the effect of common everyday drugs on automobile drivers and their contribution to traffic accidents.
LC NO. FIA67-1124
Prod-CINEA Dist-CINEA 1967

Post-Natal Care C 14 MIN
16MM FILM, 3/4 OR 1/2 IN VIDEO H-C A
Explains how it is important to get back into good physical condition after the birth of a baby. States that the first couple of months can be very tiring as the new mother adjusts to a new schedule and additional household duties. A mime demonstrates several post-natal exercises which can be started right in the hospital bed.
From The Woman Talk Series.
Prod-CORF Dist-CORF 1983

Post-Natal Care Of A Song C 29 MIN
3/4 INCH VIDEO CASSETTE
Demonstrates the many steps between the birth of the song and the royalty checks.
From The Song Writer Series.
Prod-UMITV Dist-UMITV 1977

Post-Placement Counseling C 25 MIN
16MM FILM OPTICAL SOUND PRO
Illuminates the problems of retarded persons in social and work situations in the community through interviews with teachers, counselors, employers and parents of retarded persons.
From The Counseling The Mentally Retarded Series. No. 5
LC NO. 72-702022
Prod-UKANBC Dist-NMAC 1968

Post-Prostatectomy Urinary Incontinence C 20 MIN
16MM FILM OPTICAL SOUND PRO
Presents a cine-cystourethrographic demonstration of the mechanism of continence and incontinence and the endoscopic findings in a patient with postprostatectomy urinary incontinence. Discusses methods of treatment and illustrates a recommended procedure in detail.
LC NO. 75-702294
Prod-EATONL Dist-EATONL 1968

Post-Reconstruction Era, The C 30 MIN
1 INCH VIDEOTAPE J-H
Describes barriers confronting the Black in his growing fight for equal rights and justice. Shows the development of segregation and public education and examines the lives of Booker T Washington and W E B DuBois.
From The Odyssey In Black Series.
Prod-KLVXTV Dist-GPITVL

Post-Reinforcement - Principles And Armamentarium C 14 MIN
3/4 INCH VIDEO CASSETTE PRO
Explains how the use of post-reinforcement, techniques of root-canal therapy and methods of periodontal surgery can contribute to preventive dentistry procedures. Describes the different sizes of color-coded drills and the variety of mated accessories and lists their indications and use.
LC NO. 79-707260
Prod-VADTC Dist-USNAC 1978

Post-Trial Motions B 10 MIN
16MM FILM OPTICAL SOUND C
Deals with various aspects of a civil lawsuit involving an automobile case. Demonstrates the argument of post-trial motion for a new trial, or in the alternative for judgement notwithstanding the verdict.
From The Civil Advocates Series. No. 24
LC NO. 75-714032
Prod-ATLA Dist-RPATLF 1967

Post-Trial Motions And Review B 20 MIN
16MM FILM OPTICAL SOUND
Deals with various aspects of a criminal lawsuit involving a liquor store robbery case. Includes defense motions after conviction and sentencing on the trial court level with argument by counsel.
From The Criminal Law Series. No. 14
LC NO. 77-714046
Prod-RPATLF Dist-RPATLF 1968

Post-Video C 30 MIN
3/4 OR 1/2 INCH VIDEO CASSETTE
Presents a collection of new videotapes, radio broadcasts and performances that move in a new direction, toward narrative, allegory and unabashed humor.
Prod-EAI Dist-EAI

Post-War Era, The - Film Noir And The Hollywood Ten C 20 MIN
16MM FILM, 3/4 OR 1/2 IN VIDEO
Discusses films that reflected the cynicism and concerns of the postwar era by exploring themes such as crime, prejudice, mental illness, alcoholism and drugs. Examines the effects of the Cold War and Mc Carthyism on the entertainment industry, including the arrest of the Hollywood Ten by the House Un-American Activities Committee.
From The Life Goes To The Movies Series. Pt 3
LC NO. 79-707675
Prod-TIMLIF Dist-TIMLIF 1976

Post-War Years - The Far East C 30 MIN
3/4 OR 1/2 INCH VIDEO CASSETTE H
Reviews Mao's peasant-based communist revolution in China, Western reaction to the wars in Korea and Vietnam, Gandhi's non-violent movement in India and problems resulting from India's independence.
From The Historically Speaking Series. Part 24
Prod-KRMATV Dist-AITECH 1983

Post-War Years - The West C 30 MIN
3/4 OR 1/2 INCH VIDEO CASSETTE H
Analyzes the Soviet Union and the United States as superpowers in the cold war. Looks at the problem of Berlin and the Berlin Wall, and problems in the Near East and their significance in international affairs.
From The Historically Speaking Series. Part 23
Prod-KRMATV Dist-AITECH 1983

Postal And Musical Contributions To American History C 28 MIN
16MM FILM OPTICAL SOUND J-C A
Portrays the influence that the Postal Service together with music has had on American history. Explains that the Postal Service has made a contribution to the history and growth of the U S particularly as the means of communication between the 13 original states at the crucial period of the inception of the new nation.
Prod-DANA Dist-DANA

Postal Service - A Letter To A Football Hero (3rd Ed) C 17 MIN
16MM FILM, 3/4 OR 1/2 IN VIDEO P-I
A revised edition of the 1966 motion picture Our Post Office. Demonstrates the workings of the U S postal system by telling a true story about a boy with a hearing disability and his correspondence with a professional football player with the same problem. Shows the correct way to address letters and highlights that postal workers and machinery perform.
Prod-EBEC Dist-EBEC Prodn-RUSIRV 1977

Posterior Abdominal Wall - Unit 19 C 19 MIN
3/4 OR 1/2 INCH VIDEO CASSETTE PRO
Depicts the lecturer gaining access to the posterior abdominal wall, pointing out various structures along the way, (several of which are related to the kidney). Shows the muscles and nerves of the posterior abdominal wall.
From The Gross Anatomy Prosection Demonstration Series.
Prod-HSCIC Dist-HSCIC

Posterior Abdominal Wall, The C 17 MIN
16MM FILM, 3/4 OR 1/2 IN VIDEO C A
Focuses on the abdominal region. Demonstrates the dissection of the posterior abdominal wall.
From The Guides To Dissection Series.
Prod-UCLA Dist-TEF

Posterior And Superior Mediastina, The C 10 MIN
16MM FILM, 3/4 OR 1/2 IN VIDEO C A
Focuses on the thoracic region. Demonstrates the dissection of the posterior and superior mediastina.
From The Guides To Dissection Series.
Prod-UCLA Dist-TEF

Posterior Aspect Of The Leg (Calf) C 9 MIN
16MM FILM, 3/4 OR 1/2 IN VIDEO C A
Demonstrates the dissection of the posterior aspect of the leg.
From The Guides To Dissection Series.
Prod-UCLA Dist-TEF

Posterior Aspect Of The Thigh C 10 MIN
16MM FILM, 3/4 OR 1/2 IN VIDEO C A
Demonstrates the dissection of the posterior aspect of the thigh.
From The Guides To Dissection Series.
Prod-UCLA Dist-TEF

Posterior Dissection Of The Pharynx C 19 MIN
3/4 OR 1/2 INCH VIDEO CASSETTE PRO
Demonstrates the anatomy of the pharynx as seen in posterior dissection and identifies the anatomical relationship of nerves and blood vessels to the pharynx. Shows anatomical features from different perspectives.
From The Hollinshead Dissection Series.
Prod-HSCIC Dist-HSCIC

Posterior Resection Of The Rectum For Large Villous Adenoma C 19 MIN
16MM FILM OPTICAL SOUND PRO
Presents resection and end-to-end anastomosis of lower and middle third of rectum for the large benign villous adenoma by means of a modified kraske posterior transcoccygeal approach.
Prod-ACYDGD Dist-ACY 1968

Posterior Triangle Of The Neck, The C 12 MIN
16MM FILM, 3/4 OR 1/2 IN VIDEO C A
Focuses on head and neck. Demonstrates the dissection of the posterior triangle of the neck.
From The Guides To Dissection Series.
Prod-UCLA Dist-TEF

Posters C 15 MIN
16MM FILM, 3/4 OR 1/2 IN VIDEO I-C A
Explains the basic concepts and methods of poster design.
From The Rediscovery - Art Media Series.
Prod-ACI Dist-AIMS 1968

Posters (French) C 15 MIN
16MM FILM, 3/4 OR 1/2 IN VIDEO I-C A
Provides an orientation to the problems and possibilities of making posters. Shows the application of design principles.
From The Rediscovery - Art Media (French) Series.
Prod-ACI Dist-AIMS 1968

Posters (Spanish) C 15 MIN
16MM FILM, 3/4 OR 1/2 IN VIDEO I-C A
Provides an orientation to the problems and possibilities of making posters. Shows the application of design principles.
From The Rediscovery - Art Media (Spanish) Series.
Prod-ACI Dist-AIMS 1968

Posters Speak Out C 25 MIN
2 INCH VIDEOTAPE I
Illustrates lettering and poster design.

From The Art Has Many Forms Series.
Prod-CVETVC Dist-GPITVL

Postmark - Terror C 15 MIN
16MM FILM, 3/4 OR 1/2 IN VIDEO
Discusses package bombs, providing definitions and diagrams of letter and package bombs. Shows how to recognize these devices and what to do with suspected material.
Prod-MTI Dist-MTI

Postmark - Terror (Arabic) C 15 MIN
16MM FILM OPTICAL SOUND
Deals with all aspects of package bombs. Helps develop proper awareness and attitudes that could save lives.
Prod-MTI Dist-MTI

Postmark - Terror (French) C 15 MIN
16MM FILM OPTICAL SOUND
Deals with all aspects of package bombs. Helps develop proper awareness and attitudes that could save lives.
Prod-MTI Dist-MTI

Postmark - Terror (Spanish) C 15 MIN
16MM FILM, 3/4 OR 1/2 IN VIDEO
Deals with all aspects of package bombs. Helps develop proper awareness and attitudes that could save lives.
Prod-MTI Dist-MTI

Postmark Impressions C 22 MIN
16MM FILM OPTICAL SOUND J-C A
Shows Papua and New Guinea through its stamps.
Prod-ANAIB Dist-AUIS 1971

Postmenopausal Vaginitis C 7 MIN
3/4 OR 1/2 INCH VIDEO CASSETTE
Explains the symptoms and treatment for postmenopausal vaginitis and encourages patient compliance in treatment.
From The Take Care Of Yourself Series.
Prod-UARIZ Dist-UARIZ

Postmortem Employee Benefit Planning, Including IRAs And IRC section 403(b) Plans C 53 MIN
3/4 OR 1/2 INCH VIDEO CASSETTE PRO
Gives an overview of postdeath planning opportunities, explains the impact of TEFRA and discusses what facts must be obtained for effective planning.
From The Postmortem Tax Planning After ERTA Series.
Prod-ABACPE Dist-ABACPE

Postmortem Income Tax Planning And How It Fits Into The Overall Planning Picture C 55 MIN
3/4 OR 1/2 INCH VIDEO CASSETTE PRO
Provides a guide for the tax planner who must prepare a decedent's return. Discusses relationship between decedent's income and the marital deduction and shows the impact of choice of accounting period and alternative valuation elections.
From The Postmortem Tax Planning After ERTA Series.
Prod-ABACPE Dist-ABACPE

Postmortem Tax Planning After ERTA—A Series
PRO
Provides complete overview of the impact of recent changes in tax laws under ERTA, TEFRA and the Subchapter S Revision Act. Concentrates on a particular aspect of the postdeath picture in each of the six programs, providing concrete strategies, specific examples and warnings of potential pitfalls.
Prod-ABACPE Dist-ABACPE

Postmortem Employee Benefit Planning,
Postmortem Income Tax Planning And How It 055 MIN
Postmortem Tax Strategies For Paying The Tax 050 MIN
Postmortem Tax Strategies For The Surviving 056 MIN
Special Use Of Valuation - How And When To 051 MIN
Use Of Disclaimer In Postmortem Planning 054 MIN

Postmortem Tax Strategies For Paying The Tax Which Is Due C 50 MIN
3/4 OR 1/2 INCH VIDEO CASSETTE PRO
Discusses sections 302 and 303 redemptions and the impact of the Subchapter S Revision Act. Explains tax deferral periods and sections 6161 and 6166 and looks at the relationship between sections 6166 and 303.
From The Postmortem Tax Planning After ERTA Series.
Prod-ABACPE Dist-ABACPE

Postmortem Tax Strategies For The Surviving Spouse's Estate And The Next Generation C 56 MIN
3/4 OR 1/2 INCH VIDEO CASSETTE PRO
Provides postmortem tax strategies for the surviving spouse and the next generation. Enumerates seven reasons for moving from the deferral option to payment or partial payment of estate taxes.
From The Postmortem Tax Planning After ERTA Series.
Prod-ABACPE Dist-ABACPE

Postnatal Development Of The Skeleton, Pt 1 - The Skull C 21 MIN
16MM FILM, 3/4 OR 1/2 IN VIDEO C A
See series title for descriptive statement.
From The Skeletal And Topographic Anatomy Series.
Prod-UTEXMH Dist-TEF

Postnatal Development Of The Skeleton, Pt 2 - Vertebral Column And Extremities C 22 MIN
16MM FILM, 3/4 OR 1/2 IN VIDEO C A
See series title for descriptive statement.
From The Skeletal And Topographic Anatomy Series.
Prod-UTEXMH Dist-TEF

Postnatal Development Of The Skeleton, Pt 3 - Deciduous And Permanent Dentition C 21 MIN
16MM FILM, 3/4 OR 1/2 IN VIDEO C A
See series title for descriptive statement.
From The Skeletal And Topographic Anatomy Series.
Prod-UTEXMH Dist-TEF

Postoperative Care B 14 MIN
16MM FILM OPTICAL SOUND
Describes the duties and responsibilities of hospital corpsmen in caring for patients immediately after surgery.
LC NO. FIE60-90
Prod-USN Dist-USNAC 1959

Postoperative Disturbances Of Visually Controlled Behavior In The Cat B 14 MIN
16MM FILM SILENT C T
Shows that cats deprived of visual projection areas display no impairment of pupillary reflexes, blinking, righting reactions or optic movements. The cats, however, lose visual placing reactions and cannot descend from a slightly elevated surface or avoid obstructions. They also lose the ability to discriminate brightness under conditions of light adaptation but, retain the ability to discriminate brightness under conditions of low illumination.
Prod-PSUPCR Dist-PSUPCR 1936

Postoperative Patient, The - Nursing Assessment C 15 MIN
3/4 OR 1/2 INCH VIDEO CASSETTE PRO
Presents guidelines for assessment of the patient who is returning from surgery. Outlines signs and symptoms of postoperative complications and gives guidelines for nurse's initial observations and interactions with the patient. Gives examples of systematic assesssment the nurse can use in the care of the patient following surgery.
LC NO. 81-730133
Prod-TRAINX Dist-TRAINX

Postpartum C 14 MIN
3/4 OR 1/2 INCH VIDEO CASSETTE
Stresses new mother's need for rest, proper diet, adequate amount of fluids and moderate exercise following delivery. Covers common problems such as urinating difficulty, constipation, and 'after-pains', and explains breast care for both nursing and non-nursing mothers. Gives special attention to the importance of the six-week checkup.
LC NO. 77-73135
Prod-TRAINX Dist-TRAINX

Postpartum (Spanish) C 14 MIN
3/4 OR 1/2 INCH VIDEO CASSETTE
Stresses new mother's need for rest, proper diet, adequate amount of fluids and moderate exercise following delivery. Covers common problems such as urinating difficulty, constipation, and 'after-pains', and explains breast care for both nursing and non-nursing mothers. Gives special attention to the importance of the six-week checkup.
LC NO. 77-73135
Prod-TRAINX Dist-TRAINX

Postpartum Care C
3/4 OR 1/2 INCH VIDEO CASSETTE
Gives practical care guidelines to the new mother from delivery through postpartum check-up. Covers pains and discomforts immediately following birth.
Prod-MIFE Dist-MIFE

Postpartum Care (Arabic) C
3/4 OR 1/2 INCH VIDEO CASSETTE
Give practical care guidelines to the new mother from delivery through postpartum check-up. Covers pains and discomforts immediately following birth.
Prod-MIFE Dist-MIFE

Postpartum Care (Spanish) C
3/4 OR 1/2 INCH VIDEO CASSETTE
Give practical care guidelines to the new mother from delivery through postpartum check-up. Covers pains and discomforts immediately following birth.
Prod-MIFE Dist-MIFE

Postpartum Care - Hospital To Home B 44 MIN
16MM FILM OPTICAL SOUND PRO
Shows how the nurse meets the teaching needs of families during the postpartum period, with emphasis on the discharge procedure. Follows the family to the pediatrician's office for examination of the baby and to the obstetrician for the six week postpartum examination. Includes explanation of birth control techniques and community resources.
From The Maternity Nursing Series.
LC NO. 70-703392
Prod-VDONUR Dist-AJN Prodn-WTTWTV 1966

Postscript C 15 MIN
16MM FILM OPTICAL SOUND
Studies the discrepancy between the image of reality presented by the mass media and the reality actually experienced by presenting the story of a young couple trying to get an apartment.
LC NO. 74-703437
Prod-YORKU Dist-YORKU 1973

Postscript (French) C 15 MIN
16MM FILM OPTICAL SOUND
Studies the discrepancy between the image of reality presented by the mass media and the reality actually experienced by presenting the story of a young couple trying to get an apartment.
LC NO. 74-703437
Prod-YORKU Dist-YORKU 1973

Postural Drainage - Patient Positioning C 9 MIN
16MM FILM OPTICAL SOUND
Demonstrates the various positions of the body which are used to drain the lung segments of the patient with chronic obstructive pulmonary disease.
LC NO. 74-705387
Prod-NMAC Dist-NMAC 1968

Postural Drainage And Percussion C 16 MIN
16MM FILM, 3/4 OR 1/2 IN VIDEO C A
Teaches proper positions and techniques used in postural drainage, clapping and vibrating. Includes correct terminology, precautions, indications and contraindications.
From The Physical Respiratory Therapy Series.
Prod-VISCI Dist-TEF

Posture C 29 MIN
2 INCH VIDEOTAPE
See series title for descriptive statement.
From The Maggie And The Beautiful Machine - Backs Series.
Prod-WGBHTV Dist-PUBTEL

Posture - Thinking Tall C 12 MIN
16MM FILM, 3/4 OR 1/2 IN VIDEO I-H
Uses examples of excellent body control in a variety of human activities to demonstrate that good posture contributes to performance, well-being and durability. Shows what is important in developing concepts and habits of good posture.
Prod-WINTNC Dist-PHENIX 1978

Posture And The Keyboard C 15 MIN
16MM FILM, 3/4 OR 1/2 IN VIDEO J-H
Shows the fine points and adjustments to good posture, demonstrating the interrelationship between the typist, the typewriter and the copy as well as the position of the hands on the keyboard and striking action of the fingers. Uses examples to dramatize the importance of posture, the home row, rhythmic speed and striking action.
Prod-SF Dist-SF 1969

Posture Perfect With Harv And Marv C 11 MIN
16MM FILM, 3/4 OR 1/2 IN VIDEO P-I
Explains how a young boy learns to develop good posture habits and tells why good posture is important in helping him to look, feel and perform better.
Prod-HIGGIN Dist-HIGGIN 1979

Postwar Hopes, Cold War Fears C 58 MIN
3/4 OR 1/2 INCH VIDEO CASSETTE
Tells that the 1950's was a time of nostalgia and neuroses. Factories were pouring out goods, the dollar was strong and the United States was filled with optimism. The 1950's also saw the lowering of the Iron Curtain in Eastern Europe, the loss of China to communism, the Korean War and the Red Scare dividing Americans at home.
From The Walk Through The 20th Century With Bill Moyers Series.
Prod-CORPEL Dist-PBS 1982

Postwar Politics And Art C 30 MIN
3/4 OR 1/2 INCH VIDEO CASSETTE H-C A
Examines the influence of Regionalists, Precisionists and Magic Realists on American art.
From The Art America Series.
Prod-CTI Dist-CTI

Postwar Society C 30 MIN
2 INCH VIDEOTAPE
Looks at the Populist Party and third parties in general. Covers life in the slums, Western badmen and political corruption. Includes a set of Thomas Nast's cartoons on the Tweed ring.
From The American History II Series.
Prod-KRMATV Dist-GPITVL

Pot C 30 MIN
3/4 OR 1/2 INCH VIDEO CASSETTE
Details the effect of THC on the human body. Explains the altered time perception and apparent need for higher sensory input of chronic marijuana users.
Prod-WHITEG Dist-WHITEG

Pot Bellies C 29 MIN
2 INCH VIDEOTAPE
See series title for descriptive statement.
From The Maggie And The Beautiful Machine - Bellies Series.
Prod-WGBHTV Dist-PUBTEL

Pot Problem, The C 30 MIN
2 INCH VIDEOTAPE
Features Thalassa Cruso discussing different aspects of gardening. Shows various types and sizes of pets and matches them with appropriate plants.
From The Making Things Grow I Series.
Prod-WGBHTV Dist-PUBTEL

Pot's A Put-On C 10 MIN
16MM FILM OPTICAL SOUND I-J
Presents a parody of the arguments in favor of marijuana use and satirizes those who smoke it.
Prod-PROART Dist-PROART 1969

Potassium C 34 MIN
3/4 OR 1/2 INCH VIDEO CASSETTE PRO
Describes importance of potassium as a vehicle for maintaining smoothly functioning neuromuscular system. Discusses location and function of this vital element and the pathophysiology of potassium imbalances.
From The Fluids And Electrolytes Series.
Prod-BRA Dist-BRA

Potassium-Induced Ulcer-Strictures Of The Small Intestine C 28 MIN
16MM FILM OPTICAL SOUND PRO
Illustrates the operative findings of a potassium-induced ulcer-stricture in the small intestine, which had caused vague symptoms of anemia and small bowel obstruction. Presents other benign and malignant ulcer strictures.
Prod-ACYDGD Dist-ACY 1967

Potato Appeal C 10 MIN
16MM FILM OPTICAL SOUND H-C A
Discusses the versatility of potatoes in the menu. Emphasizes the

appeal of dishes made from procssed potatoes in frozen and in dehydrated form.
LC NO. FIA63-1235
Prod-UPR Dist-UPR 1962

Potato Late Blight - Epidemiology C 13 MIN
3/4 OR 1/2 INCH VIDEO CASSETTE C A
Introduces concepts of plant disease epidemiology. Uses potato late blight to illustrate the dynamics of the development of epidemics.
LC NO. 82-707063
Prod-CUETV Dist-CUNIV 1982

Potato Planters C 17 MIN
16MM FILM OPTICAL SOUND
Shows an Aymara Indian family planting potatoes, preparing and eating a meal, and discussing the religious and astronomical forces that control their destiny. Contrasts the stark routine of a typical planting day with the complexity of their beliefs.
From The Faces Of Change - Bolivia Series.
Prod-AUFS Dist-WHEELK

Potatoes C 27 MIN
16MM FILM, 3/4 OR 1/2 IN VIDEO J-C A
Presents a documentary which takes a look at potato farmers in New Brunswick, Canada, and focuses on huge food processors as the cause of the farmers' increasing financial problems.
LC NO. 82-707178
Prod-NFBC Dist-BULFRG 1977

Potemkin B 50 MIN
16MM FILM SILENT
Depicts a mutiny aboard one of the Czar's battleships in 1905. Directed by Sergei Eisenstein.
Prod-ESNSTN Dist-REELIM 1925

Potemkin - A Multi-Media Film Study B 10 MIN
16MM FILM SILENT J-C
Presents the Odessa steps sequence from Eisenstein's 1925 motion picture Potemkin and offers an analysis of the cinematic content of the sequence.
LC NO. 76-700268
Prod-LSEC Dist-LSEC 1976

Potential Applications And Limitations Of Microprocessors C 30 MIN
3/4 OR 1/2 INCH VIDEO CASSETTE PRO
Defines types of systems suitable for microprocessor applications. Discusses main parameters of several equipment types now on market designed with microprocessors. Shows how microprocessors can lower costs, shorten design cycles, and improve performance and reliability in practical applications.
From The Designing With Microprocessors Series.
Prod-TXINLC Dist-TXINLC

Potential Energy C 30 MIN
16MM FILM, 3/4 OR 1/2 IN VIDEO C A
Explains potential energy as a clue to understanding why the world has worked the some way since the beginning of time.
From The Mechanical Universe Series.
Prod-ANNCPB Dist-FI

Potential Transformers C 7 MIN
3/4 OR 1/2 INCH VIDEO CASSETTE IND
Cites electrical backfeed as major hazard associated with PTs. Details recommended steps for clearing ALL energy sources from the circuit.
From The Electrical Safety Series.
Prod-GPCV Dist-GPCV

Potentially Yours C 31 MIN
3/4 OR 1/2 INCH VIDEO CASSETTE
Presents techniques for developing human potential through humanistic psychology.
Prod-HP Dist-HP

Potentiometric Titrations / Hydrolysis / Acids And Bases C 57 MIN
3/4 OR 1/2 INCH VIDEO CASSETTE
Discusses potentiometric titrations, hydrolysis and acids and bases.
From The Electrochemistry, Pt III - Thermodynamics Of Galvanic Cells Series.
Prod-MIOT Dist-MIOT

Potentiometric Titrations, Hydrolysis, Acids And Bases C 57 MIN
3/4 OR 1/2 INCH VIDEO CASSETTE
See series title for descriptive statement.
From The Electrochemistry Series.
Prod-KALMIA Dist-KALMIA

Potlatch Country C 28 MIN
3/4 OR 1/2 INCH VIDEO CASSETTE P-H A
Views the scenic primitive wilderness known as Potlatch country in north central Idaho. Depicts wildlife in diverse habitats.
Prod-POTFOR Dist-FO Prodn-FO

Potlatch People C 26 MIN
16MM FILM, 3/4 OR 1/2 IN VIDEO
Focuses on the Indians of the Pacific Northwest and describes the ceremonial potlatch feast. Discusses attempts to reconstruct this culture as it was before the coming of the white man.
From The Native Americans Series.
Prod-BBCTV Dist-CNEMAG

Potlatch Story, The C
3/4 OR 1/2 INCH VIDEO CASSETTE
Prod-FO Dist-FO

Potluck C 21 MIN
16MM FILM OPTICAL SOUND P-I
Reveals that the Chiffy kids decide to go camping near a haunted house. Shows that as they busy themselves around the campsite, Magpie disappears and someone's bones are found cooking in the pot.
Prod-LUF Dist-LUF 1979

Poto And Cabengo C 77 MIN
16MM FILM OPTICAL SOUND
Focuses on twin girls who converse in their own imaginary language. Describes the media attention given to these girls. Directed by Jean-Pierre Gorin.
Prod-UNKNWN Dist-NYFLMS 1979

Potomac Fever C 58 MIN
3/4 OR 1/2 INCH VIDEO CASSETTE
Follows two newly-elected Congressmen from their homes to Washington where they experience the rewards and the frustrations of making the transition from citizen to Congressman.
From The Frontline Series.
Prod-DOCCON Dist-PBS

Potpourri B 9 MIN
16MM FILM OPTICAL SOUND J-C
Presents a psychedelic animated film.
Prod-CFS Dist-CFS 1969

Potpourri C 29 MIN
3/4 INCH VIDEO CASSETTE
Exhibits and discusses a variety of unrelated house plants.
From The House Botanist Series.
Prod-UMITV Dist-UMITV 1978

Potpourri - The Many Views Of Marijuana, Pt 1 B 88 MIN
2 INCH VIDEOTAPE
Presents the social and economic facts of marijuana and its impact on society. Includes satirical essays, a picture history of the use of the plant and panel discussions.
Prod-KCET Dist-PUBTEL

Potpurri - The Many Views Of Marijuana–A Series

Prod-KCET Dist-PUBTEL

Potpurri - The Many Views Of Marijuana, Pt 1 88 MIN
Potpurri - The Many Views Of Marijuana, Pt 2 90 MIN

Potpurri - The Many Views Of Marijuana, Pt 2 C 90 MIN
2 INCH VIDEOTAPE
Presents the social and economic facts on marijuana and its impact on society. Includes satirical essays, a picture history of the use of the plant and panel discussions.
From The Potpurri - The Many Views Of Marijuana Series.
Prod-KCET Dist-PUBTEL

Potter And His Craft, The B 20 MIN
16MM FILM OPTICAL SOUND I-C A
Shows how the potter, who has carried on his craft from time immemorial, is keeping abreast with the times by joining potters' co-operatives, thereby gaining the latest know-how and improving his products.
Prod-INDIA Dist-NEDINF

Potter's Song, A - The Art And Philosophy Of Paul Soldner C 16 MIN
16MM FILM - 3/4 IN VIDEO J-C A
Explores the life of Paul Soldner, one of the better known ceramic artists and educators of the day. Discusses the changing course of his ceramic art and its relationship to the environment.
Prod-CRYSP Dist-CRYSP

Potter's Wheel, The C 10 MIN
16MM FILM OPTICAL SOUND J-C A
Richard Petterson, head of Ceramic Studio, Scripps College, shows the method of throwing a pitcher and other shapes on a potter's wheel. The process is described in detail from hollowing-out the clay to the final glaze firing.
Prod-ALLMOR Dist-AVED 1951

Potter's Wheel, The C 28 MIN
2 INCH VIDEOTAPE
Features Mrs Peterson describing certain ceramic processes for her classroom at the University of Southern California. Illustrates the potter's wheel.
From The Wheels, Kilns And Clay Series.
Prod-USC Dist-PUBTEL

Potters At Work C 29 MIN
16MM FILM, 3/4 OR 1/2 IN VIDEO H-C A
Examines the pottery of Japanese craftsmen, focusing on the daily circumstances out of which the pieces emerge.
Prod-GROSSM Dist-PHENIX 1977

Potters Of Hebron C 30 MIN
16MM FILM, 3/4 OR 1/2 IN VIDEO J-C A
A short version of the film Potters Of Hebron. Shows potters demonstrating their crafts in a workshop in the Hebron Hills, southeast of Jerusalem. Focuses on processes employed by the potters in making earthenware water jugs, called zirs.
Prod-HABERR Dist-PHENIX 1976

Potters Of Hebron C 53 MIN
16MM FILM, 3/4 OR 1/2 IN VIDEO J-C A
Shows potters demonstrating their crafts in a workshop in the Hebron Hills, southeast of Jerusalem. Focuses on processes employed by the potters in making earthenware water jugs called zirs.
Prod-HABERR Dist-PHENIX 1976

Pottery C 28 MIN
3/4 INCH VIDEO CASSETTE
Shows many varieties of Southwestern Indian pottery, all handmade without a potter's wheel. Illustrates different tribes' methods, including imprints, carving and firing methods. Also available in two-inch quad and one-inch videotape.
From The Indian Arts At The Phoenix Heard Museum Series.
Prod-KAETTV Dist-NAMPBC

Pottery - An Introduction C 17 MIN
16MM FILM OPTICAL SOUND
Provides an introduction to the techniques of making pottery.
LC NO. 75-701915
Prod-MORLAT Dist-MORLAT 1973

Pottery Making (Tajik) B 15 MIN
16MM FILM, 3/4 OR 1/2 IN VIDEO
See series title for descriptive statement.
From The Mountain Peoples Of Central Asia (Afghanistan) Series.
Prod-IFF Dist-IFF

Pottery Techniques - Slab Building B 17 MIN
3/4 OR 1/2 INCH VIDEO CASSETTE
Shows a potter demonstrating hand building by slab construction and lists the tools needed.
Prod-BU Dist-BU

Pottery Techniques - Surface Decoration B 11 MIN
3/4 OR 1/2 INCH VIDEO CASSETTE
Shows a potter demonstrating methods of surface decoration such as mishima, incision and slip decoration.
Prod-BU Dist-BU

Pottery Techniques - The Pinch Pot B 16 MIN
3/4 OR 1/2 INCH VIDEO CASSETTE
Shows a potter demonstrating pinch pot (hand building) techniques and lists the tools needed.
Prod-BU Dist-BU

Pottery, Stoneware And The Southern Crafts C 30 MIN
3/4 INCH VIDEO CASSETTE
See series title for descriptive statement.
From The Antiques Series.
Prod-NHMNET Dist-PUBTEL

Potting C 30 MIN
2 INCH VIDEOTAPE
Features Thalassa Cruso discussing different aspects of gardening. Shows how to pot plants.
From The Making Things Grow I Series.
Prod-WGBHTV Dist-PUBTEL

Potting Houseplants C 30 MIN
3/4 OR 1/2 INCH VIDEO CASSETTE
Discusses the potting of houseplants.
From The Even You Can Grow Houseplants Series.
Prod-WGTV Dist-MDCPB

Potting Mixes For Houseplants C 30 MIN
3/4 OR 1/2 INCH VIDEO CASSETTE
Discusses potting mixes for houseplants.
From The Even You Can Grow Houseplants Series.
Prod-WGTV Dist-MDCPB

Poultry C
3/4 INCH VIDEO CASSETTE H A
Introduces poultry as a complete protein food. Explains that poultry is classified according to age. Demonstrates how to cut poultry into individual serving pieces.
From The Matter Of Taste Series. Lesson 14
Prod-COAST Dist-CDTEL

Poultry - Laying It On The Line C 11 MIN
16MM FILM, 3/4 OR 1/2 IN VIDEO I-J
Examines the processing procedures of the automated poultry industry in the United States. Traces the development of specialized breeds of chickens and shows work in a modern hatchery, brooder, egg factory and processing plant.
Prod-CENTEF Dist-CORF 1975

Poultry Cookery C 21 MIN
16MM FILM, 3/4 OR 1/2 IN VIDEO
Illustrates how to cook poultry.
LC NO. 80-707634
Prod-USN Dist-USNAC 1980

Poultry Processing Inspection C 18 MIN
16MM FILM OPTICAL SOUND
Outlines poultry processing procedures required by the U S Department of Agriculture, U S Public Health Service and medical services of the Army and Air Force. Explains duties of Air Force veterinary officers in checking cleanliness and handling of birds.
LC NO. FIE56-308
Prod-USAF Dist-USNAC 1956

Poultry-Killing And Dressing C 56 MIN
3/4 INCH VIDEO CASSETTE J-C A
Shows how to kill, scald, pluck, eviscerate and package poultry in a small-scale operation. Explains in detail each step in the processing procedure and gives reasons for processing in a particular way.
LC NO. 81-707367
Prod-NYSTAL Dist-CUNIV Prodn-CUETV 1979

Pound Theory, The - Why Everyone's Special C 12 MIN
16MM FILM, 3/4 OR 1/2 IN VIDEO I-H
Presents an animated fable featuring storks-in-training, who learn why every baby is different, but equally valuable. Shows a stuffy flight instructor and his star pupil, visiting the baby factory and being shown that everyone has desirable traits.
Prod-CREEDM Dist-PHENIX 1977

Pour It On C 29 MIN
16MM FILM, 3/4 OR 1/2 IN VIDEO PRO
Feature hockey star Bobby Hull in a story that teaches principles of success that motivate salesmen and stimulates them to achieve more than ever before.
Prod-DARTNL Dist-DARTNL 1972

Pouring Babbitt Bearings C 17 MIN
3/4 OR 1/2 INCH VIDEO CASSETTE IND
Focuses on how to pour a perfect bearing the first time. Shows how to pour, bore and scrape the bearing and how to cut the oil grooves and finger slots. Includes safety practices.
From The Marshall Maintenance Training Programs Series. Tape 6
Prod-LEIKID Dist-LEIKID

Pouring Babbitt Bearings C 17 MIN
16MM FILM, 3/4 OR 1/2 IN VIDEO IND
Shows how to pour a perfect bearing the first time. Discusses melting out the old bearings, the clean-up, good safety practices, installing the wood plugs, spaces and fillers, pre-heating, blackening and preventing leaks. Details how to pour, how to bore and scrape the bearing, and how to cut the oil grooves and the finger slots.
Prod-MOKIN Dist-MOKIN

Pourquoi N'Est-Il Pas La B 13 MIN
16MM FILM OPTICAL SOUND I-H
See series title for descriptive statement.
From The Les Francais Chez Vous Series. Set II, Lesson 22
LC NO. 73-704477
Prod-PEREN Dist-CHLTN 1967

Poussaint, Alvin C 30 MIN
3/4 INCH VIDEO CASSETTE
Discusses the negative psychological effects of discrimination on blacks.
From The Like It Is Series.
Prod-OHC Dist-HRC

Poverty C 30 MIN
3/4 OR 1/2 INCH VIDEO CASSETTE C
Discusses the character and limitations of poverty.
From The Focus On Society Series.
Prod-DALCCD Dist-DALCCD

Poverty - Closing The Gap C 18 MIN
16MM FILM, 3/4 OR 1/2 IN VIDEO
Discusses aspects of poverty and shows how the poor have begun to mobilize themselves.
Prod-DOCUA Dist-CNEMAG

Poverty - The Great Obstacle C 56 MIN
16MM FILM, 3/4 OR 1/2 IN VIDEO H-C
Deals with the effect of poverty on human welfare and urban development.
Prod-SF Dist-SF 1973

Poverty In America C 30 MIN
3/4 OR 1/2 INCH VIDEO CASSETTE C
Offers historical analyses of poverty in America in 'hard times' as well as 'good times.'
America - The Second Century Series.
Prod-DALCCD Dist-DALCCD

Poverty Showdown, The C 56 MIN
3/4 OR 1/2 INCH VIDEO CASSETTE
Features Dr Joseph Lowery and Dr Walter Williams in a panel discussion on poverty, allowing professors and students to ask the speakers provocative questions about poverty and its solutions.
From The Poverty Trilogy Series.
Prod-WORLDR Dist-WORLDR

Poverty Trap, The C 30 MIN
16MM FILM OPTICAL SOUND H-C A
Exposes how the agencies which work with the poor present regulatory obstacles which keep their clients poor by limiting job opportunities, encouraging dependency, and controlling their economic and personal freedoms.
Prod-WORLDR Dist-WORLDR 1982

Poverty Trap, The C 28 MIN
3/4 OR 1/2 INCH VIDEO CASSETTE
Exposes the workings of the poverty industry, the regulatory obstacles it creates to limit job opportunities for the poor, the dependency it encourages among its recipients and its control of the economic and personal freedoms of those caught in its trap.
From The Poverty Trilogy Series.
Prod-WORLDR Dist-WORLDR

Poverty Trilogy—A Series

Presents the faults of various poverty programs, offers alternatives to government programs of social welfare and a panel discussion by recognized experts.
Prod-WORLDR Dist-WORLDR

Dignity	020 MIN
Poverty Showdown, The	056 MIN
Poverty Trap, The	028 MIN

Pow-Wow C 16 MIN
16MM FILM, 3/4 OR 1/2 IN VIDEO J-C A
Offers a display of North American Indian dances. Features participants telling what it means to be an Indian.
LC NO. 80-706875
Prod-CENTRO Dist-CORF 1980

Powder Hound C 14 MIN
16MM FILM OPTICAL SOUND
Introduces Powder Hound plummeting down high mountain ridges and plunging into deep powder chutes doing the 'Ski Wheelie.' Tells how he lives in a tent in the high mountains for peaceful solitude and the perfect descent. Shows how, in the end, Powder Hound is tamed by the charms of a local ski instructor who irreverently plants her tent next to his.
Prod-EDFLM Dist-EDFLM

Powder Keg In The Congo - A Special Report B 5 MIN
16MM FILM OPTICAL SOUND J-H
Reports on the crisis in the Congo which occurred when it received its independence from Belgium in 1960. Follows the crisis from the seating of the new parliament to the military revolt and subsequent U N intervention, renewed violence and U N discussion.
From The Screen News Digest Series. Vol 3, Issue 8
Prod-HEARST Dist-HEARST 1961

Powder Keg In The Dominican Republic B 6 MIN
16MM FILM OPTICAL SOUND
Depicts the revolution in the Dominican Republic in 1965 and the resulting evacuation of U S citizens. Shows the United States' stand against the Communist influences in the revolt.
LC NO. 70-700505
Prod-HEARST Dist-HEARST 1965

Powder Metallurgy C 15 MIN
16MM FILM OPTICAL SOUND
Describes the science of powder metallurgy and its applications. Shows the advantages of the use of metal in a powder form.
Prod-MTP Dist-MTP

Powder Metallurgy C 14 MIN
3/4 OR 1/2 INCH VIDEO CASSETTE
Covers steps in conventional powder metallurgy, its advantages and disadvantages and typical defects.
From The Manufacturing Materials And Processes Series.
Prod-GE Dist-WFVTAE

Powder Metallurgy - Manufacture Of Porous Bronze Bearings B 15 MIN
3/4 INCH VIDEO CASSETTE
Discusses the manufacturing process by which metal powders are fabricated into porous bronze bearings and impregnated with oil. Issued in 1945 as a motion picture.
From The Engineering Series.
LC NO. 79-706437
Prod-USOE Dist-USNAC Prodn-AUDIO 1979

Powder Metallurgy - Principles And Uses B 19 MIN
16MM FILM - 3/4 IN VIDEO
Describes the principles of powder metallurgy, including powder, pressure and heat. Deals with major industrial applications of powder metallurgy and the laboratory process of combining silver and nickel powders. Issued in 1945 as a motion picture.
From The Engineering Series.
LC NO. 79-706436
Prod-USOE Dist-USNAC Prodn-AUDIO 1979

Powder Metallurgy - The Better Way C 16 MIN
16MM FILM OPTICAL SOUND IND
Presents the history of powder metallurgy, compacting the part, sintering the green part, and hot forming for more demanding applications. Emphasizes that most individuals relate to the end use product and know very little about powder metallurgy as a method of part fabrication.
Prod-CINSHA Dist-CINSHA

Powder Metallurgy, Pt 2 - Manufacture Of Porous Bronze Bearings B 15 MIN
16MM FILM OPTICAL SOUND
Shows how metal powders are fabricated into porous bronze bearings and impregnated with oil.
From The Engineering Series.
LC NO. FIE52-175
Prod-USOE Dist-USNAC Prodn-AUDIO 1945

Powell Conjugate Direction Method And Introduction To OPTLIB C 60 MIN
3/4 OR 1/2 INCH VIDEO CASSETTE
See series title for descriptive statement.
From The Engineering Design Optimization II Series. Pt 11
Prod-UAZMIC Dist-UAZMIC

Powell's Conjugate Direction Method And Introduction To Gradient Methods B 60 MIN
3/4 OR 1/2 INCH VIDEO CASSETTE
See series title for descriptive statement.
From The Engineering Design Optimization I Series. Pt 8
Prod-UAZMIC Dist-UAZMIC

Power B 15 MIN
16MM FILM, 3/4 OR 1/2 IN VIDEO
Examines the relationship of voltage, current, resistance and power in a series resistive circuit.
Prod-USAF Dist-USNAC

Power B 15 MIN
2 INCH VIDEOTAPE P-I
See series title for descriptive statement.
From The Our Changing Community Series.
Prod-VITA Dist-GPITVL 1967

Power C 34 MIN
16MM FILM, 3/4 OR 1/2 IN VIDEO H-C A
Documents the essence of a hypnotist's skill, showing the amount of punishment man can endure and inflict.
Prod-DUNAV Dist-PHENIX 1973

Power Across The Sound C 23 MIN
16MM FILM OPTICAL SOUND I-H A
Shows the fabrication of worlds longest underwater cable in a factory in Italy, the transporting of the cables to New York and its installation between Norwalk, CoNN and Northport, LI.
Prod-LILC Dist-LILC

Power Amplifier IC Applications C 30 MIN
3/4 OR 1/2 INCH VIDEO CASSETTE PRO
Shows how integrated circuit power amplifiers increase output power. Accomplishes variations by adjusting bandwidth for good communications, head phone and stereo amplifiers.
From The Linear And Interface Integrated Circuits, Part I - Linear Integrated Circuits Series.
Prod-TXINLC Dist-TXINLC

Power And Conflict In The Organization - We Can Work It Out C 26 MIN
16MM FILM, 3/4 OR 1/2 IN VIDEO
Describes the skills needed for managing power struggles within organizations.
From The Human Resources And Organizational Behavior Series.
Prod-DOCUA Dist-CNEMAG

Power And Corruption C 34 MIN
16MM FILM, 3/4 OR 1/2 IN VIDEO H-C A
Presents an edited version of the film Macbeth directed by Roman Polanski. Explores the theme of why men are attracted to power and the influence power, once gained, has upon their natures.
From The Great Themes Of Literature Series.
Prod-LCOA Dist-LCOA 1973

Power And Pleasure - Shakespeare C 45 MIN
2 INCH VIDEOTAPE
See series title for descriptive statement.
From The Humanities Series. Unit I - Persons, Places And Events
Prod-WTTWTV Dist-GPITVL

Power And Power Factor B 34 MIN
16MM FILM, 3/4 OR 1/2 IN VIDEO
Explains the difference between true power and apparent power in a series RC or RL circuit. Gives the power factor, with the equations for both true and apparent power. (Kinescope)
Prod-USAF Dist-USNAC

Power And The Glory, The C 30 MIN
3/4 OR 1/2 INCH VIDEO CASSETTE
Profiles six prominent Washingtonians who have left positions of authority in government. Features Clark Clifford, Stuart Eizenstat, Edmund Muskie, Lyn Nofziger, Elliot Richardson and Robert Strauss.
Prod-WETATV Dist-PBS 1982

Power And The Land B 40 MIN
16MM FILM - 3/4 IN VIDEO
Portrays a farm family in Pennsylvania before and after electrification of their farm. Contrasts farm duties and tasks with and without electricity and discusses how to form a farmers' electrical cooperative. Issued in 1951 as a motion picture.
LC NO. 79-706462
Prod-USDA Dist-USNAC 1979

Power And The Press B 24 MIN
16MM FILM OPTICAL SOUND
Uses an extract from the motion picture Citizen Kane to illustrate the use, misuses and power of the newspaper medium. Shows how Kane uses the press as an instrument of reform and power. Stars Orson Welles and Joseph Cotton.
From The American Challenge Series.
Prod-RKOP Dist-FI 1975

Power And The Quest, The C 27 MIN
16MM FILM OPTICAL SOUND
Gives a history of the American aircraft industry as seen through the eyes of pioneer engine manufacturers. Shows how aircraft progressed from piston engines up to the present-day jet aircraft manufactured by Pratt and Whitney Aircraft.
LC NO. 75-700315
Prod-PTRSEN Dist-PWA 1975

Power And Wheels C 17 MIN
16MM FILM, 3/4 OR 1/2 IN VIDEO I-H
Surveys the social and cultural impact of the car and investigates its relationship to the American economy.
Prod-EBEC Dist-EBEC 1972

Power Basics Of Baseball C
1/2 IN VIDEO CASSETTE BETA/VHS A
See series title for descriptive statement.
From The Sports - Power Basics Series.
Prod-RMI Dist-RMI

Power Basics Of Baseball C 80 MIN
3/4 OR 1/2 INCH VIDEO CASSETTE
Features demonstrations by Jerry Reuss and others of basics such as pitching windup and grip, batting stance and pivot, baserunning, stealing, infield and outfield. Includes pitching, batting and fielding/baserunning.
From The Power Basics Of Sports Series.
Prod-ATHI Dist-ATHI

Power Basics Of Basketball C
1/2 IN VIDEO CASSETTE BETA/VHS A
See series title for descriptive statement.
From The Sports - Power Basics Series.
Prod-RMI Dist-RMI

Power Basics Of Basketball C 80 MIN
3/4 OR 1/2 INCH VIDEO CASSETTE
Demonstrations include stance, passing, types of shot, block and roll for offense and defense and rebounding. Features instruction by Walt Hazzard and others. Includes ball handling, shooting, and the complete player.
From The Power Basics Of Sports Series.
Prod-ATHI Dist-ATHI

Power Basics Of Football C
1/2 IN VIDEO CASSETTE BETA/VHS A
See series title for descriptive statement.
From The Sports - Power Basics Series.
Prod-RMI Dist-RMI

Power Basics Of Football C 80 MIN
3/4 OR 1/2 INCH VIDEO CASSETTE
Covers basics including stance, drive block, power block and pass block. Includes conditioning, coming off the line and catching the pass. Includes formations, the drop back, passing

and the handoff. Features demonstrations by Andrew Gissenger and others. Includes lineplay, receiving and quarterback.
From The Power Basics Of Sports Series.
Prod-ATHI Dist-ATHI

Power Basics Of Soccer C
1/2 IN VIDEO CASSETTE BETA/VHS A
See series title for descriptive statement.
From The Sports - Power Basics Series.
Prod-RMI Dist-RMI

Power Basics Of Soccer C 80 MIN
3/4 OR 1/2 INCH VIDEO CASSETTE
Includes instruction in instep drives, volley kicks, juggling, body traps, dribbling, feinting and other basics. Features demonstrations by Hubert Vogelsinger.
From The Power Basics Of Sports Series.
Prod-ATHI Dist-ATHI

Power Basics Of Sports—A Series

Features one-on-one instruction by leading athletes, coaches and players in football, basketball, soccer and baseball.
Prod-ATHI Dist-ATHI

Power Basics Of Baseball 080 MIN
Power Basics Of Basketball 080 MIN
Power Basics Of Football 080 MIN
Power Basics Of Soccer 080 MIN

Power Bending Conduit B 17 MIN
16MM FILM - 3/4 IN VIDEO IND
Explains how to assemble and operate a floor bender and a portable bender, make an offset in a one and one half inch conduit, and make an offset in a conduit already installed. Issued in 1945 as a motion picture.
From The Electrical Work - Wiring Series. No. 13
LC NO. 79-707487
Prod-USOE Dist-USNAC Prodn-RAYBEL 1979

Power Beneath The Land, The - A Portrait Of Power C 15 MIN
16MM FILM OPTICAL SOUND
Focuses on techniques used in surface and deep mining of coal in the Midwest and shows how land is reclaimed.
LC NO. 79-701307
Prod-AMAX Dist-VISION Prodn-VISION 1979

Power Beneath The Land, The - Westward Coal C 14 MIN
16MM FILM OPTICAL SOUND
Shows the techniques involved in surface mining of coal, reclamation of land, and transportation of coal.
LC NO. 79-701308
Prod-AMAX Dist-VISION Prodn-VISION 1979

Power Distribution Systems C 8 MIN
3/4 OR 1/2 INCH VIDEO CASSETTE IND
Shows how to be sure a circuit is de-energized before work begins, and how one-lines, work orders and communication are all essential for maintenance of distribution systems.
From The Electrical Safety Series.
Prod-GPCV Dist-GPCV

Power Drills For Woodwork C 13 MIN
16MM FILM, 3/4 OR 1/2 IN VIDEO J-C A
Presents seven concepts dealing with power drills-drill press - parts, drill press - bits, drill press - adjustments, drill press - operation, drill press - sanding drums, portable drill - parts and bits, and portable drill - operation. The projector may be stopped after each concept.
From The Woodwork - Machine Tools Series.
Prod-SF Dist-SF 1967

Power For The Moonship B 28 MIN
16MM FILM OPTICAL SOUND J-C A
Shows working models of the fuel cell for the Apollo spacecraft and discusses possible uses of the cell here on Earth.
LC NO. 78-708122
Prod-NASA Dist-USNAC 1966

Power From Coal C 24 MIN
16MM FILM OPTICAL SOUND
Shows the resurrection of the New South Wales coal industry from a strife-ridden and backward assortment of coal producers into an efficient and highly productive coal industry. Discusses the vital role of coal as the cornerstone of civilization and living standards.
LC NO. 80-700864
Prod-IMPACT Dist-TASCOR 1978

Power From Fusion - The Principles C 29 MIN
16MM FILM OPTICAL SOUND J-C A
Discusses the principles of the production of energy by nuclear fusion, including problems still to be solved. Covers thermonuclear research in Britain.
Prod-UKAEA Dist-UKAEA 1964

Power From Fusion, Pt 2 - The Problem Of Containment C 40 MIN
16MM FILM OPTICAL SOUND
Describes the theory of the fusion process and the nature of a plasma. Defines the required conditions in terms of the temperature and the density times time product for the containment of the plasma. Illustrates a number of experiments, starting with the pinch effect, and considers in detail the instabilities which arise. Considers the thetatron system, followed by magnetic cages and the Phoenix experiment. Warns that although the major instabilities appear to have been overcome, other less violent instabilities may now be revealed.
Prod-UKAEA Dist-UKAEA 1965

Power From The Atom C 30 MIN
2 INCH VIDEOTAPE I-J
Discusses ecology, the atom, fusion, use of nuclear power, elements of a power plant, safeguards in a power plant, desalinization and possibilities of agri-nuclear complex.
From The Living In A Nuclear Age Series.
Prod-GPITVL Dist-GPITVL

Power From The Earth C 13 MIN
16MM FILM, 3/4 OR 1/2 IN VIDEO I-C A
Surveys the geothermal resources available from the Earth's interior and shows how they may be used for the production of electric power.
Prod-NSF Dist-AMEDFL 1974

Power From The Earth C 13 MIN
16MM FILM, 3/4 OR 1/2 IN VIDEO
Shows eight scientists, engineers and managers describing various aspects of obtaining thermal energy from the earth for the production of electrical power.
Prod-USERD Dist-USNAC

Power From The Sun B 5 MIN
16MM FILM OPTICAL SOUND J-H
Describes experiments to find new ways of harnessing solar power. Shows America's first solar home in which sun rays serve as the source of heat and power.
From The Screen News Digest Series. Vol 4, Issue 4
Prod-HEARST Dist-HEARST 1961

Power Generators, Pt 1 C
3/4 OR 1/2 INCH VIDEO CASSETTE IND
Includes principles, frequency, construction and excitation of power generators.
From The Industrial Training, Module 4 - Power Production Series.
Prod-LEIKID Dist-LEIKID

Power Generators, Pt 2 C
3/4 OR 1/2 INCH VIDEO CASSETTE IND
Studies several aspects of power generators including cooling, hydrogen cooling and operation.
From The Industrial Training, Module 4 - Power Production Series.
Prod-LEIKID Dist-LEIKID

Power Hacksaw And Band Saw C 12 MIN
16MM FILM, 3/4 OR 1/2 IN VIDEO J-H A
Demonstrates the correct technique for accurate cutting with each machine and emphasizes the safety practices and proper maintenance of the band saw blades. Discusses the kinds of blades available and their safe installation.
Prod-BROSEB Dist-PHENIX 1969

Power Hacksaw And Band Saw (Spanish) C 12 MIN
16MM FILM, 3/4 OR 1/2 IN VIDEO J-H A
Demonstrates the correct technique for accurate cutting with each machine and emphasizes the safety practices and proper maintenance of the band saw blades. Discusses the kinds of blades available and their safe installation.
Prod-BROSEB Dist-PHENIX 1969

Power Lawn Mower Safety C
16MM FILM, 3/4 OR 1/2 IN VIDEO J-C A
Explains and illustrates safety precautions that could help avert power lawn mower accidents. Deals with safety features and the design of the mower, proper attire for operating a rotary power mower, removing safety hazards from the area to be mowed, safe fueling and refueling and maintaining the mower for safety.
Prod-CENTRO Dist-CORF 1982

Power Mechanics—A Series
16MM FILM, 3/4 OR 1/2 IN VIDEO J-C A
Covers topics in power mechanics.
Prod-THIOKL Dist-CAROUF

Air-Vane Governor, The 007 MIN
Carburetor, The 008 MIN
Four-Cycle Engine, The 009 MIN
How To Adjust The Breaker Points 007 MIN
How To Inspect And Replace The Valves 008 MIN
How To Remove The Valves 008 MIN
How To Time The 2-Cycle Engine 008 MIN
How To Trouble-Shoot A Small Engine 009 MIN
Magneto Ignition 006 MIN
Reading The Micrometer 010 MIN
Taking Inside Measurements 009 MIN
Two-Cycle Engine, The 004 MIN
Use Of The Torque Wrench 004 MIN
Use Of Thickness Gauges 010 MIN
Valve Timing The 4-Cycle Engine 008 MIN

Power Network, Pt 1 C
3/4 OR 1/2 INCH VIDEO CASSETTE IND
Covers load and demand, synchronising and reactance.
From The Industrial Training, Module 4 - Power Production Series.
Prod-LEIKID Dist-LEIKID

Power Network, Pt 2 C
3/4 OR 1/2 INCH VIDEO CASSETTE IND
Includes the Power factor, generators in parallel, sharing load, and reactive and three phase connections.
From The Industrial Training, Module 4 - Power Production Series.
Prod-LEIKID Dist-LEIKID

Power Of Involvement C 30 MIN
3/4 OR 1/2 INCH VIDEO CASSETTE T
Points out that through involvement with a caring person, a weak individual can be helped toward a strong, successful identity.
From The Developing Discipline Series.
Prod-SDPT Dist-GPITVL 1983

Power Of Listening, The C 26 MIN
16MM FILM, 3/4 OR 1/2 IN VIDEO H-C A
Describes the impact of active listening and shows how to make listening a more effective method of receiving messages. Demonstrates the benefits in productivity and morale that improved listening habits can bring.
LC NO. 81-706743
Prod-CRMP Dist-CRMP 1981

Power Of Listening, The (Spanish) C 26 MIN
16MM FILM, 3/4 OR 1/2 IN VIDEO H-C A
Explores the meaning and benefits of active listening and points out the deterrents to good listening.
Prod-MGHT Dist-MGHT Prodn-CRMP 1978

Power Of Objective Setting, The C 30 MIN
3/4 OR 1/2 INCH VIDEO CASSETTE
See series title for descriptive statement.
From The Decision Analysis By Kepner-Tregoe Series.
Prod-KEPTRG Dist-DELTAK

Power Of People, The C 28 MIN
16MM FILM OPTICAL SOUND
Traces the relationship of all links of the cooperative system to the system as a whole and describes its relationship to individual members.
LC NO. 73-702359
Prod-FAMACO Dist-FAMACO 1973

Power Of Positive Reinforcement, The C 28 MIN
16MM FILM, 3/4 OR 1/2 IN VIDEO H-C A
Demonstrates behavior modification techniques and documents their successful use in organizations.
Prod-CRMP Dist-CRMP 1978

Power Of Positive Reinforcement, The (Spanish) C 27 MIN
16MM FILM, 3/4 OR 1/2 IN VIDEO C A
Documents the systematic on-site application of behavior management and its emphasis on positive reinforcement. Examines its use in the Valley Fair Amusement Park in Minnesota, on the defensive line of the Minnesota Vikings and in the streets of Detroit, Michigan, with the Sanitation Department. Portrays behavior modification as a powerful tool for managing human performance.
Prod-MGHT Dist-MGHT Prodn-CRMP 1978

Power Of Speech C 25 MIN
16MM FILM, 3/4 OR 1/2 IN VIDEO H-C A
Discusses the development of language in the child.
From The Children Growing Up Series.
Prod-BBCTV Dist-FI 1981

Power Of Stories, The C 17 MIN
16MM FILM, 3/4 OR 1/2 IN VIDEO T
Underscores the importance of literature in children's educational, artistic and intellectual growth. Shows nursery rhymes and poetry being shared to the delight of children in a variety of settings.
Prod-IECS Dist-WWS 1984

Power Of The Market (Discussion) C 30 MIN
16MM FILM, 3/4 OR 1/2 IN VIDEO H-C A
Offers a debate on the relative benefits of free market capitalism conducted by Dr Milton Friedman and others.
From The Free To Choose (Discussion) Series.
Prod-EBEC Dist-EBEC 1983

Power Of The Market, The C 60 MIN
16MM FILM, 3/4 OR 1/2 IN VIDEO H-C A
Describes the benefits of free market capitalism and surveys successful examples of the system around the globe. Offers a debate between Dr Milton Friedman and others on the relative importance of these benefits.
From The Free To Choose Series.
Prod-EBEC Dist-EBEC 1983

Power Of The Market, The (Documentary) C 30 MIN
16MM FILM, 3/4 OR 1/2 IN VIDEO H-C A
Describes the benefits of free market capitalism and surveys successful examples of the system around the globe.
From The Free To Choose (Documentary) Series.
Prod-EBEC Dist-EBEC 1983

Power Of The Resurrection X 60 MIN
16MM FILM OPTICAL SOUND H A
Shows Peter, in a Roman prison awaiting death, consoling an anxious young fellow-prisoner by telling of the time he failed Jesus, and of the renewed power that came with the Resurrection appearance. Covers the events of the passion from Jesus' entry into Jerusalem at Passover, through Pentecost.
Prod-YALEDV Dist-YALEDV

Power Of The Resurrection, The B 60 MIN
16MM FILM OPTICAL SOUND
Pictures the aged Peter in prison with other Christians, awaiting unknown tortures and possible death, comforting and reassuring a young man by telling him the story of his own faith. Portrays the proud, boastful Peter, turning into a coward and a traitor the night he betrays his beloved Lord. Shows the fearful man becoming Peter, the rock, as the power of the Holy Spirit comes upon him and the true meaning of the Resurrection becomes a living reality in his life.
Prod-FAMF Dist-FAMF

Power Of The Team, The C 28 MIN
16MM FILM OPTICAL SOUND
Uses scenes of football plays to express the idea that teamwork can also be found throughout the Navy.
LC NO. 76-701539
Prod-USN Dist-USNAC 1975

Power Of The Tongue, The B 30 MIN
16MM FILM OPTICAL SOUND H-C A
Tells the story of Eliezer-Ben-Yehuda, presented in commemoration of the forty-fifth anniversary of his death. Portrays

Ben-Yehuda's efforts to revive the Hebrew language. (Kinescope)
From The Eternal Light Series.
LC NO. 70-700974
Prod-JTS Dist-NAAJS 1968

Power Operated Hoists And Cranes C 60 MIN
3/4 OR 1/2 INCH VIDEO CASSETTE IND
See series title for descriptive statement.
From The Mechanical Equipment Maintenance, Module 1 Rigging And Lifting Series.
Prod-LEIKID Dist-LEIKID

Power Pinch, The C 26 MIN
16MM FILM, 3/4 OR 1/2 IN VIDEO A
Illustrates behavior which is defined as sexually harassing with emphasis on the economic, legal and economic implications. Explains the underlying causes of such behavior and shows what all involved parties can do to prevent it.
Prod-MTI Dist-MTI Prodn-IVS 1981

Power Plant Fire Fighting C 60 MIN
3/4 INCH VIDEO CASSETTE IND
Describes fire safety procedures for power plants, covering topics such as extinguisher systems, personnel and housekeeping safety, fire strategies, foam selection, and fire suppression.
From The Fire Protection Training Series. Tape 2
LC NO. 80-706024
Prod-ITCORP Dist-ITCORP 1977

Power Plant Fire Fighting C 60 MIN
3/4 OR 1/2 INCH VIDEO CASSETTE IND
Includes fire prevention, fire fighting, and strategies for gas, oil and electrical fires.
From The Fire Fighting Training Series.
Prod-LEIKID Dist-LEIKID

Power Play C 15 MIN
16MM FILM, 3/4 OR 1/2 IN VIDEO I
Examines the concept of power and how it relates to the capabilities of students and the careers they will someday choose.
From The Bread And Butterflies Series.
LC NO. 74-703189
Prod-AITV Dist-AITECH Prodn-KETCTV 1973

Power Plays C 30 MIN
3/4 OR 1/2 INCH VIDEO CASSETTE
Investigates the relationship between Art and Power, how political regimes use art-power to affect and involve us to further their own purposes.
From The Eye To Eye Series.
Prod-WGBHTV Dist-EAI Prodn-MOFAB

Power Press Guarding - Yours To Keep And Protect C 16 MIN
16MM FILM, 3/4 OR 1/2 IN VIDEO
Examines protective devices for punch and power presses beginning with the commonly used fixed barrier guard. Emphasizes the guarding of foot treadles, proper lighting of the die area and the position of the control panel. Shows and explains the gate guard, pull-back devices, two-handed controls, and electronic sensing devices.
Prod-IAPA Dist-IFB 1978

Power Series Solutions B 33 MIN
3/4 OR 1/2 INCH VIDEO CASSETTE
See series title for descriptive statement.
From The Calculus Of Differential Equations Series.
Prod-MIOT Dist-MIOT

Power Shift - The Soviet Arms Build-Up C 29 MIN
3/4 OR 1/2 INCH VIDEO CASSETTE
Presents Ben Wattenberg visiting a U S aircraft carrier and viewing Soviet ships in the Mediterranean. Includes a discussion with Henry Jackson and Daniel P Moynihan covering the implications of this power shift and proposing possible corrective measures.
From The Ben Wattenberg's 1980 Series.
LC NO. 80-707698
Prod-WETATV Dist-PBS

Power Shovel Productivity C 30 MIN
16MM FILM OPTICAL SOUND
Highlights the job conditions that determine the yardage output of power shovels on highway grading work and demonstrates how production is affected by the speed of the dipper cycle, size of dipper load and frequency and duration of delays.
LC NO. 73-703379
Prod-USDTFH Dist-USNAC 1969

Power Supplies B 20 MIN
16MM FILM OPTICAL SOUND
Solves for peak inverse voltage in half and full wave rectifier circuits using a capacitor input filter. Defines bleeder resistor and states the purpose of a permanent load. (Kinescope)
LC NO. 74-705391
Prod-USAF Dist-USNAC

Power Supplies And Filters - Troubleshooting B 25 MIN
16MM FILM, 3/4 OR 1/2 IN VIDEO
Discusses problems in three commonly used power supply circuits, half-wave, full-wave and bridge rectifier. Explains the effects of open and shorted components on output voltage, ripple amplitude and ripple frequency.
Prod-USAF Dist-USNAC 1983

Power System C
3/4 OR 1/2 INCH VIDEO CASSETTE IND
Discusses the basic network, distribution system and the in-house generator.
From The Industrial Training, Module 4 - Power Production Series.
Prod-LEIKID Dist-LEIKID

Power Systems Planning And Resources—A Series
C A
Includes major decision making and economic factors in electric energy systems, planning and resource selection and future resource potential. Contains 44 fifty-minute videotapes.
Prod-UIDEEO Dist-UIDEEO

Power Systems Transients I—A Series

Presents the theory and the physical mechanisms of electromagnetic transients in power networks. Emphasizes digital computation of transients with EMTP program.
Prod-UAZMIC Dist-UAZMIC

Power Systems Transients II C 36 MIN
3/4 OR 1/2 INCH VIDEO CASSETTE
Exposes the theory and state-of-the-art methods for insulation coordination in high voltage (HV) and extra high voltage (EHV) power systems.
Prod-UAZMIC Dist-UAZMIC

Power Take Off (PTO) C 21 MIN
3/4 OR 1/2 INCH VIDEO CASSETTE
Dramatizes a scene where a farmer slips and is entangled in the power take off. Shows how the difficult disentanglement process is complicated by the tractor's three-point hitch.
From The Agricultural Accidents And Rescue Series.
Prod-PSU Dist-PSU

Power To Change, The C 28 MIN
16MM FILM - 3/4 IN VIDEO C A
Demonstrates alternatives to the traditional patterns of production, distribution and use of energy. Focuses on existing projects throughout the United States, including urban composting, solar energy on the farm and wind-powered automobiles.
LC NO. 81-707314
Prod-SIMONJ Dist-THIRD 1980

Power To Save C 15 MIN
16MM FILM, 3/4 OR 1/2 IN VIDEO P-C A
Reports on controlling power consumption and costs. Provides examples of waste.
Prod-KLEINW Dist-KLEINW

Power To Tax, The B 30 MIN
16MM FILM OPTICAL SOUND
Discusses the conflict between State and federal government which has arisen over the concurrent powers of taxation.
From The Structure And Functions Of American Government. Part VI, Lesson 5 - Second Semester
LC NO. 70-700008
Prod-NBCTV Dist-NBC 1963

Power To The People B 10 MIN
16MM FILM OPTICAL SOUND
Shows a machine that goes nowhere. Concludes with one of the workers walking away, carelessly kicking the electric plug that supplies power to the machine.
Prod-UPENN Dist-UPENN 1970

Power To The People C 30 MIN
16MM FILM - 3/4 IN VIDEO J-C A
Explains that in the next 30 years man will use as much power as all the humans who ever lived, despite the fact that two-thirds of the world's population has no electricity. Discusses how this demand for energy is doubling every ten years. Reviews all aspects of the energy shortage and sources.
From The Man Builds - Man Destroys Series.
Prod-UN Dist-GPITVL

Power Train C 13 MIN
16MM FILM, 3/4 OR 1/2 IN VIDEO J-C A
A fully animated explanation of the working of each of the components of the autombile transmission system—clutch, gearbox, drive shaft and differential.
Prod-FILMSW Dist-FLMFR 1968

Power Train (Spanish) C 13 MIN
16MM FILM, 3/4 OR 1/2 IN VIDEO H-C A
Uses animation to explain the workings of the automotive power train, including the clutch, gearbox, universal joint, drive shaft and differential.
Prod-FILMSW Dist-FLMFR 1968

Power Train, The B 5 MIN
16MM FILM OPTICAL SOUND J
Discusses the method of transmission of power in a car, showing how it gets from engine to road surface. Uses animation to describe the hydraulic brake system.
From The Driver Education Series.
LC NO. FIA66-1008
Prod-AMROIL Dist-AMROIL 1964

Power Transformers C 10 MIN
3/4 OR 1/2 INCH VIDEO CASSETTE IND
Presents basics of power transformer design and applica- tion, and details the safe work practices that maintenance and operation personnel should follow when working with this equipment.
From The Electrical Safety Series.
Prod-GPCV Dist-GPCV

Power Transmission - Mechanical C 180 MIN
3/4 OR 1/2 INCH VIDEO CASSETTE PRO
Covers, in three one-hour lectures, power producer coupling device, power user, examples with steam turbines, IC engines, hydraulic turbine and electric motors in drives involving fans, pumps, conveyors, hoist, trucks and power generators when coupled with gears, belts, chains, couplings, clutches and brakes.
From The Professional Engineer Review Series.
Prod-UILU Dist-AMCEE

Power Under Control C 22 MIN
16MM FILM, 3/4 OR 1/2 IN VIDEO H-C A
Shows the director of a driving school for racers discussing defensive driving techniques and giving other safe driving tips. Presents demonstrations that illustrate difficult driving conditions and the actual scene of a near head-on collision between an automobile and a large truck.
From The Three For The Road Series.
Prod-OMTC Dist-IFB 1982

Power Volleyball - Individual Defensive Skills C 11 MIN
16MM FILM, 3/4 OR 1/2 IN VIDEO J-C A
Offers a look at the techniques top women volleyball players use when executing a block, dig, dive, roll or sprawl.
From The Women's Power Volleyball Series.
Prod-ATHI Dist-ATHI

Power Volleyball - Individual Offensive Skills C 11 MIN
16MM FILM, 3/4 OR 1/2 IN VIDEO J-C A
Examines the individual skills of volleyball offense and shows how to improve techniques on the serve, the serve reception, the set and the attack.
From The Women's Power Volleyball Series.
Prod-ATHI Dist-ATHI

Power Vs The People C 36 MIN
16MM FILM, 3/4 OR 1/2 IN VIDEO H-C A
Presents a record of the hearings conducted by the Equal Employment Opportunity Commission in Houston Texas. Records the testimonies of workers and officials of several corporations whose hiring and promotion practices violate Title vii of the Civil Rights Act, which prohibits discrimination against individuals based on race, ethnic origin, sex or religion.
Prod-USEEOC Dist-GREAVW Prodn-GREAVW 1975

Power Without End (2nd Ed) C 16 MIN
3/4 INCH VIDEO CASSETTE I-H
Explores energy sources which cannot be exhausted, such as the sun, wind, geothermal energy and the tides. Shows current efforts to harness these energy sources.
LC NO. 77-703420
Prod-XEROXF Dist-GA 1977

Power, Control, And Decision Making C 40 MIN
3/4 OR 1/2 INCH VIDEO CASSETTE
See series title for descriptive statement.
From The Missiles Of October - A Case Study In Decision Making Series.
Prod-LCOA Dist-DELTAK

Power, Network, Pt 3 C
3/4 OR 1/2 INCH VIDEO CASSETTE IND
Covers direct current supply, motor and generator protection, and network protection.
From The Industrial Training, Module 4 - Power Production Series.
Prod-LEIKID Dist-LEIKID

Power, Power Costs And Building Energy Management Control Systems (Adamczyk), Pt 1 B 60 MIN
3/4 OR 1/2 INCH VIDEO CASSETTE
See series title for descriptive statement.
From The How To Save Energy Dollars In Industrial And Commercial Facilities Series. Pt 8
Prod-UAZMIC Dist-UAZMIC 1978

Power, Power Costs And Building Energy Management Control Systems (Adamczyk), Pt 2 B 60 MIN
3/4 OR 1/2 INCH VIDEO CASSETTE
See series title for descriptive statement.
From The How To Save Energy Dollars In Industrial And Commercial Facilities Series. Pt 9
Prod-UAZMIC Dist-UAZMIC 1978

Powerhead B 5 MIN
16MM FILM OPTICAL SOUND
Shows adjustment of the speeder spring and construction and operation of the powerhead. Demonstrates the speed-setting control of the governor.
LC NO. FIE52-1085
Prod-USN Dist-USNAC 1943

Powerhouse—A Series
3/4 OR 1/2 INCH VIDEO CASSETTE I-J
Presents short stories dealing with how young people should deal with such issues as drug and alcohol abuse, sex equity, prejudice, obesity, physical disability and stress.
Prod-EFCVA Dist-GA

Big Devil	030 MIN
Celebration	030 MIN
Cheers	030 MIN
Fit To Be Tied	030 MIN
Help Wanted	030 MIN
Life Or Breath	030 MIN
Master Of The Art	030 MIN
Name Of The Game	030 MIN
One Of The Gang	030 MIN
Short Life Of Lolo Knopke, The	030 MIN
Something For Nothing	030 MIN
Something Ventured	030 MIN
What Have You Got To Lose	030 MIN
With A Little Help From My Friends, Pt 1	030 MIN
With A Little Help From My Friends, Pt 2	030 MIN
You Make Me Sick	030 MIN

Powering Apollo C 5 MIN
3/4 INCH VIDEO CASSETTE
Explains the major parts of the Saturn 5 rocket. Issued in 1969 as a motion picture.
From The Apollo Digest Series.
LC NO. 79-706986
Prod-NASA Dist-USNAC 1979

Powerless Politics C 30 MIN
3/4 INCH VIDEO CASSETTE
Deals with impact of BIA on all aspects of reservation life. Part of KNBC series of life of modern American Indians.
Prod-KNBCTV Dist-ADL

Powerlessness Corrupts C 20 MIN
3/4 OR 1/2 INCH VIDEO CASSETTE
See series title for descriptive statement.
From The Productivity / Quality Of Work Life Series.
Prod-GOODMI Dist-DELTAK

Powers And Roots C 12 MIN
3/4 OR 1/2 INCH VIDEO CASSETTE
Covers exponential form, multiplying and dividing in exponential form, zero power and fractions with exponents.
From The Using Mathematics In The Plant Series.
Prod-TPCTRA Dist-TPCTRA

Powers And Roots (Spanish) C 12 MIN
3/4 OR 1/2 INCH VIDEO CASSETTE
Covers exponential form, multiplying and dividing in exponential form, zero power and fractions with exponents.
From The Using Mathematics In The Plant Series.
Prod-TPCTRA Dist-TPCTRA

Powers Of Ten (Finnish) C 9 MIN
16MM FILM, 3/4 OR 1/2 IN VIDEO J-C A
Presents an adventure in magnitudes, starting at a picnic by the lakeside in Chicago, and progressing to the edges of the universe and into the micro-world of cells, molecules, and atoms. Describes the universe, using the best available evidence and scientific speculation.
Prod-EAMES Dist-PFP

Powers Of Ten (French) C 9 MIN
16MM FILM, 3/4 OR 1/2 IN VIDEO J-C A
Presents an adventure in magnitudes, starting at a picnic by the lakeside in Chicago, and progressing to the edges of the universe and into the micro-world of cells, molecules, and atoms. Describes the universe, using the best available evidence and scientific speculation.
Prod-EAMES Dist-PFP

Powers Of Ten (German) C 9 MIN
16MM FILM, 3/4 OR 1/2 IN VIDEO J-C A
Presents an adventure in magnitudes, starting at a picnic by the lakeside in Chicago, and progressing to the edges of the universe and into the micro-world of cells, molecules, and atoms. Describes the universe, using the best available evidence and scientific speculation.
Prod-EAMES Dist-PFP

Powers Of Ten (Spanish) C 9 MIN
16MM FILM, 3/4 OR 1/2 IN VIDEO J-C A
Presents an adventure in magnitudes, starting at a picnic by the lakeside in Chicago, and progressing to the edges of the universe and into the micro-world of cells, molecules, and atoms. Describes the universe, using the best available evidence and scientific speculation.
Prod-EAMES Dist-PFP

Powers Of Ten (Swedish) C 9 MIN
16MM FILM, 3/4 OR 1/2 IN VIDEO J-C A
Presents an adventure in magnitudes, starting at a picnic by the lakeside in Chicago, and progressing to the edges of the universe and into the micro-world of cells, molecules, and atoms. Describes the universe, using the best available evidence and scientific speculation.
Prod-EAMES Dist-PFP

Powers Of Ten - A Rough Sketch C 8 MIN
16MM FILM, 3/4 OR 1/2 IN VIDEO I-C A
Presents a linear view of our universe from the human scale to the sea of galaxies, then directly down to the nucleus of a carbon atom. Uses an image, a narration and a dashboard, to give a clue to the relative size of things and what it means to add another zero to any number.
Prod-EAMES Dist-PFP 1968

Powers Of Ten - Decimal Conversion And Multiplication B 20 MIN
16MM FILM - 3/4 IN VIDEO
Demonstrates the use of powers of ten, shows procedures for converting large and small numbers to powers of ten and explains the rules for multiplying powers of ten.
LC NO. 78-706288
Prod-USAF Dist-USNAC 1978

Powers Of Ten - Division And Prefixes B 25 MIN
16MM FILM - 3/4 IN VIDEO
States rules of division of powers of ten and introduces prefixes for powers of ten. Shows how to convert from prefix to power of ten and from power of ten to standard prefix.
LC NO. 78-706289
Prod-USAF Dist-USNAC 1978

Powers Of Ten, 1978 C 9 MIN
16MM FILM, 3/4 OR 1/2 IN VIDEO J-C A
A revised edition of the 1968 motion picture Powers Of Ten. Shows a linear view of the universe, increasing time and distance in increments of ten. Travels into the microworld of cells, DNA molecules and the nucleus of an atom.
Prod-EAMES Dist-PFP 1978

Powers Of The Presidency, The - Armed Intervention C 23 MIN
16MM FILM, 3/4 OR 1/2 IN VIDEO J-H
Examines when, if ever, the interests of the United States are so vitally affected by events in another country that military intervention is required. Shows how the President must choose a course of action in an international crisis quickly and on the basis of swiftly changing and often conflicting information.
Prod-WILETS Dist-BARR 1973

Powers Of The Presidency, The - Economic Controls C 23 MIN
16MM FILM, 3/4 OR 1/2 IN VIDEO J-C A
Examines the extent of the President's constitutional authority to order wage and price controls without the sanction of Congress. Raises questions concerning potential effects of such controls on America's complex economy.
Prod-WILETS Dist-BARR 1975

Powers Of Trig Functions, Pt 1 C
3/4 INCH VIDEO CASSETTE
See series title for descriptive statement.
From The Calculus Series.
Prod-MDDE Dist-MDCPB

Powers Of Trig Functions, Pt 2 C
3/4 INCH VIDEO CASSETTE
See series title for descriptive statement.
From The Calculus Series.
Prod-MDDE Dist-MDCPB

Powers That Be, The C 52 MIN
16MM FILM, 3/4 OR 1/2 IN VIDEO C A
Examines Western art during the period after World War I, including Dada And German Expressionism. Points out that some artists sought an active political role.
From The Shock Of The New Series.
Prod-BBCTV Dist-TIMLIF 1980

PR C 24 MIN
3/4 OR 1/2 INCH VIDEO CASSETTE
Depicts the life of a Puerto Rican boy in New York. Explores the reasons for his immigration from an island to crowded city streets.
From The Young People's Specials Series.
Prod-MULTPP Dist-MULTPP

Practical Application Of Modern Urodynamic Equipment In The Urologist's Office C 25 MIN
16MM FILM OPTICAL SOUND PRO
Shows the practical application, in an office setting, of cystometric equipment and tests to determine problems of patients who have underlying urological dysfunction problems.
LC NO. 78-701377
Prod-EATONL Dist-EATONL Prodn-AEGIS 1978

Practical Applications Of Sensitometry C 29 MIN
3/4 OR 1/2 INCH VIDEO CASSETTE C A
From The Automatic Film Processor Quality Control Series.
Prod-BCAMRT Dist-TEF

Practical Approach To Acid-Base Balance, A C 22 MIN
3/4 OR 1/2 INCH VIDEO CASSETTE PRO
Discusses the delicate balance of acid-base chemistry in the blood. Outlines a very practical and clinically useful technique of managing patients with acid-base disorders.
Prod-UMICHM Dist-UMICHM 1973

Practical Approach To Understanding C 20 MIN
3/4 OR 1/2 INCH VIDEO CASSETTE
Presents an understanding of the forces that shape behavior. Describes why people respond as they do when a situation becomes stressful or antagonistic and why these same people can operate differently when a situation becomes favorable. Describes behavioral response in a four-dimensional model including dominance, inducement, steadiness and compliance.
From The Personality Styles Series.
Prod-AMA Dist-AMA

Practical Complete Denture Reline Technique C 11 MIN
3/4 OR 1/2 INCH VIDEO CASSETTE PRO
Demonstrates a laboratory technique for relining complete dentures that can be done in a dental office using autopolymerizing acrylic and a reline jig.
Prod-VADTC Dist-USNAC

Practical Computing Systems - Operating Systems And Procedures C
16MM FILM OPTICAL SOUND
Looks at the operating system and the sort of computing procedures used in a large company.
Prod-OPENU Dist-OPENU

Practical Examination In Neuroanatomy, Pt I C 56 MIN
3/4 OR 1/2 INCH VIDEO CASSETTE C A
From The Neuroanatomy Series.
Prod-UWO Dist-TEF

Practical Examination In Neuroanatomy, Pt II C 34 MIN
3/4 OR 1/2 INCH VIDEO CASSETTE C A
From The Neuroanatomy Series.
Prod-UWO Dist-TEF

Practical Film Making C 19 MIN
16MM FILM, 3/4 OR 1/2 IN VIDEO J-C A
Traces the essential elements of filmmaking by presenting the steps to the production of a film. Emphasizes ways to cut costs. Presents the importance of well coordinated production and preproduction preparation.
Prod-JULF Dist-EBEC 1972

Practical Information For Job Hunters C 20 MIN
3/4 OR 1/2 INCH VIDEO CASSETTE
Gives practical information to job hunters via phone calls from viewers to a panel of three experts.
Prod-WCCOTV Dist-WCCOTV 1982

Practical M B O—A Series

Deals with the concepts of Management By Objectives, with emphasis on practice and application of ideas to the job. Includes a student text and workbook, a discussion leader's guide, and a Train-the-Trainer session.
Prod-DELTAK Dist-DELTAK

Analyzing Problems And Alternatives 010 MIN
Are You Ready For It 015 MIN
Categories Of Objectives 008 MIN
Identifying Key Result Areas 006 MIN
New Or Innovative Areas 010 MIN
Obtaining Agreement On Objectives 010 MIN
Personal Development Objectives / Appraisal 012 MIN
Regular-Routine Responsibilities 007 MIN
Setting Overall Objectives 007 MIN
Starting The System 013 MIN
Step-By-Step Process, The 006 MIN
What Is M B O 013 MIN

Practical Participation—A Series
16MM FILM, 3/4 OR 1/2 IN VIDEO C A
Promotes better ways of working together and better ways of problem solving in a business environment.
Prod-MILLBK Dist-IFB

More We Are Together, The 021 MIN
On The Right Course 021 MIN

Practical Planning C 15 MIN
3/4 OR 1/2 INCH VIDEO CASSETTE H A
Shows Mary learning to plan ahead to prevent babysitting emergencies while Connie helps Lucy understand why others resent her behavior on the job and helps her plan how to do better.
From The Making It Work Series.
Prod-ERF Dist-AITECH 1983

Practical Prevention For A Healthy You C 55 MIN
3/4 INCH VIDEO CASSETTE
Discusses fact and fiction about commerical products that are said to produce cancer and offers tips on how to keep healthy.
Prod-UTAHTI Dist-UTAHTI

Practical Princess, The C 10 MIN
16MM FILM, 3/4 OR 1/2 IN VIDEO P-I
Uses animation to tell the story of a princess blessed with beauty, brains and common sense. Shows how she outsmarts a dragon, her royal father and an unacceptable suitor. Based on the children's book The Practical Princess by Jay Williams.
LC NO. 82-706522
Prod-BOSUST Dist-CF 1980

Practical Princess, The C 20 MIN
16MM FILM, 3/4 OR 1/2 IN VIDEO K-I
Presents the story 'The Practical Princess' by Jay Williams. Stimulates reading and classroom discussion of plot, character development, emotions and other elements of writing. Filmed in and around a castle in Llewellyn Park, New Jersey.
Prod-SF Dist-SF 1973

Practical Procedures Of Measurement B 48 MIN
16MM FILM OPTICAL SOUND
Discusses purposes of measurement, operational principles of the electroscope, ionization chamber, proportional counter and the Geiger-Muller counter.
From The Radioisotope Series. No. 3
LC NO. FIE53-26
Prod-USA Dist-USNAC 1953

Practical Prosthodontic Procedures C 180 MIN
3/4 INCH VIDEO CASSETTE
Offers an unedited presentation by Jack M Buchman, DDS, Bridgeport, Connecticut, giving some unique but practical and effective procedures that have been used in prosthodontic dentistry.
Prod-AMDA Dist-AMDA 1978

Practical Reading—A Series

Introduces reading comprehension skills developed and reinforced in the instructional videotexts. Gives information on a variety of subjects.
Prod-CAMB Dist-CAMB

Finding An Unstated Main Idea 030 MIN
Finding The Main Idea (Practical Reading) 030 MIN
Making Inferences (Practical Reading) 030 MIN
Reading For Facts (Practical Reading) 030 MIN
Using Sources Of Information 030 MIN

Practical Rheumatology C
3/4 OR 1/2 INCH VIDEO CASSETTE
Discusses a comprehensive approach to all aspects of the patient with a rheumatic disease. Discusses the soft tissue rheumatic syndromes.
Prod-AMEDA Dist-AMEDA

Practical Stress Management With Dr Barry Alberstein—A Series

Teaches practical, specific skills for coping with stress, approaches stress management from both the physical and mental sides of the problem, and presents all aspects of stress management in a clear manner. Discusses practical techniques for handling stress and the individual's role in creating and controlling stress, as well as the role of the environment. Includes a discussion group leader's guide and a participant's kit.
Prod-DELTAK Dist-DELTAK

Assertiveness For Stress Management 032 MIN
Introduction To Stress Management, An 037 MIN
Relaxation As A Form Of Stress Management 032 MIN
Straight Thinking For Stress Management 032 MIN
Time Management For Managing Stress 027 MIN

Practical Suggestions And Personal Stories C 45 MIN
3/4 OR 1/2 INCH VIDEO CASSETTE
See series title for descriptive statement.
From The Dizziness And Related Balance Disorders Series.
Prod-GSHDME Dist-GSHDME

Practical Tax Shelters, Pt I C 25 MIN
3/4 OR 1/2 INCH VIDEO CASSETTE
Answers commonly asked questions about individual retirement and Keogh accounts. Features banker and tax attorney.
From The Your Money Matters Series.
Prod-FILMID Dist-FILMID

Practical Tax Shelters, Pt II C 25 MIN
3/4 OR 1/2 INCH VIDEO CASSETTE
Discusses oil and gas, equipment leasing and real estate partnerships as tax shelters for those in the 50 per cent tax bracket.
From The Your Money Matters Series.
Prod-FILMID Dist-FILMID

Practical Tips On Organizing C 15 MIN
3/4 OR 1/2 INCH VIDEO CASSETTE
See series title for descriptive statement.
From The Put It In Writing Series.
Prod-DELTAK Dist-DELTAK

Practical Use Of Logarithms B 30 MIN
16MM FILM OPTICAL SOUND H
Describes the rule for the characteristic of a logarithm of a number less than one. Shows the technique of adding and subtracting 10 to obtain a positive characteristic. Presents various applications of the use of logarithms.
From The Trigonometry Series.
Prod-CALVIN Dist-MLA Prodn-UNIVFI 1959

Practical Uses Of Multi-Media Techniques C
3/4 OR 1/2 INCH VIDEO CASSETTE PRO
See series title for descriptive statement.
From The Independent Study In Human Sexuality Series.
Prod-MMRC Dist-MMRC

Practical View Of Syphilis, A X 30 MIN
16MM FILM OPTICAL SOUND PRO
Presents significant aspects of modern syphilis diagnosis and management.
LC NO. FIE65-90
Prod-USPHS Dist-USNAC 1963

Practical-Performance Examination For Emergency Medical Technicians (Basic Level), A C 92 MIN
3/4 INCH VIDEO CASSETTE
Offers instructions for the organization and execution of the standardized practical-performance examination for basic level emergency medical technicians.
LC NO. 78-706079
Prod-USHRA Dist-USNAC Prodn-NREMT 1977

Practice For Success C 14 MIN
16MM FILM, 3/4 OR 1/2 IN VIDEO I
Describes Jack's frustration about his beginning tennis lessons. Shows how he remembers that skill requires time and practice and how he begins working step-by-step on his basic tennis.
From The Thinkabout Series. Generalizing
LC NO. 81-706119
Prod-OECA Dist-AITECH 1979

Practice Makes Perfect (French) C 13 MIN
3/4 OR 1/2 INCH VIDEO CASSETTE H-C A
Features an engineer in the Allevard steel works and a village blacksmith who has run out of horses to shoe.
From The En Francais Series. Part 2 - Temporal Relationships, Logical Relationships
Prod-MOFAFR Dist-AITECH 1970

Practice Of Supervision—A Series
16MM FILM - 3/4 IN VIDEO C
Prod-BNA Dist-BNA Prodn-GELLES 1975

Planning, Organizing And Controlling, Pt 1 021 MIN
Planning, Organizing And Controlling, Pt 2 021 MIN
Planning, Organizing And Controlling, Pt 3 020 MIN

Practicing Mathmatical Skills C 18 MIN
16MM FILM OPTICAL SOUND
Illustrates suitable materials for practicing mathimatical skills, describes use of a computer terminal, and deals with techniques for promoting interest and ways of identifying appropriate items for drill.
From The Project On Interpreting Mathematics Education Research Series.
LC NO. 74-705395
Prod-USOE Dist-USNAC 1970

Practitioner's Guide To Determining Beneficiaries, A C 35 MIN
3/4 OR 1/2 INCH VIDEO CASSETTE PRO
Examines how to prevent malpractice exposure in intestate distribution. Gives a lesson in genealogy and proof of heirship.
From The Practitioner's Guide To Preventing Probate Litigation Series.
Prod-ABACPE Dist-ABACPE

Practitioner's Guide To Preventing Probate Litigation—A Series
PRO
Gives advice on preparing wills that will withstand the challenge of litigation. Points out situations connected with the distribution of intestate estates where attorneys can inadvertently commit malpractice.
Prod-ABACPE Dist-ABACPE

Anticipating The Defense Of Will Contests 042 MIN
Practitioner's Guide To Determining 035 MIN

Pragmatic Development C 112 MIN
3/4 OR 1/2 INCH VIDEO CASSETTE
Describes the normal sequences of pragmatic development and their relationship to Piaget's stages of sensorimotor development. Explores the application of pragmatics to communication assessment and intervention with severely/profoundly handicapped individuals.
From The Meeting The Communications Needs Of The Severely/Profoundly Handicapped 1980 Series.
Prod-PUAVC Dist-PUAVC

Pragmatic Development C 146 MIN
3/4 OR 1/2 INCH VIDEO CASSETTE
Addresses the central role of pragmatics in communication development and intervention. Describes normal sequences of pragmatic development and their relationship to Piaget's stages of sensorimeter development.
From The Meeting The Communication Needs Of The Severely/Profoundly Handicapped 1981 Series.
Prod-PUAVC Dist-PUAVC

Prague Castle C 13 MIN
16MM FILM, 3/4 OR 1/2 IN VIDEO
Features the Prague Castle, one of the oldest and best-preserved castles in Europe.
Prod-KAWVAL Dist-KAWVAL

Prairie Coulee C 15 MIN
16MM FILM, 3/4 OR 1/2 IN VIDEO J-C A
Shows the plants and animals that inhabit the 'prairie coulee,' a steep-walled valley made by water during a glacial period.
From The Animals And Plants Of North America Series.
LC NO. 81-707418
Prod-KARVF Dist-LCOA 1981

Prairie Fire B 30 MIN
3/4 OR 1/2 INCH VIDEO CASSETTE
Brings to life a time in American history when farmers organized to protect their way of life and fight against the abuses of Eastern grain, banking and railroad trusts.
Prod-NFPS Dist-NFPS

Prairie Giant C 21 MIN
16MM FILM, 3/4 OR 1/2 IN VIDEO J-H
Introduces the giant Canada goose in its natural habitat of prairies and tall grass plains.
Prod-COTTER Dist-IFB 1968

Prairie Giant (Geant De La Prairie, Le) C 21 MIN
16MM FILM, 3/4 OR 1/2 IN VIDEO J-H
A French language version of the film Prairie Giant. Details the life of the Canada goose in its natural habitat of prairies and tall grass plains. Includes other wild birds.
Prod-COTTER Dist-IFB

Prairie Killers C 30 MIN
16MM FILM, 3/4 OR 1/2 IN VIDEO H-C A
Describes the white man's invasion of the Great Plains, the displacement of the Indians and the annihilation of the buffalo. Explains how ranchers are changing the ecological balance by killing coyotes and prairie dogs. Points out how the destruction of one part of life relates to the eventual extermination of the whole.
From The Our Vanishing Wilderness Series. No. 2
LC NO. 80-707021
Prod-NETRC Dist-IU 1971

Prairie Pronghorn C 13 MIN
16MM FILM OPTICAL SOUND
Shows much of the wildlife in the regions of the plains of central Wyoming.
Prod-SFI Dist-SFI

Prairie Pronghorns C 15 MIN
16MM FILM OPTICAL SOUND
Archer stalks fleet antelope through sparse cover in central Wyoming.
Prod-SFI Dist-SFI

Prairie Roadsides C 14 MIN
16MM FILM OPTICAL SOUND J-C
Describes an experimental program using native prairie plants to control weeds and erosion on roadsides. Shows that the reintroduction of native plants can provide functional, low-maintenance roadside cover vegetation. Illustrates the advantages of a more ecological approach to the maintenance of highway right-of-way.
LC NO. 74-700139
Prod-IOWA Dist-IOWA 1973

Prairie School Architecture C 28 MIN
3/4 OR 1/2 INCH VIDEO CASSETTE H-C A
Capsulizes the principles of the Prairie School of Architecture. Visits the midwestern heartland to buildings sparked by the vision of master architect Louis Sullivan under the influence of Frank Lloyd Wright.
LC NO. 84-707061
Prod-UCV Dist-UCV 1984

Prairie Slough C 15 MIN
16MM FILM, 3/4 OR 1/2 IN VIDEO J-C A
Describes the role of prairie marshes in providing food and sanctuary for thousands of waterfowl as they migrate to and from breeding grounds.
From The Animals And Plants Of North America Series.
LC NO. 81-707420
Prod-KARVF Dist-LCOA 1981

Prairie Storm C 57 MIN
3/4 OR 1/2 INCH VIDEO CASSETTE
Discusses the issue of abortion and the effect the opening of North Dakota's first abortion clinic has on one midwestern community.
Prod-WCCOTV Dist-WCCOTV 1982

Prairie That Was, The C 19 MIN
16MM FILM, 3/4 OR 1/2 IN VIDEO I-C
Takes a look at the grasslands and wildlife found in parks and wildlife refuges which preserve the North American prairie in its original habitat.
Prod-GALATR Dist-AIMS 1975

Prairie Towns A-Boomin' B 30 MIN
16MM FILM OPTICAL SOUND H-C A
Describes the life of the agricultural state as reflected in its towns. Discusses the county seat struggles, the urban boom, and the cities, schools and churches. Pictures social life in Omaha and on the farm.
From The Great Plains Trilogy, 3 Series. Explorer And Settler - The White Man Arrives
Prod-KUONTV Dist-UNL 1954

Prairie War C 29 MIN
16MM FILM OPTICAL SOUND
Portrays Al Oeming's journey to southern Saskatchewan in an experiment to introduce two kit foxes, bred at his game farm, back into the wilderness.
From The Al Oeming - Man Of The North Series.
LC NO. 77-702872
Prod-NIELSE Dist-NIELSE 1977

Prairie, The C 18 MIN
16MM FILM, 3/4 OR 1/2 IN VIDEO J-H
Studies the animals that inhabit the North American prairie, such as the porcupine, prairie rattler, burrowing owl and the dung-feeders. Also examines the plants, grasses and forbs found in the prairie. Shows the prairie as it first appeared to pioneers. Explains how man has changed it to make it serve his needs.
From The Living Science Series.
Prod-CAMPF Dist-IFB 1963

Prairie, The (3rd Ed) C 15 MIN
16MM FILM, 3/4 OR 1/2 IN VIDEO J-H
Surveys the various types of animals, plants and insects which inhabit the prairie grasslands, explaining the interrelationship between each. Describes the natural forces which have created and maintain the fertile prairie ecosystem.
From The Natural Science Series.
Prod-BARR Dist-BARR 1980

Prairie, The - America's Grassland C 12 MIN
3/4 OR 1/2 INCH VIDEO CASSETTE
Explores both tall and short-grass prairies with a close look at virgin prairie areas.
Prod-CBSC Dist-CBSC

Prairies To Peaktops C 22 MIN
3/4 OR 1/2 INCH VIDEO CASSETTE I-H
Introduces important concepts in ecology and behavior of wildlife by exploring the life zones of the Rocky Mountains.
From The Aerie Nature Series.
Prod-CEPRO Dist-CEPRO 1982

Praise C 60 MIN
16MM FILM - 1/2 IN VIDEO, VHS
Portrays Praise, a young, black street boy with incredible raw intelligence, who is haunted by peer pressure and his own heritage.
Prod-TLECUL Dist-TLECUL

Praisin' His Name - The Gospel Soul Children Of New Orleans C 60 MIN
3/4 OR 1/2 INCH VIDEO CASSETTE
Presents the Gospel Soul Children who perform such gospel favorites as Wounded For Me, Call Him Up, If Jesus Goes With Me and I Love The Lord.
Prod-WYESTV Dist-MDCPB

Prayer C 2 MIN
16MM FILM OPTICAL SOUND I-H A R
Touches on every form of prayer through the quiet reflections of a young woman.
From The Meditation Series.
LC NO. 80-700755
Prod-IKONOG Dist-IKONOG 1974

Prayer C 5 MIN
16MM FILM OPTICAL SOUND
Shows the movements and atmosphere in Jewish prayer. Includes a morning service in a synagogue of a chassidic community, the welcoming of the Sabbath and a cantorial psalm.
LC NO. 76-700407
Prod-URIELI Dist-URIELI 1975

Prayer Of The Ages—A Series
R
Prod-FAMLYT Dist-FAMLYT

By The Wayside 5 MIN
Once Upon A Morning 5 MIN
Wonder 5 MIN

Pre And Post Conferences B 30 MIN
16MM FILM OPTICAL SOUND C A
Employs dramatization to illustrate pre and post conference teaching principles.
From The Nursing - Where Are You Going, How Will You Get There Series.
LC NO. 74-700184
Prod-NTCN Dist-NTCN 1971

Pre And Post Operative Breathing Exercises C
3/4 OR 1/2 INCH VIDEO CASSETTE
Explains how patients can help insure their own recovery by practicing respiratory exercises before their operation.
Prod-MIFE Dist-MIFE

Pre And Post Operative Breathing Exercises (Spanish) C
3/4 OR 1/2 INCH VIDEO CASSETTE
Explains how patients can help insure their own recovery by practicing respiratory exercises before their operation.
Prod-MIFE Dist-MIFE

Pre And Post Operative Breathing Exercises (Arabic) C
3/4 OR 1/2 INCH VIDEO CASSETTE

Explains how patients can help insure their own recovery by practicing respiratory exercises before their operation.
Prod-MIFE Dist-MIFE

Pre-Cleaning C 7 MIN
1/2 IN VIDEO CASSETTE BETA/VHS
Deals with auto body repair. Discusses entry level masking techniques, including different tape widths and the use of an apron taper.
Prod-RMI Dist-RMI

Pre-Columbian Art Of Costa Rica C 15 MIN
16MM FILM OPTICAL SOUND J-C
Deals with an extensive panorama of pre-Columbian art objects of Costa Rica.
Prod-PAN Dist-PAN

Pre-Columbian Art Of Costa Rica (Spanish) C 15 MIN
16MM FILM OPTICAL SOUND J-C
Deals with an extensive panorama of pre-Columbian art objects of Costa Rica.
Prod-PAN Dist-PAN

Pre-Columbian Civilizations C 30 MIN
3/4 OR 1/2 INCH VIDEO CASSETTE H
Looks at the first arrivals to America. Studies the Olmecs, the Mayas, the Aztecs and the Incas.
From The Historically Speaking Series. Part 2
Prod-KRMATV Dist-AITECH 1983

Pre-Delivery Adjustment Of Casting - Laboratory Procedure C 10 MIN
16MM FILM - 3/4 IN VIDEO PRO
Explains that certain arbitrary relief procedures should be accomplished on the removable partial denture casting to remove potential interferences that may resist complete sealing of the appliance. Describes area adjustment problems and methods to obtain necessary alterations. Issued in 1967 as a motion picture.
From The Removable Partial Dentures, Clasp Type - Clinical And Laboratory Procedures Series.
LC NO. 78-706182
Prod-USVA Dist-USNAC Prodn-VADTC 1978

Pre-Delivery And Casting Adjustment C 9 MIN
3/4 OR 1/2 INCH VIDEO CASSETTE
Points out that certain arbitrary relief procedures should be accomplished on the removable partial denture casting to remove any potential interferences that may resist complete seating on the appliance. Describes the area that requires adjustment and the methods to obtain the necessary alterations.
From The Removable Partial Dentures, Clasp Type Clinical And Laboratory Procedures Series.
Prod-VADTC Dist-AMDA 1969

Pre-Extraction Record Of Vertical Dimension Using Plaster Bandage, A C 9 MIN
16MM FILM, 3/4 OR 1/2 IN VIDEO
Demonstrates a simple procedure using plaster bandage to obtain accurate, permanent, pre-extraction records of vertical dimension.
Prod-USVA Dist-USNAC 1968

Pre-Flight C 29 MIN
2 INCH VIDEOTAPE
See series title for descriptive statement.
From The Discover Flying - Just Like A Bird Series.
Prod-WKYCTV Dist-PUBTEL

Pre-Game Stretch, The C 25 MIN
3/4 OR 1/2 INCH VIDEO CASSETTE
Shows California Angel Bill Singer and his teammates detailing a new form of stretching exercises that can be useful for everyone.
Prod-TRAINX Dist-TRAINX

Pre-Kindergarten Program, A - A Camera Visit To New Haven B 30 MIN
16MM FILM OPTICAL SOUND
Describes a Head Start-like program for disadvantaged children operated by a public school system in a community center. Follows the childrens' unrehearsed activities while the director of the program is being interviewed.
Prod-VASSAR Dist-NYU 1965

Pre-Malignant And Malignant Lesions Of The Breast And Colon B 90 MIN
16MM FILM OPTICAL SOUND PRO
Presents a panel of doctors discussing simple versus radical mastectomy, surgical procedures, radiation therapy and opinions about biopsies. Shows three actual breast and colon cases and a neurosurgeon demonstrating a hypophysectomy.
Prod-UPJOHN Dist-UPJOHN

Pre-Manufacture Notification Rule (EPA, May 1983)—A Series
A
Presents a panel discussion of the EPA's May 13, 1983 ruling on final Premanufacture Notification. Includes highlights of the PMN seminar in Washington, DC and discusses how to complete the PMN form.
Prod-USEPA Dist-USNAC 1983

Highlights Of The June 23, 1983 PMN Seminar
How To Complete The PMN Form 018 MIN
Questions And Answers About EPA's Final PMN 021 MIN

Pre-Miranda Interrogation B 21 MIN
16MM FILM OPTICAL SOUND C
Deals with various aspects of a criminal lawsuit involving a liquor store robbery case. Shows the adult suspect being questioned in a manner indicating potential police abuses. Includes the search of the impounded automobile.
From The Criminal Series. No. 3
LC NO. 76-714035
Prod-RPATLF Dist-RPATLF 1968

Pre-Natal Care C 10 MIN
16MM FILM OPTICAL SOUND H-C A
Presents information for the mother-to-be, including basic concepts of the physiology of pregnancy. Explains the physical needs and responsibilities of pregnancy.
From The Obstetrics And Gynecology Series.
LC NO. 75-700042
Prod-MIFE Dist-MIFE 1974

Pre-Natal Care C
3/4 OR 1/2 INCH VIDEO CASSETTE
Describes what happens on the first pre-natal care visit. Covers history taking, examination, various tests, diet and health care tips, activities, what to expect and what to be concerned about.
Prod-MIFE Dist-MIFE

Pre-Natal Care C 15 MIN
16MM FILM, 3/4 OR 1/2 IN VIDEO H-C A
Emphasizes the role of the doctor in pre-natal counseling, and also the importance of good nutrition and moderation in drinking, smoking and use of medications. Features a mime demonstrating several simple exercises useful in alleviating some of the discomfort usually associated with an advancing pregnancy.
From The Woman Talk Series.
Prod-CORF Dist-CORF 1983

Pre-Natal Care (Arabic) C
3/4 OR 1/2 INCH VIDEO CASSETTE
Describes what happens on the first pre-natal care visit. Covers history taking, examination, various tests, diet and health care tips, activities, what to expect and what to be concerned about.
Prod-MIFE Dist-MIFE

Pre-Natal Care (French) C
3/4 OR 1/2 INCH VIDEO CASSETTE
Describes what happens on the first pre-natal care visit. Covers history taking, examination, various tests, diet and health care tips, activities, what to expect and what to be concerned about.
Prod-MIFE Dist-MIFE

Pre-Natal Care (Spanish) C
3/4 OR 1/2 INCH VIDEO CASSETTE
Describes what happens on the first pre-natal care visit. Covers history taking, examination, various tests, diet and health care tips, activities, what to expect and what to be concerned about.
Prod-MIFE Dist-MIFE

Pre-Natal Care/Vaccinations C 30 MIN
3/4 OR 1/2 INCH VIDEO CASSETTE
See series title for descriptive statement.
From The Health, Safety And Well-Being Series.
Prod-MAETEL Dist-CAMB

Pre-Natal Diagnosis - To Be Or Not To Be C 45 MIN
16MM FILM, 3/4 OR 1/2 IN VIDEO A
Shows the scientific techniques involved in prenatal diagnosis of genetic abnormalities and examines the responsibilities and decisions facing both physicians and parents as they weigh the risks of the tests against the findings. Includes interviews with parents of children afflicted with genetic abnormalities and observations of genetic specialists.
LC NO. 82-706298
Prod-CANBC Dist-FLMLIB 1981

Pre-Natal Diagnosis By Amniocentesis C 26 MIN
16MM FILM OPTICAL SOUND
Portrays two genetic counseling situations in which amniocentesis is suggested, one concerning the risk of biochemical defect and the other concerning the risk of a chromosomal defect. Shows the actual technique used to withdraw amniotic fluid from the uterus and illustrates the complex laboratory procedures used to evaluate the fluid.
From The Human Genetics Series. No. 10
LC NO. 75-700026
Prod-NFMD Dist-MIFE Prodn-MIFE 1972

Pre-Natal Diagnosis By Amniocentesis (Spanish) C 26 MIN
16MM FILM OPTICAL SOUND
Portrays two genetic counseling situations in which amniocentesis is suggested, one concerning the risk of biochemical defect and the other concerning the risk of a chromosomal defect. Shows the actual technique used to withdraw amniotic fluid from the uterus and illustrates the complex laboratory procedures used to evaluate the fluid.
From The Human Genetics (Spanish) Series. No. 10
LC NO. 75-700026
Prod-NFMD Dist-MIFE Prodn-MIFE 1972

Pre-Number Ideas C 30 MIN
16MM FILM OPTICAL SOUND A
Provides an overview of modern mathematics, and presents some fundamental concepts about sets.
From The Mathematics For Elementary School Teachers Series. No. 1
Prod-SMSG Dist-MLA 1963

Pre-op C 29 MIN
16MM FILM, 3/4 OR 1/2 IN VIDEO A
Brings attention to the emotional needs of children when they are ill and need hospitalization. Dramatizes the situation in the fictional Tristero family, in which Ann Marie's own fears of sickness and hospitals frighten her young son Paul. Includes a brief introduction and commentary by real-life families and child development experts.
From The Footsteps Series.
LC NO. 80-707203
Prod-USDED Dist-USNAC Prodn-EDFCEN 1980

Pre-Op - Illness And Hospitalization C 23 MIN
16MM FILM - VIDEO, ALL FORMATS
Deals with helping sick or injured children understand what is happening to their bodies. Shows that easing fears and anxieties is as important as providing physical care.
From The Footsteps Series.
Prod-PEREN Dist-PEREN

Pre-Operative And Post-Operative Thoracotomy Care C 47 MIN
3/4 OR 1/2 INCH VIDEO CASSETTE
Emphasizes the importance of good preoperative teaching by the nursing staff. Discusses the care needed during the early post-operative period of a thoracotomy patient.
LC NO. 81-706298
Prod-USVA Dist-USNAC 1980

Pre-operative Instruction C 20 MIN
3/4 INCH VIDEO CASSETTE
Provides general information for the patient having general elective surgery, management of pain and excercises to improve recovery following surgery.
Prod-UWISN Dist-UWISN

Pre-Operative Interviews C 35 MIN
16MM FILM OPTICAL SOUND
Clarifies for the nursing staff what can be accomplished via the pre-operative visit. Focuses on three patient interviews, identified by operating room nurses as being difficult to manage, the hostile patient, the depressed patient and the patient who denies illness.
LC NO. 74-702664
Prod-ACYDGD Dist-AMCSUR 1974

Pre-Operative Problems In Regional Enteritis C 26 MIN
16MM FILM OPTICAL SOUND PRO
Explains that regional enteritis should be treated medically until complication of obstruction, fistula formation, hemorrhage or recurrent attacks require operation. Points out that recurrence is common and illustrates various late complications.
Prod-ACYDGD Dist-ACY 1961

Pre-Participation Physical Examination Of The Athlete C
3/4 OR 1/2 INCH VIDEO CASSETTE
Offers a guide to conducting a thorough examination of aspiring athletes before actual participation. Discusses specifics to look for and presents the physical examination as an important tool for the prevention of injury to athletes.
From The Sports Medicine Series.
Prod-VTRI Dist-VTRI

Pre-Primer Sanding Of Fill Material C 7 MIN
1/2 IN VIDEO CASSETTE BETA/VHS
Deals with auto body repair. Covers the proper leveling and feathering of fill material in relationship to the panel itself.
Prod-RMI Dist-RMI

Pre-Raphaelite Revolt, The C 30 MIN
16MM FILM, 3/4 OR 1/2 IN VIDEO
Traces the movement of the pre-Raphaelite Brotherhood, which protested the outmoded academic conventions of the day and wanted to emulate the naturalism of the Italian Renaissance painters before Raphael. Studies the early works of Ford Madox Brown, John Everett Millais, John Ruskin, Holman Hunt, Arthur Hughs and Dante Gabriel Rossetti.
Prod-BCACGB Dist-FI 1967

Pre-Retirement Planning C 25 MIN
3/4 OR 1/2 INCH VIDEO CASSETTE
Outlines steps that lead to a leisurely and worry-free retirement. Presented by a Social Security representative and a planning firm.
From The Your Money Matters Series.
Prod-FILMID Dist-FILMID

Pre-Retirement Planning - It Makes A Difference C 15 MIN
16MM FILM, 3/4 OR 1/2 IN VIDEO A
Uses four examples of retirees to illustrate the need to plan ahead for a successful retirement.
Prod-USSSA Dist-USNAC

Pre-School Readiness - Foundation For Learning C
3/4 OR 1/2 INCH VIDEO CASSETTE A
Suggests ways parents can prepare children for experiences encountered in school.
From The Vital Link Series.
Prod-EDCC Dist-EDCC

Pre-School, The C 22 MIN
16MM FILM, 3/4 OR 1/2 IN VIDEO H-C A
Presents a day's visit to a pre-school, illustrating the positive learning environment and long term benefits that can result from pre-school education.
Prod-JARBRI Dist-AIMS 1973

Pre-Speech Evaluation And Therapy B 17 MIN
16MM FILM OPTICAL SOUND PRO
Illustrates the techniques utilized by Miss Helen Mueller of Switzerland for evaluation of lip, tongue, jaw control, sucking, swallowing and chewing and breathing problems in the young child. Demonstrates procedures aimed to overcome deficits. Presents the findings in the abnormal child as compared to those in the normal child.
Prod-UCLA Dist-UCLA 1970

Pre-Supervisory Training—A Series

Promotes the concept of pre-supervisory training for employees before they actually assume supervisory roles.
Prod-RESEM Dist-RESEM

Determing Pay-Off Areas 012 MIN
Need For Pre-Supervisory Training, The 012 MIN

Training Activity, The 011 MIN

Pre-Vasectomy Family Consultation C 13 MIN
3/4 OR 1/2 INCH VIDEO CASSETTE PRO
See series title for descriptive statement.
From The Urology Series.
Prod-MSU Dist-MSU

Pre-Verbal Communication C 16 MIN
16MM FILM, 3/4 OR 1/2 IN VIDEO C A
Shows how dependent an eight-month-old baby is on her mother to interpret her gestures and noises. Demonstrates that they can still communicate even when they can only see each other on a television monitor.
From The Under Fives Series.
Prod-GRATV Dist-FLMLIB 1982

Pre-War German Featurettes—A Series

Documents pre-war Nazi Germany dealing with the political issues of the period. Examines the policies and conduct of Adolf Hitler as he fashions the embryo of a swift and terrible war machine.
Prod-IHF Dist-IHF

Becoming An Army
Honor Of Work
Three Years Of Adolf Hitler
Yesterday And Today

Pre/Post Test C 19 MIN
3/4 OR 1/2 INCH VIDEO CASSETTE J-H
Contains a test of 21 questions which is given to students before viewing the series and then again after they have seen the series.
From The Reading Approach To Math Series.
Prod-WNVT Dist-GPITVL 1979

Preacher, The C 1 MIN
16MM FILM OPTICAL SOUND J-C A
Satirizes the communication gap between the Church and the world and the problems of misguided though wellintentioned communication of any kind.
LC NO. 74-702119
Prod-MMA Dist-MMA 1972

Preamble, The C 3 MIN
3/4 OR 1/2 INCH VIDEO CASSETTE I
Sets the Constitution's preamble to music, showing America growing from a nation of 13 to 50 states under the protection of the Constitution.
From The America Rock Series.
Prod-ABCTV Dist-GA Prodn-SCOROC 1976

Precast Concrete Bridge C 18 MIN
16MM FILM, 3/4 OR 1/2 IN VIDEO
Uses construction scenes and animated drawings to show casting of beams, deck slabs and curb sections, driving of piles and construction of bent caps, placement of precast units and final operations in completing a three-span bridge structure.
LC NO. 82-706164
Prod-USDTFH Dist-USNAC 1955

Precautionary Measures In Isolation C
3/4 OR 1/2 INCH VIDEO CASSETTE
Presents the rationale and illustrates four precautionary measures in isolation, namely handwashing, assigning an appropriate room, protective apparel and handling of contaminated items.
From The Infection Control III Series.
Prod-CONMED Dist-CONMED

Precautions Against Fanatics (German) B 11 MIN
16MM FILM OPTICAL SOUND
Presents an elaborate on-camera practical joke involving German celebrities and a one-armed, self-appointed protector of racehorses. Directed by Werner Herzog. With English subtitles.
Prod-UNKNWN Dist-NYFLMS 1969

Precautions In The Resection Of The Colon For Carcinoma C 29 MIN
16MM FILM OPTICAL SOUND PRO
Illustrates two precautions in resection of the colon which might minimize the possibility of recurrence. Deals with the possibility of implantation of cancer cells in the suture line and with prevention of venous metastasis incident to manipulation of the tumor during the resection.
Prod-ACYDGD Dist-ACY 1954

Precinct 94-142 C 22 MIN
16MM FILM, 3/4 OR 1/2 IN VIDEO T
Looks at how attitudes, feelings and interpersonal communication can affect education for the handicapped.
Prod-MTI Dist-MTI

Precious Cargo C 15 MIN
16MM FILM OPTICAL SOUND
Illustrates and interprets the inter-country adoption program supported by WAIF/ISS.
Prod-HF Dist-HF

Precious Tissue C 10 MIN
16MM FILM OPTICAL SOUND PRO
Depicts the uses of blood components and derivatives in highly technical terms.
Prod-ARMPHC Dist-ARMPHC 1970

Precipitation Equilibria C 9 MIN
3/4 INCH VIDEO CASSETTE
Introduces solubility, precipitation and saturated solution equilibria. Demonstrates common ion effect.
From The Chemistry Videotape Series.
Prod-UMITV Dist-UMITV

Precipitation Hardening C 30 MIN
3/4 OR 1/2 INCH VIDEO CASSETTE PRO
Presents the process of forming a supersaturated solid solution and subsequent inducement of precipitation.
From The Elements Of Physical Metallurgy Series.
Prod-AMCEE Dist-AMCEE

Precipitation Hardening C 35 MIN
3/4 INCH VIDEO CASSETTE C A
See series title for descriptive statement.
From The Elements Of Metallurgy Series.
LC NO. 81-706194
Prod-AMCEE Dist-AMCEE 1980

Precipitation Of Hardening C 45 MIN
3/4 OR 1/2 INCH VIDEO CASSETTE PRO
See series title for descriptive statement.
From The Elements Of Metallurgy Series.
Prod-ICSINT Dist-ICSINT

Precisely So B 20 MIN
16MM FILM OPTICAL SOUND H-C A
Traces the development of modern standards of accuracy from ancient times. Illustrates scientific instruments which measure time to the thousandth part of a second, weigh a dot of a lead pencil on a piece of paper and split a hair-breadth measurement into hundreds of parts.
Prod-HANDY Dist-GM 1940

Precision C 12 MIN
16MM FILM OPTICAL SOUND
Explains why the manufacture of computer tape must be precise and demonstrates the accomplishments of IBM in their production facility.
LC NO. 70-702529
Prod-IBUSMA Dist-IBUSMA Prodn-STEEGP 1968

Precision Casting For High Performance C 18 MIN
16MM FILM OPTICAL SOUND
Examines the production of Jet Engine Turbine Blades from the first to final steps in their manufacture.
Prod-GM Dist-GM

Precision Football C 29 MIN
16MM FILM, 3/4 OR 1/2 IN VIDEO
Designed to provide an understanding of the rules and officiating procedures used in football by focusing on such topics as pass interference, encroachment and free kicks.
LC NO. 79-707710
Prod-NFSHSA Dist-NFSHSA Prodn-CALPRO 1979

Precision Gage Blocks B 18 MIN
16MM FILM, 3/4 OR 1/2 IN VIDEO
Discusses the various uses of gage blocks in setting inspection gages. Shows how to calculate, clean and assemble gage blocks.
From The Machine Shop Work - Operations On The Vertical Milling Machine Series. No. 6
Prod-USOE Dist-USNAC Prodn-NEMETH 1945

Precision Measuring Instruments, The Micrometer Caliper - (ITP Practical Project... C 30 MIN
3/4 OR 1/2 INCH VIDEO CASSETTE IND
Acquaints students with the most popular precision measuring instument, the micrometer caliper. Shows how the instrument is made and how it is used, especially in conjunction with the telescoping and ball gauge. Includes, also, explanations of use of the inside and depth micrometers plus care and handling of these precision instruments.
From The Aviation Technician Training Program Series.
Prod-AVIMA Dist-AVIMA

Precision Measuring Instruments, The Vernier Caliper - (ITP Practical Project Series) C 30 MIN
3/4 OR 1/2 INCH VIDEO CASSETTE IND
Explains how use of the vernier caliper is one of the fastest methods of obtaining precision measurements. Shows how it is made, how and why it works, and how to use it. Includes use of spring and firm joint calipers in conjunction with the vernier caliper. Stresses care and handling of all precision instruments.
From The Aviation Technician Training Program Series.
Prod-AVIMA Dist-AVIMA

Precision Measurment Tools C 16 MIN
3/4 OR 1/2 INCH VIDEO CASSETTE IND
Teaches how to read precision measurement tools such as the micrometer, vernier caliper and depth gauge.
From The Introduction To Machine Technology, Module 1 Series.
Prod-LEIKID Dist-LEIKID

Precision Of Articulation In Hearing Children C 17 MIN
16MM FILM, 3/4 OR 1/2 IN VIDEO
Presents an interpretation of a sound spectrogram in order to analyze the precision of a child's speech, represented as a function of age.
LC NO. 80-707426
Prod-USDHEW Dist-USNAC 1980

Precision Wood Machining - Operations On The Band Saw—A Series

Prod-USOE Dist-USNAC 1945

Sawing A Reverse Curve And A Bevel
Sawing With Jig And Changing Band 020 MIN

Precision Wood Machining - Operations On The Jointer—A Series

Prod-USOE Dist-USNAC 1945

Beveling, Stop Chamfering And Tapering
Face Planing Uneven Surfaces 013 MIN
Jointing An Edge for Gluing - Installing 021 MIN
Jointing Edges And Ends 90 Degrees To Face 017 MIN

Precision Wood Machining - Operations On The Spindle Shaper—A Series

Prod-USOE Dist-USNAC 1945

Cutting Grooves With Circular Saw Blades 022 MIN
Rabbeting And Shaping An Edge On Straight Stock 018 MIN
Shaping After Template And Shaping Curved Edges 017 MIN

Precision Wood Machining - Operations On The Variety Saw—A Series

Prod-USOE Dist-USNAC 1945

Beveling, Mitering, Rabbeting And Dadoing 019 MIN
Cutting Cove Molding And A Corebox 019 MIN
Cutting Tenons And Segments 015 MIN
Ripping And Crosscutting 019 MIN

Preconception Care And Diagnosis Of Pregnancy B 29 MIN
16MM FILM OPTICAL SOUND C A
Tells about annual physical examinations, cancer detection by cytology, prevention of fetal loss and mental retardation by optimal health at time of conception, physiologic changes of early pregnancy and older biologic and newer imminologic pregnancy tests.
From The Nine To Get Ready Series. No. 1
LC NO. 73-704217
Prod-KUONTV Dist-UNEBR 1965

Preconception Care And Diagnosis Of Pregnancy C 29 MIN
2 INCH VIDEOTAPE
See series title for descriptive statement.
From The Nine To Get Ready Series.
Prod-NETCHE Dist-PUBTEL

Precursors, The - Cezanne, Gauguin, Van Gogh C 26 MIN
16MM FILM, 3/4 OR 1/2 IN VIDEO H-C
Explains how Cezanne, Gauguin and Van Gogh contributed to the development of modern painting. Studies the artistic influences they received from other painters and looks at the development of their own personalities.
Prod-IFB Dist-IFB 1971

Predators And Prey C 9 MIN
16MM FILM, 3/4 OR 1/2 IN VIDEO P-I
Examines the predator and prey relationships among a variety of animals, including a fox, roadrunner, pocket gopher and striped skunk.
From The Life Science For Elementary Series.
Prod-PEDF Dist-AIMS 1976

Predators And Prey (Spanish) C 9 MIN
16MM FILM, 3/4 OR 1/2 IN VIDEO P-I
Examines the predator and prey relationships among a variety of animals, including a fox, roadrunner, pocket gopher and striped skunk.
From The Life Science For Elementary Series.
Prod-PEDF Dist-AIMS 1976

Predators Of North America C 12 MIN
16MM FILM, 3/4 OR 1/2 IN VIDEO I-J
Looks at North American animals that must kill to survive. Reveals some of the adaptations that aid predators in obtaining prey and the tremendous diversity among predators.
Prod-NGS Dist-NGS 1981

Predators Of The Desert C 22 MIN
16MM FILM, 3/4 OR 1/2 IN VIDEO I-H
Edited from the 1953 motion picture The Living Desert. Shows confrontations between predator and prey in a struggle for survival in the desert.
From The Living Desert Series.
Prod-DISNEY Dist-WDEMCO 1974

Predators Of The Desert (French) C 22 MIN
16MM FILM, 3/4 OR 1/2 IN VIDEO I-H
Views desert predators.
From The Living Desert (French) Series.
Prod-WDEMCO Dist-WDEMCO 1974

Predators, The C 26 MIN
16MM FILM, 3/4 OR 1/2 IN VIDEO
A shortened version of the videocassette The Predators. Observes North America's wild predators. Shows them doing what nature intended them to do killing to eat. Narrated by Robert Redford.
Prod-STOUFP Dist-STOUFP

Predators, The C 50 MIN
16MM FILM, 3/4 OR 1/2 IN VIDEO
Observes North America's wild predators. Shows them doing what nature intended them to do - killing to eat. Narrated by Robert Redford.
Prod-STOUFP Dist-STOUFP

Predators, The C 58 MIN
16MM FILM, 3/4 OR 1/2 IN VIDEO A
Discusses the discovery of oil in the Middle East and the raids by the West on the resources of the East. Examines the possibility of overcoming the gulf between East and West, and Persia's survival of the ambitions of British and Russian imperialism.
From The Crossroads Of Civilization Series.
Prod-CNEMAG Dist-CNEMAG 1978

Predatory Behavior Of Snakes C 16 MIN
16MM FILM, 3/4 OR 1/2 IN VIDEO
Demonstrates the highly specialized mechanisms of snakes for sensing, capturing and ingesting prey. Examines the roles of vision, olfaction and heat-sensing in locating prey. Discusses the adaptations of the skulls of pythons and pit vipers for capturing and swallowing prey. Explores the procedures of seizing, striking, invenomating and constricting prey.
From The Aspects Of Animal Behavior Series.
Prod-UCLA Dist-UCEMC 1978

Predatory Behavior Of The Grasshopper Mouse C 10 MIN
16MM FILM, 3/4 OR 1/2 IN VIDEO H-C A
Uses slow-motion photography to examine how the grasshopper mouse attacks its prey. Evaluates the role of experience in its handling of beetles, crickets and scorpions.
From The Aspects Of Animal Behavior Series.
Prod-UCLA Dist-UCEMC 1974

Predictable Disaster, A C 32 MIN
16MM FILM, 3/4 OR 1/2 IN VIDEO H-C A
Focuses on the development of techniques to predict earthquakes.
From The Nova Series.
LC NO. 79-707239
Prod-WGBHTV Dist-TIMLIF 1976

Predicting At Random C 43 MIN
16MM FILM OPTICAL SOUND H-C T
Professor David Blackwell solves a problem in which a source sequentially generates 0's or 1's and one must predict against it, with a knowledge of success or failure after each prediction.
From The MAA Individual Lecturers Series.
LC NO. FIA66-1271
Prod-MAA Dist-MLA 1966

Predicting Electric Circuits C 15 MIN
3/4 OR 1/2 INCH VIDEO CASSETTE I
Gives experience in predicting electric circuits.
From The Hands On, Grade 4 - Cars, Cartoons, Etc Series. Unit 4 - Inferring/Predicting
Prod-WHROTV Dist-AITECH 1975

Predicting Here, There, And Everywhere C 15 MIN
3/4 OR 1/2 INCH VIDEO CASSETTE I
Gives experience in predicting future events.
From The Hands On, Grade 4 - Cars, Cartoons, Etc Series. Unit 4 - Inferring/Predicting
Prod-WHROTV Dist-AITECH 1975

Predicting In Science C 14 MIN
3/4 OR 1/2 INCH VIDEO CASSETTE J
Shows an astrophysicist predicting the discovery of a galaxy between earth and the quasar he is studying.
From The Whatabout Series.
Prod-AITV Dist-AITECH 1983

Predicting Oscillations B
16MM FILM OPTICAL SOUND
Looks at differential equations that describe free and forced oscillations of an undamped mass spring system.
Prod-OPENU Dist-OPENU

Predicting Outcome Of Experiments B 15 MIN
2 INCH VIDEOTAPE P
See series title for descriptive statement.
From The Just Inquisitive Series. No. 22
Prod-EOPS Dist-GPITVL Prodn-KOACTV

Predicting Plant Growth C 15 MIN
3/4 OR 1/2 INCH VIDEO CASSETTE P
See series title for descriptive statement.
From The Hands On, Grade 3 Series. Unit 4 - Inferring, Predicting
Prod-VAOG Dist-AITECH Prodn-WHROTV 1975

Predicting Reliability During Development Test C 30 MIN
3/4 OR 1/2 INCH VIDEO CASSETTE IND
Describes use of Duane plots to predict reliability at customer release from failure data obtained during development test.
From The Reliability Engineering Series.
Prod-COLOSU Dist-COLOSU

Predicting Shadow Lengths C 15 MIN
3/4 OR 1/2 INCH VIDEO CASSETTE P
See series title for descriptive statement.
From The Hands On, Grade 3 Series. Unit 4 - Inferring, Predicting
Prod-VAOG Dist-AITECH Prodn-WHROTV 1975

Predicting The Weather C 30 MIN
3/4 OR 1/2 INCH VIDEO CASSETTE C
Explains how television weathermen collect data and organize their weather reports. Discusses the ways the weather affects different people and businesses.
From The Earth, Sea And Sky Series.
Prod-DALCCD Dist-DALCCD

Predicting Through Sampling C 10 MIN
16MM FILM, 3/4 OR 1/2 IN VIDEO I-H
Develops the basic principles of good sampling through a practical problem.
Prod-BOUNDY Dist-PHENIX 1969

Predicting Tracks C 14 MIN
3/4 OR 1/2 INCH VIDEO CASSETTE I
Gives experience in predicting tracks.
From The Hands On, Grade 4 - Cars, Cartoons, Etc Series. Unit 4 - Inferring/Predicting
Prod-WHROTV Dist-AITECH 1975

Predicting Weather C 15 MIN
3/4 OR 1/2 INCH VIDEO CASSETTE P
See series title for descriptive statement.
From The Hands On, Grade 3 Series. Unit 4 - Inferring, Predicting
Prod-VAOG Dist-AITECH Prodn-WHROTV 1975

Predicting Your Change C 13 MIN
3/4 OR 1/2 INCH VIDEO CASSETTE I
Explains that being shortchanged teaches George and Ingrid the importance of predicting change. Includes an animated segment that shows that when Pinocchio learns to keep the Shady Character from cheating him, he turns into a real boy.
From The It Figures Series. No. 15
Prod-AITV Dist-AITECH Prodn-NJN 1982

Prediction C 18 MIN
16MM FILM - 3/4 IN VIDEO I-J
Explains how prediction in scientific investigation helps to foresee and manipulate consequences in order to get a headstart on a future problem.
From The Search For Solutions Series.
LC NO. 80-706247
Prod-PLYBCK Dist-KAROL 1979

Prediction - A Tool For Safe And Reliable Operation C
16MM FILM - 3/4 IN VIDEO A
Outlines a three-phase ongoing program of safe and reliable operation of equipment, describes the different detection instruments and delves into the cooperation needed between workers and the specialists who perform the tests.
Prod-BNA Dist-BNA 1983

Prediction Initiative - Cerebral Cortex And Its Areas C 18 MIN
16MM FILM, 3/4 OR 1/2 IN VIDEO PRO
See series title for descriptive statement.
From The Anatomical Basis Of Brain Function Series.
Prod-AVCORP Dist-TEF

Prediction Of Dangerousness C 30 MIN
3/4 OR 1/2 INCH VIDEO CASSETTE
Presents a two-part program on the prediction of dangerousness in a violent patient. Takes a look at the current state of the art of predicting violence in the future in the first part. Identifies dangerous patient in the second part.
Prod-HEMUL Dist-HEMUL

Prediction Of Wound Disruption By The Use Of The Healing Ridge C 16 MIN
16MM FILM OPTICAL SOUND PRO
Explains that a reliable harbinger of wound disruption would be of considerable clinical value since this complication usually presents as a precipitous calamity. Points out that the state of the indurated ridge, palpable beneath healing laparotomy wounds, may be depended upon to accurately forbode the probability or improbability of wound disruption.
Prod-ACYDGD Dist-ACY 1962

Predictions And Reflections C 15 MIN
3/4 OR 1/2 INCH VIDEO CASSETTE P
Presents a space robot and his puppet assistant as they explore the concept of prediction through examples of geometric properties found in designs on a balloon and a piece of paper. Shows how they decide which designs are symmetrical.
From The Math Mission 2 Series.
LC NO. 82-706355
Prod-WCVETV Dist-GPITVL 1980

Predominantly Black College, A C 13 MIN
16MM FILM OPTICAL SOUND J-C A
Presents black students who talk about how their education helps them to succeed in a white world, and discuss how they can serve the black community. Filmed at Hampton Institute.
From The College Selection Film Series.
LC NO. 79-713044
Prod-VISEDC Dist-VISEDC 1971

Preemies - The Price Tag C 16 MIN
3/4 OR 1/2 INCH VIDEO CASSETTE
Probes the delicate, difficult ethical issues surrounding saving the prematurely born. Brings up crucial issues of who decides to begin treatment and discontinue treatment.
Prod-CANBC Dist-AJN

Preferential Treatment For High Occupancy Vehicle C 21 MIN
16MM FILM OPTICAL SOUND
Shows systematic ways to make more efficient use of urban highways, including special lanes for buses and carpools, curb lanes on arterial streets and parking facilities outside congested areas for commuters. Illustrates a design of interchanges and approaches which allows limited access to reversible lanes.
LC NO. 74-706182
Prod-USDTFH Dist-USNAC 1973

Preferred Stock C 25 MIN
16MM FILM OPTICAL SOUND
Depicts the growth of stock car racing from its beginnings in cow pasture dirt tracks to the Silver Anniversary 500 at Daytona International Speedway.
Prod-SEARS Dist-MTP

Prefixes C 20 MIN
3/4 INCH VIDEO CASSETTE J-C A
Features the most common metric prefixes, including milli, centi, deci, deka, hecto, and kilo.
From The Metric System Series.
Prod-MAETEL Dist-GPITVL 1975

Prefixes / Suffixes C 23 MIN
1/2 IN VIDEO CASSETTE BETA/VHS
Teaches basic vocabulary skills. Uses stories and visuals.
Prod-BFA Dist-BFA

Preflight Inspection - A Series

Prod-USOE Dist-USNAC

Airplane 17 MIN
Engine 13 MIN

Prefrontal Lobotomy In Chronic Schizophrenia X 21 MIN
16MM FILM SILENT PRO
Illustrates improvement that may be obtained by prefrontal lobotomy in chronic schizophrenia. Presents our cases and shows behavior before and after lobotomy. The film does not show operation itself. Showings restricted.
Prod-PSUPCR Dist-PSUPCR 1943

Prefrontal Lobotomy In The Treatment Of Mental Disorders 'PSYCHOSURGERY' B 13 MIN
16MM FILM OPTICAL SOUND PRO
Shows the locations of incisions and structures encountered in a prefrontal lobotomy on skull and brain specimens. The operation is shown in full detail. Showings restricted.
Prod-PSUPCR Dist-PSUPCR 1942

Pregnancy C
3/4 OR 1/2 INCH VIDEO CASSETTE
Explains the three trimesters of pregnancy and the changes in both mother and fetus. Expectant parents relate their anxieties and emotional changes, and feelings of expectancy and worry in the later stages.
From The Parenthood - Bringing New Life Into The World Series.
Prod-GA Dist-GA

Pregnancy C 30 MIN
3/4 OR 1/2 INCH VIDEO CASSETTE
Presents tips on maintaining health during pregnancy.
From The Consumer Survival Series. Health
Prod-MDCPB Dist-MDCPB

Pregnancy After Thirty-Five C 30 MIN
3/4 OR 1/2 INCH VIDEO CASSETTE C T
Examines the positive and negative aspects of pregnancy after thirty-five. Presents benefits as well as risks. Explains social, environmental and physical aspects of a pregnancy 'later in the female cycle.'
From The Here's To Your Health Series.
Prod-DALCCD Dist-DALCCD

Pregnancy After 35 C 22 MIN
16MM FILM OPTICAL SOUND A
Uses statistics and interviews with middle-aged mothers, along with information from Carole S Mc Cauley's book Pregnancy After 35, to discuss the effects of pregnancy during middle age. Shows women's emotional and physical reactions to pregnancy and motherhood at this time of life. Explains Down's syndrome and demonstrates an amniocentesis which is performed in testing the fetus for chromosomal normalcy.
LC NO. 79-700440
Prod-POLYMR Dist-POLYMR 1978

Pregnancy After 35 C 14 MIN
3/4 OR 1/2 INCH VIDEO CASSETTE
Deals with the physical and emotional aspects of late pregnancy.
Prod-POLYMR Dist-POLYMR

Pregnancy After 35 C 14 MIN
16MM FILM, 3/4 OR 1/2 IN VIDEO A
Discusses concerns and misconceptions facing women past 35 who decide to have children. Provides information about prenatal care, amniocentesis, relative risks to mother and child and personal adjustment after birth.
Prod-PRORE Dist-PRORE

Pregnancy After 35 C 29 MIN
3/4 INCH VIDEO CASSETTE
Takes a look at the facts, myths and misunderstandings about the pregnancies of women over 35.
From The Woman Series.
Prod-WNEDTV Dist-PUBTEL

Pregnancy And Birth C 12 MIN
16MM FILM, 3/4 OR 1/2 IN VIDEO J-H
Traces the process of conception and birth. Includes a sequence showing the birth of a baby.
Prod-NFBC Dist-TEXFLM 1969

Pregnancy And Birth C 29 MIN
3/4 OR 1/2 INCH VIDEO CASSETTE
Demonstrates a pregnancy test and describes some of the emotions surrounding the first knowlege of pregnancy. Shows a normal delivery and natural childbirth exercises, such as the La Maze method, and breast feeding, including the La Leche League techniques.
From The Human Sexuality Series.
Prod-KHETTV Dist-PBS

Pregnancy And Childbirth C 1 MIN
16MM FILM OPTICAL SOUND
Discusses pregnancy and childbirth.
LC NO. 77-702616
Prod-DALHSU Dist-CRAF Prodn-CRAF 1976

Pregnancy And Childbirth C 60 MIN
16MM FILM OPTICAL SOUND
Discusses pregnancy and childbirth.
LC NO. 77-702616
Prod-DALHSU Dist-CRAF Prodn-CRAF 1976

Pregnancy And Childbirth C 30 MIN
3/4 OR 1/2 INCH VIDEO CASSETTE C A
Describes the functions of the female body during pregnancy and the stages of fetal development. Stresses that the mother's diet, health, age and emotional condition are important factors in childbirth.

From The Family Portrait - A Study Of Contemporary Lifestyles Series. Lesson 25
Prod-SCCON Dist-CDTEL

Pregnancy And Childbirth—A Series
16MM FILM, 3/4 OR 1/2 IN VIDEO H-C A
Answers questions about pregnancy and childbirth.
Prod-DALHSU Dist-IFB Prodn-CRAF 1977

Before Pregnancy 9 MIN
Labor And Delivery 19 MIN
Prenatal 21 MIN
Special Cases 13 MIN

Pregnancy And Lactation C 30 MIN
3/4 INCH VIDEO CASSETTE H-C A
Outlines desirable eating patterns for pregnant and nursing mothers. Points out that biological youth in the mother and poor prenatal nutrition are often responsible for low birth weight.
From The Changing Nutritional Needs Series.
Prod-UWISCA Dist-GPITVL 1976

Pregnancy And The Family C 20 MIN
3/4 OR 1/2 INCH VIDEO CASSETTE PRO
Discusses changes in the role of the maternity nurse. Explains the increasing emphasis now placed on nursing care to meet the needs of the pregnant woman. Describes the many variations in the form and structure of the family.
LC NO. 81-730246
Prod-TRAINX Dist-TRAINX

Pregnancy And The Newborn Child C 72 MIN
1/2 IN VIDEO CASSETTE BETA/VHS
Demonstrates pregnancy exercises and care of a newborn baby. Deals with choosing a doctor, labor and birthing.
Prod-VIPRO Dist-VIPRO

Pregnancy Occurs C 29 MIN
3/4 OR 1/2 INCH VIDEO CASSETTE H-C A
Describes why becoming a parent is an emotional and physiological event that begins with conception.
From The Tomorrow's Families Series.
LC NO. 80-706999
Prod-MSDOE Dist-AITECH 1980

Pregnancy On The Rocks C 25 MIN
3/4 OR 1/2 INCH VIDEO CASSETTE J A
Focuses on birth defects caused by liquor intake of pregnant women. Explains that even moderate intake can precipitate defects.
LC NO. 84-707293
Prod-SUTHRB Dist-SUTHRB

Pregnancy Prevention - Options C 17 MIN
16MM FILM, 3/4 OR 1/2 IN VIDEO J-H
Presents interviews with typical teenagers to reveal the misconceptions about birth control that are widely held. Explains available techniques and gives arguments for exercising responsibility.
LC NO. 81-706721
Prod-CAHILL Dist-AIMS 1980

Pregnancy Prevention And Sex Hygiene—A Series

Explains conception and birth control options and stresses the need for early VD medical care.
Prod-USA Dist-USNAC 1983

Contraception - Alternatives For Today 019 MIN
VD - It Is Your Problem 014 MIN

Pregnant But Equal C 24 MIN
16MM FILM, 3/4 OR 1/2 IN VIDEO
Interviews doctors, lawyers, workers and union officials who discuss the problems of enforcing the Pregnancy Discrimination Act which makes it illegal for employers to discriminate against pregnant workers in hiring, firing, seniority or benefits.
Prod-POMRJ Dist-ICARUS 1983

Pregnant Teens - Taking Care C 22 MIN
16MM FILM, 3/4 OR 1/2 IN VIDEO H
Offers complete prenatal care information for pregnant teenagers. Covers such topics as nutrition, fetal development and the effects of drug and alcohol use. Emphasizes regular medical attention during pregnancy.
LC NO. 84-706101
Prod-PEREN Dist-PEREN 1983

Prehistoric Animals Of The Tar Pits C 14 MIN
16MM FILM, 3/4 OR 1/2 IN VIDEO I-H
Introduces the tar pits at Rancho La Brea and the skeletons of some of the animals taken from them. Illustrates the methods used by paleontologists in identifying and assembling fossil materials.
Prod-FA Dist-PHENIX 1957

Prehistoric Animals Of The Tar Pits (French) C 14 MIN
16MM FILM, 3/4 OR 1/2 IN VIDEO I-H
Introduces the tar pits at Rancho La Brea and the skeletons of some of the animals taken from them. Illustrates the methods used by paleontologists in identifying and assembling fossil materials.
Prod-FA Dist-PHENIX 1957

Prehistoric Farmers B 30 MIN
16MM FILM OPTICAL SOUND H-C A
Describes native crops, new types of houses and specialized tools brought in by new groups of people pushing into the plains. Takes a look at primitive social organization as suggested by archeology.
From The Great Plains Trilogy, 2 Series. Nomad And Indians - Early Man On The Plains
Prod-KUONTV Dist-UNL 1954

Prehistoric Fish C 22 MIN
16MM FILM OPTICAL SOUND
Depicts Homer Circle angling for some fish which are prehistoric throwbacks, such as the bowfin, alligator gar, paddlefish and sturgeon.
Prod-BRNSWK Dist-KAROL

Prehistoric Humans C 17 MIN
16MM FILM, 3/4 OR 1/2 IN VIDEO J-C A
Focuses on several prehistoric relatives of modern man.
Prod-MATVCH Dist-PHENIX 1980

Prehistoric Images - The First Art Of Man C 17 MIN
16MM FILM, 3/4 OR 1/2 IN VIDEO I-C
An exploration of the prehistoric caves of France and Spain, examination of the paintings found there and some conjecture as to the character of the men who created the paintings. Produced in France.
Prod-ROWETL Dist-FI

Prehistoric Magic C 14 MIN
3/4 OR 1/2 INCH VIDEO CASSETTE P-I
Discusses prehistoric art.
From The Young At Art Series.
Prod-WSKJTV Dist-AITECH 1980

Prehistoric Mammals C 16 MIN
16MM FILM, 3/4 OR 1/2 IN VIDEO I-H
Describes the large mammals which once roamed the Earth.
Prod-MATVCH Dist-PHENIX 1981

Prehistoric Man C 17 MIN
3/4 INCH VIDEO CASSETTE H
Traces the development of the Indians in the American West from prehistoric times until the Spanish arrived in the 16th century.
Prod-BARBRE Dist-GA

Prehistoric Man In Europe C 23 MIN
16MM FILM, 3/4 OR 1/2 IN VIDEO H-C
Surveys the early development of mankind in Europe, from the first traces of worked tools to the establishment of a metallurgical industry.
Prod-BHA Dist-IFB 1965

Prehistoric Times (Rev Ed) C 10 MIN
16MM FILM, 3/4 OR 1/2 IN VIDEO J-H
Deals with the eras on earth before human existence. Uses dioramas, fossil remains, examples of terrain and models to help re-construct prehistoric times and the beginnings of life.
Prod-CORF Dist-CORF

Prejudice B 58 MIN
16MM FILM OPTICAL SOUND H-C A
A businessman deludes himself into thinking that he is unprejudiced, but basic psychological insecurity creates a situation which reveals his latent prejudice.
Prod-ADL Dist-ADL

Prejudice C 25 MIN
3/4 OR 1/2 INCH VIDEO CASSETTE J-C A
Examines the modern day exploits of the Ku Klux Klan. Features interviews with the chief counsel and Grand Wizard of the KKK, James R Venable, and with a Nashville reporter who infiltrated the Klan and authored a book, My Life With The Clan.
Prod-SIRS Dist-SIRS

Prejudice - A Lesson To Forget C 16 MIN
16MM FILM, 3/4 OR 1/2 IN VIDEO J-C A
Attempts to separate discrimination, a symptom, from prejudice, its cause. Illustrates a general history of the prejudices that scorched the American melting pot. Uses vignettes to demonstrate how children learn prejudice from each other and from their parents and teachers.
Prod-DUNLF Dist-AMEDFL 1973

Prejudice - Causes, Consequences, Cures C 24 MIN
16MM FILM, 3/4 OR 1/2 IN VIDEO H-C A
Takes a look at the nature of prejudice in its many forms, including racial, sexual, educational and economic prejudice, and delves into the root causes of this devastating social illness. Demonstrates the various ways in which our need to classify groups can be subverted into negative prejudice. Presents examples of prejudice including the problems of double standards, overgeneralized observations, territorial and economic group conflicts, severe and punitive upbringing and conformity and socialization.
From The Social Science Film Series.
Prod-CRMP Dist-CRMP 1974

Prejudice - Perceiving And Believing C 28 MIN
16MM FILM, 3/4 OR 1/2 IN VIDEO H-C A
Shows that stereotyped classification by race, religion, ethnicity and sex, rather than by individual worth, prevents positive personal interactions. Reveals that prejudice is seen as prejudgment based upon what one expects to perceive, rather than what exists in reality. Narrated by Ed Asner.
Prod-MTVTM Dist-MTI 1977

Prejudice Film, The C 29 MIN
16MM FILM, 3/4 OR 1/2 IN VIDEO
Provides the reasons to arrive at positive non-judgmental conclusions about people as individuals, not as groups. Deals with the most prevalent personal hang-ups which interfere with effective Affirmative Action Programs. With David Hartman.
Prod-MTVTM Dist-MTVTM

Prejudice In Humor / Locked In These Rooms / Pat And Evy C 29 MIN
3/4 INCH VIDEO CASSETTE
Presents three looks at racial issues. Shows how ethnic humor perpetuates misunderstandings. Profiles Asian-American parents who don't want their children to leave San Francisco's Chinatown. Features a young woman's fantasy that she can eliminate people she doesn't like by snapping her fingers, and describes her realization that she has too many prejudices.
From The As We See It Series.
Prod-WTTWTV Dist-PUBTEL

Prejudice Test, The C 1 MIN
3/4 INCH VIDEO CASSETTE
Shows several examples of bigoted remarks. Asks each viewer to decide whether or not he or she is a bigot. Made in TV Spot announcement form.
Prod-ADL Dist-ADL

Prejudices, Stereotyping, Biases C 30 MIN
3/4 OR 1/2 INCH VIDEO CASSETTE T
Analyzes prejudices, stereotypes and biases in an educational setting.
From The Interaction - Human Concerns In The Schools Series.
Prod-MDDE Dist-MDCPB

Preliminary Design B 420 MIN
3/4 OR 1/2 INCH VIDEO CASSETTE PRO
See series title for descriptive statement.
From The Spacecraft System Design Series.
Prod-USCITV Dist-AMCEE

Preliminary Examination B 39 MIN
16MM FILM OPTICAL SOUND C
Deals with various aspects of a criminal lawsuit involving a liquor store robbery case. Shows the adult suspect's first appearance before the magistrate. Includes the examination of the officers to determine whether a prima facie case exists.
From The Criminal Law Series. No. 7
LC NO. 70-714039
Prod-RPATLF Dist-RPATLF 1968

Preliminary Examination And Procedures For Diagnosis C 12 MIN
16MM FILM - 3/4 IN VIDEO PRO
Presents extra-oral inspection and examines soft and hard intraoral tissues, preliminary impressions and the interocclusal record to mount the study casts. Issued in 1967 as a motion picture.
From The Removable Partial Dentures, Clasp Type - Clinical And Laboratory Procedures Series.
LC NO. 78-706183
Prod-USVA Dist-USNAC Prodn-VADTC 1978

Preliminary Examination And Procedures For Diagnosis C 13 MIN
3/4 OR 1/2 INCH VIDEO CASSETTE
Presents the extraoral inspection, as well as careful examination of the soft and hard intraoral tissues, the preliminary impressions and the interocclusal record to mount the study casts.
From The Removable Partial Dentures, Clasp Type Clinical And Laboratory Procedures Series.
Prod-VADTC Dist-AMDA 1969

Preliminary Hearing Of A Criminal Case C 161 MIN
3/4 OR 1/2 INCH VIDEO CASSETTE PRO
Covers preliminary hearing of a criminal case.
From The Trial Of A Criminal Case Series.
Prod-SBWI Dist-ABACPE

Preliminary Impressions For Complete Dentures C 14 MIN
16MM FILM - 3/4 IN VIDEO
Demonstrates a method of using wax modifications of stock trays to obtain preliminary denture impressions with alginate.
LC NO. 78-706208
Prod-VADTC Dist-USNAC 1978

Preliminary Impressions In Complete Denture Prosthodontics C 22 MIN
16MM FILM, 3/4 OR 1/2 IN VIDEO PRO
Presents a technique for obtainining physiologically acceptable preliminary impressions using four different commercially, available impression trays and an alginate substitute that consists of two pastes.
Prod-USVA Dist-USNAC 1984

Preliminary Survey Of Study Casts, Tentative Design And Detailed Treatment Planning C 11 MIN
16MM FILM - 3/4 IN VIDEO PRO
Discusses the kinds of information upon which planning for treatment is based, including that achieved from mounted study casts, oral examination, radiographs, general patient information and accurate survey of casts. Covers tentative design of the appliance compatible with the oral conditions and biological requirement. Issued in 1967 as a motion picture.
From The Removable Partial Dentures, Clasp Type - Clinical And Laboratory Procedures Series.
LC NO. 78-706184
Prod-USVA Dist-USNAC Prodn-VADTC 1978

Preliminary, Beginning, And Work Phases C 96 MIN
3/4 INCH VIDEO CASSETTE C A
Tells how social workers can tune in, respond to indirect communication, contract, elaborate, empathize, and share worker feelings.
From The Skills Of Helping Series. Program 1
LC NO. 80-707458
Prod-MCGILU Dist-SYRCU 1980

Prelude C 4 MIN
16MM FILM OPTICAL SOUND J-C
Presents an abstract film exercise using colored lights, wire forms and abstract sculpture.
Prod-CFS Dist-CFS 1954

Prelude To Conflict C 30 MIN
2 INCH VIDEOTAPE
Reviews the events 10 years prior to the outbreak of the Civil War. Includes the Kansas-Nebraska Act, creation of the Republican Party, the Dred Scott case, and the election of Lincoln.
From The American History I Series.
Prod-DENVPS Dist-GPITVL

Prelude To Power B 25 MIN
16MM FILM, 3/4 OR 1/2 IN VIDEO H-C
Traces the work of 19th century scientist Michael Faraday in the field of electromagnetism.
Prod-EFVA Dist-IFB 1965

Prelude To Revolution C 13 MIN
16MM FILM, 3/4 OR 1/2 IN VIDEO J-H
Uses watercolors by A N Wyeth to recount events that slowly transformed the American colonists' limited resistance to British rule into a struggle for the rights and principles outlined in the Declaration of Independence.
Prod-EBEC Dist-EBEC 1975

Prelude To Revolution C 17 MIN
16MM FILM, 3/4 OR 1/2 IN VIDEO I-J
Describes the two years of peace that followed the Boston Massacre and the repeal of the Townshend Acts.
From The American History - Birth Of A Nation Series.
Prod-AIMS Dist-AIMS 1967

Prelude To Revolution C 30 MIN
2 INCH VIDEOTAPE
Combines a discussion of the historical theories concerning the causes of the American Revolution with some of the specific factors which led to rebellion.
From The American History I Series.
Prod-DENVPS Dist-GPITVL

Prelude To Taps B 11 MIN
16MM FILM OPTICAL SOUND
Presents a display of military pageantry in commemoration of two centuries of American heroes who died fighting for their country.
LC NO. 75-701196
Prod-USDD Dist-USNAC 1964

Prelude To The Civil War - 'A House Divided' - 1848-1860 X 24 MIN
16MM FILM OPTICAL SOUND I-C A
Discusses events leading up to the Civil War, such as slavery in the territories, The Great Compromise, the transcontinental railroad, the Dred Scott decision, Lincoln's election and the secession of the South.
From The Exploring - The Story Of America, Set 1 Series.
LC NO. FIA68-1056
Prod-NBCTV Dist-GRACUR 1968

Prelude To The Tempest C 15 MIN
3/4 INCH VIDEO CASSETTE
Presents an art video by Doug Hall, whose imagery alludes to the crises of society, the individual's struggle for equilibrium, and a premonition of upheaval.
Prod-EAI Dist-EAI

Prelude To War B 54 MIN
3/4 OR 1/2 INCH VIDEO CASSETTE
Portrays the events leading up to World War II, including Japanese attacks on Manchuria.
From The Frank Capra's 'Why We Fight' Series.
Prod-IHF Dist-IHF

Prelude To War B 54 MIN
16MM FILM - 3/4 IN VIDEO
Reviews events from 1933 to 1939, including the Japanese conquest of Manchuria, the Italian conquest of Ethiopia, and the rise of Hitler. Discusses the Axis plan of world conquest. Issued in 1949 as a motion picture.
From The Why We Fight Series.
LC NO. 79-706286
Prod-USWD Dist-USNAC 1979

Premature C 55 MIN
16MM FILM, 3/4 OR 1/2 IN VIDEO H-C A
Records the personal crisis endured by a family when their first child was born prematurely by cesarean section and given a one percent chance of surviving without physical or mental defects. Tells how an unexpected pregnancy six months later and a second cesarean birth caused further stress.
Prod-PARRYD Dist-BNCHMK 1981

Premature Burial C 79 MIN
16MM FILM OPTICAL SOUND H A
Tells the tale of a man who fears being buried alive but suffers that very fate. Directed by Roger Corman. Stars Ray Milland.
Prod-AIP Dist-TIMLIF 1961

Premature Ejaculation C
3/4 OR 1/2 INCH VIDEO CASSETTE
Outlines a 12 to 15 visit treatment program for a husband's premature ejaculation. Includes education on the male and female reproductive organs, genitalia, arousal cycles and a progressive series of home exercises including 'sensate Focus' training and the 'Squeeze Technique.'
Prod-MIFE Dist-MIFE

Premature Infant B 44 MIN
16MM FILM OPTICAL SOUND PRO
A discussion of the causes and problems of prematurity, emphasizing the role of the nurse in caring for the infant. Shows the care of the infant at a premature center and demonstrates nursing care of a premature infant in an isolette. Explains the causes of premature mortality.
From The Maternity Nursing Series.
LC NO. 74-703393
Prod-VDONUR Dist-AJN Prodn-WTTWTV 1966

Premature Infant With Esophageal Atresia And Tracheoesophageal Fistula, The C 17 MIN
3/4 OR 1/2 INCH VIDEO CASSETTE PRO
Describes the premature infant with esophageal atresia and tracheoesophageal fistula.
Prod-WFP Dist-WFP Prodn-UKANMC

Prematurely Yours - Premature Infant Behavior And Personality C 15 MIN
3/4 OR 1/2 INCH VIDEO CASSETTE PRO
Provides encouragement for parents and hospital staff by showing how one can respond in a positive manner to the premature infant. Examines both the needs of the newborn and of the parents.
LC NO. 83-706810
Prod-POLYMR Dist-POLYMR 1983

Prematurity C 29 MIN
3/4 OR 1/2 INCH VIDEO CASSETTE
Focuses on neonatology, a speciality dedicated to insuring the health survival of pre-term infants. Includes a tour of the Parkland Memorial Hospital nurseries.
From The Daniel Foster, MD Series.
Prod-KERA Dist-PBS

Premiere B 10 MIN
16MM FILM OPTICAL SOUND
Uses an applause and 'AFTER THE OPENING' party to frame a view of the inner conflicts of an actress who is in search of her own sense of self as she wanders through the city trying to 'SEE' herself in windows, museums and cameras.
Prod-UPENN Dist-UPENN 1971

Prenatal C 21 MIN
16MM FILM, 3/4 OR 1/2 IN VIDEO H-C A
Examines changes in the mother's body and the development of the fetus during pregnancy. Demonstrates the techniques of correct breathing and proper posture and details the usual indications that the time for delivery is approaching.
Prod-DALHSU Dist-IFB Prodn-CRAF 1977

Prenatal Care B 29 MIN
16MM FILM OPTICAL SOUND C A
Tells about prenatal care, mortality and morbidity rates, nutrition, dental care, emotional aspects, physical aspects and prenatal visit to the the doctor.
From The Nine To Get Ready Series. No. 4
LC NO. 77-704218
Prod-KUONTV Dist-UNL 1965

Prenatal Care C 24 MIN
16MM FILM, 3/4 OR 1/2 IN VIDEO A
Presents basic information on prenatal care. Covers normal body changes during pregnancy, medical care, necessary precautions, preparations for birth and possible complications. Features an obstetrician and a childbirth specialist demonstrating what to do, from the first indications of pregnancy to the onset of labor.
LC NO. 77-701104
Prod-BURN Dist-PFP 1977

Prenatal Care C 29 MIN
2 INCH VIDEOTAPE
See series title for descriptive statement.
From The Nine To Get Ready Series.
Prod-NETCHE Dist-PUBTEL

Prenatal Care (Arabic) C 25 MIN
16MM FILM, 3/4 OR 1/2 IN VIDEO A
An Arabic language version of the film, Prenatal Care. Explains and demonstrates the essentials of a healthy pregnancy and birth.
Prod-BURN Dist-PFP

Prenatal Care (Spanish) C 25 MIN
16MM FILM, 3/4 OR 1/2 IN VIDEO A
A Spanish language version of the film, Prenatal Care. Explains and demonstrates the essentials of a healthy pregnancy and birth.
Prod-BURN Dist-PFP

Prenatal Care - The Early Months C 12 MIN
16MM FILM, 3/4 OR 1/2 IN VIDEO
Explores the importance of proper medical care, nutrition and dealing with common annoyances during the first few months of pregnancy.
From The Prepared Childbirth And Parenting Series.
Prod-JOU Dist-JOU 1979

Prenatal Detection Of Genetic Disorders In Man C 30 MIN
3/4 OR 1/2 INCH VIDEO CASSETTE
Discusses genetic amniocentesis, through which doctors are learning more about genetic disease than ever before. Outlines several genetic diseases and provides a detailed demonstration of genetic amniocentesis.
From The Choice To Know Series.
Prod-NETCHE Dist-NETCHE 1976

Prenatal Development C 23 MIN
16MM FILM, 3/4 OR 1/2 IN VIDEO H-C A
Explores the biology and the psychology of the developing fetus. Presents the latest theories and information about the fetus and the environmental influences within the mother's uterus.
From The Developmental Psychology Today Film Series.
Prod-CRMP Dist-CRMP 1974

Prenatal Development C 30 MIN
3/4 INCH VIDEO CASSETTE
Presents the stages of prenatal development and the environmental influences on the infant-to-be.
From The Growing Years Series.
Prod-COAST Dist-CDTEL

Prenatal Exercises C 19 MIN
16MM FILM, 3/4 OR 1/2 IN VIDEO A
Presents a planned program of exercise, breathing and movement to help achieve physical and psychological conditioning during pregnancy.
Prod-PRORE Dist-PRORE

Prenatal Management C 8 MIN
16MM FILM, 3/4 OR 1/2 IN VIDEO
Portrays the physical changes that develop as pregnancy advances. Discusses normal discomforts, danger signals and substances to be avoided.
From The Prepared Childbirth And Parenting Series.
Prod-JOU Dist-JOU 1969

Prenatal Management (Spanish) C 8 MIN
16MM FILM, 3/4 OR 1/2 IN VIDEO
Portrays the physical changes that develop as pregnancy advances. Discusses normal discomforts, danger signals and substances to be avoided.
From The Prepared Childbirth And Parenting Series.
Prod-JOU Dist-JOU 1969

Preoperative Care B 16 MIN
16MM FILM OPTICAL SOUND
Presents the duties and responsibilities of hospital corpsmen in preparing a patient for surgery in the 16 to 24 hour period immediately preceding the operation.
LC NO. FIE60-91
Prod-USN Dist-USNAC 1952

Preoperative Evaluation Of Cancer Patients At M D Anderson C 45 MIN
3/4 INCH VIDEO CASSETTE
Dr Hollis Bivens discusses preoperative requirements, evaluation and patient information for patients at the University of Texas M D Anderson Hospital.
Prod-UTAHTI Dist-UTAHTI

Preoperative Patient, The - Consent, Preparation And Transfer C 13 MIN
3/4 OR 1/2 INCH VIDEO CASSETTE PRO
Explains guidelines to planning and implementing of the patient's preparation for surgery. Identifies such nursing responsibilities as helping prepare the patient for surgical consent, coordinating surgical preparation, orienting the patient to surgical preparation and preparing the patient for transfer to the operating room.
LC NO. 80-730132
Prod-TRAINX Dist-TRAINX

Preoperative Patient, The - Nursing Assessment C 19 MIN
3/4 OR 1/2 INCH VIDEO CASSETTE PRO
Explains the nurse's preoperative assessment of the surgical patient. Presents the nurse's data collection and analysis and goals of the preoperative assessment. Describes the methods for obtaining information about the patient's physical needs, emotional needs and learning needs in preparation for surgery.
LC NO. 80-730130
Prod-TRAINX Dist-TRAINX

Preoperative Patient, The - Nursing Care C 18 MIN
3/4 OR 1/2 INCH VIDEO CASSETTE PRO
Presents guidelines for nursing care of the surgical patient during postoperative recovery. Presents specific responsibilities to promote the patient's participation in care, to promote adequate ventilation and circulation, to promote wound healing, to promote elimination and nutrition and to plan for the patient's discharge.
LC NO. 80-730134
Prod-TRAINX Dist-TRAINX

Preoperative Patient, The - Teaching And Anticipatory Guidance C 15 MIN
3/4 OR 1/2 INCH VIDEO CASSETTE PRO
Explains guidelines for planning and implementing preoperative teaching and anticipatory guidance. Identifies elements of the nurse's written teaching plan and shows guidelines for meeting individual learning needs.
LC NO. 80-730131
Prod-TRAINX Dist-TRAINX

Prepackaged Liquid Rocket Motor C 26 MIN
16MM FILM OPTICAL SOUND
Shows how a prepackaged liquid motor works and how it is fitted to the missile.
Prod-THIOKL Dist-THIOKL 1967

Preparation C
16MM FILM - 3/4 IN VIDEO A
Goes into fact finding, hidden assumptions, the opening and closing, subject matter objectives, issues, positions, team composition, agenda, implementation, self-evaluation, checklists, preparation and applications of negotiations.
From The Art Of Negotiating Series. Module 2
Prod-BNA Dist-BNA 1983

Preparation - Developing A Quality Assurance, Risk Management Program, Pt I C 20 MIN
3/4 OR 1/2 INCH VIDEO CASSETTE
Provides practical how-to methodologies to help small or rural hospitals systematically develop a program that meets current quality assurance requirements.
Prod-AHOA Dist-AHOA

Preparation - Developing A Quality Assurance, Risk Management Program, Pt II C 20 MIN
3/4 OR 1/2 INCH VIDEO CASSETTE
Continues the discussion on how to help small or rural hospitals develop a program that meets current quality assurance requirements.
Prod-AHOA Dist-AHOA 1981

Preparation - Financing Capital Investments C 20 MIN
3/4 OR 1/2 INCH VIDEO CASSETTE
Addresses the unique financing problems faced by small or rural hospitals.
Prod-AHOA Dist-AHOA 1981

Preparation - Governance In Small Rural Hospital C 20 MIN
3/4 OR 1/2 INCH VIDEO CASSETTE

Focuses on the role of trustees in small or rural hospitals and illustrates how corporate board management techniques can be used to meet the trustees' increasing responsibilities.
Prod-AHOA Dist-AHOA 1980

Preparation - Improving Hospital Management Board, Medical Staff, And Administrative-- C 20 MIN
3/4 OR 1/2 INCH VIDEO CASSETTE
Discusses problems in managerial relationships and methods for promoting better relationships between members of hospital board, medical staff and administrative staff.
Prod-AHOA Dist-AHOA 1981

Preparation - New Responsibilities For Middle Management C 19 MIN
3/4 OR 1/2 INCH VIDEO CASSETTE
Shows how hospital department managers can prepare for their responsibilities as leaders. Focuses on how to set goals, reach objectives and evaluate performance. Stresses communication skills and personal motivation techniques.
Prod-AHOA Dist-AHOA 1980

Preparation - Performance Measurements C 20 MIN
3/4 OR 1/2 INCH VIDEO CASSETTE
Presents successful methods for measuring performance and quality control in a small or rural hospital.
Prod-AHOA Dist-AHOA 1980

Preparation - Physician Recruitment C 18 MIN
3/4 OR 1/2 INCH VIDEO CASSETTE
Offers practical recruitment and retention methods to enhance the present physician recruitment process.
Prod-AHOA Dist-AHOA 1980

Preparation - Sharing And Diversifying Hospital Services C 20 MIN
3/4 OR 1/2 INCH VIDEO CASSETTE
Presents a nationwide perspective on activities and arrangements that small or rural hospitals are implementing. Discusses how a particular hospital is diversifying its services.
Prod-AHOA Dist-AHOA 1981

Preparation - The Chief Executive Officer As A Professional C 19 MIN
3/4 OR 1/2 INCH VIDEO CASSETTE
Discusses the role of the chief executive officer of a small or rural hospital. Outlines methods for transferring responsibilities and developing management skills at department levels.
Prod-AHOA Dist-AHOA 1980

Preparation - The Hospital As A Center For Community Health C 20 MIN
3/4 OR 1/2 INCH VIDEO CASSETTE
Demonstrates how a hospital offering health awareness and promotion programs can become a center for community health.
Prod-AHOA Dist-AHOA 1981

Preparation And Staining Of Blood Films C 17 MIN
16MM FILM OPTICAL SOUND
Illustrates smearing and staining procedures for preparing thick and thin blood films for use by technicians in ascertaining presence of malaria parasites. Includes technique of preparing giemsa and Wright's stains.
From The Malaria Control Series.
Prod-USPHS Dist-USPHS 1946

Preparation And Staining Of Fecal Smears For Parasitological Examination, The C 8 MIN
16MM FILM - 3/4 IN VIDEO PRO
Demonstrates the trichrome staining technique for the detection of intestinal parasites.
LC NO. 77-706128
Prod-USPHS Dist-USNAC Prodn-NMAC 1977

Preparation And Use Of Graphics C 30 MIN
3/4 OR 1/2 INCH VIDEO CASSETTE
Lists the dimensional limitations required of television. Discusses devices including marker pens and computerized graphics. Explains how to combine words and pictures for best effect.
From The Video - A Practical Guide...and More Series.
Prod-VIPUB Dist-VIPUB

Preparation For Docking With Keel And Bilge Blocks B 14 MIN
16MM FILM OPTICAL SOUND
Examines the graving dock and demonstrates the placement of keel and bilge blocks according to the docking plan.
LC NO. FIE52-1196
Prod-USN Dist-USNAC 1944

Preparation For Functional Activities- Exercise And Ambulation C 28 MIN
3/4 OR 1/2 INCH VIDEO CASSETTE
Prod-UMDSM Dist-UMDSM

Preparation For Home Care C 30 MIN
16MM FILM - 3/4 IN VIDEO PRO
Suggests methods of helping the neurologically disabled patient and his family cope with his disability. Discusses the issue of sexuality and its relation to neurological disability.
From The Neurologically Disabled Patient, Pt 2 - Nursing During The Rehabilitative... Series.
LC NO. 77-700611
Prod-AJN Dist-AJN Prodn-TVPC 1977

Preparation For Homecoming C 29 MIN
3/4 OR 1/2 INCH VIDEO CASSETTE H-C A
Points out that equipment for the baby's needs and a support system for the mother's recovery must be ready by the time the baby is born.
From The Tomorrow's Families Series.
LC NO. 81-706902
Prod-MSDOE Dist-AITECH 1980

Preparation For Mainstreaming C 60 MIN
3/4 OR 1/2 INCH VIDEO CASSETTE
Shows development of listening skills for the classroom. Depicts kindergarten child with severe to profound hearing loss participating in activities such as phonics and use of tape recorder. Shows his eight year old brother, who has a profound hearing loss and is mainstreamed, demonstrating the same activities on a second to third grade level.
From The Teaching Strategies For The Development Of Auditory Verbal Communication Series. Tape 5
Prod-BELLAG Dist-BELLAG 1981

Preparation For Negotiations C 26 MIN
3/4 INCH VIDEO CASSETTE
Shows how to prepare documentation and strategies in anticipation of negotiations on federal government contracts.
From The Basic Procurement Course Series.
LC NO. 80-706737
Prod-USGSFC Dist-USNAC Prodn-ADSAV 1978

Preparation For Overnight Camping C 30 MIN
3/4 OR 1/2 INCH VIDEO CASSETTE
Discusses preparation for overnight camping as an outdoor activity that requires 'roughing it.'
From The Roughing It Series.
Prod-KYTV Dist-KYTV 1984

Preparation For Parenthood B 44 MIN
16MM FILM OPTICAL SOUND PRO
Shows classes in prenatal exercises and relaxation techniques, discusses the husband's role during the wife's labor period, and explains natural childbirth, psychoprophylactic and psychophysical methods of analgesia.
From The Maternity Nursing Series.
LC NO. 78-703394
Prod-VDONUR Dist-AJN Prodn-WTTWTV 1966

Preparation For Permanent Waving (2) C
3/4 OR 1/2 INCH VIDEO CASSETTE
Covers all areas of preparation, such as analysis for lotion strength, the ruffle test, porosity and condition- ing, elasticity, density and blocking patterns and rod selection for the wave form desired. Explains all supplies and equipment needed.
Prod-MPCEDP Dist-MPCEDP 1984

Preparation For Spring C 30 MIN
1/2 IN VIDEO CASSETTE BETA/VHS
Shows how to prepare the garden for spring planting using cold frames and cloches. Introduces cool weather vegetables such as cabbage and broccoli.
From The Victory Garden Series.
Prod-WGBHTV Dist-MTI

Preparation For Study C 20 MIN
3/4 INCH VIDEO CASSETTE I
Introduces the topic of study skills. Examines specific study habits and activities in school, at the library and at home.
From The Study Skills Series.
Prod-WCVETV Dist-GPITVL 1979

Preparation Of A Culture Medium B 14 MIN
16MM FILM, 3/4 OR 1/2 IN VIDEO
Shows the necessity for bacteriologic diagnosis of TB. Discusses the Lowenstein medium--its advantages, ingredients, preparation, tubing, inspissating, testing and storing. Shows the appearance of colonies on the medium.
From The Laboratory Diagnosis Of Tuberculosis Series.
Prod-USPHS Dist-USNAC 1949

Preparation Of Cards And Labels B 60 MIN
3/4 OR 1/2 INCH VIDEO CASSETTE
See series title for descriptive statement.
From The Library Organization Series. Pt 6
Prod-UAZMIC Dist-UAZMIC 1977

Preparation Of Immediate Denture For Delivery C 13 MIN
3/4 OR 1/2 INCH VIDEO CASSETTE
Demonstrates the selective grinding to develop a smooth, free articulation of the teeth and corrections of the periphery and the tissue surface to permit proper seating of the denture.
Prod-VADTC Dist-AMDA 1971

Preparation Of Items For Sterilization In The Dental Office C 16 MIN
1/2 IN VIDEO CASSETTE BETA/VHS PRO
Discusses dental instruments and sterilization.
Prod-RMI Dist-RMI

Preparation Of Less Tender Beef Cuts C 7 MIN
16MM FILM OPTICAL SOUND J-C A
Identifies the less tender wholesale cuts of beef. Demonstrates two methods of cooking with moist heat and shows three methods of tenderizing by physically altering the tissue.
From The Food And Nutrition Series.
LC NO. 72-702650
Prod-IOWA Dist-IOWA 1971

Preparation Of Medication - Ampule C 5 MIN
3/4 OR 1/2 INCH VIDEO CASSETTE PRO
Demonstrates how to prepare medication in an ampule.
From The Basic Skills - Nursing Series.
Prod-NICEPR Dist-IU

Preparation Of Medication - Oral C 5 MIN
3/4 OR 1/2 INCH VIDEO CASSETTE PRO
Demonstrates how to prepare oral medication.
From The Basic Skills - Nursing Series.
Prod-NICEPR Dist-IU

Preparation Of Medication - Reconstitution C 5 MIN
3/4 OR 1/2 INCH VIDEO CASSETTE PRO
Demonstrates how to prepare medication which is to be reconstituted.
From The Basic Skills - Nursing Series.
Prod-NICEPR Dist-IU

Preparation Of Medication - Vial C 4 MIN
3/4 OR 1/2 INCH VIDEO CASSETTE PRO
Demonstrates how to prepare medication in a vial.
From The Basic Skills - Nursing Series.
Prod-NICEPR Dist-IU

Preparation Of Primary Mammalian Kidney Cell Cultures C 13 MIN
16MM FILM - 3/4 IN VIDEO PRO
Demonstrates a procedure for preparing primary cell cultures from monkey kidney tissue. Shows preparation of the animal, removal of the kidneys, dissection of the tissue and treatment of the tissue with trypsin to obtain a cell suspension. Explains the method of determining the cell concentration by microscopic means.
LC NO. 77-706129
Prod-USPHS Dist-USNAC Prodn-NMAC 1977

Preparation Of Sputum Specimens B 16 MIN
16MM FILM OPTICAL SOUND
Shows the technique of sputum preparation used in laboratory diagnosis of TB to simplify diagnostic methods and to supplement mass X-ray programs.
From The Laboratory Diagnosis Of Tuberculosis Series.
LC NO. FIE53-196
Prod-USPHS Dist-USNAC 1949

Preparation Of Surfaces (Planing) C 63 MIN
1/2 INCH VIDEOTAPE
Suggests staying with hand planing, rather than using power tools. Demonstates the technique.
From The Woodworking Series.
Prod-ANVICO Dist-ANVICO

Preparation Of Tender Beef Cuts C 11 MIN
16MM FILM OPTICAL SOUND J-C A
Identifies the tender wholesale cuts of beef and demonstrates five methods of cooking with dry heat.
From The Food And Nutrition Series.
LC NO. 72-702649
Prod-IOWA Dist-IOWA 1971

Preparation Of The Immediate Denture For Delivery C 13 MIN
16MM FILM OPTICAL SOUND PRO
Points out that the immediate denture promotes the continued health of the tissues and reduces postdelivery problems. Demonstrates the grinding process and shows corrections of the periphery and the tissue surface to permit proper seating of the denture.
LC NO. 74-706382
Prod-USVA Dist-USNAC 1971

Preparation Of The Newborn For Transport (2nd Ed) C 14 MIN
3/4 OR 1/2 INCH VIDEO CASSETTE PRO
Covers communication between community hospital and referral center ICU, care of the infant prior to trans- port, preparing the parents for infant transfer and transfer of information and interactions among community hospital staff and the transfer team.
Prod-UMICHM Dist-UMICHM 1983

Preparation Of Thick And Thin Blood Films C 6 MIN
16MM FILM OPTICAL SOUND
Demonstrates techniques of preparing blood films for detection of blood parasites and shows examples of good and poor films.
LC NO. 74-705404
Prod-USPHS Dist-USNAC 1967

Preparation/Administration Of Oral Medication C 8 MIN
3/4 OR 1/2 INCH VIDEO CASSETTE PRO
See series title for descriptive statement.
From The Basic Nursing Skills Series.
Prod-BRA Dist-BRA

Preparation/Administration Of Oral Medication C 8 MIN
3/4 OR 1/2 INCH VIDEO CASSETTE PRO
See series title for descriptive statement.
From The Basic Nursing Skills Series. Tape 13
Prod-MDCC Dist-MDCC

Preparation, The C 21 MIN
3/4 OR 1/2 INCH VIDEO CASSETTE
Exposes and analyzes the most frequent and costly errors of untrained negotiators and establishes four basic principles for successful negotiating.
From the Negotiating Sales Series. Pt I
Prod-VISUCP Dist-VISUCP

Preparation, The C 25 MIN
3/4 OR 1/2 INCH VIDEO CASSETTE
Reveals the work and techniques required for one to sell effectively. Covers research, setting objectives and using proper questioning.
From The So You Want To Be A Success At Selling Series. Pt I
Prod-VIDART Dist-VISUCP

Preparatory Techniques For Gravlee Jet Washer Endometrial Specimens C 17 MIN
16MM FILM OPTICAL SOUND
Features obstetrician-gynecologist-pathologist Dr George Wied and cytotechnologist, Margaret Harris of the University of Chicago who demonstrate various laboratory procedures for preparing endometrial specimens for both histologic and cytologic analysis.
From The Upjohn Vanguard Of Medicine Series.
LC NO. 73-701867
Prod-UPJOHN Dist-UPJOHN 1973

Preparatory, The C 24 MIN
16MM FILM OPTICAL SOUND
Deals with life in a Catholic boys boarding school, demonstrating

a boy's adaptation to that life and the interpersonal relationships that develop between him and the older students and teacher-priests.
Prod-USC Dist-USC

Prepare The Learner B 29 MIN
16MM FILM OPTICAL SOUND IND
See series title for descriptive statement.
From The Job Instructor Training Series.
LC NO. 77-703324
Prod-EDSD Dist-EDSD

Prepare The Man C 25 MIN
16MM FILM OPTICAL SOUND
Explains new concepts in selective recruiting, proper replacement and specialized training of personnel. Points out the continuing need for missile crews, pilot, electronic specialists, scientists and related high level personnel.
LC NO. 74-706183
Prod-USDD Dist-USNAC 1962

Prepare To Win C 18 MIN
16MM FILM, 3/4 OR 1/2 IN VIDEO J-C
Introduces the 1984 U S Olympic team's basketball coach. Reveals his secrets for winning championships.
Prod-KLEINW Dist-KLEINW

Prepare With Care C 15 MIN
16MM FILM OPTICAL SOUND
Provides an informational and motivational look at modern main handling machines used in many U S Post Offices. Explains the importance of preparing U S Government mail properly for maximum service.
LC NO. 74-705405
Prod-USPOST Dist-USNAC 1969

Prepare Your Halter Horse For Show C 61 MIN
1/2 IN VIDEO CASSETTE BETA/VHS
Covers the feeding, conditioning and training necessary to prepare a horse to compete at halter in the show ring. Demonstrates how to work with a horse in the ring. Shows how to attain the ideal head and neck position for the Arabian horse.
From The Horse Care And Training Series.
Prod-MOHOMV Dist-MOHOMV

Prepared Childbirth C 16 MIN
16MM FILM, 3/4 OR 1/2 IN VIDEO
Uses animation, dialogue scenes and documentary footage to explain the advantages and leading methods of prepared childbirth.
From The Prepared Childbirth And Parenting Series.
Prod-PRORE Dist-JOU Prodn-TCON 1979

Prepared Childbirth And Parenting—A Series
16MM FILM, 3/4 OR 1/2 IN VIDEO
Discusses childbirth and parenting. Points out that during pregnancy and after birth, both parents face many decisions, from how lifestyles must be adjusted to deciding on a course of childcare.
Prod-JOU Dist-JOU

Anatomy And Physiology Of Pregnancy	006 MIN
And Spare The Child	011 MIN
Birth Of Your Baby, The	014 MIN
Cesarean Childbirth	016 MIN
Fathers	016 MIN
It's Not An Illness	024 MIN
Moveable Feast, A - A Film About Breastfeeding	022 MIN
New Baby Care	018 MIN
Prenatal Care - The Early Months	012 MIN
Prenatal Management	008 MIN
Prepared Childbirth	016 MIN
Stress And The Child	010 MIN
Understanding Labor	011 MIN
Weight, Nutrition And Exercise During	008 MIN

Preparing A Child For A Renal Transplant C
3/4 INCH VIDEO CASSETTE PRO
Provides a program for showing how to teach a child who is about to undergo renal transplant what the operation is like. Includes kidney anatomy and functions, the use of dramatic play techniques, the question of kidney donors and post-operative appearance.
From The Staff Development Series.
Prod-CFDC Dist-CFDC

Preparing A Child For An Appendectomy C
3/4 INCH VIDEO CASSETTE PRO
Presents a program of teaching children about having an appendectomy. Discusses collecting teaching aids, the function of an appendix, post-operative appearance, physiology of the GI tract and the use of a body outline.
From The Staff Development Series.
Prod-CFDC Dist-CFDC

Preparing A Child For Anesthesia, OR, Recovery Room And ICU C
3/4 INCH VIDEO CASSETTE PRO
Presents the essential points to be covered in a pre-operative teaching session for preparing a child for anesthesia. Treats such topics as no food before the operation, scrubbing, hospital clothing, parent participation and recovery room. The first of two parts.
From The Staff Development Series.
Prod-CFDC Dist-CFDC

Preparing A Child For Herniorrhaphy C
3/4 INCH VIDEO CASSETTE PRO
Presents a program for teaching the parents of a child about to undergo a herniorrhaphy how to teach their child about it. Demonstrates the use of teaching equipment, including the use of a body outline for discussing anatomy, operative site and post-operative appearance.
From The Staff Development Series.
Prod-CFDC Dist-CFDC

Preparing A Crystalline Candy - Fondant C 3 MIN
16MM FILM SILENT J-C S
Demonstrates the preparation of a kneaded fondant and compares crystalline and amorphous microstructures.
From The Food And Nutrition Series.
LC NO. 71-710170
Prod-IOWA Dist-IOWA 1971

Preparing A Cupola For Charging B 21 MIN
16MM FILM OPTICAL SOUND
Explains how to recognize the end of a heat. Follows the procedure for dropping bottom and for preparing a cupola for its next heat.
LC NO. FIE52-146
Prod-USOE Dist-USNAC 1945

Preparing A Custody Case C 51 MIN
3/4 OR 1/2 INCH VIDEO CASSETTE PRO
Shares insights from two experienced family lawyers on how to prepare a custody case. Explores how to conduct the initial interview, obtain a case history and evaluate a case.
From The Preparing And Trying A Custody Case Series.
Prod-ABACPE Dist-ABACPE

Preparing A Hem C 5 MIN
16MM FILM SILENT J-C A
Demonstrates the necessary first steps for achieving an inconspicuous hem on the right side of a garment. Shows how to keep an even and appropriate width that is parallel to the floor.
From The Clothing Construction Techniques Series.
LC NO. 77-701231
Prod-IOWA Dist-IOWASP 1976

Preparing A Roast C 20 MIN
1/2 IN VIDEO CASSETTE BETA/VHS
Explains how to ready a rib roast for the oven, and provides a detailed description of the three types of heat transfer and the steps used to prepare a meat product for the roasting process.
Prod-RMI Dist-RMI

Preparing A Technical Presentation C 15 MIN
3/4 OR 1/2 INCH VIDEO CASSETTE
See series title for descriptive statement.
From The Effective Technical Presentations Series.
Prod-DELTAK Dist-DELTAK Prodn-TRESA

Preparing An Amorphous Candy - Butterscotch C 2 MIN
16MM FILM SILENT
Demonstrates the preparation of butterscotch and compares amorphous and crystalline microstructures.
From The Food And Nutrition Series.
LC NO. 75-710171
Prod-IOWA Dist-IOWA 1971

Preparing And Evaluating Reports Systematically B 55 MIN
3/4 OR 1/2 INCH VIDEO CASSETTE IND
See series title for descriptive statement.
From The Technical And Professional Writing For Industry, Government And Business Series.
Prod-UMICE Dist-AMCEE

Preparing And Setting A Keelblock And Bottom Cradle B 18 MIN
16MM FILM OPTICAL SOUND
Demonstrates the use of base line, vertical centerline, buttock lines, waterlines and frame lines in checking dimensions during ship construction. Shows how to lay a keelblock, use templates to make spauls and erect a ship cradle.
LC NO. FIE52-191
Prod-USOE Dist-USNAC 1942

Preparing And Trying A Custody Case—A Series
PRO
Provides attorneys with a practical guide to the task of preparing and trying a child custody case.
Prod-ABACPE Dist-ABACPE

Developing Trial Strategy In A Custody Case	046 MIN
Preparing A Custody Case	051 MIN
Trial Techniques In A Custody Case	074 MIN

Preparing And Trying A Medical Malpractice Case—A Series
PRO
Reviews trial preparation, strategies and tactics from the perspective of both plaintiff and defendant in medical malpractice case.
Prod-ABACPE Dist-ABACPE

Cross-Examination Of The Medical Expert	044 MIN
Direct Examination Of The Medical Expert	066 MIN
Evaluation And Preparation Of A Malpractice	082 MIN
Evaluation And Preparation Of A Malpractice1	076 MIN
Substantive Law - Consent To Treatment	051 MIN
Substantive Law - Vicarious Liability And	099 MIN
Substantive Law Of The Physician-Patient	050 MIN

Preparing Chicken Cordon Bleu C 20 MIN
1/2 IN VIDEO CASSETTE BETA/VHS
Describes the step-by-step preparation of chicken Cordon Bleu, including how to fill, roll and present this entree.
Prod-RMI Dist-RMI

Preparing Fabric C 4 MIN
16MM FILM SILENT J-C A
Identifies grain and bias directions and illustrates straightening of the fabric ends by tearing or pulling a crosswise yarn. Discusses preshrinking washable and nonwashable fabrics.
From The Clothing Construction Techniques Series.
LC NO. 77-701168
Prod-IOWA Dist-IOWASP 1976

Preparing Flatfish To Be Served Whole C
3/4 OR 1/2 INCH VIDEO CASSETTE
See series title for descriptive statement.
From The How To Fillet Fish Series.
Prod-CULINA Dist-CULINA

Preparing For And Conducting Effective Performance Reviews C 40 MIN
3/4 OR 1/2 INCH VIDEO CASSETTE
Demonstrates how the performance review can be handled effectively, using positive role models and to plan future improvement in job expectations and requirements.
From The Performance Improvement Program Series.
Prod-PRODEV Dist-PRODEV

Preparing For Bed C 16 MIN
16MM FILM MAGNETIC SOUND K-C A S
See series title for descriptive statement.
From The PANCOM Beginning Total Communication Program For Hearing Parents Of... Series. Level 2
LC NO. 77-700504
Prod-CSDE Dist-JOYCE Prodn-CSFDF 1977

Preparing For Childbirth (A Family Affair) C 26 MIN
16MM FILM OPTICAL SOUND H-C A
Shows how both a mother and father train and prepare for the birth of the family's third child. Emphasizes the role of both parents in making the birth a success.
LC NO. 75-702602
Prod-CINEMN Dist-CRTVLC 1975

Preparing For Childbirth - A Nine month Experience C
3/4 OR 1/2 INCH VIDEO CASSETTE
Emphasizing pre-natal visits and covers birth preparation classes on diet, exercise and relaxation techniques. Concludes with labor onset, birth and bonding.
Prod-MIFE Dist-MIFE

Preparing For Childbirth - A Nine Month Experience (Arabic) C
3/4 OR 1/2 INCH VIDEO CASSETTE
Emphasizes pre-natal visits and covers birth preparation classes on diet, exercise and relaxation techniques. Concludes with labor onset, birth and bonding.
Prod-MIFE Dist-MIFE

Preparing For Childbirth - A Nine Month Experience (Spanish) C
3/4 OR 1/2 INCH VIDEO CASSETTE
Emphasizes pre-natal visits and covers birth preparation classes on diet, exercise and relaxation techniques. Concludes with labor onset, birth and bonding.
Prod-MIFE Dist-MIFE

Preparing For College C 20 MIN
16MM FILM, 3/4 OR 1/2 IN VIDEO J-H
Presents interviews with five college freshmen who discuss how well they were prepared for college. Offers information on college applications and admissions.
LC NO. 81-706011
Prod-CBSNEW Dist-CRMP 1981

Preparing For Dinner C 16 MIN
16MM FILM MAGNETIC SOUND K-C A S
See series title for descriptive statement.
From The PANCOM Beginning Total Communication Program For Hearing Parents Of... Series. Level 2
LC NO. 77-700504
Prod-CSDE Dist-JOYCE Prodn-CSFDF 1977

Preparing For Negotiation C 42 MIN
3/4 OR 1/2 INCH VIDEO CASSETTE
See series title for descriptive statement.
From The Art Of Negotiating Series.
Prod-DELTAK Dist-DELTAK

Preparing For Negotiations C 50 MIN
3/4 OR 1/2 INCH VIDEO CASSETTE PRO
Explains the benefit of getting background information, holding practice negotiation sessions and creating the proper atmosphere for negotiation.
From The Negotiation Lectures Series.
Prod-NITA Dist-ABACPE

Preparing For Parenthood C
3/4 OR 1/2 INCH VIDEO CASSETTE
Presents the feelings, beliefs, attitudes and experiences of a diverse group of parents. Compares and contrasts varied concepts of parental responsibilities and roles, discusses financial and emotional problems and examines the child-parent relationship during the formative years.
From The Parenthood - Bringing New Life Into The World Series.
Prod-GA Dist-GA

Preparing For The Conference C 19 MIN
3/4 OR 1/2 INCH VIDEO CASSETTE
Covers the four steps of preplanning a conference and outlines steps for pinpointing precise conference objectives.
From The Conference Leading Skills Series.
Prod-RESEM Dist-RESEM

Preparing For The Interview C 30 MIN
3/4 OR 1/2 INCH VIDEO CASSETTE
Discusses how students of all disciplines and levels can get ready for job interviews.
From The Where The Jobs Are Series.
Prod-IVCH Dist-IVCH

Preparing For The Jobs Of The 1990's - What You Should Know C
3/4 OR 1/2 INCH VIDEO CASSETTE H
Explores factors that change the job market and the computer

revolution, and tells how to keep pace with expanding technology. Attempts to develop a flexible approach to career preparation and outlines informational resources.
Prod-GA Dist-GA

Preparing For The Review C 35 MIN
3/4 OR 1/2 INCH VIDEO CASSETTE
Focuses on the 'how' of the appraisal process. Prepares both employee and manager for the appraisal. Shows how to write specific objectives.
From The Appraisals In Action Series. Session 2
Prod-PRODEV Dist-DELTAK

Preparing For The Unexpected C 10 MIN
16MM FILM - 3/4 IN VIDEO
Presents the humorous experiences of one employee to show his change in attitude towards emergency preparedness. Illustrates the importance of every individual's role in responding to an emergency.
Prod-ALLIED Dist-BNA

Preparing For Tomorrow's World C 26 MIN
16MM FILM OPTICAL SOUND
Discusses the education necessary for a career in the nuclear field. Stresses the value of building a firm foundation in science, mathematics and English. States that government agencies, industry, and educational and research institutions engaged in a wide variety of projects all need nuclear scientists and engineers.
From The Careers In Nuclear Science And Nuclear Engineering Series.
LC NO. 70-706769
Prod-USAEC Dist-USNAC 1970

Preparing For Troubleshooting C 12 MIN
3/4 OR 1/2 INCH VIDEO CASSETTE
Discusses troubleshooting responsibility, tools, parts and supplies.
From The Developing Troubleshooting Skills Series.
Prod-TPCTRA Dist-TPCTRA

Preparing For Variable Modular Scheduling C 25 MIN
16MM FILM OPTICAL SOUND C T
Discusses considerations in planning for the implementation of a variable program. Portrays the changes in learning behavior, teaching method, curriculum and facility design that have taken place in schools across the country on this type of schedule. Emphasizes the structural concepts of variable scheduling, the ways that time can be varied, performance and demand curriculum, individualized learning and the concept of teacher as director of learning.
LC NO. 76-710821
Prod-EDUC Dist-EDUC 1970

Preparing For Winter C 9 MIN
16MM FILM, 3/4 OR 1/2 IN VIDEO K-I
Presents scenes of animals preparing for winter.
From The Primary Language Development Series.
Prod-PEDF Dist-AIMS 1975

Preparing For Your Surgery C 11 MIN
3/4 OR 1/2 INCH VIDEO CASSETTE
Introduces the patient to the basic feature of this preoperative care and describes the operating room environment. Discusses the consent form, preoperative testing and preparations immediately before a surgery.
LC NO. 81-730135
Prod-TRAINX Dist-TRAINX

Preparing Meals C 13 MIN
16MM FILM OPTICAL SOUND J-C A
Presents five concepts dealing with meal preparation-planning the menu, breakfast, luncheon, dinner and snacks. The projector may be stopped after each part.
From The Cooking, Home Economics Series.
LC NO. FIA68-1376
Prod-MORLAT Dist-SF 1968

Preparing Meals - The Last Step C 26 MIN
3/4 OR 1/2 INCH VIDEO CASSETTE J-H A
See series title for descriptive statement.
From The Food For Youth Series.
Prod-CUETV Dist-CUNIV 1975

Preparing Meals - The Last Step C 27 MIN
16MM FILM, 3/4 OR 1/2 IN VIDEO
Outlines quantity food preparation techniques and offers basic school lunch program aids aimed at making sure that maximum nutritional value gets to the children.
From The Food For Youth Series.
LC NO. 81-706396
Prod-USFNS Dist-USNAC Prodn-WGBH 1981

Preparing Old Buildings For Wiring B 21 MIN
16MM FILM - 3/4 IN VIDEO IND
Tells how to plan wiring paths, visualizing the obstructions, and then prepare the paths for the wiring runs. Issued in 1945 as a motion picture.
From The Electrical Work - Wiring Series. No. 7
LC NO. 79-707488
Prod-USOE Dist-USNAC Prodn-RAYBEL 1979

Preparing Pattern For Layout C 29 MIN
2 INCH VIDEOTAPE
Features Mrs Ruth Hickman demonstrating how to prepare the pattern for layout.
From The Sewing Skills - Tailoring Series.
Prod-KRMATV Dist-PUBTEL

Preparing Professional Notes And Reports C 15 MIN
3/4 OR 1/2 INCH VIDEO CASSETTE
Teaches the legal and operational importance of accurate notes and reports.
From The Health Care Security Training Series.
Prod-GREESM Dist-MTI

Preparing Ration-Dense Foods C 17 MIN
16MM FILM OPTICAL SOUND
Shows how to prepare ration-dense food items using standard Navy galley equipment afloat or ashore.
LC NO. 76-700475
Prod-USN Dist-USNAC 1976

Preparing The Burn Patient For Transport C 19 MIN
3/4 OR 1/2 INCH VIDEO CASSETTE PRO
Identifies the nurse's role in continuing physical support and preparation for transport of the burn patient. Discusses continuing physical support in terms of respiratory support, cardiovascular support, gastrointestinal support and other support measures which will assist the patient before transport.
LC NO. 81-730383
Prod-TRAINX Dist-TRAINX

Preparing The Dancer For Broadway C 30 MIN
3/4 OR 1/2 INCH VIDEO CASSETTE
See series title for descriptive statement.
From The Broadway Dance Series.
Prod-ARCVID Dist-ARCVID

Preparing The Loom C 29 MIN
2 INCH VIDEOTAPE
See series title for descriptive statement.
From The Exploring The Crafts - Weaving Series.
Prod-NHN Dist-PUBTEL

Preparing The Patient For Normal Delivery C 13 MIN
3/4 OR 1/2 INCH VIDEO CASSETTE PRO
Shows how to prepare a patient for normal delivery of the infant.
Prod-HSCIC Dist-HSCIC 1977

Preparing The Sensory And Visual Perceptual Motor Prerequisites For Communication C 50 MIN
3/4 OR 1/2 INCH VIDEO CASSETTE
Discusses various abnormal reflexes that interfere with the communication development of cerebral palsied individuals.
From The Meeting The Communications Needs Of The Severely/Profoundly Handicapped 1980 Series.
Prod-PUAVC Dist-PUAVC

Preparing Theatre Dance Productions C 30 MIN
3/4 OR 1/2 INCH VIDEO CASSETTE
See series title for descriptive statement.
From The Broadway Dance Series.
Prod-ARCVID Dist-ARCVID

Preparing Thickening Agents, Making A Roux C 20 MIN
1/2 IN VIDEO CASSETTE BETA/VHS
Discusses roux and cornstarch, the basic thickening agents used in food service, and describes the distinctive properties of both.
Prod-RMI Dist-RMI

Preparing To Coach An Effective Offense C 27 MIN
3/4 OR 1/2 INCH VIDEO CASSETTE T
Features Coaches Joe Paterno and Dick Anderson develop the important but overlooked details that are necessary for an efficient football offense.
From The Joe Paterno - Coaching Winning Football Series.
Prod-UNIDIM Dist-EBEC 1982

Preparing To Cook C 13 MIN
16MM FILM OPTICAL SOUND I-C A
Presents five concepts dealing with preparation for cooking--selection of foods, cleanliness and storage, measuring and terms, ways of cooking and steps in getting ready to cook. The projector may be stopped after each concept.
From The Cooking, Home Economics Series.
LC NO. FIA68-1377
Prod-MORLAT Dist-SF 1967

Preparing To Dance C 15 MIN
16MM FILM, 3/4 OR 1/2 IN VIDEO J-C
Deals with the preparation of the dancer in studio classes that will develop technique and awareness of space, time and energy.
From The Dance Experience - Training And Composing Series.
Prod-ATHI Dist-ATHI 1984

Preparing To Give Birth C
3/4 OR 1/2 INCH VIDEO CASSETTE
Reviews, through case histories, pregnancy testing, childbirth, methods of delivery, the father's involvement and selection of a medical facility and personnel. Shows a childbirth education class and discusses the importance of psychological preparation.
From The Parenthood - Bringing New Life Into The World Series.
Prod-GA Dist-GA

Preparing To Perform Shakespeare C 50 MIN
3/4 OR 1/2 INCH VIDEO CASSETTE
Shows director John Barton of the Royal Shakespeare Company working on a scene from Troilus And Cressida with actors Alan Howard, Michael Pennington, Ian McKellen, Patrick Stewart and David Suchet. Presents Ian McKellen describing the thoughts and ideas that run through an actor's mind as he prepares for a major soliloquy.
Prod-FOTH Dist-FOTH 1984

Preparing To Speak C 17 MIN
3/4 OR 1/2 INCH VIDEO CASSETTE
Discusses the tools of development, organization and method of delivery of a speech. Offers six steps for preparing an oral presentation.
From The Effective Speaking Series.
Prod-RESEM Dist-RESEM

Preparing Training Objectives C 12 MIN
3/4 OR 1/2 INCH VIDEO CASSETTE
Shows supervisors how to develop sound training objectives with emphasis on preplanning and the significance of carefully stated objectives that cover action, standards and conditions.
From The Supervisor And OJT Series. Module 2
Prod-RESEM Dist-RESEM

Preparing Witnesses For Deposition And Trial C 160 MIN
3/4 OR 1/2 INCH VIDEO CASSETTE
Discusses various considerations in preparing lay witnesses for deposition and trial, and methods for preparing expert witnesses.
Prod-CCEB Dist-ABACPE

Preparing Your Speech C 28 MIN
3/4 OR 1/2 INCH VIDEO CASSETTE
Tells how to prepare a business-related speech.
From The Business Of Effective Speaking Series.
Prod-KYTV Dist-KYTV

Preparing Your Students For The A C T C 120 MIN
3/4 OR 1/2 INCH VIDEO CASSETTE
See series title for descriptive statement.
From The A C T Exam Preparation Series.
Prod-KRLSOF Dist-KRLSOF 1985

Preparing Your Students For The SAT C 120 MIN
3/4 OR 1/2 INCH VIDEO CASSETTE
See series title for descriptive statement.
From The SAT Exam Preparation Series.
Prod-KRLSOF Dist-KRLSOF 1985

Prepartion C 8 MIN
3/4 OR 1/2 INCH VIDEO CASSETTE H-C A
Highlights the importance of being prepared for a job interview. Includes resumes, references, school reports, and knowing about the job and company.
From The Young Job Seekers Series.
Prod-SEVDIM Dist-SEVDIM

Preplanning C 28 MIN
3/4 OR 1/2 INCH VIDEO CASSETTE
Suggests preplanning makes business-related speeches more effective.
From The Business Of Effective Speaking Series.
Prod-KYTV Dist-KYTV

Preplanning And Objectives C 11 MIN
3/4 OR 1/2 INCH VIDEO CASSETTE
Stresses the importance of formulating a set of objectives before starting any training session. Offers some practical help on developing sound objectives.
From The Supervisor As A Classroom Instructor Series. Module 3
Prod-RESEM Dist-RESEM

Prepositions C 10 MIN
16MM FILM, 3/4 OR 1/2 IN VIDEO P-I
Explains the basics of using prepositions.
From The Wizard Of Words Series.
Prod-MGHT Dist-MGHT 1976

Preprocessor C
3/4 OR 1/2 INCH VIDEO CASSETTE
Defines the preprocessor in 'C' language and how it works, what its effects are and how it performs these effects. Describes the syntax and usage of preprocessor token replacement and illustrates the syntax and use of conditional compilations.
From The 'C' Language Programming Series.
Prod-COMTEG Dist-COMTEG

Preprosthetic Surgery C 3 MIN
3/4 OR 1/2 INCH VIDEO CASSETTE
Offers a presentation by Lee Getter, DDS, Wheatop, Maryland, on oral surgery and sedation. Demonstrates tooth removal, bone contour and soft tissue handling and shows methods of anxiety control and uses of local anesthesia applicable to general practice.
Prod-AMDA Dist-AMDA 1977

Preschool Articulation Screening C 18 MIN
16MM FILM - 3/4 IN VIDEO
Provides practice exercise for administering the Denver articulation screening exam. Supplements the slide-tape program Preschool Articulation Screening.
LC NO. 78-706280
Prod-NMAC Dist-USNAC 1977

Preschool Child C 41 MIN
3/4 OR 1/2 INCH VIDEO CASSETTE
Shows the rapid development of gross motor skills and beginning development of fine motor skills through the medium of play activities. Discusses the emergence of the child as a social being.
From The Infancy Through Adolescence Series.
Prod-WSUN Dist-AJN

Preschool Experience, The C 30 MIN
3/4 INCH VIDEO CASSETTE
Discusses the effect of early schooling on a child's development and the role of preschools in society.
From The Growing Years Series.
Prod-COAST Dist-CDTEL

Preschool Experience, The - Four Programs C 22 MIN
16MM FILM, 3/4 OR 1/2 IN VIDEO H-C A
Describes the programs and goals of four preschools.
From The Growing Years (CRMP) Series.
Prod-COAST Dist-CRMP 1978

Preschool Lesson In Cued Speech, A C 7 MIN
16MM FILM, 3/4 OR 1/2 IN VIDEO
Presents a short teaching segment that incorporates manipulative visuals, hand signs and language to two- to three-year-old hearing impaired children.
LC NO. 80-707427
Prod-USBEH Dist-USNAC 1972

Preschool Mental Development C 30 MIN
3/4 INCH VIDEO CASSETTE
Shows the preschool child's growing ability to use symbols and manipulate information. Discusses Piaget's stage of pre-operational thought.
From The Growing Years Series.
Prod-COAST Dist-CDTEL

Preschool Personality C 30 MIN
3/4 INCH VIDEO CASSETTE
Discusses the personality development of the three-to six-year-old child.
From The Growing Years Series.
Prod-COAST Dist-CDTEL

Preschool Physical Development C 30 MIN
3/4 INCH VIDEO CASSETTE
Shows the physical growth of the three- to six-year-old child and discusses motor skills and physical and perceptual coordination.
From The Growing Years Series.
Prod-COAST Dist-CDTEL

Preschool Story Programs C 20 MIN
3/4 INCH VIDEO CASSETTE T
Presents basic techniques for working with preschoolers in a library. Discusses how to select materials, present a story program and deal with problems that might arise.
From The Access Series.
LC NO. 76-706250
Prod-UDEN Dist-USNAC 1976

Preschool Vision Screening C 10 MIN
16MM FILM, 3/4 OR 1/2 IN VIDEO PRO
Provides practice exercises for those who will be administering the Denver eye screening test. Supplements the slide/tape program Preschool Vision Screening.
LC NO. 82-707313
Prod-NMAC Dist-USNAC Prodn-UCOLO 1977

Preschooler - Concept Development B 44 MIN
16MM FILM OPTICAL SOUND
Discusses factors influencing concept development-conditions of sense organs, intelligence, opportunity for learning, types of experience, amount of guidance, sex of child and personality.
From The Man - His Growth And Development, Birth Through Adolescence Series.
LC NO. 76-703687
Prod-VDONUR Dist-AJN Prodn-WTTWTV 1967

Preschooler - Psycho-Sexual Development B 44 MIN
16MM FILM OPTICAL SOUND
Describes developmental stages of the preschooler in his psycho-sexual development.
From The Man - His Growth And Development, Birth Through Adolescence Series.
LC NO. 70-703688
Prod-VDONUR Dist-AJN Prodn-WTTWTV 1967

Prescribing Fluoride Supplements In Dental Practice C 16 MIN
16MM FILM OPTICAL SOUND
Describes the rationale for prescribing dietary fluoride supplements for children in areas with fluoride deficient drinking water, ways to maximize longterm compliance and recommended dosages.
Prod-MTP Dist-MTP

Prescription B 7 MIN
16MM FILM OPTICAL SOUND
Describes the hospitals in New York City in need of volunteer services and discusses their physical plants and locations, and explains the procedures to follow in applying for volunteer assignments.
From The Bellevue Volunteers Series.
Prod-NYU Dist-NYU

Prescription And Over-The-Counter Drugs C 30 MIN
3/4 OR 1/2 INCH VIDEO CASSETTE C A
Examines the rapidly growing drug industry in the United States. Investigates the effectiveness of government regulation of the drug industry. Studies the role of the physician in prescribing drugs. Gives special attention to the responsibility of the patient.
From The Contemporary Health Issues Series. Lesson 18
Prod-SCCON Dist-CDTEL

Prescription Drugs / Advertising / Adoption C
3/4 OR 1/2 INCH VIDEO CASSETTE
Discusses various aspects of prescription drugs, advertising and adoption.
From The Consumer Survival Series.
Prod-MDCPB Dist-MDCPB

Prescription Drugs / Travel Tips / Air Conditioning C
3/4 OR 1/2 INCH VIDEO CASSETTE
Discusses various aspects of prescription drugs, travel tips and air conditioning.
From The Consumer Survival Series.
Prod-MDCPB Dist-MDCPB

Prescription For A Profession - A Program On Physician Well-Being C 16 MIN
3/4 OR 1/2 INCH VIDEO CASSETTE PRO
Stimulates discussion of causes, identification and prevention of physician impairment. Explores attitudes of affected colleagues and family.
Prod-HSCIC Dist-HSCIC 1984

Prescription For Complaints C 20 MIN
3/4 OR 1/2 INCH VIDEO CASSETTE
Illustrates the six stages for handling complaints with special focus on the danger points.
Prod-VISUCP Dist-VISUCP

Prescription For Complaints C 21 MIN
3/4 OR 1/2 INCH VIDEO CASSETTE A
C668 Gives employees a 6-stage strategy for handling any complaint. Uses a light touch to show right and wrong ways of dealing with complaints in the business world.
Prod-XICOM Dist-XICOM

Prescription For Life C 15 MIN
16MM FILM OPTICAL SOUND
Demonstrates the use of lifesaving resuscitation techniques in reviving unconscious persons.
LC NO. 73-700473
Prod-BANDEL Dist-BANDEL 1967

Prescription For Life C 27 MIN
16MM FILM OPTICAL SOUND H-C A
Presents detailed instructions in cardiopulmonary resuscitation, including artificial respiration, artificial circulation and definite treatment of all forms of cardiac arrest.
LC NO. 73-700183
Prod-BANDEL Dist-BANDEL 1967

Prescription For Life C 48 MIN
16MM FILM OPTICAL SOUND PRO
Presents detailed instructions in cardiopulmonary resuscitation, including artificial respiration, artificial circulation, and definitive treatment of all forms of cardiac arrest.
LC NO. FIA67-564
Prod-AHA Dist-BANDEL Prodn-BANDEL 1967

Prescription For Profit C 35 MIN
3/4 OR 1/2 INCH VIDEO CASSETTE
Examines what contributes to the rising costs which threaten to crush the health care system.
Prod-WCCOTV Dist-WCCOTV 1981

Prescription O T B 22 MIN
3/4 INCH VIDEO CASSETTE PRO
Orients resident physicians to occupational therapy, giving the prescription and explaining how occupational therapy carries out the prescription.
Prod-USNAC Dist-USNAC 1972

Prescription Trap, The C 38 MIN
3/4 OR 1/2 INCH VIDEO CASSETTE
Demonstrates that prescription drugs can be addictive and recovering alcoholics and drug abusers must avoid taking any mood altering chemical, whether wet or dry.
Prod-WHITEG Dist-WHITEG

Prescriptions For Learning C 30 MIN
16MM FILM OPTICAL SOUND C A
Pictures Navajo Indian children in special learning situations in order to show methods used in evaluating, testing and correcting learning disabilities.
LC NO. 75-702927
Prod-USBIA Dist-AVED Prodn-BAILYL 1975

Presence Of Self, The C
3/4 INCH VIDEO CASSETTE
Describes growth and development of a child from 15 to 16 months.
From The Growth And Development - A Chronicle Of Four Children Series. Series 5
Prod-JUETHO Dist-LIP

Presence Of Self, The - Gregory, 15 Months C 7 MIN
16MM FILM OPTICAL SOUND
See series title for descriptive statement.
From The Growth And Development - A Chronicle Of Four Children Series. Series 5
LC NO. 78-700686
Prod-JUETHO Dist-LIP Prodn-CONCOM 1976

Presence Of Self, The - Joseph, 16 Months C 7 MIN
16MM FILM OPTICAL SOUND
See series title for descriptive statement.
From The Growth And Development - A Chronicle Of Four Children Series. Series 5
LC NO. 78-700686
Prod-JUETHO Dist-LIP Prodn-CONCOM 1976

Presence Of Self, The - Melissa, 15 Months C 6 MIN
16MM FILM OPTICAL SOUND
See series title for descriptive statement.
From The Growth And Development - A Chronicle Of Four Children Series. Series 5
LC NO. 78-700686
Prod-JUETHO Dist-LIP Prodn-CONCOM 1976

Presence Of Self, The - Terra, 16 Months C 7 MIN
16MM FILM OPTICAL SOUND
See series title for descriptive statement.
From The Growth And Development - A Chronicle Of Four Children Series. Series 5
LC NO. 78-700686
Prod-JUETHO Dist-LIP Prodn-CONCOM 1976

Present C 6 MIN
16MM FILM, 3/4 OR 1/2 IN VIDEO H-C A
Presents an animated film in which a bottle of liquid serves as payment for services. Shows how the bottle is passed along from one person to another without ever being opened. Tells of the tragic results when the bottle is finally opened.
Prod-SFTB Dist-PHENIX

Present The Operation B 29 MIN
16MM FILM OPTICAL SOUND IND
See series title for descriptive statement.
From The Job Instructor Training Series.
LC NO. 77-703324
Prod-EDSD Dist-EDSD

Present Worth Method C 30 MIN
3/4 OR 1/2 INCH VIDEO CASSETTE IND
Introduces evaluation method which converts all cash flows to an equivalent amount today. Uses present value of U S Treasury Bond as example.
From The Engineering Econony Series.
Prod-COLOSU Dist-COLOSU

Present Worth Method (Japanese) C 30 MIN
3/4 OR 1/2 INCH VIDEO CASSETTE IND
Introduces evaluation method which converts all cash flows to an equivalent amount today. Uses present value of U S Treasury Bond as example.
From The Engineering Economy Series.
Prod-COLOSU Dist-COLOSU

Presentation C
3/4 INCH VIDEO CASSETTE H A
Shows viewers how to develop their own original ideas for presenting food with style. Discusses simple methods of stylish presentation. Demonstrates preparation of a meal served in edible containers.
From The Matter Of Taste Series. Lesson 20
Prod-COAST Dist-CDTEL

Presentation C 8 MIN
3/4 OR 1/2 INCH VIDEO CASSETTE H-C A
Shows several young interviewees. Assesses suitability of their appearance and manner.
From The Young Job Seekers Series.
Prod-SEVDIM Dist-SEVDIM

Presentation C 50 MIN
3/4 OR 1/2 INCH VIDEO CASSETTE IND
Looks at lesson plans, classroom equipment, classroom presentation and using the overhead projector.
From The Training The Trainer Series.
Prod-LEIKID Dist-LEIKID

Presentation And Application Protocols C 50 MIN
3/4 OR 1/2 INCH VIDEO CASSETTE PRO
Describes virtual terminal and file transfer protocols.
From The Computer Communications - Protocols And Architectures, Pt 2 Series.
Prod-AMCEE Dist-AMCEE

Presentation Design C 45 MIN
3/4 OR 1/2 INCH VIDEO CASSETTE PRO
See series title for descriptive statement.
From The Making More Effective Technical Presentations Series.
Prod-ICSINT Dist-ICSINT

Presentation Excellence C 77 MIN
3/4 OR 1/2 INCH VIDEO CASSETTE A
Features Walter Cronkite, former CBS national news anchor, explaining techniques for making presentations, both to individuals and to large groups.
Prod-CBSFOX Dist-CBSFOX

Presentation Phase, The C 60 MIN
3/4 OR 1/2 INCH VIDEO CASSETTE IND
See series title for descriptive statement.
From The Value Engineering Series.
Prod-NCSU Dist-AMCEE

Presentation Reel Of Films On Smoking And Health C 19 MIN
16MM FILM OPTICAL SOUND H-C A
Presents highlights of American Cancer Society films on smoking and health.
Prod-AMCS Dist-AMCS

Presentation Reel Of Public Education Films C 21 MIN
16MM FILM OPTICAL SOUND H-C A
Promotes a broader use of films on cancer by showing a presentation of short excerpts from selected American Cancer Society public education films.
Prod-AMCS Dist-AMCS

Presentation Reel Of School Films C 20 MIN
16MM FILM OPTICAL SOUND H-C A
Presents footage put together by the national office of the American Cancer Society related to cigarette smoking and health.
Prod-AMCS Dist-AMCS

Presentation Skills C 30 MIN
3/4 OR 1/2 INCH VIDEO CASSETTE A
Demonstrates how to make a presentation and gives many pointers on projecting an overall favorable image in any business situation. Gives principles for preparing and conducting a formal presentation. Hosted by Richard Benjamin and Paula Prentiss.
From The Communication Skills For Managers Series.
Prod-TIMLIF Dist-TIMLIF 1981

Presentation Techniques, Pt 1 - Presentation By B 23 MIN
16MM FILM OPTICAL SOUND
Deals with the performance and appearance of the presenter when addressing the camera directly or when showing the television audience some small object.
From The CETO Television Training Films Series.
Prod-CETO Dist-GPITVL

Presentation Techniques, Pt 2 - Presenter And Studio B 23 MIN
16MM FILM OPTICAL SOUND
Deals with demonstrations of situations in which the presenter is required to walk around a large object or along a series of displays.
From The CETO Television Training Films Series.
Prod-CETO Dist-GPITVL

Presentation, The C 26 MIN
3/4 OR 1/2 INCH VIDEO CASSETTE

Illustrates techniques for dealing with sales objections and points out the importance of watching for buying signals and then asking for the order.
From The So You Want To Be A Success At Selling Series. Pt II
Prod-VIDART Dist-VISUCP

Presente—A Series

Presents one science fiction adventure and documentaries dealing with Hispanic cultures and history including the countries of Puerto Rico, Cuba, Mexico, Peru and Nicaragua.
Prod-KCET Dist-KCET

Alpaca Breeders Of Chimboya	029 MIN
First Look - Pt I	029 MIN
First Look - Pt II	029 MIN
Manos A La Obra - The Story Of Operation	028 MIN
Manos A La Obra - The Story Of Operation	029 MIN
Manuel Jimenez - Woodcarver	029 MIN
Mexican Tapes, The - A Chronicle Of Life	029 MIN
Mexican Tapes, The - A Chronicle Of Life	029 MIN
Mexican Tapes, The - A Chronicle Of Life	029 MIN
Mexican Tapes, The - A Chronicle Of Life	029 MIN
Moon Shadows	029 MIN
Nicaragua - The Other Invasion	029 MIN
Sojourn Earth	029 MIN

Presenting Documentary And Demonstrative Evidence Effectively C 120 MIN
3/4 OR 1/2 INCH VIDEO CASSETTE
Covers collection of evidence, getting evidence admitted and employing the evidence most effectively during trial.
Prod-CCEB Dist-ABACPE

Presenting One-Third C 15 MIN
3/4 INCH VIDEO CASSETTE P
Introduces the concepts of thirds and their relationship to a whole.
From The Math Factory, Module V - Fractions Series.
Prod-MAETEL Dist-GPITVL 1973

Presenting The Case C 32 MIN
16MM FILM - 3/4 IN VIDEO
Dramatizes a social worker's testimony in a child abuse hearing before the juvenile court.
From The We Can Help Series.
LC NO. 79-706247
Prod-NCCAN Dist-USNAC 1979

Presenting The Story C 14 MIN
3/4 OR 1/2 INCH VIDEO CASSETTE
Focuses on the best way to communicate benefits to the customer. Emphasizes careful preparation and practice as keys to success.
From The Basic Sales Series.
Prod-RESEM Dist-RESEM

Presents C 15 MIN
3/4 OR 1/2 INCH VIDEO CASSETTE P
Presents the children's stories Ask Mr Bear by Marjorie Flack and Mr Rabbit And The Lovely Present by Charlotte Zolotow.
From The Picture Book Park Series. Brown Module
Prod-WVIZTV Dist-AITECH 1974

Preservation Of Bacteria By Desiccation In Vacuo B 11 MIN
16MM FILM OPTICAL SOUND
Demonstrates the technique for desiccation in vacuo as a method of preservation for most bacteria. For professional use.
LC NO. FIE52-2233
Prod-USPHS Dist-USNAC 1949

Preserve B 5 MIN
16MM FILM OPTICAL SOUND
Presents a treatment of wild African animals in a game preserve and the reactions to human visitation. Explores commerical values and the peculiar relationship of 'CAGED' people viewing 'FREE' wildelife.
LC NO. 72-702419
Prod-USC Dist-USC 1972

Preserving Egypt's Past C 23 MIN
16MM FILM, 3/4 OR 1/2 IN VIDEO J-C A
Looks at the monuments, temples and tombs that have survived since the days of ancient Egypt. Shows how agriculture, population, changing weather conditions and even tourists are endangering the monuments.
LC NO. 83-706456
Prod-NGS Dist-NGS 1982

Preserving Flowers And Foliages C 61 MIN
1/2 IN VIDEO CASSETTE BETA/VHS
Demonstrates pressing flowers. Shows how to preserve flowers in silica gel using a microwave oven. Tells how to preserve foliages in glycerine solution.
From The Crafts And Decorating Series.
Prod-MOHOMV Dist-MOHOMV

Preserving Flowers And Foliages C 61 MIN
1/2 IN VIDEO CASSETTE BETA/VHS
Explains how to preserve garden flowers in silica gel using a new microwave oven technique, with tips on preserving foliage in glycerine solution and the art of pressing flowers.
Prod-RMI Dist-RMI

Preserving The Landscape C 30 MIN
3/4 OR 1/2 INCH VIDEO CASSETTE H-C A
Examines the development of Luminism in American art and the interest in the preservation of the land.
From The Art America Series.
Prod-CTI Dist-CTI

Presidency—A Series
16MM FILM, 3/4 OR 1/2 IN VIDEO J-C A
Looks at great moments in the United States Presidency from the time of Teddy Roosevelt to the mid-sixties.
Prod-LUF Dist-LUF 1976

Perfect President, The - A Man For	
Possible Presidents, The - Vice Presidents	052 MIN
Private President, The - The Man And	052 MIN
Public President, The - Wit And Warmth	052 MIN

Presidency, The C 12 MIN
16MM FILM OPTICAL SOUND J-H
Discusses Article II of the Constitution, which deals with Executive powers.
From The Senator Sam Ervin, Jr - The Constitution Series.
Prod-CHILBE Dist-COUNFI

Presidency, The B 28 MIN
16MM FILM OPTICAL SOUND
Depicts the evolution of the constitutional powers and day-to-day duties of the President of the United States. Explains how presidential decision making has become almost too burdensome for one person. Discusses the relationship of the executive, legislative and judicial branches of government.
LC NO. 74-705409
Prod-USDD Dist-USNAC 1967

Presidency, The B 28 MIN
3/4 INCH VIDEO CASSETTE
Presents the evolution of the constitutional powers and day-to-day duties of the President of the United States. Shows how presidential decisions have shaped the character of the nation and created turning points in history. Describes the relationship of the executive, legislative and judicial branches of government and the system of checks and balances.
Prod-USNAC Dist-USNAC 1972

Presidency, The - How Much Alone C 60 MIN
3/4 OR 1/2 INCH VIDEO CASSETTE
Presents an analysis of how the Presidential office of the United States is affected by its own limitations and by the strength of other political forces.
Prod-WGBHTV Dist-PBS 1978

Presidency, The - Search For A Candidate X 29 MIN
16MM FILM, 3/4 OR 1/2 IN VIDEO J
Presents a case study of the variety of strategies a contestant can employ to become his party's candidate for president and shows the importance of choosing 'THE MAN WHO CAN WIN.' Includes original footage of the Republican Convention in 1952 and the Democratic Convention in 1960.
From The American Experience - Case Studies In 20th Century American History Series.
Prod-UPI Dist-EBEC 1969

President Gerald Ford, The Oath And Straight Talk Among Friends C 12 MIN
16MM FILM OPTICAL SOUND J-C A
Documents the inauguration of Gerald Ford as president. Includes the oath of office and the acceptance speech.
From The Great Decisions Series.
LC NO. 75-702938
Prod-ACME Dist-AMEDFL 1974

President Of The United States - Too Much Power X 25 MIN
16MM FILM, 3/4 OR 1/2 IN VIDEO J-H
Examines the powers and the constitutional limits on the powers of the president, as well as the ways in which presidents have used and extended their powers. Emphasizes the structure of the government, the way the balance of power works and the ultimate power of the people.
Prod-CNCPTF Dist-EBEC 1971

President Remembered, A B 5 MIN
16MM FILM OPTICAL SOUND J A
A tribute to the late President Kennedy. Reveals plans for his permanent grave marker at Arlington National Cemetery.
From The Screen News Digest Series. Vol 7, Issue 5.
LC NO. FIA68-2098
Prod-HEARST Dist-HEARST 1964

President Versus Congress, The - Executive Privilege And The Delegation Of Power C 60 MIN
3/4 OR 1/2 INCH VIDEO CASSETTE
Questions whether a President is bound by congressional limits he does not choose to honor and what Congress can do if he ignores them. Offers a hypothetical case concerning presidential appointees whose views conflict with congressional intentions for their agencies.
From The Constitution - That Delicate Balance Series.
Prod-WTTWTV Dist-FI 1984

President Versus Congress, The - War Powers And Covert Action C 60 MIN
3/4 OR 1/2 INCH VIDEO CASSETTE
Offers a hypothetical case involving the War Powers Act which explores whether the Constitution has - or has ever had - relevance in the implementation of foreign policy.
From The Constitution - That Delicate Balance Series.
Prod-WTTWTV Dist-FI 1984

President, Press And Public C 29 MIN
16MM FILM OPTICAL SOUND
Discusses the ways in which the President communicates with the public through the press and broadcast media, and examines such questions as the credibility gap, the white lie and managed news.
From The Government Story Series. No. 33
LC NO. 71-707185
Prod-WBCPRO Dist-WBCPRO 1968

President's Budget, The C 30 MIN
3/4 OR 1/2 INCH VIDEO CASSETTE C
Looks at the budget as an important political statement disguised as a dull economic document. Provides insight into the way the budget influences government.
From The American Government 2 Series.
Prod-DALCCD Dist-DALCCD

President's Committee On Mental Retardation In Action C 9 MIN
16MM FILM OPTICAL SOUND PRO
Describes the work and the mission of the President's Committee on Mental Retardation.
LC NO. 78-701606
Prod-UKANS Dist-UKANS 1974

President's Program, The C 29 MIN
16MM FILM OPTICAL SOUND
Discusses how the President chooses his program and the political and personal factors which affect his choice. points to the President's State of the Union Address and the executive budget as reflections of his program.
From The Government Story Series. No. 27
LC NO. 79-707187
Prod-WBCPRO Dist-WBCPRO 1968

President's Scientist - A Conversation With Dr Frank Press C 30 MIN
3/4 OR 1/2 INCH VIDEO CASSETTE
Features the Director of the White House Office of Science and Technology Policy discussing national security, energy and the environment. Reveals his opinions on weapons technology, arms control, nuclear detonation detection, earthquake mitigation and climate control as national policy.
From The Synthesis Series.
Prod-KPBS Dist-KPBS 1978

Presidential Campaign Of 1952 B 9 MIN
16MM FILM MAGNETIC SOUND C
See series title for descriptive statement.
From The U S Presidential Elections 1928-1968 Series.
LC NO. 75-703328
Prod-KRAUS Dist-KRAUS Prodn-AMSLFM 1975

Presidential Campaign Of 1956 B 9 MIN
16MM FILM MAGNETIC SOUND C
See series title for descriptive statement.
From The U S Presidential Elections 1928-1968 Series.
LC NO. 75-703330
Prod-KRAUS Dist-KRAUS Prodn-AMSLFM 1975

Presidential Campaigns And The Influence Of Music, 1840-1916 C 27 MIN
16MM FILM OPTICAL SOUND
Shows what Presidential campaigning was like before the advent of radio and television. Explains how music was an integral part of campaigning by influencing the emotions of the voters.
LC NO. 76-702870
Prod-DANA Dist-DANA 1976

Presidential Character C 30 MIN
3/4 OR 1/2 INCH VIDEO CASSETTE C
Discusses a theory that childhood, relationships with parents and peers and successes and failures make permanent imprints on leaders. Examines several Presidents.
From The American Government 1 Series.
Prod-DALCCD Dist-DALCCD

Presidential Election Of 1928 B 7 MIN
16MM FILM MAGNETIC SOUND C
See series title for descriptive statement.
From The U S Presidential Elections 1928-1968 Series.
LC NO. 75-703322
Prod-KRAUS Dist-KRAUS Prodn-AMSLFM 1975

Presidential Election Of 1932 B 16 MIN
16MM FILM MAGNETIC SOUND C
See series title for descriptive statement.
From The U S Presidential Elections 1928-1968 Series.
LC NO. 75-703323
Prod-KRAUS Dist-KRAUS Prodn-AMSLFM 1975

Presidential Election Of 1936 B 7 MIN
16MM FILM MAGNETIC SOUND C
See series title for descriptive statement.
From The U S Presidential Elections 1928-1968 Series.
LC NO. 75-703324
Prod-KRAUS Dist-KRAUS Prodn-AMSLFM 1975

Presidential Election Of 1940 B 6 MIN
16MM FILM MAGNETIC SOUND C
See series title for descriptive statement.
From The U S Presidential Elections 1928-1968 Series.
LC NO. 75-703325
Prod-KRAUS Dist-KRAUS Prodn-AMSLFM 1975

Presidential Election Of 1944 B 9 MIN
16MM FILM MAGNETIC SOUND C
See series title for descriptive statement.
From The U S Presidential Elections 1928-1968 Series.
LC NO. 75-703326
Prod-KRAUS Dist-KRAUS Prodn-AMSLFM 1975

Presidential Election Of 1948 B 10 MIN
16MM FILM MAGNETIC SOUND C
See series title for descriptive statement.
From The U S Presidential Elections 1928-1968 Series.
LC NO. 75-703327
Prod-KRAUS Dist-KRAUS Prodn-AMSLFM 1975

Presidential Election Of 1960 B 16 MIN
16MM FILM MAGNETIC SOUND C
See series title for descriptive statement.
From The U S Presidential Elections 1928-1968 Series.
LC NO. 75-703331
Prod-KRAUS Dist-KRAUS Prodn-AMSLFM 1975

Presidential Election Of 1964 B 10 MIN
16MM FILM MAGNETIC SOUND C
See series title for descriptive statement.
From The U S Presidential Elections 1928-1968 Series.
LC NO. 75-703332
Prod-KRAUS Dist-KRAUS Prodn-AMSLFM 1975

Presidential Election Of 1968 B 9 MIN
16MM FILM MAGNETIC SOUND C
See series title for descriptive statement.
From The U S Presidential Elections 1928-1968 Series.
LC NO. 75-703333
Prod-KRAUS Dist-KRAUS Prodn-AMSLFM 1975

Presidential Persuaders, The C 29 MIN
16MM FILM OPTICAL SOUND
Stephen horn Talks with Presidential special assistants, Joseph A Califano and Bryce Harlow about the ways in which the President leads and lobbies Congress to get his program enacted into law.
From The Government Story Series. No. 28
LC NO. 75-707186
Prod-WBCPRO Dist-WBCPRO 1968

Presidential Power C 30 MIN
3/4 OR 1/2 INCH VIDEO CASSETTE C
Explores the ability of the President to control and shape government activity. Shows how personality, political environment and external factors, such as war and Watergate, affect a President's power.
From The American Government 2 Series.
Prod-DALCCD Dist-DALCCD

Presidential Race Review B 9 MIN
16MM FILM OPTICAL SOUND
Experpts from Screen News Digest showing election of Presidential canditates for 1952, Stassen, Taft, Truman, Eisenhower, Kefaufer and Stevenson.
From The News Magazine Of The Screen Series. Vol 2, No. 8
Prod-PATHE Dist-HEARST 1952

Presidential Summer C 14 MIN
16MM FILM OPTICAL SOUND
Focuses on the preparations made for the 1972 Democratic and Republican Presidential Conventions in Miami Beach, Florida.
Prod-FLADC Dist-FLADC

Presidential Tour C 28 MIN
16MM FILM OPTICAL SOUND J-C A
Records the visit to Australia in 1966 by United States President Lyndon B Johnson, from touch down at Canberra to his departure from Townsville, Queensland.
LC NO. FIA68-1746
Prod-ANAIB Dist-AUIS 1966

Presidents And Politics With Richard Strout C 58 MIN
3/4 OR 1/2 INCH VIDEO CASSETTE
Focuses on newsman Richard Strout, who has covered Washington and the White House since the administration of Warren G Harding. Strout reflects about presidents from Harding to Reagan, Congressional lions and famous speeches.
From The Walk Through The 20th Century With Bill Moyers Series.
Prod-CORPEL Dist-PBS 1982

Presidents And Power, Pt 1 C 60 MIN
3/4 OR 1/2 INCH VIDEO CASSETTE
Presents an interview with Clark Clifford, former Secretary of State and advisor to Presidents Harry Truman, John Kennedy and Lyndon Johnson. Clifford talks about the men for whom he worked, looking at their contributions and weaknesses, their use and abuse of power, their characters and personalities, and their place in history.
From The Bill Moyers' Journal Series.
Prod-WNETTV Dist-WNETTV 1981

Presidents And Power, Pt 2 C 60 MIN
3/4 OR 1/2 INCH VIDEO CASSETTE
Presents an interview with Clark Clifford, former Secretary of State and advisor to Presidents Harry Truman, John Kennedy and Lyndon Johnson. Clifford talks about the men for whom he worked, looking at their contributions and weaknesses, their use and abuse of power, their characters and personalities, and their place in history.
From The Bill Moyers' Journal Series.
Prod-WNETTV Dist-WNETTV 1981

Press And The White House C 29 MIN
3/4 OR 1/2 INCH VIDEO CASSETTE
Examines the attempt by the White House to control the flow and the content of news from the Reagan Administration. Includes Hodding Carter, Jack Anderson, Barry Dunsmore and John Lofton.
From The Inside Story Series.
Prod-PBS Dist-PBS 1981

Press Brake Changing Dies C 13 MIN
1/2 IN VIDEO CASSETTE BETA/VHS IND
Explains how a set of press brake dies are removed and different ones installed and adjusted.
Prod-RMI Dist-RMI

Press Brake Demonstration C 50 MIN
1/2 IN VIDEO CASSETTE BETA/VHS IND
Discusses the basic operating procedure for using a mechanical press brake with an air electric clutch and three-speed transmission on the drive mechanism.
Prod-RMI Dist-RMI

Press Brake Guarding - They Can Be Guarded C 16 MIN
16MM FILM, 3/4 OR 1/2 IN VIDEO
Introduces and examines safety equipment now used on press brakes including clear, acrylic fixed barrier guards, hold-back cables and two-handed control panels.
Prod-IAPA Dist-IFB 1978

Press Mold Ceramics X 10 MIN
16MM FILM OPTICAL SOUND J-C A
AdA Korsakaite, west coast artist, uses the press mold method to demonstrate the process of making a ceramic, from carving a plaster of paris slab in readiness to receive the clay, to the final bisque-firing.
Prod-ALLMOR Dist-AVED 1955

Presses C
3/4 OR 1/2 INCH VIDEO CASSETTE IND
Presents aspects of papermaking presses. Includes principles of water removal, rolls and felts and press arrangements.
From The Pulp And Paper Training, Module 3 - Papermaking Series.
Prod-LEIKID Dist-LEIKID

Pressing And Construction Details C 28 MIN
3/4 OR 1/2 INCH VIDEO CASSETTE C A
Covers pressing techniques, stay-stitching and directional stitching - making darts, tucks, and pleats - making gathers, finishing garment edges, using hand stitches - layering, trimming, clipping, and notching seam allowances - matching stitching techniques.
From The Clothing Construction Techniques Series.
Prod-IOWASP Dist-IOWASP

Pressing Defense B 11 MIN
16MM FILM OPTICAL SOUND J-H
Coach Benington explains proper techniques in use and execution of a pressing defense.
Prod-BORDEN Dist-COCA

Pressing Out Fatigue C 10 MIN
2 INCH VIDEOTAPE
See series title for descriptive statement.
From The Janaki Series.
Prod-WGBHTV Dist-PUBTEL

Pressing Techniques C 3 MIN
16MM FILM SILENT J-C A
Shows pressing darts and curved seams over a pressing cushion, seams on a seam roll, corners and points on a point presser and napped fabric on a needle board or turkish towel.
From The Clothing Construction Techniques Series.
LC NO. 77-701171
Prod-IOWA Dist-IOWASP 1976

Pressman C 15 MIN
16MM FILM, 3/4 OR 1/2 IN VIDEO I
From The Career Awareness Series.
Prod-KLVXTV Dist-GPITVL

Pressure And Current C 13 MIN
16MM FILM, 3/4 OR 1/2 IN VIDEO I-C A
Discusses the electric current in terms of amperes and volts, circuit concepts, switches and parallel series.
From The Electricity Series.
Prod-MORLAT Dist-SF 1967

Pressure And Humidity C 10 MIN
16MM FILM, 3/4 OR 1/2 IN VIDEO I-J
Studies the variations in air pressure and humidity. Explains the function of the barometer and hygrometer and describes the formation of clouds and fog.
From The Weather - Air In Action Series.
Prod-CAHILL Dist-AIMS 1965

Pressure Buildup And Drawdown Analysis C 720 MIN
3/4 OR 1/2 INCH VIDEO CASSETTE
Available to SPE organizations only. Teaches systematic analysis and design procedures for pressure buildup and drawdown tests for petroleum engineers.
Prod-SPE Dist-SPE

Pressure Control Devices C 15 MIN
16MM FILM, 3/4 OR 1/2 IN VIDEO H-C
Shows the application of pressure devices on the job. Discusses types of pressure-sensing elements, differential pressure meters, pressure controls, pilot regulators and pressure distribution systems in large installations.
Prod-SF Dist-SF 1970

Pressure Control Valves C 24 MIN
16MM FILM, 3/4 OR 1/2 IN VIDEO IND
Discusses pressure adjustment, drains and flow. Studies terms and idioms associated with pressure control valves.
From The Industrial Hydraulic Technology Series. Chapter 9
Prod-TAT Dist-TAT

Pressure Controls C 60 MIN
3/4 OR 1/2 INCH VIDEO CASSETTE
Discusses pressure control valve operation. Highlights sequence and pressure reducing valves.
From The Hydraulic Systems Series.
Prod-ITCORP Dist-ITCORP

Pressure Defensive Basketball X 17 MIN
16MM FILM OPTICAL SOUND J-C
Shows defensive basketball, starting out with the basic stance in defending and progressing through drills and the application of the skills in game situations. Highlights one-on-one drills, switching drill, trapping drills and cutting of dribbling and passing lanes.
Prod-SPORTF Dist-SPORTF

Pressure Fields And Fluid Acceleration X 30 MIN
16MM FILM, 3/4 OR 1/2 IN VIDEO C
Demonstrates by experiments in a water tunnel the connection between velocity and pressure fields in diffusers, venturis and channel bends. Considers coanda effect, bernoulli's integral, pitot tubes, cavitation, a shear layer and a rotating fluid.
From The Fluid Mechanics Series.
Prod-NCFMF Dist-EBEC 1966

Pressure Gradient Prophylaxis Of Thrombosis C 12 MIN
16MM FILM OPTICAL SOUND PRO
Gives reasons for some blood clots in veins and shows the use of reduced venous stasis stockings.
LC NO. 79-700452
Prod-HFH Dist-PD 1978

Pressure Groups In Action B 20 MIN
16MM FILM OPTICAL SOUND C A
Dr Marbury Ogle, professor of Government, Purdue University, shows the need for pressure groups in our democratic political system.
From The Government And Public Affairs Films Series.
Prod-RSC Dist-MLA 1960

Pressure Groups In Action - Dr Marbury Ogle B 20 MIN
16MM FILM OPTICAL SOUND H-C
See series title for descriptive statement.
From The Building Political Leadership Series.
Prod-RCS Dist-MLA 1960

Pressure Is On, The C 19 MIN
16MM FILM OPTICAL SOUND J-C A
Describes high blood pressure, its detection and its effects on millions of black Americans. Uses animation to show what happens in cases of heart and kidney failure due to complications caused by high blood pressure.
LC NO. 75-700597
Prod-LEECC Dist-LEECC 1975

Pressure Makes Perfect (Pressure To Achieve) C 15 MIN
16MM FILM, 3/4 OR 1/2 IN VIDEO J
Highlights the life-coping skills of fantasizing and confronting. Explores the effects of pressure to achieve.
From The Self Incorporated Series.
LC NO. 75-703954
Prod-AITV Dist-AITECH Prodn-KETCTV 1975

Pressure Measurements B 10 MIN
16MM FILM OPTICAL SOUND H-C
Depicts chemistry laboratory techniques for using such pressure measuring devices as the U-tube monometer and the barometer.
Prod-PUAVC Dist-PUAVC 1958

Pressure Of Light B 23 MIN
16MM FILM OPTICAL SOUND H-C
Discusses the role of light pressure in the universe. Shows how light pressure on a thin foil suspended in a high vacuum sets the foil into oscillation. Includes a discussion of the Crookes radiometer.
From The PSSC Physics Films Series.
Prod-PSSC Dist-MLA 1959

Pressure Point C 15 MIN
16MM FILM, 3/4 OR 1/2 IN VIDEO
Informs college-age men and women about becoming aviation officer candidates in the U S Navy. Suggests ways to select the field for which they are best suited.
LC NO. 81-706378
Prod-USN Dist-USNAC 1973

Pressure Points - Oman, South Yemen, North Yemen C 21 MIN
16MM FILM, 3/4 OR 1/2 IN VIDEO H-C A
Discusses politics and government in the Arabian Peninsula. Shows how oil has forced the United States into a relationship with countries with which it has no cultural tie and no long-standing political partnership.
From The Oil And American Power Series.
Prod-NBC Dist-FI 1979

Pressure Principle, The C 25 MIN
16MM FILM - 3/4 IN VIDEO
Describes the factors that create emotional problems and shows how to work more effectively with others. Tells why people do what they do and what factors cause success or failure.
From The Project Health Series.
Prod-SEARLE Dist-BNA

Pressure Systems And Wind C 19 MIN
16MM FILM OPTICAL SOUND
Explains how phenomena of pressure systems and wind flow, and how they affect weather and flight conditions.
LC NO. FIE64-20
Prod-USAF Dist-USNAC 1963

Pressure Testing The Cooling System C 4 MIN
16MM FILM OPTICAL SOUND
Describes the use of the pressure test pump in the discovery of leaks in the cooling system.
LC NO. FI68-210
Prod-RAYBAR Dist-RAYBAR 1966

Pressure Vessels C
3/4 OR 1/2 INCH VIDEO CASSETTE IND
See series title for descriptive statement.
From The Drafting - Piping Familiarization Series.
Prod-GPCV Dist-GPCV

Pressure, Volume And Boyle's Law C 4 MIN
16MM FILM OPTICAL SOUND H-C A
Displays impulses imparted to a wall by a single particle in a box on an oscilloscope and pressure meter. Shows that as the number of particles increases, the pressure increases and becomes steadier.
From The Kinetic Theory By Computer Animation Series.
LC NO. 73-703241
Prod-KALMIA Dist-KALMIA 1973

Pressure's On, The C 28 MIN
16MM FILM - 3/4 IN VIDEO
Dramatizes the problem of high blood pressure by showing four very different Americans all afflicted with the condition. Presents some medical solutions.
Prod-PICA Dist-MTP

Pressures To Smoke C 15 MIN
16MM FILM, 3/4 OR 1/2 IN VIDEO I-J
Features two junior high school students exploring the problems of smoking and the social, family and media pressures leading to the habit. Shows the effects of smoking on carbon monoxide levels in the body, on nicotine levels in saliva and on those who inhale the smoke of others.
LC NO. 81-706321
Prod-USNIH Dist-USNAC 1979

Pressworking C 25 MIN
3/4 OR 1/2 INCH VIDEO CASSETTE H-C A
Discusses aspects of pressworking.
From The Technical Studies Series.
Prod-BBCTV Dist-FI 1981

Prestressed Concrete Analysis And Design C 39 MIN
3/4 OR 1/2 INCH VIDEO CASSETTE PRO
Uses classroom format to videotape one one-hour and one 1 1/2 hour lectures per week for 13 weeks on 39 videocassettes. Discusses basic concepts of prestressing, study of prestressing material, flexural analysis, beam design, shear and torsion, deflections, slabs, axially loaded members and precast construction. Shows applications to bridges and buildings.
Prod-USCCE Dist-AMCEE

Prestressed Concrete Pavement Construction C 25 MIN
16MM FILM OPTICAL SOUND
Shows a pictorial record of the first substantial section of prestressed concrete highway pavement built in the United States.
LC NO. 74-705410
Prod-USDTFH Dist-USNAC 1973

Presumed Innocent B 60 MIN
16MM FILM, 3/4 OR 1/2 IN VIDEO J-C A
Exposes conditions for pre-trial jail inmates and examines how the bail system affects the poor and the consequent social, constitutional and legal implications of detention.
LC NO. 80-717184
Prod-TVGDAP Dist-CNEMAG 1980

Presumption Of Innocence C 39 MIN
16MM FILM OPTICAL SOUND J-C A
Presents an actual criminal court trial. Follows the defendant's feelings through the cross-currents of question and answer, examination and cross-examination as prosecution and defense put the case before the jury.
LC NO. 73-702516
Prod-SCREEI Dist-SCREEI 1973

Presumption Of Innocence C 89 MIN
16MM FILM OPTICAL SOUND J-C A
Presents an actual criminal court trial. Follows the defendants feelings through the cross-currents of question and answer, examination and cross-examination as prosecution and defense put the case before the jury.
LC NO. 73-702517
Prod-SCREEI Dist-SCREEI 1973

Pretend The Picture Is Rosy B 7 MIN
16MM FILM OPTICAL SOUND
Examines the life of an old man wandering alone in the inner city. Emphasizes his fight to face reality and to maintain human dignity by presenting his views and thoughts on the world around him.
Prod-USC Dist-USC

Pretend World C 25 MIN
3/4 OR 1/2 INCH VIDEO CASSETTE H-C A
Shows how to build a large playhouse and the furniture to go inside it.
From The Blizzard's Wonderful Wooden Toys Series.
Prod-BBCTV Dist-FI

Pretend You're Wearing A Barrel C 10 MIN
16MM FILM, 3/4 OR 1/2 IN VIDEO H-C A
Presents a portrait of Lynn Ryan, a woman on welfare, who learned to become a welder and found a job in order to support her five children. Emphasizes how she was able to take practical steps to achieve something better for herself and her children.
LC NO. 81-706602
Prod-NFBC Dist-PHENIX 1980

Pretending C 21 MIN
16MM FILM, 3/4 OR 1/2 IN VIDEO K-P S
Presents Mr Rogers showing how to separate fantasy and reality by trying on different hats and presenting a puppet show. Shows how make-believe can be used to have fun and to explore feelings in fanciful, yet controlled, ways.
From The I Am, I Can, I Will, Level II Series.
LC NO. 80-706548
Prod-FAMCOM Dist-HUBDSC 1979

Pretrial Conferences And Opening Statements In An Antitrust Case C 170 MIN
3/4 OR 1/2 INCH VIDEO CASSETTE PRO
Offers opening statements presented by two skilled litigators in an antitrust case. Analyzes the methodologies used by the attorneys, the judge's control of the pretrial conference and jury selection procedures.
From The Trial Of An Antitrust Case Series.
Prod-ABACPE Dist-ABACPE

Pretrial Preparations And Motions B 47 MIN
16MM FILM OPTICAL SOUND C
Deals with various aspects of a criminal lawsuit involving a liquor store robbery case. Shows the arraignment of the adult suspect and presents the hearing on the motion to suppress the alleged confession.
From The Criminal Series, No. 8
LC NO. 75-714040
Prod-RPATLF Dist-RPATLF 1968

Pretty As A Picture - Graduation And Prom Dresses C 29 MIN
2 INCH VIDEOTAPE
See series title for descriptive statement.
From The Designing Women Series.
Prod-WKYCTV Dist-PUBTEL

Pretty Good Class For A Monday, A B 25 MIN
16MM FILM, 3/4 OR 1/2 IN VIDEO T
Examines the different ways in which three pupils participate in a high school history class.
From The One To Grow On Series.
LC NO. 80-706189
Prod-NIMH Dist-USNAC Prodn-UCLA 1979

Pretty Kettle Of Fish, A C 20 MIN
16MM FILM, 3/4 OR 1/2 IN VIDEO K-J
Presents a story about a young French girl who decides to fish for her supper rather than play with the other children. Explains that when she falls asleep at the fishing place a gypsy boy helps her land her catch.
Prod-INTERA Dist-PHENIX 1974

Pretty Lady And The Electronic Musicians, The C 15 MIN
3/4 INCH VIDEO CASSETTE I-H
Uses animation to show two musicians competing for the same pretty lady by inventing and playing increasingly complex electronic instruments.
Prod-BOSUST Dist-GA

Pretty Poison C 23 MIN
3/4 OR 1/2 INCH VIDEO CASSETTE
Traces the fragile-looking Monarch Butterfly. Shows where they hibernate for the winter after a long journey.
Prod-NWLDPR Dist-NWLDPR

Preventable Forms Of Kidney Disease C 25 MIN
3/4 OR 1/2 INCH VIDEO CASSETTE PRO
Presents the fact that kidney disease can be prevented or minimized by recognition and treatment of diseases which cause it and classifies these diseases according to the specific anatomic site of the kidney they affect.
Prod-UMICHM Dist-UMICHM 1978

Preventing Burns In The Kitchen (Rev Ed) C
16MM FILM, 3/4 OR 1/2 IN VIDEO
Views the burn dangers of steam, gas, boiling, bubbling fats and hot foods. Shows how to handle steam equipment safely. Explains safe procedures at the stove and what to watch out for to avoid burns in a commercial kitchen.
From The Professional Food Preparation And Service Programs Series.
Prod-NEM Dist-NEM 1983

Preventing Childhood Poisonings C 14 MIN
3/4 OR 1/2 INCH VIDEO CASSETTE
Discusses ways to poison-proof the home and respond to emergency situations in which children have ingested harmful substances.
LC NO. 81-706269
Prod-USFDA Dist-USNAC 1981

Preventing Cross Contamination In Removable Prosthodontics - Delivery-Adjustments C 15 MIN
3/4 OR 1/2 INCH VIDEO CASSETTE
Presents and demonstrates an ordered, systematic approach to handling dentures from the insertion through the adjustment phases to prevent the possibility of cross contamination.
Prod-VADTC Dist-AMDA 1978

Preventing Cutting And Welding Fires C 14 MIN
16MM FILM, 3/4 OR 1/2 IN VIDEO
Uses live action and animation to illustrate the safety measures that should be used to prevent fires before, during and after cutting and welding operations. Covers the use of approved equipment, sprinkler systems and the use of permit systems.
Prod-FILCOM Dist-FILCOM

Preventing Electrical Injuries, Part 1 C 22 MIN
3/4 OR 1/2 INCH VIDEO CASSETTE IND
Shows the basic theory of electricity potential hazards and demonstrates proper rescue techniques in an emergency situation.
From The Safety Action For Employees Series.
Prod-GPCV Dist-GPCV

Preventing Electrical Injuries, Part 2 C 21 MIN
3/4 OR 1/2 INCH VIDEO CASSETTE IND
Discusses safety practices on the job, care and use of electrical tools, and personal protective equipment.
From The Safety Action For Employees Series.
Prod-GPCV Dist-GPCV

Preventing Employee Theft C 12 MIN
16MM FILM, 3/4 OR 1/2 IN VIDEO H-C A
Shows ways to reduce employee pilferage and embezzlement, a multibillion dollar a year problem faced by all organizations. Illustrates reducing temptation, limiting opportunity, establishing controls and communicating. Emphasizes a coordinated program of prevention involving communication and control on every level, from use of simple locks to proper accounting procedures.
From The Professional Management Program Series.
LC NO. 74-700228
Prod-NEM Dist-NEM 1972

Preventing Fires In The Hospital C 16 MIN
3/4 OR 1/2 INCH VIDEO CASSETTE PRO
Explains principles of fire prevention, beginning with the conditions necessary for a fire to start in a hospital. Presents examples of combustible and flammable materials in the hospital and sources of fire ignition and support. Emphasizes the importance of applying fire prevention guidelines.
LC NO. 80-731001
Prod-TRAINX Dist-TRAINX

Preventing Food Spoilage C 14 MIN
16MM FILM - 3/4 IN VIDEO IND
Discusses the causes of food spoilage and tells what the food service worker can do to prevent it.
From The Food Service Employee Series.
Prod-COPI Dist-COPI 1969

Preventing Legal Malpractice C 4 MIN
3/4 OR 1/2 INCH VIDEO CASSETTE PRO
Presents dramatizations followed by panel discussion of typical problems and pitfalls faced by attorneys which could lead to malpractice.
Prod-ABACPE Dist-ABACPE

Preventing Legal Malpractice - A Practitioner's Guide—A Series
PRO
Discusses the causes of malpractice. Assists in designing and implementing malpractice prevention programs.
Prod-ABACPE Dist-ABACPE

Preventing Legal Malpractice - A Guide For
Preventing Legal Malpractice - A Guide For I- 050 MIN
Preventing Legal Malpractice - A Guide For 055 MIN

Preventing Legal Malpractice - A Guide For Litigators C 50 MIN
3/4 OR 1/2 INCH VIDEO CASSETTE PRO
Explores the issues surrounding the case of an employer being sued by an employee who has been fired. Includes work control calendaring and potential conflicts of interest. Suggests ways litigators can reduce malpractice vulnerability.
From The Preventing Legal Malpractice - A Practitioner's Guide Series.
Prod-ABACPE Dist-ABACPE

Preventing Legal Malpractice - A Guide For General Practitioners C 50 MIN
3/4 OR 1/2 INCH VIDEO CASSETTE PRO
Dramatizes a client asking his lawyer to draft an agreement transferring partial ownership of the client's company to the business manager. Covers such issues as deciding when to refer a case and recognizing conflicts of interest.
From The Preventing Legal Malpractice - A Practitioner's Guide Series.
Prod-ABACPE Dist-ABACPE

Preventing Legal Malpractice - A Guide For Real Property Probate And Trust Practitioners C 55 MIN
3/4 OR 1/2 INCH VIDEO CASSETTE PRO
Dramatizes the sale of an apartment building. Includes discussion about the use of checklists in real estate transactions and the doctrine of judgmental immunity.
From The Preventing Legal Malpractice - A Practitioner's Guide Series.
Prod-ABACPE Dist-ABACPE

Preventing Legal Malpractice, Pt 1 - Client Relations C 29 MIN
3/4 INCH VIDEO CASSETTE PRO
Presents dramatizations of typical malpractice problems faced by practicing attorneys, followed by analyses by a panel of experts.
LC NO. 80-707193
Prod-ABACPE Dist-ABACPE 1978

Preventing Legal Malpractice, Pt 2 - Office Procedures C 28 MIN
3/4 INCH VIDEO CASSETTE PRO
Presents dramatizations of typical malpractice problems faced by practicing attorneys, followed by analyses by a panel of experts.
LC NO. 80-707193
Prod-ABACPE Dist-ABACPE 1978

Preventing Legal Malpractice, Pt 3 - Conflicting Interests C 28 MIN
3/4 INCH VIDEO CASSETTE PRO
Presents dramatizations of typical malpractice problems faced by practicing attorneys, followed by analyses by a panel of experts.
LC NO. 80-707193
Prod-ABACPE Dist-ABACPE 1978

Preventing Legal Malpractice, Pt 4 - Standard Of Care C 30 MIN
3/4 INCH VIDEO CASSETTE PRO
Presents dramatizations of typical malpractice problems faced by practicing attorneys, followed by analyses by a panel of experts.
LC NO. 80-707193
Prod-ABACPE Dist-ABACPE 1978

Preventing Malnutrition By Reinforcing Improved Diets C 28 MIN
16MM FILM OPTICAL SOUND C
Documents a field experiment in the Philippines in which mothers are reinforced for helping improve their children's growth rate.
LC NO. 80-701546
Prod-GUTHGH Dist-PSUPCR 1980

Preventing Patient Falls In A Health Care Facility C 30 MIN
3/4 OR 1/2 INCH VIDEO CASSETTE
Illustrates a 'safe-environment awareness' on the part of all health care personnel. Identifies patients most likely to fall and the precautions that will reduce incidents.
Prod-FAIRGH Dist-FAIRGH

Preventing Pressure Sores C 21 MIN
16MM FILM OPTICAL SOUND PRO
Uses clinical examples to illustrate preventive measures against pressure sores in immobile patients.

LC NO. 76-702871
Prod-MMAMC Dist-MMAMC Prodn-WFP 1976

Preventing Pressure Sores C 20 MIN
3/4 OR 1/2 INCH VIDEO CASSETTE PRO
Shows the importance of recognition of the immobile patient and encouraging the use of measures to prevent the formation of pressure sores in such a patient by means of clinical examples.
Prod-WFP Dist-WFP

Preventing Pressure Sores (Spanish) C 21 MIN
16MM FILM OPTICAL SOUND PRO
Uses clinical examples to illustrate preventive measures against pressure sores in immobile patients.
LC NO. 76-702871
Prod-MMAMC Dist-MMAMC Prodn-WFP 1976

Preventing Probate Litigation C
3/4 OR 1/2 INCH VIDEO CASSETTE PRO
Serves as a practical guide for attorneys involved in will preparation and probate administration. Discusses how to prepare a will in such a way as to prevent later litigation. Contains a sample of a videotaped will.
Prod-ABACPE Dist-ABACPE

Preventing Reading Failure C 28 MIN
16MM FILM, 3/4 OR 1/2 IN VIDEO C
Shows a reading lesson conducted at the Marianne Frostig Center of Educational Therapy with a group of young children who have reading problems.
Prod-AIMS Dist-AIMS 1971

Preventing Reading Failure (Spanish) C 29 MIN
16MM FILM, 3/4 OR 1/2 IN VIDEO C T
Covers a reading lesson for young children with reading problems. Involves both group and individual work, demonstrating Dr Frostig's remedial approach, which can be used in regular classrooms as well as special groups.
Prod-HORNE Dist-AIMS 1971

Preventing Sexual Harassment C
16MM FILM - 3/4 IN VIDEO
Explores sexual harassment from innuendo to blatant attack, presenting vignettes based on actual cases. Points out management responsibilities and employee rights, provides guidelines for dealing with incidents involving sexual harassment, emphasizes the need to act promptly and correctly, and stresses the importance of practicing the principles of good management to prevent such incidents in the first place.
From The Fair Employment Practice Series.
Prod-BNA Dist-BNA

Preventing The Reality Of Rape C 53 MIN
16MM FILM, 3/4 OR 1/2 IN VIDEO H-C A
Shows a positive approach to preventing rape in America. Profiles typical assailants and typical victims, examines the most frequent times and places where rape occurs and tells what a person can do if assaulted.
Prod-PROSOR Dist-FI 1983

Prevention C 30 MIN
16MM FILM OPTICAL SOUND
Offers sensible decisions for those who choose to drink.
Prod-FMARTN Dist-KELLYP

Prevention C
1/2 IN VIDEO CASSETTE (VHS)
Describes the warning signs of potential suicide. Provides guidelines for intervention to help a potential suicide.
From The Suicide - Causes And Prevention Series.
Prod-IBIS Dist-IBIS

Prevention C 30 MIN
3/4 OR 1/2 INCH VIDEO CASSETTE H-C A
See series title for descriptive statement.
From The Fundamentals Of Alcohol Problems Series.
Prod-UMINN Dist-GPITVL 1978

Prevention And Care Of Decubiti C 17 MIN
16MM FILM OPTICAL SOUND IND
Describes the appearance of decubiti (bedsores), the types of patients who are prone to develop decubiti and the methods for prevention and care of decubiti.
From The Nurse's Aide, Orderly And Attendant Series.
LC NO. 73-701054
Prod-COPI Dist-COPI 1971

Prevention And Control Of Air Leaks Following Segmental Pulmonary Resection C 20 MIN
16MM FILM OPTICAL SOUND PRO
Presents a modification of conventional pulmonary segmental resection techniques both in cadavers and during an operation. Shows that air spaces and leaks have been almost completely eliminated.
Prod-ACYDGD Dist-ACY 1967

Prevention And Field Management Of Head And Neck Injuries C 23 MIN
3/4 OR 1/2 INCH VIDEO CASSETTE T
Stresses the life-threatening potential of head and neck injuries and demonstrates examination, emergency treatment and preventative measures available through conditioning and use of proper equipment.
From The Sports Medicine Series.
Prod-UNIDIM Dist-EBEC 1982

Prevention And Identification Of Premature Labor (2nd Ed) C 12 MIN
3/4 OR 1/2 INCH VIDEO CASSETTE PRO
Discusses identification of true premature labor, medical and obstetric conditions which cause premature labor, indications for intervention, arrest of labor with ritadrine and the use of cerclage.
Prod-UMICHM Dist-UMICHM 1983

Prevention And Therapy Of Infectious Complications Of Cancer And Their Treatment C 50 MIN
3/4 INCH VIDEO CASSETTE
Discusses prophylactic management of infection for patients undergoing cancer chemotherapy.
Prod-UTAHTI Dist-UTAHTI

Prevention And Treatment Of Ankle Injuries C 20 MIN
3/4 OR 1/2 INCH VIDEO CASSETTE T
Examines the causes, diagnosis, treatment, rehabilitation and prevention of ankle injuries. Demonstrates exercises designed to rehabilitate injured ankles and shows various taping procedures.
From The Sports Medicine Series.
Prod-UNIDIM Dist-EBEC 1982

Prevention And Treatment Of Decubitus Ulcers C 15 MIN
16MM FILM OPTICAL SOUND
Defines decubitus ulcers, shows how they develop and describes what specific measures to follow in order to prevent their occurrence.
LC NO. 76-712972
Prod-TRNAID Dist-TRNAID 1970

Prevention And Treatment Of Five Complications Of Diabetes C 14 MIN
3/4 OR 1/2 INCH VIDEO CASSETTE PRO
Describes the usefulness of the publication, The Prevention and Treatment of Five Complications of Diabetes - A Guide for Primary Care Practitioners, in the day to day management of the patient with diabetes. Demonstrates clinical applications of the principles advocated in the Guide in five brief case studies. Discusses visual impairment, adverse pregnancy outcome, foot problems, kidney problems and acute hyperglycemia and ketoacidosis, all complications of diabetes.
Prod-UMICHM Dist-UMICHM 1983

Prevention And Treatment Of Foot Injuries C 25 MIN
3/4 OR 1/2 INCH VIDEO CASSETTE T
Illustrates techniques for diagnosing and treating a variety of foot disorders caused by flat feet, high arches, blisters, callouses, nail hypertrophy and shin splints.
From The Sports Medicine Series.
Prod-UNIDIM Dist-EBEC 1982

Prevention And Work With Natural Helpers C 7 MIN
3/4 INCH VIDEO CASSETTE
Introduces the idea that prevention should be aimed at the person-at-risk in child welfare situations. Emphasizes the use of informal and semi-formal helpers in social work.
From The Child Welfare Learning Laboratory Materials Series.
Prod-UMITV Dist-UMITV

Prevention Factor, The C 27 MIN
16MM FILM OPTICAL SOUND
Uses flashbacks to tell a story about a man who neglects to take care of himself when he catches a cold and develops pneumonia as a result.
LC NO. 79-700453
Prod-KNIFED Dist-WSTGLC 1979

Prevention Is Better Than Cure C 19 MIN
16MM FILM, 3/4 OR 1/2 IN VIDEO A
Shows examples of industrial occupational hazards such as fumes, noise, toxic material and more. Gives suggestions on elimination, isolation or substitution of these hazards, and stresses worker protection.
Prod-MILLBK Dist-IFB

Prevention Of Cancer Dissemination In The Operating Room C 24 MIN
3/4 INCH VIDEO CASSETTE
Discusses various methods which are employed in the operating room to avoid spreading cancer during surgery.
Prod-UTAHTI Dist-UTAHTI

Prevention Of Child Abuse And Neglect C 30 MIN
3/4 OR 1/2 INCH VIDEO CASSETTE H-C A
See series title for descriptive statement.
From The Child Abuse And Neglect Series.
Prod-UMINN Dist-GPITVL 1983

Prevention Of Complications Of Bed Rest B 29 MIN
16MM FILM OPTICAL SOUND PRO
Identifies changes which predispose to complications involving the pulmonary, circulatory, musculo-skeletal system, and mental processes brought about by bed rest. Demonstrates motion exercises and the use of footboard, hand roll and trochanter roll.
From The Directions For Education In Nursing Via Technology Series. Lesson 11
LC NO. 74-701785
Prod-DENT Dist-WSU 1974

Prevention Of Contamination In Removable Posthodontics Delivery Adjustments C 14 MIN
16MM FILM OPTICAL SOUND PRO
Demonstrates a systematic method of handling dentures from the insertion through the adjustment phases, emphasizing simple precautions for preventing cross-contamination.
LC NO. 78-701359
Prod-VADTC Dist-USNAC 1978

Prevention Of Cross-Contamination In Removable Prosthodontics Delivery Adjustments C 14 MIN
3/4 INCH VIDEO CASSETTE PRO
Demonstrates a systematic method of handling dentures from the insertion through the adjustment phases, emphasizing simple precautions for preventing cross-contamination.
LC NO. 78-706209
Prod-USVA Dist-USNAC Prodn-DTC 1978

Prevention Of Drowning C 26 MIN
16MM FILM, 3/4 OR 1/2 IN VIDEO A
Describes how to avoid getting into tactical military or recreational situations that might lead to drowning. Shows the drown-proof method of staying afloat.
Prod-USA Dist-USNAC 1984

Prevention Of Heat Casualties C 25 MIN
16MM FILM OPTICAL SOUND
Introduces the problem of heat stress and the principal types of heat illness that may occur when men are subjected to heavy work output in conditions of severe climatic heat.
LC NO. FIE60-82
Prod-USN Dist-USNAC 1959

Prevention Of Heat Injury C 21 MIN
16MM FILM, 3/4 OR 1/2 IN VIDEO
Covers troop operations in jungle and desert environments and gives proper dress and other precautions to prevent heat injury.
Prod-USA Dist-USNAC 1976

Prevention Of Learning Disabilities C 30 MIN
3/4 OR 1/2 INCH VIDEO CASSETTE C A
Discusses the value of early recognition of learning disorders.
From The Characteristics Of Learning Disabilities Series.
Prod-WCVETV Dist-FI 1976

Prevention Of Occupational Injury And Disease Through Control Technology C 40 MIN
3/4 OR 1/2 INCH VIDEO CASSETTE IND
Shows Walter Haag, who describes the National Institute for Occupational Safety and Health's hazard control technology program as it relates to occupational safety. Describes the impact of engineering and monitoring controls, personal protective equipment and improved work practices.
From The Safety, Health, and Loss Control - Managing Effective Programs Series.
LC NO. 81-706518
Prod-AMCEE Dist-AMCEE 1980

Prevention Of Pulmonary Embolism By Partial Occlusion Of Inferior Vena Cava C 18 MIN
16MM FILM OPTICAL SOUND PRO
Illustrates the application of a smooth edged, partially occluding teflon clip to the inferior vena cava and types of venous pathology sometimes encountered.
Prod-ACYDGD Dist-ACY 1968

Prevention Of Stuttering, Pt 1 - Identifying The Danger Signs C 33 MIN
16MM FILM OPTICAL SOUND T
Introduces and distinguishes normal from abnormal disfluencies in the speech of young children. Points out danger signs of developing stuttering behavior, indicating the severity of the problem.
LC NO. 75-703894
Prod-SOP Dist-SOP 1975

Prevention Of Stuttering, Pt 2 - Parent Counseling And Elimination Of The Problem C 44 MIN
16MM FILM OPTICAL SOUND T
Shows stutterers, from two to six years of age, interacting in stressful situations with parents and shows counseling sessions with parents which emphasize the parent's role in helping to eliminate the problem.
LC NO. 75-703895
Prod-SOP Dist-SOP 1975

Prevention Of Suicide C 28 MIN
3/4 OR 1/2 INCH VIDEO CASSETTE PRO
Discusses how nursing staffs can recognize and prevent the suicide-prone patient. Presents a 'psychogical autopsy' of such patients, and advises on how to assess and manage the depressed inpatient.
Prod-VAMCSL Dist-USNAC 1984

Preventive And Predictive Maintenance C 30 MIN
3/4 OR 1/2 INCH VIDEO CASSETTE
Deals with balancing preventive and corrective maintenance. Identifies critical equipment. Highlights predictive maintenance.
From The Maintenance Management Series.
Prod-ITCORP Dist-ITCORP

Preventive Antitrust - Corporate Compliance Programs—A Series
PRO
Focuses on institution of corporate compliance programs, correction of antitrust problems and containment of exposure to litigation. Demonstrates techniques for presenting to management an antitrust compliance program. Explores responsibilities of counsel when problems are discovered.
Prod-ABACPE Dist-ABACPE

Corporate Antitrust Compliance Programs	187 MIN
Negotiating With The Government	072 MIN
Overview Of Preventive Antitrust Activities	089 MIN
Uncovering, Remedying And Reporting Antitrust	176 MIN

Preventive Dental Care C 15 MIN
16MM FILM, 3/4 OR 1/2 IN VIDEO J-C A
Describes methods of keeping teeth healthy and preventing serious dental problems. Stresses the importance of careful and proper brushing and flossing of the teeth, cutting down on sweets and regular dental examinations as ways of achieving dental health.
Prod-PRORE Dist-PRORE 1978

Preventive Dental Care For The Handicapped Child C 17 MIN
16MM FILM - 3/4 IN VIDEO A
Describes preventive dental techniques for handicapped children, including tooth treatment, bacteria removal, food choice and positioning techniques for brushing and flossing.

LC NO. 78-700007
Prod-VCI Dist-VCI 1974

Preventive Dentistry - A Hospital Based Program C 18 MIN
16MM FILM - 3/4 IN VIDEO PRO
Describes the approach and methodology of formulating a preventive dentistry program in a hospital.
LC NO. 80-706830
Prod-VADTC Dist-USNAC 1980

Preventive Dentistry - The Prevention Of Oral Disease C 16 MIN
16MM FILM, 3/4 OR 1/2 IN VIDEO
Discusses prevention of tooth decay and gum disease as well as beginning, progression and destruction of healthy tissue resulting from neglect.
LC NO. 79-707567
Prod-USN Dist-USNAC 1979

Preventive Dentistry - The Prevention Of Oral Disease (Spanish) C 16 MIN
16MM FILM, 3/4 OR 1/2 IN VIDEO
Shows prevention of tooth decay and gum disease as well as beginning, progression and destruction of healthy tissue resulting from neglect.
Prod-USN Dist-USNAC 1963

Preventive Dentistry For The Handicapped Patient C 17 MIN
16MM FILM - 3/4 IN VIDEO PRO
Focuses on oral hygiene problems of the severely handicapped, with emphasis on education and encouragement of the patient by the health-care team.
LC NO. 79-708029
Prod-VADTC Dist-USNAC 1978

Preventive Dentistry In B Sharp C 14 MIN
3/4 OR 1/2 INCH VIDEO CASSETTE J-H A
Stresses preventive dentistry as a zany composer dedicates his latest symphony to this cause.
Prod-AMDA Dist-AMDA 1975

Preventive Dentistry, Pt 2 - Professional Responsibility C 24 MIN
16MM FILM OPTICAL SOUND PRO
Discusses how the U S Navy's preventive dentistry program enables its professional dental staff to cope with the demands for adequate dental care for Navy personnel.
LC NO. 74-706557
Prod-USN Dist-USNAC 1966

Preventive Discipline (2nd Ed)—A Series
16MM FILM - 3/4 IN VIDEO
Uses actual cases to show managers and supervisors how to enforce organization rules by creating a climate which ends the vicious cycle of disruption that breeds employee problems and leads to loss of productivity and morale.
Prod-BNA Dist-BNA

Absenteeism (2nd Ed)
Alcoholism And Drug Abuse
Insubordination (2nd Ed)
Misconduct On And Off The Job
Unsatisfactory Work (2nd Ed)
What Is Preventive Discipline

Preventive Discipline—A Series
16MM FILM - 3/4 IN VIDEO
Shows supervisors how to use the principles of good management to boost productivity and enforce organization rules without resorting to punishment. Discusses how to act quickly and correctly, maintain authority and prevent incidents from turning into confrontations that can lead to grievances and costly, time-consuming arbitrations.
Prod-BNA Dist-BNA

Absenteeism 018 MIN
Insubordination 018 MIN
Unsatisfactory Work 018 MIN

Preventive Health Care C 20 MIN
16MM FILM, 3/4 OR 1/2 IN VIDEO H-C A
Describes breast self-examination, pelvic examination and pap smear and emphasizes the importance of their regular application. Includes a section on venereal disease and discusses the various forms of the disease, from herpes and venereal warts to syphilis. Discusses measures that should be taken to prevent their spreading.
From The Woman Talk Series.
Prod-CORF Dist-CORF 1983

Preventive Lifeguarding C 9 MIN
16MM FILM - 3/4 IN VIDEO
Points out that while rescues are vital, a lifeguard's main function is to prevent accidents, injuries and aquatic emergencies.
From The Lifesaving And Water Safety Series.
Prod-AMRC Dist-AMRC 1975

Preventive Maintenance For Pilots And Aircraft Owners C 99 MIN
3/4 OR 1/2 INCH VIDEO CASSETTE IND
Shows pilots and aircraft owners what to inspect on their aircraft between inspection periods and how to interpret their findings, to help them decide whether a problem should be corrected before the new inspection period or it can wait until the next 100-hour annual inspection.
From The Aviation Technician Training Program Series.
Prod-AVIMA Dist-AVIMA 1978

Preventive Maintenance Of Signal Equipment For Commanders B 15 MIN
16MM FILM OPTICAL SOUND
Explains the procedures to be followed in the maintenance of ground signal equipment when in storage at Army depots.
Prod-USA Dist-USNAC 1951

Preventive Maintenance, Pt 1 C 60 MIN
3/4 OR 1/2 INCH VIDEO CASSETTE IND
See series title for descriptive statement.
From The Mechanical Equipment Maintenance, Module 12 - Diesel Engines Series.
Prod-LEIKID Dist-LEIKID

Preventive Maintenance, Pt 2 C 60 MIN
3/4 OR 1/2 INCH VIDEO CASSETTE IND
See series title for descriptive statement.
From The Mechanical Equipment Maintenance, Module 12 - Diesel Engines Series.
Prod-LEIKID Dist-LEIKID

Preview C 30 MIN
3/4 OR 1/2 INCH VIDEO CASSETTE
See series title for descriptive statement.
From The Rebop Series.
Prod-WGBHTV Dist-MDCPB

Preview Program C 30 MIN
3/4 OR 1/2 INCH VIDEO CASSETTE
See series title for descriptive statement.
From The Meeting Leading Series.
Prod-PRODEV Dist-PRODEV

Preview/Overview Of Learning System Design C
3/4 OR 1/2 INCH VIDEO CASSETTE T
See series title for descriptive statement.
From The Learning System Design Series. Unit 1
Prod-MSU Dist-MSU

Prewriting, Pt 1 C 29 MIN
3/4 OR 1/2 INCH VIDEO CASSETTE
Provides a structure for organizing thought before the writer begins to write. Examines the first three of five stages in prewriting - why, what and who.
From The Teaching Writing - A Process Approach Series.
Prod-MSITV Dist-PBS 1982

Prewriting, Pt 2 C 29 MIN
3/4 OR 1/2 INCH VIDEO CASSETTE
Emphasizes that by approaching writing as a process, the fears, hesitation and obstacles to writing become diminished. Examines the last two of five stages in prewriting - where and how.
From The Teaching Writing - A Process Approach Series.
Prod-MSITV Dist-PBS 1982

Prey Capture By Terrestrial Toads And Frogs C 11 MIN
16MM FILM, 3/4 OR 1/2 IN VIDEO
Analyzes the feeding behavior of toads and frogs. Emphasizes the use of the tongue for prey capture.
From The Aspects Of Animal Behavior Series.
Prod-UCEMC Dist-UCEMC

Preying Mantis, The X 7 MIN
16MM FILM OPTICAL SOUND
Tennessee Charlie discusses the living habits of the common preying mantis, showing birth of the young.
From The World Outdoors Series. No. 4
Prod-TGAFC Dist-TGAFC

Price Of Change, The C 26 MIN
16MM FILM, 3/4 OR 1/2 IN VIDEO
Examines the consequences of employment for five Egyptian women and presents a picture of changing attitudes regarding work, the family, sex and women's place in society.
From The Women In The Middle East Series.
Prod-ICARUS Dist-ICARUS 1982

Price Of Free Speech C 29 MIN
3/4 OR 1/2 INCH VIDEO CASSETTE
Focuses on the use of libel suits that threaten many small town newspapers.
From The Inside Story Series.
Prod-PBS Dist-PBS 1981

Price Of Freedom, The C 28 MIN
16MM FILM OPTICAL SOUND
Gives some historical background on ideas behind battle monuments. Presents scenes of World War I and World War II, along with current footage of various battle monuments maintained by the American Battle Monuments Commission.
LC NO. 75-703837
Prod-AMBAT Dist-USNAC 1973

Price Of Gold, The C 60 MIN
16MM FILM, 3/4 OR 1/2 IN VIDEO H-C A
Reveals that when the Sierra Nevada was pushed upward, minerals were exposed and sediments from the mountain ranges eventually filled the shallow sea that became California's central valley. Shows that some of the minerals washed into the valley included the small amount of gold that resulted in the 1849 gold rush.
From The Making Of A Continent Series.
Prod-BBCTV Dist-FI 1983

Price Of Hunger, The C 21 MIN
16MM FILM, 3/4 OR 1/2 IN VIDEO H-C A
Discusses hunger and the Third World governments that trade the lives and health of their people for personal gain.
Prod-SMITHK Dist-BARR 1982

Price Of Imperialism, The C 30 MIN
3/4 OR 1/2 INCH VIDEO CASSETTE C
Comments on significant diplomatic happenings of the pre-World War 1 years in America.
America - The Second Century Series.
Prod-DALCCD Dist-DALCCD

Price Of Peace And Freedom, The C 28 MIN
16MM FILM OPTICAL SOUND
Compares the military defense of the United States with that of the Soviet Union. Includes interviews with military and civilian leaders and scientists of the United States and Europe as well as documentary footage from the Soviet Union.
LC NO. 77-700179
Prod-ASCEF Dist-ASCEF Prodn-WNTWRF 1976

Price Of Survival C 27 MIN
3/4 INCH VIDEO CASSETTE PRO
Presents a discussion of community disaster programs.
From The Emergency Techniques Series.
Prod-PRIMED Dist-PRIMED

Price Of Survival, The C 28 MIN
16MM FILM OPTICAL SOUND
Depicts the reactions of a hospital staff and local citizens to disaster. Portrays the preparation and planning neccssary to correct the weak points in a hospital's disaster plan and illustrates a successful test of an improved disaster plan.
LC NO. 75-701357
Prod-USDEHS Dist-USNAC

Price-Quality Relationship / Speed Reading / Retirement Homes C
3/4 OR 1/2 INCH VIDEO CASSETTE
Deals with various aspects of price-quality relationship, speed reading and retirement homes.
From The Consumer Survival Series.
Prod-MDCPB Dist-MDCPB

Priceless Laboratory, The C 25 MIN
16MM FILM OPTICAL SOUND H-C A
Records the activity of men and equipment dispatched to the frozen laboratory of Antarctica. Explores the animal life and land of the area and emphasizes the rewards in terms of scientific research and historical significance.
Prod-MCDO Dist-MCDO 1963

Priceless Treasures Of Dresden, The C 59 MIN
16MM FILM, 3/4 OR 1/2 IN VIDEO H-C A
Examines the rich array of art and artifacts gathered by Saxon kings and the wealthy merchants of Dresden over a 500-year period. Reviews the many perils which have threatened the survival of the collection over the years.
LC NO. 79-700098
Prod-WNETTV Dist-IU 1978

Prices C 15 MIN
3/4 OR 1/2 INCH VIDEO CASSETTE P
Looks at the elements that determine how much goods and services cost. Introduces the concept of expenses, supply and demand, and competition, and considers how prices change.
From The Common Cents Series.
Prod-KETCTV Dist-AITECH 1977

Pricing C 30 MIN
3/4 OR 1/2 INCH VIDEO CASSETTE C
Discusses pricing as it applies to accounting.
From The Accounting Series. Pt 11
Prod-UMA Dist-GPITVL 1980

Pricing And Promotional Decisions - Legal Implications Of Alternative Approaches C 120 MIN
3/4 OR 1/2 INCH VIDEO CASSETTE PRO
Explores the legal implications of a manager's pricing and promotional strategies, focusing on the Robinson-Patman Act. Covers issues relating to price and promotional discrimination.
From The Antitrust Counseling And The Marketing Process Series.
Prod-ABACPE Dist-ABACPE

Pricing Financial Services C
3/4 OR 1/2 INCH VIDEO CASSETTE PRO
Presents lecture by banking expert on pricing financial services.
Prod-PROEDS Dist-PROEDS

Pricing Strategies C 30 MIN
3/4 OR 1/2 INCH VIDEO CASSETTE
Focuses on the role of price in the marketing mix, product pricing sequence, effects on pricing of the product's position in the product lifecylce, corporate pricing objectives and other pricing strategies.
From The Marketing Perspectives Series.
Prod-MATC Dist-WFVTAE

Pricing Theories C 30 MIN
3/4 OR 1/2 INCH VIDEO CASSETTE
Correlates the supply and the demand curve. Covers the benefits of multiple-point pricing, break-even concept and marginal cost theory.
From The Marketing Perspectives Series.
Prod-MATC Dist-WFVTAE

Pride C 29 MIN
2 INCH VIDEOTAPE
See series title for descriptive statement.
From The Our Street Series.
Prod-MDCPB Dist-PUBTEL

Pride - Preface To Politics C 29 MIN
2 INCH VIDEOTAPE
See series title for descriptive statement.
From The Black Experience Series.
Prod-WTTWTV Dist-PUBTEL

Pride And Prejudice B 44 MIN
16MM FILM OPTICAL SOUND I-H
Portrays Jane Austen's comedy of 18th-century provincial England society. Stars Greer Garson, Laurence Olivier and Maureen O'Sullivan.
LC NO. FIA52-4976
Prod-PMI Dist-FI 1940

Pride And Principle C 17 MIN
16MM FILM, 3/4 OR 1/2 IN VIDEO J-C A
Tells how under the extreme conditions of a Japanese prison

camp, two intransigent men meet and clash over the question of principle, leaving questionable the 'RIGHTNESS' of the winner's behavior.
From The Searching For Values - A Film Anthology Series.
Prod-LCOA Dist-LCOA 1972

Pride And Workmanship C 9 MIN
16MM FILM, 3/4 OR 1/2 IN VIDEO I-C
Examines the work of an immigrant woodcarver whose life work has been devoted to carving animals for carousels.
Prod-WSMRCB Dist-AIMS 1975

Pride In Belonging, A C 28 MIN
16MM FILM OPTICAL SOUND
Depicts the changing role of women and the occupations available for women in today's military. Presents women discussing the benefits of military life and the changes that have taken place.
LC NO. 75-704424
Prod-USOIAF Dist-USNAC 1975

Pride Of Norway - The Edvard Grieg Story X 30 MIN
2 INCH VIDEOTAPE P-I
Presents a celebration in honor of Edvard Grieg during which his career is recapitulated and the Peer Gynt tale is recited, while Solveig's Song is sung and dances are performed to In The Hall Of The Mountain King and Anitra's Dance. Includes new lyrics to Grieg's Ich Liebe Song and Pal Pa Haugen, to which some of the youngsters dance. (Broadcast quality)
From The Masters Of Our Musical Heritage Series. No. 5
Prod-KTCATV Dist-GPITVL

Pride On Parade C 13 MIN
16MM FILM OPTICAL SOUND
Offers a look at the Oscar Mayer Company by juxtaposing day-to-day operations against the disciplines of a musical art form.
LC NO. 79-701188
Prod-OMAY Dist-MTP Prodn-CORPOR 1979

Pride, Purpose And Promise - Paiutes Of The Southwest C 29 MIN
3/4 INCH VIDEO CASSETTE
Presents a view of the three Paiute reservations in Arizona, Utah and Nevada. Discusses the effects of federal termination and restoration of tribal lands, as well as tribal history, education and economic development. Provides the non-Indian audience with a look at life on a present-day Indian reservation. Also available in two-inch quad and one-inch videotape.
Prod-KLVXTV Dist-NAMPBC

Priest And The Girl, The (Portuguese) B 89 MIN
16MM FILM OPTICAL SOUND
An English subtitle version of the Portuguese language film. Tells the story of a country priest who falls in love with a young girl who is jealously guarded by her stepfather. Follows the couple from their elopement to their tragic end.
Prod-NYFLMS Dist-NYFLMS 1966

Priest In Israel, A C
16MM FILM OPTICAL SOUND
Features Costa Rica's ambassador to Israel, Father Benjamin Nunez, who talks of religion and politics in describing his reactions, as both Catholic priest and ambassador, to life in a Jewish state.
From The Dateline Israel, 1973 Series.
Prod-ADL Dist-ADL

Priest Know-All, The C 27 MIN
16MM FILM, 3/4 OR 1/2 IN VIDEO
Present the Norwegian tale of a simple peasant who is mistaken for a priest and is taken to a royal convention of ecclesiastes. Shows that when he is made to predict the sex of the queen's unborn child and she luckily gives birth to twins, he is ordained a bishop.
From The Storybook International Series.
Prod-JOU Dist-JOU 1982

Priesthood To People - Transer Of Prayer From The Priesthood To The People C 15 MIN
3/4 OR 1/2 INCH VIDEO CASSETTE
Discusses the right of a single individual to approach God after identifying with the structure of the community. Focuses on prayer book.
From The Tradition And Contemporary Judaism - Prayer And The Jewish People Series. Program 1
Prod-ADL Dist-ADL

Primal Mind, The C 58 MIN
16MM FILM, 3/4 OR 1/2 IN VIDEO
Identifies the important distinctions between Native American and Western or European-based people. Looks at some of their shared legacies.
Prod-BERMNL Dist-CNEMAG

Primal Therapy - In Search Of The Real You C 19 MIN
16MM FILM, 3/4 OR 1/2 IN VIDEO
Interviews Arthur Janov, developer of primal therapy. Explains how this therapy emphasizes the importance of uncovering and reliving the hurts of childhood.
Prod-DOCUA Dist-CNEMAG

Primarily Speaking C 6 MIN
3/4 OR 1/2 INCH VIDEO CASSETTE
Prod-EAI Dist-EAI

Primary C 2 MIN
3/4 OR 1/2 INCH VIDEO CASSETTE
See series title for descriptive statement.
From The Gary Hill, Part 2 Series.
Prod-EAI Dist-EAI

Primary B 54 MIN
16MM FILM, 3/4 OR 1/2 IN VIDEO H-C A
An example of the 'CINEMA VERITE' approach to filmmaking which gives a behind-the-scenes account of the primary fight in Wisconsin between candidates John Kennedy and Hubert Humphrey. The emotional reactions of the candidates and of the public are emphasized.
From The Living Camera Series.
Prod-DREW Dist-DIRECT 1961

Primary Adventure C 42 MIN
16MM FILM OPTICAL SOUND C T
Depicts life in the primary schools of England. Emphasizes the 'OPEN PLAN' principle, the easy relationship between children and teachers and the variety of successful teaching methods.
LC NO. 73-700971
Prod-TARAL Dist-NYU 1972

Primary Art—A Series
P
Considers the important artistic concepts and presents a variety of artistic examples and methods for achieving self-expression. Examines a variety of subjects, ranging from the changing seasons to the differences in people, from a view of life in the ocean to a greater awareness of such common objects as houses and hats.
Prod-WETATV Dist-AITECH

Animals	15 MIN
Art In Motion	15 MIN
Bugs, Bees And Butterflies	15 MIN
Changing Faces	15 MIN
Cloth, Yarn And Stitches	15 MIN
Collections	15 MIN
Color All Around Us	15 MIN
Come To The Circus	15 MIN
Crayon	15 MIN
Deep Down	15 MIN
Designers	15 MIN
Fantasy	15 MIN
Finding Design	15 MIN
Follow A Line	15 MIN
From The Earth	15 MIN
Hats	15 MIN
House Of Dreams	15 MIN
Let's Really Look	15 MIN
Make It Your Way	15 MIN
Meeting Artists	15 MIN
Odds And Ends	15 MIN
Paint	15 MIN
Paint To Music	15 MIN
Paper	15 MIN
Portraits	15 MIN
Printmaking	15 MIN
Puppets	15 MIN
Shapes	15 MIN
Touch And Feel	15 MIN
What Do You See	15 MIN

Primary Batteries - Secondary Batteries (Storage Cells, Accumulators) - Fuel Cells C 52 MIN
3/4 OR 1/2 INCH VIDEO CASSETTE
See series title for descriptive statement.
From The Electrochemistry, Pt V - Electrokinetics Series.
Prod-MIOT Dist-MIOT

Primary Batteries, Secondary Batteries, Fuel Cells C 52 MIN
3/4 OR 1/2 INCH VIDEO CASSETTE
See series title for descriptive statement.
From The Electrochemistry Series.
Prod-KALMIA Dist-KALMIA

Primary Cancer Of Bone C 22 MIN
16MM FILM OPTICAL SOUND PRO
Surveys the five most important classes of malignant bone tumors and outlines how they are differentiated. Emphasizes the importance of early diagnosis and treatment in improving the chance of successful outcome.
LC NO. 77-701317
Prod-AMCS Dist-AMCS 1973

Primary Care Management Of Common Eye Problems C
3/4 OR 1/2 INCH VIDEO CASSETTE
Reviews the correlation of the anatomy and functions of the eye with frequently seen disorders. Outlines relevant medical information to be elicited from the patient. Offers guidelines to the physician in performing physical examinations of the eye and its related structures.
Prod-AMEDA Dist-AMEDA

Primary Care Nursing II C 119 MIN
3/4 OR 1/2 INCH VIDEO CASSETTE PRO
Presents reasons for and against going to another system of nursing care. Discusses the pros and cons of primary care.
LC NO. 81-706299
Prod-USVA Dist-USNAC 1980

Primary Cementing C 24 MIN
3/4 OR 1/2 INCH VIDEO CASSETTE IND
Explains the procedures and equipment used to properly cement casing in an oil or gas well.
Prod-UTEXPE Dist-UTEXPE 1976

Primary Cementing (Rev Ed) C 21 MIN
16MM FILM, 3/4 OR 1/2 IN VIDEO IND
Covers the basic theory and the latest equipment and procedures involved in cementing an oil or gas well.
Prod-UTEXPE Dist-UTEXPE 1982

Primary Circuit, The C 10 MIN
16MM FILM OPTICAL SOUND
Illustrates the assembly of the primary circuit of the steam generating heavy water reactor at Winfrith, Dorset.
Prod-UKAEA Dist-UKAEA 1966

Primary Closure Of The Perineal Wound In Abdominiperineal Resections C 27 MIN
16MM FILM OPTICAL SOUND PRO
Illustrates the operative method used for primary closure of the perineal wound in abdominoperineal resections and the results obtained.
Prod-ACYDGD Dist-ACY 1966

Primary Colors C 7 MIN
3/4 OR 1/2 INCH VIDEO CASSETTE
From The Nan Hoover - Selected Works I Series.
Prod-EAI Dist-EAI

Primary Distribution Systems C
3/4 OR 1/2 INCH VIDEO CASSETTE IND
Examines the primary distribution system in detail. Describes its function, design and features of construction. Includes substations, overhead primary and underground primary.
From The Distribution System Operation Series. Topic 4
Prod-LEIKID Dist-LEIKID

Primary Health—A Series
16MM FILM, 3/4 OR 1/2 IN VIDEO P-I
Presents information on good health.
Prod-AIMS Dist-AIMS

Health - Communicable Diseases	011 MIN
Health - Ear Care	009 MIN
Health - Exercise, Rest And Sleep	010 MIN
Health - Eye Care	011 MIN
Health - Food And Nutrition	011 MIN
Health - Our Picture Of Ourselves	011 MIN
Health - Personal Cleanliness (2nd Ed)	008 MIN
Health - Your Senses And Their Care	011 MIN

Primary Isolation Of Mycobacteria Using The N-acetyl-L Cysteine-Na-Oh Method. C 10 MIN
3/4 INCH VIDEO CASSETTE
Demonstrates the laboratory technique for the primary isolation of mycobacteria using the N-acetyl-L cysteine-Na-Oh method.
LC NO. 80-706597
Prod-CFDISC Dist-USNAC 1979

Primary Language Development—A Series
16MM FILM, 3/4 OR 1/2 IN VIDEO K-I
Presents animal stories designed for active audience participation.
Prod-PEDF Dist-AIMS 1975

Gila Monster, The	9 MIN
Ground Squirrel Family, The	9 MIN
Mouse Takes A Chance, The	9 MIN
Preparing For Winter	9 MIN
Spider Takes A Trip, The	9 MIN

Primary Nursing - Accountability For Care C 14 MIN
3/4 OR 1/2 INCH VIDEO CASSETTE PRO
Demonstrates elements of nursing care that promote accountability of the primary nurse, such as direct provision of care, patient evaluation, nursing-care review and discharge summary.
LC NO. 80-730070
Prod-TRAINX Dist-TRAINX

Primary Nursing - Continuity Of Care C 14 MIN
3/4 OR 1/2 INCH VIDEO CASSETTE PRO
Demonstrates methods for achieving continuity of care in primary nursing. Explains and illustrates important factors such as nursing orders for associate nurses, communication with other hospital departments and with the patient's attending physician, nursing-care conferences and discharge planning.
LC NO. 80-730070
Prod-TRAINX Dist-TRAINX

Primary Nursing - Planning And Validation C 12 MIN
3/4 OR 1/2 INCH VIDEO CASSETTE PRO
Illustrates cooperative planning in primary nursing. Demonstrates important features of nurse-patient communications.
LC NO. 80-730070
Prod-TRAINX Dist-TRAINX

Primary Pilot Navigation C 27 MIN
16MM FILM OPTICAL SOUND
Emphasizes the importance of a flying cadet's first cross-country solo. Includes the pre-flight preparations and all details of the flight plan and the flight.
LC NO. FIE56-195
Prod-USAF Dist-USNAC 1955

Primary Pulmonary Hypertension - Diagnosis And Treatment C 36 MIN
3/4 OR 1/2 INCH VIDEO CASSETTE PRO
Covers the major clinical features of primary pulmonary hypertension. Reviews current thoughts about the pathogenesis of this condition and these are linked to the major therapeutic efforts available. Presents the rationale for and initial results with the therapeutic use of calcium channel blockers. Emphasizes the importance of recognizing and treating right heart failure. Discusses special issues in the etiology and treatment of primary pulmonary hypertension.
Prod-UMICHM Dist-UMICHM 1982

Primary Safety - School And Playground (2nd Ed) C 11 MIN
16MM FILM, 3/4 OR 1/2 IN VIDEO P
Demonstrates safety practices to use on the way to school and on the playground.
LC NO. 80-707368
Prod-CORF Dist-CORF Prodn-CLNTCR 1980

Primary School Bus Safety C 15 MIN
16MM FILM, 3/4 OR 1/2 IN VIDEO P-I
Introduces rules of safe conduct for young children traveling to and from school by bus. Uses the concept of an invisible safety circle in which children apply safety rules to the area surrounding them.
Prod-CENTRO Dist-CORF 1976

Primary School Bus Safety (Captioned) C 15 MIN
16MM FILM, 3/4 OR 1/2 IN VIDEO P-I
Introduces rules of safe conduct for young children traveling to and from school by bus. Uses the concept of an invisible safety circle in which children apply safety rules to the area surrounding them.
Prod-CENTRO Dist-CORF 1976

Primary Tenorrhaphy In No Man's Land C 39 MIN
3/4 OR 1/2 INCH VIDEO CASSETTE PRO
Shows symptoms and diagnosis of primary tenorrhaphy in no man's land, as well as surgical repair and post-operative care.
Prod-HSCIC Dist-HSCIC 1984

Primary, Total And Near Total Colectomy For Cancer Of The Colon Including Experiences ... C 29 MIN
16MM FILM OPTICAL SOUND PRO
Explains that occult polyps and silent colic cancers are encountered beyond the reach of the conventional hemicolectomy or segmental colic resection frequently enough to justify the performance of total or near total colectomy as a primary operative procedure in most colic cancers.
Prod-ACYDGD Dist-ACY 1955

Primate C 105 MIN
16MM FILM, 3/4 OR 1/2 IN VIDEO
Presents the daily activities of Yerkes Primate Research Center. Deals with capacity to learn, remember and apply language and manual skills. Shows effect of alcohol and drugs on behavior, control of aggressive and sexual behavior and other neural and physiological determinants of behavior.
Prod-WISEF Dist-ZIPRAH

Primate Growth And Development - A Gorilla's First Year C 22 MIN
16MM FILM OPTICAL SOUND
A record of the growth and development during the first year of a gorilla raised by the attendants at the San Diego Zoo. Presents comparisons to chimpanzee and human children.
Prod-PH Dist-PHM 1968

Primates C 24 MIN
16MM FILM OPTICAL SOUND I-C
Traces the rise of the primates. Examines the anatomical changes, the beginnings of sociality and speech, the more complex brain, the semi-erect posture and other human-like characteristics.
From The Animal Secrets Series.
LC NO. FIA68-1033
Prod-NBC Dist-GRACUR 1967

Primates C 15 MIN
3/4 INCH VIDEO CASSETTE P
Presents an examination of a Capuchin monkey and a comparison of the skeletons of monkey and man.
From The Tell Me What You See Series.
Prod-WVIZTV Dist-GPITVL

Primates, The C 20 MIN
16MM FILM OPTICAL SOUND
Traces the origin of man two million years ago until the dawn of civilization.
Prod-BARSUM Dist-BARSUM

Prime Time C 16 MIN
16MM FILM OPTICAL SOUND
Offers a large-scale, role-playing simulation of the business of television. Counterpoints the simulation with the activities of a professional television executive.
Prod-UPITTS Dist-UPITTS 1974

Prime Time C 10 MIN
3/4 INCH VIDEO CASSETTE P
Describes the multi-headed residents of the planet Herkey, explaining that only the creatures with a prime number of heads are peaceful. Demonstrates a method of testing for primeness and distinguishing between prime and composite numbers.
Prod-DAVFMS Dist-GA

Prime Time—A Series

Covers aspects of aging, pointing out that old people can enjoy their later years.
Prod-SEARS Dist-MTP Prodn-UPCI 1979

Coping With Change 028 MIN
Inner Strengths 028 MIN
Interdependent Relationships 028 MIN
Learning To Enjoy 028 MIN

Primel - Kleines Madchen Zu Verleihen C 86 MIN
16MM FILM OPTICAL SOUND
A German language film with English subtitles. Tells the story of Primel, a nine-year-old girl, who is cared for by the seven tenants of a house when her mother visits her sick grandmother. Continues as the tenants describe how Primel brightens their lives, gets to know each one of them well, and, in the end, creates a togetherness and friendship hitherto unknown in this house community.
Prod-WSTGLC Dist-WSTGLC 1971

Primer For Professionals C 19 MIN
16MM FILM OPTICAL SOUND
Deals with nitrogen fertility in the soil, one of agriculture's most basic topics. Explains the use of anhydrous ammonia as the source of nitrogen for crop growth.
Prod-DCC Dist-DCC 1957

Primer Of Poison Ivy, A C 18 MIN
16MM FILM, 3/4 OR 1/2 IN VIDEO I-J
Offers information about poison ivy, poison oak and poison sumac, explaining how to avoid harmful contact with these plants.
Prod-CHVANP Dist-TEXFLM 1979

Primeros Alimentos C 14 MIN
3/4 OR 1/2 INCH VIDEO CASSETTE
A Spanish language version of the film First Foods. Offers information on how to introduce semi-solid foods to babies. Portrays parents and babies from a variety of ethnic and social groups.
Prod-SNUTRE Dist-SNUTRE

Primeros Auxilios Orientados Hacia La Prevencion De Accidentes—A Series
16MM FILM, 3/4 OR 1/2 IN VIDEO C A
A Spanish-language version of the motion picture series Safety-Oriented First Aid Multimedia Course. Deals with injury prevention and the causes and effects of accidents.
Prod-CRAF Dist-IFB

Primeros Auxilios Orientados Hacia La
Primeros Auxilios Orientados Hacia La 022 MIN
Primeros Auxilios Orientados Hacia La 028 MIN
Primeros Auxilios Orientados Hacia La 010 MIN

Primeros Auxilios Orientados Hacia La Prevencion De Accidentes, Unidad 1 C 29 MIN
16MM FILM, 3/4 OR 1/2 IN VIDEO C A
A Spanish-language version of the motion picture Safety-Oriented First Aid Multimedia Course, Unit 1. Deals with such first aid topics as respiratory emergencies and artificial respiration, indirect methods of artificial respiration, bleeding, embedded foreign objects, dressings and bandages.
From The Primeros Auxilios Orientados Hacia La Prevencion De Accidentes Series.
Prod-CRAF Dist-IFB

Primeros Auxilios Orientados Hacia La Prevencion De Accidentes, Unidad 2 C 22 MIN
16MM FILM, 3/4 OR 1/2 IN VIDEO C A
A Spanish-language version of the motion picture Safety-Oriented First Aid Multimedia Course, Unit 2. Deals with such first aid topics as shock, fractures and dislocations of the upper and lower limbs, and chest injuries.
From The Primeros Auxilios Orientados Hacia La Prevencion De Accidentes Series.
Prod-CRAF Dist-IFB

Primeros Auxilios Orientados Hacia La Prevencion De Accidentes, Unidad 3 C 28 MIN
16MM FILM, 3/4 OR 1/2 IN VIDEO C A
A Spanish-language version of the motion picture Safety-Oriented First Aid Multimedia Course, Unit 3. Deals with such first aid topics as head, neck and back injuries, burns and scalds, eye injuries, handling and moving casualties, and poisoning.
From The Primeros Auxilios Orientados Hacia La Prevencion De Accidentes Series.
Prod-CRAF Dist-IFB

Primeros Auxilios Orientados Hacia La Prevencion De Accidentes, Unidad 4 C 10 MIN
16MM FILM, 3/4 OR 1/2 IN VIDEO C A
A Spanish-language version of the motion picture Safety-Oriented First Aid Multimedia Course, Unit 4. Deals with casualty management.
From The Primeros Auxilios Orientados Hacia La Prevencion De Accidentes Series.
Prod-CRAF Dist-IFB

Primers, Surfacers, Sealers C 10 MIN
1/2 IN VIDEO CASSETTE BETA/VHS
Deals with auto body repair. Explains the applications of primers, surfacers and sealers.
Prod-RMI Dist-RMI

Priming And Block Sanding C 20 MIN
1/2 IN VIDEO CASSETTE BETA/VHS
Deals with auto body work. Explains proper methods of priming and block-sanding a repair.
Prod-RMI Dist-RMI

Priming The Productivity Engine - The Federal Rule In Advanced Electronics C 29 MIN
3/4 OR 1/2 INCH VIDEO CASSETTE A
Discusses the development of the micro-electronics and computer industries and their influence on the American economy, and the potential threat of foreign competition and its impact an U S markets.
Prod-USNAC Dist-USNAC 1985

Primitive Beliefs C 29 MIN
2 INCH VIDEOTAPE
Features Dr Puryear and Dr Van de Castle who examine the origins and consequences of the beliefs of certain primitive tribes and early man. Shows Dr Van de Castle displaying and explaining a number of artifacts he collected while studying a Central American Indian tribe.
From The Who Is Man Series.
Prod-WHROTV Dist-PUBTEL

Primitive Man In A Modern World C 23 MIN
16MM FILM, 3/4 OR 1/2 IN VIDEO J-H
Acquaints the student with data concerning the Mayan and Inca civilizations. Shows small, isolated groups of people living virtually untouched by progress surrounding them in the modern world.
Prod-MIS Dist-MIS 1969

Primitives C 30 MIN
3/4 OR 1/2 INCH VIDEO CASSETTE
Presents guests who are experts in their respective fields who share tips on collecting and caring for primitive antiques.
From The Antique Shop Series.
Prod-WVPTTV Dist-MDCPB

Primordial Soup C 10 MIN
3/4 OR 1/2 INCH VIDEO CASSETTE
Features Julia Child preparing a primordial soup. The recipe shows how simple inorganic chemicals may have been transformed into complex organic chemicals, the building blocks of life. This batch is mixed in a special laboratory apparatus made to simulate the conditions of ancient Earth.
Prod-NASM Dist-USNAC

Primum Non Nocere C 18 MIN
16MM FILM OPTICAL SOUND
Demonstrates an alternative to hospital childbirth by showing a woman giving birth to her first child at home.
LC NO. 77-702124
Prod-CINMD Dist-CINMD 1976

Prince And The Pauper, The C 28 MIN
16MM FILM, 3/4 OR 1/2 IN VIDEO
Presents a shortened version of the motion picture The Prince And The Pauper. Relates the experiences of two look-alike boys, in very different social positions, who change places. Based on the novel THE PRINCE AND THE PAUPER by Mark Twain.
From The Films As Literature, Series 1 Series.
Prod-DISNEY Dist-WDEMCO

Prince Hazelnut C 13 MIN
16MM FILM OPTICAL SOUND
A story about a king who must decide which of his sons will inherit his crown is used to stimulate oral language skills.
LC NO. 73-706881
Prod-DBA Dist-MLA 1969

Prince Of The Piano, The - Frederic Chopin Story X 30 MIN
2 INCH VIDEOTAPE P-I
Features Franz Liszt, George Sand, Heinrich Heine and Eugene Delocroix. Plays four of Chopin's compositions including Revolutionary Etude, Military Polonaise in A Major, Nocturne No. 2, Op 27 and Mazurka in B-Flat, Op 7, No. 1. (Broadcast quality)
From The Masters Of Our Musical Heritage Series. No. 4
Prod-KTCATV Dist-GPITVL

Prince Who Learned A Trade, The C 7 MIN
16MM FILM, 3/4 OR 1/2 IN VIDEO P-I
Shows what happens when a princess refuses to marry a prince until he learns a trade.
Prod-SF Dist-SF 1980

Prince, The C 58 MIN
2 INCH VIDEOTAPE
Features Dean Robert A Goldwin of St John's College of Annapolis and three of his students discussing The Prince with a special guest.
From The Dialogue Of The Western World Series.
Prod-MDCPB Dist-PUBTEL

Princely Troll, The B 15 MIN
2 INCH VIDEOTAPE P
See series title for descriptive statement.
From The Sounds Like Magic Series.
Prod-MOEBA Dist-GPITVL Prodn-KYNETV

Princes And Prelates C 41 MIN
16MM FILM, 3/4 OR 1/2 IN VIDEO H A
Discusses the Council of Constance in 1415 where an emperor deposed of three popes and arranged the coronation of a fourth. Describes the Renaissance period which gave the world the work of Michelangelo and da Vinci and ended with the sacking of Rome in 1527.
From The Christians Series.
Prod-GRATV Dist-MGHT 1978

Princess C 28 MIN
16MM FILM, 3/4 OR 1/2 IN VIDEO J-C A
Examines the way in which the divorce of her parents shatters the life of a girl whose life until then had been unusually happy. Demonstrates that divorce can strengthen the lives of the children involved. Stars Lenora May and Richard Jaeckel.
From The Reflections Series.
Prod-PAULST Dist-MEDIAG

Princess And The Pea, The C 15 MIN
3/4 OR 1/2 INCH VIDEO CASSETTE K-P
See series title for descriptive statement.
From The Gather Round Series.
Prod-CTI Dist-CTI

Princess And The Pea, The C 15 MIN
16MM FILM, 3/4 OR 1/2 IN VIDEO K-I
Dramatizes the Hans Christian Andersen story of a princess who proves she is as delicate as royalty should be.
From The Children's Classic Story Series.
Prod-SCHWAR Dist-MGHT Prodn-JOSHUA 1966

Princess Margaret B 26 MIN
16MM FILM OPTICAL SOUND I-C A
Views the life of Princess Margaret.
From The History Makers Of The 20th Century Series.
LC NO. FI67-267
Prod-WOLPER Dist-SF 1965

Princess Of The Full Moon, The C 15 MIN
3/4 INCH VIDEO CASSETTE P
Presents a West African folk tale.
From The Magic Carpet Series.
Prod-SDCSS Dist-GPITVL 1977

Princess Yang Kwei Fei (Japanese) C 91 MIN
16MM FILM OPTICAL SOUND
Takes place in eighth century China as it unfolds the love story between a servant girl and Huan Tsuang, the last great emperor of the T'ang Dynasty. Focuses on court intrigue and efforts to break the lovers apart.
Prod-NYFLMS Dist-NYFLMS 1955

Principal Dimensions - Reference Surfaces, And Tolerances B 12 MIN
16MM FILM - 3/4 IN VIDEO
Explains the relationship between a blueprint and a rough and finished casting. Shows how to use a blueprint to select reference surfaces, interpret tolerances, and check the accuracy of finished product. Issued in 1945 as a motion picture.
From The Machine Shop Work - Fundamentals Of Blueprint Reading Series.
LC NO. 79-707977
Prod-USOE Dist-USNAC Prodn-RAYBEL 1979

Principle Of Moments B 23 MIN
16MM FILM - 3/4 IN VIDEO
Explains the concept of moment of a force, the formula for finding its numerical value, and the principle of moments as applied to all coplanar force systems. Issued in 1945 as a motion picture.
From The Engineering - Fundamentals Of Mechanics Series.
LC NO. 79-706243
Prod-USOE Dist-USNAC Prodn-LNS 1979

Principles C 57 MIN
3/4 OR 1/2 INCH VIDEO CASSETTE
See series title for descriptive statement.
From The Proprioceptive Neuromuscular Facilitation Series.
Prod-UMDSM Dist-UMDSM

Principles And Body Movement B 13 MIN
16MM FILM OPTICAL SOUND
Shows parrying, striking and throwing in defensive and counteroffensive grappling in judo.
From The Combative Measures - Judo Series.
LC NO. 75-700827
Prod-USAF Dist-USNAC 1955

Principles And Metallurgy C 60 MIN
3/4 OR 1/2 INCH VIDEO CASSETTE IND
Goes into basic definition, metallurgy, effects of heat and weld defects.
From The Welding Training Series.
Prod-ITCORP Dist-ITCORP

Principles And Operation Of Glcol Dehydrators C 26 MIN
3/4 OR 1/2 INCH VIDEO CASSETTE IND
Explains the basic principles of glycol dehydration. Describes a typical flow pattern of a glycol dehydration system.
Prod-UTEXPE Dist-UTEXPE 1973

Principles And Operation Of Production Separators, Pts 1 And 2 C 35 MIN
3/4 OR 1/2 INCH VIDEO CASSETTE IND
Shows construction, operation and troubleshooting problems with production separators. Covers procedures an operator should follow to overcome the problems of high and low liquid level and high or low pessure in the separator.
Prod-UTEXPE Dist-UTEXPE 1973

Principles And Selected Procedures For Eye Care B 27 MIN
16MM FILM OPTICAL SOUND PRO
Reviews the anatomy and physiology of the eye and identifies guidelines for procedures performed on the eye. Demonstrates eversion of the eye lid, irrigation, instillation of liquid and ointment medications, application of eye compresses and the use of eye pads and shields.
From The Directions For Education In Nursing Via Technology Series. Lesson 66
LC NO. 74-701842
Prod-DENT Dist-WSU 1974

Principles And Techniques Of MIG C 60 MIN
3/4 OR 1/2 INCH VIDEO CASSETTE IND
Covers safety, equipment, plate welding and pipe welding.
From The Welding Training Series.
Prod-ITCORP Dist-ITCORP

Principles In Practice - Standards Of Conduct For Federal Procurement Personnel C 39 MIN
3/4 OR 1/2 INCH VIDEO CASSETTE
Dramatizes some of the common ways Federal Government procurement workers might unknowingly develop practices of fraud and waste.
LC NO. 80-707195
Prod-USFAI Dist-USNAC 1980

Principles Of Administration Of Medications B 26 MIN
16MM FILM OPTICAL SOUND PRO
Demonstrates the basic principles related to the administration of medications.
From The Directions For Education In Nursing Via Technology Series. Lesson 16
LC NO. 74-701791
Prod-DENT Dist-WSU 1974

Principles Of Alternating Current C 30 MIN
3/4 OR 1/2 INCH VIDEO CASSETTE IND
Provides theory and functions of AC in simple, logical steps. Begins with introduction to alternation and frequency and continues through effective values of current, voltage and apparent and true power. Uses animation to explain concept of phase angle.
From The Basic Electricity, AC Series.
Prod-AVIMA Dist-AVIMA

Principles Of Bed Exercising With The Arthritis Patient, The C 8 MIN
16MM FILM OPTICAL SOUND
Demonstrates exercises for regaining and maintaining body use. Presents exercises which can be performed by the patient alone and those which require nurse or therapist assistance.
LC NO. 75-704049
Prod-ARHEUM Dist-USNAC Prodn-AZTECP 1968

Principles Of Body Mechanics / Moving The Patient In Bed / Assisting The Patient Out... C
3/4 OR 1/2 INCH VIDEO CASSETTE
Demonstrates how to understand good posture and how to lift and move patients and objects in a safe and correct manner, illustrates how to change the position of the patient and shows proper procedures for assisting a patient in and out of bed.
From The 'We Care' Series. Pt. 2
Prod-VTRI Dist-VTRI

Principles Of Boiler Safety Systems C 18 MIN
16MM FILM, 3/4 OR 1/2 IN VIDEO IND
Covers some of the important dynamics of boiler safety, including fuel valve position, purging, air/fuel flow, water level, pressure limits, flame detection and ignition. Depicts control permissives and various safety interlock systems as part of practical approach to proper safety measures.
From The Boiler Control Series.
Prod-ISA Dist-ISA

Principles Of Caste C 24 MIN
16MM FILM, 3/4 OR 1/2 IN VIDEO
Interprets the principles of caste held in the central India village of Singhara. Pictures the caste system as rules derived from the polar concepts of purity and pollution, whereby people whose traditional occupations are considered low are themselves tainted.
Prod-OPENU Dist-MEDIAG Prodn-BBCTV 1982

Principles Of Cross-Examination C 39 MIN
3/4 OR 1/2 INCH VIDEO CASSETTE PRO
See series title for descriptive statement.
From The Principles Of Examination - Lectures By John A Burgess Series.
Prod-ABACPE Dist-ABACPE

Principles Of Democracy C 30 MIN
3/4 OR 1/2 INCH VIDEO CASSETTE C
Discusses the basic American democratic values of individualism, liberty, equality and majority rule. Considers these issues from contrasting philosophical viewpoints.
From The American Government 1 Series.
Prod-DALCCD Dist-DALCCD

Principles Of Design C 30 MIN
2 INCH VIDEOTAPE C A
Looks at proportion, scale, balance, rhythm, emphasis and harmony. Shows how these six principles of design were used in designing a model home.
From The Designing Home Interiors Series. Unit 4
Prod-COAST Dist-CDTEL Prodn-RSCCD

Principles Of Diagnosis And Treatment, The C 30 MIN
3/4 OR 1/2 INCH VIDEO CASSETTE
Presents an introduction of orthopaedic medicine diagnosis and treatment. Covers passive movements, resisted movements, specimen examination, referred pain, palpation, extrasegementally referred pain/spinal pain, history, treatment.
From The Cyriax On Orthopaedic Medicine Series.
Prod-VTRI Dist-VTRI

Principles Of Direct Examination C 44 MIN
3/4 OR 1/2 INCH VIDEO CASSETTE PRO
See series title for descriptive statement.
From The Principles Of Examination - Lectures By John A Burgess Series.
Prod-ABACPE Dist-ABACPE

Principles Of Dry Friction B 17 MIN
16MM FILM - 3/4 IN VIDEO
Defines friction and explains the advantages and disadvantages of friction. Discusses the force involved in friction, static and kinetic friction, and the calculation of the coefficients of static and kinetic friction. Issued in 1945 as a motion picture.
From The Engineering Series.
LC NO. 79-706438
Prod-USOE Dist-USNAC Prodn-GRAF 1979

Principles Of Electricity (2nd Ed) C 20 MIN
16MM FILM OPTICAL SOUND J-C
Uses animation to describe basic concepts of electrons and electron flow, positive and negative charges, current, voltage, resistance, and fundamental methods of generating electricity.
LC NO. FIA66-758
Prod-GE Dist-GE 1966

Principles Of Endocrine Activity C 16 MIN
16MM FILM, 3/4 OR 1/2 IN VIDEO H-C
Introduces the endocrine system and indicates the better known glands and the effects of gland secretions. Studies the chemical coordination in man, animals and plants. Uses roosters and a pea plant to show the effects of hormones.
From The Human Physiology Series.
LC NO. 80-707068
Prod-IU Dist-IU 1960

Principles Of Ethylene Oxide Gas Sterilization And Aeration C 18 MIN
3/4 OR 1/2 INCH VIDEO CASSETTE PRO
Gives comprehensive overview of proper ethylene oxide (EO) gas sterilization in the hospital. Discusses how EO works, preparing items for EO sterilization, how to aerate and operator safety.
Prod-MMAMC Dist-MMAMC

Principles Of Evaluation B 28 MIN
16MM FILM OPTICAL SOUND C A
Reviews general principles of evaluation. Stresses the relationship of behavioral objectives to evaluation and sources of unreliability.
From The Nursing - Effective Evaluation Series.
LC NO. 74-700189
Prod-NTCN Dist-NTCN 1971

Principles Of Examination - Lectures By John A Burgess—A Series
PRO
Outlines principles of effective direct and cross-examination in lectures by John A. Burgess. Reviews witness preparation and courtroom practices and rules for cross-examining hostile adverse witness.
Prod-ABACPE Dist-ABACPE

Principles Of Cross-Examination 039 MIN
Principles Of Direct Examination 044 MIN

Principles Of Flying C 9 MIN
16MM FILM, 3/4 OR 1/2 IN VIDEO P-I
Uses animation to give an overview of the history of aviation and the principles of flight.
Prod-FLMFR Dist-FLMFR

Principles Of Foundry Work B 23 MIN
16MM FILM OPTICAL SOUND C A
Shows the operations of molding, core making, smelting and pouring applied to the production of a water jacketed gas engine cylinder.
Prod-PUAVC Dist-PUAVC 1959

Principles Of Fracture Reduction C 30 MIN
3/4 OR 1/2 INCH VIDEO CASSETTE PRO
See series title for descriptive statement.
From The Fracture Management Series.
Prod-WFP Dist-WFP

Principles Of Fracture Reduction C 31 MIN
3/4 INCH VIDEO CASSETTE PRO
Uses animation to show the anatomy in various fractures of the long bones. Demonstrates methods of reduction on individual fractures by traction, countertraction and suspension. Emphasizes that the principles of fracture reduction can be applied in any farmhouse with the materials at hand.
LC NO. 77-706145
Prod-USVA Dist-USNAC Prodn-CW

Principles Of Frequency Response C 37 MIN
16MM FILM OPTICAL SOUND IND
Explores the basic elements of frequency responses. Gives a practical example showing how a frequency response analysis is performed.
LC NO. FIA65-22
Prod-ISA Dist-ISA Prodn-PILOT 1958

Principles Of Gas-Filled Tubes B 15 MIN
16MM FILM - 3/4 IN VIDEO
Explains the theory of ionization as it applies to gas-filled tubes. Discusses control of currents in circuits employing gas-filled tubes, use of the gas diode as a rectifier, action of the grid in a gas triode and application of the gas triode as a grid-controlled rectifier. Issued in 1945 as a motion picture.
From The Engineering - Electronics Series. No. 4
LC NO. 79-706283
Prod-USOE Dist-USNAC Prodn-LNS 1979

Principles Of Gearing - An Introduction B 18 MIN
16MM FILM OPTICAL SOUND
Discusses friction gears and toothed gears. Explains the law of gearing, positive driving, pressure angle, involute profiles, cycloid profiles, velocity rates and circular pitch.
From The Engineering Series. Fundamentals Of Mechanics
LC NO. FIE52-172
Prod-USOE Dist-USNAC Prodn-LNS 1945

Principles Of Heterocyclic Chemistry C
16MM FILM OPTICAL SOUND C
Explains the difference between heterocycles and homocycles and examines the relationship between structural, chemical and physical properties of heterocyclic compounds. Contains 24 reels totalling 1,260 minutes.
LC NO. 79-701625
Prod-KODAKC Dist-AMCHEM 1974

Principles Of Human Communication—A Series
H-C A
Studies the origins and nature of language, and the relationships between culture and the meaning of words. Includes nonverbal communication, listening, role playing, interpersonal communication and communication games.
Prod-UMINN Dist-GPITVL 1983

And The People Merely Players 030 MIN
First Steps, The 030 MIN
Interpersonal Bond, The 030 MIN
Knowing The Rules 030 MIN
Learning The Process 030 MIN
Playing Communication Games 030 MIN
Sound And Movement 030 MIN
Space And Touch 030 MIN
What Do You Mean 030 MIN
Who Listens 030 MIN

Principles Of Indexing C 86 MIN
3/4 OR 1/2 INCH VIDEO CASSETTE
Discusses the principles and techniques of indexing journal articles for input to the Medline data base and explains how these same theories and practices may be used in searching Medline.
Prod-USDHEW Dist-USNAC

Principles Of Investment C 25 MIN
3/4 OR 1/2 INCH VIDEO CASSETTE H-C A
Shows methods of evaluating financial vehicles and developing financial strategies.
From The Money Smart - A Guide To Personal Finance Series.
Prod-SOMFIL Dist-BCNFL 1985

Principles Of Ladder Diagrams C 30 MIN
3/4 OR 1/2 INCH VIDEO CASSETTE
Sketches principles of ladder diagrams. Covers switches, relays and symbols.
From The Programmable Controllers Series.
Prod-ITCORP Dist-ITCORP

Principles Of Ladder Logic Programming C 30 MIN
3/4 OR 1/2 INCH VIDEO CASSETTE
Introduces principles of ladder logic programming. Points out limitations.
From The Programmable Controllers Series.
Prod-ITCORP Dist-ITCORP

Principles Of Learning B 23 MIN
16MM FILM OPTICAL SOUND
Explains six principles of learning–motivation, objective, doing, realism, background and appreciation-emphasizing the importance of understanding and applying them during all phases of instruction.
From The Military Instruction Series. No. 1
LC NO. FIE56-248
Prod-USA Dist-USNAC 1956

Principles Of Learning B 30 MIN
16MM FILM OPTICAL SOUND C A
Describes essential principles related to patient learning. Examines learning levels which patients may be capable of achieving.
From The Nursing - Patient Teaching, Pt 1 Series.
LC NO. 74-700200
Prod-NTCN Dist-NTCN 1971

Principles Of Learning C 50 MIN
3/4 OR 1/2 INCH VIDEO CASSETTE IND
See series title for descriptive statement.
From The Task Analysis And Job Instructor Training Series.
Prod-NCSU Dist-AMCEE

Principles Of Learning And Instruction C 30 MIN
3/4 OR 1/2 INCH VIDEO CASSETTE C A
Defines the application of educational pyschology to the use of learning materials, wherein four mental processes come are developed: cognition, memory, motivation and attitude. Lists external conditions affecting the learning process, including stating objectives, establishing content, guiding learning, providing practice and giving feedback. Documents how such 'learning events' create learning sequences that guide students' integration of knowledge, and how the concepts work in both teacher-based and media-based instruction.
From The Instructional Technology Introduction Series.
Prod-MCGILU Dist-BCNFL

Principles Of Lubrication B 16 MIN
16MM FILM - 3/4 IN VIDEO
Discusses the need for lubrication, properties of lubricants, the action of lubricants, viscosity of lubricants, and conditions that determine proper viscosity. Issued in 1945 as a motion picture.
From The Engineering Series.
LC NO. 79-706439
Prod-USOE Dist-USNAC Prodn-GRAF 1979

Principles Of Lubrication C 23 MIN
16MM FILM, 3/4 OR 1/2 IN VIDEO H-C
Shows the major principles involved when two moving surfaces meet. Demonstrates simple laws of friction experimentally and explains them in terms of the geometric nature of solid surfaces. Explores three ways of reducing friction and wear.
LC NO. 83-706697
Prod-BARRAN Dist-IFB 1978

Principles Of Lubrication (Captioned) C 23 MIN
16MM FILM, 3/4 OR 1/2 IN VIDEO H-C
Shows the major principles involved when two moving surfaces meet. Demonstrates simple laws of friction experimentally and explains them in terms of the geometric nature of solid surfaces. Explores three ways of reducing friction and wear.
Prod-BARRAN Dist-IFB 1978

Principles Of Management–A Series

Presents core competencies in management. Includes self-study packets for individual and group instruction.
Prod-RMI Dist-RMI

Approaches To Management Thought
Change And Conflict
Communication - The Thread Of Unity
Controlling - The Thermostat
Informal Organization, The
Job Of Management, The
Leadership - Working With People
Manager's Environment, The
Managerial Decision Making
Motivation - Why Employees Work
Organizing - The Structuring Function
Planning - The Primary Function
Planning - The Process
Staffing - Developing The Employee
Staffing - Matching People To Jobs

Principles Of Marketing–A Series

C
Consists of 20 hours of videotapes of 22 classroom format lectures. Covers nature of activities to be dealt with during the exchange process in the market place. Provides information about consumers, some theories that attempt to explain the behavior of such consumers, and the impact of social, cultural, economic, technological and political systems in the market place.
Prod-UIDEEO Dist-AMCEE

Principles Of Mechanical Troubleshooting C 60 MIN
3/4 OR 1/2 INCH VIDEO CASSETTE
Outlines principles of troubleshooting. Stresses preventing future trouble. Deals with troubleshooting under pressure.
From The Troubleshooting Series.
Prod-ITCORP Dist-ITCORP

Principles Of MRO Inventory Management C
3/4 OR 1/2 INCH VIDEO CASSETTE IND
Discusses objectives of inventory management, identifies most important questions a manager considers when setting up a system and defines performance measures. Considers prerequisites for successful inventory management and explains importance of a good classification or numbering system.
From The Effective Inventory Control Series.
Prod-GPCV Dist-GPCV

Principles Of Neurological Epidemiology–A Series

PRO
Prod-NINDIS Dist-USNAC 1978

General Concepts Of Analytic Epidemiology	55 MIN
General Concepts Of Descriptive Epidemiology	48 MIN
General Concepts Of Experimental And	31 MIN
Investigating An Epidemic - Cohort Analysis	42 MIN

Principles Of Neuromotor Assessment C 19 MIN
3/4 OR 1/2 INCH VIDEO CASSETTE
See series title for descriptive statement.
From The Pediatric Assessment Series.
Prod-UMDSM Dist-UMDSM

Principles Of Orbit C 11 MIN
16MM FILM, 3/4 OR 1/2 IN VIDEO I-H
Investigates how the laws of inertia and universal gravitation govern the flight of an orbiting satellite, demonstrating the behavior of a satellite, both in circular and elliptical orbits.
From The Space Science Series.
Prod-ALTPRO Dist-JOU 1984

Principles Of Paper Work Management - Managing Your Forms C 17 MIN
16MM FILM, 3/4 OR 1/2 IN VIDEO
Describes the efficient design and use of Navy forms and shows common errors. Outlines the procedures for obtaining well-designed forms.
Prod-USN Dist-USNAC 1960

Principles Of Paperwork Management C 13 MIN
16MM FILM OPTICAL SOUND
Describes the qualities of efficient, effective letterwriting and suggests ways of obtaining these qualities.
LC NO. FIE61-111
Prod-USN Dist-USNAC 1960

Principles Of Paperwork Management - Better Correspondence Practices C 11 MIN
16MM FILM OPTICAL SOUND
Describes nine ways of saving time and money in correspondence management.
LC NO. 74-705416
Prod-USN Dist-USNAC 1960

Principles Of Paperwork Management - Managing Your Reports C 11 MIN
16MM FILM OPTICAL SOUND
Describes common deficiencies that occur in reports and in reporting procedures. Describes areas of possible improvements such as quality of content, frequency and timing, preparation procedures and cost.
LC NO. FIE61-107
Prod-USN Dist-USNAC 1961

Principles Of Paperwork Management - Moving The Mail C 14 MIN
16MM FILM OPTICAL SOUND
Describes common deficiencies which occur in reports and in reporting procedures. Describes areas of possible improvement such as quality of content, frequency and timing, preparation procedures and cost.
LC NO. FIE61-110
Prod-USN Dist-USNAC

Principles Of Paperwork Management - Records Disposal C 15 MIN
16MM FILM OPTICAL SOUND
Discusses the administrative and supervisory problem of moving mail quickly and economically. Shows 15 ways of improving mail movement.
LC NO. FIE61-106
Prod-USN Dist-USNAC

Principles Of Parent - Child Programs For The Pre-School Hearing Impaired B 28 MIN
16MM FILM OPTICAL SOUND C T S
Illustrates pre-school programs for children with impaired hearing. Indicates the importance of parental cooperation in these programs.
LC NO. FIA68-1959
Prod-PSU Dist-PSUPCR 1967

Principles Of Pharmacokinetics C 40 MIN
3/4 INCH VIDEO CASSETTE PRO
Presents basic principles associated with the process of absorption, distribution, metabolism, and excretion of drugs and other chemicals.
LC NO. 79-707946
Prod-ORMAC Dist-USNAC Prodn-OHIOSU 1978

Principles Of Polymer Systems–A Series

C
Uses classroom format of taping two lectures per week, one of 1 hour and one of 1 1/2 hours. Goes into the theory and applications of polymer systems. Shows structure, physical properties, rheological and mechanical behavior of polymers. Includes polymerization reactions and industrial process and fabrication techniques.
Prod-USCCE Dist-AMCEE

Principles Of Professional Salesmanship–A Series

Offers live and filmed instruction on tested selling principles, methods and techniques to help new and veteran salespeople shape and revitalize their selling styles.
Prod-AMA Dist-AMA

Principles Of Professional Salesmanship (French)–A Series

Offers live and filmed instruction on tested selling principles, methods and techniques to help new and veteran salespeople shape and revitalize their selling styles.
Prod-AMA Dist-AMA

Principles Of Professional Salesmanship (Spanish)–A Series

Offers live and filmed instruction on tested selling principles, methods and techniques to help new and veteran salespeople shape and revitalize their selling styles.
Prod-AMA Dist-AMA

Principles Of Quality Concrete C 26 MIN
16MM FILM, 3/4 OR 1/2 IN VIDEO
Tells how concrete is made, what it is and its hydration process. Explains the water/cement ratio theory. Shows how to design concrete mixes for different conditions. Illustrates the effects of aggregates on concrete quality and the importance of air entrainment for durability.
Prod-PRTLND Dist-PRTLND

Principles Of Quality Concrete (2nd Ed) C 26 MIN
16MM FILM, 3/4 OR 1/2 IN VIDEO
Deals with the fundamental principles of quality concrete and procedures for the design of mixes. Explains and illustrates the water-cement-ratio hypothesis, the process of hydration, and the effects of aggregates and air entrainment on concrete.
LC NO. 82-706082
Prod-PRTLND Dist-PRTLND 1980

Principles Of Refrigeration B 20 MIN
16MM FILM - 3/4 IN VIDEO IND
Explains the basic physics of heat transfer. Uses animation to show the compression of the absorption systems of refrigeration.
From The Engineering Series.
LC NO. 77-706083
Prod-USOE Dist-USNAC 1944

Principles Of Respiratory Mechanics, Pt 1 C 22 MIN
16MM FILM OPTICAL SOUND PRO
Demonstrates the process of breathing using a healthy subject in contrast to one with various functional and organic disorders. Explains basic concepts such as elastic and resistive properties of the lungs and pressure-volume relationships.
Prod-HSPUBH Dist-AMEDA 1954

Principles Of Respiratory Mechanics, Pt 2 C 21 MIN
16MM FILM OPTICAL SOUND PRO
Demonstrates the process of breathing using a healthy subject in contrast to one with various functional and organic disorders. Explains basic concepts such as work of breathing and the value of mechanical measurements.
Prod-HSPUBH Dist-AMEDA 1956

Principles Of Seed Processing–A Series

H-C A
Discusses various methods of seed processing and the machinery involved.
Prod-EVERSL Dist-IOWA Prodn-IOWA 1975

Air Screen Cleaner	5 MIN
Indent Disk Separator, The	3 MIN
Specific Gravity Separator	3 MIN
Spiral Separator	3 MIN
Velvet Roll Separator	3 MIN

Principles Of SNA C 35 MIN
3/4 OR 1/2 INCH VIDEO CASSETTE
Presents the concepts, structure and components of System Network Architecture (SNA) and the relationship of SNA to other IBM products and to non-IBM products as well.
From The SNA Management Considerations Series.
Prod-DELTAK Dist-DELTAK

Principles Of Statistics–A Series

C A
Studies empirical frequency distribution, descriptive measures, elementary probability, population samples and distribution, multinomial data and analysis of variance. Contains 42 one-hour videotapes.
Prod-UIDEEO Dist-UIDEEO

Principles Of Teaching Speech After Laryngectomy C 21 MIN
16MM FILM OPTICAL SOUND PRO
Discusses the advantages and disadvantages of various methods of teaching speech after laryngectomy. Explores the anatomical and physiological changes that result from larynegectomy and examines the associated psychological, social and economic aspects of total rehabilitation.
Prod-AMCS Dist-AMCS 1970

Principles Of TIG C 60 MIN
3/4 OR 1/2 INCH VIDEO CASSETTE IND
Focuses on safety, equipment, electrodes, shield gas, starting arc, techniques and shutdown.
From The Welding Training Series.
Prod-ITCORP Dist-ITCORP

Principles Of Time Management C 30 MIN
3/4 OR 1/2 INCH VIDEO CASSETTE A
Explains a time management process which can be followed to help meet goals in the time available. Emphasizes the need to distinguish between goals and activities.
From The Time Management For Management Series. Pt 1
Prod-TIMLIF Dist-TIMLIF 1981

Principles Of Tracheal Care C 19 MIN
16MM FILM OPTICAL SOUND
Explores and explains the principles of tracheal care, emphasizing the neurological, anatomical and physiological implications of breathing. Covers the anatomy of the lungs and the tracheobronchial structures, nasotracheal suctioning and tracheostomy care.
From The Patient With A Respiratory Disease Series.
LC NO. 72-712971
Prod-TRNAID Dist-TRNAID 1970

Principles Of Traction C 20 MIN
3/4 OR 1/2 INCH VIDEO CASSETTE
Reviews the basics of traction. Discusses the three classifications of traction, including skin, skeletal and manual, along with a review of the principles of traction a application.
From The Traction Series.
Prod-FAIRGH Dist-FAIRGH

Principles Of Translation C 50 MIN
3/4 OR 1/2 INCH VIDEO CASSETTE
Discusses relation of translation to interpretation, efficiency advantages of translation and translation of AEs to LISP in computer languages.
From The Computer Languages - Pt 1 Series.
Prod-MIOT Dist-MIOT

Principles Of Visual Training C 30 MIN
3/4 OR 1/2 INCH VIDEO CASSETTE T
Describes types of visual aids used in training. Discusses principles of visual learning.
From The Training The Trainer Series.
Prod-ITCORP Dist-ITCORP

PRINT Again, Finding Largest Values And String Variables C 60 MIN
3/4 OR 1/2 INCH VIDEO CASSETTE
See series title for descriptive statement.
From The Introduction To BASIC Series. Lecture 7
Prod-UIDEEO Dist-UIDEEO

Print Reading, No. 1 C 30 MIN
2 INCH VIDEOTAPE IND
Illustrates functions and reading and drawing of blueprints.
From The Basic Machine Shop Practices Series.
Prod-VTETV Dist-GPITVL

Print Reading, No. 2 C 30 MIN
2 INCH VIDEOTAPE IND
Illustrates dimensioning, print notes, symbols and print revisions.
From The Basic Machine Shop Practices Series.
Prod-VTETV Dist-GPITVL

Print Shop C 3 MIN
16MM FILM OPTICAL SOUND
Presents the day-to-day workings of a small print shop owned and operated by poet-printer Tim Inkster.
LC NO. 77-702617
Prod-MIRUS Dist-CANFDC 1976

Printed Circuit Boards C 12 MIN
3/4 OR 1/2 INCH VIDEO CASSETTE
Defines printed circuits. Covers materials for boards and conductors, single-sided PC boards, double-sided PC boards, mounting components, repairing PC assemblies and tools.
From The Industrial Electronics-- Semiconductors Series.
Prod-TPCTRA Dist-TPCTRA

Printed Circuit Boards (Spanish) C 12 MIN
3/4 OR 1/2 INCH VIDEO CASSETTE
Defines printed circuits. Covers materials for boards and conductors, single-sided PC boards, double-sided PC boards, mounting components, repairing PC assemblies and tools.
From The Industrial Electronics - Semiconductors (Spanish) Series.
Prod-TPCTRA Dist-TPCTRA

Printed Circuits And Their Repair C 28 MIN
16MM FILM, 3/4 OR 1/2 IN VIDEO
Explains that the accomplishment of many Air Force missions is dependent upon the reliability of printed circuits. Shows how to manufacture, clean, coat and dry printed circuits. Describes methods and tools used in their repair. Demonstrates how to remove and replace a faulty transistor and some types of emergency repair.
Prod-USAF Dist-USNAC 1961

Printed Flowers C 10 MIN
16MM FILM, 3/4 OR 1/2 IN VIDEO P-I
Depicts the situation which occurs when Boy decides to paint a house and gets some clumsy help from a friend. Shows that by turning mistakes into advantages and by putting some common materials to inventive use, he finds a way to make his task easier.
From The Inventive Child Series.
Prod-POLSKI Dist-EBEC 1983

Printing C 15 MIN
3/4 OR 1/2 INCH VIDEO CASSETTE P-I
Describes glue printing and object printing and shows how to design a pattern to be printed or stamped.
From The Art Cart Series.
LC NO. 79-708040
Prod-WBRATV Dist-AITECH 1979

Printing C 20 MIN
2 INCH VIDEOTAPE I
Helps students learn the techniques of printing and how these can be utilized for visual expressions.
From The Creating Art, Pt 2 - Learning To Create Art Forms Series.
Prod-GPITVL Dist-GPITVL

Printing - Printed Capital Letters A-M C 30 MIN
3/4 OR 1/2 INCH VIDEO CASSETTE
See series title for descriptive statement.
From The Printing And Writing Series.
Prod-KITTLC Dist-KITTLC

Printing - Printed Capital Letters N-Z C 30 MIN
3/4 OR 1/2 INCH VIDEO CASSETTE
See series title for descriptive statement.
From The Printing And Writing Series.
Prod-KITTLC Dist-KITTLC

Printing - Printed Small Letters a-m C 30 MIN
3/4 OR 1/2 INCH VIDEO CASSETTE
See series title for descriptive statement.
From The Printing And Writing Series.
Prod-KITTLC Dist-KITTLC

Printing - Printed Small Letters n-z C 30 MIN
3/4 OR 1/2 INCH VIDEO CASSETTE
See series title for descriptive statement.
From The Printing And Writing Series.
Prod-KITTLC Dist-KITTLC

Printing And Fractur C 29 MIN
2 INCH VIDEOTAPE
See series title for descriptive statement.
From The Commonwealth Series.
Prod-WITFTV Dist-PUBTEL

Printing And Writing—A Series

Teaches printing and writing of the alphabet to adult basic education students and English-as-a-second-language students.
Prod-KITTLC Dist-KITTLC

Printing - Printed Capital Letters A-M 030 MIN
Printing - Printed Capital Letters N-Z 030 MIN
Printing - Printed Small Letters a-m 030 MIN
Printing - Printed Small Letters n-z 030 MIN
Writing - Cursive Capital Letters A-M 030 MIN
Writing - Cursive Capital Letters N-Z 030 MIN
Writing - Cursive Small Letters a-m 030 MIN
Writing - Cursive Small Letters n-z 030 MIN

Printing Card Punch C 15 MIN
16MM FILM, 3/4 OR 1/2 IN VIDEO H-C A
Follows a card through the entire process of recording data on the key punch machine. Indicates the design, purpose and function of the keyboard, its keys, switches and other manipulative parts. Describes the hopper, stacker, feeding station and reading station. Demonstrates card duplication and shows how data can be printed as the card is punched.
Prod-SF Dist-SF 1968

Printing Is Fun C 25 MIN
2 INCH VIDEOTAPE I
Describes salvage printing and repeats patterns.
From The Art Has Many Forms Series.
Prod-CVETVC Dist-GPITVL

Printing The Positive B 19 MIN
16MM FILM OPTICAL SOUND
Shows hand and machine methods of making photographic prints. Emphasizes cleanliness, timing, temperature, testing of solutions and drying.
From The Fundamentals Of Photography Series.
Prod-USN Dist-USNAC Prodn-LNS 1950

Printmaking C 15 MIN
3/4 OR 1/2 INCH VIDEO CASSETTE P
Discusses printmaking as an art form. Illustrates the usefulness of printmaking. Demonstrates stamping, roller printing and stenciling techniques.
From The Primary Art Series.
Prod-WETATV Dist-AITECH

Printmaking - Four Artists, Four Media C 19 MIN
16MM FILM, 3/4 OR 1/2 IN VIDEO A
Explains that printmaking can be divided into four basic methods--serigraph, woodcut, lithograph and intaglio. Shows four printmakers in their workshop. Pictures how each method progresses from sketch to finished print, including the special equipment and skills required by each method. Contrasts the differences in producing each kind of print and the differences in appearance of the finished artwork.
Prod-EDDLES Dist-PHENIX 1968

Prints C 15 MIN
16MM FILM, 3/4 OR 1/2 IN VIDEO I-C A
Illustrates print-making processes involving simple materials like vegetables, string, crayon graffito and cardboard. Emphasizes each method's potential in stimulating creativity and individual exploration.
From The Rediscovery - Art Media Series.
Prod-ACI Dist-AIMS 1966

Prints C 30 MIN
3/4 OR 1/2 INCH VIDEO CASSETTE
Presents guests who are experts in their respective fields who share tips on collecting and caring for antique prints.
From The Antique Shop Series.
Prod-WVPTTV Dist-MDCPB

Prints (French) C 15 MIN
16MM FILM, 3/4 OR 1/2 IN VIDEO I-C A
Presents a number of printmaking processes that can be carried out with the use of readily available materials.
From The Rediscovery - Art Media (French) Series.
Prod-ACI Dist-AIMS 1966

Prints (Spanish) C 15 MIN
16MM FILM, 3/4 OR 1/2 IN VIDEO I-C A
Presents a number of printmaking processes that can be carried out with the use of readily available materials.
From The Rediscovery - Art Media (Spanish) Series.
Prod-ACI Dist-AIMS 1966

Prioress' Tale, The B 30 MIN
1 INCH VIDEOTAPE A
See series title for descriptive statement.
From The Canterbury Tales Series.
Prod-UMITV Dist-UMITV 1967

Priorities C 12 MIN
16MM FILM, 3/4 OR 1/2 IN VIDEO J-C A
Presents three vignettes leading to an assessment of personal values.
From The Vignettes Series.
Prod-PAULST Dist-PAULST 1973

Priorities In Hospital Fire Procedure C 13 MIN
3/4 OR 1/2 INCH VIDEO CASSETTE PRO
Defines priorities for action during a hospital fire. Emphasizes the importance of using good judgement and explains factors which influence appropriate actions. Reviews an evacuation procedure.
LC NO. 80-731001
Prod-TRAINX Dist-TRAINX

Prioritization Of Treatments In Gully Networks C 31 MIN
3/4 OR 1/2 INCH VIDEO CASSETTE
See series title for descriptive statement.
From The Gully Control By Check Dams Series. Pt 3.
Prod-UAZMIC Dist-UAZMIC

Priority Highway Facilities For Carpools And Buses C 28 MIN
16MM FILM OPTICAL SOUND A
Shows how urban traffic congestion can be solved with the use of bus priority projects and special facilities for carpools.
LC NO. 77-702238
Prod-USDTFH Dist-USNAC 1977

Priory - The Only Home I've Got C 29 MIN
16MM FILM, 3/4 OR 1/2 IN VIDEO H-C A
Focuses on the Priory, a public extended-care hospital in Victoria, British Columbia, which helps those suffering from chronic geriatic illnesses to regenerate some physical independence and find a sense of self-worth.
Prod-NFBC Dist-PHENIX Prodn-WHELRA 1980

Prisms - Some Properties C 12 MIN
16MM FILM, 3/4 OR 1/2 IN VIDEO I-J
Reviews the basic properties of three-dimensional objects. Uses an examination of a conventional triangular glass prism, to introduce the viewer to the basic properties of prisms. Shows other prisms and examines their properties.
Prod-BOUNDY Dist-PHENIX 1968

Prison Break, The C 1 MIN
16MM FILM, 3/4 OR 1/2 IN VIDEO A
Presents a funny announcement which lets professionals break out of the room and head for the coffee pots during business meetings.
From The Coffee Breaks I Series.
Prod-MBACC Dist-MTI 1983

Prison Guards C 28 MIN
3/4 INCH VIDEO CASSETTE J-C A
Features a group of North Carolina prison guards speaking about the changes they have noticed in the prison system and about how their jobs have altered as a result.
From The Are You Listening Series.
LC NO. 80-707151
Prod-STURTM Dist-STURTM 1973

Prison Reform - Gruvberget C 15 MIN
3/4 OR 1/2 INCH VIDEO CASSETTE H-C A
Looks at a prison without guards, where inmates live with their wives and children in order to acclimate them to living in society. Explains that no one has ever tried to escape.
Prod-UPI Dist-JOU

Prison Without Bars C 27 MIN
2 INCH VIDEOTAPE
Explains that alternatives to prison are being tried in Pennsylvania. Explores the pros and cons offered by community treatment centers, including supervised homes in the neighborhood where non-dangerous offenders learn to adjust to society.
Prod-WLVTTV Dist-PUBTEL

Prisoner Counseling C 26 MIN
16MM FILM, 3/4 OR 1/2 IN VIDEO
Explains the different phases of confinement and the counseling used as a major part of the Army rehabilitation program.
Prod-USA Dist-USNAC

Prisoner, The B 91 MIN
16MM FILM OPTICAL SOUND J-C A
Stars Alec Guinness and Jack Hawkins. Portrays the conflict between two strong-willed, brilliant minds a cardinal and former resistance leader who is arrested and charged with treason and an interrogator determined to extract a confession.
Prod-CPC Dist-TWYMAN 1955

Prisoner, The B 27 MIN
16MM FILM, 3/4 OR 1/2 IN VIDEO H-C A
Tells the true story of a concentration camp prisoner who gave his life to save a condemned man. Stars Jack Klugman and Werner Klemperer.

From The Insight Series.
Prod-PAULST Dist-PAULST

Prisoners C 28 MIN
16MM FILM - 3/4 IN VIDEO J-C A
Presents black and white inmates of a North Carolina prison giving their personal testimony about how prisons strip a man of dignity and self-respect. Focuses on racism, parole boards, sex and homosexuality, violence, family, and prison conditions.
From The Are You Listening Series.
LC NO. 80-707150
Prod-STURTM Dist-STURTM 1973

Prisoners Of Chance C 23 MIN
16MM FILM, 3/4 OR 1/2 IN VIDEO J-C A
Dramatizes the problems, philosophies and lifestyles of several teenagers who became parents due to their lack of sexual responsibility. Emphasizes their unrealistic views toward their futures.
Prod-FLMFR Dist-FLMFR Prodn-VITASC 1979

Prisoners Of Chance (Captioned Version) C 23 MIN
16MM FILM, 3/4 OR 1/2 IN VIDEO J-C A
Dramatizes the problems, philosophies and lifestyles of several teenagers who became parents due to their lack of sexual responsibility. Emphasizes their unrealistic views toward their futures.
Prod-FLMFR Dist-FLMFR Prodn-VITASC 1979

Prisoners Of Conscience B 45 MIN
16MM FILM OPTICAL SOUND
Examines the human rights situation in India, focusing on the State of Emergency imposed by Indira Gandhi from June, 1975, to March, 1977.
Prod-ICARUS Dist-ICARUS 1977

Prisoners Of Conscience C 30 MIN
16MM FILM, 3/4 OR 1/2 IN VIDEO
Dramatizes international human rights with the story of Gustavo Westerkamp in Argentina and Danylo Shumuk in the Soviet Union, both imprisoned for their beliefs. Shows efforts of Amnesty International to help obtain release of these two prisoners.
Prod-AMNSTY Dist-CNEMAG

Prisoners Of Hope - Multiple Sclerosis C 50 MIN
16MM FILM, 3/4 OR 1/2 IN VIDEO C A
Looks at multiple sclerosis, a major crippling disease which is difficult to diagnose in its early stages.
Prod-BBCTV Dist-FI 1980

Prisoners Of The Dunes C 23 MIN
3/4 OR 1/2 INCH VIDEO CASSETTE K-C A
Focuses on a strange community of insects, lizards and primitive mammals. Shows how these life forms have survived since prehistoric times.
Prod-NWLDPR Dist-NWLDPR 1982

Pritikin Way, The C 30 MIN
3/4 OR 1/2 INCH VIDEO CASSETTE A
Presents an interview with Dr Nathan Pritikin, who discusses his program for diet and exercise.
LC NO. 80-707547
Prod-EAI Dist-EAI 1980

Privacy - Can You Buy It C 20 MIN
16MM FILM, 3/4 OR 1/2 IN VIDEO
Explores the increasing rate of privacy invasions. Outlines the various types of bugging devices, the use of lie detectors, and widespread industrial spying.
Prod-DOCUA Dist-CNEMAG

Privacy - The Press At Your Door C 29 MIN
3/4 OR 1/2 INCH VIDEO CASSETTE
Discusses the question of invasion of privacy by the press. Includes the parents of former hostage Richard Queen talking about how the press invaded their privacy when the news broke that their son was to be released from Iran.
From The Inside Story Series.
Prod-PBS Dist-PBS 1981

Privacy / Homebuying / Hotels-Motels C
3/4 OR 1/2 INCH VIDEO CASSETTE
Discusses various aspects of privacy, homebuying, and hotels and motels.
From The Consumer Survival Series.
Prod-MDCPB Dist-MDCPB

Privacy Act Of 1974 And Its Relevancy To Medical Records, The C 16 MIN
3/4 INCH VIDEO CASSETTE
Gives an overview of the Privacy Act of 1974, explaining how it affects access to medical records and what its implications are for the staffs of VA health care facilities.
LC NO. 79-708081
Prod-VAHSL Dist-USNAC 1976

Privacy And The Right To Know B 30 MIN
2 INCH VIDEOTAPE C T
Discusses the struggle between privacy and electronic devices as an ever-increasing problem. Emphasizes the the climate of opinion and the role of mass media as they set a tone of decent regard for the rights of the individual are key factors in the problem. (Broadcast quality)
From The Communications And Education Series. No. 11
Prod-NYSED Dist-GPITVL Prodn-WNDTTV

Private Contentment C 90 MIN
3/4 OR 1/2 INCH VIDEO CASSETTE H-C A
Deals with the conflicts and emotions experienced by a young GI in 1945, who discovers his father's secret when he returns home for his mother's funeral before he is shipped overseas to fight the war.
LC NO. 84-706189
Prod-WNETTV Dist-FI 1983

Private Eyes, The C 97 MIN
3/4 OR 1/2 INCH VIDEO CASSETTE H-C A
Portrays two bumbling detectives, Doctor Tart and Inspector Winslip as they try to solve a complex double murder. Shows what happens when the two bumblers receive a letter from the victims authorizing them to investigate the homicide. Stars Tim Conway and Don Knotts.
Prod-TIMLIF Dist-TIMLIF 1982

Private Fire Brigades C 60 MIN
3/4 OR 1/2 INCH VIDEO CASSETTE IND
See series title for descriptive statement.
From The Industrial Fire Hazard Recognition And Control Series.
Prod-NCSU Dist-AMCEE

Private Junior College, A C 12 MIN
16MM FILM OPTICAL SOUND J-C A
Presents students of Mitchell Junior College who discuss the heavy academic support and structured lifestyle at a two-year school which serves as a stepping stone to four-year colleges. Shows that close student-teacher relationships and minimal social activities predominate.
From The College Selection Film Series.
LC NO. 70-713110
Prod-VISEDC Dist-VISED 1971

Private Life (Russian) C 102 MIN
16MM FILM OPTICAL SOUND C A
A Russian-language film with English subtitles. Presents the story of a manager of a large Soviet factory who has spent all his time and energy on work and is now facing retirement. Shows him taking stock of his role as husband and father and of the many things he has neglected as he attempts to acquire a private life.
LC NO. 83-700202
Prod-MOSFLM Dist-IFEX Prodn-SOVEXP 1983

Private Life Of A Cat B 20 MIN
16MM FILM SILENT P-C A
Shows the female cat approaching labor and the birth of her five kittens, and then as she feeds and cares for them in the learning and growing process.
Prod-HAMMID Dist-GROVE 1947

Private Life Of A Kingfisher, A C 26 MIN
16MM FILM, 3/4 OR 1/2 IN VIDEO J-H A
Reviews the feeding habits, courtship rituals and family life of the European kingfisher.
Prod-BBCTV Dist-FI 1965

Private Life Of Henry VIII, The B 95 MIN
16MM FILM OPTICAL SOUND
Features Charles Laughton as King Henry VIII. Directed by Sir Alexander Korda.
Prod-LONDON Dist-TWYMAN 1933

Private Life Of Henry VIII, The B 92 MIN
1/2 IN VIDEO CASSETTE (BETA)
Features an inside look at Henry VIII, one of England's livelier monarchs. Stars Charles Laughton.
Prod-UNKNWN Dist-VIDIM 1933

Private Or Public - Public Goods And Services C 15 MIN
3/4 OR 1/2 INCH VIDEO CASSETTE J-H
Explains that the sophomore class has created a park on a private lot and considers whether it should be sold to a private concessionaire or to the city. Deals with basic economic concepts dealing with land ownership.
From The Give And Take Series. Pt 7
LC NO. 83-706375
Prod-AITV Dist-AITECH 1982

Private Pilot B 15 MIN
3/4 INCH VIDEO CASSETTE
Covers the business and pleasure trip taken by a family flying a small aircraft cross-country. Illustrates the role of the various FAA facilities utilized by private pilots and general aviation.
Prod-USNAC Dist-USNAC 1972

Private Places C 30 MIN
3/4 OR 1/2 INCH VIDEO CASSETTE C
See series title for descriptive statement.
From The In Our Own Image Series.
Prod-DALCCD Dist-DALCCD

Private Practices C 20 MIN
3/4 OR 1/2 INCH VIDEO CASSETTE C A
Documents the experiences of a sexual surrogate and two of her clients. Profiles each client's progress.
Prod-KIRBDP Dist-MMRC

Private President, The - The Man And His Family C 52 MIN
16MM FILM, 3/4 OR 1/2 IN VIDEO J-C A
Presents the wives of six presidents offering their behind-the-scenes views of life in the White House. Depicts some of the famous and infamous moments involving the women who have shared the office of the President.
From The Presidency Series.
Prod-LUF Dist-LUF 1976

Private Property C 20 MIN
16MM FILM, 3/4 OR 1/2 IN VIDEO S
Uses a TV game show format to stress the importance of respecting other's possessions and taking care of one's own.
From The Good Life Series.
LC NO. 81-706179
Prod-DUDLYN Dist-HUBDSC 1981

Private University, A C 15 MIN
16MM FILM OPTICAL SOUND J-H A
Explores the strong influences of locale and climate on the atmosphere and programs of a university, using the University of Miami as an example. Shows that where the surrounding area offers interesting activities, students tend to use them for educational and extracurricular activities.
From The College Selection Film Series.
LC NO. 75-713106
Prod-VISEDC Dist-VISEDC 1971

Private Yankee Doodle C 30 MIN
3/4 OR 1/2 INCH VIDEO CASSETTE
Discusses the American Revolution with special emphasis on the daily routine of the common soldier. Recreates an entire Continental Army Camp with 250 soldiers.
Prod-MDCPB Dist-MDCPB

Privilege C 26 MIN
3/4 OR 1/2 INCH VIDEO CASSETTE
Presents the story of a dealer in rare stamps who takes the law into his own hands when he is libeled by an unscrupulous newspaper columnist. Stars Milo O'Shea and Patrick Bedford.
From The Two By Forsyth Series.
Prod-FOTH Dist-FOTH 1984

Privilege Of Walking, The B 50 MIN
16MM FILM OPTICAL SOUND PRO
Shows several children undergoing procedures to help them walk normally, including a boy with scoliosis who has a cast applied to help straighten his spine, a baby with congenital hip dislocation who is placed in traction, a boy with Perthes disease who must wear a shoebar to help restore his hip joint and a boy with osteochondroma who has bony growths removed surgically.
Prod-CMA Dist-LAWREN

Privileges For The Trial And Business Lawyer C 120 MIN
3/4 OR 1/2 INCH VIDEO CASSETTE
Explains how to preserve and assert major evidentiary privileges for the trial and business lawyer during trial.
Prod-CCEB Dist-ABACPE

Prize, The C 15 MIN
3/4 OR 1/2 INCH VIDEO CASSETTE K-P
Deals with French-Americans. Focuses on family rivalries.
From The La Bonne Aventure Series.
Prod-MPBN Dist-GPITVL

Prize, The C 73 MIN
16MM FILM, 3/4 OR 1/2 IN VIDEO R
Uses a story about professional skiing to discuss the importance of winning.
Prod-OUTRCH Dist-OUTRCH

Prizewinners, The C 59 MIN
16MM FILM - 3/4 IN VIDEO
Focuses on 1977 Veterans Administration Nobel laureates Rosalyn Yalow, Roger Guillemin and Andrew Schally. Presents a portrait of their personalities and describes their scientific backgrounds, research methods and the impact of their research on patient care.
LC NO. 79-706010
Prod-USVA Dist-USNAC Prodn-SCIPG 1978

Pro Arte String Quartet In Rehearsal, The C 15 MIN
3/4 OR 1/2 INCH VIDEO CASSETTE I-H
See series title for descriptive statement.
From The Chamber Music - The String Quartet Series.
Prod-NETCHE Dist-AITECH 1977

Pro Bowl Classic C 27 MIN
16MM FILM OPTICAL SOUND J-C A
Highlights the activities surrounding the 1967 NFL Pro Bowl game in which the East defeated the West by a score of 20 to 10.
LC NO. FIA68-1409
Prod-NFL Dist-NFL 1967

Pro Bowl Classic - 1960 B 30 MIN
16MM FILM OPTICAL SOUND
See series title for descriptive statement.
From The Pro Bowl Classic - 1959 Through 1962 Series.
Prod-NBC Dist-NBC

Pro Driving Attitudes C 16 MIN
16MM FILM, 3/4 OR 1/2 IN VIDEO H-C A
Shows why professional automobile drivers have better safety records and demonstrates four attitudes characteristic of professional drivers.
Prod-PORTA Dist-AIMS 1977

Pro Driving Attitudes (Spanish) C 16 MIN
16MM FILM, 3/4 OR 1/2 IN VIDEO H-C A
Shows why professional automobile drivers have better safety records and demonstrates four attitudes characteristic of professional drivers.
Prod-AIMS Dist-AIMS 1977

Pro Driving Tactics C 15 MIN
16MM FILM, 3/4 OR 1/2 IN VIDEO H-C A
Uses animation to dramatize tactics that can be used to avoid hazardous driving situations.
Prod-PORTA Dist-AIMS 1977

Pro Driving Tactics (Spanish) C 15 MIN
16MM FILM, 3/4 OR 1/2 IN VIDEO H-C A
Uses animation to dramatize tactics that can be used to avoid hazardous driving situations.
Prod-PORTA Dist-AIMS 1977

Pro Football - Mayhem On A Sunday Afternoon C 58 MIN
16MM FILM OPTICAL SOUND
Surveys the history of football as a game, a business and a sociological phenomenon from 14th-century England to the present. Shows football teams in their training camps, class sessions and locker rooms. Includes highlights of a game between the Cleveland Browns and the San Francisco Forty-niners.

LC NO. FIA66-1728
Prod-MMAMC Dist-WOLPER 1965

Pro Ski Racers C 13 MIN
16MM FILM OPTICAL SOUND
Shows Spider Sabich and others competing in the world championship dual slalom and giant slalom ski races in Montreal.
LC NO. 77-702618
Prod-FLTHMK Dist-CANFDC 1975

Pro Ten - Different And Better C 8 MIN
16MM FILM OPTICAL SOUND
Explains the research, development and testing of Pro Ten pre-tendered beef products.
LC NO. 77-700403
Prod-CINEMR Dist-CINEMR 1976

Pro-Karate Championships C
3/4 OR 1/2 INCH VIDEO CASSETTE
Prod-MSTVIS Dist-MSTVIS

Probabilistic Design—A Series

Reviews some of the recent theoretical and practical developments in the application of probability theory and statistics to engineering design. Presented by Paul H Wirsching, Professor of Aerospace and Mechanical Engineering at the University of Arizona.
Prod-UAZMIC Dist-UAZMIC 1976

General Approach To Design, A 050 MIN
How To Describe Variability In Design Factors 050 MIN
Observed Variability In Design Factors 050 MIN
Review Of Design Theory And Second Moment 050 MIN

Probabilities Of Zero And One, The C 11 MIN
16MM FILM, 3/4 OR 1/2 IN VIDEO I-J
Demonstrates how situations which involve chance are stated as probabilities. Presents basic concepts of probability.
Prod-BAILEY Dist-PHENIX 1969

Probabilities, Pt 1 C 20 MIN
3/4 INCH VIDEO CASSETTE H-C
Discusses the various conditions and characteristics of probabilities. Identifies the value of using numbers to predict occurrences and extend statistics.
From The Mainly Math Series.
Prod-WCVETV Dist-GPITVL 1977

Probabilities, Pt 2 C 20 MIN
3/4 INCH VIDEO CASSETTE H-C
Introduces probabilities and the Fundamental Counting Principle.
From The Mainly Math Series.
Prod-WCVETV Dist-GPITVL 1977

Probability B 30 MIN
16MM FILM OPTICAL SOUND PRO
Presents the meanings of probability, frequency distributions, the normal curve, types of data and cross tabulation. Introduces the presentation of data in graphic and tabular form.
From The Public Health Science - Biostatistics Series.
Prod-KUHTTV Dist-GPITVL

Probability C
3/4 OR 1/2 INCH VIDEO CASSETTE IND
Reveals a practical discussion of go/no-go evaluation. Discusses elementary probability definitions and concepts. Covers binomial distribution and expected value as well.
From The Statistics For Managers Series.
Prod-COLOSU Dist-COLOSU

Probability C
16MM FILM, 3/4 OR 1/2 IN VIDEO H
Shows how a race horse owner keeps records to predict the odds on her horse. Depicts a rock band which studies a radio station's history to compute whether a fast or a slow song has a greater probability of being aired.
From The Math Wise Series. Module 3 - Locating/Interpreting
Prod-KOCETV Dist-AITECH 1981

Probability C 30 MIN
3/4 OR 1/2 INCH VIDEO CASSETTE
See series title for descriptive statement.
From The Infinity Factory Series.
Prod-EDFCEN Dist-MDCPB

Probability B 45 MIN
2 INCH VIDEOTAPE H-C
See series title for descriptive statement.
From The Fundamentals Of Mathematics Series. Unit 10 Statistics
Prod-CHITVC Dist-GPITVL Prodn-WTTWTV

Probability - An Introduction C 9 MIN
16MM FILM, 3/4 OR 1/2 IN VIDEO I-J
Explains some of the fundamental principles of probability, using a disc, a lettered cube, a set of numbered cards and several everyday situations. Demonstrates how the verbal description of a probability may be written as a simple equation.
Prod-BOUNDY Dist-PHENIX 1969

Probability - Possible Outcomes C 15 MIN
3/4 OR 1/2 INCH VIDEO CASSETTE I
Looks at relationship between possible outcome and probability in examples that include both one out of five and two out of five.
From The Math Works Series.
Prod-AITECH Dist-AITECH

Probability And Its Uses C 13 MIN
16MM FILM, 3/4 OR 1/2 IN VIDEO I-J
Discusses mathematical probability and its use in predicting the likelihood of future events. Defines such probability terms as event, outcome, sample space, tree diagram and sampling.
Prod-CORF Dist-CORF

Probability And Random Processes - Introduction To Random Processes—A Series
PRO
Discusses probability and random processes.
Prod-MIOT Dist-MIOT

Binary Transmission Wave 032 MIN
Fixed-Form Random Processes 034 MIN
Introduction To Random Processes 033 MIN
Random Processes - Basic Concepts And 028 MIN
Random Telegraph Wave 024 MIN
Role Of The Covariance Function In 022 MIN
Second-Moment Characterization 038 MIN

Probability And Random Processes - Statistical Averages—A Series
PRO
Discusses statistical averages.
Prod-MIOT Dist-MIOT

Characteristic Functions 025 MIN
Chebyshev Inequality, The 029 MIN
Conditional Expectation 013 MIN
Estimation Of Random Variables 023 MIN
Expectations Of Functions Of A Random 023 MIN
Joint Characteristic Functions 025 MIN
Joint Moments - Correlation 027 MIN
Linear Estimation 044 MIN
Minimum Mean-Square Error Estimation 018 MIN
Moments Of A Random Variable 018 MIN
Statistical Averages - Expectation Of A 019 MIN

Probability And Random Processes - Elementary Probability Theory—A Series
PRO
Reveals the widespread applicability of probability theory.
Prod-MIOT Dist-MIOT

Conditional Probability 018 MIN
Conditional Probability (2) 026 MIN
Conditional Probability - A Digital 029 MIN
Elementary Set Theory 029 MIN
Formulation Of Mathematical Models (1) 022 MIN
Formulation Of Mathematical Models (2) 022 MIN
Introduction To Probability 035 MIN
Joint Probability 019 MIN
Probablistic Models 045 MIN
Product Spaces And Statistically Independent 017 MIN
Proof By Induction 016 MIN
Statistical Independence 019 MIN
Theorem Proving 018 MIN

Probability And Random Processes - Limit Theorems And Statistics—A Series
PRO
Discusses limit theorems and statistics.
Prod-MIOT Dist-MIOT

Central Limit Theorem 035 MIN
Estimation Of The Moments Of A Random 037 MIN
Estimation Of The Parameter Of A Probability 027 MIN
Estimation Of The Probability Density Of A 036 MIN
Gaussian Approximation, The 033 MIN
Introduction To Statistical Inference 018 MIN
Performance Bounds - The Cramer Rao 028 MIN
Relative Frequency 018 MIN
Sample Means And The Weak Law Of Large Numbers 030 MIN

Probability And Random Processes - Linear Systems—A Series
PRO
Discusses linear systems.
Prod-MIOT Dist-MIOT

Complex Exponential Inputs - Frequency Domain
Convolution Integral 016 MIN
Fourier Series Demonstration 015 MIN
Fourier Transform Properties 042 MIN
Fourier Transforms 033 MIN
Linear System Descriptions 040 MIN
Measurement Of Impulse Response 011 MIN
Periodic Inputs And Fourier Series 028 MIN
Sampling Theorem 028 MIN
System Classification 027 MIN
System Descriptions 022 MIN
System Functions 035 MIN

Probability And Random Processes - Random Variables—A Series
PRO
Discusses probability and random processes.
Prod-MIOT Dist-MIOT

Canonical Random Variables 030 MIN
Conditioning 015 MIN
Conditioning By Sets 016 MIN
Continuous Random Variables 034 MIN
Digital Communication Application, A 049 MIN
Functions Of A Random Variable 022 MIN
Functions Of Vector Random Variables (1) 019 MIN
Functions Of Vector Random Variables (2) 011 MIN
Impulsive Densities 018 MIN
Mixed Random Variables 011 MIN
Multiple Random Variables - Discrete 034 MIN
Point Conditioning 017 MIN
Random Variables (1) 026 MIN
Random Variables (2) 020 MIN
Reliability Applications 030 MIN
Statistically-Independent Random Variables 025 MIN

Probability And Statistics C
3/4 OR 1/2 INCH VIDEO CASSETTE
Teaches the computation of chance or probability. Discusses predicting events using probability. Describes how to collect and organize data and present information on charts, tables and graphs.
Prod-EDUACT Dist-EDUACT

Probability And The Binomial Distribution C 30 MIN
3/4 OR 1/2 INCH VIDEO CASSETTE IND
Incorporates a general introduction to probability rules, and discusses development of the binomial probability distribution and the underlying distribution for the proportion defective in a process.
From The Engineering Statistics Series.
Prod-COLOSU Dist-COLOSU

Probability And Uncertainty C 45 MIN
3/4 OR 1/2 INCH VIDEO CASSETTE IND
Discusses working capital requirements, inherent uncertainty in new product development, gives as a way to portray uncertainty, two ways to calculate ogives and significance of ogives.
From The New Product Development Series.
Prod-AMCEE Dist-AMCEE

Probability And Uncertainty B 57 MIN
3/4 INCH VIDEOTAPE
Considers the behavior of electrons and photon according to the theories of quantum mechanics. Discusses single and double slit experiments.
From The Feynman Lectures - The Character Of Physical Law Series.
Prod-EDC Dist-EDC

Probability Distributions C
3/4 OR 1/2 INCH VIDEO CASSETTE IND
Continues discussion of go/no-go data where sample sizes are large or small. Discusses use of the normal and Poisson distributions to approximate the binomial, along with general use of the Poisson and hypergeometric distributions.
From The Statistics For Managers Series.
Prod-COLOSU Dist-COLOSU

Probability For Decision Analysis 1 - Fundamentals C 55 MIN
3/4 OR 1/2 INCH VIDEO CASSETTE
See series title for descriptive statement.
From The Decision Analysis Series.
Prod-MIOT Dist-MIOT

Probability For Decision Analysis 2 - Random Variables C 57 MIN
3/4 OR 1/2 INCH VIDEO CASSETTE
See series title for descriptive statement.
From The Decision Analysis Series.
Prod-MIOT Dist-MIOT

Probability I C 14 MIN
3/4 OR 1/2 INCH VIDEO CASSETTE I-J
Presents the basic concepts of probability using a gumball machine, a gypsy fortuneteller and a probability counseling booth.
From The Math Matters Series. Green Module
Prod-KRLNTV Dist-AITECH 1975

Probability I C 20 MIN
3/4 OR 1/2 INCH VIDEO CASSETTE J-C
See series title for descriptive statement.
From The Math Topics - Statistics Series.
Prod-BBCTV Dist-FI

Probability II C 14 MIN
3/4 OR 1/2 INCH VIDEO CASSETTE I-J
Shows how the possibility of winning a free meal at a restaurant called Fat Chance draws the characters into a challenging probability exercise.
From The Math Matters Series. Green Module
Prod-KRLNTV Dist-AITECH 1975

Probability II C 20 MIN
3/4 OR 1/2 INCH VIDEO CASSETTE J-C
See series title for descriptive statement.
From The Math Topics - Statistics Series.
Prod-BBCTV Dist-FI

Probable Cause - Search And Seizure C 25 MIN
16MM FILM, 3/4 OR 1/2 IN VIDEO PRO
Covers how police can determine probable cause to search, seize and arrest with or without a warrant. Shows how to obtain eyewitness information, use a police informant and obtain a warrant.
From The Law Enforcement - Patrol Procedures Series.
Prod-MTROLA Dist-MTI Prodn-WORON 1973

Probable Cause And The Scope Of Searches C 50 MIN
3/4 OR 1/2 INCH VIDEO CASSETTE PRO
Explains the requirements of a valid warrant, probable cause and the scope of a search. Discusses who may issue the warrant and the implications of a flaw in the warrant.
From The Criminal Procedure And The Trial Advocate Series.
Prod-ABACPE Dist-ABACPE

Probable Passing Of Elk Creek, The C 60 MIN
16MM FILM, 3/4 OR 1/2 IN VIDEO J-C A
Portrays a controversy in Elk Creek, California, in which the state government plans to build a reservoir in a valley that would force the white people and the Indians to leave their homes. Reveals that the Indians have the power to decide whether the the dam is built.
LC NO. 84-707124
Prod-TOCAYO Dist-CNEMAG 1982

Probableman C 14 MIN
3/4 INCH VIDEO CASSETTE P
Explores the exploits of a part-time superhero named Probableman. Introduces the relative frequency notion of probability.
Prod-DAVFMS Dist-GA

Probablistic Models B 45 MIN
3/4 OR 1/2 INCH VIDEO CASSETTE PRO
Covers the five basic axioms of probability theory.
From The Probability And Random Processes - Elementary Probability Theory Series.
Prod-MIOT Dist-MIOT

Probe C 7 MIN
3/4 OR 1/2 INCH VIDEO CASSETTE
Introduces a group of women discussing personal sexual experiences related to vibrators. Presented by Carol Porter and Joan Valdes.
Prod-ARTINC Dist-ARTINC

PROBE - Pattern Recognition Of Behavioral Events C 14 MIN
16MM FILM OPTICAL SOUND H-C
Describes the application of computer pattern recognition programs to the study of primate behavior and shows how such data can be correlated with morphological changes. Demonstrates the sensitivity of the method in detecting alterations of spontaneous behavior by toxicologic and pharmacologic insults.
LC NO. 80-700557
Prod-ISURF Dist-IOWA Prodn-IOWA 1979

Probing - Questions That Help You Sell C 10 MIN
16MM FILM, 3/4 OR 1/2 IN VIDEO
Demonstrates a technique of asking questions to find out why, what and how much a prospective customer will buy.
LC NO. 79-706195
Prod-SALENG Dist-SALENG 1979

Probing A New Domain C 33 MIN
3/4 OR 1/2 INCH VIDEO CASSETTE C
See series title for descriptive statement.
From The Artificial Intelligence, Pt 1 - Fundamental Concepts Series.
Prod-MIOT Dist-AMCEE

Probing A New Domain C 45 MIN
3/4 OR 1/2 INCH VIDEO CASSETTE PRO
Helps in understanding success and failure, moving from ad hoc heuristics to constraint-based algorithms, and an illustration.
From The Artificial Intelligence - Pt 1, Fundamental Concepts Series.
Prod-MIOT Dist-MIOT

Probing For The Sale C 20 MIN
16MM FILM, 3/4 OR 1/2 IN VIDEO H-C A
Offers an example of probing for the sale by telling how Art sells Claire on the idea of a miniature computerized telephone.
LC NO. 81-706213
Prod-CRMP Dist-CRMP 1981

Probing For The Sale (Spanish) C 21 MIN
16MM FILM, 3/4 OR 1/2 IN VIDEO C A
Depicts Art asking Claire, a successful salesperson, about her selling style and customer contacts.
Prod-CRMP Dist-CRMP 1981

Probing Mind B 29 MIN
16MM FILM - 3/4 IN VIDEO
Describes the uses of new educational media, such as films, television, recordings, teaching machines and well equipped laboratories in the teaching of high school science.
Prod-USOE Dist-USNAC 1972

Probing Ones' Feelings About Superstition C 30 MIN
2 INCH VIDEOTAPE J
See series title for descriptive statement.
From The Summer Journal, Unit 1 - You Are What You Feel Series.
Prod-WNINTV Dist-GPITVL

Probing Planetary Processes C 15 MIN
16MM FILM OPTICAL SOUND C
Examines the possible explanations for the formation and evolution of the earth and moon. Utilizes data provided by the Apollo Lunar Missions and the Glomar Challenger Drilling Project.
From The Science In Action Series.
Prod-ALLFP Dist-COUNFI

Probing Storms Over And Under The Sea C 13 MIN
16MM FILM OPTICAL SOUND
Discusses two scientific projects carried out at sea. Tells how Project GATE and Project MODE study various aspects of oceanography.
Prod-ALLFP Dist-NSTA 1977

Probing The Continental Margin C 23 MIN
16MM FILM OPTICAL SOUND J-C A
Describes life and work on board two ships as men survey the Australian continental shelf and slopes.
LC NO. 72-701524
Prod-ANAIB Dist-AUIS 1971

Probing The Mysteries Of Planet Venus C 14 MIN
16MM FILM OPTICAL SOUND
Tells how the Pioneer Venus space mission and the Venus Orbiting Imaging Radar will add to scientific knowledge of the planet Venus.
Prod-ALLFP Dist-NSTA

Probing The Mysteries Of Sleep C
1/2 IN VIDEO CASSETTE (VHS)
Examines sleep deprivation, REM and non-REM sleep, and myths about normal lengths of sleep. Traces the progress of a volunteer through a night at a sleep lab.
From The Theater Of The Night - The Science Of Sleep And Dreams Series.
Prod-IBIS Dist-IBIS

Probing The Mysteries Of The Brain C 14 MIN
16MM FILM OPTICAL SOUND
Shows how researchers probe and monitor single brain cells of simple life forms. Tells how they study the mental processes of primates, use X-rays to map the brain, and prepare three-dimensional blueprints of brain structures.
Prod-ALLFP Dist-NSTA 1975

Probing The Secrets Of The Stomach C 18 MIN
16MM FILM OPTICAL SOUND
Depicts the functions and organisms of the stomach of a mammal using a microscope. Shows the secretions of gastric acid by the mucous membrane and hydrochloric acid and pepsinogen by the cells. Follows the changes that occur in the secretions when acetylcholine and gastrin come into contact with these cells.
Prod-UNIJAP Dist-UNIJAP 1969

Problem Children B 20 MIN
16MM FILM OPTICAL SOUND C
Presents the story of two junior high school boys and how their personalities are affected by their relationships in home and school. Illustrates how parents and teachers can and should work together.
Prod-ODPW Dist-PSUPCR 1947

Problem Class, The B 30 MIN
16MM FILM OPTICAL SOUND T
Records the strategies used by a University Elementary School staff teacher to overcome severe behavior problems in an inner-city classroom. Includes Dr Madeline Hunter's comments on the episodes to point out the power of basic learning principles in the hands of a teacher who understands how to use those principles.
Prod-SPF Dist-SPF

Problem Diagnosis C 35 MIN
3/4 OR 1/2 INCH VIDEO CASSETTE
See series title for descriptive statement.
From The Situation Management Series.
Prod-EXECDV Dist-DELTAK

Problem Dogs C 30 MIN
3/4 OR 1/2 INCH VIDEO CASSETTE H-C A
Shows Barbara Woodhouse's method of handling problem dogs.
From The Training Dogs The Woodhouse Way.
Prod-BBCTV Dist-FI 1982

Problem Drinker-Driver C 6 MIN
16MM FILM OPTICAL SOUND
Shows how a center in Nassau County, New York, aids drivers who have drinking problems. Discusses several cases and suggests how they can be helped.
LC NO. 75-703699
Prod-USHTSA Dist-USNAC Prodn-MITCHS 1974

Problem Identification - Determining The Underlying Issues Of A Conflict C 22 MIN
16MM FILM, 3/4 OR 1/2 IN VIDEO PRO
Explains how to identify the underlying causes of disputes by calm, orderly information gathering.
From The Officer Survival - An Approach To Conflict Management Series.
Prod-HAR Dist-MTI 1976

Problem Of Acceptance, A B 47 MIN
16MM FILM OPTICAL SOUND
Features the psychodramatic exploration of a teenager's attempt to deal with her homosexuality.
From The Psychodrama In Group Process Series.
Prod-NYU Dist-NYU

Problem Of Evil C 25 MIN
3/4 OR 1/2 INCH VIDEO CASSETTE C
See series title for descriptive statement.
From The Introduction To Philosophy Series.
Prod-UDEL Dist-UDEL

Problem Of Evil, The C 30 MIN
3/4 OR 1/2 INCH VIDEO CASSETTE C
See series title for descriptive statement.
From The Art Of Being Human Series. Module 6
Prod-MDCC Dist-MDCC

Problem Of Feelings, A C 15 MIN
3/4 OR 1/2 INCH VIDEO CASSETTE K-P
Deals with French-American culture. Focuses on caring for others and self.
From The La Bonne Aventure Series.
Prod-MPBN Dist-GPITVL

Problem Of Hookworm Infection, The C 8 MIN
16MM FILM OPTICAL SOUND
Pictures the life cycle of the hookworm and shows the conditions in a rural home conducive to hookworm infection. Depicts the effects of hookworm disease in a young girl.
LC NO. FIE54-126
Prod-USPHS Dist-USNAC 1954

Problem Of Power, A C 45 MIN
16MM FILM OPTICAL SOUND
Illustrates the general social and economic situation in Latin America, using Colombia as the representative nation. Includes views of the agrarian culture, the urban poor, and various individuals working for change in Latin America.
LC NO. 79-705001
Prod-CCNCC Dist-CCNCC Prodn-CMC 1970

Problem Of Water, The C 15 MIN
3/4 OR 1/2 INCH VIDEO CASSETTE I
Visits California's Mojave Desert and recounts the explorations of Jedediah Smith. Examines the water dependence of the Imperial Valley and of Los Angeles.
From The American Legacy Series. Program 13
Prod-KRMATV Dist-AITECH 1983

Problem On Our Hands, The C 19 MIN
16MM FILM OPTICAL SOUND
Presents unrehearsed interviews with nurses, doctors, aids and personnel of the U S Public Health Service discussing the problem of inadequate hand decontamination in hospitals.
Prod-JAJ Dist-JAJ 1967

Problem Oriented Languages - Cobol B 45 MIN
2 INCH VIDEOTAPE
See series title for descriptive statement.
From The Data Processing, Unit 3 - Instructing The Computer Series.
Prod-GPITVL Dist-GPITVL

Problem Oriented Languages - Fortran B 45 MIN
2 INCH VIDEOTAPE
See series title for descriptive statement.
From The Data Processing, Unit 3 - Instructing The Computer Series.
Prod-GPITVL Dist-GPITVL

Problem Oriented Languages - Report Program Generator RPG B 45 MIN
2 INCH VIDEOTAPE
See series title for descriptive statement.
From The Data Processing, Unit 3 - Instructing The Computer Series.
Prod-GPITVL Dist-GPITVL

Problem Oriented Medical Record C 25 MIN
3/4 OR 1/2 INCH VIDEO CASSETTE
Describes and demonstrates the components of Problem Oriented Medical Record (POMR). Utilizes actual patient interview and develops a care plan centered on real patient needs.
Prod-WSUN Dist-AJN

Problem Oriented Record C 16 MIN
3/4 OR 1/2 INCH VIDEO CASSETTE PRO
Provides a detailed description of the use of the problem oriented record and details its use in individualizing patient care.
Prod-UMICHM Dist-UMICHM 1978

Problem Prevention C 26 MIN
3/4 OR 1/2 INCH VIDEO CASSETTE
See series title for descriptive statement.
From The Situation Management Series.
Prod-EXECDV Dist-DELTAK

Problem Soliving - Calculating Formatting And Filing C 60 MIN
3/4 OR 1/2 INCH VIDEO CASSETTE
Teaches math functions, explains formatting data, teaches writing to disk and recovering data from text files and presents overview of VisiCalc and Apple Writer (R).
From The Computer Tutor Series.
Prod-FILMID Dist-FILMID 1983

Problem Solvers, The C 13 MIN
16MM FILM OPTICAL SOUND
Explains the collector's role in the consumer credit community and emphasizes the professional character of the collection business.
LC NO. 80-701373
Prod-ACOLLA Dist-ACOLLA Prodn-JAMIE 1979

Problem Solvers, The - An Opportunity C 11 MIN
16MM FILM OPTICAL SOUND
Looks at the profession of internal auditing providing an overview of responsibilities and activities by visiting a practicing internal auditor.
Prod-IIA Dist-MTP

Problem Solving B 10 MIN
16MM FILM OPTICAL SOUND
See series title for descriptive statement.
From The Parent Education - Attitude Films Series.
Prod-TC Dist-TC

Problem Solving C 20 MIN
16MM FILM OPTICAL SOUND
A teacher-training film in which Ernest Duncan discusses the importance of working with concrete objects and sets and set language in the early problem-solving process. Points out how reading difficulties can be reduced by using problems which picture the objects.
From The Duncan - Modern School Math Films Series.
LC NO. 72-701745
Prod-HMC Dist-HMC 1971

Problem Solving B 29 MIN
16MM FILM OPTICAL SOUND IND
See series title for descriptive statement.
From The Interviewing For Results Series.
LC NO. 73-703323
Prod-EDSD Dist-EDSD 1968

Problem Solving C
3/4 OR 1/2 INCH VIDEO CASSETTE
Provides ten steps to problem solving. Addresses pitfalls and teamwork.
From The Organizational Quality Improvement Series.
Prod-BNA Dist-BNA

Problem Solving C
3/4 OR 1/2 INCH VIDEO CASSETTE
See series title for descriptive statement.
From The Asset Series.
Prod-RESPRC Dist-RESPRC

Problem Solving C 8 MIN
3/4 OR 1/2 INCH VIDEO CASSETTE J-H
Presents problem-solving techniques which adolescents can use in their dealings with parents, teachers, peers and others.
From The ASSET - A Social Skills Program For Adolescents Series. Session 5

LC NO. 81-706054
Prod-HAZLJS Dist-RESPRC Prodn-BAXLEN 1981

Problem Solving C 20 MIN
2 INCH VIDEOTAPE P
See series title for descriptive statement.
From The Mathemagic, Unit II - Addition And Subtraction Series.
Prod-WMULTV Dist-GPITVL

Problem Solving - A Case Study C 22 MIN
16MM FILM, 3/4 OR 1/2 IN VIDEO
Explains how to apply basic problem-solving techniques in order to obtain information essential to making clear decisions. Presents a case study of a company that loses the business of one of its oldest customers due to severe quality control problems and shows how the problem is solved.
LC NO. 74-700689
Prod-RANKAV Dist-RTBL 1972

Problem Solving - A Process For Managers C 20 MIN
16MM FILM, 3/4 OR 1/2 IN VIDEO A
Shows eight young managers who gather in a theater setting to role-play problems they have faced and to share principles they have learned. Demonstrates a simple process for solving the problems of managers and supervisors.
Prod-NEM Dist-NEM 1981

Problem Solving - A Process For Managers (Spanish) C 16 MIN
16MM FILM, 3/4 OR 1/2 IN VIDEO
Teaches problem-solving methods for managers and supervisors.
From The Professional Management Program (Spanish) Series.
Prod-NEM Dist-NEM

Problem Solving - Acting It Out C 15 MIN
3/4 OR 1/2 INCH VIDEO CASSETTE I
Presents Elaine, Nisha, Cliff and Roger using everyday objects to set up a mock race-course and discover the secret of winning a problem-solving race. Includes an animated segment which has Sherlock Holmes showing Watson how to let convenient objects stand for things to solve a problem.
From The It Figures Series. No. 3
Prod-AITV Dist-AITECH Prodn-NJN 1982

Problem Solving - Calculating, Formatting And Filing C 57 MIN
3/4 OR 1/2 INCH VIDEO CASSETTE
Covers math functions, formats, filing and word processing. Teaches writing to disk and recovering data from text files. Gives applications for the Apple II and IIe.
From The Computer Tutor Series.
Prod-PSU Dist-PSU 1984

Problem Solving - Drawing A Picture C 14 MIN
3/4 OR 1/2 INCH VIDEO CASSETTE I
Utilizes a combination of realistic dramatizations and animated tales to demonstrate how to use mathematical strategies to solve problems. Shows Ingrid calling upon diagrams to provide directions for a stranger and to set up a contest.
From The It Figures Series. No. 8
LC NO. 82-707005
Prod-AITV Dist-AITECH Prodn-NJN 1982

Problem Solving - Identifying The Problem C 15 MIN
3/4 OR 1/2 INCH VIDEO CASSETTE I
Teaches problem solving by re-stating the problem, changing the context, discarding unnecessary information and indicating what is given and what is needed.
From The Math Works Series.
Prod-AITECH Dist-AITECH

Problem Solving - Keep On Trying C 14 MIN
3/4 OR 1/2 INCH VIDEO CASSETTE I
Reveals that Mary and Robert need flexibility and persistence when trying to train a pet and organize a bedroom. Includes an animated segment in which the hungry fox tries several ploys before getting the crow to drop a piece of cheese.
From The It Figures Series. No. 26
Prod-AITV Dist-AITECH Prodn-NJN 1982

Problem Solving - Looking For A Pattern C 15 MIN
3/4 OR 1/2 INCH VIDEO CASSETTE I
Explains how a pattern helps solve a problem and how to find a pattern by looking at data from different perspectives.
From The Math Works Series.
Prod-AITECH Dist-AITECH

Problem Solving - Making A Table C 14 MIN
3/4 OR 1/2 INCH VIDEO CASSETTE I
Explains how George helps Ned and Jessica keep track of their progress toward making the swim team by making a table. Includes an animated segment in which Cinderella's table shows how long she can dance.
From The It Figures Series. No. 12
Prod-AITV Dist-AITECH Prodn-NJN 1982

Problem Solving - Many Ways To Go C 15 MIN
3/4 OR 1/2 INCH VIDEO CASSETTE I
Shows how Kaylin and Chenetta discover different paths to solving a problem in their dog-walking business. Includes an animated segment in which the master shows himself to be wiser than his best students because he sees that there is seldom only one way to solve a problem.
From The It Figures Series. No. 27
Prod-AITV Dist-AITECH Prodn-NJN 1982

Problem Solving - Recognizing Necessary Information C 15 MIN
3/4 OR 1/2 INCH VIDEO CASSETTE I
Explains how sorting relevant from irrelevant information in a word problem lets Mrs Murphy's students track down a prize. Includes an animated segment in which St Georgina fights through a thicket of irrelevancies to rescue a young man in distress.
From The It Figures Series. No. 18
Prod-AITV Dist-AITECH Prodn-NJN 1982

Problem Solving - Simplifying The Problem C 15 MIN
3/4 OR 1/2 INCH VIDEO CASSETTE I
Shows how to simplify a problem by decreasing the size of numbers or the number of variables or by taking one step at a time.
From The Math Works Series.
Prod-AITECH Dist-AITECH

Problem Solving - Some Basic Principles C 18 MIN
16MM FILM, 3/4 OR 1/2 IN VIDEO
Presents a systematic approach to problem solving and decision making for managers.
LC NO. 74-700690
Prod-RANKAV Dist-RTBL 1972

Problem Solving - Unit IV C 20 MIN
2 INCH VIDEOTAPE P
See series title for descriptive statement.
From The Mathemagic, Unit II - Addition And Subtraction Series.
Prod-WMULTV Dist-GPITVL

Problem Solving - Unit V C 20 MIN
2 INCH VIDEOTAPE P
See series title for descriptive statement.
From The Mathemagic, Unit V - Addition And Subtraction series.
Prod-WMULTV Dist-GPITVL

Problem Solving - Unit VIII C 20 MIN
2 INCH VIDEOTAPE P
See series title for descriptive statement.
From The Mathemagic, Unit VIII - Multiplication And Division Series.
Prod-WMULTV Dist-GPITVL

Problem Solving - Using A Guide C 14 MIN
3/4 OR 1/2 INCH VIDEO CASSETTE I
Explains that when Andy is locked out, he remembers Eva's way of dealing with a problem she had. Includes an animated segment in which Jill suggests that Jack use the 'Hey, Wait!-Think-See-So' problem-solving guide to deal with a leaky bucket.
From The It Figures Series. No. 28
Prod-AITV Dist-AITECH Prodn-NJN 1982

Problem Solving - Using Diagrams And Models C 15 MIN
3/4 OR 1/2 INCH VIDEO CASSETTE I
Shows how flow charts, models, assembly plans and blueprints simplify, clarify, abstract or make concrete.
From The Math Works Series.
Prod-AITECH Dist-AITECH

Problem Solving - Using Graphs C 15 MIN
3/4 OR 1/2 INCH VIDEO CASSETTE I
Focuses on how to choose the right kind of graph to convey a particular point. Compares situations in which bar, circle or line graphs are most appropriate.
From The Math Works Series.
Prod-AITECH Dist-AITECH

Problem Solving - Using Maps C 15 MIN
3/4 OR 1/2 INCH VIDEO CASSETTE I
Focuses on reading and interpreting a map that someone else has prepared. Shows how to find a particular location, to determine the distance between two points and to plan a route by noting the region covered, the directions, the coordinates, the scale and the key to symbols.
From The Math Works Series.
Prod-AITECH Dist-AITECH

Problem Solving - Using Tables C 15 MIN
3/4 OR 1/2 INCH VIDEO CASSETTE I
Reviews different kinds of tables and explains how to read and how to make a table.
From The Math Works Series.
Prod-AITECH Dist-AITECH

Problem Solving - Using The Hen As An Educational Tool C 29 MIN
3/4 OR 1/2 INCH VIDEO CASSETTE J-H A
Demonstrates a technique for solving problems using a real life problem - whether or not a hen is in laying condition at a given time. Describes the five basic steps taken in solving this problem.
Prod-CUETV Dist-CUNIV 1974

Problem Solving And Decision Making C 17 MIN
3/4 OR 1/2 INCH VIDEO CASSETTE
See series title for descriptive statement.
From The Applied Management Series.
Prod-ORGDYN Dist-DELTAK

Problem Solving And Decision Making C 20 MIN
3/4 OR 1/2 INCH VIDEO CASSETTE
See series title for descriptive statement.
From The Effective Manager Series.
Prod-DELTAK Dist-DELTAK

Problem Solving By Objectives B 29 MIN
16MM FILM OPTICAL SOUND IND
See series title for descriptive statement.
From The Management By Objectives Series.
LC NO. 70-703325
Prod-EDSD Dist-EDSD

Problem Solving In Groups B 25 MIN
16MM FILM, 3/4 OR 1/2 IN VIDEO C A
Outlines functions of management committees. Describes methods of improving group problem-solving procedure and decision-making procedure. Illustrates advantages and difficulties of group problem solving.
From The Mangement Development Series.
Prod-UCLA Dist-UCEMC 1961

Problem Solving In Mathematics C
3/4 OR 1/2 INCH VIDEO CASSETTE J
Presents strategies for solving math problems that cover five categories - whole numbers, fractions, decimals, percent and combined computational skills. Uses everyday problems to help students find hidden questions and key words to simplify problem solving.
Prod-PATED Dist-GA

Problem Solving Methods In Artificial Intelligence—A Series
PRO
Uses classroom format to videotape two 75-minute lectures weekly for 14 weeks on 56 cassettes. Shows underlying theoretical concepts in solving problems by heuristically guided trial and error search methods. Covers state-space problem reduction and first-order predicate calculus representations for solving problems search algorithms and their 'optimality' proofs.
Prod-UMD Dist-AMCEE

Problem Solving Process C
3/4 OR 1/2 INCH VIDEO CASSETTE
Shows how to establish and use standard guidelines for problem solving.
From The Implementing Quality Circles Series.
Prod-BNA Dist-BNA

Problem Solving Selling C
3/4 OR 1/2 INCH VIDEO CASSETTE
Introduces 19 vignettes that depict situations using problem solving, preventive problem solving and contingency planning. Includes kinds of obstacles, responses to obstacles, the 'lost order,' problem solving methods and competitor-prepared specs.
From The Making Of A Salesman Series. Session 5
Prod-PRODEV Dist-PRODEV

Problem Solving Strategies - The Synectics Approach C 28 MIN
16MM FILM, 3/4 OR 1/2 IN VIDEO C A
Shows a problem-solving session held at Synectics, Inc, a consulting firm specializing in helping clients explore creative alternatives and solutions. Presents strategies to stimulate organizational creativity and streamline problem solving.
LC NO. 79-707397
Prod-CRMP Dist-CRMP 1980

Problem With Bears, The - Number Patterns And Problem Solving C 14 MIN
3/4 OR 1/2 INCH VIDEO CASSETTE P
Features Uncle Estill translating a word problem into a number sequence.
From The Math Country Series.
Prod-KYTV Dist-AITECH 1979

Problem With Exhaustion C 30 MIN
3/4 OR 1/2 INCH VIDEO CASSETTE P-I
See series title for descriptive statement.
From The Sonrisas Series.
Prod-KRLNTV Dist-MDCPB

Problem With Water Is People, The C 30 MIN
16MM FILM, 3/4 OR 1/2 IN VIDEO I-H A
Traces the Colorado River watershed from the snowcovered Rockies to the delta in Baja California. Discusses water usage and equitable division of water, especially between California and Arizona. Narrated by Chet Huntley.
Prod-NBCTV Dist-MGHT 1964

Problem Witness Tactics - A Lecture With Demonstrations C 28 MIN
3/4 OR 1/2 INCH VIDEO CASSETTE PRO
Presents 12 common problems and possible solutions that lawyers face during trial. Discusses and demonstrates different methods for resolving problems and methods by which a witness' recollection can be refreshed.
Prod-ABACPE Dist-ABACPE

Problem-Oriented Medical Record C 30 MIN
16MM FILM OPTICAL SOUND PRO
Defines and demonstrates the problem-oriented medical record as a systemic process for documenting, monitoring and evaluating the quality of health care provided by nursing service.
From The Directions For Education In Nursing Via Technology Series.
LC NO. 76-703340
Prod-DENT Dist-WSU Prodn-CENIT 1976

Problem-Oriented Medical Record C 4 MIN
1/2 IN VIDEO CASSETTE BETA/VHS
From The Typing - Medical Series.
Prod-RMI Dist-RMI

Problem-Oriented Medical Record, The - Dental Utilization C 18 MIN
16MM FILM OPTICAL SOUND
Describes the method by which the Veterans Administration Dental Services utilizes and implements the medical records of its patients. Shows how this system permits recording of the patient's history, problems, assessment, plan for treatment and continuing treatment record on the same medical record chart.
LC NO. 75-703838
Prod-USVA Dist-USNAC 1975

Problem-Solving And Approximation C 30 MIN
3/4 OR 1/2 INCH VIDEO CASSETTE
See series title for descriptive statement.
From The Infinity Factory Series.
Prod-EDFCEN Dist-MDCPB

Problem-Solving And Decision-Making C 30 MIN
3/4 OR 1/2 INCH VIDEO CASSETTE
Demonstrates the opportunity for release of leadership potential in problem-solving and decision activities. Develops basic functions and requirements of organizations. Identifies crucial requirements which must be met for the functions to be effectively carried out.
From The Organizational Transactions Series.
Prod-PRODEV Dist-PRODEV

Problem-Solving And Math Strategies C 30 MIN
3/4 OR 1/2 INCH VIDEO CASSETTE
See series title for descriptive statement.
From The Infinity Factory Series.
Prod-EDFCEN Dist-MDCPB

Problem-Solving In Groups B 25 MIN
3/4 OR 1/2 INCH VIDEO CASSETTE
Brings a situation to a problem-solving group in which in-laws have decided to visit a student for the first time. Helps to develop a satisfactory plan to deal with student's stressful situation.
Prod-VRL Dist-UWISC 1980

Problem-Solving Strategies And Arithmetic Shortcuts C 30 MIN
3/4 OR 1/2 INCH VIDEO CASSETTE
See series title for descriptive statement.
From The Infinity Factory Series.
Prod-EDFCEN Dist-MDCPB

Problem-Solving Unit C
3/4 OR 1/2 INCH VIDEO CASSETTE A
Shows how managers can identify a problem, determine what has gone wrong, decide what to do about it and take corrective action. Gives specifics for anticipating difficulties, stating goals, brainstorming and other problem-solving skills and techniques.
From The Management Skills For Supervisors Series.
Prod-TIMLIF Dist-TIMLIF 1984

Problem-Solving 1 - The Basic Skill C
3/4 OR 1/2 INCH VIDEO CASSETTE T
Focuses on variety of problem-solving processes and strategies. Features five elementary school children applying these strategies.
From The Third R - Teaching Basic Mathematics Skills Series.
Prod-EPCO Dist-EDCORP

Problem, The C 13 MIN
16MM FILM, 3/4 OR 1/2 IN VIDEO
An animated puppet film that centers on the question of what color the trash box in a large organization should be painted. Examines the dehumanizing effect of bureaucracies and raises questions concerning the nature of responsibility and the individual's reaction to it.
Prod-BF Dist-FI 1966

Problem, The C 30 MIN
3/4 OR 1/2 INCH VIDEO CASSETTE
Discusses the complexity of contemporary environmental problems, for example, man's use of chemical pesticides which are beginning to have effects they were never intended to have on the environment.
From The Ecology - Our Road To Survival Series.
Prod-NETCHE Dist-NETCHE 1971

Problems And Challenges For Office Support C 30 MIN
3/4 OR 1/2 INCH VIDEO CASSETTE
Examines how office automation is changing the office support function and the attitudes and abilities of people in support positions. Points out steps that mangement must take to avoid the serious problems that may arise with the introduction of automated technologies.
From The Impact Of Office Automation On People Series.
Prod-DELTAK Dist-DELTAK

Problems And Practices For The Disadvantaged C 30 MIN
3/4 OR 1/2 INCH VIDEO CASSETTE
Examines government programs for the disadvantaged, beginning with emergency nursery care during the Depression and the growth of the Head Start program.
From The Educating The Disadvantaged Series.
Prod-NETCHE Dist-NETCHE 1972

Problems Communities Face B 15 MIN
2 INCH VIDEOTAPE P-I
See series title for descriptive statement.
From The Our Changing Community Series.
Prod-VITA Dist-GPITVL 1967

Problems Encountered By The Home Visitor B 15 MIN
3/4 OR 1/2 INCH VIDEO CASSETTE PRO
Shows typical problems encountered by the home visitor, such as a mother annoyed because the visitor arrives late, constant interruptions by the father and absence of the parent at the appointed time.
Prod-HSERF Dist-HSERF

Problems In Academic Task Performance C 6 MIN
16MM FILM OPTICAL SOUND
Illustrates problems of the physically, multiply handicapped and demonstrates supportive devices for task performance. Includes auditory sound production of written letter cues, letter production of auditory cues, blending sound and word reading.
From The Systems For Precise Observations For Teachers Series. Part 1
LC NO. 74-705419
Prod-USOE Dist-USNAC 1970

Problems In Academic Tasks Performance, Pt 1 C 7 MIN
16MM FILM OPTICAL SOUND
Presents portions of one student's verbal and written response to alphabet symbols represented orally or visually.
From The Systems For Precise Observations For Teachers Series.
LC NO. 74-705420
Prod-USOE Dist-USNAC 1970

Problems In Diagnosis And Management Of Hypothyroidism B 40 MIN
16MM FILM OPTICAL SOUND
Presents a patient with severe myxedema secondary to pituitary tumor. Describes the clinical procedure and laboratory findings common to primary and pituitary myxedema. Explains etiologies and importance of differential diagnosis. (Kinescope)
From The Boston Medical Reports Series.
LC NO. 74-705421
Prod-NMAC Dist-USNAC 1964

Problems In Job Enrichment C 13 MIN
3/4 OR 1/2 INCH VIDEO CASSETTE
Covers the many problems that arise when a job enrichment program is installed and suggests some ways to prevent them.
From The Job Enrichment Series.
Prod-RESEM Dist-RESEM

Problems In Supervision (Spanish)—A Series

Discusses various problem areas of supervision.
Prod-USOE Dist-USNAC 1979

Buenas Condiciones En El Trabajo	009 MIN
Conserve El Interes De Sus Empleados	013 MIN
Instructing The Worker On The Job (Spanish)	014 MIN
Maintaining Quality Standards (Spanish)	010 MIN
Placing The Right Man On The Job (Spanish)	013 MIN
Relaciones Entre Supervisores	008 MIN
Safety In The Shop (Spanish)	012 MIN

Problems In Supervision—A Series

Discusses various problem areas of supervision.
Prod-USOE Dist-USNAC 1979

Employing Blind Workers In Industry	017 MIN
Employing Disabled Workers In Industry	020 MIN
Establishing Working Relations For The	014 MIN
Every Minute Counts	010 MIN
Improving The Job	009 MIN
Instructing The Blind Worker On The Job	017 MIN
Instructing The Disabled Worker On The Job	014 MIN
Instructing The Worker On The Job	014 MIN
Introducing The New Worker To His Job	016 MIN
Maintaining Good Working Conditions	009 MIN
Maintaining Quality Standards	010 MIN
Maintaining Workers' Interest	013 MIN
New Supervisor Takes A Look At His Job, A	013 MIN
Placing The Right Man On The Job	013 MIN
Planning And Laying Out Work	010 MIN
Safety In The Shop	012 MIN
Supervising Women Workers	011 MIN
Supervising Workers On The Job	010 MIN
Supervisor As A Leader, The	027 MIN
Using Visual Aids In Training	014 MIN
Working With Other Supervisors	008 MIN

Problems In The Surgical Management Of Hyperparathyroidism C 19 MIN
16MM FILM OPTICAL SOUND PRO
Points cut that when the diagnosis of primary hyperparathyroidism has been made, many of the surgeon's problems have really just begun. Explains that the obscure and variable positions of the parathyroid glands require for their search and identification adequate exposure, meticulous hemostasis, careful dissection and a detailed working knowledge of the anatomical relationships and anomalies of the neck and mediastinum.
Prod-ACYDGD Dist-ACY 1962

Problems In Transporting The Handicapped C 27 MIN
16MM FILM OPTICAL SOUND A
Discusses problems in transporting the physically handicapped.
Prod-VISUCP Dist-VISUCP 1978

Problems Of Conservation - Air X 15 MIN
16MM FILM, 3/4 OR 1/2 IN VIDEO J A
Studies adverse effects of air pollution. Discusses technological and legislative controls. Specifies the percentages of various gases that make up the troposphere.
From The Environmental Studies Series.
Prod-EBEC Dist-EBEC 1968

Problems Of Conservation - Air (Spanish) C 15 MIN
16MM FILM, 3/4 OR 1/2 IN VIDEO J-H
Explains causes of man-made air pollution, outlining its effects on health and property and reporting on what is being done to help solve the problem.
From The Environmental Studies (Spanish) Series.
Prod-EBEC Dist-EBEC

Problems Of Conservation - Forest And Range X 14 MIN
16MM FILM, 3/4 OR 1/2 IN VIDEO J-C A
Emphasizes how the encroachment of a growing world population upon forest and range poses a serious problem and examines the part played by the U S Forest Service in protecting forest lands. Shows how forest land furnishes wood for lumber and paper, and prevents erosion.
From The Environmental Studies Series.
Prod-EBEC Dist-EBEC 1969

Problems Of Conservation - Forest And Range (Spanish) C 14 MIN
16MM FILM, 3/4 OR 1/2 IN VIDEO J-H
Describes the struggle to retain large areas of undeveloped forest and range while the demands of rapidly expanding population press upon these areas. Illustrates the 'multiple use' programs of protection and management that lead to effective use of resources.
From The Environmental Studies (Spanish) Series.
Prod-EBEC Dist-EBEC

Problems Of Conservation - Minerals X 16 MIN
16MM FILM, 3/4 OR 1/2 IN VIDEO J-H
Introduces a variety of mineral resources vital to the economy and way of life in the United States. Desscribes the non-renewable features of mineral resources and the current efforts directed toward conserving mineral resources.
From The Environmental Studies Series.
Prod-EBEC Dist-EBEC 1969

Problems Of Conservation - Minerals (Spanish) C 16 MIN
16MM FILM, 3/4 OR 1/2 IN VIDEO J-H
Gives examples of man's reliance on non-renewable minerals and presents several possible conservation measures.
From The Environmental Studies (Spanish) Series.
Prod-EBEC Dist-EBEC

Problems Of Conservation - Our Natural Resources X 11 MIN
16MM FILM, 3/4 OR 1/2 IN VIDEO J-H
Discusses pollution of water and air, depletion of natural resources, dwindling food supplies for an exploding population, destruction of forests and wildlife, consumption of non-renewable resources and other problems of conservation that must be faced. Presents a broad overview of the developing problem in natural resources. Establishes man's reliance on natural resources and his misuse of them. Gives current efforts in conservation.
From The Environmental Studies Series.
Prod-EBEC Dist-EBEC 1970

Problems Of Conservation - Our Natural Resources (Spanish) C 11 MIN
16MM FILM, 3/4 OR 1/2 IN VIDEO J-H
Explains that man must control population growth and pollution in order to keep the Earth habitable.
From The Environmental Studies (Spanish) Series.
Prod-EBEC Dist-EBEC

Problems Of Conservation - Soil X 14 MIN
16MM FILM, 3/4 OR 1/2 IN VIDEO J-H
Discusses the nature of soil, what it is and how it was formed. Illustrates the damaging effects of water and wind erosion when the ground cover of vegetation is stripped away and the loss of nutrients in the soil. Describes the origin of the U S Soil Conservation Service which was established by Congress to help combat these problems. Shows on-the-spot examples of its technical assistance of projects that range from tour plowing to land-use planning.
From The Environmental Studies Series.
Prod-EBEC Dist-EBEC 1969

Problems Of Conservation - Water X 16 MIN
16MM FILM, 3/4 OR 1/2 IN VIDEO J-H
Emphasizes the importance of conserving water for use in areas with little rainfall. Discusses problems of water pollution in lakes, rivers and bays and suggests solutions. Demonstrates how drinking water can be obtained from the ocean.
From The Environmental Studies Series.
Prod-EBEC Dist-EBEC 1969

Problems Of Conservation - Water (Spanish) C 16 MIN
16MM FILM, 3/4 OR 1/2 IN VIDEO J-H
Emphasizes the importance of conserving water for use in areas with little rainfall. Discusses problems of water pollution in lakes, rivers and bays and suggests solutions. Demonstrates how drinking water can be obtained from the ocean.
Prod-EBEC Dist-EBEC 1969

Problems Of Conservation - Wildlife C 13 MIN
16MM FILM, 3/4 OR 1/2 IN VIDEO J A
Establishes the importance of every species to the biosphere in which we all live. Points out the crucial need to manage our entire ecosystem. Describes the natural process of decline and extinction among species. Identifies endangered species of wildlife. Examines current efforts in ecology to conserve wildlife.
From The Environmental Studies Series.
Prod-EBEC Dist-EBEC 1970

Problems Of Conservation - Wildlife (Spanish) C 13 MIN
16MM FILM, 3/4 OR 1/2 IN VIDEO J-H
Identifies endangered species, examines efforts to conserve wildlife and emphasizes the importance of every species to the biosphere.
From The Environmental Studies (Spanish) Series.
Prod-EBEC Dist-EBEC

Problems Of Emerging Nations C 11 MIN
16MM FILM OPTICAL SOUND I-C A
Explores social and economic problems of the emerging African nations, such as communication, education, national unity, cultural conflict and poverty.
Prod-CBF Dist-AVED 1962

Problems Of Flight - Control C 20 MIN
2 INCH VIDEOTAPE I
See series title for descriptive statement.
From The Exploring With Science, Unit VI - Flight Series.
Prod-MPATI Dist-GPITVL

Problems Of Scarcity And Choice C 45 MIN
3/4 OR 1/2 INCH VIDEO CASSETTE
Deals with the economic problems of scarcity and choice.
From The Economic Perspectives Series.
Prod-MDCPB Dist-MDCPB

Problems Of The Allocation Of Scarce Life-Saving Therapy C 59 MIN
3/4 INCH VIDEO CASSETTE
Discusses who should have access to scarce life-saving therapies. Covers the pros and cons of various solutions.

From The Ethics And Medicine Series.
Prod-OHC Dist-HRC

Problems Of The G-Machine C 50 MIN
3/4 OR 1/2 INCH VIDEO CASSETTE
Gives review of G-machine algorithms in computer languages.
From The Computer Languages - Pt 1 Series.
Prod-MIOT Dist-MIOT

Problems Of The Middle East C 22 MIN
3/4 INCH VIDEO CASSETTE J-C A
Depicts the history and culture of the Middle East area from antiquity to the present, explaining the basic forces molding its fragile destiny. Provides essential concepts of principal problems - minorities, Arab unity, agriculture, industrialization, Westernization and education.
Prod-ATLAP Dist-ATLAP 1967

Problems Of The Middle East (2nd Ed) C 21 MIN
16MM FILM OPTICAL SOUND J-H
Depicts the history and culture of the Middle East area from antiquity to the present resurgence of nationalism and unrest. Examines four main problems--the role of minorities and the state of Israel, the introduction of modern agricultural methods that are gradually changing relationships between peasants and feudal landlords, the increasing industrialization which means westernization and education's slow progress toward literacy.
LC NO. 77-704660
Prod-ATLAP Dist-ATLAP 1967

Problems Of The Therapeutic Symbiosis-Helplessness, Self-Doubt And Feelings Of... C 16 MIN
3/4 OR 1/2 INCH VIDEO CASSETTE
Points out that borderline patients provoked by the calmness of the therapist are driven to knock him off his omnipotent pedestal that can lead the therapist to feel irrelevant. Presents the implications of therapeutic symbiosis.
From The Treatment Of The Borderline Patient Series.
Prod-HEMUL Dist-HEMUL

Problems Of The Twenties, The B 30 MIN
16MM FILM OPTICAL SOUND H-C A
Dr St Clair Drake discusses the diverse occurrences that were eventually to forge the fabric of Afro-American cultural, economic, social and political direction. He describes especially the conditions which existed in New Orleans, Birmingham, Atlanta, Durham, Chicago, New York City and Detroit. He analyzes Booker T Washington's philosophy and the impact of the 1929 stock market crash.
From The Black History, Section 12 - World War I And The Post War Series.
LC NO. 70-704077
Prod-WCBSTV Dist-HRAW 1969

Problems Of The Young Married B 30 MIN
16MM FILM OPTICAL SOUND J-H T R
Tells a story to point out the dangers of over emphasis on material things during the first years of marriage.
Prod-FAMF Dist-FAMF

Problems Of Urbanization, The C 20 MIN
3/4 INCH VIDEO CASSETTE H-C
See series title for descriptive statement.
From The Geography For The '70's Series.
Prod-KLRNTV Dist-GPITVL

Problems Of World Order--A Series
J-H
Prod-VISNEW Dist-AGAPR 1972

Communication Satellites 10 MIN
Hijacking 10 MIN
Our Cultural Heritage 10 MIN
World Health 10 MIN

Problems That Inhibit Or Delay Learning C 30 MIN
2 INCH VIDEOTAPE T
Focuses on cultural, instructional and neurological factors which may inhibit or delay success in learning to read.
From The Child Reads Series.
Prod-WENHTV Dist-GPITVL

Problems To Solve C 20 MIN
3/4 INCH VIDEO CASSETTE I
Discusses some of the problems confronting large cities in America. Focuses on inadequate housing, unemployment, pollution and transportation. Proposes a number of solutions to each problem.
From The Exploring Our Nation Series.
Prod-KRMATV Dist-GPITVL 1975

Problems, Crises And Opportunities C 13 MIN
3/4 OR 1/2 INCH VIDEO CASSETTE A
Shows how problems can be solved in a business environment by defining them, breaking them down and looking beyond the first and most obvious adequate answer.
From The Thinking In Action Series. Module 4
Prod-BBCTV Dist-FI 1983

Problems, Problems, Problems C 30 MIN
16MM FILM, 3/4 OR 1/2 IN VIDEO I-H
Discusses how the computer solves problems, using information and following certain rules, and whether or not computers can make mistakes.
From The Mr Microchip Series.
Prod-JOU Dist-JOU

Procainamide In The Management Of Acute Ventricular Arrhythmias - Pharmacodynamic... C 30 MIN
16MM FILM OPTICAL SOUND PRO
Studies ventricular arrhythmias that occur in almost 90 percent of the patients who survive myocardial infarction long enough to reach a hospital. Examines the effectiveness of Procainamide as a highly useful and versatile agent in the management of these ventricular arrhythmias.
Prod-SQUIBB Dist-SQUIBB

Procedure For Permanent Waving C
3/4 OR 1/2 INCH VIDEO CASSETTE
Covers the entire permanent wave procedure, from the client consultation to after-care advice. Details wrapping techniques, including angle, end papers, control and place- ment. Outlines processing and neutralizing. Gives specifics of test curling. Shows all client protection measures and illustrates all working sequences.
Prod-MPCEDP Dist-MPCEDP 1984

Procedure Of Choice In Duodenal Ulcer Problems C 23 MIN
16MM FILM OPTICAL SOUND PRO
Explains that time has clarified the relative advantages and disadvantages of the newer procedures for duodenal ulcer. Discusses the physiological basis of ulcer surgery and the choice of procedure indicated in specific situations.
Prod-ACYDGD Dist-ACY 1960

Procedures C
3/4 OR 1/2 INCH VIDEO CASSETTE
Introduces modular programming concept, global vs local variables, passing parameters, value vs variable parameters, and comments.
From The PASCAL - A Modern Programming Language Series.
Prod-EDUACT Dist-EDUACT

Procedures C 30 MIN
3/4 OR 1/2 INCH VIDEO CASSETTE H-C A
Introduces the generalized Pascal subprogram, the PROCEDURE. Discusses actual arguments and formal para- meters, and variables. Provides examples. Concludes with discussion of Pascal block structure and scope of variables.
From The Pascal, Pt 1 - Beginning Pascal Series.
LC NO. 81-706049
Prod-COLOSU Dist-COLOSU 1980

Procedures Common To Most Pyeloplasties, Pt 1 C 15 MIN
16MM FILM OPTICAL SOUND
Illustrates the steps required in a pyeloplasty operation including patient positioning and draping, incision and kidney exposure, evaluation of obstruction, the importance of ureteral length, pyelotomy placement and division of the ureter.
From The Surgical Correction Of Hydronephrosis, Pt 3 - Procedures Common To Most Pyeloplasties Series.
LC NO. 75-702266
Prod-EATONL Dist-EATONL 1972

Procedures Common To Most Pyeloplasties, Pt 2 C 15 MIN
16MM FILM OPTICAL SOUND
Discusses the technique of ureteral calibration and its value in splint selection and placement.
From The Surgical Correction Of Hydronephrosis, Pt 3 - Procedures Common To Most Pyeloplasties Series.
LC NO. 75-702267
Prod-EATONL Dist-EATONL 1972

Procedures Common To Most Pyeloplasties, Pt 3 C 15 MIN
16MM FILM OPTICAL SOUND
Illustrates the steps required in a pyeloplasty operation including nephrostomy technique, ureteral splint placement, surgical pelvic reduction, nephropexy, drain placement, wound closure and the tube fixation.
From The Surgical Correction Of Hydronephrosis, Pt 3 - Procedures Common To Most Pyeloplasties Series.
LC NO. 75-702268
Prod-EATONL Dist-EATONL 1972

Procedures For Entering And Leaving The Isolation Unit C 13 MIN
16MM FILM - 3/4 IN VIDEO IND
Illustrates the care and procedures entailed in entering and leaving the isolation unit.
From The Housekeeping Personnel Series.
Prod-COPI Dist-COPI 1970

Procedures For Mixing Dental Cements C 13 MIN
3/4 OR 1/2 INCH VIDEO CASSETTE
Shows methods for mixing cements for use as temporary cements, permanent cements and base material and demonstrates using the chemical preparations zinc phosphate, polycarboxylate, zinc oxide eugenol and calcium hydroxide (Dycal). Manual included.
Prod-UWASH Dist-UWASH

Procedures For Monitoring The Preterm Infant (2nd Ed) C 15 MIN
3/4 OR 1/2 INCH VIDEO CASSETTE PRO
Details principles and techniques of monitoring and interpreting temperature, heart rate, respiratory rate, blood pressure, skin color, oxygenation, and activity level and urine output in the preterm infant.
Prod-UMICHM Dist-UMICHM 1983

Procedures For Rat Muscle Experiments C 15 MIN
3/4 OR 1/2 INCH VIDEO CASSETTE PRO
Shows how to perform a rat muscle experiment, together with the set-up, calibration, and operation of a polygraph.
Prod-HSCIC Dist-HSCIC 1981

Procedures For Using Shop Equipment And Hand- Tools For Electric Arc Welding C 15 MIN
3/4 OR 1/2 INCH VIDEO CASSETTE
See series title for descriptive statement.
From The Welding II - Basic Shielded Metal Arc Welding series.
Prod-CAMB Dist-CAMB

Procelain C 28 MIN
2 INCH VIDEOTAPE
Features Mrs Peterson describing certain ceramic processes for her classroom at the University of Southern California. Demonstrates how to work with porcelain.
From The Wheels, Kilns And Clay Series.
Prod-USC Dist-PUBTEL

Procelain Jacket Crown, Pt I - The Matrix C 9 MIN
3/4 OR 1/2 INCH VIDEO CASSETTE
Depicts the various laboratory steps involved in the fabrication of a porcelain jacket crown.
Prod-VADTC Dist-AMDA 1977

Process Analysis C
3/4 OR 1/2 INCH VIDEO CASSETTE
Shows how to uncover hidden costs, delays and shortages using process analysis.
From The Implementing Quality Circles Series.
Prod-BNA Dist-BNA

Process And Analysis C
3/4 OR 1/2 INCH VIDEO CASSETTE C
Shows the second of four lessons on how to write a practical paper using the process and analysis pattern. Explores the uses of the process/analysis pattern for writing outside of the classroom.
From The Write Course - An Introduction To College Composition Series.
Prod-DALCCD Dist-DALCCD

Process And Analysis C 30 MIN
3/4 OR 1/2 INCH VIDEO CASSETTE C A
Discusses uses of the process/analysis pattern for writing outside of the classroom.
From The Write Course - An Introduction To College Composition Series.
Prod-FI Dist-FI 1984

Process And Proof--A Series
I
Studies the solution of scientific problems through legitimate investigative processes and the proofs which lead to and culminate in those solutions. (Broadcast quality)
Prod-MCETV Dist-GPITVL Prodn-WVIZTV

Air Movement 20 MIN
Artificial Satellites I 20 MIN
Artificial Satellites II 20 MIN
Atoms And Molecules I 20 MIN
Atoms And Molecules II 20 MIN
Characteristics Of Magnetism 20 MIN
Conservation I 20 MIN
Conservation II 20 MIN
Conservation III 20 MIN
Conservation IV 20 MIN
Conservation V 20 MIN
Disposers, The 20 MIN
Earth And Its Parts, The 20 MIN
Electric Motors 20 MIN
Food Web, The 20 MIN
Forces In Space 20 MIN
Generating Electricity Chemically 20 MIN
Generating Electricity Mechanically 20 MIN
Greenhouse Effect, The 20 MIN
Inertia 20 MIN
Luminescence And Incandescence 20 MIN
Nature Of Light, The 20 MIN
Refraction 20 MIN
Rocket Propulsion 20 MIN
Solar Spectrum, The 20 MIN
Symbiosis - Mutualism, Parasitism, 20 MIN
Symbiosis - Mutualism, Parasitism, 20 MIN
Terrestrial Magnetism 20 MIN
Transparency And Translucency 20 MIN
Vital Gases 20 MIN
Weather And Climate 20 MIN
Weather Measurements 20 MIN

Process Control C 20 MIN
3/4 OR 1/2 INCH VIDEO CASSETTE IND
Introduces the concepts of X, R and P control charts. Notes how these charts are most informative as to manufacturing processes, and emphasizes chart interpretation.
From The Statistics For Technicians Series.
Prod-COLOSU Dist-COLOSU

Process Control C 30 MIN
3/4 OR 1/2 INCH VIDEO CASSETTE IND
Concludes UNIX lecture series with following commands - ps, kill, sleep, wait, and at.
From The UNIX Series.
Prod-COLOSU Dist-COLOSU

Process In Music - Tonality, Rhythm, Space B 45 MIN
2 INCH VIDEOTAPE C
See series title for descriptive statement.
From The General Humanities Series. Unit 3 - The Auditory Arts
Prod-CHITVC Dist-GPITVL Prodn-WTTWTV

Process Library Function C
3/4 OR 1/2 INCH VIDEO CASSETTE
Discusses the concept and use of the standard library functions in 'C' language programs and describes the relationship of standard library functions to actual libraries.
From The 'C' Language Programming Series.
Prod-COMTEG Dist-COMTEG

Process Of Becoming, The B 30 MIN
2 INCH VIDEOTAPE PRO
Helps nursing students understand how the process of becoming can help their abilities in treating patients.
From The Mental Health Concepts For Nursing, Unit 1 - Self-Understanding Series.

LC NO. 73-702635
Prod-GPITVL Dist-GPITVL 1971

Process Of Catherization With A Foley Catheter C 25 MIN
3/4 OR 1/2 INCH VIDEO CASSETTE
Presents the indications for catherization of the urinary bladder using a Foley catheter and shows the equipment used in the process. Demonstrates techniques used for male and female patients.
Prod-WSUN Dist-AJN

Process Of Catheterization With A Foley Catheter B 28 MIN
16MM FILM OPTICAL SOUND PRO
Demonstrates the process of catheterization with a Foley catheter on a female and a male patient.
From The Directions For Education In Nursing Via Technology Series. Lesson 108
LC NO. 74-701887
Prod-DENT Dist-WSU 1974

Process Of Communication, The B 46 MIN
16MM FILM - 3/4 IN VIDEO
Depicts a theoretical model of the communication process and presents illustrations of communication from industry training models, military models, school administrators' training, teacher training and computer-based systems.
From The Communication Theory And The New Educational Media Series.
LC NO. 79-706671
Prod-OSUPD Dist-USNAC 1979

Process Of Communication, The (Spanish) B 46 MIN
16MM FILM OPTICAL SOUND
Explores the process of communication beginning with an animated theoretical model, followed by sequences that progressively elaborate and illuminate the theory through illustrations drawn from communications networks in military, industrial, research and teaching setting.
From The Communication Theory And The New Educational Media Series.
LC NO. 74-705427
Prod-USOE Dist-USNAC 1966

Process Of Engineering Production C 20 MIN
3/4 OR 1/2 INCH VIDEO CASSETTE H-C A
See series title for descriptive statement.
From The Engineering Crafts Series.
Prod-BBCTV Dist-FI 1981

Process Of Growth (Section A), The C 48 MIN
3/4 OR 1/2 INCH VIDEO CASSETTE
See series title for descriptive statement.
From The Management By Responsibility Series.
Prod-TRAINS Dist-DELTAK

Process Of Growth (Section B), The C 28 MIN
3/4 OR 1/2 INCH VIDEO CASSETTE
See series title for descriptive statement.
From The Management By Responsibility Series.
Prod-TRAINS Dist-DELTAK

Process Of Newspaper Production, The C 13 MIN
16MM FILM OPTICAL SOUND
Gives a brief history of printing and explains the steps in publishing a newspaper, from writing the story to publishing the paper.
LC NO. 80-701374
Prod-COLOSU Dist-COLOSU 1980

Process Of Taking Temperature, Pulse And Respiration B 27 MIN
16MM FILM OPTICAL SOUND PRO
Demonstrates methods of taking oral, axillary and rectal temperatures, as well as apical rate and apical-radial pulse. Discusses the parts, types and operational principles of equipment.
From The Directions For Education In Nursing Via Technology Series. Lesson 9
LC NO. 74-701783
Prod-DENT Dist-WSU 1974

Process Of Television News, The C 15 MIN
16MM FILM OPTICAL SOUND
Reveals the people and forces at work behind a television news show. Examines the role of anchormen, reporters, producers, editors and minicams.
Prod-COLOSU Dist-COLOSU 1977

Process-Capability Analysis C 30 MIN
3/4 OR 1/2 INCH VIDEO CASSETTE
Discusses how Q C affects process capability analysis. Describes the steps in performing a process-capability analysis.
From The Quality Control Series.
Prod-MIOT Dist-MIOT

Process-Centered Composition—A Series
16MM FILM, 3/4 OR 1/2 IN VIDEO T
Presents methods for teaching composition.
Prod-IU Dist-IU 1977

Nine-Step Writing Process In Class	37 MIN
Organizing Your Writing Course	31 MIN
Poet's Journal	25 MIN
Professional Talks About Interviewing, A	25 MIN
Report, Analyze, Evaluate	58 MIN
Student As Interviewer, The	53 MIN
Students As Their Own Editors	40 MIN
Using The Journal	94 MIN

Processes C 29 MIN
3/4 OR 1/2 INCH VIDEO CASSETTE
Presents a group discussion concerning genital sexuality versus love and emotion. Features Milton Diamond, Ph D, a biologist at the University of Hawaii, along with several college students and a married, middle-aged couple for conversation about the phases of sexual response, the use of artificial devices to stimulate sexual interaction and personal interpretations of the meaning of orgasm.
From The Human Sexuality Series.
Prod-KHETTV Dist-PBS

Processing C 30 MIN
3/4 OR 1/2 INCH VIDEO CASSETTE T
Shows how processing is done in an educational setting.
From The Interaction - Human Concerns In The Schools Series.
Prod-MDDE Dist-MDCPB

Processing Files B
16MM FILM OPTICAL SOUND
Explores the nature of computer files. Illustrates how files can be organized on tape and discs and shows a simple model of sequential updating.
Prod-OPENU Dist-OPENU

Processing States And Exception C 30 MIN
3/4 OR 1/2 INCH VIDEO CASSETTE IND
Describes three system control systems in the 68000 HALT, RESET, and bus error (BERR). Discusses normal, halted and exception processing states including privileged states and interrupts.
From The MC68000 Microprocessor Series.
Prod-COLOSU Dist-COLOSU

Procession - Contemporary Directions In American Dance B 19 MIN
16MM FILM, 3/4 OR 1/2 IN VIDEO J-C
Presents Ann Halpern and the Dancers Workshop Company of San Francisco performing selections from Procession, a dance from their experimental repertoire. Examines the group's theory of the dance and 'total theater' as the dancers adapt to their constantly changing environment, collaborating with all of its elements and accompanied by electronic sound.
Prod-UCEMC Dist-UCEMC 1967

Processual Video B 11 MIN
3/4 OR 1/2 INCH VIDEO CASSETTE
See series title for descriptive statement.
From The Gary Hill, Part 4 Series.
Prod-EAI Dist-EAI

Proclaim Christ Lord C 15 MIN
3/4 OR 1/2 INCH VIDEO CASSETTE A
Presents a documentary shot on location at the 1979 General Assembly of the Christian Church (Disciples of Christ). Uses action shot, interviews and comments on the delegates to show the expectations of those who attended and how the expectations were fulfilled by the assembly.
Prod-DCCMS Dist-ECUFLM 1979

Proctosigmoidoscopy C 9 MIN
3/4 OR 1/2 INCH VIDEO CASSETTE PRO
See series title for descriptive statement.
From The Medical Skills Films Series.
Prod-WFP Dist-WFP

Proctosigmoidoscopy - A Part Of The Physical Examination C 22 MIN
16MM FILM OPTICAL SOUND PRO
Presents a convincing case for extensive use of proctosigmoidoscopy to detect asymptomatic cancer of the colon and rectum. Demonstrates technical points and safeguards of the examination using endoscopic photography.
Prod-AMCS Dist-AMCS 1963

Proctosigmoidoscopy - A Part Of The Routine Physical Examination C 23 MIN
3/4 OR 1/2 INCH VIDEO CASSETTE PRO
Attempts to persuade physicians in general practice to use the proctosigmoidoscope as part of the routine physical examination. Shows endoscopic views of areas of the colon as the physician sees them.
Prod-WFP Dist-WFP

Procurement Source Selection C 20 MIN
16MM FILM OPTICAL SOUND
Explains how the Defense Department and the Army select the source of a major procurement.
LC NO. 74-705428
Prod-USA Dist-USNAC 1967

Prodigal Father, The X 27 MIN
16MM FILM, 3/4 OR 1/2 IN VIDEO H-C A
Tells how a son's childhood hatred of his father is transformed when he encounters his father years later. Shows that forgiveness is a Christian mandate.
From The Insight Series.
Prod-PAULST Dist-PAULST

Prodigal Son C 15 MIN
16MM FILM OPTICAL SOUND P-J
Presents the Parable of the Prodigal Son, dramatized with the use of puppets.
Prod-YALEDV Dist-YALEDV

Producers And Consumers C 15 MIN
3/4 OR 1/2 INCH VIDEO CASSETTE P
Compares the roles of producers and consumers, defines income, and discusses the value of productive work.
From The Common Cents Series.
Prod-KETCTV Dist-AITECH 1977

Producers And Consumers C 20 MIN
3/4 INCH VIDEO CASSETTE T
Illustrates how children can come to understand the interactions that exist among the various organisms making up a community. Defines producers, consumers and decomposers.
From The Science In The Elementary School - Life Science Series.
Prod-UWKY Dist-GPITVL 1980

Producing A Videotape C 30 MIN
3/4 OR 1/2 INCH VIDEO CASSETTE
Follows a production from conceptualization through post-production. Explains story treatments, scripts, storyboards, budgets, production boards, shooting schedules and more.
From The Video - A Practical Guide...and More Series.
Prod-VIPUB Dist-VIPUB

Producing An Ad C 23 MIN
16MM FILM, 3/4 OR 1/2 IN VIDEO
Demonstrates the production of an advertisement as it concerns the commercial artist. Shows the five layout steps followed in producing an ad, using the creation of a school poster as an example.
From The Introduction To Commercial Art Series.
Prod-SF Dist-SF Prodn-ACORN 1979

Producing Better Learning—A Series

Provides a short course in fundamental teaching theory and practice to help instructors make 'better learning' happen in their classrooms.
Prod-RESEM Dist-RESEM

Good Techniques For Teaching	007 MIN
Helping Learning Happen	006 MIN
Let The Student Come First	007 MIN

Producing Dance Documentaries C 30 MIN
3/4 OR 1/2 INCH VIDEO CASSETTE
See series title for descriptive statement.
From The Glances At The Past Series.
Prod-ARCVID Dist-ARCVID

Producing Dance Specials For The Mass Market C 30 MIN
3/4 OR 1/2 INCH VIDEO CASSETTE
See series title for descriptive statement.
From The Dance On Television - Lorber Series.
Prod-ARCVID Dist-ARCVID

Producing Oil C 26 MIN
16MM FILM, 3/4 OR 1/2 IN VIDEO IND
Shows in a nontechnical manner how oil and gas are formed, produced and processed for delivery from the well to the pipeline.
Prod-UTEXPE Dist-UTEXPE 1974

Producing The Product C 29 MIN
3/4 OR 1/2 INCH VIDEO CASSETTE
See series title for descriptive statement.
From The Business File Series.
Prod-PBS Dist-PBS

Product And Competitive Knowledge C 9 MIN
3/4 OR 1/2 INCH VIDEO CASSETTE
See series title for descriptive statement.
From The Telemarketing For Better Business Results Series.
Prod-COMTEL Dist-DELTAK

Product Costs - What's In Them C 14 MIN
16MM FILM, 3/4 OR 1/2 IN VIDEO H-C A
Shows some of the costs that go into the final price of a product. Uses the situation of a shopper at his local grocery store to demonstrate why the same or similar products can have widely varying prices.
Prod-GREENF Dist-PHENIX 1979

Product Development C 30 MIN
3/4 OR 1/2 INCH VIDEO CASSETTE
Covers primary sources for new product concepts, product development sequences, ways that product introductions affect existing product lines and role of corporate management in product development.
From The Marketing Perspectives Series.
Prod-MATC Dist-WFVTAE

Product Development C 58 MIN
3/4 OR 1/2 INCH VIDEO CASSETTE
Lectures on information sources, the project team and management guidelines in product development.
From The Management Of Microprocessor Technology Series.
Prod-MIOT Dist-MIOT

Product Liability C 26 MIN
3/4 OR 1/2 INCH VIDEO CASSETTE
Describes the current status of product liability in the U S and the impacts on quality control specifications and procedures.
From The Quality Control Series.
Prod-MIOT Dist-MIOT

Product Liability - Loss Prevention And Control—A Series
16MM FILM - 3/4 IN VIDEO
Discusses product liability and shows how to institute an action plan.
Prod-KACC Dist-BNA

Product Liability - Loss Prevention And
Product Liability - Loss Prevention And

Product Liability - Loss Prevention And Control, Pt 1 C
16MM FILM - 3/4 IN VIDEO
Provides a nontechnical explanation of the law of product liability and how it evolved. Explains the Deep Pocket theory and presents court decisions concerning product liability.
From The Product Liability - Loss Prevention And Control Series.
Prod-KACC Dist-BNA

Product Liability - Loss Prevention And Control, Pt 2 C
16MM FILM - 3/4 IN VIDEO

Recommends the establishment of a company policy on product liability and tells who should be involved in its implementation.
From The Product Liability - Loss Prevention And Control Series.
Prod-KACC Dist-BNA

Product Liability And The Reasonably Safe Product C 55 MIN
3/4 OR 1/2 INCH VIDEO CASSETTE
Stresses that designing for safety from the start avoids product liability suits and rising insurance rates. Explains the definitions of defects, warnings, and disclaimers in today's legal system.
Prod-SME Dist-SME

Product Management C 30 MIN
3/4 OR 1/2 INCH VIDEO CASSETTE
Shows five stages of the product lifecycle. Compares the growth curve to the profit-loss curve in the product lifecycle. Shows ways to expand the product line and to extend the product's lifecycle.
From The Marketing Perspectives Series.
Prod-MATC Dist-WFVTAE

Product Spaces And Statistically Independent Experiments B 17 MIN
3/4 OR 1/2 INCH VIDEO CASSETTE PRO
Extends the concept of statistical independence.
From The Probability And Random Processes - Elementary Probability Theory Series.
Prod-MIOT Dist-MIOT

Product, The C 45 MIN
3/4 OR 1/2 INCH VIDEO CASSETTE IND
Discusses finding solutions to market needs with case history, sources of ideas with three case histories, brainstorming, two crucial questions of can it be made and can it be sold at a profit, evaluation issues and case history, and checklists uses and abuses with case history.
From The New Product Development Series.
Prod-AMCEE Dist-AMCEE

Production C 15 MIN
3/4 OR 1/2 INCH VIDEO CASSETTE P
Uses the format of a television program to explain the basic economic principle of production. Demonstrates that both goods and services are produced and that their production is carried out by people for the most part.
From The Pennywise Series. No. 5
LC NO. 82-706007
Prod-MAETEL Dist-GPITVL 1980

Production C 30 MIN
3/4 INCH VIDEO CASSETTE
See series title for descriptive statement.
From The It's Everybody's Business Series. Unit 5, Operating A Business
Prod-DALCCD Dist-DALCCD

Production And General Control C 30 MIN
3/4 OR 1/2 INCH VIDEO CASSETTE C A
Focuses on control devices, methods and procedures that are used to collect and distribute information to various management information systems. Discusses new trends in control and management information systems today.
From The Business Of Management Series. Lesson 20
Prod-SCCON Dist-SCCON

Production And Inventory Control C 15 MIN
16MM FILM OPTICAL SOUND A
Introduces the American Production And Inventory Control Society, emphasizing its history, why it developed and what it does.
LC NO. 80-701484
Prod-APICS Dist-MTP Prodn-HMF 1979

Production And Printing C 30 MIN
3/4 INCH VIDEO CASSETTE
Explains early processes such as wood blocks and copper plates and the more recent use of offset lithography in map making.
From The Maps - Horizons To Knowledge Series.
Prod-UMITV Dist-UMITV 1980

Production Engineering—A Series
C A
Includes planning, analysis and control of engineering design, processes, decision models, planning models and linear programming. Contains 43 one-hour videotape lectures.
Prod-UIDEEO Dist-UIDEEO

Production Of Poliomyelitis Vaccine C 12 MIN
16MM FILM, 3/4 OR 1/2 IN VIDEO H-C
Shows the production of poliomyelitis vaccine from the receipt of the monkeys to the final packaging of the vaccine after passing 43 separate tests for safety, potency and sterility.
From The Microbiology Teaching Series.
Prod-UCEMC Dist-UCEMC 1961

Production Process C 15 MIN
3/4 OR 1/2 INCH VIDEO CASSETTE P
Introduces the concept of risk and profit, explains assembly line production, looks at some responsibilities of producers, and reinforces the theme of economic interdependence.
From The Common Cents Series.
Prod-KETCTV Dist-AITECH 1977

Production-Minded Management—A Series

Views efficient production as an essential goal of all management functions. Examines productivity in its relation to inflation. Explores ways of improving production and changing it.
Prod-RESEM Dist-RESEM

Attitudes Toward Production 014 MIN
How To Improve Production 013 MIN
Inflation And Productivity 012 MIN
What Difference Does It Make? 013 MIN

Productive Discipline—A Series

Teaches supervisors a practical and realistic approach to learning the fine art of discipline.
Prod-RESEM Dist-RESEM

How To Do Productive Discipline 010 MIN
Why Discipline? 010 MIN
Why Employees Don't Perform 012 MIN

Productivity C 20 MIN
16MM FILM OPTICAL SOUND
See series title for descriptive statement.
Prod-CINE Dist-CINE

Productivity C
3/4 OR 1/2 INCH VIDEO CASSETTE
Satirizes well-known rules for improving employee productivity.
Prod-BBB Dist-MEETS Prodn-CFDC

Productivity C 30 MIN
3/4 OR 1/2 INCH VIDEO CASSETTE T
Presents Dr Willard M Kniep of Arizona State University instructing teachers in the strategies and skills of teaching children economics and consumer education concepts. Focuses on the topic of productivity by explaining it and then demonstrating specific approaches that teachers can use in their classrooms.
From The Economics Exchange Series. Program 5
LC NO. 82-706417
Prod-KAETTV Dist-GPITVL 1981

Productivity - An American Challenge C 18 MIN
16MM FILM, 3/4 OR 1/2 IN VIDEO C A
Presents Dr Frank Wagner analyzing the Hawthorne studies film and commenting on America's failure in recent years to match the productivity levels of other nations.
LC NO. 84-706179
Prod-SALENG Dist-SALENG 1984

Productivity - Can We Get More For Less C 30 MIN
3/4 OR 1/2 INCH VIDEO CASSETTE C
See series title for descriptive statement.
From The Economics USA Series.
Prod-WEFA Dist-ANNCPB

Productivity - It's A Personal Matter C 19 MIN
16MM FILM, 3/4 OR 1/2 IN VIDEO IND
Explores the idea of work, what it means to people, how its meaning has changed for many and how that change has hurt some people. Argues that people need to rediscover the value of work for their own individual benefit as well as that of their company and their country.
LC NO. 84-7067178
Prod-CCS Dist-SALENG 1983

Productivity - Key To America's Economic Growth X 28 MIN
16MM FILM OPTICAL SOUND H
Provides an introduction to the American economic system. Explains the relationship between productivity and wages and between productivity and the standard of living. Cites causes of economic growth.
LC NO. FIA65-567
Prod-SLOAN Dist-SUTHLA 1965

Productivity - Key To Progress B 20 MIN
16MM FILM OPTICAL SOUND H A
Discusses the factors of productivity as related to economic growth. Illustrates how savings and investments create capital and how increasingly efficient tools add to increased productivity.
From The Exploring Basic Economics Series.
LC NO. FI67-368
Prod-RSC Dist-MLA 1964

Productivity / Quality Of Work Life—A Series

Increases the understanding of managers in the ways people succeed or fail, and discusses some of the specific steps that can be taken to increase employees' productivity and quality of work life. Includes a training manual, which contains complete scripts and a bibliography, discussion questions, exercises and activities, handouts, and full details of scheduling, timing, room set-up, opening and closing remarks.
Prod-GOODMI Dist-DELTAK

Getting Them Moving 020 MIN
Human Resources In The 1980s 020 MIN
Moving And The Stuck, The 020 MIN
Organizing For Productivity 020 MIN
Powerlessness Corrupts 020 MIN
Turning On The Power 020 MIN
Twelve Minutes A Day 020 MIN

Productivity And Performance Improvement - Management And...—A Series

Presents three one-hour recording of a live teleconference held September 30, 1982. Helps educators develop strategies and action plans for improving productivity and performance in a health care setting.
Prod-AHOA Dist-AHOA

Productivity And Performance By Alex K C 24 MIN
16MM FILM, 3/4 OR 1/2 IN VIDEO
Presents the story of Alex K, who strives to become a highly motivated human being. Explains that productivity, usually thought of in relation to the workplace, is of little value unless understood and adopted at a personal level.
From The Developing Your Potential Series.
Prod-SCCL Dist-JOU

Productivity And The Self-Fulfilling Prophecy - The Pygmalion Effect C 28 MIN
16MM FILM, 3/4 OR 1/2 IN VIDEO H-C A
Explains how a manager's expectations alone can actually influence a worker's performance.
Prod-CRMP Dist-CRMP 1975

Productivity Breakthroughs - Begin With Results Instead Of Preparation C 28 MIN
3/4 OR 1/2 INCH VIDEO CASSETTE
Explains why managers can't wait for more motivated employees, increasingly cooperative unions, newer equipment or low cost power, but must make dramatic productivity gains with resources available now.
Prod-SME Dist-SME

Productivity Challenge In The Decade Of The 80's C 43 MIN
3/4 OR 1/2 INCH VIDEO CASSETTE
Identifies some of the changes companies can make to dramatically increase productivity. Discusses the part that a sense of a national spirit, unity and pride plays in effectively dealing with lagging productivity.
Prod-SME Dist-SME

Productivity Dilemma, The C 30 MIN
3/4 OR 1/2 INCH VIDEO CASSETTE C A
Features academicians and managers as they discuss the dimensions of productivity and the numerous factors that have contributed to the productivity slowdown in the United States.
From The Business Of Management Series. Lesson 25
Prod-SCCON Dist-SCCON

Productivity In Motion C 14 MIN
16MM FILM OPTICAL SOUND
Documents the importance of the conveyor industry to America's industrialization.
Prod-CEMA Dist-MTP

Productivity Of Japanese Industry C 30 MIN
3/4 OR 1/2 INCH VIDEO CASSETTE A
See series title for descriptive statement.
From The Business Nippon Series.
LC NO. 85-702162
Prod-JAPCTV Dist-EBEC 1984

Products, People And Ideas C 15 MIN
16MM FILM OPTICAL SOUND
Tells the story of the National Housewares Manufacturers Association through its annual exposition. Stresses marketing and merchandising in the housewares industry.
Prod-NATHMA Dist-MTP 1982

Profession Of Accounting Is..., The C 25 MIN
3/4 INCH VIDEO CASSETTE
Describes the challenges and rewards of the accounting profession. Discusses the skills and education needed. Narrated by Ed Herlihy.
Prod-AICPA Dist-MTP

Profession Of Arms, The C 60 MIN
16MM FILM, 3/4 OR 1/2 IN VIDEO C A
Deals with the professional soldier, career officers in every country who devote their lives to maintaining military organizations. Features officers from the Israeli, American, Soviet and Canadian forces describing battles they have fought and the special characteristics needed to pursue their career, discussing how they reconcile themselves to their mandate to kill and the knowledge that they may be killed.
From The War Series.
Prod-NFBC Dist-FI

Professional Attitudes C 15 MIN
3/4 OR 1/2 INCH VIDEO CASSETTE
Presents the story of a man with a hangover who comes to work on heavy equipment, doing about everything wrong, no hard-hat, improper equipment sense and finally the tragic end.
From The Safety For Oilfield Contractors Series.
Prod-FLMWST Dist-FLMWST

Professional Counselor In School Settings, The C 33 MIN
3/4 OR 1/2 INCH VIDEO CASSETTE A
Discusses through panel guests the problems and future challenges that school counselors are facing.
Prod-AACD Dist-AACD 1984

Professional Development In The Fire Service C
3/4 OR 1/2 INCH VIDEO CASSETTE
See series title for descriptive statement.
From The Fire Away Series.
Prod-NFPA Dist-NFPA

Professional Drug Films—A Series

Prod-NIMH Dist-USNAC 1980

Bunny 016 MIN
Confrontation - A Nurse And A Drug Addict 010 MIN
Counseling - A Critical Incident 008 MIN
Drug Dialogue - Involvement 010 MIN
Drug Dialogue - Orientation 016 MIN
Rick, File X-258375 011 MIN
Treatment - New Teams 010 MIN

Professional Education Program Of The American Cancer Society, The C 22 MIN
16MM FILM OPTICAL SOUND
Shows the roles of volunteers from health professions and American Cancer Society staff members in planning and carrying out cancer education by and for professionals. Shows this program in action at unit, division and national levels. Examines projects conducted for developing attitudes and clinical techniques to promote the early detection of cancer and its prompt

and adequate treatment. Demonstrates the effective uses of professional publications, films and exhibits and shows how programs are adapted to local community needs.
Prod-AMCS Dist-AMCS 1973

Professional Engineer Review—A Series
PRO
Includes topics covering basic engineering and professional practice to assist graduate engineer or equivalent in reviewing engineering basics. Presented by University of Illinois at Urbana-Champaign and other qualified professional engineers through the Office of Continuing Education and Public Service.
Prod-UILU Dist-AMCEE

Alternating Circuits And Equipment 180 MIN
Chemistry And Chemical Interaction 180 MIN
Communication And Electronics 180 MIN
Dynamics 180 MIN
Economic Alternatives - Engineering Practice 180 MIN
Electrical Circuits And D C Motors 180 MIN
Electrical Power Circuits 180 MIN
Engineering Mathematics 180 MIN
Engineering Measurements And Layout - Materials 180 MIN
Fluids 180 MIN
Heat-Power Generation 180 MIN
Mechanical Design 180 MIN
Municipal Water Resources 180 MIN
Power Transmission - Mechanical 180 MIN
Statics 180 MIN
Strength Of Materials 180 MIN
Structures - Foundations 180 MIN
Thermodynamics 180 MIN

Professional Engineer's Exam Refresher Course—A Series
PRO
Uses classroom format to videotape two fifty-minute lectures weekly for 13 weeks on 26 cassettes. Emphasizes rapid solution of basic problems in mathematics, statics, dynamics, fluid mechanics, strength of materials, electrical theory, thermodynamics and engineering economy. Guides students in reviewing theory and typical problem solving, and includes material in both parts I and II of the exam.
Prod-UMICE Dist-AMCEE

Dynamics 150 MIN
Electrical Theory 150 MIN
Engineering Economy 150 MIN
Final Review 050 MIN
Fluid Mechanics 150 MIN
Introduction 050 MIN
Mathematics 150 MIN
Mechanics Of Materials 150 MIN
Statics 150 MIN
Thermodynamics 150 MIN

Professional Engineering Review—A Series
PRO
Consists of 63 one-hour lectures on videotape cassettes and organized in the four principal engineering disciplines, (CHE) chemical, (CE) civil, (EE) electrical (currently under development), and (ME) mechanical, as well as (EEC) engineering economics. Prepares engineers, by individual discipline or as generalists, to take state examinations to certify as professional engineers.
Prod-NCSU Dist-AMCEE

CE 1 007 MIN
CE 2 007 MIN
CE 3 009 MIN
CHE 1 009 MIN
CHE 2 009 MIN
EEc 1 006 MIN
ME 1 006 MIN
ME 2 007 MIN

Professional Food Preparation And Service Program—A Series
16MM FILM, 3/4 OR 1/2 IN VIDEO J-C A
Prod-NEM Dist-NEM 1972

Braising And Stewing 10 MIN
Broiling 10 MIN
Cafeteria Service 10 MIN
Carving The Rib Roast 10 MIN
Cool Head For Salads, A 10 MIN
Courtesy - Food Service Is People Service 10 MIN
Courtesy - The Inside Story 10 MIN
Deep Fat Frying 10 MIN
Dining Room Safety 10 MIN
Dining Room Sanitation 10 MIN
Fast Sandwich Making 10 MIN
Give Your Eggs A Break 10 MIN
Hamburger Sandwich, The 10 MIN
How Do You Look When It Counts 10 MIN
Kitchen Safety - Preventing Burns 10 MIN
Kitchen Safety - Preventing Cuts And Strains 10 MIN
Kitchen Safety - Preventing Falls 10 MIN
Kitchen Safety - Preventing Fires 10 MIN
Kitchen Safety - Preventing Machine Injuries 10 MIN
Mr Busboy 10 MIN
Mr Dish Machine Operator 10 MIN
New System, The 10 MIN
Presentation Of Food And Beverage 10 MIN
Preventing Waste 10 MIN
Receiving And Storing 10 MIN
Roasting 10 MIN
Rush Hour Service 10 MIN
Sandwich Preparation And Presentation 10 MIN
Sanitation - Rodent And Insect Control 10 MIN
Sanitation - Rules Make Sense 10 MIN
Sanitation - Why All The Fuss 10 MIN
Selling Wine And Liquor 10 MIN
Short Order Cookery 10 MIN
Simmering And Poaching 10 MIN
Table Settings 10 MIN
Taking The Order 10 MIN
Using Standarized Recipes 10 MIN
Vegetable Preparation 10 MIN

Professional Hospitality Program—A Series
16MM FILM, 3/4 OR 1/2 IN VIDEO H-C A
Prod-NEM Dist-NEM 1972

Bellman, The 10 MIN
Front Desk, The 10 MIN
Maid, The - Cleaning The Bathroom 10 MIN
Maid, The - Making Up The Room 10 MIN
Room Service 10 MIN
Telephone Manners 10 MIN

Professional Hotel And Tourism Programs—A Series
16MM FILM, 3/4 OR 1/2 IN VIDEO A
Focuses on methods of providing superior hotel service and obtaining better guest relations.
Prod-NEM Dist-NEM

Bellman, The 010 MIN
Cleaning The Bathroom 009 MIN
Courtesy Is The Answer 017 MIN
Front Desk Courtesy 011 MIN
Hotel Fire Safety 030 MIN
Hotel Security 025 MIN
Making Up The Room 009 MIN
Personal Grooming And Hygiene 011 MIN
Room Service 010 MIN

Professional Image, The C 20 MIN
3/4 OR 1/2 INCH VIDEO CASSETTE A
Shows how to create an effective business wardrobe for both men and women. Based on book The Professional Image by Susan Bixler.
Prod-AMEDIA Dist-AMEDIA

Professional Management Program (Spanish)—A Series

Presents a series of programs for the training and development of supervisors, department heads and managers at all levels.
Prod-NEM Dist-NEM

Delegate - Don't Abdicate (Spanish) 012 MIN
Discipline - A Matter Of Judgement (Spanish) 011 MIN
Eye Of The Supervisor (Spanish) 012 MIN
Flight Plan (Spanish) 014 MIN
Increasing Productivity (Spanish) 014 MIN
Manager And The Law, The (Spanish) 019 MIN
Managerial Control (Spanish) 020 MIN
Peter Hill Puzzle, The (Spanish) 032 MIN
Problem Solving - A Process For Managers 020 MIN
Profile Of A Manager (Spanish) 014 MIN
Strategy For Winning (Spanish) 020 MIN
Supervisor, The - Motivating Through Insight 011 MIN
Time Game, The (Spanish) 014 MIN
Training Memorandum, The (Spanish) 010 MIN

Professional Management Program—A Series
16MM FILM, 3/4 OR 1/2 IN VIDEO J-C A
Prod-NEM Dist-NEM

Delegate - Don't Abdicate 012 MIN
Discipline - A Matter Of Judgment 012 MIN
Eye Of The Supervisor 013 MIN
Fine Art Of Keeping Your Cool 020 MIN
Flight Plan 013 MIN
Increasing Productivity 012 MIN
Manager And The Law, The 019 MIN
Managerial Control 020 MIN
Peter Hill Puzzle, The 031 MIN
Problem Solving - A Process For Managers 020 MIN
Profile Of A Manager 014 MIN
Strategy For Winning 020 MIN
Supervisor - Motivating Through Insight 013 MIN
Time Game, The 014 MIN
Training Memorandum, The 012 MIN

Professional Nature Of Selling, The C
3/4 OR 1/2 INCH VIDEO CASSETTE
Identifies the main elements that must be managed in all selling situations.
From The Strategies For Successful Selling Series. Module 1
Prod-AMA Dist-AMA

Professional Patrol C 14 MIN
3/4 OR 1/2 INCH VIDEO CASSETTE
Stresses the importance of the routine patrol, illustrating proper tactics and procedures. Covers various patrol requirements and decision-making skills.
From The Professional Security Training Series. Module 2
Prod-MTI Dist-MTI

Professional Photography B 29 MIN
16MM FILM, 3/4 OR 1/2 IN VIDEO H-C A
Presents Ansel Adams and Milton Halberstadt discussing photography as a profession. Mr Adams applies his imagination and techniques to industrial, promotional and portrait photography.
From The Photography - The Incisive Art Series.
LC NO. 80-707012
Prod-NET Dist-IU Prodn-KQEDTV 1960

Professional Planning For Pairs C 27 MIN
3/4 INCH VIDEO CASSETTE H-C A
Explores how married couples cope with the difficulties encountered with dual careers. Interviews three couples who discuss such topics as children, part-time employment and problems presented by new job opportunities.
LC NO. 81-707368
Prod-CUETV Dist-CUNIV 1979

Professional Planting C
3/4 OR 1/2 INCH VIDEO CASSETTE
Prod-MSTVIS Dist-MSTVIS

Professional Scientists C 15 MIN
2 INCH VIDEOTAPE J-H
Illustrates some of the specialty-area collegiate studies available for those aspiring to be professional scientists.
From The Work Is For Real Series.
Prod-STETVC Dist-GPITVL

Professional Security Training—A Series
16MM FILM, 3/4 OR 1/2 IN VIDEO
Presents essential background information about the security profession.
Prod-MTI Dist-MTI

Fire 014 MIN
Notes, Reports, And Communications 014 MIN
Plan For Security 012 MIN
Professional Patrol 014 MIN
Public Relations In Security 012 MIN
Security And The Law 014 MIN
Security Story, The 012 MIN

Professional Selling C 20 MIN
16MM FILM OPTICAL SOUND H
Stimulates the thinking of high school students toward possible careers in sales and marketing. Acquaints young people with what men and women in professional selling believe about their jobs and the kind of opportunity available for youth.
From The Career Guidance Series.
Prod-KRMATV Dist-GPITVL

Professional Selling Practices, Series 1—A Series
H-C A
Prod-SAUM Dist-SAUM Prodn-CALPRO 1967

Know Your Facts 9 MIN
Moment Of Decision 11 MIN
One Minute Please 8 MIN
Personalize Your Presentation 9 MIN

Professional Selling Practices, Series 2—A Series
H-C A
Gives examples of productive retail selling practices.
Prod-SAUM Dist-SAUM Prodn-CALPRO 1968

No One Told Me 8 MIN
Test Your Suggestability 8 MIN
They Know What They Want 8 MIN
Think Tall - Sell Up To Quality 8 MIN

Professional Shoplifting C 18 MIN
16MM FILM, 3/4 OR 1/2 IN VIDEO A
Discusses the psychology of the shoplifter. Demonstrates the shopping bag, garment hanger and other concealment methods used by the shoplifter. Alerts to the team techniques used by thieves.
Prod-RTBL Dist-RTBL

Professional Skills For Secretaries—A Series
16MM FILM, 3/4 OR 1/2 IN VIDEO A
Shows how secretaries can improve their performance and, as a result, that of their bosses. Explores the changing roles, skill requirements and career opportunities for the secretary.
LC NO. 81-707648
Prod-TIMLIF Dist-TIMLIF 1981

Coping With Change 030 MIN
Getting The Job Done 030 MIN
We're Counting On You 030 MIN
Working With Others 030 MIN

Professional Talks About Interviewing, A C 25 MIN
3/4 OR 1/2 INCH VIDEO CASSETTE T
Discusses techniques for interviewing, including the structuring of questions and taking notes.
From The Process-Centered Composition Series.
LC NO. 79-706302
Prod-IU Dist-IU 1977

Professional Techniques C
3/4 OR 1/2 INCH VIDEO CASSETTE
Prod-MSTVIS Dist-MSTVIS

Professional Teller, The C
3/4 OR 1/2 INCH VIDEO CASSETTE PRO
Presents lecture by banking expert on The Professional Teller.
Prod-PROEDS Dist-PROEDS

Professional, The C 30 MIN
16MM FILM, 3/4 OR 1/2 IN VIDEO PRO
No descriptive information available.
Prod-DARTNL Dist-DARTNL 1969

Professionals, The C 27 MIN
16MM FILM OPTICAL SOUND
Takes a look at the work of firemen and considers a number of fire prevention tips.
LC NO. 76-701356
Prod-OMSG Dist-OOFM 1975

Professionals, The C 117 MIN
16MM FILM OPTICAL SOUND H-C A
Gives an account of what happens when a band of adventurers is hired to rescue a railroad tycoon's daughter from her kidnapper. Stars Burt Lancaster, Lee Marvin and Robert Ryan.
Prod-CPC Dist-TIMLIF 1966

Professor B 20 MIN
16MM FILM OPTICAL SOUND
Presents a psychology professor at the University of Pennsylvania who declares himself a revolutionary. Shows him in class, at home with his wife and children, and interacting with his students in his office and on campus. Explores the professor's view of what it means to be a revolutionary in today's academic context, his relations with his faculty colleagues and the nature of his choices between normal academic pursuits, and the values of revolutionary behavior as he sees them.
Prod-UPENN Dist-UPENN 1971

Professor Bonner And The Slime Molds C 50 MIN
3/4 OR 1/2 INCH VIDEO CASSETTE H-C A
Introduces slime molds, simple soil-dwelling protozoans with properties of both plants and animals, that aggregate together to form slugs. Shows these slugs metamorphosing into plant-like stalks which split open and discharge thousands of new one-celled slime molds. Explains how the development of these molds may teach us more about the development of the human embryo.
Prod-BBCTV Dist-FI

Professor Ya-Ya's Memoirs C 8 MIN
16MM FILM, 3/4 OR 1/2 IN VIDEO
Takes a sentimental journey in animated fashion with Professor Ya-Ya who, on his birthday, sits down on his favorite easy chair to peruse his family photograph album and recall all his charming and unusual relatives. Based on the cartoons by Gerald Hoffnung.
From The Tales Of Hoffnung Series.
Prod-HALAS Dist-PHENIX 1981

Profile - Health—A Series

Prod-BRGNHS Dist-BRGNHS

Eat Defensively 029 MIN

Profile - The Petroleum Industry C 30 MIN
16MM FILM, 3/4 OR 1/2 IN VIDEO
Presents a fundamental overview of the petroleum industry from exploration to refining.
Prod-UTEXPE Dist-UTEXPE 1981

Profile - Three Nurses C 25 MIN
3/4 OR 1/2 INCH VIDEO CASSETTE
Explores the responsibilities and emotions involved in being a nurse. Follows three nurses, one who cares for children, another who cares for critically ill patients in the Intensive Care Unit, and one who is the head nurse on a medical-surgical floor.
Prod-TRAINX Dist-TRAINX

Profile Descent And Metering C 13 MIN
3/4 OR 1/2 INCH VIDEO CASSETTE A
Describes new operational procedures in effect as of 1979 at terminals serving high performance aircraft. Shows profile descent and metering program as an air traffic management concept for safety enhancement.
Prod-FAAFL Dist-AVIMA

Profile Descent And Metering C 20 MIN
16MM FILM, 3/4 OR 1/2 IN VIDEO PRO
Offers a look at the profile descent and metering program, a comprehensive air traffic management concept designed to enhance safety and efficiency in air traffic handling, conserve fuel and reduce noise over airport communities. Describes new operational procedures that are expected to be in effect at all terminals served by high performance aircraft by 1979.
LC NO. 82-707228
Prod-USFAA Dist-USNAC 1977

Profile Of A Dropout, The C 20 MIN
2 INCH VIDEOTAPE J-H
Discusses the merits of acquiring sufficient training and skills to be acceptable in this modern working world.
From The Our World Of Economics Series.
Prod-MPATI Dist-GPITVL

Profile Of A Manager C 14 MIN
16MM FILM, 3/4 OR 1/2 IN VIDEO H-C A
Explores the attitudes, skills and knowledge required of an effective manager.
From The Professional Management Program Series.
LC NO. 77-700929
Prod-NEM Dist-NEM 1977

Profile Of A Manager (Spanish) C 14 MIN
16MM FILM, 3/4 OR 1/2 IN VIDEO
Dramatizes the experiences of a new manager. Shows basic management skills.
From The Professional Management Program (Spanish) Series.
Prod-NEM Dist-NEM

Profile Of A President - Richard Milhous Nixon B 15 MIN
16MM FILM OPTICAL SOUND J-H
Presents a biographical sketch of America's 37th President, Richard Nixon.
From The Screen News Digest Series. Vol 11, Issue 4
LC NO. 77-703470
Prod-HEARST Dist-HEARST 1968

Profile Of A Winning Competitor C 30 MIN
3/4 OR 1/2 INCH VIDEO CASSETTE
Examines the critical factors of success and looks at what the winners are doing with their new systems and technology for manufacturing and materials.
From The Successful Strategies For Manufacturing Management Series.
Prod-DELTAK Dist-DELTAK

Profile Of An Accident - And Then There Were Two C 13 MIN
16MM FILM, 3/4 OR 1/2 IN VIDEO
Depicts two helicopter crashes which happen on the same day, not because of chance or fate, but because of carelessness and hastiness. Outlines procedures by the accident investigation board as to why the mishaps occurred and how they could have been prevented.
LC NO. 82-706270
Prod-USA Dist-USNAC 1980

Profile Of An Aging Person, A B 30 MIN
16MM FILM OPTICAL SOUND PRO
Demonstrates that the aging process is an individual matter. Provides a profile of the aged person in American society.
From The Directions For Education In Nursing Via Technology Series. Lesson 82
LC NO. 74-701860
Prod-DENT Dist-WSU 1974

Profile Of Community C 42 MIN
16MM FILM OPTICAL SOUND
Looks at a group called the Community of the Christian Spirit, in which the liturgy, written by the members, is the focal point. Shows people celebrating God and each other as they explain their reasons for participating in the Community.
LC NO. 80-700441
Prod-TEMPLU Dist-TEMPLU Prodn-SCHUMJ 1979

Profile Of Paul Robeson, A C 60 MIN
3/4 OR 1/2 INCH VIDEO CASSETTE
Documents the life and achievements of Paul Robeson.
From The Interface Series.
Prod-WETATV Dist-PBS

Profile Of The Real Mounties B 4 MIN
16MM FILM SILENT H
See series title for descriptive statement.
From The Reading Films - High School Level Series. No. 10
Prod-PUAVC Dist-PUAVC 1957

Profiles In American Art—A Series

Documents the ideas and work of some of today's painters and sculptors. Involves history, philosophy and geography. Highlights commitment, hard work and creation.
Prod-KAWVAL Dist-KAWVAL

Bob Kuhn 030 MIN
Conrad Schwiering 030 MIN
Donald Teague 030 MIN
Edward Fraughton 030 MIN
Eric Sloane 030 MIN
George Carlson 030 MIN
Glenna Goodacre 030 MIN
John Clymer 030 MIN
John Stobart 030 MIN
Sergei Bongart 030 MIN
William Whitaker 030 MIN
Wilson Hurley 030 MIN

Profiles In Courage—A Series
I-C A
Presents a series of films portraying significant incidents in American history, the men and women who played a major role in them and how it affected their lives. Based on the book Profiles In Courage by John F Kennedy.
Prod-SAUDEK Dist-SSSSV

Anne Hutchinson 50 MIN
Chief Justice Charles Evans Hughes 50 MIN
Chief Justice John Marshall 50 MIN
Frederick Douglass 50 MIN
General Alexander William Doniphan 50 MIN
George Mason 50 MIN
Governor John M Slaton 50 MIN
Governor Peter Altgeld 50 MIN
Governor Sam Houston 50 MIN
John Adams 50 MIN
John Quincy Adams 50 MIN
Judge Ben B Lindsey 50 MIN
Mary S Mc Dowell 50 MIN
President Grover Cleveland 50 MIN
President Woodrow Wilson 50 MIN
Prudence Crandall 50 MIN
Richard T Ely 50 MIN
Secretary Of State Hamilton Fish 50 MIN
Senator Andrew Johnson 50 MIN
Senator Daniel Webster 50 MIN
Senator Edmund Ross 50 MIN
Senator George W Norris 50 MIN
Senator Oscar W Underwood 50 MIN
Senator Robert A Taft 50 MIN
Senator Thomas Corwin 50 MIN
Senator Thomas Hart Benton 50 MIN

Profiles In Courage—A Series
I-H
Presents segments from the NBC television program Profiles In Courage. Based on book with same title by John F Kennedy. Selects biographical data of various Americans.
Prod-SAUDEK Dist-SSSSV

Profiles In Journalism—A Series

Interviews well-known journalists who provide insights and anecdotes about their careers and the publications they mold.
Prod-UMITV Dist-UMITV 1975

Alfred Balk 029 MIN
Arnold Gingrich 029 MIN
Francoise Giroud 029 MIN

Profiles In Power (Spanish)—A Series
H-C A
Dramatizes men and women who shaped history. Interviews leading actors who portray these men and women.
Prod-LCOA Dist-LCOA Prodn-MCADLT 1977

Catherine The Great - A Profile In Power
Gandhi - A Profile In Power (Spanish) 025 MIN
Hitler - A Profile In Power (Spanish) 026 MIN
Joan Of Arc - A Profile In Power (Spanish) 025 MIN
Queen Victoria - A Profile In Power (Spanish) 026 MIN
Sitting Bull - A Profile In Power (Spanish) 026 MIN

Profiles In Power—A Series
16MM FILM, 3/4 OR 1/2 IN VIDEO H-C A
Prod-LCOA Dist-LCOA Prodn-MCADLT 1976

Catherine The Great - A Profile In Power 26 MIN
Gandhi - A Profile In Power 25 MIN
Hitler - A Profile In Power 26 MIN
Joan Of Arc - A Profile In Power 25 MIN
Queen Victoria - A Profile In Power 26 MIN
Sitting Bull - A Profile In Power 26 MIN

Profiling The Blade C 30 MIN
3/4 OR 1/2 INCH VIDEO CASSETTE
Shows how to profile a blade when building a knife.
From The How To Build A Knife Series.
Prod-UGATV Dist-MDCPB

Profit C 20 MIN
16MM FILM OPTICAL SOUND
See series title for descriptive statement.
Prod-CINE Dist-CINE

Profit - A Lure, A Risk C 8 MIN
16MM FILM, 3/4 OR 1/2 IN VIDEO J-H
Explains principles of financial investment, profit and risk using a song-and-dance extravaganza.
Prod-SUTHLA Dist-EBEC 1977

Profit Forecasting C 30 MIN
16MM FILM - 3/4 IN VIDEO
Revised version of the 1977 videorecording Forecasting Profit And The Cash Flow. Explains the concepts of gross profit, pre-tax profit, net profit and overhead. Shows how to calculate and forecast profit and elaborates on the accrual concept of matching revenues with expenses to determine profit. Based on the book Profit And Cash Flow Management For Non-Financial Managers by John Welsh and Jerry White.
From The That's Business Series.
LC NO. 79-706418
Prod-WELSHJ Dist-OWNMAN 1978

Profit Plan C 45 MIN
3/4 OR 1/2 INCH VIDEO CASSETTE IND
Covers financial measures, return on investment not appropriate, discounted cash flow, the profit map and how to make money, significance of internal rate of return (IRR), how to calculate the IRR and assessment of inadequate after tax income.
From The New Product Development Series.
Prod-AMCEE Dist-AMCEE

Profitable Direct Mail Programs C 30 MIN
3/4 OR 1/2 INCH VIDEO CASSETTE
Gives the characteristics of profitable direct mail programs.
From The Business Of Direct Mail Series.
Prod-KYTV Dist-KYTV 1983

Profitable Pork Selection C 12 MIN
16MM FILM OPTICAL SOUND
Describes what to look for in a modern meat hog. Features 'JASPER,' a 225 pound chest white-Hampshire cross - bred barrow, donated to Purdue University for study and carcass evaluation.
Prod-ADAC Dist-MTP

Profits And Bosses C 25 MIN
16MM FILM OPTICAL SOUND
Examines regimented forms of management that are used by Japanese firms to pursue the highest profit margins possible. Notes that these and related mind-conforming techniques are widely copied and enforced by North American business firms.
LC NO. 77-702520
Prod-CTV Dist-CTV 1976

Profits And Interest - Where Is The Best Return C 30 MIN
3/4 OR 1/2 INCH VIDEO CASSETTE C
See series title for descriptive statement.
From The Economics USA Series.
Prod-WEFA Dist-ANNCPB

Profits In The Bag C 9 MIN
16MM FILM OPTICAL SOUND I-H
Demonstrates the fundamentals of proper grocery bag packing through animation and 'HIP' narration.
Prod-CALVIN Dist-CALVIN 1966

Profits, Capital, Equipment And Economic Growth B 17 MIN
16MM FILM OPTICAL SOUND H A
Tells how professional management of labor and capital can make wages, productive output and profits increase simultaneously. Gives the factors needed for growth. Emphasizes the role of manager and entrepreneur.
From The Exploring Basic Economics Series.
LC NO. FI67-367
Prod-RSC Dist-MLA 1963

Progeny C 18 MIN
3/4 OR 1/2 INCH VIDEO CASSETTE
Involves the subjective framing of space. Presented by Steina and Woody Vasulka and Barbara Smith.
Prod-ARTINC Dist-ARTINC

Progeny C 19 MIN
3/4 OR 1/2 INCH VIDEO CASSETTE
Prod-EAI Dist-EAI

Prognosis - Fire C 20 MIN
3/4 OR 1/2 INCH VIDEO CASSETTE
Presents employee's responsibilities for fire prevention, fire control and emergency action.
Prod-FPF Dist-FPF

Prognosis - Safety C 22 MIN
3/4 OR 1/2 INCH VIDEO CASSETTE
Teaches employees how to prevent occupational injuries or illness from falls, strains, electric shock, needle punctures and other hazards.
Prod-FPF Dist-FPF

Program Acquisition C
3/4 INCH VIDEO CASSETTE T
Explains how to preview and acquire television programs for classroom use. Discusses the media-related services available to schools.
From The Visual Learning Series. Session 5
Prod-NYSED Dist-NYSED

Program Conception/Development C 60 MIN
3/4 OR 1/2 INCH VIDEO CASSETTE IND
See series title for descriptive statement.
From The Microprocessor Fundamentals For Decision Makers Series.
Prod-NCSU Dist-AMCEE

Program Control C 30 MIN
3/4 OR 1/2 INCH VIDEO CASSETTE IND
Demonstrates JMP.RTR and RESET instructions. Shows how main program FLASHAWORD calls subroutine FLASH to illustrate simple program control features of the 68000.
From The Hands-On With The 68000 Series.
Prod-COLOSU Dist-COLOSU

Program Development C 30 MIN
3/4 INCH VIDEO CASSETTE C
Discusses negative reinforcement, extinction, spontaneous recovery, target behavior and baseline.
From The Behavioral Revolution Series.
Prod-WPSXTV Dist-GPITVL 1978

Program Development Conference C 29 MIN
3/4 INCH VIDEO CASSETTE
Outlines the events leading to the passage of the Civil Service Reform Act and explains the purpose of the Ocean City, Maryland, program development conference. Includes excerpts from addresses on the issues and points out the challenges of civil service reform.
From The Launching Civil Service Reform Series.
LC NO. 79-706272
Prod-USOPMA Dist-USNAC 1978

Program Development In The Kindergarten—A Series

Acquaints teachers of kindergarten children with the content of various teaching programs. Describes current theories about learning and explains how such theories are related to the selection of programs in kindergarten.
Prod-GPITVL Dist-GPITVL

Art - A Way Of Learning 30 MIN
First Day In Kindergarten, A 30 MIN
Implications For Language Development 30 MIN
Implications For Planning A Total 30 MIN
Learning Environment, The 30 MIN
Literature In The Kindergarten 30 MIN
Mathematics In The Kindergarten, Pt 1 30 MIN
Mathematics In The Kindergarten, Pt 2 30 MIN
Music In The Kindergarten 30 MIN
Outdoor Activities 30 MIN
Self-Chosen Activities, Pt 1 30 MIN
Self-Chosen Activities, Pt 2 30 MIN
Social Studies - Science, Pt 1 30 MIN
Social Studies - Science, Pt 2 30 MIN
Social Studies - Science, Pt 3 30 MIN
Spying Out The Course 30 MIN

Program Documentation C 30 MIN
3/4 OR 1/2 INCH VIDEO CASSETTE
Examines the function and procedures of program documentation. Reports on types of documents.
From The Programmable Controllers Series.
Prod-ITCORP Dist-ITCORP

Program Examples B 60 MIN
3/4 OR 1/2 INCH VIDEO CASSETTE
See series title for descriptive statement.
From The Understanding Microprocessors Series. Pt 12
Prod-UAZMIC Dist-UAZMIC 1979

Program Execution - A Grey Code-Counter Implementation C 30 MIN
3/4 OR 1/2 INCH VIDEO CASSETTE IND
Describes program execution, and shows how a simple counting program is designed and a delay used to slow down program operation. Notes that Grey counter is designed as Class 2 machine and program is provided for implementation.
From The Microprocessors For Monitoring And Control Series.
Prod-COLOSU Dist-COLOSU

Program Exercises C 30 MIN
3/4 OR 1/2 INCH VIDEO CASSETTE IND
Examines four problems and various solutions to each, using bytes, words and long words, making a good working demonstration of the 68000.
From The MC68000 Microprocessor Series.
Prod-COLOSU Dist-COLOSU

Program For Grades K-3, A C 30 MIN
16MM FILM, 3/4 OR 1/2 IN VIDEO K-P T
Teaches children about touching, the meaning of good touches, bad touches, or touches that may be uncomfortable or confusing. Prescreening advised.
From The Child Sexual Abuse - What Your Child Should Know Series.
Prod-WTTWTV Dist-IU 1983

Program For Grades 4-7, A C 30 MIN
16MM FILM, 3/4 OR 1/2 IN VIDEO J-C T
Tells children about problem situations involving touching. Explores problems with babysitters, sex role stereotypes, and communications. Prescreening advised.
From The Child Sexual Abuse - What Your Child Should Know Series.
Prod-WTTWTV Dist-IU 1983

Program for Grades 7-12, A C 60 MIN
16MM FILM, 3/4 OR 1/2 IN VIDEO J-C T
Illustrates the problems of adolescence. Helps growing people to examine the risks in dating and the growing up process that may leave them vulnerable to sexual assault and abuse. Prescreening advised.
From The Child Sexual Abuse - What Your Child Should Know Series.
Prod-WTTWTV Dist-IU 1983

Program For Parents, A C 90 MIN
16MM FILM, 3/4 OR 1/2 IN VIDEO C A
Explains sexual abuse of children, who falls victim, who are the perpetrators, and what the viewer can do to prevent it. Prescreening advised.
From The Child Sexual Abuse - What Your Child Should Know Series.
Prod-WTTWTV Dist-IU 1983

Program For Senior High, A C 60 MIN
16MM FILM, 3/4 OR 1/2 IN VIDEO H-C T
Explores issues confronting adolescents. Discusses understanding of sexual assault, how it happens, who is the victim, and who is the assailant. Prescreening advised.
From The Child Sexual Abuse - What Your Child Should Know Series.
Prod-WTTWTV Dist-IU 1983

Program For Training In Human Sexuality, A C 60 MIN
3/4 OR 1/2 INCH VIDEO CASSETTE
Describes a conceptual approach for training in sexuality for practioners in medicine, psychology, social work, nursing and education. Presents a training design which examines the cognitive, affective and communication skills necessary for preparing health professionals for effective delivery of sexual health care.
Prod-HEMUL Dist-HEMUL

Program For Victory C 10 MIN
3/4 OR 1/2 INCH VIDEO CASSETTE A
Presents Tom Osborne, football coach at Nebraska and holder of a PhD in psychology, explaining the importance of sound preparation in motivating a team. Stresses care, understanding and sharing goals.
Prod-SFTI Dist-SFTI

Program Four C 30 MIN
2 INCH VIDEOTAPE J-H
Presents discussions among students, teachers, a parent and doctors about the drug problem and alternatives to taking drugs.
From The Drugs Use And Abuse Series.
Prod-WGBHTV Dist-GPITVL

Program Manipulation Instructions C 30 MIN
3/4 OR 1/2 INCH VIDEO CASSETTE IND
Describes very special instructions including the decrement and branch until condition true. Tells about LINK and UNLINK, powerful subroutine instructions, in a typical compiler exercise.
From The MC68000 Microprocess Series.
Prod-COLOSU Dist-COLOSU

Program Of Satire, A C 30 MIN
3/4 INCH VIDEO CASSETTE H-C A
Centers around poets who have trained their wits on a wide variety of targets, from postmasters and politicians to war and religion. Presents poems by Richard Armour, John Betjeman, Alexander Pope, Edith Sitwell and Jonathan Swift.
From The Anyone For Tennyson Series.
Prod-NETCHE Dist-GPITVL

Program Of Songs By Lightnin' Sam Hopkins, A B 8 MIN
16MM FILM, 3/4 OR 1/2 IN VIDEO
Shows Lightnin' Sam Hopkins, a country-blues guitarist performing three songs on unamplified guitar.
Prod-UWASHP Dist-UWASHP

Program One C 14 MIN
16MM FILM - VIDEO, ALL FORMATS
Teaches children basic skills to protect themselves against sexual assault. Differentiates good touching and bad touching. Encourages children to use their right to say NO.
From The Feeling Yes, Feeling No Series.
Prod-NFBC Dist-PEREN

Program One C 30 MIN
2 INCH VIDEOTAPE J-H
Presents discussions among students, teachers, a parent and doctors about the drug problems and alternatives to taking drugs.
From The Drugs Use And Abuse Series.
Prod-WGBHTV Dist-GPITVL

Program Planning C 30 MIN
3/4 OR 1/2 INCH VIDEO CASSETTE T
Discusses program planning when teaching adult basic education students.
From The Basic Education - Teaching The Adult Series.
Prod-MDDE Dist-MDCPB

Program Planning, Pt 1 C 12 MIN
3/4 INCH VIDEO CASSETTE
Focuses on the planning of instructional programs. Discusses identifying and developing objectives.
LC NO. 79-708057
Prod-VAHSL Dist-USNAC 1976

Program Planning, Pt 2 C 11 MIN
3/4 INCH VIDEO CASSETTE
Focuses on the planning of instructional programs. Discusses developing an instructional task analysis.
LC NO. 79-708057
Prod-VAHSL Dist-USNAC 1976

Program Preparation C 15 MIN
3/4 OR 1/2 INCH VIDEO CASSETTE PRO
See series title for descriptive statement.
From The Numerical Control/Computer Numerical Control, Pt 1 - Fundamentals Series.
Prod-ICSINT Dist-ICSINT

Program Preparation C 16 MIN
3/4 OR 1/2 INCH VIDEO CASSETTE IND
Focuses on required operations, selecting appropriate tools and identifying methods to fix the parts.
From The Numerical Control/Computerized Numerical Control, Module 1 - Fundamentals Series.
Prod-LEIKID Dist-LEIKID

Program Structures C 20 MIN
3/4 OR 1/2 INCH VIDEO CASSETTE H-C A
Examines some fundamental structures. Shows how to create branching and looping structures.
From The Basic Power Series.
Prod-VANGU Dist-UCEMC

Program Testing, Pt 1 C 30 MIN
3/4 OR 1/2 INCH VIDEO CASSETTE IND
Defines some program-testing terminology. Distinguishes various types of testing. Discusses unit-testing concepts of functional testing, structural testing and test-coverage criteria.
From The Software Engineering - A First Course Series.
Prod-COLOSU Dist-COLOSU

Program Testing, Pt 2 C 30 MIN
3/4 OR 1/2 INCH VIDEO CASSETTE IND
Covers system-integration strategies and testing techniques, including structural walk-through, static analysis and dynamic testing. Concludes with discussion of current issues in testing.
From The Software Engineering - A First Course Series.
Prod-COLOSU Dist-COLOSU

Program Three C 16 MIN
16MM FILM - VIDEO, ALL FORMATS
Deals with the subject of the sexual assault of children by family members or other trusted persons.
From The Feeling Yes, Feeling No Series.
Prod-NFBC Dist-PEREN

Program Three C 30 MIN
2 INCH VIDEOTAPE J-H
Presents information on drug users. Includes young people who have used drugs talking with doctors about some of their experiences, feelings and attitudes.
From The Drugs Use And Abuse Series.
Prod-WGBHTV Dist-GPITVL

Program Two C 14 MIN
16MM FILM - VIDEO, ALL FORMATS
Shows children how to recognize sexual assault by strangers. Shows how children can ensure their safety before saying yes or no to a request from a stranger.
From The Feeling Yes, Feeling No Series.
Prod-NFBC Dist-PEREN

Program Two C 30 MIN
2 INCH VIDEOTAPE J-H
Presents information on drug users. Includes young people who have used drugs talking with doctors about some of their experiences, feelings and attitudes.
From The Drugs Use And Abuse Series.
Prod-WGBHTV Dist-GPITVL

Program Types / Stereotyping C 15 MIN
3/4 OR 1/2 INCH VIDEO CASSETTE J-H
Explains why information in television news stories is often edited out. Reveals that the ninth-grade students come to the conclusion that this editing may be a plot against kids and are therefore challenged to produce better television, complete with drama, news and commercials.
From The Tuned-In Series. Lesson 4
Prod-WNETTV Dist-FI 1982

Programmable Controllers—A Series

Provides instruction on programmable controllers. Contains student workbooks, instructor's guides and overhead transparencies.
Prod-ITCORP Dist-ITCORP

Analog And Special Input, Output Modules 030 MIN
Central Processing Unit 030 MIN
Communication Fundamentals 030 MIN
Developing A Program 030 MIN
Discrete Input, Output Modules 030 MIN
Installation Considerations 030 MIN
Interpreting Ladder Diagrams 030 MIN
Introduction To Programmable Controllers 030 MIN
Networking 030 MIN
Numbering Systems, Numbering Codes, And Logic 030 MIN
Principles Of Ladder Diagrams 030 MIN
Principles Of Ladder Logic Programming 030 MIN
Program Documentation 030 MIN

Programming 030 MIN
Programming - Analog And PID 030 MIN
Programming - Data Comparison And Arithmetic 030 MIN
Programming - Times And Counters 030 MIN
Programming Devices And Peripheral Equipment 030 MIN
Sizing And Selection 030 MIN
Troubleshooting Field Device Malfunctions 030 MIN
Troubleshooting P C Malfunctions 030 MIN
Troubleshooting Techniques 030 MIN

Programmed Instruction - The Development Process C 19 MIN
16MM FILM - 3/4 IN VIDEO
Introduces the major stages in the development of programmed instructional materials with primary emphasis on student tryouts and revisions leading to lasting and influential effects on education.
LC NO. 79-706672
Prod-USOE Dist-USNAC 1979

Programmed Instruction - The Development Process (Spanish) B 19 MIN
16MM FILM - 3/4 IN VIDEO
Introduces the major stages in the development of programmed instructional materials, emphasizing the importance of student tryouts and revisions. Issued in 1966 as a motion picture.
LC NO. 79-706672
Prod-USOE Dist-USNAC 1979

Programmed Instruction - The Teacher's Role–A Series
C T
Stimulates teacher discussion of the various uses of programmed instruction in teaching.
LC NO. 74-705431
Prod-USOE Dist-USNAC 1968

Eighth Grade Mathematics 10 MIN
Fifth Grade Geography 10 MIN
First Grade Reading 10 MIN
Fourth Grade Vocabulary 13 MIN
Third Grade Science 11 MIN

Programmed Instruction - The Teacher's Role (Spanish)–A Series
T
Discusses various aspects of programmed instruction. Issued in 1966 as a motion picture.
Prod-USOE Dist-USNAC 1979

First Grade Reading (Spanish) 010 MIN
Third Grade Science (Spanish) 011 MIN

Programmed Instruction In Medical Interviewing–A Series

Prod-USCSM Dist-NMAC 1970

Programmed Interview Instruction, No. 1 - Mrs
Programmed Interview Instruction, No. 10 - 15 MIN
Programmed Interview Instruction, No. 11 - Mr 14 MIN
Programmed Interview Instruction, No. 12 - Mr 15 MIN
Programmed Interview Instruction, No. 2 - Mr 20 MIN
Programmed Interview Instruction, No. 3 - Mrs 18 MIN
Programmed Interview Instruction, No. 4 - Mr 17 MIN
Programmed Interview Instruction, No. 5 - Mr 20 MIN
Programmed Interview Instruction, No. 6 - 18 MIN
Programmed Interview Instruction, No. 7 - Mrs 20 MIN
Programmed Interview Instruction, No. 8 - 20 MIN
Programmed Interview Instruction, No. 9 - 12 MIN

Programmed Instruction In Medical Interviewing–A Series

Prod-USCSM Dist-USNAC Prodn-NMAC 1970

Programmed Interview Instruction - Mrs Goodrich 20 MIN

Programmed Interview Instruction - Mrs Goodrich B 20 MIN
3/4 INCH VIDEO CASSETTE
Demonstrates how the interviewer discourages an overtalkative patient from communicating redundant or irrelevant information in the interest of permitting the emergence of new or more relevant information within the time limits of the interview.
From The Programmed Instruction In Medical Interviewing Series. No. 7
LC NO. 77-706098
Prod-USCSM Dist-USNAC Prodn-NMAC 1970

Programmed Interview Instruction, No. 1 - Mrs Adams B 20 MIN
16MM FILM OPTICAL SOUND
Demonstrates the technique of facilitation in an interview with a patient who complains of chronic fatigue. Shows how the interviewer encourages the flow of information from the patient without requiring him to speak or to specify the content expected.
From The Programmed Instruction In Medical Interviewing Series.
LC NO. 74-706188
Prod-USCSM Dist-NMAC 1970

Programmed Interview Instruction, No. 10 - Mrs Jackson B 15 MIN
16MM FILM OPTICAL SOUND
Demonstrates how the interviewer arouses the patient's confidence in the physician and his recommendations, as well as limits the patient's dependency on the physician.
From The Programmed Instruction In Medical Interviewing Series.
LC NO. 74-706198
Prod-USCSM Dist-NMAC 1970

Programmed Interview Instruction, No. 11 - Mr King B 14 MIN
16MM FILM OPTICAL SOUND
Follows an interview with a patient, pausing at intervals to ask a multiple-choice question on the correct response for each situation. Serves as a test film to measure cognitive learning.
From The Programmed Instruction In Medical Interviewing Series.
LC NO. 74-706199
Prod-USCSM Dist-NMAC 1970

Programmed Interview Instruction, No. 12 - Mr Lloyd B 15 MIN
16MM FILM OPTICAL SOUND
Follows an interview with a patient, pausing at intervals to give the audience a multiple-choice question on the correct response for each situation.
From The Programmed Instruction In Medical Interviewing Series.
LC NO. 74-706200
Prod-USCSM Dist-NMAC 1970

Programmed Interview Instruction, No. 2 - Mr Barrett B 20 MIN
16MM FILM OPTICAL SOUND
Demonstrates the technique of confrontation designed to elicit significant verbal and nonverbal information from a businessman who tries to discuss only his peptic ulcer and denies that he has emotional problems.
From The Programmed Instruction In Medical Interviewing Series.
LC NO. 74-706189
Prod-USCSM Dist-NMAC 1970

Programmed Interview Instruction, No. 3 - Mrs Carson B 18 MIN
16MM FILM OPTICAL SOUND
Demonstrates the effective use of silence to permit a harassed housewife with continuous headaches to speak on her own initiative and contribute to an understanding of her complaint.
From The Programmed Instruction In Medical Interviewing Series.
LC NO. 74-706190
Prod-USCSM Dist-NMAC 1970

Programmed Interview Instruction, No. 4 - Mr Dunn B 17 MIN
16MM FILM OPTICAL SOUND
Combines the use of confrontation, facilitation and silence to show that relevant communication occurs when opportunity is provided for it to emerge. Deals with an anxious, overweight professional man who reports two recent cases of tachycardia.
From The Programmed Instruction In Medical Interviewing Series.
LC NO. 74-706191
Prod-USCSM Dist-NMAC 1970

Programmed Interview Instruction, No. 5 - Mr Egan B 20 MIN
16MM FILM OPTICAL SOUND
Reviews a case of an industrial accident victim to demonstrate that accuracy in communication is facilitated when the interviewer avoids suggesting patient responses by wording and by demeanor, tone of voice and other nonverbal acts.
From The Programmed Instruction In Medical Interviewing Series.
LC NO. 74-706192
Prod-USCSM Dist-NMAC 1970

Programmed Interview Instruction, No. 6 - Miss Frazer B 18 MIN
16MM FILM OPTICAL SOUND
Points out how the interviewer avoids suggesting patient responses by the timing of his participation. Involves the case of a suggestive young woman who has developed conversion reaction on the job.
From The Programmed Instruction In Medical Interviewing Series.
LC NO. 74-706193
Prod-USCSM Dist-NMAC 1970

Programmed Interview Instruction, No. 7 - Mrs Goodrich B 20 MIN
16MM FILM OPTICAL SOUND
Demonstrates how the interviewer discourages an overtalkative patient from communicating redundant or irrelevant information in the interest of permitting the emergence of new or more relevant information within time limits of the interview.
From The Programmed Instruction In Medical Interviewing Series.
LC NO. 74-706195
Prod-USCSM Dist-NMAC 1970

Programmed Interview Instruction, No. 8 - Miss Hadkell B 20 MIN
16MM FILM OPTICAL SOUND
Demonstrates how the interviewer selects and sequences interventions to exercise the least possible explicit control over the patient and to obtain medical information which is difficult for the patient to talk about.
From The Programmed Instruction In Medical Interviewing Series.
LC NO. 74-706196
Prod-USCSM Dist-NMAC 1970

Programmed Interview Instruction, No. 9 - Miss Ingram B 12 MIN
16MM FILM OPTICAL SOUND
Demonstrates the technique of creation of an emotional climate conducive to a successful interview in the case of a hostile patient.
From The Programmed Instruction In Medical Interviewing Series.
LC NO. 74-706197
Prod-USCSM Dist-NMAC 1970

Programmed Learning C 33 MIN
16MM FILM - 3/4 IN VIDEO
Deals with the philosophy, practicalities and some of the hardware of a system that introduces a learning package through which individuals work at their own pace making responses to various stimuli until they can show what they have learned. Points out the advantages which include improved results because of the individual approach, quality control and better use of staff and better allocation of time to the needs of the individual.
Prod-BNA Dist-BNA

Programmed Learning In The United States Air Force C 26 MIN
16MM FILM OPTICAL SOUND
Describes principles of programmed learning and explains how the Air Force is using this revolutionary teaching method to increase quality and quantity of Air Force instructions with a decrease in training cost.
LC NO. 74-705433
Prod-USAF Dist-USNAC 1963

Programmed Preventive Maintenance C 27 MIN
3/4 OR 1/2 INCH VIDEO CASSETTE IND
Discusses the advantages, scope, design, implementation, follow-up and modification of a programmed preventive maintenance plan for a well production system.
Prod-UTEXPE Dist-UTEXPE 1974

Programmer's Workbench C
3/4 OR 1/2 INCH VIDEO CASSETTE
Describes the four major UNIX applications, the five primary stages of the application development cycle, the four major programmer's workbench tools and shows how major tools can be applied to office automation, engineering and management information applications.
From The UNIX Overview Series. Unit 5
Prod-COMTEG Dist-COMTEG

Programming C 30 MIN
3/4 OR 1/2 INCH VIDEO CASSETTE IND
Explains position-independent coding, stack programming and other real-time profitably oriented techniques. Covers important stack-mark concept which implements modular structured code. Describes ROM example for various printer-motor devices with portable code techniques.
From The Interface Programming (6809) Series.
Prod-COLOSU Dist-COLOSU

Programming C 30 MIN
3/4 OR 1/2 INCH VIDEO CASSETTE
Considers logical operations and data manipulation.
From The Programmable Controllers Series.
Prod-ITCORP Dist-ITCORP

Programming - Analog And PID C 30 MIN
3/4 OR 1/2 INCH VIDEO CASSETTE
Deals with analog and PID.
From The Programmable Controllers Series.
Prod-ITCORP Dist-ITCORP

Programming - Data Comparison And Arithmatic Functions C 30 MIN
3/4 OR 1/2 INCH VIDEO CASSETTE
Covers data comparison and arithmatic functions.
From The Programmable Controllers Series.
Prod-ITCORP Dist-ITCORP

Programming - Times And Counters C 30 MIN
3/4 OR 1/2 INCH VIDEO CASSETTE
Examines programming timers and counters. Describes cascading functions.
From The Programmable Controllers Series.
Prod-ITCORP Dist-ITCORP

Programming C N C - Absolute C 14 MIN
1/2 IN VIDEO CASSETTE BETA/VHS IND
See series title for descriptive statement.
From The Machine Shop - C N C Machine Operations Series.
Prod-RMI Dist-RMI

Programming C N C - Incremental C 23 MIN
1/2 IN VIDEO CASSETTE BETA/VHS IND
See series title for descriptive statement.
From The Machine Shop - C N C Machine Operations Series.
Prod-RMI Dist-RMI

Programming C N C, Circular Interpolation C 20 MIN
1/2 IN VIDEO CASSETTE BETA/VHS IND
See series title for descriptive statement.
From The Machine Shop - C N C Machine Operations Series.
Prod-RMI Dist-RMI

Programming C N C, Drilling Cycles C 19 MIN
1/2 IN VIDEO CASSETTE BETA/VHS IND
See series title for descriptive statement.
From The Machine Shop - C N C Machine Operations Series.
Prod-RMI Dist-RMI

Programming C N C, Special Milling Cycles C 16 MIN
1/2 IN VIDEO CASSETTE BETA/VHS IND
See series title for descriptive statement.
From The Machine Shop - C N C Machine Operations Series.
Prod-RMI Dist-RMI

Programming Devices And Peripheral Equipment C 30 MIN
3/4 OR 1/2 INCH VIDEO CASSETTE
Explores programming devices and peripheral equipment. Highlights I O simulators.
From The Programmable Controllers Series.
Prod-ITCORP Dist-ITCORP

Programming Dilemma C 30 MIN
3/4 OR 1/2 INCH VIDEO CASSETTE

Describes how application development tools can help meet the increasing demand for computer application that directly affect a business' growth.
From The Application Development Without Programmers Series.
Prod-DELTAK Dist-DELTAK

Programming For Microcomputers—A Series
16MM FILM, 3/4 OR 1/2 IN VIDEO J-C A
Shows how to write structured programs in BASIC.
Prod-IU Dist-IU 1983

Alphanumeric Expressions / Numeric Operations	030 MIN
Branching And Looping	029 MIN
Designing A Program	029 MIN
Double Subscripted Variables	029 MIN
Format And Edit Commands / Storing And Functions	030 MIN 029 MIN
Introduction / Getting Started	030 MIN
More About Program Construction	029 MIN
Nested Loops / More About Program Design	030 MIN
READ - DATA Statements / Strings	030 MIN
Single Subscripted Variables	029 MIN
Subroutines / Program Construction	030 MIN
Variables / Input Statements	030 MIN

Programming Language - Understanding BASIC C
3/4 OR 1/2 INCH VIDEO CASSETTE
Illustrates the computer language BASIC for use in programming computers.
From The Computer Literacy/Computer Language Series.
Prod-LIBFSC Dist-LIBFSC

Programming Languages - Apple Logo C
3/4 OR 1/2 INCH VIDEO CASSETTE
Contains the common primitive LOGO and TURTLE commands and gives demonstration programs and examples in computer programming.
From The Computer Literacy/Computer Language Series.
Prod-LIBFSC Dist-LIBFSC

Programming Languages - Apple Logo C 29 MIN
1/2 IN VIDEO CASSETTE BETA/VHS
See series title for descriptive statement.
From The Computer Education / Programming / Operations Series.
Prod-RMI Dist-RMI

Programming Languages - Apple Pascal C
3/4 OR 1/2 INCH VIDEO CASSETTE
Offers an introductory overview of the Apple II adaptation of the UCSD Pascal Operating System.
From The Computer Literacy/Computer Language Series.
Prod-LIBFSC Dist-LIBFSC

Programming Languages - Apple Pascal C 25 MIN
1/2 IN VIDEO CASSETTE BETA/VHS
See series title for descriptive statement.
From The Computer Education / Programming / Operations Series.
Prod-RMI Dist-RMI

Programming Languages - Atari Pilot-Text C
3/4 OR 1/2 INCH VIDEO CASSETTE
Introduces PILOT programming language and covers the basic CORE PILOT commands required to write text programs (without graphics). Explains and demonstrates all commands.
From The Computer Literacy/Computer Language Series.
Prod-LIBFSC Dist-LIBFSC

Programming Languages - Atari Pilot-Turtle Graphics And Sound C
3/4 OR 1/2 INCH VIDEO CASSETTE
Presents all necessary commands needed to create interesting and exciting color graphics displays. Covers PILOT sound capabilities to add a dimension to TEXT and TURTLE graphic programs using Atari PILOT. Explains the commands and shows the programs and examples.
From The Computer Literacy/Computer Language Series.
Prod-LIBFSC Dist-LIBFSC

Programming Languages - Basic C 22 MIN
1/2 IN VIDEO CASSETTE BETA/VHS
See series title for descriptive statement.
From The Computer Education / Programming / Operations Series.
Prod-RMI Dist-RMI

Programming Microprocessors—A Series
IND
Shows in four modules and 30 videotapes how to assess current technology, operate a microprocessor, learn rapid design techniques, participate in design applications, generate machine-language codes, produce efficient debugging software, develop broad-based understanding of microprocessors, and originate new product applications.
Prod-COLOSU Dist-COLOSU

AMD/Motorola 6800 Architecture System, The	030 MIN
Input/Output	030 MIN
Software	030 MIN
What Is A Microprocessor?	030 MIN

Programming Perspectives C 28 MIN
3/4 OR 1/2 INCH VIDEO CASSETTE T
See series title for descriptive statement.
From The Next Steps With Computers In The Classroom Series.
Prod-PBS Dist-PBS

Programming Style And Documentation C 35 MIN
3/4 INCH VIDEO CASSETTE C A
See series title for descriptive statement.
From The Software Management For Small Computers Series.
LC NO. 81-706201
Prod-AMCEE Dist-AMCEE 1980

Programming The Key Punch C 14 MIN
16MM FILM, 3/4 OR 1/2 IN VIDEO H-C A
Illustrates the preparation of different program cards for the key punch. Shows how the star wheels of the program unit read the cards and cause the keypunch to change shifts, ship or duplicate. Introduces the verifier, which checks punched cards to detect errors.
Prod-SF Dist-SF 1968

Programs - Helicopter Example C 45 MIN
3/4 OR 1/2 INCH VIDEO CASSETTE PRO
See series title for descriptive statement.
From The Modern Control Theory - Deterministic Optimal Linear Feedback Series.
Prod-MIOT Dist-MIOT

Progress Against Cancer C 28 MIN
16MM FILM OPTICAL SOUND
Explains how modern research has solved many of the mysteries of cancer and improved the cancer victim's chance to survive.
LC NO. 74-706560
Prod-USDHEW Dist-USNAC 1974

Progress In All Traffic Control C 20 MIN
16MM FILM OPTICAL SOUND
Reviews the history of air traffic control and depicts techniques and systems presently in operation. Describes plans for improved future control and conservation of air space to handle increasing air traffic.
LC NO. 74-705435
Prod-USAF Dist-USNAC 1966

Progress Through Performance - Iowa's Swine Testing Stations C 14 MIN
16MM FILM OPTICAL SOUND H-C
Illustrates how the four Iowa Swine Testing Stations identify genetically superior pigs by measuring feed efficiency, average daily weight gain and back fat levels under carefully controlled environmental conditions.
LC NO. 83-700621
Prod-IOWA Dist-IOWA 1982

Progress Towards Mach 3 C 11 MIN
16MM FILM OPTICAL SOUND J-C A
Highlights the first 9 XB-0a test flights.
Prod-NAA Dist-RCKWL

Progress, But Who Is It For C 20 MIN
16MM FILM, 3/4 OR 1/2 IN VIDEO J-H
Points out that coffee used to dominate the Brazilian economy, but the products of a growing industrial sector are just as important, if not more so. Discusses who benefits from progress in Brazil, showing that the production line worker at the Fiat plant outside Belo Horizonte can rarely afford a car and that plantation workers are the people who gain the least from the sugar cane being made into motor fuel.
From The Brazil Series.
Prod-BBCTV Dist-FI 1982

Progressions C 2 MIN
16MM FILM OPTICAL SOUND
To be used as an opening and a tail for old films that still show the old logo and the old name of the Pittsburg Plate Glass Company.
LC NO. 76-702533
Prod-PPG Dist-PPGC Prodn-TORCEL 1969

Progressions, Sequences And Series B 29 MIN
16MM FILM OPTICAL SOUND H
Develops the law of formation for arithmetic and geometric progressions and shows how to find a series from known terms. The problem of finding the sum of N terms in a series is worked out analytically for both arithmetic and geometric progressions.
From The Intermediate Algebra Series.
Prod-CALVIN Dist-MLA Prodn-UNIVFI 1959

Progressive Development Of Movement Abilities In Children, The C 13 MIN
16MM FILM, 3/4 OR 1/2 IN VIDEO C A
Defines the three developmental stages of children's physical maturity. Uses high-speed, normal, and stop-action cinematography to show individuals at each of the three stages engaged in a variety of activities. Emphasizes a hierarchical approach to categorizing children's development and identifies developmental anomalies.
Prod-IU Dist-IU 1982

Progressive Era, The - Reform Works In America X 23 MIN
16MM FILM, 3/4 OR 1/2 IN VIDEO J-H
Examines politics in the early 1900's. Describes the government then, and how it has affected government and politics in the 1970's.
Prod-UPITN Dist-EBEC 1971

Progressive Muscular Dystrophies, The C 48 MIN
3/4 INCH VIDEO CASSETTE PRO
Presents Dr Lewis P Rowland lecturing on the progressive muscular dystrophies.
From The Intensive Course In Neuromuscular Diseases Series.
LC NO. 76-706077
Prod-NINDIS Dist-USNAC 1974

Progressive Relaxation Training C 20 MIN
16MM FILM, 3/4 OR 1/2 IN VIDEO
Portrays the subtleties of progressive relaxation procedures while observing the therapist directing a client in the stages of relaxation.
Prod-RESPRC Dist-RESPRC

Progressives, Populists And Reform In America (1890-1917) C 32 MIN
3/4 OR 1/2 INCH VIDEO CASSETTE
Presents reform activists Jesse Jackson and Heather Booth relating past social problems and reformers to modern-day struggles for racial justice and to other contemporary social conditions.
LC NO. 81-706676
Prod-GA Dist-GA 1981

Progressives, The C 25 MIN
16MM FILM, 3/4 OR 1/2 IN VIDEO H-C A
Examines the progressive movement in America, telling how it responded to the conditions of poverty and squalor that existed at the turn of the century.
From The American History Series.
Prod-CRMP Dist-CRMP 1969

Progressives, The C 30 MIN
3/4 OR 1/2 INCH VIDEO CASSETTE C
Shows how the Progressives became an important political force in the pre-World War 1 years as they tried to alleviate some of the societal inequities that industrialization in America had created.
America - The Second Century Series.
Prod-DALCCD Dist-DALCCD

Progressives, The - Foreign Policy C 30 MIN
2 INCH VIDEOTAPE
Reviews the Open Door Policy, the Russo-Japanese War, the Panama Canal and the outbreak of war in Europe.
From The American History II Series.
Prod-KRMATV Dist-GPITVL

Progressives, The - Taft And Wilson C 30 MIN
2 INCH VIDEOTAPE
Examines the progressive programs of Taft and Wilson. Concludes with our growing involvement in foreign affairs.
From The American History II Series.
Prod-KRMATV Dist-GPITVL

Progressives, The - Theodore Roosevelt C 30 MIN
2 INCH VIDEOTAPE
Illustrates the possibility for non-violent change in society. Covers the progressive goals implemented by Roosevelt.
From The American History II Series.
Prod-KRMATV Dist-GPITVL

Prohibition And Pot C 15 MIN
16MM FILM OPTICAL SOUND
Discusses whether the parallels in public attitudes toward prohibition in the 20's and toward pot now are valid comparisons.
Prod-INTEXT Dist-REAF

Prohibition Days, With William Temple C 15 MIN
3/4 OR 1/2 INCH VIDEO CASSETTE
Recalls the days of prohibition as one of the most successful periods in Ontario's history. Reflects on the issues of alcohol propoganda, prevention versus treatment, and the policies of alcohol use today.
Prod-ARFO Dist-ARFO 1981

Project Apollo C 15 MIN
16MM FILM OPTICAL SOUND
Shows pre-Apollo flight plans and animated drawings of how Apollo flights will be made by manned space vehicles.
Prod-THIOKL Dist-THIOKL 1965

Project Apollo - Manned Flight To The Moon C 13 MIN
16MM FILM OPTICAL SOUND J-C
Shows the Gemini spacecraft and Titan booster, and the Apollo spacecraft and the Saturn 1, ñb and 5 boosters. Depicts the sequence of events for a manned lunar landing using Saturn 5 booster and Apollo spacecraft.
LC NO. 74-704125
Prod-NASA Dist-USNAC 1963

Project Apollo - Mission To The Moon B 18 MIN
16MM FILM OPTICAL SOUND
Reports on the rendezvous in space between Geminis 6 and 7, and explains its relation to America's proposed manned flight to the moon.
From The Screen News Digest Series. Vol 10, Issue 5
Prod-HEARST Dist-HEARST

Project Aware C 27 MIN
16MM FILM, 3/4 OR 1/2 IN VIDEO J-H
Presents ex-felon David Crawford who relates his experiences and mistakes both on the streets and in prison. Encourages people to think twice before engaging in unlawful behavior.
Prod-CRAWDA Dist-PEREN

Project Bilingual—A Series

Prod-SANISD Dist-SUTHLA 1972

Everything You Do	007 MIN
Fiesta	008 MIN
Happy	008 MIN
How Do We Look	007 MIN
Other People At School	007 MIN
Temores	008 MIN
Un Viaje A Mexico	009 MIN
Unpleasant Feelings	007 MIN

Project Children—A Series

Focuses on children of the 1980's.
Prod-WCCOTV Dist-WCCOTV

Project Children, Pt 1	060 MIN
Project Children, Pt 2	023 MIN

Project Children, Pt 1 C 60 MIN
3/4 OR 1/2 INCH VIDEO CASSETTE

Deals with the problems of children such as growing up in the eighties, divorce, new family structures, changing culture, stress, the punk subculture, changing schools, juvenile justice and rejection.
From The Project Children Series.
Prod-WCCOTV Dist-WCCOTV

Project Children, Pt 2 C 23 MIN
3/4 OR 1/2 INCH VIDEO CASSETTE
Focuses on mental health, spare time, children and Reaganomics, and looking to the future for the children of the 80's.
From The Project Children Series.
Prod-WCCOTV Dist-WCCOTV

Project Compassion C 29 MIN
16MM FILM OPTICAL SOUND
Presents a young woman who panics when her grandmother suffers a stroke and the ensuing personality change. Shows how working in a volunteer program in a nursing home helps the young woman deal with her feelings.
From The This Is The Life Series.
Prod-LUTTEL Dist-LUTTEL 1982

Project Deep Probe C 28 MIN
16MM FILM, 3/4 OR 1/2 IN VIDEO H-C A
Describes the work of scientists associated with the deep sea drilling project as they work aboard the ship Glomar Challenger, which is capable of sending a probe 20,000 feet to retrieve samples of the ocean floor for analysis, in an attempt to determine what the earth looked like millions of years ago. Hypothesizes that the earth was once a single body of land.
Prod-NET Dist-IU 1969

Project Discovery - A Demonstration In Education C 28 MIN
16MM FILM, 3/4 OR 1/2 IN VIDEO C
Describes project discovery, an examination of audiovisual materials as the primary element of instruction. Describes classroom utilization of audio-visual materials.
Prod-EBF Dist-EBEC 1965

Project Earth - Airports (Kennedy And La Guardia) C 9 MIN
16MM FILM OPTICAL SOUND
Documents the environmental impact of jet noise and traffic congestion surrounding John F Kennedy and La Guardia airports near New York City and explores alternative solutions to the problem.
LC NO. 74-700365
Prod-WNETTV Dist-WNETTV 1974

Project Famous C 24 MIN
16MM FILM OPTICAL SOUND
Uses an animated model to illustrate findings about the processes of sea floor spreading discovered by Project Famous. Describes how the Woods Hole Institute of Oceanography set up the project, the technology involved and what has been learned.
Prod-BBCTV Dist-OPENU 1979

Project Famous C 24 MIN
16MM FILM, 3/4 OR 1/2 IN VIDEO
Uses an animated model to illustrate findings about the processes of sea floor spreading discovered by Project Famous. Describes how the Woods Hole Institute of Oceanography set up the project, the technology involved and what has been learned.
Prod-OPENU Dist-MEDIAG Prodn-BBCTV 1979

Project G B 15 MIN
16MM FILM OPTICAL SOUND C T
Consists of a documentary record of gambling behavior in a variety of situations which include teen-age groups in tenement districts and pool rooms and adults at race tracks. Attempts to indicate some of the psychological causes of gambling.
Prod-PSUPCR Dist-CCNY 1956

Project Gemini - The Next Step In Space B 9 MIN
16MM FILM OPTICAL SOUND J A
Animated. Explains Project Gemini, America's next step into space. Introduces astronauts who will fly Gemini missions.
From The Screen News Digest Series. Vol 6, Issue 2
LC NO. FIA68-2074
Prod-HEARST Dist-HEARST 1963

Project Gemini And Sea Lab II B 18 MIN
16MM FILM OPTICAL SOUND
Reports on America's astronauts and aquanauts as they explore the sky and sea in Project Gemini and Sea Lab II.
From The Screen News Digest Series.
Prod-HEARST Dist-HEARST

Project Gemini Mission Review 1965 C 20 MIN
3/4 INCH VIDEO CASSETTE
Highlights the six Gemini missions in 1965, including the Gemini II verification of spacecraft reentry, the first manned mission by astronauts Grissom and Young in Gemini III, the stroll in space by astronaut White of Gemini V and the first dual missions of Gemini VII in which two spacecrafts rendezvoused in space.
Prod-NASA Dist-NASA 1972

Project Hardsite C 14 MIN
16MM FILM OPTICAL SOUND
Depicts the launching of the rocket-like F-100 A/C.
Prod-NAA Dist-RCKWL

Project Health—A Series
16MM FILM - 3/4 IN VIDEO
Discusses how illness costs an organization and presents information on eight health hazards.
Prod-SEARLE Dist-BNA

Alcohol - Drug Of Choice	027 MIN
Ashes To Ashes	024 MIN
Cancer - Common And Curable	025 MIN
Fat Of The Land, The	026 MIN
Gift Of Energy, The	026 MIN
Healthy Heart, The	027 MIN
Just One More Time	024 MIN
Pressure Principle, The	025 MIN

Project Management C 50 MIN
3/4 OR 1/2 INCH VIDEO CASSETTE C
Covers project casts, hardware and software, program environments, product, instrumentation and process control.
From The Microcomputers - An Overview For Managers And Engineers Series.
Prod-GMIEMI Dist-AMCEE

Project Management - Cash Flow B 60 MIN
3/4 OR 1/2 INCH VIDEO CASSETTE
See series title for descriptive statement.
From The Project Management And CPM Series. Pt 6
Prod-UAZMIC Dist-UAZMIC 1977

Project Management And CPM—A Series

Consists of a short course on project management and CPM taught by Robert H Wortman, Associate Professor of Civil Engineering at the University of Arizona.
Prod-UAZMIC Dist-UAZMIC 1977

Development And Use Of Bar Charts	060 MIN
Float Computations	060 MIN
Model Development	060 MIN
Network Computations	060 MIN
PERT Computations and Analysis	060 MIN
Project Management - Cash Flow	060 MIN
Resource Management	060 MIN

Project Management For Engineers—A Series
PRO
Tells how successful project managers get things done on schedule and within budget.
Prod-AMCEE Dist-AMCEE

Completing And Summary	050 MIN
Introduction And Defining	050 MIN
Leading	050 MIN
Monitoring	050 MIN
Planning, Pt 1	050 MIN
Planning, Pt 2	050 MIN

Project Management Techniques—A Series
PRO
Uses classroom format to videotape 28 one-hour lectures. Discusses concepts needed to understand and use PERT and CPM scheduling techniques as applied to construction and management problems. Includes network cost accounting, time cost tradeoffs and network scheduling with limited resources.
Prod-UIDEEO Dist-AMCEE

Project Management—A Series
IND
Details a step-by-step course focusing on the skills and techniques required for successful project management.
LC NO. 81-707501
Prod-AMCEE Dist-AMCEE 1981

Project Management—A Series

Shows techniques for successful project management. Presented by A Richard De Luca. Includes participant manual and facilitator's guide.
Prod-ITCORP Dist-ITCORP

Implementing And Controlling Your Project	030 MIN
Managing People For Project Success	030 MIN
Manloading And Budgeting In Project Planning	030 MIN
Organizing For Successful Project Management	030 MIN
Planning A Project And Building Your Project	030 MIN
Using Networking And Bar Charting In Project	030 MIN

Project Management—A Series
PRO
Provides an introduction to the successful management of customer contract programs, computer contract programs, computer programming projects, facility and relocation projects and other similar projects.
Prod-MIOT Dist-MIOT

Completion	034 MIN
Control	042 MIN
Definition	048 MIN
Implementation	040 MIN
Planning - Pt 1	043 MIN
Planning - Pt 2	045 MIN

Project Management—A Series
PRO
Uses classroom format to videotape 42 hours of lectures on 42 cassettes. Covers organizing, planning, scheduling and controlling projects. Discusses use of CPM and PERT, computer applications, and case studies of project management problems and solutions.
Prod-UAKEN Dist-AMCEE

Project Manager Or Product Manager? C 30 MIN
3/4 OR 1/2 INCH VIDEO CASSETTE
Points out that the Information Systems manager must function as a product manager as well as a project manager. Reveals that a product manager takes a broader perspective, considering issues such as operational costs, maintenance, enhancement, marketing and education as they relate to products and services.
From The Changing Role Of The Information Systems Manager Series.
Prod-DELTAK Dist-DELTAK

Project Mercury C 28 MIN
16MM FILM OPTICAL SOUND
Presents animated sequences of a Mercury orbital manned mission, demonstrating the rigors of astronaut training and the complexities of the program.
Prod-NASA Dist-NASA

Project Middle East—A Series
I-J
Offers a look at life in the Arab world and Israel.
Prod-UNICEF Dist-GPITVL

Different Path, A	30 MIN
Economy, The	20 MIN
Kibbutz	30 MIN
People, The	20 MIN
Place, The	20 MIN

Project Operations, Pt 1 C 45 MIN
3/4 OR 1/2 INCH VIDEO CASSETTE PRO
Discusses team building. Covers projects and matrices. Comments on planning and problem solving meetings.
From The Advanced Project Management Series.
Prod-AMCEE Dist-AMCEE

Project Operations, Pt 2 C 45 MIN
3/4 OR 1/2 INCH VIDEO CASSETTE PRO
Shows how to design project reporting formats. Stresses the right way to close the project.
From The Advanced Project Management Series.
Prod-AMCEE Dist-AMCEE

Project ORBIS In Ankara, Turkey - A Secondary Implant C 17 MIN
3/4 OR 1/2 INCH VIDEO CASSETTE PRO
Demonstrates Dr Leiske technique for secondary lens implantation.
From The Project ORBIS Videotape Subscription Series.
Prod-HSCIC Dist-HSCIC 1982

Project ORBIS In Berlin - Corneal Wedge Resection C 30 MIN
3/4 OR 1/2 INCH VIDEO CASSETTE PRO
Shows corneal wedge resection performed by Dr Troutman. Demonstrates the use of a prototypical, double-bladed diamond knife.
From The Project ORBIS Videotape Subscription Series.
Prod-HSCIC Dist-HSCIC 1982

Project ORBIS In Berlin - Penetrating Keratoplasty C 28 MIN
3/4 OR 1/2 INCH VIDEO CASSETTE PRO
Shows a corneal transplant performed by Dr Troutman and provides surgeons with the rationale behind each of the steps performed.
From The Project ORBIS Videotape Subscription Series.
Prod-HSCIC Dist-HSCIC 1982

Project ORBIS In Birmingham, England - Molteno Long Tube Implant C 26 MIN
3/4 OR 1/2 INCH VIDEO CASSETTE PRO
Discusses Dr Cairns' technique for inserting the Molteno tube and anchoring it at the back of the eye.
From The Project ORBIS Videotape Subscription Series.
Prod-HSCIC Dist-HSCIC 1982

Project ORBIS In Birmingham, England - Clear Corneal Iridectomy And... C 25 MIN
3/4 OR 1/2 INCH VIDEO CASSETTE PRO
Complete title is Project ORBIS In Birmingham, England - Clear Corneal Iridectomy And Trabeculectomy. Shows Dr Cairns performing a clear corneal iridectomy on one patient and a trabeculectomy on a second.
From The Project ORBIS Videotape Subscription Series.
Prod-HSCIC Dist-HSCIC 1982

Project ORBIS In Birmingham, England - Two Methods Of Cataract Extraction And ... C 24 MIN
3/4 OR 1/2 INCH VIDEO CASSETTE PRO
Complete Title is Project ORBIS In Birmingham, England - Two Methods of Cataract Extraction And Intraocular Lens Implantation. Features Dr Barnet implanting an iris clip intraocular lens, while Dr McCannel implants a Leiske-type anterior chamber lens.
From The Project ORBIS Videotape Subscription Series.
Prod-HSCIC Dist-HSCIC 1982

Project ORBIS In Canton, China - Silica Bead Cataract Extraction C 20 MIN
3/4 OR 1/2 INCH VIDEO CASSETTE PRO
Demonstrates Dr McIntyre performing a simple Chinese method of cataract extraction.
From The Project ORBIS Videotape Subscription Series.
Prod-HSCIC Dist-HSCIC 1982

Project ORBIS In Cartagena, Colombia - Vitrectomy For Cysticercus C 39 MIN
3/4 OR 1/2 INCH VIDEO CASSETTE PRO
Demonstrates Dr Ronald Michels performing the removal of a retinal cysticercus.
From The Project ORBIS Videotape Subscription Series.
Prod-HSCIC Dist-HSCIC 1982

Project ORBIS In Kingston - Extracapsular Cataract Extraction With Intraocular Lens... C 33 MIN
3/4 OR 1/2 INCH VIDEO CASSETTE PRO
Complete title is Project ORBIS In Kingston Extracapsular Cataract Extraction With Intraocular Lens Implantation. Demonstrates Dr Praeger's techniques for performing an extracapsular cataract extraction and intraocular lens implantation.
From The Project ORBIS Videotape Subscription Series.
Prod-HSCIC Dist-HSCIC 1982

Project ORBIS In Kingston - Senile Ptosis Repair C 30 MIN
3/4 OR 1/2 INCH VIDEO CASSETTE PRO

Demonstrates Dr Iliff's technique for ptosis repair. Provides ongoing commentary on the anatomical and technical aspects of the procedure.
From The Project ORBIS Videotape Subscription Series.
Prod-HSCIC Dist-HSCIC 1982

Project ORBIS In Munich - Extracapsular Cataract Extraction With Intraocular Lens... C 20 MIN
3/4 OR 1/2 INCH VIDEO CASSETTE PRO
Complete title is Project ORBIS In Munich Extracapsular Cataract Extraction With Intraocular Lens Implantation. Demonstrates Dr McIntyre's microsurgical technique for extracapsular cataract extraction.
From The Project ORBIS Videotape Subscription Series.
Prod-HSCIC Dist-HSCIC 1982

Project ORBIS In Munich - Phacoemulsification Of A Cataract With Posterior Chamber... C 17 MIN
3/4 OR 1/2 INCH VIDEO CASSETTE PRO
Complete title is Project ORBIS In Munich Phacoemulsification OfCataract With Posterior Chamber Intraocular Lens Implantation. Introduces medical students, residents in ophthalmology, and ophthalmologists to a technique for phacoemulsification of a cataract.
From The Project ORBIS Videotape Subscription Series.
Prod-HSCIC Dist-HSCIC 1982

Project ORBIS Videotape Subscription—A Series
PRO
Takes you around the world for various ophthalmologic projects.
Prod-HSCIC Dist-HSCIC 1982

Project ORBIS In Ankara, Turkey - A Secondary
Project ORBIS In Berlin - Corneal Wedge 030 MIN
Project ORBIS In Berlin - Penetrating 028 MIN
Project ORBIS In Birmingham, 026 MIN
Project ORBIS In Birmingham, 025 MIN
Project ORBIS In Birmingham, England - Two 024 MIN
Project ORBIS In Canton, China - Silica Bead 020 MIN
Project ORBIS In Cartagena, 039 MIN
Project ORBIS In Kingston - Extracapsular 033 MIN
Project ORBIS In Kingston - Senile Ptosis 030 MIN
Project ORBIS In Munich - Extracapsular 020 MIN
Project ORBIS In Munich - Phacoemulsification 017 MIN

Project Pride - A Positive Approach To Vandalism C 17 MIN
16MM FILM - 3/4 IN VIDEO
Shows how one elementary school district cut vandalism costs in half or more. Explains how students were involved in school improvement projects.
Prod-PARKRD Dist-LAWREN

Project Puffin C 13 MIN
16MM FILM, 3/4 OR 1/2 IN VIDEO J-C A
Shows the effort being made to induce the puffin to recolonize their former breeding sites.
LC NO. 82-706571
Prod-NAS Dist-LCOA 1982

Project Self Discovery—A Series
K-P
Includes 32, 15-minute Language Arts lessons. Follows the children's sequential development of understanding and use of symbols to represent their actions in time and space. Teaches children that through their senses, as they act upon their environment, words, numbers and the visual arts of movement, music and drama are communicative symbols which can represent ideas, actions, people and objects far removed in time and place.
Prod-WESTEL Dist-WESTEL

Project Shoal C 18 MIN
16MM FILM OPTICAL SOUND
A non-technical film on the underground Project Shoal detonation, an experiment conducted by the Department of Defense with the participation of the Atomic Energy Commission. Describes the selection of the test site near Fallon, Nevada, the pre-shot preparations to insure public safety and the efforts to inform the citizens of Fallon of the proposed shot, the reaction of various city groups to the test, the Seismic Station Program, instrumentation and the results of the detonation.
LC NO. FIE64-144
Prod-USAEC Dist-USNAC Prodn-USDD 1964

Project Skill C 15 MIN
16MM FILM OPTICAL SOUND
Shows how a two-year project in the state of Wisconsin has developed, tested and demonstrated methods and procedures for employing less severely mentally and emotionally handicapped persons. Points out that state agencies are using the hire first, train later concept and that such employees will be absorbed in regular work settings with the nonhandicapped.
LC NO. 76-701596
Prod-USETA Dist-USNAC 1975

Project Slush C 21 MIN
16MM FILM OPTICAL SOUND
Reports tests conducted at NAFEC using the 850 jet aircraft to determine the effects of slush on jet aircraft accelerating for take off.
LC NO. 74-705438
Prod-FAAFL Dist-USNAC 1963

Project Solo C 28 MIN
16MM FILM OPTICAL SOUND
Presents a look at a new program that uses individualized computer programming to expand the horizons of high school math, physics and chemistry. Features students who demonstrate and explain their programs and give spontaneous reactions to the new technology. Discusses Project Solo's design, its aims and the role of staff members and teachers in making the project work.
Prod-MATHWW Dist-MATHWW 1971

Project Stormfury Studies Hurricanes C 4 MIN
16MM FILM OPTICAL SOUND
Profiles Project Stormfury, which is seeking to decrease the destructive wind velocity of hurricanes.
Prod-ALLFP Dist-NSTA 1973

Project STRETCH (Strategies To Train Regular Educators To Teach Children With...)—A Series
T S
Presents a program developed by project STRETCH (Strategies To Train Regular Educators To Teach Children With Handicaps). Covers special education inservice training for regular classroom teachers where good instruction for students is the basic approach, with emphasis on handicaps only where they make an instructional difference. Contains three broad categories, including general teaching strategies and techniques, teaching strategies and techniques specific to instructional areas, and information relevant to handicapping conditions.
Prod-METCO Dist-HUBDSC

Art And The Exceptional 030 MIN
Assessment 030 MIN
Behavior Modification 030 MIN
Career Education 030 MIN
Classroom Management 030 MIN
Counseling Parents 030 MIN
Exceptional Child, The 030 MIN
Grouping And Special Students 030 MIN
Individualized Instruction 030 MIN
Language Experience Approach 030 MIN
Learning Centers 030 MIN
Learning Styles 030 MIN
Mainstreaming 030 MIN
Mathematics And The Special Student 030 MIN
Peer Tutoring 030 MIN
Questioning Skills 030 MIN
Reading In The Content Area 030 MIN
Simulation 030 MIN
Spelling 030 MIN
Value Clarification 030 MIN

Project STRETCH—A Series
T
Presents an education program which explains how to facilitate the mainstreaming of exceptional children into a regular classroom.
Prod-METCO Dist-HUBDSC Prodn-GAEDTN 1980

Art And The Exceptional Child 30 MIN
Assessment 30 MIN
Behavior Modification 30 MIN
Career Education 30 MIN
Classroom Management 30 MIN
Counseling Parents Of Exceptional Children 30 MIN
Grouping 25 MIN
Increasing Teacher Effectiveness Through Peer 29 MIN
Individualized Instruction 30 MIN
Label The Behavior, Not The Child 30 MIN
Language Experience Approach 30 MIN
Learning Centers 27 MIN
Learning Styles 30 MIN
Mainstreaming 30 MIN
Mathematics And The Special Child 29 MIN
Questioning Skills 30 MIN
Reading In The Content Area 30 MIN
Simulation - The Next Best Thing To Being There 30 MIN
Spelling - Visualization, The Key To Spelling 30 MIN
Value Clarification 30 MIN

Project Survival—A Series
I-J
Assists students in building upon basic map and globe skills.
Prod-GPITVL Dist-GPITVL

Angleland 20 MIN
Art Of Earth Travel - Interpreting Road Maps 20 MIN
Art Of Earth Travel - Many Maps To Use 20 MIN
Art Of Earth Travel - Review 20 MIN
Attitude On Latitude 20 MIN
Case For Maps And Globes, The 20 MIN
Knowing Where You're Going 20 MIN
Lines To Find 20 MIN
Looking Northward 20 MIN
Map Scales - How And Why 20 MIN
Pole To Pole 20 MIN

Project Survival—A Series
I-J
Prod-MAETEL Dist-GPITVL

Angleland 20 MIN
Art Of Earth Travel - Interpreting Road Maps 20 MIN
Art Of Earth Travel - Many Maps To Use 20 MIN
Art Of Earth Travel - Review 20 MIN
Attitude On Latitude 20 MIN
Case For Maps And Globes, The 20 MIN
Knowing Where You're Going 20 MIN
Lines To Find 20 MIN
Looking Northward 20 MIN
Map Scales - How And Why 20 MIN
Pole To Pole 20 MIN

Project The Right Image C 14 MIN
3/4 INCH VIDEO CASSETTE H-C A
Discusses the proper techniques of running a film projector.
Prod-CHERIO Dist-GPITVL 1977

Project Universe - Astronomy—A Series
C A
Covers several aspects of astronomy including the history of astronomy, characteristics of the solar system, and extraterrestrial communication.
Prod-COAST Dist-CDTEL Prodn-SCCON

Astronomer's Universe, The 029 MIN
Astronomical Observation 029 MIN
Big Bang, The 029 MIN
Binary Stars 029 MIN
Black Holes 029 MIN
Earth - The Water Planet 029 MIN
Electromagnetic Radiation 029 MIN
Expanding Universe, The 029 MIN
Extraterrestrial Communication 029 MIN
Galaxies 029 MIN
Historical Perspectives 029 MIN
Jupiter 029 MIN
Lunar Aspects 029 MIN
Lunar Geology 029 MIN
Mars 029 MIN
Mercury And Venus 029 MIN
Message Of Starlight, The 029 MIN
Milky Way Discovered, The 029 MIN
Milky Way Structure, The 029 MIN
Quasars 029 MIN
Relativity 029 MIN
Saturn 029 MIN
Solar Image, The 029 MIN
Solar Interior, The 029 MIN
Solar System Debris 029 MIN
Stars - The Nuclear Furnace 029 MIN
Supernova And Pulsars 029 MIN
Surveying The Stars 029 MIN
Uranus, Neptune, Pluto 029 MIN
White Dwarfs And Red Giants 029 MIN

Project 20—A Series
16MM FILM, 3/4 OR 1/2 IN VIDEO H-C A
Looks at aspects of America's past, from the mid-18th century to 1950.
Prod-NBC Dist-CRMP

End Of The Trail - The American Plains Indian 053 MIN
Great War, The - 1914-1917 052 MIN
Innocent Years, The - 1901-1914 054 MIN
Island Called Ellis, The 053 MIN
Jazz Age, The - 1919-1929 050 MIN
Life In The Thirties 052 MIN
Mark Twain's America 054 MIN
Not So Long Ago - 1945-1950 054 MIN
Real West, The 054 MIN

Project, The C 30 MIN
16MM FILM OPTICAL SOUND J-H T R
Dramatizes two high school boys who are undertaking a science project in a garage. Shows the importance of friendship.
LC NO. FIA66-1335
Prod-FAMF Dist-FAMF 1966

Project, The C 6 MIN
16MM FILM, 3/4 OR 1/2 IN VIDEO I-J
Depicts how to work on a project with others and how not to end with a few doing the work and the rest giving orders.
From The What Should I Do Series.
Prod-DISNEY Dist-WDEMCO 1970

Project, The C 35 MIN
3/4 OR 1/2 INCH VIDEO CASSETTE
Points out the keys to successful project management using an entertaining vehicle of a band of white-collar criminals planning and carrying out a crime.
Prod-MELROS Dist-VISUCP

Project, The (French) C 6 MIN
16MM FILM, 3/4 OR 1/2 IN VIDEO P
Helps develop attitudes about the need for mutual cooperation.
From The What Should I Do (French) Series.
Prod-WDEMCO Dist-WDEMCO 1970

Projectile Motion C
3/4 OR 1/2 INCH VIDEO CASSETTE
Shows interesting examples of flight in a weightless space.
From The Experiments In Space Series.
Prod-EDMEC Dist-EDMEC

Projecting National Images C 30 MIN
3/4 OR 1/2 INCH VIDEO CASSETTE
Focuses on how several countries present themselves to the rest of the world through print and broadcast journalism. Hosted by Daniel Schorr and featuring several foreign correspondents and media representatives from around the world.
From The Issues In World Communications, 1979 Series.
Prod-OHUTC Dist-OHUTC

Projecting The Ball C 15 MIN
3/4 OR 1/2 INCH VIDEO CASSETTE T
Explains how to teach primary students to strike a ball with various parts of their body and about the application of force, and about the relationship of impact to desired direction.
From The Leaps And Bounds Series. No. 14
Prod-HSDE Dist-AITECH 1984

Projection Of Australia, The C 59 MIN
16MM FILM OPTICAL SOUND J-C A
Presents a compilation of excerpts from productions of the Commonwealth Film Unit made over the past 21 years.
Prod-ANAIB Dist-AUIS

Projections C 35 MIN
16MM FILM OPTICAL SOUND H-C A
Tells a story about a photographer who discovers he is dying of cancer and dreams that all his photographs of children turn into symbols of death. Concludes with his discovery of life's possibilities after he is visited by his niece.
LC NO. 79-701622
Prod-JURMAR Dist-JURMAR 1979

Projections For The Future In Nursing B 30 MIN
16MM FILM OPTICAL SOUND C

Shows three young graduates as they listen to and discuss various views of nursing. Presents legislative and healthcare leaders as they comment on the national philosophy of health care, the extension of government control, the changing roles of health professionals, community health services and new concepts in nursing education.
From The Nursing Perspectives Series.
LC NO. 75-706828
Prod-VDONUR Dist-AJN Prodn-WTTWTV 1969

Projections For The Future—A Series J-C A
Consists of futurists Willis Harman, Frank Herbert, Dennis Meadows and John Platt presenting their views and a scenario showing what life might be like if their ideas became reality.
Prod-BSCS Dist-CRYSP

Behavior Model, A 018 MIN
Growth Model, A 017 MIN
Humanist Model, A 020 MIN

Projective Generation Of Conics C 16 MIN
16MM FILM, 3/4 OR 1/2 IN VIDEO H-C
Focuses on the several projective definitions and demonstrates the logical relationship between the methods.
From The Geometry Series.
Prod-UMINN Dist-IFB 1971

Projects Mean People C
16MM FILM OPTICAL SOUND
Looks at three case studies involving computers and business.
Prod-OPENU Dist-OPENU

Prolog C 60 MIN
3/4 OR 1/2 INCH VIDEO CASSETTE C
Introduces programming in Logic, language of the Japanese fifth generation effort. Covers constants, variables, and compound terms, facts, rules and clauses, commands and questions, the database, factors and predicates, lists, recursion, backtracking, elements of predicate calculus and applications.
From The Introduction To Artificial--Intelligence Series.
Prod-UAZMIC Dist-AMCEE

Prologue - The Lion And The Crown C 7 MIN
16MM FILM OPTICAL SOUND J-C A
A revised version of the 1964 film Of Stars And Men. Presents a fable about forest animals who observe the miracles of man and are so awed by him that they present him with a crown. Shows how he gives up his hum-drum existence to seek truth through a philosophical quest.
From The Of Stars And Men (2nd Ed) Series.
LC NO. 76-701274
Prod-HUBLEY Dist-RADIM 1976

Prologue In Masonry B 24 MIN
16MM FILM OPTICAL SOUND H-C A
Explores some of the history of bricklaying and clay masonry structures made from brick.
LC NO. 75-701979
Prod-BRICKI Dist-BRICKI Prodn-ROSNER

Prologue To Peace B 16 MIN
16MM FILM OPTICAL SOUND
Shows a delegation of peace from Malaysia, headed by Malaysian Deputy Premier Tun Abdul Razak, arriving in Bangkok, Thailand, on May 29, 1966, to meet with an Indonesian delegation, headed by Indonesian Deputy Premier Adam Malik. Tells how they were hosted by Thai Foreign Minister Tun Thanat Khoman and met to discuss ways and means of ending the Indonesian confrontation and to restore friendly relations between the two countries.
Prod-FILEM Dist-PMFMUN 1966

Prologue To Tomorrow C 19 MIN
16MM FILM OPTICAL SOUND
Shows how advance planning helped provide sufficient energy during an extremely harsh winter.
LC NO. 77-701829
Prod-CONPOW Dist-CONPOW Prodn-FARTC 1977

Prolonging The Life Of Your Vegetable C 29 MIN
3/4 OR 1/2 INCH VIDEO CASSETTE
See series title for descriptive statement.
From The Crockett's Victory Garden Series.
Prod-WGBHTV Dist-KINGFT

Promedia - Microcomputer Applications—A Series
Offers five half hour videotapes teaching the basics of software categories, including word processing, database management, spreadsheets, communications and graphics. Uses examples and applications in the workplace.
Prod-DSIM Dist-DSIM

Computer Calc - Electronic Spreadsheets And 030 MIN
Computer Images - Computer Graphics 030 MIN
Computer Talk - Microcomputer Applications 030 MIN
Electronic Words - Word Processing And 030 MIN
Keeping Track - Data Base Management And 030 MIN
Microcomputer - Applications Series, The 030 MIN

Promedia 1 - The Video Computer Primer C 60 MIN
3/4 OR 1/2 INCH VIDEO CASSETTE A
Demostrates the capabilities of a personal computer. Includes segments on data base information and an introduction to programming and computer languages.
Prod-DSIM Dist-DSIM

Promise C 14 MIN
16MM FILM OPTICAL SOUND P-H
Various Girl Scout community service projects are used to show that scouting is a significant influence in the lives of girls and that it deserves community support.
LC NO. FIA68-1542
Prod-GSUSA Dist-GSUSA 1968

Promise C 14 MIN
16MM FILM OPTICAL SOUND I-H A R
Tells how a young woman looks back in her life and realizes that the promises of others to her and her promises to others have given her a fuller life. States that God has also used promises to enrich human life.
LC NO. 80-700758
Prod-IKONOG Dist-IKONOG 1974

Promise And Danger Of Genetic Engineering, The C
1/2 IN VIDEO CASSETTE (VHS)
Weighs potential benefits and risks of genetic engineering. Explores ethical ramifications of eugenics, cloning and genetic screening.
From The Genetic Engineering - Prospects Of The Future Series.
Prod-IBIS Dist-IBIS

Promise And The Challenge, The C 18 MIN
16MM FILM OPTICAL SOUND
Discusses Dow's Texas division and how it produces many basic intermediates that serve as working tools for chemists and manufacturers.
Prod-DCC Dist-DCC

Promise City B 29 MIN
2 INCH VIDEOTAPE
Portrays a small Iowa farming community and explores its past, present and people that are a part of both.
From The Synergism - Cities And Towns Series.
Prod-IEBNTV Dist-PUBTEL

Promise For The Future C 16 MIN
16MM FILM OPTICAL SOUND
Uses split-screen opticals to show division of work, employees and products of Rockwell International. Includes information on the company's space shuttle and B-1 bomber.
LC NO. 76-703154
Prod-RCKWL Dist-RCKWL Prodn-PTRSEN 1976

Promise For The Future (French) C 16 MIN
16MM FILM OPTICAL SOUND
Uses split-screen opticals to show division of work, employees and products of Rockwell International. Includes information on the company's space shuttle and B-1 bomber.
LC NO. 76-703154
Prod-RCKWL Dist-RCKWL Prodn-PTRSEN 1976

Promise For The Future (German) C 16 MIN
16MM FILM OPTICAL SOUND
Uses split-screen opticals to show division of work, employees and products of Rockwell International. Includes information on the company's space shuttle and B-1 bomber.
LC NO. 76-703154
Prod-RCKWL Dist-RCKWL Prodn-PTRSEN 1976

Promise For The Future (Italian) C 16 MIN
16MM FILM OPTICAL SOUND
Uses split-screen opticals to show division of work, employees and products of Rockwell International. Includes information on the company's space shuttle and B-1 bomber.
LC NO. 76-703154
Prod-RCKWL Dist-RCKWL Prodn-PTRSEN 1976

Promise For The Future (Spanish) C 16 MIN
16MM FILM OPTICAL SOUND
Uses split-screen opticals to show division of work, employees and products of Rockwell International. Includes information on the company's space shuttle and B-1 bomber.
LC NO. 76-703154
Prod-RCKWL Dist-RCKWL Prodn-PTRSEN 1976

Promise Fulfilled And The Promise Broken, The C 52 MIN
16MM FILM, 3/4 OR 1/2 IN VIDEO J-C A
Presents Alistair Cooke who shows how the Depression came after the war to end all wars and after the promise of unlimited prosperity symbolized by a Model-T Ford and a mail order catolog. Explains how the mills stayed closed until the United States returned to war.
From The America - A Personal History Of The United States Series. No. 10
LC NO. 79-707145
Prod-BBCTV Dist-TIMLIF 1972

Promise Of Life, The C 29 MIN
3/4 INCH VIDEO CASSETTE
Describes the history and purpose of the Knights of Columbus. Emphasizes its social and humanitarian works throughout the western hemisphere.
Prod-KNICOL Dist-MTP

Promise Of Plato C 7 MIN
16MM FILM, 3/4 OR 1/2 IN VIDEO I-C A
Shows the diversity of learning experiences possible with computer-assisted education and points out that this individualized instruction helps to meet the needs of each student.
Prod-NSF Dist-AMEDFL 1974

Promise Of Sociology, The C 30 MIN
3/4 OR 1/2 INCH VIDEO CASSETTE C
Examines the discipline of sociology, one which examines the many groups and relationships in which individuals participate.
From The Focus On Society Series.
Prod-DALCCD Dist-DALCCD

Promise Of Space, The C 14 MIN
16MM FILM OPTICAL SOUND A
Describes the diverse activities of the Marshall Space Flight Center in Alabama.
LC NO. 77-700778
Prod-NASA Dist-USNAC 1976

Promise Of Spring C 18 MIN
16MM FILM OPTICAL SOUND C A
Demonstrates how to get best results from world famous imported Holland spring flowering bulbs.
Prod-NATDIS Dist-NATDIS 1955

Promise Of Spring C 26 MIN
16MM FILM OPTICAL SOUND I-C A
Shows plants, animals and elements as they are affected by the changing patterns of spring in British Columbia, Canada.
From The Audubon Wildlife Theatre Series.
LC NO. 73-703231
Prod-KEGPL Dist-AVEXP 1973

Promise Of Spring C 26 MIN
16MM FILM OPTICAL SOUND
Shows the changing patterns of plants, animals and elements in the spring from the shores of Vancouver Island to the alpine meadows of the Canadian Rockies and the rich valleys of the interior.
LC NO. 76-702046
Prod-WILFGP Dist-KEGPL 1975

Promise Shared, A C 29 MIN
2 INCH VIDEOTAPE
Documents the status of women in Israel.
Prod-WOSUTV Dist-PUBTEL

Promise Shared, A - Women In Israeli Society C 25 MIN
16MM FILM OPTICAL SOUND
Presents working women in Israel, including labor union officials, a kibbutz secretary, an attorney and a newspaper publisher, who takes a hard look at the legal and social status of women in their country. Features divergent opinions based on differences in age, experience and expectation and an analysis of the women's movement in the United States as it affects Israel.
Prod-ADL Dist-ADL

Promise, The C 15 MIN
16MM FILM, 3/4 OR 1/2 IN VIDEO I-J
Presents a story about a girl and her unhappiness when she learns that the horse she has been caring for is to be sold.
From The Bloomin' Human Series.
Prod-PAULST Dist-MEDIAG 1977

Promise, The C 17 MIN
16MM FILM, 3/4 OR 1/2 IN VIDEO P-I
Deals with the topic of responsibility through the story of a young girl who takes care of her blind neighbor's guide dog in order to earn money to buy her own puppy.
Prod-BARR Dist-BARR Prodn-ARMUND 1982

Promise, The C 29 MIN
3/4 INCH VIDEO CASSETTE
Focuses on problems faced by Native American students in South Dakota.
From The As We See It Series.
Prod-WTTWTV Dist-PUBTEL

Promise, The (Captioned) C 17 MIN
16MM FILM - VIDEO, ALL FORMATS P-I
Tells the story of a little girl who takes care of a blind man's guide dog in order to earn money to buy a puppy. Deals with what happens when she leaves the gate open and the dog gets out. Examines promises, responsibility and love.
Prod-BARR Dist-BARR Prodn-ARMUND

Promised Land, Troubled Land B 14 MIN
16MM FILM, 3/4 OR 1/2 IN VIDEO
Tells of major events during the centuries of smouldering conflict that have shaped history in the Middle East from ancient days to modern times.
From The Screen News Digest Series. Vol 16, No. 4
Prod-HEARST Dist-HEARST 1973

Promised Lands C 55 MIN
16MM FILM OPTICAL SOUND
Documents the October, 1973, war between Israel and its Arab neighbors. Emphasizes the Jewish struggle for survival throughout history. Explains that Israel is a land promised to many peoples.
Prod-NYFLMS Dist-NYFLMS 1973

Promised Lands C 87 MIN
16MM FILM OPTICAL SOUND
Documents the October, 1973, war between Israel and its Arab neighbors. Emphasizes the Jewish struggle for survival throughout history. Explains that Israel is a land promised to many peoples.
Prod-NYFLMS Dist-NYFLMS 1973

Promised People, The C 15 MIN
16MM FILM OPTICAL SOUND
Tells the story of Kiryat-Gat, a typical Israeli town, as a microcosm of Israel's hopes and problems.
Prod-UJA Dist-ALDEN

Promises C 21 MIN
16MM FILM, 3/4 OR 1/2 IN VIDEO J A
Explores advertising and its influence on our lives through a series of satires on television commercials.
Prod-SUTHRB Dist-SUTHRB

Promises - Profile Of An Alcoholic C 30 MIN
16MM FILM, 3/4 OR 1/2 IN VIDEO
Tells the true story of a successful theater producer during one crucial period in his life. Shows that he cannot control his drinking and that his problems with alcohol are slowly beginning to destroy every facet of his life. Demonstrates that his wife also has serious emotional problems that contribute to her husband's drinking.

LC NO. 83-706744
Prod-ELKIND Dist-PFP 1982

Promises To Keep–A Series
16MM FILM, 3/4 OR 1/2 IN VIDEO T
Offers inservice training for professionals who work with children with various types of handicaps.
Prod-VPISU Dist-LUF 1979

Behavior Disorders 030 MIN
Classroom Assessment Of Student Needs 030 MIN
Guidelines For Teaching The Handicapped Child 030 MIN
Hearing Impaired Child, The 030 MIN
Instructional And Behavior Management 030 MIN
Introduction To Teaching The Handicapped, An 030 MIN
Mentally Retarded And Slow Learning Child, The 030 MIN
Physically Handicapped And Health Impaired 030 MIN
Related Services For The Handicapped 030 MIN
Specific Learning Disabilities 030 MIN
Speech And Language Disorders 030 MIN
Visually Impaired, The 030 MIN

Promises, Promises C 30 MIN
3/4 OR 1/2 INCH VIDEO CASSETTE K-P
See series title for descriptive statement.
From The Villa Alegre Series.
Prod-BCTV Dist-MDCPB

Promotion And Transfer C 23 MIN
16MM FILM - 3/4 IN VIDEO
Analyzes the requirements of equal employment laws regarding promoting or transferring personnel within an organization.
From The Fair Employment Practice Series.
Prod-BNA Dist-BNA 1979

Promotion Of Q C Circle Activities C 30 MIN
3/4 OR 1/2 INCH VIDEO CASSETTE
Discusses Q C circle activities, unique to Japan and the key to success of T Q C, covering explanations of 'voluntarism', 'total participation', 'improving the physical constitution of a company' and 'respecting humanity'.
From The Seven Steps To T Q C Promotion Series.
Prod-TOYOVS Dist-TOYOVS

Promotional Strategy–A Series
C
Covers gamut of marketing and sales promotion in 30 videotapes of 30 classroom lectures. Includes marketing management point of view, objective, methods, strategies, budgets, and measures effectiveness of campaign management including advertising, public relations, sales promotion, reseller support and personal selling.
Prod-UIDEEO Dist-AMCEE

Pronunciation Difficulties C 8 MIN
3/4 OR 1/2 INCH VIDEO CASSETTE
See series title for descriptive statement.
From The Better Spelling Series.
Prod-TELSTR Dist-DELTAK

Pronunciation Of Medical Terminology C 15 MIN
3/4 OR 1/2 INCH VIDEO CASSETTE PRO
Discusses and demonstrates pronunciation of medical terminology and gives viewers examples to follow. Helps the learner feel comfortable pronouncing medical terminology by showing the similarities between the medical vocabulary and the English language.
From The Medical Terminology Series.
Prod-HSCIC Dist-HSCIC

Proof C 24 MIN
16MM FILM OPTICAL SOUND
Relates how a young man surprises his friends by parachuting out of an airplane and proving his manhood.
LC NO. 81-701143
Prod-USC Dist-USC 1981

Proof By Induction B 16 MIN
3/4 OR 1/2 INCH VIDEO CASSETTE PRO
Continues theorem proving. Illustrates in detail proof by induction.
From The Probability And Random Processes - Elementary Probability Theory Series.
Prod-MIOT Dist-MIOT

Proofs Of Claims Hearing C 58 MIN
3/4 OR 1/2 INCH VIDEO CASSETTE PRO
Presents a hypothetical formal hearing on proof of claims. Covers the language and form of the notice, the best methods of its distribution and the proper stage at which plaintiff's attorney can contact unnamed class members. Includes cost considerations and discouraging of fraudulent claims.
From The Remedies Phase Of An EEO Case - Class Back Pay And Proof Of Claims Series. Pt 1
Prod-ALIABA Dist-ABACPE

Propaganda - International And Domestic B 30 MIN
2 INCH VIDEOTAPE C T
Discusses international propaganda and compares it to the clarity of domestic propaganda. Discusses whether politics can be merchandised like products.
From The Communications And Education Series. No. 15
Prod-NYSED Dist-GPITVL Prodn-WNDTTV

Propaganda - Its Power B 30 MIN
2 INCH VIDEOTAPE C T
Propaganda can result in four outcomes–nothing, conversion, precipitation or confirmation. The outcome is achieved through success of saturation, repetition and association with the receiver's susceptibilities. In a large measure, the success of propaganda is related to education's failure to teach logic. (Broadcast quality)
From The Communications And Education Series. No. 14
Prod-NYSED Dist-GPITVL Prodn-WNDTTV

Propaganda - Meaning And Significance B 30 MIN
2 INCH VIDEOTAPE C T
Propaganda has become a dirty word because of its misuse. We must be aware of it, however, because of its power. (Broadcast quality)
From The Communications And Education Series. No. 13
Prod-NYSED Dist-GPITVL Prodn-WNDTTV

Propaganda - Section 315 B 30 MIN
2 INCH VIDEOTAPE C T
The equal time provision of the Communications Act creates a sensitive issue especially at election time. Section 315 and its implications are related to the larger social problems of the cost of running for office and the whole question of controversial issues. (Broadcast quality)
From The Communications And Education Series. No. 16
Prod-NYSED Dist-GPITVL Prodn-WNDTTV

Propaganda Detectives C 15 MIN
2 INCH VIDEOTAPE I
Provides illustration examples and explanations of propaganda techniques.
From The Images Series.
Prod-CVETVC Dist-GPITVL

Propaganda Message, A (Un Message De Propagande) C 13 MIN
16MM FILM, 3/4 OR 1/2 IN VIDEO H-C A
Presents a cartoon film about the whole heterogenous mixture of Canada and Canadians. Views the way the invisible, adhesive force called federalism makes it all cling together.
Prod-NFBC Dist-PHENIX 1973

Propaganda Parade B 55 MIN
3/4 OR 1/2 INCH VIDEO CASSETTE
Looks at various propaganda shorts from the 1940s and 1950s including some recently declassified footage.
Prod-IHF Dist-IHF

Propagation 1 C 30 MIN
3/4 OR 1/2 INCH VIDEO CASSETTE C A
Discusses plant reproduction. Demonstrates simpler methods of propogation such as layering methods.
From The Home Gardener With John Lenanton Series. Lesson 27
Prod-COAST Dist-CDTEL

Propellant-Plus Heat C 20 MIN
16MM FILM OPTICAL SOUND
A safety film on the handling characteristics of propellants.
Prod-THIOKL Dist-THIOKL 1962

Propellorband (The Propeller Tape) C 30 MIN
3/4 INCH VIDEO CASSETTE
Uses archival World War II footage intercut with the faces of the artist, Klaus Vom Bruch, and an Oriental woman, to suggest futility.
Prod-EAI Dist-EAI

Proper Dressing Of The Football Player C 22 MIN
3/4 OR 1/2 INCH VIDEO CASSETTE T
Describes the football uniform and the function of each piece, with emphasis on the importance of a good fit and the role of the regulation helmet in preventing head injuries.
From The Sports Medicine Series.
Prod-UNIDIM Dist-EBEC 1982

Proper Laboratory Techniques C 59 MIN
3/4 OR 1/2 INCH VIDEO CASSETTE PRO
See series title for descriptive statement.
From The Digital Electronics Series.
Prod-MIOT Dist-MIOT

Proper Operating Room Attire C 24 MIN
16MM FILM OPTICAL SOUND PRO
Explains the controversy over what is worn in the operating room. Designed to inform persons who must enter a surgical suite area with the proper policies and procedures relating to operating room dress.
From The AORN Film Series.
LC NO. 75-703020
Prod-AORN Dist-ACY 1975

Proper Place For Women In The Church, The C 29 MIN
3/4 INCH VIDEO CASSETTE
Discusses the changing role of women in the Catholic church.
From The Woman Series.
Prod-WNEDTV Dist-PUBTEL

Proper Summer Bush Clothing C 10 MIN
16MM FILM, 3/4 OR 1/2 IN VIDEO I-C A
Shows two boys who dress differently for a fishing trip and the resulting differences in comfort and well-being.
From The Survival In The Wilderness Series.
Prod-MORLAT Dist-SF 1967

Proper Training And Hole Fill Procedure C 9 MIN
3/4 OR 1/2 INCH VIDEO CASSETTE IND
Details procedure before tripping out, keeping the fluid level from falling below 30 meters from the top of the hole, and minimum intervals when flow checks should be performed.
From The Blowout Prevention And Well Control Series.
Prod-CAODC Dist-GPCV

Proper Winter Clothing C 13 MIN
16MM FILM, 3/4 OR 1/2 IN VIDEO I-C A
Shows that skiers, hikers and other winter outdoor people learn quickly that it is not how much you have on but what you wear and how you wear it. Provides the necessary clues to keeping warm during outdoor travel in the winter.
From The Outdoor Recreation - Winter Series.
Prod-SF Dist-SF 1967

Properties B 15 MIN
2 INCH VIDEOTAPE P
See series title for descriptive statement.
From The Just Curious Series. No. 1
Prod-EOPS Dist-GPITVL Prodn-KOACTV

Properties And Conditions B 15 MIN
2 INCH VIDEOTAPE P
See series title for descriptive statement.
From The Just Inquisitive Series. No. 1
Prod-EOPS Dist-GPITVL Prodn-KOACTV

Properties And Grain Structure C 20 MIN
3/4 OR 1/2 INCH VIDEO CASSETTE H-C A
See series title for descriptive statement.
From The Engineering Crafts Series.
Prod-BBCTV Dist-FI 1981

Properties And Uses Of Redwood C 25 MIN
16MM FILM OPTICAL SOUND I-C A
Explores the properties of the redwood tree, including its durability, fire-resistance and beauty. Illustrates the architectural uses of different redwood grades, patterns and grains.
Prod-CRA Dist-CRA

Properties Of Air C 15 MIN
3/4 INCH VIDEO CASSETTE I
Shows that although air is a colorless fluid, it exerts force and has weight.
From The Search For Science (2nd Ed.) Unit VI - Air And Weather Series.
Prod-WVIZTV Dist-GPITVL

Properties Of Cardiac Muscle, Pt 1 - Heart Responses To Stimuli C 2 MIN
16MM FILM SILENT
Uses electrical stimulation of an isolated turtle heart to demonstrate the all or nothing response of cardiac muscle, the induction of premature beats and the compensatory pauses.
From The Dukes Physiology Film Series. No. 6
LC NO. 71-710197
Prod-IOWA Dist-IOWA 1971

Properties Of Cardiac Muscle, Pt 2 - Isolation Of The Cardiac Pacemaker C 2 MIN
16MM FILM SILENT
Demonstrates the location and function of the cardiac pacemaker in an isolated turtle heart by successively separating less rhythmic parts from those in which auto-rhythm is most developed.
From The Dukes Physiology Film Series. No. 7
LC NO. 78-710196
Prod-IOWA Dist-IOWA 1971

Properties Of Cardiac Muscle, Pt 3 - Cardiac Muscle Contrasted With Skeletal Muscle C 2 MIN
16MM FILM SILENT
Uses the ventricle muscle from a turtle heart and the gastronemius muscle of the frog to compare the latent periods and the contraction and relaxation periods of cardiac and skeletal muscles under various rates of stimulation. Suggests physiological advantages for each type of muscle response.
From The Dukes Physiology Film Series. No. 8
LC NO. 74-710195
Prod-IOWA Dist-IOWA 1971

Properties Of Cardiac Muscle, Pt 4 - Cardiac Response To An Artificial Pacemaker C 2 MIN
16MM FILM SILENT
Demonstrates the response of an isolated turtle ventricle to artificial stimulation. Illustrates the staircase effect as the degree of response to rhythmical application of stimuli.
From The Dukes Physiology Film Series. No. 9
LC NO. 70-710194
Prod-IOWA Dist-IOWA 1971

Properties Of Cardiac Muscle, Pt 5 - Sino-Atrial Block In The Frog Heart C 2 MIN
16MM FILM SILENT
Demonstrates a blocking of excitatory impulses from the sinus venosus in a frog heart and compares the normal heart beat, the beat with a sino-atrial block and the impaired beat with the blocking ligature removed.
From The Dukes Physiology Film Series. No. 10
LC NO. 77-710193
Prod-IOWA Dist-IOWA 1971

Properties Of Enzymes I - Flexibility C 24 MIN
16MM FILM, 3/4 OR 1/2 IN VIDEO
Presents eminent biochemist Daniel Koshland's work in the field of enzymes. Postulates the concept of the flexible enzyme, called the induced fit theory of enzyme action.
Prod-OPENU Dist-MEDIAG Prodn-BBCTV 1978

Properties Of Enzymes II - Cooperativity C 24 MIN
16MM FILM, 3/4 OR 1/2 IN VIDEO
Develops the idea of the flexible enzyme in connection with the cooperativity factor of enzymes, an important factor in the regulation of enzyme activity. Details the two major theories about the various kinds of cooperativity, the sequential or concerted model and the symmetry model.
Prod-OPENU Dist-MEDIAG Prodn-BBCTV 1978

Properties Of Heat, The C 21 MIN
3/4 OR 1/2 INCH VIDEO CASSETTE H-C A
Introduces the subject of heat, the BTU, calorie and kilocalorie. Rates various substances in terms of their abilities to absorb and store heat. Shows the ways heat is transferred from one place to another.
From The Introduction To Energy And Heat Series.
Prod-NCDCC Dist-MOKIN

Properties Of I And O In Multiplication And Division C 20 MIN
2 INCH VIDEOTAPE P
See series title for descriptive statement.

From The Mathemagic, Unit VIII - Multiplication And Division Series.
Prod-WMULTV Dist-GPITVL

Properties Of Light C 20 MIN
2 INCH VIDEOTAPE I
See series title for descriptive statement.
From The Adventure Of Science, Unit II - Matter And Energy Series.
Prod-MPATI Dist-GPITVL

Properties Of Matter B 15 MIN
16MM FILM, 3/4 OR 1/2 IN VIDEO
Defines matter and shows examples of matter in different states. Shows how a material can be tested to see if it is a conductor or insulator, and how materials exhibit different characteristics when subjected to extreme voltages or when impurities are added.
Prod-USAF Dist-USNAC 1983

Properties Of Metals C 12 MIN
3/4 OR 1/2 INCH VIDEO CASSETTE
Covers the mechanical properties of metals such as hardness, ductility, malleability, toughness, strength and compression.
From The Working With Metals In The Plant Series.
Prod-TPCTRA Dist-TPCTRA

Properties Of Petroleum Fluids C 300 MIN
3/4 OR 1/2 INCH VIDEO CASSETTE
Available to SPE organizations only. Provides a better understanding of the properties that characterize oil, gas and water encountered in the oil patch, and the ability to estimate values of these properties for use in other engineering calculations.
Prod-SPE Dist-SPE

Properties Of Plastics C 25 MIN
3/4 OR 1/2 INCH VIDEO CASSETTE H-C A
Discusses the properties of plastics.
From The Technical Studies Series.
Prod-BBCTV Dist-FI 1981

Properties Of Radiation B 68 MIN
16MM FILM OPTICAL SOUND
Explains the characteristics and properties of primary and secondary nuclear radiations in terms of their ionizing effects. Describes the effect of matter on radiation, showing that absorbing materials can be used to measure radiation characteristics or to shield against their biological effects.
From The Radioisotope Series. No. 2
Prod-USA Dist-USNAC 1953

Properties Of Zero And One C 15 MIN
3/4 OR 1/2 INCH VIDEO CASSETTE I-J
Expresses the concept of an additive identity and multiplicative identity by demonstrating their existence and illustrating with examples. Shows how to change fractions to equivalent fractions.
From The Math Matters Series. Blue Module
Prod-STETVC Dist-AITECH Prodn-KLRNTV 1975

Property C 89 MIN
3/4 OR 1/2 INCH VIDEO CASSETTE
Depicts long-haired inhabitants of a particular city block in Portland, Oregon. Shows how some members of the youth culture of the sixties functioned twenty years later.
Prod-MEDIPR Dist-MEDIPR 1978

Property C 92 MIN
16MM FILM - 3/4 IN VIDEO C A
Focuses on a group of eccentrics who get together and buy their block from real estate developers and secure their way of life within the mainstream.
Prod-FIRS Dist-FIRS

Property And Liability Insurance C 25 MIN
3/4 OR 1/2 INCH VIDEO CASSETTE H-C A
Outlines methods of avoiding financial loss due to property damage or suit for negligence.
From The Money Smart - A Guide To Personal Finance Series.
Prod-SOMFIL Dist-BCNFL 1985

Property And Liability Insurance C 29 MIN
3/4 INCH VIDEO CASSETTE
See series title for descriptive statement.
From The You Owe It To Yourself Series.
Prod-WITFTV Dist-PUBTEL

Property Identification And Theft Insurance C 30 MIN
3/4 OR 1/2 INCH VIDEO CASSETTE
Discusses property identification in the event of theft insurance.
From The Burglar-Proofing Series.
Prod-MDCPB Dist-MDCPB

Property Rights And Pollution C 19 MIN
16MM FILM, 3/4 OR 1/2 IN VIDEO H A
Shows how the exchange of well-defined property rights can direct goods to their highest valued applications. Contrasts this situation with one in which difficulties are encountered because property rights are not well defined or exchangeable. Illustrates these principles in the context of air and water usage.
From The People On Market Street Series.
Prod-FNDREE Dist-WDEMCO Prodn-KAHNT 1977

Prophecy C 40 MIN
16MM FILM OPTICAL SOUND
Shows the effects of the atomic bombing of Japan. Uses footage from the U S government and the Hiroshima-Nagasaki Publishing Committee.
Prod-PSR Dist-PSR 1982

Prophecy C 48 MIN
16MM FILM, 3/4 OR 1/2 IN VIDEO A
Presents views of the explosions and the aftermath of the atomic bombing of Hiroshima and Nagasaki. Views the anguish of the survivors and the horror of the 90,000 people who were killed.
LC NO. 84-706163
Prod-FI Dist-FI 1983

Prophecy, A C 54 MIN
16MM FILM, 3/4 OR 1/2 IN VIDEO
Focuses on the Dalai Lama and the changing nature of his theocracy. Deals with the Dalai Lama's flight to India following the Chinese annexation of Tibet in 1959 and examines his establishment of a society based on the intermingling of theocratic, democratic and socialistic policies.
From The Tibet - A Buddhist Trilogy Series. Part 1
Prod-COLLAS Dist-UCEMC 1981

Prophet For All Seasons - Aldo Leopold C 59 MIN
3/4 OR 1/2 INCH VIDEO CASSETTE
Presents Lorne Greene narrating a biography of Aldo Leopold, following his life and career as a naturalist, biologist and agriculturalist.
Prod-WETN Dist-PBS 1980

Prophet From Tekoa C 30 MIN
16MM FILM OPTICAL SOUND R
Shows how God punishes a nation that fails to heed warnings to overcome evil and renew allegiance to God. Describes how Amos went to Israel, witnessed against the people's sins and lashed out against them. Shows people in modern-day America committing the particular sin of which Amos speaks.
Prod-BROADM Dist-BROADM 1961

Prophets And Promise Of Classical Capitalism C 60 MIN
16MM FILM, 3/4 OR 1/2 IN VIDEO H-C A
Discusses the birth of classical capitalism in Britain and France generated by the theories of Adam Smith. Based on the book The Age Of Uncertainty by John Kenneth Galbraith.
From The Age Of Uncertainty Series.
LC NO. 77-700660
Prod-BBCL Dist-FI 1977

Prophets, The - Pont-Aven, The Nabis, Toulouse-Lautrec C 18 MIN
16MM FILM, 3/4 OR 1/2 IN VIDEO H-C
Explains that the Nabis saw their movement as a development of the work of their predecessors. Includes work by Gauguin, Serusier and Vuillard.
Prod-IFB Dist-IFB 1971

Propogation 2 C 30 MIN
3/4 OR 1/2 INCH VIDEO CASSETTE C A
Discusses some of the more difficult techniques of plant reproduction including stem cuttings, root cuttings and leaf-bud cuttings. Includes suggestions for easy ways to create a humid environment for newly planted cuttings.
From The Home Gardener With John Lenanton Series. Lesson 28
Prod-COAST Dist-CDTEL

Proportion C 15 MIN
16MM FILM, 3/4 OR 1/2 IN VIDEO H
Shows how proportions are useful in the daily operation of a bakery and a rock band.
From The Math Wise Series. Module 2 - Comparing
Prod-KOCETV Dist-AITECH 1981

Proportion C 29 MIN
3/4 INCH VIDEO CASSETTE C A
Considers how relative size of body parts affects the size of an entire creature. Shows how relative size is used to inject humor. Demonstrates the use of proportion.
From The Sketching Techniques Series. Lesson 9
Prod-COAST Dist-CDTEL

Proportion At Work C 12 MIN
16MM FILM, 3/4 OR 1/2 IN VIDEO H
Introduces ratio and proportion as practical tools for solving problems by indirect measurement.
Prod-IFB Dist-IFB 1960

Proposal For 'QUBE' C 10 MIN
3/4 OR 1/2 INCH VIDEO CASSETTE
Concerns the QUBE system - two-way cable television in Columbus, Ohio.
Prod-KITCHN Dist-KITCHN

Proposal For Expansion C 30 MIN
1/2 IN VIDEO CASSETTE BETA/VHS
Presents a 1950s ranch-style tract house. Discusses possibilities for creating space in it.
From The This Old House, Pt 2 - Suburban '50s Series.
Prod-WGBHTV Dist-MTI

Proposal, The C 24 MIN
3/4 OR 1/2 INCH VIDEO CASSETTE A
Shows salespersons the crucial selling advantage of an organized proposal over a cold quotation. Explains five simple headings that make a proposal clear and convincing in order to ensure a sale.
Prod-XICOM Dist-XICOM

Proposal, The C 25 MIN
3/4 OR 1/2 INCH VIDEO CASSETTE
Shows how a salesman makes all of the most common mistakes in proposal writing before he learns the simple five-part structure and sees how to present the proposal in terms of the needs of a customer.
Prod-VIDART Dist-VISUCP

Proprioceptive Neuromuscular Facilitation—A Series
PRO
Provides an introduction to proprioceptive neuromuscular facilitation (PNF) and applications to occupational therapy. Emphasizes diagonal patterns and assisting to postures. Intended for use by Occupational Therapy students as an adjunct to classroom instruction.
Prod-RICHGO Dist-RICHGO

PNF - Assisting To Postures And Application	
PNF - Diagonal Patterns And Their Application	045 MIN
PNF - Patterns And Applications In	045 MIN

Proprioceptive Neuromuscular Facilitation—A Series

Describes the Proprioceptive Neuromuscular Facilitation Treatments and Exercises.
Prod-UMDSM Dist-UMDSM

Geriatric CVA - Resistive Gait Program	026 MIN
Geriatric CVA - Resistive Mat Exercises	030 MIN
Geriatric CVA - Table Exercises	039 MIN
History And Philosophy	026 MIN
Principles	057 MIN
Resistive Gait Program	026 MIN
Resistive Mat Exercises I	033 MIN
Resistive Mat Exercises II	032 MIN
Table Treatment	041 MIN

Propulsion Systems C 16 MIN
16MM FILM, 3/4 OR 1/2 IN VIDEO I-J
Discusses propulsion systems, pointing out that the history of man is closely correlated to the history of propulsion. Tells how the horse-drawn vehicle opened up the American West and the steam engine in locomotives welded the entire continent. Describes how the gasoline engine of the Model T Ford revolutionized transportation, how the gasoline engine spawned air transportation and how rockets made it possible to leave the earth's gravity and conquer space.
Prod-HANDEL Dist-HANDEL 1981

Pros And Cons C 28 MIN
3/4 OR 1/2 INCH VIDEO CASSETTE
Addresses teacher attitudes towards the metric system and promotes the generation of a positive attitude.
From The Metric Education Video Tapes For Pre And Inservice Teachers (K-8) Series.
Prod-PUAVC Dist-PUAVC

Prose Literature—A Series

Demonstrates acquired reading skills and resolves various situations which were introduced earlier in the series.
Prod-CAMB Dist-CAMB

Finding The Main Idea (Prose Literature)	030 MIN
Making Inferences (Prose Literature)	030 MIN
Reading For Details	030 MIN
Understanding Figurative Language	030 MIN

Prospect Of Turkey C 32 MIN
16MM FILM - 3/4 IN VIDEO
Examines conditions in Turkey and discusses its successive cultures throughout history, its technological and economic development and its military contribution to Western security. Issued in 1967 as a motion picture.
LC NO. 79-706673
Prod-NATO Dist-USNAC 1979

Prospecting And Planning C 7 MIN
3/4 OR 1/2 INCH VIDEO CASSETTE
See series title for descriptive statement.
From The Telemarketing For Better Business Results Series.
Prod-COMTEL Dist-DELTAK

Prospective Application, The B 45 MIN
2 INCH VIDEOTAPE C
See series title for descriptive statement.
From The Business Writing Series. Unit IV - Letters About Employment - Reports
Prod-CHITVC Dist-GPITVL Prodn-WTTWTV

Prospective Pricing - Management Strategies C 10 MIN
3/4 OR 1/2 INCH VIDEO CASSETTE
Offers the management team a comprehensive review of the major events and key legislative provisions leading to Medicare payment on a cost-per-case basis. Addresses such issues as hospitals' financial concerns and the impact of the Prospective Payment Commission and Professional Review Board on the new Medicare payment system.
Prod-AHOA Dist-AHOA

Prospects For Humanity—A Series

Features participants in the World Symposium on Humanity. Discusses prospects for humanity.
Prod-OHC Dist-HRC

Community And Culture	059 MIN
Consciousness And Health	059 MIN
Energy And Technology	059 MIN
Evolution And Education	060 MIN
Justice And Religion	060 MIN

Prospects For Survival In The Post-Attack World C 30 MIN
3/4 OR 1/2 INCH VIDEO CASSETTE
Presents a speech by Dr Jennifer Leaning to a 1982 Symposium of Physicians For Social Responsibility. Discusses the issue of prospects for survival in a world after nuclear attack.
Prod-PSR Dist-PSR 1982

Prostaglandins - Tomorrow's Physiology C 22 MIN
16MM FILM OPTICAL SOUND PRO
Examines the discovery, current status and clinical potential of prostaglandins.
LC NO. 74-702505
Prod-UPJOHN Dist-UPJOHN 1974

Prostate Surgery B 18 MIN
16MM FILM OPTICAL SOUND H-C A
Shows how an X-ray pyelogram reveals an enlargement of the prostate gland in an elderly man. Describes corrective surgery for the prostate condition, including a discussion on the anatomy of the prostate gland, and a clarification of misconceptions concerning the disorder.
From The Doctors At Work Series.
LC NO. FIA65-1358
Prod-CMA Dist-LAWREN Prodn-LAWREN 1961

Prostate Surgery C 9 MIN
3/4 OR 1/2 INCH VIDEO CASSETTE
Describes the two most common 'open' procedures for prostate surgery. Prepares the patient both for hospitalization and operative procedures.
Prod-TRAINX Dist-TRAINX

Prostate, A Patient's View, The C 19 MIN
16MM FILM OPTICAL SOUND
Encourages early diagnosis and treatment for prostate conditions.
LC NO. 78-701378
Prod-EATONL Dist-EATONL Prodn-AEGIS 1978

Prostatitis C 7 MIN
3/4 OR 1/2 INCH VIDEO CASSETTE
Alerts the adult male population to this very common problem among men. Discusses medical intervention, including antibiotic therapy, sitz baths, and the need for diminished activity during the acute phase.
Prod-TRAINX Dist-TRAINX

Prosthesis Films—A Series
PRO
Details the use of various protheses to correct orthopedic disabilities.
Prod-WFP Dist-WFP

Shoulder Prosthesis For Four Part Fracture	019 MIN
Surgical Technique For Multiple Total Knee	032 MIN
Universal Proximal Femur Prothesis	020 MIN

Prosthesis Implant, The - A Surgical Treatment For Temporomandibular Joint Disease C 19 MIN
16MM FILM OPTICAL SOUND
Describes the headaches, dizziness and other symptoms of jaw joint disease and shows X-rays of the surgical repair of the jaw by a metal prosthesis.
LC NO. 77-702408
Prod-WFP Dist-WFP 1977

Prosthesis Plus Technique Equals Independence, Pt 1 C 30 MIN
3/4 INCH VIDEOTAPE
Features a bilateral upper extremity amputee explaining and demonstrating techniques for bathing, shampooing, dressing and other personal hygiene activities.
Prod-UNDMC Dist-UNDMC

Prosthesis Plus Technique Equals Independence, Pt 2 C 37 MIN
3/4 INCH VIDEOTAPE
Features a bilateral upper extremity amputee explaining and demonstrating techniques for cooking, driving, working and participating in leisure time activities.
Prod-UNDMC Dist-UNDMC

Prosthetic Above-Knee Sockets C 9 MIN
16MM FILM OPTICAL SOUND
Describes the quadrilateral or anatomical socket used with above-knee amputations and shows the importance of having the socket fit the stump correctly. Shows three different methods of suspension.
LC NO. 74-705441
Prod-NYUIMR Dist-USNAC Prodn-NMAC 1969

Prosthetic Below-Knee Sockets C 6 MIN
16MM FILM OPTICAL SOUND
Explains the various qualities of three different below-knee prosthetic sockets and shows each of these being worn by a patient.
LC NO. 74-705443
Prod-NYUIMR Dist-USNAC Prodn-NMAC 1969

Prosthetic Checkout B 12 MIN
3/4 OR 1/2 INCH VIDEO CASSETTE
Shows step-by-step checkouts of two below knee prostheses, one a PTS prothesis and the other a PTB prosthesis.
Prod-BU Dist-BU

Prosthetic Foot Components C 7 MIN
16MM FILM OPTICAL SOUND
Reviews the various aspects of four types of foot-ankle components and presents patients wearing each of these types.
LC NO. 74-705444
Prod-NYUIMR Dist-USNAC Prodn-NMAC 1969

Prosthetic Knee Components C 8 MIN
16MM FILM OPTICAL SOUND
Describes the various qualities of five different knee joints that may be used by the patient with an above-knee amputation.
LC NO. 74-705445
Prod-NYUIMR Dist-USNAC Prodn-NMAC 1969

Protect The Patient C 12 MIN
16MM FILM OPTICAL SOUND
Presents six methods of carrying a hospital patient from a room in an emergency. Includes information on notifying the fire department.
Prod-UIOWA Dist-UIOWA 1976

Protected School, The B 6 MIN
16MM FILM OPTICAL SOUND
Tells the story of the United Consolidated High School in Webb County, Texas--about the architects, school board, teachers, administrators and the students who work in this fallout protected school. Emphasizes the advantages of this two-story type building.
Prod-USOCD Dist-USNAC 1965

Protecting Endangered Animals C 15 MIN
16MM FILM, 3/4 OR 1/2 IN VIDEO I-J
Discusses animals that have become extinct or are in danger of extinction such as the dinosaur, the passenger pigeon, the black-footed ferret, the Devil's Hole pupfish, the manatee and the bald eagle. Looks at animals that have been saved from extinction such as the bison and the whooping crane.
Prod-NGS Dist-NGS 1984

Protecting The Family Members From Germs And Infection C 8 MIN
3/4 OR 1/2 INCH VIDEO CASSETTE
Provides a clear, easily understood definition of microorganisms and preventing the spread of infection. Explains difference between harmless and harmful microorganisms and conditions required for growth of microorganisms. Shows ways how germ may be spread from person to person and step-by-step instruction for preventing such spread.
LC NO. 77-731356
Prod-TRAINX Dist-TRAINX

Protecting The Family Members From Germs And Infection (Spanish) C 8 MIN
3/4 OR 1/2 INCH VIDEO CASSETTE
Provides a clear, easily understood definition of microorganisms and preventing the spread of infection. Explains difference between harmless and harmful microorganisms and conditions required for growth of microorganisms. Shows ways how germs may be spread from person to person and step-by-step instructions for preventing such spread.
LC NO. 77-731353
Prod-TRAINX Dist-TRAINX

Protecting Your Hearing In A Noisy World C 13 MIN
3/4 OR 1/2 INCH VIDEO CASSETTE A
Explains the nature of sound and its transmission, pointing out how exposure to very loud noise can cause hearing loss. Demonstrates sound-insulated booths and protection devices such as ear muffs and plugs. Recommends yearly testing.
LC NO. 84-707798
Prod-KOHLER Dist-IFB

Protecting Your Safety And Health In The Plant (Spanish)—A Series

Introduces the subject of safety and its importance in the work environment. Explains how to recognize safety hazards and techniques for working safely.
Prod-TPCTRA Dist-TPCTRA

Electrical Safety (Spanish)	012 MIN
Fire Protection (Spanish)	012 MIN
Government Safety Regulations (Spanish)	012 MIN
Handling Materials Safely (Spanish)	012 MIN
Introduction To Safety (Spanish)	012 MIN
Other Hazards (Spanish)	012 MIN
Personal Protective Equipment (Spanish)	012 MIN
Recognizing Hazards (Spanish)	012 MIN
Using Machinery Safely (Spanish)	012 MIN
Working Safely (Spanish)	012 MIN

Protecting Your Safety And Health In The Plant—A Series

Introduces the subject of safety and its importance in the work environment. Explains how to recognize safety hazards and techniques for working safely.
Prod-TPCTRA Dist-TPCTRA

Electrical Safety	012 MIN
Fire Protection	012 MIN
Government Safety Regulations	012 MIN
Handling Materials Safely	012 MIN
Introduction To Safety	012 MIN
Other Hazards	012 MIN
Personal Protective Equipment	012 MIN
Recognizing Hazards	012 MIN
Using Machinery Safely	012 MIN
Working Safely	012 MIN

Protection Against Nuclear Radiation C 8 MIN
16MM FILM OPTICAL SOUND
Examines factors that reduce the hazards of nuclear radiation. Emphasizes the value of fallout shelters in a nuclear emergency.
LC NO. 74-706202
Prod-USOCD Dist-USNAC 1968

Protection Against Radioactivity In Uranium Mines C 27 MIN
16MM FILM OPTICAL SOUND
Presents a general description of the radon daughter hazards in uranium mines and outlines the environmental control, principles and procedures that have proven effective in mitigating the hazard.
LC NO. 74-705447
Prod-USBM Dist-USNAC 1969

Protection Equipment C
3/4 OR 1/2 INCH VIDEO CASSETTE IND
Introduces the concept of electrical faults. Shows details of operation of various types of protective relays and devices. Includes maintenance considerations.
From The Distribution System Operation Series. Topic 8
Prod-LEIKID Dist-LEIKID

Protection For Sale - The Insurance Industry C 52 MIN
16MM FILM, 3/4 OR 1/2 IN VIDEO H-C A
Looks at the vastness of the insurance industry and questions whether the public needs more federal protection from their supposed protectors.
Prod-NBCNEW Dist-FI 1982

Protection In Neighborhoods C 15 MIN
3/4 OR 1/2 INCH VIDEO CASSETTE P
Looks at the issue of protection in neighborhoods.
From The Neighborhoods Series.
Prod-NEITV Dist-GPITVL 1981

Protection In The Nuclear Age C 24 MIN
16MM FILM - 3/4 IN VIDEO
Uses artwork and animation to show what individuals can do to improve chances for survival if a nuclear crisis or enemy attack should occur. Covers aspects of protection, from avoidance of blast effects and fallout to emergency shelter and supplies.
LC NO. 78-706221
Prod-USDCPA Dist-USNAC Prodn-TRIOPR 1978

Protection Of People And Structures From Fire C 60 MIN
3/4 OR 1/2 INCH VIDEO CASSETTE IND
See series title for descriptive statement.
From The Industrial Fire Hazard Recognition And Control Series.
Prod-NCSU Dist-AMCEE

Protection Of Proprietary Information (POPI) C 23 MIN
16MM FILM, 3/4 OR 1/2 IN VIDEO
Discusses employees' important role in protecting their organization's intellectual assets including patents, trade secrets and commercial information. Includes a discussion of classification, marking and duplication of sensitive materials, access control, confidentiality procedures, handling the press, and employee and family gossip.
Prod-SOREG Dist-MTI

Protection Of Proprietary Information (POPI) (French) C 23 MIN
16MM FILM, 3/4 OR 1/2 IN VIDEO
Points to employees' role in protecting their organization's intellectual assets - patents, trade secrets and commercial information.
Prod-SOREG Dist-MTI

Protection Of Proprietary Information (POPI) (Spanish) C 23 MIN
16MM FILM, 3/4 OR 1/2 IN VIDEO
Points to employees' role in protecting their organization's intellectual assets - patents, trade secrets and commercial information.
Prod-SOREG Dist-MTI

Protective Clothing And Breathing Apparatus C
3/4 OR 1/2 INCH VIDEO CASSETTE
Emphasizes proper use and maintenance of protective clothing for fire fighters and self-contained breathing apparatus, illustrating how it is designed as a system for protection of the individual.
From The Safety Series.
Prod-NFPA Dist-NFPA 1980

Protective Coloration C 13 MIN
16MM FILM, 3/4 OR 1/2 IN VIDEO
Shows the relationships between an animal's coloration and its habitat and behavior. Discusses camouflage, disguise, warning, coloration and Batesian mimicry.
From The Many Worlds Of Nature Series.
Prod-MORALL Dist-MTI 1975

Protective Relaying, Tape 16A C
3/4 OR 1/2 INCH VIDEO CASSETTE IND
Covers fundamentals, overcurrent, voltage, pilot wire, primary and backup, targets, distance relays, phase and ground faults, load shedding and trip and block relays.
From The Electric Power System Operation Series.
Prod-LEIKID Dist-LEIKID

Protective Relaying, Tape 16B C
3/4 OR 1/2 INCH VIDEO CASSETTE IND
Covers fundamentals, overcurrent, voltage, pilot wire, primary and backup, targets, distance relays, phase and ground faults, load shedding and trip and block relays.
From The Electric Power System Operation Series.
Prod-LEIKID Dist-LEIKID

Protective Relays, Tape 1 - Protective Relaying Fundamentals, Relay Testing C 60 MIN
3/4 OR 1/2 INCH VIDEO CASSETTE IND
See series title for descriptive statement.
From The Electrical Equipment Maintenance Series.
Prod-ITCORP Dist-ITCORP

Protective Relays, Tape 1 - Protective-Relaying Fundamentals, Relay Testing (Spanish) C 60 MIN
3/4 OR 1/2 INCH VIDEO CASSETTE IND
See series title for descriptive statement.
From The Electrical Equipment Maintenance (Spanish) Series.
Prod-ITCORP Dist-ITCORP

Protective Services C 58 MIN
3/4 OR 1/2 INCH VIDEO CASSETTE
Focuses on due process rights for parents, protective proceedings, jurisdictional and residency requirements, problems in dealing with emotional neglect, psychological abuse in the legal system and the child abuse reporting laws.
From The Legal Training For Children Welfare Workers Series. Pt III
Prod-UWISC Dist-UWISC 1975

Protein - Structure And Function C 16 MIN
16MM FILM, 3/4 OR 1/2 IN VIDEO C A
Shows how proteins work in our bodies. Explains the structure

of protein and illustrates the interactions that bring about three-dimensiomal proteins and how enzymes work. Describes how proteins play a major part in the structure of living things and how, as catalysts, they control life's chemical reactions.
Prod-WILEYJ Dist-MEDIAG 1972

Protein Food Foams C 3 MIN
16MM FILM SILENT J-C A
Illustrates the preparation, stabilization and structure of foams of gelatin, evaporated milk, non-fat milk solids and whipping cream. Compares butterfat, stabilized and protein-stabilized foams.
From The Food And Nutrition Series.
LC NO. 74-710179
Prod-IOWA Dist-IOWA 1971

Protein From The Sea C 26 MIN
16MM FILM OPTICAL SOUND
Documents the construction of a seafood processing ship in Seattle which is owned by a Native American organization and stationed in Cold Bay, Alaska.
LC NO. 81-700425
Prod-ANFP Dist-ANFP 1980

Protein Quality Of Foods - James Adkins, PHD C 20 MIN
3/4 INCH VIDEO CASSETTE PRO
Discusses aspects of the Food and Drug Administration's regulations governing labeling of food and nutritional quality guidelines.
From The Food And Nutrition Seminars For Health Professionals Series.
LC NO. 78-706164
Prod-USFDA Dist-USNAC 1976

Protein Synthesis C 12 MIN
16MM FILM OPTICAL SOUND
Uses a dance by 200 students to symbolize the intracellular process which produces proteins.
From The Protein Primer Series.
LC NO. 72-713585
Prod-UCSD Dist-HAR 1971

Protein, Pt 1 C 30 MIN
3/4 OR 1/2 INCH VIDEO CASSETTE
See series title for descriptive statement.
From The Food For Life Series.
Prod-MSU Dist-MSU

Protein, Pt 2 C 30 MIN
3/4 OR 1/2 INCH VIDEO CASSETTE
See series title for descriptive statement.
From The Food For Life Series.
Prod-MSU Dist-MSU

Proteins, Immunoglobulins And Antibodies C 22 MIN
3/4 OR 1/2 INCH VIDEO CASSETTE C A
From The Immunology Series.
Prod-ESSMED Dist-TEF

Protest And Communication C 52 MIN
16MM FILM, 3/4 OR 1/2 IN VIDEO J-C A
Surveys the development of Western civilization in the 16th century in the north as evidenced in the use of the printing press, in the Reformation and Protestantism and in the works of Erasmus, Sir Thomas Moore, Durer, Holbein, Luther, Cranach and Shakespeare.
From The Civilisation Series. No. 6
LC NO. 79-707046
Prod-BBCTV Dist-FI 1970

Protest And Reform C 40 MIN
16MM FILM, 3/4 OR 1/2 IN VIDEO H-C A
Surveys the history of the Reformation, focusing on developments within the Christian church.
From The Christians Series. Episode 7
Prod-GRATV Dist-MGHT 1978

Protest On The Campus - Columbia University 1968 C 15 MIN
16MM FILM OPTICAL SOUND H
What is the meaning of the extreme behavior of students at the ivy-covered Columbia campus. This film puts your class in the arena for a first-hand view of the age-old conflict between generations. Helps the young discover for themseleves a broadened viewpoint of how a faculty and administration reacted to the passion and needs of their students.
From The Protest Series.
Prod-INTEXT Dist-REAF

Protest—A Series

Prod-INTEXT Dist-REAF

All Of The People Against Some Of The Anti-War Protest	15 MIN
Assassins - The Ultimate Protest, The	15 MIN
Black Power - The Spokesmen	15 MIN
Black Protest - The Quest For Civil Liberties	15 MIN
Chicago 1968 - Rights In Conflict	15 MIN
Confrontation In Washington - Resurrection City	15 MIN
March On Washington - The Bonus March	15 MIN
Non-Violence - Mahatma Gandhi And Martin	15 MIN
Political Protest - The Splinter Groups	15 MIN
Political Protest - Within A Party	15 MIN
Prohibition And Pot	15 MIN
Protest On The Campus - Columbia University	15 MIN
Quiet Protestors - Mothers And The Church,	15 MIN
Strikes - Protesting To Gain Power As Well As	15 MIN

Protest's New Prophets B 30 MIN
16MM FILM OPTICAL SOUND H-C A
Benjamin Quarles, Vincent Harding and Sterling Stuckey discuss the notion that most abolitionists-including William Lloyd Garrison-were white. They describe the role of the 'OLD' black abolitionists who preceded them and the 'NEW' abolitionists who are credited with the thrust that brought symbolic emanicipation-Charles Remond, Samuel R Ward, William Wells Brown, Frederick Douglass and others.
From The Black History, Section 07 - Black Radicals And Abolitionists Series.
LC NO. 71-704053
Prod-WCBSTV Dist-HRAW 1969

Protestant Spirit USA C 52 MIN
16MM FILM, 3/4 OR 1/2 IN VIDEO H-C A
Visits various Protestant churches in Indianapolis and observes how services are conducted. Examines the reasons for the vigor of religious expression among both black and white American Protestants.
From The Long Search Series. No. 1
LC NO. 79-707790
Prod-BBCTV Dist-TIMLIF 1977

Protist Behavior C 11 MIN
16MM FILM OPTICAL SOUND J-C
Shows avoidance reactions, mechanisms for aggregation in favorable environments, predator-prey relationships, light reactions and escape responses in free-living protists.
From The Inhabitants Of The Planet Earth Series.
LC NO. 75-701960
Prod-RUSB Dist-MLA 1975

Protist Ecology C 12 MIN
16MM FILM OPTICAL SOUND J-C
Discusses the vital role played by the protists in the ecology of the planet earth. Examines the commensal, parasitic and mutualistic life styles practiced by a large number of protist species.
From The Inhabitants Of The Planet Earth Series.
LC NO. 75-701961
Prod-RUSB Dist-MLA 1975

Protist Kingdom, The C 14 MIN
16MM FILM, 3/4 OR 1/2 IN VIDEO I-C A
Discusses protists, one-celled animals or plants, which scientists have divided into six major groups-sarcodina, ciliates, flagellates, slime mold, sporozoa and bacteria.
Prod-FA Dist-PHENIX Prodn-BEAN 1965

Protist Kingdom, The (Spanish) C 14 MIN
16MM FILM, 3/4 OR 1/2 IN VIDEO I-C A
Discusses protists, one-celled animals or plants, which scientists have divided into six major groups-sarcodina, ciliates, flagellates, slime mold, sporozoa and bacteria.
Prod-FA Dist-PHENIX Prodn-BEAN 1965

Protist Physiology C 13 MIN
16MM FILM OPTICAL SOUND J-C
Examines the internal processes of independently living cells, including mechanisms for phagocytosis and digestion, and for saprozoic and autotrophic nutrition. Describes symbiotic associations between autotrophs and heterotrophs and methods of water balance.
From The Inhabitants Of The Planet Earth Series.
LC NO. 75-701962
Prod-RUSB Dist-MLA 1975

Protist Reproduction C 10 MIN
16MM FILM OPTICAL SOUND J-C
Shows the reproductive methods of protists, including fission with replication of organelles and subcellular particles, specialized forms of budding in suctorians, sexual reproductive processes including conjugation in ciliates and algae and the production of eggs and sperm by colonial protists.
From The Inhabitants Of The Planet Earth Series.
LC NO. 75-701963
Prod-RUSB Dist-MLA 1975

Protista - Protozoa And Algae C 14 MIN
16MM FILM, 3/4 OR 1/2 IN VIDEO H-C
Reveals that protista are a new kingdom of organisms in addition to plants and animals and that they consist of single-celled organisms, including protozoa and the higher-order protistans.
Prod-BNCHMK Dist-BNCHMK

Protists - Form, Function, and Ecology (2nd Ed) C 23 MIN
16MM FILM, 3/4 OR 1/2 IN VIDEO J-H
Guides viewers through the kingdom protista with light and electron microscopes. Examines distinguishing behavior and physiology of this kingdom which includes protozoa, algae, and slime molds. Includes teachers guide.
Prod-EBEC Dist-EBEC 1984

Protists - Threshold Of Life C 12 MIN
16MM FILM, 3/4 OR 1/2 IN VIDEO
Presents the tiny organisms called protists, including the euglena, amoeba and paramecium. Shows how thousands of single cells join together to form the colonial protist volvox.
From The Bio-Science Series.
LC NO. 80-706312
Prod-NGS Dist-NGS 1974

Protocol Materials In Teacher Education Interpersonal Communication Skills—A Series
T
Presents a series of filmed episodes which illustrate specific learning concepts in a real world setting. Focuses on responsible feedback in interpersonal communication.
Prod-MSU Dist-MSU

Responsible Feedback, Pt 1	015 MIN
Responsible Feedback, Pt 2	015 MIN

Protocol Materials In Teacher Education - The Process Of Teaching, Pt 1—A Series
T
Presents a series of filmed episodes which illustrate specific learning concepts in a real world setting. Includes assessment, goal setting, strategies and evaluation.
Prod-MSU Dist-MSU

Tasks Of Teaching, Pt 1	030 MIN
Tasks Of Teaching, Pt 2	020 MIN

Protocol Materials In Teacher Education - The Process Of Teaching, Pt 2—A Series
T
Presents a series of filmed episodes which illustrates specific learning concepts in a real world setting. Includes model, respondent and operant learning.
Prod-MSU Dist-MSU

Modeling	010 MIN
Negative Reinforcement	005 MIN
Operant Learning	010 MIN
Positive Reinforcement	010 MIN
Respondent Learning	010 MIN
Shaping	005 MIN

Protocols C 50 MIN
3/4 OR 1/2 INCH VIDEO CASSETTE PRO
Involves file transfer, flow and error control, sequencing and multiplexing.
From The Computer Communications - Protocols And Architectures, Pt 2 Series.
Prod-AMCEE Dist-AMCEE

Protozoa C 15 MIN
3/4 OR 1/2 INCH VIDEO CASSETTE
Presents representative members of the four groups of protozoa in photomicrographs of both living and stained specimens, as well as electron micrographs and artwork. Shows how protozoa regulate their internal environment, get food, move and reproduce.
Prod-CBSC Dist-CBSC

Protozoa - Structures And Life Functions C 16 MIN
16MM FILM, 3/4 OR 1/2 IN VIDEO J-C
Uses photomicrography to show the living specimens of the four classes of protozoa—rhizopods, flagellates, ciliates and sporozoans. Pictures structural adaptations which enable these animals to get food, reproduce and respond to stimuli.
From The Major Phyla Series.
Prod-CORF Dist-CORF 1965

Protozoa, The C 30 MIN
3/4 OR 1/2 INCH VIDEO CASSETTE
Depicts the micro-world of the protozoa. Captures the structures and functions of four of the main phyla represented by the Amoeba, Paramecium, Euglena and Plasmodium. Includes ten follow-up questions at the end of the program.
Prod-EDMEC Dist-EDMEC

Proud Barns Of North America C 8 MIN
16MM FILM OPTICAL SOUND
Examines the architecture, construction and use of several old barns in North America.
LC NO. 79-700362
Prod-DEERE Dist-DEERE Prodn-CENTEF 1978

Proud Breed, The C
1/2 IN VIDEO CASSETTE BETA/VHS
Depicts Arabian horses. Hosted by Wayne Newton.
Prod-EQVDL Dist-EQVDL

Proud Girl And Bold Eagle C 20 MIN
3/4 INCH VIDEO CASSETTE I
Offers an adaptation of a Cherokee Indian legend about a princess whose vanity leads to misfortune.
From The Wonderama Of The Arts Series.
Prod-WBRATV Dist-GPITVL 1978

Provence And The Riviera C 20 MIN
3/4 OR 1/2 INCH VIDEO CASSETTE J-C A
Shows the romantic and enchanting regions of Provence and the Riviera that once attracted artists, such as Picasso, Cezanne and Fragonard. Visits the cities of Saint Tropez, Cannes and Marseilles. Also shows the native flower markets and cafes which help to make this area a special place to visit.
LC NO. 82-706760
Prod-AWSS Dist-AWSS 1981

Provide For The Common Defense B 24 MIN
16MM FILM OPTICAL SOUND
Discusses national defense. Emphasizes its importance to security.
LC NO. FIE58-80
Prod-USDD Dist-USNAC 1957

Providence B 5 MIN
16MM FILM OPTICAL SOUND P-H
Features a modern interpretation of Psalm 112 using scenes of a farm family as they go about their daily chores.
From The Song Of The Ages Series.
LC NO. 74-702136
Prod-FAMLYT Dist-FAMLYT 1964

Providing Feedback C 19 MIN
3/4 OR 1/2 INCH VIDEO CASSETTE
See series title for descriptive statement.
From The Videosearch Behavior Skill Model Series.
Prod-DELTAK Dist-DELTAK

Providing For Family Needs C 15 MIN
3/4 OR 1/2 INCH VIDEO CASSETTE I
Shows how family needs are met by the Tarahumara Indians of Mexico, the Baoule of West Africa and the Japanese. Reveals that the Tarahumara and the Baoule grow their own food or grow cash crops which can be sold for money to buy goods. Contrasts this with the Japanese who must buy all their goods, either on the local or international market.

From The Across Cultures Series.
Prod-POSIMP Dist-AITECH Prodn-WETN 1983

Provinces And People (2nd Ed) C 14 MIN
16MM FILM, 3/4 OR 1/2 IN VIDEO I-H
The second edition of Canada - Geography Of The Americas. Shows the land and people of Canada. Emphasizes the relation of Canada's natural resources to the lives of its people.
From The Canada's Provinces And People Series.
Prod-CORF Dist-CORF

Proving Meters With Pipe Provers C 34 MIN
3/4 OR 1/2 INCH VIDEO CASSETTE IND
Describes the components in a bidirectional U-type pipe prover and their functions. Shows a typical meter proving with a pipe prover and covers filling out a proving report. Conforms to current API Manual of Petroleum Measurement Standards.
Prod-UTEXPE Dist-UTEXPE

Provisions Affecting Qualified Plans C 30 MIN
3/4 OR 1/2 INCH VIDEO CASSETTE PRO
See series title for descriptive statement.
From The Tax Reform Act Of 1984 Series.
Prod-ALIABA Dist-ALIABA

Prowler, The Lone Trailer Story C 12 MIN
16MM FILM OPTICAL SOUND
Documents how the first Prowler Travel Trailer television commercial was made.
LC NO. 76-702608
Prod-FLTWDE Dist-FLTWDE Prodn-EJLAD 1976

Proxemics - Distance C 30 MIN
3/4 OR 1/2 INCH VIDEO CASSETTE C
See series title for descriptive statement.
From The Language And Meaning Series.
Prod-WUSFTV Dist-GPITVL 1983

Proxemics-Spacing, And Touching-Haptics C 30 MIN
3/4 OR 1/2 INCH VIDEO CASSETTE
Demonstrates communication through sitting and standing, using space to reject someone, fear of touch and joy of touch.
From The Nonverbal Communication Series.
Prod-IVCH Dist-IVCH

Proxyhawks B 80 MIN
16MM FILM OPTICAL SOUND
Presents a story about the anger, brutality, softness and vulnerability reverberating between a woman, a man and their animals.
LC NO. 74-701248
Prod-CFDEVC Dist-CANFDC 1971

Prudence Crandall B 51 MIN
16MM FILM, 3/4 OR 1/2 IN VIDEO I-H
Describes Prudence Crandall's importance in civil rights activities on the behalf of black Americans in the 1783 to 1860 period. Based on book Profiles In Courage by John F Kennedy.
From The Profiles In Courage Series.
LC NO. 83-706542
Prod-SAUDEK Dist-SSSSV 1965

Prudhoe Bay - Or Bust C 30 MIN
16MM FILM, 3/4 OR 1/2 IN VIDEO J-H A
Points out that monetary interests and ecological and conservation interests are at odds over the issue of building 800 miles of hot oil pipeline through the Arctic tundra in Alaska.
From The Our Vanishing Wilderness Series.
LC NO. 80-707022
Prod-NET Dist-IU 1970

Pruning C 29 MIN
2 INCH VIDEOTAPE
Features Tom Lied detailing what should be done with various types of woody plants to give them better appearance and better health.
From The Dig It Series.
Prod-WMVSTV Dist-PUBTEL

Pruning C 47 MIN
1/2 IN VIDEO CASSETTE BETA/VHS
Shows how to prune a variety of trees and bushes. Demonstrates the proper tools to use. Explains when to prune trees.
From The Lawn And Garden Series.
Prod-MOHOMV Dist-MOHOMV

Pruning C 48 MIN
1/2 IN VIDEO CASSETTE BETA/VHS
Explains how, when and where to prune trees. Describes the proper tools to use.
Prod-RMI Dist-RMI

Pruning Mature Fig Trees C 11 MIN
3/4 INCH VIDEO CASSETTE
Shows how to prune a mature fig tree and describes the necessary tools.
Prod-TUCPL Dist-GPITVL

Pruning Mature Peach Trees C 11 MIN
3/4 INCH VIDEO CASSETTE
Explains how to prune a mature peach tree and points out that these techniques can be used for pruning many types of fruit trees.
Prod-TUCPL Dist-GPITVL

Pruning Of Woody Plants C 29 MIN
3/4 INCH VIDEO CASSETTE
Demonstrates how to prune shrubs, small trees, vines, hedges and evergreens. Includes definitions, identification of pruning tools and when to use them.
From The Grounds Maintenance Training Series.
Prod-UMITV Dist-UMITV 1978

Pruning Rose Bushes C 19 MIN
3/4 INCH VIDEO CASSETTE
Demonstrates how and when to prune roses.
Prod-TUCPL Dist-GPITVL

Pruning Young Fruit Trees C 11 MIN
3/4 INCH VIDEO CASSETTE
Demonstrates how to prune all young fruit trees, with the exception of citrus trees.
Prod-TUCPL Dist-GPITVL

Prurient Interest B 20 MIN
3/4 OR 1/2 INCH VIDEO CASSETTE
Presents a video-play which revolves around a movie producer's jousting with the local Board of Censors.
Prod-EAI Dist-EAI

Psalm 104 C 7 MIN
16MM FILM OPTICAL SOUND I-C A
Presents an iconographic interpretation of a time painting to show Psalm 104 as an esthetic, visual, verbal and musical experience.
LC NO. 71-705156
Prod-SCHNDL Dist-SIM 1969

PSAT And National Merit Scholarship Qualifying Test Preparation—A Series

Offers tutoring for the PSAT and National Merit Scholarship Qualifying Test exam, in two versions. The school version consists of nine 2 hr lessons. The home version consists of the first five lessons.
Prod-KRLSOF Dist-KRLSOF 1985

Math - All Skill Areas And Problem Types	120 MIN
Math - Quantitative Comparison	120 MIN
Model Examination - I With Explanations	120 MIN
Model Examination - II With Explanations	120 MIN
Model Examination - III With Explanations	120 MIN
Preparing Your Students For The SAT	120 MIN
PSAT And NMSQT Overview And Test Taking	120 MIN
Reading Comprehension	120 MIN
Vocabulary And Word Analogies	120 MIN

PSAT And NMSQT Overview And Test Taking Strategy C 120 MIN
3/4 OR 1/2 INCH VIDEO CASSETTE
See series title for descriptive statement.
From The PSAT And National Merit Scholarship Qualifying Test Preparation Series.
Prod-KRLSOF Dist-KRLSOF

PSI - Boundaries Of The Mind C 17 MIN
16MM FILM, 3/4 OR 1/2 IN VIDEO H-C A
Presents experiments being conducted to explore and define the phenomena of PSI, an unexplained, extra sensory type of communication.
From The Science - New Frontiers Series.
Prod-BFA Dist-PHENIX Prodn-CREEDM 1976

Psoriasis C 21 MIN
3/4 OR 1/2 INCH VIDEO CASSETTE PRO
Provides information which differentiates psoriasis from eczema, pityriasis rosea, syphilis, and Bowen's carcinoma. Describes the clinical course of the disease, including time of onset, hereditary factors, waxing and waning course and exacerbation following trauma. Includes treatment with topical steroids, occlusion, intralesional injections of steroids, tar therapy and maintenance with methotrexate.
Prod-UMICHM Dist-UMICHM 1976

Psoriasis C 25 MIN
3/4 OR 1/2 INCH VIDEO CASSETTE PRO
Describes the lesions of psoriasis and defines treatment procedures.
Prod-PRIMED Dist-PRIMED

Psoroptic Sheep And Cattle Scabies C 12 MIN
16MM FILM OPTICAL SOUND C A
Describes the history of the disease in the United States, showing symptoms in cattle and sheep affected with psoroptic scabies, loss of wool and hair, evidence of itching and irritation and demonstration of causative mites, including photomicrography of the mite.
LC NO. FIE58-162
Prod-USDA Dist-AMVMA 1956

PSSC College Physics Films—A Series

Prod-PSSC Dist-MLA

Angular Momentum - A Vector Quantity	27 MIN
Time Dilation - An Experiment With Mu-Mesons	36 MIN
Ultimate Speed, The - An Exploration With	38 MIN

Psst - Hammerman's After You C 28 MIN
16MM FILM, 3/4 OR 1/2 IN VIDEO I-H
Adapted from the novel THE 18TH EMERGENCY by Betsy Byars, about Mouse, a timid 11-year-old boy who provokes the school bully. Shows how Mouse learns a lesson in honor and self-respect when he faces the consequences of his actions.
From The Afterschool Specials, Series 1 Series.
Prod-TAHSEM Dist-WDEMCO 1977

Psychedelic Wet C 8 MIN
16MM FILM, 3/4 OR 1/2 IN VIDEO J-C A
Presents an impressionistic view of water. Views reflections on the ceiling of the sea off the Bahamas, a pretty girl in a pool and great waves off the north shore in Oahu, Hawaii.
Prod-GROENG Dist-AIMS 1968

Psychiatric Emergencies C 30 MIN
16MM FILM OPTICAL SOUND PRO
Discusses the meaning of a psychiatric emergency. Presents principles of assessment and nursing intervention in psychiatric emergencies, giving examples of a variety of settings.
From The Psychiatric-Mental Health Nursing Series.
LC NO. 76-701622
Prod-AJN Dist-AJN Prodn-WGNCP 1976

Psychiatric Emergencies - Therapeutic Intervening C 30 MIN
3/4 INCH VIDEO CASSETTE PRO
Discusses the meaning of a psychiatric emergency. Presents principles of assessment and nursing intervention in psychiatric emergencies, giving examples of a variety of settings.
LC NO. 76-701622
Prod-AJN Dist-AJN Prodn-WGNCP 1976

Psychiatric Evaluation C 41 MIN
3/4 OR 1/2 INCH VIDEO CASSETTE PRO
Gives Norman Kagan's view to assessment and the mental status examination.
From The Psychiatry Learning System, Pt 1 - Assessments Series.
Prod-HSCIC Dist-HSCIC 1982

Psychiatric Medical Records - Treatment Plan C 27 MIN
3/4 INCH VIDEO CASSETTE PRO
Presents a basic review of the essential content of psychiatric medical records. Features Dr George J Weinstein and a resident psychiatrist discussing medical records and their role in quality of care, research and avoidance of litigation.
LC NO. 77-706084
Prod-USVA Dist-USNAC 1977

Psychiatric Nursing - Past And Present B 44 MIN
16MM FILM OPTICAL SOUND PRO
Traces the development of psychiatric nursing to the present-day concern for a therapeutic nurse-patient relationship.
From The Nursing In Psychiatry Series.
LC NO. 73-703437
Prod-VDONUR Dist-AJN Prodn-WTTWTV 1968

Psychiatric Problems Of The Aged B 30 MIN
16MM FILM OPTICAL SOUND
Describes organic brain syndrome with emphasis upon hypoxia and the impairment of utilization of oxygen. Illustrates some of the nursing measures which can assist patients to cope with this type of disability.
From The Gerontological Nursing Series. No. 7
LC NO. 73-710011
Prod-VDONUR Dist-AJN Prodn-WTTWTV 1970

Psychiatric-Mental Health Nursing—A Series
PRO
Presents psychotherapeutic methodology for all nurses.
Prod-AJN Dist-AJN Prodn-WGNCP 1976

Acute Alcoholic Intoxication	30 MIN
Adolescent Drug Abuse	30 MIN
Anxiety - Concept And Manifestations	30 MIN
Crisis Intervention - Theory And Application	30 MIN
Crisis Of Loss, The	30 MIN
Depressed Client, The	30 MIN
Facilitating Self-Disclosure	30 MIN
Family Therapy, Pt 1	30 MIN
Family Therapy, Pt 2	30 MIN
Long-Term Psychiatric Patient, The	40 MIN
Manipulative Client, The	30 MIN
Nurse In Child Abuse Prevention, The	30 MIN
Nursing In A Multi-Cultural Society	30 MIN
Psychiatric Emergencies	30 MIN
Psychogeriatrics	40 MIN
Psychosocial Assessment, Pt 1	30 MIN
Psychosocial Assessment, Pt 2	30 MIN
Psychotherapeutic Interview	30 MIN
Suicide Intervention	30 MIN
Suspicious Client, The	30 MIN
Withdrawn Client, The	30 MIN

Psychiatrist, The C 2 MIN
16MM FILM, 3/4 OR 1/2 IN VIDEO A
Offers a humorous tale designed to introduce coffee breaks in which a man on the psychiatrist's couch thinks he's a cup of coffee, and the doctor helps couch an ordinary announcement in unusual terms.
From The Coffee Breaks I Series.
Prod-MBACC Dist-MTI 1983

Psychiatry And Law - How Are They Related, Pt 1 B 29 MIN
16MM FILM OPTICAL SOUND
Presents Dr Thomas S Szasz, Dr Bernard Diamond and Dr Alexander D Brooks discussing the role of the psychiatrist in the courtroom and in prison.
From The Concepts And Controversies In Modern Medicine Series.
LC NO. 75-701277
Prod-NMAC Dist-USNAC 1970

Psychiatry And Law - How Are They Related, Pt 2 B 29 MIN
3/4 INCH VIDEO CASSETTE
Presents Dr Thomas S Szasz, Dr Bernard Diamond and Dr Alexander D Brooks discussing the role of the psychiatrist in the courtroom and in prison.
From The Concepts And Controversies In Modern Medicine Series.
LC NO. 74-706203
Prod-NMAC Dist-USNAC 1970

Psychiatry And The System C 25 MIN
3/4 OR 1/2 INCH VIDEO CASSETTE
Examines the psychiatrists's role as well as that of the doctor in society, using Dr Seymour Pollack, Professor of Psychiatry at USC School of Medicine, and John Miner, a lawyer who was formerly Deputy DA in charge of medical legal matters in Los Angeles. Shows them, with host Mario Machado, as they discuss the ways doctors are involved in practicing medicine in

deciding who is a threat to society because of mental illness, as well as the psychiatrist's function in court.
Prod-TRAINX Dist-TRAINX

Psychiatry Learning System, Pt 1 - Assessments—A Series
PRO
Contains a complete course in basic concepts of psychiatry, designed specifically for medical students doing a psychiatry clerkship. Includes a 1000 page text and 22 clinical videotapes for 19 lessons.
Prod-HSCIC Dist-HSCIC 1982

Psychiatric Evaluation 041 MIN
Psychodynamic Considerations And Defense 023 MIN
Psychological Evaluation 021 MIN
Psychosocial Factors in Physical Illness 027 MIN

Psychiatry Learning System, Pt 2 - Disorders—A Series
PRO
Continues from Part 1.
Prod-HSCIC Dist-HSCIC 1982

Affective Disorders 062 MIN
Anxiety Disorders 034 MIN
Behavioral Treatment 056 MIN
Disorders Of Infancy, Childhood, And 085 MIN
Impulse Control Disorders 027 MIN
Organic Mental Disorders 030 MIN
Other Treatment Modalities 018 MIN
Personality Disorders 066 MIN
Psychopharmacology 000 MIN
Psychosexual Disorders 078 MIN
Psychosocial Treatments 000 MIN
Schizophrenic Disorders, Psychoses Not 066 MIN
Sleep Disorders 000 MIN
Somatoform And Dissociative Disorders 070 MIN
Substance Use Disorders 000 MIN

Psychic Parrot, The C 19 MIN
16MM FILM, 3/4 OR 1/2 IN VIDEO J-C A
Deals with a TV-viewing family of apartment dwellers watching the drama unfolding of portended end of the world as forefold by a psychic parrot. Focuses on a group of people selected by the President to rocket to the moon to permit survival of the human race which is treated as a news event by TV reporters. Shows reactions of apartment dwellers to TV reporting as 'the end' nears.
Prod-PARROT Dist-BCNFL 1979

Psychic Phenomena And The Occult C 30 MIN
3/4 OR 1/2 INCH VIDEO CASSETTE H-C A
Shows professional conjurer James Randi, professor of psychology Ray Hayman, author Ethel Grodzins and psycho-physicist Wilbur Franklin discussing paranormal and psychic phenomena, and taking sides in regard to its validity.
From The Ethics In America Series.
Prod-AMHUMA Dist-AMHUMA

Psychics, Saints And Scientists C 35 MIN
16MM FILM, 3/4 OR 1/2 IN VIDEO
Covers spiritual healing, biofeedback, ESP training, brain-wave conditioning and Kirlian photography.
Prod-HP Dist-HP

Psychling C 25 MIN
16MM FILM, 3/4 OR 1/2 IN VIDEO H-C A
Chronicles a cross-country bicycle trip made by a man whose doctors told him he would never again participate in sports. Explains how his personal motivation and goal setting strategies helped him build himself up.
LC NO. 80-706457
Prod-CRMP Dist-CRMP 1981

Psycho-Educational Assessment C 24 MIN
16MM FILM OPTICAL SOUND
Shows how children are admitted to the League School for seriously disturbed children and tells how they are initially and progressively evaluated by staff clinicians representing a variety of disciplines.
From The League School For Seriously Disturbed Children Series.
LC NO. 75-702424
Prod-USBEH Dist-USNAC 1973

Psychoactive C 29 MIN
16MM FILM, 3/4 OR 1/2 IN VIDEO J-C A
Uses actor George Carlin's comedy routine to show how the nine systems of the human body are affected by each of the five classifications of psychoactive drugs. Explores tolerance, withdrawal and dependence.
Prod-COHNW Dist-PFP 1976

Psychodrama In Group Process—A Series

Shows the application of psychodrama techniques to deal with various situations.
Prod-NYU Dist-NYU

Interstaff Communications 042 MIN
Problem Of Acceptance, A 047 MIN

Psychodynamic Considerations And Defense Mechanisms C 23 MIN
3/4 OR 1/2 INCH VIDEO CASSETTE PRO
Deals with theories of the unconscious and with some of the ways the unconscious is manifested verbally and behaviorally.
From The Psychiatry Learning System, Pt 1 - Assessments Series.
Prod-HSCIC Dist-HSCIC 1982

Psychodynamics Of Pain C 19 MIN
3/4 INCH VIDEO CASSETTE PRO
See series title for descriptive statement.
From The Management Of Pain Series. Module 2
LC NO. 80-707393
Prod-BRA Dist-BRA 1980

Psychogenic Diseases In Infancy B 20 MIN
16MM FILM SILENT C T
Illustrates a series of psychogenic diseases and attempts to relate them to the infants' relationships with their mothers.
From The Film Studies Of The Psychoanalytic Research Project On Problems In Infancy Series.
Prod-SPITZ Dist-NYU 1952

Psychogeriatrics C 40 MIN
16MM FILM OPTICAL SOUND PRO
Presents interviews with patients of nursing homes which illustrate the dynamics of two major psychiatric syndromes of the elderly, chronic brain syndrome and depression. Discusses nursing assessment and related planning for care of the elderly to minimize these problems.
From The Psychiatric-Mental Health Nursing Series.
LC NO. 76-701624
Prod-AJN Dist-AJN Prodn-WGNCP 1976

Psychogeriatrics - Mental Health Problems Of The Aged C 40 MIN
3/4 INCH VIDEO CASSETTE PRO
Presents interviews with patients of nursing homes which illustrate the dynamics of the two major psychiatric syndromes of the elderly, chronic brain syndrome and depression. Discusses nursing assessment and related planning for care of the elderly to minimize these problems.
LC NO. 76-701624
Prod-AJN Dist-AJN Prodn-WGNCP 1976

Psychokinesis (Russia And Here) C 29 MIN
2 INCH VIDEOTAPE
Features Dr Charles Thomas Cayce and Dr Puryear who show and explain a film made on a recent research trip when Dr Puryear met and observed at work two women especially gifted in the practice of psychokinesis.
From The Who Is Man Series.
Prod-WHROTV Dist-PUBTEL

Psychologic Stress In Critical Illness C 26 MIN
3/4 INCH VIDEO CASSETTE PRO
Reviews physiologic responses identified with stress and discusses the stages of the psychologic general adaptation syndrome. Describes appropriate nursing intervention during this stage.
From The Stress In Critical Illness Series. Module 2
LC NO. 80-707622
Prod-BRA Dist-BRA 1980

Psychological Adjustment To College B 43 MIN
16MM FILM OPTICAL SOUND
Frederick Coons describes for beginnng college students the major developmental tasks that they will encounter during their college years.
LC NO. 77-714204
Prod-IU Dist-IU 1971

Psychological Adjustment To Dizziness C 50 MIN
3/4 OR 1/2 INCH VIDEO CASSETTE
See series title for descriptive statement.
From The Dizziness And Related Balance Disorders Series.
Prod-GSHDME Dist-GSHDME

Psychological And Emotional Habits C
1/2 IN VIDEO CASSETTE BETA/VHS
See series title for descriptive statement.
From The R M I Stress Management Series Series.
Prod-RMI Dist-RMI

Psychological Aspects C 25 MIN
3/4 OR 1/2 INCH VIDEO CASSETTE
Tells how to cope with emotional reactions and frustrating situations while driving.
From The Right Way Series.
Prod-SCETV Dist-PBS 1982

Psychological Aspects C 28 MIN
3/4 OR 1/2 INCH VIDEO CASSETTE J A
Explores the thinking and psychology of the heavy drinker.
Prod-SUTHRB Dist-SUTHRB

Psychological Aspects Of Coma C 22 MIN
3/4 OR 1/2 INCH VIDEO CASSETTE PRO
Studies psychological and emotional needs of comatose patient, family, and health professionals.
From The Comatose Patient Series.
Prod-BRA Dist-BRA

Psychological Aspects Of Dance Performance And Competition C 30 MIN
3/4 OR 1/2 INCH VIDEO CASSETTE
See series title for descriptive statement.
From The Dancers' Bodies Series.
Prod-ARCVID Dist-ARCVID

Psychological Evaluation C 21 MIN
3/4 OR 1/2 INCH VIDEO CASSETTE PRO
Reviews the use of various psychological tests in assessment evaluation. Addresses issues of reliability and validity of tests.
From The Psychiatry Learning System, Pt 1 - Assessments Series.
Prod-HSCIC Dist-HSCIC 1982

Psychological Evaluation Of Patients With Cerebral Dysfunction—A Series
PRO
Prod-UOKLA Dist-UOKLA 1966

Interviewing An Adult Male Aphasic Patient 18 MIN
Interviewing And Testing A 'MOTOR' Aphastic 21 MIN
Testing An Adult Male Aphasic Patient 20 MIN

Psychological Factors and Ethical Considerations In Negotiations C 50 MIN
3/4 OR 1/2 INCH VIDEO CASSETTE PRO
Explains how to handle racial, ethnic, gender and age differences that may affect negotiations. Includes discussion of provisions of the ABA Code Of Professional Responsibility.
From The Negotiation Lectures Series.
Prod-NITA Dist-ABACPE

Psychological Factors Applied To Public Health B 30 MIN
2 INCH VIDEOTAPE PRO
Discusses some of the psychological factors influencing the kinds of things people do or fail to do about their health. (Broadcast quality)
From The Public Health Science Series. Unit I - Introduction To Foundations Of Public Health
Prod-TEXWU Dist-GPITVL Prodn-KUHTTV

Psychological Factors Applied To Public Health B 30 MIN
16MM FILM OPTICAL SOUND PRO
Discusses some of the psychological factors influencing the kinds of things people do or fail to do about their health.
From The Public Health Science - Foundations Of Public health Series.
Prod-KUHTTV Dist-GPITVL

Psychological Hazards In Infancy C 22 MIN
16MM FILM OPTICAL SOUND
Shows that in group care and at home, the vital experiences and learnings of infancy may be hampered by inadequte stimulation, insuffieient warm attention from adults or inappropriate handling which is not geared to changing developmental needs. Shows both mild and severe psychological damage and suggests means of prevention.
LC NO. 73-700108
Prod-USDHEW Dist-USNAC 1970

Psychological Hazards In Infancy B 22 MIN
16MM FILM OPTICAL SOUND J-C T
Describes the types of psychological damage that may be done to infants and suggests means of prevention.
From The Head Start Training Series.
Prod-VASSAR Dist-NYU

Psychological Implications Of Behavior During The Clinical Visit B 20 MIN
16MM FILM SILENT C T
Illustrates that clues to a child's emotional attitudes are seen from its overt behavior while awaiting examination, during physical and dental examinations and at play.
From The Film Studies On Integrated Development Series.
Prod-FRIWOL Dist-NYU 1944

Psychological Implications Of Divorce C 30 MIN
3/4 OR 1/2 INCH VIDEO CASSETTE C A
Examines major problems faced by divorced persons and their families.
From The Family Portrait - A Study Of Contemporary Lifestyles Series. Lesson 22
Prod-SCCON Dist-CDTEL

Psychological Limitations C 11 MIN
16MM FILM, 3/4 OR 1/2 IN VIDEO
Explores emotional limits and how they affect people. Shows that caution is a psychological process that evolves through learning, and that humans can only learn so much so fast. Points out that knowing psychological limitations can help prevent accidents.
From The Safety And You Series.
Prod-FILCOM Dist-FILCOM

Psychological Make-Up Of A Customer, The C
3/4 OR 1/2 INCH VIDEO CASSETTE
Stresses that people don't buy from people they don't trust and that sales success depends heavily on one's ability to build a personal rapport with the customer.
From The Strategies For Successful Selling Series. Module 2
Prod-AMA Dist-AMA

Psychological Romance C 10 MIN
16MM FILM OPTICAL SOUND
Concerns a young man's fantasies about a girl he wants to date. Shows his reactions when he finally meets her.
LC NO. 81-700392
Prod-NUCCI Dist-NUCCI 1981

Psychological Testing C 30 MIN
3/4 OR 1/2 INCH VIDEO CASSETTE
Focuses on achievement tests, aptitude tests, cognitive style mapping, criteria of a good test and other psychological testing.
From The Psychology Of Human Relations Series.
Prod-MATC Dist-WFVTAE

Psychology C 29 MIN
3/4 OR 1/2 INCH VIDEO CASSETTE
See series title for descriptive statement.
From The Vic Braden's Tennis For The Future Series.
Prod-WGBHTV Dist-PBS 1981

Psychology C 48 MIN
3/4 OR 1/2 INCH VIDEO CASSETTE
Includes 48 half-hour videotape lessons on several aspects of psychology.
Prod-TELSTR Dist-TELSTR

Psychology And Movement C 30 MIN
3/4 OR 1/2 INCH VIDEO CASSETTE
See series title for descriptive statement.

From The Health And Well-Being Of Dancers Series.
Prod-ARCVID Dist-ARCVID

Psychology And The World Of Work C 30 MIN
3/4 OR 1/2 INCH VIDEO CASSETTE
Focuses on applications of psychological theory in work settings, elements of rational-emotive therapy applied to work-related problems, positive reinforcement in work situations and psychological consulting in business and industry.
From The Psychology Of Human Relations Series.
Prod-MATC Dist-WFVTAE

Psychology Of Aging, The B 30 MIN
16MM FILM OPTICAL SOUND C
Discusses the psychological changes which occur in old age, such as difficulty in recall, disengagement and increasing dependence.
From The Growth And Development, The Adult Years Series.
LC NO. 71-706819
Prod-VDONUR Dist-AJN Prodn-WTTWTV 1969

Psychology Of Human Relations--A Series

Features interviews with renowned psychologists. Presents basic psychological theory and research about the ways human beings behave and relate to each other.
Prod-MATC Dist-WFVTAE

Abnormal Behavior	030 MIN
Adult Life Stages	030 MIN
Aggression	030 MIN
Aging And Death	030 MIN
Applied Learning	030 MIN
Assertiveness Training	030 MIN
Attitudes And Actions	030 MIN
B F Skinner On Behaviorism	030 MIN
Career Choice	030 MIN
Career Development	030 MIN
Communication And Language	030 MIN
Conditioning	030 MIN
Coping	030 MIN
Emotion, Mind And Body	030 MIN
Groups In Action	030 MIN
How Do We Feel?	030 MIN
Information Processing	030 MIN
Intergroup Relations	030 MIN
Interpersonal Relations	030 MIN
Moral Development	030 MIN
Motives In Our Lives, The	030 MIN
Perception	030 MIN
Personality	030 MIN
Psychological Testing	030 MIN
Psychology And The World Of Work	030 MIN
Psychology, A Science	030 MIN
Psychotherapy	030 MIN
Social Roles	030 MIN
What Is Psychology?	030 MIN
Why We Do What We Do	030 MIN

Psychology Of Personal And Professional Goal Setting C 30 MIN
3/4 OR 1/2 INCH VIDEO CASSETTE
Illustrates company, professional and personal goal setting as healthy processes which benefit all.
From The High Performance Leadership Series.
Prod-PRODEV Dist-PRODEV

Psychology Of Personal And Professional Goal Setting C 30 MIN
3/4 OR 1/2 INCH VIDEO CASSETTE
See series title for descriptive statement.
From The High Performance Leadership Series.
Prod-VIDAI Dist-DELTAK

Psychology Of Persuasion, The C
3/4 OR 1/2 INCH VIDEO CASSETTE
Introduces sales people to the master methods of overcoming a customer's objection.
From The Strategies For Successful Selling Series. Module 6
Prod-AMA Dist-AMA

Psychology Of Sport C 19 MIN
16MM FILM OPTICAL SOUND
Introduces applications of sports psychology.
From The Coaching Development Programme Series. No. 3
LC NO. 76-701040
Prod-SARBOO Dist-SARBOO Prodn-SVL 1974

Psychology Of Sports C 25 MIN
3/4 OR 1/2 INCH VIDEO CASSETTE T
Discusses the importance of psychological factors in motivating athletes to perform at their best, how to communicate through positive reinforcement, how to be a good listener and the importance of skill improvement.
From The Sports Medicine Series.
Prod-UNIDIM Dist-EBEC 1982

Psychology Of The Bible, The, Pt 1 B 30 MIN
16MM FILM OPTICAL SOUND
Maurice Samuel and Mark Van Doren discuss the psychological connotations of various episodes in the Bible. (Kinescope)
Prod-JTS Dist-NAAJS Prodn-NBCTV 1963

Psychology Of The Bible, The, Pt 2 B 30 MIN
16MM FILM OPTICAL SOUND
Features Maurice Samuel and Mark Van Doren discussing the psychological connotations of several biblical episodes.
LC NO. FIA65-1101
Prod-JTS Dist-NAAJS Prodn-NBCTV 1965

Psychology Of Trading C 30 MIN
3/4 OR 1/2 INCH VIDEO CASSETTE C A
Presents experts discussing the use of discipline in overcoming emotions which interfere with objective trading.
From The Commodities -- The Professional Trader Series.
Prod-VIPUB Dist-VIPUB

Psychology Of Winning, The C 20 MIN
16MM FILM OPTICAL SOUND
Explores the characteristics of successful people in all walks of life, including astronauts, returning POW's, and sports figures.
LC NO. 81-700722
Prod-SOLIL Dist-SOLIL 1981

Psychology Of Winning, The C 20 MIN
3/4 OR 1/2 INCH VIDEO CASSETTE A
Presents Dr Denis Waitley, Chairman of Psychology for the U S Olympic Committee's Sports Medicine Council, describing the personal characteristics common to winners. Emphasizes the principle that winning is a matter of fully developing the potential that one is born with.
Prod-SFTI Dist-SFTI

Psychology Today Films--A Series
16MM FILM, 3/4 OR 1/2 IN VIDEO
Prod-CRMP Dist-CRMP

Abnormal Behavior - A Mental Hospital	028 MIN
Aspects Of Behavior	031 MIN
Development	033 MIN
Information Processing	028 MIN
Learning	030 MIN
Methodology - The Psychologist And The	031 MIN
Personality	030 MIN
Sensory World, The	033 MIN
Social Psychology	033 MIN

Psychology, A Science? C 30 MIN
3/4 OR 1/2 INCH VIDEO CASSETTE
Outlines the applications of the scientific method in psychology and the purposes of psychological research.
From The Psychology Of Human Relations Series.
Prod-MATC Dist-WFVTAE

Psychopathology - Diagnostic Vignettes--A Series
C A
Presents brief excerpts from diagnostic interviews with patients who exhibit characteristic symptoms of schizophrenic and affective disorders.
Prod-IU Dist-IU 1984

Bipolar Affective Disorders (Case Numbers 5-8)	032 MIN
Dysthymic Disorder And Major Affective	038 MIN
Schizophrenic Disorders (Case Numbers 9-12)	035 MIN

Psychopharmacological Drugs, Pt 1 C 30 MIN
16MM FILM OPTICAL SOUND C
See series title for descriptive statement.
From The Pharmacology Series.
LC NO. 73-703336
Prod-MVNE Dist-TELSTR 1971

Psychopharmacological Drugs, Pt 2 C 30 MIN
16MM FILM OPTICAL SOUND C
See series title for descriptive statement.
From The Pharmacology Series.
LC NO. 73-703337
Prod-MVNE Dist-TELSTR 1971

Psychopharmacology C
3/4 OR 1/2 INCH VIDEO CASSETTE PRO
Serves as a good guide to the use of psychoactive drugs.
From The Psychiatry Learning System, Pt 2 - Disorders Series.
Prod-HSCIC Dist-HSCIC 1982

Psychosexual Disorders C 78 MIN
3/4 OR 1/2 INCH VIDEO CASSETTE PRO
Teaches how to recognize common myths about sexuality and to recall information to dispel these myths. Identifies the gender identity disorders, paraphilias, and psychosexual dysfunctions. Considers diagnosis and treatment.
From The Psychiatry Learning System, Pt 2 - Disorders Series.
Prod-HSCIC Dist-HSCIC 1982

Psychosis - A Family Intervention C 13 MIN
3/4 OR 1/2 INCH VIDEO CASSETTE PRO
Tells of the methods emergency medical technicians employ to calm a psychotic who is threatening family members.
From The Crisis Intervention Series.
Prod-SBG Dist-GPITVL 1983

Psychosocial Adaptation To Illness C 13 MIN
16MM FILM OPTICAL SOUND
Reveals the patient's psychological and sociological needs to the nurse and shows her the ways in which she can help meet these needs.
From The Patient As A Person Series.
LC NO. 70-712973
Prod-TRNAID Dist-TRNAID 1970

Psychosocial And Sexual Involvement C 30 MIN
3/4 OR 1/2 INCH VIDEO CASSETTE
Explores the effects of renal dysfunction on the sexual psychosocial functioning of a patient and his family. Shows patient, his wife and a group of other patients comparing their experiences and problems in adjusting to the illness.
From The Individuals With Renal Dysfunction Series.
Prod-AJN Dist-AJN

Psychosocial Aspects Of Death B 39 MIN
16MM FILM, 3/4 OR 1/2 IN VIDEO
Presents a dramatized story about a nurse who faces the death of a patient for the first time, in order to show the impact of the death of a patient on a nurse and to examine the nurse-patient relationship.
Prod-IU Dist-IU 1971

Psychosocial Assessment, Pt 1 C 30 MIN
16MM FILM - 3/4 IN VIDEO PRO
Surveys the aims, content areas and methods of obtaining data for a nursing psychosocial assessment. Shows the importance of the initial psychiatric interview.
From The Psychiatric-Mental Health Nursing Series.
LC NO. 76-701626
Prod-AJN Dist-AJN Prodn-WGNCP 1976

Psychosocial Assessment, Pt 2 C 30 MIN
16MM FILM - 3/4 IN VIDEO PRO
Explores the initial psychiatric interview as an investigative and therapeutic method in the nurse's assessment of psychosocial problems. Illustrates and evaluates four common interview techniques.
From The Psychiatric-Mental Health Nursing Series.
LC NO. 76-701626
Prod-AJN Dist-AJN Prodn-WGNCP 1976

Psychosocial Factors In Physical Illness C 27 MIN
3/4 OR 1/2 INCH VIDEO CASSETTE PRO
Contains material on the relationship between the mind and the body.
From The Psychiatry Learning System, Pt 1 - Assessments Series.
Prod-HSCIC Dist-HSCIC 1982

Psychosocial Sexual Development Infant-Preadolescent C 24 MIN
3/4 OR 1/2 INCH VIDEO CASSETTE
Defines sexuality and describes what constitutes being sexually healthy. Presents the biological determinants of sexuality from conception through birth.
From The Human Sexuality Series.
Prod-WSUN Dist-AJN

Psychosocial Sexual Development Adolescent-Aged C 20 MIN
3/4 OR 1/2 INCH VIDEO CASSETTE
Presents the development of sexuality from adolescence through old age. Emphasizes behavioral aspects.
From The Human Sexuality Series.
Prod-WSUN Dist-AJN

Psychosocial Sexual Development - Adolescent, Aged C 30 MIN
16MM FILM OPTICAL SOUND PRO
Presents the development of sexuality from adolescence through adult age, with emphasis on behavioral aspects of sexual development.
From The Directions For Education In Nursing Via Technology Series. Human Sexuality
LC NO. 76-703344
Prod-DENT Dist-WSU Prodn-CENIT 1976

Psychosocial Sexual Development - Infant, Pre-Adolescent C 30 MIN
16MM FILM OPTICAL SOUND PRO
Defines what constitutes being sexually healthy. Depicts the development of sexuality in children from birth through preadolescence, with emphasis on behavioral components that are characteristic of each phase.
From The Directions For Education In Nursing Via Technology Series. Human Sexuality
LC NO. 76-703343
Prod-DENT Dist-WSU Prodn-CENIT 1976

Psychosocial Survival In Burn Trauma C 26 MIN
3/4 OR 1/2 INCH VIDEO CASSETTE PRO
Reveals effects of burn trauma in terms of sudden, catastrophic, physiologic or psychologic assault on patient. Shows two main sections, each dealing in detail with massive psychologic and sociologic insults to burn victims life-style and personal integrity.
From The Burn Trauma Series.
Prod-BRA Dist-BRA

Psychosocial Treatments C
3/4 OR 1/2 INCH VIDEO CASSETTE PRO
Goes beyond the traditional individual psychotherapy to include family therapy and group therapies.
From The Psychiatry Learning System, Pt 2 - Disorders Series.
Prod-HSCIC Dist-HSCIC 1982

Psychosomatics Of Experimental Drug Dissociation B 14 MIN
16MM FILM SILENT C T
Presents an experiment in which conditioned responses to tone and light stimuli are developed in dogs given erythroidine, a curare-like drug which produces paralysis. An electric shock is used as an unconditioned stimulus. Conditioned responses produced during the drug state cannot be elicited after recovery but reappear spontaneously when the animal is again given the drug.
Prod-PSUPCR Dist-PSUPCR 1946

Psychotherapeutic Interview C 30 MIN
16MM FILM - 3/4 IN VIDEO PRO
Uses the beginning and middle stages of an actual therapy relationship to present the nurse's conduct of individual psychotherapy. Describes the process by which the patient is helped to observe personal behavior, identify patterns of experience and make connections between present and past life events.
LC NO. 76-701625
Prod-AJN Dist-AJN Prodn-WGNCP 1976

Psychotherapeutic Interviewing--A Series

Prod-USVA Dist-USNAC

Approach To Understanding Dynamics, An	32 MIN
Clinical Picture Of Anxiety Hysteria, A	26 MIN
Clinical Picture Of Claustrophobia, A	31 MIN
Introduction	10 MIN

Method Of Procedure, A 32 MIN
Non-Verbal Communication 27 MIN

Psychotherapeutic Interviewing—A Series
PRO
Prod-USVA Dist-USNAC 1977

Approach To Understanding Dynamics, An 34 MIN

Psychotheraphy II C 29 MIN
3/4 INCH VIDEO CASSETTE C A
Describes group and environmental therapies. Compares types of therapies in terms of claims for success, cost, duration and basis for choice.
From The Understanding Human Behavior - An Introduction To Psychology Series. Lesson 26
Prod-COAST Dist-CDTEL

Psychotherapy C 26 MIN
16MM FILM, 3/4 OR 1/2 IN VIDEO H-C A
Discusses the reasons for psychotherapy and provides an overview of the basic process of psychotherapy.
Prod-DAVFMS Dist-CRMP 1979

Psychotherapy And Medication C 30 MIN
3/4 OR 1/2 INCH VIDEO CASSETTE
Presents a two-part program on working with violent persons. Discusses psychotherapy treatment in the first part and medication in the second part.
From The Management And Treatment Of The Violent Patient Series.
Prod-HEMUL Dist-HEMUL

Psychotherapy Begins - The Case Of Mr Lin B 53 MIN
16MM FILM OPTICAL SOUND C T
Documents the first interview with a young male student concerned about his homosexuality. Shows him exploring his problem and beginnint to realize that perhaps homosexuality is not the central difficulty. He realizes he has many personality difficulties and reviews some of his attempts to resolve these problems.
Prod-PSUPCR Dist-PSUPCR 1955

Psychotherapy I C 29 MIN
3/4 INCH VIDEO CASSETTE C A
Illustrates and evaluates wide range of therapies being used to treat mental disorders. Focuses on and critically examines the psychoanalytic and humanistic approaches.
From The Understanding Human Behavior - An Introduction To Psychology Series. Lesson 25
Prod-COAST Dist-CDTEL

Psychotherapy In Process - The Case Of Miss Mun B 57 MIN
16MM FILM OPTICAL SOUND C T
Follows a complete therapeutic interview of a young woman client who is suffering from fatigue, depression, tenseness and psychosomatic ailments. She is deeply involved in therapy and her emotional responses are supplemented by spontaneous reactions from the therapist. The client weeps as she expresses her complete aloneness in her fears and expresses positive feelings as she realizes that the therapist understands her. The reactions of the therapist are recorded at the end.
Prod-PSUPCR Dist-PSUPCR 1955

Psychotherapy Of The Schizophrenic C 60 MIN
3/4 OR 1/2 INCH VIDEO CASSETTE
Gives the step-by-step approach used by Dr Silvano Arieti with patients suffering with hallucinations, delusions and thought disorders. Integrates his theories and techniques with traditional psychodynamics.
From Schizophrenia Series.
Prod-HEMUL Dist-HEMUL

Psychotic Assaultive Patient, The C
3/4 OR 1/2 INCH VIDEO CASSETTE
Shows how the violent patient can be controlled by applying expert technique. Places emphasis on verbal, personal intervention to help the patient regain internal control. Presents recommended applications and appropriate cautions in the administration of medication.
From The Crisis Intervention Series.
Prod-VTRI Dist-VTRI

Psychotic Assaultive Patient, The C 20 MIN
3/4 OR 1/2 INCH VIDEO CASSETTE PRO
Show how to effectively and efficiently recognize and provide initial treatment and disposition of psychotic assaultive patients. Discusses typical precipitating factors, management techniques, how to test patient's level and control and behavioral characteristics.
From The Medical Crisis Intervention Series.
Prod-LEIKID Dist-LEIKID

Psychotic Child, The B 25 MIN
16MM FILM OPTICAL SOUND C A
Pictures a seven-year-old psychotic child who actively resists a variety of relationships, displaying autistic defenses and ritualistic, compulsive behavior. Indicates that his motor skill has developed to that of a two or three year-old. Shows the child exhibiting rebellious and frustrated behavior.
LC NO. FIA68-2699
Prod-PSU Dist-PSUPCR 1967

Psychotropic Drugs And The Health Care Professional—A Series

Presents different drug therapies available to health care professionals for different mental illnesses.
Prod-UWASHP Dist-UWASHP

Adjunctive Medications 022 MIN
Antidepressants And Lithium 024 MIN
Anxiolytic Sedatives 011 MIN
Introduction 010 MIN
Management Issues 028 MIN
Neuroleptic Drugs And Adjunctive Medications 029 MIN

Psychotropic Drugs And The Hyperkinetic Syndrome B 24 MIN
16MM FILM OPTICAL SOUND PRO
Focuses on a research project conducted at the Kansas Center for Mental Retardation and Human Development, which examines psychotropic drug effects on the memory and academic performance of hyperactive, mentally retarded children.
LC NO. 78-701607
Prod-UKANS Dist-UKANS 1974

Psychotropics C 20 MIN
3/4 OR 1/2 INCH VIDEO CASSETTE PRO
Defines psychotropic drugs and briefly reviews the nervous system. Employs a case-study technique to demonstrate the use of psychotropic drugs in treating anxiety, depression and psychosis. Introduces the patient for each of these conditions, describes his complaints, specifies the types of drugs that might be used, explains their intended actions and depicts important nursing considerations.
LC NO. 77-730541
Prod-TRAINX Dist-TRAINX

Pterodactyls Alive C 25 MIN
16MM FILM, 3/4 OR 1/2 IN VIDEO J-C A
Explores the possibility of the existence of pterodactyls, the prehistoric flying reptiles from the age of dinosaurs. Presents living clues among reptiles, bats and birds around the world which exhibit similar characteristics.
Prod-BBCTV Dist-FI

Pterygoid Muscles And Infrapterygoid Structures C 17 MIN
3/4 INCH VIDEO CASSETTE PRO
Illustrates the anatomy of the lateral aspects of the head to the pterygoid muscles, and shows the nerves and vessels to the base of the skull.
From The Anatomy Of The Head And Neck Series.
LC NO. 78-706252
Prod-USVA Dist-USNAC Prodn-VADTC 1978

Pterygoid Muscles And Infrapterygoid Structures C 17 MIN
16MM FILM OPTICAL SOUND PRO
Presents Dr Harry Sicher, professor emeritus of dentistry, illustrating the anatomy of the lateral aspects of the head deep to the pterygoid muscles and showing the nerves and vessels to the base of the skull.
From The Anatomy Of The Head And Neck Series.
LC NO. 75-702081
Prod-USVA Dist-USNAC Prodn-LUSD 1969

Pterygopalatine Fossa C 9 MIN
3/4 OR 1/2 INCH VIDEO CASSETTE C A
Describes the boundaries, demonstrates the bones and identifies the boney regions of the pterygopalatine fossa.
From The Skull Anatomy Series.
Prod-UTXHSA Dist-TEF

Pterygopalatine Fossa, The C 16 MIN
16MM FILM, 3/4 OR 1/2 IN VIDEO PRO
Points out the distribution of nerves and vessels of the middle face.
From The Cine-Prosector Series.
Prod-AVCORP Dist-TEF

Puberty In Boys C 10 MIN
16MM FILM, 3/4 OR 1/2 IN VIDEO J-H
Discusses the physical changes occurring in boys during puberty. Shows how sperm is created and explores the effects of the endocrine system in the development of secondary sexual characteristics.
Prod-NFBC Dist-TEXFLM 1969

Public Data Networks C 45 MIN
3/4 OR 1/2 INCH VIDEO CASSETTE
Covers such topics as the structure of an Advanced Communications Service (ACS) network, ACS services, possible uses for ACS, relationship between ACS and other architectures and the storage of programs and data in an ACS network.
From The Network Architectures - A Communications Revolution Series.
Prod-DELTAK Dist-DELTAK

Public Education - At Whose Expense C 29 MIN
2 INCH VIDEOTAPE
Examines methods of public school financing in light of the 1971 California Supreme Court ruling which declared revenue raised from property taxes unconstitutional as a source of funds for public education.
From The Turning Points Series.
Prod-NETCHE Dist-PUBTEL

Public Education After The Civil War B 30 MIN
16MM FILM OPTICAL SOUND H-C A
Horace Mann Bond discusses the exclusion of black children from public education after the Civil War, the schools operated by missionary groups and the Freedman's Bureau, and the foundation of the first black colleges.
From The Black History, Section 10 - New South And New North Series.
LC NO. 76-704065
Prod-WCBSTV Dist-HRAW 1969

Public Enemy Number One C 55 MIN
16MM FILM, 3/4 OR 1/2 IN VIDEO A
Introduces 70-year-old Australian journalist Wilfred Burchett, who has found himself unwelcome in his own country because of his unconventional reporting on World War II, Korea and Vietnam.
LC NO. 81-707568
Prod-FLMLIB Dist-FLMLIB 1981

Public Goods And Responsibilities - How Far Should We Go C 30 MIN
3/4 OR 1/2 INCH VIDEO CASSETTE C
See series title for descriptive statement.
From The Economics USA Series.
Prod-WEFA Dist-ANNCPB

Public Health C
3/4 OR 1/2 INCH VIDEO CASSETTE
See series title for descriptive statement.
From The Pest Control Technology Correspondence Course Series.
Prod-PUAVC Dist-PUAVC

Public Health And The U S Army Veterinarian C 15 MIN
16MM FILM OPTICAL SOUND
Explains the role played by United States Army veterinarians in maintaining public health. Shows the interrelationship between human and animal well-being.
LC NO. 78-700253
Prod-USA Dist-USNAC 1977

Public Health Aspects Of The Residential Environment B 30 MIN
16MM FILM OPTICAL SOUND
Discusses the relationship between the elements of the residential environment and health. Describes the responsibilities of health agencies in programs of housing improvement.
From The Public Health Science - Bioenvironmental Health Series.
Prod-KUHTTV Dist-GPITVL

Public Health Aspects Of The Residential Environment C 30 MIN
2 INCH VIDEOTAPE PRO
Discusses the relationship between the elements of the residential environment and health which are the responsibilities of health agencies in programs of housing improvement. (Broadcast quality)
From The Public Health Science Series. Unit V - Introduction To Bioenvironmental Health
Prod-TEXWU Dist-GPITVL Prodn-KUHTTV

Public Health Nurse And The Mentally Retarded Child, The C 24 MIN
16MM FILM, 3/4 OR 1/2 IN VIDEO C T
Shows how a public health nurse can help the parents of retarded children. Traces one case from the detection of the abnormal condition to the education given parents to cope with training situations.
Prod-UOKLA Dist-IFB 1959

Public Health Problems In Mass Evacuation B 13 MIN
16MM FILM OPTICAL SOUND
Explains the public health problems attending the mass evacuation of an urban population, including mass feeding, water supply, medical care, waste and sewage disposal and disease outbreaks. Supplement with current data.
LC NO. FIE57-85
Prod-USPHS Dist-USNAC 1957

Public Health Science - Bioenvironmental Health—A Series
PRO
Looks at environmental health from an ecological point of view. Gives attention to selected environmental health concerns and problems.
Prod-KUHTTV Dist-GPITVL

Air And Water Pollution 30 MIN
Man And His Environment 30 MIN
Migrant Health 30 MIN
Occupational Health 30 MIN
Public Health Aspects Of The Residential 30 MIN
Survival 30 MIN

Public Health Science - Biostatistics—A Series
PRO
Presents some basic statistical concepts and methods and their application in community health by the health practitioner.
Prod-KUHTTV Dist-GPITVL

Basic Measurement Tools 30 MIN
Estimation 30 MIN
Health Information Systems 30 MIN
More Basic Tools 30 MIN
People And Statistics 30 MIN
Probability 30 MIN
Tests Of Hypotheses 30 MIN

Public Health Science - Community Organization For Health Services—A Series
PRO
Provides a view of the systems of community forces related to contemporary community health problems. Focuses on the nature of contemporary health problems, a systems approach to analysis and planning and management as related to these problems.
Prod-KUHTTV Dist-GPITVL

Agency Structure And Health Service Delivery 30 MIN
Community Development For Community Health 30 MIN
Contemporary Community Scene, The 30 MIN
Framework For Viewing Contemporary Health 30 MIN
Model For Community Health Problem Analysis 30 MIN

Public Health Science - Epidemiology—A Series
PRO
Discusses the epidemiological concept and its applications in community health practive. Presents the application of epidemiological methods in clinical situations with emphasis on its use to evaluate the outcome of nursing processes.
Prod-KUHTTV Dist-GPITVL

Associates Can Cause Happenings - Control Them 30 MIN
Epidemiology - What's That 30 MIN
Future Health Happenings 30 MIN
Glimpse Of Reality, A 30 MIN
Way It Is, The 30 MIN
We Need From Time To Time 30 MIN
When Is A Case A Case 30 MIN

Public Health Science - Foundations Of Public Health—A Series
PRO
Explores the meaning of health, individual health and community health, the health enterprise, and the individual's interaction therein. Demonstrates some of the effects of change as they relate to the individual, his family and his community.
Prod-KUHTTV Dist-GPITVL

Emergence Of Comprehensive Health Services
High-Level Wellness In The World Of Today 30 MIN
Psychological Factors Applied To Public Health 30 MIN
Scope And Goals Of The Health Enterprise 30 MIN
Social Forces And Their Implications To 30 MIN

Public Health Science—A Series
PRO
Provides instruction in public health science, including specialized teaching resources, for the baccalaureate nursing program. Contains 12 authorities in the field of public health that were secured to teach the series because of the specialization inherent in each of the areas. Organizes the course in five sections, foundations of public health, biostatistics, epidemiology, community organization and bioenvironmental health. (Broadcast quality)
Prod-TEXWU Dist-GPITVL Prodn-KUHTTV

Agency Structure And Health Service Delivery 30 MIN
Air And Water Pollution 30 MIN
Associates Can 'Cause' Happenings - Control 30 MIN
Basic Measurement Tools 30 MIN
Community Development For Community Health 30 MIN
Contemporary Community Scene, The 30 MIN
Emergence Of Comprehensive Health Services 30 MIN
Epidemiology - What's That 30 MIN
Estimation 30 MIN
Framework For Viewing Contemporary Health 30 MIN
Future Health Happenings 30 MIN
Glimpse Of Reality, A 30 MIN
Health Information Systems 30 MIN
High-Level Wellness In The World Today 30 MIN
Man And His Environment 30 MIN
Migrant Health 30 MIN
Model For Community Health Problem Analysis 30 MIN
More Basic Tools 30 MIN
Occupational Health 30 MIN
People And Statistics 30 MIN
Probability 30 MIN
Psychological Factors Applied To Public 30 MIN
Public Health Aspects Of The Residential 30 MIN
Scope And Goals Of The Health Enterprise 30 MIN
Social Forces And Their Implications To 30 MIN
Survival 30 MIN
Tests Of Hypotheses 30 MIN
Way It Is, The 30 MIN
We Need From Time To Time 30 MIN
When Is A Case A Case 30 MIN

Public Language B 15 MIN
2 INCH VIDEOTAPE I
Explains the nature of public language and the importance of having minimum skills in using public language. (Broadcast quality)
From The Bill Martin Series. No. 12
Prod-BRITED Dist-GPITVL Prodn-KQEDTV

Public Man And Private Man C 29 MIN
3/4 INCH VIDEO CASSETTE
Examines public roles and private roles that each person has.
From The Social Animal Series.
Prod-UMITV Dist-UMITV 1974

Public Opinion C 30 MIN
3/4 OR 1/2 INCH VIDEO CASSETTE C
Reviews the origin, nature and impact of public opinion on political matters.
From The American Government 1 Series.
Prod-DALCCD Dist-DALCCD

Public President, The - Wit And Warmth In The White House C 52 MIN
16MM FILM, 3/4 OR 1/2 IN VIDEO J-C A
Focuses on the wit and charm of Presidents Roosevelt, Truman, Eisenhower and Kennedy.
From The Presidency Series.
Prod-CORPEL Dist-LUF 1976

Public Relations C 20 MIN
3/4 INCH VIDEO CASSETTE T
Stresses that good public relations are a matter of filling unmet needs of the community. Shows how, in different ways, four libraries have done this and as a consequence have earned strong community support.
From The Access Series.
LC NO. 76-706251
Prod-UDEN Dist-USNAC 1976

Public Relations In Security C 12 MIN
3/4 OR 1/2 INCH VIDEO CASSETTE
Shows the importance of courtesy, good manners, tact and personal deportment in dealing with the public as a security officer.
From The Professional Security Training Series. Module 1C
Prod-MTI Dist-MTI

Public Relations With Kalman B Druck C 32 MIN
3/4 OR 1/2 INCH VIDEO CASSETTE
Presents the history and future of public relations in marketing and its meaning for all executives.
From The Contemporary Issues In Marketing Series.
Prod-CANTOR Dist-IVCH

Public Schools - How Are They Doing? C 29 MIN
3/4 INCH VIDEO CASSETTE
Discusses racism in the schools, sexism, teacher accountability, and the causes of vandalism and violence.
From The Issue At Hand Series.
Prod-UMITV Dist-UMITV 1976

Public Sculpture - The Piazza Della Signoria C 24 MIN
16MM FILM OPTICAL SOUND
Uses extensive color film of the statues commissioned for Florence's Piazza della Signoria to demonstrate sculpture's public symbolic significance. Explains how political change and patronage influenced individual sculptors through new commissions, the movements of statues and the reversal of symbolism in these works to suit those in power.
Prod-BBCTV Dist-OPENU 1981

Public Sculpture - The Piazza Della Signoria C 24 MIN
16MM FILM, 3/4 OR 1/2 IN VIDEO
Uses extensive color film of the statues commissioned for Florence's Piazza della Signoria to demonstrate sculpture's public symbolic significance. Explains how political change and patronage influenced individual sculptors through new commissions, the movements of statues and the reversal of symbolism in these works to suit those in power.
Prod-OPENU Dist-MEDIAG Prodn-BBCTV 1981

Public Sector I, The C 45 MIN
3/4 OR 1/2 INCH VIDEO CASSETTE
Discusses the effect of the public sector on the economy.
From The Economic Perspectives Series.
Prod-MDCPB Dist-MDCPB

Public Sector II, The C 45 MIN
3/4 OR 1/2 INCH VIDEO CASSETTE
Discusses the effect of the public sector on the economy.
From The Economic Perspectives Series.
Prod-MDCPB Dist-MDCPB

Public Sector Integrity Program, The C 50 MIN
3/4 OR 1/2 INCH VIDEO CASSETTE
Trains federal employees to be more aware of waste, fraud and abuse in their jobs and identifies their responsibilities as public servants working under standards of conduct.
Prod-USDJ Dist-USNAC

Public Service C 6 MIN
16MM FILM, 3/4 OR 1/2 IN VIDEO K-I
See series title for descriptive statement.
From The Kingdom Of Could Be You Series.
Prod-EBEC Dist-EBEC 1974

Public Service C 10 MIN
3/4 INCH VIDEO CASSETTE P
Presents a National Weather Service forecaster explaining the detailed work behind local and national weather reports.
Prod-MINIP Dist-GA

Public Service - Federal C 15 MIN
2 INCH VIDEOTAPE J-H
Explains that becoming an employee of the Federal government is dependent upon one's initiative and ability to meet the qualifications necessary for a particular job.
From The Work Is For Real Series.
Prod-STETVC Dist-GPITVL

Public Service - State And Local C 15 MIN
2 INCH VIDEOTAPE J-H
Points out that state and local governments have openings in the field of public service for persons with almost any kind of talent and training.
From The Work Is For Real Series.
Prod-STETVC Dist-GPITVL

Public Service Announcement C 2 MIN
16MM FILM OPTICAL SOUND
Presents am experimental film which shows an expert negro soccer player, representing all men, kicking a ball, symbolizing the world. Uses titles to convey the uniqueness of each moment and the world itself. Includes a musical background consisting of a plaintive Zulu chant.
LC NO. FIA67-572
Prod-GROENG Dist-GROENG 1966

Public Spaces C 30 MIN
3/4 OR 1/2 INCH VIDEO CASSETTE C
See series title for descriptive statement.
From The In Our Own Image Series.
Prod-DALCCD Dist-DALCCD

Public Speaking C 16 MIN
3/4 OR 1/2 INCH VIDEO CASSETTE H-C A
Teaches the characteristics of a purpose sentence as a preliminary step in the creation of a public speech. Provides students practice in critiquing sample purpose sentences.
From The Communication Series.
Prod-MSU Dist-MSU

Public-School Library Cooperation C 40 MIN
3/4 INCH VIDEO CASSETTE T
Presents experiences and ideas on cooperative library programs. Discusses issues, trends and possible programs involved with public-school library cooperation.
From The Access Series.
LC NO. 76-706253
Prod-UDEN Dist-USNAC 1976

Public's View, The C 60 MIN
3/4 OR 1/2 INCH VIDEO CASSETTE H-C A
Examines public perceptions of the presidency and the kind of person people say they want in that office. Focuses on the 1980 political campaign.
From The Every Four Years Series.
LC NO. 81-706050
Prod-WHYY Dist-AITECH 1980

Publicity C 20 MIN
3/4 INCH VIDEO CASSETTE T
Discusses the different ways local radio and newspapers can be used to publicize the library.
From The Access Series.
LC NO. 76-706256
Prod-UDEN Dist-USNAC 1976

Publish And Print C 15 MIN
3/4 OR 1/2 INCH VIDEO CASSETTE P-I
Shows the complex process of preparing and printing a magazine.
From The Explorers Unlimited Series.
Prod-WVIZTV Dist-AITECH 1971

Publisher Is Known By The Company He Keeps, A (2nd Ed) B 25 MIN
16MM FILM, 3/4 OR 1/2 IN VIDEO
Presents a series of sequences about famous writers using footage from the personal film library of Alfred A Knopf.
Prod-DEROCH Dist-PHENIX 1974

Puddling And Running Beads With Oxy-Acetylene C 15 MIN
3/4 OR 1/2 INCH VIDEO CASSETTE
See series title for descriptive statement.
From The Welding I - Basic Oxy-Acetylene Welding Series.
Prod-CAMB Dist-CAMB

Puddling And Running Beads With Oxy-Acetylene C 15 MIN
3/4 OR 1/2 INCH VIDEO CASSETTE IND
See series title for descriptive statement.
From The - Oxy-Acetylene Welding Series.
Prod-ICSINT Dist-ICSINT

Puddling And Running Beads With Oxy-Acetylene (Spanish) C
3/4 OR 1/2 INCH VIDEO CASSETTE
See series title for descriptive statement.
From The Oxy-Acetylene Welding (Spanish) Series.
Prod-VTRI Dist-VTRI

Pueblo Affair, The C 106 MIN
16MM FILM, 3/4 OR 1/2 IN VIDEO J-C A
Looks at the seizure of the American intelligence ship Pueblo by North Korean gunboats. Examines the treatment of the captain and crew as well as the tangled bureaucracy that precipitated the affair. Stars Hal Holbrook.
Prod-LUF Dist-LUF 1976

Pueblo Andaluz X 14 MIN
16MM FILM, 3/4 OR 1/2 IN VIDEO J-H A
A Spanish language film. Depicts life in a southern village through the eyes of a young boy. To be used after lesson 10 of level II, 'EMILIO EN ESPANA.'
From The Viajando Por Mexico Y Espana Series.
Prod-EBF Dist-EBEC 1966

Pueblo Arts C 11 MIN
16MM FILM, 3/4 OR 1/2 IN VIDEO I-H
Shows that the soil used by the Pueblos to build homes is also used to create objects of art. Reveals that by using the coil technique, a pot is built up, shaped, smoothed and polished and subsequently painted using an artist's brush made from the Yucca tree using minerals ground into powder and mixed with water.
Prod-WEBALB Dist-IFB Prodn-UMINN

Pueblo Of Laguna - Elders Of The Tribe C 14 MIN
16MM FILM OPTICAL SOUND
Documents the development and delivery of the Laguna tribe's comprehensive program of services to the elderly, including transportation, housing, nutrition, health, recreation, social services and community involvement.
LC NO. 81-700733
Prod-USDHEW Dist-USNAC 1981

Pueblo Renaissance C 26 MIN
16MM FILM, 3/4 OR 1/2 IN VIDEO
Discusses social and religious practices among the Indians of the Southwest. Explains that unlike other American Indians, these tribes were never removed from their homeland and therefore retain many ancient traditions.
From The Native Americans Series.
Prod-BBCTV Dist-CNEMAG

Pueden Ser Protegidos C 16 MIN
16MM FILM, 3/4 OR 1/2 IN VIDEO IND
A Spanish language film. Trains workers to use press brakes safely. Introduces safety equipment used on press brakes. Examines fixed barrier guards, hold-back cables, two-handed control panels and electronic sensing devices.
Prod-BLLHOW Dist-IFB

Puerto Rican Folkart Expression - Las Artesanias De Puerto Rico—A Series

Prod-CASPRC Dist-CASPRC 1979

Life Of Christ As Seen By A Puerto Rican 047 MIN

Puerto Rican Folkart Expression - Las Artesanias De Puerto Rico (Spanish)—A Series

Prod-CASPRC Dist-CASPRC 1979

Life Of Christ As Seen By A Puerto Rican 047 MIN

Puerto Rican Women's Federation C 29 MIN
3/4 INCH VIDEO CASSETTE
Examines the goals of the Puerto Rican Women's Foundation, which is intended to change discriminatory laws and eradicate social inequities in Puerto Rico.
From The Woman Series.
Prod-WNEDTV Dist-PUBTEL

Puerto Rico (Captioned) C 28 MIN
16MM FILM, 3/4 OR 1/2 IN VIDEO A
Presents a socio-economic analysis of Puerto Rico, and discusses the history of U S involvement in Puerto Rico and the anti-colonialist struggle. Spanish dialog with English subtitles. In two parts.
Prod-CUBAFI Dist-CNEMAG 1975

Puerto Rico - A Colony The American Way C 27 MIN
16MM FILM, 3/4 OR 1/2 IN VIDEO
Portrays Puerto Rico and its long relationship with the U S. Examines Puerto Rico's emerging economic crisis, reviews the transformation of the island in the 50's under Operation Bootstrap and shows demonstrators protesting U S naval bombardment and artillery practice on the off-shore islands.
Prod-TERRP Dist-CNEMAG

Puerto Rico - Migration C 9 MIN
16MM FILM OPTICAL SOUND I-H
Explains that large numbers of Puerto Ricans left their homeland to settle in some of the larger cities in the United States. Depicts the problems these people faced in the course of their migration. Parallels the Puerto Ricans with the Europeans who came to the United States during the late 19th and early 20th century.
Prod-SF Dist-SF 1972

Puerto Rico - More Or Less C 22 MIN
16MM FILM, 3/4 OR 1/2 IN VIDEO
Shows the many beauties of Puerto Rico and the work of the Institute of Tropical Forestry and the research that is being carried on to improve the forests of Puerto Rico.
LC NO. 82-707220
Prod-USDA Dist-USNAC 1972

Puerto Rico - More Or Less (Spanish) C 22 MIN
16MM FILM OPTICAL SOUND
Shows many natural features of Puerto Rico. Describes the work of the Institute of Tropical Forestry and the research that is being conducted to improve the forests of Puerto Rico.
LC NO. 76-703678
Prod-USDA Dist-USNAC 1972

Puerto Rico - Our Right To Decide C 28 MIN
16MM FILM, 3/4 OR 1/2 IN VIDEO
Examines the social reality behind most Americans' image of Puerto Rico, primarily as a pleasant vacation spot. Describes Puerto Ricans as disenfranchised US Citizens who cannot vote in national elections and have no representation in the Congress. Traces the island's history from Spanish colonials' destruction of Indian natives to revolts quelled by US troops to the unsolved questions of today - Puerto Rican destiny and right to determine their own future.
Prod-UMCBGM Dist-CNEMAG 1981

Puerto Rico - Paradise Invaded (Captioned) C 30 MIN
16MM FILM, 3/4 OR 1/2 IN VIDEO A
Portrays the history and present-day reality of Puerto Rico. Discusses the relationship with the United States, the impact of industrialization, the economic exile and life in New York City, and the Puerto Rican independence movement. Includes interviews with Puerto Ricans and rare documentary and news reel footage of the 1898 invasion by the Marines. Spanish dialog with English subtitles.
Prod-BEATOA Dist-CNEMAG 1977

Puerto Rico - The Caribbean Americans C 22 MIN
16MM FILM, 3/4 OR 1/2 IN VIDEO I-H
Describes the land and people of Puerto Rico. Introduces Rafael Gonzalez, one of many Puerto Ricans who came to the United States to make a better life, then returned to the island of his birth.
Prod-ABCNEW Dist-IFB Prodn-WILSND 1970

Puerto Rico Es Asi C 22 MIN
16MM FILM, 3/4 OR 1/2 IN VIDEO I-H
A Spanish language version of Puerto Rico - The Caribbean Americans. Describes the land and people of Puerto Rico. Introduces Rafael Gonzalez, one of many Puerto Ricans who came to the United States to make a better life, then returned to the island of his birth.
Prod-ABCNEW Dist-IFB Prodn-WILSND 1970

Puerto Rico Libre C 26 MIN
3/4 INCH VIDEO CASSETTE
Asks whether Puerto Rico should remain a Commonwealth of the United States or become independent.
From The Interface Series.
Prod-WETATV Dist-PUBTEL

Puerto Rico USA C 24 MIN
16MM FILM OPTICAL SOUND
Looks at the Puerto Rican people, discussing culture, lifestyles, spirit, and commitment. Emphasizes the benefits of investing in Puerto Rico.
LC NO. 80-701557
Prod-EDAPR Dist-EDAPR Prodn-GUG 1980

Puerto Rico, Isle Of Guernsey, United States C 27 MIN
16MM FILM OPTICAL SOUND P-I
Describes sports activities of children in Puerto Rico, the Isle of Guernsey and New Jersey. Presents a Puerto Rican folk tale about a red hat.
From The Big Blue Marble - Children Around The World Series. Program M
LC NO. 76-700624
Prod-ALVEN Dist-VITT 1975

Puerto Rico, USA - Profile Of A People C 23 MIN
16MM FILM OPTICAL SOUND
Pictures Puerto Rico as a land where economic growth has created a unique partnership between government and industry. Shows that the family remains the centerpiece of life in Puerto Rico.
Prod-PROT Dist-MTP

Pues, Alfredo B 28 MIN
16MM FILM, 3/4 OR 1/2 IN VIDEO
Describes basic requirements and opportunities available in apprenticeship. Issued in 1969 as a motion picture.
From The Career Job Opportunity Film Series.
LC NO. 79-707887
Prod-USDLMA Dist-USNAC 1979

Puff And The Incredible Mr Nobody C 24 MIN
16MM FILM, 3/4 OR 1/2 IN VIDEO K-I
When Terry needed a friend who thought in the same intellectual way he did, he invented Nobody - a duck with a sauce-pan hat and a wild imagination. When Terry's parents urged him to let Nobody go, he felt lost without his friend. Puff, the Magic Dragon took Terry on a fantastic odyssey through the Fantaverse, and he realized that the children at school didn't understand how special he was. He found Nobody and learned something about Somebody.
From The Puff Series.
Prod-PERSPF Dist-CORF 1984

Puff Pastry Dough C 9 MIN
3/4 OR 1/2 INCH VIDEO CASSETTE PRO
Demonstrates the long method and the Blitz or Scottish Method of making puff pastry.
Prod-CULINA Dist-CULINA

Puff Pastry—A Series

Prod-CULINA Dist-CULINA

Puff Pastry, Pt 1
Puff Pastry, Pt 2

Puff Pastry, Pt 1 C
3/4 OR 1/2 INCH VIDEO CASSETTE
See series title for descriptive statement.
From The Puff Pastry Series.
Prod-CULINA Dist-CULINA

Puff Pastry, Pt 2 C
3/4 OR 1/2 INCH VIDEO CASSETTE
See series title for descriptive statement.
From The Puff Pastry Series.
Prod-CULINA Dist-CULINA

Puff The Magic Dragon C 24 MIN
16MM FILM, 3/4 OR 1/2 IN VIDEO K-I
Presents an animated story with the voice of Burgess Meredith as Puff. Tells how doctors despair of ever curing Jackie of his shyness until Puff takes him on an incredible journey to the land of Hona Lee. Eventually Jackie makes contact with the real world again so he no longer needs to retreat into the world of his imagination to cover his shyness.
From The Puff Series.
Prod-PERSPF Dist-CORF 1984

Puff The Magic Dragon In The Land Of Living Lies C 24 MIN
16MM FILM, 3/4 OR 1/2 IN VIDEO K-I
Tells how when Sandy's parents were divorced, she assumed guilt and responsibility and resolved these feelings by telling fictitious tales which appeared to be lies. When Puff, a genuine imaginary dragon, took her on a magical journey to the Land of Living Lies, Sandy realized that the divorce wasn't her fault and learned the difference between harmless fantasy and falsehood.
From The Puff Series.
Prod-PERSPF Dist-CORF 1984

Puff—A Series
16MM FILM, 3/4 OR 1/2 IN VIDEO K-I
Presents colorful adventures woven around the classic children's song about Puff. Because children deal with different issues through fantasy, these stories of positive child development use the imagination of the children involved.
Prod-PERSPF Dist-CORF 1984

Puff And The Incredible Mr Nobody 024 MIN
Puff The Magic Dragon 024 MIN
Puff The Magic Dragon In The Land Of 024 MIN

Puffed Out C 7 MIN
16MM FILM - 3/4 IN VIDEO P-J
Uses animation to show how everything is harder for a smoker who is exercising.
LC NO. 81-706511
Prod-VICCOR Dist-TASCOR 1981

Puffed-Up Dragon, The C 10 MIN
16MM FILM, 3/4 OR 1/2 IN VIDEO K-I
The story of a friendly, vegetarian dragon, who visits a medieval kingdom and eats wagon-loads of food each day while the townspeople try to get rid of him. The story is told with animated paper cut-outs and music.
Prod-VIKING Dist-SF 1966

Puffins, Predators And Pirates C 28 MIN
16MM FILM OPTICAL SOUND I-H
Views the struggle between two species, the North American Puffin and the Herring Gull. Describes their life on the Great Island near Newfoundland and explains that their delicate population balance has been upset by man's pollution of the coastal waters.
From The Nature Of Things Series.
LC NO. 79-700961
Prod-CANBC Dist-FLMLIB 1979

Pugnacious Sailing Master, The B 30 MIN
16MM FILM OPTICAL SOUND
Presents the story of Uriah P Levy, who was responsible for the elimination of corporal punishment in the U S Navy, and who refused to conceal his Jewish origin in the face of anti-semitic taunting from members of the crew. Tells how Levy later become a commodore. (Kinescope)
Prod-JTS Dist-NAAJS Prodn-NBCTV 1954

Puhipau - Blown Away C 29 MIN
3/4 OR 1/2 INCH VIDEO CASSETTE
Juxtaposes physicians' explanations of the medical effects of nuclear weapons with the natural beauty of Hawaii.
Prod-PSR Dist-PSR 1982

Pulaskis, Shovels And Men C 25 MIN
16MM FILM OPTICAL SOUND PRO
Tells the story of the organization of a crew for the suppression of a watershed fire.
Prod-LAFIRE Dist-LAFIRE

Pulcinella C 11 MIN
16MM FILM OPTICAL SOUND
Presents an animated cartoon about the uproarious adventures of Pulcinella, the Tuscan version of the puppet Punch.
LC NO. 74-701037
Prod-CONNF Dist-CONNF 1973

Pulitzer Prize Poets, Pt 1 C 30 MIN
3/4 INCH VIDEO CASSETTE H-C A
Features selections of the works of poets who won the Pulitzer Prize between 1922 and 1950. Includes poems by Robinson, Frost, Brooks, Shapiro and Benet.
From The Anyone For Tennyson Series.
Prod-NETCHE Dist-GPITVL

Pulitzer Prize Poets, Pt 2 C 30 MIN
3/4 INCH VIDEO CASSETTE H-C A
Offers selections of the works of poets who won the Pulitzer Prize between 1950 and 1975. Includes poems by Mc Ginley, Snyder, Sandurg, Moore and Mac Leish.
From The Anyone For Tennyson Series.
Prod-NETCHE Dist-GPITVL

Pull My Daisy B 29 MIN
16MM FILM OPTICAL SOUND A
Presents a slice of beatnik life in a New York Bowery loft with Allan Ginsberg, Gregory Corso, Peter Orlovsky and Larry Rivers. Documents the subculture of the 1950's and features narration by author Jack Kerouac.
Prod-NYFLMS Dist-NYFLMS 1959

Pull Ourselves Up Or Die Out C 26 MIN
3/4 OR 1/2 INCH VIDEO CASSETTE
Documents the situation of the Kung San people at Tshum Kwi. Includes issues affecting the economy of the Kung and confrontations with South African administration officials.
Prod-DOCEDR Dist-DOCEDR

Pull Through Intra-Urethral Bladder Flap - A New Surgical Treatment Of Post... C 25 MIN
3/4 INCH VIDEO CASSETTE PRO
Shows an intra-urethral bladder flap operation on a patient who is incontinent after a suprapubic prostatectomy and who has perineal urethral fistula due to erosion of a bulbous urethra after using a Kaufman III prothesis.
Prod-VAHSL Dist-USNAC 1976

Pulley - A Simple Machine C 15 MIN
3/4 OR 1/2 INCH VIDEO CASSETTE P-I
Discusses the characteristics of a pulley.
From The Why Series.
Prod-WDCNTV Dist-AITECH 1976

Pulley Bar C 15 MIN
3/4 OR 1/2 INCH VIDEO CASSETTE IND
Shows basics of reading blueprints. Demonstrates how to identify dimensions and other vital characteristics of the part to be produced.
From The Blueprint Reading For Machinists Series.
Prod-LEIKID Dist-LEIKID

Pulley Bar (Basic) C
3/4 OR 1/2 INCH VIDEO CASSETTE
See series title for descriptive statement.
From The Blueprint Reading Series.
Prod-VTRI Dist-VTRI

Pulley Bar (Basic) (Spanish) C
3/4 OR 1/2 INCH VIDEO CASSETTE
See series title for descriptive statement.
From The Blueprint Reading (Spanish) Series.
Prod-VTRI Dist-VTRI

Pulley System, A - Focusing On Discovery C 20 MIN
3/4 INCH VIDEO CASSETTE T
Demonstrates the five levels of discovery through the use of a pulley system. Presents classroom scenes providing examples of each level as one teacher might implement it.
From The Science In The Elementary School - Physical Science Series.
Prod-UWKY Dist-GPITVL 1979

Pulleys And Work Load C 14 MIN
16MM FILM, 3/4 OR 1/2 IN VIDEO I-C A
Explores what the pulley, a typical, simple machine, can and cannot do. Shows that pulleys do not create energy, but can be used to make a small force exert a large force.
Prod-IWANMI Dist-PHENIX 1968

Pulling And Installing Cable And Packing Terminal Tubes B 16 MIN
16MM FILM OPTICAL SOUND
Demonstrates how to pull, strap and straighten cable, prepare cable for pushing and for pulling with a rope and how to pack terminal tubes.
LC NO. FIE52-210
Prod-USOE Dist-USNAC 1945

Pulling It All Together C 30 MIN
2 INCH VIDEOTAPE C A
Discusses when architectural changes are appropriate in the sequence of an interior design plan.
From The Designing Home Interiors Series. Unit 28
Prod-COAST Dist-CDTEL Prodn-RSCCD

Pulling Together C 9 MIN
16MM FILM, 3/4 OR 1/2 IN VIDEO P-I
Tells the story of a little boy and his friend, the Squiggle, and how they rescue their friend, the Puffy, from a bubble gum pond. Focuses on individual strengths and working together.
Prod-BARR Dist-BARR 1978

Pullorum Disease Control C 10 MIN
16MM FILM OPTICAL SOUND C A
Portrays the proper sanitary measures necessary to control pullorum disease in turkeys. Documents the story from farm to hatchery and shows the technique for drawing blood samples and the tube-agglutination test for pullorum disease.
Prod-CDADAB Dist-AMVMA

Pulmonary Anastomosis C 33 MIN
16MM FILM OPTICAL SOUND PRO
Illustrates the operative technique of aortic-pulmonary anastomosis for tetralogy of fallot. Summarizes follow-up results in the first 100 patients operated upon six to eight years ago.
Prod-ACYDGD Dist-ACY 1955

Pulmonary And Cardiovascular Systems C 31 MIN
3/4 OR 1/2 INCH VIDEO CASSETTE
Shows a patient deviating from his diet and experiencing pulmonary edema. Assesses and explains his signs and symptoms.
From The Individuals With Renal Dysfunction Series.
Prod-AJN Dist-AJN

Pulmonary Arterial Catheterization C 9 MIN
3/4 OR 1/2 INCH VIDEO CASSETTE PRO
Demonstrates pulmonary catheterization in the intraoperative and postoperative monitoring of a critically ill patient using the Swan-Ganz, flow directed catheter. Utilizes an oscilloscope to determine its location.
Prod-UARIZ Dist-UARIZ

Pulmonary Artery Banding C 24 MIN
3/4 OR 1/2 INCH VIDEO CASSETTE
See series title for descriptive statement.
From The Cardiovascular Series.
Prod-SVL Dist-SVL

Pulmonary Complications In Shock C 17 MIN
16MM FILM OPTICAL SOUND PRO
Demonstrates the shock lung phenomenon, using in vivo cinematography of a dog's lung. Explains the correct step-by-step program required to prevent this pulmonary edema in a human patient in severe shock.
From The Upjohn Vanguard Of Medicine Series.
LC NO. 75-700366
Prod-UPJOHN Dist-UPJOHN 1974

Pulmonary Complications Of Fire And Smoke C 22 MIN
3/4 OR 1/2 INCH VIDEO CASSETTE PRO
Provides information which aids physicians in diagnosing smoke inhalation from the minute signs and symptoms, determining the severity of pulmonary damage from the physical exam, determining the existence of carbon monoxide intoxication, managing the airway, treating progressive bronchiolitis and infections if pulmonary infiltrates appear on chest x-rays and performing pulmonary hygiene to treat accompanying bronchospasm.
Prod-UMICHM Dist-UMICHM 1976

Pulmonary Cryptococcosis B 16 MIN
16MM FILM - 3/4 IN VIDEO PRO
Presents a brief review of the epidemiology of pulmonary cryptococcosis as well as the clinical and radiologic findings. Discusses techniques for the isolation and identification of the etiologic agent, crytpococcus neoformans and the significance of the serologic studies in the diagnosis and treatment of the disease.
From The Clinical Pathology Series.
LC NO. 76-706080
Prod-NMAC Dist-USNAC 1969

Pulmonary Disease - The Hidden Enemy C 25 MIN
3/4 OR 1/2 INCH VIDEO CASSETTE
Looks at America's most deadly, yet most preventable illness, pulmonary disease. Explains what causes respiratory disease, who's likely to be afflicted and what can be done to prevent it. Fosters new understanding, through on-the-scene reports from clinics and hospitals and respect for the efforts and achievements of science in combating pulmonary ailments.
From The Killers Series.
Prod-TRAINX Dist-TRAINX

Pulmonary Embolism C 18 MIN
3/4 OR 1/2 INCH VIDEO CASSETTE
Discusses pulmonary embolism, including pre-disposing factors, signs of thrombophlebitis, ventilation perfusion lung scan, pulmonary angiography, arterial blood gas analysis and treatment with heparin therapy.
From The Emergency Management - The First 30 Minutes, Vol II Series.
Prod-VTRI Dist-VTRI

Pulmonary Function Testing 1 - Lung Volumes And Capacities Using 'Collins' Spirometer C 14 MIN
1/2 IN VIDEO CASSETTE BETA/VHS PRO
Prod-RMI Dist-RMI

Pulmonary Histoplasmosis B 30 MIN
16MM FILM OPTICAL SOUND
Discusses pulmonary histoplasmosis, its spectrum etiology, epidemiology, distribution, clinical forms and radiologic findings. Shows techniques for the isolation and identification of H capsulatum and treatment. (Kinescope)
From The Clinical Pathology Series.
LC NO. 74-705453
Prod-NMAC Dist-USNAC 1969

Pulmonary Mycoisis, Pt 1 - Blastomycosis B 12 MIN
16MM FILM OPTICAL SOUND
Defines blastomycosis as a chronic granulomatous mycosis primarily in the lungs. Presents early symptomatology. Discusses epidemiology and concurrent factors, such as race, sex and age. (Kinescope)
From The Clinical Pathology Series.
LC NO. 74-705454
Prod-NMAC Dist-USNAC 1969

Pulmonary Mycosis B 12 MIN
3/4 INCH VIDEO CASSETTE PRO
Discusses epidemiology, symptomatology, differential diagnosis and therapy.
From The Clinical Pathology Series.
LC NO. 76-706082
Prod-NMAC Dist-USNAC 1969

Pulmonary Resection C 29 MIN
16MM FILM OPTICAL SOUND PRO
Explains that meticulous dissection of the vascular and bronchial anatomy at the pulmonary hilum greatly increases the safety of pulmonary resectional procedures. Shows a number of techniques, including a rapid pneumonectomy utilizing vascular clamps.
Prod-ACYDGD Dist-ACY 1967

Pulp B 7 MIN
16MM FILM OPTICAL SOUND
Satirizes the content of modern 'PULP' magazines. Shows the effect of these magazines' exaggerated style of writing on a leather jacketed youth who is viewing the world as the magazine writers do.
LC NO. 75-703222
Prod-USC Dist-USC

Pulp And Paper Training - Thermo-Mechanical Pulping—A Series
IND
Designed to teach the thermo mechanical pulping process to operating personnel who already have a basic familiarity with the pulp and paper industry.
Prod-LEIKID Dist-LEIKID

Introduction To TMP
Materials Handling
Operation And Process Control
Pulp Treatment
Refining Principles
Steam And Water Recovery And Effluent Treatment
TMP Equipment

Pulp And Paper Training, Module - Kraft Pulping—A Series
IND
Traces the Kraft pulping process from the wood stage through preparation, digesting and pulp treatment. Covers terminology, basic chemistry, variable factors in controlling the kraft process, the batch digester and pulp treatment such as screening and refining.
Prod-LEIKID Dist-LEIKID

Kraft Pulping, Pt 1
Kraft Pulping, Pt 2
Kraft Pulping, Pt 3
Kraft Pulping, Pt 4
Kraft Treatment, Pt 1
Kraft Treatment, Pt 2
Kraft Treatment, Pt 3
Wood, Pt 1
Wood, Woodyard And Pulping

Pulp And Paper Training, Module 2 - Chemical Recovery—A Series
IND
Discusses the complete chemical recovery process used in making paper. Gives an overview and details the black liquor system, evaporators, recovery boiler operation, boiler safety of white liquor. Provides an introduction to the subject of chemical recovery as well as information for operators and maintenance personnel.
Prod-LEIKID Dist-LEIKID

Black Liquor Systems Operation
Black Liquor Systems, Pt 1
Black Liquor Systems, Pt 2
Recovery Boiler Operation
Recovery Boiler, Pt 1
Recovery Boiler, Pt 2
Recovery Process, The
Smelt Recovery Operation
Smelt Recovery, Pt 1
Smelt Recovery, Pt 2

Pulp And Paper Training, Module 3 - Papermaking—A Series
PRO
Discusses and demonstrates the basic paper making process from stock preparation through to shipping the final product. Includes chemical additives, color, deposits, cleaners and screens, the Fourdrinier machine, head boxes, suction boxes, and the cylinder machine.
Prod-LEIKID Dist-LEIKID

Cylinder Machine
Dryers
Finishing And Shipping
Fourdrinier Machine, Pt 1
Fourdrinier Machine, Pt 2
Papermaking, Pt 1
Papermaking, Pt 2
Papermaking, Pt 3
Presses
Stock Preparation Equipment
White Water And Broke

Pulp Treament, Pt 2 C
3/4 OR 1/2 INCH VIDEO CASSETTE IND
Covers refiners, handling rejects and pulp washers.
From The Pulp And Paper Training, Moduel 1 - Kraft Pulping Series.
Prod-LEIKID Dist-LEIKID

Pulp Treatment C
3/4 OR 1/2 INCH VIDEO CASSETTE IND
Shows treatment of pulp after refining. Includes screening and cleaning, objectives, latency treatment, handling and refining of rejects, and thickening of the pulp for storage.
From The Pulp And Paper Training - Thermo-Mechanical Pulping Series.
Prod-LEIKID Dist-LEIKID

Pulp Treatment, Pt 1 C
3/4 OR 1/2 INCH VIDEO CASSETTE IND
Covers several aspects of the pulp treatment process such as the purpose, coarse and fine screens and knot breakers.
From The Pulp And Paper Training, Module 1 - Kraft Pulping Series.
Prod-LEIKID Dist-LEIKID

Pulp Treatment, Pt 3 C
3/4 OR 1/2 INCH VIDEO CASSETTE IND
Includes several aspects of pulp treatment such as wash water, thickeners, pulp storage and treatment systems.
From The Pulp And Paper Training, Module 1 - Kraft Pulping Series.
Prod-LEIKID Dist-LEIKID

Pulse C
16MM FILM OPTICAL SOUND
Presents an experimental film done entirely in animation.
Prod-CANCIN Dist-CANCIN

Pulse B 11 MIN
16MM FILM OPTICAL SOUND P-C
An experimental film which combines a succession of still drawings of abstract shapes with a sound track of electronic synthesized sounds.
LC NO. 72-702045
Prod-BYMPRO Dist-CFS 1972

Pulse And Digital Circuits—A Series
C A
Covers electronic switching, timing and pulse-shaping techniques, logic functions, and realization with diodes, transistors and FETs. Focuses on modeling of devices in the switching mode. Contains 44 videotape lectures.
Prod-UIDEEO Dist-UIDEEO

Pulse Modulation B 26 MIN
16MM FILM OPTICAL SOUND
Discusses the basic principles of pulse modification with emphasis on these terms - pulse repetition frequency, pulse width, peak power, average power, duty cycle and pulse repetition time. Explains the block diagram of a pulse modulated transmitter showing the waveshapes out of each block. (Kinescope)
LC NO. 74-705455
Prod-USAF Dist-USNAC 1965

Pump And Valve Packing C 60 MIN
3/4 OR 1/2 INCH VIDEO CASSETTE IND
See series title for descriptive statement.
From The Mechanical Equipment Maintenance, Module 3 - Packing And Seals Series.
Prod-LEIKID Dist-LEIKID

Pump Assembly C 60 MIN
3/4 OR 1/2 INCH VIDEO CASSETTE IND
See series title for descriptive statement.
From The Mechanical Equipment Maintenance, Module 5 - Centrifugal Pumps Series.
Prod-LEIKID Dist-LEIKID

Pump Disassembly C 60 MIN
3/4 OR 1/2 INCH VIDEO CASSETTE IND
See series title for descriptive statement.
From The Mechanical Equipment Maintenance, Module 5 - Centrifugal Pumps Series.
Prod-LEIKID Dist-LEIKID

Pump Failure C 30 MIN
3/4 INCH VIDEO CASSETTE PRO
Describes normal and abnormal left ventricular function curves and explains the importance of measuring the pulmonary capillary wedge pressure, cardiac output and systemic resistance in patients with acute myocardial infarction complicated by pump failure.
From The Acute Myocardial Infarction Series. Unit 2
LC NO. 77-706060
Prod-NMAC Dist-USNAC 1977

Pump Operations, Centrifugal Pumps C 60 MIN
3/4 OR 1/2 INCH VIDEO CASSETTE IND

Identifies the major parts of a centrifugal pump and tells how it works. Defines Net Positive Suction, Head available and Suction Head required. Shows how to read and interpret a pump normal operating curve as well as a pump system characteristic curve.
From The Equipment Operation Training Program Series.
Prod-ITCORP Dist-ITCORP

Pump Operations, Positive Displacement Pumps C 60 MIN
3/4 OR 1/2 INCH VIDEO CASSETTE IND
Describes the operation of a rotary positive displacement pump. Highlights performing an emergency pump shutdown. Tells how a reciprocating positive displacement pump works.
From The Equipment Operation Training Program Series.
Prod-ITCORP Dist-ITCORP

Pump Operator C 26 MIN
16MM FILM, 3/4 OR 1/2 IN VIDEO PRO
Depicts the development of the pump apparatus, how it is placed in service, how men are trained to use it, spotting for hookups, routine, and fire maintenance, driving, and handling and tips on drafting and firefighting procedures.
Prod-LACFD Dist-FILCOM 1955

Pump Packing C 7 MIN
3/4 OR 1/2 INCH VIDEO CASSETTE IND
Demonstrates how to remove old ring packing, how to cut new packing rings and install them and how to tighten packing glands. Discusses what the function of the lantern ring is.
From The Marshall Maintenance Training Programs Series. Tape 3
Prod-LEIKID Dist-LEIKID

Pump Packing C 7 MIN
16MM FILM, 3/4 OR 1/2 IN VIDEO IND
Shows how to remove old ring packing, how to cut new packing rings, how to install new rings for long life, what the function of the lantern ring is and how to tighten packing glands.
Prod-MOKIN Dist-MOKIN

Pump, The C 13 MIN
16MM FILM, 3/4 OR 1/2 IN VIDEO
Tells a story about a caretaker and his ancient water pump.
Prod-PRELJ Dist-CAROUF

Pumpdown, Evacuation And Charging C 60 MIN
3/4 OR 1/2 INCH VIDEO CASSETTE IND
Teaches about systempump down, system evacuation and charging.
From The Air Conditioning And Refrigeration-- Training Series.
Prod-ITCORP Dist-ITCORP

Pumpkin Who Couldn't Smile, The C 23 MIN
16MM FILM, 3/4 OR 1/2 IN VIDEO K-I
Describes what happens when Raggedy Ann and Raggedy Andy bring together a glum pumpkin and a sad boy during the Halloween season.
Prod-CORF Dist-CORF 1981

Pumps And Compressors C
3/4 OR 1/2 INCH VIDEO CASSETTE IND
See series title for descriptive statement.
From The Drafting - Piping Familiarization Series.
Prod-GPCV Dist-GPCV

Pumps—A Series
J-C A
Deals with the design and operation of pumps.
Prod-TAT Dist-TAT 1979

Centrifugal Pumps, Pt 1 24 MIN
Centrifugal Pumps, Pt 2 23 MIN

Punch And Jonathan C 9 MIN
16MM FILM OPTICAL SOUND P-I
Describes how a young boy's desire to play with the puppet Punch which he sees in a show on an English beach leads him to an adventure.
LC NO. 72-702191
Prod-CONNF Dist-CONNF 1972

Punching And Editing C 15 MIN
3/4 OR 1/2 INCH VIDEO CASSETTE PRO
See series title for descriptive statement.
From The Numerical Control/Computer Numerical Control, Part I - Fundamentals Series.
Prod-ICSINT Dist-ICSINT

Punching And Editing C 16 MIN
3/4 OR 1/2 INCH VIDEO CASSETTE IND
Discusses operating the terminal in the local mode, loading a program through the terminal and editing a program.
From The Numerical Control/Computerized Numerical Control, Module 1 - Fundamentals series.
Prod-LEIKID Dist-LEIKID

Punctuation - Colon, Semicolon, And Quotation Marks C 14 MIN
16MM FILM, 3/4 OR 1/2 IN VIDEO I-J
Describes the uses of colons, semicolons and quotation marks.
Prod-CENTRO Dist-CORF

Punctuation - Mark Your Meaning (2nd Ed) C 14 MIN
16MM FILM, 3/4 OR 1/2 IN VIDEO I-J
Points out the importance of punctuation and why it is needed to reveal the meaning intended by the writer.
Prod-CORF Dist-CORF 1968

Punctuation - Mischievous Marks - ()'s C 15 MIN
16MM FILM, 3/4 OR 1/2 IN VIDEO I-J
Uses innovative visuals and effects to illustrate the uses of dashes and parentheses to interrupt a sentence and the use of the apostrophe in contractions and in forming possessives.
Prod-CENTRO Dist-CORF 1977

Punctuation - Putting Commas Between C 16 MIN
16MM FILM, 3/4 OR 1/2 IN VIDEO I-J
Introduces Dr O G Whiz, who describes the various uses of commas.
Prod-CENTRO Dist-CORF

Punctuation - Stop That Period, Period That Stop C 18 MIN
16MM FILM, 3/4 OR 1/2 IN VIDEO I-J
Focuses on the use of periods, exclamation points and question marks.
Prod-CENTRO Dist-CORF

Punctuation - Taking Commas Aside C 18 MIN
16MM FILM, 3/4 OR 1/2 IN VIDEO I-J
Explains how commas are used to set off parenthetical statements and non-restrictve subordinate clauses.
Prod-CENTRO Dist-CORF

Punctuation With Ralph And Stanley C 14 MIN
16MM FILM, 3/4 OR 1/2 IN VIDEO P-I
Tells a story about a boy who makes arrangements to take a UFO to Jupiter until he receives extraterrestrial messages that are missing punctuation marks. Teaches how various types of punctuation marks give meaning to the written word.
From The Writing Skills Series.
Prod-BEAN Dist-PHENIX 1978

Punctuation Wizard, The C 24 MIN
16MM FILM - VIDEO, ALL FORMATS P-I
Teaches the basics of punctuation in a story about a kingdom where punctuation is not allowed.
Prod-BARR Dist-BARR

Punishment C 44 MIN
3/4 OR 1/2 INCH VIDEO CASSETTE T
Covers the effects of punishment. Examines whether or not a teacher should use it.
From The Learning And Liking It Series.
Prod-MSU Dist-MSU

Punitive Damages C 120 MIN
3/4 OR 1/2 INCH VIDEO CASSETTE PRO
Discusses the kinds of cases in which punitive damages may be available, and focuses on the pleading and proof of punitive damages and the arguments for and against them.
Prod-CCEB Dist-ABACPE

Punk Rock And The Elvis Legend C 15 MIN
3/4 OR 1/2 INCH VIDEO CASSETTE
Focuses on the Elvis Presley legend, discusses the Elvis imitators and the mini-industry of Presley mementos, and looks at the devotees of punk rock.
Prod-UPI Dist-JOU

Punking Out B 25 MIN
16MM FILM OPTICAL SOUND
Documents the punk rock music scene at the CBGB club in New York City.
LC NO. 79-700263
Prod-CARMAG Dist-CARMAG 1978

Punktlichkeit Ist Alles C 15 MIN
16MM FILM, 3/4 OR 1/2 IN VIDEO
See series title for descriptive statement.
From The Guten Tag Wie Geht's Series. Part 8
Prod-BAYER Dist-IFB 1973

Punt Gunning For Ducks C 29 MIN
16MM FILM OPTICAL SOUND J-C A
Examines many aspects of punt-gunning for ducks, including the preparation and loading of shot, the mounting of the stanchion gun on the punt, the stalking of water fowl and the firing of the large gun at a flock of ducks.
LC NO. 74-703695
Prod-ASHLEY Dist-VEDO 1975

Punt, A Pass And A Prayer, A C 76 MIN
3/4 OR 1/2 INCH VIDEO CASSETTE
Offers a play written by David Mark about the aspirations, obsessions and ironic conflicts that delineate the life of a star quarterback seeking to make a comeback. Stars Hugh O'Brien and Betsy Palmer.
Prod-FOTH Dist-FOTH 1984

Punto De Encuentro C 15 MIN
16MM FILM OPTICAL SOUND
Surveys pre-Columbian culture in Costa Rica.
LC NO. 74-700625
Prod-OOAS Dist-PAN 1973

Punto De Ignicion C 21 MIN
16MM FILM, 3/4 OR 1/2 IN VIDEO IND
A Spanish-language version of the motion picture Flashpoint. Dramatizes the events leading to a chemical explosion and fire in a chemical laboratory. Shows the safety precautions which should have been taken.
Prod-MILLBK Dist-IFB 1980

Puny Petunia, A Canine Venus B 16 MIN
16MM FILM OPTICAL SOUND
Presents five visual 'STORIES' in a surrealistic manner--scenes about a young girl who finds and cherishes a clothing store dummy, a man who gets caught and strangles in the strings growing on an abacus, a nude girl who rides a unicycle, a photographer who tries to pose his model and a dancer who does a dance to a cook book recipe.
Prod-UPENN Dist-UPENN 1967

Pupil Interactions C 30 MIN
3/4 OR 1/2 INCH VIDEO CASSETTE T
Looks at pupil interactions in an educational setting.
From The Interaction - Human Concerns In The Schools Series.
Prod-MDDE Dist-MDCPB

Puppet Magic C 12 MIN
16MM FILM, 3/4 OR 1/2 IN VIDEO P-I
Offers a short history of puppets which ends with marionettes coming to life.
LC NO. 80-706701
Prod-INTNEW Dist-IFB 1977

Puppet On A String C 15 MIN
16MM FILM, 3/4 OR 1/2 IN VIDEO
Provides consumer information on batteries, telling how to buy them for each use, how to store them, and what to expect of them. Discusses their diversity and battery safety and convenience.
Prod-KLEINW Dist-KLEINW 1979

Puppet Preparation For Surgery C 10 MIN
16MM FILM OPTICAL SOUND
Demonstrates modes of operation as hospital employees, including doctors, nurses, recreation workers and others work with the hospitalized child. Shows the interaction between volunteer and patient, and explains the surgical procedure by using puppets and mock-ups of the equipment.
LC NO. 71-711407
Prod-CMHOSP Dist-AMEDA 1970

Puppet Proposition, The C 26 MIN
16MM FILM OPTICAL SOUND
Takes a look at several kinds of puppets used in marionette theater and how a puppet show is planned and performed.
LC NO. 76-700411
Prod-LMT Dist-LMT 1976

Puppet Show B 15 MIN
2 INCH VIDEOTAPE P
See series title for descriptive statement.
From The Language Corner Series.
Prod-CVETVC Dist-GPITVL Prodn-WCVETV

Puppet's Dream C 9 MIN
16MM FILM MAGNETIC SOUND K-C A
Presents motion, light and shadow effects with the linear shapes of puppet-like figures on evolving plane and surfaces.
LC NO. FIA68-636
Prod-SIGMA Dist-FILCOM 1967

Puppetry C 15 MIN
3/4 INCH VIDEO CASSETTE
Shows a portion of a puppet show and explains how the puppets were made. Presents a collection of puppets from around the world.
From The Look And A Closer Look Series.
Prod-WCVETV Dist-GPITVL

Puppets B 11 MIN
16MM FILM OPTICAL SOUND
Presents a puppet actor who steps out of his role in a marionette performance of 'JULIUS CAESAR' to provide a lesson on totalitariansm and conformity. Introduces infamous charlatans and despots and the victims who suffered through their treachery. Reveals how these villains used the scapegoat technique to gain adherence from their followers while duping them into relinquishing their freedom.
Prod-ADL Dist-ADL

Puppets C 15 MIN
16MM FILM, 3/4 OR 1/2 IN VIDEO K-C T
Presents various methods of making puppets ranging from simple stick puppets to more involved processes including the use of sawdust and glue, shaped cloth, and paper mache.
From The Rediscovery - Art Media Series.
Prod-ACI Dist-AIMS 1967

Puppets C 15 MIN
3/4 OR 1/2 INCH VIDEO CASSETTE P-I
Tells how to construct and animate puppets.
From The Art Cart Series.
Prod-WBRATV Dist-AITECH 1979

Puppets C 15 MIN
3/4 OR 1/2 INCH VIDEO CASSETTE P
Shows the use of puppets in performances at the Bunraku Theatre, Osaka, Japan, and at the Norwood Puppet Theatre, Denver, Colorado. Explains that throughout the ages people have made puppets and have used them to tell stories. Shows ways to make puppets.
From The Primary Art Series.
Prod-WETATV Dist-AITECH

Puppets (French) C 15 MIN
16MM FILM, 3/4 OR 1/2 IN VIDEO I-C A
Presents a number of puppet-making techniques varying in levels of difficulty and complexity. Describes simple stick puppets and more elaborate creations of paper mache.
From The Rediscovery - Art Media (French) Series.
Prod-ACI Dist-AIMS 1967

Puppets (Spanish) C 15 MIN
16MM FILM, 3/4 OR 1/2 IN VIDEO K-C
Presents various methods of making puppets ranging from simple stick puppets to more involved processes including the use of sawdust and glue, shaped cloth and paper mache.
From The Rediscovery - Art Media (Spanish) Series.
Prod-ACI Dist-AIMS 1967

Puppets And The Poet C 59 MIN
2 INCH VIDEOTAPE
Features the National Theatre of Puppet Arts in an adaptation of Excerpts From Shakespeare. Includes dramatizations of scenes from Macbeth, Taming of the Shrew, Richard III and Hamlet.
Prod-MAETEL Dist-PUBTEL

Puppets Are Fun C 15 MIN
2 INCH VIDEOTAPE P

Provides an enrichment program in the communitive arts area by the use of puppets and imagination.
From The Word Magic (2nd Ed) Series.
Prod-CVETVC Dist-GPITVL

Puppets Come Alive C 25 MIN
2 INCH VIDEOTAPE I
Shows hand puppets and marionettes.
From The Art Has Many Forms Series.
Prod-CVETVC Dist-GPITVL

Puppets Of Jiri Trnka C 26 MIN
16MM FILM, 3/4 OR 1/2 IN VIDEO K-C A
Brings to life several puppets in the world of fairy tale, using various film techniques.
Prod-CFET Dist-PHENIX 1973

Puppets You Can Make C 16 MIN
16MM FILM, 3/4 OR 1/2 IN VIDEO I-H
Demonstrates how to make workable hand puppets using assorted odds and ends and shows how to work the puppets.
Prod-NILLU Dist-CORF 1971

Puppies C 30 MIN
3/4 OR 1/2 INCH VIDEO CASSETTE H-C A
Shows Barbara Woodhouse's method of handling puppies.
From The Training Dogs The Woodhouse Way.
Prod-BBCTV Dist-FI 1982

Puppy Dogs' Tails C 29 MIN
16MM FILM OPTICAL SOUND
A promotional and fund raising film for the Crippled Children's Society of Los Angeles County which shows a group of crippled children, aged seven to nine years, going to camp for the first time.
LC NO. 75-711408
Prod-CCSLAC Dist-CCSLAC 1971

Puppy Saves The Circus, The C 23 MIN
16MM FILM, 3/4 OR 1/2 IN VIDEO K-I
Presents an animated film about Petey, the circus elephant, who has amnesia, and his owner Tommy. Tells how villain clowns plot to destroy the circus but the circus animals unite to catch the culprits.
Prod-CORF Dist-CORF 1983

Puppy Who Wanted A Boy, The C 23 MIN
16MM FILM, 3/4 OR 1/2 IN VIDEO K-I
Tells a story about a puppy who waits impatiently for the day he will be adopted and who watches as his brothers and sisters are carried off while he is left behind. Shows his adventures when he runs off to the city to find a boy of his own.
Prod-RSPRO Dist-CORF 1978

Puppy's Amazing Rescue C 23 MIN
16MM FILM, 3/4 OR 1/2 IN VIDEO K-I
Presents the animated story of two puppies who save their master and his father after they are trapped on a mountain by an avalanche.
Prod-RSPRO Dist-CORF 1980

Puppy's Great Adventure - Further Adventures Of Petey C 24 MIN
16MM FILM, 3/4 OR 1/2 IN VIDEO K-I
Tells how a puppy is separated from his young master and sets out to find him, encountering diamond thieves and puppy love along the way.
Prod-RSPRO Dist-CORF 1979

Pups Is Pups B 19 MIN
16MM FILM OPTICAL SOUND
Describes how the Gang enters their unruly pets in a posh hotel pet show, while one of the kids scours the city for his missing flock of puppies. A Little Rascals film.
Prod-ROACH Dist-BHAWK 1930

Purcell, The Trumpet And John Wilbraham And Michael Laird C 26 MIN
16MM FILM, 3/4 OR 1/2 IN VIDEO J-C A
States that British composer Henry Purcell (1659-1695) held the prestigious post of organist at London's Westminster Abbey for several years. Presents professional musicians John Wilbraham and Michael Laird playing Purcell's trumpet music.
From The Musical Triangle Series.
Prod-THAMES Dist-MEDIAG 1975

Purchasing (Resupply) Lead Time C
3/4 OR 1/2 INCH VIDEO CASSETTE IND
Discusses components and statistics of lead time and a system for tracking and forecasting. Cites importance of understanding combined effects of usage and lead time uncertainty.
From The Effective Inventory Control Series.
Prod-GPCV Dist-GPCV

Purdue Eye Camera B 10 MIN
16MM FILM SILENT C T
Photographs the eye movements of a person looking at advertisements. Special drawings show localization of eyes, experienced investigators indicate the areas of the advertisement to which the person devoted time and the subject verifies these interpretations by saying which elements interested him.
Prod-PSUPCR Dist-PSUPCR 1940

Pure Dance - A Demonstration C 58 MIN
3/4 OR 1/2 INCH VIDEO CASSETTE
Demonstrates 'pure dance' as performed by Barbara Mettler and her five-member dance company.
Prod-METT Dist-METT

Purification By Fire - The Passage Through Pain C 26 MIN
3/4 OR 1/2 INCH VIDEO CASSETTE
Describes fear of physical and emotional pain. Recounts work with a young man immobilized and in intractable pain who was able to use the pain to transform his life.
From The Conscious Living/Conscious Dying - The Work Of A Lifetime Series.
Prod-ORGNLF Dist-PELICN

Purification Of Amphibian Oovacyte Promoting Factor C 60 MIN
3/4 INCH VIDEO CASSETTE
Studies the human cell cycles and amphibian cell cycles to show the changes that occur in cancer cells.
Prod-UTAHTI Dist-UTAHTI

Purim C 15 MIN
16MM FILM OPTICAL SOUND
Shows how the festival of Purim is celebrated in Israel.
Prod-ALDEN Dist-ALDEN

Puritan Experience, The - Forsaking England C 28 MIN
16MM FILM, 3/4 OR 1/2 IN VIDEO I-C A
Presents the story of one family, the Higgins, and their decision to leave the land they love and head for America. Describes the main ideas of Puritanism and depicts the experiences lived by many immigrants.
Prod-LCOA Dist-LCOA 1975

Puritan Experience, The - Forsaking England (Spanish) C 28 MIN
16MM FILM, 3/4 OR 1/2 IN VIDEO J-C A
Uses the experience of the Higgins family to represent the lives 20,000 Puritans who fled England in the 1630's to migrate to America.
Prod-LCOA Dist-LCOA 1975

Puritan Experience, The - Making A New World C 31 MIN
16MM FILM, 3/4 OR 1/2 IN VIDEO I-C A
Describes Puritan Massachusetts in 1640 and the plight of Charity Higgins, who was captured by the Indians and forcibly returned to the Puritan community. Depicts how Charity becomes outraged by the Puritans' treatment of the Indians and rebels against Puritan doctrine.
Prod-LCOA Dist-LCOA 1975

Puritan Experience, The - Making A New World (Spanish) C 31 MIN
16MM FILM, 3/4 OR 1/2 IN VIDEO J-C A
Continues the Higgins' chronicle in Massachusetts. Presents factual information on Puritan beliefs, culture and life.
Prod-LCOA Dist-LCOA 1975

Puritan Family Of Early New England (2nd Ed) C 11 MIN
16MM FILM, 3/4 OR 1/2 IN VIDEO I
Describes the life of a Puritan family.
LC NO. 80-707369
Prod-CORF Dist-CORF 1980

Puritan Revolution, The - Cromwell And The Rise Of Parliamentary Democracy C 33 MIN
16MM FILM, 3/4 OR 1/2 IN VIDEO H-C
Shows how the revolt of Parliament against Charles I in the 1640's, under the leadership of Oliver Cromwell and the Puritans, destroyed the absolute power of the English monarchy and directed the country on the road to parliamentary democracy.
From The Western Civilization - Majesty And Madness Series.
Prod-LCOA Dist-LCOA 1972

Purlie Victorious, Daris, Dee And Alda C
3/4 OR 1/2 INCH VIDEO CASSETTE
Prod-MSTVIS Dist-MSTVIS

Purloined Letter, The C 30 MIN
2 INCH VIDEOTAPE J-H
Presents the short story The Purloined Letter by Edgar Allan Poe.
From The From Franklin To Frost - Edgar Allan Poe Series.
Prod-MPATI Dist-GPITVL

Purple Adventures Of Lady Elaine Fairchilde—A Series
K-P
Presents Mr Rogers talking, singing and using puppets to present the story of Lady Elaine Fairchilde's trip into space and her visit to a purple planet. Discusses individual differences, including handicaps, uniqueness and change.
LC NO. 80-706562
Prod-FAMCOM Dist-HUBDSC 1979

Lady Elaine Discovers Planet Purple 025 MIN
Lady Elaine Flies For Jupiter 029 MIN
Lady Elaine Wants Everything To Be As It Is 024 MIN
Purple Visitors To The Neighborhood Of 025 MIN
Things Begin To Change On Planet Purple 028 MIN

Purple Adventures Of Lady Elaine Fairchilde C
3/4 OR 1/2 INCH VIDEO CASSETTE K-P
Explores individual differences with Mister Rogers. Presented in 5 parts.
Prod-FAMCOM Dist-FAMCOM

Purple Gang, The B 85 MIN
16MM FILM OPTICAL SOUND H-C A
Dramatizes the career of the Purples, a gang that terrorized Detroit in the prohibition era.
Prod-CINEWO Dist-CINEWO 1960

Purple Heart C 1 MIN
16MM FILM OPTICAL SOUND J-C A
Presents an anti-war comment.
Prod-CFS Dist-CFS 1970

Purple Turtle C 14 MIN
16MM FILM, 3/4 OR 1/2 IN VIDEO K-P T
Shows kindergarten children at work with various art mediums. Captures the intensity, delight and skill with which four-and five-year-olds take to paint. Shows why art is one of the most important means of development.
Prod-ACI Dist-AIMS 1962

Purple Visitors To The Neighborhood Of Make-Believe C 25 MIN
16MM FILM, 3/4 OR 1/2 IN VIDEO K-P
Presents Mr Rogers talking and singing about differences making people interesting. Reveals what happens when Purple Panda, Paul and Pauline arrive from Planet Purple.
From The Purple Adventures Of Lady Elaine Fairchilde Series. Program 4
LC NO. 80-706562
Prod-FAMCOM Dist-HUBDSC 1979

Purpose And Audience C 30 MIN
3/4 OR 1/2 INCH VIDEO CASSETTE C A
Focuses on techniques involved in planning and getting started writing correspondence. Shows how to define the purpose of correspondence and where to place important ideas to get the reader's attention, taking into account his needs. Describes those situations in which it is more desirable to call or see someone in person. Hosted by Ed Asner.
From The Effective Writing For Executives Series.
LC NO. 80-707552
Prod-TIMLIF Dist-TIMLIF 1980

Purpose Of Satsang C 60 MIN
3/4 OR 1/2 INCH VIDEO CASSETTE
Presents Sri Gurudev answering a series of questions including 'what is the difference between needs and desires?' and 'how can love grow without attachment?'
Prod-IYOGA Dist-IYOGA

Purposes And Techniques Of Joint Aspiration C 20 MIN
3/4 OR 1/2 INCH VIDEO CASSETTE PRO
Demonstrates the technique for aspiration of the knee, ankle, wrist and shoulder. Emphasizes aseptic technique, anatomical landmarks, positioning of the patient and handling of the specimen in order to obtain maximum diagnostic information. Gives special consideration to identification of crystals and to noting the pressure of cells associated with specific disease.
Prod-UMICHM Dist-UMICHM 1974

Purposes Of Family Planning C 15 MIN
16MM FILM, 3/4 OR 1/2 IN VIDEO H-C A
Presents the different reasons why people choose to practice family planning. Points out that among the motivations for choosing to practice family planning are health, emotional maturity, economic stability and the need to provide each child with individual love and attention.
From The Family Planning And Sex Education Series.
Prod-MORLAT Dist-AIMS 1973

Purposes Of Family Planning (Spanish) C 15 MIN
16MM FILM, 3/4 OR 1/2 IN VIDEO H-C A
Presents reasons for practicing family planning. Includes motivations of health, emotional maturity, economic stability and the need to provide each child with individual love and attention.
Prod-MORLAT Dist-AIMS 1973

Purse, The B 13 MIN
16MM FILM, 3/4 OR 1/2 IN VIDEO H-C A
Dramatizes the discovery of a lost purse containing a large sum of money to stimulate discussion about conscience and its motivation and principles of honesty and integrity.
Prod-NFBC Dist-IFB 1967

Pursuit Of Cleanliness, The C 14 MIN
16MM FILM OPTICAL SOUND J-H A
Depicts the evolution and importance of cleanliness from ancient Rome to today. Traces the history of soap.
Prod-SOAPDS Dist-MTP

Pursuit Of Efficiency, The C 25 MIN
16MM FILM, 3/4 OR 1/2 IN VIDEO A
Tells the story of a tea lady who pushes her cart through an office, dispensing observations on office management along with the refreshments. Stresses the importance of taking a fresh and critical look at one's duties.
Prod-RANKAV Dist-RTBL 1980

Pursuit Of Excellence, The C 50 MIN
16MM FILM OPTICAL SOUND
Profiles two of America's top long-distance runners, Bill Rodgers and Frank Shorter, as they prepare for the 1978 Boston Marathon.
LC NO. 79-701054
Prod-WQED Dist-WQED 1978

Pursuit Of Happiness, The C 52 MIN
16MM FILM, 3/4 OR 1/2 IN VIDEO J-C A
Surveys the development of Western civilization during the 18th century as evidenced in the music of Bach, Handel, Mozart and Haydn, the architecture of Neumann and the paintings and etchings of Tiepolo.
From The Civilisation Series. No. 9
LC NO. 79-707053
Prod-BBCTV Dist-FI 1971

Pursuit Of Peace (History Of The U N) B 20 MIN
16MM FILM OPTICAL SOUND I-C A
Provides a history of th United Nations - from the Atlantic Conference in 1941 until today, in a documentary report on the world organization's pursuit of peace. Shows great figures from present and past and gives a first-hand look at the successes and failures of the United Nations. Reports comprehensively, on the President's three-continent, eleven-nation-mission of peace - that is climaxed by the crucial Big Four Western Summit Conference in Paris. Shows President Eisenhower visiting South America on Operation Amigo.
Prod-HEARST Dist-HEARST

Pursuit Of The Ideal, The C 30 MIN
3/4 OR 1/2 INCH VIDEO CASSETTE C
See series title for descriptive statement.
From The Art Of Being Human Series. Module 11
Prod-MDCC Dist-MDCC

Push And Pull B 15 MIN
2 INCH VIDEOTAPE I
Discusses the importance of making useful definitions. (Broadcast quality)
From The Let's Explore Science Series. No. 8
Prod-POPS Dist-GPITVL Prodn-KOAPTV

Push Button Film C
16MM FILM OPTICAL SOUND
Takes a look at funking around in Venice, California, a Sunday afternoon and the kites, a stereopticon dream and old ladies playing cards.
Prod-CANCIN Dist-CANCIN

Push-Pull Amplifier B 32 MIN
16MM FILM, 3/4 OR 1/2 IN VIDEO
Lists the requirements for push-pull operation. Explains how bias affects class of operation and compares classes as to fidelity, harmonics and efficiency. (Kinescope)
Prod-USAF Dist-USNAC

Pushed To The Limit C 28 MIN
16MM FILM, 3/4 OR 1/2 IN VIDEO
Shows how the speed of light was measured and that Newton's universal laws have certain limitations.
From The Understanding Space And Time Series.
Prod-BBCTV Dist-UCEMC 1980

Pushing The Limits - An IBM Information Technology Report C 27 MIN
16MM FILM OPTICAL SOUND
Presents a view of computer technology research and development in IBM laboratories around the world.
LC NO. 78-701347
Prod-IBMCOP Dist-MTP Prodn-MURPHO 1978

Pushmi-Pullyu C 11 MIN
16MM FILM OPTICAL SOUND P-I
An excerpt from the motion picture Doctor Dolittle. Tells how Doctor Dolittle receives a pushmi-pullyu, a rare llama with a head on each end, as a gift to help him raise money for his search for the great pink sea snail. Based on the book Doctor Dolittle by Hugh Lofting.
From The Peppermint Stick Selection Series.
LC NO. 76-701277
Prod-FI Dist-FI 1976

Puss In Boots B 10 MIN
16MM FILM OPTICAL SOUND
Uses animated paper silhouettes to illustrate the children's story Puss In Boots. Based on live shadow plays produced by Lotte Reiniger for BBC Television.
From The Lotte Reiniger's Animated Fairy Tales Series.
Prod-PRIMP Dist-MOMA 1934

Puss In Boots C 15 MIN
3/4 OR 1/2 INCH VIDEO CASSETTE K-P
See series title for descriptive statement.
From The Gather Round Series.
Prod-CTI Dist-CTI

Puss In Boots C 15 MIN
3/4 OR 1/2 INCH VIDEO CASSETTE P
Presents the children's story Puss in Boots by Charles Perrault, retold by Ann Mc Gregor.
From The Tilson's Book Shop Series.
Prod-WVIZTV Dist-GPITVL 1975

Puss In Boots B 16 MIN
16MM FILM, 3/4 OR 1/2 IN VIDEO P-I
Retells the fairy tale with animated puppets made by the Dietz Brothers. Uses stop-motion photography.
Prod-EBF Dist-EBEC 1958

Puss In Boots (Spanish) B 16 MIN
16MM FILM, 3/4 OR 1/2 IN VIDEO P-I
Uses animated puppets to retell the story of Puss In Boots.
Prod-EBEC Dist-EBEC

Puss In Boots - A French Fairy Tale C 11 MIN
16MM FILM, 3/4 OR 1/2 IN VIDEO K-P
Presents the French fairy tale Puss In Boots. Tells the story of Jacques, who has nothing to his name by the clothes on his back, a pair of old, red boots and the loyalty of Puss, his very clever cat. Shows how, with Puss' help, Jacques becomes a rich, landowning noble.
From The Favorite Fairy Tales And Fables Series.
Prod-CORF Dist-CORF 1980

Pussycat That Ran Away C 21 MIN
16MM FILM, 3/4 OR 1/2 IN VIDEO P-I
Gives an impression of life on a farm and views of the Norwegian countryside. Includes importance of obeying parents and being kind to little brothers.
Prod-SVEK Dist-PHENIX 1958

Pustular Psoriasis C 14 MIN
16MM FILM OPTICAL SOUND PRO
Describes and illustrates an atypical form of psoriasis vulgaris through the use of charts and a case history.
From The Case Presentations On Film Series.
LC NO. 70-701966
Prod-SQUIBB Dist-SQUIBB Prodn-AUDIO 1966

Put A Medal On The Man C 5 MIN
16MM FILM OPTICAL SOUND H-C A
Presents a scathing political-social commentary to the words of Phil Ochs' 'IS THERE ANYBODY HERE.'
Prod-UWFKD Dist-UWFKD

Put It In Writing—A Series

Improves written communications by developing clarity in writing, speed in composing written communications, organization skills, professional image, grammar and awareness of different purposes of writing. Includes student text and workbook, a discussion leader's guide and a train-the-trainer session.
Prod-DELTAK Dist-DELTAK

Changing Some Old Attitudes 020 MIN
Clarity - Your First Objective 027 MIN
Finishing Touches Of The Pros, The 020 MIN
How To Outsmart The Deadline 015 MIN
Measuring Your Clarity 013 MIN
Practical Tips On Organizing 015 MIN

Put It On Poles C 18 MIN
16MM FILM OPTICAL SOUND
Illustrates the problem of space including space for display, raw material storage and servicing extensive machines. Offers an answer in pole building.
Prod-DCC Dist-DCC

Put More Leadership Into Your Style C 30 MIN
16MM FILM, 3/4 OR 1/2 IN VIDEO
Deals with the development of leadership qualities.
Prod-BARR Dist-BARR

Put The Kettle On C 11 MIN
16MM FILM, 3/4 OR 1/2 IN VIDEO P
Uses vignettes of train trips, boat rides, amusement park attractions, a kettle, a clown and a magician to reinforce the words get, find, put, on, off and help.
From The Reading And Word Play Series.
Prod-PEDF Dist-AIMS 1976

Put Them Together - A Saturday Adventure C 11 MIN
16MM FILM, 3/4 OR 1/2 IN VIDEO P
Uses a story about a young boy's adventures in an imaginary jungle to encourage the use of descriptive words and phrases in describing experiences.
From The Read On Series.
Prod-ACI Dist-AIMS 1971

Put Wings On Your Career C 15 MIN
3/4 OR 1/2 INCH VIDEO CASSETTE A
Encourages careers in aviation maintenance. Illustrates diversity of jobs associated with it, both in government and private industry.
Prod-FAAFL Dist-AVIMA

Put Wings On Your Career C 15 MIN
16MM FILM, 3/4 OR 1/2 IN VIDEO
Illustrates the diversity of jobs associated with aviation maintenance, both in government and in private industry. Outlines the basic technical requirements of this field and enumerates various sources of more specific career information.
Prod-USFAA Dist-USNAC 1978

Put Your Hand In My Hand C 15 MIN
16MM FILM OPTICAL SOUND I-H
Shows several foreign youths on a cultural exchange program to the United States discussing differences in customs and explains how visiting their American peers has affected their perception of the country.
LC NO. 77-701857
Prod-CASTOP Dist-CASTOP 1975

Put Your Hands On The Top Of Your Head C 4 MIN
16MM FILM, 3/4 OR 1/2 IN VIDEO K
Presents a song game where the hands are put on top of the head and the body moves to a rousing song, to learn the parts of the body and just for action.
From The Most Important Person - Body Movement Series.
Prod-EBEC Dist-EBEC 1972

Put-Down C 3 MIN
16MM FILM OPTICAL SOUND H-C A
Presents three short vignettes about the ways in which society discriminates against women.
LC NO. 74-701531
Prod-FRACOC Dist-FRACOC 1973

Put-Together Look, The C 29 MIN
2 INCH VIDEOTAPE
See series title for descriptive statement.
From The Designing Women Series.
Prod-WKYCTV Dist-PUBTEL

Put-Togetherer C 15 MIN
3/4 OR 1/2 INCH VIDEO CASSETTE P
See series title for descriptive statement.
From The Strawberry Square II - Take Time Series.
Prod-NEITV Dist-AITECH 1984

Putting - Golf's End Game C 12 MIN
16MM FILM - 3/4 IN VIDEO H-C A
Explains geometrical factors of putting and fundamentals for developing a dependable putting technique. Demonstrates methods of stroking and putting across, up and down slopes.
From The Modern Golf Instruction In Motion Pictures Series. Unit 5
LC NO. 76-703596
Prod-NGF Dist-NGF Prodn-GOLF 1944

Putting Animals In Groups C 13 MIN
16MM FILM, 3/4 OR 1/2 IN VIDEO I-J
Explains how animals are classified according to their structure. Points out the distinctive characteristics of mammals, birds, reptiles, amphibians, fishes and insects.
Prod-IFB Dist-IFB 1956

Putting Art To Work C 25 MIN
2 INCH VIDEOTAPE I
Demonstrates school beautification.
From The Art For Every Day Series.
Prod-CVETVC Dist-GPITVL

Putting Food By - The Canning Way C 55 MIN
16MM FILM, 3/4 OR 1/2 IN VIDEO
Demonstrates how to can tomatoes and green beans.
Prod-ODECA Dist-BULFRG

Putting Food By - The Solar Way C 12 MIN
16MM FILM, 3/4 OR 1/2 IN VIDEO
Shows the steps for dehydrating vegetables, from building a solar box to storing the product.
Prod-ODECA Dist-BULFRG

Putting Fruit By - The Solar Way C 15 MIN
16MM FILM, 3/4 OR 1/2 IN VIDEO
Shows the steps for dehydrating fruits, from building a solar box to storing the product.
Prod-ODECA Dist-BULFRG

Putting It All Together C 15 MIN
16MM FILM OPTICAL SOUND J-C A
Explores different attitudes toward music and presents interviews with people whose interests in the musical world range from student teaching to performing, including jazz musicians and Clark Terry and Bobby Columbi of the rock group Blood, Sweat and Tears.
Prod-MAGSD Dist-MTP

Putting It All Together C
3/4 OR 1/2 INCH VIDEO CASSETTE
Examines how to reduce costs and increase quality. Shows how to set up a system of checks and balances with quality audits. Deals with establishing goals.
From The Organizational Quality Improvement Series.
Prod-BNA Dist-BNA

Putting It All Together C 18 MIN
3/4 OR 1/2 INCH VIDEO CASSETTE PRO
Provides an orientation to community health nursing through a typical student's experiences as she visits several families. Utilizes interviewing and interpersonal skills with a broad range of families and ages. Emphasizes nursing experiences to which students are exposed and the personal and professional growth that results.
Prod-UMICHM Dist-UMICHM 1975

Putting It All Together - Action Plans C 26 MIN
16MM FILM - 3/4 IN VIDEO
Illustrates how definable steps in a chosen strategy are put into the work stream of an organization. Examines two new activities for their fiscal and manpower implications.
LC NO. 76-706083
Prod-USOE Dist-USNAC 1973

Putting It All Together - Evaluation C 30 MIN
16MM FILM - 3/4 IN VIDEO
Discusses principles of evaluation in a managerial context with programs, students, teachers and administrators as a part of the total system. Emphasizes that evaluation is corrective and not punitive.
LC NO. 76-706084
Prod-USOE Dist-USNAC 1973

Putting It All Together - Farmers And Their Cooperatives C 22 MIN
16MM FILM OPTICAL SOUND
Explains the cooperative system in American agriculture and the significance of this system to the family farmer and the consumer.
LC NO. 79-701239
Prod-AMIC Dist-AMIC Prodn-VISION 1979

Putting It All Together - Integrating Your Objectives C 22 MIN
16MM FILM - 3/4 IN VIDEO
Demonstrates a top-down, deductive means of developing a hierarchy of objectives. Shows that a hierarchy is useful to relate objectives to the fundamental purpose of a school system.
LC NO. 76-706085
Prod-USOE Dist-USNAC 1973

Putting It All Together - Introduction To Planning C 12 MIN
16MM FILM - 3/4 IN VIDEO
Points up the consequences of the absence of planning and indicates the necessity for a rational approach to planning.
LC NO. 76-706087
Prod-USOE Dist-USNAC 1973

Putting It All Together - It All Depends C 18 MIN
16MM FILM - 3/4 IN VIDEO
Stresses the importance of understanding the situation before setting objectives or committing resources when planning. Provides guidance for structuring analysis of the situation to make it useful in decisionmaking.
LC NO. 76-706088
Prod-USOE Dist-USNAC 1973

Putting It All Together - Organization C 22 MIN
16MM FILM - 3/4 IN VIDEO
Describes the concepts of organization, the tools for organizing and the impact of good organization.
LC NO. 76-706089
Prod-USOE Dist-USNAC 1973

Putting It All Together - Pitfalls Of Planning C 29 MIN
16MM FILM - 3/4 IN VIDEO
Discusses seven of the most critical reasons why planning fails and offers suggestions to prevent failure.
LC NO. 76-706090
Prod-USOE Dist-USNAC 1973

Putting It All Together - Planning C 57 MIN
16MM FILM - 3/4 IN VIDEO
Presents principles of management, emphasizing the differences between management activities and technical activities. In-

cludes concepts of a system of management in which planning is stressed.
LC NO. 76-706091
Prod-USOE Dist-USNAC 1973

Putting It All Together - Policies C 16 MIN
3/4 INCH VIDEO CASSETTE
Shows how an organization analyzes its goals and chooses to channel its activities in one direction rather than another. Demonstrates how articulating such policies can avoid conflict.
LC NO. 76-706092
Prod-USOE Dist-USNAC 1973

Putting It All Together - Summary And Conclusion C 15 MIN
3/4 OR 1/2 INCH VIDEO CASSETTE P
Presents a summary of how to use The Clyde Frog Show Series.
From The Clyde Frog Show Series.
Prod-MAETEL Dist-GPITVL 1977

Putting It All Together - The Concept Of Strategy C 25 MIN
16MM FILM - 3/4 IN VIDEO
Shows how alternative means may be devised to achieve management objectives. Describes ways of developing priorities among the strategies.
LC NO. 76-706093
Prod-USOE Dist-USNAC 1973

Putting It All Together - The Nature Of Objectives C 14 MIN
16MM FILM - 3/4 IN VIDEO
Presents the criteria for evaluating a management objective. Emphasizes the problem of evaluating the validity of an objective and the problem of tying an objective to a specific position in the organization.
LC NO. 76-706095
Prod-USOE Dist-USNAC 1973

Putting It All Together - Values In Planning C 14 MIN
16MM FILM - 3/4 IN VIDEO
Demonstrates the value of a visible system of beliefs and assumptions in the management of a school system. Provides a discussion of the basic issues involved in the management of a school system.
LC NO. 76-706096
Prod-USOE Dist-USNAC 1973

Putting It Together C 30 MIN
3/4 OR 1/2 INCH VIDEO CASSETTE K-P
See series title for descriptive statement.
From The Villa Alegre Series.
Prod-BCTV Dist-MDCPB

Putting Learning Back In The Classroom C 45 MIN
3/4 OR 1/2 INCH VIDEO CASSETTE C
Presents economist Milton Friedman examining schooling in the United States.
From The Milton Friedman Speaking Series. Lecture 11
LC NO. 79-708071
Prod-HBJ Dist-HBJ Prodn-WQLN 1980

Putting Microbes To Work C
1/2 IN VIDEO CASSETTE (VHS)
Focuses on the role of bacteria in genetic engineering and the creation of new kinds of bacteria by scientists. Examines recombinant DNA techniques used in producing insulin and interferon.
From The Genetic Engineering - Prospects Of The Future Series.
Prod-IBIS Dist-IBIS

Putting On The Dog C 8 MIN
16MM FILM OPTICAL SOUND J-C A
Dramatizes the importance of perseverance, as well as occasional compromise in the pursuit of happiness. Tells the story of a woman who dresses up in odds and ends and waltzes around town, fantasizing that she is a beautiful lady. Shows how she accidentally finds a solution and dances happily away to the country.
LC NO. 80-700737
Prod-INSDEA Dist-KINMIK 1980

Putting Sleeves On The Coat C 29 MIN
2 INCH VIDEOTAPE
Features Mrs Ruth Hickman demonstrating how to put sleeves on a coat.
From The Sewing Skills - Tailoring Series.
Prod-KRMATV Dist-PUBTEL

Putting The Atom To Work C 25 MIN
16MM FILM OPTICAL SOUND
Presents basic information on nuclear fission, how this is applied to generate power, the present nuclear generating stations now operating or under construction for Britain's power program, the advanced gas-cooled reactor, the Dounreay fast breeder reactor and what radioisotopes are and how they are used.
Prod-UKAEA Dist-UKAEA 1966

Putting The One Minute Manager To Work C 60 MIN
3/4 OR 1/2 INCH VIDEO CASSETTE A
Presents Dr Ken Blanchard and Dr Robert Lorber, business consultants, explaining how to implement management theory in a work setting. Expands on the ideas of the book The One Minute Manager. Emphasizes goal setting and judicious praising and reprimands.
Prod-CBSFOX Dist-CBSFOX

Putting The Rules Together C 14 MIN
16MM FILM, 3/4 OR 1/2 IN VIDEO P-I
Shows that the rules for pronouncing the long and short sounds of a single vowel can be put together and reduced to a few simple understandings.
From The Reading Skills, Set 2 Series. No. 3
Prod-GLDWER Dist-JOU 1972

Putting The Sun To Work C 5 MIN
16MM FILM, 3/4 OR 1/2 IN VIDEO I-C A
Describes the work of scientists and engineers from government and private industry in their search for ways to produce electrical energy from the sun.
From The Search - Encounters With Science Series.
Prod-NSF Dist-AMEDFL 1973

Putting Up The Pickles C 29 MIN
16MM FILM, 3/4 OR 1/2 IN VIDEO J-C A
Shows the members of the Pickle Family Circus, including jugglers, trapeze and tightrope artists, acrobats and clowns as they rehearse and at actual performances. Tells how they travel together and of their unusual rapport with their audience.
LC NO. 81-707571
Prod-AGINP Dist-AGINP 1981

Putting Your Financial Plan Into Action C 25 MIN
3/4 OR 1/2 INCH VIDEO CASSETTE H-C A
Explains how individuals set aside money for investment. Includes budgeting, developing good spending habits, finding suitable investments and using professional help.
From The Money Smart - A Guide To Personal Finance Series.
Prod-SOMFIL Dist-BCNFL 1984

Putting Your Money To Work C 18 MIN
16MM FILM OPTICAL SOUND
Examines some of the ways in which money can be invested.
From The Consumer Game Series.
LC NO. 74-701249
Prod-OECA Dist-OECA 1972

Puzzle Children, The C 59 MIN
16MM FILM OPTICAL SOUND H-C A
Discusses learning disabilities in children and identifies some of the myths that prevent an accurate understanding of these problems. Profiles four children with specific learning handicaps, including comments by their parents, teachers and special educators. Hosted by Julie Andrews and Bill Bixby.
LC NO. 77-701035
Prod-WQED Dist-IU 1977

Puzzle Children, The C 59 MIN
3/4 OR 1/2 INCH VIDEO CASSETTE H-C A
Discusses learning disabilities in children and identifies some of the myths that prevent an accurate understanding of these problems. Profiles four children with specific learning handicaps and includes comments by their parents, teachers and special educators. Hosted by Julie Andrews and Bill Bixby.
LC NO. 77-701035
Prod-WQED Dist-PBS 1977

Puzzle, The C 6 MIN
16MM FILM, 3/4 OR 1/2 IN VIDEO IND
Discusses the problem of dealing with a good employee who suddenly becomes hard to get along with and sloppy when he transfers to another department.
From The This Matter Of Motivation Series.
Prod-CTRACT Dist-DARTNL Prodn-CALVIN 1971

Puzzling Problems C 15 MIN
3/4 OR 1/2 INCH VIDEO CASSETTE P
Tells how a space robot and his detective friend help unravel mysterious numbers and a secret message by translating and finding the answers to several different types of word problems, picture problems, and number stories.
From The Math Mission 2 Series.
LC NO. 82-706317
Prod-WCVETV Dist-GPITVL 1980

Pychotherapy C 30 MIN
3/4 OR 1/2 INCH VIDEO CASSETTE
Presents the psychoanalytic approach, client-centered therapy, gestalt therapy, transactional analysis, psychiatric drugs, services offered by counselor, psychologists, clinical social workers and psychiatrists.
From The Psychology Of Human Relations Series.
Prod-MATC Dist-WFVTAE

Pyeloplasty By Modified Ureteroneopyelostomy C 25 MIN
16MM FILM OPTICAL SOUND
Presents three cases to illustrate that the method of pyeloplasty best suited to the individual case must be determined at the time of surgical intervention. Illustrates the classical approach, in case one, used with high ureteral insertion with no intrinsic stricture at the uretero-pelvic junction. Portrays the preservation of an aberrant blood vessel supplying a major portion of the kidney in case two. Depicts the utilization of the Schwyzer-Foley modification combined with ureteroneopyelostomy in the correction of a uretero-pelvic junction stricture.
LC NO. 75-702300
Prod-EATONL Dist-EATONL 1966

Pygmalion B 96 MIN
16MM FILM OPTICAL SOUND
Presents the classic story of Professor Henry Higgins, who bets his companion Colonel Pickering that he can transform a Cockney flower girl into a lady after only a few months instruction. Shows what happens when Higgins chooses hapless Eliza Doolittle as his subject. Features Leslie Howard, Wendy Hiller and Wilfrid Lawson. Directed by Anthony Asquith. Based on the play Pygmalion by George Bernard Shaw.
Prod-MGM Dist-LCOA 1938

Pygmalion B
1/2 IN VIDEO CASSETTE BETA/VHS
Presents a 1938 adaptation of Shaw's play Pygmalion, starring Wendy Miller and Leslie Howard.
Prod-GA Dist-GA

Pygmies Of The Ituri Forest, The C 19 MIN
16MM FILM, 3/4 OR 1/2 IN VIDEO J-H
Examines the life and customs of the Efe Pygmies as observed and photographed by the anthropologist Jean-Pierre Hallet.
Prod-HALLTJ Dist-EBEC 1974

Pygmies Of The Rain Forest C 51 MIN
16MM FILM, 3/4 OR 1/2 IN VIDEO I-C A
Portrays the life of the nomadic Mbuti pygmies of Zaire, Africa. Shows their primal world of hut building, food gathering and bull elephant hunting.
LC NO. 77-701105
Prod-DUFFY Dist-PFP 1976

Pygmies, The - People Of The Forest C 14 MIN
16MM FILM, 3/4 OR 1/2 IN VIDEO I-J
Examines the life and customs of Pygmies in the African forest. Shows how they adapt their way of life to their environment from which they take all their basic supplies and materials.
Prod-HALLTJ Dist-EBEC 1975

Pyloric Stenosis B 13 MIN
16MM FILM OPTICAL SOUND PRO
Uses drawings and a stomach model to explain the anatomy of the stomach region and the area involved in the treatment of pyloric stenosis. Shows a pediatrician performing surgery on a six-week old infant.
From The Doctors At Work Series.
LC NO. FIA65-1359
Prod-CMA Dist-LAWREN Prodn-LAWREN 1962

Pyloric Stenosis C 28 MIN
16MM FILM OPTICAL SOUND PRO
Points out that the modern operative technique for pyloroplasty varies little from that described by Conrad Ramstedt in 1912. Explains that improved preparation for operation coupled with improved anesthesia and after-care are the major factors contributing to a now extremely low mortality.
Prod-ACYDGD Dist-ACY 1963

Pyloric Stenosis C 9 MIN
3/4 OR 1/2 INCH VIDEO CASSETTE
See series title for descriptive statement.
From The Pediatric Series.
Prod-SVL Dist-SVL

Pyramid Layout Radial Line Method C 7 MIN
1/2 IN VIDEO CASSETTE BETA/VHS IND
Demonstrates the application of the radial line method for developing the patterns for pyramid shapes.
Prod-RMI Dist-RMI

Pyramid Probe C 6 MIN
16MM FILM, 3/4 OR 1/2 IN VIDEO
Focuses on a search for an Egyptian pharoah's secret burial chamber. Explains how cosmic radiation from space was used to X-ray the pyramid.
Prod-NSF Dist-AMEDFL 1975

Pyramid Puzzle C 15 MIN
16MM FILM OPTICAL SOUND C A
Explains the significance of the scientific method, showing practical as well as theoretical implications which can be made by the research scientist.
LC NO. FIA65-573
Prod-NSTA Dist-UOKLA Prodn-UOKLA 1964

Pyramids Of The Sun And The Moon C 20 MIN
3/4 OR 1/2 INCH VIDEO CASSETTE
Presents a comprehensive panorama of Teotihuacan and the Aztec art.
Prod-MOMALA Dist-MOMALA

Pyramids Of The Sun And The Moon (Spanish) C 20 MIN
3/4 OR 1/2 INCH VIDEO CASSETTE
Presents a comprehensive panorama of Teotihuacan and the Aztec art.
Prod-MOMALA Dist-MOMALA

Pyramids Of The Sun And The Moon, The C 20 MIN
16MM FILM OPTICAL SOUND
Offers a panorama of Teotihuacan and the Aztec art, filmed on location and at the Museum of Anthropology of Mexico City.
Prod-OOAS Dist-MOMALA 1983

Pyramids Of The Sun And The Moon, The (Spanish) C 20 MIN
16MM FILM OPTICAL SOUND
Offers a panorama of Teotihuacan and the Aztec art, filmed on location and at the Museum of Anthropology of Mexico City.
Prod-OOAS Dist-MOMALA 1983

Pysanka - The Ukrainian Easter Egg C 14 MIN
16MM FILM, 3/4 OR 1/2 IN VIDEO
Explains the myth and magic behind the craft of Easter egg design. Follows an artist as she creates a design on a naked egg.
Prod-NOWYTS Dist-CORF 1975

P4W - Prison For Women C 81 MIN
16MM FILM - 3/4 IN VIDEO J-C A
Looks at Canada's only federal penitentiary for women. Centers on five women, discussing their stories, their relationships with the other inmates and family and how they cope with their lives in prison. Reveals the inadequacy of a rehabilitation system which cannot provide skills for useful re-entry into society.
Prod-FIRS Dist-FIRS

Q

Q A Documentation C 60 MIN
3/4 OR 1/2 INCH VIDEO CASSETTE IND
Presents vendor qualification, traceability, document control and conducting an audit.

From The Quality Assurance Series.
Prod-LEIKID Dist-LEIKID

Q A Programs C 60 MIN
3/4 OR 1/2 INCH VIDEO CASSETTE IND
Presents details of management's responsibility, regulatory bodies and standards. Discusses dominance, inspection and nonconformance.
From The Quality Assurance Series.
Prod-LEIKID Dist-LEIKID

Q Is For Quest C 20 MIN
16MM FILM OPTICAL SOUND I-J
Tells of 10-year-old Kathy who feels that her dreams of knighthood will never come true after she goes to live with an embittered old aunt who vows to turn her into a proper young lady. Shows how she gets her opportunity for knighthood and in the process revises her aunt's opinions on the roles of men and women.
Prod-USC Dist-USC 1983

Q, U And V C 15 MIN
3/4 INCH VIDEO CASSETTE P
From The Writing Time Series.
Prod-WHROTV Dist-GPITVL

Qeros - The Shape Of Survival C 50 MIN
16MM FILM, 3/4 OR 1/2 IN VIDEO H-C A
Looks at the lifestyle of the Qeros Indian who have lived in the Peruvian Andes for over 3,000 years. Shows their ecological consciousness as they adapt crops to different altitudes, use natural materials and play flutes which echo Andean winds.
Prod-COHEN Dist-FI 1979

Qeros - The Shape Of Survival C 53 MIN
16MM FILM, 3/4 OR 1/2 IN VIDEO
Illustrates the life of the Qeros Indians in the high Andes Mountains of Peru. Describes their culture as far older than that of the Incas. Portrays them as rural and agricultural and doomed to extinction, primarily because of vulnerability to disease.
Prod-CNEMAG Dist-CNEMAG 1979

Qu'est-Ce Qu'il Y A B 13 MIN
16MM FILM OPTICAL SOUND I-H
See series title for descriptive statement.
From The Les Francais Chez Vous Series. Set I, Lesson 06
Prod-PEREN Dist-CHLTN 1967

Qu'est-Ce Que C'Est B 13 MIN
16MM FILM OPTICAL SOUND I-H
See series title for descriptive statement.
From The Les Francais Chez Vous Series. Set I, Lesson 03
Prod-PEREN Dist-CHLTN 1967

Quackery - A Side Effect Of Arthritis C 12 MIN
3/4 INCH VIDEO CASSETTE
Features discussions between patients and health professionals regarding the hazards of quackery and patients' reasons for trying unproven remedies.
From The Arthritis Series.
LC NO. 79-707861
Prod-UMICH Dist-UMICH 1978

Quackgrass - The Perennial Guest C 17 MIN
16MM FILM OPTICAL SOUND
Explains that quackgrass is a difficult and costly problem for farmers. Shows how scientific development can increase yields, improve crop quality and facilitate crop tillage.
Prod-DCC Dist-DCC

Quadragla B 3 MIN
16MM FILM OPTICAL SOUND
Presents an experimental film with action and stop-action effects.
LC NO. 74-703007
Prod-UTORMC Dist-CANFDC 1973

Quadratic Equations B 29 MIN
16MM FILM OPTICAL SOUND H
Analyzes the standard form for the quadratic expression in order to find various conditions that make it solvable. Describes a second way of solving by completing the square.
From The Intermediate Algebra Series.
Prod-CALVIN Dist-MLA Prodn-UNIVFI 1959

Quadratic Forms B
16MM FILM OPTICAL SOUND
Looks at the problem of classifying stationary values of a function of two variables. Introduces Taylor's series for a function of two variables by demonstrating how to find linear and quadratic approximations to a surface at a point.
Prod-OPENU Dist-OPENU

Quadratic Functions, Pt 1 C 30 MIN
3/4 INCH VIDEO CASSETTE C
See series title for descriptive statement.
From The Introduction To Mathematics Series.
Prod-MDCPB Dist-MDCPB

Quadratic Functions, Pt 2 C 30 MIN
3/4 INCH VIDEO CASSETTE C
See series title for descriptive statement.
From The Introduction To Mathematics Series.
Prod-MDCPB Dist-MDCPB

Quadricepsplasty - A Technique For Restoration Of Muscle Function In Cases Of... C 18 MIN
16MM FILM OPTICAL SOUND PRO
Examines quadricepsplasty, a technique for restoration of muscle function in cases of fibrous adhesions following injury. Presents the case study of a patient with a 'stiff knee' gait who undergoes surgery and regains 90 degrees of flexion at the knee through the quadricepsplasty technique.
Prod-SQUIBB Dist-SQUIBB

Quadrilaterals C 15 MIN
3/4 OR 1/2 INCH VIDEO CASSETTE I-J
Identifies, squares, rectangles and rhombi and points out the special characteristics of each. Distinguishes between parallelograms, trapezoids and other quadrilaterals.
From The Math Matters Series. Blue Module
Prod-STETVC Dist-AITECH Prodn-KLRNTV 1975

Quadriplegia - Car Transfer C 15 MIN
3/4 OR 1/2 INCH VIDEO CASSETTE
Deals with car transfer of quadriplegics, but can be applied to persons with other disabilities. Focuses on making the patient completely independent in transferring himself and his wheelchair in and out of a standard automobile.
Prod-PRIMED Dist-PRIMED

Quadriplegia - Driver Training C 15 MIN
3/4 OR 1/2 INCH VIDEO CASSETTE
Demonstrates the type of equipment needed for quadraplegic driver and begins the process of teaching the patient to drive.
Prod-PRIMED Dist-PRIMED

Quadriplegia Car Transfer, Pt 3 C 15 MIN
16MM FILM OPTICAL SOUND PRO
Shows the complete independence of a patient transferring himself and his wheelchair in and out of a standard production automobile.
Prod-RLAH Dist-RLAH

Quadriplegia Driver Training, Pt 4 C 15 MIN
16MM FILM OPTICAL SOUND PRO
Demonstrates the potential for training the quadriplegic to drive an automobile. Shows the actual training of the quadriplegic.
Prod-RLAH Dist-RLAH

Quadriplegic Functional Skills - Bowel And Bladder Techniques C 14 MIN
16MM FILM - 3/4 IN VIDEO
Presents methods that may be utilized by the quadriplegic to achieve independence in the management of bowel and bladder functions. Shows variation in drainage clamps and urinary connectors, management of catheter irrigation and external collectors and adaptations in clothing.
LC NO. 79-706718
Prod-UILLAV Dist-USNAC 1979

Quadriplegic Functional Skills - Dressing C 18 MIN
16MM FILM, 3/4 OR 1/2 IN VIDEO
Demonstrates ways for quadriplegics to achieve independence in clothing themselves.
Prod-UILL Dist-USNAC 1974

Quadriplegic Functional Skills - Driving C 19 MIN
16MM FILM - 3/4 IN VIDEO
Demonstrates methods quadriplegics can use in transferring to and from a car and in getting a wheelchair in and out of a car without assistance. Show driving with hand controls and adaptations.
LC NO. 79-706719
Prod-UILLAV Dist-USNAC 1979

Quadriplegic Functional Skills - Showering And Grooming C 16 MIN
16MM FILM, 3/4 OR 1/2 IN VIDEO
Demonstrates ways for the quadriplegic to achieve independence in personal hygiene. Shows how to transfer to and from a wheelchair to a shower seat in a tub and a shower stall. Illustrates bathing, shaving and dental and hair care.
Prod-UILL Dist-USNAC 1974

Quadruparetic Patient, The - Changing Position And Sitting Up In Bed C 7 MIN
16MM FILM OPTICAL SOUND
Depicts how the quadruparetic patient can move to one side and roll over in bed. Shows how a patient can learn to sit up.
LC NO. 74-705459
Prod-USPHS Dist-USNAC 1968

Quadruparetic Patient, The - Sitting Balance In Bed C 9 MIN
16MM FILM OPTICAL SOUND
Illustrates how the quadruparetic patient can learn to move his extremities and trunk while sitting in bed.
LC NO. 74-705460
Prod-USPHS Dist-USNAC 1968

Quadruparetic Patient, The - Transfer From Bed To Wheelchair Using A Sliding Board C 7 MIN
16MM FILM - 3/4 IN VIDEO PRO
Shows techniques used in transferring the quadruparetic patient between bed and wheelchair with the use of a sliding board. Issued in 1968 as a motion picture.
LC NO. 79-706720
Prod-NYUMC Dist-USNAC Prodn-NMAC 1979

Quadruparetic Patient, The - Transfer From Wheelchair To Car And Reverse Using Sliding... C 8 MIN
16MM FILM - 3/4 IN VIDEO PRO
Demonstrates use of the sliding board for transfer of the quadruparetic patient between wheelchair and car. Issued in 1970 as a motion picture.
LC NO. 79-706721
Prod-NYUMC Dist-USNAC Prodn-NMAC 1979

Quaint Cafe C 10 MIN
3/4 OR 1/2 INCH VIDEO CASSETTE H-C A
Presents comedy by the Brave New World Workshop of the Twin Cities.
Prod-BRVNP Dist-UCV

Qualification Test Programs C 30 MIN
3/4 OR 1/2 INCH VIDEO CASSETTE IND
Describes test programs to estimate mean time to failure of devices that fail according to either the normal (wearout) or exponential (chance) distributions. Presents confidence limits for MTTF as well.
From The Reliability Engineering Series.
Prod-COLOSU Dist-COLOSU

Qualification Tests--Examples C 30 MIN
3/4 OR 1/2 INCH VIDEO CASSETTE IND
Contains numerical examples to estimate parameters of the normal and exponential distributions and their confidence intervals.
From The Reliability Engineering Series.
Prod-COLOSU Dist-COLOSU

Qualitative Analytical Techniques C 17 MIN
3/4 OR 1/2 INCH VIDEO CASSETTE C A
Demonstrates some of the basic techniques of semimicro qualitative analysis, including techniques relevant to transfer, addition and mixing of chemicals and techniques related to precipitation.
From The Chemistry - Master/Apprentice Series. Program 8
LC NO. 82-706042
Prod-CUETV Dist-CUNIV 1981

Qualitatively Different Program C 30 MIN
3/4 OR 1/2 INCH VIDEO CASSETTE T
See series title for descriptive statement.
From The Simple Gifts Series. No. 6
Prod-UWISC Dist-GPITVL 1977

Quality And Productivity In Service Organizations C
3/4 OR 1/2 INCH VIDEO CASSETTE
Discusses the differences between and similarities of service industries and manufacturing concerns.
From The Deming Videotapes - Quality, Productivity, And Competitive...Series.
Prod-MIOT Dist-MIOT

Quality And Productivity In Service Organizations C 50 MIN
3/4 OR 1/2 INCH VIDEO CASSETTE
See series title for descriptive statement.
From The Deming Video Tapes - Quality, Productivity And The Competitive...Series.
Prod-MIOT Dist-SME

Quality And The Consumer C 50 MIN
3/4 OR 1/2 INCH VIDEO CASSETTE
See series title for descriptive statement.
From The Deming Video Tapes - Quality, Productivity And The Competitive...Series.
Prod-MIOT Dist-SME

Quality Assurance Is The Essence Of T Q C C 28 MIN
3/4 OR 1/2 INCH VIDEO CASSETTE
Explains the thinking behind quality assurance, the essence of T Q C. Outlines progress in quality control as it leads to a philosophy stressing process control and new product development. Describes the basic theory of 'quality'.
From The Seven Steps To T Q C Promotion Series.
Prod-TOYOVS Dist-TOYOVS

Quality Assurance--A Series
IND
Provides instruction which will enable manufacturers and contractors to meet current international standards regarding quality assurance programs. Shows how to implement procedures to assure a quality product.
Prod-LEIKID Dist-LEIKID

International Standards	060 MIN
Measuring And Calibration	060 MIN
Q A Documentation	060 MIN
Q A Programs	060 MIN
Testing	060 MIN
Why Q A?	060 MIN

Quality Assurance--A Series
PRO
Includes four main aspects, including construction quality control, process control, product or lot control and control charts for variables, attibutes and defects. Studies measurement of significance of control factors, statistical sampling by attributes and variables for product and lot conformance. Includes multiple and sequential sampling plans and study of statistical and mathematical techniques involved in analyzing data and establishing reliability, and applications in complex system design.
Prod-UAKEN Dist-AMCEE

Quality Audits C 30 MIN
3/4 OR 1/2 INCH VIDEO CASSETTE
Discusses how audits can make the success difference. Describes the purposes of quality audits and lists some items for audit.
From The Quality Control Series.
Prod-MIOT Dist-MIOT

Quality Circle Concepts--A Series
IND
Cites 'quality circle concept' as being used by hundreds of U S organizations to provide opportunity to realize full potential of its greatest resource, the employees. Defines a 'quality circle' as a small group of employees from the same work area who meet together voluntarily on regular basis to identify and analyze work-related problems in their area, recommend solutions to management and, when possible, implement those solutions.
Prod-NCSU Dist-AMCEE

Definition	060 MIN
Introduction	060 MIN
Key Elements	060 MIN

Measurement And Results 060 MIN
Objectives 060 MIN
Operation Of Quality Circle Programs 060 MIN
Structure Of Successful Programs 060 MIN
Training 060 MIN

Quality Circles C
3/4 OR 1/2 INCH VIDEO CASSETTE
Describes how to involve employees in the program for organizational quality improvement.
From The Organizational Quality Improvement Series.
Prod-BNA Dist-BNA

Quality Circles - First Year In Review C 42 MIN
3/4 OR 1/2 INCH VIDEO CASSETTE
Explains a tried and proven concept, 'people involvement', which has added to employee morale and productivity improvement. Discusses why management must listen to, as well as direct, the work force.
Prod-SME Dist-SME

Quality Control Circles - A Lasting Impact? C 70 MIN
3/4 OR 1/2 INCH VIDEO CASSETTE A
Features Robert Cole, sociology professor at the University of Michigan, discussing quality control circles as a key factor in Japan's phenomenal productivity. Explains how they can be adopted in American business.
Prod-CBSFOX Dist-CBSFOX

Quality Control—A Series

Presents the essentials of a modern quality control program, control charts, acceptance sampling plans, specifications and tolerances and product liability.
Prod-MIOT Dist-MIOT

Attribute Sampling (MIL-STD-105D) 030 MIN
Concepts Of Acceptance Sampling Plans 033 MIN
Continuous Sampling Plans 029 MIN
Control Charts For Defectives 031 MIN
Control Charts For Mean And Range 035 MIN
Control Of Continuous Processes 030 MIN
Dodge-Romig Sampling Plans 037 MIN
Process-Capability Analysis 030 MIN
Product Liability 026 MIN
Quality Audits 030 MIN
Specifications And Tolerances 032 MIN
Variable Sampling (MIL-STD-414) 030 MIN
Vendor Certification And Rating 033 MIN

Quality Data Collection And Analysis C 30 MIN
3/4 OR 1/2 INCH VIDEO CASSETTE
Reviews several forms used by a company to collect and analyze quality data.
From The Quality Planning Series.
Prod-MIOT Dist-MIOT

Quality Difference, The C 14 MIN
16MM FILM OPTICAL SOUND
Advises on the assessment and selection of quality and confidence-building clothing by showing the artistry and craftsmanship that goes into the creation of a finely-tailored suit.
LC NO. 82-700179
Prod-MTP Dist-MTP Prodn-INSIGH 1981

Quality For All Seasons C 18 MIN
16MM FILM OPTICAL SOUND J-C A
Presents an overview of fruit and vegetable marketing, from harvest through packing, grading and distribution to wholesale markets. Shows how fresh fruits and vegetables are inspected for quality by the U S Department of Agriculture and cooperating state departments of agriculture.
LC NO. 76-703702
Prod-USDA Dist-USNAC 1974

Quality In Design C 29 MIN
3/4 INCH VIDEO CASSETTE
See series title for descriptive statement.
From The Kirk - American Furniture Series.
Prod-WGBHTV Dist-PUBTEL

Quality In The Making C 23 MIN
16MM FILM OPTICAL SOUND
Highlights the production and quality control of ball bearings at General Motors, New Departure Division.
Prod-GM Dist-GM

Quality Man, The C 30 MIN
16MM FILM, 3/4 OR 1/2 IN VIDEO C A
Presents the views of Philip B Crosby, who has been associated with quality in business and industry for 30 years, on the need for effective quality management. Lays out the philosophy that the key to quality is an attitude that must be generated from those at the top and points the way to quality improvements.
Prod-BBCTV Dist-FI

Quality Of A Nation, The C 30 MIN
16MM FILM OPTICAL SOUND
Celebrates Canada's 100th anniversary of confederation.
Prod-CRAF Dist-CFI

Quality Of Care, The C 35 MIN
16MM FILM OPTICAL SOUND PRO
Examines British attempts to find more humane ways to deal with the problems of the chronic schizophrenic. Focuses on the new and different problems created by the advent of antipsychotic drugs and discusses the long-acting fluphenazine decanoate known in the United States as Prolixin Decanoate.
Prod-SQUIBB Dist-SQUIBB

Quality Of Life C 20 MIN
3/4 OR 1/2 INCH VIDEO CASSETTE I-J
Deals with the effects of noise, air and visual pollution.
From The Terra - Our World Series.
Prod-MSDOE Dist-AITECH 1980

Quality Of Life C 30 MIN
3/4 OR 1/2 INCH VIDEO CASSETTE
Discusses the extent to which quality of life in any society is dependent on the society's population density. Explains how the decision to change the ideal family size affects lifestyles, patterns of behavior, birth control methods and sex education.
From The Family Planning Series.
Prod-NETCHE Dist-NETCHE 1970

Quality Of Life, The C 58 MIN
3/4 INCH VIDEO CASSETTE
Examines the influence of economics on the overall quality of life in America.
From The Moneywatchers Series.
Prod-SCIPG Dist-PUBTEL

Quality Planning—A Series

Emphasizes the philosophy of quality control, what quality is, its economics and organization and the development of quality consciousness.
From The Quality Control Series.
Prod-MIOT Dist-MIOT

Designing Quality Into A Product 026 MIN
Developing Quality Mindedness 031 MIN
Diagnostic Techniques To Identify The Causes 031 MIN
Economics Of Quality 031 MIN
Improving The Quality Image By Customer 023 MIN
Interfacing Quality And Reliability 032 MIN
Organization 031 MIN
Quality Data Collection And Analysis 030 MIN
Selling Quality To Management 032 MIN
What Is Quality? 030 MIN

Quality Practice C 56 MIN
3/4 OR 1/2 INCH VIDEO CASSETTE PRO
Responds to 1979 poll which found that almost half of all lawyers face difficulties in operating and managing their practices. Includes interviews with consumers, a dramatized lawyer-client consultation and a display of modern office equipment.
Prod-ABACPE Dist-ABACPE

Quality Programs And Inspection System Requirements - Quality Program... B 29 MIN
16MM FILM OPTICAL SOUND
Shows the military and civilian panel review Department of Defense specifications for a contractor's quality program and inspection system.
LC NO. 74-705462
Prod-USAF Dist-USNAC 1964

Quality, Our Competitive Edge C 28 MIN
16MM FILM OPTICAL SOUND
Explains the problem of terminal maintenance that was causing severe interruption in phone service in New York City and gives instructions for repair by telephone company service people.
LC NO. 77-700570
Prod-NYTELE Dist-NILCOM Prodn-NILCOM 1976

Quality, Productivity And Me—A Series
16MM FILM, 3/4 OR 1/2 IN VIDEO A
Shows how supervisors can make sure employees develop to maximum potential and that lines of communication are open.
Prod-PORTA Dist-RTBL 1982

Me And We 017 MIN
Me And You 012 MIN

Quantitative Approaches To Decision Making—A Series
IND
Introduces participants to quantitive approaches to decision making and assists in examination of individual decision making processes.
LC NO. 74-703326
Prod-EDSD Dist-EDSD 1969

Assessing The Value Of Information 29 MIN
Decision Making - Rationality Or Intuition 29 MIN
Decision Making Under Risk 29 MIN
Decision Making Under Uncertainty 29 MIN
Key Elements In The Decision Making Process 29 MIN
Systems Analysis - Means-Ends Diagnosis 29 MIN

Quantitative Transfer C 4 MIN
16MM FILM SILENT H-C A
Demonstrates three types of transfer involving precipitates, liquids and solids. Concentrates on maximum precipitate retention rather than filter preparation and the transference of the liquid from the beaker to volumetric flask. Includes rinsing the underside of the beaker lip and outside of funnel tip. Concludes with the reaction residue transfering from the beaker to the flask by dissolving in volatile solvent.
From The General Chemistry Laboratory Techniques Series.
LC NO. 79-708614
Prod-KALMIA Dist-KALMIA 1970

Quantum Numbers C 20 MIN
3/4 OR 1/2 INCH VIDEO CASSETTE
Illustrates the four quantum numbers. Develops possible values for the quantum numbers.
Prod-EDMEC Dist-EDMEC

Quarks C 8 MIN
3/4 OR 1/2 INCH VIDEO CASSETTE
Analyzes broadcast television in a series of 30 second intervals of layers of sounds. Juxtaposes images and written texts with TV patter.
Prod-EAI Dist-EAI

Quarks C 8 MIN
3/4 OR 1/2 INCH VIDEO CASSETTE
Analyzes broadcast television. Presents layers of sounds, images and written texts ironically juxtaposed with TV patter.
Prod-KITCHN Dist-KITCHN

Quarter Horses C 3 MIN
16MM FILM OPTICAL SOUND P-I
Discusses the horses known as quarter horses.
From The Of All Things Series.
Prod-BAILYL Dist-AVED

Quarter Panel Replacement, Pt 1 C 30 MIN
1/2 IN VIDEO CASSETTE BETA/VHS
Deals with auto body repair.
Prod-RMI Dist-RMI

Quarter Panel Replacement, Pt 2 C 42 MIN
1/2 IN VIDEO CASSETTE BETA/VHS
Deals with auto body repair.
Prod-RMI Dist-RMI

Quarterbacking To Win C 56 MIN
1/2 IN VIDEO CASSETTE BETA/VHS
Demonstrates such details of quarterbacking as the drop back pass, the rollout, handing off, and faking and reading the defense.
From The Football Fundamentals Series.
Prod-MOHOMV Dist-MOHOMV

Quartermaster Quality Control For Clothing And Textile Items B 17 MIN
16MM FILM OPTICAL SOUND
Discusses a new system of quality control inspection of the U S Army and describes its application to the manufacture of clothing and textile items.
LC NO. FIE59-262
Prod-USA Dist-USNAC 1959

Quartermaster Quality Control For General Supplies And Parts B 17 MIN
16MM FILM OPTICAL SOUND
Discusses a new system of quality control inspection of the U S Army and describes its application to the manufacture of general supplies and equipment.
LC NO. FIE59-263
Prod-USA Dist-USNAC 1959

Quartermaster Quality Control For Subsistence Items B 18 MIN
16MM FILM OPTICAL SOUND
Discusses a new system of quality control inspection of the U S Army and describes its application to the production of food and other subsistence items.
LC NO. FIE59-264
Prod-USA Dist-USNAC 1959

Quarters Guard, The C 4 MIN
16MM FILM OPTICAL SOUND
Demonstrates the military drill known as the Quarters Guard.
From The Ceremonial Drill Series.
LC NO. 77-702844
Prod-CDND Dist-CDND Prodn-FLMSMI 1976

Quasars C 29 MIN
3/4 INCH VIDEO CASSETTE C A
Reviews initial discovery of quasi-stellar radio objects, or quasars. Describes radio and Suzfert galaxies.
From The Project Universe - Astronomy Series. Lesson 28
Prod-COAST Dist-CDTEL Prodn-SCCON

Quasi At The Quackadero C 10 MIN
16MM FILM OPTICAL SOUND H-C A
Features Quasi, a science fiction boy who lives in a progressive household with his grownup friend Anita and little robot friend Rollo. Follows them on a day's outing to Quackadero, the Coney Island of the future.
LC NO. 76-700714
Prod-CRUIKS Dist-SERIUS 1976

Quaternions - A Herald Of Modern Algebra C 25 MIN
16MM FILM OPTICAL SOUND
Points out that one of the key mathematical developments on the path to modern algebraic ideas was the discovery of non-commutative algebra. Tells how the work of William Rowan Hamilton contributed to this field.
Prod-OPENU Dist-GPITVL

Que Fais-Tu Aujourd'hui C 10 MIN
3/4 OR 1/2 INCH VIDEO CASSETTE
Focuses on pastimes, intonation questions, inversion questions, and question formulas with inversion.
From The Salut - French Language Lessons Series.
Prod-BCNFL Dist-BCNFL 1984

Que Hacer C 90 MIN
16MM FILM OPTICAL SOUND
A Spanish language film. Depicts the different roads to revolution including the reality of Chile, Allende's election victory and the CIA, and a fictional story about a Peace Corps girl, a murdered priest and a political kidnapping.
Prod-LOBO Dist-IMPACT 1972

Que Hacer C 90 MIN
16MM FILM, 3/4 OR 1/2 IN VIDEO
Deals with the Salvador Allende election campaign in Chile. Combines fiction and documentary technique. Filmed during the 1970 elections in Chile.
Prod-NEWTIM Dist-NEWTIM

Que Hacer (English) C 90 MIN
16MM FILM OPTICAL SOUND
Depicts the different roads to revolution including the reality of Chile, Allende's election victory and the CIA and a fictional story about a Peace Corps girl, a murdered priest and a political kidnapping.
Prod-LOBO Dist-IMPACT 1972

Que Pasa USA—A Series
H-C A
Centers on a three generation Cuban-American family trying to bridge the generation gaps.
Prod-QUEPAS Dist-GPITVL 1978

Que Pasa, U S A—A Series

Features a bilingual sitcom that centers on three generations of a Cuban-American family living in Miami. Attempts to lessen the isolation that Hispanic teens might feel living in a cultural environment different from their own.
Prod-WPBTTV Dist-MDCPB

Ay, Abuela	030 MIN
Bad News	030 MIN
Bodas De Porcelana	030 MIN
Carmen Runs Away	030 MIN
Carmen's Night Out	030 MIN
Citizenship	030 MIN
Computer Friend	030 MIN
Confession, The	030 MIN
Dream, The	030 MIN
Encounter, The	030 MIN
Farewell Party, The	030 MIN
Fiesta De Quince	030 MIN
First Move, The	030 MIN
Garage Sale, The	030 MIN
Gato Encerrado	030 MIN
Growing Pains	030 MIN
Here Comes The Bride	030 MIN
Joe Goes To Heaven	030 MIN
Joe Goes To The Hospital	030 MIN
Juana Gets Smart	030 MIN
Los Novios	030 MIN
Malas Companias	030 MIN
Mi Abuelo	030 MIN
Nephew From New Jersey	030 MIN
Nirvana	030 MIN
Noche Cubana	030 MIN
Patria And Company	030 MIN
Que Paso	030 MIN
Se Necesita Ser Bilingue	030 MIN
Spring Cleaning	030 MIN
Super Chaperone	030 MIN
TV Interview	030 MIN
Vacation Pena Style	030 MIN
We Speak Spanish	030 MIN

Que Paso C 30 MIN
3/4 OR 1/2 INCH VIDEO CASSETTE
See series title for descriptive statement.
From The Que Pasa, U S A Series.
Prod-WPBTTV Dist-MDCPB

Que Viva Mexico (Russian) B 85 MIN
16MM FILM, 3/4 OR 1/2 IN VIDEO H-C A
A Russian language film with English subtitles. Presents a history of Mexico, divided into four separate novellas. Includes an exposition of the Tehuantepec jungles and the peculiarly quiet and peaceful lifestyles of the inhabitants, a love story of a poor peon and his wife, a novel devoted to bullfighting and romantic love, and a view of the 1910 Revolution.
Prod-MOSFLM Dist-IFEX 1931

Quebec - Ski C 5 MIN
16MM FILM OPTICAL SOUND
Depicts the superb terrain and beauty of winter in Quebec, Canada, where the snow falls abundantly and the ski season is long.
Prod-CTFL Dist-CTFL

Quebec - The Citadel City C 14 MIN
16MM FILM OPTICAL SOUND
Surveys Quebec and its surroundings and points out why the city is a tourist attraction.
From The New Candian City Series.
LC NO. FIA68-1224
Prod-MORLAT Dist-MORLAT 1968

Quebec - The French Disconnection C 28 MIN
16MM FILM, 3/4 OR 1/2 IN VIDEO H-C A
Features Canada's province of Quebec, which has a past with French and English nationalistic rivalry and a present with growing French separatist sentiments. An 80 percent majority has a specific viewpoint that will have an effect on the British community and on the future of the province.
Prod-THAMES Dist-MEDIAG 1977

Quebec In The Colder Months C 15 MIN
16MM FILM OPTICAL SOUND
Depicts winter sports in Canada.
LC NO. 76-702047
Prod-QDTFG Dist-CTFL Prodn-SDAPRO 1975

Quebec Kandahar B 23 MIN
16MM FILM OPTICAL SOUND
Presents a film on skiing in French and English.
LC NO. 76-702048
Prod-RYERC Dist-RYERC 1975

Quebec Kandahar (French) B 23 MIN
16MM FILM OPTICAL SOUND
Presents a French language film on skiing.
LC NO. 76-702048
Prod-RYERC Dist-RYERC 1974

Quebec Winter Carnival - Carnaval D'Hiver De Quebec C 10 MIN
16MM FILM OPTICAL SOUND
Surveys, without commentary, various activities associated with the Quebec Winter Carnival. Includes scenes of the street parade, ice sculptures, canoe and toboggan races, and the festivities of the participants.
LC NO. 70-705259
Prod-MORLAT Dist-CTFL 1969

Quebec, La Belle Province C 11 MIN
16MM FILM, 3/4 OR 1/2 IN VIDEO H-C
A French language film. Follows four Canadian students as they tour their native province of Quebec. Shows two boys on a motorcycle who travel the south bank of the St Lawrence while their two sisters ride in a car along the north bank in a race to Perce on the Gaspe Peninsula.
From The Pays Francophones Series.
Prod-EBEC Dist-EBEC

Queen And Prince Philip, The C 60 MIN
16MM FILM, 3/4 OR 1/2 IN VIDEO H-C A
Reviews the history of the collections of Queen Elizabeth and her family. Features Prince Philip talking about the modernization of the royal farms and the redecoration of the Edward III tower. Presents Prince Charles showing his collection of Eskimo sculpture.
From The Royal Heritage Series.
Prod-BBCTV Dist-FI 1981

Queen Bea C 14 MIN
16MM FILM OPTICAL SOUND
Presents the story of Bea Farber, who abandoned her career as a legal secretary to enter the sport of harness racing.
LC NO. 80-701258
Prod-USTROT Dist-LANGED Prodn-LANGED 1980

Queen Elizabeth II B 26 MIN
16MM FILM OPTICAL SOUND
Highlights the life of Queen Elizabeth II of England. Includes her life as a princess of the royal family, her marriage to Philip Mountbatten and her coronation in 1952.
From The Biography Series.
LC NO. FI67-269
Prod-WOLPER Dist-SF 1962

Queen Esther B 50 MIN
16MM FILM OPTICAL SOUND J-C A
Describes religious misunderstanding and prejudice and presents the message that God never fails those who love and serve him. Presents the book of Esther.
Prod-CAFM Dist-CAFM

Queen For A Day C 30 MIN
16MM FILM - 3/4 IN VIDEO
Shows how young children go about defining themselves and how this effort can affect their relationships with other family members. Tells how parents can ease this process.
From The Footsteps Series.
LC NO. 79-707257
Prod-USOE Dist-USNAC 1976

Queen Isabel And Her Spain C 32 MIN
16MM FILM, 3/4 OR 1/2 IN VIDEO J-H A
Studies key events during the reign of Isabel I of Spain, centering on the year 1492, when she consolidated her power. Shows palaces, monasteries and towns that were constructed during this era.
LC NO. 79-706408
Prod-PFMP Dist-IFB 1979

Queen Of Apollo C 12 MIN
16MM FILM OPTICAL SOUND
Features the 1970 debutante-queen of Apollo, an Exclusive New Orleans Mardi Gras ball, on her big night. By Richard Leacock.
Prod-PENNAS Dist-PENNAS

Queen Of Autumn - The Chrysanthemum In Japan C 22 MIN
16MM FILM, 3/4 OR 1/2 IN VIDEO H-C A
Depicts the various forms of chrysanthemum as they are grown and displayed in competition each year in Japan.
Prod-GREL Dist-IFB 1969

Queen Of Hearts B 60 MIN
16MM FILM OPTICAL SOUND
Presents a profile of Argentine political leader Eva Peron.
LC NO. 74-701024
Prod-CTV Dist-CTV 1972

Queen Of Heaven C 60 MIN
16MM FILM, 3/4 OR 1/2 IN VIDEO C A
Relates how Tiberius' empire declines and Claudius learns all of Livia's secrets, including his own eventual rule as Emperor.
From The I, Claudius Series. Number 7
Prod-BBCTV Dist-FI 1977

Queen Of Outer Space C 80 MIN
16MM FILM OPTICAL SOUND J-C A
Features Zsa Zsa Gabor in a science fiction tale of a planet populated and ruled by beautiful women.
Prod-CINEWO Dist-CINEWO 1958

Queen Of Spades By Alexander Pushkin, The C 15 MIN
16MM FILM, 3/4 OR 1/2 IN VIDEO J-C A
Presents a tale of the supernatural in which a greedy gambler meets a fitting fate at the hands of a former victim. Based on the short story The Queen Of Spades by Alexander Pushkin.
From The Short Story Series.
LC NO. 83-706230
Prod-IITC Dist-IU 1982

Queen Of The Cascades C 26 MIN
16MM FILM OPTICAL SOUND I-C A
Presents Mount Rainier, the superb landmark towering 14,410 feet above the Pacific Northwest, which allows Ty Hotchkiss to photograph wildlife in four different life zones without leaving the mountain environment. Reveals a broad range of plants and animals that otherwise would be spread across hundreds of miles of northward travel.
From The Audubon Wildlife Theatre Series.
Prod-AVEXP Dist-AVEXP

Queen Of The Cascades C 26 MIN
16MM FILM OPTICAL SOUND J-C
Illustrates the kinds of plants and animals found in the four life zones of the Canadian climate - the low level zone, the Canadian zone, the Hudsonian Zone and the Arctic Zone.
From The Audubon Wildlife Theatre Series.
LC NO. 72-701989
Prod-KEGPL Dist-AVEXP 1970

Queen Victoria - A Profile In Power C 26 MIN
16MM FILM, 3/4 OR 1/2 IN VIDEO H-C A
Explores, through the use of an imaginary historical interview, the life and role of Queen Victoria of England.
From The Profiles In Power Series.
Prod-LCOA Dist-LCOA Prodn-MCADLT 1976

Queen Victoria - A Profile In Power (Spanish) C 26 MIN
16MM FILM, 3/4 OR 1/2 IN VIDEO H-C A
Portrays Queen Victoria and her accomplishments.
From The Profiles In Power (Spanish) Series.
Prod-LCOA Dist-LCOA Prodn-MCADLT 1977

Queen Victoria And British History (1837-1901) C 28 MIN
16MM FILM, 3/4 OR 1/2 IN VIDEO H-C A
Features a biography of Queen Victoria and a global view of the changes that occurred during her reign.
From The World Leaders Series.
Prod-CFDLD Dist-CORF

Queen, The C 68 MIN
16MM FILM OPTICAL SOUND H-C A
A documentary film about a transvestite beauty pageant. Includes scenes of the contestants as they prepare for the pageant.
LC NO. 73-707582
Prod-LITVIS Dist-GROVE 1968

Queena Stovall - Life's Narrow Space C 19 MIN
16MM FILM OPTICAL SOUND J-C A
Presents 90-year-old Queena Stovall reminiscing about her life and the rural Virginia atmosphere captured in her paintings.
LC NO. 80-701591
Prod-BOWGRN Dist-BOWGRN 1980

Quenelles And Meat Dumplings C 30 MIN
1/2 IN VIDEO CASSETTE BETA/VHS
Shows how to prepare dumplings using pork, liver and fish.
From The Frugal Gourmet Series.
Prod-WTTWTV Dist-MTI

Quest C 30 MIN
16MM FILM, 3/4 OR 1/2 IN VIDEO
Presents a short fiction story by Ray Bradbury.
Prod-BASSS Dist-PFP 1983

Quest For Excellence C 18 MIN
3/4 OR 1/2 INCH VIDEO CASSETTE
Describes design and testing of new and improved equipment by Caterpillar Vice President.
Prod-IVCH Dist-IVCH

Quest For Flight C 23 MIN
16MM FILM, 3/4 OR 1/2 IN VIDEO I-J
Uses animation in simulating scenes from aviation history. Includes an account of Leonardo da Vinci's 15th-century helicopter.
From The Wide World Of Adventure Series.
Prod-AVATLI Dist-EBEC 1976

Quest For Food C 30 MIN
3/4 OR 1/2 INCH VIDEO CASSETTE C A
Shows the interconnections of science, technology and society as they relate to world food problems. Interviews Sterling Wortman, acting president of the Rockefeller Foundation and Frances Moore Lappe, director of the Institute for Food and Development Policy.
Prod-PSU Dist-GPITVL 1981

Quest For Humaness, The B 15 MIN
2 INCH VIDEOTAPE I
Attempts to form an appreciation of books and poetry. Tries to release the reader to the excellence of his spirit, to the uniqueness of his life and to the amazing panorama of human existence that surrounds him. Features selections such as 'RIKKI-TIKKI-TAVI' by Rudyard Kipling. (Broadcast quality)
From The Bill Martin Series. No. 10
Prod-BRITED Dist-GPITVL Prodn-KQEDTV

Quest For Integration In Europe, The C 29 MIN
2 INCH VIDEOTAPE
See series title for descriptive statement.
From The Course Of Our Times III Series.
Prod-WGBHTV Dist-PUBTEL

Quest For Peace—A Series
A
Presents a series of interviews with individuals who are knowledgeable about the nature of the human condition and what must be done differently in years ahead to reduce risk of nuclear war. Stimulates people to think about how they can contribute their own lives to achieve an enduring peace.
Prod-AACD Dist-AACD 1984

Albert Ellis, Psychology	029 MIN
B F Skinner, Psychology	029 MIN
Carl R Rogers, Psychology, Pt 1	029 MIN
Carl R Rogers, Psychology, Pt 2	029 MIN
Daniel Ellsberg, Government, Education	029 MIN
F Sherwood Rowland, Chemistry	029 MIN
H Jack Geiger, Community Medicine, Pt 1	029 MIN
H Jack Geiger, Community Medicine, Pt 2	029 MIN
Harold Willens, Business	029 MIN
Helen Caldicott, Pediatrics	029 MIN
Herbert F York, Physics, Government	029 MIN
Jerome D Frank, Psychology, Psychiatry	029 MIN
Jessie Bernard, Sociology	029 MIN
John Kenneth Galbraith, Economics, Government	029 MIN

John Marshall Lee, Military 029 MIN
John W Gardner, Psychology, Government, 029 MIN
Julian Bond, Government 029 MIN
Karl Menninger, Psychiatry, Education 029 MIN
Kenneth B Clark, Psychology 029 MIN
Norman Cousins, Education, Public Service 029 MIN
Paul R Ehrlich, Biology 029 MIN
Rollo May, Psychology 029 MIN
Sheila Tobias, Political Science, Education 029 MIN
Theodore M Hesburgh, Education, Religion, Pt 1 029 MIN
Theodore M Hesburgh, Education, Religion, Pt 2 029 MIN
William Sloane Coffin, Jr, Religion 029 MIN

Quest For Perfection C 10 MIN
16MM FILM OPTICAL SOUND
Presents the story of Linda Fratianne's hard work and efforts to win the gold medal in women's figure skating at the 1980 Winter Olympics. Emphasizes her achievements although she did not win the gold medal.
LC NO. 80-701485
Prod-IBM Dist-STEEGP 1980

Quest For Power - Sketches Of The American New Right C 50 MIN
16MM FILM, 3/4 OR 1/2 IN VIDEO
Examines the radical right-wing movement in the United States.
Prod-STDC Dist-NEWTIM

Quest For Self, The C 30 MIN
3/4 INCH VIDEO CASSETTE C A
Studies how values are revealed in seven different art forms. Defines terms used in critical evaluation of art forms.
From The Humanities Through The Arts With Maya Angelou Series. Lesson 1
Prod-COAST Dist-CDTEL Prodn-CICOCH

Quest For The Best C 10 MIN
3/4 OR 1/2 INCH VIDEO CASSETTE
Goes into women's track and field as top amateur athletes tell their stories of dedication to the accomplishment of their goals.
Prod-KAROL Dist-KAROL

Quest For The Best–A Series
I
Encourages the pupil to read widely and with discrimination, develop a greater appreciation of books and to think and to write creatively. (Broadcast quality)
Prod-DENVPS Dist-GPITVL Prodn-KRMATV

Adventure 20 MIN
Adventure, Real And Otherwise 20 MIN
Animal Stories 20 MIN
Animals - Snake, Llama 20 MIN
Biography 20 MIN
Book Week 20 MIN
December Days 20 MIN
Exploring New Fields 20 MIN
Fairy And Folk Tales 20 MIN
Family, No. 1 20 MIN
Family, No. 2 20 MIN
Famous Voyages 20 MIN
Fantasy 20 MIN
Find The Facts 20 MIN
Find The Facts - Television 20 MIN
Harvest Time 20 MIN
Historical Fiction, No. 1 20 MIN
Historical Fiction, No. 2 20 MIN
Humor, No. 1 20 MIN
Humor, No. 2 20 MIN
Let's Read Together 20 MIN
Myths, Legends And Folktales, No. 1 20 MIN
Myths, Legends And Folktales, No. 2 20 MIN
Myths, Legends And Folktales, No. 3 20 MIN
Other Lands And People 20 MIN
People And Events - Major Powell 20 MIN
Pioneering, No. 1 20 MIN
Pioneering, No. 2 20 MIN
Poetry 20 MIN
Suspense And Mystery 20 MIN
Too Good To Miss - Suggestions For Summer 20 MIN
Winter In Stories 20 MIN

Quest For The Killers–A Series

Documents the achievements, tragedies, triumphs and visions of doctors and scientists whose breakthroughs in disease research have helped change the face of modern medicine. Probes five different illnesses, illustrating the complex process of identifying, treating and ultimately eradicating disease. Features medical writer Dr June Goodfield.
Prod-PBS Dist-PBS

Kuru Mystery, The 060 MIN
Last Outcasts, The 060 MIN
Last Wild Virus, The 060 MIN
Three Valleys Of Saint Lucia, The 060 MIN
Vaccine On Trial 060 MIN

Quest Into Matter C 30 MIN
16MM FILM, 3/4 OR 1/2 IN VIDEO H-C
Describes how man's interest in shape and form is related to his study of molecules, the building blocks of nature. Explains the significance of symmetry and shape at the molecular level. Points out the relationship between the molecular structure of materials and their general properties.
From The Dimensions In Science, Series 1 Series.
Prod-OECA Dist-FI 1978

Quest Of Robert Goddard, The C 24 MIN
16MM FILM OPTICAL SOUND
Presents Robert Goddard, pioneer genius of rocketry, and his wife Ester and combines their color photography of space flights with records of experiments they have done over a 30-year period.
Prod-INTEXT Dist-REAF

Quest Of Robert Goddard, The X 24 MIN
16MM FILM OPTICAL SOUND H
Presents the compelling and exciting story of Robert Goddard, pioneer genius of rocketry. Combines the color photography of space flight with the record of his experiment photographed by Goddard's wife, Esther, over a thirty-year period.
Prod-REAF Dist-REAF 1968

Quest, A C 8 MIN
16MM FILM, 3/4 OR 1/2 IN VIDEO K A
Discusses how people can evaluate their personal goals and learn to feel good. Narrated by Hugh O'Brian.
Prod-SUTHRB Dist-SUTHRB

Quest, The C 28 MIN
16MM FILM OPTICAL SOUND
Explores the progress in the field of medicine during the last 25 years, which has been the result of the work of many scientists, including those in the pharmaceutical industry.
LC NO. 80-700072
Prod-HOFLAR Dist-GOLDST Prodn-THOMPN 1979

Quest, The C 15 MIN
3/4 OR 1/2 INCH VIDEO CASSETTE K-P
Deals with the history of French-Americans.
From The La Bonne Aventure Series.
Prod-MPBN Dist-GPITVL

Quest, The - An Artist And His Prey C 22 MIN
16MM FILM OPTICAL SOUND
Accompanies artist Guy Coheleach as he watches lions and leopards, giraffes and gazelles, bison and elk. Examines his wildlife paintings.
Prod-ACORN Dist-ACORN

Quest, The - An Artist And His Prey C 22 MIN
16MM FILM OPTICAL SOUND J-C A
Shows how artist Guy Coheleach derives his inspiration from his contacts with wild animals in their natural habitats.
LC NO. 74-703669
Prod-UONEFP Dist-ACORN 1974

Question Of Attitude, A C 12 MIN
16MM FILM OPTICAL SOUND H-C A
Examines the reluctance that many firms have towards the employment of physically hanicapped people. Shows that once the initial reluctance is overcome, it is found that the handicapped become loyal and productive employees who are capable of doing a fine job without any special considerations.
LC NO. 70-709831
Prod-ANAIB Dist-AUIS 1970

Question Of Balance, A C 29 MIN
16MM FILM OPTICAL SOUND J-H
Explains the role of the electric power industry in maintaining an adequate power supply in an era of increasing demand, fuel shortage, opposition to nuclear power and the need to protect the environment.
From The Energy - An Overview Series.
Prod-CENTRO Dist-CONPOW

Question Of Chairs, A - The Challenge To American Education B 45 MIN
16MM FILM OPTICAL SOUND H-C A
Deals in dramatic form with the problems faced and overcome by the American education system in its three-century evolution. Traces the growth and development of American education as a way of training people for citizenship in a democracy. Features Everett Sloane, Maureen Stapleton and Walter Abel.
Prod-ADL Dist-ADL

Question Of Consent - Rape C 20 MIN
16MM FILM, 3/4 OR 1/2 IN VIDEO
Looks at a court case in which a rape victim's inviting her assailant into her apartment causes the attorneys to argue over the issue of consent.
Prod-WORON Dist-MTI

Question Of Custody, A C 19 MIN
3/4 OR 1/2 INCH VIDEO CASSETTE
Attempts to determine what is in the best interests of the child when it comes to custody. Shows an interview between a social worker and a father who is filing for custody of his son, presently in custody of the mother.
From The Child Training Tapes Series.
Prod-OHIOSU Dist-UWISC

Question Of Duty, A C 26 MIN
16MM FILM, 3/4 OR 1/2 IN VIDEO
Describes humans' responsibility to all wildlife.
Prod-KAWVAL Dist-KAWVAL

Question Of Growth, A C 30 MIN
3/4 OR 1/2 INCH VIDEO CASSETTE C
See series title for descriptive statement.
From The Time's Harvest - Exploring The Future Series.
Prod-MDCPB Dist-MDCPB

Question Of Heating, The C 30 MIN
1/2 IN VIDEO CASSETTE BETA/VHS
Looks at the bedroom closets of an old house being renovated and at the heating plant in the basement. Discusses baseboard heat.
From The This Old House, Pt 1 - The Dorchester Series.
Prod-WGBHTV Dist-MTI

Question Of Hunting, A C 29 MIN
16MM FILM OPTICAL SOUND
Examines the controversies surrounding hunting for sport in America. Presents the arguments used by the critics of hunting and shows, from the point of view of the defenders, the contributions of sportsmen to wildlife conservation.
LC NO. 75-700156
Prod-RARMS Dist-MTP Prodn-MADISN 1974

Question Of Intimacy, A C 19 MIN
16MM FILM, 3/4 OR 1/2 IN VIDEO A
Shows author and lecturer Keith Miller as he leads a group of people in a thought-provoking discussion of intimate relationships in our society. Discusses what intimacy means and implies.
Prod-UMCOM Dist-ECUFLM 1981

Question Of Justice, A B 28 MIN
16MM FILM OPTICAL SOUND
Considers several recent court cases and studies which dramatize the problem of unpunished rapes. Shows that society and the criminal justice system often punish women for using violence in defending themselves against assaults.
LC NO. 76-702200
Prod-WNETTV Dist-WNETTV 1975

Question Of Learning, A C 60 MIN
3/4 OR 1/2 INCH VIDEO CASSETTE H-C A
Re-creates Ivan Pavlov's experiments which led to the discovery of the conditioned reflex. Looks at the investigation by Otto Pfungst of Clever Hans, a horse whose apparent knowledge of arithmetic was actually a response to subtle signals from his trainer.
From The Discovery Of Animal Behavior Series.
Prod-WNETTV Dist-FI 1982

Question Of Life, A C 29 MIN
16MM FILM - 3/4 IN VIDEO
Reviews the natural history of Mars, describes its present surface topography and considers its capacity to sustain life.
LC NO. 78-706268
Prod-NASA Dist-USNAC Prodn-WHROTV 1978

Question Of Loyalty, A C 50 MIN
16MM FILM, 3/4 OR 1/2 IN VIDEO H-C A
Describes the internment of Japanese-Americans in camps during World War II out of fear that they might help the enemy. Presents interviews with people who were actually interned at the Manzanar camp in California.
From The Yesterday's Witness In America Series.
Prod-BBCTV Dist-TIMLIF 1982

Question Of May, A C 22 MIN
16MM FILM - 3/4 IN VIDEO
Provides guidelines for clear communication between individuals.
From The Communication Series.
Prod-BNA Dist-BNA

Question Of Quality, A C 29 MIN
16MM FILM - 3/4 IN VIDEO
Stresses the importance of humankind's effect upon forest and wilderness areas. States that the quality of the wilderness experience, the quality of land resources and the quality of human life depend upon an awareness of this fact.
LC NO. 79-706154
Prod-USNPS Dist-USNAC 1979

Question Of Re-Election, The C 29 MIN
16MM FILM OPTICAL SOUND
Discusses how campaigning for election and re-election affects the working Congress, pointing out the advantages of the incumbents over the challengers.
From The Government Story Series. No. 4
LC NO. 76-707189
Prod-OGCW Dist-WBCPRO 1968

Question Of Survival, A C 30 MIN
16MM FILM, 3/4 OR 1/2 IN VIDEO
Presents a discussion by physicians and academics of the medical and economic effects of the arms race and of nuclear war.
Prod-PSR Dist-PSR 1982

Question Of Television Violence, The C 56 MIN
16MM FILM, 3/4 OR 1/2 IN VIDEO H-C A
Reports on the hearings of the United States Senate Subcommittee on Communications investigating the effects of televised violence. Explains that the hearings confirmed a correlation between violence on the screen and violence in real life.
Prod-NFBC Dist-PHENIX 1973

Question Of Values, A C 28 MIN
16MM FILM OPTICAL SOUND I-C A
Probes the attitudes of people in Searsport, Maine, as they confront a proposal to build an oil refinery on their bay. Presents arguments from both proponents and opponents of the refinery.
LC NO. 74-701899
Prod-NEWFLM Dist-NEWFLM 1972

Question Of Values, A C 24 MIN
16MM FILM, 3/4 OR 1/2 IN VIDEO H-C A
Describes Down's syndrome and some of the moral problems it raises. Presents three infants and three children, ranging in age from five years to 21 years, with their families. Includes information about the physical and psychological characteristics and the range of variation in a population of persons with Down's syndrome.
Prod-CWRU Dist-FEIL Prodn-FEIL 1973

Question Of Video Display Terminals, The C 27 MIN
3/4 OR 1/2 INCH VIDEO CASSETTE IND
Prod-PLACE Dist-PLACE 1982

Question Of War, The C 19 MIN
16MM FILM, 3/4 OR 1/2 IN VIDEO I-H
Uses animation to trace the history of war from the first armed conflict between primitive men to the highly complex nature of war in the 1970's.
LC NO. 81-706009
Prod-CGWEST Dist-CGWEST 1980

Question 7 B 107 MIN
16MM FILM OPTICAL SOUND H-C A

Sets an example for every young person who must someday decide between what is easy and expedient and what is right and honorable, and for every parent who wishes to instill faith in God and respect for the freedom and dignity of man.
Prod-CONCOR Dist-CPH

Questioning B 29 MIN
16MM FILM OPTICAL SOUND
Features a dialog between Indian spiritual leader Krishnamurti and the boys of Thacher school, Ojai, California. Contains his encouragement to question life and understand themselves, warns them against the traditional intellectual and argumentative approach to questioning. Comments on war as a way of life and acceptance of death and world problems such as hunger and poverty.
From The Real Revolution - Talks By Krishnamurti Series.
LC NO. 73-703037
Prod-KQEDTV Dist-IU 1968

Questioning In Science C 14 MIN
3/4 OR 1/2 INCH VIDEO CASSETTE J
Reveals that a research horticulturist is making progress toward more salt-tolerant crops because he learned to ask the right questions.
From The Whatabout Series.
Prod-AITV Dist-AITECH 1983

Questioning Skills C 30 MIN
3/4 OR 1/2 INCH VIDEO CASSETTE T
Shows questioning builds concept formation through increased involvement.
From The Stretch Strategies For Teaching Handicapped Children Series.
Prod-HUBDSC Dist-HUBDSC

Questioning Skills C 30 MIN
16MM FILM, 3/4 OR 1/2 IN VIDEO T S
Demonstrates types of creative questions that require students to formulate ideas reather than simply recall facts.
From The Project STRETCH (Strategies To Train Regular Educators To Teach Children With...) Series. Module 1
LC NO. 80-706637
Prod-METCO Dist-HUBDSC 1980

Questioning Techniques And Probing C 29 MIN
3/4 OR 1/2 INCH VIDEO CASSETTE T
Deals with a teaching strategy called probing, which is aimed at increasing reflexive thinking in students. Demonstrates different types of probing questions.
From The Strategies Of Effective Teaching Series.
Prod-GSDE Dist-AITECH 1980

Questions C 20 MIN
16MM FILM OPTICAL SOUND
Presents a high school student discussion on smoking. Focuses on the social pressures that impel them to smoke and the emotional attitudes that make them receptive to those pressures.
LC NO. 74-706384
Prod-USDHEW Dist-USNAC 1969

Questions C
16MM FILM - 3/4 IN VIDEO A
Deals with how to formulate and use questions, the five functions of questions, the question matrix, the question map for preparation and applications.
From The Art Of Negotiating Series. Module 5
Prod-BNA Dist-BNA 1983

Questions C 29 MIN
2 INCH VIDEOTAPE
Presents information on teenage smoking.
From The Synergism - In Today's World Series.
Prod-WETATV Dist-PUBTEL

Questions - Answers—A Series
16MM FILM, 3/4 OR 1/2 IN VIDEO I-J
Presents a series of open-ended films dealing with values and decisions faced by young people.
Prod-DISNEY Dist-WDEMCO

Being Right - Can You Still Lose 021 MIN
Death - How Can You Live With It 019 MIN

Questions And Answers C 15 MIN
2 INCH VIDEOTAPE I
Discusses interviewer and interviewee responsibilities and shows an interview of a well-known personality.
From The Images Series.
Prod-CVETVC Dist-GPITVL

Questions And Answers B 29 MIN
3/4 OR 1/2 INCH VIDEO CASSETTE IND
Deals with understanding the nature of questions from the audience, and techniques for fielding questions accurately.
From The Making More Effective Technical Presentations Series.
Prod-UMCEES Dist-AMCEE

Questions And Answers C 33 MIN
16MM FILM, 3/4 OR 1/2 IN VIDEO
Provides answers from experts on many of the questions people ask about career education.
From The School Board Debates - Career Education Series.
Prod-NSBA Dist-SWRLFF

Questions And Answers - Globes C 13 MIN
3/4 OR 1/2 INCH VIDEO CASSETTE P
Presents an interview show in which a panel of experts provides information on the globe.
From The Under The Blue Umbrella Series.
Prod-SCETV Dist-AITECH 1977

Questions And Answers - Making Things Grow I C 30 MIN
2 INCH VIDEOTAPE
Features Thalassa Cruso discussing different aspects of gardening and answering questions.
From The Making Things Grow I Series.
Prod-WGBHTV Dist-PUBTEL

Questions And Answers - Making Things Grow II C 30 MIN
2 INCH VIDEOTAPE
Features Thalassa Cruso discussing different aspects of gardening and answering questions.
From The Making Things Grow II Series.
Prod-WGBHTV Dist-PUBTEL

Questions And Answers - Maps C 14 MIN
3/4 OR 1/2 INCH VIDEO CASSETTE P
Offers information on maps.
From The Under The Blue Umbrella Series.
Prod-SCETV Dist-AITECH 1977

Questions And Answers About EPA's Final PMN Rule C 21 MIN
3/4 OR 1/2 INCH VIDEO CASSETTE A
Jack McCarthy, director of the Toxic Substances Control Act Assistance Office of the Environmental Protection Agency, chairs a panel discussion of the EPA's May 1983 ruling on final Premanufacture Notification. Covers the most important elements of the rule, information changes, requirements for importers and exporters, and how a manufacturer can determine whether or not a specific chemical substance is on the inventory.
From The Pre-Manufacture Notification Rule (EPA, May 1983) Series.
LC NO. 84-706424
Prod-USEPA Dist-USNAC 1983

Questions And Answers I C 29 MIN
2 INCH VIDEOTAPE
Features Dr Puryear who examines and answers questions sent by viewers from all over the country during the broadcast of the Who Is Man series.
From The Who Is Man Series.
Prod-WHROTV Dist-PUBTEL

Questions And Answers II C 29 MIN
2 INCH VIDEOTAPE
Features Dr Puryear who examines and answers questions sent by viewers from all over the country during the broadcast of the Who Is Man series.
From The Who Is Man Series.
Prod-WHROTV Dist-PUBTEL

Questions And Answers III - Making Things Grow III C 29 MIN
2 INCH VIDEOTAPE
See series title for descriptive statement.
From The Making Things Grow III Series.
Prod-WGBHTV Dist-PUBTEL

Questions And Answers IV - Making Things Grow III C 29 MIN
2 INCH VIDEOTAPE
See series title for descriptive statement.
From The Making Things Grow III Series.
Prod-WGBHTV Dist-PUBTEL

Questions For The Statistician B
16MM FILM OPTICAL SOUND
Underlines the need for sampling. Chooses a sample statistic from a population of 52 permutations of a pack of playing cards and concludes by proving the formula for the variance of the binomial distribution using the new viewpoint of a sampling distribution.
Prod-OPENU Dist-OPENU

Questions For Thinking C 28 MIN
16MM FILM, 3/4 OR 1/2 IN VIDEO C A
Explores what schools are doing, not doing or could be doing to encourage students to think.
From The Survival Skills For The Classroom Teacher Series.
Prod-MFFD Dist-FI 1972

Questions Most Frequently Asked C 30 MIN
16MM FILM, 3/4 OR 1/2 IN VIDEO H-C A
Provides information about funerals, telling which questions to ask funeral directors, various ways of dealing with arrangements, and other death customs.
Prod-KLEINW Dist-KLEINW 1979

Questions Of Hamlet - Why Does Hamlet Delay C 45 MIN
3/4 OR 1/2 INCH VIDEO CASSETTE
Strives to answer the question of why Hamlet delayed in Shakespeare's play Hamlet.
From The Survey Of English Literature I Series.
Prod-MDCPB Dist-MDCPB

Questions Of Time C 30 MIN
16MM FILM, 3/4 OR 1/2 IN VIDEO I-H
Tells the story of time as the most elusive of all man's measurements.
From The World We Live In Series.
Prod-TIMELI Dist-MGHT 1968

Questors, The C 17 MIN
16MM FILM OPTICAL SOUND
Uses a story about a man and what happens to him during a family vacation to explain the need of man to give in order to receive even though giving is a matter of choice.
LC NO. 77-711411
Prod-MATTCO Dist-MATTCO 1971

Quetzalcoatl B 20 MIN
16MM FILM OPTICAL SOUND
Presents the legend of Quetzalcoatl, the fairest god of the Aztecs. Gods and mortals are portrayed by masks, statuettes and other artifacts made by preColumbian Indians of Mexico.
LC NO. FIA52-424
Prod-USC Dist-USC 1951

Quetzalcoatl (Spanish) B 20 MIN
16MM FILM OPTICAL SOUND
Presents the legend of Quetzalcoatl, the fairest god of the Aztecs. Gods and mortals are portrayed by masks, statuettes and other artifacts made by preColumbian Indians of Mexico.
LC NO. 75-703224
Prod-USC Dist-USC 1954

Qui A Casse... C 13 MIN
16MM FILM OPTICAL SOUND J A
From The En Francais, Set 1 Series.
Prod-PEREN Dist-CHLTN 1969

Qui Est-Ce B 13 MIN
16MM FILM OPTICAL SOUND I-H
See series title for descriptive statement.
From The Les Francais Chez Vous Series. Set I, Lesson 01
Prod-PEREN Dist-CHLTN 1967

Quiche Lorraine C 29 MIN
2 INCH VIDEOTAPE
A French language videotape. Features Julia Child of Haute Cuisine au Vin demonstrating how to prepare Quiche Lorraine. With captions.
From The French Chef (French) Series.
Prod-WGBHTV Dist-PUBTEL

Quiche Lorraine And Co C 30 MIN
3/4 OR 1/2 INCH VIDEO CASSETTE H-C
Julia Child demonstrates how to bake a quiche.
From The French Chef Series.
Prod-WGBH Dist-KINGFT

Quick B 98 MIN
16MM FILM OPTICAL SOUND
A German language film with English subtitles. Tells the story of a young girl who falls in love with a clown without ever having seen his face, and as a result of mixups and mistaken identities, the original love story turns into a comedy with a very happy ending.
Prod-WSTGLC Dist-WSTGLC 1932

Quick As Light C 25 MIN
16MM FILM, 3/4 OR 1/2 IN VIDEO I-H
Shows experiments which explain wavelength and color.
From The Start Here - Adventure Into Science Series.
Prod-LANDMK Dist-LANDMK

Quick Esthetic Provisionalization During Crown And Bridge Therapy C 10 MIN
16MM FILM, 3/4 OR 1/2 IN VIDEO PRO
Demonstrates how a preformed polypropylene splint is used to fabricate a temporary bridge intraorally. Discusses the principles of temporization.
Prod-USVA Dist-USNAC 1984

Quick Flicks—A Series
I-C A S
Teaches the American sign language alphabet.
Prod-JOYCE Dist-JOYCE 1975

Numbers In Sign Language 15 MIN
Sign Language Alphabet, The 15 MIN

Quick Relaxation C 10 MIN
2 INCH VIDEOTAPE
See series title for descriptive statement.
From The Janaki Series.
Prod-WGBHTV Dist-PUBTEL

Quick Rise C 5 MIN
16MM FILM OPTICAL SOUND K-C A
Uses stop-motion techniques to show the complete construction of a high rise office building.
LC NO. 78-714049
Prod-GERGOR Dist-VIEWFI 1971

Quick-Witted Hikoichi C 16 MIN
16MM FILM OPTICAL SOUND
A Japanese language film. Tells the story of Japan's feudal age Hikoichi, the quick witted who saves his lord and province.
Prod-UNIJAP Dist-UNIJAP 1970

Quickest Draw In The West C 12 MIN
16MM FILM OPTICAL SOUND J-C A
Portrays the Strategic Air Command as sheriff guarding over the west, stretching from the Berlin Wall to the China coast.
Prod-NAA Dist-RCKWL

Quickie, A C 2 MIN
16MM FILM, 3/4 OR 1/2 IN VIDEO
Shows a couple race from the point of meeting through lovemaking in less than two minutes.
Prod-MMRC Dist-MMRC

Quidditas C 30 MIN
3/4 OR 1/2 INCH VIDEO CASSETTE
Captures the restless spirit and elusive light of the different modes of Outer Cape Cod. Video artist Frank Gillette adds a new dimension to landscape painting through video art.
Prod-EAI Dist-EAI

Quiddity Tree C 17 MIN
16MM FILM OPTICAL SOUND I-C A
Presents a fantasy film which illustrates the history of man's relationship with nature from the time of the Garden of Eden to the future.
LC NO. 75-700000
Prod-WASDE Dist-MARALF Prodn-MARALF 1975

Quiescence C 10 MIN
16MM FILM OPTICAL SOUND I-H

Uses a sailing voyage among the islands and waterways of Northwestern Washington and British Columbia as the setting for a visual poem.
LC NO. 72-709994
Prod-SOUND Dist-SOUND 1970

Quiet Afternoon C 20 MIN
3/4 OR 1/2 INCH VIDEO CASSETTE C A
Shows an interracial couple sharing an afternoon of music, massage and sexuality.
Prod-NATSF Dist-MMRC

Quiet Champion, The (Captioned) C 59 MIN
3/4 OR 1/2 INCH VIDEO CASSETTE P A
Presents Gallaudet College student Danny Fitzpatrick as he trains for and competes in World Games for the Deaf in Romania.
Prod-GALCO Dist-GALCO 1978

Quiet Crisis, The C 55 MIN
3/4 OR 1/2 INCH VIDEO CASSETTE J-C A
Examines the use of water resources in transportation, industry, recreation, energy and food production. Discusses the issue of of a water crisis and emphasizes the need to attend to and correct negative trends before an irreversible freshwater shortage occurs.
From The Moore Report Series.
LC NO. 81-707441
Prod-WCCOTV Dist-IU 1981

Quiet Evening With Mother Goose, A C 30 MIN
3/4 INCH VIDEO CASSETTE H-C A
Presents the First Poetry Quartet reading children's poetry.
From The Anyone For Tennyson Series.
Prod-NETCHE Dist-GPITVL

Quiet Life C 27 MIN
16MM FILM OPTICAL SOUND
Shows how the Japanese try to keep protecting beauty and a tranquil mind in the midst of this mechanical civilization. Points out that these attempts to regain a quiet life can be found in offices, urban construction sites, plants and in the lives of citizens. Explains that loving nature and a sense of beauty helps them understand the charms of the world, gives them composure of mind and increases their reserve of energy.
Prod-KAJIMA Dist-UNIJAP 1970

Quiet Man, The C 129 MIN
16MM FILM OPTICAL SOUND
Tells the story of a fighter who goes back to his hometown in Ireland to forget the tragic fight in which he killed a man. Stars John Wayne.
Prod-REP Dist-TWYMAN 1952

Quiet Nacelle C 17 MIN
16MM FILM OPTICAL SOUND
Depicts flight tests, complete with noise level recordings, which compare a 707 with untreated nacelles and an identical aircraft complete with treated nacelles. Uses animation to illustrate noise comparisons for approach and takeoff operations.
LC NO. 75-701730
Prod-BOEING Dist-USNAC 1974

Quiet One, The B 67 MIN
16MM FILM, 3/4 OR 1/2 IN VIDEO
Presents the story of an unloved Negro child lost in loneliness and delinquency, who is rehabilitated at the Wiltwyck School for Boys, founded by the Protestant Episcopal Church.
Prod-FDOC Dist-TEXFLM 1948

Quiet Revolution C 15 MIN
16MM FILM OPTICAL SOUND H-C A
Depicts the revolution which has occurred in the Jacksonville area with the merging of the county and city government and other aspects of Florida living.
Prod-FLADC Dist-FLADC

Quiet Revolution Of Mrs Harris, The C 20 MIN
16MM FILM, 3/4 OR 1/2 IN VIDEO H-C A
Gives a housewife's account of her gradual self-realization in becoming a person. Features Gloria Harris, talking about her dissatisfaction with her roles as mother, wife and housekeeper. Follows her efforts to establish her own identity by attending college and becoming a professional.
Prod-CINELO Dist-MEDIAG 1976

Quiet Revolution, The C 28 MIN
16MM FILM OPTICAL SOUND K-H T
Depicts staffing patterns in five different schools that have initiated team teaching, flexible scheduling, non-graded elementary programs and other innovations. Explains that improvement in American education can only follow when the teacher has time to plan, analyze and teach. Suggests some alternatives for educators who desire action.
LC NO. FIA67-1626
Prod-NEA Dist-EDUC Prodn-STNFRD 1967

Quiet Summer, The B 28 MIN
16MM FILM OPTICAL SOUND
Describes how in 1965 a summer project operated by youths ended annual youth rioting in Hampton Beach, New Hampshire.
LC NO. 74-705463
Prod-USOJD Dist-USNAC 1965

Quiet Too Long B 29 MIN
16MM FILM OPTICAL SOUND A
Studies the new militancy of teachers who are rising in protest against poor school facilities. Observes the work of two teachers in the classroom, on the streets, in budget meetings and at a space center.
LC NO. 77-706448
Prod-NEA Dist-NEA Prodn-GUG 1967

Quiet Victory C 35 MIN
16MM FILM OPTICAL SOUND PRO
Shows the responsibilites of four nurses in four diabetes cases--in the detection center, outpatient department, hospital and a patients home.
From The Diabetes Nursing Series.
LC NO. 67-5617
Prod-ANANLN Dist-AJN 1967

Quiet Warrior, The C 28 MIN
16MM FILM OPTICAL SOUND
Tells the story of a Naval Air Reserve squadron. Shows how the reservist-citizens keep in readiness by training on weekends.
LC NO. 74-705463
Prod-USN Dist-USNAC 1968

Quiet, Please C 22 MIN
16MM FILM OPTICAL SOUND
Prod-FENWCK Dist-FENWCK

Quieting A Noisy Refrigerator B 16 MIN
16MM FILM, 3/4 OR 1/2 IN VIDEO
Shows how to check and correct compressor and motor noises, noises caused by wear or looseness of parts and noises caused by high head pressure or an oillogged evaporator.
From The Refrigeration Service - Domestic Units Series. No. 10
LC NO. 81-707341
Prod-USOE Dist-USNAC Prodn-ROCKT 1945

Quilted Friendship C 6 MIN
3/4 OR 1/2 INCH VIDEO CASSETTE
Shows two women who have almost completed a quilt together when they discover that they have completely different views of their friendship.
Prod-WMEN Dist-WMEN

Quilting C 30 MIN
3/4 OR 1/2 INCH VIDEO CASSETTE
Demonstrates the basic quilting process, including showing how to add unique details, patchwork, applique, lazy daisy stitches and the Italian technique of trapunto.
From The Erica Series.
Prod-WGBHTV Dist-KINGFT

Quilting - Patterns Of Love C 20 MIN
3/4 INCH VIDEO CASSETTE
Traces the evolution of quilting from a necessary skill to a highly prized folk art. Takes a look at the use of quilts to express social concerns as well as the resurgence of quilting as a creative craft.
Prod-LAURON Dist-LAURON

Quilting Party C 2 MIN
16MM FILM OPTICAL SOUND
Presents an artistic view of quilting patterns set to the fiddle music of the Red Clay Ramblers.
Prod-TRIF Dist-TRIF

Quilting Women C 28 MIN
16MM FILM - 3/4 IN VIDEO
Focuses on women artists who create works of art in textile. Traces the entire process of quiltmaking.
Prod-APPAL Dist-APPAL 1976

Quinceaneras C 23 MIN
3/4 OR 1/2 INCH VIDEO CASSETTE
Explores the traditional ceremony and party held when a Chicana comes into womanhood.
From The Images / Imagenes Series.
Prod-TUCPL Dist-LVN

Quingalik And The Sea C 6 MIN
16MM FILM, 3/4 OR 1/2 IN VIDEO K-P
Tells how the Eskimo hunter is accidentally set adrift on an ice floe during the Arctic spring. Shows how he remembers what an old hunter told him, improvises a raft and reaches home safely.
From The Inuit Legends Series.
Prod-ANIMET Dist-BCNFL 1982

Quinkins, The C 11 MIN
16MM FILM, 3/4 OR 1/2 IN VIDEO
Presents the story of two groups of Quinkins, the spirit people of the country of Cape York. Explains that one group consists of small, fat-bellied bad fellows who steal children and the other is comprised of humorous, whimsical spirits. Based on the book The Quinkins by Percy Trezise and Dick Roughsey.
Prod-WWS Dist-WWS Prodn-SCHNDL 1982

Quit Kicking Sand In Our Faces C 20 MIN
3/4 OR 1/2 INCH VIDEO CASSETTE
Presents vignettes which illustrate and satirize sexual stereotyping.
Prod-KITCHN Dist-KITCHN

Quitting - Tips For Smokers C 28 MIN
16MM FILM - 3/4 IN VIDEO H-C A
Presents an interview with the Director of the New York City Smoking Withdrawal Clinic.
Prod-LAWREN Dist-LAWREN

Quiver Of Life, The C 57 MIN
16MM FILM, 3/4 OR 1/2 IN VIDEO H-C A
Explores the evolution of music by looking at how the ancient civilizations of China, Japan, Sumeria and Greece created music. Presents the primeval rhythms of Africa and shows the recent discoveries of prehistoric instruments. Demonstrates a soundscape, a gigantic mobile that emits a cacophony of unique sounds.
From The Music Of Man Series.
Prod-CANBC Dist-TIMLIF 1981

Quo Vadis C 3 MIN
16MM FILM, 3/4 OR 1/2 IN VIDEO H-C A
Emphasizes the problem of overpopulation and an insufficient food supply. Shows cells dividing into more complex forms of life, culminating in the human face, which turns into many faces and then just many mouths. Pictures the earth being devoured by such hungry mouths.
Prod-ZAGREB Dist-MGHT 1974

Quotations From Chairman Stu B 22 MIN
16MM FILM OPTICAL SOUND
Presents a story about an aluminum powder factory in New Jersey that is importing and exploiting Haitians. Tells how chaos ensues when the youngest son of the factory owner returns home from college espousing Maoist ideals and discovers the injustice.
Prod-USC Dist-USC 1980

Quote, Unquote C 15 MIN
3/4 OR 1/2 INCH VIDEO CASSETTE P
Employs a magician named Amazing Alexander and his assistants to explore the use of quotation marks.
From The Magic Shop Series. No. 13
LC NO. 83-706158
Prod-CVETVC Dist-GPITVL Prodn-WCVETV 1982

Quyhn Lap Leprosorium C 10 MIN
16MM FILM OPTICAL SOUND
Shows a leprosorium in Vietnam that has been the frequent target of United States bombings.
Prod-NEWSR Dist-NEWSR

Quynh Leprosarium B 10 MIN
16MM FILM OPTICAL SOUND
Shows Quynh leprosarium in Vietnam that has been bombed 106 times by U S planes. Shows the continued devastation of Vietnam.
Prod-UNKNWN Dist-SFN 1967

R

R A / Osteo - Two Different Diseases C 17 MIN
16MM FILM OPTICAL SOUND
Deals with rheumatoid arthritis and osteoarthritis, two different diseases which attack different age groups. Defines both types of arthritis, appropriate techniques of diagnosis, and a general professional overview of current methods of treatment.
Prod-WSTGLC Dist-WSTGLC

R And D And Innovation C 45 MIN
3/4 OR 1/2 INCH VIDEO CASSETTE
See series title for descriptive statement.
From The Technology, Innovation, And Industrial Development Series.
Prod-MIOT Dist-MIOT

R Buckminster Fuller - Prospects For Humanity B 30 MIN
16MM FILM OPTICAL SOUND H-C A
Presents excerpts from speeches by R Buckminster Fuller during which Dr Fuller predicts the unification of mankind as a result of technology derived from space exploration, computer applications and systems analysis.
From The Spectrum Series.
Prod-NET Dist-IU 1967

R C Gorman C 20 MIN
3/4 OR 1/2 INCH VIDEO CASSETTE
Profiles American Indian artist R C Gorman, a Navajo painter and printmaker.
From The American Indian Artists Series.
Prod-KAETTV Dist-PBS

R D Laing - A Dialog On Mental Illness And Its Treatment C 22 MIN
16MM FILM OPTICAL SOUND H-C
Presents R D Laing answering Dr Desmond Kelly's interview queries concerning the success of his career in psychiatry. Discusses schizophrenia, Freud's studies on hysteria, the semantics of psychiatry, the Kingsley Hall therapeutic experiment, the birth ritual and his criticism of psychiatry.
LC NO. 76-702269
Prod-HAR Dist-HAR Prodn-MELTZN 1976

R D Laing On R D Laing C 15 MIN
16MM FILM OPTICAL SOUND H-C
Presents psychiatrist R D Laing discussing his career with Dr Desmond Kelly. Reveals the influence of his childhood, family life and teenage scientific interests on his decision to enter medicine and psychiatry. Includes Laing's view of his career future.
LC NO. 76-702268
Prod-HAR Dist-HAR Prodn-MELTZN 1976

R D Laing's Glasgow C 25 MIN
16MM FILM, 3/4 OR 1/2 IN VIDEO H-C A
A shortened version of the motion picture R D Laing's Glasgow. Presents psychiatrist R D Laing on a tour of the city of Glasgow.
From The Cities Series.
Prod-NIELSE Dist-LCOA Prodn-MCGREE 1980

R D Laing's Glasgow C 51 MIN
16MM FILM, 3/4 OR 1/2 IN VIDEO I-C A
Presents R D Laing, psychiatrist and poet, as he tours his native city of Glasgow, Scotland.
From The Cities Series.
Prod-NIELSE Dist-LCOA Prodn-MCGREE 1978

R H And Left Shift Keys B 30 MIN
2 INCH VIDEOTAPE
From The Typewriting, Unit 1 - Keyboard Control Series.
Prod-GPITVL Dist-GPITVL

R I P Harry Sparks C 21 MIN
16MM FILM, 3/4 OR 1/2 IN VIDEO IND
Stresses safety precautions such as inspecting tools and tagging those which are defective before tackling electrical repair jobs.
Prod-IAPA Dist-IFB 1972

R I P Harry Sparks (Spanish) C 21 MIN
16MM FILM, 3/4 OR 1/2 IN VIDEO IND
Stresses safety precautions such as inspecting tools and tagging those which are defective before tackling electrical repair jobs.
Prod-IAPA Dist-IFB 1972

R M I Stress Management Series—A Series

Covers stress relief techniques, information on health, nutrition, exercise and recreation, progressive relaxation, self-hypnosis and meditation, as well as body stretching and realignment exercises.
Prod-RMI Dist-RMI

Health And Nutrition Habits
Introduction And Overview
Personal Stress Management
Psychological And Emotional Habits
Stress Relief Techniques

R Sound, The C 15 MIN
3/4 INCH VIDEO CASSETTE P
Explains the pronunciation of the r sound.
From The New Talking Shop Series.
Prod-BSPTV Dist-GPITVL 1978

R Sound, The - Reddy Rooster's New Tail C 15 MIN
2 INCH VIDEOTAPE P
Introduces some of the consonant sounds met in early reading. Identifies the written letter with the spoken sound.
From The Listen And Say Series.
Prod-MPATI Dist-GPITVL

R T Gribbon - Interview On Campus Ministry C 29 MIN
3/4 OR 1/2 INCH VIDEO CASSETTE A
Features R T Gribbon as he addresses the role of higher education and how churches can help students who are entering college.
Prod-WHSPRO Dist-ECUFLM 1981

R T Techniques C 30 MIN
3/4 OR 1/2 INCH VIDEO CASSETTE T
See series title for descriptive statement.
From The Dealing In Discipline Series.
Prod-UKY Dist-GPITVL 1980

R W (Real World) (French) C 26 MIN
16MM FILM, 3/4 OR 1/2 IN VIDEO I-J
The French version of the film and videorecording R W (Real World).
Prod-ATLAF Dist-BCNFL 1983

R.W. C 26 MIN
16MM FILM, 3/4 OR 1/2 IN VIDEO I-J
Shows how people of all ages sometimes have difficulty grappling with their real worlds. Looks at an eleven-year old boy who was advanced to high school and is unable to fit in, his mother who has self doubts about returning to work, and his father who masks his own insecurities in a blustery, go-get-'em attitude. Shows how they confront their problems.
LC NO. 83-707158
Prod-ATLAF Dist-BCNFL 1981

R-A-P - Radiological Assistance Program C 27 MIN
16MM FILM OPTICAL SOUND
Re-enacts three radiological emergencies to show the readiness and proficiency of radiological assistance teams as they put to work their specialized professional skills and equipment in dealing with accidents involving radiological materials.
LC NO. FIE66-12
Prod-USAEC Dist-USNAC 1965

R-Blends, The - Brooms And Crutches, Using The Structure Of The Word C 18 MIN
3/4 OR 1/2 INCH VIDEO CASSETTE J-H
See series title for descriptive statement.
From The Getting The Word Series. Unit II
Prod-SCETV Dist-AITECH 1974

R-G-B C 11 MIN
3/4 OR 1/2 INCH VIDEO CASSETTE
Shows a performer exploring the color system in which he is trapped.
From The Three Short Tapes Series.
Prod-EAI Dist-EAI

RAAF Heritage C 28 MIN
16MM FILM OPTICAL SOUND J-C A
Presents the history of the first fifty years of the Royal Australian Air Force. Includes scenes of action in World Wars I and II, Korea and Vietnam.
LC NO. 71-713558
Prod-ANAIB Dist-AUIS 1971

Rabbeting And Shaping An Edge On Straight Stock B 18 MIN
16MM FILM, 3/4 OR 1/2 IN VIDEO
Explains the principles of the shaper operation. Shows how to set up a machine for cutting rabbets and for shape molding, and describes the process.
From The Precision Wood Machining - Operations On The Spindle Shaper Series. No. 1
Prod-USOE Dist-USNAC Prodn-RCM 1945

Rabbit And Foxes On Wheels C 13 MIN
16MM FILM OPTICAL SOUND H-C A
Describes the U S Cycling Federation Competitive Stock-Bike Program, a nationwide program involving all municipalities in an amateur competitive cycling network.
LC NO. 79-700088
Prod-MENCI Dist-MENCI 1979

Rabbit Ears C 33 MIN
3/4 OR 1/2 INCH VIDEO CASSETTE
Obscures that fine balance which separates a child's imagination and the realities of adulthood.
Prod-EAI Dist-EAI

Rabbit For Alice, A C 15 MIN
16MM FILM, 3/4 OR 1/2 IN VIDEO P-I
Presents the story of Alice, who is lonely in the new neighborhood she and her family have moved to. Tells how her father buys her a rabbit named Peter and recounts the adventures they have together.
Prod-AMITAI Dist-FLMFR 1984

Rabbit Hill C 53 MIN
16MM FILM, 3/4 OR 1/2 IN VIDEO K-P S
Tells how the small animals who live on Rabbit Hill are affected by the new owners who move into the big house and plant a garden.
Prod-NBC Dist-MGHT 1968

Rabbit Hill, Pt 1 C 26 MIN
16MM FILM, 3/4 OR 1/2 IN VIDEO K-P S
Tells how the small animals who live on Rabbit Hill are affected by the new owners who move into the big house and plant a garden.
Prod-NBC Dist-MGHT 1968

Rabbit Hill, Pt 2 C 27 MIN
16MM FILM, 3/4 OR 1/2 IN VIDEO K-P S
Tells how the small animals who live on Rabbit Hill are affected by the new owners who move into the big house and plant a garden.
Prod-NBC Dist-MGHT 1968

Rabbit Stew C 7 MIN
16MM FILM OPTICAL SOUND
Presents an animated story in which a brash, fearless rabbit is pitted against a human landowner.
Prod-PORTER Dist-BHAWK

Rabbits C 11 MIN
16MM FILM, 3/4 OR 1/2 IN VIDEO P-I
Offers a closeup look at the domestic rabbit.
Prod-FILMSW Dist-FLMFR

Rabbits C 15 MIN
3/4 OR 1/2 INCH VIDEO CASSETTE P
See series title for descriptive statement.
From The Let's Draw Series.
Prod-OCPS Dist-AITECH Prodn-KOKHTV 1976

Rabbits And Hares C 11 MIN
16MM FILM, 3/4 OR 1/2 IN VIDEO I-H
Compares and contrasts rabbits and hares and discusses the burrowing, nesting and feeding habits of each.
From The Looking At Animals Series.
Prod-BHA Dist-IFB 1966

Rabbits, Rabbits And More Rabbits B 15 MIN
2 INCH VIDEOTAPE P
See series title for descriptive statement.
From The Sounds Like Magic Series.
Prod-MOEBA Dist-GPITVL Prodn-KYNETV

Rabies C 13 MIN
3/4 OR 1/2 INCH VIDEO CASSETTE
Demonstrates, through a story of a rabies incident, the actions taken to save a child's life. Portrays current ways to curtail exposure to rabies disease and to discourage its existence.
LC NO. 83-706974
Prod-AMVMA Dist-MTP Prodn-MOTIVI 1983

Rabies Can Be Controlled C 20 MIN
16MM FILM OPTICAL SOUND
Emphasizes the importance of protecting dogs against rabies by means of vaccination. Shows clinical cases of rabies in both humans and dogs and demonstrates methods of producing rabies vaccine for dogs as well as its use in mass vaccination programs.
Prod-ACYLLD Dist-LEDR 1954

Rabies Control In The Community B 11 MIN
16MM FILM - 3/4 IN VIDEO PRO
Shows cases of rabies in humans and dogs. Considers how apathy of dog owners can permit rabies to become a community problem and how concerted community action can prevent rabies. Issued in 1956 as a motion picture.
LC NO. 78-706236
Prod-USPHS Dist-USNAC Prodn-NMAC 1978

Rabies F-A Staining C 8 MIN
16MM FILM - 3/4 IN VIDEO
Demonstrates the technique of staining brain impressions with fluorescent antibodies for the detection of Negri bodies. Issued in 1966 as a motion picture.
LC NO. 80-706280
Prod-USPHS Dist-USNAC 1980

Rabies In A Human Patient B 4 MIN
16MM FILM, 3/4 OR 1/2 IN VIDEO H-C A
Shows clinical symptoms in an Iranian patient as rabies proceeds through its course.
From The Microbiology Teaching Series.
Prod-UCEMC Dist-UCEMC 1961

Rabies Threat, The C 15 MIN
16MM FILM OPTICAL SOUND J-C A
Deals with rabies, an animal disease which is foreign to Australia and outlines the work of the Animal Quarantine Service which functions to keep Australia free of all exotic animal diseases.
LC NO. 74-703290
Prod-ANAIB Dist-AUIS Prodn-FLMAUS 1974

Rabindranath Tagore B 22 MIN
16MM FILM OPTICAL SOUND I-C A
Presents a biography of the Nobel laureate Rabindranath Tagore narrated through live shots, sketches, photographs, paintings and a dramatic impersonation of his early life. Shows the many-sided life of Gurudev Tagore as poet, painter, composer of songs and dances, educationist and patriot.
Prod-INDIA Dist-NEDINF

Raccoon C 11 MIN
16MM FILM, 3/4 OR 1/2 IN VIDEO P-J
Describes how raccoons have good brains and nimble feet and manage to survive well in an assortment of environments, from forest den to the chimney of a suburban home.
Prod-CENTRO Dist-CORF 1982

Raccoon Story - A Menomini Indian Folktale C 9 MIN
16MM FILM, 3/4 OR 1/2 IN VIDEO P
Features two old blind men who live by a lake. Shows how a playful raccoon tricks the men and gets their food. Concludes with the blind men learning that if they had trusted each other the raccoon would not have been able to trick them.
Prod-SCHLAT Dist-LUF 1974

Raccoons Are For Loving C 15 MIN
3/4 INCH VIDEO CASSETTE K-P
See series title for descriptive statement.
From The Storytime Series.
Prod-WCETTV Dist-GPITVL 1976

Raccoons' Picnic, The X 5 MIN
16MM FILM, 3/4 OR 1/2 IN VIDEO P-I
Shows two baby raccoons in their natural habitat.
Prod-EBF Dist-EBEC 1955

Race Against Death C 15 MIN
3/4 OR 1/2 INCH VIDEO CASSETTE I
Tells of a true life heroic mission to bring antitoxin to a remote Alaskan village struck by diptheria. From the book by Seymour Reit.
From The Book Bird Series.
Prod-CTI Dist-CTI

Race Against Time (Introduction) B 30 MIN
2 INCH VIDEOTAPE C A
Discusses significant changes of atomic energy, increased leisure time, a moral vaccum and the compression of time necessary for change to occur. Describes these changes' relation to the functioning of education and communications. (Broadcast quality)
From The Communications And Education Series. No. 1
Prod-NYSED Dist-GPITVL Prodn-WNDTTV

Race And Residence - The Shaker Heights Model C 30 MIN
3/4 INCH VIDEO CASSETTE
Describes how the people of Shaker Heights, Ohio, have encouraged integration maintenance instead of resegregation.
Prod-OHC Dist-HRC

Race For Gold C 57 MIN
16MM FILM, 3/4 OR 1/2 IN VIDEO H-C A
Discusses government-sponsored training for Olympic competitors. Considers whether new training programs could help American amateur athletes, who only receive a ticket to the games and a uniform, and asks who should be responsible for the costs of these new programs.
From The Nova Series.
LC NO. 79-708058
Prod-WGBHTV Dist-TIMLIF

Race For Number One C 52 MIN
16MM FILM, 3/4 OR 1/2 IN VIDEO H-C A
Relates the spills, laughs and strange twists which occur in a Yukon dog sled race between Big Olaf and Smoke with a million dollars in gold waiting at the finish line. Based on the short story Race For Number One by Jack London.
From The Jack London's Tales Of The Klondike Series.
LC NO. 84-706231
Prod-NORWK Dist-EBEC 1982

Race For Professionals, A C 25 MIN
16MM FILM OPTICAL SOUND
Shows the 59th running of the Indianapolis 500 in which Bobby Unser took the checkered flag. Includes the spectacular crash survived by Tom Sneva and memories of earlier races that are now part of Indy lore.
Prod-GTARC Dist-GTARC

Race Of Horses, A C 10 MIN
16MM FILM, 3/4 OR 1/2 IN VIDEO J-H
Shows the sport of horse racing which involves many people, such as strappers, trainers, jockeys, veterinarians and breeders. Features all of these people at work as the pace of the race and the quiet of routine are undercut.
Prod-JOU Dist-JOU 1976

Race Of The Century, The C 46 MIN
16MM FILM - 1/2 IN VIDEO
Deals with the 1983 America's Cup races.
Prod-SILVER Dist-OFFSHR

Race Relations B 15 MIN
16MM FILM OPTICAL SOUND A
Explores today's Christian biggest problems - does the Christian attitude toward other races mean more than toleration and sympathetic understanding of national background, how and where do racial prejudice and bigotry begin and how can they be combated in the Christian home.
Prod-CONCOR Dist-CPH

Race Symphony / Two-Penny Magic B 10 MIN
16MM FILM OPTICAL SOUND
Features Race Symphony, an excerpt from Hans Richter's study of a day at the races, in pre-Nazi Germany, and Two-Penny Magic, Richter's essay in rhyming images, made to advertise a picture magazine. Produced 1928-29.
Prod-STARRC Dist-STARRC

Race To Oblivion C 28 MIN
16MM FILM, 3/4 OR 1/2 IN VIDEO H-C A
Documents nuclear war. Features Burt Lancaster interviewing a Hiroshima survivor.
Prod-PSR Dist-CF

Race To Oblivion C 49 MIN
16MM FILM, 3/4 OR 1/2 IN VIDEO
Presents a symposium of Physicians For Social Responsibility. Includes an interview with a survivor of Hiroshima.
Prod-PSR Dist-PSR 1982

Race With Death, A C 30 MIN
16MM FILM OPTICAL SOUND
Shows the work of the Maryland Institute for Emergency Medical Service Systems in Baltimore in combating trauma, the leading killer of people under 40. Follows several victims from rescue in police helicopters through the trauma emergency rooms and postoperative critical care.
LC NO. 79-701012
Prod-WJLATV Dist-WJLATV 1978

Race, The C 10 MIN
16MM FILM, 3/4 OR 1/2 IN VIDEO C A
Shows how a bike race through beautiful mountain vistas becomes the occasion for a champion's momentous decision regarding the need always to win.
Prod-ZAGREB Dist-WOMBAT

Race, The - Trans-Am C 15 MIN
16MM FILM, 3/4 OR 1/2 IN VIDEO J-H
Presents one of America's major series of auto racing, the Trans-Am. Builds excitingly from the arrival of the festive and excited spectators and the intense concentration of the drivers to the split-second precision of the pit crews and the sounds of the cars through high speed turns.
Prod-COUKLA Dist-AIMS 1972

Racer That Lost His Edge, The C 30 MIN
16MM FILM - 3/4 IN VIDEO I
Tells the story of a fat race driver and his new bride who learn why a healthy diet is for champions.
From The Mulligan Stew Series.
Prod-GPITVL Dist-GPITVL

Racetrack Chaplain C 25 MIN
16MM FILM OPTICAL SOUND
Follows Reverend Izzy Vega as he ministers to the needs of his unique congregation, the exercise boys, grooms, and stablehands on a thoroughbred racetrack. Describes special ministries and areas in which there are physical and spiritual needs.
LC NO. 79-701337
Prod-FAMF Dist-FAMF 1979

Rachel C 3 MIN
16MM FILM OPTICAL SOUND I-C A
Uses a Jewish man who is mourning his daughter's 'death' as the hour of her church wedding approaches as the basis for discussing intermarriage.
Prod-JEWMED Dist-NJWB 1974

Rachel At School B 11 MIN
16MM FILM OPTICAL SOUND J-C A
Shows Rachel and two of her friends engaged in a mild clash over who is to be included in their small group. Shows how the three solve their problem with little adult intervention.
From The Exploring Childhood Series.
LC NO. 76-701895
Prod-EDC Dist-EDC Prodn-FRIEDJ 1975

Rachel Runs For Office C 26 MIN
16MM FILM, 3/4 OR 1/2 IN VIDEO I-J
Describes the differing campaign strategies of Rachel Hewitt and Billy Martin, opposing candidates in a school election. Shows how Rachel refuses to use personal information against Billy.
Prod-PLAYTM Dist-BCNFL 1985

Racial Relationships C 29 MIN
16MM FILM OPTICAL SOUND
Features representatives of groups who have suffered discrimination. Looks at the problem of racial discrimination from a Christian perspective.
From The We're Number One Series.
LC NO. 79-701398
Prod-AMERLC Dist-AMERLC 1979

Racing - The Will To Win C 17 MIN
16MM FILM, 3/4 OR 1/2 IN VIDEO I-H
Shows competitors of all ages learning about the preparation, discipline, knowledge and endurance needed to compete successfully in a race. Emphasizes that the rewards in racing are more than just winning.
From The Wide World Of Adventure Series.
Prod-AVATLI Dist-EBEC 1978

Racing Cars C 7 MIN
16MM FILM OPTICAL SOUND J-C A
Shows five-year-old Enroue painting cars on an easel for the first time, although he has drawn cars with pencils, crayons or magic markers on horizontal surfaces. Illustrates his ability to conceive and follow a plan and to improvise when the plan runs into problems.
From The Exploring Childhood Series.
LC NO. 76-701896
Prod-EDC Dist-EDC 1974

Racing On Thin Air B 30 MIN
2 INCH VIDEOTAPE
Relates the external challenge of Pikes Peak through its history and excitement of the Pikes Peak Auto Hill Climb. Interviews the winners of the 1966 race.
From The Synergism - The Challenge Of Sports Series.
Prod-KRMATV Dist-PUBTEL

Racing Revolution C 22 MIN
16MM FILM OPTICAL SOUND I-H
A documentary account of the development and use of gas turbine engines in vehicles. Includes the controversy over the use of turbine engines in automobile racing which resulted in barring turbine engines in competition at the Indianapolis Motor Speedway.
LC NO. 72-702855
Prod-STP Dist-STP Prodn-AP 1968

Racing Tradition C 14 MIN
16MM FILM OPTICAL SOUND
Features the Hialeah Park Racetrack in Florida.
Prod-FLADC Dist-FLADC

Racism - How Pervasive Is It C 30 MIN
3/4 OR 1/2 INCH VIDEO CASSETTE C
Discusses the pervasiveness of racism in America.
From The Afro-American Perspectives Series.
Prod-MDDE Dist-MDCPB

Racism And Education B 30 MIN
16MM FILM OPTICAL SOUND H-C A
William Strickland serves as moderator as James Garrett, James Turner, Linda Housh and Ray Brown discuss the contribution of Malcolm X as a teacher, the failure of educational institutions and teachers' unions to serve the needs of the Black community, and the need for the conditioning of Black children.
From The Black History, Section 24 - New Roles For Black Students Series.
LC NO. 75-704125
Prod-WCBSTV Dist-HRAW 1969

Racism, Disfranchisement And Jim Crow B 30 MIN
2 INCH VIDEOTAPE H-C A
See series title for descriptive statement.
From The Americans From Africa - A History Series. No. 20
Prod-CVETVC Dist-GPITVL Prodn-WCVETV

Rack And Pinion Power Steering Gears And Pumps C 25 MIN
3/4 OR 1/2 INCH VIDEO CASSETTE
Covers the operation, diagnosis and repair of rack and pinion steering systems used on Ford and other domestic vehicles. Describes use of special tools.
Prod-FORDSP Dist-FORDSP

Racquetball C 15 MIN
16MM FILM, 3/4 OR 1/2 IN VIDEO I-C A
Looks at advanced racquetball. Uses voice-over commentaries by players Mike Yellen and Lindsay Myers to accompany scenes of their intense concentration during warm-up exercises and a game. Shows the manufacture of racquets and balls.
LC NO. 82-706709
Prod-MERPI Dist-DIRECT 1981

Racquetball - Moving Fast C 15 MIN
16MM FILM, 3/4 OR 1/2 IN VIDEO J-C A
Explains the rules for playing racquetball and provides step-by-step instruction in the basic skills of the game. Demonstrates strokes, serves and returns, illustrating the strategic function of each.
Prod-CREEDM Dist-PHENIX 1978

Racquetball Fundamentals C 11 MIN
16MM FILM, 3/4 OR 1/2 IN VIDEO J-C A
Discusses the basic concepts of the sport of racquetball. Covers such topics as the ball, the racquet, the court, the basic grip, playing strokes, service and strategies.
LC NO. 81-706580
Prod-ASSOCF Dist-AIMS 1980

Racquetball Serves And Serve Returns C 10 MIN
16MM FILM, 3/4 OR 1/2 IN VIDEO I-C A
Focuses on racquetball serves and serve returns.
From The Racquetball Series. No. 3
LC NO. 81-706055
Prod-ATHI Dist-ATHI 1979

Racquetball Shots C 10 MIN
16MM FILM, 3/4 OR 1/2 IN VIDEO I-C A
Focuses on techniques for racquetball shots.
From The Racquetball Series. No. 2
LC NO. 81-706055
Prod-ATHI Dist-ATHI 1979

Racquetball With Dave Peck C 60 MIN
1/2 IN VIDEO CASSETTE BETA/VHS
Offers neuro-muscular programming, using Dave Peck as the model for perfecting racquetball skills. Comes with four audiocassettes and personal training guide.
Prod-SYBVIS Dist-SYBVIS

Racquetball–A Series
16MM FILM, 3/4 OR 1/2 IN VIDEO I-C A
Describes precise racquetball techniques, including fundamentals.
LC NO. 81-706055
Prod-ATHI Dist-ATHI 1979

Fundamentals Of Racquetball 10 MIN
Racquetball Serves And Serve Returns 10 MIN
Racquetball Shots 10 MIN
Strategy For Singles, Doubles, Cut-Throat 10 MIN

Radar Contact C 28 MIN
3/4 OR 1/2 INCH VIDEO CASSETTE A
Shows how radar operates, its capabilities and limitations, and cautions that radar does not replace pilot responsibility.
Prod-FAAFL Dist-AVIMA

Radar Eyes The Weather, Pt A - Fundamentals Of Radar Meteorology B 25 MIN
16MM FILM OPTICAL SOUND
Discusses the basic principles of radar meteorology. Explains reflectivity and factors affecting it, such as hydrometers and precipitation attentuation. Shows various types of clouds and describes their characteristics.
LC NO. FIE61-199
Prod-USAF Dist-USNAC 1961

Radar Eyes The Weather, Pt B - Analysis Of Severe Weather B 21 MIN
16MM FILM OPTICAL SOUND
Explains the necessary use of weather data from other sources in addition to radar scope readings when the approach of severe weather seems imminent. Shows how the meteorologist must be alert for areas of deception.
LC NO. FIE61-200
Prod-USAF Dist-USNAC 1961

Radar Refraction And Weather - The Radar Weather Problem C 15 MIN
16MM FILM OPTICAL SOUND
Explains how weather information is used at three different levels - operational radar site, division or sector control center and staff level for planning purposes. Emphasizes the importance of teamwork at each level with the weather station.
LC NO. FIE56-361
Prod-USAF Dist-USNAC 1956

Radar Set AN - PPS-5 - Operation And Manpacking C 25 MIN
16MM FILM OPTICAL SOUND
Shows components, assembly and replacement of the set. Tells how it is operated to detect, locate and identify moving targets through visual and aural radar signals. Shows disassembly and manpacking the equipment for movement to the next surveillance site.
LC NO. 74-705467
Prod-USA Dist-USNAC 1968

Radha's Day - Hindu Family Life C 17 MIN
16MM FILM OPTICAL SOUND H-C
Shows a Hindu girl in her late teens during a typical day doing such things as getting up, decorating the threshold, putting on her make-up and jewelry, shopping, cooking and performing other typical middle-class activities.
From The Hindu Religion Series. No. 5
LC NO. 77-712494
Prod-SMTHHD Dist-SYRCU 1969

Radial Artery Cannulation C 7 MIN
3/4 OR 1/2 INCH VIDEO CASSETTE PRO
Reviews pertinent anatomy and essential equipment. Presents step-by-step analysis of cannulation procedure on a critically ill patient.
Prod-UWASH Dist-UWASH

Radial Drill No. 1 - Familiarization And Basic Drill Operations C 22 MIN
1/2 IN VIDEO CASSETTE BETA/VHS IND
Discusses methods of mounting work and drills, machine functions and controls. Explains the procedure for positioning the drill for spotting and drilling through and blind holes.
From The Machine Shop - Drill Press, Radial Drill, Drill Grinder Series.
Prod-RMI Dist-RMI

Radial Drill No. 2 - Production, Drilling, Reaming And Tapping C 22 MIN
1/2 IN VIDEO CASSETTE BETA/VHS IND
Explains methods of locating and drilling a series of holes with emphasis on speed and accuracy. Includes reaming and tapping techniques.
From The Machine Shop - Drill Press, Radial Drill, Drill Grinder Series.
Prod-RMI Dist-RMI

Radial Line - 180 Degree Shortcut Method C 12 MIN
1/2 IN VIDEO CASSETTE BETA/VHS IND
See series title for descriptive statement.
From The Metal Fabrication - Round Tapers Series.
Prod-RMI Dist-RMI

Radial Line Theory For Cone Or Frustrum Of Cone - Parallel Openings C 20 MIN
1/2 IN VIDEO CASSETTE BETA/VHS IND
See series title for descriptive statement.
From The Metal Fabrication - Round Tapers Series.
Prod-RMI Dist-RMI

Radiance - The Experience Of Light C 21 MIN
3/4 OR 1/2 INCH VIDEO CASSETTE
Relates the insight felt by Dorothy Fadiman after her 'experience of light'.
Prod-HP Dist-HP

Radiance, The Experience Of Light C 22 MIN
16MM FILM, 3/4 OR 1/2 IN VIDEO I-C A
Uses nature photography, religious art, video images and kinetic mandalas to provide a visual illustration of the experience of inner light, a recurrent theme in religious and spiritual trends throughout the world.
LC NO. 78-701047
Prod-FADMND Dist-PFP Prodn-WIESEM 1978

Radiant Energy - More Than Meets The Eye C 17 MIN
16MM FILM, 3/4 OR 1/2 IN VIDEO I-H

Gives an overview of visible light as a source of radiant energy within the electromagnetic spectrum. Examines various aspects of radiant energy, including its major forms, and tells how the relationship between wavelengths and frequency of light waves determines their color and how the reflection of light affects people's ability to see objects.
Prod-MIS Dist-MIS 1978

Radiant Energy And The Electromagnetic Spectrum C 11 MIN
16MM FILM, 3/4 OR 1/2 IN VIDEO J-H
Presents re-enacted experiments of discovery and modern sensing devices introduce the various forms of radiant energy, giving insights into concepts of waves, wave-lengths and energy. Includes sources and uses of radio waves, micro-waves, infra-red waves, light waves, ultra-violet waves, X-rays and gamma rays.
Prod-CORF Dist-CORF 1968

Radiating The Fruit Of Truth C 129 MIN
16MM FILM, 3/4 OR 1/2 IN VIDEO
Presents an exposition of the Tantric view of the world and the mind, documenting a 2,000-year-old Buddhist ritual of pacification. Follows the lamas through their spiritual preparations in remote Nepalese mountain retreats and also through their study and practices within their monastery.
From The Tibet - A Buddhist Trilogy Series. Part 2
Prod-COLLAS Dist-UCEMC 1981

Radiation - Can We Control It? (Safety Precautions) C 15 MIN
3/4 OR 1/2 INCH VIDEO CASSETTE H-C A
Tells how many occupations involve exposure to potentially harmful radiation. Notes that advisory bodies and regulatory commissions have established safety standards and procedures.
From The Story Of Radiation Series.
Prod-EDMI Dist-EDMI 1981

Radiation - Can We Use It? (Risks vs Benefits) C 15 MIN
3/4 OR 1/2 INCH VIDEO CASSETTE H-C A
Gives examples to help define what is meant by 'risk' and 'benefit.' Tells how risk factor is quantifiable to some extent, but often remains subjective. Notes that attempts are being made to analyze radiation effects to provide a sound basis for legislative control.
From The Story Of Radiation Series.
Prod-EDMI Dist-EDMI 1981

Radiation - Does It Affect Us? (Human Effects) C 15 MIN
3/4 OR 1/2 INCH VIDEO CASSETTE H-C A
Shows how humans are exposed to approximately 100 millirads per year from both background of radiation and man-made radiation. Notes how knowledge of human effects is based on cases of severe exposure and that effects of small doses are still difficult to measure.
From The Story Of Radiation Series.
Prod-EDMI Dist-EDMI 1981

Radiation - Impact On Life C 23 MIN
16MM FILM, 3/4 OR 1/2 IN VIDEO H-C A
Presents three experts who explain the most important physical and biological concepts regarding radiation, including stable and unstable elements, ionizing radiation, the half-life of radioactive materials, how radiation affects DNA and how its levels can be concentrated in the food chain.
LC NO. 82-707099
Prod-PUBCOM Dist-BULFRG 1982

Radiation - In Sickness And In Health C 28 MIN
16MM FILM OPTICAL SOUND H-C A
Studies the constructive applications of radiation, explaining what radioactivity and ionizing radiation are. Examines the use of radiation for diagnostic purposes, in which radioactive materials are injected into the patient's body.
Prod-CANBC Dist-FI

Radiation - Is It Safe? (Interpretation Of Dose) C 15 MIN
3/4 OR 1/2 INCH VIDEO CASSETTE H-C A
Tells how government committees try to assess results of low-level radiation on health, genetic inheritance and the unborn fetus. Notes how study of Hiroshima victims helped our knowledge of injuries resulting from radiation exposure. Explains how maximum doses are established.
From The Story Of Radiation Series.
Prod-EDMI Dist-EDMI 1981

Radiation - Naturally C 29 MIN
16MM FILM OPTICAL SOUND
Explores radiation, its sources, applications, effects, benefits and risks. Includes an historical perspective, an animated trip from space to the heart of the atom, and visits nuclear research reactors and nuclear power generating plants.
LC NO. 81-701372
Prod-AIF Dist-MTP Prodn-FILMGR 1981

Radiation - Physician And Patient C 45 MIN
16MM FILM OPTICAL SOUND
Demonstrates biological effects of large doses of ionizing radiation and shows clinical ways to minimize radiation exposures in X-ray examinations. Demonstrates the proper use of the fluoroscope and shows how to shield gonads. For professional use.
Prod-AMCRAD Dist-AMCRAD 1959

Radiation - What Does It Do? (Inter-reaction With Matter) C 15 MIN
3/4 OR 1/2 INCH VIDEO CASSETTE H-C A
Outlines the basic idea of ionization through animation and interviews with experts, and reveals that harmful effects from radiation were discovered over the years. Explains how radiation interacts with matter and how it can be used.
From The Story Of Radiation Series.
Prod-EDMI Dist-EDMI 1981

Radiation - What Effect Does It Have? (Biological Effects) C 15 MIN
3/4 OR 1/2 INCH VIDEO CASSETTE H-C A
Shows how differing life forms all have cells, whose characteristics are encoded in DNA, a chemical substance which may be affected by radiation. Notes how different radiation forms affect cells differently and shows radiation's role in causing leukemia.
From The Story Of Radiation Series.
Prod-EDMI Dist-EDMI 1981

Radiation - What Is It Made Of? (Particles And Waves) C 15 MIN
3/4 OR 1/2 INCH VIDEO CASSETTE H-C A
Explains that radiation is the result of unstable atoms. Illustrates and describes gamma rays, x-rays, alpha and beta particles and neutron radiation. Notes how radiation in form of x-ray photos has been used since end of 19th century, but first self-sustaining nuclear reaction took place in 1942.
From The Story Of Radiation Series.
Prod-EDMI Dist-EDMI 1981

Radiation - What Is It? (Energy In Motion) C 15 MIN
3/4 OR 1/2 INCH VIDEO CASSETTE J-C A
Defines radiation as a form of energy, like sunlight, which can be natural or man-made. Shows how radiation can change living cells either harmfully or beneficially. Deals with alpha, beta, gamma and x-rays, and concludes it is up to us how we control and use radiation.
From The Story Of Radiation Series.
Prod-EDMI Dist-EDMI 1981

Radiation - Where Do We Go From Here? (Issues) C 15 MIN
3/4 OR 1/2 INCH VIDEO CASSETTE H-C A
Notes how some interest groups are concerned about nuclear safety, disposal of radioactive waste and limitation of nuclear arms, and that many radiation questions are unresolved. Explains how Congressional committees reconcile the interests of the public, industry, science and medicine.
From The Story Of Radiation Series.
Prod-EDMI Dist-EDMI 1981

Radiation - Where Is It? (Measurement And Detection) C 15 MIN
3/4 OR 1/2 INCH VIDEO CASSETTE H-C A
Describes how radiation detecting instruments such as the Geiger Counter work. Examines others, too, such as scintillation detectors and personal monitoring devices.
From The Story Of Radiation Series.
Prod-EDMI Dist-EDMI 1981

Radiation Accident Patients C 17 MIN
16MM FILM, 3/4 OR 1/2 IN VIDEO J-H A
describes how workers suffering from radioactive contamination can be effectively and safely treated within existing medical facilities. Presents techniques for proper handling of radiation accident patients, shows how to use simple detection instruments and discusses radiation injury aspects of first aid.
Prod-USAEC Dist-USNAC 1969

Radiation And Your Environment C 25 MIN
3/4 OR 1/2 INCH VIDEO CASSETTE
Introduces radioactive emissions. Provides an understanding of radiation concepts essential to informed decisions on related energy, health and environmental issues. Includes ten review questions at the end of the program.
Prod-EDMEC Dist-EDMEC

Radiation Carcinogenesis C 59 MIN
3/4 INCH VIDEO CASSETTE
Discusses radiation-related malignancies resulting from the Hiroshima and Nagasaki bombings.
Prod-UTAHTI Dist-UTAHTI

Radiation Damage In Solids B 30 MIN
16MM FILM OPTICAL SOUND C A
Develops an understanding of the nature of solids using the simple atomic theory of matter. Discusses the use of radiation to investigate the properties of solids. Presents an experiment in which a sodium chloride is bombarded with three billionths of a second pulse of 600 kilovolt electrons.
LC NO. 74-700176
Prod-UNL Dist-UNL 1969

Radiation Hygiene - Double Collimation C 7 MIN
16MM FILM - 3/4 IN VIDEO PRO
Explains the advantages of double collimation as a means of reducing the field of radiation in dental X-rays. Shows how an intraoral positioner provides an effective means of placing the radiographic film and projecting the reduced size X-ray beam, thus minimizing the amount of radiation exposure.
LC NO. 78-706222
Prod-USVA Dist-USNAC Prodn-VADTC 1978

Radiation Losses C 34 MIN
3/4 OR 1/2 INCH VIDEO CASSETTE C
Discusses the radiation losses which occur in waveguides, especially in curved waveguides. Gives examples of the techniques used to measure waveguide losses.
From The Integrated Optics Series.
Prod-UDEL Dist-UDEL

Radiation Processing - A New Industry C 14 MIN
16MM FILM OPTICAL SOUND PRO
Provides several examples--including radiation sterilization, chemical processing and electron beam treatment of durable-press fabrics--of the use of radiation for industrial processing and states the reasons for the rapid increase of its use.
LC NO. 70-714174
Prod-BATELL Dist-USERD 1971

Radiation Protection In Nuclear Medicine C 43 MIN
16MM FILM OPTICAL SOUND
Demonstrates the procedures devised for naval hospitals to protect against the gamma radiation emitted from materials used in radiation therapy. Shows that the principles are applicable in all hospitals.
LC NO. FIE62-21
Prod-USN Dist-SQUIBB 1961

Radiation Safety - Emergency Procedures C 16 MIN
3/4 OR 1/2 INCH VIDEO CASSETTE C A
Contains re-enactments of a variety of laboratory accidents illustrating the basic principles for coping with emergency situations, including assist people first, monitor personnel, control area and call radiation safety.
From The Radiation Safety Series.
LC NO. 83-706046
Prod-IU Dist-IU 1982

Radiation Safety - Introduction C 16 MIN
3/4 OR 1/2 INCH VIDEO CASSETTE C A
Deals with the properties of radiation, its biololgical effects and the regulations governing the use of radioactive materials in the laboratory.
From The Radiation Safety Series.
LC NO. 83-706044
Prod-IU Dist-IU 1982

Radiation Safety - Laboratory Techniques C 16 MIN
3/4 OR 1/2 INCH VIDEO CASSETTE C A
Describes a program for laboratory safety to be used when working with radioactive materials. Notes that such a program involves careful planning, safe working habits, routine monitoring, proper disposal of radioactive waste and utilization of radiation safety personnel.
From The Radiation Safety Series.
LC NO. 83-706045
Prod-IU Dist-IU 1982

Radiation Safety In Nuclear Energy Explorations C 24 MIN
16MM FILM OPTICAL SOUND
Depicts the activities of the division of radiological health of the Public Health Service, showing health programs designed for protection against radiation.
LC NO. FIE62-7
Prod-USPHS Dist-USNAC 1962

Radiation Safety--A Series
16MM FILM, 3/4 OR 1/2 IN VIDEO C A
Presents safety procedures for using radioactive materials in research.
Prod-IU Dist-IU 1982

Radiation Safety - Emergency Procedures 016 MIN
Radiation Safety - Introduction 016 MIN
Radiation Safety - Laboratory Technique 016 MIN

Radiation Therapy For Cancer C 25 MIN
16MM FILM OPTICAL SOUND PRO
Demonstrates the biophysical principles involved in radiation therapy dosage for cancer. Shows treatment planning and the clinical management of various cancer sites.
LC NO. 78-711414
Prod-AMCS Dist-AMCS 1970

Radical Freedom - Strauss, Existentialism Is Humanism C 45 MIN
2 INCH VIDEOTAPE
See series title for descriptive statement.
From The Humanities Series. Unit III - The Realm Of Idea And Speculation
Prod-WTTWTV Dist-GPITVL

Radical Hysterectomy Following Central Irradiation For Carcinoma Of The Cervix C 29 MIN
16MM FILM OPTICAL SOUND PRO
Gives a resume of the method used in the central irradiation. Depicts the details of the lymph node dissection, emphasizing the removal of the obturator group with reference to the prevention of troublesome bleeding.
Prod-ACYDGD Dist-ACY 1962

Radical Mastectomy C 23 MIN
16MM FILM OPTICAL SOUND PRO
Deals with policy in the treatment of primary carcinoma of the breast. Illustrates briefly the place of mammography and details the technical operation of the conventional radical mastectomy.
Prod-ACYDGD Dist-ACY 1965

Radical Mastectomy C 27 MIN
3/4 OR 1/2 INCH VIDEO CASSETTE
See series title for descriptive statement.
From The Breast Series.
Prod-SVL Dist-SVL

Radical Mastectomy For Carcinoma Of The Breast C 26 MIN
16MM FILM OPTICAL SOUND
Depicts the technique of doing a biopsy in carcinoma of the breast and methods that decrease the likelihood of dissemination by biopsy. Shows the technique of radical mastectomy and excision of an internal mammary lymph node for biopsy.
Prod-ACYDGD Dist-ACY 1956

Radical Neck Dissection And Epiglottidectomy C 36 MIN
3/4 OR 1/2 INCH VIDEO CASSETTE
See series title for descriptive statement.
From The Head And Neck Series.
Prod-SVL Dist-SVL

Radical Operation For Carcinoma Of The Vulva During Pregnancy C 15 MIN
16MM FILM OPTICAL SOUND
Describes the treatment of a patient who was found to have invasive carcinoma of the vulva in the 24th week of pregnancy. Ex-

plains that she was treated with radical vulvectomy and bilateral groin lymphadenectomy at this stage in pregnancy and at the 38th week of pregnancy a Cesarean hysterectomy with bilateral pelvic lymphadenectomy was performed. Discusses the use of lymphography in the mangement of this patient.
LC NO. 75-702325
Prod-EATONL Dist-EATONL 1967

Radical Pneumonectomy For Carcinoma Of Lung C 33 MIN
16MM FILM OPTICAL SOUND PRO
Explains that radical pneumonectomy, as described by Brock and others, follows accepted principles of cancer surgery, and makes even extensive tumor resectable with an accepted mortality. Depicts the technique for this procedure.
Prod-ACYDGD Dist-ACY 1969

Radical Reformation, The B 30 MIN
16MM FILM OPTICAL SOUND H-C A
J H O'Dell discusses the major reformation in labor in America occasioned by the passing of the Wagner Act in 1935 and by the activities of the Congress of Industrial Organizations, and evidenced in the emergence of Black leadership and political awareness.
From The Black History, Section 16 - Depression, Blacks And The Labor Series.
LC NO. 77-704092
Prod-WCBSTV Dist-HRAW 1969

Radical Reformer, The C 29 MIN
3/4 INCH VIDEO CASSETTE
Looks at Charles Dickens as the radical defender of the poor and attacker of the law, church and schools.
From The Dickens World Series.
Prod-UMITV Dist-UMITV 1973

Radical Republicans, The B 30 MIN
16MM FILM OPTICAL SOUND H-C A
Professor James Shenton analyzes the motives of President Andrew Johnson and of the majority of the whites who became identified with the black struggle during the Reconstruction Period, describing them as brutal, hypocritical, and corrupt men who used Blacks for personal advancement.
From The Black History, Section 09 - Home Rule And Reconstruction Series.
LC NO. 79-704063
Prod-WCBSTV Dist-HRAW 1969

Radical Resection Of The Ischial Tuberosity C 15 MIN
16MM FILM OPTICAL SOUND
Illustrates the technique used in radical resection of the ischial tuberosity in a 21-year-old paraplegic with a large ulcer proved to be refractory to healing for a year. Points out that the operation does not interfere with the use of braces and hastens rehabilitation.
LC NO. FIA66-59
Prod-EATONL Dist-EATONL Prodn-AVCORP 1963

Radical Skull Resection For Congenital Skull Defects C 24 MIN
3/4 OR 1/2 INCH VIDEO CASSETTE PRO
Demonstrates a radical skull resection in treating an infant with premature skull base and vault suture fusion known as kleeblatt-schadel or Cloverleaf skull. Shows the three-month follow-up.
Prod-UARIZ Dist-UARIZ

Radical Therapy - Techniques For Directed Change With Will Handy C 49 MIN
3/4 OR 1/2 INCH VIDEO CASSETTE
Presents guidelines for changing reactions to individual/internal and societal/external reinforcement patterns.
Prod-NOTTH Dist-UWISC 1982

Radical Vulvectomy With Posterior Exenteration For Carcinoma Of The Vulva C 15 MIN
16MM FILM OPTICAL SOUND
Shows the technique of radical vulvectomy with bilateral pelvic inguinal lymphadenectomy. Shows preand post-operative lymphangiograms.
LC NO. 75-702324
Prod-EATONL Dist-EATONL 1967

Radical Wertheim Operation C 26 MIN
16MM FILM OPTICAL SOUND PRO
Depicts in detail a personal technique of radical abdominal hysterectomy and bilateral pelvic lymphadenectomy as it has evolved over the last 20 years.
Prod-ACYDGD ' Dist-ACY 1960

Radicals And Conservatives C 29 MIN
2 INCH VIDEOTAPE
See series title for descriptive statement.
From The Black Experience Series.
Prod-WTTWTV Dist-PUBTEL

Radicals And The Real Number System B 29 MIN
16MM FILM OPTICAL SOUND H
Defines the concept of irrational numbers and lists some. Explains that the real number system includes all irrational and rational numbers, but does not include radicals of negative numbers.
From The Intermediate Algebra Series.
Prod-CALVIN Dist-MLA Prodn-UNIVFI 1959

Radio C 60 MIN
16MM FILM OPTICAL SOUND
Takes an up-tempo look at today's large radio fad. Emphasizes the radio's message and its influence on its youthful owners. Asks such questions as 'Can you own the big box and still succeed at your career objectives'.
Prod-BLKFMF Dist-BLKFMF

Radio B 29 MIN
16MM FILM, 3/4 OR 1/2 IN VIDEO H-C A
Features Dr Dodds discussing how the 'RADIO ERA' revolutionized life. Explains that from the 20s to the early 30s, radio was emerging as the 'POOR MAN'S' entertainment and that in the 30s radio entered the realm of serious programing. Concludes that today, in the era of television, radio has lost much of its mass appeal.
From The American Memoir Series.
Prod-WTTWTV Dist-IU 1961

Radio - New Life For An Old Medium C 30 MIN
3/4 OR 1/2 INCH VIDEO CASSETTE
Describes how all radio stations were alike in the 50's and 60's and how the president of ABC radio pioneered the position of KABC in Los Angeles to make it different from the competition.
From The Contemporary Issues In Marketing Series.
Prod-CANTOR Dist-IVCH

Radio Antennas, Creation And Behavior Of Radio Waves B 12 MIN
16MM FILM - 3/4 IN VIDEO
Explains electric and magnetic fields, generation of electromagnetic waves, behavior of radio waves in space, ground wave, reflection and refraction, the ionosphere and causes of fading.
LC NO. 78-706317
Prod-USAF Dist-USNAC 1978

Radio Astronomers Probe The Universe C 15 MIN
16MM FILM OPTICAL SOUND C
Shows how the study of radio signals given off in space is already transforming our picture of the universe. Explains that the sun emits blasts of radio energy which can be linked to disruptions of radio and TV communications. Tells how the Crab Nebula in the constellation Taurus gives off a pulsating signal generated by the imploded star within it.
From The Science In Action Series.
Prod-ALLFP Dist-COUNFI

Radio Astronomy Explorer C 30 MIN
16MM FILM OPTICAL SOUND J-C
Describes the new radio astronomy spacecraft, whose 1500-foot antennas will detect radio waves of various frequencies emitted by the sun, the earth and Jupiter.
LC NO. FIE68-93
Prod-NASA Dist-NASA 1968

Radio Drama - Life And Rebirth C 30 MIN
3/4 INCH VIDEO CASSETTE
Focuses on the art of radio drama, its life in Europe and its revival in the United States.
Prod-UMITV Dist-UMITV 1974

Radio Dynamics B 4 MIN
16MM FILM OPTICAL SOUND
Presents an interplay of shapes, colors and movement visualizing color-keyed moods, recurrent themes, contrapuntal melodies and staccato chords without the accompaniment of music.
LC NO. 73-700559
Prod-PFP Dist-CFS 1972

Radio Frequency Heater/Sealer Surveys C 27 MIN
3/4 OR 1/2 INCH VIDEO CASSETTE A
Discusses a radio frequency heater/sealer survey. Emphasizes field measurement techniques. Introduces the basic methods of controlling employee exposure.
Prod-USNAC Dist-USNAC 1983

Radio Frequency Radiation Hazards C 18 MIN
16MM FILM, 3/4 OR 1/2 IN VIDEO
Explains the biological (personnel) and nonbiological (EED and fuel) effects of RF radiation. Explains the frequency spectrum and shows the difference between ionizing and non-ionizing radiation.
Prod-USAF Dist-USNAC

Radio Goes After Its Audience C 15 MIN
3/4 OR 1/2 INCH VIDEO CASSETTE J-H
Examines efforts by two radio stations to cater to their individual audiences.
From The Media Machine Series.
Prod-WVIZTV Dist-GPITVL 1975

Radio Interference B 60 MIN
3/4 INCH VIDEO CASSETTE
Explains the significance of radio interference in military operations and describes the nature and theory of radio interference. Shows how radio interference can be tracked down and how various kinds of interference can be suppressed. Issued in 1958 as a motion picture.
LC NO. 78-706293
Prod-USA Dist-USNAC 1978

Radio Interference From Rural Power Lines B 45 MIN
16MM FILM OPTICAL SOUND
Demonstrates, using models, charts and blackboard, the causes of radio interference from power lines in rural areas. For the training of employees of rural electrification co-operatives.
LC NO. FIE53-631
Prod-USDA Dist-USNAC 1953

Radio Mathematics In Nicaragua C 20 MIN
3/4 OR 1/2 INCH VIDEO CASSETTE
Explores a project in Nicaragua that combines radio and systematic instructional design to teach primary school mathematics in rural parts of the country. Shows how curriculum and lesson plans are developed and how Nicaraguan teachers support the project.
LC NO. 81-707240
Prod-USAID Dist-USNAC 1980

Radio Of The Universe, A C 29 MIN
16MM FILM OPTICAL SOUND
Dr Morton S Roberts of the National Radio Astronomy Observatory in Green Bank, West Virginia, explains the use of the radio line of atomic hydrogen in determining the total hydrogen content of galaxies external to the Milky Way system. Dr Roberts then establishes the strong correlation between hydrogen content and galactic shape and raises the question as to whether this correlation can be used as an indicator of galactic evolution.
Prod-MLA Dist-MLA

Radio Relay Equipment An-Trc35 And 36, Pt 4 - System Lineup Procedures B 24 MIN
16MM FILM OPTICAL SOUND
Describes the features and function of AN-TRC35 and 36. Gives procedures for radio system lineup and overall system lineup when radio relay equipment is used with telephone carrier equipment.
LC NO. FIE60-170
Prod-USA Dist-USNAC 1959

Radio Sets AN-GRC 3, 4, 5, 6, 7, And 8 B 17 MIN
16MM FILM OPTICAL SOUND
Explains the characteristics, components and mechanical operation of the Army-Navy radio sets in the GRC classification.
LC NO. FIA53-126
Prod-USA Dist-USNAC 1952

Radio Shack TRS-80 Model 2 C
3/4 OR 1/2 INCH VIDEO CASSETTE
Presents basic operation procedures for use of the Radio Shack micro-computer TRS-80 Model II.
From The Basic Computer Operations Series.
Prod-LIBFSC Dist-LIBFSC

Radio Shack TRS-80 Model 3 C
3/4 OR 1/2 INCH VIDEO CASSETTE
Presents basic operation procedures for use of the Radio Shack micro-computer TRS-80 Model III.
From The Basic Computer Operations Series.
Prod-LIBFSC Dist-LIBFSC

Radio Shop Techniques B 38 MIN
16MM FILM - 3/4 IN VIDEO
Shows tools used by a radio technician and demonstrates orthographic projection, layouts, sawing and filing, drilling, bending metal, wiring and soldering in making a regenerative receiver. Issued in 1943 as a motion picture.
From The Radio Technician Training Series.
LC NO. 78-706299
Prod-USN Dist-USNAC Prodn-HOLMES 1978

Radio Technician Training - Elementary Electricity—A Series

Prod-USN Dist-USNAC 1978

Amperes, Volts And Ohms 8 MIN
Current And Electromotive Force 11 MIN

Radio Technician Training—A Series

Prod-USN Dist-USNAC 1978

Audio Oscillator Operation And Use 9 MIN
Capacitance 31 MIN
Inductance 31 MIN
Oscillators 13 MIN
Periodic Functions 17 MIN
Radio Shop Techniques 38 MIN
RCL 34 MIN
Rectangular Coordinates 13 MIN
Signal Generator Operation 9 MIN
Standing Waves On Transmission Lines 23 MIN
Synchro Systems 28 MIN
Tube Tester Operation 9 MIN
Vectors 12 MIN
Volt Ohmmeter Operation 12 MIN

Radio View Of The Universe, A C 29 MIN
16MM FILM OPTICAL SOUND
Dr Morton S Roberts explains his methods of studying the age and evolution of galaxies. The film was shot on location at the Harvard College Observatory and the National Radio Astronomy Observatory, Greenbank, West Virginia.
Prod-MLA Dist-MLA 1967

Radio, Racism And Foreign Policy C 26 MIN
16MM FILM, 3/4 OR 1/2 IN VIDEO H-C
Describes how the United States tried to isolate herself after being disillusioned by the horrors of the First World War. Explains that there was a period of racism and ethnic discrimination during the 1920's.
From The Between The Wars Series.
Prod-LNDBRG Dist-FI 1978

Radioactive Clocks B 30 MIN
2 INCH VIDEOTAPE J
See series title for descriptive statement.
From The Investigating The World Of Science, Unit 1 - Matter And Energy Series.
Prod-MPATI Dist-GPITVL

Radioactive Dating C 13 MIN
16MM FILM, 3/4 OR 1/2 IN VIDEO J-C
Describes radioactive dating and how carbon-14 and potassium-40 is used to date materials from recent past to times over 4.5 billion years ago.
Prod-CORF Dist-CORF 1981

Radioactive Decay A-1 C 3 MIN
16MM FILM SILENT H-C
Uses time-lapse photography to study radioactive decay. Shows a gamma-ray display of a 400-channel analyzer indicating simultaneous decay of 12.8 hour CU-64 for 1 half life, and 2.6 hour MN-56 for 5 half lives.
From The Single-Concept Films In Physics Series.
Prod-OSUMPD Dist-OSUMPD 1963

Radioactive Fallout And Shelter C 28 MIN
16MM FILM OPTICAL SOUND
Discusses the effects of radiation on people and emphasizes protective procedures against radiation. To be used with the course 'MEDICAL SELF-HELP TRAINING.'
From The Medical Self-Help Series.
LC NO. 74-705471
Prod-USDHEW Dist-USNAC Prodn-USOCD 1965

Radioactive Fallout And Shelter (Spanish) C 28 MIN
16MM FILM OPTICAL SOUND
Teaches the individual how to take care of his medical and health needs in time of disaster when medical assistance might not be readily available. Presents instructions on radioactive fallout and shelter.
From The Medical Self-Help Series.
LC NO. 75-702548
Prod-USPHS Dist-USNAC 1965

Radioactive Medicine B 50 MIN
16MM FILM OPTICAL SOUND PRO
Details the use of radioisotopes in diagnosis and treatment. Shows a scintillation scanner providing a picture of a patient's thyroid gland as it detects radioactivity from the isotope, iodine 193. Depicts the use of isotopes in diagnosing blood diseases and in researching metabolic processes.
Prod-CMA Dist-LAWREN

Radioactivity C 18 MIN
16MM FILM, 3/4 OR 1/2 IN VIDEO J-C
Creates a short-lived radioactive isotope and shows how to plot its decay curve. Introduces the Diffusion Cloud Chamber.
From The Physics In Action Series.
Prod-LUF Dist-LUF

Radioactivity C 29 MIN
3/4 INCH VIDEO CASSETTE
Explains the nature, uses and perils of nuclear radioactivity. Shows the physiological dangers of radiation and the extraordinary measures taken by atomic power stations to contain the toxicity of atom fuels and wastes.
From The Nuclear Power And You Series.
LC NO. 79-706951
Prod-UMAVEC Dist-UMAVEC 1979

Radioactivity C 29 MIN
3/4 INCH VIDEO CASSETTE
Describes radioactivity and how it works for and against people.
From The Nuclear Power And You Series.
Prod-UMITV Dist-UMITV 1979

Radioactivity And The Environment C 15 MIN
3/4 OR 1/2 INCH VIDEO CASSETTE I
Explores the properties of radioactive materials.
From The Matter And Motion Series. Module Blue
Prod-WHROTV Dist-AITECH 1973

Radiocarbon Dating B 27 MIN
16MM FILM OPTICAL SOUND
Discusses radioactive materials and their decay and describes the application of the radiocarbon count in dating archaeological materials.
Prod-NYU Dist-NYU

Radiochromatography - Testing For Radiochemical Purity C 18 MIN
3/4 OR 1/2 INCH VIDEO CASSETTE PRO
Discusses the factors involved in choosing a radiochromatography procedure, and the technique and methodology of various kits. Explores the evaluation of radiopharmaceutical quality and alternatives for reporting product defects.
LC NO. 83-706072
Prod-USDHEW Dist-USNAC 1982

Radiographic Processing—A Series
C
Deals with various aspects of radiographic processing.
Prod-USVA Dist-USNAC 1975

Artifact Film Interpretation	29 MIN
Basic Sensitometry	29 MIN
Basics Of Consistent Sensitometric Quality	29 MIN
Chemistry System, Archival Quality And Safety	29 MIN
Chemistry System, Developer	29 MIN
Chemistry System, Fixer And Wash	29 MIN
Circulation - Filtration System	29 MIN
Drying System	29 MIN
Electrical System, The	30 MIN
Function Of Processing	29 MIN
Maintenance, Lubrication And Troubleshooting	29 MIN
Replenishment System	29 MIN
Short Story History Of Processors, A	29 MIN
Temperature Control System	29 MIN
Theory Of Processing	29 MIN
Transport System	29 MIN

Radiography Of The Mandibular Ramus With The Panorex Unit C 9 MIN
16MM FILM OPTICAL SOUND PRO
Demonstrates a method of obtaining conventional panoramic radiographs of the maxillo-mandibular regions.
LC NO. 75-701672
Prod-USVA Dist-USNAC 1973

Radiography Of The Temporomandibular Joints C 20 MIN
16MM FILM, 3/4 OR 1/2 IN VIDEO
Demonstrates three techniques utilizing conventional dental radiographic units for radiographing the temporomandibular joints from their lateral and inferior aspects.
Prod-AMDA Dist-AMDA 1973

Radioisotope Scanning In Medicine C 16 MIN
16MM FILM, 3/4 OR 1/2 IN VIDEO J-C
Explains the principle of scanning with radioactive tracers for diagnostic purposes. Presents a case history of a lung scanning. Illustrates both photoscans and dot scans. Discusses future developments.
From The Magic Of The Atom Series. No. 30
Prod-HANDEL Dist-HANDEL 1965

Radioisotopes C 30 MIN
2 INCH VIDEOTAPE I-J
Defines radioisotopes and describes their uses, including tracing, dating, half life and decay and systems for nuclear auxiliary power.
From The Living In A Nuclear Age Series.
Prod-GPITVL Dist-GPITVL

Radioisotopes - Tools Of Discovery X 11 MIN
16MM FILM, 3/4 OR 1/2 IN VIDEO H
Demonstrates the proper techniques for handling radioactive materials in the classroom. Procedures emphasize safety in handling, recording and disposition of radioactive materials as well as accuracy in recording data. Establishes the usefulness of radioisotopes in the laboratory by pursuing investigations with both plants and animals.
Prod-EBF Dist-EBEC 1968

Radioisotopes - Tools Of Discovery (Spanish) C 11 MIN
16MM FILM, 3/4 OR 1/2 IN VIDEO H
Demonstrates techniques for handling radioactive materials. Emphasizes safety in handling, recording and disposing of radioactive materials as well as accuracy in recording data. Establishes the usefulness of radioisotopes in the laboratory by showing investigations with plants and animals.
Prod-EBEC Dist-EBEC

Radioisotopes For Medicine C 11 MIN
16MM FILM OPTICAL SOUND PRO
Using a flow chart as a guide, depicts the main steps in the manufacturing of medotopes at the Squibb Radiopharmaceuticals Plant in New Brunswick, N. J. And traces events taking place when an order is received. Stresses testing for quality control.
LC NO. FI68-220
Prod-SQUIBB Dist-SQUIBB Prodn-STGT 1965

Radioisotopes In Agricultural Research B 41 MIN
16MM FILM OPTICAL SOUND
Traces the utilization of chemicals by plants and animals, and explains how the exact amounts needed are determined by radioactive chemicals. Shows the manufacture and uses of radioactive phosphate.
From The Radioisotopes Series. No. 12
LC NO. FIE53-494
Prod-USA Dist-USNAC 1952

Radioisotopes In General Science B 46 MIN
16MM FILM OPTICAL SOUND
Gives nine illustrations of the radioisotope as an important research tool adaptable to tracer investigations in all branches of general science.
From The Radioisotope Series. No. 13
LC NO. FIE52-2009
Prod-USA Dist-USNAC 1952

Radioisotopes In Medical Diagnosis And Investigation C 30 MIN
16MM FILM OPTICAL SOUND
Shows the present day uses of radioisotopes in medical diagnosis and investigation, including dilution analysis, tracing studies, scanning and renography.
Prod-UKAEA Dist-UKAEA 1967

Radioisotopes In The Diagnosis Of Cancer C 22 MIN
16MM FILM OPTICAL SOUND PRO
Uses animation to describe to members of the medical profession the nature of radioisotopes. Shows through clinical photography how radioisotopes are used in cancer detection.
LC NO. 72-700180
Prod-AMCS Dist-AMCS 1971

Radioisotopes In The Diagnosis Of Cancer(2nd Edition) C 23 MIN
3/4 OR 1/2 INCH VIDEO CASSETTE
Describes the nature of radioisotopes and how their properties are applied in the diagnosis of cancer, by means of animation. Discusses and illustrates the most common clinical applications.
Prod-WFP Dist-WFP

Radiological Reporting - A New Approach C 13 MIN
16MM FILM OPTICAL SOUND
Discusses a computerized radiological reporting system which eliminates the risk of lost X-ray records.
LC NO. 78-701565
Prod-JHH Dist-JHH Prodn-PAPPVA 1978

Radiology Factor To DRGs, The C 30 MIN
3/4 OR 1/2 INCH VIDEO CASSETTE PRO
Reveals ways to manage radiology cooperatively with physicians in the hospital.
Prod-AMCRAD Dist-AMCRAD

Radiology Practice In A Small Community C 23 MIN
16MM FILM OPTICAL SOUND
Presents four practicing radiologists from small towns in Nebraska, New York and Pennsylvania who offer their impressions concerning practice in their areas.
LC NO. 76-702198
Prod-AMCRAD Dist-FILAUD 1976

Radiometric Laws C 60 MIN
3/4 OR 1/2 INCH VIDEO CASSETTE
See series title for descriptive statement.
From The Advanced Remote Sensing Techniques Series. Section I, Pt 2
Prod-UAZMIC Dist-UAZMIC

Radiometry Of Optical Systems C 60 MIN
3/4 OR 1/2 INCH VIDEO CASSETTE
See series title for descriptive statement.
From The Advanced Remote Sensing Techniques Series. Section I, Pt 3
Prod-UAZMIC Dist-UAZMIC

Radiotherapy - High Dosage Treatment B 17 MIN
16MM FILM OPTICAL SOUND
Shows nature and physiological effects of high dosage X-rays, administration of X-ray treatment for carcinoma of the tongue, function and administration of radon seeds and factors in care of patients receiving X-ray therapy.
From The Nursing Series.
LC NO. FIE52-361
Prod-USOE Dist-USNAC Prodn-WILLRD 1945

Radiotherapy Of Breast Cancer C 31 MIN
3/4 INCH VIDEO CASSETTE
Summarizes the effectiveness of control dosages of radiation in the treatment of breast cancer.
Prod-UTAHTI Dist-UTAHTI

Radium Decontamination C 8 MIN
16MM FILM OPTICAL SOUND
Tells the story of the decontamination of a radium contaminated basement in a duplex frame house by the Pennsylvania Health Department and the U S Public Health Service during the summer of 1964 at Lansdowne, Pennsylvania.
LC NO. 74-705472
Prod-USPHS Dist-USNAC

Rafer Johnson Story, The B 55 MIN
16MM FILM OPTICAL SOUND I-C A
The story of Rafer Johnson, world decathlon champion, captain of the 1960 U S Olympic Team, honor student, president of his grade school, high school and college classes and first member of the Peace Corps.
Prod-SF Dist-SF 1963

Raft, The C 29 MIN
16MM FILM, 3/4 OR 1/2 IN VIDEO C A
Tells how a family travels on a raft down the Parnaiba River in Brazil to sell their homemade earthenware and other merchandise in the city of Teresina, the journey taking approximately a month.
Prod-SLUIZR Dist-PHENIX 1974

Rafter Construction C 13 MIN
16MM FILM, 3/4 OR 1/2 IN VIDEO J-H A
Explains rafter construction, including basic roof types, roof members and all types of rafters. Defines rafter layout terminology and presents layout of the common rafter with the framing square.
Prod-SF Dist-SF 1969

Rafting The Whitewater—A Series

Shows how to increase the skills, knowledge and enthusiasm of novice and intermediate river rafters.
Prod-KWSU Dist-PBS 1981

Rafting The Whitewater, Pt 1
Rafting The Whitewater, Pt 2
Rafting The Whitewater, Pt 3
Rafting The Whitewater, Pt 4

Rafting The Whitewater, Pt 1 C
3/4 OR 1/2 INCH VIDEO CASSETTE
Shows what to look for in a raft, the pro's and con's of various raft designs and the advantages of different rafting materials.
From The Rafting The Whitewater Series.
Prod-KWSU Dist-PBS 1981

Rafting The Whitewater, Pt 2 C
3/4 OR 1/2 INCH VIDEO CASSETTE
Shows how to equip a raft, taking a careful look at the difference in paddles.
From The Rafting The Whitewater Series.
Prod-KWSU Dist-PBS 1981

Rafting The Whitewater, Pt 3 C
3/4 OR 1/2 INCH VIDEO CASSETTE
Demonstrates the maintenance of a raft with a step-by-step look at the repair of tears, a common occurence in the whitewater rafting.
From The Rafting The Whitewater Series.
Prod-KWSU Dist-PBS 1981

Rafting The Whitewater, Pt 4 C
3/4 OR 1/2 INCH VIDEO CASSETTE
Summarizes the information in the first three programs, and prepares viewers for an extended trip on the river.
From The Rafting The Whitewater Series.
Prod-KWSU Dist-PBS 1981

Rag Rugs C 14 MIN
2 INCH VIDEOTAPE
Shows how to make a throw rug from strips of old clothing and burlap. Explains that the cloth strips are sewn to the burlap backing with a running stitch and additional information is given on hooking the rug.
From The Living Better II Series.
Prod-MAETEL Dist-PUBTEL

Rag Tag Champs, The C 48 MIN
16MM FILM, 3/4 OR 1/2 IN VIDEO
Tells how young Jake finds a solution that helps his baseball team win games in a spectacular manner. Based on the book Jake by Alfred Slote. Originally shown on the television series ABC Weekend Specials.
LC NO. 79-707133
Prod-ABCTV Dist-MTI Prodn-ABCCIR 1978

Rag Tapestry C 11 MIN
16MM FILM, 3/4 OR 1/2 IN VIDEO
Shows 24 children, ages 8-12, at a series of Saturday workshops at the Metropolitan Museum of Art, learning how to make a rag tapestry. Reveals how the children, after choosing their subject, New York City, made line drawings, then transferred them to a large piece of rug backing, and then, using wool scraps, created a colorful 3 x 10 foot tapestry.
Prod-IFF Dist-IFF

Rage C 20 MIN
16MM FILM OPTICAL SOUND I-C A
See series title for descriptive statement.
From The Cellar Door Cine Mites Series.
LC NO. 74-701552
Prod-CELLAR Dist-CELLAR 1972

Ragged Ragamuffins Of The Continental Army, The C 8 MIN
16MM FILM, 3/4 OR 1/2 IN VIDEO P-I
Explains the beginnings of the Revolutionary War period, and the adoption of the Declaration of Independence on July 4, 1776. Shows the Colonists' long struggle for what they wanted - freedom from British rule and the freedom to build a life of their own.
From The A Nation Is Born Series.
Prod-PIC Dist-LUF 1973

Ragged Revolution, The - The Romance And The Reality Of The Mexican Revolution,... C 37 MIN
16MM FILM, 3/4 OR 1/2 IN VIDEO
Looks at the realities behind the romantic myths of the Mexican Revolution. States that it was a brutal war between weak and disorganized Federal troops and rebel armies led by illiterate peasants and opportunistic bandits.
Prod-YORKTV Dist-CNEMAG

Raging Bull B 129 MIN
16MM FILM OPTICAL SOUND
Stars Robert DeNiro as middle-weight boxing champion Jake La Motta. Directed by Martin Scorsese.
Prod-UAA Dist-UAE 1980

Raglan Shoulder Shaping And Decreasing B 29 MIN
2 INCH VIDEOTAPE
See series title for descriptive statement.
From The Busy Knitter I Series.
Prod-WMVSTV Dist-PUBTEL

Rags - 100 Years Of The Apparel Industry In Northeastern Ohio C 29 MIN
3/4 INCH VIDEO CASSETTE
Presents a documentary about the apparel industry in northeastern Ohio for the past 100 years. Discusses its prospects for the future.
Prod-OHC Dist-HRC

Ragtime King C 20 MIN
3/4 INCH VIDEO CASSETTE I
Explores the life of ragtime composer Scott Joplin.
From The Truly American Series.
Prod-WVIZTV Dist-GPITVL 1979

Raguira C 9 MIN
3/4 OR 1/2 INCH VIDEO CASSETTE P-H
Shows a remote mountain village, Raguira, in Colombia, where an old man reflects on his youth. Reliving the old man's reminiscing, a small boy shows that things have changed little as major daily activites still include selling wood, making pottery, going to market and playing music. Exhibits the first effects of modernization on an old way of life.
From The Life In Colombia Series.
Prod-IFF Dist-IFF

Rahway - Stay 'Way C 27 MIN
16MM FILM, 3/4 OR 1/2 IN VIDEO H-C A
Looks at the Juvenile Awareness Project at Rahway State Prison, where teenagers are brought to the jail to learn what confinement is really like.
Prod-WNETTV Dist-FI 1977

Raices De Felicidad B 25 MIN
16MM FILM, 3/4 OR 1/2 IN VIDEO J-C
A Spanish language film. Describes the nature of family relationships, particularly the role of the father in building and maintaining a happy family environment. Shows a family in Puerto Rico where mutual love and respect provide the mortar to build a firm structure of self-respect, independence and productivity.
Prod-MHFB Dist-IFB 1955

Raid Commercial C 1 MIN
3/4 OR 1/2 INCH VIDEO CASSETTE
Shows a classic animated television commercial.
Prod-BROOKC Dist-BROOKC

Railroad Builders, The X 14 MIN
16MM FILM, 3/4 OR 1/2 IN VIDEO I-H
Uses live photography, original prints and photographs to present an account of the building of the first continental railroad. Explains how the railroad builders contributed to westward expansion.
Prod-EBF Dist-EBEC 1963

Railroad Safety B 34 MIN
16MM FILM OPTICAL SOUND
Points out the importance of safety in all phases of railroad work, in the yards, on the trains, along the right-of-way and in the shops.
LC NO. FIE52-2092
Prod-PENNRR Dist-USNAC 1952

Railroad Songs, Pt 1 C 15 MIN
3/4 OR 1/2 INCH VIDEO CASSETTE P
Shows how to clap a steady beat and an off beat pattern, and recognize a tempo change. Presents the songs I've Been Working On The Railroad, Down At The Station and Get On Board.
From The Song Sampler Series.
LC NO. 81-707034
Prod-JCITV Dist-GPITVL 1981

Railroad Songs, Pt 2 C 15 MIN
3/4 OR 1/2 INCH VIDEO CASSETTE P
Shows how to clap a steady beat and an offbeat pattern, and recognize a tempo change. Presents the songs I've Been Working On The Railroad, Down At The Station and Get On Board.
From The Song Sampler Series.
LC NO. 81-707034
Prod-JCITV Dist-GPITVL 1981

Railroaders B 22 MIN
16MM FILM, 3/4 OR 1/2 IN VIDEO I-C A
Shows how railroaders of the Rockies battle the elements to keep open a vital link between the Pacific and Atlantic shores of Canada.
Prod-NFBC Dist-IFB

Railroads C 20 MIN
3/4 OR 1/2 INCH VIDEO CASSETTE
Presents a documentary on the Soviet railroad system.
Prod-IHF Dist-IHF

Railroads And Westward Expansion - 1800-1845 C 14 MIN
16MM FILM, 3/4 OR 1/2 IN VIDEO I-C A
Examines America's need for improved transportation in the early 19th century, discusses the industrial revolution and its effect on the development of the railroad, and shows the impact of the railroad on commerce, westward expansion and jobs in the first half of the 19th century.
Prod-CALVIN Dist-PHENIX 1978

Railroads And Westward Expansion - 1845-1865 C 14 MIN
16MM FILM, 3/4 OR 1/2 IN VIDEO I-C A
Examines the role of the railroad in the settlement of the prairies, the growth of cities and immigration during the period 1845-1865. Explains how the growth of the frontier led to the growth of the railroad and discusses the impact of rail power on the Civil War.
Prod-CALVIN Dist-PHENIX 1978

Railroads And Westward Expansion, 1865-1900 C 16 MIN
16MM FILM, 3/4 OR 1/2 IN VIDEO I-C A
Explains how the desire for the resources of the West led to the building of the transcontinental railroad after the Civil War. Discusses the importance of the railroad in settling the Great Plains and Western states and its significance in unifying the nation. Examines the ways in which the transcontinental railroad affected commerce and the fabric of daily life in America.
Prod-CALVIN Dist-PHENIX 1978

Railrodder, The C 25 MIN
16MM FILM, 3/4 OR 1/2 IN VIDEO J-C A
Presents Buster Keaton as the 'RAILRODDER,' crossing Canada east to west on a railway track speeder.
Prod-NFBC Dist-NFBC 1965

Rails Across The Summit C 28 MIN
16MM FILM, 3/4 OR 1/2 IN VIDEO
Presents sights and sounds recorded on the 64-mile narrow gage railroad line between Chama, New Mexico and Antonito, Colorado, in the San Juan Mountains.
Prod-MARLOV Dist-MCFI 1976

Railway With A Heart Of Gold C 15 MIN
16MM FILM, 3/4 OR 1/2 IN VIDEO
An account of the Talyllyn Railroad, a historic narrow-gauge slate carrier in northern Wales, and its operation by interested inhabitants in the area who saved it from being sold for scrap.
Prod-DAVC Dist-TEXFLM 1965

Rain C 6 MIN
16MM FILM, 3/4 OR 1/2 IN VIDEO P
Uses everyday situations in familiar environments to encourage the development of language skills. Teaches basic words through song, melody and repetition.
From The Starting To Read Series.
Prod-BURGHS Dist-AIMS 1971

Rain - A First Film C 10 MIN
16MM FILM, 3/4 OR 1/2 IN VIDEO
Presents visual experiences which encourage students to look for interesting patterns in clouds and rain, while learning about the water cycle. Considers the information that can be gained from watching clouds and winds and the good and bad effects of rainstorms.
Prod-BFA Dist-PHENIX 1973

Rain And Shine (Hungarian) C 103 MIN
16MM FILM OPTICAL SOUND
Details the encounter between dyspeptic city bureaucracy and voracious peasantry. Directed by Ferenc Andras. With English subtitles.
Prod-UNKNWN Dist-NYFLMS 1977

Rain Forest C 59 MIN
16MM FILM, 3/4 OR 1/2 IN VIDEO
Looks at moist tropical forests in Costa Rica where a rich ecosystem is sustained by an impoverished forest. Reveals the inhabitants of the area, including the ants, the rare golden toad and the quetzal, a bird sacred to the ancient Maya.
LC NO. 83-706453
Prod-NGS Dist-NGS 1983

Rain Forest, The C 12 MIN
3/4 OR 1/2 INCH VIDEO CASSETTE
Takes a tour of the South American rain forest and discusses many of the interesting plants and animals, as well as man's impact on the area.
Prod-CBSC Dist-CBSC

Rain People, The C 106 MIN
16MM FILM OPTICAL SOUND
Follows the fortunes of a housewife who escapes to California. Directed by Francis Ford Coppola. Stars Shirley Knight, James Caan and Robert Duvall.
Prod-WB Dist-TWYMAN 1969

Rain, Rain Go Away C 11 MIN
16MM FILM, 3/4 OR 1/2 IN VIDEO P
Shows how a rainy morning turns into an action-packed sunshiny day where children, adults and animals work and play with the joy of language. Designed to reinforce the words work, play, hands, feet, big and little.
From The Reading And Word Play Series.
Prod-PEDF Dist-AIMS 1976

Rain, The B 8 MIN
16MM FILM OPTICAL SOUND
Tells the story of a pregnant woman who, after the death of her husband, struggles with the decision to keep or abort her unborn child.
Prod-USC Dist-USC 1981

Rainbow Acres C 26 MIN
16MM FILM - 3/4 IN VIDEO
Depicts life in a farm community called Rainbow Acres which is run and inhabited by mentally retarded adults. Includes comments by founder Reverend Ralph Showers, who discusses the advantages of a self-help environment for handicapped individuals.
LC NO. 79-706856
Prod-FMSP Dist-FMSP 1979

Rainbow Bear, The C 6 MIN
16MM FILM, 3/4 OR 1/2 IN VIDEO K-I
Uses animation to tell the story about the rainbow bear who awakes after several hundred years of slumber, returns to a world of warmth and sunshine to play a green flute and then vanishes into space and time.
Prod-MELNDZ Dist-AMEDFL 1971

Rainbow Black C 31 MIN
16MM FILM OPTICAL SOUND H-C A
Presents a portrait of Black poet, critic and historian Sarah Webster Fabio. Includes readings of her works and interviews in which she discusses her approaches to writing, the relationship of the Black experience to her work and her early influences.
LC NO. 77-701039
Prod-FABIOC Dist-UCEMC 1976

Rainbow Movie Of The Week–A Series
J A
Presents dramas dealing with racial, cultural and social problems.
Prod-RAINTV Dist-GPITVL 1981

Ann Of The Wolf Clan	060 MIN
Billy Loves Ali	060 MIN
College	060 MIN
JOB	060 MIN
Keiko	060 MIN
Mariposa	060 MIN
Pals	060 MIN
Silver City	060 MIN
Two Of Hearts	060 MIN
Weekend	060 MIN

Rainbow Pass C 6 MIN
16MM FILM OPTICAL SOUND J-C A
Presents an experimental film in which immobile shapes are combined with moving patterns to create a feeling of endless depth.
LC NO. 75-704206
Prod-DEMOS Dist-CFS 1975

Rainbow Quest–A Series

Contains a wide assortment of songs, languages, dances, instruments and humor. Hosted by Pete Seeger, who participates in the singing and playing.
Prod-SEEGER Dist-CWATER

Alexander Zelkin	052 MIN
Beers Family, The	052 MIN
Bessie Jones And Children From The Downtown	052 MIN
Bessie Jones And Children From The Downtown	052 MIN
Buffy Sainte-Marie	042 MIN
Cajun Band, The	052 MIN
Clinch Mountain Boys And Cousin Emmy	052 MIN
Doc Watson, Clint Howard and Fred Price	052 MIN
Donovan And Rev Gary Davis	052 MIN
Elizabeth Cotton, Rosa Valentin And Rafael	052 MIN
Frank Warner	052 MIN
Greenbriar Boys, The	052 MIN
Herbert Levy, K L Wong And Hilanders	052 MIN
Herbert Manana	052 MIN
Jean Ritchie And Bernice Reagon	052 MIN
Jim And Hazel Garland	052 MIN
Judy Collins	052 MIN
Leadbelly	052 MIN
Len Chandler	052 MIN
Lino Manocchia, Ralph Marino And Federico	052 MIN
Malvina Reynolds And Jack Elliot	052 MIN
Martha Schlamme	052 MIN
Mimi And Richard Farina	052 MIN
New Lost City Ramblers	052 MIN
Norman Studer And Grant Rogers	052 MIN
Pat Sky And The Pennywhistlers	052 MIN
Paul Cadwell, Mississippi John Hurt	052 MIN
Paul Draper	052 MIN

Penny And Sonya Cohen 052 MIN
Pete Seeger - Solo 052 MIN
Roscoe Holcomb And Jean Redpath 052 MIN
Ruth Rabin 052 MIN
Sonia Malkine 052 MIN
Sonny Terry And Brownie McGhee 052 MIN
Steve Addiss And Bill Crofut With Phan Duy 052 MIN
Theodore Bikel And Rashid Hussein 052 MIN
Tom Paxton, The Clancy Brothers And Tommy Makem 052 MIN
Woody Guthrie 052 MIN

Rainbow Reel C 15 MIN
16MM FILM OPTICAL SOUND K-J
Presents a series of animated designs made by children, including flip cards, cells and cut-outs.
Prod-YELLOW Dist-YELLOW 1968

Rainbow Road - Overview C 30 MIN
3/4 OR 1/2 INCH VIDEO CASSETTE A
Surveys the various factors that make for a solid foundation in reading readiness such as visual and auditory discrimination, directionality, eye-hand coordination, attention span, teaching the alphabet, and physical, emotional and social awareness.
From The Rainbow Road Series. Pt 1
LC NO. 82-707393
Prod-KAIDTV Dist-GPITVL 1982

Rainbow Road - Review C 30 MIN
3/4 OR 1/2 INCH VIDEO CASSETTE A
Relates oral and written language with the development of a background of information and experiences on the part of the young child.
From The Rainbow Road Series. Pt 4
LC NO. 82-707396
Prod-KAIDTV Dist-GPITVL 1982

Rainbow Road—A Series
A
Demonstrates the ways parents can help their children develop a solid foundation of basic reading readiness skills.
Prod-KAIDTV Dist-GPITVL 1982

Oral Language 030 MIN
Rainbow Road - Overview 030 MIN
Rainbow Road - Review 030 MIN
Written Language 030 MIN

Rainbow Serpent, The C 11 MIN
16MM FILM, 3/4 OR 1/2 IN VIDEO P-I
Retells the aboriginal legend of creation. Explains how a giant serpent named Goorialla journeyed across Australia and created the topographical features and animal life. Based on the book The Rainbow Serpent by Dick Roughsey.
LC NO. 79-707206
Prod-WWS Dist-WWS 1979

Rainbow Stroke - B And K C 15 MIN
3/4 INCH VIDEO CASSETTE P
From The Writing Time Series.
Prod-WHROTV Dist-GPITVL

Rainbowland C 14 MIN
16MM FILM, 3/4 OR 1/2 IN VIDEO I-C A
Presents an animated allegory which follows the adventures of two characters in order to present the concept that the United States is a good place to live.
Prod-ARTASI Dist-LCOA 1978

Rainbowland (Captioned) C 14 MIN
16MM FILM, 3/4 OR 1/2 IN VIDEO I-C A
Presents Philip Harmonic, the best harmonica player in Rainbowland, who is disgusted with the pollution, graffiti and noise that surround him. His journeys through other lands convince him, finally, that his home land is special, after all.
Prod-ARTASI Dist-LCOA 1979

Raindrops And Soil Erosion C 21 MIN
16MM FILM OPTICAL SOUND
Shows the action of individual raindrops on uncovered soil and emphasizes the need for soil and water conservation methods.
LC NO. FIE52-420
Prod-USDA Dist-USNAC 1947

Rainforest C 27 MIN
16MM FILM OPTICAL SOUND
Presents the premiere performance at the 1968 Buffalo Festival of the Arts of the Merce Cunningham ballet, with music by John Cage. By Richard Leacock and D A Pennebaker.
Prod-PENNAS Dist-PENNAS

Rainforest People C 14 MIN
16MM FILM, 3/4 OR 1/2 IN VIDEO I-C A
Examines the isolation of people who live behind the barrier of dense vegetation. Tells how the tropical rainforest provides the pygmies of the Congo with all their basic needs. Shows the Waika indians who live along the Orinoco River in the rainforests of Southern Venezuela. Discusses their crops and points out that the river is their sole means of transportation to the outside world.
From The Places People Live Series.
Prod-SF Dist-SF 1970

Rainmaking C 17 MIN
16MM FILM OPTICAL SOUND
Revised edition of THE RAINMAKERS. Shows the history of cloud seeding in Australia from early experiments to the present.
Prod-CSIROA Dist-CSIROA 1968

Rainmaking C 29 MIN
2 INCH VIDEOTAPE
Features meteorologist Frank Sechrist explaining how man can and does make rain through cloud seeding. Introduces a couple of theories, such as supercooling and coalescence showing how clouds can produce freezing water drops and then considers the moral and economic aspects of weather modification.
From The Weather Series.
Prod-WHATV Dist-PUBTEL

Rainshower C 15 MIN
16MM FILM, 3/4 OR 1/2 IN VIDEO P-I
Presents the sights, sounds, beauty and rhythm of rain. Explains that it is a source of the water which we use, and that it affects plants and other living things as well as people working in the community.
Prod-CF Dist-CF 1965

Rainshower (Rev Ed) C 15 MIN
16MM FILM, 3/4 OR 1/2 IN VIDEO P-I
Explores the sights and sounds of rain coming to plants and animals. Includes no narration.
Prod-CF Dist-CF

Rainshower (Spanish) C 15 MIN
16MM FILM, 3/4 OR 1/2 IN VIDEO P-I
Shows a rainshower which comes to the plants and animals on a farm and to the people in a community.
Prod-CF Dist-CF 1965

Rainy Day Story, A C 13 MIN
16MM FILM, 3/4 OR 1/2 IN VIDEO P-J
Describes a step-by-step procedure for writing original stories.
Prod-PHENIX Dist-CORF

Rainy Day, A C 14 MIN
3/4 OR 1/2 INCH VIDEO CASSETTE P
See series title for descriptive statement.
From The Strawberry Square Series.
Prod-NEITV Dist-AITECH 1982

Rainy Day, A C 35 MIN
16MM FILM, 3/4 OR 1/2 IN VIDEO H-C A
Tells the story of a famous actress who returns home for her father's funeral and reminisces about the horrors of her overprotected childhood.
Prod-AMERFI Dist-LCOA 1979

Rainy Night, A Sick Computer, An Estimate, A - Estimating To Tens And Hundreds C 15 MIN
3/4 OR 1/2 INCH VIDEO CASSETTE I
Tells how Alice estimates prices to see if she has enough money for spare parts.
From The Figure Out Series.
Prod-MAETEL Dist-AITECH 1982

Rainy Season In West Africa C 14 MIN
16MM FILM, 3/4 OR 1/2 IN VIDEO P
Portrays the lives, religion and dress of West African villagers. Follows the planting and harvesting of crops in this dry land using centuries-old methods.
From The Man And His World Series.
Prod-FI Dist-FI 1969

Raised In Anger C 54 MIN
16MM FILM, 3/4 OR 1/2 IN VIDEO H-C A
Explains aspects of child abuse, including how it touches families throughout society and programs available to help parents deal with stress.
Prod-WQED Dist-MEDIAG 1979

Raisin In The Sun B 128 MIN
16MM FILM OPTICAL SOUND H
Tells what happens to the dreams of a Chicago black family when they receive a life insurance check for 10,000 dollars. Stars Sidney Poitier and Ruby Dee.
LC NO. 82-700882
Prod-CPC Dist-TIMLIF 1961

Raisin Wine C 15 MIN
3/4 OR 1/2 INCH VIDEO CASSETTE
Reviews the day-to-day life of a 79-year-old man in a retirement facility. Emphasizes what is positive rather than what is negative about old age. Illustrates the need for continuation of previous life style, aspects of normal aging and common human needs of the aged.
Prod-INLL Dist-AJN

Raising And Lowering Our Flag C 11 MIN
16MM FILM OPTICAL SOUND I-J
Shows the correct way to handle the American flag. Depicts a Marine Corps color detail in the traditional ceremonies of raising and of lowering the flag.
LC NO. FIA65-1157
Prod-SIGMA Dist-FILCOM 1964

Raising Children C 59 MIN
3/4 OR 1/2 INCH VIDEO CASSETTE
Explores contrasting views on discipline, religion, parental authority, and youthful rebellion.
From The Young And Old - Reaching Out Series.
LC NO. 80-707699
Prod-CRFI Dist-PBS 1979

Raising Children C 60 MIN
3/4 OR 1/2 INCH VIDEO CASSETTE J-C A
Presents the views of eight persons, half in their twenties and half over 60, as they discuss with their host various aspects of child rearing. Contrasts views on discipline, religion, parental authority, youthful rebellion and personal tragedy.
LC NO. 80-707699
Prod-WINFBC Dist-WINFBC 1979

Raising Dairy Calves C 10 MIN
16MM FILM OPTICAL SOUND I-H
Shows the recommended steps for raising dairy calves for herd replacements.
Prod-HUNTER Dist-UPR 1959

Raj Gonds C 55 MIN
16MM FILM, 3/4 OR 1/2 IN VIDEO H-C A
Explains that the Raj Gonds were once a rich and powerful people in Central India, but now live as a tribal group outside the mainstream of Indian life on land owned by landlords. Portrays their annual festival of Dandari in which they cover themselves in dust and ashes and take a bemused and self-deprecating look at their present low status, as landlords, Gods and bridegrooms are all made fun of.
From The Worlds Apart Series.
Prod-BBCTV Dist-FI 1982

Rajvinder - An East Indian Family C 16 MIN
16MM FILM, 3/4 OR 1/2 IN VIDEO J-C
Documents the marriage preparations and wedding of Rajvinder, a young Sikh woman who lives in an East Indian community in North America. Reveals the Sikh culture through traditional activities as well as different stages of the wedding ceremony. Shows the couple's adaptation to living between two cultures.
Prod-BCNFL Dist-BCNFL 1984

Raku - The Ancient Art Of Japanese Ceramics C 10 MIN
16MM FILM, 3/4 OR 1/2 IN VIDEO J-C A
Covers the basic techniques involved in the ancient Raku process of making pottery.
Prod-CAHILL Dist-AIMS Prodn-LEVING 1972

Raku Glaze Firing C 28 MIN
2 INCH VIDEOTAPE
Features Mrs Peterson describing certain ceramic processes for her classroom at the University of Southern California. Demonstrates raku glaze firing.
From The Wheels, Kilns And Clay Series.
Prod-USC Dist-PUBTEL

Rally - A Race Against Time C 19 MIN
16MM FILM OPTICAL SOUND
Depicts a road rally from San Francisco to Sacramento to Reno showing the drivers, navigators and their equipment pitted against unrelenting terrain under the most demanding and varied conditions available.
Prod-GC Dist-MTP

Rally Around The Flag C 10 MIN
16MM FILM OPTICAL SOUND
Describes a training program for personnel who conduct company Payroll Savings Plan campaigns.
Prod-USSBD Dist-USSBD

Ralph Bunche B 20 MIN
2 INCH VIDEOTAPE I
See series title for descriptive statement.
From The Americans All Series.
Prod-DENVPS Dist-GPITVL Prodn-KRMATV

Ralph Fasanella, Song Of The City C 25 MIN
16MM FILM OPTICAL SOUND H-C A
Describes the life and works of self-taught painter Ralph Fasanella. Emphasizes the themes that make up his work, including his troubled youth, hard-working immigrant parents and labor organizing activities.
LC NO. 79-701720
Prod-BOWGRN Dist-BOWGRN 1979

Ralph Nader - Opinion Leader C 30 MIN
3/4 OR 1/2 INCH VIDEO CASSETTE C
Illustrates the way consumer advocate Ralph Nader rose from relative obscurity to his position as a national opinion leader, as well as the reasons he is able to command national attention.
From The American Government 1 Series.
Prod-DALCCD Dist-DALCCD

Ralph Stanley's Bluegrass Festival C 15 MIN
3/4 OR 1/2 INCH VIDEO CASSETTE
Captures Bluegrass performer Ralph Stanley's foot stomping, hand clapping, outdoor music festival and pays tribute to the Stanley family.
LC NO. 84-707294
Prod-AMBERO Dist-AMBERO 1984

Ralph Votapek - Pianist C 29 MIN
2 INCH VIDEOTAPE
Presents the music of pianist Ralph Votapek.
From The Young Musical Artists Series.
Prod-WKARTV Dist-PUBTEL

Ralph Waldo Emerson - Emerson's Critical Theory B 30 MIN
2 INCH VIDEOTAPE J-H
From The Franklin To Frost Series.
Prod-GPITVL Dist-GPITVL

Ralph Waldo Emerson - Emerson's Disciple, Thoreau B 30 MIN
2 INCH VIDEOTAPE J-H
From The Franklin To Frost Series.
Prod-GPITVL Dist-GPITVL

Ralph Waldo Emerson - Introduction B 30 MIN
2 INCH VIDEOTAPE J-H
From The Franklin To Frost Series.
Prod-GPITVL Dist-GPITVL

Ralph Waldo Emerson - Introduction C 30 MIN
2 INCH VIDEOTAPE J-H
See series title for descriptive statement.
From The From Franklin To Frost - Ralph Waldo Emerson Series.
Prod-MPATI Dist-GPITVL

Ralph Waldo Emerson - Meter-Making Arguments B 30 MIN
2 INCH VIDEOTAPE J-H

From The Franklin To Frost Series.
Prod-GPITVL Dist-GPITVL

Ralph Waldo Emerson - Self-Reliance, Emerson's Philosophy B 30 MIN
2 INCH VIDEOTAPE J-H
Prod-GPITVL Dist-GPITVL

Rameau, The Harpsichord, And George Malcolm C 26 MIN
16MM FILM, 3/4 OR 1/2 IN VIDEO J-C A
Presents French composer and theorist Jean Philippe Rameau (1683-1764), who composed both suites and operas for the harpsichord. Features professional musician George Malcolm who describes the harpsichord and plays several selections from some of Rameau's compositions.
From The Musical Triangle Series.
Prod-THAMES Dist-MEDIAG 1975

Rameau's Nephew, By Diderot C 240 MIN
16MM FILM OPTICAL SOUND
Presents an adaptation of Diderot's book RAMEAU'S NEPHEW.
LC NO. 74-703008
Prod-SNOWM Dist-CANFDC 1973

Ramifications Of Normal Value C 50 MIN
3/4 OR 1/2 INCH VIDEO CASSETTE
Discusses relativity of privileged names and implications of changes in order of evaluation in computer languages.
From The Computer Languages - Pt 1 Series.
Prod-MIOT Dist-MIOT

Ramlila B 13 MIN
16MM FILM OPTICAL SOUND I-C A
Presents the Ramlila celebrations as performed in Delhi where the legend of Rama and Sita is unfolded. Includes recitations from Tulsidas' 'RAMAYANA.'
Prod-INDIA Dist-NEDINF

Ramona B 93 MIN
16MM FILM OPTICAL SOUND
A Spanish language film. Explores the story of an adopted Indian girl and the problems that develop when she falls in love and marries a young Indian man.
Prod-TRANSW Dist-TRANSW

Rampaging Carbons C 27 MIN
16MM FILM, 3/4 OR 1/2 IN VIDEO J-C A
Discusses the 'Greenhouse Effect' - the increase in the carbon dioxide content of the air - and its cause and its potential effects.
From The Perspective Series.
Prod-LONTVS Dist-STNFLD

Ramsey Trade Fair C 18 MIN
16MM FILM - 3/4 IN VIDEO
Visits the Ramsey Trade Fair where people from the Virginia community of Ramsey gather to socialize and trade.
Prod-APPAL Dist-APPAL 1973

Ramus Endosseous Implant C 20 MIN
16MM FILM OPTICAL SOUND PRO
Examines the use of the ramus endosseous implant and presents patients who have been using them for as many as three years.
Prod-LOMAM Dist-LOMAM

Rana C 19 MIN
16MM FILM, 3/4 OR 1/2 IN VIDEO J-C A
Profiles a 21-year-old Moslem college student living in Old Delhi. Tells how she accepts the opportunities and restrictions of her life.
Prod-FLMAUS Dist-WOMBAT

Ranch Girl C 16 MIN
16MM FILM, 3/4 OR 1/2 IN VIDEO P-J
Uses the snow capped Teton peaks as a background for a portrait of a self-reliant girl who helps with her family's occupation, ranching. Shows her spending the day riding, exploring and looking for Indian relics.
Prod-GORKER Dist-AIMS 1972

Ranch Hand C 15 MIN
16MM FILM, 3/4 OR 1/2 IN VIDEO I
From The Career Awareness Series.
Prod-KLVXTV Dist-GPITVL

Ranch, The, Pt 1 C 14 MIN
2 INCH VIDEOTAPE
See series title for descriptive statement.
From The Muffinland Series.
Prod-WGTV Dist-PUBTEL

Ranch, The, Pt 2 C 14 MIN
2 INCH VIDEOTAPE
See series title for descriptive statement.
From The Muffinland Series.
Prod-WGTV Dist-PUBTEL

Rancher Glen's Secrets C 10 MIN
16MM FILM OPTICAL SOUND P-H A
Rancher Glen, the healthy cowboy of the Tuberculosis Association, explains why and how the tuberculin skin test is given.
Prod-WSU Dist-WSU 1961

Ranchero And Gauchos In Argentina C 17 MIN
16MM FILM, 3/4 OR 1/2 IN VIDEO P-C
Describes the ranch life on a beef ranch. Shows gauchos working with the herd and the use of scientific farming methods. Trasts the affluence and poverty on the ranch. Views Spanish architecture and furnishings.
From The Man And His World Series.
Prod-FI Dist-FI 1969

Random Access Memory Applications, Pt 1 C 60 MIN
1 INCH VIDEOTAPE IND
Gives application examples of systems ranging in size from small scratch pad memory systems to a minicomputer mainframe.
From The Semiconductor Memories Course Series. No. 9
Prod-TXINLC Dist-TXINLC

Random Access Memory Applications, Pt 2 C 60 MIN
1 INCH VIDEOTAPE IND
Details MOS random access memory applications. Emphasizes considerations unique to MOS including drive requirements, refresh and clock timing.
From The Semiconductor Memories Course Series. No. 10
Prod-TXINLC Dist-TXINLC

Random Access Memory Applications, Pt 3 C 60 MIN
1 INCH VIDEOTAPE IND
Describes thoroughly the level cache, core, MOS, ECL and TTL memory systems. Emphasizes the comparison of these memory systems.
From The Semiconductor Memories Course Series. No. 11
Prod-TXINLC Dist-TXINLC

Random Events B 31 MIN
16MM FILM OPTICAL SOUND H-C
Shows how the over-all effect of a very large number of random events can be very predictable. Several unusual games are played to bring out the statistical nature of this predictability. The predictable nature of radioactive decay is explained.
From The PSSC Physics Films Series.
Prod-PSSC Dist-MLA 1962

Random Processes - Basic Concepts And Definitions C 28 MIN
3/4 OR 1/2 INCH VIDEO CASSETTE PRO
See series title for descriptive statement.
From The Probability And Random Processes Introduction To Random Processes Series.
Prod-MIOT Dist-MIOT

Random Telegraph Wave B 24 MIN
3/4 OR 1/2 INCH VIDEO CASSETTE PRO
Considers the random telegraph wave and uses that example to introduce the minimum mean-square error (MMSE) prediction problem.
From The Probability And Random Processes Introduction To Random Processes Series.
Prod-MIOT Dist-MIOT

Random Variables (1) B 26 MIN
3/4 OR 1/2 INCH VIDEO CASSETTE PRO
Introduces random variables. Defines probability distributions and probability distribution functions.
From The Probability And Random Processes - Random Variables Series.
Prod-MIOT Dist-MIOT

Random Variables (2) B 20 MIN
3/4 OR 1/2 INCH VIDEO CASSETTE PRO
Discusses random variables and probability density functions and their properties.
From The Probability And Random Processes - Random Variables Series.
Prod-MIOT Dist-MIOT

Randy B 27 MIN
16MM FILM OPTICAL SOUND
Shows an emotionally disturbed eleven-year-old boy at Camp Wedico to illustrate the difficulty of meeting the needs of an emotionally handicapped child.
From The Wediko Series.
LC NO. 71-711415
Prod-MASON Dist-DOCUFL 1973

Randy C 15 MIN
3/4 OR 1/2 INCH VIDEO CASSETTE J-H
Tells how a boy's loneliness leads him to join a gang that goes in for vandalism.
From The Changing Series.
Prod-WGTETV Dist-AITECH 1980

Randy B 27 MIN
3/4 OR 1/2 INCH VIDEO CASSETTE T
Presents the ways that, due to beguiling but inconsistent behavior, a more seriously disturbed eleven-year-old camper is treated by four different staff members with varying degrees of success.
From The Wediko Series - Emotionally Disturbed-- Children At Camp Series.
Prod-DOCUFL Dist-DOCUFL

Randy's Thanksgiving C 15 MIN
3/4 INCH VIDEO CASSETTE K-P
See series title for descriptive statement.
From The Storytime Series.
Prod-WCETTV Dist-GPITVL 1976

Randy's Up - Randy's Down C 22 MIN
16MM FILM OPTICAL SOUND C A
Depicts a child's progress and regressions during the administration of contingent shock therapy for controlling self-abusive behavior in an institutional environment. Focuses on the child's behavior as well as the moods and attitudes of the workers and psychologists dealing with him day to day.
LC NO. 78-701608
Prod-UKANS Dist-UKANS 1977

Range Allotment Analysis C 47 MIN
16MM FILM OPTICAL SOUND
Shows the systematic method used by range managers in the U S Forest Service to collect information on which to base their management plans and decisions for the National Forests and National Grasslands.
LC NO. 75-701372
Prod-USDA Dist-USNAC 1965

Range Determination B 21 MIN
16MM FILM OPTICAL SOUND
Describes various range determination methods, such as binoculars, registration maps, and observation of flash and sound.
LC NO. 80-701839
Prod-USA Dist-USNAC 1980

Range Of Motion - The Lower Extremity B 19 MIN
3/4 OR 1/2 INCH VIDEO CASSETTE
Shows a step-by-step demonstration of the range of motion exercises for the joints of the lower extremity.
Prod-BU Dist-BU

Range Of Motion - The Upper Extremity B 24 MIN
3/4 OR 1/2 INCH VIDEO CASSETTE
Shows a step-by-step demonstration of motion exercises for the joints of the upper extremity.
Prod-BU Dist-BU

Rangelands - An American Heritage C 24 MIN
16MM FILM OPTICAL SOUND
Emphasizes the importance of the American rangelands in providing clean water, recreational areas, vegetation for livestock and other natural resources.
LC NO. 77-702409
Prod-SOCRM Dist-SOCRM Prodn-MONTFP 1977

Rangelands - The Silent Resources C 24 MIN
16MM FILM OPTICAL SOUND
Stresses the importance of the American rangelands as a natural resource and explains techniques for proper range management.
LC NO. 77-702410
Prod-SOCRM Dist-SOCRM Prodn-MONTFP 1977

Ranger C 29 MIN
16MM FILM OPTICAL SOUND
Points out how the small unit leader must be resourceful and capable of directing operations under many types of geographic and climatic conditions. Shows how rangers are trained at Fort Benning, Georgia.
From The Big Picture Series.
LC NO. 74-705476
Prod-USA Dist-USNAC 1968

Ranger - The Ultimate Soldier C 32 MIN
16MM FILM OPTICAL SOUND A
Describes the objectives and nature of ranger training offered in the U S Army, including physical conditioning, military mountaineering and guerilla warfare.
LC NO. 77-700728
Prod-USA Dist-USNAC 1968

Ranger 7 - Photographs Of The Moon B 8 MIN
16MM FILM OPTICAL SOUND
Describes the photographs of the moon taken by Ranger 7 on July 31, 1964. Gives a detailed description of selected photographs.
LC NO. 74-706385
Prod-NASA Dist-USNAC 1964

Ranger 8 - Television Pictures Of The Moon B 8 MIN
16MM FILM OPTICAL SOUND
Shows the photographs of the moon taken by Ranger 8 on February 17, 1965. Gives a detailed description of selected photographs.
LC NO. 74-706386
Prod-NASA Dist-USNAC 1965

Rangi And Papa (Maori Creation Myth) C 8 MIN
3/4 OR 1/2 INCH VIDEO CASSETTE J-C A
Shows in animation the story of the creation, based on ancient wood and stone carvings. Tells of the gods' struggle to separate themselves from their parents and, once free, to develop their creative powers and shape the universe.
Prod-IFF Dist-IFF

Ransom C 5 MIN
16MM FILM OPTICAL SOUND
Uses animation in a story in which the kidnappers of a young girl struggle to spell a word in their ransom note, with a series of rather humorous variants resulting.
Prod-USC Dist-USC

Ransom Of Red Chief C 24 MIN
16MM FILM, 3/4 OR 1/2 IN VIDEO I-J
Recounts the tale of two scoundrels who kidnap a young boy with the hope of collecting a large ransom for his return. Reveals, however, that the boy turns out to be more trouble than they bargained for and the abductors gladly pay the boy's father to take back the mischievous child. Based on a short story by O Henry and produced for the ABC Weekend Specials.
LC NO. 84-706106
Prod-ABCLR Dist-MTI 1983

Rap About Risk C 20 MIN
3/4 INCH VIDEO CASSETTE J-H
Explains the nature and purpose of insurance as a risk. Describes insurance as a sharing proposition in which many people pay relatively little for protection against serious financial loss.
From The Dollar Data Series.
Prod-WHROTV Dist-GPITVL

Rape C 25 MIN
3/4 OR 1/2 INCH VIDEO CASSETTE
Includes interviews with four rape victims who explain their ordeal and how they dealt with it. Shows how to defend oneself when in a rape situation.
Prod-TRAINX Dist-TRAINX

Rape - A Matter Of Survival C 28 MIN
16MM FILM, 3/4 OR 1/2 IN VIDEO
Explodes myths regarding rape, describes types of rapists and challenges women to develop their own prevention and survival plan.
Prod-ODECA Dist-BULFRG

Rape - A Preventive Inquiry C 18 MIN
16MM FILM, 3/4 OR 1/2 IN VIDEO J-C A
Portrays four rape victims, a college student, a businesswoman, a secretary and a mother, who relate the circumstances surrounding their attacks and methods of escape in what police call the four most common cases - hitchhiking, casual acquaintance, hot prowl and kidnapping.
Prod-MITCHG Dist-MTI 1974

Rape - A Preventive Inquiry (Spanish) C 18 MIN
16MM FILM, 3/4 OR 1/2 IN VIDEO J-C A
Portrays four rape victims, a college student, a businesswoman, a secretary and a mother, who relate the circumstances surrounding their attacks and methods of escape in what the police call the four most common cases - hitchhiking, casual acquaintance, hot prowl and kidnapping.
Prod-MITCHG Dist-MTI 1974

Rape - Caring For The Adult Female Victim C 29 MIN
3/4 INCH VIDEO CASSETTE PRO
Portrays the experience of a rape victim and illustrates procedure and approaches that should be used during initial contact with the patient, as well as taking the history, general physical and pelvic examinations, evidence collection, treatment and aftercare instructions.
Prod-NCPCR Dist-MTP

Rape - Caring For The Adult Female Victim C 29 MIN
16MM FILM, 3/4 OR 1/2 IN VIDEO PRO
Portrays the trauma of rape and demonstrates the procedures and approaches to be used by emergency room personnel in treating rape victims, emphasizing sensitivity to the needs of the victim.
Prod-USNAC Dist-USNAC

Rape - Escape Without Violence C 18 MIN
16MM FILM, 3/4 OR 1/2 IN VIDEO J-C A
Shows women how to stop a rapist in a non-violent manner. Emphasizes home security and planning travel routes for optimum safety.
Prod-COXBAR Dist-PEREN

Rape - Face To Face C
3/4 OR 1/2 INCH VIDEO CASSETTE
Features a remarkable confrontation between four female rape victims and four young who are undergoing treatment in a sex offenders program.
Prod-FLMLIB Dist-FLMLIB 1984

Rape - It Can Happen To You C 17 MIN
16MM FILM, 3/4 OR 1/2 IN VIDEO J-C A
Presents dramatic vignettes showing how five women were raped in ordinary circumstances in which they behaved naturally, but too trustingly. Helps teach women how to develop a self-protection program against rape.
LC NO. 84-706022
Prod-GORKER Dist-AIMS 1983

Rape - The Community Viewpoint B 20 MIN
3/4 OR 1/2 INCH VIDEO CASSETTE
Examines public sentiment about rape, raises questions about the treatment of rape victims and tackles some of the myths about rape.
Prod-NOVID Dist-NOVID

Rape - The Right To Resist C 17 MIN
16MM FILM, 3/4 OR 1/2 IN VIDEO J-C A
Presents the positive options that a woman has available to her under attack or attempted rape conditions. Shows how to face an assailant and strategies to use in evading and escaping.
Prod-AIMS Dist-AIMS 1975

Rape - Victim Or Victor C 17 MIN
16MM FILM, 3/4 OR 1/2 IN VIDEO H-C A
Deals with situations in which rapes occur and demonstrates precautions which women can take to reduce the risk of attack. Explains how to avoid vulnerability, how to prevent an intruder from entering a home or automobile and how, if trouble arises, to attract attention and to escape.
LC NO. 79-700092
Prod-LACSD Dist-MTI 1978

Rape / Crisis C 87 MIN
16MM FILM, 3/4 OR 1/2 IN VIDEO J-C A
Investigates the trauma of rape, documents the experience of the rape victim and provides insight into the root causes of sexual violence in society.
LC NO. 84-707172
Prod-SAMHUN Dist-CNEMAG 1983

Rape Alert C 17 MIN
16MM FILM, 3/4 OR 1/2 IN VIDEO J-C A
Offers hints to women on defense against rape, including how to make the home secure, how to avoid hazards, how to use available weapons in case of attack and how to try to escape.
Prod-CAHILL Dist-AIMS 1975

Rape Alert (Spanish) C 17 MIN
16MM FILM, 3/4 OR 1/2 IN VIDEO J-C A
Offers hints to women on defense against rape, including how to make the home secure, how to avoid hazards, how to use available weapons in case of attack and how to try to escape.
Prod-CAHILL Dist-AIMS 1975

Rape And The Rapist C 15 MIN
16MM FILM, 3/4 OR 1/2 IN VIDEO PRO
Uses a series of vignettes to examine the psychology of the rapist, including research which indicates that rapists are primarily motivated by the desire to dominate and to inflict suffering.
Prod-DAVP Dist-MTI 1978

Rape Culture C 35 MIN
16MM FILM - 3/4 IN VIDEO
Examines popular films, advertising, music and 'adult entertainment,' and records the insights of rape crisis workers and prisoners working against rape. Establishes the connections between violence and 'nomal' patterns of male-female behavior. Attempts to expand society's narrow and sexist concept of rape to its real and accurate limits.
Prod-CMBRD Dist-CMBRD

Rape Culture (2nd Ed) C 35 MIN
16MM FILM OPTICAL SOUND
Considers the phenomenon of rape in relation to the cultural and social forces that produce rapists and rape victims. Includes the opinions of convicted rapists, rape crisis center workers and others associated with the problem.
Prod-CMBRD Dist-CMBRD 1983

Rape Is A Social Disease C 28 MIN
3/4 INCH VIDEO CASSETTE
Looks at the image of women and rape presented in classical art and modern day advertising. Dramatizes some of the most common myths surrounding rape to dispel the myths and pinpoint the facts. Analyzes how males are socialized into aggressive roles and women into passive roles.
Prod-WMENIF Dist-WMENIF

Rape Prevention—A Series

Discusses various aspects of rape prevention.
Prod-USA Dist-USNAC

He Loves Me Not 29 MIN

Rape Prevention—A Series

Deals with ways of preventing rape.
Prod-USA Dist-USNAC

He Loves Me Not 029 MIN

Rape Relief C 28 MIN
3/4 INCH VIDEO CASSETTE
Presents a member of the Vancouver Rape Relief talking about the problem of rape and the work done by Rape Relief.
Prod-WMENIF Dist-WMENIF

Rape Victims, The C 22 MIN
16MM FILM, 3/4 OR 1/2 IN VIDEO
Presents information on rape and an assessment of the act as a social problem. Includes a discussion of punishment for rapists, the history of rape and the psychology of the act of rape.
Prod-MEDIAG Dist-MEDIAG Prodn-ABCTV 1978

Rape, Pt 1 C 29 MIN
3/4 OR 1/2 INCH VIDEO CASSETTE
Features Susan Brownmiller discussing her book Against Our Will, a study of rape.
From The Woman Series.
Prod-WNEDTV Dist-PBS

Rape, Pt 2 C 29 MIN
3/4 OR 1/2 INCH VIDEO CASSETTE
Features Susan Brownmiller discussing her book Against Our Will, a study of rape.
From The Woman Series.
Prod-WNEDTV Dist-PBS

Raphael / Bolognese C 30 MIN
1/2 IN VIDEO CASSETTE BETA/VHS K-I
See series title for descriptive statement.
From The Jump Over The Moon - Sharing Literature With Young Children Series.
Prod-HRAW Dist-HRAW

Rapid Frozen Section Techniques C 6 MIN
16MM FILM OPTICAL SOUND
A training film for hospital medical technologists in a rapid method of preparing tissue sections for examination by the hospital pathologists. Demonstrates how the specimen is identified, trimmed for sectioning, placed on the microtome and frozen. Shows how th frozen specimen is cut into thin sections, stained and finally prepared for examination by the pathologist.
LC NO. FIE67-512
Prod-USPHS Dist-USNAC 1966

Rapid Reading C 27 MIN
3/4 OR 1/2 INCH VIDEO CASSETTE
See series title for descriptive statement.
From The Art Of Reading/Speed Learning Series.
Prod-LEARNI Dist-DELTAK

Rapid Reading C 29 MIN
3/4 OR 1/2 INCH VIDEO CASSETTE J-H
Emphasizes the importance of pacing while reading. Shows that pacing retrains the eyes so that they don't have to see all the words on the page.
From The Speed Learning Series.
Prod-LEARNI Dist-AITECH 1982

Rapid Reading C 30 MIN
3/4 OR 1/2 INCH VIDEO CASSETTE
Discusses the place of rapid reading within the confines of learning, and demonstrates steps to developing reading rate as one part of overall reading efficiency. Uses runners as an analogy.
From The Speed Learning Video Series. Show 8
Prod-LEARNI Dist-LEARNI

Rapid Runway Repair Procedures C 15 MIN
16MM FILM OPTICAL SOUND
Demonstrates how to repair a bomb-damaged runway in four hours or less. Shows how to clean the area around a crater and how to top it off with gravel and a metal patch that has been assembled beside it. Introduces new engineering techniques for performing these jobs.
LC NO. 76-703704
Prod-USAF Dist-USNAC 1975

Rapid Transit C 10 MIN
16MM FILM, 3/4 OR 1/2 IN VIDEO
Offers an impressionistic view of the 1979 Transpac on board the 61-foot sloop Rapid Transit.
Prod-OFFSHR Dist-OFFSHR 1979

Rappaccini's Daughter C 57 MIN
16MM FILM, 3/4 OR 1/2 IN VIDEO J-C A
Tells a story set in 18th century Italy about a young man's romantic entanglement with a beautiful, forbidden woman in a poisonous garden. Based on the short story Rappaccini's Daughter by Nathaniel Hawthorne.
From The American Short Story Series.
LC NO. 80-706663
Prod-LEARIF Dist-CORF 1979

Rapping C 15 MIN
16MM FILM, 3/4 OR 1/2 IN VIDEO J-H S
Features a discussion of teenagers about why they take drugs and why they want to stop.
From The Drug Films - Alternatives To Drugs Series.
Prod-FLMFR Dist-FLMFR 1969

Rapping And Tripping—A Series
J-H
Confronts the problem of drugs at the junior high and high school levels.
Prod-FLMFR Dist-FLMFR

Rapping 015 MIN
Tripping 015 MIN

Rapport C 12 MIN
16MM FILM, 3/4 OR 1/2 IN VIDEO J-C A
Presents three vignettes exploring the dynamics of the man-woman relationship to encourage reflection on the deeper aspects of contemporary marriage.
From The Vignettes Series.
Prod-PAULST Dist-PAULST 1973

Raptors - Birds Of Prey C 14 MIN
16MM FILM, 3/4 OR 1/2 IN VIDEO I-H
Shows birds of prey such as the golden eagle, sparrow hawk, great horned owl, red tail hawk, falcon and osprey. Discusses their flying, nesting and feeding habits.
Prod-AFAI Dist-PHENIX 1976

Rapture Family, The C 30 MIN
16MM FILM OPTICAL SOUND H-C A
Discusses the history and meaning of a traditional black form of worship known as 'in the rapture,' which dramatizes man's struggle to resist the temptations of Satan.
LC NO. 79-700101
Prod-IU Dist-IU 1978

Rapture Of The Deep End B 15 MIN
16MM FILM OPTICAL SOUND
Presents a story about a young man employed as a lifeguard at an indoor swimming pool and the strange woman who uses her attractiveness to lure the lifeguard to the pool for a midnight swim.
LC NO. 78-700215
Prod-ROSNFJ Dist-ROSNFJ 1977

Rapture, The C 42 MIN
16MM FILM OPTICAL SOUND R
Portrays how a television network might handle the news events one day after Christ returns. Reveals what happens to those who are not ready for the return.
Prod-GF Dist-GF

Rapunzel B 17 MIN
16MM FILM OPTICAL SOUND
Tells how a young girl uses her long hair to help her rescuer climb into the tower where she has been imprisoned by a wicked witch. Based on the story Rapunzel by the Brothers Grimm.
LC NO. 78-701445
Prod-HOOVJ Dist-HOOVJ 1978

Rapunzel C 10 MIN
16MM FILM, 3/4 OR 1/2 IN VIDEO K-P
Recounts the tale of a girl with long blonde hair who is kept imprisoned in a tower by a witch. Tells how the girl falls in love with a young prince who climbs her braided hair to be with her until he is blinded by the witch.
LC NO. 81-706934
Prod-PERSPF Dist-CORF 1980

Rapunzel X 11 MIN
16MM FILM, 3/4 OR 1/2 IN VIDEO P-I
Uses puppets to visualize this well-known fairy tale.
Prod-HARRY Dist-PHENIX 1955

Rapunzel C 15 MIN
3/4 OR 1/2 INCH VIDEO CASSETTE K-P
See series title for descriptive statement.
From The Gather Round Series.
Prod-CTI Dist-CTI

Rapunzel, Rapunzel C 15 MIN
16MM FILM, 3/4 OR 1/2 IN VIDEO P-H A
Tells the famous Grimm Brothers folktale of Rapunzel.
From The Brothers Grimm Folktales Series.
Prod-DAVT Dist-DAVT

Rapunzel, Rapunzel C 15 MIN
3/4 OR 1/2 INCH VIDEO CASSETTE
Reveals a young girl's struggle with independence.
From The Children's Folktales Series.
Prod-FILMID Dist-FILMID

Rarefied Gas Dynamics X 33 MIN
16MM FILM, 3/4 OR 1/2 IN VIDEO C
Explains that gases of very low density are often encountered in

high-altitude flights, in industrial vacuum processes and in laboratory experiments. Shows the evolution of flow fields as density is varied from continuum levels to the rarefield levels of free-molecule flow. Shows the role of the molecular mean-freepath as a natural scale for shock wave thickness and molecular-beam attenuation, and the interaction of free-molecular flows with molecular beams which are made visible by fluorescence and resonant-scattering techniques.
From The Fluid Mechanics Series.
Prod-NCFMF Dist-EBEC 1968

Rascal C 15 MIN
16MM FILM, 3/4 OR 1/2 IN VIDEO I-H
Tells the story of a young boy, his pet raccoon and their striving to get along with each other.
From The Film As Literature, Series 3 Series.
Prod-DISNEY Dist-WDEMCO 1982

Rasgos Culturales—A Series
16MM FILM, 3/4 OR 1/2 IN VIDEO
A Spanish language motion picture series. Examines the dance and art of Spain and Mexico.
Prod-EBEC Dist-EBEC

Danzas Regionales Espanolas 14 MIN
Maestros De La Pintura 9 MIN
Siqueiros, El Maestro - March Of Humanity In 14 MIN

Rashomon B 83 MIN
3/4 OR 1/2 INCH VIDEO CASSETTE
A Japanese language motion picture. Delves into the mysteries of truth by examining the contradictory stories of a murder and rape recounted by the murdered man, his ravished wife, the murderer, the arresting constable and a neutral bystander. Directed by Akira Kurosawa. Stars Toshiro Mifune, Machiko Kyo and Masayuki Mori. With English Subtitles.
Prod-IHF Dist-IHF

Raspberry High C 10 MIN
3/4 OR 1/2 INCH VIDEO CASSETTE J A
Represents a new concept for getting an audience to examine their own behavior. Shows a young man being urged by his fellow workers to drink more than he can hold.
Prod-SUTHRB Dist-SUTHRB

Rat Attack C
16MM FILM OPTICAL SOUND
See series title for descriptive statement.
From The Rats Series.
Prod-MLA Dist-MLA

Rat Life And Diet In North America C 14 MIN
16MM FILM OPTICAL SOUND
Presents a parable on political and economic repression in the United States and liberation in Canada.
LC NO. 75-704332
Prod-CANFDC Dist-CANFDC 1973

Rate Concepts C 30 MIN
3/4 OR 1/2 INCH VIDEO CASSETTE
See series title for descriptive statement.
From The Infinity Factory Series.
Prod-EDFCEN Dist-MDCPB

Rate Of Change B
16MM FILM OPTICAL SOUND
Shows how the concepts of function, limit, and limit of a function can be drawn together to make a mathematical definition of instantaneous velocity.
Prod-OPENU Dist-OPENU

Rate Of Return Method C 30 MIN
3/4 OR 1/2 INCH VIDEO CASSETTE IND
Introduces evaluation method which solves for the prospective rate of return or invested capital. Uses a share of American Telephone and Telegraph Co common stock as basis for analysis as example problem.
From The Engineering Economy Series.
Prod-COLOSU Dist-COLOSU

Rate Of Return Method (Japanese) C 30 MIN
3/4 OR 1/2 INCH VIDEO CASSETTE IND
Introduces evaluation method which solves for the prospective rate of return or invested capital. Uses a share of American Telephone and Telegraph Co. common stock as basis for analysis as example problem.
From The Engineering Economy Series.
Prod-COLOSU Dist-COLOSU

Rates Of Change C 45 MIN
2 INCH VIDEOTAPE
See series title for descriptive statement.
From The Fundamentals Of Mathematics (2nd Ed.) Unit III - Linear And Quadratic Functions Series.
Prod-CHITVC Dist-GPITVL

Rates Over Time C 30 MIN
3/4 OR 1/2 INCH VIDEO CASSETTE
See series title for descriptive statement.
From The Infinity Factory Series.
Prod-EDFCEN Dist-MDCPB

Ratio - Forming Ratios C 15 MIN
3/4 OR 1/2 INCH VIDEO CASSETTE I
Demonstrates what a ratio is, how to express ratio in particular examples, when ratio might be used and what specific ratios mean in specific situations.
From The Math Works Series.
Prod-AITECH Dist-AITECH

Ratio And Trend Analysis C 15 MIN
3/4 OR 1/2 INCH VIDEO CASSETTE
See series title for descriptive statement.
From The Finance For Nonfinancial Managers Series.
Prod-DELTAK Dist-DELTAK

Ratio, Rate, Percent C 30 MIN
16MM FILM OPTICAL SOUND T
Shows the techniques to be used in determining ratio, rate and per cent. Explores the use of decimals. To be used following 'DECIMALS.'
From The Mathematics For Elementary School Teachers Series. No. 24
Prod-SMSG Dist-MLA 1963

Rational - Emotive Therapy - A Documentary Film Featuring Dr Albert Ellis C 30 MIN
16MM FILM OPTICAL SOUND
Discusses Rational-Emotive Therapy's basic tenets and their evolution and shows live counseling sessions by Albert Ellis and other therapists. Demonstrates R E T's applications to guilt, anxiety and jealousy in an overview of R E T.
Prod-IRL Dist-IRL 1982

Rational Approach To Newly Discovered Hypertension, A C 18 MIN
3/4 OR 1/2 INCH VIDEO CASSETTE PRO
Presents the diagnostic criteria for the various types of hypertension, indications for differing forms of anti- hypertensive therapy, the potential morbidity and mortality associated with diagnostic procedures and the concept of utilizing the cost/benefit ratio in making diagnostic and therapeutic decisions.
Prod-UMICHM Dist-UMICHM 1974

Rational Approach To The Patient With Azotemia, TheThe C 12 MIN
3/4 OR 1/2 INCH VIDEO CASSETTE PRO
Uses logical procedures, including four major diagnostic categories, to lead the viewer to a definitive physio- logical diagnosis. Discusses the common causes and the historical, physical, physiological and biochemical findings which suggest a diagnosis of pre-renal azotemia. Shows the historical physical and roentgenographic findings which suggest post renal azotemia, and the means to differentiate between acute and chronic renal failure.
Prod-UMICHM Dist-UMICHM 1973

Rational Approach To The Square Root Of 2, A B
16MM FILM OPTICAL SOUND
Explains the algebraic techniques needed for finding the root of a polynomial which is irreducible over the rational numbers. Shows how a quotient field can be constructed in which a root lies.
Prod-OPENU Dist-OPENU

Rational Emotive Therapy C 30 MIN
16MM FILM, 3/4 OR 1/2 IN VIDEO C A
Presents a documentary overview of rational emotive therapy, a form of psychotherapy developed in the 1950's by Dr Albert Ellis. Discusses the evolution of RET and shows it in practice at a public workshop and in unstaged counseling sessions.
LC NO. 82-706484
Prod-RESPRC Dist-RESPRC Prodn-BAXLEN 1982

Rational Numbers C 45 MIN
2 INCH VIDEOTAPE
See series title for descriptive statement.
From The Fundamentals Of Mathematics (2nd Ed.) Unit I - Number Theory Series.
Prod-CHITVC Dist-GPITVL

Rational Numbers And The Square Root Of Two C 24 MIN
16MM FILM, 3/4 OR 1/2 IN VIDEO
Asks what sort of number is the square root of two, from the viewpoint of geometry and the veiwpoint of calculation.
Prod-OPENU Dist-MEDIAG Prodn-BBCTV 1979

Rational Suicide C 15 MIN
16MM FILM, 3/4 OR 1/2 IN VIDEO C A
Examines the idea of suicide as an option for terminally ill people. Narrated by Mike Wallace. Originally shown on the CBS television program 60 Minutes.
LC NO. 82-706507
Prod-CBSNEW Dist-CAROUF

Rational, Irrational And Real Numbers C 45 MIN
2 INCH VIDEOTAPE
See series title for descriptive statement.
From The Fundamentals Of Mathematics (2nd Ed.) Unit I - Number Theory Series.
Prod-CHITVC Dist-GPITVL

Rationale For Seeking Solutions C 30 MIN
3/4 OR 1/2 INCH VIDEO CASSETTE T
Reveals the rationale for seeking solutions in an educational setting.
From The Interaction - Human Concerns In The Schools Series.
Prod-MDDE Dist-MDCPB

Ratios C 18 MIN
3/4 INCH VIDEO CASSETTE
See series title for descriptive statement.
From The Basic Math Skills Series. Proportions
Prod-TELSTR Dist-TELSTR

Ratios And Proportion (Spanish) C 12 MIN
3/4 OR 1/2 INCH VIDEO CASSETTE
Covers ratios, expressing, writing and units in ratios and proportion.
From The Using Mathematics In The Plant Series.
Prod-TPCTRA Dist-TPCTRA

Ratios And Proportions C 12 MIN
3/4 OR 1/2 INCH VIDEO CASSETTE
Covers ratios, expressing, writing and units in ratios and proportion.
From The Using Mathematics In The Plant Series.
Prod-TPCTRA Dist-TPCTRA

Ratios And Proportions C 20 MIN
3/4 INCH VIDEO CASSETTE H-C
Uses the dimensions of a television screen to illustrate ratios and proportions.
From The Mainly Math Series.
Prod-WCVETV Dist-GPITVL 1977

Ratopolis C 57 MIN
16MM FILM OPTICAL SOUND H-C A
Studies the rat, focusing on its origins and its role in maintaining an ecological balance.
LC NO. 74-702413
Prod-NFBC Dist-NFBC 1973

Ratopolis (French) C 57 MIN
16MM FILM, 3/4 OR 1/2 IN VIDEO H-C A
Studies the rat, focusing on its origins and its role in maintaining an ecological balance.
Prod-NFBC Dist-NFBC 1973

Rats C
16MM FILM OPTICAL SOUND
See series title for descriptive statement.
From The Rats Series.
Prod-MLA Dist-MLA

Rats C
3/4 OR 1/2 INCH VIDEO CASSETTE
See series title for descriptive statement.
From The Pest Control Technology Correspondence Course Series.
Prod-PUAVC Dist-PUAVC

Rats And Mice C 17 MIN
16MM FILM OPTICAL SOUND
Describes how rats and mice spread disease and what the hospital worker can do to make the hospital safe from these threats to the patient and to the worker.
From The Control Of Pests For Food Service And Housekeeping Personnel Series.
LC NO. 73-704828
Prod-COPI Dist-COPI 1969

Rats—A Series

Introduces the viewer to rats, their threat to the health and welfare of individuals and to society. Illustrates methods of detection and control.
Prod-MLA Dist-MLA

Minus One
Rat Attack
Rats

Rattlesnakes C 8 MIN
3/4 INCH VIDEO CASSETTE
Discusses the characteristics and habits of rattlesnakes.
Prod-TUCPL Dist-GPITVL

Rattlesnakes (Spanish) C 8 MIN
3/4 INCH VIDEO CASSETTE
Discusses the characteristics and habits of rattlesnakes.
Prod-TUCPL Dist-GPITVL

Rauchen Ist Ungesund C 15 MIN
16MM FILM, 3/4 OR 1/2 IN VIDEO
See series title for descriptive statement.
From The Guten Tag Series. Part 14
Prod-BAYER Dist-IFB 1968

Ravaged Land, The C 15 MIN
16MM FILM, 3/4 OR 1/2 IN VIDEO C A
Juxtaposes the unspoiled beauty of our land with the widespread devastation created by monstrous earthmoving machines that ravage the earth in search of coal. Describes three efforts to reclaim surface mining areas in the mountains. Interviews conservationist, Harry Caudill, who calls for enactment by Congress of national laws to solve the problems caused by surface mining.
Prod-WILEYJ Dist-MEDIAG 1971

Raven By Edgar A Poe, The C 11 MIN
16MM FILM, 3/4 OR 1/2 IN VIDEO I-C
Revised version of the 1951 film, The Raven. Uses the engravings of Gustave Dore to illustrate Poe's poem, The Raven.
Prod-JACOBS Dist-TEXFLM 1976

Raven, The C 84 MIN
16MM FILM OPTICAL SOUND H A
Describes two 15th century conjurers who fight a deadly duel of magic. Stars Vincent Price, Peter Lorre, Boris Karloff and Jack Nicholson.
Prod-AIP Dist-TIMLIF 1963

Raven's End (Swedish) B 99 MIN
16MM FILM OPTICAL SOUND
Looks at Raven's End, a slum area of Sweden, in 1936, focusing on one family. Tells of the son who wants to become a writer and of the father who has lost hope for the future.
Prod-NYFLMS Dist-NYFLMS 1964

Ravens Remain, The B 26 MIN
16MM FILM OPTICAL SOUND
Uses documentary footage to describe the Battle of Britain. Includes scenes of the Luftwaffe Blitz on RAF installations and industrial cities of northern England, the bombing of London and the resistance of members of the R A F.
From The Winston Churchill - The Valiant Years Series. No. 6
LC NO. FI67-2111
Prod-ABCTV Dist-SG 1961

Raw Fish And Pickle - Traditional Rural And Seafaring Life C 28 MIN
16MM FILM OPTICAL SOUND H-C A

Looks At Iwate, a rural area of Japan which has been transformed through the country's technological boom and new found prosperity.
From The Human Face Of Japan Series.
LC NO. 82-700642
Prod-FLMAUS Dist-LCOA 1982

Raw Fish And Pickle - Traditional Rural And Seafaring Life C 28 MIN
16MM FILM, 3/4 OR 1/2 IN VIDEO H-C A
Looks at Iwate, a rural area of Japan which has been transformed through the country's technological boom and new found prosperity.
From The Human Face Of Japan Series.
LC NO. 82-707153
Prod-FLMAUS Dist-LCOA 1982

Raw Mash C 30 MIN
16MM FILM - 3/4 IN VIDEO H-C A
Portrays moonshiner, storyteller and traditional balladeer Hamper McBee. Follows his building of a still and the production of 'Christmas whiskey.' Captures the spirit of the Tennessee Mountains which has helped mold McBee's character.
Prod-SOFOLK Dist-SOFOLK

Raw Materials C 20 MIN
3/4 INCH VIDEO CASSETTE H-C
See series title for descriptive statement.
From The Geography For The '70's Series.
Prod-KLRNTV Dist-GPITVL

Raw Stock C 27 MIN
16MM FILM OPTICAL SOUND
Explains the making of a motion picture.
LC NO. 76-701358
Prod-SFRASU Dist-SFRASU 1975

Ray Bradbury B 30 MIN
16MM FILM OPTICAL SOUND H-C A
Ray Bradbury, magazine writer and Oscar winner for a screen play of 'MOBY DICK,' gives an interpretation of the creative writer's place in life and describes how the writer's role relaxes tensions formed in man by the demands of modern civilization. (Kinescope)
From The Sun And The Substance Series.
LC NO. FIA67-5004
Prod-USC Dist-MLA 1964

Ray Bradbury On Fantasy And Reality C 29 MIN
3/4 OR 1/2 INCH VIDEO CASSETTE
Presents an interview with science fiction writer Ray Bradbury, author of The Martian Chronicles and Fahrenheit 451. Bradbury talks about his craft and the elusive spark which he compares to a hummingbird that comes and goes.
Prod-KPBS Dist-PBS 1975

Ray Bradbury On Fantasy And Reality C 29 MIN
16MM FILM, 3/4 OR 1/2 IN VIDEO
Presents Ray Bradbury discussing the joys of writing, the techniques of his craft and creativity. Tells how he developed some of his stories.
Prod-UCEMC Dist-UCEMC

Ray Lum - Mule Trader C 18 MIN
16MM FILM - 3/4 IN VIDEO J-C A
Shows a day in the life of trader, storyteller and auctioneer Ray Lum.
LC NO. 81-707515
Prod-SOFOLK Dist-SOFOLK 1980

Ray Of Hope, A C 10 MIN
16MM FILM OPTICAL SOUND
Describes positive results achieved in the treatment of Hodgkin's disease by means of radiation therapy. Follows two young mothers' experiences as patients and after recovery. Shows their family lives, medical examinations and treatments.
LC NO. 78-700301
Prod-AMCS Dist-AMCS Prodn-TAPPRO 1977

Raybestos Brake Service Clinic C 40 MIN
16MM FILM OPTICAL SOUND
Discusses various aspects of automotive brake systems, including discs and drums, calipers, valves, master cylinder and power brakes, hydraulic systems, rotors and asbestos linings. Includes multiple choice tests.
Prod-MTP Dist-MTP

Raymond Loewy - Father Of Industrial Design C 15 MIN
16MM FILM, 3/4 OR 1/2 IN VIDEO J-C
Presents Morley Safer as he interviews Raymond Loewy, who discusses elements of good design, his design of NASA's Skylab capsule and the philosophy behind his work. Shows some of his designs, such as the original Coca-Cola dispenser and the Greyhound bus. Originally shown on the CBS television program 60 Minutes.
LC NO. 80-707735
Prod-CBSNEW Dist-CAROUF 1979

Rays And Angles C 20 MIN
2 INCH VIDEOTAPE P
See series title for descriptive statement.
From The Mathemagic, Unit III - Geometry Series.
Prod-WMULTV Dist-GPITVL

RBS Express, The C 19 MIN
16MM FILM OPTICAL SOUND
Presents operation of SAC mobile RADAR Bomb Scoring (RBS) trains. Reviews site selection and preparation and features crew accommodations and community relations.
LC NO. 74-706208
Prod-USAF Dist-USNAC 1965

RC And RL Time Constants C
3/4 OR 1/2 INCH VIDEO CASSETTE
See series title for descriptive statement.
From The Basic Electricity - AC Series.
Prod-VTRI Dist-VTRI

RC Circuit Analysis C
3/4 OR 1/2 INCH VIDEO CASSETTE
See series title for descriptive statement.
From The Basic Electricity - AC Series.
Prod-VTRI Dist-VTRI

RC Method Of Smoking C 14 MIN
3/4 OR 1/2 INCH VIDEO CASSETTE
Tells how most smokers are used to having a cigarette with coffee, a drink or while working. Teaches how to break these associations, helping to think in terms of a non-smoker.
From The RC Methods Series.
Prod-MLKVTH Dist-PBS 1981

RC Method Of Stress Control C 14 MIN
3/4 OR 1/2 INCH VIDEO CASSETTE
Explains that a minimal amount of stress is normal, however excessive stress can limit your ability to deal effectively with daily matters. Instructs on how to recognize excess stress situations and how to redirect that energy towards productive thoughts and actions.
From The RC Methods Series.
Prod-MLKVTH Dist-PBS 1981

RC Method Of Weight Control C 14 MIN
3/4 OR 1/2 INCH VIDEO CASSETTE
Describes how to lose weight without a diet. By being aware of your eating habits, you can control your weight, experiencing a steady, permanent loss of weight.
From The RC Methods Series.
Prod-MLKVTH Dist-PBS 1981

RC Methods—A Series

Presents the RC method of relaxation and concentration which has helped many to achieve their goals through positive hypnosis. First developed for use with Olympic athletes.
Prod-MLKVTH Dist-PBS 1981

RC Method Of Smoking 014 MIN
RC Method Of Stress Control 014 MIN
RC Method Of Weight Control 014 MIN

RC Time Constants C
3/4 OR 1/2 INCH VIDEO CASSETTE
See series title for descriptive statement.
From The Basic DC Circuits Series.
Prod-VTRI Dist-VTRI

RC Time Constants C 15 MIN
3/4 OR 1/2 INCH VIDEO CASSETTE
See series title for descriptive statement.
From The Basic Electricity And D.C. Circuits, Laboratory Series.
Prod-TXINLC Dist-TXINLC

RC Time Constants C 20 MIN
3/4 OR 1/2 INCH VIDEO CASSETTE
See series title for descriptive statement.
From The Basic AC Circuits, Laboratory--Sessions--A Series.
Prod-TXINLC Dist-TXINLC

RC Time Constants (Basic AC Circuits) C
3/4 OR 1/2 INCH VIDEO CASSETTE
See series title for descriptive statement.
From The Basic AC Circuits Series.
Prod-VTRI Dist-VTRI

RC Transients B 34 MIN
16MM FILM, 3/4 OR 1/2 IN VIDEO
Gives several illustrations showing the importance of timing in radar circuits. Provides definitions for transient voltage, transient current, transient interval and waveshape. Illustrates the meaning of each of these terms, using a simple circuit consisting of a battery, switch, resistor and capacitor. Demonstrates the effect on charge time when the value of capitance and resistance is charged and briefly explains the universal time constant chart.
Prod-USAF Dist-USNAC

RCA Victor Portable Radio C 1 MIN
3/4 OR 1/2 INCH VIDEO CASSETTE
Shows a classic television commercial with the famous dog logo.
Prod-BROOKC Dist-BROOKC

RCL B 34 MIN
3/4 INCH VIDEO CASSETTE
Explains current and voltage in relation to time and discusses voltage and current curves, the relationship of current and voltage, the measurement of voltage at source, the addition of phase components and the effect of impedance on resonance. Issued in 1943 as a motion picture.
From The Radio Technician Trainiing Series.
LC NO. 78-706298
Prod-USN Dist-USNAC Prodn-HOLMES 1978

RCL - Resistance Capacitance B 34 MIN
16MM FILM OPTICAL SOUND
Explains current and voltage in relation to time. Voltage and current curves, how current leads voltage and voltage leads current in different instances and the relation of current to voltage are shown.
From The Radio Technician Training Series.
LC NO. FIE52-915
Prod-USN Dist-USNAC 1943

RCMP Musical Ride, The C 12 MIN
16MM FILM OPTICAL SOUND
Presents a look at the precision and horsemanship of the Royal Canadian Mounted Police in their famous musical ride.
Prod-CTFL Dist-CTFL

Re-Discovering America—A Series
16MM FILM, 3/4 OR 1/2 IN VIDEO I-C A
Prod-COP Dist-AIMS 1973

Goldrush Country 18 MIN
St Augustine - The Oldest City 14 MIN
Washington, DC 20 MIN
West Point On The Hudson 17 MIN

Re-Making Of Work—A Series
C A
Updates developments which may have major impact on current business practices. Provides alternative to assembly lines. Offers innovative concepts including quality circles, alternative work-sites, and flex time. Described by actual workers and managers in U S and foreign markets.
Prod-BLCKBY Dist-EBEC 1983

At Home, At Work - Alternative Work Sites 030 MIN
For My Own Cause - Quality Circles 027 MIN
Modern Times - Revisited - Alternatives To 029 MIN
More Time To Live - Flexible Working Time 030 MIN
Responsibility Shared - Autonomous Production 028 MIN
Smarter Together - Autonomous Working Groups 029 MIN
Terminal On My Desk, A - The Impact Of Data 029 MIN

Reach Beyond The Horizon - A History Of Edwards Air Force Base C 40 MIN
16MM FILM OPTICAL SOUND
Traces the history of Edwards Air Force Base in California. Shows many unusual aircraft in flight, including the XP-59, the X-1, the X-15 mach 6 rocket plane, the X-13 tail sitter, and the XC-142 tilt wing.
LC NO. 79-701538
Prod-USAF Dist-USNAC

Reach Far Out C 15 MIN
3/4 OR 1/2 INCH VIDEO CASSETTE I
Deals with the search for life in outer space.
From The L-Four Series.
Prod-CTI Dist-CTI

Reach For The Summit C 30 MIN
16MM FILM OPTICAL SOUND R
Introduces Lou Zamperini, who was unable to adjust to post-war life because of some horrifying experiences in a Japanese prisoner-of-war camp. Shows how a Billy Graham crusade changed his life.
Prod-OUTRCH Dist-OUTRCH

Reach For Tomorrow C 14 MIN
16MM FILM OPTICAL SOUND
Traces the history of United Way of Los Angeles through five decades. Discusses the growth and social changes of the Los Angeles area and considers how these will affect the future.
LC NO. 75-700157
Prod-UWAMER Dist-UWAMER Prodn-MASCOT 1974

Reach For Tomorrow C 15 MIN
16MM FILM OPTICAL SOUND
Shows Girl Scout participation in activities ranging from high ropes to bread baking. Represents all levels from Daisy Girl Scouts to adults. Filmed on location at four different Girl Scout Councils.
Prod-GSUSA Dist-GSUSA 1984

Reach Into Silence C 15 MIN
16MM FILM OPTICAL SOUND
Attempts to recruit workers to work with handicapped children especially those with defective hearing.
LC NO. FIA63-1077
Prod-USC Dist-USC 1956

Reach Into Space C 16 MIN
16MM FILM OPTICAL SOUND
Explains the military and scientific significance of space research. Describes the progress of various space projects and examines their future requirements.
LC NO. 74-706209
Prod-USAF Dist-USNAC 1964

Reach Out C 5 MIN
16MM FILM, 3/4 OR 1/2 IN VIDEO K-I
Explores the concept of open mind to accept new sights, sounds and people to counteract the urge to settle for the comfort of the familiar.
From The Bill Martin's Freedom Series.
Prod-LAWTNM Dist-FLMFR 1971

Reach Out C 15 MIN
3/4 OR 1/2 INCH VIDEO CASSETTE I
Shows how explorations of space have changed the dimensions of environmental research.
From The L-Four Series.
Prod-CTI Dist-CTI

Reach Out - Occupational Therapy In The Community C 20 MIN
3/4 INCH VIDEO CASSETTE
Presents occupational therapists providing services in the community. Includes home health services for the elderly, the progress of an adolescent spinal cord injury patient from the hospital to recovery, identification of developmental disabilities and living skills programs in special education.
Prod-AOTA Dist-AOTA 1977

Reach Out And Grow C 28 MIN
16MM FILM OPTICAL SOUND R
Discusses why some churches are more successful than others and why some Christians seem to enjoy more useful and effective lives. Presents comments by Christian leaders on principles and practical applications of Biblical messages.
Prod-GF Dist-GF

Reach Out And Touch C 15 MIN
16MM FILM OPTICAL SOUND
Shows the human side of a hospital, emphasizing staff attitude rather than medical care.
LC NO. 74-700524
Prod-VISION Dist-VISION 1973

Reach Out And Touch C 14 MIN
3/4 OR 1/2 INCH VIDEO CASSETTE
Focuses on community health, showing nursing programs and services in several towns and cities.
Prod-AMRC Dist-AMRC 1974

Reach Out For Life C 11 MIN
16MM FILM OPTICAL SOUND A
Relates the story of an elderly man who realizes that his preoccupation with job advancement and family expenses in his youth has prevented him from enjoying life. Shows that after attempting suicide and gaining control of his life, he comes to believe that people should not harbor unrealistic expectations about themselves and others.
LC NO. 80-701099
Prod-EPIDEM Dist-FLMLIB 1980

Reach Out To Help Someone—A Series
A
Presents information on telemarketing. Includes techniques for handling outbound sales and incoming customer calls.
Prod-AMEDIA Dist-AMEDIA

Dealing With People On The Telephone 020 MIN
Handling Incoming Calls 020 MIN
Selling On The Telephone 020 MIN

Reach Up C 15 MIN
3/4 OR 1/2 INCH VIDEO CASSETTE I
Demonstrates how space exploration has increased our kKnowledge of the environment.
From The L-Four Series.
Prod-CTI Dist-CTI

Reaching For Reality C
3/4 INCH VIDEO CASSETTE
Describes growth and development of a child from seven and a half to nine months.
From The Growth And Development - A Chronicle Of Four Children Series. Series 3
Prod-JUETHO Dist-LIP

Reaching For Reality - Gregory, 7 1/2 Months C 6 MIN
16MM FILM OPTICAL SOUND
See series title for descriptive statement.
From The Growth And Development - A Chronicle Of Four Children Series. Series 3
LC NO. 78-700684
Prod-JUETHO Dist-LIP Prodn-CONCOM 1976

Reaching For Reality - Joseph, 9 Months C 7 MIN
16MM FILM OPTICAL SOUND
See series title for descriptive statement.
From The Growth And Development - A Chronicle Of Four Children Series. Series 3
LC NO. 78-700684
Prod-JUETHO Dist-LIP Prodn-CONCOM 1976

Reaching For Reality - Melissa, 7 1/2 Months C 6 MIN
16MM FILM OPTICAL SOUND
See series title for descriptive statement.
From The Growth And Development - A Chronicle Of Four Children Series. Series 3
LC NO. 78-700684
Prod-JUETHO Dist-LIP Prodn-CONCOM 1976

Reaching For Reality - Terra, 9 Months C 7 MIN
16MM FILM OPTICAL SOUND
See series title for descriptive statement.
From The Growth And Development - A Chronicle Of Four Children Series. Series 3
LC NO. 78-700684
Prod-JUETHO Dist-LIP Prodn-CONCOM 1976

Reaching For The Gold, Pt 1 C 60 MIN
1/2 IN VIDEO CASSETTE BETA/VHS
Deals with horsemanship. Discusses posture, lunging, dressage saddles, breeds, gaits, training tests and transitions.
Prod-EQVDL Dist-EQVDL

Reaching For The Gold, Pt 2 C 52 MIN
1/2 IN VIDEO CASSETTE BETA/VHS
Covers transitions, levels, piaf, passage and stretching involved in horsemanship.
Prod-EQVDL Dist-EQVDL

Reaching For The Stars, And Life Beyond Earth—A Series

Illustrates the infinite curiosity of man, from the desire to fly, to the search for life on other worlds.
Prod-IVCH Dist-IVCH

Life? / Mars - Is There Life? 030 MIN
Man's Reach Should Exceed His Grasp 030 MIN
Universe 030 MIN
We Came In Peace 038 MIN
Who's Out There? 030 MIN

Reaching Orgasm C 17 MIN
16MM FILM, 3/4 OR 1/2 IN VIDEO
Trains pre-orgasmic women and their counselors.
From The Women's Issues - Sexuality Series.
Prod-DAVFMS Dist-DAVFMS

Reaching Out C 32 MIN
16MM FILM, 3/4 OR 1/2 IN VIDEO H-C A
Presents the story of two teenagers, one physically handicapped and the other emotionally handicapped, who learn to accept each other and themselves at the same time and fall in love.
Prod-CINEFL Dist-LCOA 1980

Reaching Out - A Story About Mainstreaming C 13 MIN
16MM FILM, 3/4 OR 1/2 IN VIDEO P-I
Portrays the first days of school for Mary Rivera, a multiply-handicapped girl who is entering a regular classroom for the first time. Shows both Mary's reactions and those of her classmates.
Prod-BELLDA Dist-WDEMCO 1982

Reaching Out - Ken Tyler, Master Printer C 28 MIN
16MM FILM, 3/4 OR 1/2 IN VIDEO
Shows the lithographer Ken Tyler at work with other artists. Discusses artistic philosophies and demonstrates techniques.
Prod-UCEMC Dist-UCEMC

Reaching Out - The Library And The Exceptional Child C 25 MIN
16MM FILM OPTICAL SOUND P
Shows how children with various handicaps respond to books and other materials and how the use of these materials can contribute to their development.
LC NO. 72-701728
Prod-CHCPL Dist-CONNF Prodn-CONNF 1968

Reaching Potential C 26 MIN
16MM FILM, 3/4 OR 1/2 IN VIDEO T
Shows the integration into a regular school system of four children who are visually impaired to different degrees. Assesses the value of integration of visually impaired children from the point of view of teachers, school administrators, parents and other children. Stresses the importance of integration into a regular school system as a learning system that will facilitate the later adjustment of the visually impaired to life in the community at large.
Prod-EBEC Dist-EBEC 1981

Reaching Your Reader (2nd Ed) C 10 MIN
16MM FILM, 3/4 OR 1/2 IN VIDEO I-C A
Discusses how to make written material more interesting to the reader. Suggests using words that stimulate the reader's memory, appeal to the five senses and create images with feeling and movement.
From The Effective Writing Series.
Prod-CENTRO Dist-CORF 1983

REACT - Review Of Emergency Aid And CPR Training—A Series
H-C A
Dramatizes injuries and illnesses and offers instructions for emergency treatments.
Prod-MTI Dist-MTI

Accident Prevention And Safety 015 MIN
Bandaging 015 MIN
Care For Choking Victim Who Is Conscious 015 MIN
Care For Choking Victim Who Is Unconscious 015 MIN
CPR For Babies And Children 015 MIN
Emergency Action Principles 015 MIN
Emergency Rescue And Transfer 015 MIN
First Aid For Burns 015 MIN
First Aid For Injuries To Bones, Muscles And 015 MIN
First Aid For Specific Injuries 015 MIN
First Aid For Sudden Illness 015 MIN
First Aid For Wounds 015 MIN
Mouth-To-Mouth Breathing 015 MIN
One Rescuer CPR 015 MIN
Respiratory Emergencies 015 MIN
Respiratory Emergencies - Babies And Children 015 MIN
Two Rescuer CPR 015 MIN

Reactance Tube Modulator B 24 MIN
16MM FILM OPTICAL SOUND
Points out the principles of operation of the reactance tube modulator and identifies and states the purpose of each component. (Kinescope)
LC NO. 74-705480
Prod-USAF Dist-USNAC 1963

Reaction - Molecules - Molecular Symbols C 60 MIN
3/4 OR 1/2 INCH VIDEO CASSETTE IND
Shows sulphur as an energy-rich raw material, the symbol for the molecules in water, how molecular symbols confirm one another, the size of the molecules in olive oil, the vaporization and electrolysis of water and its energy requirements.
From The Chemistry Training Series.
Prod-ITCORP Dist-ITCORP

Reaction Overpotential - Crystallization Overpotential C 51 MIN
3/4 OR 1/2 INCH VIDEO CASSETTE
See series title for descriptive statement.
From The Electrochemistry, Pt V - Electrokinetics Series.
Prod-MIOT Dist-MIOT

Reaction Overpotential, Crystallization Overpotential C 51 MIN
3/4 OR 1/2 INCH VIDEO CASSETTE
See series title for descriptive statement.
From The Electrochemistry Series.
Prod-KALMIA Dist-KALMIA

Reaction Rates And Equilibrium C 20 MIN
16MM FILM, 3/4 OR 1/2 IN VIDEO J-C
Discusses factors which influence the rates at which chemical reactions take place. Explores these factors and their roles. Shows equilibrium, how it can be upset and its role in the chemical industry.
From The Chemistry Series.
Prod-CORF Dist-CORF

Reaction, Brakes, Time And Space (2nd Ed) C 9 MIN
16MM FILM, 3/4 OR 1/2 IN VIDEO H-C A
Illustrates reaction, brakes, time and space.
Prod-AIMS Dist-AIMS 1964

Reaction, Braking And Stopping Distances B 30 MIN
16MM FILM - 3/4 IN VIDEO C A
See series title for descriptive statement.
From The Sportsmanlike Driving Series. Refresher Course
Prod-AAAFTS Dist-GPITVL Prodn-SCETV

Reactive Displays C 6 MIN
16MM FILM OPTICAL SOUND C A
Describes the General Motors Research Laboratory computer which processes pictures instead of digits. Provides designers flexibility in manipulating shapes and forms on a readout screen to determine the best possible dimensions for a part. Represents a blend of human skill and judgment with computer precision for product design.
Prod-GM Dist-GM

Reactor Safety Research C 15 MIN
16MM FILM OPTICAL SOUND C A
Shows the characteristics, conservative design of nuclear power reactors and the elaborate safeguards that are incorporated into the design. Examines the progress of reactor safety research in studies of abnormal nuclear behavior, fission product release, chemical reactions, containment and vapor cleanup systems.
LC NO. FIE64-147
Prod-ANL Dist-USNAC 1964

Reactor, The C 29 MIN
3/4 INCH VIDEO CASSETTE
Tours the Enrico Fermi Nuclear Power Generating Plant II. Discusses the energy process.
From The Nuclear Power And You Series.
Prod-UMITV Dist-UMITV 1979

Reactors At Calder Hall B 35 MIN
16MM FILM OPTICAL SOUND
Presents a survey of the work carried out inside the reactor pressure vessel, including cleaning, laying the graphite and installing the gas-sampling equipment.
Prod-UKAEA Dist-UKAEA 1957

READ - DATA Statements / Strings C 30 MIN
3/4 OR 1/2 INCH VIDEO CASSETTE J-C A
Teaches how to use 'read..data' statements and explains the data pointer. Discusses how 'data' statements may be written and suggests their placement at the end of a program. Reveals how certain functions can be used to manipulate strings. Explains a number of these functions and introduces the ASCII character code. Shows a program illustrating the use of quotation marks and brackets.
From The Programming For Microcomputers Series. Unit 14 And 15
LC NO. 83-707132
Prod-IU Dist-IU 1983

Read Before You Write C 7 MIN
16MM FILM, 3/4 OR 1/2 IN VIDEO J-C A
Presents a young couple considering a typical installment purchase, a TV set. Follows them from their obvious enchantment outside the store window to a new awareness when they learn to really examine a contract before they sign it.
From The Consumer Education Series.
Prod-FLMFR Dist-FLMFR 1972

Read Before You Write (Captioned Version) C 7 MIN
16MM FILM, 3/4 OR 1/2 IN VIDEO J-C A
Presents a young couple considering a typical installment purchase, a TV set. Follows them from their obvious enchantment outside the store window to a new awareness when they learn to really examine a contract before they sign it.
From The Consumer Education Series.
Prod-FLMFR Dist-FLMFR 1972

Read Before You Write (Spanish) C 7 MIN
16MM FILM, 3/4 OR 1/2 IN VIDEO J-C A
Shows a couple in the midst of signing an installment contract for a new television until a program appears on the set's screen and makes them aware of the points they should clarify before signing the contract.
Prod-FLMFR Dist-FLMFR 1972

Read My Arm C 17 MIN
16MM FILM OPTICAL SOUND
Relates the actual experience of administering the Lederle Tuberculine Tine Test to several hundred migratory farm workers on a large farm. Demonstrates how state and local agencies can help to protect the health of migratory farm workers by bringing services directly into the field and indicates how a cooperative project, involving employers, churches, voluntary agencies and government agencies, can be applied to control other infectious diseases in both urban and rural situations.
Prod-ACYLLD Dist-LEDR 1962

Read On—A Series
16MM FILM, 3/4 OR 1/2 IN VIDEO P
Tells children's stories.
Prod-ACI Dist-AIMS 1971

And Then What Happened, Starring Donna, Alice
From Left To Right - Inversions And Reversals 11 MIN
From Start To Finish - The Nature Trail 11 MIN
One And More Than One - Birthday On A Farm 8 MIN
Put Them Together - A Saturday Adventure 11 MIN
Tell Me All About It - What Makes A Friend 9 MIN

Read Read Read C 15 MIN
2 INCH VIDEOTAPE I
Presents a number of recommended books in a variety of ways to stimulate literary appreciation and to increase awareness and understanding of different people and situations.

From The Images Series.
Prod-CVETVC Dist-GPITVL

Read The Label - And Live (2nd Ed) C 13 MIN
16MM FILM, 3/4 OR 1/2 IN VIDEO I-H
Stresses reading the labels of commonly used household products. Details safe handling practices for foods, aerosol products, insecticides, paint thinners and medicines.
Prod-HIGGIN Dist-HIGGIN 1977

Read The Label, Set A Better Table C 14 MIN
16MM FILM - 3/4 IN VIDEO
Shows how to get more value for the food dollar by reading the food labels. Explains that food packages list many nutrients. Encourages the preparation of more nutritious meals.
LC NO. 79-706001
Prod-USFDA Dist-USNAC 1978

Read The Label, Set A Better Table (Spanish) C 14 MIN
16MM FILM OPTICAL SOUND
Shows consumers how they can get more value for their food dollar by reading the new food labels. Explains that food packages now list many nutrients and encourages viewers to learn to set a better table.
LC NO. 75-702479
Prod-USFDA Dist-USNAC 1974

Readability C 30 MIN
3/4 OR 1/2 INCH VIDEO CASSETTE
See series title for descriptive statement.
From The Effective Writing Series.
Prod-TWAIN Dist-DELTAK

Reader's Digest In America C 20 MIN
16MM FILM OPTICAL SOUND
Uses facts and figures to illustrate the impact of an advertising campaign in a national magazine of popular appeal. Shows how a selected readership in a specific economic level brings in a high rate of sales' return for the advertising dollar.
Prod-READER Dist-CCNY

Readers' Cube—A Series
I
Puts emphasis on the recreational reading of ten- to thirteen-year-olds, presenting dramatizations of works that deal with universal feelings and experiences.
Prod-MDDE Dist-AITECH 1977

Be A Friend	20 MIN
Dimensions	20 MIN
Here's How	20 MIN
Me Of The Moment, The	20 MIN
My World	20 MIN
One Can Be A Lonely Number	20 MIN
Scene Now, The	20 MIN
Something To Do	20 MIN
Sorcerers, Spells, Suspense	20 MIN
Touch Of Humor, A	20 MIN
Trouble With Life, The	20 MIN
Troubles And Triumphs	20 MIN
Under The Sky	20 MIN
Winning Combination	20 MIN
Without Words	20 MIN

Readers's Guide To Periodical Literature C 7 MIN
3/4 OR 1/2 INCH VIDEO CASSETTE
Shows how to locate magazine articles on a particular subject by using Reader's Guide to Periodical Literature.
From The Library Skills Tapes Series.
Prod-MDCC Dist-MDCC

Readin' And Writin' Ain't Everything C 25 MIN
16MM FILM, 3/4 OR 1/2 IN VIDEO A
Presents a community-oriented view of mental retardation through the personal account of a retarded adult and three families with retarded children.
Prod-KCCMHS Dist-STNFLD Prodn-DETCOL 1975

Readiness - Audience And Persona C 30 MIN
3/4 OR 1/2 INCH VIDEO CASSETTE C
See series title for descriptive statement.
From The Writing For A Reason Series.
Prod-DALCCD Dist-DALCCD

Readiness For Addition And Subtraction C 15 MIN
3/4 INCH VIDEO CASSETTE P
Introduces basic aspects of addition and subtraction.
From The Measure Up Series.
Prod-WCETTV Dist-GPITVL 1977

Readiness For Learning B 30 MIN
16MM FILM OPTICAL SOUND C A
Differentiates between student readiness for learning to teach patients and patient readiness to learn self-care.
From The Nursing - Patient Teaching, Pt 1 Series.
LC NO. 74-700201
Prod-NTCN Dist-NTCN 1971

Reading B 20 MIN
16MM FILM OPTICAL SOUND
Demonstrates the direct teaching method for disadvantaged children, developed at the University of Illinois by Dr Carl Bereiter and Siegfried Engelmann, with two groups of four-year-olds mastering the sub-skills necessary for reading.
Prod-ADL Dist-ADL

Reading - A Language Experience Approach C 33 MIN
16MM FILM - VIDEO, ALL FORMATS
Presents the teaching of reading through resources such as dictated stories, experience charts, talking murals, word walls and book publishing to help develop the child's progression from speaking, to writing, to reading. Discusses the idea that reading skills are not sequenced, but develop best in clusters.
Prod-PROMET Dist-PROMET

Reading - An Introduction C 25 MIN
16MM FILM OPTICAL SOUND C T
Presents examples of each of the four basic methods of teaching children to read as observed in actual classroom situations. Emphasizes reading on the elementary level.
From The Jab Reading Series.
LC NO. 75-701423
Prod-JABP Dist-JBFL 1974

Reading - Assessment And Programming C 29 MIN
3/4 OR 1/2 INCH VIDEO CASSETTE T
Discusses reading assessment and programming in a mainstreaming situation.
From The Mainstreaming The Exceptional Child Series.
Prod-MFFD Dist-FI

Reading - The American Dinosaur C 26 MIN
16MM FILM, 3/4 OR 1/2 IN VIDEO C A
Features English headmistress-teacher Lillian Thompson in a discussion of her approach to the teaching of reading, raising questions about contemporary practices. Filmed at the Claremont Reading Conference.
From The Dealing With Social Problems In The Classroom Series.
Prod-MFFD Dist-FI 1976

Reading - Who Needs It C 19 MIN
16MM FILM, 3/4 OR 1/2 IN VIDEO J-H
Dramatizes the common plight of high school students whose career ambitions are stymied by their illiteracy. Includes adults offering advice on how to overcome this problem.
LC NO. 82-706613
Prod-ALLEND Dist-PHENIX 1981

Reading - Why - The Ice Cream Stand C 13 MIN
16MM FILM, 3/4 OR 1/2 IN VIDEO K-P
Illustrates the importance of learning to read by presenting a story about two children whose desire to open an ice cream and cookie stand runs into trouble when the boy uses the wrong ingredients because of his reading problem.
Prod-HANDEL Dist-HANDEL 1978

Reading A Drawing Of A Valve Bonnet B 20 MIN
16MM FILM - 3/4 IN VIDEO
Explains how to interpret conventional blueprint symbols tolerance specifications. Illustrates the use of a blueprint in planning machine operations. Issued in 1944 as a motion picture.
From The Machine Shop Work - Fundamentals Of Blueprint Reading Series.
LC NO. 79-707978
Prod-USOE Dist-USNAC Prodn-ATLAS 1979

Reading A Lecture C 16 MIN
3/4 OR 1/2 INCH VIDEO CASSETTE H-C
Outlines the different forms a lecture may take. Explains the necessity for students to assess the lecture and determine to what extent they are expected to participate. Presents an approach to effective note-taking.
From The Developing Your Study Skills Series.
Prod-UWO Dist-BCNFL 1985

Reading A Map C 20 MIN
3/4 INCH VIDEO CASSETTE I
Features host John Rugg discussing basic concepts in map reading.
From The Understanding Our World, Unit I - Tools We Use Series.
Prod-KRMATV Dist-GPITVL

Reading A Story To Extend Thinking C 30 MIN
3/4 OR 1/2 INCH VIDEO CASSETTE
Demonstrates teachers' use of the six levels of thinking to extend students' thinking while listening to a story.
From The Aide-ing In Education Series.
Prod-SPF Dist-SPF

Reading A Story To Students To Extend Their Thinking C 30 MIN
16MM FILM OPTICAL SOUND T
Presents two annotated lessons which demonstrate teachers' use of the six levels of thinking to extend students' thinking while listening to a story.
From The Aide-Ing In Education Series.
Prod-SPF Dist-SPF

Reading A Thermometer C 20 MIN
2 INCH VIDEOTAPE P
See series title for descriptive statement.
From The Mathemagic, Unit VI - Measurement Series.
Prod-WMULTV Dist-GPITVL

Reading A Three-View Drawing B 10 MIN
16MM FILM OPTICAL SOUND
Describes how to interpret and use a blueprint. Shows how to make a tool block according to specifications written on a blueprint.
From The Machine Shop Work Series. Fundamentals Of Blueprint Reading
LC NO. FIE51-502
Prod-USOE Dist-USNAC 1945

Reading A Three-View Drawing B 10 MIN
3/4 INCH VIDEO CASSETTE
Explains how to use a blueprint for visualizing an object and tells how to interpret a blueprint. Demonstrates the construction of a tool block according to specifications shown on a blueprint. Issued in 1945 as a motion picture.
From The Machine Shop Work - Fundamentals Of Blueprint Reading Series.
LC NO. 79-707979
Prod-USOE Dist-USNAC Prodn-RAYBEL 1979

Reading A Three-View Drawing (Spanish) B 10 MIN
16MM FILM OPTICAL SOUND
Describes how to interpret and use a blueprint. Shows how to make a tool block according to specifications written on a blueprint.
From The Machine Shop Work Series. Fundamentals Of Blueprint Reading
LC NO. FIE62-66
Prod-USOE Dist-USNAC 1945

Reading And Learning Styles C 28 MIN
3/4 OR 1/2 INCH VIDEO CASSETTE
Presents a program for elementary school children with learning disabilities. Emphasizes auditory and visual learning. Discusses remedial activities for the classroom.
From The Integration Of Children With Special Needs In A Regular Classroom Series.
Prod-LPS Dist-AITECH Prodn-WGBHTV 1975

Reading And Sorting Mail Automatically C 10 MIN
16MM FILM OPTICAL SOUND
Examines the operation of the new optical character reader used by the U S Post Office Department to recognize typed addresses and sort mail at high speeds.
LC NO. 75-700574
Prod-USPOST Dist-USNAC 1970

Reading And Word Play—A Series
16MM FILM, 3/4 OR 1/2 IN VIDEO P
Uses action, songs, active audience participation, reiteration and visualization of words on the screen to reinforce approximately 100 words.
Prod-PEDF Dist-AIMS 1976

Around You Go	11 MIN
Come Out To Play	11 MIN
Day Begins, The	11 MIN
How Do You Do	11 MIN
Jack Be Quick	11 MIN
Ladybug, Ladybug	11 MIN
Put The Kettle On	11 MIN
Rain, Rain Go Away	11 MIN
Some Like It Cold	11 MIN
Up To The Moon	11 MIN

Reading and Writing / Five Basic Skills C 30 MIN
1/2 IN VIDEO CASSETTE BETA/VHS
Uses skits to demonstrate the importance of skills in reading, writing, speaking, listening and non-verbal communication.
Prod-BFA Dist-BFA

Reading Approach To Math—A Series
J-H
Tells how to interpret and solve written mathematical problems.
Prod-WNVT Dist-GPITVL 1979

Estimating, Pt 1	019 MIN
Estimating, Pt 2	019 MIN
How To Read A Math Problem, Pt 1	019 MIN
How To Read A Math Problem, Pt 2	019 MIN
In Service Program	029 MIN
Pre/Post Test	019 MIN
Words And Symbols	020 MIN

Reading As A Part Of Life C 29 MIN
16MM FILM, 3/4 OR 1/2 IN VIDEO T
Identifies and discusses key thoughts on reading's broad context. Examines reading as a natural part of language development rather than as an isolated skill.
From The Teaching Children To Read Series.
Prod-MFFD Dist-FI 1975

Reading Blood Pressure C 10 MIN
3/4 INCH VIDEO CASSETTE PRO
Discusses the method for reading blood pressure, including the palpation and audition of pulsating sounds in the brachial artery. Explains the sphygmomanometer.
From The Human Sexuality Series.
Prod-PRIMED Dist-PRIMED

Reading Blueprints (Spanish)—A Series

Cover all types of blueprints used in industrial plants. Discusses machine parts and machine drawings, concentrating on compound rest and clutch-brake control.
Prod-TPCTRA Dist-TPCTRA

Air Conditioning And Refrigeration Drawings	012 MIN
Building Drawings	012 MIN
Electrical Drawings	012 MIN
Hydraulic And Pneumatic Drawings	012 MIN
Introduction To Blueprints	012 MIN
Machine Drawings	012 MIN
Machine Parts	012 MIN
Piping And Plumbing Drawings	012 MIN
Sheet Metal Drawings	012 MIN
Sketching	012 MIN

Reading Blueprints—A Series

Covers all types of blueprints used in industrial plants. Discusses machine parts and machine drawings, concentrating on compound rest and clutch-brake control.
Prod-TPCTRA Dist-TPCTRA

Air Conditioning And Refrigeration Drawings	012 MIN
Building Drawings	012 MIN
Electrical Drawings	012 MIN
Hydraulic And Pneumatic Drawings	012 MIN
Introduction To Blueprints	012 MIN
Machine Drawings	012 MIN
Machine Parts	012 MIN
Piping And Plumbing Drawings	012 MIN
Sheet Metal Drawings	012 MIN
Sketching	012 MIN

Reading Comprehension C 120 MIN
3/4 OR 1/2 INCH VIDEO CASSETTE
See series title for descriptive statement.
From The SAT Exam Preparation Series.
Prod-KRLSOF Dist-KRLSOF 1985

Reading Comprehension - The Instructional Connection C 29 MIN
3/4 OR 1/2 INCH VIDEO CASSETTE T
See series title for descriptive statement.
From The Reading Comprehension Series.
Prod-IU Dist-HNEDBK

Reading Comprehension From The Child's Perspective C 29 MIN
3/4 OR 1/2 INCH VIDEO CASSETTE T
See series title for descriptive statement.
From The Reading Comprehension Series.
Prod-IU Dist-HNEDBK

Reading Comprehension I C 30 MIN
3/4 OR 1/2 INCH VIDEO CASSETTE H-C A
Presents reading comprehension skills dealing with main idea, supporting idea, relationship, cause and effect.
From The Reading Series.
Prod-KYTV Dist-CAMB

Reading Comprehension II C 30 MIN
3/4 OR 1/2 INCH VIDEO CASSETTE H-C A
Presents reading comprehension skills dealing with inference, author's point of view, application of idea and words in context.
From The KET / Cambridge GED Videotapes Series.
Prod-KYTV Dist-CAMB

Reading Comprehension Introduction, Preview C 29 MIN
3/4 OR 1/2 INCH VIDEO CASSETTE T
See series title for descriptive statement.
From The Reading Comprehension Series.
Prod-IU Dist-HNEDBK

Reading Comprehension—A Series
T
Provides a conceptual framework for understanding the role of comprehension in the reading process. Discusses specific techniques to aid children in understanding what they read.
Prod-IU Dist-HNEDBK

Children's Literature In A
Comprehension-Centered Classroom, The - 029 MIN
Comprehension-Centered Reading Curriculum 029 MIN
First Encounters With Written Language 029 MIN
Learning About The Reader 029 MIN
Reading Comprehension - The Instructional 029 MIN
Reading Comprehension From The Child's 029 MIN
Reading Comprehension Introduction, Preview 029 MIN
Strategies For A Comprehension-Centered 029 MIN
Teacher Variable, The - An Interview With 029 MIN

Reading Comprehension, Analysis Of Situations, Lesson 2 C
3/4 OR 1/2 INCH VIDEO CASSETTE C A
See series title for descriptive statement.
From The GMAT/Graduate Management Admission Test Series.
Prod-COMEX Dist-COMEX

Reading Comprehension, Analytical Reasoning, Lesson 1 C
3/4 OR 1/2 INCH VIDEO CASSETTE H A
See series title for descriptive statement.
From The GRE/Graduate Record Examination Series.
Prod-COMEX Dist-COMEX

Reading Difficulties B 30 MIN
2 INCH VIDEOTAPE
Gives accounts of many children who have failed because they have not learned how to read. Explains that personality characteristics must be examined along with reading problems. Features a teacher who concentrates her efforts toward the elimination of previous failures and who builds up the child.
From The Motivating Children To Learn Series.
Prod-VTETV Dist-GPITVL

Reading Disabilities C 30 MIN
3/4 OR 1/2 INCH VIDEO CASSETTE C A
Characterizes various reading disorders.
From The Characteristics Of Learning Disabilities Series.
Prod-WCVETV Dist-FI 1976

Reading Drawings C
3/4 OR 1/2 INCH VIDEO CASSETTE IND
See series title for descriptive statement.
From The Drafting - Blueprint Reading Basics Series.
Prod-GPCV Dist-GPCV

Reading Efficiency System—A Series
16MM FILM, 3/4 OR 1/2 IN VIDEO A
Shows how to improve reading efficiency. Emphasizes comprehension skills, critical thought skills, vocabulary skills and rate improvement skills.
LC NO. 79-707448
Prod-TIMLIF Dist-TIMLIF 1979

Reading Electrical Drawings C
3/4 OR 1/2 INCH VIDEO CASSETTE IND
Covers indication and alarm diagrams, set-in-circuit and control diagrams.
From The Industrial Training, Module 3 - Electrical And Instrumentation Fundamentals Series.
Prod-LEIKID Dist-LEIKID

Reading Enrichment - The Fun Way To Grow C 30 MIN
3/4 OR 1/2 INCH VIDEO CASSETTE T
Uses interviews and candid scenes from the classroom to show how teachers help children learn to express themselves through the creative arts.
From The Reading Is Power Series. No. 7
LC NO. 81-707522
Prod-NYCBED Dist-GPITVL 1981

Reading Films - College Level (2nd Ed)—A Series
C A
Provides material to be used in a developmental reading program, ranging in speed from 190 to 760 words per minute in 32 steps.
Prod-PUAVC Dist-PUAVC 1962

Art And Meaning Of Fiction, The (2nd Ed) 8 MIN
Automobile Revolution, The (2nd Ed) 8 MIN
Billy The Kid (2nd Ed) 8 MIN
Cheerful Songster, The - The Robin (2nd Ed) 8 MIN
College Athletics - Education Or Show 8 MIN
Contortionist, The (2nd Ed) 8 MIN
Crazy Bet - Union Spy (2nd Ed) 8 MIN
Impressions Of America (2nd Ed) 8 MIN
Introduction (2nd Ed) 8 MIN
Land Of The Sun, The (2nd Ed) 8 MIN
New Hope For Older People (2nd Ed) 8 MIN
No Panacea For College Cheating (2nd Ed) 8 MIN
Race (2nd Ed) 8 MIN
Range Of The Normal Heart Rate, The (2nd Ed) 8 MIN
Robert E Lee - The Guardian Angel Myth (2nd Ed) 8 MIN
Unpopular Passenger, The (2nd Ed) 8 MIN
Wreck And The Crown (2nd Ed) 8 MIN

Reading Films - High School Level—A Series
H
Provides selections to be used in a developmental reading program, ranging in speed from 160 to 700 words per minute in 32 steps.
Prod-PUAVC Dist-PUAVC 1957

Best Advice I Ever Had, The 4 MIN
Generation Of Spectators, A 4 MIN
I Become A Horseman 4 MIN
Iron Horse, The 4 MIN
Is Sleep A Waste Of Time 4 MIN
Little Runt 4 MIN
Marvel Of An Insect, The 4 MIN
Outlaw, The 4 MIN
Piece Of The Moon, A 4 MIN
Profile Of The Real Mounties 4 MIN
Rabbit In Australia, The 4 MIN
Red Snow, The 4 MIN
Shoot'em If They Don't Wear A Hat 4 MIN
Stonewall - A Rare And Eminent Christian 4 MIN
Two Were Left 4 MIN
Under The Sea Wind 4 MIN

Reading Films - Junior High School Level—A Series
J
Provides selections for a developmental reading program, ranging in speed from 90 to 300 words per minute
Prod-PUAVC Dist-PUAVC 1961

Booker T Washington 5 MIN
Caribou, The 5 MIN
Castle, The 5 MIN
Comets From Afar 5 MIN
How Would You Decide The Case 5 MIN
Mountains Under The Sea 5 MIN
Peking Man 5 MIN
Reign Of Reptiles, The 5 MIN
Socrates 5 MIN
Spinning Jennies 5 MIN
Using Your Eyes 5 MIN
Why The British Burned Washington 5 MIN

Reading Financial Reports - The Balance Sheet C 13 MIN
16MM FILM, 3/4 OR 1/2 IN VIDEO J-H
Explains graphically how to read an annual report, including assets, liabilities, capital, accounts receivable and earned surplus.
Prod-CENTRO Dist-CORF 1984

Reading For A Reason—A Series
J
Introduces students to strategies and techniques for getting the most out of expository texts. Follows a cast of eight junior high school students as they struggle with the sometimes uninspiring prose of their textbooks.
Prod-WETN Dist-AITECH Prodn-GBCTP 1983

Different Kind Of Reading, A 015 MIN
Different Subjects, Different Messages 015 MIN
Everything Means Something 015 MIN
I Already Knew That 015 MIN
I Know The Reason 015 MIN
Is That A Fact 015 MIN
There's A Message For You 014 MIN
Way I Remember It, The 015 MIN

Reading For Analysis B 13 MIN
16MM FILM OPTICAL SOUND T
A shortened version, without commentary, of the film Reading For Analysis. Presents a reading lesson in an upper grade classroom which provides examples of how a skillful teacher adjusts his expectations and instructional techniques to meet the individual needs of students.
From The Individualizing In A Group Series.
Prod-SPF Dist-SPF

Reading For Analysis B 30 MIN
16MM FILM OPTICAL SOUND T
Presents a reading lesson in an upper grade classroom which provides examples of how a skillful teacher adjusts his expectations and instructional techniques to meet the individual needs of students.
From The Individualizing In A Group Series.
Prod-SPF Dist-SPF

Reading For Details C 30 MIN
3/4 OR 1/2 INCH VIDEO CASSETTE
See series title for descriptive statement.
From The Prose Literature Series.
Prod-CAMB Dist-CAMB

Reading For Facts C 30 MIN
3/4 OR 1/2 INCH VIDEO CASSETTE
See series title for descriptive statement.
From The General Reading Series.
Prod-CAMB Dist-CAMB

Reading For Facts (Practical Reading) C 30 MIN
3/4 OR 1/2 INCH VIDEO CASSETTE
See series title for descriptive statement.
From The Practical Reading Series.
Prod-CAMB Dist-CAMB

Reading In The Content Area C 26 MIN
3/4 OR 1/2 INCH VIDEO CASSETTE T
Introduces teacher and reading specialist Norma McClean who demonstrates how she helps teachers fuse course content and the reading content into a holistic unit through remodeling existing activities, recognition, dealing with reading problems in the classroom and designing activities that encourage success.
From The Successful Teaching Practices Series.
Prod-UNIDIM Dist-EBEC 1982

Reading In The Content Area C 30 MIN
3/4 OR 1/2 INCH VIDEO CASSETTE T
Presents the importance of preteaching, comprehension improvement and patterns and skills relating to content area. Suggests techniques to adopt.
From The Stretch Subject Matter Materials For Teaching Handicapped Children Series.
Prod-HUBDSC Dist-HUBDSC

Reading In The Content Area C 30 MIN
16MM FILM, 3/4 OR 1/2 IN VIDEO T S
Shows a teacher viewing a videotape of an in-service session which gives practical suggestions for analyzing and adapting any reading task for maximum effectiveness.
From The Project STRETCH (Strategies To Train Regular Educators To Teach Children With...) Series. Module 13
LC NO. 80-706649
Prod-METCO Dist-HUBDSC 1980

Reading In The Content Areas - Interaction C 22 MIN
16MM FILM OPTICAL SOUND
Demonstrates how student interaction with other students help clarify their own ideas. Shows students working cooperatively on tasks and learning to help each other as well as learning from one another.
Prod-SYRCU Dist-SYRCU 1978

Reading In The Content Areas - Preparation C 22 MIN
16MM FILM OPTICAL SOUND C T
Focuses on preparing students for reading a selection or performing some related task. Demonstrates a lesson that teaches reading skills functionally and simultaneously with course content.
Prod-HERBH Dist-SYRCU 1976

Reading In The Content Areas - Process C 21 MIN
16MM FILM OPTICAL SOUND C T
Demonstrates the development of four general processes, including vocabulary, comprehension, organization and reasoning.
Prod-HERBH Dist-SYRCU 1976

Reading Is Power—A Series
T
Explains how to satisfy the individual needs of reading pupils and strategies to use in developing pupils' skills. Shows how teachers can develop strategies which are directed toward students functioning at their own pace and level.
Prod-NYCBED Dist-GPITVL 1981

Comprehension - The Early Stages 030 MIN
Content Area Reading - Getting It All Together 030 MIN
Diagnosis - Getting To Know You 030 MIN
Meeting Individual Needs 030 MIN
Organization - Stations, Everyone 030 MIN
Reading Enrichment - The Fun Way To Grow 030 MIN
Words, Words, Words 030 MIN

Reading Is The Way To Grow C 15 MIN
16MM FILM - VIDEO, ALL FORMATS K-J
Presents A Fat Albert cartoon on the importance of knowing how to read.
From The Fat Albert And The Cosby Kids IV Series.
Prod-BARR Dist-BARR Prodn-FLMTON

Reading Is... C 25 MIN
16MM FILM, 3/4 OR 1/2 IN VIDEO I
Tells the story of a young girl who finds that she can find release from her personal problems through reading.
LC NO. 83-706062
Prod-BARR Dist-BARR 1982

Reading Matters—A Series

Involves parents and other concerned adults in supporting the efforts of classroom teachers to promote reading success.
Prod-HRAW Dist-HRAW

Everyday At Home
Everyday At School
From Day One

Reading Motivation—A Series
16MM FILM, 3/4 OR 1/2 IN VIDEO P-I
Prod-BFA Dist-PHENIX 1972

Elephant Eats, The Penguin Eats, The - Nouns	010 MIN
Frogs Are Funny, Frogs Are Fat - Adjectives	010 MIN
Monkey See, Monkey Do - Verbs	010 MIN
Squirrels Are Up, Squirrels Are Down -	010 MIN
What Are Letters For - Initial Consonants	012 MIN
What Are Letters For - Vowels	012 MIN

Reading Nonverbal Communications C
16MM FILM - 3/4 IN VIDEO A
Shows how to understand hidden verbal and nonverbal responses, gestures, gesture clusters and the nonverbal communications of environment, furniture, sitting arrangements and rooms.
From The Art Of Negotiating Series. Module 8
Prod-BNA Dist-BNA 1983

Reading Nonverbal Communications C 42 MIN
3/4 OR 1/2 INCH VIDEO CASSETTE
See series title for descriptive statement.
From The Art Of Negotiating Series.
Prod-DELTAK Dist-DELTAK

Reading On, And On C 15 MIN
3/4 OR 1/2 INCH VIDEO CASSETTE P
Reviews the kinds of print and nonprint material presented in the Spinning Stories series, and relates student growth to independence in reading.
From The Spinning Stories Series.
Prod-MDDE Dist-AITECH 1977

Reading Photographs C 30 MIN
3/4 OR 1/2 INCH VIDEO CASSETTE
See series title for descriptive statement.
From The Photographic Vision - All About Photography Series.
Prod-COAST Dist-CDTEL

Reading Piping Drawings C 17 MIN
3/4 OR 1/2 INCH VIDEO CASSETTE IND
Reduces complicated piping drawings to simple terms. Covers symbols and notations, dimensional, elevation and plan drawings, and spool drawing. Designed for the pipefitter or millwright.
From The Marshall Maintenance Training Programs Series. Tape 44
Prod-LEIKID Dist-LEIKID

Reading Poetry—A Series
16MM FILM, 3/4 OR 1/2 IN VIDEO
Prod-EVANSA Dist-AIMS

Annabel Lee	10 MIN
Casey At The Bat	12 MIN
Creation, The	12 MIN
Haiku	7 MIN
Mending Wall	10 MIN
O Captain, My Captain	12 MIN

Reading Rainbow—A Series
P
Promotes a positive self-concept and literacy skills. Includes an adaptation of a children's picture book and a field trip segment illustrating the use of the library as a vital resource.
Prod-WNEDTV Dist-GPITVL 1982

Arthur's Eyes	030 MIN
Bea And Mr Jones	030 MIN
Bringing The Rain To Kapiti Plain	030 MIN
Chair For My Mother, A	030 MIN
Day Jimmy's Boa Ate The Wash, The	030 MIN
Digging Up Dinosaurs	030 MIN
Gift Of The Sacred Dog, The	030 MIN
Gila Monsters Meet You At The Airport	030 MIN
Gregory The Terrible Eater	030 MIN
Hot-Air Henry	030 MIN
Liang And The Magic Paintbrush	030 MIN
Louis The Fish	030 MIN
Miss Nelson Is Back	030 MIN
Mystery On The Docks	030 MIN
Ox-Cart Man	030 MIN
Simon's Book	030 MIN
Three By The Sea	030 MIN
Three Days On a River In A Red Canoe	030 MIN
Tight Times	030 MIN
Ty's One Man Band	030 MIN

Reading Readiness C 30 MIN
2 INCH VIDEOTAPE T
Discusses the various factors that influence a child's reading readiness.
From The Child Reads Series.
Prod-WENHTV Dist-GPITVL

Reading Schematics And Symbols—A Series

Covers all types of schematics and symbols used in industrial plants. Examines symbols on schematics, electrical symbols and diagrams.
Prod-TPCTRA Dist-TPCTRA

Air Conditioning And Refrigeration Systems	012 MIN
Electrical Diagrams	012 MIN
Electrical Symbols	012 MIN
Hydraulic And Pneumatic Diagrams	012 MIN
Hydraulic And Pneumatic Symbols	012 MIN
Introduction To Schematics And Symbols	012 MIN
Piping Diagrams	012 MIN
Piping Symbols	012 MIN
Symbols On Schematics	012 MIN
Welding And Joining Symbols	012 MIN

Reading Schematics And Symbols—A Series (Spanish)

Covers all types of schematics and symbols used in industrial plants. Examines symbols on schematics, electrical symbols and diagrams.
Prod-TPCTRA Dist-TPCTRA

Air Conditioning And Refrigeration Systems	012 MIN
Electrical Diagrams	012 MIN
Electrical Symbols	012 MIN
Hydraulic And Pneumatic Diagrams	012 MIN
Hydraulic And Pneumatic Symbols	012 MIN
Introduction To Schematics And Symbols	012 MIN
Piping Diagrams	012 MIN
Piping Symbols	012 MIN
Symbols On Schematics	012 MIN
Welding And Joining Symbols	012 MIN

Reading Self-Improvement - Interpretation C 13 MIN
16MM FILM, 3/4 OR 1/2 IN VIDEO I-H
Explores how to search for unstated meanings when reading. Tells how to understand the difference between denotive and connotative meanings, recognize figures of speech, identify assumptions and draw inferences.
From The Reading Self-Improvement Series.
Prod-CORF Dist-CORF 1979

Reading Self-Improvement—A Series
16MM FILM, 3/4 OR 1/2 IN VIDEO I-H
Discusses self-improvement techniques in reading.
Prod-CORF Dist-CORF 1979

Reading Self-Improvement - Competency Skills	012 MIN
Reading Self-Improvement - Comprehension	012 MIN
Reading Self-Improvement - Interpretation	013 MIN
Reading Self-Improvement - Variable Speeds	013 MIN
Reading Self-Improvement - Word Recognition	011 MIN
Reading Self-Improvement - Word Understanding	014 MIN

Reading Short Stories—A Series
16MM FILM, 3/4 OR 1/2 IN VIDEO P-J
Presents famous short stories to motivate reading in students.
Prod-MORLAT Dist-AIMS

Big Red Barn, The	8 MIN
Dead Bird, The	13 MIN
Just Awful	8 MIN
One Kitten For Kim	16 MIN
Right Thumb, Left Thumb	9 MIN

Reading Skills, Set 1 (2nd Ed)—A Series
16MM FILM, 3/4 OR 1/2 IN VIDEO P
Focuses on the unique part that vowels play in the pronunciation of words and presents the patterns of letters which produce the familiar sounds of reading.
Prod-JOU Dist-JOU

Find The Vowels (2nd Ed)	011 MIN
Vowel A, The (2nd Ed)	013 MIN
Vowel E, The (2nd Ed)	013 MIN
Vowel I, The (2nd Ed)	013 MIN
Vowel O, The (2nd Ed)	014 MIN
Vowel U, The (2nd Ed)	013 MIN
Vowels And Their Sounds (2nd Ed)	012 MIN

Reading Skills, Set 2—A Series
16MM FILM, 3/4 OR 1/2 IN VIDEO P-I
Prod-GLDWER Dist-JOU 1972

Long Vowel Sounds, The	15 MIN
Phonics And Word Structure	15 MIN
Putting The Rules Together	14 MIN
Short Vowel Sounds, The	12 MIN

Reading Skills, Set 3—A Series
16MM FILM, 3/4 OR 1/2 IN VIDEO P-I
Prod-GLDWER Dist-JOU 1974

Double Vowel Rule, The	14 MIN
Semi-Vowel Rule, The	15 MIN

Reading Stories - Characters And Settings C 11 MIN
16MM FILM, 3/4 OR 1/2 IN VIDEO I
Shows how a good storyteller makes both characters and settings become real, using examples from Onion John, Captains Courageous, and Fawn in the Forest.
Prod-CORF Dist-CORF 1969

Reading Stories - Plots And Themes C 14 MIN
16MM FILM, 3/4 OR 1/2 IN VIDEO I
Shows the interrelationship between a story's plot and its theme by using examples from 'A DOG ON BARKHAM STREET,' 'THE BORROWERS,' 'A SUMMER ADVENTURE' and 'MY BROTHER STEVIE.'
Prod-CORF Dist-CORF 1969

Reading Ternary Phase Diagrams C 8 MIN
16MM FILM OPTICAL SOUND C
Uses computer animation to show how to decipher data in a ternary phase diagram. Includes obtaining information about composition, primary fields of crystalization for each component and temperature in its relationship to isothermal lines.
From The Phase Equilibria Series.
LC NO. 78-700706
Prod-NSF Dist-PSU Prodn-MSRL 1976

Reading The Blood Pressure Manometer C 6 MIN
16MM FILM OPTICAL SOUND PRO
Shows six different 100 pressure readings - the viewer records his readings, and compares them to the correct readings given at the end of the film.
LC NO. 74-705481
Prod-USA Dist-USNAC 1971

Reading The Micrometer C 10 MIN
16MM FILM, 3/4 OR 1/2 IN VIDEO J-C A
See series title for descriptive statement.
From The Power Mechanics Series.
Prod-THIOKL Dist-CAROUF

Reading The Moon's Secrets C 16 MIN
16MM FILM - 3/4 IN VIDEO
Presents basic information about the moon.
LC NO. 79-706028
Prod-NASA Dist-USNAC Prodn-AVCORP 1978

Reading The Sky C 20 MIN
3/4 OR 1/2 INCH VIDEO CASSETTE J-C A
Discusses how the changing patterns and colors of the sky help make weather forecasts. Shows what different types of clouds mean and how to identify them.
LC NO. 82-706783
Prod-AWSS Dist-AWSS 1981

Reading Through Television—A Series

Develops a pictorial language to accompany, support and control the beginning stages in reading and learning a language. Provides means by which these early stages can lead to a broadening of man's capacity to read and understand.
Prod-GPITVL Dist-GPITVL

Reading To Develop Sight Vocabulary B 13 MIN
16MM FILM OPTICAL SOUND T
A shortened version, without commentary, of the film Reading To Develop Sight Vocabulary. Depicts the initial stages of developing sight vocabulary with a group of inner-city children who don't learn to read automatically, but who are successful when taught by a skillful teacher.
From The Individualizing In A Group Series.
Prod-SPF Dist-SPF

Reading To Develop Sight Vocabulary B 30 MIN
16MM FILM OPTICAL SOUND T
Depicts the initial stages of developing sight vocabulary with a group of inner-city children who don't learn to read automatically, but who are successful when taught by a skillful teacher.
From The Individualizing In A Group Series.
Prod-SPF Dist-SPF

Reading Vocabulary—A Series
16MM FILM, 3/4 OR 1/2 IN VIDEO P-J
Presents original tales designed to motivate and promote the desire to read.
Prod-KINGSP Dist-PHENIX 1971

Boat That Jack Sailed, The	11 MIN
Dog Gone	11 MIN
They Were Cars	11 MIN

Reading With Sparkle B 20 MIN
2 INCH VIDEOTAPE P
Stresses techniques of oral reading. (Broadcast quality)
From The Language Lane Series. Lesson 24
Prod-CVETVC Dist-GPITVL Prodn-WCVETV

Reading Your Tires C 30 MIN
1/2 IN VIDEO CASSETTE BETA/VHS
Demonstrates how to 'read' tires. Discusses headlight alignment and rack-and-pinion steering. Features a 1926 Pierce Arrow.
From The Last Chance Garage Series.
Prod-WGBHTV Dist-MTI

Reading—A Series

Presents lessons in reading skills, comprehension, social studies, science and literature.
Prod-KYTV Dist-CAMB

Orientation/Test Taking Skills	030 MIN
Reading Comprehension I	030 MIN
Reading Comprehension II	030 MIN
Reading/Literature I	030 MIN
Reading/Literature II	030 MIN
Reading/Literature III	030 MIN
Reading/Literature IV	030 MIN
Reading/Science I	030 MIN
Reading/Science II	030 MIN
Reading/Science III	030 MIN
Reading/Social Studies I	030 MIN
Reading/Social Studies II	030 MIN
Reading/Social Studies III	030 MIN

Reading/Liteature IV C 30 MIN
3/4 OR 1/2 INCH VIDEO CASSETTE
Presents reading skills in Literature dealing with poetry, identifying poetic devices, drama, identifying plot, dialogue characterization setting and climax.
From The Reading Series.
Prod-KYTV Dist-CAMB

Reading/Literature I C 30 MIN
3/4 OR 1/2 INCH VIDEO CASSETTE
Presents reading skills in literature dealing with style and tone.
From The Reading Series.
Prod-KYTV Dist-CAMB

Reading/Literature II C 30 MIN
3/4 OR 1/2 INCH VIDEO CASSETTE
Presents reading skills in Literature dealing with figurative language, simile, metaphor and personification.
From The Reading Series.
Prod-KYTV Dist-CAMB

Reading/Literature III C 30 MIN
3/4 OR 1/2 INCH VIDEO CASSETTE
Presents reading skills in literature dealing with poetry,
From The Reading Series.
Prod-KYTV Dist-CAMB

Reading/Science I C 30 MIN
3/4 OR 1/2 INCH VIDEO CASSETTE
Presents reading skills in science dealing with the heart, blood vessels, heart disorders and treatment.
From The Reading Series.
Prod-KYTV Dist-CAMB

Reading/Science II C 30 MIN
3/4 OR 1/2 INCH VIDEO CASSETTE
Presents reading skills in science dealing with the blood, the circulatory and respiratory systems, diseases and treatments.
From The Reading Series.
Prod-KYTV Dist-CAMB

Reading/Science III C 30 MIN
3/4 OR 1/2 INCH VIDEO CASSETTE
Presents reading skills in Science dealing with the atom and atomic energy.
From The Reading Series.
Prod-KYTV Dist-CAMB

Reading/Social Studies I C 30 MIN
3/4 OR 1/2 INCH VIDEO CASSETTE
Presents reading skills in Social Studies dealing with the government, constitutional convention, principles of the Constitution, three branches of Government.
From The Reading Series.
Prod-KYTV Dist-CAMB

Reading/Social Studies II C 30 MIN
3/4 OR 1/2 INCH VIDEO CASSETTE
Presents reading skills in Social Studies dealing with different economic systems, role of Government and graphs.
From The Reading Series.
Prod-KYTV Dist-CAMB

Reading/Social Studies III C 30 MIN
3/4 OR 1/2 INCH VIDEO CASSETTE
Presents reading skills in social studies dealing with anthropology, geography, map reading, sociology, and varying viewpoints.
From The Reading Series.
Prod-KYTV Dist-CAMB

Reading, Writing And Reefer C 52 MIN
16MM FILM, 3/4 OR 1/2 IN VIDEO J-C A
Reports on the use of marijuana among teenagers in the 1970's. Presents a simplified chemical breakdown of the weed and describes its illegal routes into U S schoolyards. Includes remarks by teenage marijuana smokers, their parents and professional authorities.
LC NO. 79-706325
Prod-NBCTV Dist-FI 1978

Readit—A Series
P-I
Presents stories with cliff-hanger endings designed to get reluctant readers to read.
Prod-POSIMP Dist-AITECH 1982

Ben And Me 014 MIN
Blue Moose And Return Of The Moose 015 MIN
Boxcar Children, The 015 MIN
Comeback Dog, The 015 MIN
Deadwood City And The Third Planet From Altair 015 MIN
Give Us A Great Big Smile, Rosy Cole 014 MIN
Grandmother For The Orphelines, A 014 MIN
Groundhog's Horse 015 MIN
Have You Seen Hyacinth Macaw 015 MIN
My Father's Dragon 015 MIN
My Robot Buddy And My Trip To Alpha I 014 MIN
Rise And Fall Of Ben Gizzard, The Parrot And 015 MIN
Trouble For Lucy 014 MIN
Twenty And Ten 015 MIN
Whistling Teakettle And The Witch Of Fourth 014 MIN
Who's In Charge Of Lincoln And The Lucky Stone 014 MIN

Ready - Story Of The Marine Corps Reserves C 15 MIN
16MM FILM OPTICAL SOUND
Documents the 50-year history of the Marine Corps Reserves from World War I to World War II and Korea.
LC NO. 74-705482
Prod-USMC Dist-USNAC 1966

Ready For A Small Disaster C 21 MIN
3/4 OR 1/2 INCH VIDEO CASSETTE
Provides information tool for all chapters that want to pre-plan and coordinate their disaster relief efforts and resources for greater effectiveness.
Prod-AMRC Dist-AMRC 1981

Ready For Edna B 29 MIN
16MM FILM OPTICAL SOUND
Examines, through the experiences of a stroke victim, the range of health services needed to protect and promote the physical and mental health of the aged. Points out that the number of aged is increasing.
LC NO. FIE67-59
Prod-USPHS Dist-USNAC 1965

Ready For Sea B 14 MIN
16MM FILM OPTICAL SOUND
Follows the training necessary to make a young civillan into a sailor ready for sea. Shows scenes of the work, study, play and companionship which comprises 'BOOT CAMP.'
LC NO. 74-706210
Prod-USN Dist-USNAC 1966

Ready For Sea C 29 MIN
16MM FILM OPTICAL SOUND
Presents a story of the preparation of navy supply officers through OCS and the Naval Supply Officer School at Athens, Georgia, ending with shipboard assignments showing the application of their training.
Prod-USN Dist-USNAC 1966

Ready For The Worst C 40 MIN
3/4 OR 1/2 INCH VIDEO CASSETTE
Explains why the Red Cross has become a major force in disaster relief and what the future may hold in store. Features action, pathos, tragedy and ironic humor.
Prod-AMRC Dist-AMRC

Ready Or Not C 23 MIN
16MM FILM OPTICAL SOUND C A
Describes the follow-through projects in Wichita and Topeka, Kansas. Explains that two different instructional models are used in the Kansas program. Shows children working under the models and describes the facets of the follow-through program which are carried on outside the classroom.
LC NO. 72-702021
Prod-UKANBC Dist-UKANS 1972

Ready Or Not—A Series
T
Presents information to help educators plan for and use microcomputers in the schools.
Prod-NCSDPI Dist-PCATEL

Administrative Management In Schools - Case
Administrative Management In Schools - Software 030 MIN
Courseware Review - The Criteria 030 MIN
Courseware Review - The Process 030 MIN
Managing Microcomputers - The Microcomputer 030 MIN
Micros And The Arts 030 MIN
Micros And The Writing Process 030 MIN
Planning For Microcomputers 030 MIN

Ready Or Not, Here I Come C 4 MIN
3/4 OR 1/2 INCH VIDEO CASSETTE P-I
Uses songs and cartoons to explore the mathematical possibilities of the number five.
From The Multiplication Rock Series.
Prod-ABCTV Dist-GA 1974

Ready Or Not, Here I Come C 52 MIN
3/4 OR 1/2 INCH VIDEO CASSETTE H-C A
Probes the psychological and physical abuse of the elderly. Profiles the elderly through four tragic cases - lonely, helpless, isolated elderly people often mistreated to the point of death in nursing homes and by members of their family. Features a panel discussion by several experts on aging.
Prod-FI Dist-FI

Ready To Grow C 29 MIN
3/4 OR 1/2 INCH VIDEO CASSETTE
Contains three segments about inexpensive activities for parents and their preschool-age children.
Prod-LVN Dist-LVN

Ready To Strike C 29 MIN
16MM FILM OPTICAL SOUND
Shows the actions of the Tropic Lightning 25th Infantry Division in Vietnam.
From The Big Picture Series.
LC NO. 74-706211
Prod-USA Dist-USNAC 1967

Ready...Or Not C 14 MIN
16MM FILM OPTICAL SOUND
Urges individuals to take basic first aid training so they will be prepared if they happen upon the scene of a serious accident before professional help arrives.
Prod-EMW Dist-EMW

Ready-Made Programs C 30 MIN
3/4 OR 1/2 INCH VIDEO CASSETTE A
Examines ready-made computer programs, shows everyday applications of computers, such as accounting, and introduces the computer as a teaching aid. Explains the differences between RAM and ROM.
From The Bits And Bytes Series. Pt 2
Prod-TVOTAR Dist-TIMLIF 1984

Ready, Get Set, Go - Subtraction Via Time B 20 MIN
3/4 INCH VIDEO CASSETTE P
See series title for descriptive statement.
From The Let's Figure It Out Series.
Prod-WNYETV Dist-NYSED 1968

Ready, Sing—A Series
P-I
Introduces basic musical principles and emphasizes the fun of singing. Explores harmony, melody, rhythm and syncopation and shows how to identify tonalities, describe melodic contours, and execute changes in dynamics and tempo.
Prod-ARKETV Dist-AITECH 1979

All Through The Night 013 MIN
America - Thanksgiving 014 MIN
Are You Sleeping 014 MIN
Autumn 014 MIN
Crawdad Hole 014 MIN
Crocodile Song 014 MIN
Down The River 013 MIN
Frosty The Snowman - Christmas 015 MIN
Go Tell Aunt Rhody 015 MIN
Hawaiian Rainbows 015 MIN
Hiking Song, The 014 MIN
Home On The Range 012 MIN
I Love The Mountains 015 MIN
Land Of The Silver Birch 015 MIN
Lonely Dove, The 012 MIN
Long John 015 MIN
Michael, Row The Boat Ashore 014 MIN
More We Get Together, The 015 MIN
Oh Come, All Ye Faithful - Christmas 015 MIN
Polly Wolly Doodle 014 MIN
Sarasponda 015 MIN
Semester Review, Pt 1 015 MIN
Semester Review, Pt 2 014 MIN
Skin And Bones - Halloween 014 MIN
Stars And Stripes Forever 014 MIN
Stevedore's Song 014 MIN
Sweet Betsy From Pike 015 MIN
There Was An Old Woman 014 MIN
Tinga Layo 014 MIN
When Johnny Comes Marching Home 014 MIN
Wonderful Day 014 MIN
Wondering 015 MIN

Ready, Wrestle - The Rules Of Wrestling C 17 MIN
16MM FILM OPTICAL SOUND I-C A
Describes rules and procedures used in judging interscholastic wrestling competitions. Includes takedowns, reverses, technical violations, escapes, potentially dangerous holds, stalling, pinning situations and illegal holds.
From The National Federation Sports Films Series.
LC NO. 77-700469
Prod-NFSHSA Dist-NFSHSA Prodn-CALVIN 1976

Reagan At Midterm C 52 MIN
3/4 OR 1/2 INCH VIDEO CASSETTE J-C A
Assesses the presidency of Ronald Reagan at its halfway point, analyzing the president's effect on national defense, foreign affairs and economics. Includes interviews with politicians, economists, businesspersons and private citizens, as well as footage of the president in various settings.
LC NO. 83-706396
Prod-NBCNEW Dist-FI 1983

Real Estate B 29 MIN
16MM FILM OPTICAL SOUND
Predicts the role of the corporation, one of the largest landowners in Quebec, in shaping the future of the cities and the way of life of their dwellers.
From The Corporation Series.
LC NO. 74-702415
Prod-NFBC Dist-NFBC 1973

Real Estate C 30 MIN
16MM FILM, 3/4 OR 1/2 IN VIDEO H-C A
Looks at a real estate developer interested in drawing show business to Texas.
From The Enterprise Series.
Prod-MTI Dist-MTI

Real Estate Broker C 15 MIN
3/4 OR 1/2 INCH VIDEO CASSETTE I
Explains the qualifications and personal qualities required for a successful career as a real estate broker.
From The Career Awareness Series.
Prod-KLVXTV Dist-GPITVL 1973

Real Estate Investments C 25 MIN
3/4 OR 1/2 INCH VIDEO CASSETTE
Outlines the groundwork for those thinking about owning or investing in income producing property.
From The Your Money Matters Series.
Prod-FILMID Dist-FILMID

Real Estate Investments C 30 MIN
3/4 OR 1/2 INCH VIDEO CASSETTE C A
Describes the myths and facts about investing in real estate, including factors that can affect investments in income-producing property, vacant land and mortgages.
From The Personal Finance Series. Lesson 18
Prod-SCCON Dist-CDTEL

Real Estate—A Series
16MM FILM, 3/4 OR 1/2 IN VIDEO A
Presents a comprehensive training program developed by the Realtors National Marketing Institute of the National Association of Realtors.
Prod-CORF Dist-CORF 1984

Real Estate, Pt 1 - Getting Started
Real Estate, Pt 2 - The Real Estate Success
Real Estate, Pt 3 - The Real Estate

Real Estate, Pt 1 - Getting Started C
3/4 OR 1/2 INCH VIDEO CASSETTE A
Includes multiple learning techniques, visual instruction, written workbook exercises, related readings, job aids and follow-up checklists for retention.
From The Real Estate Series.
Prod-CORF Dist-CORF 1984

Real Estate, Pt 2 - The Real Estate Success Series C
3/4 OR 1/2 INCH VIDEO CASSETTE A
Demonstrates solutions for the real estate salesperson in any situation. Stresses solid training and includes lectures, video instructions, dramatizations, written exercises and group discussion.
From The Real Estate Series.
Prod-CORF Dist-CORF 1984

Real Estate, Pt 3 - The Real Estate Executive Series C
3/4 OR 1/2 INCH VIDEO CASSETTE A
Presents a management program that heightens the ability to organize, prepare and direct a high-yield sales force. This program would be useful for a single office firm or a multi-office organization as part of a management training program.
From The Real Estate Series.
Prod-CORF Dist-CORF 1984

Real Inside C 12 MIN
16MM FILM, 3/4 OR 1/2 IN VIDEO C A
Presents a cartoon character tired of the animated life applying for an executive assistant position.
Prod-NFBC Dist-MTI

Real Mr Ratty, The C 25 MIN
16MM FILM, 3/4 OR 1/2 IN VIDEO K-J
Features the life-style of one of Kenneth Grahame's characters from The Wind In The Willows, Ratty, the Water Vole. Shows the animal underground and underwater, among the wild creatures of the Devon river bank in western England and through the changing seasons.
Prod-BBCTV Dist-FI

Real Naked Lady, A C 13 MIN
16MM FILM, 3/4 OR 1/2 IN VIDEO
Tells how three young boys visit an art school in order to satisfy their longing to see a nude woman.
Prod-EISBEN Dist-FI 1980

Real Numbers, The C 30 MIN
16MM FILM OPTICAL SOUND T
Reviews the properties of rational numbers, and provides an introduction to irrational numbers. Restates the three major aspects of the arithmetic program-concepts, computations and application. To be used following 'NEGATIVE RATIONAL NUMBERS.'
From The Mathematics For Elementary School Teachers Series. No. 30
Prod-SMSG Dist-MLA 1963

Real People—A Series

Focuses on the Indian tribes of the Northwestern United States.
Prod-KSPSTV Dist-GPITVL 1976

Awakening 30 MIN
Buffalo, Blood, Salmon And Roots 30 MIN
Circle Of Song, Pt 1 30 MIN
Circle Of Song, Pt 2 30 MIN
Legend Of The Stick Game 30 MIN
Mainstream 30 MIN
Season Of Grandmothers, A 30 MIN
Spirit Of The Wind 30 MIN
Words Of Life, People Of Rivers 30 MIN

Real Rookies, The C 28 MIN
16MM FILM, 3/4 OR 1/2 IN VIDEO A
Follows a group of recruits from the time they enter the police academy through their first year on the force. Shows how police officers and their families respond to the rigors of training and the threat of violence on the job.
Prod-BELLDA Dist-MTI 1979

Real Security, The C 24 MIN
16MM FILM - 3/4 IN VIDEO IND
An illustrated lecture by J Lewis Powell, nationally known management consultant, on the causes and cures of 'MENTAL RETIREMENT' and organizational lethargy.
Prod-BNA Dist-BNA 1963

Real Self B 14 MIN
16MM FILM OPTICAL SOUND T
Looks at the cultural differences of 'MINORITY GROUPS,' the people of the black ghetto and those of the Chicano barrio. Describes the feelings of parents and children about the present educational system.
LC NO. 79-711417
Prod-NEA Dist-NEA 1970

Real Star Wars, The - Defense In Space C 50 MIN
3/4 OR 1/2 INCH VIDEO CASSETTE H-C A
Discusses Reagan's Star Wars proposal and studies the exotic weapons involved, including the x-ray laser developed by Dr Edward Teller, father of the H-bomb. Presents a three-dimensional animation process using models of new weapons systems. Features several mini-debates between Secretary of Defense Weinberger, Robert McNamara, physicist Richard Garwin and scientist Robert Jastrow.
Prod-NBCNEW Dist-FI

Real Talking Singing Action Movie About Nutrition C 14 MIN
16MM FILM, 3/4 OR 1/2 IN VIDEO P-J
Discusses the impact of food and food choices on body development.
Prod-SUNKST Dist-AIMS 1973

Real Talking Singing Action Movie About Nutrition (French) C 14 MIN
16MM FILM, 3/4 OR 1/2 IN VIDEO P-J
Discusses the impact of food and food choices on body development.
Prod-SUNKST Dist-AIMS 1973

Real Talking, Singing Action Movie About Nutrition (Spanish) C 14 MIN
16MM FILM, 3/4 OR 1/2 IN VIDEO P-J
Presents the impact of food choice on body development, personality and self-image.
Prod-SUNKST Dist-AIMS 1973

Real Thing By Henry James, The C 15 MIN
16MM FILM, 3/4 OR 1/2 IN VIDEO J-C A
Explores the nature of reality through a story of artists' models who can create illusions with ease and and upper-class couples who cannot even gracefully portray people of their own status. Based on the short story The Real Thing by Henry James.
From The Short Story Series.
LC NO. 83-706131
Prod-IITC Dist-IU 1978

Real Thing, The C 20 MIN
16MM FILM, 3/4 OR 1/2 IN VIDEO H-C A
Discusses television documentary and current affairs programs. Points out that the usefulness of concepts such as balance and bias are questionable when media continually restructure reality in the light of a given set of beliefs and values.
From The Viewpoint Series.
Prod-THAMES Dist-MEDIAG 1975

Real Time Systems C 45 MIN
3/4 OR 1/2 INCH VIDEO CASSETTE IND
See series title for descriptive statement.
From The Management Of Microprocessor Technology Series.
Prod-ICSINT Dist-ICSINT

Real Time Systems C 57 MIN
3/4 OR 1/2 INCH VIDEO CASSETTE
Discusses real time interrupts, human interaction considerations, developments in the man-machine interface and intelligent safeguards.
From The Management Of Microprocessor Technology Series.
Prod-MIOT Dist-MIOT

Real Time Teletype C 19 MIN
16MM FILM OPTICAL SOUND
Describes the use by Chrysler Corporation of a GE Datanet 30 system as a communication processor in worldwide data communications. Explains that the system serves as a message switching center, replacing a tape system.
Prod-GE Dist-HONIS

Real War In Space, The C 52 MIN
3/4 OR 1/2 INCH VIDEO CASSETTE H-C A
Presents General George Keegan, former Chief of U S Air Force Intelligence, who believes the Russians are developing the capacity to destroy intercontinental ballistic missiles by using high-energy lasers. Discusses the discovery that the Russians have been testing hunter-killer satellites capable of seeking out and destroying other satellites in space. Explains that both America and Russia may be on the verge of a costly arms race for the domination of space.
LC NO. 80-706910
Prod-BBCTV Dist-FI 1980

Real West, The B 54 MIN
16MM FILM, 3/4 OR 1/2 IN VIDEO H-C A
Explores the social and economic development of the American West between 1849 and 1900. Debunks the legends of the famous gunfighters and brings to life the conquest of the proud Plains Indians. Narrated by Gary Cooper.
From The Project 20 Series.
Prod-NBC Dist-CRMP 1962

Real World Of Insects (Spanish)—A Series
P-C A
Presents habits of some of the world's most industrious and destructive creatures.
Prod-PEGASO Dist-LCOA

Dragonflies - Flying Hunters Of The Waterside
Dragonflies - Flying Hunters Of The Waterside 013 MIN
Gypsy Moths - Vandals Of The Forest (Spanish) 010 MIN
Locusts - The Now And Ancient Plague 010 MIN
Locusts - The Now And Ancient Plague I- 010 MIN
Termites - Architects Of The Underground 009 MIN
Termites - Architects Of The Underground 009 MIN
Wasps - Paper Makers Of The Summer 010 MIN
Wasps - Paper Makers Of The Summer 010 MIN

Real World Of Insects—A Series
16MM FILM, 3/4 OR 1/2 IN VIDEO I-C A
Prod-PEGASO Dist-LCOA 1973

Dragonflies - Flying Hunters Of The Waterside 013 MIN
Gypsy Moths - Vandals Of The Forest 010 MIN
Locusts - The Now And Ancient Plague 009 MIN
Termites - Architects Of The Underground 009 MIN
Wasps - Paper Makers Of The Summer 010 MIN

Real World Of Selling, The C
3/4 OR 1/2 INCH VIDEO CASSETTE
Gives numerous examples of customer contact problems in both plant penetration and account building. Aimed at projecting salespeople into a variety of field situations to develop strategies. Includes cold call strategies, tools for territory management, purchasing authority conflicts and the entertainment entrapment.
From The Making Of A Salesman Series. Session 2
Prod-PRODEV Dist-PRODEV

Real World Of TV, The C 12 MIN
16MM FILM, 3/4 OR 1/2 IN VIDEO I-J
Examines the various types of news programs available on TV and analyzes how television news programming compares with coverage in magazines, newspapers and other formats.
From The Getting The Most Out Of TV Series.
LC NO. 81-706062
Prod-TAPPRO Dist-MTI 1981

Real You, The C 15 MIN
3/4 OR 1/2 INCH VIDEO CASSETTE P-I
Shows how others see us and how we see ourselves. Demonstrates how self-concept affects our lives.
From The Safer You Series.
Prod-WCVETV Dist-GPITVL 1984

Real-Time Microcomputer Applications I C 45 MIN
3/4 OR 1/2 INCH VIDEO CASSETTE IND
See series title for descriptive statement.
From The Microprocessors - Fundamental Concepts And Applications Series.
Prod-ICSINT Dist-ICSINT

Real-Time Microcomputer Applications II C 45 MIN
3/4 OR 1/2 INCH VIDEO CASSETTE IND
See series title for descriptive statement.
From The Microprocessors - Fundamental Concepts And Applications Series.
Prod-ICSINT Dist-ICSINT

Real-Time Microcomputer Applications III C 45 MIN
3/4 OR 1/2 INCH VIDEO CASSETTE IND
See series title for descriptive statement.
From The Microprocessors - Fundamental Concepts And Applications Series.
Prod-ICSINT Dist-ICSINT

Realities Of Blindness - The Perkins Experience C 29 MIN
16MM FILM OPTICAL SOUND I-C A
Shows how the staff and pupils at the Perkins School for the Blind correct the opposing myths that the blind person is capable of anything or that he is helpless. Discusses the nature of blindness and various activities that make up a well-rounded education for blind children.
LC NO. 72-702330
Prod-CMPBL Dist-CAMPF 1972

Realities Of Change, The C 29 MIN
16MM FILM, 3/4 OR 1/2 IN VIDEO T
Describes techniques, ideas and tips which have made change a positive experience for some teachers. Includes ideas on what to do about tests, texts and troublemakers, and on the creative uses of curriculum. Offers suggestions on how new ideas and techniques can most effectively be introduced into a school.
From The Dealing With Classroom Problems Series.
Prod-MFFD Dist-FI 1976

Realities Of Recycling, The C 38 MIN
16MM FILM OPTICAL SOUND J A
Points out that recycling our solid wastes is basic to the protection of our environment, showing the inadequacy of many of today's systems. Discusses new ideas being developed, such as the CPU-400 which is designed to burn 400 tons of refuse a day to produce up to 15,000 kilowatts of electricity and the zig-zag air classifier which sorts and separates refuse into specific categories. Intended for use by leaders and technicians who need a more comprehensive grasp of the potentials of recycling.
LC NO. 71-714058
Prod-USEPA Dist-FINLYS 1971

Reality And Hallucinations C 23 MIN
3/4 OR 1/2 INCH VIDEO CASSETTE J-C A
Shows the life and work of renowned Mexican artist Jose Luis Cueva.
LC NO. 82-707009
Prod-MOMALA Dist-MOMALA

Reality And Hallucinations (Spanish) C 23 MIN
3/4 OR 1/2 INCH VIDEO CASSETTE J-C A
Shows the life and work of the renowned Mexican artist Jose Luis Cueva.
Prod-MOMALA Dist-MOMALA

Reality And Hallucinations Of Jose Luis Cuevas (Spanish) C 23 MIN
16MM FILM OPTICAL SOUND
Focuses on the life and works of Mexican artist Jose Luis Cuevas. Explores Cuevas' artistic beliefs through his commentary on the various themes that characterize his drawings.
LC NO. 78-701324
Prod-OOAS Dist-MOMALA 1978

Reality And Hallucinations Of Jose Luis Cuevas C 23 MIN
16MM FILM OPTICAL SOUND
Focuses on the life and works of Mexican artist Jose Luis Cuevas. Explores Cuevas' artistic beliefs through his commentary on the various themes that characterize his drawings.
LC NO. 78-701324
Prod-OOAS Dist-MOMALA 1978

Reality And The Also-Ran Van C 22 MIN
3/4 OR 1/2 INCH VIDEO CASSETTE H
Presents high school senior Jerry Malone giving tips on being a wise consumer.
From The Dollar Scholar Series. Pt 2
LC NO. 82-707401
Prod-BCSBIT Dist-GPITVL 1982

Reality Of Dreams, The C 22 MIN
3/4 INCH VIDEO CASSETTE
Illustrates the World of Motion Pavillion at Disney World's Epcot Center. Focuses on transportation systems of the future.
Prod-GM Dist-MTP

Reality Of Rape C 10 MIN
16MM FILM, 3/4 OR 1/2 IN VIDEO
Recounts how a rapist negotiates for powerful control of his victim. Shows two police officers of varying sensitivity interviewing the victim after the rape.
Prod-FILMA Dist-MTI

Reality Therapy Approach To School Discipline, The C 29 MIN
16MM FILM, 3/4 OR 1/2 IN VIDEO C
Documents teachers successfully using concepts developed by Dr William Glasser to achieve effective school discipline, along with a full explanation by Dr Glasser of his five-part approach to discipline and the seven steps of reality therapy.
From The Human Relations And School Discipline Series.
Prod-MFFD Dist-FI 1974

Reality Therapy In High School C 29 MIN
16MM FILM, 3/4 OR 1/2 IN VIDEO T
Discusses Dr William Glasser's Reality Therapy approach to discipline as it is used at the Jersey Village High School in Hous-

ton, Texas. Presents the principal and staff describing how the use of Reality Therapy was introduced into the school and how discipline problems were reduced by over 80 percent the first year.
From The Dealing With Classroom Problems Series.
Prod-MFFD Dist-FI 1976

Reality, Truth, And Temporality C 120 MIN
3/4 OR 1/2 INCH VIDEO CASSETTE A
See series title for descriptive statement.
From The Beyond Philosophy - The Thought Of Martin Heidegger Series. Program 9
Prod-UCEMC Dist-UCEMC

Really And Truly C 20 MIN
2 INCH VIDEOTAPE P-I
See series title for descriptive statement.
From The Learning Our Language, Unit V - Exploring With Books Series.
Prod-MPATI Dist-GPITVL

Really Rosie C 26 MIN
16MM FILM, 3/4 OR 1/2 IN VIDEO P-I
Uses animation to tell the story of Rosie who challenges all to believe that she's a star, terrific at everything and a fascinating personality. Shows how make-believe is not just a pastime, but a lifestyle.
Prod-WWS Dist-WWS 1976

Realm Of Birds, The C 25 MIN
16MM FILM, 3/4 OR 1/2 IN VIDEO J-H A
Explores the social behavior, mating habits and navigational abilities of various species of birds.
LC NO. 79-707891
Prod-NGS Dist-NGS 1979

Realm Of The Wild C 28 MIN
16MM FILM, 3/4 OR 1/2 IN VIDEO
Shows scenes of wildlife in the National Forests - big game, small animals and birds. Emphasizes the relationship between the wildlife population and the available food supply.
Prod-USDA Dist-USNAC

Reamer Sharpening Between Centers C
3/4 OR 1/2 INCH VIDEO CASSETTE
See series title for descriptive statement.
From The Milling And Tool Sharpening Series.
Prod-VTRI Dist-VTRI

Reamer Sharpening Between Centers C 15 MIN
3/4 OR 1/2 INCH VIDEO CASSETTE
See series title for descriptive statement.
From The Machine Technology IV - Milling Series
Prod-CAMB Dist-CAMB

Reamer Sharpening Between Centers (Spanish) C
3/4 OR 1/2 INCH VIDEO CASSETTE
See series title for descriptive statement.
From The Milling And Tool Sharpening (Spanish) Series.
Prod-VTRI Dist-VTRI

Reaming With Straight Hand Reamers B 20 MIN
16MM FILM - 3/4 IN VIDEO IND
Shows types of reamers, how to check the size of reamers, and how to ream straight holes with straight-fluted helical-fluted, and adjustable reamers. Issued in 1942 as a motion picture.
From The Machine Shop Work - Bench Work Series. Number 4
LC NO. 80-706758
Prod-USOE Dist-USNAC Prodn-RAYBEL 1980

Reaming With Taper Hand Reamers B 15 MIN
16MM FILM - 3/4 IN VIDEO IND
Shows how to hand ream a tapered hole through a shaft and collar, fit a taper pin in the reamed hole, and ream bearing caps for fitting dowel pins. Issued in 1942 as a motion picture.
From The Machine Shop Work - Bench Work Series. Number 5
LC NO. 80-706759
Prod-USOE Dist-USNAC Prodn-RAYBEL 1980

Rear End Collision, Unitized Body C 14 MIN
1/2 IN VIDEO CASSETTE BETA/VHS
Deals with auto body repair. Shows body and uniframe deflection, using a Ford Pinto as an example.
Prod-RMI Dist-RMI

Rearing And Handling Of Anopheles Mosquitoes X 16 MIN
16MM FILM OPTICAL SOUND
Depicts the insectary techniques used at the U S Public Health Service Malaria Research Laboratory, Columbia, S C, in supplying anopheles mosquitoes to health laboratories studying transmission of foreign types of malaria.
From The Malaria Control Series.
LC NO. FIE52-2262
Prod-USNAC Dist-USNAC 1945

Rearing Kibbutz Babies C 27 MIN
16MM FILM OPTICAL SOUND C T
Observes infant rearing in an Israeli kibbutz organized around the activities of Hannah, seen both as a young mother and as a metapelet (care-giver) for four infants. Follows her weekday work as she cares for four under-a-year-old infants in their baby house from early morning to mid-afternoon and as she takes scheduled breaks to visit her own children in their nearby children's houses. Depicts Hannah's adroit blending of household tasks with tender, expert infant care and upbringing.
LC NO. 74-701433
Prod-VASSAR Dist-NYU 1973

Reason For Confidence, A C 28 MIN
16MM FILM OPTICAL SOUND
Depicts a day in the life of Nancy Taylor, homemaker and mother of three, as she and her family use a variety of foods, drugs, cosmetics and household chemicals. Takes the viewer behind the scenes to see what the food and drug administration does to protect the health and safety of every American.
Prod-USPHS Dist-USPHS

Reason Why, The C 14 MIN
16MM FILM, 3/4 OR 1/2 IN VIDEO J-C A
Presents two cronies who sit before an isolated country house and gradually spill forth their personal feelings about the things they have killed during their lifetimes. Deals with the impulses of the human animal toward war, violence and murder. Features Eli Wallach and Robert Ryan. Written by Arthur Miller.
Prod-BFA Dist-PHENIX 1970

Reasons For Caring C 21 MIN
16MM FILM, 3/4 OR 1/2 IN VIDEO IND
Describes correct fire prevention and emergency action procedures for hospital employees. Illustrates how a fire safety program applies to their work.
Prod-NFPA Dist-NFPA 1975

Reasons For Implementing T Q C C 27 MIN
3/4 OR 1/2 INCH VIDEO CASSETTE
Examines the reasons that Deming Award-winning companies have implemented T Q C. Points out problems encountered when promoting T Q C, and urges companies to 'break down the walls of growth by promoting T Q C'.
From The Seven Steps To T Q C Promotion Series.
Prod-TOYOVS Dist-TOYOVS

Reasons for Knocking At An Empty House C 19 MIN
3/4 OR 1/2 INCH VIDEO CASSETTE
Prod-EAI Dist-EAI

Reasons For Law - Le Cafe Politic C 19 MIN
3/4 OR 1/2 INCH VIDEO CASSETTE H
Examines in depth, exactly why we need laws.
From The Ways Of The Law Series.
Prod-SCITV Dist-GPITVL 1980

Reassembling The Engine B 22 MIN
16MM FILM OPTICAL SOUND
Shows how to reassemble the crankshaft and camshaft assemblies, crankcase section and gear case cover assembly, how to reinstall the oil sump and how to completely reassemble the engine.
From The Aircraft Work Series. Power Plant Maintenance
LC NO. FIE52-148
Prod-USOE Dist-USNAC Prodn-AUDIO 1945

Reassembly Of Cylinder Head B 14 MIN
16MM FILM OPTICAL SOUND
Demonstrates how to reassemble and install the cylinder head. Explains each operation and the use of proper tools.
LC NO. FIE52-1241
Prod-USN Dist-USNAC 1944

Reassembly Of The 8-268A Engine B 36 MIN
16MM FILM OPTICAL SOUND
Demonstrates how to reassemble the General Motors 8-268A diesel engine.
LC NO. FIE52-1050
Prod-USN Dist-USNAC 1943

Rebecca B
1/2 IN VIDEO CASSETTE BETA/VHS
Presents Daphne DuMaurier's thriller, directed by Alfred Hitchcock and starring Lawrence Olivier and Joan Fontaine.
Prod-GA Dist-GA

Rebecca Allen And Dianne McIntyre C 30 MIN
3/4 OR 1/2 INCH VIDEO CASSETTE
Discusses the interface of the choreographer and the new technology. Presents excerpts from the works of Allen and McIntyre. Shows Dianne McIntyre in 'Esoterica.'
From The Eye On Dance - Dance On TV Series.
Prod-ARTRES Dist-ARTRES

Rebel Earth B 50 MIN
3/4 OR 1/2 INCH VIDEO CASSETTE
Chronicles a prairie voyage as a 97-year-old man goes out with a young farmer to look for the sites of his past.
Prod-NFPS Dist-NFPS

Rebel Slave, The C 24 MIN
3/4 OR 1/2 INCH VIDEO CASSETTE
Focuses on a young slave boy's involvement in the Civil War.
From The Young People's Specials Series.
Prod-MULTPP Dist-MULTPP

Rebids C 30 MIN
3/4 OR 1/2 INCH VIDEO CASSETTE A
See series title for descriptive statement.
From The Bridge Basics Series.
Prod-KYTV Dist-KYTV 1982

Rebirth Of A Nation C 30 MIN
3/4 OR 1/2 INCH VIDEO CASSETTE H-C A
See series title for descriptive statement.
From The Japan - The Changing Tradition Series.
Prod-UMA Dist-GPITVL 1978

Rebop—A Series
16MM FILM, 3/4 OR 1/2 IN VIDEO I-H
Relates the personal experiences of three children which emphasize the importance of personal courage, dedication and interpersonal relationships.
Prod-WGBHTV Dist-IU 1979

Kelly	9 MIN
Michael	9 MIN
Thanh	9 MIN

Rebop—A Series
P-J
Shows how young people ages 7 to 14 from diverse backgrounds deal with problems, plan for the future and relate to their families.
Prod-WGBHTV Dist-MDCPB 1977

Cultures To Share	030 MIN
Darlene And Tommy	030 MIN
Experiences To Learn	030 MIN
Family	030 MIN
Finding Their Path	030 MIN
Friends	030 MIN
Gabe And Alice	030 MIN
Heritage	030 MIN
Holding Their Own	030 MIN
In My School We Don't Have Grades	030 MIN
It's Easier When Someone Helps	030 MIN
Knowing Who You Are	030 MIN
Language To Share	030 MIN
Learn To Deal	030 MIN
Leaving Home, Going Home	030 MIN
Livin' In The City	030 MIN
Looking Forward To The Future	030 MIN
Making It - They Tell Their Stories	030 MIN
Mixed Bag, A	030 MIN
Movin' On Up	030 MIN
Music	030 MIN
Preview	030 MIN
She Ain't Heavy	030 MIN
Surrounded By Life	030 MIN
Taking Aim	030 MIN
Two Names - Jose	030 MIN

Rebuilding A Master Cylinder C 4 MIN
16MM FILM OPTICAL SOUND
Shows the method of disassembling the master cylinder, inspecting and honing the bore, installing new parts and refilling the reservoir before reinstalling the cylinder unit in the automobile.
LC NO. FI68-222
Prod-RAYBAR Dist-RAYBAR 1966

Rebuilding Of Jerusalem, The C
16MM FILM OPTICAL SOUND
Features his honor, Mayor Teddy Kollek of Jerusalem, who tells what his country has created in the last 25 years in the world's holiest city and how Israel plans to make Jerusalem the most beautiful city of all.
From The Dateline Israel, 1973 Series.
Prod-ADL Dist-ADL

Rebuilding The Union C 30 MIN
3/4 OR 1/2 INCH VIDEO CASSETTE C
See series title for descriptive statement.
From The American Story - The Beginning To 1877 Series.
Prod-DALCCD Dist-DALCCD

Rebuttal Of The Selling Of The Pentagon B 22 MIN
16MM FILM, 3/4 OR 1/2 IN VIDEO J-C A
Offers a follow-up to the documentary The Selling Of The Pentagon, with Vice-President Agnew, Secretary of Defense Laird, and others speaking on behalf of the Pentagon.
Prod-CBSNEW Dist-CAROUF

Recall And Testing C 20 MIN
3/4 INCH VIDEO CASSETTE I
Explains that memory relates to non-academic as well as academic situations. Discusses association, mnemonics and preparation for tests.
From The Study Skills Series.
Prod-WCVETV Dist-GPITVL 1979

Received With Interest C 14 MIN
16MM FILM, 3/4 OR 1/2 IN VIDEO C A
Presents a coaching session in which a manager works through an action plan with two of his subordinates in order to develop their skills more fully.
From The Coaching For Results Series.
Prod-MILLBK Dist-IFB

Receiver Alignment B 37 MIN
16MM FILM OPTICAL SOUND
Demonstrates the troubleshooting of a superheterodyne receiver. Shows how, after finding and replacing the defective component, the receiver is aligned using a signal generator for the signals. Explains proper test equipment and how alignment is reaccomplished. (Kinescope)
LC NO. 74-705486
Prod-USAF Dist-USNAC

Receiver Troubleshooting Procedure B 21 MIN
16MM FILM OPTICAL SOUND
Explains general troubleshooting procedures for receivers, stage-by-stage and half-split methods of troubleshooting and identifies basic test equipment. (Kinescope)
LC NO. 74-705487
Prod-USAF Dist-USNAC 1965

Receiving And Storing C 10 MIN
16MM FILM, 3/4 OR 1/2 IN VIDEO I-C A
Presents basic principles of receiving and storing foods. Shows the importance of proper procedures in checking quality and quantity of received goods. Includes detailed explanation of both dry and refrigerator storage to prevent contamination, waste and pilferage. Explains how to maintain control of merchandise.
From The Professional Food Preparation And Service Program Series.
LC NO. 74-700220
Prod-NEM Dist-NEM 1973

Receiving And Storing (Spanish) C 10 MIN
16MM FILM, 3/4 OR 1/2 IN VIDEO J A
Presents basic principles of receiving and storing foods. Shows

the importance of proper procedures in checking quality and quantity of received goods and points out the necessity of dry and refrigerator storage to prevent contamination.
From The Professional Food Preparation And Service Program (Spanish) Series.
Prod-NEM Dist-NEM 1973

Receiving Feedback Non-Defensively C 17 MIN
2 INCH VIDEOTAPE C A
Features a humanistic psychologist who, by analysis and examples, discusses that receiving feedback is essential to self-improvement provided that it is done in a non-defensive manner.
From The Interpersonal Competence, Unit 02 - Communication Series.
Prod-MVNE Dist-TELSTR 1973

Receiving Help And Manipulating C 27 MIN
2 INCH VIDEOTAPE C A
Features a humanistic psychologist who, by analysis and examples, discusses that it is as important to be capable of receiving help as giving it.
From The Interpersonal Competence, Unit 04 - Helping Series.
Prod-MVNE Dist-TELSTR 1973

Recent Advances In Folate-Antagonist Pharmacology C 40 MIN
3/4 INCH VIDEO CASSETTE
Discusses new developments in antifolate intercellular metabolism.
Prod-UTAHTI Dist-UTAHTI

Recent Advances In Gastrointestinal Endoscopy C 30 MIN
3/4 OR 1/2 INCH VIDEO CASSETTE
Describes the state of the art of gastrointestinal endoscopy. Reviews the techniques and usefulness of esophagogastroduodenoscopy, endoscopic retrograde cholangiopancreatography and colonoscopy with polypectomy.
Prod-ROWLAB Dist-ROWLAB

Recent Advances In Reproductive Physiology B 29 MIN
16MM FILM OPTICAL SOUND C A
Discusses research in reproductive physiology, including biochemistry, endocrinology, electron microscopy, genetics and clinical pathology. Features Dr J Robert Bragonier and Leta Powell Drake.
From The Nine To Get Ready Series. No. 12
LC NO. 70-704219
Prod-KUONTV Dist-UNL 1965

Recent Advances In Reproductive Physiology C 29 MIN
2 INCH VIDEOTAPE
See series title for descriptive statement.
From The Nine To Get Ready Series.
Prod-NETCHE Dist-PUBTEL

Recent Cartoon Innovations C 15 MIN
2 INCH VIDEOTAPE
See series title for descriptive statement.
From The Charlie's Pad Series.
Prod-WSIU Dist-PUBTEL

Recent Developments In Our Knowledge Of Serum Hepatitis B 30 MIN
3/4 INCH VIDEO CASSETTE PRO
Reviews developments in our knowledge of serum hepatitis resulting from the discovery of the serum hepatitis virus specific antigen (SH) or Australia antigen.
From The Clinical Pathology Series.
LC NO. 76-706098
Prod-NMAC Dist-USNAC 1970

Recent Developments In Programming Languages—A Series
C A
Traces the roots of current programming languages. Focuses on aspects of each language that has been significant on modern programming languages. Contains 42 one-hour videotapes.
Prod-UIDEEO Dist-UIDEEO

Recent Modifications Of Convulsive Shock Therapy X 20 MIN
16MM FILM SILENT C T
Demonstrates the use of curare and quinine methochloride in protecting patients from spinal fractures in metrazol and electrical convulsion therapies. Curare is administered to a young woman in extreme manic excitement and the result is a 'SOFT' convulsion. An X-ray photograph shows a fracture which occurred when older methods were used.
Prod-PSUPCR Dist-PSUPCR 1941

Recent Results In X-Ray Astronomy C 30 MIN
3/4 OR 1/2 INCH VIDEO CASSETTE
Discusses how x-ray astronomy has been able to pinpoint sources of x-radiation and information from the satellite 'Uhuru', which some consider to be strong evidence for the existence of black holes.
From The Astronomy Series.
Prod-NETCHE Dist-NETCHE 1973

Recent Trends In Manual Communication C 60 MIN
3/4 OR 1/2 INCH VIDEO CASSETTE S
Discusses major characteristics of sign language systems and reviews research of recent trends. Signed.
Prod-GALCO Dist-GALCO 1983

Recette D'Abidjan, Une C 11 MIN
16MM FILM, 3/4 OR 1/2 IN VIDEO H-C
Prod-EBEC Dist-EBEC 1974

Recidivist, The B 15 MIN
16MM FILM OPTICAL SOUND J-C A
Points out factors which could cause a man to become a repeated criminal offender by telling a story about a man, who was faced with loneliness and desperation after being released from prison. Shows how he steals a car, unconsciously hoping to be caught.
LC NO. 72-700409
Prod-MMA Dist-MMA 1969

Recipe For Happy Children, A C 26 MIN
3/4 OR 1/2 INCH VIDEO CASSETTE H-C A
Presents Reynelda Muse explaining how to guide children's behavior and stresses the necessity of having expectations that children can live up to. Shows day-care providers using supervisory skills to create stimulating environments for their charges.
From The Spoonful Of Lovin' Series. No. 4
LC NO. 82-706064
Prod-KRMATV Dist-AITECH 1981

Recipe for Marriage-Minded Career Women C 30 MIN
3/4 OR 1/2 INCH VIDEO CASSETTE
Studies the problems of working women. Provides data regarding the conflicts which build up between marriage and career. Presents views of researcher Dr Sandra S Tangri, Professor of Psychology, Howard University. From the Syl Watkins television program.
Prod-RCOMTV Dist-SYLWAT

Recipe For Results - The Nuts And Bolts Of Managing By Objectives C 30 MIN
3/4 OR 1/2 INCH VIDEO CASSETTE
Deals with a specific function of supervisory management, and provides specific skills in planning effectively, setting objectives, motivating employees and making MBO a workable, usable system. Includes a training leader's guide and a student text.
Prod-CREMED Dist-DELTAK

Reciprocal Function, The - An Area For Revision C 24 MIN
16MM FILM, 3/4 OR 1/2 IN VIDEO
Describes weighing shapes cut from the area under the graph of the reciprocal (1 over X) function. Explains that such areas add like logarithms.
Prod-OPENU Dist-MEDIAG Prodn-BBCTV 1979

Reciprocating Air Compressor Operation C 60 MIN
3/4 OR 1/2 INCH VIDEO CASSETTE IND
Identifies components and describes how an air compression system works. Covers monitoring of oil level and how to perform startup checks.
From The Equipment Operation Training Program Series.
Prod-LEIKID Dist-LEIKID

Reciprocating Air Compressor Operations C 60 MIN
3/4 OR 1/2 INCH VIDEO CASSETTE IND
Identifies the components of a reciprocating air compressor and describes how it works. Demonstrates how to perform periodic operational checks. Tells how to recognize an abnormally operating compressor.
From The Equipment Operation Training Program Series.
Prod-ITCORP Dist-ITCORP

Reciprocating Gas Compressors C 29 MIN
3/4 OR 1/2 INCH VIDEO CASSETTE IND
Explains compression fundamentals, operating principles and troubleshooting procedures for reciprocating compressors.
Prod-UTEXPE Dist-UTEXPE 1973

Reciprocating Pump Opening For Inspection B 21 MIN
16MM FILM OPTICAL SOUND
Demonstrates, on a vertical simplex reciprocating pump, the proper procedures, marking of parts, use of standard machinist's tools and safety precautions.
LC NO. FIE52-1233
Prod-USN Dist-USNAC 1943

Reckless Years, The (1919-1929) C
3/4 OR 1/2 INCH VIDEO CASSETTE H
Demonstrates how corruption, government inaction and a laissez-faire economic policy contributed to the worst depression in the nation's history. Discusses the profound changes that took place during that time.
Prod-GA Dist-GA

Reckless Years, The - 1919-1929 C 39 MIN
3/4 OR 1/2 INCH VIDEO CASSETTE
Explores the post-World War I depression, crime, prohibition, growth of the middle class, jazz, the automotive industry and the events of the years between 1919 and 1929. Explains the causes that led to the eventual collapse of the American economy.
LC NO. 81-706675
Prod-GA Dist-GA 1981

Reckon With The Wind C 28 MIN
16MM FILM, 3/4 OR 1/2 IN VIDEO
Documents the 1976 Victoria to Maui race on board the sailboat Impossible, captained by mountaineer Jim Whittaker.
Prod-OFFSHR Dist-OFFSHR 1976

Reckoning - 1945 And After C 52 MIN
16MM FILM, 3/4 OR 1/2 IN VIDEO H-C A
Tells how after the war, world governments attempted to restore civilization. The order of the day included revenge, brutality and displaced and missing persons throughout the world who numbered in the tens of millions in Europe alone.
From The World At War Series.
Prod-THAMES Dist-MEDIAG 1973

Reckoning, The C 26 MIN
16MM FILM OPTICAL SOUND
Traces the research of Dr. Harvey Brenner of John Hopkins University which shows a frightening correlation between joblessness and an increase in mortality from heart attacks, liver disease, suicide and other stress-related ailments.
Prod-GRATV Dist-CANWRL 1979

Reclaimed B 11 MIN
16MM FILM OPTICAL SOUND A
Portrays the Christian Witness Pavilion of the Seattle World's Fair.
Prod-CONCOR Dist-CPH

Recognition And Management Of Valvular Heart Disease C 54 MIN
3/4 INCH VIDEO CASSETTE PRO
Discusses mitral stenosis and describes aortic stenosis. Includes signs and symptoms, electrocardiographic features, radiographic features, catheterization and angiocardiography.
LC NO. 76-706099
Prod-WARMP Dist-USNAC 1969

Recognition And Prevention Of Bedsores C 8 MIN
3/4 OR 1/2 INCH VIDEO CASSETTE PRO
Defines the conditions under which bed sores may develop and describes those persons most susceptible to the development of bed sores. Explains the stages of development of bed sores. Emphasizes the relative ease with which bed sores are prevented and the relative difficulty with which they are cured. Concludes with steps required to prevent the development of bed sores.
LC NO. 77-731353
Prod-TRAINX Dist-TRAINX

Recognition And Prevention Of Bedsores (Spanish) C 8 MIN
3/4 OR 1/2 INCH VIDEO CASSETTE PRO
Defines the conditions under which bed sores may develop and describes those persons most susceptible to the development of bed sores. Explains the stages of development of bed sores. Emphasizes the relative ease with which they are cured. Concludes with steps required to prevent the development of bed sores.
LC NO. 77-731353
Prod-TRAINX Dist-TRAINX

Recognition and Prevention Of Child Abuse C 18 MIN
3/4 OR 1/2 INCH VIDEO CASSETTE PRO
Details the shared characteristics of abusive parents, the means to follow up the suspicion that abuse has occurred, the way to determine the triad of 'special parents,' 'special child,' and 'stressful home environ- ment' and an effective way to encourage local supports to initiate a community-based child abuse prevention program.
Prod-UMICHM Dist-UMICHM 1975

Recognition And Treatment Of Arrhythmias C 76 MIN
3/4 INCH VIDEO CASSETTE PRO
Discusses recognition and treatment of arrhythmias, including chronotropic agents, myocardial depressants, cardioversion and pacemaker therapy. Describes early recognition of the common arrhythmias associated with myocardial infarction, including observations which enable classification of arrhythmias.
LC NO. 76-706100
Prod-WARMP Dist-USNAC 1968

Recognition Of Defects C 24 MIN
3/4 OR 1/2 INCH VIDEO CASSETTE
Explores the realistic application of the federal Food, Drug and Cosmetic Act and the Good Manufacturing Practice regulation. Reviews handling of commodities, storage temperatures, and protection of facility and stock from adulteration.
From The Supervisor's Role In Food Distribution Series.
Prod-PLAID Dist-PLAID

Recognition Of Leprosy C 13 MIN
16MM FILM OPTICAL SOUND
Illustrates the clinical manifestations of leprosy. Shows the technique of taking and staining skin scrapings to demonstrate the etiologic agent, mycobacterium leprae, and the technique of taking skin biopsies to determine pathology of peripheral nerves.
LC NO. FIE59-254
Prod-USPHS Dist-USNAC 1959

Recognition Of Leprosy (Spanish) C 13 MIN
16MM FILM OPTICAL SOUND
Illustrates the clinical manifestations of leprosy, using patients from the Public Health Service hospital at Carville, Louisiana. Shows the technique of taking and staining skin scrapings to demonstrate the etiologic agent, Mycobacterium leprae, and the technique of taking skin biopsies to determine pathology of peripheral nerves.
LC NO. 74-705490
Prod-USPHS Dist-USNAC 1959

Recognition Of Man - The Renaissance C 18 MIN
16MM FILM OPTICAL SOUND J-H A
Shows that the main Renaissance contribution to Western culture was the recognition of the individual in life and art. Explains that one of the most significant creations of the Renaissance was portraiture, a new cateogry of art which reveals man's developing awareness of his active destiny in life.
From The History Through Art Series.
LC NO. FIA68-115
Prod-ALEF Dist-ALEF 1968

Recognition Of Russia, The - A Climate Of Mutual Distrust C 26 MIN
16MM FILM, 3/4 OR 1/2 IN VIDEO H-C
Traces the relationship between the United States and Russia from 1917 to 1933. Explains that Cold War attitudes can be linked to this period and the national paranoia over Bolshevism.
From The Between The Wars Series.
Prod-LNDBRG Dist-FI 1978

Recognizing A Failure Identity C 30 MIN
3/4 OR 1/2 INCH VIDEO CASSETTE T
Tells how to become aware of negative addictive behaviors in our self and others.

From The Developing Discipline Series.
Prod-SDPT Dist-GPITVL 1983

Recognizing Alcoholism In The Hospitalized Patient C 25 MIN
3/4 OR 1/2 INCH VIDEO CASSETTE
See series title for descriptive statement.
Alcohol - A Critical Illness Series.
Prod-BRA Dist-BRA

Recognizing And Reacting C 22 MIN
3/4 OR 1/2 INCH VIDEO CASSETTE
Assists the supervisor with applied knowledge in the trained observation of food plant problems, emphasizing the coupling of seemingly unrelated problems to arrive at common sense corrections which save in terms of cost of repairs and down time.
From The Food Plant Supervisor - Understanding And Performing Inplant Food Safety Insp Series.
Prod-PLAID Dist-PLAID

Recognizing Common Communicable Diseases C
3/4 OR 1/2 INCH VIDEO CASSETTE PRO
Helps the viewer gain skill and confidence in recognizing common communicable diseases of children. Focuses on the differentiation between measles, ruhella, chickenpox, smallpox and scarlet fever.
Prod-UMICHM Dist-UMICHM 1976

Recognizing Fact And Opinion C 30 MIN
3/4 OR 1/2 INCH VIDEO CASSETTE
See series title for descriptive statement.
From The General Reading Series.
Prod-CAMB Dist-CAMB

Recognizing Food Spoilage C 14 MIN
16MM FILM - 3/4 IN VIDEO IND
Points out factors that indicate food spoilage and shows ways to prevent possible food poisoning.
From The Food Service Employee Series.
Prod-COPI Dist-COPI 1969

Recognizing Hazards C 12 MIN
3/4 OR 1/2 INCH VIDEO CASSETTE
Discusses the recognition of hazards in the plant such as safely using tools and elevated working surfaces such as ladders and scaffolds.
From The Protecting Your Safety And Health In the Plant Series.
Prod-TPCTRA Dist-TPCTRA

Recognizing Hazards (Spanish) C 12 MIN
3/4 OR 1/2 INCH VIDEO CASSETTE
Discusses the recognition of hazards in the plant such as safely using tools and elevated working surfaces such as ladders and scaffolds.
From The Protecting Your Safety And Health In The Plant Series.
Prod-TPCTRA Dist-TPCTRA

Recognizing Intervals C 29 MIN
3/4 INCH VIDEO CASSETTE H A
Introduces D-major scale and principal dynamic indication in music notation. Presents intervals of the sixth to the tenth.
From The Beginning Piano - An Adult Approach Series. Lesson 11
Prod-COAST Dist-CDTEL

Recognizing Misbehavior Goals B 30 MIN
2 INCH VIDEOTAPE T
Offers an understanding of the motivation of the individual child according to Dr Dreikurs, also shows his analysis of the misbehavior of children. Shows Dr Dreikurs discussing four misbehavior goals, desire for attention, power revenge and desire to be left alone. (Broadcast quality)
From The Dynamics Of Classroom Behavior Series.
Prod-VTETV Dist-GPITVL Prodn-WETKTV

Recognizing The Obvious C 25 MIN
3/4 OR 1/2 INCH VIDEO CASSETTE H-C A
Discusses the systems approach to a complex problem and the kind of sophisticated software which can be introduced in the more advanced systems. Concludes with a look at the future of robotics.
From The Computers In Control Series.
Prod-BBCTV Dist-FI 1984

Recognizing, Confronting, And Helping The Alcoholic C 40 MIN
3/4 OR 1/2 INCH VIDEO CASSETTE PRO
Acquaints users with principles of diagnosing and confronting the alcoholic. Excerpts the interview session and demonstrates the four CAGE questions to determine the alcoholic condition.
Prod-HSCIC Dist-HSCIC 1982

Recommendations For A More Rational Use Of Antipsychotic Drugs—A Series
PRO
Describes the use of antipsychotic drugs.
Prod-VAHSL Dist-USNAC 1979

Antipsychotics And Acute Psychosis 20 MIN
Recommendations For A More Rational Use Of 5 MIN

Recommendations For A More Rational Use Of Antipsychotic Drugs - Overview To The Series C 5 MIN
3/4 INCH VIDEO CASSETTE PRO
Emphasizes the importance of the sensible use of antipsychotic drugs, stating that physicians should reexamine their drug administration practices.
From The Recommendations For A More Rational Use Of Antipsychotic Drugs Series.
LC NO. 80-706126
Prod-VAHSL Dist-USNAC 1979

Reconciliation And Justice C 30 MIN
16MM FILM OPTICAL SOUND R
Explores life in Zaire, the heartland of Africa, and the home of the largest independent African church, the Kimbanguist. Discusses the problems of ecumenism, tribal unity and Africanization.
Prod-CBSTV Dist-CCNCC

Reconditioning A Cultivator B 14 MIN
16MM FILM OPTICAL SOUND
Demonstrates replacement of a worn wheel boring. Explains how to adjust the yoke, check and adjust the shovels, check and lubricate the gang expansion and steering assemblies and lubricate all parts of a cultivator.
From The Farm Work Series.
LC NO. FIE52-326
Prod-USOE Dist-USNAC 1944

Reconditioning A Cylinder With A Portable Boring Bar B 36 MIN
16MM FILM OPTICAL SOUND
Traces a typical boring job to illustrate various checks, adjustments and alignments required to operate the boring bar. Covers types, uses, nomenclature, set-up and operation of the portable bar while demonstrating the reconditioning of a cylinder.
LC NO. FIE52-1213
Prod-USN Dist-USNAC 1944

Reconditioning A Grain Drill B 31 MIN
16MM FILM OPTICAL SOUND
Shows how to inspect, repair and recondition a typical grain drill.
From The Farm Work Series. Equipment Maintenance, No. 4
LC NO. FIE52-359
Prod-USOE Dist-USNAC Prodn-CALVIN 1943

Reconditioning A Grain Drill (French) B 31 MIN
16MM FILM OPTICAL SOUND H-C A
Tells how to inspect and repair a typical grain drill, clean and lubricate the fertilizer and seeding mechanism, repair the disc furrow openers, drive chains, assemble a pawl and calibrate the seeding mechanism.
Prod-USOE Dist-USNAC 1943

Reconditioning A Mower, Pt 1 - Cutter Bar B 21 MIN
16MM FILM OPTICAL SOUND
Shows how to recondition, check and repair the cutter bar mechanism.
From The Farm Work Series. Equipment Maintenance, No. 1
LC NO. FIE52-324
Prod-USOE Dist-USNAC Prodn-CALVIN 1943

Reconditioning A Mower, Pt 2 - Drive System B 21 MIN
16MM FILM OPTICAL SOUND
Shows how to clean, inspect and lubricate a reconditioned mower.
From The Farm Work Series. Equipment Maintenance, No. 2
LC NO. FIE52-325
Prod-USOE Dist-USNAC Prodn-CALVIN 1943

Reconditioning The Fuel Pump B 17 MIN
16MM FILM OPTICAL SOUND
Shows how to install seal assembly, diaphragm, copper seal gasket, shim, setting bar and spacer in the fuel pump.
LC NO. FIE52-1364
Prod-USN Dist-USNAC 1945

Reconductoring Or Upgrading Voltage C
3/4 OR 1/2 INCH VIDEO CASSETTE IND
Demonstrates procedures for grounding an overhead disbtribution line on a tangent structure, a vertical running corner, and a vertical deadend.
From The Live Line Maintenance Series.
Prod-LEIKID Dist-LEIKID

Reconnaissance Pilot B 35 MIN
3/4 OR 1/2 INCH VIDEO CASSETTE
Features William Holden as a P-38 Lightning reconnaissanse pilot in the South Pacific in 1942.
Prod-IHF Dist-IHF

Reconnective Surgery C 20 MIN
16MM FILM, 3/4 OR 1/2 IN VIDEO
Discusses reconnective surgery. Describes the achievements of Dr Chen Chung Wei of China in reconstructing usable limbs after accidents and the work of Dr Ralph Mankeltow of Toronto General Hospital who performs intricate microsurgery. Presents a young man who has regained the use of his damaged hand telling about the dramatic change in his life since the surgery.
LC NO. 83-706225
Prod-CANBC Dist-FLMLIB

Reconstructing The Nation - The Crucial Years C 29 MIN
2 INCH VIDEOTAPE
See series title for descriptive statement.
From The Black Experience Series.
Prod-WTTWTV Dist-PUBTEL

Reconstruction C 30 MIN
3/4 OR 1/2 INCH VIDEO CASSETTE C
See series title for descriptive statement.
From The American Story - The Beginning To 1877 Series.
Prod-DALCCD Dist-DALCCD

Reconstruction Of Early Ballet Repertory C 30 MIN
3/4 OR 1/2 INCH VIDEO CASSETTE
See series title for descriptive statement.
From The Passing On Dance Series.
Prod-ARCVID Dist-ARCVID

Reconstruction Of The Breast After Mastectomy C 27 MIN
3/4 INCH VIDEO CASSETTE
Discusses the advances made in breast reconstruction. Looks at the different methods of reconstruction after mastectomy.
Prod-UTAHTI Dist-UTAHTI

Reconstruction Of The Cervical Esophagus C 25 MIN
16MM FILM OPTICAL SOUND PRO
Presents a technique of total excision of the laryngo-esophageal complex, with or without radical neck dissection and thyroidectomy, with a staged reconstruction as the most satisfactory method of obtaining significant cure rate and maintaining adequate patency.
Prod-ACYDGD Dist-ACY 1967

Reconstruction Of The Common Bile Duct C 26 MIN
16MM FILM OPTICAL SOUND PRO
Explains that if the two ends of the common bile duct can be found, an end-to-end anastomosis should be performed. Shows the techniques for two or three different types of anastomoses.
Prod-ACYDGD Dist-ACY 1965

Reconstruction Of The Thumb C 30 MIN
16MM FILM OPTICAL SOUND PRO
Illustrates transplantation of an index finger and utilization of a vestigial thumb to reconstruct the first web.
From The Cine Clinic Series.
Prod-ACYDGD Dist-NMAC 1970

Reconstruction, Pt 1 C 30 MIN
2 INCH VIDEOTAPE
Looks briefly at the Civil War as a turning point in U S history. Covers the political side of Reconstruction.
From The American History II Series.
Prod-KRMATV Dist-GPITVL

Reconstruction, Pt 2 C 30 MIN
2 INCH VIDEOTAPE
Emphasizes social reconstruction as it applied to former slaves. Analyzes the 'radical Republicians,' rule of the court and the ultimate failure of social reconstruction.
From The American History II Series.
Prod-KRMATV Dist-GPITVL

Reconstruction, The - A Changing Nation - 1865-1880 X 24 MIN
16MM FILM OPTICAL SOUND I-C A
Discusses aspects of the Reconstruction, such as the black codes, the conflict between Congress and the President, the 14th amendment, carpetbaggers, tariffs, sharecropping, railroad rates, banking, immigration, unionization and industrialization.
From The Exploring - The Story Of America, Set 2 Series.
LC NO. FIA68-1059
Prod-NBCTV Dist-GRACUR 1968

Reconstructive And Cosmetic Surgery C 29 MIN
3/4 OR 1/2 INCH VIDEO CASSETTE
Describes the techniques of cosmetic surgery and shows an operation which rebuilt a young boy's entire facial skeleton with rib and hip grafts.
From The Daniel Foster, MD Series.
Prod-KERA Dist-PBS

Record Layout And Print Chart B 45 MIN
2 INCH VIDEOTAPE
See series title for descriptive statement.
From The Data Processing, Unit 3 - Instructing The Computer Series.
Prod-GPITVL Dist-GPITVL

Record Of A Tenement Gentleman, The (Japanese) B 72 MIN
16MM FILM OPTICAL SOUND
Deals with the relationship between an aging woman and an abandoned child. Tells of the difficulties of their life together, the hostility of the woman and the exasperating ungratefulness of the child.
Prod-NYFLMS Dist-NYFLMS 1947

Record Of The Rocks, The C 20 MIN
3/4 OR 1/2 INCH VIDEO CASSETTE
Discusses determining the age of rocks and how to evaluate the results, Miller's experiment simulating the conditions of early Earth and ascending the layers of sedimentary rock in the Grand Canyon.
From The Evolution Series.
Prod-FOTH Dist-FOTH 1984

Record Ride For The Pony Express, The C 22 MIN
16MM FILM, 3/4 OR 1/2 IN VIDEO I-H
Shows how hostile Indians, the refusal of a relief rider to take his turn and other emergencies do not keep Bob Haslam, one of the teen-age Pony Express riders, from riding 380 miles in 36 hours - a record ride for the Pony Express.
From The You Are There Series.
Prod-CBSTV Dist-PHENIX 1972

Record Show, A C 30 MIN
3/4 OR 1/2 INCH VIDEO CASSETTE P-I
Presents young performers Ocie Davis and Robert Chen, who show that there are two sides to a record and that music is music whether it be rock, country, gospel, jazz or classical. Features violinist Nina Bodnar, winner of the Jacques Thibaud prize. Hosted by Florence Henderson.
From The Musical Encounter Series.
Prod-KLCSTV Dist-GPITVL 1983

Record Structures C 30 MIN
3/4 OR 1/2 INCH VIDEO CASSETTE H-C A
Introduces the RECORD data structure. Describes variables of RECORD type as well as RECORD TYPES. Includes examples of code segments using records. Concludes with description of WITH statement.
From The Pascal, Pt 2 - Intermediate Pascal Series.
LC NO. 81-706049
Prod-COLOSU Dist-COLOSU 1980

Recorded Live C 8 MIN
16MM FILM, 3/4 OR 1/2 IN VIDEO

Follows a young man's efforts to answer a invitation to a job interview at a forbidding mansion. Shows how the young man searches for some signs of life in the place, but instead is eaten up by a slithering mass of carnivorous videotape.
LC NO. 76-700414
Prod-USC Dist-PFP 1978

Recorders C
16MM FILM - 3/4 IN VIDEO IND
Covers drive and balance motors and multipoint, strip and circular recorders.
From The Instrumentation Maintenance Series.
Prod-ISA Dist-ISA

Recording And Measuring Lengths C 15 MIN
3/4 OR 1/2 INCH VIDEO CASSETTE P
See series title for descriptive statement.
From The Hands On, Grade 3 Series. Unit 2 - Measuring
Prod-VAOG Dist-AITECH Prodn-WHROTV 1975

Recording Centric Relation Graphic Methods, Pt II - Extraoral Tracer C 10 MIN
3/4 OR 1/2 INCH VIDEO CASSETTE
Demonstrates in detail the clinical use of an extraoral tracing device for recording centric relation during the fabrication of complete dentures.
Prod-VADTC Dist-AMDA 1980

Recording Centric Relation Graphic Methods, Pt I - Intraoral Tracer C 14 MIN
3/4 OR 1/2 INCH VIDEO CASSETTE
Demonstrates in detail the clinical use of an intraoral tracing device for recording centric relation during the fabrication of complete dentures.
Prod-VADTC Dist-AMDA 1980

Recording Centric Relation, Graphic Methods—A Series
PRO
Shows the clinical use of intraoral and extraoral tracing devices for recording centric relation for denture fabrication.
Prod-VADTC Dist-USNAC

Recording Centric Relation, Graphic Methods,
Recording Centric Relation, Graphic Methods, 010 MIN

Recording Centric Relation, Graphic Methods, Pt 1, Intraoral Tracer C 14 MIN
16MM FILM, 3/4 OR 1/2 IN VIDEO PRO
Details the clinical use of an intraoral tracing device for recording centric relations during the fabrication of complete dentures. Demonstrates the fabrication of accurate stable record bases.
From The Recording Centric Relation, Graphic Methods Series.
Prod-VADTC Dist-USNAC

Recording Centric Relation, Graphic Methods, Pt 2, Extraoral Tracer C 10 MIN
16MM FILM, 3/4 OR 1/2 IN VIDEO PRO
Details the clinical use of the extraoral tracing device for recording centric relation during the fabrication of complete dentures. Compares intraoral and extraoral tracing devices.
From The Recording Centric Relation, Graphic Methods Series.
Prod-VADTC Dist-USNAC

Recording Data In Science C 14 MIN
3/4 OR 1/2 INCH VIDEO CASSETTE J
Shows a marine biologist recording data about a coral reef in hope of learning how to farm reefs for food.
From The Whatabout Series.
Prod-AITV Dist-AITECH 1983

Recording Edentulous Ridge Contour - Correctable Wax Impressions C 16 MIN
16MM FILM - 3/4 IN VIDEO PRO
Shows the methodology for fluid wax impressions of the edentulous ridges in distal extension removable partial dentures. Shows how this procedure enhances the stability and retention of the prosthesis and reduces the stress on the remaining teeth. Issued in 1967 as a motion picture.
From The Removable Partial Dentures, Clasp Type - Clinical And Laboratory Procedures Series.
LC NO. 78-706185
Prod-USVA Dist-USNAC Prodn-VADTC 1978

Recording Edentulous Ridge Contour And Correctable Wax Impression C 16 MIN
3/4 OR 1/2 INCH VIDEO CASSETTE
Demonstrates the methodology for fluid wax impressions of the edentulous ridges in distal extension for removable partial dentures.
From The Removable Partial Dentures, Clasp Type Clinical And Laboratory Procedures Series.
Prod-VADTC Dist-AMDA 1969

Recording Industry, The C 30 MIN
3/4 OR 1/2 INCH VIDEO CASSETTE J-H
Looks at the influence Black artists have had on the recording industry by focusing on the contributions of George Benson and Quincy Jones.
From The From Jumpstreet Series.
Prod-WETATV Dist-GPITVL 1979

Recording Machines, The B 45 MIN
2 INCH VIDEOTAPE
See series title for descriptive statement.
From The Data Processing, Unit 1 - Introduction To Data Processing Series.
Prod-GPITVL Dist-GPITVL

Recording Observations C 14 MIN
3/4 OR 1/2 INCH VIDEO CASSETTE P
See series title for descriptive statement.
From The Hands On, Grade 1 Series. Unit 1 - Observing
Prod-VAOG Dist-AITECH Prodn-WHROTV 1975

Recording Observations C 15 MIN
3/4 OR 1/2 INCH VIDEO CASSETTE P
See series title for descriptive statement.
From The Hands On, Grade 3 Series. Unit 1 - Observing
Prod-VAOG Dist-AITECH Prodn-WHROTV 1975

Records In The Rocks C 29 MIN
2 INCH VIDEOTAPE
See series title for descriptive statement.
From The Observing Eye Series.
Prod-WGBHTV Dist-PUBTEL

Recourse For The Consumer C 18 MIN
16MM FILM, 3/4 OR 1/2 IN VIDEO J-H
Shows available alternatives when purchased merchandise proves to be defective.
LC NO. 81-707265
Prod-CENTRO Dist-CORF 1981

Recovery After Mastectomy C 17 MIN
16MM FILM OPTICAL SOUND PRO
Presents a nurse and a volunteer visitor who has undergone mastectomy demonstrating exercises and prostheses to aid mastectomy patients in quickly recovering to a full and normal life.
LC NO. 78-701059
Prod-AMCS Dist-AMCS 1970

Recovery After Mastectomy (2nd Ed) C 16 MIN
16MM FILM OPTICAL SOUND
Shows a Reach To Recovery volunteer visiting hospitalized mastectomy patients. Explains her role in helping patients to recuperate and demonstrates Reach To Recovery exercises.
Prod-AMCS Dist-AMCS 1971

Recovery Boiler Operation C
3/4 OR 1/2 INCH VIDEO CASSETTE IND
Includes startup and operation, operating problems and emergencies and safety procedures of recovery boiler operation.
From The Pulp And Paper Training, Module 2 - Chemical Recovery series
Prod-LEIKID Dist-LEIKID

Recovery Boiler, Pt 1 C
3/4 OR 1/2 INCH VIDEO CASSETTE IND
Includes boiler construction, auxiliary fuel, air/gas flowpath and precipitator.
From The Pulp And Paper Training, Module 2 - Chemical Recovery series.
Prod-LEIKID Dist-LEIKID

Recovery Boiler, Pt 2 C
3/4 OR 1/2 INCH VIDEO CASSETTE IND
Covers sootblowers, water and steam flowpath, steam and drum, and desuperheater.
From The Pulp And Paper Training, Module 2 - Chemical Recovery Series.
Prod-LEIKID Dist-LEIKID

Recovery From A Heart Attack C 16 MIN
3/4 OR 1/2 INCH VIDEO CASSETTE
Presents a typical recovery from a heart attack, beginning in the hospital and concluding six months afterward. Shows what one's own recovery will involve and why, and that recovery will take time, patience and restraint but, more importantly, that he/she can recover and return to a normal life.
LC NO. 77-730434
Prod-TRAINX Dist-TRAINX

Recovery From Major Disasters C
3/4 OR 1/2 INCH VIDEO CASSETTE IND
Includes sectionalization, cold load pick-up, resynchronization of islands, black start, operator co-ordination and frequency-volt-age control.
From The Electric Power System Operation Series. Tape 19
Prod-LEIKID Dist-LEIKID

Recovery Process, The C
3/4 OR 1/2 INCH VIDEO CASSETTE IND
Covers making pulp, black liquor, recovery boiler and smelt recovery.
From The Pulp And Paper Training, Module 2 - Chemical Recovery Series.
Prod-LEIKID Dist-LEIKID

Recovery Room Care C 22 MIN
3/4 OR 1/2 INCH VIDEO CASSETTE PRO
Indicates a rationale for development of the recovery room. Identifies patients needing recovery room care. Discusses cardio-respiratory problems. Considers differential diagnosis of the anxious or restless recovery room patient, with special emphasis on postanesthetic pain relief.
From The Anesthesiology Clerkship Series.
Prod-UMICHM Dist-UMICHM 1982

Recreating The Earliest Modern Dance C 30 MIN
3/4 OR 1/2 INCH VIDEO CASSETTE
See series title for descriptive statement.
From The Passing On Dance Series.
Prod-ARCVID Dist-ARCVID

Recreation - Hospitality - Tourism C 6 MIN
16MM FILM, 3/4 OR 1/2 IN VIDEO K-I
See series title for descriptive statement.
From The Kingdom Of Could Be You Series.
Prod-EBEC Dist-EBEC 1974

Recreation - The Japanese Way C 30 MIN
16MM FILM OPTICAL SOUND
Depicts the various recreational activities enjoyed by the Japanese including sumo wrestling, the Kabuki theatre and cherry blossom viewing.
Prod-MTP Dist-MTP

Recreation Leadership B 23 MIN
16MM FILM OPTICAL SOUND
Portrays the procedures used by an army captain in developing a recreational program for a newly formed company.
LC NO. FIE55-26
Prod-USA Dist-USNAC 1953

Recreational And Occupational Therapy B 13 MIN
16MM FILM OPTICAL SOUND
Points out recreational and occupational activities fitted to the patient's condition—passive diversion during an immobile state, limited physical activities carried on in bed, individualized occupational therapy and social recreation projects.
LC NO. FIE52-333
Prod-USOE Dist-USNAC 1945

Recruiting - Search And Interviewing Techniques C 60 MIN
3/4 OR 1/2 INCH VIDEO CASSETTE
Discusses the use of selection effectiveness when expanding or replacing members of a sales force in order to lessen the training time needed in the future. Clarifies the 'can-do' versus the 'will-do' components of the job matching. Includes cost of open territories, sales personnel planning, recruiting sources and how to avoid the ten biggest mistakes of interviewing.
From The Dynamics Of Sales Management Series. Session 6
Prod-PRODEV Dist-PRODEV

Recruiting And Developing The D P Professional—A Series

Presents some alternative ideas for addressing the need for highly qualified systems professionals, and includes a variety of tools for persons involved in the recruitment and development of DP professionals. Features Tom Lutz, writer and lecturer.
Prod-DELTAK Dist-DELTAK

Decision To Build Or Buy Systems Talent, The 030 MIN
Interview Process, The 030 MIN
Mark Of The D P Professional, The 030 MIN
Recruiting And Hiring 030 MIN
Staff Development 030 MIN

Recruiting And Hiring C 30 MIN
3/4 OR 1/2 INCH VIDEO CASSETTE
See series title for descriptive statement.
From The Recruiting And Developing The D P Professional Series.
Prod-DELTAK Dist-DELTAK

Recruiting Life At Sea C 20 MIN
16MM FILM OPTICAL SOUND H-C
Depicts the life of men aboard ships, including their living quarters, chow call, recreation, medical care, religious services, military activities and drills.
LC NO. 77-703235
Prod-USN Dist-USNAC 1948

Recruiting Step By Step C 13 MIN
16MM FILM OPTICAL SOUND
Demonstrates the six key steps for recruiting volunteers, and the benefits they gain by working with Girl Scout troops.
Prod-GSUSA Dist-GSUSA 1980

Recruiting Talented People, J Kenneth Lund C
3/4 OR 1/2 INCH VIDEO CASSETTE PRO
See series title for descriptive statement.
From The Management Skills Series.
Prod-AMCEE Dist-AMCEE

Recruitment And Retention C 30 MIN
3/4 OR 1/2 INCH VIDEO CASSETTE T
Explains how to recruit and retain adult basic education students.
From The Basic Education - Teaching The Adult Series.
Prod-MDDE Dist-MDCPB

Recruitment, Selection And Placement C 23 MIN
16MM FILM - 3/4 IN VIDEO
Presents an overview of the spirit and intent of equal employment laws as they relate to the recruitment, selection and placement of new personnel.
From The Fair Employment Practice Series.
Prod-BNA Dist-BNA 1979

Recrystallization C 21 MIN
3/4 OR 1/2 INCH VIDEO CASSETTE
Presents the theory and methods of selecting a solvent or solvent pair for a laboratory recrystallization.
From The Organic Chemistry Laboratory Techniques Series.
Prod-UCLA Dist-UCEMC

Recrystallization, Pt 1 C 3 MIN
16MM FILM SILENT H-C A
Demonstrates techniques for purifying a substance containing soluble and insoluble impurities. Shows preparation of solution and removal of insoluble impurities, the filtering of the hot solution through a funnel and flask and the ice bath where the filtrate and solvent bottle are placed to cool.
From The General Chemistry Laboratory Techniques Series.
LC NO. 72-708615
Prod-KALMIA Dist-KALMIA 1970

Recrystallization, Pt 2 C 3 MIN
16MM FILM SILENT H-C A
Shows the cold filtrate resulting from the procedure in part 1 which is now supersaturated. Shows the adding of seed crystals and the spreading of beautiful crystal 'NEEDLES.' Illustrates vacuum filtration and the cold solvent stage of the crystals. Concludes with the removing of the filter cake for viewing and drying.
From The General Chemistry Laboratory Techniques Series.
LC NO. 76-708616
Prod-KALMIA Dist-KALMIA 1970

Rectal Bleeding C 17 MIN
3/4 OR 1/2 INCH VIDEO CASSETTE
Presents evaluation, physical examination, diagnostic procedures and diagnostic techniques of rectal bleeding.
From The Emergency Management - The First 30 Minutes, Vol III Series.
Prod-VTRI Dist-VTRI

Rectal Flap Repair (Beneventi-Cassebaum) Of Prostato-Rectal Fistula C 14 MIN
16MM FILM OPTICAL SOUND
Demonstrates rectal flap repair of the prostato-rectal fistula. Shows that with the patient in the jack knife position wide exposure of the fistula is obtained by linear incision of the posterior or rectal wall and rectal sphincters.
LC NO. 75-702244
Prod-EATONL Dist-EATONL 1973

Rectal Polyp Regression With Surgical Management Of Multiple Familial Polyposis C 27 MIN
16MM FILM OPTICAL SOUND PRO
Illustrates the technique of colectomy and the need for low ileo-rectal anastomosis. Shows regression of rectal polyps after colectomy through the proctoscope and discusses the mechanism for polyp disappearance.
Prod-ACYDGD Dist-ACY 1967

Rectal Prolapse, Enterocele, And Uterine Prolapse Repair Through Rectal And... C 23 MIN
16MM FILM OPTICAL SOUND PRO
Explains that complete rectal prolapse in women is associated with pelvic floor relaxation, sliding of the cul-de-sac, and uterine descensus. Presents a technique of repair, using a combined rectal and transvaginal approach.
Prod-ACYDGD Dist-ACY 1965

Rectangles And Right Angle C 20 MIN
2 INCH VIDEOTAPE P
See series title for descriptive statement.
From The Mathemagic, Unit III - Geometry Series.
Prod-WMULTV Dist-GPITVL

Rectangular Coordinates B 13 MIN
16MM FILM, 3/4 OR 1/2 IN VIDEO
Demonstrates how to use coordinates in solving problems of time and distance. Shows how to locate a point using two coordinates. Issued in 1944 as a motion picture.
From The Radio Technician Training Series.
LC NO. 78-706300
Prod-USN Dist-USNAC Prodn-LNS 1978

Rectangular To Larger Round Transition - Centered C 15 MIN
1/2 IN VIDEO CASSETTE BETA/VHS IND
See series title for descriptive statement.
From The Metal Fabrication - Square To Round Layout Series.
Prod-RMI Dist-RMI

Rectangular To Round Transition - Centered C 20 MIN
1/2 IN VIDEO CASSETTE BETA/VHS IND
See series title for descriptive statement.
From The Metal Fabrication - Square To Round Layout Series.
Prod-RMI Dist-RMI

Rectangular To Round Transition - Double Offset C 37 MIN
1/2 IN VIDEO CASSETTE BETA/VHS IND
See series title for descriptive statement.
From The Metal Fabrication - Square To Round Layout Series.
Prod-RMI Dist-RMI

Rectangular To Round Transition - Offset One-Way C 34 MIN
1/2 IN VIDEO CASSETTE BETA/VHS IND
See series title for descriptive statement.
From The Metal Fabrication - Square To Round Layout Series.
Prod-RMI Dist-RMI

Rectangular To Round Transition - Offset Two-Way C 44 MIN
1/2 IN VIDEO CASSETTE BETA/VHS IND
See series title for descriptive statement.
From The Metal Fabrication - Square To Round Layout Series.
Prod-RMI Dist-RMI

Rectangular To Triangular Transition - One Elevation, Sides Of Openings Parallel C 23 MIN
1/2 IN VIDEO CASSETTE BETA/VHS IND
See series title for descriptive statement.
From The Exercise In Triangulating One-Piece Patterns Series.
Prod-RMI Dist-RMI

Rectifiers C 12 MIN
3/4 OR 1/2 INCH VIDEO CASSETTE
Covers diode rectifiers, half-wave, full-wave, bridge, three-phase and other types of rectifiers.
From The Industrial Electronics - Power Supplies Series.
Prod-TPCTRA Dist-TPCTRA

Rectifiers And Power Supplies C 60 MIN
3/4 OR 1/2 INCH VIDEO CASSETTE IND
See series title for descriptive statement.
From The Electrical Maintenance Training, Module 7 - Solid-State Devices Series.
Prod-LEIKID Dist-LEIKID

Recurrence In Inguinal Hernia C 21 MIN
16MM FILM OPTICAL SOUND PRO
Indicates the causes of recurrence in inguinal hernia and emphasizes the need for repair of the anatomical defects in the transversalis fascia as well as the inguinal canal. Demonstrates the use of a rectus sheath.
Prod-ACYDGD Dist-ACY 1960

Recurrent Anterior Dislocation Of The Shoulder - Simplified Surgical Repair C 13 MIN
16MM FILM OPTICAL SOUND PRO
Shows surgical techniques for repairing anterior dislocation of the shoulder. Explains the advantages of this method of operation and shows the postoperative recovery of a patient.
LC NO. 74-706213
Prod-USAF Dist-USNAC 1968

Recurrent Inguinal Hernia Repair With Fascial Sutures C 26 MIN
16MM FILM OPTICAL SOUND PRO
Explains that recurrent inguinal hernia is the surgeon's bete noire. Demonstrates repairing recurrent inguinal hernia with fascial sutures.
Prod-ACYDGD Dist-ACY 1963

Recurrent Parotidectomy C 20 MIN
3/4 OR 1/2 INCH VIDEO CASSETTE
See series title for descriptive statement.
From The Head And Neck Series.
Prod-SVL Dist-SVL

Recurring Idea, A B
16MM FILM OPTICAL SOUND
Revises the way in which the theory of linear problems helps solve differential equations and systems of algebraic equations. Presents a banking problem and expresses it in terms of a recurrence relation.
Prod-OPENU Dist-OPENU

Recursion C 30 MIN
3/4 OR 1/2 INCH VIDEO CASSETTE H-C A
Introduces recursion as used in the Pascal compiler itself and user-written recursive algorithms. Describes execution of recursive code and defines variable scope in recursive procedures.
From The Pascal, Pt 3 - Advanced Pascal Series.
LC NO. 81-706049
Prod-COLOSU Dist-COLOSU 1980

Recursion C 40 MIN
3/4 OR 1/2 INCH VIDEO CASSETTE
Explains and demonstrates the process of writing recursive programs, i.e., programs that invoke themselves in computer languages.
From The Computer Languages - Pt 2 Series.
Prod-MIOT Dist-MIOT

Recursion In G And S C 50 MIN
3/4 OR 1/2 INCH VIDEO CASSETTE
Gives examples demonstrating the implementation of recursive programs in global and stack environments in computer languages.
From The Computer Languages - Pt 1 Series.
Prod-MIOT Dist-MIOT

Recursive Function Theory C 50 MIN
3/4 OR 1/2 INCH VIDEO CASSETTE
Continues the subject of computability by defining the computing scheme known as the recursive functions.
From The Computer Languages - Pt 1 Series.
Prod-MIOT Dist-MIOT

Recycled Reflections C 12 MIN
16MM FILM, 3/4 OR 1/2 IN VIDEO
Explains how automobile bumpers are recycled, thereby saving a great deal of waste. Points out one way industry can help conserve natural resources.
Prod-FLMFR Dist-FLMFR

Recycling C 21 MIN
16MM FILM OPTICAL SOUND J A
Shows the inadequacy of today's systems for reclaiming and re-using steel, aluminum, glass, paper and others. Points out that recycling is the most important single principle which must be incorporated into tomorrow's solid waste management systems to permit conservation of our resources and easy and economical solid waste disposal. Discusses new ideas being developed. Intended for use by the general public, including con servationists and students.
LC NO. 73-714061
Prod-FINLYS Dist-FINLYS 1971

Recycling C 15 MIN
3/4 OR 1/2 INCH VIDEO CASSETTE K-P
Discusses paper and how it is made and why recycling is important.
From The Pass It On Series.
Prod-WKNOTV Dist-GPITVL 1983

Recycling - A Way Of Life C 14 MIN
16MM FILM OPTICAL SOUND
Presents the story of aluminum recycling and its importance in a world where conservation of energy and material resources is a must. Shows facets of aluminum recycling from consumer collection to recycling of auto parts.
Prod-ALUMA Dist-MTP

Recycling - Waste Into Wealth C 29 MIN
16MM FILM, 3/4 OR 1/2 IN VIDEO I-C A
Features recycling techniques.
Prod-PATH Dist-BULFRG

Recycling / Furniture Buying / Marriage Counselors C
3/4 OR 1/2 INCH VIDEO CASSETTE
Discusses various aspects of recycling, furniture buying and picking a marriage counselor.
From The Consumer Survival Series.
Prod-MDCPB Dist-MDCPB

Recycling In Action C 14 MIN
16MM FILM, 3/4 OR 1/2 IN VIDEO
Establishes the need for recycling solid waste products and introduces community reclamation centers.
Prod-FLMFR Dist-FLMFR

Recycling Our Resources C 10 MIN
16MM FILM, 3/4 OR 1/2 IN VIDEO I-J
Shows why conservation is important and some significant ways that recycling contributes.
Prod-COLLRD Dist-AIMS 1973

Recycling Roads With Asphalt Emulsions C 22 MIN
16MM FILM OPTICAL SOUND
Highlights the methods and materials used throughout the United States to recycle low-volume roads' materials to construct asphalt-strengthened pavement bases. Shows both central plant and in-place operations.
Prod-AI Dist-AI 1982

Recycling Waste C 12 MIN
16MM FILM, 3/4 OR 1/2 IN VIDEO
Shows how raw materials can be conserved and pollution curbed by turning waste materials back into useful products. Illustrates how paper, glass and metal can be recycled.
Prod-WER Dist-JOU 1971

Recycling Waste (Captioned) C 12 MIN
16MM FILM, 3/4 OR 1/2 IN VIDEO
Shows how raw materials can be conserved and pollution curbed by turning waste materials back into useful products. Illustrates how paper, glass and metal can be recycled.
Prod-WER Dist-JOU 1971

Red C 6 MIN
16MM FILM OPTICAL SOUND
A departure from the traditional Little Red Ridinghood tale in which a little girl falls in love with a red wolf.
LC NO. 74-713398
Prod-GCCED Dist-GCCED 1971

Red Alert C 16 MIN
16MM FILM - 3/4 IN VIDEO
Describes Federal Aviation Administration regulations relating to airplane crash and fire rescue operations. Illustrates basic principles and techniques and demonstrates equipment, protective suits and agents to extinguish fires.
LC NO. 80-707126
Prod-USFAA Dist-USNAC Prodn-COMCRP 1980

Red And Black C 6 MIN
16MM FILM, 3/4 OR 1/2 IN VIDEO K-I
A parody of a bullfight, effected through tricks of animation, color and light and accompanied by lively Spanish music.
Prod-MINFS Dist-SF 1965

Red And Black C 7 MIN
16MM FILM, 3/4 OR 1/2 IN VIDEO P-I
Uses unexpected plot twists and lively Spanish music to convert a funny parody of a bullfight into a setting for imagination.
Prod-LUF Dist-LUF

Red Army, The B 22 MIN
3/4 OR 1/2 INCH VIDEO CASSETTE
Portrays the Soviet armed forces on the eve of World War II. Includes recruit training, Army, Navy and Air Force maneuvers, a performance by the Red Army Ensemble conducted by Professor Alexandrov and a military parade in Red Square.
Prod-IHF Dist-IHF

Red Army, The C 58 MIN
3/4 OR 1/2 INCH VIDEO CASSETTE
Looks at the men and equipment that comprise the modern Soviet military, showing how the weapons and training of the NATO Bloc prove equal or superior to their Soviet counterparts.
From The World Series.
LC NO. 81-707250
Prod-WGBHTV Dist-PBS 1981

Red Auerbach C 20 MIN
16MM FILM OPTICAL SOUND I-J
Features Red Auerbach, coach of the Boston Celtics, speaking candidly about his philosophy, some of the great players he has coached and other provocative issues in professional basketball.
From The Sports Legends Series.
Prod-COUNFI Dist-COUNFI

Red Badge Of Courage, The, Pt 1 C 30 MIN
2 INCH VIDEOTAPE J-H
Presents the novel THE RED BADGE OF COURAGE by Stephen Crane.
From The From Franklin To Frost - Stephen Crane Series.
Prod-MPATI Dist-GPITVL

Red Badge Of Courage, The, Pt 2 C 30 MIN
2 INCH VIDEOTAPE J-H
Presents the novel THE RED BADGE OF COURAGE by Stephen Crane.
From The From Franklin To Frost - Stephen Crane Series.
Prod-MPATI Dist-GPITVL

Red Ball Attacks, The - 34th Infantry Division B 21 MIN
16MM FILM, 3/4 OR 1/2 IN VIDEO H A
Discusses the history of the 34th Infantry Division, from its origin as Minnesota volunteers in the Civil War to division action in World Wars I and II.
Prod-USA Dist-USNAC 1950

Red Ball Express C 4 MIN
16MM FILM, 3/4 OR 1/2 IN VIDEO
Uses animation to show a train changing shape and color. Describes how this is achieved by drawing directly on the film, a technique for fast-paced animated short films.
Prod-PERSPF Dist-CORF 1975

Red Balloon, The C 34 MIN
16MM FILM, 3/4 OR 1/2 IN VIDEO P-C
A boy makes friends with a balloon and the balloon begins to live a life of its own. They play together in the streets of Montmartre and try unsuccessfully to elude the urchins who want to destroy the balloon.
Prod-LAM Dist-FI 1956

Red Blood Cell Development C 30 MIN
3/4 OR 1/2 INCH VIDEO CASSETTE
Deals with red blood cell development as a complex, vitally important phase of development in the embryo.
From The Developmental Biology Series.
Prod-NETCHE Dist-NETCHE 1971

Red Bowmen, The C 58 MIN
3/4 INCH VIDEO CASSETTE
Explores the fertility ritual of the Umeda people of Papua, New Guinea. Describes the ritual transformation of the cassowaries during the 'Ida' ceremony. Filmed by Chris Oowens.
Prod-IPANGS Dist-DOCEDR

Red Box, The B 30 MIN
16MM FILM OPTICAL SOUND
Dramatizes an episode in the life of Gershom Seixas, a rabbi who lived during the American Revolution and fought for freedom through his religious beliefs. (Kinescope)
Prod-JTS Dist-NAAJS Prodn-NBCTV 1958

Red Carpet, The C 10 MIN
16MM FILM, 3/4 OR 1/2 IN VIDEO K-P
An iconographic motion picture based on the children's book of the same title. Tells the story of a carpet that ran away to greet the Duke of Sultana. Camera techniques are used to give an illusion of motion to the original illustrations.
Prod-WWS Dist-WWS 1955

Red Cell Preservation C 19 MIN
3/4 OR 1/2 INCH VIDEO CASSETTE
Explains principles of blood preservation as related to red cell metabolism.
Prod-AMRC Dist-AMRC

Red China Diary With Morley Safer X 54 MIN
16MM FILM, 3/4 OR 1/2 IN VIDEO H-C A
Takes a first-hand look at the cultural revolution of Chairman Mao Tse-tung. Examines the impact of Maoism and covers the five principal cities in Red China. Interviews students, factory workers and aggressive members of the Red Guard.
Prod-CBSTV Dist-PHENIX 1968

Red Cross First Aid Course—A Series

Prod-AMRC Dist-AMRC

First Aid For Shock And Artificial Respiration 28 MIN
Why And How Of Standard First Aid, The 28 MIN

Red Danube, The C 25 MIN
16MM FILM OPTICAL SOUND
Presents correspondent Michael Maclear's examination of the Hungarian freedom fighters who rebelled against Soviet oppression in 1956. Discusses how these individuals have unwittingly become supporters of the Soviet regime.
LC NO. 77-702521
Prod-CTV Dist-CTV 1976

Red Dawn C 20 MIN
3/4 OR 1/2 INCH VIDEO CASSETTE
Recounts the abdication of Czar Nicholas and Lenin's seizure of power.
From The History In Action Series.
Prod-FOTH Dist-FOTH 1984

Red Deer Valley C 26 MIN
16MM FILM OPTICAL SOUND I-C A
Shows many plants and animals of Red Deer Valley in Central Alberta. Portrays an unusual number of rare creatures and includes many sequences of seldom seen animal behavior.
From The Audubon Wildlife Theatre Series.
Prod-AVEXP Dist-AVEXP

Red Deer, The C 25 MIN
16MM FILM, 3/4 OR 1/2 IN VIDEO J-C A
Uses the red deer of New Zealand as an example of man's folly in introducing an animal into an environment that isn't ready for it.
Prod-SPRKTF Dist-JOU 1980

Red Dress, The C 28 MIN
16MM FILM, 3/4 OR 1/2 IN VIDEO
Tells the story of an Indian trapper and his daughter, illustrating both culture conflict and parental misunderstanding.
Prod-NFBC Dist-FI 1979

Red Eye, Pt 1 C 20 MIN
3/4 OR 1/2 INCH VIDEO CASSETTE PRO
Presents information to assist the primary care physician in recognizing and treating simple cases of red eye and indications for referral to an opthalmologist.
Prod-UMICHM Dist-UMICHM 1976

Red Eye, Pt 2 C 16 MIN
3/4 OR 1/2 INCH VIDEO CASSETTE PRO
Discusses the symptoms, causes and treatment of keratitis, keratoconjunctivitis sicca, iritis and acute angle closure glaucoma.
Prod-UMICHM Dist-UMICHM 1976

Red Flag - To Fly And To Fight C 25 MIN
16MM FILM, 3/4 OR 1/2 IN VIDEO
Depicts the importance of Tactical Air Command training programs. Shows how these programs attempt to help air crews and support personnel maintain a constant state of readiness.
LC NO. 82-707215
Prod-USAF Dist-USNAC 1978

Red Fox - Second Hanging C 90 MIN
1/2 IN VIDEO CASSETTE BETA/VHS
Features a live performance of the play Red Fox / Second Hangin' written and produced by the Appalshop Roadside Theater. Presents a classic of Southern storytelling, based on oral history and trial transcripts from the 1880's. Evokes the history of Southern rural America.
Prod-APPAL Dist-APPAL

Red Fox, The - A Predator X 10 MIN
16MM FILM, 3/4 OR 1/2 IN VIDEO I
Follows the activities of a red fox and its family showing how they live, how they are adapted to be predators, and the characteristics of a red fox that place it in the group called mammals.
Prod-EBEC Dist-EBEC 1967

Red Hen, The (3rd Ed) C 11 MIN
16MM FILM, 3/4 OR 1/2 IN VIDEO K-P
Presents the experience of a young boy who monitors the development of his red hen's baby chicks. Shows how the chicks learn to eat, drink and play.
Prod-BARR Dist-BARR 1979

Red Hen, The (3rd Ed) (Captioned) C 11 MIN
16MM FILM - VIDEO, ALL FORMATS K-I
Shows the process of baby chickens being hatched. Tells of a boy and his red hen.
Prod-BARR Dist-BARR

Red Light Return C 14 MIN
16MM FILM, 3/4 OR 1/2 IN VIDEO H-C A
Studies impacts of collisions with windshields, doors flung open and ejected bodies.
Prod-CAHILL Dist-AIMS 1966

Red Man And The Red Cedar C 12 MIN
16MM FILM OPTICAL SOUND I-C A
Shows how the coastal Indians used the Western red cedar for food, clothing, shelter, transportation and art. Portrays the relationship of present day Indians to the old culture through demonstrations of how things were done in the old culture.
From The Man And The Forest Series.
LC NO. 78-707902
Prod-MMP Dist-MMP 1969

Red Metal Of Amarillo, The C 24 MIN
16MM FILM OPTICAL SOUND
Shows the construction and operation of Asarco's new copper refinery.
LC NO. 77-700404
Prod-BECHTL Dist-BECHTL 1976

Red Nightmare B 25 MIN
3/4 OR 1/2 INCH VIDEO CASSETTE
Presents anti-Communist propaganda in a story of a small-town American who finds his community taken over by Communists. Narrated by Jack Webb.
Prod-IHF Dist-IHF

Red Nightmare B 25 MIN
16MM FILM - 3/4 IN VIDEO
Depicts the nightmare of an American citizen who finds himself in a mockup of a Communist village. Shows how this experience awakens him to his obligations to his family and his country. Issued in 1965 as a motion picture.
LC NO. 79-706481
Prod-USDD Dist-USNAC 1979

Red Plague, The C 21 MIN
16MM FILM OPTICAL SOUND P-I
Presents an adventure set in the time of the Saxons which tells how old Wulfric is taking his sick granddaughter to the Friar when he is caught by the Baron's men, who accuse him of poaching. Relates how the men scramble for cover when convinced that the granddaughter's illness is catching.
From The Unbroken Arrow Series.
Prod-LUF Dist-LUF 1977

Red Planet, The C 52 MIN
16MM FILM - 3/4 IN VIDEO H-C A
Traces 300 years of speculation, investigation and discoveries about the planet Mars.
From The Nova Series.
Prod-WGBHTV Dist-PBS 1977

Red Pony, The C 101 MIN
16MM FILM, 3/4 OR 1/2 IN VIDEO I-C A
Based on the book THE RED PONY by John Steinbeck. Tells a story of a young boy and life on his father's ranch. Stars Henry Fonda and Maureen O'Hara.
Prod-PHENIX Dist-PHENIX 1976

Red Ribbon, A C 10 MIN
16MM FILM, 3/4 OR 1/2 IN VIDEO P-I
Chronicles, without words, the making and testing of a kite by a small boy, as observed by a little girl, whom he ignores. Reveals that when he runs into problems, her hair ribbon saves the day.
LC NO. 82-706531
Prod-TEXFLM Dist-TEXFLM 1981

Red River, The C
3/4 OR 1/2 INCH VIDEO CASSETTE
Looks inside the heart and bloodstream of a human fetus, examines human lungs and provides a guided tour through the inside of a 'hardened' artery. Includes cases of a 41-year old man undergoing a delicate triple-bypass operation, a six-year-old girl with a leaking malformed heart undergoing surgery wherein her heart is stopped, rebuilt, and started again, a 16-year-old girl, paralyzed and facing death from a rare growth of blood vessels obstructing her spinal cord, and a 61-year-old man, with severe blockage of his brain arteries
From The Body Human Series,
Prod-TRAINX Dist-TRAINX

Red Room Riddle C 24 MIN
16MM FILM, 3/4 OR 1/2 IN VIDEO I
Tells what happens when two children visit a haunted mansion and encounter a strange boy who traps them in a glowing red room peopled by menacing transparent people. Reveals that when the adventure is over, the boys admit that sometimes it feels good to say you're scared. Produced for the ABC Weekend Specials.
LC NO. 84-706257
Prod-ABCLR Dist-MTI 1983

Red Sea Case Study 1, The - The Geology C 24 MIN
16MM FILM OPTICAL SOUND
Investigates the principal physiographic and geological features of the Red Sea to explain how and why continents split to form new oceans. Studies the geological history and the sedimentary evidence of the region that clearly indicates the Red Sea was formed in the last 30 million years, but identifies no particular mechanism for formation.
Prod-BBCTV Dist-OPENU 1981

Red Sea Case Study 1, The - The Geology C 24 MIN
16MM FILM, 3/4 OR 1/2 IN VIDEO
Investigates the principal physiographic and geological features of the Red Sea to explain how and why continents split to form new oceans. Studies the geological history and the sedimentary evidence of the region that clearly indicates the Red Sea was formed in the last 30 million years, but identifies no particular mechanism for formation.
Prod-OPENU Dist-MEDIAG Prodn-BBCTV 1981

Red Sea Case Study 2, The - The Geophysics C 24 MIN
16MM FILM OPTICAL SOUND
Presents a causative model, based on deductions from geological evidence of how and why the Red Sea formed, which may be used to study older oceans on earth. Summarizes the evidence that the entire Red Sea marine area is underlain by ocean crust by assessing the aeromagnentic survey data across the Red Sea.
Prod-BBCTV Dist-OPENU 1981

Red Sea Case Study 2, The - The Geophysics C 24 MIN
16MM FILM, 3/4 OR 1/2 IN VIDEO
Presents a causative model, based on deductions from geological evidence of how and why the Red Sea formed, which may be used to study older oceans on earth. Summarizes the evidence that the entire Red Sea marine area is underlain by ocean crust by assessing the aeromagnentic survey data across the Red Sea.
Prod-OPENU Dist-MEDIAG Prodn-BBCTV 1981

Red Shoes, The C 134 MIN
16MM FILM OPTICAL SOUND
Tells the story of ballerina Victoria Page, who is catapulted to stardom in the Ballet Russes. Shows the conflict which arises when she falls in love with the company's composer and must choose between art and romance. Stars Moira Shearer and Leonide Massine. Directed by Michael Powell and Emeric Pressburger.
Prod-RANK Dist-LCOA 1948

Red Shoes, The C 10 MIN
16MM FILM, 3/4 OR 1/2 IN VIDEO P-I
Presents the Hans Christian Andersen story about a girl obsessed with obtaining a pair of red shoes.
From The Classic Tales Retold Series.
Prod-BFA Dist-PHENIX 1981

Red Squad B 45 MIN
16MM FILM, 3/4 OR 1/2 IN VIDEO
Presents a study of the New York Police Department's red squad and various agencies involved in domestic intelligence gathering. Depicts the filmmakers themselves as they become the target of investigation, harrassment and intimidation.
Prod-PACSFM Dist-CNEMAG 1972

Red Star C 60 MIN
16MM FILM OPTICAL SOUND H-C A
From The World At War Series.
LC NO. 76-701778
Prod-THAMES Dist-USCAN 1975

Red Star - The Soviet Union, 1941-1943 C 52 MIN
16MM FILM, 3/4 OR 1/2 IN VIDEO H-C A
Describes Russia's massive, lonely war against Germany from 1941 to 1943, resulting in twenty million military and civilian casualties and equally staggering material losses. Russian military men demonstrated a heroic fighting spirit that became legendary.
From The World At War Series.
Prod-THAMES Dist-MEDIAG 1973

Red Star Over Kyber C 58 MIN
1/2 IN VIDEO CASSETTE BETA/VHS
Examines the complex and politically charged situation in Afghanistan and Pakistan. Traces the relationship between the two countries and the two superpowers behind them, Russia and the U S.
From The Frontline Series.
Prod-DOCCON Dist-PBS

Red Sunday C 28 MIN
16MM FILM, 3/4 OR 1/2 IN VIDEO
Studies the Battle of Little Big Horn.
Prod-HGFP Dist-PFP

Red Tape—A Series

Includes work by video artist Bill Viola who uses the language of experience, the sounds and images of the real world, imagination, dreams and memory.
Prod-EAI Dist-EAI

Million Other Things, A (2)

Non-Dairy Creamer, A
Playing Soul Music To My Freckles
Return
Semi-Circular Canals, The

Red Tapes—A Series

Investigates the myth of American self-hood in the film noir and gallery idioms.
Prod-KITCHN Dist-KITCHN

Common Knowledge 045 MIN
Local Color
Time Lag

Red Trap, The B 30 MIN
16MM FILM OPTICAL SOUND H A
Exposes some of the subtle methods used by communist agents.
LC NO. 72-701643
Prod-CONCOR Dist-CPH 1961

Red Tsar C 20 MIN
3/4 OR 1/2 INCH VIDEO CASSETTE
Documents how Stalin took power after the death of Lenin and eliminated his rivals and former comrades.
From The History In Action Series.
Prod-FOTH Dist-FOTH 1984

Red-White Struggle, The B 30 MIN
16MM FILM OPTICAL SOUND H-C A
Discusses the Indian barrier to white settlement, the methods used to subdue the red man, military expeditions and posts and the Indian wars. Describes the Grattan Massacre and the conflict between military and civilian authority.
From The Great Plains Trilogy, 3 Series. Explorer And Settler - The White Man Arrives
Prod-KUONTV Dist-UNL 1954

Red-Winged Blackbirds C 3 MIN
16MM FILM OPTICAL SOUND P-I
Discusses the birds known as red-winged blackbirds.
From The Of All Things Series.
Prod-BAILYL Dist-AVED

Red, White And Blue C 1 MIN
3/4 INCH VIDEO CASSETTE
Discusses prejudice in America by use of animation. Made in a television spot announcement format.
Prod-ADL Dist-ADL

Red, White, Blue And Brown C 29 MIN
16MM FILM OPTICAL SOUND
Briefs government supervisors, personnel directors, ethnic groups and the general public on the President's 16-point program. Defines some of the problems faced by the Spanish surname minority.
LC NO. 75-701278
Prod-USN Dist-USNAC Prodn-NVMC 1972

Redecorating The House Before Crystal's Girlfriends Arrive C 8 MIN
16MM FILM OPTICAL SOUND K-P
Shows how Crystal's friends cooperate in redecorating the house before her girlfriends arrive to help her choose a dress for a party.
From The Crystal Tipps And Alistair Series.
LC NO. 73-700452
Prod-BBCTV Dist-VEDO 1972

Redemption Of Space, The C 5 MIN
16MM FILM OPTICAL SOUND J-H A
Tells how churches can use their buildings to meet the needs of the community for worship and for cultural, social and educational purposes.
LC NO. 80-700761
Prod-IKONOG Dist-IKONOG 1979

Redesigning Appliances C 30 MIN
3/4 INCH VIDEO CASSETTE
Discusses the appliance industry's focus on efficiency of units versus sleek appearance.
From The Rethinking America Series.
Prod-UMITV Dist-UMITV 1979

Redevelopment B 15 MIN
2 INCH VIDEOTAPE P-I
See series title for descriptive statement.
From The Our Changing Community Series.
Prod-VITA Dist-GPITVL 1967

Redi-Temp (Superscript R) Is Ready C 8 MIN
16MM FILM OPTICAL SOUND
Provides nurses and medical personnel with instructions for using improved short-term dry heat and cold therapy. Contrasts ready-to-use hot and cold packs with hot water bottles and ice packs.
LC NO. 75-715458
Prod-WYETH Dist-WYLAB 1971

Rediscover The Safety Belt C 9 MIN
16MM FILM, 3/4 OR 1/2 IN VIDEO H A
Former Mercury astronaut Wally Schirra illustrates why business and community leaders will benefit from encouraging employees, constituents and others to wear safety belts. Features driving risks, safety belt facts and myths, and personal commentary.
Prod-NHTSA Dist-USNAC 1982

Rediscovering America C 30 MIN
3/4 OR 1/2 INCH VIDEO CASSETTE C
See series title for descriptive statement.
From The American Story - The Beginning To 1877 Series.
Prod-DALCCD Dist-DALCCD

Rediscovering Herbs - Overview C 28 MIN
16MM FILM, 3/4 OR 1/2 IN VIDEO H-C A
Describes the role of herbs in home remedies, cookies, potpourris, pest control in the garden, dyeing and home decorating.
From The Rediscovering Herbs Series.
LC NO. 82-707364
Prod-RPFD Dist-BULFRG 1981

Rediscovering Herbs—A Series
16MM FILM, 3/4 OR 1/2 IN VIDEO H-C A
Gives an overview of the various uses of herbs not only in cooking, but also in dyeing and home decoration.
Prod-RPFD Dist-BULFRG 1981

Culinary Herbs 015 MIN
Dried Flower Arrangements 015 MIN
Rediscovering Herbs - Overview 028 MIN

Rediscovery - Art Media (French)—A Series
16MM FILM, 3/4 OR 1/2 IN VIDEO I-C A
Explores art materials for their creative and expressive possibilities.
Prod-ACI Dist-AIMS

Clay (French) 015 MIN
Collage (French) 016 MIN
Crayon (French) 015 MIN
Enameling (French) 015 MIN
Paper Construction (French) 014 MIN
Papier Mache (French) 015 MIN
Posters (French) 015 MIN
Prints (French) 015 MIN
Puppets (French) 015 MIN
Silkscreen (French) 014 MIN
Stitchery (French) 014 MIN
Watercolor (French) 014 MIN

Rediscovery - Art Media (Spanish)—A Series
16MM FILM, 3/4 OR 1/2 IN VIDEO I-C A
Explores art materials for their creative and expressive possibilities.
Prod-ACI Dist-AIMS

Clay (Spanish) 015 MIN
Collage (Spanish) 016 MIN
Crayon (Spanish) 015 MIN
Enameling (Spanish) 015 MIN
Paper Construction (Spanish) 014 MIN
Papier Mache (Spanish) 015 MIN
Posters (Spanish) 015 MIN
Prints (Spanish) 015 MIN
Puppets (Spanish) 015 MIN
Silkscreen (Spanish) 014 MIN
Stitchery (Spanish) 014 MIN
Watercolor (Spanish) 014 MIN
Weaving (Spanish) 014 MIN

Rediscovery - Art Media—A Series
16MM FILM, 3/4 OR 1/2 IN VIDEO I-J A
Explores art materials for their creative and expressive possibilities.
Prod-ACI Dist-AIMS

Basketry 015 MIN
Clay 015 MIN
Collage 015 MIN
Crayon 015 MIN
Enameling 015 MIN
Leather 015 MIN
Macrame 015 MIN
Paper Construction 015 MIN
Papier Mache 015 MIN
Posters 015 MIN
Prints 015 MIN
Puppets 015 MIN
Silkscreen 015 MIN
Stitchery 015 MIN
Watercolor 015 MIN
Weaving 015 MIN

Rediscovery—A Series

Discusses various natural disasters. Shows how NASA provides early weather warning data from space observations to reduce casualties and property loss from hurricanes, floods, tornadoes, earthquakes and other natural disasters.
Prod-NASA Dist-USNAC 1977

Earthquake Below 15 MIN
Flood Below 14 MIN
Hurricane Below 14 MIN
Pollution Below 14 MIN
Tornado Below 15 MIN

Redox Titration C 16 MIN
3/4 OR 1/2 INCH VIDEO CASSETTE C A
Uses a Fisher Scientific Company Model 230 pH/ion meter as a potentiometer in the titration of ferrous ion with ceric using calomel and platinum electrodes.
From The Chemistry - Master/Apprentice Series. Program 17
LC NO. 82-706044
Prod-CUETV Dist-CUNIV 1981

Reds, Whites And Booze C 29 MIN
16MM FILM OPTICAL SOUND H-C
Explores a few days in the life of a high school senior to examine cultural forces and everyday stimuli that help individual attitudes regarding drugs.
Prod-LYNVIL Dist-NINEFC

Redtail - The Story Of A Hawk C 25 MIN
16MM FILM, 3/4 OR 1/2 IN VIDEO J-C A
Covers a year in the life of a hawk from his birth in an oak tree to his migration to the Caribbean for winter in an environment of humming-birds, orchids and palm trees to his return to his birthplace, a freezing wilderness where he must find food until spring comes.
Prod-BBCTV Dist-FI

Reduced Gradient Method, The C 60 MIN
3/4 OR 1/2 INCH VIDEO CASSETTE
See series title for descriptive statement.
From The Engineering Design Optimization II Series. Pt 27
Prod-UAZMIC Dist-UAZMIC

Reduced Voltage Starters B 23 MIN
16MM FILM - 3/4 IN VIDEO
Demonstrates the principle of the transformer and shows the operation of a manual starting compensator, a thermal overload relay and an automatic starting compensator.
From The Electrical Work - Motor Control Series. No. 3
LC NO. 79-707497
Prod-USOE Dist-USNAC Prodn-CALVCO 1979

Reducers And Gearmotors C 25 MIN
3/4 OR 1/2 INCH VIDEO CASSETTE IND
Gives introduction and requirements for reducers. Discusses advantages and disadvantages of parallel reducers and gear motors.
Prod-TAT Dist-TAT

Reducers And Generators (Spanish) C 25 MIN
3/4 OR 1/2 INCH VIDEO CASSETTE IND
Gives introduction and requirements for reducers. Discusses advantages and disadvantages of parallel reducers and gear motors.
Prod-TAT Dist-TAT

Reducing Conflict In The Organization C 14 MIN
3/4 OR 1/2 INCH VIDEO CASSETTE
Shows supervisors how to remove the threats, uncertainties and other causes of conflict in the work group. Deals with problems of competition and conflict between work groups.
From The Supervisor And Interpersonal Relations Series. Module 5
Prod-RESEM Dist-RESEM

Reducing Equipment And Piping Losses C 35 MIN
3/4 INCH VIDEO CASSETTE C A
See series title for descriptive statement.
From The Energy Conservation In Industrial Plants Series.
LC NO. 81-706196
Prod-AMCEE Dist-AMCEE 1979

Reducing Fractions C 11 MIN
3/4 INCH VIDEO CASSETTE
See series title for descriptive statement.
From The Basic Math Skills Series. Multiplying Fractions And Reducing
Prod-TELSTR Dist-TELSTR

Reducing Poverty - What Have We Done C 30 MIN
3/4 OR 1/2 INCH VIDEO CASSETTE C
See series title for descriptive statement.
From The Economics USA Series.
Prod-WEFA Dist-ANNCPB

Reducing Sentences B 15 MIN
2 INCH VIDEOTAPE I
Warns that in linguistic trimming, the sentence meaning may be destroyed or altered, or the author's style may be ruined. Features selections, such as Pumpkins by David Mc Cord, Mool The Mole, a German language poem adapted by Bill Martin and words by Robert Louis Stevenson. (Broadcast quality)
From The Bill Martin Series. No. 6
Prod-BRITED Dist-GPITVL Prodn-KQEDTV

Reduction And Fixation Of Middle Third Fractures Of The Face - Lateral Orbital Rim... C 13 MIN
16MM FILM - 3/4 IN VIDEO PRO
Demonstrates the reduction of a fracture of the middle third of the face by the lateral orbital rim approach.
LC NO. 78-706007
Prod-USVA Dist-USNAC 1977

Reduction Of Radio Interference - Shipboard Installation B 17 MIN
16MM FILM OPTICAL SOUND
Shows how poor installation practices contribute to radio interference and how good installation practices can eliminate such interferences.
From The Machine Workshop Series.
Prod-USN Dist-USNAC

Reduction Of Zygomatic Arch Fracture, Gillies Approach C 7 MIN
16MM FILM - 3/4 IN VIDEO PRO
Demonstrates reduction of a zygomatic arch fracture. Points out how access to the fracture is gained through an aurinculotemporal incision and how reduction is achieved by blind manipulation and touch.
LC NO. 76-706221
Prod-USVA Dist-USNAC Prodn-VADTC 1969

Redwoods, The B 6 MIN
16MM FILM OPTICAL SOUND
Presents excerpts of 1952 Screen News Digest films showing the most ancient living thing, the giant redwood in California and on the Pacific West Coast. Depicts the petrified forest in Arizona with its landscape and petrified objects.
From The News Magazine Of The Screen Series. Vol 3, No. 4
Prod-PATHE Dist-HEARST 1952

Redwoods, The C 20 MIN
16MM FILM, 3/4 OR 1/2 IN VIDEO I-C A
Surveys the future of a vanishing forest of Sequoia sempervirens, a link to the age of the dinosaurs and a testament to nature's power to create and of man's power to destroy.
Prod-SIERRA Dist-PHENIX Prodn-KINGSP 1972

Reed - Insurgent Mexico (Spanish) B 110 MIN
16MM FILM OPTICAL SOUND
An English subtitle version of the Spanish language film. Accompanies a left-wing American journalist, John Reed, on a tour through modern Mexico. Shows how he begins participating in revolutionary events, rather than merely reporting them.
Prod-NYFLMS Dist-NYFLMS 1971

Reed Instruments C 30 MIN
3/4 OR 1/2 INCH VIDEO CASSETTE
Shows the development of reeds from those played by the Saracens to frighten the Crusaders' horses, to the 17th-century forerunners of modern orchestral reed instruments.
From The Early Musical Instruments Series.
Prod-GRATV Dist-FOTH

Reef At Heron Island C 10 MIN
16MM FILM OPTICAL SOUND I-H A
Describes a reef as an intricate accumulation of organism whose symbiotic relationships result in a seemingly indestructible barrier to sea and surf.
From The Ecology Of The Ocean Series.
LC NO. 77-710536
Prod-AMEDFL Dist-AMEDFL

Reef At Michaelmas Cay C 10 MIN
16MM FILM OPTICAL SOUND I-H T
Shows the beauty and importance of reefs through their evolution and formation throughout geologic history.
From The Ecology Of The Ocean Series.
LC NO. 70-712314
Prod-AMEDFL Dist-AMEDFL 1970

Reefer Madness B 67 MIN
16MM FILM OPTICAL SOUND J-C A
Explains the evils of marijuana, previously called 'the devil's weed.' Discusses out-moded views that marijuana may lead to either insanity or death.
Prod-NLC Dist-KITPAR 1936

Reefer Madness B 71 MIN
3/4 OR 1/2 INCH VIDEO CASSETTE
Features a government sponsored anti-marijuana propaganda piece. Shows kids smoking pot, which results in murder, suicide and comical nonsense.
Prod-ADVCAS Dist-ADVCAS

Reefs B 27 MIN
16MM FILM OPTICAL SOUND C A
Describes reefs, along with accompanying environment. Utilizes submarine photography to show various portions of a reef. Uses the late Paleozoic Horseshoe Atoll of West Texas as an example.
Prod-UTEX Dist-UTEX 1960

Reefs - Past To Present C 28 MIN
3/4 OR 1/2 INCH VIDEO CASSETTE
Explores the 250 million-year history of the Capitan Reef in Texas, with geologists using microscopic analysis, topographic maps and cross-sectional drawings.
From The Earth Explored Series.
Prod-BBCTV Dist-PBS

Reefs, Deltas And Channels C 30 MIN
3/4 OR 1/2 INCH VIDEO CASSETTE IND
See series title for descriptive statement.
From The Basic And Petroleum Geology For Non-Geologists - Sedimentary Rocks Series.
Prod-PHILLP Dist-GPCV

Reel Estate C 30 MIN
3/4 OR 1/2 INCH VIDEO CASSETTE H-C A
Looks at the plans of a Texas real estate tycoon to lure movie production companies to Texas by building a one-billion dollar soundstage and office complex.
From The Enterprise III Series.
Prod-WGBHTV Dist-KINGFT

Reel Way To Lay Pipe, The C 17 MIN
16MM FILM OPTICAL SOUND
Uses live action and animation to show the advantages of laying pipe on the ocean floor using the reel system.
LC NO. 79-700266
Prod-SFINTL Dist-MARTB Prodn-MARTB 1978

Reel World Of News, The C 58 MIN
3/4 OR 1/2 INCH VIDEO CASSETTE
Looks at newsreels, first seen in 1911, and their role in the evolution to televised news. Tells that newsreels disappeared in the mid-1960's as televised news took over.
From The Walk Through The 20th Century With Bill Moyers Series.
Prod-CORPEL Dist-PBS 1982

Reelfoot Lake X 13 MIN
16MM FILM OPTICAL SOUND
Visits 'CRANETOWN,' a rookery located at Tennessee's Earthquake Lake. Explains the siltation problem that is endangering Reelfoot Lake.
From The World Outdoors Series. No. 5
Prod-TGAFC Dist-TGAFC

Reeving C 15 MIN
3/4 OR 1/2 INCH VIDEO CASSETTE IND
Defines reeving and discusses components of a reeved block system,mechanical advantages and friction, reeving methods and inspection methods.
From The Safety In Rigging Series.
Prod-CSAO Dist-CSAO

Referee C 30 MIN
1/2 IN VIDEO CASSETTE BETA/VHS
Deals with the work of Jess Kersey, who has been blowing a whistle and calling the shots for basketball games across the country as a National Basketball Association Referee.
From The American Professionals Series.
Prod-WTBS Dist-RMI

Reference Collection C
3/4 OR 1/2 INCH VIDEO CASSETTE
See series title for descriptive statement.
From The College Library Series.
Prod-NETCHE Dist-NETCHE 1973

Reference Frame B 15 MIN
2 INCH VIDEOTAPE P
See series title for descriptive statement.
From The Just Curious Series. No. 19
Prod-EOPS Dist-GPITVL Prodn-KOACTV

Reference Section, The C 22 MIN
16MM FILM, 3/4 OR 1/2 IN VIDEO I-J
Tells how a talking almanac teaches Glenn about the various reference books.
From The Library Skills Series.
Prod-BARR Dist-BARR 1980

Referral Process, The C 30 MIN
3/4 OR 1/2 INCH VIDEO CASSETTE T
Discusses the referral process used when dealing with children with special needs.
From The Teaching Children With Special Needs Series.
Prod-MDDE Dist-MDCPB

Refiner's Fire, The C 6 MIN
16MM FILM, 3/4 OR 1/2 IN VIDEO P-C A
Presents an animated abstract ballet, without narration, which depicts the conflict that arises between an established society and its idealistic members who discover and preach a new truth. Uses squares and circles which take on human characteristics in the portrayal of the conflict.
Prod-BGH Dist-PHENIX 1977

Refinery C 14 MIN
16MM FILM OPTICAL SOUND
Uses animation to explain how crude oil is broken down into useful components.
LC NO. 76-702465
Prod-IMO Dist-IMO Prodn-CRAF 1975

Refinery C 14 MIN
16MM FILM - 3/4 IN VIDEO
Describes the process of refining crude oil into useful petroleum products. Emphasizes the scientific and economic principles underlying refining. Uses animation to show how molecules are changed and reformed.
Prod-EXXON Dist-MTP

Refinery And Petrochemical Plant Fire Fighting C 60 MIN
3/4 OR 1/2 INCH VIDEO CASSETTE IND
Covers special strategies and techniques, hose handling and tank fires.
From The Fire Fighting Training Series.
Prod-LEIKID Dist-LEIKID

Refinery And Petrochemical Plant Fires C 60 MIN
3/4 OR 1/2 INCH VIDEO CASSETTE
See series title for descriptive statement.
From The Fire Protection Training Series.
Prod-ITCORP Dist-ITCORP

Refining Principles C
3/4 OR 1/2 INCH VIDEO CASSETTE IND
Details refiner operation, loading, axial thrust, steam generation, feed problems, consistency and refiner plates.
From The Pulp And Paper Training - Thermo-Mechanical Pulping Series.
Prod-LEIKID Dist-LEIKID

Refining Your Search Techniques C 35 MIN
3/4 OR 1/2 INCH VIDEO CASSETTE PRO
Explains advanced computer searching techniques for law-related material. Suggests ways of reducing the costs of computer research.
From The Computers In Legal Research Series.
Prod-ABACPE Dist-ABACPE

Refinishing Antiques - Refinishing Antiques, Varnish / Refinishing Antiques, Paint C 30 MIN
1/2 IN VIDEO CASSETTE BETA/VHS
See series title for descriptive statement.
From The Wally's Workshop Series.
Prod-KARTES Dist-KARTES

Reflect On Your Grandparents C 30 MIN
2 INCH VIDEOTAPE J
See series title for descriptive statement.
From The Summer Journal, Unit 1 - You Are What You Feel Series.
Prod-WNINTV Dist-GPITVL

Reflectance Map, The C 45 MIN
3/4 OR 1/2 INCH VIDEO CASSETTE PRO
Features the reflectance map, properties of Lambertian surfaces, the photometric stereo technique, and needle diagrams and depth maps.
From The Artificial Intelligence - Pt 3, Computer Vision Series.
Prod-MIOT Dist-MIOT

Reflectance Map, The C 46 MIN
3/4 OR 1/2 INCH VIDEO CASSETTE C
See series title for descriptive statement.
From The Artificial Intelligence, Pt III - Computer Vision Series.
Prod-MIOT Dist-AMCEE

Reflectant Spectroscopy C 9 MIN
3/4 OR 1/2 INCH VIDEO CASSETTE
Uses diagrams and actual equipment to teach the principles of operating a chemical reflectant photometer. Describes calibration and maintenance procedures.
LC NO. 80-706814
Prod-CFDISC Dist-USNAC Prodn-NMAC 1979

Reflected Light C 15 MIN
3/4 OR 1/2 INCH VIDEO CASSETTE P-I
Discusses reflected light.
From The Why Series.
Prod-WDCNTV Dist-AITECH 1976

Reflecting On The Life Career Of A Dancer C 30 MIN
3/4 OR 1/2 INCH VIDEO CASSETTE
See series title for descriptive statement.
From The Dancers' Survival Tactics Series.
Prod-ARCVID Dist-ARCVID

Reflecting On The Moon C 15 MIN
16MM FILM, 3/4 OR 1/2 IN VIDEO P-I
Deals with the moon's composition, gravity, lack of atmosphere, orbit, phases, exploration and effect on earth.
Prod-NGS Dist-NGS 1982

Reflecting Pool, The C 7 MIN
3/4 OR 1/2 INCH VIDEO CASSETTE
See series title for descriptive statement.
From The Reflecting Pool Series.
Prod-EAI Dist-EAI

Reflecting Pool, The—A Series

Represents the stages of a personal journey from birth to death to rebirth.
Prod-EAI Dist-EAI

Reflection B 22 MIN
16MM FILM OPTICAL SOUND H
Covers the laws of reflection and the formation and characteristics of the virtual image formed in a plane mirror.
From The Optics Series.
Prod-CETO Dist-GPITVL

Reflection - A Metaphoric Journey C 9 MIN
16MM FILM OPTICAL SOUND
Presents a fable about one man's struggle to find meaning in life.
Prod-HP Dist-HP

Reflections B 10 MIN
16MM FILM OPTICAL SOUND
Shows the United States of America through the metaphor of a used car junk heap. Begins with 'ARTISTIC' close-ups of parts of old cars, and the huge machinery needed to make scrape out of them. Concludes with the steel teeth of the scrap derrick across a highway and the American flag waving in the midst of grain and storage tanks.
Prod-UPENN Dist-UPENN 1970

Reflections C 29 MIN
16MM FILM OPTICAL SOUND
Presents a documentary on American life by examining the beliefs and values of residents of a seven-county region of Pennsylvania, with narrative in the words of the people themselves.
LC NO. 76-702875
Prod-GITTFI Dist-GITTFI 1976

Reflections C 16 MIN
16MM FILM, 3/4 OR 1/2 IN VIDEO H-C A
Presents astronaut Rusty Schweickart's philosophical reactions to the grandeur of viewing the Earth during his incredible journey.
Prod-VARDIR Dist-LCOA 1980

Reflections B 17 MIN
3/4 OR 1/2 INCH VIDEO CASSETTE J-C A
Presents survivors of the Jewish Holocaust reflecting on such questions as how the scope of Nazi atrocities grew beyond the Jewish question to include non-Jews and what universal lessons can be learned from the Holocaust.
From The Witness To The Holocaust Series.
Prod-HORECE Dist-CNEMAG 1983

Reflections C 20 MIN
3/4 OR 1/2 INCH VIDEO CASSETTE P
Features folktales from Japan, Russia and Korea.
From The Folk Book Series.
Prod-UWISC Dist-AITECH 1980

Reflections C 25 MIN
16MM FILM, 3/4 OR 1/2 IN VIDEO C A
Shows what group sex is really like, what happens and how people feel about it. Demystifies an aspect of human sexual behavior that many people have fantasized about.
Prod-NATSF Dist-MMRC

Reflections C 60 MIN
3/4 OR 1/2 INCH VIDEO CASSETTE
Presents Dr Carl Rogers discussing his development. Also presents Dr Warren Bennis, an expert in the field of group dynamics and organizational development.
Prod-PSYCHD Dist-PSYCHD

Reflections - A Cultural History C 30 MIN
3/4 OR 1/2 INCH VIDEO CASSETTE
See series title for descriptive statement.
From The Kaleidoscope Series.
Prod-KTEHTV Dist-SCCOE

Reflections - A Japanese Folk Tale C 19 MIN
16MM FILM, 3/4 OR 1/2 IN VIDEO P-I
Presents an Oriental folk tale, showing different human re-

sponses to an unfamiliar experience, which exemplifies unresolved or unresolvable dilemmas.
Prod-EBEC Dist-EBEC 1975

Reflections - A Metaphoric Journey C 9 MIN
3/4 OR 1/2 INCH VIDEO CASSETTE
Presents one woman's struggle to find meaning in life. Told as a fable.
Prod-HP Dist-HP

Reflections - George Meany C 52 MIN
16MM FILM, 3/4 OR 1/2 IN VIDEO
Focuses on American labor leader George Meany.
LC NO. 80-706468
Prod-USINCA Dist-USNAC 1979

Reflections - George Meany (Spanish) C 52 MIN
16MM FILM OPTICAL SOUND C A
Focuses on American labor leader George Meany.
LC NO. 80-700514
Prod-USINCA Dist-USNAC 1979

Reflections - Ireland C 17 MIN
16MM FILM OPTICAL SOUND H-C A
Depicts the sights of Ireland, showing landscape, greenery, animal life and sea.
LC NO. 79-701091
Prod-ITO Dist-CECROP 1979

Reflections - Margaret Mead C 58 MIN
16MM FILM - 3/4 IN VIDEO H-C A
Presents anthropologist Margaret Mead discussing a wide range of subjects, including her childhood, her studies of primitive peoples, the evolution of women's suffrage, World War II, the atomic bomb, mental health and the environment.
LC NO. 80-706290
Prod-ICA Dist-USNAC 1975

Reflections - Samuel Eliot Morison C 58 MIN
16MM FILM, 3/4 OR 1/2 IN VIDEO
Profiles Samuel Eliot Morison, historian, discussing his early years, his 40-year relationship with Harvard University and the influences that led him to become the biographer of Columbus, Magellan, John Paul Jones and others. Explores his interest in maritime history.
Prod-USIA Dist-USNAC 1982

Reflections In A Golden Eye C 109 MIN
16MM FILM OPTICAL SOUND
Tells how an Army colonel hides his impotence from his nymphomaniacal wife, who in turn has an affair with another officer whose wife is losing her mind. Stars Marlon Brando, Julie Harris, Elizabeth Taylor and Brian Keith. Based on the novel REFLECTIONS IN A GOLDEN EYE by Carson McCullers. Directed by Carson McCullers.
Prod-WB Dist-TWYMAN 1967

Reflections In A Pond C 10 MIN
16MM FILM, 3/4 OR 1/2 IN VIDEO K-C
Presents a story about animal life of the pond, using free form music and sound effects to show a pair of swans during their courtship-nest building and other activities.
Prod-WER Dist-JOU 1971

Reflections In Limestone C 28 MIN
16MM FILM OPTICAL SOUND
Presents the history of Kingston, Ontario, as related by Professor A R M Lower.
From The Education Showcase Series.
LC NO. 74-701252
Prod-OECA Dist-OECA 1972

Reflections Of A Good Life C 15 MIN
16MM FILM OPTICAL SOUND
Points out the social and business opportunities available in Palm Beach, Florida.
Prod-FLADC Dist-FLADC

Reflections Of Man C 13 MIN
16MM FILM OPTICAL SOUND
Explores the basic universal nature of all men through an examination of chess pieces from all over the world.
LC NO. 74-702846
Prod-USC Dist-USC 1974

Reflections Of Reality C 45 MIN
16MM FILM OPTICAL SOUND H-C A
Discusses the reasons that could dictate an artist's choice of subject. Points out that nudes, landscapes and still lifes are the most familiar artistic subjects.
From The Man And His Art Series.
Prod-WTTWTV Dist-GPITVL

Reflections Of Spinal Cord Injuries B 60 MIN
3/4 OR 1/2 INCH VIDEO CASSETTE
Interviews a quadraplegic man and a paraplegice woman, both of whom were injured in their teens. Discusses their experiences as hospital patients undergoing rehabilitation and their lives since then.
Prod-UWISC Dist-UWISC 1979

Reflections Of The Old Student Movement B 30 MIN
16MM FILM OPTICAL SOUND H-C
William Strickland serves as moderator as leaders of student rebellions–James Turner, James Garrett, Linda Housh and Ray Brown discuss the origin, growth and accomplishments of the student movement.
LC NO. 71-704124
Prod-WCBSTV Dist-HRAW 1969

Reflections On Suffering C 20 MIN
16MM FILM, 3/4 OR 1/2 IN VIDEO
Presents a conversation between a doctor and a cancer victim who has come to terms with her illness.
Prod-NFBC Dist-NFBC 1982

Reflections On The Long Search C 52 MIN
16MM FILM, 3/4 OR 1/2 IN VIDEO H-C A
Presents theater director Ronald Eyre discussing some personal reflections on his pilgrimage throughout the world in which he explored the religious beliefs and experiences of various peoples.
From The Long Search Series. No. 13
LC NO. 79-707792
Prod-BBCTV Dist-TIMLIF 1978

Reflections On Time C 22 MIN
16MM FILM, 3/4 OR 1/2 IN VIDEO I-H
Discusses subjective, objective and geological time. Follows a geologist down the Grand Canyon as he records his interpretation of the significance of each layer within the millions of years locked inside the rock formation.
From The Earth Science Program Series.
Prod-EBEC Dist-EBEC 1969

Reflections On Waves C 24 MIN
3/4 OR 1/2 INCH VIDEO CASSETTE H-C
Introduces key concepts about electromagnetism, waves, and resonance using a case study of a new airfield surveillance radar system under development. Describes how radar works and defines a radar signal.
From The Discovering Physics Series.
Prod-BBCTV Dist-MEDIAG Prodn-OPENU 1983

Reflections–A Series
16MM FILM, 3/4 OR 1/2 IN VIDEO J-C
Presents dramatizations which deal with various moral and religious questions.
Prod-PAULST Dist-PAULST

Chicken	028 MIN
Courage	027 MIN
Family Of Winners, A	028 MIN
Friend In Deed, A	030 MIN
Girl On The Edge Of Town	025 MIN
Grandpa's Day	025 MIN
Hang Tight, Willy-Bill	027 MIN
High Powder	027 MIN
It Can't Happen To Me	025 MIN
Josie	025 MIN
Leadfoot	027 MIN
Loser Take All	015 MIN
Princess	028 MIN
Rocco's Star	027 MIN
Seventeen Going On Nowhere	028 MIN
Sex Game, The	020 MIN
Soupman	025 MIN
Step Too Slow, A	025 MIN
Things Are Different Now	015 MIN
This One For Dad	018 MIN
To Climb A Mountain	025 MIN
When, Jenny, When	025 MIN
Who Loves Amy Tonight	025 MIN

Reflections, No. 2 C 7 MIN
16MM FILM OPTICAL SOUND
Shows a moulding of light patterns into a controlled artistic expression. Presents an interplay of shapes and colors in building complexity.
Prod-DAVISJ Dist-RADIM

Reflets De La Vie Intellectuelle C 19 MIN
16MM FILM OPTICAL SOUND
A French language film. Traces France's intellectual creativity and expression through the centuries.
From The Aspects De France Series.
Prod-WSU Dist-MLA Prodn-BORGLM 1966

Reflex Klystron B 40 MIN
16MM FILM OPTICAL SOUND
Uses a mock-up to give a pictorial view of the construction and components of the reflex klystron. Shows the operation of the tube, emphasizing the bunching and catching action of the cavity. Shows how repeller plate voltage can be changed to obtain the different modes of operation. (Kinescope)
LC NO. 74-705496
Prod-USAF Dist-USNAC

Reflexes C
3/4 OR 1/2 INCH VIDEO CASSETTE
See series title for descriptive statement.
From The Physical Assessment - Neurologic System Series.
Prod-CONMED Dist-CONMED

Reflexes In The Cerebral Palsied Child B 23 MIN
3/4 OR 1/2 INCH VIDEO CASSETTE
Discusses the effect of the cortical, midbrain, brainstem and spiral level reflexes on the child with cerebral palsy.
Prod-BU Dist-BU

Reflexions C 4 MIN
3/4 OR 1/2 INCH VIDEO CASSETTE
Presents an abstract of nighttime water reflections. Uses hand-colored imagery. An experimental film.
Prod-MEDIPR Dist-MEDIPR 1979

Reflexives, The (Los Refexivos) C 30 MIN
3/4 INCH VIDEO CASSETTE H-C
See series title for descriptive statement.
From The Telespanol Uno Series.
Prod-WUSFTV Dist-GPITVL 1979

Reflux (Peptic) Esophagitis C 30 MIN
3/4 OR 1/2 INCH VIDEO CASSETTE
Discusses causes and treatment of reflux esophagitis.
Prod-ROWLAB Dist-ROWLAB

Reflux In Duplicated Ureters - Modern Surgical Techniques C 18 MIN
16MM FILM OPTICAL SOUND
Depicts embryologic development of ureteral duplication, leading to increased susceptibility to reflux. Describes modern methods of diagnosis of ureteral duplication, including excretory urography, cystography, cystoscopy and the cystoscopic indigo carmine test for the detection of associated reflux. Shows two surgical techniques for correction of reflux in duplicated ureters and discusses the results and complications of these operations.
LC NO. 75-702273
Prod-EATONL Dist-EATONL 1971

Reform And Reaction C 30 MIN
3/4 OR 1/2 INCH VIDEO CASSETTE C
Discusses the political swings involved in reform and reaction in American politics.
America - The Second Century Series.
Prod-DALCCD Dist-DALCCD

Reform Movements C 30 MIN
2 INCH VIDEOTAPE
Discusses specific reforms in the area of education, care for the insane, women's rights and abolition.
From The American History I Series.
Prod-DENVPS Dist-GPITVL

Reformation, The C 30 MIN
16MM FILM OPTICAL SOUND
Surveys the contributions of the Reformation towards a reestablishment of man's spiritual integrity which had been threatened by the worldliness of the Renaissance. Based on the book How Should We Then Live by Francis A Schaeffer.
From The How Should We Then Live Series. No. 4
LC NO. 77-702366
Prod-GF Dist-GF 1977

Reformation, The C 45 MIN
16MM FILM, 3/4 OR 1/2 IN VIDEO H A
Discusses the Reformation of the church by such men as Luther and Calvin. Shows how although the Reformation movement had many great leaders, it did not have a consistent view.
From The Christians Series.
Prod-GRATV Dist-MGHT 1978

Reformation, The (Dutch) C 30 MIN
16MM FILM OPTICAL SOUND
Surveys the contributions of the Reformation towards a reestablishment of man's spiritual integrity which had been threatened by the worldliness of the Renaissance. Based on the book How Should We Then Live by Francis A Schaeffer.
From The How Should We Then Live (Dutch) Series. No. 4
LC NO. 77-702366
Prod-GF Dist-GF 1977

Reformation, The (2nd Ed) C 14 MIN
16MM FILM, 3/4 OR 1/2 IN VIDEO J-C
Discusses how criticism of the Catholic Church, the cultural rebirth brought about by the Renaissance, the emergence of national states and new interpretations of the Scriptures combined to bring about the Reformation. Focuses on Martin Luther and the Protestant Reformation in Germany.
Prod-CORF Dist-CORF 1979

Reformation, The - Age Of Revolt C 24 MIN
16MM FILM, 3/4 OR 1/2 IN VIDEO H-C
Introduces the political, social and religious climate that existed in Europe during the 16th century. Emphasizes the religious reforms of Martin Luther as indicators of the future trend and reflection of their historical context.
From The Humanities - Philosophy And Political Thought Series.
Prod-EBEC Dist-EBEC 1973

Reformation, The, Pt 1 C 26 MIN
16MM FILM, 3/4 OR 1/2 IN VIDEO H-C A
Explores the factors which prompted the development of the schism between Protestants and Roman Catholics during the 16th century.
Prod-NBCTV Dist-MGHT 1967

Reformation, The, Pt 2 C 26 MIN
16MM FILM, 3/4 OR 1/2 IN VIDEO H-C A
Explores the factors which prompted the development of the schism between Protestants and Roman Catholics during the 16th century.
Prod-NBCTV Dist-MGHT 1967

Refracted Image, The C
1/2 IN VIDEO CASSETTE BETA/VHS
Examines representations of the human figure in Greek, Renaissance, and modern visual arts, and discusses the images of adulthood in these historical periods. Explores the role of the arts in conveying these images.
From The Adult Years - Continuity And Change Series.
Prod-OHUTC Dist-OHUTC

Refraction X 20 MIN
2 INCH VIDEOTAPE I
See series title for descriptive statement.
From The Process And Proof Series. No. 16
Prod-MCETV Dist-GPITVL Prodn-WVIZTV

Refraction Of Light By Spherical Lenses C 10 MIN
16MM FILM, 3/4 OR 1/2 IN VIDEO H-C A
From The Optics Of The Human Eye Series.
Prod-BAYCMO Dist-TEF

Refraction Of Light By Spherocylindrical Lenses C 10 MIN
16MM FILM, 3/4 OR 1/2 IN VIDEO H-C A
From The Optics Of The Human Eye Series.
Prod-BAYCMO Dist-TEF

Refraction, Pt 1 B 22 MIN
16MM FILM OPTICAL SOUND H

Deals with the general effects of refraction at plane interfaces and teaches the laws of refraction.
From The Optics Series.
Prod-CETO Dist-GPITVL

Refraction, Pt 2 B 22 MIN
16MM FILM OPTICAL SOUND H
Continues the investigation of refraction beginning with the path of rays of light through a prism, followed by total internal reflection.
From The Optics Series.
Prod-CETO Dist-GPITVL

Refractions, No. 1 C 7 MIN
16MM FILM OPTICAL SOUND
Shows how light passes through the transparent material of objects and is bent or refracted in a spectrum of colors.
Prod-DAVISJ Dist-RADIM

Refractive Errors C 25 MIN
3/4 OR 1/2 INCH VIDEO CASSETTE PRO
Defines preshyopia, myopia, hyperopia, astigmatism and cataracts and describes how these conditions affect vision. Discusses corrective procedures to modify these conditions, including the use of glasses and contact lenses.
Prod-UMICHM Dist-UMICHM 1976

Refractory Cast In Removable Partial Denture Construction, The C 5 MIN
16MM FILM, 3/4 OR 1/2 IN VIDEO PRO
Demonstrates the transfer of design, steps involved in modifying the master cast, surveying, block out, and duplication for accurate removable partial denture casting.
LC NO. 81-706309
Prod-USVA Dist-USNAC 1980

Refractory Cast In Removable Partial Denture Construction, The, Pt I - Construction Of... C 15 MIN
3/4 OR 1/2 INCH VIDEO CASSETTE
Demonstrates the various steps involved in modifying the master cast, surveying, block out and its duplication, stressing the importance of this procedure in the production of accurate removable partial denture casting.
Prod-VADTC Dist-AMDA 1979

Refractory Cast In Removable Partial Denture Construction, The, Pt II - Developing The... C 13 MIN
3/4 OR 1/2 INCH VIDEO CASSETTE
Illustrates the waxing procedures incident to developing the wax pattern for a maxillary removable partial denture with a design which includes circumferential clasps and a palatal strap major connector.
Prod-VADTC Dist-AMDA 1979

Refrains Of Paris B 16 MIN
16MM FILM OPTICAL SOUND J-C A
Presents Jacqueline Francois, French Chanteuse, singing three songs against a Parisian background. 'DE LA MADELEIN A L'OPERA,' A satirical present-day ballad, is pantomimed as Georgette Plana sings.
Prod-ART Dist-RFL 1955

Refrigerated Ammonia Spill Tests C 22 MIN
16MM FILM OPTICAL SOUND
Shows controlled one-ton and ten-ton low-temperature spills designed to determine evaporation rates, concentration and spread of vapors, reaction to water and flammability under the test conditions.
LC NO. FI68-223
Prod-PHILLP Dist-PHILLP 1965

Refrigeration - Compressor Controls B 6 MIN
16MM FILM, 3/4 OR 1/2 IN VIDEO
Depicts how the low pressure switch turns on and off the compressor motor via motor controller and how safety controls protect compressor and motor.
LC NO. 82-706151
Prod-USN Dist-USNAC 1957

Refrigeration - Condenser Controls B 5 MIN
16MM FILM, 3/4 OR 1/2 IN VIDEO
Shows controls for the condenser of a refrigeration system. Demonstrates how the refrigeration pressure in the high pressure line is used by the water-regulating valve to control the flow of water through the condenser. Tells how use of the water failure switch serves as protection for the compressor.
LC NO. 82-706092
Prod-USN Dist-USNAC 1957

Refrigeration - Evacuating And Charging C 13 MIN
16MM FILM, 3/4 OR 1/2 IN VIDEO
Demonstrates procedures for removing air and moisture from refrigeration lines and charging the unit with fresh refrigerant. Shows how to attach the manifold gauge assembly, evacuate the system and conduct a leak test prior to charging.
LC NO. 82-706150
Prod-USAF Dist-USNAC 1957

Refrigeration - Evaporator Controls B 8 MIN
16MM FILM, 3/4 OR 1/2 IN VIDEO
Examines how the thermostatic switch and solenoid valve work to deliver full flow refrigerant to the thermal expansion valve. Shows how the super head is used by the thermal expansion valve to control the flow of refrigerant into the evaporator coil and how the evaporator pressure regulator works to release refrigerant from the evaporator to the compressor.
LC NO. 82-706152
Prod-USN Dist-USNAC 1957

Refrigeration - Introduction To Control Mechanisms B 10 MIN
16MM FILM, 3/4 OR 1/2 IN VIDEO
Explains the function of the automatic controls in the refrigeration cycle and use of the manual control in emergencies.
LC NO. 82-706148
Prod-USN Dist-USNAC 1970

Refrigeration - Motors, Controls And Testing Them C 16 MIN
3/4 OR 1/2 INCH VIDEO CASSETTE H-C A
Shows the single phase motor compressors, single phase motors, capacitor start run, permanent split capacitor, meters and how to use them, locating terminals on unmarked dome, testing relays, capacitors and fuses.
Prod-SF Dist-SF 1970

Refrigeration - Multiple Temperature Evaporator C 16 MIN
3/4 OR 1/2 INCH VIDEO CASSETTE H-C A
Presents an instructional film on installation and valves, surge tank and oil separator, thermostat and solenoid valve, short cycling of compressor and the sizing liquid reservoirs.
Prod-SF Dist-SF 1970

Refrigeration Service - Domestic Units—A Series

Prod-USOE Dist-USNAC 1945

Adding Or Removing Refrigeration	017 MIN
Adjusting And Checking The Expansion Valve	021 MIN
Checking And Replacing A Float Valve	019 MIN
Checking The Electrical System	017 MIN
Checking The System, Pt 1 - General Procedure	017 MIN
Checking The System, Pt 2 - Trouble Shooting	017 MIN
Locating And Repairing Leaks	017 MIN
Quieting A Noisy Refrigerator	016 MIN
Removing And Installing A Compressor	017 MIN
Removing And Installing A Cooling Unit	019 MIN

Refuelling C 32 MIN
16MM FILM OPTICAL SOUND PRO
Illustrates the fuel channels in a Calder Hall reactor discharging spent fuel, preparation of new fuel elements and refuelling.
From The Operating A Calder Hall Reactor Series.
Prod-UKAEA Dist-UKAEA 1959

Refugee Road C 59 MIN
16MM FILM OPTICAL SOUND
Portrays the life of a Laotian family from their life in a refugee camp on the Cambodian border through their first year in America. Presents an understanding of the refugee experience and provides a perspective on the culture into which they must find their way. Includes some dialogue in Lao with English subtitles.
LC NO. 82-700140
Prod-FOGLIT Dist-FOGLIT 1981

Refugee Road C 59 MIN
16MM FILM OPTICAL SOUND
Follows a Laotian family from a refugee camp in Thailand to the United States. Illustrates the differences in cultures.
Prod-OHC Dist-HRC

Refugees C 23 MIN
3/4 OR 1/2 INCH VIDEO CASSETTE
Shows the arrival of the Hmong family in Minnesota, pointing out the difficulties of adapting to life in a new country.
Prod-WCCOTV Dist-WCCOTV 1979

Refuse Disposal By Sanitary Landfills C 13 MIN
16MM FILM OPTICAL SOUND
Describes the faults of disposal methods such as open dumps and compares the hazards of these methods to those of landfills. Shows how to select a site and procedures to use.
LC NO. FIE57-8
Prod-USPHS Dist-USNAC 1956

Refuse Disposal By Sanitary Landfills (Spanish) C 13 MIN
16MM FILM OPTICAL SOUND
Discusses the faults of disposal methods, such as open dumps, and compares the vector-borne disease and nuisance hazards of these methods to those of landfills. Shows how to select a site, types of equipment used, how to construct a landfill, different types of operating procedures and overall contributions of sanitary landfills to public health.
LC NO. 74-705501
Prod-NMAC Dist-USNAC 1956

Refuse Problem, The C 14 MIN
16MM FILM OPTICAL SOUND J-H A
Presents the problems of refuse storage, collection and disposal. Suggests how the individual can act to help solve some of these problems.
Prod-VADE Dist-VADE 1963

Refusing Credit B 45 MIN
2 INCH VIDEOTAPE C
See series title for descriptive statement.
From The Business Writing Series. Unit II - Disappointing Messages
Prod-CHITVC Dist-GPITVL Prodn-WTTWTV

Refusing The Adjustment B 45 MIN
2 INCH VIDEOTAPE C
See series title for descriptive statement.
From The Business Writing Series. Unit II - Disappointing Messages
Prod-CHITVC Dist-GPITVL Prodn-WTTWTV

Refusing The Request B 45 MIN
2 INCH VIDEOTAPE C
See series title for descriptive statement.
From The Business Writing Series. Unit II - Disappointing Messages
Prod-CHITVC Dist-GPITVL Prodn-WTTWTV

Regen B 14 MIN
16MM FILM, 3/4 OR 1/2 IN VIDEO H-C
A German language film. Presents the various activities which occupy the people in a typical German city during the rain.
From The German Cities Series.
Prod-IFB Dist-IFB 1969

Regeneration B 30 MIN
2 INCH VIDEOTAPE J
See series title for descriptive statement.
From The Investigating The World Of Science, Unit 2 - Energy Within Living Systems Series.
Prod-MPATI Dist-GPITVL

Regentropfen B 89 MIN
16MM FILM OPTICAL SOUND
A German language film with English subtitles. Deals with the hardships of an integrated Jewish family in a small German town at the beginning of the Nazi regime, and ending with the family being allowed to immigrate to the United States, leaving the father behind because he cannot pass the necessary health examination.
Prod-WSTGLC Dist-WSTGLC 1980

Reggae C 25 MIN
3/4 OR 1/2 INCH VIDEO CASSETTE J-C A
Shows how the rise of reggae, based on a perfect symmetrical relationship between guitar, bass and drums, has influenced rock music. Explains the importance of a sense of discipline and precision to reggae musicians. Looks at the 'dub' technique.
From The Rockschool Series.
Prod-BBCTV Dist-FI

Regina - Gift Of Vision C 11 MIN
16MM FILM, 3/4 OR 1/2 IN VIDEO P-I
Focuses on an 11-year-old blind girl who explains how she has learned to function effectively in the everyday world.
Prod-LOYUDC Dist-LRF 1978

Reginald Parse C 5 MIN
3/4 OR 1/2 INCH VIDEO CASSETTE J-H
Teaches correct word usage. Explains 'Imply' and 'Infer' and 'Continual' and 'Continuous'. Shows the distinction between 'Differ with' and 'Differ from'.
From The Write On, Set 1 Series.
Prod-CTI Dist-CTI

Region Of Tanach C 28 MIN
16MM FILM OPTICAL SOUND
Tells the story of the Atlas Mountains Jews living in Israel.
Prod-ALDEN Dist-ALDEN

Regional Enteritis C 19 MIN
16MM FILM OPTICAL SOUND PRO
Describes the etiology, surgical anatomy and symptoms of regional ileitis. Presents the indications and contraindications for surgery. Illustrates microscopic and gross findings in diseased bowel.
Prod-ACYDGD Dist-ACY 1960

Regional Ileitis Treatment By Resection And Primary Anastomosis Between The Ilium And ... C 40 MIN
16MM FILM OPTICAL SOUND PRO
Demonstrates surgical problems encountered with the marked involvement of the terminal ileum, perforation and thickening of the mesentery. Shows the salient pathologic and X-ray features of regional ileitis as well as the clinical symptoms and course of the disease.
Prod-ACYDGD Dist-ACY 1952

Regional Intervention Program—A Series

Prod-USBEH Dist-USNAC Prodn-AIRLIE 1973

Individual Tutoring	18 MIN
Language Preschool	19 MIN
That's What It's All About	29 MIN
Toddler Management	19 MIN

Regional Perfusion For Malignant Melanoma C 15 MIN
16MM FILM OPTICAL SOUND PRO
Explains that a patient with melanoma of calf with clinically negative lymph nodes had extremity perfusion with phenylalanine nitrogen mustard and wide local excision of the melanoma.
From The Cine Clinic Series.
Prod-ACYDGD Dist-NMAC 1970

Regional Seminar On Development B 10 MIN
16MM FILM OPTICAL SOUND
Presents a seminar on economic development in Malaysia.
Prod-FILEM Dist-PMFMUN 1968

Regional Variations C 28 MIN
16MM FILM OPTICAL SOUND J-C T
Dr Frederic Cassidy, professor of English at the University of Wisconsin, and Dr Hood Roberts, of the Center for Applied Linguistics, discuss the major regional dialects in the United States.
From The Language - The Social Arbiter Series. No. 4
LC NO. FIA67-5264
Prod-FINLYS Dist-FINLYS Prodn-CALING 1966

Register And Vote C 1 MIN
16MM FILM OPTICAL SOUND H-C A
Encourages members of the black community in the United States to register and vote.
LC NO. 75-701514
Prod-LEECC Dist-LEECC 1975

Regitel Training At Bullock's C 16 MIN
16MM FILM OPTICAL SOUND
Presents the basic operational methodology of the American Regitel Corporation electronic computer-controlled point-of-sale cash register at Bullock's, a high-fashion department store.

LC NO. 72-700038
Prod-CANCIN Dist-CANCIN 1971

Regression Analysis C
3/4 OR 1/2 INCH VIDEO CASSETTE IND
Gives detailed explanation of the linear trend between one independent and dependent variable. Develops, discusses and tests the least square line. Makes predictions for mu sub-y/x, Y sub-x and Y sub-x. Cites possible problems relating to data gathered.
From The Statistics For Managers Series.
Prod-COLOSU Dist-COLOSU

Regrouping Tens In Subtraction C 20 MIN
2 INCH VIDEOTAPE P
See series title for descriptive statement.
From The Mathemagic, Unit II - Addition And Subtraction Series.
Prod-WMULTV Dist-GPITVL

Regular Homotopies In The Plane, Pt 1 C 14 MIN
16MM FILM, 3/4 OR 1/2 IN VIDEO C
Records the deformation of regular closed curves and the rotation of tangent vectors. Demonstrates the theorem that two regular curves in the plane which are regularly homotopic must have the same rotation number.
From The Topology Series.
LC NO. 81-706243
Prod-EDC Dist-IFB 1975

Regular Homotopies In The Plane, Pt 2 C 19 MIN
16MM FILM, 3/4 OR 1/2 IN VIDEO C
Illustrates the Whitney-Graustein Theorem.
From The Topology Series.
LC NO. 81-706244
Prod-EDC Dist-IFB 1975

Regular Kid, A C 15 MIN
16MM FILM OPTICAL SOUND A
Presents four vignettes involving children who have asthma to explain what causes the disease, how it affects children's lives, and how the child and parents cope with the disease.
LC NO. 81-700361
Prod-AMLUNG Dist-GEIGY Prodn-NOWAKA 1981

Regular Kid, A C 16 MIN
3/4 INCH VIDEO CASSETTE
Documents parents' and children's views on asthma. Explains how medicine and medical equipment help treat the problem.
Prod-GEIGYP Dist-MTP

Regular Stochastic Matrices C 30 MIN
3/4 INCH VIDEO CASSETTE C
See series title for descriptive statement.
From The Introduction To Mathematics Series.
Prod-MDCPB Dist-MDCPB

Regular-Routine Responsibilities C 7 MIN
3/4 OR 1/2 INCH VIDEO CASSETTE
See series title for descriptive statement.
From The Practical M B O Series.
Prod-DELTAK Dist-DELTAK

Regulating Body Temperature (2nd Ed) C 22 MIN
16MM FILM, 3/4 OR 1/2 IN VIDEO J-H
Presents the development, importance and physiology of body temperature regulation. Compares man's heat-regulating responses with that of other animals. Introduces the variety of physiological and behavior mechanisms that balance heat and cold in the body.
From The Biology Series, Unit 8 - Human Physiology.
Prod-EBEC Dist-EBEC 1972

Regulation And Innovation C 51 MIN
3/4 OR 1/2 INCH VIDEO CASSETTE
See series title for descriptive statement.
From The Technology, Innovation, And Industrial Development Series.
Prod-MIOT Dist-MIOT

Regulation Of Atomic Radiation, The C 29 MIN
16MM FILM OPTICAL SOUND
Surveys the work of the Atomic Energy Commission in licensing and regulating the use of nuclear materials. Examines the close control of radioactive materials from the time they leave the mines to be processed until they are again returned to the earth or to the sea as waste materials.
LC NO. FIE64-190
Prod-USAEC Dist-USNAC 1963

Regulation Of Heart Beat In The Mammal C 4 MIN
16MM FILM SILENT C
Illustrates the relationship of nerve impulses to neurocellular junctions in the heart as regulators of the heart beat.
From The Dukes Physiology Series.
LC NO. 73-710192
Prod-IOWA Dist-IOWA 1971

Regulation Of Normal And Leukemic Hematopoiesis In Humans C 60 MIN
3/4 INCH VIDEO CASSETTE
Discusses the regulation of normal and leukemic hematopoiesis in humans.
Prod-UTAHTI Dist-UTAHTI

Regulation Of The Microcirculation C 50 MIN
3/4 OR 1/2 INCH VIDEO CASSETTE PRO
Familiarizes students with mechanisms of flow regulation in microcirculation.
Prod-HSCIC Dist-HSCIC 1982

Regulations C 19 MIN
3/4 OR 1/2 INCH VIDEO CASSETTE H
Tells how a worker balks at a tyrannical boss's order and is then fired. Explains how he gets his job back by going through grievance procedures.
From The Jobs - Seeking, Finding, Keeping Series.
Prod-MSDOE Dist-AITECH 1980

Regulator Fundamentals C 25 MIN
3/4 OR 1/2 INCH VIDEO CASSETTE IND
Describes the most common kinds of regulators and controllers used in the gas industry to control the pressure of gas. Tells how the regulators and controllers work.
Prod-UTEXPE Dist-UTEXPE 1978

Regulators, Excess Flow Valves, Boosters, Sequence Valves C 26 MIN
3/4 OR 1/2 INCH VIDEO CASSETTE IND
Illustrates and explains the operations of sequence values, pressure regulators, venting type regulators, pilot controlled regulators, differential pressure circuits, dual pressure circuits, air-to-oil booster circuits and excess flow values.
From The Industrial Pneumatic Technology Series. Chapter 10
Prod-TAT Dist-TAT

Regulators, The C 29 MIN
16MM FILM OPTICAL SOUND
A discussion of the role of the independent regulatory agencies created by Congress and staffed by the President. Includes a picture history of the creation of the first agency, the Interstate Commerce Commission and the development of the seven major commissions and agencies which followed.
From The Government Story Seroes. No. 34
LC NO. 70-707190
Prod-OGCW Dist-WBCPRO 1968

Regulators, The - Our Invisible Government C 50 MIN
16MM FILM, 3/4 OR 1/2 IN VIDEO H-C A
Looks at the regulatory function of the U S government by focusing on the Environmental Protection Agency's drafting of one regulation which carries out a provision of the Clean Air Act. Illustrates the role of citizens in establishing governmental policy.
LC NO. 82-707151
Prod-WVIATV Dist-LCOA 1982

Regulatory Mechanisms - Biosphere B 30 MIN
2 INCH VIDEOTAPE J
See series title for descriptive statement.
From The Investigating The World Of Science, Unit 2 - Energy Within Living Systems Series.
Prod-MPATI Dist-GPITVL

Regulatory Mechanisms - Endocrine Glands B 30 MIN
2 INCH VIDEOTAPE J
See series title for descriptive statement.
From The Investigating The World Of Science, Unit 2 - Energy Within Living Systems Series.
Prod-MPATI Dist-GPITVL

Regulatory Mechanisms - Environment B 30 MIN
2 INCH VIDEOTAPE J
See series title for descriptive statement.
From The Investigating The World Of Science, Unit 2 - Energy Within Living Systems Series.
Prod-MPATI Dist-GPITVL

Rehabilitation C 10 MIN
16MM FILM OPTICAL SOUND J-C A
Defines rehabilitation as it relates to the offender and stresses modern concepts and different types of programs currently in operation.
From The Criminal Justice Series.
Prod-GCCED Dist-GCCED 1971

Rehabilitation - A Patient's Perspective C 26 MIN
16MM FILM, 3/4 OR 1/2 IN VIDEO
Examines the psychological and emotional aspects of rehabilitation from the patient's point of view.
Prod-TOGGFI Dist-FLMLIB 1973

Rehabilitation - An Inside View B 29 MIN
16MM FILM OPTICAL SOUND PRO
Demonstrates facets of rehabilitation of patients with musculo-skeletal and visual problems and the laryngectomized patient. Shows activities of physical therapy, hydrotherapy and occupational therapy. Includes interviews with patients, a psychologist, a social worker and therapists.
From The Directions For Education In Nursing Via Technology Series. Lesson 81
LC NO. 74-701859
Prod-DENT Dist-WSU 1974

Rehabilitation - The Miracle In Us All C 28 MIN
16MM FILM OPTICAL SOUND C A
Demonstrates the Liberty Mutual Insurance Company's commitment to provide the best medical care and to return the injured worker to a productive life. Portrays case histories and features actual claimants, rehabilitation nurses and four physicians associated with well-known hospitals and rehabilitation facilities.
Prod-LIBMIC Dist-MTP Prodn-CRABRO

Rehabilitation After Myocardial Infarction C
3/4 OR 1/2 INCH VIDEO CASSETTE
Provides detailed clinical guidelines for the rehabilitation of myocardial infarction patients, both during and after hospitalization. Presents the principles of patient selection and outlines a comprehensive rehabilitation program.
Prod-AMEDA Dist-AMEDA

Rehabilitation Center C 14 MIN
3/4 OR 1/2 INCH VIDEO CASSETTE H-C A
Views a rehabilitation center with all its services and separate parts. Shows how a physician can help his patients with physical handicaps to return to job and family, with a new education in self care. Describes the overall concept of rehabilitation rather than specific methods of treatment.
Prod-FO Dist-FO

Rehabilitation Management Of Below Knee Amputation C 13 MIN
16MM FILM OPTICAL SOUND PRO
Discusses the amputation, beginning with the preoperative evaluation and following through to the postsurgical prosthetic training. Describes surgical techniques, application of rigid dressing, controlled weight-bearing and progressive ambulation.
LC NO. 74-706388
Prod-USVA Dist-USNAC 1971

Rehabilitation Of Dancer's Injuries C 30 MIN
3/4 OR 1/2 INCH VIDEO CASSETTE
See series title for descriptive statement.
From The Care And Feeding Of Dancers Series.
Prod-ARCVID Dist-ARCVID

Rehabilitation Of The Forequarter Amputee C 12 MIN
3/4 OR 1/2 INCH VIDEO CASSETTE PRO
Describes a forequarter amputation and various aspects of rehabilitation for patients who have had one. Includes a description of a post-operative program, a pre-prosthetic program, and the initial checkout of the prosthesis, as well as demonstrating a patient putting on the prosthesis and a description of prosthetic training programs.
Prod-HSCIC Dist-HSCIC

Rehabilitation Team Conference, A C 20 MIN
3/4 OR 1/2 INCH VIDEO CASSETTE PRO
Concerns the rehabilitation of a 48-year-old male stroke patient. Shows how a rehabilitation team consisting of an occupational therapist, physical therapist, speech therapist, nurse, social worker, psychologist, and physician identify and rank the patient's problems and treatment.
Prod-UMICHM Dist-UMICHM 1979

Rehabilitation, Essential To Patient Care C 60 MIN
3/4 OR 1/2 INCH VIDEO CASSETTE PRO
Emphasizes the three phases of rehabilitation. Illustrates the basic concepts of positioning, bowel and bladder training, and range of motion.
LC NO. 81-706300
Prod-USVA Dist-USNAC 1980

Rehabilitative Patient Care Planning - A Team Approach C 27 MIN
3/4 INCH VIDEO CASSETTE PRO
Demonstrates the interaction and decision-making processes of a multidisciplinary stroke rehabilitation team. Shows how the team identifies the patient's needs and establishes goals for the treatment plan in order to insure effective rehabilitation.
LC NO. 80-706787
Prod-VAHSL Dist-USNAC 1980

Rehearsal B 17 MIN
16MM FILM OPTICAL SOUND C A
Dramatizes the story of a woman directing a play in a theater where actuality, memory and fantasy all intertwine.
Prod-VIERAD Dist-CANCIN 1976

Rehearsal C 28 MIN
16MM FILM, 3/4 OR 1/2 IN VIDEO H-C A
Describes how teenage members of a therapy group use role-playing to learn more about their parents.
Prod-PAULST Dist-MEDIAG

Rehearsal C 29 MIN
3/4 INCH VIDEO CASSETTE
Gives an insider's look at a rehearsal for a recording session.
From The Music Shop Series.
Prod-UMITV Dist-UMITV 1974

Rehearsal - Strindberg's Miss Julie C 60 MIN
3/4 OR 1/2 INCH VIDEO CASSETTE C
See series title for descriptive statement.
From The Drama - Play, Performance, Perception Series. Module 1
Prod-MDCC Dist-MDCC

Rehearsal For The Moon C 7 MIN
3/4 INCH VIDEO CASSETTE
Reports on the complex simulators used to train astronauts for the Apollo mission. Issued in 1969 as a motion picture.
From The Apollo Digest Series.
LC NO. 79-706987
Prod-NASA Dist-USNAC 1979

Rehearsal, The C 23 MIN
3/4 OR 1/2 INCH VIDEO CASSETTE
Follows hospital staff and community emergency personnel as they rehearse together various methods of moving both ambulatory and bedfast patients.
Prod-FPF Dist-FPF

Rehearsing A Dance Company C 30 MIN
3/4 OR 1/2 INCH VIDEO CASSETTE
See series title for descriptive statement.
From The Behind The Scenes Series.
Prod-ARCVID Dist-ARCVID

Rehearsing The Text C 53 MIN
3/4 OR 1/2 INCH VIDEO CASSETTE
Employs a scene from Twelfth Night to search for Shakespeare's clues to character, language and staging. Discusses text and subtext and how the verse itself is a clue to the meaning.
From The Royal Shakespeare Company Series.
Prod-FOTH Dist-FOTH 1984

Reign Of Terror C 60 MIN
16MM FILM, 3/4 OR 1/2 IN VIDEO C A
Describes how Claudius helps remove Sejanus as a threat to Tiberius and how the bloodbath that follows almost destroys him.
From The I, Claudius Series. Number 8
Prod-BBCTV Dist-FI 1977

Reincarnation C 29 MIN
2 INCH VIDEOTAPE
Features Dr Puryear looking at the possibilities and beliefs with regard to theories of reincarnation and examines a number of documented case histories.
From The Who Is Man Series.
Prod-WHROTV Dist-PUBTEL

Reinforced Plastics - Inspection And Quality Control C 20 MIN
16MM FILM OPTICAL SOUND
Demonstrates inspection procedures, showing examples of various common defects and procedures leading to final acceptance of the finished parts by naval inspectors.
LC NO. FIE58-24
Prod-USN Dist-USNAC 1957

Reinforced Plastics - Introduction B 20 MIN
16MM FILM OPTICAL SOUND
Explains in general the nature of reinforced plastics and their composition and fabrication.
LC NO. FIE58-23
Prod-USN Dist-USNAC 1957

Reinforcement Show, The C 28 MIN
16MM FILM OPTICAL SOUND P-I
Shows handicapped people achieving difficult goals and effectively interacting with their nonhandicapped peers.
From The Special Delivery Series.
LC NO. 79-701078
Prod-WNVT Dist-LAWREN 1979

Reinforcement Show, The C 28 MIN
3/4 INCH VIDEO CASSETTE P-I
Shows handicapped people achieving difficult goals and effectively interacting with their nonhandicapped peers.
From The Special Delivery Series.
LC NO. 79-706882
Prod-WNVT Dist-LAWREN 1979

Reinforcement Theory For Teachers B 28 MIN
16MM FILM OPTICAL SOUND C
Features Dr Madeline Hunter discussing positive reinforcement, negative reinforcement, extinction and schedule of reinforcement. Suggests how the theory behind reward and punishment can be applied effectively in daily teaching.
From The Translating Theory Into Classroom Practices Series.
Prod-SPF Dist-SPF 1963

Reinheit Des Herzens C 104 MIN
16MM FILM OPTICAL SOUND
A German language film with English subtitles. Shows how violence affects human relationships, through the story of a couple who had formerly lived together harmoniously but who are suddenly torn apart by an outside force. Describes how the partner who, during good times, was the strong one, falls apart, with the formerly dependent one taking over.
Prod-WSTGLC Dist-WSTGLC 1980

Reining Horse, The C 25 MIN
16MM FILM, 3/4 OR 1/2 IN VIDEO
Discusses the reining horse, the foundation for any performance event. Offers a definition of a reining horse, basic training, and the difference between East and West coast styles of competition. Deals with the snaffle-bit, hackamore and bit reining.
Prod-AQHORS Dist-AQHORS

Reins Of Command, The - Air Force Communications Service C 28 MIN
16MM FILM OPTICAL SOUND
Portrays the mission of the Air Force Communications Service and its role in air force operations. Presents the highly complex and sophisticated techniques, equipment, global communications network and air traffic control system.
LC NO. 74-705508
Prod-USAF Dist-USNAC

Rejected C 30 MIN
16MM FILM OPTICAL SOUND H A
John Stubbins refuses to help Cliff Brown, a former friend, who has just completed a prison term for embezzlement. A tragic chain of events ensues for which John blames himself.
LC NO. FIA68-1494
Prod-CONCOR Dist-CPH 1968

Rejection Of Renal Transplant B 18 MIN
16MM FILM OPTICAL SOUND PRO
Provides a general review of rejection theory followed by a discussion concerning types of rejections of renal homografts in man. Includes a brief survey of statistical data. (Kinescope)
From The Clinical Pathology Series.
LC NO. 74-705509
Prod-NMAC Dist-USNAC 1969

Relaciones Entre Supervisores B 8 MIN
3/4 INCH VIDEO CASSETTE
A Spanish language version of Working With Other Supervisors. Discusses the importance of working harmoniously with other people. Issued in 1959 as a motion picture.
From The Problems In Supervision (Spanish) Series.
LC NO. 79-706960
Prod-USOE Dist-USNAC 1979

Related Rates C
3/4 INCH VIDEO CASSETTE
See series title for descriptive statement.
From The Calculus Series.
Prod-MDDE Dist-MDCPB

Related Services For The Handicapped C 30 MIN
3/4 OR 1/2 INCH VIDEO CASSETTE T
Defines related services for the handicapped and the benefits from effective coordination for the handicapped child. Gives attention to selected specialists, their role and the services which each might provide. Presents a professional panel discussing the procedures for determining eligibility for Special Education services.
From The Promises To Keep Series. Module 9
Prod-VPISU Dist-LUF 1979

Relating Addition To Multiplication C 20 MIN
2 INCH VIDEOTAPE P
See series title for descriptive statement.
From The Mathemagic, Unit VIII - Multiplication And Division Series.
Prod-WMULTV Dist-GPITVL

Relating Division To Multiplication C 20 MIN
2 INCH VIDEOTAPE P
See series title for descriptive statement.
From The Mathemagic, Unit VIII - Multiplication And Division Series.
Prod-WMULTV Dist-GPITVL

Relating Facts C 15 MIN
16MM FILM MAGNETIC SOUND K-C A S
See series title for descriptive statement.
From The PANCOM Beginning Total Communication Program For Hearing Parents Of... Series. Level 1
LC NO. 77-700504
Prod-CSDE Dist-JOYCE Prodn-CSFDF 1977

Relating Fractions And Decimals C 14 MIN
3/4 OR 1/2 INCH VIDEO CASSETTE I
Relates that for his initiation, David unravels decimal clues with some advice from a canny granny. Includes an animated segment which shows that Romeo Fraction's and Juliet Decimal's families find common ground on a region diagram.
From The It Figures Series. No. 14
Prod-AITV Dist-AITECH Prodn-NJN 1982

Relating Multiplication And Division C 15 MIN
3/4 INCH VIDEO CASSETTE P
Presents multiplication and division as inverse operations.
From The Math Factory, Module IV - Problem Solving Series.
Prod-MAETEL Dist-GPITVL 1973

Relating Semiconductors To Systems C 60 MIN
1 INCH VIDEOTAPE IND
Discusses electronic circuits by describing how their frequency, power and other requirements affect the choice of semiconductor devices used in the circuits. Includes explanations of inductance and capacitance.
From The Understanding Semiconductors Course Outline Series. No. 04
Prod-TXINLC Dist-TXINLC

Relating Sets To Numbers C 11 MIN
16MM FILM OPTICAL SOUND I-H
Shows the meaning of a 'WELL-DEFINED SET' and 'MEMBER OF A SET.' Demonstrates methods of writing sets using braces to enclose a listing of the members. Emphasizes the meaning of 'EMPTY SET,' 'FINITE SETS' and 'INFINITE SETS,' and the meaning and difference between the concepts of number and numerals.
From The Pathways To Modern Math Series.
LC NO. FIA64-1444
Prod-GE Dist-GE

Relating Sound And Movement, Pt 1 C 6 MIN
16MM FILM OPTICAL SOUND P-I
Presents a program that interrelates the music and physical education experiences in a seven year old's school day.
Prod-VIP Dist-VIP Prodn-CEMREL 1974

Relating Sound And Movement, Pt 2 C 5 MIN
16MM FILM OPTICAL SOUND P-I
Presents a program that interrelates the music and physical education experiences in a seven year old's school day.
Prod-VIP Dist-VIP Prodn-CEMREL 1974

Relating Subtraction To Division C 20 MIN
2 INCH VIDEOTAPE P
See series title for descriptive statement.
From The Mathemagic, Unit VIII - Multiplication And Division Series.
Prod-WMULTV Dist-GPITVL

Relation Between Impulse And Change In Momentum, The X 13 MIN
16MM FILM OPTICAL SOUND C
Depicts a physics demonstration which shows relation between impulse and change in momentum using forces applied to a cart rolling on a horizontal track.
Prod-PUAVC Dist-PUAVC 1961

Relation Of Mathematics To Physics, The B 55 MIN
16MM FILM - 3/4 IN VIDEO
Presents examples of how the logic of mathematics aids us in describing nature, as well as in using models to formulate laws. Emphasizes the contrasts between physical laws and mathematical theorems.
From The Feynman Lectures - The Character Of Physical Law Series.
Prod-EDC Dist-EDC

Relation Of Transfer Functions And State Variable Representations, The C 53 MIN
3/4 OR 1/2 INCH VIDEO CASSETTE
See series title for descriptive statement.
From The Modern Control Theory - Systems Analysis Series.
Prod-MIOT Dist-MIOT

Relational Data Base C 30 MIN
3/4 OR 1/2 INCH VIDEO CASSETTE
Provides a basic introduction to relational data base systems. Discusses current trends in data processing suggesting the need for improved data management tools and techniques and looks at various data base structures and the advantages and disadvantages associated with each.
From The SQL/DS And Relational Data Base Systems Series.
Prod-DELTAK Dist-DELTAK

Relational Database C 180 MIN
3/4 OR 1/2 INCH VIDEO CASSETTE PRO
Describes relational database and discusses its importance. Covers basic concepts, terminology, programmer and end-user access, data definition and manipulation, views, application programming, security and integrity, transaction processing, frontend systems and storage structures.
Prod-AMCEE Dist-AMCEE

Relational Growth Group--A Series

Presents a series of lectures by Dr Donald R Bardhill, ACSW, on relational family therapy.
Prod-WRAMC Dist-UWISC

Family Genogram, The, Pt 2	045 MIN
Family Grid Demonstration, The, Pt 4	044 MIN
Family Grid Discussion, The, Pt 3	032 MIN
Family Interpersonal Development, Family	042 MIN
Life Stances Genogram, Pt 7	041 MIN
Life Stances, Pt 6	045 MIN
Setting The Context, Pt 1	042 MIN
Termination, Pt 8	050 MIN

Relations B
16MM FILM OPTICAL SOUND
Introduces the concept of a relation on a set and considers equivalence relations. Illustrates the partition of a set into disjoining equivalence classes under an equivalence relation.
Prod-OPENU Dist-OPENU

Relations C 48 MIN
16MM FILM, 3/4 OR 1/2 IN VIDEO T
Shows the relationship between students and teachers in the arts, using the examples of a Kentucky mountain fiddler, an instructor in primitive art and the conductor of the Seattle Youth Symphony.
Prod-FERTIK Dist-PHENIX 1975

Relations - Ringing The Changes C 25 MIN
16MM FILM, 3/4 OR 1/2 IN VIDEO
Discusses the 'Trinitas' symbol found in 13th century manuscripts, which depicts three rings locked together. Asks whether four rings can be linked in the same manner.
Prod-OPENU Dist-MEDIAG Prodn-BBCTV 1979

Relations With The World C 30 MIN
3/4 INCH VIDEO CASSETTE
Examines China's place in the world and its relationship with other countries.
From The China After Mao Series.
Prod-UMITV Dist-UMITV 1980

Relationship Among Protocols C 50 MIN
3/4 OR 1/2 INCH VIDEO CASSETTE PRO
Provides a rationale for the OSI model. Compares it with other approaches.
From The Computer Communications - Protocols And Architectures, Pt 2 Series.
Prod-AMCEE Dist-AMCEE

Relationship And Evolutionary Trends C 45 MIN
3/4 OR 1/2 INCH VIDEO CASSETTE C
Discusses evolutionary trends.
From The Biology I Series.
Prod-MDCPB Dist-MDCPB

Relationship Of Conformation To Lameness C 56 MIN
1/2 IN VIDEO CASSETTE BETA/VHS
Deals with plating, fractures, hoof wall wear, knock knees and other causes of lameness in a horse.
Prod-EQVDL Dist-EQVDL

Relationship Of Problems, The C 22 MIN
3/4 OR 1/2 INCH VIDEO CASSETTE
Instructs the supervisor in determining the seriousness of observed food protection problems, determination of the sources, and establishing priorities for correction.
From The Food Plant Supervisor - Understanding And Performing Inplant Food Safety Insp Series.
Prod-PLAID Dist-PLAID

Relationship Styles C 23 MIN
2 INCH VIDEOTAPE C A
Features a humanistic psychologist who, by analysis and examples, discusses interpersonal relationships.
From The Interpersonal Competence, Unit 01 - The Self Series.
Prod-MVNE Dist-TELSTR 1973

Relationships Among Solids, Liquids, Gases B 15 MIN
2 INCH VIDEOTAPE P
See series title for descriptive statement.
From The Just Wondering Series.
Prod-EOPS Dist-GPITVL Prodn-KOACTV

Relationships Among Structued Techniques C 30 MIN
3/4 OR 1/2 INCH VIDEO CASSETTE
Continues the introductory overview of structured techniques by investigating the relationships among the various structured techniques.
From The Structured Techniques - An Overview Series.
Prod-DELTAK Dist-DELTAK

Relationships Among Structured Techniques C 30 MIN
3/4 OR 1/2 INCH VIDEO CASSETTE
Continues the introductory overview of structured techniques by investigating the relationships among the various structured techniques.

From The Structured Techniques - An Overview Series.
Prod-DELTAK Dist-DELTAK

Relationships And Stress C 30 MIN
16MM FILM, 3/4 OR 1/2 IN VIDEO H-C A
Explains how serious illness can materially change relationships and how people can cope with the emotion and strain that invariably follow the diagnosis of a serious illness.
From The Coping With Serious Illness Series. Number 4
Prod-TIMLIF Dist-TIMLIF 1980

Relationships Of The Elderly C 30 MIN
3/4 OR 1/2 INCH VIDEO CASSETTE C A
Presents the three phases of aging. Considers the physiological realities of aging and changes brought about by retirement in the individual and in the marriage relationship.
From The Family Portrait - A Study Of Contemporary Lifestyles Series. Lesson 29
Prod-SCCON Dist-CDTEL

Relative Age Dating C 33 MIN
3/4 OR 1/2 INCH VIDEO CASSETTE IND
See series title for descriptive statement.
From The Basic And Petroleum Geology For Non-Geologists - Geologic Age Series.
Prod-PHILLP Dist-GPCV

Relative And Absolute Age Dating C 27 MIN
3/4 OR 1/2 INCH VIDEO CASSETTE IND
See series title for descriptive statement.
From The Basic Geology Series.
Prod-GPCV Dist-GPCV

Relative Frequency B 18 MIN
3/4 OR 1/2 INCH VIDEO CASSETTE PRO
Defines relative frequency. Shows that the relative frequency of an event converges to the probability of that event.
From The Probability And Random Processes - Limit Theorems And Statistics Series.
Prod-MIOT Dist-MIOT

Relative Motion B
16MM FILM OPTICAL SOUND
Discusses relative motion in the context of the observed retrograde motion of a planet, and introduces the concept of the derivative of a vector.
Prod-OPENU Dist-OPENU

Relative Movement, Pt 1 - Relative Movement And Interception B 14 MIN
16MM FILM, 3/4 OR 1/2 IN VIDEO
Shows the basic principles of relative movement and interception between planes and ships.
From The Navigation Series.
LC NO. 81-706352
Prod-USN Dist-USNAC 1944

Relative Movement, Pt 2 - Out And In Search, Relative Wind B 13 MIN
16MM FILM, 3/4 OR 1/2 IN VIDEO
Covers relative movement, computing time speed when leaving and returning to a carrier, searching on a relative bearing to a carrier and relative wind.
From The Navigation Series.
LC NO. 81-706353
Prod-USN Dist-USNAC 1944

Relative Position C 14 MIN
3/4 OR 1/2 INCH VIDEO CASSETTE P
Gives experience in observing relative position.
From The Hands On, Grade 2 - Lollipops, Loops, Etc Series. Unit 1 - Observing
Prod-WHROTV Dist-AITECH 1975

Relative Position And Motion C 20 MIN
3/4 INCH VIDEO CASSETTE T
Tells how teachers can instill the ability to accurately locate and describe the motion of objects using time/space relationship terms.
From The Science In The Elementary School - Physical Science Series.
Prod-UWKY Dist-GPITVL 1979

Relativity C 29 MIN
3/4 INCH VIDEO CASSETTE C A
Explains features of Einstein's special theory of relativity. Uses hypothetical examples and scientific observations to illustrate effects of uniform relative motion.
From The Project Universe - Astronomy Series. Lesson 22
Prod-COAST Dist-CDTEL Prodn-SCCON

Relax, Take It Easy C 25 MIN
3/4 OR 1/2 INCH VIDEO CASSETTE
Focuses on stress and the stress-triggered diseases of high blood pressure, headaches and stomach upsets. Suggests that tension may be linked to everything from cancer to stiff necks.
Prod-TRAINX Dist-TRAINX

Relaxation And Imagination C 20 MIN
3/4 OR 1/2 INCH VIDEO CASSETTE I
Introduces drama as a means of communication, begins the relaxation process, and provides several imagination-stretching experiences.
From The Creative Dramatics Series.
Prod-NEWITV Dist-AITECH 1977

Relaxation And Imagination (Teacher) C 30 MIN
3/4 OR 1/2 INCH VIDEO CASSETTE T
Shows classroom demonstrations of beginning creative drama techniques.
From The Creative Dramatics (Teacher) Series.
Prod-NEWITV Dist-AITECH 1977

Relaxation As A form Of Stress Management C 32 MIN
3/4 OR 1/2 INCH VIDEO CASSETTE
See series title for descriptive statement.
From The Practical Stress Management With Dr Barry Alberstein Series.
Prod-DELTAK Dist-DELTAK

Relaxation Oscillations B 30 MIN
3/4 OR 1/2 INCH VIDEO CASSETTE
See series title for descriptive statement.
From The Nonlinear Vibrations Series.
Prod-MIOT Dist-MIOT

Relaxation Tape, The C 30 MIN
3/4 OR 1/2 INCH VIDEO CASSETTE
Presents soothing music and sounds and a narration to help focus the mind for point by point relaxation, controlled breathing, autogenic training, meditation and concentration exercises.
Prod-HP Dist-HP

Relaxation Techniques C 11 MIN
16MM FILM OPTICAL SOUND H-C A
Presents methods of meditation, biofeedback and relaxation therapy that are effective means of reducing stress and keeping its negative effects to a minimum.
From The Stress And You Series.
LC NO. 78-701903
Prod-MAWBYN Dist-AMEDFL Prodn-AMEDFL 1978

Relaxation Techniques B 45 MIN
3/4 OR 1/2 INCH VIDEO CASSETTE
Discusses various types of stress and the effects of stress on muscle tensions. Offers techniques for relieving stress.
Prod-UWISC Dist-UWISC 1979

Relay, The C 11 MIN
16MM FILM, 3/4 OR 1/2 IN VIDEO H-C A
Shows a relay training session and reveals the details of high-speed baton exchange. Depicts a complete race in the European Cup Semi-Finals.
From The Athletics Series.
LC NO. 80-706585
Prod-GSAVL Dist-IU 1980

Relays B 18 MIN
16MM FILM - 3/4 IN VIDEO
Discusses some uses of relays and explains their construction, purpose and operation. Depicts the symbols used to identify various types of relays.
LC NO. 79-707700
Prod-USAF Dist-USNAC 1979

Relays And Vibrators B 18 MIN
16MM FILM, 3/4 OR 1/2 IN VIDEO
Discusses the principles, use and operation of a relay. Shows troubleshooting a relay for an open or shorted coil with an ohmmeter. Describes the vibrator as an intermittent relay and shows its operation and output waveshape. Includes animated sequences.
Prod-USAF Dist-USNAC 1983

Release Of Burn Scar Contracture Of The Knee C 10 MIN
16MM FILM OPTICAL SOUND
Demonstrates the correction of an early post-burn contracture of the popliteal space. Shows that an excellent cosmetic and functional result is obtained by excision of the contracture and coverage of the defect with thick split thickness skin.
LC NO. 75-702315
Prod-EATONL Dist-EATONL 1969

Release Of Information - Or Knowing When To Open Your Mouth And Close The File C 39 MIN
3/4 INCH VIDEO CASSETTE
Deals with the Privacy act, the Freedom of information act, statutes on drugs, alcohol and sickle cell anemia and the Veterans Administration confidentiality statute, 38 USC 3301.
LC NO. 79-707304
Prod-VAHSL Dist-USNAC 1978

Release Of The Inner-Self - Hesse C 45 MIN
2 INCH VIDEOTAPE
See series title for descriptive statement.
From The Humanities Series. Unit III - The Realm Of Idea And Speculation
Prod-WTTWTV Dist-GPITVL

Relevance And Witnesses C 33 MIN
3/4 OR 1/2 INCH VIDEO CASSETTE PRO
Analyzes prohibition against evidence of subsequent remedial measures and discusses exceptions offered to prove ownership and control or feasability of precautionary measures.
From The Evidence Update Series.
Prod-ABACPE Dist-ABACPE

Reliability - Economic Considerations In Reliability C 20 MIN
16MM FILM, 3/4 OR 1/2 IN VIDEO
Shows applications of break-even analysis for use in selection from competing systems and for economic decisions when changes to a system are considered.
LC NO. 81-706753
Prod-USN Dist-USNAC 1965

Reliability - Elements Of Reliability Prediction C 30 MIN
16MM FILM, 3/4 OR 1/2 IN VIDEO
Shows how prediction techniques are used on major components of a weapon system. Describes how predictions are made in drawing-board phase and refined in bench test and prototype test phase.
LC NO. 81-706751
Prod-USN Dist-USNAC 1964

Reliability - Fundamental Concepts, Pt 1 C 30 MIN
16MM FILM, 3/4 OR 1/2 IN VIDEO
Presents some of the fundamental concepts of reliability engineering that shall be used by designers of national weapons systems to achieve maximum inherent reliability in the design.
LC NO. 81-706744
Prod-USN Dist-USNAC 1961

Reliability - Fundamental Concepts, Pt 2 C 30 MIN
16MM FILM, 3/4 OR 1/2 IN VIDEO
Presents fundamentals of engineering that should be used by designers of naval weapons systems to achieve the maximum inherent reliability in the design.
LC NO. 81-706745
Prod-USN Dist-USNAC 1961

Reliability - Part And Parcel C 28 MIN
16MM FILM, 3/4 OR 1/2 IN VIDEO
Describes reliability standards established within Air Force Systems and Logistics Commands. Explains how the standards serve as production requirements and management tools in procurement of electronic replacement parts. Shows how the standards reduce costs and increase product reliability.
Prod-USAF Dist-USNAC 1963

Reliability - Reliability Analysis C 30 MIN
16MM FILM, 3/4 OR 1/2 IN VIDEO
Presents advanced methods and techniques of reliability analysis. Studies an actual problem and demonstrates regression techniques, design improvement analysis and the Monte Carlo technique.
Prod-USN Dist-USNAC

Reliability - Reliability Monitoring C 20 MIN
16MM FILM, 3/4 OR 1/2 IN VIDEO
Shows how a program is monitored from concept through use phase and shows how data is used.
LC NO. 81-706752
Prod-USN Dist-USNAC 1964

Reliability - Reliability Testing C 25 MIN
16MM FILM, 3/4 OR 1/2 IN VIDEO
Depicts fundamentals of reliability testing design.
LC NO. 81-706748
Prod-USN Dist-USNAC 1962

Reliability - Specifications And Reliability Assurance C 25 MIN
16MM FILM, 3/4 OR 1/2 IN VIDEO
Describes the philosophy and function of specifications in relation to achievement of reliability assurance, general and detailed specifications, environment, interferences, interactions and interfaces affecting system performance requirements.
LC NO. 81-706749
Prod-USN Dist-USNAC 1963

Reliability - Statistical Concepts C 25 MIN
16MM FILM, 3/4 OR 1/2 IN VIDEO
Describes reliability engineering methods and demonstrates the basic concepts on which the analytical methods are based.
LC NO. 81-706746
Prod-USN Dist-USNAC 1961

Reliability - The Application Of Reliability Data C 21 MIN
16MM FILM, 3/4 OR 1/2 IN VIDEO
Shows application of feedback to the solution of problems arising during the life cycle of a weapon system.
LC NO. 81-706750
Prod-USN Dist-USNAC 1964

Reliability Applications B 30 MIN
3/4 OR 1/2 INCH VIDEO CASSETTE PRO
Introduces computation of reliability, standard configurations of networks and components in series and in parallel.
From The Probability And Random Processes - Random Variables Series.
Prod-MIOT Dist-MIOT

Reliability Apportionment And Growth C 30 MIN
3/4 OR 1/2 INCH VIDEO CASSETTE IND
Describes how the reliability of successive generations of a product should improve. Shows a dynamic programming procedure to direct efforts to activities with greatest reliability payoffs.
From The Reliability Engineering Series.
Prod-COLOSU Dist-COLOSU

Reliability Approach To Safety - A Management Introduction C
16MM FILM - 3/4 IN VIDEO A
Describes the reliability approach to safety, illustrates its effectiveness, the techniques used and shows how it anticipates potential trouble spots before they become serious.
Prod-BNA Dist-BNA 1983

Reliability Engineering C 25 MIN
3/4 OR 1/2 INCH VIDEO CASSETTE
Covers Reliability Engineering principles, times-to-failure acquisition, failure rate calculation, reliability, time-to-failure, and failure rate function determination for early, useful and wearout life periods.
Prod-UAZMIC Dist-UAZMIC

Reliability Engineering - Introduction C 30 MIN
3/4 OR 1/2 INCH VIDEO CASSETTE IND
Provides introduction by defning reliability and describing various models to predict mode of failure. Describes graphical techniques to estimate failure distribution.
From The Reliability Engineering Series.
Prod-COLOSU Dist-COLOSU

Reliability Engineering - Reliability Testing C 30 MIN
16MM FILM, 3/4 OR 1/2 IN VIDEO
Presents advanced methods of techniques of reliability analysis.
LC NO. 81-706747
Prod-USN Dist-USNAC 1961

Reliability Engineering Principles And Benefits With Applications—A Series

Provides an overview of the techniques for predicting the reliability of components, equipment and systems, the determination of the failure rate of components and other methodologies regarding product reliability and assurance.
Prod-UAZMIC Dist-UAZMIC

Course Objectives, Reliability And	
Early, Chance, And Wearout Reliability -	060 MIN
Failure Identification, Actual Failure Rate	060 MIN
Reliability Engineering Program Functions,	060 MIN
Standby, Load-Sharing, Multimode Function,	060 MIN

Reliability Engineering Program Functions, Reliability Data Feedback And Corrective... B 60 MIN
3/4 OR 1/2 INCH VIDEO CASSETTE
Discusses reliability engineering program functions, reliability data feedback and corrective action system, reliability growth, cost benefits of implementing reliability and maintainability engineering programs and how to reduce equipment cost while increasing its reliability.
From The Reliability Engineering Principles And Benefits With Applications Series. Pt 5
Prod-UAZMIC Dist-UAZMIC

Reliability Engineering—A Series
IND
Reveals that most field problems with either electronic or mechanical systems are reliability problems. Points out that Reliability Engineering course should help to both predict and improve product liability.
Prod-COLOSU Dist-COLOSU

Chance Failures	030 MIN
Chance Failures - Examples	030 MIN
Comparison Test Programs	030 MIN
Comparison Tests - Examples	030 MIN
Designing Reliability Into A Product	030 MIN
Lot Acceptance Sampling	030 MIN
Mil-STD-781C - Examples	030 MIN
Nonparametric Tests - Examples	030 MIN
Optimum Burn-In	030 MIN
Predicting Reliability During Development Test	030 MIN
Qualification Test Programs	030 MIN
Qualification Tests - Examples	030 MIN
Reliability Apportionment And Growth	030 MIN
Reliability Engineering - Introduction	030 MIN
Series, Parallel And Standby - Examples	030 MIN
Series, Parallel And Standby Systems	030 MIN
Software Reliability	030 MIN
Wearout Failure	030 MIN
Wearout Failure - Examples	030 MIN
Weibull Failure Model	030 MIN
Weibull Probability Paper - Example	030 MIN

Reliability Of Inferences Based On Number Of Observations B 15 MIN
2 INCH VIDEOTAPE P
See series title for descriptive statement.
From The Just Inquisitive Series. No. 24
Prod-EOPS Dist-GPITVL Prodn-KOACTV

Reliability Of Semiconductor Memories C 60 MIN
1 INCH VIDEOTAPE IND
Establishes failure rates of future semiconductor memory systems using basic reliability information on integrated circuits.
From The Semiconductor Memories Course Series. No. 7
Prod-TXINLC Dist-TXINLC

Reliability Testing C 28 MIN
3/4 OR 1/2 INCH VIDEO CASSETTE
Covers Reliability Testing principles, the failure rate concept, time-to-failure distribution, failure rate function and reliability function determination.
Prod-UAZMIC Dist-UAZMIC

Reliable Software C 35 MIN
3/4 INCH VIDEO CASSETTE C A
See series title for descriptive statement.
From The Software Management For Small Computers Series.
LC NO. 81-706201
Prod-AMCEE Dist-AMCEE 1980

Relief Carving C 29 MIN
3/4 OR 1/2 INCH VIDEO CASSETTE
See series title for descriptive statement.
From The Woodcarver's Workshop Series.
Prod-WOSUTV Dist-PBS

Relief Of Obstruction Of Superior Vena Cava By Venous Autografts C 31 MIN
16MM FILM OPTICAL SOUND PRO
Shows excision of benign, calcific obstruction of the superior vena cava in a young woman. Shows that continuity is restored by femoral vein autografts between innominate veins and intra-pericardial vena cava.
Prod-ACYDGD Dist-ACY 1956

Relief Printing C 25 MIN
3/4 OR 1/2 INCH VIDEO CASSETTE H-C A
Demonstrates a method of making a lino-cut flower print. Shows cutting, inking and printing cardboard to make a brightly colored interior scene.
From The Artist In Print Series.
Prod-BBCTV Dist-FI

Relief Valves C 120 MIN
3/4 OR 1/2 INCH VIDEO CASSETTE IND
Features steam and gas safety valves. Highlights electrically operated relief valves.
From The Mechanical Equipment Maintenance Series.
Prod-ITCORP Dist-ITCORP

Relief Valves (Spanish) C 120 MIN
3/4 OR 1/2 INCH VIDEO CASSETTE IND
Features steam and gas safety valves. Highlights electrically operated relief valves.
From The Mechanical Equipment Maintenance (Spanish) Series.
Prod-ITCORP Dist-ITCORP

Relieve Stress And Anxiety B 30 MIN
3/4 OR 1/2 INCH VIDEO CASSETTE
Relieves stress and anxiety through subliminal suggestions.
Prod-ADVCAS Dist-ADVCAS

Relieving Your Pain With Brain Stimulation C 18 MIN
3/4 INCH VIDEO CASSETTE A
Presents patient information on deep brain stimulation. Includes techniques, hospital stay and recovery for one method of pain relief.
Prod-KRI Dist-KRI

Relieving Your Pain With Spinal Cord Stimulation C 16 MIN
3/4 INCH VIDEO CASSETTE A
Provides patient information on spinal cord stimulation. Includes techniques and hospital stay and recovery.
Prod-KRI Dist-KRI

Religion - Life After Death C 25 MIN
3/4 OR 1/2 INCH VIDEO CASSETTE J-C A
Discusses religion with the Rev Pat Fenske in Philadelphia and Rabbi Ephraim Buchwald in New York. Describes a first-hand 'near death' experience.
Prod-SIRS Dist-SIRS

Religion And Magic C 30 MIN
3/4 INCH VIDEO CASSETTE C A
Describes a variety of religious practices. Includes the roles of gods and goddesses, worship of ancestral spirits, animism, and various rituals and ceremonies.
From The Faces Of Culture - Studies In Cultural Anthropology Series. Lesson 19
Prod-COAST Dist-CDTEL Prodn-HRAW

Religion And Politics B 30 MIN
16MM FILM OPTICAL SOUND H-C A
Dr C Eric Lincoln discusses the role of ministers in the social protest of Black Americans in urban ghettos during the period 1945-1954, and the effect of two wars, the N A A C P, and other factors in shaping political ideologies.
From The Black History, Section 18 - A Period Of Transition, 1945-1954 Series.
LC NO. 72-704099
Prod-WCBSTV Dist-HRAW 1969

Religion And Resistance B 30 MIN
16MM FILM OPTICAL SOUND H-C A
Vincent Harding exposes the spiritual undercurrent which aided and abetted the active resistance of blacks to enslavement, including the revolutionary messages shrouded in religion that revolt leaders such as Nat Turner and Denmark Vesey used. He discusses such hymns as Steal Away in which the slaves secretly encouraged one another to quit the services of the master and either live a life of rebellion in the South or escape to the North.
From The Black History, Section 05 - Rebellion And Resistance Series.
LC NO. 76-704049
Prod-WCBSTV Dist-HRAW 1969

Religion And The Clergy B 35 MIN
3/4 INCH VIDEO CASSETTE
See series title for descriptive statement.
From The Terminal Illness Series.
Prod-UWASHP Dist-UWASHP

Religion In A Post-Holocaust World—A Series

Discusses various aspects of religion in a post-holocaust world.
Prod-OHC Dist-HRC

Anti-Semitism In The New Testament	141 MIN
Defining The Holocaust	155 MIN
German Church, The	120 MIN
Reshaping Values After The Holocaust	180 MIN

Religion In America C 30 MIN
3/4 OR 1/2 INCH VIDEO CASSETTE C
Discusses the status and history of religion in America. Examines secularization as a complex and important process affecting organized religion.
From The Focus On Society Series.
Prod-DALCCD Dist-DALCCD

Religion In Indonesia - The Way Of The Ancestors C 52 MIN
16MM FILM, 3/4 OR 1/2 IN VIDEO H-C A
Visits the Torajas of Indonesia to investigate the experience of primal worship. Explores the reasons for the survival of the Torajas' religion at a time when other primal religions are dying out as a result of contact with the outside world.
From The Long Search Series. No. 8
LC NO. 79-707795
Prod-BBCTV Dist-TIMLIF 1978

Religion In Nigeria - Christianity C 28 MIN
16MM FILM - 1/2 IN VIDEO, VHS A
Presents a documentary depicting conversations with church leaders, people at worship and commentators on the interaction of religions in Nigeria. Explores such issues as indigenization (bringing more African cultural influence into the church), secularization of education, provision of social services, the role of women and contributions of Christianity to contemporary Nigerian society and world culture.
Prod-CBSTV Dist-ECUFLM 1982

Religion In Nigeria - Islam C 28 MIN
1/2 IN VIDEO CASSETTE (VHS) A
Looks at Islam, the dominant religion in Nigeria. Discusses its hundreds of year history and the varied ethnic groups that practice Islam in Nigeria today.
Prod-CBSTV Dist-ECUFLM 1982

Religion In Russia C 21 MIN
16MM FILM, 3/4 OR 1/2 IN VIDEO J-C A
See series title for descriptive statement.
From The Russia Today Series.
Prod-IFF Dist-IFF

Religion, Pt 1 B 15 MIN
16MM FILM OPTICAL SOUND I-C A
Shows Murphy, North Carolina where the Bible laws are engraved in letters sic feet high at Ten Commandment mountain. Shows a devout band of Pilgrims winding toward Mecca - birthplace of Mohammedanism.
Prod-HEARST Dist-HEARST

Religion, Pt 2 B 14 MIN
16MM FILM OPTICAL SOUND J-C A
Shows the ancient documents now know as the 'DEAD SEA SCROLLS' fround in a cave near the Dead Sea. Shows two of the most famous rituals of the Roman Catholic church recorded - the burial of a Pope, and the selection and crowning of his successor, Pope John XXIII. Shows the dedication of the American Memorial Chapel at St Paul's Cathedral in London.
Prod-HEARST Dist-HEARST

Religion, The C 15 MIN
3/4 OR 1/2 INCH VIDEO CASSETTE I
Examines the very special place religion has in the cultures of the Baoule of West Africa, the Tarahumara of Mexico and the Japanese.
From The Across Cultures Series.
Prod-POSIMP Dist-AITECH Prodn-WETN 1983

Religious Experience C 25 MIN
3/4 OR 1/2 INCH VIDEO CASSETTE C
See series title for descriptive statement.
From The Introduction To Philosophy Series.
Prod-UDEL Dist-UDEL

Religious Experience, Pt 1 C 30 MIN
3/4 OR 1/2 INCH VIDEO CASSETTE H-C A
Examines the major religions in Japan.
From The Japan - The Living Tradition Series.
Prod-UMA Dist-GPITVL 1976

Religious Experience, Pt 2 C 30 MIN
3/4 OR 1/2 INCH VIDEO CASSETTE H-C A
Examines the major religions in Japan.
From The Japan - The Living Tradition Series.
Prod-UMA Dist-GPITVL 1976

Religious Experience, The C 17 MIN
16MM FILM, 3/4 OR 1/2 IN VIDEO H-C A
Explores the various facets of the religious experience, discusses the meaning of religion to man and portrays the forms and rituals of several religions.
From The Humanities Series.
Prod-MGHT Dist-MGHT 1971

Religious Laws As The Source Of Joy C 28 MIN
3/4 OR 1/2 INCH VIDEO CASSETTE
Discusses three liberating experiences gained through observance of religious law. Features Rabbi David Hartman.
From The Tradition And Contemporary Judaism - Joy And Responsibility Series. Program 1
Prod-ADL Dist-ADL

Religious Liberty C 30 MIN
3/4 OR 1/2 INCH VIDEO CASSETTE J-C A
Presents Glenn L Archer of Americans United Foundation and C Stanley Lowell, Associate Director of Church And State magazine, talking about religious liberty.
From The Moral Values In Contemporary Society Series.
Prod-AMHUMA Dist-AMHUMA

Religious Neighborhoods - City C 15 MIN
3/4 OR 1/2 INCH VIDEO CASSETTE P
Looks at religious neighborhoods in cities.
From The Neighborhoods Series.
Prod-NEITV Dist-GPITVL 1981

Religious Neighborhoods - Rural C 15 MIN
3/4 OR 1/2 INCH VIDEO CASSETTE P
Looks at rural religious neighborhoods.
From The Neighborhoods Series.
Prod-NEITV Dist-GPITVL 1981

Religious Neighborhoods - Town C 15 MIN
3/4 OR 1/2 INCH VIDEO CASSETTE P
Looks at religious neighborhoods in towns.
From The Neighborhoods Series.
Prod-NEITV Dist-GPITVL 1981

Relocation C 22 MIN
3/4 OR 1/2 INCH VIDEO CASSETTE H
Presents high school senior Jerry Malone discussing home ownership.
From The Dollar Scholar Series. Pt 8
LC NO. 82-707406
Prod-BCSBIT Dist-GPITVL 1982

Reluctant Astronaut, The C 102 MIN
16MM FILM OPTICAL SOUND
Presents Don Knotts as an astronaut in an amusement park. Deals with a funny situation that arises when Knotts is sent to Washington for space duty.
Prod-SWAMD Dist-SWANK

Reluctant Braider, The C 8 MIN
16MM FILM OPTICAL SOUND IND
Studies the development and recognition of attitudes and attitude changes that vitally affect any kind of production. Asks how much to monitor the work of the old hand who has an enviable work record and how to motivate this 'EXPERT' into changing the technique.
From The Human Side Of Supervision Series.
LC NO. 73-701928
Prod-VOAERO Dist-VOAERO 1972

Reluctant Delinquent, The C 24 MIN
16MM FILM, 3/4 OR 1/2 IN VIDEO C A
Examines the high correlation between learning disabilities and juvenile delinquency. Presents a positive case history of what can be done to help young people with undiagnosed learning disabilities avoid problems with the law.
Prod-EISBGI Dist-MTI 1978

Reluctant Delinquent, The C 24 MIN
16MM FILM - 3/4 IN VIDEO
Shows the relationship between learning disabilities and delinquency. Tells the story of a 17-year-old boy who stays in Juvenile Hall on weekends and attends a special school on weekdays.
Prod-LAWREN Dist-LAWREN

Reluctant Dragon, The C 12 MIN
16MM FILM, 3/4 OR 1/2 IN VIDEO P-J
Recounts the story of a boy who discovers that the terrifying dragon who lives in a cave near his village wants nothing more than to live peacefully and write poetry. Reveals that when a famous dragon slayer appears in the village, both he and the boy visit the dragon and agree to stage a mock battle in order to save their reputations and appease the villagers.
From The Misunderstood Monsters Series.
Prod-BOSUST Dist-CF 1981

Reluctant Dragon, The C 19 MIN
16MM FILM, 3/4 OR 1/2 IN VIDEO K-I
An edited version of the 1941 motion picture The Reluctant Dragon. Uses animation to tell the story of a dragon who is shy and poetic rather than ferocious. Based on the story The Reluctant Dragon by Kenneth Grahame.
Prod-DISNEY Dist-WDEMCO 1979

Reluctant Politician, The - The Life And Presidency Of William Howard Taft C 28 MIN
3/4 INCH VIDEO CASSETTE
Dramatizes the life and political career of former President William Howard Taft.
Prod-OHC Dist-HRC

Reluctant World Power, The C 29 MIN
16MM FILM, 3/4 OR 1/2 IN VIDEO J-C A
Portrays the agonizing process by which the United States assumed, then rejected, and then finally was obliged to accept the role of a major power.
From The History Of U S Foreign Relations Series.
Prod-USDS Dist-MTI 1972

Remarkable Mountain Goat, The C 20 MIN
3/4 OR 1/2 INCH VIDEO CASSETTE J-C A
Shows the mountain goat in the highest crags of the Rocky Mountains where no other large mammal lives year around. Depicts this remote home in the alpine areas where the mountain goats feeling the pressures of modern civilization as people seek minerals, timber and recreation.
Prod-BERLET Dist-BERLET

Remarkable Phagocyte, The C 22 MIN
3/4 OR 1/2 INCH VIDEO CASSETTE
Shows actions of granulocytes in response to various foreign bodies and micro-organisms by means of animation and scenes through a microscope.
Prod-WFP Dist-WFP

Remarkable Riderless Runaway Tricycle, The C 11 MIN
16MM FILM, 3/4 OR 1/2 IN VIDEO P
Tells a story of a tricycle whose young owner distractedly abandons it. Shows how it ends up in a dump, escapes, careens around town in a series of humorous hijinks and then returns, at last, to its downcast owner. Based on the book The Remarkable Riderless Runaway Tricycle by Bruce McMillan.
LC NO. 82-706508
Prod-EVRGRN Dist-PHENIX 1982

Remarkable Rocket, The C 25 MIN
16MM FILM, 3/4 OR 1/2 IN VIDEO
Tells the story of a pompous-looking rocket who feels he is the most important part of a lavish fireworks display until he dampens his own fuse with his tears of pride. Features David Niven as narrator of this Oscar Wilde short story.
Prod-READER Dist-PFP 1975

Remarriage C 30 MIN
3/4 OR 1/2 INCH VIDEO CASSETTE C A
Discusses the readjustment of the family when a remarriage occurs following a divorce or death of a spouse.
From The Family Portrait - A Study Of Contemporary Lifestyles Series. Lesson 23
Prod-SCCON Dist-CDTEL

Remarrieds, The C 29 MIN
3/4 OR 1/2 INCH VIDEO CASSETTE
Suggests how people who want to remarry can prevent the problems that broke up their first marriages.
From The Woman Series.
Prod-WNEDTV Dist-PBS

Rembitika C 50 MIN
16MM FILM, 3/4 OR 1/2 IN VIDEO J-C A
Introduces Rembitika, the often-melancholy music brought to Greece after the 1921 tragedy at Smyrna, Turkey and the subsequent Greek and Turkish exchange of minority religious groups. Presents the music being performed by master musicians and by contemporary groups, who have adopted past performers' styles or added new interpretations of the bousouki-accompanied songs.
LC NO. 84-706001
Prod-MONROS Dist-WOMBAT 1983

Rembrandt C 27 MIN
16MM FILM OPTICAL SOUND J-C A
Presents the life of Rembrandt from his childhood to his successful elder years. Shows many of his paintings and masterpieces.
From The Human Dimension Series.
LC NO. 73-700906
Prod-GRACUR Dist-GRACUR 1972

Rembrandt C 7 MIN
16MM FILM, 3/4 OR 1/2 IN VIDEO J-C
Concentrates on Rembrandt's aesthetic and dramatic use of light and shade. Considers Rembrandt's richly painted and sensitive portraits, then progresses to his etchings of New Testament scenes.
From The Art Awareness Collection Series.
Prod-USNGA Dist-EBEC 1974

Rembrandt B 29 MIN
3/4 INCH VIDEO CASSETTE
Discusses Rembrandt's genius. Reproduces a portion of Man in the Gold Helmet to show the master's technique.
From The Meet The Masters Series.
Prod-UMITV Dist-UMITV 1966

Rembrandt - Painter Of Man C 20 MIN
16MM FILM OPTICAL SOUND J-C A
Presents selected canvases gathered from twenty-nine museums in twelve countries. These show Rembrandt's amazing ability in the use of light and shadow and his genius in expressing human compassion for his subjects. Made in commemoration of the 350th anniversary of Rembrandt's birth.
Prod-NETHIS Dist-CORF Prodn-HA 1958

Rembrandt Van Rijn - A Self-Portrait C 27 MIN
16MM FILM, 3/4 OR 1/2 IN VIDEO J-C
Uses Rembrandt's self-portraits to depict his life from the time he was a young cavalier to when he was an old man. Explains that he was one of Holland's most popular portrait painters, but gave up fame and wealth to follow his true artistic inclinations.
Prod-EBF Dist-EBEC 1955

Rembrandt's Christ (1606-1669) B 40 MIN
16MM FILM OPTICAL SOUND
Depicts the story of Christ as drawn by Rembrandt. Takes place in the houses, towns, canals, streets and fields of 17th century Holland.
Prod-ROLAND Dist-ROLAND 1964

Remedial Reading - Who, What, Why And How C 23 MIN
16MM FILM OPTICAL SOUND C S
Offers explanations of corrective and remedial reading programs for students in elementary and secondary school levels, as well as possible causative factors leading to reading disability. Features Dr Albert J Mazurkiewicz in a reading clinic to show diagnosis and remedial situations in action. Shows examples of VAK VAKT and neurological impress techniques.
From The Jab Reading Series.
LC NO. 75-701424
Prod-JABP Dist-JBFL 1975

Remedial Typing C 11 MIN
16MM FILM, 3/4 OR 1/2 IN VIDEO J-H
Demonstrates clear and concise information concerning reading, rhythm and pre-positioning, showing that the most common typing errors result from poor posture and finger positioning, a bad striking action and carriage return, unrhythmic typing and a generally careless attitude.
Prod-SF Dist-SF 1969

Remedies Phase Of An EEO Case - Class Back Pay And Proof Of Claims—A Series
PRO
Comprises the first in a three series seminar. Focuses on what happens after a finding of liability. Features conferences, hearings and trial demonstrations.
Prod-ALIABA Dist-ABACPE

Class Back Pay 057 MIN
Panel Discussions 049 MIN
Proof Of Claims Hearing 058 MIN

Remedies Phase Of An EEO Case - Contested Settlement And Attorneys' Fees Trial—A Series
PRO
Comprises the third in a three series law seminar. Presents conferences, hearings and trial demonstrations. Covers a contested settlement through the attorneys' fees trial.
Prod-ALIABA Dist-ABACPE

Attorneys' Fees Trial 055 MIN
Closing Arguments And Panel Discussion 042 MIN
Contested Settlement 057 MIN

Remedies Phase Of An EEO Case - Individual Determinations—A Series
PRO
Comprised the second program in a three series seminar. Focuses on a hypothetical trial based on a sex and race discrimination class action suit. Includes witness examination and a panel discussion.
Prod-ALIABA Dist-ABACPE

Opening Statements And First Witness 043 MIN
Panel Discussion 037 MIN
Second And Third Witnesses 044 MIN

Remedy For Riot B 37 MIN
3/4 INCH VIDEO CASSETTE
Examines 1967 riots. Explores problems within the ghetto and and role of law enforcement. Based on a report of the National Advisory Commission on Civil Disorders.
Prod-CBSNEW Dist-ADL 1968

Remember C 60 MIN
16MM FILM OPTICAL SOUND H-C A
From The World At War Series.
LC NO. 76-701778
Prod-THAMES Dist-USCAN 1975

Remember C 52 MIN
16MM FILM, 3/4 OR 1/2 IN VIDEO H-C A
States that the war is the most memorable experience in the lives of many men and women all over the world. Many veterans feel alienated from those who did not experience the war because they cannot or prefer not to understand it.
From The World At War Series.
Prod-THAMES Dist-MEDIAG 1973

Remember Me C 10 MIN
16MM FILM, 3/4 OR 1/2 IN VIDEO H A
Looks at several typical examples of salesperson-customer interface and shows that it is not whether the customer's desired service can be fulfilled that is important, but the attitude with which the customer is treated.
LC NO. 81-707267
Prod-CRMP Dist-CRMP 1981

Remember Me C 15 MIN
16MM FILM, 3/4 OR 1/2 IN VIDEO
Presents portraits of children from around the world and the environments in which they live. Emphasizes the influence of environment on daily life.
Prod-UNICEF Dist-PFP Prodn-DYP 1979

Remember Me (Spanish) C 10 MIN
16MM FILM, 3/4 OR 1/2 IN VIDEO H A
Looks at several typical examples of salesperson-customer interface and shows that it is not whether the customer's service can be fulfilled that is important, but the attitude with which the customer is treated.
Prod-CRMP Dist-CRMP 1981

Remember My Name C 18 MIN
16MM FILM OPTICAL SOUND
Illustrates the frustrations of employees in lower level, deadended jobs. Stresses the need for management and supervisory actions to bring about equality of opportunity in employment and upward mobility within the Federal Government.
LC NO. 75-700575
Prod-USCSC Dist-USNAC 1972

Remember Pearl Harbor - America At War, 1941-45 B 17 MIN
16MM FILM OPTICAL SOUND J-C A
Recalls America's entry into World War II with the attack on Pearl Harbor, and her subsequent involvement in Guadalcanal, Europe and the Pacific. Shows effects of the war at home and the final Allied victories.
From The Screen New Digest Series. Vol 9, Issue 5
LC NO. 70-700284
Prod-HEARST Dist-HEARST 1966

Remember The Audience C 14 MIN
16MM FILM, 3/4 OR 1/2 IN VIDEO I
Tells how three young filmmakers make a film that will be shown around the world, taking into account that most of the viewers will speak no English.
From The Thinkabout Series. Giving And Getting Meaning
LC NO. 81-706120
Prod-KERA Dist-AITECH 1979

Remember The Ladies - Women In America 1750- 1815 C 25 MIN
16MM FILM OPTICAL SOUND
Documents the exhibition Remember The Ladies held at the Corcoran Art Gallery. Traces the changing lifestyle, position and concerns of colonial women through the art, artifacts and documents of the period.
LC NO. 77-702130
Prod-PHILMO Dist-MTP Prodn-CUNLIM 1977

Remember The Main - An Introduction To Commercial Arbitration C 22 MIN
16MM FILM OPTICAL SOUND A
Shows the arbitration which occurs when a construction company applies to the city for permission to move a water main, the city delays and construction costs back up.
Prod-AARA Dist-AARA 1981

Remembering C 15 MIN
3/4 OR 1/2 INCH VIDEO CASSETTE P
See series title for descriptive statement.
From The Strawberry Square Series.
Prod-NEITV Dist-AITECH 1982

Remembering C 57 MIN
16MM FILM, 3/4 OR 1/2 IN VIDEO H-C A
Gives a broad overview of historic and modern China.
From The Heart Of The Dragon Series. Pt 1
Prod-ASH Dist-TIMLIF 1984

Remembering Happy Times C 29 MIN
16MM FILM, 3/4 OR 1/2 IN VIDEO
Looks at the images artists create to portray the happy, exciting or tender moments of an earlier day. Considers how art preserves the scenes of people enjoying and cherishing life.
From The Images And Things Series.
LC NO. 73-702108
Prod-NITC Dist-AITECH

Remembering Jack Cole C 30 MIN
3/4 OR 1/2 INCH VIDEO CASSETTE
See series title for descriptive statement.
From The Broadway Series.
Prod-ARCVID Dist-ARCVID

Remembering Jackie Robinson C 14 MIN
3/4 OR 1/2 INCH VIDEO CASSETTE
Examines the historical implications and social significance of Jackie Robinson's breaking the color barrier to become the first black man to play in the major leagues.
Prod-KINGFT Dist-KINGFT 1983

Remembering Life C 28 MIN
16MM FILM, 3/4 OR 1/2 IN VIDEO H-C A
Documents the history of Life magazine. Presents photographers and editors of Life who describe their experiences and Life's impact on the country and on modern journalism.
Prod-VARDIR Dist-MTI

Remembering Names And Faces C 17 MIN
16MM FILM, 3/4 OR 1/2 IN VIDEO A
Portrays a salesman who cannot recall the name of an important customer. Shows him going to a memory expert who demonstrates how to fix a name firmly in the mind so that it can be recalled easily.
Prod-RTBL Dist-RTBL

Remembering Names And Faces (Dutch) C 17 MIN
16MM FILM, 3/4 OR 1/2 IN VIDEO A
Portrays a salesman who cannot recall the name of an important customer. Shows him going to a memory expert who demonstrates how to fix a name firmly in the mind so that it can be recalled easily.
Prod-RTBL Dist-RTBL

Remembering Thelma C 15 MIN
16MM FILM OPTICAL SOUND
Documents the late dance instructor and performer, Thelma Hill, and her influence on the development of black dance in America. Includes film footage and photographs of her performances.
Prod-BLKFMF Dist-BLKFMF

Remembering Winsor Mc Cay C 20 MIN
16MM FILM, 3/4 OR 1/2 IN VIDEO J-C T
Profiles American animation pioneer Winsor Mc Cay, including excerpts from his classics, Gertie The Dinosaur, The Sinking Of The Lusitania, and the rare hand-colored version of Little Nemo.
LC NO. 81-706790
Prod-CANEJ Dist-PHENIX 1978

Remembrance Of Toribio, A C 30 MIN
3/4 OR 1/2 INCH VIDEO CASSETTE
See series title for descriptive statement.
From The Mundo Real Series.
Prod-CPT Dist-MDCPB

Remington And AVA - American Art C
3/4 OR 1/2 INCH VIDEO CASSETTE
Prod-MSTVIS Dist-MSTVIS

Remington Shaver Shaving A Peach C 1 MIN
3/4 OR 1/2 INCH VIDEO CASSETTE
Shows a classic television commercial.
Prod-BROOKC Dist-BROOKC

Remnants Of A Race C 18 MIN
16MM FILM, 3/4 OR 1/2 IN VIDEO I-H
Explores the life of the Bushmen who live in the desolate Kalahari Desert of South-Central Africa. Shows these people in their search for food. Presents examples of their local art work.
Prod-KALAHR Dist-EBEC 1953

Remote Possibilities C 15 MIN
3/4 OR 1/2 INCH VIDEO CASSETTE
Explains the functions of NASA's 'Spy in the Sky,' the satellite LANDSAT program in terms of its non-military applications.
From The LANDSAT Series.
Prod-IVCH Dist-IVCH

Remote Possibilities C 15 MIN
16MM FILM - 3/4 IN VIDEO
Discusses the concept of remote sensing and explains how the Landsat satellite's remote sensing capabilities can aid in the management of Earth's natural resources.
From The Environmental Series - Landsat - Satellite For All Seasons Series.
LC NO. 78-706008
Prod-NASA Dist-USNAC Prodn-NVETA 1977

Remote Sensing C 30 MIN
3/4 OR 1/2 INCH VIDEO CASSETTE C
Explains the process and the value of remote sensing. Demonstrates some work with crop analysis, thermatic mapping, forestry, perma frost, hurricane damage and urban sprawl using Landsat images.
From The Earth, Sea And Sky Series.
Prod-DALCCD Dist-DALCCD

Remote Sensing Detectors C 60 MIN
3/4 OR 1/2 INCH VIDEO CASSETTE
See series title for descriptive statement.
From The Advanced Remote Sensing Techniques Series. Section I, Pt 9
Prod-UAZMIC Dist-UAZMIC

Remote Sensing Information System, The C 30 MIN
3/4 OR 1/2 INCH VIDEO CASSETTE
Provides a non-mathematical description of the multispectral technique and how it can be applied to obtain information from current satellite data as well as future satellites with more advanced sensors.
From The Introduction To Quantitative Analysis Of Remote Sensing Data Series.
Prod-PUAVC Dist-PUAVC

Remote Sensing Instruments C 60 MIN
3/4 OR 1/2 INCH VIDEO CASSETTE
See series title for descriptive statement.
From The Advanced Remote Sensing Techniques Series. Section I, Pt 8
Prod-UAZMIC Dist-UAZMIC

Remote Sensing Systems, Pt 1 C 60 MIN
3/4 OR 1/2 INCH VIDEO CASSETTE
See series title for descriptive statement.
From The Advanced Remote Sensing Techniques Series. Section I, Pt 10
Prod-UAZMIC Dist-UAZMIC

Remote Sensing Systems, Pt 2 C 60 MIN
3/4 OR 1/2 INCH VIDEO CASSETTE
See series title for descriptive statement.
From The Advanced Remote Sensing Techniques Series. Section I, Pt 11
Prod-UAZMIC Dist-UAZMIC

Remotely Piloted Vehicle C 7 MIN
16MM FILM OPTICAL SOUND
Introduces the QF86H target system with details of the first successful flight as a real-size, all-attitude, highly-maneuverable, remotely-piloted vehicle.
LC NO. 74-706563
Prod-USN Dist-USNAC 1973

Removable Partial Denture Design - The RPI Clasp Assembly C 14 MIN
16MM FILM, 3/4 OR 1/2 IN VIDEO PRO
Demonstrates use of the RPI clasp assembly, which exhibits minimal tooth and gingival coverage and provides stress relief for abutment teeth that support extension base partial dentures.
LC NO. 81-706533
Prod-VADTC Dist-USNAC 1979

Removable Partial Dentures C 20 MIN
16MM FILM OPTICAL SOUND PRO
Describes how to develop wax-up for partial denture casting from a plain refractory cast. Emphasizes the important construction details.
LC NO. 74-706564
Prod-USN Dist-USNAC 1963

Removable Partial Dentures C 7 MIN
16MM FILM, 3/4 OR 1/2 IN VIDEO A
Discusses application of a removable partial denture in replacing diseased or missing teeth. Covers the anatomy of teeth and gums, study casts, radiographs, design, materials, types, occlusion, food impaction, period of adjustment, home care, repairs, appearance, cleaning do's and don'ts and professional treatment.
Prod-PRORE Dist-PRORE

Removable Partial Dentures, Clasp Type - Clinical And Laboratory Procedures—A Series
PRO
Prod-USVA Dist-USNAC Prodn-VADTC 1978

Constructing The Occlusal Template,	-
Finishing, Occlusal Correction, Insertion,	13 MIN
Impression And Preparation Of The Master	13 MIN
Mouth Preparation Procedures	13 MIN
Occlusal Path Record, The	15 MIN
Pre-Delivery Adjustment Of Casting -	10 MIN
Preliminary Examination And Procedures For	12 MIN
Preliminary Survey Of Study Casts, Tentative	11 MIN
Recording Edentulous Ridge Contour -	16 MIN

Removable Partial Dentures, Clasp Type - Clinical And Laboratory Procedures—A Series

Presents a series on the removable partial dentures, clasp type.
Prod-VADTC Dist-AMDA 1969

Constructing The Occlusal Template And	-
Finishing, Occlusal Correction, Insertion And	013 MIN
Impression And Preparation Of The Master Cast	012 MIN
Occlusal Path Record, The	015 MIN
Pre-Delivery And Casting Adjustment	009 MIN
Preliminary Examination And Procedures For	013 MIN
Preliminary Survey Of Study Cast - Tentative	011 MIN
Recording Edentulous Ridge Contours And	016 MIN

Removal From The Water C 6 MIN
16MM FILM - 3/4 IN VIDEO
Illustrates that the lifesaver's job doesn't end when he has the victim in tow, but that knowing how to remove the victim from the water is important too.
From The Lifesaving And Water Safety Series.
Prod-AMRC Dist-AMRC 1975

Removal Of A Superficial Foreign Body From The Eye C 9 MIN
3/4 OR 1/2 INCH VIDEO CASSETTE PRO
Presents a concise demonstration of removal of a superficial foreign body from the eye.
From The Medical Skills Films Series.
Prod-WFP Dist-WFP

Removal Of Corneal And Scleral Contact Lenses C 9 MIN
16MM FILM OPTICAL SOUND
Uses close-up photography to demonstrate emergency manual or suction cup removal of a patient's corneal or scleral contact lenses.
From The Nursing Techniques For The Care Of Patients With Impaired Vision Series.
LC NO. 72-700351
Prod-OHIOSU Dist-OSUMPD 1971

Removal Of Double Gallbladder - Technique Of Sphincterotomy And Pancreatogram C 26 MIN
16MM FILM OPTICAL SOUND PRO
Demonstrates removal of double gallbladders, cholangiogram through the two cystic ducts, a reliable simple method to facilitate transduodenal sphincterotomy and the technique of pancreatogram.
From The Cine Clinic Series.
Prod-ACYDGD Dist-NMAC 1970

Removal Of The Brain C 18 MIN
16MM FILM, 3/4 OR 1/2 IN VIDEO PRO
Demonstrates step-by-step procedures for dissection of the brain, from initial incision to total removal. Identifies the pituitary stalk and gland, various arteries and nerves, and the sinuses.
From The Autopsy Dissection Technique - A Cinematographic Atlas Series.
LC NO. 78-706034
Prod-MFIORH Dist-USNAC

Removal Of The Eye C 8 MIN
16MM FILM - 3/4 IN VIDEO PRO
Demonstrates the removal of an eye during an autopsy. Demonstrates reconstruction of a closed eye for embalming and viewing by mourners.
From The Autopsy Dissection Technique - A Cinematographic Atlas Series.
LC NO. 78-706035
Prod-MFIORH Dist-USNAC

Removal Of The Spinal Cord C 18 MIN
16MM FILM, 3/4 OR 1/2 IN VIDEO PRO
Demonstrates a technique for removing the spinal cord, emphasizing the way in which the individual vertebral pedicles are identified and cut to facilitate the removal of the vertebrate column.
From The Autopsy Dissection Technique - A Cinematographic Atlas Series.
LC NO. 78-706036
Prod-MFIORH Dist-USNAC

Removal Of The Spinal Cord - Anterior Approach C 18 MIN
16MM FILM OPTICAL SOUND PRO
Demonstrates the technique for removing the spinal cord by exposing it anteriorly after removal of the vertebral column from C4 to T5 inclusive. Emphasizes the way in which the individual vertebral pedicles are identified and cut to facilitate the removal of the vertebrate column.
From The Autopsy Dissection Technique - A Cinematographic Atlas Series.
LC NO. 74-706219
Prod-HASSJ Dist-NMAC 1971

Removing A Section Of Piping Aboard Ship B 13 MIN
16MM FILM OPTICAL SOUND
Explains the purpose of the piping system. Shows how to remove a section of pipe aboard ship and defines outside diameter, pitch diameter, pitch cord, bleeding point and backing-off.
LC NO. FIE52-1189
Prod-USN Dist-USNAC 1943

Removing And Inspecting Cylinders B 18 MIN
16MM FILM OPTICAL SOUND
Shows how to remove the cylinder assemblies from the engine, disassemble the cylinder assemblies, and clean, inspect and recondition the cylinders.
From The Aircraft Work Series. Power Plant Maintenance
LC NO. FIE52-253
Prod-USOE Dist-USNAC Prodn-AUDIO 1945

Removing And Installing A Compressor Or Condenser B 17 MIN
16MM FILM, 3/4 OR 1/2 IN VIDEO
Shows how to evacuate and remove a compressor in a domestic refrigerator, evacuate a stuck compressor, install a compressor and remove and install a condenser.
From The Refrigeration Service - Domestic Units Series. No. 5
LC NO. 81-707342
Prod-USOE Dist-USNAC Prodn-ROCKT 1945

Removing And Installing A Cooling Unit B 19 MIN
16MM FILM, 3/4 OR 1/2 IN VIDEO
Discusses cooling unit disorders in a domestic refrigerator. Shows how to evacuate valved evaporators, remove an oil-logged evaporator, install the evaporator and install a direct expansion cooling unit.
From The Refrigeration Service - Domestic Units Series. No. 6
LC NO. 81-707322
Prod-USOE Dist-USNAC Prodn-ROCKT 1945

Removing And Replacing Seat Backrest Trim C 19 MIN
1/2 IN VIDEO CASSETTE BETA/VHS
Deals with auto body repair. Describes complete removal and replacement of a seat backrest, using a G M bucket seat to illustrate.
Prod-RMI Dist-RMI

Removing And Replacing Seat Cushion Trim C 18 MIN
1/2 IN VIDEO CASSETTE BETA/VHS
Deals with auto body repair. Explains removal and replacement of seat cushions, using a G M seat with jack stringers and complete envelope repair.
Prod-RMI Dist-RMI

Removing Defective Rivets B 15 MIN
16MM FILM OPTICAL SOUND
Pictures how an inspector marks defective rivets. Demonstrates

how to drill the head of flushtype and brazier head rivets and remove the shand and head after drilling.
From The Aircraft Work Series.
LC NO. FIE52-34
Prod-USOE Dist-USNAC

Remy Charlip And Elaine Summers C 30 MIN
3/4 OR 1/2 INCH VIDEO CASSETTE
Focuses on experimenting with the design of dance in different media. Hosted by Celia Ipiotis.
From The Eye On Dance - Dance And The Plastic Art Series.
Prod-ARTRES Dist-ARTRES

Remy/Grand Central - Trains And Boats And Planes C 4 MIN
3/4 OR 1/2 INCH VIDEO CASSETTE
See series title for descriptive statement.
From The Five Short Works By Dana Birnbaum Series.
Prod-EAI Dist-EAI

Remy, Grand Central - Trains And Boats And Planes C 4 MIN
3/4 OR 1/2 INCH VIDEO CASSETTE
Involves a pretty girl, animated trains, updated Bacharach Muzak and pouring Remy.
Prod-KITCHN Dist-KITCHN

Renaissance B 10 MIN
16MM FILM OPTICAL SOUND J-C A
An art film in which a mysterious piece of junk which has been filmed in monochrome vanishes with a flash and turns into a spectrum of colors, then explodes in various shades of blue.
LC NO. 77-708686
Prod-FORGJ Dist-VIEWFI 1970

Renaissance C 6 MIN
3/4 INCH VIDEO CASSETTE
Presents art video using computer imagery. Features a journey through cityscapes with spinning pyramids and cubes with musical background by Jamaladeen Tacuma.
From The John Sanborn And Dean Winkler - Selected Works Series.
Prod-EAI Dist-EAI

Renaissance And Resurrection, The, Pt 1 C 26 MIN
16MM FILM, 3/4 OR 1/2 IN VIDEO J-C A
Presents author-historian Luigi Barzini discussing the artistic achievements of the Renaissance and how these works reflected the glory of God.
Prod-ABCTV Dist-MGHT 1978

Renaissance And Resurrection, The, Pt 2 C 29 MIN
16MM FILM, 3/4 OR 1/2 IN VIDEO J-C A
Presents author-historian Luigi Barzini discussing the artistic achievements of the Renaissance and how these works reflected the glory of God.
Prod-ABCTV Dist-MGHT 1978

Renaissance And The Resurrection, The C 55 MIN
16MM FILM, 3/4 OR 1/2 IN VIDEO J-C A
Presents author-historian Luigi Barzini discussing the artistic achievements of the Renaissance and how these works reflected the glory of God.
Prod-ABCTV Dist-MGHT 1978

Renaissance Architecture In Slovakia (1500 - 1600) B 40 MIN
16MM FILM OPTICAL SOUND
Presents the architecture of the High Renaissance that is often overwhelming in its perfection but shows how on the edge of the then civilized world the Slovaks softened the style to human scale, adding charming touches of their own.
Prod-ROLAND Dist-ROLAND

Renaissance Band, The B 30 MIN
16MM FILM OPTICAL SOUND J-C A
Presents music of the Renaissance played by the New York Pro Musica using authentic instruments of that period. Demonstrates these instruments using woodcuts and the instruments of the individual band members.
From The World Of Music Series.
LC NO. 73-703490
Prod-NET Dist-IU 1965

Renaissance Center C 9 MIN
16MM FILM OPTICAL SOUND
Shows the construction of the Detroit Renaissance Center and several models of the finished structures.
LC NO. 76-702877
Prod-RCP Dist-FORDFL Prodn-FORDFL 1976

Renaissance Of A River C 20 MIN
16MM FILM OPTICAL SOUND J A
Shows that the Susquehanna River from its headwater tributaries to its mouth at the head of Chesapeake Bay has various specific problems which are to be solved by a proposed interstate compact.
Prod-FINLYS Dist-FINLYS 1965

Renaissance Pleasure Fair C 20 MIN
16MM FILM, 3/4 OR 1/2 IN VIDEO
Features the Renaissance Pleasure Fair, which recreates the spirit and atmosphere of medieval and Renaissance England.
Prod-UCEMC Dist-UCEMC

Renaissance Show C 24 MIN
3/4 OR 1/2 INCH VIDEO CASSETTE
Takes a trip to the Renaissance Fair in Shakopee, Minnesota, to meet the kids there, including a group of unicycling youngsters, a kid dj and kids who eat bugs as a source of protein.
Prod-WCCOTV Dist-WCCOTV 1981

Renaissance, The C 30 MIN
16MM FILM OPTICAL SOUND
Juxtaposes the artistic accomplishments of the Renaissance with its spiritual bankruptcy, which resulted from an emphasis on humanism and a deemphasis of religion. Based on the book How Should We Then Live by Francis A Schaeffer.
From The How Should We Then Live Series. Episode 3
LC NO. 77-702365
Prod-GF Dist-GF 1977

Renaissance, The C 60 MIN
3/4 OR 1/2 INCH VIDEO CASSETTE J-C A
Presents flutist James Galway discussing the importance of wealthy nobles, kings and the church as patrons of music. Shows how music moved away from the elaborate formality of the Gothic and found newer and purer forms.
From The James Galway's Music In Time Series.
LC NO. 83-706264
Prod-POLTEL Dist-FOTH 1982

Renaissance, The (Dutch) C 30 MIN
16MM FILM OPTICAL SOUND
Juxtaposes the artistic accomplishments of the Renaissance with its spiritual bankruptcy, which resulted from an emphasis on humanism and a deemphasis of religion. Based on the book How Should We Then Live by Francis A Schaeffer.
From The How Should We Then Live (Dutch) Series. Episode 3
LC NO. 77-702365
Prod-GF Dist-GF 1977

Renaissance, The (2nd Ed) C 13 MIN
16MM FILM, 3/4 OR 1/2 IN VIDEO I-H
Examines the renewed interest in art and architecture, the discoveries in science and technology, the spirit of exploration and learning and the sense of the importance and potential of human beings that characterized the Renaissance. Discusses the men and women whose ideas were the backbone of this period.
Prod-CORF Dist-CORF 1978

Renaissance, The - Its Beginnings In Italy X 26 MIN
16MM FILM, 3/4 OR 1/2 IN VIDEO J-C
Photographed entirely in Italy and France. Pictures the achievements of the Renaissance by showing paintings, sculpture and architecture of the period.
Prod-EBF Dist-EBEC 1957

Renaissance, The - Its Beginnings In Italy (Spanish) C 26 MIN
16MM FILM, 3/4 OR 1/2 IN VIDEO J-C
Portrays the rise of the Renaissance, when Europe awoke to a new awareness of man and his surroundings. Includes examples of Renaissance painting, sculpture and architecture.
Prod-EBEC Dist-EBEC

Renal Angiography C 19 MIN
16MM FILM OPTICAL SOUND PRO
Shows the preparation of the patient for a renal angiography and the proper technique for performing the procedure.
Prod-CORDIS Dist-CORDIS

Renal Biopsy, A C 6 MIN
16MM FILM OPTICAL SOUND PRO
Shows the technic of renal biopsy in a pediatric patient. Describes preoperative sedation and positioning technics. Points out that the same processes are applicable for adults.
LC NO. 74-703666
Prod-MCGA Dist-WYLAB 1963

Renal Hypertension / Bilateral Nephrectomy Kidney Transplantation C 23 MIN
16MM FILM OPTICAL SOUND PRO
Features three outstanding authorities in the field of renal hypertension, Dr William Kolff, Dr Irvine Page and Dr Harry Goldblatt.
Prod-UPJOHN Dist-UPJOHN

Renal System Involvement C 24 MIN
3/4 OR 1/2 INCH VIDEO CASSETTE
Explains the effects of renal dysfunction. Explains the role of the kidney in maintaining the body's acid-base balance. Discusses related problems resulting from renal failure.
From The Individuals With Renal Dysfunction Series.
Prod-AJN Dist-AJN

Renal Transplantation C 15 MIN
3/4 OR 1/2 INCH VIDEO CASSETTE PRO
Demonstrates an actual renal transplantation. Covers anatomy and explains details of operation.
Prod-HSCIC Dist-HSCIC 1984

Renal Vascular Access In Hemodialysis C 39 MIN
3/4 OR 1/2 INCH VIDEO CASSETTE
Reviews the causes of kidney failure and the purposes of hemodialysis. Discusses internal and external access devices, such as the Scribner shunt, femoral vein catheter, subclavian vein catheter, A-V fistula and A-V graft.
Prod-UMCSN Dist-AJN

Renal Vascular Hypertension C 26 MIN
3/4 INCH VIDEO CASSETTE PRO
Discusses etiology and methods of diagnosing renal vascular hypertension. Describes surgical management and arteriography.
LC NO. 76-706101
Prod-WARMP Dist-USNAC 1969

Renaming Fractions And Addition Of Fractions C 12 MIN
16MM FILM, 3/4 OR 1/2 IN VIDEO
Presents an animated story dealing with the renaming and addition of fractions.
From The Mathematics - An Animated Approach To Fractions Series. Part 2
Prod-FI Dist-FI

Renaming In Addition C 15 MIN
3/4 INCH VIDEO CASSETTE P
Introduces addition when regrouping of ones is required.
From The Math Factory, Module IV - Problem Solving Series.
Prod-MAETEL Dist-GPITVL 1973

Renaming In Addition C 16 MIN
3/4 OR 1/2 INCH VIDEO CASSETTE P
Discusses renaming the ones and tens place.
From The Math Cycle Series.
Prod-WDCNTV Dist-GPITVL 1983

Renaming In Subtraction C 16 MIN
3/4 OR 1/2 INCH VIDEO CASSETTE P
Discusses renaming the tens place.
From The Math Cycle Series.
Prod-WDCNTV Dist-GPITVL 1983

Renaming Numbers C 20 MIN
2 INCH VIDEOTAPE P
See series title for descriptive statement.
From The Mathemagic, Unit II - Addition And Subtraction Series.
Prod-WMULTV Dist-GPITVL

Renaming Olympics C 15 MIN
3/4 INCH VIDEO CASSETTE I
Discusses renaming in mathematics.
From The Math - No Mystery Series.
Prod-WCETTV Dist-GPITVL 1977

Renaming Ones In Addition C 20 MIN
2 INCH VIDEOTAPE P
See series title for descriptive statement.
From The Mathemagic, Unit II - Addition And Subtraction Series.
Prod-WMULTV Dist-GPITVL

Renault Dauphin C 1 MIN
3/4 OR 1/2 INCH VIDEO CASSETTE
Shows a classic television commercial that uses fast action and the line 'a better way to get around.'
Prod-BROOKC Dist-BROOKC

Rendering Plant Safety C 12 MIN
3/4 OR 1/2 INCH VIDEO CASSETTE A
Discusses safety and health issues in the animal rendering industry.
Prod-USNAC Dist-USNAC 1981

Rendevous 90 Degrees South C 28 MIN
16MM FILM OPTICAL SOUND
Depicts the role of the C-130 Hercules in blazing an unrestricted supply line to the South Pole, heart of Antarctica.
LC NO. 74-705523
Prod-USAF Dist-USNAC 1961

Rendezvous C 9 MIN
16MM FILM, 3/4 OR 1/2 IN VIDEO H-C A
Takes the viewer on a high-speed Ferrari ride through the early morning streets of Paris, passing its most famous districts and giving a split second glimpse of well-known monuments and buildings.
Prod-LFILMT Dist-PFP 1977

Rendezvous C 10 MIN
16MM FILM, 3/4 OR 1/2 IN VIDEO A
Presents the frontier life of American fur trappers in the 1820's with a description of trappers living in Teton Canyon, Wyoming, during that time.
LC NO. 77-706024
Prod-USIA Dist-USNAC 1976

Rendezvous C 11 MIN
16MM FILM, 3/4 OR 1/2 IN VIDEO I-H
Presents a complete rendezvous maneuver when two spacecraft are in different orbits and on different planes. Discusses the similarities between the rendezvous maneuver and flight to the moon.
From The Space Science Series.
Prod-ALTPRO Dist-JOU 1984

Rendezvous X 27 MIN
16MM FILM, 3/4 OR 1/2 IN VIDEO H-C A
Reveals how a man encounters a woman who shows him that he has suppressed the feminine side of himself all his life. Stars James Farentino and Melinda Dillon.
From The Insight Series.
Prod-PAULST Dist-PAULST

Rene And George Magritte C 4 MIN
3/4 INCH VIDEO CASSETTE
Presents a music video by Joan Logue for the Paul Simon song, Rene And George Magritte With Their Dog After The War.
Prod-AEI Dist-AEI

Renegade, The C 19 MIN
16MM FILM, 3/4 OR 1/2 IN VIDEO J-C A
Presents an adaptation of a short story by Shirley Jackson. Concerns the trouble that results in a Vermont town when a family's dog begins killing neighbors' chickens.
Prod-BFA Dist-BFA

Renewable Energy Resources - Wind, Water, And Solar Rays C 48 MIN
3/4 OR 1/2 INCH VIDEO CASSETTE
Provides information about possible solutions to the energy problem.
LC NO. 81-706669
Prod-SCIMAN Dist-GA 1981

Renewable Resources C 20 MIN
3/4 OR 1/2 INCH VIDEO CASSETTE I-J
Describes resources that can maintain themselves or be replenished if managed wisely. Discusses the delicate balance that lets certain wildlife species survive.

From The Terra - Our World Series.
Prod-MSDOE Dist-AITECH 1980

Renewable Sources Of Energy C 13 MIN
16MM FILM OPTICAL SOUND H-C A
Deals with German research into renewable sources of energy, and provides examples of government-supported research.
Prod-WSTGLC Dist-WSTGLC

Renewable Tree, The C 59 MIN
16MM FILM, 3/4 OR 1/2 IN VIDEO H-C A
Explores solutions to the problem of conserving trees while meeting economic and social demands for paper.
From The Nova Series.
LC NO. 78-700590
Prod-WGBHTV Dist-TIMLIF 1976

Renewal And Evaluation Of Teaching, The - Preparing A Teaching Dossier C 37 MIN
3/4 OR 1/2 INCH VIDEO CASSETTE C A
Presents Kenneth Gros Louis, a university executive officer with extensive experience helping faculty document their professional achievements, providing a detailed review of what a useful dossier should include and how faculty can prepare materials pertinent to reappointment, promotion and tenure decisions.
LC NO. 83-706043
Prod-IU Dist-IU 1982

Renewal Of Our Rangelands C 30 MIN
3/4 OR 1/2 INCH VIDEO CASSETTE
Documents a cooperative venture in which industry and ranchers under direction of the Soil Conservation Service treated eleven widely varying test plots to evaluate the practicability of wholesale range renovation in areas of meager rainfall.
Prod-IVCH Dist-IVCH

Renewing Your Motivation C 20 MIN
16MM FILM - 3/4 IN VIDEO
Shows how salespeople can get derailed and thrown into a slump by many things that have nothing to do with sales, such as personal, family, financial or health problems. Describes how Tom handled his situation and became an inspiration to younger salespeople. Points out that the best thing about selling is selling itself and tells how it can help salespeople to work off disappointments and keep feeling good about themselves.
From The Self-Motivation In Selling Series.
Prod-BNA Dist-BNA

Rennsymphonie / Zweigroschenzauber B 10 MIN
16MM FILM OPTICAL SOUND
Features Race Symphony, an excerpt from Hans Richter's study of a day at the races, in pre-Nazi Germany, and Two-Penny Magic, Richter's essay in rhyming images, made to advertise a picture magazine. Produced 1928-29.
Prod-STARRC Dist-STARRC

Renoir C 7 MIN
16MM FILM, 3/4 OR 1/2 IN VIDEO J-C
Presents fifteen Renoir works, Uses narration adapted from Renoir's own observations about art.
From The Art Awareness Collection Series.
Prod-USNGA Dist-EBEC 1974

Renovation, The C 30 MIN
3/4 OR 1/2 INCH VIDEO CASSETTE
See series title for descriptive statement.
From The Mundo Real Series.
Prod-CPT Dist-MDCPB

Renting C 30 MIN
3/4 OR 1/2 INCH VIDEO CASSETTE C A
Stresses financial and legal factors that are involved in renting. Provides guidelines for assessing the pros and cons of renting versus buying, with regard to taxes, types of leases and rent control legislation.
From The Personal Finance Series. Lesson 11
Prod-SCCON Dist-CDTEL

Renting Your Money For Profit C 25 MIN
3/4 OR 1/2 INCH VIDEO CASSETTE H-C A
Features use of debt instruments for financial growth.
From The Money Smart - A Guide To Personal Finance Series.
Prod-SOMFIL Dist-BCNFL 1985

Reorienting Occlusal Relationships, Pt 2 C 27 MIN
16MM FILM OPTICAL SOUND
Presents a clinical demonstration of a correctly engineered restoration of a patient's upper teeth, with stress on accomplishment of proper occlusal balance.
LC NO. 74-705524
Prod-USA Dist-USNAC 1963

Repainting A Frame Building B 18 MIN
16MM FILM, 3/4 OR 1/2 IN VIDEO
Shows how to determine repairs on a building before painting and how to prepare a building for painting.
From The Farm Work Series. Painting, No. 1
Prod-USOE Dist-USNAC Prodn-CALVIN 1944

Repair Cluster C 15 MIN
3/4 OR 1/2 INCH VIDEO CASSETTE
Discusses the requirements and duties for such jobs as heating/air conditioning repairer, appliance/refrigeration repairer and radio/TV repairer.
From The Vocational Visions Series.
Prod-GA Dist-GA

Repair Of Esophageal Hiatal Hernia Using The Abdominal Approach, The C 28 MIN
16MM FILM OPTICAL SOUND PRO
Shows that the abdominal approach for the repair of an esophageal hiatus hernia offers distinct advantages in selected patients. Illustrates the steps in operative technique employed in accomplishing the repair of such a hernia in an elderly patient with concomitant chronic cholecystitis and cholelithiasis.
Prod-ACYDGD Dist-ACY 1957

Repair Of Flexor Tendon Injuries C 60 MIN
3/4 OR 1/2 INCH VIDEO CASSETTE PRO
Presents a discussion of flexor tendon injuries and the method of repair. Uses diagrams and selected cases to present the principles involved in management of one of the most difficult problems in treatment of the injured hand.
Prod-ASSH Dist-ASSH

Repair Of Inguinal Hernia C
3/4 OR 1/2 INCH VIDEO CASSETTE
Explains both congenital and direct hernias including a warning on incarcerated hernia. Discusses the choice of living with a hernia or having it surgically repaired.
Prod-MIFE Dist-MIFE

Repair Of Inguinal Hernia (Arabic) C
3/4 OR 1/2 INCH VIDEO CASSETTE
Explains both congenital and direct hernias including a warning on incarcerated hernia. Discusses the choice of living with a hernia or having it surgically repaired.
Prod-MIFE Dist-MIFE

Repair Of Inguinal Hernia (Spanish) C
3/4 OR 1/2 INCH VIDEO CASSETTE
Explains both congenital and direct hernias including a warning on incarcerated hernia. Discusses the choice of living with a hernia or having it surgically repaired.
Prod-MIFE Dist-MIFE

Repair Of Inguinal Hernia In Infancy C 31 MIN
16MM FILM OPTICAL SOUND PRO
Presents the repair of inguinal hernia in infancy to show the pre-operative and operative findings and the technique of repair of a variety of infantile hernias, hydrocoeles and undescended testes.
Prod-ACYDGD Dist-ACY 1968

Repair Of Median Episiotomies Including Third Degree Lacerations C 28 MIN
16MM FILM OPTICAL SOUND PRO
Shows a method of repairing midline episiotomies with emphasis upon technical simplicity and the relief of postpartum pain. Explains the many advantages of midline episiotomy. Includes an anatomical technique for the repair of third degree lacerations.
Prod-ACYDGD Dist-ACY 1960

Repair Of Old Complete Perineal Lacerations C 14 MIN
16MM FILM OPTICAL SOUND
Demonstrates the classical layer type of repair of an old complete perineal laceration with careful anatomical restoration of the entire perineal body. Emphasizes the use of the paradoxical incision or anal sphincterotomy allowing partial decompression and careful pre-operative mechanical and antimicrobial bowel preparation.
LC NO. 75-702323
Prod-EATONL Dist-EATONL 1973

Repair Of Penoscrotal Urethral Fistula And Diverticulum C 16 MIN
16MM FILM OPTICAL SOUND PRO
Illustrates a technique for treating diverticulum and fistula of the male urethra by urethrostomy or cystostomy drainage.
LC NO. 75-702241
Prod-EATONL Dist-EATONL 1974

Repair Of Recurrent Urethrovaginal Fistula By Bladder Flap Advancement Technique C 20 MIN
16MM FILM OPTICAL SOUND
Explains that the successful repair of recurrent urethrovaginal fistula requires the mobilization of tissue which contains a good blood supply. Shows that the advancement of a bladder flap by the technique illustrated provides tissue with excellent blood supply, normal urothelium and obviates a suture line in the area of repair. Points out that this technique also lends itself to the reconstruction of the urethra and to repair of urethral and vesical-rectal fistulae.
LC NO. 75-702252
Prod-EATONL Dist-EATONL 1973

Repair Of The Injured Common Duct C 30 MIN
16MM FILM OPTICAL SOUND PRO
Shows the steps in performing end-to-end anastomosis. Identifies, and frees the duct ends as the reconstruction of the duct is accomplished over a T-tube.
Prod-ACYDGD Dist-ACY 1959

Repair Of Urethane Bumpers And Grills C 21 MIN
1/2 IN VIDEO CASSETTE BETA/VHS
Deals with auto body repair. Shows gauge repair on a 'soft' bumper, using a 1976 Mustang bumper.
Prod-RMI Dist-RMI

Repair Of Ventral Hernia C 25 MIN
16MM FILM OPTICAL SOUND PRO
Explains that the majority of incisional herniae occur in obese persons through vertical incisions. Emphasizes the fact that each repair is an individual problem and that no one method of repair is universally satisfactory.
Prod-ACYDGD Dist-ACY 1956

Repair Of Vesicovaginal Fistula, The - Transperitoneal Transvesical Approach C 15 MIN
16MM FILM OPTICAL SOUND
Demonstrates a surgical procedure which produced cures with a single operation in 32 cases of complicated vesicovaginal fistula. Emphasizes the value of the transperitoneal, transvesical exposure, which allows complete visualization of all important structures, mobilization of fistula tract under direct vision, simplified closure of vaginal defect with peritonealization, closure of bladder without tension and deperitonealization of anterior vaginal wall to prevent recurrent fistula formation.
LC NO. 75-702326
Prod-EATONL Dist-EATONL 1959

Repairing A Wooden Rib B 24 MIN
16MM FILM - 3/4 IN VIDEO IND
Shows how to remove gussets and broken rib parts from an airplane, how to splice a section of cap strip, cut and finish a scarf joint, make a new truss member, and make and assemble gussets and reinforcement plates. Issued in 1945 as a motion picture.
From The Aircraft Work - Aircraft Maintenance Series.
LC NO. 79-706791
Prod-USOE Dist-USNAC Prodn-HANDY 1979

Repairing Aircraft Tires B 22 MIN
16MM FILM - 3/4 IN VIDEO IND
Tells how to inspect an airplane tire, remove the tire and the tube, vulcanize the tube, repair a cut in the tire and reinstall the wheel. Issued in 1945 as a motion picture.
From The Aircraft Work - Aircraft Maintenance Series.
LC NO. 79-706792
Prod-USOE Dist-USNAC Prodn-NEMETH 1979

Repairing And Relining Mechanical Brakes B 21 MIN
16MM FILM - 3/4 IN VIDEO IND
Describes how to check brake action on an airplane, how to remove a wheel and inspect the brakes, disassemble a wheel and remove the brake lining, replace brake cables, and adjust brakes. Issued in 1945 as a motion picture.
From The Aircraft Work - Aircraft Maintenance Series.
LC NO. 79-706793
Prod-USOE Dist-USNAC Prodn-NEMETH 1979

Repairing Door Damage Using The Door Stretcher C 25 MIN
1/2 IN VIDEO CASSETTE BETA/VHS
Deals with auto body repair.
Prod-RMI Dist-RMI

Repairing Structural Tubing B 20 MIN
16MM FILM - 3/4 IN VIDEO IND
Shows how to straighten a bent tube, round out a tube, remove a damaged section of tube, prepare a replacement section and internal reinforcing sleeves, and how to assemble and weld the replacement section and sleeves. Issued in 1945 as a motion picture.
From The Aircraft Work - Aircraft Maintenance Series.
LC NO. 79-706794
Prod-USOE Dist-USNAC Prodn-HANDY 1979

Repeat Yourself, Please C 15 MIN
3/4 OR 1/2 INCH VIDEO CASSETTE I
Emphasizes using repetition and colorful words in writing.
From The Tyger, Tyger Burning Bright Series.
Prod-CTI Dist-CTI

Repertory Styles - How Different Is One Ballet From Another - A Series

Presents programs from the New York City cable TV series Eye On Dance.
Prod-ARCVID Dist-ARCVID

All-Round Dancer, The - Swinging From Jazz To
Demands Placed On Principal Dancers By 030 MIN
Small Repertory Companies And The Importance 030 MIN

Repetition And Contrast C 30 MIN
2 INCH VIDEOTAPE J-H
See series title for descriptive statement.
From The From Franklin To Frost - Narrative Fiction Series.
Prod-MPATI Dist-GPITVL

Repetition In Sketching C 29 MIN
3/4 INCH VIDEO CASSETTE C A
Illustrates that repetition is one of the most prevalent and basic of all art elements. Shows examples of repetition in nature as well as in man-made objects.
From The Sketching Techniques Series. Lesson 14
Prod-COAST Dist-CDTEL

Repetitive Programming C 15 MIN
1/2 IN VIDEO CASSETTE BETA/VHS IND
See series title for descriptive statement.
From The Machine Shop - C N C Machine Operations Series.
Prod-RMI Dist-RMI

Replacement Of The Aortic Valve With A Homograft C 28 MIN
16MM FILM OPTICAL SOUND PRO
Depicts the operative treatment of acquired aortic valve disease with a homograft. Presents certain other sequences illustrating ancillary material.
Prod-ACYDGD Dist-ACY 1968

Replacement Studies C 30 MIN
3/4 OR 1/2 INCH VIDEO CASSETTE IND
Introduces methodology necessary to calculate the economic time to replace an asset that still has remaining physical life. Utilizes replacement of an automobile as example problem.
From The Engineering Economy Series.
Prod-COLOSU Dist-COLOSU

Replacement Studies (Japanese) C 30 MIN
3/4 OR 1/2 INCH VIDEO CASSETTE IND
Introduces methodology necessary to calculate the economic time to replace an asset that still has remaining physical life. Utilizes replacement of an automobile as example problem.
From The Engineering Economy Series.
Prod-COLOSU Dist-COLOSU

Replantation Techniques - Indications And Contraindications C 60 MIN
3/4 OR 1/2 INCH VIDEO CASSETTE PRO

Presents the techniques of replantation of the amputated extremity and revascularization of the partially severed extremity. Discusses the indications and contraindications for replantation. Narrated by Dr Harold E Kleinert.
Prod-ASSH Dist-ASSH

Replay C 8 MIN
16MM FILM, 3/4 OR 1/2 IN VIDEO J-C A
Documents the existence of the generation link. Shows that history repeats itself and change is very often a replay of past events.
Prod-CUNLIM Dist-MGHT 1971

Replenishment System C 29 MIN
3/4 INCH VIDEO CASSETTE C
Shows how replenishing is necessary to sustain the chemical volume and activity in the radiographic processor. Discusses equipment function and problems, emphasizing factors involved in the calculation of correct replenishment rates. Describes replenishment pumps and those used in popular X-ray processors.
From The Radiographic Processing Series. Pt 10
LC NO. 77-706079
Prod-USVA Dist-USNAC 1975

Replies To Inquiries B 45 MIN
2 INCH VIDEOTAPE C
See series title for descriptive statement.
From The Business Writing Series. Unit I - Neutral Good-News Messages
Prod-CHITVC Dist-GPITVL Prodn-WTTWTV

Repolarization Alterations C 51 MIN
3/4 OR 1/2 INCH VIDEO CASSETTE PRO
Emphasizes the lability of the ventricular repolarization phase (S-T segment and T wave) and illustrates factors that create ventricular repolarization alterations.
From The Electrocardiogram Series.
Prod-HSCIC Dist-HSCIC 1982

Report - Endeavour Anchor C 14 MIN
16MM FILM OPTICAL SOUND J-C A
Covers the recovery and restoration of the anchor abandoned by Captain James Cook on Australia's Great Barrier Reef in 1770.
LC NO. 76-700570
Prod-FLMAUS Dist-AUIS 1975

Report And Proposal Writing C
3/4 OR 1/2 INCH VIDEO CASSETTE C
Studies how to write proposals and reports using proper format, audience appeal and occasion.
From The Write Course - An Introduction To College Composition Series.
Prod-DALCCD Dist-DALCCD

Report And Proposal Writing C 30 MIN
3/4 OR 1/2 INCH VIDEO CASSETTE C A
Discusses how to write proposals and reports using proper format. Studies audience appeal and occasion.
From The Write Course - An Introduction To College Composition Series.
Prod-FI Dist-FI 1984

Report Card, The - How Does Ricardo Feel C 5 MIN
16MM FILM, 3/4 OR 1/2 IN VIDEO P
Tells a story about Ricardo, who gets a scolding instead of expected praise for a good report card. How could it happen. Shows Ricardo busy at school and proud of a good report card he knows will please his mother. But she is having a frustrating day little brother is in her way, she pricks her finger, a pot boils over. So when Ricardo bursts into the kitchen and knocks over the scrub bucket, he becomes the target of an emotional tirade. The last scene shows Ricardo clutching his report card as he listens in hurt, confused astonishment. By using the empathy young viewers will have for Ricardo, teachers can help them see that people do not always control their emotions, that anger can be misdirected.
Prod-EBEC Dist-EBEC 1970

Report From Beirut - Summer Of '82 C 20 MIN
16MM FILM, 3/4 OR 1/2 IN VIDEO
Documents the experiences of the people of Beirut, under siege by Israeli forces in the summer of 1982.
Prod-NEWTIM Dist-NEWTIM

Report From China C 90 MIN
16MM FILM OPTICAL SOUND
Portrays the apparent success of Mao Tse-Tung's cultural revolution in China. Explains Mao's philosophy and stresses the vast economic development that has occurred as a result of educating peasants and city workers to accept and participate in various degrees of industrialization.
LC NO. 70-710762
Prod-IWANMI Dist-RADIM 1970

Report From The Aleutians C 47 MIN
3/4 OR 1/2 INCH VIDEO CASSETTE
Portrays the lives of the soldiers in the most remote outpost in World War II, the Aleutian Islands in the North Pacific. Shows the bombings of the area and the loneliness of the troops. Directed by John Huston.
Prod-IHF Dist-IHF

Report From The Aleutians C 47 MIN
16MM FILM, 3/4 OR 1/2 IN VIDEO
Documents the lives of soldiers in the Aleutians during World War II, and the bad weather, boredom and loneliness they encountered. Concludes with a bombing raid against Japanese-held Kiska Island. Written, narrated and directed by John Huston.
Prod-USAPS Dist-USNAC

Report From Thiokol - Polysulfide Base Industrial Sealants C 13 MIN
16MM FILM OPTICAL SOUND IND
Reviews the properties of polysulfide base sealants and discusses their applications in industry, in architecture and in marine and highway situations.
LC NO. FI67-949
Prod-THIOKL Dist-THIOKL 1963

Report From Wounded Knee C 11 MIN
3/4 OR 1/2 INCH VIDEO CASSETTE J-C A
Presents a short history of the government's attitude towards the American Indian culminating in the infamous massacre of Wounded Knee.
Prod-SF Dist-SF

Report Of The National Advisory Commission On Civil Disorders B 29 MIN
16MM FILM OPTICAL SOUND
Dore Schary, producer-playwright, and Father Theodore Hesburgh, president of Notre Dame University, discuss civil disorders. They plead for integration as the best hope for America and call for individual commitment to purge prejudice from the country.
Prod-ADL Dist-ADL

Report On Civilization C 8 MIN
16MM FILM, 3/4 OR 1/2 IN VIDEO J-C
Presents an animated report on the negative aspects of humanity and the state of mankind today, told in a cartoon-like fashion.
LC NO. 84-706802
Prod-KRATKY Dist-PHENIX 1983

Report On CORA C 30 MIN
16MM FILM OPTICAL SOUND R
Reports on the Commission on Religion in Appalachia, CORA. Tries to instill an awareness of welfare rights and calls attention to the problem of strip mining in West Virginia.
Prod-CBSTV Dist-CCNCC

Report On Down's Syndrome C 22 MIN
16MM FILM, 3/4 OR 1/2 IN VIDEO A
A clinical film report with observations by Richard Koch. Outlines the general characteristics of Down's syndrome, previously called mongolism, and describes methods of treatment and diagnosis. Points out the advantages of warm family life, early diagnosis and the cooperation of physician, public health nurse, social worker, psychologist, educator and all disciplines interested in the field of mental retardation.
Prod-IFB Dist-IFB 1964

Report On Drought B 21 MIN
16MM FILM OPTICAL SOUND I-C A
Reports on the drought conditions of 1966-1967 in Bihar and Uttar Pradesh.
Prod-INDIA Dist-NEDINF

Report On German Morale, A B 21 MIN
3/4 OR 1/2 INCH VIDEO CASSETTE
Purports to examine methods used by the Nazi to control morale and includes original Nazi footage.
Prod-IHF Dist-IHF

Report To The Nation B 14 MIN
16MM FILM OPTICAL SOUND
Presents a picture of United Cerebral Palsy's research, training and treatment program.
Prod-UCPA Dist-UCPA

Report Writing C 27 MIN
16MM FILM, 3/4 OR 1/2 IN VIDEO
Shows how to write clear and accurate reports. Uses hospital and industry security as well as police training.
Prod-MTROLA Dist-MTI 1973

Report, Analyze, Evaluate C 58 MIN
3/4 OR 1/2 INCH VIDEO CASSETTE T
Shows methods for teaching students to analyze and discuss writing.
From The Process-Centered Composition Series.
LC NO. 79-706299
Prod-IU Dist-IU 1977

Report, The C 30 MIN
3/4 OR 1/2 INCH VIDEO CASSETTE C
See series title for descriptive statement.
From The Writing For A Reason Series.
Prod-DALCCD Dist-DALCCD

Reportage (Report) B 10 MIN
16MM FILM OPTICAL SOUND
A Danish language film. Presents an experimental film based on the expressive prints of the young Danish painter, Soren Hansen. Portrays the cruel, tragic story of Jeftha, who, returning home victorious from war, must sacrifice his daughter to fulfill a promise to the Lord, which is taken from the book of Judges, chapter 11.
Prod-STATNS Dist-STATNS 1968

Reporter's Eye, The C 29 MIN
3/4 INCH VIDEO CASSETTE
Discusses several aspects of news reporting.
From The City Desk Series.
Prod-UMITV Dist-UMITV

Reporters (Captioned) C 101 MIN
16MM FILM, 3/4 OR 1/2 IN VIDEO A
Portrays the lives of Parisian photojournalists in a humorous light. French dialog with English subtitles.
Prod-CNEMAG Dist-CNEMAG 1983

Reporting And Briefing C 16 MIN
16MM FILM, 3/4 OR 1/2 IN VIDEO H-C A
Points out the importance of effective informative discourse. Highlights characteristics of successful reporting.
From The Art Of Communication Series.
LC NO. 79-701659
Prod-CENTRO Dist-CORF 1979

Reporting Of The Economy - The Numbers Game C 29 MIN
3/4 OR 1/2 INCH VIDEO CASSETTE
Tells how press coverage of the economy is improving but still lacks economic literacy on the part of both the press and its audience.
From The Inside Story Series.
Prod-PBS Dist-PBS 1981

Reports From Iran And Afghanistan C 30 MIN
3/4 OR 1/2 INCH VIDEO CASSETTE
Depicts life in Tehran and other areas of Iran (circa the hostage crisis at the United States Embassy in Tehran). Portrays the Iranian culture as still pervaded by western influence and drug addiction despite the Shah's departure and Ayatolloh Khomenini's teaching. Includes footage shot while traveling with an Afghan rebel unit in Afghanistan.
Prod-DCTVC Dist-DCTVC

Representation Of Linear Digital Networks C 52 MIN
3/4 OR 1/2 INCH VIDEO CASSETTE PRO
See series title for descriptive statement.
From The Digital Signal Processing Series.
Prod-GPCV Dist-GPCV

Representation Of Linear Digital Networks C 52 MIN
3/4 OR 1/2 INCH VIDEO CASSETTE
See series title for descriptive statement.
From The Digital Signal Processing - An Introduction Series.
Prod-MIOT Dist-MIOT

Representative Beef Brisket, Short Plate And Flank Breakdown C 5 MIN
16MM FILM OPTICAL SOUND J-C A
Shows a representative breakdown of the beef shank, brisket, short plate and flank, providing a basis for the indentification of retail cuts in the grocery store.
From The Food And Nutrition Series.
LC NO. 72-702641
Prod-IOWA Dist-IOWA 1971

Representative Beef Carcass Breakdown, A C 9 MIN
16MM FILM OPTICAL SOUND J-C A
Shows a representative breakdown of a beef carcass half into the nine most common wholesale cuts. Gives the yield figures for the demonstration carcass and points out the tender wholesale cuts.
From The Food And Nutrition Series.
LC NO. 72-702637
Prod-IOWA Dist-IOWA 1971

Representative Beef Chuck Breakdown, A C 7 MIN
16MM FILM OPTICAL SOUND J-C A
Shows a representative beef chuck breakdown of the wholesale cuts into the most common retail cuts, providing a basis for the identification of retail cuts in the grocery store.
From The Food And Nutrition Series.
LC NO. 72-702639
Prod-IOWA Dist-IOWA 1971

Representative Beef Rib Breakdown, A C 4 MIN
16MM FILM OPTICAL SOUND J-C A
Shows a representative breakdown of the beef rib into the most common retail cuts, providing a basis for the identification of retail cuts in the grocery store.
From The Food And Nutrition Series.
LC NO. 72-702630
Prod-IOWA Dist-IOWA 1971

Representative Beef Round Breakdown, A C 7 MIN
16MM FILM OPTICAL SOUND J-C A
Shows a representative breakdown of the beef round providing a basis for the identification of retail cuts in the grocery store.
From The Food And Nutrition Series.
LC NO. 72-702648
Prod-IOWA Dist-IOWA 1971

Representative Beef Short Loin Breakdown, A C 5 MIN
16MM FILM OPTICAL SOUND J-C A
Shows a representative breakdown of the beef short loin providing a basis for the identification of retail cuts in the grocery store.
From The Food And Nutrition Series.
LC NO. 72-702645
Prod-IOWA Dist-IOWA 1971

Representative Beef Sirloin Breakdown, A C 5 MIN
16MM FILM OPTICAL SOUND J-C A
Shows a representative breakdown of the beef sirloin providing a basis for the identification of retail cuts in the grocery store.
From The Food And Nutrition Series.
LC NO. 72-702647
Prod-IOWA Dist-IOWA 1971

Representative Hog Carcass Breakdown, A C 5 MIN
16MM FILM OPTICAL SOUND
Describes typical breakdown of a hog carcass into primal cuts. Shows which cuts must be skinned and stresses the economic importance of skinning for gelatin production.
LC NO. 70-710222
Prod-IOWA Dist-IOWA 1970

Representing A Client Before A Grand Jury—A Series
PRO
Provides lawyers with a comprehensive checklist of issues and options to be considered before advising clients subpoenaed by a grand jury. Demonstrates what actually takes place in a grand jury room when witnesses have to face tough prosecutors without counsel at their side.
Prod-ABACPE Dist-ABACPE

Client Interviews - Demonstration And Grand Jury Lecture Series 130 MIN

Grand Jury Room - Demonstration And Discussion 201 MIN
Witness Preparation For The Grand Jury 175 MIN

Representing The Individual Debtor C 60 MIN
3/4 OR 1/2 INCH VIDEO CASSETTE PRO
See series title for descriptive statement.
From The Modern Bankruptcy Practice Series.
Prod-ABACPE Dist-ABACPE

Representing The State In Child Abuse And Neglect Proceedings C 60 MIN
3/4 OR 1/2 INCH VIDEO CASSETTE PRO
Designed for training of attorneys representing child protective services agencies in court cases brought under state civil code child protective laws.
Prod-ABACPE Dist-ABACPE

Reprieve B 105 MIN
16MM FILM OPTICAL SOUND H-C A
Traces John Resko's actual rehabilitation at Dannemora prison through the efforts of the dedicated prison staff. Shows how Resko's aggressiveness was channelled into the study of art.
Prod-CINEWO Dist-CINEWO 1962

Reprieve C 22 MIN
16MM FILM - 3/4 IN VIDEO
Features former President Dwight D Eisenhower and other heart patients relating their return to active and useful living with adherence to doctor's orders and sensible living habits.
Prod-USNAC Dist-USNAC 1972

Reproducer, The C 15 MIN
16MM FILM, 3/4 OR 1/2 IN VIDEO H-C A
Demonstrates several card reproducing techniques to show the integral functions of the reproducer. Examines the gang punch operation and the method of verifying matching cards and detecting and correcting unmatched cards. Discusses mark sensing, alone and in combination with gang punching and the method, purpose and application of end printing and summary punching. Introduces the principle of control panel wiring as it applies to the reproducer.
Prod-SF Dist-SF 1968

Reproduction C 60 MIN
3/4 OR 1/2 INCH VIDEO CASSETTE A
Presents biologist Humberto Maturana discussing reproduction.
From The Biology Of Cognition And Language Series. Program 6
Prod-UCEMC Dist-UCEMC

Reproduction - A New Life C 26 MIN
3/4 OR 1/2 INCH VIDEO CASSETTE
Looks at the events that lead from the fertilized cell to a human baby. Uses film of living fetuses in the womb to show how the familiar human shape is 'sculpted' out of the basic cell mass.
From The Living Body - An Introduction To Human Biology Series.
Prod-FOTH Dist-FOTH 1985

Reproduction - Cell Mitosis B 30 MIN
2 INCH VIDEOTAPE J
See series title for descriptive statement.
From The Investigating The World Of Science, Unit 2 - Energy Within Living Systems Series.
Prod-MPATI Dist-GPITVL

Reproduction - Coming Together C 29 MIN
3/4 OR 1/2 INCH VIDEO CASSETTE
Discusses the physiological events that underly the process of reproduction.
From The Living Body - An Introduction To Human Biology Series.
Prod-FOTH Dist-FOTH 1985

Reproduction - Into The World C 26 MIN
3/4 OR 1/2 INCH VIDEO CASSETTE
Covers the tumultuous events of birth, using fetoscopy and models to show what happens from the baby's viewpoint. Shows the physiological events immediately following the birth.
From The Living Body - An Introduction To Human Biology Series.
Prod-FOTH Dist-FOTH 1985

Reproduction - Other Means B 20 MIN
2 INCH VIDEOTAPE I
See series title for descriptive statement.
From The Science Room Series.
Prod-MCETV Dist-GPITVL Prodn-WVIZTV

Reproduction - Seeds B 30 MIN
2 INCH VIDEOTAPE J
See series title for descriptive statement.
From The Investigating The World Of Science, Unit 2 - Energy Within Living Systems Series.
Prod-MPATI Dist-GPITVL

Reproduction - Shares In The Future C 26 MIN
3/4 OR 1/2 INCH VIDEO CASSETTE
Looks at how the male and female bodies are prepared for their task of increasing the human race. Shows the characteristics of sperm and ova and how each contains a partial blueprint for the future offspring. Uses micro-photography to show the mechanism of cell vision and describes the mechanisms of heredity.
From The Living Body - An Introduction To Human Biology Series.
Prod-FOTH Dist-FOTH 1985

Reproduction - The Continuity Of Life C
3/4 OR 1/2 INCH VIDEO CASSETTE H
Shows how living organisms reproduce both sexually and asexually. Studies fission, mitotic cell division, budding, spore formation and propagation by runners, and illustrates evolutionary changes with comparisons of external and internal fertilization.
Prod-SCIMAN Dist-GA

Reproduction And Birth B 25 MIN
16MM FILM OPTICAL SOUND T
Presents an in-service program for elementary school teachers on the introduction of sex education.
From The Starting Tomorrow Series. Unit 5 - Introducing Sex Education.
Prod-EALING Dist-WALKED 1969

Reproduction And Meiosis C 29 MIN
3/4 INCH VIDEO CASSETTE C A
Presents first of four lectures on reproduction in series. Provides overview of reproduction. Explains meiosis, the process underlying all forms of sexual reproduction. Defines chromosome.
From The Introducing Biology Series. Program 26
Prod-COAST Dist-CDTEL

Reproduction Cycle Of Angel Fish C 10 MIN
16MM FILM, 3/4 OR 1/2 IN VIDEO H-C
Details the reproduction of the angel fish. Documents the development of the fish during the six weeks they remain under their parents' care.
Prod-IFB Dist-IFB 1971

Reproduction Cycle Of Angel Fish (Danish) C 10 MIN
16MM FILM, 3/4 OR 1/2 IN VIDEO P-H
Explains the reproduction cycle of an angel fish. Begins with the courtship and proceeds through the egg-laying, fertilization and incubation stages to the development of the newly-hatched fry.
Prod-IFB Dist-IFB 1971

Reproduction In Organisms C 16 MIN
3/4 OR 1/2 INCH VIDEO CASSETTE J-C A
Shows the constant reproductive activity of creatures everywhere, including turtles, garden snails, insects and spiders as examples. Reinforces the point that all life is dependent on reproduction for its continued existence. Uses close-up shots to show spiders laying eggs, nudibranch eggs hatching and also beetles and butterflies.
Prod-EDMI Dist-EDMI 1982

Reproduction In The Collared Lemming B 13 MIN
16MM FILM OPTICAL SOUND C
Shows the mating behavior of collared lemmings and the birth of a litter. Includes sequences on the growth of the young and retrieval behavior by the mother.
Prod-UILL Dist-PSUPCR 1967

Reproduction Of Life C
3/4 OR 1/2 INCH VIDEO CASSETTE
Prod-MSTVIS Dist-MSTVIS

Reproductive And Social Behavior Of Belding's Ground Squirrel C 18 MIN
16MM FILM, 3/4 OR 1/2 IN VIDEO
Follows the annual cycle of Belding's ground squirrel in the alpine environments of the Sierra Nevada and documents hibernation, aggressive behavior between males, female territoriality, feeding, copulation, nest construction, behavior of the young, the effects of predation and altruistic predator-warning behavior.
From The Aspects Of Animal Behavior Series.
Prod-UCLA Dist-UCEMC 1979

Reproductive Behavior In The African Mouth-Breeding Fish C 35 MIN
16MM FILM SILENT C T
Points out characteristic markings which identify male and female African mouth-breeding fish (Tilapia macrocephilia). illustrates courtship patterns and the laying of eggs. Shows the eggs, stored in the male's mouth, at various stages of development—eight days, ten days, two months, four months and eight months. Pictures the ovulation process in detail.
Prod-PSUPCR Dist-PSUPCR 1959

Reproductive Behavior Of The Brook Trout C 24 MIN
16MM FILM OPTICAL SOUND C
Demonstrates all behavioral activity leading up to, including, and following spawning of brook trout in their natural environment.
Prod-PSUPCR Dist-PSUPCR 1971

Reproductive Behavior Of The Brook Trout, Salvelinus Fontinalis C 24 MIN
16MM FILM OPTICAL SOUND H-C A
Shows the spawning of brook trout in their natural environment. Explains how phenologic environmental changes are related to the spawning period. Illustrates the initiatory cutting and probing of the female and her preparation of the redd. Shows the competitive behavior of males, the spawning act and the postnuptial dance.
LC NO. 76-713858
Prod-SPTFRF Dist-PSUPCR 1971

Reproductive Behavior Of The Guppy Poecilia Reticulata Peters B 17 MIN
16MM FILM SILENT C
Shows, using normal and slow-motion photographs, the movement patterns, displays and copulatory behavior of unreceptive and receptive female and normal and gonopodectomized male guppies.
Prod-UBC Dist-PSUPCR 1967

Reproductive Or Sexual Cycles In The Female I C 11 MIN
16MM FILM, 3/4 OR 1/2 IN VIDEO C A
From The Human Embryology Series.
Prod-UTORMC Dist-TEF

Reproductive Or Sexual Cycles In The Female II C 11 MIN
16MM FILM, 3/4 OR 1/2 IN VIDEO C A
From The Human Embryology Series.
Prod-UTORMC Dist-TEF

Reproductive System, The C 7 MIN
16MM FILM, 3/4 OR 1/2 IN VIDEO J-C
Defines reproduction and then dissects a rat to show the major components of the system.
Prod-CFDLD Dist-CORF

Reptiles C 10 MIN
16MM FILM, 3/4 OR 1/2 IN VIDEO P
Shows the characteristics of reptiles through nature photography.
From The All About Animals Series.
Prod-BURGHS Dist-AIMS 1978

Reptiles X 14 MIN
16MM FILM, 3/4 OR 1/2 IN VIDEO I-C
Introduces the five orders of reptiles remaining on earth - lizards, turtles, tautaras, crocodilians and serpents. Describes the physical characteristics, reproductive processes, feeding habits and habitats.
Prod-EBF Dist-EBEC Prodn-ANDERS 1955

Reptiles C 15 MIN
3/4 OR 1/2 INCH VIDEO CASSETTE K
Illustrates reptiles having scaly skin and laying their eggs with shells.
From The Let's Go Sciencing, Unit III - Life Series.
Prod-DETPS Dist-GPITVL

Reptiles C 15 MIN
3/4 OR 1/2 INCH VIDEO CASSETTE I
See series title for descriptive statement.
From The Discovering Series. Unit 1 - Vertebrate Animals
Prod-WDCNTV Dist-AITECH 1978

Reptiles C 20 MIN
16MM FILM, 3/4 OR 1/2 IN VIDEO I-C A
Presents a program on reptiles taken from the TV special 'REPTILES AND AMPHIBIANS.'
LC NO. 80-706301
Prod-NGS Dist-NGS 1973

Reptiles C 29 MIN
2 INCH VIDEOTAPE
See series title for descriptive statement.
From The Observing Eye Series.
Prod-WGBHTV Dist-PUBTEL

Reptiles - A First Film C 12 MIN
16MM FILM, 3/4 OR 1/2 IN VIDEO P-J
Introduces the reptile family, which includes snakes, turtles and lizards, filmed in each species' natural habitat.
Prod-BEAN Dist-PHENIX 1983

Reptiles And Amphibians C 52 MIN
16MM FILM, 3/4 OR 1/2 IN VIDEO J-H
Explores the world of reptiles and amphibians, and compares their prehistoric existence with their existence today as lower life forms.
LC NO. 80-706365
Prod-NGS Dist-NGS 1969

Reptiles And Birds C 30 MIN
3/4 OR 1/2 INCH VIDEO CASSETTE
Looks at the three families of marine reptiles in the world today. Discusses the common ancestry of reptiles and birds. Compares the behavior and habits of several oceanic birds.
From The Oceanus - The Marine Environment Series. Lesson 17
Prod-SCCON Dist-CDTEL

Reptiles Are Interesting C 10 MIN
16MM FILM, 3/4 OR 1/2 IN VIDEO I-C
Pictures various kinds of reptiles and the characteristics of each including the crocodilians, turtles, lizards, snakes and the group represented by the tautara.
Prod-FA Dist-PHENIX 1955

Reptiles Are Interesting (French) C 10 MIN
16MM FILM, 3/4 OR 1/2 IN VIDEO I-C
Pictures various kinds of reptiles and the characteristics of each including the crocodilians, turtles, lizards, snakes and the groups represented by the tautara.
Prod-FA Dist-PHENIX 1955

Reptiles, Pt 1 - Snakes C 20 MIN
2 INCH VIDEOTAPE I
See series title for descriptive statement.
From The Exploring With Science, Unit XI - Vertebrates series.
Prod-MPATI Dist-GPITVL

Reptiles, Pt 2 - Turtles, Lizards, Alligators And Crocodiles C 20 MIN
2 INCH VIDEOTAPE I
See series title for descriptive statement.
From The Exploring With Science, Unit XI - Vertebrates series.
Prod-MPATI Dist-GPITVL

Repulsion Motor Principles B 11 MIN
16MM FILM - 3/4 IN VIDEO IND
Explains the construction of a repulsion motor, rotor circuits and the effect of the brush position, short-circuiting and the brush-lifting mechanism, and applications of repulsion motors. Issued in 1945 as a motion picture.
From The Electrical Work - Electrical Machinery Series. No. 5
LC NO. 79-706240
Prod-USOE Dist-USNAC Prodn-RAYBEL 1979

Repulsion-Induction Motor - General Overhaul B 25 MIN
16MM FILM - 3/4 IN VIDEO
Explains how to check a repulsion-induction motor for electrical and mechanical faults. Demonstrates how to dismantle, assemble, and lubricate the motor, remove a damaged coil, and wind and insulate a new coil. Issued in 1945 as a motion picture.
From The Electrical Work - Motor Maintenance And Repair Series. Number 6

LC NO. 79-707705
Prod-USOE Dist-USNAC Prodn-CALVCO 1979

Requiem C 4 MIN
16MM FILM OPTICAL SOUND
A tribute to Martin Luther King. Portrays the shame and horror of his death.
LC NO. 73-702858
Prod-DELL Dist-MMM 1968

Requiem For A Faith C 28 MIN
16MM FILM, 3/4 OR 1/2 IN VIDEO
Tells the story of Tibetan Buddhism, presents ancient rituals, continuous meditation, deep compassion and a profound faith in the divinity of man.
Prod-HP Dist-HP

Requiem For A Heavyweight B 18 MIN
16MM FILM OPTICAL SOUND
An abridged version of the motion picture Requiem For A Heavyweight. Gives a grim account of an honest, proud champion prizefighter forced into corruption and degradation when his ring career ends. Stars Anthony Quinn and Jackie Gleason.
Prod-CPC Dist-TIMLIF 1982

Requiem For A Heavyweight B 100 MIN
16MM FILM OPTICAL SOUND
Features the story of the decline of an ex-champion prize fighter and his inability to adjust to the loss of fame, glory and dignity. Stars Mickey Rooney, Jackie Gleason and Jack Dempsey.
Prod-CPC Dist-TIMLIF 1962

Requiem For A Race Track C 21 MIN
16MM FILM OPTICAL SOUND
Presents the last endurance race around the airport road course at Sebring, Florida. Features Peter Revson expressing his views on racing at Sebring and how not to get along with the SCCA stewards. Hosted by Jackie Stewart and Keith Jackson.
Prod-GTARC Dist-GTARC

Requiem For An Alcoholic C 19 MIN
16MM FILM OPTICAL SOUND
Portrays the desperate and purposeless existence of a hardened alcoholic.
LC NO. 77-700036
Prod-AFFAC Dist-CFS Prodn-MAISNA 1976

Required Dives, The C 20 MIN
16MM FILM, 3/4 OR 1/2 IN VIDEO
Covers required dives, including forward, back and reverse dives.
From The Diving Series. No 2
Prod-ATHI Dist-ATHI 1977

Requirements Analysis C 30 MIN
3/4 OR 1/2 INCH VIDEO CASSETTE IND
Discusses system analysis, software requirements, analysis, analysis tools and techniques, and form and content of requirements documents.
From The Software Engineering - A First Course Series.
Prod-COLOSU Dist-COLOSU

Requirements For Television Bronchoscopy C 15 MIN
16MM FILM - 3/4 IN VIDEO
Discusses equipment requirements for two types of television bronchoscopy systems, a high-quality system for teaching programs and a more economical system for in-house use. Covers topics such as bronchoscopes, light sources, cameras, test and monitoring equipment, videotape recorders and tape storage.
LC NO. 78-706080
Prod-VAHLCF Dist-USNAC 1977

Resale Price Maintenance - Legal Issues In Developing Pricing Policies C 58 MIN
3/4 OR 1/2 INCH VIDEO CASSETTE PRO
Reviews the state of the law after a marketing manager requests legal help on how to respond to price cutting by distributors.
From The Antitrust Counseling And The Marketing Process Series.
Prod-ABACPE Dist-ABACPE

Rescue C 20 MIN
3/4 OR 1/2 INCH VIDEO CASSETTE
Shows approved procedures for locating and rescuing people in burning structures. Demonstrates carries, drags, life nets, stretchers, life belts and other rescue equipment and techniques.
Prod-IFSTA Dist-IFSTA

Rescue Breathing C 22 MIN
16MM FILM OPTICAL SOUND
Uses laboratory experiments to explain the superiority of mouth-to-mouth or mouth-to-nose breathing techniques over manual methods of artificial respiration.
Prod-HERMAN Dist-RBFA 1958

Rescue From Isolation C 22 MIN
16MM FILM OPTICAL SOUND A
Depicts the activities of geriatric day hospitals which offer medical, social and psychiatric rehabilitation for elderly persons whose physical disabilities, negative outlook and personal loneliness have caused them to become increasingly isolated.
LC NO. 79-700592
Prod-BLUMNO Dist-POLYMR 1978

Rescue From Isolation C 22 MIN
3/4 OR 1/2 INCH VIDEO CASSETTE
Documents the problem of isolation among the elderly and presents an answer in the form of a geriatric day hospital.
Prod-POLYMR Dist-POLYMR

Rescue From Isolation - The Role Of A Psychogeriatric Day Hospital C 22 MIN
16MM FILM OPTICAL SOUND C A
Uses a series of interviews with old people to establish the need for some sort of half-way house between total isolation and total institutionalization. Points out that one answer to this need is a day hospital, an out-patient facility connected with a geriatric day hospital. Documents the activities of one such organization in the areas of physiotherapy and psychiatry.
LC NO. 73-703365
Prod-TRNSIT Dist-TRNSIT 1973

Rescue Of A River C 29 MIN
2 INCH VIDEOTAPE
Looks at one of the nation's environmental success stories - the clean-up of Oregon's Willamette River, once one of the filthiest waterways in the Northwest. Traces the industrial and agricultural growth of the rich Willamette River, fabled in historic monographs as a land of milk and honey, and shows in vivid detail how man had polluted the river.
From The Turning Points Series.
Prod-KOAPTV Dist-PUBTEL

Rescue Party C 20 MIN
16MM FILM, 3/4 OR 1/2 IN VIDEO I-C
Presents a story about a spaceship from the Galactic Federation which is given a mission to rescue the inhabitants of Earth before the Sun explodes.
Prod-WILETS Dist-BARR 1978

Rescue Squad C 14 MIN
16MM FILM, 3/4 OR 1/2 IN VIDEO I-H
Describes the danger, excitement and responsibility of a large city rescue team. Shows the squad as it is called to a fire and to assist in health emergencies.
From The World Of Work Series.
Prod-EBEC Dist-EBEC 1971

Rescue Team Alert C 21 MIN
16MM FILM, 3/4 OR 1/2 IN VIDEO IND
Tells how two men are trapped in a pit by a load of drums containing acid waste. Depicts their rescue, which is hampered because the rescue team lacks training. Encourages the establishment of factory rescue teams.
LC NO. 81-706566
Prod-MILLBK Dist-IFB 1980

Research - The Challenge To Survival C 24 MIN
16MM FILM OPTICAL SOUND H-C A
Studies the advances being made in the fight against leukemia.
LC NO. 83-700682
Prod-LEUSA Dist-LEUSA 1983

Research And Development C 30 MIN
3/4 INCH VIDEO CASSETTE
See series title for descriptive statement.
From The It's Everybody's Business Series. Unit 5, Operating A Business
Prod-DALCCD Dist-DALCCD

Research And Development - Interactive Computer Graphics For Intuitional Problem... C 41 MIN
3/4 OR 1/2 INCH VIDEO CASSETTE J-C A
Complete title is Research And Development Interactive Computer Graphics For Intuitional Problem Solving. Shows computer systems which explore the possibility that the skillful use of dynamic graphics may bring about qualitative changes in the educational process. Shows a system for animating algebra word problems that exercises intuitional rather than analytical problem solving.
From The New Technology In Education Series.
Prod-USDOE Dist-USNAC 1983

Research And Development Perspective, A C 25 MIN
16MM FILM OPTICAL SOUND
Highlights research and development efforts of the U S Department of Transportation. Shows projects, such as a microwave landing system, vessel traffic control radar, linear induction motored rail vehicles and nondestructive tire testing.
LC NO. 78-700819
Prod-USDT Dist-USNAC 1978

Research And Development Progress Report Number Nine - Delong Piers C 12 MIN
16MM FILM OPTICAL SOUND
Discusses the construction and installation of Delong piers to relieve logistical problems in Vietnam.
LC NO. 76-701540
Prod-USA Dist-USNAC 1967

Research And Planning C 30 MIN
3/4 OR 1/2 INCH VIDEO CASSETTE
Examines profiling customers, preparing the message and selecting the media that best fits a particular business. Discusses the various methods of advertising, including radio, newspapers, direct mail, television, outdoor and point-of-purchase.
From The Advertising The Small Business Series.
Prod-NETCHE Dist-NETCHE 1981

Research And Preparation C 50 MIN
3/4 OR 1/2 INCH VIDEO CASSETTE IND
Includes the trainer's role, job and task analysis and the course outline.
From The Training The Trainer Series.
Prod-LEIKID Dist-LEIKID

Research At The Interface C 19 MIN
16MM FILM OPTICAL SOUND
Shows a scientific research expedition in the North Atlantic.
LC NO. 80-700444
Prod-GOLDMN Dist-WOODHO 1980

Research In Animal Behavior C 18 MIN
16MM FILM, 3/4 OR 1/2 IN VIDEO
Discusses six experiments in animal behavior in order to introduce significant research in this field, interdisciplinary methodology and experimental procedures.
Prod-HAR Dist-MTI 1978

Research In Metal Turning C
16MM FILM OPTICAL SOUND
Presents a study of the process of metal turning.
Prod-MASTER Dist-MASTER

Research In Multiple Sclerosis C 15 MIN
16MM FILM OPTICAL SOUND
Details how the National Multiple Sclerosis Society allocates three million dollars a year for research into the cause, prevention and cure of MS. Explains in lay terms some of the unsolved mysteries surrounding the virology, immunology and epidemology of MS Demonstrates how antibodies form in humans and animals and how they may contribute to the demyelination process in the central nervous system.
Prod-FLEMRP Dist-NMSS 1972

Research In Nursing C 62 MIN
3/4 OR 1/2 INCH VIDEO CASSETTE PRO
Reviews the definition and purpose of research in nursing. Demonstrates the 16 major steps involved in the research process by using the hypothetical research study.
LC NO. 81-706301
Prod-USVA Dist-USNAC 1980

Research Interview Module, Session 1 C 20 MIN
3/4 OR 1/2 INCH VIDEO CASSETTE H A
Covers basic techniques and how to handle an interview. Tells how to gain entry, begin the interview and conduct the actual interview.
From The Interview Techniques Series.
Prod-CUETV Dist-CUNIV 1978

Research Interview Module, Session 2 C 20 MIN
3/4 OR 1/2 INCH VIDEO CASSETTE H A
Emphasizes how to record verbatim when the interviewer is writing and the subject is talking quickly. Includes simulated interviews demonstrating what the interviewer is doing correctly and not so correctly.
From The Interview Techniques Series.
Prod-CUETV Dist-CUNIV 1978

Research Interview Module, Session 3 C 20 MIN
3/4 OR 1/2 INCH VIDEO CASSETTE H A
Features three different interviewers handling three specific problems. Includes entry problem, how to probe and stress questions.
From The Interview Techniques Series.
Prod-CUETV Dist-CUNIV 1978

Research Into Controlled Fusion C 55 MIN
16MM FILM OPTICAL SOUND
A technical report of fusion research programs at Princeton University, Oak Ridge National Laboratory, Los Alamos scientific laboratory and the University of California radiation laboratory. Outlines principal problems encountered and uses animation to explain research devices in detail.
LC NO. FIE63-184
Prod-USAEC Dist-USERD Prodn-USA 1958

Research Into Genetics C 13 MIN
16MM FILM OPTICAL SOUND I-H
Discusses research into genetics which could lead to benefits in health, agriculture and the environment.
Prod-ALLFP Dist-NSTA 1978

Research Into High Blood Pressure C 15 MIN
16MM FILM OPTICAL SOUND C
Deals with high blood pressure. Explains that this condition has no characteristic symptoms and in most cases the cause is unknown. Tells of the dangers of untreated high blood pressure including stroke, kidney failure and congestive heart failure.
From The Science In Action Series.
Prod-ALLFP Dist-COUNFI

Research Methods And Probability C 29 MIN
2 INCH VIDEOTAPE
Examines methods for scientific research with emphasis on mathematical probability as it applies to investigations into psychic phenomena.
From The Who Is Man Series.
Prod-WHROTV Dist-PUBTEL

Research On Family And Marital Therapy With Alan Gurman B 60 MIN
3/4 OR 1/2 INCH VIDEO CASSETTE
Discusses with Proffessor Alan Gurman his research on family and marital therapy. Presents information taken from an article he co-authored and includes a discussion of the pros and cons of statistical analysis.
Prod-UWISC Dist-UWISC 1978

Research On Survival In Bushfires C 17 MIN
16MM FILM OPTICAL SOUND
Describes the scientific approach and research work of the bushfire research team of the commonwealth scientific and industrial research organization division of physical chemistry, leading up to the development of a prototype survival tent for use by trained personnel in emergencies.
LC NO. FIA65-1071
Prod-CSIROA Dist-CSIROA Prodn-AVCORP 1964

Research On The Disadvantaged C 30 MIN
3/4 OR 1/2 INCH VIDEO CASSETTE
Focuses on language skills, intelligence tests and the self-concept of the disadvantaged. Discusses recent concern with problems of health as a prerequisite for learning.
From The Educating The Disadvantaged Series.
Prod-NETCHE Dist-NETCHE 1972

Research Paper Made Easy, The - From Assignment To Completion C 55 MIN
3/4 OR 1/2 INCH VIDEO CASSETTE
Offers instruction in writing a research paper by focusing on such skills as defining a topic, making a thesis statement, preparing

a bibliography, outlining, writing a draft and preparing the final paper.
LC NO. 81-706679
Prod-CHUMAN Dist-GA 1981

Research Problem, A - Inert Gas Compounds C 19 MIN
16MM FILM OPTICAL SOUND H
Conveys the excitement and personal involvement of research involved in the synthesis of one of the inert gas compounds, krypton difluoride.
From The CHEM Study Films Series.
Prod-CHEMS Dist-MLA 1962

Research Process, The C 30 MIN
3/4 OR 1/2 INCH VIDEO CASSETTE
Offers an in-depth look at research itself, a well-organized process that is still open enough to allow for the unexpected.
From The Innovation Series.
Prod-WNETTV Dist-WNETTV 1983

Research Project X-15 C 27 MIN
16MM FILM OPTICAL SOUND
Shows the development of the experimental X 15 research airplane which took test pilots to the edge of space.
LC NO. FIE67-116
Prod-NASA Dist-NASA 1966

Research Reactors - U S A C 38 MIN
16MM FILM OPTICAL SOUND
Uses live action and animation to present a semitechnical summary of the major types of research reactors and their uses in industry, chemistry, physics, metallurgy, biology and medicine.
Prod-USAEC Dist-USERD Prodn-LYTLE 1958

Research To Reality C 29 MIN
16MM FILM OPTICAL SOUND
Shows the many capabilities of the Naval Ship Research and Development Center.
LC NO. 75-700576
Prod-USN Dist-USNAC 1973

Research With Disadvantaged Preschool Children C 11 MIN
16MM FILM OPTICAL SOUND C T
Demonstrates research at the Juniper Gardens Children's Project of the University of Kansas Bureau of Child Research. Explains that the Turner House Preschool is designed to develop and investigate child behavior, particularly language behavior.
LC NO. 72-702020
Prod-UKANBC Dist-UKANS 1969

Research, The Challenge Of Survival C 24 MIN
3/4 INCH VIDEO CASSETTE H-C A
Spotlights the work of four researchers supported by the Leukemia Society of America. Discusses their work, and offers a positive approach to fighting both the childhood and adult forms of leukemia.
LC NO. 83-706829
Prod-METROM Dist-LEUSA Prodn-HMS 1983

Resection Of Abdominal Aneurysm C 23 MIN
16MM FILM OPTICAL SOUND PRO
Demonstrates the technique of resection of an abdominal aortic aneurysm. Discusses specific areas of technical difficulty as well as pre-and postoperative management.
Prod-ACYDGD Dist-ACY 1970

Resection Of An Adrenal Tumor C 10 MIN
3/4 OR 1/2 INCH VIDEO CASSETTE
See series title for descriptive statement.
From The Pediatric Series.
Prod-SVL Dist-SVL

Resection Of Arteriosclerotic Aneurysms Of The Abdominal Aorta And Replacement By... C 26 MIN
16MM FILM OPTICAL SOUND PRO
Demonstrates two cases of arteriosclerotic aneurysm of the abdominal aorta and principles of excision therapy of aortic aneurysm. Considers technical aspects of the procedure and the method of preparation and use of vascular homografts for aortic replacement.
Prod-ACYDGD Dist-ACY 1953

Resection Of Right Colon For Carcinoma C 14 MIN
16MM FILM OPTICAL SOUND PRO
Points out that malignant lesions of the right colon should never have less than a resection of the entire right colon, with approximately 25 centimeters of the terminal ileum.
Prod-ACYDGD Dist-ACY 1950

Reservations In The Southwest X 30 MIN
2 INCH VIDEOTAPE I
Visits Indian reservations in the Southwest. Features governors of three of the 19 pueblos and shows Indian life in the home and at school, the ways Indians make their living, how they gain understanding of the Indian governmental system and their feelings about the future of their people. (Broadcast quality)
From The Cultural Understandings Series. No. 5
Prod-DENVPS Dist-GPITVL Prodn-KRMATV

Reserve For Tomorrow C 13 MIN
16MM FILM, 3/4 OR 1/2 IN VIDEO
Discusses the Strategic Petroleum Reserve, a supply of crude oil stored underground for emergency use in the event of an oil embargo.
LC NO. 81-706426
Prod-USERD Dist-USNAC 1981

Reserved For Tomorrow / Coal - The Other Energy C 28 MIN
3/4 OR 1/2 INCH VIDEO CASSETTE
Describes the U S crude oil stockpile of up to one billion barrels in underground salt domes one mile wide and 1000 feet deep. Reveals the amount of coal that is available to the U S over the next 200 years for electricity and petro-chemical derivatives by converting coal to gas or liquid.
Prod-IVCH Dist-IVCH

Reservoir Fluids And Pressures C 60 MIN
3/4 OR 1/2 INCH VIDEO CASSETTE IND
See series title for descriptive statement.
From The Basic And Petroleum Geology For Non-Geologists - Reservoirs And...-Series.
Prod-PHILLP Dist-GPCV

Reservoir In The Sky C 5 MIN
16MM FILM OPTICAL SOUND
Discusses studies to regulate snow and hail formation.
Prod-ALLFP Dist-NSTA 1973

Reservoir Mechanics C 33 MIN
3/4 OR 1/2 INCH VIDEO CASSETTE IND
See series title for descriptive statement.
From The Basic And Petroleum Geology For Non-Geologists - Drilling And...-Series.
Prod-PHILLP Dist-GPCV

Reservoir Mechanics And Secondary And Tertiary Recovery C 27 MIN
3/4 OR 1/2 INCH VIDEO CASSETTE IND
See series title for descriptive statement.
From The Petroleum Geology Series.
Prod-GPCV Dist-GPCV

Reservoir Rocks C 37 MIN
3/4 OR 1/2 INCH VIDEO CASSETTE IND
See series title for descriptive statement.
From The Petroleum Geology Series.
Prod-GPCV Dist-GPCV

Reservoir Rocks - Limestones C 39 MIN
3/4 OR 1/2 INCH VIDEO CASSETTE IND
See series title for descriptive statement.
From The Basic And Petroleum Geology For Non-Geologists - Hydrocarbons And...-Series.
Prod-PHILLP Dist-GPCV

Reservoir Rocks - Sandstones C 36 MIN
3/4 OR 1/2 INCH VIDEO CASSETTE IND
See series title for descriptive statement.
From The Basic And Petroleum Geology For Non-Geologists - Hydrocarbons And...-Series.
Prod-PHILLP Dist-GPCV

Reshape, Remake C 15 MIN
3/4 OR 1/2 INCH VIDEO CASSETTE I
Deals with common writing errors and with rewriting.
From The Tyger, Tyger Burning Bright Series.
Prod-CTI Dist-CTI

Reshaping Aquatic Environments C 15 MIN
16MM FILM OPTICAL SOUND C
Examines the attempts of marine ecologists, scientists and engineers to regulate and understand various life-systems within aquatic environments. Includes the investigation of the energy systems of the Chesapeake Estuary, an attempt to monitor the migration of the shad and an examination of the experiment to control life-destroying pollution.
From The Science In Action Series.
Prod-ALLFP Dist-COUNFI

Reshaping Values After The Holocaust B 180 MIN
1/2 IN VIDEO CASSETTE (VHS)
Discusses the re-defining of post-Holocaust values.
From The Religion In A Post-Holocaust World Series.
Prod-OHC Dist-HRC

Reshaping, Characterization And Glazing Of Anterior Ceramometal Restorations C 21 MIN
3/4 INCH VIDEO CASSETTE
Demonstrates and explains each step in the procedure for reshaping, characterizing and glazing the porcelain in an anterior ceramo-metal restoration.
LC NO. 79-706755
Prod-MUSC Dist-USNAC 1978

Residential Fire Problem, The, Pt 1 C
3/4 OR 1/2 INCH VIDEO CASSETTE
See series title for descriptive statement.
From The International Fire Protection Organizations Conference Series.
Prod-NFPA Dist-NFPA

Residential Fire Problem, The, Pt 2 C
3/4 OR 1/2 INCH VIDEO CASSETTE
See series title for descriptive statement.
From The International Fire Protection Organizations Conference Series.
Prod-NFPA Dist-NFPA

Residential Styles C 30 MIN
3/4 INCH VIDEO CASSETTE
See series title for descriptive statement.
From The Growing Old In Modern America Series.
Prod-UWASHP Dist-UWASHP

Residenz- Und Wagnerstadt Bayreuth C 5 MIN
16MM FILM, 3/4 OR 1/2 IN VIDEO H-C A
A German-language version of the motion picture Bayreuth, Royal Residence And Wagner City. Examines Bayeuth, noted not only for Richard Wagner's festival hall, but for other historic and artistic landmarks as well.
From The European Studies - Germany (German) Series.
Prod-MFAFRG Dist-IFB Prodn-BAYER 1973

Residual Exceptions C 57 MIN
3/4 OR 1/2 INCH VIDEO CASSETTE PRO
Explains erosion of the rule against hearsay. Points out that the federal rules provide for the admissibility of hearsay not falling within other exceptions.
From The Evidence Update Series.
Prod-ABACPE Dist-ABACPE

Resist-Resistance B 10 MIN
16MM FILM OPTICAL SOUND
Gives a general outline of the anti-draft work being done in the Boston-Cambridge area by National Resist and the New England Resistance.
Prod-SFN Dist-SFN 1967

Resistance B 16 MIN
16MM FILM, 3/4 OR 1/2 IN VIDEO
Shows how changes in length, diameter and temperature of a material affect its resistance. Shows the construction of several different resistors and their use in circuits.
Prod-USAF Dist-USNAC

Resistance B 17 MIN
3/4 OR 1/2 INCH VIDEO CASSETTE J-C A
Explores spiritual and armed resistance by the Jews to Nazi tyranny during World War II.
From The Witness To The Holocaust Series.
LC NO. 84-706508
Prod-HORECE Dist-CNEMAG 1983

Resistance Welding B 12 MIN
16MM FILM OPTICAL SOUND
Shows aluminum welds made under heat and pressure, two types of spot-welding machines, the use of carbon electrodes in high-speed resistance welding and tests for checking the size and strength of welds.
From The How To Weld Aluminum Series.
Prod-USDIBM Dist-USDIBM 1946

Resistance, The C 7 MIN
16MM FILM, 3/4 OR 1/2 IN VIDEO
Presents an animated story about conformity and rebellion which is expressed in the struggle of a hammer and other hand tools to force a nail into a piece of wood.
Prod-ZAGREB Dist-IFB 1980

Resisting Peer Pressure C
3/4 OR 1/2 INCH VIDEO CASSETTE
See series title for descriptive statement.
From The Asset Series
Prod-RESPRC Dist-RESPRC

Resisting Peer Pressure C 8 MIN
3/4 OR 1/2 INCH VIDEO CASSETTE J-H
Presents methods of resisting peer pressure which adolescents can use in their dealings with peers.
From The ASSET - A Social Skills Program For Adolescents Series. Session 4
LC NO. 81-706054
Prod-HAZLJS Dist-RESPRC Prodn-BAXLEN 1981

Resisting Pressures To Smoke C 9 MIN
16MM FILM, 3/4 OR 1/2 IN VIDEO J-H
Presents strategies for students to resist the pressure to smoke, be it peer pressure, parental modeling or media advertising.
Prod-USDHEW Dist-USNAC

Resistive Bridge Circuits B 26 MIN
16MM FILM - 3/4 IN VIDEO
Identifies a simple, resistive bridge circuit and discusses the specific characteristics of resistance ratio, voltage distribution and current flow.
LC NO. 79-707520
Prod-USAF Dist-USNAC 1979

Resistive Circuit Analysis C
3/4 OR 1/2 INCH VIDEO CASSETTE
See series title for descriptive statement.
From The Basic AC Circuits Series.
Prod-VTRI Dist-VTRI

Resistive Circuit Analysis C 20 MIN
3/4 OR 1/2 INCH VIDEO CASSETTE
See series title for descriptive statement.
From The Basic AC Circuits, Laboratory--Sessions--A Series.
Prod-TXINLC Dist-TXINLC

Resistive Circuits C
3/4 OR 1/2 INCH VIDEO CASSETTE
See series title for descriptive statement.
From The Basic Electricity - AC Series.
Prod-VTRI Dist-VTRI

Resistive Gait Program C 26 MIN
3/4 OR 1/2 INCH VIDEO CASSETTE
See series title for descriptive statement.
From The Proprioceptive Neuromuscular Facilitation Series.
Prod-UMDSM Dist-UMDSM

Resistive Mat Exercises I C 33 MIN
3/4 OR 1/2 INCH VIDEO CASSETTE
See series title for descriptive statement.
From The Proprioceptive Neuromuscular Facilitation Series.
Prod-UMDSM Dist-UMDSM

Resistive Mat Exercises II C 32 MIN
3/4 OR 1/2 INCH VIDEO CASSETTE
See series title for descriptive statement.
From The Proprioceptive Neuromuscular Facilitation Series.
Prod-UMDSM Dist-UMDSM

Resistor Color Code C 8 MIN
16MM FILM, 3/4 OR 1/2 IN VIDEO H-C A
Shows how to identify the resistors in a circuit and explains color bands, tolerances and identification bands.
From The Basic Electricity Series.
Prod-STFD Dist-IFB 1979

Resistors - Color Code B 33 MIN
16MM FILM - 3/4 IN VIDEO
Explains why electric resistors are color coded and provides the value indicated by each color. Illustrates how to use the color code chart and how to read the color code on a resistor.
LC NO. 79-707701
Prod-USAF Dist-USNAC 1979

Resistors - Construction B 21 MIN
16MM FILM - 3/4 IN VIDEO
States the purpose of resistors and describes various types. Demonstrates the construction and uses of fixed, adjustable and variable resistors.
LC NO. 79-707521
Prod-USAF Dist-USNAC 1979

Resolution Of Mossie Wax, The C 89 MIN
3/4 OR 1/2 INCH VIDEO CASSETTE
Illustrates the problems of the welfare system for the elderly and in particular one woman's struggle for a dignified old age. Features the life of Mossie Wax, a widow determined to survive in spite of her difficulties.
Prod-WITFTV Dist-PBS 1972

Resolution Of The Eye C 40 MIN
3/4 OR 1/2 INCH VIDEO CASSETTE
A collection of five self-contained abstract allegories which offer variations on the processes of seeking, receiving, retaining and recalling information.
Prod-EAI Dist-EAI

Resolution Of The Eye C 40 MIN
3/4 OR 1/2 INCH VIDEO CASSETTE
Presents themes and variations concerning perception, time and television. Originally aired on the Video-Film Review Series on PBS.
Prod-KITCHN Dist-KITCHN

Resolution On Saturn C 57 MIN
3/4 OR 1/2 INCH VIDEO CASSETTE H-C A
Shows pictures of Saturn and its moons taken on the Voyager I mission. Uses interviews with scientists, along with computer graphics and animation to explain such phenomena as why there are numerous rings around Saturn and how tiny moons help keep the rings in place.
From The Nova Series.
LC NO. 83-706022
Prod-BBCTV Dist-TIMLIF 1982

Resolved To Be Free C 29 MIN
16MM FILM OPTICAL SOUND
Chronicles Connecticut's role in the American Revolution from 1765 to 1781, includes glimpses of Israel Putnam defending Bunker Hill, Benedict Arnold assaulting Fort Ticonderoga and the sacrifice of Nathan Hale. Features Katharine Hepburn as narrator.
LC NO. 76-701168
Prod-FENWCK Dist-FENWCK 1975

Resolving Conflicts C 22 MIN
16MM FILM, 3/4 OR 1/2 IN VIDEO C A
Teaches supervisors and managers how to respond to conflict in the most productive way. Illustrates five conflict resolution strategies - avoidance, giving it back to those involved, imposing a solution, compromise and collaboration.
LC NO. 82-706569
Prod-CRMP Dist-CRMP 1982

Resolving Conflicts Through Counseling C 70 MIN
3/4 INCH VIDEO CASSETTE H-C A
Shows the integrative approach that can be used by equal employment opportunity counselors in resolving discrimination complaint problems.
LC NO. 77-706017
Prod-USIRS Dist-USNAC 1976

Resolving Interpersonal Conflicts C 11 MIN
3/4 OR 1/2 INCH VIDEO CASSETTE
Alerts supervisors to some common conflict situations that may arise when disadvantaged workers are introduced into the work group and describes some actions that can substantially reduce or eliminate these troublesome areas.
From The Supervising The Disadvantaged Series. Module 3
Prod-RESEM Dist-RESEM

Resolving Power L-3 C 3 MIN
16MM FILM SILENT H-C
Shows a pinhold source viewed through a telescope variable aperture. Discusses the rayleigh criterion.
From The Single-Concept Films In Physics Series.
Prod-OSUMPD Dist-OSUMPD 1963

Resonance C
3/4 OR 1/2 INCH VIDEO CASSETTE
See series title for descriptive statement.
From The Basic Electricity - AC Series.
Prod-VTRI Dist-VTRI

Resonance C 20 MIN
3/4 OR 1/2 INCH VIDEO CASSETTE
See series title for descriptive statement.
From The Basic AC Circuits, Laboratory--Sessions--A Series.
Prod-TXINLC Dist-TXINLC

Resonance C 30 MIN
16MM FILM, 3/4 OR 1/2 IN VIDEO C A
Explains resonance as the cause of a swaying bridge collapsing in a high wind and a wineglass shattering with a higher octave.
From The Mechanical Universe Series.
Prod-ANNCPB Dist-FI

Resonance (Basic AC Circuits) C
3/4 OR 1/2 INCH VIDEO CASSETTE
See series title for descriptive statement.
From The Basic AC Circuits Series.
Prod-VTRI Dist-VTRI

Resonant Lines B 30 MIN
16MM FILM - 3/4 IN VIDEO
Explains open and shorted resonant lines. Focuses on standing waves and shows the phase of relationship of the incident and reflected waves of current and voltage.
LC NO. 79-707777
Prod-USAF Dist-USNAC 1979

Resonant Sections And Matching Devices B 25 MIN
16MM FILM - 3/4 IN VIDEO
Discusses the use of resonant sections of transmission lines. Explains the operation and gives applications of harmonic filters, metallic insulators, quarter-wave matching transformers, half-wave matching transformers, line balance converters, and capacitive coupled joints.
LC NO. 79-707778
Prod-USAF Dist-USNAC 1979

Resource Center C 28 MIN
16MM FILM OPTICAL SOUND
Dr Dwight Allen, professor of education at Stanford University, presents the functions and uses of resource centers for students in various academic areas, and mentions the operation, staffing and administration of such centers.
From The Innovations In Education Series.
Prod-STNFRD Dist-EDUC 1966

Resource Geology C 25 MIN
16MM FILM, 3/4 OR 1/2 IN VIDEO H-C
Uses animated graphics to provide a comprehensive overview of the rock cycle, demonstrating the combination of natural forces at work over millions of years which redistributed chemical elements to form deposits of coal, iron and gypsum and other ores. Describes means of extracting these minerals.
Prod-BBCTV Dist-MEDIAG Prodn-OPENU 1985

Resource Management B 60 MIN
3/4 OR 1/2 INCH VIDEO CASSETTE
See series title for descriptive statement.
From The Project Management And CPM Series. Pt 5
Prod-UAZMIC Dist-UAZMIC 1977

Resource Recovery C 25 MIN
16MM FILM OPTICAL SOUND
Shows the recovery and remanufacturing of glass, metal, paper and plastics.
LC NO. 76-703799
Prod-BCDA Dist-BCDA 1974

Resource Recovery C 14 MIN
16MM FILM, 3/4 OR 1/2 IN VIDEO J-C
Describes the search for ways to recycle raw materials and energy from garbage.
From The Screen News Digest Series. Volume 20, Issue 8
Prod-HEARST Dist-HEARST 1978

Resource Sharing In Networks C 55 MIN
3/4 OR 1/2 INCH VIDEO CASSETTE C
Discusses evolution of the information society, point to point versus switched service, economic factors, types of user demand and role and impact of satellites.
From The Distributed Telecommunications Networks Series.
Prod-AMCEE Dist-AMCEE

Resources C 10 MIN
16MM FILM, 3/4 OR 1/2 IN VIDEO P-I
Portrays America as rich in natural resources such as forests, minerals, agricultural land and human potential. Presents conflicting points of view in order to raise questions, stimulate thinking, present alternatives and inspire interest on the part of the student.
From The Economics For Elementary Series.
Prod-OF Dist-AIMS 1971

Resources And Scarcity - What Is Economics All About C 30 MIN
3/4 OR 1/2 INCH VIDEO CASSETTE C
See series title for descriptive statement.
From The Economics USA Series.
Prod-WEFA Dist-ANNCPB

Resources And World Trade C 14 MIN
16MM FILM, 3/4 OR 1/2 IN VIDEO I-H
Explains how resources are used around the world to provide goods for home needs and for trade. Uses maps to show where some of the world's most important resources are located and illustrates the role of rivers and harbors in establishing trade centers.
Prod-BEAN Dist-PHENIX 1978

Resources And World Trade (Swedish) C 14 MIN
16MM FILM, 3/4 OR 1/2 IN VIDEO I-H
Explains how resources are used around the world to provide goods for home needs and for trade. Uses maps to show where some of the world's most important resources are located and illustrates the role of rivers and harbors in establishing trade centers.
Prod-BEAN Dist-PHENIX 1978

Resources Make It Happen C 19 MIN
16MM FILM OPTICAL SOUND T
Examines effective ways and means of using professional and financial resources in adult education courses.
From The Further Education Series.
LC NO. 77-702846
Prod-ADEAV Dist-CENTWO Prodn-CENTWO 1976

Resources Of 20th-Century Music B 45 MIN
2 INCH VIDEOTAPE C
See series title for descriptive statement.
From The General Humanities Series. Unit 3 - The Auditory Arts
Prod-CHITVC Dist-GPITVL Prodn-WTTWTV

Respectable Lie, A C 30 MIN
3/4 OR 1/2 INCH VIDEO CASSETTE
Examines the imagery and messages of pornography and its connection to violence against women, stating that in fact one doesn't have to accept this propaganda. Discusses pornography, what it is, how it has affected and continues to affect women.
Prod-WMENIF Dist-WMENIF

Respecting Differences C 11 MIN
16MM FILM OPTICAL SOUND
Deals with the cultural stresses on the Australian migrant child in the community. Presents the view that if a child is given a bad self-image by his environment, it is difficult, if not impossible, to eradicate it.
LC NO. 80-700834
Prod-NSWF Dist-TASCOR 1978

Respecting Others Game, The C 11 MIN
16MM FILM, 3/4 OR 1/2 IN VIDEO P
Tells of a young boy's realization of the importance of respecting others when his friend shows him how he would feel if his rights were not respected.
From The Learning Responsibility Series.
Prod-HIGGIN Dist-HIGGIN 1978

Respirando Por Otros C 14 MIN
16MM FILM, 3/4 OR 1/2 IN VIDEO C A
A Spanish-language version of the motion picture Breathing For Others. Shows many situations where exhaled air resuscitation may save a life, including asphyxia, drowning, gassing, electric shock and suffocation. Demonstrates the mouth-to-mouth and mouth-to-nose techniques.
From The Emergency Resuscitation (Spanish) Series.
Prod-UKMD Dist-IFB

Respiration C 29 MIN
3/4 INCH VIDEO CASSETTE C A
Overviews ways in which simpler organisms such as amoebas exchange oxygen and carbon dioxide. Presents various repiratory structures. Focuses on human respiration.
From The Introducing Biology Series. Program 14
Prod-COAST Dist-CDTEL

Respiration - Energy For Life C
3/4 OR 1/2 INCH VIDEO CASSETTE H
Explains the related processes of breathing and cell respiration. Reviews the major experiments that have enabled the relationship between bodily activity and cell chemistry to be understood.
Prod-GA Dist-GA

Respiration And Circulation C 26 MIN
16MM FILM OPTICAL SOUND PRO
Explains the functions of the circulatory and respiratory systems within the human body and shows how they work together under the direction of the brain through reflex chemoreceptor control. Depicts how these complex systems affect the physiological problems of flight.
LC NO. FIE61-13
Prod-USAF Dist-USNAC 1961

Respiration And Transpiration C 15 MIN
3/4 INCH VIDEO CASSETTE I
Shows that respiration is vital to the existence of green plants.
From The Search For Science (2nd Ed.) Unit VIII - Plants Series.
Prod-WVIZTV Dist-GPITVL

Respiration During And After Anesthesia C 21 MIN
16MM FILM OPTICAL SOUND PRO
Presents principles of respiratory care during preoperative, intraoperative and postoperative periods. Utilizes dramatizations during which the viewer is asked to interpret findings and decide on a course of action.
LC NO. 72-700350
Prod-AYERST Dist-AYERST 1973

Respiration In Man X 26 MIN
16MM FILM, 3/4 OR 1/2 IN VIDEO H-C
Describes the structure and functions of the respiratory system. Provides visual proof of the exchange of carbon dioxide for oxygen. Raises the question of air pollution and how long man will tolerate it.
From The Biology Series. Unit 8 - Human Biology
Prod-EBF Dist-EBEC 1969

Respiration In Man (Spanish) C 25 MIN
16MM FILM, 3/4 OR 1/2 IN VIDEO H-C
Analyzes the structure and function of the respiratory system.
From The Biology (Spanish) Series. Unit 8 - Human Physiology
Prod-EBEC Dist-EBEC

Respirators For Health And Safety C 10 MIN
16MM FILM - 3/4 IN VIDEO
Shows how to set up an effective respirator program, including matching respirators to hazards, writing procedures, fitting, training and maintenance.
Prod-ALLIED Dist-BNA

Respiratory Acidosis And Alkalosis C 19 MIN
3/4 OR 1/2 INCH VIDEO CASSETTE PRO
Explains causes and identifies acute and chronic diseases associated with respiratory acid-base problems. Shows proper health-team action to be taken.
From The Fluids And Electrolytes Series.
Prod-BRA Dist-BRA

Respiratory Care C 60 MIN
3/4 OR 1/2 INCH VIDEO CASSETTE PRO
Describes how to formulate a care approach for a patient with chronic obstructive pulmonary disease.
LC NO. 81-706302
Prod-USVA Dist-USNAC 1980

Respiratory Distress - Auscultation (2nd Ed) C 13 MIN
3/4 OR 1/2 INCH VIDEO CASSETTE PRO
Demonstrates proper auscultatory techniques. Discusses abnormal breath and cardiac sounds and their underlying causes. Notes the limitations of auscultation and the indications for other diagnostic techniques.
Prod-UMICHM Dist-UMICHM 1983

Respiratory Distress - Clinical Identification C 15 MIN
3/4 OR 1/2 INCH VIDEO CASSETTE PRO
Shows how to identify respiratory distress in the newborn infant by demonstrating the observation and identification of abnormalities in respiratory rate, respiratory effort, expiratory effort and skin coloration.
From The Michigan Perinatal Education, Instructional Unit B - Respiratory Distress Series.
LC NO. 79-707740
Prod-UMICH Dist-UMICH 1978

Respiratory Distress - Diagnosis By Inspection And Arterial Blood Analysis C 18 MIN
16MM FILM OPTICAL SOUND PRO
Presents case studies of four patients who suffer from respiratory distress and how diagnosis is determined by inspection and arterial blood analysis.
Prod-SQUIBB Dist-SQUIBB

Respiratory Distress - Size/Maturity Factors (2nd Ed) C 13 MIN
3/4 OR 1/2 INCH VIDEO CASSETTE PRO
Covers determining a newborn's gestational age, weight and size, classifying infants by gestational age and size and risk factors related to gestational age and size.
Prod-UMICHM Dist-UMICHM 1983

Respiratory Distress Syndrome C 15 MIN
3/4 OR 1/2 INCH VIDEO CASSETTE PRO
Reviews the clinical factors related to the causes of respiratory distress syndrome, clinical management of the condition in both primary care settings and regional perinatal centers and the clinical course.
From The Michigan Perinatal Education, Instructional Unit B - Respiratory Distress Series.
LC NO. 79-707743
Prod-UMICH Dist-UMICH 1978

Respiratory Emergencies C 15 MIN
16MM FILM, 3/4 OR 1/2 IN VIDEO H-C A
See series title for descriptive statement.
From The REACT - Review Of Emergency Aid And CPR Training Series.
Prod-MTI Dist-MTI

Respiratory Emergencies - Babies And Children C 15 MIN
16MM FILM, 3/4 OR 1/2 IN VIDEO H-C A
See series title for descriptive statement.
From The REACT - Review Of Emergency Aid And CPR Training Series.
Prod-MTI Dist-MTI

Respiratory Emergencies And Artificial Respiration C 10 MIN
16MM FILM, 3/4 OR 1/2 IN VIDEO A
Describes first aid procedures to use with a person who has stopped breathing.
From The Emergency First Aid Training Series.
LC NO. 81-706710
Prod-CRAF Dist-IFB 1980

Respiratory Exercises For The Parkinson Patient C 13 MIN
16MM FILM OPTICAL SOUND
Demonstrates respiratory exercises designed to enhance the diaphragmatic breathing and lateral costal expansion of the Parkinson patient.
LC NO. 74-705531
Prod-USPHS Dist-USNAC

Respiratory Failure C 22 MIN
3/4 INCH VIDEO CASSETTE PRO
Discusses factors which may precipitate respiratory failure, symptoms and signs of respiratory acidosis and treatment of respiratory failure.
LC NO. 76-706102
Prod-WARMP Dist-USNAC 1970

Respiratory Failure - Etiology And Management C 21 MIN
3/4 INCH VIDEO CASSETTE
Presents lung cancer mortality statistics and describes paraneoplastic syndromes.
Prod-UTAHTI Dist-UTAHTI

Respiratory Protection C 8 MIN
3/4 OR 1/2 INCH VIDEO CASSETTE A
Explains the need for respiratory protection when airborne hazardous materials are in excess of safe levels. Shows the use of cartridge and single-use respirators.
LC NO. 84-707799
Prod-KOHLER Dist-IFB

Respiratory Protection C 60 MIN
3/4 OR 1/2 INCH VIDEO CASSETTE
See series title for descriptive statement.
From The Fire Protection Training Series.
Prod-ITCORP Dist-ITCORP

Respiratory System - Unit 10 C 40 MIN
3/4 OR 1/2 INCH VIDEO CASSETTE PRO
Covers prominent features of the respiratory system and lungs.
From The Histology Review Series.
Prod-HSCIC Dist-HSCIC

Respiratory System, The C 9 MIN
16MM FILM, 3/4 OR 1/2 IN VIDEO J-C
Shows a dissected rat and traces the path of air through the respiratory system.
Prod-CFDLD Dist-CORF

Respiratory Systems In Animals C 14 MIN
16MM FILM, 3/4 OR 1/2 IN VIDEO H-C
Compares the respiratory systems of a variety of phyla, examining the intake of oxygen by gills, membranes and lungs.
From The Animal Systems Series.
LC NO. 80-707017
Prod-IU Dist-IU 1971

Respiratory Therapy - Basic Principles Of Ventilators (2nd Ed) C 12 MIN
3/4 OR 1/2 INCH VIDEO CASSETTE PRO
Describes the classification of the commonly available positive pressure ventilators. Considers the relationship between ventilator characteristics and pulmonary gas exchange.
From The Anesthesiology Clerkship Series.
Prod-UMICHM Dist-UMICHM 1982

Respiratory Therapy - Clinical Applications Of Mechanical Ventilators C 40 MIN
3/4 OR 1/2 INCH VIDEO CASSETTE PRO
Discusses the clinical use of positive pressure ventilators. Describes the types of patients requiring mechanical ventilation. Discusses both invasive and noninvasive monitoring. Considers methods of weaning from ventilator support.
From The Anesthesiology Clerkship Series.
Prod-UMICHM Dist-UMICHM 1982

Respiratory Therapy - Humidity Aerosol Treatment (2nd Ed) C 16 MIN
3/4 OR 1/2 INCH VIDEO CASSETTE PRO
Defines both relative and absolute humidity and the calculation of humidity deficit. Indicates the differences between humidifiers and nebulizers, and describes their advantages and disadvantages in clinical use.
From The Anesthesiology Clerkship Series.
Prod-UMICHM Dist-UMICHM 1982

Respiratory Therapy - Oxygen Administration (2nd Ed) C 15 MIN
3/4 OR 1/2 INCH VIDEO CASSETTE PRO
Discusses equipment available for the administration of oxygen therapy. Provides guidelines for the clinical use of this equipment in patients requiring various inspired oxygen concentrations.
From The Anesthesiology Clerkship Series.
Prod-UMICHM Dist-UMICHM 1982

Respiratory Tract, The C 30 MIN
3/4 OR 1/2 INCH VIDEO CASSETTE
Presents the respiratory system and how it works. Discusses the problems of pneumonia, puncture, emphysema and air pollution. Looks at how individuals can protect their respiratory system.
Prod-UILCCC Dist-AL

Respond - On-Site Assistance C 23 MIN
16MM FILM OPTICAL SOUND
Designed to motivate local government officials to participate in on-site assistance. Shows how a Federal-State team surveys local government agencies to check their emergency readiness plans and procedures.
LC NO. 74-706390
Prod-USDCPA Dist-USNAC 1974

Respondent Learning C 10 MIN
3/4 OR 1/2 INCH VIDEO CASSETTE T
See series title for descriptive statement.
From The Protocol Materials In Teacher Education - The Process Of Teaching, Pt 2 Series.
Prod-MSU Dist-MSU

Responding C 6 MIN
3/4 OR 1/2 INCH VIDEO CASSETTE C A
Portrays hetorosexual, bisexual, and homosexual lovemaking. Conveys that human lovemaking is essentially the same regardless of sexual orientation.
Prod-MMRC Dist-MMRC

Responding At Appropriate Levels C 29 MIN
2 INCH VIDEOTAPE C A
Features a humanistic psychologist who, by analysis and examples, discusses responding at appropriate levels.
From The Interpersonal Competence, Unit 02 - Communication Series.
Prod-MVNE Dist-TELSTR 1973

Responding Positively To Change C 30 MIN
3/4 OR 1/2 INCH VIDEO CASSETTE
Focuses on relating positively to stress or change which can be vital to a company experiencing organizational, technical, growth or profitability changes.
From The High Performance Leadership Series.
Prod-PRODEV Dist-PRODEV

Responding Positively To Change C 30 MIN
3/4 OR 1/2 INCH VIDEO CASSETTE
See series title for descriptive statement.
From The High Performance Leadership Series.
Prod-VIDAI Dist-DELTAK

Responding To A Baby's Actions B 24 MIN
3/4 OR 1/2 INCH VIDEO CASSETTE PRO
Follows adults interacting with babies, as in imitating the baby's sounds, exploring toys with baby, joining in game baby has started. Presents three un-narrated examples of interaction for group discussions.
Prod-HSERF Dist-HSERF

Responding To Light C 30 MIN
3/4 OR 1/2 INCH VIDEO CASSETTE
See series title for descriptive statement.
From The Photographic Vision - All About Photography Series.
Prod-COAST Dist-CDTEL

Responding To New Incentives - The Role Of Hospital Managers C 20 MIN
3/4 OR 1/2 INCH VIDEO CASSETTE
Helps hospital managers look at new ways of getting the job done in response to changing financial incentives. Examines examples of hospital-wide changes that have been implemented to achieve increased cost-effectiveness and efficiency.
Prod-AHOA Dist-AHOA

Response And Implementation Of The 1954 Decision B 30 MIN
16MM FILM OPTICAL SOUND H-C A
Dr Vincent Browne discusses the types of plans that were supposed to implement school desegregation in the Southern and border states after 1954, the efforts of whites to evade implementation, De Facto segregation in Northern schools and other aspects of the problem.
LC NO. 73-704103
Prod-WCBSTV Dist-HRAW 1969

Response Of A Resonant System To A Frequency Step B 11 MIN
16MM FILM - 3/4 IN VIDEO
Presents a computer-generated film that visualizes fundamental concepts relevant to linear system theory and frequency modulation.
Prod-NCEEF Dist-EDC

Response Of Linear Systems To White Noise Inputs - Discrete Time Case C 46 MIN
3/4 OR 1/2 INCH VIDEO CASSETTE PRO
See series title for descriptive statement.
From The Modern Control Theory - Stochastic Estimation Series.
Prod-MIOT Dist-MIOT

Response Of Linear Systems To White Noise Inputs - Continuous Time Case C 52 MIN
3/4 OR 1/2 INCH VIDEO CASSETTE PRO
See series title for descriptive statement.
From The Modern Control Theory - Stochastic Estimation Series.
Prod-MIOT Dist-MIOT

Response Spectrum Analysis C 60 MIN
3/4 OR 1/2 INCH VIDEO CASSETTE C
Discusses use of response spectrum curves and effects of ductility as well as accounting for damping effects during dynamic analysis.
From The Fundamentals Of Dynamic Analysis For Structural Design Series.
Prod-USCCE Dist-AMCEE

Response To Mechanical Shock C 18 MIN
16MM FILM OPTICAL SOUND
Illustrates several types of mechanical shock, showing the shock signature generated by each. Defines and explains the interdependence of the parameters of mechanical shock--acceleration, velocity and displacement. Tells how different degrees of damping affect the motion of the spring-mass system during shock response.
LC NO. 70-700217
Prod-USAEC Dist-USNAC Prodn-SANDIA 1968

Response To Misbehavior C 9 MIN
16MM FILM, 3/4 OR 1/2 IN VIDEO I-J
Gives students an opportunity to evaluate and discuss possible choices of action in the area of responsibility.
From The Moral Decision Making Series.
Prod-MORLAT Dist-AIMS 1972

Response To Stress C 29 MIN
3/4 OR 1/2 INCH VIDEO CASSETTE
Presents information on stress.
From The Daniel Foster, MD Series.
Prod-KERA Dist-PBS

Response To The Challenge C 30 MIN
16MM FILM OPTICAL SOUND H-C
Presents a speech by Bob Richards, twice Olympic pole vault champion. Outlines the problems confronting society and gives a description of the ways persons must respond to these problems. Motivates the individual into positive action.
Prod-GEMILL Dist-NINEFC

Responsibile Assertion C 28 MIN
16MM FILM, 3/4 OR 1/2 IN VIDEO H-C A
Tells that people who are insufficiently assertive find find themselves continually manipulated by others, frustrated in their desires and aspirations and even emotionally incapacitated because of their inhibitions. Reveals that effective assertion training demonstrates that although such training is not intended to cure behavioral dysfunction, it can be a potent coping mechanism for most individuals who learn to use it responsibly.
Prod-WILEYJ Dist-MEDIAG 1978

Responsibilities And Rewards Of Parenting C 30 MIN
16MM FILM, 3/4 OR 1/2 IN VIDEO H-C A
Summarizes the importance of a parent's role and retraces the steps in a young child's development.
From The Look At Me Series.
Prod-WTTWTV Dist-FI 1980

Responsibilities Of The Contracting Officer C 10 MIN
16MM FILM OPTICAL SOUND
Discusses contracts, purchase orders and unilateral agreements in business.
LC NO. 74-706391
Prod-USFSS Dist-USNAC 1966

Responsibility C
3/4 OR 1/2 INCH VIDEO CASSETTE T
Presents Dr Ed Frierson lecturing on how to help students develop personal responsibility. Contains three videotapes.
From The School Inservice Videotape Series.
Prod-TERRAS Dist-SLOSSF

Responsibility C 30 MIN
3/4 OR 1/2 INCH VIDEO CASSETTE
Discusses the responsibility of both the sender and receiver in personal communication. Looks at the communication circle from the listener's point of view.
From The Effective Listening Series. Tape 2
Prod-TELSTR Dist-TELSTR

Responsibility - The Gang And I C 14 MIN
16MM FILM, 3/4 OR 1/2 IN VIDEO I-J
Relates the recollections of David, who tries to convince himself that being part of a gang when he was younger was the only way. Shows David slowly coming to see the irresponsibility and lack of concern for others in the gang's selfish and sometimes dangerous acts.
Prod-AIMS Dist-AIMS 1977

Responsibility - The Key To Freedom C 30 MIN
3/4 OR 1/2 INCH VIDEO CASSETTE
See series title for descriptive statement.
From The Personal Development And Professional Growth - Mike McCaffrey's Focus Seminar Series.
Prod-DELTAK Dist-DELTAK

Responsibility - The Only Way C 15 MIN
16MM FILM - VIDEO, ALL FORMATS K-J
Presents a Fat Albert cartoon teaching a lesson about money and responsibility.
From The Fat Albert And The Cosby Kids IV Series.
Prod-BARR Dist-BARR Prodn-FLMTON

Responsibility - Work Or Home B 15 MIN
16MM FILM OPTICAL SOUND A
Deals with how far company loyalty should go and where the dividing line between work obligations and home stands. Explains when one's job should take priority over family and when family comes before the job.
From The Discussion Series.
LC NO. 72-701677
Prod-CONCOR Dist-CPH 1962

Responsibility For The Future C 27 MIN
16MM FILM, 3/4 OR 1/2 IN VIDEO J-H A
Examines the consequences of decimating the earth's resources, both mineral and biological.
From The Of Energy, Minerals, And Man Series.
Prod-GAZEL Dist-JOU

Responsibility Shared - Autonomous Production Groups C 28 MIN
3/4 OR 1/2 INCH VIDEO CASSETTE C A
Offers examples of businesses that are being run by their employees. Describes how motivation and profits increase when employees organize and impose their own regulations.
From The Re-Making Of Work Series.
Prod-BLCKBY Dist-EBEC 1983

Responsibility To Act C 19 MIN
16MM FILM, 3/4 OR 1/2 IN VIDEO
Tells a true, tragic school fire story and then examines how several occupational hazards could have been avoided.
Prod-VISUCP Dist-VISUCP

Responsible Assertion - A Model For Personal Growth C 28 MIN
16MM FILM OPTICAL SOUND
Demonstrates the different consequences of nonassertive, aggressive and assertive behaviors by using dramatic scenes of a graduate student confronting her advisor about the demanding requirements of her assistantship.
Prod-RESPRC Dist-RESPRC

Responsible Assertions C 28 MIN
3/4 OR 1/2 INCH VIDEO CASSETTE
Examines different styles of behavior through dramatic scenes in which a graduate student confronts her advisor about the demanding requirements of her assistantship.
Prod-RESPRC Dist-RESPRC

Responsible Caring—A Series
J-C A
Deals with various problems faced by teenagers.
Prod-MEMAPP Dist-MEMAPP Prodn-VISCNT 1980

Adrianne's Man 005 MIN
Boy's Don't Do That 006 MIN
Wayne's Decision 006 MIN
What's To Understand 004 MIN

Responsible Consumer, The C 29 MIN
3/4 OR 1/2 INCH VIDEO CASSETTE H-C A
Deals with consumers' responsibilities, both to themselves in terms of getting the best food buy, and to society in terms of dealing fairly and honestly in the marketplace.
From A Be A Better Shopper Series. Program 13
LC NO. 81-707313
Prod-CUETV Dist-CUNIV 1978

Responsible Feedback, Pt 1 C 15 MIN
3/4 OR 1/2 INCH VIDEO CASSETTE T
See series title for descriptive statement.
From The Protocol Materials In Teacher Education - Interpersonal Communication Skills Series.
Prod-MSU Dist-MSU

Responsible Feedback, Pt 2 C 15 MIN
3/4 OR 1/2 INCH VIDEO CASSETTE T
See series title for descriptive statement.
From The Protocol Materials In Teacher Education - Interpersonal Communication Skills Series.
Prod-MSU Dist-MSU

Responsible Level, The C 40 MIN
3/4 OR 1/2 INCH VIDEO CASSETTE
See series title for descriptive statement.
From The Management By Responsibility Series.
Prod-TRAINS Dist-DELTAK

Responsible Pricing Of Services C
3/4 OR 1/2 INCH VIDEO CASSETTE
Explains pricing health care services with financial survival in mind. Illustrates the five financing requirements basic to all successful pricing structures, direct expenses, indirect expenses, working capital, capital and profit.
From The Revenues, Rates And Reimbursements Series.
Prod-TEACHM Dist-TEACHM

Responsive Health Care - One Patient's Search C 34 MIN
3/4 OR 1/2 INCH VIDEO CASSETTE PRO
Describes a man's positive and negative experiences while seeking diagnosis through a maze of medical specialties and undergoing subsequent treatment for a brain tumor. Views a life-threatening illness from a patient's perspective, covering such topics as pre-surgical fears, postoperative confusion, social support systems, heightened sense of vulnerability and altered body image.
Prod-UMICHM Dist-UMICHM 1984

Responsive Parenting Program, The C 30 MIN
16MM FILM OPTICAL SOUND C A
Focuses on a parent training program in Kansas, in which parents learn to use positive behavior management techniques to improve the management of their children and the general quality of their homelife.
LC NO. 78-701609
Prod-UKANS Dist-UKANS 1978

Rest C 3 MIN
3/4 INCH VIDEO CASSETTE
Shows the New Mexican landscape as viewed from a hammock.
From The South-Western Landscape Series.
Prod-EAI Dist-EAI

Rest And Leisure In The USSR C 14 MIN
16MM FILM, 3/4 OR 1/2 IN VIDEO H-C
A Russian language film. Views the way Soviet citizens enjoy leisure activities.
From The Russian Language Series.
Prod-IFB Dist-IFB 1963

Rest Of Your Life, The C 28 MIN
16MM FILM, 3/4 OR 1/2 IN VIDEO H-C A
Identifies and examines some of the problems related to retirement. Raises pertinent questions and explains the need for planning for retirement.
Prod-ALTSUL Dist-JOU 1967

Restarts Of Beads C 13 MIN
3/4 OR 1/2 INCH VIDEO CASSETTE IND
See series title for descriptive statement.
From The Electric Arc Welding Series. Chapter 8
Prod-TAT Dist-TAT

Restless City Speaks, The B 15 MIN
16MM FILM OPTICAL SOUND H-C A
Studies complexities of life in a vast urban area, showing their causes and effects.
Prod-WSU Dist-WSU 1958

Restless Earth—A Series
16MM FILM, 3/4 OR 1/2 IN VIDEO H-C A
Prod-WNETTV Dist-IU 1972

Restless Earth, The - Earthquakes 26 MIN
Restless Earth, The - Evidence From Ancient 11 MIN
Restless Earth, The - Geology And Man 19 MIN
Restless Earth, The - Plate Tectonics Theory 58 MIN

Restless Earth, The - Earthquakes C 26 MIN
16MM FILM, 3/4 OR 1/2 IN VIDEO H-C A
Examines theories explaining causes of earthquake and methods of 'DEFUSING' earthquakes.
From The Restless Earth Series.
LC NO. 80-707036
Prod-WNETTV Dist-IU 1972

Restless Earth, The - Evidence From Ancient Life C 11 MIN
16MM FILM, 3/4 OR 1/2 IN VIDEO H-C A
Presents the relationships between the evolution of plant and animal life and the history of our changing earth. Explains that some species of worms are known to be 600 million years old and some plant life dates back 3,400 million years.
From The Restless Earth Series.
LC NO. 80-707037
Prod-WNETTV Dist-IU 1972

Restless Earth, The - Geology And Man C 19 MIN
16MM FILM, 3/4 OR 1/2 IN VIDEO H-C A
Explains that life began to evolve more than 100 million years ago, but at man's present rate of consumption and waste production, his effect on future geological history is yet to be determined.
From The Restless Earth Series.
LC NO. 80-707038
Prod-WNETTV Dist-IU 1973

Restless Earth, The - Plate Tectonics Theory C 58 MIN
16MM FILM, 3/4 OR 1/2 IN VIDEO H-C A
Explains plate theory through the use of models, examining scientific experiments and visiting geological sites throughout the world.
From The Restless Earth Series.
LC NO. 80-707039
Prod-WNETTV Dist-IU 1973

Restless Earth, The - Understanding The Theory Of Plate Tectonics C 43 MIN
3/4 OR 1/2 INCH VIDEO CASSETTE
Describes the theory of plate tectonics and explains where the material comes from to create a new ocean floor. Explains the source of the force which is able to move continents and change the contours of the ocean floors.
LC NO. 81-706668
Prod-SCIMAN Dist-GA 1981

Restless Ocean Of Air, The C 20 MIN
16MM FILM, 3/4 OR 1/2 IN VIDEO I-J T
Shows a student participation film in which students are challenged to form their own answers to the question 'WHAT MAKES THE AIR SO RESTLESS.'
From The Science Twenty Series.
Prod-PRISM Dist-SF 1969

Restless Ones, The C 105 MIN
16MM FILM OPTICAL SOUND
Presents a portrayal of today's teenagers, set to the heartbeat of their trials and triumphs.
Prod-WWP Dist-NINEFC

Restless Sea, The C 36 MIN
16MM FILM, 3/4 OR 1/2 IN VIDEO J-H
A revised version of the 1964 motion picture The Restless Sea. Uses animation to examine various aspects of the sea, including waves and tides, marine life, erosion of land, the nature of the sea bottom, analysis of sea water and tracing of storms.
Prod-DISNEY Dist-WDEMCO 1979

Restoration In Bedford Stuyvesant C 15 MIN
16MM FILM OPTICAL SOUND
Focuses on efforts to improve the Bedford Stuyvesant neighborhood of Brooklyn, New York, using community resources and outside help.
LC NO. 77-700025
Prod-BUGAS Dist-BEMPS Prodn-BAILYB 1976

Restoration In Bedford Stuyvesant C 15 MIN
3/4 OR 1/2 INCH VIDEO CASSETTE
Takes a look at Bedford Stuyvesant restoration's economic, cultural and housing rehabilitation.
Prod-IVCH Dist-IVCH

Restoration Of A Class I Facial Pit Cavity Preparation With Amalgam C 12 MIN
16MM FILM - 3/4 IN VIDEO PRO
Demonstrates placing copal varnish, condensing, carving, burnishing, finishing and polishing an amalgam restoration in a manikin. Shows, in a cross-sectional view, the causes and effects of improper and proper condensing. Presents four-handed procedures.
From The Restoration Of Cavity Preparations With Amalgam And Tooth - Colored Materials Series. Module
LC NO. 76-706184
Prod-USBHRD Dist-USNAC Prodn-NMAC 1974

Restoration Of A Class I Occlusal Cavity Preparation With Amalgam C 11 MIN
16MM FILM - 3/4 IN VIDEO PRO
Demonstrates placing varnish, condensing, carving, burnishing, occlusal adjustment, finishing and polishing an amalgam restoration in a manikin. Shows four-handed procedures.
From The Restoration Of Cavity Preparations With Amalgam And Tooth-Colored Materials Series. Module 10
LC NO. 76-706185
Prod-USBHRD Dist-USNAC Prodn-NMAC 1974

Restoration Of A Class I Occluso-Lingual Cavity Preparation With Amalgam C 9 MIN
16MM FILM - 3/4 IN VIDEO
Demonstrates placing a secondary metal matrix, condensing, carving, burnishing and polishing in a manikin. Shows four-handed procedures.
From The Restoration Of Cavity Preparations With Amalgam And Tooth-Colored Materials Series. Module 13
LC NO. 76-706186
Prod-USBHRD Dist-USNAC Prodn-NMAC 1974

Restoration Of A Class II Mesio-Occlusal Cavity Preparation With Amalgam C 18 MIN
16MM FILM - 3/4 IN VIDEO PRO
Demonstrates condensing, carving, burnishing, occlusal adjustment, finishing and polishing an amalgam restoration in a manikin. Shows four-handed procedures.
From The Restoration Of Cavity Preparations With Amalgam And Tooth-Colored Materials Series. Module 12
LC NO. 76-706187
Prod-USBHRD Dist-USNAC Prodn-NMAC 1974

Restoration Of A Class III Distal Cavity Preparation With Silicate Cement C 10 MIN
16MM FILM - 3/4 IN VIDEO PRO
Demonstrates placing a calcium hydroxide liner, adapting a plastic matrix strip, placing silicate cement using the bulk pack technic and finishing in a manikin. Shows four-handed procedures.
From The Restoration Of Cavity Preparations With Amalgam And Tooth-Colored Materials Series. Module 6
LC NO. 76-706188
Prod-USBHRD Dist-USNAC Prodn-NMAC 1974

Restoration Of A Class III Disto-Lingual Cavity Preparation With Amalgam C 18 MIN
16MM FILM - 3/4 IN VIDEO PRO
Demonstrates placing varnish, preparing and placing a custom

metal matrix strip, condensing, carving, burnishing, finishing and polishing an amalgam restoration in a manikin. Shows four-handed procedures.
From The Restoration Of Cavity Preparations With Amalgam And Tooth-Colored Materials Series. Module 9
LC NO. 76-706189
Prod-USBHRD Dist-USNAC Prodn-NMAC 1974

Restoration Of A Class III Mesial Cavity Preparation With Filled Resin C 10 MIN
16MM FILM - 3/4 IN VIDEO PRO
Demonstrates placing calcium hydroxide liner, adapting a plastic matrix strip, placing filled resin with a syringe and finishing in a manikin. Shows four-handed procedures.
From The Restoration Of Cavity Preparations With Amalgam And Tooth-Colored Materials Series. Module 7
LC NO. 76-706190
Prod-USBHRD Dist-USNAC Prodn-NMAC 1974

Restoration Of A Class IV Mesio-Incisal Cavity Preparation With Filled Resin C 17 MIN
16MM FILM - 3/4 IN VIDEO PRO
Demonstrates placing a dead soft metal matrix, placing a filled resin with a syringe, finishing and adjustment of occlusion in a manikin. Shows four-handed procedures.
From The Restoration Of Cavity Preparations With Amalgam And Tooth-Colored Materials Series. Module 8
LC NO. 76-706191
Prod-USBHRD Dist-USNAC Prodn-NMAC 1974

Restoration Of A Class V Disto-Facial Cavity Preparation With Amalgam C 15 MIN
16MM FILM - 3/4 IN VIDEO PRO
Demonstrates placing a calcium hydroxide base, placing a custom metal matrix, condensing, carving, burnishing, finishing and polishing in a manikin. Shows four-handed procedures.
From The Restoration Of Cavity Preparations With Amalgam And Tooth-Colored Materials Series. Module 14
LC NO. 76-706192
Prod-USBHRD Dist-USNAC Prodn-NMAC 1974

Restoration Of A Class V Facial Cavity Preparation With Amalgam C 12 MIN
16MM FILM - 3/4 IN VIDEO PRO
Demonstrates placing varnish, condensing, carving, finishing and polishing in a manikin. Emphasizes the polishing procedure with proper and improper technic. Shows four-handed procedures.
From The Restoration Of Cavity Preparations With Amalgam And Tooth-Colored Materials Series. Module 4
LC NO. 76-706193
Prod-USBHRD Dist-USNAC Prodn-NMAC 1974

Restoration Of A Class V Facial Cavity Preparation With Unfilled Resin C 11 MIN
16MM FILM - 3/4 IN VIDEO PRO
Demonstrates placing calcium hydroxide liner, placing unfilled resin with the brush-in technique, finishing and polishing in a manikin. Shows four-handed procedures.
From The Restoration Of Cavity Preparations With Amalgam And Tooth-Colored Materials Series. Module 5
LC NO. 76-706194
Prod-USBHRD Dist-USNAC Prodn-NMAC 1974

Restoration Of Cavity Preparations With Amalgam And Tooth-Colored Materials--A Series

Prod-USBHRD Dist-USNAC Prodn-NMAC 1974

Assembly Of A Matrix Band And Mechanical
Isolation Of A Class V Facial Lesion With A 5 MIN
Restoration Of A Class I Facial Pit Cavity 12 MIN
Restoration Of A Class I Occlusal Cavity 11 MIN
Restoration Of A Class I Occluso-Lingual 9 MIN
Restoration Of A Class II Mesio-Occlusal 18 MIN
Restoration Of A Class III Distal Cavity 10 MIN
Restoration Of A Class III Disto-Lingual 18 MIN
Restoration Of A Class III Mesial Cavity 10 MIN
Restoration Of A Class IV Mesio-Incisal 17 MIN
Restoration Of A Class V Disto-Facial 15 MIN
Restoration Of A Class V Facial Cavity 12 MIN
Restoration Of A Class V Facial Cavity 11 MIN
Temporary Restoration Of A Class II 10 MIN

Restoration Of Equestrain Statues At The Memorial Bridge Plaza C 16 MIN
16MM FILM OPTICAL SOUND J-C A
Examines the techniques used in the restoration of the equestrain statues at Memorial Bridge Plaza in Washington, DC. Follows the entire restoration process of two statues from the initial cleaning to the final application of gold using the brush electroplating technique.
LC NO. 74-701403
Prod-USNBOS Dist-USNBOS 1972

Restoration Of The Nightwatch, The C 26 MIN
3/4 OR 1/2 INCH VIDEO CASSETTE J A
Shows the months of effort necessary to restore a famous Rembrandt painting after it was seriously damaged.
Prod-SUTHRB Dist-SUTHRB

Restoration Wits, The C 30 MIN
3/4 INCH VIDEO CASSETTE H-C A
Features Cyril Ritchard as the Earl of Rochester in a dramatization of 17th century light verse and poetry.
From The Anyone For Tennyson Series.
Prod-NETCHE Dist-GPITVL

Restore Breathing - Mouth-To-Mouth Resuscitation C 6 MIN
3/4 OR 1/2 INCH VIDEO CASSETTE PRO
Presents methods for determining when mouth-to-mouth resuscitation is required, how it is administered and how to stop the procedure.
From The EMT Video - Group Three Series.
Prod-USA Dist-USNAC 1979

Restore Breathing - Opening The Airway C 8 MIN
3/4 OR 1/2 INCH VIDEO CASSETTE PRO
Describes procedures for positioning the patient, checking for injuries, selecting the method, and properly opening the airway. Illustrates head tilt, thumb jaw lift, two-hand jaw lift, and modified jaw thrust methods. Also describes how to resuscitate an unconscious, nonbreathing patient by first attempting mouth-to-mouth resuscitation, and then by using the oral pharyngeal airway (j-tube).
From The EMT Video - Group Three Series.
LC NO. 84-706484
Prod-USA Dist-USNAC 1983

Restoring Confidence In Our Schools C 30 MIN
3/4 OR 1/2 INCH VIDEO CASSETTE T
Excerpts from interviews with various individuals concerning current attitudes about public schools in the United States. Includes comments and suggestions for improvements. Intended to stimulate discussions which will lead educators to develop a written plan of action.
LC NO. 82-706447
Prod-AFSCD Dist-AFSCD 1980

Restoring Harmony In Marriage C 28 MIN
16MM FILM OPTICAL SOUND
Presents the advice of personal and marriage counselor Henry Brandt that an effective marriage relationship contains no competition. Points out hindrances to cooperation between couples and guidelines for them to follow.
From The Christian Home Series. No. 8
LC NO. 73-701560
Prod-CCFC Dist-CCFC 1972

Restoring The Environment C 30 MIN
3/4 OR 1/2 INCH VIDEO CASSETTE
Examines how technology can be helpful in alleviating the problems of pollution in the environment.
From The Innovation Series.
Prod-WNETTV Dist-WNETTV 1983

Restraint For Survival C 8 MIN
16MM FILM OPTICAL SOUND
Demonstrates the life-saving potential of shoulder harnesses and seat belts. Documents FAA aeromedical research which simulates aircraft accidents using electronically outfitted 'DUMMIES.'
LC NO. 74-705533
Prod-FAAFL Dist-USFAA 1967

Restraints On Technology Access - Employment Agreements And Protection Of Trade Secrets C 22 MIN
3/4 OR 1/2 INCH VIDEO CASSETTE PRO
Examines the legal opportunities and pitfalls associated with technology access and effective protection of trade secrets.
From The Antitrust Counseling And The Marketing Process Series.
Prod-ABACPE Dist-ABACPE

Restraints, Seclusion And A Demonstration Of Applying Restraints C 30 MIN
3/4 OR 1/2 INCH VIDEO CASSETTE
Illustrates the need for emergency rooms and psychiatric facilities to have practiced, effective non-assualtive team restraint procedures.
From The Management And Treatment Of The Violent Patient Series.
Prod-HEMUL Dist-HEMUL

Restricted U S And British Training Films - World War II B 110 MIN
3/4 OR 1/2 INCH VIDEO CASSETTE
Consists of six short films which are restricted U S and British training films used during World War II. Includes Parachute Training in the German Army, U-Boat Identification and others.
Prod-IHF Dist-IHF

Restroom Cleaning Procedures C 12 MIN
16MM FILM - 3/4 IN VIDEO IND
Presents procedures and materials used in cleaning and maintaining a health care facility restroom.
From The Housekeeping Personnel Series.
Prod-COPI Dist-COPI 1973

Restructuring The Global Economy C 30 MIN
3/4 OR 1/2 INCH VIDEO CASSETTE
Discusses the changing nature of the world's economy. Pictures a Third World 'debtor's cartel' and collective default. Presented by Drs Lester Thurow, Sidney Dell and Howard Perlmutter.
From The Creating Alternative Futures Series.
Prod-BULFRG Dist-BULFRG

Results Of War, The - Are We Making A Good Peace C 52 MIN
16MM FILM - 1/2 IN VIDEO
Analyzes the considerations that affected the formulation of the Treaty of Versailles. Discusses the civil war and the counter-revolution in Russia.
From The Europe, The Mighty Continent Series. No. 6
LC NO. 79-707421
Prod-BBCTV Dist-TIMLIF 1976

Resume Preparation B 50 MIN
3/4 OR 1/2 INCH VIDEO CASSETTE
Shows James L Lewis, placement specialist, giving advice on writing a resume. Treats who the person is, what he knows, what he has done, what he can do, what kind of work he wants and why he should be hired.
Prod-UAZMIC Dist-UAZMIC 1977

Resume Preparation (Captioned) C 17 MIN
3/4 OR 1/2 INCH VIDEO CASSETTE S
Presents talk with student and placement counselor about how to prepare a resume. Signed.
Prod-GALCO Dist-GALCO 1980

Resume Workshop, Pt 1 B 60 MIN
3/4 OR 1/2 INCH VIDEO CASSETTE
Discusses and answers questions concerning resumes. Includes such topics as resume sections on education, field and volunteer experience, interests and references.
Prod-UWISC Dist-UWISC 1979

Resume Workshop, Pt 2 B 12 MIN
3/4 OR 1/2 INCH VIDEO CASSETTE
Continues a discussion on resume writing and what an employer looks for in a job application. Tells when to send resumes and where they should be sent and discusses responses to unfair questions and the use of cover letters.
Prod-UWISC Dist-UWISC 1979

Resume, The C 15 MIN
3/4 INCH VIDEO CASSETTE H-C A
Describes the successful resume.
From The Job Seeking Series.
Prod-WCETTV Dist-GPITVL 1979

Resumes And Interviews B 60 MIN
3/4 OR 1/2 INCH VIDEO CASSETTE
Discusses the tactics for handling two types of interviews. Demonstrates the difference between ineffectual and successful interviews.
Prod-UWISC Dist-UWISC 1979

Resurgence - The Movement For Equality Vs The Ku Klux Klan C 27 MIN
3/4 INCH VIDEO CASSETTE
A shortened version of the videocassette Resurgence The Movement For Equality Vs The Ku Klux Klan. Juxtaposes two sides of a political battle now raging in the United States - efforts of union and civil rights activists to achieve social and economic justice with the upsurge in activiity of the Ku Klux Klan and the American Nazi Party. Examines the complex issues of race relations and economic growth.
Prod-SKYLN Dist-FIRS

Resurgence - The Movement For Equality Vs The Ku Klux Klan C 54 MIN
16MM FILM - 3/4 IN VIDEO
Juxtaposes two sides of a political battle now raging in the United States which are efforts of union and civil rights activists to achieve social and economic justice with the upsurge in activity of the Ku Klux Klan and the American Nazi Party. Examines the complex issues of race relations and economic growth.
Prod-SKYLN Dist-FIRS

Resurrection C 27 MIN
16MM FILM, 3/4 OR 1/2 IN VIDEO H-C A
Discusses the mission of Jesus and the meaning of his resurrection. Presents a series of vignettes in which Jesus is a hospital patient, a vacationer, a rock star, a parish priest and a peasant leader, showing how he is tempted by demons in a variety of disguises. Stars James Farentino, Richard Beymer and Joanna Cassidy.
From The Insight Series.
Prod-PAULST Dist-PAULST

Resurrection C 27 MIN
3/4 OR 1/2 INCH VIDEO CASSETTE J A
Dramatizes the story of the Resurrection. Stars James Farentino.
Prod-SUTHRB Dist-SUTHRB

Resurrection Of Bronco Billy C 21 MIN
16MM FILM OPTICAL SOUND
A story of Billy who has his boots, spurs and hat, but no prairie to ride.
LC NO. 79-711425
Prod-USC Dist-USC 1970

Resurrection Of Turkey C 29 MIN
2 INCH VIDEOTAPE
See series title for descriptive statement.
From The Course Of Our Times I Series.
Prod-WGBHTV Dist-PUBTEL

Resurrection, The C 30 MIN
16MM FILM OPTICAL SOUND
Tells the story of a young black executive who visits his old neighborhood and finds himself having to re-examine his identity. Shows him chased, hunted and shot by the surrealistic figures of THEM. Combines fantasy and realistic situations to tell the story.
Prod-BLKFMF Dist-BLKFMF

Resuscitation C 7 MIN
16MM FILM, 3/4 OR 1/2 IN VIDEO A
Gives a description of the technique of mouth-to-mouth and mouth-to-nose resuscitation of patients who have stopped breathing. Explains how to carry out external cardiac compression on a patient whose heart has stopped beating.
From The First Aid Series.
LC NO. 81-707495
Prod-HBL Dist-IFB 1977

Resuscitation - Bag And Mask Technique C 15 MIN
3/4 OR 1/2 INCH VIDEO CASSETTE PRO
Explains indications for bag and mask ventilation of the newborn, shows appropriate equipment necessary, demonstrates how to perform and evaluate ventilation, and discusses complications and their management.
From The Michigan Perinatal Education, Instructional Unit C - Resuscitation Series.
LC NO. 79-707745
Prod-UMICH Dist-UMICH 1978

Resuscitation In The Operating Room C 22 MIN
16MM FILM OPTICAL SOUND PRO

Dramatizes problems of cardiopulmonary arrest during operations. Stresses the need of teamwork for early detection and remedial action.
LC NO. 72-700349
Prod-AYERST Dist-AYERST 1973

Resuscitation Of Infants And Children C 18 MIN
3/4 OR 1/2 INCH VIDEO CASSETTE PRO
Shows how to manage airway obstruction on an infant or child.
From The Cardiopulmonary Resuscitation Series.
Prod-HSCIC Dist-HSCIC 1984

Resuscitation Of The Newborn C 21 MIN
3/4 OR 1/2 INCH VIDEO CASSETTE PRO
Describes and demonstrates routine and emergency treatment for neo-natal depression in new born infants.
Prod-WFP Dist-WFP

Resuscitation Of The Newborn C 22 MIN
3/4 OR 1/2 INCH VIDEO CASSETTE
Demonstrates the principles and practices for resuscitation of the newborn. Emphasizes early recognition of problem babies by appropriate parental history taking and testing.
Prod-AMCOG Dist-AMCOG

Resuscitative Care Of The Severely Wounded B 24 MIN
16MM FILM OPTICAL SOUND
Describes first aid procedures and corrective surgery to revive severely wounded patients and to counteract injurious results of a wound.
LC NO. FIE57-79
Prod-USA Dist-USNAC 1957

RET Demonstration With Self-Acceptance And Assertiveness Problems C 40 MIN
3/4 OR 1/2 INCH VIDEO CASSETTE
Demonstrates cognitive rehearsal, rational-emotive imagery and other techniques. Includes post-session client interview.
Prod-IRL Dist-IRL

RET Demonstrations With Female Student With Social Anxiety C 40 MIN
3/4 OR 1/2 INCH VIDEO CASSETTE
Demonstrates how to combine cognitive restructuring, imagery techniques and behavior rehearsal into a plan for a female with social anxiety.
Prod-IRL Dist-IRL

Retail Location C 30 MIN
3/4 OR 1/2 INCH VIDEO CASSETTE
Classifies consumer products based upon purchasing patterns. Covers key criteria in developing a shopping center, advantages and disadvantages of developing a specialty product image.
From The Marketing Perspectives Series.
Prod-MATC Dist-WFVTAE

Retail Sales Power—A Series

Presents ways to help move more merchandise off store shelves for the paying customer and minimize the shrinkage problem. Develops key ideas with discussion breaks provided in order to allow flexibility.
Prod-PRODEV Dist-PRODEV

Improving Customer Relations 022 MIN
Shrink Or Swim/In-Store Theft 008 MIN

Retailing C 30 MIN
3/4 OR 1/2 INCH VIDEO CASSETTE
Covers the characteristics of a retail chain, types of retail chain stores, advantages of franchising, advantages, of general merchandising and comparison of advantages of small single store operations to large chain store operations.
From The Marketing Perspectives Series.
Prod-MATC Dist-WFVTAE

Retailing - Sears C 20 MIN
3/4 OR 1/2 INCH VIDEO CASSETTE
Interviews a representative from Sears, Roebuck and Company in order to describe the jobs available in the retailing field for college graduates with liberal arts degrees. Discusses initial interviews, hiring practices and advancement opportunities.
From The Clues To Career Opportunities For Liberal Arts Graduates Series.
LC NO. 79-706056
Prod-IU Dist-IU 1978

Retailing Fish C 21 MIN
16MM FILM OPTICAL SOUND
Shows the selection, handling, display and selling of fresh and frozen fish at a retail fish store.
Prod-USBCF Dist-USNOAA Prodn-SUN 1948

Retaining The Land - Containing The Water C 13 MIN
16MM FILM OPTICAL SOUND
Discusses coastal erosion and flooding and scientific efforts to predict, forestall and hold back these processes.
Prod-ALLFP Dist-NSTA 1977

Retardation Research C 7 MIN
16MM FILM OPTICAL SOUND T
Describes a research program to test the Doman-Delacato theory of neuropsychology.
LC NO. FIA67-5259
Prod-FINLYS Dist-FINLYS 1967

Retarded Client And His Family, The C 20 MIN
3/4 OR 1/2 INCH VIDEO CASSETTE
Shows how enlightened family help can shape the future of a retarded person.
Prod-PRIMED Dist-PRIMED

Retention C 30 MIN
16MM FILM OPTICAL SOUND T
Provides a summary of principles of learning that should be present in every student-teacher interaction.
From The Aide-Ing In Education Series.
Prod-SPF Dist-SPF

Retention Theory For Teachers B 28 MIN
16MM FILM OPTICAL SOUND C T
Features Dr Madeline Hunter discussing the factors that facilitate remembering. Suggests how to incorporate these factors in daily teaching to increase the long term economy and effectiveness of learning.
From The Translating Theory Into Classroom Practices Series.
Prod-SPF Dist-SPF 1967

Rethinking America—A Series

Focuses on conservation as an energy resource. Discusses several ways of rethinking our attitudes about energy use and wastes.
Prod-UMITV Dist-UMITV 1979

Conservation And The Car 030 MIN
Energy And Housing 030 MIN
Energy And Industry 030 MIN
Redesigning Appliances 030 MIN

Rethinking Tomorrow C 28 MIN
16MM FILM, 3/4 OR 1/2 IN VIDEO
Shows growing national concern for energy conservation. Discusses how citizens have adopted comprehensive energy programs in various cities.
LC NO. 81-706312
Prod-USDOE Dist-USNAC 1980

Retinacular System Of The Digits Of The Hand, The C 30 MIN
3/4 OR 1/2 INCH VIDEO CASSETTE PRO
Presents an anatomical study of the small ligaments underlying the skin at the level of the finger joints. Attempts to identify and document their relationship to one another by color photographs of dissection of frozen specimens.
Prod-ASSH Dist-ASSH

Retinitis Pigmentosa C 12 MIN
16MM FILM OPTICAL SOUND
Explains in lay language what is known of retinitis pigmentosa and tells of research in progress.
LC NO. 75-703261
Prod-ITTCMD Dist-RETIN 1975

Retinoids And Cancer Prevention C 48 MIN
3/4 INCH VIDEO CASSETTE
Discusses the role of retinoids in the prevention and treatment of cancer.
Prod-UTAHTI Dist-UTAHTI

Retirement C 29 MIN
3/4 INCH VIDEO CASSETTE C A
Discusses the basic workings of recent laws pertaining to retirees and older citizens. Describes retirement plans for savings, selling a business or home and moving.
From The You And The Law Series. Lesson 25
Prod-COAST Dist-CDTEL Prodn-SADCC

Retirement Income Security C
16MM FILM OPTICAL SOUND
Considers retirement income during the stages of life, social security, the individual's responsibility for maintaining retirement income and the adjustments older people can make for inflation. Urges people in both the pre-retirement and retirement years to consider ways that purchasing power can be maintained.
From The Aging In The Future Series.
Prod-UMICH Dist-UMICH

Retirement Income Security C 14 MIN
3/4 INCH VIDEO CASSETTE
Shows young people worrying about whether or not there will be Social Security when they want to retire. Discusses the roles of society and the older citizen.
From The Aging In The Future Series.
Prod-UMITV Dist-UMITV 1981

Retirement Of The Hallam Nuclear Power Facility C 35 MIN
16MM FILM OPTICAL SOUND C A
Shows the decommissioning of the 254 MWT sodium cooled graphite-moderated nuclear power reactor located at Nebraska Public Power District's Sheldon station. Stresses the safety procedures necessary for the handling of sodium and radioactive materials.
LC NO. 72-708997
Prod-USAEC Dist-USERD 1970

Retirement Planning C 30 MIN
3/4 OR 1/2 INCH VIDEO CASSETTE
Presents tips on retirement planning.
From The Consumer Survival Series. Personal Planning
Prod-MDCPB Dist-MDCPB

Retirement Planning / Batteries / Water Filter Systems C
3/4 OR 1/2 INCH VIDEO CASSETTE
Discusses various aspects of retirement planning, batteries and water filter systems.
From The Consumer Survival Series.
Prod-MDCPB Dist-MDCPB

Retirement Plans For Small Business And Professionals - Entering The Top-Heavy And... C 210 MIN
3/4 OR 1/2 INCH VIDEO CASSETTE PRO
Presents an advanced program focused on the implementation of parity and top-heavy rules enacted by the Tax Equity and Fiscal Responsibility Act of 1982 (TEFRA).
Prod-ALIABA Dist-ALIABA

Retour A La Terre C 10 MIN
16MM FILM OPTICAL SOUND
A French language film. Reports on Canada's National Capital Commission's management of gardens in the Ottawa region.
LC NO. 76-703504
Prod-NATCAP Dist-MTS Prodn-MCTOSD 1975

Retratos (Captioned) C 53 MIN
16MM FILM, 3/4 OR 1/2 IN VIDEO A
Portrays the life stories of four New York Puerto Ricans and their attempt to assimilate themselves into American life while maintaining their cultural heritage. Spanish dialog with English subtitles.
Prod-BRSOKS Dist-CNEMAG 1980

Retreat C 11 MIN
16MM FILM OPTICAL SOUND H-C A
Tells the story of a young man, with backpack and fishing rod, who hikes through the autumn countryside. Points out that everything is pastoral and serene until his war experiences are suddenly awakened in him, turning his retreat into a nightmare.
From The Revelation Series.
LC NO. 72-703104
Prod-FRACOC Dist-FRACOC 1970

Retreat C 39 MIN
3/4 INCH VIDEO CASSETTE
Depicts students from Austin, Texas, discovering that rugged outdoor retreats can encourage understanding among people of different races and backgrounds.
From The As We See It Series.
Prod-WTTWTV Dist-PUBTEL

Retreat And Decision X 30 MIN
16MM FILM OPTICAL SOUND J-C A
Includes the transfiguration of Jesus, followed by more healing miracles.
From The Living Christ Series.
Prod-CAFM Dist-ECUFLM

Retrograde Amalgam In Endodontics, The C 15 MIN
16MM FILM - 3/4 IN VIDEO PRO
Discusses indications and demonstrates procedures for retrograde root canal filling. Issued in 1970 as a motion picture.
LC NO. 78-706127
Prod-USVA Dist-USNAC 1978

Retrolabyrinthine Approach To The Cerebellopontine Angle C 55 MIN
3/4 OR 1/2 INCH VIDEO CASSETTE PRO
Shows the excellent exposure of the cerebellopontine angle by an approach through the mastoid posterior to the labyrinth. This retrolabyrinthine approach has been used primarily for selective partial section of the trigeminal nerve for tic douloureaux.
Prod-HOUSEI Dist-HOUSEI

Retrolabyrinthine Selective Section Of The Trigeminal Nerve (Posterior) For Intractable... C 10 MIN
3/4 OR 1/2 INCH VIDEO CASSETTE PRO
Demonstrates the suboccipital approach to the retrolabyrinthine technique combined with the lower complication rate of the transtemporal approach.
Prod-HOUSEI Dist-HOUSEI

Retromandibular Structures And Infratemporal Fossa - Unit 4 C 15 MIN
3/4 OR 1/2 INCH VIDEO CASSETTE PRO
Shows the muscles, nerves, arteries, and other structures that compose the area posterior to the jaw, including the maxillary artery and its branches.
From The Gross Anatomy Prosection Demonstration Series.
Prod-HSCIC Dist-HSCIC

Retroperitoneal Ultrasonography C 18 MIN
3/4 INCH VIDEO CASSETTE PRO
Explains how ultrasound can be used to distinguish renal abnormalities such as cysts, abscesses, tumors and hydronephrosis. Presents an evaluation of a renal transplant.
From The Ultrasound In Diagnostic Medicine Series.
LC NO. 80-706125
Prod-USVA Dist-USNAC 1979

Retropubic Prostatovesiculectomy C 10 MIN
16MM FILM OPTICAL SOUND
Demonstrates the operative technique of retropubic prostatovesiculectomy. Emphasizes the ideal visualization afforded by the retropubic approach, which assures optimum hemostasis, obviates damage to the lower ureters and rectum and facilitates accurate revisions of the bladder neck and precise vesicourethral anastomosis.
LC NO. 75-702307
Prod-EATONL Dist-EATONL 1958

Retter Aus Bergnot C 5 MIN
16MM FILM, 3/4 OR 1/2 IN VIDEO H-C A
A German-language version of the motion picture Mountain Rescue Workers. Shows the operation of a typical German rescue effort following an avalanche.
From The European Studies - Germany (German) Series.
Prod-MFAFRG Dist-IFB Prodn-BAYER 1973

Return C
3/4 OR 1/2 INCH VIDEO CASSETTE
Concerns the advance of an individual towards an unseen goal.
From The Red Tape Series.
Prod-EAI Dist-EAI

Return From Foster Care Through Task Centered Casework B 55 MIN
3/4 OR 1/2 INCH VIDEO CASSETTE
Explains and demonstrates techniques of the middle phase of 'task centered casework.' Identifies problems and tasks in returning children to mother from foster homes.
Prod-UCHI Dist-UWISC

Return From Witch Mountain C 93 MIN
16MM FILM OPTICAL SOUND
Tells how two youngsters from outer space arrive in Los Angeles and encounter a fanatical scientific genius. Stars Bette Davis and Christopher Lee.
Prod-DISNEY Dist-UAE 1978

Return Of Count Spirochete, The C 21 MIN
16MM FILM - 3/4 IN VIDEO
Uses animation to give medical facts about venereal diseases. Describes symptoms, course of infection and the effects of syphilis and gonorrhea on the human body. Emphasizes diagnosis and treatment by a physician as the only means of eradicating the infection. Issued in 1973 as a motion picture.
LC NO. 79-706060
Prod-USN Dist-USNAC 1979

Return Of Juan Peron, The - 'El Caudillo' Tries Again C 15 MIN
16MM FILM OPTICAL SOUND I-C
Features Juan Domingo Peron who first comes to power as President of Argentina in 1946. Explains that he patterns his policies after those of Adolf Hitler and Benito Musolini, promising to avoid their mistakes as he establishes an inflexible dictatorship.
Prod-HEARST Dist-HEARST

Return Of Milton Whitty, The C 17 MIN
16MM FILM, 3/4 OR 1/2 IN VIDEO IND
Presents a sequel to the Inner Mind Of Milton Whitty. Shows that prevention of accidents costs less than compensation. Illustrates the steps that should be taken to help eliminate hazards at a construction site.
Prod-CSAO Dist-IFB

Return Of The Allies B 27 MIN
16MM FILM, 3/4 OR 1/2 IN VIDEO J-H
Recounts the liberation of the Philippines during World War II.
From The Victory At Sea Series.
Prod-NBCTV Dist-LUF

Return Of The Black Stallion C
1/2 IN VIDEO CASSETTE BETA/VHS
Features the return of the Black Stallion.
Prod-EQVDL Dist-EQVDL

Return Of The Child, The C 26 MIN
16MM FILM, 3/4 OR 1/2 IN VIDEO
Dramatizes an Algonquin Indian legend about a young man who lost both his wife and his child. Tells of the child freed from the bonds of death by the sap of the fir tree.
Prod-FOTH Dist-FOTH

Return Of The Daylight C 30 MIN
1/2 IN VIDEO CASSETTE BETA/VHS
Presents the Daylight, a well-known steam locomotive numbered 4449 and built in 1941 by the Lima Locomotive Works.
Prod-DELUZ Dist-DELUZ 1981

Return Of The Elephant Seal, The C 29 MIN
16MM FILM, 3/4 OR 1/2 IN VIDEO H-C A
Discusses elephant seals who were near extinction, but have made a miraculous recovery, doubling their population every ten years and reclaiming most of their original territory on California coastal islands. Traces the nineteenth-century seal hunts through archival footage, records the immense animals' breeding behavior, and traces their annual migration patterns. Ponders and depicts the problems of expanding animal populations.
LC NO. 82-707298
Prod-PERSPF Dist-CORF 1982

Return Of The Kingpin C 30 MIN
3/4 OR 1/2 INCH VIDEO CASSETTE
See series title for descriptive statement.
From The Up And Coming Series.
Prod-KQEDTV Dist-MDCPB

Return Of The Kiteman C 30 MIN
16MM FILM, 3/4 OR 1/2 IN VIDEO I-C A
Tells the story of a 45-year-old man and his efforts trying to fly a kite. Takes place in the future where a large bureaucratic government has declared kiteflying illegal because it is oriented to the self and not to society.
Prod-PHENIX Dist-PHENIX 1975

Return Of The Nene C 9 MIN
16MM FILM OPTICAL SOUND I-C A
Tells the story of the nene, Hawaii's state bird. The nene is a nearly extinct goose that inhabits waterless uplands and feeds on berries and vegetation.
LC NO. FIA67-1764
Prod-STUTP Dist-SF 1967

Return Of The Sea Elephant C 20 MIN
16MM FILM, 3/4 OR 1/2 IN VIDEO I-C A
A shortened version of Return Of The Sea Elephant. Studies the life cycle of the sea elephant.
From The Undersea World Of Jacques Cousteau Series.
Prod-METROM Dist-CF 1970

Return Of The Sea Elephant, The C 52 MIN
16MM FILM, 3/4 OR 1/2 IN VIDEO
Shows Jacques Cousteau's group observing the behavior of a herd of nomadic sea elephants, including the care of the young, the pre-mating rituals and the battles of the bulls.
From The Undersea World Of Jacques Cousteau Series.
Prod-METROM Dist-CF 1971

Return Of The Serve, The C 29 MIN
3/4 OR 1/2 INCH VIDEO CASSETTE
Features Lew Gerrard and Don Candy giving tennis instructions, emphasizing the return of the serve.
From The Love Tennis Series.
Prod-MDCPB Dist-MDCPB

Return To Appalachia C 28 MIN
16MM FILM, 3/4 OR 1/2 IN VIDEO
Offers a warm portrait of three sisters in rural America and shows how each has found fulfillment despite differences in temperaments and need.
LC NO. 83-707173
Prod-MARKSC Dist-FLMLIB 1982

Return To Everest C 59 MIN
16MM FILM, 3/4 OR 1/2 IN VIDEO
Looks at the efforts of Sir Edmund Hillary, the first man to climb Mount Everest, to help the people who live in the shadow of the mountain by building hospitals, schools and bridges.
Prod-NGS Dist-NGS 1984

Return To Holyoke C 15 MIN
16MM FILM OPTICAL SOUND
Depicts the visit of the director of Women Marines to Mt Holyoke to commemorate the establishment of the Women's Reserve Officer Training School on campus in 1943.
LC NO. 74-705534
Prod-USN Dist-USNAC 1969

Return To Improvisation, A C 30 MIN
3/4 INCH VIDEO CASSETTE
See series title for descriptive statement.
From The Changing Music Series.
Prod-WGBHTV Dist-PUBTEL

Return To Isolationism C 26 MIN
16MM FILM, 3/4 OR 1/2 IN VIDEO H-C
Points out that President Woodrow Wilson destroyed his health in his desperate struggle for the League of Nations. Explains that his refusal to compromise led to the League's defeat.
From The Between The Wars Series.
Prod-LNDBRG Dist-FI 1978

Return To Masada B 25 MIN
16MM FILM OPTICAL SOUND
Depicts the excavations of Masada, the last Jewish stronghold that resisted the Roman legions in the first millennium.
Prod-ALDEN Dist-ALDEN

Return To Michigan C 28 MIN
16MM FILM, 3/4 OR 1/2 IN VIDEO H-C A
Gives an account of a shipping error in 1976 that resulted in cattle in Michigan eating feed that caused health problems for humans who ate the beef and drank the milk from disfigured cows that went to market. Government agencies were reluctant to admit the widespread nature of the problem.
Prod-THAMES Dist-MEDIAG 1978

Return To Nazareth X 30 MIN
16MM FILM OPTICAL SOUND J-C A
Contrasts the attitude of Jesus' contemporaries toward Him. Includes the healing of the centurion's servant, the marriage at Cana, the rejection at Nazareth, the midnight visit of Nicodemus and the parable of the Good Samaritan.
From The Living Christ Series.
Prod-CAFM Dist-ECUFLM

Return To Nursing–A Series
PRO
Helps the inactive graduate nurse resume her profession, hospital classroom and supervised care experience.
Prod-SUNY Dist-AJN

Care Of The Aging Patient	30 MIN
Changing Role Of The Nurse, The	30 MIN
Comprehensive Nursing Care, Pt 1	30 MIN
Comprehensive Nursing Care, Pt 2	30 MIN
Comprehensive Nursing Care, Pt 3	30 MIN
Fluid And Electrolytes	30 MIN
Inhalation Therapy	30 MIN
Intramuscular Injections	30 MIN
Intravenous Therapy	30 MIN
Legal Aspects Of Nursing	30 MIN
Medications	30 MIN
Nurse And New Equipment, The	30 MIN
Nurse-Patient Relation, The	30 MIN
Nursing Care Plan, The	30 MIN
Nursing Team, The	30 MIN
Patient With Cancer, The	30 MIN
Patient With CVA, The, Pt 1	30 MIN
Patient With CVA, The, Pt 2	30 MIN
Patient With Diabetes, The	30 MIN
Patient With Peptic Ulcer, The - Diagnosis	30 MIN
Patient With Peptic Ulcer, The - Nursing Care	30 MIN
Post-Operative Care	30 MIN
Pre-Operative Care	30 MIN
Problem With Infection, The	30 MIN
What's Ahead For Nursing	30 MIN

Return To Oz C 57 MIN
16MM FILM OPTICAL SOUND
Presents an animated version of L Frank Baum's 'THE WIZARD OF OZ.'
Prod-UPA Dist-TWYMAN 1970

Return To Pelican Island C 26 MIN
16MM FILM OPTICAL SOUND I-C A
Explains that each spring the great white pelicans return from the south to a small island in the Great Salt Lake of Utah, a lake devoid of fish, to breed. Follows the development of the young pelicans from birth, to feather and wing development, and to the time in late summer when the fledglings have at last learned to fly.
From The Audubon Wildlife Theatre Series.
Prod-AVEXP Dist-AVEXP

Return To Pelican Island C 26 MIN
16MM FILM OPTICAL SOUND J-C A
Depicts the breeding and growth of great white pelicans in the Great Salt Lake in Utah. Follows the development of the young birds from their birth in the spring, through their feather and wing development, to the fledglings' first flights in late summer.
From The Audubon Wildlife Theatre Series.
LC NO. 72-701990
Prod-KEGPL Dist-AVEXP 1971

Return To Poland C 58 MIN
3/4 OR 1/2 INCH VIDEO CASSETTE
Features former journalist Marion Marzunski, who in 1980 returned home to her native Poland. Reveals a penetrating profile of the Polish people and the influence of the Catholic Church and the then growing Solidarity Labor Movement.
From The World Series.
Prod-WGBHTV Dist-PBS 1981

Return To Reality C 35 MIN
16MM FILM - 3/4 IN VIDEO
Deals with the problems of confusion in an elderly stroke patient and demonstrates a technique of reality orientation as practiced at the Veterans Administration Hospital in Tuscaloosa, Alabama. Shows how this program affects the lives of the patient and his family. Issued in 1972 as a motion picture.
LC NO. 78-706259
Prod-VAHT Dist-USNAC 1978

Return To Space C 59 MIN
3/4 OR 1/2 INCH VIDEO CASSETTE
Examines the first space shuttle mission factors involved in its heavily military role, and the opportunities to use it for the long-term good of mankind.
LC NO. 81-707289
Prod-KTEHTV Dist-KTEHTV 1981

Return To The Philippines C 30 MIN
3/4 OR 1/2 INCH VIDEO CASSETTE H-C A
See series title for descriptive statement.
From The World War II - GI Diary Series.
Prod-TIMLIF Dist-TIMLIF 1980

Return To The River C 29 MIN
16MM FILM OPTICAL SOUND
Deals with the Connecticut River. Records the progress against pollution of the river. Shows the varied uses of the river, including the annual Sunfish Race and the Goodspeed Opera House.
Prod-GRANTE Dist-FENWCK

Return To The Rocks, The C 17 MIN
16MM FILM OPTICAL SOUND
Describes the birth of the Australian nation in 1788 and the attempts of early settlers and convicts to survive in the harsh new land.
LC NO. 80-700835
Prod-IMPACT Dist-TASCOR 1976

Return, The C 23 MIN
16MM FILM OPTICAL SOUND
Tells of the struggle of Soviet Jewry for freedom and relates the personal experiences of Soviet Jews as they adjust to their new lives in Israel.
Prod-UJA Dist-ALDEN

Return, The C 27 MIN
16MM FILM, 3/4 OR 1/2 IN VIDEO
A documentary of Biblical prophesies. Filmed in Israel.
Prod-PFP Dist-PFP 1972

Return, The C 30 MIN
3/4 OR 1/2 INCH VIDEO CASSETTE P-I
See series title for descriptive statement.
From The Sonrisas Series.
Prod-KRLNTV Dist-MDCPB

Return, The C 30 MIN
16MM FILM, 3/4 OR 1/2 IN VIDEO
Presents an adaptation of the short story The Return by Ambrose Bierce and A M Burrage. Offers a tale about a murdered woman's ghost in a brooding country mansion.
Prod-MCKAYE Dist-PFP

Return, The (German) C 27 MIN
16MM FILM, 3/4 OR 1/2 IN VIDEO J-C A
Discusses the predictions of the Old Testament prophets, retelling and foretelling the events leading to the final hours in world history. Introduced and narrated by Hal Lindsay, author of The Late Great Planet Earth.
Prod-PFP Dist-PFP

Return, The (Japanese) C 27 MIN
16MM FILM, 3/4 OR 1/2 IN VIDEO J-C A
Discusses the predictions of the Old Testament prophets, retelling and foretelling the events leading to the final hours in world history. Introduced and narrated by Hal Lindsay, author of The Late Great Planet Earth.
Prod-PFP Dist-PFP

Returning From The Moon B 29 MIN
16MM FILM - 3/4 IN VIDEO
Describes the problem of getting the Apollo Command Module safely back through the atmosphere to earth. Discusses the problems of guidance and heating and the manufacturing process for the ablative heat shield.
Prod-USNAC Dist-USNAC 1972

Returning To Fuji C 8 MIN
3/4 INCH VIDEO CASSETTE
Presents the perception of a mountain swathed in misty clouds.
From The Nan Hoover - Selected Works 2 Series.
Prod-EAI Dist-EAI

Reunion C 28 MIN
16MM FILM OPTICAL SOUND
Shows how an ex-soldier released from prison for his wife's funeral cannot cope with the situation and tries to retreat to a vanished past.

LC NO. 76-703075
Prod-YORKU Dist-CANFDC 1974

Reunion B 48 MIN
16MM FILM OPTICAL SOUND C A
A documentary film in cinema verite style which consists of interviews with alumni of Yale University combined with an impressionistic study of class reunions ranging from the class of 1909 to the class of 1964.
LC NO. 72-711426
Prod-MCQLKN Dist-MCQLKN 1970

Reunion B 21 MIN
16MM FILM - 3/4 IN VIDEO
Presents an account of the liberation of French prisoners from Nazi concentration camps. Shows the removal of the prisoners to temporary hospitals and pictures joyful reunions with families and friends in Paris. Directed and photographed by Henri Cartier-Bresson. Issued in 1946 as a motion picture.
LC NO. 79-706582
Prod-USOWI Dist-USNAC 1979

Revelation—A Series
H-C A
Prod-FRACOC Dist-FRACOC 1970

Come To Life 11 MIN
Epiphania - The Manifestation 15 MIN
Let The Rain Settle It 13 MIN
Retreat 11 MIN
Right Here, Right Now 15 MIN
Turned Round To See 11 MIN

Revenge Of The Nerd C 31 MIN
16MM FILM, 3/4 OR 1/2 IN VIDEO J-H
A shortened version of the motion picture Revenge Of The Nerd. Presents the story of high school computer genius Bertram Cummings, who has the reputation of being a 'nerd.' Tells how Bertram seeks revenge against three classmates who try to make a fool out of him. Shows that Bertram's victory is not long-lasting and demonstrates that being yourself is the most important way to behave.
LC NO. 83-707148
Prod-HGATE Dist-LCOA 1982

Revenge Of The Nerd C 45 MIN
16MM FILM, 3/4 OR 1/2 IN VIDEO J-H
Presents the story of high school computer genius Bertram Cummings, who has the reputation of being a 'nerd.' Tells how Bertram seeks revenge against three classmates who try to make a fool out of him. Shows that Bertram's victory is not long-lasting and demonstrates that being yourself is the most important way to behave.
LC NO. 83-707149
Prod-HGATE Dist-LCOA 1982

Revengers, The C 5 MIN
3/4 OR 1/2 INCH VIDEO CASSETTE J-H
Deals with the use of 'Could have' and 'Should have' in writing.
From The Write On, Set 2 Series.
Prod-CTI Dist-CTI

Revenues, Rates And Reimbursements—A Series

Presents a series explaining the pricing and financial problems confronting hospitals as they strive to control costs.
Prod-TEACHM Dist-TEACHM

Financial Sensibilities And Responsibilities
Responsible Pricing Of Services
Toward Price-Based Reimbursement
Validating Pricing Strategies

Revere The Emperor, Expel The Barbarian C 30 MIN
3/4 OR 1/2 INCH VIDEO CASSETTE H-C A
See series title for descriptive statement.
From The Japan - The Changing Tradition Series.
Prod-UMA Dist-GPITVL 1978

Reverence Day C 29 MIN
2 INCH VIDEOTAPE
See series title for descriptive statement.
From The Our Street Series.
Prod-MDCPB Dist-PUBTEL

Reverend Al Carmines, Carla de Sola And Bill Cordh C 30 MIN
3/4 OR 1/2 INCH VIDEO CASSETTE
Discusses dance in the Christian tradition. Hosted by Julinda Lewis.
From The Eye On Dance - Dance In Religion And Ritual Series.
Prod-ARTRES Dist-ARTRES

Reverse Bevel Flap C 19 MIN
3/4 INCH VIDEO CASSETTE PRO
Shows how a reverse bevel flap is used to remove crevicular epithelium from periodontal pockets and to provide adequate access for subsequent scaling and root planing.
LC NO. 77-706187
Prod-USVA Dist-USNAC 1972

Reverse Dive, Layout Position C 4 MIN
16MM FILM OPTICAL SOUND
From The Diving - For Fun And Fame Series.
LC NO. 73-702915
Prod-PART Dist-PURPOS 1972

Reverse Dive, Pike Position C 4 MIN
16MM FILM OPTICAL SOUND
From The Diving - For Fun And Fame Series.
LC NO. 73-702915
Prod-PART Dist-PURPOS 1972

Reverse Osmosis C 29 MIN
2 INCH VIDEOTAPE
See series title for descriptive statement.
From The Interface Series.
Prod-KCET Dist-PUBTEL

Reverse Side Of The Eye, The C 29 MIN
3/4 INCH VIDEO CASSETTE
Discusses the inner fantasies and visions of artists that are made visible on canvas.
From The Creation Of Art Series.
Prod-UMITV Dist-UMITV 1975

Reverse Television - Portraits Of Viewers C 15 MIN
3/4 INCH VIDEO CASSETTE
Presents 15-second portraits of television viewers in their homes by Bill Viola. Originally aired as station breaks on WGBH Boston.
Prod-EAI Dist-EAI

Reverse The Charges - How To Save Money On Your Phone Bill C 49 MIN
3/4 OR 1/2 INCH VIDEO CASSETTE H-C A
Explains how changes in the phone industry are affecting the consumer. Emphasizes how consumers can capitalize on the AT&T breakup and save money on their monthly phone bill. Examines three areas - local calls, equipment selection, and long distance calls.
Prod-TAG Dist-FI 1989

Reverse Three-Quarter Crown For Non-Parallel Abutments—A Series
3/4 OR 1/2 INCH VIDEO CASSETTE PRO
Discusses treating nonparallel abutments with a reverse three-quarter crown.
Prod-VADTC Dist-USNAC 1977

Reverse Three-Quarter Crown For Non-Parallel
Reverse Three-Quarter Crown For Non-Parallel 6 MIN
Reverse Three-Quarter Crown For Non-Parallel 12 MIN

Reverse Three-Quarter Crown For Non-Parallel Abutments, A - Treatment Planning And Tooth... C 12 MIN
16MM FILM, 3/4 OR 1/2 IN VIDEO PRO
Demonstrates the appropriate instrumentation, procedures and tooth preparation used in treating non-parallel abutments with a reverse three-quarter crown.
From The Reverse Three-Quarter Crown For Non-Parallel Abutments Series. Part 1
Prod-VADTC Dist-USNAC 1977

Reverse Three-Quarter Crown For Non-Parallel Abutments, A - Jaw Relation Record And... C 6 MIN
16MM FILM, 3/4 OR 1/2 IN VIDEO PRO
Demonstrates the procedures for making impressions, jaw relation records and temporary coverage in treating a lingually inclined molar abutment with a reverse three-quarter crown.
From The Reverse Three-Quarter Crown For Non-Parallel Abutments Series. Part 2
Prod-VADTC Dist-USNAC 1977

Reverse Three-Quarter Crown For Non-Parallel Abutments, Pt II - Impression Jaw Relation... C 7 MIN
3/4 OR 1/2 INCH VIDEO CASSETTE
Demonstrates the various steps involved in the procedures of impression making, jaw relation record and temporary coverage for a reverse three-quarter crown for a lingually-inclined molar abutment.
Prod-VADTC Dist-AMDA 1976

Reverse Three-Quarter Crown For Non-Parallel Abutments, A - Fabrication And Insertion... C 12 MIN
16MM FILM, 3/4 OR 1/2 IN VIDEO PRO
Demonstrates the laboratory fabrication and insertion procedures used in treating a lingually inclined molar abutment with a reverse three-quarter crown. Illustrates the preparation of the master cast with removable dyes, articulation of the master and opposing casts and fabrication of the wax patterns and metal castings.
From The Reverse Three-Quarter Crown For Non-Parallel Abutments Series. Part 3
Prod-VADTC Dist-USNAC 1977

Reverse Three-Quarter Crown For Non-Parallel Abutments, Pt III - Laboratory Fabrication... C 13 MIN
3/4 OR 1/2 INCH VIDEO CASSETTE
Demonstrates some of the steps of laboratory fabrication of a reverse three-quarter crown for a lingually inclined molar abutment as well as the insertion procedures.
Prod-VADTC Dist-AMDA 1976

Reversed Jejunal Segment For Disabling Post-Vagotomy Diarrhea C 18 MIN
16MM FILM OPTICAL SOUND PRO
Explains that a reversed jejunal segment constructed approximately 100 centimeters distal to Treitz's ligament will effectively retard the passage of food stuffs in the proximal small intestine and will serve to correct post-vagotomy diarrhea and intestinal hurry.
Prod-ACYDGD Dist-ACY 1969

Reversible And Irreversible Events C 8 MIN
16MM FILM OPTICAL SOUND J-C A
Portrays perceptual events which can proceed in a forward direction as well as in a backward direction and events that are not reversible or do not appear normal when reversed.
LC NO. 76-703732
Prod-GIBSOJ Dist-PSUPCR 1973

Reversible And Irreversible Processes B 21 MIN
16MM FILM OPTICAL SOUND H-C
Shows how a large air-filled cylinder is closed with a heavy piston and when the piston is displaced from equilibrium the system oscillates. Explains two conditions for long oscillations (reversibility) when the surface area approaches zero, the temperature changes in the gas are high (adiabatic,) and when the surface area becomes very large, there are no measurable temperature changes (isothermal.)
From The College Physics Film Program Series.
LC NO. 74-709338
Prod-ESSOSI Dist-MLA 1970

Review C 15 MIN
2 INCH VIDEOTAPE P
See series title for descriptive statement.
From The Avenida De Ingles Series.
Prod-SDITVA Dist-GPITVL

Review C 15 MIN
3/4 INCH VIDEO CASSETTE P
Discusses the pronunciation of v, f, t, d, m, n, l and p.
From The New Talking Shop Series.
Prod-BSPTV Dist-GPITVL 1978

Review C 29 MIN
3/4 INCH VIDEO CASSETTE
See series title for descriptive statement.
From The Woodcarver's Workshop Series.
Prod-WOSUTV Dist-PUBTEL

Review - H, W, HW, S, Z, K, G C 15 MIN
3/4 INCH VIDEO CASSETTE P
Reviews the pronunciation of the letters h, w, s, z, k and g.
From The New Talking Shop Series.
Prod-BSPTV Dist-GPITVL 1978

Review - L, T, R, H, M, N C 15 MIN
3/4 INCH VIDEO CASSETTE P
Reviews the sounds of the letters l, t, r, h, m and n.
From The New Talking Shop Series.
Prod-BSPTV Dist-GPITVL 1978

Review - Letter, Table Manuscript B 30 MIN
2 INCH VIDEOTAPE
From The Typewriting, Unit 5 - Correspondence, Tabulations And Manuscripts Series.
Prod-GPITVL Dist-GPITVL

Review - Letters, Forms, Reports B 30 MIN
2 INCH VIDEOTAPE
From The Typewriting, Unit 7 - Postal Cards, Forms, Manuscripts Series.
Prod-GPITVL Dist-GPITVL

Review - R, SH, ZH, CH, J C 15 MIN
3/4 INCH VIDEO CASSETTE P
Reviews the sounds of r, SH, ZH, CH and j.
From The New Talking Shop Series.
Prod-BSPTV Dist-GPITVL 1978

Review - Six Word-Attack Skills, Consonant Combinations, Short And Long Vowel Sounds... C 20 MIN
3/4 OR 1/2 INCH VIDEO CASSETTE J-H
Presents a review, including six word-attack skills, consonant combinations, short and long vowel sounds, R-influenced vowel sounds and beginning syllabication.
From The Getting The Word Series. Unit IV
Prod-SCETV Dist-AITECH 1974

Review 'Cane' Letters And I And J C 15 MIN
3/4 INCH VIDEO CASSETTE P
From The Writing Time Series.
Prod-WHROTV Dist-GPITVL

Review 'The Great Search' C 30 MIN
2 INCH VIDEOTAPE J
See series title for descriptive statement.
From The Summer Journal, Unit 1 - You Are What You Feel Series.
Prod-WNINTV Dist-GPITVL

Review And Preview C 30 MIN
3/4 OR 1/2 INCH VIDEO CASSETTE H-C A
Examines data processing installations. Tours two processing centers to examine the roles of personnel and equipment, security and privacy problems, the selection of computer systems and services, and projections for the future.
From The Making It Count Series.
LC NO. 80-707571
Prod-BCSC Dist-BCSC 1980

Review And Rewrite C 30 MIN
3/4 OR 1/2 INCH VIDEO CASSETTE C A
Applies the principles of organization, use of language, style and tone in writing a first draft and rewrite. Shows how to frame a negative message. Hosted by Ed Asner.
From The Effective Writing For Executives Series.
LC NO. 80-707555
Prod-TIMLIF Dist-TIMLIF 1980

Review And The Future C 30 MIN
3/4 OR 1/2 INCH VIDEO CASSETTE H-C A
Reviews the Making It Count course and speculates on future computer developments. Discusses hardware and software, operating systems, multiprogramming, system analysis in computer applications, the selection and use of computer resources, special uses in management decision making and the impact of computers on society.
From The Making It Count Series.
LC NO. 80-707584
Prod-BCSC Dist-BCSC 1980

Review Number One C 29 MIN
3/4 OR 1/2 INCH VIDEO CASSETTE P-I
See series title for descriptive statement.
From The USS Rhythm Series.
Prod-ARKETV Dist-AITECH 1977

Review Number Two C 19 MIN
3/4 OR 1/2 INCH VIDEO CASSETTE P-I
See series title for descriptive statement.
From The USS Rhythm Series.
Prod-ARKETV Dist-AITECH 1977

Review Of Addition C 20 MIN
2 INCH VIDEOTAPE P
See series title for descriptive statement.
From The Mathemagic, Unit VIII - Multiplication And Division Series.
Prod-WMULTV Dist-GPITVL

Review Of All Capital Letters C 15 MIN
3/4 INCH VIDEO CASSETTE P
From The Writing Time Series.
Prod-WHROTV Dist-GPITVL

Review Of All 13 Lower Case Letters Previously Learned C 15 MIN
3/4 INCH VIDEO CASSETTE P
From The Writing Time Series.
Prod-WHROTV Dist-GPITVL

Review Of Capital Letters C 18 MIN
3/4 OR 1/2 INCH VIDEO CASSETTE J-H
See series title for descriptive statement.
From The Getting The Word Series. Unit I
Prod-SCETV Dist-AITECH 1974

Review Of Combinatorial Logic C 30 MIN
3/4 OR 1/2 INCH VIDEO CASSETTE
Reviews basic logic elements of NOT, AND, OR, NOR, and NAND. Discusses basic rules of Boolean algebra, and examples of both minimized and non-minimized design.
From The Digital Sub-Systems Series.
Prod-TXINLC Dist-TXINLC

Review Of Design Theory And Second Moment Code Formats, A B 50 MIN
3/4 OR 1/2 INCH VIDEO CASSETTE
See series title for descriptive statement.
From The Probabilistic Design Series. Pt 3
Prod-UAZMIC Dist-UAZMIC 1976

Review Of Electrical Fundamentals C
3/4 OR 1/2 INCH VIDEO CASSETTE IND
Aims at ensuring the participant has sufficient familiarity with basic electrical theory to understand concepts which will be used throughout the training program. Includes topics such as basic electricity, frequency transformers and current flow in multiple circuits.
From The Distribution System Operation Series. Topic 2
Prod-LEIKID Dist-LEIKID

Review Of Electrical Fundamentals 1 C
3/4 OR 1/2 INCH VIDEO CASSETTE IND
Covers voltage generation, frequency, current, power, reactive, power factor, three-phase operation, power and energy, watts and vars.
From The Electric Power System Operation Series. Tape 1
Prod-LEIKID Dist-LEIKID

Review Of Electrical Fundamentals 2 C
3/4 OR 1/2 INCH VIDEO CASSETTE IND
Includes inductance, impedance, capacitance, voltage drop, line charging and per unit calculations.
From The Electric Power System Operation Series. Tape 2
Prod-LEIKID Dist-LEIKID

Review Of Electrical Fundamentals—A Series
IND
Reviews material for those who have already undergone some training in electrical technology, and for others who want to increase their knowledge of electrical theory. Focuses on power applications with particular emphasis on such areas as AC generation, reactive components and power factor. Explains material with animated graphics.
Prod-LEIKID Dist-LEIKID

Electrical Fundamentals 1 060 MIN
Electrical Fundamentals 2 060 MIN

Review Of Human Biology - Design For Living C 26 MIN
3/4 OR 1/2 INCH VIDEO CASSETTE
Summarizes the functions and designs of the body's major systems and organs and the methods by which they interact.
From The Living Body - An Introduction To Human Biology Series.
Prod-FOTH Dist-FOTH 1985

Review Of One Rescuer And Two Rescuer CPR / First Aid For Foreign Body Obstruction Of... C 13 MIN
3/4 OR 1/2 INCH VIDEO CASSETTE H-C A
Reviews the principles of one rescuer and two rescuer CPR and shows first aid for foreign body obstruction of the airway.
From The CPR - Yours For Life (Rev Ed) Series.
Prod-KUONTV Dist-GPITVL 1982

Review Of One Rescuer And Two Rescuer CPR / Review Of First Aid For Foreign Body... C 15 MIN
3/4 OR 1/2 INCH VIDEO CASSETTE H-C A
Provides a review of one rescuer CPR, two rescuer CPR and first aid for foreign body obstruction of the airway. Discusses infant resuscitation and special resuscitation situations.
From The CPR - Yours For Life (Rev Ed) Series.
Prod-KUONTV Dist-GPITVL 1982

Review Of One Rescuer CPR / Two Rescuer CPR / 911 And The EMS System C 11 MIN
3/4 OR 1/2 INCH VIDEO CASSETTE H-C A
Reviews one rescuer CPR and presents the basics of two rescuer CPR and the 911 and EMS system.
From The CPR - Yours For Life (Rev Ed) Series.
Prod-KUONTV Dist-GPITVL 1982

Review Of Previews - 31 Lessons C 15 MIN
3/4 INCH VIDEO CASSETTE P
Uses a newscast format to review the Studio M series.
From The Studio M Series.
Prod-WCETTV Dist-GPITVL 1979

Review Of Probablistic Concepts C 50 MIN
3/4 OR 1/2 INCH VIDEO CASSETTE PRO
See series title for descriptive statement.
From The Modern Control Theory - Stochastic Estimation Series.
Prod-MIOT Dist-MIOT

Review Of Safety And Electronic Mathematics B 12 MIN
3/4 OR 1/2 INCH VIDEO CASSETTE
Reviews the safety precautions to be observed when working on electrical equipment. Also reviews the conversion of numbers to powers of 10 and the addition, subtraction, multiplication and division of powers.
LC NO. 84-706408
Prod-USAF Dist-USNAC 1983

Review Of Sequential Logic C 30 MIN
3/4 OR 1/2 INCH VIDEO CASSETTE
Gives basic elements required for sequential logic design as well as their truth tables, and follows with development of state diagram, excitation tables, and output tables. Summarizes by reviewing basic sequential design method.
From The Digital Sub-Systems Series.
Prod-TXINLC Dist-TXINLC

Review Of Series Parallel Circuits B 24 MIN
3/4 OR 1/2 INCH VIDEO CASSETTE
Reviews series-parallel circuit problem solving, including measuring current, voltage and resistance. Discusses practical troubleshooting.
LC NO. 84-706410
Prod-USAF Dist-USNAC 1983

Review Of Skills In Relation To Types Of Readers B 30 MIN
2 INCH VIDEOTAPE J-H
Demonstrates how a writer must adjust his styles of writing to suit his reader. (Broadcast quality)
From The English Composition Series. Exposition
Prod-GRETVO Dist-GPITVL Prodn-KUHTTV

Review Of Subtraction C 20 MIN
2 INCH VIDEOTAPE P
See series title for descriptive statement.
From The Mathemagic, Unit VIII - Multiplication And Division Series.
Prod-WMULTV Dist-GPITVL

Review Of The Course, A - Language Corner B 15 MIN
2 INCH VIDEOTAPE P
See series title for descriptive statement.
From The Language Corner Series.
Prod-CVETVC Dist-GPITVL Prodn-WCVETV

Review Of The Evidence Associating Herpes Type II Virus With Cervical Cancer, A C 40 MIN
3/4 INCH VIDEO CASSETTE
Discusses the relationship between Herpes II and cervical cancer and the problems that have arisen in this association.
Prod-UTAHTI Dist-UTAHTI

Review Of The Report Of The National Commission On Marijuana C 29 MIN
16MM FILM OPTICAL SOUND H-C A
Presents a synopsis of the report of the National Commission on Marijuana. Includes interviews with sociologists, psychiatrists and other professionals who indicate that it is neither physically nor psychologically addictive and may be unfavorable only when used in higher doses.
LC NO. 73-702925
Prod-NOLAN Dist-HAASF 1973

Review Of The Seventies C 44 MIN
16MM FILM, 3/4 OR 1/2 IN VIDEO
Focuses on major events and trends during the 1970's.
Prod-DOCUA Dist-CNEMAG

Review Of The Sixties C 44 MIN
16MM FILM, 3/4 OR 1/2 IN VIDEO
Explores the major events and trends of the 1960's.
Prod-DOCUA Dist-CNEMAG

Review Of The Year 1955 B 15 MIN
16MM FILM OPTICAL SOUND
Gives an account of the first general elections ever held in Malaysia.
Prod-FILEM Dist-PMFMUN 1956

Review Of The Year 1959 B 21 MIN
16MM FILM OPTICAL SOUND
Shows the significant events in the federation of Malaysia and highlights the steady progress made by the government in all fields in 1959.
Prod-FILEM Dist-PMFMUN 1960

Review Of The Year 1961 B 27 MIN
16MM FILM OPTICAL SOUND
Discusses the installation of a new king, rural development, the Association of Southeast Asia, the concept of Malaysia making a resounding impact all over the world and her overseas reputation remaining high in 1961.
Prod-FILEM Dist-PMFMUN 1962

Review Of The Year 1962 B 25 MIN
16MM FILM OPTICAL SOUND
Shows the Malaysian royal visit to India and Pakistan and discusses 1962 as the year where all facets of the National Second Five Year Development Plan were successfully carried out in Malaysia.
Prod-FILEM Dist-PMFMUN 1963

Review Of Unit I C 45 MIN
2 INCH VIDEOTAPE
See series title for descriptive statement.
From The Fundamentals Of Mathematics (2nd Ed.) Unit I - Number Theory Series.
Prod-CHITVC Dist-GPITVL

Review Of Unit II C 45 MIN
2 INCH VIDEOTAPE
See series title for descriptive statement.
From The Fundamentals Of Mathematics (2nd Ed.) Unit II - Relations And Functions Series.
Prod-CHITVC Dist-GPITVL

Review Of Unit III C 45 MIN
2 INCH VIDEOTAPE
Presents a review of linear and quadratic functions.
From The Fundamentals Of Mathematics (2nd Ed.) Unit III - Linear And Quadratic Functions Series.
Prod-CHITVC Dist-GPITVL

Review Of Writing Position And The Last 13 Lower Case Letters Learned C 15 MIN
3/4 INCH VIDEO CASSETTE P
From The Writing Time Series.
Prod-WHROTV Dist-GPITVL

Review Of Writing Position, Indirect And Direct Ovals, Cane Stroke, Rocker For... C 15 MIN
3/4 INCH VIDEO CASSETTE P
From The Writing Time Series.
Prod-WHROTV Dist-GPITVL

Review Process, Policies Of Grants B 50 MIN
3/4 OR 1/2 INCH VIDEO CASSETTE
See series title for descriptive statement.
From The Looking For A Grant? Here's What You Should Know Series. Pt 5
Prod-UAZMIC Dist-UAZMIC 1978

Review That Builds Commitment, The C 30 MIN
3/4 OR 1/2 INCH VIDEO CASSETTE
Provides an integrated review and basis for continuing growth of managerial skill in the performance appraisal process.
From The Performance Reviews That Build Commitment Series.
Prod-PRODEV Dist-DELTAK

Review, Microprocessor Architecture (Continued) B 50 MIN
3/4 OR 1/2 INCH VIDEO CASSETTE
See series title for descriptive statement.
From The Microprocessors And Applications Series. Pt 3
Prod-UAZMIC Dist-UAZMIC 1976

Reviewing Past Efforts C 22 MIN
16MM FILM - 3/4 IN VIDEO
Provides a technique for finding the true cause of any program failure and presents ten points for better productivity.
From The Increasing Productivity And Efficiency Series.
Prod-BNA Dist-BNA

Reviewing Past Efforts (Dutch) C 120 MIN
16MM FILM, 3/4 OR 1/2 IN VIDEO
Examines the failure to profit from experience or past mistakes.
From The Increasing Productivity And Efficiency (Dutch) Series.
Prod-BNA Dist-BNA

Reviewing Past Efforts (Norwegian) C 120 MIN
16MM FILM, 3/4 OR 1/2 IN VIDEO
Examines the failure to profit from experience or past mistakes.
From The Increasing Productivity And Efficiency (Norwegian) Series.
Prod-BNA Dist-BNA

Reviewing Performance B 29 MIN
16MM FILM OPTICAL SOUND IND
See series title for descriptive statement.
From The Interviewing For Results Series.
LC NO. 73-703323
Prod-EDSD Dist-EDSD 1968

Reviews And Criticisms C 6 MIN
3/4 OR 1/2 INCH VIDEO CASSETTE
Enables students to find reviews and criticisms of plays, poems, short stories and novels through the use of special reference tools.
From The Library Skills Tapes Series.
Prod-MDCC Dist-MDCC

Reviews Of Series And Parallel Resistive Circuits B 23 MIN
3/4 OR 1/2 INCH VIDEO CASSETTE
Reviews current, voltage and resistance characteristics in series and parallel circuits and reviews balanced and unbalanced bridge circuits.
LC NO. 84-706409
Prod-USAF Dist-USNAC 1983

Revised Gesell And Amatruda Developmental And Neurologic Examination In Infancy, The C 29 MIN
3/4 OR 1/2 INCH VIDEO CASSETTE PRO
Shows how to present each of the exam materials to the infant, to describe what the infant does, and to give an interpretation of the behaviors observed.
From The Developmental - Neurologic Approach To Assessment In Infancy And Early Childhood Series.
Prod-HSCIC Dist-HSCIC 1982

Revised Gesell And Amatruda Developmental And Neurologic Examination (With Interview) At... C 75 MIN
3/4 OR 1/2 INCH VIDEO CASSETTE PRO
Complete title is Revised Gesell And Amatruda Developmental And Neurologic Examination (With Interview) At 18, 24, And 36 Months. Contains interviews with a mother to get information about the child's current behavior. On 3 tapes.
From The Developmental - Neurologic Approach To Assessment In Infancy And Early Childhood Series.
Prod-HSCIC Dist-HSCIC 1982

Revising And Editing C 30 MIN
3/4 OR 1/2 INCH VIDEO CASSETTE A
Explains how to place oneself in the reader's place when editing a written communication. Describes how to check for errors in grammar and spelling and how to be critical of words, thoughts, order and meaning.
From The Writing For Work Series. Pt 7
LC NO. 81-706734
Prod-TIMLIF Dist-TIMLIF 1981

Revision B
16MM FILM OPTICAL SOUND
Explores the role of boundary conditions in the subject of partial differential equations and discusses methods available for their solution. Talks about the numerical approach.
Prod-OPENU Dist-OPENU

Revision Marks, Unbound Reports, How To Erase B 30 MIN
2 INCH VIDEOTAPE
From The Typewriting, Unit 7 - Postal Cards, Forms, Manuscripts Series.
Prod-GPITVL Dist-GPITVL

Revision Stapedectomy C 55 MIN
3/4 OR 1/2 INCH VIDEO CASSETTE PRO
Shows examples of displaced protheses, incus necrosis, slipped strut, fistulae, idiopathic malleus head fixation and exposed overhanging facial nerve as causes of failure in stapedectomies, and consequently the need for revision stapedectomies. Demonstrates the technique for use of an IRP (wire from the malleus handle) on a case with both incus necrosis and fistula.
Prod-HOUSEI Dist-HOUSEI 1982

Revision Strategies C
3/4 OR 1/2 INCH VIDEO CASSETTE C
Focuses solely on the revision stage of the writing process. Treats revision as more than proofreading and editing.
From The Write Course - An Introduction To College Composition Series.
Prod-DALCCD Dist-DALCCD

Revision Strategies C 30 MIN
3/4 OR 1/2 INCH VIDEO CASSETTE C A
Focuses on the revision stage of writing and goes beyond the concept of revision as merely proofreading and editing.
From The Write Course - An Introduction To College Composition Series.
LC NO. 85-700989
Prod-FI Dist-FI 1984

Revival Of Victorianism, The C 29 MIN
2 INCH VIDEOTAPE
See series title for descriptive statement.
From The University Of Chicago Round Table Series.
Prod-WTTWTV Dist-PUBTEL

Revocable Trust, The C 150 MIN
3/4 OR 1/2 INCH VIDEO CASSETTE PRO
Analyzes and explains changes in the Economic Recovery Act of 1981 and the Tax Equity and Fiscal Responsibility Act of 1982. Replaces ABA Video Law Seminar.
Prod-ABACPE Dist-ABACPE

Revolution C 16 MIN
16MM FILM OPTICAL SOUND
Traces important events, such as the Boston Massacre and Boston Tea Party, which led to the American Revolution, highlights the significant battles of the Revolutionary War, and examines the American victory in the struggle for independence.
LC NO. 74-702508
Prod-SCHMAG Dist-SCHMAG Prodn-STRHAY 1974

Revolution In Nicaragua C 58 MIN
3/4 OR 1/2 INCH VIDEO CASSETTE A
Traces the evolution of U S involvement in Nicaragua and the struggle for control of the revolution. Describes the overthrow of the 50-year-old Somoza dynasty by the Sandinistas in 1979 which the U S tried to prevent, then tried to court and then tried to undermine.
From The Crisis In Central America Series.
Prod-WGBHTV Dist-FI

Revolution In Russia, 1917 B 19 MIN
16MM FILM, 3/4 OR 1/2 IN VIDEO H-C
Depicts the March Revolution in Russia and describes the toppling of the Provisional Government by the Bolsheviks.
From The World War I Series.
Prod-CBSTV Dist-FI 1967

Revolution In The Paint Locker C 18 MIN
16MM FILM OPTICAL SOUND IND
Shows the impact of paints and coatings on the operation and maintenance of naval ships.
LC NO. 77-700078
Prod-USN Dist-USNAC 1975

Revolution In The World Of Work C 7 MIN
16MM FILM OPTICAL SOUND
Shows how vocational and career education can provide a saleable skill, as well as give personal security and a sense of relevance and opportunity to the individual.
LC NO. 73-702917
Prod-PART Dist-PART 1973

Revolution Is Advancing, The C 26 MIN
16MM FILM OPTICAL SOUND
Deals less with the legacies of the Mozambican past, and more with the outlook for the future. Emphasizes the priority given to educational work, both adult literacy programs and childhood education, and shows some of the steps under way to develop a culture drawing on the strengths of the Mozambican people.
Prod-ICARUS Dist-ICARUS

Revolution Or Evolution - Music In Progress C 30 MIN
3/4 INCH VIDEO CASSETTE
See series title for descriptive statement.
From The Changing Music Series.
Prod-WGBHTV Dist-PUBTEL

Revolution Until Victory B
16MM FILM OPTICAL SOUND
Presents the story of the Palestinian people and the rise of Fateh, the leading guerrilla organization.
Prod-SFN Dist-SFN 1970

Revolution, The C 30 MIN
2 INCH VIDEOTAPE
Discusses the meaning of the declaration of independence, the suffering at Valley Forge, and George Washington as a war leader.
From The American History I Series.
Prod-DENVPS Dist-GPITVL

Revolution, The - 1775-1783 X 24 MIN
16MM FILM OPTICAL SOUND I-C A
Reviews the efforts of the untrained citizen soldiers of the revolution at such places as Breed and Bunker Hills, Camden and Yorktown. Explores the responsibility of independence.
From The Exploring - The Story Of America, Set 1 Series.
LC NO. FIA68-1051
Prod-NBCTV Dist-GRACUR 1968

Revolution's Orphans C 28 MIN
16MM FILM, 3/4 OR 1/2 IN VIDEO J-C A
Presents a drama which meshes fact and fiction in a study of the 1956 Hungarian Revolution as seen from the point of view of a young woman, who searches her past to understand those catastrophic days.
From The Adventures In History Series.
LC NO. 82-706168
Prod-NFBC Dist-FI 1981

Revolutionary Age, The C 30 MIN
16MM FILM OPTICAL SOUND
Attributes the tyranny and revolutions of the post-Reformation era to the rejection of the spiritual and religious values embraced during the Reformation. Based on the book How Should We Then Live by Francis A Schaeffer.
From The How Should We Then Live Series. Episode 5
LC NO. 77-702367
Prod-GF Dist-GF 1977

Revolutionary Age, The (Dutch) C 30 MIN
16MM FILM OPTICAL SOUND
Attributes the tyranny and revolutions of the post-Reformation era to the rejection of the spiritual and religious values embraced during the Reformation. Based on the book How Should We Then Live by Francis A Schaeffer.
From The How Should We Then Live (Dutch) Series. Episode 5
LC NO. 77-702367
Prod-GF Dist-GF 1977

Revolutionary Regulations C 19 MIN
16MM FILM OPTICAL SOUND
Explains the new Federal regulations for personal flotation devices on recreational boats.
LC NO. 74-706397
Prod-USCG Dist-USNAC 1973

Revolutionary, The C 60 MIN
3/4 OR 1/2 INCH VIDEO CASSETTE J-C A
Presents flutist James Galway discussing Beethoven, the man who changed the course of music. Provides movements or significant extracts from the 3rd, 6th and 9th Symphonies.
From The James Galway's Music In Time Series.
Prod-POLTEL Dist-FOTH 1982

Revolutions Go Backwards I - The South C 29 MIN
2 INCH VIDEOTAPE
See series title for descriptive statement.
From The Black Experience Series.
Prod-WTTWTV Dist-PUBTEL

Revolutions Go Backwards II - The Nation C 29 MIN
2 INCH VIDEOTAPE
See series title for descriptive statement.
From The Black Experience Series.
Prod-WTTWTV Dist-PUBTEL

Revolutions Go Backwards III - Redemption C 29 MIN
2 INCH VIDEOTAPE
See series title for descriptive statement.
From The Black Experience Series.
Prod-WTTWTV Dist-PUBTEL

Revolutions In Science C 30 MIN
3/4 INCH VIDEO CASSETTE J-C A
Discusses aspects of man's technological knowledge, showing how he has learned to prolong and destroy life more efficiently.
From The Jacob Bronowski - 20th Century Man Series.
Prod-KPBS Dist-GPITVL 1976

Revue Des Forces Canadiennes C 5 MIN
16MM FILM OPTICAL SOUND
A French language version of the film Canadian Forces Year End Review. Shows the major activities of the Canadian Forces in 1973.
LC NO. 75-701445
Prod-CDND Dist-CDND Prodn-NIMBUS 1974

Reward And Punishment C 14 MIN
16MM FILM, 3/4 OR 1/2 IN VIDEO J-C A
Discusses principles underlying the two major influences in human development, reward and punishment. Shows guidelines for their use in developing new behaviors of changing existing ones in young children.
Prod-CRMP Dist-CRMP 1974

Reward Of Champions C 14 MIN
16MM FILM OPTICAL SOUND
Presents the Pan American Turf Handicap, Canadian Turf Handicap and the Florida Derby at Gulfstream Park in Florida.
Prod-FLADC Dist-FLADC

Reward, Punishment And Responsibility C 25 MIN
3/4 OR 1/2 INCH VIDEO CASSETTE C
See series title for descriptive statement.
From The Introduction To Philosophy Series.
Prod-UDEL Dist-UDEL

Rewards And Reinforcements B 26 MIN
16MM FILM OPTICAL SOUND C T
Points out that economically underprivileged children must often be provided with motives for learning, that the value systems of these children may differ from those of the economically satisfied child, and that behavior may need to be reinforced with rewards such as candy, money, clothes, or other material objects.
LC NO. 76-700843
Prod-CINPS Dist-IU 1968

Rewards Of Rewarding, The C 24 MIN
16MM FILM, 3/4 OR 1/2 IN VIDEO
Explains how supervisors can use rewards as a management tool. Tells about a ranch foreman who is out of touch with a worker's real needs. Shows how a wise and experienced ranch cook teaches how and when to show appreciation to subordinates.
From The Thanks A'Plenty Boss Series.
LC NO. 74-700244
Prod-RTBL Dist-RTBL 1973

Rewards Of Rewarding, The (Captioned) C 24 MIN
16MM FILM, 3/4 OR 1/2 IN VIDEO
Explains to supervisors how to use rewards as a management tool. Tells about a ranch foreman who is out of touch with a worker's real needs. Shows how a wise and experienced ranch cook teaches when and how to show appreciation to subordinates.
From The Thanks A' Plenty Boss Series.
Prod-RTBL Dist-RTBL 1973

Rewards Of Rewarding, The (French) C 24 MIN
16MM FILM, 3/4 OR 1/2 IN VIDEO
Explains to supervisors how to use rewards as a management tool. Tells about a ranch foreman who is out of touch with a worker's real needs. Shows how a wise and experienced ranch cook teaches how and when to show appreciation to subordinates.
From The Thanks A' Plenty Boss Series.
Prod-RTBL Dist-RTBL 1973

Rewards Of Rewarding, The (Spanish) C 24 MIN
16MM FILM, 3/4 OR 1/2 IN VIDEO
Explains to supervisors how to use rewards as a management tool. Tells about a ranch foreman who is out of touch with a worker's real needs. Shows how a wise and experienced ranch cook teaches how and when to show appreciation to subordinates.
From The Thanks A' Plenty Boss Series.
Prod-RTBL Dist-RTBL 1973

Rewriting - Proofreading C 29 MIN
3/4 OR 1/2 INCH VIDEO CASSETTE
Emphasizes that the mechanics of writing must be taught within the context of the writing process. Explains that when students understand that the correct punctuation in writing clarifies their message, they refine their writing by using correct mechanical conventions.
From The Teaching Writing - A Process Approach Series.
Prod-MSITV Dist-PBS 1982

Rewriting - Revising C 29 MIN
3/4 OR 1/2 INCH VIDEO CASSETTE
Examines the distinction between revising and proofreading and offers teachers several methods of working with students to revise their initial written work.
From The Teaching Writing - A Process Approach Series.
Prod-MSITV Dist-PBS 1982

Rex Harrison C 29 MIN
2 INCH VIDEOTAPE
Presents exchanges and arguments between the dean of American theatre critics, Elliot Norton, and Rex Harrison.
From The Elliot Norton Reviews II Series.
Prod-WGBHTV Dist-PUBTEL

Reye's Syndrome C 18 MIN
3/4 OR 1/2 INCH VIDEO CASSETTE PRO
Covers the diagnosis, treatment and effects of Reye's syndrome through presentation of a five-year-old patient. Includes presenting symptoms, probable triggering events, four stages of the disease, suggested laboratory work and results that lead to diagnosis and therapy. Emphasizes early detection of the disease.
Prod-UMICHM Dist-UMICHM 1978

Reyes Syndrome - The Child Killer C 29 MIN
3/4 INCH VIDEO CASSETTE A

Describes the symptoms and treatment of the children's disease known as Reyes Syndrome.
LC NO. 81-707485
Prod-FITZJ Dist-PBS 1981

Reynolds Aluminum Recycling Pays C 10 MIN
16MM FILM OPTICAL SOUND
Shows the benefits of the Reynolds Metals aluminum recycling program. Demonstrates the program's success in fighting litter, saving energy and conserving natural resources.
LC NO. 76-702315
Prod-REYMC Dist-REYMC 1975

RF And IF Amplifiers, Pt 1 B 21 MIN
16MM FILM OPTICAL SOUND
Discusses the single tuned RF amplifier using capacitive and transformer coupling. Explains circuit operation with respect to a parallel resonant tank in the plate circuit of the capacitance coupled amplifier and in the grid circuit of the transformer coupled amplifier's second stage. (Kinescope)
LC NO. 74-705536
Prod-USAF Dist-USNAC

RF Glow Discharges C 35 MIN
3/4 OR 1/2 INCH VIDEO CASSETTE IND
Studies and compares RF to DC discharges. Notes that RF includes frequencies from 50 kiloherz to 50 megaherz, and that electron temperature in RF discharge is derived in terms of the applied frequency and voltage as well as gas pressure.
From The Plasma Sputtering, Deposition And Growth Of Microelectronic Films For VLSI Series.
Prod-COLOSU Dist-COLOSU

Rh - The Disease And Its Conquest C 18 MIN
16MM FILM OPTICAL SOUND
Explains the complex genetic nature of the Rh factor and the Rh negative problem. Discusses the cause and development of antibodies, the immunization process in the mother and the effects on the fetus. Provides a description of the development of anti-Rh globulin.
From The Human Genetics Series. No. 12
LC NO. 75-700028
Prod-NFMD Dist-MIFE Prodn-MIFE 1974

Rh - The Disease And Its Conquest (Spanish) C 18 MIN
16MM FILM OPTICAL SOUND
Explains the complex genetic nature of the Rh factor and the Rh negative problem. Discusses the cause and development of antibodies, the immunization process in the mother and the effects on the fetus. Provides a description of the development of anti-Rh globulin.
From The Human Genetics (Spanish) Series. No. 12
LC NO. 75-700028
Prod-NFMD Dist-MIFE Prodn-MIFE 1974

Rh Testing C 10 MIN
3/4 OR 1/2 INCH VIDEO CASSETTE
Reviews Rh testing procedures with special emphasis on Du testing.
Prod-AMRC Dist-AMRC 1977

Rh-Negative Mother C
3/4 OR 1/2 INCH VIDEO CASSETTE
Addresses the natural concern of the Rh-negative mother. Explains how Anti-Rh Globular Serum and 'exchange transfusions' have made it possible for 98% of all Rh incompatible babies to live.
Prod-MIFE Dist-MIFE

Rh-Negative Mother (Arabic) C
3/4 OR 1/2 INCH VIDEO CASSETTE
Addresses the natural concern of the Rh-negative mother. Explains how Anti-Rh Globular Serum and 'exchange transfusions' have made it possible for 98% of all Rh incompatible babies to live.
Prod-MIFE Dist-MIFE

Rh-Negative Mother (French) C
3/4 OR 1/2 INCH VIDEO CASSETTE
Addresses the natural concern of the Rh-negative mother. Explains how Anti-Rh Globular Serum and 'exchange transfusions' have made it possible for 98% of all Rh incompatible babies to live.
Prod-MIFE Dist-MIFE

Rh-Negative Mother (Spanish) C
3/4 OR 1/2 INCH VIDEO CASSETTE
Addresses the natural concern of the Rh-negative mother. Explains how Anti-Rh Globular Serum and 'exchange transfusions' have made it possible for 98% of all Rh incompatible babies to live.
Prod-MIFE Dist-MIFE

Rhapsody Of A River C 12 MIN
16MM FILM OPTICAL SOUND
Presents a picture set to music of one day in the life of the countryside and of the city of Cork, Ireland, showing both traditional and modern aspects of life in the region.
Prod-CONSUI Dist-CONSUI

Rhapsody On A Theme From A House Movie B 7 MIN
16MM FILM OPTICAL SOUND
Uses experimental techniques to create a world of temporal and spatial relationships that could only exist in dream or memory.
LC NO. 77-702627
Prod-MARINL Dist-CANFDC 1972

Rheinberg, A Small Town On The Outskirts Of The Ruhr C 5 MIN
16MM FILM, 3/4 OR 1/2 IN VIDEO
Offers a brief history of the area around Rheinberg, Germany, and explains how its picturesque tranquility is being threatened by its own economic success.
From The European Studies - Germany Series. Part 11
Prod-BAYER Dist-IFB 1973

Rheinberg, Eine Kleinstadt Am Rande Des Ruhrgebiets C 5 MIN
16MM FILM, 3/4 OR 1/2 IN VIDEO H-C A
A German-language version of the motion picture Rheinberg, A Small Town On The Outskirts Of The Ruhr. Gives a brief history of the Ruhr area and shows how its picturesque tranquility is being threatened by its own economic success.
From The European Studies - Germany (German) Series.
Prod-MFAFRG Dist-IFB Prodn-BAYER 1973

Rheingold C 91 MIN
16MM FILM OPTICAL SOUND
A German language film with English subtitles. Travels alongside its namesake, the renowned city train, and relates two love stories, one the legend of beautiful Lorelei, the other a modern melodrama in which the wife of a diplomat loves her former boyfriend, a waiter in the dining car. She is caught by her husband, mortally wounded, and, during the remaining trip through Germany, dies a slow death filled with fragmented memories.
Prod-WSTGLC Dist-WSTGLC 1977

Rheingold C 1 MIN
3/4 OR 1/2 INCH VIDEO CASSETTE
Shows a classic television commercial with moving bottles, cans and toy trains.
Prod-BROOKC Dist-BROOKC

Rheological Behavior Of Fluids X 22 MIN
16MM FILM, 3/4 OR 1/2 IN VIDEO C
Contrasts non-Newtonian to Newtonian viscous fluid behavior. Illustrates effects of non-linearity on shear and normal stresses.
From The Fluid Mechanics Series.
Prod-NCFMF Dist-EBEC 1964

Rheology—A Series
C
Uses classroom format of taping two lectures per week, one of one hour and one of 1 1/2 hours. Covers rheological characteristics of viscous, elastic, viscoelastic and plastic substances, non-Neutonian fluid flow, viscometry and rheogoniometry, rheological equations of state and engineering applications.
Prod-USCCE Dist-AMCEE

Rheostats And Potentiometers B 23 MIN
16MM FILM, 3/4 OR 1/2 IN VIDEO
Defines a rheostat and potentiometer. Discusses the characteristics of a rheostat and how it can be used. Gives the characteristics and use of a potentiometer. Concludes with a demonstration of how each of these units are connected in a circuit. (Kinescope)
Prod-USAF Dist-USNAC

Rhesus Monkey Births C 12 MIN
16MM FILM OPTICAL SOUND C
Features five birth sequences in rhesus monkeys at the California Primate Research Center. Includes normal deliveries by experienced mothers, a breech delivery and a normal delivery by an inexperienced female.
LC NO. 75-702187
Prod-MITG Dist-PSUPCR 1975

Rhesus Monkey In India C 22 MIN
16MM FILM OPTICAL SOUND C T
Presents a general introduction to the ecology and behavior of the rhesus monkey in northern India—data on abundance, distribution, habitat preferences, group sizes, sex and age ratios, population trends and interrelationships with humans shows the basic patterns of social behavior of four groups inhabiting a Hindu temple area.
Prod-JHU Dist-PSUPCR 1962

Rhesus Monkey Infant's First Four Months, A C 32 MIN
16MM FILM OPTICAL SOUND C
Records the social and physical development of a Rhesus monkey from birth through the infant's first 16 weeks.
LC NO. 80-701578
Prod-HOWES Dist-PSUPCR 1980

Rhesus Play C 23 MIN
16MM FILM, 3/4 OR 1/2 IN VIDEO
Studies the question of why animals play by describing and analyzing aggressive play among free-ranging rhesus monkeys on La Cueva Island, Puerto Rico.
Prod-HUFSC Dist-UCEMC 1977

Rhetoric Of War C 29 MIN
3/4 INCH VIDEO CASSETTE
Gives a reenactment of the verbal battles that preceded the American Revolution. Looks at letters, newspaper accounts and speeches before the Continental Congress.
Prod-UMITV Dist-UMITV 1974

Rheumatic Pain Syndrome C 30 MIN
3/4 OR 1/2 INCH VIDEO CASSETTE
Uses graphic illustrations to describe and explain bursitis, tendinitis and rheumatic diseases which occur outside the joints.
Prod-PRIMED Dist-PRIMED

Rheumatoid Arthritis B 17 MIN
16MM FILM OPTICAL SOUND H-C A
A doctor explains ways to keep joints from deteriorating in a condition of rheumatoid arthritis and exposes quack devices for the cure of arthritis.
From The Doctors At Work Series.
LC NO. FIA65-1360
Prod-CMA Dist-LAWREN Prodn-LAWREN 1962

Rheumatoid Arthritis C
3/4 OR 1/2 INCH VIDEO CASSETTE
Covers the causes of rheumatoid arthritis and basic elements of a conservative management program. Emphasizes therapy to help prevent damaging changes and help restore function under close medical supervision.
Prod-MIFE Dist-MIFE

Rheumatoid Arthritis C 29 MIN
3/4 OR 1/2 INCH VIDEO CASSETTE
Describes the causes, symptoms and treatment of rheumatoid arthritis.
From The Daniel Foster, MD Series.
Prod-KERA Dist-PBS

Rheumatoid Arthritis (Rev Ed) C 21 MIN
16MM FILM, 3/4 OR 1/2 IN VIDEO PRO
Discusses the ways in which rheumatoid arthritis affects the body and explains the goals of treatment and the roles of rest, heat, exercise and medication in treatment.
Prod-PRORE Dist-PRORE

Rheumatoid Arthritis (Spanish) C
3/4 OR 1/2 INCH VIDEO CASSETTE
Covers the causes of rheumatoid arthritis and basic elements of a conservative management program. Emphasizes therapy to help prevent damaging changes and helps restore function under close medical supervision.
Prod-MIFE Dist-MIFE

Rheumatoid Arthritis (Spanish) C 21 MIN
16MM FILM, 3/4 OR 1/2 IN VIDEO J-C A
Explores rheumatoid arthritis, discussing how it affects people differently and the various treatments available. Warns against the many 'miracle' cures that promise the impossible and could be harmful.
Prod-JOU Dist-PRORE 1974

Rhine Valley And The North, The, Pt 1 C 40 MIN
16MM FILM OPTICAL SOUND H-C A
Focuses on a variety of scenes, and animates them with commentary. Presents a rounded view of Germans as members of a particular culture.
Prod-WSTGLC Dist-WSTGLC

Rhine-Main Airport, Frankfurt C 5 MIN
16MM FILM, 3/4 OR 1/2 IN VIDEO
Examines the operation of Germany's largest airport, Rhine-Main.
From The European Studies - Germany Series. Part 19
Prod-BAYER Dist-IFB 1973

Rhine, The - A European River C 29 MIN
16MM FILM OPTICAL SOUND H-C A
Traces the history of the Rhine River as a vehicle of trade and commerce, an instrument of political change and a stage for drama, literature and art. Shows Rhine landmarks from Switzerlandto Holland.
Prod-WSTGLC Dist-WSTGLC

Rhino Rescue C 22 MIN
16MM FILM, 3/4 OR 1/2 IN VIDEO
Shows the care of rhinoceros in wildlife preservation.
Prod-IFB Dist-PHENIX 1974

Rhino, The - Giant On Land B 30 MIN
16MM FILM OPTICAL SOUND H-C A
Traces the origin of the rhinoceros forty-five million years ago in the Rocky Mountain areas and its migration to the plains some ten million years ago.
From The Great Plains Trilogy, 1 Series. In The Beginning - The Primitive Man
Prod-KUONTV Dist-UNL 1954

Rhinoceros C 12 MIN
16MM FILM, 3/4 OR 1/2 IN VIDEO P A
Shows the African rhinoceros through its daily routine of browsing, sleeping, wallowing and drinking. Explores why this animal is the target of hunters and poachers.
From The Silent Safari Series.
Prod-CHE Dist-EBEC 1984

Rhinoplasty C 15 MIN
16MM FILM, 3/4 OR 1/2 IN VIDEO A
Covers the physical and psychological aspects of rhinoplasty surgery. Features people who have had the surgery and discusses the reasons for having it, reactions to the experience and feelings about the results.
Prod-PRORE Dist-PRORE

Rhinos C 8 MIN
16MM FILM, 3/4 OR 1/2 IN VIDEO P-I
Compares the African and Indian varieties of rhinoceros including their physical make up, their native habitats and their methods of caring for the young.
From The Looking At Animals Series.
Prod-IFB Dist-IFB 1973

Rhinos And Hippos C 6 MIN
16MM FILM, 3/4 OR 1/2 IN VIDEO K-P
Looks at the habits of rhinos and hippos. Shows rhinos rolling in the mud to protect their hairless skin from insects and hippos running gracefully on lake or stream bottoms.
From The Zoo Animals In The Wild Series.
Prod-CORF Dist-CORF 1981

Rhoda Grauer And John Job Christian Holder C 30 MIN
3/4 OR 1/2 INCH VIDEO CASSETTE
Looks at the opportunities for dancers presented by television. Includes a performance of 'Esoterica' with Dianne McIntyre. Hosted By Celia Ipiotis.
From The Eye On Dance - Dancing Families Series.
Prod-ARTRES Dist-ARTRES

Rhubarb Power C 5 MIN
3/4 OR 1/2 INCH VIDEO CASSETTE J-H
Teaches pronoun reference.
From The Write On, Set 1 Series.
Prod-CTI Dist-CTI

Rhyme C 30 MIN
2 INCH VIDEOTAPE J-H
Presents the components of poetry, emphasizing rhyme.

From The From Franklin To Frost - Poetry Series.
Prod-MPATI Dist-GPITVL

Rhyme And Reason C 28 MIN
3/4 OR 1/2 INCH VIDEO CASSETTE C
Focuses on the process of cognitive development in children.
From The Learning Through Play - Programs Series. Program 1
Prod-UTORMC Dist-UTORMC 1976

Rhyme And Reason Of Politics, The C 30 MIN
3/4 OR 1/2 INCH VIDEO CASSETTE
See series title for descriptive statement.
From The Language - Thinking, Writing, Communicating Series.
Prod-MDCPB Dist-MDCPB

Rhyme Time C 15 MIN
3/4 OR 1/2 INCH VIDEO CASSETTE T
Uses the adventures of a pirate and his three friends to explore the many facets of language arts. Focuses on poetry writing and encourages the use of this form.
From The Hidden Treasures Series. No. 11
LC NO. 82-706551
Prod-WCVETV Dist-GPITVL 1980

Rhymes In Clay C 10 MIN
16MM FILM - VIDEO, ALL FORMATS P
Uses clay animation to present the rhymes Simple Simon, The Owl And The Pussycat and I Saw A Ship A'Sailing.
Prod-WATTGO Dist-WATTGO

Rhyming Dictionary Of Boats, A C 11 MIN
16MM FILM, 3/4 OR 1/2 IN VIDEO P
Uses songs and rhymes to introduce different types of boats.
From The Rhyming Dictionary Series.
Prod-ALTSUL Dist-JOU 1978

Rhyming Dictionary Of Planes, A C 11 MIN
16MM FILM, 3/4 OR 1/2 IN VIDEO P
Uses songs and rhymes to introduce different types of airplanes and their functions.
From The Rhyming Dictionary Series.
Prod-ALTSUL Dist-JOU 1978

Rhyming Dictionary Of Shapes And Sizes, A C 11 MIN
16MM FILM, 3/4 OR 1/2 IN VIDEO P
Visits playgrounds, food stands and toy rooms to show that geometric shapes are everywhere.
Prod-ALTSUL Dist-JOU 1981

Rhyming Dictionary Of Trucks, A C 11 MIN
16MM FILM, 3/4 OR 1/2 IN VIDEO P
Uses songs and rhymes to introduce different types of trucks and their functions.
From The Rhyming Dictionary Series.
Prod-ALTSUL Dist-JOU 1978

Rhyming Dictionary Of Zoo Animals, A C 10 MIN
16MM FILM, 3/4 OR 1/2 IN VIDEO K-P
Explains scientific facts about animals by using songs and rhymes while taking a tour of a zoo.
Prod-ALTSUL Dist-JOU 1977

Rhyming Dictionary—A Series
16MM FILM, 3/4 OR 1/2 IN VIDEO P-I
Introduces concepts about the world of transportation.
Prod-ALTSUL Dist-JOU 1978

Rhyming Dictionary Of Boats, A 011 MIN
Rhyming Dictionary Of Planes, A 011 MIN
Rhyming Dictionary Of Shapes And Sizes, A 011 MIN
Rhyming Dictionary Of Trucks, A 011 MIN
Rhyming Dictionary Of Zoo Animals, A 010 MIN

Rhyming Words C 15 MIN
3/4 OR 1/2 INCH VIDEO CASSETTE P
Employs a magician named Amazing Alexander and his assistants to explore rhyme.
From The Magic Shop Series. No. 2
LC NO. 83-706147
Prod-CVETVC Dist-GPITVL Prodn-WCVETV 1982

Rhythm B 1 MIN
16MM FILM OPTICAL SOUND
Shows Len Lye's remarkable sense of motion applied to the editing of live footage, with the footage becoming a kinetic composition, synchonised to the rhythms of African drum music. Commissioned as a commercial for the Chrysler Corporation.
Prod-STARRC Dist-STARRC Prodn-LYEL 1957

Rhythm B 20 MIN
16MM FILM OPTICAL SOUND C A
See series title for descriptive statement.
From The All That I Am Series.
Prod-MPATI Dist-NWUFLM

Rhythm C 15 MIN
3/4 OR 1/2 INCH VIDEO CASSETTE K-J
See series title for descriptive statement.
From The Arts Express Series.
Prod-KYTV Dist-KYTV 1983

Rhythm C 30 MIN
2 INCH VIDEOTAPE J-H
Presents the components of poetry, emphasizing rhythm.
From The From Franklin To Frost - Poetry Series.
Prod-MPATI Dist-GPITVL

Rhythm And Blues C 15 MIN
3/4 OR 1/2 INCH VIDEO CASSETTE P
See series title for descriptive statement.
From The Strawberry Square II - Take Time Series.
Prod-NEITV Dist-AITECH 1984

Rhythm And Blues C 30 MIN
3/4 OR 1/2 INCH VIDEO CASSETTE J-H
Focuses on rhythm and blues artists The Dells and Bo Diddley.
From The From Jumpstreet Series.
Prod-WETATV Dist-GPITVL 1979

Rhythm And Blues Review B 90 MIN
16MM FILM OPTICAL SOUND
Presents a musical review starring such greats of the as Lionel Hampton, Count Basie and Duke Ellington.
Prod-STDIOF Dist-KITPAR 1955

Rhythm And Movement In Art C 19 MIN
16MM FILM, 3/4 OR 1/2 IN VIDEO I-C
Explains the place of rhythm and movement in art.
Prod-BURN Dist-PHENIX 1969

Rhythm And Pulse C 11 MIN
16MM FILM OPTICAL SOUND
Shows how children develop their natural expressions in music. Includes examples which illustrate rhythm and pulse.
From The Music With Children Series. No. 1
LC NO. 75-700737
Prod-NASHGC Dist-SWRTWT Prodn-SWRTWT 1967

Rhythm Around You C 4 MIN
16MM FILM, 3/4 OR 1/2 IN VIDEO K-I
Portrays the rhythm that's in the rain, in the sea, in the traffic in the street and even inside people.
From The Most Important Person - Creative Expression Series.
Prod-EBEC Dist-EBEC 1972

Rhythm Method - Natural Family Planning C 9 MIN
3/4 OR 1/2 INCH VIDEO CASSETTE
Explains ovulation, menstruation and fertilization. Describes methods of recognizing ovulation.
Prod-MEDFAC Dist-MEDFAC 1972

Rhythm Of Africa B 17 MIN
16MM FILM OPTICAL SOUND H-C
Presents traditional ceremonial dances of the Chad. Recorded and photographed in Equatorial Africa.
Prod-VILLIE Dist-RADIM 1947

Rhythm Of Gujarat C 17 MIN
16MM FILM OPTICAL SOUND I-C A
Shows the colorful folk dances of the Gujarat region in India. Presents the story of Radha and Krishna as told in the Raas and Garba dances.
Prod-INDIA Dist-NEDINF

Rhythm 21 / Diagonal Symphony B 8 MIN
16MM FILM SILENT
Presents pioneer works by two artists, Viking Eggeling and Hans Richter, who first made the transition from abstract painting to abstract film. Includes Eggeling's Diagonal Symphony, which moves hieroglyphic forms along an invisible diagonal, and Richter's Rhythm 21, which orchestrates the squares and rectangles of the film and screen. Produced 1921-24.
Prod-STARRC Dist-STARRC

Rhythm 23 B 3 MIN
16MM FILM SILENT
Presents criss-cross patterns, negative reversals, intercut stringed forms, and further variations of the rectangle and square. By Hans Richter, 1923.
Prod-STARRC Dist-STARRC 1923

Rhythm, Rhythm Everywhere C 11 MIN
16MM FILM, 3/4 OR 1/2 IN VIDEO K-P
Shows children jumping rope to rhymes and introduces many lively examples to the rhythms of everyday life. Depicts the youngsters creating rhythms in pantomime to express their inner feelings.
Prod-CORF Dist-CORF 1974

Rhythm, Speed And Accuracy In Hand Sending B 12 MIN
16MM FILM OPTICAL SOUND
Discusses rhythm and timing and points out that clear, distinct sending is essential in order to assure proper receiving at destination.
From The Radio Technician Training Series.
LC NO. FIE52-1102
Prod-USN Dist-USNAC 1947

Rhythm's The Name Of The Game C 30 MIN
3/4 OR 1/2 INCH VIDEO CASSETTE
See series title for descriptive statement.
From The Third World Dance - Tracing Roots Series.
Prod-ARCVID Dist-ARCVID

Rhythmetron C 40 MIN
16MM FILM, 3/4 OR 1/2 IN VIDEO I-H A
Introduces the basics of ballet in terms of daily activities, sports, and popular dance steps. Features Arthur Mitchell and the Dance Theatre of Harlem.
Prod-CAPCBC Dist-CRMP 1973

Rhythmic Ball Skills For Perceptual-Motor Development C 11 MIN
16MM FILM OPTICAL SOUND P-I T
Introduces activities using the perceptual-motor approach to learning directional concepts.
LC NO. 76-714784
Prod-MMP Dist-MMP 1971

Rhythmic Composition In Yellow Green Minor C 9 MIN
16MM FILM OPTICAL SOUND
Discusses one of the first abstract paintings produced in Australia.
From The Australian Eye Series.
LC NO. 80-700788
Prod-FLMAUS Dist-TASCOR 1978

Rhythmic Gymnastics - The Perfect New Women's Sport C
3/4 OR 1/2 INCH VIDEO CASSETTE
Demonstrates movements and techniques of beginning rhythmic gymnastics and covers all apparatus. Produced by the coaches of the Penn State University women's gymnastic team.
Prod-ATHI Dist-ATHI

Rhythmical Gymnastics C 22 MIN
16MM FILM OPTICAL SOUND
Demonstrates Liss Burmester's modern rhythmic exercises for women.
Prod-RDCG Dist-AUDPLN

Rhythms And Drives C 60 MIN
3/4 OR 1/2 INCH VIDEO CASSETTE C A
Discusses subconscious, instinctive rhythms and drives.
From The Brain, Mind And Behavior Series.
Prod-WNETTV Dist-FI

Rhythms From Africa C 15 MIN
16MM FILM, 3/4 OR 1/2 IN VIDEO
Shows different types of rhythm instruments from Africa. Demonstrates various ways of performing with each of the instruments and invites children to add their hands, feet and voices to the rhythmic musical aggregate.
From The Ripples Series.
LC NO. 73-702151
Prod-NITC Dist-AITECH

Rhythms Of Haiti C 25 MIN
16MM FILM, 3/4 OR 1/2 IN VIDEO J-C A
Shows the cultural, folklife and tourist aspects of Haiti.
LC NO. 82-707000
Prod-MOMALA Dist-MOMALA

Rhythms Of Haiti (French) C 25 MIN
16MM FILM, 3/4 OR 1/2 IN VIDEO J-C A
Shows the cultural, folklife and tourist aspects of Haiti.
Prod-MOMALA Dist-MOMALA

Rhythms Of Haiti (Spanish) C 25 MIN
3/4 OR 1/2 INCH VIDEO CASSETTE J-C A
Shows the cultural, folklife and tourist aspects of Haiti.
Prod-MOMALA Dist-MOMALA

Rhythms Of Paris C 9 MIN
16MM FILM, 3/4 OR 1/2 IN VIDEO I-H
Captures the excitement of Paris and its people. Contrasts rush-hour jams and bustling cafe-lined streets with serene parks and the quiet of fishing along the Seine. Explores couturier shops along the Place Royale, small boutiques in the Latin Quarter, famous historical sites and night club life.
From The Life In Modern France Series.
Prod-EBEC Dist-EBEC 1971

Rhythms Of The Universe C 24 MIN
16MM FILM OPTICAL SOUND I-C
Studies the rhythmic patterns which living things seem to follow and examines various theories that explain these patterns.
From The Animal Secrets Series.
LC NO. FIA68-1038
Prod-NBC Dist-GRACUR 1967

Rhythms, Pt 1 C 15 MIN
3/4 OR 1/2 INCH VIDEO CASSETTE P
Introduces rhythm and rhythm notations. Presents the songs Bingo, Chicka Hanka and Riding In The Buggy.
From The Song Sampler Series.
LC NO. 81-707072
Prod-JCITV Dist-GPITVL 1981

Rhythms, Pt 2 C 15 MIN
3/4 OR 1/2 INCH VIDEO CASSETTE P
Introduces rhythm and rhythm notations. Presents the songs Bingo, Chicka Hanka and Riding In The Buggy.
From The Song Sampler Series.
LC NO. 81-707072
Prod-JCITV Dist-GPITVL 1981

Rhythmus 21 / Symphonie Diagonale B 8 MIN
16MM FILM SILENT
Presents pioneer works by two artists, Viking Eggeling and Hans Richter, who first made the transition from abstract painting to abstract film. Includes Eggeling's Diagonal Symphony, which moves hieroglyphic forms along an invisible diagonal, and Richter's Rhythm 21, which orchestrates the squares and rectangles of the film and screen. Produced 1921-24.
Prod-STARRC Dist-STARRC

Rhythmus 23 B 3 MIN
16MM FILM SILENT
Presents criss-cross patterns, negative reversals, intercut stringed forms, and further variations of the rectangle and square. By Hans Richter, 1923.
Prod-STARRC Dist-STARRC 1923

Ribbon Bridge - Launching And Retrieval C 17 MIN
16MM FILM, 3/4 OR 1/2 IN VIDEO A
Discusses two types of bridge bays and connecting hardware. Demonstrates the procedure for launching and retrieving bridge bays.
Prod-USA Dist-USNAC 1978

Ribosome, The C 24 MIN
16MM FILM OPTICAL SOUND
Relates details of ribosome structure to the cell's functional role in protein synthesis. Uses models to interpret the latest experimental work of Charles Kurland and George Stoffler, especially ribosome function and structure.
Prod-BBCTV Dist-OPENU 1978

Ribosome, The C 24 MIN
16MM FILM, 3/4 OR 1/2 IN VIDEO

Relates details of ribosome structure to the cell's functional role in protein synthesis. Uses models to interpret the latest experimental work of Charles Kurland and George Stoffler, especially ribosome function and structure.
Prod-OPENU Dist-MEDIAG Prodn-BBCTV 1978

Ribs C 5 MIN
16MM FILM SILENT
Examines the problems of sexual identity in as abstract manner through a series of drawings and paintings super-imposed on x-ray film.
Prod-HEARST Dist-HEARST

Riccio - Bronze Statuettes C 24 MIN
16MM FILM OPTICAL SOUND
Uses bronze statuettes of both large and small scale by sculptor Andrea Riccio to illustrate an approach to art history used when origins of works are undocumented. Explains the contrasts between Riccio's smaller works and monumental bronzes attributed to him on such aspects as technique, style, function and type of patronage.
Prod-BBCTV Dist-OPENU 1981

Riccio - Bronze Statuettes C 24 MIN
16MM FILM, 3/4 OR 1/2 IN VIDEO
Uses bronze statuettes of both large and small scale by sculptor Andrea Riccio to illustrate an approach to art history used when origins of works are undocumented. Explains the contrasts between Riccio's smaller works and monumental bronzes attributed to him on such aspects as technique, style, function and type of patronage.
Prod-OPENU Dist-MEDIAG Prodn-BBCTV 1981

Rice C 26 MIN
16MM FILM, 3/4 OR 1/2 IN VIDEO I-C A
Stresses the world-wide importance of rice and describes methods of growing it. Shows measures taken to improve the quantity and quality of rice.
Prod-ROCKE Dist-MGHT 1965

Rice - Biggest Small Grain On Earth C 12 MIN
16MM FILM, 3/4 OR 1/2 IN VIDEO I-J
Shows different methods of planting and harvesting rice. Emphasizes the importance of rice as a basic food and source of energy for more than half the world's people.
LC NO. 81-706038
Prod-CENTRO Dist-CORF 1980

Rice And Tea C 29 MIN
2 INCH VIDEOTAPE
Features Joyce Chen showing how to adapt Chinese recipes so that they can be prepared in the American kitchen and still retain the authentic flavor. Demonstrates how to prepare rice and tea.
From The Joyce Chen Cooks Series.
Prod-WGBHTV Dist-PUBTEL

Rice Farmers In Thailand C 19 MIN
16MM FILM, 3/4 OR 1/2 IN VIDEO P-C
Contrasts the old and the new way of rice farming in Thailand. Shows ancient ceremonies at the beginning of planting season and when the harvest is in. Depicts rice farmers learning to irrigate land to increase their harvest.
From The Man And His World Series.
Prod-FI Dist-FI 1969

Rice Ladle, The - The Changing Role Of Women C 28 MIN
16MM FILM, 3/4 OR 1/2 IN VIDEO H-C A
Discusses the status of women in Japan by focusing on Fumiko Sawada, a would-be pop star and Hatsumi Suda, a widow who supports herself as a cook's assistant in a sushi shop.
From The Human Face Of Japan Series.
LC NO. 82-707081
Prod-FLMAUS Dist-LCOA 1982

Rice, America's Food For The World C 13 MIN
16MM FILM OPTICAL SOUND I-J
Shows the use of machines in preparing soil, planting and harvesting the crop. Scientific research to improve crops and land conservation are illustrated.
Prod-DAGP Dist-MLA 1962

Rich B 20 MIN
16MM FILM OPTICAL SOUND
Tells the story of a young man determined to go to college despite his depressed environment and his mother's desire for him to go to work.
Prod-BLKFMF Dist-BLKFMF

Rich And Judy C 12 MIN
16MM FILM, 3/4 OR 1/2 IN VIDEO C A
Shows a married couple as they explore and fondle one another in two different settings.
Prod-NATSF Dist-MMRC

Rich And Poor - North-South Dialogue C 27 MIN
3/4 OR 1/2 INCH VIDEO CASSETTE J-H
Discusses the summit held in Cancun, Mexico in October,1981, where 22 world leaders met to discuss common problems afflicting their nations in light of global interdependence in the world economy. Describes the issues that prompted this meeting and explores the solutions that might be implemented to advance the cause of global and political stability.
Prod-JOU Dist-JOU

Rich Country, Strong Military C 30 MIN
3/4 OR 1/2 INCH VIDEO CASSETTE H-C A
See series title for descriptive statement.
From The Japan - The Changing Tradition Series.
Prod-UMA Dist-GPITVL 1978

Rich Dummy, The C 30 MIN
3/4 OR 1/2 INCH VIDEO CASSETTE P-I
See series title for descriptive statement.
From The Sonrisas Series.
Prod-KRLNTV Dist-MDCPB

Rich Young Ruler, The B 27 MIN
16MM FILM OPTICAL SOUND J-C A
Portrays the human story of Azor, rich young ruler of Judea. And his search for eternal values.
Prod-CAFM Dist-CAFM

Rich, Thin, And Beautiful C 58 MIN
16MM FILM, 3/4 OR 1/2 IN VIDEO H-C A
Takes a look at America's obsession with money and thin, beautiful bodies. Interviews people who make it apparent that in the race for the American Dream, there isn't any finish.
Prod-BELLDA Dist-FI 1983

Richard Chase - Storyteller, Pt 2 C 35 MIN
3/4 INCH VIDEO CASSETTE
Presents Richard Chase telling the stories Jack In The Giant's New Ground and Old Roaney.
Prod-BLUHER Dist-BLUHER

Richard Hunt - Outdoor Sculpture C 29 MIN
3/4 INCH VIDEO CASSETTE
Follows the artist from studio to site during the development of an outdoor sculpture. Explores the importance of public art.
Prod-UMITV Dist-UMITV 1975

Richard Hunt - Sculptor X 14 MIN
16MM FILM, 3/4 OR 1/2 IN VIDEO J-H
A study of sculptor Richard Hunt, showing how he utilizes the resources of his urban environment to create fantastic structures in welded metals. Follows Hunt as he collects junk, welds, brazes, files and sketches.
From The Black Achievements In America Series.
Prod-EBEC Dist-EBEC 1970

Richard II C 12 MIN
16MM FILM, 3/4 OR 1/2 IN VIDEO H-C
See series title for descriptive statement.
From The Shakespeare Series.
Prod-IFB Dist-IFB 1974

Richard II C 157 MIN
3/4 OR 1/2 INCH VIDEO CASSETTE
Presents Shakespeare's play about an uprising to replace an unjust king with a just one. Stars Derek Jacobi, Jon Finch and John Gielgud.
From The Shakespeare Plays Series.
LC NO. 79-706937
Prod-BBCTV Dist-TIMLIF 1979

Richard III B
1/2 IN VIDEO CASSETTE BETA/VHS
Presents Sir Lawrence Olivier starring in Shakespeare's tragedy.
Prod-GA Dist-GA

Richard III C 12 MIN
16MM FILM, 3/4 OR 1/2 IN VIDEO H-C
See series title for descriptive statement.
From The Shakespeare Series.
Prod-IFB Dist-IFB 1974

Richard III C 29 MIN
2 INCH VIDEOTAPE
Features Alan Levitan, associate professor of English at Brandeis University discussing Richard III by Shakespeare.
From The Feast Of Language Series.
Prod-WGBHTV Dist-PUBTEL

Richard III C 120 MIN
3/4 OR 1/2 INCH VIDEO CASSETTE H-C A
Presents William Shakespeare's play about Richard of Gloucester, a self-proclaimed villain, who usurps the crown of King Edward IV.
From The Shakespeare Plays Series.
LC NO. 82-707360
Prod-BBCTV Dist-TIMLIF 1982

Richard James Martin C
3/4 OR 1/2 INCH VIDEO CASSETTE
Portrays Richard James Martin, British Columbian filmmaker with interviews and film clips.
From The Filmmakers' Showcase Series.
Prod-CANFDW Dist-CANFDW

Richard Landry - Divided Alto C 15 MIN
3/4 OR 1/2 INCH VIDEO CASSETTE
Presented by Richard Landry.
Prod-ARTINC Dist-ARTINC

Richard Landry - One Two Three Four B 8 MIN
3/4 OR 1/2 INCH VIDEO CASSETTE
Presents four clapping hands with a strobe light on them.
Prod-ARTINC Dist-ARTINC

Richard Landry - Quad Suite, Six Vibrations For Agnes Martin, Hebes Grande Bois, 4th... B 35 MIN
3/4 OR 1/2 INCH VIDEO CASSETTE
Complete title reads Richard Landry - Quad Suite, Six Vibrations For Agnes Martin, Hebes Grande Bois, 4th Register.
Prod-ARTINC Dist-ARTINC

Richard M Nixon, Gerald Ford C 90 MIN
3/4 OR 1/2 INCH VIDEO CASSETTE
Presents biographies tracing the private and public lives of Nixon and Ford up to the year 1973. Features Nixon's 'Checkers' speech and 1974 resignation speech.
Prod-IHF Dist-IHF

Richard Nixon B 15 MIN
3/4 OR 1/2 INCH VIDEO CASSETTE
Portrays Richard Milhous Nixon and his journey to the White House, from his birth in Yorba Linda, California in 1913 to his election as the thirty-seventh President of the United States. Important for understanding the man behind the Watergate affair.
Prod-KINGFT Dist-KINGFT

Richard Patton C
3/4 OR 1/2 INCH VIDEO CASSETTE
Portrays Richard Patton, British Columbian filmmaker with interviews and film clips.
From The Filmmakers' Showcase Series.
Prod-CANFDW Dist-CANFDW

Richard Payment C
3/4 OR 1/2 INCH VIDEO CASSETTE
Portrays Richard Payment, British Columbian filmmaker with interviews and film clips.
From The Filmmakers' Showcase Series.
Prod-CANFDW Dist-CANFDW

Richard Prince, Editions C 8 MIN
3/4 OR 1/2 INCH VIDEO CASSETTE
See series title for descriptive statement.
From The Cross-Overs - Photographers Series.
Prod-ARTINC Dist-ARTINC

Richard Rogers C 58 MIN
3/4 OR 1/2 INCH VIDEO CASSETTE
See series title for descriptive statement.
From The Evening At Pops Series.
Prod-WGBHTV Dist-PBS 1978

Richard Serra - Anxious Automation B 5 MIN
3/4 OR 1/2 INCH VIDEO CASSETTE
Presented by Richard Serra.
Prod-ARTINC Dist-ARTINC

Richard Serra - Boomerang C 10 MIN
3/4 OR 1/2 INCH VIDEO CASSETTE
Presented by Richard Serra.
Prod-ARTINC Dist-ARTINC

Richard Serra - Prisoner's Dilemma B 60 MIN
3/4 OR 1/2 INCH VIDEO CASSETTE
Criticizes television. Features cops and robbers.
Prod-ARTINC Dist-ARTINC

Richard Serra - Surprise Attack B 2 MIN
3/4 OR 1/2 INCH VIDEO CASSETTE
Presented by Richard Serra.
Prod-ARTINC Dist-ARTINC

Richard Serra - Television Delivers People C 6 MIN
3/4 OR 1/2 INCH VIDEO CASSETTE
Focuses on broadcasting as corporate czar.
Prod-ARTINC Dist-ARTINC

Richard Serra, An Interview C 28 MIN
3/4 OR 1/2 INCH VIDEO CASSETTE
Interviews Richard Serra. Produced by Liza Bear, Ales Susteric, Michael McClard and C Arcache.
Prod-ARTINC Dist-ARTINC

Richard T Ely B 51 MIN
16MM FILM, 3/4 OR 1/2 IN VIDEO I-H
Describes the activities of Richard T Ely in the post-Civil War period. Based on book Profiles In Courage by John F Kennedy. Stars Ed Asner, Marsha Hunt and Leonard Nimoy.
From The Profiles In Courage Series.
LC NO. 83-706543
Prod-SAUDEK Dist-SSSSV 1964

Richard Wagner - The Man And His Music C 58 MIN
3/4 OR 1/2 INCH VIDEO CASSETTE
Offers both a biography of Richard Wagner and a guide to his Ring Cycle. Traces his development as a composer and theatrical visionary, his relationship with his patron King Ludwig of Bavaria, the Wagner family and homes and the years in Venice which inspired and solaced Wagner during a tempestuous career.
Prod-FOTH Dist-FOTH 1984

Richard Watson C
3/4 OR 1/2 INCH VIDEO CASSETTE
Portrays Richard Watson, British Columbian filmmaker with interviews and film clips.
From The Filmmakers' Showcase Series.
Prod-CANFDW Dist-CANFDW

Richard Williams B 30 MIN
16MM FILM OPTICAL SOUND H-C A
Studies the training and work of animator Richard Williams. Shows him in his studio in London performing tasks ranging from preliminary storyboarding to the finishing touches on a nearly completed product.
LC NO. FIA68-3221
Prod-NET Dist-IU 1968

Richard's Totem Pole C 25 MIN
16MM FILM, 3/4 OR 1/2 IN VIDEO J-C A
Introduces Richard Harris, a Gitskan Indian living in British Columbia, who helps his father carve a 30 foot totem pole. Shows that while researching symbols to carve on the pole, he gains a new respect for his family's cultural heritage.
From The World Cultures And Youth Series.
Prod-SUNRIS Dist-CORF 1981

Richardson Goes Five For Five C 5 MIN
16MM FILM OPTICAL SOUND
Highlights one of baseball's great players, Richardson of the New York Yankees, speaking to the young men at a Fellowship of Christian Athletes huddle about his faith.
Prod-FELLCA Dist-FELLCA

Richer Harvest, A C 22 MIN
16MM FILM OPTICAL SOUND
Examines the problems faced by the farmer and demonstrates the scope of an American business company's involvement in world agriculture as exemplified by the world-wide research and distribution of Merck Sharp Dohme.
LC NO. FIA67-582
Prod-MESHDO Dist-MESHDO Prodn-VISION 1966

Riches From The Earth C 23 MIN
16MM FILM, 3/4 OR 1/2 IN VIDEO I-C A
Looks at the earth's resources with scenes of man's first formation of instruments of copper, the industrial revolution, islanders mining their lands in the Pacific Ocean and the clamor of the New York Commodities Exchange.
LC NO. 83-706363
Prod-PLATTS Dist-NGS 1982

Riches From The Sea C 23 MIN
16MM FILM, 3/4 OR 1/2 IN VIDEO J-H A
Depicts the importance of the sea as a source of food, minerals, energy and salt.
Prod-NGS Dist-NGS 1984

Riches Of The Earth (2nd Ed) C 17 MIN
16MM FILM, 3/4 OR 1/2 IN VIDEO I-C A
Depicts with animation the formation of the earth's crust by fire, water, wind and ice. Explains that this crust holds our wealth of minerals, oil, coal, arable land and water power.
Prod-NFBC Dist-SF 1966

Riches Or Happiness C 27 MIN
16MM FILM, 3/4 OR 1/2 IN VIDEO
Presents the Indian story of a young man who offers himself to a goddess. Relates that she in turn offers him riches or enjoyment. Tells how he does not know the difference until she shows him two merchants, one who is rich and not happy and the other who has enjoyment and is very happy.
From The Storybook International Series.
Prod-JOU Dist-JOU 1982

Richest Land, The C 23 MIN
16MM FILM OPTICAL SOUND
Deals with agriculture in California, focusing on Sibu subsidies, politics and battles among small farmers, big farmers, international oil companies and farmworkers. Points out how California agriculture relates to the livelihood, struggles and ideals of many Americans.
LC NO. 74-700145
Prod-BALLIS Dist-BALLIS 1973

Richie C 31 MIN
16MM FILM, 3/4 OR 1/2 IN VIDEO J-C A
Tells the story of a teenage boy who becomes deeply involved with drugs and a series of family conflicts and crises. Shows how the struggle with his family and drugs leads to his death by his father's hand. Based on the book Richie by Thomas Thompson.
Prod-JAFFE Dist-LCOA 1978

Richness Of Activity, The C 17 MIN
3/4 INCH VIDEO CASSETTE PRO
Demonstrates theoretical concepts, activity history, activity analysis and activity process in mental health using case histories as examples.
Prod-AOTA Dist-AOTA 1980

Richter On Film C 14 MIN
16MM FILM OPTICAL SOUND
Presents Hans Richter at age 83, who appears on camera at his Connecticut home and talks about his early experimental films and their relationship to his paintings, scrolls and collages. Includes excerpts from Rhythm 21, Ghosts Before Breakfast and Race Symphony. Produced by Cecile Starr.
Prod-STARRC Dist-STARRC 1972

Rick Amputee - Part I C 15 MIN
3/4 OR 1/2 INCH VIDEO CASSETTE
Shows the training of a 20-year-old male who has sustained a traumatic right shoulder and left above elbow amputation. Demonstrates the use of numerous adaptive devices and techniques in order to attain maximum independence in daily activities.
Prod-UWASH Dist-UWASH

Rick Amputee - Part II C 22 MIN
3/4 OR 1/2 INCH VIDEO CASSETTE
Shows aspects of the comprehensive rehabilitation program for the patient in Part I. Demonstrates measuring and fitting of the protheses, and the occupational therapist is shown performing a functional check-out.
Prod-UWASH Dist-UWASH

Rick, File X-258375 C 11 MIN
3/4 OR 1/2 INCH VIDEO CASSETTE
Shows how the probation service responds to a youthful narcotics offender. Issued in 1971 as a motion picture.
From The Professional Drug Films Series.
LC NO. 80-707346
Prod-NIMH Dist-USNAC 1980

Rick, You're In - A Story About Mainstreaming C 20 MIN
16MM FILM, 3/4 OR 1/2 IN VIDEO J-H T
Depicts the experiences of Rick Rehaut, a handicapped youth who is entering a regular high school for the first time.
Prod-WDEMCO Dist-WDEMCO

Rick, You're In - A Story About Mainstreaming (French) C 20 MIN
16MM FILM, 3/4 OR 1/2 IN VIDEO J-H
Explores the problems, hopes and interests of disabled people. Tells the story of Rick and his efforts to be accepted when he enters a regular high school.
Prod-WDEMCO Dist-WDEMCO

Ricky C 15 MIN
3/4 OR 1/2 INCH VIDEO CASSETTE P
See series title for descriptive statement.
From The Strawberry Square II - Take Time Series.
Prod-NEITV Dist-AITECH 1984

Ricky Raccoon Shows The Way C 15 MIN
16MM FILM, 3/4 OR 1/2 IN VIDEO K-P
Teaches safety rules concerning how to drive bicycles in traffic, how to refuse strangers' offers, how to obey signal lights, how to understand street signs and how to wait at bus stops.
Prod-KLEINW Dist-KLEINW 1978

Ricky's Great Adventure C 11 MIN
16MM FILM - 3/4 IN VIDEO P
Presents the story of a small boy deprived of his sight to motivate students to become better observers of nature by making better use of their senses of touch, taste, smell and hearing.
Prod-ATLAP Dist-ATLAP 1969

Rico Carty - An Interview C 5 MIN
16MM FILM OPTICAL SOUND H-C A
Features baseball player Rico Carty and his victorious struggle against TB. Explains chemotherapy treatment for the disease.
Prod-NTBA Dist-AMLUNG 1971

Rico-Union - Urban Community Development C
16MM FILM OPTICAL SOUND A
Highlights PUnc's citizen involvement activities, especially techniques for promoting involvement in urban renewal planning, designing low-income housing, community surveying and the design and building of a west pocket park.
LC NO. 72-702860
Prod-UCLA Dist-UCLA 1971

RIDAC Process, The C 8 MIN
16MM FILM OPTICAL SOUND
Deals with the Rehabilitation Initial Diagnosis and Assessment process. Explains program principles and organizational structure for teams which perform the initial assessment of vocational rehabilitation applicants.
From The Audio Visual Research Briefs Series.
LC NO. 75-702425
Prod-USSRS Dist-USNAC Prodn-DRU 1974

Riddle Of Photosynthesis, The (2nd Ed) B 15 MIN
16MM FILM, 3/4 OR 1/2 IN VIDEO J-H A
Visits the AEC's radiation laboratory at Berkeley. Shows how radioactive carbon is incorporated in algae in order to make it possible to follow the photosynthetic process in plants. Uses chromatography and radioautography to pinpoint compounds.
From The Magic Of The Atom Series. No. 24
Prod-HANDEL Dist-HANDEL 1965

Riddle Of The Rook, The C 25 MIN
16MM FILM, 3/4 OR 1/2 IN VIDEO H-C A
Points out that rooks do great damage to farmlands. Shows what is known about the rook's feeding habits, its annual movements and its behavior. Points out that rooks protect themselves from over-population and make up for their losses, making bullets ineffective as a means for getting rid of them.
From The Behavior And Survival Series.
Prod-MGHT Dist-MGHT 1973

Riddle, The B 20 MIN
3/4 INCH VIDEO CASSETTE
Deptcts the use of narcotics and drugs by young people in New York City. Focuses on the attempt of a young man to make his way instead of 'COPPING OUT' with drugs.
Prod-USNAC Dist-USNAC 1972

Ride A Mile In My Seat C 25 MIN
16MM FILM OPTICAL SOUND C A
Emphasizes the complexities of driving a school bus safely. Points out that safe transportation is a collective effort involving students and drivers.
Prod-VISUCP Dist-VISUCP 1979

Ride A Turquoise Pony X 28 MIN
16MM FILM, 3/4 OR 1/2 IN VIDEO H-C A
Tells how a young woman learns to know God by loving and suffering with other people. Stars Belinda Montgomery and Jan Clayton.
From The Insight Series.
Prod-PAULST Dist-PAULST

Ride A Turquoise Pony (Spanish) X 28 MIN
16MM FILM, 3/4 OR 1/2 IN VIDEO H-C A
Tells how a young woman learns to know God by loving and suffering with other people. Stars Belinda Montgomery and Jan Clayton.
From The Insight Series.
Prod-PAULST Dist-PAULST

Ride A Turquoise Pony (Spanish) C 28 MIN
3/4 OR 1/2 INCH VIDEO CASSETTE J A
Tells the story of a girl who learns from a Navajo the meaning of suffering and love.
Prod-SUTHRB Dist-SUTHRB

Ride A Wagon Train C 15 MIN
16MM FILM, 3/4 OR 1/2 IN VIDEO I-J
Captures a day in the week-long journey of modern adventurers on the Fort Seward Wagon Train in North Dakota. Records the routine along an eleven-mile route as well as the varied wildlife of the countryside.
LC NO. 83-706711
Prod-BERLET Dist-IFB 1983

Ride And Tie C 22 MIN
1/2 IN VIDEO CASSETTE BETA/VHS
Combines endurance riding, marathon running, horsemanship, physical conditioning and strategy in 31 miles of trail.
Prod-LEVI Dist-EQVDL

Ride Lonesome C 73 MIN
16MM FILM OPTICAL SOUND
Stars Randolph Scott as a man seeking revenge on the man who raped and murdered his wife.
Prod-CPC Dist-KITPAR 1959

Ride On C 14 MIN
16MM FILM, 3/4 OR 1/2 IN VIDEO P
Offers a light-hearted history of the bicycle and highlights the do's and don'ts of bicycle safety.
Prod-CRMP Dist-CRMP 1973

Ride Safe C 16 MIN
16MM FILM OPTICAL SOUND
Describes several riding techniques designed to keep motorcyclists out of accidents. Includes countersteering, combination braking, crossing obstacles and counterweighting.
Prod-NILLU Dist-NILLU 1982

Ride Safe C
3/4 OR 1/2 INCH VIDEO CASSETTE
Describes several riding techniques designed to keep motorcyclists out of accidents. Analyzes the techniques of countersteering, combination braking, crossing obstacles and counter-weighting.
Prod-NILLU Dist-NILLU

Ride The Reading Rocket–A Series
P
Presents a summer reading program for children who have just completed first grade to maintain reading skills over the summer months.
Prod-GPITVL Dist-GPITVL

Ride The Wind - Moods Of Hang-Gliding C 24 MIN
16MM FILM - 3/4 IN VIDEO P-C A
Projects the excitement of the sport of hang-gliding. Shows many of the best hang-glider pilots soaring the beach ridges or flying thousands of feet in the air over rugged mountains.
Prod-CRYSP Dist-CRYSP

Ride This Way Grey Horse C 5 MIN
16MM FILM OPTICAL SOUND
Shows John Huston at work in Austria directing the motion picture, 'A WALK WITH LOVE AND DEATH.' Shows Huston working with his daughter Anjelica and Assaf Dayan, the son of the Israeli defense minister.
LC NO. 79-710436
Prod-KNP Dist-TWCF 1970

Ride, The C 7 MIN
16MM FILM, 3/4 OR 1/2 IN VIDEO A
Presents a slapstick comedy in which a portly tycoon takes a wild ride in his Rolls Royce, which becomes a toboggan and escapes from the chauffeur in the snowclad Laurentians.
Prod-NFBC Dist-NFBC 1968

Rider In Jumping C
1/2 IN VIDEO CASSETTE BETA/VHS
See series title for descriptive statement.
From The Captain Mark Phillips Horsemanship Training Series.
Prod-EQVDL Dist-EQVDL

Rider On The Flat C
1/2 IN VIDEO CASSETTE BETA/VHS
See series title for descriptive statement.
From The Captain Mark Phillips Horsemanship Training Series.
Prod-EQVDL Dist-EQVDL

Rider's Aids, The C 21 MIN
16MM FILM, 3/4 OR 1/2 IN VIDEO H-C A
Demonstrates how a rider signals a horse to move or change direction using natural and artificial aids. Shows how the aids are first employed in conjunction with voice commands and then used alone. Emphasizes correct application of the aids and describes the use of aids in combination. Introduced by Princess Anne of Great Britain.
From The Riding Training Series.
LC NO. 80-707108
Prod-BHORSE Dist-IU Prodn-GSAVL 1979

Riders Of The Purple Sage B 56 MIN
16MM FILM SILENT
Tells a story of the Old West of a man who sets out to unravel and avenge the kidnapping of his sister. Stars Tom Mix and Marion Nixon. Directed by Lynn Reynolds.
Prod-UNKNWN Dist-KILLIS 1925

Riders To The Sea B 27 MIN
16MM FILM OPTICAL SOUND
Presents a tragedy set on one of the Aran Isles off the coast of Ireland concerning an old woman who becomes resigned to death after losing her husband and all her sons to the sea.
LC NO. FI68-648
Prod-CBSF Dist-CBSF 1959

Riders To The Sea C 30 MIN
3/4 OR 1/2 INCH VIDEO CASSETTE C
See series title for descriptive statement.
From The Communicating Through Literature Series.
Prod-DALCCD Dist-DALCCD

Riders To The Sea C 30 MIN
3/4 OR 1/2 INCH VIDEO CASSETTE
Presents the one-act drama by Irish playwright John Millington Synge (1871-1909) which is set in a small Irish fishing village in the early 1900's. The play is symbolic of life in the village where the people must make their livings from the sea.
Prod-WQLN Dist-PBS

Riders To The Stars B 81 MIN
16MM FILM OPTICAL SOUND J-C A
Stars William Lundigan in the science fiction story of three space pilots who attempt to capture a meteor and return it to earth for scientific inspection.
Prod-UNKNWN Dist-UAE

Rides And Escapes C 22 MIN
16MM FILM, 3/4 OR 1/2 IN VIDEO
Illustrates rides, breakdowns, escapes and reversals in the sport of wrestling. Focuses on the referee's positions.
From The Wrestling Series. No. 3
Prod-ATHI Dist-ATHI 1976

Ridin' Cool To School C 16 MIN
16MM FILM, 3/4 OR 1/2 IN VIDEO K-P
Uses puppets and live action to delineate safety rules, from bus stop to boarding, riding and getting off bus.
Prod-BORTF Dist-BCNFL 1983

Riding For America C 58 MIN
1/2 IN VIDEO CASSETTE BETA/VHS
Shows men and women competing in the final selection for the U S Equestrian Team.
Prod-INSILC Dist-EQVDL

Riding For America C 60 MIN
3/4 INCH VIDEO CASSETTE
Illustrates the sport of horseback riding. Features interviews with members of the United States Equestrian team. Focuses on the dedication, teamwork, discipline and effort needed to become an Olympic rider.
Prod-USEQT Dist-MTP Prodn-INSILC

Riding Out C
16MM FILM OPTICAL SOUND
Examines water, weeds, mist, rooms, meadows, hills, corrals, dirt roads, old bones and reflections.
Prod-CANCIN Dist-CANCIN

Riding Position, The C 18 MIN
16MM FILM, 3/4 OR 1/2 IN VIDEO H-C A
Focuses on the classical riding position, emphasizing its practicality and efficiency. Uses closeups of body movement and position during the application of aids to illustrate the most efficient use of legs, seat, and hands while guiding the horse. Concludes with variations of the basic position that are shown during walking, trotting, cantering, galloping and jumping. Introduced by Princess Anne of Great Britain.
From The Riding Training Series.
LC NO. 80-707110
Prod-BHORSE Dist-IU Prodn-GSAVL 1979

Riding The Pulpit C 80 MIN
16MM FILM OPTICAL SOUND
Tells the story of Jess Moddy, whose persistence, courage, and sense of humor are combined with a deep love for God.
Prod-YOUTH Dist-GF

Riding The Space Range C 18 MIN
16MM FILM OPTICAL SOUND
Demonstrates how NASA calibrates the equipment in its world-wide net of tracking stations.
Prod-NASA Dist-NASA 1966

Riding Training—A Series
16MM FILM, 3/4 OR 1/2 IN VIDEO H-C A
Presents basic training in horsemanship, focusing on the classic English style.
Prod-BHORSE Dist-IU Prodn-GSAVL 1979

Basic Paces Of The Horse 024 MIN
Dressage Movements 023 MIN
Rider's Aids, The 021 MIN
Riding Position, The 018 MIN
Training The Young Horse 027 MIN

Riding Your School Bus C 9 MIN
16MM FILM OPTICAL SOUND K-I
An elementary teacher discusses school bus safety with her class, and children are shown demonstrating bus safety practices.
LC NO. 72-700614
Prod-VADE Dist-VADE 1972

Riemann Integration B
16MM FILM OPTICAL SOUND
Deals with the definition of the Riemann integral.
Prod-OPENU Dist-OPENU

Riff '65 B 12 MIN
16MM FILM OPTICAL SOUND J-C T
A documentary that projects the character of Riff, a resourceful underprivileged youngster who is in conflict with his environment.
LC NO. FIA67-583
Prod-NYU Dist-NYU 1966

Rifle Platoon In Night Attack C 21 MIN
16MM FILM OPTICAL SOUND
Shows how to lead troops in planning and executing a night attack and how a platoon operates during a surprise assault to seize an assigned objective.
LC NO. 80-701840
Prod-USA Dist-USNAC 1980

Rifle Shooting Fundamentals - Firing The Shot C 13 MIN
16MM FILM, 3/4 OR 1/2 IN VIDEO J-C A
Presents two-time Olympic Rifle Gold Medalist Lones Wigger reviewing the fundamentals of aiming, breath control, hold control, trigger pull and follow through.
From The Rifle Shooting Fundamentals Series.
Prod-ATHI Dist-ATHI 1981

Rifle Shooting Fundamentals - Kneeling And Sitting C 14 MIN
16MM FILM, 3/4 OR 1/2 IN VIDEO J-C A
Presents two-time Olympic Rifle Gold Medalist Gary Anderson and four-time National Rifle Champion Carl Bernosky reviewing the fundamentals necessary for developing the kneeling and sitting shooting positions.
From The Rifle Shooting Fundamentals Series.
Prod-ATHI Dist-ATHI 1981

Rifle Shooting Fundamentals - Standing And Prone C 13 MIN
16MM FILM, 3/4 OR 1/2 IN VIDEO J-C A
Presents World Rifle Champion Sue Ann Sandusky and U S Shooting Team Coach William Krilling reviewing the fundamentals necessary for developing the standing and prone shooting positions.
From The Rifle Shooting Fundamentals Series.
Prod-ATHI Dist-ATHI 1981

Rifle Shooting Fundamentals—A Series
16MM FILM, 3/4 OR 1/2 IN VIDEO J-C A
Presents technical knowledge on the fundamentals of rifle and pistol shooting.
Prod-ATHI Dist-ATHI

Pistol Shooting Fundamentals 015 MIN
Rifle Shooting Fundamentals - Firing The Shot 013 MIN
Rifle Shooting Fundamentals - Kneeling And 014 MIN
Rifle Shooting Fundamentals - Standing And 013 MIN
Shotgun Shooting Fundamentals 015 MIN

Rifle Squad, The - Dismounted Movement Techniques C 21 MIN
16MM FILM OPTICAL SOUND
Shows how two fire teams use various techniques to achieve positions of cover and to suppress enemy fire and emplacement.
LC NO. 80-701841
Prod-USA Dist-USNAC 1980

Rifle, M16A1, Pt 1 - Care, Cleaning And Lubrication B 33 MIN
16MM FILM OPTICAL SOUND
Teaches riflemen of the U S Army how to clean, lubricate and care for the M16A1 rifle in the field to prevent weapon failure and keep it in optimum condition ready for use.
LC NO. 75-702895
Prod-USA Dist-USNAC 1968

Rifle, M16A1, Pt 2 - Field Expedients B 17 MIN
16MM FILM OPTICAL SOUND
Teaches riflemen of the U S Army how to clean wet and dirty rifles and ammunition. Shows the use of cleaning expedients and of SLA to prevent weapon failures. Stresses the importance of emergency action when weapons fail to fire.
LC NO. 75-702897
Prod-USA Dist-USNAC 1968

Rig Floor Safety C
3/4 OR 1/2 INCH VIDEO CASSETTE IND
Demonstrates basic safety practices of work on the rig floor while emphasizing what can occur if safe techniques are not used.
From The Rig Orientation For New Hands Series.
Prod-CAODC Dist-GPCV

Rig Inspections C 19 MIN
3/4 OR 1/2 INCH VIDEO CASSETTE IND
Offers several guidelines for setting up a rig inspection program in order to protect employees and equipment from accidents that could be caused by unsafe conditions.
Prod-UTEXPE Dist-UTEXPE 1979

Rig Orientation For New Hands—A Series
IND
Covers in two parts the basics for new employees working on a drilling rig, including maintenance, safety, making hole and working the monkey board. Developed and produced by the Canadian Association Of Oilwell Drilling Contractors.
Prod-CAODC Dist-GPCV

It Ain't Easy 033 MIN
Rig Floor Safety 000 MIN

Rigging - Wire Rope Slings C 18 MIN
3/4 OR 1/2 INCH VIDEO CASSETTE IND
Presents safe, recommended methods for securing maximum use from wire rope slings. Stresses safe and proper rigging procedures. Uses animation.
From The Marshall Maintenance Training Programs Series. Tape 26
Prod-LEIKID Dist-LEIKID

Rigging - Wire Rope Slings C 18 MIN
16MM FILM, 3/4 OR 1/2 IN VIDEO IND
Presents recommended methods for securing maximum use from wire rope slings. Portrays the skills required to select and properly use slings.
Prod-MOKIN Dist-MOKIN

Rigging And Lifting C 240 MIN
3/4 OR 1/2 INCH VIDEO CASSETTE IND
Deals with rigging and lifting. Discusses hand and power operated hoists, forklifts, cranes, ladders and scaffolds.
From The Mechanical Equipment Maintenance Series.
Prod-ITCORP Dist-ITCORP

Rigging And Lifting (Spanish) C 240 MIN
3/4 OR 1/2 INCH VIDEO CASSETTE IND
Deals with rigging and lifting. Discusses hand and power operated hoists, forklifts, cranes, ladders and scaffolds.
From The Mechanical Equipment Maintenance (Spanish) Series.
Prod-ITCORP Dist-ITCORP

Rigging Blocks B 11 MIN
3/4 INCH VIDEO CASSETTE
Shows how various types of tackle pulleys operate, including whip, gun, luff, and two-fold purchase tackle pulleys. Explains the mechanical advantage obtained from using this equipment. Issued in 1944 as a motion picture.
From The Shipbuilding Skills - Rigging Series.
LC NO. 80-707050
Prod-USN Dist-USNAC 1980

Rigging Equipment Over The Floor C 16 MIN
3/4 OR 1/2 INCH VIDEO CASSETTE IND
Shows common rigging practices of moving equipment using rollers, dollies, roller casters, skids, air jacks and wooden skids.
From The Marshall Maintenance Training Programs Series. Tape 41
Prod-LEIKID Dist-LEIKID

Rigging Up - The Safe Way C 23 MIN
3/4 OR 1/2 INCH VIDEO CASSETTE IND
Covers several safety procedures the rig crew should be aware of and practice during a rig-up in order to prevent accidents during this critical time in the drilling process.
Prod-UTEXPE Dist-UTEXPE 1981

Right Angle Intraoral Radiography With Rinn Rectangular Positioning In Dictating...Pt II... C 11 MIN
3/4 OR 1/2 INCH VIDEO CASSETTE
Demonstrates the use of a rectangular tube to decrease the amount of x-radiation received by a patient in dental radiography.
Prod-VADTC Dist-AMDA 1973

Right Angle Radiography With Rinn Rectangular Positioning Indicating Device... C 11 MIN
3/4 INCH VIDEO CASSETTE
Demonstrates that the dental patient receives 50 percent less radiation with the rectangular tube than with the conventional circular tube. Discusses its use on anterior teeth and describes right angle accessories and beam-directing instruments. Issued in 1973 as a motion picture.
LC NO. 80-706831
Prod-USVA Dist-USNAC Prodn-VADTC 1980

Right Angle Radiography With Rinn Rectangular Positioning Indicating Device... C 11 MIN
3/4 INCH VIDEO CASSETTE
Demonstrates the use of a recctangular tube to decrease the amount of radiation received by a patient in dental radiography. Shows instruments used to achieve perfect alignment of the posterior teeth. Issued in 1973 as a motion picture.
LC NO. 80-706832
Prod-USVA Dist-USNAC Prodn-VADTC 1980

Right Angle Radiography With Rinn Circular Positioning Indicating Device - Anterior... C 9 MIN
16MM FILM, 3/4 OR 1/2 IN VIDEO PRO
Demonstrates the use of the Rinn circular positioning indicating device for anterior teeth. Shows how a long, cylindrical tube with instruments positions the film parallel to the long axes of the teeth and how guiding devices direct the x-ray beam at right angles to the film.
Prod-USVA Dist-USNAC 1973

Right Angle Radiography With Rinn Circular Positioning Indicating Device - Posterior... C 9 MIN
16MM FILM, 3/4 OR 1/2 IN VIDEO PRO
Shows how a long, cylindrical tube, a directing circle and an alignment rod are used to direct the x-ray beam at a right angle to the film, producing more anatomically accurate radiographs of posterior teeth.
Prod-USVA Dist-USNAC 1973

Right Angle Radiography With Rinn Rectangular Positioning Indicating Device - Posterior... C 11 MIN
16MM FILM OPTICAL SOUND PRO
Demonstrates the use of a rectangular tube to decrease the amount of radiation received by a patient in dental radiography. Shows instruments used to achieve perfect alignment of the posterior teeth.
LC NO. 75-701266
Prod-USVA Dist-USNAC 1973

Right Angle Radiography With The Versatile Intra-Oral Positioner—A Series
PRO
Discusses various aspects of radiography with the versatile intra-Oral positioner.
Prod-VADTC Dist-USNAC 1977

Right Angle Radiography With The Versatile
Right Angle Radiography With The Versatile 11 MIN
Right Angle Radiography With The Versatile 16 MIN
Right Angle Radiography With The Versatile 12 MIN

Right Angle Radiography With The Versatile Intra-Oral Positioner, Pt 1 - Principles C 14 MIN
16MM FILM - 3/4 IN VIDEO PRO
Illustrates how right angle, parallel plane radiographic technique minimizes dimensional distortion and how use of the versatile intraoral positioner (VIP) instrument prevents elongation, shortening and overlapping.
LC NO. 78-706227
Prod-VADTC Dist-USNAC 1978

Right Angle Radiography With The Versatile Intra-Oral Positioner, Pt 2 - Anterior C 11 MIN
16MM FILM - 3/4 IN VIDEO PRO
Shows how to use a versatile intraoral positioner (VIP) to radiography the anterior teeth. Illustrates procedures graphically and follows with demonstrations on a skull and with a patient.
LC NO. 78-706224
Prod-VADTC Dist-USNAC 1978

Right Angle Radiography With The Versatile Intra-Oral Positioner, Pt 3 - Posterior C 16 MIN
16MM FILM - 3/4 IN VIDEO PRO
Demonstrates use of the versatile intraoral positioner (VIP) to record radiographic images of the posterior teeth. Shows how the VIP instrument facilitates placement of the film parallel to

the long axes of the posterior teeth, as well as correct direction of an X-ray beam at right angles to the radiographic film.
LC NO. 78-706226
Prod-VADTC Dist-USNAC 1978

Right Angle Radiography With The Versatile Intra-Oral Positioner, Pt 4 - Bite Wings C 12 MIN
16MM FILM - 3/4 IN VIDEO PRO
Demonstrates a method bite wing radiography that positions the film vertically and provides adequate coverage of height of the crest of the alveolar bone and minimizes deficiencies such as obliteration of embrasure space.
LC NO. 78-706225
Prod-VADTC Dist-USNAC 1978

Right At The Typewriter B 27 MIN
16MM FILM OPTICAL SOUND
Discusses the place of the typewriter in modern business. Describes posture, proper key stroking, letter form, carbon copies, typing of forms, carbon paper, stencils and the new IBM selective typewriter.
LC NO. FIA67-100
Prod-IBUSMA Dist-IBUSMA 1962

Right Book For You, The B 20 MIN
2 INCH VIDEOTAPE P
Stresses how to choose a book when a child goes to the library. (Broadcast quality)
From The Language Lane Series. Lesson 12
Prod-CVETVC Dist-GPITVL Prodn-WCVETV

Right Book For You, The C 20 MIN
2 INCH VIDEOTAPE P-I
See series title for descriptive statement.
From The Learning Our Language, Unit V - Exploring With Books Series.
Prod-MPATI Dist-GPITVL

Right Choice, The C 6 MIN
16MM FILM - 3/4 IN VIDEO PRO
Discusses oral hygiene. Shows the relationship between the ingestion of sucrose and the conversion of sucrose to dextran and acid by oral bacteria. Issued in 1972 as a motion picture.
LC NO. 78-706243
Prod-USVA Dist-USNAC Prodn-VADTC 1978

Right Container, The C 29 MIN
3/4 OR 1/2 INCH VIDEO CASSETTE
Features Mrs Ascher showing how to choose or make the correct container and using containers to make two arrangements.
From The Flower Show Series.
Prod-MDCPB Dist-MDCPB

Right Exposure, The C 29 MIN
3/4 OR 1/2 INCH VIDEO CASSETTE
Explains that the most critical factor in getting a technically good photograph is proper exposure. Shows that the first step for proper exposure is choosing the correct film.
From The Photo Show Series.
Prod-WGBHTV Dist-PBS 1981

Right From The Start C 55 MIN
16MM FILM OPTICAL SOUND H-C A
Looks at the important relationship between parent and child that begins at birth. Shows how, moments after a child is born, a parent and child make important connections through touching, responding and eye contact. Illustrates the surprising capabilities and personalites of infants and explains how to interpret a baby's signals.
Prod-PTST Dist-FILAUD Prodn-CRASCO 1983

Right From The Start C 58 MIN
3/4 OR 1/2 INCH VIDEO CASSETTE
Takes a look at the important relationship between parent and child which begins at birth. Documents the importance of bonding for both the care giver and child, and focuses on some of the practices and institutions in society that can either encourage or hinder this attachment process.
Prod-CRASCO Dist-FILAUD

Right Good Thing, A C 12 MIN
16MM FILM, 3/4 OR 1/2 IN VIDEO
Focuses on tax problems frequently encountered by older people, such as tax benefits for people over 65, consequences of selling a home after age 55 and treatment of Social Security benefits as taxable income. Discusses the free tax counseling services available to older citizens from the U S Internal Revenue Service.
LC NO. 81-707710
Prod-USIRS Dist-USNAC 1980

Right Hand Of Congress, The C 29 MIN
16MM FILM OPTICAL SOUND H-C
Discusses the role of congressional assistants and staff members on Capitol Hill and explains the differences between committee staff members and personal staff members of Senators and Representatives.
From The Government Story Series. No. 10
LC NO. 74-707191
Prod-OGCW Dist-WBCPRO 1968

Right Hand Of The Court, The C 26 MIN
16MM FILM OPTICAL SOUND J-C A
Demonstrates the role of the court clerk and shows that he dispenses general information and acts as a training aid for new court personnel.
LC NO. 77-715508
Prod-LAC Dist-IA 1970

Right Hand Of The Court, The C 20 MIN
3/4 OR 1/2 INCH VIDEO CASSETTE
Describes the functions and duties of the office of the Court Clerk, while demonstrating the daily workings of a court of law.
Prod-LACFU Dist-IA

Right Hand Of The President, The C 29 MIN
16MM FILM OPTICAL SOUND H-C
Describes the creation, growth and duties of the White House staff. Explains the relationship between the White House staff, the Cabinet and the Congress.
From The Government Story Series. No. 25
LC NO. 78-707192
Prod-OGCW Dist-WBCPRO 1968

Right Heart Catheterization C 13 MIN
3/4 OR 1/2 INCH VIDEO CASSETTE PRO
Includes a review of pertinent intrathoracic anatomy, visualization, and demonstration of pressure wave form transitions.
Prod-HSCIC Dist-HSCIC 1982

Right Hemicolectomy For Carcinoma C 21 MIN
16MM FILM OPTICAL SOUND PRO
Presents the procedure of right colectomy for a malignant lesion of the ascending colon. Emphasizes the blood supply and its treatment early in the operation. Demonstrates a palliative prodecure.
Prod-ACYDGD Dist-ACY 1963

Right Here, Right Now C 15 MIN
16MM FILM OPTICAL SOUND H-C A
A dramatization about a janitor in an apartment house who reaches out to help those around him, is used to explore the mystery of Christ present today in one's fellowman.
From The Revelation Series.
LC NO. 72-700510
Prod-FRACOC Dist-FRACOC 1970

Right Hose And Fuel Tanks C 30 MIN
1/2 IN VIDEO CASSETTE BETA/VHS
Explores picking the right hose. Describes the workings of the fuel tank. Features a 1931 Ford Model A Roadster.
From The Last Chance Garage Series.
Prod-WGBHTV Dist-MTI

Right Location, The C 16 MIN
16MM FILM OPTICAL SOUND
Uses the experiences of a small businessman who tries to select a site for his first menswear store to dramatize the relationship of site selection to the success of a business and to identify some of the important factors in selecting a business site.
LC NO. 74-702883
Prod-USSBA Dist-USSBA Prodn-VAVPRO 1974

Right Location, The C 14 MIN
3/4 OR 1/2 INCH VIDEO CASSETTE
Designed to inform small business owners faced with relocation problems, or new businesses, of the importance of site selection.
From The Small Business Administration Series.
Prod-IVCH Dist-IVCH

Right Lower Lobectomy C 18 MIN
3/4 OR 1/2 INCH VIDEO CASSETTE
See series title for descriptive statement.
From The Thoracic Series.
Prod-SVL Dist-SVL

Right Man, The C 28 MIN
16MM FILM OPTICAL SOUND
Examines the career of Dr Robert Hayes, black president of Wiley College in Marshall, Texas. Shows how Hayes escaped from the black ghetto, was able to get an education and became a college president.
LC NO. 74-703235
Prod-KPRCTV Dist-KPRCTV 1974

Right Move, The C 15 MIN
16MM FILM, 3/4 OR 1/2 IN VIDEO
Discusses the problems of moving to a new city. Shows how children should be prepared as well as one's possessions for the important move to a new location. Answers such questions as how to pack and move pets, plants, and valuables, how to sell what you leave behind, when to move, which professional movers to use, what tax advantages, and what troubles to avoid.
Prod-KLEINW Dist-KLEINW

Right Not To Be A Patient, The C 60 MIN
3/4 INCH VIDEO CASSETTE
Describes the difference between having a disease and the role of being a patient. Discusses individual freedom and medical care, as well as involuntary confinement in psychiatric hospitals.
From The Ethics And Medicine Series.
Prod-OHC Dist-HRC

Right Of Privacy B 59 MIN
16MM FILM OPTICAL SOUND H-C A
Reports on the governmental and business activities which pose a threat to individual privacy today. Discusses the National Data Bank as a collection of statistics and as a potential threat to individual freedom. Documents pre-employment investigations, lie detector tests, credit checks and personality tests. Interviews congressmen and other public officials.
From The Net Journal Series.
LC NO. FIA68-580
Prod-NET Dist-IU 1968

Right Of Way C 14 MIN
16MM FILM OPTICAL SOUND
Explains the need for reforms in urban highway planning. Shows how mass transit can balance transportation needs, reveals examples of functional and beautiful urban highway planning, outlines new methods of solving such problems, and emphasizes the role of the city as a place for people.
LC NO. 73-702551
Prod-AIA Dist-AIA Prodn-KAUFMH 1968

Right On C 14 MIN
16MM FILM OPTICAL SOUND
Demonstrates the varied aspects of archery as a competitive and fun sport.
LC NO. 74-703216
Prod-BEARAC Dist-MTP Prodn-CRSP 1973

Right On C 78 MIN
16MM FILM OPTICAL SOUND J-C A
Presents David Nelson, Felipe Luciano and Gylau Kair, black revolutionary and self-professed original last poets, photographed against their ghetto backgrounds, reciting their poetry.
Prod-NLC Dist-NLC 1971

Right On - Be Free C 15 MIN
16MM FILM, 3/4 OR 1/2 IN VIDEO
Shows the energy, vitality and sense of identity of the black American artist.
Prod-FLMFR Dist-FLMFR

Right On - Poetry On Film C 77 MIN
16MM FILM OPTICAL SOUND
Features a performance by the Last Poets, three young black men, reciting their poems on rooftops and in the streets of New York City. Presents a poetry based in the vernacular of the black working class, in street language and the rhythms of the ghetto.
Prod-BLKFMF Dist-BLKFMF

Right On Course C 30 MIN
1/2 IN VIDEO CASSETTE BETA/VHS
Describes how to sail a course. Discusses wind direction and knot tying.
From The Under Sail Series.
Prod-WGBHTV Dist-MTI

Right Out Of History - The Making Of Judy Chicago's Dinner Party C 75 MIN
16MM FILM, 3/4 OR 1/2 IN VIDEO
Follows the creation of the Dinner Party, a monumental artistic tribute to women of achievement throughout history.
Prod-PHENIX Dist-PHENIX 1980

Right Partial Mastectomy C 41 MIN
3/4 OR 1/2 INCH VIDEO CASSETTE
See series title for descriptive statement.
From The Breast Series.
Prod-SVL Dist-SVL

Right Role, The C 30 MIN
3/4 OR 1/2 INCH VIDEO CASSETTE P-I
See series title for descriptive statement.
From The Sonrisas Series.
Prod-KRLNTV Dist-MDCPB

Right Start, The C 30 MIN
3/4 OR 1/2 INCH VIDEO CASSETTE H-C A
See series title for descriptive statement.
From The Training Dogs The Woodhouse Way.
Prod-BBCTV Dist-FI 1982

Right Thumb C 9 MIN
16MM FILM OPTICAL SOUND
Tells the story of a young boy who is sent to the store on his own for the first time. Shows how he learns the value of being attentive and following directions. Based on the book Right Thumb - Left Thumb by Osmond Molarsky.
LC NO. 74-703751
Prod-MORLAT Dist-MORLAT 1973

Right Thumb, Left Thumb C 9 MIN
16MM FILM, 3/4 OR 1/2 IN VIDEO K-I
Presents a story about a little boy's adventures along the road to growing up. Encourages the relating of viewers' own early experiences at accepting responsibility.
From The Reading Short Stories Series.
Prod-MORLAT Dist-AIMS 1970

Right Thumb, Left Thumb (Spanish) C 9 MIN
16MM FILM, 3/4 OR 1/2 IN VIDEO P-I
Tells about a little boy's adventures when he goes to the store alone for the first time.
Prod-MORLAT Dist-AIMS 1970

Right To Be Desperate, The C 52 MIN
16MM FILM OPTICAL SOUND A
Observes how Carl Rogers works as a therapist. Comments on what transpires in an initial counseling session, and how to work with clients who are struggling with issues of living and dying. Provides evidence that a clid is open to all experiencing. On two (2) reels.
Prod-AACD Dist-AACD 1977

Right To Be, The B 30 MIN
2 INCH VIDEOTAPE PRO
Helps nursing students understand how acceptance of others can help improve their abilities to treat patients.
From The Mental Health Concepts For Nursing, Unit 3 - Acceptance Of Others Series.
LC NO. 73-702642
Prod-GPITVL Dist-GPITVL 1971

Right To Believe, Pt 1 C 30 MIN
3/4 OR 1/2 INCH VIDEO CASSETTE H-C A
Shows how early Americans won religious freedom.
Prod-ABCTV Dist-GA 1983

Right To Believe, Pt 2 C 30 MIN
3/4 OR 1/2 INCH VIDEO CASSETTE H-C A
Shows how early Americans won religious freedom.
Prod-ABCTV Dist-GA 1983

Right To Die C 25 MIN
3/4 OR 1/2 INCH VIDEO CASSETTE
Examines the right to die controversy. Shows two doctors debating the issue.
Prod-TRAINX Dist-TRAINX

Right To Die, The C 56 MIN
16MM FILM OPTICAL SOUND H-C A
Touches on such questions as hopeless medical situations, recent technical means for prolonging biological existence, solutions such as mercy killing and suicide and the ability and best means for physicians and clergymen to deal with dying patients.
LC NO. 74-701428
Prod-AJM Dist-FI 1974

Right To Health, A C 34 MIN
16MM FILM OPTICAL SOUND H-C A
Gives an overview of the Office of Economic Opportunity's neighborhood health center. Examines the concept of community medicine and the neighborhood health center function.
LC NO. 77-700084
Prod-USOEO Dist-USNAC Prodn-PROART 1969

Right To Know, The C 17 MIN
16MM FILM, 3/4 OR 1/2 IN VIDEO J-C A
Documents the hazards of an uninformed citizenry through an historical examination of basic democratic principles and a view of local and national contemporary events. Discusses the personal and institutional obstacles to understanding and points out that unless citizens have access to information, democracy ceases to function.
Prod-ALTSUL Dist-JOU 1973

Right To Legal Counsel, The C 14 MIN
16MM FILM, 3/4 OR 1/2 IN VIDEO J-C
Gives a dramatic telling of the 1963 Supreme Court decision from the Gideon vs Wainright case, that ruled that indigent defendants, accused of serious crimes, must be offered the assignment of counsel. In making this decision, the Supreme Court overruled the Betts vs Brady decision. When tried, with adequate legal representation, Gideon was found innocent. Presents a vivid demonstration of the citizen's use of the 5th, 6th and 14th amendments to the Bill of Rights.
Prod-VIGNET Dist-PHENIX 1968

Right To Live And The Right To Die, The C 60 MIN
3/4 INCH VIDEO CASSETTE
Covers three areas of medical ethics - scarce life-saving therapies, euthanasia and defining death.
From The Ethics And Medicine Series.
Prod-OHC Dist-HRC

Right To Live, The - Who Decides B 17 MIN
16MM FILM, 3/4 OR 1/2 IN VIDEO J-C A
Tells how in the face of general condemnation and at great personal risk, a ship's captain obeys his conscience and makes the agonizing decision to sacrifice some lives in order to save others.
From The Searching For Values - A Film Anthology Series.
Prod-LCOA Dist-LCOA 1972

Right To Lobby, The C 28 MIN
16MM FILM OPTICAL SOUND H-C
Traces the history of lobbying and explains the techniques and effects of contemporary lobbyists.
From The Government Story Series. No. 14
LC NO. 71-707193
Prod-OGCW Dist-WBCPRO 1968

Right To Read, The C 28 MIN
16MM FILM OPTICAL SOUND
Shows the problem of illiteracy in human terms, what is being done and can be done to improve the reading ability of illiterates from all walks of life in communities everywhere in the nation.
Prod-USOE Dist-USOE

Right Track, The C 30 MIN
3/4 OR 1/2 INCH VIDEO CASSETTE J-H
Presents a fictional story of a talented teenager and two friends who are running a television station while the owner is recovering from an illness. Discusses nonrestrictive adjective phrases in a story dealing with an athlete involved in an accident. Shows that good writing skills are necessary in real-life experiences.
From The Edit Point Series. Pt 4
LC NO. 83-706609
Prod-MAETEL Dist-GPITVL 1983

Right Triangles And Trigonometric Ratios B 29 MIN
16MM FILM OPTICAL SOUND H
Presents Thales' method for finding the height of a pyramid, by using the definitions of sine, cosine and tangent of an angle as ratios of corresponding sides of a right triangle. Derives the values of the sine, cosine and tangent of 30, 45 and 60 degrees.
From The Trigonometry Series.
Prod-CALVIN Dist-MLA Prodn-UNIVFI 1959

Right Upper Lobectomy C 39 MIN
3/4 OR 1/2 INCH VIDEO CASSETTE
See series title for descriptive statement.
From The Thoracic Series.
Prod-SVL Dist-SVL

Right Ventricular Hypertrophy C 49 MIN
3/4 OR 1/2 INCH VIDEO CASSETTE PRO
Teaches the criteria for electro-cardiographic diagnosis of right ventricular hypertrophy. Includes a discussion of presumptive evidence of right ventricular hypertrophy and numerous sample ECGs.
From The Electrocardiogram Series.
Prod-HSCIC Dist-HSCIC 1982

Right Way—A Series

Explores fundamental concepts and basic safety principles of driving.
Prod-SCETV Dist-PBS 1982

Adverse Driving Conditions	027 MIN
Alcohol And Other Drugs	026 MIN
Basic Car Controls	027 MIN
Basic Maneuvers	029 MIN
Buying A New Or Used Car	029 MIN
City And Town Driving	024 MIN
Collision Involvement	026 MIN
Emergency Situations	029 MIN
Expressway Driving	027 MIN
Highway Driving	022 MIN
Highway Transportation System	028 MIN
Insuring A Car	025 MIN
Licensing And Traffic Laws	029 MIN
Maintenance	026 MIN
Motorcycles	029 MIN
Natural Laws	029 MIN
Parking	024 MIN
Physical Conditions	026 MIN
Psychological Aspects	025 MIN
Vehicle Interaction	021 MIN

Right Way, The C 21 MIN
16MM FILM OPTICAL SOUND
Highlights the annual Marine Corps physical fitness program for high school students.
LC NO. 74-705539
Prod-USN Dist-USNAC 1972

Right Whale, The - An Endangered Species C 23 MIN
16MM FILM, 3/4 OR 1/2 IN VIDEO J-C A
Studies the southern right whale, the rarest of the ten species of great whales. Describes their feeding and communication habits.
LC NO. 80-706304
Prod-NGS Dist-NGS 1976

Right-Of-Way For Highways C 26 MIN
16MM FILM - 3/4 IN VIDEO
Shows how a State highway department studies, evaluates and selects the route for a highway. Describes the various steps in the appraisal of a property needed for right-of-way and the negotiations for purchase of the property. Issued in 1961 as a motion picture.
LC NO. 79-707544
Prod-USFHAD Dist-USNAC 1979

Right-On Roofer Safework—A Series
16MM FILM, 3/4 OR 1/2 IN VIDEO IND
Presents safety guidelines to be followed by roofers.
Prod-SAFSEM Dist-IFB 1980

Flag Warning Lines	006 MIN
Right-On Roofer, Pt 1	015 MIN
Right-On Roofer, Pt 2	012 MIN
Right-On Roofer, Pt 3	012 MIN
Right-On Roofer, Pt 4	009 MIN

Right-On Roofer, Pt 1 C 15 MIN
16MM FILM, 3/4 OR 1/2 IN VIDEO IND
Deals with such aspects of roofing safety as the correct methods of melting and pouring asphalt, moving filled containers, adjusting temperature and the wearing of a hardhat.
From The Right-On Roofer Safework Series.
LC NO. 81-706768
Prod-SAFSEM Dist-IFB 1980

Right-On Roofer, Pt 2 C 12 MIN
16MM FILM, 3/4 OR 1/2 IN VIDEO IND
Shows the procedures for working near the edges or openings in a roof, for bringing materials up to the roof, and for tearing off and disposing of the old roof.
From The Right-On Roofer Safework Series.
LC NO. 81-706768
Prod-SAFSEM Dist-IFB 1980

Right-On Roofer, Pt 3 C 12 MIN
16MM FILM, 3/4 OR 1/2 IN VIDEO IND
Describes the proper use of a ladder on roofing jobs, the proper way to lift materials and the proper housekeeping procedures to facilitate finding things.
From The Right-On Roofer Safework Series.
LC NO. 81-706768
Prod-SAFSEM Dist-IFB 1980

Right-On Roofer, Pt 4 C 9 MIN
16MM FILM, 3/4 OR 1/2 IN VIDEO IND
Provides special safety precautions to be followed when working on steep, shake or tile roofs.
From The Right-On Roofer Safework Series.
LC NO. 81-706768
Prod-SAFSEM Dist-IFB 1980

Righteous Rumors C 30 MIN
3/4 OR 1/2 INCH VIDEO CASSETTE
See series title for descriptive statement.
From The Up And Coming Series.
Prod-KQEDTV Dist-MDCPB

Rights And Citizenship—A Series

Covers life skills in rights and citizenship regarding credit cards, credit ratings, citizenship and voting.
Prod-MAETEL Dist-CAMB

Citizenship And Voting	030 MIN
Consumer Complaints	030 MIN
Credit Cards	015 MIN
Credit Ratings	015 MIN
Legal Rights	030 MIN

Rights And Responsibilities C 15 MIN
16MM FILM OPTICAL SOUND I-J
Examines the dual concept of rights and privileges by using various groups and organizations to demonstrate the privileges gained by memberships in those groups. Describes what is expected of the members in turn for these privileges.
From The Florida Elementary Social Studies Series.
Prod-DADECO Dist-DADECO 1973

Rights And Responsibilities C 29 MIN
3/4 INCH VIDEO CASSETTE
Recounts the struggle at North Carolina high school to set up a system of school government fair to students, faculty and administrators alike.
From The As We See It Series.
Prod-WTTWTV Dist-PUBTEL

Rights And Responsibilities—A Series
J-H
Examines the duties and privileges of the individual in a free and stable society. Presents case studies and examples of real situations to explore the complex legal interplay of privileges, obligations and limitations inherent in citizenship. Deals with rights and responsibilities in school, at work and in society as a whole.
Prod-VAOG Dist-AITECH Prodn-WHROTV 1975

At Work	020 MIN
Change	020 MIN
Dead Path	020 MIN
I Didn't Care	020 MIN
In-School, Pt 1	020 MIN
In-School, Pt 2	020 MIN
Interview With Larry, An	020 MIN
Open Mind, An	020 MIN
Police Officer	020 MIN
Sign Here	020 MIN
Voting Machine, The	020 MIN

Rights Of Age, The B 28 MIN
16MM FILM, 3/4 OR 1/2 IN VIDEO C A
Describes the many benefits available to the aged who are in need of either physical, psychological or legal assistance, as portrayed in a dramatization about a recluse who becomes physically disabled and discovers the various benefits available to her.
From The Emotions Of Every-Day Living Series.
Prod-PASDPW Dist-IFB Prodn-AFF 1967

Rights Of Children, The C 30 MIN
3/4 OR 1/2 INCH VIDEO CASSETTE H-C A
See series title for descriptive statement.
From The Child Abuse And Neglect Series.
Prod-UMINN Dist-GPITVL 1983

Rights Of Patients B 44 MIN
16MM FILM OPTICAL SOUND
Illustrates the basic elements of legal consent and discusses mental health codes and their provisions for assuring the civil rights of mental patients.
From The Nursing And The Law Series.
LC NO. 73-703374
Prod-VDONUR Dist-AJN Prodn-WTTWTV 1968

Rights Of Patients, No. 1 C 30 MIN
16MM FILM - 3/4 IN VIDEO PRO
Discusses the legal rights of all patients, emphasizing the special civil rights of the mentally ill.
From The Nurse And The Law Series.
LC NO. 76-701554
Prod-AJN Dist-AJN Prodn-WGNCP 1974

Rights Of Patients, No. 2 C 30 MIN
16MM FILM - 3/4 IN VIDEO PRO
Presents course instructor Eugene I Pavalon discussing a patient's rights to refuse treatment and to refuse an invasion of privacy resulting from student participation in care and treatment. Examines the latest legal decisions on the cessation of life sustaining equipment.
From The Nurse And The Law Series.
LC NO. 77-700130
Prod-AJN Dist-AJN Prodn-WGNCP 1977

Rights Of Reproduction C 60 MIN
3/4 INCH VIDEO CASSETTE
Discusses a couple's reproductive rights in terms of the legal, cultural and medical aspects.
From The Ethics And Medicine Series.
Prod-OHC Dist-HRC

Rights Of The Accused, The C 30 MIN
3/4 OR 1/2 INCH VIDEO CASSETTE C
Examines the constitutional amendments which protect the rights of those accused of crimes from the time a search warrant is issued through court proceedings.
From The American Government 2 Series.
Prod-DALCCD Dist-DALCCD

Rights, Wrongs And The First Amendment C 28 MIN
16MM FILM, 3/4 OR 1/2 IN VIDEO
Traces the history in the United States of freedom of speech, freedom of the press and freedom of assembly from the Declaration of Independence to the exposure of Watergate. Points out that though personal freedom has often seemed to be in jeopardy, the democratic political process in America has displayed a remarkable resilience.
Prod-REPRO Dist-SF

Rigid And Swinging Staging B 18 MIN
16MM FILM, 3/4 OR 1/2 IN VIDEO
Shows how to set up rigid staging, using A-frame stage and extension, overlapped double boards and a lifeline. Issued in 1944 as a motion picture.
From The Shipbuilding Skills - Rigging Series.
LC NO. 80-707051
Prod-USN Dist-USNAC 1980

Rigid Bodies B
16MM FILM OPTICAL SOUND

Illustrates the principles of mathematical modelling and underlines the significance of the rigid body model.
Prod-OPENU Dist-OPENU

Rigid Heddle Frame, The C 12 MIN
3/4 OR 1/2 INCH VIDEO CASSETTE H-C
Describes how the rigid heddle frame provides the simple solution for weaving cloth. Shows an experienced weaver with the complete sequence of threading and getting ready to weave, and the loom in operation, producing an attractive woven jacket.
Prod-EDMI Dist-EDMI 1976

Rigid Heddle Looms And How To Warp Them For Fabric Weaving C 29 MIN
3/4 INCH VIDEO CASSETTE
Tells how the rigid heddle loom can be used for weaving scarves, shawls, and upholstery or pillow fabric.
From The Your Weekly Weaver Series.
Prod-GAEDTN Dist-PUBTEL

Rigid Medullary Fixation Of Forearm Fractures C 16 MIN
16MM FILM OPTICAL SOUND
Describes the principles, technique and advantage of rigid medullary fixation of forearm fractures.
LC NO. FIE62-2
Prod-USA Dist-USNAC 1961

Rigid Pavement Design And Methods, Pt 1 B 60 MIN
3/4 OR 1/2 INCH VIDEO CASSETTE
See series title for descriptive statement.
From The Bases For Several Pavement Design Methods Series. Pt 8
Prod-UAZMIC Dist-UAZMIC 1977

Rigid Pavement Design And Methods, Pt 2 B 60 MIN
3/4 OR 1/2 INCH VIDEO CASSETTE
See series title for descriptive statement.
From The Bases For Several Pavement Design Methods Series. Pt 9
Prod-UAZMIC Dist-UAZMIC 1977

Rigid Transformations B
16MM FILM OPTICAL SOUND
Defines a rigid transformation and investigates its geometric properties in two and three dimensions.
Prod-OPENU Dist-OPENU

Rigoletto C 30 MIN
16MM FILM, 3/4 OR 1/2 IN VIDEO J-C A
Presents Joan Sutherland singing the opera Rigoletto. Features puppets in an opera box acting as a reviewing audience conversing with the performers as they enter or leave front stage.
From The Who's Afraid Of Opera Series.
Prod-PHENIX Dist-PHENIX 1973

Rikki-Tikki-Tavi C 26 MIN
3/4 INCH VIDEO CASSETTE E
Tells how a mongoose saves a British family from two dreaded cobras. Based on the story Rikki-Tikki Tavi by Rudyard Kipling. Narrated by Orson Welles.
Prod-CJE Dist-GA

Rillettes And Terrines C 30 MIN
1/2 IN VIDEO CASSETTE BETA/VHS
Looks at the differences among pates, terrines and rillettes. Shows how to prepare beef terrine and pork rillette.
From The Frugal Gourmet Series.
Prod-WTTWTV Dist-MTI

Rin Tin Tin B 28 MIN
16MM FILM OPTICAL SOUND P-C A
Stars the dog hero Rin Tin Tin, of the 1920's in scenes from one of his films Tracked By The Police.
From The History Of The Motion Picture Series.
Prod-KILLIS Dist-KILLIS 1927

Rincon - Island Paradox C 25 MIN
3/4 OR 1/2 INCH VIDEO CASSETTE
Shows marine biology classes conducting research on a man-made island between Ventura and Santa Barbara off the California coast.
Prod-HBS Dist-IVCH

Ring And Circle Shear Operation C 9 MIN
1/2 IN VIDEO CASSETTE BETA/VHS IND
Presents the application of the ring and circle shear for cutting out circles or rings from sheet metal.
Prod-RMI Dist-RMI

Ring For Television, A C 58 MIN
3/4 OR 1/2 INCH VIDEO CASSETTE
Documents how Richard Wagner's Ring Cycle was filmed offering a fascinating behind the facade view of the creation of this epic production.
Prod-FOTH Dist-FOTH 1984

Ring Modulation C 4 MIN
3/4 OR 1/2 INCH VIDEO CASSETTE
See series title for descriptive statement.
From The Gary Hill, Part 2 Series.
Prod-EAI Dist-EAI

Ring Of Gyges, The C 30 MIN
3/4 OR 1/2 INCH VIDEO CASSETTE C
See series title for descriptive statement.
From The Art Of Being Human Series. Module 5
Prod-MDCC Dist-MDCC

Ring Of Lakes C 24 MIN
16MM FILM OPTICAL SOUND
Shows the lake and parkland region in central Alberta, Canada, around the capital city of Edmonton.
From The Heading Out Series.
LC NO. 76-702049
Prod-CENTWO Dist-CENTWO 1975

Ring-A-Jing-Jing C 20 MIN
2 INCH VIDEOTAPE P
See series title for descriptive statement.
From The Learning Our Language, Unit III - Creative Writing Series.
Prod-MPATI Dist-GPITVL

Ring, Ring C 15 MIN
3/4 OR 1/2 INCH VIDEO CASSETTE K-P
Discusses the telephone, telephone numbers and using the telephone in an emergency.
From The Pass It On Series.
Prod-WKNOTV Dist-GPITVL 1983

Ringer, The C 20 MIN
16MM FILM OPTICAL SOUND
A dramatic story which shows how drug pushers use high pressure advertising techniques to sell their drugs to young people.
LC NO. 72-702334
Prod-HEARST Dist-HEARST 1972

Ringovelser (Flying Ring Exercises) B 29 MIN
16MM FILM SILENT
Presents a systematic demonstration of a number of flying ring exercises.
Prod-STATNS Dist-STATNS 1962

Rings C 11 MIN
16MM FILM, 3/4 OR 1/2 IN VIDEO J-C A
Introduces the beginning gymnast to the rings.
Prod-AIMS Dist-AIMS 1971

Rings Around Rabaul B 27 MIN
16MM FILM, 3/4 OR 1/2 IN VIDEO J-H
Presents highlights of the struggle for the Solomon Islands.
From The Victory At Sea Series.
Prod-NBCTV Dist-LUF

Rings I - The Axiom B
16MM FILM OPTICAL SOUND
Examines number systems, polynomials, matrices, and functions. Sets up a formal axiom system which reflects the properties common to all these structures. Explores the internal structure of rings, drawing analogies with group theory.
Prod-OPENU Dist-OPENU

Ringsiders C 28 MIN
2 INCH VIDEOTAPE
Shows thousands of people going each week to the Friday night wrestling matches to cheer and jeer their boys, to take out their frustrations and to add a little excitement to their lives. Features Paul Boesch, Houston wrestling promoter and former wrestler himself, explaining why wrestling matches attract so many fans.
From The Bayou City And Thereabouts People Show Series.
Prod-KUHTTV Dist-PUBTEL

Ringstealer C 23 MIN
16MM FILM, 3/4 OR 1/2 IN VIDEO I-J
Presents a mystery story about a boy named Brian, whose experiences point out the importance of values and beliefs, self-esteem and self-image, honesty, truthfulness, friendships and making the right decisions.
Prod-SWAIN Dist-MCFI 1984

Ringtail C 9 MIN
16MM FILM OPTICAL SOUND
Tells a story about a young boy and his pet raccoon, and their adventures in the wilds of Algonquin Park.
LC NO. 75-701920
Prod-GIB Dist-EFD 1973

Rio De Janeiro C 3 MIN
16MM FILM OPTICAL SOUND P-I
Discusses the city of Rio De Janeiro in Brazil.
From The Of All Things Series.
Prod-BAILYL Dist-AVED

Rio Escondido (Hidden River) B 100 MIN
16MM FILM OPTICAL SOUND
A Spanish language film. Explores the struggle between a young school teacher and a tyrannical, self-appointed ruler of a village who keeps the villagers in ignorance to enforce his power over them.
Prod-TRANSW Dist-TRANSW

Rio Grande C 40 MIN
16MM FILM OPTICAL SOUND
Follows the course of the Rio Grande River from its headwaters in Colorado to the Texas border. Shows Indian pueblos, hispanic villages, ranches, the city of Albuquerque and deserts along the route.
LC NO. 76-702610
Prod-NMARBC Dist-BLUSKY Prodn-BLUSKY 1976

Rio Grande - Where Four Cultures Meet C 16 MIN
16MM FILM, 3/4 OR 1/2 IN VIDEO I-H
Explores the cultural and economic interdependence and interaction of Mexican, Spanish, Indian and Anglo-American peoples of the Rio Grande Valley.
Prod-EVANSA Dist-PHENIX 1972

Rios Del Mundo C 30 MIN
3/4 OR 1/2 INCH VIDEO CASSETTE K-P
See series title for descriptive statement.
From The Villa Alegre Series.
Prod-BCTV Dist-MDCPB

Riot Control Formations C 24 MIN
16MM FILM OPTICAL SOUND
Shows the composition and application of basic wedge, line and echelon formations in riot control operations. Illustrates commands, hand signals and steps in executing these formations and their variants at the squad, platoon and company level.
LC NO. 74-705541
Prod-USA Dist-USNAC 1967

Riot-Control Weapons C 6 MIN
16MM FILM OPTICAL SOUND
Documents the weapons the government has specifically designed to paralyze mass resistance in the cities.
Prod-NEWSR Dist-NEWSR

Riot-Control Weapons B 6 MIN
16MM FILM OPTICAL SOUND
Views new weapons that the police are using and have available for use in riots.
Prod-SFN Dist-SFN 1968

Rip Van Winkle C 27 MIN
16MM FILM OPTICAL SOUND
Uses clay animation to present an adaptation of Washington Irving's tale Rip Van Winkle. Includes a dream sequence in which Rip gradually discovers the secret of life. Narrated by Will Geer.
LC NO. 79-700271
Prod-VINTN Dist-BBF 1978

Rip Van Winkle C 15 MIN
16MM FILM, 3/4 OR 1/2 IN VIDEO P
Presents the American legend of Rip Van Winkle.
From The Magic Carpet Series.
Prod-SDCSS Dist-GPITVL 1979

Rip Van Winkle C 18 MIN
16MM FILM, 3/4 OR 1/2 IN VIDEO
Retells the tale of a man who escaped into the hills, fell into a magical sleep and awoke to find that many years had passed. Based on the story Rip Van Winkle by Washington Irving.
Prod-BFA Dist-BARR 1980

Rip Van Winkle C 24 MIN
16MM FILM, 3/4 OR 1/2 IN VIDEO P-J
Presents cartoon character Mr Magoo as Rip Van Winkle in an animated version of Washington Irving's story of a man who sleeps for 20 years.
Prod-UPAPOA Dist-MCFI 1976

Rip Van Winkle (Spanish) C 27 MIN
16MM FILM OPTICAL SOUND
Presents an animated adaptation of Washington Irving's Rip Van Winkle. Tells the story of a free spirit who preferred telling stories to tilling soil.
Prod-VINTN Dist-BBF

Rip-Off C 94 MIN
16MM FILM OPTICAL SOUND
Presents the story of four high-spirited boys in their last year of high school who play very hard at being 'in' and making the groovy scene.
LC NO. 74-701648
Prod-PHENIX Dist-CFDEVC

Riparian Vegetation C 14 MIN
3/4 INCH VIDEO CASSETTE J-C A
Highlights vegetation growing along California's waterways. Discusses management necessary to strike a balance between wildlife habitats controlling floodwater and farming interests.
Prod-CSDWR Dist-CALDWR

Ripoff, The C 15 MIN
16MM FILM, 3/4 OR 1/2 IN VIDEO J-C
Tells a story about a young boy who is a habitual thief and his friend whom he persuades to act as decoy while he attempts to steal. Shows how, when the young thief draws a real but unloaded gun and threatens the salesman's life, both boys are arrested and petitions are filed in juvenile court for robbery and burglary.
From The Under The Law, Pt 1 Series.
Prod-USNEI Dist-WDEMCO 1974

Ripping And Crosscutting B 19 MIN
16MM FILM, 3/4 OR 1/2 IN VIDEO
Shows how each working part of the variety saw functions. Demonstrates how to check saw blades, set the fence, changes saw blades, use a cutoff gage and use a hinged block in crosscutting.
From The Precision Wood Machining - Operations On The Variety Saw Series. No. 1
Prod-USOE Dist-USNAC Prodn-RCM 1945

Ripple C 29 MIN
16MM FILM MAGNETIC SOUND J-C A
An introductory film for United States Coast Guard Auxiliary and the United States Power Squadron Boating Safety courses. Tells the story about a boat that describes her life to a small boy, pointing out the boat's fear of fire, collision and leaks.
LC NO. 72-701608
Prod-SAFECO Dist-LAWJ 1971

Ripple Effect, The C 12 MIN
16MM FILM OPTICAL SOUND
Presents a poetic essay about some of the qualities required for leadership. Pictures four accomplished individuals and explores the qualities exemplified by each of them that have made it possible for them to become leaders.
LC NO. 74-702865
Prod-GITTFI Dist-GITTFI 1974

Ripple Of Time, A C 24 MIN
3/4 OR 1/2 INCH VIDEO CASSETTE C A
Alternates interludes of conversation with leisurely and active lovemaking to paint a beautiful and moving picture of mature sexuality.
Prod-NATSF Dist-MMRC

Ripple Tank Wave Phenomena 3 - Barrier Penetration B 8 MIN
16MM FILM OPTICAL SOUND C
Shows how a wide channel of deep water between two shallow regions in a ripple tank will act to prevent wave movement between the shallow regions. Demonstrates that the narrowing of the channel increases wave transmission.
From The College Physics Film Program.
LC NO. FIA68-1437
Prod-EDS Dist-MLA 1962

Ripple Tank Wave Phenomena 4 - Bragg Reflection B 10 MIN
16MM FILM OPTICAL SOUND C
Examines the reflection of waves by a lattice of small objects and demonstrates that the reflection changes as the wavelength and angle of incidence are varied.
From The College Physics Film Program Series.
LC NO. FIA68-1436
Prod-EDS Dist-MLA 1962

Ripple Tank Wave Phenomena 5 - Doppler Effect And Shock Waves B 8 MIN
16MM FILM OPTICAL SOUND C
Demonstrates the effects of a wave source in a ripple tank, including the Doppler effect and the formation of shock wave and shock cone.
From The College Physics Film Program Series.
LC NO. FIA68-1435
Prod-EDS Dist-MLA 1962

Ripples—A Series

Prod-NITC Dist-AITECH

About Ripples 15 MIN
All By Myself 15 MIN
Animals Need You 15 MIN
Body Talk 15 MIN
Caring For The World 15 MIN
Checkup 15 MIN
Dad And I 15 MIN
Everybody's Different 15 MIN
Eyes And Lenses 15 MIN
Feeling Spaces 15 MIN
Fifty-Five To Get Ready 15 MIN
Fire 15 MIN
Friends 15 MIN
Going Home To Earth 15 MIN
Going To The Hospital 15 MIN
Hands 15 MIN
How Did I Get To Be Me 15 MIN
How Do You Know 15 MIN
How It Used To Be 15 MIN
How Will I Grow 15 MIN
I Found It 15 MIN
Lost 15 MIN
Millions Of Pies 15 MIN
Movement 15 MIN
Out To The Moon 15 MIN
Overnight At The Hospital 15 MIN
People Make Music 15 MIN
Playing Where You Are 15 MIN
Rhythms From Africa 15 MIN
Seeds 15 MIN
Shadows 15 MIN
Sounds Of Myself 15 MIN
Take A Good Look 15 MIN
Talking Round The World 15 MIN
To Make A Dance 15 MIN
Touching The World 15 MIN
Using Ripples - Change And Aesthetics 15 MIN
Using Ripples - Values And Knowledge 15 MIN
You're It 15 MIN

Risa Friedman And Peter Justice C 30 MIN
3/4 OR 1/2 INCH VIDEO CASSETTE
Discusses warm-up and conditioning
From The Eye On Dance - Health And Well-Being Of Dancers Series.
Prod-ARTRES Dist-ARTRES

Rise And Fall Of Ben Gizzard, The Parrot And The Thief And The Contests At Cowlick, The C 15 MIN
3/4 OR 1/2 INCH VIDEO CASSETTE P-I
Presents three stories in which an old Indian predicts the death of a scoundrel, a thief who steals a parrot finds it to be an awkward eyewitness, and Wally challenges Hogbone and his cutthroats to one contest after another and wins by losing. Based on the books The Rise And Fall Of Ben Gizzard, The Parrot And The Thief and The Contests At Cowlick by Richard Kennedy.
From The Readit Series.
Prod-POSIMP Dist-AITECH 1982

Rise And Fall Of Cyrus, The C 30 MIN
3/4 INCH VIDEO CASSETTE
Focuses on Persian king Cyrus the Great as seen through the eyes of Herodotus.
From The Herodotus - Father Of History Series.
Prod-UMITV Dist-UMITV 1980

Rise And Fall Of Money, The C 57 MIN
16MM FILM, 3/4 OR 1/2 IN VIDEO H-C A
Focuses on the history and function of money in society. Based on the book The Age Of Uncertainty by John Kenneth Galbraith.
From The Age Of Uncertainty Series.
LC NO. 77-701493
Prod-BBCL Dist-FI 1977

Rise And Fall Of The Great Lakes C 17 MIN
16MM FILM, 3/4 OR 1/2 IN VIDEO J-C A
Uses animation, ballad singing, trick photography, and a canoe trip through the Great Lakes in showing how profoundly the last ice age affected the face of the land and how the Great Lakes system which was created continues to change, largely through the intervention of man.
Prod-NFBC Dist-PFP 1970

Rise And Fall Of The Third Reich—A Series
16MM FILM, 3/4 OR 1/2 IN VIDEO H-C A
Prod-MGMD Dist-FI 1974

Gotterdammerung - Collapse Of The Third Reich 28 MIN
Nazi Germany - Years Of Triumph 28 MIN
Rise Of Hitler 28 MIN

Rise Of Adolph Hitler, The B 27 MIN
16MM FILM, 3/4 OR 1/2 IN VIDEO J-C
Reconstructs the events of September 9, 1938, at Nuremberg, the climax of Adolph Hitler's rise to power.
From The You Are There Series.
Prod-MGHT Dist-MGHT 1957

Rise Of Big Business, The X 27 MIN
16MM FILM, 3/4 OR 1/2 IN VIDEO J-H
Studies the values, aspirations and achievements of Andrew Carnegie, John D Rockefeller and J P Morgan. Shows the effect these men had on the growth of great business enterprises and the further effect these enterprises had on American society.
From The Rise Of Industrial America Series.
Prod-EBF Dist-EBEC 1970

Rise Of Big Business, The - Part 1 C 30 MIN
3/4 OR 1/2 INCH VIDEO CASSETTE C
Supplies perspective on issues involved in the rapid industrialization of the U S between the Civil War and the Great Crash.
America - The Second Century Series.
Prod-DALCCD Dist-DALCCD

Rise Of Big Business, The - Part 2 C 30 MIN
3/4 OR 1/2 INCH VIDEO CASSETTE C
Contributes historical perspectives on Big Business after the Great Crash.
America - The Second Century Series.
Prod-DALCCD Dist-DALCCD

Rise Of Europe, The - 1000-1500 A D C 23 MIN
16MM FILM, 3/4 OR 1/2 IN VIDEO J-C
Traces the major social economic and philosophic developments in Europe between 1000 and 1500 A D. Uses representative art forms to exemplify historical events.
Prod-MGHT Dist-MGHT Prodn-MUR 1968

Rise Of Greek Tragedy, The - Sophocles, Oedipus The King C 45 MIN
16MM FILM, 3/4 OR 1/2 IN VIDEO H-C A
Presents Sophocles' Oedipus The King, performed in a 5th-century Greek theater, with the use of masks made after ancient models. Shows how this drama developed from primeval sacrifical ceremonies to Dionysius.
From The History Of The Drama Series. Unit 1
LC NO. 75-700102
Prod-MANTLH Dist-FOTH 1975

Rise Of Hitler B 28 MIN
16MM FILM, 3/4 OR 1/2 IN VIDEO H-C A
Discusses Hitler's youth and career.
From The Rise And Fall Of The Third Reich Series.
Prod-MGMD Dist-FI 1972

Rise Of Industrial America—A Series
16MM FILM, 3/4 OR 1/2 IN VIDEO J-H
Traces the evolution of Industrial America, telling how it came about, how it transformed American society and how it continues to shape American life-styles.
Prod-EBEC Dist-EBEC

Farmer In A Changing America, The 27 MIN
Industrial Revolution, The - Beginnings In 23 MIN
Rise Of Big Business, The 27 MIN
Rise Of Labor, The 30 MIN
Rise Of The American City, The 32 MIN

Rise Of Labor, The X 30 MIN
16MM FILM, 3/4 OR 1/2 IN VIDEO J-H
Traces the history of the American labor movement. Discusses the working conditions from the 1800's to the present, the effects of early strikes in changing governmental attitudes toward labor and the organization of the American federation of labor and the congress of industrial organizations.
From The Rise Of Industrial America Series.
Prod-EBEC Dist-EBEC 1969

Rise Of Mammals, The C 58 MIN
3/4 OR 1/2 INCH VIDEO CASSETTE J-C A
Offers a detailed study of the many marsupial species, paying special to the primitive marsupials found in Australia.
From The Life On Earth Series. Program 9
LC NO. 82-706681
Prod-BBCTV Dist-FI 1981

Rise Of Minna Nordstrom, The C 30 MIN
3/4 OR 1/2 INCH VIDEO CASSETTE C A
Presents an adaptation of the short story The Rise Of Minna Nordstrom by P G Wodehouse.
From The Wodehouse Playhouse Series.
Prod-BBCTV Dist-TIMLIF 1980

Rise Of Modernism In Music—A Series
16MM FILM, 3/4 OR 1/2 IN VIDEO
Looks at various composers and the music they created.
Prod-BBCTV Dist-MEDIAG 1982

Are My Ears On Wrong - A Profile Of Charles 024 ...
Paris - La Belle Epoque 024 MIN
Vienna - Stripping The Facade 025 MIN

Rise Of Nations In Europe (2nd Ed) C 13 MIN
16MM FILM, 3/4 OR 1/2 IN VIDEO J-C
Traces the rise of European nations from feudal beginnings to the highly centralized states of the 17th century.
Prod-CORF Dist-CORF 1978

Rise Of The American City, The C 32 MIN
16MM FILM, 3/4 OR 1/2 IN VIDEO J-C A
Presents John Lindsay, mayor of New York, and Godfrey Cambridge, well-known black comedian and social observer, commenting on the problems of pollution, poverty, hunger, violence and social change. Searches the heart of the city and of the men and women who are its strength and future.
From The Rise Of Industrial America Series.
Prod-EBEC Dist-EBEC 1970

Rise Of The Cotton Kingdom B 30 MIN
2 INCH VIDEOTAPE H-C A
See series title for descriptive statement.
From The Americans From Africa - A History Series. No. 9
Prod-CVETVC Dist-GPITVL Prodn-WCVETV

Rise Of The Dictators, The - Form, Riflemen, Form C 52 MIN
16MM FILM - 1/2 IN VIDEO
Analyzes conditions in Europe that made Hitler's and Mussolini's rise to power possible. Discusses Stalin's five-year plans in the Soviet Union, the civil war in Spain and the signing of the Nazi-Soviet Pact of 1939.
From The Europe, The Mighty Continent Series.
LC NO. 79-707423
Prod-BBCTV Dist-TIMLIF 1976

Rise Of The Horsemen, The B 30 MIN
16MM FILM OPTICAL SOUND J-C A
Describes the new plains life resulting from the spread of Spanish horses. Discusses the change from agriculture to bison hunting (1650-1750), the movement of Indian tribes and typical plains Indian culture (1750-1850.)
From The Great Plains Trilogy, 2 Series. Nomad And Indians - Early Man On The Plains
Prod-UNEBR Dist-UNEBR 1954

Rise Of The Industrial Giants, The C 25 MIN
16MM FILM, 3/4 OR 1/2 IN VIDEO J-C A
Spotlights the rise of trusts and monopolies and the powerful group of men who controlled the newly industrialized and urbanized America.
From The American History Series.
Prod-CRMP Dist-CRMP 1968

Rise Of The Nazis B 20 MIN
3/4 OR 1/2 INCH VIDEO CASSETTE J-C A
Shows how a violent, extralegal group of outsiders and fringe elements rose to power in a democracy and established political and economic institutions of legitimized terror and mass murder in Nazi Germany. Documents the economic, political and attitudinal factors which contributed to the rise of Naziism.
From The Witness To The Holocaust Series.
LC NO. 84-706506
Prod-HORECE Dist-CNEMAG 1983

Rise Of The Red Navy, The C 57 MIN
16MM FILM, 3/4 OR 1/2 IN VIDEO H-C A
Documents the growth of the Russian Navy, focusing on warships and submarines, fishing fleets, an oceanographic research fleet larger than that of all other nations together, a merchant fleet second only to that of Japan and a unique flotilla of more than 50 intelligence and surveillance vessels.
LC NO. 80-706906
Prod-BBCTV Dist-FI 1980

Rise Of The Soviet Navy, The C 28 MIN
16MM FILM - 3/4 IN VIDEO
Traces the rise of Soviet sea power from the Imperial Navy of the czar to the navy of the 1960's. Narrated by Richard Basehart. Issued in 1969 as a motion picture.
LC NO. 79-706675
Prod-USN Dist-USNAC 1979

Rise Up And Walk C 28 MIN
16MM FILM, 3/4 OR 1/2 IN VIDEO C A
Explores the beliefs and practices of a variety of independent African Christian churches, showing how they interpret and live the Christian faith in the context of their own pre-Christian religious and cultural traditions.
Prod-ANKELE Dist-UCEMC 1982

Rise Up And Walk C 55 MIN
16MM FILM, 3/4 OR 1/2 IN VIDEO
Explores the beliefs and practices of independent African Christian churches. Shows how they interpret the Christian faith in the context of their own pre-Christian religions and cultural traditions.
Prod-ANKELE Dist-UCEMC

Rishost Hos Bontoc-Igoroterne (Rice Harvest Among The Bontoc Igorots) C 20 MIN
16MM FILM SILENT
Portrays a rice harvest among the Bontoc Igorots. Describes the rice being harvested in accordance with the traditional ceremonies. Includes Danish subtitles.
Prod-STATNS Dist-STATNS 1954

Rising Expectations C 28 MIN
16MM FILM OPTICAL SOUND
Explores the ways in which people with disabilities are making advances in American society in such areas as employment, housing, education, transportation and recreation.
LC NO. 79-701240
Prod-UCPA Dist-UCPA 1978

Rising High And Beautiful C 14 MIN
16MM FILM OPTICAL SOUND
Takes a look at the scenic highlights of the Niagara Falls area of southern Ontario.
From The Journal Series.
LC NO. 74-703753
Prod-FIARTS Dist-CANFDC 1973

Rising Of The Moon, The B 81 MIN
16MM FILM OPTICAL SOUND
Presents a trilogy of Irish comedy and drama.
Prod-WB Dist-TWYMAN 1957

Rising Tide, A C 30 MIN
16MM FILM OPTICAL SOUND
Shows how New Bedrod is experiencing a rising economic tide, spurred by the area redevelopment and administration. Shows how a combination of local, state and federal resources can be used to develop community facilities, create jobs, attract new industry and train workers.
Prod-USARA Dist-AFLCIO 1965

Risk C 29 MIN
3/4 INCH VIDEO CASSETTE
Focuses on the risks and safety factors in nuclear power reactor operations.
From The Nuclear Power And You Series.
Prod-UMITV Dist-UMITV 1979

Risk Analysis And The EDP Security Assurance Review C 30 MIN
3/4 OR 1/2 INCH VIDEO CASSETTE
Discusses risk analysis and outlines several methods for conducting a risk analysis while stressing that companies must determine the risks which face their computer systems
From The Auditing EDP Systems Series.
Prod-DELTAK Dist-DELTAK

Risk Factors In Heart Disease C 30 MIN
3/4 OR 1/2 INCH VIDEO CASSETTE C T
Discusses hypertension, smoking and high levels of cholesterol in the bloodstream as dangerous health risk factors. Shows how to recognize these dangers and why we should avoid them.
From The Here's To Your Health Series.
Prod-DALCCD Dist-DALCCD

Risk Factors Of Coronary Disease C
3/4 OR 1/2 INCH VIDEO CASSETTE
Explains how one can reduce the major risk factors that lead to heart disease. Deals with smoking, hypertension, cholesterol as well as such probable factors as diabetes, obesity, stress and inactivity.
Prod-MIFE Dist-MIFE

Risk Factors Of Coronary Disease (Arabic) C
3/4 OR 1/2 INCH VIDEO CASSETTE
Explains how one can reduce the major risk factors that lead to heart disease. Deals with smoking, hypertension, cholesterol as well as such probable factors as diabetes, obesity, stress and inactivity.
Prod-MIFE Dist-MIFE

Risk Factors Of Coronary Disease (Spanish) C
3/4 OR 1/2 INCH VIDEO CASSETTE
Explains how one can reduce the major risk factors that lead to heart disease. Deals with smoking, hypertension, cholesterol as well as such probable factors as diabetes, obesity, stress and inactivity.
Prod-MIFE Dist-MIFE

Risk Management C 11 MIN
16MM FILM OPTICAL SOUND
Discusses business risks and how to deal with them.
From The Running Your Own Business Series.
Prod-EFD Dist-EFD

Risk Management/Reliability Approach - A Successful Combination C
16MM FILM - 3/4 IN VIDEO A
Presents two logical tools to help people and equipment perform efficiently and safely, prevent breakdowns, plus five major causes of breakdowns.
Prod-BNA Dist-BNA 1983

Risky Business C 30 MIN
1/2 IN VIDEO CASSETTE BETA/VHS
Explores the world of bartering. Provides tax tips. Describes how money affects emotions.
From The On The Money Series.
Prod-WGBHTV Dist-MTI

Rite Of Renewal C
1/2 IN VIDEO CASSETTE BETA/VHS
Explores the need for rites of passage to mark important transitions in adult lives. Presents examples of such rituals, including a Bat Mitzvah for adult women, a therapy group and a religious divorce service.
From The Adult Years - Continuity And Change Series.
Prod-OHUTC Dist-OHUTC

Ritual B 4 MIN
16MM FILM OPTICAL SOUND
Presents a visual exploration of the ritual involved in the application of eye make-up and the elaborate materials used.
LC NO. 75-703226
Prod-USC Dist-USC 1966

Ritual C 30 MIN
16MM FILM, 3/4 OR 1/2 IN VIDEO J-C A
Tells how the Japanese have survived as a people, linked to their traditions and each other despite the demands of a highly industrialized society.
Prod-PSYMED Dist-WOMBAT

Ritual Dance In Three Oriental Cultures C 30 MIN
3/4 OR 1/2 INCH VIDEO CASSETTE
See series title for descriptive statement.
From The Dance In Religion And Ritual Series.
Prod-ARCVID Dist-ARCVID

Ritual Vs Social Dance In The Indigenous Lifestyle C 30 MIN
3/4 OR 1/2 INCH VIDEO CASSETTE
See series title for descriptive statement.
From The Dance In Religion And Ritual Series.
Prod-ARCVID Dist-ARCVID

Ritualistic Patient, The B 44 MIN
16MM FILM OPTICAL SOUND PRO
Discusses the message character of ritualistic behavior with regard to anxiety and conflict and its implications for nursing intervention.
From The Nursing In Psychiatry Series.
LC NO. 77-703438
Prod-VDONUR Dist-AJN Prodn-WTTWTV 1968

Rituel C 30 MIN
16MM FILM OPTICAL SOUND
Presents composer Pierre Boulez conducting his own composition Rituel before the New York Philharmonic Orchestra. Uses computer graphics by artist L Schwartz to accompany the musical composition.
Prod-LILYAN Dist-LILYAN

Ritz Crackers C 1 MIN
3/4 OR 1/2 INCH VIDEO CASSETTE
Shows a classic television commercial with still frame action.
Prod-BROOKC Dist-BROOKC

Ritz, The C 91 MIN
16MM FILM OPTICAL SOUND
Stars Jack Weston as a man on the run from the mob who hides out in a gay bathhouse. Directed by Richard Lester.
Prod-WB Dist-TWYMAN 1976

Rivals, The C 12 MIN
16MM FILM OPTICAL SOUND
Presents the story of a blacksmith and a tailor who despise each other's job and argue about an accident in which their displays for a fair were destroyed. Explains that a judge makes them settle their argument by exchanging jobs. Shows how they learn to live happily side by side.
From The Animatoons Series.
LC NO. FIA67-5506
Prod-ANTONS Dist-RADTV 1968

River (Planet Earth) C 27 MIN
16MM FILM, 3/4 OR 1/2 IN VIDEO J-C A
Takes a look at the Saskatchewan-Nelson river in order to examine the impact which a water system has upon the economy, sociology and ecology of a nation.
Prod-NFBC Dist-MGHT 1978

River - A First Film C 10 MIN
16MM FILM, 3/4 OR 1/2 IN VIDEO P-I
Follows the formation of a river from melting snow, which forms streams that join together and flow into the ocean. Explains that cities are often located along a river bank to take advantage of the river waters. Shows river ports and ships.
Prod-FA Dist-PHENIX 1969

River - A First Film (French) C 10 MIN
16MM FILM, 3/4 OR 1/2 IN VIDEO P-I
Follows the formation of a river from melting snow, which forms streams that join together and flow into the ocean. Explains that cities are often located along a river bank to take advantage of the river waters. Shows river ports and ships.
Prod-FA Dist-PHENIX 1969

River - An Allegory C 11 MIN
16MM FILM, 3/4 OR 1/2 IN VIDEO H-C A
Depicts the quickening life and movement of a great river.
Prod-HARL Dist-IFB 1968

River - Where Do You Come From C 10 MIN
16MM FILM, 3/4 OR 1/2 IN VIDEO K-P
Follows a river's full cycle from its origin to its final return to the sea. Shows the numerous ways in which water benefits man and, by contrast, its destructive potential.
Prod-LCOA Dist-LCOA 1969

River Body B 8 MIN
16MM FILM, 3/4 OR 1/2 IN VIDEO C A
Shows eighty-seven male and female bodies in continuous dissolve.
Prod-MMRC Dist-MMRC

River Called Potomac, A C 29 MIN
16MM FILM OPTICAL SOUND
Examines the numerous natural resources provided by the Potomac River, such as water for cities and industries, food, and recreational opportunities. Looks at water resource management programs that protect the quality and quantity of water in the river.
LC NO. 79-700272
Prod-USDENV Dist-FINLYS Prodn-FINLYS 1979

River Channel Forms C 20 MIN
3/4 OR 1/2 INCH VIDEO CASSETTE
Discusses the dynamic nature of rivers and the relationship between their forms and their processes. Deals with river function, the transport of water and sediment, river form and cross-section shape.
From The Earth Science Series.
Prod-FOTH Dist-FOTH 1984

River Characteristics B 27 MIN
16MM FILM OPTICAL SOUND C A
Features a discussion of tributaries and the interrelationship of width, depth, velocity and quantity of various rivers. Explains problems of pools and ripples in streams. Demonstrates meanders and shows flash floods. Utilizes a glass-fronted sand model to visualize maintenance of streams by ground water during the dry season.
Prod-UTEX Dist-UTEX 1960

River Flows North C 15 MIN
16MM FILM OPTICAL SOUND
Presents an informative view of Sanford, Florida, which is centrally situated on the St Johns River near numerous attractions.
Prod-FLADC Dist-FLADC

River Insects C 20 MIN
16MM FILM OPTICAL SOUND
A Japanese language film. Observes the interesting existence and reproduction of various insects in the swift mountain streams. Shows the various species of mole crickets living in such surroundings. Points out how the river insects live by adjusting themselves according to their environments.
Prod-TOEI Dist-UNIJAP 1967

River Journey On The Upper Nile C 18 MIN
16MM FILM, 3/4 OR 1/2 IN VIDEO P-C
Discusses government priority given to education and training in skills for the inhabitants of the Sudan who at present live as primitive farmers.
From The Man And His World Series.
Prod-FI Dist-FI 1969

River Kwai Expedition, The C 12 MIN
16MM FILM OPTICAL SOUND
Presents the find of prehistoric cave pictures at the River Kwai by the Thai-Danish Expedition. Shows some extensive settlements from the Bronze Age in Bang Khao.
Prod-RDCG Dist-AUDPLN

River Logging C 3 MIN
16MM FILM OPTICAL SOUND P-I
Discusses river logging.
From The Of All Things Series.
Prod-BAILYL Dist-AVED

River Museum, A C 15 MIN
3/4 OR 1/2 INCH VIDEO CASSETTE K-P
Discusses rivers and their uses and takes a trip to a museum to observe river boats.
From The Pass It On Series.
Prod-WKNOTV Dist-GPITVL 1983

River Nile, The X 34 MIN
16MM FILM, 3/4 OR 1/2 IN VIDEO J-C A
A short version of the film, 'THE RIVER NILE.' Pictures the physical characteristics of the river. Discusses its role in history and in the economy of the regions.
Prod-NBCTV Dist-MGHT 1965

River Of Grass C 26 MIN
16MM FILM OPTICAL SOUND I-C A
Examines man's encroachment on the Florida Everglades and his devastating destruction of land, water and wildlife as nature struggles to balance her scales in one of the few tropical wildernesses surviving in North America.
From The Audubon Wildlife Theatre Series.
Prod-AVEXP Dist-AVEXP

River Of Grass C 26 MIN
16MM FILM OPTICAL SOUND
Examines the Florida Everglades and the struggle to balance nature while man is destroying it. Includes scenes of the blue heron, alligators, the anhinga and snakes. Shows the metamorphosis of the helconius caterpillar into a butterfly.
From The Audubon Wildlife Theatre Series.
LC NO. 74-710207
Prod-KEGPL Dist-AVEXP 1969

River Of Ice - Life Cycle Of A Glacier (2nd Ed) C 10 MIN
16MM FILM, 3/4 OR 1/2 IN VIDEO I-H
Uses scenes of such glaciers as the Knik and Columbian ice field, to show the source, structure and movement of a typical Alpine glacier, the relationship of climate to ice formation and the effect of glaciation upon the land, fauna and flora of the Alpine region.
Prod-BAILEY Dist-PHENIX 1964

River Of Life, The C 22 MIN
3/4 OR 1/2 INCH VIDEO CASSETTE J-H
See series title for descriptive statement.
From The Phenomenal World Series.
Prod-EBEC Dist-EBEC 1983

River Of Mail C 9 MIN
16MM FILM OPTICAL SOUND
A study of complexities of mail handling. Shows how new methods and new equipment are being used to cope with the constantly increasing flow of mail.
LC NO. 77-702859
Prod-USPOST Dist-USPOST Prodn-AUDIO 1968

River Of Power C 21 MIN
16MM FILM, 3/4 OR 1/2 IN VIDEO J-H
Traces the history of the oil well in the United States. Demonstrates the many ways in which oil is used, and describes some of the by-products of petroleum, including plastics, fibers and industrial raw materials.
Prod-ALTSUL Dist-JOU 1968

River Of Time C 8 MIN
16MM FILM OPTICAL SOUND I-C A
Explains that the Colorado River, surely a river of time, has carved one of nature's greatest monuments, the Grand Canyon. Reveals life from the past preserved in the rock and life in its constant struggle today.
Prod-AVEXP Dist-AVEXP

River Of Wealth, River Of Freedom C 24 MIN
16MM FILM OPTICAL SOUND
Looks at America's highway system and shows how a mobile population must learn to share the road.
Prod-GM Dist-MTP

River Patrol C 28 MIN
16MM FILM OPTICAL SOUND
Presents one aspect of the American Navy's operations in the Mekong Delta, South Vietnam.
LC NO. 74-706227
Prod-USN Dist-USNAC 1968

River People C 12 MIN
16MM FILM, 3/4 OR 1/2 IN VIDEO I-C A
Tells how the river determines the lives of the people living along the Magdelena River in Columbia. Describes how their houses are built on stilts, how they travel by boat and how the river is their principal source of food. Compares the Mopti living on the Niger River in Mali whose habits vary with the season. Explains that during the wet season they live in their boats and during the dry season they build settlements of thatched huts on the shore.
From The Places People Live Series.
Prod-SF Dist-SF 1970

River People Of Chad C 20 MIN
16MM FILM, 3/4 OR 1/2 IN VIDEO P-C
Contrasts the modern city of Fort Lamy with the villages of Chad where men, women and children use primtive tools for farming, fishing and cooking in a communal effort at existence.
From The Man And His World Series.
Prod-PMI Dist-FI 1969

River Rain - Gift Of Passage C 26 MIN
16MM FILM OPTICAL SOUND
Documents a visit to the Painted Stone at the Echimamish River of northern Manitoba. Recalls how Indian and white traders stopped there for brief celebrations of thanksgiving.
LC NO. 76-703255
Prod-CANFDC Dist-CANFDC 1975

River Rhine, The C 22 MIN
16MM FILM, 3/4 OR 1/2 IN VIDEO I-J
Studies the area around the Rhine River, describes the traffic using this busy waterway, and looks at the development of Europoort.
Prod-BHA Dist-IFB 1968

River Riders C 20 MIN
3/4 INCH VIDEO CASSETTE I-J A
Describes the work of river riders, 86 men hired by the Department of Agriculture, who patrol the Texas border and inspect cattle crossing over from Mexico for ticks. Talks with some riders and their families. Discusses danger in this job.
LC NO. 82-707072
Prod-SWINS Dist-SWINS 1982

River Spirit C 36 MIN
16MM FILM OPTICAL SOUND
Shows white water rafting on three American rivers.
LC NO. 78-701567
Prod-COFP Dist-COFP 1978

River Town C 28 MIN
16MM FILM, 3/4 OR 1/2 IN VIDEO J-C A
Records the building of the nation's first solar town in Soldier's Grove, Wisconsin. Recounts the flooding that led to moving the town to higher ground.
Prod-BULFRG Dist-BULFRG

River Valley X 11 MIN
16MM FILM, 3/4 OR 1/2 IN VIDEO P-J
Tells the story of a river which flows through a river valley. Explains how a river valley is formed and how river valley people depend on the river for water, food, minerals, power and transportation.
Prod-EBF Dist-EBEC 1964

River Valley Archeology C 14 MIN
16MM FILM OPTICAL SOUND J-C A
Shows the work of archaeologists in creating and under standing of ancient civilizations. Centers on the work of the University of Georgia archeology department in cooperation with the Smithsonian Institute in excavating an ancient Indian Fort site soon to be buried under the water of a new dam.
Prod-UGA Dist-UGA 1951

River Watchers C 20 MIN
16MM FILM OPTICAL SOUND J-C A
Explains that river surveillance data is needed to provide modern water quality management systems.
Prod-FINLYS Dist-FINLYS 1962

River, The C 29 MIN
16MM FILM, 3/4 OR 1/2 IN VIDEO H-C A
Tells how a neglected four-year-old finds his way back to the river where he was baptized in an effort to recapture the self-esteem he felt there. Based on the short story The River by Flannery O'Connor.
Prod-NOBLEB Dist-PHENIX 1978

River, The C 32 MIN
16MM FILM, 3/4 OR 1/2 IN VIDEO
Traces the history of the Mississippi River and its tributaries. Shows the consequences of sharecropping, soil exhaustion, unchecked erosion and flooding. Concludes with scenes of regional planning, Tennessee Valley Authority development and correlated Federal efforts. Directed by Pare Lorentz. Issued in 1937 as a motion picture.
LC NO. 76-706167
Prod-USDA Dist-USNAC Prodn-LORNTZ 1975

River, The (Der Fluss) C 4 MIN
16MM FILM, 3/4 OR 1/2 IN VIDEO H-C A
Uses a combination of still photography, rough sketch animation and dissolving images to project a melancholic look not only at young love but also at the other kinds of separation, physical and emotional that exist in any sphere of human existence.
Prod-TRICFD Dist-PHENIX

River's Legacy, A C 25 MIN
16MM FILM OPTICAL SOUND
Investigates the agricultural and industrial activities of the Chilliwack area and shows the results from the fertile soil of the Fraser River, British Columbia.
LC NO. 76-703800
Prod-BCDA Dist-BCDA 1974

Rivers C 12 MIN
16MM FILM OPTICAL SOUND P-I
Discusses how rivers develop, their behavior and their importance to man.
LC NO. FIA66-1122
Prod-IU Dist-IU 1965

Rivers C 16 MIN
16MM FILM OPTICAL SOUND I-C A
Presents a montage of scenes which show that rivers are important resources. Shows various activities, including boating, fishing, transporting goods, dam building, operating a water-powered mill, baptism by immersion and painting riverside scenery on canvas.
LC NO. 76-702879
Prod-IU Dist-UMISS 1977

Rivers C 17 MIN
16MM FILM OPTICAL SOUND
Tells how since the industrial revolution Western man has harnessed rivers to his needs as a producer. Shows that by an historical coincidence, the ravages of industrialization bypass most of the 13,750 miles of rivers in Victoria.
LC NO. 80-700875
Prod-VICCOR Dist-TASCOR 1978

Rivers - The Work Of Running Water C 22 MIN
16MM FILM, 3/4 OR 1/2 IN VIDEO I-H
Compares the Colorado and Mississippi Rivers and reveals how running water sculpts the geologic features of the land. Documents the impact of the rivers' flooding on the surrounding terrain. Uses animation in defining terms associated with erosion and sedimentation. Highlights the natural and economic roles of these important bodies of water.
LC NO. 82-706265
Prod-EBEC Dist-EBEC Prodn-BORKBV 1981

Rivers - The Work Of Running Water (Spanish) C 22 MIN
16MM FILM, 3/4 OR 1/2 IN VIDEO I-H
A Spanish language version of the film and videorecording Rivers - The Work Of Running Water.
Prod-EBEC Dist-EBEC

Rivers And Our History X 10 MIN
16MM FILM, 3/4 OR 1/2 IN VIDEO I-H A
Depicts a boy's trip down a river and uses this trip as a basis for an analysis of early trips on rivers during the exploration period in America. Explains how early river settlements grew into vast cities.
Prod-JOU Dist-JOU 1966

Rivers At Work C 20 MIN
16MM FILM, 3/4 OR 1/2 IN VIDEO J-C
Introduces the basic concepts of fluvial geomorphology, the science which seeks to understand the ways in which running water contributes to the creation of landforms.
Prod-LUF Dist-LUF 1983

Rivers Of America - The Hudson, A History B 17 MIN
16MM FILM OPTICAL SOUND I A
Presents the history of the Hudson River from its discovery in 1609 by Henry Hudson, through its role as a source of water power and an artery of commerce. Touches upon the river's geological past and traces its source to kae tear-of-the-clouds in the Adirondack mountains.
Prod-PATHE Dist-HEARST

Rivers Of Fire - An Eruption Of Hawaii's Mauna Loa Volcano C
3/4 OR 1/2 INCH VIDEO CASSETTE P-C A
Presents 1984 eruption of Mauna Loa volcano, on Big Island of Hawaii.
Prod-HNHIST Dist-HNHIST 1984

Rivers Of Kyoto C 34 MIN
16MM FILM OPTICAL SOUND
Pictures four rivers (Kamo, Uji, Katsura and Kitsu) which run through the city of Kyoto and suggests that culture and history are closely associated with rivers.
Prod-UNIJAP Dist-UNIJAP 1971

Rivers Of Sand C 83 MIN
16MM FILM, 3/4 OR 1/2 IN VIDEO H-C A
Portrays the people called the Hamar, who live in the scrubland of southwestern Ethiopia. Points out that in this society, the men are the masters and the women are slaves and shows how this sexual inequality affects the mood and behavior of the people.
Prod-GARDNR Dist-PHENIX 1974

Rivers Of The Rockies C 16 MIN
16MM FILM, 3/4 OR 1/2 IN VIDEO I-H
Shows how high mountain rivers provide attractive habitats for a remarkable and diverse number of living creatures. Illustrates the dipper bird, harlequin duck and osprey, also known as the sea eagle, and mountain lions and mountain sheep as well.
From The Mountain Habitat Series.
Prod-KARVF Dist-BCNFL 1982

Rivers Of The Sea C 52 MIN
16MM FILM, 3/4 OR 1/2 IN VIDEO
Joins scientists working at sea and in land-based laboratories who are working on a large-scale oceanographic survey to gain knowledge vital to the prevention of ocean pollution, improved commercial fishing and better understanding of climatic conditions.
Prod-NSF Dist-USNAC 1981

Rivers, Floods And People C 11 MIN
16MM FILM, 3/4 OR 1/2 IN VIDEO J-H
Shows how fighting the flood has minimized losses and how wise use of the flood plain can let it serve both man and its natural purpose.
Prod-COUKLA Dist-AIMS 1973

Rivet Identification - (ITP Practical Project Series) C 17 MIN
3/4 OR 1/2 INCH VIDEO CASSETTE IND
Treats in entertaining manner the tedious and monotonous subject of aircraft rivet identification. Gives subject an interesting and attention-getting twist while providing a wealth of information about the most common aircraft fastener, the rivet.
From The Aviation Technician Training Program Series.
Prod-AVIMA Dist-AVIMA 1980

RL Circuit Analysis C
3/4 OR 1/2 INCH VIDEO CASSETTE
See series title for descriptive statement.
From The Basic Electricity - AC Series.
Prod-VTRI Dist-VTRI

RL Time Constants C
3/4 OR 1/2 INCH VIDEO CASSETTE
See series title for descriptive statement.
From The Basic AC Circuits Series.
Prod-VTRI Dist-VTRI

RL Time Constants C 20 MIN
3/4 OR 1/2 INCH VIDEO CASSETTE
See series title for descriptive statement.
From The Basic AC Circuits, Laboratory--Sessions--A Series.
Prod-TXINLC Dist-TXINLC

RL Transients B 13 MIN
16MM FILM, 3/4 OR 1/2 IN VIDEO
Determines the values of voltage and current at various time intervals in a series RL circuit with a DC voltage applied. Shows time constant chart. (Kinescope)
Prod-USAF Dist-USNAC

RL Transients And Waveshaping B 20 MIN
16MM FILM, 3/4 OR 1/2 IN VIDEO
Uses a series RL circuit with a DC voltage applied and a universal time constant chart to determine values of voltage and current at various time intervals. Defines time constants and draws output wave forms for RC and RL circuits. Illustrates integrated and differentiated wave forms.
Prod-USAF Dist-USNAC 1983

RLC Circuit Analysis C
3/4 OR 1/2 INCH VIDEO CASSETTE
See series title for descriptive statement.
From The Basic Electricity - AC Series.
Prod-VTRI Dist-VTRI

RM Connection, The C 24 MIN
16MM FILM OPTICAL SOUND
Tells how a chemical plant supervisor is annoyed by the extra work required to support a computerized reliability maintenance program until he realizes the system's value when two dangerous failures occur.
LC NO. 78-700214
Prod-UCC Dist-UCC Prodn-TIMMAR 1977

RM Fischer, An Industrial C 4 MIN
3/4 OR 1/2 INCH VIDEO CASSETTE
Spotlights R M Fisher's baroque futuristic lamp sculptres. Presented by Carole Ann Klonarides and Michael Owen.
Prod-ARTINC Dist-ARTINC

Road Ahead, The C 17 MIN
16MM FILM - 3/4 IN VIDEO H A
Presents the new or prospective civil service employee with information on performance requirements, within-grade increases, incentive awards, training and development, upward mobility and merit promotion.
From The Working For The United States Series.
LC NO. 77-706027
Prod-USCSC Dist-USNAC Prodn-LOUISP 1976

Road Ahead, The C 30 MIN
3/4 INCH VIDEO CASSETTE
Speculates about the future paths of Chinese society, politics, science, art and law. Summarizes the China After Mao Series.
From The China After Mao Series.
Prod-UMITV Dist-UMITV 1980

Road And The Wind, The - Destination Gold C 23 MIN
16MM FILM OPTICAL SOUND
Depicts a tour through California gold rush country on a motorcycle.
LC NO. 80-701375
Prod-USSUZ Dist-EJLAD Prodn-HANSED 1980

Road Back, The B 49 MIN
3/4 OR 1/2 INCH VIDEO CASSETTE
Follows Jim Blattie, boxer, as he struggled to save his life in the midst of drugs, alcohol and high stakes. Takes him through his own treatment and then to counseling youths at a residential drug center.
Prod-UCV Dist-UCV

Road From Montgomery, The B 30 MIN
16MM FILM OPTICAL SOUND H-C A
Dr Vincent Harding discusses the significance of the South in the

civil rights movement, traces the various trains of thought that evolved during this period and describes these attitudes as being typified by such terminology as legal defense, integration, unarmed direct action and armed self-defense.
From The Black History, Section 20 - Freedom Movement Series.
LC NO. 70-704105
Prod-WCBSTV Dist-HRAW 1969

Road In The Forest, A C 14 MIN
16MM FILM OPTICAL SOUND
Explores the challenge of building new roads that will have the least impact on the environment. Stresses design criteria which will provide service, safety, beauty, economy and harmony with the landscape.
LC NO. 76-703706
Prod-USDA Dist-USNAC 1974

Road Map B 24 MIN
16MM FILM OPTICAL SOUND I-J
Pictures the development of California's network of roads and highways from the rutted El Camino Real of mission days to the eight-lane super freeways of the 1960's. Traces the change in vehicles over the years and portrays the role played by Californians in state highway development programs.
Prod-ABCTV Dist-MLA 1963

Road Never Ends, The C 15 MIN
16MM FILM, 3/4 OR 1/2 IN VIDEO
Tells the story of a truckdriver as a man, a worker and as the head of a family. Follows him on a trip from his home factory in Massachusetts to a New York City pier to an Ohio plant and back. Includes comments by the trucker on his life and career, an explanation by his boss of his value to the firm and the trucker's wife's observations on the precarious state of their homelife and marriage.
Prod-ASDA Dist-TEXFLM 1976

Road Signs On A Merry-Go-Round C 57 MIN
16MM FILM, 3/4 OR 1/2 IN VIDEO H-C A
Discusses man's search for self, communion with his brother, and relationship with nature and God. Based on the writings of Martin Buber, Pierre Teilhard de Chardin, and Dietrich Bonhoeffer.
Prod-CBSNEW Dist-CAROUF

Road Talk C 10 MIN
16MM FILM OPTICAL SOUND
Examines road talk, the language drivers use to communicate whenever they're behind the wheel.
Prod-GM Dist-GM

Road To Appomattox C 30 MIN
3/4 OR 1/2 INCH VIDEO CASSETTE C
See series title for descriptive statement.
From The American Story - The Beginning To 1877 Series.
Prod-DALCCD Dist-DALCCD

Road To Berlin C 30 MIN
3/4 OR 1/2 INCH VIDEO CASSETTE H-C A
See series title for descriptive statement.
From The World War II - GI Diary Series.
Prod-TIMLIF Dist-TIMLIF 1980

Road To Berlin, The C 20 MIN
16MM FILM, 3/4 OR 1/2 IN VIDEO H-C A
Covers the major events in the European theater of war between 1943 and 1945.
From The Twentieth Century History Series.
Prod-BBCTV Dist-FI 1981

Road To Charlie, The C 11 MIN
16MM FILM, 3/4 OR 1/2 IN VIDEO J-C A
Uses animation to tell how many different people demand things of Charlie but how not one of them cares about what Charlie wants.
Prod-FLMAUS Dist-WOMBAT

Road To Disaster, The C 30 MIN
3/4 OR 1/2 INCH VIDEO CASSETTE H-C A
See series title for descriptive statement.
From The Japan - The Changing Tradition Series.
Prod-UMA Dist-GPITVL 1978

Road To Emancipation B 30 MIN
16MM FILM OPTICAL SOUND H-C A
Professor E A Toppin discusses the role of blacks in the Civil War, explaining why they fought for both the Union and Confederate forces, and analyzes Abraham Lincoln's policies leading to the Emancipation Proclamation.
From The Black History, Section 08 - Civil War, Afro-Americans Series.
LC NO. 72-704056
Prod-WCBSTV Dist-HRAW 1969

Road To Energy, USA, The C 29 MIN
16MM FILM OPTICAL SOUND
Presents the people whose efforts help supply and conserve energy in the United States. Features Bob Hope.
Prod-TEXACO Dist-MTP

Road To Gettysburg, The - Civil War, Pt 1, 1861-1863 X 24 MIN
16MM FILM OPTICAL SOUND I-C A
Reviews the early part of the Civil War, depicting the Battle of Bull Run, the Monitor and the Merrimac, the Emancipation Proclamation, the telegraph and the railroads. Discusses leading men, such as Jackson, Lee, Grant, Mc Clellan and Farragut.
From The Exploring - The Story Of America, Set 2 Series.
LC NO. FIA68-1057
Prod-NBCTV Dist-GRACUR 1968

Road To Happiness C 59 MIN
16MM FILM, 3/4 OR 1/2 IN VIDEO H-C A
Uses archival footage to explore the life and work of Henry Ford.
From The Nova Series.
Prod-WGBHTV Dist-FI 1978

Road To Interdependence, The C 30 MIN
16MM FILM, 3/4 OR 1/2 IN VIDEO J-H
Follows the development of U S foreign policy from 1945 up to the mid-1970's. Describes the onset of the nuclear age and the cold war and underlines the growing significance of our relations with the Third World. Uses documentary footage.
From The History Of U S Foreign Relations Series.
Prod-USDS Dist-MTI 1976

Road To Liberty, The C 65 MIN
16MM FILM, 3/4 OR 1/2 IN VIDEO A
Portrays the new society being created in El Salvador in the third of the country controlled by the Farabundo Marti National Liberation Front.
Prod-FIRES Dist-CNEMAG 1984

Road To Mandalay, The B 27 MIN
16MM FILM, 3/4 OR 1/2 IN VIDEO J-H
Views highlights of the China, Burma, India and the Indian Ocean campaigns during World II.
From The Victory At Sea Series.
Prod-NBCTV Dist-LUF

Road To Mandalay, The - China, Burma, India, And Indian Ocean B 30 MIN
16MM FILM OPTICAL SOUND I-C
Follows the war in Asia, as the Japanese capture Shangai, Hankow and Nanking and the Chinese nationalists flee to Chungking. Explains the significance of the closing of the Burma road. Describes the fall of Mandalay, the arrival of British troops and eventual allied victory.
From The Victory At Sea Series.
Prod-GRACUR Dist-GRACUR

Road To Peace B 9 MIN
16MM FILM OPTICAL SOUND
Explains that the people of the East stand at a crossroads with one of two paths to follow, peace or war, and that the road to peace lies in the program of the United Nations.
LC NO. FIE52-1937
Prod-USA Dist-USNAC 1951

Road To Progress, The C 5 MIN
16MM FILM OPTICAL SOUND
Tells the story of those people in desperate need of both food and the means to grow their own food. Suggests the need for water that is fit to drink, adequate medical care, education and economic development to increase family incomes that are often less than $200 a year.
Prod-CARE Dist-CARE

Road To Progress, The C 20 MIN
16MM FILM OPTICAL SOUND
A combined version of four shorter films, Road To Progress, Food Or Famine, Water Means Life and Medical Aid. Tells the story of those people in desperate need of both food and the means to grow their own food. Suggests the need for water that is fit to drink, adequate medical care, education and economic development to increase family incomes that are often less than $200 a year.
Prod-CARE Dist-CARE

Road To Recovery, The C 21 MIN
16MM FILM OPTICAL SOUND
Shows how C and P Telephone Company repair personnel responded to a flood in West Virginia which wiped out all communications. Points out that lines were restored and a new office established within six days.
LC NO. 78-700382
Prod-CPTEL Dist-CPTEL 1977

Road To Revolution C 30 MIN
3/4 OR 1/2 INCH VIDEO CASSETTE C
See series title for descriptive statement.
From The American Story - The Beginning To 1877 Series.
Prod-DALCCD Dist-DALCCD

Road To Santiago C 52 MIN
16MM FILM, 3/4 OR 1/2 IN VIDEO H-C A
Describes the journey of three young Britons who walk the ancient symbolic four-week pilgrimage from Jaca in the Pyrenees to Santiago de Compostela through the Spanish countryside. In a medieval spirit, they stay at inns or monasteries relying on the Codex Calixtinus, the pilgrim guide from the twelfth century.
Prod-THAMES Dist-MEDIAG 1973

Road To Santiago - France C 30 MIN
16MM FILM, 3/4 OR 1/2 IN VIDEO H-C
Describes the road traveled by 12th century pilgrims through France on their way to the Shrine of St James the Greater at Santiago de Compostela. Explores the four roads through France and includes examples of art and architecture.
Prod-KIRBY Dist-IFB 1968

Road To Santiago - Spain C 21 MIN
16MM FILM, 3/4 OR 1/2 IN VIDEO H-C
Describes the road taken by 12th century pilgrims as they travelled through Spain to the Shrine of St James the Greater at Santiago de Compostela.
Prod-KIRBY Dist-IFB 1968

Road To Success, The C 15 MIN
16MM FILM OPTICAL SOUND
Shows methods of building wooden roads in Nova Scotia.
LC NO. 76-702050
Prod-NSFPA Dist-NSFPA Prodn-NSDLF 1975

Road To The Wall B 29 MIN
16MM FILM - 3/4 IN VIDEO
Documents the rise of communism, from the early days of Lenin and Trotsky to Berlin and Cuba under the influence of Krushchev. Issued in 1963 as a motion picture.
From The Big Picture Series.
LC NO. 79-706482
Prod-USA Dist-USNAC 1979

Road To The White House, Pt 1 C 29 MIN
16MM FILM OPTICAL SOUND H-C
Discusses how candidates for the office of President of the United States are created and developed. Explains the role of state primaries and describes the strategies employed by candidates at the national nominating conventions.
From The Government Story Series. No. 21
LC NO. 75-707194
Prod-OGCW Dist-WBCPRO 1968

Road To The White House, Pt 2 C 29 MIN
16MM FILM OPTICAL SOUND H-C
Describes the campaign for the presidency from the nominating conventions to the White House. Discusses campaign strategies and the problems of the electoral college system.
From The Government Story Series. No. 22
LC NO. 79-707195
Prod-OGCW Dist-WBCPRO 1968

Road To Total War, The C 60 MIN
16MM FILM, 3/4 OR 1/2 IN VIDEO C A
Charts how the major social, economic and technological developments of the last two centuries have changed warfare to the point of being able to destroy totally. Covers 200 year of world military history with anecdotes from past wars.
From The War Series.
Prod-NFBC Dist-FI

Road To Wigan Pier, The C 52 MIN
16MM FILM, 3/4 OR 1/2 IN VIDEO H-C A
Presents a musical documentary about the British working class based on a 1936 book by George Orwell. It opened the eyes of the world to a scene of appalling human suffering and degradation, slum housing and unemployment. Contrasts modern conditions with life in the thirties.
Prod-THAMES Dist-MEDIAG 1973

Road To World War I, The C 29 MIN
2 INCH VIDEOTAPE
See series title for descriptive statement.
From The Course Of Our Times I Series.
Prod-WGBHTV Dist-PUBTEL

Road To World War II, The C 29 MIN
2 INCH VIDEOTAPE
See series title for descriptive statement.
From The Course Of Our Times I Series.
Prod-WGBHTV Dist-PUBTEL

Road To 1984, The - A Biography Of George Orwell C
1/2 IN VIDEO CASSETTE BETA/VHS
Presents James Fox starring in the story of the true-life experiences that led to Orwell's vision of 'Big Brother'.
Prod-GA Dist-GA

Road-Eo C 22 MIN
16MM FILM OPTICAL SOUND
Shows how a truck road-eo, or a demonstration and test of skillful driving of large trucks, is conducted. Shows how road-eos contribute to safe driving attitudes and procedures.
LC NO. 75-700476
Prod-APATC Dist-APATC Prodn-THOMB 1974

Road, The B 28 MIN
16MM FILM, 3/4 OR 1/2 IN VIDEO H-C A
Looks at the Frontier Nursing Service in Appalachia.
Prod-FNSI Dist-CAROUF

Roadblock, The C 6 MIN
16MM FILM, 3/4 OR 1/2 IN VIDEO PRO
Discusses the problem of dealing with an elder employee of the company who's lost interest in new ideas, resists changes of any kind, is not performing up to par and is a roadblock to the younger men in the department.
From The This Matter Of Motivation Series.
Prod-CTRACT Dist-DARTNL Prodn-CALVIN 1971

Roadblocks To Communication B 30 MIN
16MM FILM OPTICAL SOUND H-C A
Distinguishes between disagreements and misunderstandings. Explores the concept of 'feedback' as one of the ways to improve communication. Explains the use of watchdog, reaction and audience panels.
From The Dynamics Of Leadership Series.
Prod-NET Dist-IU Prodn-WGBHTV 1963

Roadbuilders, The C 20 MIN
16MM FILM, 3/4 OR 1/2 IN VIDEO IND
Tells a story that demonstrates the different safety precautions that must be observed by roadbuilding crews.
Prod-CSAO Dist-IFB

Roadmap For Change - The Deming Approach C 29 MIN
16MM FILM, 3/4 OR 1/2 IN VIDEO C A
Uses a case study to examine how Dr W Edwards D Deming's fourteen obligations of management are being implemented at the Pontiac Motor Division of General Motors and shows the reactions of managers and employees to the Deming approach.
Prod-EBEC Dist-EBEC 1984

Roadmap To Control, The C 17 MIN
3/4 OR 1/2 INCH VIDEO CASSETTE
Tells what diabetes is, how insufficient insulin affects various body functions, and stresses the importance of good general health habits.

From The Understanding Diabetes Series.
Prod-FAIRGH Dist-FAIRGH

Roadmap To Less Effort - The Flow Process Chart B 15 MIN
16MM FILM, 3/4 OR 1/2 IN VIDEO
Illustrates the use, preparation and analysis of the flow process chart, a device for the solution of work efficiency problems. Shows that an analysis of the chart enables actions to be eliminated, combined, changed or reassigned.
LC NO. 81-707137
Prod-USA Dist-USNAC 1973

Roads Across The Bay B 24 MIN
16MM FILM OPTICAL SOUND I-J
Traces the history behind the building of the great bridges of San Francisco Bay, showing the need for bridges, proposals made over the years and the actual construction of the Bay Bridge.
Prod-ABCTV Dist-MLA 1963

Roads, Roads, Roads C 27 MIN
16MM FILM OPTICAL SOUND H-C A
Provides information on transport policy and strategy in the Federal Republic of Germany, the funding of road construction and maintenance, and the growing understanding of the impact this is having on the environment.
Prod-WSTGLC Dist-WSTGLC

Roald Amundsen C 30 MIN
16MM FILM, 3/4 OR 1/2 IN VIDEO
A shortened version of the 1976 film Roald Amundsen. Dramatizes Amundsen's victory over England's Captain Robert Smith in their 1911 race to the South Pole, the last terrestrial frontier.
From The Ten Who Dared Series.
LC NO. 79-707390
Prod-BBCTV Dist-TIMLIF 1976

Roald Amundsen C 52 MIN
16MM FILM, 3/4 OR 1/2 IN VIDEO
Dramatizes Roald Amundsen's victory over England's Captain Robert Smith in their 1911 race to the South Pole, the last terrestrial frontier.
From The Ten Who Dared Series.
LC NO. 79-707389
Prod-BBCTV Dist-TIMLIF 1976

Roald Amundsen - South Pole, 1911, Pt 1 C 26 MIN
16MM FILM OPTICAL SOUND I A
Special classroom version of the film and videorecording Roald Amundsen - South Pole, 1911.
From The Ten Who Dared Series.
Prod-BBCTV Dist-TIMLIF 1977

Roald Amundsen - South Pole, 1911, Pt 2 C 26 MIN
16MM FILM OPTICAL SOUND I A
Special classroom version of the film and videorecording Roald Amundsen - South Pole, 1911.
From The Ten Who Dared Series.
Prod-BBCTV Dist-TIMLIF 1977

Roald Hoffmann C
3/4 OR 1/2 INCH VIDEO CASSETTE
Reflects on some of the key accomplishments of Dr Roald Hoffmann, including his work on quantum mechanical studies of chemical reactivity.
From The Eminent Chemists - The Interviews Series.
Prod-AMCHEM Dist-AMCHEM 1984

Roald Hoffmann, Lecture 1 - The Isolobal Analogy C
3/4 OR 1/2 INCH VIDEO CASSETTE
Discusses the bridge between inorganic and organic chemistry by Dr Roald Hoffmann.
From The Eminent Chemists - The Lectures Series.
Prod-AMCHEM Dist-AMCHEM

Roald Hoffmann, Lecture 2 - Conservation Of Orbital Symmetry C
3/4 OR 1/2 INCH VIDEO CASSETTE
Features Dr Roald Hoffman in a personal, historical perspective on the development of conservation of orbital symmetry concept and its consequences.
From The Eminent Chemists - The Lectures Series.
Prod-AMCHEM Dist-AMCHEM

Roamin' Holiday B 11 MIN
16MM FILM OPTICAL SOUND
Tells how Spanky and the gang leave home in order to avoid babysitting chores. A Little Rascals film.
Prod-UNKNWN Dist-BHAWK 1937

Roamin' I C 15 MIN
3/4 INCH VIDEO CASSETTE
Presents documentary scenes, shot during the production of the filmdance 'locale,' as well as outtakes from the film itself.
Prod-CUNDAN Dist-CUNDAN

Roar Of Power C 15 MIN
16MM FILM OPTICAL SOUND
Presents the how and why of tractor pulling contests.
Prod-ALLISC Dist-IDEALF

Roar Of The Gods, The C 20 MIN
16MM FILM, 3/4 OR 1/2 IN VIDEO J-C A
Examines various pre-Colombian stone monoliths found in the area of San Agustin, Colombia and explains their anthropological meaning.
LC NO. 82-707010
Prod-MOMALA Dist-MOMALA

Roar Of The Gods, The (Spanish) C 20 MIN
3/4 OR 1/2 INCH VIDEO CASSETTE J-C A
Examines various pre-Colombian stone monoliths found in the area of San Agustin, Colombia, and explains their anthropological meaning.
Prod-MOMALA Dist-MOMALA

Roaring Silence, The C 24 MIN
16MM FILM OPTICAL SOUND
Explains that the Buddhist spiritual experience of Nirvana is often referred to as a roaring silence and seen as evidence of the essentially incommunicable nature of the religion. Documents the spiritual and secular life of the Buddhist monastery of Tangboche in Nepal.
Prod-BBCTV Dist-OPENU 1979

Roaring Silence, The C 24 MIN
16MM FILM, 3/4 OR 1/2 IN VIDEO
Explains that the Buddhist spiritual experience of Nirvana is often referred to as a roaring silence and seen as evidence of the essentially incommunicable nature of the religion. Documents the spiritual and secular life of the Buddhist monastery of Tangboche in Nepal.
Prod-OPENU Dist-MEDIAG Prodn-BBCTV 1979

Roaring Twenties, The C 30 MIN
2 INCH VIDEOTAPE
Views the Twenties as both the age of disillusionment and the age of wonderful nonsense.
From The American History II Series.
Prod-KRMATV Dist-GPITVL

Roasting C 10 MIN
16MM FILM, 3/4 OR 1/2 IN VIDEO J-C A
Demonstrates a basic cooking method to show procedures to assure perfect roasting results. Shows use of racks, pans, thermometer and ovens in preparation of beef roasts and turkey. Includes pros and cons of high temperature searing. Stresses that low temperatures cause minimum shrinkage.
From The Professional Food Preparation And Service Program Series.
LC NO. 74-700407
Prod-NEM Dist-NEM 1972

Rob B 30 MIN
2 INCH VIDEOTAPE
Presents an interview with a 16-year-old boy who is having academic and behavioral difficulties in school.
From The Counseling The Adolescent Series.
Prod-GPITVL Dist-GPITVL

Rob McLachlan C
3/4 OR 1/2 INCH VIDEO CASSETTE
Portrays Rob McLachlan, British Columbian filmmaker with interviews and film clips.
From The Filmmakers' Showcase Series.
Prod-CANFDW Dist-CANFDW

Robber's Guide, The C 5 MIN
3/4 OR 1/2 INCH VIDEO CASSETTE J-H
Consists of a lesson on correlative conjunctions.
From The Write On, Set 1 Series.
Prod-CTI Dist-CTI

Robbers, Rooftops And Witches C 46 MIN
16MM FILM, 3/4 OR 1/2 IN VIDEO I-H
Discusses various aspects of story telling and writing using excerpts from The Chaparral Prince by O Henry, Antaeus by Borden Deal and The Invisible Boy by Ray Bradbury. Includes interviews with an actor portraying writer Washington Irving.
From The LCA Short Story Library Series.
LC NO. 82-707256
Prod-HGATE Dist-LCOA 1982

Robbery, The B 19 MIN
16MM FILM OPTICAL SOUND C
Deals with various aspects of a criminal lawsuit involving a liquor store robbery case. Shows the robbery by an adult and a juvenile offender.
From The Criminal Law Series. No. 1
LC NO. 79-714033
Prod-RPATLF Dist-RPATLF 1968

Robbie - A Teenage Quadriplegic C 30 MIN
3/4 OR 1/2 INCH VIDEO CASSETTE
Presents the story of a 17-year-old quadriplegic. Shares his intimate thoughts, wishes, struggles and hopes. Provides a courageous story of a grave disability.
Prod-MONTV Dist-AJN

Robe, The C 133 MIN
1/2 IN VIDEO CASSETTE (BETA)
Tells the story of a Greek slave and a Roman officer who are affected by Christianity. Stars Richard Burton, Jean Simmons and Victor Mature.
Prod-UNKNWN Dist-BHAWK 1953

Robert C 23 MIN
3/4 INCH VIDEO CASSETTE H-C A
Tells how a successful young man must choose between his invalid mother and his anxious fiancee, who wants him to accept a lucrative job offer in another city.
From The Handle With Care Series.
Prod-CHERIO Dist-GPITVL

Robert A Taft B 51 MIN
16MM FILM, 3/4 OR 1/2 IN VIDEO I-H
Describes the activities of Robert A Taft with regard to international law. Based on book Profiles In Courage by John F Kennedy. Stars Lee Tracy.
From The Profiles In Courage Series.
LC NO. 83-706544
Prod-SAUDEK Dist-SSSSV 1965

Robert A Taft - Mr Republican B 15 MIN
1/2 IN VIDEO CASSETTE BETA/VHS
Presents Robert A Taft, a leader of the Republican party.
Prod-STAR Dist-STAR

Robert And Elizabeth Browning C 30 MIN
3/4 INCH VIDEO CASSETTE H-C A
Examines the poetry of Robert and Elizabeth Browning.
From The Anyone For Tennyson Series.
Prod-NETCHE Dist-GPITVL

Robert Bly C 29 MIN
3/4 INCH VIDEO CASSETTE
See series title for descriptive statement.
From The Poets Talking Series.
Prod-UMITV Dist-UMITV 1975

Robert Browning - His Life And Poetry C 21 MIN
16MM FILM, 3/4 OR 1/2 IN VIDEO H-C
Examines the life and work of Victorian poet Robert Browning.
Prod-ARMADA Dist-IFB 1972

Robert Burns Cigars C 1 MIN
3/4 OR 1/2 INCH VIDEO CASSETTE
Shows a classic television commercial where memories make a man smoke Burns cigars.
Prod-BROOKC Dist-BROOKC

Robert Clark - An American Realist C 19 MIN
16MM FILM, 3/4 OR 1/2 IN VIDEO
Presents a study of the American landscape painter, Robert Clark, showing his paintings and the real scenes they depict. Shows him discussing his artistic style and philosophy and demonstrating egg tempera techniques.
Prod-TAYLWF Dist-UCEMC 1974

Robert Clary - A5174, A Memoir Of Liberation C 57 MIN
1/2 IN VIDEO CASSETTE (VHS)
Provides an autobiographical account of actor Robert Clary's capture, imprisonment and liberation from a German concentration camp.
Prod-OHC Dist-HRC

Robert Duncan C 29 MIN
16MM FILM, 3/4 OR 1/2 IN VIDEO
Provides a look at the life and work of American poet Robert Duncan.
From The Writer In America Series.
Prod-PERSPF Dist-CORF

Robert E Lee B 20 MIN
2 INCH VIDEOTAPE I
See series title for descriptive statement.
From The Americans All Series.
Prod-DENVPS Dist-GPITVL Prodn-KRMATV

Robert E Lee - A Background Study C 16 MIN
16MM FILM, 3/4 OR 1/2 IN VIDEO J-C A
Traces the life of Robert E Lee and analyzes the reasons for his decision to lead the army of the Confederacy. Includes an explanation of his battle strategy and photographs of his birthplace, of his home overlooking the Potomac river, of the countryside which he knew as a youth and of his personal effects.
Prod-CORF Dist-CORF 1953

Robert Farber C 60 MIN
3/4 OR 1/2 INCH VIDEO CASSETTE
Shows top New York photographer, Robert Farber, in behind-the-scenes view of fashion and fine art photography.
From The Famous Photographer Series.
Prod-SHERVP Dist-SHERVP

Robert Frost C 10 MIN
16MM FILM, 3/4 OR 1/2 IN VIDEO I-H
Presents a biography of Robert Frost, followed by a reading of his poem 'MENDING WALL,' by Leonard Nimoy.
From The Poetry By Americans Series.
Prod-EVANSA Dist-AIMS 1972

Robert Frost - A First Acquaintance C 16 MIN
16MM FILM, 3/4 OR 1/2 IN VIDEO I-H
Explores American poet Robert Frost's relationship with children. Shows the poet's daughter, Lesley Frost, at the Frost farm in New Hampshire, where neighboring children interpret the action of Frost's poems at the farm spot which inspired the poet to write them.
Prod-MANTLH Dist-FOTH 1974

Robert Frost - A Lover's Quarrel With The World B 52 MIN
16MM FILM OPTICAL SOUND
Presents two views of the poet Robert Frost--his public performance and his private thoughts. Shows Frost at Sarah Lawrence College with a large appreciative crowd, at Amherst with a more awkward, intimate group and alone at his home in Ripton, Vermont.
LC NO. FIA67-1098
Prod-WGBH Dist-HRAW 1963

Robert Frost - A Sampling B 30 MIN
2 INCH VIDEOTAPE J-H
From The Franklin To Frost Series.
Prod-GPITVL Dist-GPITVL

Robert Frost - Fact, Form, Process And Meaning B 30 MIN
2 INCH VIDEOTAPE J-H
From The Franklin To Frost Series.
Prod-GPITVL Dist-GPITVL

Robert Frost - Perspectives B 30 MIN
2 INCH VIDEOTAPE J-H
From The Franklin To Frost Series.
Prod-GPITVL Dist-GPITVL

Robert Frost - Simplicity And Complexity B 30 MIN
2 INCH VIDEOTAPE J-H
From The Franklin To Frost Series.
Prod-GPITVL Dist-GPITVL

Robert Frost's New England C 22 MIN
16MM FILM, 3/4 OR 1/2 IN VIDEO J-C A

Presents a selection of Frost's poetry relating to New England and its seasons. Describes how he uses the rocks, leaves and snows of Vermont as metaphors to lead the reader into deeper reaches of the mind.
Prod-JONESD Dist-CF 1976

Robert Frost's The Death Of The Hired Man C 22 MIN
16MM FILM, 3/4 OR 1/2 IN VIDEO J-C A
Dramatizes Robert Frost's poem The Death Of The Hired Man.
From The Humanities - Poetry Series.
Prod-EBEC Dist-EBEC

Robert Fulton C 15 MIN
3/4 OR 1/2 INCH VIDEO CASSETTE P
Illustrates how Robert Fulton developed his early interest in painting and boats.
From The Stories Of America Series.
Prod-OHSDE Dist-AITECH Prodn-WVIZTV 1976

Robert Hall Commercial C 1 MIN
3/4 OR 1/2 INCH VIDEO CASSETTE
Shows a classic television commercial with blackbirds singing.
Prod-BROOKC Dist-BROOKC

Robert Hayden C 29 MIN
3/4 INCH VIDEO CASSETTE
See series title for descriptive statement.
From The Poets Talking Series.
Prod-UMITV Dist-UMITV 1975

Robert MacGregor, PhD, Mary MacGregor, MPsych - Single Parent Struggle C 60 MIN
3/4 OR 1/2 INCH VIDEO CASSETTE PRO
Demonstrates the multiple impact approach to therapy for a single parent family. Shows the effect of a series of interviews with the whole family and with parent and children separately.
From The Perceptions, Pt A - Interventions In Family Therapy Series. Vol IV, Pt A7.
Prod-BOSFAM Dist-BOSFAM

Robert MacGregor, PhD, Mary MacGregor, 1 MPsych - Private Practice, Chicago C 60 MIN
3/4 OR 1/2 INCH VIDEO CASSETTE PRO
Stimulates discussion about working couples and the Multiple Impact Therapy espoused by the MacGregors.
From The Perceptions, Pt B - Dialogues With Family Therapists Series. Vol IV, Pt B7.
Prod-BOSFAM Dist-BOSFAM

Robert Mc Closkey X 18 MIN
16MM FILM, 3/4 OR 1/2 IN VIDEO C A
Robert Mc Closkey, who draws picture books, tells how he works, showing not only his craftsmanship but also how he gets his inspiration.
Prod-WWS Dist-WWS 1965

Robert Morris - Exchange B 32 MIN
3/4 OR 1/2 INCH VIDEO CASSETTE
Represents a response to Lynda Benglis' videotape Mumble. Speculates about work, travel and relationships.
Prod-ARTINC Dist-ARTINC

Robert P Soup Anderson For Anderson Pea Soup C 1 MIN
3/4 OR 1/2 INCH VIDEO CASSETTE
Shows a classic animated television commercial.
Prod-BROOKC Dist-BROOKC

Robert Reed And Phyllis Mark C 29 MIN
3/4 INCH VIDEO CASSETTE
Focuses on painter Robert Reed and sculptor Phyllis Mark who exhibit and describe their work.
From The Art Show Series.
Prod-UMITV Dist-UMITV

Robert Taft B 26 MIN
16MM FILM, 3/4 OR 1/2 IN VIDEO I-C A
Uses rare actuality footage to portray the personal life and history-making deeds of Robert Taft.
From The History Makers Of The 20th Century Series.
Prod-WOLPER Dist-SF 1966

Robert Taft (January 7, 1951) B 28 MIN
16MM FILM OPTICAL SOUND
U S Senator Robert Taft of Ohio, discusses nationalism with Martha Rountree, moderator, Ned Brooks, Marshall Mc Neil, James Reston and Lawrence Spivak.
From The Meet The Press Series.
LC NO. FI68-561
Prod-NBCTV Dist-NBC 1951

Robert Wall - Ex FBI Agent B 28 MIN
16MM FILM OPTICAL SOUND H-C A
Tells how Robert Wall, an idealistic FBI agent, underwent a crisis of conscience as a result of the Vietnamese war and resigned from the bureau. Shows how he was then subject to wiretapping and spying.
Prod-NYFLMS Dist-NYFLMS

Robert, Suzanne, Et La Boite De Carton C 15 MIN
16MM FILM OPTICAL SOUND P-I
A French language version of Tommie, Suzie And The Cardboard Box. Uses three stories about a young boy and girl and their cardboard box to illustrate story structure.
From The Creative Writing Skills Series.
LC NO. 74-703611
Prod-MORLAT Dist-MORLAT 1973

Robert's Second Chance C 30 MIN
3/4 INCH VIDEO CASSETTE
Introduces a boy who has a hearing impairment, but wants a career in baseball. Shows how he meets a magical creature who points out the successes of other disabled people.
From The Knan Du Series.

LC NO. 78-706322
Prod-USOE Dist-USNAC Prodn-KRLNTV 1978

Robin - A Runaway C 32 MIN
16MM FILM, 3/4 OR 1/2 IN VIDEO J-C A
Uses flashbacks to show why Robin, a 14-year-old, ran away from home.
Prod-VITASC Dist-FLMFR

Robin Hood Junior C 62 MIN
16MM FILM OPTICAL SOUND P-I
Presents what happens when a Norman baron usurps Locksay Castle in 12th century England and the daughter of the rightful heir escapes to the forest. Reveals that the village children will be held hostage by the baron unless she surrenders and shows how Robin saves them all.
Prod-LUF Dist-LUF 1977

Robin Hood With Mr Magoo C 105 MIN
16MM FILM OPTICAL SOUND P-I
Prod-FI Dist-FI

Robin Redbreast (2nd Ed) X 11 MIN
16MM FILM, 3/4 OR 1/2 IN VIDEO P-I
The story of a robin family from the time the parents build their nest until the baby robins are old enough to take care of themselves.
Prod-EBF Dist-EBEC 1957

Robins And Rainbows B 15 MIN
2 INCH VIDEOTAPE P
See series title for descriptive statement.
From The Children's Literature Series. No. 23
Prod-NCET Dist-GPITVL Prodn-KUONTV

Robinson C 30 MIN
16MM FILM OPTICAL SOUND
Shows the adventures and preparation of Jacky and Hermine who live in southwestern France on the Bay of Biscay, as they experience 'ROBINSON CRUSOE.'
Prod-BEAUVA Dist-RADIM

Robinson Jeffers B 30 MIN
16MM FILM OPTICAL SOUND H-C A
An introduction to the poetry, philosophy and environment of Robinson Jeffers. Novelist Walter Clark and Dame Judith Anderson assess the poet and his works. Dame Anderson presents a passage from Jeffers' 'THE POWER BEYOND TRAGEDY.' Matches recordings of the poems made by Jeffers in 1941 with scenes illustrating the poems.
From The Creative Person Series.
Prod-NET Dist-IU 1967

Robinson-Turpin B 30 MIN
16MM FILM OPTICAL SOUND
From The IBC Championship Fights, Series 2 Series.
Prod-SFI Dist-SFI

Robinson, Wilhelmena C 29 MIN
3/4 INCH VIDEO CASSETTE
Discusses Black female leaders involved in the struggle for equal rights.
From The Like It Is Series.
Prod-OHC Dist-HRC

Robinson's Place (French) B 38 MIN
16MM FILM OPTICAL SOUND
Features one of two short stories combined in the film, Bad Company. Tells of two petty con-artists who cruise the boulevards of Paris in search of girls.
Prod-NYFLMS Dist-NYFLMS 1966

Robot (Japanese) C 27 MIN
16MM FILM OPTICAL SOUND
Explains that about 200 years ago, a Japanese man wrote a book about a mechanical doll. Shows how Professor Tachikawa of Kitazato University made a doll which could serve tea. Points out that an artificial hand called a 'WASEDA-HAND' has been improved at Waseda University, which can grasp a paper glass of water. Emphasizes that improvement in robotizing, leads mechanical engineering and industry towards a highly mechanized civilization.
Prod-IWANMI Dist-UNIJAP 1970

Robot Dynamics And Control C 270 MIN
3/4 OR 1/2 INCH VIDEO CASSETTE PRO
Emphasizes various dynamic methods for control of general purpose robotic manipulators. Examines different strategies for accomplishing accurate robot arm control. Includes coarse and finite sensing.
Prod-AMCEE Dist-AMCEE

Robot Moles, The C 15 MIN
16MM FILM OPTICAL SOUND
Features a girl named Hanaka, who thinks of a mole to cultivate beautiful flowers all over the land. Pictures some laboratory men taking over her project.
Prod-GAKKEN Dist-UNIJAP 1970

Robot Revolution, The C 14 MIN
3/4 OR 1/2 INCH VIDEO CASSETTE H
Documents the growing importance and significance of robots in speeding up production and relieving workers of tedious and dangerous jobs on assembly lines.
From The Screen News Digest Series.
Prod-HEARST Dist-HEARST 1981

Robot Revolution, The C 19 MIN
16MM FILM, 3/4 OR 1/2 IN VIDEO J
Shows that civilization is fast becoming the driving force behind a new technological revolution.
LC NO. 83-707267
Prod-EBEC Dist-EBEC 1984

Robot Revolution, The C 26 MIN
3/4 OR 1/2 INCH VIDEO CASSETTE
Explores the robot world, how they are used today, their history, how they might be used tomorrow and how we have come to accept and sometimes love them.
Prod-JOU Dist-JOU

Robot Revolution, The C 58 MIN
3/4 OR 1/2 INCH VIDEO CASSETTE H-C A
Shows how American manufacturers are turning to computers and robots to increase productivity. Explores the workplace of the future and the role of advanced automation in altering the way people work. Originally a NOVA television program.
From The Nova Series.
Prod-WGBHTV Dist-CORF 1985

Robot Safety At Caterpillar C 12 MIN
3/4 OR 1/2 INCH VIDEO CASSETTE
Demonstrates the hazardous elements present in most robotic systems. Points out safety devices and procedures necessary to protect workers.
Prod-CTRACT Dist-SME

Robotics C 30 MIN
3/4 OR 1/2 INCH VIDEO CASSETTE
Explores the potentials and limitations of artificial intelligence and the more exotic applications of robatic technology.
From The Innovation Series.
Prod-WNETTV Dist-WNETTV 1983

Robotics C 41 MIN
3/4 OR 1/2 INCH VIDEO CASSETTE
Presents the topic of robotics to a general audience requiring no previous knowledge. Show how robotics is dependent on various engineering disciplines.
Prod-FLMWST Dist-FLMWST

Robotics - Isaac Asimov's Artificial Man C 20 MIN
16MM FILM, 3/4 OR 1/2 IN VIDEO
Features Isaac Asimov discussing robot technology.
Prod-DOCUA Dist-CNEMAG

Robotics - Research And Business Opportunities C 300 MIN
3/4 OR 1/2 INCH VIDEO CASSETTE PRO
Pinpoints current and future robot applications, tradeoffs, basics of control, vision and tonch sensing, programming, human interfacing and economic considerations.
Prod-AMCEE Dist-AMCEE

Robots - Intelligent Machines Serving Mankind C 13 MIN
16MM FILM OPTICAL SOUND
Tells how intelligent machines are taking over more and more jobs performed by human workers.
Prod-ALLFP Dist-NSTA

Robots Get Smarter C 29 MIN
2 INCH VIDEOTAPE
See series title for descriptive statement.
From The Interface Series.
Prod-KCET Dist-PUBTEL

Robots Get Smarter C 30 MIN
16MM FILM, 3/4 OR 1/2 IN VIDEO
Features three robots under development at Stanford Research Institute.
Prod-UCEMC Dist-UCEMC

Robots 6 - Tomorrow's Technology On Display C 30 MIN
3/4 OR 1/2 INCH VIDEO CASSETTE
Gives an update on the state-of-the-art industrial robot capabilities, demonstrates laser and video sensing equipment, examines many recently introduced robot systems and explores small robots designed specifically for training and educational purposes.
Prod-SME Dist-SME

Rocco's Star C 27 MIN
16MM FILM, 3/4 OR 1/2 IN VIDEO J-H A
Describes the conflict which ensues when a young man tells his father that he wants to pursue a career as a singer. Shows that out of this tension, both grow to be better men. Stars Billy Hufsey and Al Ruscio.
Prod-PAULST Dist-PAULST 1984

Rochester Philharmonic Orchestra - Unlikely Sources Of Symphonic Music B 60 MIN
2 INCH VIDEOTAPE
Presents the words of Dr Samuel Jones of the Rochester Philharmonic, and uses the music of the orchestra to demonstrate some unlikely sources of symphonic music.
From The Synergism - Command Performance Series.
Prod-WXXITV Dist-PUBTEL

Rock - The Beat Goes On C 20 MIN
16MM FILM, 3/4 OR 1/2 IN VIDEO I-H
Presents an historical review of rock 'n roll, exploring the musical styles of major performers and speculating on the future directions rock will take. Includes historical clips of famous stars, such as the Beatles and Elvis Presley.
From The Wide World Of Adventure Series.
Prod-AVATLI Dist-EBEC 1979

Rock - Tilt With A Lilt C 29 MIN
3/4 INCH VIDEO CASSETTE
Focuses on the popularity of rock music.
From The Music Shop Series.
Prod-UMITV Dist-UMITV 1974

Rock And Roll With The Safety Patrol C 15 MIN
16MM FILM OPTICAL SOUND P-I
Rocky and Rollo, a hippy-like animated twosome, cavort against live-action photography in a futile campaign to 'free' school children from control by School safety patrols.

LC NO. 73-711429
Prod-AAAFTS Dist-AAAFTS 1971

Rock Bolting In Ore Mines C 24 MIN
16MM FILM OPTICAL SOUND
Points up the safe methods of rock bolting practiced in the underground mineral mines of the western part of the United States. Shows various installations and bolting patterns.
LC NO. 74-705546
Prod-USBM Dist-USNAC 1964

Rock Bolting Safety (Rev Ed) C 17 MIN
16MM FILM, 3/4 OR 1/2 IN VIDEO
Uses live-action photography, animation and working models to explain rock bolting as a means of maintaining mine openings. Traces the history and development of ground support methods, materials and equipment from the earliest timbering practices to today's improved rock bolting techniques.
Prod-USDL Dist-USNAC 1982

Rock Climbing And Rappelling C 30 MIN
3/4 OR 1/2 INCH VIDEO CASSETTE
Discusses rock climbing and rappelling as an outdoor activity that requires 'roughing it.'
From The Roughing It Series.
Prod-KYTV Dist-KYTV 1984

Rock Climbing, Rigging, Running C 30 MIN
1/2 IN VIDEO CASSETTE BETA/VHS
Describes basic rock climbing and rigging. Examines the cause, prevention and treatment of blisters. Discusses trail food.
From The Great Outdoors Series.
Prod-WGBHTV Dist-MTI

Rock Concert Violence C 25 MIN
3/4 OR 1/2 INCH VIDEO CASSETTE J-C A
Takes a look at the causes and solutions to violence erupting at rock concerts. Features interviews with behind-the-scenes people.
Prod-SIRS Dist-SIRS

Rock Creek Park C 16 MIN
16MM FILM, 3/4 OR 1/2 IN VIDEO
Visits the recreational facilities, historical points and nature settings of Rock Creek Park in metropolitan Washington, DC.
Prod-USNPS Dist-USNAC 1982

Rock Cycle B 45 MIN
2 INCH VIDEOTAPE C
See series title for descriptive statement.
From The Physical Science Series. Unit 1 - Geology
Prod-CHITVC Dist-GPITVL Prodn-WTTWTV

Rock Cycle, The C 22 MIN
16MM FILM, 3/4 OR 1/2 IN VIDEO J-C A
Examines the importance of the rock cycle as a fundamental natural process and key factor in geologic change. Identifies the basic rock classifications and describes their origins and composition. Explores the relationship of energy to the processes by which rock is created, altered and destroyed.
LC NO. 83-707265
Prod-EBEC Dist-EBEC 1982

Rock Cycle, The (Spanish) C 22 MIN
16MM FILM, 3/4 OR 1/2 IN VIDEO J A
A Spanish language version of the film and videorecording The Rock Cycle.
Prod-EBEC Dist-EBEC 1982

Rock In The Road, A C 6 MIN
16MM FILM, 3/4 OR 1/2 IN VIDEO P-J
Uses animation to present a story about a man coming down the road, tripping over a rock and plunging into a hole. Pictures him, in his fury, replacing the rock and hiding as he spots someone else coming down the road. Shows that the second and third men do the same but that the fourth man removes the rock, fills the hole and departs happily.
Prod-FA Dist-PHENIX Prodn-BEAUXA 1968

Rock In The Road, A (Captioned) C 6 MIN
16MM FILM, 3/4 OR 1/2 IN VIDEO P-J
Uses animation to present a story about a man coming down the road, tripping over a rock and plunging into a hole. Pictures him, in his fury, replacing the rock and hiding as he spots someone else coming down the road. Shows that the second and third men do the same but that the fourth man removes the rock, fills the hole and departs happily.
Prod-FA Dist-PHENIX Prodn-BEAUXA 1968

Rock Paintings Of Baja California C 25 MIN
16MM FILM, 3/4 OR 1/2 IN VIDEO
Describes the environmental and cultural setting within which the natives of Baja California developed their rock art work.
Prod-UCEMC Dist-UCEMC

Rock Paintings Of Baja California (2nd Ed) C 17 MIN
16MM FILM, 3/4 OR 1/2 IN VIDEO H-C A
Examines the rock paintings at a recently discovered site in a remote area of Baja California. Provides a brief introduction to prehistoric rock paintings in various parts of the world and compares the style of the Baja paintings to those found elsewhere. Explains their age, how they were painted and their significance to the Indians who painted them.
Prod-MEIC Dist-UCEMC 1975

Rock Weathering - Origin Of Soils B 26 MIN
16MM FILM OPTICAL SOUND C A
Discusses mechanical disintegration and chemical decomposition of soil. Describes development of soil and factors in soil formation. Outlines soil zones and illustrates profiles of laterites, podsols, chernozem and sierozem.
Prod-UTEX Dist-UTEX 1960

Rock Your Baby C 12 MIN
16MM FILM OPTICAL SOUND
Presents a film about filmmakers and the scenes they shoot.
LC NO. 76-703849
Prod-CONCRU Dist-CONCRU 1976

Rock-A-Bye Baby C 30 MIN
16MM FILM, 3/4 OR 1/2 IN VIDEO J-C A
Presents some of the techniques that psychologists use to measure mothering practices in the human and animal world during the important infant years.
From The Life Around Us Series.
Prod-TIMLIF Dist-TIMLIF 1971

Rock-A-Bye Baby (Spanish) C 30 MIN
16MM FILM OPTICAL SOUND
Presents techniques that psychologists use to measure mothering practices in the human and animal world during the important infant years.
From The Life Around Us (Spanish) Series.
LC NO. 78-700060
Prod-TIMLIF Dist-TIMLIF 1971

Rock-A-Bye Baby - A Group Projective Test For Children B 35 MIN
16MM FILM OPTICAL SOUND C
Presents a puppet show designed to elicit projective responses of children from ages five to ten years. Taps the areas of sibling rivalry, aggressions, fears, guilt feelings and attitudes toward parents.
Prod-PSUPCR Dist-PSUPCR 1956

Rock, Revere And Revolution C 24 MIN
3/4 OR 1/2 INCH VIDEO CASSETTE K-J
Shows a group of young people reviewing Paul Revere and the American Revolution through a musical presentation.
Prod-SUTHRB Dist-SUTHRB

Rockaby C 60 MIN
16MM FILM, 3/4 OR 1/2 IN VIDEO
Presents the play Rockaby by Samuel Beckett. Follows the British actress Billie Whitelaw, and American director Alan Schneider as they create, rehearse and premiere Rockaby. By D A Pennebaker and Chris Hegedus.
Prod-PENNAS Dist-PENNAS

Rocker C 9 MIN
16MM FILM - 3/4 IN VIDEO I-C A
Presents an experimental film which uses video effects to show kinetic sculptures of dance.
LC NO. 77-703398
Prod-CHASED Dist-CHASED 1977

Rocker Curve - And W C 15 MIN
3/4 INCH VIDEO CASSETTE P
From The Writing Time Series.
Prod-WHROTV Dist-GPITVL

Rockers C 99 MIN
16MM FILM OPTICAL SOUND
Presents a celebration of Jamaica's Rastafarian culture. Directed by Theodoros Bafaloukos. In Rasta patois with English subtitles.
Prod-UNKNWN Dist-NYFLMS 1978

Rocket Mice On A Record Ride B 5 MIN
16MM FILM OPTICAL SOUND
Records the story of three mice who traveled higher into the heavens than an creature ever has gone. Shows that the mice have brought man a step closer to his journey into space.
From The Screen News Digest Series. Vol 3, Issue 4
Prod-HEARST Dist-HEARST 1960

Rocket Power For Manned Flight C 17 MIN
16MM FILM OPTICAL SOUND
Presents the X1R99-RM-1 Throttlable Rocket Engine which powers the X-15 and the X-20. Includes historic flight scenes of early Bell X-1 and Douglas X-4 rocket ships to the present X-15.
Prod-THIOKL Dist-THIOKL 1960

Rocket Propulsion X 20 MIN
2 INCH VIDEOTAPE I
See series title for descriptive statement.
From The Process And Proof Series. No. 8
Prod-MCETV Dist-GPITVL Prodn-WVIZTV

Rocket Safety C 27 MIN
16MM FILM OPTICAL SOUND
Demonstrates the safe handling and packaging of rockets and motors. Considers what happens when amateurs work with materials of unknown quality and illustrates several spectacular rocket-test failures. Includes remarks on rocket safety by Dr H W Ritchey.
Prod-THIOKL Dist-THIOKL 1962

Rocket That Guards Our Skies, The B 9 MIN
16MM FILM OPTICAL SOUND
A 1954 Screen News Digest excerpt shows the NIKE intercept system through guided missiles used for warfare. Includes first films from rockets as they travel into space.
From The News Magazine Of The Screen Series. Vol 4, No. 6
Prod-PATHE Dist-HEARST 1954

Rocket To Nowhere B 79 MIN
16MM FILM OPTICAL SOUND P-I
Prod-FI Dist-FI

Rockets - How They Work C 16 MIN
16MM FILM, 3/4 OR 1/2 IN VIDEO
Discusses the principles of rocket propulsion, construction of a rocket, the need for an internal oxygen supply, fuels and oxidants, the multi-stage rocket and guidance and steering.
Prod-EBEC Dist-EBEC 1958

Rockets - How They Work (Captioned) C 16 MIN
16MM FILM, 3/4 OR 1/2 IN VIDEO I-H
Discusses the principles of rocket propulsion, construction of a rocket, the need for an internal oxygen supply, fuels and oxidants, the multi-stage rocket and guidance and steering.
Prod-EBEC Dist-EBEC 1958

Rockets - How They Work (Spanish) C 16 MIN
16MM FILM, 3/4 OR 1/2 IN VIDEO I-H
Explains how rockets achieve motion and how their power compares with other types of motive power. Demonstrates the principles of rocket propulsion, fuels, rocket engines, multi-stage rockets and guidance systems.
Prod-EBEC Dist-EBEC

Rockets And Space Exploration, Pt 1 B 30 MIN
2 INCH VIDEOTAPE J
See series title for descriptive statement.
From The Investigating The World Of Science, Unit 5 - Life In The Universe Series.
Prod-MPATI Dist-GPITVL

Rockets And Space Exploration, Pt 2 B 30 MIN
2 INCH VIDEOTAPE J
See series title for descriptive statement.
From The Investigating The World Of Science, Unit 5 - Life In The Universe Series.
Prod-MPATI Dist-GPITVL

Rocking Chair Rebellion, The C 30 MIN
16MM FILM, 3/4 OR 1/2 IN VIDEO I-H A
Tells the story of a young girl who finds her initial reluctance to have anything to do with elderly people gradually replaced by a growing respect for their abilities and needs, as well as a conviction about their rights as individuals. Based on the novel THE ROCKING CHAIR REBELLION by Eth Clifford. Originally shown on the television series NBC Special Treats.
From The Teenage Years Series.
LC NO. 80-706671
Prod-WILSND Dist-TIMLIF 1980

Rocking Horse Cowboy C 24 MIN
16MM FILM, 3/4 OR 1/2 IN VIDEO J-C
Presents a character study recording the true story of a modern day cowboy facing the problems of old age. Tells the story in the man's own words and voice, revealing the life of a person who followed his romantic dreams, only to find the life of a real cowboy is bittersweet.
Prod-ALTUSF Dist-EBEC 1976

Rocking Horse Writer, The C 5 MIN
3/4 OR 1/2 INCH VIDEO CASSETTE J-H
Demonstrates how to achieve proper emphasis in writing. See also the title Their Finest Paragraph.
From The Write On, Set 2 Series.
Prod-CTI Dist-CTI

Rocking-Horse Winner, The C 30 MIN
16MM FILM, 3/4 OR 1/2 IN VIDEO H-C A
Presents an adaptation of the novel THE ROCKING-HORSE WINNER by D H Lawrence, about a young, sensitive English boy whose rocking horse empowers him to predict winning racehorses at the eventual cost of his life.
From The Classics, Dark And Dangerous Series.
Prod-LCOA Dist-LCOA 1977

Rocking-Horse Winner, The (Captioned) C 30 MIN
16MM FILM, 3/4 OR 1/2 IN VIDEO P-C A
Tells the story a of young boy who predicts the winners of horse-races by riding on a wooden rocking horse. Based on a story by D H Lawrence.
From The Classics Dark And Dangerous (Captioned) Series.
Prod-LCOA Dist-LCOA 1977

Rocking-Horse Winner, The (Spanish) C 30 MIN
16MM FILM, 3/4 OR 1/2 IN VIDEO P-C A
Tells story of a boy who picks the winners at the horseraces by mounting and riding his wooden rocking-horse. Based on a story by D H Lawrence.
From The Classics Dark And Dangerous (Spanish) Series.
Prod-LCOA Dist-LCOA 1977

Rocks B 10 MIN
3/4 INCH VIDEO CASSETTE P
Shows different kinds of rocks and their importance to scientists and humanity.
From The Two For Tomorrow Series.
Prod-BEOC Dist-GPITVL

Rocks B 15 MIN
2 INCH VIDEOTAPE P
Develops a method for classifying a group of assorted rocks. (Broadcast quality)
From The Land And Sea Series.
Prod-TTOIC Dist-GPITVL Prodn-WGBHTV

Rocks And Gems C 3 MIN
16MM FILM OPTICAL SOUND P-I
Shows rocks and gems.
From The Of All Things Series.
Prod-BAILYL Dist-AVED

Rocks And Gems X 11 MIN
16MM FILM OPTICAL SOUND I-H A
Uses animation to explain the basic principles of the formation of rocks and gems. Describes how to recognize the different types by color, luster, weight, hardness and crystal formations. Shows where to find gems and names many ways rocks and minerals are used.
Prod-AVED Dist-AVED 1960

Rocks And Minerals C 28 MIN
3/4 OR 1/2 INCH VIDEO CASSETTE
Covers the differences in the three basic kinds of rocks, and characteristics for classification. Uses animation, site visits and rock examples.

From The Earth Explored Series.
Prod-BBCTV Dist-PBS

Rocks And Minerals (2nd Ed) C 17 MIN
16MM FILM, 3/4 OR 1/2 IN VIDEO I-J
Describes how rocks are formed, what shapes rocks take, and how the form of rocks help in the understanding of their history.
Prod-BFA Dist-PHENIX 1978

Rocks And Minerals - Formation C 15 MIN
3/4 OR 1/2 INCH VIDEO CASSETTE P
Tells a story about a boy who marries a beautiful princess after successfully answering a riddle about how various rocks and minerals are formed.
From The Featherby's Fables Series.
Prod-WVUTTV Dist-GPITVL 1983

Rocks And Minerals - How We Identify Them C 14 MIN
16MM FILM, 3/4 OR 1/2 IN VIDEO I-J
Shows how common rocks and minerals can be identified by color, texture, hardness, streak and other standard procedures.
Prod-CORF Dist-CORF 1971

Rocks And Minerals - Properties C 15 MIN
3/4 OR 1/2 INCH VIDEO CASSETTE P
Tells a story which reveals the use of simple tests that show the difference between various rocks and minerals.
From The Featherby's Fables Series.
Prod-WVUTTV Dist-GPITVL 1983

Rocks And Minerals - Uses C 15 MIN
3/4 OR 1/2 INCH VIDEO CASSETTE P
Tells how certain rocks relate to things like pencils, talcum powder and statues.
From The Featherby's Fables Series.
Prod-WVUTTV Dist-GPITVL 1983

Rocks And Their Meaning C 40 MIN
3/4 OR 1/2 INCH VIDEO CASSETTE IND
See series title for descriptive statement.
From The Basic And Petroleum Geology For Non-geologists - Fundamentals And...--Series.
Prod-PHILLP Dist-GPCV

Rocks And Time B 26 MIN
16MM FILM OPTICAL SOUND C A
Considers the relationship of a sequence of formations at an outcrop to similar formations many miles away. Outlines a transgressive cycle to illustrate that as deposition at one place changes from sand to finer materials, the shoreline has moved landward. Shows how this is followed by a regressive cycle, illustrating the entire sequence with a model experiment.
Prod-UTEX Dist-UTEX 1960

Rocks For Beginners C 16 MIN
16MM FILM OPTICAL SOUND I-J
Presents fundamentals of rock classification. Explains origin and characteristics of different classes of rocks.
LC NO. 70-701209
Prod-JHP Dist-MLA 1968

Rocks In the Heart Surgical Excision Of Multifaceted Calcified Right Ventricular Mass C 11 MIN
16MM FILM, 3/4 OR 1/2 IN VIDEO PRO
Discusses the diagnosis and testing (echo and angiograms) of a patient with pulmonary emboli, contracardiac calcifications and obstructive cardiac failure. Demonstrates surgical management.
Prod-USVA Dist-USNAC

Rocks That Form On The Earth's Surface X 16 MIN
16MM FILM, 3/4 OR 1/2 IN VIDEO I-H
Uses examples and demonstrations to explain how sediments are produced, transported, accumulated and hardened into sedimentary rock.
From The Earth Science Program Series.
Prod-EBEC Dist-EBEC 1964

Rocks That Form On The Earth's Surface (Spanish) C 17 MIN
16MM FILM, 3/4 OR 1/2 IN VIDEO I-H
Investigates the nature of sedimentary rocks, asking where they come from, what they are made of and how they are formed.
Prod-EBEC Dist-EBEC

Rocks That Originate Underground X 23 MIN
16MM FILM, 3/4 OR 1/2 IN VIDEO I-H
Explores the origin of igneous and metamorphic rocks and investigates the requirements for the formation of intergrown crystalline mineral grains, a common characteristic of igneous and metamorphic rocks.
From The Earth Science Program Series.
Prod-EBEC Dist-EBEC 1966

Rocks That Originate Underground (Spanish) C 23 MIN
16MM FILM, 3/4 OR 1/2 IN VIDEO I-H
Proves that igneous and metamorphic rocks must be formed within the Earth's crust. Shows that both types of rocks are composed of intergrown crystalline mineral grains.
Prod-EBEC Dist-EBEC

Rocks That Reveal The Past C 12 MIN
16MM FILM, 3/4 OR 1/2 IN VIDEO I-C
By studying fossils found in layers of sedimentary rocks, scientists reconstruct the plant and animal life of the past. A demonstration to explain how sedimentary rocks are formed and examples of fossils found in certain layers of the Grand Canyon are shown.
Prod-FA Dist-PHENIX 1962

Rocks, Fossils And Earth History C 17 MIN
16MM FILM, 3/4 OR 1/2 IN VIDEO J-H
Shows several different kinds of fossils and discusses how fossils are formed, the rock cycle and the earth forces that act on them.
From The Natural Phenomena Series.
Prod-GLDWER Dist-JOU 1981

Rockschool--A Series
J-C A
Helps young musicians who have mastered the basics of traditional rock instruments - the guitar, bass and drums - to develop their skills. Demonstrates how a musical vocabulary of chords, riffs, licks and fills, as used in the major rock styles from blues and heavy metal to funk and reggae, can be built up.
Prod-BBCTV Dist-FI

Basic Technique 025 MIN
Blues And Rock 'N' Roll 025 MIN
Contemporany 025 MIN
Funk 025 MIN
Hardware 025 MIN
Heavy Metal 025 MIN
Reggae 025 MIN
Tuning 025 MIN

Rocky - The American Dream Continues C 26 MIN
16MM FILM, 3/4 OR 1/2 IN VIDEO I-C A
Merges film clips from the Rocky trilogy with the real life and screen life stories of Sylvester Stallone and the character he created, Rocky Balboa, to create a personal film record of Stallone's achievements.
Prod-DIRECT Dist-DIRECT 1982

Rocky Mountain Empire C 29 MIN
16MM FILM OPTICAL SOUND
A pictorial and musical portrayal of Colorado with emphasis on scenery, sports, Western living, crafts, industry and natural resources. Explains the role of Union Pacific in the development and progress of the state.
LC NO. 78-702555
Prod-UPR Dist-UPR 1968

Rocky Mountain Rails C 60 MIN
1/2 IN VIDEO CASSETTE BETA/VHS
Follows The Cumbres and Toltec Railroad, the nation's longest and highest steam narrow gauge railroad, which runs from Antonito, Colorado, to Chama, New Mexico. Shows other Rocky Mountain railroads, including the Silverton, near Durango, Colorado, and the Rio Grande Zephyr.
Prod-DELUZ Dist-DELUZ 1981

Rocky Mountain Town, A - Revelstoke C 14 MIN
16MM FILM, 3/4 OR 1/2 IN VIDEO P-I
Shows how a community changes its environment to provide services to other communities. Accompanies a child and her friends to a dam site where concerned biologists describe minimizing damage to fish populations. Accompanies a train conductor through his duties linking Revelstoke to other communities.
From The This Is My Home Series.
Prod-BCNFL Dist-BCNFL 1984

Rocky Mountains, The (2nd Ed) C 17 MIN
16MM FILM, 3/4 OR 1/2 IN VIDEO J-H
Surveys the various types of plants and animals which thrive in the Rocky Mountains, explaining the interrelationship between each. Describes the food chain of the ecosystem and discusses the geological processes which formed the Rockies.
From The Natural Science Series.
Prod-BARR Dist-BARR 1980

Rocky Mountains, The - The Last Stand C 30 MIN
3/4 OR 1/2 INCH VIDEO CASSETTE
Examines the debate between naturalists, tourists and industry regarding the use of the Rocky Mountain National Parks.
Prod-CANBC Dist-JOU

Rod Cell, The C 24 MIN
16MM FILM OPTICAL SOUND
Demonstrates the relationship between form and function in retinal rod cells, energy transducers that convert energy received as photons of dim light into changes in electrical currents, resulting in nerve impulses leading from the retina to the brain.
Prod-BBCTV Dist-OPENU 1982

Rod Cell, The C 24 MIN
16MM FILM, 3/4 OR 1/2 IN VIDEO
Demonstrates the relationship between form and function in retinal rod cells, energy transducers that convert energy received as photons of dim light into changes in electrical currents, resulting in nerve impulses leading from the retina to the brain.
Prod-OPENU Dist-MEDIAG Prodn-BBCTV 1982

Rod Mill Trimmers C 5 MIN
3/4 OR 1/2 INCH VIDEO CASSETTE IND
Explains the trimmers' job of cutting scrap and test samples from the hot coils. Emphasizes safety. Covers cleaning reel tangles.
From The Steel Making Series.
Prod-LEIKID Dist-LEIKID

Rodeo C 3 MIN
16MM FILM OPTICAL SOUND P-I
Discusses the sport of rodeo.
From The Of All Things Series.
Prod-BAILYL Dist-AVED

Rodeo C 15 MIN
16MM FILM, 3/4 OR 1/2 IN VIDEO I
Explains that a rodeo is not only an entertainment but a testing place for the skills of a working cowboy. Traces the history of rodeos.
From The American Scrapbook Series.
Prod-WVIZTV Dist-GPITVL 1977

Rodeo C 20 MIN
16MM FILM, 3/4 OR 1/2 IN VIDEO P-H
Uses slow motion to emphasize the danger and loneliness that a cowboy experiences as he attempts to win a rodeo event by riding a bull for eight seconds.
Prod-CUNLIM Dist-PHENIX 1969

Rodeo C 29 MIN
2 INCH VIDEOTAPE
Explains that small town weekend rodeoing still happens all over the country and is considered a family recreation for many families. Features host Demaret talking to the weekend participants at the Lucky Lady Arena in Spring, Texas.
From The Bayou City And Thereabouts People Show Series.
Prod-KUHTTV Dist-PUBTEL

Rodeo Boy C 28 MIN
16MM FILM OPTICAL SOUND J-H
Introduces Duane Daines, a youth from a small Alberta, Canada town who has wanted to be a professional cowboy ever since he entered his first rodeo at the age of five. Highlights activities at a rodeo school run by Duane's uncle.
Prod-CANBC Dist-FI

Rodeo Clown - The Daring Breed C 25 MIN
16MM FILM - 3/4 IN VIDEO
Focuses on rodeo clown Bill Lane, showing him at work in the hazardous rodeo arena and revealing his attitudes toward his job.
LC NO. 79-706409
Prod-CHPRL Dist-ADAMSF 1978

Rodeo Cowboy C 22 MIN
16MM FILM, 3/4 OR 1/2 IN VIDEO J-C A
Offers an intimate look at the men who make their living riding in rodeos.
Prod-FRIDBR Dist-BARR

Rodeo Girl C 24 MIN
3/4 OR 1/2 INCH VIDEO CASSETTE
Looks at the true story of a 13-year old girl whose determination and skill made her the youngest world champion barrel racer.
From The Young People's Specials Series.
Prod-MULTPP Dist-MULTPP

Rodeo Red And The Runaway C 33 MIN
16MM FILM, 3/4 OR 1/2 IN VIDEO I-C A
A shortened version of the motion picture Rodeo Red And The Runaway. Shows how a young girl refuses to accept her stepmother and runs away from home. Tells how she meets 'Big Red,' a former rodeo horse who becomes her companion. Based on the book Shelter From The Wind by Marion Dane Bauer. An NBC Special Treat.
Prod-LCOA Dist-LCOA 1979

Rodeo Red And The Runaway C 49 MIN
16MM FILM, 3/4 OR 1/2 IN VIDEO I-C A
Shows how a young girl refuses to accept her stepmother and runs away from home. Tells how she meets 'Big Red,' a former rodeo horse who becomes her companion. Based on the book Shelter From The Wind by Marion Dane Bauer. An NBC Special Treat.
Prod-LCOA Dist-LCOA 1979

Rodeo Red And The Runaway (Captioned) C 33 MIN
16MM FILM, 3/4 OR 1/2 IN VIDEO P-H A
Tells the story of a young girl who runs away from her stepmother only to run into a strong-willed woman and a rodeo horse. Edited version.
Prod-LCOA Dist-LCOA 1979

Rodeo Red And The Runaway (Captioned) C 49 MIN
16MM FILM, 3/4 OR 1/2 IN VIDEO P-H A
Tells the story of a young girl who runs away from her stepmother only to run into a strong-willed woman and a rodeo horse. Full version.
Prod-LCOA Dist-LCOA 1979

Rodeo Red And The Runaway (French) C 33 MIN
16MM FILM, 3/4 OR 1/2 IN VIDEO P-H A
Tells the story of a young girl who runs away from her stepmother only to run into a strong-willed woman and a rodeo horse. Edited version.
Prod-LCOA Dist-LCOA 1979

Rodeo Red And The Runaway (French) C 49 MIN
16MM FILM, 3/4 OR 1/2 IN VIDEO P-H A
Tells the story of a young girl who runs away from her stepmother only to run into a strong-willed woman and a rodeo horse. Full version.
Prod-LCOA Dist-LCOA 1979

Rodeo Red And The Runaway (Spanish) C 33 MIN
16MM FILM, 3/4 OR 1/2 IN VIDEO P-H A
Tells the story of a young girl who runs away from her stepmother only to run into a strong-willed woman and a rodeo horse. Edited version.
Prod-LCOA Dist-LCOA 1979

Rodeo Red And The Runaway (Spanish) C 49 MIN
16MM FILM, 3/4 OR 1/2 IN VIDEO P-H A
Tells the story of a young girl who runs away from her stepmother only to run into a strong-willed woman and a rodeo horse. Full version.
Prod-LCOA Dist-LCOA 1979

Rodney Fails To Qualify C 30 MIN
3/4 OR 1/2 INCH VIDEO CASSETTE C A
Presents an adaptation of the short story Rodney Fails To Qualify by P G Wodehouse.
From The Wodehouse Playhouse Series.
Prod-BBCTV Dist-TIMLIF 1980

Roentgen Anatomy Of The Normal Alimentary Canal B 27 MIN
16MM FILM OPTICAL SOUND PRO

Uses cineflourographic sequences to show functioning anatomy from mouth to bowel, including throat, esophagus, stomach, duodenum, small and large intestine.
From The Normal Roentgen Anatomy Series.
LC NO. FIA67-585
Prod-AMCRAD Dist-AMEDA 1966

Roentgen Anatomy Of The Normal Bones And Joints B 19 MIN
16MM FILM OPTICAL SOUND PRO
Uses cinefluoroscopy to show the shape, location and movement of the principle joints of the human body as they are seen by radiologists and other physicians. Demonstrates the movements of these joints in normal exercise and then the interior movement of the bones and joints as seen by cinefluoroscopy.
From The Normal Roentgen Anatomy Series.
LC NO. 78-711430
Prod-GEXRAY Dist-AMEDA 1970

Roentgen Anatomy Of The Normal Genito-Urinary System C 29 MIN
16MM FILM OPTICAL SOUND PRO
Demonstrates the function of the normal genito-urinary system.
From The Normal Anatomy Series.
LC NO. FIA67-5313
Prod-AMCRAD Dist-AMCRAD Prodn-KEYFP 1967

Roentgen Anatomy Of The Normal Heart B 27 MIN
16MM FILM OPTICAL SOUND PRO
Uses segments of cineflourographic studies plus animation to depict the flow of blood through the heart and the coronary arteries.
From The Normal Roentgen Anatomy Series.
LC NO. FIA66-621
Prod-AMCRAD Dist-AMEDA 1965

Roger Baldwin C 22 MIN
3/4 OR 1/2 INCH VIDEO CASSETTE
Presents an intimate biography of Roger Baldwin, founder and former director of the American Civil Liberties Union.
Prod-MEDIPR Dist-MEDIPR 1978

Roger Berg Story, The C 15 MIN
16MM FILM, 3/4 OR 1/2 IN VIDEO H-C A
Illustrates the role values play in the decision-making process. Shows that values also influence the way people deal with the consequences of their decisions.
From The Focus On Ethics Series.
LC NO. 77-700213
Prod-SALENG Dist-SALENG 1977

Roger Mc Gough And The Liverpool Lads C 30 MIN
3/4 INCH VIDEO CASSETTE H-C A
Offers readings from the humorous poems and songs of British television personality Roger Mc Gough.
From The Anyone For Tennyson Series.
Prod-NETCHE Dist-GPITVL

Roger Ward C 20 MIN
16MM FILM OPTICAL SOUND I-J
Features Roger Ward discussing his career through film clips of some great and harrowing racing moments.
From The Sports Legends Series.
Prod-COUNFI Dist-COUNFI

Roger Williams B 20 MIN
2 INCH VIDEOTAPE I
See series title for descriptive statement.
From The Americans All Series.
Prod-DENVPS Dist-GPITVL Prodn-KRMATV

Roger Williams - Founder Of Rhode Island B 28 MIN
16MM FILM, 3/4 OR 1/2 IN VIDEO J-C
Shows the trial of Roger Williams by the magistrate of Massachusetts colony and his banishment for preaching religious freedom. Illustrates the importance of the separation of Church and State.
Prod-EBF Dist-EBEC 1956

Roi, Chevalier Et Saint - King, Knight And Saint C 52 MIN
16MM FILM OPTICAL SOUND
Visits Europe during the 13th century when Gothic and Art Nouveau develop in Italy, Louis XI tries to bring the knighthood to perfection and La Sainte Chapelle is built. Deals with such events as the papacy moving to Avignon and the publication of Marco Polo's book of wonders.
From The Le Temp Des Cathedrales Series.
Prod-FACSEA Dist-FACSEA 1979

Roland Kirk C 30 MIN
2 INCH VIDEOTAPE
Presents the jazz music of Roland Kirk. Features host Jim Rockwell interviewing the artist.
From The People In Jazz Series.
Prod-WTVSTV Dist-PUBTEL

Role Enactment In Children's Play - A Developmental Overview C 29 MIN
16MM FILM OPTICAL SOUND A
Functions as the main film in a training module of six films on role enactment in children's play. Presents the developmental aspects of role enactment in children 2 to 10 years of age, focusing on four basic concepts, verbal and motoric elements, role perception, age differences in styles of role enactment and thematic content.
From The Training Module On Role Enactment In Children's Play Series. One
LC NO. 76-700936
Prod-UPITTS Dist-CFDC Prodn-CFDC 1974

Role Of Coal, The C 17 MIN
16MM FILM, 3/4 OR 1/2 IN VIDEO J-C A
Explains the role of coal as an energy source in the past, present and future. Contrasts coal with other energy sources and notes that the scarcity and expense of petroleum necessitates consideration of developing alternative sources.
Prod-IU Dist-IU 1980

Role Of Department Chairpersons C 28 MIN
3/4 OR 1/2 INCH VIDEO CASSETTE T
Examines the rationale for an expanded role of department chairperson as liaison assisting the administration and faculty.
From The On And About Instruction Series.
Prod-VADE Dist-GPITVL 1983

Role Of Everyday Movement Habits In Chronic Injuries C 30 MIN
3/4 OR 1/2 INCH VIDEO CASSETTE
See series title for descriptive statement.
From The Care And Feeding Of Dancers Series.
Prod-ARCVID Dist-ARCVID

Role Of Fire Testing Organizations, The C
3/4 OR 1/2 INCH VIDEO CASSETTE
See series title for descriptive statement.
From The Fire Away Series.
Prod-NFPA Dist-NFPA

Role of Government C 20 MIN
16MM FILM OPTICAL SOUND
See series title for descriptive statement.
Prod-CINE Dist-CINE

Role Of Government In A Free Society, The C 76 MIN
3/4 OR 1/2 INCH VIDEO CASSETTE C
Presents economist Milton Friedman examining the role of the U S government in economic and political contexts. Notes that the government's actions have exceeded proper limitations.
From The Milton Friedman Speaking Series. Lecture 4
LC NO. 79-708063
Prod-HBJ Dist-HBJ Prodn-WQLN 1980

Role Of Hemodynamic Monitoring In The Critically Ill C 39 MIN
3/4 OR 1/2 INCH VIDEO CASSETTE PRO
Presents a brief look at the history of the Swan-Ganz catheter. Details major issues related to this procedure, such as decision making, indications for monitoring and interpretation of data. Discusses the relationship of cardiac index to performance, pre-load and after-load and the lack of correlation between the wedge pressure and the CVP. Discussion by Dr H J C Swan on complications.
Prod-AMCARD Dist-AMCARD

Role Of Hygienist In Dental Care, Pt 1, History And Examination C 11 MIN
3/4 OR 1/2 INCH VIDEO CASSETTE PRO
Demonstrates the procedures involved in recording a patient's medical and dental history, as well as the findings of an extraoral and intraoral examination. Shows positioning and palpation techniques in detail.
From The Role Of The Hygienist In Dental Care Series.
Prod-VADTC Dist-USNAC 1982

Role Of Hygienist In Dental Care, Pt 2, Scaling And Root Planing C 15 MIN
3/4 OR 1/2 INCH VIDEO CASSETTE PRO
Demonstrates scaling and root planing, the instruments used, and the proper finger placement and instrument grasp. Shows techniques for instrument sharpening.
From The Role Of The Hygienist In Dental Care Series.
LC NO. 82-707251
Prod-VADTC Dist-USNAC 1982

Role Of Numerial Analysis In Forest Management, The C 30 MIN
3/4 OR 1/2 INCH VIDEO CASSETTE
Shows how current accurate information about forest resources can be obtained through analysis of satellite collected data.
From The Introduction To Quantitative Analysis Of Remote Sensing Data Series.
Prod-PUAVC Dist-PUAVC

Role Of Others, The C 29 MIN
3/4 OR 1/2 INCH VIDEO CASSETTE H-C A
Describes how siblings, members of the extended family, and others in the community affect a child's development.
From The Tomorrow's Families Series.
LC NO. 81-706914
Prod-MSDOE Dist-AITECH 1980

Role Of Pattern Recognition In Remote Sensing, The C 30 MIN
3/4 OR 1/2 INCH VIDEO CASSETTE
Discusses the role of pattern recognition in remote sensing. Describes how a statistical approach is used to improve decision making in the face of uncertainty.
From The Introduction To Quantitative Analysis Of Remote Sensing Data Series.
Prod-PUAVC Dist-PUAVC

Role Of Phonics, The C 29 MIN
16MM FILM, 3/4 OR 1/2 IN VIDEO C A
Explores the role of phonics and puts it in perspective in an overall reading program.
From The Teaching Children To Read Series.
Prod-MFFD Dist-FI 1976

Role Of Racial Differences In Therapy, The B 70 MIN
3/4 OR 1/2 INCH VIDEO CASSETTE
Discusses the often avoided issue of social differences that is avoided by patient and therapist alike. Includes excerpts from therapy sessions with a biracial couple.
Prod-PSU Dist-PSU

Role Of Research, The C 20 MIN
16MM FILM, 3/4 OR 1/2 IN VIDEO
Describes research carried on by the U S Fish and Wildlife Service, including environmental contaminant evaluation, endangered species recovery, control of wildlife damage to crops, fish husbandry and genetics, habitat preservation and more.
Prod-USBSFW Dist-USNAC

Role Of Surgery In The Management Of Ovarian Cancer C 60 MIN
3/4 INCH VIDEO CASSETTE
Discusses the various treatments for primary carcinoma of the ovary, emphasizing the role of surgery.
Prod-UTAHTI Dist-UTAHTI

Role Of Surgical Adjuvant Therapy In The Management Of Lung Cancer C 45 MIN
3/4 INCH VIDEO CASSETTE
Demonstrates the expected results of surgery used in conjunction with other modalities in treating lung cancer.
Prod-UTAHTI Dist-UTAHTI

Role Of The Black Inventors, The C 29 MIN
3/4 OR 1/2 INCH VIDEO CASSETTE
From The Black Inventors Series.
Prod-RCOMTV Dist-SYLWAT 1982

Role Of The Cello In A String Quartet, The C 15 MIN
3/4 OR 1/2 INCH VIDEO CASSETTE I-H
See series title for descriptive statement.
From The Chamber Music - The String Quartet Series.
Prod-NETCHE Dist-AITECH 1977

Role Of The Clavicle And Its Surgical Significance, The C 24 MIN
3/4 OR 1/2 INCH VIDEO CASSETTE PRO
Discusses function of the clavicle and demonstrates excision of the medial two-thirds, tip and entire clavicle.
Prod-WFP Dist-WFP

Role Of The Coach C 12 MIN
16MM FILM OPTICAL SOUND
Outlines the role of the school sports coach.
From The Coaching Development Programme Series. No. 2
LC NO. 76-701042
Prod-SARBOO Dist-SARBOO Prodn-SVL 1974

Role Of The Covariance Function In Estimation, The B 22 MIN
3/4 OR 1/2 INCH VIDEO CASSETTE PRO
Returns to the MMSE prediction problem for the case in which the predictor is constrained to be linear.
From The Probability And Random Processes Introduction To Random Processes Series.
Prod-MIOT Dist-MIOT

Role Of The Engineer Manager C 30 MIN
3/4 OR 1/2 INCH VIDEO CASSETTE
See series title for descriptive statement.
From The Management For Engineers Series.
Prod-UKY Dist-SME

Role Of The Family In Rehabilitation Of The Physically Disabled - A Personal Statement... B 26 MIN
3/4 OR 1/2 INCH VIDEO CASSETTE
Describes the personal tragedy of a mother of four children after the deaths of three of her children as a result of Smith-Opitz Syndrome. Describes the lack of support from some medical personnel in attending to parents in crisis.
Prod-BU Dist-BU

Role Of The Father, The C 29 MIN
3/4 OR 1/2 INCH VIDEO CASSETTE H-C A
Discusses how men can define the economic and nurturing elements of their fathering to suit their personal preferences and their relationships with their partners.
From The Tomorrow's Families Series.
LC NO. 81-706897
Prod-MSDOE Dist-AITECH 1980

Role Of The First Violin In A String Quartet, The C 15 MIN
3/4 OR 1/2 INCH VIDEO CASSETTE I-H
See series title for descriptive statement.
From The Chamber Music - The String Quartet Series.
Prod-NETCHE Dist-AITECH 1977

Role Of The Home Visitor, The B 23 MIN
3/4 OR 1/2 INCH VIDEO CASSETTE PRO
Emphasizes key elements of a successful home visit program. Shows importance of respecting the ideas, suggestions and beliefs of parents, and need for sharing information and experiences. Indicates importance of early stages of screening and training potential home visitors.
Prod-HSERF Dist-HSERF

Role Of The Hygienist In Dental Care—A Series
PRO
Discusses techniques and procedures for dental hygienists.
Prod-VADTC Dist-USNAC

Role Of Hygienist In Dental Care, Pt 1,
Role Of Hygienist In Dental Care, Pt 2, 015 MIN

Role Of The Hypothalamus In Emotion And Behavior, Pt 1 B 54 MIN
16MM FILM SILENT C T
Shows that environmental stimuli associated as many as 480 times with 'SHAM RAGE' reactions due to hypothalamic stimulation fail to induce affective states. Points out that, in contrast, recovery animals continue feeding or other adaptative behavior during stimulation and show normal fear and rage despite extensive hypothalamic lesions. Shows that cardiac and vasomotor accompaniments of hypothalamic 'CONDITIONING' are not produced in anesthetized animals.
Prod-PSUPCR Dist-PSUPCR 1943

Role Of The Instructor X 30 MIN
16MM FILM OPTICAL SOUND C T
Discusses the essential features of the instructor-student relationship.
From The Teaching Role Series.
LC NO. 73-703318
Prod-MVNE Dist-TELSTR 1968

Role Of The Medical Department In Hearing Conservation C 28 MIN
16MM FILM OPTICAL SOUND
Presents the U S Navy Medical Department's program of hearing conservation with examples of applicable conditions. Explains the use of noise measurement and analysis, engineering control, audiometry, protective devices and education. Emphasizes hearing-loss prevention through periodic audiograms and wearing hearing protection devices.
LC NO. 75-703072
Prod-USN Dist-USNAC 1973

Role Of The MLR LAB Procedure In Organ Transplantation, The C 20 MIN
3/4 OR 1/2 INCH VIDEO CASSETTE PRO
Presents detailed methods used in the selection of prospective graft donors. Demonstrates the techniques used in obtaining lymphoid cells and performing the MLR procedure. Includes basic immunological concepts as they apply to this laboratory exercise.
Prod-UMICHM Dist-UMICHM 1981

Role Of The Mother, The C 29 MIN
3/4 OR 1/2 INCH VIDEO CASSETTE H-C A
Discusses some aspects of motherhood which are determined biologically and others which vary according to culture and social milieu.
From The Tomorrow's Families Series.
LC NO. 81-706909
Prod-MSDOE Dist-AITECH 1980

Role Of The Natural Parent C 30 MIN
3/4 OR 1/2 INCH VIDEO CASSETTE
Presents a program specialist, foster parents and a natural parent sharing their natural experiences in working together to help children face a changing family structure.
From The Home Is Where The Care Is Series. Module 3
Prod-MTI Dist-MTI 1984

Role Of The Nurse Specialist, The B 30 MIN
16MM FILM OPTICAL SOUND C
Discusses the expanded role of nurse-midwives and pediatric nurse practitioners. Shows the training which prepares them for these professions.
From The Nursing Perspectives Series.
LC NO. 71-706827
Prod-VDONUR Dist-AJN Prodn-WTTWTV 1969

Role Of The Occupational Therapist In The Public School, The, Tape I C 25 MIN
3/4 INCH VIDEO CASSETTE PRO
Begins a discussion of the role of the occupational therapist in the public school. Narrated by Virginia Scardina.
Prod-AOTA Dist-AOTA 1979

Role Of The Occupational Therapist In The Public School, The, Tape II C 20 MIN
3/4 INCH VIDEO CASSETTE PRO
Concludes a discussion of the role of the occupational therapist in the public school. Narrated by Virginia Scardina.
Prod-AOTA Dist-AOTA 1979

Role Of The Office Worker, The C 9 MIN
3/4 OR 1/2 INCH VIDEO CASSETTE
Shows the office staff where they fit into the overall organization and points out that they are an important part of the team.
From The Effective Office Worker Series
Prod-RESEM Dist-RESEM

Role Of The Operating Room Nurse In Cardiovascular Surgery, The C 19 MIN
16MM FILM OPTICAL SOUND PRO
Demonstrates the duties and requirements placed upon the nurse from the time the patient enters the operating room until completion of the operative procedure. Emphasizes the necessity for skill, dedication and the ability to work effectively in an active and demanding environment where success depends upon coordinated teamwork.
Prod-ACYDGD Dist-ACY 1968

Role Of The Parents, The (2nd Ed) C 11 MIN
3/4 OR 1/2 INCH VIDEO CASSETTE PRO
Discusses the impact of preterm delivery on parents, interactions between parents, infant and nursery personnel and ways in which staff can facilitate parents' emotional adjustments.
Prod-UMICHM Dist-UMICHM 1983

Role Of The Physician, The C 41 MIN
3/4 OR 1/2 INCH VIDEO CASSETTE
See series title for descriptive statement.
From The Terminal Illness Series.
Prod-UWASHP Dist-UWASHP

Role Of The Police Officer, The C 27 MIN
3/4 OR 1/2 INCH VIDEO CASSETTE I-J
Follows a police officer as he performs such duties as telling a father that his son was killed while leaning from a car and warns a car full of young people of that danger.
From The Cop Talk Series.
Prod-UTSBE Dist-AITECH 1981

Role Of The President's Cabinet, The C 20 MIN
3/4 INCH VIDEO CASSETTE H-C A
Presents the highlights of a panel discussion concerning the role of the President's cabinet. Discusses the answers to such issues as direct access to the president, role of the office of management and budget and the dilemma of time in managing a government department.
LC NO. 76-706257
Prod-USCSC Dist-USNAC 1976

Role Of The Second Violin In A String Quartet, The C 15 MIN
3/4 OR 1/2 INCH VIDEO CASSETTE I-H
See series title for descriptive statement.
From The Chamber Music - The String Quartet Series.
Prod-NETCHE Dist-AITECH 1977

Role Of The Supervisor, The C 17 MIN
3/4 OR 1/2 INCH VIDEO CASSETTE
See series title for descriptive statement.
From The Leadership Link - Fundamentals Of Effective Supervision Series.
Prod-CHSH Dist-DELTAK

Role Of The Supreme Court, The B 20 MIN
16MM FILM OPTICAL SOUND H A
Dr David Fellman, professor of political science, University of Wisconsin, analyzes the history, power and judicial procedures of our highest court.
From The Government And Public Affairs Films Series.
Prod-RSC Dist-MLA 1960

Role Of The Supreme Court, The - Dr David Fellman B 20 MIN
16MM FILM OPTICAL SOUND H-C
See series title for descriptive statement.
From The Building Political Leadership Series.
Prod-RSC Dist-MLA 1960

Role Of The VA Police Officer, The C 14 MIN
3/4 OR 1/2 INCH VIDEO CASSETTE PRO
Discusses the responsibilities of the Veterans Administration police officer.
Prod-VAMSLC Dist-USNAC 1984

Role Of The Viola In A String Quartet, The C 15 MIN
3/4 OR 1/2 INCH VIDEO CASSETTE I-H
See series title for descriptive statement.
From The Chamber Music - The String Quartet Series.
Prod-NETCHE Dist-AITECH 1977

Role Of The Witness C 42 MIN
16MM FILM OPTICAL SOUND
Offers instruction on being an expert witness in a court action on air pollution.
LC NO. 75-700695
Prod-USEPA Dist-USNAC 1969

Role Of Videotape In The Diagnosis And Management Of Laryngeal Cancer C 11 MIN
3/4 OR 1/2 INCH VIDEO CASSETTE PRO
Focuses on using videotape in the outpatient clinic, in the operating room and for instructional purpose.
Prod-HSCIC Dist-HSCIC 1984

Role Of Women In American Society—A Series

Prod-EDC Dist-EDC 1974

Clorae And Albie 36 MIN
Girls At 12 30 MIN

Role Of Women Project—A Series

Prod-EDC Dist-EDC

Clorae And Albie 36 MIN

Role Playing For Social Values B 16 MIN
16MM FILM OPTICAL SOUND P-I
Presents role-playing as one aspect of the TABA in-service education program.
Prod-AWPC Dist-AWPC 1968

Role-Play, Simulations And Evaluating Classroom Environment C 30 MIN
3/4 OR 1/2 INCH VIDEO CASSETTE
See series title for descriptive statement.
From The Creating A Learning Environment Series.
Prod-NETCHE Dist-NETCHE 1975

Roles And Goals In High School C 29 MIN
16MM FILM, 3/4 OR 1/2 IN VIDEO T
Presents Dr William Glasser who extends the application of his Identity Society and Schools Without Failure concepts to the secondary level. Shows how reality therapy can be used to handle discipline problems.
From The Dealing With Classroom Problems Series.
Prod-MFFD Dist-FI 1976

Roles And Services C 30 MIN
3/4 OR 1/2 INCH VIDEO CASSETTE
Covers three major topics, beginning with the need for schools to provide a continuum of educational services for the handicapped, including the various types of programs ranging from mainstreaming to special schools. Illustrates identification and placement procedures for students with special needs, especially those who remain in regular school programs. Describes the role of classroom teachers and support personnel as they work together on programming for handicapped students and communicate with parents about their programs.
From The Educational Alternatives For Handicapped Students Series.
Prod-NETCHE Dist-NETCHE 1977

Roles Of The President, The C 30 MIN
3/4 OR 1/2 INCH VIDEO CASSETTE C
Presents the parts the President must play, how each role evolved to what it is today and how several Presidents have used these roles to suit their own personalities.
From The American Government 2 Series.
Prod-DALCCD Dist-DALCCD

Roles We Play C 30 MIN
3/4 OR 1/2 INCH VIDEO CASSETTE C
See series title for descriptive statement.
From The Art Of Being Human Series. Module 10
Prod-MDCC Dist-MDCC

Rolf Harris In Tasmania C 27 MIN
16MM FILM OPTICAL SOUND
Presents Rolf Harris, who takes a look at the wide variety of scenery in Tasmania.
LC NO. 80-700915
Prod-TASCOR Dist-TASCOR 1976

Roll 'Em Lola C 5 MIN
16MM FILM OPTICAL SOUND
Presents an animated film depicting the fantasy of an eternal Hollywood chase which communicates images of psychic unrest.
LC NO. 75-700478
Prod-USC Dist-USC

Roll Of Thunder, Hear My Cry C 110 MIN
16MM FILM, 3/4 OR 1/2 IN VIDEO J-C A
Tells the story of a Black family in the poverty-stricken South of 1933, who struggle to hold on to the land they have owned for three generations. Based on the book Roll Of Thunder, Hear My Cry by Mildred D Taylor.
Prod-TOMENT Dist-LCOA 1979

Roll Out C 5 MIN
16MM FILM OPTICAL SOUND
Shows a group of people who get together to play a new game called racquetball. Examines the details of how the game is played and encourages other people to play the game themselves.
LC NO. 75-700479
Prod-AMFVOI Dist-AMFVOI Prodn-MOVPIT 1975

Roll Over C 10 MIN
16MM FILM OPTICAL SOUND J-C A
Presents a montage of scenes that expose oppression and celebrate the liberation of women. Includes views of sex role stereotyping and of women working in professions previously restricted to men. Features many feminist businesses and shows scenes about housework, motherhood and working for men, ending with a glance at women in the future.
LC NO. 74-703029
Prod-HERFLM Dist-HERFLM 1974

Roll Threading Setup Procedures C 14 MIN
3/4 OR 1/2 INCH VIDEO CASSETTE IND
Presents a detailed procedure for the setup and change of rolls on a Hartford roll threading machine. Covers feed way assembly timer adjustments.
From The Steel Making Series.
Prod-LEIKID Dist-LEIKID

Rolle's Theorem, Mean Value Theorem C
3/4 INCH VIDEO CASSETTE
See series title for descriptive statement.
From The Calculus Series.
Prod-MDDE Dist-MDCPB

Roller Chain C 22 MIN
3/4 OR 1/2 INCH VIDEO CASSETTE IND
Explains basic components of roller chain, pin link and roller link. Discusses pitch, links and clearances. Includes a section on special chains.
Prod-TAT Dist-TAT

Roller Cone Bits C 27 MIN
3/4 OR 1/2 INCH VIDEO CASSETTE IND
Examines the parts, features and proper techniques for running steel-tooth and carbide-insert bits to bottom.
Prod-UTEXPE Dist-UTEXPE 1977

Roller Cone Bits (Spanish) C 27 MIN
3/4 OR 1/2 INCH VIDEO CASSETTE
Examines the parts, features and proper techniques for running steel-tooth and carbide-insert bits to bottom.
Prod-UTEXPE Dist-UTEXPE 1977

Roller Skate Fever C 10 MIN
16MM FILM, 3/4 OR 1/2 IN VIDEO
Shows roller skaters in Venice, California, performing dizzying stunts to the accompaniment of rambunctious rock music.
LC NO. 82-706493
Prod-SHAPP Dist-PFP 1981

Roller Skate Safely C 15 MIN
16MM FILM, 3/4 OR 1/2 IN VIDEO
Illustrates the importance of roller skating safety equipment and stresses the need for routine safety and maintenance checks. Shows a variety of skates and makes recommendations on equipment purchase versus rental. Deals with basic skating safety on sidewalks and streets.
LC NO. 80-707492
Prod-FIESTF Dist-FIESTF 1980

Roller Skating Safety C 15 MIN
16MM FILM, 3/4 OR 1/2 IN VIDEO
Discusses safety and etiquette in roller skating.
LC NO. 81-706586
Prod-CAHILL Dist-AIMS 1980

Rolligon - All-Terrain Vehicle C 3 MIN
16MM FILM OPTICAL SOUND
Shows the road tests for the Rolligon, an all-terrain vehicle.
Prod-ALLFP Dist-NSTA 1973

Rollin' With Love C 6 MIN
3/4 OR 1/2 INCH VIDEO CASSETTE H-C A

Provides a relaxed lighter side introduction to a discussion on same-sex lifestyles. Uses animation
Prod-MMRC Dist-MMRC

Rolling C 11 MIN
3/4 OR 1/2 INCH VIDEO CASSETTE
Covers steps in rolling and kinds of rolling processes.
From The Manufacturing Materials And Processes Series.
Prod-GE Dist-WFVTAE

Rolling C 25 MIN
3/4 OR 1/2 INCH VIDEO CASSETTE H-C A
Discusses aspects of industrial rolling.
From The Technical Studies Series.
Prod-BBCTV Dist-FI 1981

Rolling Home C 15 MIN
1/2 IN VIDEO CASSETTE BETA/VHS I-J
Describes how radio contact is made with the Coast guard, as the crew decides to repair the Mimi and rescue themselves. Includes a trip to a Maine shipbuilder, which illustrates the physical and mathematical principles that keep a boat afloat.
From The Voyage Of The Mimi Series.
Prod-HRAW Dist-HRAW

Rolling Plant-Mixed Asphalt Pavements C 12 MIN
16MM FILM OPTICAL SOUND
Presents the recommended procedure for rolling plant-mixed asphalt and the correct use of steel-wheeled, vibratory and pneumatic-tired rollers.
Prod-AI Dist-AI

Rolling Rice Ball, The C 11 MIN
16MM FILM, 3/4 OR 1/2 IN VIDEO P
Presents an animated film version of a Japanese fairy tale about a Japanese woodcutter who shares his rice balls with the mice and is rewarded and a grasping hunter who learns the folly of greed when he receives no treasure from the mice.
Prod-GAKKEN Dist-CORF 1967

Rolling South C 15 MIN
16MM FILM OPTICAL SOUND
Presents visual imagery with minimum narration to create a picture of a railroad constantly on the move around the clock.
LC NO. 80-700073
Prod-SR Dist-SR Prodn-THOMPN 1979

Rolling Steel C 14 MIN
16MM FILM, 3/4 OR 1/2 IN VIDEO I-H
Shows a field trip to a plant where construction steel is manufactured from scrap iron. Reveals giant electric furnaces, searing heat of molten metal and ear piercing din of a steel plant. Explains the elements necessary to produce steel in a variety of shapes for industrial use.
Prod-BORTF Dist-BCNFL 1983

Rolling Stone C 27 MIN
16MM FILM OPTICAL SOUND
Follows two itinerant sportsmen in the Alaska Panhandle as they fish for salmon, camp in the wilderness and explore remote regions.
Prod-MERMAR Dist-TELEFM

Rollo May And Human Encounter, Pt 1 - Self-Self Encounter And Self-Other Encounter C 30 MIN
16MM FILM OPTICAL SOUND
Features Dr Rollo May who describes man's dilemma as having to see himself as both subject and object in life. Discusses the four elements of human encounter including empathy, eros, friendship and agape. Points out that if any of the four elements is absent, human encounter does not exist.
Prod-PSYCHF Dist-PSYCHD

Rollo May And Human Encounter, Pt 2 - Manipulation And Human Encounter,... C 30 MIN
16MM FILM OPTICAL SOUND
Features Dr Rollo May who discusses how man is manipulated when any of the four elements of human encounter is missing. Describes the problems of transference in psychotherapy as a distortion of human encounter. Explains the exploitation of eros, describing modern man's fixation on sexuality and relating this to man's fear of death.
Prod-PSYCHF Dist-PSYCHD

Rollo May On Creativity And The Tragic C 30 MIN
16MM FILM OPTICAL SOUND
Discusses Dr Rollo May's early education, theological and graduate training, and onset of tuberculosis. Shows how creativity derives from coming to grips with adversity and death, and rebelling against it.
Prod-AACD Dist-AACD 1976

Rollo May, Psychology C 29 MIN
3/4 OR 1/2 INCH VIDEO CASSETTE A
See series title for descriptive statement.
From The Quest For Peace Series.
Prod-AACD Dist-AACD 1984

Rollos / Roles C 30 MIN
3/4 OR 1/2 INCH VIDEO CASSETTE H-C A
Uses a story to try to reduce the minority isolation of Mexican-American students by showing the teenager as an individual, as a member of a unique cultural group and as a member of a larger complex society.
From The La Esquina (English) Series.
Prod-SWEDL Dist-GPITVL 1976

Roly Poly Blues C 42 MIN
16MM FILM, 3/4 OR 1/2 IN VIDEO
Gives information and personal testimonial on obesity and excess weight.
Prod-PEREN Dist-PEREN

Roma Barocca C 10 MIN
16MM FILM OPTICAL SOUND I-C
Depicts Roman fountains to present an exercise in how to isolate a single concept from a conglomeration of materials. Shows the importance of being able to discern and to separate what one sees from its surroundings.
LC NO. 76-703637
Prod-GREGGB Dist-MALIBU 1974

Roman Age, The C 30 MIN
16MM FILM OPTICAL SOUND
Interprets the collapse of Rome as being the result of the Romans' failure to embrace Christianity. Attributes the survival of the early Christians to their belief in God's existence. Based on the book How Should We Then Live by Francis A Schaeffer.
From The How Should We Then Live Series.
LC NO. 77-702363
Prod-GF Dist-GF 1977

Roman And Egyptian - Shakespeare C 45 MIN
2 INCH VIDEOTAPE
See series title for descriptive statement.
From The Humanities Series. Unit I - Persons, Places And Events
Prod-WTTWTV Dist-GPITVL

Roman Banquet Stretch C 10 MIN
2 INCH VIDEOTAPE
See series title for descriptive statement.
From The Janaki Series.
Prod-WGBHTV Dist-PUBTEL

Roman Life In Ancient Pompeii C 16 MIN
16MM FILM OPTICAL SOUND I-J
The voice of a young girl recounts the story of her life in Pompeii before the eruption of Vesuvius. The camera retraces her steps through the silent ruins as she helps with family tasks, shops, visits friends and goes to the amphitheater.
Prod-SUEF Dist-SUTHLA 1962

Roman Renaissance B 27 MIN
16MM FILM, 3/4 OR 1/2 IN VIDEO J-H
Views the Sicilian and Italian campaigns during World War II.
From The Victory At Sea Series.
Prod-NBCTV Dist-LUF

Roman Renaissance - Sicily And The Italian Campaign B 30 MIN
16MM FILM OPTICAL SOUND I-C
Pictures the invasion of Sicily, the resignation of Mussolini and the signing of an armistice. Describes Germany's defensive reaction which left the Italian people confused and divided. Shows Allied attacks on Salerno, Naples, Anzio and Cassino and describes the entry into Rome on June 4, 1944.
From The Victory At Sea Series.
Prod-GRACUR Dist-GRACUR

Roman Riviera - The Art Of Pompeii C 45 MIN
2 INCH VIDEOTAPE
See series title for descriptive statement.
From The Humanities Series. Unit II - The World Of Myth And Legend
Prod-WTTWTV Dist-GPITVL

Roman World, The C 23 MIN
16MM FILM, 3/4 OR 1/2 IN VIDEO H-C
Tours the cities which exist today and which existed during the period of the Roman empire.
Prod-BHA Dist-IFB 1963

Romance B 134 MIN
3/4 OR 1/2 INCH VIDEO CASSETTE
Conjoins extreme sexual ambiguity with narrative breakdown.
Prod-KITCHN Dist-KITCHN

Romance And Reality C 52 MIN
16MM FILM, 3/4 OR 1/2 IN VIDEO J-C A
Surveys the development of Western civilization during the 13th century. Depicts a world of chivalry, courtesy and romance as evidenced in the emergence of courtly love as the ultimate in aesthetic and ascetic devotion and as reflected in the poetry of Dante and the Anjou tapestries. Points out the spiritual happiness of the period as seen in the life of St Francis and in the work The Little Flowers.
From The Civilisation Series. No. 3
LC NO. 79-707043
Prod-BBCTV Dist-FI 1970

Romance At Droitwich Spa C 30 MIN
3/4 OR 1/2 INCH VIDEO CASSETTE C A
Presents an adaptation of the short story Romance At Droitwich Spa by P G Wodehouse.
From The Wodehouse Playhouse Series.
Prod-BBCTV Dist-TIMLIF 1980

Romance In Snow Country C 25 MIN
16MM FILM OPTICAL SOUND C A
Tells the true story of Shoshin, who lived in northern Japan's snowladen mountains. Explains that he was destined to become a Shinto priest like his father until a Christian radio program changed the course of his life.
Prod-CBFMS Dist-CBFMS

Romance Of A Horsethief C 101 MIN
16MM FILM OPTICAL SOUND H-C A
Presents a folk tale set in a small Polish border town in 1904 as a young revolutionary woman is torn between her love for her fiance and fellow revolutionary and her handsome childhood sweetheart. Stars Yul Brynner and Eli Wallach.
Prod-CINEWO Dist-CINEWO 1971

Romance Of Transportation, The C 11 MIN
16MM FILM, 3/4 OR 1/2 IN VIDEO
Uses animation to show the growth of transportation in North America. Comments on the development of the canoe, oxcart, barge, steamboat, railroad, automobile, and airplane.
Prod-NFBC Dist-IFB 1954

Romance To Recovery C 34 MIN
16MM FILM - 3/4 IN VIDEO
Explains how alcohol abuse can lead to the disintegration of the family unit. Emphasizes the importance of rehabilitation for the 'co-alcoholic' as well as the alcoholic.
LC NO. 79-706857
Prod-FMSP Dist-FMSP 1979

Romance, Sex, And Marriage - All The Guys Ever Want Is S-E-X C 26 MIN
16MM FILM, 3/4 OR 1/2 IN VIDEO
Records the conversations of high school students as they describe their feelings about sex. Covers birth control, virginity, physical appearance, emotional involvement, acceptance, sexual abuse, masturbation and self-confidence.
Prod-DOCUA Dist-CNEMAG

Romanesque Painters (1000 - 1200 A D) C 11 MIN
16MM FILM OPTICAL SOUND
Discusses Romanesque painters from 1000 to 1200 A D. Shows 12th century church murals that use color and design to create a universe of pure symbols around the figure of a tender and mystical Jesus which are startlingly modern in their stylized, almost abstract imagery.
Prod-ROLAND Dist-ROLAND

Romania C 20 MIN
16MM FILM OPTICAL SOUND I-C A
Describes the character of the people of Romania and the strength and dignity of their culture. Emphasizes the historical importance of both the land and its major waterway, the Danube. Discusses the political turmoil resulting from today's communist domination.
Prod-WIANCK Dist-AVED 1962

Romania C 25 MIN
16MM FILM OPTICAL SOUND
Presents a view of Romania, the ancient land of Eastern Europe whose traditions and name stem from a time before the ancient Romans.
From The Eye Of The Beholder Series.
LC NO. 75-701922
Prod-RCPDF Dist-VIACOM 1974

Romania C 18 MIN
16MM FILM, 3/4 OR 1/2 IN VIDEO I-J
Describes the way of life of the Romaian people, the basis of the agricultural economy and the geographical location of Romania. Shows the home of one of the workers and discusses the change from a rural-agricultural society to an urban-industrial society.
From The Man And His World Series.
Prod-IFFB Dist-FI 1970

Romanian Village Life - On The Danube Delta C 15 MIN
16MM FILM, 3/4 OR 1/2 IN VIDEO
Follows the varied daily activities of a family in a small Romanian village. Shows farming activities, kneading dough for apple pastry and baking it in an old clay oven, washing laundry in a basin in the yard and rinsing it in the Danube river, catching frogs, embroidering, fishing, preparing lunch over an open fire, and eating a crayfish dinner in a small peasant home. Unnarrated.
Prod-IFF Dist-IFF

Romans, The C 24 MIN
16MM FILM, 3/4 OR 1/2 IN VIDEO H-C
Describes how the Romans imitated the Greek ideal of the city-state and how they emerged as the ruling force of the ancient world. Uses models of Rome and photographs of amphitheaters, aqueducts and roads to demonstrate the brilliance of Roman architecture and indicate the relationship between engineering and military accomplishments.
Prod-IFB Dist-IFB

Romans, The C 24 MIN
16MM FILM, 3/4 OR 1/2 IN VIDEO H-C
Presents the origins, growth and collapse of the Roman Empire, using animated maps, artwork and live footage.
From The Outline History Of Europe Series.
LC NO. 80-706988
Prod-POLNIS Dist-IFB 1976

Romans, The (French) C 24 MIN
16MM FILM, 3/4 OR 1/2 IN VIDEO H-C
Describes how the Romans imitated the Greek ideal of the city-state and how they emerged as the ruling force of the ancient world. Uses models of Rome and photographs of amphitheaters, aqueducts and roads to demonstrate the brilliance of Roman architecture and indicate the relationship between engineering and military accomplishments.
Prod-IFB Dist-IFB

Romans, The (Greek) C 24 MIN
16MM FILM, 3/4 OR 1/2 IN VIDEO H-C
Describes how the Romans imitated the Greek ideal of the city-state and how they emerged as the ruling force of the ancient world. Uses models of Rome and photographs of amphitheaters, aqueducts and roads to demonstrate the brilliance of Roman architecture and indicate the relationship between engineering and military accomplishments.
Prod-IFB Dist-IFB

Romans, The (Swedish) C 24 MIN
16MM FILM, 3/4 OR 1/2 IN VIDEO H-C A
Presents the origins, growth and collapse of the Roman Empire. Describes how the Roman initiated the Greek ideal of the city-state and how they expanded over a period of 400 years, emerging as the ruling force of the world.
Prod-IFB Dist-IFB 1975

Romans, The - Life, Laughter And Law C 22 MIN
16MM FILM, 3/4 OR 1/2 IN VIDEO J-C A
Recreates the human side of the Roman empire by showing excerpts from Roman writings.
From The Western Civilization - Majesty And Madness Series.
Prod-SCNDRI Dist-LCOA 1971

Romans, The - Life, Laughter And Law (Captioned) C 22 MIN
16MM FILM, 3/4 OR 1/2 IN VIDEO J-C A
Brings Rome's Golden Age to life through writings of the time.
Prod-SCNDRI Dist-LCOA 1971

Romans, The - Life, Laughter and Law (Spanish) C 22 MIN
16MM FILM, 3/4 OR 1/2 IN VIDEO J-C A
Brings Rome's Golden Age to life through writings of the time.
Prod-SCNDRI Dist-LCOA 1971

Romantic Age In English Literature, The C
3/4 OR 1/2 INCH VIDEO CASSETTE H
Explores the literary themes and social currents of the Romantic Age through the works of Wordsworth, Shelley, Byron and Keats. Gives biographical notes on each poet with an analysis of their works. Includes original illustrations and paintings from the period.
Prod-GA Dist-GA

Romantic Ballet, The C 52 MIN
16MM FILM, 3/4 OR 1/2 IN VIDEO J-C A
Traces the story of the Romantic Ballet and its greatest exponents.
From The Magic Of Dance Series.
Prod-BBCTV Dist-TIMLIF 1980

Romantic Days Of Fire Horses, The B 10 MIN
16MM FILM OPTICAL SOUND
Presents edited biograph and Edison footage from the paperprint collection and from the George Kleine collection, in the library of Congress. Shows an exhibition drill of New York firemen in Union Square, which was photographed in 1904, a run of the New York Fire Department in 1903 and exhibitions of efficiency by the fire departments of Schennectady, New York and Chelsea, Massachusetts.
LC NO. 72-700770
Prod-BHAWK Dist-BHAWK 1972

Romantic Rebellion, The (Spanish) C 50 MIN
16MM FILM, 3/4 OR 1/2 IN VIDEO H-C A
Outlines the historic background of the Romantic movement and illustrates the general principles of Romantic and Classic art with illustrations from the work of individual artists.
From The Romantic Vs Classic Art (Spanish) Series.
Prod-VPSL Dist-PFP

Romantic Versus Classic Art - Auguste Rodin C 26 MIN
16MM FILM, 3/4 OR 1/2 IN VIDEO J-C A
Presents the works of sculptor Auguste Rodin (1840-1917.) Includes the statue of Balzac.
From The Romantic Versus Classic Art Series.
Prod-VPSL Dist-PFP 1974

Romantic Versus Classic Art - Edgar Degas C 26 MIN
16MM FILM, 3/4 OR 1/2 IN VIDEO J-C A
Features Kenneth Clark discussing the classical paintings of French artist Edgar Degas. Televised in the series THE ROMANTIC REBELLION.
From The Romantic Versus Classic Art Series.
Prod-VPSL Dist-PFP 1974

Romantic Versus Classic Art - Eugene Delacroix C 26 MIN
16MM FILM, 3/4 OR 1/2 IN VIDEO J-C A
Features Kenneth Clark discussing the underlying themes in the paintings of French artist Eugene Delacroix. Televised in the series THE ROMANTIC REBELLION.
From The Romantic Versus Classic Art Series.
Prod-VPSL Dist-PFP 1974

Romantic Versus Classic Art - Francisco Goya Y Lucientes C 26 MIN
16MM FILM, 3/4 OR 1/2 IN VIDEO J-C A
Features Kenneth Clark discussing Goya's transition from the classic tradition in painting to that of Romanticism. Televised in the series THE ROMANTIC REBELLION.
From The Romantic Versus Classic Art Series.
Prod-VPSL Dist-PFP 1974

Romantic Versus Classic Art - Gian-Battista Piranesi - Henry Fuseli C 26 MIN
16MM FILM, 3/4 OR 1/2 IN VIDEO J-C A
Features Kenneth Clark discussing the art works of Giambattista Piranesi and Henry Fuseli. Televised in the series THE ROMANTIC REBELLION.
From The Romantic Versus Classic Art Series.
Prod-VPSL Dist-PFP 1974

Romantic Versus Classic Art - Jacques Louis David C 26 MIN
16MM FILM, 3/4 OR 1/2 IN VIDEO J-C A
Features Kenneth Clark discussing the classical paintings of French artist Jacques Louis David. Televised in the series THE ROMANTIC REBELLION.
From The Romantic Versus Classic Art Series.
Prod-VPSL Dist-PFP 1974

Romantic Versus Classic Art - James William Mallord Turner, Pt 1 C 26 MIN
16MM FILM, 3/4 OR 1/2 IN VIDEO J-C A
Features Kenneth Clark tracing Turner's development from traditional Romantic paintings to works composed of swirling color forms. Televised in the series THE ROMANTIC REBELLION.
From The Romantic Versus Classic Art Series.
Prod-VPSL Dist-PFP 1974

Romantic Versus Classic Art - James William Mallord Turner, Pt 2 C 26 MIN
16MM FILM, 3/4 OR 1/2 IN VIDEO J-C A
Features Kenneth Clark tracing Turner's development from traditional Romantic paintings to works composed of swirling forms. Televised in the series THE ROMANTIC REBELLION.
From The Romantic Versus Classic Art Series.
Prod-VPSL Dist-PFP 1974

Romantic Versus Classic Art - Jean Auguste Dominique Ingres, Pt 1 C 26 MIN
16MM FILM, 3/4 OR 1/2 IN VIDEO J-C A
Features Kenneth Clark discussing the classic tradition of the paintings of French artist Jean Auguste Dominique Ingres. Televised in the series THE ROMANTIC REBELLION.
From The Romantic Versus Classic Art Series.
Prod-VPSL Dist-PFP 1974

Romantic Versus Classic Art - Jean Auguste Dominique Ingres, Pt 2 C 26 MIN
16MM FILM, 3/4 OR 1/2 IN VIDEO J-C A
Features Kenneth Clark discussing the classic tradition of the paintings of French artist Jean Auguste Dominique Ingres. Televised in the series THE ROMANTIC REBELLION.
From The Romantic Versus Classic Art Series.
Prod-VPSL Dist-PFP 1974

Romantic Versus Classic Art - Jean Francois Millet C 26 MIN
16MM FILM, 3/4 OR 1/2 IN VIDEO J-C A
Features Kenneth Clark discussing the paintings of French artist Jean Francois Millet. Televised in the series THE ROMANTIC REBELLION.
From The Romantic Versus Classic Art Series.
Prod-VPSL Dist-PFP 1974

Romantic Versus Classic Art - John Constable C 26 MIN
16MM FILM, 3/4 OR 1/2 IN VIDEO J-C A
Features Kenneth Clark discussing the paintings of English artist John Constable. Televised in the series THE ROMANTIC REBELLION.
From The Romantic Versus Classic Art Series.
Prod-VPSL Dist-PFP 1974

Romantic Versus Classic Art - The Romantic Rebellion C 50 MIN
16MM FILM, 3/4 OR 1/2 IN VIDEO J-C A
Features Kenneth Clark discussing the basic principles of classic and Romantic art and demonstrates how they have been in conflict. Televised in the series THE ROMANTIC REBELLION.
From The Romantic Versus Classic Art Series.
Prod-VPSL Dist-PFP 1974

Romantic Versus Classic Art - Theodore Gericault C 26 MIN
16MM FILM, 3/4 OR 1/2 IN VIDEO J-C A
Features Kenneth Clark discussing the paintings of French artist Theodore Gericault. Televised in the series THE ROMANTIC REBELLION.
From The Romantic Versus Classic Art Series.
Prod-VPSL Dist-PFP 1974

Romantic Versus Classic Art - William Blake C 26 MIN
16MM FILM, 3/4 OR 1/2 IN VIDEO J-C A
Features Kenneth Clark discussing the art of William Blake, focusing on the drawings and engravings which expressed the need for a new religion in the Romantic period. Televised in the series THE ROMANTIC REBELLION.
From The Romantic Versus Classic Art Series.
Prod-VPSL Dist-PFP 1974

Romantic Versus Classic Art—A Series
16MM FILM, 3/4 OR 1/2 IN VIDEO I-C A
Prod-VPSL Dist-PFP 1974

Romantic Versus Classic Art - Auguste Rodin	26 MIN
Romantic Versus Classic Art - Edgar Degas	26 MIN
Romantic Versus Classic Art - Eugene Delacroix	26 MIN
Romantic Versus Classic Art - Francisco Goya	26 MIN
Romantic Versus Classic Art - Giambattista	26 MIN
Romantic Versus Classic Art - Jacques Louis	26 MIN
Romantic Versus Classic Art - James William	26 MIN
Romantic Versus Classic Art - James William	26 MIN
Romantic Versus Classic Art - Jean Auguste	26 MIN
Romantic Versus Classic Art - Jean Auguste	26 MIN
Romantic Versus Classic Art - Jean Francois	26 MIN
Romantic Versus Classic Art - John Constable	26 MIN
Romantic Versus Classic Art - The Romantic	50 MIN
Romantic Versus Classic Art - Theodore	26 MIN
Romantic Versus Classic Art - William Blake	26 MIN

Romantic Vs Classic Art (Spanish)—A Series
H-C A
Analyzes the personalities of the major Romantic and Classic artists and examines the characteristics of their work. Features art historian, Lord Kenneth Clark.
Prod-VPSL Dist-PFP

Auguste Rodin (Spanish)	026 MIN
Edgar Degas (Spanish)	026 MIN
Eugene Delacroix (Spanish)	026 MIN
Francisco Goya (Spanish)	026 MIN
Gian-Battista Piranesi/Henry Fuseli	026 MIN
Jacques Louis David (Spanish)	026 MIN
Jean-Auguste Dominique Ingres, Pt I (Spanish)	026 MIN
Jean-Auguste Dominique Ingres, Pt II (Spanish)	026 MIN
Jean-Francois Millet (Spanish)	026 MIN
John Constable (Spanish)	026 MIN
Joseph Mallord-William Turner, Pt I (Spanish)	026 MIN
Joseph Mallord-William Turner, Pt II(Spanish)	026 MIN
Romantic Rebellion, The (Spanish)	026 MIN
Theodore Gericault (Spanish)	026 MIN
William Blake (Spanish)	026 MIN

Romanticism - The Revolt Of The Spirit C 27 MIN
16MM FILM, 3/4 OR 1/2 IN VIDEO J-C A
Presents the romantic movement as an era much like our own, an era of spiraling technology and bewildering change. Dramatizes excerpts from the works of Hugo, Shelley, Byron, Emily Bronte and others who spoke out for individuality, freedom, sentiment and revolt.
Prod-SCNDRI Dist-LCOA 1971

Romanticism - The Revolt Of The Spirit (Spanish) C 24 MIN
16MM FILM, 3/4 OR 1/2 IN VIDEO J-C A
Illustrates 19th century romanticism through excerpts from Les Miserables and Wuthering Heights.
Prod-SCNDRI Dist-LCOA 1971

Romantics, The C 60 MIN
3/4 OR 1/2 INCH VIDEO CASSETTE J-C A
Presents flutist James Galway discussing the Romantic movement in music that strove for music and self-expression. Includes music from Chopin's Polonaise in A-Flat, Mendelssohn's Elijah and Brahms' German Requiem.
From The James Galway's Music In Time Series.
Prod-POLTEL Dist-FOTH 1982

Rome C 3 MIN
16MM FILM OPTICAL SOUND P-I
Discusses the city of Rome in Italy.
From The Of All Things Series.
Prod-BAILYL Dist-AVED

Rome C 13 MIN
16MM FILM, 3/4 OR 1/2 IN VIDEO I-H A
Capsulizes the early growth of the city of Rome, which became a metropolis of the ancient world and describes the life and times of the Caesars.
Prod-LUF Dist-LUF 1981

Rome - City Eternal X 11 MIN
16MM FILM, 3/4 OR 1/2 IN VIDEO I-H
Pictures the glories of Rome—the Colosseum, Saint Peter's Square, the Villa d'Este fountains, the Forum, Hadrian's Villa and the Piazza Navona. Shows the city by the light of a fireworks display.
Prod-EBF Dist-EBEC 1951

Rome - City Eternal (Spanish) C 11 MIN
16MM FILM, 3/4 OR 1/2 IN VIDEO I-H
Portrays the glories of Rome, including the Colosseum, St Peter's Square, the art treasures of the Basilica of St Peter, the fountains of the Villa d'Este and the Piazza Navona, the ruins of the Forum and Hadrian's villa.
Prod-EBEC Dist-EBEC

Rome - Impact Of An Idea C 27 MIN
16MM FILM, 3/4 OR 1/2 IN VIDEO H-C A
Examines the design of Rome by Pope Sixtus V. Shows that Sixtus was the first to see the city as a system.
From The Understanding Cities Series.
Prod-FI Dist-FI 1983

Rome - Sacred City C 13 MIN
16MM FILM OPTICAL SOUND
Takes a reverent look at the eternal city as the camera spans the centuries.
Prod-PANWA Dist-PANWA

Rome - The Eternal City C 21 MIN
16MM FILM, 3/4 OR 1/2 IN VIDEO I-H A
Deals with the history of Rome from the time it was founded to the 1970's.
Prod-HOE Dist-MCFI 1977

Rome - The Fading Glory C 12 MIN
3/4 OR 1/2 INCH VIDEO CASSETTE
Shows how the ancient city of Rome has begun to show the effects of modern pollution.
Prod-UPI Dist-JOU

Rome And The Vatican - Pope John Paul II C 26 MIN
16MM FILM, 3/4 OR 1/2 IN VIDEO I-J A
Follows the visit of six British school children to Rome and films their meeting with Pope John Paul II.
Prod-THAMES Dist-MEDIAG 1984

Rome, City Of Fountains C 3 MIN
16MM FILM OPTICAL SOUND P-I
Discusses the city of Rome in Italy.
From The Of All Things Series.
Prod-BAILYL Dist-AVED

Romeo And Juliet B 40 MIN
16MM FILM OPTICAL SOUND
An excerpt from the feature film of the same title. Includes the duel scene, the death scene, Friar Lawrence's cell and flashes of the Capulet-Montague feud. Stars John Barrymore, Leslie Howard and Norma Shearer.
LC NO. FIA52-4977
Prod-PMI Dist-FI 1936

Romeo And Juliet C 142 MIN
16MM FILM OPTICAL SOUND
Presents a version of Romeo and Juliet, William Shakespeare's Mediterranean tragedy of blood feuds and star-crossed lovers. Stars Laurence Harvey, Susan Shentall and Flora Robson.
Prod-UNKNWN Dist-LCOA 1954

Romeo And Juliet C 8 MIN
16MM FILM, 3/4 OR 1/2 IN VIDEO H-C
See series title for descriptive statement.
From The Shakespeare Series.
Prod-IFB Dist-IFB 1974

Romeo And Juliet C 30 MIN
3/4 OR 1/2 INCH VIDEO CASSETTE J-C A

Presents an adaptation of Shakespeare's play Romeo And Juliet, a tragedy of circumstance where love chooses as its object its own hated enemy. Includes the plays Macbeth, Julius Caesar and Hamlet on the same tape.
From The Shakespeare In Perspective Series.
Prod-FI Dist-FI 1984

Romeo And Juliet C 36 MIN
16MM FILM, 3/4 OR 1/2 IN VIDEO
Presents an adaptation of William Shakespeare's play Romeo And Juliet cut to preserve the story line and famous passages.
From The World Of William Shakespeare Series.
LC NO. 80-706327
Prod-NGS Dist-NGS 1978

Romeo And Juliet C 45 MIN
16MM FILM, 3/4 OR 1/2 IN VIDEO H-C A
A shortened version of the 1968 Franco Zeffirelli film Romeo And Juliet, based on the play by Shakespeare. Traces Romeo and Juliet's love from their first meeting to their self-inflicted deaths.
Prod-ZEFFIF Dist-AIMS 1968

Romeo And Juliet C 124 MIN
16MM FILM, 3/4 OR 1/2 IN VIDEO J-C A
Stars the Royal Ballet with Margot Fonteyn and Rudolf Nureyev in the ballet with musical score provided by Serge Prokofiev.
Prod-IDEAL Dist-FI 1966

Romeo And Juliet C 165 MIN
3/4 OR 1/2 INCH VIDEO CASSETTE
Presents Shakespeare's play of young love and death in medieval Italy. Stars Sir John Gielgud, Rebecca Saire and Patrick Ryecart.
From The Shakespeare Plays Series.
LC NO. 79-706938
Prod-BBCTV Dist-TIMLIF 1979

Romeo And Juliet (1595) B 45 MIN
16MM FILM OPTICAL SOUND J-C A
Presents Otto Krejca's production of William Shakespeare's tragedy performed in Prague's National Theatre and shows actors in rehearsal.
Prod-ROLAND Dist-ROLAND

Romeo And Juliet - Act II, Scene II C 9 MIN
16MM FILM, 3/4 OR 1/2 IN VIDEO J-C A
Presents a dramatization of Act II, Scene II of Shakespeare's play Romeo And Juliet.
From The Great Scenes From Shakespeare Series.
Prod-SEABEN Dist-PHENIX 1971

Romeo And Juliet - Poet Versus Playwright B 45 MIN
2 INCH VIDEOTAPE C
See series title for descriptive statement.
From The Shakespeare Series.
Prod-CHITVC Dist-GPITVL Prodn-WTTWTV

Romeo And Juliet - Tragedy Of Coincidence And Accident B 45 MIN
2 INCH VIDEOTAPE C
See series title for descriptive statement.
From The Shakespeare Series.
Prod-CHITVC Dist-GPITVL Prodn-WTTWTV

Romeo And Juliet Ballet C
1/2 IN VIDEO CASSETTE BETA/VHS
Presents Prokofiev's Romeo And Juliet danced by the Bolshoi Ballet Company.
Prod-GA Dist-GA

Romeo And Juliet In Kansas City C 28 MIN
16MM FILM, 3/4 OR 1/2 IN VIDEO I A
Features Tchaikovsky's Romeo and Juliet Overture, played by the Kansas City Philharmonic, interspersed with quotations from Shakespeare's play Romeo and Juliet.
LC NO. 76-700076
Prod-MUSICP Dist-PFP 1975

Romeros, The C 58 MIN
3/4 OR 1/2 INCH VIDEO CASSETTE
See series title for descriptive statement.
From The Evening At Pops Series.
Prod-WGBHTV Dist-PBS 1978

Romie-O And Julie-8 C 25 MIN
16MM FILM, 3/4 OR 1/2 IN VIDEO
Shows two robots falling in love, though supposedly without feelings. Teaches their human creators about feeling and caring for one another. Animated.
Prod-NELVNA Dist-BCNFL 1980

Ron Brooks And Group C 29 MIN
2 INCH VIDEOTAPE
Presents the jazz music of Ron Brooks and group. Features host Jim Rockwell interviewing these artists.
From The People In Jazz Series.
Prod-WTVSTV Dist-PUBTEL

Ron Palelek - Feeding Your Horse C 28 MIN
1/2 IN VIDEO CASSETTE BETA/VHS
Addresses the proper use of roughage and concentrates in feeding horses. Points out differences between feeding young and older horses.
From The Ron Palelek Training Series.
Prod-VDTECH Dist-EQVDL

Ron Palelek - Grooming Your Horse C 61 MIN
1/2 IN VIDEO CASSETTE BETA/VHS
Discusses horse grooming. Describes equipment, brushing techniques, bathing and hoof care, among other things.
From The Ron Palelek Training Series.
Prod-VDTECH Dist-EQVDL

Ron Palelek - Leading Your Horse C 62 MIN
1/2 IN VIDEO CASSETTE BETA/VHS
Shows how to lead a horse. Involves halterbreaking.
From The Ron Palelek Training Series.
Prod-VDTECH Dist-EQVDL

Ron Palelek - Preparing The Halter Horse For Show C 61 MIN
1/2 IN VIDEO CASSETTE BETA/VHS
Discusses preparing the halter horse for show, including hoof care, feeding and exercising.
From The Ron Palelek Training Series.
Prod-VDTECH Dist-EQVDL

Ron Palelek Training–A Series

Describes the training of horses. Presented by Ron Palelek.
Prod-VDTECH Dist-EQVDL

Ron Palelek - Feeding Your Horse 028 MIN
Ron Palelek - Grooming Your Horse 061 MIN
Ron Palelek - Leading Your Horse 062 MIN
Ron Palelek - Preparing The Halter Horse For 061 MIN

Ronald Reagan C 12 MIN
3/4 OR 1/2 INCH VIDEO CASSETTE H-C A
Follows Ronald Reagan's career from its Hollywood beginnings to his candidacy in the 1980 elections.
Prod-UPI Dist-JOU

Ronald Reagan - Identification Of The Japanese Zero B 24 MIN
3/4 OR 1/2 INCH VIDEO CASSETTE
Focuses on the necessity of American pilots' recognizing the difference between a P-40 and a Japanese Zero. Made by young Ronald Reagan.
Prod-IHF Dist-IHF

Ronald W Estabrook C 50 MIN
3/4 OR 1/2 INCH VIDEO CASSETTE
Reviews the research events of the 60s leading to the discovery of the significance of cytochrome P-450 to chemical carcinogenesis, featuring Dr Ronald W Estabrook.
From The Eminent Chemists - The Interviews Series.
Prod-AMCHEM Dist-AMCHEM 1982

Ronnie's Tune C 18 MIN
16MM FILM, 3/4 OR 1/2 IN VIDEO J-C A
Tells how 11-year-old Julie must deal with the suicide of her teenaged cousin.
Prod-WOMBAT Dist-WOMBAT

Roof Bolting In Coal Mines (Rev Ed) C 19 MIN
16MM FILM, 3/4 OR 1/2 IN VIDEO
Explains the principles and purposes of roof bolting in coal mining. Coordinates mining operations and bolting methods, and stresses safety throughout the roof control process.
Prod-USDL Dist-USNAC

Roof Check C 30 MIN
1/2 IN VIDEO CASSETTE BETA/VHS
Checks the condition of a house's roof. Considers installing a wood burning stove and a new bathroom.
From The This Old House, Pt 2 - Suburban '50s Series.
Prod-WGBHTV Dist-MTI

Roofer's Pitch - Safety In Roofing C 21 MIN
16MM FILM, 3/4 OR 1/2 IN VIDEO IND
Covers all facets of safety for roofers.
Prod-CSAO Dist-IFB

Roofing C 30 MIN
16MM FILM, 3/4 OR 1/2 IN VIDEO
Provides basic information on roofing repairs.
From The Do It Yourself Home Repairs Series.
Prod-ODECA Dist-BULFRG

Rooftop Odyssey C 10 MIN
16MM FILM, 3/4 OR 1/2 IN VIDEO J-C A
Surveys the thoughts, symbols, irony and anguish which go through the mind of a man about to commit suicide.
LC NO. 80-707630
Prod-CSAKYA Dist-CSAKYA 1970

Rooftop Road C 8 MIN
16MM FILM, 3/4 OR 1/2 IN VIDEO J-C A
Presents a montage of Chicago's major transportation system, the elevated CTA. Captures the many moods of the city.
Prod-IFB Dist-IFB 1974

Rooftopics C 11 MIN
16MM FILM OPTICAL SOUND J A
Provides a different perspective on Australia's largest city with views of rooftops in Sydney.
LC NO. 72-702256
Prod-ANAIB Dist-AUIS 1971

Rookie Of The Year C 47 MIN
16MM FILM, 3/4 OR 1/2 IN VIDEO
Deals with the problems of identity and sex discrimination among adolescents, focusing on the controversy triggerd when a girl plays on her brother's baseball team. Based on the book Not Bad For A Girl by Isabella Taves. Originally shown on the television series ABC Afterschool Specials.
From The Teenage Years Series.
LC NO. 79-707363
Prod-WILSND Dist-TIMLIF 1975

Rookies, The C 1 MIN
16MM FILM OPTICAL SOUND
Provides a lead-in without narration to the television show The Rookies.
LC NO. 78-700377
Prod-VIACOM Dist-VIACOM Prodn-BUNINE 1978

Room And Board C 5 MIN
16MM FILM OPTICAL SOUND H-C
Presents an animated film depicting man's quest for the unattainable. Shows a cartoon character placed in an empty room with a single golden door knob. Shows how he grows, matures, withers and dies as all the while he tries to open the door with the golden knob.
LC NO. 76-703638
Prod-CARTR Dist-MALIBU 1976

Room At The Top B 28 MIN
16MM FILM OPTICAL SOUND I-H
Explains that at the top of the Saturn-Apollo is the command module, the crew quarters, flight center and command post for the flight to the moon.
LC NO. 71-708123
Prod-NASA Dist-USNAC 1966

Room At The Top B 115 MIN
16MM FILM OPTICAL SOUND
Focuses on a factory worker who tries to court the boss's daughter but ends up with another woman. Stars Laurence Harvey and Simone Signoret.
Prod-UNKNWN Dist-KITPAR 1958

Room At The Top C 30 MIN
16MM FILM, 3/4 OR 1/2 IN VIDEO H-C A
Discusses the decision to build the Westin Hotel in Boston.
From The Enterprise Series.
Prod-MTI Dist-MTI

Room At The Top C 30 MIN
3/4 OR 1/2 INCH VIDEO CASSETTE H-C A
Describes Westin Hotel's gamble as it opened a new hotel in Boston, a city already well supplied with hotels. Follows the hotel's executives as they plan the opening of the 125 million dollar New England flagship hotel.
From The Enterprise III Series.
Prod-WGBHTV Dist-KINGFT

Room Check, A C 30 MIN
2 INCH VIDEOTAPE C A
Explains how all the small, individual plans discussed throughout the telecourse work together to create a complete design plan. Details importance of utilizing extended living spaces in a home.
From The Designing Home Interiors Series. Unit 26
Prod-COAST Dist-CDTEL Prodn-RSCCD

Room For A Stranger C 25 MIN
16MM FILM OPTICAL SOUND
Shows Indochinese refugees languishing in refugee camps and depicts Lutheran congregations examining conflicts between a humanitarian response and economic burdens for the Nation. Explores myths about refugees. Explains how refugee families can be resettled by parishes rather than by individual sponsors.
LC NO. 80-700407
Prod-LCUSA Dist-LCUSA 1979

Room For Heroes C 14 MIN
16MM FILM, 3/4 OR 1/2 IN VIDEO
Explains that legendary heroes have traditionally grown out of the needs of the people, and have represented the ideals and distinguishing characteristics of particular groups or nations. Describes the exploits of such heroes as Johnny Appleseed, Pecos Bill, Casey Jones, Davy Crockett and others who became legends in their own time.
Prod-DISNEY Dist-WDEMCO 1971

Room For Us C 30 MIN
3/4 OR 1/2 INCH VIDEO CASSETTE P-I
See series title for descriptive statement.
From The Sonrisas Series.
Prod-KRLNTV Dist-MDCPB

Room Service C 15 MIN
16MM FILM OPTICAL SOUND
Presents a filmed version of the dance piece by Yvonne Rainer, as performed at the 81st St Theatre Rally.
Prod-VANBKS Dist-VANBKS 1965

Room Service C 8 MIN
3/4 INCH VIDEO CASSETTE
Deals with the arrival of the Cuban boat people and the language barriers most immigrants must overcome, interspersed with the artist telling a classic Lenny Bruce immigrant joke. By Tony Labat.
Prod-EAI Dist-EAI

Room Service C 10 MIN
16MM FILM, 3/4 OR 1/2 IN VIDEO J-C A
Deals with special problems of room service, including duties of waiter or waitress and order taker. Stresses the importance of getting the order complete and having exact identification of the guest and room. Explains that servers must check trays, make sure the order is complete, give instruction for entering a room, serve guests and observe discretion and courtesy throughout.
From The Professional Hospitality Program Series.
LC NO. 74-700224
Prod-NEM Dist-NEM 1973

Room To Learn C 22 MIN
16MM FILM OPTICAL SOUND
Shows a preschool facility based on the Montessori methods, with children playing and learning in an environment that encourages participation in the learning process.
Prod-NYU Dist-NYU

Room To Let C 20 MIN
16MM FILM OPTICAL SOUND P-I
Shows what happens when the Chiffy Kids befriend a friendly but crafty hobo by allowing him to use their den for temporary shelter. Relates how the old man then refuses to leave.
Prod-LUF Dist-LUF 1979

Room To Live C 27 MIN
16MM FILM OPTICAL SOUND
Deals with the importance of wearing seatbelt safety restraints when riding in an automobile.
LC NO. 80-701376
Prod-MEGROU Dist-MEGROU 1979

Room 10 - Ramsey Hospital Emergency C 24 MIN
3/4 OR 1/2 INCH VIDEO CASSETTE
Shows the dramatic efforts of an emergency team to save the life of an auto accident victim. Reveals the thoughts and attitudes of people who work daily with death.
Prod-WCCOTV Dist-WCCOTV 1972

Roommates On A Rainy Day X 26 MIN
16MM FILM, 3/4 OR 1/2 IN VIDEO H-C A
Looks at the relationship between a woman who wants a deeper commitment and a man who is afraid of marriage. Tells how the man's encounter with a jaded swinger forces him to reexamine his priorities. Stars Martin Sheen.
Prod-PAULST Dist-MEDIAG

Roommates On A Rainy Day (Spanish) X 26 MIN
16MM FILM, 3/4 OR 1/2 IN VIDEO H-C A
Looks at the relationship between a woman who wants a deeper commitment and a man who is afraid of marriage. Tells how the man's encounter with a jaded swinger forces him to reexamine his priorities. Stars Martin Sheen.
From The Insight Series.
Prod-PAULST Dist-PAULST

Roomnastics—A Series
P
Presents exercises which can be done in the classroom.
Prod-WVIZTV Dist-GPITVL 1976

Arm Pull / Bend And Twist / Side Straddle Jump 015 MIN
Arm Stretcher / Forward And Backward 015 MIN
Arm Twister / Alternate Toe Touching / Sprinter 015 MIN
Arms Circles / Back Stretcher / Hopping 015 MIN
Backward Stretcher / Toe Touching / Strider 015 MIN
Breast Stroke And Double Arm Lift / Swing And 015 MIN
Chain Breaker / Forward Lunge And Turn / 015 MIN
Crawl Stroke / Body Bend And Reverse Arm 015 MIN
Cross Chest Arm Swing / Trunk Circles / 015 MIN
Double Arm Coordinators / Toe Touch And Leg 015 MIN
Double Armlifts Forward / Front And Back Bend 015 MIN
Double Armlifts Sideward / Sideward Bend With 015 MIN
Double Armstretchers / Sideward Bend And 015 MIN
Elbow Bender / Sideward Bending / Blast-Off 015 MIN
Forward Stretcher / Trunk Rotation / Knee 015 MIN
Giant Circles / Trunk Twister / Knee Lifts 015 MIN
Overarm Sweep And Shoulder Shrug / Trunk 015 MIN
Rope Pull / Swing And Bend / Double Heel Lifts 015 MIN
Rower / Sideward Lunge And Bend / Lower Leg 015 MIN
Signaler / Forward Lunge And Bend / Siam Squat 015 MIN
Single Arm Coordinators / Front And Back Knee 015 MIN
Single Armlifts Forward / Sideward Bend With 015 MIN
Single Armlifts Sideward / Trunk Twist With 015 MIN
Single Armstretchers / Trunk Twist And 015 MIN

Roosevelt - Hail To The Chief C 24 MIN
16MM FILM, 3/4 OR 1/2 IN VIDEO H-C A
Shows President Franklin Roosevelt as he offered leadership and a New Deal during the depths of the Depression.
From The Leaders Of The 20th Century - Portraits Of Power Series.
Prod-NIELSE Dist-LCOA 1979

Roosevelt - Hail To The Chief (Spanish) C 24 MIN
16MM FILM, 3/4 OR 1/2 IN VIDEO H-C A
Features Roosevelt's leadership, vigor and courage that helped restore a sense of purpose to a whole nation.
Prod-NIELSE Dist-LCOA 1979

Roosevelt - Manipulator-In-Chief C 24 MIN
16MM FILM, 3/4 OR 1/2 IN VIDEO H-C A
Shows how Franklin Roosevelt dealt with the problems of leading America into another world war.
From The Leaders Of The 20th Century - Portraits Of Power Series.
Prod-NIELSE Dist-LCOA 1979

Roosevelt - Manipulator-In-Chief (Spanish) C 24 MIN
16MM FILM, 3/4 OR 1/2 IN VIDEO H-C A
Shows how Roosevelt took a united nation into a foreign land.
Prod-NIELSE Dist-LCOA 1979

Roosevelt And The New Deal C 20 MIN
16MM FILM, 3/4 OR 1/2 IN VIDEO H-C A
Examines Franklin Roosevelt's New Deal, a set of programs designed to end the Great Depression. Describes the process and the main aims of the programs which brought about profound changes in the United States.
From The Twentieth Century History Series.
Prod-BBCTV Dist-FI 1981

Roosevelt And U S History (1882-1929) B 28 MIN
16MM FILM, 3/4 OR 1/2 IN VIDEO H-C A
Gives an overview of life in the United States during the time of Franklin Roosevelt's childhood. Traces the youth and early political career of the future president.
From The World Leaders Series.
Prod-CFDLD Dist-CORF

Roosevelt And U S History (1930-1945) B 32 MIN
16MM FILM, 3/4 OR 1/2 IN VIDEO H-C A
Focuses on the White House years of Franklin D Roosevelt. Contrasts the private man and the public personality.
From The World Leaders Series.
Prod-CFDLD Dist-CORF

Roosevelt Vs Isolation B 25 MIN
16MM FILM, 3/4 OR 1/2 IN VIDEO J-C
Describes the conflict in America between pacifist isolationists and President F D Roosevelt, who favored lend-lease and military aid to Britain and France. Discusses the first peace-time draft in U S history, and the 50 destroyers sent to England. Shows Roosevelt's war plant tours.
From The Men In Crisis Series.
Prod-WOLPER Dist-FI 1965

Roosevelt, New Jersey - Visions Of Utopia C 52 MIN
16MM FILM, 3/4 OR 1/2 IN VIDEO J-C A
Tells the history of Roosevelt, New Jersey, an experimental project set up by the Theodore Roosevelt administration which resettled Jewish immigrants from the Lower East Side of New York into a cooperative in the Jersey countryside.
LC NO. 83-707109
Prod-LUMEN Dist-CNEMAG 1984

Rooster C 20 MIN
16MM FILM OPTICAL SOUND
Tells about a boy who finds his father's expectations to be too much too soon when he is taken to a brothel.
LC NO. 79-701294
Prod-USC Dist-USC Prodn-FRANCR 1979

Rooster And Mice Have A Race, The C 8 MIN
16MM FILM OPTICAL SOUND P-I
Tells the story of a race between a rooster and some mice to stimulate oral language skills.
LC NO. 75-706879
Prod-DBA Dist-MLA 1969

Rooster And Mice Make Pretzels, The C 10 MIN
16MM FILM OPTICAL SOUND P-I
Shows all the steps necessary in order to bake pretzels or bread. Stimulates oral language skills.
LC NO. 70-706880
Prod-DBA Dist-MLA 1969

Root Amputation Of First Maxillary Molar Mesial Buccal Root C 9 MIN
16MM FILM - 3/4 IN VIDEO PRO
Presents a demonstration by Robert A Uchin of the treatment of a patient with localized periodontal disease of a maxillary first molar by removal of the mesial buccal root. Describes the access, separation of the root from the remaining tooth structure and the contouring of the crown.
LC NO. 78-706129
Prod-USVA Dist-USNAC 1978

Root Amputation Of Maxillary Molar Distal Buccal Root C 10 MIN
16MM FILM - 3/4 IN VIDEO PRO
Presents a demonstration by Robert A Uchin of procedures for treatment of a molar with advanced periodontal disease by means of surgery, endodontics and reconstruction with a crown.
LC NO. 78-706130
Prod-USVA Dist-USNAC 1978

Root Canal Therapy C 10 MIN
16MM FILM OPTICAL SOUND P-H
Portrays the treatment of a typical abscess. Shows the dentist performing the treatment while using animation to describe what happens inside the tooth.
From The Dental Health Series.
LC NO. 75-700036
Prod-MIFE Dist-MIFE 1973

Root Canal Therapy On An Extracted Lower Molar - Access And Length Determination C 10 MIN
3/4 INCH VIDEO CASSETTE
Describes the armamentarium needed to perform root canal therapy, explains the three stages of access preparation and demonstrates the procedures for determining the length of roots.
LC NO. 79-706767
Prod-MUSC Dist-USNAC 1978

Root Canal Therapy On An Extracted Lower Molar - Instrumentation C 14 MIN
3/4 INCH VIDEO CASSETTE
Describes the armamentarium needed for root canal therapy and demonstrates the cleaning and instrumentation of a root canal.
LC NO. 79-706768
Prod-MUSC Dist-USNAC 1978

Root Canal Therapy On An Extracted Lower Molar - Obturation C 10 MIN
3/4 INCH VIDEO CASSETTE
Demonstrates obturation of the root canal using the softened gutta-percha techniques. Describes the rationale for recapitulation and the procedure for filling the canal.
LC NO. 79-706769
Prod-MUSC Dist-USNAC 1978

Root Hog Or Die C 59 MIN
16MM FILM - 3/4 IN VIDEO
Documents farm life in New England through several seasons.
Prod-WGBYTV Dist-DOCEDR

Root Of The Neck And The Thorax - Unit 14 C 23 MIN
3/4 OR 1/2 INCH VIDEO CASSETTE PRO
Introduces the anterior chest wall, the organs and vessels of the thorax, and the structures in the posterior mediastinum.
From The Gross Anatomy Prosection Demonstration Series.
Prod-HSCIC Dist-HSCIC

Root Planing And Gingival Curettage—A Series
PRO
Presents the rationale and techniques for root planing and gingival curettage. Describes therapeutic modalities in the management of periodontal disease.
Prod-VADTC Dist-USNAC 1982

Root Planing And Gingival Curettage, Pt 1,
Root Planing And Gingival Curettage, Pt 2, 014 MIN

Root Planing And Gingival Curettage, Pt 1, Rationale And Instrumentation C 16 MIN
3/4 OR 1/2 INCH VIDEO CASSETTE PRO
Describes the histopathologic changes which occur in diseased gingiva following root planing and curettage. Describes the recommended instrumentation and demonstrates techniques on typodont models.
From The Root Planing And Gingival Curettage Series.
LC NO. 83-706069
Prod-VADTC Dist-USNAC 1982

Root Planing And Gingival Curettage, Pt 2, Clinical Demonstrations C 14 MIN
3/4 OR 1/2 INCH VIDEO CASSETTE PRO
Demonstrates scaling, root planing and gingival curettage on a patient with gingival inflammation associated with heavy hard and soft deposits on his teeth. Shows a prearranged sterile tray setup and demonstrates instrumentation of one quadrant. Shows postoperative results.
From The Root Planing And Gingival Curettage Series.
LC NO. 83-706069
Prod-VADTC Dist-USNAC 1982

Root Two, Geometry Or Arithmetic C 25 MIN
16MM FILM OPTICAL SOUND
Focuses on a mathematical problem in which a length was discovered which did not correspond to a number which could be represented by the length of a line or the ratio between two lengths. Tells how the problem of irrational numbers undermined the development of calculus in the 17th and 18th centuries. Explains how these problems were solved by Eudoxus and Richard Dedekind respectively.
Prod-OPENU Dist-GPITVL

Rooted In The Past C 13 MIN
16MM FILM, 3/4 OR 1/2 IN VIDEO P-I
Features a boy living in an Indian village and a boy who visits his grandfather's cattle ranch.
From The Zoom Series.
Prod-WGBHTV Dist-FI

Roots / Races C 30 MIN
3/4 OR 1/2 INCH VIDEO CASSETTE H-C A
Presents a story centering on a real Mexican celebration. Uses the story to try to reduce the minority isolation of Mexican-American students by showing the teenager as an individual, as a member of a unique cultural group and as a member of a larger complex society.
From The La Esquina (English) Series.
Prod-SWEDL Dist-GPITVL 1976

Roots Of Black Resistance, The B 30 MIN
16MM FILM OPTICAL SOUND H-C A
Dr earl E Thorpe describes the efforts of Dubois and other blacks to form progressive movements and work for their rights as Americans during the early years of the century, as evidenced by the formation of such groups as the N A A C P, the National Negro Business League and the Niagara movement. He describes the conflict between W E B Dubois and Booker T Washington.
From The Black History, Section 11 - W E B Dubois And The New Century Series.
LC NO. 72-704072
Prod-WCBSTV Dist-HRAW 1969

Roots Of Change, The C 30 MIN
16MM FILM OPTICAL SOUND
Concentrates on Ghana and records the changes occurring there, especially in the cities. Deals with the Christian self-help projects in Accra and Kumasi where the Ashanti culture is being threatened by the break-up of tribal and family customs.
Prod-CBSTV Dist-CCNCC

Roots Of Dance On Television And Film, The C 30 MIN
3/4 OR 1/2 INCH VIDEO CASSETTE
See series title for descriptive statement.
From The Dance On Television - Ipiotis Series.
Prod-ARCVID Dist-ARCVID

Roots Of Democracy, The C
3/4 OR 1/2 INCH VIDEO CASSETTE
Prod-MSTVIS Dist-MSTVIS

Roots Of Disbelief, The C 37 MIN
16MM FILM, 3/4 OR 1/2 IN VIDEO H A
Discusses the factors which have reduced the power of the Christian church, such as scientific discoveries which have disproven church dogma and the stripping of the church of political power in Rome in 1848.
From The Christians Series.
Prod-GRATV Dist-MGHT 1978

Roots Of Happiness C 21 MIN
16MM FILM, 3/4 OR 1/2 IN VIDEO I-H
Uses the character of Phil the philodendron to explain plant care. Emphasizes that water, air and light are the three basic necessities in producing healthy plants.
Prod-LUF Dist-LUF 1977

Roots Of Happiness B 25 MIN
16MM FILM, 3/4 OR 1/2 IN VIDEO C A
The story of a family living in a poor rural area of Puerto Rico. Points out the recognizable elements that make a happy atmosphere for family living, particularly the role of the father.
From The Emotions Of Everyday Living Series.
Prod-MHFB Dist-IFB Prodn-SUN 1953

Roots Of High Order B 28 MIN
16MM FILM OPTICAL SOUND H
Discusses radicals of higher order than two, explaining that odd roots, not even roots, of negative numbers are real numbers.

Describes the complex number system, which includes all real and imaginary numbers, and illustrates the use of these numbers.
From The Intermediate Algebra Series.
Prod-CALVIN Dist-MLA Prodn-UNIVFI 1959

Roots Of Plants (2nd Ed) X 11 MIN
16MM FILM, 3/4 OR 1/2 IN VIDEO I-C
Shows the structure and growth patterns of various forms of plant roots, and explains the functions of root-cap and hair-roots. Illustrates osmosis.
Prod-EBF Dist-EBEC 1957

Roots Of Plants (2nd Ed) (Spanish) C 11 MIN
16MM FILM, 3/4 OR 1/2 IN VIDEO I-C
Shows the structure and growth patterns of various forms of plant roots and explains the functions of root-caps and half-roots. Illustrates osmosis.
Prod-EBF Dist-EBEC

Roots Of The Nation C 29 MIN
16MM FILM - 3/4 IN VIDEO
Shows how forests have influenced the development of America.
Prod-USFS Dist-USNAC 1976

Roots Of The Tree B 32 MIN
16MM FILM OPTICAL SOUND J-C A
Portrays three centuries of the history of the Oregon country and shows the period of exploration of the Northwest coast by sea, the charting of the land by fur traders and explorers, the arrival of the settlers and typical scenes of life in the area during the early years of the 20th century.
Prod-OREGHS Dist-OREGHS 1959

Roots Of War, The C 60 MIN
3/4 OR 1/2 INCH VIDEO CASSETTE H-C A
Offers a short history of the century during which France dominated Vietnam under the colonial tradition leading up to the rise of Ho Chi Minh. Shows that at the end of World War II Ho, flanked by U S officers, declared independence in Hanoi, but that the British helped the French regain control of Saigon.
From The Vietnam - A Television History Series. Episode 1
Prod-WGBHTV Dist-FI 1983

Roots To Cherish C 30 MIN
16MM FILM, 3/4 OR 1/2 IN VIDEO
Identifies and illustrates the consequences of cultural differences on school performance, ways to conduct a more appropriate evaluation and suggestions for program modifications to improve individual pupil achievement.
Prod-SHENFP Dist-SHENFP

Roots, Episode 01 - The African, Pt 1 C 47 MIN
16MM FILM OPTICAL SOUND J-C A
Describes the birth of Kunta Kinte in the West African village of Juffere. Tells how 15 years later Kunta and his friends are beginning their manhood rites, while the slave ship Lord Ligonier nears the African shore.
Prod-WOLPER Dist-FI

Roots, Episode 02 - The African, Pt 2 C 50 MIN
16MM FILM OPTICAL SOUND J-C A
Depicts the completion of Kunta Kinte's rites of manhood. Describes how the joy of the village is shortlived when Kunta and other villagers are captured by slavers and chained in the hold of the Lord Ligonier.
Prod-WOLPER Dist-FI

Roots, Episode 03 - The Slave, Pt 1 C 53 MIN
16MM FILM OPTICAL SOUND J-C A
Explains that the slave rebellion aboard the Lord Ligonier is quickly put down. Tells how the ship anchors in Annapolis and Kunta Kinte is bought by plantation owner John Reynolds.
Prod-WOLPER Dist-FI

Roots, Episode 04 - The Slave, Pt 2 C 48 MIN
16MM FILM OPTICAL SOUND J-C A
Shows how Fiddler, an older slave, is put in charge of training Kunta Kinte. Focuses on Kunta's rebellious attitude, which leads him to an unsuccessful escape attempt.
Prod-WOLPER Dist-FI

Roots, Episode 05 - The Escape C 48 MIN
16MM FILM OPTICAL SOUND J-C A
Tells how Kunta Kinte makes one last try for freedom, which results in his captors chopping off half of his foot to prevent future escapes.
Prod-WOLPER Dist-FI

Roots, Episode 06 - The Choice C 49 MIN
16MM FILM OPTICAL SOUND J-C A
Revolves around Kunta Kinte's marriage to Bell and the birth of his daughter, Kizzy. Describes how Kunta is given the opportunity to escape but chooses to remain with his wife and baby.
Prod-WOLPER Dist-FI

Roots, Episode 07 - The Uprooted C 48 MIN
16MM FILM OPTICAL SOUND J-C A
Tells how Kizzy's happiness at being in love with handsome young Noah is shattered when Noah is captured during an escape attempt and implicates her as well. Shows Kizzy and Noah being sold to the evil Tom Moore, who later rapes Kizzy, and depicts Kizzy's pledge that she will have a son who will grow up and exact vengeance on her new owner.
Prod-WOLPER Dist-FI

Roots, Episode 08 - Chicken George, Pt 1 C 48 MIN
16MM FILM OPTICAL SOUND J-C A
Focuses on Kizzy's son, Chicken George, who is a game cocker and a special favorite of their debauched owner, Tom Moore. Tells how George looks forward to buying his freedom and marrying Tildy.
Prod-WOLPER Dist-FI

Roots, Episode 09 - Chicken George, Pt 2 C 48 MIN
16MM FILM OPTICAL SOUND J-C A
Explains that the aristocratic Squire James offers to buy Chicken George and his family from Tom Moore, promising the family's freedom after five years of service. Describes George's rage when Moore flatly refuses, and tells how George is sent to England to pay off Moore's gambling debts.
Prod-WOLPER Dist-FI

Roots, Episode 10 - The War C 52 MIN
16MM FILM OPTICAL SOUND J-C A
Tells how Chicken George returns to his family as a free man but soon leaves, promising to return with enough money to free them all. Shows how the family befriends a young white couple who have lost their farm to the ravages of the Civil War.
Prod-WOLPER Dist-FI

Roots, Episode 11 - Freedom, Pt 1 C 52 MIN
16MM FILM OPTICAL SOUND J-C A
Describes the family's attempts to sharecrop the land after the war, until rampaging nightriders destroy their crops. Tells how Tom manages to identify the criminals. Explains that wily Senator Justin takes control of the plantation and announces that Tom cannot leave because of an outstanding debt.
Prod-WOLPER Dist-FI

Roots, Episode 12 - Freedom, Pt 2 C 44 MIN
16MM FILM OPTICAL SOUND J-C A
Relates how Chicken George and his family concoct a plan to leave slavery forever and fulfill Kunta Kinte's abiding dream of freedom.
Prod-WOLPER Dist-FI

Rooty Toot Toot C 8 MIN
16MM FILM OPTICAL SOUND
Presents an animated story based on the song Frankie And Johnny.
Prod-TIMLIF Dist-TIMLIF 1982

Rope Jumping C 15 MIN
3/4 OR 1/2 INCH VIDEO CASSETTE T
Explains how to teach primary students to turn a long rope, jump inside a long rope, jump in rhythm, turn a short rope, jump a short rope turning forward and backward, and jump to a rhyme.
From The Leaps And Bounds Series. No. 11
Prod-HSDE Dist-AITECH 1984

Rope Pull / Swing And Bend / Double Heel Lifts C 15 MIN
3/4 OR 1/2 INCH VIDEO CASSETTE P
Presents several exercises which can be performed in a classroom setting.
From The Roomnastics Series.
Prod-WVIZTV Dist-GPITVL 1979

Rope Skipping - Basic Steps C 16 MIN
16MM FILM OPTICAL SOUND I-H
Describes the purposes of rope skipping in maintaining physical fitness. Demonstrates eleven basic steps of jump roping, done in various tempos.
LC NO. FIA66-1088
Prod-MMP Dist-MMP 1965

Ropes And Knots C 20 MIN
3/4 OR 1/2 INCH VIDEO CASSETTE
Shows how a firefighter uses ropes and knots to secure and hoist personnel and equipment. All knots are clearly demonstrated.
Prod-IFSTA Dist-IFSTA

Ropin' Fool, The B 20 MIN
16MM FILM SILENT
Features Will Rogers as Ropes Reilly, a cowhand who gets fired because he likes roping more than eating and even ropes in his sleep.
Prod-UNKNWN Dist-REELIM 1921

Rordrum - Botaurus Stellaris (Bittern) C 10 MIN
16MM FILM OPTICAL SOUND
Describes the bittern in its natural surroundings, accompanied by sound effects.
Prod-STATNS Dist-STATNS 1969

Rorskoven (Forest Of Reeds) C 18 MIN
16MM FILM OPTICAL SOUND
Describes animal life among the reeds of a woodland lake. Includes music and sound effects.
Prod-STATNS Dist-STATNS 1964

Rosa - An Editing Exercise C 33 MIN
16MM FILM OPTICAL SOUND H-C A
Presents an editing exercise which consists of unedited scenes that are designed to be edited into various narrative and non-narrative works.
LC NO. 78-701186
Prod-MARBLO Dist-TEMPLU Prodn-TEMPLU 1978

Roscoe Holcomb And Jean Redpath C 52 MIN
3/4 OR 1/2 INCH VIDEO CASSETTE
Shows Pete Seeger and Roscoe Holcomb trading traditional American songs. Features Jean Redpath singing several songs from her native Scotland.
From The Rainbow Quest Series.
Prod-SEEGER Dist-CWATER

Roscoe's Rules C 10 MIN
16MM FILM, 3/4 OR 1/2 IN VIDEO K-P
Presents Roscoe the Drumming Bear as the symbol for the four basic safety rules for avoiding molestation. Depicts a police officer talking to a class of second graders and introducing them to Roscoe's four special safety rules. Shows that during the next few days, some of the children are tempted to forget one of Roscoe's rules until the little drumming bear pops into their minds and triggers a recollection of the rule.
Prod-DAVP Dist-AIMS 1973

Rose (French) C 13 MIN
3/4 OR 1/2 INCH VIDEO CASSETTE H-C A
Takes place in a small country restaurant and in an elegant restaurant along the Seine.
From The En Francais Series. Part 1 - Essential Elements
Prod-MOFAFR Dist-AITECH 1970

Rose And The Mignonette, The B 8 MIN
16MM FILM OPTICAL SOUND
Interprets a poem by Louis Aragon, a noted French poet. Illustrates the thesis that unified faith, regardless of individual beliefs, forms a bond against invading forces.
Prod-FILIM Dist-RADIM

Rose Bowl, The - Granddaddy Of Them All (History Of The Rose Bowl 'Til 1969) C 54 MIN
16MM FILM OPTICAL SOUND H-C A
Presents the complete history of the Rose Bowl through 1969. Includes capsule interviews of famous coaches and their teams through the years. Shows many of the famous plays and older uniforms.
LC NO. 73-702565
Prod-TRA Dist-TRA 1969

Rose By Any Other Name C 15 MIN
16MM FILM OPTICAL SOUND H-C A
Presents a dramatization about a 79-year-old woman resident of a nursing home who is found in the bed of a male resident. Shows how their warm, intimate and fulfilling relationship is threatened by the administration, the staff, the residents and her family.
LC NO. 80-700446
Prod-ADELPH Dist-ADELPH 1979

Rose By Any Other Name C 15 MIN
3/4 OR 1/2 INCH VIDEO CASSETTE C A
Explores the reactions of other people to a loving relationship between an aging pair and the pressures that are brought to end it in a nursing home.
Prod-MMRC Dist-MMRC

Rose For Emily, A C 27 MIN
16MM FILM, 3/4 OR 1/2 IN VIDEO
Presents the tale of an indomitable Southern woman who clutched the past so resolutely that life itself was denied. Based on the short story A Rose For Emily by William Faulkner.
LC NO. 83-706940
Prod-CHBDYL Dist-PFP 1982

Rose Parade (Pasadena) C 3 MIN
16MM FILM OPTICAL SOUND P-I
Discusses the Rose Parade in the city of Pasadena, California.
From The Of All Things Series.
Prod-BAILYL Dist-AVED

Rose, The C 10 MIN
16MM FILM, 3/4 OR 1/2 IN VIDEO
Features a poetic account set in ancient Greece about the love of a girl and shepherd and a magic rose which grew from a drop of blood.
Prod-MINFS Dist-PHENIX 1974

Rosedale - The Way It Is C 57 MIN
16MM FILM, 3/4 OR 1/2 IN VIDEO H-C A
Captures the sights, sounds and tensions of Rosedale, a New York community fighting to keep from becoming a slum area.
Prod-WNETTV Dist-IU 1976

Rosemary Dunleavy, Mary Barnett And Alan Lewis C 30 MIN
3/4 OR 1/2 INCH VIDEO CASSETTE
Focuses on rehearsing a dance company. Looks at excerpts of 'Esoterica' with Christine Spizzo. Hosted by Celia Ipiotis.
From The Eye On Dance - Behind The Scenes Series.
Prod-ARTRES Dist-ARTRES

Rosen Incontinence Procedure, The C 10 MIN
3/4 OR 1/2 INCH VIDEO CASSETTE PRO
Shows silicone prothesis implantaion to allow patients to control incontinence.
Prod-WFP Dist-WFP

Roses C 29 MIN
2 INCH VIDEOTAPE
Features Tom Lied explaining the types of roses and where they will grow best. Gives tips on the handling, planting, pruning, fertilizing and watering of roses.
From The Dig It Series.
Prod-WMVSTV Dist-PUBTEL

Roses C 30 MIN
3/4 OR 1/2 INCH VIDEO CASSETTE C A
Tells how and when to select healthy roses. Recommends nine step-by-step pruning procedures. Explains rose grading and selection processes
From The Home Gardener With John Lenanton Series. Lesson 18
Prod-COAST Dist-CDTEL

Roses C 47 MIN
1/2 IN VIDEO CASSETTE BETA/VHS
Deals with roses, the most popular flowers in the world. Explains the differences between the hybrid teas, grandifloras, pillars and the miniature roses, and describes how to grow climbing and tree roses. Discusses fertilization and insect control.
Prod-RMI Dist-RMI

Roses In December C 55 MIN
16MM FILM - 3/4 IN VIDEO J-C A
Chronicles the life of Jean Donovan, a lay missioner who was murdered by members of the government security forces in El Salvador. Raises questions about the relationship that exists between the U S government and the military leaders of El Salvador.

LC NO. 83-706613
Prod-FIRS Dist-FIRS 1982

Rosey Grier - The Courage To Be Me C 23 MIN
16MM FILM, 3/4 OR 1/2 IN VIDEO J-C
Presents a profile of Rosey Grier and details how he overcame shyness, rejection and failures and achieved success in sports, politics, entertainment and service to young people.
Prod-CF Dist-CF 1978

Rosh Hashana / Yom Kippur C 15 MIN
3/4 INCH VIDEO CASSETTE P
See series title for descriptive statement.
From The Celebrate Series.
Prod-KUONTV Dist-GPITVL 1978

Rosie The Riveter C 65 MIN
3/4 INCH VIDEO CASSETTE
Relates the experience of women workers during World War II as told by the women themselves and interwoven with rare archival recruitment films.
Prod-FIRS Dist-FIRS

Rosie's Walk C 5 MIN
16MM FILM, 3/4 OR 1/2 IN VIDEO K-P
Tells the story about Rosie, a hen, who went for a walk across the yard, around the pond, over the haystack, past the mill, through the fence, under the beehives and got back in time for dinner. A fox stalks close behind the proud little hen. Rosie struts across the barnyard, to the tune of 'TURKEY IN THE STRAW,' keeping her country-cool and unwittingly leading the fox into one disaster after another.
Prod-WWS Dist-WWS

Roslyn Migration, The C 30 MIN
3/4 INCH VIDEO CASSETTE
Focuses on the tough coal mining town of Roslyn, Washington, established by the Northern Pacific Railroad around 1886. Tells about the Black strike breakers who were brought in to mine after the 1888 miner's strike. Focuses on the role of James E Sheppardson.
From The South By Northwest Series.
Prod-KWSU Dist-GPITVL

Ross Bridge C 18 MIN
16MM FILM OPTICAL SOUND
Takes a close look at the intricate symbolic carving on both sides of the Ross Bridge in Tasmania, with an explanation of the possible reasons for the work behind this Australian landmark.
LC NO. 80-700919
Prod-TASCOR Dist-TASCOR 1977

Ross Mac Donald C 29 MIN
16MM FILM, 3/4 OR 1/2 IN VIDEO
Focuses on Ross Mac Donald, author of detective stories. Tells how he draws extensively on his own background for situations and locations.
From The Writer In America Series.
Prod-PERSPF Dist-CORF

Ross Taylor C
3/4 OR 1/2 INCH VIDEO CASSETTE
Emphasizes that specialized skills for a technology-centered society are becoming increasingly important. Emphasizes the use of calculators and computers in the mathematics classroom.
From The Third R - Teaching Basic Mathematics Skills Series.
Prod-EDCPUB Dist-EDCPUB

Rotameter Equipment C 10 MIN
3/4 OR 1/2 INCH VIDEO CASSETTE A
Illustrates the calibration of a rotameter by the assignment of flow rate values to the rotameter's scale markings. Includes information on primary, secondary and intermediate standards and a listing of equipment set-up interconnection and operation, as well as how to pilot the flow chart for the rotameter.
LC NO. 84-706453
Prod-USNAC Dist-USNAC 1978

Rotaries, Blocks And Swivels, Pt 1 - The Swivel C 19 MIN
3/4 OR 1/2 INCH VIDEO CASSETTE IND
Explains the function, workings and maintenance of the swivel. Focuses on longer equipment life and increased personal safety on the rig.
Prod-UTEXPE Dist-UTEXPE 1980

Rotaries, Blocks And Swivels, Pt 2 - The Rotary Table C 20 MIN
3/4 OR 1/2 INCH VIDEO CASSETTE IND
Shows the rotary table broken down into its component parts. Gives the table construction, workings and basic maintenance. Stresses a well-planned preventive maintenance program.
Prod-UTEXPE Dist-UTEXPE 1981

Rotary - Engine Of The Future C 11 MIN
16MM FILM, 3/4 OR 1/2 IN VIDEO J-C A
Uses live action and animation to illustrate the workings of the rotary engine, pointing out the advantages of only seven moving parts, lightness, greater efficiency and less polluting emissions than the piston engine.
Prod-IFFB Dist-FI 1973

Rotary Combustion Engine, The C 29 MIN
2 INCH VIDEOTAPE
See series title for descriptive statement.
From The Interface Series.
Prod-KCET Dist-PUBTEL

Rotary Compressors C 60 MIN
3/4 OR 1/2 INCH VIDEO CASSETTE IND
See series title for descriptive statement.
From The Mechanical Equipment Maintenance, Module 9 - Air Compressors Series.
Prod-LEIKID Dist-LEIKID

Rotary Drilling Fluids C 24 MIN
16MM FILM, 3/4 OR 1/2 IN VIDEO IND
Deals with the use, testing and treatment of water-base drilling muds. Emphasizes the role mud plays in well control.
Prod-UTEXPE Dist-UTEXPE 1973

Rotary Drilling Fluids, Pt 1 - Functions C 19 MIN
3/4 OR 1/2 INCH VIDEO CASSETTE IND
Discusses in a basic manner the ten functions of drilling mud in rotary drilling.
Prod-UTEXPE Dist-UTEXPE 1983

Rotary Drilling Fluids, Pt 2 - Water-Base Muds (Spanish) C 29 MIN
3/4 OR 1/2 INCH VIDEO CASSETTE IND
Covers each phase of water-base muds. Gives the purpose and control of each.
Prod-UTEXPE Dist-UTEXPE

Rotary Drilling Fluids, Pt 2 - Water-Base Muds C 29 MIN
3/4 OR 1/2 INCH VIDEO CASSETTE IND
Covers each phase of water-base muds. Gives the purpose and control of each.
Prod-UTEXPE Dist-UTEXPE

Rotary Drilling Fluids, Pt 3 - Oil Muds C 24 MIN
3/4 OR 1/2 INCH VIDEO CASSETTE IND
Discusses uses, composition and precautions to exercise when using oil-base and inverted muds.
Prod-UTEXPE Dist-UTEXPE 1976

Rotary Drilling Fluids, Pt 4 - Field Testing C 21 MIN
3/4 OR 1/2 INCH VIDEO CASSETTE IND
Tells how to run each test on the API mud report form. Discusses why tests are valuable.
Prod-UTEXPE Dist-UTEXPE 1977

Rotary Drilling Fluids, Pt 5 - Hole Problems C 22 MIN
3/4 OR 1/2 INCH VIDEO CASSETTE IND
Tells how to detect, prevent and correct differential pressure sticking and lost circulation.
Prod-UTEXPE Dist-UTEXPE 1976

Rotary Gear Pumps, Pt 1 C 14 MIN
3/4 OR 1/2 INCH VIDEO CASSETTE IND
Outlines installation and maintenance procedures showing the importance of installing base plate on a solid foundation. Discusses recommended piping methods, the necessity of safety relief valves on positive displacement pumps, start-up procedures and preventive maintenance procedures using vacuum and pressure gauges.
From The Marshall Maintenance Training Programs Series. Tape 45
Prod-LEIKID Dist-LEIKID

Rotary Gear Pumps, Pt 2 C 14 MIN
3/4 OR 1/2 INCH VIDEO CASSETTE IND
Covers inspection and repair of rotary gear pumps. Emphasizes importance of locking out the main disconnect and venting the pump chamber.
From The Marshall Maintenance Training Programs Series. Tape 46
Prod-LEIKID Dist-LEIKID

Rotary Joints - Installation And Maintenance C 13 MIN
3/4 OR 1/2 INCH VIDEO CASSETTE IND
Shows the function of the joint that connect a stationary supply pipe to a rotating machine part to cool or heat the unit. Demonstrates how the joint is repaired and installed.
From The Marshall Maintenance Training Programs Series. Tape 43
Prod-LEIKID Dist-LEIKID

Rotating Flows C 29 MIN
16MM FILM, 3/4 OR 1/2 IN VIDEO H-C
Illustrates the phenomena associated with rotation of homogenous fluids, including horizontal trajectories in surface gravity waves, low and high-Rossby-number flows around spheres, Taylor walls, normal modes of inertia oscillation and rossby waves in a cylindrical annulus.
From The Fluid Mechanics Films Series.
Prod-EDS Dist-EBEC 1968

Rotating Magnetic Fields B 13 MIN
16MM FILM - 3/4 IN VIDEO IND
Discusses the rotating magnetic field pattern, three-phase winding in a demonstration stator, factors that cause rotation of the magnetic field, and the construction of polyphase motors. Issued in 1945 as a motion picture.
From The Electrical Work - Electrical Machinery Series.
LC NO. 78-706141
Prod-USOE Dist-USNAC Prodn-RAYBEL 1978

Rotation C 15 MIN
3/4 OR 1/2 INCH VIDEO CASSETTE PRO
See series title for descriptive statement.
From The Numerical Control/Computer Numerical Control, Part 2 - Advanced Programming Series.
Prod-ICSINT Dist-ICSINT

Rotation C 18 MIN
3/4 OR 1/2 INCH VIDEO CASSETTE IND
Includes rotation and its rules, rotating a program and terminating rotation.
From The Numerical Control/Computerized Numerical Control - Advanced Programming Series. Module 2
Prod-LEIKID Dist-LEIKID

Rotation C 30 MIN
3/4 OR 1/2 INCH VIDEO CASSETTE H
Presents physics professor Jearl Walker offering graphic and unusual demonstrations exemplifying the principles of the rotation of solids.
From The Kinetic Karnival Of Jearl Walker. Pt 2

LC NO. 83-706116
Prod-WVIZTV Dist-GPITVL 1982

Rotation Of The Earth, The B 15 MIN
2 INCH VIDEOTAPE P
Acquaints children with the concept of apparent motion as opposed to real motion. (Broadcast quality)
From The Land And Sea Series.
Prod-TTOIC Dist-GPITVL Prodn-WGBHTV

Rotational Dynamics - Kinetic Energy X 9 MIN
16MM FILM OPTICAL SOUND C A
Presents a physics laboratory demonstration. Uses the results to establish the expression for kinetic energy of rotation.
Prod-PUAVC Dist-PUAVC 1961

Rotational Dynamics - Newton's Second Law X 18 MIN
16MM FILM OPTICAL SOUND C A
Demonstrates that the angular acceleration is proportional to the force applied, proportional to the lever arm, inversely proportional to the mass of the ring and inversely proportional to the ring's radius.
Prod-PUAVC Dist-PUAVC 1961

Rotational Path Concept In Removable Partial Denture Design—A Series
PRO
Describes the use of the rotational path in maxillary Class IV partially edentulous arches and maxillary and mandibular Class III bilateral partially edentulous arches.
Prod-VADTC Dist-USNAC

Rotational Path Concept In Removable Partial
Rotational Path Concept In Removable Partial 012 MIN

Rotational Path Concept In Removable Partial Denture Design, Pt 1 C 12 MIN
3/4 OR 1/2 INCH VIDEO CASSETTE PRO
Describes the use of the rotational path of insertion in designing removable partial dentures for maxillary class IV partially edentulous arches. Eliminates clasps to improve aesthetics and minimize plaque accumulation.
From The Rotational Path Concept In Removable Partial Denture Design Series.
Prod-VADTC Dist-USNAC

Rotational Path Concept In Removable Partial Denture Design, Pt 2 C 12 MIN
3/4 OR 1/2 INCH VIDEO CASSETTE PRO
Describes the use of the rotational path concept in the maxillary and mandibular Class III bilateral partially edentulous arches. Eliminates clasps to improve aesthetics and minimize plaque accumulation.
From The Rotational Path Concept In Removable Partial Denture Design Series.
Prod-VADTC Dist-USNAC

ROTC B 20 MIN
16MM FILM OPTICAL SOUND
Explains that ROTC is a primary issue on many college campuses and is a major focus of anti-war activity. Shows the university's ties to the military-industrial complex and shows how ROTC serves this relationship.
Prod-SFN Dist-SFN

Rothko Conspiracy, The C 90 MIN
3/4 OR 1/2 INCH VIDEO CASSETTE H-C A
Recounts the tragedy of artist Mark Rothko, who became insane and committed suicide at the age of 66. Tells that when he died, the people he had depended on to handle his legacy unscrupulously emptied his estate of most of his assets including over 1,000 paintings.
Prod-FI Dist-FI

Rotor Assembly C 60 MIN
3/4 OR 1/2 INCH VIDEO CASSETTE IND
See series title for descriptive statement.
From The Mechanical Equipment Maintenance, Module 5 - Centrifugal Pumps Series.
Prod-LEIKID Dist-LEIKID

Rotor Repair C 60 MIN
3/4 OR 1/2 INCH VIDEO CASSETTE IND
See series title for descriptive statement.
From The Mechanical Equipment Maintenance, Module 5 - Centrifugal Pumps Series.
Prod-LEIKID Dist-LEIKID

Rotten World About Us, The C 50 MIN
16MM FILM, 3/4 OR 1/2 IN VIDEO H-C A
Unravels the mysteries of mushrooms and molds, showing how fungi feed, grow and multiply.
Prod-BBCTV Dist-FI 1981

Rotterdam - Europort Gateway To Europe C 20 MIN
16MM FILM, 3/4 OR 1/2 IN VIDEO I-H
Studies life in Rotterdam. Includes views of the city and its people.
Prod-EBEC Dist-EBEC 1971

Rouad - Island Of The Crusaders B 10 MIN
16MM FILM OPTICAL SOUND
Examines the anachronistic life of the fishermen on Rouad, a tiny Mediterranean island. Shows the simplicity of life that takes place in this 20th century community which still works and lives under conditions which prevailed during the Crusades.
Prod-FILIM Dist-RADIM 1945

Rough Grinding By Pin-Bar B 19 MIN
16MM FILM OPTICAL SOUND
Demonstrates how to use the job card, select and adjust the grinding tool, use abrasive, perform the grinding operation, clean the grinding tool and correct worn grinding tools.
From The Optical Craftsmanship Series. Spherical Surfaces
LC NO. FIE52-350
Prod-USOE Dist-USNAC

Rough Grinding With Vertical Surface Grinder Flat Surfaces B 26 MIN
16MM FILM OPTICAL SOUND
Describes machine grinding flat surfaces and methods of blocking to grind all surface with a minimum of changes in position.
LC NO. FIE52-1106
Prod-USN Dist-USNAC 1944

Rough Line-Boring B 19 MIN
16MM FILM - 3/4 IN VIDEO
Describes how to install the boring bar and cutters and how to bore, counterbore and spot-face holes. Explains how to reposition from one hole to another. Issued in 1945 as a motion picture.
From The Machine Shop Work - Operations On The Horizontal Boring Mill Series. Number 5
LC NO. 80-706608
Prod-USOE Dist-USNAC Prodn-ESCAR 1980

Rough Turning Between Centers B 15 MIN
16MM FILM - 3/4 IN VIDEO
Shows how to set up an engine lathe, operate the controls, grind clearances on cutting tools and rough-turn round bar stock to a specified diameter. Issued in 1941 as a motion picture.
From The Machine Shop Work - Operations On The Engine Lathe Series. No. 1
LC NO. 79-707089
Prod-USOE Dist-USNAC Prodn-HANDY 1979

Rough-Facing, Boring And Turning A Shoulder B 22 MIN
16MM FILM, 3/4 OR 1/2 IN VIDEO
Demonstrates how to set up a rough casting on a vertical turret lathe, face a flange and turn a shoulder with the sidehead turret, and face a flange and bore a hole with the vertical turret.
From The Machine Shop Work - Operations On The Vertical Boring Mill Series. No. 2
Prod-USOE Dist-USNAC Prodn-AUDIO 1942

Rough-Facing, Turning And Drilling B 31 MIN
16MM FILM, 3/4 OR 1/2 IN VIDEO
Tells how to operate the controls of a vertical turret lathe, set up tools in the main turret head, rough-face and rough-turn an aluminum casting and drill the center hole.
From The Machine Shop Work - Operations On The Vertical Boring Mill Series. No. 1
Prod-USOE Dist-USNAC 1942

Roughing And Finishing External Threads On The Lathe C
3/4 OR 1/2 INCH VIDEO CASSETTE
See series title for descriptive statement.
From The Intermediate Engine Lathe Operation Series.
Prod-VTRI Dist-VTRI

Roughing And Finishing External Threads On The Lathe C 15 MIN
3/4 OR 1/2 INCH VIDEO CASSETTE IND
See series title for descriptive statement.
From The Machining And The Operation Of Machine Tools, Module 3 - Intermediate Engine Lathe Series.
Prod-LEIKID Dist-LEIKID

Roughing And Finishing External Threads On The Lathe (Spanish) C
3/4 OR 1/2 INCH VIDEO CASSETTE
See series title for descriptive statement.
From The Intermediate Engine Lathe Operation (Spanish) Series.
Prod-VTRI Dist-VTRI

Roughing And Finishing External Threads On A Die C 15 MIN
3/4 OR 1/2 INCH VIDEO CASSETTE
See series title for descriptive statement.
From The Machine Technology III - Intermediate Engine Lathe Series.
Prod-CAMB Dist-CAMB

Roughing It—A Series

Presents the favorite outdoor activities of Carroll Tichenor, with tips on camping, rock climbing, kayaking, rafting and canoeing.
Prod-KYTV Dist-KYTV 1984

Bicycle Touring 030 MIN
Canoeing 030 MIN
Cave Exploration 030 MIN
Day Hiking 030 MIN
Family Camping 030 MIN
Kayaking And Rafting 030 MIN
Nature Photography 030 MIN
Outdoor Cooking 030 MIN
Outdoor Gear 030 MIN
Overnight Camping 030 MIN
Preparation For Overnight Camping 030 MIN
Rock Climbing And Rappelling 030 MIN
Wildflowers 030 MIN

Roughing-In Nonmetallic Sheathed Cable B 24 MIN
16MM FILM - 3/4 IN VIDEO IND
Shows how to determine the location of required runs, install an offset bar hanger and ceiling outlet box, rough-in a circuit run and make up connections for switches, receptacles and fixtures. Issued in 1945 as a motion picture.
From The Electrical Work - Wiring Series. No. 3
LC NO. 79-707489
Prod-USOE Dist-USNAC Prodn-RAYBEL 1979

Roughneck Training—A Series
IND
Aimed at assisting entry-level rotary helpers to learn about proper care and handling of the drill stem. Describes equipment and demonstrates drilling techniques.
Prod-UTEXPE Dist-UTEXPE 1983

Care And Use Of Tongs 012 MIN
Laying Down Pipe 011 MIN
Making A Connection 012 MIN
Making A Trip 018 MIN
What Are Slips? 012 MIN

Round Around, A C 9 MIN
16MM FILM OPTICAL SOUND
Presents a turn dance on the streets of New York with different voices in different languages counting the turns. Emphasizes the disinterest of the people on the streets to the dance.
Prod-FINLYS Dist-FINLYS

Round Elbow Pattern Layout Using End Gore Template C 17 MIN
1/2 IN VIDEO CASSETTE BETA/VHS IND
See series title for descriptive statement.
From The Metal Fabrication - Parallel Line Development Series.
Prod-RMI Dist-RMI

Round Pipe Different Diameters 45 Degree Intersection Offset C 21 MIN
1/2 IN VIDEO CASSETTE BETA/VHS IND
See series title for descriptive statement.
From The Metal Fabrication - Parallel Line Development Series.
Prod-RMI Dist-RMI

Round Pipe Different Diameters 90 Degree Intersection Offset C 22 MIN
1/2 IN VIDEO CASSETTE BETA/VHS IND
See series title for descriptive statement.
From The Metal Fabrication - Parallel Line Development Series.
Prod-RMI Dist-RMI

Round Pipe Fabrication - Grooved Lock Seam C 19 MIN
1/2 IN VIDEO CASSETTE BETA/VHS IND
See series title for descriptive statement.
From The Metal Fabrication - Round Pipe Fabrication Series.
Prod-RMI Dist-RMI

Round Pipe Fabrication - Machine Formed Seam C 9 MIN
1/2 IN VIDEO CASSETTE BETA/VHS IND
See series title for descriptive statement.
From The Metal Fabrication - Round Pipe Fabrication Series.
Prod-RMI Dist-RMI

Round Pipe Intersected By Rectangular Pipe Centered At 45 Degree C 20 MIN
1/2 IN VIDEO CASSETTE BETA/VHS IND
See series title for descriptive statement.
From The Metal Fabrication - Parallel Line Development Series.
Prod-RMI Dist-RMI

Round Pipe Intersecting A Round Taper At 90 Degrees C 18 MIN
1/2 IN VIDEO CASSETTE BETA/VHS IND
See series title for descriptive statement.
From The Metal Fabrication - Parallel Line Development Series.
Prod-RMI Dist-RMI

Round Pipe Intersecting A Round Taper At 45 Degrees C 13 MIN
1/2 IN VIDEO CASSETTE BETA/VHS IND
See series title for descriptive statement.
From The Metal Fabrication - Parallel Line Development Series.
Prod-RMI Dist-RMI

Round Pipe Mitered End C 32 MIN
1/2 IN VIDEO CASSETTE BETA/VHS IND
See series title for descriptive statement.
From The Metal Fabrication - Parallel Line Development Series.
Prod-RMI Dist-RMI

Round Pipe Same Diameter 45 Degree Intersection C 24 MIN
1/2 IN VIDEO CASSETTE BETA/VHS IND
See series title for descriptive statement.
From The Metal Fabrication - Parallel Line Development Series.
Prod-RMI Dist-RMI

Round Pipe Same Diameter 90 Degree Intersection C 40 MIN
1/2 IN VIDEO CASSETTE BETA/VHS IND
See series title for descriptive statement.
From The Metal Fabrication - Parallel Line Development Series.
Prod-RMI Dist-RMI

Round Robin C 15 MIN
16MM FILM, 3/4 OR 1/2 IN VIDEO K-J
Depicts British robins (a different species than the American robin), their lifestyle, how they live, how males and females form pair bonds, and the roles each sex plays in raising young.
From The RSPB Collection Series.
Prod-RSFPB Dist-BCNFL 1980

Round Seven Months, A C 29 MIN
2 INCH VIDEOTAPE
See series title for descriptive statement.
From The Maggie And The Beautiful Machine - Pregnancy Series.
Prod-WGBHTV Dist-PUBTEL

Round Shapes C 15 MIN
3/4 OR 1/2 INCH VIDEO CASSETTE K-P
Identifies round shapes and discusses alike and different in shapes.
From The Pass It On Series.
Prod-WKNOTV Dist-GPITVL 1983

Round Tap Collar Formed With Beader And Notcher C 8 MIN
1/2 IN VIDEO CASSETTE BETA/VHS IND
Explains the application of a tap collar, and use of the beading machine and a hand notcher.
Prod-RMI Dist-RMI

Round Tap Collar Formed With Dovetail Hand Tool C 5 MIN
1/2 IN VIDEO CASSETTE BETA/VHS IND
Illustrates the use of the dovetail hand tool for forming the tap collar connection.
Prod-RMI Dist-RMI

Round Tap Collar Formed With Elbow Edge C 9 MIN
1/2 IN VIDEO CASSETTE BETA/VHS IND
Illustrates the use of the elbow edge wheels for forming a screw in the round tap collar.
Prod-RMI Dist-RMI

Round Tap Collar Formed With Hand Tap-In Tool C 6 MIN
1/2 IN VIDEO CASSETTE BETA/VHS IND
Discusses the use of a hand tap-in tool for forming the tap collar connection.
Prod-RMI Dist-RMI

Round Taper Intersecting A Round Pipe At 90 Degrees C 14 MIN
1/2 IN VIDEO CASSETTE BETA/VHS IND
See series title for descriptive statement.
From The Metal Fabrication - Round Tapers Series.
Prod-RMI Dist-RMI

Round Taper Intersecting A Round Pipe At 45 Degrees C 32 MIN
1/2 IN VIDEO CASSETTE BETA/VHS IND
See series title for descriptive statement.
From The Metal Fabrication - Round Tapers Series.
Prod-RMI Dist-RMI

Round Tapers - Internal Or External Offset C 19 MIN
1/2 IN VIDEO CASSETTE BETA/VHS IND
See series title for descriptive statement.
From The Metal Fabrication - Round Tapers Series.
Prod-RMI Dist-RMI

Round The Bend C 50 MIN
16MM FILM - 3/4 IN VIDEO PRO
Dramatizes the case history of a schizophrenic patient in a psychiatric hospital.
LC NO. 81-706512
Prod-TASCOR Dist-TASCOR 1981

Round Trip C 8 MIN
16MM FILM, 3/4 OR 1/2 IN VIDEO P-I
Presents a children's story about human kindness and equality, which involves three snowmen who, at various stages, get covered with soot and realize that color is unimportant.
Prod-WHTF Dist-FI 1977

Round Up C 15 MIN
3/4 INCH VIDEO CASSETTE I
Shows how to round off numbers.
From The Math - No Mystery Series.
Prod-WCETTV Dist-GPITVL 1977

Round Y - Branch Layout C 57 MIN
1/2 IN VIDEO CASSETTE BETA/VHS IND
See series title for descriptive statement.
From The Metal Fabrication - Round Tapers Series.
Prod-RMI Dist-RMI

Roundabout C 19 MIN
16MM FILM, 3/4 OR 1/2 IN VIDEO P-I
Presents a story about a young boy's experience with an old man who owns a magical toy merry-go-round. Tells what happens when it is stolen by the boy's friends. Focuses on responsibility and consideration for others.
Prod-CF Dist-CF 1977

Rounded Vowels And Labio-Dentals C 10 MIN
1/2 IN VIDEO CASSETTE BETA/VHS A
See series title for descriptive statement.
From The Speech Reading Materials Series.
Prod-RMI Dist-RMI

Rounders, The B 8 MIN
16MM FILM SILENT J-C A
Charlie Chaplin, Fatty Arbuckle and Minta Durfee star in a slapstick comedy. The story revolves around two men who arrive home 'TIPSY' and are met by irate wives.
Prod-SENN Dist-BHAWK 1914

Rounds, Pt 1 C 15 MIN
3/4 OR 1/2 INCH VIDEO CASSETTE P
Demonstrates how to sing a round and play an instrumental ostinato accompaniment. Presents the songs The Donkey and Scotland's Burning.
From The Song Sampler Series.
LC NO. 81-707073
Prod-JCITV Dist-GPITVL 1981

Rounds, Pt 2 C 15 MIN
3/4 OR 1/2 INCH VIDEO CASSETTE P
Demonstrates how to sing a round and play an instrumental ostinato accompaniment. Presents the songs The Donkey and Scotland's Burning.
From The Song Sampler Series.

LC NO. 81-707073
Prod-JCITV Dist-GPITVL 1981

Route Du Champagne C
3/4 OR 1/2 INCH VIDEO CASSETTE
See series title for descriptive statement.
From The Tableside Series.
Prod-CULINA Dist-CULINA

Route One C 15 MIN
16MM FILM, 3/4 OR 1/2 IN VIDEO J
Shows an eighth grade science class and its study of different kinds of alcohol. Presents factual information on alcohol and discusses hangover cures. Uses animation to show how alcohol travels through the body and how it effects the brain and other systems.
From The Jackson Junior High Series.
Prod-USOLLR Dist-USNAC Prodn-NVETA 1976

Route 1 C 15 MIN
3/4 OR 1/2 INCH VIDEO CASSETTE I-J
Shows an eighth grade science class studying alcohol. Includes an animated segment showing the route alcohol takes through the body.
From The Jackson Junior High Series.
Prod-EFLMC Dist-GPITVL

Router And Shaper C 14 MIN
1/2 IN VIDEO CASSETTE BETA/VHS IND
See series title for descriptive statement.
From The Woodworking Power Tools Series.
Prod-RMI Dist-RMI

Router, The C 13 MIN
3/4 INCH VIDEO CASSETTE
Shows how the high speed power tool is used for cutting and shaping wood plastic and non-ferrous metals. Presents the nomenclature of parts of the router, their functions, how the router is set up and adjusted and the actual cutting operations.
From The Woodworking Series
Prod-VISIN Dist-VISIN

Routers And Planes C 12 MIN
3/4 OR 1/2 INCH VIDEO CASSETTE
Covers routers and planes, their characteristics, use, accessories and safety.
From The Using Portable Power Tool Series.
Prod-TPCTRA Dist-TPCTRA

Routers And Planes (Spanish) C 12 MIN
3/4 OR 1/2 INCH VIDEO CASSETTE
Covers routers and planes, their characteristics, use accessories and safety.
From The Using Portable Power Tool Series.
Prod-TPCTRA Dist-TPCTRA

Routes Of Exile - A Moroccan Jewish Odyssey C 90 MIN
16MM FILM - 3/4 IN VIDEO J-C A
Explores the controversial issues of whether Jews and Arabs can live together in the Middle East and whether the Sephardi and Ashkenazi Jews can live together in Israel. Portrays the ongoing odyssey of a 2000 year old community whose remarkable journey is still unfolding.
Prod-FIRS Dist-FIRS

Routine Abdominal Skin Prep (Gel) C 10 MIN
3/4 OR 1/2 INCH VIDEO CASSETTE PRO
Demonstrates a step-by-step procedure for performing an abdominal skin prep using a gel prepping agent. Emphasizes maintenance of aseptic technique and careful handling of supplies to prevent contamination.
Prod-UMICHM Dist-UMICHM 1983

Routine Abdominal Skin Prep (Wet) C 10 MIN
3/4 OR 1/2 INCH VIDEO CASSETTE PRO
Demonstrates a step-by-step procedure for performing an abdominal skin prep using a wet prepping agent. Emphasizes maintenance of aseptic technique and careful handling of supplies to prevent contamination.
Prod-UMICHM Dist-UMICHM 1983

Routine Anorectal And Signoidoscopic Examination With Differential Diagnosis C 30 MIN
16MM FILM OPTICAL SOUND PRO
Stresses the value of routine anorectal and sigmoidoscopic examination in general practice by the internist, pediatrician and general surgeon, as well as the proctologist. Shows various aspects of this examination.
Prod-LOMAM Dist-LOMAM

Routine Compliance Testing For Diagnostic X-Ray Machines—A Series

Shows the individual test steps to be performed in determining the compliance of seven different X-ray systems to the federal performance standards.
Prod-USDHEW Dist-USNAC

Routine Compliance Testing For Diagnostic
Routine Compliance Testing For Diagnostic 030 MIN
Routine Compliance Testing For Diagnostic 012 MIN
Routine Compliance Testing For Diagnostic 013 MIN
Routine Compliance Testing For Diagnostic 016 MIN
Routine Compliance Testing For Diagnostic 010 MIN
Routine Compliance Testing For Diagnostic 028 MIN

Routine Compliance Testing For Diagnostic X-Ray Machines - Abovetable X-Ray Source... C 14 MIN
3/4 OR 1/2 INCH VIDEO CASSETTE
Complete title is Routine Compliance Testing For Diagnostic X-Ray Machines - Abovetable X-Ray Source Fluoroscopic And Spot Film Systems. Shows the test steps to be performed in determining the compliance of abovetable source fluoroscopic X-ray systems to federal performance standards. Shows a remote controlled system with automatic and manual technique factor selection.
From The Routine Compliance Testing For Diagnostic X-Ray Machines Series.
Prod-USDHEW Dist-USNAC

Routine Compliance Testing For Diagnostic X-Ray Machines - Abovetable X-Ray Source... C 30 MIN
3/4 OR 1/2 INCH VIDEO CASSETTE
Complete title is Routine Compliance Testing For Diagnostic X-Ray Machines - Abovetable X-Ray Source Radiographic Systems. Shows the test steps to be performed on stationary, mobile, abovetable, fluoroscopic, mammographic and dental X-ray equipment, and how to determine peak kilovoltage for compliance with PL 90-602.
From The Routine Compliance Testing For Diagnostic X-Ray Machines Series.
Prod-USDHEW Dist-USNAC

Routine Compliance Testing For Diagnostic X-Ray Machines - Dental Radiographic Systems C 12 MIN
3/4 OR 1/2 INCH VIDEO CASSETTE
Shows test steps to be performed to determine the compliance of intraoral dental X-ray systems to the federal performance standards. Shows testing of a system with both fixed KVP and MA.
From The Routine Compliance Testing For Diagnostic X-Ray Machines Series.
Prod-USDHEW Dist-USNAC

Routine Compliance Testing For Diagnostic X-Ray Machines - Mammographic Systems C 13 MIN
3/4 OR 1/2 INCH VIDEO CASSETTE
Shows the test steps to be performed in determining the compliance of mobile or stationary special-purpose mammographic X-ray systems to federal performance standards. Shows testing of a stationary system with fixed SID and variable KVP.
From The Routine Compliance Testing For Diagnostic X-Ray Machines Series.
Prod-USDHEW Dist-USNAC

Routine Compliance Testing For Diagnostic X-Ray Machines - Mobile Radiographic System C 16 MIN
3/4 OR 1/2 INCH VIDEO CASSETTE
Shows the test steps to be performed to determine the compliance of mobile and/or portable X-ray systems to the federal performance standards. Shows tests on a battery powered mobile system with various KVP and 'MA's only' selection.
From The Routine Compliance Testing For Diagnostic X-Ray Machines Series.
Prod-USDHEW Dist-USNAC

Routine Compliance Testing For Diagnostic X-Ray Machines - Peak Kilovoltage Determination C 10 MIN
3/4 OR 1/2 INCH VIDEO CASSETTE
Shows the test steps to be performed to determine the compliance of the tube potential (KVP) for stationary and mobile radiographic systems to the federal performance standards. This test method is to be employed routinely by both state and federal investigators.
From The Routine Compliance Testing For Diagnostic X-Ray Machines Series.
Prod-USDHEW Dist-USNAC

Routine Compliance Testing For Diagnostic X-Ray Machines - Undertable Source... C 28 MIN
3/4 OR 1/2 INCH VIDEO CASSETTE
Complete title is Routine Compliance Testing For Diagnostic X-Ray Machines - Undertable Source Fluoroscopic And Spot Film Systems. Shows the test steps to be performed to determine the compliance of conventional undertable source fluoroscopic X-ray systems. Shows tests on a combination radioscopic/fluoroscopic system with a spot film capability and automatic technique factor selection.
From The Routine Compliance Testing For Diagnostic X-Ray Machines Series.
Prod-USDHEW Dist-USNAC

Routine Dental Care Of The Equine C 33 MIN
1/2 IN VIDEO CASSETTE BETA/VHS
Provides an overview of dental needs and problems of the horse.
Prod-MSU Dist-EQVDL

Routine Female Physical Examination, The C 26 MIN
3/4 OR 1/2 INCH VIDEO CASSETTE PRO
Covers instruments and techniques used in the general physical exam of a female patient.
Prod-HSCIC Dist-HSCIC 1982

Routine General Physical Examination, The C 22 MIN
3/4 OR 1/2 INCH VIDEO CASSETTE PRO
Demonstrates the general physical examination, which is aimed at detecting conditions that are not producing symptoms.
Prod-HSCIC Dist-HSCIC 1977

Routine Health Examination C 10 MIN
16MM FILM OPTICAL SOUND H-C A
Emphasizes the importance of routine health examinations.
From The Obstetrics And Gynecology Series.
LC NO. 75-700058
Prod-MIFE Dist-MIFE 1974

Routine Maintenance Of Hypodermic Jet Injection Apparatus C 27 MIN
16MM FILM OPTICAL SOUND PRO
Demonstrates maintenance procedures for the hypodermic jet injection apparatus. Discusses the components and the functioning of the injector.
LC NO. 74-706228
Prod-USA Dist-USNAC 1972

Routine Pelvic Examination And The Cytologic Method C 15 MIN
16MM FILM OPTICAL SOUND PRO
Illustrates the technique of bimanual physical examination of the pelvis, using both a live model and a rubber model. Shows the technique of obtaining cellular material from the vagina, cervix and endocervix for use in cytologic testing. Demonstrates how specimen material may be obtained with various standard sampling tools and how specimens may be transferred to slides.
Prod-AMCS Dist-AMCS 1958

Routine Physical Examination, The - The Adult Male C 26 MIN
3/4 OR 1/2 INCH VIDEO CASSETTE PRO
Illustrates correct techniques to use in the general physical exam of an adult male.
Prod-HSCIC Dist-HSCIC 1982

Routine Stops (2nd Ed) C 18 MIN
16MM FILM, 3/4 OR 1/2 IN VIDEO
Presents procedures for law enforcement officers to use in making traffic stops. Uses vignettes to demonstrate what to do and how to handle vehicle stops properly. Gives specific instructions for one-officer and two-officer patrol cars, and notes that no vehicle stop is routine.
LC NO. 81-706587
Prod-CAHILL Dist-AIMS 1980

Routine Work C 26 MIN
3/4 OR 1/2 INCH VIDEO CASSETTE
Chronicles the filming of a modern dance routine. Shows that while the production team is working on the studio's sound stage, a second unit is filming them.
Prod-BBCTV Dist-FI

Row C 15 MIN
16MM FILM, 3/4 OR 1/2 IN VIDEO J-C A
Explores crew racing. Details the skill, dedication and training necessary for participation in crew racing. Shows men and women from rowing clubs and universities in the United States and Canada as they train for a 200-meter race.
LC NO. 77-701107
Prod-AMSAL Dist-PFP 1977

Rowe String Quartet, The C 60 MIN
3/4 OR 1/2 INCH VIDEO CASSETTE
Presents members of the Rowe String Quartet discussing their individual musical backgrounds, their instruments and their positions in the group.
Prod-WTVITV Dist-MDCPB

Rower / Sideward Lunge And Bend / Lower Leg Stretcher C 15 MIN
3/4 OR 1/2 INCH VIDEO CASSETTE P
Presents several exercises which can be performed in a classroom setting.
From The Roomnastics Series.
Prod-WVIZTV Dist-GPITVL 1979

Rowing - A Symphony In Motion C 26 MIN
16MM FILM, 3/4 OR 1/2 IN VIDEO J-C A
Surveys the different varieties of rowing, from sport with a single oarsman to competition with an eight-oar crew.
Prod-DOCU Dist-PHENIX 1974

Roy Campanella C 20 MIN
16MM FILM OPTICAL SOUND I-J
Interviews Roy Campanella, one of the greatest catchers in baseball history. Includes film footage of Campy, Jackie Robinson, Gil Hodges and other Brooklyn Dodger players. Covers the career of this Hall Of Fame member during the Dodgers' great years in New York.
From The Sports Legends Series.
Prod-COUNFI Dist-COUNFI

Roy Clark C 58 MIN
3/4 OR 1/2 INCH VIDEO CASSETTE
See series title for descriptive statement.
From The Evening At Pops Series.
Prod-WGBHTV Dist-PBS 1978

Roy Harris B 30 MIN
16MM FILM OPTICAL SOUND R
Roy Harris, music composer and teacher, relates his creative capacity to the larger values he finds in human life—the moral laws of the universe and the renewal he sees in nature and in each successive generation of students. (Kinescope)
From The Sum And Substance Series.
LC NO. FIA67-5267
Prod-USC Dist-MLA 1964

Roy Lichtenstein C 52 MIN
16MM FILM OPTICAL SOUND
Features Roy Lichtenstein working on a series of paintings in his Long Island, New York, studio. Records his view on color and abstraction and his position in the Pop Art movement. Includes appearances and comments by art critics Lawrence Alloway and John Coplans as well as fellow artists Rivers, Rauschenberg, Odenburg and Rosenquist.
LC NO. 76-703156
Prod-BLACKW Dist-BLACKW 1976

Roy Obi B 13 MIN
16MM FILM OPTICAL SOUND
Tells the story of a factory worker who seems to go insane, locking himself in his room and refusing to come out for anyone or anything.
LC NO. 79-700849
Prod-KRUSNK Dist-KRUSNK 1977

Roy Wilkins - The Right To Dignity C 20 MIN
16MM FILM, 3/4 OR 1/2 IN VIDEO H-C A
Provides a history of the civil rights movement in the United States from the turn-of-the-century to the present. Focuses on the dramatic rise of Roy Wilkins' from humble beginnings to the post of executive director of the NAACP.
Prod-USIA Dist-CAROUF Prodn-ROPE

Roy Wilkins - The Right To Dignity C 20 MIN
16MM FILM - 3/4 IN VIDEO
Reviews the career of Black activist Roy Wilkins with the National Association for the Advancement of Colored People. Outlines the growth and impact of the organization, including its role in the 1954 Supreme Court ruling on school desegregation and the landmark civil rights legislation of the 1960's.
LC NO. 79-706708
Prod-USINCA Dist-USNAC 1978

Royal Albatross, The C 32 MIN
16MM FILM, 3/4 OR 1/2 IN VIDEO J-C A
Shows the world's only albatross colony on the island of Taiaroa in New Zealand. Captures the elaborate courting dance which culminates with the pairing of two birds throughout their 50-year lifespans.
LC NO. 84-707030
Prod-NZNFU Dist-EBEC 1982

Royal Archives Of Ebla, The C 58 MIN
16MM FILM, 3/4 OR 1/2 IN VIDEO H-C A
Examines the archeological finds at Ebla in Syria, where 17,000 clay tablets covered in cuneiform writing were unearthed.
LC NO. 81-706801
Prod-FI Dist-FI 1980

Royal Bed, The B 73 MIN
1/2 IN VIDEO CASSETTE (BETA)
Offers a comedy-drama about the foibles of royalty.
Prod-UNKNWN Dist-VIDIM 1930

Royal Boy Of Samoa C 30 MIN
16MM FILM OPTICAL SOUND
Recounts the life of a Samoan boy, including his birth, boyhood, manhood and marriage.
Prod-CINEPC Dist-CINEPC 1975

Royal Dancers And Musicians From The Kingdom Of Bhutan, The C 29 MIN
16MM FILM OPTICAL SOUND
Documents an important Bhutanese festival in which masked dancers are the central feature. Shows preparations for the festival and provides a brief overview of daily life in Bhutan.
LC NO. 80-701261
Prod-AS Dist-AS 1979

Royal Heritage—A Series
16MM FILM, 3/4 OR 1/2 IN VIDEO H-C A
Journeys through the castles, palaces and churches of England's royalty and offers a close-up view of treasures which have accrued to the Crown since the Middle Ages.
Prod-BBCTV Dist-FI 1977

Charles I	060 MIN
Edward VII And The House Of Windsor	060 MIN
First Three Georges, The	060 MIN
George IV	060 MIN
Medieval Kings, The	060 MIN
Queen And Prince Philip, The	060 MIN
Stuarts Restored, The	060 MIN
Tudors, The	060 MIN
Victoria And Albert	060 MIN
Victoria, Queen And Empress	060 MIN

Royal Hudson C 12 MIN
16MM FILM OPTICAL SOUND
Presents a documentary on the Royal Hudson, Pacific Great Eastern's show locomotive that runs between North Vancouver and Squamish during the summer.
LC NO. 76-703256
Prod-BCPEMC Dist-BCPEMC 1976

Royal Ontario Museum B 11 MIN
16MM FILM OPTICAL SOUND
Focuses on the contents of the Royal Ontario Museum.
LC NO. 77-702630
Prod-CANFDC Dist-CANFDC 1972

Royal Palace, Stockholm, The C 26 MIN
16MM FILM, 3/4 OR 1/2 IN VIDEO H-C A
Features Swedish history and culture as represented in the imposing Royal Palace in Stockholm, a seven-hundred-room edifice whose small royal apartment houses the world's youngest monarch, Karl XVI Gustav, descendant of one of Napoleon's marshalls who became king of Sweden.
From The Place In Europe Series.
Prod-THAMES Dist-MEDIAG 1975

Royal Province, The C 21 MIN
16MM FILM OPTICAL SOUND
Portrays the colorful early history of Nova Scotia from its earliest colonizers in 1605 through the struggle of Louisbourg to its entrance into confederation. Pictures the many races that settled in Nova Scotia and the contributions they made through their varied cultures and customs and social and political achievements.
Prod-NOSIS Dist-CTFL 1967

Royal Road C 28 MIN
16MM FILM, 3/4 OR 1/2 IN VIDEO
Retraces Einstein's logic to demonstrate that space and time are curved or warped by the distribution of matter in the universe and that matter and energy move along this curvature of space/time.
From The Understanding Space And Time Series.
Prod-BBCTV Dist-UCEMC 1980

Royal Rococo (1725 - 1750) C 12 MIN
16MM FILM OPTICAL SOUND
Shows an Archbiship's palace that is an example of the gaiety and elegance of the 18th century churchmen who decorated their splendid homes with pagan scenes in glowing shell-like polychrome.
Prod-ROLAND Dist-ROLAND

Royal Shakespeare Company—A Series

Explores facets of William Shakespeare's works including language, meter and verse, the force of blank verse, broken lines and heightened language, how characters are defined, irony and amiguity, and soliloquies and choric speeches.
Prod-FOTH Dist-FOTH 1983

Exploring A Character	053 MIN
Irony And Ambiguity	051 MIN
Language And Character	051 MIN
Passion And Coolness	052 MIN
Poetry And Hidden Poetry	053 MIN
Rehearsing The Text	053 MIN
Set Speeches And Soliloquies	052 MIN
Two Traditions, The	050 MIN
Using The Verse	050 MIN

Royal Silk Of Thailand, The C 14 MIN
16MM FILM OPTICAL SOUND C A
A study of hand-woven Thai silk, Thailand's fastest growing export commodity. Follows the process of the creation of silk from the tiny bombyx-mori moth to the finished product. Includes scenes of temples, waterways, the villages and the inhabitants of Thailand.
LC NO. 75-702557
Prod-THAI Dist-MCDO Prodn-MCDO 1968

Royal Silver Jubilee C 26 MIN
3/4 OR 1/2 INCH VIDEO CASSETTE
Presents an overview of Queen Elizabeth II's first twenty-five years of rule in Britain. Documents the many changes made not only in the Monarchy but also in the British Empire.
Prod-JOU Dist-JOU

Royal Tour Of South Africa B 30 MIN
3/4 OR 1/2 INCH VIDEO CASSETTE
Documents the historic Royal Family tour of South Africa. Show Zulu tribesmen performing dances in their honor.
Prod-IHF Dist-IHF

Royal Visit, The C 28 MIN
16MM FILM OPTICAL SOUND
Looks at the 1976 visit of Queen Elizabeth II and Prince Philip to the Washington Cathedral on the occasion of the dedication of the nave for the reconciliation of the people's of the earth.
Prod-NCATHA Dist-NCATHA

RSPB Collection—A Series
16MM FILM, 3/4 OR 1/2 IN VIDEO I-C A
Includes a variety of natural history films about birds collected by the Royal Society For the Protection of Birds (RSPB). Captures rare, uninhibited moments of bird wildlife.
Prod-RSFPB Dist-BCNFL

Heron Named Bill, A	025 MIN
Kingfisher	020 MIN
Masterbuilders	015 MIN
Osprey	035 MIN
Pinkfoot	019 MIN
Round Robin	015 MIN
Seabirds	017 MIN
Short Eared Owl	017 MIN
Talons	022 MIN

Rub-A-Dub-Dub C 10 MIN
3/4 OR 1/2 INCH VIDEO CASSETTE K-P
Points out that one story may be illustrated in many ways.
From The Book, Look And Listen Series.
Prod-MDDE Dist-AITECH 1977

Rubber C 12 MIN
3/4 OR 1/2 INCH VIDEO CASSETTE
Covers the nature of rubber, its processing, properties, uses and treatment.
From The Working With Nonmetals In The Plant Series.
Prod-TPCTRA Dist-TPCTRA

Rubber Boots C 5 MIN
16MM FILM OPTICAL SOUND K-I
Portrays an insect community in puppet animation.
From The Adventures In The High Grass Series.
LC NO. 74-702125
Prod-MMA Dist-MMA 1972

Rubber Dam Application C 35 MIN
3/4 OR 1/2 INCH VIDEO CASSETTE PRO
Introduces the use of the rubber dam as a means of operative field isolation. Includes specific instruction for those restorative procedures requiring gingival tissue retraction and tooth separation. Includes the working field preparation, dam application to maxillary anterior teeth using a wizard rubber dam holder or a Young's frame, the application of a Ferrier separator interproximally on anterior teeth, dam application to posterior areas and demonstration of the use of the Ferrier 212 gingival clamp.
Prod-UWASH Dist-UWASH

Rubber Dam Application And Removal C 7 MIN
16MM FILM OPTICAL SOUND PRO
Demonstrates a method of assisting the application and removal of a rubber dam in dentistry.
From The Four-Handed Dentistry Series.
LC NO. 75-704335
Prod-SAIT Dist-SAIT 1973

Rubber Dam In Dentistry, The C 19 MIN
16MM FILM OPTICAL SOUND
Illustrates the use of the rubber dam in restorative dentistry and shows techniques of its application.
LC NO. FIE56-126
Prod-USN Dist-USNAC 1955

Rubber Elasticity C 39 MIN
3/4 OR 1/2 INCH VIDEO CASSETTE
See series title for descriptive statement.
From The Colloid And Surface Chemistry - Lyophilic Colloids Series.
Prod-KALMIA Dist-KALMIA

Rubber Elasticity B 39 MIN
3/4 OR 1/2 INCH VIDEO CASSETTE
See series title for descriptive statement.
From The Colloids And Surface Chemistry - Lyophilic Colloids Series.
Prod-MIOT Dist-MIOT

Rubber Plantation (Southeast Asia) C 10 MIN
16MM FILM, 3/4 OR 1/2 IN VIDEO J-C A
Shows that natural rubber production is a time-consuming process. Explains that it has become a major factor in the national economy of Malaysia due to the scarcity of petroleum.
Prod-ASIABU Dist-LUF 1979

Rubber-Tired Haulage In Underground Coal Mining C 14 MIN
16MM FILM OPTICAL SOUND
Shows six of the most frequently occuring haulage accidents, explaining why they happened and what could have been done to prevent them. Points out the need for closer supervision and more adequate employee job and safety training.
LC NO. 75-702460
Prod-USMESA Dist-USNAC 1974

Rubbish To Riches C 11 MIN
16MM FILM, 3/4 OR 1/2 IN VIDEO J
Shows various ways that refuse can be processed to extract usable by-products, contending that this is a practical way to save both money and resources.
LC NO. 81-706570
Prod-LINDH Dist-AIMS 1979

Rubble Trouble C 11 MIN
16MM FILM, 3/4 OR 1/2 IN VIDEO I-C A
Uses live action and animation to show how to prevent fires by using the most efficient methods of collecting, storing and removing industrial wastes.
Prod-FACTMS Dist-FILCOM 1972

Rubens C 6 MIN
16MM FILM OPTICAL SOUND
Reflects the richness and exuberance of both the art and the life reflected in Ruben's portraits, classical themes and religious paintings.
Prod-USNGA Dist-USNGA

Rubens C 26 MIN
16MM FILM, 3/4 OR 1/2 IN VIDEO H-C A
Documents the life and artistic philosophy of Flemish artist, Rubens. Shows examples of the portraits and baroque works commissioned while he was a court painter and diplomat. Emphasizes Rubens' message of personal and artistic freedom.
Prod-IFB Dist-IFB 1974

Ruby Shang And Mel Wong C 30 MIN
3/4 OR 1/2 INCH VIDEO CASSETTE
Draws parallels between dance, the visual arts and environments. Features 'Esoterica' with Ohad Naharin. Hosted by Celia Ipiotis.
From The Eye On Dance - Dance And The Plastic Arts Series.
Prod-ARTRES Dist-ARTRES

Rudiments Of Self Concept B 44 MIN
16MM FILM OPTICAL SOUND
Discusses the physical and social influences related to the emergence of a self-concept.
From The Man - His Growth And Development, Birth Through Adolescence Series.
LC NO. 71-703689
Prod-VDONUR Dist-AJN Prodn-WTTWTV 1967

Rudolf Nureyev's Film Of Don Quixote—A Series
3/4 OR 1/2 INCH VIDEO CASSETTE
Features Rudolf Nureyev, Robert Helpmann, Lucette Aldous and the dancers of the Australian Ballet in an excerpt from the film version of the ballet Don Quixote.
Prod-WRO Dist-SF Prodn-IARTS 1978

Basilio And Kitri, The Lovers	15 MIN
Marketplace In The Port Of Barcelona, The	15 MIN
Tavern Celebration, A	15 MIN
Wedding Reception, The - The Grand Pas De Deux	15 MIN

Rudolph And Frosty's Christmas In July C 97 MIN
3/4 OR 1/2 INCH VIDEO CASSETTE
Recounts the story of how Rudolph the Red-Nosed Reindeer and his pal Frosty The Snowman try to save an impoverished circus by making guest appearances on the Fourth of July weekend. Features the voices of Mickey Rooney, Ethel Merman and Jackie Vernon.
Prod-TIMLIF Dist-TIMLIF 1982

Rudolph, The Red-Nosed Reindeer C 50 MIN
16MM FILM OPTICAL SOUND K-H A
Presents the puppet-animated TV special of Rudolph The Red-Nosed Reindeer, narrated by Burl Ives.
Prod-PERSPF Dist-CORF

Rudyard Kipling - The Road From Mandalay C 30 MIN
16MM FILM, 3/4 OR 1/2 IN VIDEO J-C A

Re-creates one day in the life of Rudyard Kipling, when the unassuming author is informed he has been awarded the Nobel Prize for literature.
From The Nobel Prizewinners Series.
Prod-CFDLD Dist-CORF

Rufus M, Try Again C 13 MIN
16MM FILM, 3/4 OR 1/2 IN VIDEO P
Dramatizes chapter one of the book Rufus M by Eleanor Estes, where Rufus Moffat learns about the library. Tells how his older brother and sister taunt him because he can't read, so he goes to the library to check out a book, only to run into difficulties.
Prod-BFA Dist-PHENIX 1977

Rufus M, Try Again / Ira Sleeps Over C 20 MIN
1/2 IN VIDEO CASSETTE BETA/VHS
Tells about Rufus M, a little boy who can't get a library card because he can't write his name. Based on the book by Eleanor Estes. Tells the story of Ira's first night away from home, based on the book by Bernard Waber.
Prod-BFA Dist-BFA

Rufus Xavier Sarsaparilla C 3 MIN
3/4 OR 1/2 INCH VIDEO CASSETTE P-I
Illustrates the need for pronouns.
From The Grammar Rock Series.
Prod-ABCTV Dist-GA Prodn-SCOROC 1978

Rug Maker, The - A Folktale Of Africa C 10 MIN
16MM FILM, 3/4 OR 1/2 IN VIDEO P-I
An animated East African folktale which shows the benefits, even for a chief's son, of knowing a trade.
Prod-LCOA Dist-LCOA Prodn-BOSUST 1970

Rug Spots C 15 MIN
2 INCH VIDEOTAPE
See series title for descriptive statement.
From The Making Things Work Series.
Prod-WGBHTV Dist-PUBTEL

Ruggie And The Momma Junkie B 10 MIN
16MM FILM OPTICAL SOUND
Tells the story of a young man who wanders into an auto junkyard and encounters its lone female resident.
Prod-NYU Dist-NYU

Ruggles Of Red Gap B 90 MIN
16MM FILM OPTICAL SOUND
Tells the story of a gentleman butler thrown out of his element into the American wild west. Stars Charles Laughton, Charlie Ruggles, Zasu Pitts and Mary Boland. Directed by Leo Mc Carey.
Prod-UPCI Dist-TWYMAN

Rugmaker, The - A Folktale Of Africa (Spanish) C 8 MIN
16MM FILM, 3/4 OR 1/2 IN VIDEO P A
Features story of Kamalo a rugmaker who doesn't care about having an occupation until he meets the woman he wants to marry.
Prod-LCOA Dist-LCOA 1970

Rugs C 25 MIN
3/4 OR 1/2 INCH VIDEO CASSETTE J-C A
Portrays the making of plain weave rag rugs and demonstrates twill weave. Discusses woolen rugs and the considerations when weaving for the floor. Explains the operation of the Dobby loom in making patterned weaves. Illustrates the variety of design, color and texture of rugs from around the world.
From The Craft Of The Weaver Series.
Prod-BBCTV Dist-FI 1983

Ruins Of Athens C 20 MIN
3/4 OR 1/2 INCH VIDEO CASSETTE J-C A
Visits Athens, showing the Parthenon, the acropolis and other ancient ruins.
LC NO. 82-706784
Prod-AWSS Dist-AWSS 1981

Ruins, The C 19 MIN
16MM FILM, 3/4 OR 1/2 IN VIDEO H-C
Describes the creative processes involved in creating a breakthrough style of painting. Follows the artist as he searches for the right subjects which will reflect his present passion for the visual aspects and evocations of ruins.
Prod-SF Dist-SF 1972

Rule Bound Behavior C 42 MIN
3/4 INCH VIDEO CASSETTE PRO
Presents a theoretical discussion of rule bound behavior and defines rules as one classification of symbol. Suggests implications for treatment, specifically the teaching-learning process. Narrated by Ann Robinson Popper.
Prod-AOTA Dist-AOTA 1977

Rule By Consent B 22 MIN
16MM FILM OPTICAL SOUND I-C A
Depicts the recent electioneering spirit in India and includes a few striking events which have occurred during the last 20 years.
Prod-INDIA Dist-NEDINF

Rule Of Thumb C 16 MIN
16MM FILM, 3/4 OR 1/2 IN VIDEO J-C A
Treats the dangerous side of hitchhiking, depicting the robber, the junkie and the rapist. Stresses the importance of thinking hard before picking up a hitchhiker or thumbing a ride.
Prod-DAVP Dist-AIMS 1972

Rules C 24 MIN
16MM FILM OPTICAL SOUND K-I
Reveals how Josh is worried because he has gotten in trouble in school. Tells how Mickey explains to him that all people have broken God's rules and that all can be forgiven. Looks at how Boaz decides to make up his own rules because everyone else seems to have rules. Shows him God's rules are for the good of humanity.
From The Good Time Growing Show Series. Show 5
Prod-WHTLIN Dist-WHTLIN

Rules And Regulations B 20 MIN
16MM FILM OPTICAL SOUND T
Discusses how a teacher's application of school rules concerning matters such as dress codes or hair styles might affect teacher-student relations.
From The Human Relations Training Unit - Confrontations Series.
Prod-ADL Dist-ADL

Rules Are For Everyone C 29 MIN
3/4 OR 1/2 INCH VIDEO CASSETTE T
See series title for descriptive statement.
From The Coping With Kids Series.
Prod-MFFD Dist-FI

Rules Are For Everyone C 30 MIN
3/4 OR 1/2 INCH VIDEO CASSETTE
Presents the principles of allowing children to learn by the consequences of their actions and how to help children experience the logic of social living.
From The Coping With Kids Series.
Prod-OHUTC Dist-OHUTC

Rules Are Good Directions (2nd Ed) C 13 MIN
16MM FILM, 3/4 OR 1/2 IN VIDEO P-I
Presents the reasons behind various safety rules.
Prod-SAIF Dist-BARR 1983

Rules In Fog B 17 MIN
16MM FILM OPTICAL SOUND
Explains when to use fog and danger signals, the meaning of fog signals under inland and international rules and how to determine safe speed in fog.
LC NO. 74-705550
Prod-USN Dist-USNAC 1943

Rules Of The Game B 108 MIN
16MM FILM OPTICAL SOUND
A French language motion picture. Presents Jean Renoir's strange, subtle and dreamlike study of a society in collapse on the eve of a war. Tells the story of an aviator who lands in Paris after a kind of Lindbergian solo flight. Includes English subtitles.
Prod-UNKNWN Dist-KITPAR 1939

Rules Of The Game C 19 MIN
16MM FILM, 3/4 OR 1/2 IN VIDEO H-C A
Dramatizes aspects of work habits, deadlines, loyalty and business etiquette and examines the power structure.
From The Working Series.
Prod-JOU Dist-JOU Prodn-INCC 1980

Rules Of The Game (French) B 110 MIN
3/4 OR 1/2 INCH VIDEO CASSETTE
Depicts a social world where pleasure is the prize and intrigue and guile are the rules. Directed by Jean Renoir with English subtitles.
Prod-IHF Dist-IHF

Rules Of The Nautical Road - Introduction B 22 MIN
16MM FILM OPTICAL SOUND
Describes international rules of navigation, the importance of taking bearings and selected nautical terms.
LC NO. FIE52-932
Prod-USN Dist-USNAC

Rules Of The Road C 24 MIN
16MM FILM OPTICAL SOUND
Shows how the Honolulu Marathon Clinic teaches individuals to prepare for, and finish, a running marathon. Presents the rules for healthy running.
Prod-MTP Dist-MTP

Rules Of The Road For Boatmen, The C 16 MIN
16MM FILM - 3/4 IN VIDEO
Presents the inland rules applicable to all vessels, including small craft regulations (except those under international rules), Western rivers rules and the Great Lakes rules. Presents meeting, passing and overtaking situations, small craft versus large vessels and proper procedures for boating in fog.
LC NO. 79-706676
Prod-USCG Dist-USNAC 1979

Rules Of The Road, International - Restricted Visibility Situations B 10 MIN
16MM FILM OPTICAL SOUND
Shows what to do in situations when visibility is restricted.
LC NO. FIE56-256
Prod-USN Dist-USNAC 1955

Rules Of The Road, International - Special Daytime Situations C 11 MIN
16MM FILM OPTICAL SOUND
Shows how to tell the status, occupation or degree of maneuverability of vessels not in independent operation in daylight.
LC NO. FIE56-257
Prod-USN Dist-USNAC 1955

Rules Of The Road, International - Vessel Crossing, Daytime B 21 MIN
16MM FILM OPTICAL SOUND
Shows what should be done when vessels cross in the daytime.
LC NO. 74-705551
Prod-USN Dist-USNAC 1956

Rules Of The Road, International - Vessels Overtaking, Daytime B 19 MIN
16MM FILM OPTICAL SOUND
Shows what should be done when vessels are overtaking in daytime and stresses the obligation of all vessels in obeying the rule that the overtaking vessel must keep out of the way of the overtaken vessel.
LC NO. FIE56-214
Prod-USN Dist-USNAC 1956

Rules Rules Rules C 10 MIN
3/4 INCH VIDEO CASSETTE I-H
Explains how the children in Ms Krumsky's class decide to set up their own system of 'backwards' rules and then determine to abolish them when they become too confusing. Tells how they come to appreciate the importance of rational rules.
Prod-GA Dist-GA

Rules To The Rescue C
16MM FILM, 3/4 OR 1/2 IN VIDEO
Shows the advantages of following rules, as well as the natural consequences of not following them.
Prod-HIGGIN Dist-HIGGIN

Ruling Houses, The - 1900 - The Day Of Empires Has Arrived, Pt 1 C 26 MIN
3/4 OR 1/2 INCH VIDEO CASSETTE H-C A
Special two-part version of the film and videorecording The Ruling Houses - 1900 - The Day Of Empires Has Arrived.
From The Europe - The Mighty Continent Series.
Prod-BBCTV Dist-TIMLIF 1976

Ruling Houses, The - 1900 - The Day Of Empires Has Arrived, Pt 2 C 26 MIN
3/4 OR 1/2 INCH VIDEO CASSETTE H-C A
Special two-part version of the film and videorecording The Ruling Houses - 1900 - The Day Of Empires Has Arrived.
From The Europe - The Mighty Continent Series.
Prod-BBCTV Dist-TIMLIF 1976

Ruling Houses, 1900, The - The Day Of Empires Has Arrived C 52 MIN
16MM FILM, 3/4 OR 1/2 IN VIDEO
Discusses the forces of unrest threatening the European empires at the turn of the century, including revolutionaries in Russia, the theories of Marx and Engels and the weakening of the Austro-Hungarian and Ottoman empires.
From The Europe, The Mighty Continent Series. No. 2
Prod-BBCTV Dist-TIMLIF 1976

Rumania On The Tightrope C 29 MIN
2 INCH VIDEOTAPE
See series title for descriptive statement.
From The Course Of Our Times III Series.
Prod-WGBHTV Dist-PUBTEL

Rumble Of Wheels C 19 MIN
1/2 IN VIDEO CASSETTE BETA/VHS
Discusses the heritage, training and appearance of the Budweiser Clydesdales.
Prod-EQVDL Dist-EQVDL

Rumble Of Wheels, The Jingle Of Chain, The C 14 MIN
16MM FILM OPTICAL SOUND
Tells the story of the Clydesdale horse from birth, training and eventually as a member of the famous team which pulls the Budweiser wagon.
LC NO. 78-700303
Prod-ANHBUS Dist-MTP 1978

Rumblefish C
1/2 IN VIDEO CASSETTE BETA/VHS
Presents S E Hinton's story of a young tough's adoration of his even tougher older brother, starring Matt Dillon and Mickey Rourke.
Prod-GA Dist-GA

Rumen Ciliate Protozoa B 15 MIN
16MM FILM, 3/4 OR 1/2 IN VIDEO H-C A
Rumen is the first stomach of grazing animals such as cattle, deer and camels. The rume ciliate protozoas found in the rumen help the ruminants, as the grazing animals are called, digest the cellulose and other fibrous materials in their food. How the rumen ciliate protozoas move, what they look like and what they feed on is shown. The way protozoa are transferred from mother to offspring in ruminants to assure continuity within the species is discussed.
From The Microbiology Teaching Series.
Prod-UCEMC Dist-UCEMC 1966

Rumor B 6 MIN
16MM FILM OPTICAL SOUND H-C A
Traces the course of a rumor, how it starts, spreads and its results. Discusses ways of dealing with rumors.
From The Challenge Series.
Prod-CMC Dist-ADL 1954

Rumor Clinic B 2(MIN
16MM FILM OPTICAL SOUND J-C A
Presents an entertainment show with a message stating the necessity of getting facts rather than rumors.
Prod-NBC Dist-ADL

Rumors / Black History / Sex Discrimination C 29 MIN
3/4 INCH VIDEO CASSETTE
Presents Portland, Oregon, students showing how the old game of 'telephone' illustrates the realities of their desegregated high school. Asks whether a high school in Harrisburg, Pennsylvania, should give special emphasis to black history. Focuses on Latino girls in Chicago for whom old-world standards suddenly seem oppressive.
From The As We See It Series.
Prod-WTTWTV Dist-PUBTEL

Rumpelstiltskin C 8 MIN
16MM FILM, 3/4 OR 1/2 IN VIDEO P
Presents adaptation of the fairy tale by the Brothers Grimm about

the strange little man who agreed to teach the miller's daughter how to spin straw into gold.
From The Halas And Batchelor Fairy Tale Films Series.
Prod-HALAS Dist-EBEC 1969

Rumpelstiltskin C 10 MIN
16MM FILM, 3/4 OR 1/2 IN VIDEO K-I
all roles in a live version of the fairy tale Rumpelstiltskin.
Presents a group of Connecticut school children who play
Prod-SF Dist-SF 1963

Rumpelstiltskin C 17 MIN
16MM FILM, 3/4 OR 1/2 IN VIDEO K-I
Dramatizes Grimm's fairy tale about the dwarf with magic powers and a funny name and a queen who has to guess his name or lose her infant son.
From The Children's Classics Story Series.
Prod-SCHWAR Dist-MGHT Prodn-JOSHUA 1966

Rumpelstiltskin (Spanish) C 8 MIN
16MM FILM, 3/4 OR 1/2 IN VIDEO P
Tells how a miller boasts too much about the weaving skill of his daughter and how Rumpelstiltskin helps the daughter fulfill these boastful predictions.
Prod-HALAS Dist-EBEC

Rumpelstiltskin (2nd Ed) C 12 MIN
16MM FILM, 3/4 OR 1/2 IN VIDEO K-I
Relates the story of a queen who has promised her first born child to a little man who has spun her straw into gold. Describes how the queen gets out of the bargain by guessing the little man's name.
LC NO. 81-707453
Prod-PERSPF Dist-CORF 1981

Rumpelstilzchen C 88 MIN
16MM FILM OPTICAL SOUND
Presents Grimm's fairy tale of the poor miller whose daughter could presumably spin straw into gold.
Prod-WSTGLC Dist-WSTGLC 1955

Rumplestiltskin C 15 MIN
16MM FILM, 3/4 OR 1/2 IN VIDEO P-I
Tells about a queen who outsmarts a little man and guesses his name - Rumplestiltskin.
From The Timeless Tales Series.
Prod-WESFAL Dist-LUF

Rumplestiltzkin C 28 MIN
16MM FILM OPTICAL SOUND
Presents the Cosmic Box Players of Kenyon College, Gambier, Ohio, in their stage production of the Grimm Brothers' classic, Rumplestiltzkin. Features characters who are neither hero nor villain, allowing each child to make his own judgments and react in his own individual way.
Prod-ASPTEF Dist-ASPTEF

Rums Paradise C 25 MIN
16MM FILM OPTICAL SOUND
Takes a close look at Grand Cayman, a Caribbean tax haven for both individuals and multinational corporations. Notes that these tax havens provide a tax dodge that creates financial hardship for the rest of the taxpaying population.
LC NO. 77-702522
Prod-CTV Dist-CTV 1976

Run Dick, Run Jane C 20 MIN
16MM FILM OPTICAL SOUND
Illustrates through laboratory statistics and case studies, the benefits of a personal fitness program. Includes views of Larry Lewis, a 104-year-old runner, and of Peter Strudwick, who jogs with no feet.
LC NO. 72-700176
Prod-BYU Dist-BYU 1971

Run For Life C 24 MIN
16MM FILM OPTICAL SOUND
Depicts a young married couple who begin the Run for Life educational fitness program under the guidance of marathon runner Frank Shorter and Dr Lenore R Zohman. Emphasizes guidelines for graduated exercise and offers motivational advice to help new runners stay with running.
LC NO. 79-701117
Prod-CONNML Dist-CONNML Prodn-CORPEL 1978

Run For The Money C 22 MIN
16MM FILM OPTICAL SOUND
Shows how the urgency of team effort creates a special relationship among race drivers and crewmen. Examines this cooperative spirit against the background of the Indianapolis 500. Includes highlights of the 54th running of the Memorial Day classic.
Prod-GTARC Dist-GTARC

Run For The Trees C 7 MIN
16MM FILM OPTICAL SOUND
Documents a ten kilometer race in Los Angeles in which every runner received a smog-tolerant tree.
LC NO. 80-700409
Prod-LOUPAC Dist-LOUPAC Prodn-BIGGSD 1979

Run For Your Life C 15 MIN
16MM FILM, 3/4 OR 1/2 IN VIDEO J-C A
Shows a group of high school students as they participate in a three month training program including running and other endurance sports. Emphasizes the role of exercise in the prevention of cardiovascular disease.
From The World Of Health Series.
Prod-INFORP Dist-SF 1975

Run For Your Life C 16 MIN
16MM FILM, 3/4 OR 1/2 IN VIDEO A
Emphasizes the importance of physical activity for all ages to promote cardiac fitness. Features a marathon race by ex-cardiac arrest victims and a fitness program for high school students to portray the importance of keeping fit for life.
Prod-PRORE Dist-PRORE

Run For Your Life C 17 MIN
16MM FILM, 3/4 OR 1/2 IN VIDEO
Investigates aspects of running and jogging. Presents interviews with those who have taken up this activity.
Prod-PERSPF Dist-CORF

Run For Your Money, A C 30 MIN
3/4 OR 1/2 INCH VIDEO CASSETTE
Presents the workings of the banking system, showing the importance of loans and pointing out how one loan can create billions of dollars.
From The Money Puzzle - The World Of Macroeconomics Series. Module 11
Prod-MDCC Dist-MDCC

Run For Yourself C 26 MIN
16MM FILM OPTICAL SOUND
Follows doctors as they prepare for the grueling, 26-mile City Of Lakes Big Green Team Marathon. Scans the training regimen, pros and cons of running and the actual performance of the doctors in the race, one of whom was himself a heart attack victim. Contains a note of optimism for those who think they're beyond the athletic age.
Prod-NCRENT Dist-MTP

Run Sunward C 54 MIN
16MM FILM OPTICAL SOUND
Follows ocean powerboat racers as they battle each other and the elements from Italy to England and points beyond.
Prod-MERMAR Dist-TELEFM

Run The Team C 10 MIN
16MM FILM OPTICAL SOUND
See series title for descriptive statement.
From The Safety Management Series.
Prod-NSC Dist-NSC

Run To Live C 22 MIN
3/4 OR 1/2 INCH VIDEO CASSETTE J A
Presents a documentary which studies Dr Dorothy Brow, surgeon, educator and civic leader, whose life reflects the promise of the American dream. Shows her as she reflects on her past and accepts the challenges of the present. Follows her through her professional day.
Prod-UMCOM Dist-ECUFLM 1980

Run To Live (2nd Ed) C 22 MIN
16MM FILM OPTICAL SOUND
Describes the philosophy and life of Dr Dorothy L Brown, a black woman who became a surgeon, educator and civic leader.
LC NO. 81-700441
Prod-UMCOM Dist-ECUFLM 1980

Run Wild, Run Free C 100 MIN
16MM FILM OPTICAL SOUND
Tells what happens when a mute boy befriends a white colt.
Prod-CPC Dist-TIMLIF 1969

Run-A-Ways C 10 MIN
16MM FILM OPTICAL SOUND J
Endeavors to show teenagers the folly of the immature act of running away from home.
LC NO. 76-709317
Prod-DAVP Dist-DAVP 1969

Run, America, Run C 60 MIN
3/4 OR 1/2 INCH VIDEO CASSETTE
Examines America's mania for running and physical fitness. Features health professionals who are also runners discussing the medical and psychological benefits of running and also how to take care of your feet.
Prod-KINGFT Dist-KINGFT

Run, Appaloosa, Run C 48 MIN
16MM FILM, 3/4 OR 1/2 IN VIDEO
Presents a story about an Indian girl and her love for an Appaloosa colt. Shows how together they bring honor and glory to the Nez Perce Indian nation.
From The Animal Featurettes, Set 2 Series.
Prod-DISNEY Dist-WDEMCO

Runaround, The C 12 MIN
16MM FILM OPTICAL SOUND J-C A
Searches for those responsible for air pollution.
Prod-NTBA Dist-AMLUNG 1969

Runaway C 33 MIN
3/4 OR 1/2 INCH VIDEO CASSETTE I-J
Relates the story of 15-year-old Karen who runs away from the problems she faces with an alcoholic mother and finds herself having to cope with hunger, cold, disorientation and danger. Shows that when the police pick her up for a curfew violation, she and her mother receive joint counseling.
From The Cop Talk Series.
Prod-UTSBE Dist-AITECH 1981

Runaway C 54 MIN
16MM FILM, 3/4 OR 1/2 IN VIDEO A
Tells what happens to the nearly one million children who run away from home each year. Looks at the runaway shelters which have sprung up since the passage of the Runaway and Homeless Youth Act of 1974. Includes interviews with runaways, parents, police and counselors.
Prod-MEDIAG Dist-MEDIAG 1981

Runaway - Freedom Or Fright C 10 MIN
16MM FILM, 3/4 OR 1/2 IN VIDEO J
Explores the problems and dangers connected with running away from home. Suggests that family problems aren't solved by running away.
LC NO. 81-706720
Prod-CAHILL Dist-AIMS 1980

Runaway Camel C 15 MIN
3/4 OR 1/2 INCH VIDEO CASSETTE I
Shows the life of Bedouin nomads. Tells of recapturing an escaped camel.
From The Encounter In The Desert Series.
Prod-CTI Dist-CTI

Runaway Problem, The (2nd Ed) C 13 MIN
16MM FILM, 3/4 OR 1/2 IN VIDEO I-C A
Offers information on teenage runaways and tells how the Runaway Hotline serves to comfort and inform families.
Prod-MILPRO Dist-CORF 1980

Runaway Slave C 15 MIN
3/4 OR 1/2 INCH VIDEO CASSETTE P
Tells the story of the life of Harriet Tubman.
From The Stories Of America Series.
Prod-OHSDE Dist-AITECH Prodn-WVIZTV 1976

Runaway, The C 30 MIN
3/4 OR 1/2 INCH VIDEO CASSETTE I-H
See series title for descriptive statement.
From The Gettin' To Know Me Series.
Prod-CTI Dist-MDCPB 1979

Runaways C 10 MIN
3/4 OR 1/2 INCH VIDEO CASSETTE J
Follows the separate cases of two teenage runaways, Danny and Alice.
Prod-DAVP Dist-AIMS

Runaways C 24 MIN
16MM FILM, 3/4 OR 1/2 IN VIDEO J-C A
Presents the story of a girl who ran away from home after a breakdown in family communications. Shows what it is like to be a runaway trying to survive on the streets. Examines the very limited facilities available to help these children.
Prod-LRF Dist-LRF 1975

Rund Um Den Munchner Marienplatz C 5 MIN
16MM FILM, 3/4 OR 1/2 IN VIDEO H-C A
A German-language version of the motion picture Around And About The Marienplatz In Munich. Explores the history and economy of Munich, the most famous of Germany's state capitals.
From The European Studies - Germany (German) Series.
Prod-MFAFRG Dist-IFB Prodn-BAYER 1973

Running - Short Course On The Long Run C 18 MIN
16MM FILM, 3/4 OR 1/2 IN VIDEO H-C A
Explains how to begin a running program, from first introduction to the point of running 30 minutes at a time, every other day.
Prod-ATHI Dist-ATHI 1982

Running A Dance Company C 30 MIN
3/4 OR 1/2 INCH VIDEO CASSETTE
See series title for descriptive statement.
From The Update - Topics Of Current Concern Series.
Prod-ARCVID Dist-ARCVID

Running A Small Business—A Series
16MM FILM, 3/4 OR 1/2 IN VIDEO H-C A
Shows basic principles of small business operations and basic skills and research methods. Teaches principles of organizing and sorting data relative to successful ventures.
Prod-MVM Dist-BCNFL 1982

Basic Records For A Small Business 018 MIN
Credit And Collections For A Small Business 015 MIN
Evaluating A Small Business 017 MIN
Financing A Small Business 018 MIN
Insurance Needs For A Small Business 017 MIN
Inventory Control For Manufacturers 012 MIN
Merchandise Control For Retailers 014 MIN

Running A Stringer Bead In Flat Position/ Running Weave Beads In Flat Position/Padding C 28 MIN
3/4 OR 1/2 INCH VIDEO CASSETTE H-C A
See series title for descriptive statement.
From The Arc Welding Series.
Prod-CUETV Dist-CUNIV 1981

Running And Handling Of Tubular Goods C 18 MIN
16MM FILM, 3/4 OR 1/2 IN VIDEO IND
Tells in a practical way how to successfully run and handle oil field tubular goods in the field.
Prod-HYDRIL Dist-UTEXPE 1982

Running And Riding Smooth - Tune-Up And Shocks C 60 MIN
1/2 IN VIDEO CASSETTE BETA/VHS
Shows how to perform an engine tune-up. Demonstrates changing spark plugs, points and condensers. Covers servicing a car's PCV System and timing an engine.
From The Car Care Series.
Prod-MOHOMV Dist-MOHOMV

Running Back, The B 11 MIN
16MM FILM OPTICAL SOUND J-H
Stance, running forward, right and left receiving the hand-off, fanking on receiving the ball, following the blocker and changing pace and direction while running with the ball.
Prod-BORDEN Dist-COCA

Running Continuous Bead In Horizontal And Vertical Down Position (Spanish) C
3/4 OR 1/2 INCH VIDEO CASSETTE
See series title for descriptive statement.
From The Shielded Metal Arc Welding (Spanish) Series.
Prod-VTRI Dist-VTRI

Running Continuous Bead In Horizontal And Vertical Down Position C 15 MIN
3/4 OR 1/2 INCH VIDEO CASSETTE IND
See series title for descriptive statement.
From The Welding - Shielded Metal-Arc Welding Series.
Prod-ICSINT Dist-ICSINT

Running Continuous Beads Flat Position, Flat Butt Welds, Horizontal Butt Welds With... C 15 MIN
3/4 OR 1/2 INCH VIDEO CASSETTE
See series title for descriptive statement.
From The Welding III - TIG and MIG (Industry) Welding series.
Prod-CAMB Dist-CAMB

Running Continuous Beads Flat Position, Flat Butt Welds, Horizontal Butt Welds With Steel C 15 MIN
3/4 OR 1/2 INCH VIDEO CASSETTE
See series title for descriptive statement.
From The Welding III - TIG and MIG (Industry) Welding series.
Prod-CAMB Dist-CAMB

Running Continuous Beads Flat Position, Flat Butt Welds, Horizontal Butt Welds With Aluminum C 15 MIN
3/4 OR 1/2 INCH VIDEO CASSETTE
See series title for descriptive statement.
From The Welding III - TIG and MIG (Industry) Welding series.
Prod-CAMB Dist-CAMB

Running Continuous Beads Flat Position,- Including Flat Butt And Horiztontal Butt Welds C 15 MIN
3/4 OR 1/2 INCH VIDEO CASSETTE
See series title for descriptive statement.
From The Welding II - Basic Shielded Metal Arc Welding series.
Prod-CAMB Dist-CAMB

Running Continuous Beads In Vertical Up And Overhead Position (Spanish) C
3/4 OR 1/2 INCH VIDEO CASSETTE
See series title for descriptive statement.
From The Shielded Metal Arc Welding (Spanish) Series.
Prod-VTRI Dist-VTRI

Running Continuous Beads In Vertical Up And Overhead Position C 15 MIN
3/4 OR 1/2 INCH VIDEO CASSETTE IND
See series title for descriptive statement.
From The Welding - Shielded-Arc Welding Series.
Prod-ICSINT Dist-ICSINT

Running Events, The - Men C 21 MIN
16MM FILM, 3/4 OR 1/2 IN VIDEO J-C
Examines the running events at all distances plus hurdling and sprint relay techniques.
From The LeRoy Walker Track And Field - Men Series.
Prod-ATHI Dist-ATHI 1976

Running Events, The - Women C 21 MIN
16MM FILM, 3/4 OR 1/2 IN VIDEO J-C
Develops and studies sprints, middle distance, hurdling and sprint relays.
From The LeRoy Walker Track And Field - Women Series.
Prod-ATHI Dist-ATHI 1976

Running Fence C 60 MIN
16MM FILM OPTICAL SOUND
Looks at an artist's struggle to plan and construct a 24 mile long fence of white fabric through the hills of California. Reveals that the heart of his struggle is his attempt to communicate his concept of art to the ranchers and local governments involved.
Prod-MAYSLS Dist-MAYSLS 1978

Running For Life C 28 MIN
16MM FILM, 3/4 OR 1/2 IN VIDEO H-C
Discusses the U S Office of Public Health's two-year experiment to determine the effects of exercise on middle-aged persons and whether such exercising can reduce the chances of heart disease. Shows faculty members of the University of Wiscosin exercising and reporting on their experiences.
Prod-NET Dist-IU 1970

Running Gear C 14 MIN
16MM FILM, 3/4 OR 1/2 IN VIDEO H
Uses a specially prepared chassis to demonstrate the qualities of frame design and development. Shows integral body and frame construction and emphasizes the types and functions of springs, shackles and shock absorbers. Examines independent suspension systems and demonstrates mechanical and hydraulic braking systems.
Prod-SF Dist-SF 1969

Running Ground C 29 MIN
3/4 INCH VIDEO CASSETTE H
Dramatizes one high school student's choices as he examines the directionless lives of his friends, many of whom are involved in drugs and alcohol. Shows how he is able to set a clearer direction in his own life by running and writing.
LC NO. 80-707476
Prod-MESJ Dist-MESJ 1980

Running Hard, Breathing Easy - The Jeanette Bolden Story C 13 MIN
3/4 INCH VIDEO CASSETTE
Tells the story of Jeanette Bolden, a young woman who overcame asthma to become a world-class sprinter and a member of the 1980 U.S. Olympic team. Stresses how she was helped by good medical treatment.
Prod-SCHPLO Dist-MTP

Running I C 30 MIN
3/4 OR 1/2 INCH VIDEO CASSETTE
Discusses various aspects of running.
From The Bodyworks Series.
Prod-KTXTTV Dist-MDCPB

Running II C 30 MIN
3/4 OR 1/2 INCH VIDEO CASSETTE
Discusses various aspects of running.
From The Bodyworks Series.
Prod-KTXTTV Dist-MDCPB

Running My Way C 28 MIN
16MM FILM OPTICAL SOUND I-J A
Depicts various ways teenagers struggle with their maturing sexuality.
LC NO. 82-700197
Prod-CHSCA Dist-CHSCA Prodn-LITMAN 1981

Running On Empty - The Fuel Economy Challenge C 27 MIN
3/4 OR 1/2 INCH VIDEO CASSETTE
Gives tips on fast starts, highway speed, accelerating before hills and wind drag while meeting a fuel economy challenge.
Prod-IVCH Dist-IVCH

Running On Empty - The Fuel Economy Challenge C 27 MIN
16MM FILM - 3/4 IN VIDEO
Illustrates various driving and fuel economy techniques used during a 90-mile rally. Shows how drivers can practice ways to achieve maximum savings in gasoline and money while traveling city streets, country roads and major highways.
LC NO. 79-706061
Prod-USDOE Dist-USNAC 1979

Running On The Edge Of The Rainbow - Laguna Stories And Poems C 28 MIN
3/4 OR 1/2 INCH VIDEO CASSETTE
Reflects on the nature of Laguna storytelling, its functions and the problems she has faced as an Indian poet. Discusses how these stories are current versions of traditional tales.
From The Words And Place Series.
Prod-CWATER Dist-CWATER

Running Out Of Water C 30 MIN
3/4 OR 1/2 INCH VIDEO CASSETTE C
See series title for descriptive statement.
From The Time's Harvest - Exploring The Future Series.
Prod-MDCPB Dist-MDCPB

Running Programs, Mathematical Expressions C 60 MIN
3/4 OR 1/2 INCH VIDEO CASSETTE
See series title for descriptive statement.
From The Introduction To BASIC Series. Lecture 2
Prod-UIDEEO Dist-UIDEEO

Running Start, A C 28 MIN
1/2 IN VIDEO CASSETTE BETA/VHS
Highlights 30 years of California's history in horse racing and breeding.
Prod-CTBRDA Dist-EQVDL

Running Start, A - Preparing For Participation C 12 MIN
16MM FILM, 3/4 OR 1/2 IN VIDEO I-H
Stresses the importance of pre-season football conditioning and the need for emphasizing building endurance and weight training.
From The Football Injury Prevention Series.
Prod-ATHI Dist-ATHI

Running The Show C 30 MIN
16MM FILM, 3/4 OR 1/2 IN VIDEO C A
See series title for descriptive statement.
From The Case Studies In Small Business Series.
Prod-UMA Dist-GPITVL 1979

Running Wild C 50 MIN
3/4 OR 1/2 INCH VIDEO CASSETTE H-C A
Features a scheme devised by the organization Visionquest for rehabilitating tough young offenders in which they face the challenge of breaking a wild mustang. Tells the history of the wild mustang in America, brought over from Spain. Portrays the respect that develops between the youth and the horse resulting in taming them both.
Prod-BBCTV Dist-FI

Running Your Own Business—A Series

Explains the role of accountancy and financial administration in successful business management.
Prod-EFD Dist-EFD

Accounting - The Language Of Business	11 MIN
Bankruptcy	11 MIN
Capital Gains	11 MIN
Capital Investments	11 MIN
Inventory Management	11 MIN
Management Controls	11 MIN
Planning For Profit	11 MIN
Risk Management	11 MIN
Sources Of Capital	11 MIN
Taxation	11 MIN

Running, Jumping And Standing Still Film B 10 MIN
16MM FILM OPTICAL SOUND J-C A
Presents, in the style of silent comedy, Peter Sellers and his 'GOON SHOW' troupe as they pursue their eccentric courses across the British countryside.
LC NO. 77-709667
Prod-PFP Dist-VIEWFI 1970

Runoff, Land Use And Water Quality C 21 MIN
16MM FILM, 3/4 OR 1/2 IN VIDEO
Explores the ways in which land use affects water quality.
Prod-UWISCA Dist-MCFI 1978

Runt Of The Litter C 13 MIN
16MM FILM OPTICAL SOUND P-I
An excerpt from the motion picture Charlotte's Web. Tells how a pig named Wilbur is desolate when he discovers he is destined to be the farmer's Christmas dinner, until his spider friend, Charlotte, decides to help him. Based on the book Charlotte's Web by E B White.
From The Peppermint Stick Selection Series.
LC NO. 77-701720
Prod-FI Dist-FI 1976

Runt, The C 14 MIN
16MM FILM, 3/4 OR 1/2 IN VIDEO P-I
Relates how Pee Wee feels inferior because of his size until he joins the kids in a football game and saves the day.
From The Learning Values With Fat Albert Series.
Prod-FLMTON Dist-CRMP 1977

Ruptured Lumbar Discs - Treatment By Vertebral Body Fusion C 20 MIN
16MM FILM OPTICAL SOUND PRO
Examines the steps of discography employed to demonstrate the etiology of low back pain and its relation to the intervertebral discs. Shows the entire surgical procedure for the removal of a pathological lumbar disc and replacement with bone grafts.
Prod-SQUIBB Dist-SQUIBB

Rural America C 18 MIN
16MM FILM, 3/4 OR 1/2 IN VIDEO H-C A
Presents a documentary on the effects of a recession on the people of Pecatonica, Illinois. Shows how the economic survival of the city depends on the surrounding farm community and the availability of jobs in two industrial centers that are 15 miles away. Records what people can and cannot afford in a recession and what they think about America's promise for the future.
From The American Condition Series.
Prod-ABCTV Dist-MGHT 1976

Rural Cooperative, The C 15 MIN
16MM FILM OPTICAL SOUND
Presents a portrait of the Tsao Tun Farmers' Association, which typifies rural cooperatives in Taiwan. Show it as being the center of social, leisure and economic activities for the 9,600 families who own the cooperative and rely on it for services ranging from irrigation, provision of seeds, farm implements and fertilizers to crop storage and marketing.
From The Faces Of Change - Taiwan Series.
Prod-AUFS Dist-WHEELK

Rural Crime - They're Stealin' The Farm C 18 MIN
16MM FILM, 3/4 OR 1/2 IN VIDEO H-C A
Explains how to protect equipment, animals and crops on the farm.
Prod-CAGO Dist-AIMS 1982

Rural Crime Prevention C 16 MIN
16MM FILM, 3/4 OR 1/2 IN VIDEO
Points out the special vulnerability of rural property to crime and the steps people who live and work in sparsely populated areas can take to minimize opportunity for crime.
Prod-HAR Dist-MTI 1984

Rural Driving C 35 MIN
16MM FILM OPTICAL SOUND H
Depicts country and mountain road conditions as they affect the driver. Illustrates crash-producing situations and how to avoid them.
From The To Get From Here To There Series.
Prod-PROART Dist-PROART

Rural Driving C 10 MIN
16MM FILM, 3/4 OR 1/2 IN VIDEO
Discusses speed relationships with other vehicles and roadway elements.
From The Driver Education Series.
Prod-FMCMP Dist-FORDFL 1969

Rural Land Use And Settlement Patterns C 20 MIN
3/4 INCH VIDEO CASSETTE H-C
See series title for descriptive statement.
From The Geography For The '70's Series.
Prod-KLRNTV Dist-GPITVL

Rural Mental Health Practice C 23 MIN
3/4 INCH VIDEO CASSETTE
Interviews four mental health professionals who have made the transition from urban to rural practice. Discusses their transition in terms of an impractical romanticizing about rural life.
Prod-UWASHP Dist-UWASHP

Rural Migrants - No Place To Live C 20 MIN
16MM FILM, 3/4 OR 1/2 IN VIDEO J-C
Revised version of the 1975 motion picture No Place To Go. Explores the problems in Africa, Latin America and Asia caused by the influx of rural migrants into the cities.
Prod-UN Dist-BARR 1977

Rural Neighborhood - A Beautiful Place C 15 MIN
3/4 OR 1/2 INCH VIDEO CASSETTE P
Explains how beautiful a rural neighborhood can be.
From The Neighborhoods Series.
Prod-NEITV Dist-GPITVL 1981

Rural Neighborhood - A General Description C 15 MIN
3/4 OR 1/2 INCH VIDEO CASSETTE P
Provides a general description of rural neighborhoods.
From The Neighborhoods Series.
Prod-NEITV Dist-GPITVL 1981

Rural Neighborhood - Good Neighbors Help Each Other C 15 MIN
3/4 OR 1/2 INCH VIDEO CASSETTE P
Shows good neighbors help each other in a rural environment.

From The Neighborhoods Series.
Prod-NEITV Dist-GPITVL 1981

Rural Nurse B 20 MIN
16MM FILM OPTICAL SOUND J-C A
Shows the work of a rural nurse of the United Nations Integral Demonstration Headquarters in El Salvador. Explains how, as a nurse-midwife, she helps the people of the area assigned to her, who live under primitive conditions. Illustrates the need for sanitation and more medical services in the area.
Prod-UN Dist-UN 1954

Rural Politics C 30 MIN
3/4 OR 1/2 INCH VIDEO CASSETTE C
Details some of the political problems faced by rural Americans, a new minority group lacking the political clout farmers once enjoyed.
From The American Government 1 Series.
Prod-DALCCD Dist-DALCCD

Rural Rat Control B 16 MIN
16MM FILM OPTICAL SOUND
Explains how a farmer who understands rat habits can free his farm of rats through ratproofing buildings and food sources, burying garbage in a one-man land fill and using approved poisons.
LC NO. FIE53-204
Prod-USPHS Dist-USNAC 1951

Rural Rat Control (Spanish) B 16 MIN
16MM FILM OPTICAL SOUND
Explains how a farmer who understands rat habits can free his farm of rats through ratproofing buildings and food sources, burying garbage in a one-man landfill and using approved poisons.
LC NO. 74-705553
Prod-NMAC Dist-USNAC 1951

Rural Recreations B 23 MIN
16MM FILM OPTICAL SOUND I-C A
Presents simple pastimes of rural Indian folk and highlights festivals like Gokul Astami and Diwali and Kerala's boat races.
Prod-INDIA Dist-NEDINF

Rural Youth C 30 MIN
3/4 OR 1/2 INCH VIDEO CASSETTE H-C A
Describes common themes among Maine's rural youth, including poverty, broken families, disinterest in and dropping out of school.
From The Can I Get There From Here? Series.
Prod-MESETC Dist-UMEA 1981

Rush C 3 MIN
16MM FILM OPTICAL SOUND J-C
Presents a rapid fire, humorous comment on the pace of our lives today.
Prod-NWSWGR Dist-SLFP 1968

Rush Hour Service C 9 MIN
16MM FILM, 3/4 OR 1/2 IN VIDEO J-C A
Illustrates techniques for properly confronting the rush hour in dining rooms and coffee shops stressing that this is the time for the greatest profits and the greatest losses.
From The Professional Food Preparation And Service Program Series.
Prod-NEM Dist-NEM 1971

Rush Hour Service C 10 MIN
16MM FILM, 3/4 OR 1/2 IN VIDEO J-C A
Illustrates how to properly confront the rush hour in dining rooms and coffee shops. Shows the basic responsibilities of hostesses, waitresses and busboys during this critical time. Stresses importance of the rush hour as the time when chances for profits or losses are greatest and when employees must perform courteously and efficiently under pressure.
From The Professional Food Preparation And Service Program Series.
LC NO. 74-700218
Prod-NEM Dist-NEM 1971

Rush To Judgment B 110 MIN
16MM FILM OPTICAL SOUND
Disputes the findings and conclusions of the Warren Commission's report on the assassination of President John F Kennedy. Directed by Emile de Antonio.
Prod-NYFLMS Dist-NYFLMS Prodn-DEANTE 1967

Rushcape C 20 MIN
3/4 INCH VIDEO CASSETTE I
Presents an Appalachian folktale staged with rod puppets.
From The Wonderama Of The Arts Series.
Prod-WBRATV Dist-GPITVL 1979

Rushes C 56 MIN
16MM FILM, 3/4 OR 1/2 IN VIDEO
Presents a self-destructive filmmaker who proposes to film the last 24 hours of his life. Reveals his relationships through telephone conversations, confrontations and interviews. Shows that despite the threats and pleading of those who care, he poisons himself.
Prod-SPINLB Dist-DIRECT 1979

Russia C 24 MIN
16MM FILM OPTICAL SOUND I-C
Shows present day Russia with a few flash backs of the Czar and his family. Includes scenes of industries, collective farms, churches, recreation, shopping, the Kremlin and Red Square.
Prod-IFF Dist-IFF 1958

Russia C 18 MIN
16MM FILM, 3/4 OR 1/2 IN VIDEO J-C A
Provides an overview of the Soviet Union from the last of the czars to Lenin. Shows today's Russians at work and play.
Prod-LUF Dist-LUF

Russia - A Cultural Revolution C 27 MIN
16MM FILM OPTICAL SOUND J-H A
Tells the effect of the Russian Revolution in 1917 on Russian culture. Explains that the revolution ended a period of brilliant creativity in the Russian arts by using these arts solely to sell the dream of a worker's paradise to the people in order to inspire them to work harder toward communist goals. Relates the Russian definition of the word 'CULTURE.'
LC NO. 79-701203
Prod-AVED Dist-AVED 1967

Russia - Czar To Lenin B 29 MIN
16MM FILM, 3/4 OR 1/2 IN VIDEO J-C
Uses actual footage to document the causes and outbreak of the Russian Revolution.
Prod-MGHT Dist-MGHT Prodn-AXELBK 1966

Russia - The Unfinished Revolution B 60 MIN
16MM FILM OPTICAL SOUND J-C A
Discusses the thesis that Russia's Revolution is unfinished, since it has not yet come into harmony with the talents of the Russian people. Shows scenes of life in Russia today and presents interviews with leading persons in economics, medicine, science, children's literature and poetry.
From The New Journal Series.
LC NO. FIA68-579
Prod-NET Dist-IU 1968

Russia Crushes Hungary B 8 MIN
16MM FILM OPTICAL SOUND
Presents excerpts of 1956 Screen News Digest films which recall the assault of rebels of communist control in Hungary and the ensuing communist tyranny in Budapest under the Soviets. Shows the flight of 125,000 Hungarian refugees into Austria and the entrance of 21,000 into the United States.
From The News Magazine Of The Screen Series. Vol 7, No. 4
Prod-PATHE Dist-HEARST 1956

Russia In Europe C 19 MIN
16MM FILM, 3/4 OR 1/2 IN VIDEO I-J
Studies White Russia, the Ukraine and the Crimea. Discusses Russia's one-party system and gives examples of propaganda.
Prod-DOOLYJ Dist-IFB 1961

Russia In World War I B 20 MIN
16MM FILM, 3/4 OR 1/2 IN VIDEO
Covers the Russian declaration of war on Germany in the first World War, a major defeat of Russia in its first battle, and the 'NO SURRENDER' policy of the Tsar which contributed to the overthrow of the Tsar and his government.
From The Russian Revolution Series.
Prod-GRATV Dist-FI 1971

Russia Today–A Series
J-C A
Depicts principal aspects of life in the U.S.S.R. today, including use of leisure time, religion, the Russian consumer, the peasant and the women of Russia.
Prod-IFF Dist-IFF

Leisure Time, U.S.S.R.	012 MIN
Religion In Russia	021 MIN
Russian Consumer, The	014 MIN
Russian Peasant, The - The Story Of Russian	019 MIN
Women Of Russia	011 MIN

Russia Under Stalin C 29 MIN
2 INCH VIDEOTAPE
See series title for descriptive statement.
From The Course Of Our Times I Series.
Prod-WGBHTV Dist-PUBTEL

Russia, Siberia - The Way It Is C 16 MIN
16MM FILM OPTICAL SOUND I-C A
Shows the people, cities, country, art and architecture of russia, giving a feeling for the present as well as a sense of history.
LC NO. 73-702808
Prod-PORTIN Dist-SCREEI 1973

Russian And The Tartar, The C 27 MIN
16MM FILM, 3/4 OR 1/2 IN VIDEO
Presents the Russian story of a Russian and a Tartar who are traveling together and argue over who will watch the horses. Shows them trying to trick each other throughout the night.
From The Storybook International Series.
Prod-JOU Dist-JOU 1982

Russian Athlete, The C 50 MIN
16MM FILM OPTICAL SOUND
Presents a television special from the CTV program Olympiad, which examines the performances of Soviet athletes in Olympic competition.
LC NO. 77-702543
Prod-CTV Dist-CTV 1976

Russian Chinese Rupture, The C 29 MIN
2 INCH VIDEOTAPE
See series title for descriptive statement.
From The Course Of Our Times II Series.
Prod-WGBHTV Dist-PUBTEL

Russian Connection, The C 50 MIN
16MM FILM, 3/4 OR 1/2 IN VIDEO H-C A
Tells about the backing of terrorist organizations by the USSR and includes interviews with two members of the PLO. Explains that once the Soviets have trained and aided such groups, they can then require them to carry out actions on their behalf in trouble spots throughout the world without being directly linked to their activities.
Prod-CANBC Dist-PHENIX 1980

Russian Consumer, The C 14 MIN
3/4 OR 1/2 INCH VIDEO CASSETTE J-C A
See series title for descriptive statement.
From The Russia Today Series.
Prod-IFF Dist-IFF

Russian Consumer, The - Rubles And Kopecks C 13 MIN
16MM FILM OPTICAL SOUND J-H
Shows the progress which has been made over the last twenty years in furnishing better consumer goods to the Russian city dweller, but not to the peasant.
From The Russia Today Series.
LC NO. 70-701844
Prod-IFF Dist-IFF 1968

Russian Language And People–A Series
16MM FILM, 3/4 OR 1/2 IN VIDEO
A series of 20 videocassettes which presents lessons on the Russian language while introducing aspects of Russian life.
Prod-FI Dist-FI

Russian Language–A Series
16MM FILM, 3/4 OR 1/2 IN VIDEO H-C A
A series of Russian-language films dealing with the geography of Russia and the lifestyle of its people.
Prod-IFB Dist-IFB 1963

From Moscow To The Baykal	014 MIN
Moscow And Leningrad	014 MIN
Rest And Leisure In The USSR	014 MIN
Science, Technology And Art In The USSR	013 MIN

Russian Life Today - Inside The Soviet Union C 21 MIN
16MM FILM, 3/4 OR 1/2 IN VIDEO J-C A
Reveals what life is like in Russia, where the central government controls all aspects of economic, cultural and social life. Provides information about the Communist party, religion, transportation, education, culture and the arts, business, health and climate.
Prod-IFADV Dist-MCFI

Russian Lubok C 10 MIN
16MM FILM, 3/4 OR 1/2 IN VIDEO J-C A
Shows examples of Russian woodcarving and sculpture that exemplify the charm and vivid color of the folklore styles that have endured into the 20th century.
Prod-FMPORT Dist-CAROUF

Russian Peasant, The - The Story Of Russian Agriculture C 19 MIN
16MM FILM, 3/4 OR 1/2 IN VIDEO
See series title for descriptive statement.
From The Russia Today Series.
Prod-IFF Dist-IFF

Russian Revolution C 30 MIN
3/4 OR 1/2 INCH VIDEO CASSETTE H
Recounts the tzar's attempts at reform, Russia's 1905 defeat by Japan and the causes of the February Revolution of 1917. Describes the radical demands of the Soviets and Lenin's return.
From The Historically Speaking Series. Part 20
Prod-KRMATV Dist-AITECH 1983

Russian Revolution And The 50 Years That Followed, The B 16 MIN
16MM FILM OPTICAL SOUND
Analyzes the origins, objectives, strengths and weaknesses of international communism.
From The Screen News Digest Series. Vol 10, Issue 4
LC NO. FIA68-1665
Prod-HEARST Dist-HEARST 1967

Russian Revolution 1917-1967, The B 20 MIN
16MM FILM OPTICAL SOUND
Presents a timely and penetrating analysis of the origins and objectives, strengths and weaknesses of international communism.
From The Screen News Digest Series. Vol 10, Issue 4
Prod-HEARST Dist-HEARST 1967

Russian Revolution–A Series
16MM FILM, 3/4 OR 1/2 IN VIDEO
Prod-GRATV Dist-FI 1971

Bolshevik Victory, The	20 MIN
Last Years Of The Tsar	19 MIN
Lenin Prepares For Revolution	22 MIN
Russia In World War I	20 MIN

Russian Revolution, The C 29 MIN
2 INCH VIDEOTAPE
See series title for descriptive statement.
From The Course Of Our Times I Series.
Prod-WGBHTV Dist-PUBTEL

Russian Rooster C 4 MIN
16MM FILM, 3/4 OR 1/2 IN VIDEO
Combines the music of Rimsky-Korsakov with an animated story about a group of hunters frantically chasing a rooster.
Prod-PERSPF Dist-CORF 1975

Russian Soul C 29 MIN
3/4 OR 1/2 INCH VIDEO CASSETTE
Dimitri Devytakin uses his heritage to uncover the emotional and psychological aspects of the Russian character. He converses with various Soviet citizens.
Prod-EAI Dist-EAI

Russians Are Here, The C 58 MIN
3/4 OR 1/2 INCH VIDEO CASSETTE
Investigates a community of Russian immigrants who have recently arrived in the United States.
From The Frontline Series.
Prod-DOCCON Dist-PBS

Russians–A Series
16MM FILM, 3/4 OR 1/2 IN VIDEO H-C A

Offers information on the people and government of the Soviet Union.
Prod-FLMAUS Dist-LCOA 1979

People Of Influence 30 MIN
People Of The Cities 30 MIN
People Of The Country 30 MIN

Rustic Delights B 9 MIN
16MM FILM OPTICAL SOUND I-C A
Describes how puppet shows have delighted rural Indian audiences for centuries, especially in Rajasthan and South India. Shows select scenes from the puppet play 'HARISCHANDRA' and provides glimpses of behind-the-scene activities of puppeteers.
Prod-INDIA Dist-NEDINF

Rutabagas - The Root Of Good Eating C 14 MIN
16MM FILM, 3/4 OR 1/2 IN VIDEO H-C A
Shows a girl visiting her uncle on a farm and learning how the rutabaga travels from the planting and harvesting in the fields to the processing plant and then to the table.
Prod-LOCKF Dist-MCFI 1984

Ruth Ellen Patton/Helen Ross C 28 MIN
3/4 OR 1/2 INCH VIDEO CASSETTE
Features two women reflecting on their lives, the daughter of General George S Patton, sister of General George S Patton III, and the wife of General James W Totten and a descendent of generations of military families. Helen Ross talks about her work with children and her remembrances of her own childhood.
From The Old Friends - New Friends Series.
Prod-FAMCOM Dist-PBS 1981

Ruth Page - An American Original C 59 MIN
16MM FILM, 3/4 OR 1/2 IN VIDEO J-C A
Describes the career of dancer-choreographer Ruth Page.
Prod-HAHND Dist-TEXFLM 1978

Ruth Rubin C 52 MIN
3/4 OR 1/2 INCH VIDEO CASSETTE
Presents Ruth Rubin performing several well-known Yiddish songs.
From The Rainbow Quest Series.
Prod-SEEGER Dist-CWATER

Ruth St Denis By Baribault C 24 MIN
16MM FILM OPTICAL SOUND J-C A
Presents five dances performed by Ruth St Denis filmed in the 1940's and early 1950's by her friend and photographer, Phillip Baribault. Includes White Jade, Dance Of The Red And Gold Saree, Gregorian Chant, Tillers Of The Soil and Incense.
LC NO. 78-701822
Prod-UR Dist-UR 1978

Ruth Stout's Garden C 23 MIN
16MM FILM, 3/4 OR 1/2 IN VIDEO A
Journeys into the life of a woman who, from a perspective of more than 90 years, has a great deal to offer young and old on subjects ranging from growing vegetables to growing old.
Prod-MOKIN Dist-MOKIN 1976

Rutherford Atom B 40 MIN
16MM FILM OPTICAL SOUND H-C
Uses a cloud chamber and gold foil in a simple alphaparticle scattering experiment to illustrate the historic Rutherford experiment which led to the nuclear model of the atom. Uses scale models to illustrate the nuclear atom and coulomb scattering.
From The PSSC Physics Films Series.
Prod-PSSC Dist-MLA 1961

Ruthie Gordon - Folk Singer C 30 MIN
3/4 INCH VIDEO CASSETTE
Features feminist folk singer Ruthie Gordon singing a selection of folk songs concerning the struggles of women, third world people and workers to change their situations. Gives background history to the songs and talks about how the songs reflect her experience and feelings as a woman and as a singer.
Prod-WMENIF Dist-WMENIF

Rx For Drug Abuse C 26 MIN
3/4 OR 1/2 INCH VIDEO CASSETTE
Provides some answers to the questions of what pharmacists should know about prescription drug abuse and what steps can be taken to eliminate it.
Prod-ARFO Dist-ARFO 1977

Rx For Flight C 18 MIN
3/4 OR 1/2 INCH VIDEO CASSETTE
Shows some of the aeromedical problems that face general aviation pilots, including alcohol, drugs, hypoxia, disorientation, smoking and safety equipment.
LC NO. 80-706841
Prod-USFAA Dist-USNAC 1980

Rx For Hope C 15 MIN
16MM FILM OPTICAL SOUND
Explains how non-addictive, anti-depressant drug therapy can be used to treat depression.
Prod-CIBA Dist-MTP

Rx Understanding C 16 MIN
16MM FILM OPTICAL SOUND H-C
Shows a skillful pediatrician as he works with three children and their mothers. Discusses clinical aspects, such as interview techniques and routines for physical examinations. Also emphasizes the art of dealing with people, especially when offering advice.
LC NO. FIA66-20
Prod-OSUMPD Dist-OSUMPD 1958

Ryan C 26 MIN
16MM FILM OPTICAL SOUND

Uses the subjective camera technique to portray the systems approach to apprehending, identifying and rehabilitating problem drinking drivers. Follows a problem drinker from the time of arrest through jail and court and eventually to a rehabilitation program.
LC NO. 76-701541
Prod-SEKCAS Dist-USNAC Prodn-CAMERN 1973

Rythmes De Paris C 9 MIN
16MM FILM, 3/4 OR 1/2 IN VIDEO
A French language film. Explores the principal points of interest in various sections of Paris and presents a cultural portrait of the Parisian citizenry.
From The La France Contemporaine Series.
Prod-EBEC Dist-EBEC 1971

Rythmetic C 9 MIN
16MM FILM, 3/4 OR 1/2 IN VIDEO I-J
Uses animation to show digits meeting, adding, subtracting, jostling, and attacking.
Prod-NFBC Dist-IFB 1957

Rytmisk Pigegymnastik (Rhythmic Gymnastics For Girls) B 16 MIN
16MM FILM SILENT
Describes various rhythmic exercises for girls. Includes Danish subtitles.
Prod-STATNS Dist-STATNS 1961

S

S A T Exam Preparation—A Series

Offers preparation for the student planning to take the S A T exam, in a ten module School Version, or the Home Version with modules.
Prod-KRLSOF Dist-KRLSOF 1985

Math - All Skill Areas And Problem Types 120 MIN
Math - Quantitative Comparison 120 MIN
Model Examination I With Explanations 120 MIN
Model Examination II With Explanations 120 MIN
Model Examination III With Explanations 120 MIN
Preparing Your Students For The S A T 120 MIN
Reading Comprehension 120 MIN
SAT Overview And Test Taking Strategy 120 MIN
Test Of Standard Written English 120 MIN
Vocabulary And Word Analogies 120 MIN

S A T Overview And Test Taking Strategy C 120 MIN
3/4 OR 1/2 INCH VIDEO CASSETTE
See series title for descriptive statement.
From The S A T Exam Preparation Series.
Prod-KRLSOF Dist-KRLSOF 1985

S Is For Single Parent C 8 MIN
16MM FILM, 3/4 OR 1/2 IN VIDEO
Looks at the men and women who raise their children alone and the many difficulties they face in terms of finances, finding adequate housing and daycare, and coping with loneliness.
From The ABC's Of Canadian Life Series.
Prod-UTORMC Dist-UTORMC

S Sound C 14 MIN
3/4 OR 1/2 INCH VIDEO CASSETTE K
See series title for descriptive statement.
From The I-Land Treasure Series.
Prod-NETCHE Dist-AITECH 1980

S Sound, The C 15 MIN
3/4 INCH VIDEO CASSETTE P
Discusses various spellings of the s sound.
From The New Talking Shop Series.
Prod-BSPTV Dist-GPITVL 1978

S Sound, The - Mr Sam's Little Tire C 15 MIN
2 INCH VIDEOTAPE P
Introduces some of the consonant sounds met in early reading. Identifies the written letter with the spoken sound.
From The Listen And Say Series.
Prod-MPATI Dist-GPITVL

S W L A C 8 MIN
16MM FILM OPTICAL SOUND H-C A
Presents an abstract interpretation of the Industrial area of Southwest Los Angeles. Includes music which emphasizes the continual activity and the ceaseless pulsation of modern machinery.
LC NO. 70-713816
Prod-THOMPR Dist-CFS 1971

S.he C 12 MIN
3/4 INCH VIDEO CASSETTE
Presents a spoken and visual poem that contemplates male and female elements in the universe, by Bill Seaman.
Prod-EAI Dist-EAI

S-Blends - Stars And Stripes In Scouting C 20 MIN
3/4 OR 1/2 INCH VIDEO CASSETTE J-H
See series title for descriptive statement.
From The Getting The Word Series. Unit II
Prod-SCETV Dist-AITECH 1974

S-Expressions C 50 MIN
3/4 OR 1/2 INCH VIDEO CASSETTE
Discusses S-expressions and the functions which operate on them in computer languages.
From The Computer Languages - Pt 1 Series.
Prod-MIOT Dist-MIOT

S-M B 50 MIN
16MM FILM OPTICAL SOUND C A

Presents an insightful document about a real world of deviant sex in hidden behind artificial taboos.
Prod-GROVE Dist-GROVE

S-Offset Change Cheeks (Same Depth) C 22 MIN
1/2 IN VIDEO CASSETTE BETA/VHS IND
Presents a mechanical layout method of drawing an S-offset when the cheek dimensions change size.
Prod-RMI Dist-RMI

S-Offset Same Size Cheeks (Same Size Openings) C 16 MIN
1/2 IN VIDEO CASSETTE BETA/VHS IND
Presents a mechanical layout method of drawing an accurate O gee curve for an S-offset.
Prod-RMI Dist-RMI

S-100 Bus, The C 60 MIN
3/4 OR 1/2 INCH VIDEO CASSETTE C
See series title for descriptive statement.
From The Microcomputer Bus Structures Series.
Prod-NEU Dist-AMCEE

S-8 Logger C 8 MIN
16MM FILM OPTICAL SOUND
Describes the International Harvester S-8 logger.
LC NO. 75-703533
Prod-IH Dist-IH Prodn-IPHC 1974

S, L, R C
3/4 OR 1/2 INCH VIDEO CASSETTE
See series title for descriptive statement.
From The Educational Video Concepts For Early Childhood Language Development Series.
Prod-ECCOAZ Dist-ECCOAZ

Sa Sa Di C 29 MIN
2 INCH VIDEOTAPE
Presents Sa Sa Di, a group of nine instrumentalists, ranging from flugelhorn to electric piano, performing the instrumental piece, 200, Freddie's Dead and other selections.
From The Changing Rhythms Series.
Prod-KRMATV Dist-PUBTEL

Sabato Fiorello C 9 MIN
16MM FILM OPTICAL SOUND C A
Features a surrealist who use the underpinnings of the old art movement to rationalize his compulsion for collecting thousands of unwanted objects to furnish his house. Roams about the rooms of a cluttered mansion, while its artist-owner engages in a one-way conversation with the viewer, asking him if he believes in his own reality.
LC NO. 72-702044
Prod-CFS Dist-CFS 1971

Sabda C 15 MIN
3/4 INCH VIDEO CASSETTE
Presents an experimental video poem inspired by the Indian poet Kabir and other mystical poets. The imagery and sound were taped in India. By Dan Reeves.
Prod-EAI Dist-EAI

Sabertooth C 9 MIN
16MM FILM OPTICAL SOUND
Describes the ancient sabertooth tigers' weaponry as evidenced by remains found in tar pits. Discusses the weaponry of today's cats and raises the question of man's aberrant use of weapons.
LC NO. 80-701377
Prod-HARTK Dist-HARTK 1980

Sabina Lietzmann C 29 MIN
3/4 INCH VIDEO CASSETTE
Interviews a West German correspondent who covers the United States for Frankfurter Allgemeine Zeitung.
From The Foreign Assignment - U S A Series.
Prod-UMITV Dist-UMITV 1978

Sabina Sanchez - Artesana Bordadora C 22 MIN
16MM FILM OPTICAL SOUND
A Spanish language version of the motion picture Sabina Sanchez - The Art Of Embroidery. Shows the life and work of Sabina Sanchez, a Zapotec woman who still makes the embroidered blouses of her traditional village costume.
From The Artesano Mexicanos Series.
Prod-WORKS Dist-WORKS 1976

Sabina Sanchez - The Art Of Embroidery C 22 MIN
16MM FILM OPTICAL SOUND
Shows the life and work of Sabina Sanchez, a Zapotec woman who still makes the embroidered blouses of her traditional village costume.
From The Mexico's Folk Artists Series.
Prod-WORKS Dist-WORKS 1976

Sable Island C 20 MIN
16MM FILM OPTICAL SOUND
Tells the story of the animals and people of Sable Island, an area off Nova Scotia composed of nothing but sand and grass.
LC NO. 74-702419
Prod-DALHSU Dist-FI 1973

Sabotage B 77 MIN
1/2 IN VIDEO CASSETTE BETA/VHS
Tells how the manager of a small British cinema is suspected of disrupting the supply of electricity to the city and setting off a time bomb. Directed by Alfred Hitchcock.
Prod-UNKNWN Dist-VIDIM 1936

Sabu And The Magic Ring C 62 MIN
16MM FILM OPTICAL SOUND I-J
Tells of Sabu, the Caliph's elephant boy, who finds a ring which he need only rub to summon a huge genie ready to answer his every wish.
Prod-CINEWO Dist-CINEWO 1957

SAC Command Post C 20 MIN
16MM FILM OPTICAL SOUND
Presents physical characteristics of the Strategic Air Command's air defense and communications network. Points out the command post's control over SAC operations during peacetime and in event of enemy air attack.
LC NO. 74-706229
Prod-USAF Dist-USNAC 1966

SAC Numbered Air Forces - This Is The 8th Air Force C 13 MIN
16MM FILM, 3/4 OR 1/2 IN VIDEO
Explains the mission of the 8th Air Force, a major arm of the Strategic Air Command. Reviews its missile and aircraft inventory and shows the readiness of its personnel and equipment.
LC NO. 81-707723
Prod-USAF Dist-USNAC 1967

Sacajawea C 24 MIN
3/4 OR 1/2 INCH VIDEO CASSETTE
Tells the true story of the young Indian girl who guided the Lewis and Clark Expedition.
From The Young People's Specials Series.
Prod-MULTPP Dist-MULTPP

Sachiyo Ito, Ritha Devi And Sun Ock Lee C 30 MIN
3/4 OR 1/2 INCH VIDEO CASSETTE
Looks at ethnic dance. Discusses how those of other cultures see ethnic dances.
From The Eye On Dance - Third World Dance, Beyond The White Stream Series.
Prod-ARTRES Dist-ARTRES

Sacra Biblia C 60 MIN
3/4 OR 1/2 INCH VIDEO CASSETTE
Looks at the care, long-range planning and thought processes used by scribes of the Middle Ages to create the manuscript for a 13th century Bible. Features Frank Fielder, Ohio University professor of English, as he looks at what has happened to the Bible in the centuries since it was first made.
Prod-OHUTC Dist-OHUTC

Sacrament—A Series
P-C
Prod-FRACOC Dist-FRACOC

Baptism - Sacrament Of Belonging 8 MIN
Confirmation - Sacrament Of Witness 11 MIN
Eucharist - Sacrament Of Life 10 MIN
Penance - Sacrament Of Peace 11 MIN

Sacraments, The C 11 MIN
16MM FILM OPTICAL SOUND
Celebrates the joys of the sacraments and of life.
Prod-LUTHER Dist-LUTHER

Sacred Ground C 52 MIN
16MM FILM OPTICAL SOUND
Presents a documentary look at the geographical locations within North America that are considered sacred to the American Indian.
LC NO. 77-700408
Prod-FFL Dist-FFL 1977

Sacred Trances In Bali And Java C 30 MIN
16MM FILM, 3/4 OR 1/2 IN VIDEO
Shows sacred rituals of Bali and Java in which invisible spirits are brought down to enter the bodies of trancers, who perform supernormal feats such as walking on fire, piercing cheeks with pins and palling on broken glass.
Prod-HP Dist-HP

Sacrificial Burnings C 40 MIN
3/4 INCH VIDEO CASSETTE
Explores how patriarchal authority vested in the institutions of Church, State and Marriage has suppressed dissident female voices.
Prod-WMENIF Dist-WMENIF

Sacroiliac, Buttock And Hip, The C 30 MIN
3/4 OR 1/2 INCH VIDEO CASSETTE
Examines the sacroiliac, buttock and hip, covering the sign of the buttock, gluteal bursitis, psoas bursitis, osteoarthrosis, rheumatoid arthritis, loose body, hamstrings and rectus femoris.
From The Cyriax On Orthopaedic Medicine Series.
Prod-VTRI Dist-VTRI

Sad Balloon, The C 15 MIN
3/4 INCH VIDEO CASSETTE P
Features Benny, Fran and Joy who explore the feeling of sadness and shows how it can be turned to happiness by illustrating how people can help change the way they feel.
From The Think Fine - Feel Fine Series.
Prod-KTCATV Dist-GPITVL

Sad Clowns B 27 MIN
16MM FILM OPTICAL SOUND
Pictures styles and techniques that made Charlie Chaplin, Buster Keaton and Harry Langdon great comedians.
From The History Of The Motion Picture Series.
Prod-SF Dist-KILLIS 1960

Sad Song Of Touha B 12 MIN
16MM FILM OPTICAL SOUND
Comments on the poverty and desperation of street performers, jugglers, contortionists and fire eaters. Filmed in one of the poorest sections of Cairo.
Prod-ICARUS Dist-ICARUS 1971

Sad Song Of Yellow Skin C 58 MIN
16MM FILM, 3/4 OR 1/2 IN VIDEO
Presents a different view of Saigon, as seen by three young Americans working for peace in a city where bombs seldom fall, but all of life is shaped by decades of war. Includes nostalgic Vietnamese street ballads and close-up views of the people of Saigon, emphasizing the children.
Prod-NFBC Dist-FI 1970

Sadat - The Presidency And The Legacy C 26 MIN
3/4 OR 1/2 INCH VIDEO CASSETTE J-H
Documents Anwar Sadat's presidency and those events which assure him a prominent place in 20th century history. Charts the problems his successor, Hosni Mubarak, must address if order is to be maintained in his country and the Sadat legacy realized.
Prod-JOU Dist-JOU

Sadat's Eternal Egypt C 45 MIN
16MM FILM, 3/4 OR 1/2 IN VIDEO H-C
Examines the treasures that remain from the reign of the Pharoahs. Presents Egyptian president Anwar Sadat reflecting on the society and people who produced these works of art. Narrated by Walter Cronkite.
LC NO. 80-707721
Prod-CBSNEW Dist-CAROUF 1980

Saddle Bronc Clinic C 30 MIN
1/2 IN VIDEO CASSETTE BETA/VHS
Presents a saddle bronc clinic. Ranges from chute to whistle.
From The Western Training Series.
Prod-EQVDL Dist-EQVDL

Saddle Up C 15 MIN
16MM FILM OPTICAL SOUND P-H
Reveals the past and present importance of the horse. Illustrates the different kinds of horses and the purposes to which each is best suited. Shows how and why a well-handled horse responds to command.
Prod-MALIBU Dist-MALIBU

Saddleback C 25 MIN
16MM FILM, 3/4 OR 1/2 IN VIDEO J-C A
Discusses the rescue mission which saved the Saddleback bird from extinction in New Zealand.
Prod-SPRKTF Dist-JOU 1980

Saddling The Finest C
1/2 IN VIDEO CASSETTE BETA/VHS
Demonstrates what to look for in a dressage saddle and how to fit it. Shows how to saddle up.
Prod-ELCMR Dist-EQVDL

Sadrina Project, The C
16MM FILM, 3/4 OR 1/2 IN VIDEO
Presents an intermediate level series aimed at those who need to use English when they travel.
Prod-NORTNJ Dist-NORTNJ

SAF Story, The - Together We Serve C 18 MIN
3/4 OR 1/2 INCH VIDEO CASSETTE
Shows how military service members throughout the world seek out the Red Cross' services to the armed forces and veterans in the face of personal emergencies.
Prod-AMRC Dist-AMRC 1977

Safari Drums B 71 MIN
16MM FILM OPTICAL SOUND I-C A
See series title for descriptive statement.
From The Bomba, The Jungle Boy Series.
Prod-CINEWO Dist-CINEWO 1953

Safari Rally C 12 MIN
3/4 OR 1/2 INCH VIDEO CASSETTE
Views an auto rally set in the heart of Africa. Shows how the rough roads and trails test the skill of the most accomplished drivers.
Prod-UPI Dist-JOU

Safari To Tsavo C 28 MIN
16MM FILM OPTICAL SOUND
Presents a documentary on Tsavo, the largest game reserve in Kenya.
LC NO. 76-702467
Prod-RUDDEL Dist-RUDDEL 1975

Safe Altitude Warning C 8 MIN
3/4 OR 1/2 INCH VIDEO CASSETTE A
Explains the safe altitude warning system. Covers Arch 3 and the air traffic controller, MSAW features and functions, including various types of terrain monitoring and system responses to differing circumstances.
Prod-FAAFL Dist-AVIMA

Safe And Conservative Treatment Of Lesions Of The Female Breast C 32 MIN
16MM FILM OPTICAL SOUND
Demonstrates the safe substitution of aspiration for biopsy in fibrocystic mastitis. Includes the ease and simplicity of this maneuver, cosmetic incisions for biopsy of clinically benign solid masses and avoidance of recurrence in scar of radical mastectomy.
Prod-ACYDGD Dist-ACY 1957

Safe And Effective Pest Management C 19 MIN
3/4 INCH VIDEO CASSETTE J-H
Shows how safe and effective pest management can be provided while still protecting and enhancing the environment. Focuses on controlling the damage plants and animals can cause to dams, aqueducts and levees.
Prod-CSDWR Dist-CALDWR

Safe Area Operating Limits For Power Transistors C 28 MIN
3/4 INCH VIDEO CASSETTE
Suggests improvements in methods for measuring and specifying transistor power limits for forward bias operation.
Prod-USNBOS Dist-MTP

Safe As You Know How B 10 MIN
16MM FILM OPTICAL SOUND
Shows unsafe acts and conditions and how they cause accidents. Urges action towards safety.
Prod-DUNN Dist-NSC 1960

Safe As You Make It B
16MM FILM OPTICAL SOUND
Contrasts the safety of the high rides at amusement parks with the hazards of the safe-appearing things we encounter every day.
Prod-NSC Dist-NSC

Safe At Home C 10 MIN
3/4 OR 1/2 INCH VIDEO CASSETTE
Shows Bill Kunkel, American League Umpire, who is back in the game after an operation for colorectal cancer. Tells story in his own words and those of his peers, including Reggie Jackson, George Steinbrenner, Carlton Fisk, and Bucky Dent and his wife and children.
Prod-AMCS Dist-AMCS 1982

Safe Bicycling C 13 MIN
16MM FILM, 3/4 OR 1/2 IN VIDEO P-J
Illustrates the basic instructions in bicycle safety. Stresses the need for parents to see that children have a properly equipped bicycle in good mechanical working condition.
Prod-CRAF Dist-IFB 1959

Safe Bicycling (Hebrew) C 13 MIN
16MM FILM, 3/4 OR 1/2 IN VIDEO P-J
Illustrates the basic rules of bicycle safety. Stresses the need for parents to see that children have a properly equipped bicycle in good mechanical working condition.
Prod-CRAF Dist-IFB 1959

Safe Bicycling In Traffic C 19 MIN
16MM FILM, 3/4 OR 1/2 IN VIDEO J-C A
Shows experienced bicyclists how to become a predictable part of the normal traffic flow. Gives examples of anticipating motorists' errors, performing basic traffic manuevers, approaching intersections, riding safely with cars, and riding in a group.
LC NO. 81-707487
Prod-IOWA Dist-CORF 1981

Safe Child—A Series

Presents fire prevention and safety training for children.
Prod-FPF Dist-FPF

Burns 007 MIN
Fire 008 MIN
Smoke 008 MIN

Safe Diving C 22 MIN
3/4 OR 1/2 INCH VIDEO CASSETTE
Stresses numerous safety measures for diving in offshore oil operations.
From The Offshore Safety Series.
Prod-FLMWST Dist-FLMWST

Safe Handling And Storage Of Combustibles On Drilling Rigs C 25 MIN
3/4 OR 1/2 INCH VIDEO CASSETTE IND
Defines flammables and combustibles. Details the procedures needed for proper use and care of such materials on the drilling rig.
Prod-UTEXPE Dist-UTEXPE 1977

Safe Handling Of Compressed Gas Cylinders C 32 MIN
3/4 OR 1/2 INCH VIDEO CASSETTE IND
Covers safe storage, inspection, transportation and use of metal cylinders that contain various gases under pressure.
Prod-UTEXPE Dist-UTEXPE 1978

Safe Handling Of Diving Injuries C 20 MIN
3/4 OR 1/2 INCH VIDEO CASSETTE
Depicts the critical aspects of a spinal cord injury. Shows how it should be handled after the diving accident.
Prod-PRIMED Dist-PRIMED

Safe Handling Of Enriched Uranium, The C 22 MIN
16MM FILM OPTICAL SOUND H-C A
Introduces the concept of nuclear fission and criticality, and explains the reasons for safety procedures that are observed in the handling of enriched uranium and other fissionalbe materials.
LC NO. 71-703797
Prod-USAEC Dist-USERD Prodn-UCC 1969

Safe Handling Of Foals And Yearlings C 51 MIN
1/2 IN VIDEO CASSETTE BETA/VHS
Shows methods of working with new foals to accustom them to haltering, handling, loading, trailering and training.
Prod-CSPC Dist-EQVDL

Safe Handling Of Foods In Quantity C 17 MIN
16MM FILM, 3/4 OR 1/2 IN VIDEO IND
A dietician discussing with her food-service personnel the precautions to take in order to prevent contaminations of cooked foods by staphylococci and salmonells. Shows positive methods used to avoid intestinal illnesses.
Prod-NYSCHE Dist-CUNIV Prodn-CUNIV 1964

Safe Handling Of Laboratory Animals C 14 MIN
16MM FILM - 3/4 IN VIDEO
Demonstrates techniques of handling laboratory animals. Emphasizes methods of avoiding injury and infection to the caretaker, as well as to the animals.
LC NO. 77-706130
Prod-USPHS Dist-USNAC 1977

Safe Handling Of Medical Gases C
3/4 OR 1/2 INCH VIDEO CASSETTE
Prod-NFPA Dist-NFPA

Safe Handling Of Medical Gases C 19 MIN
3/4 OR 1/2 INCH VIDEO CASSETTE
Explains fire hazards associated with storage and handling of oxygen, nitrous oxide and other gases that are commonly used in health care facilities. Discusses safety features of gas dispensing equipment, as well as proper maintenance and testing procedures. Also provides information on correct procedures for the safety of patients in the event of fire in areas where medical gases are used.
LC NO. 82-707080
Prod-NFPA Dist-NFPA 1982

Safe Handling Of Oxy Fuel Gas Heating Equipment, The C 14 MIN
3/4 OR 1/2 INCH VIDEO CASSETTE IND
Includes details on protective clothing, procedures for the safe handling of propane and oxygen cylinders, regulators, hoses and torches. Covers proper start-up and shutdown techniques as well as the procedure to follow in the event of a blow back.
From The Steel Making Series.
Prod-LEIKID Dist-LEIKID

Safe Harbor C 25 MIN
16MM FILM, 3/4 OR 1/2 IN VIDEO H A
Discusses the effect of fear of nuclear war on teenage depression, leading to drug and alcohol abuse and even suicide. Presents the story of three unemployed school dropouts.
Prod-PAULST Dist-MEDIAG 1985

Safe In Nature C 20 MIN
16MM FILM, 3/4 OR 1/2 IN VIDEO I-H
Dramatizes two examples of young people getting lost. Shows how to survive in the woods and in the desert by making shelters and giving distress signals. Touches on nature lore and first aid basics.
Prod-FLMFR Dist-FLMFR

Safe In Recreation C 15 MIN
16MM FILM, 3/4 OR 1/2 IN VIDEO P-J
Dramatizes typical accidents that can happen to children during common recreation activities around the home, on the playground and outdoors.
Prod-FLMFR Dist-FLMFR

Safe In The Water C 15 MIN
16MM FILM, 3/4 OR 1/2 IN VIDEO P-J
Shows the most frequent causes of water accidents involving children in both moving and still bodies of water.
Prod-FLMFR Dist-FLMFR

Safe Living At School (2nd Ed) C 11 MIN
16MM FILM, 3/4 OR 1/2 IN VIDEO I
Teaches safety rules and different safety devices in schools. Emphasizes a child's responsibility for accident prevention.
Prod-CORF Dist-CORF 1969

Safe Methods For Canning (Captioned) C 25 MIN
3/4 OR 1/2 INCH VIDEO CASSETTE S
Discusses methods of home food canning, equipment, and precautions.
From The Consumer Education For The Deaf Adult Series.
Prod-GALCO Dist-GALCO Prodn-MCES 1975

Safe Operation Of Farm Tractors C 14 MIN
16MM FILM, 3/4 OR 1/2 IN VIDEO J-C A
Outlines a daily service routine which helps to insure a safe tractor. Shows the use of protective equipment, road and field hazards, hydraulics and necessary skills to become a certified operator.
Prod-CUNIV Dist-CUNIV 1973

Safe Operation Of The Backhoe And Bulldozer C 14 MIN
16MM FILM, 3/4 OR 1/2 IN VIDEO H-C A
Emphasizes service checks and operative procedures for the backhoe and bulldozer.
Prod-CUETV Dist-CUNIV 1977

Safe Operation Of The Forklift Truck C 17 MIN
16MM FILM - 3/4 IN VIDEO
Provides guidelines on how to operate forklifts safely. Includes pretrip examination, operating forklifts in warehouses, trucks and box cars, on loading docks, ramps and outside ground, as well as proper lifting procedures. Discusses OSHA, visual, written and weekly checks.
Prod-ALLIED Dist-BNA

Safe Place For Children, A C 10 MIN
3/4 OR 1/2 INCH VIDEO CASSETTE C A
Presents a psychologist who looks at the activities on orthopedic day in a clinic waiting room and helps the children there explore their fantasies about the plaster casts they've placed on dolls. Shows the children learning how the noisy cast-cutting machine operates as a doctor saws the casts off their dolls.
From The Emotional Factors Affecting Children And Parents In The Hospital Series.
LC NO. 81-707458
Prod-LRF Dist-LRF 1979

Safe Practices In Marine And Offshore Drilling And Workover C 27 MIN
3/4 OR 1/2 INCH VIDEO CASSETTE IND
Covers safe and proper techniques personnel should use when going offshore. Explains personal protection devices and practices that should be used on offshore rigs.
Prod-UTEXPE Dist-UTEXPE 1978

Safe Practices In Marine And Offshore Drilling And Workover (Spanish) C 27 MIN
3/4 OR 1/2 INCH VIDEO CASSETTE IND
A Spanish language version of Safe Practices In Marine And Offshore Drilling And Workover.
Prod-UTEXPE Dist-UTEXPE

Safe Practices In Well Drilling And Workover C 30 MIN
3/4 OR 1/2 INCH VIDEO CASSETTE IND
Introduces new personnel to many of the techniques and components of land rotary drilling and workover rigs. Explains safe procedures to be used.
Prod-UTEXPE Dist-UTEXPE 1977

Safe Practices In Well Drilling And Workover (Spanish) C 30 MIN
3/4 OR 1/2 INCH VIDEO CASSETTE IND
Introduces new personnel to many of the techniques and components of land rotary drilling and workover rigs. Explains safe procedures to be used.
Prod-UTEXPE Dist-UTEXPE 1977

Safe Ride On Your School Bus, A C 14 MIN
16MM FILM OPTICAL SOUND K-I
Reviews safety and courtesy standards for school bus uses. Suggests practices for safe walking to bus stop, waiting for the bus, boarding, riding and leaving the bus. Shows driver training and bus maintenance.
LC NO. 79-714782
Prod-MMP Dist-MMP 1970

Safe Skateboarding C 15 MIN
16MM FILM OPTICAL SOUND
Outlines safety procedures and regulations regarding skateboard use. Includes information on maintenance of the board, riding techniques and protective clothing.
LC NO. 77-702137
Prod-AMEDFL Dist-AMEDFL 1977

Safe Summer Fun C 15 MIN
3/4 OR 1/2 INCH VIDEO CASSETTE K-P
Identifies the summer season, safety rules and things to do in summer.
From The Pass It On Series.
Prod-WKNOTV Dist-GPITVL 1983

Safe Transport Of Radioactive Materials C 20 MIN
16MM FILM OPTICAL SOUND
Describes radioactivity and shows the comparatively simple transport of unused fuel elements compared to the special means needed for transporting fuel elements under special supervision after they have been used in a reactor. Illustrates the transport of radioisotopes, starting with their preparation and shows some of the many ways in which they are used.
Prod-UKAEA Dist-UKAEA 1964

Safe Use Of Catheads And Air Hoists C 20 MIN
3/4 OR 1/2 INCH VIDEO CASSETTE IND
Explains the proper procedures for making a safe lift using a cathead or an air hoist on the drilling or workover rig.
Prod-UTEXPE Dist-UTEXPE 1979

Safe Use Of Catheads And Air Hoists (Spanish) C 20 MIN
3/4 OR 1/2 INCH VIDEO CASSETTE IND
Explains the proper procedures for making a safe lift using a cathead or an air hoist on the drilling or workover rig.
Prod-UTEXPE Dist-UTEXPE 1979

Safe Use Of Drill Pipe Tongs C
3/4 OR 1/2 INCH VIDEO CASSETTE IND
Looks at various roughneck duties associated with drill pipe tongs and emphasizing safety. Covers installation of tongs, safe procedures for work when using wire rope, cleaning and maintenance and inserting tong dies.
From The Working Offshore Series.
Prod-GPCV Dist-GPCV

Safe Use Of Drill Pipe Tongs C 17 MIN
3/4 OR 1/2 INCH VIDEO CASSETTE IND
Covers the correct and safe installation, maintenance and use of drill pipe tongs.
Prod-UTEXPE Dist-UTEXPE 1978

Safe Use Of Drill Pipe Tongs (Spanish) C 17 MIN
3/4 OR 1/2 INCH VIDEO CASSETTE IND
Covers the correct and safe installation, maintenance and use of drill pipe tongs.
Prod-UTEXPE Dist-UTEXPE 1978

Safe Use Of Hand Tools C 18 MIN
3/4 OR 1/2 INCH VIDEO CASSETTE IND
Focuses on several aspects of safety in the use of hand tools. Includes need for prior inspection before using any tools, proper use, power tool safety and techniques to avoid electrical shock. Discusses what to do if a fellow worker receives an electric shock.
From The Industrial Safety Series.
Prod-LEIKID Dist-LEIKID

Safe Use Of Low Energy X-Rays For The Treatment Of Skin Cancer C 29 MIN
3/4 OR 1/2 INCH VIDEO CASSETTE PRO
Presents advantages and disadvantages of low energy X-rays for the treatment of skin cancer. Gives indications and methods for treatment, and safety procedures. Creates an understanding of the applicability of physics for therapy.
Prod-USNAC Dist-USNAC

Safe Use Of Non-Prescription Drugs C 4 MIN
3/4 OR 1/2 INCH VIDEO CASSETTE
Describes how non-prescription drugs can be useful in relieving ailments.
Prod-TRAINX Dist-TRAINX

Safe Use Of Pesticides, The C 21 MIN
16MM FILM OPTICAL SOUND
Explains the proper use of pesticides, emphasizing the importance of following instructions on the labels to avoid seizure of crops because of harmful residue.
LC NO. FIE64-105
Prod-USDA Dist-USNAC 1964

Safe Winter Driving B 10 MIN
16MM FILM OPTICAL SOUND
Discusses the hazards of winter driving and shows steps to follow in order to drive safely.
LC NO. FIA67-2018
Prod-GTARC Dist-GTARC Prodn-IVC 1962

Safeguard C 22 MIN
16MM FILM, 3/4 OR 1/2 IN VIDEO
Views the variety of attitudes that workers and management have toward safety matters. Shows the necessity for machine guards and their benefits. Points out that innocent bystanders may be hurt by non-compliance with safety regulations.
Prod-MILLBK Dist-IFB

Safeguarding C 11 MIN
3/4 OR 1/2 INCH VIDEO CASSETTE A
Discusses the storage, control, access, reproduction, disposal and transmission of National Security Information. Discusses leaks and precautions to minimize compromise.
From The Information Security Briefing Series.
Prod-USISOO Dist-USNAC 1983

Safeguarding Military Information B 16 MIN
16MM FILM OPTICAL SOUND
Stresses the importance of safeguarding military information for both military and civilian personnel.
LC NO. FIE62-2091
Prod-USA Dist-USNAC 1952

Safeguarding Our Highways C 15 MIN
16MM FILM OPTICAL SOUND H-C A
Describes how steel median guard rail increases highway safety and the role local groups can play in improving area road safety.
Prod-AIAS Dist-AIAS

Safeguarding Your Patient C 15 MIN
3/4 OR 1/2 INCH VIDEO CASSETTE
Reviews basic safety concepts for health care personnel so injuries and accidents to patients can be prevented. Emphasizes the prevention of burns, decubiti, treatment errors and property loss or damage.
Prod-FAIRGH Dist-FAIRGH

Safely Walk To School (2nd Ed) C 12 MIN
16MM FILM, 3/4 OR 1/2 IN VIDEO P
Presents guidelines for walking to school safely. Stresses the importance of remembering to look both ways before going into the street and crossing streets and driveways.
LC NO. 83-706214
Prod-AIMS Dist-AIMS 1983

Safer Game, A - A Better Game C 12 MIN
16MM FILM, 3/4 OR 1/2 IN VIDEO I-H
Explains the importance of many different elements of football safety practice and procedure, proper conditioning, good coaching, competent officiating, improved equipment and facilities, and adequate medical precautions and supervision.
From The Football Injury Prevention Series.
Prod-ATHI Dist-ATHI

Safer Place To Eat, A C 15 MIN
16MM FILM, 3/4 OR 1/2 IN VIDEO A
Points out the dangers of food contamination from several types of bacteria and shows how to prevent contamination by keeping food stored in a cold environment.
Prod-USFDA Dist-USNAC 1976

Safer Way Down - Sky Genie C 23 MIN
16MM FILM OPTICAL SOUND H-C A
Describes the characteristics of the sky genie, a safety device for the controlled safe descent of personnel. Illustrates some of its uses in rescue operations.
LC NO. 76-701749
Prod-USFC Dist-FILCOM Prodn-FILCOM 1976

Safer You, A—A Series
P-I
Demonstrates proper safety practices for the school bus, playground and home. Includes matters such as self-concept, physical fitness, traveling, moving, consumer decision-making and playing at home.
Prod-WCVETV Dist-GPITVL 1984

Bicycle Safety	015 MIN
Consumer Decisions	015 MIN
Fire Safety	015 MIN
Fitness For Everybody	015 MIN
Home Play	015 MIN
Home Safety	015 MIN
How Can I Help	015 MIN
Moving	015 MIN
Pedestrian Safety	015 MIN
Playground Safety	015 MIN
Real You, The	015 MIN
School Bus Safety	015 MIN
Traveling	015 MIN

Safest Place, The C 14 MIN
3/4 INCH VIDEO CASSETTE
Shows how to choose the safest place around the farm for atomic survival and how to lessen the danger from radioactive fallout. Issued in 1963 as a motion picture.
LC NO. 79-706677
Prod-USDA Dist-USNAC 1979

Safest Way, The C 15 MIN
3/4 OR 1/2 INCH VIDEO CASSETTE P
Shows how David walks to the theater and encounters some hazards at an intersection and a railroad crossing.
From The It's Your Move Series.
Prod-WETN Dist-AITECH 1977

Safest Way, The (2nd Ed) X 15 MIN
16MM FILM OPTICAL SOUND
Shows a teacher explaining to children the value of selecting the safest route between home and school. Shows the cooperation of parents and the activities of the children as they follow the advice of the teacher and plan their own routes.
LC NO. FIA66-646
Prod-AAAFTS Dist-AAAFTS Prodn-CALVIN 1962

Safety C 6 MIN
3/4 OR 1/2 INCH VIDEO CASSETTE IND
Emphasizes the fact that safety on the job is a matter of professional attitude, communications, paying attention and good housekeeping.
From The Steel Making Series.
Prod-LEIKID Dist-LEIKID

Safety B 9 MIN
16MM FILM, 3/4 OR 1/2 IN VIDEO
Depicts the dangers of the electronic environment, showing the causes of electrical shock, how to avoid shock and what to do for a shock victim. Describes how to fight an electrical fire.
Prod-USAF Dist-USNAC 1983

Safety C 19 MIN
3/4 OR 1/2 INCH VIDEO CASSETTE
Illustrates safety rules and procedures common to all laboratory situations.
From The General Chemistry Laboratory Techniques Series.
Prod-UCEMC Dist-UCEMC

Safety C 20 MIN
3/4 OR 1/2 INCH VIDEO CASSETTE H-C A
See series title for descriptive statement.
From The Engineering Crafts Series.
Prod-BBCTV Dist-FI 1981

Safety C 30 MIN
3/4 OR 1/2 INCH VIDEO CASSETTE C A
See series title for descriptive statement.
From The Pests, Pesticides And Safety Series.
Prod-UMA Dist-GPITVL 1976

Safety C 30 MIN
2 INCH VIDEOTAPE IND
Illustrates the five-point plant safety program.
From The Basic Machine Shop Practices Series.
Prod-VTETV Dist-GPITVL

Safety - Harm Hides At Home C 16 MIN
16MM FILM, 3/4 OR 1/2 IN VIDEO P-I
Uses a story about children who are rescued from accidents at home to create an awareness of home safety and provides examples for accident prevention.
From The Safety Series.
Prod-FILMCO Dist-BARR 1977

Safety - Home, Safe Home C 14 MIN
16MM FILM, 3/4 OR 1/2 IN VIDEO P-I
Utilizes 'INQUIRY' mode of stop-projector technique for teaching basic concepts of home safety. Presents typical household hazards and situations for student discussion.
Prod-CAHILL Dist-AIMS 1972

Safety - In Danger Out Of Doors C 15 MIN
16MM FILM, 3/4 OR 1/2 IN VIDEO P-I
Shows how Safety Woman comes to the rescue of children in hazardous situations. Presents basic rules of water safety and other basic safety rules.
From The Safety Series.
Prod-FILMCO Dist-BARR 1977

Safety - Isn't It Worth It C 15 MIN
16MM FILM, 3/4 OR 1/2 IN VIDEO A
Stresses the importance of safety in biological labs. Demonstrates the consequences of negligence. Narrated by Jack Klugman.
Prod-FISHSC Dist-FILCOM 1981

Safety - Mrs Andrews / Attending To Tasks - Miss George C 35 MIN
3/4 INCH VIDEO CASSETTE PRO
Assists nurses in developing awareness of the specific subtleties related to assessment and clinical management of right and left stroke patients. Discusses the issues of safety and attending to the daily task of eating.
Prod-RICHGO Dist-RICHGO

Safety - Peril Rides The Roads C 15 MIN
16MM FILM, 3/4 OR 1/2 IN VIDEO P-I
Presents Safety Woman who rescues children from perilous situations. Provides examples of street, bicycle and traffic safety rules.
From The Safety Series.
Prod-FILMCO Dist-BARR 1977

Safety - Playground Spirits C 9 MIN
16MM FILM, 3/4 OR 1/2 IN VIDEO P-I
Presents good and bad playground spirits to show social problems and safety hazards that exist in recreational areas. Stresses the importance of safety, consideration of others and the right to privacy.
From The Joy Of Growing Series.
Prod-EBEC Dist-EBEC 1971

Safety - Proper Use C 20 MIN
2 INCH VIDEOTAPE I
See series title for descriptive statement.
From The Exploring With Science, Unit VIII - Electricity Series.
Prod-MPATI Dist-GPITVL

Safety - Second To None C 15 MIN
16MM FILM OPTICAL SOUND
A number of experts in atomic safety point out the elaborate safety precautions and procedures required by the AEC for the nuclear power industry.
LC NO. 74-703764
Prod-USAEC Dist-USNAC Prodn-STARIP 1974

Safety - The Helpful Burglars C 11 MIN
16MM FILM, 3/4 OR 1/2 IN VIDEO P
Points out the important lesson that household hazards are a threat to everyone.
From The Joy Of Growing Series.
Prod-EBEC Dist-EBEC 1971

Safety - The Traffic Jungle C 7 MIN
16MM FILM, 3/4 OR 1/2 IN VIDEO P
Teaches children how to avoid injury in the urban 'TRAFFIC JUNGLE' by learning and observing traffic safety rules.
Prod-EBEC Dist-EBEC 1971

Safety - Total Loss Control C 9 MIN
16MM FILM OPTICAL SOUND IND
Uses animation to point out hazardous situations in the plant. Emphasizes fire prevention, theft, pollution (noise), and industrial health and hygiene.
Prod-CRAF Dist-CRAF 1971

Safety - Total Loss Control C 10 MIN
16MM FILM, 3/4 OR 1/2 IN VIDEO IND
Points out that industry must direct its accident prevention efforts toward all incidents which might eventually lead to injury of employees. Notes that fire prevention, theft prevention, reduction in pollution and improvement of industrial health and hygiene are of particular importance to loss control.
Prod-IAPA Dist-IFB Prodn-CRAF 1972

Safety Action For Employees—A Series
IND
Shows how these videotape training programs fit right in with weekly safety melting can be viewed by individual worker when time permits. Covers specific job responsibilities and demonstrates how to prepare them safely.
Prod-GPCV Dist-GPCV

Cleaning With Hot Water And Steam 015 MIN
Fire Protection Awareness 017 MIN
Guide To Industrial Housekeeping 000 MIN
Handling Compressed Gas Cylinders 024 MIN
Handling Flammables and Combustibles 029 MIN
Machine Shop Safety 017 MIN
Manual Lifting 019 MIN
Personal Protective Equipment 000 MIN
Preventing Electrical Injuries, Part 1 012 MIN
Working Safely With Scaffolds 019 MIN

Safety Afloat C 21 MIN
16MM FILM OPTICAL SOUND P-C T
Demonstrates some of the potential dangers on the water, rescue techniques and the pleasures that can be derived from water sports if safety rules are obeyed.
LC NO. FIA66-647
Prod-TGAFC Dist-TGAFC 1965

Safety Aloft C 20 MIN
16MM FILM, 3/4 OR 1/2 IN VIDEO A
Highlights the proper use of safety equipment in tower erection. Describes two key components of safety - the Fall Arrester and Life Line.
Prod-OHMPS Dist-BCNFL 1984

Safety And Basic Fundamentals On The Engine Lathe, Pt 1 C 11 MIN
16MM FILM, 3/4 OR 1/2 IN VIDEO J A
Demonstrates the basic safety points and basic processes in engine lathe operation.
From The Metal Shop - Safety And Operations Series.
Prod-EPRI Dist-AIMS Prodn-EPRI 1970

Safety And Basic Fundamentals On The Engine Lathe, Pt 2 C 13 MIN
16MM FILM, 3/4 OR 1/2 IN VIDEO J A
Demonstrates the basic safety points and processes in engine lathe operation.
From The Metal Shop - Safety And Operations Series.
Prod-EPRI Dist-AIMS Prodn-EPRI 1970

Safety And Basic Fundamentals On The Engine Lathe, Pt 1 (Arabic) C 11 MIN
16MM FILM, 3/4 OR 1/2 IN VIDEO J A
Demonstrates the basic safety points and basic processes in engine lathe operation.
From The Metal Shop - Safety And Operations Series.
Prod-EPRI Dist-AIMS Prodn-EPRI 1970

Safety And Basic Fundamentals On The Engine Lathe, Pt 2 (Arabic) C 13 MIN
16MM FILM, 3/4 OR 1/2 IN VIDEO J A
Demonstrates the basic safety points and processes in engine lathe operation.
From The Metal Shop - Safety And Operations Series.
Prod-EPRI Dist-AIMS Prodn-EPRI 1970

Safety And Basic Fundamentals On The Engine Lathe, Pt 1 (Spanish) C 11 MIN
16MM FILM, 3/4 OR 1/2 IN VIDEO J A
Demonstrates the basic safety points and basic processes in engine lathe operation.
From The Metal Shop - Safety And Operations Series.
Prod-EPRI Dist-AIMS Prodn-EPRI 1970

Safety And Basic Fundamentals On The Engine Lathe, Pt 2 (Spanish) C 13 MIN
16MM FILM, 3/4 OR 1/2 IN VIDEO J A
Demonstrates the basic safety points and processes in engine lathe operation.
From The Metal Shop - Safety And Operations Series.
Prod-EPRI Dist-AIMS Prodn-EPRI 1970

Safety And Equipment For Gas Shielded Arc-Welding C 15 MIN
3/4 OR 1/2 INCH VIDEO CASSETTE IND
See series title for descriptive statement.
From The Welding - MIG And TIG Welding Series.
Prod-ICSINT Dist-ICSINT

Safety And Equipment For Gas Shielded Arc Welding (Spanish) C
3/4 OR 1/2 INCH VIDEO CASSETTE
See series title for descriptive statement.
From The MIG And TIG Welding (Spanish) Series.
Prod-VTRI Dist-VTRI

Safety And Equipment For Gas Shielded Arc Welding (MIG) C 15 MIN
3/4 OR 1/2 INCH VIDEO CASSETTE
See series title for descriptive statement.
From The Welding III - TIG And MIG (Industry) Welding series.
Prod-CAMB Dist-CAMB

Safety And Familiarization On Radial Arm Drill Press C 26 MIN
1/2 IN VIDEO CASSETTE BETA/VHS IND
See series title for descriptive statement.
From The Machine Shop - Drill Press, Radial Drill, Drill Grinder Series.
Prod-RMI Dist-RMI

Safety And Familiarization On The Horizontal Bandsaw C 18 MIN
1/2 IN VIDEO CASSETTE BETA/VHS IND
See series title for descriptive statement.
From The Machine Shop - Bandsaw Series.
Prod-RMI Dist-RMI

Safety And Familiarization On The Horizontal Boring Mill C 24 MIN
1/2 IN VIDEO CASSETTE BETA/VHS IND
See series title for descriptive statement.
From The Machine Shop - Milling Machine Series.
Prod-RMI Dist-RMI

Safety And Familiarization On The Bridgeport Series I Milling Machine C 23 MIN
1/2 IN VIDEO CASSETTE BETA/VHS IND
See series title for descriptive statement.
From The Machine Shop - Milling Machine Series.
Prod-RMI Dist-RMI

Safety And Familiarization On The Bridgeport Series II Milling Machine C 21 MIN
1/2 IN VIDEO CASSETTE BETA/VHS IND
See series title for descriptive statement.
From The Machine Shop - Milling Machine Series.
Prod-RMI Dist-RMI

Safety And Familiarization On The Clausing Colchester Engine Lathe C 25 MIN
1/2 IN VIDEO CASSETTE BETA/VHS IND
See series title for descriptive statement.
From The Machine Shop - Engine Lathe Series.
Prod-RMI Dist-RMI

Safety And Familiarization On The Kearney And Trecher Milling Machine, Pt 1 C 22 MIN
1/2 IN VIDEO CASSETTE BETA/VHS IND
See series title for descriptive statement.
From The Machine Shop - Milling Machine Series.
Prod-RMI Dist-RMI

Safety And Familiarization On The Kearney And Trecher Milling Machine, Pt 2 C 17 MIN
1/2 IN VIDEO CASSETTE BETA/VHS IND
See series title for descriptive statement.
From The Machine Shop - Milling Machine Series.
Prod-RMI Dist-RMI

Safety And Familiarization On the LeBlond Engine Lathe C 22 MIN
1/2 IN VIDEO CASSETTE BETA/VHS IND
See series title for descriptive statement.
From The Machine Shop - Engine Lathe Series.
Prod-RMI Dist-RMI

Safety And Familiarization On The South Bend Engine Lathe C 30 MIN
1/2 IN VIDEO CASSETTE BETA/VHS IND
See series title for descriptive statement.
From The Machine Shop - Engine Lathe Series.
Prod-RMI Dist-RMI

Safety And Familiarization On The Surface Grinder C 33 MIN
1/2 IN VIDEO CASSETTE BETA/VHS IND
See series title for descriptive statement.
From The Machine Shop - Surface Grinder Series.
Prod-RMI Dist-RMI

Safety And Familiarization On The Vertical Bandsaw C 25 MIN
1/2 IN VIDEO CASSETTE BETA/VHS IND
See series title for descriptive statement.
From The Machine Shop - Bandsaw Series.
Prod-RMI Dist-RMI

Safety And Instrumentation Grounding Problems C 60 MIN
3/4 OR 1/2 INCH VIDEO CASSETTE IND
See series title for descriptive statement.
From The Instrumentation Basics - Instrumentation Electrical And Mechanical Connections Series. Tape 2
Prod-ISA Dist-ISA

Safety And Operation Of Faceplate Turning, Pt 1 (Arabic) C 8 MIN
16MM FILM, 3/4 OR 1/2 IN VIDEO J A
Covers the basic techniques and safety points to follow in the operation of faceplate turning.
From The Wood Shop - Safety And Operations Series.
Prod-EPRI Dist-AIMS 1971

Safety And Operation Of Faceplate Turning, Pt 2 (Arabic) C 12 MIN
16MM FILM, 3/4 OR 1/2 IN VIDEO J A
Covers the basic techniques and safety points to follow in the operation of faceplate turning.
From The Wood Shop - Safety And Operations Series.
Prod-EPRI Dist-AIMS 1971

Safety And Operation Of Faceplate Turning, Pt 1 (Spanish) C 8 MIN
16MM FILM, 3/4 OR 1/2 IN VIDEO J A
Covers the basic techniques and safety points to follow in the operation of faceplate turning.
From The Wood Shop - Safety And Operations Series.
Prod-EPRI Dist-AIMS 1971

Safety And Operation Of Faceplate Turning, Pt 2 (Spanish) C 12 MIN
16MM FILM, 3/4 OR 1/2 IN VIDEO J A
Covers the basic techniques and safety points to follow in the operation of faceplate turning.
From The Wood Shop - Safety And Operations Series.
Prod-EPRI Dist-AIMS 1971

Safety And Operation Of Faceplate Turning, Pt 1 C 8 MIN
16MM FILM, 3/4 OR 1/2 IN VIDEO J A
Covers the basic techniques and safety points to follow in the operation of faceplate turning.
From The Wood Shop - Safety And Operations Series.
Prod-EPRI Dist-AIMS 1971

Safety And Operation Of Faceplate Turning, Pt 2 C 12 MIN
16MM FILM, 3/4 OR 1/2 IN VIDEO J A
Covers the basic techniques and safety points to follow in the operation of faceplate turning.
From The Wood Shop - Safety And Operations Series.
Prod-EPRI Dist-AIMS 1971

Safety And The Foreman—A Series

Prod-NSC Dist-NSC

Fact Finding, Not Fault Finding 10 MIN
Foresight - Not Hindsight 10 MIN
No One Else Can Do It 10 MIN
What They Don't Know Can Hurt 10 MIN

Safety And The Supervisor C 22 MIN
16MM FILM - 3/4 IN VIDEO
Points out that pressure to meet delivery dates or production quotas often causes supervisors to bend or ignore safety rules. Shows what happens when a supervisor succumbs to these pressures and discusses management's responsibility for safety. Provides examples of potential safety hazards in plants, offices, canteens, loading areas and stores.
Prod-MTLTD Dist-BNA

Safety And The Supervisor - Positive Attitudes Pay Off C 20 MIN
3/4 OR 1/2 INCH VIDEO CASSETTE
Reveals the steps supervisors must take to reduce lost-time injuries and prevent insurance premiums from climbing out of sight.
Prod-BBP Dist-BBP

Safety And You—A Series
3/4 OR 1/2 INCH VIDEO CASSETTE
Discusses risk control issues in the work environment.
Prod-FILCOM Dist-FILCOM

Communications 009 MIN
Motivation 009 MIN
Physical Limitations 010 MIN
Physiological Limitations 011 MIN
Psychological Limitations 011 MIN
Supervision 008 MIN
Tools 006 MIN

Safety And Your Car C 20 MIN
16MM FILM, 3/4 OR 1/2 IN VIDEO H-C A
Presents race driver Mark Donohue and other noted personalities discussing the differences among street automobiles and demonstrating how these differences affect safe driving. Shows how improper alterations to tires and chassis can have serious results.
Prod-SCCA Dist-AIMS 1976

Safety As We Play C 7 MIN
16MM FILM, 3/4 OR 1/2 IN VIDEO K-P
No descriptive information available.
From The Starting To Read Series.
Prod-ACI Dist-AIMS 1971

Safety At School C 9 MIN
16MM FILM, 3/4 OR 1/2 IN VIDEO K-I
Depicts children following practices of safety and courtesy for hall and stairway travel, for lunchtime eating habits, for play in the yard and for drinking fountain use. Illustrates what can occur when students 'forget' their manners.
Prod-TFBCH Dist-AIMS 1974

Safety At School (Spanish) C 9 MIN
16MM FILM, 3/4 OR 1/2 IN VIDEO K-I
Depicts children following practices of safety and courtesy for hall and stairway travel, for lunchtime eating habits, for play in the yard and for drinking fountain use. Illustrates what can occur when students 'forget' their manners.
Prod-TFBCH Dist-AIMS 1974

Safety At Work C 19 MIN
16MM FILM OPTICAL SOUND C A
Shows the precautions that should be taken in industry to prevent industrial accidents that cost Americans four billion dollars a year.
Prod-AETNA Dist-AETNA

Safety Belt For Susie C 11 MIN
16MM FILM, 3/4 OR 1/2 IN VIDEO H-C A
Demonstrates that children, one year and older, should wear safety belts.
Prod-AIMS Dist-AIMS 1964

Safety Belt For Susie (Spanish) C 11 MIN
16MM FILM, 3/4 OR 1/2 IN VIDEO P-I A
Uses anthropometric dummies and dolls to show what could happen to children not wearing safety belts in collisons. Emphasizes that children, one-year-old and older, should wear safety belts.
From The Automobile Safety Series.
Prod-CAHILL Dist-AIMS 1963

Safety Belts C 24 MIN
16MM FILM, 3/4 OR 1/2 IN VIDEO IND
Presents falls using safety belts and lanyards to convince workers of the importance of wearing safety belts for high construction site work. Shows how to choose and wear a belt correctly and demonstrates the triple rolling hitch knot.
Prod-CSAO Dist-IFB

Safety Belts - A Smashing Success C 14 MIN
16MM FILM, 3/4 OR 1/2 IN VIDEO J-C A
Presents data from tests and statistics and shows automobile collision experiments at UCLA in order to solidify the arguments for the use of safety belts and harnesses.
Prod-CAHILL Dist-AIMS 1975

Safety Belts - A Smashing Success (Spanish) C 14 MIN
16MM FILM, 3/4 OR 1/2 IN VIDEO J-C A
Presents data from tests and statistics and shows automobile collision experiments at UCLA in order to solidify the arguments for the use of safety belts and harnesses.
Prod-CAHILL Dist-AIMS 1975

Safety Belts - Short Version C 9 MIN
16MM FILM, 3/4 OR 1/2 IN VIDEO IND
Demonstrates the correct use of nylon webbing safety belts and lanyard. A shortened version of the film Safety Belts.
Prod-CSAO Dist-IFB

Safety Belts And You C 9 MIN
16MM FILM, 3/4 OR 1/2 IN VIDEO
Shows what happens to belted and unbelted drivers and passengers in fast-moving automobile crashes.
Prod-FORDFL Dist-FORDFL

Safety By The Numbers C 32 MIN
16MM FILM OPTICAL SOUND P-J
A safety-education film for pilots and aviation groups. A lumberman searching for a lost barge is introduced to safety by the numbers in a twin engine aircraft.
LC NO. 71-702860
Prod-FAAFL Dist-USFAA Prodn-FAIRKS 1969

Safety Check Your Car C 15 MIN
16MM FILM OPTICAL SOUND
Discusses the importance of a simple safety check and how to conduct such a check in less than 15 minutes per month.
Prod-BUMPA Dist-BUMPA

Safety Check Your Car C 16 MIN
16MM FILM, 3/4 OR 1/2 IN VIDEO H-C A
Explains how to safety check a car. Points out potential problem areas and shows how to recognize signs of potential trouble for brakes, mufflers, shock absorbers, tires and other automobile systems.
LC NO. 77-701108
Prod-STNLYL Dist-PFP 1976

Safety Consciousness C 10 MIN
16MM FILM, 3/4 OR 1/2 IN VIDEO
Demonstrates how to develop safe attitudes in daily activities by clarity in thinking, acting and outlook on life.
From The Foremanship Training Series.
LC NO. 82-706279
Prod-USBM Dist-USNAC 1969

Safety Considerations C 37 MIN
3/4 OR 1/2 INCH VIDEO CASSETTE IND
Presents differences between robots and conventional equipment. Focuses on several safety methods and devices currently used in industry.
From The Industrial Robotics Series.
Prod-GMIEMI Dist-AMCEE

Safety Demonstration On The Band Saw C 14 MIN
16MM FILM, 3/4 OR 1/2 IN VIDEO J-H A
Demonstrates close-up photography of basic safety procedures and operational points on the table saw.
From The Wood Shop - Safety And Operations Series.
Prod-EPRI Dist-AIMS 1970

Safety Demonstration On The Band Saw (Arabic) C 14 MIN
16MM FILM, 3/4 OR 1/2 IN VIDEO J-H A
Demonstrates close-up photography of basic safety procedures and operational points on the table saw.
From The Wood Shop - Safety And Operations Series.
Prod-EPRI Dist-AIMS 1970

Safety Demonstration On The Band Saw (Spanish) C 14 MIN
16MM FILM, 3/4 OR 1/2 IN VIDEO J-H A
Demonstrates close-up photography of basic safety procedures and operational points on the table saw.
From The Wood Shop - Safety And Operations Series.
Prod-EPRI Dist-AIMS 1970

Safety Demonstration On The Jointer C 12 MIN
16MM FILM, 3/4 OR 1/2 IN VIDEO J A
Demonstrates the basic safety points and basic processes of operating the jointer.
From The Wood Shop - Safety And Operations Series.
Prod-EPRI Dist-AIMS Prodn-EPRI 1970

Safety Demonstration On The Jointer (Arabic) C 12 MIN
16MM FILM, 3/4 OR 1/2 IN VIDEO J A
Demonstrates the basic safety points and processes of operating the jointer.
From The Wood Shop - Safety And Operations Series.
Prod-EPRI Dist-AIMS Prodn-EPRI 1970

Safety Demonstration On The Jointer (Spanish) C 12 MIN
16MM FILM, 3/4 OR 1/2 IN VIDEO J A
Demonstrates the basic safety points and processes of operating the jointer.
From The Wood Shop - Safety And Operations Series.
Prod-EPRI Dist-AIMS Prodn-EPRI 1970

Safety Demonstration On The Radial Saw C 12 MIN
16MM FILM, 3/4 OR 1/2 IN VIDEO IND
Shows close-up photography of basic safety procedures and operational points in using the radial saw.
From The Wood Shop - Safety And Operations Series.
Prod-EPRI Dist-AIMS 1971

Safety Demonstration On The Radial Saw (Spanish) C 12 MIN
16MM FILM, 3/4 OR 1/2 IN VIDEO IND
Shows close-up photography of basic safety procedures and operational points in using the radial saw.
From The Wood Shop - Safety And Operations Series.
Prod-EPRI Dist-AIMS 1971

Safety Demonstration On The Radial Saw (Arabic) C 12 MIN
16MM FILM, 3/4 OR 1/2 IN VIDEO IND
Shows close-up photography of basic safety procedures and operational points in using the radial saw.
From The Wood Shop - Safety And Operations Series.
Prod-EPRI Dist-AIMS 1971

Safety Demonstration On The Single Surface Planer C 15 MIN
16MM FILM, 3/4 OR 1/2 IN VIDEO J-C
Demonstrates the basic safety points and the basic operations on the single-surface planer.
From The Wood Shop - Safety And Operations Series.
Prod-EPRI Dist-AIMS Prodn-EPRI 1970

Safety Demonstration On The Single Surface Planer (Arabic) C 15 MIN
16MM FILM, 3/4 OR 1/2 IN VIDEO J-C
Demonstrates the basic safety points and the basic operations on the single-surface planer.
From The Wood Shop - Safety And Operations Series.
Prod-EPRI Dist-AIMS Prodn-EPRI 1970

Safety Demonstration On The Single Surface Planer (Spanish) C 15 MIN
16MM FILM, 3/4 OR 1/2 IN VIDEO J-C
Demonstrates the basic safety points and the basic operations on the single-surface planer.
From The Wood Shop - Safety And Operations Series.
Prod-EPRI Dist-AIMS Prodn-EPRI 1970

Safety Demonstration On The Table Saw, Pt 1 C 11 MIN
16MM FILM, 3/4 OR 1/2 IN VIDEO J-C A
Demonstrates close-up photography of basic safety procedures and operational points on the table saw.
From The Wood Shop - Safety And Operations Series.
Prod-EPRI Dist-AIMS 1970

Safety Demonstration On The Table Saw, Pt 1 (Arabic) C 11 MIN
16MM FILM, 3/4 OR 1/2 IN VIDEO J-C A
Demonstrates close-up photography of basic safety procedures and operational points on the table saw.
From The Wood Shop - Safety And Operations Series.
Prod-EPRI Dist-AIMS 1970

Safety Demonstration On The Table Saw, Pt 1 (Spanish) C 11 MIN
16MM FILM, 3/4 OR 1/2 IN VIDEO J-C A
Demonstrates close-up photography of basic safety procedures and operational points on the table saw.
From The Wood Shop - Safety And Operations Series.
Prod-EPRI Dist-AIMS 1970

Safety Demonstration On The Table Saw, Pt 2 C 9 MIN
16MM FILM, 3/4 OR 1/2 IN VIDEO J-C A
Demonstrates close-up photography of basic safety procedures and operational points on the table saw.
From The Wood Shop - Safety And Operations Series.
Prod-EPRI Dist-AIMS 1970

Safety Demonstration On The Table Saw, Pt 2 (Arabic) C 9 MIN
16MM FILM, 3/4 OR 1/2 IN VIDEO J-C A
Demonstrates close-up photography of basic safety procedures and operational points on the table saw.
From The Wood Shop - Safety And Operations Series.
Prod-EPRI Dist-AIMS 1970

Safety Demonstration On The Table Saw, Pt 2 (Spanish) C 9 MIN
16MM FILM, 3/4 OR 1/2 IN VIDEO J-C A
Demonstrates close-up photography of basic safety procedures and operational points on the table saw.
From The Wood Shop - Safety And Operations Series.
Prod-EPRI Dist-AIMS 1970

Safety Demonstration On The Wood Lathe C 11 MIN
16MM FILM, 3/4 OR 1/2 IN VIDEO J-C A
Shows close-up photography of basic safety points and operational procedures in using the wood lathe.
From The Wood Shop - Safety And Operations Series.
Prod-EPRI Dist-AIMS 1971

Safety Demonstration On The Wood Lathe (Spanish) C 11 MIN
16MM FILM, 3/4 OR 1/2 IN VIDEO J-C A
Shows close-up photography of basic safety points and operational procedures in using the wood lathe.
From The Wood Shop - Safety And Operations Series.
Prod-EPRI Dist-AIMS 1971

Safety Demonstration On The Wood Shaper, Pt 1 C 11 MIN
16MM FILM, 3/4 OR 1/2 IN VIDEO J-C A
Describes the uses of the wood shaper, showing a variety of spindles and cutter shapes and sizes. Tells how to install and align the fence and discusses how to select correct cutter rotation and how to reverse direction.
From The Wood Shop - Safety And Operations Series.
Prod-AIMS Dist-AIMS 1970

Safety Demonstration On The Wood Shaper, Pt 1 (Arabic) C 11 MIN
16MM FILM, 3/4 OR 1/2 IN VIDEO J-C A
Describes the uses of the wood shaper, showing a variety of spindles and cutter shapes and sizes. Tells how to install and align the fence and discusses how to select correct cutter rotation and how to reverse direction.
From The Wood Shop - Safety And Operations Series.
Prod-AIMS Dist-AIMS 1970

Safety Demonstration On The Wood Shaper, Pt 1 (Spanish) C 11 MIN
16MM FILM, 3/4 OR 1/2 IN VIDEO J-C A
Describes the uses of the wood shaper, showing a variety of spindles and cutter shapes and sizes. Tells how to install and align the fence and discusses how to select correct cutter rotation and how to reverse direction.
From The Wood Shop - Safety And Operations Series.
Prod-AIMS Dist-AIMS 1970

Safety Demonstration On The Wood Shaper, Pt 2 C 10 MIN
16MM FILM, 3/4 OR 1/2 IN VIDEO J-C A
Discusses the use of the wood shaper, explaining that steady feed is best and that stopping and backing up are dangerous. Shows how to feed for straight facing, how to use rub collar for irregular shaping, and how to feed stock using a starting pin and rub collar. Illustrates use of spring ring guard, pressure bar, tall fence, and bevel fence. Explains how to minimize end-grain chipping and how to shape short ends. Describes the procedure for internal shaping.
From The Wood Shop - Safety And Operations Series.
Prod-AIMS Dist-AIMS 1970

Safety Demonstration On The Wood Shaper, Pt 2 (Arabic) C 10 MIN
16MM FILM, 3/4 OR 1/2 IN VIDEO J-C A
Discusses the use of the wood shaper, explaining that steady feed is best and that stopping and backing up are dangerous. Shows how to feed for straight facing, how to use rub collar for irregular shaping, and how to feed stock using a starting pin and rub collar. Illustrates use of spring ring guard, pressure bar, tall fence, and bevel fence. Explains how to minimize end-grain chipping and how to shape short ends. Describes the procedure for internal shaping.
From The Wood Shop - Safety And Operations Series.
Prod-AIMS Dist-AIMS 1970

Safety Demonstration On The Wood Shaper, Pt 2 (Spanish) C 10 MIN
16MM FILM, 3/4 OR 1/2 IN VIDEO J-C A
Discusses the use of the wood shaper, explaining that steady feed is best and that stopping and backing up are dangerous. Shows how to feed for straight facing, how to use rub collar for irregular shaping, and how to feed stock using a starting pin and rub collar. Illustrates use of spring ring guard, pressure bar, tall fence, and bevel fence. Explains how to minimize end-grain chipping and how to shape short ends. Describes the procedure for internal shaping.
From The Wood Shop - Safety And Operations Series.
Prod-AIMS Dist-AIMS 1970

Safety Depends On You C 9 MIN
16MM FILM, 3/4 OR 1/2 IN VIDEO H-C A
Demonstrates the safe and proper use of tools in firefighting and other work.
Prod-PUBSF Dist-FILCOM

Safety Doesn't Happen B
16MM FILM OPTICAL SOUND
Shows how accidents result in production lags, slowing up shipments and disrupting employee efficiency.
Prod-NSC Dist-NSC

Safety Elements In Laboratory Practice C 20 MIN
3/4 OR 1/2 INCH VIDEO CASSETTE
Illustrates eye protection, protective clothing, toxicity, flammability and other safety elements in laboratory practice.
Prod-FPF Dist-FPF

Safety Factor, The C 58 MIN
3/4 INCH VIDEO CASSETTE
Explores the subject of air travel safety. Joins the pilot and crew on the flight of a Laker Airways DC-10 as it crosses the Atlantic from London to Los Angeles. Points out that the advances in technology must coincide with an understanding of human factors if safety is to be further improved.
From The Nova Series.
LC NO. 80-707185
Prod-BBCTV Dist-PBS 1980

Safety First C
3/4 OR 1/2 INCH VIDEO CASSETTE
Makes use of humor in a review of safety rules for a business organization.
Prod-BBB Dist-MEETS Prodn-CFDC

Safety First C 29 MIN
2 INCH VIDEOTAPE
See series title for descriptive statement.
From The Discover Flying - Just Like A Bird Series.
Prod-WKYCTV Dist-PUBTEL

Safety For Elementary—A Series
16MM FILM, 3/4 OR 1/2 IN VIDEO H-C A
Prod-MORLAT Dist-AIMS 1976

Safety In The Home	009 MIN
Safety In The Street	010 MIN
Safety In Transit	008 MIN
School Safety	009 MIN

Safety For Oilfield Contractors—A Series

Presents a series on safety for oilfield contractors.
Prod-FLMWST Dist-FLMWST

Breakout	015 MIN
Professional Attitudes	015 MIN
Trenching - A Grave Affair	015 MIN
Wide World Of Records	017 MIN

Safety For Special Needs Children C 14 MIN
3/4 INCH VIDEOTAPE
Shows special considerations for children who are disabled with visual, lower extremity and developmental impairments.
Prod-UNDMC Dist-UNDMC

Safety For The New Employee C 20 MIN
3/4 OR 1/2 INCH VIDEO CASSETTE IND
Shows major safety hazards a new employee will be exposed to in an industrial plant or maintenance shop. Includes housekeeping, ladders, welding flashes, grinders and improperly grounded electrical tools. Stresses the importance of safety glasses, hard hats and safety shoes.
From The Marshall Maintenance Training Programs Series. Tape 22
Prod-LEIKID Dist-LEIKID

Safety For The New Employee C 20 MIN
16MM FILM, 3/4 OR 1/2 IN VIDEO IND
Shows major safety hazards a new employee will be exposed to in an industrial plant or maintenance shop. Covers housekeeping, ladders, welding flashes and improperly grounded electrical tools. Stresses the importance of safety glasses, hard hats and safety shoes.
Prod-MOKIN Dist-MOKIN

Safety In Construction—A Series
16MM FILM, 3/4 OR 1/2 IN VIDEO
Discusses safety in various types of construction settings involving excavations, scaffolding, lifting equipment and mechanical aids.
Prod-NFBTE Dist-IFB

Cost Of Chaos	011 MIN
Excavations	009 MIN
Lifting Equipment	010 MIN
Mechanical Aids	010 MIN
Scaffolding	011 MIN

Safety In Electric-Arc Welding C 15 MIN
3/4 OR 1/2 INCH VIDEO CASSETTE
See series title for descriptive statement.
From The Welding II - Basic Shielded Metal Arc Welding series.
Prod-CAMB Dist-CAMB

Safety In Electric-Arc Welding And Terms C 15 MIN
3/4 OR 1/2 INCH VIDEO CASSETTE IND
See series title for descriptive statement.
From The Welding - Shieldd Metal-Arc Welding Series.
Prod-ICSINT Dist-ICSINT

Safety In Electric-Arc Welding And Terms (Spanish) C
3/4 OR 1/2 INCH VIDEO CASSETTE
See series title for descriptive statement.
From The Shielded Metal Arc Welding (Spanish) Series.
Prod-VTRI Dist-VTRI

Safety In Gas Tungsten Arc Welding C 15 MIN
3/4 OR 1/2 INCH VIDEO CASSETTE IND
See series title for descriptive statement.
From The Welding - MIG And TIG Welding Series.
Prod-ICSINT Dist-ICSINT

Safety In Gas Tungsten Arc Welding (Spanish) C
3/4 OR 1/2 INCH VIDEO CASSETTE
See series title for descriptive statement.
From The MIG And TIG Welding (Spanish) Series.
Prod-VTRI Dist-VTRI

Safety In Hospitals B 27 MIN
16MM FILM OPTICAL SOUND
Discusses major aspects of the safety program required in Army hospitals.
LC NO. 74-706232
Prod-USA Dist-USNAC 1967

Safety In Mountain Surveying C 27 MIN
16MM FILM, 3/4 OR 1/2 IN VIDEO
Introduces some of the basic techniques of safe mountain climbing to Federal Highway Administration personnel. Covers knot tying, rope testing, proper equipment and basic safe methods of moving on rock.
LC NO. 82-706110
Prod-USDTFH Dist-USNAC 1969

Safety In Plywood Operations C 10 MIN
16MM FILM OPTICAL SOUND J-C A
Points out specific things to watch for in plywood manufacturing for both new and experienced plywood employees. Illustrates principles of individual and managerial responsibility.
Prod-RARIG Dist-RARIG 1970

Safety In Rigging—A Series
IND
Trains new crane operators and reviews crane components and operating techniques for all operators. Includes instructor's booklet.
Prod-CSAO Dist-IFB

Chain	013 MIN
Cranes - Types And Components Case Histories	019 MIN
Hardware	020 MIN
Hazard Awareness In Crane Operating Areas	015 MIN
International Hand Signals	007 MIN
Reeving	015 MIN
Slings	021 MIN
Wire Rope	019 MIN

Safety In Strip Mining C 24 MIN
16MM FILM OPTICAL SOUND
Presents a general treatment of surface mining operations and the hazards connected with truck haulage, blasting, falling material, power cables, ect.
LC NO. 74-705568
Prod-USBM Dist-USNAC 1961

Safety In Surface Coal Mining C 22 MIN
16MM FILM, 3/4 OR 1/2 IN VIDEO
Presents a history and overall view of surface coal mining operations with a close look at some of most common hazards connected with specific jobs and working environments. Points out dangers in the use of bulldozers, power shovels, dump trucks and other mining equipment. Demonstrates appropriate safety practices and operating procedures to eliminate or reduce possible accidents.
LC NO. 82-706909
Prod-USDL Dist-USNAC 1982

Safety In The Balance C 23 MIN
16MM FILM, 3/4 OR 1/2 IN VIDEO IND
Crane safety is highlighted by showing various hazards encountered on the job. Warns crane operators about the many factors that must be taken into account to insure safe operation of the equipment and successful completion of the job.
Prod-CSAO Dist-IFB

Safety In The Health Care Environment C 15 MIN
3/4 OR 1/2 INCH VIDEO CASSETTE
Covers the health care facility's moral, legal and economic responsibility to maintain safety standards.
From The Health Care Security Training Series.
Prod-GREESM Dist-MTI

Safety In The Home C 9 MIN
16MM FILM, 3/4 OR 1/2 IN VIDEO K-I
Identifies home safety hazards and shows how to correct them.
From The Safety For Elementary Series.
Prod-MORLAT Dist-AIMS 1974

Safety In The Home (Spanish) C 9 MIN
16MM FILM, 3/4 OR 1/2 IN VIDEO K-I
Identifies home safety hzards and shows how to correct them.
From The Safety For Elementary Series.
Prod-MORLAT Dist-AIMS 1974

Safety In The Home (3rd Ed) X 12 MIN
16MM FILM, 3/4 OR 1/2 IN VIDEO I
Demonstrates the need of making common sense decisions for safety in the home. Depicts causes of accidents.
Prod-EBF Dist-EBEC 1965

Safety In The Home (3rd Ed) (Captioned) C 12 MIN
16MM FILM, 3/4 OR 1/2 IN VIDEO I
Demonstrates the need for making common sense decisions for safety in the home. Depicts causes of accidents.
Prod-EBEC Dist-EBEC 1965

Safety In The Kitchen C 14 MIN
16MM FILM, 3/4 OR 1/2 IN VIDEO
Covers 18 major hazard areas in the kitchen. Discusses knives and utensils, matches, gas and electric ranges, electric appliances, hot objects, deep fat frying, fire and escaping gas, glassware, food storage and kitchen cleanliness.
Prod-GRDNHN Dist-FILCOM 1969

Safety In The Laboratory—A Series
IND
Prod-KALMIA Dist-KALMIA 1972

Chemical Hazards	4 MIN
Fire In The Laboratory	4 MIN
Personal Safety	3 MIN

Safety In The Plowshare Program C 22 MIN
16MM FILM OPTICAL SOUND
Documents the safety precautions which are taken during experiments or projects in the U S program to develop peaceful uses

of nuclear explosives. Shows how radioactivity and other effects of nuclear explosions are controlled in order to insure the public safety.
LC NO. FIE66-13
Prod-USAEC Dist-USNAC 1966

Safety In The Science Lab C 30 MIN
3/4 OR 1/2 INCH VIDEO CASSETTE
Clarifies safety procedures for fire emergencies and other lab activities. Emphasizes dangerous lab practices. Includes ten follow-up questions.
Prod-EDMEC Dist-EDMEC

Safety In The Shop B 12 MIN
3/4 INCH VIDEO CASSETTE
Dramatizes three typical shop accidents. Shows how poor supervision or inadequate training may have been the real cause behind the accidents.
Prod-USNAC Dist-USNAC 1972

Safety In The Shop C 12 MIN
16MM FILM - 3/4 IN VIDEO
Dramatizes the relationship between poor supervision or inadequate training and shop accidents. Issued in 1944 as a motion picture.
From The Problems In Supervision Series.
LC NO. 78-706061
Prod-USOE Dist-USNAC Prodn-CENTRY 1978

Safety In The Shop (Spanish) C 12 MIN
16MM FILM - 3/4 IN VIDEO
Dramatizes three typical shop accidents and shows how poor supervision or inadequat training may have been the real cause behind these accidents. Issued in 1944 as a motion picture.
From The Problems In Supervision (Spanish) Series.
LC NO. 79-706678
Prod-USOE Dist-USNAC Prodn-CENTRY 1979

Safety In The Shop - Basic Practices C 13 MIN
16MM FILM, 3/4 OR 1/2 IN VIDEO H-C A
Emphasizes the worker's responsibility for safety in using hand and power tools in both wood and metal shops. Shows the importance of proper clothing, the safe way to lift and carry, the value of tidiness in a shop and ways to guard against possible fires.
From The Safety In The Shop Series.
Prod-CORF Dist-CORF 1970

Safety In The Shop - Hand Tools C 13 MIN
16MM FILM, 3/4 OR 1/2 IN VIDEO H-C A
Shows the value of keeping hand tools in good condition. Emphasizes the importance of protective clothing and demonstrates safe use of the forge and welding equipment.
From The Safety In The Shop Series.
Prod-CORF Dist-CORF 1970

Safety In The Shop - Power Tools C 13 MIN
16MM FILM, 3/4 OR 1/2 IN VIDEO H-C A
Stresses common sense practices with power saws, lathes and other woodworking and metalworking machine tools, proper clothing, adjusting machine before starting, and dealing with broken blades.
From The Safety In The Shop Series.
Prod-CORF Dist-CORF 1970

Safety In The Shop—A Series
16MM FILM, 3/4 OR 1/2 IN VIDEO H-C A
Prod-CORF Dist-CORF 1970

Safety In The Shop - Basic Practices 013 MIN
Safety In The Shop - Hand Tools 012 MIN
Safety In The Shop - Power Tools 013 MIN

Safety In The Street C 10 MIN
16MM FILM, 3/4 OR 1/2 IN VIDEO K-I
Explains how accidents can happen to pedestrians and stresses how alertness and patience are essential for safety in the street.
From The Safety For Elementary Series.
Prod-MORLAT Dist-AIMS 1974

Safety In The Street (Spanish) C 10 MIN
16MM FILM, 3/4 OR 1/2 IN VIDEO K-I
Stages scenes with dangerous traffic situations, then restages safe ones.
Prod-MORLAT Dist-AIMS 1974

Safety In Transit C 8 MIN
16MM FILM, 3/4 OR 1/2 IN VIDEO K-I
Discusses safety measures to practice when traveling.
From The Safety For Elementary Series.
Prod-MORLAT Dist-AIMS 1974

Safety In Transit (Spanish) C 8 MIN
16MM FILM, 3/4 OR 1/2 IN VIDEO K-I
Depicts accidents which occur in business, commuter stations and subways.
Prod-MORLAT Dist-AIMS 1974

Safety In Your Home C 14 MIN
16MM FILM, 3/4 OR 1/2 IN VIDEO I-J
Features a house that talks back as it instructs a family on ways to prevent accidents involving falls, fires, misplaced tools, electric shock and poisons.
Prod-GREENF Dist-PHENIX 1979

Safety Instruction—A Series

Presents a series for use in industry to help prevent serious injury by demonstrating approved safety measures.
Prod-VTRI Dist-VTRI

Application And Use Of Breathing Apparatus
CPR
Fire Protection Training
First Aid To Industry 012 MIN
Hydrogen Sulphide Alert

Safety Is A Full Time Job - Rules For Tools C
3/4 OR 1/2 INCH VIDEO CASSETTE
Tackles the problem of safety awareness and accident prevention on the job and in educational programs using tools. Includes humorous dialogue and step-by-step demonstrations.
Prod-EDUACT Dist-EDUACT

Safety Is In Order C 10 MIN
16MM FILM OPTICAL SOUND
See series title for descriptive statement.
From The Safety Management Series.
Prod-NSC Dist-NSC

Safety Management Course—A Series

Shows how to search for safety around every corner and make the safety, investigation count.
Prod-EDRF Dist-EDRF

Chemicals Under Control 017 MIN
Path Of Least Resistance, The 015 MIN
Shape Up! 017 MIN

Safety Management—A Series

Provides training for foremen and supervisors in eight basic areas of accident prevention.
Prod-NSC Dist-NSC

Bare Minimum 10 MIN
Guard Duty 10 MIN
Let Them Know 10 MIN
Mind Over Matter 10 MIN
Plan For Prevention 10 MIN
Run The Team 10 MIN
Safety Is In Order 10 MIN
Sell Safety 10 MIN

Safety Of Being Understood, The C
16MM FILM - 3/4 IN VIDEO A
Demonstrates how to give clear orders and make certain they are understood so there is no room for assumptions or misunderstandings which so often lead to accidents.
Prod-BNA Dist-BNA 1983

Safety On Our School Bus (2nd Ed) C 13 MIN
16MM FILM, 3/4 OR 1/2 IN VIDEO P-I
Illustrates proper conduct for riding in a school bus.
Prod-EBEC Dist-EBEC 1980

Safety On Street And Sidewalk C 11 MIN
16MM FILM, 3/4 OR 1/2 IN VIDEO P-I
Provides background on pedestrian safety techniques.
Prod-CENTRO Dist-CORF

Safety On Street And Sidewalk (Spanish) C 11 MIN
16MM FILM, 3/4 OR 1/2 IN VIDEO P-I
Provides background on pedestrian safety techniques.
Prod-CENTRO Dist-CORF

Safety On The Farm C 8 MIN
16MM FILM OPTICAL SOUND
Cites possible dangers around the farm and discusses common causes of accidents.
Prod-TASCOR Dist-TASCOR 1976

Safety On The Job - Accident Causes And Prevention C 17 MIN
16MM FILM, 3/4 OR 1/2 IN VIDEO H A
Looks at the behaviors that cause accidents. Examines stress, negligence, recklessness, over-exertion and fatigue as causes of accidents on the job. Offers techniques for preventing potentially dangerous situations.
Prod-AIMS Dist-AIMS 1984

Safety On The Job - The Hazards Of Substance Abuse C 18 MIN
16MM FILM, 3/4 OR 1/2 IN VIDEO H-C A
Discusses and demonstrates the safety hazards caused by misuse of drugs in the workplace.
Prod-AIMS Dist-AIMS 1983

Safety On The Move - Truck Haulage Safety C 16 MIN
16MM FILM, 3/4 OR 1/2 IN VIDEO A
Portrays frequent accidents which truck operators encounter. Emphasizes corrective and preventive action.
Prod-MSHA Dist-USNAC 1976

Safety On The Move - Truck Haulage Safety C 16 MIN
16MM FILM, 3/4 OR 1/2 IN VIDEO IND
Focuses on an open-pit mining operation. Shows huge haulage trucks, pointing out existing and potential hazards involved in their operation. Reenacts common accidents, explains their causes and outlines the steps necessary to prevent their reoccurrence.
Prod-USDL Dist-USNAC 1982

Safety On The Playground (2nd Ed) X 13 MIN
16MM FILM, 3/4 OR 1/2 IN VIDEO I
Points up safe practices in catching and batting softballs, and playing on see-saws, slides and swings. Emphasizes that consideration for others on the playground results in a good time for all.
Prod-EBF Dist-EBEC 1966

Safety On The Street (2nd Ed) X 11 MIN
16MM FILM, 3/4 OR 1/2 IN VIDEO I
Places the responsibility for safety on children. Explains why they must be alert and why safety is their own decision.
Prod-EBF Dist-EBEC 1965

Safety On The Way To School C 7 MIN
16MM FILM, 3/4 OR 1/2 IN VIDEO P-I
Emphasizes the importance of following safety rules while crossing streets and obeying traffic signals on the way to school. Reinforces the idea that it takes time for vehicles to stop.
Prod-LUF Dist-LUF 1983

Safety On-The-Job At Sea B 17 MIN
16MM FILM OPTICAL SOUND
Describes the organization for shipboard safety, how shipboard accidents can occur, accident prevention measures and the importance of crew safety consciousness.
LC NO. FIE58-11
Prod-USN Dist-USNAC

Safety Or Slaughter C 14 MIN
16MM FILM, 3/4 OR 1/2 IN VIDEO P-H A
Presents the reasons why industry should be concerned with traffic accidents. Illustrates safe driving techniques and stresses courtesy.
Prod-CRAF Dist-IFB 1958

Safety Pipetting C 5 MIN
16MM FILM OPTICAL SOUND
Presents three commonly used instruments that are employed in the laboratory for safety pipetting. Demonstrates the operation of these instruments in detail.
LC NO. 74-705569
Prod-USPHS Dist-USNAC 1965

Safety Plays And End Plays C 30 MIN
3/4 OR 1/2 INCH VIDEO CASSETTE A
See series title for descriptive statement.
From The Play Bridge Series.
Prod-KYTV Dist-KYTV 1983

Safety Practices In Dredging Operations C 16 MIN
16MM FILM, 3/4 OR 1/2 IN VIDEO IND
Shows that underwater mining for sand and gravel presents safety problems. Shows the tasks performed on a modern dredge and the hazards involved, and stresses the need for employees to be alert to the dangers and to work safely.
Prod-USDL Dist-USNAC 1982

Safety Practices In Low-Coal Mining C 15 MIN
16MM FILM OPTICAL SOUND
Shows the special hazards workmen must guard against in thin-seam mines. Illustrates how restricted work space, curtailed field of vision and cramped body position can intensify the dangers involved in working with fast-moving, high-powered machines.
LC NO. 74-705570
Prod-USBM Dist-USNAC 1971

Safety Practices, Pt 1 - Tag Out, Personnel Protective Gear, Voltage Limitations C 60 MIN
3/4 OR 1/2 INCH VIDEO CASSETTE IND
See series title for descriptive statement.
From The Electrical Maintenance Basics Series.
Prod-ITCORP Dist-ITCORP

Safety Practices, Pt 1 - Tag Out, Personnel-Protective Gear, Voltage Limitations (Spanish) C 60 MIN
3/4 OR 1/2 INCH VIDEO CASSETTE IND
See series title for descriptive statement.
From The Electrical Maintenance Basics (Spanish) Series.
Prod-ITCORP Dist-ITCORP

Safety Precautions And Work Habits C 30 MIN
3/4 OR 1/2 INCH VIDEO CASSETTE
Teaches the student to recognize safety hazards and describes precautions to take to minimize the possibility of injury. Describes basic safety equipment available to the weekend mechanic.
From The Keep It Running Series.
Prod-NETCHE Dist-NETCHE 1982

Safety Precautions For Electronics Personnel C 18 MIN
16MM FILM, 3/4 OR 1/2 IN VIDEO
Shows electrical and mechanical hazards which technicians encounter in their normal work and stresses precautions which should be used to prevent accidents.
LC NO. 82-706093
Prod-USN Dist-USNAC Prodn-ROUSHP 1952

Safety Procedures And Guidelines For Machine Technology C
3/4 OR 1/2 INCH VIDEO CASSETTE
See series title for descriptive statement.
From The Basic Machine Technology Series.
Prod-VTRI Dist-VTRI

Safety Procedures And Guidelines For Machine Technology C 15 MIN
3/4 OR 1/2 INCH VIDEO CASSETTE
See series title for descriptive statement.
From The Machine Technology II - Engine Lathe Accessories Series.
Prod-CAMB Dist-CAMB

Safety Procedures And Guidelines For Machine Technology C 15 MIN
3/4 OR 1/2 INCH VIDEO CASSETTE IND
See series title for descriptive statement.
From The Machining And The Operation Of Machine Tools, Module 1 - Basic Machine Technology Series.
Prod-LEIKID Dist-LEIKID

Safety Procedures And Guidelines For Machine Technology (Spanish) C
3/4 OR 1/2 INCH VIDEO CASSETTE
See series title for descriptive statement.
From The Basic Machine Technology (Spanish) Series.
Prod-VTRI Dist-VTRI

Safety Record B 10 MIN
16MM FILM OPTICAL SOUND
Shows how each employee has a role in achieving a good safety record.
From The Personal Side Of Safety Series.
Prod-NSC Dist-NSC

Safety Sense—A Series
J-C A
Emphasizes injury prevention and planning what to do in case of mishaps in such areas as jogging, hunting, camping, bicycling and boating.
Prod-WCVETV Dist-GPITVL 1981

Babysitting Safety 020 MIN
Bicycle Safety 020 MIN
Boating Safety 020 MIN
Camping Safety 020 MIN
Consumer Safety 020 MIN
Drug Effects 020 MIN
Fire Safety 020 MIN
Home Safety 020 MIN
Hunting Safety 020 MIN
In-Service Program For Teachers 020 MIN
Jogging Safety 020 MIN
Mental Health 020 MIN
School Safety 020 MIN
Self-Protection 020 MIN
Survival 020 MIN

Safety Times Three C 16 MIN
16MM FILM OPTICAL SOUND J-C
Explains that the three elements which make up safe driving are the driver, the car and the road. Discusses the need for courtesy and attentiveness on the part of the driver and details the skills and knowledge needed to be a good defensive driver.
LC NO. 74-703048
Prod-GM Dist-GM Prodn-IMPCTP 1972

Safety Training—A Series
IND
Presents programs on various aspects of industrial safety.
Prod-LEIKID Dist-LEIKID

Application And Use Of Breathing Apparatus 030 MIN
Cardio-Pulmonary Resuscitation 045 MIN
Hydrogen Sulphide Alert 060 MIN

Safety Week C 30 MIN
3/4 OR 1/2 INCH VIDEO CASSETTE K-P
See series title for descriptive statement.
From The Villa Alegre Series.
Prod-BCTV Dist-MDCPB

Safety Wise—A Series

Prod-BSC Dist-NSC

Help Yourself To Safety 10 MIN
Not Even One Chance 10 MIN
Safe As You Know How 10 MIN

Safety With Electricity X 10 MIN
16MM FILM, 3/4 OR 1/2 IN VIDEO P
Demonstrates that electricity can be dangerous, shows how these dangers can be minimized by simple safety precautions and illustrates some of the uses of electricity. Shows the nature and sources of electicity.
Prod-EBF Dist-EBEC 1963

Safety—A Series
16MM FILM, 3/4 OR 1/2 IN VIDEO P-I
Uses stories about children who are rescued from a variety of hazardous situations to create an awareness of the necessity of safety practices.
Prod-FILMCO Dist-BARR 1977

Safety - Harm Hides At Home 16 MIN
Safety - In Danger Out Of Doors 15 MIN
Safety - Peril Rides The Roads 15 MIN

Safety—A Series

Presents a series on how to fight fires safely and efficiently.
Prod-NFPA Dist-NFPA

Basic Fire Fighting Machine, The
Danger - Fire Fighters At Work
Emergency Vehicle Operation
Fire Department Safety Program, The
Fire Ground Operations
Organizing The Fire Ground
Protective Clothing And Breathing Apparatus
Structural Collapse

Safety-Oriented First Aid Multimedia Course—A Series
16MM FILM, 3/4 OR 1/2 IN VIDEO C A
Deals with injury prevention and the causes and effects of injuries.
Prod-CRAF Dist-IFB

Safety-Oriented First Aid Multimedia Course,
Safety-Oriented First Aid Multimedia Course, 022 MIN
Safety-Oriented First Aid Multimedia Course, 028 MIN
Safety-Oriented First Aid Multimedia Course, 010 MIN

Safety-Oriented First Aid Multimedia Course, Unit 1 C 29 MIN
16MM FILM, 3/4 OR 1/2 IN VIDEO C A
Deals with such first aid topics as respiratory emergencies and artificial respiration, indirect methods of artificial respiration, bleeding, embedded foreign objects, dressings and bandages.
From The Safety-Oriented First Aid Multimedia Course Series.
Prod-CRAF Dist-IFB

Safety-Oriented First Aid Multimedia Course, Unit 2 C 22 MIN
16MM FILM, 3/4 OR 1/2 IN VIDEO C A
Deals with such first aid topics as shock, fractures and dislocations of the upper and lower limbs, and chest injuries.
From The Safety-Oriented First Aid Multimedia Course Series.
Prod-CRAF Dist-IFB

Safety-Oriented First Aid Multimedia Course, Unit 3 C 28 MIN
16MM FILM, 3/4 OR 1/2 IN VIDEO C A
Deals with such first aid topics as head, neck and back injuries, burns and scalds, eye injuries, handling and moving casualties, and poisoning.
From The Safety-Oriented First Aid Multimedia Course Series.
Prod-CRAF Dist-IFB

Safety-Oriented First Aid Multimedia Course, Unit 4 C 10 MIN
16MM FILM, 3/4 OR 1/2 IN VIDEO C A
Deals with casualty management.
From The Safety-Oriented First Aid Multimedia Course Series.
Prod-CRAF Dist-IFB

Safety, Health And Discipline C 30 MIN
3/4 OR 1/2 INCH VIDEO CASSETTE J
Uses several vignettes to help students become aware that discipline helps people adjust to different situations and that parents must take certain measures to provide a healthy and safe environment for their children.
From The Middle Road Traveler Series.
LC NO. 80-707469
Prod-BAYUCM Dist-GPITVL 1979

Safety, Health And Environmental Concerns C
3/4 OR 1/2 INCH VIDEO CASSETTE
See series title for descriptive statement.
From The Pest Control Technology Correspondence Course Series.
Prod-PUAVC Dist-PUAVC

Safety, Health, And Discipline C 30 MIN
16MM FILM OPTICAL SOUND J-H
Discusses the importance of discipline and safety in child-rearing.
From The Middle Road Traveler Series.
LC NO. 80-701709
Prod-GRETVO Dist-GPITVL 1978

Safety, Health, And Loss Control - Managing Effective Programs—A Series
IND
Discusses all main aspects of the OSHA act, new regulations by the Occupational Safety and Health Administration, industry's reaction to them, safety and cost considerations and security measures.
LC NO. 81-706200
Prod-AMCEE Dist-AMCEE 1979

Behavior Management For Safety 040 MIN
Establishing An Effective Executive Security 040 MIN
Establishing And Implementing An Effective 040 MIN
Health Compliance For Small Industries 040 MIN
Impact Of New Government Regulations On 040 MIN
Industry's Reaction To A Changing OSHA 040 MIN
Loss Control, Impact 1980 040 MIN
Management, Impact 1980 040 MIN
Management's Safety Mirror 040 MIN
Monitoring The Work Environment 040 MIN
Occupational Safety, Impact 1980 040 MIN
On Responsibility 040 MIN
Prevention Of Occupational Injury And Disease 040 MIN

Safety, Nurturance And Expectations C 30 MIN
16MM FILM, 3/4 OR 1/2 IN VIDEO J
Uses several vignettes to create an awareness that parental expectations, nurturing and concern for safety all contribute to the development of normal, healthy children.
From The Middle Road Traveler Series.
LC NO. 80-707470
Prod-BAYUCM Dist-GPITVL 1979

Safety, Second To None C 15 MIN
3/4 INCH VIDEO CASSETTE
Points out the safety precautions and procedures required by the Atomic Energy Commission for the nuclear power industry. Issued in 1974 as a motion picture.
LC NO. 79-706188
Prod-USAEC Dist-USNAC Prodn-STARIF 1979

Saffron - Autumn Gold C 26 MIN
3/4 OR 1/2 INCH VIDEO CASSETTE J A
Discloses the secrets of saffron in the preparation of select dishes from bouillabaisse to saffron buns.
From The Spice Of Life Series.
Prod-BLCKRD Dist-BCNFL 1985

Saga Of Mink C 28 MIN
16MM FILM OPTICAL SOUND
Deals with the Scandinavian mink ranching industry and the manufacture and marketing of mink garments.
LC NO. 80-701334
Prod-SMINK Dist-TARGET Prodn-GOLDST

Saga Of Progress B 15 MIN
16MM FILM OPTICAL SOUND I-C A
Presents the achievements of the five-year plans in the urban areas of India. Shows the major projects set up according to the plans and the progress made by them.
Prod-INDIA Dist-NEDINF

Saga Of Safety Sam B 15 MIN
16MM FILM, 3/4 OR 1/2 IN VIDEO J-C
Employs a folk song to stress the importance of using safety shoes, non-slip gloves, goggles, a non-sinkable jacket and a safety hat in situations where necessary.
Prod-CRAF Dist-IFB 1959

Saga Of The Semis C 25 MIN
16MM FILM OPTICAL SOUND
Focuses on the capabilities of the Rowan Companies' semi-submersible oil drilling platforms.
LC NO. 77-702138
Prod-ROWAN Dist-ROWAN Prodn-RAMSEY 1977

Saga Of The Whale / Too Many Elephants C 46 MIN
3/4 OR 1/2 INCH VIDEO CASSETTE
Traces the annual migration of the gray whale from Alaska to Baja California where they court and calve in the warm winter waters. Examines the elephant's family and herd structures and the life cycle of this long-living animal with particular attention to the consequences a herd has on its environment.
Prod-TIMLIF Dist-TIMLIF 1979

Saga Of Western Man—A Series
16MM FILM, 3/4 OR 1/2 IN VIDEO
Prod-ABCTV Dist-MGHT

Beethoven - Ordeal And Triumph 052 MIN
Cortez And The Legend 052 MIN
Custer - The American Surge Westward 033 MIN
Eighteen Ninety-Eight 054 MIN
Fourteen Ninety-Two 054 MIN
I Am A Soldier 051 MIN
I, Leonardo Da Vinci 054 MIN
Legacy Of Rome, The 053 MIN
Nineteen Sixty-Four 054 MIN
Pilgrim Adventure, The 054 MIN
Seventeen Seventy-Six 054 MIN

Saga Of Windwagon Smith C 13 MIN
16MM FILM, 3/4 OR 1/2 IN VIDEO I-J
Presents a tale about Captain Windwagon Smith, who blew into a Kansas town in a prairie schooner, outfitted with mast, sails, and other seagoing equipment. The townspeople helped build a super windwagon to haul freight, but it was blown away by a Kansas twister.
Prod-DISNEY Dist-WDEMCO 1971

SAGE - Semi-Automatic Ground Environment System C 19 MIN
16MM FILM OPTICAL SOUND
Describes the mission, operations, capabilities and military importance of the SAGE system. Shows how SAGE sectors electronically compute aircraft movement information which is received from the observer agencies.
LC NO. 74-706233
Prod-USAF Dist-USNAC 1964

Sage And The Sayer, The - Ralph Waldo Emerson And Henry David Thoreau C 20 MIN
3/4 OR 1/2 INCH VIDEO CASSETTE H-C A
Presents conversations and soliloquies excerpted from Ralph Waldo Emerson's and Henry David Thoreau's essays and other writings.
From The American Literature Series.
LC NO. 83-706252
Prod-AUBU Dist-AITECH 1983

Sage Of Monticello And Old Hickory, The C 20 MIN
3/4 INCH VIDEO CASSETTE I
Offers information on Thomas Jefferson and Andrew Jackson.
From The Truly American Series.
Prod-WVIZTV Dist-GPITVL 1979

Sahara Fantasia - A Desert Festival Of Morocco C 9 MIN
16MM FILM, 3/4 OR 1/2 IN VIDEO P-C
Features nomadic desert tribes coming together in Southern Morocco to celebrate their Moussem, a unique Saharan festival. Covers music and dancing, colorful tents of trade, highlighted by the celebration of 'fantasia', a traditional event combining ancient musketry and skilled horsemanship. Unnarrated.
Prod-IFF Dist-IFF 1970

Sahel - Struggle For Survival C 18 MIN
16MM FILM OPTICAL SOUND
Shows the Catholic Relief Services teaching Africans how to combat the long-term effects of drought.
Prod-CATHRS Dist-MTP

Sahuaroland C 15 MIN
16MM FILM OPTICAL SOUND
Karl Maslowski tells amusing story of Chipmunk and an egg, including many birds in natural Arizona habitat.
Prod-SFI Dist-SFI

Said The Whiting To The Snail C 15 MIN
3/4 OR 1/2 INCH VIDEO CASSETTE P
Explains the process of commercial fishing in Maine.
From The Other Families, Other Friends Series. Blue Module - Maine
Prod-WVIZTV Dist-AITECH 1971

Sail Away C 14 MIN
16MM FILM OPTICAL SOUND
Takes a look at the sport of sailboat racing.
From The Journal Series.
LC NO. 74-703754
Prod-FIARTS Dist-CANFDC 1973

Sail Away C 18 MIN
16MM FILM, 3/4 OR 1/2 IN VIDEO I-J
Documents the adventures of a young boy who goes sailing in a trimaran with a friend and encounters different forms of marine life and a dramatic storm.
Prod-NFBC Dist-MOKIN 1978

Sail The Ocean Blue C 8 MIN
16MM FILM, 3/4 OR 1/2 IN VIDEO I-J
Points out that few sports offer such a unique sense of individual satisfaction as does sailing. Captures a succession of striking

images which transmits some of the feeling encountered by the crew of a racing sail boat. Serves as a springboard to both written and oral expression.
Prod-EVANSA Dist-AIMS 1973

Sail To Glory C 50 MIN
16MM FILM OPTICAL SOUND
Dramatizes the first America's Cup Race and traces the history of the winning sailing vessel, the America.
Prod-COUNFI Dist-COUNFI 1977

Sailfish Ho C 15 MIN
16MM FILM OPTICAL SOUND
Shows champions George and phyllis Bass catch sailfish off Florida and the Gulf Stream.
Prod-SFI Dist-SFI

Sailing C 3 MIN
16MM FILM OPTICAL SOUND P-I
Discusses the sport of sailing.
From The Of All Things Series.
Prod-BAILYL Dist-AVED

Sailing - Do It Right, Keep It Safe C 28 MIN
16MM FILM OPTICAL SOUND
Reviews the terms, techniques and equipment used in sailing. Highlights the camaraderie and teamwork that can be developed in the sport.
Prod-MICLOB Dist-MTP

Sailing Above The Alps C 28 MIN
16MM FILM, 3/4 OR 1/2 IN VIDEO H-C A
Shows a group of hang-gliding enthusiasts on the Alpine peaks of Switzerland. Features photographer Eric Jones receiving elementary hang-gliding lessons.
LC NO. 83-706848
Prod-GSAVL Dist-IU 1981

Sailing With The Clouds C 9 MIN
16MM FILM, 3/4 OR 1/2 IN VIDEO P-C
Depicts the experience of soaring through the sky in a sailplane. Portrays the visual and emotional experience from the point of view of the pilot.
Prod-GLDWER Dist-JOU 1974

Sailing, Pt 1 B 28 MIN
16MM FILM OPTICAL SOUND I-C A
Explains and demonstrates the principles and terminology of sailing. Emphasizes that each person on a sailboat must know how to swim and the correct way to use a life preserver. Explains the major parts of a sailboat, the mast, boom and centerboard housing. Shows how responses to wind should be made before going out in a sailboat, and demonstrates the effects of wind upon the sail.
LC NO. 78-704655
Prod-NET Dist-IU 1969

Sailing, Pt 2 B 27 MIN
16MM FILM OPTICAL SOUND I-C A
Investigates the effects of weight placement, wind and sail adjustment to gain smooth and efficient sailing. Shows that the sail must be let in and out and the tension changed for different kinds of wind. Demonstrates the rules of navigation using sailboat models to show which boat would have the right of way under certain conditions. Compares these demonstrations with live scenes of the same maneuvers using real sailboats.
LC NO. 71-704656
Prod-NET Dist-IU 1969

Sailor With A Future C 21 MIN
16MM FILM OPTICAL SOUND
Deals with the naval nuclear propulsion program. Shows a young nuclear propulsion plant operator aboard the USS Long Beach as he looks back at the training that prepared him for a career in the Navy.
LC NO. 74-706567
Prod-USN Dist-USNAC 1968

Sailor-Made Man, A / Grandma's Boy C 83 MIN
16MM FILM, 3/4 OR 1/2 IN VIDEO
Reissue of the 1921 silent Harold LLoyd comedy A Sailor-Made Man. Tells the story of a young man who joins the Navy in order to impress his girlfriend's father. Includes the 1922 Harold Lloyd comedy about a timid young man who, with the help of a lucky charm, manages to capture the local bandit, thrash his bullying rival and win the affection of his girlfriend.
From The Harold Lloyd Series.
Prod-ROACH Dist-TIMLIF 1976

Sailors In Green C 28 MIN
16MM FILM OPTICAL SOUND
Describes the founding of the Navy Seabees and highlights their participation in the Pacific and European theaters during World War II, Korea and Vietnam. Shows Seabee assistance as disaster teams during Hurricane Camille and taking part in civic action in Micronesia and in underwater construction in naval research projects.
LC NO. 74-706568
Prod-USN Dist-USNAC 1972

Sails And Sailors - J Boats '37 B
1/2 IN VIDEO CASSETTE BETA/VHS
Shows a glimpse of Newport and the Cup race of 1937 between J's Ranger and Endeavor II.
Prod-MYSTIC Dist-MYSTIC 1983

Saint Augustine C 57 MIN
16MM FILM, 3/4 OR 1/2 IN VIDEO
Deals with the life and thought of St Augustine. Tells how he provided the classic analysis between man in time and man in eternity and compares St Augustine's writings after the sack of Rome with the great disarray of society in the 70's. Written and narrated by Malcolm Muggeridge.
From The Third Testament Series.
LC NO. 79-707924
Prod-CANBC Dist-TIMLIF Prodn-RAYTAF 1976

Saint Louis - Gateway To The West C 25 MIN
16MM FILM OPTICAL SOUND I-C A
Describes the results of the bicentennial celebration of Saint Louis, which led to the rebuilding of much of the city, beginning in 1955. Includes views of the city's industries, universities, hospitals, museums, zoo and attractive living areas.
LC NO. FI68-235
Prod-SWBELL Dist-SWBELL Prodn-CONDOR 1966

Saint-Urbain In Troyes C 28 MIN
16MM FILM, 3/4 OR 1/2 IN VIDEO H-C A
Explores the history of the cathedral of Saint-Urbain de Troyes in France. Details its Gothic architecture and looks at other French cathedrals in comparison.
Prod-NFBC Dist-IFB 1973

Saints And Spirits C 26 MIN
16MM FILM, 3/4 OR 1/2 IN VIDEO H-C A
Looks at one group of Moroccan Muslims, telling how they view their worship of saints and spirits as part of the wider Islamic tradition. Shows them visiting shrines in Marrakech and in the Atlas Mountains.
Prod-UTEX Dist-ICARUS Prodn-DAVML 1980

Salad Nicoise C 30 MIN
3/4 OR 1/2 INCH VIDEO CASSETTE H-C
Tells how to make a Mediterranean salad with lettuce, tomatoes, potatoes, beans, eggs, tuna fish, capers and anchovies with the authentic flavor of the Riviera.
From The French Chef Series.
Prod-WGBH Dist-KINGFT

Salad Preparation C 16 MIN
16MM FILM - 3/4 IN VIDEO IND
Stresses the importance of salads in the diet, and shows the correct procedures to follow in their preparation and serving.
From The Food Service Employee Series.
Prod-COPI Dist-COPI 1969

Salad Presentation C
3/4 OR 1/2 INCH VIDEO CASSETTE
Prod-CULINA Dist-CULINA

Salads C
3/4 INCH VIDEO CASSETTE H A
Suggests that salads have potential for greater variety than many other foods because many kinds of foods can be combined. Demonstrates how to make a basic salad which can be made into a main dish.
From The Matter Of Taste Series. Lesson 6
Prod-COAST Dist-CDTEL

Salamanders - A Night At The Phi Delt House C 14 MIN
3/4 OR 1/2 INCH VIDEO CASSETTE
Looks at a fraternity at a major state university which celebrates the end of the school year by ritually capturing and eating live salamanders.
Prod-HRNBIG Dist-FLMLIB 1984

Salamanders And Lizards C 11 MIN
3/4 INCH VIDEO CASSETTE P
Depicts salamanders and chameleons in a tank. Explains how life evolved from water to land and emphasizes the similarity between lizards and the dinosaurs.
Prod-BOBWIN Dist-GA

Salary Administration, James F Carey C
3/4 OR 1/2 INCH VIDEO CASSETTE PRO
See series title for descriptive statement.
From The Management Skills Series.
Prod-AMCEE Dist-AMCEE

Salem Witch Trials B 28 MIN
16MM FILM, 3/4 OR 1/2 IN VIDEO J-C
Reconstructs two witch trials and depicts hysterical young girls accusing innocent people of being witches.
From The You Are There Series.
Prod-CBSTV Dist-MGHT 1957

Sales C 21 MIN
3/4 OR 1/2 INCH VIDEO CASSETTE C A
Presents a representative from a major corporation who defines sales and outlines some of the advantages of a career in sales. Discusses salaries, working conditions, and opportunities for advancement.
From The Clues To Career Opportunities For Liberal Arts Graduates Series.
LC NO. 80-706236
Prod-IU Dist-IU 1979

Sales / Marketing C 30 MIN
3/4 OR 1/2 INCH VIDEO CASSETTE
See series title for descriptive statement.
From The Videosearch Performance Appraisal (Case Studies) Series.
Prod-DELTAK Dist-DELTAK

Sales And Income Tax C 15 MIN
3/4 OR 1/2 INCH VIDEO CASSETTE
See series title for descriptive statement.
From The Consumer Education Series.
Prod-MAETEL Dist-CAMB

Sales And Service C 27 MIN
3/4 OR 1/2 INCH VIDEO CASSETTE
Looks at the kinds of effort needed to keep blood donors coming back. Draws analogy between an auto dealer's sales and service efforts and what a blood center must do after recruitment of donors.
Prod-AMRC Dist-AMRC

Sales Building Role, The C 7 MIN
16MM FILM OPTICAL SOUND H A
Depicts how to satisfy the customer's wants in both quantity and quality. Shows how sales and service can be increased through intelligent and appropriate suggestions of additional or higher priced merchandise.
From The People Sell People Series.
LC NO. FI68-236
Prod-SAUM Dist-MLA 1965

Sales Communications—A Series

Discusses sales communications.
Prod-VISUCP Dist-VISUCP

In Two Minds 019 MIN
Meetings Of Minds, The 014 MIN

Sales Film, The C 27 MIN
3/4 OR 1/2 INCH VIDEO CASSETTE A
Focuses on sales training. Includes customer relations, overcoming objections and other sales techniques. Uses story format.
Prod-AMEDIA Dist-AMEDIA

Sales Grid—A Series
16MM FILM - 3/4 IN VIDEO IND
Features Drs Blake and Mounton discussing and giving examples of the Grid approach to selling. Based on the book The Grid For Sales Excellence by Robert R Blake and Jane Srygley Mouton.
Prod-BNA Dist-BNA

Sales Grid, The - What It Is And How It Works 30 MIN
Sales Grid, The - 9, 9 Solution Selling 30 MIN

Sales Grid, The - What It Is And How It Works C 30 MIN
16MM FILM - 3/4 IN VIDEO IND
Presents the basic concepts pertaining to the sales and customer grids. Features Drs Blake and Mouton discussing their ideas with four salesmen who question them on various aspects of the selling relationship. Based on the book The Grid For Sales Excellence by Robert R Blake and Jane Srygley Mouton.
From The Sales Grid Series. Part 1
Prod-BNA Dist-BNA

Sales Grid, The - 9, 9 Solution Selling C 30 MIN
16MM FILM - 3/4 IN VIDEO IND
Features Drs Blake and Moution who use vignettes to criticize principal seller sytles. Focuses on the Sales Grid approach to selling. Based on the book The Grid For Sales Excellence by Robert Blake and Jane Srygley Mouton.
From The Sales Grid Series. Part 2
Prod-BNA Dist-BNA

Sales Meeting Films—A Series
16MM FILM, 3/4 OR 1/2 IN VIDEO C A
Offers brief stories which may be used as links between meeting speakers and the meeting elements.
Prod-MBACC Dist-MTI 1983

Building For Success 002 MIN
Demonstration - A Selling Technique 003 MIN
Efficiency In The Field 003 MIN
Selling As A Profession 002 MIN

Sales Talk C 25 MIN
16MM FILM, 3/4 OR 1/2 IN VIDEO A
Dramatizes a true-life case involving two salespeople and their unintentional misrepresentation of their products and services. Shows the result of these misrepresentations in the loss of business and goodwill.
Prod-RTBL Dist-RTBL

Sales Tax - Yes Or No? C
3/4 OR 1/2 INCH VIDEO CASSETTE
Prod-FO Dist-FO

Salesman B 90 MIN
16MM FILM OPTICAL SOUND
Uses cinema verite style to follow the activities of four door-to-door Bible salesmen on their routes.
LC NO. 72-710820
Prod-MAYSLS Dist-MAYSLS 1969

Salesman C 29 MIN
16MM FILM, 3/4 OR 1/2 IN VIDEO
Features a salesman who likes his job, telling why he likes it. Reveals the challenge of selling, the satisfaction of doing the job right and the rewards that the dedicated salesman receives.
Prod-DARTNL Dist-DARTNL

Salesmanship - Career Opportunities C 15 MIN
16MM FILM, 3/4 OR 1/2 IN VIDEO H-C
Presents vocational opportunities available in a sales career. Discusses qualifications, techniques, compensation methods, training and sales tools needed in this career. Shows the importance of the salesman in the marketing and industrial complex.
Prod-ALTSUL Dist-JOU 1968

Salesmanship - Career Opportunities (Spanish) C 15 MIN
16MM FILM, 3/4 OR 1/2 IN VIDEO H-C
Presents vocational opportunities available in a sales career. Discusses qualifications, techniques, compensation methods, training and sales tools needed in this career. Shows the importance of the salesman in the marketing and industrial complex.
Prod-ALTSUL Dist-JOU 1968

Sallie 1893-1974 C 54 MIN
16MM FILM OPTICAL SOUND H-C A
Records a funeral as it is occurring. Suggests that the ceremony is really a celebration of the life of Sallie Mc Ginnis, who died at age 81.
Prod-OSSHE Dist-OSSHE 1974

Sally C 8 MIN
16MM FILM, 3/4 OR 1/2 IN VIDEO K-P
Tells how a local wizard teaches a little girl the importance of telling the truth.
Prod-KRATKY Dist-LCOA 1978

Sally At 13 C 18 MIN
16MM FILM, 3/4 OR 1/2 IN VIDEO J
Deals with the concerns most girls face as they enter puberty.
Prod-RUSELP Dist-PEREN

Sally Garcia And Family C 35 MIN
16MM FILM OPTICAL SOUND
Presents a profile of Sally Garcia, a 40-year-old wife and mother of five children, who counsels women and adolescents in career planning while attending school in the evenings to obtain her BA. Deals with the issues that surround the separate demands of children, a husband, work and continuing education.
LC NO. 78-700304
Prod-EDC Dist-EDC 1977

Sally Had A Sweet Tooth, Now It's Gone B 15 MIN
2 INCH VIDEOTAPE P-I
Discusses diet and how what you eat affects the health of your teeth. Considers problems resulting from bad food choices or from being a nervous nibbler who eats often and brushes seldom.
From The Dental Health Series.
Prod-GPITVL Dist-GPITVL

Sally Of The Sawdust B 92 MIN
16MM FILM SILENT
Introduces Eustace McGargle, a carnival barker who has adopted Sally and enjoys an occasional nip or two, yet is on record as being none too fond of children or dogs. Stars W C Fields. Directed by D W Griffith.
Prod-GFITH Dist-KILLIS 1925

Sally Osborne - Mechanical Engineer C 10 MIN
16MM FILM OPTICAL SOUND
Follows a mechanical engineer through her day's work and examines the diversity of her job. Shows how this mechanical engineer manages both home and career.
Prod-POLARD Dist-MTP

Sally Ride - Lady Astronaut C 14 MIN
3/4 OR 1/2 INCH VIDEO CASSETTE
Profiles Sally Ride, a 30-year-old astro-physicist who became the first American woman in space when she flew in the space shuttle Challenger in 1983.
Prod-KINGFT Dist-KINGFT 1983

Sally Sommer And Beate Gordon C 30 MIN
3/4 OR 1/2 INCH VIDEO CASSETTE
Focuses on obtaining a broader understanding of ethnic dance.
From The Eye On Dance - Third World Dance, Beyond The White Stream Series.
Prod-ARTRES Dist-ARTRES

Salmon - Catch To Can C 14 MIN
16MM FILM OPTICAL SOUND P-C
Depicts the return of salmon from sea to fresh water streams where they spawn and die. Shows methods used to catch the fish, such as trolling, seining and gill netting, and pictures machinery used for processing.
LC NO. FIE64-202
Prod-USBCF Dist-USNOAA 1960

Salmon - Catch To Can C 14 MIN
3/4 OR 1/2 INCH VIDEO CASSETTE
Discusses the life of the Pacific salmon and describes the commercial fishery activities involved in taking it from the sea and putting it into a can. Issued as a motion picture in 1960.
LC NO. 80-707616
Prod-USBSFW Dist-USNAC 1980

Salmon - Life Cycle C 3 MIN
16MM FILM OPTICAL SOUND P-I
Discusses the life cycle of the salmon fish.
From The Of All Things Series.
Prod-BAILYL Dist-AVED

Salmon For All Seasons C 23 MIN
16MM FILM OPTICAL SOUND
Discusses the problem of declining natural salmon runs and explains how ocean ranching can benefit both man and nature.
LC NO. 78-701568
Prod-WEYCO Dist-ODS Prodn-ODYSSP 1978

Salmon On The Run C 57 MIN
3/4 OR 1/2 INCH VIDEO CASSETTE H-C A
Shows how business and technology are changing the future of the fishing industry, with salmon now 'farmed' on 'ranches.' Presents an argument to let salmon remain as wild as possible.
From The Nova Series.
Prod-WGBHTV Dist-TIMLIF 1982

Salomon 727 C 6 MIN
16MM FILM OPTICAL SOUND
Discusses the technical features of the Salomon 727 ski binding.
LC NO. 78-701483
Prod-SALNA Dist-SALNA 1978

Salomon 727 (French) C 6 MIN
16MM FILM OPTICAL SOUND
Discusses the technical features of the Salomon 727 ski binding.
LC NO. 78-701483
Prod-SALNA Dist-SALNA 1978

Salomon 727 (German) C 6 MIN
16MM FILM OPTICAL SOUND
Discusses the technical features of the Salomon 727 ski binding.
LC NO. 78-701483
Prod-SALNA Dist-SALNA 1978

Salomon 727 (Italian) C 6 MIN
16MM FILM OPTICAL SOUND
Discusses the technical features of the Salomon 727 ski binding.
LC NO. 78-701483
Prod-SALNA Dist-SALNA 1978

Salon Esso De Artistas Jovenes C 16 MIN
16MM FILM OPTICAL SOUND
Discusses a selection of works by prize-winning Latin American artists at the 1964 Esso Salon of Young Artists.
LC NO. 75-700282
Prod-OOAS Dist-PAN 1970

Salp'uri - Korean Improvisational Dance B 15 MIN
16MM FILM, 3/4 OR 1/2 IN VIDEO
Includes two separate performances of an improvisational dance of Korea called Salp'uri.
From The Ethnic Music And Dance Series.
Prod-UWASHP Dist-UWASHP

Salt - The Essence Of Life C 28 MIN
16MM FILM OPTICAL SOUND
Tells the story of salt and its importance to man and animals. Demonstrates its production through the mining of rocksalt and the evaporation of brine either mechanically or by the sun. Explores the principle and varied uses of salt and how salt affects every aspect of human life.
Prod-SALTI Dist-MTP 1982

Salt - The Hidden Threat C 21 MIN
16MM FILM, 3/4 OR 1/2 IN VIDEO J-C A
Explores the problems caused by people eating too much salt. Provides examples of sodium contents of certain foods and shows ways in which salt intake can be reduced.
Prod-HIGGIN Dist-HIGGIN 1983

Salt And Hypertension - How To Save Your Own Life C 26 MIN
16MM FILM, 3/4 OR 1/2 IN VIDEO J-C A
Discusses the causes and effects of hypertension, pointing out that high blood pressure can be controlled by reducing the intake of salt. Shows how to limit salt intake by revealing the often surprising salt content of many foods. Presents strategies for shopping and food preparation and discusses the dangers of high blood pressure and the effectiveness of a low salt diet as a treatment.
LC NO. 83-706302
Prod-IA Dist-PFP 1982

Salt Marsh, The - A Question Of Values C 22 MIN
16MM FILM, 3/4 OR 1/2 IN VIDEO J-C A
Shows researchers from the University of Georgia as they examine the complex ecological system of a salt marsh. Shows how marshland provides an important link in the ecological system of the neighboring ocean.
From The Environmental Studies Series.
Prod-EBEC Dist-EBEC 1975

Salt Marshes, The - Border Between Land And Sea C 23 MIN
16MM FILM OPTICAL SOUND
Describes the importance of salt marshes as breeding and feeding grounds of birds, fish and crustaceans and as a protective barrier against storm damage to the mainland. Documents the destruction of salt marshes by pollution and urban development and pleads for the preservation of those that remain. Focuses on East Coast marshes but is relevant to all.
Prod-UCEMC Dist-HAR 1973

Salt Of The Earth C 50 MIN
16MM FILM OPTICAL SOUND J A
Shows how a miner who has never taken God seriously inadvertently causes a fellow miner to become critically injured. Explains that the man changes his outlook, and through the local pastor and church, finds the meaning of Christian stewardship.
Prod-YALEDV Dist-YALEDV

Salt Of The Earth C 15 MIN
3/4 OR 1/2 INCH VIDEO CASSETTE P-I
Visits a salt mine in Cleveland to examine methods of extracting salt.
From The Explorers Unlimited Series.
Prod-WVIZTV Dist-AITECH 1971

Salt Or Sugar C 20 MIN
16MM FILM, 3/4 OR 1/2 IN VIDEO P-J T
Presents a student participation film in which students observe and record the physical and chemical properties of two common materials, salt and sugar.
From The Science Twenty Series.
Prod-PRISM Dist-SF 1969

Salts And Oxidizers C 30 MIN
3/4 OR 1/2 INCH VIDEO CASSETTE PRO
See series title for descriptive statement.
From The HTM - Hazardous Toxic Materials Series. Unit II
Prod-FILCOM Dist-FILCOM

Salty C 93 MIN
3/4 OR 1/2 INCH VIDEO CASSETTE
Reveals that when a lovable but mischievous sea lion, formerly with a circus, becomes the pet of two brothers, its escapades manage to complicate the boys' lives when they volunteer to help a friend renovate a Florida marina.
Prod-TIMLIF Dist-TIMLIF 1982

Salut - French Language Lessons—A Series

Designed to enrich and reinforce the basic materials taught in beginning French. Programs consist of four segments featuring live performers in amusing situations. Spoken in clear dialogue and explained by visuals. Includes program guide and teaching handbook. Each segment is self-contained.
Prod-BCNFL Dist-BCNFL 1984

A La Ville 010 MIN
Bonjour 010 MIN
C'est Le Premier Juillet 010 MIN
C'est Un Sac D'ecole 010 MIN
De La Creme Glacee 010 MIN
Est-Ce Que Vous Etes Bucheron 010 MIN
Il Fait Beau 010 MIN
Il Frappe La Balle 010 MIN
Il Y A Trois Chiens 010 MIN
J'ai Hate 010 MIN
J'ai Vingt Robes 010 MIN
J'aime La Campagne 010 MIN
Je Fais Mes Devoirs 010 MIN
Je Me Leve A Sept Heures 010 MIN
Je Parle, Tu Encoutes 010 MIN
Je Peus Vous Aider 010 MIN
Je Vaise En Auto 010 MIN
Lancez 010 MIN
Les Belles Couleurs 010 MIN
Mon Bras, Ton Nez 010 MIN
Nous Jouons 010 MIN
Pas De Moutarde 010 MIN
Que Fais-Tu Aujourd'hui 010 MIN
Son Pantalon 010 MIN
Tu Es Dans La Maison 010 MIN

Salut, Montreal C 12 MIN
16MM FILM, 3/4 OR 1/2 IN VIDEO H-C A
A French language motion picture. Shows two Quebec students taking two exchange students on a tour of Montreal to see sights, sounds and atmosphere of the city.
From The Connaissons-Nous Series.
Prod-INCC Dist-BCNFL 1982

Salute To A Crusader - Dwight Eisenhower Portrait Of A Patriot B 14 MIN
16MM FILM OPTICAL SOUND J-H
Traces the career of a Kansas farm boy, Dwight David Eisenhower, who served his country in war as a great military commander and in peace as its 34th President.
From The Screen News Digest Series. Vol 11 Issue 9
LC NO. 70-703471
Prod-HEARST Dist-HEARST 1969

Salute To The American Theatre, A C 40 MIN
16MM FILM OPTICAL SOUND H-C A
Presents scenes from 'THE OCTOROON,' 'WAITING FOR LEFTY,' 'THE MALE ANIMAL,' 'CALL ME MISTER,' 'HOME OF THE BRAVE,' 'THE CRUCIBLE,' 'SOUTH PACIFIC,' 'RAISIN IN THE SUN' and other dramas whose theme is freedom and anti-discrimination.
Prod-CBSTV Dist-ADL 1960

Salvador Minuchin, MD - Anorexia Is A Greek Word C 60 MIN
3/4 OR 1/2 INCH VIDEO CASSETTE PRO
Defines the steps in treating a family whose fourteen-year-old daughter has been anorexic.
From The Perceptions, Pt A - Interventions In Family Therapy Series. Vol VIII, Pt A16.
Prod-BOSFAM Dist-BOSFAM

Salvador Minuchin, MD, Director, Philadelphia Child Guidance Clinic C 60 MIN
3/4 OR 1/2 INCH VIDEO CASSETTE PRO
Features Frederick J Duhl interviewing Salvador Minuchin concerning his background in Argentina, Israel and New New York as it affects his approach to family therapy.
From The Perceptions, Pt B - Dialogues With Family Therapists Series. Vol VIII, Pt B16.
Prod-BOSFAM Dist-BOSFAM

Salvage C 15 MIN
3/4 OR 1/2 INCH VIDEO CASSETTE PRO
Presents on-scene footage to show how buildings and contents are salvaged after a fire. Emphasizes protection of public and private property.
Prod-IFSTA Dist-IFSTA

Salvage Of The Gunboat Cairo C 26 MIN
16MM FILM - 3/4 IN VIDEO
Documents the raising of the Civil War gunboat Cairo from the river bed of the Mississippi. Issued in 1969 as a motion picture.
LC NO. 79-706156
Prod-USNPS Dist-USNAC Prodn-PARKS 1979

Salvage Of The Sub Squalus B 45 MIN
16MM FILM OPTICAL SOUND
Shows the salvage of the submarine USS Squalus.
LC NO. 74-706569
Prod-USN Dist-USNAC 1968

Salvage Of The USS Lafayette B 35 MIN
16MM FILM OPTICAL SOUND
Shows salvage operations from time of fire to drydocking of the ship USS Lafayette. Demonstrates the work of salvage engineers and divers, shows the design and placement of patches, demonstrates how to shore decks and bulkheads, how to place pumps, how to stop leaks with concrete and how to moor the ship during pumping.
LC NO. 74-706570
Prod-USN Dist-USNAC 1944

Salvage Picture, A B 15 MIN
2 INCH VIDEOTAPE P
Details creating designs or pictures using feathers, cloth, yarn, buttons, seeds, bark and other salvage or nature materials.
From The Art Corner Series.
Prod-CVETVC Dist-GPITVL Prodn-WCVETV

Salvage Printing, Collage And Care Of Materials C 15 MIN
3/4 INCH VIDEO CASSETTE P-I
See series title for descriptive statement.

From The Look And A Closer Look Series.
Prod-WCVETV Dist-GPITVL 1976

Salvaging American Prehistory, Pt 1 C 28 MIN
16MM FILM OPTICAL SOUND C A
Treats the general subject of archeology and reservoir salvage and travels over the whole United States.
From The Spadework For History Series.
Prod-UTEX Dist-UTEX 1964

Salvaging Texas Prehistory C 28 MIN
16MM FILM OPTICAL SOUND C A
Tells of the problems faced in a site in central Texas as seen against the varied background of archeological effort in Texas as a whole. Shows how the scientific process takes place--how the information from one project serves to check the hypotheses formed from the earlier ones, resulting in further hypotheses to be checked by further work.
From The Spadework For History Series.
Prod-UTEX Dist-UTEX 1964

Salvation And Christian Fellowship X 17 MIN
16MM FILM OPTICAL SOUND J-H T R
Explains that many of the early jewish Christians found it difficult to accept Gentiles into the fellowship. Shows Paul and Barnabas called to Jerusalem to report on the work in Antioch. Stresses salvation by grace through faith.
From The Book Of Acts Series.
Prod-BROADM Dist-FAMF 1957

Salvation, Pt II C 26 MIN
3/4 OR 1/2 INCH VIDEO CASSETTE
Offers plans for organizing, delegating, setting priorities, scheduling time for active tasks and allocating time for reactive tasks.
From The Unorganized Manager Series.
Prod-VIDART Dist-VISUCP

Sam C 14 MIN
16MM FILM OPTICAL SOUND P-I
Uses the dialogue of the television show Dragnet to show a case officer introducing and investigating the circumstances surrounding the abandonment and abuse of a dog named Sam. Emphasizes the responsibilities involved in pet ownership.
LC NO. 81-701248
Prod-ASPCA Dist-ADELPH 1981

Sam B 20 MIN
16MM FILM, 3/4 OR 1/2 IN VIDEO
Explores culture and class through the portrayal of a Japanese-American. Recounts his World War II detention and his wife's survival of the atomic bombing of Hiroshima.
Prod-UCEMC Dist-UCEMC

Sam C 25 MIN
16MM FILM, 3/4 OR 1/2 IN VIDEO I-J
Tells the story of a young boy who has cerebral palsy and how he copes with his handicap.
Prod-BARR Dist-BARR Prodn-HOFD 1981

Sam X 29 MIN
16MM FILM, 3/4 OR 1/2 IN VIDEO J-C A
Presents a futuristic story about the last man on earth, an old vaudeville comedian who is still alive because he is impossible to program. Tells what happens when a little boy appears. Stars Jack Albertson.
From The Insight Series.
Prod-PAULST Dist-PAULST

Sam (Captioned) C 25 MIN
16MM FILM - VIDEO, ALL FORMATS I-J
Tells the story of a child with cerebral palsy. Adapted from the book Sam And His Cart by Arthur Honeyman, about his own childhood.
Prod-BARR Dist-BARR

Sam Daggett's House C 28 MIN
16MM FILM, 3/4 OR 1/2 IN VIDEO H-C A
Looks at the history of an 18th-century house, and at the life of the man who built it.
Prod-JOU Dist-JOU

Sam Francis C 52 MIN
16MM FILM OPTICAL SOUND
Features Sam Francis, an American artist, in Paris, Tokyo and Los Angeles, where he lives and works. Shows him talking about his career, the importance of dreams in his paintings and his relationship with color.
LC NO. 76-703157
Prod-BLACKW Dist-BLACKW 1976

Sam Houston B 20 MIN
2 INCH VIDEOTAPE I
See series title for descriptive statement.
From The Americans All Series.
Prod-DENVPS Dist-GPITVL Prodn-KRMATV

Sam Houston C 51 MIN
16MM FILM, 3/4 OR 1/2 IN VIDEO I-H
Describes the military and political career of Sam Houston. Emphasizes his life as governor and his fight to keep Texas in the Union. Based on book Profiles In Courage by John F Kennedy.
From The Profiles In Courage Series.
LC NO. 83-706545
Prod-SAUDEK Dist-SSSSV 1964

Sam Maloof - Woodworker C 17 MIN
16MM FILM, 3/4 OR 1/2 IN VIDEO
Observes Sam Maloof making furniture and commenting on his work and philosophy.
Prod-ORMEN Dist-AIMS 1973

Sam On The Busses C 15 MIN
16MM FILM, 3/4 OR 1/2 IN VIDEO I-H
Introduces Sam The Safety Duck who shows what can happen to children as the result of inconsiderate or wrongful behavior on the school bus and illustrates rules to prevent injuries while riding the school bus.
LC NO. 82-706407
Prod-OMTC Dist-FIESTF 1982

Sam On Winter Safety C 18 MIN
16MM FILM, 3/4 OR 1/2 IN VIDEO P-J
Shows the animated character Sam the Safety Duck taking a helicopter ride to spot the dangers of winter for winter sports enthusiasts. Discusses preventive measures and emergency care directions for winter accidents.
LC NO. 82-706408
Prod-OMTC Dist-FIESTF 1982

Sam Seagull Presents Cape Cod C 28 MIN
16MM FILM OPTICAL SOUND
Explores the countryside, culture and recreation available in Cape Cod, Massachusetts.
Prod-CCCOC Dist-MTP

Sam Snead C 20 MIN
16MM FILM OPTICAL SOUND I-J
Tells how Sam Snead was a hillbilly from Hot Springs, Virginia, who came to the game a barefoot caddy, and now over 60, is still playing golf competitively on the pro circuit. Features Snead reviewing more than half a century of golf.
From The Sports Legends Series.
Prod-COUNFI Dist-COUNFI

Sam The Safety Duck Learns To Drive A Bicycle C 5 MIN
16MM FILM, 3/4 OR 1/2 IN VIDEO P
Presents Sam the Safety Duck in an animated sequence illustrating basic techniques of bicycling safety. Compares cycling with automobile driving. Lists necessary safety equipment.
Prod-CMT Dist-FIESTF 1984

Sam, Bangs And Moonshine C 15 MIN
16MM FILM, 3/4 OR 1/2 IN VIDEO P-I
Presents an adaptation of the children's story Sam, Bangs And Moonshine by Evaline Ness, about a young girl whose habit of pretending causes unexpected troubles.
Prod-JOHR Dist-PHENIX 1976

Sam's Secret C 10 MIN
16MM FILM, 3/4 OR 1/2 IN VIDEO K-C A
Presents a successful salesman who reveals the secret of his success to his colleagues at a sales meeting.
Prod-PORTA Dist-RTBL 1965

Sam's Secret (Dutch) C 10 MIN
16MM FILM, 3/4 OR 1/2 IN VIDEO
Presents a successful salesman who reveals the secret of his success to his colleagues at a sales meeting.
Prod-PORTA Dist-RTBL 1965

Sam's Secret (Norwegian) C 10 MIN
16MM FILM, 3/4 OR 1/2 IN VIDEO
Presents a successful salesman who reveals the secret of his success to his colleagues at a sales meeting.
Prod-PORTA Dist-RTBL 1965

Sam's Secret (Portuguese) C 10 MIN
16MM FILM, 3/4 OR 1/2 IN VIDEO
Presents a successful salesman who reveals the secret of his success to his colleagues at a sales meeting.
Prod-PORTA Dist-RTBL 1965

Sam's Secret (Spanish) C 10 MIN
16MM FILM, 3/4 OR 1/2 IN VIDEO
Presents a successful salesman who reveals the secret of his success to his colleagues at a sales meeting.
Prod-PORTA Dist-RTBL 1965

Sam's Secret (Swedish) C 10 MIN
16MM FILM, 3/4 OR 1/2 IN VIDEO
Presents a successful salesman who reveals the secret of his success to his colleagues at a sales meeting.
Prod-PORTA Dist-RTBL 1965

Sam's Song - The Legacy Of A Free Economy / Business Money- Where It Comes From And... C 27 MIN
16MM FILM OPTICAL SOUND
Presents the films Sam's Song - The Legacy Of A Free Economy and Business Money - Where It Comes From And Where It Goes. Introduces in Sam's Song the role of supply and demand and in Business Money tells about capital and profit.
Prod-SUNCO Dist-KAROL

Samal Dances From Taluksangay C 12 MIN
16MM FILM, 3/4 OR 1/2 IN VIDEO J-C A
Shows examples of the Samal dances from Taluksangay village which is at the northern end of the Sulu Archipelago on the island of Mindanao.
From The Ethnic Music And Dance Series.
Prod-UWASH Dist-UWASHP 1971

Samantha Gets A Visitor C 26 MIN
16MM FILM, 3/4 OR 1/2 IN VIDEO I-J
Tells how country-girl Samantha learns to like camping after she, her younger brother and her city cousin lose their way in the woods.
Prod-PLAYTM Dist-BCNFL 1985

Samantha Rastles The Woman Question C 50 MIN
3/4 OR 1/2 INCH VIDEO CASSETTE J-C A
Presents a one-woman performance in which Jane Curry portrays Samantha Smith Allen, a character created by author Marietta Holley. Deals with questions concerning women, such as rights denied them by the church, powerlessness before the law, their social status and role assumptions in the 19th century.
LC NO. 83-707104
Prod-CUETV Dist-CUNIV 1983

Samaritans, The C 30 MIN
16MM FILM OPTICAL SOUND J-C A
Looks at the Samaritans, people who separated themselves from the Jewish people 2,500 years ago and consider themselves Hebrew, not Jewish. Reveals how their ritual practices are derived from the Samaritan Pentateuch, not the Torah.
Prod-SPECJO Dist-NJWB 1971

Sambizanga (Portuguese) C 102 MIN
16MM FILM OPTICAL SOUND
An English subtitle version of the Portuguese language film. Focuses on a young black couple who bask in each other's presence until the husband, a tractor driver is suddenly arrested as a political prisoner in Angola. Portrays the relationship between white and black Africans.
Prod-NYFLMS Dist-NYFLMS 1972

Same And Different C 15 MIN
3/4 OR 1/2 INCH VIDEO CASSETTE T
Uses the adventures of a pirate and his three friends to explore the many facets of language arts. Focuses on synonyms and antonyms, shows what they are, and how they are used in oral and written expression.
From The Hidden Treasures Series. No. 4
LC NO. 82-706528
Prod-WCVETV Dist-GPITVL 1980

Same But Different C 4 MIN
16MM FILM OPTICAL SOUND I-C A
Uses cartoon characters to tell the story of Percy, a conformist and his friend Sidney, a nonconformist. Describes the resulting frustration as Percy copies Sidney until Sidney cannot succeed in being different.
LC NO. 72-700407
Prod-PHID Dist-MMA 1970

Same But Different, The C 15 MIN
3/4 OR 1/2 INCH VIDEO CASSETTE K-P
Shows how each human being is a unique individual.
From The Dragons, Wagons And Wax, Set 2 Series.
Prod-CTI Dist-CTI

Same Inside C 13 MIN
16MM FILM, 3/4 OR 1/2 IN VIDEO K-I
Presents four children with birth defects who talk about what they like to do and how they cope with their handicaps. Demonstrates that feelings can transcend external differences.
Prod-NFMD Dist-NFMD 1982

Same Subject, Different Treatment C 11 MIN
16MM FILM, 3/4 OR 1/2 IN VIDEO J-C A
Explains that in nature and in art the same objects are seen in many different ways. Uses the example of the sun at dawn to show these differences and to demonstrate that each artist has his own way of portraying it.
From The Art Of Seeing Series.
Prod-AFA Dist-FI 1972

Same Time, Next Year C 119 MIN
16MM FILM OPTICAL SOUND
Tells how a man and a woman, both married to other people, meet every year for 26 years. Stars Ellen Burstyn and Alan Alda.
Prod-UPCI Dist-TWYMAN 1978

Sami Herders C 28 MIN
16MM FILM, 3/4 OR 1/2 IN VIDEO I-H
Traces the life, over a 12-month period, of a family of Laplanders traveling from Norway up the Arctic coast with their herd of reindeer.
Prod-NFBC Dist-BNCHMK 1979

Sami, The - Four Lands, One People C 24 MIN
16MM FILM, 3/4 OR 1/2 IN VIDEO J-C A
Focuses on the life styles of four Sami families at the crossroads of modernity and tradition.
Prod-NFBC Dist-BNCHMK 1979

Sammy Mayfield And The Outcasts C 29 MIN
2 INCH VIDEOTAPE
Features Sammy and the Outcasts playing some hard-driving blues that contrasts with the easy sounds of vocalist Dee Dee Walker and Howard Bomar.
From The Changing Rhythms Series.
Prod-KRMATV Dist-PUBTEL

Sammy Williams, Bill Bradley And Gloria Rosenthal C 30 MIN
3/4 OR 1/2 INCH VIDEO CASSETTE
Presents the tale of the gypsy robe. Looks at 'Esoterica' with Helen Gueditis. Hosted by Celia Ipiotis.
From The Eye On Dance - Broadway Series.
Prod-ARTRES Dist-ARTRES

Sammy, Sammy C 20 MIN
16MM FILM OPTICAL SOUND
Presents the meaningless and pointless existence of a young man named Sammy.
LC NO. 76-701362
Prod-SFRASU Dist-SFRASU 1975

Sammy's Super T-Shirt C 58 MIN
16MM FILM OPTICAL SOUND P-I
Tells the story of pint-sized Sammy who possesses a T-shirt which endows him with great physical strength. Shows what happens when a friend convinces him to run a race without it.
Prod-CHILDF Dist-LUF 1979

Samoa I Sisifo (Western Samoa) C 26 MIN
16MM FILM, 3/4 OR 1/2 IN VIDEO
Demonstrates how traditional values and progressive develop-

ment are interwoven in Western Samoa. Shows how limited resources have brought about new methods of poultry raising, food gathering and fishing.
From The Village Life Series.
Prod-IFF Dist-JOU

Sampan Family C 16 MIN
16MM FILM, 3/4 OR 1/2 IN VIDEO P-H
Follows a day in the life of a Chinese family which lives and works on a tiny sampan in a harbor on the coast in Fukien province near Foochow. Shows how the children help in fishing, rowing the boat and other daily tasks.
Prod-IFF Dist-IFF 1949

Sample Bus Transactions C 30 MIN
3/4 OR 1/2 INCH VIDEO CASSETTE IND
Shows how addresses and command messages are differentiated from data, and how this information is used by all participants on the Bus. Uses block diagrams and byte-by-byte examples and timing diagrams to show actual data sent in Bus transactions. Explains ASCH table and IEEE commands.
From The IEEE 488 Bus Series.
Prod-COLOSU Dist-COLOSU

Sample Means And The Weak Law Of Large Numbers B 30 MIN
3/4 OR 1/2 INCH VIDEO CASSETTE PRO
Presents the sample mean as an estimator of expectation. Discusses different types of convergence.
From The Probability And Random Processes - Limit Theorems And Statistics Series.
Prod-MIOT Dist-MIOT

Sample Mounting Techniques, Evaporation C 6 MIN
16MM FILM OPTICAL SOUND PRO
Demonstrates three methods for mounting solid samples by evaporation–pouring a slurry, pipetting a slurry and pouring a dissolved solution.
LC NO. 74-705571
Prod-USPHS Dist-USNAC 1966

Sample Mounting Techniques, Filtration C 7 MIN
16MM FILM OPTICAL SOUND PRO
Illustrates in mounting solid samples that filtration is a common technique used to mount precipitated samples by the use of a vacuum, suction flash, filter paper and filter tower. Depicts 3 types of filter towers–glass, teflon and stainless steel. Shows filter paper placed in a counting dish and dried under a heat lamp and more permanently mounted with a ring and disk.
LC NO. 74-705573
Prod-USPHS Dist-USNAC 1966

Sampler Of Selections From Favorite Authors, A C 29 MIN
2 INCH VIDEOTAPE
From The One To One Series.
Prod-WETATV Dist-PUBTEL

Sampling And Descriptive Statistics C 30 MIN
3/4 OR 1/2 INCH VIDEO CASSETTE IND
Begins by discussing first step in a practical situation, that of taking a sample from a population. Cites examples relating to particular problems on a production line. Describes graphical display techniques.
From The Engineering Statistics Series.
Prod-COLOSU Dist-COLOSU

Sampling And Estimation C 23 MIN
16MM FILM, 3/4 OR 1/2 IN VIDEO C
Introduces basic concepts in statistics such as sample, random sample, sample bias, point estimation and confidence intervals.
From The Inferential Statistics Series.
Prod-WILEYJ Dist-MEDIAG Prodn-JHNSNR 1977

Sampling Respirable Dusts - Key Words C 7 MIN
1/2 IN VIDEO CASSETTE BETA/VHS
Discusses dust control, dust measurement and environmental health.
Prod-RMI Dist-RMI

Sampling Respirable Dusts - Sample Records C 14 MIN
1/2 IN VIDEO CASSETTE BETA/VHS
Discusses dust control, dust measurement and environmental health.
Prod-RMI Dist-RMI

Sampling Theorem B 28 MIN
3/4 OR 1/2 INCH VIDEO CASSETTE PRO
Discusses the presentation of a bandlimited waveform by its time samples.
From The Probability And Random Processes - Linear Systems Series.
Prod-MIOT Dist-MIOT

Sampling, A B 30 MIN
2 INCH VIDEOTAPE J-H
From The Franklin To Frost Series.
Prod-GPITVL Dist-GPITVL

Sampling, A C 30 MIN
2 INCH VIDEOTAPE J-H
See series title for descriptive statement.
From The From Franklin To Frost - Introduction Series.
Prod-MPATI Dist-GPITVL

Sampling, Aliasing And Frequency Response C 28 MIN
3/4 OR 1/2 INCH VIDEO CASSETTE PRO
See series title for descriptive statement.
From The Digital Signal Processing Series.
Prod-GPCV Dist-GPCV

Sampling, Aliasing, And Frequency Response C 28 MIN
3/4 OR 1/2 INCH VIDEO CASSETTE
Demonstrates sampling and aliasing with a sinusoidal signal, sinusoidal response of a digital filter and dependence of frequency response on sampling period.
From The Digital Signal Processing - An Introduction Series.
Prod-MIOT Dist-MIOT

Samson And Delilah C 52 MIN
16MM FILM, 3/4 OR 1/2 IN VIDEO I-C A
Accounts for Samson's great strength by showing that God gave it to him with the condition that he never touch unclean food, never take wine or drink, and never let a razor touch his hair. Re-enacts how Samson meets his downfall when Delilah seduces him and cuts off his hair, rendering him powerless. Stars John Beck and Victor Jory.
From The Greatest Heroes Of The Bible Series.
Prod-LUF Dist-LUF 1979

Samuel Gompers B 20 MIN
2 INCH VIDEOTAPE I
See series title for descriptive statement.
From The Americans All Series.
Prod-DENVPS Dist-GPITVL Prodn-KRMATV

Samuel Slater And The Industrial Revolution C 30 MIN
3/4 OR 1/2 INCH VIDEO CASSETTE C A
See series title for descriptive statement.
From The American Business History Series.
Prod-UMINN Dist-GPITVL 1981

Samurai Toys C 3 MIN
3/4 OR 1/2 INCH VIDEO CASSETTE
Presents a music video guide to psychic self-defense. Features music by the Ballistic Kisses.
Prod-KITCHN Dist-KITCHN

San (Bushmen)–A Series

Prod-DOCEDR Dist-DOCEDR Prodn-MRSHL

Argument About A Marriage, An	018 MIN
Baobab Play	008 MIN
Bitter Melons	030 MIN
Children Throw Toy Assegais	004 MIN
Curing Ceremony, A	008 MIN
Debe's Tantrum	007 MIN
Group Of Women, A	005 MIN
Joking Relationship, A	013 MIN
Kung Bushmen Hunting Equipment	037 MIN
Lion Game, The	004 MIN
Meat Fight, The	014 MIN
Melon Tossing Game, The	015 MIN
Men Bathing	014 MIN
N/um Tchai - The Ceremonial Dance of the Kung	020 MIN
Playing With Scorpions	004 MIN
Tug-Of-War, Bushmen	006 MIN
Wasp Nest, The	020 MIN

San Andreas Fault, The C 21 MIN
16MM FILM, 3/4 OR 1/2 IN VIDEO J-H
Shows the mapping of the geologic history of the fault region and scientists engaged in monitoring current conditions. Explains that elaborate sensing equipment has been distributed along the faultline of San Andreas in an effort to coordinate data about the forces at work in the fault system.
From The Earth Science Program Series.
Prod-EBEC Dist-EBEC 1974

San Antonio Talk, Pt 1 C 60 MIN
3/4 OR 1/2 INCH VIDEO CASSETTE
Covers true happiness, unchanging One in the changing Universe, selfless living, endless nature of desires and coming into life and leaving with nothing.
Prod-IYOGA Dist-IYOGA

San Antonio Talk, Pt 2 C 60 MIN
3/4 OR 1/2 INCH VIDEO CASSETTE
Covers the function of pain, how man has created his own health problems, and the purpose and benefit of yoga communities in correcting health problems and in strengthening the mind.
Prod-IYOGA Dist-IYOGA

San Antonio, The Heart Of Texas C 28 MIN
16MM FILM OPTICAL SOUND
Presents a look at the historic past and colorful present of San Antonio, Texas.
LC NO. 79-701192
Prod-MFCFP Dist-MFCFP 1979

San Diego Children's Center B 20 MIN
3/4 OR 1/2 INCH VIDEO CASSETTE
Shows how the San Diego Children's Center helps the parent adjust to the child being at the center. Includes such children's problems as introversion, mild retardation, hyperactivity and being 'uncontrollable.'
Prod-SDCC Dist-UWISC 1977

San Diego Zoo C 17 MIN
16MM FILM, 3/4 OR 1/2 IN VIDEO P-I A
Visits the San Diego Zoo which covers 100 acres with large outdoor enclosures that simulate natural environments. Shows that the park allows the animals to live as they would in their natural environments.
Prod-LUF Dist-LUF 1970

San Francisco C 13 MIN
16MM FILM, 3/4 OR 1/2 IN VIDEO I-H A
Views San Francisco which has cable cars, hills and unmatched beauty at every turn.
Prod-LUF Dist-LUF 1980

San Francisco - City Of Bridges C 3 MIN
16MM FILM OPTICAL SOUND P-I
Discusses the city of San Francisco, California.
From The Of All Things Series.
Prod-BAILYL Dist-AVED

San Francisco - City Of Hills C 3 MIN
16MM FILM OPTICAL SOUND P-I
Discusses the city of San Francisco, California.
From The Of All Things Series.
Prod-BAILYL Dist-AVED

San Francisco Bay C 53 MIN
1/2 IN VIDEO CASSETTE BETA/VHS
Presents sailing and racing in San Francisco Bay. Combines the shorter titles 'Big Boats,' 'Eyedeen (18) Footers' and 'Heavy Weather Slalom.'
Prod-OFFSHR Dist-OFFSHR

San Francisco Bay Area Filmmakers–A Series
H-C A
Presents interviews with filmmakers working in the San Francisco area.
Prod-DANKAR Dist-DANKAR 1979

Diane Li	030 MIN
Fred Padula	030 MIN
Seth Hill	028 MIN

San Francisco Good Times B 60 MIN
16MM FILM, 3/4 OR 1/2 IN VIDEO
Chronicles life in San Francisco between the years 1968 and 1972 as seen in the pages of Good Times, San Francisco's underground newspaper. Provides a colorful portrait of the culture and lifestyles of the era, including rock music, brown rice, organic gardens, astrology, communes and collectives, and assorted chemical contraband.
Prod-FARE Dist-CNEMAG

San Francisco State Sit-In B 22 MIN
16MM FILM OPTICAL SOUND
Presents a critical account of the spring 1968 student take-over of the Administration Building at San Francisco State College.
Prod-SFN Dist-SFN 1968

San Francisco, The City By The Bay C 20 MIN
3/4 OR 1/2 INCH VIDEO CASSETTE J-C A
Takes viewers to San Francisco. Discusses the gold rush and the 1906 earthquake and shows the cable car, Chinatown and Alcatraz.
LC NO. 82-706785
Prod-AWSS Dist-AWSS 1980

San Jose Dance Theatre/Sam Richardson Profile C 30 MIN
3/4 OR 1/2 INCH VIDEO CASSETTE
See series title for descriptive statement.
From The Kaleidoscope Series.
Prod-KTEHTV Dist-SCCOE

San Juan Islands, The C 26 MIN
16MM FILM OPTICAL SOUND I-J
Presents a family which discovers sites of historical interest and observes the natural beauty of the San Juan islands and waterways of Northwest Washington.
LC NO. 77-709387
Prod-SOUND Dist-SOUND 1970

Sanaguagat - Inuit Masterworks Of 1000 Years C 25 MIN
16MM FILM, 3/4 OR 1/2 IN VIDEO J-C A
Explains that the Inuit are inhabitants of the Artic. Discusses their philosophy and life-style.
Prod-CDIAND Dist-NFBC 1975

Sanctuary C 14 MIN
16MM FILM OPTICAL SOUND
Presents a study of the interaction between wild animals and people at the Okanagan Game Farm near Pentiction, British Columbia. Tells how the farm was designed as an experiment to protect, preserve and perpetuate endangered species.
LC NO. 76-702053
Prod-BRCOL Dist-CTFL Prodn-PACMP 1975

Sanctuary C 58 MIN
3/4 OR 1/2 INCH VIDEO CASSETTE
Observes the new 'underground system' in the United States. This is a network of individuals and organizations providing shelter, food and hope for illegal aliens fleeing oppression.
From The Frontline Series.
Prod-DOCCON Dist-PBS

Sanctuary - The Great Smoky Mountains C 10 MIN
16MM FILM - 3/4 IN VIDEO
Examines the landscape, foliage and wildlife of the Great Smoky Mountains National Park during the changing seasons.
LC NO. 79-708131
Prod-USNPS Dist-USNAC 1979

Sanctuary Of The Sea C 22 MIN
16MM FILM OPTICAL SOUND
Describes in depth the behind the scenes action at Miami Seaquarium, from the capture of certain sea animals to the return of others to the sea.
Prod-MIAMIS Dist-MIAMIS

Sand C 10 MIN
16MM FILM OPTICAL SOUND
Features, without narration, sculptor Saul Leyton creating a sand sculpture at the beach. Shows an assembling crowd which aids in the construction of reclining human figures. Views the impermanence of the creation when an afternoon tide begins to destroy the completed work.
LC NO. 77-701109
Prod-LEYTNS Dist-VIEWFI 1973

Sand C 10 MIN
16MM FILM, 3/4 OR 1/2 IN VIDEO J-C A
Shows the graphic possibilities of one of nature's most ordinary substances, sand. Shows sand images as a medium of expression photographed in moving silhouette to interpret the fa-

ble of Peter and the Wolf as a shadow-world in which a small boy's fear of the dark, the woods and the wolf are confronted and finally resolved.
Prod-PHENIX Dist-PHENIX 1973

Sand C 12 MIN
16MM FILM, 3/4 OR 1/2 IN VIDEO C
Demonstrates how play with sand provides children with new sensory and perceptual experiences including those involving weight, texture and quantity.
From The Early Childhood Education Series.
Prod-MEDIAG Dist-MEDIAG 1976

Sand - The Desert In Motion C 11 MIN
16MM FILM, 3/4 OR 1/2 IN VIDEO I-H
Examines the origin and distribution of desert sands. Pictures deserts of many regions and explains the effects of water, wind and the sharp edges of the grains of sand on the rocky surfaces. Concludes that in some areas man has been able to bring water to the desert and convert sandy wasteland to productive drop-growing soil.
Prod-BYE Dist-PHENIX 1969

Sand And Imagination B 30 MIN
16MM FILM OPTICAL SOUND I-H A
Visits the corning glass works where scientists discuss the analysis of glass structure and properties and demonstrate new developments, such as glass ceramics, photochromic glass and thin-walled and strengthened glass.
Prod-NET Dist-CORGLW 1964

Sand And Snow B 26 MIN
16MM FILM OPTICAL SOUND
Documentary footage of the establishment of the free French government, the successful conclusion of the North African campaign, the Roosevelt-Churchill meeting at Casablanca in 1943 and the Battle of Stalingrad.
From The Winston Churchill - The Valiant Years Series. No. 12
LC NO. FI67-2112
Prod-ABCTV Dist-SG 1961

Sand And Steel B 16 MIN
16MM FILM OPTICAL SOUND
Describes the construction of the Marine airfield at Chu Lai in Vietnam.
LC NO. 74-706234
Prod-USMC Dist-USNAC 1966

Sand Casting C 25 MIN
3/4 OR 1/2 INCH VIDEO CASSETTE H-C A
Discusses aspects of sand casting.
From The Technical Studies Series.
Prod-BBCTV Dist-FI 1981

Sand Casting - An Art Adventure C 10 MIN
16MM FILM, 3/4 OR 1/2 IN VIDEO
Tells how to make original sand castings from simple materials.
From The Art Adventure Series.
Prod-EASY Dist-CORF

Sand Castle, The C 14 MIN
16MM FILM, 3/4 OR 1/2 IN VIDEO K-I
Uses animation to show fantasy creatures transforming sand into a community of sand structures only to have the wind destroy them.
Prod-NFBC Dist-NFBC 1978

Sand County Almanac C 16 MIN
16MM FILM, 3/4 OR 1/2 IN VIDEO J-C A
Presents the writings of Aldo Leopold, a professor of biology who wrote about the natural environment throughout America, but especially his Sand County farm in Wisconsin. Explores Leopold's ideas on ecology and his concept for land use called 'land ethic.'
Prod-JANOFF Dist-PHENIX 1979

Sand Drains C 24 MIN
16MM FILM, 3/4 OR 1/2 IN VIDEO
Explains the sand drain method of consolidating swampy areas for the construction of highways. Uses animation and scenes of an actual project to show preparation of the site, driving the sand drains, placing the control devices and overload, final preparation of the roadway and paving.
LC NO. 82-706143
Prod-USDTFH Dist-USNAC 1965

Sand Dune Erosion Project C 14 MIN
3/4 OR 1/2 INCH VIDEO CASSETTE H A
Points out the value of sand dunes to the environment and to people. Describes the growth pattern of beach grass which helps to control sand dune erosion.
Prod-CUETV Dist-CUNIV

Sand Dunes B 27 MIN
16MM FILM OPTICAL SOUND C A
Outlines stokes law and visualizes transportation by suspension, saltation and traction as being size controlled. Pictures actual sand transport and illustrates development of transverse, barchan and longitudinal dunes and sand avalanches. Summarizes the inter-relationship of wind and sand, as well as water and vegetation.
Prod-UTEX Dist-UTEX 1960

Sand Fishermen C 9 MIN
3/4 OR 1/2 INCH VIDEO CASSETTE
Illustrates the gathering of sand near Bogota with which to make cement by 'fishing' river bottoms. Shows how required sand is necessary for Colombia's skyscrapers and modern roads. No narration.
Prod-IFF Dist-IFF

Sand In Art C 12 MIN
16MM FILM, 3/4 OR 1/2 IN VIDEO
Shows how sand can be molded and combined with different tools and substances to create permanent works of art.
LC NO. 81-707171
Prod-AMBELH Dist-FLMFR 1981

Sand In Art (French) C 12 MIN
16MM FILM, 3/4 OR 1/2 IN VIDEO
Shows how sand can be molded and combined with different tools and substances to create permanent works of art.
Prod-AMBELH Dist-FLMFR 1981

Sand Pebbles, The C 195 MIN
1/2 IN VIDEO CASSETTE (BETA)
Involves the crew of an American gunboat caught between Chinese war lords and foreign powers. Stars Steve McQueen, Richard Crenna and Candice Bergen.
Prod-UNKNWN Dist-BHAWK 1966

Sandbox B 10 MIN
16MM FILM OPTICAL SOUND
A screen adaptation of the play of the same name by Edward Albee. Uses abstract dialogue and setting to comment on contemporary American family relationships and particularly their attitude towards the elderly.
LC NO. 75-703228
Prod-USC Dist-USC 1965

Sandbox, The C 25 MIN
3/4 OR 1/2 INCH VIDEO CASSETTE H-C A
Demonstrates how to make a sandbox and toys that can be used in and around it - a crane, a sand hopper and a dump truck. Shows how to design a model from the original.
From The Blizzard's Wonderful Wooden Toys Series.
Prod-BBCTV Dist-FI

Sandcastles C 30 MIN
16MM FILM OPTICAL SOUND R
Presents psychologist Dr Bruce Narramore explaining the role of Christ in family relationships and communication.
Prod-GF Dist-GF

Sanders Of The River B 80 MIN
16MM FILM OPTICAL SOUND
Depicts the adventures of a black chief who comes to the aid of a British district head in Africa. Stars Paul Robeson and Leslie Banks.
Prod-UNKNWN Dist-REELIM 1935

Sandfly Control C 32 MIN
16MM FILM OPTICAL SOUND
Explains the symptoms and treatment of diseases transmitted by the sandfly. Describes the principles and methods of sanitation essential to control.
LC NO. FIE52-1723
Prod-USA Dist-USNAC 1950

Sandi Mehring - A Special Kind Of Drive C 6 MIN
16MM FILM OPTICAL SOUND
Introduces Sandi Mehring, a bright young woman who found a career as a truckdriver.
Prod-ATA Dist-MTP

Sandia Spinoff C 11 MIN
16MM FILM OPTICAL SOUND H-C
Illustrates the Sandia Laminar flow cleanroom principle with live action and animation. Indicates its industrial and medical applications. Describes an iron plating process and an automated method of producing printed circuits.
LC NO. FIA67-592
Prod-SANDIA Dist-SANDIA 1966

Sanding Machines C 13 MIN
1/2 IN VIDEO CASSETTE BETA/VHS IND
See series title for descriptive statement.
From The Woodworking Power Tools Series.
Prod-RMI Dist-RMI

Sanding Methods C 8 MIN
1/2 IN VIDEO CASSETTE BETA/VHS
Deals with auto body work. Shows proper methods of feathering a repair to eliminate bullseyes.
Prod-RMI Dist-RMI

Sanding Techniques C 14 MIN
1/2 IN VIDEO CASSETTE BETA/VHS
Explains the various methods of sanding a surface for refinishing. Deals with auto body work.
Prod-RMI Dist-RMI

Sandino, Today And Forever C 55 MIN
16MM FILM, 3/4 OR 1/2 IN VIDEO
Studies the tremendous social changes which have taken place in Nicaragua since the overthrow of Somoza as seen through the life of Pedro Pablo, a small farmer and member of a recently founded agricultural cooperative.
Prod-TERCIN Dist-ICARUS 1981

Sandpipers, Pt 1 C 3 MIN
16MM FILM OPTICAL SOUND P-I
Discusses the birds known as sandpipers.
From The Of All Things Series.
Prod-BAILYL Dist-AVED

Sandpipers, Pt 2 C 3 MIN
16MM FILM OPTICAL SOUND P-I
Discusses the birds known as sandpipers.
From The Of All Things Series.
Prod-BAILYL Dist-AVED

Sandra And Her Kids C 28 MIN
16MM FILM, 3/4 OR 1/2 IN VIDEO
Tells of a dynamic woman who has adopted 20 handicapped children from around the world. Reveals how she organized Families For Children, an agency which has handled over 2,000 adoptions.
Prod-CANBC Dist-FLMLIB 1982

Sandra Jamrog, Dr Hans Kraus And Priscilla Tablante C 30 MIN
3/4 OR 1/2 INCH VIDEO CASSETTE
Focuses on exercise for pregnant women. Includes demonstrations.
From The Eye On Dance - Health And Well-Being Of Dancers Series.
Prod-ARTRES Dist-ARTRES

Sands Of Time C 14 MIN
16MM FILM OPTICAL SOUND
Uses extreme closeup and microphotography to provide a view of the manufacturing techniques and skills required in the production of solid state devices and integrated circuits that are revolutionizing many products.
LC NO. 76-702882
Prod-HONEYW Dist-HONEYW 1976

Sandsong C 18 MIN
16MM FILM, 3/4 OR 1/2 IN VIDEO J-C A
Introduces Gerry Lynas, an artist who sculpts in sand at the edge of the sea. Shows him creating a sculpture which is eventually reclaimed by the ocean.
LC NO. 81-706228
Prod-MMMAST Dist-WOMBAT 1981

Sandstone Deposition - Rivers And Deltas C 53 MIN
3/4 OR 1/2 INCH VIDEO CASSETTE IND
See series title for descriptive statement.
From The Basic Geology Series.
Prod-GPCV Dist-GPCV

Sandstone Depostion - Dunes, Beaches, And Submarine Fans C 43 MIN
3/4 OR 1/2 INCH VIDEO CASSETTE IND
See series title for descriptive statement.
From The Basic Geology Series.
Prod-GPCV Dist-GPCV

Sandstone Secrets C 28 MIN
3/4 OR 1/2 INCH VIDEO CASSETTE
Covers the various sampling and observation techniques for the interpretation of sediments.
From The Earth Explored Series.
Prod-BBCTV Dist-PBS

Sandwich Preparation And Presentation C 8 MIN
16MM FILM, 3/4 OR 1/2 IN VIDEO J-C A
Discusses how to achieve variety in sandwiches. Shows the actual preparation of distinctive open and closed sandwiches by a professional. Demonstrates how a clean, efficient sandwich area is organized.
From The Professional Food Preparation And Service Program Series.
Prod-NEM Dist-NEM 1969

Sandwich Preparation And Presentation (German) C 8 MIN
16MM FILM, 3/4 OR 1/2 IN VIDEO J-C A
Discusses how to achieve variety in sandwiches. Shows the actual preparation of distinctive open and closed sandwiches by a professional. Demonstrates how a clean, efficient sandwich area is organized.
From The Professional Food Preparation And Service Program (German) Series.
Prod-NEM Dist-NEM 1969

Sandwich Preparation And Presentation (Spanish) C 8 MIN
16MM FILM, 3/4 OR 1/2 IN VIDEO J-C A
Discusses how to achieve variety in sandwiches. Shows the actual preparation of distinctive open and closed sandwiches by a professional. Demonstrates how a clean, efficient sandwich area is organized.
From The Professional Food Preparation And Service Program (Spanish) Series.
Prod-NEM Dist-NEM 1969

Sandwich Savvy C 11 MIN
3/4 OR 1/2 INCH VIDEO CASSETTE PRO
Examines the basic elements of any sandwich and shows how to build upon these to make a variety, including hearty closed sandwiches, canapes, and Scandinavian-style open-faced sandwiches.
Prod-CULINA Dist-CULINA

Sandwich Stuff C 15 MIN
16MM FILM, 3/4 OR 1/2 IN VIDEO P-I
Covers the manufacture of each ingredient of a peanut butter and jam sandwich. Children's observations informs viewer about each stage in process.
From The Let's Visit Series.
Prod-BCNFL Dist-BCNFL 1984

Sandwiches - Dinner, Tea And Canape, Scandinavian C 26 MIN
3/4 OR 1/2 INCH VIDEO CASSETTE PRO
Shows how to make ham on rye, turkey club, grilled cheese and Reuben sandwiches, also tunafish concolaise canapes, salami canapes twisted into cornucopias and tea sandwiches. Emphasizes Scandinavian-style sandwiches.
Prod-CULINA Dist-CULINA

Sandy And Madeleine's Family C 30 MIN
16MM FILM, 3/4 OR 1/2 IN VIDEO C A
Documents a child custody case where children were awarded to mothers even though they openly admitted their homosexual relationship. Anthropologist Margaret Mead expresses her view that the welfare of of the children will depend on the love and warmth of their family environment and not on the sexual orientation of the parents.
Prod-FARELS Dist-MMRC 1973

Sandy Wilson C
3/4 OR 1/2 INCH VIDEO CASSETTE

Portrays Sandy Wilson, British Columbian filmmaker with interviews and film clips.
From The Filmmakers' Showcase Series.
Prod-CANFDW Dist-CANFDW

Sanford Meisner - The Theater's Best-Kept Secret C 56 MIN
3/4 OR 1/2 INCH VIDEO CASSETTE
Portrays acting teacher Sanford Meisner. Interviews Meisner students such as Robert Duvall, Tony Randall and Joanne Woodward.
Prod-FOTH Dist-FOTH

Sanitary Inspection, The C 18 MIN
3/4 OR 1/2 INCH VIDEO CASSETTE PRO
Looks at a foodservice establishment through the eyes of a sanitarinspector. The building is inspected inside and out, and procedures are observed to make sure food handlers are following the rules for sound hygiene.
Prod-CULINA Dist-CULINA

Sanitary Landfill - One Part Earth To Four Parts Refuse C 24 MIN
3/4 INCH VIDEO CASSETTE
Presents details for the design and operation of sanitary landfills. Issued in 1969 as a motion picture.
LC NO. 78-706325
Prod-USBSM Dist-USNAC 1978

Sanitary Landfill - You're The Operator C 22 MIN
16MM FILM OPTICAL SOUND
Demonstrates that a sanitary landfill can be a good neighbor and a community asset. Illustrates the careful planning and precise techniques required to achieve maximum standards.
LC NO. 75-701731
Prod-USEPA Dist-USNAC 1973

Sanitary Landfill - You're The Operator (Spanish) C 22 MIN
16MM FILM, 3/4 OR 1/2 IN VIDEO
Demonstrates that a sanitary landfill can be a community asset. Illustrates the careful planning and precise techniques required to achieve maximum standards.
Prod-USEPA Dist-USNAC 1979

Sanitation C
3/4 OR 1/2 INCH VIDEO CASSETTE
See series title for descriptive statement.
From The Pest Control Technology Correspondence Course Series.
Prod-PUAVC Dist-PUAVC

Sanitation - Rodent And Insect Control C 10 MIN
16MM FILM, 3/4 OR 1/2 IN VIDEO
Discusses the ways in which food service workers can control and eliminate rodent and insect infestation of food preparation areas.
From The Professional Food Preparation And Service Program Series.
Prod-NEM Dist-NEM 1972

Sanitation - Rodent And Insect Control (Spanish) C 8 MIN
16MM FILM, 3/4 OR 1/2 IN VIDEO J-C A
Discusses the ways in which food service workers can control and eliminate rodent and insect infestations of food preparation areas.
From The Professional Food Preparation And Service Program (Spanish) Series.
Prod-NEM Dist-NEM

Sanitation And Food Safety - K J Baker, MS C 32 MIN
3/4 INCH VIDEO CASSETTE PRO
Discusses the extent of the foodborne illness program, covering the causes as well as the preventive measures that can be taken to reduce contamination of food.
From The Food And Nutrition Seminars For Health Professionals Series.
LC NO. 78-706166
Prod-USFDA Dist-USNAC 1976

Sanitation And Hygiene - Basic Rules C
16MM FILM, 3/4 OR 1/2 IN VIDEO
Emphasizes basic rules of kitchen sanitation and hygiene including how to handle potentially hazardous foods including fowl, seafood and custards. Illustrates control of pests, personal cleanliness and proper techniques for cooling, storage and refrigeration. Emphasizes the importance of clean hands and proper washing methods.
From The Professional Food Preparation And Service Programs Series.
Prod-NEM Dist-NEM 1983

Sanitation And Hygiene - Why The Importance C
16MM FILM, 3/4 OR 1/2 IN VIDEO
Introduces kitchen sanitation and hygiene. Shows biological reasons for sanitation and hygiene and the conditions for controlling bacterial growth. Explains the danger of bacteria, how bacteria spread from place to place and how their growth can be accelerated or retarded. Demonstrates how hands, clothing, kitchen tools, unclean surfaces, rats, roaches and flies can carry germs.
From The Professional Food Preparation And Service Programs Series.
Prod-NEM Dist-NEM 1983

Sanitation And Hygiene For Dining Room Personnel (Rev Ed) C
16MM FILM, 3/4 OR 1/2 IN VIDEO
Demonstrates techniques of sanitary food handling for dining room personnel. Emphasizes the importance of the servers' personal cleanliness, hygiene and grooming. Includes sanitary practices necessary before reporting for work, as well as dining practices that inhibit growth of germs.
From The Professional Food Preparation And Service Programs Series.
Prod-NEM Dist-NEM 1983

Sanitation For Food Service Workers / Housekeeping And Safety In The... C
3/4 OR 1/2 INCH VIDEO CASSETTE
Describes germs that can cause food-borne disease, shows how to keep the kitchen and equipment clean and suggests practical assembly-line methods that function best for preparing patient trays and/or table service.
From The 'We Care' Series. Pt. 7
Prod-VTRI Dist-VTRI

Sanjo - Korean Improvisational Music C 31 MIN
16MM FILM, 3/4 OR 1/2 IN VIDEO
Presents a performance of sanjo, an improvisational style of music that developed in southwestern Korea.
Prod-UWASH Dist-UWASHP

Santa Barbara - Everybody's Mistake C 30 MIN
16MM FILM, 3/4 OR 1/2 IN VIDEO H-C A
Examines the controversies behind the two-million gallon oil leak off the shore of California in 1969. Points out that the smog created by the oil is killing pine trees 6,000 feet above sea level.
From The Our Vanishing Wilderness Series. No. 6
LC NO. 80-707023
Prod-NETRC Dist-IU 1970

Santa Claus C 15 MIN
3/4 OR 1/2 INCH VIDEO CASSETTE P
See series title for descriptive statement.
From The Let's Draw Series.
Prod-OCPS Dist-AITECH Prodn-KOKHTV 1976

Santa Claus Has Blue Eyes (French) B 45 MIN
16MM FILM OPTICAL SOUND
Features one of two short stories combined in the film, Bad Company. Tells of a youth in a provincial French town who finally lands a job posing as Santa Claus at Christmas time.
Prod-NYFLMS Dist-NYFLMS 1966

Santa Claus Will Soon Be Here C 19 MIN
3/4 OR 1/2 INCH VIDEO CASSETTE P-I
Introduces the musical rest.
From The USS Rhythm Series.
Prod-ARKETV Dist-AITECH 1977

Santa Fe C 16 MIN
16MM FILM - 3/4 IN VIDEO
Discusses Santa Fe, New Mexico, in terms of its Indian, Spanish and Mexican heritage. Interweaves historical scenes and scenes of 1970's to show the richness of the tradition and heritage of the Southwest.
LC NO. 77-706000
Prod-USIA Dist-USNAC Prodn-RASHBP 1974

Santa Fe And The Trail X 20 MIN
16MM FILM, 3/4 OR 1/2 IN VIDEO I-J
Pictures life in the Spanish settlements of the old Southwest. Shows the impact of the American migration on the region in the early 1800's. Explains the fusion of the American and Spanish cultures which gives the Southwest its unique character.
Prod-EBF Dist-EBEC 1963

Santa Fe Trail C 16 MIN
16MM FILM, 3/4 OR 1/2 IN VIDEO I-C A
Traces the history of the Santa Fe Trail.
Prod-CALPRO Dist-PHENIX 1978

Santa Monica Project, The C 30 MIN
16MM FILM OPTICAL SOUND
Depicts the engineered classroom for educationally handicapped children as described in Dr Frank W Hewett's book, 'THE EMOTIONALLY DISTURBED CHILD IN THE CLASSROOM.'
Prod-NYSED Dist-NYSED

Santa Monica Project, The C 28 MIN
16MM FILM, 3/4 OR 1/2 IN VIDEO H-C A
Describes the hierarchy of educational goals, means of promoting attention and response for emotionally disturbed children.
Prod-AIMS Dist-AIMS

Santa's Toys C 8 MIN
16MM FILM, 3/4 OR 1/2 IN VIDEO K-I
Presents an animated film which tells the story of Christmas Eve. Shows how the toys that Santa Claus has left come to life, decorate the tree, fill the stockings and make everything ready for Christmas day.
Prod-DISNEY Dist-WDEMCO 1974

Santiago's Ark C 47 MIN
16MM FILM, 3/4 OR 1/2 IN VIDEO P-J
Describes the attempts of a young Puerto Rican boy to build a ship on a tenement roof.
Prod-ACW Dist-CAROUF

Santiago's Ark (Captioned) C 47 MIN
16MM FILM, 3/4 OR 1/2 IN VIDEO P-J
Shows that dreams, even in a ghetto, can become reality with encouragement and persistence. Tells the story of a Puerto Rican boy who inspires a Spanish Harlem neighborhood by building a boat on a tenement rooftop. Follows the boy, Santiago, as he gathers materials from the street and alleys and pursues his project with fervor.
Prod-ACW Dist-CAROUF 1972

Sao Paulo High Rise Building Fires B
3/4 OR 1/2 INCH VIDEO CASSETTE
Prod-NFPA Dist-NFPA

Saps At Sea B 61 MIN
16MM FILM OPTICAL SOUND
Presents the story of two hard-working homtesters who decide they need a vacation and buy a leaky sail boat for a cruise.
Prod-ROACH Dist-BHAWK 1940

SAR Mission Coordinator - Search And Rescue C 27 MIN
16MM FILM OPTICAL SOUND
Describes how a mission coordinator in the Air Force organizes and conducts an inland search and rescue mission. Shows how search crews are instructed on the types of flight patterns and the areas to be covered and demonstrates a successful rescue.
LC NO. 74-706235
Prod-USAF Dist-USNAC 1966

Sara And Maybelle B 10 MIN
16MM FILM, 3/4 OR 1/2 IN VIDEO A
Presents two members from the original Carter family singing 'Sweet Fern' and 'Solid Gone,' two songs which demonstrate their famous guitar picking style and harmony singing.
Prod-CNEMAG Dist-CNEMAG 1981

Sara Has Down's Syndrome B 17 MIN
16MM FILM OPTICAL SOUND
Shows a six-year-old child suffering from Down's syndrome as she interacts with her family and works in school. Shows how her family copes with this form of mongoloidism.
From The Exploring Childhood Series.
LC NO. 74-702512
Prod-USOCHD Dist-EDC 1974

Sara's Summer Of The Swans C 33 MIN
16MM FILM, 3/4 OR 1/2 IN VIDEO
Tells how a teenage girl gains new insight into herself and her family when her five-year-old brother gets lost. Based on the book The Summer Of The Swans by Betsy Byars. Originally shown on the television series ABC Afterschool Specials.
From The Teenage Years Series.
LC NO. 79-707360
Prod-TAHSEM Dist-TIMLIF 1976

Sarah C 27 MIN
16MM FILM OPTICAL SOUND
Tells the story of a woman in her forties who invites a man to her home, along with her family, for Thanksgiving. Shows her family being scornful and abusive and her turning to a friend for understanding. Tells of a woman seeking affirmation in mid-life.
Prod-BLKFMF Dist-BLKFMF

Sarah C 10 MIN
16MM FILM, 3/4 OR 1/2 IN VIDEO T
Examines the problems which arise between a teacher, a pupil and a counselor over an issue of confidential information.
From The One To Grow On Series.
LC NO. 80-706190
Prod-NIMH Dist-USNAC Prodn-UCLA 1979

Sarah At 2-1/2 C 17 MIN
16MM FILM OPTICAL SOUND
Portrays the talents and interests of a child at age two and a half years.
Prod-URBNIM Dist-URBNIM 1978

Sarah Rudner C 30 MIN
3/4 OR 1/2 INCH VIDEO CASSETTE
Features dancer/choreographer Sarah Rudner in three video variations.
From The Doris Chase Dance Series.
Prod-CHASED Dist-CHASED

Sarah Vaughn C 58 MIN
3/4 OR 1/2 INCH VIDEO CASSETTE
See series title for descriptive statement.
From The Evenings At Pops Series.
Prod-WGBHTV Dist-PBS 1978

Sarah Wilson C 8 MIN
16MM FILM - 3/4 IN VIDEO
Focuses on a health office personnel meeting and the conflicts which arise in discussing business. Presents an open-end situation aimed at promoting guided group discussion.
Prod-USPHS Dist-USNAC 1972

Sarah's War C 30 MIN
16MM FILM OPTICAL SOUND
Presents the story of a young woman who is separated from her husband. Shows that when obliged to make money to support herself and her child, she becomes involved in crime and ends up in prison.
LC NO. 74-703439
Prod-JUNGR Dist-CFDEVC 1973

Sarasponda C 15 MIN
3/4 OR 1/2 INCH VIDEO CASSETTE P-I
See series title for descriptive statement.
From The Ready, Sing Series.
Prod-ARKETV Dist-AITECH 1979

Sarcoma C 55 MIN
3/4 INCH VIDEO CASSETTE
Describes the different ways soft-tissue sarcomas are treated. Shows how they were previously managed with radical surgery and how physicians are now combining radiotherapy with more conservative surgery.
Prod-UTAHTI Dist-UTAHTI

Sardines From Maine - Down East Style C 13 MIN
16MM FILM OPTICAL SOUND P-H A
Explains how Maine sardines are prepared in many parts of the country and in various seasons of the year.
Prod-USBCF Dist-USNOAA

Sargent Swell C 16 MIN
16MM FILM OPTICAL SOUND P-C

Presents a satire involving a Canadian mountie, a gay Indian chief, an alcoholic father and tomboy daughter all living up to their expected roles in the Wild West.
Prod-JANMEN Dist-CFS 1973

Sartre, Pt 1 - Existentialism, Development From Kierkegaard And Nietzsche C 30 MIN
3/4 INCH VIDEO CASSETTE
Discusses the existentialist theory and its development from Kierkegaard and Nietzsche.
From The From Socrates To Sartre Series.
Prod-MDCPB Dist-MDCPB

Sartre, Pt 2 - Bad Faith, Ethics, Freedom Dread And Nothingness C 30 MIN
3/4 INCH VIDEO CASSETTE
Examines the concepts of bad faith, ethics, freedom, dread and nothingness in the work of Sartre.
From The From Socrates To Sartre Series.
Prod-MDCPB Dist-MDCPB

Sartre, Pt 3 - Metaphysics, Influence Of Descartes, Hegel, Husserle C 30 MIN
3/4 INCH VIDEO CASSETTE
Discusses metaphysics in the philosophy of Sartre. Considers the influence of Hegel, Descartes and Husserle.
From The From Socrates To Sartre Series.
Prod-MDCPB Dist-MDCPB

Sartre, Pt 4 - Masochism And Sadism, Extremities Of Hatred C 30 MIN
3/4 INCH VIDEO CASSETTE
Describes the concepts of masochism and sadism in the philosophy of Sartre.
From The From Socrates To Sartre Series.
Prod-MDCPB Dist-MDCPB

Sarvapalli Radhakrishnan - President Of India C 94 MIN
16MM FILM OPTICAL SOUND I-C A
Presents a biographical documentary on ex-President Sarvapalli Radhakrishnan. Portrays his earlier life as a Professor of philosophy, educationist, writer, lecturer and diplomat. Includes passages spoken by the President himself on various occasions.
Prod-INDIA Dist-NEDINF

SAS - Understanding Its Capabilities C 20 MIN
3/4 OR 1/2 INCH VIDEO CASSETTE
Provides potential SAS (statistical analysis system) users with an understanding of what SAS is and what SAS can do for them and gives a unique way of thinking about the language of SAS as an introduction to further training they'll need to become effective users.
Prod-DELTAK Dist-DELTAK

Sasha, Yasha, Yakov And The Wolf C 11 MIN
16MM FILM, 3/4 OR 1/2 IN VIDEO K-P
Uses animation to describe the adventures of a hare, a pig, and a little black goat.
Prod-PSFS Dist-CAROUF

Saskatchewan - Faces, Places, Memories C 13 MIN
16MM FILM OPTICAL SOUND
Shows Saskatchewan as it might be discovered by a family on a camping vacation.
LC NO. 74-701650
Prod-SASKAT Dist-CTFL Prodn-ARMADL 1973

Saskatchewan Off The Straight And Narrow C 14 MIN
16MM FILM OPTICAL SOUND
Presents a travelog of tourist sites in Saskatchewan.
LC NO. 77-702633
Prod-DTRRS Dist-CTFL Prodn-ARMADL 1976

SAT Exam Preparation—A Series

Offers preparation for the student planning to take the SAT exam, in a ten module School Version, or the Home Version with the first six modules.
Prod-KRLSOF Dist-KRLSOF 1985

Math - All Skill Areas And Problem Types	120 MIN
Math - Quantitative Comparison	120 MIN
Model Examination I With Explanations	120 MIN
Model Examination II With Explanations	120 MIN
Model Examination III With Explanations	120 MIN
Preparing Your Students For The SAT	120 MIN
Reading Comprehension	120 MIN
SAT Overview And Test Taking Strategy	120 MIN
Test Of Standard Written English	120 MIN
Vocabulary And Word Analogies	120 MIN

SAT Overview And Test Taking Strategy C 120 MIN
3/4 OR 1/2 INCH VIDEO CASSETTE
See series title for descriptive statement.
From The SAT Exam Preparation Series.
Prod-KRLSOF Dist-KRLSOF 1985

SAT Review - Math C
1/2 IN VIDEO CASSETTE BETA/VHS H
Reviews the math skills tested on SAT and PSAT exams. Offers creative problem-solving and test-taking techniques, time-saving hints and multiple-choice strategies.
Prod-GA Dist-GA

SAT Review - Verbal C
1/2 IN VIDEO CASSETTE BETA/VHS H
Reviews the verbal skills tested on SAT and PSAT exams. Offers creative problem-solving and test-taking techniques, time-saving hints and multiple-choice strategies.
Prod-GA Dist-GA

SAT/ACT Examination Video Review—A Series
H A

Discusses the importance of test scores and shows how to get the most out of subject matter knowledge when taking the SAT/ACT exam.
Prod-COMEX Dist-COMEX

Mathematics Reivew, Tape 5	045 MIN
Mathematics Review, Tape 1	045 MIN
Mathematics Review, Tape 2	045 MIN
Mathematics Review, Tape 3	045 MIN
Mathematics Review, Tape 4	045 MIN
Mathematics Review, Tape 6	045 MIN
Mathematics Review, Tape 7	045 MIN
Verbal Review, Tape 1	045 MIN
Verbal Review, Tape 2	045 MIN
Verbal Review, Tape 3	045 MIN
Verbal Review, Tape 4	045 MIN
Verbal Review, Tape 5	045 MIN
Verbal Review, Tape 6	045 MIN
Verbal Review, Tape 7	045 MIN
Verbal Review, Tape 8	045 MIN

Satan In The Church C 9 MIN
16MM FILM OPTICAL SOUND C A R
Uses animation to show a battle of good and evil, as the Devil disrupts a group of monks who are worshipping in a church sanctuary. Shows how the mass becomes an orgiastic affair with Satan emerging victorious.
LC NO. 72-700406
Prod-IVANOV Dist-MMA 1971

Satan On The Loose C 30 MIN
16MM FILM OPTICAL SOUND R
Tells of the early life of former New York hoodlum, Nicky Cruz. Traces his upbringing in Puerto Rico where his parents were Satan worshippers.
Prod-GF Dist-GF

Satan's Brew (German) C 110 MIN
16MM FILM OPTICAL SOUND
Presents a comedy centering around a so-called revolutionary poet who hasn't written a word in two years. Explains that he will do anything to get money or to write again. Directed by Rainer Werner Fassbinder. With English subtitles.
Prod-UNKNWN Dist-NYFLMS 1976

Satellite Aids Education C 2 MIN
16MM FILM OPTICAL SOUND
Describes how a satellite can relay educational television to remote areas of the world.
Prod-ALLFP Dist-NSTA 1973

Satellite And Earth Station Technology C 30 MIN
3/4 OR 1/2 INCH VIDEO CASSETTE
Introduces the components of the satellite and earth station and explores the impact of future technology on communications satellite systems.
From The Communications Satellite Systems Series.
Prod-DELTAK Dist-DELTAK

Satellite Applications And Demand Assignment For Data, Pt I C 50 MIN
3/4 OR 1/2 INCH VIDEO CASSETTE C
Includes satellite cost trends, information capacity, purely random access, the ALOHA technique, ALOHA channel capacity and delay and the Slotted ALOHA channel.
From The Packet Switching Networks Series.
Prod-AMCEE Dist-AMCEE

Satellite Applications And Demand Assignment For Data, Pt 1 C 53 MIN
3/4 OR 1/2 INCH VIDEO CASSETTE
See series title for descriptive statement.
From The Packet Switching Series.
Prod-MIOT Dist-MIOT

Satellite Applications And Demand Assignment For Data, Pt 2 C 55 MIN
3/4 OR 1/2 INCH VIDEO CASSETTE
See series title for descriptive statement.
From The Packet Switching Series.
Prod-MIOT Dist-MIOT

Satellite Applications And Demand Assignment For Data, Pt II C 50 MIN
3/4 OR 1/2 INCH VIDEO CASSETTE C
Covers satellite capacity reservation techniques, terrestrial packet radio, carrier sense multiple access (CSMA), integrated satellite/terrestrial networks and random network optimization.
From The Packet Switching Networks Series.
Prod-AMCEE Dist-AMCEE

Satellite House Call C 21 MIN
16MM FILM, 3/4 OR 1/2 IN VIDEO H-C A
Documents how the NASA experimental satellite, ATS-1 is used to provide a voice link between native health aides in central Alaska and a consulting doctor at the Indian Health Service Hospital at Tanana.
Prod-STANDC Dist-UCEMC 1975

Satellite Links - Problems And Solutions C 30 MIN
3/4 OR 1/2 INCH VIDEO CASSETTE
Discusses the problems of delay, outages, noise, satellite failures and security risks in satellite links. Points out that good design can overcome all of them. 81-403.
From The Communications Satellite Systems Series.
Prod-DELTAK Dist-DELTAK

Satellite Networks C 50 MIN
3/4 OR 1/2 INCH VIDEO CASSETTE PRO
Covers satellite communications. Describes properties and configurations, as well as centralized and distributed reservation.
From The Communication Networks Series.
Prod-AMCEE Dist-AMCEE

Satellite Rescue In Space C
3/4 OR 1/2 INCH VIDEO CASSETTE P-J
Introduces children to the marvels of the world.
Prod-CNVID Dist-KTVID

Satellite TV - Birth Of An Industry, Pts 1 And 2 C 56 MIN
3/4 OR 1/2 INCH VIDEO CASSETTE
Presented by Liza Bear and Michael McClard in conjunction with Willoughby Sharp.
Prod-ARTINC Dist-ARTINC

Satellites B 30 MIN
2 INCH VIDEOTAPE J
See series title for descriptive statement.
From The Investigating The World Of Science, Unit 5 - Life In The Universe Series.
Prod-MPATI Dist-GPITVL

Satellites - Reporters In Space C 20 MIN
2 INCH VIDEOTAPE I
See series title for descriptive statement.
From The Exploring With Science, Unit VI - Flight Series.
Prod-MPATI Dist-GPITVL

Satellites And Men In Orbit (2nd Ed) C 24 MIN
16MM FILM, 3/4 OR 1/2 IN VIDEO I-C A
Discusses 'near space,' including atmosphere, the effects of gravity and the physics of achieving orbit. Describes the operation, discoveries and types of satellites and depicts man in orbit.
From The Man Into Space - The Story Of Rockets And Space Science Series.
Prod-ACI Dist-AIMS 1974

Satellites Of The Sun C 12 MIN
16MM FILM, 3/4 OR 1/2 IN VIDEO I-C A
Uses animation in order to explore the characteristics of the solar system.
Prod-NFBC Dist-PHENIX 1975

Satiemania C 15 MIN
16MM FILM, 3/4 OR 1/2 IN VIDEO H-C A
Presents complex animated images set to the music of Erik Satie and which change in moods from satirical to abrasive to introspective to lyrical. Uses cel animation to present the themes art movements, morality and values in Western civilization, and the divergence between men and women.
LC NO. 81-707638
Prod-ZAGREB Dist-IFB 1981

Satire C 30 MIN
2 INCH VIDEOTAPE J-H
Discusses satire in American literature.
From The From Franklin To Frost - Humor Series.
Prod-MPATI Dist-GPITVL

Satisfaction - A Job Well Done C 9 MIN
16MM FILM, 3/4 OR 1/2 IN VIDEO C A
Interviews a master shipbuilder and illustrates how a master craftsman motivates his employees by setting high standards, giving continuous honest feedback and providing encouragement and praise. Originally shown on the CBS program On The Road With Charles Kuralt.
LC NO. 84-700176
Prod-CBSNEW Dist-SALENG 1984

Satsang With Sri Swami Satchidananda, SAYVA C 50 MIN
3/4 OR 1/2 INCH VIDEO CASSETTE
Answers questions on how to lose attachment to the body and how to increase faith.
Prod-IYOGA Dist-IYOGA

Satsang With Sri Swami Satchidananda, SAYVA C 50 MIN
3/4 OR 1/2 INCH VIDEO CASSETTE
Answers questions on how to increase faith and how can one conquer restlessness.
Prod-IYOGA Dist-IYOGA

Satsang With Sri Swami Satchidananda, SAYVA C 52 MIN
3/4 OR 1/2 INCH VIDEO CASSETTE
Explains that both pleasure and pain are one's own creation. Speaks on reincarnation and the three rare qualities.
Prod-IYOGA Dist-IYOGA

Satsang With Sri Swami Satchidananda, SAYVA C 50 MIN
3/4 OR 1/2 INCH VIDEO CASSETTE
Answers questions on understanding a friend's unhappiness. Tells story of a blind beggar calling for God.
Prod-IYOGA Dist-IYOGA

Satsang With Sri Swami Satchidanada, Washington DC C 50 MIN
3/4 OR 1/2 INCH VIDEO CASSETTE
Explains we are essentially one in spirit and variety is for our fun. Tells about our first and foremost duty in life.
Prod-IYOGA Dist-IYOGA

Satsang With Sri Swami Satchidanada, Washington DC C 50 MIN
3/4 OR 1/2 INCH VIDEO CASSETTE
Explains how religions are different approaches in different languages to help us recognize our spiritual oneness.
Prod-IYOGA Dist-IYOGA

Satsang With Sri Gurudev SAY VA C
3/4 OR 1/2 INCH VIDEO CASSETTE
Presents Sri Gurudev speaking on realization, being God's instrument and the present state of the world.
Prod-IYOGA Dist-IYOGA

Satsang With Sri Gurudev SAY VA C 60 MIN
3/4 OR 1/2 INCH VIDEO CASSETTE
Presents Sri Gurudev speaking on work and play and the story of the pariah farm worker going to a festival.
Prod-IYOGA Dist-IYOGA

Satsang With Sri Gurudev SAY VA C 60 MIN
3/4 OR 1/2 INCH VIDEO CASSETTE
Presents Sri Gurudev speaking on how to share peace within marriage and how to determine if one's decisions are selfish.
Prod-IYOGA Dist-IYOGA

Satsang With Sri Gurudev SAY VA C 60 MIN
3/4 OR 1/2 INCH VIDEO CASSETTE
Presents Sri Gurudev speaking on the use of the mantra. Unveils an original oil painting of the LOTUS.
Prod-IYOGA Dist-IYOGA

Satsang With Sri Gurudev SAY VA C 60 MIN
3/4 OR 1/2 INCH VIDEO CASSETTE
Presents Sri Gurudev speaking on love and peace and how one can exercise one's will without developing egoism.
Prod-IYOGA Dist-IYOGA

Satsang With Sri Gurudev SAY VA C 60 MIN
3/4 OR 1/2 INCH VIDEO CASSETTE
Presents Sri Gurudev speaking on the goal and the planning of one's journey to reach the goal.
Prod-IYOGA Dist-IYOGA

Satsang With Sri Gurudev Satchidananda Ashram Yogaville East C 60 MIN
3/4 OR 1/2 INCH VIDEO CASSETTE
Addresses vegetarian cats and dogs, value of abstaining from meat, alcohol and cigarettes, growing spiritually at one's own speed and dangers of acquiring supernatural powers with an impure attitude.
Prod-IYOGA Dist-IYOGA

Satsang With Sri Gurudev Satchidananda Ashram Yogaville Virginia C 60 MIN
3/4 OR 1/2 INCH VIDEO CASSETTE
Presents Sri Gurudev speaking on prostrating to the Guru and rising above the pleasure and pain of worldly happiness.
Prod-IYOGA Dist-IYOGA

Satsang With Sri Gurudev SAYE C 30 MIN
3/4 OR 1/2 INCH VIDEO CASSETTE
Presents Sri Gurudev speaking on Lord Jesus, the crucifixion and ahimsa, simplicity, control of the mind and death of John Lennon.
Prod-IYOGA Dist-IYOGA

Satsang With Sri Swami Satchindananda SAYVA C 50 MIN
3/4 OR 1/2 INCH VIDEO CASSETTE
Explains the unifying aspect of diversity. Explains all religions have the same essence and goal.
Prod-IYOGA Dist-IYOGA

Satsang With Sri Swami Satchidananda, SAYVA C 50 MIN
3/4 OR 1/2 INCH VIDEO CASSETTE
Explains Navaratri. Talks tamas, rajas, sattwa, suddhamaya and the pure and impure gunas.
Prod-IYOGA Dist-IYOGA

Satsang With Sri Swami Satchindananda SAYVA C 50 MIN
3/4 OR 1/2 INCH VIDEO CASSETTE
Answers questions regarding ego and the relationship between myself and yourself.
Prod-IYOGA Dist-IYOGA

Satsang With Sri Swami Satchidananda, SAYVA C 50 MIN
3/4 OR 1/2 INCH VIDEO CASSETTE
Answers questions regarding personal guidance of the inner guru. Tells two stories of two Indian saints adamant in their vows.
Prod-IYOGA Dist-IYOGA

Satsang With Sri Swami Satchidananda, SAYVA C 50 MIN
3/4 OR 1/2 INCH VIDEO CASSETTE
Speaks about education and use of the brain. Refers to memorizing the Vedas and the capacity of the mind. Tells a story of the Banyan tree.
Prod-IYOGA Dist-IYOGA

Satsang With Sri Swami Satchidananda, SAYVA C 50 MIN
3/4 OR 1/2 INCH VIDEO CASSETTE
Answers questions on how a parent should deal with a child who no longer enjoys attending satsang and other ashram activities.
Prod-IYOGA Dist-IYOGA

Satsang With Sri Swami Satchidananda, SAYVA C 50 MIN
3/4 OR 1/2 INCH VIDEO CASSETTE
Answers questions regarding the pause between birth and death. Asks how one builds devotion in God and Guru.
Prod-IYOGA Dist-IYOGA

Satsang With Sri Swami Satchidananda, SAYVA C 50 MIN
3/4 OR 1/2 INCH VIDEO CASSETTE
Addresses indebtedness and giving what you can. Talks about making offerings to ancestors.
Prod-IYOGA Dist-IYOGA

Satsang With Sri Swami Satchidananda, SAYVA C 50 MIN
3/4 OR 1/2 INCH VIDEO CASSETTE
Answers questions on the benefit of going to school. Tells of a king who was trying to become a spiritual disciple.
Prod-IYOGA Dist-IYOGA

Satsang With Sri Swami Satchidananda, SAYVA C 50 MIN
3/4 OR 1/2 INCH VIDEO CASSETTE
Presents Sri Gurudev speaking about cleaning your attachments. Tells about the two times God laughs.
Prod-IYOGA Dist-IYOGA

Satsang With Sri Swami Satchidananda, SAYVA C 50 MIN
3/4 OR 1/2 INCH VIDEO CASSETTE
Answers questions on controlling the senses and how important is body purity through diet.
Prod-IYOGA Dist-IYOGA

Satsang With Sri Swami Satchidananda C 30 MIN
3/4 OR 1/2 INCH VIDEO CASSETTE
Answers questions regarding deities existing on this plane on just in the mind. Explains how God is superior, unconditional love.
Prod-IYOGA Dist-IYOGA

Satsang With Sri Swami Satchidananda SAY VA C 30 MIN
3/4 OR 1/2 INCH VIDEO CASSETTE
Presents Sri Gurudev speaking on student-Teacher relationship and what to do with a mind that vacillates.
Prod-IYOGA Dist-IYOGA

Satsang With Sri Swami Satchidananda SAY VA C 45 MIN
3/4 OR 1/2 INCH VIDEO CASSETTE
Presents Sri Gurudev giving his first satsang after returning from 1981 India trip.
Prod-IYOGA Dist-IYOGA

Satsang With Sri Swami Satchidananda SAY VA C 60 MIN
3/4 OR 1/2 INCH VIDEO CASSETTE
Presents Sri Gurudev speaking on the role of parents.
Prod-IYOGA Dist-IYOGA

Satsang With Sri Swami Satchidananda SAY VA C 100 MIN
3/4 OR 1/2 INCH VIDEO CASSETTE
Presents Sri Gurudev speaking on the purpose of human endeavor, renunciation and attachment and the importance of knowing the goal of one's path.
Prod-IYOGA Dist-IYOGA

Satsang With Sri Swami Satchidananda SAY VA C 60 MIN
3/4 OR 1/2 INCH VIDEO CASSETTE
Presents Sri Gurudev speaking on the necessity and benefits of doing the yoga practices.
Prod-IYOGA Dist-IYOGA

Satsang With Sri Swami Satchidananda SAY VA C 30 MIN
3/4 OR 1/2 INCH VIDEO CASSETTE
Presents Sri Gurudev speaking on faith, how to prevent the ego from growing when one surrenders to God and benefit of group sanga.
Prod-IYOGA Dist-IYOGA

Satsang With Sri Swami Satchidananda SAY VA C 60 MIN
3/4 OR 1/2 INCH VIDEO CASSETTE
Presents Sri Gurudev speaking on how to receive guidance for making decisions and how the Guru differs from God.
Prod-IYOGA Dist-IYOGA

Satsang With Sri Swami Satchidananda SAY VA C 30 MIN
3/4 OR 1/2 INCH VIDEO CASSETTE
Presents Sri Gurudev speaking on how to deal with negative energy and the nature of the physical universe as we perceive it.
Prod-IYOGA Dist-IYOGA

Satsang With Sri Swami Satchidananda SAY VA C 60 MIN
3/4 OR 1/2 INCH VIDEO CASSETTE
Presents Sri Gurudev speaking on Saint Pulusar who built a mental temple, work, attitude and fatigue.
Prod-IYOGA Dist-IYOGA

Satsang With Sri Swami Satchidananda SAY VA C 60 MIN
3/4 OR 1/2 INCH VIDEO CASSETTE
Presents Sri Gurudev speaking on how a spiritual seeker makes progress, nature of a contented mind, discrimination and helping one's parents.
Prod-IYOGA Dist-IYOGA

Satsang With Sri Swami Satchidananda SAY VA C 60 MIN
3/4 OR 1/2 INCH VIDEO CASSETTE
Presents Sri Gurudev speaking on what to do while waiting for spiritual maturity.
Prod-IYOGA Dist-IYOGA

Satsang With Sri Swami Satchidananda SAY VA C 60 MIN
3/4 OR 1/2 INCH VIDEO CASSETTE
Presents Sri Gurudev speaking on fasting, proper attitude and how to make the feeling last that everything is perfect.
Prod-IYOGA Dist-IYOGA

Satsang With Sri Swami Satchidananda SAY VA C 60 MIN
3/4 OR 1/2 INCH VIDEO CASSETTE
Presents Sri Gurudev speaking on the development and importance of will power, how to develop a sense of humor and how God gives us all we need.
Prod-IYOGA Dist-IYOGA

Satsang With Sri Swami Satchidananda SAY VA C 60 MIN
3/4 OR 1/2 INCH VIDEO CASSETTE
Presents Sri Gurudev speaking on the difference between Atman, Jiva and the mind.
Prod-IYOGA Dist-IYOGA

Satsang With Sri Swami Satchidananda SAY VA C 60 MIN
3/4 OR 1/2 INCH VIDEO CASSETTE
Presents Sri Gurudev speaking on the significance of the lotus flower in Hindu Theology.
Prod-IYOGA Dist-IYOGA

Satsang With Sri Swami Satchidananda At SAYE C 50 MIN
3/4 OR 1/2 INCH VIDEO CASSETTE
Answers questions about God's will and ours, and how does one function on the earthly plane having reached the highest level of samadhi.
Prod-IYOGA Dist-IYOGA

Satsang With Sri Swami Satchidananda SAYE C
3/4 OR 1/2 INCH VIDEO CASSETTE
Answers questions about hell and the cause of excessive worry. Explains how picking flowers is not a violent act.
Prod-IYOGA Dist-IYOGA

Satsang With Sri Swami Satchidananda SAYE C 40 MIN
3/4 OR 1/2 INCH VIDEO CASSETTE
Answers questions about the soul and the mind. Talks about detachment and renunciation and making yourself strong.
Prod-IYOGA Dist-IYOGA

Satsang With Sri Swami Satchidananda SAYVA C 45 MIN
3/4 OR 1/2 INCH VIDEO CASSETTE
Answers questions regarding the difference between deep sleep and samadhi. Talks about training the mind.
Prod-IYOGA Dist-IYOGA

Satsang With Sri Swami Satchidananda SAYVA C 46 MIN
3/4 OR 1/2 INCH VIDEO CASSETTE
Presents Sri Gurudev answering questions on how far into pregnancy can one do the shoulder stand and how to teach beginning students.
Prod-IYOGA Dist-IYOGA

Satsang With Sri Swami Satchidananda, SAYVA C 52 MIN
3/4 OR 1/2 INCH VIDEO CASSETTE
Presents Sri Gurudev speaking on happiness as a common desire. Explains how we once were happy and lost it. Tells about how without peace there is no happiness.
Prod-IYOGA Dist-IYOGA

Satsang With Sri Swami Satchidananda, SAYVA C 55 MIN
3/4 OR 1/2 INCH VIDEO CASSETTE
Tells how we all must renounce to know permanent peace. Speaks on free will vs God's will. Tells how work is worship.
Prod-IYOGA Dist-IYOGA

Satsang With Swami Chidananda And Sri Gurudev at SAYE C 60 MIN
3/4 OR 1/2 INCH VIDEO CASSETTE
Presents Swami Chidananda giving a talk on our divine path and the four qualities of the spiritual aspirant according to Master Sivananda.
Prod-IYOGA Dist-IYOGA

Saturable Reactors B 23 MIN
16MM FILM - 1/2 IN VIDEO, BETA
Develops a hysteresis loop through the use of an applied AC sine wave to a coil containing a core material. Describes the core's control on the loop shape, the effect on switching action and how the loop is associated with the operation of a saturable reactor. Issued in 1970 as a motion picture.
LC NO. 79-707522
Prod-USAF Dist-USNAC 1979

Saturation Diving C 20 MIN
3/4 OR 1/2 INCH VIDEO CASSETTE
Explains that, under pressure, gas dissolves in the bloodstream, something all divers should know. Illustrates diving equipment.
Prod-FLMWST Dist-FLMWST

Saturday C 5 MIN
16MM FILM OPTICAL SOUND I-C A
Shows the art of the dance as executed at the Lexington School of Modern Dance. Emphasizes the grace of movement in the performance of the dancers.
LC NO. 74-701546
Prod-CELLAR Dist-CELLAR 1970

Saturday Afternoon C 11 MIN
16MM FILM OPTICAL SOUND
Demonstrates, through pantomime, a young couple depicting what happens when husband and wife develop roles that block real communication and personal growth.
From The Contemporary Family Series.
LC NO. 75-700480
Prod-FRACOC Dist-FRACOC 1975

Saturday Afternoon B 27 MIN
16MM FILM SILENT I-C
Stars Harry Langdon as a hen-pecked foundry worker whose every move must be reported to his domineering wife.
Prod-UNKNWN Dist-TWYMAN 1926

Saturday Club, The - James Russell Lowell, Henry Wadsworth Longfellow, John Greenleaf... C 20 MIN
3/4 OR 1/2 INCH VIDEO CASSETTE H-C A
Offers a dramatic re-creation of a meeting in which members of the Saturday Club including James Russell Lowell, Henry Wadsworth Longfellow, John Greenleaf Whittier and Oliver Wendell Holmes discuss an early edition of The Atlantic Monthly in a posh Boston eating club and recite from their works.
From The American Literature Series.
LC NO. 83-706253
Prod-AUBU Dist-AITECH 1983

Saturday Morning C 88 MIN
16MM FILM, 3/4 OR 1/2 IN VIDEO J-C A
Discusses adolescent issues which young people find most urgent - their feelings about parents, sex, morality and their search for identity and love.
Prod-DF Dist-CF 1972

Saturday's Children C 36 MIN
16MM FILM, 3/4 OR 1/2 IN VIDEO H-C A
Documents four prepared, unmedicated births that took place in one day in a traditional, but progressive, hospital delivery room. Follows the mothers through labor and delivery with examples of labor coaching and support by fathers and staff.
LC NO. 83-70603
Prod-COURTR Dist-PARPIC 1982

Saturn C 29 MIN
3/4 INCH VIDEO CASSETTE C A
Describes characteristics of Saturn and its ring system. Discusses nature of the atmospheres of Jovian planets. Shows excerpts from two NASA films of Saturn.
From The Project Universe - Astronomy Series. Lesson 11
Prod-COAST Dist-CDTEL Prodn-SCCON

Saturn First Stage C 5 MIN
16MM FILM - 3/4 IN VIDEO
Looks at the first stage of the Saturn 5 rocket. Issued in 1969 as a motion picture.
From The Apollo Digest Series.
LC NO. 79-706988
Prod-NASA Dist-USNAC 1979

Saturn Second Stage C 5 MIN
16MM FILM - 3/4 IN VIDEO
Describes the second stage of the Saturn 5 rocket, including scenes of manufacturing and testing. Issued in 1969 as a motion picture.
From The Apollo Digest Series.
LC NO. 79-706989
Prod-NASA Dist-USNAC 1979

Saturn Third Stage C 5 MIN
16MM FILM - 3/4 IN VIDEO
Deals with the final stage of the Saturn 5 rocket, including scenes of test firings. Issued in 1969 as a motion picture.
From The Apollo Digest Series.
LC NO. 79-706990
Prod-NASA Dist-USNAC 1979

Saturn 3 C 95 MIN
16MM FILM OPTICAL SOUND
Stars Kirk Douglas and Farrah Fawcett as scientists living on a research station in space, 400 years in the future.
Prod-UNKNWN Dist-SWANK

Saturnus Alchimia C 18 MIN
3/4 OR 1/2 INCH VIDEO CASSETTE
Uses color, shape, texture and rhythm to form visual music compositions.
Prod-KITCHN Dist-KITCHN

Satyajit Ray B 28 MIN
16MM FILM OPTICAL SOUND H-C A
Satyajit Ray, noted Indian film maker, explains the underlying philosophy guiding him in the production of his films, which he sees as a confluence of Eastern and Western cultures. Ray's main objective is to make his audiences see and think about issues such as poverty and politics.
LC NO. 74-705974
Prod-NET Dist-IU 1970

Sauce For The Gander C 22 MIN
16MM FILM OPTICAL SOUND
Examines attitudes of a man who expects perfection from others. Shows importance of a right-the-first-time attitude, which also applies to him.
LC NO. 74-705581
Prod-USN Dist-USNAC 1963

Sauce Preparation - Veloute C 20 MIN
1/2 IN VIDEO CASSETTE BETA/VHS
Describes the important steps involved in the incorporation of roux into a liquid. Discusses the four basic mother sauces. Features Chef Paul, who uses a blonde roux and light stock to show how a veloute sauce is created.
Prod-RMI Dist-RMI

Saudi Arabia C 18 MIN
16MM FILM, 3/4 OR 1/2 IN VIDEO H-C A
Explains that the crude oil resources of Saudi Arabia make it a world power and a key factor in America's economic well-being.
From The Oil And American Power Series.
Prod-NBC Dist-FI 1979

Saudi Arabia C 25 MIN
3/4 OR 1/2 INCH VIDEO CASSETTE H-C A
Focuses on the cultural clash which has occurred as Saudi Arabia emerges as a major power of the 20th century. Contrasts the country's wealth with its traditional culture.
Prod-UPI Dist-JOU

Saudi Arabia (International Byline) C 28 MIN
3/4 INCH VIDEOTAPE
Interviews His Royal Highness Prince Mohamed Al-Faisal, son of the late King Faisal, on Islam, oil, women, economic development and the Middle East. Hosted by Marilyn Perry.
From The International Byline Series.
Prod-PERRYM Dist-PERRYM

Saudi Arabia (Marilyn's Manhatten) C 28 MIN
3/4 INCH VIDEOTAPE
Features an interview with Mr Saud Shawwaf, Special Representative on a people to people tour of the United States from Saudi Arabia. Hosted by Marilyn Perry.
From The Marilyn's Manhatten Series.
Prod-PERRYM Dist-PERRYM

Saudi Arabia - The Oil Revolution C 25 MIN
16MM FILM, 3/4 OR 1/2 IN VIDEO H-C A
Probes the internal tension of Saudia Arabia, in transition since the oil boom of the mid-1960's and the reforms of King Faisal.
From The Arab Experience Series.
Prod-LCOA Dist-LCOA Prodn-YORKTV 1976

Saudi Arabia - The Oil Revolution (Spanish) C 25 MIN
16MM FILM, 3/4 OR 1/2 IN VIDEO H-C A
Looks at the world's richest oil-producing country and its diverseculture, ranging from extreme orthodoxy to influences of Western modernization.
From The Arab Experience Series.
Prod-LCOA Dist-LCOA Prodn-YORKTV 1976

Saudi Arabia Today C 28 MIN
16MM FILM - 3/4 IN VIDEO
Depicts the scenic and cultural variety of modern Saudi Arabia, including mountains, deserts, farms, construction sights, villages and suburbs. Treats concerns of individual Saudis.
Prod-EXXON Dist-MTP Prodn-GRAHMR 1981

Saudis, The C 49 MIN
16MM FILM, 3/4 OR 1/2 IN VIDEO J-C A
Presents a documentary report on America's largest oil supplier and tenuous ally, Saudi Arabia. Discusses government, customs, business methods, law, religion, modernization and the relationship of the sexes in that country.
Prod-CBSNEW Dist-PHENIX 1980

Sauerkraut C 3 MIN
16MM FILM - 3/4 IN VIDEO
Suggests making sauerkraut from red cabbage. Demonstrates the steps in the process and gives instructions on the preparation of the cabbage, storing of the mixture for fermentation to take place and caring for it during fermentation. Shows how it looks when it is ready to eat.
From The Beatrice Trum Hunter's Natural Foods Series.
Prod-WGBH Dist-PUBTEL 1974

Saugus Ironworks Restoration, The C 15 MIN
16MM FILM OPTICAL SOUND
Presents a description of the discovery, excavation and rebuilding of an ironworks, dated about 1650, at Saugus, Massachusetts.
Prod-AIAS Dist-AIAS 1954

Saul Alinsky Went To War C 57 MIN
16MM FILM, 3/4 OR 1/2 IN VIDEO H-C A
Presents a documentary on Saul Alinsky and his work with minority groups. Shows how he hires himself out to the poor and oppressed, instructs them in the art of protest and sends them to do battle against the establishment.
Prod-NFBC Dist-NFBC 1969

Sausalito B 9 MIN
16MM FILM OPTICAL SOUND H-C
Utilizes textures, sounds and pieces of visual experience to create a 'POETIC FABRIC' of the atmosphere of Sausalito, a small village on the shore of the San Francisco bay.
LC NO. FIA52-704
Prod-FILIM Dist-RADIM 1952

Sauteeing And White Searing C 20 MIN
1/2 IN VIDEO CASSETTE BETA/VHS
Describes the cooking techniques of white searing and sauteeing, and discusses the effects of each process.
Prod-RMI Dist-RMI

Sauteing And Pan Frying C 12 MIN
16MM FILM, 3/4 OR 1/2 IN VIDEO A
Presents the subtleties of two classic cooking techniques, sauteing and pan frying. Describes skillets, frying pans and saute pans and when the different types should be used. Demonstrates correct procedures with thin, tender foods as well as thicker, slower cooking items.
From The Professional Food Preparation And Service Programs Series.
Prod-NEM Dist-NEM

Savage C 25 MIN
3/4 OR 1/2 INCH VIDEO CASSETTE
Portrays the world of live professional wrestling. Focuses on the ritualistic acting aspect of the phenomenon.
Prod-MEDIPR Dist-MEDIPR 1978

Savage Flame (Mission Call-South America) C 30 MIN
16MM FILM OPTICAL SOUND J-C A
Shows the strangest tribes of primitive natives. Dramatizes the Church's true mission of a missionary family service--its healing ministry, its teaching mission and its Gospel preaching.
Prod-CAFM Dist-CAFM

Savage Iron C 21 MIN
16MM FILM OPTICAL SOUND
Shows development of the iron ore mine at Savage River in Australia, including construction of a complete township, mill, ore slurry, pipeline pelletising plant at Port Latta and offshore loading facilities for bulk ore carriers of up to 100,000 tons.
LC NO. 80-700920
Prod-TASCOR Dist-TASCOR 1968

Savage Love C 26 MIN
3/4 OR 1/2 INCH VIDEO CASSETTE
Prod-EAI Dist-EAI

Savage River Iron C 22 MIN
16MM FILM OPTICAL SOUND H-C A
Tells the story of Savage River Mines, the only iron ore mining operation in Australia's island state of Tasmania. Explains in detail the development of the modern mining and processing facilities as well as the world's longest iron slurry pipeline and unique offshore loading system extending a mile out to sea.
Prod-PICMAT Dist-PICMAT

Savage Road To China C 30 MIN
3/4 OR 1/2 INCH VIDEO CASSETTE H-C A
See series title for descriptive statement.
From The World War II - GI Diary Series.
Prod-TIMLIF Dist-TIMLIF 1980

Save A Bit Hop, The C 30 MIN
16MM FILM OPTICAL SOUND J-H
Shows how Tommy and his classmates use ridesharing and other energy-conservation techniques to raise money for the big senior class dance.
Prod-GRAVAR Dist-SUNCO

Save It, Food, Fiber And Environment C 28 MIN
16MM FILM OPTICAL SOUND J-C A
Tells how men in the sheep industry in the United States work to conserve water, soil and wildlife, the elements upon which they rely upon for their existence.
LC NO. 75-701973
Prod-ASPC Dist-AUDPLN 1972

Save Our Soil - Save Our Streams C 20 MIN
16MM FILM, 3/4 OR 1/2 IN VIDEO H A
Discusses soil erosion from cropland and construction sites and how this relates to the nation's clean water goals. Shows how local government, cooperating with landowners and conservation groups, can stop almost all erosion problems, saving both soil and streams.
Prod-UWISC Dist-USNAC 1983

Save The Children C 29 MIN
3/4 OR 1/2 INCH VIDEO CASSETTE
See series title for descriptive statement.
From The All About Welfare Series.
Prod-WITFTV Dist-PBS

Save The Panda C 59 MIN
16MM FILM, 3/4 OR 1/2 IN VIDEO
Looks at the panda and it's only known home in the People's Republic of China.
LC NO. 83-706734
Prod-NGS Dist-NGS 1983

Save The Planet C 18 MIN
3/4 OR 1/2 INCH VIDEO CASSETTE
Presents the origins and key pressure points of the nuclear debate.
Prod-MUSEI Dist-GMPF Prodn-GMPF

Save Water C 5 MIN
3/4 INCH VIDEO CASSETTE K-I
Shows how children, their families and friends and neighbors can avoid wasting water.
Prod-CSDWR Dist-CALDWR

Saved By The Bell C 10 MIN
3/4 OR 1/2 INCH VIDEO CASSETTE
Explains how many home fires can be avoided by using common sense.
LC NO. 81-707124
Prod-CPSAFC Dist-USNAC Prodn-KUEHL 1981

Saved From The Pound C 30 MIN
3/4 OR 1/2 INCH VIDEO CASSETTE I-J
Focuses on the parallel between one's responsibility to take care of a pet and one's responsibility to eat properly.
From The High Feather Series. Pt 9
LC NO. 83-706055
Prod-NYSED Dist-GPITVL 1982

Saving A Big Land C 30 MIN
16MM FILM - 3/4 IN VIDEO J-C A
Recounts the environmental controversy over the ways and means of using oil from Alaska's north slope, suggesting that satisfactory environmental solutions found there might be applied elsewhere.
From The Man Builds - Man Destroys Series.
LC NO. 75-704154
Prod-UN Dist-GPITVL 1975

Saving Energy And Money Too C 25 MIN
3/4 OR 1/2 INCH VIDEO CASSETTE
Offers low cost or no cost tips for reducing energy usage in the home.
Prod-ODECA Dist-BULFRG

Saving Energy At Home C 13 MIN
16MM FILM, 3/4 OR 1/2 IN VIDEO I A
Illustrates the major sources of energy waste around the house. Gives specific tips on how to reduce energy consumption.
Prod-RAMFLM Dist-SUTHRB 1975

Saving Energy On The Road C 15 MIN
3/4 OR 1/2 INCH VIDEO CASSETTE I A
Presents an entertaining but practical guide to better gas mileage. Presents facts that can save drivers money.
Prod-SUTHRB Dist-SUTHRB

Saving Lives In High-Rise Fires C 14 MIN
16MM FILM OPTICAL SOUND C
Tells how today's high-rise buildings pose unique problems to those involved in fire prevention, fire protection and fire suppression. Shows some of the latest methods and techniques developed to prevent and control future high-rise fires.
From The Science In Action Series.
Prod-ALLFP Dist-NSTA

Saving Of The President, The C 31 MIN
16MM FILM OPTICAL SOUND
Presents a documentary drama covering the events immediately following the assassination attempt on President Ronald Reagan's life in Washington, DC, on March 30, 1981. Recreates the events with the actual doctors and nurses and others who were part of the effort to save President Reagan's life on that day and into the night. Shares the events and feelings of those involved through the unscripted recollections of the President, the U S Secret Service and staff of the George Washington University Medical Center.
LC NO. 82-700378
Prod-GWASHU Dist-GWASHU 1982

Saving Our Wildlife - Conservation C 20 MIN
2 INCH VIDEOTAPE I
See series title for descriptive statement.
From The Exploring With Science, Unit XII - Prehistory series.
Prod-MPATI Dist-GPITVL

Saving Teeth For Lifetime Service—A Series
PRO
Discusses restorative dentistry, conservation dentistry and patient hygiene education.
Prod-USAF Dist-USNAC 1983

Saving Teeth For Lifetime Service,	
Saving Teeth For Lifetime Service,	058 MIN
Saving Teeth For Lifetime Service,	101 MIN
Saving Teeth For Lifetime Service, Pin	107 MIN
Saving Teeth For Lifetime Service, Prevention	059 MIN
Saving Teeth For Lifetime Service, Restoring	014 MIN

Saving Teeth For Lifetime Service, Conservative Class I And II Amalgam Restoration C 263 MIN
3/4 OR 1/2 INCH VIDEO CASSETTE PRO
Presents Dr Miles Markley's philosophy of restorative dentistry, discussing the purposes and techniques of conservative dentistry.
From The Saving Teeth For Lifetime Service Series.
LC NO. 84-706519
Prod-USAF Dist-USNAC 1983

Saving Teeth For Lifetime Service, Foundations For Restorations And Cavity Liners C 58 MIN
3/4 OR 1/2 INCH VIDEO CASSETTE PRO
Discusses Dr Miles Markley's philosophy of restorative dentistry, with information on intermediary bases and cavity liners.
From The Saving Teeth For Lifetime Service Series.
LC NO. 84-706520
Prod-USAF Dist-USNAC 1983

Saving Teeth For Lifetime Service, Restoration And Maintenance Of Class V Or... C 101 MIN
3/4 OR 1/2 INCH VIDEO CASSETTE PRO
Complete title is Saving Teeth For Lifetime Service, Restoration And Maintenance Of Class V Or Gingival Third Areas. Discusses Dr Miles Markley's philosophy of restorative dentistry and presents techniques of class V restorations.
From The Saving Teeth For Lifetime Service Series.
LC NO. 84-706523
Prod-USAF Dist-USNAC 1983

Saving Teeth For Lifetime Service, Pin Retention Of Amalgam Foundations And... C 107 MIN
3/4 OR 1/2 INCH VIDEO CASSETTE PRO
Complete title is Saving Teeth For Lifetime Service, Pin Retention Of Amalgam Foundations And Restorations - Pin Reinforcement Of Weakened Teeth. Shows advantages of and techniques for using cemented pins in restorative dentistry.
From The Saving Teeth For Lifetime Service Series.
LC NO. 84-706521
Prod-USAF Dist-USNAC 1983

Saving Teeth For Lifetime Service, Prevention Is A Prerequisite To Dental Health C 59 MIN
3/4 OR 1/2 INCH VIDEO CASSETTE PRO
Presents Dr Miles Markley's philosophy of restorative dentistry. Promotes an awareness of the need and method for educating patients in oral hygiene.
From The Saving Teeth For Lifetime Service Series.
LC NO. 84-706522
Prod-USAF Dist-USNAC 1983

Saving Teeth For Lifetime Service, Restoring The Distal Of Cuspids C 14 MIN
3/4 OR 1/2 INCH VIDEO CASSETTE PRO
Discusses Dr Miles Markley's philosophy of restorative dentistry. Presents a technique for conservative restoration of cuspids.
From The Saving Teeth For Lifetime Service Series.
LC NO. 84-706524
Prod-USAF Dist-USNAC 1983

Saving The Gorilla C 23 MIN
16MM FILM, 3/4 OR 1/2 IN VIDEO J-C A
Documents the work of Dr Dian Fossey with the endangered mountain gorilla in Rwanda, Africa.
LC NO. 83-706617
Prod-NGS Dist-NGS 1982

Saving Your Own Life C 1 MIN
3/4 OR 1/2 INCH VIDEO CASSETTE
Features a fireman and his concerned wife regarding fears about checkups for colorectal cancer. Quotes wife who says 'he risks his life for strangers' but was afraid of a checkup for colorectal cancer. Carries message aimed at over-50 viewers. Uses TV spot format.
Prod-AMCS Dist-AMCS 1984

Saving Yourself A Lot Of Grief! Or How To Complete Form 5074 C 11 MIN
3/4 OR 1/2 INCH VIDEO CASSETTE
Offers instructions on how to fill out the activities report Form 5074 for nursing and health services.
Prod-AMRC Dist-AMRC 1977

Saw Timber (2nd Ed) C 22 MIN
16MM FILM, 3/4 OR 1/2 IN VIDEO J-C A
Shows forestry and logging work in central Idaho.
Prod-BOISE Dist-FO 1966

Sawing A Reverse Curve And A Bevel Reverse Curve C 18 MIN
16MM FILM, 3/4 OR 1/2 IN VIDEO
Shows how to select and lay out stock to avoid waste, reverse curves to contour lines, use the table tilting gage, saw a beveled reverse curve, prepare a template for a newel post and saw a newel post.
From The Precision Wood Machining - Operations On The Band Saw Series. No. 2
Prod-USOE Dist-USNAC Prodn-RCM 1945

Sawing An Internal Irregular Shape C 32 MIN
16MM FILM, 3/4 OR 1/2 IN VIDEO
Shows how to drill the saw-starting hole, make the saw selection, set up a band saw machine, weld saw bands, saw an internal contour shape and store a band saw.
From The Machine Shop Work - Operations On The Metal Cutting Band Saw Series. No. 1
Prod-USOE Dist-USNAC Prodn-RAYBEL 1944

Sawing Template Metal B 17 MIN
16MM FILM OPTICAL SOUND
Demonstrates the mounting of the saw blade on a band saw, selecting the adjusting blade guides, sawing to a layout line, 'CHEWING OUT' metal from a notch and removing burrs.
LC NO. FIE52-33
Prod-USOE Dist-USNAC 1943

Sawing With Jig And Changing Band C 20 MIN
16MM FILM, 3/4 OR 1/2 IN VIDEO
Shows how to select proper band saw blades for the job, adjust saw guides, mark stock and cut to the mark, prepare a jig, and cut discs using a jig.
From The Precision Wood Machining - Operations On The Band Saw Series. No. 1
Prod-USOE Dist-USNAC Prodn-RCM 1945

Saxophone X 24 MIN
16MM FILM OPTICAL SOUND J-C T
Sigurd Rascher, saxophone virtuoso and teacher, demonstrates the fundamentals of saxophone playing, good playing posture, phrasing, dynamics, types of mouthpieces and their effect on tone quality, attaining speed and the importance of practice. The Oklahoma City University symphonic band accompanies rascher in introductory and concluding solo passages.
Prod-UOKLA Dist-UOKLA Prodn-CF 1958

Say Amen, Somebody C
1/2 IN VIDEO CASSETTE BETA/VHS
Presents a documentary about gospel music, featuring performances and interviews with gospel greats.
Prod-GA Dist-GA

Say Goodbye C 51 MIN
16MM FILM OPTICAL SOUND K-P A
Examines man's careless arrogance toward the delicate balance of his relationship to the wildlife on earth and shows the necessity of sharing life with the wild creatures.
LC NO. 76-711435
Prod-QUO Dist-WOLPER 1971

Say Goodbye - America's Endangered Species C 50 MIN
16MM FILM OPTICAL SOUND J-H
Shows how humans are damaging the delicate balance of nature in North America.
Prod-WOLPER Dist-FI 1973

Say Goodbye Again - Children Of Divorce C 26 MIN
16MM FILM, 3/4 OR 1/2 IN VIDEO C A
Analyzes the impact of divorce on the young people involved. Focuses on three families over a two-year period illustrating how children from different age groups deal with the social and psychological effects of each phase of the divorce process. Interviews various experts to examine several programs designed to help both parents and children cope with the feelings, attitudes and concerns arising from a divorce.
LC NO. 83-706915
Prod-CINSF Dist-MTI 1981

Say In Your Community With The Australian Assistance Plan, A C 31 MIN
16MM FILM OPTICAL SOUND
Profiles a large, complex Australian community in terms of its social and welfare needs and illustrates the benefits available to community groups throughout the country under the Australian Assistance Plan.
LC NO. 76-701870
Prod-FLMAUS Dist-AUIS 1975

Say It Again C 15 MIN
2 INCH VIDEOTAPE J
Uses restatement as one way of developing a topic sentence.
From The From Me To You...In Writing, Pt 2 Series.
Prod-DELE Dist-GPITVL

Say It Again, Sam C 15 MIN
3/4 OR 1/2 INCH VIDEO CASSETTE J-H
Examines the manipulation of picture and sound to create mood in motion pictures.
From The Movies, Movies Series.
Prod-CTI Dist-CTI

Say It By Signing C 60 MIN
1/2 IN VIDEO CASSETTE BETA/VHS
Provides instruction in basic sign language.
Prod-CROWNP Dist-CROWNP

Say It Right C 14 MIN
3/4 OR 1/2 INCH VIDEO CASSETTE IND
Helps standardize radio procedure for communicating patient information to the emergency department of a hospital or to a doctor.
From The Emergency Medical Training Series. Lesson 7
Prod-LEIKID Dist-LEIKID

Say It Right C 14 MIN
3/4 OR 1/2 INCH VIDEO CASSETTE
Shows how to obtain the essential information about a patient, how to communicate that information to the doctor or nurse at the hospital and how to communicate confidence and give reassurance to the patient and the patient's family.
From The Emergency Medical Training Series.
Prod-VTRI Dist-VTRI

Say It With Hands—A Series
I-C A
Introduces basic sign language. Adapted from the book Say It With Hands by Louis J Fant, Jr. Issued 1973 as a motion picture.
LC NO. 78-706143
Prod-USBEH Dist-USNAC 1978

Say It With Sign - Review, Parts 1-4 C 30 MIN
3/4 OR 1/2 INCH VIDEO CASSETTE H-C A
Presents Lawrence Solow and Sharon Neumann Solow introducing American Sign Language used by the hearing-impaired. Reviews the contents of parts 1 through 4 of the Say It With Sign Series.
From The Say It With Sign Series. Part 5
Prod-KNBCTV Dist-FI 1982

Say It With Sign - Review, Parts 11-14 C 30 MIN
3/4 OR 1/2 INCH VIDEO CASSETTE H-C A
Presents Lawrence Solow and Sharon Neumann Solow introducing American Sign Language used by the hearing-impaired. Reviews the contents of parts 11 through 14 of the Say It With Sign Series.
From The Say It With Sign Series. Part 15
Prod-KNBCTV Dist-FI 1982

Say It With Sign - Review, Parts 16-19 C 30 MIN
3/4 OR 1/2 INCH VIDEO CASSETTE H-C A
Presents Lawrence Solow and Sharon Neumann Solow introducing American Sign Language used by the hearing-impaired. Reviews the contents of parts 16 through 19 of the Say It With Sign Series.
From The Say It With Sign Series. Part 20
Prod-KNBCTV Dist-FI 1982

Say It With Sign - Review, Parts 21-24 C 30 MIN
3/4 OR 1/2 INCH VIDEO CASSETTE H-C A
Presents Lawrence Solow and Sharon Neumann Solow introducing American Sign Language used by the hearing-impaired. Reviews the contents of parts 21 through 24 of the Say It With Sign Series.
From The Say It With Sign Series. Part 25
Prod-KNBCTV Dist-FI 1982

Say It With Sign - Review, Parts 26-29 C 30 MIN
3/4 OR 1/2 INCH VIDEO CASSETTE H-C A
Presents Lawrence Solow and Sharon Neumann Solow introducing American Sign Language used by the hearing-impaired. Reviews the contents of parts 26 through 29 of the Say It With Sign Series.
From The Say It With Sign Series. Part 30
Prod-KNBCTV Dist-FI 1982

Say It With Sign - Review, Parts 31-34 C 30 MIN
3/4 OR 1/2 INCH VIDEO CASSETTE H-C A
Presents Lawrence Solow and Sharon Neumann Solow introducing American Sign Language used by the hearing-impaired. Reviews the contents of parts 31 through 34 of the Say It With Sign Series.
From The Say It With Sign Series. Part 35
Prod-KNBCTV Dist-FI 1982

Say It With Sign - Review, Parts 36-39 C 30 MIN
3/4 OR 1/2 INCH VIDEO CASSETTE H-C A
Presents Lawrence Solow and Sharon Neumann Solow introducing American Sign Language used by the hearing-impaired. Reviews the contents of parts 36 through 39 of the Say It With Sign Series.
From The Say It With Sign Series. Part 40
Prod-KNBCTV Dist-FI 1982

Say It With Sign - Review, Parts 6-9 C 30 MIN
3/4 OR 1/2 INCH VIDEO CASSETTE H-C A
Presents Lawrence Solow and Sharon Neumann Solow introducing American Sign Language used by the hearing-impaired. Reviews the contents of parts 6 through 9 of the Say It With Sign Series.
From The Say It With Sign Series. Part 10
Prod-KNBCTV Dist-FI 1982

Say It With Sign—A Series
16MM FILM, 3/4 OR 1/2 IN VIDEO H-C A
Presents American Sign Language dealing with various topics.
Prod-KNBCTV Dist-FI 1982

Around The House	030 MIN
Basic Conversation	030 MIN

Beauty Parlor / Occupations	030 MIN
Colors	030 MIN
Decoder	030 MIN
Emergency Signs	030 MIN
Emotions	030 MIN
Family	030 MIN
Family II	030 MIN
Family III	030 MIN
Family Vacation	030 MIN
Food	030 MIN
Fruits And Colors	030 MIN
Furniture	030 MIN
General Health	030 MIN
Golf	030 MIN
Holidays And Seasons	030 MIN
Megan At 2	030 MIN
More Signs You Already Know	030 MIN
Numbers	030 MIN
Say It With Sign - Review, Parts 1-4	030 MIN
Say It With Sign - Review, Parts 11-14	030 MIN
Say It With Sign - Review, Parts 16-19	030 MIN
Say It With Sign - Review, Parts 21-24	030 MIN
Say It With Sign - Review, Parts 26-29	030 MIN
Say It With Sign - Review, Parts 31-34	030 MIN
Say It With Sign - Review, Parts 36-39	030 MIN
Say It With Sign - Review, Parts 6-9	030 MIN
Signs You Already Know	030 MIN
Sports	030 MIN
Still More Signs You Already Know	030 MIN
Time I	030 MIN
Time II	030 MIN
Time III	030 MIN
TTY/Telephone	030 MIN
Vacationing	030 MIN
Vehicles	030 MIN
Weather I	030 MIN
Weather II	030 MIN
Wonderful Baby	030 MIN

Say It With Words C 10 MIN
3/4 OR 1/2 INCH VIDEO CASSETTE H-C A
Explains difference between private writing and public speaking. Demonstrates speech preparation and rehearsal. Includes use of visual aids.
Prod-SEVDIM Dist-SEVDIM

Say No—A Series
16MM FILM, 3/4 OR 1/2 IN VIDEO I-J
Encourages young people to think for themselves and emphasizes that it's all right to say no under peer pressure.
Prod-NEWMNS Dist-CF 1982

Deciso 3003	008 MIN
Doin' What The Crowd Does	005 MIN
Jojo's Blues	006 MIN

Say Old Man, Can You Play The Fiddle B 20 MIN
16MM FILM, 3/4 OR 1/2 IN VIDEO
Portrays an old man in Downey, California, who plays a fiddle made by his blind father.
Prod-HAWESB Dist-UCEMC 1974

Say That One More Time C 14 MIN
3/4 OR 1/2 INCH VIDEO CASSETTE H A
Presents two versions of Jane's first day showing that when Jane asks and answers questions, pays attention and takes notes, she learns. Shows Paula demonstrating poor and good telephone communication skills.
From The Making It Work Series.
Prod-ERF Dist-AITECH 1983

Say What We Feel, Not What We Ought To Say C 60 MIN
16MM FILM - 3/4 IN VIDEO P A
Dramatizes the need for group-sensitivity as members of a community confront each other on drug-related issues.
From The Turned On Crisis Series.
Prod-WQED Dist-GPITVL

Say What You Mean C 20 MIN
2 INCH VIDEOTAPE P
See series title for descriptive statement.
From The Learning Our Language, Unit IV - Speaking And Spelling Series.
Prod-MPATI Dist-GPITVL

Say Yes C 17 MIN
16MM FILM OPTICAL SOUND H-C A
Emphasizes the importance of immunizing children against measles, polio, rubella, mumps, diptheria, whooping cough and tetanus.
LC NO. 79-700538
Prod-BLONDL Dist-BLONDL 1978

Saybrook - The Colony 1635 - 1985 C 23 MIN
16MM FILM OPTICAL SOUND
Shows how Saybrook Colony, the third oldest settlement in Connecticut, and the seven towns that developed from it represent a microcosm of American society in a river-oriented environment. Begins with the Mehantics, the river Indians who first occupied Pashbeshauke, 'the place at the river's mouth.'
Prod-GRANTE Dist-FENWCK

Saydu - Conflict Of Commitment C 28 MIN
16MM FILM OPTICAL SOUND J-H
Tells the story of Saydu, a teenager who is caught in changing Africa and finds his allegiance divided between the traditional ways of his father's village and life in the bustling city of Abidjan.
Prod-CBFMS Dist-CBFMS

Saying 'Goodbye' To Our Losses C 30 MIN
3/4 OR 1/2 INCH VIDEO CASSETTE
Examines idea that letting go of, saying 'goodbye' to hurts and losses is essential to healing. Shows how expressing our feelings and encouraging others to do so helps bring a release from old feelings and pain.
From The Growing Through Grief - Personal Healing Series.
Prod-UMCOM Dist-ECUFLM

Saying No C 17 MIN
16MM FILM, 3/4 OR 1/2 IN VIDEO
Presents young women talking about their personal decisions regarding sexuality, how they have been affected by their decisions, and how they respect themselves for having the courage and will-power to abstain from sex.
Prod-PEREN Dist-PEREN

Saying No - A Few Words To Young Women About Sex C 17 MIN
16MM FILM OPTICAL SOUND J-H A
Presents young women talking about their personal decisions regarding sexuality, how they have been affected by their decisions, how they feel about themselves and how much they respect themselves for having the courage and willpower to abstain from sex.
Prod-CROMIE Dist-CROMIE 1983

Sayings Of The Fathers, The B 30 MIN
16MM FILM OPTICAL SOUND
Uses dramatic readings from a collection of Rabbinical sayings, Pirke Avot, to explain the meaning of life to a disillusioned businessman.
LC NO. FIA64-1140
Prod-JTS Dist-NAAJS Prodn-NBC 1955

Scabies C 5 MIN
16MM FILM OPTICAL SOUND
Explores problems associated with the affliction of scabies.
Prod-VICCOR Dist-TASCOR 1978

Scabies (The Itch) C 7 MIN
16MM FILM OPTICAL SOUND J-C A
A commentary on the composition of society and the irritants of life as revealed by a story about a man whose composure is interrupted by itching sensations and a cough, which he traces to little men inside his clothing.
LC NO. 72-700405
Prod-ZAGREB Dist-MMA 1971

Scaffolding C 11 MIN
16MM FILM, 3/4 OR 1/2 IN VIDEO
Covers setting out and erecting scaffolds safely, including mobile scaffolds. Explains the main causes of scaffold collapse.
From The Safety In Construction Series.
Prod-NFBTE Dist-IFB

Scag C 21 MIN
16MM FILM, 3/4 OR 1/2 IN VIDEO J-C
Shows what it is like to be addicted to heroin by presenting two young people who were addicts and are now trying to rid themselves of their habits. Discusses the background of these addicts and examines the physical, emotional and social consequences of shooting heroin.
From The Drug Abuse Education Series.
Prod-CONFI Dist-EBEC

Scale Drawings C 30 MIN
3/4 OR 1/2 INCH VIDEO CASSETTE
See series title for descriptive statement.
From The Infinity Factory Series.
Prod-EDFCEN Dist-MDCPB

Scale Drawings, Models And Maps C 30 MIN
3/4 OR 1/2 INCH VIDEO CASSETTE
See series title for descriptive statement.
From The Infinity Factory Series.
Prod-EDFCEN Dist-MDCPB

Scale Factor C 20 MIN
3/4 OR 1/2 INCH VIDEO CASSETTE J-C
See series title for descriptive statement.
From The Math Topics - Trigonometry Series.
Prod-BBCTV Dist-FI

Scale Models B 15 MIN
2 INCH VIDEOTAPE P
See series title for descriptive statement.
From The Just Curious Series. No. 18
Prod-EOPS Dist-GPITVL Prodn-KOACTV

Scale Models And Representation B 15 MIN
2 INCH VIDEOTAPE P
See series title for descriptive statement.
From The Just Inquisitive Series. No. 11
Prod-EOPS Dist-GPITVL Prodn-KOACTV

Scales And Scale Bowings C 30 MIN
3/4 OR 1/2 INCH VIDEO CASSETTE J-H A
See series title for descriptive statement.
From The Cello Sounds Of Today Series.
Prod-IU Dist-IU 1984

Scales Of Justice, The - Our Court System C
3/4 OR 1/2 INCH VIDEO CASSETTE H
Describes the court system and trial procedures and considers problems facing the court system today.
Prod-GA Dist-GA

Scaling C 15 MIN
3/4 OR 1/2 INCH VIDEO CASSETTE PRO
See series title for descriptive statement.
From The Numerical Control/Computer Numerical Control, Part 2 - Advanced Programming Series.
Prod-ICSINT Dist-ICSINT

Scaling C 16 MIN
3/4 OR 1/2 INCH VIDEO CASSETTE IND
Includes scaling limits and rules, how to write a scaling statement and terminating a scaling statement.
From The Numerical Control/Computerized Numerical Control - Advanced Programming Series. Module 2
Prod-LEIKID Dist-LEIKID

Scaling And Root Planing, Pt 1 - Maxillary Teeth C 13 MIN
16MM FILM - 3/4 IN VIDEO PRO
Presents a demonstration by Robert R Nissle and Sigurd P Ramfjord of a method of scaling and root planing. Uses one representative tooth from each segment of the dental arch. Stresses the necessity for removal of supra- and subgingival calculus deposits and subsequent smoothing of these tooth surfaces.
LC NO. 77-706188
Prod-USVA Dist-USNAC 1974

Scaling And Root Planing, Pt 2 - Mandibular Teeth C 11 MIN
16MM FILM - 3/4 IN VIDEO PRO
Describes the advantages of using planned procedures for removal of subgingival calculus and planing of root surfaces.
LC NO. 77-706189
Prod-USVA Dist-USNAC 1974

Scaling Techniques—A Series
PRO
Prod-UTENN Dist-USNAC 1976

Fulcrums And Vision	27 MIN
Introduction To Basic Skills	21 MIN
Operator-Patient And Light Positions	9 MIN
Polishing	15 MIN
Use Of Sickle Scalers	21 MIN
Use Of The Explorer	15 MIN
Use Of The Gracey Curet No. 07-08	21 MIN
Use Of The Gracey Curet No. 11-12	13 MIN
Use Of The Gracey Curet No. 13-14	12 MIN
Use Of The Periodontal Probe	11 MIN

Scalp As A Skin Donor Site, The C 10 MIN
3/4 OR 1/2 INCH VIDEO CASSETTE PRO
Presents transparent dressings as a means of promoting rapid healing of skin graft donor sites with virtually no pain.
Prod-MMAMC Dist-MMAMC

Scan Reading Materials C 30 MIN
2 INCH VIDEOTAPE J
See series title for descriptive statement.
From The Summer Journal, Unit 2 - You Are What You Can Do Series.
Prod-WNINTV Dist-GPITVL

Scandal Sheet B 82 MIN
16MM FILM OPTICAL SOUND
Tells how a new editor turns a conservative newspaper into a yellow journal until the circulation quadruples. Shows how a reporter and his photographer unravel the murder of a woman. Stars Broderick Crawford, Donna Reed and John Derek.
Prod-CPC Dist-KITPAR 1952

Scandals At The Check-Out Counter C 29 MIN
3/4 OR 1/2 INCH VIDEO CASSETTE
Examines the journalistic practices and philosophy behind supermarket tabloids. Looks at how one company, Globe Communications, develops its stories and the impact such tabloids have had on other forms of popular communication.
From The Inside Story Series.
LC NO. 83-706853
Prod-PBS Dist-PBS 1981

Scandinavia C 24 MIN
16MM FILM OPTICAL SOUND I-C A
Introduces the geography, people and industry of Denmark, Sweden, Norway, Finland and Iceland.
LC NO. 76-702867
Prod-IFF Dist-IFF Prodn-BRYANS 1976

Scandinavia - A Place Apart C 28 MIN
16MM FILM OPTICAL SOUND C A
Explains how the people and scenery of Scandinavia separate those Nordic nations from other parts of the world, and focuses on the specific differences among the five countries. A new film by Fritz and Ingaborg Kahlenberg.
Prod-WSTGLC Dist-WSTGLC

Scandinavia - Nations Of The North (2nd Ed) C 21 MIN
16MM FILM, 3/4 OR 1/2 IN VIDEO I-H
Focuses on Denmark, Sweden and Norway, providing information on their systems of social service
Prod-SVEK Dist-PHENIX 1981

Scandinavia - Norway, Sweden, Denmark (2nd Ed) (Spanish) C 22 MIN
16MM FILM, 3/4 OR 1/2 IN VIDEO I-H
Points out how the people of Scandinavia have created a high standard of living. Shows their physical geography, natual resources, agriculture, commerce and industry.
Prod-EBEC Dist-EBEC

Scandinavia - Norway, Sweden, Denmark (2nd Ed) X 22 MIN
16MM FILM, 3/4 OR 1/2 IN VIDEO I-H
Explains how the Scandinavians, through cooperation and industrial development, have created a high living standard. Also provides an overview of each country-the physical geography, natural resources, industry and culture.
Prod-EBF Dist-EBEC 1962

Scandinavia - Unique Northern Societies C 24 MIN
3/4 OR 1/2 INCH VIDEO CASSETTE J-C A
Surveys Scandinavia as a whole, with emphasis on the industrial aspects of life. Deals also with geography and climate, lifestyle of the Lapps, education, art, and government. Points out the

problems that may arise in such a system, even though living standards are high.
Prod-IFF Dist-IFF

Scandinavia, In Short C 15 MIN
16MM FILM OPTICAL SOUND C A
Highlights five Scandinavian countries. Discusses the architecture of Finland, the hot tubs of Iceland, the Denmark home of Hans Christian Andersen, the elegance of Sweden and the castles of Norway.
Prod-WSTGLC Dist-WSTGLC

Scandinavian Saga C 27 MIN
16MM FILM OPTICAL SOUND
Features more than 50 species of Scandinavian birds and other animals. Depicts other colorful aspects of life in Denmark, Finland, Norway and Sweden.
Prod-SWNTO Dist-SWNTO 1968

Scandinavian Sketchbook C 20 MIN
16MM FILM OPTICAL SOUND
Follows a family which is interested in tracing its ancestry in Sweden as it travels by car through Denmark, Sweden and Norway.
LC NO. FIA66-1391
Prod-GOFFD Dist-SWNTO 1965

Scapemates C 29 MIN
3/4 OR 1/2 INCH VIDEO CASSETTE
Presents a combination of computer animation, video synthesizers, art work and an electronic music score.
Prod-EAI Dist-EAI

Scapular And Deltoid Regions - Unit 9 C 16 MIN
3/4 OR 1/2 INCH VIDEO CASSETTE PRO
Describes the musculature of the scapular and deltoid regions, the boundries and contents of the subdivisions of those regions, and the dorsal scapular region and its muscles, arteries, nerves, and other related structures.
From The Gross Anatomy Prosection Demonstration Series.
Prod-HSCIC Dist-HSCIC

Scar Beneath, The C 32 MIN
16MM FILM - 3/4 IN VIDEO PRO
Describes the vocational rehabilitation of a prison inmate arrested for his first offense.
Prod-USOVR Dist-USNAC Prodn-USPHS 1972

Scar Of Shame, The B 69 MIN
16MM FILM SILENT
Presents a noted production made by blacks, considered to be the equivalent of Hollywood productions made during the same period.
Prod-UNKNWN Dist-KITPAR 1927

Scarborough - Ontario, Canada C 13 MIN
16MM FILM OPTICAL SOUND
Describes daily life in Scarborough, Ontario. Includes topics such as housing, recreation, business and industry, municipal government and education. Presents the Scarborough Civic Centre.
LC NO. 77-702634
Prod-SCARCC Dist-SCARCC Prodn-CRAF 1975

Scarcity C 30 MIN
3/4 OR 1/2 INCH VIDEO CASSETTE T
Presents Dr Willard M Kniep of Arizona State University instructing teachers in the strategies and skills of teaching children economics and consumer education concepts. Focuses on the topic of scarcity by explaining it and then demonstrating specific approaches that teachers can use in their classrooms.
From The Economics Exchange Series. Program 1
LC NO. 82-706413
Prod-KAETTV Dist-GPITVL 1981

Scarcity And Planning C 16 MIN
16MM FILM, 3/4 OR 1/2 IN VIDEO H A
Introduces the concept of scarcity, explaining that want more and better goods than are available. Relates the economic problem of organizing and coordinating the work of many people to produce desired goods.
From The People On Market Street Series.
Prod-FNDREE Dist-WDEMCO Prodn-KAHNT 1977

Scare Me C 20 MIN
3/4 OR 1/2 INCH VIDEO CASSETTE P-I
Presents literary selections that deal with the excitement of fantasy and the supernatural.
From The Once Upon A Town Series.
Prod-MDDE Dist-AITECH 1977

Scarecrow C 115 MIN
16MM FILM OPTICAL SOUND
Stars Gene Hackman and Al Pacino as a couple of drifters who team up.
Prod-WB Dist-TWYMAN 1973

Scarecrow Man C 8 MIN
16MM FILM OPTICAL SOUND
Explains that Scarecrow Man is a person who has taken it upon himself to expose a person's worst character trait to the community in an attempt to help that person see what he really looks like to his friends and neighbors. Demonstrates that if everyone could see themselves as others do, then they would probably not continue their bad behavioral habits.
Prod-ECI Dist-ECI

Scarecrow, The B 17 MIN
16MM FILM SILENT J-C A
Stars Buster Keaton.
Prod-MGM Dist-TWYMAN 1920

Scarecrow, The C 10 MIN
16MM FILM, 3/4 OR 1/2 IN VIDEO K-P
Uses animation to describe the adventures of two cuckoo birds and a scarecrow.
Prod-CAROUF Dist-CAROUF

Scared Straight C 54 MIN
16MM FILM, 3/4 OR 1/2 IN VIDEO
Documents a visit by adolescent offenders to Rahway Prison in New Jersey, where they experience the realities of life in a maximum security prison. Shows how they are intimidated, sexually taunted and warned by prisoners.
LC NO. 79-700008
Prod-GWB Dist-PFP 1978

Scarfing Safely C 7 MIN
3/4 OR 1/2 INCH VIDEO CASSETTE IND
Discusses necessity of understanding the job and procedures of scarfing in order to know how to react to a problem in scarfing.
From The Steel Making Series.
Prod-LEIKID Dist-LEIKID

Scariest Place On Earth, The C 23 MIN
3/4 OR 1/2 INCH VIDEO CASSETTE K-C A
Visits the deep Columbian rainforest where a variety of animals reside, including the anaconda, cayman crocodile and piranha.
Prod-NWLDPR Dist-NWLDPR 1982

Scarlet And Gold C 14 MIN
16MM FILM OPTICAL SOUND
Traces the early history of the North-West Mounted Police of Canada.
From The Journal Series.
LC NO. 76-702093
Prod-FIARTS Dist-CANFDC 1975

Scarlet Letter And The Fortunate Fall, The C 30 MIN
2 INCH VIDEOTAPE J-H
Presents the novel THE SCARLET LETTER by Nathaniel Hawthorne.
From The From Franklin To Frost - Nathaniel Hawthorne Series.
Prod-MPATI Dist-GPITVL

Scarlet Letter, The C 240 MIN
16MM FILM - 3/4 IN VIDEO
Presents a four-part dramatization of Nathaniel Hawthorne's classic novel, THE SCARLET LETTER. Tells the story of Hester Prynne, a woman condemned for a sin of passion who must forever wear a scarlet letter 'A' on her breast. Set in Puritan America. Features Meg Foster as Hester Prynne.
Prod-PBS Dist-PBS

Scarlet Letter, The C 240 MIN
16MM FILM, 3/4 OR 1/2 IN VIDEO
Presents the story of an adulteress in puritanical, 18th-century New England. Based on the novel THE SCARLET LETTER by Nathaniel Hawthorne.
Prod-WGBHTV Dist-KINGFT 1979

Scarlet Pen Pal, The C 5 MIN
3/4 OR 1/2 INCH VIDEO CASSETTE J-H
Shows how to develop paragraphs through the use of contrast.
From The Write On, Set 2 Series.
Prod-CTI Dist-CTI

Scarlet Pimpernel, The B 95 MIN
3/4 OR 1/2 INCH VIDEO CASSETTE
Stars Leslie Howard aiding victims of the French revolution while posing as a foppish member of British society.
Prod-ADVCAS Dist-ADVCAS

Scarlet Pimpernel, The B 95 MIN
1/2 IN VIDEO CASSETTE (BETA)
Follows the adventures of a man who masquerades as an ineffectual member of the royalty during the day and who works for the French Revolution at night. Stars Leslie Howard and Merle Oberon.
Prod-UNKNWN Dist-BHAWK 1935

Scarlet Street B 103 MIN
16MM FILM OPTICAL SOUND
Tells the tragic story of a middle-aged cashier who falls in love with a golddigger. Stars Edward G Robinson and Joan Bennett.
Prod-UPCI Dist-REELIM 1945

Scars On The Surface C 30 MIN
16MM FILM - 3/4 IN VIDEO J-C A
Views the earth as seen by the Appollo astronauts - an earth that is blue, beautiful and unscarred. Shows a montage of mined areas, scars on the planet's surface inflicted by man in his search for minerals and energy. Reports on two techniques of restoration used in West Germany, noting that such land rehabilitation and reduction of extravagant and trivial uses of resources can eliminate some of the environmental impact of mining.
From The Man Builds - Man Destroys Series.
Prod-UN Dist-GPITVL 1972

Scary Sounds - H, W, HW C 15 MIN
3/4 INCH VIDEO CASSETTE P
Discusses the proper pronunciation of the h, w and HW sounds. Studies words that sound alike but are spelled differently and words that start with the same sound but begin with different letters, such as one and way.
From The New Talking Shop Series.
Prod-BSPTV Dist-GPITVL 1978

Scattering And Absorption Loses C 40 MIN
3/4 OR 1/2 INCH VIDEO CASSETTE C
Discusses the scattering and absorption losses experienced by waves propagating in various waveguides. Deals with theoretical expressions for loss derived and illustrated with experimentally measured data.
From The Integrated Optics Series.
Prod-UDEL Dist-UDEL

Scattering Demonstrations Using Microwaves B 14 MIN
16MM FILM OPTICAL SOUND C
Demonstrates the polarization and intensity of 12mm microwaves scattered by various metallic objects, some much larger, others much smaller, than the microwavelength. Uses flat surfaces, wire grating, wires and small beads. Shows radiation scattered from the small beads to be linearly polarized, even when the incident radiation is circularly polarized. Also shows how light is polarized as it is scattered by the air molecules in the atmosphere.
From The College Physics Film Series.
LC NO. 78-709339
Prod-EDS Dist-MLA 1970

Scattering From Impurities B 4 MIN
16MM FILM SILENT C
Shows the effect of a narrow singularity in an otherwise perfect periodic potential on a moving wave packet.
From The College Physics - Quantum Physics Series. No. 8
LC NO. 72-709340
Prod-ERCMIT Dist-EDC 1970

Scenario Du Film 'Passion' (French) C 53 MIN
3/4 OR 1/2 INCH VIDEO CASSETTE
A french language version of the videotape Scenario of the Film 'Passion.' Subtitles in English. Provides a tour of Jean-Luc Godard's production facility. Describes his methods.
Prod-KITCHN Dist-KITCHN

Scene - Politic 68, An Artist's Report C 59 MIN
16MM FILM OPTICAL SOUND J-C A
Artist-reporter Franklin Mc Mahon presents a review of the presidential campaign of 1968. Follows the candidates from the primary campaigns in New Hampshire, Wisconsin, Indiana, Oregon, California and to both political conventions, and through the final campaigns to the election.
From The Artist As A Reporter Series.
LC NO. 71-701733
Prod-ROCSS Dist-ROCSS 1968

Scene Changes, The C 52 MIN
16MM FILM, 3/4 OR 1/2 IN VIDEO J-C A
Presents Margot Fonteyn exploring her own world of dance, from the dominance of the ballerina in the 1930's to the great male dancers of the 60's and 70's.
From The Magic Of Dance Series.
Prod-BBCTV Dist-TIMLIF 1980

Scene Is Set, The C
16MM FILM OPTICAL SOUND
Introduces set theory, algebra, topology, and finite machine computations. Highlights the relationship between set theory and the rest of mathematics.
Prod-OPENU Dist-OPENU

Scene Now, The C 20 MIN
3/4 OR 1/2 INCH VIDEO CASSETTE I
Presents dramatizations of literary works that deal with how involvement in social issues can effect change.
From The Readers' Cube Series.
Prod-MDDE Dist-AITECH 1977

Scene Of The Crime C 30 MIN
3/4 OR 1/2 INCH VIDEO CASSETTE
See series title for descriptive statement.
From The Burglar-Proofing Series.
Prod-MDCPB Dist-MDCPB

Scene Playing C 15 MIN
3/4 OR 1/2 INCH VIDEO CASSETTE P
See series title for descriptive statement.
From The Word Shop Series.
Prod-WETATV Dist-WETATV

Scenery C 30 MIN
2 INCH VIDEOTAPE
See series title for descriptive statement.
From The Trains, Tracks And Trestles Series.
Prod-WMVSTV Dist-PUBTEL

Scenes From A Divorce B 20 MIN
3/4 OR 1/2 INCH VIDEO CASSETTE
Follows a couple working through stages encountered during the course of a divorce, including a typical argument and early realization of questions about custody.
Prod-UWISC Dist-UWISC 1978

Scenes From The Workplace C 23 MIN
16MM FILM - 3/4 IN VIDEO
Illustrates different grievances and how they are handled by presenting eight grievances in various types of state and local public employment.
LC NO. 77-706146
Prod-USDELR Dist-USNAC Prodn-MONUMT 1975

Scenes From The Workplace C 30 MIN
3/4 OR 1/2 INCH VIDEO CASSETTE
Consists of eight vignettes of actual and potential management-employee conflict situations.
From The Labor Relations Series.
Prod-IVCH Dist-IVCH

Scenes From Travel In Colombia C 26 MIN
16MM FILM, 3/4 OR 1/2 IN VIDEO J-C A
Presents a sampler of the lives, places and events which make up Colombia, South America. Provides insights into the look and feel of Colombia, as well as Latin America as a whole.
LC NO. 81-706875
Prod-SMITD Dist-PHENIX 1978

Scenes Of Natural Reserve C 13 MIN
16MM FILM OPTICAL SOUND
Shows rare animal and bird species roaming freely in Israel's natural reserves.
Prod-ALDEN Dist-ALDEN

Scenic Route, The C 76 MIN
3/4 INCH VIDEO CASSETTE C A

Deals with a melodramatic universe of three characters: two sisters and the man caught between them. Explores romantic myths in the context of an urban '70s environment.
Prod-FIRS Dist-FIRS

Schechter Revisited At Cambridge University B 30 MIN
16MM FILM OPTICAL SOUND H-C A
Presents a panel discussion of Solomon Schechter and his discovery of the Cairo Genizah manuscripts. (Kinescope)
From The Eternal Light Series.
LC NO. 71-700953
Prod-JTS Dist-NAAJS 1966

Schedule Masters, The C 25 MIN
16MM FILM OPTICAL SOUND
Traces the development of the 40 series tractors and introduces each model. Emphasizes Deere and Company's commitment to its European farming customers.
LC NO. 80-700412
Prod-DEERE Dist-DEERE Prodn-SCHAR 1979

Schedule Masters, The (Danish) C 25 MIN
16MM FILM OPTICAL SOUND
Traces the development of the 40 series tractors and introduces each model. Emphasizes Deere and Company's commitment to its European farming customers.
LC NO. 80-700412
Prod-DEERE Dist-DEERE Prodn-SCHAR 1979

Schedule Masters, The (Dutch) C 25 MIN
16MM FILM OPTICAL SOUND
Traces the development of the 40 series tractors and introduces each model. Emphasizes Deere and Company's commitment to its European farming customers.
LC NO. 80-700412
Prod-DEERE Dist-DEERE Prodn-SCHAR 1979

Schedule Masters, The (French) C 25 MIN
16MM FILM OPTICAL SOUND
Traces the development of the 40 series tractors and introduces each model. Emphasizes Deere and Company's commitment to its European farming customers.
LC NO. 80-700412
Prod-DEERE Dist-DEERE Prodn-SCHAR 1979

Schedule Masters, The (German) C 25 MIN
16MM FILM OPTICAL SOUND
Traces the development of the 40 series tractors and introduces each model. Emphasizes Deere and Company's commitment to its European farming customers.
LC NO. 80-700412
Prod-DEERE Dist-DEERE Prodn-SCHAR 1979

Schedule Masters, The (Italian) C 25 MIN
16MM FILM OPTICAL SOUND
Traces the development of the 40 series tractors and introduces each model. Emphasizes Deere and Company's commitment to its European farming customers.
LC NO. 80-700412
Prod-DEERE Dist-DEERE Prodn-SCHAR 1979

Schedule Masters, The (Norwegian) C 25 MIN
16MM FILM OPTICAL SOUND
Traces the development of the 40 series tractors and introduces each model. Emphasizes Deere and Company's commitment to its European farming customers.
LC NO. 80-700412
Prod-DEERE Dist-DEERE Prodn-SCHAR 1979

Scheduling C 30 MIN
3/4 OR 1/2 INCH VIDEO CASSETTE
Delineates principles of scheduling. Explores scheduling techniques. Covers emergency maintenance.
From The Maintenance Management Series.
Prod-ITCORP Dist-ITCORP

Scheduling C 30 MIN
3/4 OR 1/2 INCH VIDEO CASSETTE A
Relates that to schedule effectively, managers must distinguish between initiated items and response items. Emphasizes the need for making a 'to do' list, itemizing exactly what the manager wishes to accomplish, establishing priorities, estimating the time required to execute the task and assigning the tasks.
From The Time Management For Management Series. Pt 4
Prod-TIMLIF Dist-TIMLIF 1981

Scheduling Your Time C 29 MIN
3/4 OR 1/2 INCH VIDEO CASSETTE
See series title for descriptive statement.
From The Personal Time Management Series.
Prod-TELSTR Dist-DELTAK

Scheduling Your Time and Others' Time C 30 MIN
3/4 OR 1/2 INCH VIDEO CASSETTE
Helps the viewer examine a personal time schedule. Gives consideration to the scheduling time of others.
From The Personal Time Management Series.
Prod-TELSTR Dist-TELSTR

Schematic Diagrams C 60 MIN
3/4 OR 1/2 INCH VIDEO CASSETTE IND
See series title for descriptive statement.
From The Electrical Maintenance Training, Module C - Electrical Print Reading Series.
Prod-LEIKID Dist-LEIKID

Schempp Case, The - Bible Reading In Public Schools X 35 MIN
16MM FILM, 3/4 OR 1/2 IN VIDEO J-C
Presents issues and background of the Supreme Court decision concerning whether or not Bible reading in public schools is a violation of the first amendment of the Constitution. Points out the complications in maintaining separation of church and state.
From The Our Living Bill Of Rights Series.
Prod-EBEC Dist-EBEC 1969

Scherben B 48 MIN
16MM FILM SILENT
A silent motion picture with German subtitles. Tells the story of a railway inspector, who arrives at a lonely block station and seduces the signalmaster's daughter. Relates how they are discovered by the suspicious mother who, brokenhearted, walks into the snow to pray and freezes to death. Continues as the daughter implores the inspector to take her to town but is rejected, and ends with the daughter taking revenge by asking her father to demand satisfaction.
Prod-WSTGLC Dist-WSTGLC 1921

Schistosomes In The Primary Host B 7 MIN
16MM FILM SILENT
Shows through photomicrography the development of male and female schistosomes in various stages of growth in rabbit and mouse. For professional use.
From The Schistosomiasis Mansoni Study Films Series.
LC NO. FIE53-186
Prod-USPHS Dist-USNAC 1948

Schizophrenia - Removing The Veil C 30 MIN
1/2 IN VIDEO CASSETTE (VHS) J-C A
Explores the symptoms, causes and treatment of schizophrenia. Defines the term, dispels misconceptions and provides examples of the major types.
LC NO. 85-703934
Prod-HRMC Dist-HRMC

Schizophrenia - Removing The Veil–A Series

Explores the symptoms, causes and treatment of schizophrenia. Defines the term, dispels misconceptions and provides examples of the major types.
Prod-IBIS Dist-IBIS

Causes And Treatment
What Is Schizophrenia

Schizophrenia - The Shattered Mirror B 60 MIN
16MM FILM, 3/4 OR 1/2 IN VIDEO C A
Examines some experiences of victims of schizophrenia. Reviews the research being conducted toward developing a better knowledge of the disease.
LC NO. 80-707099
Prod-NET Dist-IU Prodn-MAYER 1967

Schizophrenia–A Series

Presents a series on schizophrenia with Dr Silvano Arieti.
Prod-HEMUL Dist-HEMUL

Interview With A Patient Discussing Her Psychotherpay Of The Schizophrenic 060 MIN

Schizophrenic Disorders (Case Numbers 9-12) C 35 MIN
3/4 OR 1/2 INCH VIDEO CASSETTE C A
Represents classic patterns of schizophrenia, emphasizing the heterogeneity of this category. Shows patients exhibiting various signs of formal thought disorder, including derailment, tangentiality, neologisms, poverty of content of speech, and illogicality.
From The Psychopathology - Diagnostic Vignettes Series.
Prod-IU Dist-IU 1984

Schizophrenic Disorders, Psychoses Not Elsewhere Classified, And Paranoid Disorders C 66 MIN
3/4 OR 1/2 INCH VIDEO CASSETTE PRO
Teaches how to diagnose schizophrenia, paranoid disorders, and some psychoses.
From The Psychiatry Learning System Pt 2 - Disorders Series.
Prod-HSCIC Dist-HSCIC 1982

Schizophrenic Superman C 5 MIN
16MM FILM OPTICAL SOUND
Discusses sex and violence in comic books.
LC NO. 77-702636
Prod-PSYMED Dist-CANFDC 1973

Schlock It To 'Em C 25 MIN
16MM FILM OPTICAL SOUND
Shows correspondent Michael Maclear in Hollywood, California, where he reports on the film and television industry. Notes what he considers to be the increasing cultural mindlessness of an industry where mediocrity abounds with violence and sadistic sex and with exploitation films which seem to reflect the general malaise of North America.
LC NO. 77-702524
Prod-CTV Dist-CTV 1976

Schloss Johannisberg, Germany C 26 MIN
16MM FILM, 3/4 OR 1/2 IN VIDEO H-C A
Presents Schloss Johannisberg in Germany, which was built as a small monastery in the year 860. It was destroyed by Royal Air Force bombers during the second World War and reconstructed on the original foundations by the castle's present-day owners, descendants of Prince Metternich, who appreciate their heritage.
From The Place In Europe Series.
Prod-THAMES Dist-MEDIAG 1975

Schloss Valduz - Liechtenstein C 26 MIN
16MM FILM, 3/4 OR 1/2 IN VIDEO H-C A
Shows the descendants of Liechtenstein's ruling family living in a small apartment within their huge thirteenth-century castle, which houses the world's largest private art collection. The income of this smallest country in the world is from forestry, agriculture and banking.
From The Place In Europe Series.
Prod-THAMES Dist-MEDIAG 1975

Schloss Vogeloed B 60 MIN
16MM FILM SILENT
A silent motion picture with German subtitles. Tells the story Of Count Oetsch, who is suspected of having murdered his brother, and in the disguise of a priest is able to expose the real murderer.
Prod-WSTGLC Dist-WSTGLC 1921

Schmid Membrane Model - Non-Equilibrium Thermodynamics Of Electrophoresis And... B 30 MIN
3/4 OR 1/2 INCH VIDEO CASSETTE
Shows Schmid membrane model. Teaches non-equilibrium thermodynamics of electrophoresis and sedimentation potential.
From The Colloids And Surface Chemistry Electrokinetics And Membrane...–Series.
Prod-MIOT Dist-MIOT

Schmid Membrane Model, Non-Equilibrium Thermodynamics Of Electrophoresis And... C 30 MIN
3/4 OR 1/2 INCH VIDEO CASSETTE
Discusses the Schmid membrane model, non-equilibrium thermodynamics of electrophoresis and sedimentation potential.
From The Colloid And Surface Chemistry - Electrokinetics And Membrane...Series.
Prod-KALMIA Dist-KALMIA

Schneeweisschen Und Rosenrot C 62 MIN
16MM FILM OPTICAL SOUND
An English language film. Relates the fairytale by the Grimm brothers called Snow White And Rose Red.
Prod-WSTGLC Dist-WSTGLC 1955

School C 15 MIN
16MM FILM OPTICAL SOUND P-J
See series title for descriptive statement.
From The Off To Adventure Series.
Prod-YALEDV Dist-YALEDV

School - Community B 30 MIN
16MM FILM OPTICAL SOUND T
Depicts ways in which institutional procedures and the attitudes of school personnel might alienate visitors to a school.
From The Human Relations Training Unit - Confrontations Series.
Prod-ADL Dist-ADL

School - Obstacle Or Opportunity? Coping With Chronic Illness In The Secondary Classroom C 25 MIN
3/4 INCH VIDEO CASSETTE C S
Presents students with cancer discussing issues relevant to many chronic life-threatening illnesses such as confronting personal feelings about illness, communicating with family and colleagues, designing academic goals, preparing classmates, reaching out to siblings and dealing with death.
LC NO. 84-706061
Prod-CHMCHO Dist-CHMCHO 1983

School - The Child's Community B 15 MIN
16MM FILM OPTICAL SOUND C T
Compares the adult-dominated world where the child has no opportunity to help make decisions with the classroom situation where the child is encouraged to share in the decisions.
Prod-WSU Dist-WSU 1959

School And Classrooms C 29 MIN
3/4 OR 1/2 INCH VIDEO CASSETTE T
See series title for descriptive statement.
From The Mainstreaming The Exceptional Child Series.
Prod-MFFD Dist-FI

School And Jobs C 15 MIN
16MM FILM, 3/4 OR 1/2 IN VIDEO I
Investigates the similarities and differences between school and work activities.
From The Bread And Butterflies Series.
LC NO. 74-703179
Prod-AITV Dist-AITECH Prodn-UTSBE 1973

School And The Child B 44 MIN
16MM FILM OPTICAL SOUND
Discusses the child's initial attitude toward school, relevance of material presented, teacher expectations, influence of cultural differences and cultural inconsistencies. Presents a brief history of educational changes in America since 1836.
From The Man - His Growth And Development, Birth Through Adolescence Series.
LC NO. 78-703690
Prod-VDONUR Dist-AJN Prodn-WTTWTV 1967

School Board Debates - Career Education–A Series

Addresses major concepts involved in career education. Points out that career education is an emotionally-charged issue.
Prod-NSBA Dist-SWRLFF

Career Education 037 MIN
Ken Hoyt Comments I 020 MIN
Ken Hoyt Comments II 020 MIN
Questions And Answers 033 MIN

School Bus Driver, The C 15 MIN
16MM FILM OPTICAL SOUND H A
Describes the school bus drivers's duties and responsibilities. Demonstrates driving skills and safety practices in city traffic and in rural areas.
LC NO. 72-700613
Prod-VADE Dist-VADE 1972

School Bus Driving - Special Education Transportation C 14 MIN
16MM FILM, 3/4 OR 1/2 IN VIDEO A
Discusses the talents and attitudes helpful in transporting handi-

capped school children. Describes the techniques and equipment used in driving children who are blind, orthopedically handicapped, retarded or those with epilepsy or cerebral palsy.
Prod-CAHILL Dist-AIMS 1977

School Bus Driving Tactics C 22 MIN
16MM FILM, 3/4 OR 1/2 IN VIDEO A
Shows, through the solo trip of a new driver, basic duties and responsibilities of driving a school bus. Includes pre-trip bus inspection, safety practices during loading and unloading, actual driving techniques and simulated incidents. Dramatizes the need for safe driving practices with a staged crash of a school bus and automobile, filmed in slow motion.
Prod-CAHILL Dist-AIMS 1976

School Bus Driving Tactics (Spanish) C 22 MIN
16MM FILM, 3/4 OR 1/2 IN VIDEO A
Shows, through the solo trip of a new driver, basic duties and responsibilities of driving a school bus. Includes pre-trip bus inspection, safety practices during loading and unloading, actual driving techniques and simulated incidents. Dramatizes the need for safe driving practices with a staged crash of a school bus and automobile, filmed in slow motion.
Prod-CAHILL Dist-AIMS 1976

School Bus Driving, Pt 1 C 10 MIN
16MM FILM, 3/4 OR 1/2 IN VIDEO A
Introduces techniques of safe school bus driving. Stresses defensive driving techniques. Shows proper multiple mirror usage, stop light measures and procedures for determining correct following distance, reaction time and stopping distances along with methods for turning and evaluating turns.
Prod-CAHILL Dist-AIMS 1976

School Bus Driving, Pt 1 (Spanish) C 10 MIN
16MM FILM, 3/4 OR 1/2 IN VIDEO A
Introduces techniques of safe school bus driving. Stresses defensive driving techniques. Shows proper multiple mirror usage, stop light measures and procedures for determining correct following distance, reaction time and stopping distances along with methods for turning and evaluating turns.
Prod-CAHILL Dist-AIMS 1976

School Bus Driving, Pt 2 C 10 MIN
16MM FILM, 3/4 OR 1/2 IN VIDEO A
Introduces techniques of safe school bus driving. Stresses safety, not schedules as the first priority. Demonstrates left turn situations, backing and downhill parking and stopping.
Prod-CAHILL Dist-AIMS 1976

School Bus Driving, Pt 2 (Spanish) C 10 MIN
16MM FILM, 3/4 OR 1/2 IN VIDEO A
Introduces techniques of safe school bus driving. Stresses safety, not schedules as the first priority. Demonstrates left turn situations, backing and downhill parking and stopping.
Prod-CAHILL Dist-AIMS 1976

School Bus Emergencies And Evacuation Procedures C 13 MIN
16MM FILM, 3/4 OR 1/2 IN VIDEO A
Builds on the theme of safety, not speed, in school bus emergencies and evacuation procedures. Demonstrates skids and skid control and the use of flares and reflectors. Shows evacuation procedures and the importance of choosing student assistants.
Prod-CAHILL Dist-AIMS 1976

School Bus Emergencies And Evacuation Procedures (Spanish) C 13 MIN
16MM FILM, 3/4 OR 1/2 IN VIDEO A
Builds on the theme of safety, not speed, in school bus emergencies and evacuation procedures. Demonstrates skids and skid control and the use of flares and reflectors. Shows evacuation procedures and the importance of choosing student assistants.
Prod-CAHILL Dist-AIMS 1976

School Bus Evacuation For Students C 9 MIN
16MM FILM, 3/4 OR 1/2 IN VIDEO I
Shows students how to deal with school bus evacuation during an emergency. Demonstrates how to shut off the engine, set brakes and open the front door, emergency doors and exits. Emphasizes quick access to emergency phone numbers, along with orderliness and cooperation with student bus leaders.
Prod-CAHILL Dist-AIMS 1976

School Bus Evacuation For Students (Captioned) C 9 MIN
16MM FILM, 3/4 OR 1/2 IN VIDEO I
Shows students how to deal with school bus evacuation during an emergency. Demonstrates how to shut off the engine, set brakes and open the front door, emergency doors and exits. Emphasizes quick access to emergency phone numbers, along with orderliness and cooperation with student bus leaders.
Prod-CAHILL Dist-AIMS 1976

School Bus Evacuation For Students (Spanish) C 9 MIN
16MM FILM, 3/4 OR 1/2 IN VIDEO I
Shows students how to deal with school bus evacuation during an emergency. Demonstrates how to shut off the engine, set brakes and open the front door, emergency doors and exits. Emphasizes quick access to emergency phone numbers, along with orderliness and cooperation with student bus leaders.
Prod-CAHILL Dist-AIMS 1976

School Bus Loading And Unloading C 11 MIN
16MM FILM, 3/4 OR 1/2 IN VIDEO A
Shows the need for cooperation between bus drivers and passengers during loading and unloading of buses. Demonstrates how to stop for loading, maintain order prior to boarding and use red flashers. Stresses the importance of counting and controlling passengers and shows the correct way for children to cross the street after unloading.
Prod-CAHILL Dist-AIMS 1976

School Bus Patrol X 15 MIN
16MM FILM OPTICAL SOUND P-J
Dramatizes the experience of a typical school as it improves school bus transportation by establishing school bus patrols. Shows how a school bus patrol operates and presents safety values of a good program.
Prod-AAAFTS Dist-AAAFTS 1963

School Bus Pre-Trip Inspection, The C 14 MIN
16MM FILM, 3/4 OR 1/2 IN VIDEO A
Shows bus drivers how to inspect a school bus for safe driving. Covers dashboard instruments, air brakes, lights and emergency equipment plus underthe-hood items. Teaches a driver, in a circle tour of a bus, how to check mirrors, wheels, tires, brake lights, flashers and turn signals. Presents also a condensed version of a complete brake system check.
Prod-CAHILL Dist-AIMS 1976

School Bus Safety C 15 MIN
3/4 OR 1/2 INCH VIDEO CASSETTE P-I
Emphasizes the importance of following the rules for school bus safety by contrasting the right and wrong ways of walking to school, waiting for the bus, boarding, riding and leaving the bus.
From The Safer You Series.
Prod-WCVETV Dist-GPITVL 1984

School Bus Safety - A Schmoadle Nightmare C 9 MIN
16MM FILM, 3/4 OR 1/2 IN VIDEO P
Shows how to behave on a school bus.
Prod-CROCUS Dist-CRMP 1975

School Bus Safety - With Strings Attached B 28 MIN
16MM FILM, 3/4 OR 1/2 IN VIDEO I-H A
Re-creates a bus hootenanny assembly program, showing student volunteers in an unrehearsed demonstration of the basic principles of school bus safety. Made in collaboration with the National Safety Council.
Prod-JOU Dist-JOU 1964

School Bus Safety And Courtesy (2nd Ed) C 15 MIN
16MM FILM, 3/4 OR 1/2 IN VIDEO P-J
Covers safety rules such as proper conduct to and from the bus stop, proper behavior while riding the bus, respect for the bus driver and orderly boarding and leaving of the bus. Includes a demonstration of emergency evacuation procedures.
Prod-CENTRO Dist-CORF 1983

School Citizenship—A Series
P-I
Discusses various aspects of proper deportment in school situations.
Prod-CENTRO Dist-CENTEF 1979

School Lunchroom Manners 010 MIN
Taking Care Of Your School Building 015 MIN
Use And Care of Books 013 MIN
Using And Caring For Art Materials 011 MIN

School Day In Japan C 10 MIN
16MM FILM, 3/4 OR 1/2 IN VIDEO P-I
Illustrates the typical school day in the life of a young Japanese boy and his sister. Presents the children's attitudes as an interesing contrast from the American school system.
Prod-FI Dist-FI 1970

School Day, A C 24 MIN
16MM FILM OPTICAL SOUND
Follows a bright, well-adjusted nine-year-old girl, who is congenitally blind, during her usual day. Portrays her as she arrives at her neighborhood school, goes to special instruction for the visually handicapped and participates in class with sighted peers.
Prod-VASSAR Dist-NYU

School Days C
16MM FILM OPTICAL SOUND
Documents the radical high school students organizing in New York City. Shows how they begin to use newspapers an an organizing tool, struggle to develop ways to protect themselves against repression and attempt to counteract tendencies toward insignificant reform.
Prod-SBARGE Dist-NEWSR

School Days C 15 MIN
2 INCH VIDEOTAPE
Demonstrates the relationship between the school and the city and reinforces the importance of education.
From The Let's Build A City Series.
Prod-WVIZTV Dist-GPITVL

School Days (Green Module - Quebec) C 15 MIN
3/4 OR 1/2 INCH VIDEO CASSETTE P
Presents a tour of carpenter, guide and cooking schools established by the Canadian government.
From The Other Families, Other Friends Series. Green Module - Quebec
Prod-WVIZTV Dist-AITECH 1971

School Daze - The Teacher Talks To OTs C 18 MIN
3/4 OR 1/2 INCH VIDEO CASSETTE PRO
Presents personal accounts of teachers who have worked with occupational therapists (OTs) in public schools.
Prod-BU Dist-BU

School Desegregation Missed, The C 29 MIN
3/4 INCH VIDEO CASSETTE
Describes an all-black school in Memphis, Tennessee, which was not desegregated by court order. Shows how students from a low income area lack the same opportunities as students in desegregated schools.
From The As We See It Series.
Prod-WTTWTV Dist-PUBTEL

School District Experiences In Implementing Technology C 65 MIN
3/4 OR 1/2 INCH VIDEO CASSETTE J-C A
Presents a panel of representatives from five school districts discussing the experiences of their districts in implementing technology and identifying some of the issues which emerged.
From The New Technology In Education Series.
Prod-USDOE Dist-USNAC 1983

School Excursion C 8 MIN
16MM FILM, 3/4 OR 1/2 IN VIDEO
Tells the animated story of two children who, fearing that their teacher won't allow them to bring their neighbor's dog on a school trip, use a magic earphone to turn him into a boy who walks on all fours.
Prod-KRATKY Dist-PHENIX 1978

School Experiences C 10 MIN
3/4 OR 1/2 INCH VIDEO CASSETTE
Features Fred Rogers discussing experiences children have at school.
From The You (Parents) Are Special Series.
Prod-FAMCOM Dist-FAMCOM

School For Clowns C 11 MIN
16MM FILM OPTICAL SOUND
A story about a boy who runs away from school to be a clown is used to stimulate oral language skills.
LC NO. 77-706882
Prod-DBA Dist-MLA 1969

School For Fours B 27 MIN
16MM FILM OPTICAL SOUND C T
Shows how play can become a learning experience for a four-year-old. Illustrates seven typical play activities, for both indoor and outdoor learning. Discusses the effects of teaching and discipline on the child's behavior.
LC NO. FIA68-2412
Prod-OHIOSU Dist-OSUMPD 1967

School For Me, A C 30 MIN
16MM FILM OPTICAL SOUND C A
Shows the techniques and methods employed by special education teachers in the field of teaching mentally retarded children, using the example of children from Navajo Indian reservations.
LC NO. 75-702928
Prod-USBIA Dist-AVED Prodn-BAILYL 1975

School For Playing C 25 MIN
16MM FILM, 3/4 OR 1/2 IN VIDEO H-C A
Features the school for gifted young musicians, run by world-renowned violinist Yehudi Menuhin. Shows how he views music as relaxation with a purpose and attempts to impart this philosophy to beginners on the violin, cello and piano. Discusses the importance of practice and music's role in life.
Prod-THAMES Dist-MEDIAG 1975

School Helpers C 9 MIN
16MM FILM OPTICAL SOUND K-P
Shows the teacher, the principal, school nurse and other helpful people. Suggests the ways in which boys and girls can help the school to run more smoothly and safely.
LC NO. FIA68-637
Prod-SIGMA Dist-FILCOM 1967

School Inservice Videotape—A Series
T
Provides instruction for teachers and educational administrators on a variety of topics including computers, teacher evaluation and special student problems.
Prod-TERRAS Dist-SLOSSF

Discipline
Effective Principal, The
Evaluation Of Teacher Performance
Gifted And The Talented, The
Microcomputers In Your School
Responsibility
Success Oriented Schools

School Is For Children C 17 MIN
16MM FILM OPTICAL SOUND
Shows the exceptional child being prepared for his first trip to school. Shows children participating in school activities designed to help them achieve self-confidence, social and motor skills and enthusiasm for learning.
LC NO. 75-701322
Prod-USBEH Dist-USNAC

School Lab Safety C 20 MIN
16MM FILM, 3/4 OR 1/2 IN VIDEO
Points out the potential hazards in school labs and shows ways to prevent accidents.
Prod-HANDEL Dist-HANDEL 1980

School Lab Safety (Captioned) C 20 MIN
16MM FILM, 3/4 OR 1/2 IN VIDEO
Points out the potential hazards in school labs and shows ways to prevent accidents.
Prod-HANDEL Dist-HANDEL 1980

School Law C 29 MIN
2 INCH VIDEOTAPE H-C A
Discusses laws that directly affect young people, the laws that govern education. Shows the Ace Trucking Company satirizing dress codes and discussion progresses from dress codes to students' rights.
From The Just Generation Series.
Prod-WITFTV Dist-PUBTEL 1972

School Libraries In Action C 18 MIN
16MM FILM OPTICAL SOUND
Illustrates major areas of a school library program-planning for library use, guiding reading, teaching library skills, supplying instructional materials and guiding reference work.
Prod-NCDPI Dist-UNC 1960

School Lunchroom Manners C 10 MIN
16MM FILM, 3/4 OR 1/2 IN VIDEO P-I
Uses examples of a pigpen, an elegant formal dining room and a battlefield to examine proper deportment in the school lunchroom. Addresses such problems as crowding, rowdy behavior, handling lunch coupons or money, courtesy to lunchroom workers and good table manners.
From The School Citizenship Series.
LC NO. 79-707212
Prod-CENTRO Dist-CORF 1979

School Of Physic C 18 MIN
16MM FILM - 3/4 IN VIDEO J-C A
Demonstrates research in such areas as solar energy, plasma physics, astronomy, astrophysics, and environmental physics.
LC NO. 81-706513
Prod-SYDUN Dist-TASCOR 1977

School Of The Sky - Parachuting At The U S Air Force Academy C 12 MIN
16MM FILM OPTICAL SOUND
Discusses the basic parachute training program used by the military forces, focusing on the program of the U S Air Force Academy.
LC NO. 74-706238
Prod-USAF Dist-USNAC 1969

School Otological-Audiological Follow-Up C 10 MIN
16MM FILM, 3/4 OR 1/2 IN VIDEO
Presents otological and audiological assessment within the School for the Partially Hearing. Describes a hearing aid check at the School for the Deaf in Stockholm.
From The International Education Of The Hearing Impaired Child Series.
LC NO. 80-707412
Prod-USBEH Dist-USNAC Prodn-AIRLIE 1980

School Prayer, Gun Control And The Right To Assemble C 60 MIN
3/4 OR 1/2 INCH VIDEO CASSETTE
Debates what the courts' role is in determining policy on school prayer, gun control and the right to assemble. Visits a hypothetical town beset by First and Second Amendment controversies.
From The Constitution - That Delicate Balance Series.
Prod-WTTWTV Dist-FI 1984

School Professionals And Parents C 22 MIN
16MM FILM, 3/4 OR 1/2 IN VIDEO A
Presents 12 vignettes which demonstrate typical situations parents might encounter when dealing with school professionals such as parents who need but reject the assistance of a psychologist or social worker, parents who reject advice about their child or request inappropriate placement, parents who ask the school to be responsible for something outside its domain and parents who object to the presence of the teacher or the child in discussions about the child's problem.
Prod-MTI Dist-MTI

School Readiness C 25 MIN
3/4 OR 1/2 INCH VIDEO CASSETTE PRO
Shows a variety of tests administered to children by a pediatrician to determine their psychological as well as physical readiness to enter the school world.
Prod-WFP Dist-WFP

School Safety C 9 MIN
16MM FILM, 3/4 OR 1/2 IN VIDEO K-I
Presents ways to help insure safety when playing in the schoolyard, when using supplies in the classroom and when responding to emergency drills at schools.
From The Safety For Elementary Series.
Prod-MORLAT Dist-AIMS 1974

School Safety C 20 MIN
3/4 OR 1/2 INCH VIDEO CASSETTE J-C A
Discusses various aspects of school safety.
From The Safety Sense Series. Pt. 10
Prod-WCVETV Dist-GPITVL 1981

School Safety (Spanish) C 9 MIN
16MM FILM, 3/4 OR 1/2 IN VIDEO K-I
Presents ways to help insure safety when playing in the schoolyard, when using supplies in the classroom and when responding to emergency drills at school.
From The Safety For Elementary Series.
Prod-MORLAT Dist-AIMS 1974

School Shop Safety X 15 MIN
16MM FILM, 3/4 OR 1/2 IN VIDEO J-H
Emphasizes basic safety practices to be observed when handling various materials, hand tools, and machine tools and electricity. Points out that paying careful attention to safety rules is the first good habit of safety in any school shop.
Prod-FA Dist-PHENIX Prodn-FA 1968

School Shop Safety (Spanish) X 15 MIN
16MM FILM, 3/4 OR 1/2 IN VIDEO J-H
Exphasizes basic safety practices to be observed when handling various materials, hand tools, and machine tools and electricity. Points out that paying careful attention to safety rules is the first good habit of safety in any school shop.
Prod-FA Dist-PHENIX 1968

School Survival Skills - How To Study Effectively C 57 MIN
3/4 OR 1/2 INCH VIDEO CASSETTE
Shows how students can budget their time and study effectively.
LC NO. 81-706694
Prod-CHUMAN Dist-GA 1981

School That Went To Town, The B 15 MIN
16MM FILM OPTICAL SOUND
Records health-related activities in an elementary school classroom over the course of a year.
Prod-VTDH Dist-VTDH

School Vandalism C 9 MIN
16MM FILM, 3/4 OR 1/2 IN VIDEO I-J
Explores school vandalism through the actions and laments of four trouble-making youths. Uses flashback techniques to unfold the story of breaking in and accidental fire.
Prod-EVANSA Dist-AIMS 1972

School Volunteers - A New Dimension For Learning C 9 MIN
16MM FILM OPTICAL SOUND
Shows how four people became interested in school volunteer work and how their services contribute to the quality of children's education.
LC NO. 76-702139
Prod-FSDOE Dist-FSDOE Prodn-ORANGE 1977

School-Age Child C 41 MIN
3/4 OR 1/2 INCH VIDEO CASSETTE
Shows the refinement of motor skills and continuous activity of the child aged six to 12. Demonstrates continual socialization activities via play activities.
From The Infancy Through Adolescence Series.
Prod-WSUN Dist-AJN

School's Environment, The C 30 MIN
16MM FILM OPTICAL SOUND T
Provides lesson ideas dealing with the investigation of the school's environment.
From The Starting Tomorrow Series. Unit 2 - Understanding The School's Neighborhood
Prod-EALING Dist-WALKED 1968

School's In - Soviet Style C 27 MIN
16MM FILM, 3/4 OR 1/2 IN VIDEO J-C A
Follows the progress of Soviet students in a rural and urban school. Examines student-teacher attitudes, the curricula and aspirations.
From The Soviet Style Series.
LC NO. 84-707068
Prod-JOU Dist-JOU 1982

Schoolboy Father C 30 MIN
16MM FILM, 3/4 OR 1/2 IN VIDEO J-H
Tells a story about an unplanned, teenage pregnancy and the father's attempt to raise the child. Shows him finally realizing that he should give the child up for adoption. Originally shown as an ABC Afterschool Special.
LC NO. 81-707016
Prod-TAHSEM Dist-LCOA 1980

Schools C 29 MIN
3/4 OR 1/2 INCH VIDEO CASSETTE A
Discusses whether children are learning what they are being taught in schools or if they are getting different messages.
From The Feelings Series.
Prod-SCETV Dist-PBS 1979

Schools That Care C
16MM FILM, 3/4 OR 1/2 IN VIDEO T
See series title for descriptive statement.
From The Dealing With Social Problems In The Classroom Series.
Prod-MFFD Dist-FI 1983

Schubert C 27 MIN
16MM FILM, 3/4 OR 1/2 IN VIDEO H-C A
Describes the composer, Franz Schubert, as a quiet, unassuming man who lived in the classical era, but whose orchestral and piano works had a romantic strain that anticipated the light-hearted spirit of the 19th century. Focuses on some of his most famous compositions.
Prod-SEABEN Dist-IFB 1974

Schubert, The Piano Trio, And Peter Frankl, Gyorgy Pauk And Ralph Kirshbaum C 26 MIN
16MM FILM, 3/4 OR 1/2 IN VIDEO J-C A
States that Austrian composer Franz Schubert (1797-1828) is noted for chamber works, symphonies, overtures, masses and piano music in the romantic style. Presents a trio composed of Peter Frankl playing the piano, Gyorgy Paul playing the violin and Ralph Kirshbaum playing the cello performing some of Schubert's music.
From The Musical Triangle Series.
Prod-THAMES Dist-MEDIAG 1975

Schuster / Issacson Family, The C 9 MIN
16MM FILM, 3/4 OR 1/2 IN VIDEO H-C A
Introduces a lesbian couple who have kept their children.
From The American Family - An Endangered Species Series.
Prod-NBC Dist-FI 1979

Schweinfurt And Regensburg C 14 MIN
3/4 OR 1/2 INCH VIDEO CASSETTE
Records the famous bombing mission over Germany's ball-bearing plants, August 17, 1943.
Prod-IHF Dist-IHF

Schwepps Tonic Water C 1 MIN
3/4 OR 1/2 INCH VIDEO CASSETTE
Shows a classic television commercial with a dignified woman and man trying to find out where they met each other.
Prod-BROOKC Dist-BROOKC

Sci-Fair—A Series J
Shows how to plan a science fair and how to research and present science experiments.
Prod-MAETEL Dist-GPITVL

Application 015 MIN
At The Fair 015 MIN
Conducting Research 015 MIN
Selecting An Investigation 015 MIN
Teacher, The (Inservice) 015 MIN

Sciatic Pain And The Intervertebral Disk C 33 MIN
16MM FILM OPTICAL SOUND PRO
Explains symptoms and treatment of functional and organic rupturing of the spine in the lower lunbar region, especially at the intervertebral disk.
LC NO. FIE52-1072
Prod-USN Dist-USNAC

Science - New Frontiers—A Series
16MM FILM, 3/4 OR 1/2 IN VIDEO J-C A
Prod-CREEDM Dist-PHENIX 1974

Exploring The Human Brain 18 MIN
Extending Life 15 MIN
Hungry World 13 MIN
Is The Weather Changing 16 MIN
No Easy Answers 14 MIN
PSI - Boundaries Of The Mind 18 MIN

Science - Woman's Work C 27 MIN
16MM FILM, 3/4 OR 1/2 IN VIDEO
Looks at the various science careers available to women. Emphasizes the need for a strong science and math background in high school coursework.
Prod-NSF Dist-USNAC 1982

Science Aids The Mariner C 13 MIN
16MM FILM OPTICAL SOUND
Shows several innovations in technology aimed at making the seas safer, including the automated mutual assistance rescue system, communications satellites which are major improvements on radio telegraphy, an augmented international ice patrol and an ocean-weather satellite monitor.
Prod-ALLFP Dist-NSTA 1976

Science Aids The Visually Handicapped C 13 MIN
16MM FILM OPTICAL SOUND
Profiles scientific approaches toward meeting the needs of the blind and visually impaired, including therapies and training systems and advanced mobility and vision aids.
Prod-ALLFP Dist-NSTA 1978

Science And Metrics C 20 MIN
3/4 INCH VIDEO CASSETTE I
Introduces the term ampere and shows the passage of current from battery to light bulb. Demonstrates volume of solid objects by their displacement in water.
From The Metric Marmalade Series.
Prod-WCVETV Dist-GPITVL 1979

Science And Society C 18 MIN
16MM FILM, 3/4 OR 1/2 IN VIDEO J-C
Presents an introduction to science and its role in society.
From The Humanities Series.
Prod-MGHT Dist-MGHT Prodn-CLAIB 1971

Science And Society C 30 MIN
3/4 OR 1/2 INCH VIDEO CASSETTE
Explores the mechanical worldview of a clockwork universe and the emerging view of an ecological, biological and living-systems paradigm. Presented by Dr Fritjof Capra, author of The Tao Of Physics.
From The Creating Alternative Futures Series.
Prod-BULFRG Dist-BULFRG

Science And Society - A Race Against Time B 30 MIN
16MM FILM OPTICAL SOUND H-C A
Discusses the social problems created by technology and the probability of correction in the near future. Points out that social problems have resulted not from knowledge but from the application of that knowledge. Predicts that problems will be solved but that they will first become worse.
From The Spectrum Series.
LC NO. FIA68-414
Prod-NET Dist-IU 1968

Science And Superstition (2nd Ed) C 10 MIN
16MM FILM, 3/4 OR 1/2 IN VIDEO I-H A
Compares common beliefs from the world of superstition with scientifically tested ideas. Illustrates similarities and differences between science and superstition.
Prod-CORF Dist-CORF 1973

Science And Technology C 30 MIN
3/4 INCH VIDEO CASSETTE
Discusses the effect of the Cultural Revolution on Chinese science and technology.
From The China After Mao Series.
Prod-UMITV Dist-UMITV 1980

Science And Technology Advisory Committee - The Future In Focus C 20 MIN
16MM FILM - 3/4 IN VIDEO
Depicts the story of the STAC group from its inception by James Webb in 1964 to its climatic meeting in 1969. Stresses contributions made by this group to manned space flight program in the various scientific areas.
Prod-NASA Dist-NASA 1972

Science And The Free Mind C 30 MIN
3/4 OR 1/2 INCH VIDEO CASSETTE J-C A
Presents Nobel Laureate Sir John Eccles discussing science and the free mind.
From The Moral Values In Contemporary Society Series.
Prod-AMHUMA Dist-AMHUMA

Science And The Metric System C 20 MIN
3/4 INCH VIDEO CASSETTE J-C A
Presents the seven base units of the metric system. Includes a segment on scientific notation.
From The Metric System Series.
Prod-MAETEL Dist-GPITVL 1975

Science And The Sea, Pt 1 C 30 MIN
3/4 INCH VIDEO CASSETTE J
Depicts a cruise aboard the Duke University research vessel Eastward. Describes the ship's operation, navigation, physical oceanography and microbiological studies.
From The What On Earth Series.
Prod-NCSDPI Dist-GPITVL 1979

Science And The Sea, Pt 2 C 30 MIN
3/4 INCH VIDEO CASSETTE J
Follows the cruise of the research vessel Eastward, showing how scientists study plankton and bottom communities and sample water and air pollution.
From The What On Earth Series.
Prod-NCSDPI Dist-GPITVL 1979

Science Animal Life—A Series

Discusses various wild and domesticated animals.
Prod-MORLAT Dist-MORLAT

Buffalo 010 MIN
Cattle 010 MIN

Science At Kew Gardens C 27 MIN
16MM FILM, 3/4 OR 1/2 IN VIDEO J-C A
Explores the behind-the-scenes scientific work and research at Kew Gardens in London.
From The Perspective Series.
Prod-LONTVS Dist-STNFLD

Science Communications Speeded C 14 MIN
16MM FILM OPTICAL SOUND
Profiles methods which scientific investigators can use to keep abreast of new research breakthroughs and to study swiftly occurring events in remote regions.
Prod-ALLFP Dist-NSTA 1975

Science Corner I, Unit I - Living Things In Autumn—A Series
P
Stimulates children to investigate in their own backyard or park the many changes that take place in the autumn. Discusses migration and hibernation as well as the cycle of plant growth.
Prod-MPATI Dist-GPITVL

How Are Seeds Scattered In Autumn 20 MIN
How Can We Help Birds In Autumn And Winter 20 MIN
How Do People Get Ready For Winter 20 MIN
What Can We Do With A Pumpkin 20 MIN
What Can You Discover In A Vacant Lot 20 MIN
What Can You Discover In A Wooded Area 20 MIN
What Do Some Birds Do In Autumn And Winter 20 MIN
What Do Some Other Animals Do In Autumn And 20 MIN
What Happens To Some Furry Animals In Autumn 20 MIN
What Happens To Trees In Autumn 20 MIN

Science Corner I, Unit II - Studying Rocks—A Series
P
Helps children find out how rocks help form the surface of the earth, observes the constant change in rocks and observes the wealth we take from the earth for use in our lives.
Prod-MPATI Dist-GPITVL

How Are Rocks Formed 20 MIN
How Are Stones Formed From Seashells 20 MIN
How Can Rocks Be Identified 20 MIN
How Was Coal Formed 20 MIN
What Breaks Rocks 20 MIN
What Can We Learn By Looking At Rocks 20 MIN
What Rocks Can We Collect 20 MIN

Science Corner I, Unit III - Looking At Things Around Us—A Series
P
Investigates some simple problems involving everyday things. Draws attention to the materials of the earth and how they are changed to fill some basic needs.
Prod-MPATI Dist-GPITVL

How Do We Use Rubber 20 MIN
What Can We Find Out About Paper 20 MIN
What Do We Put Under Our Streets 20 MIN
What Do We Use To Make Our Streets 20 MIN
What Happens When We Mix Things With Water 20 MIN
What Makes Things Dry Up 20 MIN
Where Do Some Classroom Materials Come From 20 MIN

Science Corner I, Unit IV - Protection Against The Weather—A Series
P
Illustrates the way science helps man protect himself from the extremes of weather.
Prod-MPATI Dist-GPITVL

How Do Buildings Help To Keep Us Warm And Dry 20 MIN
How Does Clothing Help To Keep Us Dry 20 MIN
How Does Clothing Help To Keep Us Warm 20 MIN
What Does Fire Need To Burn 20 MIN

Science Corner I, Unit IX - Transportation—A Series
P
Illustrates moving of products and people from place to place. Treats the principle of transportation with the integration of social studies.
Prod-MPATI Dist-GPITVL

How Are Boats Moved Through The Water 20 MIN
How Can We Use Wheels Safely 20 MIN
How Do We Use Moving Water 20 MIN
How Does A Glider Fly 20 MIN
How Does An Airplane Fly 20 MIN
What Happens When Things Fall Through The Air 20 MIN
What Is Ocean Water Like 20 MIN
What Makes Wheels Move 20 MIN
Why Do Boats Float 20 MIN
Why Do We Use Wheels 20 MIN

Science Corner I, Unit V - Your Body And How It Works—A Series
P
Develops the interest that children have in the human body. Explains how energy is obtained from food and how the body accommodates itself to the stresses placed on it.
Prod-MPATI Dist-GPITVL

What Happens When We Exercise 20 MIN
Where Does Your Body Get Its Energy 20 MIN

Science Corner I, Unit VI - Class Science Fair—A Series
P
Illustrates classroom displays and how they can be a source of great satisfaction to the originators.
Prod-MPATI Dist-GPITVL

How Can We Have A Class Science Fair 20 MIN

Science Corner I, Unit VII - Obtaining And Preserving Foods—A Series
P
Illustrates the story of how the foods we eat are secured, prepared and preserved.
Prod-MPATI Dist-GPITVL

How Do Canning And Cooling Preserve Foods 20 MIN
How Do We Make Bread 20 MIN
How Do We Preserve Foods 20 MIN
What Foods Do We Get From The Sea 20 MIN
Where Does Your Breakfast Come From 20 MIN

Science Corner I, Unit VIII - Communication—A Series
P
Introduces children to the many different kinds of sound impressions. Experiments with sound interpretation that can extend a child's acquaintance with the world.
Prod-MPATI Dist-GPITVL

How Can We Make High And Low Sounds 20 MIN
How Can We Make Rhythm Instruments 20 MIN
How Do We Make Sounds 20 MIN
How Do We Make Sounds Louder 20 MIN
How Do We Make Sounds Softer 20 MIN
How Do We Record Sounds 20 MIN
How Does Sound Travel 20 MIN
Why Do We Use Mirrors 20 MIN

Science Corner I, Unit X - Simple Machines—A Series
P
Experiments with devices of the home and school to discover how they operate and how they make work easier.
Prod-MPATI Dist-GPITVL

How Are Levers Helpful To Us 20 MIN
How Are Pulleys Useful To Us 20 MIN
How Do Gears Help Us 20 MIN
Why Do We Use Kitchen Tools 20 MIN

Science Corner I, Unit XI - Young Animals—A Series
P
Experiences an understanding of birth and growth patterns of baby animals. Comprehends the miracle of growth in all living things.
Prod-MPATI Dist-GPITVL

How Are Young Farm Animals Cared For 20 MIN
How Are Young Zoo Animals Cared For 20 MIN
How Do Animals Take Care Of Their Young 20 MIN
How Do Frogs Change As They Grow 20 MIN
What Happens Inside An Egg 20 MIN

Science Corner II, Unit I - Animals—A Series
I
Gives an opportunity for children to observe what one kind of animal needs in order to live and grow. Presents a better understanding of animals that will help the pupil learn to enjoy the outdoors.
Prod-MPATI Dist-GPITVL

How Are Bees Important To Us 20 MIN
How Are Fish Fitted To Live Under Water 20 MIN
How Are Turtles Fitted To The Places Where 20 MIN
How Can We Keep A Pet Hamster 20 MIN
How Can We Learn To Recognize Birds 20 MIN
How Can We Make A Good Home For Water-Living 20 MIN
How Can We Take Care Of Puppies And Kittens 20 MIN
How Do Ants Live Together 20 MIN
How Do Spiders Live 20 MIN
How Do Wasps Live 20 MIN
What Are Salamanders Like 20 MIN
What Can We Learn About Butterflies And Moths 20 MIN
What Can We Learn About The Crayfish And Its 20 MIN
What Can We Learn By Studying Snakes 20 MIN
What Is An Insect 20 MIN
Where Do Animals Live 20 MIN

Science Corner II, Unit II - The Earth In Space—A Series
I
Develops fundamental concepts of the sun, moon and stars and of such phenomena as sunset and sunrise, shadows and night and day.
Prod-MPATI Dist-GPITVL

How Are Shadows Made Indoors 20 MIN
What Are The Planets Like 20 MIN
What Are The Stars Like 20 MIN
What Can The Sun Do 20 MIN
What Can We See After Sunset 20 MIN
What Causes Night And Day 20 MIN
What Is It Like On The Moon 20 MIN
What Makes The Moon Seem To Change Its Shape 20 MIN
Why Do Shadows Change Outdoors 20 MIN

Science Corner II, Unit III - Journey In Space—A Series
I
Furnishes an opportunity to develop important science concepts of flight, gravity and the conditions man needs to live.
Prod-MPATI Dist-GPITVL

How Are Space Rockets Made 20 MIN
How Can We Live In Space 20 MIN
What Are Man-Made Satellites Like 20 MIN
What Will Space Stations Be Like 20 MIN

Science Corner II, Unit IV - Scientific Instruments—A Series
I
Uses everyday instruments such as the ruler, thermometer, carpenter's level and the kitchen measuring cups for scientific investigation that children can understand.
Prod-MPATI Dist-GPITVL

How Can We Make And Use Scientific Instruments 20 MIN
What Can You Discover With A Magnifying Glass 20 MIN

Science Corner II, Unit IX - Exploring Our Country—A Series
I
Provides an insight into the various areas of this country and the living problems that each particular place presents. Discusses how plants, animals, weather, climate, soil and water are related to human life.
Prod-MPATI Dist-GPITVL

What Living Things Can Be Found In Ponds,
What Living Things Can Be Found In Swamps And 20 MIN
What Living Things Can Be Found On The Desert 20 MIN
What Plants And Animals Can Be Found Along 20 MIN
Why Do We Need Animal Refuges 20 MIN

Science Corner II, Unit V - School Science Fair Series
I
Discusses the effectiveness found in the organization of a school fair on one or more grade levels.
Prod-MPATI Dist-GPITVL

How Can We Plan A School Science Fair 20 MIN

Science Corner II, Unit VI - Magnetism And Electricity—A Series
I
Examines magnetism and electricity, makes compasses, uses dry cells in simple circuits, and makes switches, electromagnets and telegraph sets.
Prod-MPATI Dist-GPITVL

For What Things Do We Use Electricity 20 MIN
How Are All Magnets Alike 20 MIN
How Can We Make A Simple Telegraph 20 MIN
How Can We Make An Electromagnet 20 MIN
How Can We Make And Use A Compass 20 MIN
How Do We Get Light From Electricity 20 MIN
How Does Electricity Travel 20 MIN
What Can Magnets Do 20 MIN
What Happens When Electricity Travels Through 20 MIN

Science Corner II, Unit VII - Understanding Weather—A Series
I
Provides opportunities for first-hand experiences with the forces of nature. Includes experimentation on the changing weather as well as a construction of a simple weather instrument.
Prod-MPATI Dist-GPITVL

How Do We Measure The Wind 20 MIN
What Are The Different Forms That Water Takes 20 MIN
What Causes Thunder And Lightning 20 MIN
What Does The Wind Do 20 MIN
What Happens At A Weather Station 20 MIN
What Happens On A Freezing Day 20 MIN
What Makes Clouds And Rain 20 MIN
What Makes Static Electricity 20 MIN
Why Is Rain Important To Us 20 MIN

Science Corner II, Unit VIII - Plants In Spring—A Series
I
Directs a child's observations to the many ways in which plants propagate themselves from seeds, roots, stems, leaves and bulbs.
Prod-MPATI Dist-GPITVL

How Are Plants Fitted To Grow In Different
How Can We Make A Terrarium 20 MIN
How Can We Plant And Care For A Garden 20 MIN
How Do We Get New Plants 20 MIN
What Are Spring Days Like 20 MIN

What Are The Important Parts Of A Plant 20 MIN
What Do Farm Crops Need In Order To Grow 20 MIN
What Do Seeds Need In Order To Sprout 20 MIN
What Kind Of Soil Do We Need For Planting 20 MIN

Science Education In Tropical Africa B 55 MIN
16MM FILM OPTICAL SOUND
A lecture by an African professor on the necessity for advanced education in the fields of science and technology to enable African nations to meet the demands of the present-day world.
Prod-EDS Dist-EDC 1962

Science Fairs C 20 MIN
16MM FILM, 3/4 OR 1/2 IN VIDEO
Shows how science fairs can be set up within a school district and how some projects can gain wider recognition. Provides examples of student-built science experiments.
Prod-HANDEL Dist-HANDEL 1984

Science Fiction - Jules Verne To Ray Bradbury C 51 MIN
3/4 OR 1/2 INCH VIDEO CASSETTE
Tells how science fiction continues to frighten and entertain readers but is being taken more seriously. Distinguishes between science fiction and fantasy.
LC NO. 81-706689
Prod-CHUMAN Dist-GA 1981

Science Fiction Films C 30 MIN
16MM FILM OPTICAL SOUND H-C T
Forrest Ackerman, major historian of science fiction and horror films, discusses the development of science fiction films according to the subject or themes.
From The Literature Of Science Fiction Series.
LC NO. 72-700534
Prod-UKANBC Dist-UKANS 1971

Science Fiction Highlights No. 2 B 30 MIN
16MM FILM OPTICAL SOUND
Presents excerpts from science fiction films.
Prod-CFS Dist-CFS 1975

Science For The Future - Implications C 20 MIN
2 INCH VIDEOTAPE I
See series title for descriptive statement.
From The Exploring With Science, Unit XIII - Conclusion Series.
Prod-MPATI Dist-GPITVL

Science Friction C 9 MIN
16MM FILM OPTICAL SOUND C A
Presents a satire on mass society, conformism, and today's infatuation with rockets.
Prod-VANBKS Dist-VANBKS 1959

Science Goes Underground - Japan's Road-Builders Beat The Swampland C 15 MIN
16MM FILM OPTICAL SOUND
Explains that the Sendai By-pass was constructed to relieve traffic congestion on the national road, route number four, which passes through Sendai City. Introduces the sand and paper drain methods and various types of experiments to improve the foundation of the road to be constructed on marsh land. Documents construction progress from start to completion.
Prod-UNIJAP Dist-UNIJAP 1967

Science In Action—A Series
C
Prod-ALLFP Dist-COUNFI

Advances In Bio-Medical Engineering 15 MIN
Agricultural Genetics Improves Yields 15 MIN
Environmental Impact Study Safeguards 15 MIN
Glacier Research 15 MIN
Manmade Extinction 15 MIN
Mars - The Search For Life Begins 15 MIN
New Solar System, The 15 MIN
New Ways To Disseminate Scientific Knowledge 15 MIN
Probing Planetary Processes 15 MIN
Radio Astronomers Probe The Universe 15 MIN
Research Into High Blood Pressure 15 MIN
Reshaping Aquatic Environments 15 MIN
Search For New Energy, The, Pt 1 15 MIN
Search For New Energy, The, Pt 2 15 MIN
Secrets Of The Brain 15 MIN
Shark - Ancient Mystery Of The Sea 15 MIN
Studies In Meteorology 15 MIN
Studying The Big Cats Of Africa 15 MIN
To Save A Speicies 15 MIN
Towers Without Infernos 15 MIN
Upwelling Phenomenon, The 15 MIN
Water For A Thirsty World 15 MIN

Science In Museums C 27 MIN
16MM FILM, 3/4 OR 1/2 IN VIDEO J-C A
Explores the role of Britain's museums in scientific research.
From The Perspective Series.
Prod-LONTVS Dist-STNFLD

Science In Our Space Age—A Series

Prod-ACA Dist-ACA

Portrait Of The Sun 18 MIN
Sun's Energy, The 17 MIN
Trees - Our Plant Giants 14 MIN
Water In The Weather 17 MIN

Science In The Elementary School - Life Science—A Series
T
Focuses on the teaching of life sciences.
Prod-UWKY Dist-GPITVL 1980

Animals And Environment 20 MIN
Animals On The School Grounds 20 MIN
Biotic Potential And Genetic Identity 20 MIN
Environmental Cycles 20 MIN
Food Webs And Chains 20 MIN
Formal Operations And Classroom Management 20 MIN
Interdependent Populations 20 MIN
Interrupted Cycles 20 MIN
Introduction - Building An Aquarium 20 MIN
Life Cycles 20 MIN
Observations In The Aquarium 20 MIN
Plant Eaters And Animal Eaters 20 MIN
Producers And Consumers 20 MIN
Seeds And Plants 20 MIN

Science In The Elementary School - Physical Science—A Series
T
Explains how teachers can teach physical sciences, illustrating communication skills, teaching tactics, and evaluation strategies.
Prod-UWKY Dist-GPITVL 1979

Collecting Evidence Of Energy Transfer 20 MIN
Energy Transfer - The Rotoplane 20 MIN
Exploring Classroom Strategies 20 MIN
Extending The Exploration Lesson 20 MIN
Interaction - Exploration Of The Invention 20 MIN
Interpreting Models - Magnetic And Electric 20 MIN
Introduction, An 20 MIN
Locating Objects By Coordinates 20 MIN
Measuring Electrical Flow 20 MIN
Mystery Systems And Mental Models 20 MIN
Pulley System, A - Focusing On Discovery 20 MIN
Relative Position And Motion 20 MIN
Subsystems And Variables - The Whirly Bird 20 MIN
System In Solution, A 20 MIN

Science In The Seventies C 52 MIN
3/4 INCH VIDEO CASSETTE
Discusses the relevance of science to problems of the 1970's, summarizing the goals, orientation and activities of the research and development community. Issued in 1973 as a motion picture.
LC NO. 79-706062
Prod-NSF Dist-USNAC Prodn-BMICRL 1979

Science In Your Classroom—A Series

Prod-WENHTV Dist-GPITVL

Activity-Centered Science 30 MIN
Collecting And Classifying 30 MIN
Elementary Science Today 30 MIN
Evaluating Pupil Progress 30 MIN
Evaluating Your Science Program 30 MIN
Experiments 30 MIN
Field Trip, The 30 MIN
Living Things In The Classroom 30 MIN
Measurement 30 MIN
Models And Audio-Visual Aids 30 MIN
New Programs In Elementary Science 30 MIN
Observation 30 MIN
Outdoor Laboratory, The 30 MIN
Planning Science Activities 30 MIN
Supplementing Direct Experiences 30 MIN

Science Investigates Energy Fields Of Life C 14 MIN
16MM FILM OPTICAL SOUND
Discusses Kirlian photography, which depicts the auras of light surrounding living objects. Shows how these images appear to change due to the presence of alcohol, drugs, emotional stress or psychic healers.
Prod-ALLFP Dist-NSTA 1977

Science Is Discovery—A Series
P
Prod-DETPS Dist-GPITVL

Are All Stars Alike 15 MIN
How Are Animals Adapted For Survival 15 MIN
How Are Animals Classified 15 MIN
How Are Atoms Combined 15 MIN
How Are Green Plants Alike 15 MIN
How Are Non-Green Plants Alike 15 MIN
How Are Plants Classified 15 MIN
How Big Is The Universe 15 MIN
How Big Is Your World 15 MIN
How Can Electrical Energy Make Things Move 15 MIN
How Does Temperature Affect Matter 15 MIN
How Is Balance In An Environment Maintained 15 MIN
How Is The Earth's Surface Changed By 15 MIN
How Is The Earth's Surface Changed By Water 15 MIN
How Is The Earth's Surface Changed By Wind 15 MIN
How Many Kinds Of Atoms Exist 15 MIN
What Animals Live In Communities 15 MIN
What Are Planets 15 MIN
What Are Some Special Forms Of Behavior 15 MIN
What Are The Characteristics Of Living Things 15 MIN
What Are The Properties Of Matter 15 MIN
What Green Plants Reproduce By Other Means 15 MIN
What Green Plants Reproduce By Seeds 15 MIN
What Happens When Environmental Conditions 15 MIN
What Is In A Pond 15 MIN
What Is Matter 15 MIN
What Is The Earth's Surface Like 15 MIN
What Is The Water Cycle 15 MIN
What Makes Air Move 15 MIN
What Makes Electric Current Flow 15 MIN
What Makes Water Move 15 MIN
Where Are Living Things Found 15 MIN
Why Do Eclipses Occur 15 MIN
Why Do Temperatures Of Planets Vary 15 MIN
Why Does The Sun's Position Seem To Change 15 MIN

Science Is Everywhere—A Series
P
Prod-DETPS Dist-GPITVL

Animals Live And Grow, Pt 1 15 MIN
Animals Live And Grow, Pt 2 15 MIN
Animals Live And Grow, Pt 3 15 MIN
Animals Live And Grow, Pt 4 15 MIN
Darkness And Light, Pt 1 15 MIN
Darkness And Light, Pt 2 15 MIN
Darkness And Light, Pt 3 15 MIN
Fuels At Work, Pt 1 15 MIN
Fuels At Work, Pt 2 15 MIN
Fuels At Work, Pt 3 15 MIN
Millions Of Years Ago And Now 15 MIN
Molecules At Work, Pt 1 15 MIN
Molecules At Work, Pt 2 15 MIN
Molecules At Work, Pt 3 15 MIN
Plants Live And Grow, Pt 1 15 MIN
Plants Live And Grow, Pt 2 15 MIN
Plants Live And Grow, Pt 3 15 MIN
Plants Live And Grow, Pt 4 15 MIN
Silence And Sound, Pt 1 15 MIN
Silence And Sound, Pt 2 15 MIN
Silence And Sound, Pt 3 15 MIN
Silence And Sound, Pt 4 15 MIN
Stories For A New View - The Earth's Plants, 15 MIN
Stories For A New View - The Earth's Plants, 15 MIN
Very Large, The, Pt 1 15 MIN
Very Large, The, Pt 2 15 MIN
Very Large, The, Pt 3 15 MIN
Very Large, The, Pt 4 15 MIN
Very Large, The, Pt 5 15 MIN
Very Small, The, Pt 1 15 MIN
Very Small, The, Pt 2 15 MIN
Very Small, The, Pt 3 15 MIN

Science Is Searching—A Series
P
Evolves around large, relatively stable ideas in science. Explores the material universe, and seeks an orderly explanation of the objects and events therein. Allows small children to test these explanations and make every lesson an experience in search of meaning.
Prod-DETPS Dist-GPITVL

Animal Development 15 MIN
Animal Eggs 15 MIN
Animals Need Food 15 MIN
Changes In The State Of Matter 15 MIN
Clouds 15 MIN
Condensation 15 MIN
Day And Night 15 MIN
Dinosaur Fossils 15 MIN
Energy And Motion 15 MIN
Evaporation 15 MIN
Food Chain 15 MIN
Fossil Preservation 15 MIN
Friction And Motion 15 MIN
Growth 15 MIN
Living Things Grow, Pt 1 15 MIN
Living Things Grow, Pt 2 15 MIN
Magnetic Force 15 MIN
Mammal Fossils 15 MIN
Mammal Young 15 MIN
Matter 15 MIN
Moon, The 15 MIN
Non-Green Plants 15 MIN
Plants Need Energy 15 MIN
Plants Need Water 15 MIN
Seeds And Cutting 15 MIN
Shadows 15 MIN
Sources Of Evergy 15 MIN
Thermometers 15 MIN
We Grow 15 MIN
Weather Cycle 15 MIN
Work 15 MIN
Working Against The Force Of Gravity 15 MIN

Science Island B 5 MIN
16MM FILM OPTICAL SOUND
Portrays a unique natural science school on Toronto Island in Canada where children can learn science through first hand experience with nature.
From The Screen News Digest Series. Vol 4, Issue 7
Prod-HEARST Dist-HEARST 1962

Science Laboratory Safety, Pt 1 C 18 MIN
16MM FILM OPTICAL SOUND J-H
Emphasizes the importance of safety measures in using lab equipment and performing experiments in the school science lab.
LC NO. 79-709019
Prod-VADE Dist-VADE 1970

Science Laboratory Safety, Pt 2 C 15 MIN
16MM FILM OPTICAL SOUND J-C
Discusses the importance of using proper safety measures while performing experiments or using equipment in the biology laboratory.
Prod-VADE Dist-VADE 1975

Science Of Chemistry, The C 10 MIN
16MM FILM OPTICAL SOUND J-H
Helps take the mystery out of chemistry for the beginning student. Uses diagrammatic animation to explain simple atomic and molecular processes in the formation of compounds.
LC NO. FIA61-806
Prod-CLI Dist-CLI Prodn-CLI 1960

Science Of Cooking, The C 30 MIN
3/4 OR 1/2 INCH VIDEO CASSETTE H
Presents physics professor Jearl Walker offering graphic and unusual demonstrations exemplifying the principles of heat through the science of cooking.

From The Kinetic Karnival Of Jearl Walker. Pt 6
LC NO. 83-706120
Prod-WVIZTV Dist-GPITVL 1982

Science Of Energy—A Series

Prod-FINLYS Dist-FINLYS 1976

Breeder, The 023 MIN
Energy Consequences 021 MIN
Solar Generation, The 021 MIN
Which Energy 023 MIN

Science Of Hitting, The C 28 MIN
16MM FILM OPTICAL SOUND
Reveals baseball super-star Ted Williams' secrets of being a good hitter.
Prod-SEARS Dist-MTP

Science Of Life—A Series
J-C A
Offers an interdisciplinary approach to the life sciences.
Prod-CRIPSE Dist-WARDS 1981

Animal Worldsense, The 025 MIN
Ascent Of Man, The 024 MIN
Check And Balance In Nature (2nd Ed) 022 MIN
Death - An Invention Of Life 023 MIN
Energy In Life (2nd Ed) 022 MIN
Man, The Symbol Maker 025 MIN
Man's Impact On The Environment 020 MIN
Technological Man 025 MIN

Science Of Murder, The C 57 MIN
16MM FILM, 3/4 OR 1/2 IN VIDEO H-C A
Examines the reality of murder, including the social distress it causes and the clinical expertise needed to determine responsibility. Studies the work of a medical examiner, the police, a pathologist and laboratory technicians. Includes discussions by forensic psychiatrists, convicted murderers and former U S Attorney-General Ramsey Clark as to the motives which lead people to mortal violence.
From The Nova Series.
LC NO. 83-706023
Prod-WGBHTV Dist-TIMLIF 1981

Science Of Musical Sounds, The C 11 MIN
16MM FILM OPTICAL SOUND I-H
Explores the basic principles of sound production, using the harp, flute and xylophone. Shows that sound is produced when something is made to vibrate, and illustrates pitch and volume. Uses an oscilloscope to show sound vibrations.
LC NO. FIA64-1450
Prod-ACA Dist-ACA 1964

Science Of Orbiting B 28 MIN
16MM FILM OPTICAL SOUND I-J
Uses a tub, a swing and a carbon dioxide fire extinguisher to explain such things as weightlessness, telemetry, heat shield and retro rockets.
From The Mr Wizard Series.
Prod-PRISM Dist-MLA 1963

Science Of Pitching, The C 60 MIN
1/2 IN VIDEO CASSETTE BETA/VHS
Demonstrates pitching technique in baseball. Features slow motion and stop action photography.
Prod-MOHOMV Dist-MOHOMV

Science Of Sport C 30 MIN
3/4 OR 1/2 INCH VIDEO CASSETTE
Discusses sports medicine, pointing out that a team physician can be as important to its players as the coach.
From The Innovation Series.
Prod-WNETTV Dist-WNETTV 1983

Science Of The Sea C 19 MIN
16MM FILM, 3/4 OR 1/2 IN VIDEO H-C
Stresses the importance of the sea to life on Earth. Records the efforts of oceanographers to comprehend the physical, geological, meteorological, chemical and biological aspects of the ocean.
Prod-IFB Dist-IFB 1958

Science Of Wellness, The C 30 MIN
3/4 OR 1/2 INCH VIDEO CASSETTE
Points out that a great deal of attention is being placed on preventive medicine, instead of treating diseases after they occur.
From The Innovation Series.
Prod-WNETTV Dist-WNETTV 1983

Science On The Light C 29 MIN
2 INCH VIDEOTAPE
See series title for descriptive statement.
From The Observing Eye Series.
Prod-WGBHTV Dist-PUBTEL

Science Probes Desertification C 12 MIN
16MM FILM OPTICAL SOUND
Reports on efforts to sustain and cultivate desert margins.
Prod-ALLFP Dist-NSTA

Science Processes—A Series
16MM FILM, 3/4 OR 1/2 IN VIDEO P
Introduces science through a process-inquiry approach.
Prod-MGHT Dist-MGHT Prodn-HANBAR

Classifying 10 MIN
Experimenting 10 MIN
Measuring 10 MIN
Observing And Describing 10 MIN
Time 14 MIN

Science Questions Sometimes Are Issue Questions C 20 MIN
3/4 INCH VIDEO CASSETTE T
Points out that what may appear to be a science question may really be a question about a current issue.
From The Access Series.
LC NO. 76-706258
Prod-UDEN Dist-USNAC 1976

Science Rock—A Series
3/4 OR 1/2 INCH VIDEO CASSETTE P-I
Presents animated films dealing with scientific topics.
Prod-ABCTV Dist-GA Prodn-SCOROC

Body Machine, The 003 MIN
Do The Circulation 003 MIN
Electricity, Electricity 003 MIN
Energy Blues, The 003 MIN
Interplanet Janet 003 MIN
Telegraph Line 003 MIN
Them Not-So-Dry Bones 003 MIN
Victim Of Gravity, A 003 MIN
Weather 003 MIN

Science Room—A Series
I
Introduces science as a discipline, defines that discipline generates a respect for it and encourages its continued use. Arouses the spirit of inquiry through discovery. Stimulates an interest in science, showing that it is an exciting, absorbing field of study. (Broadcast quality)
Prod-MCETV Dist-GPITVL Prodn-WVIZTV

Airplane Engines - Jets 20 MIN
Atom And Current Electricity, The 20 MIN
Atom And Static Electricity, The 20 MIN
Atoms And Their Fundamental Particles 20 MIN
Cell, The 20 MIN
Diving Devices 20 MIN
Earth, The - Fossils 20 MIN
Earth, The - Geological Time Scale 20 MIN
Earth, The - Its Beginning And Basic Parts 20 MIN
Element, The - Atomic Number And 20 MIN
Heat - Atoms And Molecules 20 MIN
Heat - Capacity 20 MIN
Heat - Conduction - Convection 20 MIN
Heat - Expansion And Contraction 20 MIN
Heat As A Form Of Energy 20 MIN
Internal Combustion Engine, The 20 MIN
Microscopic Plants 20 MIN
Minerals In The Sea 20 MIN
Moon, The 20 MIN
Ocean, The - Microscopic Plants And Animals 20 MIN
Plant Growth - Hormones 20 MIN
Plants - Reproduction-Pollination 20 MIN
Plants As Food Makers - Photosynthesis 20 MIN
Reproduction - Other Means 20 MIN
Solar System, The 20 MIN
Sound And Communications 20 MIN
Steam Engine And Turbine, The 20 MIN
Sun And Other Stars, The 20 MIN
Telescope, The 20 MIN
Television 20 MIN
Vertebrates And Invertebrates In The Sea 20 MIN
What Is Sound 20 MIN

Science Screen Report—A Series

Presents dramatic and contemporary happenings in all branches of science. Reports the most recent developments in research and technology from the ocean depths to outer space. Includes stories dealing with such topics as shark control research, the National Observatory, molecular biology, laser technology prosthetics, the Lunar Rover and many more.
Prod-ALLFP Dist-SF

Science Screen Report, No. 01 17 MIN
Science Screen Report, No. 02 17 MIN
Science Screen Report, No. 03 14 MIN
Science Screen Report, No. 04 17 MIN
Science Screen Report, No. 05 17 MIN
Science Screen Report, No. 06 18 MIN
Science Screen Report, No. 07 16 MIN
Science Screen Report, No. 08 16 MIN
Science Screen Report, No. 09 20 MIN
Science Screen Report, No. 10 17 MIN
Science Screen Report, No. 11 18 MIN
Science Screen Report, No. 12 17 MIN
Science Screen Report, No. 13 16 MIN
Science Screen Report, No. 14 14 MIN
Science Screen Report, No. 15 15 MIN
Science Screen Report, No. 16 15 MIN
Science Screen Report, No. 17 15 MIN
Science Screen Report, No. 18 15 MIN

Science Screen Report, No. 01 C 17 MIN
16MM FILM OPTICAL SOUND
Presents a detailed preview of an exciting new space concept, the reusable space shuttle. Features Deepstar 4000 and an all-seas survival system, a development in research and rescue vehicles. Describes how a pressure cell creates new forms of matter. Lists new applications of computers and electric motors, latest teaching aids to driver education and environmental data buoys to chart the oceans.
From The Science Screen Report Series.
Prod-ALLFP Dist-SF

Science Screen Report, No. 02 C 17 MIN
16MM FILM OPTICAL SOUND
Illustrates the importance of science in protecting man from the menace of shark attacks. Depicts scientific efforts to find ecologically sound disposal methods for waste. Shows scientists' efforts in striving to conquer the problem of insect control without polluting the atmosphere with poisons. Reports on a new method used by engineers to determine and solve problems connected with automobile safety. Demonstrates the versatility and capability of space technologists in developing the Lunar Rover, which can perform all tasks necessary to the moon mission.
From The Science Screen Report Series.
Prod-ALLFP Dist-SF

Science Screen Report, No. 03 C 14 MIN
16MM FILM OPTICAL SOUND
Reports on sulfur mining off the Louisiana coast and the removal of sulfur from fuel oils. Shows two instruments which aid man in extending his senses into the realm of the large and small, the macrocosm and microcosm. Presents a report on a systematic data collection and flood warning system. Describes the selection and breeding of tomatoes for easier machine harvesting. Tests the effects of impact, using a live human subject.
From The Science Screen Report Series.
Prod-ALLFP Dist-SF

Science Screen Report, No. 04 C 17 MIN
16MM FILM OPTICAL SOUND
Investigates the web of life in arid lands. Presents a new temperature-controlled method to grow near perfect crystals. Features researchers who have created an automated wheel chair and voice-dial telephone to aid the handicapped. Introduces a new triple-control autopilot which can land a jetliner perfectly in the case of an emergency.
From The Science Screen Report Series.
Prod-ALLFP Dist-SF

Science Screen Report, No. 05 C 17 MIN
16MM FILM OPTICAL SOUND
Theorizes new answers to noise pollution. Analyzes the atmosphere of the different planets through the use of spectroscopy. Describes an astronaut's wardrobe where each spacesuit is individually designed and precision-built to protect him in an airless, hostile environment. Features sea lions which have been taught underwater recovery.
From The Science Screen Report Series.
Prod-ALLFP Dist-SF

Science Screen Report, No. 06 C 18 MIN
16MM FILM OPTICAL SOUND
Investigates research into trace elements' relations to heart disease and the development of two new heart pacers. Features a tornado watch of the severe storms forecasting program and weather phenomena viewed from orbit. Explains that a laser's energy can be measured by means of torsion pendulum. Describes tests made on a new twin-hulled, semi-submerged, high-speed ship.
From The Science Screen Report Series.
Prod-ALLFP Dist-SF

Science Screen Report, No. 07 C 16 MIN
16MM FILM OPTICAL SOUND
Explains that chemicals provide one way to check crop destruction. Describes stimulation by computers that help study complex effects of fluid flow.
From The Science Screen Report Series.
Prod-ALLFP Dist-SF

Science Screen Report, No. 08 C 16 MIN
16MM FILM OPTICAL SOUND
Ivestigates the structure and function of the cell. Describes new 'VOCODERS' that help the deaf by converting sound to other forms of energy. Features a tiny new laser, lasers to aid the ecologist and lasers to aid the blind. Introduces a three-dimensional lunar relief map to help simulate moon landings. Reveals a spacecraft that is investigating Jupiter, the largest planet. Includes scenes of a school for chimpanzees that prepares them to be subjects in scientific research.
From The Science Screen Report Series.
Prod-ALLFP Dist-SF

Science Screen Report, No. 09 C 20 MIN
16MM FILM OPTICAL SOUND
Views researchers who study arid expanses of sargassum weed in the Atlantic. Presents Mariner orbiters and Viking landers who investigated Mars in the 1970's. Features a magnetic separation which may extract resources and decontaminate oil and water. Analyzes a new national astronomical observatory which is studying the universe.
From The Science Screen Report Series.
Prod-ALLFP Dist-SF

Science Screen Report, No. 10 C 17 MIN
16MM FILM OPTICAL SOUND
Explains that Skylab, the first U S space station, will probe earth resources, materials processing, biomedical reactions and stellar phenomena. Describes a new way to obtain germfree animals for medical research. Reports on leukemia study with cattle. Reveals steel crash cushions which promise to improve automobile safety and new experimental safety vehicles.
From The Science Screen Report Series.
Prod-ALLFP Dist-SF

Science Screen Report, No. 11 C 18 MIN
16MM FILM OPTICAL SOUND
Examines Antarctic research to study world environmental history, continental drift, polar life forms and weather origins. Focuses on grooving as an answer to hydroplaning accidents. Explains how space technology is applied to keep operating rooms sterile, help the handicapped get around, enhance x-rays and move a bullet in a man's brain.
From The Science Screen Report Series.
Prod-ALLFP Dist-SF

Science Screen Report, No. 12 C 17 MIN
16MM FILM OPTICAL SOUND
Examines recycling research in progress on garbage, paper, glass and water. Features the first laser lighthouse, which has a beam visible for 22 miles. Describes ERTS, Earth Resources Technology Satellite, designed to inventory this planet's natural resources.
From The Science Screen Report Series.
Prod-ALLFP Dist-SF

Science Screen Report, No. 13 C 16 MIN
16MM FILM OPTICAL SOUND
Probes noise pollution, unwanted sound that is a growing national problem. Presents new facts about metal crystal structures that lead to better bearings. Features researchers who study photos and simulate whirlwinds to learn about tornados.
From The Science Screen Report Series.
Prod-ALLFP Dist-SF

Science Screen Report, No. 14 C 14 MIN
16MM FILM OPTICAL SOUND
Presents researchers who investigate possible medicines that can be derived from sea life. Establishes different life surrounding off-shore drilling platforms. Features a pilot whale who was taught to recover objects 1500 feet down.
From The Science Screen Report Series.
Prod-ALLFP Dist-SF

Science Screen Report, No. 15 C 15 MIN
16MM FILM OPTICAL SOUND
Establishes the clean air cycle and describes how man-made pollution has overloaded this cycle. Views chick embryos which are X-rayed to study the effects on the vascular system.
From The Science Screen Report Series.
Prod-ALLFP Dist-SF

Science Screen Report, No. 16 C 15 MIN
16MM FILM OPTICAL SOUND
Features a deep sea drilling vessel that finds evidence of continental drift. Describes studies using anthropometric dummies and computers that promote auto safety.
From The Science Screen Report Series.
Prod-ALLFP Dist-SF

Science Screen Report, No. 17 C 15 MIN
16MM FILM OPTICAL SOUND
Evaluates a new approach to ocean research, FLARE, which investigates reefs using mobile habitat. Features unmanned space probes which study Venus, Mercury, the asteroids and Jupiter.
From The Science Screen Report Series.
Prod-ALLFP Dist-SF

Science Screen Report, No. 18 C 15 MIN
16MM FILM OPTICAL SOUND
Explores the scientific uses of photography exemplified in space exploration. Features telephoned drawings of liquid crystals. Analyzes a new approach to diagnosing deafness in children using computer-recorded brainwaves.
From The Science Screen Report Series.
Prod-ALLFP Dist-SF

Science Seeks Answers To Ocean Pollution C 13 MIN
16MM FILM OPTICAL SOUND
Profiles scientific research efforts to safeguard the seas.
Prod-ALLFP Dist-NSTA 1977

Science Skills (Spanish)—A Series
16MM FILM, 3/4 OR 1/2 IN VIDEO I-J
Introduces basic science skills.
Prod-GLDWER Dist-JOU

Science Skills Film No. 1 - Observing
Science Skills Film No. 2 - Controlling 015 MIN
Science Skills Film No. 3 - Defining, 016 MIN
Science Skills Film No. 4 - Interpreting 016 MIN
Science Skills Film No. 5 - Conducting An 015 MIN

Science Skills Film No. 1 - Observing, Recording, Mapping And Graphing C 16 MIN
16MM FILM, 3/4 OR 1/2 IN VIDEO I-H
Introduces basic skills needed to conduct a scientific investigation by studying a swarm of honeybees being handled by a beekeeper. Emphasizes the proper way to observe the action of bees and the way to record these observations.
From The Science Skills Series.
Prod-GLDWER Dist-JOU 1975

Science Skills Film No. 1 - Observing, Recording, Mapping And Graphing (Spanish) C 16 MIN
16MM FILM, 3/4 OR 1/2 IN VIDEO I-H
Introduces basic skills needed to conduct a scientific investigation by studying a swarm of honeybees being handled by a beekeeper. Emphasizes the proper way to observe the action of bees and the way to record these observations.
From The Science Skills (Spanish) Series.
Prod-GLDWER Dist-JOU 1975

Science Skills Film No. 2 - Controlling Variables, Making Measurements C 15 MIN
16MM FILM, 3/4 OR 1/2 IN VIDEO I-H
Introduces basic skills needed to conduct a scientific investigation by observing an experiment in which sunflower seeds are grown under controlled conditions. Demonstrates that by controlling the variables and making measurements of the plants as they grow, the effect of chemical nutrients can be learned.
From The Science Skills Series.
Prod-GLDWER Dist-JOU 1975

Science Skills Film No. 2 - Controlling Variables, Making Measurements (Spanish) C 15 MIN
16MM FILM, 3/4 OR 1/2 IN VIDEO I-H
Introduces basic skills needed to conduct a scientific investigation by observing an experiment in which sunflower seeds are grown under controlled conditions. Demonstrates that by controlling the variables and making measurements of the plants as they grow, the effect of chemical nutrients can be learned.
From The Science Skills (Spanish) Series.
Prod-GLDWER Dist-JOU 1975

Science Skills Film No. 3 - Defining, Classifying And Identifying C 16 MIN
16MM FILM, 3/4 OR 1/2 IN VIDEO I-H
Introduces basic skills needed to conduct a scientific investigation by conducting tests on three unknown materials. Explains the process of defining the properties of the minerals and shows how classifying and identifying are important to the scientific inquiry.
From The Science Skills Series.
Prod-GLDWER Dist-JOU 1975

Science Skills Film No. 3 - Defining, Classifying And Identifying (Spanish) C 16 MIN
16MM FILM, 3/4 OR 1/2 IN VIDEO I-H
Introduces basic skills needed to conduct a scientific investigation by conducting tests on three unknown materials. Explains the process of defining the properties of the minerals and shows how classifying and identifying are important to the scientific inquiry.
From The Science Skills (Spanish) Series.
Prod-GLDWER Dist-JOU 1975

Science Skills Film No. 4 - Interpreting Data, Testing Hypotheses (Spanish) C 16 MIN
16MM FILM, 3/4 OR 1/2 IN VIDEO I-J
Introduces basic skills needed to conduct a scientific investigation by studying data on the pollution of a pond to determine if there are any fish in it.
From The Science Skills (Spanish) Series.
Prod-GLDWER Dist-JOU 1975

Science Skills Film No. 4 - Interpreting Data, Testing Hypotheses C 16 MIN
16MM FILM, 3/4 OR 1/2 IN VIDEO I-J
Introduces basic skills needed to conduct a scientific investigation by studying data on the pollution of a pond to determine if there are any fish in it.
From The Science Skills Series.
Prod-GLDWER Dist-JOU 1975

Science Skills Film No. 5 - Conducting An Experiment In Cleaning Our Air C 15 MIN
16MM FILM, 3/4 OR 1/2 IN VIDEO I-J
Shows how the basic science skills are used in a scientific investigation. Uses an experiment on particles in the air to show how these skills are employed in scientific experimentation.
From The Science Skills Series.
Prod-GLDWER Dist-JOU 1975

Science Skills Film No. 5 - Conducting An Experiment In Cleaning Our Air (Spanish) C 15 MIN
16MM FILM, 3/4 OR 1/2 IN VIDEO I-J
Shows how the basic science skills are used in a scientific investigation. Uses an experiment on particles in the air to show how these skills are employed in scientific investigation.
From The Science Skills (Spanish) Series.
Prod-GLDWER Dist-JOU 1975

Science Skills—A Series
16MM FILM, 3/4 OR 1/2 IN VIDEO I-J
Introduces basic science skills.
Prod-GLDWER Dist-JOU

Science Skills Film No. 1 - Observing
Science Skills Film No. 2 - Controlling 015 MIN
Science Skills Film No. 3 - Defining, 016 MIN
Science Skills Film No. 4 - Interpreting 016 MIN
Science Skills Film No. 5 - Conducting An 015 MIN

Science Studies The Africanized Bee C 13 MIN
16MM FILM OPTICAL SOUND
Studies the killer bee and its potential to harm man.
Prod-ALLFP Dist-NSTA 1978

Science Technicians C 15 MIN
2 INCH VIDEOTAPE J-H
Covers semi-professional jobs, such as dental technicians, fish culturist, salesman of scientific equipment, nurseryman and optometrist.
From The Work Is For Real Series.
Prod-STETVC Dist-GPITVL

Science Through Discovery B 28 MIN
16MM FILM OPTICAL SOUND T
Demonstrates the use of modern teaching techniques in science teaching, including audio-visual illustration. Considers the parts played by outside specialists as consultants, the committee project and report system, and individual student-teacher conferences.
LC NO. FIE63-28
Prod-USOE Dist-USNAC Prodn-NET 1972

Science Unlimited C 15 MIN
2 INCH VIDEOTAPE J-H
Discusses the role of science-based industry in our economy. Covers nonprofessional but vital jobs in this category, such as process workers, equipment operators, material handlers and truck drivers.
From The Work Is For Real Series.
Prod-STETVC Dist-GPITVL

Science—A Series
3/4 OR 1/2 INCH VIDEO CASSETTE K-I
Prod-MORLAT Dist-SF

Exploring The Moon 9 MIN
Heat And Hemispheres 8 MIN
Light And Shadow 7 MIN
Size Of The Moon, The 8 MIN
Sun, The 9 MIN
Time And Direction 7 MIN
What Is Autumn 7 MIN
What Is Spring 7 MIN
What Is Summer 7 MIN
What Is Winter 8 MIN

Science, Pt 2 B 23 MIN
16MM FILM OPTICAL SOUND J-C A
Shows a Frenchman removing the heart from a chicken embryo, coating it with a filmy substance and freezing it at minus 200 degress centigrade. Explains how collecting the sun's energy and converting it directly into electricity is the function of this cluster of small aluminum reflectors in a special science report on the worldwide search for new ways of harnessing power form the sun.
Prod-HEARST Dist-HEARST

Science, Technology And Art In The USSR C 13 MIN
16MM FILM, 3/4 OR 1/2 IN VIDEO H-C
A Russian language film. Depicts the uses of atomic energy in power stations, steel mills and cultural activities of Russians. Shows how young people study.
From The Russian Language Series.
Prod-IFB Dist-IFB 1963

Scienceland—A Series
P
Prod-MPATI Dist-GPITVL

How Can You Make Water Move 20 MIN
How Can You Send Messages Through The Air 20 MIN
How Can You Send Something Into Space 20 MIN
How Do Different Things Mix With Water 20 MIN
How Do Tools Help 20 MIN
How Does A Glider Work 20 MIN
How Does A Magnifying Glass Help You Find Out 20 MIN
How Does A Music Box Work 20 MIN
How Does A Parachute Work 20 MIN
How Does Heat Help You 20 MIN
How Strong Is The Wind 20 MIN
What Are The Sounds Around You 20 MIN
What Can A Frog Do 20 MIN
What Can A Turtle Do 20 MIN
What Can You Find In A Pond 20 MIN
What Does A Fish Do 20 MIN
What Does The Earth Look Like From Space 20 MIN
What Floats On Water 20 MIN
What Goes On In Scienceland 20 MIN
What Happens At Night 20 MIN
What Happens In Scienceland 20 MIN
What Happens To Leaves 20 MIN
What Kinds Of Coats Do Animals Wear 20 MIN
What Kinds Of Homes Do Animals Live In 20 MIN
What Lights Up The Darkness 20 MIN
What Stories Can Rocks Tell 20 MIN
What's In A Fallen Log 20 MIN
What's In The Snow 20 MIN
Where Can You Find Seeds Inside Your House 20 MIN
Where Do Evergreen Trees Come From 20 MIN
Where Do Shadows Come From 20 MIN
Where Do The Raindrops Go 20 MIN

Scientific Age, The C 30 MIN
16MM FILM OPTICAL SOUND
Contends that the theories of Galileo, Bacon and Copernicus have a Biblical interpretation of the universe as their foundation. Warns that a departure from such a Biblical framework can make science a threat to man. Based on the book How Should We Then Live by Francis A Schaeffer.
From The How Should We Then Live Series. No. 6
LC NO. 77-702368
Prod-GF Dist-GF 1977

Scientific Age, The (Dutch) C 30 MIN
16MM FILM OPTICAL SOUND
Contends that the theories of Galileo, Bacon and Copernicus have a Biblical interpretation of the universe as their foundation. Warns that a departure from such a Biblical framework can make science a threat to man. Based on the book How Should We Then Live by Francis A Schaeffer.
From The How Should We Then Live (Dutch) Series. No. 6
LC NO. 77-702368
Prod-GF Dist-GF 1977

Scientific Evidence - The Polygraph—A Series
PRO
Gives an understanding of proper polygraph examination procedures and the legal and scientific issues surrounding its use.
Prod-ABACPE Dist-ABACPE

Polygraph, The - Demonstration And Discussion 043 MIN
Polygraph, The - Useful Tool Or Dangerous 058 MIN

Scientific Fact And Fun—A Series
16MM FILM, 3/4 OR 1/2 IN VIDEO P-I
Describes basic scientific investigative skills and looks at some common scientific phenomena.
Prod-JOU Dist-JOU

Arcs And Sparks 013 MIN
Everything Is Something 013 MIN
How Much Does The Earth Weigh 013 MIN
Looking Into Things 013 MIN
Machines, Engines And Motors 013 MIN
Making Sense Of It 013 MIN
Seeds And Weeds 013 MIN
Water Runs Downhill 013 MIN
What's In A Rainbow 013 MIN
What's In A Shadow 013 MIN
What's In A Spider Web 013 MIN
What's In An Egg 013 MIN

Scientific Graphs - How To Make Them And Make Sense Of Them C
3/4 OR 1/2 INCH VIDEO CASSETTE H
Uses video segments and computer graphics to explain bar, line and pie graphs. Teaches how to construct an appropriate graph form, plot data and interpret finished graphs correctly.
Prod-GA Dist-GA

Scientific Investigation—A Series
16MM FILM, 3/4 OR 1/2 IN VIDEO I-H
Prod-GLDWER Dist-JOU 1977

Studying Chemical Interactions 17 MIN
Studying Electricity 16 MIN
Studying Fluid Behavior 17 MIN
Studying Gravitation And Mass 16 MIN
Studying Heat And Its Behavior 17 MIN
Studying The Behavior Of Light 16 MIN

Scientific Literacy C 30 MIN
3/4 OR 1/2 INCH VIDEO CASSETTE
Looks at the role of computers and how this role conflicts with the traditional notions of a 'good' education.
From The Innovation Series.
Prod-WNETTV Dist-WNETTV 1983

Scientific Method C 15 MIN
3/4 OR 1/2 INCH VIDEO CASSETTE I
Presents TV teacher Robert Crumpler investigating the scientific method.
From The Search For Science Series.
Prod-WVIZTV Dist-GPITVL 1972

Scientific Method In Action C 19 MIN
16MM FILM, 3/4 OR 1/2 IN VIDEO J-H
Shows how the scientific method has contributed to the advancement of scientific knowledge and to a better understanding of the world. Re-creates Galileo's experiments with gravity and Salk's conquest of polio. Analyzes the six formal steps of the scientific method.
Prod-VEF Dist-IFB 1960

Scientific Method In Action (Captioned) C 19 MIN
16MM FILM, 3/4 OR 1/2 IN VIDEO J-H
Shows how the scientific method has contributed to the advancement of scientific knowledge and to a better understanding of the world. Re-creates Galileo's experiments with gravity and Salk's conquest of polio. Analyzes the six formal steps of the scientific method. Captioned for the hearing impaired.
Prod-VEF Dist-IFB 1960

Scientific Method, The X 12 MIN
16MM FILM, 3/4 OR 1/2 IN VIDEO J-H
Explains the steps of the scientific method, demonstrates the way this method of problem solving is applied by scientists and discusses the value of scientific thinking in dealing with problems of everyday life. Features the discovery of penicillin by Sir Alexander Fleming.
Prod-EBF Dist-EBEC 1954

Scientific Noise B 28 MIN
16MM FILM OPTICAL SOUND I-J
Explains that sound changed in volume and frequency becomes noise. Shows how scrambled letters may be unscrambled with a filter and how a screened photograph with 'INTERFERENCE' removed may be identified.
From The Mr Wizard Series.
Prod-PRISM Dist-MLA 1964

Scientific Notation C 20 MIN
3/4 INCH VIDEO CASSETTE H-C
Emphasizes the importance of scientific notation in astronomy, physics and economics.
From The Mainly Math Series.
Prod-WCVETV Dist-GPITVL 1977

Scientific Notation And Metric Prefixes C
3/4 OR 1/2 INCH VIDEO CASSETTE
See series title for descriptive statement.
From The Basic Electricity - DC Series.
Prod-VTRI Dist-VTRI

Scientific Notation And Metric Prefixes C 30 MIN
3/4 OR 1/2 INCH VIDEO CASSETTE
Introduces simple 'metric chart' to help master number conversions from decimal form to scientific notation and metric prefixed format or vice versa. Discusses addition, subtraction, multiplication and division of numbers written in scientific notation.
From The Basic Electricity And D.C. Circuits Series.
Prod-TXINLC Dist-TXINLC

Scientific Revolution C 30 MIN
3/4 OR 1/2 INCH VIDEO CASSETTE H
Discusses Ptolemy's view of the universe and how it was challenged by Copernicus and Galileo. Shows that mathematics is the language of science and deals with Newton's contributions, the beginnings of scientific medicine and the concept of natural laws.
From The Historically Speaking Series. Part 4
Prod-KRMATV Dist-AITECH 1983

Scientific Super Sleuths C 10 MIN
16MM FILM, 3/4 OR 1/2 IN VIDEO
Shows different scientific methods used in identifying criminals, including handwriting analysis, voice print identification, gunshot residue identification, ballistic testing, fingerprinting and identification of moonshine samples.
LC NO. 83-706090
Prod-USBATF Dist-USNAC 1975

Scientific Wildlife Management Safeguards Endangered Species C 13 MIN
16MM FILM OPTICAL SOUND
Shows how the nation of Botswana in southern Africa is carrying out programs to manage its wildlife heritage, including elephants, lions, antelope, giraffes and other exotic species.
Prod-ALLFP Dist-NSTA 1979

Scientist In The Sea C 16 MIN
16MM FILM OPTICAL SOUND
Tells how an oceanographer, skilled in the use of scuba gear, utilizes his scientific knowledge to aid in the study of the ocean.
LC NO. FIE68-28
Prod-USN Dist-USNAC 1967

Scientists In Blue Jeans B 5 MIN
16MM FILM OPTICAL SOUND
Surveys the work being done by the Future Engineers of America, an organization sponsoring scientific talent at the pre-college level. Presents some of the projects underway at an experimental E center in California.
From The Screen News Digest Series. Vol 3, Issue 2
Prod-HEARST Dist-HEARST 1960

Scintillation Spectrometry A-2 C 3 MIN
16MM FILM SILENT H-C
Pictures the assembly of a detector. Identifies the single gamma-ray displayed with various statistics, photo-peak, Compton edge and backscatter.
From The Single-Concept Films In Physics Series.
Prod-OSUMPD Dist-OSUMPD 1963

Scoffer, The C 8 MIN
16MM FILM, 3/4 OR 1/2 IN VIDEO J A
Shows that the scoffer is acting out an inferiority complex (he tries to make himself bigger by belittling the rules) or a superiority complex (he usually thinks he is above such childish nonsense as regulations.) Indicates that either way he is a problem.
From The Dealing With Problem People Series.
Prod-JOU Dist-JOU 1969

Scoffer, The (Captioned) C 8 MIN
16MM FILM, 3/4 OR 1/2 IN VIDEO J A
Shows that the scoffer is acting out an inferiority complex (he tries to make himself bigger by belittling the rules) or a superiority complex (he usually thinks he is above such childish nonsense as regulations.) Indicates that either way he is a problem.
From The Dealing With Problem People Series.
Prod-JOU Dist-JOU 1969

Scoliosis C 8 MIN
16MM FILM OPTICAL SOUND I-C A
Defines scoliosis and kyphosis and describes how these conditions are treated.
LC NO. 82-700300
Prod-HFHSC Dist-HFHSC Prodn-HFH 1981

Scoliosis C 30 MIN
3/4 OR 1/2 INCH VIDEO CASSETTE PRO
Focuses on diagnostic and therapeutic aspects of scoliosis and presents case studies to highlight discussions by specialists in the field.
Prod-HSCIC Dist-HSCIC 1980

Scoliosis Screening For Early Detection C 14 MIN
16MM FILM OPTICAL SOUND PRO
Demonstrates step-by-step techniques for scoliosis screening, focusing on when and who to screen, what to look for, what to do if scoliosis is found and why early detection is crucial. Describes the establishment and evaluation of community screening programs, their facilities and staff.
LC NO. 75-703774
Prod-MVI Dist-EMCOM 1974

Scope And Goals Of The Health Enterprise B 30 MIN
16MM FILM - 3/4 IN VIDEO PRO
Reviews the dimensions of the health enterprise, including finances, personnel and organizational approach. (Broadcast quality)
From The Public Health Science Series. Unit I - Introduction To Foundations Of Public Health
Prod-TEXWU Dist-GPITVL Prodn-KUHTTV

Scope Of Practice And Standards Of Care C 30 MIN
16MM FILM OPTICAL SOUND PRO
Discusses the relationship between nursing practice and the definitions contained in nurse practice acts. Emphasizes the effect legal definitions can have on the emerging roles in nursing.
From The Nurse And The Law Series.
LC NO. 76-701555
Prod-AJN Dist-AJN Prodn-WGNCP 1974

Scope Of Systems Engineering Problem C 53 MIN
3/4 OR 1/2 INCH VIDEO CASSETTE
Provides a picture of the overall systems engineering problem, its common characteristics and procedures for engineering a system.
From The Systems Engineering And Systems Management Series.
Prod-MIOT Dist-MIOT

Scope Of The Problem C 28 MIN
3/4 OR 1/2 INCH VIDEO CASSETTE J A
Presents a discussion of alcohol abuse and alcoholism. Features former United States Senator Harold Hughes.
Prod-SUTHRB Dist-SUTHRB

Scope Two C 3 MIN
16MM FILM OPTICAL SOUND J-C
Presents an audio-visual performance which exemplifies the modern age - an age in which both the painter and compser use the tools of the scientist to create their artistry.
Prod-STOCH Dist-CFS

Scoraform C 10 MIN
16MM FILM, 3/4 OR 1/2 IN VIDEO J-C A
Follows the design and construction processes of scoraform sculpture, showing a variety of an artist's works. Explains that scoraform sculpture is created by scoring the surface of paper, cardboard or plastic and then bending the material into an original design.
Prod-MCCBUR Dist-AIMS

Score Offshore, The C 20 MIN
16MM FILM OPTICAL SOUND
Provides current Federal legal requirements for boat operators. Informs new boat owners about the requirements which all boat operators must fulfill before they are allowed to leave the dock.
LC NO. 75-702461
Prod-USCG Dist-USNAC 1974

Score Yourself C 30 MIN
3/4 OR 1/2 INCH VIDEO CASSETTE
Discusses nine traits or habits which characterize an individual who may develop CHD.
From The CHD And You Series.
Prod-NETCHE Dist-NETCHE 1976

Scorn Of Women, The C 52 MIN
16MM FILM, 3/4 OR 1/2 IN VIDEO H-C A
Introduces Floyd Vanderlipp, a manly hero much admired for his prowess in overcoming the perils of the frozen North. Shows how a comedy of errors leads Floyd to meet his match as three ladies from one of the Yukon's more civilized outposts attempt to ensnare him in a web of feminine intrigue. Based on the short story The Scorn Of Women by Jack London.
From The Jack London's Tales Of The Klondike Series.
LC NO. 84-706232
Prod-NORWK Dist-EBEC 1982

Scorpion C 25 MIN
16MM FILM, 3/4 OR 1/2 IN VIDEO H-C A
Observes the private world of the scorpion, one of the oldest creatures on earth.
Prod-BBCTV Dist-FI 1981

Scotchcast Casting Tape Techniques C 10 MIN
3/4 INCH VIDEO CASSETTE PRO
Presents step-by-step instructions on how to apply a cast using water-activated fiberglass casting tape.
Prod-MMAMC Dist-MMAMC

Scotland Oil Report C 11 MIN
3/4 OR 1/2 INCH VIDEO CASSETTE H-C A
Examines the development of Scottish off-shore oil fields and describes the methods being implemented to ensure safe delivery.
Prod-UPI Dist-JOU

Scots, The C 50 MIN
16MM FILM OPTICAL SOUND
Explores Scotland's contributions to Canada. Traces the history of the Scottish people in Canada. Points out that the people of Scottish descent in Canada have a strong identity and are a proud, hard-working, cultural group.
From The Heritage Series.
LC NO. 77-702837
Prod-CTV Dist-CTV 1976

Scott Goes To The Hospital C 11 MIN
16MM FILM, 3/4 OR 1/2 IN VIDEO P
Follows Scott, who requires a tonsillectomy, through a typical day in the hospital. Depicts the friendly nurses, doctors and assistants and shows how his room, equipped with television, night-lights and call-button helps to reassure him.
Prod-HIGGIN Dist-HIGGIN 1973

Scott Joplin C 15 MIN
16MM FILM, 3/4 OR 1/2 IN VIDEO I-C A
Presents the life and music of ragtime musician Scott Joplin, narrated by Eartha Kitt. Follows his discovery and initial success to the failure of his opera Treemonisha and his early death in poverty and obscurity. Includes examples of his music and excerpts from the posthumous performance of Treemonisha.
LC NO. 77-701111
Prod-ANDSNA Dist-PFP 1977

Scott O'Dell In His Home C 15 MIN
3/4 OR 1/2 INCH VIDEO CASSETTE
Features children's author Scott O'Dell talking about his writing and his books for children and young adults,
LC NO. 83-707202
Prod-HMC Dist-CLRFLM 1983

Scott's Old New Friend C 22 MIN
16MM FILM, 3/4 OR 1/2 IN VIDEO I
Presents Scott, who stops off at the park to play ball with classmates every day after school. Tells how he meets an old lady in the park and although his classmates ignore her, Scott makes friends with her and learns that a difference in age is no reason not to make friends.
From The If You Know How I Feel Series.
Prod-CENTRO Dist-CORF 1983

Scottish Symphony C 30 MIN
16MM FILM, 3/4 OR 1/2 IN VIDEO I-C A
Traces the journey of the young German composer, Felix Mendelssohn, as he traveled throughout Scotland in 1829. Includes movements of the 'SCOTTISH SYMPHONY,' and accompanying scenes of the sights that moved him to compose the symphony. Features the London Philharmonic, conducted by Otto Klemperer.
Prod-DKMNH Dist-BNCHMK 1972

Scottish Tragedy, The C 30 MIN
3/4 OR 1/2 INCH VIDEO CASSETTE
Highlights the problems which can so easily overwhelm a badly organized film unit on location. Reveals that the efforts of the long-suffering production manager to run an efficient unit are continually thwarted by the determined, but inexperienced, young director.
Prod-BBCTV Dist-FI

Scouring, Bleaching, Dyeing, Printing, Finishing C
3/4 OR 1/2 INCH VIDEO CASSETTE
See series title for descriptive statement.
From The ITMA 1983 Review Series.
Prod-NCSU Dist-NCSU

Scout Squad Operations C 26 MIN
16MM FILM OPTICAL SOUND
Shows how a scout squad prepares for and conducts patrols while the parent platoon performs reconnaissance and security operations in support of a task force tank battalion.
LC NO. 80-701842
Prod-USA Dist-USNAC 1980

Scout, The C 10 MIN
16MM FILM, 3/4 OR 1/2 IN VIDEO J-C A
Captures the tragic inevitability of an unidentified war by telling how a chance act of humanity seals a man's fate. Based on the short story The Scout by Jack London.
Prod-UONEFP Dist-WOMBAT

Scouting For Giant Bass C 22 MIN
16MM FILM OPTICAL SOUND
Follows outdoor sports writer Homer Circle on a fishing expedition deep in Ocala National Forest.
LC NO. 79-701446
Prod-IH Dist-IPHC Prodn-IPHC 1979

Scouting Of Old Sandy C 22 MIN
16MM FILM OPTICAL SOUND
Shows how champion skier Billy Kidd and a friend take a four-wheel-drive Scout to the top of Sand Mountain to ski.
LC NO. 79-701448
Prod-IH Dist-IPHC Prodn-IPHC 1979

Scram C 20 MIN
16MM FILM OPTICAL SOUND I-C A
See series title for descriptive statement.
From The Cellar Door Cine Mites Series.
LC NO. 74-701552
Prod-CELLAR Dist-CELLAR 1972

Scramble C 43 MIN
16MM FILM OPTICAL SOUND P-J
Tells about Jimmy, who has been in trouble with the police, trying to start a new life.
Prod-LUF Dist-LUF

Scramble, The C 22 MIN
16MM FILM OPTICAL SOUND
Features former football quarterback Fran Tarkenton, who presents a plan for achieving top individual performance. Stresses the importance of defining and developing one's own strengths through a five-point program.
Prod-PROIC Dist-PROIC 1979

Scrambled Eggs And Canned Meat C 14 MIN
2 INCH VIDEOTAPE
Prepares a dish made with the commodity foods, dried eggs and canned meats. Discusses tips for using eggs and what can be used if not on the commodity program. Emphasizes eggs as a source of protein and shows many ways eggs can be prepared.
From The Living Better II Series.
Prod-MAETEL Dist-PUBTEL

Scranton Fire Test C 30 MIN
3/4 OR 1/2 INCH VIDEO CASSETTE
SHows a full-scale fire test which was conducted in a modern, operating, multi-story open-air parking structure in order to study the effects of an uncontrolled fire in an automobile on the integrity of the exposed steel frame.
Prod-ALSC Dist-MPS

Scrap Of Paper And A Piece Of String, A C 6 MIN
16MM FILM, 3/4 OR 1/2 IN VIDEO P-I
Uses animation to tell of the friendship between a scrap of paper and a piece of string. Points out the significance of paper and string to the economy.
Prod-NBCTV Dist-MGHT Prodn-KORTY 1964

Scrapbook Experience, The C 16 MIN
16MM FILM, 3/4 OR 1/2 IN VIDEO
Shows a social worker and a child gathering photos, documents, remembrances and souvenirs into a scrapbook of a foster child's life in order to create a self-identity and personal history.
Prod-LACFU Dist-IA

Scrapbook Experience, The C 17 MIN
3/4 OR 1/2 INCH VIDEO CASSETTE J A
Shows one way a foster child develops a sense of identity by writing his own biographical scrapbook under the guidance of a social worker.
Prod-SUTHRB Dist-SUTHRB

Scrapers And Abrasives C 13 MIN
16MM FILM, 3/4 OR 1/2 IN VIDEO H-C A
Describes concepts in scrapers and abrasives for woodwork, such as using cabinet and hand scrapers, sharpening scrapers, preparing wood surfaces and sandpapers and sanding.
From The Hand Tools For Wood Working Series.
Prod-MORLAT Dist-SF 1967

Scraping Flat Surfaces B 14 MIN
16MM FILM - 3/4 IN VIDEO IND
Shows how surface plates are used to check the flatness of surfaces, types of scrapers, how to remove high spots, and how to determine when a surface is scraped flat. Issued in 1942 as a motion picture.
From The Machine Shop Work - Bench Work Series. Number 2
LC NO. 80-706760
Prod-USOE Dist-USNAC Prodn-RAYBEL 1980

Scraps C 5 MIN
3/4 INCH VIDEO CASSETTE K-P
Documents how poor women in Amedabad, India, recylce scraps of trash into toy birds. Features Bangali flute music instead of narration.
Prod-HANMNY Dist-HANMNY 1971

Scratch C 6 MIN
3/4 OR 1/2 INCH VIDEO CASSETTE
Presents work by Yugoslavian born video artist Ante Bozanich as he uses sound to juxtapose and create mood and feeling.
Prod-EAI Dist-EAI

Scratch Pad C 7 MIN
16MM FILM OPTICAL SOUND J-C A
Presents a collage film.
Prod-CFS Dist-CFS 1960

Scratching Pole, The C 30 MIN
16MM FILM - 3/4 IN VIDEO
Discusses the concept of developmental tasks and explains how parents can interpret their child's behavior in terms of developmental tasks. Points out that parents can be more tolerant of what their children are trying to accomplish by behaving in a certain manner.
From The Footsteps Series.
LC NO. 79-707630
Prod-USOE Dist-USNAC 1978

Scratching Where It Itches C 28 MIN
16MM FILM, 3/4 OR 1/2 IN VIDEO A
See series title for descriptive statement.
From The Care And Maintenance Of A Good Marriage Series. Program 3
Prod-UMCOM Dist-ECUFLM 1982

Scream From Silence, A C 96 MIN
16MM FILM, 3/4 OR 1/2 IN VIDEO C A
Documents the rape and eventual suicide of Suzanne, a nurse whose physical and emotional health deteriorates beyond repair as a result of the violence inflicted on her. Explores society's attitudes which cause women to feel guilty for being raped. Touches upon the physical, emotional, spiritual and legal aspects of this crime.
Prod-NFBC Dist-NFBC 1979

Screaming Eagles In Vietnam C 29 MIN
16MM FILM OPTICAL SOUND
Shows some of the activities of the Screaming Eagles, the 101st Division of the Army, in Vietnam.
From The Big Picture Series.
LC NO. 74-706239
Prod-USA Dist-USNAC 1967

Screaming Eagles In Vietnam C 30 MIN
3/4 OR 1/2 INCH VIDEO CASSETTE
Shows the exploits of the U S 101st Airborne Division (Screaming Eagles) in Vietnam.
Prod-IHF Dist-IHF

Screen News Digest, Vol 18, Issue 07 C 15 MIN
16MM FILM OPTICAL SOUND I-H
Father Of The Space Age - Robert Hutchings Goddard documents the life and works of Robert Goddard, the man who launched the world's first liquid-propellant rocket.
LC NO. 76-701852
Prod-HEARST Dist-HEARST 1976

Screen News Digest, Vol 18, Issue 08 C 12 MIN
16MM FILM OPTICAL SOUND J-H
Caribbean Powder Keg - The Panama Canal examines the history and present conflicts of the Panama Canal. Discusses how the canal was made, the many treaties between the United States and Panama and the present negotiations.
Prod-HEARST Dist-HEARST 1976

Screen Play, The C 13 MIN
16MM FILM, 3/4 OR 1/2 IN VIDEO J-C A
Presents the fundamentals of writing for the screen. Encourages people of all ages and backgrounds to try their hand at script writing.
Prod-PFP Dist-PFP 1972

Screening And Management Of Plasma Lipids C 21 MIN
3/4 OR 1/2 INCH VIDEO CASSETTE PRO
Discusses questions that the physician must consider in developing a rational approach to the prevention of arteriosclertic disease.
Prod-UMICHM Dist-UMICHM 1977

Screening For Driver Limitations - Cardiovascular C 18 MIN
16MM FILM - 3/4 IN VIDEO A
Presents information on such cardiovascular conditions as coronary disease, hypertension, arterial disorders, coronary bypass surgery and pacemakers. Gives clues to identify drivers whose degree of impairment should be medically evaluated before they are licensed.
LC NO. 77-706152
Prod-USHTSA Dist-USNAC Prodn-MONUMT 1976

Screening For Driver Limitations - Aging C 19 MIN
16MM FILM - 3/4 IN VIDEO A
Presents adverse medical conditions which may be more common in older drivers.
LC NO. 77-706151
Prod-USHTSA Dist-USNAC Prodn-MONUMT 1976

Screening For Driver Limitations - General Medicine C 16 MIN
16MM FILM - 3/4 IN VIDEO A
Presents a wide variety of medical conditions, such as metabolic disorders, diabetes, orthopedic problems, hearing and respiratory disorders. Shows the signs of these disorders, which will help driver examiners identify those drivers whose impairment should be medically evaluated before they are licensed.
LC NO. 77-706154
Prod-USHTSA Dist-USNAC Prodn-MONUMT 1976

Screening For Driver Limitations - Introduction C 8 MIN
16MM FILM - 3/4 IN VIDEO A
Presents signs and symptoms of conditions which may impair a driver's ability to safely operate a motor vehicle.
LC NO. 77-706153
Prod-USHTSA Dist-USNAC Prodn-MONUMT 1976

Screening For Driver Limitations - Mental And Emotional C 21 MIN
16MM FILM - 3/4 IN VIDEO A
Presents a wide range of mental and emotional disorders, including alcoholism, drug abuse and suicide, which driver examiners need to identify in order that medical evaluation can be made before the individual is licensed.
LC NO. 77-706155
Prod-USHTSA Dist-USNAC Prodn-MONUMT 1976

Screening For Driver Limitations - Neurological C 16 MIN
16MM FILM - 3/4 IN VIDEO A
Presents information on such neurological diseases as epilepsy and other central nervous system and neuromuscular disorders. Gives clues to identify drivers whose degree of impairment should be medically evaluated before they are licensed.
LC NO. 77-706156
Prod-USHTSA Dist-USNAC Prodn-MONUMT 1976

Screening For Driver Limitations - Vision C 21 MIN
16MM FILM - 3/4 IN VIDEO A
Shows the importance of good vision to the ability to drive safely and describes visual diseases and disorders which should be evaluated by a specialist.
LC NO. 77-706157
Prod-USHTSA Dist-USNAC Prodn-MONUMT 1976

Screening For Glaucoma In Your Office - Tonometry C 15 MIN
3/4 OR 1/2 INCH VIDEO CASSETTE PRO
Gives a brief overview of intraocular pressure. Presents standards for normal and elevated pressure and a step-by- step description of how to perform tonometry.
Prod-UMICHM Dist-UMICHM 1973

Screening Technique For Colon Cancer, A (2nd Ed) C 9 MIN
3/4 OR 1/2 INCH VIDEO CASSETTE
Discusses the prevalence of colon cancer, explains what it is, and demonstrates a self-administered test for its early detection.
LC NO. 81-706285
Prod-VAHSL Dist-USNAC 1980

Screening Test For Sensory Integrative Dysfunction, A B 27 MIN
3/4 OR 1/2 INCH VIDEO CASSETTE
Demonstrates ways of screening children for sensory-integrative problems, using performances by children illustrating these problems.
Prod-BU Dist-BU

Screenprinting C 25 MIN
3/4 OR 1/2 INCH VIDEO CASSETTE H-C A
Shows an artist in her studio using hand-cut stencils and photographic techniques to make a print of Al Capone. Shows a German artist, a student of master printer, Chris Prater, making a screenprint of an Arabian wall.
From The Artist In Print Series.
Prod-BBCTV Dist-FI

Screenwriter, The C 29 MIN
3/4 INCH VIDEO CASSETTE
Interviews screenwriter Rob Thompson. Focuses on the role of the screenwriter today in the development and production of a major motion picture.
From The Directions - The Cinema Series.
Prod-UMITV Dist-UMITV 1976

Screwdrivers, Nutrunners, And Wrenches C 12 MIN
3/4 OR 1/2 INCH VIDEO CASSETTE
Covers power screwdrivers, nutrunners and wrenches, their mechanisms, accessories, maintenance and safety.
From The Using Portable Power Tool Series.
Prod-TPCTRA Dist-TPCTRA

Screwdrivers, Nutrunners, And Wrenches (Spanish) C 12 MIN
3/4 OR 1/2 INCH VIDEO CASSETTE
Covers power screwdrivers, nutrunners and wrenches, their mechaniisms, accessories, maintenance and safety.
From The Using Portable Power Tool Series.
Prod-TPCTRA Dist-TPCTRA

Screws And Screwdrivers C 13 MIN
16MM FILM, 3/4 OR 1/2 IN VIDEO H-C A
Discusses the woodscrew and screwdrivers. Demonstrates the use of flat blade, phillips, socket and special purpose screwdrivers.
From The Hand Tools For Wood Working Series.
Prod-MORLAT Dist-SF 1967

Scribbling Beauty C 5 MIN
3/4 OR 1/2 INCH VIDEO CASSETTE J-H
Continues the lesson on coherence in writing.
From The Write On, Set 2 Series.
Prod-CTI Dist-CTI

Scribbling Beauty, Pt 1 C 5 MIN
3/4 OR 1/2 INCH VIDEO CASSETTE J-H
Deals with coherence in writing.
From The Write On, Set 2 Series.
Prod-CTI Dist-CTI

Scribe, The C 30 MIN
16MM FILM, 3/4 OR 1/2 IN VIDEO IND
Stars Buster Keaton as an investigative reporter who serves as an illustration of the importance of construction safety rules by unwittingly breaking them. A comedic pantomime with a serious message.
Prod-CSAO Dist-IFB

Script For Scandinavia (German) C 27 MIN
16MM FILM, 3/4 OR 1/2 IN VIDEO C A
An air-travel film about Denmark, Sweden, Finland and Norway. Includes scenes of the beauty and exhilaration of Nordic winter life as contrasted with the pastoral loveliness of summer. Shows cosmopolitan centers such as Copenhagen, Gothenburg, Stockholm, Helsinki and Bergen.
Prod-DAC Dist-MCDO 1966

Script For Scandinavia, A C 27 MIN
16MM FILM OPTICAL SOUND C A
An air-travel film about Denmark, Sweden, Finland and Norway. Includes scenes of the beauty and exhilaration of Nordic winter life as contrasted with the pastoral loveliness of summer. Shows cosmopolitan centers such as Copenhagen, Gothenburg, Stockholm, Helsinki and Bergen.
LC NO. FIAL7-597
Prod-DAC Dist-MCDO 1966

Script Writing C 15 MIN
3/4 OR 1/2 INCH VIDEO CASSETTE I
Provides an introduction to a study unit on filming and videotaping. Explains and illustrates camera movements, sound and picture alignment, and the addition of music and sound effects.
From The Zebra Wings Series.
Prod-NITC Dist-AITECH Prodn-MAETEL 1975

Scroll Saw, The C 13 MIN
16MM FILM, 3/4 OR 1/2 IN VIDEO H-C A
Presents instruction in the properties and use of a scroll saw. Illustrates parts of the saw, the blades to be selected and inserted and the tension and machine speed when the saw is in use. Shows the type of table, hold-down and operation.
From The Woodwork - Machine Tools Series.
Prod-MORLAT Dist-SF Prodn-MORLAT 1967

Scrooge Mc Duck And Money C 15 MIN
16MM FILM, 3/4 OR 1/2 IN VIDEO I-J
Uses a cartoon featuring Scrooge Mc Duck and a variety of songs, dances and choruses in order to help young people understand the concept of money, money flow, inflation and deflation. Outlines the uses of money throughout history and relates some of the money words and phrases in use today.
Prod-DISNEY Dist-WDEMCO 1974

Scrotal Hydrocele C 15 MIN
3/4 OR 1/2 INCH VIDEO CASSETTE
See series title for descriptive statement.
From The Pediatric Series.
Prod-SVL Dist-SVL

Scrubbing, Gowning And Gloving C 20 MIN
3/4 OR 1/2 INCH VIDEO CASSETTE PRO
Demonstrates in detail, basic surgical scrubbing techniques and illustrates assisted and unassisted methods of gowning and gloving.
From The Basic Clinical Skills Series.
Prod-HSCIC Dist-HSCIC 1984

Scrubbing, Gowning, and Gloving C 21 MIN
3/4 OR 1/2 INCH VIDEO CASSETTE PRO
Demonstrates and explains an anatomical stroke count scrub, hand drying, gowning and gloving unassisted and assisted, as well as proper techniques for removing gown and gloves.
Prod-PRIMED Dist-PRIMED

Scruffy C 7 MIN
16MM FILM, 3/4 OR 1/2 IN VIDEO H-C A
Scruffy Kitten runs away from home to find a sunbeam and is joined by other small animals of the woods. Grandfather Hare saves them when their boat is carried over a water fall, and they return home much wiser.
Prod-SF Dist-SF 1959

Scuba C 22 MIN
16MM FILM, 3/4 OR 1/2 IN VIDEO A
Provides an introduction to the sport of scuba diving. Observes a scuba class in which basic diving is learned.
Prod-KROWN Dist-MCFI 1975

Sculpting On The Square C 15 MIN
3/4 OR 1/2 INCH VIDEO CASSETTE P
See series title for descriptive statement.
From The Strawberry Square II - Take Time Series.
Prod-NEITV Dist-AITECH 1984

Sculptor, The C 15 MIN
16MM FILM OPTICAL SOUND J-C A
Shows the sources of the sculptor's inspiration in the world around him and describes how he adapts materials and equipment to the medium at hand. Covers the process whereby a group of birds in flight is sculptured in welded brass.
LC NO. 74-705585
Prod-AVED Dist-AVED 1963

Sculpture B 17 MIN
16MM FILM, 3/4 OR 1/2 IN VIDEO J-C
A basic introduction to the materials and techniques used in sculpting. Shows sculptors George Grard and Rik Poot at work on various materials such as clay, stone, wood and plaster. Compares the sculpted forms of ancient civilization and the emerging shapes of today, with Rodin as a kind of link between the two. Uses time - lapse photography of clay forms to demonstrate the transition from realism to cubism.
Prod-BELMNE Dist-IFB Prodn-IFB 1969

Sculpture - Elements Of Dimension C 30 MIN
3/4 INCH VIDEO CASSETTE C A
Studies elements of sculpture as an art form. Explores relief and monolith forms of sculpture that preceded modern sculpture.
From The Humanities Through The Arts With Maya Angelou Series. Lesson 23
Prod-COAST Dist-CDTEL Prodn-CICOCH

Sculpture - Meaning Through The Body's Form C 30 MIN
3/4 INCH VIDEO CASSETTE C A
Explores unique ways in which sculpture conveys meaning through three-dimensional form. Focuses on life and works of August Rodin.
From The Humanities Through The Arts With Maya Angelou Series. Lesson 24
Prod-COAST Dist-CDTEL Prodn-CICOCH

Sculpture - Mirror Of Man's Being C 30 MIN
3/4 INCH VIDEO CASSETTE C A
Outlines the history of sculpture. Offers understanding of diverse ways humans have expressed their perception through three-dimensional forms. Shows representative works of sculpture.
From The Humanities Through The Arts With Maya Angelou Series. Lesson 22
Prod-COAST Dist-CDTEL Prodn-CICOCH

Sculpture - Most Difficult Of Arts C 30 MIN
3/4 INCH VIDEO CASSETTE C A
Discusses personal reactions to minimal sculpture, the roles of the critic in sculpture and the responsibility of the critic for informing and encouraging the sculptor. Features Maya Angelou, curator Donna Stein, and sculptor Oliver Andrews.
From The Humanities Through The Arts With Maya Angelou Series. Lesson 25
Prod-COAST Dist-CDTEL Prodn-CICOCH

Sculpture - Process Of Discovery C 11 MIN
16MM FILM, 3/4 OR 1/2 IN VIDEO J-C A
Presents sculptor Norm Hines discussing his approach to creativity, explaining how he works with no preconceived form but follows the shape which is indicated by the rock itself.
Prod-BARR Dist-BARR 1975

Sculpture - The Forms Of Life C 18 MIN
16MM FILM, 3/4 OR 1/2 IN VIDEO J-H
Shows the materials of the sculptor, the wide range of techniques and many examples of works from around the the world.
From The Humanities Series.
Prod-MGHT Dist-MGHT 1971

Sculpture At The Middelheim C 11 MIN
16MM FILM, 3/4 OR 1/2 IN VIDEO H-C
Presents the works of outstanding twentieth century sculptors on display at the Middelheim Park in Antwerp, Belgium. Includes the work of Henry Moore, Giacometti, Manzu, Maillol and Gargallo.
Prod-BELMNE Dist-IFB Prodn-GEIL 1969

Sculpture Australia C 30 MIN
16MM FILM OPTICAL SOUND H-C A
A survey of contemporary Australian sculpture in which some sculptors, working in Australia and overseas, discuss and show some of their work.
LC NO. 75-709227
Prod-ANAIB Dist-AUIS 1969

Sculpture By Isaac Witkin C 22 MIN
16MM FILM OPTICAL SOUND
Explores the philosophy, artistic methods and abstract sculpture of Isaac Witkin.
LC NO. 76-702668
Prod-CINETU Dist-CINETU 1976

Sculpture From Life X 11 MIN
16MM FILM OPTICAL SOUND J-C A
Grant Beach of the Grant Beach Arts and Crafts School creates a life-sized head, working from a posed model. Starting with the armature, he adds clay, constructs the head and details of the face and forms the hair.
Prod-AVED Dist-AVED 1957

Sculpture In The City - Spoleto (1960's) C 11 MIN
16MM FILM OPTICAL SOUND
Presents the anguished imagery of modern sculpture that invades the serene old Lombard town of Spoleto each year, disturbing the piazzas with metal monsters.
Prod-ROLAND Dist-ROLAND

Sculpture In The Round C 28 MIN
3/4 INCH VIDEO CASSETTE
See series title for descriptive statement.
From The Woodcarver's Workshop Series.
Prod-WOSUTV Dist-PUBTEL

Sculpture Of The Human Figure, The C 24 MIN
3/4 OR 1/2 INCH VIDEO CASSETTE H-C
Analyzes works of art from the Greek period demonstrating the changing attitude of sculptors toward the human figure.
Prod-BBCTV Dist-OPENU 1983

Sculpture Today B 19 MIN
16MM FILM, 3/4 OR 1/2 IN VIDEO J-C
Illustrates the many styles of modern sculpture, with emphasis on the expressive potential of the material. Includes examples of the work of Adam, Arp, Calder, Gabo, Giacometti, Hepworth, Laurens, Manzu, Moore, Walrauens and Zadkine.
Prod-BELMNE Dist-IFB Prodn-IFB 1967

Sculpture 58 - The Story Of A Creation C 12 MIN
16MM FILM OPTICAL SOUND
Follows a sculptor struggling with his material and inspiration to create a large sculptural group. Watches him from earliest drawings through models to the final triumph of full-scale bronze.
Prod-ROLAND Dist-ROLAND

Sculpturing C 20 MIN
2 INCH VIDEOTAPE I
Helps students build and design three-dimensional forms.
From The Creating Art, Pt 2 - Learning To Create Art Forms Series.
Prod-GPITVL Dist-GPITVL

Sculpturing Copper With A Torch C 14 MIN
16MM FILM, 3/4 OR 1/2 IN VIDEO H-C A S
Shows the use of copper tube, wire, sheets and pipes. Explains the processes of forming, patching, enameling, brazing, cleaning and oxidation.
Prod-MOTIVF Dist-IFB 1965

SDC C 14 MIN
16MM FILM OPTICAL SOUND
Shows a taxpayer questioning the role of the Social Development Commission. Uses interviews with SDC clients to explain the way it deals with various social and economic problems in Milwaukee County.
LC NO. 80-700443
Prod-CRSDC Dist-MOYA Prodn-MOYA 1980

Se Necesita Ser Bilingue C 30 MIN
3/4 OR 1/2 INCH VIDEO CASSETTE
See series title for descriptive statement.
From The Que Pasa, U S A Series.
Prod-WPBTTV Dist-MDCPB

Sea Adventures Of Sandy The Snail - A Lesson In Finger Painting X 16 MIN
16MM FILM, 3/4 OR 1/2 IN VIDEO P-I
Artist and teacher, Betty Ohlrogge, uses a series of finger paintings to tell the story of a little snail's adventures with several marine animals.
Prod-EBF Dist-EBEC 1957

Sea And Sand B 27 MIN
16MM FILM, 3/4 OR 1/2 IN VIDEO J-H
Depicts the Invasion of North Africa from 1942-1943.
From The Victory At Sea Series.
Prod-NBCTV Dist-LUF

Sea And Sand - Invasion Of North Africa, 1942 -1943 B 30 MIN
16MM FILM OPTICAL SOUND I-C
Describes the establishment of a second front against Germany while Hitler was moving against Russia. Depicts the invasion of French North Africa, commanded by Eisenhower and follows the Allied advance through Tunis, Bizerte and Suez.
From The Victory At Sea Series.
Prod-GRACUR Dist-GRACUR

Sea Animals B 15 MIN
2 INCH VIDEOTAPE P
Examines the kinds of animals living in the sea and how they are suited to this life. (Broadcast quality)
From The Land And Sea Series.
Prod-TTOIC Dist-GPITVL Prodn-WGBHTV

Sea Area Forties C 29 MIN
16MM FILM OPTICAL SOUND
Provides a look at undersea oil gathering operations in Great Britain's North Sea. Focuses on all aspects of bringing the oil ashore, from locating the oil in 400 feet of treacherous water to respecting the fragility of nature.
Prod-BPNA Dist-MTP

Sea Behind The Dunes, The C 57 MIN
16MM FILM, 3/4 OR 1/2 IN VIDEO H-C A
Looks at the ecology of an ocean inlet. Describes the interrelationship of the ocean, bay, barrier beach and salt marsh and shows the animals that inhabit this ecosystem.
From The Nova Series.
LC NO. 81-706781
Prod-WGBHTV Dist-TIMLIF 1981

Sea Beneath The Earth C 22 MIN
3/4 OR 1/2 INCH VIDEO CASSETTE J-H
See series title for descriptive statement.
From The Phenomenal World Series.
Prod-EBEC Dist-EBEC 1983

Sea Birds Of Isabela, The C 23 MIN
16MM FILM, 3/4 OR 1/2 IN VIDEO I-C A
A shortened version of Sea Birds Of Isabela. Presents a study of the habits and interrelationships of various species of birds on the island of Isabela in the Galapagos Islands as seen by Jacques Cousteau and his expedition.
From The Undersea World Of Jacques Cousteau Series.
Prod-METROM Dist-CF 1977

Sea Birds Of Isabela, The C 52 MIN
16MM FILM, 3/4 OR 1/2 IN VIDEO I-C A
Presents Jacques Cousteau's study of the frigate bird, the brown- and the blue-footed booby, the pelican and the red-billed tropic bird.
From The Undersea World Of Jacques Cousteau Series.
Prod-METROM Dist-CF 1977

Sea Can Kill, The C 27 MIN
16MM FILM, 3/4 OR 1/2 IN VIDEO A
Presents a dramatization of a crew being forced to abandon ship during a storm and the procedures which they follow afterward. Shows how to abandon ship and board a raft, how to search for survivors, care for the injured, avoid hypothermia, apportion rations and post lookouts.
LC NO. 79-707949
Prod-UKMD Dist-IFB Prodn-RANDC 1978

Sea Creatures C 12 MIN
16MM FILM, 3/4 OR 1/2 IN VIDEO P-C
Features lower-depth sea life including crabs, jellyfish, spiny urchins, zebra-striped fish, snakes and the giant manta ray.
Prod-PHENIX Dist-PHENIX 1974

Sea Dream C 6 MIN
16MM FILM, 3/4 OR 1/2 IN VIDEO P
Presents an animated story about a little girl, who after suffering through a bad day, escapes into an underwater fantasy featuring a lady octopus who comforts her. Shows how, after they

do many things together, the girl awakens, ready to start a new day.
LC NO. 81-706604
Prod-NFBC Dist-PHENIX 1980

Sea Egg, The C 15 MIN
3/4 OR 1/2 INCH VIDEO CASSETTE P
See series title for descriptive statement.
From The Best Of Cover To Cover 1 Series.
Prod-WETATV Dist-WETATV

Sea Fever C 6 MIN
16MM FILM, 3/4 OR 1/2 IN VIDEO I-C A
Shows a square-rigged clipper at sea in fair weather and foul, based upon John Masefield's poem Sea Fever.
Prod-AIMS Dist-AIMS 1966

Sea Fever (Japanese) C 6 MIN
16MM FILM, 3/4 OR 1/2 IN VIDEO I-C A
Presents a visual interpretationf of John Masefield's poem Sea Fever, which expresses his feeling about salt air, clear skies and the freedom of the sea. Narrated by Lorne Greene.
Prod-CAHILL Dist-AIMS 1966

Sea Fever (Spanish) C 6 MIN
16MM FILM, 3/4 OR 1/2 IN VIDEO I-C A
Presents a visual interpretationf of John Masefield's poem Sea Fever, which expresses his feeling about salt air, clear skies and the freedom of the sea. Narrated by Lorne Greene.
Prod-CAHILL Dist-AIMS 1966

Sea Gulls C 3 MIN
16MM FILM OPTICAL SOUND P-I
Discusses the birds known as sea gulls.
From The Of All Things Series.
Prod-BAILYL Dist-AVED

Sea Gulls, The C 10 MIN
16MM FILM, 3/4 OR 1/2 IN VIDEO P-I
Demonstrates the scientific techniques of careful observation. Explores the habitat of the sea gulls and observes the gulls in flight, noting how different parts of the body are used to 'take off,' glide, soar and land.
Prod-AIMS Dist-AIMS 1968

Sea Ice C 28 MIN
16MM FILM OPTICAL SOUND
Points out that every winter, the Sea of Okhotsk becomes the scene of a dynamic development of sea ice but that the causes of its formation, its movement and its characteristics have remained a mystery. Presents the account of scientific research conducted by Hokkaido University's Institute of Low Temperature Science with cooperation from the Maritime Safety Agency to probe into this mystery.
Prod-KAJIMA Dist-UNIJAP 1970

Sea Images C 20 MIN
16MM FILM, 3/4 OR 1/2 IN VIDEO
Explores the majesty and mystery of the sea. Considers man's fascination with and reliance on the sea and how it has been a source of imagery for artists in all times and cultures.
From The Images And Things Series.
LC NO. 73-702110
Prod-NITC Dist-AITECH 1971

Sea In The Clouds, A C 21 MIN
16MM FILM, 3/4 OR 1/2 IN VIDEO J-C A
Shows the beauty of Lake Tahoe and the Sierras and explains how the lake may die as a result of human exploitation.
Prod-PNDRGN Dist-FLMFR

Sea Life That Doesn't Crawl C 15 MIN
2 INCH VIDEOTAPE P
Observes the peculiar and adaptive qualities of the starfish, sea anemone, sea urchin, hermit crab, shark, lung fish, grouper and scavenger. Studies a large goldfish.
From The Tell Me What You See Series.
Prod-GPITVL Dist-GPITVL

Sea Lions And Fur Seals C 19 MIN
16MM FILM OPTICAL SOUND
Compares and contrasts sea lions found off California and on the Galapogos Islands.
From The Galapagos - Laboratory For Evolution Series.
LC NO. 73-702572
Prod-UCBR Dist-HAR 1971

Sea Otter, The C 3 MIN
16MM FILM OPTICAL SOUND P-I
Discusses the mammal known as the sea otter.
From The Of All Things Series.
Prod-BAILYL Dist-AVED

Sea Otters - The California Rough Riders C 23 MIN
3/4 OR 1/2 INCH VIDEO CASSETTE
Goes to the coast of California where a sea otter mother and pup evade great white sharks and ride the rough waves of the storm-tossed Pacific.
Prod-NWLDPR Dist-NWLDPR

Sea Power - A Destiny Upon The Waters C 28 MIN
16MM FILM, 3/4 OR 1/2 IN VIDEO
Shows the evolution of naval power and its impact on the development of empires and the age of exploration from the Phoenicians to the mid-18th century.
LC NO. 82-706239
Prod-USN Dist-USNAC 1968

Sea Power - Seas Of Liberty C 28 MIN
16MM FILM OPTICAL SOUND
Illustrates the impact of sea power on the national economy, geopolitical aspects of the seas from the mid-18th century and the necessity for freedom of the seas.
LC NO. 74-705587
Prod-USN Dist-USNAC 1968

Sea Power - The Sea Is A Special Place C 28 MIN
16MM FILM OPTICAL SOUND
Shows the responsibilities of command and the demands and rewards for the people who make the complex and sophisticated naval machinery work.
LC NO. 74-705588
Prod-USN Dist-USNAC 1968

Sea Power In The Pacific B 30 MIN
16MM FILM OPTICAL SOUND
Traces the history and depicts the role of American sea power in the Pacific during World War II.
LC NO. 74-705589
Prod-USN Dist-USNAC 1946

Sea Power On The Move C 28 MIN
16MM FILM, 3/4 OR 1/2 IN VIDEO
Describes the mobility, versatility and flexibility of naval forces. Explains the overall naval purpose, mission and philosophies of the use of sea power.
LC NO. 81-707724
Prod-USN Dist-USNAC 1969

Sea Search C 18 MIN
16MM FILM, 3/4 OR 1/2 IN VIDEO J
Introduces oceanography with a story about a search for sunken treasure. Reveals the complexity of the ocean environment, the effects oceans have upon earth systems and the scientific and economic potential of the oceans.
From The Universe And I Series.
LC NO. 80-706485
Prod-KYTV Dist-AITECH 1977

Sea Shell Animals C 10 MIN
16MM FILM, 3/4 OR 1/2 IN VIDEO I-H
Presents a Survey of mollusks photographed at Marineland of the Pacific, under the direction of the curator of the oceanarium.
Prod-FA Dist-PHENIX 1955

Sea Shell Animals (Spanish) C 10 MIN
16MM FILM, 3/4 OR 1/2 IN VIDEO I-H
Presents a Survey of mollusks photographed at Marineland of the Pacific, under the direction of the curator of the oceanarium.
Prod-FA Dist-PHENIX 1955

Sea Snakes Studied C 2 MIN
16MM FILM OPTICAL SOUND
Shows an American scientist doing research on sea snakes in Australia.
Prod-ALLFP Dist-NSTA 1973

Sea Squawk, The B 18 MIN
16MM FILM SILENT J-C A
Stars Harry Langdon as a kilted bagpipe carrying Scotsman aboard a ship enroute to the United States.
Prod-MGM Dist-TWYMAN 1924

Sea Survival C 21 MIN
3/4 OR 1/2 INCH VIDEO CASSETTE PRO
Demonstrates the most important points of surviving a mishap at sea. Includes information about life rafts and survival suits, and interviews with survivors at accidents at sea.
From The Fisheries Safety And Survival Series.
Prod-USCG Dist-USNAC 1983

Sea Survival - The Physical And Mental Challenge C 22 MIN
16MM FILM, 3/4 OR 1/2 IN VIDEO
Deals with the psychological and physical problems of long-term survival at sea encountered by aircrew members after ditching or ejection over water. Illustrates actual living conditions and a variety of problems.
Prod-USAF Dist-USNAC

Sea To Sea C 25 MIN
16MM FILM OPTICAL SOUND
Views the Canadian fishing industry on both the east and west coasts of Canada and the way of life of those who work in the fishing industry.
LC NO. 76-701478
Prod-WILFGP Dist-WILFGP 1975

Sea Travels C 11 MIN
3/4 OR 1/2 INCH VIDEO CASSETTE
Depicts children in beautiful land- and sea-scapes.
Prod-EAI Dist-EAI

Sea Turtles C 13 MIN
16MM FILM, 3/4 OR 1/2 IN VIDEO
Depicts the birth of sea turtles and their race for survival into the sea to escape attacking predators. Edited from the television program Wild, Wild World Of Animals.
From The Wild, Wild World Of Animals Series.
LC NO. 79-707916
Prod-TIMLIF Dist-TIMLIF 1976

Sea Un Profesional C 14 MIN
16MM FILM, 3/4 OR 1/2 IN VIDEO J-H A
A Spanish-language version of the motion picture Be A Pro. Explains that professional players use the best equipment to protect themselves from injury when playing. Discusses such techniques as applied to automobile driving and machine work.
Prod-CHET Dist-IFB 1966

Sea Water And The Floor C 17 MIN
16MM FILM, 3/4 OR 1/2 IN VIDEO J-H
Describes the composition of sea water, the variations in temperature of sea water, the substances dissolved in sea water, the sediments that cover the sea floor and the topograhy of the sea floor.
Prod-WILEYJ Dist-MEDIAG 1970

Sea We Cannot Sense, A C 28 MIN
16MM FILM - 3/4 IN VIDEO
Shows how both man-made and background radiation are measured in order to determine their prevalence and possible effects on human life.
LC NO. 79-706189
Prod-ANL Dist-USNAC 1979

Sea Witch - Esso Brussels Collision And Fire C 26 MIN
16MM FILM - 3/4 IN VIDEO A
Documents the collision and resulting fire of the underway container vessel Sea Witch and the anchored Belgian tanker Esso Brussels in 1973. Depicts the events following a steering control failure aboard the Sea Witch which was leaving New York Harbor and describes the rescue efforts, structural damage to the vessels and effects of the fire on various types of containers.
LC NO. 77-706066
Prod-USCG Dist-USNAC 1976

Sea, Ice And Fire C 26 MIN
16MM FILM OPTICAL SOUND P-C A
A study of Iceland and its people, describing their way of life within their natural heritage of glaciers, hot springs and wildlife. Includes scenes of murres, gannets, puffins and kittiwakes.
From The Audubon Wildlife Theatre Series.
LC NO. 77-709407
Prod-KEGPL Dist-AVEXP 1969

Sea, The B 15 MIN
3/4 OR 1/2 INCH VIDEO CASSETTE P
Gives the child a feeling for the vastness of the sea and knowledge of some of its basic characteristics.
From The Land And Sea Series.
Prod-TTOIC Dist-GPITVL Prodn-WGBHTV

Sea, The X 26 MIN
16MM FILM, 3/4 OR 1/2 IN VIDEO
Illustrates basic concepts of marine ecology, and shows interrelationships between living things in the sea, their dependence on each other and on the conditions of the marine environment.
From The Biology Series. Unit 2 - Ecosystems
Prod-EBF Dist-EBEC 1962

Sea, The C 30 MIN
3/4 OR 1/2 INCH VIDEO CASSETTE
Explores the relationship between what people know, see and do and the sea around them.
From The Land And The People Series.
Prod-EKC Dist-MDCPB

Sea, The (Spanish) C 27 MIN
16MM FILM, 3/4 OR 1/2 IN VIDEO H
Describes the interrelationships between living things in the sea, pointing out their dependence on each other and on the conditions of the marine environment. Illustrates basic concepts of marine ecology.
From The Biology (Spanish) Series. Unit 2 - Ecosystems
Prod-EBEC Dist-EBEC

Sea, The - Career Day C 15 MIN
16MM FILM OPTICAL SOUND
Shows Navy occupations and scenes of life at sea.
LC NO. 74-706573
Prod-USN Dist-USNAC 1971

Sea, The - Mysteries Of The Deep C 23 MIN
16MM FILM, 3/4 OR 1/2 IN VIDEO I-H
Examines some of the inhabitants of the ocean depths. Focuses on the hunter-hunted relationship that exists undersea. Discusses the threat to sea life by human beings and their endless supply of pollutants.
From The Wide World Of Adventure Series.
Prod-AVATLI Dist-EBEC 1979

Sea, The - Mysteries Of The Deep (Spanish) C 23 MIN
16MM FILM, 3/4 OR 1/2 IN VIDEO I-H
Examines some of the inhabitants of the ocean depths. Focuses on the hunter-hunted relationship that exists undersea. Discusses the threat to sea life posed by human beings and their endless supply of pollutants.
Prod-AVATLI Dist-EBEC 1979

Seabee Teams C 30 MIN
16MM FILM OPTICAL SOUND
Shows the navy 'STAT' teams training Vietnamese to build roads, homes and schools in South Vietnam.
LC NO. 74-706240
Prod-USN Dist-USNAC 1966

Seabirds C 16 MIN
16MM FILM, 3/4 OR 1/2 IN VIDEO K-H
Observes the seabirds along the shores of the British Isles, where twenty-four species nest and raise their young. Looks at their various fishing styles and techniques of cleaning and preening.
From The RSPB Collection Series.
LC NO. 83-707194
Prod-RSFPB Dist-BCNFL 1983

Seacoast People C 14 MIN
16MM FILM, 3/4 OR 1/2 IN VIDEO I-C A
Depicts a day in the life of a lobster fisherman in York Harbor, Maine. Shows how he picks up the bait early in the morning, checks and baits half of his traps, gathers his catch and returns at the end of the day to sell it to a wholesaler. Tells of the similar methods of the Norwegian crab fisherman who sells his catch directly to the people at the dock.
From The Places People Live Series.
Prod-SF Dist-SF

Seacoast Port City, A - Port Of Vancouver C 14 MIN
16MM FILM, 3/4 OR 1/2 IN VIDEO P-I
Develops an understanding of how communities interact by means of resources and transportation through the experiences of a young boy who learns the origin of some of the products his family buys.

From The This Is My Home Series.
Prod-BCNFL Dist-BCNFL 1984

Seacoast Villages Of Japan C 19 MIN
16MM FILM - 3/4 IN VIDEO I-J
Depicts seacoast village life of Japan in all its seasonal changes and stresses Japan's dependence upon the sea.
Prod-ATLAP Dist-ATLAP Prodn-CARRD 1963

Seacoasts - A First Film B 10 MIN
16MM FILM, 3/4 OR 1/2 IN VIDEO I-J
Describes the various kinds of seacoasts and the variety of animals that live in the intertidal zone.
Prod-NELLES Dist-PHENIX 1973

Seaflight C 12 MIN
16MM FILM, 3/4 OR 1/2 IN VIDEO I-C A
Presents the state of the art of surfing as well as exhibiting a new quality level of surfing film photography. Looks at wind surfing. Without narration.
LC NO. 82-706989
Prod-PFP Dist-PFP 1982

Seafood C 29 MIN
2 INCH VIDEOTAPE
Features gourmet-humorist Justin Wilson showing ways to cook seafood with various ingredients.
From The Cookin' Cajun Series.
Prod-MAETEL Dist-PUBTEL

Seafood Cookery C 21 MIN
16MM FILM OPTICAL SOUND
Shows various methods of cooking seafood.
LC NO. 74-706574
Prod-USN Dist-USNAC 1966

Seafood Cookery C 21 MIN
3/4 OR 1/2 INCH VIDEO CASSETTE
Shows various methods of cooking seafood.
LC NO. 80-707635
Prod-USN Dist-USNAC 1966

Seafood Cookery C 57 MIN
3/4 OR 1/2 INCH VIDEO CASSETTE
Demonstrates various means of preparing fish. Shows how to distinguish fresh from frozen fish, proper storage of seafood and how to determine proper cooking times. Concludes with a demonstration of salmon smoked by an altar fire. Hosted by Sharon Kramis.
Prod-CINAS Dist-CINAS 1982

Seafood Cookery C 57 MIN
1/2 IN VIDEO CASSETTE BETA/VHS
Demonstrates the preparation of a variety of fish and shellfish.
Prod-MOHOMV Dist-MOHOMV

Seafood Specialties C 12 MIN
16MM FILM - 3/4 IN VIDEO J-H
Presents recipes for seafood, a valuable source of protein.
From The Eat Right To Your Heart's Delight Series.
Prod-IPS Dist-IPS 1976

Seahorse, The - A Most Exceptional Fish C 12 MIN
16MM FILM OPTICAL SOUND J-C A
Reviews external anatomy, feeding and birth of the young through the use of time-lapse microscopic scenes of developing embryos and microscopic scenes of newborn sea horses. Shows the function of the air bladder and relates this apparatus to the countercurrent exchange system.
Prod-REELA Dist-MIAMIS 1968

Seal Island C 55 MIN
16MM FILM OPTICAL SOUND P-I
Reveals what happens when two children discover that although an island has been sold to conservationists, permission has been granted for two killers to shoot seals on the island until the sale is completed.
Prod-LUF Dist-LUF 1979

Seal Island C 27 MIN
16MM FILM, 3/4 OR 1/2 IN VIDEO I-C A
Scenes of the life of the seal colony which each year during May and June inhabits the rocky shores of the Pribilof Islands in the Bering Sea.
Prod-DISNEY Dist-WDEMCO 1953

Seal Island (Afrikaans) C 27 MIN
16MM FILM, 3/4 OR 1/2 IN VIDEO I-H
Tells the story of the fur-bearing seals of the Pribilof Islands. Teaches respect for nature's balance.
Prod-WDEMCO Dist-WDEMCO 1953

Seal Island (Danish) C 27 MIN
16MM FILM, 3/4 OR 1/2 IN VIDEO I-H
Tells the story of the fur-bearing seals of the Pribilof Islands. Teaches respect for nature's balance.
Prod-WDEMCO Dist-WDEMCO 1953

Seal Island (French) C 27 MIN
16MM FILM, 3/4 OR 1/2 IN VIDEO I-H
Tells the story of the fur-bearing seals of the Pribilof Islands. Teaches respect for nature's balance.
Prod-WDEMCO Dist-WDEMCO 1953

Seal Island (German) C 27 MIN
16MM FILM, 3/4 OR 1/2 IN VIDEO I-H
Tells the story of the fur-bearing seals of the Pribilof Islands. Teaches respect for nature's balance.
Prod-WDEMCO Dist-WDEMCO 1953

Seal Island (Spanish) C 27 MIN
16MM FILM, 3/4 OR 1/2 IN VIDEO I-H
Tells the story of the fur-bearing seals of the Pribilof Islands. Teaches respect for nature's balance.
Prod-WDEMCO Dist-WDEMCO 1953

Sealab 1 C 28 MIN
16MM FILM OPTICAL SOUND
Shows the navy's exploratory attempt to apply laboratory studies of man's ability to live and work in an artificial atmosphere at a depth of 200 feet for prolonged periods.
LC NO. 74-705590
Prod-USN Dist-USNAC 1965

Sealed In Glass C 11 MIN
16MM FILM OPTICAL SOUND PRO
Explains the manufacture of glass containers.
Prod-FPI Dist-FPI

Sealegs C 15 MIN
16MM FILM - 3/4 IN VIDEO
Discusses the carrier environment and the special aircraft on board.
Prod-WSTGLC Dist-WSTGLC

Sealing The Breach B 27 MIN
16MM FILM, 3/4 OR 1/2 IN VIDEO J-H
Documents anti-submarine warfare between 1941-1943.
From The Victory At Sea Series.
Prod-NBCTV Dist-LUF

Seals B 22 MIN
16MM FILM, 3/4 OR 1/2 IN VIDEO I-C A
A shortened version of Seals. Presents Pepito and Cristabal, two young sea lion pups taken aboard the Calypso off the coast of Africa. Records the behavior of the sea lions and the relationship that develops between the crew and the sea lions.
From The Undersea World Of Jacques Cousteau Series.
Prod-METROM Dist-CF 1970

Seals C 52 MIN
16MM FILM, 3/4 OR 1/2 IN VIDEO I-C A
Presents Pepito and Cristabal, two young sea lion pups taken aboard the Calypso off the coast of Africa. Records the behavior of the sea lions and the relationship that develops between the crew and the sea lions.
From The Undersea World Of Jacques Cousteau Series.
Prod-METROM Dist-CF 1970

Seamless Modern C 13 MIN
16MM FILM OPTICAL SOUND
Explains how seamless steel pipes are made.
LC NO. 79-702862
Prod-USSC Dist-USSC Prodn-HWP 1968

Seamless Modern (General Pipe Making) C 13 MIN
16MM FILM OPTICAL SOUND
See series title for descriptive statement.
From The Pipe And Tubing Series.
Prod-USSC Dist-USSC

Seamless Web, The C 30 MIN
3/4 INCH VIDEO CASSETTE J-C A
Examines man's relationship to his environment and the choices he must make to preserve it.
From The Man Builds - Man Destroys Series.
Prod-UN Dist-GPITVL 1974

Seamless Webb, The C 30 MIN
16MM FILM - 3/4 IN VIDEO J-C A
Examines man's relationship to his environment and the choices he must make to preserve it.
From The Man Builds - Man Destroys Series.
LC NO. 75-704153
Prod-UN Dist-GPITVL 1974

Seams And Edges C 41 MIN
1/2 IN VIDEO CASSETTE BETA/VHS IND
Deals with the application of the various seams and edges used in light gauge sheet metal fabricating. Gives seam allowances.
Prod-RMI Dist-RMI

Seams And Hems C 26 MIN
3/4 OR 1/2 INCH VIDEO CASSETTE C A
Covers making French and flat fell seams, making square or V-shaped corners, sewing unlike curved seams, sewing crotch seams, preparing a hem, finishing a hem.
From The Clothing Construction Techniques Series.
Prod-IOWASP Dist-IOWASP

Seams And Hems - Basting C 10 MIN
16MM FILM OPTICAL SOUND H-C A
Presents concepts in sewing, such as machine basting, pressing and pinning the hem and machine and hand hem stitches.
From The Sewing Series.
Prod-MORLAT Dist-SF 1967

Seamstress Of Salzburg, The C 15 MIN
3/4 OR 1/2 INCH VIDEO CASSETTE P
See series title for descriptive statement.
From The Magic Pages Series.
Prod-KLVXTV Dist-AITECH 1976

Seamus Heaney - Poet In Limboland C 29 MIN
16MM FILM, 3/4 OR 1/2 IN VIDEO H-C A
Traces the life and development of the Belfast poet who is considered the most promising young talent in Ireland today, Seamus Heaney. Explains that his poems arise from the involvement with his people.
Prod-MANTLH Dist-FOTH 1972

Sean B 15 MIN
16MM FILM OPTICAL SOUND
A four-year-old boy who lives in the Haight Ashbury district of San Francisco describes his world and the adult world as he sees it.
LC NO. 70-705007
Prod-ARRA Dist-ARRA 1969

Sean Lavery And Merrill Ashley C 30 MIN
3/4 OR 1/2 INCH VIDEO CASSETTE
See series title for descriptive statement.
From The Partners In Dance Series.
Prod-ARCVID Dist-ARCVID

Sean Lavery And Merrill Ashley C 30 MIN
3/4 OR 1/2 INCH VIDEO CASSETTE
See series title for descriptive statement.
From The Eye On Dance - Partners In Dance Series.
Prod-ARTRES Dist-ARTRES

Sean's Story C 12 MIN
16MM FILM, 3/4 OR 1/2 IN VIDEO H-C A
Focuses on a 12-year-old boy who divides his time between his mother in Los Angeles and his father in Las Vegas. Shows how the continued care and love shown by his parents and their cooperation in working out a custody arrangement has minimized his initial trauma.
From The American Family - An Endangered Species Series.
Prod-NBC Dist-FI 1979

Seaports And Ships C 15 MIN
3/4 OR 1/2 INCH VIDEO CASSETTE I
Shows fishermen along the New England coast and in the Atlantic catching lobster.
From The American Legacy Series. Program 2
LC NO. 83-706639
Prod-KRMATV Dist-AITECH 1983

Seapower C 28 MIN
16MM FILM OPTICAL SOUND
Illustrates the tasks and mission of the navy in protecting the sea lanes and the security of the free world. Shows how a strong navy should stress our nation's reliance on maritime trade and the necessity for development of the wealth of underseas' resources. Portrays the practical applications of versatile naval strength in contributing to the solution of the 1962 Cuban crisis. Narrated by Glenn Ford.
Prod-WB Dist-WB 1964

Seapower - Plymouth Rock To Polaris C 28 MIN
16MM FILM OPTICAL SOUND
Shows the history, growth and importance of American naval power.
LC NO. 74-705591
Prod-USN Dist-USNAC 1965

Seaprobe Probes Sea C 8 MIN
16MM FILM OPTICAL SOUND
Discusses Seaprobe, the first complete ocean-engineering tool.
Prod-ALLFP Dist-NSTA 1973

Search C 6 MIN
16MM FILM MAGNETIC SOUND J-C R
Shows how to discover God in human experience.
From The Christian Encounter Series,
LC NO. 72-700558
Prod-FRACOC Dist-FRACOC 1969

Search C 22 MIN
16MM FILM OPTICAL SOUND H-C
Shows the operation of the General Motors Research Laboratories, part of Saarinen's Technical Center.
LC NO. FIA66-762
Prod-GM Dist-GM Prodn-SENECA 1965

Search C 13 MIN
16MM FILM, 3/4 OR 1/2 IN VIDEO
Shows the wide range and diversity of ongoing scientific research. Examines the curiosity and motivation of scientists who are attempting to know what no one knew before.
LC NO. 81-706427
Prod-NSF Dist-USNAC 1980

Search C 60 MIN
3/4 OR 1/2 INCH VIDEO CASSETTE C
Covers dynamic programming NP-completeness and propositional calculus. Includes most computer searches, including sequential, binary and binary tree search, depth-first search, breadth-first search, steepest descent search, Heuristic search procedures, best-first search, branch and bound search and bidirectional search. Covers problem reduction by use of AND/OR trees.
From The Introduction To Artificial--Intelligence Series.
Prod-UAZMIC Dist-AMCEE

Search And Identification C 15 MIN
16MM FILM, 3/4 OR 1/2 IN VIDEO
Discusses how police officers should go about searching for and identifying physical evidence.
From The Physical Evidence Series.
Prod-WORON Dist-MTI

Search And Questioning Of Juvenile Offender B 20 MIN
16MM FILM OPTICAL SOUND C
Deals with various aspects of a criminal lawsuit involving a liquor store robbery case. Shows the interrogation of the juvenile robbery suspect and the search of his school locker and residence.
From The Criminal Law Series. No. 5
LC NO. 73-714037
Prod-RPATLF Dist-RPATLF 1968

Search And Rescue C
3/4 OR 1/2 INCH VIDEO CASSETTE PRO
Shows techniques for searching for victims in all types of occupancies, such as hotels, apartments, homes and large industrial complexes. Demonstrates tips for maintaining good communications via the buddy system and larger teams and techniques for covering all areas.
Prod-LACFD Dist-FILCOM

Search And Rescue - Pleasure Craft C 26 MIN
16MM FILM OPTICAL SOUND
Explains the operation of the search and rescue network as it ap-

plies to surface craft. Discusses the procedures to be followed by vessels in distress in order to obtain search and rescue assistance.
LC NO. FIE63-240
Prod-USGS Dist-USNAC 1960

Search And Rescue - Visual Aspects Of Search And Signalling C 19 MIN
16MM FILM OPTICAL SOUND
Shows relative merits of dye markets, various pistols, flares, smokes and mirrors. Describes air search patterns.
LC NO. 74-705592
Prod-USN Dist-USNAC 1947

Search And Rescue Scanning And Sighting Techniques C 7 MIN
16MM FILM OPTICAL SOUND
Shows the proper method for systematic scanning and sighting during search operations. Describes fixation points, clock systems and reference points.
LC NO. FIE62-76
Prod-USAF Dist-USNAC 1960

Search And Research - Hunting Animals Of The Past B 30 MIN
16MM FILM OPTICAL SOUND H-C A
Describes the methods for finding the remains of prehistoric animals, uncovering and collecting them, preparing specimens and mounting skeletons. Features a field-trip.
From The Great Plains Trilogy, 1 Series. In The Beginning - The Primitive Man
Prod-KUONTV Dist-UNL 1954

Search And Research - Psychology In Perspective B 30 MIN
16MM FILM OPTICAL SOUND H-C T
Describes through a story about a young lady who seeks psychotherapy, the three forces of psychology--experimental, psychoanalytic and existential or humanistic. Includes interviews with psychologists Harry Harlow, Rollo May and Carl Rogers.
LC NO. FIA66-1378
Prod-PSYCHF Dist-PSYCHD 1963

Search And Seizure C 19 MIN
3/4 OR 1/2 INCH VIDEO CASSETTE I-J
Uses three very different incidents to show how police handle search and seizure differently but always legally. Tackles the tricky questions of probable cause and privacy from the viewpoints of teens and the police.
From The Cop Talk Series.
Prod-UTSBE Dist-AITECH 1981

Search And Serendipity C 20 MIN
16MM FILM, 3/4 OR 1/2 IN VIDEO J-H
Follows the course of man's exploration of the skies, from Stonehenge to a contemporary observatory. Shows close-up views of some of the planets.
From The Matter Of Fact Series.
LC NO. 74-703198
Prod-NITC Dist-AITECH Prodn-WETATV 1973

Search At San Jose, The C 12 MIN
16MM FILM OPTICAL SOUND
Shows how the RAMAC computer was developed. Depicts interrelationships of market research, engineering, product development, sales and production as RAMAC evolved from an idea into production line computers. Shows the San Jose IBM plant.
Prod-ONFILM Dist-IBUSMA 1958

Search For A Cancer Cure C
16MM FILM OPTICAL SOUND
Features Professor Nathan Trainin, a member of a team of medical and biological experts at the Weitzmann Institute, who tells of his slow but exacting search for some answers about cancer.
From The Dateline Israel, 1973 Series.
Prod-ADL Dist-ADL

Search For A Century C 59 MIN
16MM FILM, 3/4 OR 1/2 IN VIDEO J-C A
Conveys the excitement of rediscovering Wolstenholme Towne, a 17th-century settlement which was left in ruins by an Indian uprising in 1622. Shows archeologists from Colonial Williamsburg uncovering artifacts in trash pits, wells and the remains of the people's homes.
Prod-CWMS Dist-CWMS 1980

Search For A New Architecture, The - 1920-1950 C 12 MIN
16MM FILM OPTICAL SOUND
See series title for descriptive statement.
From The Twelve Decades Of Concrete In American Architecture Series.
Prod-PRTLND Dist-PRTLND 1965

Search For Acadia, The C 15 MIN
16MM FILM, 3/4 OR 1/2 IN VIDEO
Shows the terrain at Acadia National Park in Maine. Reviews the history of Mt Desert Island.
LC NO. 80-707448
Prod-USNPS Dist-USNAC 1980

Search For Achievement C 27 MIN
16MM FILM OPTICAL SOUND C A
Presents Dr Jay Hall discussing the relationship between managerial behavior and managerial achievement, illustrating types of behavior that cause managers to become high achievers, moderate achievers or low achievers.
LC NO. 77-702216
Prod-TELEO Dist-TELEO Prodn-LANGLO 1976

Search For Alexander The Great--A Series
16MM FILM, 3/4 OR 1/2 IN VIDEO C A
Presents the story of Alexander the Great, who conquered most of the ancient world by the time he was 27 years old. Uses the recollections of his father, King Philip II; his mother, Olympias; his tutor, Aristotle; his enemy, Darius; his friend, Hephaiston; and his generals. Hosted by James Mason.
Prod-TIMLIF Dist-TIMLIF 1981

Last March, The 060 MIN
Lord Of Asia, The 060 MIN
Young Conqueror, The 060 MIN
Young Lion, The 060 MIN

Search For Alternate Life-Styles And Philosophies, The C 20 MIN
16MM FILM, 3/4 OR 1/2 IN VIDEO J-C A
Explores the efforts made by young people who are searching for personal harmony and a fulfilling lifestyle.
Prod-FLMFR Dist-FLMFR

Search For Antiworlds, A C 25 MIN
16MM FILM, 3/4 OR 1/2 IN VIDEO
Documents a physics research experiment at the Lawrence Berkeley Laboratory of the University of California, which seeks to determine the existence of large amounts of antimatter in the universe.
Prod-BERKFA Dist-PFP 1977

Search For Coal C 18 MIN
16MM FILM OPTICAL SOUND
Tells how coal was formed, its geological characteristics, where coal is mined and likely locations of reserves as well as exploration techiques. Stresses the continuous need for an intensive proving program in order to ensure adequate reserves of energy to sustain future natural growth.
LC NO. 80-700839
Prod-IMPACT Dist-TASCOR 1978

Search For Electromagnetic Induction, The C 43 MIN
16MM FILM OPTICAL SOUND
Recounts the story of research into methods of producing electricity with magnetism, emphasizing Oersted's chance discovery of electromagnetism in 1820.
LC NO. 81-700393
Prod-PURDEV Dist-PURDEV 1980

Search For Excellence, The B 29 MIN
16MM FILM OPTICAL SOUND
Discusses the place of the consolidated school and explores its various problems and advantages. Examines consolidation of school systems between city and county areas in Greenville, Winston-Salem, Charlotte and Waynesville North Carolina.
LC NO. FIA67-5602
Prod-NFBC Dist-UNC 1965

Search For Extra Terrestrial Life, The C 30 MIN
16MM FILM, 3/4 OR 1/2 IN VIDEO J-H
Examines the evidence for UFO's. Explains how the unlocking of the Egyptian hieroglyphic code parallels man's attempt to establish contact with extraterrestrial life. Edited from an episode of the Cosmos series.
From The Cosmos (Edited Version) Series.
Prod-SAGANC Dist-FI Prodn-KCET 1980

Search For Faith, The C 12 MIN
16MM FILM, 3/4 OR 1/2 IN VIDEO J-C A
Probes the faith experience in three vignettes in which a teenage girl discovers God through the wisdom of an old Navajo, a disillusioned advertising executive finds God through the practice of meditation and a jaded rock star meets God by writing a Jesus song.
From The Vignettes Series.
Prod-PAULST Dist-PAULST 1973

Search For Fossil Man C 24 MIN
16MM FILM, 3/4 OR 1/2 IN VIDEO H-C A
Presents Dr Phillip Tobias as he takes a team of amateur anthropologists to the famous Makapansgat fossil-hominid site in Africa. Shows how the team members continue a search for early hominid remains and how they excavate and develop the finesse necessary for chipping fossils from the rock in which they are encased.
LC NO. 80-706334
Prod-NGS Dist-NGS 1974

Search For Life--A Series
J-H
Uses photos and simulations to trace the mission of the Viking Project to seek life on Mars.
Prod-WHROTV Dist-AITECH 1977

Search For Life, The C 30 MIN
16MM FILM, 3/4 OR 1/2 IN VIDEO H-C A
Describes experiments that have been conducted which attempt to understand the origins of life.
From The Nova Series.
LC NO. 79-707227
Prod-WGBHTV Dist-TIMLIF 1976

Search For More Food, The, Pt 1 C 14 MIN
16MM FILM OPTICAL SOUND
Profiles research by scientists and engineers seeking methods of producing more food to feed the Earth's population. Discusses breeding new types of grains, more effective pest control, innovations in irrigation, ways to reverse land erosion and fresh approaches to animal agriculture.
Prod-ALLFP Dist-NSTA 1976

Search For More Food, The, Pt 2 C 14 MIN
16MM FILM OPTICAL SOUND
Profiles research by scientists and engineers seeking methods of producing more food to feed the Earth's population. Discusses combining several different species into super-food plants, controlled environment food production and fabricated indirect nutrition sources.
Prod-ALLFP Dist-NSTA 1976

Search For Moyaone, The C 5 MIN
16MM FILM OPTICAL SOUND
Demonstrates the basic techniques of archaeology. Shows University of Maryland students as they excavate a site on the Potomac River believed to be the remains of the chief village of the Piscataway Indians, last seen by Captain John Smith.
LC NO. 72-701789
Prod-UMD Dist-UMD 1972

Search For New Energy, The, Pt 1 C 15 MIN
16MM FILM OPTICAL SOUND C
Deals with the efforts of scientists and engineers to discover and develop new sources of fuel in order to solve the problems created by the energy crisis. Examines new power sources, such as the magnetohydrodynamic generator and geothermal energy.
From The Science In Action Series.
Prod-ALLFP Dist-COUNFI

Search For New Energy, The, Pt 2 C 15 MIN
16MM FILM OPTICAL SOUND C
Examines the new, sophisticated sources of power being developed for long-range usage and supply. Explains that some of these includes the breeder reactor, fusion, solar power systems, windmills, tidal power and atmospheric electricity.
From The Science In Action Series.
Prod-ALLFP Dist-COUNFI

Search For Opportunity, The C 30 MIN
3/4 OR 1/2 INCH VIDEO CASSETTE H-C A
See series title for descriptive statement.
From The Japan - The Changing Tradition Series.
Prod-UMA Dist-GPITVL 1978

Search For Permanence C
3/4 INCH VIDEO CASSETTE
Describes growth and development of a child from ten to twelve months.
From The Growth And Development - A Chronicle Of Four Children Series. Series 4
Prod-JUETHO Dist-LIP

Search For Permanence - Gregory, 10 Months C 7 MIN
16MM FILM OPTICAL SOUND
See series title for descriptive statement.
From The Growth And Development - A Chronicle Of Four Children Series. Series 4
LC NO. 78-700685
Prod-JUETHO Dist-LIP Prodn-CONCOM 1976

Search For Permanence - Joseph, 12 Months C 7 MIN
16MM FILM OPTICAL SOUND
See series title for descriptive statement.
From The Growth And Development - A Chronicle Of Four Children Series. Series 4
LC NO. 78-700685
Prod-JUETHO Dist-LIP Prodn-CONCOM 1976

Search For Permanence - Melissa, 10 Months C 6 MIN
16MM FILM OPTICAL SOUND
See series title for descriptive statement.
From The Growth And Development - A Chronicle Of Four Children Series. Series 4
LC NO. 78-700685
Prod-JUETHO Dist-LIP Prodn-CONCOM 1976

Search For Permanence - Terra, 12 Months C 7 MIN
16MM FILM OPTICAL SOUND
See series title for descriptive statement.
From The Growth And Development - A Chronicle Of Four Children Series. Series 4
LC NO. 78-700685
Prod-JUETHO Dist-LIP Prodn-CONCOM 1976

Search For Safety C 15 MIN
3/4 OR 1/2 INCH VIDEO CASSETTE
Explains the procedure of job safety analysis (JSA) in detail. Shows how JSA works to reduce accidents, increase safety, productivity and employee morale.
Prod-EDRF Dist-EDRF

Search For Sandra Laing, The C
16MM FILM OPTICAL SOUND H-C A
Tells the story of a 'colored' child born to white parents in South Africa and her rejection by a small town.
From The World Series.
Prod-INTENC Dist-INTENC 1977

Search For Science (2nd Ed) - Search For Science C 15 MIN
3/4 INCH VIDEO CASSETTE P
Demonstrates that the greater the degree of organization in scientific work, the better or more tangible the results.
Prod-WVIZTV Dist-GPITVL

Search For Science (2nd Ed,) Unit I - Living Things--A Series
I
Prod-WVIZTV Dist-GPITVL

Bird, The - Adaptation 15 MIN
Bird, The - How We Change The Numbers 15 MIN
Fish And Its Survival, The 15 MIN
Fish And Water In The Biosphere 15 MIN
Food Web And How Animals Fit Into It, The 15 MIN

Search For Science (2nd Ed,) Unit II - Space --A Series
I
Prod-WVIZTV Dist-GPITVL

Earth And The Moon, The 15 MIN
How We Get Into Space 15 MIN
Solar System, The 15 MIN

Space Exploration 15 MIN

Search For Science (2nd Ed,) Unit III - The Micro-World—A Series
I

Prod-WVIZTV Dist-GPITVL

Microscope, The 15 MIN

Search For Science (2nd Ed,) Unit IV - Life In The Ocean—A Series
I

Prod-WVIZTV Dist-GPITVL

Ocean, The - Always The Weak And The Strong 15 MIN
Ocean, The - Animal Relationships 15 MIN
Ocean, The - Animals Of A Different Kind 15 MIN

Search For Science (2nd Ed,) Unit V - Electricity—A Series
I

Prod-WVIZTV Dist-GPITVL

Chemical Electricity 15 MIN
Magnetism, Pt 1 15 MIN
Magnetism, Pt 2 15 MIN
Mechanical Electricity 15 MIN
Series And Parallel Circuits 15 MIN

Search For Science (2nd Ed,) Unit VI - Air And Weather—A Series
I

Prod-WVIZTV Dist-GPITVL

Air - Hot And Cold 15 MIN
Air In Motion 15 MIN
Conductors And Non-Conductors 15 MIN
Properties Of Air 15 MIN
Weather - The Water Cycle 15 MIN

Search For Science (2nd Ed,) Unit VII - Flight—A Series
I

Prod-WVIZTV Dist-GPITVL

Balanced Flight, Pt 1 15 MIN
Balanced Flight, Pt 2 15 MIN
Jet Engines 15 MIN

Search For Science (2nd Ed,) Unit VIII - Plants—A Series
I

Prod-WVIZTV Dist-GPITVL

Photosynthesis, Pts 1 And 2 15 MIN
Respiration And Transpiration 15 MIN
Tropism, Pt 1 15 MIN
Tropism, Pt 2 15 MIN

Search For Silence B 15 MIN
16MM FILM OPTICAL SOUND
Explains what the navy is doing to curb the noise of jet aircraft around naval air stations and follows a naval aviator as he points up the salient features of the navy's noise abatement program.
LC NO. FIE61-118
Prod-USN Dist-USNAC 1960

Search For Solid Ground, The B 45 MIN
16MM FILM OPTICAL SOUND
Presents a panel discussion in which Mark Kac, John Kemeny, Harley Rogers and Raymond Smullyan discuss recent developments in logic and their implications for modern mathematics.
From The Mathematics Today Series.
LC NO. FIA66-1278
Prod-WNDTTV Dist-MLA Prodn-MACKNZ 1963

Search For Solid Ground, The B 62 MIN
16MM FILM OPTICAL SOUND H-C T
Presents a panel discussion on various developments in logic and their implications for mathematics.
From The MAA Individual Lecturers Series.
Prod-MAA Dist-MLA 1966

Search For Solutions—A Series
I-J
Discusses the various approaches to scientific research.
Prod-PLYBCK Dist-KAROL 1979

Adaptation 018 MIN
Context 018 MIN
Evidence 018 MIN
Investigation 018 MIN
Modeling 018 MIN
Patterns 018 MIN
Prediction 018 MIN
Theory 018 MIN
Trial And Error 018 MIN

Search For Sounds C 29 MIN
3/4 INCH VIDEO CASSETTE
Focuses on how to look for the right combination of instruments to play a song.
From The Music Shop Series.
Prod-UMITV Dist-UMITV 1974

Search For The Great Apes C 52 MIN
16MM FILM, 3/4 OR 1/2 IN VIDEO
Shows women scientists studying the wild orangutans of Borneo and mountain gorillas of central Africa.
LC NO. 80-706360
Prod-NGS Dist-NGS 1975

Search For The Mind C 60 MIN
3/4 OR 1/2 INCH VIDEO CASSETTE H-C A
Reveals that Darwin's theory of natural selection was followed by Lewis Henry Morgan who discovered evidence of cogitation in beavers, George Romanes experimenting with fish, cats and dogs, Douglas Spalding working with newborn chicks and Jacques Loeb attempting to prove animals mindless.
From The Discovery Of Animal Behavior Series.
Prod-WNETTV Dist-FI 1982

Search For The Nile (Spanish)—A Series
16MM FILM, 3/4 OR 1/2 IN VIDEO
Re-creates 19th century expeditions in search of the source of the Nile.
LC NO. 77-701637
Prod-BBCTV Dist-TIMLIF 1972

Conquest And Death (Spanish) 52 MIN
Discovery And Betrayal (Spanish) 52 MIN
Dream Of The Wanderer, The (Spanish) 52 MIN
Find Livingstone (Spanish) 52 MIN
Great Debate, The (Spanish) 52 MIN
Secret Fountains, The (Spanish) 52 MIN

Search For The Nile—A Series
16MM FILM, 3/4 OR 1/2 IN VIDEO J-C A
Presents James Mason, who narrates one of the most spectacular quests of all time, the search for the source of the Nile. Depicts five men, each of whom hoped to carve a place for himself in the history books.
LC NO. 79-707465
Prod-BBCTV Dist-TIMLIF 1972

Conquest And Death 52 MIN
Discovery And Betrayal 60 MIN
Dream Of The Wanderer, The 60 MIN
Find Livingstone 60 MIN
Great Debate, The 60 MIN
Secret Fountains, The 52 MIN

Search For The Unknown C 15 MIN
16MM FILM, 3/4 OR 1/2 IN VIDEO I
Summarizes the arguments surrounding the Loch Ness monster and suggests that students come up with explanations for this or other mysteries.
From The Thinkabout Series. Finding Patterns
LC NO. 81-706121
Prod-SCETV Dist-AITECH 1979

Search For The Western Sea C 29 MIN
16MM FILM, 3/4 OR 1/2 IN VIDEO J-H
Tells the story of Alexander Mackenzie's overland expedition from Fort Chippewyan to the Pacific coast during the 18th century.
Prod-DEVGCF Dist-MGHT 1978

Search For The Whale C 20 MIN
16MM FILM OPTICAL SOUND PRO
Explains the U S Navy's continuing research into the sounds of ocean mammals, their effects on sonar and the benefits of new knowledge for fleet operations.
LC NO. 77-701400
Prod-USN Dist-USNAC 1976

Search For Ulysses, The C 53 MIN
16MM FILM, 3/4 OR 1/2 IN VIDEO H-C A
Describes a journey aimed at discovering where Ulysses went after leaving Troy.
Prod-CBSNEW Dist-CAROUF

Search For Understanding, The C 18 MIN
16MM FILM OPTICAL SOUND
Explains the operation of the Clinton P Anderson Meson Physics Facility in Los Alamos, New Mexico.
LC NO. 79-700053
Prod-LASL Dist-LASL 1978

Search For Unity, A - A European Idea C 52 MIN
16MM FILM - 1/2 IN VIDEO
Analyzes developments in Europe during the 1960's and 1970's. Describes the Soviet invasion of Czechoslovakia, the weakening of the European Economic Community by the Middle East War and the subsequent oil crisis, and the evolution of detente relations between East and West. Discusses prospects for Europe's future.
From The Europe, The Mighty Continent Series. No. 13
LC NO. 79-707429
Prod-BBCTV Dist-TIMLIF 1976

Search For Water, The C 21 MIN
16MM FILM OPTICAL SOUND J-C A
Uses the city of Boston as a model to explain ways in which cities secure suitable water supplies. Shows that environmental disruption associated with the process may be minimized by water recycling.
LC NO. 76-700244
Prod-HANOVC Dist-HANOVC 1975

Search Of Zubin Mehta—A Series
J-C A
Looks at the life and music of musician and conductor Zubin Mehta.
Prod-ESMRDA Dist-ESMRDA 1978

Education Of Zubin Mehta In The Eastern And ---
Zubin Mehta - Commitment And Fulfillment As A 22 MIN
Zubin Mehta - If You Are Going To Lead, Lead 36 MIN
Zubin Mehta And His Masters - Piatigorsky And 29 MIN
Zubin Mehta Rocks The Gospel 21 MIN

Search Operations B 29 MIN
16MM FILM OPTICAL SOUND
Demonstrates the systematic search and rescue operations conducted according to the National Search and Rescue Plan and the National Search and Rescue Agreement. Depicts areas of responsibility delegated to the armed forces, Civil Air Patrol and local authorities.
LC NO. FIE63-271
Prod-USDD Dist-USNAC 1961

Search To Survive, The C 24 MIN
16MM FILM OPTICAL SOUND I-C
Describes the adaptation of animals to different surroundings. Distinguishes the special characteristics of man—erect posture, free moving arms and hands, sharp focusing eyes, a brain and speech which allow him to change his environment and to survive in such unfriendly environments as outer space.
From The Animal Secrets Series.
LC NO. FIA68-1028
Prod-NBC Dist-GRACUR 1967

Search Warrant B 9 MIN
16MM FILM OPTICAL SOUND C
Deals with various aspects of a criminal lawsuit involving a liquor store robbery case. Shows police officers seeking and obtaining a warrant from the magistrate to search the premises of the adult suspect.
From The Criminal Law Series. No. 6
LC NO. 77-714038
Prod-RPATLF Dist-RPATLF 1968

Search, The C 13 MIN
16MM FILM OPTICAL SOUND
Blends poetry, sculpture and music with the sounds and the beauty of a far north river bank in the spring.
LC NO. FIA68-1777
Prod-CALCAG Dist-RADIM 1968

Search, The C 29 MIN
16MM FILM OPTICAL SOUND
Explains the difference between Congressional hearings and investigations, pointing out that hearings become investigations when a committee uses its power to subpoena witnesses and demand testimony.
From The Government Story Series. No. 15
LC NO. 70-707198
Prod-OGCW Dist-WBCPRO 1968

Search, The C 30 MIN
16MM FILM OPTICAL SOUND J-C
Explores what is the fragment of the planet Earth that nourishes leaders who would forever alter the course of mankind.
From The Human Dimension Series.
Prod-GRACUR Dist-GRACUR

Search, The B 30 MIN
16MM FILM OPTICAL SOUND
Illustrates how the inner drive and compassion of Lillian Wald led her to establish the world's first visiting nurse service and the Henry Street settlement, an important social force in New York. (Kinescope)
Prod-JTS Dist-NAAJS Prodn-NBCTV 1961

Search, The C 30 MIN
16MM FILM OPTICAL SOUND J A
Documents the process of racial integration in Baltimore, Maryland and the role citizens play to make this possible.
Prod-YALEDV Dist-YALEDV

Search, The C 15 MIN
3/4 INCH VIDEO CASSETTE H
Shows ways of locating jobs. Examines the letter of application and the process of making telephone contact. Offers advice on self-preparation for a personal interview.
From The Success In The Job Market Series.
Prod-KUONTV Dist-GPITVL 1980

Search, The C 27 MIN
3/4 INCH VIDEO CASSETTE
Traces the development of the drug Reglan. Describes how the scientific research community, individual physicians and a pharmaceutical company joined forces in the effort.
Prod-ROBINA Dist-MTP

Search, The (Spanish) C 19 MIN
16MM FILM, 3/4 OR 1/2 IN VIDEO H-C
Depicts scenes of Mexico as Joselito and Pulgarcito search for Joselito's father. Follows the boys as they visit the bullring, the Church of the Virgin of Guadalupe and the newspaper office.
From The Aventuras De Joselito Y Pulgarcito Series. No. 4
Prod-IFB Dist-TRANSW 1961

Searches Incident To Lawful Arrests C 50 MIN
3/4 OR 1/2 INCH VIDEO CASSETTE PRO
Examines the search incident to lawful arrest. Raises questions on how far the search can extend, what is necessary to protect the arresting officer, what is meant by wingspan and how far the search of an automobile may extend.
From The Criminal Procedure And The Trial Advocate Series.
Prod-ABACPE Dist-ABACPE

Searching Eye, The C 18 MIN
16MM FILM, 3/4 OR 1/2 IN VIDEO P-C A
Views the world under the sea, the world of past geological formations, the inner world of microscopic creatures, the process of growth and fruition, the world of outer space and the world of imagination.
Prod-BASSS Dist-PFP 1964

Searching Eye, The (French) C 18 MIN
16MM FILM, 3/4 OR 1/2 IN VIDEO I-C A
Deals with the art of seeing and the power of observation. Describes the actions of a young boy at the beach, with the camera showing what the boy cannot see, providing a visual metaphor for the normally unseen world.
Prod-BASSS Dist-PFP

Searching Eye, The (German) C 18 MIN
16MM FILM, 3/4 OR 1/2 IN VIDEO I-C A

Deals with the art of seeing and the power of observation. Describes the actions of a young boy at the beach, with the camera showing what the boy cannot see, providing a visual metaphor for the normally unseen world.
Prod-BASSS Dist-PFP

Searching For Fish C 29 MIN
16MM FILM OPTICAL SOUND
A Japanese language film. Emphasizes the important significance of marine resources by way of depicting the mutual relations between seaweed and the life of fish.
Prod-UNIJAP Dist-UNIJAP 1968

Searching For My Picture C 29 MIN
3/4 INCH VIDEO CASSETTE
Demonstrates posing and re-posing a model.
From The Artist At Work Series.
Prod-UMITV Dist-UMITV 1973

Searching For Solutions C 30 MIN
3/4 OR 1/2 INCH VIDEO CASSETTE T
See series title for descriptive statement.
From The Eager To Learn Series.
Prod-KTEHTV Dist-KTEHTV

Searching For Some Love And Care C 11 MIN
16MM FILM, 3/4 OR 1/2 IN VIDEO K-P
Explores emotions and feelings toward one's parents and reflections on what parents expect of children.
From The Growing Up With Sandy Offenheim Series
LC NO. 82-707059
Prod-PLAYTM Dist-BCNFL 1982

Searching For Values - A Film Anthology—A Series
16MM FILM, 3/4 OR 1/2 IN VIDEO J-C A
Prod-LCOA Dist-LCOA 1972

Dehumanizing City And Hymie Schultz, The 015 MIN
Fine Art Of Aggression, The 016 MIN
I Who Am, Who Am I 017 MIN
Loneliness - And Loving 017 MIN
Love To Kill 015 MIN
My Country Right Or Wrong 015 MIN
Politics, Power And The Public Good 020 MIN
Pride And Principle 017 MIN
Right To Live, The - Who Decides 017 MIN
Sense Of Purpose, A 014 MIN
Spaces Between People 018 MIN
Trouble With The Law 016 MIN
Violence - Just For Fun 015 MIN
When Parents Grow Old 015 MIN
Whether To Tell The Truth 018 MIN

Searching Heart, The - A Medieval Legend B 20 MIN
16MM FILM OPTICAL SOUND
Describes the early Renaissance conception of life. Suggests the later Pilgrim's Progress and tells the travels of a human heart in its search for maturity and a place for the traditional 'GIRL WITH YELLOW HAIR.'
Prod-FILIM Dist-RADIM

Seas Of Grass C 55 MIN
16MM FILM, 3/4 OR 1/2 IN VIDEO H-C A
Visits the African grasslands which are home to the greatest collections of savannah animals. Shows how the antelope, zebra and wildebeest reside with their predators, lions and cheetahs.
From The Living Planet Series. Pt 5
Prod-BBCTV Dist-TIMLIF 1984

Seas Of Infinity C 15 MIN
16MM FILM OPTICAL SOUND H-C A
Reviews the planning, development, launching and function of the orbiting astronomical observatory, a series of orbiting telescopes which are being used to study the solar system and the stars. Features comments by leading scientists on the potential of this advancement in astronomy.
LC NO. 72-701239
Prod-NASA Dist-NASA Prodn-FILMG 1969

Seas Of Tomorrow C 14 MIN
16MM FILM OPTICAL SOUND
Shows a young man as he decides on a career in the Navy. Mixes scenes of Navy life and training with sailing scenes in order to convey the theme of man's ageless identity with the sea.
LC NO. 75-700577
Prod-USN Dist-USNAC 1972

Seascape C 29 MIN
3/4 INCH VIDEO CASSETTE
See series title for descriptive statement.
From The Magic Of Oil Painting Series.
Prod-KOCETV Dist-PUBTEL

Seashore C 7 MIN
16MM FILM, 3/4 OR 1/2 IN VIDEO
Views the beauties of the ocean and its wildlife. Includes super-slow motion sequences of pelicans diving for fish.
Prod-PFP Dist-PFP 1971

Seashore Community, A C 15 MIN
3/4 OR 1/2 INCH VIDEO CASSETTE P-I
Discusses the living things found at the seashore.
From The Why Series.
Prod-WDCNTV Dist-AITECH 1976

Seashore Ecology C 16 MIN
16MM FILM, 3/4 OR 1/2 IN VIDEO I-C A
Analyzes some of the flora and fauna to be found in various types of shorelines. Identifies each species and indicates the characteristic features of each.
Prod-LUF Dist-LUF 1983

Seashore Life C 10 MIN
16MM FILM, 3/4 OR 1/2 IN VIDEO P-J
Portrays life on three kinds of seashores—the sandy beach, the rock pool and the mud flat. Shows the adaptations seashore animals make to their special environments.
Prod-EBF Dist-EBEC 1950

Seashore Life C 29 MIN
2 INCH VIDEOTAPE
See series title for descriptive statement.
From The Observing Eye Series.
Prod-WGBHTV Dist-PUBTEL

Seashore, The - Atlantic Coast C 15 MIN
16MM FILM, 3/4 OR 1/2 IN VIDEO I-H
Explores the variety of shorelines that stretch from Nova Scotia south to Florida and reveals the variety of animal life that lives along the rocky coasts, the sandy beaches and salt marshes of the Atlantic coastline.
Prod-BARR Dist-BARR 1973

Seashore, The - Atlantic Coast (Captioned) C 15 MIN
16MM FILM - VIDEO, ALL FORMATS I-H A
Explores the variety of shorelines that stretch from Nova Scotia to Florida. Looks at the variety of animal life that lives along the Atlantic Coastline.
Prod-BARR Dist-BARR

Seashore, The - Challenge Between The Tides C 12 MIN
3/4 OR 1/2 INCH VIDEO CASSETTE
Offers a close look at the abundant, varied life found where the ocean meets the land. Explains special relationships between tides and shore life.
Prod-CBSC Dist-CBSC

Seashore, The - Pacific Coast C 10 MIN
16MM FILM, 3/4 OR 1/2 IN VIDEO I-J
Explores beaches and coastlines of the Pacific shore. Examines plants, birds, shells, and animals along beaches and in tide pools.
Prod-BARR Dist-BARR 1968

Season Of Fire C 15 MIN
16MM FILM OPTICAL SOUND J-C A
Shows the January 23, 1973, eruption of Helgafell Volcano on Heimaey Island, Iceland. Reports the evacuation of the area and the efforts to save the fishing port on the island from destruction.
LC NO. 74-702155
Prod-NINESP Dist-FI 1974

Season Of Grandmothers, A C 30 MIN
3/4 INCH VIDEO CASSETTE
Examines the revival of Indian traditions.
From The Real People Series.
Prod-KSPSTV Dist-GPITVL 1976

Season, The C 15 MIN
16MM FILM, 3/4 OR 1/2 IN VIDEO J-C A
Uses a serio-comic technique to contemplate certain aspects of Christmas in Los Angeles. Uses an interview with Sunday schoolers and shows scenes of stinging crassness with the relentless exploitation of innocence for a fast buck.
Prod-DONMAC Dist-LRF 1968

Seasons C 16 MIN
16MM FILM OPTICAL SOUND
Deals with the health and rehabilitation of older people, including nursing and rest home conditions and effective programs in geriatric therapy.
LC NO. 74-705594
Prod-USSRS Dist-USNAC 1971

Seasons C 15 MIN
16MM FILM, 3/4 OR 1/2 IN VIDEO J-C A
Explores the underlying reasons for marked seasonal changes during the year.
Prod-LUF Dist-LUF 1983

Seasons (2nd Ed)—A Series
16MM FILM, 3/4 OR 1/2 IN VIDEO P
Introduces the activities of people and animals and the alterations in nature as the seasons change. Explains why seasons occur.
Prod-IFB Dist-IFB Prodn-BERLET 1979

Fall Is Here (2nd Ed) 010 MIN
Spring Is Here (2nd Ed) 011 MIN
Summer Is Here (2nd Ed) 011 MIN
Winter Is Here (2nd Ed) 011 MIN

Seasons - A Year Of Change C 15 MIN
16MM FILM, 3/4 OR 1/2 IN VIDEO J
Shows the life cycles of flora and fauna in the biome of a North American deciduous forest at different times of the year.
LC NO. 81-706719
Prod-CAHILL Dist-AIMS 1980

Seasons - Latitude And Longitude B 45 MIN
2 INCH VIDEOTAPE C
See series title for descriptive statement.
From The Physical Science Series. Unit 3 - Astronomy
Prod-CHITVC Dist-GPITVL Prodn-WTTWTV

Seasons And Days C 13 MIN
16MM FILM, 3/4 OR 1/2 IN VIDEO I-H
Shows how changes in seasons and the length of daylight result from the earth revolving around the sun on an inclined axis. Explains polar circles and the tropics.
LC NO. 84-706127
Prod-IFFB Dist-CF 1984

Seasons And The Symphony, The C 60 MIN
3/4 OR 1/2 INCH VIDEO CASSETTE J-C A
Presents flutist James Galway studying the operatic developments wrought by Gluck and discussing Vivaldi and Haydn. Talks about new ideas for symphonic compositions developed at Mannheim.
From The James Galway's Music In Time Series.
LC NO. 83-706230
Prod-POLTEL Dist-FOTH 1982

Seasons Change C 10 MIN
16MM FILM, 3/4 OR 1/2 IN VIDEO P-I
Shows children and adults involved in various seasonal activities such as garden planting, going to a country fair and savoring winter weather.
LC NO. 83-706921
Prod-MOKIN Dist-MOKIN 1983

Seasons In Nature—A Series
16MM FILM, 3/4 OR 1/2 IN VIDEO P-I
Describes how the four seasons affect life in nature.
Prod-FLMFR Dist-FLMFR

Autumn In Nature 14 MIN
Spring In Nature 17 MIN
Summer In Nature 14 MIN
Winter In Nature 12 MIN

Seasons In The City—A Series
16MM FILM, 3/4 OR 1/2 IN VIDEO P
Looks at how a change of seasons affects life in the city.
Prod-CORF Dist-CORF

Autumn Comes To The City 010 MIN
Spring Comes To The City 010 MIN
Winter Comes To The City 010 MIN

Seasons Of A Navajo C 60 MIN
3/4 OR 1/2 INCH VIDEO CASSETTE
Presents an intimate portrait of a traditional Navajo Indian family, whose heritage of sacred songs, ceremonies and oral tradition comes alive through the grandparents, Chauncey and Dorothy Nehoyia, who farm, weave and tend sheep in a traditional hogan dwelling without water or electricity, while their children live in tract homes and their grandchildren attend modern public schools.
Prod-PBS Dist-PBS

Seasons Of Sexuality C 14 MIN
16MM FILM, 3/4 OR 1/2 IN VIDEO J-C A
Demonstrates the manifestations of sexuality at different stages of human development. Shows a toddler's unconcern for physical distinctions, children's dislike for members of the opposite sex, adolescents experiencing first romantic love, and an older married couple.
LC NO. 81-707565
Prod-PPSY Dist-PEREN 1980

Seasons Of Sexuality (Captioned) C 14 MIN
16MM FILM - VIDEO, ALL FORMATS H-C A
Explores sexuality throughout the life cycle. Discusses issues such as touching, privacy, body images, fantasies and values.
Prod-PPSY Dist-PEREN

Seasons Of Survival C 21 MIN
3/4 OR 1/2 INCH VIDEO CASSETTE J-H
See series title for descriptive statement.
From The Phenomenal World Series.
Prod-EBEC Dist-EBEC 1983

Seasons Of The Basque C 29 MIN
3/4 OR 1/2 INCH VIDEO CASSETTE
Traces the movements of the Basque sheepherders in Nevada throughout the seasons' changes. Records their skills and way of life.
Prod-MEDIPR Dist-MEDIPR 1978

Seasons Of The Basque C 30 MIN
3/4 OR 1/2 INCH VIDEO CASSETTE
Portrays the Basque shepherds who have brought their ancient skills and culture to the ranges of the American West.
Prod-EAI Dist-EAI

Seasons Of The Elk C 20 MIN
16MM FILM, 3/4 OR 1/2 IN VIDEO J-C A
Shows the growth of newborn elk calves and their migration.
Prod-BERLET Dist-BERLET 1981

Seasons Of The Year C 11 MIN
16MM FILM, 3/4 OR 1/2 IN VIDEO P
Shows the characteristics of each of the four seasons, including the changes in human activity.
Prod-CORF Dist-CORF

Seasons—A Series
16MM FILM, 3/4 OR 1/2 IN VIDEO K-P
Presents an overview of the natural and recreational events associated with each season.
Prod-CENTRO Dist-CORF 1980

Autumn 011 MIN
Spring 011 MIN
Summer 011 MIN
Winter 011 MIN

Seasons, The C 15 MIN
16MM FILM OPTICAL SOUND I-J A
Deals with the seasonal climates in the Western hemisphere, emphasizing that seasonal changes are due in part to the tilt of the earth on its axis and the earth's rotation around the sun. Uses animation and live photography to show examples and conditions of seasonal changes.
Prod-AVED Dist-AVED 1962

Seasons, The C 17 MIN
16MM FILM, 3/4 OR 1/2 IN VIDEO P-J
Records the cycle of the seasons on a dairy farm in the Pennsylvania Dutch country.
Prod-MOKIN Dist-MOKIN 1971

Seasons, The (Captioned) C 17 MIN
3/4 OR 1/2 INCH VIDEO CASSETTE P-J
Records the cycle of the seasons on a dairy farm in the Pennsylvania Dutch country.
Prod-MOKIN Dist-MOKIN 1971

Seasons, The - Fall And Winter C 15 MIN
3/4 OR 1/2 INCH VIDEO CASSETTE P
Tells why fall is the harvest and leaf-dropping season and why animals either hibernate or move to warmer climes during the winter.
From The Featherby's Fables Series.
Prod-WVUTTV Dist-GPITVL 1983

Seasons, The - Spring C 15 MIN
3/4 OR 1/2 INCH VIDEO CASSETTE P
Tells about spring rains, growth and new life. Describes how the tilting earth brings warmer weather.
From The Featherby's Fables Series.
Prod-WVUTTV Dist-GPITVL 1983

Seasons, The - Summer C 15 MIN
3/4 OR 1/2 INCH VIDEO CASSETTE P
Describes how people and animals keep cool in the summer and why plants grow bigger and stronger.
From The Featherby's Fables Series.
Prod-WVUTTV Dist-GPITVL 1983

Seat Belt Hernia - Price For Survival C 8 MIN
16MM FILM OPTICAL SOUND
Presents a kaleidoscopic view of the 1962 Seattle World's Fair including brief glimpses of the architecture, art, science exhibits, shops, dancers from foreign countries and midway. Natural sound and modern jazz music take the place of narration.
LC NO. FIA66-638
Prod-MFIORH Dist-AMCSUR 1965

Seat Belt Safety C 30 MIN
3/4 OR 1/2 INCH VIDEO CASSETTE PRO
Presents information on seat belt safety. Tells why people don't wear them and survival statistics that support wearing them. Focuses on the use of seat belts by firefighters and emergency personnel.
Prod-LACFD Dist-FILCOM

Seat Removal From An Automobile C 8 MIN
1/2 IN VIDEO CASSETTE BETA/VHS
Deals with auto body repair. Discusses removal procedures and necessary electrical interlocks.
Prod-RMI Dist-RMI

Seatbelt Safety C 14 MIN
16MM FILM OPTICAL SOUND
Uses animation to stress the need to use seatbelts.
LC NO. 77-702639
Prod-OECA Dist-OECA Prodn-CINEPR 1976

Seatbelts, Your Life Insurance C 9 MIN
16MM FILM OPTICAL SOUND
Emphasizes the benefits of seat belts in preventing fatalities and reducing injuries. Shows methods of installation.
LC NO. FIE64-54
Prod-USAF Dist-USNAC 1962

Seawards The Great Ships C 29 MIN
16MM FILM OPTICAL SOUND
Presents shipbuilding on the Clyde River in Scotland. Shows how the flat plates of steel are molded and shaped into various kinds of sailing vessels.
Prod-BIS Dist-SF 1961

Sebring '66 C 30 MIN
16MM FILM OPTICAL SOUND
Fords sweep 12 hours of endurance.
Prod-SFI Dist-SFI

Seclusion C 12 MIN
3/4 OR 1/2 INCH VIDEO CASSETTE PRO
Provides basic information on seclusion. Defines seclusion and the kinds of situations that call for its use.
Prod-HSCIC Dist-HSCIC 1985

Second American Revolution, The, Pt 1 C 58 MIN
3/4 OR 1/2 INCH VIDEO CASSETTE
Presents Ossie Davis and Ruby Dee who re-create and dramatize the world of blacks whose lives and ideas marked the struggle for equality in the 1900's to 1920. Looks at the lives of Booker T Washington, W E B DuBois, Marcus Garvey, Jack Johnson and Langston Hughes.
From The Walk Through The 20th Century With Bill Moyers Series.
LC NO. 84-707295
Prod-CORPEL Dist-PBS 1983

Second American Revolution, The, Pt 2 C 58 MIN
3/4 OR 1/2 INCH VIDEO CASSETTE
Tells how the New Deal, World War II and postwar social changes set the stage for the 1954 Supreme Court decision to outlaw racial segregation in schools. Shows how the decision sparked a decade of continuing nonviolent revolution, leading to the Voting Rights Act of 1965. Depicts Thurgood Marshall, Rosa Parks, Martin Luther King, Malcolm X, Kenneth Clark, Daisy Bates and others. Features Ossie Davis, Ruby Dee and Bill Moyers.
From The Walk Through The 20th Century With Bill Moyers Series.
LC NO. 84-707295
Prod-CORPEL Dist-PBS 1983

Second And Third Witnesses C 44 MIN
3/4 OR 1/2 INCH VIDEO CASSETTE PRO
Demonstrates the testimony of two defense witnesses. Focuses on promotion policy of the hypothetical defendant.
From The Remedies Phase Of An EEO Case - Individual Determinations Series. Pt 2
Prod-ALIABA Dist-ABACPE

Second Battle Of Britain, The C 49 MIN
16MM FILM, 3/4 OR 1/2 IN VIDEO H-C A
Documents Britain's social and economic decline and her fight for survival. Explains that the slow death of private industry and the rapid growth of powerful labor unions has dealt Britain's economy a crippling blow.
Prod-CBSNEW Dist-CAROUF

Second Breath, A - A Guide For Home Tracheostomy Care C 12 MIN
3/4 OR 1/2 INCH VIDEO CASSETTE PRO
Provides nurses with information to convey to tracheostomy patients and their families concerning basic home care procedures.
Prod-HSCIC Dist-HSCIC 1982

Second Career, A - Dentistry In The U S Army Reserve C 16 MIN
16MM FILM OPTICAL SOUND
Describes the role of reserve and active Army dental personnel in implementing the dental care system.
LC NO. 80-701967
Prod-USA Dist-USNAC 1979

Second Chance C 10 MIN
16MM FILM OPTICAL SOUND H-C A
Shows the actual experiences of a heart attack victim, describing the recovery period after the attack, the modification of the life-style upon returning home from the hospital and the proper care that will help the victim lead a long and full life.
From The Heart Series. No. 1
LC NO. 75-700038
Prod-MIFE Dist-MIFE 1974

Second Chance C 12 MIN
16MM FILM OPTICAL SOUND
Shows how a twenty-two-month-old child who is severely retarded mentally, physically and emotionally was helped through the Mother Bank Volunteer Program.
LC NO. FIA68-161
Prod-CMHOSP Dist-CMHOSP Prodn-SCHMNJ 1967

Second Chance C 13 MIN
16MM FILM - 3/4 IN VIDEO
Presents the case of a child admitted to the hospital with a diagnosis of maternal deprivation and emotional maltreatment. Shows the six-week treatment course provided by the hospital involving staff and a volunteer foster grandparent.
From The We Can Help Series.
LC NO. 79-707561
Prod-NCCAN Dist-USNAC Prodn-CMHOSP 1979

Second Chance - Sea C 11 MIN
16MM FILM, 3/4 OR 1/2 IN VIDEO
Presents, without narration, an animated film which examines many aspects and meanings of the sea and the relationship of man to it.
Prod-HUBLEY Dist-PFP 1976

Second Chance, A C 25 MIN
16MM FILM OPTICAL SOUND
Illustrates the problems encountered between court volunteers and their wards. Dramatizes an actual case study which provides an overall view of the many phases of the problem.
LC NO. 75-700578
Prod-USSRS Dist-USNAC 1970

Second Chance, A - Consumers Guide To Fire Extinguishers C 15 MIN
16MM FILM, 3/4 OR 1/2 IN VIDEO
Discusses fire safety, covering escape planning, fire protection and control, kitchen discipline, electrical responsibility, what extinguishers to buy, where to place them, how to operate them, and how to maintain them.
Prod-KLEINW Dist-KLEINW

Second Chance, A - Protecting Endangered Species C 27 MIN
16MM FILM OPTICAL SOUND
Describes how some wildlife, including some endangered species, are attracted to and benefited by electrical operations.
Prod-EEI Dist-MTP

Second Childhood B 19 MIN
16MM FILM OPTICAL SOUND
Describes grouchy Zeffie Tilbury's disgust at turning 66 and shows what happens when Alfalfa, Porky, Darla, Spanky and Buckwheat pitch in to cheer her up. A Little Rascals film.
Prod-ROACH Dist-BHAWK 1936

Second Chorus B 90 MIN
16MM FILM OPTICAL SOUND
Relates the story of two hot trumpeters who try to keep their band together amidst rivalry for the same girl. Stars Fred Astaire.
Prod-PARACO Dist-REELIM 1940

Second Chorus C 25 MIN
16MM FILM, 3/4 OR 1/2 IN VIDEO
Tells how a divorced couple meet at their son's marriage and how they begin to reflect on the nature of their own marriage.
LC NO. 79-706589
Prod-PAULST Dist-MEDIAG 1978

Second Chorus C 25 MIN
3/4 OR 1/2 INCH VIDEO CASSETTE J A
Tells the story a divorced couple who later discover they may have been more successful than they had thought. Stars John Astin and Patty Duke Astin.
Prod-SUTHRB Dist-SUTHRB

Second Chorus B 83 MIN
3/4 OR 1/2 INCH VIDEO CASSETTE
Features a musical. Stars Fred Astaire, Paulette Goddard and Artie Shaw.
Prod-ADVCAS Dist-ADVCAS

Second Chorus B 84 MIN
1/2 IN VIDEO CASSETTE (BETA)
Describes how two trumpet players compete for the same girl and a job with the Artie Shaw orchestra. Stars Fred Astaire and Paulette Goddard.
Prod-UNKNWN Dist-VIDIM

Second City Comedy Special C 60 MIN
1/2 IN VIDEO CASSETTE (VHS)
Showcases the comedy talents of the Second City Comedy characters, such as John Candy and Fred Willard.
Prod-KARLVI Dist-KARLVI

Second Class Passenger C 11 MIN
16MM FILM, 3/4 OR 1/2 IN VIDEO J-H
Presents a metaphor for life by showing a man on a train who encounters a progression of strange characters. Shows how he remains optimistic in spite of the fact that things get worse.
Prod-ZAGREB Dist-MGHT 1974

Second Collision, The C 30 MIN
3/4 OR 1/2 INCH VIDEO CASSETTE H
Demonstrates the results of the 'second collision' within a vehicle in an accident when safety belts are not used. Stresses the importance of using safety restraints.
From The Behind The Wheel Series.
Prod-WCVETV Dist-GPITVL 1983

Second Commandment, The B 30 MIN
16MM FILM OPTICAL SOUND
Explains the meaning of the commandment against idolatry, a frequently misunderstood passage in the Bible. (Kinescope)
Prod-JTS Dist-NAAJS Prodn-NBCTV 1955

Second Edition C 20 MIN
3/4 OR 1/2 INCH VIDEO CASSETTE
Covers such stories as housing renovation in Manhattan, the subway rate hike, the Guardian Angels, The New York Met's batboys, an interview with Dick Cavett and a look at the teenagers in the summer youth employment program who made this videotape.
Prod-DCTVC Dist-DCTVC

Second Effort C 28 MIN
16MM FILM, 3/4 OR 1/2 IN VIDEO PRO
Vince Lombardi, the former Green Bay Packer coach, shows how the five motivational principles he used so successfully to build great football teams, can be used with equal success in improving the performance of any salesman.
Prod-DARTNL Dist-DARTNL 1968

Second Generation Microelectronics C 25 MIN
16MM FILM OPTICAL SOUND J-C A
Depicts the research, development and systems applications of advanced microelectronics. Describes the evolution of integrated circuits, thin films, ceramic printed circuits to multi-functional Ic's, metal oxide semiconductors and silicon-on-sapphire devices and their applications. Discusses the future use of epitaxial ferrite micro-memory, silicon-on-sapphire stripline waveguides and Gunn-effect oscillators.
Prod-NAA Dist-RCKWL

Second Golden Age, The C 25 MIN
16MM FILM OPTICAL SOUND
Shows the world of wine tasting throughout the country in preparation for an annual wine auction.
Prod-MTP Dist-MTP

Second Grade Embarassment C 5 MIN
16MM FILM SILENT I-H A S
Presents Willard Madsen relating in American sign language a personal experience of what it was like to be a deaf boy in second grade attending a public school for the deaf where the teacher did not know enough sign language to understand an urgent request.
LC NO. 76-701701
Prod-JOYCE Dist-JOYCE 1976

Second Homes / Calculators / Medical Insurance C
3/4 OR 1/2 INCH VIDEO CASSETTE
Presents tips on buying second homes, calculators and medical insurance.
From The Consumer Survival Series.
Prod-MDCPB Dist-MDCPB

Second Order Methods B 60 MIN
3/4 OR 1/2 INCH VIDEO CASSETTE
See series title for descriptive statement.
From The Engineering Design Optimization I Series. Pt 9
Prod-UAZMIC Dist-UAZMIC

Second Pollution, The C 22 MIN
16MM FILM OPTICAL SOUND
Discusses air pollution. Examines the problem which exists in Los Angeles and Chicago.
LC NO. 73-702056
Prod-FINLYS Dist-FINLYS 1973

Second Sitting C 29 MIN
3/4 INCH VIDEO CASSETTE
Discusses reappraising the painting and making changes.
From The Artist At Work Series.
Prod-UMITV Dist-UMITV 1973

Second Thoughts On Being Single C 52 MIN
3/4 OR 1/2 INCH VIDEO CASSETTE A
Reveals that women who formerly shunned monogamous relationships for sexual liberation or who postponed marriage to further careers are adopting more conservative sexual values and seeking marriage. Considers reasons for this change of heart and for the frustrating elusiveness of husband and family.
LC NO. 84-707302
Prod-NBCNEW Dist-FI Prodn-ROGERR 1984

Second Time Around C 60 MIN
3/4 OR 1/2 INCH VIDEO CASSETTE J-C A
Presents a picture of the issues and complexities of contemporary marriage by focusing on a couple in which the man is getting married because everyone is doing it yet wants a church wedding.
From The Middletown Series.
Prod-WQED Dist-FI 1982

Second Time Around - Career Options For Dancers—A Series

Presents programs from the New York City Cable TV series Eye On Dance, dealing with career options for dancers.
Prod-ARCVID Dist-ARCVID

Deborah Jowitt, Sally Brayley-Bliss And Helen
Ellen Jacob, Jo Ellen Grzyb And Mara Greenbert 030 MIN
Laura Reitman And Nancy Reynolds 030 MIN
Stuart Hodes, Liz Thompson And Brann Wry 030 MIN

Second To Nobody C 25 MIN
16MM FILM OPTICAL SOUND
Analyzes the role of management, union and public opinion in the daily life of New York City sanitation workers.
Prod-SCHLP Dist-RBFLM 1983

Second Trimester, The C 29 MIN
3/4 OR 1/2 INCH VIDEO CASSETTE H-C A
Discusses the development of the fetus during the second trimester of pregnancy. States that the parents must now make decisions about delivery.
From The Tomorrow's Families Series.
LC NO. 81-706900
Prod-MSDOE Dist-AITECH 1980

Second Voice, A C 13 MIN
16MM FILM OPTICAL SOUND H-C A
Portrays the services of the International Association of Laryngectomees (IAL) beginning with surgery on a patient and ending with his participation in the national convention in Chicago.
Prod-AMCS Dist-AMCS

Second World Conference C 28 MIN
16MM FILM - 3/4 IN VIDEO A
Documents the Second World Conference on National Parks held at Yellowstone and Grand Teton National Parks in October, 1972. Shows representatives from over 90 countries in the process of developing an international philosophy on conservation and park management. Includes speeches on the world environmental crisis. Issued in 1973 as a motion picture.
LC NO. 79-706157
Prod-USNPS Dist-USNAC 1979

Second World War, The - Allied Victory B 28 MIN
16MM FILM, 3/4 OR 1/2 IN VIDEO J-H
Uses newsreels, captured Axis films and armed forces' footage to document key events of World War II from 1944 to Japan's surrender in 1945. Explains how total mobilization of manpower and resources was achieved.
Prod-EBF Dist-EBEC 1963

Second World War, The - Allied Victory (Spanish) C 28 MIN
16MM FILM, 3/4 OR 1/2 IN VIDEO J-H
Reviews key events in World War II from early 1944 to the surrender of Japan in 1945. Explains how total mobilization of manpower and resources was achieved and how strategic coordination of fighting forces made the Allies victorious.
Prod-EBEC Dist-EBEC

Second World War, The - D-Day B 26 MIN
16MM FILM, 3/4 OR 1/2 IN VIDEO H-C
Shows the invasion of Europe on June 6, 1944. Examines the anxiety of two million soldiers as they prepare for D-Day. Pictures both the leaders of the invasion - Eisenhower, Patton and Bradley and the German High Command. Edited version of the 52 minute film D-Day.
Prod-WOLPER Dist-FI 1967

Second World War, The - Prelude To Conflict B 29 MIN
16MM FILM, 3/4 OR 1/2 IN VIDEO J-H
Uses newsreels, captured Axis films and armed forces' footage to document causes of World War II. Depicts the failure of the Versailles Peace Treaty, the political crisis which resulted from economic chaos in Germany and the isolationism of the United States.
Prod-EBF Dist-EBEC 1964

Second World War, The - Triumph Of The Axis B 25 MIN
16MM FILM, 3/4 OR 1/2 IN VIDEO J-H
Shows how Germany and Japan conceived and nearly carried out their bold plan for world conquest. Explains how Allied indecision and military unpreparedness resulted in Axis aggression.
Prod-EBEC Dist-EBEC 1963

Second-Moment Characterizations B 38 MIN
3/4 OR 1/2 INCH VIDEO CASSETTE PRO
Relaxes the constraint of complete characterization by introducing the concept of partial characterization by the mean function and correlation function.
From The Probability And Random Processes Introduction To Random Processes Series.
Prod-MIOT Dist-MIOT

Secondary Distribution Systems C
3/4 OR 1/2 INCH VIDEO CASSETTE IND
Aquaints participants with the features and operating characteristics of various types of secondary distribution. Includes spot and distributed loads in overhead secondary and underground secondary.
From The Distribution System Operation Series. Topic 5
Prod-LEIKID Dist-LEIKID

Secondary Flow X 30 MIN
16MM FILM, 3/4 OR 1/2 IN VIDEO C
Introduces the idea of secondary flow with the classical teacup experiment. Demonstrates secondary flow in a sink-vortex tank, a bend in an open channel and at the base of a strut in a shear flow. Explains in terms of pressure fields on boundary layers and vorticity conservation theorems.
From The Fluid Mechanics Series
Prod-NCFMF Dist-EBEC 1966

Secondary Impressions For The Distal Extension Base Removable Partial Denture C 15 MIN
3/4 INCH VIDEO CASSETTE PRO
Demonstrates dental procedures for obtaining impressions of edentulous areas made on bases attached to the removable partial denture framework.
LC NO. 78-706200
Prod-USVA Dist-USNAC Prodn-VADTC 1978

Secondary Impressions For The Distal Extension Base, Removable Partial Denture C 15 MIN
3/4 OR 1/2 INCH VIDEO CASSETTE
Demonstrates the procedures incident to obtaining impressions of edentulous areas made on bases attached to the removable partial denture framework.
Prod-VADTC Dist-AMDA 1970

Secondary Lens Implantation C 17 MIN
3/4 OR 1/2 INCH VIDEO CASSETTE PRO
Demonstrates implantation procedure using a newly developed intraocular lens called Stable Flex.
Prod-HSCIC Dist-HSCIC 1984

Secondary Particle Emissions From Surfaces, I C 35 MIN
3/4 OR 1/2 INCH VIDEO CASSETTE IND
Notes how secondary particle emission from surfaces after bombardment may be used for both qualitative and quantitative surface analysis. Points out that the bombardment/emission sequence is basis for various surface analysis techniques that allow categorization and measurement of atomic and compound species concentrations in a solid sample.
From The Plasma Sputtering, Deposition And Growth Of Microelectronic Films For VLSI Series.
Prod-COLOSU Dist-COLOSU

Secondary Particle Emissions From Surfaces, II C 35 MIN
3/4 OR 1/2 INCH VIDEO CASSETTE IND
Discusses specific examples of Auger analysis, energy dispersive x-ray analysis, ESCA or XPS analysis and SIMS probing of surfaces. Describes and compares various surface analytical techniques.
From The Plasma Sputtering, Deposition And Growth Of Microelectronic Films For VLSI Series.
Prod-COLOSU Dist-COLOSU

Secondary School Safety—A Series

Prod-NSC Dist-NSC

Noontime Nonsense 13 MIN
You're In Charge 12 MIN

Secondary Storage C
3/4 OR 1/2 INCH VIDEO CASSETTE
Discusses information storage, introducing such terms as random access, parity and byte, which provides a sound basis for evaluating the magnetic storage media with reference to an ideal device. Uses a combination of diagrams which explain how information is stored on the various media, and photographs which illustrate the full range of equipment within a typical computer system.
From The Audio Visual Library Of Computer Education Series.
Prod-PRISPR Dist-PRISPR

Secondary Surgery For Recurrent Ulcer C 28 MIN
16MM FILM OPTICAL SOUND PRO
Outlines the major physiological patterns responsible for recurrent ulcer. Includes examples of secondary pyloric obstruction, continued vagal activity after simple gastric resection and hypersecretion due to the activity of a portion of retained antrum.
Prod-ACYDGD Dist-ACY 1966

Secondary Survey, Control Points And Hydrographic Developments C 18 MIN
16MM FILM OPTICAL SOUND
Describes secondary signals building, sounding and wire dragging operations and other miscellaneous survey work.
LC NO. FIE52-1268
Prod-USN Dist-USNAC 1950

Seconds Count C
16MM FILM - 3/4 IN VIDEO A
Explains how to motivate workers to go to the nearest emergency shower and shed their contaminated clothes if they become victims of a chemical spill or thermal burn.
Prod-BNA Dist-BNA 1983

Seconds Count C 15 MIN
16MM FILM, 3/4 OR 1/2 IN VIDEO C A
Emphasizes the need for speed in applying emergency resuscitation by the mouth-to-mouth method using incidents stemming from drowning and asphyxia.
From The Emergency Resuscitation Series.
Prod-UKMD Dist-IFB

Seconds To Play C 28 MIN
16MM FILM, 3/4 OR 1/2 IN VIDEO J-C
Examines technical and human factors involved in the production of a major television sports event. Shows the broadcast of a football game to demonstrate the electronic equipment, advance planning, tensions and split-second decisions involved in televising the event.
Prod-CROWLP Dist-FI 1976

Secret Agent, The B 84 MIN
16MM FILM OPTICAL SOUND
Presents a mystery story involving fake funerals, a one-armed man and the inadvertent of the wrong man. Stars John Geilgud, Peter Lorre and Robert Young. Directed by Alfred Hitchcock.
Prod-GBIF Dist-REELIM 1936

Secret Agent, The C 57 MIN
3/4 INCH VIDEO CASSETTE A
Looks at dioxin, the contaminant of the herbicide 2, 4, 5-T, a main ingredient of the defoliant code named Agent Orange used during the Vietnam War. Documents the extraordinary history of chemical warfare and agricultural herbicides.
LC NO. 84-706035
Prod-FIRS Dist-FIRS 1983

Secret Agent, The C 57 MIN
3/4 OR 1/2 INCH VIDEO CASSETTE
Uses war footage in support of interviews with veterans, scientists, attorneys and representatives of the U S Air Force, Veterans Administration and Dow Chemical Company regarding the use of chemical warfare and agricultural herbicides in Vietnam.
Prod-HAAP Dist-GMPF 1983

Secret Fountains, The C 52 MIN
16MM FILM, 3/4 OR 1/2 IN VIDEO J-C A
Follows Speke as he is appointed leader of a second journey into the jungles to reaffirm his Lake Victoria theory about the Nile's source. Describes how he makes another discovery, the Ripon Falls, where the Nile leaves the lake.
From The Search For The Nile Series. No. 3
LC NO. 79-707461
Prod-BBCTV Dist-TIMLIF 1972

Secret Fountains, The (Spanish) C 52 MIN
16MM FILM OPTICAL SOUND
Dramatizes the story of John Speke's discovery of Ripon Falls, the point at which the Nile flows from Lake Victoria.
From The Search For The Nile (Spanish) Series. No. 3
LC NO. 77-701628
Prod-BBCTV Dist-TIMLIF 1972

Secret Horror C 14 MIN
3/4 INCH VIDEO CASSETTE
Presents Mike, alterego of artist Michael Smith, who, in a comic narrative, is whisked off to an absurd version of This Is Your Life by ghostly creatures. Satirizes television and suspense films.
Prod-EAI Dist-EAI

Secret Horror, The C 14 MIN
3/4 OR 1/2 INCH VIDEO CASSETTE
Features a surrealistic comedy involving the kidnapping of Mike. Presents a thematic journey to a place somewhere between initiation and renovation.
Prod-KITCHN Dist-KITCHN

Secret In The White Cell B 11 MIN
16MM FILM OPTICAL SOUND J-H
Pictures how the enzymes in the granules within white cells are released to kill and digest microbes.
From The Science Close-Up Series.
LC NO. FIA67-5013
Prod-PRISM Dist-SF 1967

Secret Life Of A Trout River C 10 MIN
16MM FILM, 3/4 OR 1/2 IN VIDEO
Shows the complex, delicately balanced ecological system found in a trout river. Includes studies of the relationship between the brown trout and the mayfly, the water ouzel and the pike, and depicts mating and reproductive behavior of the brown trout.
From The Bio-Science Series.
LC NO. 80-706314
Prod-NGS Dist-NGS 1974

Secret Life Of An Orchestra, The C 28 MIN
16MM FILM, 3/4 OR 1/2 IN VIDEO
Shows the Denver Symphony as they rehearse and perform the overture from Wagner's Die Meistersinger. Includes film images which take the viewer into the minds of the musicians, in their conscious and unconscious focus upon performance.
Prod-MUSICP Dist-PFP 1975

Secret Life Of T K Dearing, The C 47 MIN
16MM FILM, 3/4 OR 1/2 IN VIDEO I-H A
Presents the story of a teenage girl's relationship with her grandfather and the lessons which she learns as a result. Based on the book The Secret Life Of T K Dearing by Jean Robinson.
From The Teenage Years Series.
LC NO. 80-706925
Prod-WILSND Dist-TIMLIF 1980

Secret Love Of Sandra Blain, The C 22 MIN
3/4 OR 1/2 INCH VIDEO CASSETTE
Tells the story of a wife and mother who finds a seductive but treacherous solution for frustration and loneliness in alcohol. Reveals the facilities and treatment centers available to the woman alcoholic.
Prod-LACFU Dist-IA

Secret Love Of Sandra Blain, The C 28 MIN
16MM FILM, 3/4 OR 1/2 IN VIDEO H-C A
Shows the progression into alcoholism of a wife and mother. Focuses attention on the facilities and treatments available for the successful treatment and recovery of victims of the disease of alcoholism.
Prod-AIMS Dist-AIMS 1971

Secret Love Of Sandra Blain, The (Spanish) C 27 MIN
16MM FILM, 3/4 OR 1/2 IN VIDEO H-C A
Presents the expericnces of a wife and mother who turns to alcohol to escape frustration, boredom, anxiety and loneliness.
Prod-LAC Dist-AIMS 1971

Secret Of Little Ned, The C 30 MIN
16MM FILM - 3/4 IN VIDEO
Discusses the different types of ideas, feelings, and concerns which children may express in ways other than speaking. Shows how parents can determine and respond to what is being expressed.
From The Footsteps Series.
LC NO. 79-707631
Prod-USOE Dist-USNAC 1978

Secret Of Michelangelo, The - Every Man's Dream C 60 MIN
16MM FILM OPTICAL SOUND
Shows details of the Sistine Chapel fresco by Michelangelo.
LC NO. 73-702673
Prod-MMAMC Dist-CAPCBC Prodn-CAPCBC 1968

Secret Of Pushbuttons, The C 4 MIN
16MM FILM OPTICAL SOUND
Explains how to use the pedestrian crosswalk pushbuttons.
From The Otto The Auto Series.
Prod-AAAFTS Dist-AAAFTS 1971

Secret Of The Universe, The C 2 MIN
16MM FILM OPTICAL SOUND
Attempts to explain allegorically how a basketball player shoots an impossible shot.
LC NO. 73-702202
Prod-GROENG Dist-GROENG 1973

Secret Of The Waterfall C 29 MIN
3/4 OR 1/2 INCH VIDEO CASSETTE
Presents a dancing weekend at Martha's Vineyard, in a garden, street, living room, patio, chapel, bedroom and at the beach. Involves two poets.
Prod-WGBH Dist-KITCHN

Secret Of The White Cell B 30 MIN
16MM FILM OPTICAL SOUND J-C A
Reports on the successful search for the way in which white cells kill germs in the body. Depicts a method of separating and analyzing subcellular components of the white cell, cinephotomicrography of white cells ingesting germs, and electron microscope photos of internal structures which release germicidal materials.
From The Experiment Series.
Prod-PRISM Dist-IU 1966

Secret Of Wendel Samson, The C 31 MIN
16MM FILM OPTICAL SOUND H-C
Presents a Freudian psychodrama dealing with homosexuality.
Prod-CFS Dist-CFS

Secret Return, The C 10 MIN
16MM FILM OPTICAL SOUND
Looks at the nesting habits of the sea turtle which sometimes travels hundreds of miles to reach a particular beach where their ancestors hatched eons earlier.
Prod-UGAIA Dist-UGAIA

Secret Seller, The C 15 MIN
3/4 INCH VIDEO CASSETTE K-P
See series title for descriptive statement.
From The Storytime Series.
Prod-WCETTV Dist-GPITVL 1976

Secret Sharer, The C 30 MIN
16MM FILM, 3/4 OR 1/2 IN VIDEO H-C A
Presents a haunting tale of a captain whose inner conflicts pit his conscience against the safety of the ship he commands and the men he leads - a struggle precipitated by the secret sharer.
From The Humanities - Short Story Showcase Series.
Prod-EBEC Dist-EBEC 1973

Secret World Of Odilon Redon, The C 30 MIN
16MM FILM, 3/4 OR 1/2 IN VIDEO H-C A
Examines the life, work and techniques of 19th century artist Odilon Redon. Includes Redon's own comments on his work.
Prod-ACOGRB Dist-FI 1973

Secret, The C 15 MIN
16MM FILM, 3/4 OR 1/2 IN VIDEO
Tells how a group of children accidently chase a stray dog off a cliff and agree not to tell anyone. Explains how one boy goes back, discovers the dog alive and nurses it back to health.
From The Bloomin' Human Series.
Prod-PAULST Dist-MEDIAG 1977

Secretarial Work Sampling C 18 MIN
16MM FILM OPTICAL SOUND
Introduces methods of work observation to management. Explains that each member of the audience keeps an account of the work done by a secretary each day of the week. Measures these samplings against the actual record of her achievements to increase efficiency in observation.
LC NO. 72-701955
Prod-VOAERO Dist-VOAERO 1971

Secretariat - Big Red's Last Race C 24 MIN
16MM FILM, 3/4 OR 1/2 IN VIDEO C A
Takes a look at the horse named Secretariat through the eyes of jockeys, grooms, trainers, owners and fans.
Prod-INST Dist-WOMBAT

Secretary And Her Boss, The, Pt 1 - Try To See It My Way C 28 MIN
3/4 OR 1/2 INCH VIDEO CASSETTE A
Employs humor to show the quirks, mannerisms, demands and actions that destroy the mutual respect of a secretary and her boss and bring productivity to a halt. Focuses on routines, mail, appointments and filing.
Prod-XICOM Dist-XICOM

Secretary And Her Boss, The, Pt 2 - We Can Work It Out C 28 MIN
3/4 OR 1/2 INCH VIDEO CASSETTE A
Uses the somewhat humorous characters of John and Adrienne to illustrate good techniques for interaction between bosses and secretaries. Focuses on three main areas - visitors, telephone callers and dictation.
Prod-XICOM Dist-XICOM

Secretary And Management Relationship—A Series

Focuses on the management of the manager's office, one of the principal areas of inefficiency and time wasting.
Prod-VIDART Dist-VISUCP

Try To See It My Way 027 MIN
We Can Work It Out 029 MIN

Secretary General Of The United Nations C 28 MIN
3/4 INCH VIDEOTAPE
Interviews Kurt Waldheim, Secretary General of the United Nations. Discusses his varied and unique responsibilities. Hosted by Marilyn Perry.
From The International Byline Series.
Prod-PERRYM Dist-PERRYM

Secretary To Hitler C 26 MIN
3/4 OR 1/2 INCH VIDEO CASSETTE H-C A
Relates that Hitler's private secretary, Traudi Junge, was with Hitler at his death in his private bunker. Her extensive information about Hitler during the war years and in defeat illuminate what he was like as a man and how he reacted to adversity.
From The World At War Specials Series.
Prod-THAMES Dist-MEDIAG 1974

Secretary—A Series
16MM FILM, 3/4 OR 1/2 IN VIDEO H-C
Describes the day-to-day activities and duties of a secretary, emphasizing the skills needed for this job.
Prod-CORF Dist-CORF 1966

Secretary, The - A Normal Day (2nd Ed) 11 MIN
Secretary, The - Taking Dictation (2nd Ed) 11 MIN
Secretary, The - Transcribing (2nd Ed) 11 MIN

Secretary, The - A Normal Day (2nd Ed) C 11 MIN
16MM FILM, 3/4 OR 1/2 IN VIDEO H-C
Shows a secretary's normal day in a modern office, pointing out her responsibilities for making appointments, greeting visitors, processing mail, supervising files, organizing a business trip, taking dictation and transcribing. Emphasizes personal qualities.
From The Secretary Series.
Prod-CORF Dist-CORF 1966

Secretary, The - Taking Dictation (2nd Ed) C 11 MIN
16MM FILM, 3/4 OR 1/2 IN VIDEO H-C
Shows good secretarial practices for taking dictation, such as organizing materials, assuming a correct posture, knowing how to indicate special instructions and how to key dictation to letters being answered, and determining when to interrupt and when not to.
From The Secretary Series.
Prod-CORF Dist-CORF 1966

Secretary, The - Transcribing (2nd Ed) C 11 MIN
16MM FILM, 3/4 OR 1/2 IN VIDEO H-C
Shows good secretarial practices for transcribing, such as organizing materials, establishing priorities so that rush items get out first and typing faster, neater letters. Discusses basic letter forms and procedures for transcribing from a dictating machine.
From The Secretary Series.
Prod-CORF Dist-CORF 1966

Secretion Of Insulin, The C 23 MIN
3/4 OR 1/2 INCH VIDEO CASSETTE PRO
Describes a poineer research project which seeks to determine how insulin is secreted from the pancreas into the blood stream.
Prod-WFP Dist-WFP

Secretony Otitis Media (Arabic) C
3/4 OR 1/2 INCH VIDEO CASSETTE
Shows how the ear works, why the middle ear needs air furnished by the Eustachian tubes, and the various way blockage occurs. Explains various diagnostic procedures and treatment.
Prod-MIFE Dist-MIFE

Secretory Otitis Media C
3/4 OR 1/2 INCH VIDEO CASSETTE
Shows how the ear works, why the middle ear needs air furnished by the Eustachian tubes, and the various way blockage occurs. Explains various diagnostic procedures and treatment.
Prod-MIFE Dist-MIFE

Secrets C 8 MIN
16MM FILM OPTICAL SOUND
Presents an elegant 80-year-old man whose daily life consists of work in a well-furnished office, attention by a chauffeur and secretary and lunch with a lovely lady. Demonstrates that there are no stereotypes in considering the lifestyles of the aged.
Prod-THOMAC Dist-FLMLIB 1980

Secrets C 13 MIN
16MM FILM OPTICAL SOUND H-C A
Presents artist Phillip Jones' character study of a girl combining paintings, sketches, anatomical cross sections, photographs and colored washes of a pretty girl's face with ominous orchestral background music and sounds of the night to invoke his subject's hidden identity.
LC NO. 73-700756
Prod-PFP Dist-VIEWFI 1973

Secrets For A Happy Hostess C 13 MIN
16MM FILM OPTICAL SOUND
Presents Patty and Susie planning the menu, shopping, preparing and serving the 20th anniversary dinner for their parents and family. Illustrates time and appliance-use management, highlighting the dishwasher and the food waste disposer.
Prod-MAY Dist-MAY

Secrets In Your Cells C 15 MIN
3/4 OR 1/2 INCH VIDEO CASSETTE P
Introduces the idea of genetic inheritance.
From The All About You Series.
Prod-WGBHTV Dist-AITECH Prodn-TTOIC 1975

Secrets Of A Brook B 30 MIN
16MM FILM OPTICAL SOUND P-J
Presents a view of the travels of a brook as seen through the eyes of a ten-year-old girl.
LC NO. 79-700344
Prod-KVIETV Dist-IU 1967

Secrets Of A Brook (Award Series 1967) B 30 MIN
2 INCH VIDEOTAPE
Presents a glimpse through the eyes of a youngster to whom a brook seems to speak of the meaning of life.
From The Synergism - Gallimaufry Series.
Prod-KVIETV Dist-PUBTEL

Secrets Of Cancer, The C 26 MIN
3/4 INCH VIDEO CASSETTE
Explains how cancer develops and how it could possibly be prevented. Describes a preventive technique called chemo-prevention.
Prod-NFCR Dist-MTP

Secrets Of Life (Afrikaans)—A Series
I-H
Examines various life forms.
Prod-WDEMCO Dist-WDEMCO 1961

Secrets Of The Ant And Insect World (Afrikaans) 013 MIN
Secrets Of The Bee World (Afrikaans) 013 MIN
Secrets Of The Underwater World (Afrikaans) 016 MIN

Secrets Of Life (French)—A Series
I-H
Examines various life forms.
Prod-WDEMCO Dist-WDEMCO 1961

Secrets Of The Ant And Insect World (French) 013 MIN
Secrets Of The Bee World (French) 013 MIN
Secrets Of The Plant World (French) 015 MIN
Secrets Of The Underwater World (French) 016 MIN

Secrets Of Life (German)—A Series
I-H
Examines various life forms.
Prod-WDEMCO Dist-WDEMCO 1961

Secrets Of The Ant And Insect World (German) 013 MIN
Secrets Of The Bee World (German) 013 MIN
Secrets Of The Underwater World (German) 016 MIN

Secrets Of Life (Norwegian)—A Series
I-H
Examines various life forms.
Prod-WDEMCO Dist-WDEMCO 1961

Secrets Of The Ant And Insect World (Norwegian) 013 MIN
Secrets Of The Bee World (Norwegian) 013 MIN
Secrets Of The Plant World (Norwegian) 015 MIN
Secrets Of The Underwater World (Norwegian) 016 MIN

Secrets Of Life (Portuguese)—A Series
I-H
Examines various life forms.
Prod-WDEMCO Dist-WDEMCO 1961

Secrets Of The Plant World (Portuguese) 015 MIN
Secrets Of The Underwater World (Portuguese) 016 MIN

Secrets Of Life (Spanish)—A Series
I-H
Examines various life forms.
Prod-WDEMCO Dist-WDEMCO 1961

Secrets Of The Bee World (Spanish) 013 MIN
Secrets Of The Plant World (Spanish) 015 MIN
Secrets Of The Underwater World (Spanish) 016 MIN

Secrets Of Life (Swedish)—A Series
I-H
Examines various life forms.
Prod-WDEMCO Dist-WDEMCO 1961

Secrets Of The Ant And Insect World (Swedish) 013 MIN
Secrets Of The Bee World (Swedish) 013 MIN
Secrets Of The Plant World (Swedish) 015 MIN
Secrets Of The Underwater World (Swedish) 016 MIN

Secrets Of Life—A Series
16MM FILM, 3/4 OR 1/2 IN VIDEO I-C A
Prod-DISNEY Dist-WDEMCO 1961

Secrets Of The Ant And Insect World 013 MIN
Secrets Of The Bee World 013 MIN
Secrets Of The Plant World 015 MIN
Secrets Of The Underwater World 016 MIN

Secrets Of Limestone Groundwater C 14 MIN
16MM FILM, 3/4 OR 1/2 IN VIDEO H-C
Shows how groundwater from springs, wells, and underground rivers in limestone country may well be polluted by human sewage and garbage that was unintentionally allowed to filter down into the water table.
Prod-INERTH Dist-IU Prodn-FBFP 1980

Secrets Of Making Good Grades, The C 15 MIN
16MM FILM, 3/4 OR 1/2 IN VIDEO J-C
Tells the secrets six successful students have used to achieve good grades. Offers tips on lecture note taking, reviewing, reading textbooks and test-taking.
LC NO. 83-707236
Prod-CROMIE Dist-CORF 1983

Secrets Of Nikola Tesla, The C 120 MIN
3/4 OR 1/2 INCH VIDEO CASSETTE
Features Orson Welles, Strother Martin and Dennis Patrick in a film about clean energy.
Prod-ZAGREB Dist-PLACE

Secrets Of Seed Growth X 8 MIN
16MM FILM OPTICAL SOUND
Tennessee Charlie reveals the growth of a seed by means of time-lapse photography.
From The World Outdoors Series. No. 9
Prod-TGAFC Dist-TGAFC

Secrets Of Sleep C 52 MIN
16MM FILM, 3/4 OR 1/2 IN VIDEO H-C A
Uses animation and documentary footage of experiments conducted to study the effects of sleep. Considers what happens during sleep, how much sleep is needed by the average person, the quality of sleep induced by pills and the importance of dreaming and interpreting dreams.
From The Nova Series.
LC NO. 79-707241
Prod-WGBHTV Dist-TIMLIF 1976

Secrets Of Sleep, The C 60 MIN
3/4 INCH VIDEO CASSETTE
Examines some of the theories of sleep and the reason for dreams. Shows the kinds of sleep research being conducted and looks at a group session in which the hidden meanings that dreams may have are unravelled.
Prod-WGBH Dist-PUBTEL 1974

Secrets Of The Ant And Insect World C 13 MIN
16MM FILM, 3/4 OR 1/2 IN VIDEO I-C A
Presents facts about the subterranean world of the ant, including a description of the warfare that persists between rival tribes of ants and their desperate struggle to protect their nests from invasion. Discusses in detail the honeycast, hunting and leaf-cutter ants.
From The Secrets Of Life Series.
Prod-DISNEY Dist-WDEMCO 1961

Secrets Of The Ant And Insect World (Afrikaans) C 13 MIN
16MM FILM, 3/4 OR 1/2 IN VIDEO I-H
Reveals the highly structured, specialized ant society.
From The Secrets Of Life (Afrikaans) Series.
Prod-WDEMCO Dist-WDEMCO 1961

Secrets Of The Ant And Insect World (French) C 13 MIN
16MM FILM, 3/4 OR 1/2 IN VIDEO I-H
Reveals the highly structured, specialized ant society.
From The Secrets Of Life (French) Series.
Prod-WDEMCO Dist-WDEMCO 1961

Secrets Of The Ant And Insect World (German) C 13 MIN
16MM FILM, 3/4 OR 1/2 IN VIDEO I-H
Reveals the highly structured, specialized ant society.
From The Secrets Of Life (German) Series.
Prod-WDEMCO Dist-WDEMCO 1961

Secrets Of The Ant And Insect World (Norwegian) C 13 MIN
16MM FILM, 3/4 OR 1/2 IN VIDEO I-H
Reveals the highly structured, specialized ant society.
From The Secrets Of Life (Norwegian) Series.
Prod-WDEMCO Dist-WDEMCO 1961

Secrets Of The Ant And Insect World (Swedish) C 13 MIN
16MM FILM, 3/4 OR 1/2 IN VIDEO I-H
Reveals the highly structured, specialized ant society.
From The Secrets Of Life (Swedish) Series.
Prod-WDEMCO Dist-WDEMCO 1961

Secrets Of The Bee World C 13 MIN
16MM FILM, 3/4 OR 1/2 IN VIDEO I-C A
Shows the many facets of life in a highly organized bee colony. Describes the construction of the comb, discusses the importance of the queen bee and explains about the work of bees in the pollination process.
From The Secrets Of Life Series.
Prod-DISNEY Dist-WDEMCO 1961

Secrets Of The Bee World (Afrikaans) C 13 MIN
16MM FILM, 3/4 OR 1/2 IN VIDEO I-H
Examines the communication and social systems of bees.
From The Secrets Of Life (Afrikaans) Series.
Prod-WDEMCO Dist-WDEMCO 1961

Secrets Of The Bee World (Dutch) C 13 MIN
16MM FILM, 3/4 OR 1/2 IN VIDEO I-H
Examines the communication and social systems of bees.
Prod-WDEMCO Dist-WDEMCO 1961

Secrets Of The Bee World (French) C 13 MIN
16MM FILM, 3/4 OR 1/2 IN VIDEO I-H
Examines the communication and social systems of bees.
From The Secrets Of Life (French) Series.
Prod-WDEMCO Dist-WDEMCO 1961

Secrets Of The Bee World (German) C 13 MIN
16MM FILM, 3/4 OR 1/2 IN VIDEO I-H
Examines the communication and social systems of bees.
From The Secrets Of Life (German) Series.
Prod-WDEMCO Dist-WDEMCO 1961

Secrets Of The Bee World (Norwegian) C 13 MIN
16MM FILM, 3/4 OR 1/2 IN VIDEO I-H
Examines the communication and social systems of bees.
From The Secrets Of Life (Norwegian) Series.
Prod-WDEMCO Dist-WDEMCO 1961

Secrets Of The Bee World (Spanish) C 13 MIN
16MM FILM, 3/4 OR 1/2 IN VIDEO I-H
Examines the communication and social systems of bees.
From The Secrets Of Life (Spanish) Series.
Prod-WDEMCO Dist-WDEMCO 1961

Secrets Of The Bee World (Swedish) C 13 MIN
16MM FILM, 3/4 OR 1/2 IN VIDEO I-H
Examines the communication and social systems of bees.
From The Secrets Of Life (Swedish) Series.
Prod-WDEMCO Dist-WDEMCO 1961

Secrets Of The Brain C 15 MIN
16MM FILM OPTICAL SOUND C
Explains that the prevention, treatment and cure of cerebral palsy are the goals of intensive research into the subtle and delicate processes of the brain. Shows methods being researched for curing such problems as headaches, muscular spasms and learning difficulties.
From The Science In Action Series.
Prod-ALLFP Dist-COUNFI

Secrets Of The City C 28 MIN
3/4 OR 1/2 INCH VIDEO CASSETTE
Depicts 16 Los Angeles and Santa Monica Bay area locations, revealing little-known anecdotes about well-known places.
Prod-WAHL Dist-WAHL 1983

Secrets Of The Plant World C 15 MIN
16MM FILM, 3/4 OR 1/2 IN VIDEO I-C A
Describes the various ways in which seeds are planted without the help of man. Uses time-lapse photography to show the growing, budding and flowering of many plants.
From The Secrets Of Life Series.
Prod-DISNEY Dist-WDEMCO 1961

Secrets Of The Plant World (French) C 15 MIN
16MM FILM, 3/4 OR 1/2 IN VIDEO I-H
Reveals nature's various methods for plant-life propagation.
From The Secrets Of Life (French) Series.
Prod-WDEMCO Dist-WDEMCO 1961

Secrets Of The Plant World (Greek) C 15 MIN
16MM FILM, 3/4 OR 1/2 IN VIDEO I-H
Reveals nature's various methods for plant-life propagation.
Prod-WDEMCO Dist-WDEMCO 1961

Secrets Of The Plant World (Norwegian) C 15 MIN
16MM FILM, 3/4 OR 1/2 IN VIDEO I-H
Reveals nature's various methods for plant-life propagation.
From The Secrets Of Life (Norwegian) Series.
Prod-WDEMCO Dist-WDEMCO 1961

Secrets Of The Plant World (Portuguese) C 15 MIN
16MM FILM, 3/4 OR 1/2 IN VIDEO I-H
Reveals nature's various methods for plant-life propagation.
From The Secrets Of Life (Portuguese) Series.
Prod-WDEMCO Dist-WDEMCO 1961

Secrets Of The Plant World (Spanish) C 15 MIN
16MM FILM, 3/4 OR 1/2 IN VIDEO I-H
Reveals nature's various methods for plant-life propagation.
From The Secrets Of Life (Spanish) Series.
Prod-WDEMCO Dist-WDEMCO 1961

Secrets Of The Plant World (Swedish) C 15 MIN
16MM FILM, 3/4 OR 1/2 IN VIDEO I-H
Reveals nature's various methods for plant-life propagation.
From The Secrets Of Life (Swedish) Series.
Prod-WDEMCO Dist-WDEMCO 1961

Secrets Of The Sea C 15 MIN
16MM FILM, 3/4 OR 1/2 IN VIDEO J-C A
Pictures two scuba divers as they explore a coral reef and observe its inhabitants. Shows views of colored fish and other sea animals, a wrecked ship, a shark and a barracuda.
Prod-DUTCHE Dist-AIMS 1974

Secrets Of The Underwater World C 16 MIN
16MM FILM, 3/4 OR 1/2 IN VIDEO I-C A
Describes many of the unusual creatures to be found in the shallow seas in the tidal fringe and in fresh water, including the stickleback, diving spider, archer fish, kelpfish, jellyfish, centophere, angler fish, decorator crab, and fiddler crab.
From The Secrets Of Life Series.
Prod-DISNEY Dist-WDEMCO 1961

Secrets Of The Underwater World (Afrikaans) C 16 MIN
16MM FILM, 3/4 OR 1/2 IN VIDEO I-H
Introduces life beneath the water's surface. Examines the habits of those animals who inhabit tidal fringes, fresh water and shallow seas.
From The Secrets Of Life (Afrikaans) Series.
Prod-WDEMCO Dist-WDEMCO 1961

Secrets Of The Underwater World (Arabic) C 16 MIN
16MM FILM, 3/4 OR 1/2 IN VIDEO I-H
Introduces life beneath the water's surface. Examines the habits of those animals who inhabit tidal fringes, fresh water and shallow seas.
Prod-WDEMCO Dist-WDEMCO 1961

Secrets Of The Underwater World (French) C 16 MIN
16MM FILM, 3/4 OR 1/2 IN VIDEO I-H
Introduces life beneath the water's surface. Examines the habits of those animals who inhabit tidal fringes, fresh water and shallow seas.
From The Secrets Of Life (French) Series.
Prod-WDEMCO Dist-WDEMCO 1961

Secrets Of The Underwater World (German) C 16 MIN
16MM FILM, 3/4 OR 1/2 IN VIDEO I-H
Introduces life beneath the water's surface. Examines the habits of those animals who inhabit tidal fringes, fresh water and shallow seas.
From The Secrets Of Life (German) Series.
Prod-WDEMCO Dist-WDEMCO 1961

Secrets Of The Underwater World (Norwegian) C 16 MIN
16MM FILM, 3/4 OR 1/2 IN VIDEO I-H
Introduces life beneath the water's surface. Examines the habits of those animals who inhabit tidal fringes, fresh water and shallow seas.
From The Secrets Of Life (Norwegian) Series.
Prod-WDEMCO Dist-WDEMCO 1961

Secrets Of The Underwater World (Portuguese) C 16 MIN
16MM FILM, 3/4 OR 1/2 IN VIDEO I-H
Introduces life beneath the water's surface. Examines the habits of those animals who inhabit tidal fringes, fresh water and shallow seas.
From The Secrets Of Life (Portuguese) Series.
Prod-WDEMCO Dist-WDEMCO 1961

Secrets Of The Underwater World (Spanish) C 16 MIN
16MM FILM, 3/4 OR 1/2 IN VIDEO I-H
Introduces life beneath the water's surface. Examines the habits of those animals who inhabit tidal fringes, fresh water and shallow seas.
From The Secrets Of Life (Spanish) Series.
Prod-WDEMCO Dist-WDEMCO 1961

Secrets Of The Underwater World (Swedish) C 16 MIN
16MM FILM, 3/4 OR 1/2 IN VIDEO I-H
Introduces life beneath the water's surface. Examines the habits of those animals who inhabit tidal fringes, fresh water and shallow seas.
From The Secrets Of Life (Swedish) Series.
Prod-WDEMCO Dist-WDEMCO 1961

Sectional Tray Impression For Maxillary Immediate Denture C 15 MIN
3/4 OR 1/2 INCH VIDEO CASSETTE
Demonstrates the construction of a sectional tray impression for maxillary immediate denture.
Prod-VADTC Dist-AMDA 1971

Sectional Views And Projections - Finish Marks B 15 MIN
16MM FILM - 3/4 IN VIDEO
Defines technical drawing terms such as dimension, center, cross section, and object lines. Discusses the projection of a section view, the uses of finish marks, and the significance of standard cross section lines. Issued in 1944 as a motion picture.
From The Machine Shop Work - Fundamentals Of Blueprint Reading Series.
LC NO. 79-707981
Prod-USOE Dist-USNAC Prodn-RAYBEL 1979

Sector Boss C 21 MIN
16MM FILM, 3/4 OR 1/2 IN VIDEO
Identifies the specific sector boss responsibilities and their critical relationship to successful and economical fire management.
LC NO. 82-706247
Prod-USDA Dist-USNAC 1970

Secular Music Of The Renaissance - Josquin Des Pres B 30 MIN
16MM FILM OPTICAL SOUND J-C A
Discusses the primacy of Josquin des Pres in Renaissance music and presents several examples of his works which are played and sung by the New York Pro Musica.
From The World Of Music Series.
Prod-NET Dist-IU 1965

Secure Society, The B 30 MIN
16MM FILM OPTICAL SOUND
Describes the Swedish welfare program.
From The Face Of Sweden Series.
Prod-SIS Dist-SIS 1963

Secure Your Child's Future C 14 MIN
16MM FILM, 3/4 OR 1/2 IN VIDEO H-C A
Explains the consequences of neglecting to use car safety restraints when children are passengers in a car. Discusses how to choose and install safety restraints.
LC NO. 81-706567
Prod-IFB Dist-IFB 1980

Securities C 19 MIN
16MM FILM OPTICAL SOUND H-C A
Explains various types of security investments, including stocks, bonds and mutual funds. Follows Jeff and a friend who meet a stockbroker at his office where they listen to an explanation of stock exchanges, tour the office and learn to read stock quotations on the financial page.
From The Money Management And Family Financial Planning Series.
Prod-AETNA Dist-AETNA

Security And 'C' Language C
3/4 OR 1/2 INCH VIDEO CASSETTE
Describes the three major areas of concern regarding security and how UNIX handles them, the four characteristics of 'C' language and identifies why 'C' language is so popular today.
From The UNIX Overview Series. Unit 6
Prod-COMTEG Dist-COMTEG

Security And Integrity C 25 MIN
16MM FILM, 3/4 OR 1/2 IN VIDEO
Offers an overview of insurance database procedures at Blue Cross/Blue Shield in Boston, demonstrating ways the system guards against unauthorized disclosure of sensitive informa-

tion. Shows controls at each of three system software levels that govern access - terminal restrictions, codes and passwords, and handling flags for specific classification of information.
Prod-OPENU Dist-MEDIAG Prodn-BBCTV 1980

Security And Loss Prevention Control C 15 MIN
3/4 OR 1/2 INCH VIDEO CASSETTE
Teaches ways to prevent, detect and investigate losses at health care facilities by means of patrol, consistent systems enforcement and parcel inspection.
From The Health Care Security Training Series.
Prod-GREESM Dist-MTI

Security And The Law C 14 MIN
3/4 OR 1/2 INCH VIDEO CASSETTE
Examines the extent and types of authority legally held by private security officers. Covers such topics as probable cause, laws of arrest, discretionary authority and law enforcement coordination.
From The Professional Security Training Series. Module 4
Prod-MTI Dist-MTI

Security And Weatherproofing - Door Locks, Burglar Alarms, Wall Safe, Garage Door... C 90 MIN
1/2 IN VIDEO CASSETTE BETA/VHS
Explains do-it-yourself procedures for the homeowner. Title continues ..Openers, Fiberglass Insulation, Weatherstripping.
From The Best Of Wally's Workshop Series.
Prod-KARTES Dist-KARTES

Security Control - You Never Can Tell B 36 MIN
16MM FILM OPTICAL SOUND
Explains the elements of security by following a Naval Security Officer through the offices, laboratory and production plant of a manufacturer producing a classified device for the U S Navy.
Prod-USN Dist-USNAC 1951

Security Council C 18 MIN
16MM FILM, 3/4 OR 1/2 IN VIDEO
Describes the role, functions, composition and activities of the Security Council within the context of the overall UN structure.
Prod-UN Dist-ICARUS 1982

Security In Data Communications C 45 MIN
3/4 OR 1/2 INCH VIDEO CASSETTE C
Defines threats, including personal authentication something you know (passwords) something you have (key, card), something you are (fingerprint, signature). Covers encryption as conventional crypto system, digital signatures and security management.
From The Telecommunications And The Computer Series.
LC NO. 81-707502
Prod-AMCEE Dist-AMCEE 1981

Security In Data Communications C 46 MIN
3/4 OR 1/2 INCH VIDEO CASSETTE
See series title for descriptive statement.
From The Telecommunications And The Computer Series.
Prod-MIOT Dist-MIOT

Security Man B 17 MIN
16MM FILM OPTICAL SOUND
Follows a government security man as he visits an industrial facility and points out some of the problems encountered.
Prod-USA Dist-USNAC 1961

Security Markets C 30 MIN
3/4 INCH VIDEO CASSETTE
See series title for descriptive statement.
From The It's Everybody's Business Series. Unit 3, Financing A Business
Prod-DALCCD Dist-DALCCD

Security Profile, A C 14 MIN
3/4 INCH VIDEO CASSETTE
Describes the responsibility of the Manned Spacecraft Center to safeguard classified information. Outlines policies and procedures in acquiring access to classified material as specified by the security manual, Safeguarding Classified Information.
Prod-NASA Dist-NASA 1972

Security Story, The C 12 MIN
3/4 OR 1/2 INCH VIDEO CASSETTE
Presents a brief history of private security in America. Explores the role of the security professional as a protector of assets. Shows modern security tools and emphasizes the need for training in their proper usage.
From The Professional Security Training Series. Module 1
Prod-MTI Dist-MTI

Security Surveys In Manufacturing C 11 MIN
16MM FILM, 3/4 OR 1/2 IN VIDEO
Deals with a clothing manufacturer's security-crime prevention plan. Uncovers weaknesses in windows, alarms and internal procedures.
Prod-WORON Dist-MTI

Security, Custody And Control B
16MM FILM OPTICAL SOUND PRO
Provides information on security, custody and control.
From The View And Do Series.
LC NO. 73-700192
Prod-SCETV Dist-SCETV 1971

Security, Privacy, Protection In Distributed Communications Networks C 55 MIN
3/4 OR 1/2 INCH VIDEO CASSETTE C
Covers information threats in distributed networks, concepts of encryption, the Data Encryptron Standard (DES) and protection from internal threats.
From The Distributed Telecommunications Networks Series.
Prod-AMCEE Dist-AMCEE

Sedatives C 5 MIN
3/4 OR 1/2 INCH VIDEO CASSETTE
Explains uses of sedatives and describes their effects on the individual personality. Discusses tolerance and physical and psychological dependence. Issued in 1971 as a motion picture.
From The Single Concept Drug Film Series.
LC NO. 80-706848
Prod-NIMH Dist-USNAC 1980

Sedatives, Hypnotics And Alcohol B 30 MIN
16MM FILM OPTICAL SOUND C
See series title for descriptive statement.
From The Pharmacology Series.
LC NO. 73-703334
Prod-MVNE Dist-TELSTR 1971

Sedimentary Rock - Composition Of The Earth C 20 MIN
2 INCH VIDEOTAPE I
See series title for descriptive statement.
From The Exploring With Science, Unit II - Geology Series.
Prod-MPATI Dist-GPITVL

Sedimentary Rock Depositional Patterns C 30 MIN
3/4 OR 1/2 INCH VIDEO CASSETTE IND
See series title for descriptive statement.
From The Basic Geology Series.
Prod-GPCV Dist-GPCV

Sedimentary Rock Lithologies C 51 MIN
3/4 OR 1/2 INCH VIDEO CASSETTE IND
See series title for descriptive statement.
From The Basic And Petroleum Geology For Non-Geologists - Sedimentary Rocks Series.
Prod-PHILLP Dist-GPCV

Sedimentary Rock Structures C 47 MIN
3/4 OR 1/2 INCH VIDEO CASSETTE IND
See series title for descriptive statement.
From The Basic And Petroleum Geology For Non-Geologists - Sedimentary Rocks Series.
Prod-PHILLP Dist-GPCV

Sedimentary Rock Textures C 36 MIN
3/4 OR 1/2 INCH VIDEO CASSETTE IND
See series title for descriptive statement.
From The Basic And Petroleum Geology For Non-Geologists - Sedimentary Rocks Series.
Prod-PHILLP Dist-GPCV

Sedimentary Rocks C 15 MIN
3/4 OR 1/2 INCH VIDEO CASSETTE I
See series title for descriptive statement.
From The Discovering Series. Unit 6 - Rocks And Minerals
Prod-WDCNTV Dist-AITECH 1978

Sedimentary Rocks C 30 MIN
3/4 INCH VIDEO CASSETTE J
Relates sedimentary rocks to the conditions under which they form. Shows how fossils were created and explains how scientists reconstruct the environment in which the plants and animals lived.
From The What On Earth Series.
Prod-NCSDPI Dist-GPITVL 1979

Seduction Of Joe Tynan, The C 107 MIN
16MM FILM OPTICAL SOUND
Stars Alan Alda as a married senator who becomes involved with another woman (Meryl Streep).
Prod-UPCI Dist-SWANK

See C 13 MIN
16MM FILM, 3/4 OR 1/2 IN VIDEO I-C A
Reveals the beauty and wonders of the sea.
Prod-OPUS Dist-PHENIX 1975

See 'N Tell—A Series
16MM FILM, 3/4 OR 1/2 IN VIDEO P-I
Prod-FI Dist-FI 1970

Australian Animals	008 MIN
Birds On A Seashore	010 MIN
Blackbird Family	012 MIN
Butterfly	008 MIN
Carp In A Marsh	007 MIN
Lizard	011 MIN
Shepherd Dog And His Flock	008 MIN
Silk Moth	007 MIN

See America—A Series
H A
Travels to California, New Orleans, and New England.
Prod-MTOLP Dist-MTOLP 1985

California Drive	028 MIN
New England, An Independence Of Spirit	030 MIN
New Orleans, The Big Easy	027 MIN

See Andy Run C 20 MIN
16MM FILM OPTICAL SOUND
Features a satirical look at the pros and cons surrounding higher education.
LC NO. 77-702640
Prod-CANFDC Dist-CANFDC 1975

See Better - Healthy Eyes (2nd Ed) C 10 MIN
16MM FILM, 3/4 OR 1/2 IN VIDEO I
Shows how eyes are used to explore, discover, work and play. Discusses eye structure, function and care and the importance of annual eye check-ups.
Prod-CORF Dist-CORF 1973

See Hear C 15 MIN
16MM FILM OPTICAL SOUND PRO
Briefly describes the hearing difficulties encountered by individuals with conductive and sensori-neural hearing impairments. Demonstrates the importance of speech by simulating these losses on the sound track of the film.
LC NO. FIA68-1198
Prod-EAR Dist-EAR 1964

See Hear C 15 MIN
16MM FILM, 3/4 OR 1/2 IN VIDEO PRO
Shows, through distortion of the sound track, what the different types of hearing losses are like including conductive losses of 20, 30 and 40 dB, and sensorineural losses in the high frequencies and speech range. Visual cues are shown to be of primary importance. Presents the response by a person using a hearing aid due to either a conductive or sensorineural hearing loss.
Prod-EAR Dist-HOUSEI

See How The Cat Walks C 10 MIN
16MM FILM OPTICAL SOUND
Presents one man's passion for life expressed through his zest for the ancient game of chess.
LC NO. 76-703801
Prod-RYERI Dist-RYERI 1975

See How They Fit C 15 MIN
3/4 OR 1/2 INCH VIDEO CASSETTE K-P
Shows how living things survive in their environment.
From The Dragons, Wagons And Wax, Set 1 Series.
Prod-CTI Dist-CTI

See How They Grow B
16MM FILM OPTICAL SOUND
Introduces the concept of differential equations. Discusses three methods of solving differential equations.
Prod-OPENU Dist-OPENU

See How They Grow C 15 MIN
3/4 OR 1/2 INCH VIDEO CASSETTE K-P
Shows that all living things undergo developmental changes.
From The Dragons, Wagons And Wax, Set 1 Series.
Prod-CTI Dist-CTI

See How They Ran, Pt 1 C 24 MIN
16MM FILM OPTICAL SOUND
Reviews William Mc Kinley's campaign and election in 1896, through the campaigns of Theodore Roosevelt, William Howard Taft, Woodrow Wilson, Warren G Harding, Calvin Coolidge and Herbert Hoover, to the 1932 election of Franklin Delano Roosevelt.
Prod-INTEXT Dist-REAF

See How They Ran, Pt 2 C 24 MIN
16MM FILM OPTICAL SOUND
Highlights the re-election of Franklin Delano Roosevelt in 1936, 1940 and 1944, Harry Truman's surprise win over Thomas E Dewey in 1948, the re-election of the late war hero Dwight D Eisenhower in 1952 and his landslide re-election in 1956.
Prod-INTEXT Dist-REAF

See How They Ran, Pt 3 C 24 MIN
16MM FILM OPTICAL SOUND
Shows the shifting trends of U S public opinion concerning the United States as a world power, the fears of an atomic holocaust and the growing impact of the electronic communications media on the U S political scene.
Prod-INTEXT Dist-REAF

See How They Run C 26 MIN
3/4 OR 1/2 INCH VIDEO CASSETTE
Features comments and analyses by medical specialists, sports personalities, coaches, team doctors and young competitors in exploring the role and control of drug administration in injured player situations, the conflicting attitudes on the status of drugs among amateur and professional sports authorities and the future role of drugs in sports.
Prod-ARFO Dist-ARFO

See How We Run C 31 MIN
16MM FILM, 3/4 OR 1/2 IN VIDEO J-C A
Explains ways to prevent common running accidents and injuries to the feet, knees, bones, tendons and ligaments. Outlines methods of diagnosis and treatment.
Prod-LUF Dist-LUF

See Is Never All The Way Up C 14 MIN
3/4 OR 1/2 INCH VIDEO CASSETTE
Presents a non-figurative painting in time where tension is sustained with the volume of the screen's surface.
Prod-EAI Dist-EAI

See It And Believe It C 10 MIN
16MM FILM OPTICAL SOUND P-I A
Hollywood's jungle compound beasts are put through their paces, apparently for their own amusement. All of the animals want to be king of the beasts and they put on their act for the approval of admiring chimps.
LC NO. FIA66-1690
Prod-AVED Dist-AVED 1961

See It My Way C 15 MIN
3/4 OR 1/2 INCH VIDEO CASSETTE I
Describes an accident involving a pedestrian, a truck driver and a bike rider. Replays the incident so that each person can see how things look from another person's perspective.
From The It's Your Move Series.
Prod-WETN Dist-AITECH 1977

See No Evil B 15 MIN
16MM FILM OPTICAL SOUND
Documents the difficulties an elderly couple have in working out their relationship. Explores their lifestyle and offers their comments on themselves, their contemporaries, aging, love, life and death.
LC NO. 77-700029
Prod-CREVAS Dist-FLMLIB Prodn-PINSKR 1976

See Saw Seems B 10 MIN
16MM FILM OPTICAL SOUND H-C A
Views a writer's portrait microscopically and slowly transforms it into other images through variances in texture and form.
Prod-UWFKD Dist-UWFKD 1972

See The Little Picture C 9 MIN
16MM FILM - 3/4 IN VIDEO
Shows workers that they must take responsibility for their own actions that could cause accidents. Discusses self-evaluation, identifying and correcting those actions that could lead to an accident. Points out that success can be achieved by concentrating on the little things and breaking big problems down to little steps.
Prod-ALLIED Dist-BNA

See What I Feel - A Blind Child C 6 MIN
16MM FILM, 3/4 OR 1/2 IN VIDEO K-P
Describes the adventures of Laura, a blind girl, as she visits the zoo.
From The Like You, Like Me Series.
Prod-EBEC Dist-EBEC 1977

See What I Say C 24 MIN
16MM FILM, 3/4 OR 1/2 IN VIDEO J-C A
Presents interviews with hearing-impaired people who reveal the frustration they feel about having limited access to cultural events.
Prod-FLMLIB Dist-FLMLIB Prodn-MICHWF 1981

See What We Have Done B 20 MIN
2 INCH VIDEOTAPE P-I
Provides guides to help students evaluate their own work so they can improve and grow in art. Demonstrates displaying students' work and arranging bulletin boards so all can enjoy and appreciate other students' and adult artists' work.
From The Art Adventures Series.
Prod-CVETVC Dist-GPITVL Prodn-WCVETV

See You Again Soon C 23 MIN
3/4 OR 1/2 INCH VIDEO CASSETTE A
See series title for descriptive statement.
From The Welcome Customer Series. Pt 2
Prod-XICOM Dist-XICOM

See You Again Soon C 24 MIN
3/4 OR 1/2 INCH VIDEO CASSETTE
See series title for descriptive statement.
From The Hotel/Restaurant Selling - Welcome Customer Series. Pt II
Prod-VIDART Dist-VISUCP

See-Touch-Feel C 31 MIN
16MM FILM, 3/4 OR 1/2 IN VIDEO J-C A
Features artists-in-residence at high schools in Pennsylvania, Minnesota and Colorado demonstrating and discussing their methods of teaching young people. Includes artists Mac Fisher, a watercolorist, Charles Huntington, a Chippewa Indian who creates metal sculpture, and Don Coel, a painter.
Prod-CEMREL Dist-AIMS 1971

See, Hear And Feel Sounds C 15 MIN
3/4 INCH VIDEO CASSETTE P
Reviews the sounds of p, b, m, n and NG.
From The New Talking Shop Series.
Prod-BSPTV Dist-GPITVL 1978

See, Saw, Seems C 12 MIN
16MM FILM OPTICAL SOUND
Presents an experiment in animation in which the eye of the viewer travels deeper and deeper into each scene, finding new relationships and visual metaphors in what appears at first sight to be a simple scene.
Prod-VANBKS Dist-VANBKS 1967

Seed Cones And Reforestation C 23 MIN
16MM FILM OPTICAL SOUND J-C A
Illustrates the need for reforestation and shows the new methods used today to speed the development of new forests, including how seed cones are collected and stored, how seedlings are started, various planting techniques, selective cross-breeding and storing and grafting.
From The Man And The Forest Series.
LC NO. 76-702995
Prod-MMP Dist-MMP 1976

Seed Dispersal C 12 MIN
3/4 OR 1/2 INCH VIDEO CASSETTE I-H A
Shows the various methods plants use to get their seeds dispersed to continue and spread their species.
From The Many Worlds Of Nature Series.
Prod-SCRESC Dist-MTI

Seed Dispersal C 15 MIN
16MM FILM, 3/4 OR 1/2 IN VIDEO I-J
Discusses such topics as why flowers exist, why there are so many flowers on one plant, what grapes and milkweed have in common, what fruit really is, the complexity of design in nature, different ways seeds are dispersed and what a symbiotic relationship is.
Prod-MIS Dist-MIS 1981

Seed Dispersal (3rd Ed) C 11 MIN
16MM FILM, 3/4 OR 1/2 IN VIDEO P-I
Presents a visual report on different types of seedcoats and shows how external agents help each kind become dispersed.
Prod-EBEC Dist-EBEC 1971

Seed Dispersal (3rd Ed) (Spanish) C 11 MIN
16MM FILM, 3/4 OR 1/2 IN VIDEO P-I
Shows how the different types of seedcoats help each kind of seed become dispersed. Portrays seeds with wings, seeds with projections which hook onto passing animals, and seeds that explode.
Prod-EBEC Dist-EBEC

Seed Germination X 15 MIN
16MM FILM, 3/4 OR 1/2 IN VIDEO H
Explains how seeds serve plants in reproduction, distribution and as a device to survive unfavorable climatic periods. Shows how seed germination studies aid biologists in understanding growth, development and metabolism. Time-lapse photography shows germination process.
From The Biology Series. Unit 6 - Plant Classification And Physiology
Prod-EBF Dist-EBEC 1960

Seed Germination (Spanish) C 15 MIN
16MM FILM, 3/4 OR 1/2 IN VIDEO H
Explains how seeds serve plants in reproduction, distribution, and survival of unfavorable climatic periods. Illustrates the importance of seeds as a source of food for man.
From The Biology (Spanish) Series. Unit 6 - Plant Classification And Physiology
Prod-EBEC Dist-EBEC

Seed Plants C 15 MIN
2 INCH VIDEOTAPE K
Illustrates seed plants having the same component parts and similar life activities, but may differ in many ways.
From The Let's Go Sciencing, Unit III - Life Series.
Prod-DETPS Dist-GPITVL

Seed Plants B 30 MIN
2 INCH VIDEOTAPE J
See series title for descriptive statement.
From The Investigating The World Of Science, Unit 4 - Plants And Their Adaptations Series.
Prod-MPATI Dist-GPITVL

Seeding And Sodding C 29 MIN
3/4 INCH VIDEO CASSETTE
Explains turf construction, grading, soil types, fertilizing, sodding and moving. Instructs in proper equipment needed.
From The Grounds Maintenance Training Series.
Prod-UMITV Dist-UMITV 1978

Seedling Gun Aids Reforestation C 2 MIN
16MM FILM OPTICAL SOUND
Shows how a seedling gun cuts the tree harvest wait to 40 years.
Prod-ALLFP Dist-NSTA 1973

Seeds B 10 MIN
3/4 INCH VIDEO CASSETTE P
Shows the parts of a seed and discusses conditions under which seeds can or cannot begin to grow.
From The Two For Tomorrow Series.
Prod-BEOC Dist-GPITVL

Seeds C 15 MIN
3/4 OR 1/2 INCH VIDEO CASSETTE
Offers an introduction to the seed method of reproduction, seed structure, dispersal, dormancy and germination. Discusses the nature of the seed plants and the significance of the seed in their success as terrestrial organisms.
Prod-CBSC Dist-CBSC

Seeds C 15 MIN
2 INCH VIDEOTAPE K
Illustrates that green plants reproduce by means of a seed.
From The Let's Go Sciencing, Unit III - Life Series.
Prod-DETPS Dist-GPITVL

Seeds C 15 MIN
16MM FILM, 3/4 OR 1/2 IN VIDEO
Shows the baby plant within a seed. Uses time-lapse photography to show a lima bean growing and compares this growth with the growth of a baby chick.
From The Ripples Series.
LC NO. 73-702153
Prod-NITC Dist-AITECH

Seeds C 29 MIN
2 INCH VIDEOTAPE
See series title for descriptive statement.
From The Making Things Grow III Series.
Prod-WGBHTV Dist-PUBTEL

Seeds - Function C 20 MIN
2 INCH VIDEOTAPE I
See series title for descriptive statement.
From The Exploring With Science, Unit X - Plants Series.
Prod-MPATI Dist-GPITVL

Seeds - How They Germinate C 11 MIN
16MM FILM, 3/4 OR 1/2 IN VIDEO I-J
Shows the various factors in the success of seed plants including the system of seed dispersal and the structure and stages in the growth of the embroyo.
Prod-CORF Dist-CORF 1971

Seeds And Cutting C 15 MIN
2 INCH VIDEOTAPE P
Shows how green plants reproduce their own kind in several ways.
From The Science Is Searching Series.
Prod-DETPS Dist-GPITVL

Seeds And Nonseeds C 15 MIN
3/4 OR 1/2 INCH VIDEO CASSETTE P
See series title for descriptive statement.
From The Hands On, Grade 1 Series. Unit 3 - Classifying
Prod-VAOG Dist-AITECH Prodn-WHROTV 1975

Seeds And Plants C 20 MIN
3/4 INCH VIDEO CASSETTE T
Shows how one teacher conducts lessons with primary grade children in a manner that allows her to examine the reasoning patterns of children.
From The Science In The Elementary School - Life Science Series.
Prod-UWKY Dist-GPITVL 1980

Seeds And Weeds C 13 MIN
16MM FILM, 3/4 OR 1/2 IN VIDEO P-I
Shows the characteristics of a weed, showing how they spread their seeds and grow.
From The Scientific Fact And Fun Series.
Prod-GLDWER Dist-JOU 1981

Seeds Grow Into Plants (2nd Ed) C 7 MIN
16MM FILM, 3/4 OR 1/2 IN VIDEO P-I
Uses time-lapse photography in tracing the life cycle of a plant. Observes seed types, methods of dispersal and stages of development to explain the basic concepts involved in plant reproduction and growth.
Prod-CORF Dist-CORF 1978

Seeds Of Cure, The C 25 MIN
3/4 OR 1/2 INCH VIDEO CASSETTE
Shows polio vaccine pioneer Dr Jonas Salk and six UC San Diego medical students discussing views on man, medicine and medical research. Presents a look at Salk's cancer research at the Salk Institute in La Jolla, who also notes that 'Although historically mankind has sown the seeds of his own destruction, we also possess the potential for sowing the seeds of cure.'
Prod-TRAINX Dist-TRAINX

Seeds Of Destiny B 21 MIN
3/4 OR 1/2 INCH VIDEO CASSETTE
Portrays the plight of the millions of children left at the end of World War II without food, shelter or clothing. Shows children in 14 countries in bombed-out cities, refugee camps and other locations. Filmed by a team of Signal Corps cameramen under the sponsorship of the United Nations Relief and Rehabilitation Administration.
Prod-IHF Dist-IHF

Seeds Of Destiny B 21 MIN
16MM FILM, 3/4 OR 1/2 IN VIDEO
Documents the plight of victims of Nazi Germany's plan to subjugate the populations of adjacent countries by starvation. By the end of the war, millions of children were left without food, clothing or medical attention.
Prod-USAPS Dist-USNAC

Seeds Of Discovery C 28 MIN
3/4 INCH VIDEO CASSETTE
Presents a view of the NASA space program and discusses the ways in which this program can benefit man. Features James Franciscus. Issued in 1970 as a motion picture.
LC NO. 79-706710
Prod-NASA Dist-USNAC Prodn-MRC 1979

Seeds Of Hate C 20 MIN
16MM FILM, 3/4 OR 1/2 IN VIDEO H-C A
Documents how religious fanatics are feeding on the farmers' financial despair and advocating white Christian supremacy.
Prod-ABCTV Dist-MTI

Seeds Of Revolution C 28 MIN
16MM FILM, 3/4 OR 1/2 IN VIDEO
Examines the various sectors of Honduran society through interviews with corporate representatives, military officials, labor leaders, missionaries and peasants. Demonstrates the conflicting demands of agribusiness concerns and the new peasant self-help cooperatives.
Prod-ABCNEW Dist-ICARUS 1979

Seeds Of Survival C 27 MIN
16MM FILM OPTICAL SOUND I-C A
Depicts the life of average Iowa farming families in the 1840's and early 1900's. Shows how various agricultural and household chores were done before the development of modern farm machinery and household appliances.
LC NO. 77-700725
Prod-MOHWKA Dist-GMRC Prodn-VF 1976

Seeds Of Survival C 27 MIN
16MM FILM, 3/4 OR 1/2 IN VIDEO H-C A
Follows a Nebraska farm family and their farming neighbors through one year in their lives, from planting through harvest.
LC NO. 84-700724
Prod-ROBPAM Dist-FLMFR 1983

Seeds Of The Revolution - Colonial America - 1763-1775 X 24 MIN
16MM FILM OPTICAL SOUND I-C A
Discusses events leading up to the revolution, such as the Mayflower Compact, the Boston Tea Party, the Continental Congress, the Battles of Lexington, Concord and Bunker Hill, the siege of Boston and the Declaration of Independence.
From The Exploring - The Story Of America, Set 1 Series.
LC NO. FIA68-1050
Prod-NBCTV Dist-GRACUR 1968

Seeds Of Tomorrow C 58 MIN
3/4 OR 1/2 INCH VIDEO CASSETTE H-C A
Shows how the 'green revolution,' a plan based on advanced agricultural technologies to ensure food for the world, now threatens the supply of food for the future. Originally a NOVA television program.
From The Nova Series.
Prod-WGBHTV Dist-CORF 1985

Seeds Of Trust C 29 MIN
16MM FILM OPTICAL SOUND
Offers a view of childbirth as a family experience. Follows four families of diverse backgrounds through the experience of childbirth and records their responses to the event. Shows how support is given to the families by trained nurse-midwives who interact with the families with sensitivity and care.
LC NO. 79-700277
Prod-VICTFL Dist-VICTFL 1979

Seeds Of Wonder - The Story Of Papermaking At Hammermill C 27 MIN
16MM FILM OPTICAL SOUND

Explains the papermaking process beginning with the planting, cultivation and harvesting of trees, the turning of trees into pulp and the turning of pulp into paper.
Prod-HMPC Dist-HMPC 1981

Seeds Scatter C 15 MIN
16MM FILM, 3/4 OR 1/2 IN VIDEO P-I
Shows the remarkable ways in which seeds scatter. Shows seeds scattered by the wind, seeds with wings and barbed seeds which are carried by animals and man. Uses remarkable time-lapse photography which show the drying of seed pods, catapulted seeds and even seeds that bore into the ground.
LC NO. 84-706128
Prod-IFFB Dist-CF 1984

Seeds To Grow C 22 MIN
16MM FILM OPTICAL SOUND I-C A
Shows several new approaches to agricultural education and research now underway in East Africa under the sponsorship of the University of West Virginia.
LC NO. 74-701236
Prod-WVAU Dist-WVAU 1973

Seeds, Indeed C 15 MIN
16MM FILM OPTICAL SOUND K-I
Shows how Yoffy illustrates an animated story about Ivan the impatient gardener with several different types of seeds.
From The Fingermouse, Yoffy And Friends Series.
LC NO. 73-700445
Prod-BBCTV Dist-VEDO 1972

Seeds, The C 60 MIN
16MM FILM OPTICAL SOUND R
Follows Hugh Downs as he visits sites which recall the first 600 years of the Christian church. Includes scenes from Rome, Pompeii, Carthage and Istanbul. Compares the similarities between issues facing Christians then and now.
Prod-NBCTV Dist-CCNCC

Seeing B 20 MIN
16MM FILM OPTICAL SOUND C A
See series title for descriptive statement.
From The All That I Am Series.
Prod-MPATI Dist-NWUFLM

Seeing C 26 MIN
16MM FILM OPTICAL SOUND
Depicts a brief episode in the life of a 35-year-old woman who learns during a routine eye examination that she may have glaucoma.
LC NO. 79-701055
Prod-NSPB Dist-WSTGLC Prodn-FORMIL 1979

Seeing C 4 MIN
16MM FILM, 3/4 OR 1/2 IN VIDEO K-I
Introduces Danny, who doesn't mind his new glasses, when he learns how important eyes are.
From The Most Important Person - Senses Series.
Prod-EBEC Dist-EBEC 1972

Seeing Eye, The C 25 MIN
3/4 OR 1/2 INCH VIDEO CASSETTE
Explains how to safeguard sight in children and adults. Warns about the adult diseases of glaucoma and cataracts and the threats to children's sight of strabismus of amblyopia.
Prod-TRAINX Dist-TRAINX

Seeing God At Christmas C 18 MIN
16MM FILM OPTICAL SOUND
Shows a variety of Christmas customs as practiced in the Moravian community in Bethlehem, Pennsylvania.
From The Seeing God Series.
LC NO. 74-702513
Prod-FAMF Dist-FAMF 1974

Seeing God In Mountain Forests C 11 MIN
16MM FILM OPTICAL SOUND P
Portrays a family spending a day together in the mountain forests. Provides a setting in which children can gain some new appreciation for the wonder of God's creation. Presents popular children's songs including All Things Bright and Beautiful and Thank You.
Prod-FAMF Dist-FAMF

Seeing God In Signs Of Love C 10 MIN
16MM FILM OPTICAL SOUND P
Celebrates the joy of family relationships.
Prod-FAMF Dist-FAMF

Seeing God In The City C 14 MIN
16MM FILM OPTICAL SOUND
Shows a group of children journeying throughout the city and experiencing elements of God's world in an urban setting.
From The Seeing God Series.
LC NO. 74-700111
Prod-FAMF Dist-FAMF 1974

Seeing God—A Series

Prod-FAMF Dist-FAMF 1974

Seeing God At Christmas 18 MIN

Seeing Is Beautiful C 10 MIN
3/4 OR 1/2 INCH VIDEO CASSETTE
Describes the plastic lens implant procedure for treatment of a cataract.
Prod-WFP Dist-WFP

Seeing Is Believing C 10 MIN
16MM FILM OPTICAL SOUND
Spoofs media reports on such topics as incredible inventions and unbelievable world records. Suggests that what is seen is not necessarily to be believed.
LC NO. 81-700421
Prod-SIPOM Dist-SIPOM 1980

Seeing Is Believing C 14 MIN
16MM FILM, 3/4 OR 1/2 IN VIDEO J-C A
Illustrates how the human eye can be deceived. Provides examples of confusing activity, optical illusion and misdirection of movement to show how visual perception can be distorted.
Prod-NILLU Dist-MCFI 1977

Seeing Is Deceiving C 29 MIN
2 INCH VIDEOTAPE
See series title for descriptive statement.
From The Observing Eye Series.
Prod-WGBHTV Dist-PUBTEL

Seeing Like An Artist - Vegetables C 10 MIN
16MM FILM, 3/4 OR 1/2 IN VIDEO
Uses macrocinematography of a variety of vegetables in order to emphasize their different kinds of color, form, shape, texture and design.
Prod-MNDLIN Dist-SF 1973

Seeing Sound - The Process Of Captioning (Captioned) C 8 MIN
3/4 OR 1/2 INCH VIDEO CASSETTE S
Depicts videotape captioning process from transcription to final production. Notes educational benefits for deaf students.
Prod-GALCO Dist-GALCO 1980

Seeing The World B 24 MIN
16MM FILM SILENT
Depicts the Little Rascals gang travelling though Europe.
Prod-ROACH Dist-BHAWK 1927

Seeing Through Commercials - A Children's Guide To TV Advertising C 15 MIN
16MM FILM, 3/4 OR 1/2 IN VIDEO
Analyzes some typical television commercials for toys, candies and cereals and points out the techniques used to make these products seem bigger, better and more fun than they really are.
Prod-VISF Dist-BARR 1976

Seeing With Sound C 8 MIN
16MM FILM, 3/4 OR 1/2 IN VIDEO
Focuses on a technique for improving tunneling methods, which uses acoustical holography to 'see' through rock.
Prod-NSF Dist-AMEDFL 1975

Seeing With The Camera C 30 MIN
3/4 OR 1/2 INCH VIDEO CASSETTE
See series title for descriptive statement.
From The Photographic Vision - All About Photography Series.
Prod-COAST Dist-CDTEL

Seeking And Conserving Mineral Resources C 13 MIN
16MM FILM OPTICAL SOUND
Tells how scientists, conservationists and engineers have devised ways of extending the Earth's mineral resources while conserving its ecosystems.
Prod-ALLFP Dist-NSTA 1976

Seeking Community I - The North 1877-1900 C 29 MIN
2 INCH VIDEOTAPE
See series title for descriptive statement.
From The Black Experience Series.
Prod-WTTWTV Dist-PUBTEL

Seeking Community II - The South 1877-1900 C 29 MIN
2 INCH VIDEOTAPE
See series title for descriptive statement.
From The Black Experience Series.
Prod-WTTWTV Dist-PUBTEL

Seeking Community III - The Exodus C 29 MIN
2 INCH VIDEOTAPE
See series title for descriptive statement.
From The Black Experience Series.
Prod-WTTWTV Dist-PUBTEL

Seeking Community IV - African Exodus C 29 MIN
2 INCH VIDEOTAPE
See series title for descriptive statement.
From The Black Experience Series.
Prod-WTTWTV Dist-PUBTEL

Seeking Community V - The Migration C 29 MIN
2 INCH VIDEOTAPE
See series title for descriptive statement.
From The Black Experience Series.
Prod-WTTWTV Dist-PUBTEL

Seeking Help - But Where? C 30 MIN
3/4 OR 1/2 INCH VIDEO CASSETTE C A
Looks at four different approaches to therapy. Includes biological, behaviorist, intrapsychic and humanist. Provides guidelines for seeking mental health services.
From The Contemporary Health Issues Series. Lesson 3
Prod-SCCON Dist-CDTEL

Seeking New Laws B 58 MIN
16MM FILM - 3/4 IN VIDEO H-C A
Summarizes the state of our knowledge of the phyusical world. Discusses the art of guessing as a useful method for seeking new laws. Uses the development and analysis of some currently accepted laws as examples.
From The Feynman Lectures - The Character Of Physical Law Series.
Prod-EDC Dist-EDC Prodn-BBCTV 1965

Seeking The First Americans C 60 MIN
16MM FILM OPTICAL SOUND
Examines the theories of archaeologists who are searching for clues to the identity of the first people to reach North America between 11,000 and 50,000 years ago.
From The Odyssey Series.
LC NO. 81-700372
Prod-PBA Dist-DOCEDR 1980

Seeking The First Americans C 60 MIN
3/4 OR 1/2 INCH VIDEO CASSETTE
Examines the theories of archaeologists who are searching for clues to the identity of the first people to reach North America between 11,000 and 50,000 years ago.
From The Odyssey Series.
LC NO. 82-706434
Prod-PBA Dist-PBS 1980

Seeking Understanding And Acceptance - Try To Tell It Like It Is C 33 MIN
16MM FILM - 3/4 IN VIDEO IND
Presents Dr David K Berlo discussing the improvement of communication skills.
From The Two-Person Communication Series.
Prod-BNA Dist-BNA

Seen But Not Heard C 13 MIN
16MM FILM OPTICAL SOUND
Focuses on the rights of children as set down by the United Nations. Explores the child's point of view and what each child would like to change.
LC NO. 80-700840
Prod-NSWF Dist-TASCOR 1978

Seesaws, Slides And Swings B 15 MIN
2 INCH VIDEOTAPE I
Uses various levers to point up the importance of space-time comparisons. (Broadcast quality)
From The Let's Explore Science Series. No. 13
Prod-POPS Dist-GPITVL Prodn-KOAPTV

Segmental Pulmonary Resection C 21 MIN
16MM FILM OPTICAL SOUND PRO
Illustrates the technique of the removal of different individual and groups of pulmonary segments of both upper and lower lobes. Shows the important steps of segmental hilar dissection, treatment of the vascular and bronchial elements and the dissection of the intersegmental plane.
Prod-ACYDGD Dist-ACY 1950

Segmental Ureteral Achalasia C 14 MIN
16MM FILM OPTICAL SOUND
Illustrates Dr Victor A Politano's method of handling a large, dilated ureter secondary to ureteral achalasia. Shows that the achalasic segment is resected, the ureter is reduced by removing a longitudinal strip from its entire length and the distal end is reimplanted into the bladder by submucosal tunnel technique.
Prod-EATONL Dist-EATONL 1971

Segmentation - The Annelid Worms C 16 MIN
16MM FILM, 3/4 OR 1/2 IN VIDEO H
Animated drawings show the structure and functions of the nervous, digestive and reproductive systems of the earthworm. Shows the annelid worm's part in evolution. Illustrates the major classes of phylum annelida.
From The Biology Series. Unit 7 - Animal Classification And Physiology
Prod-EBF Dist-EBEC 1962

Segmentation - The Annelid Worms (Spanish) C 16 MIN
16MM FILM, 3/4 OR 1/2 IN VIDEO H
Describes the structure and functions of the segmented worm body systems and shows that the segmented annelid worm represents an important evolutionary development. Illustrates the major classes of the phylum Annelida.
From The Biology (Spanish) Series. Unit 7 - Animal Classification And Physiology
Prod-EBEC Dist-EBEC

Segregation In Public Education, Pre-1954 B 30 MIN
16MM FILM OPTICAL SOUND H-C A
Dr Vincent Browne discusses the public education of black children from the period before the Civil War to the period after World War II.
From The Black Heritage, Section 19 - The 1954 Decision - Precedents And Responses Series.
LC NO. 76-704101
Prod-WCBSTV Dist-HRAW 1969

Segregation Northern Style B 30 MIN
3/4 INCH VIDEO CASSETTE
Shows prejudice against blacks trying to buy homes in middle-income neighborhoods. Originally shown as a CBS television documentary.
Prod-ADL Dist-ADL 1965

Seguridad - Control De Perdidas Totales C 10 MIN
16MM FILM, 3/4 OR 1/2 IN VIDEO IND
A Spanish-language version of the motion picture Safety - Total Loss Control. Points out that industry must direct its accident prevention efforts toward all incidents which might lead to injury of employees. Notes that fire prevention, theft prevention, reduction in pollution and improvement in industrial health and hygiene are of particular importance to loss control.
Prod-IAPA Dist-IFB Prodn-CRAF 1972

Seikan Undersea Tunnel, Pt 1 C 32 MIN
16MM FILM OPTICAL SOUND
Presents a documentary of the work involved in constructing the longest undersea tunnel in the world, designed as a fundamental solution to link Honshu and Hokkaido by rail.
Prod-UNIJAP Dist-UNIJAP 1967

Seiko At School C 7 MIN
16MM FILM OPTICAL SOUND J-C A
Shows Seiko fingerpainting and playing with friends on the school playground.
From The Exploring Childhood Series.
LC NO. 76-703946
Prod-EDC Dist-EDC Prodn-FRIEDJ 1975

Seine Insanity C 10 MIN
16MM FILM OPTICAL SOUND
Looks at the Six Hours of Paris, where top boat racing drivers battle not only each other out also barge traffic and bridges as they roar up and down the Seine River in the heart of Paris.
Prod-MERMAR Dist-TELEFM

Seins Fiction 2 - Der Unbesiegbare (The Invincible) C 20 MIN
3/4 INCH VIDEO CASSETTE
A German language tape. Tells the story of science fiction hero Flash Gordon, using original black-and-white film footage, super-8 and video techniques. By Gusztav Hamos.
Prod-EAI Dist-EAI

Seismic Design And Base Isolation C 60 MIN
3/4 OR 1/2 INCH VIDEO CASSETTE C
Outlines design approach to ductile frames, emphasizing shear, joint design and column actions. Presents principles of base isolation for protecting structures from earthquakes and illustrates these by reference to bridge and building examples. Discusses development of mechanical energy dissipaters.
From The Basic Earthquake Engineering For Structural Engineers Series.
Prod-CSU Dist-AMCEE

Seismology - Moving Earth C 18 MIN
3/4 OR 1/2 INCH VIDEO CASSETTE H-C A
Explores the science of seismology, which is helping predict earthquake and volcanic activity.
Prod-UPI Dist-JOU

Seismos '83 C 15 MIN
3/4 OR 1/2 INCH VIDEO CASSETTE PRO
Recorded during the International Earthquake Conference in Los Angeles, shows a simulated demonstration of the city emergency plan in the simulated aftermath of an earthquake.
Prod-LACFD Dist-FILCOM

Seizure C 15 MIN
3/4 OR 1/2 INCH VIDEO CASSETTE
Deals with a chronic disease, characterized by convulsions and unconsciousness. Shows a strobe light on the faceplate.
Prod-KITCHN Dist-KITCHN

Seizure - The Medical Treatment And Social Problems Of Epilepsy B 48 MIN
3/4 INCH VIDEO CASSETTE
Explains the diagnostic and therapeutic treatment of epilepsy through a dramatized story of an epileptic veteran, the background of his condition and his treatment in a Veterans Administration Hospital. Describes the physiological basis of epilepsy, clinical manifestations of seizures and the socio-economic problems facing an epileptic.
Prod-USNAC Dist-USNAC 1972

Seizure - The Story Of Kathy Morris C 104 MIN
3/4 OR 1/2 INCH VIDEO CASSETTE H-C A
Tells of a young music student suddenly afflicted with a brain tumor, the brilliant neurosurgeon in whose hands her life is placed, and the anguish and struggle both patient and doctor must endure when the patient comes out of the operation unable to read or count. Stars Leonard Nimoy and Penelope Milford.
Prod-TIMLIF Dist-TIMLIF 1983

Seizures C 10 MIN
3/4 OR 1/2 INCH VIDEO CASSETTE P-I
Explains some of the signs that may precede a seizure, what it may feel like to have a seizure and what should be done for the person having a seizure.
From The Children's Medical Series.
Prod-HFDT Dist-MTI 1982

Sejour En France—A Series
16MM FILM, 3/4 OR 1/2 IN VIDEO
A French language videocassette series. Describes the adventures of Michele and Penny in Paris.
Prod-SEABEN Dist-IFB 1970

Arrivee En France 011 MIN
L'ile De La Cite 012 MIN
Le Marais 013 MIN
Le Musee Grevin 012 MIN
Un Hotel A Paris 011 MIN
Un Repas Chez Francis 011 MIN

Selamat Datang 'WELCOME TO INDONESIA' C 27 MIN
16MM FILM OPTICAL SOUND C A
Describes the contrasts of Indonesia, a nation of old kingdoms blending with the republic's modernization. Shows views of temples, scenery, dances and gold and silver handicrafts.
LC NO. FIA68-817
Prod-GARUDA Dist-MCDO Prodn-MCDO 1967

Selected Communication Tasks During The Trial C 50 MIN
3/4 OR 1/2 INCH VIDEO CASSETTE PRO
Explores special problems trial advocates face during voir dire, opening statements, direct and cross-examination and the closing argument. Gives suggestions for making a favorable impression during jury selection establishing credibility with the jury and persuading through effective communication.
From The Effective Communication In The Courtroom Series.
Prod-ABACPE Dist-ABACPE

Selected Issues In Using Expert Witnesses C 150 MIN
3/4 OR 1/2 INCH VIDEO CASSETTE PRO
Presents lectures on and demonstrations of direct and cross-examination techniques. Cosponsored by California Continuing Education of the Bar.
Prod-ALIABA Dist-ALIABA

Selected Issues In Using Expert Witnesses C 240 MIN
3/4 OR 1/2 INCH VIDEO CASSETTE PRO
Focuses on how to secure the right person as an expert witness, preparing the expert to testify, appproaching attorney work product issues and discovering the opponent's expert witness and information.
Prod-CCEB Dist-ABACPE

Selected Short Works B 15 MIN
3/4 OR 1/2 INCH VIDEO CASSETTE
Presents selected short works by Yugoslavian born video artist Ante Bozanich where he addresses personal helplessness, despair and loneliness.
Prod-EAI Dist-EAI

Selected Sonnets By Shakespeare C 40 MIN
3/4 OR 1/2 INCH VIDEO CASSETTE
Analyzes four examples of Shakespeare's sonnets including Sonnet 65, Sonnet 66, Sonnet 94 and Sonnet 127.
Prod-FOTH Dist-FOTH 1984

Selected Speeches Of Franklin Delano Roosevelt - Navy And Total Defense Day Address B 26 MIN
16MM FILM, 3/4 OR 1/2 IN VIDEO H A
Presents a critical speech given by Roosevelt on October 27, 1941, in which he revealed information about Nazi activities. Discusses the historical significance of the speech in light of the Nazi attacks on American ships in September and October 1941.
Prod-NA Dist-USNAC 1941

Selected Speeches Of Franklin Delano Roosevelt - State Of The Union Message B 42 MIN
16MM FILM, 3/4 OR 1/2 IN VIDEO H A
Presents a speech given by Roosevelt on January 6, 1942, one month after Pearl Harbor. Discusses the history of the Axis powers and their conquests in the 1930's, the monetary cost of the war for America, and the possibility of an ultimate victory against the Axis powers.
Prod-NA Dist-USNAC 1942

Selected Surgical Approaches To Testis, Bladder, And Prostatic Cancers C 38 MIN
16MM FILM OPTICAL SOUND
Shows surgery on the bladder and prostate, demonstrating the I-25 implant. Reviews past techniques and comments on developments in the future.
From The Visits In Urology Series.
LC NO. 79-700278
Prod-EATONL Dist-EATONL Prodn-AEGIS 1978

Selected Survey Of Decision-Making Procedures For Groups C 48 MIN
3/4 OR 1/2 INCH VIDEO CASSETTE
See series title for descriptive statement.
From The Decision Analysis Series.
Prod-MIOT Dist-MIOT

Selected Tutti Passages From The Symphonic Literature C 30 MIN
3/4 OR 1/2 INCH VIDEO CASSETTE J-H A
See series title for descriptive statement.
From The Cello Sounds Of Today Series.
Prod-IU Dist-IU 1984

Selected Works 1980 - The Cough, Secrets I'll Never Tell, The Shot Heard Round The World,... C 9 MIN
3/4 OR 1/2 INCH VIDEO CASSETTE
Complete title reads Selected Works 1980 - The Cough, Secrets I'll Never Tell, The Shot Heard Round The World, Rabbit Rabid Rawbit, This Video No Good. Pokes fun at everything from medical etiquette to prevalent truisms. Presented by Teddy Dibble and Peter Keenan.
Prod-ARTINC Dist-ARTINC

Selecting A Bare Root Tree C 7 MIN
3/4 INCH VIDEO CASSETTE
Demonstrates what to look for when buying a bare root tree from a nursery.
Prod-TUCPL Dist-GPITVL

Selecting A Citrus Tree C 7 MIN
3/4 INCH VIDEO CASSETTE
Discusses qualities of various kinds of citrus trees and shows how to choose a good tree from the nursery.
Prod-TUCPL Dist-GPITVL

Selecting A Computer And Setting Up Shop C 35 MIN
3/4 INCH VIDEO CASSETTE C A
See series title for descriptive statement.
From The Software Management For Small Computers Series.
LC NO. 81-706201
Prod-AMCEE Dist-AMCEE 1980

Selecting A Good Child Care Program C 26 MIN
3/4 OR 1/2 INCH VIDEO CASSETTE C A
Presents a specialist in early childhood education defining the characteristics of quality child care outside the home and compare the features of three types of child care including the nursery school, the day-care center and the day-care home.
From The Focus On Children Series.
LC NO. 81-707445
Prod-IU Dist-IU 1981

Selecting A Jury - A Critique C 60 MIN
3/4 INCH VIDEO CASSETTE PRO
Features a panel critiquing the performances of attorneys who have just completed a voir dire. Offers suggestions on analyzing and communicating with a panel of jurors.
From The Picking And Persuading A Jury Series. Program 2
LC NO. 81-706167
Prod-ABACPE Dist-ABACPE 1980

Selecting A Jury - A Demonstration C 150 MIN
3/4 INCH VIDEO CASSETTE PRO
Shows a demonstration voir dire presented by attorneys for both sides in a case involving a civil suit.
From The Picking And Persuading A Jury Series. Program 1
LC NO. 81-706166
Prod-ABACPE Dist-ABACPE 1980

Selecting A Pattern For A Coat C 29 MIN
2 INCH VIDEOTAPE
Features Mrs Ruth Hickman showing how to select a pattern for a coat.
From The Sewing Skills - Tailoring Series.
Prod-KRMATV Dist-PUBTEL

Selecting A Pet C 9 MIN
3/4 INCH VIDEO CASSETTE
Exhibits many common domestic pets and discusses their advantages and disadvantages.
Prod-TUCPL Dist-GPITVL

Selecting An Investigation C 15 MIN
3/4 OR 1/2 INCH VIDEO CASSETTE J
Provides ideas for research projects for science fairs.
From The Sci-Fair Series.
Prod-MAETEL Dist-GPITVL

Selecting And Buying Clothes C 13 MIN
2 INCH VIDEOTAPE
See series title for descriptive statement.
From The Living Better I Series.
Prod-MAETEL Dist-PUBTEL

Selecting And Handling Glassware C
3/4 OR 1/2 INCH VIDEO CASSETTE
See series title for descriptive statement.
From The Tableside Series.
Prod-CULINA Dist-CULINA

Selecting And Managing Projects C 30 MIN
3/4 OR 1/2 INCH VIDEO CASSETTE
See series title for descriptive statement.
From The Management For Engineers Series.
Prod-UKY Dist-SME

Selecting Appropriate Leadership Styles For Instructional Improvement C 33 MIN
3/4 OR 1/2 INCH VIDEO CASSETTE T
Designed to train educators to improve their leadership behavior through the situational leadership model which explains how to choose an appropriate leadership style based on the maturity of the followers. Features Dr Gordon Cawelti.
LC NO. 82-706448
Prod-AFSCD Dist-AFSCD 1978

Selecting DeltaVision Courses C 30 MIN
3/4 OR 1/2 INCH VIDEO CASSETTE
Focuses on the different types of courses offered through the DELTAK DeltaVision library. Discusses each type, video journals, skills courses, professional development products and computer-enhanced multimedia training products.
From The Using DELTAK Courses Series.
Prod-DELTAK Dist-DELTAK

Selecting Flowering Trees C 29 MIN
2 INCH VIDEOTAPE
Features Tom Lied describing the different types of flowering trees and suggesting what to look for and which might be best suited for particular types of yards.
From The Dig It Series.
Prod-WMVSTV Dist-PUBTEL

Selecting Fruit Trees C 29 MIN
2 INCH VIDEOTAPE
Features Tom Lied offering a close look at different types of fruit trees and giving special hints on how to care for them.
From The Dig It Series.
Prod-WMVSTV Dist-PUBTEL

Selecting Houseplants C 30 MIN
3/4 OR 1/2 INCH VIDEO CASSETTE
Discusses selecting houseplants to fit individual needs.
From The Even You Can Grow Houseplants Series.
Prod-WGTV Dist-MDCPB

Selecting Media C 19 MIN
16MM FILM OPTICAL SOUND
Highlights various equipment available to support classroom audiovisual presentations and training situations.
LC NO. 81-700636
Prod-USAF Dist-USNAC 1981

Selecting Patients For Treatment C 15 MIN
3/4 OR 1/2 INCH VIDEO CASSETTE
Gives reasons therapists resist making a diagnosis on a borderline patient. Discusses evaluating severity of pathology and deciding those likely to become psychotic during treatment.
From The Treatment Of The Borderline Patient Series.
Prod-HEMUL Dist-HEMUL

Selecting Related Objects B 15 MIN
2 INCH VIDEOTAPE P
See series title for descriptive statement.
From The Just Wondering Series.
Prod-EOPS Dist-GPITVL Prodn-KOACTV

Selecting Shade Trees C 29 MIN
2 INCH VIDEOTAPE
Features Tom Lied describing what shade trees can do for a yard and offering a careful and complete explanation of the different varieties of shade trees and how they are sold.
From The Dig It Series.
Prod-WMVSTV Dist-PUBTEL

Selecting The Best Alternative C 30 MIN
3/4 OR 1/2 INCH VIDEO CASSETTE

See series title for descriptive statement.
From The Decision Analysis By Kepner-Tregoe Series.
Prod-KEPTRG Dist-DELTAK

Selecting Toys for Disabled Children C 22 MIN
3/4 INCH VIDEOTAPE
Presents suggestions for parents and caregivers of developmentally impaired children of 0-24 months. Explains the need for stimulation and proper positioning for activities. Stresses the importance of play and use of appropriate selection of educational tools to enhance development. Available in American Sign Language format.
Prod-UNDMC Dist-UNDMC

Selection And Adaptation C 20 MIN
3/4 OR 1/2 INCH VIDEO CASSETTE
Studies plants in the desert and snails in the hedgerow and woodlands to show adaptation and natural selection at work.
From The Evolution Series.
Prod-FOTH Dist-FOTH 1984

Selection And Location Of Trees C 29 MIN
2 INCH VIDEOTAPE
Features Tom Lied offering ideas for turning driveways and parking areas into inviting and necessary parts of the landscape and looking at the kinds of trees which could be added. Provides tips on effective lighting.
From The Dig It Series.
Prod-WMVSTV Dist-PUBTEL

Selection And Use Of Materials C 30 MIN
3/4 OR 1/2 INCH VIDEO CASSETTE T
Discusses the selection and use of materials when teaching adult basic education students.
From The Basic Education - Teaching The Adult Series.
Prod-MDDE Dist-MDCPB

Selection And Use Of Wrapping Materials For Sterilization C 40 MIN
3/4 INCH VIDEO CASSETTE
Demonstrates techniques for wrapping medical supplies and instruments, discussing the selection of wrapping materials, the proper size and thickness of wrappers for various trays and instruments, and the folding and taping of the finished product.
LC NO. 79-707309
Prod-USVA Dist-USNAC 1976

Selection Interview, The - Choice Or Chance C 31 MIN
3/4 OR 1/2 INCH VIDEO CASSETTE
Shows how the selection interview should be run and how different the prospective employee looks when interviewed properly. Points out several common mistakes, such as failing to prepare for the interview, failing to draw the candidate out and get him/her talking freely and failing to come out with direct, probing questions.
Prod-VIDART Dist-VISUCP

Selection Interview, The - Screening Candidates With Leo F McManus C 38 MIN
3/4 OR 1/2 INCH VIDEO CASSETTE
Deals with hiring decisions, an important aspect of any manager's job. Works as a tool for the manager who makes or contributes to employment decisions, and presents proven methods for conducting screening interviews within the selection process. Includes a student manual.
Prod-HBCORP Dist-DELTAK

Selection Of Electrode, Gas, Cups And Filler Rod For Inert Gas Tungsten (TIG) (Spanish) C
3/4 OR 1/2 INCH VIDEO CASSETTE
See series title for descriptive statement.
From The MIG And TIG Welding (Spanish) Series.
Prod-VTRI Dist-VTRI

Selection Of Electrode, Gas, Cups And Filler Rod For Gas Tungsten Arc (Tig) Welding C 15 MIN
3/4 OR 1/2 INCH VIDEO CASSETTE
See series title for descriptive statement.
From The Welding III - TIG and MIG (Industry) Welding series.
Prod-CAMB Dist-CAMB

Selection Of Electrode, Gas, Cups, And Filler Rod For Inert Gas Tungsten Arc... C 15 MIN
3/4 OR 1/2 INCH VIDEO CASSETTE IND
Explains selection of electrode, gas, cups, and filler rod for inert gas tungsten arc welding (TIG).
From The Welding - MIG And TIG Welding Series.
Prod-ICSINT Dist-ICSINT

Selection Of Electrodes For Arc Welding C 15 MIN
3/4 OR 1/2 INCH VIDEO CASSETTE
See series title for descriptive statement.
From The Welding II - Basic Shielded Metal Arc Welding series.
Prod-CAMB Dist-CAMB

Selection Of Electrodes For Shielded Metal-Arc Welding C 15 MIN
3/4 OR 1/2 INCH VIDEO CASSETTE IND
See series title for descriptive statement.
From The Welding - Shielded Metal-Arc Welding Series.
Prod-ICSINT Dist-ICSINT

Selection Of Electrodes For Shielded Metal Arc-Welding (Spanish) C
3/4 OR 1/2 INCH VIDEO CASSETTE
See series title for descriptive statement.
From The Shielded Metal Arc Welding (Spanish) Series.
Prod-VTRI Dist-VTRI

Selection Of Fables, A C 15 MIN
3/4 OR 1/2 INCH VIDEO CASSETTE P
See series title for descriptive statement.
From The Magic Pages Series.
Prod-KLVXTV Dist-AITECH 1976

Selection Of Hardware/Software C 60 MIN
3/4 OR 1/2 INCH VIDEO CASSETTE IND
See series title for descriptive statement.
From The Microprocessor Fundamentals For Decision Makers Series.
Prod-NCSU Dist-AMCEE

Selection Of Wire Type And Diameter For (MIG) Welding C 15 MIN
3/4 OR 1/2 INCH VIDEO CASSETTE
See series title for descriptive statement.
From The Welding III - TIG and MIG (Industry) Welding series.
Prod-CAMB Dist-CAMB

Selection Of Your Horse C
1/2 IN VIDEO CASSETTE BETA/VHS
See series title for descriptive statement.
From The Captain Mark Phillips Horsemanship Training Series.
Prod-EQVDL Dist-EQVDL

Selection, Order, Emphasis B 30 MIN
2 INCH VIDEOTAPE J-H
From The Franklin To Frost Series.
Prod-GPITVL Dist-GPITVL

Selection, Order, Emphasis C 30 MIN
2 INCH VIDEOTAPE J-H
See series title for descriptive statement.
From The From Franklin To Frost - Introduction Series.
Prod-MPATI Dist-GPITVL

Selective Distal Splenorenal Shunt C 20 MIN
3/4 OR 1/2 INCH VIDEO CASSETTE
Describes the selective distal splenorenal shunt procedure developed by Dr W Dean Warren and presents the surgical procedure as a more successful alternative to the commonly practiced mesocaval shunt. Shows the actual surgical procedure.
LC NO. 80-706815
Prod-VAHSL Dist-USNAC 1980

Selective Esophageal Variceal Decompression By In Situ Distal Splenorenal Shunt C 32 MIN
16MM FILM OPTICAL SOUND PRO
Demonstrates a new approach to the problem of controlling bleeding esophageal varices in the cirrhotic minimizing the risk of progressive hepatic failure, prevalent following standard portacaval shunt.
Prod-ACYDGD Dist-ACY 1969

Selective Gene Expression C 30 MIN
3/4 OR 1/2 INCH VIDEO CASSETTE
Discusses the process by which certain genes become active during embryonic development and explores the process of regulation of these genes.
From The Developmental Biology Series.
Prod-NETCHE Dist-NETCHE 1971

Selective Practice - Centering On Line B 30 MIN
2 INCH VIDEOTAPE
From The Typewriting, Unit 6 - Skill Development Series.
Prod-GPITVL Dist-GPITVL

Selective Practice - Corrections B 30 MIN
2 INCH VIDEOTAPE
From The Typewriting, Unit 6 - Skill Development Series.
Prod-GPITVL Dist-GPITVL

Selective Practice - Insertions B 30 MIN
2 INCH VIDEOTAPE
From The Typewriting, Unit 6 - Skill Development Series.
Prod-GPITVL Dist-GPITVL

Selective Practice - Word Division, Pt 1 B 30 MIN
2 INCH VIDEOTAPE
From The Typewriting, Unit 4 - Skill Development Series.
Prod-GPITVL Dist-GPITVL

Selective Practice - Word Division, Pt 2 B 30 MIN
2 INCH VIDEOTAPE
From The Typewriting, Unit 4 - Skill Development Series.
Prod-GPITVL Dist-GPITVL

Selective Practive - Margin Bell B 30 MIN
2 INCH VIDEOTAPE
From The Typewriting, Unit 4 - Skill Development Series.
Prod-GPITVL Dist-GPITVL

Selective Renal Angiography C 10 MIN
16MM FILM OPTICAL SOUND
Demonstrates the technique of selective renal angiography in obtaining diagnostic information regarding lesions of the kidney. Uses animation and slow motion cineradiology to illustrate the author's technique for percutaneous femoral puncture, catheterization of the renal artery and injection of the contrast media.
LC NO. FIA66-61
Prod-EATONL Dist-EATONL Prodn-AVCORP 1965

Selective Vagotomy And Pyloroplasty C 34 MIN
3/4 OR 1/2 INCH VIDEO CASSETTE
See series title for descriptive statement.
From The Gastrointestinal Series.
Prod-SVL Dist-SVL

Selective Vagotomy, Antrectomy And Gastroduodenostomy C 25 MIN
16MM FILM OPTICAL SOUND PRO
Shows selective gastric vagotomy in detail upon two patients. Portrays the standard technique for antrectomy and gastroduodenal anastomosis. Depicts the Strauss maneuver for the difficult posterior penetrating duodenal ulcer.
Prod-ACYDGD Dist-ACY 1968

Self C 2 MIN
16MM FILM OPTICAL SOUND I-H A R
Explores the belief that each individual is an important statement made by God.
From The Meditation Series.
LC NO. 80-700747
Prod-IKONOG Dist-IKONOG 1974

Self And Many Others, The C
3/4 INCH VIDEO CASSETTE
Describes growth and development of a child from 46 to 47 months.
From The Growth And Development - A Chronicle Of Four Children Series. Series 10
Prod-JUETHO Dist-LIP

Self And Many Others, The - Gregory, 46 Months C 6 MIN
16MM FILM OPTICAL SOUND
See series title for descriptive statement.
From The Growth And Development - A Chronicle Of Four Children Series. Series 10
LC NO. 78-700691
Prod-JUETHO Dist-LIP Prodn-CONCOM 1976

Self And Many Others, The - Joseph, 47 Months C 6 MIN
16MM FILM OPTICAL SOUND
See series title for descriptive statement.
From The Growth And Development - A Chronicle Of Four Children Series. Series 10
LC NO. 78-700691
Prod-JUETHO Dist-LIP Prodn-CONCOM 1976

Self And Many Others, The - Melissa, 46 Months C 6 MIN
16MM FILM OPTICAL SOUND
See series title for descriptive statement.
From The Growth And Development - A Chronicle Of Four Children Series. Series 10
LC NO. 78-700691
Prod-JUETHO Dist-LIP Prodn-CONCOM 1976

Self And Many Others, The - Terra, 47 Months C 6 MIN
16MM FILM OPTICAL SOUND
See series title for descriptive statement.
From The Growth And Development - A Chronicle Of Four Children Series. Series 10
LC NO. 78-700691
Prod-JUETHO Dist-LIP Prodn-CONCOM 1976

Self Blood Glucose Monitoring C 17 MIN
16MM FILM - 3/4 IN VIDEO
Discusses the benefits of self defense glucose which includes greater flexibility of lifestyle, greater accuracy and better blood glucose control.
Prod-ADAS Dist-ORACLE

Self Confidence B 30 MIN
3/4 OR 1/2 INCH VIDEO CASSETTE
Increases self-confidence by means of subliminal suggestions.
Prod-ADVCAS Dist-ADVCAS

Self Control - Learning To CARE For Yourself C 29 MIN
16MM FILM OPTICAL SOUND C A
Preeents Dr Carl E Thoresen demonstrating a model for leading group discussions in helping persons apply self-control strategies in their own lives. Depicts a group of college-age students in a discussion led by Dr Thoresen.
LC NO. 76-702687
Prod-COUNF Dist-COUNF Prodn-SOREND 1976

Self Defense C 50 MIN
1/2 IN VIDEO CASSETTE BETA/VHS
Begins with self-defense techniques that can be used by the elderly, frail or untrained. Progresses to more advanced techniques.
Prod-VIPRO Dist-VIPRO

Self Defense With Steve Powell, Pt 1 - Self Defense For Men C 60 MIN
1/2 IN VIDEO CASSETTE BETA/VHS
Provides instruction in self defense skills for men. Includes exercises for home practice.
Prod-MOHOMV Dist-MOHOMV

Self Defense With Steve Powell, Pt 2 - Self Defense For Women C 60 MIN
1/2 IN VIDEO CASSETTE BETA/VHS
Provides instruction in self defense skills for women. Includes exercises for home practice.
Prod-MOHOMV Dist-MOHOMV

Self Discovery C 16 MIN
3/4 OR 1/2 INCH VIDEO CASSETTE
Shows a woman looking at her body, exploring her genitals and discovering areas of her body that give her pleasure.
From The Becoming Orgasmic - A Sexual Growth Program Series.
Prod-MMRC Dist-MMRC

Self Incorporated—A Series
J
Focuses on the problems that arise as a result of the physical, emotional and social changes experienced by adolescents.
Prod-AIT Dist-AITECH 1975

By Whose Rules (Systems And Self)	15 MIN
Changes (Physiological Changes)	15 MIN
Clique, The (Cliques)	15 MIN
Different Folks (Sex Role Identification)	15 MIN
Double Trouble (Family Adversity)	15 MIN
Down And Back (Failure And Disappointment)	15 MIN
Family Matters (What Is A Family)	15 MIN
Getting Closer (Boy-Girl Relationships)	15 MIN
My Friend (Ethnic-Racial Differences)	15 MIN

No Trespassing (Privacy) 15 MIN
Pressure Makes Perfect (Pressure To Achieve) 15 MIN
Trying Times (Making Decisions) 15 MIN
Two Sons (Family Communications) 15 MIN
What's Wrong With Jonathan (Everyday Pressures) 15 MIN
Who Wins (Morality) 15 MIN

Self Monitoring Of The Blood Glucose C 17 MIN
3/4 OR 1/2 INCH VIDEO CASSETTE PRO
Reviews the blood sugar curve of diabetics. Discusses the shortcomings of urine testing. Focuses on self monitoring.
Prod-MEDFAC Dist-MEDFAC 1982

Self Portrait C 29 MIN
3/4 INCH VIDEO CASSETTE
Demonstrates drawing a self portrait.
From The Artist At Work Series.
Prod-UMITV Dist-UMITV 1973

Self Propelled Cotton Stripper C 8 MIN
16MM FILM OPTICAL SOUND
Tells why the 707 and 707XTB Cotton Strippers are machines that are designed to handle the new varieties of high-yielding, storm-proof cotton.
Prod-ALLISC Dist-IDEALF

Self-Acceptance - Role Of The Significant Others B 30 MIN
16MM FILM - 3/4 IN VIDEO PRO
From The Mental Health Concepts For Nursing, Unit 2 - Self-Acceptance Series.
Prod-SREB Dist-GPITVL 1971

Self-Acceptance - The Individual B 30 MIN
16MM FILM - 3/4 IN VIDEO PRO
From The Mental Health Concepts For Nursing, Unit 2 - Self-Acceptance Series.
Prod-SREB Dist-GPITVL 1971

Self-Acceptance Training With Dick Olney, Pt I B 60 MIN
3/4 OR 1/2 INCH VIDEO CASSETTE
Shows a low-key approach to self-acceptance through individual analysis of thought process. Stresses ideas which will turn nervousness into excitement, help meet fears head on and bring about mental and verbal acceptance of one's self.
Prod-UWISC Dist-UWISC 1982

Self-Acceptance Training With Dick Olney, Pt II B 60 MIN
3/4 OR 1/2 INCH VIDEO CASSETTE
Continues discussion on self-acceptance approach. Stresses use of experience to teach about the fear of the unconscious and the fear of being afraid, the idea of emotional containment versus catharsis or repression and actively accepting one's feelings.
Prod-UWISC Dist-UWISC 1982

Self-Actualization As A Life-Long Phenomenon C 30 MIN
3/4 INCH VIDEO CASSETTE
See series title for descriptive statement.
From The Growing Old In Modern America Series.
Prod-UWASHP Dist-UWASHP

Self-Awareness C 30 MIN
3/4 OR 1/2 INCH VIDEO CASSETTE
Deals with self-awareness, the beginning of effective communication.
From The Couples Communication Skills Series.
Prod-NETCHE Dist-NETCHE 1975

Self-Awareness C 30 MIN
3/4 OR 1/2 INCH VIDEO CASSETTE T
See series title for descriptive statement.
From The Simple Gifts Series. No. 5
Prod-UWISC Dist-GPITVL 1977

Self-Awareness And The Prospective Parent C 29 MIN
3/4 OR 1/2 INCH VIDEO CASSETTE H-C A
Explains that many factors of heredity and environment affect how a person reacts to parental responsibilities.
From The Tomorrow's Families Series.
LC NO. 81-706051
Prod-MSDOE Dist-AITECH 1980

Self-Awareness/Increases Independence Group With Mentally Handicapped Adults C 21 MIN
3/4 OR 1/2 INCH VIDEO CASSETTE
Teaches the importance of making decisions. Uses a consensus vote in a group to facilitate the decision-making process.
Prod-LASSWC Dist-UWISC 1979

Self-Breast Examination C 8 MIN
3/4 OR 1/2 INCH VIDEO CASSETTE
Explains reasons for self-breast exam. Presents a step-by-step demonstration.
Prod-MEDFAC Dist-MEDFAC

Self-Care For Females C
3/4 OR 1/2 INCH VIDEO CASSETTE J-H
Presents a practical guide to developing good eating habits, selecting make-up and maintaining a practical wardrobe.
Prod-GA Dist-GA

Self-Care For Males C
3/4 OR 1/2 INCH VIDEO CASSETTE J-H
Presents information on everyday grooming aids and shows how to shave and how to care for nails, hair and scalp.
Prod-GA Dist-GA

Self-Chosen Activities, Pt 1 B 30 MIN
2 INCH VIDEOTAPE
See series title for descriptive statement.
From The Program Development In The Kindergarten Series.
Prod-GPITVL Dist-GPITVL

Self-Chosen Activities, Pt 2 B 30 MIN
2 INCH VIDEOTAPE
See series title for descriptive statement.
From The Program Development In The Kindergarten Series.
Prod-GPITVL Dist-GPITVL

Self-Concept C 30 MIN
3/4 OR 1/2 INCH VIDEO CASSETTE T
Discusses the importance of self-concept in an educational setting.
From The Interaction - Human Concerns In The Schools Series.
Prod-MDDE Dist-MDCPB

Self-Defense For Girls C 16 MIN
16MM FILM, 3/4 OR 1/2 IN VIDEO J-C
Uses dramatized episodes of threatened attack to introduce fundamental self-defense techniques and to prepare girls and women to meet attacks without panic.
Prod-BFA Dist-PHENIX 1969

Self-Defense For Women - A Positive Approach C 13 MIN
16MM FILM, 3/4 OR 1/2 IN VIDEO J-C A
Looks at karate experts Kim Fritz and George A Dillman teaching a class of female students how to defend themselves successfully. Stresses the importance of a positive self-image and positive body language to destroy the helpless woman image and discourage potential attackers.
Prod-FILMPA Dist-PHENIX 1979

Self-Development - The Key To Success C 11 MIN
3/4 OR 1/2 INCH VIDEO CASSETTE
Shows that supervisors, not their organizations, are primarily responsible for their own self-development.
From The New Supervisor Series. Module 5
Prod-RESEM Dist-RESEM

Self-Disclosure C 11 MIN
2 INCH VIDEOTAPE C A
Features a humanistic psychologist who, by analysis and examples, discusses the importance of self-disclosure in communication.
From The Interpersonal Competence, Unit 02 - Communication Series.
Prod-MVNE Dist-TELSTR 1973

Self-Examination For Oral Disease C 15 MIN
16MM FILM - 3/4 IN VIDEO
Demonstrates a self-examination procedure for detecting early signs of oral cancer.
LC NO. 80-706801
Prod-VADTC Dist-USNAC 1979

Self-Examination Of The Testes For Testicular Tumor C 10 MIN
16MM FILM OPTICAL SOUND
Presents a dramatization of an actual case history of a patient with a testicular tumor, emphasizing the importance of early diagnosis and demonstrating the correct procedure for self-examination.
LC NO. 75-702662
Prod-EATONL Dist-EATONL Prodn-AEGIS 1975

Self-Fulfillment - Become The Person You Want To Be C 50 MIN
3/4 OR 1/2 INCH VIDEO CASSETTE
Emphasizes the importance of recognizing and fulfilling one's potential. Shows young people in various careers, leisure activities and volunteer programs finding self-fulfillment.
LC NO. 81-706683
Prod-CHUMAN Dist-GA 1981

Self-Health C 23 MIN
3/4 OR 1/2 INCH VIDEO CASSETTE C A
Shows women sharing their experiences and learning how to do self-examinations of the breasts and vagina and the biomanual examination. Emphasizes what is normal for your own body.
Prod-MMRC Dist-MMRC

Self-Help Housing B 45 MIN
3/4 OR 1/2 INCH VIDEO CASSETTE
Describes a relatively new government assisted housing program and current issues facing the housing market, realtors and building and lending institutions. Deals with differences between rural and urban housing and with the organization of self-help housing.
Prod-UWISC Dist-UWISC 1980

Self-Identity / Sex Roles - I Only Want You To Be Happy C 16 MIN
16MM FILM, 3/4 OR 1/2 IN VIDEO J-H
Depicts the interaction of two sisters and their mother, all sharing conflicting points of view on the role of women.
From The Conflict And Awareness Series.
Prod-CRMP Dist-CRMP 1975

Self-Image C 19 MIN
3/4 OR 1/2 INCH VIDEO CASSETTE H
Tells how Denise learns that in order to be a successful job-hunter she must know who she is and what she wants.
From The Jobs - Seeking, Finding, Keeping Series.
Prod-MSDOE Dist-AITECH 1980

Self-Image C 30 MIN
3/4 OR 1/2 INCH VIDEO CASSETTE
Focuses on an enhanced self-image that can improve interpersonal relationship skills and unleash additional capabilities in creativity and productivity. Shows that this in turn makes for productivity.
From The High Performance Leadership Series.
Prod-PRODEV Dist-PRODEV

Self-Image C 30 MIN
3/4 OR 1/2 INCH VIDEO CASSETTE
See series title for descriptive statement.
From The High Performance Leadership Series.
Prod-VIDAI Dist-DELTAK

Self-Image Concepts In Selling, The C
3/4 OR 1/2 INCH VIDEO CASSETTE
Shows how to identify and organize self-image concepts in selling and shows how they can be enhanced and/or dealt with.
From The Strategies For Successful Selling Series. Module 3
Prod-AMA Dist-AMA

Self-Image Film, The - If Mirrors Could Speak C 12 MIN
16MM FILM, 3/4 OR 1/2 IN VIDEO P
Attempts to generate an interest in building a positive self-image by telling a story about three children in the same class whose negative behavior is changed when they have an opportunity to see themselves in a talking mirror.
Prod-SAIF Dist-BARR 1976

Self-Learning C 18 MIN
2 INCH VIDEOTAPE C A
Features a humanistic psychologist who, by analysis and examples, discusses self-learning.
From The Interpersonal Competence, Unit 05 - Learning Series.
Prod-MVNE Dist-TELSTR 1973

Self-Loving C 34 MIN
3/4 OR 1/2 INCH VIDEO CASSETTE C A
Offers a positive cross-cultural statement about female sexuality. Eleven women of heterosexual, bisexual and lesbian lifestyles share their early and later experiences, current patterns, use of vibrators, fantasies and orgasmic patterns.
Prod-NATSF Dist-MMRC

Self-Management Of Behavior C 33 MIN
16MM FILM, 3/4 OR 1/2 IN VIDEO C A
Deals with the self-management of behavior. Follows the evaluation of two behavior-problem children and the ensuing development of self-intervention behavior modification programs. Includes commentary by B F Skinner.
Prod-MEDIAG Dist-MEDIAG 1976

Self-Management Training Program, The C 27 MIN
3/4 OR 1/2 INCH VIDEO CASSETTE
Teaches specific coping skills needed to function successfully in a vocational setting. Deals with negative self-concepts, motivational difficulties, overreactions to external influences and negative emotionality.
Prod-RESPRC Dist-RESPRC

Self-Motivated Achiever, The C 28 MIN
16MM FILM - 3/4 IN VIDEO IND
Dr David C Mc Clelland, chairman of the department of social relations at Harvard University, discusses the problems of identifying individuals with a high need for achievement and how to deal with them when they are discovered in an organization.
From The Motivation And Productivity Series.
Prod-BNA Dist-BNA 1967

Self-Motivation In Selling—A Series
16MM FILM - 3/4 IN VIDEO
Presents Saul Gellerman who reveals the motivational dangers that threaten salespeople in different stages of their careers and shows how to deal with them.
Prod-BNA Dist-BNA

For Managers Only 015 MIN
Maintaining Your Motivation 020 MIN
Managing Your Motivation 020 MIN
Renewing Your Motivation 020 MIN

Self-Pleasuring C 5 MIN
3/4 OR 1/2 INCH VIDEO CASSETTE
Highlights the importance of being comfortable within oneself and feeling good about giving pleasure to oneself.
From The Mutuality Series.
Prod-MMRC Dist-MMRC

Self-Preservation In An Atomic Bomb Attack B 10 MIN
16MM FILM OPTICAL SOUND
Explains individual methods of self-preservation in the event of an A-bomb attack, describing methods of protection for air or underwater explosions. Shows the effects of the blast, heat and radiation.
Prod-USDD Dist-USNAC 1951

Self-Protection C 20 MIN
3/4 OR 1/2 INCH VIDEO CASSETTE J-C A
Uses a variety of situations to demonstrate sensible techniques for protecting oneself from assault and injury. Encourages the avoidance of panic and thinking of alternatives when a threatening situation arises on the street, at home or at school.
From The Safety Sense Series. Pt. 8
LC NO. 82-706076
Prod-WCVETV Dist-GPITVL 1981

Self-Protective Level (Section A), The C 28 MIN
3/4 OR 1/2 INCH VIDEO CASSETTE
See series title for descriptive statement.
From The Management By Responsibility Series.
Prod-TRAINS Dist-DELTAK

Self-Protective Level (Section B), The C 40 MIN
3/4 OR 1/2 INCH VIDEO CASSETTE
See series title for descriptive statement.
From The Management By Responsibility Series.
Prod-TRAINS Dist-DELTAK

Self-Reliance - Emerson's Philosophy C 30 MIN
2 INCH VIDEOTAPE J-H
See series title for descriptive statement.

From The From Franklin To Frost - Ralph Waldo Emerson Series.
Prod-MPATI Dist-GPITVL

Self-Scoring Examination - Brazelton Behavioral Assessment Scale B 23 MIN
3/4 INCH VIDEOTAPE
Shows an infant being subjected to the full set of stimuli called for by the Neonatal Scale. Contains no narration, but is intended to allow the viewer to assess the performance of the infant. Must be used with the accompanying score sheet.
From The Brazelton Neonatal Behavioral Assessment Scale Films Series.
Prod-EDC Dist-EDC

Self-Service C 11 MIN
16MM FILM - 1/2 IN VIDEO H-C A
Uses animation to show mosquitoes launching an epic attack on a sleeping man.
Prod-BOZETO Dist-TEXFLM 1979

Self-Understanding C 28 MIN
16MM FILM OPTICAL SOUND H A
Discusses self-analysis, the indoor sport of the twentieth century. Presents and interprets different views of man from Socrates to Freud.
From The Tangled World Series.
Prod-YALEDV Dist-YALEDV

Self-Understanding - Developing A Self-Concept B 30 MIN
16MM FILM OPTICAL SOUND PRO
Shows nursing students how a positive self-concept can help their abilities in caring for patients.
From The Mental Health Concepts For Nursing Series.
LC NO. 73-702634
Prod-SREB Dist-GPITVL 1971

Self-Understanding - Introduction To Series B 30 MIN
16MM FILM OPTICAL SOUND PRO
Helps nursing students understand the role played in nursing by an awareness of one's emotions and attitudes.
From The Mental Health Concepts For Nursing Series.
LC NO. 73-702633
Prod-SREB Dist-GPITVL 1971

Self-Understanding - Perception Of Reality B 30 MIN
16MM FILM OPTICAL SOUND PRO
Helps nursing students understand the role an accurate perception of reality plays in their abilities in treating patients.
From The Mental Health Concepts For Nursing Series.
LC NO. 73-702637
Prod-SREB Dist-GPITVL 1971

Self-Understanding - The Autonomous Self B 30 MIN
16MM FILM OPTICAL SOUND PRO
Helps nursing students understand how the development of an autonomous self can help their abilities in treating patients.
From The Mental Health Concepts For Nursing Series.
LC NO. 73-702638
Prod-SREB Dist-GPITVL 1971

Self-Understanding - The Key To Mastery Of Environment B 30 MIN
16MM FILM OPTICAL SOUND PRO
Helps nursing students understand how self-understanding can prove the key to a mastery of the environment and a help for their abilities in treating patients.
From The Mental Health Concepts For Nursing Series.
LC NO. 73-702639
Prod-SREB Dist-GPITVL 1971

Self-Understanding - The Process Of Becoming B 30 MIN
16MM FILM OPTICAL SOUND PRO
Helps nursing students understand the process of becoming can help their abilities in treating patients.
From The Mental Health Concepts For Nursing Series.
LC NO. 73-702635
Prod-SREB Dist-GPITVL 1971

Self-Understanding - Toward An Integrated Personality B 30 MIN
16MM FILM OPTICAL SOUND PRO
Helps nursing students understand how the development of an integrated personality can help their abilities in treating patients.
From The Mental Health Concepts For Nursing Series.
LC NO. 73-702636
Prod-SREB Dist-GPITVL 1971

Selfish Giant B 14 MIN
16MM FILM, 3/4 OR 1/2 IN VIDEO P-I
Based on the short story by Oscar Wilde in which a giant who shuts his garden to prevent children from playing in it realizes that in his selfishness he has shut out happiness and sunshine.
Prod-UGA Dist-WWS 1963

Selfish Giant, The C 27 MIN
16MM FILM, 3/4 OR 1/2 IN VIDEO J-H
Uses animatiom to tell the story of a selfish giant who builds a wall around his castle garden to keep children from playing there. Explains that for being so nasty, the giant is tormented by the personifications of snow, frost, wind and hail, which finally force the giant into accepting the children when they sneak back to the garden and make it bloom.
Prod-READER Dist-PFP 1972

Selfish Giant, The (Finnish) C 27 MIN
16MM FILM, 3/4 OR 1/2 IN VIDEO P-I
A Finnish language version of the animated film, The Selfish Giant, an interpretation of Oscar Wilde's fairy tale. Relates the story of a giant who builds a wall around his garden to keep out the neighboring children and soon finds himself living in perpetual winter. Teaches an important lesson about loving and sharing.
Prod-READER Dist-PFP

Selfish Giant, The (French) C 27 MIN
16MM FILM, 3/4 OR 1/2 IN VIDEO P-I
A French language version of the animated film, The Selfish Giant, an interpretation of Oscar Wilde's fairy tale. Relates the story of a giant who builds a wall around his garden to keep out the neighboring children, and soon finds himself living in perpetual winter. Teaches an important lesson about loving and sharing.
Prod-READER Dist-PFP

Selfish Giant, The (Spanish) C 27 MIN
16MM FILM, 3/4 OR 1/2 IN VIDEO P-I
A Spanish language version of the animated film, The Selfish Giant, an interpretation of Oscar Wilde's fairy tale. Relates the story of a giant who builds a wall around his garden to keep out the neighboring children and soon finds himself living in perpetual winter. Teaches an important lesson about loving and sharing.
Prod-READER Dist-PFP

Selfish Giant, The (Swedish) C 27 MIN
16MM FILM, 3/4 OR 1/2 IN VIDEO P-I
A Swedish language version of the animated film, The Selfish Giant, an interpretation of Oscar Wilde's fairy tale. Relates the story of a giant who builds a wall around his garden to keep out the neighboring children and soon finds himself living in perpetual winter. Teaches an important lesson about loving and sharing.
Prod-READER Dist-PFP

Sell Benefits - The Key To Creative Selling C 9 MIN
16MM FILM, 3/4 OR 1/2 IN VIDEO H-C A
Focuses on creative selling. Illustrates the difference between the features of a product or service and the benefits which prospective purchasers may derive from them.
Prod-SALENG Dist-SALENG 1977

Sell Like An Ace - Live Like A King C 28 MIN
16MM FILM, 3/4 OR 1/2 IN VIDEO
Features a sales consultant explaining how to improve selling performance and close more sales. Based on the book Sell Like An Ace - Live Like A King by John Wolfe.
Prod-DARTNL Dist-DARTNL Prodn-CAPRLO 1974

Sell Safety C 10 MIN
16MM FILM OPTICAL SOUND
See series title for descriptive statement.
From The Safety Management Series.
LC NO. 74-705598
Prod-NSC Dist-NSC

Sellin Of Jamie Thomas, The, Pt 2 C 24 MIN
3/4 OR 1/2 INCH VIDEO CASSETTE
Tells of a slave family's escape through the underground railway and their settlement in a Quaker town.
From The Young People's Specials Series.
Prod-MULTPP Dist-MULTPP

Sellin' Of Jamie Thomas, The, Pt 1 C 24 MIN
3/4 OR 1/2 INCH VIDEO CASSETTE
Tells the story of a slave family's breaking apart due to a slave auction and the hardships they endure in order to reunite.
From The Young People's Specials Series.
Prod-MULTPP Dist-MULTPP

Selling C 15 MIN
16MM FILM, 3/4 OR 1/2 IN VIDEO A
Presents the five basic steps that experts generally agree are essential to success in selling. Emphasizes the importance of relating the product or service to the customer's need.
From The Communications And Selling Program Series.
Prod-NEM Dist-NEM

Selling (Spanish) C 15 MIN
16MM FILM, 3/4 OR 1/2 IN VIDEO
Illustrates the five primary steps a salesperson must know to lead a customer to a purchase. Uses three typical sales situations as examples.
From The Communications And Selling Program (Spanish) Series.
Prod-NEM Dist-NEM

Selling - The Discovery Of Willie C 45 MIN
3/4 OR 1/2 INCH VIDEO CASSETTE
Presents a lesson that establishes the universality of selling problems and the personal solutions that must be utilized to achieve objectives.
From The Introduction To Marketing, A Lecture Series.
Prod-IVCH Dist-IVCH

Selling - The Power Of Confidence C 20 MIN
16MM FILM, 3/4 OR 1/2 IN VIDEO H-C A
Shows how a salesperson can often be his or her own worst enemy. Follows one sales representative as he works through his fears toward becoming a more confident, effective and successful salesperson.
LC NO. 81-706214
Prod-CRMP Dist-MGHT 1981

Selling A Song C 29 MIN
3/4 INCH VIDEO CASSETTE
Focuses on the modern business of music.
From The Music Shop Series.
Prod-UMITV Dist-UMITV 1974

Selling As A Profession C 2 MIN
16MM FILM, 3/4 OR 1/2 IN VIDEO C A
Offers a tribute to the sales team which is the heartbeat of the corporation.

From The Sales Meeting Films Series.
Prod-MBACC Dist-MTI 1983

Selling By Telephone C 13 MIN
16MM FILM, 3/4 OR 1/2 IN VIDEO
Presents a series of vignettes demonstrating the techniques of telephone selling.
From The Communications And Selling Program Series.
Prod-NEM Dist-NEM 1980

Selling By Telephone (Spanish) C 13 MIN
16MM FILM, 3/4 OR 1/2 IN VIDEO
Demonstrates how to use the telephone effectively as a sales tool.
From The Customer Service, Courtesy And Selling Programs (Spanish) Series.
Prod-NEM Dist-NEM

Selling In Department Stores C 64 MIN
3/4 OR 1/2 INCH VIDEO CASSETTE
Covers several aspects of department store selling. Includes how to approach a customer and determine customer needs. Discusses how to present merchandise and how to make the sale.
Prod-DOUVIS Dist-TRASS

Selling In The 80's C 20 MIN
16MM FILM, 3/4 OR 1/2 IN VIDEO H-C A
Explains different attitudes towards selling and shows how a sales career can be both psychologically and economically rewarding.
Prod-CRMP Dist-CRMP 1981

Selling Jewelry C 101 MIN
3/4 OR 1/2 INCH VIDEO CASSETTE
Focuses on several aspects of selling jewelry in a store. Discusses how to approach a customer and how to determine customer needs. Covers how to present merchandise and how to make a sale.
Prod-DOUVIS Dist-TRASS

Selling Menswear C 92 MIN
3/4 OR 1/2 INCH VIDEO CASSETTE
Discusses several aspects of selling menswear. Shows how to approach a customer and how to determine customer needs. Shows how to present merchandise and how to make a sale.
Prod-DOUVIS Dist-TRASS

Selling Movies On Television C 55 MIN
1/2 IN VIDEO CASSETTE BETA/VHS
Presents 69 television commercials advertising various films.
Prod-UNKNWN Dist-VIDIM

Selling Of Local TV News C 29 MIN
3/4 OR 1/2 INCH VIDEO CASSETTE
Looks at the hotly contested ratings war in Boston's local news market. Both excesses and improvements were noted but the question remained 'Does it have to be this way?'
From The Inside Story Series.
Prod-PBS Dist-PBS 1981

Selling Of Terri Gibbs, The C 30 MIN
3/4 OR 1/2 INCH VIDEO CASSETTE C A
Delves into the marketing campaign which sought to make it possible for Terri Gibbs, a successful country and western singer, to cross over into the pop field.
From The Enterprise II Series.
LC NO. 83-706196
Prod-WGBHTV Dist-LCOA 1983

Selling Of The Pentagon, The C 52 MIN
16MM FILM, 3/4 OR 1/2 IN VIDEO H-C A
Focuses on the Pentagon's public relations activities, which cost millions of dollars annually.
Prod-CBSNEW Dist-CAROUF

Selling On The Telephone C 20 MIN
3/4 OR 1/2 INCH VIDEO CASSETTE A
Demonstrates ways of selling by telephone. Includes planning, sales methods, and closing a call.
From The Reach Out To Help Someone Series.
Prod-AMEDIA Dist-AMEDIA

Selling Our Products C 20 MIN
3/4 INCH VIDEO CASSETTE I
Investigates a large retail department store in order to illustrate buyer and market, wholesaling and retailing, advertising and display, and selling and the consumer.
From The Exploring Our Nation Series.
Prod-KRMATV Dist-GPITVL 1975

Selling Out C 30 MIN
16MM FILM OPTICAL SOUND
Shows Prince Edward Island, Canada's smallest and most picturesque province. Features Vernon Macgoughan, an elderly retired farmer, and Robert Hogg, a local auctioneer. Shows the sale by public auction of the farm and personal possessions of Vernon Macgoughan. Focuses on the gradual loss of the human, cultural and material resources of the Island.
Prod-JWSKIT Dist-COPFC

Selling Out C 35 MIN
16MM FILM OPTICAL SOUND
Dramatizes a farmer's last day at his ancestral home on Canada's Prince Edward Island. Examines some of the economic implications of the loss of the farmer's home and explores the personal implications of the loss for the farmer himself.
LC NO. 74-703468
Prod-UNPRO Dist-UNPRO 1972

Selling Power Every Hour C 15 MIN
3/4 OR 1/2 INCH VIDEO CASSETTE IND
Shows how point-of-purchase materials, lighting and case schematics can increase selling power. Discusses importance of service, even in a self-service store.
Prod-NLSAMB Dist-NLSAMB

Selling Quality To Management C 32 MIN
3/4 OR 1/2 INCH VIDEO CASSETTE
Describes several justifications for an increased management commitment to quality, including the threat of product liability.
From The Quality Planning Series.
Prod-MIOT Dist-MIOT

Selling Strategies - Steps To Sale C
3/4 OR 1/2 INCH VIDEO CASSETTE
Discusses idea that success is based on determining the right time, place and person in the right sequence and applying the appropriate strategy. Deals with the organizational aspects of selling. Illustrates twelve sales strategies.
From The Making Of A Salesman Series. Session 7
Prod-PRODEV Dist-PRODEV

Selling Techniques C 15 MIN
3/4 OR 1/2 INCH VIDEO CASSETTE
See series title for descriptive statement.
From The Consumer Education Series.
Prod-MAETEL Dist-CAMB

Selling To The Buyer's Needs C 28 MIN
16MM FILM - 3/4 IN VIDEO
Presents Dr Jack Schiff who shows how buyers give clues as to their real needs as opposed to their apparent needs. Features simulated sales situations which illustrate how clues are given, what they mean and what the salesperson should look for. Shows how to recognize prospect behavior patterns and tailor presentations to meet dominant prospect needs.
Prod-BNA Dist-BNA

Selling To Tough Customers C 23 MIN
16MM FILM, 3/4 OR 1/2 IN VIDEO H-C A
Distinguishes four hard-to-sell customer types and explains how to deal with them. Introduces The Complainer, The Know-It-All, The Indecisive Type, and The Unresponsive.
LC NO. 81-706216
Prod-CRMP Dist-CRMP 1981

Selling To Tough Customers (Spanish) C 20 MIN
16MM FILM, 3/4 OR 1/2 IN VIDEO H-C A
Demonstrates how sales can be made despite customer reluctance.
Prod-CRMP Dist-MGHT 1981

Selling Wine And Liquor C 10 MIN
16MM FILM, 3/4 OR 1/2 IN VIDEO J-C A
Encourages wine and liquor salesmanship for all waiters and waitresses. Demonstrates suggestive selling and gives instructions for keeping guests happy while enlarging size of check and tip. Includes a complete training experience from cocktails and champagne to dinner wines, dessert wines and liqueurs, showing basic rules for the wine service of each.
From The Professional Food Preparation And Service Program Series.
LC NO. 74-700219
Prod-NEM Dist-NEM 1972

Selling Wine And Liquor (Spanish) C 10 MIN
16MM FILM, 3/4 OR 1/2 IN VIDEO J A
Demonstrates suggestions for the selling of wine and liquor. Discusses serving techniques, from cocktails and champagne to dinner wines, dessert wines and liqueurs.
From The Professional Food Preparation And Service Program (Spanish) Series.
Prod-NEM Dist-NEM 1972

Selling Womenswear C 88 MIN
3/4 OR 1/2 INCH VIDEO CASSETTE
Examines several aspects of selling womenswear. Includes how to approach a customer and determine customer needs. Discusses how to present merchandise and how to make the sale.
Prod-DOUVIS Dist-TRASS

Selling Your Home C 30 MIN
3/4 OR 1/2 INCH VIDEO CASSETTE C A
Offers guidelines for selling a home, from setting the price to making the house more saleable. Explores alternatives for handling potential tax liabilities.
From The Personal Finance Series. Lesson 12
Prod-SCCON Dist-CDTEL

Selman's Justice C 12 MIN
16MM FILM OPTICAL SOUND
Tells how Marshal T J Selman and his deputy ride after his daughter's killer.
LC NO. 76-703804
Prod-CONCRU Dist-CONCRU 1976

Semantics And Communication C 47 MIN
3/4 OR 1/2 INCH VIDEO CASSETTE
Describes how words can be used or misused in promotion, advertising and selling.
From The Introduction To Marketing, A Lecture Series.
Prod-IVCH Dist-IVCH

Semantics And Syntax C 168 MIN
3/4 OR 1/2 INCH VIDEO CASSETTE
Defines the area of 'semantics and syntax' and clarifies the relationship between this and other aspects of child language development.
From The Meeting The Communication Needs Of The Severely/Profoundly Handicapped 1981 Series.
Prod-PUAVC Dist-PUAVC

Semester Review, Pt 1 C 15 MIN
3/4 OR 1/2 INCH VIDEO CASSETTE P-I
See series title for descriptive statement.
From The Ready, Sing Series.
Prod-ARKETV Dist-AITECH 1979

Semester Review, Pt 2 C 14 MIN
3/4 OR 1/2 INCH VIDEO CASSETTE P-I
See series title for descriptive statement.
From The Ready, Sing Series.
Prod-ARKETV Dist-AITECH 1979

Semi-Circular Canals, The C
3/4 OR 1/2 INCH VIDEO CASSETTE
Refers to the portion of the human ear, the cochlea, which regulates balance.
From The Red Tape Series.
Prod-EAI Dist-EAI

Semi-Direct Products B
16MM FILM OPTICAL SOUND
Presents the group theoretic ideas that lead to the general semi-direct product construction.
Prod-OPENU Dist-OPENU

Semi-Finished Steel C 8 MIN
16MM FILM OPTICAL SOUND H-C A
See series title for descriptive statement.
From The Making, Shaping And Treating Steel Series.
Prod-USSC Dist-USSC

Semi-Immediate Anterior Fixed Partial Denture With Reverse Pin Facing—A Series
PRO
Discusses esthetics and techniques of assembling semi-immediate anterior fixed partial dentures with reverse pin facing.
Prod-USVA Dist-USNAC 1978

Assembly Of Bridge And Delivery To Patient 13 MIN

Semi-Immediate Anterior Fixed Partial Denture With Reverse Pin Facing - Pontic Preparation... C 11 MIN
3/4 OR 1/2 INCH VIDEO CASSETTE
Shows the labial and gingival adaptation, essential for a harmonious relationship with the adjacent teeth and physiologic esthetic contact with ridge tissues.
Prod-VADTC Dist-AMDA 1969

Semi-Immediate Anterior Fixed Partial Denture With Reverse Pin Facing - Preparation Of... C 10 MIN
3/4 OR 1/2 INCH VIDEO CASSETTE
Shows and describes the procedures necessary to convert a denture tooth into a reverse pin pontic.
Prod-VADTC Dist-AMDA 1969

Semi-Immediate Anterior Fixed Partial Denture With Reverse Pin Facing - Assembly Of Bridge... C 13 MIN
3/4 OR 1/2 INCH VIDEO CASSETTE
Shows that the proper relationship of the retainers and pontics to the investing tissues is a most important esthetic and physiological consideration in any fixed prosthesis and demonstrates a direct and indirect assembly and finishing procedure to gain optimal appearance and function.
Prod-VADTC Dist-AMDA 1969

Semi-Immediate Anterior Fixed Partial Denture With Reverse Pin Facing - Impression... C 14 MIN
3/4 OR 1/2 INCH VIDEO CASSETTE
Depicts the methodology of securing impressions for a fixed prosthesis using mercaptan rubber following gingival retention, the procedures incident to producing accurate stone dies and development of the wax patterns for three-quarter type retainers.
Prod-VADTC Dist-AMDA 1969

Semi-Vowel Rule, The C 15 MIN
16MM FILM, 3/4 OR 1/2 IN VIDEO P-I
Uses animation, live action and a variety of commonly used words in order to show how the consonants L and R, sometimes called semi-vowels, have a special effect on the sound of single vowels in words.
From The Reading Skill, Set 3 Series.
Prod-GLDWER Dist-JOU 1974

Semiautomatic And Hand Molding Of Intricate Parts B 16 MIN
16MM FILM OPTICAL SOUND
Shows how to mold a part with undercuts, mold a part with complicated shape and assemble and disassemble a hand mold.
LC NO. FIE52-298
Prod-USOE Dist-USNAC 1945

Semiconductor Lasers C 40 MIN
3/4 OR 1/2 INCH VIDEO CASSETTE C
Discusses P-N junction laser structures, threshold conditions for lasing, effects of field confinement, optical mode characteristics, and power and efficiency relationships.
From The Integrated Optics Series.
Prod-UDEL Dist-UDEL

Semiconductor Memories - Dynamic, Prom memories C
3/4 OR 1/2 INCH VIDEO CASSETTE
See series title for descriptive statement.
From The Digital Techniques Series.
Prod-HTHZEN Dist-HTHZEN

Semiconductor Memories - Memory Basics C
3/4 OR 1/2 INCH VIDEO CASSETTE
See series title for descriptive statement.
From The Digital Techniques Series.
Prod-HTHZEN Dist-HTHZEN

Semiconductor Memories - READ, WRITE Memories. C
3/4 OR 1/2 INCH VIDEO CASSETTE
See series title for descriptive statement.
From The Digital Techniques Series.
Prod-HTHZEN Dist-HTHZEN

Semiconductor Memories 'Dynamic/PROM Memories' C
3/4 OR 1/2 INCH VIDEO CASSETTE
See series title for descriptive statement.
From The Digital Techniques Video Training Course Series.
Prod-VTRI Dist-VTRI

Semiconductor Memories 'Memory Basics' C
3/4 OR 1/2 INCH VIDEO CASSETTE
See series title for descriptive statement.
From The Digital Techniques Video Training Course Series.
Prod-VTRI Dist-VTRI

Semiconductor Memories 'Read/Write Memories' C
3/4 OR 1/2 INCH VIDEO CASSETTE
See series title for descriptive statement.
From The Digital Techniques Video Training Course Series.
Prod-VTRI Dist-VTRI

Semiconductor Memories Course—A Series
IND
Develops an understanding of the benefits of advanced and rapidly changing technology. Covers available functions, economics, design reliability and applications of semiconductor memories.
Prod-TXINLC Dist-TXINLC

Fixed Program And Sequentially Accessed
Fixed Program Semiconductor Storage Design 60 MIN
High Speed Random Access Storage Design 60 MIN
Memory Functions And Economics 60 MIN
MOS Random Access Semiconductor Storage Design 60 MIN
Random Access Memory Applications, Pt 1 60 MIN
Random Access Memory Applications, Pt 2 60 MIN
Random Access Memory Applications, Pt 3 60 MIN
Reliability Of Semiconductor Memories 60 MIN
Semiconductor Technology Arsenal For Storage 60 MIN
Sequentially Accessed Semiconductor Storage 60 MIN

Semiconductor Memory Devices C 30 MIN
3/4 OR 1/2 INCH VIDEO CASSETTE IND
Includes array of a memory chip, decoding scheme, address field and memory locations, static RAM, organization and operation, microprocessor memory interface signals, and block diagram of complete memory system.
From The Microcomputer Memory Design Series.
Prod-COLOSU Dist-COLOSU

Semiconductor Memory Driver Applications C 30 MIN
3/4 OR 1/2 INCH VIDEO CASSETTE PRO
Describes interface drivers for TTL and MOS memories as well as CMOS logic from TTL and ECL logic levels and discusses specific applications. Stresses difference between an interface with p-channel and n-channel MOS.
From The Linear And Interface Circuits, Part II - Interface Integrated Circuits Series.
Prod-TXINLC Dist-TXINLC

Semiconductor Technology Arsenal For Storage Elements C 60 MIN
1 INCH VIDEOTAPE IND
Reviews storage-element design objectives, bipolar and mos storage cells.
From The Semiconductor Memories Course Series. No. 2
Prod-TXINLC Dist-TXINLC

Seminar And Role-Playing Strategy, The B 30 MIN
16MM FILM OPTICAL SOUND C A
Illustrates the principles and techniques for conducting seminar and role playing episodes.
From The Nursing - Where Are You Going, How Will You Get There Series.
LC NO. 74-700180
Prod-NTCN Dist-NTCN 1971

Seminar For Progress B 14 MIN
16MM FILM OPTICAL SOUND
Shows the first Seminar of Afro-Asian Rural Development where delegates from Afro-Asian countries exchanged views, discussed national development and visited different levels of operation rooms, land development schemes and cottage industries in Kuala Trengganu, Malaysia.
Prod-FILEM Dist-PMFMUN 1967

Seminole Indians C 11 MIN
16MM FILM, 3/4 OR 1/2 IN VIDEO I-H
Documents the lives of Seminole Indians living in the Florida Everglades. Shows their open-sided houses with raised floors which offer protection against floods and snakes. Includes scenes of women creating souvenirs for tourists, doing washing and sewing, while the men hunt, fish and skin the frogs they will sell.
Prod-UMINN Dist-IFB Prodn-WEBALB 1951

Semiotics Of The Kitchen B 8 MIN
3/4 OR 1/2 INCH VIDEO CASSETTE
Features a woman explaining the use of a variety of kitchen tools. Contains irony.
Prod-KITCHN Dist-KITCHN

Semiprecision And Precision Layout C 15 MIN
3/4 OR 1/2 INCH VIDEO CASSETTE IND
Tells how to identify tools for semiprecision and precision layout and how to set up and perform a semiprecision layout and a precision layout.
From The Introduction To Machine Technology, Module 1 Series.
Prod-LEIKID Dist-LEIKID

Senator Sam Ervin, Jr - The Constitution—A Series
J-H
Prod-CHILBE Dist-COUNFI

Bill Of Rights, The 12 MIN
Congress, The 12 MIN
Constitution In The 21st Century, The 12 MIN
Delegates And Events Of The Constitutional 12 MIN
First Amendment, The 12 MIN
Framing Of The Constitution, The 12 MIN
Historical Origins Of The Constitution 12 MIN
Judiciary, The 12 MIN
Presidency, The 12 MIN
Separation Of Powers, The 12 MIN

Send Someone Happiness C 15 MIN
3/4 OR 1/2 INCH VIDEO CASSETTE P
Combines looking, listening, talking, writing and reading to help establish the link between oral and written language. Presents the traditional Christmas song We Wish You A Merry Christmas.
From The I Want To Read Series.
Prod-LACOS Dist-GPITVL 1976

Send-Receive I / Send Receive II C 50 MIN
3/4 OR 1/2 INCH VIDEO CASSETTE
Presented by Liza Bear and Keith Sonnier. Deals with communications technology.
Prod-ARTINC Dist-ARTINC

Sending Clear Messages C 29 MIN
2 INCH VIDEOTAPE C A
Features a humanistic psychologist who, by analysis and examples, discusses how to communicate in a manner that can be easily comprehended.
From The Interpersonal Competence, Unit 02 - Communication Series.
Prod-MVNE Dist-TELSTR 1973

Seneca Glass C 24 MIN
16MM FILM - 3/4 IN VIDEO A
Recaptures the production of early hand-blown Seneca glassware in Morgantown, West Virginia.
LC NO. 79-706158
Prod-USNPS Dist-USNAC 1979

Senior Center Programming C 30 MIN
3/4 INCH VIDEO CASSETTE
See series title for descriptive statement.
From The Growing Old In Modern America Series.
Prod-UWASHP Dist-UWASHP

Senior Executive Service, The C 30 MIN
3/4 INCH VIDEO CASSETTE
Explains the legal provisions governing the federal senior executive service under the system created by the Civil Service Reform Act.
From The Launching Civil Service Reform Series.
LC NO. 79-706273
Prod-USOPMA Dist-USNAC 1978

Senior Olympics 1980 C 10 MIN
3/4 OR 1/2 INCH VIDEO CASSETTE
Highlights events from the first Maryland Senior Olympics. Emphasizes the positive effects that physical activity has for older adults.
Prod-BCPL Dist-LVN

Senior Power And How To Use It C 19 MIN
16MM FILM OPTICAL SOUND
Points out practical ways in which older people can deter robbers both at home and on the streets. Illustrates how to foil purse snatchers, muggers, prowlers and obscene phone callers by using common sense rather than muscles or weapons.
From The Urban Crisis Series.
LC NO. 76-700422
Prod-BROSEB Dist-BROSEB 1975

Seniority And Discrimination C 26 MIN
16MM FILM OPTICAL SOUND
Deals with a black employee who requests an inter-company transfer but is turned down because he lacks experience. States the employee's position that he should have the job to make up for past discrimination. Reveals how an impartial arbitrator decides the case.
Prod-AARA Dist-AARA 1977

Seniority Vs Ability - A Promotion Grievance C 29 MIN
16MM FILM OPTICAL SOUND
Relates the story of a claims examiner who claims that he was denied a promotion on the grounds that he lacks advanced education. States the employee's position that the job does not require more than a high school education and that in any event, his seniority rights were violated when management encouraged a junior employee to pursue courses of study that would qualify her for advancement. Shows how an impartial arbiter decided the case.
Prod-AARA Dist-AARA 1978

Seniors Smile, The C 14 MIN
3/4 OR 1/2 INCH VIDEO CASSETTE PRO
Creates an awareness of the importance of daily oral health procedures for both dependent patients and those able to care for themselves. Shows examples of serious oral health conditions resulting from oral neglect and nutritional deficiencies.
Prod-AMDA Dist-AMDA 1976

Sensate Focus, Pt 1 C 11 MIN
3/4 OR 1/2 INCH VIDEO CASSETTE
Shows a couple modeling the initial phase of the sensate focus exercises. Shows each partner taking turns giving and getting nongenital sensual touching.
From The EDCOA Sexual Counseling Series.
Prod-MMRC Dist-MMRC

Sensate Focus, Pt 2 C 11 MIN
3/4 OR 1/2 INCH VIDEO CASSETTE
Continues the process in part one. Each partner teaches the other by means of direct physical guidance. Emphasizes nongenital touching.
From The EDCOA Sexual Counseling series.
Prod-MMRC Dist-MMRC

Sensate Focus, Pt 3 C 11 MIN
3/4 OR 1/2 INCH VIDEO CASSETTE
Shows each partner tactilely exploring the other's genitals under the direct physical supervision of the partner being stimulated.
From The EDCOA Sexual Counseling Series.
Prod-MMRC Dist-MMRC

Sensate Focus, Pt 4 C 6 MIN
3/4 OR 1/2 INCH VIDEO CASSETTE
Explains the 'silent vagina' form of sensate focus exercise which consists of intravaginal penile containment without any active thrusting.
From The EDCOA Sexual Counseling Series.
Prod-MMRC Dist-MMRC

Sensational Baby, The - Newborn Sensory Development, Pt 1 - The Fetus And The Newborn C 20 MIN
3/4 OR 1/2 INCH VIDEO CASSETTE PRO
Explores fetal reactions to a variety of sensory stimuli. Presented in terms of what parents actually experience during pregnancy.
Prod-POLYMR Dist-AMCOG

Sensational Baby, The - Newborn Sensory Development, Pt 2 - The First Week To Four... C 20 MIN
3/4 OR 1/2 INCH VIDEO CASSETTE
Deals with the newborn's sensory skills and ways parents and care givers can tailor their behavior to an infant's level of readiness.
Prod-POLYMR Dist-POLYMR

Sensational Five, The - The Inside Story Of Your Senses C 15 MIN
3/4 OR 1/2 INCH VIDEO CASSETTE P-I
Presents Slim Goodbody who uses models to show how the eye, ear, nose, mouth and skin work with the brain to keep a person in touch with the world. Looks at the deep senses like hunger and the muscle sense.
From The Inside Story With Slim Goodbody Series.
Prod-GBCTP Dist-AITECH Prodn-WETN 1981

Sensationalism Caused By The 19th Century Waltz And Serge Diaghilev's Productions C 30 MIN
3/4 OR 1/2 INCH VIDEO CASSETTE
See series title for descriptive statement.
From The Shaping Today With Yesterday Series.
Prod-ARCVID Dist-ARCVID

Sense Amplifiers C 30 MIN
3/4 OR 1/2 INCH VIDEO CASSETTE PRO
Establishes basic requirements and defines characteristics. Discusses system applications and performance variations for a core memory and MOS memory system. Gives direction to similar applications.
From The Linear And Interface Circuits, Part II - Interface Integrated Circuits Series.
Prod-TXINLC Dist-TXINLC

Sense And Nonsense With Linear Equations B
16MM FILM OPTICAL SOUND
Emphasizes that the formulation of a problem by a system of linear equations can suffer from ill-conditioning and therefore needs care. Reviews various methods for solving a system of linear equations and indicates that on the grounds of accuracy and efficiency the Guass elimination method looks like the best candidate.
Prod-OPENU Dist-OPENU

Sense And The Shape, The C 30 MIN
3/4 OR 1/2 INCH VIDEO CASSETTE
Examines the imagery and shape of Shakespeare, and explains balance and interance, Shakespeare's own word for the deliberate and insistent repetition of a word or phrase. Features Ronald Watkins, Shakespearean actor and director.
From The Actor And Shakespeare Series.
Prod-NETCHE Dist-NETCHE 1971

Sense In The Sun C 14 MIN
16MM FILM, 3/4 OR 1/2 IN VIDEO H-C A
Features Farrah Fawcett, Cancer Society Chairperson for Women Against Cancer, filmed on the beach and warning against sunburn and, over the long term, possible skin cancer. Uses TV spot format.
Prod-AMCS Dist-AMCS 1982

Sense Of Balance C 29 MIN
2 INCH VIDEOTAPE
See series title for descriptive statement.
From The Observing Eye Series.
Prod-WGBHTV Dist-PUBTEL

Sense Of Balance, A C 27 MIN
16MM FILM OPTICAL SOUND I-H A
Focuses on the experience of two disabled boys, one who suffered a cerebral hemorrhage and another with cerebral palsy, as they participate in a camping program in Minnesota.
LC NO. 82-700322
Prod-HALLM Dist-IMAGER 1982

Sense Of Color, A C 29 MIN
3/4 OR 1/2 INCH VIDEO CASSETTE
Features Mrs Ascher teaching the importance of color in relation to size, shape and placement in arrangement.
From The Flower Show Series.
Prod-MDCPB Dist-MDCPB

Sense Of Community, A C 34 MIN
16MM FILM OPTICAL SOUND
Presents an overview of activities of affiliated members of the National Community Education Association, telling what consitutes effective community education programs and describing their impact on the entire community.
LC NO. 75-700313
Prod-MOTTCF Dist-NCEA Prodn-VISION 1974

Sense Of Direction, A C 20 MIN
3/4 OR 1/2 INCH VIDEO CASSETTE
Shows how a serviceman is helped through his personal crisis by a team from the Red Cross' armed forces and veterans team.
Prod-AMRC Dist-AMRC 1976

Sense Of Hope, A C 13 MIN
16MM FILM - 3/4 IN VIDEO J-C A
Shows how a young leukemia patient copes with the disease.
LC NO. 83-706726
Prod-METROM Dist-LEUSA Prodn-HMS 1983

Sense Of Humor - Past And Present C 25 MIN
3/4 OR 1/2 INCH VIDEO CASSETTE J-C A
Deals with the question of whether comics have to have a special understanding of people in order to be funny.
Prod-SIRS Dist-SIRS

Sense Of Humus, A C 28 MIN
16MM FILM, 3/4 OR 1/2 IN VIDEO J-C A
Focuses on the organic farming movement in Canada today by interviewing farmers whose methods vary somewhat, but who all believe in keeping the soil healthy by natural methods to produce healthy crops.
LC NO. 82-707179
Prod-NFBC Dist-BULFRG 1977

Sense Of Joy, A C 15 MIN
16MM FILM, 3/4 OR 1/2 IN VIDEO I
Shows the joy which may be found in familiar things and in the surprises of everyday life. Presents Chuck and his sister Jean who take two different routes to the beach - she, eager to enjoy the water, goes directly while he wanders leisurely looking at the girls.
From The Inside-Out Series.
LC NO. 73-702447
Prod-NITC Dist-AITECH 1973

Sense Of Loss, A C
1/2 IN VIDEO CASSETTE BETA/VHS
Presents an insightful documentary look at the raging conflict in Northern Ireland.
Prod-GA Dist-GA

Sense Of Music, A C 28 MIN
16MM FILM, 3/4 OR 1/2 IN VIDEO P-C A
Shows that a good music education is an essential part of any child's overall learning techniques.
Prod-RHOMBS Dist-BULFRG

Sense Of Place, A C 55 MIN
2 INCH VIDEOTAPE
Explains that environmental and esthetic concerns in the township of East Hampton in Long Island, New York, are being threatened by rampant commercial interests.
Prod-WLIWTV Dist-PUBTEL

Sense Of Pride, A - Hamilton Heights C 15 MIN
16MM FILM OPTICAL SOUND
Documents the restoration of a neighborhood in Harlem. Focuses on the efforts of one man to bring about the change.
Prod-BLKFMF Dist-BLKFMF

Sense Of Privilege, A C 28 MIN
16MM FILM, 3/4 OR 1/2 IN VIDEO J-C A
Offers a plea for the preservation of the Alaskan frontier.
Prod-CAROUF Dist-CAROUF

Sense Of Purpose, A C 14 MIN
16MM FILM, 3/4 OR 1/2 IN VIDEO J-C A
Tells how basketball superstar Hector Bloom, indifferent to the forms and rhetoric of success, contemplates his future with little expectation of finding happiness and meaning.
From The Searching For Values - A Film Anthology Series.
Prod-LCOA Dist-LCOA 1972

Sense Of Responsibiity - How It Grows C
3/4 OR 1/2 INCH VIDEO CASSETTE A
Shows teachers and parents how to encourage responsible attitudes in elementary school children.
From The Vital Link Series.
Prod-EDCC Dist-EDCC

Sense Of Responsibility C 3 MIN
16MM FILM, 3/4 OR 1/2 IN VIDEO A
Offers a humorous story which demonstrates that safety on the job is everyone's personal responsibility.
Prod-SALENG Dist-SALENG

Sense Of Responsibility, A C 3 MIN
16MM FILM, 3/4 OR 1/2 IN VIDEO I-C
Uses animation to raise questions about individual responsibility. Shows how a careless mine worker starts a chain reaction of accidents which ultimately brings about the destruction of the entire country.
Prod-BFA Dist-PHENIX 1972

Sense Of The City X 27 MIN
16MM FILM OPTICAL SOUND
Explores the impressions of American poets in a visual tour of New York City, including such writers as Hart Crane, John Dos Passos, Edna St Vincent Millay, John Updike, E E Cummings, Thomas Wolfe and Walt Whitman.
From The Eye On New York Series.
LC NO. FIA66-842
Prod-WCBSTV Dist-CBSF 1966

Sense Of Touch, A C 7 MIN
3/4 OR 1/2 INCH VIDEO CASSETTE K-P S
Shows how to use powers of observation to identify and compare a variety of textures, and in doing so learn to touch, smell and taste using the eyes and ears. Explains that if we stretch the use of our senses, we can gain more information.
From The Visual Literacy Series.
Prod-NFBC Dist-MOKIN 1984

Sense Of Tragedy, A C 15 MIN
16MM FILM OPTICAL SOUND H
Shows how the play affects the student as a tragedy and how Macbeth is led inevitably by a chain of cause and effect to suffering and death.
From The Artistry Of Shakespeare - The Drama And Language Of Macbeth Series.
Prod-SINGER Dist-SVE 1968

Sense Organs And Their Sensitivity - Pt 2 C 46 MIN
3/4 OR 1/2 INCH VIDEO CASSETTE PRO
Illustrates and describes the traveling wave in the cochlea. Discusses various functions of the ear, comparing other animals to man.
Prod-HOUSEI Dist-HOUSEI

Sense Organs And Their Sensitivity, Pt 1 C 40 MIN
3/4 OR 1/2 INCH VIDEO CASSETTE PRO
Discusses the measurements of sensory thresholds, variations and contrasts of the various senses, and comparisons of visual touch and hearing perception. Uses art and history to illustrate the talk. Examines and discusses all the senses.
Prod-HOUSEI Dist-HOUSEI

Sense Perception (2nd Ed) C 28 MIN
16MM FILM, 3/4 OR 1/2 IN VIDEO J-C A R
Examines the senses of sight, hearing, touch, taste and smell in terms of structure and function. Presents demonstrations of inverted vision and odors made 'VISIBLE.' Shows that perception actually takes place in the brain, not in the sense organs. Points out how limited our senses are through demonstrations with 'SILENT' ultrasonic sound.
Prod-MIS Dist-MIS 1968

Sensei C 12 MIN
16MM FILM OPTICAL SOUND
Examines the Karate Kata using a simple story to emphasize the development of the spirit through rigorous physical training.
LC NO. 75-703229
Prod-USC Dist-USC 1966

Sensei - Master Teacher C 22 MIN
16MM FILM OPTICAL SOUND J-C A
Presents Manju Inque, a master Japanese potter, who demonstrates the Korean tradition, four hundred years old in Japan. Shows the throwing of porcelain, and the shaping and carving of a large jar.
LC NO. 72-713857
Prod-PSU Dist-PSUPCR 1971

Senses - Do You Remember C 20 MIN
3/4 OR 1/2 INCH VIDEO CASSETTE I
Introduces a game to aid in exploring the senses of taste, hearing, smell, sight and touch.
From The Creative Dramatics Series.
Prod-NEWITV Dist-AITECH 1977

Senses - Do You Remember (Teacher) C 30 MIN
3/4 OR 1/2 INCH VIDEO CASSETTE T
Demonstrtes sensory exercises and the use of sensory recall as a classroom tool in language arts and social studies.
From The Creative Dramatics (Teacher) Series.
Prod-NEWITV Dist-AITECH 1977

Senses And Perception, Links To The Outside World, The C 18 MIN
16MM FILM, 3/4 OR 1/2 IN VIDEO I
Shows differences in the process of sensory perception in higher animals and in man. Emphasizes that the senses are an animal's link to its environment and are necessary to its survival.
Prod-EBEC Dist-EBEC 1975

Senses Of Man, The C 18 MIN
16MM FILM, 3/4 OR 1/2 IN VIDEO H-C A
Reveals how external stimuli--light, sound, odor, touch and taste--are converted into nerve impulses by sense receptors. Discusses sense receptors which are stimulated by inner organs. An animated film.
From The Human Physiology Series.
LC NO. 80-707069
Prod-IU Dist-IU 1965

Senses, The C 10 MIN
16MM FILM, 3/4 OR 1/2 IN VIDEO K-I
Points out that hearing, seeing, tasting, smelling and touching are senses that help animals to know their world.
Prod-SIGMA Dist-FILCOM 1967

Senses, The C 15 MIN
3/4 OR 1/2 INCH VIDEO CASSETTE P
Urges children to pay attention to their senses. Explains eye care and eye safety rules and shows a blind person substituting other senses for sight. Explains the danger of loud noise. Talks about smell and taste and shows touch testing.
From The Well, Well, Well With Slim Goodbody Series.
Prod-AITECH Dist-AITECH

Senses, The C 29 MIN
3/4 INCH VIDEO CASSETTE C A
Provides students with understanding of importance of senses to an animal's survival. Introduces how senses function in humans.
From The Introducing Biology Series. Program 21
Prod-COAST Dist-CDTEL

Senses, The - Eyes And Ears C 26 MIN
3/4 OR 1/2 INCH VIDEO CASSETTE
Discusses the eyes and the ears. Shows a young reckless driver careening down a road, viewing the events from inside his eye where the image of the potential crash sight is pictured. Looks inside the ear, showing how the linked bones vibrate to a sound, and presents a computer graphic sequence showing how the eye focuses on an image.
From The Living Body - An Introduction To Human Biology Series.
Prod-FOTH Dist-FOTH 1985

Senses, The - Skin Deep C 26 MIN
3/4 OR 1/2 INCH VIDEO CASSETTE
Looks at the sense receptors that depend on contact with the immediate world, including taste buds, touch sensors and olfactory cells. Points out that these receptors lie in the skin, which also senses heat, pain and pressure.
From The Living Body - An Introduction To Human Biology Series.
Prod-FOTH Dist-FOTH 1985

Sensitive, The C 29 MIN
2 INCH VIDEOTAPE
Features Dr Puryear who looks at persons who are especially attuned to the psychic and whose powers of ESP far surpass those of the average individual.
From The Who Is Man Series.
Prod-WHROTV Dist-PUBTEL

Sensitivity Analysis, Review C 54 MIN
3/4 OR 1/2 INCH VIDEO CASSETTE
See series title for descriptive statement.
From The Decision Analysis Series.
Prod-MIOT Dist-MIOT

Sensitivity To The Disabled C 29 MIN
3/4 OR 1/2 INCH VIDEO CASSETTE
Gives suggestions on how library staff can better serve the those with learning, visual or physical limitations.
Prod-HCPL Dist-LVN

Sensitometry C 29 MIN
3/4 OR 1/2 INCH VIDEO CASSETTE C A
From The Automatic Film Processor Quality Control Series.
Prod-BCAMRT Dist-TEF

Sensor And Its Characteristics, The C 30 MIN
3/4 OR 1/2 INCH VIDEO CASSETTE PRO
Discusses the sensor, its structure, design objectives and tradeoffs for the diode or transistor configurations, and its characteristics to aid in sensor application.
From The Optoelectronics, Part I - Optoelectronic Emitters, Sensors And Couplers Series.
Prod-TXINLC Dist-TXINLC

Sensor Applications C 30 MIN
3/4 OR 1/2 INCH VIDEO CASSETTE PRO
Highlights sensor use for specific applications by categorizing effects of mounting tolerances, apertures, overlap, and size of openings in the transmission media.
From The Optoelectronics, Part I - Optoelectronic Emitters, Sensors And Couplers Series.
Prod-TXINLC Dist-TXINLC

Sensorineural Hearing Impairment - Patient Management C 56 MIN
3/4 OR 1/2 INCH VIDEO CASSETTE PRO
Presents a discussion of the management of otologic patients with sensorineural hearing impairment, including the use of a hearing aid and other communication devices.
Prod-HOUSEI Dist-HOUSEI

Sensory Conduction Studies Median Nerve C 10 MIN
16MM FILM OPTICAL SOUND
Demonstrates the antidromic and orthodromic techniques for recording the evoked potentials for digital sensory nerves.
LC NO. 74-705603
Prod-USPHS Dist-USNAC

Sensory Deprivation C 15 MIN
16MM FILM OPTICAL SOUND
Describes problems and anxiety-provoking situations of patients in isolation and explores the feelings of the nurses who deal with these patients.
From The The Patient In Isolation Series.
LC NO. 79-712970
Prod-TRNAID Dist-TRNAID 1969

Sensory Deprivation And Controlled Sensory Stimulation C 29 MIN
3/4 INCH VIDEO CASSETTE C A
Discusses effects of prolonged isolation from sensory input. Uses excerpts from Antarctica diary of Richard Byrd to show these effects.
From The Understanding Human Behavior - An Introduction To Psychology Series. Lesson 9
Prod-COAST Dist-CDTEL

Sensory Integration - Clinical Observations Of Normal Children To Accompnay The SCSIT, Pt 2 C 41 MIN
3/4 OR 1/2 INCH VIDEO CASSETTE
Shows Schilder's Arm Extension Test, Prone extension, Inhibition of the tonic neck reflex, Supine flexion and Equilibrium responses (sitting on a ball, walking on a balance beam).
Prod-BU Dist-BU

Sensory Integration - Clinical Observations Of Normal Children To Accompany The SCSIT, Pt 1 C 42 MIN
3/4 OR 1/2 INCH VIDEO CASSETTE
Presents visual tracking and convergence, ramp movement of the arms, Diadokokinesis, thumb finger touch, jumping, hopping and skipping.
Prod-BU Dist-BU

Sensory Integration In The Medford School System B 12 MIN
3/4 OR 1/2 INCH VIDEO CASSETTE
Demonstrates sensory-integrative therapy with a ten-year-old boy with learning disabilities, including a review of relevant embryology.
Prod-BU Dist-BU

Sensory Integration Problems In The Adult Wendy B 55 MIN
3/4 OR 1/2 INCH VIDEO CASSETTE
Presents an interview with a 24-year-old learning disabled woman who has severe sensory integration problems. Discusses how her problems have affected her social, emotional, physical and academic development from childhood. Show how she is dysproxic, tactually defensive, posturally insecure and hypersensitive to vestibular input.
Prod-BU Dist-BU

Sensory Integrative Therapy - Principles Of Treatment, Pt I C 25 MIN
3/4 INCH VIDEO CASSETTE PRO
Begins a discussion of the relationship between clinical expertise and sensory integrative theoretical constructs while paying attention to the political struggle of the occupational therapist in the school system. Narrated by Virginia Scardina.
Prod-AOTA Dist-AOTA 1979

Sensory Integrative Therapy - Principles Of Treatment, Pt II C 20 MIN
3/4 INCH VIDEO CASSETTE PRO
Concludes a discussion of the relationship between clinical expertise and sensory integrative theoretical constructs while paying attention to the political struggle of the occupational therapist in the school system. Narrated by Virginia Scardina.
Prod-AOTA Dist-AOTA

Sensory Psychology C 29 MIN
3/4 INCH VIDEO CASSETTE C A
Discusses basic skin receptors that detect pressure, temperature and pain. Includes functions of deep receptors and the role of the inner ear in balance and motion.
From The Understanding Human Behavior - An Introduction To Psychology Series. Lesson 6
Prod-COAST Dist-CDTEL

Sensory Testing C
3/4 OR 1/2 INCH VIDEO CASSETTE
See series title for descriptive statement.
From The Physical Assessment - Neurologic System Series.
Prod-CONMED Dist-CONMED

Sensory World, The C 33 MIN
16MM FILM, 3/4 OR 1/2 IN VIDEO H-C A
An animated film which shows a voyage through the human body to demonstrate the operation of the senses. Includes experiments showing sensory phenomena and confusion.
From The Psychology Today Films Series.
Prod-CRMP Dist-CRMP 1971

Sentence Clarity - Transition B 30 MIN
2 INCH VIDEOTAPE J-H
Introduces the value of clear transitions as a means of achieving effective writing. (Broadcast quality)
From The English Composition Series. Exposition
Prod-GRETVO Dist-GPITVL Prodn-KUHTTV

Sentence Patterns C
3/4 OR 1/2 INCH VIDEO CASSETTE C
Explores the sentence and its rhetorical aspects to help gain an understanding about the importance of sentence style and its relation to grammar.
From The Write Course - An Introduction To College Composition Series.
Prod-DALCCD Dist-DALCCD

Sentence Patterns C 30 MIN
3/4 OR 1/2 INCH VIDEO CASSETTE C A
Explores the sentence and its rhetorical aspects in order to gain an understanding about the importance of sentence style and its relation to grammar.
From The Write Course - An Introduction To College Composition Series.
Prod-FI Dist-FI 1984

Sentence Strategy C
3/4 OR 1/2 INCH VIDEO CASSETTE C
Emphasizes sentence revision to fit rhetorical context.
From The Write Course - An Introduction To College Composition Series.
Prod-DALCCD Dist-DALCCD

Sentence Strategy C 30 MIN
3/4 OR 1/2 INCH VIDEO CASSETTE C A
Emphasizes sentence revision to fit rhetorical context.
From The Write Course - An Introduction To College Composition Series.
LC NO. 85-700986
Prod-FI Dist-FI 1984

Sentence Structure B 30 MIN
2 INCH VIDEOTAPE J-H
Demonstrates methods of achieving more interesting and artistic sentences and calls attention to eliminating errors in sentence structure. (Broadcast quality)
From The English Composition Series. Description
Prod-GRETVO Dist-GPITVL Prodn-KUHTTV

Sentence 1, The C 30 MIN
3/4 OR 1/2 INCH VIDEO CASSETTE C
See series title for descriptive statement.
From The Writing For A Reason Series.
Prod-DALCCD Dist-DALCCD

Sentence 2, The C 30 MIN
3/4 OR 1/2 INCH VIDEO CASSETTE C
See series title for descriptive statement.
From The Writing For A Reason Series.
Prod-DALCCD Dist-DALCCD

Sentenced To Survival C 90 MIN
3/4 INCH VIDEO CASSETTE
Explores foundations of Judaism. Surveys religious, ethical and social factors of survival of Judaism.
Prod-ADL Dist-ADL

Sentences C 45 MIN
3/4 OR 1/2 INCH VIDEO CASSETTE
See series title for descriptive statement.
From The Effective Writing Series.
Prod-TWAIN Dist-DELTAK

Sentences - Many Ways To Begin C 12 MIN
16MM FILM, 3/4 OR 1/2 IN VIDEO I-H
Illustrates the effects achieved by various sentence beginnings. Quotes first lines from famous literary works and speeches to demonstrate sentence variety.
From The Sentences And Paragraphs Series.
LC NO. 81-706041
Prod-CENTRO Dist-CORF 1981

Sentences - Simple, Compound, Complex C 11 MIN
16MM FILM, 3/4 OR 1/2 IN VIDEO J-H
Illustrates uses of simple, compound and complex sentences and tells how skillful handling of clauses adds variety and clarity to writing.
Prod-CORF Dist-CORF 1960

Sentences - Subject And Predicate C 14 MIN
16MM FILM, 3/4 OR 1/2 IN VIDEO I-J
Analyzes different sentences and identifies and defines simple subjects and predicates and compound subjects and predicates. Shows how good sentence structure leads to better writing.
Prod-CORF Dist-CORF 1963

Sentences / Paragraphs C 27 MIN
1/2 IN VIDEO CASSETTE BETA/VHS
Provides instruction in basic sentence-building skills and in constructing paragraphs. Uses stories to present the lessons.
Prod-BFA Dist-BFA

Sentences That Ask And Tell C 11 MIN
16MM FILM, 3/4 OR 1/2 IN VIDEO P
Illustrates the difference between asking and telling sentences, shows how certain punctuation and capitalization are used and explains that a sentence is a complete thought.
Prod-CORF Dist-CORF 1961

Sentences With Ralph And Stanley C 15 MIN
16MM FILM, 3/4 OR 1/2 IN VIDEO P-I
Tells how two young boys learn the basic skills involved in writing a complete sentence when they set out to track down the Loch Ness Monster.
From The Writing Skills Series.
Prod-BEAN Dist-PHENIX 1978

Sentences, Number Line C 30 MIN
16MM FILM OPTICAL SOUND T
Analyzes word problems and associated number sentences. The number line is used to represent sets of admissible solutions under various operations. To be used following 'DIVISION TECHNIQUES.'
From The Mathematics For Elementary School Teachers Series. No. 12
Prod-SMSG Dist-MLA 1963

Sentencing B 19 MIN
16MM FILM OPTICAL SOUND C
Deals with various aspects of a criminal lawsuit involving a liquor store robbery case. Shows counsel participating in the sentencing procedure.
From The Criminal Law Series, No. 13
LC NO. 73-714045
Prod-RPATLF Dist-RPATLF 1968

Sentimientos Agradables C 30 MIN
3/4 OR 1/2 INCH VIDEO CASSETTE K-P
See series title for descriptive statement.
From The Villa Alegre Series.
Prod-BCTV Dist-MDCPB

Sentinel, West Face C 27 MIN
16MM FILM, 3/4 OR 1/2 IN VIDEO
Pictures two mountain climbers scaling the west face of the Sentinel, an 8100 ft peak in Glacier National Park, Montana.
Prod-SUMMIT Dist-PFP Prodn-SUMMIT 1967

Sentinels In Space C 16 MIN
16MM FILM, 3/4 OR 1/2 IN VIDEO
Shows what environmental satellites measure and explains how they transmit information.
LC NO. 80-707617
Prod-NOAA Dist-USNAC 1980

Sentinels Of Silence C 19 MIN
16MM FILM, 3/4 OR 1/2 IN VIDEO P-C A
An aerial panorama of Mexico's pre-Columbian ruins.
Prod-ARANGO Dist-EBEC 1971

Sentinels Of Silence (Spanish) C 19 MIN
16MM FILM, 3/4 OR 1/2 IN VIDEO J-C
Examines seven archeological sites in Mexico, showing massive pyramid mounds, elaborate relief carvings and other ruins of pre-Columbian civilization.
Prod-EBEC Dist-EBEC 1973

Sentinels Of Survival C 12 MIN
16MM FILM, 3/4 OR 1/2 IN VIDEO I-J
Describes residential sprinkler systems and their impact upon the fire service and public.
From The Fire Survival Series.
Prod-AREASX Dist-FILCOM 1980

Seoul Of Don Bosco - Seoul, Korea C 28 MIN
16MM FILM OPTICAL SOUND
Shows the work of the Salesian Missions in Korea where they run a trade school, taking the boys off the streets and out of unskilled jobs and preparing them for well-paid jobs in industry. Offers the story of three boys who have passed through the Don Bosco Center.
Prod-SCC Dist-MTP

Separate But Equal C 8 MIN
16MM FILM, 3/4 OR 1/2 IN VIDEO I-J
Outlines the political, economic and social position of the Negro in the South, from the time of the Civil War. Emphasizes the effect of the 'SEPARATE BUT EQUAL' policy, which was derived from the Plessy vs Ferguson decision of the Supreme Court, and the Brown vs Board of Education case.
Prod-KRANTZ Dist-EBEC 1971

Separate Peace, A C 45 MIN
16MM FILM, 3/4 OR 1/2 IN VIDEO J-C A
An edited version of the feature film A Separate Peace. Describes the friendship of two young men and tells how one eventually betrays the other.
Prod-PARACO Dist-AIMS 1979

Separate Self, The C
3/4 INCH VIDEO CASSETTE
Describes growth and development of a child from 21 to 22 months.
From The Growth And Development - A Chronicle Of Four Children Series. Series 6
Prod-JUETHO Dist-LIP

Separate Self, The - Gregory, 21 Months C 7 MIN
16MM FILM OPTICAL SOUND
See series title for descriptive statement.
From The Growth And Development - A Chronicle Of Four Children Series. Series 6
LC NO. 78-700687
Prod-JUETHO Dist-LIP Prodn-CONCOM 1976

Separate Self, The - Joseph, 22 Months C 7 MIN
16MM FILM OPTICAL SOUND
See series title for descriptive statement.
From The Growth And Development - A Chronicle Of Four Children Series. Series 6
LC NO. 78-700687
Prod-JUETHO Dist-LIP Prodn-CONCOM 1976

Separate Self, The - Melissa, 21 Months C 6 MIN
16MM FILM OPTICAL SOUND
See series title for descriptive statement.
From The Growth And Development - A Chronicle Of Four Children Series. Series 6
LC NO. 78-700687
Prod-JUETHO Dist-LIP Prodn-CONCOM 1976

Separate Self, The - Terra, 22 Momths C 7 MIN
16MM FILM OPTICAL SOUND
See series title for descriptive statement.
From The Growth And Development - A Chronicle Of Four Children Series. Series 6
LC NO. 78-700687
Prod-JUETHO Dist-LIP Prodn-CONCOM 1976

Separate Ways C 15 MIN
1/2 IN VIDEO CASSETTE BETA/VHS I-J
Describes the end of the journey, with the Mimi's crew members reviewing the accomplishments of their voyage and saying farewell. Includes a visit to the M I T Plasma Fusion Center to meet Peter Marston, who plays Captain Granville.
From The Voyage Of The Mimi Series.
Prod-HRAW Dist-HRAW

Separating Sets C 15 MIN
3/4 INCH VIDEO CASSETTE P
Relates the separation of sets to the operation of subtraction.
From The Math Factory, Module I - Sets Series.
Prod-MAETEL Dist-GPITVL 1973

Separation C 30 MIN
16MM FILM, 3/4 OR 1/2 IN VIDEO H-C A
Focuses on examples of child-parent separation and shows how parents can help ease their children's anxieties.
From The Look At Me Series.
LC NO. 82-706222
Prod-WTTWTV Dist-FI 1980

Separation / Divorce - It Has Nothing To Do With You C 14 MIN
16MM FILM, 3/4 OR 1/2 IN VIDEO J-H
Tells how 16-year-old Larry's parents separate and describes his feelings of conflicting loyalties.
From The Conflict And Awareness Series.
Prod-CRMP Dist-CRMP 1975

Separation Anxiety And Wishes To Be Rid Of Patients C 15 MIN
3/4 OR 1/2 INCH VIDEO CASSETTE
Discusses the significance of separation-anxiety as being as much a part of the therapists's contribution to the patient-therapist relationship as the patient's contribution. Relates this to the reality and frequency of threats by the borderline patient to leave treatment.
From The Treatment Of The Borderline Patient Series.
Prod-HEMUL Dist-HEMUL

Separation By Crystallization, Dissolution And Sublimation C 60 MIN
3/4 OR 1/2 INCH VIDEO CASSETTE IND
Covers evaporation and crystallization, sublimation and desublimation, freeze-drying, extraction and thin-layer chromatography.
From The Chemistry Training Series.
Prod-ITCORP Dist-ITCORP

Separation Of Dry Crushed Coals By High-Gradient Magnetic Separation C 20 MIN
16MM FILM OPTICAL SOUND IND
Describes the high-gradient magnetic separation of coal and explains the fundamentals of the process. Shows the development of this technology from the laboratory stage to its introduction in a pilot plant.
LC NO. 81-700854
Prod-USDOE Dist-USNAC Prodn-ORNLAB 1980

Separation Of Powers, A - Congress And The Bureaucracy / Congress And The Courts, Pt 1 C 30 MIN
3/4 OR 1/2 INCH VIDEO CASSETTE
Focuses on the interdependence of Congress in the goals each house pursues and in their conduct with each other.
From The Congress - We The People Series.
Prod-WETATV Dist-FI 1984

Separation Of Powers, A - Congress And The Bureaucracy / Congress And The Courts, Pt 2 C 30 MIN
3/4 OR 1/2 INCH VIDEO CASSETTE
Deals with the relationship between Congress and the courts.
From The Congress - We The People Series.
Prod-WETATV Dist-FI 1984

Separation Of Powers, The C 12 MIN
16MM FILM OPTICAL SOUND J-H
Traces the reasons for dividing the government into interdependent, but unique branches. Explains the distinct responsibilities and rights of the federal government, the state governments and the people.
From The Senator Sam Ervin, Jr - The Constitution Series.
Prod-CHILBE Dist-COUNFI

Separation Of Thoracopagus Twins C 24 MIN
16MM FILM OPTICAL SOUND PRO
Explains that successful separation of thoracopagus twins depends upon a careful preoperative evaluation of the extent of twinning and the physiological effects of the anatomical variations on each twin.
Prod-ACYDGD Dist-ACY 1960

Separations And Reunions B 36 MIN
16MM FILM OPTICAL SOUND PRO
Documents reactions of four children age 14 to 20 months, hospitalized for from five to 24 days. Points out that at reunion with parents, hostility and resentment are combined with joy and relief.
Prod-PSUPCR Dist-PSUPCR 1968

Separatory Funnel I C 10 MIN
3/4 OR 1/2 INCH VIDEO CASSETTE C A
Demonstrates a simple extraction of iodine from water, using an organic solvent in a separatory funnel.
From The Chemistry - Master/Apprentice Series. Program 9
LC NO. 82-706041
Prod-CUETV Dist-CUNIV 1981

Separatory Funnel II C 14 MIN
3/4 OR 1/2 INCH VIDEO CASSETTE C A
Demonstrates a simple extraction of iodine from water using an organic solvent in a separatory funnel. Covers extractions that result in gas formation and emulsions.
From The Chemistry - Master/Apprentice Series. Program 200
LC NO. 82-706051
Prod-CUETV Dist-CUNIV 1981

September Wheat C 96 MIN
16MM FILM, 3/4 OR 1/2 IN VIDEO
Deals with the world trade in wheat, and hunger in the poor countries of the third world. Examines the causes of hunger in a time of abundance.
Prod-KRIEGP Dist-NEWTIM

September 15 C 5 MIN
16MM FILM OPTICAL SOUND
Presents an autobiographical portrayal of the filmmaker's wedding day.
LC NO. 77-702641
Prod-HANCXR Dist-CANFDC 1972

September 30, 1955 C 101 MIN
16MM FILM OPTICAL SOUND
Tells how the death of James Dean affects a group of young people in Arkansas.
Prod-UPCI Dist-SWANK

Septic Shock C 21 MIN
3/4 OR 1/2 INCH VIDEO CASSETTE PRO
Discusses the general pathopysiology of shock, the nine basic parts of evaluation, chronic treatment and differentiation of septic shock from hypovolemia.
Prod-UMICHM Dist-UMICHM 1973

Septic Shock C 23 MIN
3/4 OR 1/2 INCH VIDEO CASSETTE
Discusses diagnosis and treatment of septic shock.
From The Emergency Management - The First 30 Minutes, Vol II Series.
Prod-VTRI Dist-VTRI

Sequence And Story C 5 MIN
3/4 OR 1/2 INCH VIDEO CASSETTE P-I
Shows how visual and verbal elements are assembled into a story and how the order of these elements affects the message. Features three youngsters who take a collection of photo-

graphs that show the sequence of a typical school day. When they rearrange the sequence of the photos, a different story can be told.
From The Visual Literacy Series.
Prod-NFBC Dist-MOKIN 1984

Sequences B
16MM FILM OPTICAL SOUND
Considers four theorems on sequences.
Prod-OPENU Dist-OPENU

Sequences - Numbers Growing C 20 MIN
16MM FILM, 3/4 OR 1/2 IN VIDEO I
Discusses aspects of sequences.
From The Mathscore Two Series.
Prod-BBCTV Dist-FI

Sequences - What Next C 20 MIN
16MM FILM, 3/4 OR 1/2 IN VIDEO I-J
Discusses aspects of sequences.
From The Mathscore One Series.
Prod-BBCTV Dist-FI

Sequences And Series B 33 MIN
3/4 OR 1/2 INCH VIDEO CASSETTE
See series title for descriptive statement.
From The Calculus Of Complex Variables Series.
Prod-MIOT Dist-MIOT

Sequencing C 50 MIN
3/4 OR 1/2 INCH VIDEO CASSETTE
Discusses the primitive PROG2, PROGN, and the PROG construct in computer languages.
From The Computer Languages - Pt 1 Series.
Prod-MIOT Dist-MIOT

Sequencing Instruction C 30 MIN
3/4 OR 1/2 INCH VIDEO CASSETTE
Covers course development, analysis of tasks, sequencing guidelines and examples of programs using task analysis sequencing.
From The Mainstreaming Secondary Special Vocational Needs Student Series.
Prod-PUAVC Dist-PUAVC

Sequential Circuits 1 C 49 MIN
3/4 OR 1/2 INCH VIDEO CASSETTE PRO
See series title for descriptive statement.
From The Digital Electronics Series.
Prod-MIOT Dist-MIOT

Sequential Circuits 2 C 49 MIN
3/4 OR 1/2 INCH VIDEO CASSETTE PRO
See series title for descriptive statement.
From The Digital Electronics Series.
Prod-MIOT Dist-MIOT

Sequential Lobic Circuits 'Binary Counters' C
3/4 OR 1/2 INCH VIDEO CASSETTE
See series title for descriptive statement.
From The Digital Techniques Video Training Course Series.
Prod-VTRI Dist-VTRI

Sequential Logic Circuits - BCD Special Counters C
3/4 OR 1/2 INCH VIDEO CASSETTE
See series title for descriptive statement.
From The Digital Techniques Series.
Prod-HTHZEN Dist-HTHZEN

Sequential Logic Circuits - Binary Counters C
3/4 OR 1/2 INCH VIDEO CASSETTE
See series title for descriptive statement.
From The Digital Techniques Series.
Prod-HTHZEN Dist-HTHZEN

Sequential Logic Circuits - Clocks C
3/4 OR 1/2 INCH VIDEO CASSETTE
See series title for descriptive statement.
From The Digital Techniques Series.
Prod-HTHZEN Dist-HTHZEN

Sequential Logic Circuits - Registers C
3/4 OR 1/2 INCH VIDEO CASSETTE
See series title for descriptive statement.
From The Digital Techniques Series.
Prod-HTHZEN Dist-HTHZEN

Sequential Logic Circuits 'BCD And Special Counters' C
3/4 OR 1/2 INCH VIDEO CASSETTE
See series title for descriptive statement.
From The Digital Techniques Video Training Course Series.
Prod-VTRI Dist-VTRI

Sequential Logic Circuits 'Clocks' C
3/4 OR 1/2 INCH VIDEO CASSETTE
See series title for descriptive statement.
From The Digital Techniques Video Training Course Series.
Prod-VTRI Dist-VTRI

Sequential Logic Circuits 'Registers' C
3/4 OR 1/2 INCH VIDEO CASSETTE
See series title for descriptive statement.
From The Digital Techniques Video Training Course Series.
Prod-VTRI Dist-VTRI

Sequential Processing Applications C
16MM FILM - 3/4 IN VIDEO H-C A
Delves into sequential file systems, data and hardware, programs and procedures, record matching, batch totals, backup and recovery, and the sequential systems at a university payroll.
From The Computers At Work - Concepts And Applications Series. Module 4
Prod-BNA Dist-BNA 1983

Sequential Processing Applications C
3/4 OR 1/2 INCH VIDEO CASSETTE
Identifies the most important characteristics of sequential file systems, discusses data representation and magnetic tape data storage and explains the procedures utilized in efficient sequential file processing applications.
From The Computers At Work Series.
Prod-COMTEG Dist-COMTEG

Sequentially Accessed Semiconductor Storage Design C 60 MIN
1 INCH VIDEOTAPE IND
Discusses the design for sequentially accessed semiconductor storage, including MOS and bipolar shift registers plus advanced concepts, such as chargecouple devices.
From The Semiconductor Memories Course Series. No. 3
Prod-TXINLC Dist-TXINLC

Ser / Estar C 30 MIN
3/4 INCH VIDEO CASSETTE H-C
See series title for descriptive statement.
From The Telespanol Uno Series.
Prod-WUSFTV Dist-GPITVL 1979

Serama's Mask C 25 MIN
16MM FILM, 3/4 OR 1/2 IN VIDEO I-J A
Introduces Serama, a Balinese boy who wants to be a dancer like his father. Shows him preparing the ceremonial mask which is a necessary part of the retirement dance.
From The World Cultures And Youth Series.
LC NO. 80-706677
Prod-SUNRIS Dist-CORF 1980

Seraphita's Diary C 90 MIN
16MM FILM, 3/4 OR 1/2 IN VIDEO
Presents a story of a famous fashion model who, unable to cope with the fantasies and pleasures her beauty induces in others, disappears. Profiles her emotional life and contrasts the fantasies she creates in other people's minds with strains of her real emotional life as revealed in her diaries.
Prod-WISEF Dist-ZIPRAH

Serenal C 5 MIN
16MM FILM, 3/4 OR 1/2 IN VIDEO H-C
Norman McLaren salutes the West Indies by painting the spirit of fiesta on film. His work is a flow of abstract images, pyrotechnics of light and color that sway and change in response to the rhythms of a Trinidad orchestra.
Prod-NFBC Dist-IFB Prodn-MCLN 1961

Serendipity B 29 MIN
16MM FILM OPTICAL SOUND
Analyzes the role and value of the drug researcher and discusses accidental discoveries of some important drugs. (Kinescope)
From The Apothecary Series.
LC NO. 75-703230
Prod-KNXT Dist-USC 1964

Serendipity Bomb, The (Une Bombe, Par Hasard) C 8 MIN
16MM FILM, 3/4 OR 1/2 IN VIDEO J-C
Uses animation to tell the story of a town, whose citizens evacuate when a bomb is dropped in the main square. Shows how they return to stone a stranger who settles in the deserted town only to be killed by the bomb's eventual explosion.
Prod-LESFG Dist-TEXFLM 1977

Serendipity Spy Glass C 30 MIN
3/4 OR 1/2 INCH VIDEO CASSETTE I-J
Describes how a pixie-like old man shows a boy the magic in the world around him.
Prod-CANBC Dist-JOU

Serendipity–A Series
16MM FILM, 3/4 OR 1/2 IN VIDEO P
Deals with the language arts for use in reading instruction.
Prod-MGHT Dist-MGHT

Follow The Reader	014 MIN
Speak Up	014 MIN
Wordly Wise	014 MIN
Write On	014 MIN

Sergeant Matlovich Vs The U S Air Force C 98 MIN
16MM FILM, 3/4 OR 1/2 IN VIDEO H-C A
Presents the story of Sergeant Leonard Matlovich, who was drummed out of the U S Air Force in 1975 because of his revealed homosexuality.
Prod-TOMENT Dist-LCOA 1979

Sergeant Swell C 16 MIN
16MM FILM, 3/4 OR 1/2 IN VIDEO J-C A
Presents a spoof on the Royal Canadian Mounties in which our hero Sergeant Swell finds himself at odds with a local Indian tribe and a key warrior who always seems to be just a few steps behind.
Prod-PFP Dist-PFP 1972

Sergeant, The C 108 MIN
16MM FILM OPTICAL SOUND
Stars Rod Steiger as a bullying army sergeant who enslaves a young private.
Prod-WB Dist-TWYMAN 1968

Sergei Bongart C 30 MIN
16MM FILM, 3/4 OR 1/2 IN VIDEO
See series title for descriptive statement.
From The Profiles In American Art Series.
Prod-KAWVAL Dist-KAWVAL

Serial Interface C 30 MIN
3/4 OR 1/2 INCH VIDEO CASSETTE IND
Analyzes serial interfaces by software-centered and hardware-centered techniques. Explains teletype interface with programs and schematics, and covers opto-isolator circuits with the MC1488.
From The 6809 Interface Programming Series.
Prod-COLOSU Dist-COLOSU

Serial Interfacing, Part 1 C 45 MIN
3/4 OR 1/2 INCH VIDEO CASSETTE IND
See series title for descriptive statement.
From The Microprocessor Interfacing Series.
Prod-ICSINT Dist-ICSINT

Serial Interfacing, Part 2 C 45 MIN
3/4 OR 1/2 INCH VIDEO CASSETTE IND
See series title for descriptive statement.
From The Microprocessor Interfacing Series.
Prod-ICSINT Dist-ICSINT

Serial Interfacing, Pt 1 C 35 MIN
3/4 INCH VIDEO CASSETTE C
See series title for descriptive statement.
From The Microprocessor Interfacing Series. Part 5
LC NO. 81-706199
Prod-AMCEE Dist-AMCEE 1980

Serial Interfacing, Pt 1 C 43 MIN
3/4 OR 1/2 INCH VIDEO CASSETTE PRO
Describes asynchronous and synchronous techniques.
From The Microprocessing Interfacing Series.
Prod-AMCEE Dist-AMCEE

Serial Interfacing, Pt 1 C 48 MIN
3/4 OR 1/2 INCH VIDEO CASSETTE
See series title for descriptive statement.
From The Microprocessor Interfacing Series.
Prod-MIOT Dist-MIOT

Serial Interfacing, Pt 2 C 35 MIN
3/4 INCH VIDEO CASSETTE C
See series title for descriptive statement.
From The Microprocessor Interfacing Series. Part 6
LC NO. 81-706199
Prod-AMCEE Dist-AMCEE 1980

Serial Interfacing, Pt 2 C 41 MIN
3/4 OR 1/2 INCH VIDEO CASSETTE
See series title for descriptive statement.
From The Microprocessor Interfacing Series.
Prod-MIOT Dist-MIOT

Serial Interfacing, Pt 2 C 43 MIN
3/4 OR 1/2 INCH VIDEO CASSETTE PRO
Covers special topics in serial I/O - Isolation. Involves buffering. Provides a case study and demonstration.
From The Microprocessing Interfacing Series.
Prod-AMCEE Dist-AMCEE

Serials, The, Pt 1 C 64 MIN
2 INCH VIDEOTAPE
See series title for descriptive statement.
From The Toys That Grew Up II Series.
Prod-WTTWTV Dist-PUBTEL

Serials, The, Pt 2 C 64 MIN
2 INCH VIDEOTAPE
See series title for descriptive statement.
From The Toys That Grew Up II Series.
Prod-WTTWTV Dist-PUBTEL

Series And Parallel Circuits B 8 MIN
16MM FILM, 3/4 OR 1/2 IN VIDEO
Illustrates series and parallel circuits, explaining current flow and voltage drop across each lamp.
From The Radio Technician Training - Elementary Electricity Series.
Prod-USN Dist-USNAC Prodn-HOLMES 1947

Series And Parallel Circuits C 15 MIN
3/4 INCH VIDEO CASSETTE I
Explains the differences between series and parallel circuits and the values of each.
From The Search For Science (2nd Ed,) Unit V - Electricity Series.
Prod-WVIZTV Dist-GPITVL

Series And Parallel Resistors C 9 MIN
16MM FILM, 3/4 OR 1/2 IN VIDEO H-C A
Deals with resistors in series, the calculation of current in a circuit of known resistance, resistors in parallel, calculation of current effect on cross-sectional area, resistance of cables and voltage drop.
From The Basic Electricity Series.
Prod-STFD Dist-IFB 1979

Series Circuits C
3/4 OR 1/2 INCH VIDEO CASSETTE
See series title for descriptive statement.
From The Basic Electricity - DC Series.
Prod-VTRI Dist-VTRI

Series Circuits C 30 MIN
3/4 OR 1/2 INCH VIDEO CASSETTE
Surveys series circuits and rules of their behavior. Teaches identifying of series circuits and calculating of their equivalent resistance, current flow, voltage at various circuit points and power dissipated by each resistor.
From The Basic Electricity And D.C. Circuits Series.
Prod-TXINLC Dist-TXINLC

Series Conclusion And Talking About Deafness C
3/4 OR 1/2 INCH VIDEO CASSETTE A
Shows Cindy Cochran becoming a 'rock star' for the upbeat song 'Hit Me With Your Best Shot.' Includes a visit with children as she sings the song 'Fire' and answers questions about deafness and deaf people, and a sing-along as well.

From The Signing With Cindy Series.
Prod-GPCV Dist-GPCV

Series Overview C 30 MIN
3/4 OR 1/2 INCH VIDEO CASSETTE
Introduces Dr Thomas J Sweeney, Professor of Guidance and Counseling at the Ohio University College of Education. Outlines each program briefly using excerpts from each of them.
From The Coping With Kids Series.
Prod-OHUTC Dist-OHUTC

Series Parallel Circuits - Analysis B 16 MIN
3/4 OR 1/2 INCH VIDEO CASSETTE
Describes the circuit analysis of series parallel circuits and discusses resistance, current and voltage distribution, and power. Demonstrates the results of changing both the number of branches and the resistance within a branch.
LC NO. 84-706411
Prod-USAF Dist-USNAC 1983

Series Parallel Circuits - Troubleshooting B 19 MIN
16MM FILM, 3/4 OR 1/2 IN VIDEO
Shows the symptoms for opens and shorts in series parallel circuits. Uses an ohmmeter and voltmeter to isolate the faulty component.
Prod-USAF Dist-USNAC 1983

Series RC Circuits C
3/4 OR 1/2 INCH VIDEO CASSETTE
See series title for descriptive statement.
From The Basic AC Circuits Series.
Prod-VTRI Dist-VTRI

Series RC Circuits B 15 MIN
16MM FILM, 3/4 OR 1/2 IN VIDEO
Reviews the use of vector analysis, the Pythagorean theorem and trig functions as applied to series RC circuits. Constructs the impedance and voltage vectors. Uses an oscilloscope to demonstrate phase relationships and relative amplitudes.
Prod-USAF Dist-USNAC 1983

Series RC Circuits C 20 MIN
3/4 OR 1/2 INCH VIDEO CASSETTE
See series title for descriptive statement.
From The Basic AC Circuits, Laboratory--Sessions--A Series.
Prod-TXINLC Dist-TXINLC

Series RC, RL and RCL Circuits B 37 MIN
16MM FILM, 3/4 OR 1/2 IN VIDEO
Defines a vector quality. Demonstrates the manner in which reactive circuits differ from resistive circuits. Explains why this difference exists and tells how it affects impedance and phases angle. Issued in 1970 as a motion picture.
LC NO. 79-707524
Prod-USAF Dist-USNAC 1979

Series RC, RL And RCL Circuits - Trigonometric Functions B 40 MIN
16MM FILM OPTICAL SOUND
Explains the method of solving for the phase angle and impedance by the use of trigonometric functions.
LC NO. 74-705605
Prod-USAF Dist-USNAC

Series RC, RL And RCL Circuits - Trigonometric Solutions B 40 MIN
1/2 IN VIDEO CASSETTE (BETA)
Explains solutions for phase angle and impedance by using trigonometric functions.
LC NO. 79-707525
Prod-USAF Dist-USNAC 1979

Series RCL Circuits B 16 MIN
16MM FILM, 3/4 OR 1/2 IN VIDEO
Constructs a parallel RCL circuit and shows how each branch current is independent of the others. Compares the time-phase relationship of branch currents with reactive components. Determines current and phase angle trigonometrically and vectorially.
Prod-USAF Dist-USNAC 1983

Series RCL Quality And Selectivity B 28 MIN
16MM FILM - 1/2 IN VIDEO, BETA
Determines the relationship between reactance and resistance in series RCL circuits. Issued in 1970 as a motion picture.
LC NO. 79-707526
Prod-USAF Dist-USNAC 1979

Series Resistive And Reactive Circuits C
3/4 OR 1/2 INCH VIDEO CASSETTE
See series title for descriptive statement.
From The Basic AC Circuits Series.
Prod-VTRI Dist-VTRI

Series Resistive And Reactive Circuits C 20 MIN
3/4 OR 1/2 INCH VIDEO CASSETTE
See series title for descriptive statement.
From The Basic AC Circuits, Laboratory--Sessions--A Series.
Prod-TXINLC Dist-TXINLC

Series Resistive Circuits B 15 MIN
16MM FILM, 3/4 OR 1/2 IN VIDEO
Shows how to analyze current, voltage and resistance in a series resistive circuit. Discusses how a change in the total resistance affects each parameter.
Prod-USAF Dist-USNAC 1983

Series Resistive Circuits - DC Power B 29 MIN
16MM FILM - 1/2 IN VIDEO, BETA
Defines electrical power in terms of work and rate. Discusses three formulas for computing power. Issued in 1970 as a motion picture.
LC NO. 79-707527
Prod-USAF Dist-USNAC 1979

Series Resistive Circuits - Troubleshooting B 35 MIN
16MM FILM - 1/2 IN VIDEO, BETA
Discusses the process of locating faults or trouble in a circuit. Shows how opens are located by using a voltmeter and ohmmeter and demonstrates the procedure for locating shorts with a voltmeter. Issued in 1970 as a motion picture.
LC NO. 79-707528
Prod-USAF Dist-USNAC 1979

Series Resonant Circuits B 31 MIN
16MM FILM - 1/2 IN VIDEO, BETA
Calculates the resonant frequency of a series RCL circuit, compares the magnitude of current and impedance and vectorially analyzes the series RCL circuit as capacitive, inductive or resistive. Issued in 1970 as a motion picture.
LC NO. 79-707529
Prod-USAF Dist-USNAC 1979

Series RL Circuits C
3/4 OR 1/2 INCH VIDEO CASSETTE
See series title for descriptive statement.
From The Basic AC Circuits Series.
Prod-VTRI Dist-VTRI

Series RL Circuits B 18 MIN
16MM FILM, 3/4 OR 1/2 IN VIDEO
Reviews the vector and trigonometric methods of computing total impedance and current, phase angle and power factor in series RL circuits. Uses an oscilloscope to show the values and phase relationships of ER, EL and EA.
Prod-USAF Dist-USNAC 1983

Series RL Circuits C 20 MIN
3/4 OR 1/2 INCH VIDEO CASSETTE
See series title for descriptive statement.
From The Basic AC Circuits, Laboratory--Sessions--A Series.
Prod-TXINLC Dist-TXINLC

Series Sur Les Manseuvres De Ceremonie C 7 MIN
16MM FILM OPTICAL SOUND
A French language version of the motion picture Ceremonial Drill. Discusses the historical value of ceremonial drills in the armed forces.
From The Ceremonial Drill (French) Series.
LC NO. 77-702843
Prod-CDND Dist-CDND Prodn-FLMSMI 1976

Series Wrap C 30 MIN
3/4 OR 1/2 INCH VIDEO CASSETTE H-C A
Reviews the programs of the New Voice series.
From The New Voice Series.
Prod-WGBHTV Dist-GPITVL

Series Wrap-Up C 30 MIN
3/4 OR 1/2 INCH VIDEO CASSETTE
Offers a wrap-up of the Bodyworks series.
From The Bodyworks Series.
Prod-KTXTTV Dist-MDCPB

Series 4 C 7 MIN
16MM FILM, 3/4 OR 1/2 IN VIDEO
Uses animation in suggesting the relationship between man and his environment.
Prod-NFBC Dist-FI 1974

Series-Parallel Circuits C
3/4 OR 1/2 INCH VIDEO CASSETTE
See series title for descriptive statement.
From The Basic Electricity - DC Series.
Prod-VTRI Dist-VTRI

Series-Parallel Circuits C 15 MIN
3/4 OR 1/2 INCH VIDEO CASSETTE
See series title for descriptive statement.
From The Basic Electricity And D.C. Circuits, Laboratory Series.
Prod-TXINLC Dist-TXINLC

Series-Parallel Circuits C 30 MIN
3/4 OR 1/2 INCH VIDEO CASSETTE
Discusses application of circuit reduction techniques and Ohm's Law to more complex, single-supply series-parallel circuits. Introduces practical 'circuit sense' methods to help analyze circuit schematics.
From The Basic Electricity And D.C. Circuits Series.
Prod-TXINLC Dist-TXINLC

Series-Parallel Circuits (Basic DC Circuits) C
3/4 OR 1/2 INCH VIDEO CASSETTE
See series title for descriptive statement.
From The Basic DC Circuits Series.
Prod-VTRI Dist-VTRI

Series-Parallel Resistive Circuits B 40 MIN
16MM FILM, 3/4 OR 1/2 IN VIDEO
Shows combinations of series, parallel and series-parallel circuits. Shows how to identify the type of circuit and solve for current, voltage and resistance.
Prod-USAF Dist-USNAC

Series-Parallel Resistive Circuits - Circuit Analysis B 40 MIN
16MM FILM OPTICAL SOUND
Shows various combinations of series, parallel and series-parallel circuits. Explains how to identify the type of circuit and how to solve for resistance of individual components and total resistance. Explains how to calculate current and describes and explains the procedure for constructing an equivalent circuit. (Kinescope)
LC NO. 74-705610
Prod-USAF Dist-USNAC 1965

Series-Parallel Resistive Circuits - Circuit Analysis B 40 MIN
3/4 INCH VIDEO CASSETTE
Shows various combinations of series, parallel and series-parallel circuits. Explains how to identify the type of circuit and how to solve for resistance, voltage and current. Issued in 1970 as a motion picture.
LC NO. 79-707523
Prod-USAF Dist-USNAC 1979

Series, Parallel And Standby - Examples C 30 MIN
3/4 OR 1/2 INCH VIDEO CASSETTE IND
Contains numerical examples of simple series, parallel and standby arrangements.
From The Reliability Engineering Series.
Prod-COLOSU Dist-COLOSU

Series, Parallel, And Standby Systems C 30 MIN
3/4 OR 1/2 INCH VIDEO CASSETTE IND
Describes the reliability calculations for series, parallel and standby systems.
From The Reliability Engineering Series.
Prod-COLOSU Dist-COLOSU

Serious Minded Stuff C 16 MIN
16MM FILM, 3/4 OR 1/2 IN VIDEO I-C A
Presents the whimsical story of 16-year-old Amanda Sharpe, who discovers her natural talent for slapstick and becomes an overnight silent film star. Relates the disappointment of her parents when she stops her ballet training in order to pursue her new career.
Prod-USC Dist-DIRECT 1983

Sermon On The Mount, Now C 19 MIN
16MM FILM OPTICAL SOUND H-C A
Presents an off-screen reading of the exact text of the Gospel of Matthew, chapters five through seven, commonly known as the Sermon on the Mount. Includes without additional comment, a collage of contemporary images relating by implication what is being heard to what is modern and relevant today.
LC NO. 73-701809
Prod-MMA Dist-MMA 1973

Sermons In Wood C 27 MIN
16MM FILM - 3/4 IN VIDEO H-C A
Examines the life and art of Elijah Pierce, a master craftsman who carves intricate relief sculpture in wood. Reveals his wide range of genius.
Prod-SOFOLK Dist-SOFOLK

Serological Technique - Venipuncture C 7 MIN
16MM FILM OPTICAL SOUND
Demonstrates how to take a blood sample from the arm.
From The Medical Laboratory Techniques Series.
LC NO. FIE54-453
Prod-USN Dist-USNAC 1954

Serous Otitis Media C 17 MIN
3/4 OR 1/2 INCH VIDEO CASSETTE PRO
Deals with the way to diagnose serous otitis media through history, an otoscopic and physical examination and hearing tests. Discusses evaluation of diagnositc findings, therapeutic considerations and procedures and follow-up care.
Prod-UMICHM Dist-UMICHM 1974

Serpent C 15 MIN
16MM FILM OPTICAL SOUND
An experimental film which uses abstract and concrete images and a composite sound track to suggest the conflict between good and evil. Without narration.
LC NO. 72-700070
Prod-BARTLS Dist-SERIUS 1971

Serpent River Paddlers C 14 MIN
16MM FILM OPTICAL SOUND
Shows the Huron Indians manufacturing canoes and snowshoes.
From The Sports Journal Series.
LC NO. 76-703330
Prod-FIARTS Dist-FIARTS 1975

Serrated Slopes For Erosion Control C 14 MIN
16MM FILM, 3/4 OR 1/2 IN VIDEO
Discusses slopes that can be prepared during highway construction that will reduce erosion and promote the growth of plant life.
LC NO. 82-706166
Prod-USDTFH Dist-USNAC 1970

Serum Cholesterol C 9 MIN
16MM FILM OPTICAL SOUND
Demonstrates a method of extracting both cholesterol and cholesterol esters from whole serum by treatment with alcohol potassium hydroxide and purification with petroleum ether.
LC NO. FIE67-63
Prod-USPHS Dist-NMAC 1965

Serum Cholesterol - Abell-Kendall Method - Manual C 9 MIN
3/4 INCH VIDEO CASSETTE PRO
Demonstrates a method of extracting both cholesterol and cholesterol esters from whole serum by treatment with alcohol potassium hydroxide and purification with petroleum ether.
LC NO. 77-706131
Prod-NMAC Dist-USNAC 1977

Servant Of The People C 15 MIN
16MM FILM OPTICAL SOUND
Features four members of the House of Representatives including Yvonne Burke of California, Norman Lent of New York, Joseph Mc Dade of Pennsylvania and William Scherle of Iowa, who provide an insight into the workings of one of the most powerful legislative bodies in the world.
LC NO. 74-701526
Prod-HEARST Dist-HEARST 1974

Servants In The Sky C 22 MIN
3/4 OR 1/2 INCH VIDEO CASSETTE J-H

Examines the man-made satellites that are changing the world.
Prod-HEARST Dist-HEARST 1976

Serve Or Preserve C 29 MIN
3/4 INCH VIDEO CASSETTE
Shows procedures for preparing wild plants for immediate use or preservation. Explores a variety of wild berries and their habitats.
From The Edible Wild Plants Series.
Prod-UMITV Dist-UMITV 1978

Serve Your Nation C 15 MIN
2 INCH VIDEOTAPE J-H
Explains that because of opportunities in education, training, travel and advancement, many young men and women are turning to the military for a permanent career.
From The Work Is For Real Series.
Prod-STETVC Dist-GPITVL

Serve, The C 20 MIN
16MM FILM, 3/4 OR 1/2 IN VIDEO J-C A
Features a clinic approach to teaching group tennis. Shows how to teach the serve.
From The Tennis Series.
Prod-ATHI Dist-ATHI 1976

Serve, The C 29 MIN
3/4 OR 1/2 INCH VIDEO CASSETTE
Features Lew Gerrard and Don Candy giving tennis instructions, emphasizing the serve.
From The Love Tennis Series.
Prod-MDCPB Dist-MDCPB

Serve, The C 29 MIN
3/4 OR 1/2 INCH VIDEO CASSETTE
See series title for descriptive statement.
From The Vic Braden's Tennis For The Future Series.
Prod-WGBHTV Dist-PBS 1981

Serve, The C 30 MIN
3/4 OR 1/2 INCH VIDEO CASSETTE H-C A
See series title for descriptive statement.
From The Tennis Anyone Series.
LC NO. 79-706889
Prod-BATA Dist-TIMLIF 1979

Service Around The Clock And Around The World C 18 MIN
3/4 OR 1/2 INCH VIDEO CASSETTE
Presents an overview of Red Cross services to the armed forces. Emphasizes the role of the organization in aiding men and women in the military.
Prod-AMRC Dist-AMRC 1976

Service Connected Priorities - An Overview C 17 MIN
3/4 INCH VIDEO CASSETTE
Shows how priority care programs have been implemented in two Veterans Administration medical centers.
LC NO. 79-706029
Prod-VAHSL Dist-USNAC 1978

Service Connected Priorities - Back To Basics C 13 MIN
3/4 INCH VIDEO CASSETTE
Provides examples of priority treatment procedures for service-connected veterans being used by two Veterans Administration health care facilities.
LC NO. 79-706030
Prod-VAHSL Dist-USNAC 1978

Service Economy, The C 30 MIN
3/4 INCH VIDEO CASSETTE
See series title for descriptive statement.
From The It's Everybody's Business Series. Unit 5, Operating A Business
Prod-DALCCD Dist-DALCCD

Service Interruptions C
3/4 OR 1/2 INCH VIDEO CASSETTE IND
Assists participant in dealing with interruptions of customer service, analyzing faults and taking action to normalize the situation. Includes planned and forced outages, customer complaints, clearance procedures and documentation.
From The Distribution System Operation Series. Topic 12
Prod-LEIKID Dist-LEIKID

Service Is The Price You Pay C 27 MIN
16MM FILM OPTICAL SOUND
Illustrates the theme, 'SERVICE IS THE PRICE YOU PAY FOR THE SPACE YOU OCCUPY IN THIS WORLD,' by showing unusual Red Cross programs in action. Provides a general orientation film for all new Red Cross stall and volunteer personnel.
Prod-AMRC Dist-AMRC 1972

Service Marketing C 30 MIN
3/4 OR 1/2 INCH VIDEO CASSETTE
Covers the characteristics of the service product, marketing of non-profit service organizations and other aspects of service marketing.
From The Marketing Perspectives Series.
Prod-MATC Dist-WFVTAE

Service Module, The C 5 MIN
16MM FILM - 3/4 IN VIDEO
Examines the unmanned portion of the Apollo spacecraft. Explains the functions of propulsion, fuel storage and advanced instrumentation. Issued in 1969 as a motion picture.
From The Apollo Digest Series.
LC NO. 79-706992
Prod-NASA Dist-USNAC 1979

Service Organizations C 20 MIN
3/4 OR 1/2 INCH VIDEO CASSETTE C A
Explains how to find out about existing jobs in the community and about the structure of community agencies.
From The Clues To Career Opportunities For Liberal Arts Graduates Series.
LC NO. 79-706057
Prod-IU Dist-IU 1978

Service Phase, The C 24 MIN
3/4 OR 1/2 INCH VIDEO CASSETTE
Presents an interview with nurses who are having difficulty communicating with a hospital administrator regarding the severe understaffing at the hospital. Shows ways they can bargain with the hospital administrator without jeopardizing their jobs.
From The Social Work Interviewing Series.
Prod-UCALG Dist-UWISC 1978

Service Procedure For Ball Bearing B 20 MIN
16MM FILM OPTICAL SOUND H-C A
Shows how to remove, service and install ball bearings.
Prod-GM Dist-GM 1950

Service Procedure For Ball Bearing (French) B 20 MIN
16MM FILM OPTICAL SOUND H-C A
Shows how to remove, service and install ball bearings.
Prod-GM Dist-GM 1950

Service Station Attendant C 15 MIN
16MM FILM, 3/4 OR 1/2 IN VIDEO I
From The Career Awareness Series.
Prod-KLVXTV Dist-GPITVL

Service, Leadership And Personal Rewards - Health Services In A Disaster C 36 MIN
3/4 OR 1/2 INCH VIDEO CASSETTE
Focuses on nursing responsibilities in time of disaster and how nurses provide for the physical and emotional needs of victims and workers.
Prod-AMRC Dist-AMRC

Services C 16 MIN
16MM FILM, 3/4 OR 1/2 IN VIDEO P-I
Shows how two children and the ghost of one of the first settlers in their town investigate the various public services offered by their community. Visits the city park, public library, fire station and city hall and tells about the services each provides.
From The Community Series. Part 3
Prod-BARR Dist-BARR 1977

Services For The Blind And Physically Handicapped C 20 MIN
3/4 INCH VIDEO CASSETTE T
Explains the range of services available to those people who are temporarily or permanently unable to read.
From The Access Series.
LC NO. 76-706259
Prod-UDEN Dist-USNAC 1976

Services To Elementary-Age Children C 20 MIN
3/4 INCH VIDEO CASSETTE T
Discusses ideas about noncompetitive participation-oriented programs for elementary-age children.
From The Access Series.
LC NO. 76-706261
Prod-UDEN Dist-USNAC 1976

Services To Young Children B 48 MIN
16MM FILM OPTICAL SOUND
Features a pediatric neurologist, nurse, therapist, speech pathologist, special educator and social worker who discuss the need for and demonstrate the techniques of serving young children (under three years of age) with cerebral dysfunction.
Prod-UCPA Dist-UCPA

Servicing A Propeller B 18 MIN
16MM FILM OPTICAL SOUND
Demonstrates how to inspect and remove a propeller, repair damage to the metal edges, check and correct for out-of-track and for out-of-balance problems and reinstall the propeller.
LC NO. FIE52-235
Prod-USOE Dist-USNAC 1945

Servicing An Airplane B 17 MIN
16MM FILM OPTICAL SOUND
Shows how to perform the various routine servicing operations on a plane on the ground--cleaning the airplane, refueling, changing the oil, inflating tires and starting the engine. Shows hand signals for guiding the pilot.
LC NO. FIE52-266
Prod-USOE Dist-USNAC 1945

Servicing And Timing Magnetos B 16 MIN
16MM FILM OPTICAL SOUND
Demonstrates how to remove magnetos from the engine, install and adjust points and reinstall and time the magnetos.
LC NO. FIE52-258
Prod-USOE Dist-USNAC 1945

Servicing Chrysler Electronic Ignition C 25 MIN
3/4 OR 1/2 INCH VIDEO CASSETTE IND
Identifes the components of the Chrysler ignition system. Explains their operating principles and outlines an on-the-car trouble shooting procedure. Covers distributor service.
From The Automechanics Series.
Prod-LEIKID Dist-LEIKID

Servicing Ford Electronic Ignition C 24 MIN
3/4 OR 1/2 INCH VIDEO CASSETTE IND
Presents the Ford system in a similar manner to the Chrylser system, showing a comprehensive on-the-car checkout and distributor test and service procedure.
From The Automechanics Series.
Prod-LEIKID Dist-LEIKID

Servicing GM Electronic Ignition C 36 MIN
3/4 OR 1/2 INCH VIDEO CASSETTE IND
Demonstrates the unique GM Hi-energy system, self-contained in the distributor, through a precise on-the-car inspection and test. Shows how to dismantle the distributor and reassemble it on the bench.
From The Automechanics Series.
Prod-LEIKID Dist-LEIKID

Servicing Spark Plugs And Ignition Wiring B 22 MIN
16MM FILM OPTICAL SOUND
Shows how to remove spark plugs and ignition wires, how to clean, inspect, adjust and reinstall the spark plugs, and how to prepare and install ignition wires.
From The Aircraft Work Series. Power Plant Maintenance
LC NO. FIE52-252
Prod-USOE Dist-USNAC Prodn-AUDIO 1945

Servicing The Automatic Choke C 4 MIN
16MM FILM OPTICAL SOUND
Points out the main operation features of the choke control, the control spring and the method of adjusting for the variance of volatility of the gasoline.
LC NO. FI68-242
Prod-RAYBAR Dist-RAYBAR 1966

Servicing The Radiator Pressure Cap C 4 MIN
16MM FILM OPTICAL SOUND
Shows cleaning and test for pressure of an old radiator cap. Includes inspection of filler neck and cams and cleaning of the overflow tube.
LC NO. FI68-243
Prod-RAYBAR Dist-RAYBAR 1966

Servicing Water-Cooled Condensers B 12 MIN
16MM FILM OPTICAL SOUND
Explains the theory of a counter-flow condenser, the essential elements of a water-cooled system and the operation and regulation of the electric water valve.
From The Refrigeration Service Series. Commercial Systems, No. 4
LC NO. FIE52-262
Prod-USOE Dist-USNAC Prodn-BONDP 1945

Serving And Feeding The Patient C 9 MIN
3/4 OR 1/2 INCH VIDEO CASSETTE PRO
Stresses basic nutritional needs and describes the four basic food groups. Explains the importance of adequate fluid intake. Emphasizes the importance of stimulating the patient's appetite with attractively prepared meals served in a pleasant atmosphere.
LC NO. 77-731353
Prod-TRAINX Dist-TRAINX

Serving And Feeding The Patient (Spanish) C 9 MIN
3/4 OR 1/2 INCH VIDEO CASSETTE PRO
Stresses basic nutritional needs and describes the four basic foods groups. Explains the importance of adequate fluid intake. Emphasizes the importance of stimulating the patient's appetite with attractively prepared meals served in a pleasant atmosphere.
LC NO. 77-731353
Prod-TRAINX Dist-TRAINX

Serving Cakes C 11 MIN
3/4 OR 1/2 INCH VIDEO CASSETTE PRO
Teaches how to cut various cakes, from sheet cake to wedding cake, with an eye toward reflecting in each slice the beauty of the whole cake.
Prod-CULINA Dist-CULINA

Serving Cheese C 9 MIN
3/4 OR 1/2 INCH VIDEO CASSETTE PRO
Introduces various types of cheese and suggests suitable accompaniments of wine, bread and fruit for each.
Prod-CULINA Dist-CULINA

Serving Food (Spanish) C 11 MIN
16MM FILM OPTICAL SOUND
Portrays the hiring of a waitress and shows the orientation and induction training given her by a restaurant hostess, including instruction in the proper storage of cups, dishes and glasses. Shows cleanliness, the correct ways of clearing tables, protecting the waitresses' health and safeguards against disease.
LC NO. 74-705612
Prod-NMAC Dist-USNAC 1954

Serving Food And Beverage (Rev Ed) C
16MM FILM, 3/4 OR 1/2 IN VIDEO
Demonstrates basic rules of serving food and beverage. Shows how professional waiters and waitresses place a wide range of menu items in front of the guest. Teaches how to add garnishments, condiments and accompaniments, stressing imaginative use of color.
From The Professional Food Preparation And Service Programs Series.
Prod-NEM Dist-NEM 1983

Serving The Four Corners Of Our Earth C 20 MIN
16MM FILM OPTICAL SOUND H-C A
Presents an overview of the National Cash Register Corporation's services and facilities throughout the world.
LC NO. 76-702105
Prod-NCR Dist-NCR 1974

Serving Those Who Have Served C 27 MIN
3/4 INCH VIDEO CASSETTE
Reviews the history of the Veterans Administration hospital system and explains the structure and organization of both the central office and local hospitals.
LC NO. 79-707305
Prod-USVA Dist-USNAC 1978

Servo Analysis B 40 MIN
16MM FILM, 3/4 OR 1/2 IN VIDEO
Shows how the need for a servo system is established and a block diagram of a system is analyzed. Discusses error voltage. (Kinescope)

LC NO. 82-706238
Prod-USAF Dist-USNAC

Sesame Street - Developing Self-Esteem—A Series

Encourages young viewers to experience pride in accomplishment, in unique aptitudes and abilities, in friends and family, and in learning new skills. Features Lily Tomlin, violinist Ithzak Perlman, NBC sportscaster Marv Albert and the Muppet gang.
Prod-CTELWO Dist-GA 1984

Sesame Street - Identifying Sounds—A Series

Presents the sounds familiar objects and animals make and provides practice in distinguishing between different sound patterns.
Prod-CTELWO Dist-GA 1984

Sesame Street - Recognizing Numerals And Number Sets, 1-12—A Series

Presents lessons on recognizing and understanding the numbers 1 to 12. Features favorite Muppets singing delightful renditions of specially created number songs.
Prod-CTELWO Dist-GA 1984

Sesame Street - Word Families—A Series

Discusses the relationships between words and discusses the basics of rhyming.
Prod-CTELWO Dist-GA 1984

Session I C 20 MIN
16MM FILM, 3/4 OR 1/2 IN VIDEO
Shows trainees how to replace schoolroom learning ideas with adult learning techniques and drives home the concept that learning extends far beyond the formal program and that each trainee is accountable for his or her results.
Prod-EFM Dist-EFM

Session With College Students, A B 60 MIN
16MM FILM OPTICAL SOUND
Shows Dr Frederick Perls, founder of Gestalt therapy, demonstrating his method for discovering and expressing the meaning of dreams of college students.
Prod-PSYCHF Dist-PSYCHD

Set Europe Ablaze B 26 MIN
16MM FILM OPTICAL SOUND
Uses documentary footage to describe Churchill's arrangements with governments-in-exile in London. Examines various underground movements in German-occupied Europe, including the ill-fated Warsaw uprising in 1944.
From The Winston Churchill - The Valiant Years Series. No. 19
LC NO. FI67-2113
Prod-ABCTV Dist-SG 1961

Set Numeration C 15 MIN
3/4 INCH VIDEO CASSETTE P
Provides a basic experience in relating number and numeral.
From The Math Factory, Module I - Sets Series.
Prod-MAETEL Dist-GPITVL 1973

Set Of Coincidence C 13 MIN
3/4 OR 1/2 INCH VIDEO CASSETTE
Shows a performer making a journey out of an obviously theatrical set through a moving corridor and into a space made of video noise.
From The Three Short Tapes Series.
Prod-EAI Dist-EAI

Set Of Slides, A B 30 MIN
16MM FILM, 3/4 OR 1/2 IN VIDEO J-C A
Uses over 400 old photographs to describe life in 19th century England. Narrated by Anthony Quayle.
Prod-BAYLSP Dist-WOMBAT

Set Sail C 30 MIN
1/2 IN VIDEO CASSETTE BETA/VHS
Tells what's required to safely take off and return a sailboat. Reviews the balance of forces involved in sailing.
From The Under Sail Series.
Prod-WGBHTV Dist-MTI

Set Speeches And Soliloquies C 52 MIN
3/4 OR 1/2 INCH VIDEO CASSETTE
Presents the rules governing a soliloquy including that it must arise out of a situation, it must have story and it must be spontaneous. Uses examples of Shakespearean soliloquies from The Merchant Of Venice, As You Like It, Richard III and Titus Andronicus.
From The Royal Shakespeare Company Series.
Prod-FOTH Dist-FOTH 1984

Set The Pace C 10 MIN
16MM FILM, 3/4 OR 1/2 IN VIDEO
Shows how the supervisor sets the pace for the workmen to follow safety practices in the coal mining industry by his sincerity and enthusiasm.
From The Foremanship Training Series.
LC NO. 82-706281
Prod-USBM Dist-USNAC 1968

Set Theory, Pt 1 C 45 MIN
2 INCH VIDEOTAPE
See series title for descriptive statement.
From The Fundamentals Of Mathematics (2nd Ed.) Unit I - Number Theory Series.
Prod-CHITVC Dist-GPITVL

Set Theory, Pt 2 C 45 MIN
2 INCH VIDEOTAPE
See series title for descriptive statement.
From The Fundamentals Of Mathematics (2nd Ed.) Unit I - Number Theory Series.
Prod-CHITVC Dist-GPITVL

Set-Up And Shut Down Of Oxy-Acetylene Welding Equipment (Spanish) C
3/4 OR 1/2 INCH VIDEO CASSETTE
See series title for descriptive statement.
From The Oxy-Acetylene Welding (Spanish) Series.
Prod-VTRI Dist-VTRI

Set-up And Shut Down Of Oxy-Acetylene Welding Equipment C 15 MIN
3/4 OR 1/2 INCH VIDEO CASSETTE
See series title for descriptive statement.
From The Welding I - Basic Oxy-Acetylene Welding Series.
Prod-CAMB Dist-CAMB

Set-Up And Shut-Down Of Oxy-Acetylene Equipment C 15 MIN
3/4 OR 1/2 INCH VIDEO CASSETTE IND
See series title for descriptive statement.
From The Welding - Oxy-Acetylene Welding Series.
Prod-ICSINT Dist-ICSINT

Set-up For Holding Work To Be Milled C 15 MIN
3/4 OR 1/2 INCH VIDEO CASSETTE IND
See series title for descriptive statement.
From The Machining And The Operation Of Machine Tools, Module 4 - Milling And Tool Series.
Prod-LEIKID Dist-LEIKID

Seth Hill C 28 MIN
3/4 INCH VIDEO CASSETTE H-C A
Interviews animator and documentary filmmaker Seth Hill. Focuses on the creative process of film production.
From The San Francisco Bay Area Filmmakers Series.
LC NO. 80-706449
Prod-DANKAR Dist-DANKAR 1979

Sets C 15 MIN
16MM FILM OPTICAL SOUND I-H T
Presents the elementary notions of sets and operations with appropriate vocabulary in four lessons—sets, elements and subsets, operation of intersection, operation of union, cardinal number, sum and product.
Prod-MMP Dist-MMP 1963

Sets C 30 MIN
3/4 OR 1/2 INCH VIDEO CASSETTE H-C A
Introduces the SET data type and operation that can be performed on variables of set type such as union, difference and intersection. Discusses relations like equality, inequality and inclusion as well as set membership.
From The Pascal, Pt 2 - Intermediate Pascal Series.
LC NO. 81-706049
Prod-COLOSU Dist-COLOSU 1980

Sets - Empty Sets C 14 MIN
3/4 OR 1/2 INCH VIDEO CASSETTE P
Gives experience in classifying sets versus empty sets.
From The Hands On, Grade 2 - Lollipops, Loops, Etc Series. Unit 3 - Classifying
Prod-WHROTV Dist-AITECH 1975

Sets And Locations For Videotape C 30 MIN
3/4 OR 1/2 INCH VIDEO CASSETTE
Demonstrates techniques to create minimum cost sets. Shows how to shoot on location and the use of props.
From The Video - A Practical Guide...and More Series.
Prod-VIPUB Dist-VIPUB

Sets And Numbers C 12 MIN
16MM FILM, 3/4 OR 1/2 IN VIDEO P-I
Discusses sets, one-to-one correspondence, cardinal numbers, and counting.
From The Modern Elementary Mathematics Series.
Prod-TMP Dist-CRMP

Sets Of Coins C 15 MIN
3/4 OR 1/2 INCH VIDEO CASSETTE P
Explains the value of the penny, nickel, dime and quarter and shows different sets of coins that have the same value.
From The Math Factory, Module VI - Money Series.
Prod-MAETEL Dist-GPITVL

Sets, Construction And Display B 21 MIN
16MM FILM OPTICAL SOUND
Concentrates on three commonly found production situations, the 'PRESENTER SET,' the 'INTERVIEW SET' and the 'DRAMA SET.'
From The CETO Television Training Films Series.
Prod-CETO Dist-GPITVL

Setting An Adjustable Articulator To Positional Records, Pt 1 C 19 MIN
16MM FILM OPTICAL SOUND PRO
Describes the modifications for the adjustable articulator. Demonstrates the methodology of recording the hinge axis on a patient and its transfer to the articulator. Shows how the patient's casts are related to the mandibular cast mounted to the maxillary in the most retruded position.
LC NO. 74-706519
Prod-USVA Dist-USNAC 1971

Setting An Adjustable Articulator To Positional Records, Pt I C 19 MIN
3/4 OR 1/2 INCH VIDEO CASSETTE
Shows and defines the armamentarium of the adjustable articulator and demonstrates the procedure through the mounting of the maxillary cast and the split mandibular cast on the articulator in the most retruded position.
Prod-VADTC Dist-AMDA

Setting An Adjustable Articulator To Positional Records, Pt 2 C 12 MIN
16MM FILM OPTICAL SOUND PRO
Shows the methods employed to obtain the patient's lateral and protrusive records after preregistration of the positions of the articulator. Shows how the procedures are helpful in diagnosing occlusal problems and in the fabrication of complicated fixed bridges.
LC NO. 74-706521
Prod-USVA Dist-USNAC 1971

Setting An Adjustable Articulator To Positional Records, Pt II C 12 MIN
3/4 OR 1/2 INCH VIDEO CASSETTE
Continues the demonstration of the adjustable articulator.
Prod-VADTC Dist-AMDA 1971

Setting Career Goals C 30 MIN
3/4 OR 1/2 INCH VIDEO CASSETTE
Discusses the importance of setting career goals, featuring recognized experts in the field of career planning.
From The Where The Jobs Are Series.
Prod-IVCH Dist-IVCH

Setting In A Regular Sleeve C 3 MIN
16MM FILM SILENT J-C A
Shows the conventional method of sewing the underarm seam of the sleeve and garment before inserting the sleeve, then shaping the sleeve cap with ease stitch, pinning, stitching and trimming.
From The Clothing Construction Techniques Series.
LC NO. 77-701205
Prod-IOWA Dist-IOWASP 1976

Setting In A Shirt Sleeve C 5 MIN
16MM FILM SILENT J-C A
Demonstrates the open or flat construction method for setting in a shirt-type sleeve. Shows how a row of ease stitches is used over the sleeve cap and how the sleeve is attached before the underarm is stitched.
From The Clothing Construction Techniques Series.
LC NO. 77-701211
Prod-IOWA Dist-IOWASP 1976

Setting In Stories C 15 MIN
3/4 OR 1/2 INCH VIDEO CASSETTE P
See series title for descriptive statement.
From The Word Shop Series.
Prod-WETATV Dist-WETATV

Setting Limits C 24 MIN
3/4 OR 1/2 INCH VIDEO CASSETTE
Highlights important themes from first two parts of the Setting Limits Series. Serves as a guide for discussing sexuality with teenagers. In sign language.
From The Setting Limits Series.
Prod-ODNP Dist-ODNP

Setting Limits—A Series
J-C S
Designed to help teenagers sort out their confusions about communicating with the opposite sex and help them consider the consequences of their behavior. Real-life sign language drama.
Prod-ODNP Dist-ODNP

A Night Out	010 MIN
More Than Friends	021 MIN
Setting Limits	024 MIN

Setting Overall Objectives C 7 MIN
3/4 OR 1/2 INCH VIDEO CASSETTE
See series title for descriptive statement.
From The Practical M B O Series.
Prod-DELTAK Dist-DELTAK

Setting Sail C 15 MIN
1/2 IN VIDEO CASSETTE BETA/VHS I-J
Teaches sailing, describes a sighting of whales, and explains data collection for further analysis. Includes a visit to the Provincetown Center For Coastal Research, which provides a first-hand look at whale researchers at work and explores the variety of whale species.
From The Voyage Of The Mimi Series.
Prod-HRAW Dist-HRAW

Setting Standards Of Performance C 20 MIN
3/4 OR 1/2 INCH VIDEO CASSETTE
Shows what performance standards can do for an organization, discusses kinds of practical performance standards and shows managers how to arrive at meaningful standards of their own.
Prod-AMA Dist-AMA

Setting The Bandsaws Up For Sawing And Use Of Accessories C
3/4 OR 1/2 INCH VIDEO CASSETTE
See series title for descriptive statement.
From The Basic Machine Technology Series.
Prod-VTRI Dist-VTRI

Setting The Bandsaws Up For Sawing And Use Of Accessories C 15 MIN
3/4 OR 1/2 INCH VIDEO CASSETTE
See series title for descriptive statement.
From The Machine Technology II - Engine Lathe Accessories Series.
Prod-CAMB Dist-CAMB

Setting The Bandsaws Up For Sawing And Use Of Accessories (Spanish) C
3/4 OR 1/2 INCH VIDEO CASSETTE
See series title for descriptive statement.
From The Basic Machine Technology (Spanish) Series.
Prod-VTRI Dist-VTRI

Setting The Context, Pt 1 B 42 MIN
3/4 OR 1/2 INCH VIDEO CASSETTE
Features lecture by Dr Donald R Bardill on relational family therapy. Focuses on the effect a member's absence has on group cohesiveness, the feeling of respect a person gains knowing that she/he is needed and each member's responsibility to the group.
From The Relationship Growth Group Series.
Prod-WRAMC Dist-UWISC 1979

Setting The Mandibular Anterior Teeth C 6 MIN
16MM FILM, 3/4 OR 1/2 IN VIDEO PRO
Discusses setting teeth for dentures. Shows how the mandibular anterior teeth are positioned after the maxillary anteriors have been set up. Issued in 1974 as a motion picture.
LC NO. 80-706795
Prod-USVA Dist-USNAC 1980

Setting The Maxillary Anterior Teeth C 9 MIN
16MM FILM, 3/4 OR 1/2 IN VIDEO PRO
Discusses setting teeth for dentures. Demonstrates fundamental techniques for setting teeth in edentulous arches. Deals with preparation of the record bases for reception of the denture teeth, and the positioning and arrangement of the anterior teeth.
LC NO. 80-706794
Prod-USVA Dist-USNAC Prodn-VADTC 1980

Setting The Posterior Teeth C 6 MIN
16MM FILM, 3/4 OR 1/2 IN VIDEO PRO
Describes the setting and articulating of the posterior teeth for dentures. Shows how the teeth are positioned and arranged to meet the requirements of occlusal balance in both the centric and eccentric positions.
LC NO. 80-706796
Prod-USVA Dist-USNAC Prodn-VADTC 1980

Setting The Right Climate C 22 MIN
16MM FILM - 3/4 IN VIDEO
Shows what teamwork is and is not, how to institute it and the climate in which it flourishes. Presents a six-point model for critiquing progress and discusses the line manager's vital role as a paraprofessional trainer.
From The Increasing Productivity And Efficiency Series.
Prod-BNA Dist-BNA

Setting The Right Climate (Dutch) C 120 MIN
16MM FILM, 3/4 OR 1/2 IN VIDEO
Examines the procedures for effective team building and management.
From The Increasing Productivity And Efficiency (Dutch) Series.
Prod-BNA Dist-BNA

Setting The Right Climate (Norwegian) C 120 MIN
16MM FILM, 3/4 OR 1/2 IN VIDEO
Examines the procedures for effective team building and management.
From The Increasing Productivity And Efficiency (Norwegian) Series.
Prod-BNA Dist-BNA

Setting Things Up B
16MM FILM OPTICAL SOUND
Discusses mapping and functions. Defines the terms domain, codomain, mapping, function, and operator.
Prod-OPENU Dist-OPENU 1979

Setting Up A Management Process C 30 MIN
3/4 OR 1/2 INCH VIDEO CASSETTE
Defines the purpose of financial management. Deals with record keeping, spending plans and net worth statements.
From The Financial Management Workshops Series.
Prod-ODECA Dist-BULFRG

Setting Up A Room - Creating An Environment For Learning X 27 MIN
16MM FILM OPTICAL SOUND C T
Uses live dialogue and narration to convey the process of planning a kindergarten classroom, establishing the basic work and play areas and arranging the supplementary materials in order to create a functional, flexible room environment for children.
LC NO. FIA67-5330
Prod-CFDC Dist-CFDC 1967

Setting Up A Worksheet C
3/4 OR 1/2 INCH VIDEO CASSETTE
Describes the layout of a MultiPlan worksheet, identifying rows, columns and cells. Describes the areas of a MultiPlan worksheet and defines the term window.
From The Using MultiPlan Series.
Prod-COMTEG Dist-COMTEG

Setting Up Aluminum Wire Feed And Running Butt, T, And Lap Joints (Spanish) C
3/4 OR 1/2 INCH VIDEO CASSETTE
See series title for descriptive statement.
From The MIG And TIG Welding (Spanish) Series.
Prod-VTRI Dist-VTRI

Setting Up Aluminum Wire Feed And Running Butt-T-, And Lap Joints C 15 MIN
3/4 OR 1/2 INCH VIDEO CASSETTE IND
See series title for descriptive statement.
From The Welding - MIG And TIG Welding Series.
Prod-ICSINT Dist-ICSINT

Setting Up An Aquarium C 9 MIN
3/4 INCH VIDEO CASSETTE P
Shows school children preparing a classroom aquarium and learning about the needs of living things in a water environment.
Prod-BOBWIN Dist-GA

Setting Up An Electrocardiograph Machine C 15 MIN
1/2 IN VIDEO CASSETTE BETA/VHS
Explains how to set up an electrocardiograph machine.
Prod-RMI Dist-RMI

Setting Up And Machining Bar Stock B 34 MIN
3/4 INCH VIDEO CASSETTE
Shows how to set up the turret lathe for the production machining of brushings from bar stock, install the collet, set up the hexagon turret and the cross slide, and machine bar stock. Issued in 1945 as a motion picture.
From The Machine Shop Work - Operations On The Turret Lathe Series. No. 4
LC NO. 79-706807
Prod-USOE Dist-USNAC Prodn-INDFLM 1979

Setting Up And Padding Of The Inert-Gas Shielded Metal-Arc Welding (Spanish) C
3/4 OR 1/2 INCH VIDEO CASSETTE
See series title for descriptive statement.
From The MIG And TIG Welding (Spanish) Series.
Prod-VTRI Dist-VTRI

Setting Up And Padding Of The Inert-Gas Shielded Metal-Arc Welding C 15 MIN
3/4 OR 1/2 INCH VIDEO CASSETTE IND
See series title for descriptive statement.
From The Welding - MIG And TIG Welding Series.
Prod-ICSINT Dist-ICSINT

Setting Up And Padding Of The Inert-Gas-Shielded Metal-Arc Welding C 15 MIN
3/4 OR 1/2 INCH VIDEO CASSETTE
See series title for descriptive statement.
From The Welding III - TIG and MIG (Industry) Welding series.
Prod-CAMB Dist-CAMB

Setting Up Flux Cored Wire And Running Continuous Beads C
3/4 OR 1/2 INCH VIDEO CASSETTE
See series title for descriptive statement.
From The MIG And TIG Welding (Spanish) Series.
Prod-VTRI Dist-VTRI

Setting Up Flux Cored Wire And Running Continuous Beads C 15 MIN
3/4 OR 1/2 INCH VIDEO CASSETTE IND
See series title for descriptive statement.
From The Welding - MIG And TIG Welding Series.
Prod-ICSINT Dist-ICSINT

Setting Up For Welding C 12 MIN
16MM FILM, 3/4 OR 1/2 IN VIDEO
Illustrates mig welding techniques. Shows how the spray arc and short arc work, how to set up the equipment and adjust the shielding gas, welding wire, welding current and torch in preparation for welding.
From The Welding Series.
Prod-UCC Dist-FI 1972

Setting Up Of A Club, The C 28 MIN
16MM FILM OPTICAL SOUND
Explains that in the Academic Club Method used at the Kingsbury Center Lab School, a club is built around a set of academic objectives woven into a dramatic theme designed to capture children's interest and involvement. Demonstrates by showing the functioning of the 'Greek Gods Club.'
From The Learning For A Lifetime - The Academic Club Method Series. Part 2
Prod-KINGS Dist-KINGS

Setting Up The Current Balance B 18 MIN
16MM FILM OPTICAL SOUND
Two teachers exhibit and discuss a rudimentary current balance made from aluminum foil and thin tubing, assemble and wire the circuits of the more advanced apparatus with which students can make quantitative measurements and discuss the adjustments and manipulations that students must make when using the balance.
From The Harvard Project Physics Teacher Briefings Series. No. 15
LC NO. 77-709142
Prod-WGBH Dist-HRAW 1969

Setting Up The Korek Frame Repair C 18 MIN
1/2 IN VIDEO CASSETTE BETA/VHS
Deals with auto body repair.
Prod-RMI Dist-RMI

Settlers - Early Pioneer Farmers Of The Great Lakes Region, The C 28 MIN
16MM FILM, 3/4 OR 1/2 IN VIDEO I-J
Will McLeod, a former shipbuilder and his wife Maggie, settle in the Great Lakes in 1835 to become farmers. Although a storm damages the first crop of oats, and a fire destroys their barn, they survive their first season in the new land.
Prod-RUDDEL Dist-CORF 1967

Settlers And The Land, The B 30 MIN
16MM FILM OPTICAL SOUND H-C A
Discusses the rapid settlement of the Great Plains after the Civil War. Describes the Union veterans and government land policies, how the railroads helped the settlers, Nebraska's advertising campaign to break the Great American Desert myth and the state's melting-pot population.
From The Great Plains Trilogy, 3 Series. Explorer And Settler - The White Man Arrives
Prod-UNEBR Dist-UNEBR 1954

Settlers, The C 22 MIN
16MM FILM, 3/4 OR 1/2 IN VIDEO I-H
Explores the reasons for and the impact of America's westward expansion.
From The Growth Of America's West Series.
Prod-AFAI Dist-PHENIX 1978

Settling Down C 55 MIN
16MM FILM, 3/4 OR 1/2 IN VIDEO H-C A
Explores the reasons why man began to plant and harvest cereals in the Fertile Crescent over 12,000 years ago. Traces the shift in mankind from nomadic hunter-gatherer to settled villager and farmer. Narrated by Richard Leakey.
From The Making Of Mankind Series.
Prod-BBCTV Dist-TIMLIF 1982

Settling Of The Plains, The C 30 MIN
16MM FILM, 3/4 OR 1/2 IN VIDEO H-C
See series title for descriptive statement.
From The Great Plains Experience Series.
Prod-UMA Dist-GPITVL 1976

Setup Electric-Arc Welding Equipment C 15 MIN
3/4 OR 1/2 INCH VIDEO CASSETTE
See series title for descriptive statement.
From The Welding II - Basic Shielded Metal Arc Welding series.
Prod-CAMB Dist-CAMB

Setup For Face Milling With A Fixture B 20 MIN
16MM FILM - 3/4 IN VIDEO
Demonstrates how the horizontal boring, drilling and milling machine operates. Tells how to install the fixture, set up the workpiece, and select and install an end mill and a face mill. Issued in 1945 as a motion picture.
From The Machine Shop Work - Operations On The Horizontal Boring Mill Series. Number 1
LC NO. 80-706609
Prod-USOE Dist-USNAC Prodn-ESCAR 1980

Setup For Hold Work To Be Milled C 15 MIN
3/4 OR 1/2 INCH VIDEO CASSETTE
See series title for descriptive statement.
From The Machine Technology IV - Milling Series
Prod-CAMB Dist-CAMB

Setup For Holding Work To Be Milled C
3/4 OR 1/2 INCH VIDEO CASSETTE
See series title for descriptive statement.
From The Milling And Tool Sharpening Series.
Prod-VTRI Dist-VTRI

Setup For Holding Work To Be Milled (Spanish) C
3/4 OR 1/2 INCH VIDEO CASSETTE
See series title for descriptive statement.
From The Milling And Tool Sharpening (Spanish) Series.
Prod-VTRI Dist-VTRI

Setup For Rough Line-Boring B 15 MIN
16MM FILM - 3/4 IN VIDEO
Demonstrates how to position the workpiece on the table and position the spindle for horizontal centers and for vertical centers. Issued in 1945 as a motion picture.
From The Machine Shop Work - Operations On The Horizontal Boring Mill Series. Number 4
LC NO. 80-706610
Prod-USOE Dist-USNAC Prodn-ESCAR 1980

Setup Of The Combination Torch And Cutting Of Sheet Metal, Sheet Plate C 15 MIN
3/4 OR 1/2 INCH VIDEO CASSETTE
See series title for descriptive statement.
From The Welding I - Basic Oxy-Acetylene Welding Series.
Prod-CAMB Dist-CAMB

Setup Of The Commercial Dishwasher C 20 MIN
1/2 IN VIDEO CASSETTE BETA/VHS
Provides useful steps in the operation of a commercial dishwasher, including the pre-wash setup and drying station. Discusses key parts and maintenance tips.
Prod-RMI Dist-RMI

Seurat B 29 MIN
3/4 INCH VIDEO CASSETTE
Features Guy Palazzola as he imitates the painting technique of Georges Seurat to illustrate this important nineteenth-century painter's use of pointillism and proportion.
From The Meet The Masters Series.
Prod-UMITV Dist-UMITV 1966

Seven Artists - Seven Spaces - In A Hospital C 20 MIN
3/4 OR 1/2 INCH VIDEO CASSETTE
Observes seven leading artists as they engage in massive installations of commissioned artworks in the Detroit Receiving Hospital and the University Health Center. A unique musical score accompanies each artist's interpretation as the work was completed in 1983.
Prod-MARXS Dist-MARXS

Seven Bridges Of Konigsberg, The C 4 MIN
16MM FILM, 3/4 OR 1/2 IN VIDEO H-C
Re-creates Leonard Euler's analysis of crossing the seven bridges of Konigsberg in a single continuous walk. Tells how he proved that this would be impossible.
Prod-CORNW Dist-IFB 1965

Seven Chances B 57 MIN
16MM FILM SILENT J-C A
Stars Buster Keaton. Tells of a young man who will inherit a fortune providing he is married before seven PM on a designated date.
Prod-MGM Dist-TWYMAN 1925

Seven Day Itch B 7 MIN
16MM FILM OPTICAL SOUND T
Views children exploring social relations at Hilltop Head Start Center.
From The Vignette Series.
LC NO. 71-707970
Prod-EDS Dist-EDC 1969

Seven Days A Week X 30 MIN
16MM FILM OPTICAL SOUND J-H T R
Attempts to motivate Christian laymen to witness to their Christian faith on the job and at work seven days a week.
LC NO. FIA68-586
Prod-FAMF Dist-FAMF 1964

Seven Days In The Life Of The President B 60 MIN
16MM FILM OPTICAL SOUND
A behind-the-scenes look at Lyndon B Johnson, President of the United States, during a crucial week of decision making.
From The March Of Time Series.
LC NO. FIA66-536
Prod-WOLPER Dist-WOLPER 1965

Seven Dietary Guidelines And Eating A Variety Of Foods C 28 MIN
3/4 OR 1/2 INCH VIDEO CASSETTE H-C A
Introduces the Seven Dietary Guidelines and features dishes emphasizing guideline No. 1 - Eat A Variety Of Foods.
From the Eat Well, Be Well Series.
Prod-JOU Dist-JOU 1983

Seven Doorways To Selling Excellence C 20 MIN
3/4 OR 1/2 INCH VIDEO CASSETTE
Takes salespeople through seven tough, challenging sales calls, showing how to put price objections in perspective, convince buyers who are sold on competitors' product and selling to those who agree to everything but seldom buy.
Prod-BBP Dist-BBP

Seven For Suzie C 14 MIN
16MM FILM OPTICAL SOUND
Presents a report on the rehabilitation of an eight year-old handicapped child by a team which includes a physical therapist, occupational therapist, social worker, speech pathologist, psychologist, recreation specialist and special education teacher. Shows how the members of the team work together and separately, and how the child is prepared for a regular classroom and for coping with her disabilities.
LC NO. 72-702993
Prod-NESSCA Dist-NESSCA Prodn-GITLNI 1968

Seven Forty-Seven, The C 28 MIN
16MM FILM OPTICAL SOUND
Tells the story of the Boeing 747 airplane as seen through the eyes of the people whose lives it affects as it circumnavigates the globe.
LC NO. 77-702291
Prod-BOEING Dist-WELBIT Prodn-WELBIT 1977

Seven Hundred And One Days, The C 13 MIN
16MM FILM OPTICAL SOUND
Features reminiscences by the development team that designed and built IBM'S first mass-produced electronic computer, the IBM 701.
LC NO. 73-702364
Prod-IBUSMA Dist-IBUSMA 1973

Seven Hundred And Thirty Days C 50 MIN
16MM FILM OPTICAL SOUND
Presents the Philippines village diary of four young overseas volunteers from Japan's Peace Corps, all of them eager to help their handicapped Asian neighbors. Explains some of their projects.
Prod-UNIJAP Dist-UNIJAP 1970

Seven Hundred Eighty-Four Days That Changed America--A Series C 4 MIN
3/4 OR 1/2 INCH VIDEO CASSETTE J-C A
Reviews the Watergate affair which brought down the presidency of Richard M Nixon. Composed chiefly of succinctly edited clips from the 1973 Senate hearings.
Prod-TCAF Dist-FI 1982

Break-In, The 025 MIN
Coverup, The 025 MIN
Crime, The 028 MIN
Impeachment, The 042 MIN

Seven Little Ducks (2nd Ed) X 11 MIN
16MM FILM, 3/4 OR 1/2 IN VIDEO P
Portrays the life habits of domesticated Muscovy ducks and shows a child can care for pets by feeding, watering and sheltering them.
Prod-BAILEY Dist-PHENIX 1967

Seven Minute Lesson - Acting As A Sighted Guide C 7 MIN
16MM FILM OPTICAL SOUND A
Demonstrates how sighted individuals can assist their blind companions in everyday activities, and notes verbal and physical cues the sighted guide should employ.
LC NO. 79-700074
Prod-AFB Dist-PHENIX Prodn-ARDEN 1978

Seven Minute Lesson, The C 7 MIN
16MM FILM, 3/4 OR 1/2 IN VIDEO J-C A
Demonstrates the proper techniques most commonly involved in acting as a sighted guide for a blind person.
Prod-AFB Dist-PHENIX

Seven North - Primary Nursing C 56 MIN
3/4 OR 1/2 INCH VIDEO CASSETTE
Focuses on the 'primary nurse' system at a major Boston hospital. Documents the common, but critical, events that any patient might experience and that any nurse might have to deal with.
Prod-FANPRO Dist-FANPRO

Seven Ravens, The C 21 MIN
16MM FILM, 3/4 OR 1/2 IN VIDEO K-P
Tells the story of a peasant family who had seven sons and a daughter. Relates how a wicked old woman casts a spell on the seven brothers, turning them into ravens. Proceeds to tell how the little girl frees her brothers.
Prod-ANIMAT Dist-LCOA 1971

Seven Samurai, The (Japanese) B 140 MIN
3/4 OR 1/2 INCH VIDEO CASSETTE
Presents Akira Kurosawa's adventure of the samurai. Features Toshiro Mifune and Takashi Shimura.
Prod-IHF Dist-IHF

Seven Simple Chicken Dishes C
1/2 IN VIDEO CASSETTE BETA/VHS
Instructs in the preparation of such recipes as stir fry chicken and shrimp, Sherry Chicken and Coq Au Vin.
From The Video Cooking Library Series.
Prod-KARTES Dist-KARTES

Seven Sins, The C 15 MIN
16MM FILM OPTICAL SOUND H-C
Combines the works of Flemish painter Peter Bruegel the Elder and the words of author H Arthur Klein to examine the question of whether man can alter his self-destructive instincts. Shows that man is a primitive being haunted by the demons of his own behavior.
Prod-MALIBU Dist-MALIBU

Seven Sixty-Five North/4501 South C 35 MIN
1/2 IN VIDEO CASSETTE BETA/VHS
Presents Fort Wayne Historical Society's Nickel Plate Berkshire No. 765 steam locomotive and Southern Railway's Virginia Green and Gold Mikado No. 4501.
Prod-DELUZ Dist-DELUZ 1980

Seven Stars C 13 MIN
16MM FILM OPTICAL SOUND
A Japanese language film. Presents Tolstoy's fairy story about the great bear made with shadow-pictures. Tells the story of a kind-hearted girl in a village where the people had been suffering from a long drought and how she prayed sincerely for rain until her long-cherished wish was at last realized. Explains that since then, the villagers believed the beautiful twinkle of the great bear in the north sky is that of this tender little girl's heart.
Prod-UNIJAP Dist-UNIJAP 1967

Seven Steps To T Q C Promotion--A Series

Presents Total Quality Control, a technique symbolizing Japan's recent company management successes. With Dr Kaora Ishikawa.
Prod-TOYOVS Dist-TOYOVS

Control Is The Way To Endless Progress 028 MIN
How To Use The Seven Q C Tools 027 MIN
Introduction And Implementation Of T Q C 027 MIN
Promotion Of Q C Circle Activities 030 MIN
Quality Assurance Is The Essence Of T Q C 028 MIN
Reasons For Implementing T Q C 027 MIN
What Is Total Quality Control 027 MIN

Seven Thousand Three Hundred Sixty-Two C 11 MIN
16MM FILM OPTICAL SOUND H-C A
Presents an abstract film exercise.
Prod-CFS Dist-CFS 1968

Seven Thousand Years New C 15 MIN
16MM FILM OPTICAL SOUND
Features Ben Johnson, who narrates the story of the Limousin cattle breed. Points out that the Limousin, which can be traced back seven thousand years, is one of the most economical and profitable breeds of cattle.
LC NO. 75-702756
Prod-MTP Dist-VENARD Prodn-SIMSP 1975

Seven Ways Of Communicating News B 20 MIN
2 INCH VIDEOTAPE P
Stresses accuracy in news reporting. (Broadcast quality)
From The Language Lane Series. Lesson 16
Prod-CVETVC Dist-GPITVL Prodn-WCVETV

Seven Wishes Of A Rich Kid, The C 30 MIN
16MM FILM, 3/4 OR 1/2 IN VIDEO P-J
A shortened version of The Seven Wishes Of A Rich Kid. Tells the story of Calvin Brundage, a kid who has everything money can buy but who wishes for friends, a special girl and closeness with his father. Shows what happens when a video fairy godmother decides to grant his wishes.
Prod-LCOA Dist-LCOA 1979

Seven Wishes Of A Rich Kid, The C 46 MIN
16MM FILM, 3/4 OR 1/2 IN VIDEO P-J
Tells the story of Calvin Brundage, a kid who has everything money can buy but who wishes for friends, a special girl and closeness with his father. Shows what happens when a video fairy godmother decides to grant his wishes.
Prod-LCOA Dist-LCOA 1979

Seven Wishes Of A Rich Kid, The (French) C 30 MIN
16MM FILM, 3/4 OR 1/2 IN VIDEO P-J A
Tells the story of a rich kid who has everything but friends. Edited version.
Prod-LCOA Dist-LCOA 1979

Seven Wishes Of A Rich Kid, The (French) C 46 MIN
16MM FILM, 3/4 OR 1/2 IN VIDEO P-J A
Tells the story of a rich kid who has everything but friends. version.
Prod-LCOA Dist-LCOA 1979

Seven Wishes Of A Rich Kid, The (Spanish) C 30 MIN
16MM FILM, 3/4 OR 1/2 IN VIDEO P-J A
Tells the story of a rich kid who has everything but friends. Edited.
Prod-LCOA Dist-LCOA 1979

Seven Wishes Of A Rich Kid, The (Spanish) C 46 MIN
16MM FILM, 3/4 OR 1/2 IN VIDEO P-J A
Tells the story of a rich kid who has everything but friends. Full version.
Prod-LCOA Dist-LCOA 1979

Seven Wishes Of Joanna Peabody, The C 29 MIN
16MM FILM, 3/4 OR 1/2 IN VIDEO I-C A
Presents a fantasy about a young girl living in an urban ghetto who has her wishes fulfilled by a fairy godmother who appears on the television. Shows that in the process of getting her wishes, Joanna learns that things work out better when she thinks of others rather than just herself. Based on G Gray's book The Seven Wishes Of Joanna Peabody.
Prod-LCOA Dist-LCOA 1978

Seven Wishes Of Joanna Peabody, The (French) C 27 MIN
16MM FILM, 3/4 OR 1/2 IN VIDEO P-H
Presents a modern-day Cinderella story. Tells of a young girl who is given seven wishes by a fairy godmother who lives in a television set.
Prod-LCOA Dist-LCOA 1978

Seven Wishes Of Joanna Peabody, The (Spanish) C 27 MIN
16MM FILM, 3/4 OR 1/2 IN VIDEO P-H
Tells a modern-day Cinderella story. Shares a story of a young girl who is given seven wishes by a fairy godmother who lives in a television set.
Prod-LCOA Dist-LCOA 1978

Seven With One Blow C 10 MIN
16MM FILM, 3/4 OR 1/2 IN VIDEO K-I
Uses animation to tell the classic fairy tale by the Brothers Grimm, about a brave little tailor who kills seven flies with one blow.
From The Grimm's Fairy Tales Series.
Prod-BOSUST Dist-CF 1978

Seven With One Blow (Spanish) C 10 MIN
16MM FILM, 3/4 OR 1/2 IN VIDEO K-I
Uses animation to tell the classic fairy tale by the Brothers Grimm about a brave little tailor who kills seven flies with one blow.
From The Grimm's Fairy Tales Series.
Prod-BOSUST Dist-CF 1978

Seven Wives Of Bahram Gur, The C 19 MIN
16MM FILM, 3/4 OR 1/2 IN VIDEO H-C A
Traces the life of the legendary Persian hero, Bahram Gur, including his rise to King, marriage to seven wives, and final marriage to Fitna. Adapted from the epic poem by Nizami and filmed from 15th and 16th century Persian miniatures.
Prod-IU Dist-IU 1961

Seven Wonders Of The Diving World C 27 MIN
16MM FILM, 3/4 OR 1/2 IN VIDEO
Shows the undersea world from archeological sites in the Red Sea to shipwrecks in the Great Lakes and the flora and fauna of the Great Barrier Reef. Features close-up underwater photography views of the denizens of the sea.
Prod-ATHI Dist-ATHI

Seven-Per-Cent Solution, The C 113 MIN
16MM FILM OPTICAL SOUND
Tells how Sherlock Holmes reappears in 1894 (after his presumed death in 1891) with a terrible narcotics addiction. Shows how Sigmund Freud tries to help him. Stars Nicol Williamson, Alan Arkin, Robert Duvall, Vanessa Redgrave and Laurence Olivier.
Prod-UPCI Dist-TWYMAN 1976

Seven-Up 'Undo It' Advertising Program C 9 MIN
16MM FILM OPTICAL SOUND
Follows the creation of a 7up advertising campaign, from statement of objectives and development of concept to execution in various advertising media, including radio, television and outdoor advertising.
LC NO. 78-700398
Prod-SEVUP Dist-SEVUP Prodn-FILMA 1977

Seven, Eight, Lay Them Straight C 8 MIN
16MM FILM, 3/4 OR 1/2 IN VIDEO A
Presents teenagers discussing their feelings about drugs. Edited from the 1980 videocassette entitled For Parents Only.
LC NO. 81-706600
Prod-NIAAA Dist-USNAC Prodn-VISION 1981

Seven, Eight, Lay Them Straight C 8 MIN
3/4 INCH VIDEO CASSETTE
Presents an overview of the problem of drug use by young people. Focuses on what they think of their own drug use, as well as how to promote discussion among parents.
Prod-NIDA Dist-MTP

Seventeen C 90 MIN
3/4 OR 1/2 INCH VIDEO CASSETTE J-C A
Looks at a group of teenagers who are finishing high school in Muncie, Indiana, and are finding themselves unshielded from the lessons of life and death. Contains strong language.
From The Middletown Series.
Prod-WQED Dist-FI 1982

Seventeen Forever X 27 MIN
16MM FILM, 3/4 OR 1/2 IN VIDEO H-C A
Centers on a family caught up in the youth cult. Shows how each family member learns about his or her true self.
Prod-PAULST Dist-MEDIAG

Seventeen Going On Nowhere C 28 MIN
16MM FILM, 3/4 OR 1/2 IN VIDEO J-C A
Describes a father's efforts to reach his son who is immersed in a life of rock music, girls and marijuana. Stars Ramon Bieri and Emilio Estevez.
From The Reflections Series.
Prod-PAULST Dist-MEDIAG

Seventeen Minutes Greenland C 17 MIN
16MM FILM OPTICAL SOUND
Illustrates life and nature in Greenland.
Prod-RDCG Dist-AUDPLN

Seventeen Seventy-Six C 148 MIN
16MM FILM OPTICAL SOUND
Features a musical version of the events surrounding the American Revolution.
Prod-CPC Dist-TWYMAN 1972

Seventeen Seventy-Six C 54 MIN
16MM FILM, 3/4 OR 1/2 IN VIDEO I-C A
Relates what happened during the 1776 American Revolution and why it happened. Filmed at Lexington, Concord, Boston, Philadelphia, Williamsburg, France and England. Narrated by Frederic March.
From The Saga Of Western Man Series.
Prod-ABCTV Dist-MGHT Prodn-SCNDRI 1964

Seventeen Seventy-Six, Pt 1 C 27 MIN
16MM FILM, 3/4 OR 1/2 IN VIDEO I-C A
Relates what happened during the 1776 American Revolution and why it happened. Filmed at Lexington, Concord, Boston, Philadelphia, Williamsburg, France and England. Narrated by Frederic March.
From The Saga Of Western Man Series.
Prod-ABCTV Dist-MGHT Prodn-SCNDRI 1965

Seventeen Seventy-Six, Pt 2 C 27 MIN
16MM FILM, 3/4 OR 1/2 IN VIDEO I-C A
Relates what happened during the 1776 American Revolution and why it happened. Filmed at Lexington, Concord, Boston, Philadelphia, Williamsburg, France and England. Narrated by Frederic March.
From The Saga Of Western Man Series.
Prod-ABCTV Dist-MGHT Prodn-SCNDRI 1965

Seventeen-Year-Old Boys And Girls Talk About Their Sexuality C 52 MIN
3/4 OR 1/2 INCH VIDEO CASSETTE
Presents differences in sources and knowledge of human sexuality obtained by 17-year-old males and females from different geographical and cultural backgrounds at home, in school or on the streets, impact of peer and parental pressures, conflicts and difficulties caused by different views and values from parents.
Prod-HEMUL Dist-HEMUL

Seventeenth Olympic Games - The Greatest Spectacle B 5 MIN
16MM FILM OPTICAL SOUND
Surveys the Olympic Games of 1960 including the opening ceremonies, eighteen days of games and closing ceremonies.
From The Screen News Digest Series. Vol 3, Issue 3
Prod-HEARST Dist-HEARST 1960

Seventh Chair, The C 13 MIN
16MM FILM OPTICAL SOUND
Dramatizes the credit and collection problems of five small business owners with a round-table discussion and flashbacks to their places of business.
LC NO. 74-705615
Prod-USSBA Dist-USNAC 1971

Seventh Chair, The C 14 MIN
3/4 OR 1/2 INCH VIDEO CASSETTE
Discusses credit and collection problems of a large department store, a food caterer, a lumber dealer, a druggist, a haberdasher and a florist.
From The Small Business Administration Series.
Prod-IVCH Dist-IVCH

Seventh Cross, The C
3/4 OR 1/2 INCH VIDEO CASSETTE IND
Looks at probable cause for an accident that seriously injured the driver while making a trip down Torrey Mountain in California. Focuses on safety, particularly while driving on mountainous terrain.
From The Driving Safety Series.
Prod-DCC Dist-GPCV

Seventh Cross, The (Arabic) C
3/4 OR 1/2 INCH VIDEO CASSETTE IND
Looks at probable cause for an accident that seriously injured the driver while making a trip down Torrey Mountain in California. Focuses on safety, particularly while driving on mountainous terrain.
From The Driving Safety Series.
Prod-DCC Dist-GPCV

Seventh Cross, The (French) C
3/4 OR 1/2 INCH VIDEO CASSETTE IND
Looks at probable cause for an accident that seriously injured the driver while making a trip down Torrey Mountain in California. Focuses on safety, particularly while driving on mountainous terrain.
From The Driving Safety Series.
Prod-DCC Dist-GPCV

Seventh Cross, The (Spanish) C
3/4 OR 1/2 INCH VIDEO CASSETTE IND
Looks at probable cause for an accident that seriously injured the driver while making a trip down Torrey Mountain in California. Focuses on safety, particularly with driving on mountainous terrain.
From The Driving Safety Series.
Prod-DCC Dist-GPCV

Seventh Day, The B 30 MIN
16MM FILM OPTICAL SOUND
Explains the significance and manner of observance of the Friday evening service, using narrations, liturgical music and the enactment of various Sabbath rituals. 'THE FOURTH COMMANDMENT' Is a sequel to this film. (Kinescope)
Prod-JTS Dist-NAAJS Prodn-NBCTV 1951

Seventh Fleet, The B 12 MIN
16MM FILM OPTICAL SOUND
Documents the operations and actions of the Seventh Fleet from August, 1949 to 1957.
LC NO. FIE63-354
Prod-USN Dist-USNAC 1957

Seventh Heaven B 119 MIN
16MM FILM SILENT
Tells the story of Diane, a Parisian street waif who is rescued from a savage beating by Chico, a sewer worker, who takes her home to his seventh floor garret dwelling. Shows that Chico's initial pity slowly turns to love and then heartbreak. Stars Janet Gaynor and Charles Farrell. Directed by Frank Borzage.
Prod-UNKNWN Dist-KILLIS 1925

Seventh Infantry Division B 22 MIN
16MM FILM, 3/4 OR 1/2 IN VIDEO H A
Presents the training of the 7th Infantry Division at Ford Ord, California, four Pacific campaigns (Attu, Leyte, Kwajalein and Okinawa), and occupational duties in Korea.
Prod-USA Dist-USNAC 1949

Seventh Mandarin, The C 13 MIN
3/4 INCH VIDEO CASSETTE P
Explains how a Chinese ruler accidentally learns that his people are living in terrible poverty. Describes how he decides to meet his people and rule them well.
Prod-BOSUST Dist-GA

Seventh Master Of The House, The C 12 MIN
16MM FILM OPTICAL SOUND P-I
The story of a traveller seeking food and lodging. Shows the necessity of assuming responsibility.
LC NO. 76-701335
Prod-MLA Dist-MLA 1968

Seventh Voyage Of Sinbad C 89 MIN
16MM FILM OPTICAL SOUND P-I
Tells of Sinbad's journey to Colossa to get a fragment of a roc's eggshell in order to restore the Princess Parisa to her normal size by breaking a magic spell. Reveals that along the way he encounters a huge man-eating cyclops, the two-headed roc, skeleton restored to life and a fire-breathing dragon. Stars Kerwin Mathews.
Prod-CPC Dist-TIMLIF 1958

Seventies—A Series
16MM FILM, 3/4 OR 1/2 IN VIDEO J-C A
Documents major events in the 1970's.
Prod-UPI Dist-JOU 1980

Great Powers, The 027 MIN
International Economy, The 027 MIN
Middle East, The 027 MIN
Politics Of Violence 027 MIN
Southern Africa 027 MIN
Trends 027 MIN

Seventy Per Cent B 6 MIN
16MM FILM OPTICAL SOUND
Shows an unusual occurrence that takes place during a card game late at night.
LC NO. 76-702887
Prod-CMBLGS Dist-CMBLGS 1975

Seventy-Seven Jamboree C 28 MIN
16MM FILM OPTICAL SOUND
Features host Burl Ives as he shows the many ways in which scouting provides opportunities for young people to develop character and expand their horizons.
LC NO. 78-701446
Prod-BSA Dist-BSA Prodn-HEN 1978

Severe Emotional Disturbance In Children C 26 MIN
3/4 INCH VIDEO CASSETTE
Presents an overview of current theories about etiology, symptomatology and treatment related to severely disturbed children. Emphasizes recognition of pathology, individualized treatment and importance of family participation in plan of care.
Prod-UWISN Dist-UWISN

Severe Weather Test C 30 MIN
3/4 OR 1/2 INCH VIDEO CASSETTE
Illustrates the hazards of severe weather and the precautions that can be taken to avoid injury. Examines tornadoes, thunderstorms, lightning and high winds.
Prod-WCCOTV Dist-WCCOTV 1982

Severely Traumatized Patient, The B 50 MIN
16MM FILM OPTICAL SOUND PRO
Describes how to care for a patient in the emergency room after a severe accident. Discusses the importance of examining for the most major injuries, clearance of air passages, and treatment for shock and chest injuries.
Prod-LOMAM Dist-LOMAM

Sevilla C 16 MIN
16MM FILM, 3/4 OR 1/2 IN VIDEO J-C
A Spanish language film for first year Spanish students. Shows the harbor, La Torre de la Giralda, the Gardens of Alcazar, Sevilla, as well as the flamenco dancers of Sevilla, Spain.
From The Spanish Language Series.
Prod-IFB Dist-IFB 1969

Sew-It-Yourself Workshop, The C 26 MIN
16MM FILM, 3/4 OR 1/2 IN VIDEO J-C A
Demonstrates tools and techniques of sewing through the situation of a sewing shop employee who helps an inexperienced young woman complete a dress. Covers construction of the garment from start to finish.
LC NO. 77-701113
Prod-READER Dist-PFP 1977

Sewage Treatment Plant C
3/4 OR 1/2 INCH VIDEO CASSETTE
Examines sewage treatment, focusing on the use of water, the collection system, and processing technologies, as used at the Akron Ohio City Water Pollution Control Station. Discusses primary and secondary treatment, sample collection, chemical testing and environmental concerns.
From The Field Trips in Environmental Geology - Technical And Mechanical Concerns Series.
Prod-KENTSU Dist-KENTSU

Seward's Folly B 12 MIN
16MM FILM OPTICAL SOUND
Shows the historical background, natural resources, scenic beauty and strategic importance of Alaska.
Prod-HEARST Dist-HEARST 1938

Seward's Folly - The Story Of Alaska B 20 MIN
16MM FILM OPTICAL SOUND J-C A
Relates the history of the discovery and purchase of Alaska. Examines highlights of Alaska's history, Eskimo life in Alaska, the Russian era in Alaska and the state's strategic importance in U S defense.
From The Screen News Digest Series. Vol 9, Issue 8
LC NO. 76-700283
Prod-HEARST Dist-HEARST 1967

Sewers C 20 MIN
16MM FILM OPTICAL SOUND
Describes the huge sewer systems that serve Washington, DC, and shows how they handle sanitary sewage, storm runoff and combined sewage.
LC NO. 78-700390
Prod-DCENVS Dist-FINLYS Prodn-FINLYS 1978

Sewing - Discovering Patterns, Fabric And Basting C 52 MIN
1/2 IN VIDEO CASSETTE BETA/VHS
Details the necessary information to begin creative sewing for a personal wardrobe. Discusses selection of patterns and fabric, as well as basting.
Prod-RMI Dist-RMI

Sewing - Making A Simple Skirt C 52 MIN
1/2 IN VIDEO CASSETTE BETA/VHS
Outlines the tailoring techniques for producing a skirt. Features Stella Warnick.
Prod-RMI Dist-RMI

Sewing - Skirts And Blouses C 62 MIN
1/2 IN VIDEO CASSETTE BETA/VHS
Discusses the simplified techniques for sewing a fashionable wardrobe. Demonstrated by Robert Krause.
Prod-RMI Dist-RMI

Sewing Crotch Seams C 5 MIN
16MM FILM SILENT J-C A
Illustrates three methods of stitching a crotch seam as one continuous seam through the front and back garment pieces. Includes both open and closed construction and construction when there is a center opening.
From The Clothing Construction Techniques Series.
LC NO. 77-701186
Prod-IOWA Dist-IOWASP 1976

Sewing Machine, The C 10 MIN
16MM FILM OPTICAL SOUND H-C A
Depicts the care and operation of a sewing machine and the threading of a bobbin, upper and lower threads.
From The Home Economics - Clothing Series.
LC NO. 73-709989
Prod-MORLAT Dist-SF 1967

Sewing Materials - Preparation C 10 MIN
16MM FILM OPTICAL SOUND H-C A
A guide to sewing preparation discusses basic weaves of fabric, grains of materials, straightening material making material grain perfect and pinning material.
From The Home Economics - Clothing Series.
LC NO. 78-709990
Prod-MORLAT Dist-SF 1967

Sewing On Buttons C 3 MIN
16MM FILM SILENT J-C A
Demonstrates how to locate buttons. Shows the attachment of both flat and shank buttons and a method for determining the amount of thread shank needed for a smooth closure.
From The Clothing Construction Techniques Series.
LC NO. 77-701202
Prod-IOWA Dist-IOWASP 1976

Sewing Unlike Curved Seams C 3 MIN
16MM FILM SILENT J-C A
Illustrates the joining of unlike curves, including staystitching and clipping the inside curve, pinning and stitching the two layers together. Shows how to notch the seam allowance of the outer curve in order to reduce bulk.
From The Clothing Construction Techniques Series.
LC NO. 77-701185
Prod-IOWA Dist-IOWASP 1976

Sex - Resetting The Thermostat C 28 MIN
16MM FILM, 3/4 OR 1/2 IN VIDEO A
See series title for descriptive statement.
From The Care And Maintenance Of A Good Marriage Series. Program 4
Prod-UMCOM Dist-ECUFLM 1982

Sex And Aging C
3/4 OR 1/2 INCH VIDEO CASSETTE PRO
See series title for descriptive statement.
From The Continuing Medical Education - Basic Sexology Series.
Prod-TIASHS Dist-MMRC

Sex And Decisions - Remember Tomorrow C 29 MIN
16MM FILM, 3/4 OR 1/2 IN VIDEO H
Dramatizes teenagers making decisions about sexual intercourse. Shows two teens who spend a day together at a beach house and, in the end, make the decision not to have sex.
Prod-BROWN Dist-PEREN Prodn-WFP

Sex And Disability C
3/4 OR 1/2 INCH VIDEO CASSETTE PRO
See series title for descriptive statement.
From The Continuing Medical Education - Basic Sexology Series.
Prod-TIASHS Dist-MMRC

Sex And Disability—A Series

Draws on current medical information to dispel several common myths regarding sex and disability. Features candid interviews with disabled patients and their partners. Discusses physical aspects, societal attitudes and special problems of parenting.
Prod-MLLRE Dist-AJN

Those People Can't Do It	021 MIN
Those People Can't Have Kids	022 MIN
Those People Don't Enjoy It	021 MIN
Those People Don't Want It	013 MIN

Sex And Ethics C 29 MIN
3/4 OR 1/2 INCH VIDEO CASSETTE
Presents a round table conversation with an attorney, a rabbi, a Roman Catholic priest and a professor of comparative religion, concentrating on issues of ethics, morality and sex. Features Milton Diamond, Ph D, a biologist at the University of Hawaii. Discusses cultural values, eccentric sexual practices, adultery, consent and the distinction between law and ethics.
From The Human Sexuality Series.
Prod-KHETTV Dist-PBS

Sex And Gender B 20 MIN
3/4 OR 1/2 INCH VIDEO CASSETTE C A
Explores the concept of sexuality through candid interviews with transvestites and sequences of professional female impersonators at work.
Prod-MMRC Dist-MMRC

Sex And Love Test C 60 MIN
1/2 IN VIDEO CASSETTE (VHS)
Offers a series of questions on common sexual problems, followed by comment and clarification by psychiatrists and sex therapists.
Prod-KARLVI Dist-KARLVI

Sex And Religion C
3/4 OR 1/2 INCH VIDEO CASSETTE PRO
See series title for descriptive statement.
From The Independent Study In Human Sexuality Series.
Prod-MMRC Dist-MMRC

Sex And Society C
3/4 OR 1/2 INCH VIDEO CASSETTE PRO
See series title for descriptive statement.
From The Independent Study In Human Sexuality Series.
Prod-MMRC Dist-MMRC

Sex And The Arts C 29 MIN
3/4 OR 1/2 INCH VIDEO CASSETTE
Presents artist Dick Priest and sculptor Ron Kent discussing how and why they use art to portray a sexual message. Interviews singer Don Ho talking about his 'sex appeal' and how it relates to his music and dancer Shalimar discussing the belly dance as an erotic art form. Features Milton Diamond, Ph D, a biologist at the University of Hawaii, speaking with art critic Prithwish Neogy about the problems of analyzing erotic art.
From The Human Sexuality Series.
Prod-KHETTV Dist-PBS

Sex And The Family C 28 MIN
16MM FILM OPTICAL SOUND H A
Portrays the Bible's positive view of sex. Discusses sex as a gift and a responsibility of human living.
From The Tangled World Series.
Prod-YALEDV Dist-YALEDV

Sex And The Handicapped C 18 MIN
3/4 OR 1/2 INCH VIDEO CASSETTE C A
Develops a forceful argument for new attitudes toward the handicapped. Focuses primarily on helping the handicapped establish sexual contacts.
Prod-TSISR Dist-MMRC

Sex And The Law C 29 MIN
3/4 OR 1/2 INCH VIDEO CASSETTE
Presents man-on-the-street interviews to illustrate pro and con views on matters of law related to sex. Includes people speaking about age and consent, prostitution, sex discrimination, pornography and censorship. Points out differences between family law and criminal law. Features Milton Diamond, Ph D, a biologist at the University of Hawaii.
From The Human Sexuality Series.
Prod-KHETTV Dist-PBS

Sex And The Professional C 25 MIN
16MM FILM, 3/4 OR 1/2 IN VIDEO C
Shows professionals in health and human services as they discuss the sexual needs and patterns of patients and clients. Helps health professionals understand and deal with their own sexuality and with that of their patients and clients.
Prod-EINSTN Dist-TEXFLM 1975

Sex And The Single Parent, The C 98 MIN
3/4 OR 1/2 INCH VIDEO CASSETTE H-C A
Offers a comedy-drama showing how parents re-establish themselves as unattached, available adults and still fulfill their responsibilities as parents. Stars Susan Saint James and Mike Farrell.
Prod-TIMLIF Dist-TIMLIF 1982

Sex Bias In Education, Pt 1 C 29 MIN
3/4 OR 1/2 INCH VIDEO CASSETTE
Focuses on a sex role bias in education.
From The Woman Series.
Prod-WNEDTV Dist-PBS

Sex Bias In Education, Pt 2 C 29 MIN
3/4 OR 1/2 INCH VIDEO CASSETTE
Discusses the challenges of ridding a school system of sexist textbooks, curriculum and teaching practices.
From The Woman Series.
Prod-WNEDTV Dist-PBS

Sex Differences In Children's Play B 27 MIN
16MM FILM OPTICAL SOUND C A
Examines the sex differences shown in the playground play of preschool and primary school children. Shows size of play groups, rank, style of play and precourtship behavior during group sessions on the playground.
LC NO. 74-702969
Prod-UCHI Dist-PSUPCR 1974

Sex Differentiation C 17 MIN
3/4 OR 1/2 INCH VIDEO CASSETTE PRO
Reviews normal sex differentiation. Synthesizes information from physiology, anatomy, genetics, and biochemistry.
Prod-HSCIC Dist-HSCIC 1977

Sex Education C 18 MIN
16MM FILM, 3/4 OR 1/2 IN VIDEO H-C A
Presents an examination of the parent's role in educating their children about sex, stating that it should begin with the pre-school child. Shows how questions can arise from typical situations, and how the parents must deal with these questions in an honest, straightforward manner.
From The Woman Talk Series.
Prod-CORF Dist-CORF 1983

Sex Education C 29 MIN
3/4 OR 1/2 INCH VIDEO CASSETTE
Features Milton Diamond, Ph D, a biologist at the University of Hawaii, giving examples of informal and formal sex education. Includes parents who express their concerns about sex education for children and presents a group of senior citizens who add their comments.
From The Human Sexuality Series.
Prod-KHETTV Dist-PBS

Sex Education For Mentally Handicapped Persons C 16 MIN
3/4 OR 1/2 INCH VIDEO CASSETTE
Discusses and demonstrates sex education for mentally retarded persons. Uses charts and dolls.
Prod-LASSWC Dist-UWISC 1979

Sex Education Programs C
3/4 OR 1/2 INCH VIDEO CASSETTE PRO
See series title for descriptive statement.
From The Independent Study In Human Sexuality Series.
Prod-MMRC Dist-MMRC

Sex Fears C 15 MIN
16MM FILM, 3/4 OR 1/2 IN VIDEO H-C A
Focuses on young people as they share their fears about sex.
From The Sex, Feelings And Values Series.
Prod-DF Dist-LRF 1977

Sex For Sale - The Urban Battleground C 45 MIN
16MM FILM, 3/4 OR 1/2 IN VIDEO C A
Visits a number of major American cities where pornography has become big business for some and a major headache for others. Explores the myth of the victimless crime and shows the decay of various neighborhoods in which sex businesses exist.
Prod-ABCTV Dist-MGHT Prodn-MGHT 1977

Sex Game, The C 20 MIN
16MM FILM, 3/4 OR 1/2 IN VIDEO
Tells about a shy girl and a boy at a slumber party who find that emotional intimacy is ultimately more satisfying than physical intimacy.
From The Reflections Series.
LC NO. 79-706604
Prod-PAULST Dist-PAULST 1977

Sex Games C 8 MIN
16MM FILM, 3/4 OR 1/2 IN VIDEO H-C A
Focuses on a young couple playing a sex game, in which each partner tries to reject the other first.
From The Sex, Feelings And Values Series.
Prod-DF Dist-LRF 1977

Sex Histories - Interviewing And Coding C
3/4 OR 1/2 INCH VIDEO CASSETTE PRO
See series title for descriptive statement.
From The Independent Study In Human Sexuality Series.
Prod-MMRC Dist-MMRC

Sex History, The C 60 MIN
3/4 OR 1/2 INCH VIDEO CASSETTE
Offers a discussion and demonstration by Wardell Pomeroy, PhD, co-author of the Kinsey Report, on the art and science of taking a sex history which he has developed in taking 35,000 sex histories. Tells how he gathers the data he is after.
Prod-HEMUL Dist-HEMUL

Sex Hormones, Oxytocics B 30 MIN
16MM FILM OPTICAL SOUND C
Describes and classifies male and female sex hormones, emphasizing their pharmacological effects and clinical uses. Discusses oral contraceptives.
From The Pharmacology Series.
LC NO. 73-703351
Prod-MVNE Dist-TELSTR 1971

Sex IQ, The C 25 MIN
16MM FILM OPTICAL SOUND
Features correspondent Michael Maclear reporting on sex education classes in Canada, emphasizing the program in London, Ontario.
LC NO. 73-702523
Prod-CTV Dist-CTV 1976

Sex Is A Beautiful Thing C 27 MIN
16MM FILM OPTICAL SOUND
A documentary filmed in the Berkeley-San Francisco area. Presents two engaged couples on the Berkeley campus giving an intimate, behind-the-scenes look at their lives as they confront the problems of sexual morality. Discusses the new morality, sexual freedom and permissiveness.
LC NO. 73-701035
Prod-FAMF Dist-FAMF 1970

Sex Mis-Education C 11 MIN
16MM FILM, 3/4 OR 1/2 IN VIDEO H-C A
Focuses on young people as they criticize sex education offered at school and at home.
From The Sex, Feelings And Values Series.
Prod-DF Dist-LRF 1977

Sex Morals C 13 MIN
16MM FILM, 3/4 OR 1/2 IN VIDEO H-C A
Focuses on young people as they express their attitudes about sex.
From The Sex, Feelings And Values Series.
Prod-DF Dist-LRF 1977

Sex Offenders C
3/4 OR 1/2 INCH VIDEO CASSETTE PRO
See series title for descriptive statement.
From The Independent Study In Human Sexuality Series.
Prod-MMRC Dist-MMRC

Sex Role Development C 23 MIN
16MM FILM, 3/4 OR 1/2 IN VIDEO H-C A
Examines male and female sex roles, focusing on how stereotypes are formed. Discusses ways to avoid transmitting these traditional stereotypes to children.
From The Developmental Psychology Today Film Series.
Prod-CRMP Dist-CRMP 1974

Sex Role Stereotyping In Schools—A Series

Prod-FAMF Dist-FAMF 1975

Hey, What About Us	15 MIN

Sex Role Stereotyping In Schools—A Series
16MM FILM, 3/4 OR 1/2 IN VIDEO
Studies the attitudes developed in schools concerning sex role stereotyping in relation to future career choices and social images.
Prod-FWLERD Dist-UCEMC

Changing Images - Confronting Career	
Hey What About Us	015 MIN
I Is For Important	012 MIN
Woman Emerging - Comparing Cultural	027 MIN

Sex Roles C 30 MIN
3/4 OR 1/2 INCH VIDEO CASSETTE C
Explores those agencies which contribute to sex role expectations in society.
From The Focus On Society Series.
Prod-DALCCD Dist-DALCCD

Sex Roles - Ages 3-13 B 44 MIN
16MM FILM OPTICAL SOUND
Discusses physical and psychological differences of boys and girls between the ages of 6 and 13, effects of certain child rearing tendencies on children of both sexes and principles of sex education.
From The Man - His Growth And Development, Birth Through Adolescence Series.
LC NO. 71-703691
Prod-VDONUR Dist-AJN Prodn-WTTWTV 1967

Sex Roles And Human Relations C 56 MIN
3/4 INCH VIDEO CASSETTE
Looks at changing sex roles and relationships between men and women.
Prod-OHC Dist-HRC

Sex Therapy And The Medical Practice C
3/4 OR 1/2 INCH VIDEO CASSETTE PRO
See series title for descriptive statement.
From The Continuing Medical Education - Basic Sexology Series.
Prod-TIASHS Dist-MMRC

Sex Therapy, Pt 1 C 29 MIN
3/4 OR 1/2 INCH VIDEO CASSETTE
Provides information on sex therapy, behavior therapy, psychoanalysis, marital therapy, and hormone therapy.
From The Woman Series.
Prod-WNEDTV Dist-PBS

Sex Therapy, Pt 2 C 29 MIN
3/4 OR 1/2 INCH VIDEO CASSETTE
Describes organic and emotional reasons for sexual problems. Explains that people who acknowledge problems and seek treatment generally find rewards.
From The Woman Series.
Prod-WNEDTV Dist-PBS

Sex, Anatomy And Physiology C
3/4 OR 1/2 INCH VIDEO CASSETTE PRO
See series title for descriptive statement.
From The Independent Study In Human Sexuality Series.
Prod-MMRC Dist-MMRC

Sex, Booze And Blues And Those Pills You Use C 12 MIN
16MM FILM OPTICAL SOUND C A
Explains in a humorous manner how abuse of alcohol and other drugs can lead to sexual dysfunction.
LC NO. 82-700512
Prod-SCHUM Dist-FMSP 1982

Sex, Feelings And Values—A Series
16MM FILM, 3/4 OR 1/2 IN VIDEO H-C A
Focuses on young people as they formulate their own values about sex.
Prod-DF Dist-LRF 1977

Early Homosexual Fears 11 MIN
Parents' Voice 12 MIN
Sex Fears 15 MIN
Sex Games 8 MIN
Sex Mis-Education 11 MIN
Sex Morals 13 MIN

Sex, Geriatrics, Illness And Disability C
3/4 OR 1/2 INCH VIDEO CASSETTE PRO
See series title for descriptive statement.
From The Independent Study In Human Sexuality Series.
Prod-MMRC Dist-MMRC

Sexes II, The C
3/4 OR 1/2 INCH VIDEO CASSETTE
Covers the whole spectrum of human sexuality. follows a young couple from first attraction through courtship to marriage, while taking a psychological look at the emotional side of sexual dysfunction. Demonstrates how sexuality begins in early embyronic life with brain wiring signaling every cell, imprinting basic sexual instincts that will utimately determine the sex for which the fetus was programmed by genes at the instant of conception. Focuses on physical and emotional maturing process in both sexes.
From The Body Human Series.
Prod-TRAINX Dist-TRAINX

Sexes, The C
3/4 OR 1/2 INCH VIDEO CASSETTE
Explores the wonders and mystique of human sexuality, the intricate mechanisms of the human reproductive systems, from gene-programmed sexual instincts through the advanced years. Covers surgical removal of a fallopian tubal blockage, making motherhood at last possible for a 29-year-old woman, corrective surgery and hormone treatments allowing normal female development for a young girl born with the genetic imprint of a male and the anatomy of a female.
From The Body Human Series.
Prod-TRAINX Dist-TRAINX

Sexes, The - Breaking The Barriers C 18 MIN
16MM FILM, 3/4 OR 1/2 IN VIDEO
Interviews Virginia Johnson and Dr William Masters, who speak about their research in the field of sex.
Prod-DOCUA Dist-CNEMAG

Sexes, The - Roles C 28 MIN
16MM FILM, 3/4 OR 1/2 IN VIDEO
Surveys the evolution of male-female roles from pre-history to the industrial age of the 1980's. Presents psychologist Judith Bardwick pointing out the stresses caused by the clash between traditional expectations and new realities, Matina Horner discussing her classic studies on women's fear of success and sociologist Jean Lipman-Blumen relating how girls are socialized to destroy their own dreams at an early age.
Prod-CANBC Dist-FLMLIB

Sexes, The - What's The Difference C 28 MIN
16MM FILM, 3/4 OR 1/2 IN VIDEO
Addresses the question of whether male and female traits are inborn or learned in childhood. Shows child development experts isolating biological from cultural factors such as the ability to perceive changes in the environment.
Prod-CANBC Dist-FLMLIB

Sexism In Religion, Another View C 29 MIN
3/4 INCH VIDEO CASSETTE
Discusses charges of sex bias in religious organizations.
From The Woman Series.
Prod-WNEDTV Dist-PUBTEL

Sexism In The School C 30 MIN
3/4 INCH VIDEO CASSETTE
Presents Linda Shuto of the British Columbia Teacher's Federation Status of Women Task Force showing evidence of sexism in the school system.
Prod-WMENIF Dist-WMENIF

Sexism, Stereotyping And Hidden Values C 29 MIN
16MM FILM, 3/4 OR 1/2 IN VIDEO T
Explores the sources of hidden sexist values in the school setting and offers ways whereby teachers can promote a climate of equal opportunity in their classrooms.
From The Survival Skills For The Classroom Teacher Series.
Prod-MFFD Dist-FI 1978

Sexological Examination, The C 28 MIN
3/4 OR 1/2 INCH VIDEO CASSETTE C A
Provides physiological information and aids in finding and exploring physical sensations which feel good to each partner. Shows couples how to begin exploration and experimentation.
Prod-MMRC Dist-MMRC

Sexual Abuse C 17 MIN
3/4 OR 1/2 INCH VIDEO CASSETTE PRO
Recognizes difficulties in diagnosing sexual abuse in children because of the stigma attached to it. Covers steps to assure a safe home environment and to rehabilitate the parents.
From The Child Abuse Series.
Prod-HSCIC Dist-HSCIC 1978

Sexual Abuse - The Family C 30 MIN
16MM FILM, 3/4 OR 1/2 IN VIDEO PRO
Presents a discussion by a physician, a social worker and a psychologist on sexual abuse of children. Includes a role play in which professionals interview a sexually abused child and her family in an emergency room setting.
From The We Can Help Series.
Prod-NCCAN Dist-USNAC 1977

Sexual Abuse Of Children C 29 MIN
3/4 OR 1/2 INCH VIDEO CASSETTE
Examines the incidence of sexual abuse of children among family members and neighbors. Suggests how to tell a child about molestation and discusses the identification of the abuser.
From The Woman Series.
Prod-WNEDTV Dist-PBS

Sexual Abuse Of Children C 30 MIN
3/4 OR 1/2 INCH VIDEO CASSETTE H-C A
See series title for descriptive statement.
From The Child Abuse And Neglect Series.
Prod-UMINN Dist-GPITVL 1983

Sexual Abuse Of Children C 54 MIN
3/4 OR 1/2 INCH VIDEO CASSETTE
Inspects the disturbing phenomenon of adults who use children for sex, revealing it is a crime being committed in Minnesota more frequently than imagined.
Prod-WCCOTV Dist-WCCOTV 1982

Sexual Abuse Of Children - America's Secret Shame C 28 MIN
16MM FILM, 3/4 OR 1/2 IN VIDEO A
Reveals the extent of sexual abuse of children, offering interviews with past victims and convicted child molesters. Describes the ploys used by the molesters and tells why victims don't report the incidents. Narrated by Peter Graves.
LC NO. 81-706569
Prod-TGL Dist-AIMS 1980

Sexual Abuse Of Children—A Series
C A
Prod-BAKRSR Dist-LAWREN Prodn-PROFPR 1979

Sexually Abused Child, The - A Protocol For
Time For Caring, A - The School's Response To 28 MIN

Sexual And Bladder Dysfunction In Spinal Cord Injury, Pt 2 B 48 MIN
3/4 OR 1/2 INCH VIDEO CASSETTE
Describes bladder and sexual dysfunction in spinal cord injured patients and various treatment methods.
Prod-BU Dist-BU

Sexual And Bladder Dysfunction In Spinal Cord Injury, Pt 1 B 52 MIN
3/4 OR 1/2 INCH VIDEO CASSETTE
Discusses the process of rehabilitation of disabled individuals. Includes diagrams on how the central nervous system affects the bladder.
Prod-BU Dist-BU

Sexual Assault - Emergency Room Procedures C 18 MIN
3/4 OR 1/2 INCH VIDEO CASSETTE
Presents a step-by-step guide to the correct evidence collection, examination and treatment of a sexual assault victim. Stresses importance of staff sensitivity.
Prod-GRANVW Dist-GRANVW

Sexual Behavior In Laboratory Monkeys (Macaca Mulatta) C 30 MIN
16MM FILM OPTICAL SOUND C T
Illustrates an investigation intended to identify and quantify the characteristics of sexual behavior in laboratory monkeys. Illustrates how sexual behavior in monkeys is influenced by individual differences in personality. Shows monkeys in pre-estrous, estrous and post estrous phases and depicts their variability of sexual behavior. Pictures vatiations in grooming, masturbation and coitus. Showings restricted.
Prod-YALEU Dist-PSUPCR 1955

Sexual Behavior In The American Bison C 9 MIN
16MM FILM OPTICAL SOUND C A
Illustrates basic patterns of sexual behavior in adult male and female American bison, largely interpreted in terms of the selective advantages they confer.
LC NO. 76-703303
Prod-LOTTD Dist-PSUPCR Prodn-UCD 1976

Sexual Behavior Of Normal, Socially Isolated And LSD-25 Injected Guinea Pigs B 17 MIN
16MM FILM SILENT C T
Shows the estrous behavior of female guinea pigs, and the various phases of sexual behavior of normal males and the reduced amount of sexual behavior of males, raised in social isolation, when in the presence of an estrous female. Illustrates how an injection of LSD25 disrupts the sexual behavior of the male.
Prod-UKANS Dist-PSUPCR 1959

Sexual Commerce C 29 MIN
3/4 OR 1/2 INCH VIDEO CASSETTE
Presents commercial aspects of sex as discussed by a prostitute, an advertising executive, a massage parlor owner and others who use sex as a sales approach or a product.
From The Human Sexuality Series.
Prod-KHETTV Dist-PBS

Sexual Compatibility C 30 MIN
3/4 OR 1/2 INCH VIDEO CASSETTE C A
Compares differences in the male and female sex drive. Deals with sexual satisfaction and adjustment.
From The Family Portrait - A Study Of Contemporary Lifestyles Series. Lesson 17
Prod-SCCON Dist-CDTEL

Sexual Counseling Of Physically Disabled C 40 MIN
3/4 INCH VIDEO CASSETTE
Discusses why it is important for rehabilitation professionals to include sexual counseling with patients. Explores personalities, attitudes and professional roles that influence their work. Features four rehabilitation professionals.
From The Sexuality And Physical Disability Series.
Prod-UMITV Dist-UMITV 1976

Sexual Counseling Of Physically Disabled Adults C 40 MIN
3/4 OR 1/2 INCH VIDEO CASSETTE C A
Compares methods of dealing with physically disabled clients with varying lifestyles. Explores ways in which rehabilitation professionals use their own personalities and attitudes to deal with their clients.
From The Sexuality and Physical Disability Video Tape Series.
Prod-MMRC Dist-MMRC

Sexual Development C 29 MIN
3/4 OR 1/2 INCH VIDEO CASSETTE
Presents various theories of sexual development, including Freudian, role-modeling, social learning, cognitive and interactional. Includes detailed anatomical drawings to illustrate prenatal physiological events which affect sexual development and raises questions regarding homosexuality and heterosexuality.
From The Human Sexuality Series.
Prod-KHETTV Dist-PBS

Sexual Development In Children C 45 MIN
3/4 OR 1/2 INCH VIDEO CASSETTE C A
Explores the developmental processes of the sexual life of boys and girls from infancy through puberty.
Prod-MMRC Dist-MMRC

Sexual Encounters Of A Floral Kind C 50 MIN
3/4 OR 1/2 INCH VIDEO CASSETTE H A
Studies the pollination of plants from five continents. Demonstrates how different species have evolved in order to lure insects and other animals to their pollen and 'recruit' them as unwitting carriers for fertilization.
Prod-WNETTV Dist-FI

Sexual Enhancement - The Sexual Realities Project C 28 MIN
3/4 OR 1/2 INCH VIDEO CASSETTE
Demonstrates methods for overcoming performance anxiety, erectile difficulties and ejaculatory and orgasmic problems.
Prod-IRL Dist-IRL

Sexual Fringes C 29 MIN
3/4 OR 1/2 INCH VIDEO CASSETTE
Features Milton Diamond, Ph D, a biologist at the University of Hawaii, covering aspects of human sexuality. Includes sexual abstention, nudism, women's liberation and intersexuality and hermaphroditism.
From The Human Sexuality Series.
Prod-KHETTV Dist-PBS

Sexual Function And Dysfunction C 29 MIN
3/4 OR 1/2 INCH VIDEO CASSETTE
Examines the concepts of normal and abnormal sexual behavior in physical and psychiatric terms. Comments on the results of sexual openness and talks about sexual identity.
From The Daniel Foster, MD Series.
Prod-KERA Dist-PBS

Sexual Harassment C 28 MIN
3/4 OR 1/2 INCH VIDEO CASSETTE
Explores the types of behavior and comments that constitute sexual harassment.
Prod-WCCOTV Dist-WCCOTV 1981

Sexual Harassment - A Manager-Employee Awareness Program—A Series
A
Educates managers and employees on responsibilities and problems in sexual harassment.
Prod-AMEDIA Dist-AMEDIA

Sexual Harassment - A Threat To Your Profits 020 MIN
Sexual Harassment - That's Not In My Job 020 MIN

Sexual Harassment - A Threat To Your Profits C 20 MIN
3/4 OR 1/2 INCH VIDEO CASSETTE A
Examines effects of sexual harassment on company productivity and profit. Explains EEOC guidelines.
From The Sexual Harassment - A Manager-Employee Awareness Program Series. Part 1
Prod-AMEDIA Dist-AMEDIA

Sexual Harassment - An Introduction C 8 MIN
3/4 OR 1/2 INCH VIDEO CASSETTE
Includes a description and example of possible sexual harassment within a mock job interview. Raises questions to initiate group discussion of sexual harassment.
Prod-UWISC Dist-UWISC 1982

Sexual Harassment - No Place In The Workplace C 30 MIN
3/4 INCH VIDEO CASSETTE
Features Gloria Steinem and Lynn Farley as they discuss issues facing working women. Offers insights and solutions to the problem of sexual harassment in the work place.
Prod-UMITV Dist-UMITV 1980

Sexual Harassment - That's Not In My Job Description C 20 MIN
3/4 OR 1/2 INCH VIDEO CASSETTE A
Addresses harassing behavior by both sexes, non-employees and employees. Offers suggestions on how to handle harassing situations.
From The Sexual Harassment - A Manager-Employee Awareness Program Series. Part 2
Prod-AMEDIA Dist-AMEDIA

Sexual Harassment On The Job C 29 MIN
3/4 OR 1/2 INCH VIDEO CASSETTE
Tells how to identify and deal with sexual harassment on the job.
From The Woman Series.
Prod-WNEDTV Dist-PBS

Sexual Health Care In The Nursing Process C 25 MIN
16MM FILM OPTICAL SOUND PRO
Defines sexual health care and applies concepts of sexual health care to each phase of the nursing process. Dramatizes four nurse-patient-family interactions within different health care settings.
From The Directions For Education In Nursing Via Technology Series. Human Sexuality
LC NO. 76-703345
Prod-DENT Dist-WSU Prodn-CENIT 1976

Sexual Health Care In The Nursing Process C 23 MIN
3/4 OR 1/2 INCH VIDEO CASSETTE
Defines sexual health care and relates to total care in each phase of the nursing process. Dramatizes four nurse-patient-family reactions.
From The Human Sexuality Series.
Prod-WSUN Dist-AJN

Sexual Impotence In The Male - The Tragedy Of The Bedroom C 15 MIN
16MM FILM OPTICAL SOUND
Uses a simulated patient situation in discussing the problems of impotence. Emphasizes obtaining proper help, evaluation and counseling.
LC NO. 80-701416
Prod-EATONL Dist-EATONL Prodn-AEGIS 1980

Sexual Intercourse C 16 MIN
3/4 OR 1/2 INCH VIDEO CASSETTE C A
Explains and demonstrates the physiology, psychology and basic technique of sexual intercourse. Comprises two naturalistically visualized episodes, each focusing on a different set of concerns.
Prod-TSISR Dist-MMRC

Sexual Motivation C 29 MIN
3/4 INCH VIDEO CASSETTE C A
Explores social and biological factors involved in sexual functioning. Describes Kinsey and Masters and Johnson research.
From The Understanding Human Behavior - An Introduction To Psychology Series. Lesson 13
Prod-COAST Dist-CDTEL

Sexual Pelvic Muscle Exercises C 10 MIN
3/4 OR 1/2 INCH VIDEO CASSETTE
Demonstrates the vaginal muscle tone exam and exercises for strengthening the pubococcygeus muscle.
From The EDCOA Sexual Counseling Series.
Prod-MMRC Dist-MMRC

Sexual Pleasure Education C
3/4 OR 1/2 INCH VIDEO CASSETTE PRO
See series title for descriptive statement.
From The Independent Study In Human Sexuality Series.
Prod-MMRC Dist-MMRC

Sexual Puzzle, The C 30 MIN
16MM FILM, 3/4 OR 1/2 IN VIDEO
Explores the options young people face. Shows how sexual intimacy gets its best start in caring values, responsible actions and healthy self-acceptance.
Prod-KAWVAL Dist-KAWVAL

Sexual Realities Project, The - A Self-Help Approach C 28 MIN
3/4 OR 1/2 INCH VIDEO CASSETTE C A
Provides guidelines to anyone who is interested in enhancing sexual relations and in clarifying sexual myths and misconceptions.
Prod-MMRC Dist-MMRC

Sexual Suicide C 29 MIN
3/4 INCH VIDEO CASSETTE
Features author George Gildre discussing single men and women, freedom, independence, and sexual diversity.
From The Woman Series.
Prod-WNEDTV Dist-PUBTEL

Sexual Variations C
3/4 OR 1/2 INCH VIDEO CASSETTE PRO
See series title for descriptive statement.
From The Independent Study In Human Sexuality Series.
Prod-MMRC Dist-MMRC

Sexual Variations C 39 MIN
3/4 INCH VIDEO CASSETTE
Deals with the variety of human sexual behavior in our society in order to dispel myths and to increase understanding and acceptance.
From The Sexuality And Physical Disability Series.
Prod-UMITV Dist-UMITV 1976

Sexual Variations C 40 MIN
3/4 OR 1/2 INCH VIDEO CASSETTE C A
Presents several aspects of the range of sexual behavior, including transvestism, exhibitionism, transsexuality, and homosexuality in order to dispel myths and to increase understanding.
From The Sexuality and Physical Disability Video Tape Series.
Prod-MMRC Dist-MMRC

Sexuality X 30 MIN
16MM FILM, 3/4 OR 1/2 IN VIDEO C A
Deals with the difficult issue of sexuality and the need for loving at critical times as well as during times of little stress. Discusses ways of showing and receiving physical expressions of love while coping with illness and what it achieves for the partners who share. Hosted by Meryl Streep.
From The Coping With Serious Illness Series. No. 3
LC NO. 80-707396
Prod-TIMLIF Dist-TIMLIF 1980

Sexuality - A Woman's Point Of View C 30 MIN
3/4 OR 1/2 INCH VIDEO CASSETTE H-C A
Focuses on how women view themselves sexually. Explores the world of women's attitudes about human sexuality. Narrated by Stephanie Powers.
Prod-MMRC Dist-MMRC

Sexuality - An Introduction For Medical Students C 21 MIN
16MM FILM OPTICAL SOUND
Portrays the difficulty of a medical student in maintaining his sensitivity throughout the experience of training to become a physician, as well as the difficulty in reacting sensitively to a patient with a sexual problem.
LC NO. 79-713391
Prod-UMIAMI Dist-UMIAMI 1971

Sexuality - The Human Heritage C 59 MIN
16MM FILM OPTICAL SOUND H-C A
Traces the development of human sexual identity from prenatal sex hormones to external influences of family and society. Presents Jerome Kagan, professor of developmental psychology at Harvard, discussing how children acquire gender and role identity. Includes interviews with teenagers and homosexuals explaining how they view themselves in regard to the sexual standards of society.
From The Thin Edge Series.
LC NO. 76-702373
Prod-EDUCBC Dist-IU 1976

Sexuality - The Human Heritage C 60 MIN
3/4 OR 1/2 INCH VIDEO CASSETTE
Examines the explosive questions of sexual identity, the most dramatic difference between human beings. Explores basic feelings, genetic determinants, importance of environment in determining male and female sexual behavior, and evaluates current social and political movements on sexual identity issues.
From The Thin Edge Series.
Prod-TRAINX Dist-TRAINX

Sexuality And Disability Adjustment C 30 MIN
3/4 INCH VIDEO CASSETTE
Discusses the relationship between sexuality and adjustment to disability. Stresses importance of understanding one's dependency, strength or assertivenes central to both sexual health and overall adjustment to a physical disability.
From The Sexuality And Physical Disability Series.
Prod-UMITV Dist-UMITV 1976

Sexuality And Disability Adjustment C 40 MIN
3/4 OR 1/2 INCH VIDEO CASSETTE C A
Presents a discussion between a psychologist and a disabled man anwoman on the relationships between sexuality and other aspects of adjustment.
From The Sexuality and Physical Disability Video Tape Series.
Prod-MMRC Dist-MMRC

Sexuality And Mentally Handicapped Persons C 16 MIN
3/4 OR 1/2 INCH VIDEO CASSETTE
Discusses myths connected with the mentally handicapped and sexuality, such as that the mentally handicapped are not sexual. Points out the need for workshops and classes for mentally handicapped regarding sexuality.
Prod-LASSWC Dist-UWISC 1979

Sexuality And Physical Disability Video Tape Program—A Series
C A
Conveys information to stimulate discussion and facilitate deeper consideration of sexuality in the lives of the physically disabled.
Prod-MMRC Dist-MMRC

Anatomy And Physiology of The Sexual Response	040 MIN
Body Image, Disability, And Sexuality	040 MIN
Medical And Institutional Aspects	040 MIN
Orientation To The Sexuality Of Physical	040 MIN
Sexual Counseling Of Physically Disabled	040 MIN
Sexual Variations	040 MIN
Sexuality And Disability Adjustment	040 MIN

Sexuality And Physical Disability—A Series

Designed to stimulate discussion and facilitate a deeper consideration of sexuality and why it may be important to the physically disabled and to those with whom they work.
Prod-UMITV Dist-UMITV 1976

Anatomy And Physiology Of Sexual Response	
Body Image	038 MIN
Medical And Institutional Aspects	040 MIN
Orientation To Sexuality Of The Physically	039 MIN
Sexual Counseling Of Physically Disabled	040 MIN
Sexual Variations	039 MIN
Sexuality And Disability Adjustment	030 MIN

Sexuality And Sexual Issues For The Severely And Profoundly Retarded, Pt I B 60 MIN
3/4 OR 1/2 INCH VIDEO CASSETTE
Presents an in-service workshop for social workers at a center for the developmentally disabled. Explores the areas of masturbation, public and private, inadvertent sexual arousal by caretakers and visitors, sex education and inappropriate dress and language. Presents innovative training materials.
Prod-CWCDD Dist-UWISC 1980

Sexuality And Sexual Issues For The Severely And Profoundly Retarded, Pt II B 12 MIN
3/4 OR 1/2 INCH VIDEO CASSETTE
Presents the conclusion to sexual issues for the severely and profoundly retarded as it brushes on the complexity of how to deal with situations such as encountering male clients in sexual activity or masturbation. Proposes an enlightened attitude of acceptance of male-male sexual contact among the retarded in contrast to the tradition of attempts at 'normalization.'
Prod-CWCDD Dist-UWISC 1980

Sexuality, Alcohol And Drugs C 26 MIN
3/4 OR 1/2 INCH VIDEO CASSETTE J A
Presents a film that explains how some people deal with tension, fear and guilt.
Prod-SUTHRB Dist-SUTHRB

Sexuality, Pt 1 C 29 MIN
3/4 OR 1/2 INCH VIDEO CASSETTE A
Explores what children know and how they feel about sex. Features Dr Salk's discussion with three young teens on subjects ranging from teen pregnancies to suggestive scenes on television.
From The Feelings Series.
Prod-SCETV Dist-PBS 1979

Sexuality, Pt 2 C 29 MIN
3/4 OR 1/2 INCH VIDEO CASSETTE A
Presents Dr Salk in discussion with three young teens regarding sexual attitudes and behavior. Covers topics ranging from homosexuality and the double standard to parents' mistaken ideas about their children's sexual knowledge and behavior.
From The Feelings Series.
Prod-SCETV Dist-PBS 1979

Sexually Abused Child, The C 30 MIN
3/4 OR 1/2 INCH VIDEO CASSETTE
Presents a program specialist, foster parent and clinical psychologist exchanging views on the foster parent's role in relation to helping the sexually abused child.
From The Home Is Where The Care Is Series. Module 8
Prod-MTI Dist-MTI 1984

Sexually Abused Child, The - Identification/Interview C 10 MIN
16MM FILM, 3/4 OR 1/2 IN VIDEO
Demonstrates various interviewing techniques to be used when sexual abuse is suspected. Examines methods of establishing rapport, interpreting nonverbal cues and dealing with the child's protective feelings toward the abuser.
Prod-CAVLCD Dist-MTI

Sexually Abused Child, The - A Protocol For Criminal Justice C 26 MIN
16MM FILM - 3/4 IN VIDEO
Describes procedures used to protect the rights of child sex abuse victims and to prosecute their offenders.
From The Sexual Abuse Of Children Series.
LC NO. 79-706034
Prod-BAKRSR Dist-LAWREN Prodn-PROFPR 1979

Sexually Mature Adult, The C 16 MIN
16MM FILM, 3/4 OR 1/2 IN VIDEO
Covers the physiology and emotions involved in mature sexual behavior during the four stages of sexual response in intercourse. Uses live photography to show responses of couples in each stage of lovemaking and animated diagrams to illustrate internal responses. Features men and women who give accounts of their sexual experiences and concludes with a look at sexual relationships in older men and women.
From The Human Sexuality Series.
Prod-WILEYJ Dist-MEDIAG 1973

Sexually Transmitted Disease C
3/4 OR 1/2 INCH VIDEO CASSETTE
Reviews the diverse clinical and laboratory manifestations of four common sexually transmitted diseases, syphillis, gonorrhea, chlamydial and herpes infections. Discusses the need for a careful sexual history with sensitive awareness of differing life styles.
Prod-AMEDA Dist-AMEDA

Sexually Transmitted Diseases C 25 MIN
16MM FILM OPTICAL SOUND J-C A
Presents information about sexually transmitted diseases. Includes animated segments as well as interviews in which young people tell of their experiences with these diseases.
LC NO. 79-701750
Prod-BHA Dist-BNCHMK 1983

Sexually Transmitted Diseases C
3/4 OR 1/2 INCH VIDEO CASSETTE
Represents a broad overview of the numerous, different diseases that can be sexually transmitted. Describes both diseases and symptoms.
Prod-MIFE Dist-MIFE

Sexually Transmitted Diseases C 30 MIN
3/4 OR 1/2 INCH VIDEO CASSETTE C T
Discusses the sex-linked diseases which are near epidemic proportions in this country today. Begins with a historical account of sexually transmitted diseases and complications. Explores the causes, symptoms and cures of various types. Discusses treatment and health maintenance.
From The Here's To Your Health Series.
Prod-DALCCD Dist-DALCCD

Sexually Transmitted Diseases C 30 MIN
3/4 OR 1/2 INCH VIDEO CASSETTE
See series title for descriptive statement.
From The Here's To Your Health Series.
Prod-PBS Dist-DELTAK

Sexually Transmitted Diseases (Spanish) C
3/4 OR 1/2 INCH VIDEO CASSETTE
Presents a broad overview on the numerous, different diseases that can be sexually transmitted. Describes both diseases and symptoms.
Prod-MIFE Dist-MIFE

Sexually Transmitted Diseases - Causes, Prevention And Cure C 65 MIN
3/4 OR 1/2 INCH VIDEO CASSETTE H-C
Discusses how and why sexually transmitted diseases have created such a complex set of social and medical problems. Describes the causes, transmissions, detection, prevention and cures of the most prevalent of these diseases - gonorrhea, herpes, genitalis and syphilis.
LC NO. 81-707056
Prod-GA Dist-GA 1982

Sexually Transmitted Diseases - Overview C
3/4 OR 1/2 INCH VIDEO CASSETTE
Discusses incidence and pattern of sexually transmitted disease. Describes pelvic inflammatory disease, including infertility, tubal pregnancies and surgery.
From The Sexually Transmitted Diseases Series.
Prod-CONMED Dist-CONMED

Sexually Transmitted Diseases - The Hidden Epidemic C 30 MIN
3/4 OR 1/2 INCH VIDEO CASSETTE C A
Discusses trends affecting major sexually transmitted diseases. Refutes numerous myths and misconceptions. Compares methods of prevention and treatment as to effectiveness and potential side effects.
From The Contemporary Health Issues Series. Lesson 23
Prod-SCCON Dist-CDTEL

Sexually Transmitted Diseases From A Sexological Viewpoint C
3/4 OR 1/2 INCH VIDEO CASSETTE PRO
See series title for descriptive statement.
From The Continuing Medical Education - Basic Sexology Series.
Prod-TIASHS Dist-MMRC

Sexually Transmitted Diseases—A Series

Focuses on the explosive epidemic of sexually transmitted diseases. Points out that the medical and societal problems of the epidemic have health and welfare professionals justifiably concerned and seeking explanations for the rise in the incidence of many of these diseases.
Prod-CONMED Dist-CONMED

Bacterial Infections
Intervention - Interviewing And Patient
Sexually Tranmitted Diseases - Overview
Syndromes
Viral Infections

Sexually-Transmitted Diseases C 30 MIN
3/4 OR 1/2 INCH VIDEO CASSETTE
States that there are three million reported cases of gonorrhea, just one of the 25 sexually-transmitted diseases in the United States. Discusses ways to control these diseases.
From The Here's To Your Health Series.
Prod-KERA Dist-PBS 1979

Sexy Transmitted Diseases C 29 MIN
3/4 OR 1/2 INCH VIDEO CASSETTE
Deals with the facts about sexually transmitted diseases, A I D S, herpes, syphilis, gonorrhea and others. Includes the risk factors, results and common-sense prevention options.
From The Here's To Your Health Series.
Prod-KERA Dist-PBS

Seyewailo - The Flower World C 51 MIN
3/4 OR 1/2 INCH VIDEO CASSETTE
Yaqui with English subtitles. Shows a skit about coyotes who chase and capture a deer. Shows Yaqui deer songs as they are sung and danced at a fiesta.
From The Words And Place Series.
Prod-CWATER Dist-CWATER

SGHWR For Nuclear Power C 20 MIN
16MM FILM OPTICAL SOUND
Describes, in animation, the design of a commercial Sghwr and the method of refuelling, which contributes to its very high availability for power generation.
Prod-UKAEA Dist-UKAEA 1968

SGHWR System, The C 25 MIN
16MM FILM OPTICAL SOUND IND
Shows the design, construction and operation of the Winfrith Prototype Reactor and the work of British scientists to develop the process.
Prod-UKAEA Dist-UKAEA 1975

SH Sound, The C 15 MIN
3/4 INCH VIDEO CASSETTE P
Discusses the use of the SH sound and explains that it's not always spelled with the letters s and h.
From The New Talking Shop Series.
Prod-BSPTV Dist-GPITVL 1978

Sh Sound, The - Sherman's Wish C 15 MIN
2 INCH VIDEOTAPE P
Introduces some of the consonant sounds met in early reading. Identifies the written letter with the spoken sound.
From The Listen And Say Series.
Prod-MPATI Dist-GPITVL

Sh-h-h - Cancer C 12 MIN
3/4 INCH VIDEO CASSETTE
Explains the nature of cancer and the methods of treatment.
Prod-UTAHTI Dist-UTAHTI

Shade Gardens C 30 MIN
3/4 OR 1/2 INCH VIDEO CASSETTE C A
Uses the Sherman Foundation Gardens of Corona Del Mar, California, to illustrate shade gardening. Describes planting and maintenance of shade-tolerant plants.
From The Home Gardener With John Lenanton Series. Lesson 23
Prod-COAST Dist-CDTEL

Shade Of A Toothpick, The C 60 MIN
16MM FILM - 3/4 IN VIDEO P A
Documents a handful of drug prevention projects in motion across the nation, presents a panel discussion by law enforcement authorities on the role of organized crime in the drug crisis and features an appeal to parents by public television's Fred Rogers.
From The Turned On Crisis Series.
Prod-WQED Dist-GPITVL

Shade Of Difference, A C 31 MIN
16MM FILM, 3/4 OR 1/2 IN VIDEO H-C A
Discusses important principles of traffic safety, stressing the extreme caution necessary at intersections. Illustrates that incorrect assumptions about traffic laws cause accidents.
Prod-BURROW Dist-IFB 1967

Shades Of Black C 28 MIN
16MM FILM, 3/4 OR 1/2 IN VIDEO
Explains how Einstein's general theory of relativity applies to the objects known as black holes.
From The Understanding Space And Time Series.
Prod-BBCTV Dist-UCEMC 1980

Shades Of Black And White C 5 MIN
16MM FILM, 3/4 OR 1/2 IN VIDEO IND
Deals with the problem of racial tension in business. Describes the dilemma of a white boss who chooses between two Black employees for a promotion. Discusses the problems of prejudice that arise when the personnel manager, also black, questions the promotion thinking it was done on grounds of prejudice.
From The This Matter Of Motivation Series.
Prod-CTRACT Dist-DARTNL Prodn-CALVIN 1970

Shades Of Gray B 66 MIN
16MM FILM OPTICAL SOUND
Portrays through dramatized situations and case histories various mental disorders of soldiers during training and combat. Relates the early life of the soldier to circumstances precipitating his mental breakdown and demonstrates methods of psychotherapy.
LC NO. FIE52-65
Prod-USA Dist-USNAC 1948

Shades Of Puffing Billy C 11 MIN
16MM FILM OPTICAL SOUND P-I
Presents a lighthearted look at the Victorian Narrow Guage Railway which runs between Emerald and Belgrave in the Dandenong Mountains.
Prod-ANAIB Dist-AUIS 1967

Shading, Strokes And Striping C 29 MIN
2 INCH VIDEOTAPE
See series title for descriptive statement.
From The Tin Lady Series.
Prod-NJPBA Dist-PUBTEL

Shadow C 15 MIN
3/4 OR 1/2 INCH VIDEO CASSETTE I-J
Deals with form shadows and cast shadows. Shows how shadows dramatize drawings and help give the illusion of depth.
From The Draw Man Series.
Prod-OCPS Dist-AITECH 1975

Shadow Catcher, The - Edward S Curtis And The North American Indian C 88 MIN
16MM FILM, 3/4 OR 1/2 IN VIDEO H-C A
Presents a critical account of the life of Edward S Curtis, a photographer and writer who worked among the Indians of the American Southwest for over 32 years.
Prod-PHENIX Dist-PHENIX 1975

Shadow Catcher, The - Edward S Curtis And The North American Indian (French) C 88 MIN
16MM FILM, 3/4 OR 1/2 IN VIDEO H-C A
Presents a critical account of the life of Edward S Curtis, a photographer and writer who worked among the Indians of the American Southwest for over 32 years.
Prod-PHENIX Dist-PHENIX 1975

Shadow Dance C 16 MIN
16MM FILM OPTICAL SOUND
Records the total eclipses of the Sun across southern Australia in 1976 and the ordinary and extraordinary events taking place during the eclipses.
LC NO. 79-700531
Prod-FLMAUS Dist-AUIS 1976

Shadow In The Sun C 90 MIN
16MM FILM, 3/4 OR 1/2 IN VIDEO
Dramatizes Queen Elizabeth I's flirtation with the Duke of Alencon, heir to the French throne, whom she refused to marry and placated with 60,000 pounds.
From The Elizabeth R Series. No. 3
LC NO. 79-707276
Prod-BBCTV Dist-FI 1976

Shadow Of A Pioneer, The C 14 MIN
16MM FILM OPTICAL SOUND
Depicts the story of an Illinois farmer who, tired of building rail fences, designed a machine to weave them of wire. Shows the founding of Keystone Steel and Wire Company.
Prod-KEYSAW Dist-VENARD

Shadow Of Doubt C 53 MIN
16MM FILM OPTICAL SOUND
Discusses Kamp Westerbork, a round-up point for Holocaust victims. Directed by Rolf Orthel.
Prod-UNKNWN Dist-NYFLMS 1975

Shadow Of God On Earth, The C 58 MIN
16MM FILM, 3/4 OR 1/2 IN VIDEO A
Discusses the spread and influence of Islam, beginning with the prophet Muhammad.
From The Crossroads Of Civilization Series.
Prod-CNEMAG Dist-CNEMAG 1978

Shadow Of The Eagle, The C 226 MIN
1/2 IN VIDEO CASSETTE BETA/VHS
Offers 12 episodes of a serial starring John Wayne. Tells how stunt flyer Craig McCoy rescues a kidnapped carnival owner and reveals the identity of the evil Eagle.
Prod-UNKNWN Dist-VIDIM 1932

Shadow Project, The C 14 MIN
3/4 OR 1/2 INCH VIDEO CASSETTE
Records the effort to paint shadows on New York City buildings similiar to those etched by the atomic blast at Hiroshima and the reactions of passers-by to the event and to the possibility of atomic conflict.
Prod-GMPF Dist-GMPF

Shadowplay C 52 MIN
16MM FILM OPTICAL SOUND
Tells how a young law school professor attempts to escape from professional pressure and loneliness through an organization that promotes suicide.
LC NO. 78-701569
Prod-CMBLGS Dist-CMBLGS 1977

Shadows C 15 MIN
2 INCH VIDEOTAPE P
Illustrates how opaque objects block light and cast shadows.
From The Science Is Searching Series.
Prod-DETPS Dist-GPITVL

Shadows C 15 MIN
16MM FILM, 3/4 OR 1/2 IN VIDEO K-P
Follows a group of children as they explore their own and other shadows, put on a shadow play and create a shadow zoo.
From The Ripples Series.
LC NO. 73-702154
Prod-NITC Dist-AITECH 1970

Shadows C 15 MIN
3/4 OR 1/2 INCH VIDEO CASSETTE P
See series title for descriptive statement.
From The Let's Draw Series.
Prod-OCPS Dist-AITECH Prodn-KOKHTV 1976

Shadows Of Sound C 5 MIN
16MM FILM OPTICAL SOUND
Presents a veteran with a service-connected hearing defect who is tested and fitted with a hearing aid at a VA audiology clinic. Features the training given at the clinic so that the veteran can receive maximum benefits from his hearing aid.
Prod-USVA Dist-USVA 1962

Shadows Of The Road C 20 MIN
16MM FILM OPTICAL SOUND
Shows the importance of good land transportation and the role of Oklahoma's Department of Transportation in fulfilling this need.
LC NO. 78-701570
Prod-OKDT Dist-TULSAS Prodn-TULSAS 1977

Shadows On Our Turning Earth C 11 MIN
16MM FILM, 3/4 OR 1/2 IN VIDEO P-J
Two primary youngsters use simple demonstrations to study shadows. They mark the position of a shadow and photograph its change of position. Models of the earth are used to show how the movement of the earth produces day and night.
Prod-FA Dist-PHENIX 1962

Shadows, Shadows Everywhere C 11 MIN
16MM FILM, 3/4 OR 1/2 IN VIDEO P
Without narration, shows the exciting shapes and patterns of shadows as two children play in the sun, make shadow 'ANIMALS' and present a shadow play.
Prod-CORF Dist-CORF 1972

Shaffle Bit Horsemanship C 30 MIN
1/2 IN VIDEO CASSETTE BETA/VHS
Demonstrates training involved in snaffle bit horsemanship.
From The Western Training Series.
Prod-EQVDL Dist-EQVDL

Shafting, Couplings And Joining Devices C 18 MIN
16MM FILM, 3/4 OR 1/2 IN VIDEO IND
Portrays the development of couplings from the early designs. Demonstrates various joining devices in their different forms of rigid and flexible construction. Shows applications of these devices to illustrate how they handle shaft misalignment using various directional flexing characteristics.
From The Mechanical Power Transmission Series.
Prod-LUF Dist-LUF 1977

Shah Of Iran, The C 12 MIN
3/4 OR 1/2 INCH VIDEO CASSETTE H-C A
Offers a 1974 interview with the Shah of Iran, giving insight into the upheaval that later befell Iran.
Prod-UPI Dist-JOU

Shake A Leg, Eat Eggs C 1 MIN
3/4 OR 1/2 INCH VIDEO CASSETTE
Shows a nest of country-fresh eggs singing a television spot about their protein value.
Prod-KIDSCO Dist-KIDSCO

Shake It Up - Gospel C 15 MIN
3/4 OR 1/2 INCH VIDEO CASSETTE P
See series title for descriptive statement.
From The Strawberry Square II - Take Time Series.
Prod-NEITV Dist-AITECH 1984

Shake The Habit - Learning To Live Without Salt C 12 MIN
3/4 OR 1/2 INCH VIDEO CASSETTE J-H A
Teaches people of all ages how to live without salt and high sodium foods and why they should. Identifies high sodium foods and suggests alternatives. Offers tips on how to prepare food without the use of salt.
Prod-POAPLE Dist-POAPLE

Shake Up In The Kremlin - America Votes - A Former President Is Mourned B 12 MIN
16MM FILM OPTICAL SOUND
Reviews the history of Russia under the rule of Lenin and Stalin. Traces the rise and fall of Khruschev and considers some of his policies. Introduces First Secretary Brezhnev and Premier Kosygin.
Prod-HEARST Dist-HEARST

Shakers In America, The C 28 MIN
16MM FILM OPTICAL SOUND J-C A
Uses animation, live footage of present-day Shakers and narration by Shakers and scholars to present the history of the Shakers and their contributions to American agriculture, architecture, design, music and technology.
LC NO. 75-702899
Prod-APPLAS Dist-VEDO 1975

Shakers, The C 30 MIN
16MM FILM - VIDEO, ALL FORMATS A
Presents an overview of America's oldest and most successful experiment in communal living. Contains interviews and performances of Shaker songs and tales.
From The American Traditional Culture Series.
Prod-DAVT Dist-DAVT

Shakespeare C 12 MIN
16MM FILM, 3/4 OR 1/2 IN VIDEO J-C A
Features actor/poet Roger Steffens acting out certain characters from the play Julius Caesar in a contemporary style, offering an understanding of Shakespeare's plays as universal and timeless.
From The Poetry For People Who Hate Poetry Series.
LC NO. 82-706516
Prod-STESHE Dist-CF 1980

Shakespeare - A Mirror To Man C 26 MIN
16MM FILM, 3/4 OR 1/2 IN VIDEO J-C A
Presents scenes from 'TAMING OF THE SHREW,' 'OTHELLO' and 'MACBETH' in an attempt to reveal the universality of England's greatest playwright, Shakespeare. Provides background on Elizabethan theatre and introduces each scene with appropriate background information.
Prod-SCNDRI Dist-LCOA 1971

Shakespeare - A Mirror To Man (Spanish) C 27 MIN
16MM FILM, 3/4 OR 1/2 IN VIDEO J-C A
Covers some of the highlights from Shakespeare's plays The Taming of the Shrew, Macbeth and Othello.
Prod-SCNDRI Dist-LCOA 1971

Shakespeare - Selection For Children C 6 MIN
16MM FILM, 3/4 OR 1/2 IN VIDEO P-J
Maurice Evans reads the 'ALL THE WORLD'S A STAGE' pasage from the Shakespearean comedy 'AS YOU LIKE IT' and two songs from 'LOVE'S LABOUR LOST.' Uses animation to illustrate the selections.
Prod-FINA Dist-SF 1965

Shakespeare - Soul Of An Age C 54 MIN
16MM FILM, 3/4 OR 1/2 IN VIDEO J-C A
Uses authentic maps and scenes of English towns and cities to point out landmarks in Shakespeare's life. Features Sir Michael Redgrave, who recites illustrative passages from key speeches in shakespeare's chronicles, comedies and tragedies.
Prod-NBCTV Dist-MGHT 1963

Shakespeare And His Stage - Approaches To Hamlet C 46 MIN
16MM FILM, 3/4 OR 1/2 IN VIDEO H-C A
Recreates the theatre of Shakespeare's day through the staging of scenes from Hamlet in an Elizabethan courtyard near Stratford, England. Contrasts styles of Shakespearean role playing with excerpts from performances by Laurence Olivier, John Gielgud, Nicol Williamson and John Barrymore. Includes views of landmarks in London, Stratford and Warwick which shaped Shakespeare's approach to theatrical practice.
From The History Of The Drama Series.
Prod-FOTH Dist-FOTH 1975

Shakespeare And His Theatre, Pt 1 C 26 MIN
16MM FILM, 3/4 OR 1/2 IN VIDEO H-C A
Presents a tour of the geography and history of Shakespeare's world which creates a vivid picture of the life and times as well as the plays and theatres of the world's greatest dramatist
Prod-THAMES Dist-MEDIAG 1977

Shakespeare And His Theatre, Pt 2 C 26 MIN
16MM FILM, 3/4 OR 1/2 IN VIDEO H-C A
Presents a tour of the geography and history of Shakespeare's world which creates a vivid picture of the life and times as well as the plays and theatres of the world's greatest dramatist
Prod-THAMES Dist-MEDIAG 1977

Shakespeare And Kronborg B 10 MIN
16MM FILM OPTICAL SOUND
Presents a series of pictures from Elsinore's famous Kronborg Castle. Shows the way Shakespeare probably would have seen the castle 300 years ago and includes scenes from Hamlet.
Prod-RDCG Dist-AUDPLN

Shakespeare In Perspective—A Series
16MM FILM, 3/4 OR 1/2 IN VIDEO J-C A
Offers perspectives of several Shakespearean plays.
Prod-FI Dist-FI

As You Like It 030 MIN
Hamlet 030 MIN
Julius Caesar 030 MIN
King Lear 030 MIN
Macbeth 030 MIN
Midsummer's Night Dream, A 030 MIN
Romeo And Juliet 030 MIN
Tempest, The 030 MIN

Shakespeare Is Alive And Well In The Modern World C
3/4 OR 1/2 INCH VIDEO CASSETTE H-C
Presents contemporary versions of Shakespearean dramas that enable students to penetrate complex Elizabethan vocabulary and experience insights into characters' feelings, motives and actions.
Prod-GA Dist-GA

Shakespeare Of Stratford And London C 32 MIN
16MM FILM, 3/4 OR 1/2 IN VIDEO
Deals with the life of William Shakespeare. Includes footage of Stratford-upon-Avon, the Warwickshire countryside, and 16th-century London.
From The World Of William Shakespeare Series.
LC NO. 80-706326
Prod-NGS Dist-NGS 1978

Shakespeare Plays—A Series
16MM FILM, 3/4 OR 1/2 IN VIDEO
Presents adaptations of William Shakespeare's plays.
Prod-BBCTV Dist-TIMLIF 1979

All's Well That Ends Well 141 MIN
Antony And Cleopatra 171 MIN
As You Like It 150 MIN
Comedy Of Errors, The 120 MIN
Coriolanus 145 MIN
Cymbeline 174 MIN
Hamlet 222 MIN
Henry IV, Pt I 147 MIN
Henry IV, Pt II 151 MIN
Henry V 163 MIN
Henry VI, Pt I 185 MIN
Henry VI, Pt II 212 MIN
Henry VI, Pt III 210 MIN
Henry VIII 165 MIN
Julius Caesar 161 MIN
King John 120 MIN
King Lear 185 MIN
Love's Labour's Lost 120 MIN
Macbeth 148 MIN
Measure For Measure 145 MIN
Merchant Of Venice, The 157 MIN
Merry Wives Of Windsor, The 167 MIN
Midsummer Night's Dream, A 112 MIN
Much Ado About Nothing 120 MIN
Othello 208 MIN
Pericles 177 MIN
Richard II 157 MIN
Richard III 228 MIN
Romeo And Juliet 167 MIN
Taming Of The Shrew, The 127 MIN
Tempest, The 150 MIN
Timon Of Athens 128 MIN
Titus Andronicus 120 MIN
Troilus And Cressida 190 MIN
Twelfth Night 124 MIN
Two Gentlemen Of Verona 137 MIN
Winter's Tale, The 173 MIN

Shakespeare—A Series
C
Features Professor Morris Tish emphasizing the historical period which produced Shakespeare and his contemporaries, Shakespeare's growth in skill and stature as a dramatist, growth of the drama as an art form and critical comprehension of their value. (Broadcast quality)
Prod-CHITVC Dist-GPITVL Prodn-WTTWTV

Elizabethan Life, No. 2 - Shakespeare's Life
Hamlet - Quantity And Quality of Critical 045 MIN
Hamlet - The Character Of Hamlet 045 MIN
Hamlet - Tragedy Of Blood - Role Of Avenger 045 MIN
King Henry IV, Pt 1 - Historical Background 045 MIN
King Henry IV, Pt 1 - Shakespeare's Theme, 045 MIN
King Henry IV, Pt 2 - Falstaff At Work 045 MIN
King Henry IV, Pt 2 - Machiavellian Politics, 045 MIN
King Lear - Shakespeare's Blending And 045 MIN
King Lear - Shakespeare's Conception Of 045 MIN
King Lear - The Most Profound Of 045 MIN
Measure For Measure - 'Judge Not, Lest 045 MIN
Measure For Measure - Vienna, That Wide 045 MIN
Merchant Of Venice, The - Incredibility Of 045 MIN
Merchant Of Venice, The - Shylock - Hero Or 045 MIN
Much Ado About Nothing - Beatrice And 045 MIN
Much Ado About Nothing - Dogberry And Verges, 045 MIN
Orientation To Course - Misconceptions About 045 MIN
Othello - Iago - Incarnation Of Evil For 045 MIN
Othello - Shakespeare's Only Domestic 045 MIN
Romeo And Juliet - Poet Versus Playwright 045 MIN
Romeo And Juliet - Tragedy Of Coincidence 045 MIN
Taming Of The Shrew, The - Katherina - The 045 MIN
Taming Of The Shrew, The - Unbalance Of Plots 045 MIN
Tempest And Summary, The - The Poetic Drama 045 MIN
Tempest, The - Shakespeare's Unique 045 MIN
Troilus And Cressida - Shakespeare's Most 045 MIN
Twelfth Night - Blend Of Romance And Realism 045 MIN
Twelfth Night - Complication Of Plot 045 MIN
Winter's Tale, The - Tell Us A Story 045 MIN

Shakespeare—A Series
16MM FILM, 3/4 OR 1/2 IN VIDEO J-C
Uses excerpts from the works of William Shakespeare to illustrate his stagecraft, his sources and the background for his plays.
Prod-CORF Dist-CORF

Understanding Shakespeare - His Sources 19 MIN
Understanding Shakespeare - His Stagecraft 25 MIN
William Shakespeare - Background For His Works 14 MIN

Shakespeare—A Series
16MM FILM, 3/4 OR 1/2 IN VIDEO H-C
Presents selections from the plays of Shakespeare, filmed in England on a stage patterned after Elizabethan theatres.
Prod-IFB Dist-IFB 1974

Antony And Cleopatra 011 MIN
Hamlet 010 MIN
Henry IV, Pt 2 006 MIN
Julius Caesar 014 MIN
Macbeth 011 MIN
Much Ado About Nothing 012 MIN
Othello 010 MIN
Richard II 012 MIN
Richard III 012 MIN
Romeo And Juliet 008 MIN
Taming Of The Shrew, The 013 MIN
Tempest, The 014 MIN

Shakespeare—A Series
16MM FILM, 3/4 OR 1/2 IN VIDEO J-C
Introduces Shakespearean plays performed by an English company. Preserves the continuity of each play and connects key scenes through brief narrative.
Prod-SEABEN Dist-PHENIX 1972

As You Like It - An Introduction 24 MIN
Julius Caesar - An Introduction 27 MIN
King Lear - An Introduction 27 MIN
Macbeth - An Introduction 26 MIN
Midsummer Night's Dream, A - An Introduction 25 MIN
Twelfth Night - An Introduction 23 MIN

Shakespeare's Country C 29 MIN
16MM FILM, 3/4 OR 1/2 IN VIDEO H-C A
Provides a foundation for the study of historical and environmental factors that may have influenced the early development of William Shakespeare. Explores the rural character and regal atmosphere of Elizabethan England.
Prod-VIDTRK Dist-EBEC 1983

Shakespeare's Heritage C 29 MIN
16MM FILM, 3/4 OR 1/2 IN VIDEO H-C A
Describes the history of Strafford-Upon-Avon, the resources and facilities available to students and visitors at the Shakespeare Centre, and the role of the Shakespeare Birthplace Trust in preserving and maintaining Shakespeare properties and other Shakespeariana.
Prod-VIDTRK Dist-EBEC 1983

Shakespeare's Macbeth C 60 MIN
3/4 OR 1/2 INCH VIDEO CASSETTE C
See series title for descriptive statement.
From The Drama - Play, Performance, Perception Series. Module 3
Prod-MDCC Dist-MDCC

Shakespeare's Sonnets C 150 MIN
3/4 OR 1/2 INCH VIDEO CASSETTE
Analyzes 15 of William Shakespeare's sonnets, some of which are dedicated to famous people and events.
Prod-FOTH Dist-FOTH 1984

Shakespeare's Stratford C 29 MIN
16MM FILM, 3/4 OR 1/2 IN VIDEO H-C A
Looks at the environment, manners and customs which influenced Shakespeare's thought and work by exploring Stratford, the borough in which he was born and educated.
Prod-EBEC Dist-EBEC 1983

Shakespeare's Theater C 13 MIN
16MM FILM OPTICAL SOUND H-C
An excerpt from the 1946 feature film 'HENRY V.' Dramatizes, against a background of Elizabethan music, activities in Shakespeare's theater centered about a presentation of 'HENRY V.'
Prod-RANK Dist-IU Prodn-NCTE 1960

Shakespeare's Theatre - The Globe Playhouse B 19 MIN
16MM FILM, 3/4 OR 1/2 IN VIDEO H-C A
A reconstruction of the Globe Playhouse is used to show how the stage may have been used for the production of Shakespeare's plays in his time.
Prod-UCLA Dist-UCEMC 1952

Shakespearean Tragedy C 40 MIN
3/4 OR 1/2 INCH VIDEO CASSETTE
Explores the nature of tragedy and the Shakespearean tragic hero. Discusses Shakespearean concepts of action, character and catharsis.
Prod-FOTH Dist-FOTH 1984

Shakiest Gun In The West, The C 101 MIN
16MM FILM OPTICAL SOUND
Stars Don Knotts as a frontier dentist who gets involved with Indians, gun runners and a beautiful redhead.
Prod-UPCI Dist-SWANK

Shaking The Foundations C 25 MIN
16MM FILM OPTICAL SOUND
Describes the work of Gottlob Frege and Georg Cantor, who arrived at paradoxes. Explains how these paradoxes can be avoided in less intuitive axiom systems.
Prod-OPENU Dist-GPITVL

Shall These Bones Live B 30 MIN
16MM FILM OPTICAL SOUND
Theodore Bikel presents dramatic readings with music to illustrate the living quality of the Hebrew language. (Kinescope)
Prod-JTS Dist-NAAJS Prodn-NBCTV 1958

Shall We Start Again C 27 MIN
16MM FILM, 3/4 OR 1/2 IN VIDEO A
Defines the critical path planning method and shows how to plan a program to carry out a specific objective. Gives an example of the process working in an office redecoration project. Includes workbook.
Prod-LIVACT Dist-IFB

Shallow Water Waves B
16MM FILM OPTICAL SOUND
Explains how to analyze shallow water waves mathematically.
Prod-OPENU Dist-OPENU

Shalom Aleichem C 15 MIN
3/4 OR 1/2 INCH VIDEO CASSETTE P
Picture a Roman fortress, a Bedouin family, the Dead Sea and a modern kibbutz in Israel.
From The Other Families, Other Friends Series. Red Module - Israel
Prod-WVIZTV Dist-AITECH 1971

Shaman C 12 MIN
16MM FILM OPTICAL SOUND
Depicts a glacial lake and the sound of a man's scream. Tells how a silver shaman appears as the scream reaches a crescendo to return the land to its magic silence.
LC NO. 76-703082
Prod-CANFDC Dist-CANFDC 1975

Shame Of A Nation, The C 27 MIN
3/4 OR 1/2 INCH VIDEO CASSETTE
Focuses on three Americans who are among 23 million who cannot read or write a simple sentence, or lack the basic skills required to function effectively in society. Documents the human and social cost of illiteracy in the United States.
Prod-BRRNA Dist-KINGA

Shame Of American Education, The C 24 MIN
16MM FILM OPTICAL SOUND A
Presents the essence of B F Skinner's faith in technology and outlines what needs to change in education.
Prod-AACD Dist-AACD 1984

Shame, Shame On The Bixby Boys C 90 MIN
3/4 OR 1/2 INCH VIDEO CASSETTE H-C A
Tells of the hilarious adventures of deputy Mordecai Murphy in the Old West as he tries to cope with the rustling Bixby Boys, the clients of a dentist who keeps taking out the wrong teeth and an aggressive young woman who has selected Mordecai as her one and only. Stars Monte Markham and Sammy Jackson.
Prod-TIMLIF Dist-TIMLIF 1982

Shameless Old Lady, The (French) B 94 MIN
16MM FILM OPTICAL SOUND
Tells how a 70-year-old widow takes her inheritance, buys a car, hires a prostitute as chaffeur, and sets out to sample worldly pleasure. Directed by Rene Allio. With English subtitles.
Prod-UNKNWN Dist-NYFLMS 1966

Shampoo C 112 MIN
16MM FILM OPTICAL SOUND
Portrays a Beverly Hills hairdresser who tries to juggle four love affairs at the same time. Stars Warren Beatty, Julie Christie, Goldie Hawn, Lee Grant and Carrie Fisher.
Prod-CPC Dist-TWYMAN 1975

Shampoo C 5 MIN
16MM FILM, 3/4 OR 1/2 IN VIDEO K-C A
See series title for descriptive statement.
From The How It's Made Series.
Prod-HOLIA Dist-LUF

Shamrock And The Rose, The C 68 MIN
2 INCH VIDEOTAPE
See series title for descriptive statement.
From The Toys That Grew Up II Series.
Prod-WTTWTV Dist-PUBTEL

Shamus C 98 MIN
16MM FILM OPTICAL SOUND
Stars Burt Reynolds as a private eye.
Prod-CPC Dist-TWYMAN 1972

Shane C 60 MIN
16MM FILM, 3/4 OR 1/2 IN VIDEO J-C A
An edited version of the feature film Shane. Relates the mythic story of a legendary gunfighter's final battle. Stars Alan Ladd, Jean Arthur and Van Heflin.
Prod-PARACO Dist-AIMS 1980

Shanghai - The New China C 33 MIN
16MM FILM, 3/4 OR 1/2 IN VIDEO J-C
Pictures Shanghai, the largest city in Red China. Captures traditional ways of life coexisting with efforts to modernize the city.
Prod-CBSNEW Dist-PHENIX 1974

Shanghai Duck C 29 MIN
2 INCH VIDEOTAPE
Features Joyce Chen showing how to adapt Chinese recipes so they can be prepared in the American kitchen and still retain the authentic flavor. Demonstrates how to prepare Shanghai duck.
From The Joyce Chen Cooks Series.
Prod-WGBHTV Dist-PUBTEL

Shannon - Portrait Of A River C 27 MIN
16MM FILM OPTICAL SOUND
Traces the course of the Shannon River in Ireland from source to estuary, including life along the river, monuments and ruins along its banks and the large industrial complex at Shannon.
Prod-CONSUI Dist-CONSUI

Shantiniketan B 12 MIN
16MM FILM OPTICAL SOUND I-C A
Presents Shantiniketan, the abode of peace founded as a school of international culture by the Nobel laureate, Rabindranath Tagore. Shows it today as VishWabharati University, where students live in communion with nature.
Prod-INDIA Dist-NEDINF

Shanwar Telis, The - Or, Bene Israel C 40 MIN
16MM FILM OPTICAL SOUND
Deals with the customs, ceremonies, rituals and education of the Shanwar Telis, descendants of Jews shipwrecked on the Konkan Coast of India 2,000 years ago.
From The About The Jews Of India Series.
LC NO. 79-701241
Prod-SPECJO Dist-NJWB 1979

Shao Ping The Acrobat C 25 MIN
16MM FILM, 3/4 OR 1/2 IN VIDEO J-C A
Introduces a Chinese boy names Shao Ping who is working hard to become an acrobat.
From The World Cultures And Youth Series.
Prod-SUNRIS Dist-CORF 1981

Shape C 10 MIN
16MM FILM, 3/4 OR 1/2 IN VIDEO I-C A
Explores shapes in nature and in art. Discusses how they function and how people perceive and interpret them.
From The Art Of Seeing Series.
Prod-AFA Dist-FI Prodn-ACI 1968

Shape And Color Game, The C 8 MIN
16MM FILM, 3/4 OR 1/2 IN VIDEO K-P
Shows how concepts of color, form, texture and structure of the physical world are learned by children playing with abstract toys.
Prod-KORTY Dist-SF 1967

Shape And Competence Of Ureteral Orifices C 17 MIN
16MM FILM OPTICAL SOUND
Shows that the causes of ureteral reflux have a direct relation to the shape and position of ureteral orifices rather than ureter length. Categorizes and correlates the shapes and positions to degrees of orifice competence for use in urological examination.
LC NO. 75-701734
Prod-EATONL Dist-EATONL Prodn-AVCORP 1968

Shape And Form C 15 MIN
3/4 OR 1/2 INCH VIDEO CASSETTE K-J
See series title for descriptive statement.
From The Arts Express Series.
Prod-KYTV Dist-KYTV 1983

Shape And Space B 20 MIN
2 INCH VIDEOTAPE I
Describes shapes which are not only the configuaration of an object or group of objects, but is also the space surrounding those objects.
From The For The Love Of Art Series.
Prod-GWTVAI Dist-GPITVL Prodn-WETATV

Shape From Shading C 45 MIN
3/4 OR 1/2 INCH VIDEO CASSETTE PRO
Features determining surface orientation from a single image, solving the image irradiance equation by integration along characteristic curves, and exploiting smoothness using pseudolocal, iterative computation.
From The Artificial Intelligence - Pt 3, Computer Vision Series.
Prod-MIOT Dist-MIOT

Shape From Shading C 56 MIN
3/4 OR 1/2 INCH VIDEO CASSETTE C
See series title for descriptive statement.
From The Artificial Intelligence, Pt III - Computer Vision Series.
Prod-MIOT Dist-AMCEE

Shape Hunting - Circles, Semicircles, Ellipses C 7 MIN
16MM FILM, 3/4 OR 1/2 IN VIDEO I
Discusses plane figures created from curves rather than line segments, such as circles, semicircles and ellipses. Introduces the concept of diameter, radius, circumference, concentric, arc and segment.
From The Shape Hunting Series.
Prod-CORF Dist-CORF 1980

Shape Hunting - Circles, Triangles, Rectangles, Squares C 7 MIN
16MM FILM, 3/4 OR 1/2 IN VIDEO K-P
Introduces the circle, the triangle, the rectangle and the square and defines the identifying characteristics of each shape.
From The Shape Hunting Series.
Prod-CORF Dist-CORF

Shape Hunting - Cylinders, Prisms, Pyramids C 8 MIN
16MM FILM, 3/4 OR 1/2 IN VIDEO I
Compares three-dimensional figures with analogous plane figures and objects in the physical world.
From The Shape Hunting Series.
Prod-CORF Dist-CORF

Shape Hunting - Lines, Angles, Triangles, Quadrilaterals C 13 MIN
16MM FILM, 3/4 OR 1/2 IN VIDEO P-I
Describes and compares lines, triangles and quadrilaterals.
From The Shape Hunting Series.
Prod-CORF Dist-CORF

Shape Hunting—A Series
16MM FILM, 3/4 OR 1/2 IN VIDEO K-I
Explores the characteristics of various geometrical shapes.
Prod-CORF Dist-CORF

Shape Hunting - Circles, Semicircles, Ellipses 007 MIN
Shape Hunting - Circles, Triangles, 007 MIN
Shape Hunting - Cylinders, Prisms, Pyramids 008 MIN
Shape Hunting - Lines, Angles, Triangles, 013 MIN

Shape Of A Leaf, The C 27 MIN
16MM FILM OPTICAL SOUND P-C A
Reveals the sensitive responses of retarded children to various types of art training. Demonstrates the artistic creativity and the individuality of style that these children possess in common with all children.
LC NO. FIA67-604
Prod-PERKNS Dist-CAMPF Prodn-UNIVC 1967

Shape Of Darkness, The - The Art Of Black Africa (1000-1900 A D) B 54 MIN
16MM FILM OPTICAL SOUND
Shows that the distinction of black African art dating from 1000 to 1900 A D was a terror of nature fused with a deep tenderness for it.
Prod-ROLAND Dist-ROLAND

Shape Of Language, The C 30 MIN
3/4 OR 1/2 INCH VIDEO CASSETTE
See series title for descriptive statement.
From The Language - Thinking, Writing, Communicating Series.
Prod-MDCPB Dist-MDCPB

Shape Of Our Vision, The C 45 MIN
16MM FILM OPTICAL SOUND H-C A
Examines the anatomy of a painting. Uses Georges Seurat's 'SUNDAY AFTERNOON ON THE GRADE JATTE,' to take the viewer inside the artist's work and discover the relationships within it and with respect to other works of art. Compares the techniques of Seurat with similar and contrasting techniques used by other artists including Picasso, Klein, da Vinci and Homer.
From The Man And His Art Series.
Prod-WTTWTV Dist-GPITVL

Shape Of Polyester, The C 15 MIN
16MM FILM OPTICAL SOUND
Shows the rapidly expanding industrial uses of polyester fibers.
LC NO. 79-701386
Prod-CCOA Dist-WRKSHP Prodn-WRKSHP 1979

Shape Of Speed, The C 53 MIN
16MM FILM, 3/4 OR 1/2 IN VIDEO
Presents boathandling techniques using a boat that is actually under sail. Covers racing tack, outside set, inside set, jiffy reefing, spinnaker handling, string takedown, staysail and blooper handling.
Prod-OFFSHR Dist-OFFSHR 1981

Shape Of The '80's, The C 20 MIN
16MM FILM OPTICAL SOUND
Uses interviews with executives and financial analysts to explore the American economy in the 1980's.
LC NO. 80-700502
Prod-BNBFW Dist-BNBFW Prodn-GLYNG 1980

Shape Of The Earth, The B 15 MIN
2 INCH VIDEOTAPE P
Teaches the child to question broad generalizations which are not self-evident and to ask for the evidence behind them. (Broadcast quality)
From The Land And Sea Series.
Prod-TTOIC Dist-GPITVL Prodn-WGBHTV

Shape Of The Land, The C 15 MIN
3/4 OR 1/2 INCH VIDEO CASSETTE
Teaches understanding of how the many shapes of the land came to be. Explains the basic geological processes of weathering, sedimentation, uplifting and more.
Prod-CBSC Dist-CBSC

Shape Of The Nation C 27 MIN
16MM FILM OPTICAL SOUND
Documents the state of physical fitness in Canada.
LC NO. 76-701364
Prod-SBRAND Dist-SBRAND Prodn-HARISD 1974

Shape Of The 70's C 28 MIN
16MM FILM OPTICAL SOUND C A
Discusses the role of small towns in rural areas in the 70's and the citizen's responsibility in public policy formation.
From The Eleventh Round Series. No. 5
Prod-UNL Dist-UNL 1969

Shape Of Things - Geometry C 14 MIN
3/4 OR 1/2 INCH VIDEO CASSETTE P
Depicts geometric shapes coming to life in a magic show.
From The Math Country Series.
Prod-KYTV Dist-AITECH 1979

Shape Of Things To Come, The C 21 MIN
16MM FILM OPTICAL SOUND J-C
Discusses the space research at three centers. Includes chemical and electrical propulsion at Lewis Research Center, miniaturization of circuitry and microelectronics at Langley Research Center and radiation reentry heat and frictional heating at Ames Research Center.
LC NO. 74-706401
Prod-NASA Dist-USNAC 1965

Shape Of Things, The C 10 MIN
16MM FILM, 3/4 OR 1/2 IN VIDEO H-C
Describes the activities and the results of the first symposium of sculpture to take place in North America. Highlights the work of eleven sculptors from nine countries who participated in the event.
Prod-NFBC Dist-IFB 1971

Shape Of Things, The C 15 MIN
3/4 OR 1/2 INCH VIDEO CASSETTE P
Presents a space robot as he shows his puppet assistant the

shapes of various items he has purchased at the grocery store. Tells how they compare the shapes to geometric models of a sphere, cone, cube, rectangular prism, and cylinder, and then discuss curved and flat surfaces, edges, and corners.
From The Math Mission 2 Series.
LC NO. 82-706328
Prod-WCVETV Dist-GPITVL 1980

Shape Relationships And The Third Dimension B 15 MIN
2 INCH VIDEOTAPE P
See series title for descriptive statement.
From The Just Wondering Series.
Prod-EOPS Dist-GPITVL Prodn-KOACTV

Shape Representation C 45 MIN
3/4 OR 1/2 INCH VIDEO CASSETTE PRO
Describes shapes using Gaussian images, extended Gaussian images to identify 3-dimensional objects, and finding collision-free paths for objects using the configuration-space transform.
From The Artificial Intelligence - Pt 3, Computer Vision Series.
Prod-MIOT Dist-MIOT

Shape Representation C 54 MIN
3/4 OR 1/2 INCH VIDEO CASSETTE C
See series title for descriptive statement.
From The Artificial Intelligence, Pt III - Computer Vision Series.
Prod-MIOT Dist-AMCEE

Shape Up C 8 MIN
16MM FILM OPTICAL SOUND P
See series title for descriptive statement.
From The Mathematics For Elementary School Students - Whole Numbers Series.
LC NO. 73-701838
Prod-DAVFMS Dist-DAVFMS 1974

Shape Up C 17 MIN
3/4 OR 1/2 INCH VIDEO CASSETTE
Teaches proper lifting methods and techniques for reducing back strain while standing and sitting on the job and at home.
From The Safety Management Course Series.
Prod-EDRF Dist-EDRF

Shape Up, Plants C 29 MIN
3/4 INCH VIDEO CASSETTE
Demonstrates indoor and outdoor pruning. Offers tips on how to prune for shape and health.
From The House Botanist Series.
Prod-UMITV Dist-UMITV 1978

Shape Your Stomach's In, The C 25 MIN
3/4 OR 1/2 INCH VIDEO CASSETTE
Examines gas pains, indigestion, the butterflies, upset stomach and ulcers.
Prod-TRAINX Dist-TRAINX

Shaped By Danish Hands B 17 MIN
16MM FILM OPTICAL SOUND
Gives examples of applied art in Denmark. Includes contemporary ceramists and furniture designers and their works, and examples of works in precious metals.
Prod-DAINFO Dist-NATDIS 1954

Shaped Up Shore Stations C 15 MIN
16MM FILM OPTICAL SOUND
Discusses problems of environmental pollution. Describes how the problems are being corrected through pollution abatement programs within the Naval Establishment centering on air, water and solid waste removal systems.
LC NO. 75-700580
Prod-USN Dist-USNAC 1972

Shaper No. 2 - Squaring A Block C 20 MIN
1/2 IN VIDEO CASSETTE BETA/VHS IND
Continues Shaper No. 1. Shows the procedure for machining all six sides of a workpiece parallel and square. Covers tool geometry and setup of tool and work for maximum rigidity.
From The Machine Shop-Shaper Series.
Prod-RMI Dist-RMI

Shaper No. 3 - Machining Angles C 11 MIN
1/2 IN VIDEO CASSETTE BETA/VHS IND
Demonstrates four methods of machining angles, swiveling vise, tilting the table, tilting work in vise, and tilting the head.
From The Machine Shop-Shaper Series.
Prod-RMI Dist-RMI

Shaper, The B 15 MIN
16MM FILM, 3/4 OR 1/2 IN VIDEO
Describes the functions, characteristics and basic operations of the shaper.
From The Machine Shop Work - Basic Machines Series.
Prod-USOE Dist-USNAC Prodn-LNS 1945

Shaper, The (Spanish) B 15 MIN
16MM FILM OPTICAL SOUND
Describes the functions, characteristics and basic operations of the shaper.
From The Machine Shop Work Series. Basic Machines
LC NO. FIE62-57
Prod-USOE Dist-USNAC

Shapes C 5 MIN
16MM FILM OPTICAL SOUND J-C A
Presents an experimental film which shows a variety of shapes and colors which move in time to a rhythmic background of electronic music.
LC NO. 75-701621
Prod-DEMOS Dist-CFS 1974

Shapes C 15 MIN
2 INCH VIDEOTAPE K
Recognizes and identifies an object by its shape.
From The Let's Go Sciencing, Unit I - Matter Series.
Prod-DETPS Dist-GPITVL

Shapes C 15 MIN
3/4 INCH VIDEO CASSETTE K-P
Reviews simple geometric shapes. Shows composite arrangements of shapes and studies organic, or moving, shapes.
From The Adventures Of Milo And Maisie Series.
Prod-KRLNTV Dist-GPITVL 1977

Shapes C 15 MIN
3/4 OR 1/2 INCH VIDEO CASSETTE P
Shows the characteristics of shapes and forms through an investigation of common objects. Discusses the use of shapes by Miro, Mondrian, Magritte and Stuart Davis.
From The Primary Art Series.
Prod-WETATV Dist-AITECH

Shapes C 30 MIN
3/4 OR 1/2 INCH VIDEO CASSETTE
See series title for descriptive statement.
From The Infinity Factory Series.
Prod-EDFCEN Dist-MDCPB

Shapes And More Shapes C 15 MIN
3/4 OR 1/2 INCH VIDEO CASSETTE P
Tells how a space robot and his puppet assistant help their friend, Mr Beetle, make his way through a maze, as they develop the concepts of flat shapes, space shapes, and a straight line. Shows how to draw and construct different patterns and shapes.
From The Math Mission 2 Series.
LC NO. 82-706327
Prod-WCVETV Dist-GPITVL 1980

Shapes And Polarities Of Molecules C 18 MIN
16MM FILM OPTICAL SOUND H
Uses electrical effects, including deflections of a stream of falling liquid by an electrically charged rod. Introduces the concept of molecular polarity. A molecular dipole model is used to explain differences in solubility, conductivity and chemical reactivity.
From The CHEM Study Films Series.
Prod-CHEMS Dist-MLA 1962

Shapes And Triangles C 30 MIN
3/4 OR 1/2 INCH VIDEO CASSETTE
See series title for descriptive statement.
From The Infinity Factory Series.
Prod-EDFCEN Dist-MDCPB

Shapes Of Geometry—A Series
H
Explores the mathematical analysis of tessellations and kaleidoscopes as well as miniature geometry and non-Euclidean geometry including spherical and hyperbolic topology.
Prod-WVIZTV Dist-GPITVL 1982

Kaleidoscope Geometry	020 MIN
Miniature Geometry	020 MIN
Non-Euclidean Geometries	020 MIN
Tesselations	020 MIN
Topology I	020 MIN
Topology II	020 MIN

Shapes We Live With, The C 14 MIN
16MM FILM, 3/4 OR 1/2 IN VIDEO P-I
Introduces the four basic shapes and demonstrates the sphere, the cylinder, the cone and the cube.
Prod-BOUNDY Dist-PHENIX 1970

Shapes, Pt 1 C 15 MIN
3/4 OR 1/2 INCH VIDEO CASSETTE P
See series title for descriptive statement.
From The Let's Draw Series.
Prod-OCPS Dist-AITECH Prodn-KOKHTV 1976

Shapes, Pt 2 C 15 MIN
3/4 OR 1/2 INCH VIDEO CASSETTE P
See series title for descriptive statement.
From The Let's Draw Series.
Prod-OCPS Dist-AITECH Prodn-KOKHTV 1976

Shapes, Surface C 14 MIN
3/4 OR 1/2 INCH VIDEO CASSETTE P
Shows how to draw surface shapes.
From The Let's Draw Series.
Prod-KOKHTV Dist-AITECH 1976

Shaping C 5 MIN
3/4 OR 1/2 INCH VIDEO CASSETTE T
See series title for descriptive statement.
From The Protocol Materials In Teacher Education - The Process Of Teaching, Pt 2 Series.
Prod-MSU Dist-MSU

Shaping After Template And Shaping Curved Edges B 17 MIN
16MM FILM, 3/4 OR 1/2 IN VIDEO
Shows how to make a template, install knives, use the template for smoothing squared edges and set up equipment for shaping a curved edge.
From The Precision Wood Machining - Operations On The Spindle Shaper Series. No. 2
Prod-USOE Dist-USNAC Prodn-RCM 1945

Shaping And Scheduling C 42 MIN
3/4 OR 1/2 INCH VIDEO CASSETTE T
Gives ways to encourage children to improve when their performance is poor and reward is not possible.
From The Learning And Liking It Series.
Prod-MSU Dist-MSU

Shaping Curriculum C 30 MIN
3/4 OR 1/2 INCH VIDEO CASSETTE T
Examines the first of three dimensions of the R H Anderson model of effective teaching.
From The On And About Instruction Series.
Prod-VADE Dist-GPITVL 1983

Shaping Instruction C 30 MIN
3/4 OR 1/2 INCH VIDEO CASSETTE T
Looks at the second of three dimensions of the R H Anderson model of effective teaching.
From The On And About Instruction Series.
Prod-VADE Dist-GPITVL 1983

Shaping News For The Consumer C 17 MIN
16MM FILM, 3/4 OR 1/2 IN VIDEO H-C A
Shows the process of preparing a television news story and discusses the capabilities and limitations of television news, newspapers and news magazines.
Prod-MEDFO Dist-PHENIX 1975

Shaping The Classroom C 30 MIN
3/4 OR 1/2 INCH VIDEO CASSETTE T
Examines the third dimension of the R H Anderson model of effective teaching.
From The On And About Instruction Series.
Prod-VADE Dist-GPITVL 1983

Shaping The Future C 60 MIN
3/4 OR 1/2 INCH VIDEO CASSETTE H-C A
Discusses what happens at the moment of conception and shows how the fertilized egg is transformed into a full-grown adult. Looks at traditional theories in this area, arguing that a conceptual leap was necessary for real progress to be made. Based on the book The Body In Question by Jonathan Miller. Narrated by Jonathan Miller.
From The Body In Question Series. Program 7
LC NO. 81-706951
Prod-BBCTV Dist-FI 1979

Shaping The Many Worlds C 28 MIN
16MM FILM OPTICAL SOUND
Shows a group of parents and educators considering styles of mothering and the role of the parent in fostering development.
From The Many Worlds Of Childhood Series.
LC NO. 74-701225
Prod-OECA Dist-OECA 1972

Shaping The Personality B 20 MIN
16MM FILM SILENT C T
Illustrates forms of mother-child relations and their influence on the child.
From The Film Studies Of The Psychoanalytic Research Project On Problems In Infancy Series.
Prod-SPITZ Dist-NYU 1953

Shaping The Residual Limb - Stump Wrapping And The Temporary Prosthesis C 23 MIN
3/4 OR 1/2 INCH VIDEO CASSETTE
Prod-UMDSM Dist-UMDSM

Shaping Today With Yesterday—A Series

Presents programs from the New York City Cable TV series Eye On Dance.
Prod-ARCVID Dist-ARCVID

Ballerinas Compare Notes On Creating Roles	030 MIN
Morris Dances - Ancient Ritual English Dances	030 MIN
Sensationalism Caused By The 19th Century	030 MIN
Tracing The Roots Of Dance With Hanya Holm	030 MIN

Shaping Up Your Geometry C 30 MIN
3/4 OR 1/2 INCH VIDEO CASSETTE A
See series title for descriptive statement.
From The Adult Math Series.
Prod-KYTV Dist-KYTV 1984

Shaping Up—A Series
J-H
Creates visuals which are accompanied by music and the narrator's advice for weight control.
Prod-POAPLE Dist-POAPLE

Diet	010 MIN
Exercise	010 MIN

Shaping, Prompting, And Fading C
3/4 OR 1/2 INCH VIDEO CASSETTE S
Offers demonstrations in eating, toileting and eye contact, for retarded persons and how to use and fade verbal, gestural and physical prompts.
From The Effective Behavioral Programming Series.
Prod-RESPRC Dist-RESPRC

Share It With Someone C 4 MIN
16MM FILM, 3/4 OR 1/2 IN VIDEO K-I
Stresses that, whether it's a toy car, sugar cookies or a super idea, it's more fun to share than to be alone.
From The Most Important Person - Getting Along With Others Series.
Prod-EBEC Dist-EBEC 1972

Share That Book B 20 MIN
2 INCH VIDEOTAPE P
Gives pointers for a good book review. (Broadcast quality)
From The Language Lane Series. Lesson 29
Prod-CVETVC Dist-GPITVL Prodn-WCVETV

Share To Communicate C 15 MIN
2 INCH VIDEOTAPE P
Provides an enrichment program in the communitive arts area by giving an oral report.
From The Word Magic (2nd Ed) Series.
Prod-CVETVC Dist-GPITVL

Share-A-Home C 9 MIN
16MM FILM, 3/4 OR 1/2 IN VIDEO H-C A
Describes the Share-A-Home concept, which brings together old people to share homes.
From The American Family - An Endangered Species Series.
Prod-NBC Dist-FI 1979

Shared Decision Making C 57 MIN
3/4 INCH VIDEO CASSETTE
Provides a generic introduction to a nondirective technique to aid clients in identifying goals and the actions necessary for achieving them.
From The Child Welfare Learning Laboratory Materials Series.
Prod-UMITV Dist-UMITV

Shared Experience, The C 29 MIN
16MM FILM OPTICAL SOUND
Examines the library as a repository for the transmission of human experience. Features Dr Lewis Thomas talking about the biological basis for culture, Noam Chomsky speculating on the origin of language, Alexander Marshack exploring the mind of ice age man, and John Kenneth Galbraith talking about contemporary information.
LC NO. 78-700306
Prod-PRATTE Dist-PRATTE Prodn-LAWFI 1978

Shared Illusion C 29 MIN
3/4 INCH VIDEO CASSETTE
Looks at the identification of the normal and abnormal in society today. Hosted by Dr William Rhodes, professor of psychology at the University of Michigan.
Prod-UMITV Dist-UMITV 1978

Shared Labor C 47 MIN
16MM FILM OPTICAL SOUND
Documents a young couple's experience with natural childbirth.
LC NO. 80-701264
Prod-FGCH Dist-RAINFI Prodn-RAINFI 1980

Shared Meaning C 30 MIN
3/4 OR 1/2 INCH VIDEO CASSETTE
Discusses skills used to reach a common understanding. Involves a process of feedback in which the listener paraphrases what he or she had heard the other say.
From The Couples Communication Skills Series.
Prod-NETCHE Dist-NETCHE 1975

Shared Realities—A Series
A
Features many artists, dancers, and musicians whose work is coordinated with efforts of the Long Beach Museum of Art.
Prod-LBMART Dist-LBMART 1985

Artist And Television 1, The 056 MIN
Artist And Television 2, The 058 MIN
Artist And The Computer, The 057 MIN
Artists And The Media 055 MIN
At Home - Part 1 055 MIN
At Home - Part 2 055 MIN
Exploring Dance 1 051 MIN
Exploring Dance 2 057 MIN
Long Beach Community Arts 053 MIN
Long Beach Museum Of Art - Video 056 MIN
Music And Performance 058 MIN
Personal Perspectives 053 MIN

Shareen Brysac C 30 MIN
3/4 OR 1/2 INCH VIDEO CASSETTE
Looks at producing dance specials for the mass market.
From The Eye On Dance - Dance On Television Series.
Prod-ARTRES Dist-ARTRES

Sharing C 14 MIN
16MM FILM OPTICAL SOUND
Shows how the United Way functions in Tarrant County, Texas, by presenting the story of a family with a handicapped child interspersed with examples of various United Way services.
LC NO. 77-700031
Prod-UWTC Dist-UWTC Prodn-SBRTC 1976

Sharing C 9 MIN
16MM FILM, 3/4 OR 1/2 IN VIDEO I-J
Presents Sally, who has been saving money to buy a transistor radio on sale. Considers the moral values involved in the concepts of sharing, and the factors which affect decision making about generosity.
From The Moral Decision Making Series.
Prod-MORLAT Dist-AIMS 1971

Sharing C 18 MIN
3/4 OR 1/2 INCH VIDEO CASSETTE
Shows intercourse with concurrent manual stimulation and demonstrates positions which facilitate this technique.
From The Becoming Orgasmic - A Sexual Growth Program Series.
Prod-MMRC Dist-MMRC

Sharing And Not Sharing Game, The C 11 MIN
16MM FILM, 3/4 OR 1/2 IN VIDEO P
Presents a story about a little girl who shares her brother's kite with a friend who breaks it. Discusses evaluating and making intelligent decisions in sharing situations.
From The Learning Responsibility Series.
Prod-HIGGIN Dist-HIGGIN 1979

Sharing Effectively B 15 MIN
2 INCH VIDEOTAPE P
See series title for descriptive statement.
From The Language Corner Series.
Prod-CVETVC Dist-GPITVL Prodn-WCVETV

Sharing Is Caring C 15 MIN
16MM FILM OPTICAL SOUND
Describes the educational and recreational opportunities made available primarily to inner-city youths through the Kids Corporation, a group of volunteers who are sponsored by business organizations in the Newark, New Jersey, area.
LC NO. 74-702887
Prod-PICA Dist-PICA 1974

Sharing Is Caring C 30 MIN
3/4 OR 1/2 INCH VIDEO CASSETTE K-P
See series title for descriptive statement.
From The Villa Alegre Series.
Prod-BCTV Dist-MDCPB

Sharing Is Fun X 15 MIN
16MM FILM OPTICAL SOUND P-I R
Tells the story of a boy who befriends a new neighbor who is recovering from polio. Shows how the boy learns Christian attitudes of sharing.
From The Our Children Series.
Prod-FAMF Dist-FAMF

Sharing Is Unity (Ushirika Ni Umoja) (Kiswahili) C 23 MIN
16MM FILM, 3/4 OR 1/2 IN VIDEO A
Explores rural life and feelings of the Iteso peoples of Kenya. Experiences African sense of community through farming and storytelling.
Prod-AFFILM Dist-AFFILM 1985

Sharing Is Unity (Ushirika Ni Umoja) (English) C 23 MIN
16MM FILM, 3/4 OR 1/2 IN VIDEO A
Explores rural life and feelings of the Iteso peoples of Kenya. Experiences African sense of community through farming and storytelling.
Prod-AFFILM Dist-AFFILM 1985

Sharing Literature With Children C 16 MIN
16MM FILM OPTICAL SOUND
Describes the program developed for children at the Orlando Public Library and gives guidelines for setting up such a program.
LC NO. 75-700159
Prod-ORPULI Dist-ORPULI Prodn-CYPRES 1974

Sharing Orgasm - Communicating Your Sexual Responses C 10 MIN
16MM FILM, 3/4 OR 1/2 IN VIDEO PRO
Trains pre-orgasmic women and their counselors.
From The Women's Issues - Sexuality Series.
Prod-DAVFMS Dist-DAVFMS 1978

Sharing Orgasm - Communicating Your Sexual Responses C 10 MIN
3/4 OR 1/2 INCH VIDEO CASSETTE C A
Shows genital pleasuring as a crucial first step within a series of exercises for women learning to have orgasms with their partners. Demonstrates sexual pleasuring and shows direct clitoral stimulation.
Prod-UCSF Dist-MMRC

Sharing Picture Books C 30 MIN
1/2 IN VIDEO CASSETTE BETA/VHS K-I
See series title for descriptive statement.
From The Jump Over The Moon - Sharing Literature With Young Children Series.
Prod-HRAW Dist-HRAW

Sharing The Experience With Gavin C 28 MIN
16MM FILM, 3/4 OR 1/2 IN VIDEO
Describes the situation when the birth of a child with Down's Syndrome resulted in the hospital and community working closely with the parents and grandparents to give the child the best start in life. Presents the parents describing the birth experience, their decision on amniocentesis and future children and their concern about being free to enjoy their child as a delightful addition to their family.
From The Sharing The Experience Series.
Prod-STNFLD Dist-STNFLD

Sharing The Experience With June C 28 MIN
16MM FILM, 3/4 OR 1/2 IN VIDEO
Documents experiences in the life of June, a mentally retarded teenager.
From The Sharing The Experience Series.
Prod-STNFLD Dist-STNFLD

Sharing The Experience With Peter C 28 MIN
16MM FILM, 3/4 OR 1/2 IN VIDEO
Documents the experiences of a young boy who is severely handicapped and shows how he is very much a part of his family. Discusses a program called Extend-A-Family which helps form friendships between handicapped and nonhandicapped children.
From The Sharing The Experience Series.
Prod-STNFLD Dist-STNFLD

Sharing The Experience With Walter C 28 MIN
16MM FILM, 3/4 OR 1/2 IN VIDEO
Documents the experiences of Walter, who lived most of his life in an institution for the mentally retarded and now has moved into the community and learned to live on his own. Discusses a group of parents of institutional residents who created a 'Community Living Board' to provide services that enable residents to move out into the community.
From The Sharing The Experience Series.
Prod-STNFLD Dist-STNFLD

Sharing The Experience—A Series
16MM FILM, 3/4 OR 1/2 IN VIDEO
Documents families that daily meet the challenge of living and working with a handicapped family member. Presents a study of mental retardation, spanning the ages of infancy, childhood, teenage and adulthood.
Prod-STNFLD Dist-STNFLD

Sharing The Experience With Gavin 28 MIN
Sharing The Experience With June 28 MIN
Sharing The Experience With Peter 28 MIN
Sharing The Experience With Walter 28 MIN

Sharing The Glory C 30 MIN
16MM FILM OPTICAL SOUND
Presents a Bible study in the home of Ron Simmons and his friends. Poses the question - 'DOESN'T EACH ONE OF US HAVE COUNTLESS OPPORTUNITIES TO WITNESS EVERYDAY.'
LC NO. 73-701033
Prod-FAMF Dist-FAMF 1971

Sharing The Leadership B 30 MIN
16MM FILM OPTICAL SOUND H-C A
Explores three categories of individual action—selfserving, task and group-serving functions—and their relationship to group leadership.
From The Dynamics Of Leadership Series.
Prod-NET Dist-IU Prodn-WGBHTV 1963

Sharing The Road C 15 MIN
16MM FILM OPTICAL SOUND
Stresses that the nation's highways can be shared by both motorists and truckers. Demonstrates the kinds of problems truckers encounter on the road.
Prod-ATA Dist-MTP

Sharing The Secret C 84 MIN
16MM FILM OPTICAL SOUND A
Documents the pride, pain, anguish and affection of homosexuality by looking at several gay men. Shows them in their homes, with their families and in their various gay relationships.
LC NO. 82-700350
Prod-CANBC Dist-IFEX 1981

Sharing The Wind C 27 MIN
16MM FILM, 3/4 OR 1/2 IN VIDEO
Captures the intensity of championship catamaran racing, hull-flying in conditions that demand perfection.
Prod-ALLNRP Dist-ALLNRP

Shark C 29 MIN
16MM FILM, 3/4 OR 1/2 IN VIDEO I-C
Shows author Peter Benchley and underwater photographer, Stan Waterman as they dive off the Great Barrier Reef. Follows their encounters with several different types of sharks, including the great white shark.
Prod-ABCSRT Dist-LCOA Prodn-SMITHP 1976

Shark - Ancient Mystery Of The Sea C 15 MIN
16MM FILM OPTICAL SOUND C
Explains the research being done on sharks. Deals with how sharks can by affected by underwater sound, their pattern of pre-attack behavior, if they can distinguish color and how the shark has survived unchained for millions of years. Examines ways of guarding against the shark while sharing his environment.
From The Science In Action Series.
Prod-ALLFP Dist-COUNFI

Shark, Danger In The Sea C 27 MIN
16MM FILM - 3/4 IN VIDEO
Discusses how the U S Navy's shark research programs help in the development of equipment and procedures useful in preventing shark attacks.
LC NO. 79-706712
Prod-USN Dist-USNAC 1979

Shark, The - Maneater Or Myth C 24 MIN
16MM FILM, 3/4 OR 1/2 IN VIDEO I-H
Investigates the latest scientific research on the behavior of sharks and examines new warning and protective devices designed to ward off sharks' infrequent but devastating attacks on humans.
From The Wide World Of Adventure Series.
Prod-AVATLI Dist-EBEC 1977

Sharks C 24 MIN
16MM FILM, 3/4 OR 1/2 IN VIDEO I-C
A shortened version of Sharks. Presents a discussion by Jacques Cousteau's oceanographers about myths associated with sharks. Studies how sharks are attracted to an alien presence, how sharks learn and make visual discriminations, how night affects shark behavior and how people can protect themselves from sharks.
From The Undersea World Of Jacques Cousteau Series.
Prod-METROM Dist-CF 1970

Sharks C 52 MIN
16MM FILM, 3/4 OR 1/2 IN VIDEO
Presents a study by Jacques Cousteau and his oceanographers on how sharks are attracted to an alien presence, how sharks make visual discriminations, how night affects their behavior and how man can protect himself from them.
From The Undersea World Of Jacques Cousteau Series.
Prod-METROM Dist-CF 1970

Sharks (Spanish) C 24 MIN
16MM FILM, 3/4 OR 1/2 IN VIDEO
Presents a study by Jacques Cousteau and his oceanographers on how sharks are attracted to an alien presence, how sharks make visual discriminations, how night affects their behavior and how man can protect himself from them.
From The Undersea World Of Jacques Cousteau Series.
Prod-METROM Dist-CF 1970

Sharks (Spanish) C 52 MIN
16MM FILM, 3/4 OR 1/2 IN VIDEO
Presents a study by Jacques Cousteau and his oceanographers on how sharks are attracted to an alien presence, how sharks make visual discriminations, how night affects their behavior and how man can protect himself from them.
From The Undersea World Of Jacques Cousteau Series.
Prod-METROM Dist-CF 1970

Sharks - Terror, Truth, Death C 28 MIN
16MM FILM, 3/4 OR 1/2 IN VIDEO J-H A
Demonstrates the remarkable sensory mechanism of sharks, as well as their attack pattern. Points out that attacks on people are extremely rare.
Prod-ABC Dist-FI 1976

Sharks, Some Facts C 17 MIN
16MM FILM, 3/4 OR 1/2 IN VIDEO J-C A
Presents factual information about sharks and their behavior patterns in an attempt to dispel common misconceptions about their potential danger to humans.
Prod-COUSJM Dist-PHENIX 1978

Sharks, The C 59 MIN
16MM FILM, 3/4 OR 1/2 IN VIDEO
Observes sharks around the world and addresses man's fear and hatred of sharks. Discusses the shark's anatomy, behavior and vulnerability to people.
LC NO. 82-707105
Prod-NGS Dist-NGS 1982

Sharon Lois And Bram At The Young People's Theatre C 30 MIN
16MM FILM, 3/4 OR 1/2 IN VIDEO P-J
Captures the three singers doing what they do best, singing in concert in a manner that establishes instant audience rapport. Shows them performing to children of all ages, moms, dads, grandparents, and in informal workshops, too. Helps young people to develop appreciation for music.
Prod-CAMBFP Dist-BCNFL 1983

Sharp As A Razor C 15 MIN
16MM FILM, 3/4 OR 1/2 IN VIDEO PRO
Illustrates the use of cutting tools in fighting watershed fires.
Prod-PUBSF Dist-FILCOM

Sharp AV500 (Audio Cassette Recorder) C 7 MIN
3/4 OR 1/2 INCH VIDEO CASSETTE
See series title for descriptive statement.
From The Audio-Visual Skills Modules Series.
Prod-MDCC Dist-MDCC

Sharp Eyes, Sharp Talons C 16 MIN
16MM FILM, 3/4 OR 1/2 IN VIDEO P-J
Describes the different forms of hawks, their adaptation for aerial hunting and their various habitats.
From The North American Species Series.
Prod-KARVF Dist-BCNFL 1984

Sharp-Tail Grouse - A Real Prairie Dandy C 8 MIN
16MM FILM OPTICAL SOUND I-C A
Provides a look at the habits of the sharp-tail grouse of North America. Shows the mating dance of the birds at close range.
Prod-COLIM Dist-COLIM

Sharpen Your Thinking C 30 MIN
2 INCH VIDEOTAPE J
See series title for descriptive statement.
From The Summer Journal, Unit 4 - You Are What You Think Series.
Prod-WNINTV Dist-GPITVL

Sharpening A Drill On The Drill Grinder C 16 MIN
1/2 IN VIDEO CASSETTE BETA/VHS IND
See series title for descriptive statement.
From The Machine Shop - Drill Press, Radial Drill, Drill Grinder Series.
Prod-RMI Dist-RMI

Sharpening A Form Relieved Cutter B 18 MIN
16MM FILM, 3/4 OR 1/2 IN VIDEO
Tells what constitutes the rake and clearance angles of the form relieved cutter. Shows how to mount the correct attachment, set up for spotting the back of teeth and grind the face of the teeth.
From The Machine Shop Work - Operations On The Cutter Grinder Series. No. 5
Prod-USOE Dist-USNAC Prodn-YORKES 1944

Sharpening A Plain Helical Milling Cutter B 16 MIN
16MM FILM, 3/4 OR 1/2 IN VIDEO
Shows how to mount the helical cutter on an arbor and sharpen the secondary clearance angle. Describes how to check and adjust for taper when grinding the primary clearance angle.
From The Machine Shop Work - Operations On The Cutter Grinder Series. No. 2
Prod-USOE Dist-USNAC Prodn-YORKES 1944

Sharpening A Reamer Between Centers C 15 MIN
3/4 OR 1/2 INCH VIDEO CASSETTE IND
See series title for descriptive statement.
From The Machining And The Operation Of Machine Tools, Module 4 - Milling And Tool Series.
Prod-LEIKID Dist-LEIKID

Sharpening A Shell End Mill B 17 MIN
16MM FILM, 3/4 OR 1/2 IN VIDEO
Shows how to select the correct arbor, mount the work head and adjust it for clearance settings, and set up for sharpening the outside diameter, corner and face.
From The Machine Shop Work - Operations On The Cutter Grinder Series. No. 3
Prod-USOE Dist-USNAC Prodn-YORKES 1944

Sharpening A Side Milling Cutter B 23 MIN
16MM FILM, 3/4 OR 1/2 IN VIDEO
Shows how to identify the parts of a cutter, select and mount the correct grinding wheel, mount the cutter, set up the grinder for sharpening, set the correct clearance angle and check for width of land.
From The Machine Shop Work - Operations On The Cutter Grinder Series. No. 1
Prod-USOE Dist-USNAC Prodn-YORKES 1944

Sharpening An Angular Cutter B 18 MIN
16MM FILM, 3/4 OR 1/2 IN VIDEO
Explains how to choose the correct grinding wheel, how to adjust the swivel table for grinding the angular teeth of the cutter, adjust for clearance angle and check the teeth for accuracy of the angle.
From The Machine Shop Work - Operations On The Cutter Grinder Series. No. 4
Prod-USOE Dist-USNAC 1944

Sharpening And Tempering Farm Tools B 12 MIN
16MM FILM OPTICAL SOUND
Demonstrates how to heat carbon steel tools for forge sharpening. Explains how to identify tempering colors.
Prod-USOE Dist-USNAC 1945

Sharpening And Tempering Farm Tools B 17 MIN
16MM FILM, 3/4 OR 1/2 IN VIDEO
Shows how to heat carbon steel tools for forge sharpening, hardening and tempering of a plowshare and a cultivator shovel.
From The Farm Work - Forging Series. No. 3
LC NO. 82-706697
Prod-USOE Dist-USNAC 1945

Sharpening Brazed Carbide Lathe Tools Using A Universal Vise C 15 MIN
3/4 OR 1/2 INCH VIDEO CASSETTE IND
See series title for descriptive statement.
From The Machining And The Operation Of Machine Tools, Module 4 - Milling And Tool Series.
Prod-LEIKID Dist-LEIKID

Sharpening Chisels, Plane Irons And Gouges C 12 MIN
16MM FILM, 3/4 OR 1/2 IN VIDEO H-C A
Demonstrates the sharpening of tools for woodwork, including chisels, plane irons and gouges using the grinder and the oilstone.
From The Hand Tools For Wood Working Series.
Prod-MORLAT Dist-SF 1967

Sharpening Drill Bits By Hand And Machine C
3/4 OR 1/2 INCH VIDEO CASSETTE
See series title for descriptive statement.
From The Basic Machine Technology Series.
Prod-VTRI Dist-VTRI

Sharpening Drill Bits By Hand And Machine C 15 MIN
3/4 OR 1/2 INCH VIDEO CASSETTE
See series title for descriptive statement.
From The Machine Technology II - Engine Lathe Accessories Series.
Prod-CAMB Dist-CAMB

Sharpening Drill Bits By Hand And Machine C 15 MIN
3/4 OR 1/2 INCH VIDEO CASSETTE IND
See series title for descriptive statement.
From The Machining And The Operation Of Machine Tools, Module 1 - Basic Machine Technology Series.
Prod-LEIKID Dist-LEIKID

Sharpening Drill Bits By Hand And Machine (Spanish) C
3/4 OR 1/2 INCH VIDEO CASSETTE
See series title for descriptive statement.
From The Basic Machine Technology (Spanish) Series.
Prod-VTRI Dist-VTRI

Sharpening Ends Of End Mills C
3/4 OR 1/2 INCH VIDEO CASSETTE
See series title for descriptive statement.
From The Milling And Tool Sharpening Series.
Prod-VTRI Dist-VTRI

Sharpening Ends Of End Mills C 15 MIN
3/4 OR 1/2 INCH VIDEO CASSETTE
See series title for descriptive statement.
From The Machine Technology IV - Milling Series
Prod-CAMB Dist-CAMB

Sharpening Ends Of End Mills C 15 MIN
3/4 OR 1/2 INCH VIDEO CASSETTE IND
See series title for descriptive statement.
From The Machining And The Operation Of Machine Tools, Module 4 - Milling And Tool Series.
Prod-LEIKID Dist-LEIKID

Sharpening Ends Of End Mills (Spanish) C
3/4 OR 1/2 INCH VIDEO CASSETTE
See series title for descriptive statement.
From The Milling And Tool Sharpening (Spanish) Series.
Prod-VTRI Dist-VTRI

Sharpening Lathe Tools Including N/C Lathe Tools C
3/4 OR 1/2 INCH VIDEO CASSETTE
See series title for descriptive statement.
From The Milling And Tool Sharpening Series.
Prod-VTRI Dist-VTRI

Sharpening Lathe Tools Including N/C Lathe Tools C 15 MIN
3/4 OR 1/2 INCH VIDEO CASSETTE
See series title for descriptive statement.
From The Machine Technology IV - Milling Series
Prod-CAMB Dist-CAMB

Sharpening Lathe Tools Including N/C Lathe Tools (Spanish) C
3/4 OR 1/2 INCH VIDEO CASSETTE
See series title for descriptive statement.
From The Milling And Tool Sharpening (Spanish) Series.
Prod-VTRI Dist-VTRI

Sharpening Periodontal Instruments C 15 MIN
3/4 INCH VIDEO CASSETTE PRO
Demonstrates techniques for sharpening periodontal instruments and presents two methods of testing instruments for sharpness.
LC NO. 79-706756
Prod-MUSC Dist-USNAC 1978

Sharpening Side Milling Cutters, Slitting Saws And Staggered Tooth Cutters C
3/4 OR 1/2 INCH VIDEO CASSETTE
See series title for descriptive statement.
From The Milling And Tool Sharpening Series.
Prod-VTRI Dist-VTRI

Sharpening Side Milling Cutters, Slitting Saws And Staggered Tooth Cutters C 15 MIN
3/4 OR 1/2 INCH VIDEO CASSETTE
See series title for descriptive statement.
From The Machine Technology IV - Milling Series
Prod-CAMB Dist-CAMB

Sharpening Side Milling Cutters, Slitting Saws And Staggered Tooth Cutters (Spanish) C
3/4 OR 1/2 INCH VIDEO CASSETTE
See series title for descriptive statement.
From The Milling And Tool Sharpening (Spanish) Series.
Prod-VTRI Dist-VTRI

Sharpening The Focus C
3/4 OR 1/2 INCH VIDEO CASSETTE C
Discusses the third of three lessons on the pre-writing stage showing how to develop a specific topic from a wide range of ideas. Reinforces the relationship of the composition to the audience.
From The Write Course - An Introduction To College Composition Series.
Prod-DALCCD Dist-DALCCD

Sharpening The Focus C 30 MIN
3/4 OR 1/2 INCH VIDEO CASSETTE C A
Discusses, in this third lesson on pre-writing, how to develop a specific topic from a wide range of ideas. Reinforces the relation of composition to the audience.
From The Write Course - An Introduction To College Composition Series.
Prod-FI Dist-FI 1984

Sharpening The Periphery Of An End Mill C 15 MIN
3/4 OR 1/2 INCH VIDEO CASSETTE IND
See series title for descriptive statement.
From The Machining And The Operation Of Machine Tools, Module 4 - Milling And Tool Series.
Prod-LEIKID Dist-LEIKID

Sharpening The Periphery Of End Mills C
3/4 OR 1/2 INCH VIDEO CASSETTE
See series title for descriptive statement.
From The Milling And Tool Sharpening Series.
Prod-VTRI Dist-VTRI

Sharpening The Periphery Of End Mills C 15 MIN
3/4 OR 1/2 INCH VIDEO CASSETTE
See series title for descriptive statement.
From The Machine Technology IV - Milling Series
Prod-CAMB Dist-CAMB

Sharpening The Periphery Of End Mills (Spanish) C
3/4 OR 1/2 INCH VIDEO CASSETTE
See series title for descriptive statement.
From The Milling And Tool Sharpening (Spanish) Series.
Prod-VTRI Dist-VTRI

Sharpening The Periphery Of Plain Milling Cutters And Side Mills C 15 MIN
3/4 OR 1/2 INCH VIDEO CASSETTE IND
See series title for descriptive statement.
From The Machining And The Operation Of Machine Tools, Module 4 - Milling And Tool Series.
Prod-LEIKID Dist-LEIKID

Sharpening-Inlaying And Detailing C 86 MIN
1/2 INCH VIDEOTAPE
Discusses how to properly sharpen woodworkng tools. Goes on into beginning inlaying and detailing.
From The Woodworking Series.
Prod-ANVICO Dist-ANVICO

Sharps, Flats, Keys And Scales C 29 MIN
2 INCH VIDEOTAPE
See series title for descriptive statement.
From The Playing The Guitar I Series.
Prod-KCET Dist-PUBTEL

Shatter The Silence C 29 MIN
16MM FILM, 3/4 OR 1/2 IN VIDEO H-C A
Presents an informative story of a young gir's experience with incest.
LC NO. 84-706804
Prod-SLFP Dist-PHENIX 1981

Shattered C 21 MIN
16MM FILM, 3/4 OR 1/2 IN VIDEO
Explores the social, emotional and legal aftermath of a rape attack. Dispels current myths about the rapist and the victim. Shows rape crisis personnel working with police, family members and prosecuters to help lessen the women's ordeal. Illustrates the role of peer counseling sessions in helping victims cope with the trauma.
Prod-MTI Dist-MTI

Shattered Badge, The C 26 MIN
16MM FILM, 3/4 OR 1/2 IN VIDEO J-C A
Deals with the problem of stress in police work and how various officers cope with it.

LC NO. 82-707062
Prod-ABCNEW Dist-LCOA 1980

Shavuoth C 15 MIN
16MM FILM OPTICAL SOUND
Shows how the Festival of Shavuoth is celebrated in Israel.
Prod-ALDEN Dist-ALDEN

Shaw Vs Shakespeare, Pt 1 - The Character Of Caesar C 33 MIN
16MM FILM, 3/4 OR 1/2 IN VIDEO H-C
Features Donald Moffatt in the character of George Bernard Shaw who analyzes Shakespeare's characterization of Julius Caesar and compares it with his own treatment. Tells how Shaw claims the character of Caesar was beyond Shakespeare, but admits that Shakespeare is still 'KING OF THE DRAMATISTS.'
From The Humanities - The Drama Series.
Prod-EBEC Dist-EBEC 1970

Shaw Vs Shakespeare, Pt 2 - The Tragedy Of Julius Caesar C 35 MIN
16MM FILM, 3/4 OR 1/2 IN VIDEO H-C
Discusses Shakespeare's 'Julius Caesar' as a tragedy of 'political idealism.' Features the character of George Bernard Shaw who claims that Shakespeare's portrayal of Brutus as 'the complete idealist' helps make this play 'the most splendidly written political melodrama that we possess.'
From The Humanities - The Drama Series.
Prod-EBEC Dist-EBEC 1970

Shaw Vs Shakespeare, Pt 3 - Caesar And Cleopatra C 33 MIN
16MM FILM, 3/4 OR 1/2 IN VIDEO H-C
Features the character of George Bernard Shaw who develops one of his favorite themes, the problem of the progress of the human species, by analyzing the four political murders in Shakespeare's 'CAESAR AND CLEOPATRA.'
From The Humanities - The Drama Series.
Prod-EBEC Dist-EBEC 1970

Shaw's Pygmalion B 20 MIN
16MM FILM OPTICAL SOUND H-C
An excerpt from the 1938 feature film 'PYGMALION' based on George Bernard Shaw's play about the transformation in speech, dress and manners of Eliza Doolittle, the cockney flower girl.
Prod-PASCAL Dist-IU Prodn-NCTE 1962

Shaw's St Joan C 60 MIN
3/4 OR 1/2 INCH VIDEO CASSETTE C
See series title for descriptive statement.
From The Drama - Play, Performance, Perception Series. Module 3
Prod-MDCC Dist-MDCC

She Ain't Heavy C 30 MIN
3/4 OR 1/2 INCH VIDEO CASSETTE
See series title for descriptive statement.
From The Rebop Series.
Prod-WGBHTV Dist-MDCPB

She Drinks A Little C 30 MIN
16MM FILM, 3/4 OR 1/2 IN VIDEO J-C A
Shows how a teenager is burdened and traumatized by an alcoholic mother. Depicts how her exposure to organizations such as Alateen helps her to cope emotionally with the situation.
Prod-TAHSEM Dist-LCOA 1981

She Had Her Gun All Ready C 30 MIN
3/4 OR 1/2 INCH VIDEO CASSETTE
Explores the relationship between two antithetical types, passive Pat Place and active Lydia Lunch. Characterized by increasingly violent animosity.
Prod-KITCHN Dist-KITCHN

She Has A Choice C 17 MIN
16MM FILM OPTICAL SOUND H-C A
Presents women of different ages and backgrounds who share their real-life experiences of dealing with alcoholism. Explores the myths and realities of alcohol and women.
LC NO. 81-701052
Prod-MTVTM Dist-MTVTM 1978

She Is Away C 14 MIN
16MM FILM OPTICAL SOUND
Presents a tone poem of waiting and anticipation which is based on time in its metaphysical aspects.
LC NO. 77-702642
Prod-LITWKS Dist-CANFDC 1975

She Stoops To Conquer C 119 MIN
3/4 OR 1/2 INCH VIDEO CASSETTE
Features Ralph Richardson and Tom Courtenay in Oliver Goldsmith's comedy She Stoops To Conquer.
From The Classic Theatre Series.
LC NO. 79-706929
Prod-BBCTV Dist-FI 1976

She Wore A Yellow Ribbon C 102 MIN
1/2 IN VIDEO CASSETTE (BETA)
Stars John Wayne as a 40-year cavalry veteran who carries out one last mission. Features Joanne Dru and John Agar. Directed by John Ford.
Prod-UNKNWN Dist-BHAWK 1949

She, He Shall Overcome C 60 MIN
3/4 INCH VIDEO CASSETTE
Examines male-female stereotyping. Discusses women's as well as men's liberation.
From The Liberation Series.
Prod-OHC Dist-HRC

She's A Railroader C 10 MIN
16MM FILM, 3/4 OR 1/2 IN VIDEO J-C A
Presents a portrait of Karen Zaitchik, who works on the railroad, a traditionally male field. Emphasizes that there are alternatives to office jobs for women.
LC NO. 81-706605
Prod-NFBC Dist-PHENIX 1980

She's In The Army Now C 26 MIN
16MM FILM OPTICAL SOUND
Shows the rigorous training of women for combat duty in the American armed forces. Visits three military bases and includes interviews with recruits, drill sergeants and officers.
LC NO. 79-701013
Prod-WJLATV Dist-WJLATV 1978

She's Nobody's Baby - A History Of American Women In The 20th Century C 55 MIN
16MM FILM, 3/4 OR 1/2 IN VIDEO J-C A
Surveys the trends in women's roles and lives through the twentieth century. Hosted by Marlo Thomas and Alan Alda.
LC NO. 82-707160
Prod-ABCNEW Dist-MTI 1982

She's Nobody's Baby - A History Of American Women In The 20th Century C 36 MIN
16MM FILM, 3/4 OR 1/2 IN VIDEO H-C A
Surveys the trends in women's roles and lives through the twentieth century. Hosted by Marlo Thomas and Alan Alda.
Prod-ABCNEW Dist-MTI 1982

She's Waiting For Us C 25 MIN
16MM FILM, 3/4 OR 1/2 IN VIDEO
Tells how a boy and a girl, killed in an automobile crash, are reunited in an after-death experience. Shows how the boy realizes how irresponsible his life has been and is sent back to his body to continue the process of growth.
From The Insight Series.
LC NO. 79-706347
Prod-PAULST Dist-PAULST 1977

Shear Strength Of Clays, Pt 1 B 60 MIN
3/4 OR 1/2 INCH VIDEO CASSETTE
See series title for descriptive statement.
From The Geotechnical Engineering Series. Pt 4
Prod-UAZMIC Dist-UAZMIC 1977

Shear Strength Of Clays, Pt 2 B 60 MIN
3/4 OR 1/2 INCH VIDEO CASSETTE
See series title for descriptive statement.
From The Geotechnical Engineering Series. Pt 5
Prod-UAZMIC Dist-UAZMIC 1977

Shear Strength Of Clays, Pt 3 B 60 MIN
3/4 OR 1/2 INCH VIDEO CASSETTE
See series title for descriptive statement.
From The Geotechnical Engineering Series. Pt 6
Prod-UAZMIC Dist-UAZMIC 1977

Shear Strength Of Sands, Pt 1 B 60 MIN
3/4 OR 1/2 INCH VIDEO CASSETTE
See series title for descriptive statement.
From The Geotechnical Engineering Series. Pt 1
Prod-UAZMIC Dist-UAZMIC 1977

Shear Strength Of Sands, Pt 2 B 60 MIN
3/4 OR 1/2 INCH VIDEO CASSETTE
See series title for descriptive statement.
From The Geotechnical Engineering Series. Pt 2
Prod-UAZMIC Dist-UAZMIC 1977

Shear Strength Of Sands, Pt 3 B 60 MIN
3/4 OR 1/2 INCH VIDEO CASSETTE
See series title for descriptive statement.
From The Geotechnical Engineering Series. Pt 3
Prod-UAZMIC Dist-UAZMIC 1977

Shearing Day C 15 MIN
3/4 OR 1/2 INCH VIDEO CASSETTE I
Deals with the lives of Bedouin nomads. Shows sheep-shearing.
From The Encounter In The Desert Series.
Prod-CTI Dist-CTI

Shearing Yaks (Tajik) B 9 MIN
16MM FILM, 3/4 OR 1/2 IN VIDEO
See series title for descriptive statement.
From The Mountain Peoples Of Central Asia (Afghanistan) Series.
Prod-IFF Dist-IFF

Sheath Nematode C 10 MIN
16MM FILM, 3/4 OR 1/2 IN VIDEO
Studies the nematode and its full life cycle, including the laying of the egg. Reports on combating this pest.
Prod-UCEMC Dist-UCEMC

Sheep In Wood C 10 MIN
16MM FILM OPTICAL SOUND J-C S
Presents Jacques Hnizdovsky working in his studio on a woodcut of two rams locked in combat. Uses close-up photography to show each step in the process of making a woodcut, from preliminary sketches to the artist's proof.
LC NO. 75-710644
Prod-ARTSCO Dist-FLMART 1971

Sheep Meet The Challenge C 28 MIN
16MM FILM OPTICAL SOUND I-C A
Presents an excellent pictorial tribute to the sheep industry. Shows the process by which lambs become sheep and the products that we gain from this industry. Features the lambs going to market and the wool being made into beautiful fabrics. Includes beautiful scenery of the Western plains and mountain areas.
Prod-UPR Dist-UPR 1965

Sheep Shearing B 21 MIN
16MM FILM OPTICAL SOUND
Explains how to handle sheep for shearing, the steps for shearing and how to roll and tie the fleece.
LC NO. FIE52-358
Prod-USOE Dist-USNAC Prodn-CALVCO 1944

Sheep Shearing (Spanish) B 21 MIN
16MM FILM OPTICAL SOUND
Illustrates how to handle sheep for shearing, shear the sheep step-by-step and roll and tie the fleece.
From The Farm Work Series. Livestock, No. 1
LC NO. 74-705631
Prod-USOE Dist-USNAC 1944

Sheep Sheep Sheep C 11 MIN
16MM FILM, 3/4 OR 1/2 IN VIDEO P-I
Illustrates the moods, rhythms and images of sheep through natural sounds without commentary. Shows sheep as they graze–eating, sleeping, waking and moving to the highlands.
From The Animals Series.
Prod-CF Dist-CF 1970

Sheep, Shearing And Spinning - A Story Of Wool C 11 MIN
16MM FILM, 3/4 OR 1/2 IN VIDEO K-I
Describes the traditional processes used to fashion a wool garment, including sheep shearing, wool spinning, dyeing, and knitting.
LC NO. 81-706948
Prod-BERLET Dist-IFB 1980

Sheepmen - Build The Land C 27 MIN
16MM FILM OPTICAL SOUND J-H
Presents the sheepman's age-old struggle against loneliness, drought, coyotes and cougars in the American West.
LC NO. 77-704983
Prod-ASPC Dist-AUDPLN 1964

Sheepshead Blues B 10 MIN
16MM FILM OPTICAL SOUND
Features Charles Mingus in a performance of his own jazz music.
Prod-NYU Dist-NYU

Sheer Craziness C 8 MIN
16MM FILM OPTICAL SOUND
Presents a brief glimpse into the motorcycle counterculture of motocross racing. Follows a race from tune-up to the checkered flag.
Prod-UPITTS Dist-UPITTS 1974

Sheet Metal - Making A Five-Piece Elbow C 13 MIN
16MM FILM, 3/4 OR 1/2 IN VIDEO H-C A
Shows the use of patterns and steps in laying out the elbow gores, types of snips and the squaring shear, as they are used in cutting the gores. Explains folding edges of the bar folder, the use of the slip-roll former, making the seams, turning and burring gore edges and the final assembly of the elbow.
Prod-SF Dist-SF 1969

Sheet Metal - Pattern Development C 13 MIN
16MM FILM, 3/4 OR 1/2 IN VIDEO J A
Shows the importance of three-dimensional visualization through demonstrations with various objects. Explains the principles of parallel line development, triangulation and radial line development.
Prod-SF Dist-SF 1969

Sheet Metal Drawings C 12 MIN
3/4 OR 1/2 INCH VIDEO CASSETTE
Covers sheet metal, ventilation systems, ductwork, sheet metal drawings, parallel development, miter development and other uses of sheet metal.
From The Reading Blueprints Series.
Prod-TPCTRA Dist-TPCTRA

Sheet Metal Drawings (Spanish) C 12 MIN
3/4 OR 1/2 INCH VIDEO CASSETTE
Covers sheet metal, ventilation systems, ductwork, sheet metal drawings, parallel development, miter development and other uses of sheet metal.
From The Reading Blueprints Series.
Prod-TPCTRA Dist-TPCTRA

Sheet Metal Processing C 19 MIN
3/4 OR 1/2 INCH VIDEO CASSETTE
Covers types of sheet metal processing, shearing, cutting, bending, drawing, spinning and expanding.
From The Manufacturing Materials And Processes Series.
Prod-GE Dist-WFVTAE

Sheet Metal Trades B 9 MIN
16MM FILM, 3/4 OR 1/2 IN VIDEO
Shows the work performed by laborers in the sheet metal trades. Issued in 1968 as a motion picture.
From The Career Job Opportunity Series.
LC NO. 79-707875
Prod-USDLMA Dist-USNAC 1979

Sheet Metal Upset C 11 MIN
1/2 IN VIDEO CASSETTE BETA/VHS
Deals with auto body repair. Shows upset in low crowned panels, and recommends a procedure for repair.
Prod-RMI Dist-RMI

Sheet Metal Working - Advanced Equipment C 9 MIN
16MM FILM, 3/4 OR 1/2 IN VIDEO J-C A
Teaches use of the floor shear, electric shears, rotex turret punch and common sheet metal stakes.
Prod-AIMS Dist-AIMS 1978

Sheet Metal Working - Advanced Equipment (Arabic) C 9 MIN
16MM FILM, 3/4 OR 1/2 IN VIDEO J-C A
Teaches use of the floor shear, electric shears, rotex turret punch and common sheet metal stakes.
Prod-AIMS Dist-AIMS 1978

Sheet Metal Working - Basic Equipment C 8 MIN
16MM FILM, 3/4 OR 1/2 IN VIDEO J-C A
Demonstrates the basic tools and techniques of working with sheet metal. Shows the purposes and operation of each piece of equipment and emphasizes efficient work practices and cleanup.
Prod-AIMS Dist-AIMS 1978

Sheet Metal Working - Basic Equipment (Arabic) C 8 MIN
16MM FILM, 3/4 OR 1/2 IN VIDEO J-C A
Demonstrates the basic tools and techniques of working with sheet metal. Shows the purposes and operation of each piece of equipment and emphasizes efficient work practices and cleanup.
Prod-AIMS Dist-AIMS 1978

Sheet Metalworking Tools C 12 MIN
3/4 OR 1/2 INCH VIDEO CASSETTE
Covers sheet metalworking tools such as dividers, punches, nibblers, rivets and riveting tools, metal-cutting chisels and their uses.
From The Using Hand Tools Series.
Prod-TPCTRA Dist-TPCTRA

Sheet Metalworking Tools (Spanish) C 12 MIN
3/4 OR 1/2 INCH VIDEO CASSETTE
Covers sheet metalworking tools such as dividers, punches, nibblers, rivets and riveting tools, metal-cutting chisels and their uses.
From The Using Hand Tools Series.
Prod-TPCTRA Dist-TPCTRA

Sheet Rock C 30 MIN
3/4 OR 1/2 INCH VIDEO CASSETTE
Discusses the installation of sheet rock.
From The You Can Fixit Series.
Prod-WRJATV Dist-MDCPB

Sheila Tobias, Political Science, Education C 29 MIN
3/4 OR 1/2 INCH VIDEO CASSETTE A
See series title for descriptive statement.
From The Quest For Peace Series.
Prod-AACD Dist-AACD 1984

Sheldon Trio, The B 29 MIN
2 INCH VIDEOTAPE
Features chamber music of the Sheldon Trio at Nebraska's Arbor Lodge State Historical Park.
Prod-NETCHE Dist-PUBTEL

Shell As A Command Language C
3/4 OR 1/2 INCH VIDEO CASSETTE
See series title for descriptive statement.
From The UNIX And 'C'Language Training - A Full Curriculum Series.
Prod-COMTEG Dist-COMTEG

Shell Files, Part I C 30 MIN
3/4 OR 1/2 INCH VIDEO CASSETTE IND
Lecture tells about shell variables, grave accents, substitution parameters, while ... do, for ... do, Command Search Strategy, and Commands - eval, sh, test, shift, and echo (-n)
From The UNIX Series.
Prod-COLOSU Dist-COLOSU

Shell Files, Part II C 30 MIN
3/4 OR 1/2 INCH VIDEO CASSETTE IND
Goes into if ... then, case, Arithmetic and Relational Operations, and following commands - read, expr, continue, and test (-f,-r,-w,-d).
From The UNIX Series.
Prod-COLOSU Dist-COLOSU

Shell Mounds In The Tennessee Valley (2nd Ed) B 15 MIN
16MM FILM OPTICAL SOUND H-C A
Describes archeological work in the Tennessee Valley Authority's reservoir area prior to impoundment. Shows excavation of shell mounds which mark prehistoric villages.
LC NO. 80-701174
Prod-TVA Dist-USNAC 1965

Shell Programming C
3/4 OR 1/2 INCH VIDEO CASSETTE
See series title for descriptive statement.
From The UNIX And 'C'Language Training - A Full Curriculum Series.
Prod-COMTEG Dist-COMTEG

Shell, The C
3/4 OR 1/2 INCH VIDEO CASSETTE
Describes the UNIX shell as a programming language and as a command interpreter. Illustrates the file name generation, pipes and filters.
From The UNIX Overview Series. Unit 4
Prod-COMTEG Dist-COMTEG

Shelley - The Idealist C 10 MIN
16MM FILM OPTICAL SOUND
Presents selected scenes of Shelly's play 'THE IDEALIST,' to illustrate original staging techiniques and the lightweight construction of set design.
Prod-SUCECC Dist-SUCECC

Shelley And Pete (And Carol) C 23 MIN
16MM FILM, 3/4 OR 1/2 IN VIDEO H
Describes the responsibilities which teenage parents must face, including their changing relationships with their parents, peers, and one another.
LC NO. 81-706322
Prod-USDHHS Dist-USNAC 1980

Shelley Finds Her Way C 30 MIN
3/4 INCH VIDEO CASSETTE
Tells about a young blind girl who wants to be a creative writer but is afraid to go to class. Explains how she meets a magical creature named Khan Du, who shows her other people with disabilities who can do many things because they have tried.
From The Khan Du Series.
LC NO. 78-706323
Prod-USOE Dist-USNAC Prodn-KRLNTV 1978

Shelley Whitebird's First Powwow C 8 MIN
16MM FILM, 3/4 OR 1/2 IN VIDEO P-I
Presents a story about a young girl who is preparing for her first powwow.
Prod-LIFSTY Dist-EBEC 1977

Shelley Without Hearing C 38 MIN
3/4 INCH VIDEO CASSETTE A
Observes a typical day for a four-year-old deaf girl at a day-care center as she interacts with other children and plays by herself.
LC NO. 80-706691
Prod-CTVS Dist-CTVS 1979

Shellfish C 20 MIN
3/4 OR 1/2 INCH VIDEO CASSETTE I A
Shows breeding, harvesting and processing shellfish.
Prod-SUTHRB Dist-SUTHRB

Shellfishing In The Chesapeake C 25 MIN
16MM FILM OPTICAL SOUND I-H A
Deals with the methods and equipment used in catching oysters, crabs and clams.
Prod-VADE Dist-VADE 1956

Shells And The Animals Inside C 20 MIN
16MM FILM OPTICAL SOUND
Demonstrates the use of specimens, discussion, art, creative writing, and fantasy to present the topic of mollusks to children.
LC NO. 80-700635
Prod-SMITHS Dist-USNAC 1979

Shelter (3rd Ed) C 11 MIN
16MM FILM, 3/4 OR 1/2 IN VIDEO P-I
Looks at the history of housing and community development. Outlines the many uses of shelter.
Prod-EBEC Dist-EBEC 1980

Shelter Around The World C 14 MIN
16MM FILM, 3/4 OR 1/2 IN VIDEO P-I
Shows how people throughout the world use the resources of their environment for shelter and how they adapt their housing to their culture and lifestyles.
From The Basic Needs Series.
Prod-MITC Dist-PHENIX 1979

Shelter Construction In Winter C 13 MIN
16MM FILM, 3/4 OR 1/2 IN VIDEO I-H
Explains that comfortable shelters can be constructed easily, even during winter's cold conditions. Shows some of the methods used to build comfortable shelters.
Prod-SF Dist-SF 1967

Shelter Management (Rev Ed) C 37 MIN
3/4 OR 1/2 INCH VIDEO CASSETTE
Presents a revised version of the 1976 disaster shelter management program. Informs disaster shelter managers and workers in overall operations and management of mass shelters.
Prod-AMRC Dist-AMRC 1981

Shelter, The - Psychological Aspects Of Disaster Nursing B 30 MIN
16MM FILM OPTICAL SOUND PRO
Discusses psychological preparedness for survival leadership in disaster situations. Makes no specific reference to the type of disaster. Depicts the unprepared basement found by a group of people seeking escape.
LC NO. FIA67-5616
Prod-ANANLN Dist-AJN Prodn-TILTON 1967

Sheltered Workshop C 5 MIN
16MM FILM, 3/4 OR 1/2 IN VIDEO C T
Shows how mentally retarded students, working on a sub-contract basis, process products that are used in the consumer market and divide their financial proceeds among all the trainees.
From The Aids For Teaching The Mentally Retarded Series.
Prod-THORNE Dist-IFB 1964

Sheltered Workshops C 26 MIN
16MM FILM OPTICAL SOUND H
Discusses the role of volunteer organizations in setting up special workshops for the training and employment of mentally and physically handicapped people.
LC NO. 70-711463
Prod-AUSCOF Dist-AUIS

Shema - An Affirmation Of Belief, Love And Trust, The C 15 MIN
3/4 OR 1/2 INCH VIDEO CASSETTE
Explores the three themes of the Shema. Discusses the centrality of learning within Judaism.
From The Tradition And Contemporary Judaism - Prayer And The Jewish People Series. Program 3
Prod-ADL Dist-ADL

Shenandoah C 105 MIN
16MM FILM OPTICAL SOUND
Stars James Stewart as an irascible widowed Virginia landowner who fights the forces that attempt to draw him and his sons into the Civil War.
Prod-UPCI Dist-TWYMAN 1965

Shenandoah - Dickey Ridge C 14 MIN
16MM FILM, 3/4 OR 1/2 IN VIDEO
Shows things to see and do in Shenandoah National Park and on Skyline Drive.
Prod-USNPS Dist-USNAC 1982

Shenandoah - The Gift C 19 MIN
16MM FILM, 3/4 OR 1/2 IN VIDEO
Traces the 40-year development of Shenandoah National Park from depleted and ravaged land into a wilderness park.
Prod-USNPS Dist-USNAC 1982

Shepherd Dog And His Flock C 8 MIN
16MM FILM, 3/4 OR 1/2 IN VIDEO P-J
Shows two German shepherd dogs as they help their masters to herd sheep.
From The See'n Tell Series.
Prod-PMI Dist-FI 1970

Shepherd Life X 14 MIN
16MM FILM OPTICAL SOUND I-H T R
Illustrates the typical shepherd life of people of Bible times by showing the life of the nomadic shepherds of Palestine, much of which remains unchanged since Biblical days.
Prod-FAMF Dist-FAMF 1960

Shepherd, The B 11 MIN
16MM FILM, 3/4 OR 1/2 IN VIDEO H-C A
Tells how the tranquil serenity of a shepherd is broken when he finds signs of a marauder.
Prod-NFBC Dist-IFB 1955

Shepherd, The C 15 MIN
3/4 OR 1/2 INCH VIDEO CASSETTE I
Deals with agriculture and livestock in the lives of Bedouin people.
From The Encounter In The Desert Series.
Prod-CTI Dist-CTI

Shepherd's Hat, The C 16 MIN
16MM FILM OPTICAL SOUND
A story about the origin of the perpetual hatred of dogs for cats which resulted after kitten hatmakers sold a shepherd dog's hat to a maharajah.
From The Animatoons Series.
LC NO. FIA68-1537
Prod-ANTONS Dist-RADTV 1968

Shepherd's Song, A C 20 MIN
3/4 OR 1/2 INCH VIDEO CASSETTE P-I
Reviews like phrases, minor tonality and the woodwinds.
From The USS Rhythm Series.
Prod-ARKETV Dist-AITECH 1977

Sheraton Reservations C 14 MIN
16MM FILM OPTICAL SOUND
Presents a series of musical vignettes and comedy sequences to describe features of a world-wide hotel reservations system.
LC NO. 76-702890
Prod-ITTSHE Dist-ITTSHE Prodn-ITTSHE 1976

Sheridan's World Of Society C 17 MIN
16MM FILM, 3/4 OR 1/2 IN VIDEO H-C
Evokes the leisurely world of 18th century English society, which enjoyed the plays of Richard Brinsley Sheridan but which never fully accepted him into its midst. Traces Sheridan's life from his success in the theatre to his death as a pauper.
Prod-SEABEN Dist-IFB 1972

Sherlock Holmes, Dressed To Kill B 72 MIN
3/4 OR 1/2 INCH VIDEO CASSETTE
Stars Basil Rathbone and Nigel Bruce as Sherlock Holmes and Dr Watson.
Prod-ADVCAS Dist-ADVCAS

Sherlock In Your Holmes, The C 20 MIN
16MM FILM, 3/4 OR 1/2 IN VIDEO J-H
Observing and interpreting accurately are basic skills for biologists. Includes a demonstration of how to become an accurate observer. Gives explanations of habitat and the importance of recording observtions with instructions for a nature trail.
From The Biology - It's Life Series.
Prod-THAMES Dist-MEDIAG 1980

Sherlock, Jr B 46 MIN
16MM FILM SILENT J-C A
Stars Buster Keaton. Tells of a projectionist in a motion picture theatre who falls asleep, enters the plot of the movie he is showing and fulfills his secret desire to become a great detective.
Prod-MGM Dist-TWYMAN 1924

Sherpa C 28 MIN
3/4 OR 1/2 INCH VIDEO CASSETTE
Examines the culture of the Sherpa who live at the base of Mount Everest. Focuses on one family.
Prod-CEPRO Dist-CEPRO

Sherpa High Country C 20 MIN
16MM FILM, 3/4 OR 1/2 IN VIDEO
Looks at the Sherpas of the Solu Khumbu highlands in Nepal, near Mt Everest. Focuses on the Mani-Rimdu ceremony, a three-day dance drama performed by monks celebrating Buddhist teachings.
Prod-LISANX Dist-UCEMC 1977

Shetland Experience, The C 27 MIN
16MM FILM OPTICAL SOUND
Depicts the care and concern for the environment which is being taken by the oil industry in building Europe's biggest transshipment point for oil at the Shetland Islands.
Prod-BPNA Dist-MTP

Shi No Zadanki C 27 MIN
3/4 INCH VIDEO CASSETTE
A Japanese language videotape. Discusses contemporary Japanese poetry with Yoshimasu Gozo and Yoshihara Sachiko, two Japanese poets visiting the International Writing Program at the University of Iowa.
Prod-UIOWA Dist-UIOWA 1980

Shield Against Invasion C 14 MIN
16MM FILM OPTICAL SOUND
Emphasizes the need for contant evaluation of America's weapons and aircraft. Shows how these evaluations are accomplished.
LC NO. FIE63-122
Prod-USDD Dist-USNAC 1959

Shield Of Freedom C 28 MIN
16MM FILM OPTICAL SOUND
Raymond Massey explains the Air Defense Command's dominant role in organizing, training and providing aerospace defense forces to NORAD. The magnitude of the Command's mission are portrayed, including the detection, identification, interception and destruction of manned bomber or missile attacks on the North American continent.
LC NO. 74-706241
Prod-USDD Dist-USNAC 1963

Shield Of Plenty C 29 MIN
16MM FILM, 3/4 OR 1/2 IN VIDEO J-C
Explores the extensive shields of Precambrian mountain remnants and demonstrates the use of radioactivity in dating.
From The Planet Of Man Series.
Prod-OECA Dist-FI 1976

Shield, The C 13 MIN
16MM FILM - 3/4 IN VIDEO
Presents the testimony of men who escaped blindness because they wore eye protection on-the-job. Encourages the use of appropriate 100 per cent eye and face protection on-the-job and for school shop safety.
Prod-NSPB Dist-HF 1972

Shielded Metal Arc Welding (Spanish)—A Series

Presents a series on shielded metal arc welding, explaining power sources, maintenance, safety and all types of electric arc welding procedures.
Prod-VTRI Dist-VTRI

Carbon Arc Cutting (Spanish)
Electric Arc welding In Flat, Horizontal,
Electric-Arc Power Sources And Minor
Multi-Pass Electric Arc Welding (Spanish)
Running Continuous Bead In Horizontal And
Running Continuous Beads In Vertical Up And
Safety In Electric-Arc Welding And Terms
Selection Of Electrodes For Shielded Metal
Striking An Arc, Restarting The Arc And
T-Joint, Lap Joint, Outside Corner Joint In
T-Joint, Lap Joint, Outside Corner Joint In
T-Joint, Lap Joint, Outside Corner Joint In A
T-Joint, Lap Joint, Outside Corner Joint In A
Welding Cast Iron In Flat Position With

Shielded Metal Arc Welding - Advanced, Pt 1—A Series
H-C A
Teaches how to develop the manual skills necessary to produce quality multipass fillet and groove welds with backing in all positions. Uses E6010 and E7018 electrodes on thick carbon steel plate similar to many structural applications. Running time 143 minutes in 4 cassettes.
LC NO. 83-706248
Prod-HBCWB Dist-HBCWB Prodn-LEOSY 1982

Shielded Metal Arc Welding - Advanced, Pt 2—A Series
H-C A
Teaches manual skills necessary to produce quality simple-v-groove welds (open root) in all positions. Uses E6010 and E7018 electrodes on medium thickness carbon steel. Includes information on welding variables and safety, destructive and undestructive testing, and procedure and welder qualification. Running time 106 minutes in 3 cassettes.
LC NO. 83-706247
Prod-HBCWB Dist-HBCWB Prodn-LEOSY 1982

Shielded Metal Arc Welding - Basic—A Series
H-C A
Provides technical instruction in arc welding fundamentals, welding safety, arc welding machines, electrode classifications, and selection. Runs 217 minutes in 5 cassettes.
LC NO. 83-706249
Prod-HBCWB Dist-HBCWB Prodn-LEOSY 1981

Shielded Metal Arc Welding, Pt 01 C 14 MIN
16MM FILM OPTICAL SOUND IND
See series title for descriptive statement.
From The Miller Module Method Series.
LC NO. 74-703671
Prod-MILEL Dist-MILEL 1975

Shielded Metal Arc Welding, Pt 02 C 14 MIN
16MM FILM OPTICAL SOUND IND
See series title for descriptive statement.
From The Miller Module Method Series.
LC NO. 74-703671
Prod-MILEL Dist-MILEL 1975

Shielded Metal Arc Welding, Pt 03 C 14 MIN
16MM FILM OPTICAL SOUND IND
See series title for descriptive statement.
From The Miller Module Method Series.
LC NO. 74-703671
Prod-MILEL Dist-MILEL 1975

Shielded Metal Arc Welding, Pt 04 C 14 MIN
16MM FILM OPTICAL SOUND IND
See series title for descriptive statement.
From The Miller Module Method Series.
LC NO. 74-703671
Prod-MILEL Dist-MILEL 1975

Shielded Metal Arc Welding, Pt 05 C 14 MIN
16MM FILM OPTICAL SOUND IND
See series title for descriptive statement.
From The Miller Module Method Series.
LC NO. 74-703671
Prod-MILEL Dist-MILEL 1975

Shielded Metal Arc Welding, Pt 06 C 14 MIN
16MM FILM OPTICAL SOUND IND
See series title for descriptive statement.
From The Miller Module Method Series.
LC NO. 74-703671
Prod-MILEL Dist-MILEL 1975

Shielded Metal Arc Welding, Pt 07 C 14 MIN
16MM FILM OPTICAL SOUND IND
See series title for descriptive statement.
From The Miller Module Method Series.
LC NO. 74-703671
Prod-MILEL Dist-MILEL 1975

Shielded Metal Arc Welding, Pt 08 C 14 MIN
16MM FILM OPTICAL SOUND IND
See series title for descriptive statement.
From The Miller Module Method Series.
LC NO. 74-703671
Prod-MILEL Dist-MILEL 1975

Shielded Metal Arc Welding, Pt 09 C 14 MIN
16MM FILM OPTICAL SOUND IND
See series title for descriptive statement.
From The Miller Module Method Series.
LC NO. 74-703671
Prod-MILEL Dist-MILEL 1975

Shielded Metal Arc Welding, Pt 10 C 14 MIN
16MM FILM OPTICAL SOUND IND
See series title for descriptive statement.
From The Miller Module Method Series.
LC NO. 74-703671
Prod-MILEL Dist-MILEL 1975

Shielded Metal Arc Welding, Pt 11 C 14 MIN
16MM FILM OPTICAL SOUND IND
See series title for descriptive statement.
From The Miller Module Method Series.
LC NO. 74-703671
Prod-MILEL Dist-MILEL 1975

Shielded Metal Arc Welding, Pt 12 C 9 MIN
16MM FILM OPTICAL SOUND IND
From The Miller Module Method Series.
LC NO. 74-703671
Prod-MILEL Dist-MILEL 1975

Shielded Metal Arc Welding, Pt 13 C 14 MIN
16MM FILM OPTICAL SOUND IND
See series title for descriptive statement.
From The Miller Module Method Series.
LC NO. 74-703671
Prod-MILEL Dist-MILEL 1975

Shielded Metal Arc Welding, Pt 14 C 14 MIN
16MM FILM OPTICAL SOUND IND
See series title for descriptive statement.
From The Miller Module Method Series.
LC NO. 74-703671
Prod-MILEL Dist-MILEL 1975

Shielded Metal Arc Welding, Pt 15 C 17 MIN
16MM FILM OPTICAL SOUND IND
From The Miller Module Method Series.
LC NO. 74-703671
Prod-MILEL Dist-MILEL 1975

Shielded Metal Arc Welding, Pt 16 C 14 MIN
16MM FILM OPTICAL SOUND IND
See series title for descriptive statement.
From The Miller Module Method Series.
LC NO. 74-703671
Prod-MILEL Dist-MILEL 1975

Shielded Metal-Arc Structural And Pipe Welding C 60 MIN
3/4 OR 1/2 INCH VIDEO CASSETTE IND
Focuses on practice beads, structural welding, carbon steel pipe, stainless steel pipe and aluminum pipe.
From The Welding Training Series.
Prod-ITCORP Dist-ITCORP

Shielded Metal-Arc Welding Principles C 60 MIN
3/4 OR 1/2 INCH VIDEO CASSETTE IND
Covers introduction and safety, equipment, polarity, voltage/current relationships, electrodes, setting up the machine, adjusting and starting the machine, striking an arc, electrode motion and shutdown.
From The Welding Training Series.
Prod-ITCORP Dist-ITCORP

Shift Of Stimulus Control - A Clinical Procedure For Articulation Therapy C 37 MIN
16MM FILM OPTICAL SOUND C T
Presents films of work with two mentally retarded children which demonstrate the general strategy of stimulus-shift techniques in which new phoneme responses are developed under precise stimulus control.
LC NO. 72-702018
Prod-UKANBC Dist-UKANS 1970

Shifting Gears C 12 MIN
16MM FILM - 3/4 IN VIDEO A
Shows how the friendship between two men ends in a personal conflict over the issue of battering women. Designed to develop positive male role models as an alternative to male-supported attitudes of physical violence towards women.
From The Time Out Series.
LC NO. 81-707273
Prod-ODNP Dist-ODNP 1981

Shifting Of Risk, A C 29 MIN
3/4 INCH VIDEO CASSETTE
Focuses on the function and operation of personal life insurance in estate planning.
From The Life, Death And Taxes Series.
Prod-UMITV Dist-UMITV 1977

Shigeko Kubota - Duchampiana, Video Installations C 42 MIN
3/4 OR 1/2 INCH VIDEO CASSETTE
Draws from the work of Marcel Duchamp.
Prod-ARTINC Dist-ARTINC

Shigeko Kubota - My Father B 15 MIN
3/4 OR 1/2 INCH VIDEO CASSETTE
Records events from Shigeko Kubota's life.
Prod-ARTINC Dist-ARTINC

Shigeko Kubota - Video Girls And Video Songs For Navajo Skies C 26 MIN
3/4 OR 1/2 INCH VIDEO CASSETTE
Involves Paik-Abe and Rutt-Etra synthesizers.
Prod-ARTINC Dist-ARTINC

Shigeko Kubota, An Interview C 28 MIN
3/4 OR 1/2 INCH VIDEO CASSETTE
Presented by D L Bean and Jeanine Mellinger.
Prod-ARTINC Dist-ARTINC

Shiloh C 16 MIN
16MM FILM, 3/4 OR 1/2 IN VIDEO J-H
Recounts the stalemated Battle of Shiloh fought at Pittsburg Landing, Tennessee, as a grim example of the misery and futility of the American Civil War.
Prod-BFA Dist-PHENIX 1975

Shiloh C 16 MIN
16MM FILM, 3/4 OR 1/2 IN VIDEO
Deals with Shiloh, a two-day battle of the Civil War.
Prod-KAWVAL Dist-KAWVAL

Shinnecock - The Story Of A People C 20 MIN
16MM FILM, 3/4 OR 1/2 IN VIDEO H-C A
Centers on the lost culture and heritage of the East Coast Indians of North America, focusing on the Shinnecock tribe.
Prod-PHENIX Dist-PHENIX 1976

Shinto - Nature, Gods And Man In Japan C 49 MIN
16MM FILM OPTICAL SOUND H-C A
Traces the development of the Shinto religion and portrays the reconstruction of one of the Shinto shrines according to the specifications of the ancient documents.
LC NO. 78-700218
Prod-GILWES Dist-JAPANS 1977

Shintoism C 15 MIN
16MM FILM OPTICAL SOUND P-J
See series title for descriptive statement.
From The Off To Adventure Series.
Prod-YALEDV Dist-YALEDV

Shiny Is Beautiful C 15 MIN
16MM FILM OPTICAL SOUND K-I
Follows Yoffy and his friends as they collect pretty and shiny objects such as bottle-tops, shells and tiny paper stars.
From The Fingermouse, Yoffy And Friends Series.
LC NO. 73-700438
Prod-BBCTV Dist-VEDO 1972

Ship Comes Home, A C 15 MIN
16MM FILM, 3/4 OR 1/2 IN VIDEO I-J
Demonstrates the exacting maneuvers, expert timing, and alertness to shifts in wind and currents which are necessary to bring a large ocean liner into port.
Prod-KIRPRO Dist-CORF 1969

Ship Of Fools C 149 MIN
16MM FILM OPTICAL SOUND
Portrays an allegorical voyage aboard a passenger freighter bound from Vera Cruz to Bremerhaven in 1933 of a confused world.
Prod-CPC Dist-TIMLIF 1965

Ship's Blueprints - Basic B 22 MIN
16MM FILM OPTICAL SOUND
Explains how to identify fundamental structural elements in ship construction by orthographic drawings and symbols, to visualize these drawings in three dimensions, to understand the use and function of dotted and hidden lines and to read a ship's blueprints.
LC NO. FIE52-1232
Prod-USN Dist-USNAC 1944

Ship's Pumps B 16 MIN
16MM FILM OPTICAL SOUND
Explains uses, functions and construction of ship pumps.
LC NO. 74-706577
Prod-USN Dist-USNAC 1951

Shipboard Helicopter Operations - Functions C 8 MIN
16MM FILM OPTICAL SOUND
Discusses the principal missions of the helicopter aboard ship as plane guard, in rescues and during mail transfers.
LC NO. FIE59-238
Prod-USN Dist-USNAC 1954

Shipboard Helicopter Operations - Landing And Take-Offs C 7 MIN
16MM FILM OPTICAL SOUND
Shows procedures to be followed in helicopter landings and take-offs during shipboard operations.

LC NO. FIE59-239
Prod-USN Dist-USNAC 1954

Shipboard Inspection By Medical Department Personnel - Food Preparation B 25 MIN
16MM FILM OPTICAL SOUND
Shows how to make an inspection of the various areas of possible contamination in the preparation of food aboard ship. Discusses sanitary equipment and spaces, sanitary personnel and sanitary work habits.
LC NO. FIE59-144
Prod-USN Dist-USNAC 1958

Shipboard Inspection By Medical Department Personnel - Food Serving B 13 MIN
16MM FILM OPTICAL SOUND
Shows how to make an inspection of such food-serving areas as the mess areas, serving line and the scullery.
LC NO. FIE59-145
Prod-USN Dist-USNAC 1958

Shipboard Inspection By Medical Department Personnel - Food Storage B 12 MIN
16MM FILM OPTICAL SOUND
Shows how to make a sanitary inspection of the storage of food aboard ship. Covers such subjects as cleanliness, air circulation, temperature and stowage.
LC NO. FIE59-146
Prod-USN Dist-USNAC 1958

Shipboard Inspection By Medical Department Personnel - Living And Working Spaces B 20 MIN
16MM FILM OPTICAL SOUND
Shows what and how to inspect in order to insure good conditions of sanitation, ventilation, lighting and safety in the living and working spaces of a ship.
LC NO. FIE59-147
Prod-USN Dist-USNAC 1958

Shipboard Inspection By Medical Department Personnel - Water Supply B 21 MIN
16MM FILM OPTICAL SOUND
Shows how and where to inspect a ship's fresh-water supply at the points of possible contamination.
LC NO. FIE59-148
Prod-USN Dist-USNAC 1958

Shipboard Vibrations, Pt 1 - Fundamental Principles Of Vibrating Systems B 22 MIN
16MM FILM OPTICAL SOUND
Explains basic concepts and principles, including longitudinal and torsional vibrations, free and forced vibrations, the time relationship between the force cycle and the amplitude cycle and the phase angle diagram.
LC NO. FIE53-516
Prod-USN Dist-USNAC 1953

Shipboard Vibrations, Pt 2 - Multi-Mass Systems B 23 MIN
16MM FILM OPTICAL SOUND
Explains basic concepts, including those of a uniform system, a lumped system, modes of vibration, relative amplitudes, harmonic analysis, orders of vibration and critical speeds.
LC NO. FIE53-517
Prod-USN Dist-USNAC 1953

Shipboard Vibrations, Pt 3 - Vibration, Excitation And Response B 15 MIN
16MM FILM OPTICAL SOUND
Shows vibration excitation in the propulsion machinery due to imbalance and to propeller thrust variation and the response of the ship's structure to this excitation.
LC NO. FIA53-518
Prod-USN Dist-USNAC 1953

Shipboard Vibrations, Pt 4 - Service Problems And Field Investigation B 13 MIN
16MM FILM OPTICAL SOUND
Explains how to report shipboard vibration problems, how they are diagnosed and remedied by vibration engineers and how vibration study as preventive engineering contributes to overall ship design and performance.
LC NO. FIE53-519
Prod-USN Dist-USNAC 1953

Shipbuilding Skills - Coppersmithing—A Series
IND
Discusses various aspects of copper tubing. Issued in 1944 as a motion picture series.
Prod-USOE Dist-USNAC Prodn-RCM 1979

Bending Copper Tubing To A Wire Template 022 MIN
Brazing Flanges With Silver Solder 013 MIN
Brazing Flanges With Spelter 019 MIN
Tinning And Solder Wiping 026 MIN

Shipbuilding Skills - Pipefitting—A Series

Discusses aspects of pipefitting when buiding ships. Issued in 1944 as a motion picture series.
Prod-USOE Dist-USNAC 1980

Cutting And Threading Pipe By Hand 012 MIN
Cutting And Threading Pipe On A Power Machine 017 MIN
Installing Valves In Engine Room Systems, 016 MIN
Installing Valves In Engine Room Systems, 012 MIN
Installing Vitreous Fixtures 019 MIN
Laying Out And Installing Hangers 019 MIN
Making A Cold Bend On A Hand Powered Machine 013 MIN
Measuring Pipe, Tubing, And Fittings 015 MIN
Pipe Fabrication With Jigs 022 MIN

Shipbuilding Skills - Rigging—A Series

Discusses techniques of rigging when building ships.
Prod-USN Dist-USNAC 1980

Rigging Blocks 011 MIN
Rigid And Swinging Staging 018 MIN
Slinging Load 017 MIN
Use And Care Of Fiber Rope 020 MIN
Use And Care Of Wire Rope 018 MIN
Wire Rope Terminal Connections 031 MIN

Shipley Street C 28 MIN
16MM FILM - 3/4 IN VIDEO
Deals with a black working-class family trying to make it in the city. Focuses on the father and his young daughter. Shows the difficulties of the college educated father in trying to get a promotion and the daughter's problems in the Catholic school she attends.
Prod-BLKFMF Dist-BLKFMF

Shipment To Saratoga, A B 20 MIN
16MM FILM, 3/4 OR 1/2 IN VIDEO
Describes how foreign aid helped the Continental Army defeat the British in the Battle of Saratoga, the turning point in the Revolutionary War.
Prod-USDD Dist-USNAC 1958

Shippensburg College - Guest Brook Zern, Program B C 29 MIN
2 INCH VIDEOTAPE
Features French folk singer Sonia Malkine and her special guest Brook Zern visiting Shippensburg College in Pennsylvania.
From The Sonia Malkine On Campus Series.
Prod-WITFTV Dist-PUBTEL

Shippensburg State College - Guest Brook Zern, Program A C 29 MIN
2 INCH VIDEOTAPE
Features French folk singer Sonia Malkine and her special guest Brook Zern visiting Shippensburg State College in Pennsylvania.
From The Sonia Malkine On Campus Series.
Prod-WITFTV Dist-PUBTEL

Shipping - The Tankard Hazard C 12 MIN
3/4 OR 1/2 INCH VIDEO CASSETTE H-C A
Explains that as more and more countries import and export crude oil, the seas have become jammed with super tanker traffic. Discusses the increased risk of oil spills and wrecks and looks at methods used to alleviate the problems.
Prod-UPI Dist-JOU

Shipping And Receiving Clerk C 15 MIN
16MM FILM, 3/4 OR 1/2 IN VIDEO I
From The Career Awareness Series.
Prod-KLVXTV Dist-GPITVL

Shipping Hooker, The C 8 MIN
3/4 OR 1/2 INCH VIDEO CASSETTE IND
Explains the job performed by the shipping hooker with emphasis on safety. Includes the loading of trucks and rail cars.
From The Steel Making Series.
Prod-LEIKID Dist-LEIKID

Ships - A First Film B 11 MIN
16MM FILM, 3/4 OR 1/2 IN VIDEO P-I
Shows the differences and similarities in large commercial vessels.
Prod-BEAN Dist-PHENIX 1970

Ships A'Sail C 14 MIN
3/4 OR 1/2 INCH VIDEO CASSETTE P
Classifies vessels from kayaks to aircraft carriers according to their source of power and their purpose.
From The Under The Yellow Balloon Series.
Prod-SCETV Dist-AITECH 1980

Ships And Seafaring C 24 MIN
16MM FILM, 3/4 OR 1/2 IN VIDEO J-C A
Focuses on the powerful ships that made Greece master of the sea around 470-333 BC, exploring Greek maritime activity in peace and war, boat and harbor construction, and naval and sailing tactics. Includes views of the ruins of a merchant ship which was excavated near Kyrenia, Cypress.
From The Ancient Greece Series.
LC NO. 82-706461
Prod-OPENU Dist-MEDIAG 1981

Ships That Flew, The C 49 MIN
16MM FILM OPTICAL SOUND J-C A
Takes a look at the history of flying boat services in Australian aviation. Considers in particular the last of these services from Sydney to Lord Howe Island which ended in 1974.
LC NO. 76-700572
Prod-FLMAUS Dist-AUIS 1974

Ships, Men And Ice C 22 MIN
3/4 INCH VIDEO CASSETTE
Traces the history of Arctic exploration, with particular attention to the development of ships for use in frozen Arctic Sea.
Prod-USNAC Dist-USNAC 1972

Shipwreck Island C 93 MIN
16MM FILM OPTICAL SOUND P-I
Prod-FI Dist-FI

Shipwrecked C 15 MIN
1/2 IN VIDEO CASSETTE BETA/VHS I-J
Describes the damaged Mimi, which has been beached on an island, with the Captain suffering from hypothermia and in jeopardy. Provides an inside look at the U S Army Environmental Research Labs, where scientists study the effects of exposure to extreme weather conditions on the human body.
From The Voyage Of The Mimi Series.
Prod-HRAW Dist-HRAW

Shipyard Fire And Explosion Hazards C 41 MIN
16MM FILM - 3/4 IN VIDEO IND
Presents the basic principles of fire through the use of laboratory experiments and simulation of four ship fires and explosions. Explains the flash point flammable limits and demonstrates sources of ignition. Describes the testing instruments for flammable vapors and the hazards of oxygen excess and deficiency.
LC NO. 77-706132
Prod-USDL Dist-USNAC Prodn-USDA 1977

Shirley C 13 MIN
16MM FILM, 3/4 OR 1/2 IN VIDEO C A
Shows a woman sharing her masturbatory pattern while a narrator describes each of the steps in self-sexual exploration.
Prod-NATSF Dist-MMRC

Shirley A Hill C
3/4 OR 1/2 INCH VIDEO CASSETTE
Provides an overview of the Third R - Teaching Basic Mathematics Series. Includes a brief segment from each of the other five programs in the series.
From The Third R - Teaching Basic Mathematics Skills Series.
Prod-EDCPUB Dist-EDCPUB

Shirley And Wilbur C 11 MIN
16MM FILM OPTICAL SOUND
Presents female masturbation in the presence of a partner and with his help. Stresses communication between the two.
Prod-MMRC Dist-MMRC

Shish Kebab And Shish Taouk C 30 MIN
3/4 OR 1/2 INCH VIDEO CASSETTE PRO
Presents techniques for making skewered lamb and skewered chicken.
Prod-CULINA Dist-CULINA

Shiver My Timbers B 21 MIN
16MM FILM OPTICAL SOUND
Features the Little Rascals in a spoof of pirate movies.
Prod-ROACH Dist-BHAWK 1931

Shivering King, The C 16 MIN
16MM FILM OPTICAL SOUND
Tells the story of a King who suffers from an unbearable cold and constant shivering until he realizes that his cold is the result of having a cold heart.
From The Animatoons Series.
LC NO. FIA68-1530
Prod-ANTONS Dist-RADTV 1968

Shivering Shakespeare B 18 MIN
16MM FILM OPTICAL SOUND
Tells how a classic recitation turns into a pie-throwing brawl. A Little Rascals film.
Prod-ROACH Dist-BHAWK 1929

Shock C 14 MIN
16MM FILM OPTICAL SOUND
Shows how to recognize and treat shock. Emphasizes the seriousness of shock and suggests methods of prevention. To be used with the course 'MEDICAL SELFHELP TRAINING.'
From The Medical Self-Help Series.
LC NO. 75-702550
Prod-USDHEW Dist-USNAC Prodn-USOCD 1960

Shock C 29 MIN
16MM FILM OPTICAL SOUND PRO
Outlines the diagnosis and treatment of shock based on hemodynamic diagnosis and emphasizes the value of measurement of central venous pressure and cardiac output.
Prod-ACYDGD Dist-ACY 1965

Shock C 4 MIN
16MM FILM, 3/4 OR 1/2 IN VIDEO A
Describes the symptoms of shock and discusses measures to prevent or control shock.
From The Emergency First Aid Training Series.
LC NO. 81-706702
Prod-CRAF Dist-IFB 1980

Shock C 13 MIN
3/4 OR 1/2 INCH VIDEO CASSETTE IND
Presents comprehensive steps in detecting the 'quiet killer' - trauma shock. Shows emergency medical treatment steps for the proper action.
From The Emergency Medical Training Series. Lesson 4
Prod-LEIKID Dist-LEIKID

Shock C 13 MIN
3/4 OR 1/2 INCH VIDEO CASSETTE
Defines shock and explains causes of shocks. Shows how to understand how shock sets in, recognize the symptoms of shock and take positive steps toward stopping shock.
From The Safety Instruction Series.
Prod-VTRI Dist-VTRI

Shock C 15 MIN
3/4 INCH VIDEO CASSETTE PRO
Depicts the signs and symptoms of shock, counter measures to be taken and complications to be avoided or treated in the case of shock.
From The Trauma Series.
Prod-PRIMED Dist-PRIMED

Shock (Rev Ed) C 7 MIN
3/4 OR 1/2 INCH VIDEO CASSETTE
Describes the characteristics of shock and the shock cycle, the causes, symptoms, and physical and emotional changes associated with physical shock. Illustrates the human nervous system, how it controls the body's vital organs, and how it is directly involved in cases of physical shock. Stresses that shock follows most serious injuries and should not be neglected.
From The First Aid (Rev Ed) Series.
Prod-USMESA Dist-USNAC 1981

Shock (Spanish) C 14 MIN
16MM FILM OPTICAL SOUND
Teaches the individual how to take care of his medical and health needs in time of disaster when medical assistance might not be readily available. Presents instructions for treating shock.
From The Medical Self-Help Series.
LC NO. 75-702551
Prod-USPHS Dist-USNAC 1960

Shock - Recognition And Management C 17 MIN
16MM FILM OPTICAL SOUND PRO
Uses animation and live-action to illustrate the physiology of shock, and to present procedures for recognizing and managing the shock patient. Explains the need for evaluation and treatment of shock, and emphasizes the importance of aggressive, but orderly, procedures. Follows step-by-step initial counter measures, fluid replacement, venous catheterization, physiological monitoring, and other necessary measures In the management of the patient in shock.
LC NO. 70-702865
Prod-SKF Dist-AMEDA 1968

Shock Corridor B 101 MIN
16MM FILM OPTICAL SOUND C A
Presents a drama starring Peter Breck, Costance Towers and James Best.
Prod-UNKNWN Dist-KITPAR 1963

Shock Excited Oscillator B 36 MIN
16MM FILM OPTICAL SOUND
Gives the purpose of each component in the shock excited oscillator circuit and explains the circuit operation and shows the input and output waveshapes graphically. Explains how L and C of the duration of the input gate determine the frequency and duration of the output. (Kinescope)
LC NO. 74-705632
Prod-USAF Dist-USNAC

Shock Lung C 17 MIN
3/4 INCH VIDEO CASSETTE PRO
Describes the clinical signs of acute respiratory failure and explores assessment and treatment.
From The Shock Series. Module 4
LC NO. 80-707733
Prod-BRA Dist-BRA 1980

Shock Of The New–A Series
16MM FILM, 3/4 OR 1/2 IN VIDEO C A
Explores social history as seen through the lens of modern art, beginning in the 1870's. Narrated by Robert Hughes.
LC NO. 80-706669
Prod-BBCTV Dist-TIMLIF 1980

Culture As Nature 052 MIN
Future That Was, The 052 MIN
Landscape Of Pleasure, The 052 MIN
Mechanical Paradise, The 052 MIN
Powers That Be, The 052 MIN
Threshold Of Liberty, The 052 MIN
Trouble In Utopia 052 MIN
View From The Edge, The 052 MIN

Shock Septico C 23 MIN
3/4 OR 1/2 INCH VIDEO CASSETTE PRO
A Spanish version of Septic Shock. Discusses the general pathophysiology of shock, the nine basic parts of evaluation (which include vital signs), cultures, CBC differential and a coagulation screen), chronologic treat- ment (which includes fluid therapy, pharmacologic agents and antibiotics) and differentiation of septic shock from hypovolemia.
Prod-UMICHM Dist-UMICHM 1975

Shock Trauma C 60 MIN
3/4 INCH VIDEO CASSETTE
Follows the progress of events from the time a patient is involved in a accident until he is released from the Shock Trauma Unit at the University of Maryland. Features doctors, nurses and patients describing their highly emotional involvement with this medical treatment program.
Prod-MDCPB Dist-MDCPB

Shock Waves C 32 MIN
16MM FILM, 3/4 OR 1/2 IN VIDEO H-C A
Explores the effects of television in our society. Asks whether nightly exposure to television changes the children watching it.
Prod-GANNET Dist-MTI

Shock–A Series
PRO
Explores the spectrum of shock phenomena and discusses the nursing treatment for this problem.
LC NO. 80-707733
Prod-BRA Dist-BRA 1980

Cerebral Perfusion Failure 016 MIN
Drug Therapy In Shock 018 MIN
Hemodynamics Of Perfusion 017 MIN
Perfusion Failure 019 MIN
Shock Lung 017 MIN
Volume Repletion In Shock 017 MIN

Shocking Accident, A C 25 MIN
16MM FILM, 3/4 OR 1/2 IN VIDEO I-C A
Tells the story of an English school boy who learns that his father has been killed in a bizarre accident. Relates that his friends tease him and only when he meets a girl who understands, can he shake off the terrible memory of his father's death. Based on the short story A Shocking Accident by Graham Greene.
LC NO. 84-706036
Prod-DIRECT Dist-DIRECT 1983

Shoemaker And The Elves C 15 MIN
16MM FILM, 3/4 OR 1/2 IN VIDEO P-I
Tells how the midnight magic of a pair of cobbler elves reverses the misfortunes of a poor shoemaker.
Prod-IFFB Dist-FI 1972

Shoemaker And The Elves, The C 14 MIN
16MM FILM, 3/4 OR 1/2 IN VIDEO P
Puppets re-create the story of the elves who slip into the shoemaker's shop and make shoes for him.
Prod-GAKKEN Dist-CORF 1962

Shoemaker And The Elves, The C 15 MIN
3/4 OR 1/2 INCH VIDEO CASSETTE K-P
See series title for descriptive statement.
From The Gather Round Series.
Prod-CTI Dist-CTI

Shoemaker And The Elves, The C 15 MIN
3/4 INCH VIDEO CASSETTE K-P
See series title for descriptive statement.
From The Storytime Series.
Prod-WCETTV Dist-GPITVL 1976

Shoemaker, The B 34 MIN
16MM FILM, 3/4 OR 1/2 IN VIDEO H-C A
Explores the effect of the rural exodus from Spain on the life of a poor Andalusian shoemaker.
LC NO. 79-706045
Prod-MINTZJ Dist-IU 1978

Shoes B 15 MIN
2 INCH VIDEOTAPE P
Pursues the staff and high and low singing.
From The Time For Music Series.
Prod-CVETVC Dist-GPITVL Prodn-WCVETV

Shoes For Children C 13 MIN
2 INCH VIDEOTAPE
See series title for descriptive statement.
From The Living Better I Series.
Prod-MAETEL Dist-PUBTEL

Shoeshine Girl C 25 MIN
16MM FILM, 3/4 OR 1/2 IN VIDEO I-J
Tells how a feisty young girl named Sarah finds a job with the town's shoeshine man. Explains how she learns the rewards of responsibility and hard work.
Prod-MACPRO Dist-LCOA 1980

Shoeshine Girl (Spanish) C 25 MIN
16MM FILM, 3/4 OR 1/2 IN VIDEO P-J A
Tells of a young, feisty daughter who goes to live with her aunt and takes a job as a shoeshine girl. Teaches responsibility.
Prod-MACPRO Dist-LCOA 1980

Shoo-Moosh C 5 MIN
16MM FILM OPTICAL SOUND
Tells the story of a stolen mysterious bag.
LC NO. 76-703805
Prod-CONCRU Dist-CONCRU 1975

Shoo, Fly, Don't Bother Me C 20 MIN
3/4 OR 1/2 INCH VIDEO CASSETTE P-I
Introduces the ABA form in music.
From The USS Rhythm Series.
Prod-ARKETV Dist-AITECH 1977

Shoot / Don't Shoot II C 25 MIN
16MM FILM, 3/4 OR 1/2 IN VIDEO
Discusses how policemen should be concerned with the finality of death and the extreme consequences of being wrong in a shooting situation. Covers essential rules for the use of legal force and a definition of local laws and requirements concerning the officer's response to a fleeing felon.
Prod-WORON Dist-MTI

Shoot/Don't Shoot C 26 MIN
16MM FILM, 3/4 OR 1/2 IN VIDEO
Analyzes what its like to be a police officer facing the deadly force dilemma. Addresses the psychological pressures created by shooting incidents, the effects on fellow officers, legal implications and alternatives to shooting.
Prod-BELLDA Dist-MTI

Shoot/Don't Shoot I C 24 MIN
16MM FILM, 3/4 OR 1/2 IN VIDEO
Presents scenes of incidents during which a police officer would have to decide to shoot or not shoot.
Prod-WORON Dist-MTI

Shooting Decisions C 25 MIN
16MM FILM, 3/4 OR 1/2 IN VIDEO
Presents 21 shooting decisions in which the decision had to be made by police officers to shoot or not shoot.
Prod-MTI Dist-MTI

Shooting For Mars B 3 MIN
16MM FILM OPTICAL SOUND J-C
Examines America's Mariner-Mars project. Explores attempts to reach remote regions of the galaxy.
From The Screen News Digest Series. Vol 7, Issue 5.
LC NO. FIA68-2099
Prod-HEARST Dist-HEARST 1964

Shooting Gallery, The C 5 MIN
16MM FILM OPTICAL SOUND J-H
Presents a mannequin-like soldier who enters a shooting gallery in full-dress uniform, and with no apparent feeling, fires at old targets found at a shooting gallery, setting each group of target characters into mechanical motion. Shows the captive figures repeating the same gestures, never quite completing their actions or reaching their goals. Illustrates what happens when a loving couple attempts to break away from the mechanism.
LC NO. 79-709260
Prod-KRATKY Dist-SIM 1970

Shooting Skills And Air Gun Competition C 10 MIN
16MM FILM, 3/4 OR 1/2 IN VIDEO I-C A
Describes the fundamentals of recreational and competitive air gun shooting, with emphasis on safety.
From The Air Gun Shooting Series. No. 3
Prod-ATHI Dist-ATHI 1979

Shootout In Paradise C 26 MIN
16MM FILM OPTICAL SOUND
Shows highlights of the 1982 Women's Kemper Open Golf Tournament held in Maui, Hawaii. Includes scenes of golfers JoAnne Carner, Nancy Lopez and Pat Bradley.
Prod-MTP Dist-MTP

Shootout On Imperial Highway C 58 MIN
1/2 IN VIDEO CASSETTE BETA/VHS
Originally shown as Warnings From Gang Land. Explores what Los Angeles is trying to do about its street gang problem, the worst in the nation, with more than 1,000 people killed in gang violence during the past three years. Looks at the personal struggle of 72-year-old Watts grocer James Hawkins against gang members in his neighborhood.
From The Frontline Series.
Prod-DOCCON Dist-PBS

Shop Assignments, Pt 1 C 14 MIN
16MM FILM, 3/4 OR 1/2 IN VIDEO J
Shows the different kinds of shop assignments--pistons and connecting rods Pt 1 and 2, cylinder head, Pt 1 and 2 and the generator.
Prod-SF Dist-SF 1968

Shop Assignments, Pt 2 C 15 MIN
16MM FILM, 3/4 OR 1/2 IN VIDEO J A
Shows the removal and replacement of a piston and connecting rod assembly and explains the required tools. Describes how to take apart and reassemble gear and rotor type oil pumps and fuel pumps.
Prod-SF Dist-SF 1969

Shop Mathematics, No. 1 C 30 MIN
2 INCH VIDEOTAPE IND
Examines decimals and decimal equivalents.
From The Basic Machine Shop Practices Series.
Prod-VTETV Dist-GPITVL

Shop Mathematics, No. 2 C 30 MIN
2 INCH VIDEOTAPE IND
Examines addition and subtraction of decimals and shows their application.
From The Basic Machine Shop Practices Series.
Prod-VTETV Dist-GPITVL

Shop Mathematics, No. 3 C 30 MIN
2 INCH VIDEOTAPE IND
Examines multiplication and division of decimals and shows their application.
From The Basic Machine Shop Practices Series.
Prod-VTETV Dist-GPITVL

Shop Mathematics, No. 4 C 30 MIN
2 INCH VIDEOTAPE IND
Uses circular measurement, applications and the Vernier scale.
From The Basic Machine Shop Practices Series.
Prod-VTETV Dist-GPITVL

Shop Safety C 22 MIN
16MM FILM, 3/4 OR 1/2 IN VIDEO
Describes common hazards in a vehicle maintenance shop, and shows what precautions should be taken to prevent accidents.
Prod-USA Dist-USNAC

Shop Safety–A Series

Begins with an explanation of the basic design of a lift truck and goes on to emphasize general shop safety procedures, safe repair procedures and special precautions required to tow or operate disabled lift trucks. Consists of three tapes.
Prod-CLARKV Dist-CLARKV

Shop Sharply, Eat Smartly C 6 MIN
3/4 OR 1/2 INCH VIDEO CASSETTE
Features a junk-food mother wheeling her baby around the grocery when the baby suddenly 'grows up' and begins giving Mom pointers on wise food shopping and eating.
Prod-NOVID Dist-NOVID

Shop Sketch Theory - One-View Working Drawings C 19 MIN
1/2 IN VIDEO CASSETTE BETA/VHS IND
Illustrates the shortcut approach to illustrating an object, such as a fitting or transition, with a one-view working drawing, instead of the typical three-view working drawing as found on most blueprints.
Prod-RMI Dist-RMI

Shop Stewards C 28 MIN
16MM FILM - 3/4 IN VIDEO J-C
Looks at the state of trade unionism in the 1970's, featuring the opinions of a group of shop stewards from different generations and working experiences.
From The Are You Listening Series.
LC NO. 80-707152
Prod-STURTM Dist-STURTM 1972

Shop Talk C 83 MIN
16MM FILM, 3/4 OR 1/2 IN VIDEO A
Examines contemporary American working class consciousness.
Prod-MACHR Dist-CNEMAG 1980

Shoplifting C 20 MIN
16MM FILM OPTICAL SOUND J-C A
Features numerous experts who discuss shoplifting while actors dramatize aspects of this type of crime.

From The Community Protection And Crime Prevention Series.
LC NO. 73-703199
Prod-SUMHIL Dist-SUMHIL 1973

Shoplifting C 19 MIN
3/4 OR 1/2 INCH VIDEO CASSETTE I-J
Depicts what happens when two teenage girls are caught and prosecuted for shoplifting, Phyllis as a first offender and Nancy as a repeated offender.
From The Cop Talk Series.
Prod-UTSBE Dist-AITECH 1981

Shoplifting C 21 MIN
16MM FILM, 3/4 OR 1/2 IN VIDEO J-C A
Explores the scope of shoplifting today, why people do it and what the results are to the thief and to society. Suggests that everyone should cooperate to reduce shoplifting for the protection of his own pocketbook.
Prod-ACI Dist-AIMS 1974

Shoplifting - It's A Crime C 12 MIN
16MM FILM, 3/4 OR 1/2 IN VIDEO I-H
Dramatizes typical shoplifting incidents with young people of elementary and high school age. Points out the cost to honest shoppers and the embarrassment and consequences of being caught.
Prod-FLMFR Dist-FLMFR

Shoplifting - It's A Steal C 15 MIN
16MM FILM OPTICAL SOUND J-C A
Warns young people against the temptation to shoplift. Shows how store personnel and police treat shoplifting as a serious crime and describes the future harm which can occur from a conviction on a shoplifting charge.
From The Consumer Center Program Series.
LC NO. 74-703152
Prod-GEMILL Dist-GEMILL 1974

Shoplifting - Sharon's Story C 26 MIN
16MM FILM, 3/4 OR 1/2 IN VIDEO J-C A
Tells the story of a young woman who steals from a department store and is subsequently arrested. Shows her reactions as well as those of her parents to the humiliation of search, interrogation, detention, family confrontation and court procedure.
Prod-AURO Dist-LCOA 1977

Shoplifting - You Pay For It C 16 MIN
16MM FILM, 3/4 OR 1/2 IN VIDEO
Deals with the shoplifting problem from a non-accusatory perspective. Points out the cost to consumers in terms of fewer jobs, lower earnings and higher store prices when shoplifting runs rampant. Emphasizes the high risk and low reward of shoplifting.
Prod-MTI Dist-MTI

Shoplifting Is Stealing C 16 MIN
16MM FILM, 3/4 OR 1/2 IN VIDEO J-H
Shows that the cost of shoplifting is passed on to all consumers, illustrates increasingly effective surveillance and other techniques to apprehend shoplifters and emphasizes that shoplifting is a serious crime punishable by law.
Prod-CAHILL Dist-AIMS 1975

Shoplifting Prevented C 25 MIN
3/4 OR 1/2 INCH VIDEO CASSETTE A
Shows how to save money by preventing shoplifting. In- structs in detection of shoplifters. Narrated by Martin Milner.
Prod-AMEDIA Dist-AMEDIA

Shopping Bag Ladies B 45 MIN
3/4 INCH VIDEO CASSETTE
Documents the lives of the Shopping Bag Ladies through the city. Presents five intimate portraits of these homeless women who live in doorways, in railway stations and bus stations, on park benches and who carry their belongings in bulging paper and plastic satchels.
Prod-WMENIF Dist-WMENIF

Shopping Bag Lady, The C 21 MIN
16MM FILM, 3/4 OR 1/2 IN VIDEO I-C A
Tells how a series of experiences of a group of typical 14-year-old girls make them more sensitive to the needs of elderly people.
Prod-LCOA Dist-LCOA 1975

Shopping Bag Lady, The (Captioned) C 21 MIN
16MM FILM, 3/4 OR 1/2 IN VIDEO P-H A
Helps in the understanding of old age, the problems of aging and the dignity of all individuals, regardless of their place in society.
Prod-LCOA Dist-LCOA 1975

Shopping Bag Lady, The (French) C 21 MIN
16MM FILM, 3/4 OR 1/2 IN VIDEO P-H A
Helps in the understanding of old age, the problems of aging and the dignity of all individuals, regardless of their place in society.
Prod-LCOA Dist-LCOA 1975

Shopping Bag Lady, The (Spanish) C 21 MIN
16MM FILM, 3/4 OR 1/2 IN VIDEO P-H A
Helps in the understanding of old age and the problems of aging, and the dignity of all individuals, regardless of their place in society.
Prod-LCOA Dist-LCOA 1975

Shopping Expedition, A / Paddington And The 'Old Masters' / A Disappearing Trick C 17 MIN
16MM FILM, 3/4 OR 1/2 IN VIDEO K-I
Presents the adventures of Paddington Bear when he goes to a department store and an antique shop. Tells how the little bear puts on a magic show. Based on chapters four, five and eight of the book A Bear Called Paddington by Michael Bond.
From The Paddington Bear, Series 1 Series.
LC NO. 80-707227
Prod-BONDM Dist-FLMFR Prodn-FILMF 1977

Shopping For Doomsday C 16 MIN
3/4 OR 1/2 INCH VIDEO CASSETTE H-C A
Presents the views of a growing number of people who call themselves Survivalists. Explores their beliefs, which include the fact that the West will experience a total breakdown of law and order and a nuclear disaster in the next decade.
Prod-JOU Dist-JOU

Shopping For Insurance C 14 MIN
2 INCH VIDEOTAPE
Examines the different types of insurance including, life, property, liability, automobile and health. Lists specific tips and insurance terms that help plan for a family's security.
From The Living Better II Series.
Prod-MAETEL Dist-PUBTEL

Shopping Sense - Self-Defense C 15 MIN
3/4 OR 1/2 INCH VIDEO CASSETTE J-H
Focuses on supermarket psychology and discusses ingredient labels, unit pricing, and open dating.
From The Soup to Nuts Series.
Prod-GSDE Dist-AITECH 1980

Shopping Strategies C 29 MIN
3/4 OR 1/2 INCH VIDEO CASSETTE H-C A
Discusses general shopping strategies, including ideas for preplanning the weekly shopping trip, ways to control impulse spending and supermarket specials.
From The Be A Better Shopper Series. Program 3
LC NO. 81-707303
Prod-CUETV Dist-CUNIV 1978

Shopping Trip, The C 15 MIN
3/4 OR 1/2 INCH VIDEO CASSETTE I-J
Illustrates how institutions, governmental and nongovernmental, vary in form and function.
From The It's All Up To You Series.
Prod-COOPED Dist-AITECH Prodn-WHATV 1978

Shopping Wisely C 14 MIN
16MM FILM, 3/4 OR 1/2 IN VIDEO
Lists practical suggestions for getting the best buy for the money spent when crisis shopping, planned shopping, gift shopping and clothes shopping.
Prod-ODECA Dist-BULFRG

Shore Survival C 22 MIN
3/4 OR 1/2 INCH VIDEO CASSETTE PRO
Discusses survival once on shore, including identifying alternative sources of food, boiling water, keeping dry, creating shelter and making signals. Includes interviews with survivors who followed these guidelines.
From The Fisheries Safety And Survival Series.
Prod-USCG Dist-USNAC 1983

Shores Of Gulf St Vincent C 24 MIN
16MM FILM OPTICAL SOUND P-H
Shows three submerged reefs off the coast of South Australia and their formation. Includes divers exploring the biological aspects of the reefs. Reveals a wide variety of unknown and interesting marine animals.
LC NO. 76-708711
Prod-STEEND Dist-AMEDFL 1970

Shores Of The Cosmic Ocean, The C 60 MIN
16MM FILM, 3/4 OR 1/2 IN VIDEO J-C A
Offers a guided tour of the universe, from clusters of galaxies to Earth. Introduces the discoveries of Eratosthenes and discusses the dawn of systematic scientfiic research and the Alexandrian library. Concludes with a 'cosmic calendar,' a journey through time from the Big Bang to the present. Based on the book Cosmos by Carl Sagan. Narrated by Carl Sagan.
From The Cosmos Series. Program 1
LC NO. 81-707178
Prod-KCET Dist-FI 1980

Short 'A' - Andy And The Apple C 15 MIN
2 INCH VIDEOTAPE P
Develops auditory awareness and discrimination of vowel sounds. Introduces a few common vowel generalizations which are an aid in learning to read.
From The Listen And Say Series.
Prod-MPATI Dist-GPITVL

Short 'E' - The Elephant Who Wanted To Go Upstairs C 15 MIN
2 INCH VIDEOTAPE P
Develops auditory awareness and discrimination of vowel sounds. Introduces a few common vowel generalizations which are an aid in learning to read.
From The Listen And Say Series.
Prod-MPATI Dist-GPITVL

Short 'I' - Inky The Imp C 15 MIN
2 INCH VIDEOTAPE P
Develops auditory awareness and discrimination of vowel sounds. Introduces a few common vowel generalizations which are an aid in learning to read.
From The Listen And Say Series.
Prod-MPATI Dist-GPITVL

Short 'O' - The Ox In The Box C 15 MIN
2 INCH VIDEOTAPE P
Develops auditory awareness and discrimination of vowel sounds. Introduces a few common vowel generalizations which are an aid in learning to read.
From The Listen And Say Series.
Prod-MPATI Dist-GPITVL

Short 'U' - Uncle Umber's Umbrella C 15 MIN
2 INCH VIDEOTAPE P
Develops auditory awareness and discrimination of vowel sounds. Introduces a few common vowel generalizations which are an aid in learning to read.
From The Listen And Say Series.
Prod-MPATI Dist-GPITVL

Short A - Andy And The Apple B 15 MIN
2 INCH VIDEOTAPE P
See series title for descriptive statement.
From The Listen And Say - Vowels Series.
Prod-GPITVL Dist-GPITVL

Short And Suite C 5 MIN
16MM FILM, 3/4 OR 1/2 IN VIDEO H-C
Norman McLaren translates into moving patterns of color and light the moods and rhythms of music written for jazz ensemble by Eldon Rathburn.
Prod-NFBC Dist-IFB Prodn-MCLN 1960

Short Approach Shots, The C 9 MIN
16MM FILM - 3/4 IN VIDEO H-C A
Identifies short approach golf swings. Demonstrates adjustments in setup and stroke and explores the results of lengthening a short approach swing.
From The Modern Golf Instruction In Motion Pictures Series. Unit 3
LC NO. 76-703597
Prod-NGF Dist-NGF Prodn-GOLF 1974

Short Circuit C 45 MIN
16MM FILM OPTICAL SOUND
Asks how an upper-middle-class liberal can make a documentary film about the black population and culture of his Manhattan neighborhood.
Prod-KIRPRO Dist-KIRPRO

Short Cuts C 29 MIN
2 INCH VIDEOTAPE
See series title for descriptive statement.
From The Making Things Grow III Series.
Prod-WGBHTV Dist-PUBTEL

Short Day Problems C 30 MIN
2 INCH VIDEOTAPE
See series title for descriptive statement.
From The Making Things Grow II Series.
Prod-WGBHTV Dist-PUBTEL

Short Distance Runner C 21 MIN
16MM FILM OPTICAL SOUND J-C
Dramatizes the story of a high school student whose increased dependency on alcohol affects his schoolwork and athletic pursuits.
LC NO. 79-700941
Prod-SIGPRS Dist-MARTC Prodn-MARTC 1978

Short E - The Elephant Who Wanted To Go Upstairs B 15 MIN
2 INCH VIDEOTAPE P
See series title for descriptive statement.
From The Listen And Say - Vowels Series.
Prod-GPITVL Dist-GPITVL

Short Eared Owl C 17 MIN
16MM FILM, 3/4 OR 1/2 IN VIDEO
Shows the owl, opening at its wintering grounds and follows its southern movements in spring. Examines the link between breeding success and population of meadow mice, its main prey. Reveals that, unlike most owls, the short eared owl often hunts in daylight over open fields and salt marshes.
From The RSPB Collection Series.
Prod-RSFPB Dist-BCNFL 1983

Short Field Procedure L-19 - Bird Dog, Pt 1 - Power Approach And Maximum Performance Takeoff B 16 MIN
16MM FILM OPTICAL SOUND
Presents a flight training film which shows the start and control of power approach, the effects of wind and temperature and landing techniques. Demonstrates preparation, start and climb for a maximum performance takeoff.
LC NO. 74-706244
Prod-USA Dist-USNAC 1960

Short Field Procedure L-19 - Bird Dog, Pt 2 - Barrier Landing And Barrier Takeoff B 10 MIN
16MM FILM OPTICAL SOUND
Shows directional control, power approach and line descent in barrier landing, maximum performance takeoff and climb and normal climb in barrier takeoff.
LC NO. 74-705634
Prod-USA Dist-USNAC 1960

Short Films Of D W Griffith, Vol 1 B 45 MIN
1/2 IN VIDEO CASSETTE BETA/VHS
Presents The Battle (1911), The Female Of The Species (1912) and The New York Hat (1912), silent films directed by D W Griffith.
Prod-UNKNWN Dist-VIDIM

Short Giraffe, A B 15 MIN
2 INCH VIDEOTAPE P
Compares shapes and textures of animals to increase students' awareness.
From The Art Corner Series.
Prod-CVETVC Dist-GPITVL Prodn-WCVETV

Short I - Inky The Imp B 15 MIN
2 INCH VIDEOTAPE P
See series title for descriptive statement.
From The Listen And Say - Vowels Series.
Prod-GPITVL Dist-GPITVL

Short Life Of Lolo Knopke, The C 30 MIN
3/4 OR 1/2 INCH VIDEO CASSETTE I-J
Reveals that the capture of a would-be killer by the smallest Powerhouse Kid shows that everyone can be big when they use their brains.

From The Powerhouse Series.
LC NO. 83-707192
Prod-EFCVA Dist-GA 1982

Short Novel, The, I B 45 MIN
2 INCH VIDEOTAPE C
See series title for descriptive statement.
From The General Humanities Series. Unit 4 - The Literary Arts
Prod-CHITVC Dist-GPITVL Prodn-WTTWTV

Short Novel, The, II B 45 MIN
2 INCH VIDEOTAPE C
See series title for descriptive statement.
From The General Humanities Series. Unit 4 - The Literary Arts
Prod-CHITVC Dist-GPITVL Prodn-WTTWTV

Short O - The Ox In The Box B 15 MIN
2 INCH VIDEOTAPE P
See series title for descriptive statement.
From The Listen And Say - Vowels Series.
Prod-GPITVL Dist-GPITVL

Short Order Cookery C 10 MIN
16MM FILM, 3/4 OR 1/2 IN VIDEO J-C A
Presents a training course to the short order cook for greater efficiency and productivity while facing particular problems of organizing work with the added challenge of often performing his duties in the public eye. Stresses ways of coping with traffic, staying ahead of the rush, various foods that must be prepared. Emphasizes details of griddle use and maintenance. Shows that appearance and cleanliness are needed for exhibition cooking.
From The Professional Food Preparation And Service Program Series.
Prod-NEM Dist-NEM 1973

Short Socks B 30 MIN
16MM FILM OPTICAL SOUND
From The Classic Christie Comedies Series.
Prod-SFI Dist-SFI

Short Stories By John Cheever And Eudora Welty C 29 MIN
2 INCH VIDEOTAPE
Presents readings from the short stories of John Cheever and Eudora Welty.
From The One To One Series.
Prod-WETATV Dist-PUBTEL

Short Story History Of Processors, A C 29 MIN
3/4 INCH VIDEO CASSETTE C
Discusses the development of radiographic processing equipment from the time of manual processing to automatic radiographic processors of the 1970's.
From The Radiographic Processing Series. Pt 3
LC NO. 77-706072
Prod-USVA Dist-USNAC 1975

Short Story I C 15 MIN
3/4 OR 1/2 INCH VIDEO CASSETTE I
Discusses the characters, setting and plot of a short story.
From The Zebra Wings Series.
Prod-NITC Dist-AITECH Prodn-MAETEL 1975

Short Story II C 15 MIN
3/4 OR 1/2 INCH VIDEO CASSETTE I
Introduces several mystery writing components, including aliteration, mood and setting.
From The Zebra Wings Series.
Prod-NITC Dist-AITECH Prodn-MAETEL 1975

Short Story—A Series
16MM FILM, 3/4 OR 1/2 IN VIDEO J-C A
Presents a series of dramatizations of some of the best short stories in world literature. Represents a wide variety of works, including humorous, allegorical, moral, suspenseful, realisic, and romantic.
Prod-IITC Dist-IU 1982

Bet By Anton Chekhov, The 015 MIN
Birthmark By Nathanial Hawthorne, The 015 MIN
Boarded Window By Ambrose Bierce, The 015 MIN
Dave's Necklace By Charles Chestnutt 015 MIN
Diary Of Adam And Eve By Mark Twain, The 015 MIN
Dilettante By Edith Wharton, The 015 MIN
Lull By Saki, The 015 MIN
Mrs Ripley's Trip By Hamlin Garland 015 MIN
Queen Of Spades By Alexander Pushkin, The 015 MIN
Real Thing By Henry James, The 015 MIN
Tell-Tale Heart by Edgar Allan Poe, The 015 MIN
Tennessee's Partner By Bret Harte 015 MIN
Two Little Soldiers By Guy De Maupassant, The 015 MIN
Two Thanksgiving Day Gentlemen By O Henry, The 015 MIN
Village Singer By Mary Wilkins Freeman, The 015 MIN
Yellow Wallpaper By Charlotte Perkins Gilman, 015 MIN

Short Story, The C
3/4 OR 1/2 INCH VIDEO CASSETTE H-C
Explains the key elements of the short story and discusses the different techniques and objectives of short story writers such as Poe, Thurber, Saroyan, Hemingway and others. Gives readings from Jean Stafford and Flannery O'Connor with the authors' own insights into their work methods and feelings.
Prod-GA Dist-GA

Short Story, The, I B 45 MIN
2 INCH VIDEOTAPE C
See series title for descriptive statement.
From The General Humanities Series. Unit 4 - The Literary Arts
Prod-CHITVC Dist-GPITVL Prodn-WTTWTV

Short Story, The, II B 45 MIN
2 INCH VIDEOTAPE C
See series title for descriptive statement.
From The General Humanities Series. Unit 4 - The Literary Arts
Prod-CHITVC Dist-GPITVL Prodn-WTTWTV

Short Tall Story C 5 MIN
16MM FILM, 3/4 OR 1/2 IN VIDEO I-C A
Presents an animated fable about a cloud-covered land inhabited by a group of tall people and a group of short people. Tells how a good fairy removes the clouds and the two groups see that, regardless of their physical differences, they are really all the same.
LC NO. 81-706608
Prod-HALAS Dist-PHENIX

Short Term Systems Intervention Model For Family Assessment And Intervention, A, Pt 1 B 60 MIN
3/4 OR 1/2 INCH VIDEO CASSETTE
Presents a short-term systems intervention model for family assessment and intervention. Discusses its development, methodology and testing as well as assessing the role and function of individual family members.
Prod-TELURN Dist-UWISC Prodn-UWISC 1978

Short Term Systems Intervention Model For Family Assessment And Intervention, A, Pt 2 B 60 MIN
3/4 OR 1/2 INCH VIDEO CASSETTE
Offers introduction and comments on segments of a videotaped family therapy session led by James Alexander of Western States Family Institute that demonstrates short-term systems intervention therapy.
Prod-VRL Dist-UWISC 1978

Short Time Intervals B 21 MIN
16MM FILM OPTICAL SOUND H-C
Presents a study of the extension of senses to deal with very short time intervals. Timing devices--moving cameras, pen recorders and an oscilloscope--are shown and explained.
From The PSSC Physics Films Series.
Prod-PSSC Dist-MLA 1960

Short U - Uncle Umber's Umbrella B 15 MIN
2 INCH VIDEOTAPE P
See series title for descriptive statement.
From The Listen And Say - Vowels Series.
Prod-GPITVL Dist-GPITVL

Short Vowel Sounds, The C 12 MIN
16MM FILM, 3/4 OR 1/2 IN VIDEO P-I
Reviews the long and short vowel sounds with emphasis on the latter using animated letter sequences.
From The Reading Skills, Set 2 Series. No. 2
Prod-GLDWER Dist-JOU 1972

Short Way Home, The C 14 MIN
16MM FILM OPTICAL SOUND PRO
Discusses how patients, who previously might have been confined to a hospital for a long period of recuperation, can be returned to their homes through the facilities provided by the home health services. Explains that the combined efforts of physicians, community nurses, therapists and technicans bring the hospital to the patient and speed his recovery in familiar surroundings.
LC NO. 74-705636
Prod-USPHS Dist-USPHS Prodn-MHWPA 1967

Short-Lived Radioisotopes In Nuclear Medicine C 27 MIN
16MM FILM OPTICAL SOUND PRO
Describes the development of a technetium-99M generator at Brookhaven National Laboratory and shows the medical applications of the generator at the Argonne Cancer Research Hospital.
LC NO. 77-714176
Prod-ANL Dist-USERD 1971

Shortest - Longest C 15 MIN
3/4 OR 1/2 INCH VIDEO CASSETTE P
See series title for descriptive statement.
From The Hands On, Grade 1 Series. Unit 2 - Measuring
Prod-VAOG Dist-AITECH Prodn-WHROTV 1975

Shortgrass Prairie, Pt 1 C 15 MIN
16MM FILM, 3/4 OR 1/2 IN VIDEO J-C A
Describes the extremes of climate on the prairie and shows the courtship ritual of the male sage grouse during a period of bitter cold.
From The Animals And Plants Of North America Series.
LC NO. 81-707424
Prod-KARVF Dist-LCOA 1981

Shortgrass Prairie, Pt 2 C 15 MIN
16MM FILM, 3/4 OR 1/2 IN VIDEO J-C A
Shows the display ritual of a lark bunting, hawks rearing their young and the habits of other animals that inhabit the prairie.
From The Animals And Plants Of North America Series.
LC NO. 81-707424
Prod-KARVF Dist-LCOA 1981

Shot Heard 'Round The World, The C 32 MIN
16MM FILM, 3/4 OR 1/2 IN VIDEO I-H
Presents an excerpt from the feature film Johnny Tremain. Describes how younger members of the Sons of Liberty supplied the information about British plans which enabled Paul Revere to alert the Minutemen.
From The Johnny Tremain Series.
Prod-DISNEY Dist-WDEMCO 1966

Shot Put C 4 MIN
16MM FILM SILENT
Presents male athletes competing in the shot put event, including Laut, Bojars, Akins, Stuart, Milic, Carter, Feuerbach, Oldfield, Anderson and Crouser.
Prod-TRACKN Dist-TRACKN 1982

Shot Put (Women) C 4 MIN
16MM FILM SILENT
Presents female athletes competing in the shot put, including Slupianek, Pufe, Krachevskaya, Wood, Lisovskaya, Sarria, Abashidze and Griffin. Includes views of the rotational technique by male throwers Oldfield, Crouser and Laut.
Prod-TRACKN Dist-TRACKN 1982

Shot, The C 12 MIN
16MM FILM, 3/4 OR 1/2 IN VIDEO H-C A
Describes techniques and training exercises for the shot put event and concludes with scenes of an international competition.
From The Athletics Series.
LC NO. 80-706586
Prod-GSAVL Dist-IU 1980

Shotgun - Second Weapon C 25 MIN
16MM FILM, 3/4 OR 1/2 IN VIDEO
Discusses the proper use of the law enforcement shotgun, styles and makes of weapons, psychology of the shotgun, car mounts, ammunition, and avoidance of lethal situations caused by an improper understanding of what the shotgun can and cannot do. Includes re-creations of incorrect use which can easily be avoided with knowledge, care and proper attitude.
Prod-WORON Dist-MTI

Shotgun Fundamentals C 45 MIN
1/2 IN VIDEO CASSETTE BETA/VHS A
Explains how to choose and fit a gun, correct gun mount, sight picture, trigger pull, dealing with recoil, target acquisition, and methods of lead. Includes an exhibition in trick shooting by the instructor, John Satterwhite - U S skeet shooting champion,dual Gold Medalist from the Pan American games and the U S Olympic Committee Athletic Advisor for shooting.
Prod-RMI Dist-RMI

Shotgun Joe C 25 MIN
16MM FILM OPTICAL SOUND J-C
A cinema verite portrait of Joe Scanlon who is serving time for armed robbert in the Connecticut State Reformatory. Includes interviews with guards, teachers, fellow inmates, family members and with Joe, himself, which reveal that he is moving toward self-destruction.
From The Jason Films Portrait Series.
LC NO. 75-705662
Prod-CAMPI Dist-JASON 1970

Shotgun Or Sidearm C 16 MIN
16MM FILM, 3/4 OR 1/2 IN VIDEO
Explores situations in which an officer must decide which weapon to use, a sidearm or a shotgun. Demonstrates the advantages and disadvantages of a shotgun and explores its capacities. Looks at what an officer should consider when making his decision and what problems arise when an error is made. Covers both tactical and psychological aspects of the weapons.
Prod-DAVP Dist-MTI

Shotgun Shooting Fundamentals C 15 MIN
16MM FILM, 3/4 OR 1/2 IN VIDEO J-C A
Presents Bill Clemmons, Skeet World Record Holder, and Don Haldeman, Olympic Trap Gold Medalist, reviewing with several young shooters the fundamentals of championship shotgun shooting with a strong emphasis on safety.
From The Rifle Shooting Fundamentals Series.
Prod-ATHI Dist-ATHI 1982

Should A Tax Or Fee On Commercial Broadcasting Help Pay For Public Broadcasting C 59 MIN
3/4 OR 1/2 INCH VIDEO CASSETTE
Asks whether commercial broadcasting should be taxed in order to help pay for public broadcasting. Features debaters Roger Fisher and William Rusher.
From The Advocates Series.
Prod-WGBHTV Dist-PBS

Should Congress Deregulate Interstate Trucking C 59 MIN
3/4 INCH VIDEO CASSETTE
Shows a debate between Bonnie Frank and Lisle Baker centering around Congressional deregulation of interstate trucking.
From The Advocates Series.
Prod-WGBHTV Dist-PUBTEL

Should Congress Pass Carter's Energy Program C 59 MIN
3/4 INCH VIDEO CASSETTE
Asks whether President Carter's energy bill should be approved. Features Morris Udall and Robert Kruger debating the issue.
From The Advocates Series.
Prod-WGBHTV Dist-PUBTEL

Should Congress Pass President Carter's Welfare/Jobs Bill C 56 MIN
3/4 INCH VIDEO CASSETTE
Presents Franklin Raines and John Kramer debating the question of the passage of President Carter's welfare/jobs bill.
From The Advocates Series.
Prod-WGBHTV Dist-PUBTEL

Should Congress Provide More Protection For Union Organizing C 59 MIN
3/4 OR 1/2 INCH VIDEO CASSETTE
From The Advocates Series.
Prod-WGBHTV Dist-PBS

Should I Believe It C 15 MIN
16MM FILM, 3/4 OR 1/2 IN VIDEO I

Tells how a student reporter judges the reliability of her sources in a story about two purple visitors from space.
From The Thinkabout Series. Judging Information
LC NO. 81-706122
Prod-EDFCEN Dist-AITECH 1979

Should I Retire Early? C 57 MIN
3/4 OR 1/2 INCH VIDEO CASSETTE
Designed to assist employees in making the decision to retire early, defer early retirement or continue working until normal retirement age.
Prod-DBMI Dist-DBMI

Should Journalists Have The Right To Protect Their Sources C 59 MIN
3/4 OR 1/2 INCH VIDEO CASSETTE
Discusses whether journalists have the right to protect their sources. Features Professor Charles Nesson as the pro advocate and Avi Nelson as the con advocate.
From The Advocates Series.
Prod-WGBHTV Dist-PBS

Should Oceans Meet C 30 MIN
16MM FILM, 3/4 OR 1/2 IN VIDEO
Shows how man's tampering with the oceans has had disasterous aftereffects.
From The Life Around Us Series.
LC NO. 79-707836
Prod-TIMLIF Dist-TIMLIF 1971

Should Oceans Meet (Spanish) C 30 MIN
16MM FILM OPTICAL SOUND
Presents a discussion by scientists on the potential ecological damage that may result from the excessive building of canals and dams.
From The Life Around Us (Spanish) Series.
LC NO. 78-700078
Prod-TIMLIF Dist-TIMLIF 1971

Should Old Acquaintance Be Forgot? C 30 MIN
3/4 OR 1/2 INCH VIDEO CASSETTE
Takes a hard look at society's plan for its elderly, the effects of retirement and a visit to KOPE (Keep Older People Employed).
Prod-WCCOTV Dist-WCCOTV 1981

Should Our Foreign Policy Include Covert Action By The CIA C 59 MIN
3/4 OR 1/2 INCH VIDEO CASSETTE
Presents attorneys Barney Frank and Margaret Marshall debating covert activities by the CIA.
From The Advocates Series.
Prod-WGBHTV Dist-PBS

Should Public Institutions Be Permitted To Give Preferential Treatment To Minorities In... C 58 MIN
3/4 OR 1/2 INCH VIDEO CASSETTE
Considers whether public institutions should be allowed to give preferential treatment to minorities in hiring and admissions. Features attorney Larry Tribe as the proponent and attorney Larry Lavinsky as the opponent.
From The Advocates Series.
Prod-WGBHTV Dist-PBS

Should Puerto Rico Be A Commonwealth, A State Or An Independent Nation C 59 MIN
3/4 INCH VIDEO CASSETTE
Presents Jaime Foster, Joachim Marquez and Fernando Martin debating whether Puerto Rico should be a commonwealth, a state or an independent nation.
From The Advocates Series.
Prod-WGBHTV Dist-PUBTEL

Should Second Class Citizens Give First Class Performances B 30 MIN
16MM FILM OPTICAL SOUND H-C A
Professor Robert Browne discusses black participation in the Korean War, the effect of the Mc Carthy hearings, the fight for justice in the armed forces and attitude of blacks toward the war.
From The Black History, Section 23 - Korea And Vietnam series.
LC NO. 70-704121
Prod-WCBSTV Dist-HRAW 1969

Should The Day Ever Come C 26 MIN
16MM FILM OPTICAL SOUND
Follows Coast Guard reservists as they develop and maintain the skills required to fulfill the missions imposed on the Reserve to meet mobilization assignments.
LC NO. 74-705637
Prod-USGS Dist-USNAC 1967

Should The Equal Rights Amendment Be Ratified C 59 MIN
3/4 OR 1/2 INCH VIDEO CASSETTE
Presents Laurence H Tribe and Jules Gerard debating the issue of the Equal Rights Amendment.
From The Advocates Series.
Prod-WGBHTV Dist-PBS

Should The Federal Government Give Tax Credits To Help Pay For School Tuition C 59 MIN
3/4 INCH VIDEO CASSETTE
Considers whether or not the federal government should give tax credits to help finance school tuition. Presents Antonin Scalia as the pro advocate and William Van Alstyne as the opponent.
From The Advocates Series.
Prod-WGBHTV Dist-PUBTEL

Should The Federal Government Reduce Everybody's Income Tax By 30 Percent Over... C 59 MIN
3/4 OR 1/2 INCH VIDEO CASSETTE
Asks whether the federal government should reduce income taxes by 30 percent over a three-year period. Features William Rusher as the pro advocate and Stephen I Schlossberg as the con advocate.
From The Advocates Series.
Prod-WGBHTV Dist-PBS

Should The Federal Trade Commission Ban Advertising On Children's Television C 59 MIN
3/4 INCH VIDEO CASSETTE
Features Nicholas Johnson and Ed Diamond debating the issue of advertising on children's television.
From The Advocates Series.
Prod-WGBHTV Dist-PUBTEL

Should The Senate Approve The SALT II Agreements C 59 MIN
3/4 OR 1/2 INCH VIDEO CASSETTE
Features Barney Frank and Avi Nelson debating Senate approval of the SALT II agreements.
From The Advocates Series.
Prod-WGBHTV Dist-PBS

Should The U S Reject Detente As Its Strategy In Dealing With The Soviet Union C 59 MIN
3/4 OR 1/2 INCH VIDEO CASSETTE
From The Advocates Series.
Prod-WGBHTV Dist-PBS

Should The United States Agree To United Nations Control Of Seabed Mining C 59 MIN
3/4 INCH VIDEO CASSETTE
Asks whether the United States should agree to UN control of seabed mining. Features pro advocate Randall Robinson and con advocate Lewis Crampton.
From The Advocates Series.
Prod-WGBHTV Dist-PUBTEL

Should The United States Break The Price-Setting Power Of OPEC C 59 MIN
3/4 INCH VIDEO CASSETTE
Features Avi Nelson and Margaret Marshall debating whether or not the United States should break OPEC's price-setting power.
From The Advocates Series.
Prod-WGBHTV Dist-PUBTEL

Should The United States Expand Its Nuclear Power Program C 59 MIN
3/4 INCH VIDEO CASSETTE
Presents Charles E Walker and Anthony Z Roisman debating the issue of nuclear power in the United States.
From The Advocates Series.
Prod-WGBHTV Dist-PUBTEL

Should The United States Support Self-Determination For Palestinians In A... C 59 MIN
3/4 INCH VIDEO CASSETTE
Presents Professor Fouad Ajami and attorney Morris Abram debating U S support of Palestinian self-determination in a Middle East peace settlement.
From The Advocates Series.
Prod-WGBHTV Dist-PUBTEL

Should There Be A Constitutional Convention Requiring A Balanced Federal Budget C 59 MIN
3/4 OR 1/2 INCH VIDEO CASSETTE
Presents Avi Nelson and Barney Frank debating the issue of a constitutional convention requiring a balanced budget.
From The Advocates Series.
Prod-WGBHTV Dist-PBS

Should U S Policy Discourage Investment In South Africa C 59 MIN
3/4 OR 1/2 INCH VIDEO CASSETTE
Presents Randall Robinson and Roger Fisher debating the issue of American investment in South Africa.
From The Advocates Series.
Prod-WGBHTV Dist-PBS

Should We C 30 MIN
3/4 OR 1/2 INCH VIDEO CASSETTE
See series title for descriptive statement.
From The Management For The '90s - Quality Circles Series.
Prod-TELSTR Dist-DELTAK

Should We Cut Back Veterans' Preference For State And Federal Jobs To Provide More... C 59 MIN
3/4 INCH VIDEO CASSETTE
Considers whether or not to cut back veterans' preference for state and federal jobs in order to provide more opportunity for women. Presents Margaret Marshall as the pro advocate and Avi Nelson as the con advocate.
From The Advocates Series.
Prod-WGBHTV Dist-PUBTEL

Should We Have Compulsory National Service For All Young Americans C 59 MIN
3/4 OR 1/2 INCH VIDEO CASSETTE
Presents Paul McCloskey and Lew Crampton debating the issue of compulsory national service in the United States.
From The Advocates Series.
Prod-WGBHTV Dist-PBS

Should We Impose Mandatory Controls On Wages And Prices To Stop Inflation C 59 MIN
3/4 INCH VIDEO CASSETTE
Focuses on mandatory controls on wages and prices to stop inflation. Features Margaret Marshall as the pro advocate and Avi Nelson as the con advocate.
From The Advocates Series.
Prod-WGBHTV Dist-PUBTEL

Should We Legalize Marijuana And/Or Cocaine C 59 MIN
3/4 OR 1/2 INCH VIDEO CASSETTE
Examines the pros and cons of legalizing marijuana and cocaine. Features debaters Margaret Marshall and William Rusher.
From The Advocates Series.
Prod-WGBHTV Dist-PBS

Should We Legislate Sexual Behavior? C 60 MIN
3/4 OR 1/2 INCH VIDEO CASSETTE
Discusses the topic of legislating sexual behavior. Concludes that no one should be discriminated against because of sexual preference in the areas of employment, housing and public accomodations.
Prod-UWISC Dist-UWISC 1980

Should We Stop Construction Of Nuclear Power Plants C 59 MIN
3/4 OR 1/2 INCH VIDEO CASSETTE
Features Anthony Roisman and Avi Nelson debating the issue of continued construction of nuclear power plants.
From The Advocates Series.
Prod-WGBHTV Dist-PBS

Should We Support The New Government Of Zimbabwe/Rhodesia C 59 MIN
3/4 INCH VIDEO CASSETTE
Presents Avi Nelson and Randall Robinson debating U S support of Zimbabwe.
From The Advocates Series.
Prod-WGBHTV Dist-PUBTEL

Should Your State Assume Financial Control Of Its Schools C 59 MIN
3/4 INCH VIDEO CASSETTE
Discusses whether states should assume financial control of schools. Presents Wendell Anderson as the pro advocate and Antonin Scalia as the con advocate.
From The Advocates Series.
Prod-WGBHTV Dist-PUBTEL

Should Your State Carry Out The Death Sentence C 59 MIN
3/4 OR 1/2 INCH VIDEO CASSETTE
Presents Margaret Marshall and Avi Nelson debating the death penalty.
From The Advocates Series.
Prod-WGBHTV Dist-PBS

Should Your State Require A Competency Test For High School Graduation C 59 MIN
3/4 INCH VIDEO CASSETTE
Presents Lewis Crampton and Renault A Robinson debating whether or not states should require competency tests for high school graduation.
From The Advocates Series.
Prod-WGBHTV Dist-PUBTEL

Should Your State Stop Prosecuting Juveniles For Status Offenses C 59 MIN
3/4 OR 1/2 INCH VIDEO CASSETTE
Considers whether states should stop prosecuting juveniles for status offenses. Presents Charles Nesson as the pro advocate and Margaret Marshall as the con advocate.
From The Advocates Series.
Prod-WGBHTV Dist-PBS

Shoulder And Arm Exercises For Baseball Players C 10 MIN
16MM FILM, 3/4 OR 1/2 IN VIDEO J-C A
Demonstrates exercises which strengthen and condition a rotator cuff and other shoulder muscles for baseball players.
Prod-ATHI Dist-ATHI 1982

Shoulder Arthoplasty C 13 MIN
3/4 OR 1/2 INCH VIDEO CASSETTE PRO
Shows shoulder arthoplasty.
Prod-WFP Dist-WFP

Shoulder Dysfunction C 10 MIN
3/4 OR 1/2 INCH VIDEO CASSETTE PRO
Discusses the functional anatomy of the shoulder, conditions which affect the shoulder, management of these conditions and differential diagnostic considerations.
Prod-UMICHM Dist-UMICHM 1977

Shoulder Joint C 12 MIN
3/4 OR 1/2 INCH VIDEO CASSETTE PRO
Enables the therapist to determine what range of motion of the shoulder a patient needs to increase. Part one of a three part series.
From The Upper Extremities Functional Range Of Motion Series.
Prod-HSCIC Dist-HSCIC

Shoulder Prosthesis For Four Part Fracture C 19 MIN
3/4 OR 1/2 INCH VIDEO CASSETTE PRO
See series title for descriptive statement.
From The Prothesis Films Series.
Prod-WFP Dist-WFP

Shoulder Prosthesis For 4-Part Fracture C 16 MIN
3/4 INCH VIDEO CASSETTE PRO
Shows surgical procedure, postoperative rehabilitation procedure and results of a case of 4-part fracture of the proximal humerus treated by prosthetic replacement of the humeral head.
Prod-MMAMC Dist-MMAMC

Shoulder Region, The C 11 MIN
16MM FILM, 3/4 OR 1/2 IN VIDEO C A
Demonstrates the dissection of the shoulder.
From The Guides To Dissection Series.
Prod-UCLA Dist-TEF

Shoulder Throw (Seoinage) B 3 MIN
16MM FILM OPTICAL SOUND
Demonstrates the shoulder throw in judo. Shows steps in maneuvering, setting up and executing a right- or left-shoulder throw.

From The Combative Measures - Judo Series.
LC NO. 75-700830
Prod-USAF Dist-USNAC 1955

Shoulder Wheel (Kataguruma) B 4 MIN
16MM FILM OPTICAL SOUND
Demonstrates the shoulder wheel in judo. Shows how to set up an opponent and follow through.
From The Combative Measures - Judo Series.
LC NO. 75-700829
Prod-USAF Dist-USNAC 1955

Shoulder, The C 32 MIN
3/4 OR 1/2 INCH VIDEO CASSETTE
Discusses the examination and treatment of the shoulder for arthritis, bursitis, tendonitis, infraspinatus and subscapularis.
From The Cyriax On Orthopaedic Medicine Series.
Prod-VTRI Dist-VTRI

Shout It Out Alphabet Film, The C 11 MIN
16MM FILM, 3/4 OR 1/2 IN VIDEO K-P T
A film game in which an audience of children tries to see how many words they can recognize by identifying the first letter in the collage of animated happenings on the screen.
Prod-CCVISA Dist-PHENIX 1969

Shout It Out Numbers, From One To Ten C 6 MIN
16MM FILM, 3/4 OR 1/2 IN VIDEO P-I
Uses animated geometric shapes and lively music to illustrate numbers from one through ten.
Prod-FILBUL Dist-PHENIX 1982

Shout Youngstown C 45 MIN
3/4 OR 1/2 INCH VIDEO CASSETTE A
Discusses the social and human implications of the closing of three major steel plants in Youngstown, Ohio. Covers 1976 to 1980
Prod-CNEMAG Dist-CNEMAG 1984

Shoutin' The Blues C 6 MIN
16MM FILM, 3/4 OR 1/2 IN VIDEO H-C A
Presents a solo portrait of blues harmonica player Sonny Terry.
Prod-AGINP Dist-AGINP

Shove Tuesday C 18 MIN
16MM FILM OPTICAL SOUND P-I
Relates that the Chiffy kids enter a pancake race in which the prize is a year's supply of groceries which they intend to give to a needy elderly lady. Explains that they need all their wits about them to win as one of their competitors is very tricky and determined to get the prize.
Prod-LUF Dist-LUF 1979

Show And Tell C 30 MIN
3/4 OR 1/2 INCH VIDEO CASSETTE A
Shows adult math students reviewing previous lessons and introduces them to the special mixed number pi.
From The Adult Math Series.
Prod-KYTV Dist-KYTV 1984

Show Biz - A Job Well Done C 12 MIN
16MM FILM, 3/4 OR 1/2 IN VIDEO P
Shows how a young boy turns a small part in the production of a class play into an important one and gains the satisfaction of a job well done.
Prod-CALLFM Dist-BARR 1975

Show Biz Is No Biz C 32 MIN
3/4 OR 1/2 INCH VIDEO CASSETTE
Describes the economics of producing, pricing, booking theatres and promoting plays.
From The Contemporary Issues In Marketing Series.
Prod-CANTOR Dist-IVCH

Show Business C 5 MIN
3/4 OR 1/2 INCH VIDEO CASSETTE J-H
Deals with varying sentence length in writing.
From The Write On, Set 2 Series.
Prod-CTI Dist-CTI

Show Business C 20 MIN
16MM FILM, 3/4 OR 1/2 IN VIDEO H-C A
Discusses how the communications industry is influenced by the same financial and political pressures experienced by other industrial conglomerates formed in society. Shows how these pressures can influence the range and content of messages selected for mass communication production.
From The Viewpoint Series.
Prod-THAMES Dist-MEDIAG 1975

Show Business, The C 24 MIN
3/4 OR 1/2 INCH VIDEO CASSETTE
Points out that the real purpose of a demonstration is to build a commitment to purchase the product.
Prod-VIDART Dist-VISUCP

Show Business, The - How To Demonstrate A Product C 23 MIN
3/4 OR 1/2 INCH VIDEO CASSETTE A
Using humor, shows how to successfully demonstrate a product. Emphasizes preparation, presentation and closing of the demonstration. Underlines the close connection between good demonstrations and sales.
Prod-XICOM Dist-XICOM

Show Handling C 30 MIN
3/4 OR 1/2 INCH VIDEO CASSETTE H-C A
Shows Barbara Woodhouse's method of handling show dogs.
From The Training Dogs The Woodhouse Way.
Prod-BBCTV Dist-FI 1982

Show Jumping World Cup C
3/4 OR 1/2 INCH VIDEO CASSETTE
Prod-MSTVIS Dist-MSTVIS

Show Me C 24 MIN
16MM FILM OPTICAL SOUND H-C A
Demonstrates the Timken Company's steelmaking capabilities, featuring its melting, strandcasting rolling, piercing, finishing, inspecting and shipping facilities.
Prod-TIMKEN Dist-TIMKEN

Show Me C 15 MIN
2 INCH VIDEOTAPE J
Shows a fifth way of developing a topic sentence by evidence or specific information.
From The From Me To You...In Writing, Pt 2 Series.
Prod-DELE Dist-GPITVL

Show You Know It C 11 MIN
16MM FILM - 3/4 IN VIDEO
Reminds workers to obey all safety rules both on and off the job.
Prod-ALLIED Dist-BNA

Showdown B 13 MIN
16MM FILM - 3/4 IN VIDEO
Describes the relationship between a new young supervisor and his problem with employees. Includes comments by co-workers and the supervisor's boss.
Prod-USPHS Dist-USNAC 1972

Showdown At Sweet Rock Gulch C 13 MIN
16MM FILM, 3/4 OR 1/2 IN VIDEO P-I
Utilizes a western background as two children fight off The Bad Health Gang with the aid of the town dentist. Shows flossing and brushing techniques.
Prod-AMDA Dist-AMDA 1973

Showdown At The Hoedown C 60 MIN
16MM FILM - 3/4 IN VIDEO
Represents performances at the Smithville, Tennesse, Fiddler's Jamboree. Suggests the living appeal that's at the heart of all music festivals.
Prod-SOFOLK Dist-SOFOLK

Shower Song, The C 12 MIN
16MM FILM OPTICAL SOUND
Illustrates the systematic training procedures of the showering program, a concise program designed to assist instructors in teaching proper showering to slow learning and mentally retarded children.
Prod-UKANS Dist-UKANS 1972

Showing initiative C 10 MIN
3/4 OR 1/2 INCH VIDEO CASSETTE H-C A
Shows how to ask relevant questions of job interviewer. Stresses importance of background information about company and job.
From The Young Job Seekers Series.
Prod-SEVDIM Dist-SEVDIM

Showmanship C 30 MIN
16MM FILM, 3/4 OR 1/2 IN VIDEO
Covers grooming and preparation of the horse and exhibitor as well as many do's and don'ts regarding showmanship rules and class routine.
Prod-AQHORS Dist-AQHORS 1979

Showmanship At Halter C 16 MIN
1/2 IN VIDEO CASSETTE BETA/VHS
Instructs how to show at halter. Includes basic rules, conditioning and grooming techniques, control and style.
Prod-AMSDHA Dist-EQVDL

Showroom To The World C 6 MIN
16MM FILM, 3/4 OR 1/2 IN VIDEO
Explains what a U S Trade Center is and what it does. Shows centers in New York, Paris, and Stockholm and tells how one company had success in utilizing this marketing service.
From The Export Development Series.
LC NO. 80-706628
Prod-USIATA Dist-USNAC Prodn-HEARST 1980

Showtime For Saddlebreds C 14 MIN
1/2 IN VIDEO CASSETTE BETA/VHS
Gives accounts of saddlebreds, including Bellissima and My My.
Prod-AMSDHA Dist-EQVDL

Shrimp Please C 21 MIN
16MM FILM OPTICAL SOUND
Shows methods used by the Louisiana and Mississippi shrimp industry in catching and processing shrimp. Includes freezing, breeding, drying and canning. Describes how to purchase, prepare and serve shrimp.
Prod-USBCF Dist-USNOAA 1954

Shrimp Tips From New Orleans C 14 MIN
16MM FILM OPTICAL SOUND
Describes New Orleans' reputation for cookery, and shows the preparation of six recipes using shrimp.
Prod-USBCF Dist-USNOAA 1956

Shrimps For A Day B 19 MIN
16MM FILM OPTICAL SOUND
Features the Little Rascals in a story about a young couple whose encounter with a magic lamp allows them to become children again.
Prod-UNKNWN Dist-BHAWK 1934

Shringar C 29 MIN
16MM FILM OPTICAL SOUND I-C A
Explains that Indian women through the centuries have been famous for their coiffeurs, as can be seen in the frescoes of Ajanta and the sculptures of Konarak and Khajuraho. Surveys the varied hair-styles from ancient times to the present.
Prod-INDIA Dist-NEDINF

Shrink Or Swim/In-Store Theft C 8 MIN
3/4 OR 1/2 INCH VIDEO CASSETTE
Focuses on shoplifting and how to prevent it. Presents cartoon sequences that leave indelible images of shoplifter's characteristic clothing, behavior and techniques. Stresses involvement in the prevention program by security people.
From The Retail Sales Power Series.
Prod-PRODEV Dist-PRODEV

Shrinking Dollar, The C 30 MIN
3/4 OR 1/2 INCH VIDEO CASSETTE
Investigates the causes of inflation. Stresses the difference between anticipated and unanticipated inflation. Discusses the relationship between inflation and increased income taxes.
From The Money Puzzle - The World Of Macroeconomics Series. Module 10
Prod-MDCC Dist-MDCC

Shrubs And Vines C 30 MIN
3/4 OR 1/2 INCH VIDEO CASSETTE C A
Focuses on how to buy and plant shrubs that are appropriate for the home garden. Demonstrates planting process.
From The Home Gardener With John Lenanton Series. Lesson 16
Prod-COAST Dist-CDTEL

Shucking Clams C
3/4 OR 1/2 INCH VIDEO CASSETTE
Prod-CULINA Dist-CULINA

Shucking Oysters C
3/4 OR 1/2 INCH VIDEO CASSETTE
Prod-CULINA Dist-CULINA

Shuk Day C 15 MIN
3/4 OR 1/2 INCH VIDEO CASSETTE I
Shows market day among Bedouin nomads.
From The Encounter In The Desert Series.
Prod-CTI Dist-CTI

Shunka's Story C 20 MIN
16MM FILM, 3/4 OR 1/2 IN VIDEO
Offers a portrait of a Tzotzil Maya woman of Zinacantan in Chiapas, Mexico, conveying her thoughts and feelings about her life, her culture and her children.
Prod-KREBS Dist-UCEMC 1977

Shunt Hartley Oscillator - VT B 28 MIN
16MM FILM, 3/4 OR 1/2 IN VIDEO
Shows the Shunt Hartley oscillator circuit, pointing out identifying features and explaining the purpose of each component. Shows its use in high power circuits and how to troubleshoot it.
Prod-USAF Dist-USNAC

Shutdown Rules For Variability And The Mean C 20 MIN
3/4 OR 1/2 INCH VIDEO CASSETTE IND
Develops shutdown rules for the variance using the chi-square distribution, and for the mean when sigma is not known using the t distribution. Discusses effect of changing sample size.
From The Statistics For Technicians Series.
Prod-COLOSU Dist-COLOSU

Shuttle To Tomorrow C 11 MIN
16MM FILM OPTICAL SOUND A
Explains the role of the space shuttle, with emphasis on the responsibility of the Marshall Space Flight Center in providing space shuttle engines and the solid rocket booster. Includes a profile of a shuttle mission.
LC NO. 76-704010
Prod-USMSFC Dist-USNAC 1976

Shy, Withdrawn And Bashful C 10 MIN
16MM FILM OPTICAL SOUND P-I
Features George Jammal and several children demonstrating in various ways shyness, withdrawal and bashfulness.
From The Psychology - The Emotions Series.
LC NO. 74-700307
Prod-SUMHIL Dist-SUMHIL 1974

Si No Es Demasiado Tarde C 9 MIN
16MM FILM, 3/4 OR 1/2 IN VIDEO IND
A Spanish-language version of the motion picture If It's Not Too Late. Shows how safety control has evolved from injury prevention to loss control management. Identifies some of the causes of incidents which may result in accidents and injury as well as loss of efficiency.
Prod-IAPA Dist-IFB 1974

Si Pitagoras No Miente C 14 MIN
16MM FILM, 3/4 OR 1/2 IN VIDEO J-H
A Spanish language version of the videocassette Possibly So, Pythagoras. Investigates the Pythagorean theorem through induction as well as through formal deductive proof.
Prod-IFB Dist-IFB 1963

Si Podemos (Yes, We Can) C 22 MIN
16MM FILM OPTICAL SOUND
Demonstrates to slum and semi-slum residents of Latin American cities what can be done to improve their lives through self-help projects.
LC NO. 77-702867
Prod-USAID Dist-HF Prodn-HF 1967

Si Quiero...But Not Now C 20 MIN
16MM FILM, 3/4 OR 1/2 IN VIDEO
Focuses on a young Spanish-American couple and the conflict of the traditional views on family planning versus their own needs. Shows how they finally receive help from a family planning clinic.
Prod-PPFRES Dist-USNAC Prodn-PAGRPH 1978

Siamese Fighting Fish C 17 MIN
3/4 INCH VIDEO CASSETTE
Examines features of agressive behavior in animals. Uses a series of balsa wood models then real fish in an aquarium with

Betta fighting fish to demonstrate the consistency of aggressive behavior patterns in these fish.
Prod-UMITV Dist-UMITV 1976

Siberia C
3/4 OR 1/2 INCH VIDEO CASSETTE
From The Antartica Series.
Prod-EAI Dist-EAI

Siberia C 25 MIN
16MM FILM, 3/4 OR 1/2 IN VIDEO
Features a journey to Siberia and shows the geography, history and people of this immense land.
LC NO. 80-706320
Prod-NGS Dist-NGS 1977

Siberia - The Endless Horizon C 51 MIN
16MM FILM, 3/4 OR 1/2 IN VIDEO I-C A
Shows the struggle for survival in 90 degrees below temperature, the battle with perma frost and the culture and entertainment of the 'REINDEER PEOPLE.' Visits the Yakee tribesmen and the towns of Irkutsk, Akademgorodak and Bratsk. Stresses the importance of the Trans-Siberian Railroad for communications and supplies to remote villages.
LC NO. 80-706388
Prod-NGS Dist-NGS 1969

Siberiade (Russian) C 210 MIN
16MM FILM OPTICAL SOUND H-C A
Offers an epic romantic drama about three generations of two feuding families, the rich Solomins and the poor Ustyuzhanins, from the time of the Russian Revolution to the present-day exploration of hidden resources in Siberian soil.
LC NO. 82-700446
Prod-MOSFLM Dist-IFEX 1982

Siblings C 10 MIN
3/4 OR 1/2 INCH VIDEO CASSETTE
Explores the subject of siblings, with Fred Rogers.
From The You (Parents) Are Special Series.
Prod-FAMCOM Dist-FAMCOM

Siblings As Behavior Modifiers C 25 MIN
16MM FILM, 3/4 OR 1/2 IN VIDEO C A
Tells the story of a mentally retarded child whose family chose to keep him at home rather than in an institution. Shows how each sibling was confronted with a different problem and how each was rewarded by their brother's positive responses to their efforts with him.
Prod-MEDIAG Dist-MEDIAG 1976

Siblings Of Children With Cancer C 30 MIN
3/4 OR 1/2 INCH VIDEO CASSETTE PRO
Presents siblings of young cancer patients discussing their experience and the effect the illness has had on the relationship between siblings.
Prod-UARIZ Dist-UARIZ

Sicily - The Yanks Are Coming C 30 MIN
3/4 OR 1/2 INCH VIDEO CASSETTE H-C A
See series title for descriptive statement.
From The World War II - GI Diary Series.
Prod-TIMLIF Dist-TIMLIF 1980

Sick Call - Introduction To Sick Call Techniques C 26 MIN
16MM FILM OPTICAL SOUND
Trains the inexperienced hospital corpsman to conduct sick call by acquainting him with the proper attitudes and procedures.
LC NO. 74-705641
Prod-USN Dist-USNAC 1970

Sick Call - Skin Diseases C 34 MIN
16MM FILM OPTICAL SOUND
Shows various skin conditions which most frequently confront the hospital corpsman. Tells how to distinguish between cases to treat and ones to refer to the medical officer.
LC NO. 74-706579
Prod-USN Dist-USNAC 1970

Sickle Cell Anaemia C 28 MIN
16MM FILM, 3/4 OR 1/2 IN VIDEO J-C A
Deals with sickle cell anaemia both on a scientific and a human level. Uses microphotography to show the transformation of a normal-looking cell into a sickle cell and the damage that clusters of sickle cells cause in the circulatory system. Presents conversations with the Williams family, who have six children, three of whom are severely affected.
LC NO. 82-706991
Prod-CANBC Dist-FLMLIB 1981

Sickle Cell Anemia C 29 MIN
3/4 OR 1/2 INCH VIDEO CASSETTE
Examines various aspects of sickle cell anemia, a disease of the blood which affects members of the black population.
From The Daniel Foster, MD Series.
Prod-KERA Dist-PBS

Sickle Cell Anemia And Other Genetic Disorders Probed C 13 MIN
16MM FILM OPTICAL SOUND
Discusses such genetic disorders as sickle cell anemia, muscular dystrophy, hemophilia and some types of mental illness.
Prod-ALLFP Dist-NSTA 1979

Sickle Cell Story C
3/4 OR 1/2 INCH VIDEO CASSETTE
Discusses hemoglobin screening, prenatal diagnosis and current research and development of medication to prevent the occurrence of sickle cell anemia.
Prod-MIFE Dist-MIFE

Sickle Cell Story (Arabic) C
3/4 OR 1/2 INCH VIDEO CASSETTE
Discusses hemoglobin screening, prenatal diagnosis and current research and development of medication to prevent the occurrence of sickle cell anemia.
Prod-MIFE Dist-MIFE

Sickle Cell Story (Spanish) C
3/4 OR 1/2 INCH VIDEO CASSETTE
Discusses hemoglobin screening, prenatal diagnosis and current research and development of medication to prevent the occurrence of sickle cell anemia.
Prod-MIFE Dist-MIFE

Sickle-Cell Anemia C 18 MIN
16MM FILM OPTICAL SOUND J-C A
Explains that Puerto Ricans, Latin Americans, Greeks, Italians, Indians from Mediterranean areas and people of African descent are all affected by sickle-cell anemia. Describes the disease and its effects.
LC NO. 72-702930
Prod-LEECC Dist-LEECC 1972

Siddhartha C 86 MIN
16MM FILM OPTICAL SOUND
Offers an adaptation of Herman Hesse's novel SIDDHARTHA.
Prod-CPC Dist-TWYMAN 1973

Side Abdominals C 29 MIN
2 INCH VIDEOTAPE
See series title for descriptive statement.
From The Maggie And The Beautiful Machine - Bellies Series.
Prod-WGBHTV Dist-PUBTEL

Side By Side - Prejudice C 15 MIN
16MM FILM, 3/4 OR 1/2 IN VIDEO J-H
Tells how Nancy, a Chinese-American girl, learns that she will be excluded from a country club party planned by her best friend. Shows how both girls must reconsider what their friendship means.
From The On The Level Series.
LC NO. 81-706941
Prod-EDFCEN Dist-AITECH 1980

Side Frames - Subassembly Of A Web Frame B 17 MIN
16MM FILM OPTICAL SOUND
Shows how to lay out the main web plate from a template, fit stiffeners to the web plate and dog the stiffeners to the plate for welding.
From The Shipbuilding Skills Series. Work Of Shipfitter And Shipwright, No. 4
LC NO. FIE52-192
Prod-USOE Dist-USNAC 1942

Side-To-Side Portacaval Anastomosis For Portal Hypertension C 24 MIN
16MM FILM OPTICAL SOUND PRO
Demonstrates the exposure, the approximation, and suture of the portal vein and inferior vena cava by the side-to-side technique.
Prod-ACYDGD Dist-ACY 1958

Side-To-Side Portacaval Shunts C 26 MIN
16MM FILM OPTICAL SOUND PRO
Presents a general discussion of both commonly used shunts and less frequently used shunts between the portal and systemic venous systems. Makes particular reference to the hemodynamics of these shunts.
Prod-ACYDGD Dist-ACY 1959

Sidehorse And Vaulting C 17 MIN
16MM FILM, 3/4 OR 1/2 IN VIDEO J-C
Demonstrates basic sidehorse vaulting and support work. Gives attention to teaching techniques, progressions and methods of spotting performers.
Prod-AIMS Dist-AIMS 1971

Sidehorse And Vaulting (Arabic) C 17 MIN
16MM FILM, 3/4 OR 1/2 IN VIDEO I-C
Demonstrates basic sidehorse vaulting and support work, with attention to teaching techniques, progressions and spotting performers.
Prod-ASSOCF Dist-AIMS 1974

Sidehorse And Vaulting (Spanish) C 17 MIN
16MM FILM, 3/4 OR 1/2 IN VIDEO I-C
Demonstrates basic sidehorse vaulting and support work, with attention to teaching techniques, progressions and spotting performers.
Prod-ASSOCF Dist-AIMS 1974

Sideshow, The C 9 MIN
16MM FILM, 3/4 OR 1/2 IN VIDEO J-C
Features Marcel Marceau performing a pantomime showing circus performers demonstrating their skills. Includes a juggler, an acrobat, clowns pulling ropes without ropes and a tightrope walker as the major performer.
From The Humanities - The Performing Arts, Art Of Silence, Pantomimes With Marcel Marceau Series.
Prod-EBEC Dist-EBEC 1975

Sidewalks And Similes C 14 MIN
16MM FILM, 3/4 OR 1/2 IN VIDEO P-I
Shows how inspiration for children's poetry can be found in common objects in the city, such as traffic signals, street lights and fire escapes.
Prod-CWRU Dist-AIMS 1973

Sidewalks Of Shade C 25 MIN
16MM FILM - 3/4 IN VIDEO J-C A
Takes a trip to the northeastern part of the United States in order to see successful neighborhood and community tree-planting programs. Deals with community organization, funding, maintenance and information about working with utility companies.
LC NO. 81-707038
Prod-NYSTAL Dist-CUNIV 1981

Sidney's Family Tree C 6 MIN
16MM FILM, 3/4 OR 1/2 IN VIDEO P
Presents the story of an elephant who is adopted by monkeys. Relates what happens when he takes a bride and the two elephants decide to live in a tree.
Prod-SF Dist-SF 1975

Sie Haben Die Prufung Bestanden C 15 MIN
16MM FILM, 3/4 OR 1/2 IN VIDEO
See series title for descriptive statement.
From The Guten Tag Series. Part 26
Prod-BAYER Dist-IFB 1968

Sieg Im Westen B 120 MIN
3/4 OR 1/2 INCH VIDEO CASSETTE
Presents a propaganda pageant shown to the German people after one of history's greatest victories by German force of arms, the Nazis' six-week invasion of Holland, Belgium and France in spring of 1940.
Prod-IHF Dist-IHF

Siege B 10 MIN
16MM FILM, 3/4 OR 1/2 IN VIDEO J-C A
Describes the frightening chain of events in Poland in September, 1939 that triggered World War II and finally resulted in the capitulation of Warsaw and Poland. Shows the early stages of the Blitzkreig, and how civilians were commanded to dig ditches, set tank traps and shore up fortifications. Illustrates the bombing and shelling of Warsaw, including hospitals and churches, and aerial machine-gunning of women digging potatoes in the field to feed their hungry families.
Prod-BRYAN Dist-IFF 1974

Siege At Powderham Castle C 25 MIN
3/4 OR 1/2 INCH VIDEO CASSETTE
Records the annual re-enactment of a 16th century British battle, capturing the customs, dress and flavor of the day. Explains the role of women in battle.
Prod-UPI Dist-JOU

Siege Of Fort Stanwix C 20 MIN
16MM FILM - 3/4 IN VIDEO
Dramatizes the 22-day siege at Fort Stanwix, New York, by the British and depicts the final surrender of General Burgoyne at Saratoga in 1777. Highlights a critical time when a British victory might have been a deathblow to the fight for American independence.
LC NO. 79-706159
Prod-USNPS Dist-USNAC 1979

Siege Of The Alamo, The C 21 MIN
16MM FILM, 3/4 OR 1/2 IN VIDEO I-J
Recounts the events leading to the Battle of the Alamo, portrays the defeat of the Texans at the Alamo, and covers the subsequent defeat of the Mexicans by Sam Houston.
From The You Are There Series.
Prod-CBSNEW Dist-PHENIX 1971

Siegfried C 253 MIN
3/4 OR 1/2 INCH VIDEO CASSETTE
See series title for descriptive statement.
From The Wagner Ring Cycle Series.
Prod-FOTH Dist-FOTH

Siena C 22 MIN
16MM FILM OPTICAL SOUND
Shows views of the palaces, piazzas and public buildings of Siena in the light of artistic style and social history, including the font in the baptistry and its sculptured panels by Donatello and Jacopo Della Quercia, filmed in Italy.
From The Treasures Of Tuscany Series.
LC NO. FIA66-1359
Prod-WESTCB Dist-RADIM 1965

SIER C 30 MIN
3/4 OR 1/2 INCH VIDEO CASSETTE
Focuses on sending, interpreting, evaluating and responding in personal communication.
From The Effective Listening Series. Tape 4
Prod-TELSTR Dist-TELSTR

SIER Formula, The C 30 MIN
3/4 OR 1/2 INCH VIDEO CASSETTE
See series title for descriptive statement.
From The Effective Listening Series.
Prod-TELSTR Dist-DELTAK

Sierpinksi's Curve Fills Space C 5 MIN
16MM FILM, 3/4 OR 1/2 IN VIDEO
See series title for descriptive statement.
From The Topology Short Films Series.
LC NO. 81-706248
Prod-NSF Dist-IFB 1979

Sierra Railroad C 27 MIN
1/2 IN VIDEO CASSETTE BETA/VHS
Features the Sierra Railroad of Jamestown, California, which supplies steam locomotives for Hollywood movie productions. Shows several steam engines performing routines.
Prod-DELUZ Dist-DELUZ 1979

Sifted Gold C 30 MIN
16MM FILM OPTICAL SOUND H-C A
Tells the story of a woman who contracts a fatal disease and is unable to tell anyone about it. Shows how, after her recovery, she relates her feelings and tells of her belief that God was by her side during the ordeal.
LC NO. 75-704231
Prod-CPH Dist-CPH 1975

Siga Las Instrucciones (Follow The Directions) - Program Number 2 C 20 MIN
3/4 OR 1/2 INCH VIDEO CASSETTE PRO
Includes colors, directions and prepositional phrases in Spanish.

Gives tips on taking control of the conversation to keep it at your level of understanding.
From The Spanish For Health Professionals Series.
Prod-HSCIC Dist-HSCIC 1982

Sigaalow - Town Of Dust C 22 MIN
16MM FILM, 3/4 OR 1/2 IN VIDEO H-C A
Examines the daily routine of the people of Sigaalow, a refugee camp on the banks of a muddy river in East Africa. Includes their farming methods, educational system and cultural practices. Discusses the problems they face as a result of their crowded, sedentary lifestyle. Produced in Switzerland in 1974.
Prod-CRMP Dist-CRMP 1983

Sight - Visual System C 18 MIN
16MM FILM, 3/4 OR 1/2 IN VIDEO PRO
See series title for descriptive statement.
From The Anatomical Basis Of Brain Function Series.
Prod-AVCORP Dist-TEF

Sight For A Lifetime C 20 MIN
16MM FILM OPTICAL SOUND H A
Dramatizes the total prevention of blindness program in order to help recruit community leadership in the development of the program and to enlist the aid of public health agencies and community organizations for support of programs in preventing blindness.
Prod-NSPB Dist-NSPB 1963

Sight Of Sound, The C 29 MIN
2 INCH VIDEOTAPE
See series title for descriptive statement.
From The Museum Open House Series.
Prod-WGBHTV Dist-PUBTEL

Sight Reading And Playing C 29 MIN
2 INCH VIDEOTAPE
See series title for descriptive statement.
From The Playing The Guitar I Series.
Prod-KCET Dist-PUBTEL

Sight Reading In Two Parts C 29 MIN
2 INCH VIDEOTAPE
See series title for descriptive statement.
From The Playing The Guitar II Series.
Prod-KCET Dist-PUBTEL

Sight Restoration - Miracles In The Making C 15 MIN
16MM FILM OPTICAL SOUND
Looks at the operation of Lions Club's eye banks. Views an actual cornea transplant and presents transplant recipients who tell how their lives have been changed by the operation.
Prod-MTP Dist-MTP

Sight Restoration - Miracles In The Making C 27 MIN
3/4 INCH VIDEO CASSETTE
Shows how thousands of people have had their sight restored as a result of eye banks and optic surgery. Documents an actual cornea transplant operation. Close-captioned.
Prod-IALC Dist-MTP

Sight Through Sound B 19 MIN
16MM FILM OPTICAL SOUND
Presents a study of a young engineering student who is shown working on the problem of devising a method, for use by the blind, through which they can hear their world. Explains the device, and allows us to hear the sound patterns which the 'SEEING' device produces. Shows the young inventor trying to act blind so as to learn the problems, and see and hear the device he develops.
Prod-UPENN Dist-UPENN 1969

Sigmund Freud - His Offices And Home, Vienna, 1938 C 17 MIN
16MM FILM OPTICAL SOUND
Uses contemporary photographs to show the interior of Freud's home in Vienna in 1938. Explores the political situation in Nazi Vienna and shows why Freud left his home to flee to London.
LC NO. 75-700367
Prod-FRIEDG Dist-FLMLIB 1974

Sign Here C 19 MIN
3/4 OR 1/2 INCH VIDEO CASSETTE J-H
Considers various types of contracts, contracts and minors, implications of reaching the age of majority, credit and commercial employment contracts, wage garnishment and the marriage contract.
From The Rights And Responsibilities Series.
Prod-WHROTV Dist-AITECH 1975

Sign Language - Exact English C 110 MIN
1/2 IN VIDEO CASSETTE BETA/VHS
Guides parents whose children are learning to sign Exact English at school. Shows vocabulary of 480 signs and practice sentences.
Prod-VIPRO Dist-VIPRO

Sign Language - The Language Of Life C 16 MIN
16MM FILM, 3/4 OR 1/2 IN VIDEO H-C A
Looks at the development of sign language for the deaf, from its earliest forms when it was used to convey basic needs to a complex form capable of expressing emotions and conveying creative thought.
Prod-JOU Dist-JOU 1981

Sign Language - The Language Of Life (Captioned) C 16 MIN
16MM FILM, 3/4 OR 1/2 IN VIDEO S
Traces development of sign language - from its earliest forms used to convey basic needs, to today's sophisticated language capable of expressing emotions and conveying creative thought.
Prod-GALCO Dist-GALCO 1981

Sign Language Alphabet, The C 15 MIN
16MM FILM OPTICAL SOUND I-C A S
Shows the American manual alphabet. Includes practice sentences which demonstrate how to form the letters with the hands and how to read the letters from another person's hands.
From The Quick Flicks Series.
LC NO. 75-700659
Prod-JOYCE Dist-JOYCE 1975

Sign Language And English C 8 MIN
16MM FILM SILENT I-H A S
Advocates the teaching of sign language in an academic setting to improve a deaf student's ability to read English. Points to comparisons of minority groups being taught in their own language when that language is related to English. Performed in American sign language by Herb Larson.
LC NO. 76-701703
Prod-JOYCE Dist-JOYCE 1975

Sign Language Practice - Paragraphs—A Series
S
Presents educational series of more than 200 practice paragraph tests. Consists of 45 videotapes and 209 answer sheets. Total time is 2,700 min. Twenty minute preview videocassette available on loan. Signed.
Prod-GALCO Dist-GALCO 1979

Sign Language Practice - Sentences—A Series
S
Presents educational series of 200 sign language practice tests. Consists of 51 videotapes and 200 answer sheets. Total time is 3,060 minutes. Twenty minute preview videocassette available on loan. Signed.
Prod-GALCO Dist-GALCO 1979

Sign Me Ivan - Elementary Russian Signs (Captioned)—A Series

Consists of 13 lessons to be used in conjunction with a computer-assisted course in the Russian language.
Prod-GALCO Dist-GALCO 1976

Sign Of The First Derivative C
3/4 INCH VIDEO CASSETTE
See series title for descriptive statement.
From The Calculus Series.
Prod-MDDE Dist-MDCPB

Sign Of Victory C 22 MIN
16MM FILM, 3/4 OR 1/2 IN VIDEO H-C A
Presents a championship high school basketball team where all the girls are deaf. Shows how these girls have overcome the isolation of their handicap by competing in the world of sports. Narrated by Al McGuire and filmed at the Rhode Island School for the Deaf.
Prod-FLMLIB Dist-FLMLIB 1982

Sign Off C 3 MIN
3/4 OR 1/2 INCH VIDEO CASSETTE
Presents apocalyptic, anti-military symbols to the Jimi Hendrix' performance of the Star Spangled Banner. Produced as the concluding segment for the Night Flight show on the USA Cable Network.
Prod-KITCHN Dist-KITCHN

Sign On - Sign Off C 24 MIN
16MM FILM OPTICAL SOUND C
A non-technical introduction to computer-assistedinstruction (CAI.) Examines the tutorial method of instruction in the classroom and at the computer terminal. Uses simple animation to show the operation of computer-assisted-instuction systems.
LC NO. FIA68-2700
Prod-PSUPCR Dist-PSUPCR 1967

Signal Conditioning For Digital Circuits C 59 MIN
3/4 OR 1/2 INCH VIDEO CASSETTE PRO
See series title for descriptive statement.
From The Digital Electronics Series.
Prod-MIOT Dist-MIOT

Signal Generator Operation B 9 MIN
16MM FILM, 3/4 OR 1/2 IN VIDEO
Shows how to use a signal generator to align a radio receiver. Issued in 1945 as a motion picture.
From The Radio Technician Training Series.
LC NO. 78-706301
Prod-USN Dist-USNAC Prodn-HOLMES 1978

Signal Processing And Control C 30 MIN
3/4 OR 1/2 INCH VIDEO CASSETTE IND
Shows how microprocessors do complicated tasks by linearizing a thermocouple. Describes digital control algorithms with low-pass filter example. Tells how proportion-al-integral-derivative control algorithms are employed in position-independent and modular structured code.
From The 6809 Interface Programming Series.
Prod-COLOSU Dist-COLOSU

Signal Syntax C 8 MIN
3/4 OR 1/2 INCH VIDEO CASSETTE H-C A
Presents comedy by the Brave New World Workshop of the Twin Cities.
Prod-JDR Dist-UCV

Signaler / Forward Lunge And Bend / Siam Squat C 15 MIN
3/4 OR 1/2 INCH VIDEO CASSETTE P
Presents several exercises which can be performed in a classroom setting.
From The Roomnastics Series.
Prod-WVIZTV Dist-GPITVL 1979

Signaling And Modulation C 30 MIN
3/4 OR 1/2 INCH VIDEO CASSETTE
See series title for descriptive statement.
From The Telecommunications And The Computer Series.
Prod-MIOT Dist-MIOT

Signalling And Modulation C 45 MIN
3/4 OR 1/2 INCH VIDEO CASSETTE C
Tells about modulation types with sine wave carrier, including amplitude modulation (AM), frequency modulation (FM), phase modulation (PM), information transfer rate, multistate signalling, Nyguists' theorem, modems and other types of modulation including pulse amplitude modulation (PAM) and pulse code modulation (PCM).
From The Telecommunications And The Computer Series.
LC NO. 81-707502
Prod-AMCEE Dist-AMCEE 1981

Signals C 3 MIN
16MM FILM OPTICAL SOUND H-C A
Emphasizes the life-saving potential of cancer's warning signals.
Prod-AMCS Dist-AMCS

Signals - Read 'Em Or Weep C 20 MIN
16MM FILM OPTICAL SOUND IND
Depicts a number of unnecessary and fairly common damage-causing situations involving construction equipment. Emphasizes the need for observing maintenance and operating instructions in order to help reduce damage to equipment.
LC NO. 82-700260
Prod-CTRACT Dist-MTP Prodn-CENTEF 1982

Signals For Survival C 51 MIN
16MM FILM, 3/4 OR 1/2 IN VIDEO H-C
Shows the various types of signals and language gulls use in communicating with each other. Includes behavioral aspects such as territoriality, aggression, courtship and mating, alarm signals and flight.
Prod-TINBGN Dist-MGHT 1970

Signals For Survival, Pt 1 C 21 MIN
16MM FILM, 3/4 OR 1/2 IN VIDEO H-C
Shows the various types of signals and language gulls use in communicating with each other. Includes behavioral aspects such as territoriality, aggression, courtship and mating, alarm signals and flight.
Prod-TINBGN Dist-MGHT 1970

Signals For Survival, Pt 2 C 30 MIN
16MM FILM, 3/4 OR 1/2 IN VIDEO H-C
Shows the various types of signals and language gulls use in communicating with each other. Includes behavioral aspects such as territoriality, aggression, courtship and mating, alarm signals and flight.
Prod-TINBGN Dist-MGHT 1970

Signals Of Change - The Junior High Child C
3/4 OR 1/2 INCH VIDEO CASSETTE A
Helps parents understand and deal with teenage development.
From The Vital Link Series.
Prod-EDCC Dist-EDCC

Signals Of Change - The Senior High Child C
3/4 OR 1/2 INCH VIDEO CASSETTE A
Helps parents understand and deal with teenage development.
From The Vital Link Series.
Prod-EDCC Dist-EDCC

Signatures Of The Soul C 59 MIN
3/4 OR 1/2 INCH VIDEO CASSETTE
Shows some of the most spectacular contemporary tattooing in the world. Introduces the artists who practice this most hidden of art forms.
Prod-FLMLIB Dist-FLMLIB 1984

Signed By A Woman C 60 MIN
3/4 INCH VIDEO CASSETTE
Attempts to define important issues in women's art and is a significant presentation on the power and skill of women artists today.
Prod-WMENIF Dist-WMENIF

Signed, Sealed And Delivered C 10 MIN
16MM FILM OPTICAL SOUND A
Points out the fact that cargo loss is a major problem in the United States and has a widespread effect.
From The Cargo Security Series.
LC NO. 78-700820
Prod-USDT Dist-USNAC Prodn-TILMON 1978

Signed, Sealed And Delivered - Labor Struggle In The Post Office C 40 MIN
3/4 OR 1/2 INCH VIDEO CASSETTE
Depicts working conditions and a wildcat strike among postal workers, following their struggle to the floor of the American Postal Workers' Union National Convention. Portrays the death of a mailhandler who was crushed to death by postal machinery as the event bringing their struggle to national attention.
Prod-DCTVC Dist-DCTVC

Signed, Sealed, And Delivered - Labor Struggle In The Post Office C 40 MIN
3/4 OR 1/2 INCH VIDEO CASSETTE H A
Deals with labor struggle within the American Postal Workers Union, providing observations of the often violent, always intense struggles of the union member for improved job conditions.
LC NO. 80-707700
Prod-TAMERP Dist-TAMERP 1980

Significance Of Malcolm X, The B 30 MIN
16MM FILM OPTICAL SOUND H-C A
Dr C Eric Lincoln discusses the life and career of the black revolu-

tionary leader Malcolm X and explains the impact of his message.
From The Black History, Section 21 - Protest And Rebellion Series.
LC NO. 78-704115
Prod-WCBSTV Dist-HRAW 1969

Significance Of The Second Derivative C
3/4 INCH VIDEO CASSETTE
See series title for descriptive statement.
From The Calculus Series.
Prod-MDDE Dist-MDCPB

Significance Testing B
16MM FILM OPTICAL SOUND
Introduces the idea of significance testing as applied to a simple industrial problem.
Prod-OPENU Dist-OPENU

Significance, Involvement, And Worldhood C 120 MIN
3/4 OR 1/2 INCH VIDEO CASSETTE A
See series title for descriptive statement.
From The Beyond Philosophy - The Thought Of Martin Heidegger Series. Program 4
Prod-UCEMC Dist-UCEMC

Significant Hazards - The Somerville DNA Debate C 24 MIN
16MM FILM, 3/4 OR 1/2 IN VIDEO A
Deals with a public and political debate over the building of a DNA Lab in Somerville, a densely populated blue-collar city bordering on Cambridge and Boston. Portrays the citizens and aldermen struggling to understand the new complex technology and the scientists struggling to explain it and their belief that it poses no hazard to the community. Stresses the importance of communication between scientists and citizens.
Prod-GALLEO Dist-FANPRO

Signing With Cindy—A Series

Features Cindy Cochran, content consultant, introducing the world of sign language. Brings together the language of words and signs in an easy to understand way. Taped before a live studio audience by KUHT-TV in Houston, Texas.
Prod-GPCV Dist-GPCV

Animal And Food Signs
Family Signs
Introduction And Beginning Sign Language
Series Conclusion And Talking About Deafness
Sports-Oriented Signs, Verbs And Personal
Time And Seasons Plus A Documentary - Miss

Signing With Cindy—A Series

Provides instruction in sign language. Looks at the people who communicate in sign language and how they live in a world without sound. Features an appearance by professional boxing champion Sugar Ray Leonard.
Prod-KUHTTV Dist-MDCPB

Animal And Food Signs 030 MIN
Family Signs 030 MIN
Introduction And Beginning Sign Language 030 MIN
Song And Dance Routines 030 MIN
Sports Oriented Signs, Verbs And Personal 030 MIN
Talking About Deafness 030 MIN
Time And Seasons / Documentary - Miss Deaf 030 MIN

Signing Your Life Away C 18 MIN
16MM FILM OPTICAL SOUND
Warns against some of the dangers posed by unfair conditions in binding contracts.
From The Consumer Game Series.
LC NO. 74-701227
Prod-OECA Dist-OECA 1972

Signposts B 15 MIN
16MM FILM OPTICAL SOUND J-C A S
Indicates that a chronic cough and shortness of breath are symptoms of respiratory disease. Shows the results of neglecting the symptoms by describing real case histories.
Prod-NTBA Dist-AMLUNG 1963

Signs C 11 MIN
16MM FILM, 3/4 OR 1/2 IN VIDEO P-I
Explains that signs warn, instruct, guide, explain and direct. Presents the many different kinds of signs. Encourages students to discover the various signs and their meanings, in a number of different environments, whether they are on their way to the library, looking for a bus stop, riding a bike in the park, or taking the dog for a walk. Stresses the fact that signs are helpful guides.
Prod-GABOR Dist-PHENIX 1969

Signs C 15 MIN
3/4 OR 1/2 INCH VIDEO CASSETTE P
See series title for descriptive statement.
From The Word Shop Series.
Prod-WETATV Dist-WETATV

Signs And Lines C 11 MIN
16MM FILM OPTICAL SOUND
Uses animated graphics to emphasize the importance of knowing and heeding traffic signs and markings wherever a person is driving. Encourages people to learn the international traffic signs and marking lines system.
LC NO. 74-700515
Prod-GM Dist-MTP 1973

Signs And Signals C 60 MIN
3/4 OR 1/2 INCH VIDEO CASSETTE H-C A
Looks at the phenomena of animal communication through the re-creations of Karl Von Frisch unraveling the language of honeybees, Julian Huxley discovering the possible language in ritual movements of great-crested grebes, Konrad Lorenz recording the visual language of geese and Niko Tinbergen studying the habits of hunting wasps and together with Esther Cullen recording the relationship of temperament in birds to their habitat.
From The Discovery Of Animal Behavior Series.
Prod-WNETTV Dist-FI 1982

Signs Are For Safety C 15 MIN
16MM FILM, 3/4 OR 1/2 IN VIDEO P-J
Shows how Fat Albert and the gang teaches Roy the importance of signs after his removal of a danger sign nearly causes Peewee's death.
From The Fat Albert And The Cosby Kids Series III Series.
Prod-BARR Dist-BARR Prodn-FLMTON 1979

Signs At The Shopping Center C 9 MIN
16MM FILM, 3/4 OR 1/2 IN VIDEO P
Presents a group of children and their mothers in a shopping mall. Shows how they go from store to store, guided by various signs, examining goods and making choices as to what to buy. Key words are flashed on the screen.
Prod-BFA Dist-PHENIX 1983

Signs For Time C 15 MIN
16MM FILM MAGNETIC SOUND K-C A S
See series title for descriptive statement.
From The PANCOM Beginning Total Communication Program For Hearing Parents Of... Series. Level 1
LC NO. 77-700504
Prod-CSDE Dist-JOYCE Prodn-CSFDF 1977

Signs Of Anxiety C 22 MIN
16MM FILM OPTICAL SOUND
Illustrates verbal and non-verbal signs of anxiety in three patients seen in a doctor's waiting room and in consultation. Features method actors who effectively demonstrate and relate their experiences with acute anxiety, chronic anxiety associated with somatic complaints and anxiety as it relates to interpersonal behavior in a geriatric patient.
Prod-HOFLAR Dist-AMEDA

Signs Of His Promise C 27 MIN
16MM FILM OPTICAL SOUND
Demonstrates how Christian care and training can help mentally retarded persons progress to more normal living opportunities.
Prod-BLH Dist-BLH

Signs Of Life C 27 MIN
16MM FILM OPTICAL SOUND H
Presents a look at the signs, signals and markings that help control traffic.
From The To Get From Here To There Series.
Prod-PROART Dist-PROART

Signs Of Life (German) B 90 MIN
16MM FILM OPTICAL SOUND
Depicts a wounded German soldier recuperating on a Greek island and staging a lyrical/mad one-man rebellion involving insects, fireworks and windmills. Directed by Werner Herzog. With English subtitles.
Prod-UNKNWN Dist-NYFLMS 1968

Signs Of The Apes, Songs Of The Whales C 57 MIN
3/4 OR 1/2 INCH VIDEO CASSETTE H-C A
Revisits Washoe, a chimpanzee who was taught American Sign Language. Examines some of the most recent language experiments being done not only with apes but also with dolphins, sea lions, gorillas and whales. Shows that some scientists are beginning to study the ways animals communicate among themselves in the wild.
From The Nova Series.
Prod-WGBHTV Dist-TIMLIF 1984

Signs Of The Times C 20 MIN
16MM FILM, 3/4 OR 1/2 IN VIDEO
Traces the development of signs and symbols in other times and cultures. Studies graphic forms and their effect on contemporary behavior.
From The Images And Things Series.
LC NO. 73-702111
Prod-NITC Dist-AITECH 1971

Signs You Already Know C 30 MIN
3/4 OR 1/2 INCH VIDEO CASSETTE H-C A
Presents Lawrence Solow and Sharon Neumann Solow introducing American Sign Language used by the hearing-impaired. Emphasizes signs that resemble gestures already used by many people in spoken conversation.
From The Say It With Sign Series. Part 1
LC NO. 83-706358
Prod-KNBCTV Dist-FI 1982

Signs, Symbols And Signals C 11 MIN
16MM FILM, 3/4 OR 1/2 IN VIDEO P-I
Reveals the rich and varied ways people send and receive communication with signs, symbols and signals.
Prod-FILMSW Dist-FLMFR

Silage Wagons C 17 MIN
3/4 OR 1/2 INCH VIDEO CASSETTE
Focuses on a rescue from the beater bars and teeth of an unloading silage wagon.
From The Agricultural Accidents And Rescue Series.
Prod-PSU Dist-PSU

Silas Marner B 65 MIN
16MM FILM OPTICAL SOUND J-H
Presents George Eliot's novel 'SILAS MARNER.'
LC NO. 73-701851
Prod-THAN Dist-FCE 1973

Silas Marner C 27 MIN
16MM FILM, 3/4 OR 1/2 IN VIDEO J-H
Dramatizes the story of the lonely weaver whose life changes when a girl called Eppie appears. Based upon SILAS MARNER by George Eliot.
Prod-LUF Dist-LUF

Silbale A Guillermito C 6 MIN
16MM FILM, 3/4 OR 1/2 IN VIDEO
A Spanish-language version of the motion picture Whistle For Willie. Tells the story of a boy who badly wants to learn to whistle so that he can call his dog. Based on the book Whistle For Willie by Ezra Jack Keats.
Prod-WWS Dist-WWS

Silence And Sound, Pt 1 B 15 MIN
2 INCH VIDEOTAPE P
Describes the characteristics of sound including its vibrations, pitch and wave patterns. Explains that sound can travel through solids, liquids and gases.
From The Science Is Everywhere Series. No. 10
Prod-DETPS Dist-GPITVL

Silence And Sound, Pt 2 B 15 MIN
2 INCH VIDEOTAPE P
Describes the characteristics of sound including its vibrations, pitch and wave patterns. Explains that sound can travel through solids, liquids and gases.
From The Science Is Everywhere Series. No. 11
Prod-DETPS Dist-GPITVL

Silence And Sound, Pt 3 B 15 MIN
2 INCH VIDEOTAPE P
Describes the characteristics of sound including its vibrations, pitch and wave patterns. Explains that sound can travel through solids, liquids and gases.
From The Science Is Everywhere Series. No. 12
Prod-DETPS Dist-GPITVL

Silence And Sound, Pt 4 B 15 MIN
2 INCH VIDEOTAPE P
Describes the characteristics of sound including its vibrations, pitch and wave patterns. Explains that sound can travel through solids, liquids and gases.
From The Science Is Everywhere Series. No. 13
Prod-DETPS Dist-GPITVL

Silences C 12 MIN
16MM FILM, 3/4 OR 1/2 IN VIDEO H-C A
Presents a film study of the moral ambiguities created by war as evidenced in the effect of war on the reactions of a Serbian peasant during World War II.
Prod-YF Dist-MGHT 1972

Silent Army C 29 MIN
3/4 OR 1/2 INCH VIDEO CASSETTE
Explores the stories and legends of China's Bronze Age. Uses original music recorded in China with 2400-year-old bronze chime bells.
Prod-WTTWTV Dist-PBS 1980

Silent Countdown C 28 MIN
16MM FILM OPTICAL SOUND
Follows five people on their way home from work, all of whom suffer from high blood pressure, one of whom will not make it home. Reveals their weaknesses and some of the reasons why they discontinued treatment through their discussions with Ben Gazzara.
LC NO. 75-703292
Prod-CINEMS Dist-CINEMS 1975

Silent Dancing C 27 MIN
3/4 OR 1/2 INCH VIDEO CASSETTE
Discusses Robert Joffrey's experimental Ballet For Deaf Children program.
From The Skyline Series.
LC NO. 80-706745
Prod-WNETTV Dist-WNETTV 1980

Silent E Rule, The C 7 MIN
3/4 OR 1/2 INCH VIDEO CASSETTE
See series title for descriptive statement.
From The Better Spelling Series.
Prod-TELSTR Dist-DELTAK

Silent Epidemic, The - Alzheimer's Disease C 26 MIN
16MM FILM, 3/4 OR 1/2 IN VIDEO A
Examines the disease of senility, Alzheimer's disease. Describes the symptoms of the disease and the difficulty of nursing such patients by family and nursing professionals.
LC NO. 82-707103
Prod-GRATV Dist-FLMLIB 1982

Silent Forest C 23 MIN
16MM FILM, 3/4 OR 1/2 IN VIDEO J-C A
Analyzes the kelp forests along the Pacific coastline where thousands of animal species eat, live and die among the towering columns.
Prod-TRUSTY Dist-BARR 1978

Silent Forest (Captioned) C 23 MIN
16MM FILM - VIDEO, ALL FORMATS I-C
Explores the kelp forest beneath the ocean's surface along the Pacific coastline of North America. Looks at the community of marine life supported by the kelp and at the pollution that threatens it.
Prod-TRUSTY Dist-BARR

Silent Guard, The C 15 MIN
16MM FILM OPTICAL SOUND
Describes the planning, design and sealing of a new Vertical Laminar Flow System for clean rooms. Illustrates proper methods for interior and exterior sealing and caulking.
Prod-THIOKL Dist-THIOKL 1966

Silent Heritage - The American Indian—A Series

Features representatives from major tribes as they express their views about what the American people have done to Native Americans. Hosted by Joseph R Julin, professor of law at the University of Michigan.
Prod-UMITV Dist-UMITV 1966

Myths And Manifest Destiny 029 MIN
Northern Plains, The 030 MIN

Silent Killer, The C 12 MIN
16MM FILM, 3/4 OR 1/2 IN VIDEO A
Explores the treatment of hypertension with regimens and medications targeted at bodily renin and sodium levels, as well as more unique causes. Cautions against the overzealous restriction of salt without first testing the patients' sensitivity to sodium.
LC NO. 84-706561
Prod-ABCTV Dist-MTI 1984

Silent Killer, The C 30 MIN
3/4 OR 1/2 INCH VIDEO CASSETTE
Presents Dr Eli Saunders, a hypertension specialist, joined by Drs Roberts and Race for an explanation of this disease, how to diagnose it and control it through diet and exercise.
From The Here's To Your Health Series.
Prod-KERA Dist-PBS 1979

Silent Killer, The C 30 MIN
3/4 OR 1/2 INCH VIDEO CASSETTE
See series title for descriptive statement.
From The Here's To Your Health Series.
Prod-PBS Dist-DELTAK

Silent Killer, The - A Call To Fitness C 20 MIN
16MM FILM OPTICAL SOUND
Explains how police officers can be aware of physical fitness. Discusses how to gauge and improve fitness.
LC NO. 79-700280
Prod-TRAVLR Dist-TRAVLR Prodn-WSTGLC 1978

Silent Letters - Different Ways To Spell The Sounds O, SH In The Medial Position Of... C 20 MIN
3/4 OR 1/2 INCH VIDEO CASSETTE J-H
Presents silent letters, including different ways to spell the sounds of O, SH in the medial position of words and N.
From The Getting The Word Series. Unit IV
Prod-SCETV Dist-AITECH 1974

Silent Life C 14 MIN
3/4 OR 1/2 INCH VIDEO CASSETTE
See series title for descriptive statement.
From The Reflecting Pool Series.
Prod-EAI Dist-EAI

Silent Minority, The C 26 MIN
3/4 OR 1/2 INCH VIDEO CASSETTE
Shows how recent surgical breakthroughs bring fresh hope to victims of Down's Syndrome. Demonstrates that while the condition remains incurable, speech and other defects can now be corrected and appearances radically changed enabling children to integrate with the community.
From The Breakthroughs Series.
Prod-NOMDFI Dist-LANDMK

Silent Movie C 20 MIN
16MM FILM OPTICAL SOUND
Re-creates the style of a 1920's tragicomedy.
LC NO. 76-702094
Prod-CANFDC Dist-CANFDC 1974

Silent Neighbor, The C 10 MIN
16MM FILM OPTICAL SOUND
Provides a capsule history of the place of abused children in ancient and modern society. Uses a series of vignettes to show typical cases of child abuse and the responsibility of neighbors to make it their business to help.
Prod-FILAUD Dist-FILAUD 1978

Silent Night C 21 MIN
16MM FILM OPTICAL SOUND
Tells how a young man, working as a psychiatric technician on Christmas Eve, defies the authority of the head nurse in a subtle way.
LC NO. 78-701627
Prod-USC Dist-USC 1978

Silent Night - Story Of The Christmas Carol C 13 MIN
16MM FILM, 3/4 OR 1/2 IN VIDEO P-H
Depicts the events which contributed to the writing of Silent Night, Holy Night in Oberndorf, Austria in 1818.
Prod-CORF Dist-CORF 1953

Silent Partner, The C 105 MIN
3/4 OR 1/2 INCH VIDEO CASSETTE C A
Introduces Miles Cullen, a bank teller who leads a humdrum life until, during a holdup at his bank, the robber unwittingly gives him a chance to pocket most of the money. Reveals that the thwarted thief escapes and then launches a campaign of terror to force Cullen to turn over the loot. Stars Elliott Gould and Christopher Plummer.
Prod-TIMLIF Dist-TIMLIF 1982

Silent Power C 27 MIN
16MM FILM, 3/4 OR 1/2 IN VIDEO
Documents the peaceful uses of nuclear power in the United States space program. Surveys the history of the nuclear power program and discusses developments for the future.
LC NO. 81-706428
Prod-USDOE Dist-USNAC 1978

Silent Rap, A B 6 MIN
16MM FILM OPTICAL SOUND
Presents a romantic encounter whose dramatic action is framed within a racial triangle and sparked by a silent dialogue and a complementary music track.
Prod-BLKFMF Dist-BLKFMF

Silent Revolution B 25 MIN
16MM FILM OPTICAL SOUND
Records the successful outcome of the First Malaysia Five Year Plan due to the formation of a committee system. Tells how this system established a two-way channel of intercommunication between government and the people, providing the rural areas with amenities not existing before.
Prod-FILEM Dist-PMFMUN 1967

Silent Revolution, The B 23 MIN
16MM FILM OPTICAL SOUND I-C A
Shows the transformation of an Indian village through cooperative endeavor and highlights the perseverance and idealism of a 'A GRAM SEVAK' (village worker.)
Prod-INDIA Dist-NEDINF

Silent Safari—A Series
P A
Studies East African wildlife. Presented without interpretive narrative by producer Peter Chermayeff. Filmed in a wildlife sanctuary in northern Tanzania.
Prod-CHE Dist-EBEC 1984

Baboon 020 MIN
Gazelle 011 MIN
Impala 011 MIN
Ostrich 012 MIN
Rhinoceros 012 MIN
Wildebeest 020 MIN

Silent Sentinel C 14 MIN
16MM FILM OPTICAL SOUND
Explains the basic concept of the fleet ballistic missile program and shows all the necessary steps which the Navy must go through to make the Polaris missile operational.
LC NO. FIE61-120
Prod-USN Dist-USNAC 1959

Silent Shame - The Sexual Abuse Of Children C 50 MIN
3/4 OR 1/2 INCH VIDEO CASSETTE H-C A
Reveals facts about the nationwide spread of child sexual abuse and pornography. Includes interviews with young victims and the people who abused them, both pedophiles and professional pornography purveyors. Shows undercover shots of the world's largest producers and distributors of child pornography in Europe. Testifies to the lasting damage and cyclical occurrence from generation to generation.
Prod-NBCNEW Dist-FI

Silent Speech C 50 MIN
16MM FILM, 3/4 OR 1/2 IN VIDEO H-C A
Studies non-verbal behavior in young children, focusing on the work of French biologist Hubert Montagner.
Prod-BBCTV Dist-FI 1981

Silent Traveler, The C 9 MIN
16MM FILM OPTICAL SOUND PRO
Demonstrates the techniques of application and interpretation of the Tuberculine Tine Test and includes a statement by Luther Terry, Surgeon General of the U S Public Health Service, on the seriousness of tuberculosis.
Prod-ACYLLD Dist-LEDR 1964

Silent Walls C 28 MIN
16MM FILM - 3/4 IN VIDEO
Examines deafness and the problems of deaf people who must adjust to a silent world. Shows how deaf people are trained to communicate, find employment, and bridge the gap of isolation and alienation. Demonstrates office equipment designed by deaf individuals for the deaf.
From The No Place Like Home Series.
LC NO. 79-708104
Prod-USSRS Dist-USNAC 1979

Silent Witness, The C 55 MIN
3/4 OR 1/2 INCH VIDEO CASSETTE
Investigates the possibility that the Shroud of Turin was the burial garment worn by Jesus Christ. Interviews experts from various fields who say that the shroud is either authentic of the most clever fraud in the history of man.
LC NO. 79-700967
Prod-SCREEP Dist-PFP 1979

Silent World Of Jim, The C 14 MIN
16MM FILM OPTICAL SOUND S
Describes, without narration, the adventures of a seven-year-old deaf boy in order to help deaf children develop an awareness of safety. Includes an introduction by Nanette Fabray.
LC NO. 74-703672
Prod-INMATI Dist-INMATI 1974

Silent World, Muffled World B 28 MIN
16MM FILM - 3/4 IN VIDEO PRO
Relates the difficulties of speech, education and normal living for the deaf. Discusses the physiology of the ear, the mechanics of the hearing process and the causes of hearing impairment. Shows the progress being made in the methods of education and rehabilitation of deaf persons.
Prod-USPHS Dist-USNAC Prodn-CF 1972

Silhouettes Of Gorden Vales, The C 26 MIN
3/4 OR 1/2 INCH VIDEO CASSETTE
Portrays Gordon Vales, an artist whose life began in a facility for the mentally handicapped but who developed a talent for tearing well-formed silhouettes from paper.
Prod-MEDIPR Dist-MEDIPR 1980

Silicon Chip, The C
3/4 OR 1/2 INCH VIDEO CASSETTE
Provides an explanation of the evolution, appearance, construction and manufacture of integrated circuits. Presents the use of computers as an example for tracing out the history of electronics and the development of miroelectronic techniques.
From The Audio Visual Library Of Computer Education Series.
Prod-PRISPR Dist-PRISPR

Silicon Factor—A Series
16MM FILM, 3/4 OR 1/2 IN VIDEO C A
Reviews the developments occurring in microelectronic technologies.
Prod-BBCTV Dist-FI 1981

And What Of The Future 040 MIN
Now The Chips Are Down 050 MIN
So What's It All About 040 MIN

Silicon Valley - The New Entrepreneurs C 29 MIN
3/4 OR 1/2 INCH VIDEO CASSETTE
Examines the electronics industry just south of San Francisco and the American entrepreneurs who created it. Emphasizes the beneficial side of industrial development and technological advancement and raises questions about government regulation of the private economy. Hosted by Ben Wattenberg.
From The Ben Wattenberg's 1980 Series.
Prod-WETATV Dist-PBS

Silicone Implant Arthoplasty C 17 MIN
3/4 OR 1/2 INCH VIDEO CASSETTE PRO
Shows silicone implant arthoplasty.
Prod-WFP Dist-WFP

Silicone Implant For The Correction Of Impotence C 10 MIN
16MM FILM OPTICAL SOUND
Demonstrates a complete repair procedure for impotence using a silicone implant. Illustrates pre- and post-operative measures.
LC NO. 75-702312
Prod-EATONL Dist-EATONL 1965

Silk C 22 MIN
16MM FILM, 3/4 OR 1/2 IN VIDEO J-H
Illustrates the production and uses of silk.
LC NO. 80-706712
Prod-BHA Dist-IFB 1977

Silk Flower Making, Pt 1 C 60 MIN
3/4 OR 1/2 INCH VIDEO CASSETTE J A
Shows Lee Maher crafting likenesses of flowers from polyester fabrics as her instructions progress in manageable steps using minimal supplies.
LC NO. 82-707302
Prod-CINAS Dist-CINAS 1981

Silk Flower Making, Pt 1 C 60 MIN
1/2 IN VIDEO CASSETTE BETA/VHS
Demonstrates making silk flowers. Includes carnations, camellias, peonies, chrysanthemums and rhododendrons.
From The Crafts And Decorating Series.
Prod-MOHOMV Dist-MOHOMV

Silk Flower Making, Pt 1 C 60 MIN
1/2 IN VIDEO CASSETTE BETA/VHS
Includes carnations, rhododendrons, camellias, chrysanthemums and peonies.
Prod-RMI Dist-RMI

Silk Flower Making, Pt 2 C 60 MIN
1/2 IN VIDEO CASSETTE BETA/VHS
Demonstrates making silk flowers. Includes roses, gardenias, tulips, daffodils and delphiniums.
From The Crafts And Decorating Series.
Prod-MOHOMV Dist-MOHOMV

Silk Flower Making, Pt 2 C 60 MIN
1/2 IN VIDEO CASSETTE BETA/VHS
Includes roses, gardenias, tulips, daffodils and delphiniums.
Prod-RMI Dist-RMI

Silk Industry In India C 28 MIN
16MM FILM OPTICAL SOUND I-C A
Reports on the silk industry of India today. Describes the scientific methods of breeding silk worms, the cultivation of mulberry leaves, the extraction of silk from cocoons and the weaving of silk.
Prod-INDIA Dist-NEDINF

Silk Moth C 7 MIN
16MM FILM, 3/4 OR 1/2 IN VIDEO K-I
Uses microphotography to reveal the egg-laying process of the silk moth and to show the caterpillars as they emerge from the egg. Follows the process of metamorphosis from the spinning of the cocoon, and the transformation into a chrysalis to the emergence of the silk moth twenty days later.
From The See 'N Tell Series.
Prod-PMI Dist-FI 1970

Silk Screen Fundamentals C 14 MIN
16MM FILM, 3/4 OR 1/2 IN VIDEO J-C
Presents an introduction to the art of paper stencil and silk screening. Step by step procedures involved in constructing a 'DO-IT-YOURSELF' stretcher frame, stretching the commerical frame, cutting paper stencils, registering the printing stock, and finally, printing the stencils are demonstrated. Pictures the tools used in silk screen, with emphasis on care and safety.
Prod-BFA Dist-PHENIX 1969

Silk Screen Printing X 10 MIN
16MM FILM OPTICAL SOUND H-C A
Demonstrates the technique whereby hand screen printing has been brought up to date. Shows preparation, washing, dyeing, printing and completion.
Prod-ALLMOR Dist-AVED 1957

Silk Screen Techniques C 14 MIN
16MM FILM, 3/4 OR 1/2 IN VIDEO J-C
Presents four professional artists, who demonstrate advanced silk-screen techniques. Includes the clay and glue tusche methods, the lacquer film method and the photo silk-screen process.
Prod-BFA Dist-PHENIX 1969

Silkmaking In China C 13 MIN
3/4 OR 1/2 INCH VIDEO CASSETTE P-J
Shows the process of silkmaking in a Chinese commune and provides an insight into village life in the People's Republic of China.
Prod-ATLAP Dist-ATLAP

Silkscreen C 15 MIN
16MM FILM, 3/4 OR 1/2 IN VIDEO I-C A
Illustrates the basic principles involved in silk screen printing, shows the building of a screen and demonstrates ways for creating silk screen stencils from simple to more complex film and tusche-and-glue methods. Shows the uses and expressive ideas to which this medium may be adapted.
From The Rediscovery - Art Media Series.
Prod-ACI Dist-AIMS 1967

Silkscreen (French) C 14 MIN
16MM FILM, 3/4 OR 1/2 IN VIDEO I-C A
Illustrates the basic principles involved in silkscreen printing and demonstrates the use of various materials for making stencils.
From The Rediscovery - Art Media (French) Series.
Prod-ACI Dist-AIMS 1967

Silkscreen (Spanish) C 14 MIN
16MM FILM, 3/4 OR 1/2 IN VIDEO I-C A
Illustrates the basic principles involved in silkscreen printing and demonstrates the use of various materials for making stencils.
From The Rediscovery - Art Media (Spanish) Series.
Prod-ACI Dist-AIMS 1967

Silkscreening C 30 MIN
3/4 OR 1/2 INCH VIDEO CASSETTE H A
Demonstrates the materials and equipment needed to develop a silkscreen print. Shows how to cut a master, adhere it to the screen, mask the screen, register the print, print the design, and clean the silkscreen frame.
From The Arts And Crafts Series.
LC NO. 81-707006
Prod-GPITVL Dist-GPITVL 1981

Silos C 30 MIN
3/4 OR 1/2 INCH VIDEO CASSETTE
Discusses removal of a patient from inside a tower silo. Covers the use of a Z-rig as well as silo gases and Farmer's Lung.
From The Agricultural Accidents And Rescue Series.
Prod-PSU Dist-PSU

Silver C 30 MIN
3/4 INCH VIDEO CASSETTE
See series title for descriptive statement.
From The Antiques Series.
Prod-NHMNET Dist-PUBTEL

Silver Bears C 113 MIN
16MM FILM OPTICAL SOUND
Centers on a financial speculator who manipulates amorous adventures and the world silver market with equal ease. Stars Michael Caine and Cybill Shepherd.
Prod-CPC Dist-SWANK

Silver Blaze C 31 MIN
16MM FILM, 3/4 OR 1/2 IN VIDEO H-C A
Presents an adaptation of the story 'Silver 'Blaze by Sir Arthur Conan Doyle, about the disappearance of a famous racing horse and the murder of his trainer which leads to an investigation by Sherlock Holmes.
From The Classics, Dark And Dangerous Series.
Prod-LCOA Dist-LCOA 1977

Silver Blaze (Spanish) C 31 MIN
16MM FILM, 3/4 OR 1/2 IN VIDEO P-C A
Tells the story of the theft of a racehorse, Silver Blaze. Based on a story by Sir Arthur Conan Doyle.
From The Classics Dark And Dangerous (Spanish) Series.
Prod-LCOA Dist-LCOA 1977

Silver Brazing And Soft Soldering C 15 MIN
3/4 OR 1/2 INCH VIDEO CASSETTE IND
See series title for descriptive statement.
From The Welding - Oxy-Acetylene Welding Series.
Prod-ICSINT Dist-ICSINT

Silver Brazing And Soft Soldering (Spanish) C
3/4 OR 1/2 INCH VIDEO CASSETTE
See series title for descriptive statement.
From The Oxy-Acetylene Welding (Spanish) Series.
Prod-VTRI Dist-VTRI

Silver Brazing And Soft Soldering With Oxy-Acetylene C 15 MIN
3/4 OR 1/2 INCH VIDEO CASSETTE
See series title for descriptive statement.
From The Welding I - Basic Oxy-Acetylene Welding Series.
Prod-CAMB Dist-CAMB

Silver City C 60 MIN
3/4 OR 1/2 INCH VIDEO CASSETTE J A
Reveals how the four, teenage members of a multi-ethnic rock and soul band pursue a recording career amid the tarnish and gleam of Hollywood.
From The Rainbow Movie Of The Week Series.
Prod-RAINTV Dist-GPITVL 1981

Silver Coho C 12 MIN
16MM FILM OPTICAL SOUND
Follows a group of fishermen 460 miles to Morsey Island, largest of the Queen Charlotte group of islands on the British Columbia coast. There they battle the 'BIG COHO' silver salmon.
LC NO. FIA67-2250
Prod-SNCLR Dist-CTFL 1966

Silver Eagle, The - Master Of The Skies B 16 MIN
16MM FILM, 3/4 OR 1/2 IN VIDEO
Presents a satirical reminder to general aviation pilots on the importance of being physically and mentally fit to fly. Uses the Silver Eagle, a pilot who believes that he has extraordinary judgment and flying prowess, to show other pilots the adverse effects of alcohol, medicines, stress and fatigue.
LC NO. 80-707125
Prod-USFAA Dist-USNAC Prodn-HELWEL 1980

Silver Fox And Sam Davenport, The C 47 MIN
16MM FILM, 3/4 OR 1/2 IN VIDEO I-H
Tells how a fox escapes a foxhunt by jumping on a farmer's haywagon in turn-of-the-century New England. Shows the pursuit that follows as the farmer recognizes the value of the stowaway and begins his own foxhunt.
From The Animal Featurettes, Set 3 Series.
Prod-DISNEY Dist-WDEMCO 1962

Silver Fox Rodeo C 8 MIN
16MM FILM OPTICAL SOUND
Shows U S Navy pilots and airmen at work and at play. Shows enlisted personnel and officers flying over the Sierras, riding broncos and wild burros and milking wild cows.
LC NO. 75-703702
Prod-USN Dist-USNAC 1974

Silver Harvest C 25 MIN
16MM FILM OPTICAL SOUND
Documents the Italian fishing families that came to Monterey, California, to fish schooling sardines in the 1930's. Shows special equipment that was designed and emphasizes the unique heritage which developed.
LC NO. 79-701015
Prod-MONSAV Dist-MONSAV Prodn-ROSENS 1979

Silver Lining C 24 MIN
16MM FILM, 3/4 OR 1/2 IN VIDEO H-C A
Surveys art works in Illinois produced under the Work Progress Administration program between 1933 and 1943. Includes scenes of the murals of the old post office building in Murphysboro and stained glass windows at the University of Illinois Medical Center. Conducts interviews with artists who participated in the program and presents archival footage of some of the WPA artists at work.
Prod-MCFI Dist-MCFI 1977

Silver Linings C 28 MIN
16MM FILM - 3/4 IN VIDEO
Features the Salvation Army's activities which help senior citizens cope with their problems. Focuses on a few members of the group whose lives were altered by the activities. Not available to school audiences.
Prod-SALVA Dist-MTP

Silver Maiden, The C 12 MIN
16MM FILM, 3/4 OR 1/2 IN VIDEO H-C A
Describes how a man and a woman meet by accident in a park and rediscover love. Based on the one act play A Sunny Morning by Joaquin and Serafin Quintero. Stars Eli Wallach and Jacqueline Brookes.
Prod-CAROUF Dist-CAROUF

Silver Nitrate Wet Treatment Of Burns C 26 MIN
16MM FILM OPTICAL SOUND PRO
Describes treatment of burns with continuously wet dressings with bacteriostatic control with five-tenths percent silver nitrate.
Prod-ACYDGD Dist-ACY 1996

Silver Pony, The C 7 MIN
16MM FILM, 3/4 OR 1/2 IN VIDEO K-I
Tells an animated story about a boy who escapes in his imagination on a winged pony, bringing joy to others. Illustrates the power of imagination. Based on the book The Silver Pony by Lynd Ward.
LC NO. 81-707559
Prod-BOSUST Dist-CF 1981

Silver Safari, The C 28 MIN
16MM FILM, 3/4 OR 1/2 IN VIDEO
Shows car racing at the 25th Safari Rally in Kenya, a five-day road race which started with 68 cars and ended with only 11 cars still running.
Prod-KLEINW Dist-KLEINW 1977

Silver Whistle, The C 17 MIN
16MM FILM, 3/4 OR 1/2 IN VIDEO P-I
Offers a fairy tale about a little girl named Prudence who has a magic whistle which summons insects and animals. Based on the book The Silver Whistle by Jay Williams.
LC NO. 80-707729
Prod-FLMFR Dist-FLMFR 1980

Silver Wings And Santiago Blue C 59 MIN
3/4 OR 1/2 INCH VIDEO CASSETTE
Uses old newsreels, Air Force films and footage of the Congressional hearing which gave recognition to the 1,000 women of the Woman's Auxiliary Ferry Squadron and the Women's Air Force Service Pilots for their service during World War II.
Prod-ADMKNG Dist-PBS 1980

Silver Wires, Golden Wings C 28 MIN
16MM FILM OPTICAL SOUND
Details the efforts of electric utilities to prevent the electrocution of birds of prey on power lines. Shows how many utilities have installed special nesting platforms on transmission towers.
Prod-EEI Dist-MTP

Silversmith Of Williamsburg C 44 MIN
16MM FILM, 3/4 OR 1/2 IN VIDEO IND
Documents the handcrafting of a 1765 coffee pot from a crucible of scrap silver to the fashioning of the product by master silversmith William De Matteo. Discusses methods employed, the properties of silver, and the evolution of design.
Prod-CWMS Dist-CWMS 1971

Similar Shapes C 20 MIN
3/4 OR 1/2 INCH VIDEO CASSETTE J-C
See series title for descriptive statement.
From The Math Topics - Trigonometry Series.
Prod-BBCTV Dist-FI

Similar Triangles C 8 MIN
16MM FILM, 3/4 OR 1/2 IN VIDEO J-H
Explores the concept of similar triangles.
From The Triangle Series.
LC NO. 81-706239
Prod-IFB Dist-IFB 1976

Similar Triangles In Use C 11 MIN
16MM FILM, 3/4 OR 1/2 IN VIDEO J-C
Presents the practical value of knowing that corresponding sides of similar triangles are proportional. Shows the use of the surveyor's quadrant and sextant.
Prod-IFB Dist-IFB 1962

Similarities In Wave Behavior B 27 MIN
3/4 INCH VIDEOTAPE
Considers the similarities in the behavior of waves of various mechanical, electrical, acoustical and optical wave systems. Demonstrates many aspects of wave behavior through the use of several specially built torsion wave machines.
Prod-NCEEF Dist-EDC

Simmering And Poaching C 10 MIN
16MM FILM, 3/4 OR 1/2 IN VIDEO J-C A
Demonstrates methods of cooking in liquids including totally submerged meats and poultry as well as poached items. Defines and differentiates various moist meat preparation techniques. Shows use of steam kettles and top-of-range cooking. Discusses boiling versus simmering and includes techniques in braising and stewing.
From The Professional Food Preparation And Service Program Series.
LC NO. 74-700232
Prod-NEM Dist-NEM 1973

Simmons USA (A Marketing Turnaround) C 30 MIN
3/4 OR 1/2 INCH VIDEO CASSETTE
See series title for descriptive statement.
From The Contemporary Issues In Marketing Series.
Prod-CANTOR Dist-IVCH

Simon Peter, Fisherman B 30 MIN
16MM FILM OPTICAL SOUND J-C A
Shows the effect of Jesus on the life of strong, impetuous Simon Peter. Shows aspects of home and social life of the time and the place.
Prod-CAFM Dist-CAFM

Simone Forti - Solo No. 1 B 8 MIN
3/4 OR 1/2 INCH VIDEO CASSETTE
Features the movements of grizzly and polar bears.
Prod-ARTINC Dist-ARTINC

Simone Forti - Three Grizzlies B 15 MIN
3/4 OR 1/2 INCH VIDEO CASSETTE
Features the movements of grizzly and polar bears.
Prod-ARTINC Dist-ARTINC

Simpatico Means Venezuela C 28 MIN
16MM FILM OPTICAL SOUND C A
Presents an air-travel film about Venezuela, its history and natural resources. Includes scenes of Caracas, the capital city, the nearby jungles and Lake Maracaibo.
LC NO. FIA67-609
Prod-DAC Dist-MCDO Prodn-VIASA 1966

Simpatico Means Venezuela (Spanish) C 28 MIN
16MM FILM OPTICAL SOUND I-C A
Presents an air-travel film about Venezuela, its history and natural resources. Includes scenes of Caracas, the capital city, the nearby jungles and Lake Maracaibo.
LC NO. FIA67-609
Prod-DAC Dist-MCDO 1966

Simple Accident, The C 10 MIN
16MM FILM, 3/4 OR 1/2 IN VIDEO P-I
A revised version of the 1952 motion picture Why Take Chances. Presents a direct, positive attack on the accident problem. Points out to boys and girls the dangers they face in living and playing. Shows how easily the accidents can be avoided merely by being smart and careful. Portrays a series of carefully selected situations where children may, through carelessness, get hurt.
Prod-DAVP Dist-AIMS 1969

Simple Addressing Modes C 30 MIN
3/4 OR 1/2 INCH VIDEO CASSETTE IND
Introduces register direct, address register indirect, absolute, immediate and program counter relative addressing modes using 68000 instruction.
From The MC68000 Microprocessor Series.
Prod-COLOSU Dist-COLOSU

Simple Ceramics X 10 MIN
16MM FILM OPTICAL SOUND I-C A
A fruit bowl is made of clay by the hammock-mold method.
Prod-ALLMOR Dist-AVED 1958

Simple Choice, A C 18 MIN
16MM FILM, 3/4 OR 1/2 IN VIDEO IND
Illustrates ways to reduce the number of job-related injuries, illnesses and deaths by changing the attitude of the worker toward safety rules.
Prod-DRUKRR Dist-JONEST

Simple Chords C 29 MIN
2 INCH VIDEOTAPE
See series title for descriptive statement.

From The Playing The Guitar I Series.
Prod-KCET Dist-PUBTEL

Simple Cup Of Tea, A B 28 MIN
3/4 INCH VIDEO CASSETTE
Introduces Ferguson, a farmer, teacher, rancher, businessman and agricultural advisor for the Agency for International Development, applying his know-how and experience in farming in Pakistan.
Prod-USNAC Dist-USNAC 1972

Simple Distillation C 12 MIN
3/4 OR 1/2 INCH VIDEO CASSETTE
Clarifies the theoretical principles behind simple distillation. Examines glassware. Shows various heat sources.
From The Organic Chemistry Laboratory Techniques Series.
Prod-UCLA Dist-UCEMC

Simple Distillation C 13 MIN
3/4 OR 1/2 INCH VIDEO CASSETTE C A
Shows the step-by-step assembly of the ground joint apparatus required to separate a mixture by simple distillation.
From The Chemistry - Master/Apprentice Series. Program 201
LC NO. 82-706052
Prod-CUETV Dist-CUNIV 1981

Simple Effects For Cinema C 26 MIN
16MM FILM, 3/4 OR 1/2 IN VIDEO I-H
Shows simple but professional visual effects that can be achieved by a novice filmmaker.
Prod-BELMNE Dist-CAROUF

Simple Energy Transformations B 30 MIN
2 INCH VIDEOTAPE J
See series title for descriptive statement.
From The Investigating The World Of Science, Unit 1 - Matter And Energy Series.
Prod-MPATI Dist-GPITVL

Simple Equations B 40 MIN
16MM FILM - 3/4 IN VIDEO
Explains axioms and algebraic rules needed to solve simple linear equations.
LC NO. 78-706291
Prod-USAF Dist-USNAC 1978

Simple Equations - Fractions B 20 MIN
16MM FILM - 3/4 IN VIDEO
Applies axioms and algebraic rules to rearrangement of several electronic formulas.
LC NO. 78-706292
Prod-USAF Dist-USNAC 1978

Simple Foundation, Pt 1 - Layout B 28 MIN
16MM FILM OPTICAL SOUND
Explains, through animation, the layout of a simple foundation, and shows a workman performing the actual operations. Explains how to mark the template with necessary directions.
From The Shipbuilding Skills Series. The Shipfitter, Part 1
LC NO. FIE52-1238
Prod-USN Dist-USNAC 1944

Simple Foundation, Pt 2 - Duplication And Fabrication B 17 MIN
16MM FILM OPTICAL SOUND
Shows how the layout man develops the job from the templates. Depicts fastening the template to the steel plate, marking the plate with the center punch or painting the billing on steel. Shows the use of shears, burning torch, cold press and punch.
From The Shipbuilding Skills Series.
LC NO. FIE52-1240
Prod-USN Dist-USNAC 1944

Simple Foundation, Pt 3 - Assembly And Installation B 23 MIN
16MM FILM OPTICAL SOUND
Demonstrates marking location aboard ship, swinging the assembly aboard and welding the deck and the bulkhead after making corrections.
From The Shipbuilding Skills Series.
LC NO. FIE52-1209
Prod-USN Dist-USNAC 1944

Simple Fractions C 12 MIN
16MM FILM OPTICAL SOUND T
Shows how the basic characteristics of fractions can be taught by cutting familiar objects into parts and then reassembling them.
Prod-SF Dist-SF 1970

Simple Gifts C 54 MIN
16MM FILM OPTICAL SOUND
Describes what people seek and the things they can find on a vacation within a 200 mile radius of New York City. Pictures the feudal setting of architect George Nakashima in Bucks County, a yacht racing champion and his sons in Barnegat Bay, a Shaker festival and fox hunt in Old Chatham, New York, the Harkness Ballet in Rhode Island and a climb to the top of the Adirondack's highest mountain.
LC NO. FIA66-843
Prod-WCBSTV Dist-CBSF 1965

Simple Gifts—A Series
T
Explores the problems and opportunities of working with the gifted and talented.
Prod-UWISC Dist-GPITVL 1977

Creativity 030 MIN
Definition Of Giftedness 030 MIN
Going Deeper 030 MIN
Going Faster 030 MIN
Going Wider 030 MIN
Helping Adult, The 030 MIN
History Of The Educational Treatment Of The 030 MIN
Identification - Convergent 030 MIN
Identification - Divergent 030 MIN
Issues 030 MIN
Qualitatively Different Program 030 MIN
Self-Awareness 030 MIN

Simple Gifts—A Series
16MM FILM, 3/4 OR 1/2 IN VIDEO I-C A
Uses animation to illustrate recollections, stories and fantasies about Christmas from notes and works of Moss Hart, Virginia Woolf, Teddy Roosevelt and other sources such as the classic Nativity story.
Prod-WNETTV Dist-TIMLIF

December 25, 1914 13 MIN
Great Frost, The 15 MIN
Memory Of Christmas 12 MIN
No Room At The Inn 13 MIN

Simple Investing C 60 MIN
3/4 OR 1/2 INCH VIDEO CASSETTE
Presents Dr Mary Elizabeth Schlayer talking with moderator Susan Wright about simple investing for women.
From The How To Be A Financially Secure Woman Series.
Prod-KUHTTV Dist-KUHTTV

Simple Lens, The - An Introduction C 12 MIN
16MM FILM, 3/4 OR 1/2 IN VIDEO J-H
Demonstrates the properties of the simple lens of the camera. Clarifies the principle of light refraction and illustrates the functions of the lens.
Prod-VEILX Dist-PHENIX 1976

Simple Linear Measure C 20 MIN
2 INCH VIDEOTAPE P
See series title for descriptive statement.
From The Mathemagic, Unit VI - Measurement Series.
Prod-WMULTV Dist-GPITVL

Simple Linear Regression With Evaluation And Predictive Techniques C 30 MIN
3/4 OR 1/2 INCH VIDEO CASSETTE IND
Describes how the best straight line may be fit to the data, when it should be fit, how well it fits and how to use the equation to make predictions.
From The Engineering Statistics Series.
Prod-COLOSU Dist-COLOSU

Simple Looms C 13 MIN
3/4 OR 1/2 INCH VIDEO CASSETTE J-C A
Shows how two round sticks, two weights (bricks or stones) and a suitable yarn for the warp and weft are all that is needed to create an attractive woven wall hanging. Demonstrates procedure, start to finish.
Prod-EDMI Dist-EDMI 1976

Simple Machine - The Lever C 10 MIN
3/4 OR 1/2 INCH VIDEO CASSETTE I-J
Describes the three parts of a lever and provides the formula for determining the movements in any lever system.
Prod-PICOLO Dist-PICOLO 1971

Simple Machines C 15 MIN
3/4 OR 1/2 INCH VIDEO CASSETTE I
Uses toys, games, recreational facilities and tools to illustrate how simple machines work.
From The Matter And Motion Series. Module Green
Prod-WHROTV Dist-AITECH 1973

Simple Machines - Inclined Planes (2nd Ed) C 12 MIN
16MM FILM, 3/4 OR 1/2 IN VIDEO I-J
Highlights the important distinction between stationary and moving inclined planes. Demonstrates how the slope of an inclined plane affects the amount of force and its direction.
From The Simple Machines Series.
Prod-CORF Dist-CORF 1984

Simple Machines - Inclined Planes And Levers (3rd Ed) C 17 MIN
16MM FILM, 3/4 OR 1/2 IN VIDEO J
Uses the ramp of a parking garage to illustrate the principles that apply to machines belonging to the lever and plane families. Discusses the concept of work in terms of force and distance.
Prod-EBEC Dist-EBEC 1983

Simple Machines - Inclined Planes And Levers (Spanish) (3rd Ed) C 17 MIN
16MM FILM, 3/4 OR 1/2 IN VIDEO J
Uses the ramp of a parking garage to illustrate the principles that apply to machines belonging to the lever and plane families. Discusses the concept of work in terms of force and distance.
Prod-EBEC Dist-EBEC 1983

Simple Machines - Levers (2nd Ed) C 12 MIN
16MM FILM, 3/4 OR 1/2 IN VIDEO I-J
Uses animation and a prehistoric human to introduce the workings of the lever. Explains that a lever can be any bar that tips back and forth on a point or fulcrum and that a lever exchanges distance for force or force for distance and speed.
From The Simple Machines Series.
Prod-CORF Dist-CORF 1984

Simple Machines - Pulleys (2nd Ed) C 12 MIN
16MM FILM, 3/4 OR 1/2 IN VIDEO I-J
Presents an analogy which makes clear now individual rope segments support part of an object's weight. Uses animation to make it clear how combinations of pulleys are brought together in a block and tackle.
From The Simple Machines Series.
Prod-CORF Dist-CORF 1984

Simple Machines - Using Mechanical Advantage C 18 MIN
16MM FILM, 3/4 OR 1/2 IN VIDEO I-J
Relates the importance of simple machines, such as levers, incline planes, wedges, screws, pulleys, wheels and axles.
From The Elementary Physical Science Series.
Prod-HALDAR Dist-BARR Prodn-BARR 1979

Simple Machines - Wheels And Axles (2nd Ed) C 12 MIN
16MM FILM, 3/4 OR 1/2 IN VIDEO I-J
Introduces animated, prehistoric characters who demonstrate simple machines. Shows how wheels and axles help reduce friction and are used in all sorts of devices to make work easier. Gives examples to depict the exchange between force and distance.
From The Simple Machines Series.
Prod-CORF Dist-CORF 1984

Simple Machines - Working Together C 12 MIN
16MM FILM, 3/4 OR 1/2 IN VIDEO I-J
Uses animated characters to show that the lever, pulley, inclined plane, wheel and axle are simple machines and are the basic building blocks of mechanical devices. Explains that the more these simple machines are used, the easier it is to understand the mechanics of input and output work.
From The Simple Machines Series.
Prod-CORF Dist-CORF 1984

Simple Machines—A Series
16MM FILM, 3/4 OR 1/2 IN VIDEO I-J
Examines pulleys, levers, planes and other simple machines and shows how they are used in everyday life.
Prod-CORF Dist-CORF

Simple Machines - Inclined Planes (2nd Ed) 012 MIN
Simple Machines - Levers (2nd Ed) 012 MIN
Simple Machines - Pulleys (2nd Ed) 012 MIN
Simple Machines - Wheels And Axles (2nd Ed) 012 MIN
Simple Machines - Working Together 012 MIN

Simple Matter Of Justice, A C 26 MIN
16MM FILM, 3/4 OR 1/2 IN VIDEO H-C A
Highlights the history of the Equal Rights Amendment. Describes the International Woman's Year Conference.
Prod-FI Dist-FI 1978

Simple Method For Tracheal Suction And Bronchoscopy C 11 MIN
16MM FILM OPTICAL SOUND
Describes the clinical requirement and prescribed method for performing safe and effective tracheal suction and bronchoscopy on patients who have undergone pulmonary surgery.
LC NO. FIE61-34
Prod-USA Dist-USNAC 1961

Simple Method Of Ureterocele Repair C 12 MIN
16MM FILM OPTICAL SOUND PRO
Presents ureterocele repair by a simple surgical technique not requiring extensive dissection or ureteral re-implantation. Points out that the method effectively prevents reflux, and there have been no complications. Includes pre- and post-operative pyelograms of illustrative cases.
Prod-ACYDGD Dist-ACY 1970

Simple Molds C 10 MIN
16MM FILM, 3/4 OR 1/2 IN VIDEO H-C A
Shows a skilled ceramist demonstrating the step-bystep process of making slipcasting, drape and press molds.
From The Craftsmanship In Clay Series.
Prod-NET Dist-IU 1969

Simple Overcall, The C 30 MIN
3/4 OR 1/2 INCH VIDEO CASSETTE A
See series title for descriptive statement.
From The Play Bridge Series.
Prod-KYTV Dist-KYTV 1983

Simple Plants - Algae B 30 MIN
2 INCH VIDEOTAPE J
See series title for descriptive statement.
From The Investigating The World Of Science, Unit 4 - Plants And Their Adaptations Series.
Prod-MPATI Dist-GPITVL

Simple Plants - Fungi B 30 MIN
2 INCH VIDEOTAPE J
See series title for descriptive statement.
From The Investigating The World Of Science, Unit 4 - Plants And Their Adaptations Series.
Prod-MPATI Dist-GPITVL

Simple Plants - The Algae X 18 MIN
16MM FILM, 3/4 OR 1/2 IN VIDEO H
Illustrates typical forms of algae, explains their structure and traces their evolutionary development. Photomicrography shows reproductive processes.
From The Biology Series. Unit 6 - Plant Classification And Physiology
Prod-EBF Dist-EBEC 1962

Simple Plants - The Algae (Spanish) C 18 MIN
16MM FILM, 3/4 OR 1/2 IN VIDEO H
Illustrates typical forms of algae, explaining their structure and describing their evolutionary development. Uses photomicrography to show the reproductive processes of algae. Emphasizes the importance of algae to aquatic animals and man.
From The Biology (Spanish) Series. Unit 6 - Plant Classification And Physiology
Prod-EBEC Dist-EBEC

Simple Plumbing Repairs C 21 MIN
16MM FILM, 3/4 OR 1/2 IN VIDEO J-C A
Illustrates several basic tools needed for simple plumbing repairs. Shows common problems and tells how to solve them.
From The Home Repairs Series.
LC NO. 81-706035
Prod-CENTRO Dist-CORF 1981

Simple Programming Example, A C 45 MIN
3/4 OR 1/2 INCH VIDEO CASSETTE IND
See series title for descriptive statement.
From The Microprocessors - Fundamental Concepts And Applications Series.
Prod-ICSINT Dist-ICSINT

Simple Silver Working X 10 MIN
16MM FILM OPTICAL SOUND J-C A
Demonstrates the method of silver decoration known as repousse, or chasing. Antonio Castillo, famous silver worker of Old Mexico, is shown translating an original design for a bar pin into a finished piece of jewelry.
Prod-ALLMOR Dist-AVED 1957

Simple Slab Methods C 10 MIN
16MM FILM, 3/4 OR 1/2 IN VIDEO J-H
Demonstrates three slab methods. Shows wedging, rolling out the piece and the correct use of basic tools.
From The Craftmanship In Clay Series.
Prod-IU Dist-IU

Simple Song Of Freedom, A C 30 MIN
16MM FILM OPTICAL SOUND J-C A
Presents an anti-war poetic documentary film.
Prod-CFS Dist-CFS

Simple Techniques In Shaping Glass C 9 MIN
16MM FILM, 3/4 OR 1/2 IN VIDEO H-C
Introduces basic tools and techniques for handling glass in a chemistry laboratory.
From The Fundamentals Of Chemistry Series.
Prod-CENTRO Dist-CORF

Simple Time-Interval Measurement System, A, Pt 1 C 30 MIN
3/4 OR 1/2 INCH VIDEO CASSETTE IND
Shows how a time interval measurement system is designed and implemented. Gives a microprocessor implementation program available in ROM for permanent storage. First of two lectures.
From The Microprocessors For Monitoring And Control Series.
Prod-COLOSU Dist-COLOSU

Simple Time-Interval Measurement System, A, Pt 2 C 30 MIN
3/4 OR 1/2 INCH VIDEO CASSETTE IND
Shows how a time interval measurement system is designed and implemented. Gives a microprocessor implementation program, available in ROM for permanent storage. Second of two lectures.
From The Microprocessors For Monitoring And Control Series.
Prod-COLOSU Dist-COLOSU

Simple Voltage Regulators B 22 MIN
16MM FILM OPTICAL SOUND
Identifies the purpose of each component in a simple voltage regulator circuit and shows the current paths. Explains the circuit operation when the input voltage and the load are changed. Discusses the effect of placing VR tubes in the series. (Kinescope)
LC NO. 74-705646
Prod-USAF Dist-USNAC

Simple Waves B 27 MIN
16MM FILM OPTICAL SOUND H-C
Shows elementary characteristics of waves by means of pulse propagation on ropes and slinkies. Effects are shown at regular speeds and in slow motion. A torsion bar wave-machine is used to demonstrate reflection.
From The PSSC Physics Films Series.
Prod-PSSC Dist-MLA 1959

Simplemente Jenny C 33 MIN
16MM FILM, 3/4 OR 1/2 IN VIDEO H-C A
Explores the varied cultural influences, from religion to advertising and popular culture, which shape the lives of women in Latin America.
Prod-IWFP Dist-CNEMAG 1977

Simpleton Peter C 27 MIN
16MM FILM, 3/4 OR 1/2 IN VIDEO
Presents the English story of Peter who is stumped by a wise woman's complicated riddles. Reveals that after he marries, he is able to answer the riddles with his wife's help, thus proving the value of a clever wife.
From The Storybook International Series.
Prod-JOU Dist-JOU 1982

Simplify, Simplify C 22 MIN
16MM FILM OPTICAL SOUND
Takes a behind-the-scenes look at the development of Metropolitan Life Insurance Company's corporate advertising campaign from conception to production of television commercials.
LC NO. 77-702492
Prod-MLIC Dist-COMCRP Prodn-COMCRP 1977

Simplifying Complex Fractions B 30 MIN
16MM FILM OPTICAL SOUND T
Shows how to manipulate algebraic complex fractions using various techniques such as inverting the divisor and multiplying, combining numerator terms or denominator terms and factoring, and cancelling. Analyzes the simple continued fraction.
From The Advanced Algebra Series.
Prod-CALVIN Dist-MLA Prodn-UNIVFI 1960

Simply Making Jewelry C 18 MIN
3/4 OR 1/2 INCH VIDEO CASSETTE
Reveals how unusual pieces can be made with easily available objects and materials, and how jewelry need not require expensive metals and gems. Shows how necklaces, pendants and earrings can be made from wood, metal grids, wire, dowels, screw eyes, suede lace, string and button blanks, all easily obtained from hardware stores, art and garment supply houses.
Prod-IFF Dist-IFF

Simply Metric C 20 MIN
16MM FILM, 3/4 OR 1/2 IN VIDEO I-J
Uses animation to give a history of the circumstances that led up to the introduction of the French metric system. Analyzes the system itself.
Prod-FLMFR Dist-FLMFR

Simply Scientific—A Series
16MM FILM, 3/4 OR 1/2 IN VIDEO P-I
Discusses certain aspects of astronomy, geology and the scientific method.
Prod-LCOA Dist-LCOA 1981

Beyond The Stars - A Space Story	012 MIN
Byron B Blackbear And The Scientific Method	015 MIN
How To Dig A Hole To The Other Side Of The	011 MIN
Lightning And Thunder Case, The	014 MIN
Microcomputers - An Introduction	015 MIN

Simpson Street C 22 MIN
16MM FILM, 3/4 OR 1/2 IN VIDEO H-C A
Examines the sociological and political reasons for the deterioration of the South Bronx.
Prod-ICARUS Dist-ICARUS 1980

Simtameciu Godos (Lithuanian) B 22 MIN
3/4 OR 1/2 INCH VIDEO CASSETTE
Documents the subject of Lithuania's centenarian citizens.
Prod-IHF Dist-IHF

Simulated Home Visits—A Series

Demonstrates actual patient visits in the home by community health nurses. Focuses on selected health problems and shows how to interview, examine and teach patients, adapt nursing interventions to home settings and incorporate family members in the case plan.
Prod-UTEXN Dist-AJN

Abuse	036 MIN
Cirrhotic Patient, The	035 MIN
Diabetic Patient, The	020 MIN
Dialyzed Patient, The	030 MIN
Myocardial Infarction Person, The	024 MIN
Stroke Patient, The	030 MIN

Simulation C 30 MIN
3/4 OR 1/2 INCH VIDEO CASSETTE T
Defines and demonstrates simulation.
From The Stretch Strategies For Teaching Handicapped Children Series.
Prod-HUBDSC Dist-HUBDSC

Simulation C 30 MIN
3/4 OR 1/2 INCH VIDEO CASSETTE T S
Presents a dream sequence in which a teacher visits a simulation factory which designs a simulation exercise for her to use in a social studies project.
From The Project STRETCH (Strategies To Train Regular Educators To Teach Children With...) Series. Module 9
LC NO. 80-706645
Prod-METCO Dist-HUBDSC 1980

Simulation C 30 MIN
3/4 INCH VIDEO CASSETTE H A
Tells how pseudorandom processes are generated for use in simulation. Analyzes the simulation of a game of chance.
From The Computing For Every Man Series.
Prod-NYSED Dist-NYSED 1973

Simulation C 60 MIN
3/4 OR 1/2 INCH VIDEO CASSETTE
See series title for descriptive statement.
From The Introduction To BASIC Series. Lecture 8
Prod-UIDEEO Dist-UIDEEO

Simulation - High Green To Training C 16 MIN
16MM FILM OPTICAL SOUND C A
Shows how Conduction-Missouri is applying its space technology and manufacturing skills to the development and manufacturing of one of the world's first railroad train simulators. Depicts and explains the operation of the various sub-systems of the simulator. Includes a live dialog sequence that portrays the use of the railroad simulator in a typical training situation.
LC NO. 71-706110
Prod-CONMIS Dist-MCDO Prodn-MCDO 1969

Simulation - The Next Best Thing To Being There C 30 MIN
16MM FILM OPTICAL SOUND T
Shows a dream in which a classroom teacher visits a simulation factory which designs a simulation exercise for her to use in a social studies project.
From The Project STRETCH Series. Module 9
LC NO. 80-700616
Prod-METCO Dist-HUBDSC Prodn-GAEDTN 1980

Simulation In Pilot Training C 20 MIN
16MM FILM, 3/4 OR 1/2 IN VIDEO
Discuses the advantages of using simulators in pilot training, describing the improvements from the days of the Blue Box Simulator of World War II. Features the moon simulator, the combat simulator, C-5 and DC-10 simulators, and the research simulator.
LC NO. 81-707725
Prod-USAF Dist-USNAC 1978

Simulation Of A Gemini Spacecraft Land Landing System, A C 17 MIN
3/4 INCH VIDEO CASSETTE
Simulates gliding parachute descent at Ft Hood and continues with analog simulation requirements, map plotting, altitude readouts and its commanding roll, pitch and yaw. Includes a simulated Gemini parasail reentry run.
Prod-NASA Dist-NASA 1972

Simulation Through Role-Playing C 13 MIN
3/4 OR 1/2 INCH VIDEO CASSETTE
Shows how to use role playing as a 'fun' exercise vs a learning process, using complex roles, simple roles, instructor controlled roles.
From The Dynamic Classroom Series.
Prod-RESEM Dist-RESEM

Simulations And Games C 30 MIN
3/4 OR 1/2 INCH VIDEO CASSETTE A
Investigates computer simulations and games, and the features that make them valuable as educational tools. Explains the concepts of digital and analog communication and 'booting DOS'.
From The Bits And Bytes Series. Pt 8
Prod-TVOTAR Dist-TIMLIF 1984

Simultaneous Drilling And Production C 20 MIN
3/4 OR 1/2 INCH VIDEO CASSETTE
Emphasizes the concepts involved in standard safety controls when both drilling and production are in progress. Illustrates the procedures which must be undertaken by those operating the systems.
Prod-FLMWST Dist-FLMWST

Simultaneous Two-Team Abdominal Perineal Resection Of The Rectum C 24 MIN
16MM FILM OPTICAL SOUND PRO
Shows a combined abdominal perineal resection of the lower sigmoid and rectum which has been carried out employing two surgical teams simultaneously. Demonstrates both the drawbacks and advantages of this procedure.
Prod-ACYDGD Dist-ACY 1961

Sin (Alpha Plus Beta) C
16MM FILM OPTICAL SOUND
Explains the equation Sin equals 1 plus root 3 over 2 root 2.
Prod-OPENU Dist-OPENU 1979

Sin Of Virtue, The B 30 MIN
16MM FILM OPTICAL SOUND
Presents the story about Rabbi Israel Salanter who convinced the surviving members of the Jewish community of Vilna, during a plague 125 years ago, to break the fast on Yom Kippur so that their lives might be saved.
LC NO. FIA64-1180
Prod-JTS Dist-NAAJS Prodn-NBC 1963

Sinaga's Family - A Batak Village C 18 MIN
16MM FILM OPTICAL SOUND H-C A
Explores the day-to-day life of a family living in a small village on Lake Taba in Indonesia.
From The Asian Neighbors - Indonesia Series.
LC NO. 75-703586
Prod-FLMAUS Dist-AVIS 1975

Sinai C 30 MIN
3/4 OR 1/2 INCH VIDEO CASSETTE
See series title for descriptive statement.
From The Arabs And Israelis Series.
Prod-WGBHTV Dist-PBS

Sinai Field Mission C 127 MIN
16MM FILM, 3/4 OR 1/2 IN VIDEO
Shows the routine activities of the diplomats and electronics technicians who operate the US Sinai Field Mission, the early warning system established in 1976 to help facilitate the disengagement between Egypt and Israel after the 1973 war.
Prod-WISEF Dist-ZIPRAH

Sinatra Live In Concert C 52 MIN
1/2 IN VIDEO CASSETTE BETA/VHS
Presents a live, one-man concert by Frank Sinatra, first presented on Japanese television. Contains Japanese subtitles, commentary and commercials, but Sinatra sings in English.
Prod-UNKNWN Dist-VIDIM 1974

Sinbad And The Eye Of The Tiger C 114 MIN
16MM FILM OPTICAL SOUND P A
Presents the continuing adventures of Sinbad in the sequel to Golden Voyage Of Sinbad. Directed by Sam Wanamaker. Stars Taryn Power, Patrick Wayne and Jane Seymour. Special effects by Ray Harryhousen.
Prod-CPC Dist-TIMLIF 1977

Sinbad The Sailor C 20 MIN
16MM FILM OPTICAL SOUND
Describes the life of the Beggar Boy of Baghdad as brought to the screen through the Mount Puppets, the creations of two San Francisco artists.
Prod-RLUCE Dist-RADIM

Since '45 C 30 MIN
16MM FILM, 3/4 OR 1/2 IN VIDEO J-C A
Uses old film clips and recollections of many notable people to take a nostalgic look at the significant national and world events of the three decades following 1945. Emphasizes those events that reflect a changing culture and the media's pervasive influence on it.
LC NO. 81-707617
Prod-KORM Dist-FI 1980

Sincerely Yours, Mrs Mitchell B 20 MIN
2 INCH VIDEOTAPE P
Helps children communicate effectively through written words via friendly letters. (Broadcast quality)
From The Language Lane Series. Lesson 18
Prod-CVETVC Dist-GPITVL Prodn-WCVETV

Sinclair Story, The C 18 MIN
16MM FILM OPTICAL SOUND
Documents the importance of data and records in comparative medicine. Presents research done with mini-swine at the Sinclair Research Farm of the University of Missouri.

LC NO. 73-700388
Prod-UMO Dist-UMO 1972

Sind Sie Herr Berger C 15 MIN
16MM FILM, 3/4 OR 1/2 IN VIDEO
See series title for descriptive statement.
From The Guten Tag Series. Part 4
Prod-BAYER Dist-IFB 1968

Sindrome De Trastorno Respiratorio Del Adulto C 19 MIN
3/4 OR 1/2 INCH VIDEO CASSETTE PRO
A Spanish version of Adult Respiratory Distress Syndrome. Describes the adult R.D.S entity and its many etiologies including the most common causes, confirming diagnosis and management.
Prod-UMICHM Dist-UMICHM 1980

Sine Graph C 20 MIN
3/4 OR 1/2 INCH VIDEO CASSETTE J-C
See series title for descriptive statement.
From The Math Topics - Trigonometry Series.
Prod-BBCTV Dist-FI

Sine Of Obtuse Angles C 20 MIN
3/4 OR 1/2 INCH VIDEO CASSETTE J-C
See series title for descriptive statement.
From The Math Topics - Trigonometry Series.
Prod-BBCTV Dist-FI

Sine Wave And Phase, The C
3/4 OR 1/2 INCH VIDEO CASSETTE
See series title for descriptive statement.
From The Basic Electricity - AC Series.
Prod-VTRI Dist-VTRI

Sinew-Backed Bow And Its Arrows C 24 MIN
16MM FILM, 3/4 OR 1/2 IN VIDEO I-C
Depicts a Yurok craftsman constructing a sinew-backed bow, the strongest and finest bow used by American Indians. Demonstrates how arrows were made, using stone arrowheads and feathers from the red tailed hawk.
From The American Indian Series.
Prod-UCEMC Dist-UCEMC 1961

Sing A Song And Work Along C 10 MIN
3/4 OR 1/2 INCH VIDEO CASSETTE K-P
Focuses on the knowledge and skill to recognize and interpret the story lines in songs.
From The Book, Look And Listen Series.
Prod-MDDE Dist-AITECH 1977

Sing A Song Of Friendship C 20 MIN
16MM FILM OPTICAL SOUND
Adapted from the book, 'SING A SONG OF FRIENDSHIP.' Presents songs on human rights written and sung by Irving Caesar. Songs are illustrated by cartoons and words are printed so the audience can participate.
Prod-ADL Dist-ADL 1949

Sing Along C 15 MIN
3/4 OR 1/2 INCH VIDEO CASSETTE P
Presents songs from the entire Song Sampler Series.
From The Song Sampler Series.
LC NO. 81-707071
Prod-JCITV Dist-GPITVL 1981

Sing An Answer C 15 MIN
3/4 OR 1/2 INCH VIDEO CASSETTE P
Combines looking, listening, talking, writing and reading to help establish the link between oral and written language. Presents the folk song Billy Boy.
From The I Want To Read Series.
Prod-LACOS Dist-GPITVL 1976

Sing Beast Sing C 9 MIN
16MM FILM, 3/4 OR 1/2 IN VIDEO J-C A
Employs a humorous animated film format to tell about a monster who plays blues music on the piano before an equally curious audience.
LC NO. 83-706784
Prod-INRCKL Dist-FLOWER 1980

Sing High, Sing Low C 19 MIN
3/4 OR 1/2 INCH VIDEO CASSETTE P-I
Introduces even and uneven rhythm and demonstrates good singing posture.
From The USS Rhythm Series.
Prod-ARKETV Dist-AITECH 1977

Sing It Again, Senor Snake C 15 MIN
3/4 OR 1/2 INCH VIDEO CASSETTE P
Combines looking, listening, talking, writing and reading to help establish the link between oral and written language. Presents the story The Snake Who Wanted To Fly, a traditional Mexican folk tale and the song I Can Fly.
From The I Want To Read Series.
Prod-LACOS Dist-GPITVL 1976

Sing Joyfully C 28 MIN
16MM FILM, 3/4 OR 1/2 IN VIDEO J-C A
Shows the work of the Choir School of St Thomas Church in New York City.
Prod-ROPE Dist-PHENIX 1976

Sing What You Say C 15 MIN
3/4 OR 1/2 INCH VIDEO CASSETTE T
Uses the adventures of a pirate and his three friends to explore the many levels of language arts. Focuses on the concept of learning to express oneself through music.
From The Hidden Treasures Series. No. 1
LC NO. 82-706525
Prod-WCVETV Dist-GPITVL 1980

Sing-Song Of Old Man Kangaroo, The C 11 MIN
16MM FILM, 3/4 OR 1/2 IN VIDEO K-P
Tells how long ago in Australia, Old Man Kangaroo was gray and woolly like all the other animals, but he wanted to be different. The Big God agreed to his request and sent the dingo to chase him. By five o'clock the kangaroo had been chased right out of his old shape and into one that was very different. Adapted from the short story The Sing-Song Of Old Man Kangaroo by Rudyard Kipling.
From The Just So Stories Series.
LC NO. 83-706961
Prod-CORF Dist-CORF 1983

Singapore C 20 MIN
16MM FILM, 3/4 OR 1/2 IN VIDEO J-C A
Visits Singapore which was first settled in 1819 as a port on the route from East Asia to Europe. Shows that it is now one of the best equipped ports of the world as well as a modern, beautiful city.
Prod-LUF Dist-LUF 1979

Singendes Deutschland B 16 MIN
16MM FILM, 3/4 OR 1/2 IN VIDEO
Features 15 German songs illustrated by appropriate German scenes and dances.
Prod-IFB Dist-IFB 1952

Singer Instaload (Sound/Filmstrip Projector/Viewer) C 11 MIN
3/4 OR 1/2 INCH VIDEO CASSETTE
See series title for descriptive statement.
From The Audio-Visual Skills Modules Series.
Prod-MDCC Dist-MDCC

Singer Not The Song, The C 129 MIN
16MM FILM OPTICAL SOUND H-C A
Presents a drama about the conflict between a Catholic priest and a murderous bandit who want to control the people of a fear-gripped Mexican village.
LC NO. FI67-1311
Prod-RANKOR Dist-WB 1961

Singhalese Fisherman Of Ceylon C 14 MIN
16MM FILM OPTICAL SOUND I-C A
Depicts life in Unakaruva, a fishing village on the southern shore of Ceylon. Tells the story of Upasena, his wife and their four children.
From The Human Family, Pt 1 - South And Southeast Asia Series.
Prod-AVED Dist-AVED 1972

Singing America's Songs—A Series
16MM FILM, 3/4 OR 1/2 IN VIDEO K-I
Presents America's patriotic songs.
Prod-EVANSA Dist-AIMS 1972

America	010 MIN
America The Beautiful	010 MIN
Battle Hymn Of The Republic, The	011 MIN
God Bless America	009 MIN
Star Spangled Banner, The	011 MIN

Singing Bone, The C 13 MIN
16MM FILM OPTICAL SOUND P-I
An excerpt from the motion picture The Wonderful World Of The Brothers Grimm. Presents an adaptation of the fairy tale about a magic flute that sings a song about a servant's unrewarded bravery and his master's treachery. Based on the story Der Singende Knochen by Jakob and Wilhelm Grimm.
From The Peppermint Stick Selection Series.
LC NO. 76-701279
Prod-FI Dist-FI 1976

Singing Frogs And Toads C 11 MIN
16MM FILM, 3/4 OR 1/2 IN VIDEO J-H
Shows five species of frogs and one species of toad. Presents the songs typical of each species.
Prod-IFB Dist-IFB 1961

Singing Marine, The B 106 MIN
16MM FILM OPTICAL SOUND J-C A
Stars Dick Powell, Doris Weston and Lee Dixon. Presents the musical numbers created and staged by Busby Berkeley, including 'CAUSE MY BABY SAYS IT'S SO,' 'I KNOW NOW,' 'SONG OF THE MARINES' and 'NIGHT OVER SHANGHAI.'
Prod-WB Dist-UAE 1937

Singing On The Mountain B 12 MIN
16MM FILM OPTICAL SOUND
Presents a photographic record of the annual Singing on the Mountain, an annual gathering of thousands of mountain folk to one of the largest community song festivals in America.
Prod-MORTON Dist-MORTON 1958

Singing To Millions, Rounding To Thousands - Estimating To Thousands C 15 MIN
3/4 OR 1/2 INCH VIDEO CASSETTE I
Shows how Alice estimates the revenues Mac will earn on a new recording contract.
From The Figure Out Series.
Prod-MAETEL Dist-AITECH 1982

Singing Tree, The C 15 MIN
16MM FILM OPTICAL SOUND P-I
Presents 100 school children and singer Billy Brennan who use songs to teach scientific concepts about the growth and and function of trees, such as photosynthesis, absorption of soil nutrients and water by roots, and the protective role of bark.
LC NO. 82-700468
Prod-UWISCA Dist-UWISCA 1980

Singing Trilogy, The C 15 MIN
3/4 OR 1/2 INCH VIDEO CASSETTE P
See series title for descriptive statement.
From The Magic Pages Series.
Prod-KLVXTV Dist-AITECH 1976

Singing Whales, The C 24 MIN
16MM FILM, 3/4 OR 1/2 IN VIDEO I-C
A shortened version of The Singing Whales. Describes the migration of the humpback whales and discusses the reasons for their annual migration.
From The Undersea World of Jacques Cousteu Series.
Prod-METROM Dist-CF 1975

Singing Whales, The C 52 MIN
16MM FILM, 3/4 OR 1/2 IN VIDEO I-C A
Reports on studies of the humpback whale by Jacques Cousteau and his oceanographers. Discusses the threatened extinction of all whales by hunters from protein-hungry nations.
From The Undersea World Of Jacques Cousteau Series.
Prod-METROM Dist-CF 1975

Singing With The Leprechauns B 15 MIN
2 INCH VIDEOTAPE P
See series title for descriptive statement.
From The Sounds Like Magic Series.
Prod-MOEBA Dist-GPITVL Prodn-KYNETV

Singing Words C 20 MIN
2 INCH VIDEOTAPE P-I
See series title for descriptive statement.
From The Learning Our Language, Unit V - Exploring With Books Series.
Prod-MPATI Dist-GPITVL

Single C 60 MIN
3/4 OR 1/2 INCH VIDEO CASSETTE
Looks at the issues faced by single people and the implications of this large and growing group.
Prod-WCCOTV Dist-WCCOTV

Single Arm Coordinators / Front And Back Knee Touch / Jumping Leg Crossovers C 15 MIN
3/4 OR 1/2 INCH VIDEO CASSETTE P
Presents several exercises which can be performed in a classroom setting.
From The Roomnastics Series.
Prod-WVIZTV Dist-GPITVL 1979

Single Armlifts Forward / Sideward Bend With Front And Back Bend / Leg Bend And Crossover C 15 MIN
3/4 OR 1/2 INCH VIDEO CASSETTE P
Presents several exercises which can be performed in a classroom setting.
From The Roomnastics Series.
Prod-WVIZTV Dist-GPITVL 1979

Single Armlifts Sideward / Trunk Twist With Front And Back Bend / Leg Coordinator C 15 MIN
3/4 OR 1/2 INCH VIDEO CASSETTE P
Presents several exercises which can be performed in a classroom setting.
From The Roomnastics Series.
Prod-WVIZTV Dist-GPITVL 1979

Single Armstretchers / Trunk Twist And Rotation / Leg Circles C 15 MIN
3/4 OR 1/2 INCH VIDEO CASSETTE P
Presents several exercises which can be performed in a classroom setting.
From The Roomnastics Series.
Prod-WVIZTV Dist-GPITVL 1979

Single Beam Spectrophotometer, Wavelength Calibration C 9 MIN
3/4 INCH VIDEO CASSETTE PRO
Demonstrates calibration of a single-beam spectrophotometer using a didymium filter at 585 nanometers.
LC NO. 79-708036
Prod-CFDISC Dist-USNAC 1979

Single Concept Drug Film—A Series

Discusses the use of various drugs. Issued in 1971 as a motion picture series.
Prod-NIMH Dist-USNAC 1980

Alcohol	005 MIN
Drug Abuse	005 MIN
Hallucinogens	005 MIN
Marihuana	005 MIN
Narcotics	005 MIN
Sedatives	005 MIN
Stimulants	005 MIN
Tobacco	005 MIN
Volatile Substances	005 MIN

Single Handed Sailing C 15 MIN
16MM FILM OPTICAL SOUND I-C A
Teaches the points of sailing in a bay and racing skills in setting sails and trimming the boat while reaching, running and beating.
From The Sports Film Olympic Promotion Series.
LC NO. 72-705664
Prod-SPORTF Dist-SPORTF 1970

Single Insulator Changeout C
3/4 OR 1/2 INCH VIDEO CASSETTE IND
Shows that the objective of a single insulator changeout is to lift and secure one conductor clear of its insulator. Demonstrates use of a temporary conductor holder, rubber gloves and an aerial device.
From The Live Line Maintenance Series.
Prod-LEIKID Dist-LEIKID

Single Light, A C 30 MIN
16MM FILM, 3/4 OR 1/2 IN VIDEO J-H A

An edited version of thw motion picture A Single Light. Presents a story which shows the importance of forgiveness. Based on the novel A SINGLE LIGHT by Maria Wojciechowska.
Prod-LCOA Dist-LCOA 1984

Single Light, A C 55 MIN
16MM FILM, 3/4 OR 1/2 IN VIDEO J-H A
Presents a story which shows the importance of forgiveness. Based on the novel A SINGLE LIGHT by Maria Wojciechowska.
Prod-LCOA Dist-LCOA 1984

Single Living C 30 MIN
3/4 OR 1/2 INCH VIDEO CASSETTE C A
Looks at social and personality characteristics, security, happiness and problems of the unmarried. Examines advantages, disadvantages, myths and stereotypes that surround the single person.
From The Family Portrait - A Study Of Contemporary Lifestyles Series. Lesson 11
Prod-SCCON Dist-CDTEL

Single Parent C 42 MIN
16MM FILM, 3/4 OR 1/2 IN VIDEO J-C A
Presents a portrait of the life of a divorced woman and the burdens she must cope with.
Prod-MEDIAG Dist-MEDIAG 1978

Single Parent Experience, The C 29 MIN
3/4 INCH VIDEO CASSETTE
Talks about the joys and pitfalls of being a single parent.
From The Woman Series.
Prod-WNEDTV Dist-PUBTEL

Single Parent Family C
3/4 OR 1/2 INCH VIDEO CASSETTE A
Explores the way in which schools and communities are responding to nearly half the nation's children.
From The Vital Link Series.
Prod-EDCC Dist-EDCC

Single Parent Family, The C 15 MIN
16MM FILM, 3/4 OR 1/2 IN VIDEO I-C A
Examines the adjustments that children and parents must make after a divorce. Follows the case of a fictional couple whose divorce results in the woman having to face the problems and issues of single parenthood.
From The Family Life - Transitions In Marriage Series.
LC NO. 81-707285
Prod-GORKER Dist-CORF 1981

Single Parent, The C 28 MIN
16MM FILM, 3/4 OR 1/2 IN VIDEO
See series title for descriptive statement.
From The Look At Me Series.
Prod-PEREN Dist-PEREN

Single Parent, The, Pt 1 C 22 MIN
16MM FILM OPTICAL SOUND A
Covers the issues of conflicts faced by single parents in responding both to needs of children and the demands of a job. Covers also the issue of establishing new relationships and loneliness.
Prod-AACD Dist-AACD 1981

Single Parent, The, Pt 2 C 22 MIN
16MM FILM OPTICAL SOUND A
Explores remarriage of an ex-spouse, social situations around a two-parent-family, and needs of a single parent for help from family and friends.
Prod-AACD Dist-AACD 1981

Single Parents C 28 MIN
3/4 INCH VIDEO CASSETTE I-C
Highlights the joys and jolts of the single parent experience.
From The Are You Listening Series.
LC NO. 80-707405
Prod-STURTM Dist-STURTM 1980

Single Parents - And Other Adults C 25 MIN
16MM FILM, 3/4 OR 1/2 IN VIDEO A
Presents 18 vignettes showing situations single parents are likely to encounter with other adults such as struggling with an ex-spouse over money and visiting arrangements, trying to find a new mate or a date at the same time that children require so much attention, making holidays festive and dealing with grandparents' concern over how a new single parent will manage.
Prod-MTI Dist-MTI

Single Parents And Their Children C 18 MIN
16MM FILM, 3/4 OR 1/2 IN VIDEO A
Presents 13 vignettes showing stressful situations faced by single parents including the need to be both mother and father, bringing other adult's into children's lives, coping with the simultaneous demands of children, work and household maintenance, and arranging children's visits.
Prod-MTI Dist-MTI

Single Pass Fillet C 3 MIN
1/2 IN VIDEO CASSETTE BETA/VHS IND
See series title for descriptive statement.
From The Welding Training (Comprehensive) - Metal Inert Gas (M I G) Welding Series.
Prod-RMI Dist-RMI

Single Pass Fillet (Vertical Down) C 2 MIN
1/2 IN VIDEO CASSETTE BETA/VHS IND
See series title for descriptive statement.
From The Welding Training (Comprehensive) - Metal Inert Gas (M I G) Welding Series.
Prod-RMI Dist-RMI

Single Pass Fillet Weld C 15 MIN
3/4 OR 1/2 INCH VIDEO CASSETTE IND
See series title for descriptive statement.
From The Arc Welding Training Series.
Prod-AVIMA Dist-AVIMA

Single Phase Boundary Potentials / Electrochemical Potentials / Half-Cells, E... C 53 MIN
3/4 OR 1/2 INCH VIDEO CASSETTE
Discusses single phase boundary potentials, electrochemical potentials, half-cells, E not accessible, standard electrode potentials and thermodynamic and other single ion properties.
From The Electrochemistry, Pt III - Thermodynamics Of Galvanic Cells Series.
Prod-MIOT Dist-MIOT

Single Phase Boundary Potentials, Electrochemical Potentials, Half-Cells,... C 53 MIN
3/4 OR 1/2 INCH VIDEO CASSETTE
Discusses single phase boundary potentials, electrochemical potentials, half-cells, standard electrode potentials and thermodynamic and other single ion properties.
From The Electrochemistry Series.
Prod-KALMIA Dist-KALMIA

Single Process Blonding (Tinting) (1) C
3/4 OR 1/2 INCH VIDEO CASSETTE
Demonstrates a variety of techniques and coloring effects. Shows how to lighten brown hair that has been permanent-waved, and how to lighten or darken several shades of graying hair while achieving natural results. Explains formulation, experimentation and swatch testing.
Prod-MPCEDP Dist-MPCEDP 1984

Single Process Tint Application C
3/4 OR 1/2 INCH VIDEO CASSETTE
Explains the concepts of 'lift' and 'deposit,' oxidation and various volumes of peroxide. Covers the entire procedure of the tinting service from client consultation to after-care advice. Details the strand test procedure, sectioning, and virgin application of tint. Outlines the correct procedure for removal of tint from the hair and finishing procedures.
Prod-MPCEDP Dist-MPCEDP 1984

Single Ram Vertical Surface Broaching B 28 MIN
16MM FILM, 3/4 OR 1/2 IN VIDEO
Shows how to install broaching inserts for straddle broaching, mount the tool-holder with its assembled broaching tool, mount and adjust the work fixture, and surface-broach at production rate.
From The Machine Shop Work - Operations On A Broaching Machine Series. No. 2
Prod-USOE Dist-USNAC Prodn-RAYBEL 1945

Single Sideband Radio - Introduction B 19 MIN
3/4 INCH VIDEO CASSETTE
Explains the theory of single sideband radio techniques and discusses SSB as compared with AM techniques. Issued in 1960 as a motion picture.
LC NO. 79-707779
Prod-USMC Dist-USNAC Prodn-USN 1979

Single Slit L-1 C 3 MIN
16MM FILM SILENT H-C
Shows variable width and variable wave length.
From The Single-Concept Films In Physics Series.
Prod-OSUMPD Dist-OSUMPD 1963

Single Stage Proctocolectomy For Ulcerative Colitis C 22 MIN
16MM FILM OPTICAL SOUND PRO
Shows a two team combined abdomino-perineal approach to proctocolectomy and ileostomy in a young man with severe ulcerative colitis.
Prod-ACYDGD Dist-ACY 1970

Single Subscripted Variables C 29 MIN
3/4 OR 1/2 INCH VIDEO CASSETTE J-C A
Introduces arrays and subscripted variables and shows how to dimension arrays. Explains the elements of a list and presents programs with one-dimensional arrays. Shows how to use more than one array, how to sort a list of numbers and how a list of names can be printed in alphabetical order.
From The Programming For Microcomputers Series. Unit 18
LC NO. 83-707136
Prod-IU Dist-IU 1983

Single Thyroid Nodule, The C 19 MIN
16MM FILM OPTICAL SOUND PRO
Presents the single thyroid nodule. Discusses the selection of cases for surgery and the methods of management including those situations where malignancy is encountered.
Prod-ACYDGD Dist-ACY 1961

Single Tuned RF Amplifier B 26 MIN
16MM FILM OPTICAL SOUND
Discusses the single tuned RF amplifiers using capacitive and transformer coupling. Explains circuit operation with respect to a parallel resonant tank in the plate circuit of the capacitance coupled amplifier. Explains circuit operation with respect to a series resonant tank in the grid circuit of the transformer coupled amplifier's second stage.
LC NO. 75-700581
Prod-USAF Dist-USNAC

Single-Celled Animals, The - Protozoa (Spanish) C 17 MIN
16MM FILM, 3/4 OR 1/2 IN VIDEO H
Illustrates the characteristics and behavior of each class of protozoans. Demonstrates the processes of digestion and reproduction in protozoans and discusses theories of protozoan evolution.
From The Biology (Spanish) Series. Unit 7 - Animal Classification And Physiology
Prod-EBEC Dist-EBEC

Single-Concept Films In Physics—A Series

Prod-OSUMPD Dist-OSUMPD

Absorption Spectra A-4	3 MIN
Coupled Oscillators - Equal Masses M-1	3 MIN
Coupled Oscillators - Unequal Masses M-2	3 MIN
Critical Temperature H-1	3 MIN
Double Slit L-2	3 MIN
Ferromagnetic Domain Wall Motion E-1	3 MIN
Inertial Forces - Centripetal Acceleration M-5	3 MIN
Inertial Forces - Translational	3 MIN
Measurement Of 'G' - Cavendish Experiment M-3	3 MIN
Michelson Interferometer L-4	3 MIN
Nonrecurrent Wavefronts W-3	3 MIN
Paramagnetism Of Liquid Oxygen E-2	3 MIN
Radioactive Decay A-1	3 MIN
Resolving Power L-3	3 MIN
Scintillation Spectrometry A-2	3 MIN
Single Slit L-1	3 MIN
Tacoma Narrows Bridge Collapse W-4	3 MIN
Temperature Waves W-1	3 MIN
Wilberforce Pendulum M-6, The	3 MIN

Single-Parent Families C 30 MIN
3/4 OR 1/2 INCH VIDEO CASSETTE C A
Profiles the relationship of adults and children in a single-parent family. Explores the legal, financial, emotional and social problems of single-parent faimlies.
From The Family Portrait - A Study Of Contemporary Lifestyles Series. Lesson 27
Prod-SCCON Dist-CDTEL

Single-Phase And Polyphase Circuits B 17 MIN
16MM FILM - 3/4 IN VIDEO IND
Explains a single-phase synchronous generator, the use of sine curves to illustrate flow changes, a two-phase system and three-phase system, and ways to simplify wiring. Issued in 1945 as a motion picture.
From The Electrical Work - Electrical Machinery Series. No. 1
LC NO. 78-706140
Prod-USOE Dist-USNAC Prodn-RAYBEL 1978

Single-Stage Amplifiers C 12 MIN
3/4 OR 1/2 INCH VIDEO CASSETTE
Covers single-stage amplifiers, operating points and load lines, biasing circuits, biasing common-collector and common-base amplifiers.
From The Industrial Electronics - Amplifiers Series.
Prod-TPCTRA Dist-TPCTRA

Single-Station Hand-Operated Bench Punch C 24 MIN
1/2 IN VIDEO CASSETTE BETA/VHS IND
Demonstrates the operation and set-up for changing punches and dies in a hand-operated single-station bench punch.
Prod-RMI Dist-RMI

Singles Strategy C 29 MIN
3/4 OR 1/2 INCH VIDEO CASSETTE
Features Lew Gerrard and Don Candy giving tennis instructions, emphasizing singles strategy.
From The Love Tennis Series.
Prod-MDCPB Dist-MDCPB

Singles Strategy, Pt 1 C 29 MIN
3/4 OR 1/2 INCH VIDEO CASSETTE
See series title for descriptive statement.
From The Vic Braden's Tennis For The Future Series.
Prod-WGBHTV Dist-PBS 1981

Singles Strategy, Pt 2 C 29 MIN
3/4 OR 1/2 INCH VIDEO CASSETTE
See series title for descriptive statement.
From The Vic Braden's Tennis For The Future Series.
Prod-WGBHTV Dist-PBS 1981

Singular Perturbation Theory And Geophysics B 50 MIN
16MM FILM OPTICAL SOUND C A
Discusses how geophysical phenomena, the wind-driven Gulf Stream in the Atlantic and the Kuroshio in the Pacific, from the point of view of singular perturbation theory with extensive comments about the boundary between applied and pure mathematics.
From The MAA Mathematics Series.
LC NO. 74-702789
Prod-MAA Dist-MLA 1974

Sink - Float C 14 MIN
3/4 OR 1/2 INCH VIDEO CASSETTE P
Gives experience in classifying things that float versus things that sink.
From The Hands On, Grade 2 - Lollipops, Loops, Etc Series. Unit 3 - Classifying
Prod-WHROTV Dist-AITECH 1975

Sink Or Swim C 15 MIN
3/4 INCH VIDEO CASSETTE J-C A
Explains the basics of floating and swimming.
From The Afloat And Aboat Series.
Prod-MDDE Dist-GPITVL 1979

Sinking Of The Lusitania, The B 17 MIN
16MM FILM, 3/4 OR 1/2 IN VIDEO H-C
Tells how the sinking of the Lusitania in 1915 turned the tide of public opinion against Germany and paved the way for America's declaration of war.
From The World War I Series.
Prod-CBSTV Dist-FI 1967

Sino-American Relations - A New Beginning C 16 MIN
3/4 OR 1/2 INCH VIDEO CASSETTE H-C A
Documents the opening of American-Chinese relations in the early 1970's. Tells how this alliance integrated China into the world community.
Prod-UPI Dist-JOU

Sins Of The Father, The C 29 MIN
16MM FILM OPTICAL SOUND
Describes how a young woman's marriage is almost destroyed by the memories of her father's incestuous relationship with her.
From The This Is The Life Series.
Prod-LUTTEL Dist-LUTTEL 1983

Sinus Or Sinusitis C 13 MIN
3/4 OR 1/2 INCH VIDEO CASSETTE PRO
Reviews the physiology of the sinuses. Provides the physician with an appropriate method of evaluation and differential diagnosis of patients who complain of 'sinus trouble.' Discusses treatment plans based on the cause of the disease for both acute and chronic infections.
Prod-UMICHM Dist-UMICHM 1976

Siobhan Mc Kenna C 29 MIN
2 INCH VIDEOTAPE
Presents exchanges and arguments between the dean of American theatre critics, Elliot Norton, and Siobhan Mc Kenna.
From The Elliot Norton Reviews II Series.
Prod-WGBHTV Dist-PUBTEL

Sioux County, Iowa, USA C 22 MIN
16MM FILM OPTICAL SOUND
Reports on the activities of farm cooperatives in Sioux County, Iowa, a county which has numerous farm cooperatives and is noted for its many residents of Dutch descent.
LC NO. FIA67-5815
Prod-FARMI Dist-FARMI 1966

Sioux Legends C 20 MIN
16MM FILM, 3/4 OR 1/2 IN VIDEO I-C A
Presents members of the Sioux tribes in South Dakota acting out some of their legends and folklores. Gives an impression of Indian culture and daily life before the arrival of the white man and shows the universality of folklore.
Prod-NAUMAN Dist-AIMS 1974

Sips And Songs C 28 MIN
3/4 OR 1/2 INCH VIDEO CASSETTE J A
Features entertainer Phil Gordon as he sings familiar songs.
Prod-SUTHRB Dist-SUTHRB

Siqueiros, El Maestro - March Of Humanity In Latin America X 14 MIN
16MM FILM, 3/4 OR 1/2 IN VIDEO J-C
Presents a documentary account of the largest mural ever created, 'THE MARCH OF HUMANITY IN LATIN AMERICA,' painted by David Siqueiros in Mexico City. Explains some of the artistic innovations of Siqueiros, emphasizing esculpto-pintura. Includes scenes of the artist as he supervises, paints, plans and discusses his techniques and his philosophy reflected in the theme of the mural.
From The Rasgos Culturales Series.
Prod-EBEC Dist-EBEC 1969

Siqueiros, El Maestro - The March Of Humanity In Latin America (Spanish) C 14 MIN
16MM FILM, 3/4 OR 1/2 IN VIDEO J-C
Focuses on The March Of Humanity In Latin America, a mural by David Siqueiros. Shows how Siqueiros employs a combination of sculpture and painting techniques in order to create his murals. Discusses the artist's philosophy and explains how it is reflected in the theme of the mural.
Prod-EBEC Dist-EBEC

Sir Arthur 'Bomber' Harris - Marshal Of The Royal Air Force C 52 MIN
16MM FILM, 3/4 OR 1/2 IN VIDEO
Describes the career of Sir Arthur Harris, who was charged with the massive bombings of German cities during World War II.
From The Commanders Series. No. 5
LC NO. 79-706895
Prod-BBCTV Dist-TIMLIF 1976

Sir Francis Drake - The Rise Of English Sea Power B 30 MIN
16MM FILM, 3/4 OR 1/2 IN VIDEO I-H
Shows how Sir Francis Drake won England the right-of-way into a new continent, captured vast treasures, terrorized the Spanish Navy and persuaded the people of England to 'look to the sea for their strength.'
Prod-EBF Dist-EBEC 1957

Sir John Peck C 29 MIN
3/4 INCH VIDEO CASSETTE
Interviews Sir John Peck, former British ambassador to Ireland. Gives his thoughts on the Irish problem and offers a tour of his home in Ireland.
From The Dana Wynter In Ireland Series.
Prod-GRIAN Dist-PUBTEL

Sir Johnny-On-The-Spot C 12 MIN
16MM FILM, 3/4 OR 1/2 IN VIDEO P-I
Uses marionettes to tell the story of a princess and the two dragons who long to carry her in a parade.
Prod-CENTRO Dist-CORF

Sir William Slim - Field Marshal, British Army C 62 MIN
16MM FILM, 3/4 OR 1/2 IN VIDEO
Discusses Sir William Slim, the British commander in the Burma-India theater during the Second World War. States that he was loved by his troops but tough enough to countermand direct orders from generals.
From The Commanders Series. No. 4
LC NO. 79-706894
Prod-BBCTV Dist-TIMLIF 1976

Sirene C 10 MIN
16MM FILM, 3/4 OR 1/2 IN VIDEO H-C
Presents the story of a mermaid in the harbor of a modern city who is charmed by a young man playing a flute and attempts to flee with him but the machines that surround the harbor destroy her. Provides a satirical story of present day commercial life.
Prod-SERVA Dist-IFB 1970

Sirens, Symbols And Glamour Girls, Pt 1 B 26 MIN
16MM FILM OPTICAL SOUND
Discusses the glamour girls of motion pictures and how the movie image of the ideal woman has changed. Includes scenes of Mary Pickford, Gloria Swanson, Greta Garbo, Jean Harlow, Mae West, Bette Davis, Lana Turner, Rita Hayworth and others.
From The Hollywood And The Stars Series.
LC NO. FI68-249
Prod-WOLPER Dist-WOLPER 1963

Sirens, Symbols And Glamour Girls, Pt 2 B 26 MIN
16MM FILM OPTICAL SOUND
Shows a view of the glamour girls of the screen - Rita Hayworth, Ava Gardner, Marilyn Monroe, Elizabeth Taylor. Analyzes their fame and power and discusses the price they pay. Includes scenes of young ingenues who hope to achieve fame.
From The Hollywood And The Stars Series.
LC NO. 79-701987
Prod-WOLPER Dist-WOLPER 1963

Sirius C 51 MIN
16MM FILM, 3/4 OR 1/2 IN VIDEO J-C A
Tells a story about a young Czechoslovakian boy, his parents and his beloved dog Sirius during the early years of World War II. Shows how the boy is forced to examine his values when the Nazis demand that all dogs be surrendered for training as attack dogs.
From The Featurettes For Children Series.
Prod-CFET Dist-FI Prodn-BARFLM 1978

Sirius And The White Dwarf C 8 MIN
16MM FILM OPTICAL SOUND H-C A
Uses computer animation to demonstrate the motions of the star system composed of Sirius and its companion Sirius B, a white dwarf star. Discusses the laws and calculations that resulted in the discovery of the first white dwarf.
From The Explorations In Space And Time Series.
LC NO. 75-703982
Prod-HMC Dist-HMC 1974

Sister C 22 MIN
16MM FILM OPTICAL SOUND
Depicts the thoughts and feelings of ten nuns on their work, the Church and modern life, and their service and commitment to God.
LC NO. 75-703003
Prod-ARCHCC Dist-CORPRO 1975

Sister Kenny B 116 MIN
1/2 IN VIDEO CASSETTE (BETA)
Stars Rosalind Russell as Sister Elizabeth Kenny, the nurse who crusaded for the treatment of infantile paralysis.
Prod-UNKNWN Dist-BHAWK 1946

Sister Of The Bride C 30 MIN
16MM FILM, 3/4 OR 1/2 IN VIDEO J-C A
Presents the story of two white, middle-class sisters whose mother, although divorced, tries to pressure them into early marriages. Follows the last few days before the elder's sister marriage, probing her doubts and uncertainties while the younger sister realizes that a career as a veterinarian is the most important thing in her life.
From The Planning Ahead Series.
LC NO. 83-706619
Prod-BERKS Dist-UCEMC 1982

Sister's Bay And Water, Water, Ice C 15 MIN
3/4 OR 1/2 INCH VIDEO CASSETTE
Consists of images of waves, ice breaking up and flowing water.
Prod-EAI Dist-EAI

Sisters In Crime C 29 MIN
3/4 INCH VIDEO CASSETTE
Explains why the crime rate among women is increasing several times faster than the male crime rate. Looks at the growing numbers of all-women gangs, the need for women in law enforcement, and the lack of rehabilitation in women's prisons.
From The Woman Series.
Prod-WNEDTV Dist-PUBTEL

Sisyphus C 10 MIN
16MM FILM OPTICAL SOUND C A
Shows the destructiveness of materialism by telling the story of a man who was driven out of his mind when his possessions took on an animate force.
LC NO. 72-700404
Prod-ZAGREB Dist-MMA 1970

Sisyphus B 3 MIN
16MM FILM, 3/4 OR 1/2 IN VIDEO J-C A
Shows a man pushing an ever-larger boulder up an ever-growing mountain with the use of animation.
Prod-JANK Dist-PFP 1975

Sit And Stay C 30 MIN
3/4 OR 1/2 INCH VIDEO CASSETTE H-C A
Shows Barbara Woodhouse's method of teaching a dog to sit and stay.
From The Training Dogs The Woodhouse Way.
Prod-BBCTV Dist-FI 1982

Sit Down - Sit Danish C 14 MIN
16MM FILM OPTICAL SOUND
Presents the story of Danish furniture and shows its role in the lives of everyday people.
Prod-RDCG Dist-AUDPLN

Sit Down, Doctor - And Live C 11 MIN
16MM FILM, 3/4 OR 1/2 IN VIDEO
Emphasizes the advantages and value of 'sit-down dentistry,' noting that dentists have been punishing their legs and backs needlessly for generations by working all day in a standing position and without adequate assistance.
Prod-VADTC Dist-USNAC 1969

Sit Down, Shut Up, Or Get Out C 58 MIN
16MM FILM, 3/4 OR 1/2 IN VIDEO H-C A
Presents an allegorical story about a gifted boy who doesn't fit the pattern at home or at school. Shows how his parents, teachers and peers react with strong emotions to this person who is determined to be himself.
Prod-NBC Dist-FI 1971

Sit Down, Stand Up, Thank You And You're Welcome C 15 MIN
2 INCH VIDEOTAPE P
See series title for descriptive statement.
From The Avenida De Ingles Series.
Prod-SDITVA Dist-GPITVL

Sit Housing Report C 9 MIN
3/4 OR 1/2 INCH VIDEO CASSETTE
Features practical advice on coping with housing problems and the local agencies where viewers can go for help.
Prod-NOVID Dist-NOVID

Sit In On Selling C 21 MIN
16MM FILM - 3/4 IN VIDEO
Presents information on how store salespeople can satisfy their customers. Explores the relationship at the point of sales, clarifies causes of dissatisfaction, outlines the sales associate's role in offering advice, as a seller, and in closing a sale in a way that will bring the customer back again.
Prod-BNA Dist-BNA

Sit-Ins, The - Students Take Direct Action B 30 MIN
16MM FILM OPTICAL SOUND H-C A
Joanne Grant describes the tactics of student demonstrators who used the sit-in to dramatize their insistence on a desegregated South and discusses the effect of the sit-ins on the civil rights movement.
From The Black Heritage, Section - The Freedom Move- Ment - America And Beyond Series.
LC NO. 75-704109
Prod-WCBSTV Dist-HRAW 1969

Sitar, The C 17 MIN
16MM FILM, 3/4 OR 1/2 IN VIDEO
Introduces Western audiences to the sitar, an Indian string instrument. Deals with the origin, history, philosophy, ritual, composition and performance of classical Indian music. Features sitarist Rooshikumar Pandya performing parts of three ragas.
Prod-HME Dist-UCEMC 1974

Site B 10 MIN
16MM FILM OPTICAL SOUND
Deals with a film-document of a dance by Bob Morris and Carolee Schneeman set in a black infinite space.
Prod-VANBKS Dist-VANBKS

Sittin' On Top Of The World - At The Fiddlers' Convention C 24 MIN
16MM FILM, 3/4 OR 1/2 IN VIDEO J-C A
Presents a documentary on the oldest and largest bluegrass music festival of the United States, held in the Smokey Mountains of North Carolina. Presents both contemporary and traditional performances of authentic American mountain music and dance, including many selections on the banjo and dulcimer.
Prod-PHENIX Dist-PHENIX 1974

Sitting Bull - A Profile In Power C 26 MIN
16MM FILM, 3/4 OR 1/2 IN VIDEO H-C A
Explores, through the use of an imaginary historical interview, the life and role of Chief Sitting Bull.
Prod-LCOA Dist-LCOA Prodn-MCADLT 1976

Sitting Bull - A Profile In Power (Spanish) C 26 MIN
16MM FILM, 3/4 OR 1/2 IN VIDEO H-C A
Produces an appreciation for the controversial and enigmatic native American, Sitting Bull.
From The Profiles In Power (Spanish) Series.
Prod-LCOA Dist-LCOA Prodn-MCADLT 1977

Sitting On Top Of The World B 5 MIN
16MM FILM OPTICAL SOUND
Sails with the nuclear submarine Sargo under the Arctic ice cap.
From The Screen News Digest Series. Vol 2, Issue 8
Prod-HEARST Dist-HEARST 1960

Sitting Too Long C 10 MIN
2 INCH VIDEOTAPE
See series title for descriptive statement.
From The Janaki Series.
Prod-WGBHTV Dist-PUBTEL

Situation Analysis C 35 MIN
3/4 OR 1/2 INCH VIDEO CASSETTE
See series title for descriptive statement.
From The Situation Management Series.
Prod-EXECDV Dist-DELTAK

Situation Ethics C 30 MIN
3/4 OR 1/2 INCH VIDEO CASSETTE J-C A
Features Joseph Fletcher of the University of Virginia Medical School talking about situation ethics.
From The Moral Values In Contemporary Society Series.
Prod-AMHUMA Dist-AMHUMA

Situation Management—A Series

Presents an approach to problem solving and decision making that is conscious, visible, systematic and repeatable. Contains a set of ideas that can be learned in a short period of time and

applied immediately on the job and in everyday life. Includes a leader's guide and a participant's guide.
Prod-EXECDV Dist-DELTAK

Decision Making	027 MIN
Problem Diagnosis	035 MIN
Problem Prevention	026 MIN
Situation Analysis	035 MIN

Situational Approach To Managing People C 8 MIN
3/4 OR 1/2 INCH VIDEO CASSETTE A
Consists of eight separate videotapes totaling five hours of lessons in managing people. Emphasizes the premise that there is no one best style of leadership but that good leadership varies with the style of the manager and with the requirements of the situation.
Prod-CBSFOX Dist-CBSFOX

Situational Leadership C
16MM FILM, 3/4 OR 1/2 IN VIDEO A
Uses the film 'Twelve O'Clock High' to learn about leadership, motivation, performance and the process of change. Includes a comprehensive leader's guide, three instructional tapes featuring Dr Paul Hershey, key graphics and tapes of 'Twelve O'Clock High.'
Prod-FI Dist-FI

Situational Leadership C 16 MIN
3/4 OR 1/2 INCH VIDEO CASSETTE
Introduces concepts of Situational Leadership a technique designed to help leaders assess the performance of others, achieve results, develop people and contribute to organizational success.
Prod-UNIVAS Dist-UNIVAS

Situational Leadership - Developing Leadership Skills C 20 MIN
3/4 OR 1/2 INCH VIDEO CASSETTE
Features Dr Paul Hersey in a presentation of his 'Situational Leadership Model.' Provides a visual presentation of the situational leadership model and a follow-up to readings on the theory. Includes a Situational Leadership handout and a Situational Leadership Summary handout.
Prod-DELTAK Dist-DELTAK

Siu Mei Wong - Who Shall I Be C 18 MIN
16MM FILM, 3/4 OR 1/2 IN VIDEO I-J
Tells the story of a young Chinese girl, living in Los Angeles' Chinatown, who yearns to become a ballerina. Describes the family's conflict when her ballet lessons infringe upon her education at the Chinese school where she has been sent by her father to make sure she retains her Chinese culture. Tells how her father decides that he must not let his own deep ties to tradition prevent his daughter from having a chance to pursue her own goals.
From The Many Americans Series.
Prod-LCOA Dist-LCOA 1971

Siu Mei Wong - Who Shall I Be (Captioned) C 17 MIN
16MM FILM, 3/4 OR 1/2 IN VIDEO I-J A
Presents the story of a young girl in Chinatown, Los Angeles, who wants to be a ballerina, against her father's wishes.
Prod-LCOA Dist-LCOA 1970

Six American Familes—A Series
A
Focuses on contemporary life and studies a month in the life of six American families. Shows them in their daily situation - living, working, relaxing and making decisions, both good and bad. Features the families as they view a replay of the ethnical choices they have made and discuss those choices with an objective observer.
Prod-GROUPW Dist-ECUFLM Prodn-UCHC 1976

Burk Family, The	052 MIN
George Family, The	052 MIN
Greenberg Family, The	052 MIN
Kennedy Family,The	052 MIN
Pasiak Family, The	052 MIN
Stephens Family, The	052 MIN

Six American Families—A Series
16MM FILM, 3/4 OR 1/2 IN VIDEO H-C A
Looks at families in six different geographical locations. Records their joys and sorrows, expectations and frustrations, hopes and fears.
Prod-GROUPW Dist-CAROUF

Burks Of Georgia, The	056 MIN
Georges Of New York City, The	053 MIN
Greenbergs Of California, The	058 MIN
Kennedys Of Albuquerque, The	059 MIN
Pasciaks Of Chicago, The	059 MIN
Stephenses Of Iowa, The	058 MIN

Six Bells—A Series

Prod-NIMBUS Dist-NIMBUS 1976

Birth Of The Haunted	27 MIN

Six Billion Dollar Sell, The C 15 MIN
16MM FILM, 3/4 OR 1/2 IN VIDEO I-C A
Examines clips from actual television commercials and makes use of animation, comedy sketches and children talking about their actual experiences to show people how not to be taken in by television commercials.
From The Consumer Reports Series.
Prod-CU Dist-FI 1977

Six Characters In Search Of An Author C 60 MIN
3/4 OR 1/2 INCH VIDEO CASSETTE H-C A
Discusses stylization, avantgardism, black theatre and realism in drama. Uses the play Six Characters In Search Of An Author as an example.
From The Drama - Play, Performance, Perception Series. Conventions Of The Theatre
Prod-BBCTV Dist-FI 1978

Six Days In June B 14 MIN
16MM FILM OPTICAL SOUND
Presents a compilation of newsreel films from Israel and documentary material from Egypt, showing the events which lead to the Six Day War in June, 1967. Depicts the fighting during the war and Jerusalem liberated and unified.
Prod-ALDEN Dist-ALDEN

Six Deadly Skids, The C 27 MIN
1 INCH VIDEOTAPE
Presents competition driver Denise Mc Cluggage demonstrating causes of skids and how to control them. Award winner.
Prod-LIBMIC Dist-MTP

Six Fathoms Deep C 30 MIN
16MM FILM - 3/4 IN VIDEO J-C A
Recounts several major oil spills and some constructive responses to them. Explains that more than half of the world's trade is in oil, some 600 million tons a year. Discusses controlling oil pollution.
From The Man Builds - Man Destroys Series.
Prod-UN Dist-GPITVL

Six Feet Of The Country C 29 MIN
16MM FILM, 3/4 OR 1/2 IN VIDEO H-C A
Tells how a husband and wife abandon the racial tensions of Johannesburg, South Africa, and escape to the country to coexist with black laborers. Based on the short story Six Feet Of The Country by Nadine Gordimer.
LC NO. 81-707202
Prod-PERSPF Dist-CORF 1980

Six Filmmakers In Search Of A Wedding C 13 MIN
16MM FILM, 3/4 OR 1/2 IN VIDEO
Presents six filmmakers. Depicts the different technical and style of each. Provides their views of a simple family wedding.
Prod-ENVIC Dist-PFP 1971

Six Fragments C 6 MIN
3/4 OR 1/2 INCH VIDEO CASSETTE
Offers a mystifying picture of an inner psyche faced with the fact of its own mortality.
From The Four Short Tapes Series.
Prod-EAI Dist-EAI

Six Great Ideas—A Series
16MM FILM, 3/4 OR 1/2 IN VIDEO
Presents philosopher Mortimer J Adler and journalist Bill Moyers as they explore western civilization's greatest concepts, including truth, beauty, goodness, liberty, equality and justice.
Prod-WNETTV Dist-FI 1982

Beauty	060 MIN
Equality	060 MIN
Goodness	060 MIN
Justice	060 MIN
Liberty	060 MIN
Truth	060 MIN

Six Heavy Fish And A Ton Of Sinkers C 16 MIN
16MM FILM OPTICAL SOUND J-C A
Portrays the discovery, recovery and restoration of six cannons jettisoned from Captain James Cook's ship 'ENDEAVOUR' on Australia's Great Barrier Reef 200 years ago.
LC NO. 72-702255
Prod-AUSCOF Dist-AUIS 1972

Six Hundred Millenia - China's History Unearthed C 89 MIN
3/4 OR 1/2 INCH VIDEO CASSETTE
Presents a documentary about the traveling exhibit of archaeological finds of the People's Republic of China. Uses exclusive film footage to show work at the excavation sites and the process of identifying and classifying the treasures.
Prod-KQEDTV Dist-PBS 1976

Six Hundred, Sixty-Six C 78 MIN
16MM FILM OPTICAL SOUND R
Describes the moral decisions faced by five men who must feed the best of what man has learned through the centuries into the memory banks of the latest computers.
Prod-GF Dist-GF

Six In Paris (French) C 93 MIN
16MM FILM OPTICAL SOUND
Features six episodes involving Parisians in different parts of the city. Includes tales set in St Germain des Pres, Gare du Nord, Rue St Denis, Place de l'Etoile and Montparnasse et Levallois.
Prod-NYFLMS Dist-NYFLMS 1966

Six Keys To Service C 16 MIN
16MM FILM, 3/4 OR 1/2 IN VIDEO
Dramatizes factors that affect the quality of service offered by a business. Shows how to use them to achieve greater customer satisfaction.
From The Customer Service, Courtesy And Selling Programs Series.
Prod-NEM Dist-NEM

Six Keys To Service (Spanish) C 16 MIN
16MM FILM, 3/4 OR 1/2 IN VIDEO
Dramatizes factors that affect the quality of service offered by a business. Shows how to use them to achieve greater customer satisfaction.
From The Customer Service, Courtesy And Selling Programs (Spanish) Series.
Prod-NEM Dist-NEM

Six Loop-Paintings C 11 MIN
16MM FILM OPTICAL SOUND
Shows how sound and image are handmade with the use of acetate adhesive patterned screens and tapes.
Prod-SPINLB Dist-FMCOOP 1970

Six Murderous Beliefs B 12 MIN
16MM FILM OPTICAL SOUND J-H
Tears down six false ideas of safety, such as 'I DON'T HAVE AN ACCIDENT BECAUSE I'M LUCKY' and 'SAFETY IS FOR SISSIES.' Teenagers dramatize the tragic results of such activities as jay walking and reckless driving.
Prod-NSC Dist-NSC 1955

Six Nations, The C 26 MIN
16MM FILM, 3/4 OR 1/2 IN VIDEO
Focuses on the Iriquois League, a group of Indian tribes in New York which rejects the American way of life in favor of a self-sufficient existence on their own land.
From The Native Americans Series.
Prod-BBCTV Dist-CNEMAG

Six O'Clock And All's Well C 60 MIN
16MM FILM, 3/4 OR 1/2 IN VIDEO H-C A
Follows the activities of New York WABC-TV's Eyewitness News team for several weeks during 1977. Shows producers, directors, editors, reporters, technicians and anchormen working on a variety of stories.
Prod-SPNCRR Dist-CNEMAG 1979

Six Penguins, The C 5 MIN
16MM FILM, 3/4 OR 1/2 IN VIDEO P-C A
An animated story in which six penguins and a whale mutually aid each other.
Prod-BULGRA Dist-MGHT 1971

Six Short Films C 7 MIN
16MM FILM, 3/4 OR 1/2 IN VIDEO H-C A
Uses animation to present a sort of contemporary American cinemagraphic primitive, full of visual incongruities in which things are what they seem and then become something else.
Prod-BFA Dist-PHENIX 1973

Six Spectacular Hours—A Series

Presents a collection of 150 songs and more than 40 folk acts garnered from the ninth annual Philadelphia Folk Festival. Features John Hartford, John Denver, Jaime Brockett, Pat and Victoria Garvey, John and Barry, Anne Byrne, Fairport Convention and others.
Prod-WITFTV Dist-PUBTEL

Six Spectacular Hours, Reel 1	2 MIN
Six Spectacular Hours, Reel 2	2 MIN
Six Spectacular Hours, Reel 3	2 MIN
Six Spectacular Hours, Reel 4	2 MIN
Six Spectacular Hours, Reel 5	2 MIN
Six Spectacular Hours, Reel 6	2 MIN
Six Spectacular Hours, Reel 7	2 MIN

Six Spectacular Hours, Reel 1 C 2 MIN
2 INCH VIDEOTAPE
See series title for descriptive statement.
From The Six Spectacular Hours Series.
Prod-WITFTV Dist-PUBTEL

Six Spectacular Hours, Reel 2 C 2 MIN
2 INCH VIDEOTAPE
See series title for descriptive statement.
From The Six Spectacular Hours Series.
Prod-WITFTV Dist-PUBTEL

Six Spectacular Hours, Reel 3 C 2 MIN
2 INCH VIDEOTAPE
See series title for descriptive statement.
From The Six Spectacular Hours Series.
Prod-WITFTV Dist-PUBTEL

Six Spectacular Hours, Reel 4 C 2 MIN
2 INCH VIDEOTAPE
See series title for descriptive statement.
From The Six Spectacular Hours Series.
Prod-WITFTV Dist-PUBTEL

Six Spectacular Hours, Reel 5 C 2 MIN
2 INCH VIDEOTAPE
See series title for descriptive statement.
From The Six Spectacular Hours Series.
Prod-WITFTV Dist-PUBTEL

Six Spectacular Hours, Reel 6 C 2 MIN
2 INCH VIDEOTAPE
See series title for descriptive statement.
From The Six Spectacular Hours Series.
Prod-WITFTV Dist-PUBTEL

Six Spectacular Hours, Reel 7 C 2 MIN
2 INCH VIDEOTAPE
See series title for descriptive statement.
From The Six Spectacular Hours Series.
Prod-WITFTV Dist-PUBTEL

Six Thousand Partners C 20 MIN
16MM FILM OPTICAL SOUND H-C A
Shows the contribution of the products and services of the 6,000 supplying firms which produce the materials and parts necessary for the production of the Ford automobile.
LC NO. FIA52-241
Prod-FMCMP Dist-FORDFL 1950

Six To Eight Months C 10 MIN
3/4 OR 1/2 INCH VIDEO CASSETTE H-C A
Shows how infants between the ages of six to eight months learn by seeing, hearing, feeling, general imitation and through spatial relationships.
From The Teaching Infants And Toddlers Series. Pt 3
Prod-BGSU Dist-GPITVL 1978

Six-Gun Territory X 16 MIN
16MM FILM OPTICAL SOUND
Shows one of Florida's newest tourist attractions, located near Silver springs. Six-gun territory offers a pioneer western town complete with gun fighters, trading post and a saloon, soft drinks and can-can dancers.
Prod-FDC Dist-FDC

Sixes And Sevens C 15 MIN
3/4 INCH VIDEO CASSETTE P
Shows the youngest peer social unit testing independence, defining leadership, exploring decision making, and experimenting with group processes.
From The Becoming Me, Unit 2 - Social Identity Series.
Prod-KUONTV Dist-GPITVL 1974

Sixteen In Webster Groves B 47 MIN
16MM FILM, 3/4 OR 1/2 IN VIDEO H-C A
Explores the social and personal values of 16-year-olds growing up in an affluent Midwestern suburb. Concludes that their attitudes stem directly from their parents' expectations.
Prod-CBSNEW Dist-CAROUF

Sixteen Leading Causes Of OSHA Citations And How To Avoid Them C 20 MIN
3/4 OR 1/2 INCH VIDEO CASSETTE
Takes supervisors on a probing camera tour of a typical plant to reveal common Occupational Safety and Health Administration (OSHA) violations.
Prod-BBP Dist-BBP

Sixteen Mm Film - Classroom Filmart B 2 MIN
16MM FILM OPTICAL SOUND
Shows simple ways of making movies without cameras.
LC NO. 73-702933
Prod-FLMMKR Dist-FLMMKR 1973

Sixteen Tales—A Series
P-I
Presents sixteen folktales from four of America's ethnic cultures - Latin and Hispanic, Black and African, Native American and Asian. Features storytellers and illustrators who reflect this diverse heritage, the former talking about the land and people who passed down the tale in the oral tradition. Introduces students to literature and folklore and leads them into a timeless world of talking animals and simple human beings.
Prod-KLCSTV Dist-AITECH

Ananse And The Golden Box 015 MIN
Angry Moon, The 015 MIN
Blind Man's Daughter, The 015 MIN
Brer Rabbit And The Tar Baby 015 MIN
Coyote And Cottontail / Coyote And The Beaver 015 MIN
Dancing Stars, The / The Friendly Wolf 015 MIN
Fire Bringer, The / How Saynday Brought The 015 MIN
Flea, The 015 MIN
How Ananse Got A Thin Waist / Ananse's 015 MIN
Jose And The Crocodile 015 MIN
Lazy Fox, The / Senor Fox And Senor Coyote 015 MIN
Ma Liang And The Magic Brush 015 MIN
Tale Of Urashima Taro, The 015 MIN
Tepozton, The Magic Boy From The Mountains 015 MIN
Tiger And The Rabbit, The 015 MIN
Wakaima And The Clay Man 015 MIN

Sixteen-Point Program For Spanish-Speaking Americans, The B 24 MIN
16MM FILM - 3/4 IN VIDEO
Shows the 16-point program for providing Spanish-speaking people equal opportunities in Federal employment. Discusses several of the 16 points, including the need for agencies to include Spanish-speaking Americans in their affirmative action programs.
LC NO. 79-706213
Prod-USCSC Dist-USNAC 1973

Sixteenth Olympiad (Australia) B 30 MIN
16MM FILM OPTICAL SOUND
Presents the highlights from all the events in six different films.
Prod-SFI Dist-SFI

Sixteenth-Century English C 12 MIN
16MM FILM OPTICAL SOUND
Features excerpts from a 16th-century book on healthy living, read in the original language of the time and illustrated by original drawings on 16th-century examples.
LC NO. 74-702765
Prod-QFB Dist-QFB Prodn-SDAPRO 1973

Sixth Continent, The C 28 MIN
3/4 OR 1/2 INCH VIDEO CASSETTE H-C A
Discusses the many secrets of man's history held by the ocean. Includes the work of international teams cooperating in marine research to discover major sources of energy in the ocean.
Prod-JOU Dist-JOU

Sixth Day C 27 MIN
3/4 OR 1/2 INCH VIDEO CASSETTE J A
Features Keenan Wynn and Marty Feldman in the story of Creation.
Prod-SUTHRB Dist-SUTHRB

Sixth Day, The C 27 MIN
16MM FILM, 3/4 OR 1/2 IN VIDEO H-C A
Depicts God's first man as a creature with angel's wings, a tail and some horns. Demonstrates God's constant evolutionary process. Stars Keenan Wynn and Marty Feldman.
From The Insight Series.
Prod-PAULST Dist-PAULST

Sixth Face Of The Pentagon, The C 28 MIN
16MM FILM OPTICAL SOUND
Follows the anti-war demonstrators during the two days in October, 1967 when they met at the Pentagon, were openly blocked by the militia and were forced to find a new strategy to make their protest real.
Prod-MARKC Dist-NEWSR

Sixth Infantry Division B 20 MIN
16MM FILM, 3/4 OR 1/2 IN VIDEO H A
Presents scenes from the 6th Infantry Division combat operations in New Guinea, including the securing of the Maffin Bay area, the amphibious landing at Sausapor and the assault at Lingayen Gulf, Luzon.
Prod-USA Dist-USNAC 1948

Sixth Sense, The C 15 MIN
16MM FILM, 3/4 OR 1/2 IN VIDEO P
Shows children how to protect themselves from child molestation.
Prod-KLEINW Dist-KLEINW

Sixth Street Meat Club C 10 MIN
16MM FILM OPTICAL SOUND
Shows the termination of the pacification program of the 'WAR ON POVERTY' as the federal government intervenes in the attempts of a Negro anti-poverty group, to set up their own independent meat cooperative.
Prod-NEWSR Dist-NEWSR

Sixth Wheel, The C 27 MIN
16MM FILM, 3/4 OR 1/2 IN VIDEO J-H A
Follows a salesman, a young mother and a teen-age boy through a day of driving. Observes their driving strengths and weaknesses.
Prod-IFB Dist-IFB 1962

Sixties, The C 15 MIN
16MM FILM, 3/4 OR 1/2 IN VIDEO
Points up the divisions and polarities that stirred the United States during the 1960's using news footage of the decade.
Prod-BRAVC Dist-PFP

Sixties, The C 30 MIN
3/4 OR 1/2 INCH VIDEO CASSETTE H-C A
Examines the emergence of the commercial image in American art. Looks at the techniques and mediums available to the contemporary artist.
From The Art America Series.
Prod-CTI Dist-CTI

Sixty Cycle Cyclops Show C 22 MIN
16MM FILM OPTICAL SOUND
Presents a statement against television's impact on children during 21 years of broadcasting in Australia.
LC NO. 80-700881
Prod-WILBRI Dist-TASCOR 1977

Sixty Days Beneath The Sea - Tektite I C 15 MIN
16MM FILM - 3/4 IN VIDEO
Shows how four aquanauts lived and conducted extensive oceanographic studies during an undersea project. Tells how their behavior in isolation was monitored by surface scientists. Issued in 1970 as a motion picture.
LC NO. 79-707568
Prod-USN Dist-USNAC 1979

Sixty Million Germans And Their Country, The C 28 MIN
16MM FILM OPTICAL SOUND H-C A
Deals with the people of the Federal Republic of Germany, and discusses who these people are and what their special joys and worries are.
Prod-WSTGLC Dist-WSTGLC

Sixty Minutes To Meltdown C 84 MIN
16MM FILM, 3/4 OR 1/2 IN VIDEO H-C A
Presents a docudrama chronicling the minute-by-minute sequence of malfunctions and mistakes at the Three Mile Island nuclear power plant and follows with a documentary examining the lessons raised by the accident and the critical economic and safety questions confronting nuclear power use.
From The Nova Series.
Prod-WGBHTV Dist-TIMLIF 1984

Sixty Second Spot C 25 MIN
16MM FILM, 3/4 OR 1/2 IN VIDEO
Gives an account of the unknown struggles behind the production of a major television commercial. Records a real production, as the producers decide to create a take-off on old desert movies and travel to the desert sands where Beau Geste was filmed.
Prod-MNDLIN Dist-PFP

Sixty-Eight Hundred I, O Operations, Interrupts C
3/4 OR 1/2 INCH VIDEO CASSETTE
See series title for descriptive statement.
From The Microprocessor Series.
Prod-HTHZEN Dist-HTHZEN

Sixty-Eight Hundred Instruction Set, Pt 1 B 60 MIN
3/4 OR 1/2 INCH VIDEO CASSETTE
See series title for descriptive statement.
From The Understanding Microprocessors Series. Pt 7
Prod-UAZMIC Dist-UAZMIC 1979

Sixty-Eight Hundred Instruction Set, Pt 2 B 60 MIN
3/4 OR 1/2 INCH VIDEO CASSETTE
See series title for descriptive statement.
From The Understanding Microprocessors Series. Pt 8
Prod-UAZMIC Dist-UAZMIC 1979

Sixty-Eight Hundred Microprocessor C
3/4 OR 1/2 INCH VIDEO CASSETTE
See series title for descriptive statement.
From The Microprocessor Series.
Prod-HTHZEN Dist-HTHZEN

Sixty-Eight Hundred Microprocessor C
3/4 OR 1/2 INCH VIDEO CASSETTE
See series title for descriptive statement.
From The Microprocessor Video Training Course Series.
Prod-VTRI Dist-VTRI

Sixty-Eight Hundred MPU I/O Operations/Interrupts C
3/4 OR 1/2 INCH VIDEO CASSETTE
See series title for descriptive statement.
From The Microprocessor Video Training Course Series.
Prod-VTRI Dist-VTRI

Sixty-Eight Hundred MPU Stack Operation/Subroutines C
3/4 OR 1/2 INCH VIDEO CASSETTE
See series title for descriptive statement.
From The Microprocessor Video Training Course Series.
Prod-VTRI Dist-VTRI

Sixty-Eight Hundred Stack Operations, Subroutines C
3/4 OR 1/2 INCH VIDEO CASSETTE
See series title for descriptive statement.
From The Microprocessor Series.
Prod-HTHZEN Dist-HTHZEN

Sixty-Four Million Years Ago C 12 MIN
16MM FILM, 3/4 OR 1/2 IN VIDEO K-P
Shows a day in the life of planet Earth when the dinosaur was king. Uses animation and models to show the great reptiles in peaceful life as well as fierce battles.
LC NO. 83-706629
Prod-NFBC Dist-BARR 1982

Sixty-Nine CR 180 - An Artist's Report C 60 MIN
16MM FILM OPTICAL SOUND
Presents a surreal reenactment of the 1968 Democratic Convention turmoil, depicting anti-war activists and cultural revolutionaries, such as Abbie Hoffman, Jerry Rubin, David Dellinger and others. Portrays William Kuntzler and Leonard Weinglass versus Thomas Foran and Richard Schultz, all under the watchful eye of Judge julius Hoffman.
From The Artist As A Reporter Series.
Prod-ROCSS Dist-ROCSS 1970

Sixty-Seven Thousand Dreams C 30 MIN
16MM FILM, 3/4 OR 1/2 IN VIDEO C A
Explains the development of the major theories and concepts of Carl Gustav Jung, including discussion of the collective unconscious, the psychology of types, the psyche in space and time and the importance of myth and intuition to the complete man.
From The Story Of Carl Gustav Jung Series.
Prod-BBCTV Dist-FI 1972

Size And Distance C 6 MIN
16MM FILM, 3/4 OR 1/2 IN VIDEO K-P
Describes the relationship of distance to size.
From The Basic Facts About The Earth, Sun, Moon And Stars Series.
Prod-MORLAT Dist-SF 1967

Size And Weight C 15 MIN
2 INCH VIDEOTAPE K
Experiments with objects having the same size but not necessarily having the same weight.
From The Let's Go Sciencing, Unit I - Matter Series.
Prod-DETPS Dist-GPITVL

Size Of The Moon, The C 8 MIN
16MM FILM, 3/4 OR 1/2 IN VIDEO K-P
Explains the calendar, phases of the moon and why the size of the moon appears to change.
From The Science Series.
Prod-MORLAT Dist-SF 1967

Size, Shape And Motions Of The Earth B 45 MIN
2 INCH VIDEOTAPE C
See series title for descriptive statement.
From The Physical Science Series. Unit 3 - Astronomy
Prod-CHITVC Dist-GPITVL Prodn-WTTWTV

Size, Shape, Color, Texture C 15 MIN
3/4 OR 1/2 INCH VIDEO CASSETTE P
See series title for descriptive statement.
From The Hands On, Grade 1 Series. Unit 1 - Observing
Prod-VAOG Dist-AITECH Prodn-WHROTV 1975

Sizing And Selection C 30 MIN
3/4 OR 1/2 INCH VIDEO CASSETTE
Deals with needs assessment and equipment considerations.
From The Programmable Controllers Series.
Prod-ITCORP Dist-ITCORP

Sizing Solar Collectors, Pt 1 C 25 MIN
3/4 OR 1/2 INCH VIDEO CASSETTE H-C A
Explains the use of the Clear Sky Daily Solar Radiation Table and Average Daily Solar Radiation Table to determine the expected average daily insolation for a tilted surface, the first step in sizing solar collectors.
From The Solar Collectors, Solar Radiation, Insolation Tables Series.
Prod-NCDCC Dist-MOKIN

Sizing Solar Collectors, Pt 2 C 25 MIN
3/4 OR 1/2 INCH VIDEO CASSETTE H-C A
Shows how to calculate the potential harvest of solar collectors. Describes how components affect efficiency and the use of efficiency charts.
From The Solar Collectors, Solar Radiation, Insolation Tables Series.
Prod-NCDCC Dist-MOKIN

Sizing Solar Collectors, Pt 3 C 25 MIN
3/4 OR 1/2 INCH VIDEO CASSETTE H-C A
Explains how to size collectors to meet various levels of estimated water and space-heating demand.
From The Solar Collectors, Solar Radiation, Insolation Tables Series.
Prod-NCDCC Dist-MOKIN

Sizwe Banzi Is Dead C 60 MIN
3/4 OR 1/2 INCH VIDEO CASSETTE H-C A
Discusses stylization, avantgardism, black theatre and realism in drama. Uses the play Sizwe Banzi Is Dead as an example.
From The Drama - Play, Performance, Perception Series. Conventions Of The Theatre
Prod-BBCTV Dist-FI 1978

Skarv - Phalacrocorax Carbo (Cormorant) C 12 MIN
16MM FILM OPTICAL SOUND
Describes the cormorant in its natural surroundings, accompanied by sound effects.
Prod-STATNS Dist-STATNS 1965

Skateboard C 12 MIN
16MM FILM OPTICAL SOUND
Highlights events from the first professional skateboard competition held in the United States. Illustrates the high jump, barrel jump, freestyle and speed slalom.
LC NO. 77-700987
Prod-IMAGEF Dist-MANNT 1976

Skateboard C 12 MIN
16MM FILM, 3/4 OR 1/2 IN VIDEO J
Relates the story of Sandy, an adventurous eight-year-old with a brand new skateboard, bored with coasting on easy hills and her driveway, who decides to ride in the street on a very steep hill that she has been told never to ride on and later runs and hides. Includes exciting motion sequences, a humorous, tough-minded conscience figure and a clear moral statement.
Prod-FRACOC Dist-FRACOC

Skateboard Craze, The C 11 MIN
3/4 OR 1/2 INCH VIDEO CASSETTE
Focuses on skateboarding, a California-initiated fad that became a worldwide sport. Shows skateboarding competitions featuring jumping, downhill racing, and gymnastics.
Prod-UPI Dist-JOU

Skateboard Fever C 12 MIN
16MM FILM OPTICAL SOUND
Presents an impressionistic musical essay on skateboarding. Shows both amateurs and professionals skateboarding to a variety of accompanying musical themes and rhythms.
LC NO. 78-700668
Prod-NFL Dist-NFL 1978

Skateboard Riding Tactics C 15 MIN
16MM FILM, 3/4 OR 1/2 IN VIDEO J-C A
Outlines elements of safe skateboarding, including proper equipment check, the advantages of a low center of gravity, why laws forbid riding in certain areas, the importance of protective gear, keeping control on steep slopes, dangerous surfaces and how to fall to avoid injury.
Prod-CAHILL Dist-AIMS 1978

Skateboard Safety C 13 MIN
16MM FILM, 3/4 OR 1/2 IN VIDEO P-H S
Points out that skateboarding is a sport and like other sports requires training skill and experience. Stresses the importance of protective clothing, how to check for safe equipment, where and how to ride and proper techniques for falling without injury.
Prod-MCDONJ Dist-PFP 1976

Skateboard Sense C 10 MIN
16MM FILM OPTICAL SOUND I-H
Presents the methods which top skateboarders use in wearing proper safety gear while skateboarding. Emphasizes the use of safe places to skateboard.
LC NO. 76-703492
Prod-DAVP Dist-DAVP 1976

Skateboard Sense C 10 MIN
16MM FILM, 3/4 OR 1/2 IN VIDEO P-H
Shows how good equipment and proper riding techniques enhance the thrill and safety of skateboarding techniques. Demonstrates the use of elbow and knee pads, helmets and gloves and shows the ways to take a fall.
Prod-AIMS Dist-AIMS 1976

Skateboarding To Safety C 9 MIN
16MM FILM, 3/4 OR 1/2 IN VIDEO P-J
Presents safety advice for practicing the sport of skateboarding.
Prod-LORIPR Dist-PHENIX 1976

Skateboarding To Safety (Swedish) C 9 MIN
16MM FILM, 3/4 OR 1/2 IN VIDEO P-J
Presents safety advice for practicing the sport of skateboarding.
Prod-LORIPR Dist-PHENIX 1976

Skater Dater C 18 MIN
16MM FILM, 3/4 OR 1/2 IN VIDEO
Portrays a boy's emergence into adolescence as he slowly realizes that his skateboard gang is part of a childhood that he has outgrown.
Prod-BACKLR Dist-PFP 1971

Skater, The C 24 MIN
3/4 OR 1/2 INCH VIDEO CASSETTE
Presents the story of a young girl who is told she can no longer skate because of something someone else did. Focuses on parent and child relationships.
From The Young People's Specials Series.
Prod-MULTPP Dist-MULTPP

Skates Of Uncle Richard, The / Song Of Trees C 15 MIN
3/4 OR 1/2 INCH VIDEO CASSETTE I
Tells of a young girl's dreams of becoming a famous ice skater and of a black family's attempts to save the singing trees. From the books by Carol Fenner and Mildred Taylor.
From The Book Bird Series.
Prod-CTI Dist-CTI

Skates, Wagons, Cycles And Subways To Far-Away Places C 8 MIN
16MM FILM OPTICAL SOUND K-P
Shows Crystal introducing Alistair to wheeled vehicles such as skates, wagons and cycles.
From The Crystal Tipps And Alistair Series.
LC NO. 73-700457
Prod-BBCTV Dist-VEDO 1972

Skating Rink, The C 27 MIN
16MM FILM, 3/4 OR 1/2 IN VIDEO I-C A
Portrays a teenage boy whose stammering and consequent difficulty in communicating his feelings were brought on by his mother's death. Shows how his skating gives him a way of demonstrating his love to his family. An ABC Afterschool Special.
Prod-LCOA Dist-LCOA 1975

Skating Rink, The (Captioned) C 27 MIN
16MM FILM, 3/4 OR 1/2 IN VIDEO P-H A
Centers around a teenager whose early childhood experiences left him with an awkward stutter.
Prod-LCOA Dist-LCOA 1975

Skating Rink, The (Spanish) C 27 MIN
16MM FILM, 3/4 OR 1/2 IN VIDEO P-H A
Centers around a teenager whose early childhood experiences left him with an awkward stutter.
Prod-LCOA Dist-LCOA 1975

Skeletal Adaptations - Variations On A Theme C 24 MIN
16MM FILM, 3/4 OR 1/2 IN VIDEO H-C
Outlines skeletal adaptation as a phenomenon of evolution, an instance of natural selection in animals. Deals with the concepts of convergence and divergence in animal skeleton adaptation, pointing out that convergence indicates that a single end has been achieved although organisms have used different methods.
LC NO. 82-706485
Prod-BBCTV Dist-MEDIAG 1981

Skeletal And Topographic Anatomy—A Series
C A
Illustrates the skeletal and topographic anatomy of the head and neck, the upper extremity, thorax, abdomen, pelvis-perineum and back. Indicates features of particular clinical importance. Reviews major skeletal landmarks. Superimposes bones on living subject. By Henry C Browning, PHD, Professor of Anatomy, University of Texas.
Prod-UTEXMH Dist-TEF

Introduction To Topographic Anatomy	019 MIN
Postnatal Development Of The Skeleton, Pt 1 -	021 MIN
Postnatal Development Of The Skeleton, Pt 2 -	022 MIN
Postnatal Development Of The Skeleton, Pt 3 -	021 MIN
Skeletal Features Of The Lower Extremity	018 MIN
Skeletal Features Of The Pelvis	016 MIN
Skeletal Features Of The Skull, Pt 1 - The	013 MIN
Skeletal Features Of The Skull, Pt 2 - The	018 MIN
Skeletal Features Of The Skull, Pt 3 -	019 MIN
Skeletal Features Of The Skull, Pt 4 -	020 MIN
Skeletal Features Of The Thorax	019 MIN
Skeletal Features Of The Upper Extremity	016 MIN
Skeletal Features Of The Vertebral Column	020 MIN
Topographic Anatomy Of Articular Sites,	020 MIN
Topographic Anatomy Of Articular Sites,	019 MIN
Topographic Anatomy Of Articular Sites,	020 MIN
Topographic Anatomy Of The Abdomen	018 MIN
Topographic Anatomy Of The Back	020 MIN
Topographic Anatomy Of The Head And Neck,	017 MIN
Topographic Anatomy Of The Head And Neck,	012 MIN
Topographic Anatomy Of The Head And Neck,	020 MIN
Topographic Anatomy Of The Head And Neck,	019 MIN
Topographic Anatomy Of The Lower Extremity,	017 MIN
Topographic Anatomy Of The Lower Extremity,	018 MIN
Topographic Anatomy Of The Pelvis,	018 MIN
Topographic Anatomy Of The Thorax, Pt 1 -	019 MIN
Topographic Anatomy Of The Thorax, Pt 2 -	018 MIN
Topographic Anatomy Of The Upper And Lower	022 MIN
Topographic Anatomy Of The Upper Extremity,	015 MIN
Topographic Anatomy Of The Upper Extremity,	015 MIN

Skeletal Features Of The Lower Extremity C 18 MIN
16MM FILM, 3/4 OR 1/2 IN VIDEO C A
See series title for descriptive statement.
From The Skeletal And Topographic Anatomy Series.
Prod-UTEXMH Dist-TEF

Skeletal Features Of The Pelvis C 16 MIN
16MM FILM, 3/4 OR 1/2 IN VIDEO C A
See series title for descriptive statement.
From The Skeletal And Topographic Anatomy Series.
Prod-UTEXMH Dist-TEF

Skeletal Features Of The Skull, Pt 1 - The Cranium C 13 MIN
16MM FILM, 3/4 OR 1/2 IN VIDEO C A
See series title for descriptive statement.
From The Skeletal And Topographic Anatomy Series.
Prod-UTEXMH Dist-TEF

Skeletal Features Of The Skull, Pt 2 - The Face C 18 MIN
16MM FILM, 3/4 OR 1/2 IN VIDEO C A
See series title for descriptive statement.
From The Skeletal And Topographic Anatomy Series.
Prod-UTEXMH Dist-TEF

Skeletal Features Of The Skull, Pt 3 - Vascular Structures C 19 MIN
16MM FILM, 3/4 OR 1/2 IN VIDEO C A
See series title for descriptive statement.
From The Skeletal And Topographic Anatomy Series.
Prod-UTEXMH Dist-TEF

Skeletal Features Of The Skull, Pt 4 - Neural Structures C 20 MIN
16MM FILM, 3/4 OR 1/2 IN VIDEO C A
See series title for descriptive statement.
From The Skeletal And Topographic Anatomy Series.
Prod-UTEXMH Dist-TEF

Skeletal Features Of The Thorax C 19 MIN
16MM FILM, 3/4 OR 1/2 IN VIDEO C A
See series title for descriptive statement.
From The Skeletal And Topographic Anatomy Series.
Prod-UTEXMH Dist-TEF

Skeletal Features Of The Upper Extremity C 16 MIN
16MM FILM, 3/4 OR 1/2 IN VIDEO C A
See series title for descriptive statement.
From The Skeletal And Topographic Anatomy Series.
Prod-UTEXMH Dist-TEF

Skeletal Features Of The Vertebral Column C 20 MIN
16MM FILM, 3/4 OR 1/2 IN VIDEO C A
See series title for descriptive statement.
From The Skeletal And Topographic Anatomy Series.
Prod-UTEXMH Dist-TEF

Skeletal Muscle Relaxants, Their Antagonists B 30 MIN
16MM FILM OPTICAL SOUND C
Describes the anatomy and physiology of skeletal muscle relaxants, focusing on central acting drugs and the peripheral acting drugs. Explains how antagonists of muscle relaxants work.
From The Pharmacology Series.
LC NO. 73-703343
Prod-MVNE Dist-TELSTR 1971

Skeletal Trauma In Commonplace Activities B 21 MIN
16MM FILM OPTICAL SOUND PRO
Surveys examples of traumatic fractures of the extremities.
LC NO. 76-700199
Prod-SIEMEN Dist-AMCRAD Prodn-TELTAC 1975

Skeleton, The (2nd Ed) C 17 MIN
16MM FILM, 3/4 OR 1/2 IN VIDEO J-H
Uses x-ray photography, diagrams and detailed close-ups of several types of bones to aid in identifying the structure, function, composition and overall coordination of the skeleton in humans and other vertebrates. Stresses the importance of proper diet and exercise to maintain healthy bones.
Prod-EBEC Dist-EBEC Prodn-MEDFO 1979

Skeleton, The - An Introduction C 46 MIN
3/4 OR 1/2 INCH VIDEO CASSETTE C A
Presents an introduction to human skeletal anatomy.
Prod-UWO Dist-TEF

Skenduolis (Lithuanian) B 11 MIN
3/4 OR 1/2 INCH VIDEO CASSETTE
Recreates life in Lithuania before Soviet rule.
Prod-IHF Dist-IHF

Sketches From The Tempest C 7 MIN
16MM FILM OPTICAL SOUND
Presents fragments of George Dunning's uncompleted animated version of Shakespeare's classic play The Tempest.
Prod-FWRGHT Dist-FWRGHT 1979

Sketches In Jazz C 30 MIN
3/4 OR 1/2 INCH VIDEO CASSETTE
Presents paintings of the pastoral American countryside with jazz background music provided by Rosemary Clooney, Johnny Hartman and the Loonis McGlohon Trio.
Prod-WNSCTV Dist-MDCPB

Sketches 1 C 3 MIN
16MM FILM OPTICAL SOUND
Presents without narration three audio-visual sketches about the sewing machine.
LC NO. FIA65-1018
Prod-SINGER Dist-SVE Prodn-TORCEL 1964

Sketching C 12 MIN
3/4 OR 1/2 INCH VIDEO CASSETTE
Covers the use of sketches, making of sketches, orthographic, isometric and perspective sketches.
From The Reading Blueprints Series.
Prod-TPCTRA Dist-TPCTRA

Sketching (Spanish) C 12 MIN
3/4 OR 1/2 INCH VIDEO CASSETTE
Covers the use of sketches, making of sketches, orthographic, isometric and perspective sketches.
From The Reading Blueprints Series.
Prod-TPCTRA Dist-TPCTRA

Sketching Eyes With Expression C 29 MIN
3/4 INCH VIDEO CASSETTE C A
Contains several pieces of information that are useful in drawing eyes. Illustrates key eye expressions.
From The Sketching Techniques Series. Lesson 18
Prod-COAST Dist-CDTEL

Sketching Flowers C 29 MIN
3/4 INCH VIDEO CASSETTE C A
Shows that almost all elements of art can be found in flowers. Discusses points to consider in flower arrangement, such as basic geometrical shapes.
From The Sketching Techniques Series. Lesson 17
Prod-COAST Dist-CDTEL

Sketching For Communication C 29 MIN
3/4 INCH VIDEO CASSETTE C A

Emphasizes communication as one of the most valuable uses of drawing. Explains need for drawing in education.
From The Sketching Techniques Series. Lesson 6
Prod-COAST Dist-CDTEL

Sketching In Architecture C 29 MIN
3/4 INCH VIDEO CASSETTE C A
Explains how to apply alignment in architectural drawings. Illustrates how art elements are added to architectural drawings more attractive.
From The Sketching Techniques Series. Lesson 7
Prod-COAST Dist-CDTEL

Sketching Interiors C 29 MIN
3/4 INCH VIDEO CASSETTE C A
Demonstrates how interiors can be suggested by objects usually found in a room. Shows how to create interiors with a few simple lines.
From The Sketching Techniques Series. Lesson 16
Prod-COAST Dist-CDTEL

Sketching Techniques—A Series
C A
Provides students with an introduction to each of the drawing elements. Presented by several artists experienced in various techniques, styles and subject matter.
Prod-COAST Dist-CDTEL

Action	029 MIN
Animals	029 MIN
Caricature	029 MIN
Creating Mood	029 MIN
Design And Decoration	029 MIN
Dominance In Composition	029 MIN
Drawing In Three Dimensions	029 MIN
Drawings By The Classic Artists	029 MIN
Elements Of Value, Color And Texture, The	029 MIN
Hands In Action	029 MIN
Heads And Faces	029 MIN
Proportion	029 MIN
Repetition In Sketching	029 MIN
Sketching Eyes With Expression	029 MIN
Sketching Flowers	029 MIN
Sketching For Communication	029 MIN
Sketching In Architecture	029 MIN
Sketching Interiors	029 MIN
Sources Of Ideas For Drawing	029 MIN
Special Effects In Sketches	029 MIN
Still-Life Sketches	029 MIN
Styles Of Sketching	029 MIN
Summary And Review Of Sketching Techniques	029 MIN
Thumbnail Sketch, The	029 MIN
Tools For Sketching	029 MIN
Two-Pencil Technique, The	029 MIN
Use Of Landscapes In A Sketch, The	029 MIN
Vehicles	029 MIN
Wood And Wooden Objects	029 MIN
Wrinkles	029 MIN

Skeye B 5 MIN
16MM FILM OPTICAL SOUND
Explores some of the aesthetic aspects of astronomical observation.
LC NO. 76-701365
Prod-YORKU Dist-YORKU 1974

Skezag C 73 MIN
16MM FILM, 3/4 OR 1/2 IN VIDEO J-C A
Presents a period of ten hours during which Wayne, a 21-year-old black living in New York City, talks at length about a variety of topics, including his use of heroin and why he won't become addicted. Shows Wayne four months later as he is preparing to leave New York. Points out that his physical deterioration and depressed attitude show a marked change in contrast to his former confidence in his ability to use heroin without becoming addicted.
Prod-CINNAP Dist-CNEMAG 1970

Ski Alberta C 28 MIN
16MM FILM OPTICAL SOUND
Explores some of the skiing thrills of Alberta's Canadian Rockies.
LC NO. 74-702766
Prod-ALBRTA Dist-CTFL Prodn-RANSOM 1973

Ski B C C 13 MIN
16MM FILM OPTICAL SOUND
Shows ski areas and facilities of British Columbia.
LC NO. FIA67-5697
Prod-BRCOL Dist-CTFL 1967

Ski Classic B
16MM FILM OPTICAL SOUND
From The Learn To Ski Series.
Prod-SFI Dist-SFI

Ski Country, USA C 28 MIN
1 INCH VIDEOTAPE
Shows sunshine, powder snow, a variety of slopes, action, expert skiing, skiers and lodges. Features some of the nations top eight major ski areas near Denver.
Prod-UAL Dist-MTP

Ski Cross Country C 22 MIN
16MM FILM, 3/4 OR 1/2 IN VIDEO I-H A
Explores the thrill and enjoyment of cross country skiing amid beautiful Rocky Mountain scenery.
Prod-LUF Dist-LUF 1981

Ski Esta B
16MM FILM OPTICAL SOUND
From The Learn To Ski Series.
Prod-SFI Dist-SFI

Ski Fever C 98 MIN
16MM FILM OPTICAL SOUND C A
Stars Martin Milner, Claudia Martin and Toni Sailer. Presents a musical comedy about fun on the ski slopes with a new twist.
Prod-CINEWO Dist-CINEWO 1968

Ski Fever C 9 MIN
16MM FILM, 3/4 OR 1/2 IN VIDEO I-C A
Portrays the beauty, sport and folly of skiing by presenting scenes of various ski activities.
Prod-LEMSST Dist-PHENIX 1971

Ski Finesse C 28 MIN
16MM FILM OPTICAL SOUND
Features Stein Ericksen, one of the all-time skiing greats, who shares the secrets of his famous style. Illustrates techniques for the beginner, intermediate and advanced jet turn skiier.
LC NO. 75-701530
Prod-BARP Dist-FFORIN 1974

Ski Injuries C 35 MIN
16MM FILM OPTICAL SOUND
Features Arthur Ellison, M D describing the nature of ski injuries and their mechanism of production. Deals mainly with sprains and fractures of the ankle, leg and knee.
Prod-JAJ Dist-JAJ 1973

Ski Instructors C 15 MIN
3/4 OR 1/2 INCH VIDEO CASSETTE I
Explains the qualifications and personal qualities required for a successful career as a ski instructor.
From The Career Awareness Series.
Prod-KLVXTV Dist-GPITVL 1973

Ski Moderne B
16MM FILM OPTICAL SOUND
From The Learn To Ski Series.
Prod-SFI Dist-SFI

Ski Moderne C 10 MIN
16MM FILM OPTICAL SOUND J-C A
Features the world renowned skier Ernie Mc Culloch and his superb demonstration team teaching the very latest techniques in parallel skiing. Shows the basic snowplow turn, traversing, side slipping, stem christies and elementary parallel exercises.
Prod-AVEXP Dist-AVEXP

Ski Mountains Of The West C 27 MIN
16MM FILM OPTICAL SOUND
Presents a guide to the ski mountains and accommodations of America's West.
LC NO. 78-701389
Prod-UAL Dist-MTP Prodn-SUMMIT 1977

Ski Party C 90 MIN
16MM FILM OPTICAL SOUND J-C A
Stars Frankie Avalon and Dwayne Hickman. Concentrates on two star athletes who seek to extend their sports conquests to a pair of luscious co-eds who have been monopolized by a decidedly non-athletic Romeo.
Prod-AIP Dist-TWYMAN 1965

Ski Sense C 27 MIN
16MM FILM OPTICAL SOUND H-C A
Describes the nature and causes of most skiing injuries and builds a strong case for year 'ROUND PHYSICAL CONDITIONING.
Prod-AETNA Dist-AETNA

Ski The Outer Limits C 25 MIN
16MM FILM, 3/4 OR 1/2 IN VIDEO
Demonstrates the essential mechanics of skiing. Depicts the inner limits of the sport, the discipline which must be learned before the skier has the capability for freedom of expression.
Prod-HRTSKI Dist-PFP Prodn-SUMMIT 1968

Ski Wheelers, The C 14 MIN
16MM FILM OPTICAL SOUND P-I
Shows how Genie has the bright idea of fixing a pair of skis to roller skates since there isn't any snow and how Our Gang ends up leaving a trail of destruction behind them as they rush through the shopping center, along the road and through various gardens.
From The Magnificent 6 And 1/2 Series.
Prod-CHILDF Dist-LUF 1972

Ski Whiz C 9 MIN
16MM FILM, 3/4 OR 1/2 IN VIDEO
Presents a fast-paced, fun-packed potpourri of snow sports and daredevil skiers.
Prod-PFP Dist-PFP 1973

Ski With Buick C 29 MIN
1 INCH VIDEOTAPE
Presents an award-winning ski instruction film starring Stein Eriksen, four-time Gold Metal Olympic winner. Shows some of the best U S skiing in the New England, Midwest and Rocky Mountains. Presents the new American system of teaching (conforming to U S Ski Association's national standards.)
Prod-GMBMD Dist-MTP

Skid Control C
3/4 OR 1/2 INCH VIDEO CASSETTE IND
Looks at the danger of driving on wet or slippery surfaces and what to do if your vehicle starts to skid.
From The Driving Safety Series.
Prod-DCC Dist-GPCV

Skid Correlation Study C 14 MIN
16MM FILM OPTICAL SOUND
Compares various techniques used in testing the coefficients of friction of five specially constructed pavements at Tappahannock, Virginia.
LC NO. 72-701966
Prod-USDTFH Dist-USNAC 1963

Skids And Skidding B 30 MIN
16MM FILM - 3/4 IN VIDEO C A
See series title for descriptive statement.
From The Sportsmanlike Driving Series.
Prod-AAAFTS Dist-GPITVL Prodn-SCETV

Skier's Choice C 29 MIN
16MM FILM OPTICAL SOUND J-C A
Stresses the importance of control in making skiing a safe, enjoyable and rewarding recreational sport.
LC NO. 77-701319
Prod-SAFECO Dist-LAWJ 1976

Skiing B
16MM FILM OPTICAL SOUND
From The Learn To Ski Series.
Prod-SFI Dist-SFI

Skiing C 3 MIN
16MM FILM OPTICAL SOUND P-I
Discusses the sport of skiing.
From The Of All Things Series.
Prod-BAILYL Dist-AVED

Skiing Above The Clouds C 13 MIN
16MM FILM OPTICAL SOUND
Follows a party of experienced outdoorsmen as they traverse glacier-clad Mt Rainier at the 10,000 foot level in mid-winter.
Prod-RARIG Dist-RARIG

Skiing Exercises C 7 MIN
16MM FILM OPTICAL SOUND J-C A
Provides amateurs with exercises to prepare for the skiing season. Shows a high school girl demonstrating her skill on Mt Werner, Steamboat Springs, Colorado.
LC NO. FIA67-612
Prod-MANSPR Dist-SCHMUN 1967

Skiing In Ontario C 9 MIN
16MM FILM OPTICAL SOUND
Views Ontario's popular ski areas, showing the comforts of hotels and restaurants, as well as the challenge and choice of ski slopes.
LC NO. 71-703588
Prod-MORLAT Dist-CTFL 1969

Skiing In Quebec C 11 MIN
16MM FILM OPTICAL SOUND C A
Shows skiers pluming through powder snow steep trails and toddlers huffing and puffing behind their parents on the nursery slopes.
Prod-CTFL Dist-MORLAT

Skiing Is Believing C 14 MIN
16MM FILM OPTICAL SOUND
Presents a water ski show featuring the Tommy Bartlett water skiers performing their precision routines.
Prod-MERMAR Dist-TELEFM

Skiing—A Series

Illustrates the fundamentals of skiing techniques at the beginning, intermediate and advanced levels. Features certified ski instructor, Cyrus F Smythe.
Prod-KTCATV Dist-PUBTEL

Children Have The Most Fun	29 MIN
Control Yourself	29 MIN
Different Techniques Are Not That Different	29 MIN
Don't Let The Bumps Get You Down	29 MIN
Eliminating The Crutch	29 MIN
Enjoy Beginning Turns	29 MIN
Getting The Skis Together	29 MIN
Move To Intermediate Level	29 MIN
Moving Toward Parallel Skiing	29 MIN
Open The Door To Advanced Skiing	29 MIN
Parallel For Variety	29 MIN
Perfecting Parallel	29 MIN
Stem Is Gone, The	28 MIN

Skill Demonstrations For Counseling Alcoholic Clients - Basic Communication Skills B 59 MIN
3/4 OR 1/2 INCH VIDEO CASSETTE
Shows how alcoholism counselors can improve their communication skills in one-on-one interactions with clients.
Prod-USNAC Dist-USNAC

Skill Drills - Paragraph Centering, Block Centering, Spread Centering B 30 MIN
2 INCH VIDEOTAPE
From The Typewriting, Unit 2 - Skill Development Series.
Prod-GPITVL Dist-GPITVL

Skill Drills - Vertical And Horizontal Centering, Typing All Capitals B 30 MIN
2 INCH VIDEOTAPE
From The Typewriting, Unit 2 - Skill Development Series.
Prod-GPITVL Dist-GPITVL

Skilled Acts C 37 MIN
16MM FILM OPTICAL SOUND
Discusses the characteristic impairment and disturbance of skilled acts produced by paresis or paralysis of the participating muscles, disorders of coordination and Parkinsonism with akinetic and ideakinetic apraxia.
Prod-CMC Dist-PSUPCR 1946

Skilled Craftsmen C 15 MIN
16MM FILM OPTICAL SOUND
Shows the lifestyle of five craftsmen, each illustrating a different facet of their craft.
LC NO. 80-700876
Prod-VICCOR Dist-TASCOR 1978

Skilled Hands And Sure Feet C 15 MIN
16MM FILM, 3/4 OR 1/2 IN VIDEO IND
Emphasizes the importance of hand and foot protection for construction workers. Illustrates the great amount of protection steel-toed boots provide, and shows people using artificial limbs, pointing out the grave danger in inadequate protection.
Prod-CSAO Dist-IFB

Skilled Swimming, Pt 1 C 13 MIN
16MM FILM OPTICAL SOUND I-C A
Shows swimming turns and starts and demonstrates the sidestroke, elementary backstroke and the breaststroke. Narrated by Murray Rose.
LC NO. 70-712949
Prod-AMRC Dist-AMRC 1971

Skilled Swimming, Pt 2 C 19 MIN
16MM FILM OPTICAL SOUND I-C A
Shows swimming turns and starts and demonstrates the crawl, back crawl and butterfly strokes. Narrated by Murray Rose.
LC NO. 76-712948
Prod-AMRC Dist-AMRC 1971

Skills C 30 MIN
3/4 OR 1/2 INCH VIDEO CASSETTE C A
Shows adults talking about the skills they use in work, education and leisure activities. Focuses on the necessity for skill identification in life/work planning.
From The Making A Living Work Series. Program 104
Prod-OHUTC Dist-OHUTC

Skills For Progress C 27 MIN
16MM FILM, 3/4 OR 1/2 IN VIDEO
Discusses apprenticeship systems, emphasizing the importance of acquiring a skill and explaining the steps involved in learning one.
From The Career Job Opportunity Series.
LC NO. 79-706109
Prod-USDL Dist-USNAC 1979

Skills For The New Technology - What A Kid Needs To Know Today–A Series
3/4 OR 1/2 INCH VIDEO CASSETTE P-I
Discusses the skills and values which will be needed to function effectively in the future.
Prod-EPCOT Dist-EPCOT 1983

Basic Communication Skills 010 MIN
Living With Change 010 MIN
Living With Computers 010 MIN

Skills For The New Technology - What A Kid Needs To Know Today–A Series
I
Points to skills needed for today's technological world.
Prod-WDEMCO Dist-WDEMCO

Basic Communication Skills 010 MIN
Living With Change 010 MIN
Living With Computers 010 MIN

Skills Of Football, The - Soccer C 20 MIN
16MM FILM OPTICAL SOUND
Presents tips and techniques of particular interest to players who are working to improve their skills on the playing field.
Prod-COCA Dist-COCA 1969

Skills Of Helping–A Series
C A
Discusses the communication skills needed in social work.
Prod-MCGILU Dist-SYRCU 1980

Leading A First Group Session 088 MIN
Preliminary, Beginning, And Work Phases 096 MIN
Working With The System 093 MIN

Skills To Build America C 20 MIN
16MM FILM OPTICAL SOUND
Portrays the Annual Apprenticeship Contest during which carpenters, cabinet makers and millrights gather to match their skills and craftsmanship.
Prod-UBCJ Dist-MTP

Skills To Live By C
16MM FILM OPTICAL SOUND
Provides an overview of individualized instruction in business education.
Prod-HBJ Dist-HBJ

Skills Training For The Special Child C 30 MIN
16MM FILM, 3/4 OR 1/2 IN VIDEO T
Explains the behavioral procedures used to teach number concepts and arithmetic to retarded and developmentally disabled children.
Prod-HUBFLM Dist-MTI 1971

Skimming-Scanning Road C 20 MIN
3/4 OR 1/2 INCH VIDEO CASSETTE
Covers reading flexibility and skimming and scanning in depth.
From The Efficient Reading - Instructional Tapes Series. Tape 7
Prod-TELSTR Dist-TELSTR

Skin C 15 MIN
16MM FILM OPTICAL SOUND
Shows how vinyl skins are made by the casting-on-paper process, and tells how they are used for fashion products.
LC NO. 72-700172
Prod-ENVIC Dist-ENVIC 1971

Skin (French) C 15 MIN
16MM FILM OPTICAL SOUND
Shows how vinyl skins are made by the casting-on-paper process, and tells how they are used for fashion products.
Prod-ENVIC Dist-ENVIC 1971

Skin (German) C 15 MIN
16MM FILM OPTICAL SOUND
Shows how vinyl skins are made by the casting-on-paper process, and tells how they are used for fashion products.
Prod-ENVIC Dist-ENVIC 1971

Skin (Italian) C 15 MIN
16MM FILM OPTICAL SOUND
Shows how vinyl skins are made by the casting-on-paper process, and tells how they are used for fashion products.
Prod-ENVIC Dist-ENVIC 1971

Skin - It's All Around You C 15 MIN
16MM FILM, 3/4 OR 1/2 IN VIDEO I-J
Explains the anatomy and function of skin. Tells how skin protects, how it heals itself and how it is constructed. Shows how to care for it.
Prod-HIGGIN Dist-HIGGIN 1979

Skin - Your Amazing Birthday Suit C 13 MIN
16MM FILM, 3/4 OR 1/2 IN VIDEO I-J
Presents information about the skin, including its functions, how pigment determines skin coloration and how fingernails are formed. Examines pores, blood vessels, sweat glands and hair follicles, and illustrates skin care.
LC NO. 81-707326
Prod-CENTRO Dist-CORF 1981

Skin And Bones - Halloween C 14 MIN
3/4 OR 1/2 INCH VIDEO CASSETTE P-I
See series title for descriptive statement.
From The Ready, Sing Series.
Prod-ARKETV Dist-AITECH 1979

Skin And Foot Care For The Diabetic C
3/4 OR 1/2 INCH VIDEO CASSETTE
Addresses the importance of skin and foot care for the diabetic. Provides step by step instructions on proper care. Shows appropriate action to take when injury occurs.
Prod-MIFE Dist-MIFE

Skin And Foot Care For The Diabetic (Spanish) C
3/4 OR 1/2 INCH VIDEO CASSETTE
Addresses the importance of skin and foot care for the diabetic. Provides step by step instructions on proper care. Shows appropriate action to take when injury occurs.
Prod-MIFE Dist-MIFE

Skin As A Sense Organ, The C 12 MIN
16MM FILM, 3/4 OR 1/2 IN VIDEO H-C
Introduces the variety, function and distribution of sensory receptors in the skin.
Prod-BFL Dist-IFB 1975

Skin Bank Storage Of Postmortem Homografts, Methods Of Preparation, Preservation And Use C 23 MIN
16MM FILM OPTICAL SOUND PRO
Explains that viable homografts are obtained from postmortem sources and used as biological dressings to save lives in severe burns. Shows details of the establishment of a skin bank and of the storage and use of the grafts.
Prod-ACYDGD Dist-ACY 1955

Skin Biopsy Techniques C 21 MIN
3/4 INCH VIDEO CASSETTE PRO
Demonstrates four techniques for biopsy of the skin. Discusses how and when to perform each of the biopsy procedures and includes a post-test.
LC NO. 79-706521
Prod-UMICH Dist-UMMCML 1978

Skin Cancer C 55 MIN
3/4 INCH VIDEO CASSETTE
Discusses common nonmelanoma skin cancers and squamous cell cancer.
Prod-UTAHTI Dist-UTAHTI

Skin Care C 30 MIN
3/4 OR 1/2 INCH VIDEO CASSETTE
Presents tips on skin care.
From The Consumer Survival Series. Health
Prod-MDCPB Dist-MDCPB

Skin Care And Diapering Your Baby C 11 MIN
3/4 OR 1/2 INCH VIDEO CASSETTE
Covers preventative measures and treatment for skin disorder which affect the infant. Discusses proper diapering and laundry techniques.
LC NO. 81-730128
Prod-TRAINX Dist-TRAINX

Skin Care And Diapering Your Baby (Spanish) C 11 MIN
3/4 OR 1/2 INCH VIDEO CASSETTE
Covers preventative measures and treatment for skin disorders which affect the infant. Discusses proper diapering and laundry techniques.
LC NO. 81-730128
Prod-TRAINX Dist-TRAINX

Skin Game, The C 25 MIN
3/4 OR 1/2 INCH VIDEO CASSETTE
Shows Mario Machado, with guest celebrities Pat McCormick and Jo Anne Worley exploring the world of skin through a game show format. Has guest authority Dr Marjorie Bauer, a dermatologist, explaining the questions designed to increase an understanding of proper skin care.
Prod-TRAINX Dist-TRAINX

Skin Grafting C 33 MIN
16MM FILM OPTICAL SOUND PRO
Demonstrates prepartation of the patient and local area, selection of the proper type of graft, the actual cutting of the graft, fixation of the graft and dressing. Includes patient follow-up.
Prod-ACYDGD Dist-ACY 1961

Skin Grafting Techniques C 28 MIN
16MM FILM OPTICAL SOUND PRO
Demonstrates the technique of application of thick split graft to face for infected wound, technique of thick split graft to face for cosmetic improvement, and technique of application of whole thickness graft to flexor surface of finger for post-traumatic scar contracture.
Prod-ACYDGD Dist-ACY 1966

Skin Matrix C 17 MIN
3/4 INCH VIDEO CASSETTE
Presents a computer art video which interweaves imagery of landscapes, faces, skin and tactile surfaces, by Ed Emshwiller.
Prod-EAI Dist-EAI

Skin Matrix S C 9 MIN
3/4 INCH VIDEO CASSETTE
Presents a shorter version of Ed Emshwiller's Skin Matrix, a computer art video which interweaves imagery of landscapes, faces, skin and tactile surfaces.
Prod-EAI Dist-EAI

Skin, Hair, And Nails Examination C 16 MIN
3/4 INCH VIDEO CASSETTE PRO
Demonstrates the inspection and palpation of the skin for color, texture, temperature, hydration, turgor and lesions. Shows examination of the hair for distribution, thickness, texture and lubrication and examination of the nails and nail beds for clubbing, appearance annd color.
LC NO. 79-707723
Prod-UMICHM Dist-UMMCML Prodn-UMISU 1976

Skin, The C
3/4 OR 1/2 INCH VIDEO CASSETTE
Presents the subject of human skin. Developed specifically for use in hairstyling and skin-care schools, the film utilizes techniques to give future practitioners a professional understanding of the basic structure, growth and physiological functions of human skin, the factors leading to skin destruction and the benefit of treatments involved in skin care and massage.
Prod-MPCEDP Dist-MPCEDP 1984

Skin, The - Its Function And Care C 16 MIN
16MM FILM - 3/4 IN VIDEO H-C A
Explains the structure and function of the skin and discusses maintaining proper cleansing, lubrication and protection of the patient's skin.
From The Nurse's Aide, Orderly And Attendant Series.
Prod-COPI Dist-COPI 1971

Skin, The - Its Structure And Function C 21 MIN
16MM FILM, 3/4 OR 1/2 IN VIDEO J-H
Examines the functions and structures of skin with the aid of reproductions from scanning electron micrographs and animation.
LC NO. 83-706234
Prod-EBEC Dist-EBEC 1982

Skin, The - Its Structure And Function (Spanish) C 20 MIN
16MM FILM, 3/4 OR 1/2 IN VIDEO J-H
A Spanish language version of the film and videorecording The Skin - Its Structure And Function.
Prod-EBEC Dist-EBEC 1983

Skinner Revolution, The C 23 MIN
16MM FILM, 3/4 OR 1/2 IN VIDEO
Examines the life of B F Skinner and his scientific and philosophical contributions in the field of psychology.
Prod-RESPRC Dist-MEDIAG Prodn-PRBP 1978

Skinny And Fatty B 45 MIN
16MM FILM, 3/4 OR 1/2 IN VIDEO P-J
Portrays the special friendship between two Japanese children, one shy and unsure of himself and the other outgoing.
From The CBS Children's Film Festival Series.
Prod-WRLDP Dist-MGHT 1969

Skip Some - Skip Counting C 14 MIN
3/4 OR 1/2 INCH VIDEO CASSETTE P
Explains how Woodford learns skip counting and ends up with seeds that grow numbers.
From The Math Country Series.
Prod-KYTV Dist-AITECH 1979

Skipjack, The C 25 MIN
16MM FILM OPTICAL SOUND
Focuses attention on the disappearing skipjack sailing fleet and its effect on the lives of the oyster fishermen in the Chesapeake Bay area of Maryland.
LC NO. 76-705665
Prod-WMALTV Dist-WMALTV 1969

Skipper Gets A Piano C 15 MIN
3/4 OR 1/2 INCH VIDEO CASSETTE P
See series title for descriptive statement.
From The Strawberry Square Series.
Prod-NEITV Dist-AITECH 1982

Skipping C 9 MIN
16MM FILM, 3/4 OR 1/2 IN VIDEO P
Shows two young children watching other kids skipping. Teaches skipping through the learning experiences of the two watchers.
LC NO. 82-706601
Prod-CF Dist-CF 1979

Skippy Peanut Butter C 2 MIN
3/4 OR 1/2 INCH VIDEO CASSETTE
Shows a classic animated television commercial tracing the history of peanut butter.
Prod-BROOKC Dist-BROOKC

Skokie C 28 MIN
16MM FILM OPTICAL SOUND I-C A

Explores the furor unleashed by the attempted march in Skokie, Illinois during June, 1978 by members of the American Nazi Party. Documents the key events preceding the march and interviews the Jewish attorney who defended the Nazis in court, Nazi leader Frank Collins, Tom Kerr of the American Civil Liberties Union and a family of Holocaust survivors from the community.
Prod-NJWB Dist-NJWB 1979

Skoven (The Forest) C 26 MIN
16MM FILM OPTICAL SOUND
Presents the things to be seen in a forest during the various seasons if you have good eyes and keep very quiet. Includes music and sound effects.
Prod-STATNS Dist-STATNS 1962

Skull Anatomy—A Series
C A
Offers a complete approach to the teaching and review of the skull. Presents an overview, defines general terminology and provides a review. Each part defines boundaries of a skull region and demonstrates bones specific to that region. By Dr Vick Williams, Professor of Anatomy, University of Texas Health Science.
Prod-UTXHSA Dist-TEF

Base Of The Skull, The 010 MIN
Cranial Cavity, The 017 MIN
Facial Region, The 014 MIN
Nasal Cavities 012 MIN
Oral Cavity, The 011 MIN
Orbit, The 010 MIN
Pterygopalatine Fossa 009 MIN
Skull, The - An Introduction 017 MIN
Temporal And Infratemporal Region, The 015 MIN

Skull, The - An Introduction C 17 MIN
3/4 OR 1/2 INCH VIDEO CASSETTE C A
Presents an overview of the skull. Defines terminology and provides a review of the skull.
From The Skull Anatomy Series.
Prod-UTXHSA Dist-TEF

Skullduggery C 5 MIN
16MM FILM OPTICAL SOUND
Uses double exposure and other methods to include animated collage of live newsreel footage, mixing the eye with living scenes and non-living scenes.
Prod-VANBKS Dist-VANBKS 1960

Sky C 10 MIN
16MM FILM, 3/4 OR 1/2 IN VIDEO P-J A
Looks at the sky over a 24-hour period, showing thunderheads, a rainstorm and the sunrise.
Prod-NFBC Dist-NFBC 1962

Sky Capers C 15 MIN
16MM FILM, 3/4 OR 1/2 IN VIDEO J A
Examines the sport of sky diving.
Prod-PFP Dist-PFP 1968

Sky Chief C 26 MIN
16MM FILM, 3/4 OR 1/2 IN VIDEO C
Shows the dramatic cultural and economic clash of different forces and resulting ecological damage. Portrays both collusion and conflict among an international petroleum consortium, a Latin American government, Mestize settlers and traders and the indigenous people.
Prod-SCOTTM Dist-UCEMC 1972

Sky Dance C 11 MIN
16MM FILM, 3/4 OR 1/2 IN VIDEO
Offers an animated depiction of man's age-old attempt to understand his role in the universe.
Prod-HUBLEY Dist-PFP 1980

Sky Dive C 15 MIN
16MM FILM, 3/4 OR 1/2 IN VIDEO
Shows skydivers taking part in group jumps and plunging off the 3,000-foot cliff of Yosemite's El Capitan.
LC NO. 79-706830
Prod-BOENIC Dist-PFP

Sky High C
3/4 OR 1/2 INCH VIDEO CASSETTE
Compares various aspects of flying. Includes aerobatics, sky diving, hang gliding, and the history of flying.
Prod-ALTI Dist-ALTI

Sky High C 3 MIN
3/4 INCH VIDEO CASSETTE
Shows the New Mexican landscape as seen from a mirrored sphere high above a moving vehicle.
From The South-Western Landscapes Series.
Prod-EAI Dist-EAI

Sky Is Falling, The C 15 MIN
3/4 OR 1/2 INCH VIDEO CASSETTE P
Combines looking, listening, talking, writing and reading to help establish the link between oral and written language. Presents the story Henny Penny by Paul Galdone.
From The I Want To Read Series.
Prod-LACOS Dist-GPITVL 1976

Sky Is Gray, The C 47 MIN
16MM FILM, 3/4 OR 1/2 IN VIDEO J-C A
Tells the story of a young black farmboy's dawning awareness of himself and society. Based on the short story The Sky Is Gray by Ernest Gaines.
From The American Short Story Series.
LC NO. 80-706665
Prod-LEARIF Dist-CORF 1979

Sky Over Holland C 22 MIN
16MM FILM OPTICAL SOUND
Pictures a potpourri of visual impressions of Holland. Contrasts the works of Dutch artists from Rembrandt to Van Gogh and Mondrian with scenes of contemporary life.
Prod-SCULMR Dist-WB 1968

Sky Snoopers B 15 MIN
2 INCH VIDEOTAPE P
See series title for descriptive statement.
From The Sounds Like Magic Series.
Prod-MOEBA Dist-GPITVL Prodn-KYNETV

Sky Surfers C 25 MIN
16MM FILM OPTICAL SOUND
Traces the history of flight and demonstrates the sport of hang gliding.
LC NO. 76-702096
Prod-FIARTS Dist-FIARTS 1975

Sky's The Limit—A Series

Covers actual sessions of Dr Wayne Dyer's corporate seminars, as he shares his dynamic philosophy of no-limit thinking. Compares the various limits beneath the no-limit ultimate to the steps of a ladder and discusses the kinds of attitudes and behavior patterns that place individuals on each of the steps. Includes a participant's workbook and a facilitator's guide.
Prod-LCOA Dist-DELTAK

Part One - Taking Charge 030 MIN
Part Two - Winning All The Time 030 MIN

Sky's The Limit, The C 23 MIN
16MM FILM, 3/4 OR 1/2 IN VIDEO
Investigates the causes and consequences of urban air pollution, using the San Francisco Bay Area as a case study. Shows the various case factors and analyzes how much each adds to the daily release of pollutants.
Prod-WHTKEN Dist-UCEMC 1980

Sky's The Limit, The C 56 MIN
16MM FILM, 3/4 OR 1/2 IN VIDEO H-C A
Introduces Dr Wayne Dyer's theory of no-limit thinking covering such topics as handling stress, dealing with anxiety, improving self-worth, making choices and thinking positively. Emphasizes that mastery is a fundamental approach to life.
Prod-LCOA Dist-LCOA

Sky's The Limit, The - With Dr Wayne Dyer (Captioned) C 56 MIN
16MM FILM, 3/4 OR 1/2 IN VIDEO H-C A
Shares Dr Dyer's -no-limit- philosophy as an approach to handling stress, making choices and improving goal setting. Can be used as a structured half-day workshop with facilitator's guide. Captioned in Swedish.
Prod-LCOA Dist-LCOA 1981

Sky's Unlimited, The C 26 MIN
3/4 OR 1/2 INCH VIDEO CASSETTE
Focuses on using the sky as a recreation vehicle, including ultra light airplanes, parachuting, hang gliding, antique and small plane flying, soaring and ballooning. Shows model planes as a hobby.
Prod-HARDAP Dist-BCNFL 1983

Skydivers C 29 MIN
2 INCH VIDEOTAPE
Explains that the people who participate in skydiving are as varied as their descriptions of the sport.
From The Bayou City And Thereabouts People Show Series.
Prod-KUHTTV Dist-PUBTEL

Skyfish C 30 MIN
3/4 OR 1/2 INCH VIDEO CASSETTE
Reveals the human change experienced by a woman artist as she paints, and her subconscious mind is made visual.
From The Doris Chase Concepts Series.
Prod-CHASED Dist-CHASED

Skyful Of Dragons, A / Soo Ling Finds A Way C 15 MIN
3/4 INCH VIDEO CASSETTE P
Presents the children's stories A Skyful Of Dragons by Mildred Wright and Soo Ling Finds A Way by June Behrens.
From The Tilson's Book Shop Series.
Prod-WVIZTV Dist-GPITVL 1975

Skylab C 27 MIN
16MM FILM, 3/4 OR 1/2 IN VIDEO
Shows the major objectives of the Skylab mission, its principal components, the four launches involved and a few of the investigations performed by Skylab.
Prod-NASA Dist-USNAC

Skylab - On The Eve Of Launch C 11 MIN
16MM FILM OPTICAL SOUND
Describes Skylab and its flight plans. Highlights the final preparation of flight articles and crew training up to the eve of launch of the first mission.
Prod-NASA Dist-NASA

Skylab And The Sun C 13 MIN
16MM FILM, 3/4 OR 1/2 IN VIDEO
Presents information gathered by the Skylab missions on the behavior of the sun, solar energy, plasma flow and mass/thermal transfer. Shows how we can use information about the sun to our advantage.
Prod-NASA Dist-USNAC

Skylab And The Sun C 13 MIN
16MM FILM, 3/4 OR 1/2 IN VIDEO
Presents information gathered from the Skylab missions about the Sun's behavior, solar energy, plasma flow and mass/thermal transfer. Shows how this information can be used to humankind's advantages.
LC NO. 79-706031
Prod-USMSFC Dist-USNAC 1978

Skylab Medical Experiments C 31 MIN
16MM FILM OPTICAL SOUND
Describes the equipment and experiments of the Skylab Medical Experiments Program. Discusses major experiment items such as the lower body negative pressure device, the ergometer, the rotating litter chair and the experiment support system.
Prod-NASA Dist-NASA

Skylab Science Demonstrations—A Series

Prod-NASA Dist-USNAC Prodn-AVCORP 1980

Fluids In Weightlessness 015 MIN
Gyroscopes In Space 015 MIN
Magnetic Effects In Space 014 MIN
Magnetism In Space 019 MIN
Zero-g 015 MIN

Skyline—A Series

Focuses on the world of dance.
Prod-WNETTV Dist-WNETTV

Basic Training - School Of American Ballet 030 MIN
Silent Dancing 027 MIN

Skylines For Tomorrow C 22 MIN
16MM FILM OPTICAL SOUND
Describes and illustrates light-weight aggregate, its deposits, mining, processing and properties. Pictures samples from different parts of the United States and Canada.
LC NO. FIA68-1860
Prod-ESCSI Dist-CINEA Prodn-CINEA 1967

Skylines Of The Northwest C 19 MIN
16MM FILM - VIDEO, ALL FORMATS
Discusses important dimensions of skyline logging in the Pacific Northwest, showing current research, innovations and a variety of skyline systems.
Prod-OSUSF Dist-OSUSF

Skylines Of The South C 20 MIN
16MM FILM OPTICAL SOUND C A
Shows that in a variety of ways the gospel message penerates the concrete jungles of the cities in southern Brazil.
Prod-CBFMS Dist-CBFMS

Skyrider C 7 MIN
16MM FILM, 3/4 OR 1/2 IN VIDEO
Offers an animated fantasy of space travel, complete with astronauts, space capsules, witches on broomsticks, flying toasters, and chandeliers.
LC NO. 81-706812
Prod-HALAS Dist-PHENIX 1978

Skyscraper C 15 MIN
3/4 OR 1/2 INCH VIDEO CASSETTE P-I
Explores the inside operation of a skyscraper in Cleveland.
From The Explorers Unlimited Series.
Prod-WVIZTV Dist-AITECH 1971

Skyscraper Age C 33 MIN
16MM FILM OPTICAL SOUND
Focuses on the new development project of highrise apartment houses as an effective means of urban redevelopment. Explains that the Kajima Corporation took the initiative in opening Japan's skyscraper age.
Prod-KAJIMA Dist-UNIJAP 1970

Skyscrapers And Slums C 20 MIN
16MM FILM, 3/4 OR 1/2 IN VIDEO J-H
Presents the story of Mauro, a 12-year-old schoolboy who works as a part-time shoe shiner in downtown Sao Paulo. Contrasts the spectacular business district where Mauro works, the result of the campaign for industrial growth, with the poverty of his home in the favela or squatter settlement.
From The Brazil Series.
Prod-BBCTV Dist-FI 1982

Skyward The Great Ships C 27 MIN
16MM FILM OPTICAL SOUND J-H A
Reports on the various kinds of propulsion being developed for space missions and the applications and advantages of each. Illustrates research in chemical, nuclear and electrical propulsion systems.
LC NO. FIE67-128
Prod-NASA Dist-USNAC

SL-1 Accident, Phase 3, The C 57 MIN
16MM FILM, 3/4 OR 1/2 IN VIDEO
Shows what was done with the SL-1 reactor and building following the accidental nuclear excursion of January 1961. Reenacts the accident using animation and presents a postulation of the cause.
Prod-USAEC Dist-USNAC

SL-1 Accident, Phases 1 And 2, The C 43 MIN
16MM FILM, 3/4 OR 1/2 IN VIDEO
Uses actual and reenacted scenes to show what happened in phases one and two following the accidental nuclear excursion of January 3, 1961.
Prod-USAEC Dist-USNAC

Sla-Hal, The Bone Game C 27 MIN
16MM FILM OPTICAL SOUND
Shows the native American Indian bone game called sla-hal, photographed at a Makah Indian celebration in the Pacific Northwest. Presents bone game songs in the context of the games being played, together with comments from game participants explaining facts of the game and its place in their contemporary American culture.
From The Native Music Of The North-West Series.
LC NO. 82-700230
Prod-WASU Dist-WASU Prodn-CHVANP 1982

Slab And Coil Pots C 29 MIN
2 INCH VIDEOTAPE
Features Mrs Vivika Heino demonstrating with various slab and coil pots.
From The Exploring The Crafts - Pottery Series.
Prod-WENHTV Dist-PUBTEL

Slab City - A Very Special Town C 29 MIN
16MM FILM, 3/4 OR 1/2 IN VIDEO J-C A
Shows the lifestyles of retired people who each winter migrate to an abandoned Marine base in California where they live rent-free in their trailers throughout the winter. Documents how the people organize brigades to handle such essentials as water retrieval, sewage and waste disposal, and mail distribution.
LC NO. 83-706027
Prod-VONWET Dist-WOMBAT 1982

Slabs And Sawdust C 20 MIN
16MM FILM OPTICAL SOUND
Presents information about safety procedures in sawmills.
LC NO. 76-701480
Prod-CENTWO Dist-CENTWO 1975

Slalom C 80 MIN
3/4 OR 1/2 INCH VIDEO CASSETTE
Focuses on equipment, training and technique for use in slalom skiing on water. Includes the slalom course, boats and driving. Stars Bob LaPoint.
From The Superstar Sports Tapes Series.
Prod-TRASS Dist-TRASS

Slams - Bidding And Play C 30 MIN
3/4 OR 1/2 INCH VIDEO CASSETTE A
See series title for descriptive statement.
From The Play Bridge Series.
Prod-KYTV Dist-KYTV 1983

Slanting C 9 MIN
16MM FILM - 3/4 IN VIDEO
Illustrates the slanting techniques used by architects to incorporate fallout shielding in new buildings. Encourages the construction of fallout shelters when planning new buildings and provides information regarding methods used which give this added protection at little or no extra cost.
Prod-USNAC Dist-USNAC 1972

Slap In The Face, A (Russian) C 87 MIN
16MM FILM OPTICAL SOUND C A
A Russian-language film with English subtitles about life, love and work in Armenia in the 1930's. Relates that following his father's death, an Armenian boy takes over his father's profession as a saddlemaker for donkeys, which leads to great difficulties in his pursuit of a bride.
LC NO. 82-700445
Prod-SOVEXP Dist-IFEX 1982

Slap Shot C 123 MIN
16MM FILM OPTICAL SOUND
Shows how a burned-out hockey coach (Paul Newman) suddenly gains fame and fortune when he recruits some new players who will stop at nothing to win.
Prod-UPCI Dist-TWYMAN 1977

Slapstick B 27 MIN
16MM FILM OPTICAL SOUND
Covers the slapstick era of visual comedy. Includes some of the top comics of the 1920's performing deathdefying stunts without benefit of doubles or trick effects. Charlie Chase, Monty Banks, Fatty Arbuckle, Larry Semon and Andy Clyde appear.
From The History Of The Motion Picture Series.
Prod-SF Dist-KILLIS 1960

Slate And Vinyl Floors - Slate Floors, Tile Floors C 30 MIN
1/2 IN VIDEO CASSETTE BETA/VHS
See series title for descriptive statement.
From The Wally's Workshop Series.
Prod-KARTES Dist-KARTES

Slave Coast, The C 50 MIN
16MM FILM OPTICAL SOUND J-H
Features narration by Maya Angleou in an exploration of the slave coast, an area where an estimated 15 million humans were enslaved and shipped to other lands between the 17th and 19th centuries. Depicts the Ashanti of Ghana, the Yoruba of Nigeria, the women warriors of Dahomey and the acrobatic Dan dancers of the Ivory Coast.
From The Black African Heritage Series.
Prod-WBCPRO Dist-WBCPRO 1972

Slave Life B 30 MIN
2 INCH VIDEOTAPE H-C A
See series title for descriptive statement.
From The Americans From Africa - A History Series. No. 11
Prod-CVETVC Dist-GPITVL Prodn-WCVETV

Slave Revolt B 30 MIN
16MM FILM OPTICAL SOUND H-C A
Lerone Bennett traces the rise of the Insurrection Movement from the time of David Walker to the modern day black freedom fighter. He discusses the contribution of 18th and 19th century black radicals in the North and the power of such leaders as Henry Garnet, Frederick Douglass, and Martin Delaney in the South.
From The Black History, Section 05 - Rebellion And Resistance Series.
LC NO. 72-704048
Prod-WCBSTV Dist-HRAW 1969

Slave Trade Begins, The B 30 MIN
16MM FILM OPTICAL SOUND H-C A
John Henrik Clarke describes conditions in Europe which gave rise to the African slave trade, and shipment of the first slaves to the New World.
From The Black History, Section 04 - Slave Trade And Slavery Series.
LC NO. 71-704037
Prod-WCBSTV Dist-HRAW 1969

Slave Trade From Africa To The Americas B 30 MIN
2 INCH VIDEOTAPE H-C A
See series title for descriptive statement.
From The Americans From Africa - A History Series. No. 3
Prod-CVETVC Dist-GPITVL Prodn-WCVETV

Slave Trade In The New World, The B 30 MIN
16MM FILM OPTICAL SOUND H-C A
John Henrik Clarke surveys the contribution of the early African explorers-including Pedro Alonzo, who piloted one of Columbus' ships-and those who settled in the area which later became known as Jamestown. He discusses the arrival of slaves in 1619, the extent of slavery, and the revolts of slaves in the West Indies and in North and South America.
From The Black History, Section 04 - Slave Trade And Slavery Series.
LC NO. 75-704038
Prod-WCBSTV Dist-HRAW 1969

Slave Who Wouldn't Give Up, The C 20 MIN
3/4 INCH VIDEO CASSETTE I
Discusses the life of Frederick Douglass.
From The Truly American Series.
Prod-WVIZTV Dist-GPITVL 1979

Slave's Story, A - Running A Thousand Miles To Freedom C 29 MIN
16MM FILM, 3/4 OR 1/2 IN VIDEO
Dramatizes an authenticated slave narrative by William and Ellen Craft about their escape from slavery in 1848. Tells the story of their flight from Macon, Georgia, to Philadelphia, Pennsylvania.
Prod-OBERCI Dist-LCOA 1972

Slave's Story, A - Running A Thousand Miles To Freedom (Captioned) C 29 MIN
16MM FILM, 3/4 OR 1/2 IN VIDEO J-C A
Dramatizes the Craft family's escape from slavery in 1848.
Prod-OBERCI Dist-LCOA 1972

Slave's Story, A - Running A Thousand Miles To Freedom (Spanish) C 29 MIN
16MM FILM, 3/4 OR 1/2 IN VIDEO J-C A
Dramatizes the Craft family's escape from slavery in 1848.
Prod-OBERCI Dist-LCOA 1972

Slave's Tale, A B 20 MIN
3/4 OR 1/2 INCH VIDEO CASSETTE J-H
Presents Erik Christian Haugaard's story A SLAVE'S TALE set in Scandinavia during the Viking Age. Concerns the misadventure of a slave girl's youthful master as he sails to Frankland to return a slave to his family. (Broadcast quality)
From The Matter Of Fiction Series. No. 2
Prod-WETATV Dist-AITECH

Slavery B 30 MIN
16MM FILM OPTICAL SOUND H-C A
Portrays life under slavery and examines the tragic and sometimes humorous experiences of life in the old South. Based on the testimony of former slaves and their memory of slavery. Features Ossie Davis.
From The History Of The Negro People Series.
LC NO. FIA68-1582
Prod-NET Dist-IU 1965

Slavery C 30 MIN
1 INCH VIDEOTAPE J-H
Describes legal and psychological methods which perpetuated the slave system, slaves in rural and urban areas and effects of slavery on the Black personality of today.
From The Odyssey In Black Series.
Prod-KLVXTV Dist-GPITVL

Slavery And Black America B 30 MIN
16MM FILM OPTICAL SOUND H-C A
Sterling Stuckey describes the sophisticated societies of Africa from which Africans were separated by slave traders, the cultural shock inflicted upon the Africans by their barbaric treatment as slaves, and the rise of resistance to racist oppression as evidenced in slave rebellions and other modes of resistance.
From The Black History, Section 04 - Slave Trade And Slavery Series.
LC NO. 71-704045
Prod-WCBSTV Dist-HRAW 1969

Slavery And Personality C 29 MIN
2 INCH VIDEOTAPE
See series title for descriptive statement.
From The Black Experience Series.
Prod-WTTWTV Dist-PUBTEL

Slavery And Racism In Historical Debate C 29 MIN
2 INCH VIDEOTAPE
See series title for descriptive statement.
From The Black Experience Series.
Prod-WTTWTV Dist-PUBTEL

Slavery And Slave Resistance C 26 MIN
16MM FILM, 3/4 OR 1/2 IN VIDEO I-C A
Traces the origins of slavery, examines the basis of racial stereotyping as it developed in the dehumanizing conditions of slave life and work, and describes the varieties of active and passive black resistance.
Prod-NYT Dist-CORF Prodn-DYN 1969

Slavery And The Building Of America B 30 MIN
16MM FILM OPTICAL SOUND H-C A
Sterling Stuckey discusses the cultural aspects of black life as it developed in reaction to slavery, with emphasis on the significance of folklore and slave songs.
From The Black History, Section 04 - Slave Trade And Slavery Series.
LC NO. 75-704046
Prod-WCBSTV Dist-HRAW 1969

Slavery And White America B 30 MIN
16MM FILM OPTICAL SOUND H-C A
Sterling Stuckey discusses the rationalizations of the founding fathers and the attitudes of 18th century whites which permitted slavery to persist.
From The Black History, Section 04 - Slave Trade And Slavery Series.
LC NO. 78-704044
Prod-WCBSTV Dist-HRAW 1969

Slavery As A Social System C 29 MIN
2 INCH VIDEOTAPE
See series title for descriptive statement.
From The Black Experience Series.
Prod-WTTWTV Dist-PUBTEL

Slavery As An Economic System C 29 MIN
2 INCH VIDEOTAPE
See series title for descriptive statement.
From The Black Experience Series.
Prod-WTTWTV Dist-PUBTEL

Slavery In The Cities C 29 MIN
2 INCH VIDEOTAPE
See series title for descriptive statement.
From The Black Experience Series.
Prod-WTTWTV Dist-PUBTEL

Slavery In The Northern Colonies, 1624-1776 B 30 MIN
16MM FILM OPTICAL SOUND H-C A
Professor Edgar A Toppin traces the development of slavery in New England and the Middle Atlantic colonies, describes conditions in the various colonies, and explains how economic conditions and the climate influenced the development of slavery in the North.
From The Black History, Section 04 - Slave Trade And Slavery Series.
LC NO. 77-704041
Prod-WCBSTV Dist-HRAW 1969

Slavery In The Southern Colonies B 30 MIN
2 INCH VIDEOTAPE H-C A
See series title for descriptive statement.
From The Americans From Africa - A History Series. No. 5
Prod-CVETVC Dist-GPITVL Prodn-WCVETV

Slavery In The Southern Colonies, 1619-1776 B 30 MIN
16MM FILM OPTICAL SOUND H-C A
Professor Edgar A Toppin reviews the origin and growth of slavery in the Southern colonies and the conditions which existed in the various areas of the South.
From The Black History, Section 04 - Slave Trade And Slavery Series.
LC NO. 73-704040
Prod-WCBSTV Dist-HRAW 1969

Slavery Issue And The Coming Of The Civil War B 30 MIN
2 INCH VIDEOTAPE H-C A
See series title for descriptive statement.
From The Americans From Africa - A History Series. No. 15
Prod-CVETVC Dist-GPITVL Prodn-WCVETV

Slaves And Freemen In The Middle And Northern Colonies B 30 MIN
2 INCH VIDEOTAPE H-C A
See series title for descriptive statement.
From The Americans From Africa - A History Series. No. 6
Prod-CVETVC Dist-GPITVL Prodn-WCVETV

Sleep C 11 MIN
16MM FILM, 3/4 OR 1/2 IN VIDEO P-I
Acquaints children with the importance of sleep. Shows different brain waves made during wakefulness, light sleep, deep sleep and dreaming. Presents a horse asleep on his feet, a bat hanging in a cave, a koala bear in a tree, a tree losing its leaves for months of dormancy and a squirrel in hibernation.
Prod-FILMSW Dist-FLMFR Prodn-LILLYL 1968

Sleep - Dream Voyage C 26 MIN
3/4 OR 1/2 INCH VIDEO CASSETTE
Discusses what happens to the body during sleep. Explores the mystery of REM sleep, presents a computer display of the waves that sweep across the brain during sleep, and shows footage of a cat 'acting out' its dreams. Uses the analogy of sleep to a ship on automatic pilot to illustrate how some functions must and do continuue while the conscious brain is asleep.
From The Living Body - An Introduction To Human Biology Series.
Prod-FOTH Dist-FOTH 1985

Sleep - The Mysterious Third Of Our Lives C 13 MIN
16MM FILM OPTICAL SOUND
Profiles notable discoveries and research regarding the phenomenon of sleep. Deals with the causes of sleep, how insomniacs can be helped, and the causes of sleep attacks and sleepwalking.
Prod-ALLFP Dist-NSTA 1977

Sleep And Dreaming In Humans C 14 MIN
16MM FILM OPTICAL SOUND H-C A
Demonstrates standarized research techniques used to specify stages of wakefulness, sleep and dreaming. Shows placement of electrodes, recording techniques and arousal from non-REM and REM stages using a human subject.
From The Films At The Frontiers Of Psychological Inquiry Series.

LC NO. 72-702268
Prod-HMC Dist-HMC 1971

Sleep And Dreams C 25 MIN
3/4 OR 1/2 INCH VIDEO CASSETTE
Notes that despite the fact one spends one third of his/her life asleep, for years almost nothing has been known about sleep. Says that sleep investigators are only just now learning about the physiological structure of sleep. Shows Dr Ernest Rossi, a psychotherapist, discussing dreams and analyzing their content.
Prod-TRAINX Dist-TRAINX

Sleep Apnea - An Overview C 29 MIN
3/4 OR 1/2 INCH VIDEO CASSETTE PRO
Describes the diagnostic procedures, signs and symptoms, causes and consequences of sleep apnea.
Prod-HSCIC Dist-HSCIC 1984

Sleep Disorders C
3/4 OR 1/2 INCH VIDEO CASSETTE PRO
Includes disorders of initiating and maintaining sleep, disorders of excessive somnolence, disorders of the sleep-wake schedule, and dysfunctions associated with sleep.
From The Psychiatry Learning System, Pt 2 - Disorders Series.
Prod-HSCIC Dist-HSCIC 1982

Sleep Of Babies, The - Spontaneous Cyclical Phenomena During Neonate Sleep B 30 MIN
16MM FILM OPTICAL SOUND C
Records observable behavior of three- to five-day-old infants sleep by means of normal speed, slowed motion, speeded motion and stop motion cinephotography. Illustrates methods of classifying and recording various types of behavior during sleep.
Prod-PSUPCR Dist-PSUPCR 1970

Sleep Well C 9 MIN
16MM FILM, 3/4 OR 1/2 IN VIDEO J-C A
Uses cut-out animation to tell the story of a man who settles into an armchair to snooze and whose sleep is filled with dreams. Each dream comments on the plight of the individual in society--bureaucracy, patriotism, jingoism...The dreams become nightmares.
Prod-GKF Dist-AIMS 1968

Sleep/Wake Disorders C
3/4 OR 1/2 INCH VIDEO CASSETTE
Revies the clinical aspects of the more common sleep/wake disorders in relation to appropriate phases of normal and circadian rhythm cycles. Identifies salient clinical features of the more common disorders of sleep in individual patients and establishes a differential diagnosis in the patient.
Prod-AMEDA Dist-AMEDA

Sleep, Stress And Relaxation C 15 MIN
3/4 OR 1/2 INCH VIDEO CASSETTE P
Explains how sleep rests the body and how to relax when negative feelings cause stress.
From The Well, Well, Well With Slim Goodbody Series.
Prod-AITECH Dist-AITECH

Sleepers C 9 MIN
16MM FILM OPTICAL SOUND
Chronicles sculptor John De Andrea's creation of plaster casts of two nude models.
Prod-TOGGFI Dist-TOGGFI 1974

Sleeping Bear Dunes C 9 MIN
16MM FILM, 3/4 OR 1/2 IN VIDEO
Shows how Sleeping Bear Dunes National Lakeshore in Frankfurt, Michigan, offers visitors an opportunity to see how the larger features of the lakeshore came to be, calls attention to the less obvious features and their formation, and tells what determines which plants will grow in a given environment.
Prod-USNPS Dist-USNAC 1982

Sleeping Beauty C 3 MIN
16MM FILM OPTICAL SOUND
Presents one of the first commercials filmed in Gasparcolor, made with Jean Aurenche for Nicolas Wines, and contains Alexander Alexeieff's only example of puppet animation.
Prod-STARRC Dist-STARRC 1934

Sleeping Beauty B 10 MIN
16MM FILM OPTICAL SOUND K-C
Tells the story of Sleeping Beauty through Lotte Reiniger's animated silhouette figures. Based on live shadow plays she produced for BBC Television.
From The Lotte Reiniger's Animated Fairy Tales Series.
Prod-PRIMP Dist-MOMA 1954

Sleeping Beauty C 75 MIN
16MM FILM OPTICAL SOUND
Recounts the adventures of Briar Rose, a beautiful princess who is put into a trance by an evil witch.
Prod-DISNEY Dist-SWANK

Sleeping Beauty C 7 MIN
16MM FILM, 3/4 OR 1/2 IN VIDEO P
An adaptation of the fairy tale by the Brothers Grimm about the wicked fairy and the princess who slept for one hundred years.
From The Halas And Batchelor Fairy Tale Films Series.
Prod-HALAS Dist-EBEC 1969

Sleeping Beauty (Spanish) C 7 MIN
16MM FILM, 3/4 OR 1/2 IN VIDEO P
Tells how a wicked fairy lays a curse on a baby princess, and how the good fairy is able to protect her and the royal court.
Prod-HALAS Dist-EBEC

Sleeping Beauty, The C 170 MIN
3/4 OR 1/2 INCH VIDEO CASSETTE A
Presents three of the Soviet Union's finest dancers in Tchaikovskys renowned ballet.
Prod-EDDIM Dist-EDDIM

Sleeping Beauty, The, Brier Rose - A German Folktale C 15 MIN
16MM FILM, 3/4 OR 1/2 IN VIDEO P-I
Features animated puppets as they dramatize the beloved tale of Sleeping Beauty.
Prod-OMEGA Dist-PHENIX 1970

Sleeping Brain, The - An Experimental Approach C 23 MIN
16MM FILM OPTICAL SOUND H-C A
Presents De Michel Jouvet who explores neurophysiology and neurospychology of sleep and dreaming and demonstrates research methodology through a series of experiments on cats. Shows how electrodes are implanted to record REM, EOG and PGO activity and explains how animal research relates to studies of human behavior.
From The Films At The Frontiers Of Psychological Inquiry Series.
LC NO. 72-702267
Prod-HMC Dist-HMC 1971

Sleeping Feel Good Movie, The C 6 MIN
16MM FILM, 3/4 OR 1/2 IN VIDEO K-P
Portrays children experiencing the effects of rest and not having enough rest.
From The Feel Good - Primary Health Series.
Prod-CF Dist-CF 1974

Sleeping Giant, The - Coal C 29 MIN
16MM FILM OPTICAL SOUND
Discusses the location of coal beds and how much time is required for exploiting them. Asks how coal's sulfur emission problems can be solved.
From The Energy Sources - A New Beginning Series.
Prod-UCOLO Dist-UCOLO

Sleeve And Increasing B 29 MIN
2 INCH VIDEOTAPE
See series title for descriptive statement.
From The Busy Knitter I Series.
Prod-WMVSTV Dist-PUBTEL

Sleeve Gastrectomy C 15 MIN
3/4 OR 1/2 INCH VIDEO CASSETTE PRO
Describes sleeve gastrectomy.
Prod-WFP Dist-WFP Prodn-UKANMC

Sleeve Special, The C 29 MIN
2 INCH VIDEOTAPE
See series title for descriptive statement.
From The Designing Women Series.
Prod-WKYCTV Dist-PUBTEL

Sleeves, Plackets, And Cuffs C 24 MIN
3/4 OR 1/2 INCH VIDEO CASSETTE C A
Covers setting a regular sleeve, making a continuous lapped placket, making cuffs, attaching a cuff to a sleeve having a continuous lapped placket, making a faced opening for a pleated sleeve closure and setting a shirt sleeve.
From The Clothing Construction Techniques Series.
Prod-IOWASP Dist-IOWASP

Sleigh Ride C 29 MIN
3/4 OR 1/2 INCH VIDEO CASSETTE P-I
Introduces the eighth note.
From The USS Rhythm Series.
Prod-ARKETV Dist-AITECH 1977

Sleight Of Hand C 60 MIN
3/4 OR 1/2 INCH VIDEO CASSETTE H-C A
Discusses the characteristics and historical backgrounds of official healers, charismatic healers and expert healers. Describes the alleged miracle cures of scrofula by the Royalty of England and France and the flamboyant healing performances during the late 18th century. Based on the book The Body In Question by Jonathan Miller. Narrated by Jonathan Miller.
From The Body In Question Series. Program 8
LC NO. 81-706952
Prod-BBCTV Dist-FI 1979

Slice Of Bread, A C 13 MIN
16MM FILM OPTICAL SOUND
Presents a story about a boy and his trip to a local bakery to discover how wheat is processed into bread.
Prod-SF Dist-SF 1971

Slick Magnetos C 20 MIN
3/4 OR 1/2 INCH VIDEO CASSETTE IND
Shows specialized training on the new Slick 4200 and 6200 magneto. Includes assembly, installation and timing tips.
From The Aviation Technician Training Program Series.
Prod-AVIMA Dist-AVIMA

Slick Stagger C 5 MIN
3/4 OR 1/2 INCH VIDEO CASSETTE J-H
Consists of a lesson on comma splices.
From The Write On, Set 1 Series.
Prod-CTI Dist-CTI

Slide Rule--A Series

Introduces the slide rule and shows how to use it in making basic calculations.
Prod-RCAHSS Dist-RCAHSS

Slide Rule, The - Proportion, Percentage, Squares And Square Roots B 21 MIN
16MM FILM - 3/4 IN VIDEO
Shows how to use the C and D scales on the slide rule to calculate proportions and percentages. Explains how to read the A and B scales and how to calculate squares and square roots. Issued in 1944 as a motion picture.
From The Engineering Series.
LC NO. 79-706440
Prod-USOE Dist-USNAC Prodn-LNS 1979

Slide Rule, The - The C And D Scales B 24 MIN
16MM FILM - 3/4 IN VIDEO
Deals with the purpose and parts of the slide rule and shows how to use the C and D scales in multiplication and division of numbers. Issued in 1943 as a motion picture.
From The Engineering Series.
LC NO. 79-706441
Prod-USOE Dist-USNAC Prodn-LNS 1979

Slides, Film Animations C 15 MIN
3/4 INCH VIDEO CASSETTE P-I
See series title for descriptive statement.
From The Look And A Closer Look Series.
Prod-WCVETV Dist-GPITVL 1976

Sliding Electric Contacts C 48 MIN
3/4 OR 1/2 INCH VIDEO CASSETTE
See series title for descriptive statement.
From The Tribology 2 - Advances In Friction, Wear, And Lubrication Series.
Prod-MIOT Dist-MIOT

Sliding Flap With Free Gingival Graft C 16 MIN
16MM FILM, 3/4 OR 1/2 IN VIDEO PRO
Demonstrates how a laterally positioned split-thickness flap and a free gingival graft are used to correct a periodontal defect on a 16-year-old patient's lower central incisor and shows post-operative results.
LC NO. 81-706828
Prod-USVA Dist-USNAC 1972

Sliding In Fractions C 30 MIN
2 INCH VIDEOTAPE
Aids students who are having difficulty in adding and subtracing fractional numbers and in finding equivalent fractions.
From The Devices In Their Hands - Math In Their Minds Series.
Prod-GPITVL Dist-GPITVL

Slight Change In Plans, A C 28 MIN
16MM FILM, 3/4 OR 1/2 IN VIDEO H-C A
Explores a young man's struggle to decide whether or not to become a priest.
From The Insight Series.
Prod-PAULST Dist-PAULST

Slight Drinking Problem, A C 25 MIN
16MM FILM, 3/4 OR 1/2 IN VIDEO
Tells how a woman denies her husband's alcohol problem until she attends an Al-Anon meeting and learns to assume responsibility for her own life. Shows how she abandons her victim's role and forces her husband to face the truth about himself.
From The Insight Series.
LC NO. 79-706349
Prod-PAULST Dist-PAULST 1977

Slim Green - Master Saddlemaker C 25 MIN
16MM FILM, 3/4 OR 1/2 IN VIDEO
Deals with the art and craft of custom saddle making. Tells how Slim Green learned his skills and shows him producing a saddle.
Prod-PMEDA Dist-ONEWST

Slima The Dhowmaker C 25 MIN
16MM FILM, 3/4 OR 1/2 IN VIDEO I-J A
Introduces Slima, a Tanzanian youth who makes wooden sailboats called dhows as his ancestors have for over 2,000 years. Relates how he picks the natural curved trees, seals the hull and secures the huge, hand-sewn sails.
From The World Cultures And Youth Series.
LC NO. 80-706676
Prod-SUNRIS Dist-CORF 1980

Slimderella C 21 MIN
16MM FILM OPTICAL SOUND P-I
Shows what happens when the Chiffy kids must share the church hall where they want to perform a pantomime with a rock group.
Prod-LUF Dist-LUF 1979

Slimming Your Waste C 15 MIN
16MM FILM OPTICAL SOUND
Defines the various ways that steel cans are being separated from household refuse by municipalities and the several end-use markets available for recycling these 'mined' cans.
Prod-AIAS Dist-AIAS

Slingerland Multi-Sensory Approach To Language Arts For Specific Language... C 38 MIN
16MM FILM OPTICAL SOUND
Discusses language training techniques for primary-aged children with specific language disabilities. Focuses on the Slingerland classroom adaptation of the Orton Gillingham method, which is based upon the simultaneous inter-sensory association of the auditory, visual and kinesthetic channels.
Prod-EDPS Dist-EDPS

Slinging C 11 MIN
16MM FILM - 3/4 IN VIDEO
Introduces the safe use of slings in hoisting equipment and material. Describes materials used in slings, shows the makeup and uses of 1-, 2-, 3- and 4-leg slings, extenders and clamps, and illustrates how to examine lifting gear for safety.
Prod-BNA Dist-BNA

Slinging Load B 17 MIN
16MM FILM - 3/4 IN VIDEO
Shows how to rig and use slings to handle various types of loads. Explains safety precautions to be observed. Issued in 1944 as a motion picture.
From The Shipbuilding Skills - Rigging Series.
LC NO. 80-707054
Prod-USN Dist-USNAC 1980

Slings C 21 MIN
3/4 OR 1/2 INCH VIDEO CASSETTE IND
Explains sling materials and configurations and points out the limitations of various slings. Discusses construction, capacity, inspection, safe working loads and special uses for each type of sling.
From The Safety In Rigging Series.
Prod-CSAO Dist-CSAO

Slinky And Blinky, The Gnomes B 15 MIN
2 INCH VIDEOTAPE P
See series title for descriptive statement.
From The Sounds Like Magic Series.
Prod-MOEBA Dist-GPITVL Prodn-KYNETV

Slip And Slide B 15 MIN
2 INCH VIDEOTAPE P
See series title for descriptive statement.
From The Children's Literature Series. No. 13
Prod-NCET Dist-GPITVL Prodn-KUONTV

Slip Covering Wooden Chairs C 13 MIN
2 INCH VIDEOTAPE
Explains the correct amount of material to buy and then shows the steps in covering the chair's seat, back, legs and the rounds. Includes tips on how to pad the chair, make homemade paste and mix material patterns.
From The Living Better II Series.
Prod-MAETEL Dist-PUBTEL

Slip Decoration C 29 MIN
2 INCH VIDEOTAPE
Features Mrs Vivika Heino introducing and demonstrating the basic techniques of slip decoration in pottery.
From The Exploring The Crafts - Pottery Series.
Prod-WENHTV Dist-PUBTEL

Slip Rings, Brushes, Single Phase (Centrifugal Switch And Capacitor) C 60 MIN
3/4 OR 1/2 INCH VIDEO CASSETTE IND
See series title for descriptive statement.
From The Electrical Maintenance Training, Module 2 - Motors Series.
Prod-LEIKID Dist-LEIKID

Slip Roll Forming Machine Operation C 22 MIN
1/2 IN VIDEO CASSETTE BETA/VHS IND
Explains the basic operation and set-up of a slip roll forming machine and discusses some of the problems inherent in its operation.
Prod-RMI Dist-RMI

Slippin' Away C 30 MIN
3/4 OR 1/2 INCH VIDEO CASSETTE
Considers the long-range view of this country's economic growth. Includes an analysis of the case for zero growth.
From The Money Puzzle - The World Of Macroeconomics Series. Module 13
Prod-MDCC Dist-MDCC

Slips And Falls C 3 MIN
16MM FILM, 3/4 OR 1/2 IN VIDEO IND
Depicts ways in which workers may injure themselves in slip-and-fall accidents by showing what happens to a plant maintenance girl when she carries a carpet incorrectly, lets a ladder slip on a soapy floor and steps on curtains she is trying to hang from a short ladder.
From The Accident Prevention Series.
Prod-IAPA Dist-IFB Prodn-CRAF 1972

Slips And Falls C 23 MIN
3/4 OR 1/2 INCH VIDEO CASSETTE IND
Addresses broad range of hazards associated with on-the-job injuries. Discusses safe use of ladders.
Prod-TAT Dist-TAT

Slips And Falls (Spanish) C 3 MIN
16MM FILM, 3/4 OR 1/2 IN VIDEO IND
Depicts ways in which workers may injure themselves in slip and fall accidents by showing what happens to a plant maintenance girl when she carries a carpet incorrectly, lets a ladder slip on a soapy floor and steps on curtains she is trying to hang from a short ladder.
From The Accident Prevention (Spanish) Series.
Prod-IAPA Dist-IFB Prodn-CRAF 1972

Slips And Falls - The Point Of No Return C
3/4 OR 1/2 INCH VIDEO CASSETTE
Addresses the hazards of slips and falls, and the techniques designed to prevent this type of recurring accident on the job.
Prod-TAT Dist-TAT

Slips And Falls—A Series

Offers suggestions on ways to avoid slips and falls, one of the greatest causes of injuries.
Prod-VISUCP Dist-VISUCP

Must We Fall 017 MIN
The First Step - An Invitation To Fall 015 MIN

Slips, Trips And Falls C 12 MIN
3/4 OR 1/2 INCH VIDEO CASSETTE
Presents a safety program about slips, trips and falls narrated by Murphy, creator of Murphy's Law.
Prod-FILCOM Dist-FILCOM

Slope C 20 MIN
16MM FILM, 3/4 OR 1/2 IN VIDEO J-C
Introduces slope form and processes with emphasis given to the slope as a product of both the balance between forces of uplift and downwearing and of the interaction between processes at the slope foot and on the slope itself.
Prod-LUF Dist-LUF 1982

Slope Of A Curve C
3/4 INCH VIDEO CASSETTE
See series title for descriptive statement.
From The Calculus Series.
Prod-MDDE Dist-MDCPB

Slope Of A Straight Line, The C 30 MIN
3/4 INCH VIDEO CASSETTE C
See series title for descriptive statement.
From The Introduction To Mathematics Series.
Prod-MDCPB Dist-MDCPB

Slow And Easy C 29 MIN
2 INCH VIDEOTAPE
See series title for descriptive statement.
From The Maggie And The Beautiful Machine - Easy Does It Series.
Prod-WGBHTV Dist-PUBTEL

Slow Death Of The Desert Water C 30 MIN
16MM FILM, 3/4 OR 1/2 IN VIDEO
Shows what is happening to Pyramid Lake, in Nevada, and its wildlife because dams divert its source of water and sonic booms frighten its wildlife.
From The Our Vanishing Wilderness Series. No. 4
LC NO. 80-707024
Prod-NETRC Dist-IU 1970

Slow Hello, A C 27 MIN
16MM FILM, 3/4 OR 1/2 IN VIDEO J-C A
Features an old-time cowboy working on a ranch in the rugged British Columbia interior.
Prod-NFBC Dist-UCEMC 1977

Slow Walker, The B 18 MIN
16MM FILM OPTICAL SOUND H-C A
Uses models and drawings to describe a congenital hip malformation. Shows how a congenital shallow hip socket in one child is helped by a putti frame traction while a similar condition in another child requires surgical correction.
From The Doctors At Work Series.
LC NO. FIA65-1361
Prod-CMA Dist-LAWREN Prodn-LAWREN 1962

Slow-Speed Flight Characteristics Of Swept-Wing Aircraft B 18 MIN
16MM FILM OPTICAL SOUND
Shows how the slow-speed flight affects the flow of air over swept-wing aircraft and how a stall originates at the wing tips instead of at the wing roots as in conventional wing aircraft.
LC NO. FIE58-26
Prod-USN Dist-USNAC 1957

Slowly The Singing Began C 23 MIN
16MM FILM, 3/4 OR 1/2 IN VIDEO C A
Highlights the poets-in-the-schools program by documenting the work of Michael Moos as poet-in-residence in the Wichita, Kansas, school system.
Prod-NENDOW Dist-MEDIAG Prodn-BAXLEN 1978

Sludge Management - An Integrated Approach C 27 MIN
16MM FILM, 3/4 OR 1/2 IN VIDEO IND
Details research into methods of managing sludge in an ecologically sound way. Shows the use of energized electrons for disinfection of sludges, their direct injection into soil and the effects on soil ecosystems.
LC NO. 81-707125
Prod-NSF Dist-USNAC 1978

Slums In The Third World C 17 MIN
16MM FILM, 3/4 OR 1/2 IN VIDEO J-C A
Follows the daily life of the Sulayta family who live in a typical slum of a large Third World city. Shows their living conditions, their attempts to find work, and their attitudes about the life they are living.
LC NO. 84-706806
Prod-BFA Dist-PHENIX 1983

Small Animals C 15 MIN
3/4 OR 1/2 INCH VIDEO CASSETTE P
See series title for descriptive statement.
From The Let's Draw Series.
Prod-OCPS Dist-AITECH Prodn-KOKHTV 1976

Small Animals Of The Plains (Dutch) C 15 MIN
16MM FILM, 3/4 OR 1/2 IN VIDEO I-H
Highlights the antics of prairie dogs. Looks at badgers, cottontails and porcupines.
Prod-WDEMCO Dist-WDEMCO 1963

Small Animals Of The Plains (French) C 15 MIN
16MM FILM, 3/4 OR 1/2 IN VIDEO I-H
Highlights the antics of prairie dogs. Looks at badgers, cottontails and porcupines.
From The Vanishing Prairie (French) Series.
Prod-WDEMCO Dist-WDEMCO 1963

Small Animals Of The Plains (German) C 15 MIN
16MM FILM, 3/4 OR 1/2 IN VIDEO I-H
Highlights the antics of prairie dogs. Looks at badgers, cottontails and porcupines.
From The Vanishing Prairie (German) Series.
Prod-WDEMCO Dist-WDEMCO 1963

Small Animals Of The Plains (Norwegian) C 15 MIN
16MM FILM, 3/4 OR 1/2 IN VIDEO I-H
Highlights the antics of prairie dogs. Looks at badgers, cottontails and porcupines.
From The Vanishing Prairie (Norwegian) Series.
Prod-WDEMCO Dist-WDEMCO 1963

Small Animals Of The Plains (Portuguese) C 15 MIN
16MM FILM, 3/4 OR 1/2 IN VIDEO I-H
Highlights the antics of prairie dogs. Looks at badgers, cottontails and porcupines.
From The Vanishing Prairie (Portuguese) Series.
Prod-WDEMCO Dist-WDEMCO 1963

Small Animals Of the Plains (Swedish) C 15 MIN
16MM FILM, 3/4 OR 1/2 IN VIDEO I-H
Highlights the antics of prairie dogs. Looks at badgers, cottontails and porcupines.
From The Vanishing Prairie (Swedish) Series.
Prod-WDEMCO Dist-WDEMCO 1963

Small Appliances C 30 MIN
3/4 OR 1/2 INCH VIDEO CASSETTE
Presents tips on the purchase and care of small appliances.
From The Consumer Survival Series. Homes
Prod-MDCPB Dist-MDCPB

Small Boat Engine Maintenance C 56 MIN
1/2 IN VIDEO CASSETTE BETA/VHS
Demonstrates maintenance of outboard and inboard marine engines.
Prod-MOHOMV Dist-MOHOMV

Small Boat Navy C 28 MIN
16MM FILM OPTICAL SOUND
Reports on the operations of the U S Navy's small boats in Vietnam. Discusses the challenges of riverine and coastal warfare. Shows these boats, accompanied by helicopters, on coastal or river patrols under enemy fire and superheading invasions into enemyheld river territory. Raymond Burr narrates.
Prod-USN Dist-USNAC 1968

Small Boats Afloat C 15 MIN
3/4 INCH VIDEO CASSETTE J-C A
Discusses how to prevent capsizing and falling overboard.
From The Afloat And Aboat Series.
Prod-MDDE Dist-GPITVL 1979

Small Boats Underway C 15 MIN
3/4 INCH VIDEO CASSETTE J-C A
Describes how to check weather and safety equipment.
From The Afloat And Aboat Series.
Prod-MDDE Dist-GPITVL 1979

Small Body Of Still Water, A C 16 MIN
16MM FILM, 3/4 OR 1/2 IN VIDEO I A
Portrays the life in ponds, including protozoa, algae, mosquitoes, damselflies, tadpoles and frogs. Explores the concepts of pond ecology, photosynthesis and metamorphosis.
Prod-NWDIMF Dist-NWDIMF

Small Bowel Resection For Post-Radiation Obstruction C 25 MIN
16MM FILM OPTICAL SOUND PRO
Depicts a segmental resection of a loop of terminal ileum which became obstructed three years after the patient, a 55 year old woman, received radiation treatment for carcinoma of the cervix.
Prod-ACYDGD Dist-ACY 1955

Small Business C 15 MIN
3/4 OR 1/2 INCH VIDEO CASSETTE I
Presents a cast of three ten-year-old children interacting with adults to demonstrate various economic concepts relating to small business.
From The Money Matters Series. Pt 5
LC NO. 83-706016
Prod-KEDTTV Dist-GPITVL 1982

Small Business C 21 MIN
3/4 OR 1/2 INCH VIDEO CASSETTE C A
Stresses that the person considering opening a small business should have significant skills developed through work experience and education. Presents a bank loan officer commenting on financing a small business.
From The Clues To Career Opportunities For Liberal Arts Graduates Series.
LC NO. 80-706235
Prod-IU Dist-IU 1979

Small Business Administration—A Series

Offers a collection of government, college and corporate programs concerned with problems confronting the small businessman.
Prod-IVCH Dist-IVCH

Advertising Question, The 015 MIN
All Or Nothing 040 MIN
Anything Is Possible With Training 015 MIN
Burglary Is Your Business 015 MIN
Business Plan, The 015 MIN
Calendar Game, The 015 MIN
Follow Up, The 014 MIN
Heartbeat Of Business, The 015 MIN
Inside Story, The 018 MIN
It Can Happen To You 018 MIN
Language Of Business, The 015 MIN
Man Or Woman For The Job, The 015 MIN
Man's Material Welfare 030 MIN
Right Location, The 014 MIN
Seventh Chair, The 014 MIN
Step In The Right Direction, A 015 MIN
They're Out To Get You 014 MIN
Three Times Three 015 MIN
Variations On A Theme 015 MIN
You And Your Customers 015 MIN

Small Business Keeps America Working C 28 MIN
16MM FILM OPTICAL SOUND
Presents small business owners discussing their experiences in business, their feelings about their work, and their problems and rewards. Features observations by an economic historian and the president of the U S Chamber of Commerce.
LC NO. 79-701387
Prod-CCUS Dist-CCUS Prodn-COE 1979

Small Business My Way C 28 MIN
3/4 INCH VIDEO CASSETTE A
Features owners and managers of small businesses in and around Buckhannon, W. Va., pondering the opportunities and obligations that spurred them on, the financial risks and hardships they endured and the dim prospects they see for the survival of enterprises such as theirs.
LC NO. 83-706798
Prod-GRIES Dist-CWVMA 1983

Small Cabbage White (Japanese) C 28 MIN
16MM FILM OPTICAL SOUND
Observes cabbage white butterflies, and analyzes their behavior through various experiments. Illustrates the behavior pattern they possess for individual and specific preservation.
Prod-UNIJAP Dist-UNIJAP 1968

Small Case Of Blackmail, A C 27 MIN
16MM FILM OPTICAL SOUND
Shows the dangers of corporate nuclear power plants and the possible lack of safeguards in the transport of fissionable material.
Prod-GRATV Dist-IMPACT

Small Cell Carcinoma Of Unknown Primary C 60 MIN
3/4 INCH VIDEO CASSETTE
Discusses small cell carcinoma from the dermatologist's point of view.
Prod-UTAHTI Dist-UTAHTI

Small Change C 7 MIN
16MM FILM OPTICAL SOUND
Tells how a young man's conscience becomes hostage to an apparently simple impulse to give change to a panhandler. Raises the question of who does the giving and who does the receiving.
LC NO. 77-702644
Prod-MCMFB Dist-CANFDC

Small Changes C 18 MIN
16MM FILM OPTICAL SOUND
Tells how a young boy goes to a nightclub with his older brother and how he sneaks backstage to meet a stripper.
LC NO. 80-700485
Prod-USC Dist-USC 1979

Small Claims Court C 30 MIN
3/4 OR 1/2 INCH VIDEO CASSETTE
Presents tips on using small claims court.
From The Consumer Survival Series. General
Prod-MDCPB Dist-MDCPB

Small Computer In The Chemical Laboratory C 30 MIN
16MM FILM OPTICAL SOUND
Introduces the mini computer in a basic manner by discussing computer architecture and operation. Explores several applications for using the mini computer in various laboratory automation schemes.
Prod-VIRGPI Dist-VIRGPI 1980

Small Diameter Thermocouples C 12 MIN
16MM FILM OPTICAL SOUND IND
Shows the special techniques, tools and accessories which have been developed to ensure reliability and accuracy in temperature measurement. Makes reference to the use of small diameter thermocouples.
Prod-UKAEA Dist-UKAEA 1975

Small Eatings C 29 MIN
2 INCH VIDEOTAPE
Features Joyce Chen showing how to adapt Chinese recipes so that they can be prepared in the American kitchen and still retain the authentic flavor. Demonstrates how to prepare small eatings.
From The Joyce Chen Cooks Series.
Prod-WGBHTV Dist-PUBTEL

Small Electrical Repairs C 15 MIN
2 INCH VIDEOTAPE
See series title for descriptive statement.
From The Making Things Work Series.
Prod-WGBHTV Dist-PUBTEL

Small Enough C 25 MIN
16MM FILM OPTICAL SOUND
Describes the intellectual challenge, social milieu, recreational opportunities and psychological ambience offered by the University of Wisconsin-Superior because of its small size.
LC NO. 76-702673
Prod-UWISCS Dist-UWISCS 1976

Small Farm C 5 MIN
16MM FILM OPTICAL SOUND
Shows the activities of farm animals on a small subsistence farm in the Precambrian Shield, a vast region of rock and forest which stretches across the north of Canada.
LC NO. 77-702645
Prod-MEPHTS Dist-MEPHTS 1977

Small Farm C 10 MIN
16MM FILM OPTICAL SOUND I-J
Shows modern small farm methods in California using a strawberry farm in Downey as an example.
LC NO. FIA67-613
Prod-FINA Dist-SF 1966

Small Group Communication C 24 MIN
3/4 OR 1/2 INCH VIDEO CASSETTE H-C A
Incorporates puppetry as an instructional device to define and analyze small group communication. Displays and examines such phenomena as the phases of group development, the levels of group conflict, the emergence of leadership and the importance of cohesiveness in a group situation.
From The Communication Series.
Prod-MSU Dist-MSU

Small Group Instruction C 28 MIN
16MM FILM OPTICAL SOUND
Dr Dwight Allen, professor of education at Stanford University, identifies decisions necessary for establishing productive small group interaction, including leadership selection and group control.
From The Innovations In Education Series.
Prod-STNFRD Dist-EDUC 1966

Small Happiness - Women Of A Chinese Village C 58 MIN
16MM FILM - 3/4 IN VIDEO J-H A
Investigates the conditions of life for Chinese village women today and in the past. Chinese women speak frankly about footbinding, the new birth control policy, work, love and marriage.
Prod-LNGBOW Dist-NEWDAY

Small Happiness - Women Of A Chinese Village, Pt 1 C 30 MIN
16MM FILM OPTICAL SOUND J-H A
Presents the first half-hour segment of Small Happiness - Women Of A Chinese Village.
Prod-LNGBOW Dist-NEWDAY

Small Happiness - Women Of A Chinese Village, Pt 2 C 30 MIN
16MM FILM OPTICAL SOUND J-H A
Presents the second half-hour segment of Small Happiness - Women Of A Chinese Village.
Prod-LNGBOW Dist-NEWDAY

Small Is Beautiful - Impressions Of Fritz Schumacher C 30 MIN
16MM FILM, 3/4 OR 1/2 IN VIDEO J-C A
Profiles British economist E F Schumacher who challenges the doctrine of unbridled economic growth.
LC NO. 83-706284
Prod-NFBC Dist-BULFRG 1981

Small Loan, The C 29 MIN
2 INCH VIDEOTAPE
See series title for descriptive statement.
From The Way It Is Series.
Prod-KUHTTV Dist-PUBTEL

Small Miracle C 14 MIN
16MM FILM OPTICAL SOUND I-C A
Examines such varied subjects as highway design, shoe retailing, teaching, and other every day endeavors in order to present a portrait of the world. Describes man's search for knowledge.
Prod-STRAUS Dist-IBUSMA 1966

Small Molecules B 4 MIN
16MM FILM SILENT C
Displays a catalog of small molecules generated by the Chempak programs.
From The Molecular Biology Films Series.
LC NO. 70-709326
Prod-ERCMIT Dist-EDC 1970

Small Muscle Development, Pt 1 C 11 MIN
16MM FILM OPTICAL SOUND I-C A
Encourages the practice of small muscle exercises as paper toys are cut out in easy-to-follow steps, since control and co-ordination of the hands so strongly influence academic and physical progress. Demonstrates the safe and correct handling of scissors, cutting along straight and curved lines and differences between cutting paper and fabric.
Prod-SF Dist-SF 1968

Small Muscle Development, Pt 2 C 12 MIN
16MM FILM OPTICAL SOUND
Shows three toys being produced by different folding techniques which require the use of small muscles. Includes folding a letter and folding grocery bags.
Prod-SF Dist-SF

Small Muscle Development, Pt 3 C 12 MIN
16MM FILM OPTICAL SOUND
Presents a series of games and activities for children which are really small muscle exercises.
Prod-SF Dist-SF

Small One, The C 26 MIN
16MM FILM, 3/4 OR 1/2 IN VIDEO P-I
Tells how a young boy goes to Bethlehem to sell his old donkey and how the auctioneer makes fun of his pet. Shows how he finally sells the donkey to Joseph, who buys him to carry Mary to the manger.
Prod-DISNEY Dist-WDEMCO 1978

Small Real Estate Deal B 10 MIN
16MM FILM OPTICAL SOUND
Features a story about a man who answers an advertisement and has the surprise of his life.
LC NO. 76-703806
Prod-SFRASU Dist-SFRASU 1976

Small Repertory Companies And The Importance Of Style C 30 MIN
3/4 OR 1/2 INCH VIDEO CASSETTE
See series title for descriptive statement.
From The Repertory Styles - How Different Is One Ballet From Another Series.
Prod-ARCVID Dist-ARCVID

Small Signs Supports C 30 MIN
16MM FILM, 3/4 OR 1/2 IN VIDEO
Points out the dangers posed by using certain types of posts for small highway signs in the event of impact by a subcompact car. Shows different kinds of supports and provides recommendations for their use.
Prod-TTI Dist-USNAC 1979

Small Steps - Giant Strides C 29 MIN
16MM FILM OPTICAL SOUND
Highlights the 15th anniversary of NASA, 1958-1973. Portrays the historic accomplishments during the period and stresses benefits gained from the new technology developed.
LC NO. 75-701279
Prod-NASA Dist-USNAC Prodn-IMAGA 1973

Small Town Library B 10 MIN
16MM FILM OPTICAL SOUND J-C A
Explains the benefits and shows some of the operations of a public library in a small town, particularly the weekly delivery of books not owned by the small library, from the library of a big city nearby.
LC NO. FIE52-2104
Prod-USA Dist-USNAC 1952

Small Town Life C 30 MIN
3/4 OR 1/2 INCH VIDEO CASSETTE C
Looks at a small town in America and at the nature of relationships, the quality of life and the effects of urbanization.
From The Focus On Society Series.
Prod-DALCCD Dist-DALCCD

Small Town, Pt II, The C 30 MIN
3/4 OR 1/2 INCH VIDEO CASSETTE
Looks in detail at the experience of one small town, Broken Bow, Nebraska, during the thirties. Concentrates on the aesthetic aspects of Depression events.
From The Legacies Of The Depression On The Great Plains Series.
Prod-NETCHE Dist-NETCHE 1978

Small Tumor Virus And The New Genetics C 60 MIN
3/4 INCH VIDEO CASSETTE
Discusses tumor viruses as model chromosomes for studying the basis of the origins of carcinogens.
Prod-UTAHTI Dist-UTAHTI

Small Wilderness C 30 MIN
16MM FILM, 3/4 OR 1/2 IN VIDEO
Shows that one of the last patches of unspoiled nature in highly industrialized Western Europe is the salty plain of the Camargue region of southern France. Presents the idea of environmental preservation and considers what the world will be like if people continue to destroy its wilderness.
From The Life Around Us Series.
Prod-TIMLIF Dist-TIMLIF

Small Wilderness (Spanish) C 30 MIN
16MM FILM OPTICAL SOUND
Focuses on the Camargue region of southern France. Examines its ecosystem of flora and fauna and the interrelationship of the many species.
From The Life Around Us (Spanish) Series.
LC NO. 78-700063
Prod-TIMLIF Dist-TIMLIF 1971

Small World C 12 MIN
16MM FILM OPTICAL SOUND
Presents a variety of opinions from adults and children about how to live the good life in today's world.
LC NO. 75-700084
Prod-CCNCC Dist-CCNCC 1974

Small World Of The Nursery School, The C 29 MIN
16MM FILM OPTICAL SOUND C T
Focuses on objectives for a nursery school. Summarized desirable experiences for the pre-school child as identified by leading nursery school educators. Discusses the child's total human make-up, including his attitude, physical development, cognitive growth, behavior, social relationships and ability to manage the elements of the environment.
Prod-EDUC Dist-EDUC

Small-Carrion Penile Implant For The Management Of Impotence C 12 MIN
3/4 OR 1/2 INCH VIDEO CASSETTE PRO
Shows a method of surgically implanting a silicone prothesis designed for use in patients with impotence stemming from a variety of causes.
Prod-WFP Dist-WFP

Smallest Elephant In The World, The C 5 MIN
16MM FILM, 3/4 OR 1/2 IN VIDEO K-P
Uses the story of a little elephant who finds acceptance and happiness in the circus to show that each individual is important no matter how different.
Prod-FINART Dist-AIMS 1977

Smallest Elephant In The World, The C 6 MIN
16MM FILM, 3/4 OR 1/2 IN VIDEO P
Tells the animated story of an elephant that was no bigger than a house cat.
Prod-LUF Dist-LUF

Smallest Elephant In The World, The C 6 MIN
16MM FILM, 3/4 OR 1/2 IN VIDEO K-P
Animated version of Alvin Tresselt's story of the adventures of an undersized elephant whose success in life is consolation for 'SMALL FRY' of the world.
Prod-NBCTV Dist-SF 1964

Smallest Foe, The B 20 MIN
16MM FILM OPTICAL SOUND
Portrays the properties and types of viruses, the manufacture of counter vaccines and antibiotics, their effects and problems involved in handling.
Prod-LEDR Dist-LEDR 1956

Smallmouth Bass C 30 MIN
16MM FILM OPTICAL SOUND
Gives details on where and how to find smallmouth bass and several methods for catching them throughout the U S and Canada.
Prod-GLNLAU Dist-GLNLAU 1982

Smallpox C 33 MIN
3/4 INCH VIDEO CASSETTE PRO
Demonstrates the differential clinical and laboratory manifestations used to diagnose smallpox and chickenpox. Shows procedures for treatment and techniques developed in the 1960's. Issued in 1968 as a motion picture.
LC NO. 78-706276
Prod-USA Dist-USNAC 1978

Smalltown, U S A C 50 MIN
16MM FILM OPTICAL SOUND
Uses representative small towns in the United States to explore the revolution which is under way in small towns in America. Pictures the life and death of small-town America in the 1950's showing how the small town is managing to exist today and how, in some cases, it is failing.
LC NO. FIA65-614
Prod-SAVLF Dist-NBC Prodn-NBCTV 1964

Smart Bear C 15 MIN
3/4 INCH VIDEO CASSETTE P
Presents the book Smart Bear by Tom Tichenor.
From The Tilson's Book Shop Series.
Prod-WVIZTV Dist-GPITVL 1975

Smart Money C 30 MIN
1/2 IN VIDEO CASSETTE BETA/VHS
Discusses hidden credit potential. Examines will writing. Looks at the relationship between money and productivity.
From The On The Money Series.
Prod-WGBHTV Dist-MTI

Smart Moves C 10 MIN
16MM FILM, 3/4 OR 1/2 IN VIDEO A
Stresses safety techniques for linemen.
Prod-OHMPS Dist-BCNFL 1984

Smart Parts, The - The Inside Story Of Your Brain And Nervous System C 15 MIN
3/4 OR 1/2 INCH VIDEO CASSETTE P-I
Presents Slim Goodbody who uses displays to illustrate the major brain regions and how impulses flash through the nervous system.
From The Inside Story With Slim Goodbody Series.
Prod-UWISC Dist-AITECH 1981

Smart Shopper, The C 30 MIN
3/4 OR 1/2 INCH VIDEO CASSETTE C A
Explains techniques that can aid the consumer in purchasing food, clothing, home furnishings and appliances. Discusses primary causes of poor shopping habits, unit pricing, brand name products versus generic and using coupons.
From The Personal Finance Series. Lesson 4
Prod-SCCON Dist-CDTEL

Smart Weapons C 26 MIN
3/4 OR 1/2 INCH VIDEO CASSETTE
Shows how the silicon chip and cathode tube are making smart weapons smarter with the awesome capability of transforming war into the ultimate video game.
From The Breakthroughs Series.
Prod-NOMDFI Dist-LANDMK

Smarter Together - Autonomous Working Groups C 29 MIN
3/4 OR 1/2 INCH VIDEO CASSETTE C A
Documents different approaches aimed at increasing productivity. Demonstrates how profits increase when employees are given a greater measure of identification with their work. Features the Mayekawa Manufacturing plant in Japan and the Berkel Company in Germany.
From The Re-Making Of Work Series.
Prod-BLCKBY Dist-EBEC 1983

Smartest Kid In Town, The C 20 MIN
16MM FILM OPTICAL SOUND
Depicts a community organized to prevent needless eye injuries after a teen-aged student is blinded in a school chemistry lab explosion. Points out hazards of fireworks, air rifles, games and athletics, laboratories and shops. Outlines the methods for setting up a community eye safety program.
LC NO. FIA64-162
Prod-NSPB Dist-HF 1963

Smash C 6 MIN
16MM FILM OPTICAL SOUND
Shows possible causes and effects of vandalism. Follows the story of one boy and links the boy's rejection by society and family to the wrecking of a classroom at night.
LC NO. 80-700922
Prod-TASCOR Dist-TASCOR 1978

Smashing Of The Reich, The B 84 MIN
3/4 OR 1/2 INCH VIDEO CASSETTE
Shows the fall of Nazi Germany. Includes the landing at Normandy Beach, bombing of German industrial centers, the liberation of Paris and the freeing of concentration camp survivors.
Prod-IHF Dist-IHF

Smell Of War, The C 20 MIN
3/4 OR 1/2 INCH VIDEO CASSETTE
Analyzes the causes of World War I.
From The History In Action Series.
Prod-FOTH Dist-FOTH 1984

Smell The Sunshine C 13 MIN
16MM FILM OPTICAL SOUND
Presents a story about a produce clerk in order to show how Sunkist oranges are grown and prepared for shipping.
LC NO. 77-701453
Prod-SUNKST Dist-SUNKST Prodn-CORPOR 1976

Smell-Brain And Ancient Cortex - Rhinencephalon C 18 MIN
16MM FILM, 3/4 OR 1/2 IN VIDEO PRO
See series title for descriptive statement.
From The Anatomical Basis Of Brain Function Series.
Prod-AVCORP Dist-TEF

Smelling C 4 MIN
16MM FILM, 3/4 OR 1/2 IN VIDEO K-I
Introduces Fumble, bird and his friends who tore the inside of a nose to examine the parts that do the smelling. Concludes the adventure when the nose sneezes.
From The Most Important Person - Senses Series.
Prod-EBEC Dist-EBEC

Smelt Recovery Operation C
3/4 OR 1/2 INCH VIDEO CASSETTE IND
Focuses on startup, normal operation and shutdown of the smelt recovery operation.
From The Pulp And Paper Training, Module 2 - Chemical Recovery Series.
Prod-LEIKID Dist-LEIKID

Smelt Recovery, Pt 1 C
3/4 OR 1/2 INCH VIDEO CASSETTE IND
Covers smelt spouts, the dissolving tank, green liquor clarifier and slaker/reaction tanks.
From The Pulp And Paper Training, Module 2 - Chemical Recovery Series.
Prod-LEIKID Dist-LEIKID

Smelt Recovery, Pt 2 C
3/4 OR 1/2 INCH VIDEO CASSETTE IND
Covers several aspects of smelt recovery including white liquor, lime mud and lime kiln.
From The Pulp And Paper Training, Module 2 - Chemical Recovery Series.
Prod-LEIKID Dist-LEIKID

Smelting And Refractories C 35 MIN
3/4 INCH VIDEO CASSETTE C A
See series title for descriptive statement.
From The Elements Of Metallurgy Series.
LC NO. 81-706194
Prod-AMCEE Dist-AMCEE 1980

Smelting And Refractories C 45 MIN
3/4 OR 1/2 INCH VIDEO CASSETTE PRO
See series title for descriptive statement.
From The Elements Of Metallurgy Series.
Prod-ICSINT Dist-ICSINT

Smile C 113 MIN
16MM FILM OPTICAL SOUND
Presents an affectionate satire on beauty pageants and small-town American life. Directed by Michael Ritchie.
Prod-UNKNWN Dist-UAE 1975

Smile - Don't Move (French) C 14 MIN
3/4 OR 1/2 INCH VIDEO CASSETTE H-C A
Shows a photographer at a village fair and a cameraman shooting a historical film at the 15th century castle at Pierrefonds.
From The En Francais Series. Part 1 - Essential Elements
Prod-MOFAFR Dist-AITECH 1970

Smile And The Sword, The B 22 MIN
16MM FILM OPTICAL SOUND
Depicts an actual case from United States Government files in order to illustrate Communist espionage methods. Designed for defense contractor employees in contact with classified information.
LC NO. 75-700583
Prod-USA Dist-USNAC 1967

Smile For Auntie C 5 MIN
16MM FILM, 3/4 OR 1/2 IN VIDEO P-I
Tells of an aunt's humorous attempts to make the baby smile. An adaptation of the book Smile For Auntie by Diane Paterson.
Prod-WWS Dist-WWS 1979

Smile Makers - Self-Applied Fluoride Programs For Schools C 26 MIN
16MM FILM, 3/4 OR 1/2 IN VIDEO
Assists in in-service training for adults involved in school fluoride programs. Gives the steps to instituting a program and raising funds. Details distribution procedures and explains the benefits.
Prod-USDHEW Dist-USNAC

Smile Of Reason, The C 52 MIN
16MM FILM, 3/4 OR 1/2 IN VIDEO J-C A
Surveys the development of Western civilization during the 18th century as shown in the art and sculpture of Van Loo, David, de Troy and Houdon. Points out the growth of humanitarianism and the prevailing belief that mankind would advance by conquering ignorance through reason and moderation.
From The Civilisation Series. No. 10
LC NO. 79-707050
Prod-BBCTV Dist-FI 1970

Smile Of The Baby, The B 30 MIN
16MM FILM SILENT C T
An experimental study showing the first stage of the infant's response to humans. Illustrates that parental love makes the child friendly and socially secure.
From The Film Studies Of The Psychoanalytic Research Project On Problems In Infancy Series.
Prod-SPITZ Dist-NYU 1948

Smile Of The Walrus, The C 22 MIN
16MM FILM, 3/4 OR 1/2 IN VIDEO I-C A
A shortened version of The Smile Of The Walrus. Features Jacques Cousteau as he studies the endangered walrus in its annual migration to the Arctic Sea as well as its vital importance to isolated Eskimos. Shows the crew as it rears an ophaned pup and teaches it to forage on the ocean floor.
From The Undersea World Of Jacques Cousteau Series.
Prod-METROM Dist-CF 1977

Smile Of The Walrus, The C 52 MIN
16MM FILM, 3/4 OR 1/2 IN VIDEO
Presents Jacques Cousteau and his son Philippe who travel to the Bering Sea with scientists and divers to film the annual migration of the Pacific walrus.
From The Undersea World Of Jacques Cousteau Series.
Prod-METROM Dist-CF 1972

Smile Please B 26 MIN
16MM FILM SILENT
Introduces a man who is both a sheriff and photographer and shows that the latter profession is the most dangerous of the two. Stars Harry Langdon.
Prod-KEYFC Dist-BHAWK 1924

Smile That Wins, The C 30 MIN
3/4 OR 1/2 INCH VIDEO CASSETTE C A
Presents an adaptation of the short story The Smile That Wins by P G Wodehouse.
From The Wodehouse Playhouse Series.
Prod-BBCTV Dist-TIMLIF 1980

Smile You're On C 18 MIN
16MM FILM OPTICAL SOUND
Presents a variety show based on the daily routines of supermarket employees, with a backstage theatrical twist. Points out that employees should adopt a friendly and helpful attitude with regard to customer service.
LC NO. 78-701325
Prod-ALPHAB Dist-ALPHAB Prodn-GORICH 1978

Smilemakers - Self-Applied Fluorides, Programs For Schools C 25 MIN
16MM FILM OPTICAL SOUND A
Shows how to plan and implement the school-based, self-applied fluoride program in a community. Discusses and demonstrates the procedure for conducting and supervising the fluoride tablet and fluoride mouth rinse procedures.
Prod-NIH Dist-MTP

Smiles C 5 MIN
16MM FILM OPTICAL SOUND
Demonstrates, in a classroom and in a dentist's office, how to brush and floss teeth properly and the importance of proper diet in preventive dentistry.
LC NO. 78-701481
Prod-ECP Dist-ECP Prodn-FNBAF 1978

Smiley C 20 MIN
16MM FILM OPTICAL SOUND P-I
Tells how a boy discovers a lost dog and tries unsuccessfully to find the dog's owner while growing more and more attached to it.
LC NO. 79-700850
Prod-SIMONJ Dist-SIMONJ 1979

Smiling B 8 MIN
16MM FILM OPTICAL SOUND
Presents a story about a down-and-out derelict sitting on a park bench ready to take his life. Shows how a curiously smiling little man teaches the derelict, through a series of adventures, how to best cope with life's endless problems and how to come through it all, happy, content and smiling.
LC NO. 75-703293
Prod-USC Dist-USC 1974

Smiling Response, The B 20 MIN
16MM FILM SILENT C T
An excerpt from 'THE SMILE OF THE BABY' which presents only the experimental part of the film.
From The Film Studies Of The Psychoanalytic Research Project On Problems In Infancy Series.
Prod-SPITZ Dist-NYU 1948

Smith Systems Of Space Cushion Driving, The C 18 MIN
16MM FILM, 3/4 OR 1/2 IN VIDEO
Presents professional driving instructor Harold Smith's five safe driving habits, including how to aim high in steering, how to get the big picture, how to keep the eyes moving, how to be seen and having an out.
Prod-FORDFL Dist-FORDFL

Smith-Martin Ambulance Service C 35 MIN
3/4 OR 1/2 INCH VIDEO CASSETTE
Investigates the possible abuse of public safety as the I-Team monitors ambulance calls for three weeks and discovers that some decisions about dispatching ambulances are made for profit, not patient safety.
Prod-WCCOTV Dist-WCCOTV

Smithsonian Folklife Studies—A Series
J-C A
Discusses the folkways of various American people.
Prod-SIFP Dist-PCRFV 1981

Drummaker, The 038 MIN
Meaders Family, The - North Georgia Potters 031 MIN

Smithsonian Institution C 15 MIN
3/4 OR 1/2 INCH VIDEO CASSETTE I-H
Presents a tour of the largest museum of its kind in the world, the Smithsonian Institution.
Prod-HEARST Dist-HEARST 1973

Smithsonian Institution With S Dillon Ripley, Secretary, The C 24 MIN
16MM FILM, 3/4 OR 1/2 IN VIDEO
Provides insight into the operations and facilities of the Smithsonian Institution, from the museums in Washington to the Tropical Research Institute in Panama. Touches on the work of the research scientists, artists and scholars employed by the Institution, as well as the secretaries who have headed the Institution since 1846.
Prod-SMITHS Dist-USNAC 1977

Smithsonian Institution, The C 21 MIN
16MM FILM, 3/4 OR 1/2 IN VIDEO J-C
Describes events leading up to the founding of the Smithsonian Institution and the work of those men who set the character of the Smithsonian as we know it.
From The Eames Film Collection Series.
Prod-EAMES Dist-EBEC 1965

Smithsonian World–A Series
J-C A
Features hour-long television programs about the work of the Smithsonian Institution. Explores subjects in the Arts, Sciences and Humanities.
Prod-WETATV Dist-WETATV Prodn-SMITHS

Crossing The Distance 060 MIN
Designs For Living 060 MIN
Desk In The Jungle 060 MIN
Filling In The Blanks 060 MIN
Heroes And The Test Of Time 060 MIN
Last Flower, The 060 MIN
On The Shoulders Of Giants 060 MIN
Speaking Without Words 060 MIN
Time And Light 060 MIN
Usable Past, A 060 MIN
Where None Has Gone Before 060 MIN

Smithsonian–A Series
16MM FILM, 3/4 OR 1/2 IN VIDEO J-H A
Looks at several Smithsonian exhibits dealing with such topics as American folk art, Indian portraits done by George Catlin, Australian aborigines, the conservation of American resources and American political campaigns.
Prod-NBCTV Dist-CRMP 1967

American Folk Art 024 MIN
Catlin And The Indians 024 MIN
Million Years Of Man, A 024 MIN
Our Vanishing Lands 024 MIN
Tippecanoe And Lyndon Too 024 MIN
World Around Us, The 025 MIN

Smoke C 8 MIN
3/4 OR 1/2 INCH VIDEO CASSETTE
Tells how smoke rises and spreads. Puppets and children demonstrate how to escape from smoke, whether at home or school.
From The Safe Child Series.
Prod-FPF Dist-FPF

Smoke And Fire - Two Steps To Survival C 20 MIN
16MM FILM OPTICAL SOUND
Explains the dangers of smoke and stresses the importance of early warning and rapid escape from a fire.
LC NO. 78-700219
Prod-AETNA Dist-AETNA 1977

Smoke Gets In Your Hair C 14 MIN
16MM FILM, 3/4 OR 1/2 IN VIDEO P-I
Relates how the gang learns that smoking isn't a sign of maturity.
From The Learning Values With Fat Albert Series.
Prod-FLMTON Dist-CRMP 1977

Smoke Screen C 5 MIN
16MM FILM, 3/4 OR 1/2 IN VIDEO I-C A
Aims to deter children from acquiring the smoking habit through the use of kinestatic images of smokers.
Prod-WARSHW Dist-PFP 1970

Smoke Testing A Wastewater Collection System C 6 MIN
1/2 IN VIDEO CASSETTE BETA/VHS
Discusses maintenance and repair, and water and wastewater technology.
Prod-RMI Dist-RMI

Smoke-Filled Rooms And Dark Horses B 30 MIN
16MM FILM OPTICAL SOUND
Describes and analyzes the role of organizations and national party conventions.
From The Structure And Functions Of American Government. Part VII, Lesson 3 - First Semester
Prod-NBCTV Dist-NBC 1963

Smoker's Luck C 50 MIN
16MM FILM, 3/4 OR 1/2 IN VIDEO C A
Explains the risks involved in tobacco smoking, including the danger of carbon monoxide, a possible major factor in heart disease, the effect of a mother's smoking on the unborn child and the danger to non-smokers from inhalation of other's smoke. Uses animation to show how blocking of the arteries can result causing loss of blood supply to the legs.
Prod-BBCTV Dist-FI

Smokers Have Rights Too C 24 MIN
16MM FILM OPTICAL SOUND A
Dramatizes the story of a congressional aide who says he has a right to smoke. Tells how he meets a man dying of emphysema who teaches him an important lesson.
LC NO. 79-700942
Prod-NARCED Dist-NARCED Prodn-MARTC 1979

Smokey And His Friends C 4 MIN
16MM FILM OPTICAL SOUND
Depicts Smokey meeting some of his wild animal and bird friends and watching them in their forest home. Reminds the viewer that fires destroy the homes of his friends.
LC NO. 74-705657
Prod-USDA Dist-USNAC 1967

Smokey Bear C 18 MIN
16MM FILM, 3/4 OR 1/2 IN VIDEO K-I
Tells how two children learn from their grandfather the true story of Smokey Bear and how he was found clinging to a burned tree after a devastating forest fire. Relates how Smokey Bear was made the national living symbol of forest fire prevention and was sent to live in Washington DC. Deals with the importance of preserving our forests and being cautious with fire hazards while outdoors.
Prod-USFS Dist-FILCOM 1977

Smokey The Bear B 5 MIN
16MM FILM, 3/4 OR 1/2 IN VIDEO
Presents Smokey Bear and Eddy Arnold reminding boys on a camping trip of their responsibility in helping to prevent forest fires.
Prod-USDA Dist-USNAC

Smokey's Story C 12 MIN
16MM FILM OPTICAL SOUND
Dennis Weaver sees a boy playing with matches in the woods, and so he retells the story of Little Smokey, the cub who survived a forest fire.
LC NO. 74-705658
Prod-USDI Dist-USNAC 1971

Smoki Snake Dance C 12 MIN
16MM FILM OPTICAL SOUND I-J
Shows activities of civic-minded Arizonians as they prepare to learn and present Indian dances in their annual Smoki Dance Festival.
Prod-DAGP Dist-MLA 1952

Smokin's Bad For You (Yogi Bear) C 1 MIN
3/4 OR 1/2 INCH VIDEO CASSETTE
Features animated cartoon favorite Yogi Bear in a TV spot produced jointly by American Cancer Society, American Lung Association and American Heart Association. Tells youngsters as new and potential smokers that 'Smokin's Bad For You.'
Prod-AMCS Dist-AMCS 1980

Smoking - A New Focus C 15 MIN
16MM FILM, 3/4 OR 1/2 IN VIDEO I-H
Examines the problem of smoking from a medical and sociological standpoint. Avoids scare tactics and didactic preaching.
Prod-AMEDFL Dist-AMEDFL 1972

Smoking - A New Focus (Spanish) C 16 MIN
16MM FILM, 3/4 OR 1/2 IN VIDEO J-C
Examines the smoking problem from a medical and sociological viewpoint in order to understand how the smoking myth evolved. Presents the viewpoints of a smoker as to why he started, why he can't stop and whether or not he really wants to quit.
Prod-AMEDFL Dist-AMEDFL

Smoking - A Report On The Nation's Habit C 17 MIN
16MM FILM, 3/4 OR 1/2 IN VIDEO J-C A
Outlines information regarding smoking trends, the tobacco industry and dangers associated with smoking. Gives a poignant example of why not to start, or if you already have, to quit.
From The Life And Breath Series.
Prod-JOU Dist-JOU 1978

Smoking - A Report On The Nation's Habit C 17 MIN
16MM FILM, 3/4 OR 1/2 IN VIDEO J-C A
Reports on the alarming health consequences of cigarette smoking. Includes an interview with a woman dying of lung cancer who had ignored the surgeon general's warning.
Prod-PELICN Dist-PELICN 1978

Smoking - Games Smokers Play C 26 MIN
16MM FILM, 3/4 OR 1/2 IN VIDEO J-C A
Points out the hazards of smoking. Shows a psychologist discussing reasons for the teenage smoking habit and shows a simulated discussion by teenagers on smoking.
Prod-HOBLEI Dist-CNEMAG 1976

Smoking - Hazardous To Your Health, Pt 1 C 29 MIN
3/4 OR 1/2 INCH VIDEO CASSETTE
Discusses the effects of smoking on the body, heart and lungs, and the diseases triggered by smoking.
From The Here's To Your Health Series.
Prod-KERA Dist-PBS

Smoking - How To Quit C
3/4 OR 1/2 INCH VIDEO CASSETTE
Relates a husband and wife who attempt to quit smoking. Includes practical tips.
Prod-MIFE Dist-MIFE

Smoking - How To Stop C 23 MIN
16MM FILM OPTICAL SOUND
Explains simple proven techniques for breaking the smoking habit.
LC NO. 77-702416
Prod-PELICN Dist-PELICN 1977

Smoking - How To Stop C 23 MIN
16MM FILM, 3/4 OR 1/2 IN VIDEO A
Examines the progress of a typical smoker as she advances through a quitters clinic. Portrays useful tips for quitting while positive, encouraging messages for the millions of smokers who would like to quit are relayed.
From The Life And Breath Series.
Prod-JOU Dist-JOU 1978

Smoking - How To Stop C 23 MIN
16MM FILM, 3/4 OR 1/2 IN VIDEO J-C A
Offers encouragement and practical suggestions for smokers who want to quit. Includes such proven methods as recording and rating every cigarette, making smoking less convenient and joining support groups.
Prod-REIDMA Dist-PFP 1977

Smoking - It's Your Choice (2nd Ed) C 17 MIN
16MM FILM, 3/4 OR 1/2 IN VIDEO I-J
Presents information on the effects of cigarette smoke and points out the risks involved for smokers. Examines the peer pressure on young people to smoke.
Prod-HIGGIN Dist-HIGGIN 1980

Smoking - Kicking The Habit, Pt 2 C 29 MIN
3/4 OR 1/2 INCH VIDEO CASSETTE
Examines some of the many programs aimed at stopping smoking, from hypnosis seminars to aversion-therapy clinics, with warnings about dubious, high-cost programs. Places emphasis on keeping teens from starting smoking.
From The Here's To Your Health Series.
Prod-KERA Dist-PBS

Smoking - Light Up, Strike Out C 11 MIN
16MM FILM, 3/4 OR 1/2 IN VIDEO I-C A
Presents a witty treatment of the claims made by advertisements for cigarettes. Points out that smoking is like gambling and that one smoker out of seven is likely to die from cancer.
Prod-NULSEN Dist-AIMS 1975

Smoking - Nico-Teen C 11 MIN
16MM FILM, 3/4 OR 1/2 IN VIDEO I-H
Interviews many teenagers regarding why they first began smoking. Shows that smokers are not proud of the habit and examines how teenage smokers work to stop. Originally shown on the CBS program 30 Minutes.
Prod-CBSNEW Dist-PHENIX 1981

Smoking - Personal Pollution C 18 MIN
16MM FILM, 3/4 OR 1/2 IN VIDEO J-H
Shows how cigarettes affect the human body and can lead to addiction. Demonstrates how even one cigarette can affect the blood pressure and circulatory system.
Prod-GOLDCF Dist-PEREN

Smoking - The Choice Is Yours C 11 MIN
16MM FILM, 3/4 OR 1/2 IN VIDEO I-J
Explains the hazards of smoking and deals with the root problems of self-image and peer pressure which influence students to begin smoking.
Prod-WDEMCO Dist-WDEMCO 1982

Smoking - The Choice Is Yours (Thai) C 11 MIN
16MM FILM, 3/4 OR 1/2 IN VIDEO I-J
Explains the hazards of smoking. Deals with the reasons students begin to smoke - self-image and peer pressure. Features animation.
Prod-WDEMCO Dist-WDEMCO 1982

Smoking / Emphysema - A Fight For Breath C 12 MIN
16MM FILM, 3/4 OR 1/2 IN VIDEO H-C A
Illustrates the difference between the functioning of healthy lungs and diseased ones. Describes the breakdowns that take place as emphysema develops.
Prod-NFBC Dist-CRMP 1975

Smoking And Health - A Report To Youth C 13 MIN
16MM FILM, 3/4 OR 1/2 IN VIDEO J-C A
Uses animation to show how the trachea, bronchi and lungs function and how they are affected by smoking. Points out that although bronchitis and emphysema are thought of as 'old folks' diseases, they are striking the younger population.
Prod-DESCEN Dist-PHENIX 1969

Smoking And Health - The Answers We Seek C 15 MIN
16MM FILM OPTICAL SOUND
Seeks to provide a full, free and informed discussion of the smoking and health controversy and to affirm the conviction that the controversy must be resolved by scientific research.
Prod-TOBCCO Dist-MTP

Smoking And Health - The Need To Know C 28 MIN
16MM FILM OPTICAL SOUND J-C A
Presents a scientific documentary on a current controversy that relates the facts about smoking and health.
Prod-TOBCCO Dist-MTP

Smoking And Heart Disease C 10 MIN
3/4 OR 1/2 INCH VIDEO CASSETTE
Uses animated drawings and diagrams to present the effects of nicotine on a smoker's heart and circulation. Shows how subtle body changes, such as narrowing of the blood vessels, become gross, with high blood pressure and heart disease diminishing a smoker's life expectancy.
Prod-PRIMED Dist-PRIMED

Smoking Spiral, The B 60 MIN
16MM FILM OPTICAL SOUND J-C A
Illustrates the possible crippling effects of smoking by showing one day in the lives of two men suffering from lung ailments linked to smoking. Points out that health education against smoking has had little effect. Interviews representatives of the tobacco industry, politicians and medical officers for comments concerning the various aspects of the problem.
From The Net Journal Series.
Prod-NET Dist-IU 1967

Smoking, Drinking And Drugs C 15 MIN
16MM FILM, 3/4 OR 1/2 IN VIDEO K-I
Shows how habits like smoking, drinking and drugs are easy to form and hard to break. Demonstrates the effects of smoking on the heart and circulation of a smoker. Explains how some people drink too much, hurting themselves and their families. Presents a puppet dinosaur who makes a statement about drugs when he eats an unfamiliar plant and gets more than he bargained.
From The Healthwise Series.
LC NO. 83-707065
Prod-CORF Dist-CORF 1982

Smoking, What Are The Facts? (3rd Ed) C 13 MIN
3/4 OR 1/2 INCH VIDEO CASSETTE
Presents the basic information about the effects of smoking as published in the 1979 Surgeon General's Report.
Prod-MEDFAC Dist-MEDFAC 1980

Smoky Mountains, Pt 1 C 14 MIN
2 INCH VIDEOTAPE
See series title for descriptive statement.
From The Muffinland Series.
Prod-WGTV Dist-PUBTEL

Smoky Mountains, Pt 2 C 14 MIN
2 INCH VIDEOTAPE
See series title for descriptive statement.
From The Muffinland Series.
Prod-WGTV Dist-PUBTEL

Smothering Dreams C 22 MIN
3/4 OR 1/2 INCH VIDEO CASSETTE
Presents an autobiographical videotape concerned with the myths and realities of organized violence as experienced through the imagination of a child and the eyes of a soldier.
Prod-EAI Dist-EAI

Smothering Dreams C 23 MIN
3/4 OR 1/2 INCH VIDEO CASSETTE
Deals with Dan Reeves' experiences as a marine in Viet Nam, as well as the childhood war play and fantasy of violence. Calls into doubt the myths of chivalry and war presented to children.
Prod-KITCHN Dist-KITCHN

Smotherly Love C 30 MIN
16MM FILM, 3/4 OR 1/2 IN VIDEO J-H A
Recounts that when Pete Wolenski receives the basketball scholarship he's dreamt about, his mother and his girlfriend put him through the hoop about leaving home.
From The Moving Right Along Series.
Prod-WQED Dist-MTI 1983

Smug Duds Suds-In C 13 MIN
16MM FILM OPTICAL SOUND
Presents twin sisters, Patty the know-how gal and Susie, the goof-off as they swim, ski, bowl, motorcycle ride, go to school and play tennis. Includes tips on wardrobe selection and care and illustrates the differences between easy care and special care fabrics. Provides tips on using laundry aids and selection of procedures for automatic care.
Prod-MAY Dist-MAY

Smush The Fire Out C 11 MIN
16MM FILM, 3/4 OR 1/2 IN VIDEO P-I
Introduces the students of a second grade class, who demonstrate fire survival basics through games and activities.
Prod-FILCOM Dist-FILCOM Prodn-SOLARI 1976

SNA - Critical Issues C 35 MIN
3/4 OR 1/2 INCH VIDEO CASSETTE
Discusses the critical issues faced by managers in using the System Network Architecture (SNA) technology. Points out the pitfalls of the product and evaluates its suitability for its intended purpose.
From The SNA Management Consideration Series.
Prod-DELTAK Dist-DELTAK

SNA Implementation And Operation Considerations C 35 MIN
3/4 OR 1/2 INCH VIDEO CASSETTE
Puts the entire issue of System Network Architecture (SNA) into management perspective. Explores planning and implementation issues, emphasizing the impact of the SNA decision on the people and the organization.
From The SNA Management Consideration Series.
Prod-DELTAK Dist-DELTAK

SNA Management Considerations—A Series

Discusses the concepts, principles of operation and implementation considerations of the Systems Network Architecture (SNA). Covers the subject of management planning considerations for SNA and gives insight into IBM's strategy for this product.
Prod-DELTAK Dist-DELTAK

Components Of SNA 035 MIN
Critical Issues 035 MIN
Principals Of SNA 035 MIN
SNA Implementation And Operation Considerations 035 MIN

Snack Cakes C 5 MIN
16MM FILM, 3/4 OR 1/2 IN VIDEO K-C A
See series title for descriptive statement.
From The How It's Made Series.
Prod-HOLIA Dist-LUF

Snacking - Garbage In Your Gut C 15 MIN
16MM FILM, 3/4 OR 1/2 IN VIDEO PRO
Examines the snacking habits of a high school class and shows the effects of both inadequate and proper nutrition.
Prod-PRORE Dist-PRORE

Snacking - Garbage In Your Gut C 15 MIN
16MM FILM, 3/4 OR 1/2 IN VIDEO I-H
Shows how simple changes in snacking habits can turn a 'bad snacker' into a 'good snacker.'
From The World Of Health Series.
Prod-SF Dist-SF 1975

Snacking Mouse Goes To School C 6 MIN
3/4 OR 1/2 INCH VIDEO CASSETTE K-P
Follows Snacking Mouse as he starts his first day of school. Shows the mouse beginning to snack excessively at the expense of regular meals.
Prod-POAPLE Dist-POAPLE

Snacking Mouse, The C 5 MIN
3/4 OR 1/2 INCH VIDEO CASSETTE K-P
Shows children what happens when a mouse becomes too fat to fit through his mouse hole as a result of consistently eating only sweet and salty snacks.
Prod-POAPLE Dist-POAPLE

Snacks C 4 MIN
16MM FILM OPTICAL SOUND
See series title for descriptive statement.
From The Beatrice Trum Hunter's Natural Foods Series.
Prod-PUBTEL Dist-PBS 1974

Snacks C 3 MIN
2 INCH VIDEOTAPE
Shows how to make a snack mixture combining all sorts of dried fruits, nuts and seeds. Demonstrates a simple method for drying fruits at home.
From The Beatrice Trum Hunter's Natural Foods Series.
Prod-WGBH Dist-PUBTEL

Snacks Count Too (2nd Ed) C 12 MIN
16MM FILM, 3/4 OR 1/2 IN VIDEO I-H
Examines the factors that lead to excess snacking and discusses the nutritive value of popular snack foods.
From The Your Diet Series.
LC NO. 84-707064
Prod-JOU Dist-JOU 1983

Snaffle Bit And Trail Horse C 52 MIN
1/2 IN VIDEO CASSETTE BETA/VHS
Demonstrates how to calm, saddle and ride an inexperienced horse.
Prod-ARABSC Dist-EQVDL

Snail And The Caterpillar, The C 15 MIN
3/4 INCH VIDEO CASSETTE K-P
See series title for descriptive statement.
From The Storytime Series.
Prod-WCETTV Dist-GPITVL 1976

Snails - Backyard Science (2nd Ed) C 12 MIN
16MM FILM, 3/4 OR 1/2 IN VIDEO P-I
Describes the physical characteristics, eating habits and behavior patterns of snails. Explains how they are helpful to man.
Prod-BEANM Dist-PHENIX 1979

Snake C 22 MIN
16MM FILM, 3/4 OR 1/2 IN VIDEO P-I
Looks at the various habitats and means of locomotion of snakes as well as some medical research being done on using venom to cure disease. Uses stories and poems to tell about the snake and his lifestyle. Hosted by Hal Linden.
From The Animals, Animals, Animals Series.
Prod-ABCNEW Dist-MEDIAG 1977

Snake Hunt C 10 MIN
16MM FILM, 3/4 OR 1/2 IN VIDEO P-J
Shows how staff members of the Lincoln Park Zoo on a 'SNAKE HUNT' in Central Florida, where they capture snakes in a variety of environments. Describes the equipment used by the hunters, the method of capture and the identification and transportation of snakes.
From The Science Close-Up Series.
Prod-PRISM Dist-SF 1967

Snake Prince, The C 18 MIN
16MM FILM, 3/4 OR 1/2 IN VIDEO P-I
Employs puppets to tell the story of a young prince who sets out to comb his kingdom for a young woman he can love.
LC NO. 84-706037
Prod-KRATKY Dist-WOMBAT 1983

Snake, The - Villain Or Victim C 24 MIN
16MM FILM, 3/4 OR 1/2 IN VIDEO I-J
Attempts to dispel, through the use of cartoons and scenes of snakes in various habitats, the myths and villainous reputation associated with serpents. Provides physiological information on snakes and demonstrates medicinal uses of their venom. Includes interviews with owners of snakes, who impart advice on the proper care, housing and handling of these animals.
From The Wide World Of Adventure Series.
Prod-AVATLI Dist-EBEC 1976

Snakebite - First Aid C 11 MIN
16MM FILM, 3/4 OR 1/2 IN VIDEO
Discusses the characteristics, habitats and geographical distribution of various species of venomous snakes. Explains the first aid measures that should be taken when treating the victim of a snakebite.
Prod-WLBPRO Dist-PHENIX 1971

Snakebites And Other Emergencies C 25 MIN
3/4 OR 1/2 INCH VIDEO CASSETTE
Shows two facets of emergency care investigated with on-the-scene filming at an urban emergency ward. Says one is an anti-venom program where patients bitten by poisonous reptiles or insects receive life-saving special care. Notes that the other is emergency medicine as a speciality that attracts young doctors, as two young physicians, a woman and a man, are followed during their tour of duty as residents in an emergency room.
Prod-TRAINX Dist-TRAINX

Snakes C 3 MIN
16MM FILM OPTICAL SOUND P-I
Discusses snakes.
From The Of All Things Series.
Prod-BAILYL Dist-AVED

Snakes (2nd Ed Rev) C 15 MIN
16MM FILM, 3/4 OR 1/2 IN VIDEO I-H
Presents a wide-ranging survey of snakes focusing on habitats and structural and behavioral adaptations. Shows a representative sampling of the 2200 species from the highly venomous rattlesnakes, copperheads and water moccasins to the gentle and helpful corn and hognose snakes.
Prod-CORF Dist-CORF 1984

Snakes Alive C 15 MIN
3/4 OR 1/2 INCH VIDEO CASSETTE K-J
Focuses on many aspects of snakes.
Prod-SUTHRB Dist-SUTHRB

Snakes And How They Live C 13 MIN
16MM FILM, 3/4 OR 1/2 IN VIDEO I-J
Reveals major key concepts about snakes. Covers different species, both helpful and harmful.
Prod-AIMS Dist-AIMS 1968

Snakes And How They Live (Captioned) C 13 MIN
16MM FILM, 3/4 OR 1/2 IN VIDEO I-J
Relates major pertinent concepts about snakes, using a great variety of types to show how they move, eat, shed skin, etc. An open-end approach stimulates class discussion.
Prod-CAHILL Dist-AIMS 1968

Snakes And How They Live (French) C 13 MIN
16MM FILM, 3/4 OR 1/2 IN VIDEO I-J
Relates major pertinent concepts about snakes, using a great variety of types to show how they move, eat, shed skin, etc. An open-end approach stimulates class discussion.
Prod-CAHILL Dist-AIMS 1968

Snakes And How They Live (Spanish) C 13 MIN
16MM FILM, 3/4 OR 1/2 IN VIDEO I-J
Relates major pertinent concepts about snakes, using a great variety of types to show how they move, eat, shed skin, etc. An open-end approach stimulates class discussion.
Prod-CAHILL Dist-AIMS 1968

Snakes And The Like C 15 MIN
3/4 OR 1/2 INCH VIDEO CASSETTE I-J
Investigates a variety of reptiles, including turtles, snakes, lizards and crocodiles.
From The Animals And Such Series. Module Brown - Types Of Vertebrates
Prod-WHROTV Dist-AITECH 1972

Snakes Are Interesting C 11 MIN
16MM FILM, 3/4 OR 1/2 IN VIDEO I-J
Describes the life cycles of snakes.
Prod-DEU Dist-IFB 1956

Snakes, Scorpions And Spiders C 15 MIN
16MM FILM, 3/4 OR 1/2 IN VIDEO J-C A
Shows the snakes, scorpions and spiders of the shortgrass prairie, with special close-ups of the animals' and insects' unusual physical features.
From The Animals And Plants Of North America Series.
LC NO. 81-707419
Prod-KARVF Dist-LCOA 1981

Snaketown C 40 MIN
16MM FILM OPTICAL SOUND C
Shows archeological tools, techniques and methods of excavation used at the snaketown site, home of the prehistoric Hohokam Indians.
LC NO. 73-702926
Prod-TEIWES Dist-UCEMC 1969

Snap Art C 14 MIN
3/4 OR 1/2 INCH VIDEO CASSETTE P-I
Discusses snap art.
From The Young At Art Series.
Prod-WSKJTV Dist-AITECH 1980

Snap Out Of It C 1 MIN
3/4 OR 1/2 INCH VIDEO CASSETTE
Shows Larry Hagman using as his pitch a rubber band which he suggests the smoker snap every time he desires a cigarette. Uses TV spot format. Also available in 10-second version.
Prod-AMCS Dist-AMCS 1982

Snapshots Of The City C 5 MIN
16MM FILM OPTICAL SOUND
Presents a black statement about the city in which two people represent the populace.
Prod-VANBKS Dist-VANBKS 1961

Snared Runner, The C 28 MIN
3/4 OR 1/2 INCH VIDEO CASSETTE
Shows emergency care given to a young family man who suffers a cerebrovascular accident. Depicts loss of speech and right-side paralysis which leaves the man handicapped and in need of an integrated rehabilitation program. Portrays community resources working together throughout the patient's recovery and rehabilitation.
Prod-PRIMED Dist-PRIMED

Snatches C 10 MIN
16MM FILM OPTICAL SOUND J-H
Presents a study of the creative sterility existing in movie making under major studio conditions.
Prod-CFS Dist-CFS 1970

Sneak Previews—A Series

Presents Gene Siskel, film critic for the Chicago Tribune and Roger Ebert, film critic of the Chicago Sun-Times reviewing movies which they feel represent social trends perceived in Hollywood and reflected by our culture.
From The Sneak Previews Series.
Prod-WTTWTV Dist-PBS 1981

Changing Hollywood Sex Roles 029 MIN
Women In Danger 029 MIN

Sneakers C 5 MIN
16MM FILM, 3/4 OR 1/2 IN VIDEO J-C A
Uuses pixillation to present an amusing story about a worn-out pair of sneakers that are joined by pairs of moccasins, boots and sandals for a merry round of square dancing on the living room floor. Without narration.
LC NO. 81-706886
Prod-JABA Dist-PHENIX 1978

Sneetches, The C 13 MIN
16MM FILM, 3/4 OR 1/2 IN VIDEO
Points out that differences are only relative. Presents an animated cartoon about various kinds of sneetches, showing that beneath their different kinds of bellies they are really quite alike.
From The Dr Seuss On The Loose Series.
Prod-CBSTV Dist-PHENIX Prodn-DEPFRE 1974

Sneezles, Wheezles And Measles C 15 MIN
3/4 OR 1/2 INCH VIDEO CASSETTE P
Describes the nature of germs and the body's natural defenses against them.
From The All About You Series.
Prod-WGBHTV Dist-AITECH Prodn-TTOIC 1975

Sniff And Snuff Animated Television Spots, Set 1 C 3 MIN
16MM FILM, 3/4 OR 1/2 IN VIDEO
Presents the exploits of Sniff and Snuff who are in constant pursuit of those who cause fires. Includes A-Hunting They Will Go, Careless Teenagers and Thoughtless Farmer Brown.
Prod-FILCOM Dist-FILCOM

Sniff And Snuff Animated Television Spots, Set 2 C 3 MIN
16MM FILM, 3/4 OR 1/2 IN VIDEO
Presents the exploits of Sniff and Snuff who are in constant pursuit of those who cause fires. Includes Find A Firebug, Make The Forest Kid-Proof and Meet The Most Dangerous Animal In The Forest.
Prod-FILCOM Dist-FILCOM

Sniff And Snuff On The Moon C 5 MIN
16MM FILM, 3/4 OR 1/2 IN VIDEO
Features Super Fire-Safe Snoopers, Sniff and Snuff as astronauts on the moon. Tells how they wonder if the moon is like it is because of fire and how they conclude that people must prevent forest fires so the earth does not look like the moon.
Prod-PUBSF Dist-FILCOM

Sniffles, Sneezes And Contagious Diseases C 14 MIN
16MM FILM, 3/4 OR 1/2 IN VIDEO K-I
Presents the Healthwise puppets who learn how people defend themselves against germs. Uses animation to discuss the body's immune system and to illustrate how the inflammatory reaction helps fight germs that survive the immune system.
From The Healthwise Series.
LC NO. 83-707064
Prod-CORF Dist-CORF 1982

Sniffy Escapes Poisoning C 6 MIN
16MM FILM, 3/4 OR 1/2 IN VIDEO P-I
Speaks to children in a language they can understand as sniffy and his young friend give an effective but non-frightening warning about the dangers behind the medicine cabinet door.
Prod-PEREN Dist-PEREN

Sniper, The B 9 MIN
16MM FILM OPTICAL SOUND
Attempts to come to terms with the intimate irony of three characters caught in a war. An experimental film produced by students in the cinema division, University of Southern California.
LC NO. 75-703233
Prod-USC Dist-USC 1964

Snips And Shears C 13 MIN
16MM FILM, 3/4 OR 1/2 IN VIDEO H-C A
Straight, combination, curved blade and aviation snips and foot squaring shears.
From The Metalwork - Hand Tools Series.
Prod-MORLAT Dist-SF 1967

Snookie, The Adventures Of A Black Bear Cub C 11 MIN
16MM FILM, 3/4 OR 1/2 IN VIDEO P
Follows the adventures of a young and playful black bear.
Prod-DEU Dist-IFB 1957

Snorkeling Skills And Rescue Techniques C 16 MIN
16MM FILM OPTICAL SOUND
Demonstrates the uses and functions of the snorkel tube both in water recreation and safety.
Prod-AMRC Dist-AMRC 1972

Snorkeling Skills And Rescue Techniques C 13 MIN
16MM FILM - 3/4 IN VIDEO I-C A
Demonstrates correct use of face mask, swim fins and snorkel. Illustrates how to select proper equipment and how to use it safely.
From The Lifesaving And Water Safety Series.
Prod-AMRC Dist-AMRC

Snort History, A C 7 MIN
16MM FILM, 3/4 OR 1/2 IN VIDEO H-C A
Uses live action and animation to show how alcohol can distort the preception of an individual to such a point that he is overly optimistic in driving situations.
Prod-CODHW Dist-AIMS 1972

Snow C 6 MIN
16MM FILM OPTICAL SOUND
Looks at the clean-up of a big city after a major snowfall.
Prod-SOLEIL Dist-IFEX 1982

Snow C 7 MIN
16MM FILM, 3/4 OR 1/2 IN VIDEO P-J
A visual poem showing the beauty of the snow when it begins to fall. As the snow grows heavier it becomes a menace which eventually turns into an avalanche.
Prod-MALONS Dist-AIMS 1975

Snow - A First Film C 9 MIN
16MM FILM, 3/4 OR 1/2 IN VIDEO P-I
Introduces the young student to a variety of observations about snow--how a snowflake is formed and how it affects plant and animal life.
Prod-NELLES Dist-PHENIX 1969

Snow Balls C 12 MIN
16MM FILM OPTICAL SOUND
Presents a spontaneous, as-it-happens account of winter fun in Quebec, Canada. Shows the Quebec City Winter Carnival and the hospitality of resort hotels and chalets throughout this winter playground.
Prod-CTFL Dist-CTFL

Snow Damage C 30 MIN
16MM FILM OPTICAL SOUND
A Japanese language film. Points out that snow, which covers 80 percent of all Japan in winter, causes great damage to railways, roads and power-transmission lines. Shows the experiments, the counterplan and the solution actually taken against snow damage, by using many new kinds of optical instruments from microscopes to aerial cameras.
Prod-UNIJAP Dist-UNIJAP 1968

Snow How C 27 MIN
16MM FILM OPTICAL SOUND J-C
Combines fun and scenic beauty with a wilderness emergency. Tells of three people who undertake a three day snowmobile trek into the rugged 'ALPS OF OREGON.' Continues with an accident resulting in the loss of the equipment sled and serious personal injury. Presents snow country survival techniques.
LC NO. 75-709018
Prod-LSTI Dist-LSTI 1969

Snow In The Winter And Flowers In The Spring C 8 MIN
16MM FILM OPTICAL SOUND K-P
Follows Crystal and her friends as they play in the snow during the winter and turn to gardening with the coming of spring.
From The Crystal Tipps And Alistair Series.
LC NO. 73-700453
Prod-BBCTV Dist-VEDO 1972

Snow Metamorphism C 9 MIN
16MM FILM, 3/4 OR 1/2 IN VIDEO
Uses time-lapse micrographs to illustrate snow compaction under load, equitemperature and temperature-gradient metamorphism, sintering, melt metamorphism and melt.
Prod-ILTS Dist-UWASHP 1973

Snow Monkeys Of Japan C 8 MIN
16MM FILM, 3/4 OR 1/2 IN VIDEO I-C A
Views a band of snow monkeys, an endangered animal species. Concentrates on the only snow monkeys in the world that have adapted to hot spring water.
Prod-MCGHRY Dist-AIMS 1975

Snow Queen, The C 21 MIN
16MM FILM, 3/4 OR 1/2 IN VIDEO P-I
Traces the adventures of a boy and a girl who grow up together, are separated by evil spirits, and are finally reunited. Based on the story The Snow Queen by Hans Christian Andersen.
Prod-BFA Dist-PHENIX 1981

Snow Spryte At Olympics C 10 MIN
16MM FILM OPTICAL SOUND
Shows 1201 Snow Spryte tracked vehicles working at grooming and repairing the ski trails for the 1968 Olympics at Grenoble, france.
Prod-THIOKL Dist-THIOKL 1968

Snow What B 9 MIN
16MM FILM OPTICAL SOUND
Explores the shapes, textures and movement inherent in the fabrication of artificial snow under artificial light.
LC NO. 76-701368
Prod-RYERC Dist-RYERC 1975

Snow White - A Lesson In Cooperation C 8 MIN
16MM FILM, 3/4 OR 1/2 IN VIDEO P-I
Tells how a young boy misses a birthday party because he procrastinates and doesn't cooperate at home. Shows how his friend Uncle Phil and a scene from the animated film Snow White And The Seven Dwarfs help him realize that cooperating with others can be a rewarding experience.
From The Disney's Animated Classics - Lessons In
Prod-DISNEY Dist-WDEMCO Prodn-WDEMCO 1978

Snow White And Rose Red B 13 MIN
16MM FILM OPTICAL SOUND K-I
Presents the fairy tale Snow White And Rose Red in animated form based on live shadow plays produced by Lotte Reiniger for BBC Television.
From The Lotte Reiniger's Animated Fairy Tales Series.
Prod-PRIMP Dist-MOMA 1954

Snow White And The Seven Dwarfs - A German Fairy Tale C 11 MIN
16MM FILM, 3/4 OR 1/2 IN VIDEO K-P
Presents the German fairy tale Snow White And The Seven Dwarfs. Tells the story of Snow White who flees to the forest and finds refuge with the seven dwarfs when the wicked queen tries to have her killed.
From The Favorite Fairy Tales And Fables Series.
Prod-CORF Dist-CORF 1980

Snow White With Mr Magoo C 52 MIN
16MM FILM OPTICAL SOUND P-I
Prod-FI Dist-FI

Snow White's Daughter C 8 MIN
16MM FILM, 3/4 OR 1/2 IN VIDEO J-C A
Uses an animated story about Snow White, Prince Charming and their little daughter to examine the needs and problems of all children. Celebrates UNICEF's International Year of the Child with an appeal to help alleviate the suffering of two-thirds of the world's children.
LC NO. 81-707219
Prod-KRATKY Dist-PHENIX 1981

Snow-Show C 7 MIN
16MM FILM OPTICAL SOUND
Reveals the heart of the symmetry of snow flakes through the center of the microscope's eye.
Prod-VANBKS Dist-VANBKS

Snowbound C 33 MIN
16MM FILM, 3/4 OR 1/2 IN VIDEO I-C
A shortened version of the 1978 motion picture Snowbound. Features two teenagers who learn to understand themselves and each other when they are caught in a desolate area during a snowstorm.
Prod-LCOA Dist-LCOA 1978

Snowbound C 50 MIN
16MM FILM, 3/4 OR 1/2 IN VIDEO I-C
Features two teenagers who learn to understand themselves and each other when they are caught in a desolate area during a snowstorm.
Prod-LCOA Dist-LCOA 1978

Snowbound (Captioned) C 32 MIN
16MM FILM, 3/4 OR 1/2 IN VIDEO J-H A
Tells about a teenager who offers a lift to a plain, insecure girl who eventually helps both of them out of a blizzard. Edited version.
Prod-LCOA Dist-LCOA 1978

Snowbound (Captioned) C 50 MIN
16MM FILM, 3/4 OR 1/2 IN VIDEO J-H A
Tells about a teenager who offers a lift to a plain, insecure girl who eventually helps them both out of a blizzard. Full version.
Prod-LCOA Dist-LCOA 1978

Snowbound (Spanish) C 32 MIN
16MM FILM, 3/4 OR 1/2 IN VIDEO J-H A
Tells the story of a teenager who offers a lift to a plain, insecure girl who eventually helps both of them out of a blizzard. Edited version.
Prod-LCOA Dist-LCOA 1978

Snowbound (Spanish) C 50 MIN
16MM FILM, 3/4 OR 1/2 IN VIDEO J-H A
Relates the story of a teenager who offers a lift to a plain, insecure girl who eventually helps both out of a blizzard. Full version.
Prod-LCOA Dist-LCOA 1978

Snowdrift Wesson Oil C 2 MIN
3/4 OR 1/2 INCH VIDEO CASSETTE
Shows a classic television commercial that uses only three words - 'John, Marcia and Snowdrift.'
Prod-BROOKC Dist-BROOKC

Snowfire B 79 MIN
16MM FILM OPTICAL SOUND P-J
Tells the story of Molly, a little girl who talks to horses and is convinced they talk to her.
Prod-CINEWO Dist-CINEWO 1958

Snowflakes C 7 MIN
16MM FILM, 3/4 OR 1/2 IN VIDEO P-I
Shows snow as a source for fun activities, winter beauty and food for plants. Studies the physical structure of snowflakes through photomicroscopy. Explains snow as a treasure which God supplies to meet man's needs.
Prod-MIS Dist-MIS 1956

Snowman And Eskimos B 29 MIN
2 INCH VIDEOTAPE K-P
See series title for descriptive statement.
From The Children's Fair Series.
Prod-WMVSTV Dist-PUBTEL

Snowman, The C 26 MIN
16MM FILM, 3/4 OR 1/2 IN VIDEO
Tells the story of a young boy's dream of his snowman coming to life. Described in muted pastels, with an orchestral score.
Prod-RH Dist-WWS

Snowman's Dilemma C 9 MIN
16MM FILM, 3/4 OR 1/2 IN VIDEO H-C
An animated film about a snowman whose tender feelings for a little girl are turned into icicles on her windowsill.
Prod-FILBUL Dist-MGHT 1969

Snowmobile Safety Savvy C 15 MIN
16MM FILM OPTICAL SOUND
Combines live action and animation in order to dramatize the pleasures of snowmobiling and to point out dangers of not conforming to established safety rules.
LC NO. 74-702669
Prod-DEERE Dist-DEERE Prodn-HANBAR 1974

Snowmobiling - Trail And Safari C 14 MIN
16MM FILM, 3/4 OR 1/2 IN VIDEO
Outlines the necessary equipment and safety precautions for trail and safari snowmobiling.
Prod-MORLAT Dist-SF 1973

Snows Of Kilimanjaro C 114 MIN
16MM FILM OPTICAL SOUND
Shows a successful but disillusioned writer who though near death from the wounds received in Africa, reminisces about his amorous intrigues and experiences as a hunter.
LC NO. FIA53-870
Prod-TWCF Dist-TWCF

Snowshoeing C 12 MIN
16MM FILM, 3/4 OR 1/2 IN VIDEO J-C A
Explains that the ungainly looking snow shoes, invented by the Indians long ago can be loads of fun as well as providing for easy walking in deep snow. Demonstrates how to use them correctly.
Prod-SF Dist-SF 1968

Snowy '69 C 24 MIN
16MM FILM OPTICAL SOUND J-C A
Presents a progress report on the Snowy Mountains hydro-electric scheme.
Prod-ANAIB Dist-AUIS 1971

Snowy Day, The C 6 MIN
16MM FILM, 3/4 OR 1/2 IN VIDEO K-P
An animated version of the picture book by Ezra Jack Keats, using the original illustrations. Tale of a small boy's delight in a city snowfall.
Prod-WWS Dist-WWS 1964

Snowy, Chilly, Motley and Me C 50 MIN
16MM FILM, 3/4 OR 1/2 IN VIDEO I-J
Presents John Paling's experiences with a German Shepherd dog, a Siamese cat and a stray cat, including scenes of the dog mating and delivering her first litter. Shows the interaction of the three pets and presents information on the unique behavior of dogs and cats.
Prod-BBCTV Dist-FI

So - What Happened To You C 14 MIN
3/4 OR 1/2 INCH VIDEO CASSETTE J-C A
See series title for descriptive statement.
From The Poetry Alive Series.
Prod-CMSS Dist-AITECH 1978

So Be It Enacted C 13 MIN
16MM FILM OPTICAL SOUND
Gives an account of the Danish parliamentary procedure. Shows an imaginary bill going through the various legislative processes.
Prod-RDCG Dist-AUDPLN

So Ein Zufall C 15 MIN
16MM FILM, 3/4 OR 1/2 IN VIDEO
See series title for descriptive statement.
From The Guten Tag Series. Part 15
Prod-BAYER Dist-IFB 1968

So Etwas Muss Man Mit Gefuhl Machen C 15 MIN
16MM FILM, 3/4 OR 1/2 IN VIDEO
See series title for descriptive statement.
From The Guten Tag Wie Geht's Series. Part 6
Prod-BAYER Dist-IFB 1973

So Fair A Land C 15 MIN
16MM FILM OPTICAL SOUND J-H
Shows the U S foreign aid program operating in the Dominican Republic and how it affects the lives of the Dominican forest people.
LC NO. 77-703238
Prod-USAID Dist-USNAC 1977

So Far Apart C 19 MIN
16MM FILM OPTICAL SOUND J-C A
Considers the problems of the runaway child. Helps stimulate thought and discussion about the forces within families which can cause children to run away.
LC NO. 74-702169
Prod-KBTV Dist-SCREEI 1974

So Far From India C 49 MIN
16MM FILM, 3/4 OR 1/2 IN VIDEO
Describes the tension which occurs in an East Indian family when the husband moves to New York seeking a better life while his wife stays behind in India, depending on her in-laws for sustenance.
LC NO. 84-706221
Prod-NAIRM Dist-FLMLIB 1982

So I Took It C 10 MIN
16MM FILM, 3/4 OR 1/2 IN VIDEO
Shows how a girl named Sally gets caught in the snowballing nightmare of shoplifting due to peer pressure and how she eventually involves her own brother in the crime.
Prod-SRSPRD Dist-MTI

So Ist Das Leben B 66 MIN
16MM FILM SILENT
A silent motion picture with German subtitles. Illustrates the life of a working class family in a Prague suburb. A significant film from the transitional period from silent to sound films.
Prod-WSTGLC Dist-WSTGLC 1929

So Kann Es Nicht Weitergehen C 15 MIN
16MM FILM, 3/4 OR 1/2 IN VIDEO
See series title for descriptive statement.
From The Guten Tag Wie Geht's Series. Part 26
Prod-BAYER Dist-IFB 1973

So Life May Continue B 18 MIN
16MM FILM OPTICAL SOUND C A
Deals with laboratory animal medicine as it applies to research on breast cancer, leukemia, the common cold and heart disease. Shows in detail the handling and care of laboratory animals, the preparation of the animals for research projects and the use of a germfree surrounding during research.
Prod-UILL Dist-AMVMA

So Little Time C 11 MIN
16MM FILM, 3/4 OR 1/2 IN VIDEO J-C A
Presents a poetic treatise on the waterfowl of the Midwestern United States that makes a plea for their preservation.
Prod-LATHAM Dist-AIMS 1974

So Little Time C 27 MIN
16MM FILM, 3/4 OR 1/2 IN VIDEO H-C A
Portrays a journalist in a civil war who knows he is about to die wishing that he could see his wife just one more time. Shows how God allows him to enter the dream she is having and apologize for his infidelity and selfishness. Stars William Devane.
From The Insight Series.
Prod-PAULST Dist-PAULST

So Little Time C 27 MIN
3/4 OR 1/2 INCH VIDEO CASSETTE J A
Tells the story of reconciliation, love and facing the truth about oneself. Stars William DeVane, Lois Nettleton and David Spielberg.
Prod-SUTHRB Dist-SUTHRB

So Long Joey C 63 MIN
16MM FILM OPTICAL SOUND R
Reveals the struggle of singer Dave Boyer whose heavy drinking led him to the brink of suicide. Details how the acceptance of Christ changed his life.
Prod-GF Dist-GF

So Long Pal C 22 MIN
16MM FILM, 3/4 OR 1/2 IN VIDEO H-C A
Uses fantasy and humor in order to break down the resistance to treatment of people arrested for drunken driving and to promote alcohol safety.
Prod-NHTSA Dist-AIMS 1974

So Long Pal C 22 MIN
3/4 OR 1/2 INCH VIDEO CASSETTE J A
Focuses on the drinking driver who refuses help. Contains fantasy, humor and animation.
Prod-SUTHRB Dist-SUTHRB

So Long Pal (Spanish) C 22 MIN
3/4 OR 1/2 INCH VIDEO CASSETTE J A
Focuses on the drinking driver who refuses help. Contains fantasy, humor and animation.
Prod-SUTHRB Dist-SUTHRB

So Long, Pal C 22 MIN
3/4 OR 1/2 INCH VIDEO CASSETTE
Reveals the story of a typical social drinker who often drives after drinking too much. Explores the attitude of the drinking driver, the penalties imposed by law and the fatal consequences of his actions.
Prod-LACFU Dist-IA

So Many Voices - A Look At Abortion In America C 30 MIN
16MM FILM, 3/4 OR 1/2 IN VIDEO H-C A
Examines both sides of the abortion issue through interviews with people personally affected by the legal right to an abortion. Notes that antiabortion legislation is being considered by the U S Congress and questions the various implications such legislation would have for American women. Hosted by Ed Asner and Tammy Grimes.
Prod-NARAL Dist-PHENIX 1982

So Many Ways To Communicate B 20 MIN
2 INCH VIDEOTAPE P
Reviews the different ways of communicating that have been presented through the years. (Broadcast quality)
From The Language Lane Series. Lesson 31
Prod-CVETVC Dist-GPITVL Prodn-WCVETV

So Many Ways... C 10 MIN
16MM FILM OPTICAL SOUND I
Discusses bodily joints, how they work and what happens when they don't. Shows children with arthritis and demonstrates that they are capable of many things despite their illness.
Prod-ARTHF Dist-ARTHF

So Nearly Distant C 30 MIN
16MM FILM OPTICAL SOUND H-C A
Studies the institution of marriage, its meaning, the hazards involved and its benefits.
Prod-FAMF Dist-FAMF

So Old The Pain C 25 MIN
3/4 OR 1/2 INCH VIDEO CASSETTE
Presents Jane Wyman and host Mario Machado in the filmed program about arthritis, the nation's number one crippler. Shows arthritis victims telling how the disease has changed their lives, and scientists, surgeons and rheumatologists explaining treatment alternatives.
Prod-TRAINX Dist-TRAINX

So Red Hot C 12 MIN
16MM FILM OPTICAL SOUND
Uses four short musical numbers to highlight Parents' Magazine's marketing outlook, their target audience of mothers and their industry status.
LC NO. 82-700538
Prod-PARENT Dist-PARENT Prodn-WINGS 1982

So That's Where It's From C 30 MIN
3/4 INCH VIDEO CASSETTE H-C A
Features the First Poetry Quartet playing a game in which they exchange quotes from the world of poetry that have been used as movie, book and song titles.
From The Anyone For Tennyson Series.
Prod-NETCHE Dist-GPITVL

So This Is Love B 60 MIN
16MM FILM SILENT
Explains what happens when a male dress designer and a hard-as-nails boxer court the same girl. Directed by Frank Capra.
Prod-CPC Dist-KITPAR 1928

So What C 15 MIN
2 INCH VIDEOTAPE J
Shows a fourth way of developing a topic sentence by giving effects.
From The From Me To You...In Writing, Pt 2 Series.
Prod-DELE Dist-GPITVL

So What If It Rains C 17 MIN
16MM FILM OPTICAL SOUND A
Interviews a retired couple, a couple not yet retired, an 80-year-old widow and a 55-year-old divorcee to address the topic of financial planning for retirement.
LC NO. 80-700532
Prod-ALTERC Dist-FLMLIB Prodn-JOHNG 1980

So What's It All About C 40 MIN
16MM FILM, 3/4 OR 1/2 IN VIDEO C A
Looks at the silicon chip and its mushrooming applications. Gives an idea of what goes on in the 'black box' of the micro-computer. Asks how far computer-controlled machines can go in imitating human functions.
From The Silicon Factor Series.
Prod-BBCTV Dist-FI 1981

So Who's Perfect - How To Give And Receive Criticism C 14 MIN
16MM FILM, 3/4 OR 1/2 IN VIDEO
Explores some of the common mistakes people make when giving or receiving criticism. Offers a step-by-step method for giving and receiving it productively. Features Dr Hendrie Weisinger and Carrie Snodgrass. Based on the book Nobody's Perfect by Dr Weisinger.
LC NO. 83-707145
Prod-SALENG Dist-SALENG 1984

So You Live By Yourself C 29 MIN
2 INCH VIDEOTAPE
See series title for descriptive statement.
From The That's Life Series.
Prod-KOAPTV Dist-PUBTEL

So You Wanna Make A Film C 9 MIN
16MM FILM, 3/4 OR 1/2 IN VIDEO J-C A
Presents the animated story of a brash businessman who wants a film on the history of aviation for a convention the following Thursday. Shows a filmmaker telling him why it's not possible to produce it so quickly.
LC NO. 80-706465
Prod-WMICHU Dist-WMICHU 1980

So You Wanna' Make A Film C 9 MIN
16MM FILM, 3/4 OR 1/2 IN VIDEO J-C A
Tells how an industrialist decides he wants to make a film about his company. Traces the filmmaking process from script through answer print.
Prod-WMUDIC Dist-CORF

So You Want To Be A Star C 15 MIN
3/4 OR 1/2 INCH VIDEO CASSETTE J-H
Examines jobs in the motion picture industry.
From The Movies, Movies Series.
Prod-CTI Dist-CTI

So You Want To Be A Success At Selling—A Series

Discusses mistakes and lessons learned in a wide variety of selling situations.
Prod-VIDART Dist-VISUCP

Preparation, The 025 MIN
Presentation, The 026 MIN

So You Want To Be A Success At Selling, Pt 1 - The Preparation C 26 MIN
3/4 OR 1/2 INCH VIDEO CASSETTE A
Illustrates, in a humorous vein, the work to be done and the techniques to be acquired before one can start to sell effectively.
Prod-XICOM Dist-XICOM

So You Want To Be A Success At Selling, Pt 2 - The Presentation C 25 MIN
3/4 OR 1/2 INCH VIDEO CASSETTE A
Shows how, using sound preparation as a foundation, to build an actual sale.
Prod-XICOM Dist-XICOM

So You Want To Be A Success At Selling, Pt 3 - Difficult Customers C 25 MIN
3/4 OR 1/2 INCH VIDEO CASSETTE A
Demonstrates how to make sales to three different types of difficult subjects - the domineering client, the super-busy decision-maker and the indecisive manager.
Prod-XICOM Dist-XICOM

So You Want To Be President C 120 MIN
1/2 IN VIDEO CASSETTE BETA/VHS
Presents an inside view of what anyone who wants to run for President must do. Follows Colorado Senator Gary Hart's campaign for the 1984 Democratic Nomination and Presidency. Provides a unique look at how the election process works, from closed door strategy sessions to debates.
From The Frontline Series.
Prod-DOCCON Dist-PBS

So You're New Around Here (New Worker) B 13 MIN
16MM FILM OPTICAL SOUND
Presents sound, understandable reasons for having a plant safety program.
Prod-NSC Dist-NSC

So You've Got Diabetes C
3/4 OR 1/2 INCH VIDEO CASSETTE
Explains the nature of diabetes, method of control and the importance of exercise and diet as well as regular office visits. Stresses that you can live a full life despite being a diabetic.
Prod-MIFE Dist-MIFE

So You've Got Diabetes (Arabic) C
3/4 OR 1/2 INCH VIDEO CASSETTE
Explains the nature of diabetes, method of control and the impor-

tance of exercise and diet as well as regular office visits. Stresses that you can live a full life despite being a diabetic.
Prod-MIFE Dist-MIFE

So You've Got Diabetes (Spanish) C
3/4 OR 1/2 INCH VIDEO CASSETTE
Explains the nature of diabetes, method of control and the importance of exercise and diet as well as regular office visits. Stresses that you can live a full life despite being a diabetic.
Prod-MIFE Dist-MIFE

So-To-Speak Telephone Boutique, The C 3 MIN
16MM FILM OPTICAL SOUND
Presents a look at the future in telecommunications.
LC NO. 75-701926
Prod-NORTEL Dist-NORTEL Prodn-GROUP 1974

So, This Is Philosophy? C 24 MIN
3/4 OR 1/2 INCH VIDEO CASSETTE I-J
A humorous treatment of the study of philosophy, pivoting on the question of what is right and wrong. Centers on a high school class discussion of the ethics involved in a true-to-life, hypothetical situation.
LC NO. 83-707155
Prod-RESPRO Dist-RESPRO 1983

So, You Want To Buy A Good Used Car C 15 MIN
16MM FILM, 3/4 OR 1/2 IN VIDEO J-C A
Outlines basic steps to follow in determining the condition of a used car. Suggests a memory aid for those elements of particular importance for safety.
Prod-FMCMP Dist-FORDFL Prodn-ALLFP 1966

Soap C 13 MIN
16MM FILM, 3/4 OR 1/2 IN VIDEO
Outlines the history of soap. Shows how it is made and how it works.
Prod-KAWVAL Dist-KAWVAL

Soap C 13 MIN
3/4 OR 1/2 INCH VIDEO CASSETTE
Deals with how soap operas glamorize everyday life. Reveals a heartbroken but not so glamorous woman.
Prod-KITCHN Dist-KITCHN

Soap Box Derby Scandal, The C 24 MIN
16MM FILM, 3/4 OR 1/2 IN VIDEO P-I
Tells the story of a boy's experience in the Soap Box Derby of 1973 and his involvement with scandal when the race was won with an illegally-designed car. Raises questions in order to promote discussion about winning, losing and cheating.
LC NO. 75-701091
Prod-CIHIB Dist-WWS 1975

Soap Bubbles And The Forces That Mould Them C 24 MIN
16MM FILM OPTICAL SOUND J-C
Actor Richard Montgomery dramatizes the 1911 Sir Charles V Boys lecture describing the phenomenon and nature of soap bubbles.
Prod-RARIG Dist-RARIG 1967

Soap Operas C 30 MIN
16MM FILM, 3/4 OR 1/2 IN VIDEO H-C A
Looks behind-the-scenes to see how the daytime soap opera All My Children is made. Shows how a dramatic scene evolves and examines the unique relationship which exists between 35 million soap-watchers and their favorite serials. Presents soap writer Pete Lemay talking about the rigors of writing for the form and expresses concern about the impact of the soap opera on American culture. Hosted by Ruth Warrick.
From The Media Probes Series.
Prod-LAYLEM Dist-TIMLIF 1982

Soap, Scents And The Hard, Hard Sell C 16 MIN
16MM FILM, 3/4 OR 1/2 IN VIDEO J A
Demonstrates good personal hygiene habits. Presents a humorous analysis of television commercials to explain why expensive, highly advertised products are unnecessarily proper hygiene.
Prod-HIGGIN Dist-HIGGIN 1975

Soaring Over The Rockies C 30 MIN
3/4 OR 1/2 INCH VIDEO CASSETTE
Helps the viewers to experience and enjoy the beauty and exhilaration that make soaring high above dark peaks one of today's most relaxing and fun-loving sports.
Prod-KRMATV Dist-PBS

Soccer C 27 MIN
16MM FILM OPTICAL SOUND J-C A
Describes the increasing popularity of soccer in Australia, emphasizing the importance of improved coaching and training methods.
From The Man And His Sport Series.
LC NO. 72-701523
Prod-ANAIB Dist-AUIS 1971

Soccer C 25 MIN
3/4 OR 1/2 INCH VIDEO CASSETTE
Witnesses this exciting sport in North America featuring Pele.
Prod-KAROL Dist-KAROL

Soccer - Goalkeeping C 20 MIN
16MM FILM, 3/4 OR 1/2 IN VIDEO J-C A
Shows positioning and catching, diving, punching, tipping, clearing, throwing and conditioning drills.
From The Soccer Series.
Prod-ATHI Dist-ATHI 1976

Soccer - Hands Off C 16 MIN
16MM FILM, 3/4 OR 1/2 IN VIDEO I-H
Introduces the game play of soccer and shows the basic moves of the game, including traps, dribbles, the instep drive, passing the ball with legs and head and techniques of goal-keeping.
Prod-BFA Dist-PHENIX 1975

Soccer - Individual Skills C 20 MIN
16MM FILM, 3/4 OR 1/2 IN VIDEO J-C A
Shows the basic kicks, trapping, heading and juggling.
From The Soccer Series.
Prod-ATHI Dist-ATHI 1976

Soccer - Let's Play C 10 MIN
16MM FILM OPTICAL SOUND I-H
Demonstrates basic skills of soccer and suggests some class drills to develop skills. Shows plays and fouls that might be encountered in playing the game.
LC NO. FIA65-1550
Prod-SLFP Dist-SLFP Prodn-SCHLLR 1964

Soccer - Offensive And Defensive Play C 21 MIN
16MM FILM, 3/4 OR 1/2 IN VIDEO J-C A
Shows feinting tackling the throw-in, the passing attack and shooting.
Prod-ATHI Dist-ATHI 1976

Soccer Clinics U S A C 60 MIN
1/2 IN VIDEO CASSETTE BETA/VHS A
Deals with ball handling and scoring. Teaches techniques needed to advance to higher levels of play. Features Clive Charles and Brian Gant, internationally recognized soccer players.
Prod-RMI Dist-RMI

Soccer Exercises And Tactics For Everyone C 20 MIN
16MM FILM, 3/4 OR 1/2 IN VIDEO I-C
Presents game-like situations in a series of soccer exercises and drills designed to improve player readiness and ball control. Includes strength- and endurance-building exercises which also increase ball control.
Prod-ASSOCF Dist-AIMS 1976

Soccer Exercises And Tactics For Everyone (Arabic) C 20 MIN
16MM FILM, 3/4 OR 1/2 IN VIDEO I-C
Presents game-like situations in a series of soccer exercises and drills designed to improve player readiness and ball control. Includes strength- and endurance-building exercises which also increase ball control.
Prod-ASSOCF Dist-AIMS 1976

Soccer Fundamentals For Everyone C 12 MIN
16MM FILM, 3/4 OR 1/2 IN VIDEO J-C
Explains the basics of soccer from the dimensions of the playing field to the techniques of ball control. Demonstrates various types of kicks, trapping, passing and heading. Shows practice techniques and drills for ball control.
Prod-ASSOCF Dist-AIMS 1976

Soccer Fundamentals For Everyone (Captioned) C 12 MIN
16MM FILM, 3/4 OR 1/2 IN VIDEO J-C
Explains the basics of soccer from the dimensions of the playing field to the techniques of ball control. Demonstrates various types of kicks, trapping, passing and heading. Shows practice techniques and drills for ball control.
Prod-ASSOCF Dist-AIMS 1976

Soccer Games C 11 MIN
16MM FILM, 3/4 OR 1/2 IN VIDEO J-C A
Introduces the game of soccer with sequences on dribbling, passing, kicking and falling. Presents the basics of the game with a motivational rather than a how-to-do-it approach.
Prod-TEXFLM Dist-TEXFLM

Soccer Rules C 14 MIN
16MM FILM, 3/4 OR 1/2 IN VIDEO I-H
Explains basic soccer rules. Demonstrates how to mark and measure the field and discusses systems of play, fouls and penalties.
LC NO. 81-706572
Prod-AIMS Dist-AIMS 1979

Soccer Scene Germany Gelsenkirch C 28 MIN
16MM FILM OPTICAL SOUND H-C A
Deals with the soccer clubs of Germany and the cities that sponsor them. Includes inside views of soccer and the cities that form the major conference of German Soccer.
Prod-WSTGLC Dist-WSTGLC

Soccer U S A C 25 MIN
16MM FILM, 3/4 OR 1/2 IN VIDEO I-C A
Documents the history of soccer from its origins on muddy fields with poor equipment to its worldwide popularity which has produced local, national and international rivalries.
Prod-SOCCER Dist-LCOA 1981

Soccer—A Series
16MM FILM, 3/4 OR 1/2 IN VIDEO
Prod-ATHI Dist-ATHI

Soccer - Goalkeeping 020 MIN
Soccer - Individual Skills 020 MIN
Soccer - Offensive And Defensive Play 021 MIN

Soccer, USA C 45 MIN
16MM FILM OPTICAL SOUND
Presents an American view of soccer, the fastest-growing spectator and participant sport in the United States. Shows how deeply and rapidly the sport has become a part of the American mainstream.
Prod-SOCCER Dist-SOCCER 1980

SOCCIS Collection—A Series

Prod-UCLA Dist-UCLA

Social Adjustment For The Aphasic C 26 MIN
3/4 OR 1/2 INCH VIDEO CASSETTE PRO
Discusses methods of reorienting the aphasic socially. Demonstrates restraining techniques through group therapy sessions.
From The Aphasia Series.
Prod-WFP Dist-WFP

Social Adjustment For The Aphasic Patient C 26 MIN
16MM FILM OPTICAL SOUND
Emphasizes the problems of social reorientation for the aphasic patient and explains the use and importance of group therapy and of corrective physical therapy for the retraining of the language function.
From The Aphasia Series. Pt 3
LC NO. FIE53-105
Prod-USVA Dist-USNAC Prodn-CW 1950

Social And Physical Space C 60 MIN
3/4 OR 1/2 INCH VIDEO CASSETTE A
Presents biologist Humberto Maturana discussing social and physical space.
From The Biology Of Cognition And Language Series. Program 13
Prod-UCEMC Dist-UCEMC

Social Animal—A Series

Explains the motivations of individuals in terms of forces imposed upon them by society.
Prod-UMITV Dist-UMITV 1974

Authority And Man 029 MIN
Becoming Human 029 MIN
Behavior And Its Consequences 029 MIN
Bureaucracy 029 MIN
Cultural Threat 029 MIN
Education And Man 029 MIN
Ideology And Ecology 029 MIN
Population 029 MIN
Public Man And Private Man 029 MIN
Social Position 029 MIN

Social Animal, The - Social Psychology B 29 MIN
16MM FILM, 3/4 OR 1/2 IN VIDEO H-C A
Investigates some of the ways in which man is influenced and changed by society. Studies group pressures to conform and shows the consequences of publicly stating ideas contrary to one's private belief.
From The Focus On Behavior Series.
Prod-NET Dist-IU 1963

Social Attitudes Toward People With Disabilities B 27 MIN
3/4 OR 1/2 INCH VIDEO CASSETTE
Presents a lecture about prejudice and negative attitudes toward physically disabled people.
Prod-BU Dist-BU

Social Behavior Of Rhesus Monkeys B 26 MIN
16MM FILM OPTICAL SOUND C T
Shows large numbers of rhesus monkeys living in a semi-natural environment. Emphasizes the social interaction of individuals and organized groups. Shows various kinds of behavior--reproductive, maternal, dominance, fighting, homosexual, play and general.
Prod-PSUPCR Dist-PSUPCR 1947

Social Behavior Of The Norwegian Lemming, Lemmus, Lemmus In Captivity C 9 MIN
16MM FILM SILENT C
Illustrates the agonistic and sexual behavior of wild Norwegian lemmings in cages. Includes male-male, male-female and male-young fighting, male-female sexual behavior, male-male homosexual behavior and defense against threat by human beings.
Prod-PSUPCR Dist-PSUPCR 1967

Social Belief And Alcohol C 30 MIN
3/4 OR 1/2 INCH VIDEO CASSETTE H-C A
See series title for descriptive statement.
From The Fundamentals Of Alcohol Problems Series.
Prod-UMINN Dist-GPITVL 1978

Social Cat, The C 25 MIN
16MM FILM, 3/4 OR 1/2 IN VIDEO I-J A
Deals with behavioral relationships between predator and prey, using the lion as an example. Shows how the social structure in a group of lions operates.
From The Behavior And Survival Series.
Prod-MGHT Dist-MGHT 1973

Social Change C 30 MIN
3/4 OR 1/2 INCH VIDEO CASSETTE C
Identifies major social changes in the United States and evaluates their consequences.
From The Focus On Society Series.
Prod-DALCCD Dist-DALCCD

Social Classes, 1900, The - A World To Win C 52 MIN
16MM FILM - 1/2 IN VIDEO
Examines the forces of unrest which disrupted European stability at the beginning of the 20th century, including colonial nationalism, industrialization, socialism, trade unionism and reform movements. Analyzes the causes and effects of the 1905 revolution in Russia.
From The Europe, The Mighty Continent Series. No. 3
LC NO. 79-707418
Prod-BBCTV Dist-TIMLIF 1976

Social Cognition - How And What The Infant Learns About Others, Pt 1 C
3/4 OR 1/2 INCH VIDEO CASSETTE
See series title for descriptive statement.
From The Human Development - A New Look At The Infant Series.
Prod-CONMED Dist-CONMED

Social Cognition - How And What The Infant Learns About Others, Pt 2 C
3/4 OR 1/2 INCH VIDEO CASSETTE

See series title for descriptive statement.
From The Human Development - A New Look At The Infant Series.
Prod-CONMED Dist-CONMED

Social Control C 30 MIN
3/4 INCH VIDEO CASSETTE C A
Studies many forms of controls found in various societies. Shows forms of conflict resolution such as the 'trial by ordeal' method used by the Kpelle of Liberia.
From The Faces Of Culture - Studies In Cultural Anthropology Series. Lesson 18
Prod-COAST Dist-CDTEL Prodn-HRAW

Social Control C 30 MIN
3/4 OR 1/2 INCH VIDEO CASSETTE C
Discusses the concepts of stigma and labeling and looks at the life and problems of an alcoholic, a hearing- impaired person, an ex-offender and a war veteran in a wheelchair.
From The Focus On Society Series.
Prod-DALCCD Dist-DALCCD

Social Dances Of The American Indian, Square Dancing And The 'Swing' Era C 30 MIN
3/4 OR 1/2 INCH VIDEO CASSETTE
See series title for descriptive statement.
From The Social Dancing Is Not Just For Fun Series.
Prod-ARCVID Dist-ARCVID

Social Dancing Is Not Just For Fun—A Series

Presents programs from the New York City Cable TV series Eye on Dance. Discusses 16th century social dance, to ballroom dance today.
Prod-ARCVID Dist-ARCVID

Ballroom Dance As An Art Form	030 MIN
Dancing At The Cotton Club And The Savoy	030 MIN
Demonstration And Discussion Of Social Dance	030 MIN
Social Dances Of The American Indian, Square	030 MIN

Social Development C 27 MIN
3/4 OR 1/2 INCH VIDEO CASSETTE C
Shows children involved in solitary play, sibling play, parallel play and informal team play.
From The Learning Through Play - Modules Series. Module 1
Prod-UTORMC Dist-UTORMC 1976

Social Development C 30 MIN
3/4 OR 1/2 INCH VIDEO CASSETTE H-C A
Discusses social development. Presents seven illustrations, including solitary play, sibling play, parallel play and informal team play.
From The Learning Through Play Series.
Prod-UTORMC Dist-UTORMC 1980

Social Development Of The Infant C 29 MIN
3/4 OR 1/2 INCH VIDEO CASSETTE H-C A
Tells how a growing child learns about other people, relationships, rules, and role behaviors.
From The Tomorrow's Families Series.
LC NO. 81-706917
Prod-MSDOE Dist-AITECH 1980

Social Dominance In The Male Black Buck B 9 MIN
16MM FILM SILENT C T
Shows how one male dominates the herd and interferes with the expression of social and sexual behavior by subordinate adult and young males. Demonstrates the gait and postures of the dominant male. Shows patterns of aggressive interaction between males (headwrestling and chasing) and of sexual interactions between male and female ('NECK-STRETCHING,' herding). photographed at the new York zoological park.
Prod-PSUPCR Dist-PSUPCR 1960

Social Drinker And Anti-Social Driver C 16 MIN
16MM FILM, 3/4 OR 1/2 IN VIDEO H A
Demonstrates the effects of alcohol on peripheral vision. Provides statistics which show that social drinkers are involved in a high percentage of traffic accidents.
Prod-CAHILL Dist-AIMS 1972

Social Drinker And Anti-Social Driver (Spanish) C 16 MIN
16MM FILM, 3/4 OR 1/2 IN VIDEO H A
Demonstrates the effects of alcohol on peripheral vision. Provides statistics which show that social drinkers are involved in a high percentage of traffic accidents.
Prod-CAHILL Dist-AIMS 1972

Social Drinking - Fun And Fatal C 14 MIN
16MM FILM, 3/4 OR 1/2 IN VIDEO H-C A
Re-creates a tragic accident in order to illustrate the results of driving under the influence of alcohol and to demonstrate the effects of liquor on the driving ability of social drinkers.
From The Alcohol Abuse Series.
Prod-NSC Dist-JOU 1979

Social Encounter C 8 MIN
16MM FILM OPTICAL SOUND I-C A
Considers the impact of personal values on various everyday situations.
From The Encounter Series.
LC NO. 72-703205
Prod-FRACOC Dist-FRACOC 1970

Social Factors In The Parenthood Decision C 29 MIN
3/4 OR 1/2 INCH VIDEO CASSETTE H-C A
Discusses the effect of a new baby on the community, family relationships, and the educational and career plans of the parents.
From The Tomorrow's Families Series.
LC NO. 81-706894
Prod-MSDOE Dist-AITECH 1980

Social Forces And Their Implications To Public Health B 30 MIN
16MM FILM - 3/4 IN VIDEO PRO
See series title for descriptive statement.
From The Public Health Science Series. Unit I - Introduction To Foundations Of Public Health
Prod-TEXWU Dist-GPITVL Prodn-KUHTTV

Social Group Work With Families Related To Problems Of Child Abuse And Neglect, Pt 2 C 20 MIN
3/4 OR 1/2 INCH VIDEO CASSETTE
Discusses the 'buddy' system of evaluation in terms of behavioral modification with children, various aspects of these modification systems and negotiations between children and adults.
Prod-VRL Dist-UWISC

Social Group Work With Families Related To Problems Of Child Abuse And Neglect, Pt 1 C 60 MIN
3/4 OR 1/2 INCH VIDEO CASSETTE
Outlines a social work program developed to help eliminate conflicts between parents and their abused children.
Prod-VRL Dist-UWISC 1976

Social Groups C 29 MIN
3/4 INCH VIDEO CASSETTE C A
Defines concept of social groups. Discusses classic research by Asch and Sherif. Focuses on manner in which social groups exert powerful influence upon individual behavior.
From The Understanding Human Behavior - An Introduction To Psychology Series. Lesson 28
Prod-COAST Dist-CDTEL

Social Inequality C 30 MIN
3/4 OR 1/2 INCH VIDEO CASSETTE C
Looks at the nature and basis of social stratification, its impact upon life chances and the moneyed nature of American society. Discusses the basis of social inequality and possible alternatives to the present system.
From The Focus On Society Series.
Prod-DALCCD Dist-DALCCD

Social Insects C 15 MIN
16MM FILM, 3/4 OR 1/2 IN VIDEO J-H
Examines the complex organization of insect communities.
From The Insect Series.
LC NO. 80-706700
Prod-BHA Dist-IFB 1977

Social Insects - The Honeybee X 24 MIN
16MM FILM, 3/4 OR 1/2 IN VIDEO H
Shows how social insects live in colonies and divide into castes. Illustrates the particular adaptation of the various castes to reproduction, population control and food gathering. Shows metamorphosis of a honeybee from egg to adult.
From The Biology Series. Unit 9 - Behavior
Prod-EBF Dist-EBEC 1960

Social Insects - The Honeybee (Spanish) C 24 MIN
16MM FILM, 3/4 OR 1/2 IN VIDEO H
Shows that social insects, including the honeybee, live in colonies and are divided into castes. Illustrates the particular adaptation of various castes to reproduction, population control and food gathering.
From The Biology (Spanish) Series. Unit 9 - Behavior
Prod-EBEC Dist-EBEC

Social Learning Approach To Family Therapy C 31 MIN
16MM FILM OPTICAL SOUND
Presents a case study involving a family with a predelinquent boy progressing through a complete treatment process using social learning-based family intervention procedures developed by Drs G Patterson and J Reid at the Oregon Research Institute.
LC NO. 74-702670
Prod-OREGRI Dist-RESPRC Prodn-PRBPRO 1974

Social Life Of Small Urban Spaces, The C 58 MIN
16MM FILM OPTICAL SOUND
Studies how people use the parks and plazas of cities. Describes the importance of seating, food, sunlight, and something to watch.
LC NO. 81-700460
Prod-MASOC Dist-MASOC 1981

Social Movements C 30 MIN
3/4 OR 1/2 INCH VIDEO CASSETTE C
Examines the various stages through which social movements progress using the women's movement as an example. Discusses the status of women and social forces affecting the movement.
From The Focus On Society Series.
Prod-DALCCD Dist-DALCCD

Social Needs As Business Opportunities C 33 MIN
16MM FILM - 3/4 IN VIDEO IND
Explains that good intentions are no substitute for competence, and businessmen should resist being pushed into projects merely because there is nobody else to do it. Covers the areas of education, vocational training, employing the disadvantaged, community rebuilding and many others.
From The Managing Discontinuity Series.
Prod-BNA Dist-BNA 1971

Social Organization In The Red Jungle Fowl C 10 MIN
16MM FILM SILENT H-C
Shows the pattern of fighting behavior which leads to dominance relations between two red jungle fowl males. Illustrates the normally aggressive interactions among an intergrated flock of eleven males during feeding and in a mixed flock of males and females. Concludes with sequences on sexual courtship and copulation.
LC NO. 76-701854
Prod-BANKSE Dist-PSUPCR 1960

Social Partnership, The C 24 MIN
16MM FILM OPTICAL SOUND H-C A
Discusses the development of social security in the Federal Republic of Germany after the Second World War, which was marked by expansion and improvement of benefits from welfare insurance programs, including health, accident, pension and unemployment insurance. Explains how these and a variety of other systems work.
Prod-WSTGLC Dist-WSTGLC

Social Position C 29 MIN
3/4 INCH VIDEO CASSETTE
Examines social position, no matter what kind of rank, as a measure of happiness.
From The Social Animal Series.
Prod-UMITV Dist-UMITV 1974

Social Primate, The - Good Timing C 24 MIN
16MM FILM, 3/4 OR 1/2 IN VIDEO
Presents contemporary research into the timing aspect of sexual behavior of rhesus monkeys living in a captive social group at the Yerkes Primate Center in Atlanta. Explains that the pattern of sexual interaction in captive, but social, rhesus monkeys is similar to their pattern in the wild, depending less on confinement than on the hormonal state of the female.
Prod-OPENU Dist-MEDIAG Prodn-BBCTV 1982

Social Problems And Classroom Guidance C 29 MIN
3/4 OR 1/2 INCH VIDEO CASSETTE T
Discusses how social problems can be handled in a classroom guidance situation.
From The Dealing With Social Problems In The Classroom Series.
Prod-MFFD Dist-FI

Social Psychology C 33 MIN
16MM FILM, 3/4 OR 1/2 IN VIDEO H-C A
Introduces the field of social psychology and defines some of the key concepts. Shows community reactions to bussing and integration in Westport, Conn, with commentary from a panel moderated by Kenneth B Clark.
From The Psychology Today Films Series.
Prod-CRMP Dist-CRMP 1971

Social Psychology—A Series

Prod-OPENU Dist-OPENU 1977

Analyzing Interaction	50 MIN
Man's Experience Of The World	25 MIN
Naughty Things	25 MIN

Social Psychology—A Series
16MM FILM, 3/4 OR 1/2 IN VIDEO C
Introduces the field of social psychology emphasizing the topics conformity and independence, human aggression and nonverbal communication.
Prod-HAR Dist-MTI

Conformity And Independence	024 MIN
Human Aggression	023 MIN
Invitation To Social Psychology	026 MIN
Nonverbal Communication	023 MIN

Social Reaction In Imprinted Ducklings C 21 MIN
16MM FILM OPTICAL SOUND C
Shows the effects of a sequence of experimental procedures in which newly hatched ducklings were first imprinted to a moving stimulus and then taught to peck a pole, using presentation of the moving stimulus as the sole response-contingent.
LC NO. 77-708678
Prod-PSUPCR Dist-PSUPCR 1968

Social Reform C 30 MIN
3/4 OR 1/2 INCH VIDEO CASSETTE C
See series title for descriptive statement.
From The American Story - The Beginning To 1877 Series.
Prod-DALCCD Dist-DALCCD

Social Rehearsal For Dying B 50 MIN
3/4 OR 1/2 INCH VIDEO CASSETTE
See series title for descriptive statement.
From The Social Responses To Aging Care And The Caring For Older People Series. Pt 5
Prod-UAZMIC Dist-UAZMIC 1976

Social Responses To Aging Care And The Caring For Older People—A Series

Explains a number of aspects of the problems of aging in contemporary society, including the increased numbers of old people, changing lifestyles, early retirement, inflation and the proliferation of medical problems. Emphasizes the need for more knowledge about the aging process and its effects.
Prod-UAZMIC Dist-UAZMIC 1976

Continuum Of Care, The - An Alternative To	
Institutionalization - Warehousing Or	050 MIN
Introduction - Overview Of The Field Of	050 MIN
Music - A Bridge To Reality	050 MIN
Social Rehearsal For Dying	050 MIN
Triple 'A' Agency, The - Anger, Advocacy,	050 MIN

Social Responsibility - It's My Hobby C 11 MIN
16MM FILM, 3/4 OR 1/2 IN VIDEO J-H
Tells how Ed, a high school student, discovers that his friend Scott is selling drugs to young students.
From The Conflict And Awareness Series.
Prod-CRMP Dist-CRMP 1975

Social Roles C 30 MIN
3/4 OR 1/2 INCH VIDEO CASSETTE
Examines the influence of genetic factors on social behavior and social development, the influences of social environment and

learning, social roles of men and women and modeling and socialization.
From The Psychology Of Human Relations Series.
Prod-MATC Dist-WFVTAE

Social Science Reading C 120 MIN
3/4 OR 1/2 INCH VIDEO CASSETTE
See series title for descriptive statement.
From The A C T Exam Preparation Series.
Prod-KRLSOF Dist-KRLSOF 1985

Social Science/History, Tape 1 C 45 MIN
3/4 OR 1/2 INCH VIDEO CASSETTE H A
Prepares students for the College Level Examination Program (CLEP) tests in Social Science and History. Focuses on United States history.
From The CLEP General Examinations Series.
Prod-COMEX Dist-COMEX

Social Science/History, Tape 2 C 45 MIN
3/4 OR 1/2 INCH VIDEO CASSETTE H A
Prepares students for the College Level Examination Program (CLEP) tests in Social Science and History. Discusses political science and American constitutional government.
From The CLEP General Examinations Series.
Prod-COMEX Dist-COMEX

Social Science/History, Tape 3 C 45 MIN
3/4 OR 1/2 INCH VIDEO CASSETTE H A
Prepares students for the College Level Examination Program (CLEP) tests in Social Science and History. Focuses on economics.
From The CLEP General Examinations Series.
Prod-COMEX Dist-COMEX

Social Science/History, Tape 4 C 45 MIN
3/4 OR 1/2 INCH VIDEO CASSETTE H A
Prepares students for the College Level Examination Program (CLE) tests in Social Science and History. Examines social psychology.
From The CLEP General Examinations Series.
Prod-COMEX Dist-COMEX

Social Science/History, Tape 5 C 45 MIN
3/4 OR 1/2 INCH VIDEO CASSETTE H A
Prepares students for the College Level Examination Program (CLEP) tests in Social Science and History. Explores several aspects of sociology.
From The CLEP General Examinations Series.
Prod-COMEX Dist-COMEX

Social Sciences, The - What Is Economics C
3/4 OR 1/2 INCH VIDEO CASSETTE H
Demonstrates that economics is a coherent science. Outlines the major economic systems and examines our own. Shows how values and priorities shape the decisions which direct our economy.
Prod-GA Dist-GA

Social Security C 30 MIN
3/4 INCH VIDEO CASSETTE
See series title for descriptive statement.
From The You Owe It To Yourself Series.
Prod-WITFTV Dist-PUBTEL

Social Seminar—A Series

Prod-NIMH Dist-USNAC

Brian At Seventeen	030 MIN
Bunny	016 MIN
Community In Quest, The	030 MIN
Drug Talk - Some Current Programs	030 MIN
Drugs And Beyond	030 MIN
Family	030 MIN
Got My Own	030 MIN
Guy	018 MIN
Jordan Paul - One Teacher's Approach	030 MIN
Meeting, The	030 MIN
Mr Edler's Class - Drug Education At The	030 MIN
News Story, A	029 MIN
Olde English	019 MIN
Teddy	017 MIN
You Got The Same Thing, Aincha	017 MIN

Social Side Of Health C 10 MIN
16MM FILM, 3/4 OR 1/2 IN VIDEO P-H
Discusses man's ability to adjust to a group without losing his right to individuality and the need for him to make a contribution to society.
From The Triangle Of Health Series.
Prod-UPJOHN Dist-WDEMCO 1969

Social Side Of Health, The (Arabic) C 10 MIN
16MM FILM, 3/4 OR 1/2 IN VIDEO I-H
Focuses on learning how to live with others while retaining one's own individuality.
From The Triangle Of Health (Arabic) Series.
Prod-WDEMCO Dist-WDEMCO 1969

Social Side Of Health, The (French) C 10 MIN
16MM FILM, 3/4 OR 1/2 IN VIDEO I-H
Focuses on learning how to live with others while retaining one's own individuality.
From The Triangle Of Health (French) Series.
Prod-WDEMCO Dist-WDEMCO 1969

Social Side Of Health, The (German) C 10 MIN
16MM FILM, 3/4 OR 1/2 IN VIDEO I-H
Focuses on learning how to live with others while retaining one's own individuality.
From The Triangle Of Health (German) Series.
Prod-WDEMCO Dist-WDEMCO 1969

Social Side Of Health, The (Spanish) C 10 MIN
16MM FILM, 3/4 OR 1/2 IN VIDEO I-H
Focuses on learning how to live with others while retaining one's own individuality.
From The Triangle Of Health (Spanish) Series.
Prod-WDEMCO Dist-WDEMCO 1969

Social Skills For The Spinal Cord Injured Patient C 28 MIN
3/4 INCH VIDEO CASSETTE S
Features eight vignettes which demonstrate how persons with severe physical disabilities can manage common social situations. Portrays aggressive, passive and assertive responses.
LC NO. 77-706068
Prod-USVA Dist-USNAC Prodn-VAHOS 1976

Social Stereotyping C 30 MIN
3/4 INCH VIDEO CASSETTE
Discusses sex and ethnic stereotyping and the factors influencing prejudice.
From The Growing Years Series.
Prod-COAST Dist-CDTEL

Social Studies - Science, Pt 1 B 30 MIN
2 INCH VIDEOTAPE
See series title for descriptive statement.
From The Program Development In The Kindergarten Series.
Prod-GPITVL Dist-GPITVL

Social Studies - Science, Pt 2 B 30 MIN
2 INCH VIDEOTAPE
See series title for descriptive statement.
From The Program Development In The Kindergarten Series.
Prod-GPITVL Dist-GPITVL

Social Studies - Science, Pt 3 B 30 MIN
2 INCH VIDEOTAPE
See series title for descriptive statement.
From The Program Development In The Kindergarten Series.
Prod-GPITVL Dist-GPITVL

Social Studies Program—A Series

Prod-EDS Dist-EDC

Corn And The Origins Of Settled Life In	
Corn And The Origins Of Settled Life In	41 MIN
Earliest Writing, The	11 MIN
Land And Water In Iraq	14 MIN
Netsilik Eskimos Fishing At The Stone Weir	58 MIN

Social Variations C 27 MIN
16MM FILM OPTICAL SOUND
Points out that the great majority of New Yorkers unconsciously shift their sound patterns as well as their grammar according to changes in situation. Notes that the shift is uniform and that there is agreement among New Yorkers on the norms of careful speech. Explains that differences among people are often revealed in their speech patterns.
From The Language - The Social Arbiter Series. No. 5
LC NO. FIA67-5265
Prod-FINLYS Dist-FINLYS Prodn-CALING 1966

Social Work C 46 MIN
3/4 OR 1/2 INCH VIDEO CASSETTE
Follows a case through the Meyer Children's Rehabilitation Institute's routine, with emphasis on the social work department's function as a family intermediary. Features a short segment on training social work graduate students at MCRI.
Prod-UNEBO Dist-UNEBO

Social Work Interviewing—A Series

Presents a series on social work interviewing.
Prod-UWISC Dist-UWISC

Exploration Phase, The - Assessment	035 MIN
Exploration Phase, The - Data Collection	035 MIN
Involvement Phase, The	022 MIN
Service Phase, The	024 MIN
Terminal Phase, The	022 MIN

Social Work Licensure C 60 MIN
3/4 OR 1/2 INCH VIDEO CASSETTE
Looks at the regulation of social work as a profession and as it relates to the mental health industry.
Prod-VRL Dist-UWISC 1983

Social Work Roles In Foster Care—A Series

Presents a series dealing with the social work roles in foster care, including the child welfare worker, the foster parent and the foster home consultant.
Prod-UWISC Dist-UWISC

Child Welfare Worker, Pt I	039 MIN
Child Welfare Worker, Pt II	062 MIN
Foster Parent Trainer, Foster Home	039 MIN
Foster Parent Trainer, Foster Home	038 MIN

Social Work With The Hearing Impaired C 18 MIN
3/4 OR 1/2 INCH VIDEO CASSETTE
Gives examples of interpersonal skills necessary in dealing with the deaf and how to use them. Shows several interviews with a deaf client and social worker.
Prod-UWISC Dist-UWISC 1980

Social Worker C 15 MIN
3/4 OR 1/2 INCH VIDEO CASSETTE I
Explains the qualifications and personal qualities required for a successful career as a social worker.
From The Career Awareness Series.
Prod-KLVXTV Dist-GPITVL 1973

Socialism C 25 MIN
16MM FILM, 3/4 OR 1/2 IN VIDEO J-H A
Discusses how socialism developed as a response to workers' abuse brought about by the Industrial Revolution. Presents Robert Owen who developed the model factory town of New Lanark in Scotland. Examines the principles of socialism at work in Sweden in a shipbuilding company and the medical system, the promotion of material equality and the attempt to spread income more evenly over a lifetime.
From The Capitalism, Socialism, Communism Series.
Prod-NGS Dist-NGS

Socialization - Moral Development C 22 MIN
16MM FILM, 3/4 OR 1/2 IN VIDEO C A
Explores theories of morality and moral development through the demonstration of classic experimental work in social and developmental psychology.
Prod-HAR Dist-MTI Prodn-MAMMEN 1980

Socially Responsible Investing C 30 MIN
3/4 OR 1/2 INCH VIDEO CASSETTE
Demonstrates that the trend to invest in companies that respect the environment and human rights and that do not produce weapons is profitable. Presented by Dr Robert Schwarz, Alice Tepper Marlin, John Westergaard and Tim Smith.
From The Creating Alternative Futures Series.
Prod-BULFRG Dist-BULFRG

Society - The Students' Places C 15 MIN
16MM FILM OPTICAL SOUND P-J
Presents society by describing it as a group of people living together and sharing ideas, customs, rules and laws.
From The Florida Elementary Social Studies Series.
Prod-DADECO Dist-DADECO 1973

Society And The Individual C 30 MIN
3/4 OR 1/2 INCH VIDEO CASSETTE H-C A
See series title for descriptive statement.
From The Japan - The Changing Tradition Series.
Prod-UMA Dist-GPITVL 1978

Society And Things Nuclear C 30 MIN
2 INCH VIDEOTAPE I-J
Covers civil defense procedures, necessity for planning and group action, results of a nuclear blast, effects of distance on radiation, principles of shielding, fallout shelters and waste disposal procedures.
From The Living In A Nuclear Age Series.
Prod-GPITVL Dist-GPITVL

Society And You C 14 MIN
16MM FILM OPTICAL SOUND J-H
Questions whether disenchantment with parents and discontentment with the way things are is considered valid without alternative initiative.
From The Family Life Education And Human Growth
LC NO. 73-703066
Prod-SF Dist-SF 1970

Society-Serving Skills C 15 MIN
2 INCH VIDEOTAPE J-H
Covers the three major groups of service works private, household workers, protective service workers and other service works, such as waiters, custodians, ushers and elevator operators.
From The Work Is For Real Series.
Prod-STETVC Dist-GPITVL

Society, The C 22 MIN
16MM FILM, 3/4 OR 1/2 IN VIDEO
Discusses the varied systemic and societal causes, settings and perpetrators of crime.
From The Every Two Seconds Series.
Prod-MTI Dist-MTI

Sociobiology - Doing What Comes Naturally C 20 MIN
16MM FILM, 3/4 OR 1/2 IN VIDEO
Discusses the evolution of man's behavior in society and tells how sociobiology can help man plan and understand his behavior.
Prod-DOCUA Dist-CNEMAG

Sociobiology - The Human Animal C 57 MIN
16MM FILM, 3/4 OR 1/2 IN VIDEO C A
Focuses on sociobiology, a controversial science which holds that behavior is biologically determined.
From The Nova Series.
LC NO. 79-707228
Prod-WGBHTV Dist-TIMLIF 1977

Sockeye Odyssey C 14 MIN
16MM FILM, 3/4 OR 1/2 IN VIDEO
Discusses the life cycle and conservation of the Alaskan sockeye salmon. Emphasizes migration, color changes, and spawning.
LC NO. 80-707618
Prod-NOAA Dist-USNAC 1980

Socks / Gorilla Gorilla C 15 MIN
3/4 OR 1/2 INCH VIDEO CASSETTE P
See series title for descriptive statement.
From The Best Of Cover To Cover 1 Series.
Prod-WETATV Dist-WETATV

Socrates (Italian) C 120 MIN
16MM FILM OPTICAL SOUND
Offers a portrait of the Greek philosopher Socrates, pointing out that he was a man of both weakness and strength. Directed by Roberto Rossellini. With English subtitles.
Prod-UNKNWN Dist-NYFLMS 1970

Sod House Frontier, The B 30 MIN
16MM FILM OPTICAL SOUND H-C A
Describes the sod house as a symbol of the frontier. Shows the food, furnishings and clothing of the settlers and mentions the

problems of wood and water. Describes the cultural, educational, religious and social life of the frontier, and discusses frontier agriculture.
From The Great Plains Trilogy, 3 Series. Explorer And Settler - The White Man Arrives
Prod-KUONTV Dist-UNEBR 1954

Sodbusters C 29 MIN
16MM FILM - 3/4 IN VIDEO
Examines the problems of how to stop the historically justified prodigal use of resources. Traces the growth of America and American values in historical photographs, paintings and early motion picture film and finds the roots of the energy crisis in the Amercan past.
From The Earthkeeping Series.
Prod-WTTWTV Dist-PUBTEL

Sodom And Gomorrah C 50 MIN
16MM FILM, 3/4 OR 1/2 IN VIDEO I-C A
Reveals that when Lot and his people find themselves in the sinful cities of Sodom and Gomorrah, an angel tells them to leave the cities and not look back, lest they be turned into pillars of salt. Stars Ed Ames and Dorothy Malone.
From The Greatest Heroes Of The Bible Series.
Prod-LUF Dist-LUF 1979

Sofa C 23 MIN
3/4 OR 1/2 INCH VIDEO CASSETTE
Documents the engineering of two collaborative performances, the Whisper Project and Freeze Frame Room For Living Room. Directed by Suzanne Lacy with Doug Smith and Eric La Brecque.
Prod-ARTINC Dist-ARTINC

Sofa-Fire Death-Song C 11 MIN
16MM FILM OPTICAL SOUND C A
Presents a psychedelic mood study of the female form.
Prod-CFS Dist-CFS 1968

Soft Is The Heart Of A Child C 27 MIN
16MM FILM - 3/4 IN VIDEO
Focus on the impact on children of parents' alcoholism. Deals with such matters as where children can turn for help and support. Close-captioned.
Prod-OPCORK Dist-MTP Prodn-GTRPRO 1979

Soft Lenses C 13 MIN
16MM FILM, 3/4 OR 1/2 IN VIDEO A
Explains how soft lenses work and demonstrates techniques of handling, inserting and removing them. Shows the proper methods of lens wear and care, including asepticizing soft lenses.
Prod-PRORE Dist-PRORE

Soft Pad C 4 MIN
16MM FILM, 3/4 OR 1/2 IN VIDEO
Describes a system of chairs, reflecting some of the design concepts and conveying the character of the pieces.
Prod-EAMES Dist-PFP 1970

Soft Pitch Peddlers C 28 MIN
3/4 OR 1/2 INCH VIDEO CASSETTE
Gives a back-stage look at how a salesperson uses psychology to move money from another's pocket to his.
Prod-WCCOTV Dist-WCCOTV 1977

Soft Sell C 30 MIN
16MM FILM, 3/4 OR 1/2 IN VIDEO H-C A
Presents various approaches to selling.
From The Enterprise Series.
Prod-MTI Dist-MTI

Soft Tissue Examination C 17 MIN
3/4 OR 1/2 INCH VIDEO CASSETTE PRO
Demonstrates a procedure for performing a systematic examination of the external lips, vestibule, frenum attachments, buccal mucosa, parotid gland and orifice, muscles of mastication, temporalis muscle, gingiva, hard and soft palate, pharynx, tongue, the floor of the mouth and sublingual and submand ibular texture of soft tissue, brimanual and bidigital palpation of muscles, tongue, salivary glands and palate, noting tenderness and/or swelling as well as saliva flow and consistently upon palpation.
Prod-UWASH Dist-UWASH

Soft Tissue Injuries To The Face C 21 MIN
3/4 OR 1/2 INCH VIDEO CASSETTE PRO
Demonstrates the procedure for a regional physical exam, the preparation of a facial wound for repair, the way to dress a wound, follow-up care and the the principles of repairing injuries of the tongue, oral mucosa, lips, nose, ears, scalp and eyelids.
Prod-UMICHM Dist-UMICHM 1977

Soft Tissue Lesions Of The Oral Cavity C 17 MIN
16MM FILM - 3/4 IN VIDEO PRO
Demonstrates how hyperplastic tissue caused by an ill-fitting denture is excised from the maxillary muco-labial area. Shows how a surgical stent is used to maintain the deepened labial sulcus. Presents preoperative results.
LC NO. 78-706009
Prod-USVA Dist-USNAC 1977

Soft White Death C 23 MIN
3/4 OR 1/2 INCH VIDEO CASSETTE
Follows a mother polar bear and her young on their traditional migratory route from hibernation out to the ice flows of Hudson Bay.
Prod-NWLDPR Dist-NWLDPR

Softball - Skills And Practice C 13 MIN
16MM FILM, 3/4 OR 1/2 IN VIDEO I-J
Illustrates the correct performance of each softball skill. Uses normal as well as slow-motion photography to give the viewer an opportunity to study each skill in detail. The plays are shown in individual and group action.
Prod-FA Dist-PHENIX 1967

Softball - Skills And Practice (Spanish) C 13 MIN
16MM FILM, 3/4 OR 1/2 IN VIDEO I-J
Illustrates the correct performance of each softball skill. Uses normal as well as slow-motion photography to give the viewer an opportunity to study each skill in detail. The plays are shown in individual and group action.
Prod-FA Dist-PHENIX 1967

Softball Fundamentals For Elementary Schools B 11 MIN
16MM FILM, 3/4 OR 1/2 IN VIDEO I
Basic rules, positions of players and teamwork are shown in a beginning class in softball. Demonstrates how to bat, pitch, catch and throw. Also stresses the importance of safety measures and good sportsmanship.
Prod-FURMAN Dist-PHENIX 1966

Softball—A Series
16MM FILM, 3/4 OR 1/2 IN VIDEO J-C A
Illustrates all of the basic techniques and strategies that make the difference between winning and losing in softball.
Prod-ATHI Dist-ATHI 1980

Basic Skills In Softbll	010 MIN
Better Hitting And Baserunning	010 MIN
Better Pitching And Defense	010 MIN

Softfire C 19 MIN
3/4 OR 1/2 INCH VIDEO CASSETTE H-C A
Covers the care of an 88-year-old widowed retired school teacher by an in-home care service that specializes in treating the elderly with dignity.
Prod-CEPRO Dist-CEPRO

Software C 30 MIN
3/4 OR 1/2 INCH VIDEO CASSETTE IND
Uses nine videotapes to bring one up to speed in programming the 6800 microprocessor through several demonstration exercises, showing good and bad practices. Utilizes twelve demonstrations to lead one through programming exercises, to build up expertise in programming microprocessors and interfacing them to real applications.
From The Programming Microprocessors Series.
Prod-COLOSU Dist-COLOSU

Software Design, Pt 1 C 30 MIN
3/4 OR 1/2 INCH VIDEO CASSETTE IND
Distinguishes between architectural and detail design. Discusses fundamental design principles. Covers method and notation of design by levels of abstraction.
From The Software Engineering - A First Course Series.
Prod-COLOSU Dist-COLOSU

Software Design, Pt 2 C 30 MIN
3/4 OR 1/2 INCH VIDEO CASSETTE IND
Depicts hierarchical structure versus tree structure, the integrated top-down approach to design, coding and testing, design of transaction-driven systems and design-representation techniques.
From The Software Engineering - A First Course Series.
Prod-COLOSU Dist-COLOSU

Software Design, Pt 3 C 30 MIN
3/4 OR 1/2 INCH VIDEO CASSETTE IND
Presents definition of the term module. Describes several modularization criteria, including the composite (or structured) design method. Concludes with discussion of detail design.
From The Software Engineering - A First Course Series.
Prod-COLOSU Dist-COLOSU

Software Development C 50 MIN
3/4 OR 1/2 INCH VIDEO CASSETTE C
Shows specifications, flow charts, structured programming, top/down programming, assembly language, editing, debugging and software management.
From The Microcomputers - An Overview For Managers And Engineers Series.
Prod-GMIEMI Dist-AMCEE

Software Development - Key Issues And Considerations C 30 MIN
3/4 OR 1/2 INCH VIDEO CASSETTE J-C A
Discusses education strategies for introducing software, development models for software, hardware choices and software policies.
From The New Technology In Education Series.
Prod-USDOE Dist-USNAC 1983

Software Engineering - A First Course—A Series
IND
Tells how to increase software quality and lower its development cost by analysis, design, implementation, and testing, and how maintenance includes enhancement, adaptation and fixing bugs.
Prod-COLOSU Dist-COLOSU

Coding Standards And Documentation Techniques	030 MIN
Coding Style And Standards	030 MIN
Design Summary And Language Features, Pt 1	030 MIN
Economic Issues In Software Engineering	030 MIN
Formal Verification	030 MIN
Introduction, Pt 1	030 MIN
Introduction, Pt 2	030 MIN
Language Features, Pt 2	030 MIN
Language Features, Pt 3	030 MIN
Program Testing Pt 1	030 MIN
Program Testing Pt 2	030 MIN
Requirements Analysis	030 MIN
Software Design, Pt 1	030 MIN
Software Design, Pt 2	030 MIN
Software Design, Pt 3	030 MIN
Software Maintenance	030 MIN
Software Requirements Analysis Techniques, Pt 1	030 MIN
Software Requirements Analysis Techniques, Pt 2	030 MIN
Summary	030 MIN
Testing, Symbolic Execution And Formal	030 MIN

Software Engineering—A Series
PRO
Uses classroom format to videotape two 60-minute lectures weekly for 14 weeks on 22 cassettes. Covers software development modeling and tools, techniques for design estimation, testing and reliability management; design and analysis techniques such as topdown, modulars, HIPO diagrams and a cause-effect graph, testing techniques such as modular integration, paths, exhaustive and regression; and regression; and management controls and productive controls.
Prod-PINY Dist-AMCEE

Software Engineering—A Series
C A
No information available.
Prod-UIDEEO Dist-UIDEEO

Software Engineering—A Series
PRO
Uses classroom format to videotape lectures on 42 cassettes. Delineates software development lifecycle into the six stages of requirement analysis, specifications, design, implementation, testing and maintenance. Examines important issues and current status of tools and techniques supporting each of these stages. Reads and discusses 'classic' software papers, and alternative techniques are described and discussed.
Prod-UMAEEE Dist-AMCEE

Software Engineering—A Series
C
Uses classroom format to videotape two 75-minute lectures weekly for 14 weeks 56 cassettes. Gives architectural aspects of software engineering, machine language and structure, assembler language and assemblers, macro- language and macro-processors, loaders and linkers, programming language and language structure, computers, interpreters and operating systems.
Prod-UMD Dist-AMCEE

Software Evaluation C 28 MIN
3/4 OR 1/2 INCH VIDEO CASSETTE T
See series title for descriptive statement.
From The Next Steps With Computers In The Classroom Series.
Prod-PBS Dist-PBS

Software For Microprocessors C 30 MIN
3/4 OR 1/2 INCH VIDEO CASSETTE PRO
Provides background and definitions in order to bring the hardware designs up to speed in software technology. Discusses alternatives in addressing modes, and direction in software usage.
From The Designing With Microprocessors Series.
Prod-TXINLC Dist-TXINLC

Software Fundamentals C 50 MIN
3/4 OR 1/2 INCH VIDEO CASSETTE C
Includes binary signals and numbers, hex representation, program counter, registers, memory reference instructions, branch and I/O instruction.
From The Microcomputers - An Overview For Managers And Engineers Series.
Prod-GMIEMI Dist-AMCEE

Software Maintenance C 30 MIN
3/4 OR 1/2 INCH VIDEO CASSETTE IND
Discusses life-cycle aspects of software maintenance tools and techniques for maintenance. Tells about personnel aspects of software maintenance.
From The Software Engineering - A First Course Series.
Prod-COLOSU Dist-COLOSU

Software Management For Small Computers—A Series
C A
Deals with various management considerations concerning computer software.
LC NO. 81-706201
Prod-AMCEE Dist-AMCEE 1980

Computer Hardware And Software Jargon	035 MIN
Computer Hardware Features	035 MIN
Contemporary Microcomputer Architecture	035 MIN
Defensive Programming	035 MIN
Fault Tolerant Software	035 MIN
Impact Of Technology, The	035 MIN
Monitoring Your Progress	035 MIN
Programming Style And Documentation	035 MIN
Reliable Software	035 MIN
Selecting A Computer And Setting Up Shop	035 MIN
Software Management Team, The	035 MIN
Software Selection	035 MIN
Testing Process, The	035 MIN
Trouble Shooting Aids	035 MIN

Software Management For Small Computers—A Series
IND
Covers an introduction to and review of how to manage software acquisition and use for small computers. Shows on camera instruction by Professor F J Mowle at Purdue University. Goes through nomenclature, architecture, necessary management teams, software selection and testing, troubles shooting and monitoring progress.
Prod-ICSINT Dist-ICSINT

Computer Hardware And Software Jargon	045 MIN
Computer Hardware Features	045 MIN
Contemporary Microcomputer Architecture	045 MIN
Defensive Programming	045 MIN

Designing Reliable Software 045 MIN
Fault Tolerant Software 045 MIN
Impact Of Technology, The 045 MIN
Monitoring Your Progress 045 MIN
Programming Style And Documentation 045 MIN
Selecting A Computer And Setting Up Shop 045 MIN
Software Management Team, The 045 MIN
Software Selection 045 MIN
Testing Process, The 045 MIN
Trouble Shooting Aids 045 MIN

Software Management Team, The C 35 MIN
3/4 INCH VIDEO CASSETTE C A
See series title for descriptive statement.
From The Software Management For Small Computers Series.
LC NO. 81-706201
Prod-AMCEE Dist-AMCEE 1980

Software Reliability C 30 MIN
3/4 OR 1/2 INCH VIDEO CASSETTE IND
Defines software reliability, and presents several models to model software reliability, mean time to failures when errors are reduced and test time is required to reduce errors.
From The Reliability Engineering Series.
Prod-COLOSU Dist-COLOSU

Software Requirements Analysis Techniques, Pt 1 C 30 MIN
3/4 OR 1/2 INCH VIDEO CASSETTE IND
Tells about software specification techniques emphasis on desired attributes, developing quality metrics, developing quality assurance procedures, and use of formal notations.
From The Software Engineering - A First Course Series.
Prod-COLOSU Dist-COLOSU

Software Requirements Analysis Techniques, Pt 2 C 30 MIN
3/4 OR 1/2 INCH VIDEO CASSETTE IND
Concludes discussion on use of formal notations with implicit equations, recurrence relations and property lists. Describes use of automated tools for software specification.
From The Software Engineering - A First Course Series.
Prod-COLOSU Dist-COLOSU

Software Selection C 28 MIN
3/4 OR 1/2 INCH VIDEO CASSETTE T
See series title for descriptive statement.
From The Next Steps With Computers In The Classroom Series.
Prod-PBS Dist-PBS

Software Selection C 35 MIN
3/4 INCH VIDEO CASSETTE C A
See series title for descriptive statement.
From The Software Management For Small Computers Series.
LC NO. 81-706201
Prod-AMCEE Dist-AMCEE 1980

Softwood Cuttings C 28 MIN
2 INCH VIDEOTAPE
See series title for descriptive statement.
From The Making Things Grow III Series.
Prod-WGBHTV Dist-PUBTEL

Soil C 15 MIN
3/4 OR 1/2 INCH VIDEO CASSETTE I
Looks at how soil, water and living things affect one another.
From The L-Four Series.
Prod-CTI Dist-CTI

Soil B 15 MIN
2 INCH VIDEOTAPE P
Teaches the value of close, careful observation as a basic scientific approach to a problem. (Broadcast quality)
From The Land And Sea Series.
Prod-TTOIC Dist-GPITVL Prodn-WGBHTV

Soil C 15 MIN
3/4 OR 1/2 INCH VIDEO CASSETTE P
Explains that when Hocus and Myrtle picnic on a rock, Myrtle predicts that over thousands of years, the rock will change to soil. Shows Hocus learning how weather, plants, water and animals make and move topsoil.
From The Let Me See Series. No. 7
Prod-WETN Dist-AITECH Prodn-STSU 1982

Soil - An Introduction C 9 MIN
16MM FILM, 3/4 OR 1/2 IN VIDEO P-I
Explores soil as an important resource. Shows that soil is renewable but in need of constant attention.
Prod-NELLES Dist-PHENIX 1976

Soil - What It Is And What It Does C 11 MIN
16MM FILM, 3/4 OR 1/2 IN VIDEO P
Points out how mixtures of sand, clay and humus make various kinds of soil. Explains how the weathering of rocks helps make soil. Uses experiments to indicate types of soils in which plants grow well.
Prod-CORF Dist-CORF 1966

Soil And Structure Response To Earthquakes--A Series
PRO
Uses classroom format to videotape four two-hour lectures on eight cassettes. Includes Understanding And Predicting Soil Behavior, Introduction To Structural Dynamics, Understanding And Predicting Structural Behavior, and Soil-Structure Interaction. Presents the fundamentals of structural dynamics as related to earthquake engineering technology.
Prod-USCITV Dist-AMCEE

Soil And Water - A Living World C 16 MIN
16MM FILM, 3/4 OR 1/2 IN VIDEO P-I
Looks at the various creatures who live in both soil and water, some of which can be seen with the naked eye and some of which require a microscope.
LC NO. 84-706648
Prod-SAIF Dist-BARR 1983

Soil Compaction On Forest Lands C 32 MIN
16MM FILM OPTICAL SOUND
Takes an in-depth look at the causes of forest soil compaction, its effects on productivity and some management alternatives for reducing compaction and restoring compacted lands.
Prod-OSUSF Dist-OSUSF

Soil Engineering II C 46 MIN
3/4 OR 1/2 INCH VIDEO CASSETTE C
Uses classroom format to videotape a series of 48 lectures. Discusses course objectives as gaining an under- standing of soil behavior by examining theories relating to earth pressure, bearing capacity, slope stability and ground water flow.
Prod-NCSU Dist-AMCEE

Soil Makers C 17 MIN
16MM FILM OPTICAL SOUND I-H
Explains the complex processes that produce fertile top soil, upon which all life on Earth is dependent.
Prod-MMP Dist-MMP 1966

Soil pH C 30 MIN
3/4 OR 1/2 INCH VIDEO CASSETTE C A
Defines pH, explains its relationship to soil nutrients and shows the student how to change the pH of garden soil to make it more acid or more basic. Includes charts and tables to help in selection of appropriate plants for various soils.
From The Home Gardener With John Lenanton Series. Lesson 4
Prod-COAST Dist-CDTEL

Soil Profiles And Factors Of Formation C 15 MIN
1/2 IN VIDEO CASSETTE BETA/VHS
Discusses soil composition.
Prod-RMI Dist-RMI

Soil Profiles And Processes C 20 MIN
3/4 OR 1/2 INCH VIDEO CASSETTE
Offers a detailed study of a large coniferous plantation surrounded by agricultural land. Discusses podzolization and the nature of pozol soil, the effect of slope position, land use drainage and soil profiles.
From The Earth Science Series.
Prod-FOTH Dist-FOTH 1984

Soil We Plough, The C 20 MIN
16MM FILM OPTICAL SOUND
Describes the automation of today's Swedish agriculture, in which cooperatives play a significant part.
Prod-ASI Dist-AUDPLN

Soil-Asphalt Stabilization, Pt 1 B 60 MIN
3/4 OR 1/2 INCH VIDEO CASSETTE
See series title for descriptive statement.
From The Geotechnical Engineering Series. Pt 20
Prod-UAZMIC Dist-UAZMIC 1977

Soil-Asphalt Stabilization, Pt 2 B 60 MIN
3/4 OR 1/2 INCH VIDEO CASSETTE
See series title for descriptive statement.
From The Geotechnical Engineering Series. Pt 21
Prod-UAZMIC Dist-UAZMIC 1977

Soil-Cement In Energy And Water Resources C 20 MIN
16MM FILM OPTICAL SOUND
Shows examples of soil-cement construction to stabilize earth dams, water storage reservoirs, waste water treatment lagoons, settling ponds, spillways and other water resource facilities, illustrating proper design and construction.
LC NO. 82-700040
Prod-PRTLND Dist-PRTLND 1980

Soil-Cement Stabilization B 60 MIN
3/4 OR 1/2 INCH VIDEO CASSETTE
See series title for descriptive statement.
From The Geotechnical Engineering Series. Pt 19
Prod-UAZMIC Dist-UAZMIC 1977

Soil-Cement Stabilization, Pt 1 B 60 MIN
3/4 OR 1/2 INCH VIDEO CASSETTE
See series title for descriptive statement.
From The Geotechnical Engineering Series. Pt 18
Prod-UAZMIC Dist-UAZMIC 1977

Soil-Lime Stabilization, Pt 1 B 60 MIN
3/4 OR 1/2 INCH VIDEO CASSETTE
See series title for descriptive statement.
From The Geotechnical Engineering Series. Pt 16
Prod-UAZMIC Dist-UAZMIC 1977

Soil-Lime Stabilization, Pt 2 B 60 MIN
3/4 OR 1/2 INCH VIDEO CASSETTE
See series title for descriptive statement.
From The Geotechnical Engineering Series. Pt 17
Prod-UAZMIC Dist-UAZMIC 1977

Soils C 30 MIN
2 INCH VIDEOTAPE
Features Thalassa Cruso discussing different aspects of gardening. Describes different types of soil.
From The Making Things Grow I Series.
Prod-WGBHTV Dist-PUBTEL

Soils 1 C 30 MIN
3/4 OR 1/2 INCH VIDEO CASSETTE C A
Stresses the importance of soil for good plant growth. Discusses physical properties of sandy, clay and loam soils. Teaches how to test soil to determine its texture.
From The Home Gardener With John Lenanton Series. Lesson 2
Prod-COAST Dist-CDTEL

Soils 2 C 30 MIN
3/4 OR 1/2 INCH VIDEO CASSETTE C A
Introduces materials that are used to turn sandy or clay soil into soil that has good structure. Discusses various soils and synthetic materials. Gives solutions for 'hardpan,' a hard layer of earth beneath the surface.
From The Home Gardener With John Lenanton Series. Lesson 3
Prod-COAST Dist-CDTEL

Sojourn Earth C 29 MIN
16MM FILM - 3/4 IN VIDEO
Presents an adventure that looks at the planet earth from an alien perspective. Features a journey across thousands of miles of the earth's surface, landing at intervals to show a variety of living creatures and structures of beauty, grace and humor. Directed by Robert Marien. No dialogue.
From The Presente Series.
Prod-KCET Dist-KCET

Sojourn In India C 13 MIN
16MM FILM OPTICAL SOUND I-C A
Presents the visit of a group of American tourists to India in 1964 in the course of their overland tour of the world. Shows the India seen by them.
Prod-INDIA Dist-NEDINF

Sol Preparation, Dialysis And Ultrafiltration C 57 MIN
3/4 OR 1/2 INCH VIDEO CASSETTE
See series title for descriptive statement.
From The Colloid And Surface Chemistry - Lyophobic Colloids Series.
Prod-KALMIA Dist-KALMIA

Sol Preparation, Dialysis And Ultrafiltration B 57 MIN
3/4 OR 1/2 INCH VIDEO CASSETTE
See series title for descriptive statement.
From The Colloid And Surface Chemistry - Lyophobic Colloids Series.
Prod-MIOT Dist-MIOT

Solar Advantage, The C 20 MIN
16MM FILM OPTICAL SOUND
Discusses passive, active and photovoltaic solar energy. Shows all three types of systems in operation in several locations across the country. Includes interviews with people who are using and installing solar systems giving the audience a good overview of how solar energy can be applied.
Prod-COPRO Dist-COPRO

Solar Atmosphere, The B 29 MIN
16MM FILM OPTICAL SOUND C A
Discusses various aspects of the solar atmosphere including granulation, development of sunspots, spicules, flares and flare waves, surges and prominences.
LC NO. 75-702360
Prod-NSF Dist-CIT 1972

Solar Collectors C 27 MIN
3/4 OR 1/2 INCH VIDEO CASSETTE H-C A
Discusses the parts of a flat-plate collector and suitable materials for each part. Shows the three types of solar collectors along with practical applications for each type. Covers methods for aiming the solar collector for maximum efficiency.
From The Solar Collectors, Solar Radiation, Insolation Tables Series.
Prod-NCDCC Dist-MOKIN

Solar Collectors, Solar Radiation, Insolation Tables—A Series
H-C A
Prod-NCDCC Dist-MOKIN

Amount And Direction Of Solar Input 026 MIN
Sizing Solar Collectors, Pt 1 025 MIN
Sizing Solar Collectors, Pt 2 025 MIN
Sizing Solar Collectors, Pt 3 025 MIN
Solar Collectors 027 MIN

Solar Comfort C 23 MIN
16MM FILM OPTICAL SOUND
Shows how proper home design can provide solar heating and cooling with a minimum of commercially produced energy. Includes interviews with owners of passive-solar homes.
LC NO. 80-701621
Prod-CALENC Dist-CALENC Prodn-CALDWR 1980

Solar Demonstration Projects C 60 MIN
3/4 OR 1/2 INCH VIDEO CASSETTE IND
Presents a lecture dealing with various solar demonstration projects. Shows schematics of typical heating and cooling systems and describes solar hot water systems and includes case studies.
From the Solar Energy - Fundamentals And Applications Series.
LC NO. 81-706412
Prod-GATECH Dist-AMCEE 1977

Solar Domestic Hot Water Heater C 24 MIN
3/4 OR 1/2 INCH VIDEO CASSETTE H-C A
Explains the basic components of a solar domestic hot water heater and illustrates the function of each.
From The Active Solar Heating And Cooling Series.
Prod-NCDCC Dist-MOKIN

Solar Eclipse '73 C 23 MIN
16MM FILM, 3/4 OR 1/2 IN VIDEO H-C A
Shows the activities of scientists in the country of Mauritania as they observe a solar eclipse which occurred in June, 1973.
LC NO. 80-706297
Prod-NGS Dist-NGS 1974

Solar Energy C 15 MIN
3/4 OR 1/2 INCH VIDEO CASSETTE P-I

Demonstrates man's dependence on the sun, explaining that it is the earth's chief source of radiant energy. Shows how the sun's light and heat provide energy for plants to grow, to make food and to create fossil fuels, such as coal and oil. Depicts how solar energy causes an evaporation-condensation rain cycle that ultimately results in electricity.
From The First Films On Science Series.
Prod-MAETEL Dist-AITECH 1975

Solar Energy - Fundamentals And Applications—A Series
IND
Discusses what is happening in the field of solar energy, and how to apply solar energy to buildings.
LC NO. 81-706202
Prod-AMCEE Dist-AMCEE 1977

Design And Installation Of Solar Heating
Design And Installation Of Solar Heating And 052 MIN
Solar Demonstration Projects 060 MIN
Solar House Design 050 MIN
Solar Voltaic Conversion 028 MIN
Thermal Storage Systems 060 MIN

Solar Energy - How It Works C 15 MIN
16MM FILM, 3/4 OR 1/2 IN VIDEO I-J
Discusses solar energy and its advantages over depletable fossil fuels. Provides scenes of solar water heating systems, a solar oven, banks of silicon solar cells and a community which is totally powered by the Sun.
LC NO. 82-706545
Prod-SMITG Dist-CF 1980

Solar Energy - How It Works (Captioned) C 16 MIN
16MM FILM, 3/4 OR 1/2 IN VIDEO I-H
Demonstrates ways to use the energy from the Sun through experiments by children and by showing commercial applications.
Prod-SMITG Dist-CF 1979

Solar Energy - Ray Of Hope C 16 MIN
3/4 OR 1/2 INCH VIDEO CASSETTE
Looks at solar housing in Minnesota, the farsighted California approach and the future hope of generating solar power.
Prod-WCCOTV Dist-WCCOTV 1979

Solar Energy - The Great Adventure C 29 MIN
3/4 OR 1/2 INCH VIDEO CASSETTE
Describes passive heating and distilling water. Shows vertical axis wind turbines and renewable energy as methane gas is made from waste products. Narrated by Eddie Albert.
Prod-IVCH Dist-IVCH

Solar Energy - To Capture The Power Of Sun And Tide C 21 MIN
16MM FILM, 3/4 OR 1/2 IN VIDEO J-C A
Looks at the potential of solar and tidal power for meeting the earth's energy needs. Gives examples of solar and tidal power stations in France and shows a man's house which uses the rain water and a solar still to heat it.
From The Coping With Tomorrow Series.
Prod-DOCUA Dist-AIMS 1975

Solar Energy - To Capture The Power Of Sun And Tide C 24 MIN
16MM FILM, 3/4 OR 1/2 IN VIDEO
Suggests that the sun and the moon may offer the most promising solutions to the energy crisis. Shows solar mirrors, a house heated by rain water and solar energy, and tidal power.
Prod-DOCUA Dist-CNEMAG

Solar Energy - Unlimited Power C 14 MIN
16MM FILM OPTICAL SOUND
Discusses the ways in which power can be obtained from the Sun, including solar water and space heating, high temperature conversion to produce electricity, solar architecture and air conditioning. Compares solar energy to other sources of power, showing its advantages and disadvantages.
LC NO. 77-700007
Prod-MNTAGE Dist-MNTAGE 1977

Solar Energy And You C 19 MIN
16MM FILM OPTICAL SOUND
Reviews the field of solar energy. Shows efforts at utilizing solar power and projected application for the future.
LC NO. 77-701834
Prod-FARTC Dist-CONPOW 1977

Solar Energy Fundamentals C 50 MIN
3/4 OR 1/2 INCH VIDEO CASSETTE
Gives the fundamental principles of solar utilization as they relate to solar thermal conversion, photovoltaics, bioconversion and heating/cooling applications. Stresses active and passive solar heating, using actual examples and applications.
From The Energy Issues And Alternatives Series.
Prod-UIDEEO Dist-UIDEEO

Solar Energy Now C 30 MIN
3/4 OR 1/2 INCH VIDEO CASSETTE
Presents a de-mystifying look at solar energy systems at work in the home. Taped at the Farallones Institute's Integral Urban House in Berkeley, California and illustrates the applications and installation of home solar energy heating units.
Prod-GOLHAR Dist-PBS 1982

Solar Energy Options C 14 MIN
16MM FILM OPTICAL SOUND
Discusses the technological and economic prospects for the development of solar energy, showing its uses in dwellings, in industry, on farms and as a source of electrical energy.
Prod-ALLFP Dist-NSTA 1979

Solar Energy Primer C 30 MIN
3/4 INCH VIDEOTAPE J A

Features Jules Bergman as he narrates a documentary which uses a question and answer format to show the efficiency and effectiveness of solar energy. Uses the National Council of Churches' Policy Statement on energy as a basis.
Prod-ABCVID Dist-ECUFLM 1979

Solar Energy Systems—A Series
C A
Discusses the availability and potential application of solar energy to domestic and commercial heating and cooling. Consists of 41 fifty-minute videotape lectures.
Prod-UIDEEO Dist-UIDEEO

Solar Energy, The Great Adventure C 28 MIN
16MM FILM, 3/4 OR 1/2 IN VIDEO
Introduces individuals who have developed their own solar energy systems. Shows how they found methods of putting the Sun to work for them. Narrated by Eddie Albert.
LC NO. 80-707731
Prod-USDOE Dist-USNAC 1978

Solar Film, The C 9 MIN
16MM FILM, 3/4 OR 1/2 IN VIDEO
Depicts the ancient relationship between the Sun and man. Explores the formation of the Earth, traces man's consumption of Sun-created fossil fuels and presents the Sun as a logical source of future power.
LC NO. 80-707480
Prod-WILDWD Dist-PFP

Solar Frontier, The C 25 MIN
16MM FILM, 3/4 OR 1/2 IN VIDEO J-C
Features architects Nick Nicholson, Greg Allen, and Doug Lorriman and residents as they discuss the cost, performance and technology of three houses in the Canadian snowbelt which are heated by solar energy.
Prod-MELFIL Dist-BULFRG 1978

Solar Generation, The C 21 MIN
16MM FILM OPTICAL SOUND J-H
Explores the possibilities, problems and successes in harnessing the Sun's power for energy.
From The Science Of Energy Series.
Prod-FINLYS Dist-FINLYS 1976

Solar Greenhouses C 20 MIN
3/4 OR 1/2 INCH VIDEO CASSETTE H-C A
Serves as an introduction to solar-heated sun spaces. Covers orientation of the greenhouse, design factors, the different glazing types, heat loss, heat storage and summer cooling.
From The Active Solar Heating And Cooling Series.
Prod-NCDCC Dist-MOKIN

Solar Horizon, The C 10 MIN
16MM FILM, 3/4 OR 1/2 IN VIDEO I-J
Shows the many ways in which solar energy is being harnessed and the new techniques that are being developed to supply man's need for a renewable source of energy.
LC NO. 81-706579
Prod-LINDH Dist-AIMS 1981

Solar House Design C 50 MIN
3/4 OR 1/2 INCH VIDEO CASSETTE IND
Presents a lecture on how to design houses so that they act as solar collectors and storage units. Discusses insulation techniques as well.
From the Solar Energy - Fundamentals And Applications Series.
LC NO. 81-706414
Prod-UILLAV Dist-AMCEE 1977

Solar Image, The C 29 MIN
3/4 INCH VIDEO CASSETTE C A
Discusses importance of sun to humanity since prehistoric times. Provides basic data on sun's composition. Uses still photographs, time-lapse photography and animation.
From The Project Universe - Astronomy Series. Lesson 14
Prod-COAST Dist-CDTEL Prodn-SCCON

Solar Interior, The C 29 MIN
3/4 INCH VIDEO CASSETTE C A
Explains fusion of hydrogen atoms into helium. Reports on observations of a slight increase in sun's rotation rates.
From The Project Universe - Astronomy Series. Lesson 15
Prod-COAST Dist-CDTEL Prodn-SCCON

Solar Percentage, The C 25 MIN
16MM FILM, 3/4 OR 1/2 IN VIDEO PRO
Describes the use of solar energy in health care facilities.
LC NO. 81-706787
Prod-USDHHS Dist-USNAC Prodn-BSIDE 1981

Solar Power C 20 MIN
16MM FILM, 3/4 OR 1/2 IN VIDEO J-C A
Shows solar power being used for passive solar heating, active thermal heating and photovoltaic production of electricity.
Prod-HANDEL Dist-HANDEL 1980

Solar Power - The Giver Of Life C 27 MIN
16MM FILM OPTICAL SOUND
Suggests that the sun's energy could supplement other fuels. Examines solar stills, cookers and collectors and the impact of commercial solar installations on the environment.
From The Energy Sources - A New Beginning Series.
Prod-UCOLO Dist-UCOLO

Solar Powered Irrigation C 29 MIN
16MM FILM OPTICAL SOUND
Traces the evolution of the solar energy applications in agriculture from its origins in the nineteenth century to the planning, construction and operation of the present demonstration project.
Prod-UARIZ Dist-UARIZ 1979

Solar Promise, The C 29 MIN
16MM FILM, 3/4 OR 1/2 IN VIDEO
Demonstrates the basic principles of available solar energy devices. Shows the difference between passive and active systems and stresses the value of passive systems and their cost effectiveness.
LC NO. 83-706296
Prod-MAYRH Dist-BULFRG 1979

Solar Radiation, Pt 1 - Sun And Earth C 18 MIN
16MM FILM OPTICAL SOUND H
Discusses the concept that the energy radiated away to space by the earth must balance the energy received from the sun.
Prod-AMS Dist-MLA 1967

Solar Radiation, Pt 2 - The Earth's Atmosphere C 21 MIN
16MM FILM OPTICAL SOUND H
Examines the effects of solar radiation on the earth. Uses instruments to study the light spectrum and light absorption.
From The Educational Films In The Atmospheric Sciences series.
LC NO. 76-702576
Prod-AMS Dist-MLA Prodn-DAVFMS 1967

Solar Scenario, The C 30 MIN
3/4 INCH VIDEO CASSETTE
Looks ahead to the time when solar power may be the only energy source man will ever need. Tells how some ideas to exploit the sun's energy border on science fiction.
Prod-KNMETV Dist-PUBTEL 1974

Solar Sea, The C 60 MIN
16MM FILM, 3/4 OR 1/2 IN VIDEO C A
Looks at the sun as a star that powers the earth, giving life, creating weather and warming the oceans, land and even ice. Shows scientists at the North Pole flying through a supercharged aurora shaped by violent solar storms and infra-red and x-ray satellite eyes peering deep into the interior of the sun. Discusses how the solar wind affects the earth.
From The Planet Earth Series.
Prod-ANNCPB Dist-FI

Solar Spectrum, The X 20 MIN
2 INCH VIDEOTAPE I
See series title for descriptive statement.
From The Process And Proof Series. No. 17
Prod-MCETV Dist-GPITVL Prodn-WVIZTV

Solar System Debris C 29 MIN
3/4 INCH VIDEO CASSETTE C A
Presents overview of objects in the solar system smaller than planets and their satellites. Discusses asteroids, meteorites and comets.
From The Project Universe - Astronomy Series. Lesson 13
Prod-COAST Dist-CDTEL Prodn-SCCON

Solar System, The C 15 MIN
3/4 OR 1/2 INCH VIDEO CASSETTE I
Uses advanced photographic techniques to explore the sun, planets, moons, asteroids and comets.
From The Matter And Motion Series. Module Brown
Prod-WHROTV Dist-AITECH 1973

Solar System, The C 15 MIN
3/4 OR 1/2 INCH VIDEO CASSETTE I
Studies the solar system and those physical forces which permit it to exist.
From The Search For Science (2nd Ed), Unit II - Space Series.
Prod-WVIZTV Dist-GPITVL

Solar System, The C 17 MIN
16MM FILM, 3/4 OR 1/2 IN VIDEO J
Introduces the solar system, indicating known facts about it and questions which remain unanswered.
From The Universe And I Series.
LC NO. 80-706486
Prod-KYTV Dist-AITECH 1977

Solar System, The B 20 MIN
3/4 OR 1/2 INCH VIDEO CASSETTE I
See series title for descriptive statement.
From The Science Room Series.
Prod-MCETV Dist-GPITVL Prodn-WVIZTV

Solar System, The C 20 MIN
16MM FILM, 3/4 OR 1/2 IN VIDEO H-C A
Describes the atmospheres, appearances, climates, moons and distinctive characteristics of each planet in the solar system.
LC NO. 80-706296
Prod-NGS Dist-NGS 1980

Solar System, The C 30 MIN
3/4 OR 1/2 INCH VIDEO CASSETTE C
Examines the evolution and composition of the planets in our solar system. Concentrates on the exploration of Mars using National Aeronautics and Space administration (NASA) footage.
From The Earth, Sea And Sky Series.
Prod-DALCCD Dist-DALCCD

Solar System, The (Spanish) C 18 MIN
16MM FILM, 3/4 OR 1/2 IN VIDEO J-H
A Spanish language version of the film and videorecording The Solar System.
Prod-EBEC Dist-EBEC 1977

Solar System, The (2nd Ed) C 18 MIN
16MM FILM, 3/4 OR 1/2 IN VIDEO J-H
Investigates the structure and composition of the solar system. Describes the origin of the sun and its planets and surveys the major planetary bodies in the solar system. From the revised edition of Our Solar Family.
Prod-EBEC Dist-EBEC 1977

Solar System, The (2nd Ed) C 28 MIN
16MM FILM, 3/4 OR 1/2 IN VIDEO J-C A

Surveys current knowledge of the sun, the nine planets and their moons, asteroids, comets and meteors. Features animated drawings, special photographs of the Sun obtained by Skylab astronauts, Mariner 10 photographs of Mercury, film of the Earth's moon surface by Apollo astronauts, and photographs of Mars, Jupiter and Saturn.
LC NO. 83-706712
Prod-ARMADA Dist-IFB

Solar System, The - And Beyond C 13 MIN
16MM FILM OPTICAL SOUND I-H
Presents knowledge gathered by space missions to study the universe.
Prod-ALLFP Dist-NSTA 1978

Solar System, The - Islands In Space C 17 MIN
16MM FILM, 3/4 OR 1/2 IN VIDEO I-J
Explains space and size relationships and combines special effects and recent research footage to amplify additional concepts. Gives the student a concise, accurate and modern viewpoint about the solar system.
Prod-AIMS Dist-AIMS 1969

Solar System, The - Islands In Space (Spanish) C 17 MIN
16MM FILM, 3/4 OR 1/2 IN VIDEO I-C A
Discusses and illustrates basic concepts about the solar system.
Prod-CAHILL Dist-AIMS 1969

Solar System, The - Its Motions C 9 MIN
16MM FILM, 3/4 OR 1/2 IN VIDEO
Traces the theories of movement of celestial objects from Ptolemy, Copernicus, Brahe, and Kepler to Isaac Newton. Examines the patterns of the planets, the sun, the moons, asteroids and comets.
From The Astronomy Series.
Prod-MGHT Dist-MGHT 1972

Solar System, The - Measuring Its Dimensions C 10 MIN
16MM FILM, 3/4 OR 1/2 IN VIDEO P-I
Uses live photography, animation and special effects to investigate methods astronomers use to determine distances between planets in the solar system and planet size. Explains one of the most important methods used, triangulation.
From The Astronomy Series.
Prod-MGHT Dist-MGHT Prodn-HABER 1970

Solar Systems Engineering—A Series
C A
No information available.
Prod-UIDEEO Dist-UIDEEO

Solar Visions C 18 MIN
16MM FILM OPTICAL SOUND
Deals with the sun as a pragmatic partial solution to an urgent energy problem. Explores the concept of solar building design, photovoltaics and solar heating.
Prod-TAPPRO Dist-MARJON 1980

Solar Visions C 24 MIN
16MM FILM OPTICAL SOUND J-C A
Focuses on the sun as a pragmatic, partial solution to the energy crisis. Explains the basic principles of solar energy and explores the concepts of solar building design, photovoltaics and solar heating.
LC NO. 79-701746
Prod-MALIBU Dist-MALIBU 1980

Solar Voltaic Conversion C 28 MIN
3/4 OR 1/2 INCH VIDEO CASSETTE IND
Presents a lecture on silicon solar cells, their cost effectiveness, array sizing and required tilt.
From the Solar Energy - Fundamentals And Applications Series.
LC NO. 81-706415
Prod-CWRU Dist-AMCEE 1977

Soldering C 13 MIN
16MM FILM, 3/4 OR 1/2 IN VIDEO H-C A
Describes soldering equipment and techniques - tinning an iron, tinning metal, soldering seams and hand soldering.
From The Metalwork - Hand Tools Series.
Prod-MORLAT Dist-SF 1967

Soldering And Brazing C 17 MIN
3/4 OR 1/2 INCH VIDEO CASSETTE
Covers steps in soldering and brazing and soldering and brazing defects.
From The Manufacturing Materials And Processes Series.
Prod-GE Dist-WFVTAE

Soldering and Brazing Copper Tubing C 13 MIN
3/4 OR 1/2 INCH VIDEO CASSETTE IND
Shows how to produce good joinings, using soft solder as well as hard solder in joining copper tubing and capillary fittings.
From The Marshall Maintenance Training Programs Series. Tape 19
Prod-LEIKID Dist-LEIKID

Soldering And Brazing Copper Tubing C 13 MIN
16MM FILM, 3/4 OR 1/2 IN VIDEO IND
Shows how to produce good joints, using soft solder as well as hard solder in joining copper tubing and capillary fittings.
Prod-MOKIN Dist-MOKIN

Soldering Inspection—A Series

Presents a visual approach to solder inspection techniques using DOD specifics.
Prod-VTRI Dist-VTRI

Inspecting Boards And Solder
Inspecting Components And Leads

Soldering Lugs And Splicing Stranded Conductors B 18 MIN
16MM FILM - 3/4 IN VIDEO IND
Shows how to solder a lug, using electric soldering tongs, a blowtorch, and solder pot and ladle. Demonstrates how to splice stranded conductors and make a served cable splice. Issued in 1945 as a motion picture.
From The Electrical Work - Wiring Series. No. 2
LC NO. 79-707490
Prod-USOE Dist-USNAC Prodn-RAYBEL 1979

Soldering Theory C 24 MIN
1/2 IN VIDEO CASSETTE BETA/VHS IND
Discusses the various considerations necessary for a student to understand what soldering is and how it takes place, with key pointo be considered.
Prod-RMI Dist-RMI

Soldier Girls C 87 MIN
16MM FILM, 3/4 OR 1/2 IN VIDEO H-C A
Captures the military experiences of a group of young women who have enlisted in the U S Army. Focuses on the women as they go through basic training and make, what is in most cases, a painful adjustment to military life.
LC NO. 81-707586
Prod-CF Dist-CF 1981

Soldier Girls C 90 MIN
3/4 INCH VIDEO CASSETTE
Follows a group of young women through basic training in the U S Army. Captures remarkable scenes of compassion.
Prod-FIRS Dist-FIRS

Soldier In Love C 76 MIN
3/4 OR 1/2 INCH VIDEO CASSETTE
Offers a story of the fascinating life of John Churchill, the First Duke of Marlborough and his wife Sarah. Stars Jean Simmons, Claire Bloom and Keith Michell.
Prod-FOTH Dist-FOTH 1984

Soldier In The Rain B 96 MIN
16MM FILM OPTICAL SOUND C A
Stars Steve Mc Queen and Jackie Gleason. Tells the story of two non-commissioned officer buddies in the peace-time army.
Prod-CINEWO Dist-CINEWO 1963

Soldier Man B 33 MIN
16MM FILM SILENT J-C A
Stars Harry Langdon as a soldier who has been forgotten at the end of World War I.
Prod-MGM Dist-TWYMAN 1926

Soldier Man B 42 MIN
16MM FILM SILENT
A comedy in which Harry Langdon plays the dual role of a World War I doughboy and a perpetually inebriated King of a small European country.
LC NO. 71-713610
Prod-SENN Dist-BHAWK 1971

Soldier Who Didn't Wash, The C 27 MIN
16MM FILM, 3/4 OR 1/2 IN VIDEO
Tells the Russian story of a soldier who makes a deal with the devil not to wash for fifteen years. Relates that when the soldier grows wealthy, a king asks for his help but the soldier demands one of the king's daughters as payment. Shows that on the wedding day, the fifteen years end and he is revealed to be quite young and handsome.
From The Storybook International Series.
Prod-JOU Dist-JOU 1982

Soldier, The B 5 MIN
16MM FILM OPTICAL SOUND H-C A
Presents a modern interpretation of Psalm 41 using a dramatization about a soldier who is shot while sharing his chocolate bar with a seagull along a deserted beach.
From The Song Of The Ages Series.
LC NO. 70-702127
Prod-FAMLYT Dist-FAMLYT 1964

Soldier's Home C 42 MIN
16MM FILM, 3/4 OR 1/2 IN VIDEO
Describes the life of a soldier returning home from World War I. Based on the short story Soldier's Home by Ernest Hemingway.
From The American Short Story Series.
Prod-LEARIF Dist-CORF

Soldier's Story, A C
1/2 IN VIDEO CASSETTE BETA/VHS
Tells the story of a murder on a black army base during World War II. Stars Howard E Rollins, Jr and Adolph Caesar.
Prod-GA Dist-GA

Soldier's Tale, A C 52 MIN
16MM FILM OPTICAL SOUND
Combines mime, melodrama and ballet, set to the musical score by Igor Stravinsky. Presents a Russian folk tale, A Soldier's Tale. Features ballet star, Robert Helpmann as the Devil.
Prod-CANTOR Dist-CANTOR

Soldiers In Greasepaint C 28 MIN
16MM FILM, 3/4 OR 1/2 IN VIDEO
Tells about entertainers who traveled wherever military personnel were stationed in World War II, bringing them a laugh and a reminder of home.
From The Big Picture Series.
Prod-USA Dist-USNAC 1980

Sole Bonne Femme C 29 MIN
2 INCH VIDEOTAPE
A French language videotape. Features Julia Child of Haute Cuisine au Vin demonstrating how to prepare sole bonne femme. With captions.
From The French Chef (French) Series.
Prod-WGBHTV Dist-PUBTEL

Sole Proprietorships And Partnerships C 30 MIN
3/4 INCH VIDEO CASSETTE
See series title for descriptive statement.
From The It's Everybody's Business Series. Unit 2, Organizing A Business
Prod-DALCCD Dist-DALCCD

Soleil-O (French) B 106 MIN
16MM FILM OPTICAL SOUND
An English subtitle version of the French language film. Considers the life of immigrant African blacks in Paris. Centers around the sad, frustrating existence of an educated immigrant from Mauritania.
Prod-NYFLMS Dist-NYFLMS 1972

Solicitation, The, Pt 1 C 24 MIN
3/4 INCH VIDEO CASSETTE
Describes the proper method for putting together a solicitation for bids on federal contracts.
From The Basic Procurement Course Series.
LC NO. 80-706738
Prod-USGSFC Dist-USNAC Prodn-ADSAV 1978

Solicitation, The, Pt 2 C 24 MIN
3/4 INCH VIDEO CASSETTE
Describes the proper method for putting together a solicitation for bids on federal contracts.
From The Basic Procurement Course Series.
LC NO. 80-706738
Prod-USGSFC Dist-USNAC Prodn-ADSAV 1978

Solid Figures C 30 MIN
16MM FILM OPTICAL SOUND T
Introduces solid figures, and discusses related geometric concepts. To be used following 'CONGRUENCE AND SIMILARITY.'
From The Mathematics For Elementary School Teachers Series. No. 26
Prod-SMSG Dist-MLA 1963

Solid Gold Cadillac, The C 99 MIN
16MM FILM OPTICAL SOUND J-C A
Stars Judy Holliday and Paul Douglas in the story of a naive young lady who is plunged into a merry tug-ofwar for control of a large corporation.
Prod-CPC Dist-TIMLIF

Solid Ground C 27 MIN
16MM FILM OPTICAL SOUND IND
Traces the development of the minuteman system from its inception to the delivery of the first operational flight to Strategic Air Command. Includes live and static minuteman missile motor firings.
LC NO. FIA67-2338
Prod-THIOKL Dist-THIOKL 1962

Solid Performance Leadership C 18 MIN
3/4 OR 1/2 INCH VIDEO CASSETTE
See series title for descriptive statement.
From The Leadership Link - Fundamentals Of Effective Supervision Series.
Prod-CHSH Dist-DELTAK

Solid Propellant Rocketry C 14 MIN
16MM FILM OPTICAL SOUND
Deals with the early history of the Thiokol Corporation, the production of various solid propellant rocket motors and basic theory with actual rocket motors being both static and flight tested.
Prod-THIOKL Dist-THIOKL 1959

Solid Punch C 27 MIN
16MM FILM OPTICAL SOUND IND
Shows and traces the development of the Army's new generation of missiles and rockets.
LC NO. FIA67-2339
Prod-THIOKL Dist-THIOKL Prodn-FILMEN

Solid Solutions C 35 MIN
3/4 INCH VIDEO CASSETTE C A
See series title for descriptive statement.
From The Elements Of Metallurgy Series.
LC NO. 81-706194
Prod-AMCEE Dist-AMCEE 1980

Solid Solutions C 45 MIN
3/4 OR 1/2 INCH VIDEO CASSETTE PRO
See series title for descriptive statement.
From The Elements Of Metallurgy Series.
Prod-ICSINT Dist-ICSINT

Solid State Electronics C 17 MIN
16MM FILM, 3/4 OR 1/2 IN VIDEO IND
Explains basic semiconductor theory. Shows types of atomic bonds. Discusses majority and minority carriers.
From The Introduction To Solid State Electronics Series. Chapter 1
LC NO. 80-707259
Prod-TAT Dist-TAT 1980

Solid State Electronics (Spanish) C 17 MIN
3/4 OR 1/2 INCH VIDEO CASSETTE IND
Explains basic semiconductor theory. Shows types of atomic bonds. Discusses majority and minority carriers.
From The Introduction To Solid State Electronics (Spanish) Series. Chapter 1
Prod-TAT Dist-TAT

Solid State Electronics—A Series
IND
Describes the basics of solid state electronics.
Prod-TAT Dist-TAT 1980

Amplifier Applications 019 MIN
Full-Wave Rectifiers, Heat Sinks, Filters, 016 MIN
Oscillators, Modulators, Demodulators 016 MIN
Solid State Electronics 017 MIN
Special Purpose Semiconductors 018 MIN
Transistor Amplifiers 018 MIN
Transistors, Semiconductor Diodes, Half-Wave 016 MIN

Solid State Principles B 26 MIN
16MM FILM, 3/4 OR 1/2 IN VIDEO
Identifies the relative energy level of electrons and identifies chemically active and chemically stable atoms. Defines electron pair band and lattice structure and differentiates between conductor, semiconductor and insulator. Describes the effect of donor and acceptor atoms on chemically stable lattice structures and defines and identifies P and N type materials. (Kinescope)
Prod-USAF Dist-USNAC 1969

Solid Waste C 30 MIN
3/4 OR 1/2 INCH VIDEO CASSETTE C
Discusses the origins and volume of solid waste material, methods of recycling waste, waste disposal methods and costs and the economic and political obstacles to recycling.
From The Living Environment Series.
Prod-DALCCD Dist-DALCCD

Solid-State Devices, Tape 1 - Basic Electronics And Diodes C 60 MIN
3/4 OR 1/2 INCH VIDEO CASSETTE IND
See series title for descriptive statement.
From The Electrical Equipment Maintenance Series.
Prod-ITCORP Dist-ITCORP

Solid-State Devices, Tape 1 - Basic-Electronics And Diodes (Spanish) C 60 MIN
3/4 OR 1/2 INCH VIDEO CASSETTE IND
See series title for descriptive statement.
From The Electrical Equipment Maintenance (Spanish) Series.
Prod-ITCORP Dist-ITCORP

Solid-State Devices, Tape 2 - Rectifiers And Power Supplies C 60 MIN
3/4 OR 1/2 INCH VIDEO CASSETTE IND
See series title for descriptive statement.
From The Electrical Equipment Maintenance Series.
Prod-ITCORP Dist-ITCORP

Solid-State Devices, Tape 2 - Rectifiers And-Power Supplies (Spanish) C 60 MIN
3/4 OR 1/2 INCH VIDEO CASSETTE IND
See series title for descriptive statement.
From The Electrical Equipment Maintenance (Spanish) Series.
Prod-ITCORP Dist-ITCORP

Solid-State Devices, Tape 3 - Transistor Theory And Testing, Silicon Controlled... C 60 MIN
3/4 OR 1/2 INCH VIDEO CASSETTE IND
Complete title reads Solid-State Devices, Tape 3 Transistor Theory And Testing, Silicon Controlled Rectifiers And Triacs. Provides training in electrical equipment maintenance.
From The Electrical Equipment Maintenance Series.
Prod-ITCORP Dist-ITCORP

Solid-State Devices, Tape 3 - Transistor-Theory And Testing, Silicon Controlled... C 60 MIN
3/4 OR 1/2 INCH VIDEO CASSETTE IND
Complete title reads Solid-State Devices, Tape 3 Transistor Theory And Testing, Silicon Controlled Rectifiers And Triacs (Spanish). Provides training in electrical equipment maintenance.
From The Electrical Equipment Maintenance (Spanish) Series.
Prod-ITCORP Dist-ITCORP

Solid-State Devices, Tape 4 - Oscilloscope Operation, Soldering And Troubleshooting... C 60 MIN
3/4 OR 1/2 INCH VIDEO CASSETTE IND
Complete title reads Solid-State Devices, Tape 4 Oscilloscope Operation, Soldering And Troubleshooting Solid-State Devices. Provides training in electrical equipment maintenance.
From The Electrical Equipment Maintenance Series.
Prod-ITCORP Dist-ITCORP

Solid-State Devices, Tape 4 - Oscilloscope-Operation, Soldering And Troubleshooting... C 60 MIN
3/4 OR 1/2 INCH VIDEO CASSETTE IND
Complete title reads Solid-State Devices, Tape 4 Oscilloscope Operation, Soldering And Troubleshooting Solid-State Devices (Spanish). Provides training in electrical equipment maintenance.
From The Electrical Equipment Maintenance (Spanish) Series.
Prod-ITCORP Dist-ITCORP

Solidarity C 11 MIN
16MM FILM OPTICAL SOUND
Commemorates a demonstration by workers at Dare Foods Ltd, a cookie factory in Kitchner, ontario. Presents an organizer's speech on the labor situation.
LC NO. 74-702767
Prod-WIELNJ Dist-CANFDC 1973

Solidification C 30 MIN
3/4 OR 1/2 INCH VIDEO CASSETTE PRO
Examines the details of solidification with particular attention to the redistribution of solute in the solidification of alloys.
From The Elements Of Physical Metallurgy Series.
Prod-AMCEE Dist-AMCEE

Solidification Of Metals C 35 MIN
3/4 INCH VIDEO CASSETTE C A
See series title for descriptive statement.
From The Elements Of Metallurgy Series.
LC NO. 81-706194
Prod-AMCEE Dist-AMCEE 1980

Solidification Of Metals C 45 MIN
3/4 OR 1/2 INCH VIDEO CASSETTE PRO
See series title for descriptive statement.
From The Elements Of Metallurgy Series.
Prod-ICSINT Dist-ICSINT

Solids B 15 MIN
2 INCH VIDEOTAPE P
See series title for descriptive statement.
From The Just Inquisitive Series. No. 4
Prod-EOPS Dist-GPITVL Prodn-KOACTV

Solids - Liquids C 14 MIN
3/4 OR 1/2 INCH VIDEO CASSETTE P
Gives experience in classifying solids versus liquids.
From The Hands On, Grade 2 - Lollipops, Loops, Etc Series. Unit 3 - Classifying
Prod-WHROTV Dist-AITECH 1975

Soliloquy Of A River C 19 MIN
16MM FILM OPTICAL SOUND I-C A
Tells the story of a river with emphasis on its continuing beauty and on the life in and around a stream during the changing seasons of the year.
LC NO. 70-702873
Prod-HDP Dist-AVEXP 1969

Soliloquy Of A River C 26 MIN
16MM FILM OPTICAL SOUND P-C A
Presents the story of a river from its spring resurgence, running through forests and meadows to its struggle for life as it moves past a city. Shows the river under the water and along its shores and how it slowly turns into a polluted waterway.
From The Audubon Wildlife Theatre Series.
LC NO. 70-709408
Prod-KEGPL Dist-AVEXP 1969

Solitary Man, The B 5 MIN
16MM FILM OPTICAL SOUND H-C A
A modern interpretation of Psalm 6 using the dramatization about a dejected, unemployed man and a little boy who gives him a toy doll.
From The Song Of The Ages Series.
LC NO. 70-702119
Prod-FAMLYT Dist-FAMLYT 1964

Solitary Man, The C 96 MIN
3/4 OR 1/2 INCH VIDEO CASSETTE H-C A
Reveals that Dave Keyes' happiness over his promotion and raise is shattered when he discovers that his wife wants a divorce. Explores the children's reactions, Dave's attempts at reconciliation and the manner in which he constructs a new life for himself. Stars Earl Holliman and Carrie Snodgrass.
Prod-TIMLIF Dist-TIMLIF 1982

Solitary Nodule Of The Thyroid C 21 MIN
16MM FILM OPTICAL SOUND PRO
Demonstrates a technique for excision of a thyroid nodule. Reviews the role of malignancy in such nodules, their diagnosis and management.
Prod-ACYDGD Dist-ACY 1964

Solitary Thyroid Nodule, The C 21 MIN
16MM FILM OPTICAL SOUND PRO
Makes a plea for the removal of the solitary nodule by complete lobectomy. Explains that occult lymphatic involvement which occurs with thyroid tumors may be recognized by careful exploration and judicious biopsy. Presents the thyroid lymphatic pathways and the operative procedure in a typical case.
Prod-ACYDGD Dist-ACY 1961

Solitary Wasps C 13 MIN
16MM FILM, 3/4 OR 1/2 IN VIDEO I-J
Shows wasps excavating and building their nests, laying eggs and providing for their young.
From The Discovering Insects Series.
Prod-MORALL Dist-MTI 1982

Solo C 15 MIN
16MM FILM, 3/4 OR 1/2 IN VIDEO
Portrays the efforts and exhilarations that are experienced by the solo mountain climber. Filmed in Mexico, the United States and Canada.
Prod-PFP Dist-PFP 1971

Solo C 29 MIN
3/4 INCH VIDEO CASSETTE
Presents a video dance piece by James Byrne of five dance solos designed specifically for video.
Prod-EAI Dist-EAI

Solo - Alone Versus Lonely C 15 MIN
16MM FILM, 3/4 OR 1/2 IN VIDEO J-H R
Describes Ben's loneliness and boredom while staying on his grandfather's farm. Tells how he eventually learns the difference between alone and lonely.
From The On The Level Series.
LC NO. 81-706940
Prod-EDFCEN Dist-AITECH 1980

Solo - Behind The Scenes C 12 MIN
16MM FILM, 3/4 OR 1/2 IN VIDEO
Features an account of the making of the motion picture Solo.
Prod-PFP Dist-PFP 1973

Solo Basic C 28 MIN
16MM FILM, 3/4 OR 1/2 IN VIDEO J-C A
Demonstrates the fundamental paddling positions, strokes and turns of solo canoeing.
From The Path Of The Paddle Series.
Prod-NFBC Dist-NFBC 1978

Solo Survival C 11 MIN
16MM FILM, 3/4 OR 1/2 IN VIDEO
Shows how a solitary hiker loses his bearings and becomes lost. Emphasizes the importance of proper hiking equipment.
From The Outdoor Education Mountaineering Series.
Prod-MORLAT Dist-SF 1973

Solo Whitewater C 28 MIN
3/4 OR 1/2 INCH VIDEO CASSETTE J-C A
Shows how a lone canoeist can read the surface of the water to determine what's underneath. Explains how to maneuver the canoe through the deepest channels and survive the swim if a canoeist wipes out.
From The Path Of The Paddle Series.
Prod-NFBC Dist-NFBC 1977

Solo-Chorus Songs, Pt 1 C 15 MIN
3/4 OR 1/2 INCH VIDEO CASSETTE P
Describes the form of the solo-chorus song and the relationship between dotted and flagged notes. Presents the songs Hoosen Johnny, I Caught A Rabbit and Michael Row The Boat Ashore.
From The Song Sampler Series.
LC NO. 81-707033
Prod-JCITV Dist-GPITVL 1981

Solo-Chorus Songs, Pt 2 C 15 MIN
3/4 OR 1/2 INCH VIDEO CASSETTE P
Describes the form of the solo-chorus song and the relationship between dotted and flagged notes. Presents the songs Hoosen Johnny, I Caught A Rabbit and Michael Row The Boat Ashore.
From The Song Sampler Series.
LC NO. 81-707033
Prod-JCITV Dist-GPITVL 1981

Solos And Ensembles B 29 MIN
2 INCH VIDEOTAPE
See series title for descriptive statement.
From The American Band Goes Symphonic Series.
Prod-WGTV Dist-PUBTEL

Solubility And Optochine Tests For Streptococcus Pneumoniae C 8 MIN
16MM FILM OPTICAL SOUND
Demonstrates the differentiation of streptococcus pneumoniae from other species by the optochin test or by the addition of sodium desoxycholate.
LC NO. 74-705660
Prod-NMAC Dist-USNAC 1969

Solution And Interpretation B 33 MIN
3/4 OR 1/2 INCH VIDEO CASSETTE
See series title for descriptive statement.
From The Nonlinear Vibrations Series.
Prod-MIOT Dist-MIOT

Solution Methods For Calculation Of Frequencies And Mode Shapes C 58 MIN
3/4 OR 1/2 INCH VIDEO CASSETTE
discusses solution methods for finite element eigen-problems.
From The Finite Element Methods In Engineering Mechanics Series.
Prod-MIOT Dist-MIOT

Solution Of Bent Wire Detour Problem By Children, Monkey And Racoon B 14 MIN
16MM FILM OPTICAL SOUND C T
Shows how to make and present various patterns of bent wire detour problems. Pictures a two-year-old child, a monkey and a raccoon having difficulty in solving simple bent wire detour problems, especially if solution requires that lure be pushed away from subject. Shows that a five-year-old child easily solves complicated problems, an adult monkey can be trained to solve complicated problems and a raccoon succeeds in solving a simple problem after 45 days of practice.
Prod-SDSU Dist-PSUPCR 1959

Solution Of Equations Beyond The Second Degree B 31 MIN
16MM FILM OPTICAL SOUND T
Applies the method of synthetic division to finding the roots of a 4th degree equation. Explains the rule of signs for finding the number of possible roots. Discusses rules for upper and lower bounds on roots.
From The Advanced Algebra Series.
Prod-CALVIN Dist-MLA Prodn-UNIVFI 1960

Solution Of Finite Element Equilibrium Equations In Dynamic Analysis C 56 MIN
3/4 OR 1/2 INCH VIDEO CASSETTE
Discusses solution of dynamic response by direct integration.
From The Finite Element Methods In Engineering Mechanics Series.
Prod-MIOT Dist-MIOT

Solution Of Finite Element Equilibrium Equations In Static Analysis C 60 MIN
3/4 OR 1/2 INCH VIDEO CASSETTE
Discusses solution of finite element equations in static analysis.
From The Finite Element Methods In Engineering Mechanics Series.
Prod-MIOT Dist-MIOT

Solution Of Salts - The Variation Of Solubility With Temperature B 12 MIN
16MM FILM OPTICAL SOUND
Prepares students to develop a detailed experimental procedure to study the effect of temperature on the solubility of salts. Illustrates the factors that influence the solubility of salts and discusses the use of Le Chateliers' principle.
From The Experimental General Chemistry Series.
Prod-MLA Dist-MLA

Solution Of The Linear-Quadratic Problem, The C 47 MIN
3/4 OR 1/2 INCH VIDEO CASSETTE PRO

See series title for descriptive statement.
From The Modern Control Theory - Deterministic Optimal Linear Feedback Series.
Prod-MIOT Dist-MIOT

Solution Preparation C 19 MIN
3/4 OR 1/2 INCH VIDEO CASSETTE
Demonstrates the preparation of four different solutions. Shows how to choose appropriate equipment and techniques.
From The General Chemistry Laboratory Techniques Series.
Prod-UCEMC Dist-UCEMC

Solutions C 13 MIN
16MM FILM, 3/4 OR 1/2 IN VIDEO J-H
Presents experiments demonstrating various characteristics of a chemical solution.
Prod-GAKKEN Dist-PHENIX 1969

Solutions (Ionic And Molecular) (2nd Ed) C 23 MIN
16MM FILM, 3/4 OR 1/2 IN VIDEO J-C
Explores the chemical nature of a solution and what happens when it forms. Illustrates the role of electrostatic forces. Shows Brownian movement, saturation, molarity and why some substances won't dissolve in others.
From The Chemistry Series.
Prod-CORF Dist-CORF

Solutions And Projections C 30 MIN
3/4 OR 1/2 INCH VIDEO CASSETTE C
Suggests some of the brighter possibilities for the coming generations on earth without attempting to project a specific future for mankind.
From The Living Environment Series.
Prod-DALCCD Dist-DALCCD

Solutions In Communications - Introductory Lesson C 30 MIN
2 INCH VIDEOTAPE T
From The Solutions In Communicating Series.
Prod-SCCOE Dist-SCCOE

Solutions In Communications—A Series
T
Designed to provide information and skills for teachers working with Mexican-American children experiencing language difficulties. Contains nine 30-minute programs.
Prod-KTEHTV Dist-SCCOE

Solutions In Communications—A Series
T
Provides knowledge and skills for teachers working with Mexican-American children experiencing language difficulties.
Prod-SCCOE Dist-SCCOE

Air Bubble, The	30 MIN
Difficult 'TH' Sound, The	30 MIN
Introduction Of 'SCHWA,' An	30 MIN
New Look At 'Jack Be Nimble,' A	30 MIN
Other Pieces Of The Puzzle	30 MIN
Solutions In Communications - Introductory	30 MIN
Spanish Smootheners	30 MIN
Thirty Demons	30 MIN
Troubles With 'S,' The - Initial 'S'	30 MIN

Solutions Of Lyophilic Colloids, Examples Of Macromolecules C 55 MIN
3/4 OR 1/2 INCH VIDEO CASSETTE
See series title for descriptive statement.
From The Colloid And Surface Chemistry - Lyophilic Colloids Series.
Prod-KALMIA Dist-KALMIA

Solutions To Images C 30 MIN
3/4 OR 1/2 INCH VIDEO CASSETTE J-H
Contains a technical survey of the major photographic processes, beginning with the daguerrotype.
From The Developing Image Series.
Prod-CTI Dist-CTI

Solutions To Pollution C 17 MIN
16MM FILM OPTICAL SOUND P-C
Discusses a few solutions to cleaning up our polluted environment.
LC NO. 72-715409
Prod-ACA Dist-ACA 1971

Solutions To Vandalism C 35 MIN
16MM FILM, 3/4 OR 1/2 IN VIDEO H-C A
Describes successful vandalism prevention programs in six U S towns, cities and counties. Includes comments by Birch Bayh.
Prod-RNBWP Dist-PEREN 1978

Solvents C
3/4 OR 1/2 INCH VIDEO CASSETTE
Concentrates on the health and safety precautions to take when working with solvents.
From The Chemsafe Series.
Prod-BNA Dist-BNA

Solving A Problem With Sedation / The Routine Administration Of Drugs / Admissions... C 14 MIN
3/4 OR 1/2 INCH VIDEO CASSETTE
Dramatizes the use of tranquilizers, other medication and the need for human interaction in nursing homes.
From The It Can't Be Home - Nursing Series.
Prod-IVCH Dist-IVCH

Solving AX Equals B C 17 MIN
3/4 INCH VIDEO CASSETTE
See series title for descriptive statement.
From The Basic Math Skills Series. Proportions
Prod-TELSTR Dist-TELSTR

Solving Calculus Problems I C 39 MIN
3/4 OR 1/2 INCH VIDEO CASSETTE C
See series title for descriptive statement.
From The Artificial Intelligence, Pt 1 - Fundamental Concepts Series.
Prod-MIOT Dist-AMCEE

Solving Calculus Problems I C 45 MIN
3/4 OR 1/2 INCH VIDEO CASSETTE PRO
Presents a fundamental paradigm - heuristic search through goal trees. Shows how heuristics can be used to measure difficulty and focus attention.
From The Artificial Intelligence - Pt 1, Fundamental Concepts Series.
Prod-MIOT Dist-MIOT

Solving Calculus Problems II C 25 MIN
3/4 OR 1/2 INCH VIDEO CASSETTE C
See series title for descriptive statement.
From The Artificial Intelligence, Pt 1 - Fundamental Concepts Series.
Prod-MIOT Dist-AMCEE

Solving Calculus Problems II C 45 MIN
3/4 OR 1/2 INCH VIDEO CASSETTE PRO
Features importance of experiment, alternative ways to measure performance. Presents searching alternatives - depth first, breadth first, and best first - and what understanding does to the appearance of intelligence.
From The Artificial Intelligence - Pt 1, Fundamental Concepts Series.
Prod-MIOT Dist-MIOT

Solving Electrical Problems C 12 MIN
3/4 OR 1/2 INCH VIDEO CASSETTE
Addresses the solutions to electrical problems. Covers power generation and distribution, service entrance equipment, fuses and circuit breakers.
From The Developing Troubleshooting Skills Series.
Prod-TPCTRA Dist-TPCTRA

Solving Employee Conflict C 15 MIN
3/4 OR 1/2 INCH VIDEO CASSETTE
Discusses conflict between two subordinates and between a supervisor and a subordinate, and suggests ways to develop patience and insight, while using sound judgment to handle personal conflict. Explains how to ask the right questions to determine the real reasons for the conflict, develop good listening skills, differentiate between giving advice and providing sound counsel, develop patience, use candor in dealing with conflict, use behavior modification in conflict situations, and resolve conflict in a healthy, positive manner where everyone wins.
Prod-CREMED Dist-DELTAK

Solving Equations Of Fractional Form B 30 MIN
16MM FILM OPTICAL SOUND H
Stresses the importance of properly handling equations in which X appears in the denominator in order that a solution does not make the denominator equal to zero. Presents techniques for manipulating fractional equations. Formulates and solves a typical work problem.
From The Intermediate Algebra Series.
Prod-CALVIN Dist-MLA Prodn-UNIVFI 1959

Solving Everday Problems C
3/4 OR 1/2 INCH VIDEO CASSETTE
Demonstrates the principles of rational-emotive therapy with a group of youngsters.
Prod-IRL Dist-IRL

Solving Mechanical Problems C 12 MIN
3/4 OR 1/2 INCH VIDEO CASSETTE
Addresses the solutions to a variety of mechanical problems such as bearing problems, pump problems, heating, ventilating and air conditioning.
From The Developing Troubleshooting Skills Series.
Prod-TPCTRA Dist-TPCTRA

Solving Money Problems C 15 MIN
3/4 INCH VIDEO CASSETTE P
Reviews addition and subtraction of two-digit numerals by using problems involving money and illustrates how to make change.
From The Math Factory, Module VI - Money Series.
Prod-MAETEL Dist-GPITVL 1973

Solving Problems C 30 MIN
3/4 OR 1/2 INCH VIDEO CASSETTE A
Shows ways a manager can handle a highly challenging job and the outside world while maintaining a sense of well-being. Covers the manager's role and responsibility in controling the stress-related aspects of relationships among staff members.
From The Stress Management - A Positive Strategy Series. Pt 4
LC NO. 82-706501
Prod-TIMLIF Dist-TIMLIF 1982

Solving Problems Creatively C 44 MIN
16MM FILM, 3/4 OR 1/2 IN VIDEO C A
Offers a training program in problem solving designed to stimulate creativity in resolving management problems and differences. Shows which techniques work best and makes participants aware that there is no one method of solving a problem.
LC NO. 81-707291
Prod-MGHT Dist-CRMP 1981

Solving Problems With The Quadratic Formula B 29 MIN
16MM FILM OPTICAL SOUND H
Uses the quadratic formula to solve for the roots of a quadratic equation. Describes three methods for extracting square roots of numbers—the square root algorithm, the slide rule and tables of square roots. Also shows the use of tables of cube roots.
From The Advanced Algebra Series.
Prod-CALVIN Dist-MLA Prodn-UNIVFI 1960

Solving Proportions In Fractions And Decimals C 10 MIN
3/4 INCH VIDEO CASSETTE
See series title for descriptive statement.
From The Basic Math Skills Series. Proportions
Prod-TELSTR Dist-TELSTR

Solving Proportions In Whole Numbers C 15 MIN
3/4 INCH VIDEO CASSETTE
See series title for descriptive statement.
From The Basic Math Skills Series. Proportions
Prod-TELSTR Dist-TELSTR

Solving Simultaneous Equations B
16MM FILM OPTICAL SOUND
Discusses the problem of solving simultaneous equations, using the engineering of the Concorde as an example.
Prod-OPENU Dist-OPENU

Solving Simultaneous Linear Equations B 29 MIN
16MM FILM OPTICAL SOUND H
Shows graphical solutions of two unknowns, X and Y. Explains that the unknowns may be subject to pointvalue conditions or to those conditions that can be expressed as linear equations and which appear as straight lines. Discusses the concept of simultaneous solution of two straight lines.
From The Intermediate Algebra Series.
Prod-CALVIN Dist-MLA Prodn-UNIVFI 1959

Solving The Energy Problem C 20 MIN
16MM FILM, 3/4 OR 1/2 IN VIDEO J-H
Traces the search for alternative sources of energy, now that stocks of coal, oil and natural gas are running short.
From The Exploring Science Series.
Prod-BBCTV Dist-FI 1982

Solving The Linear Equations L(y)–0 - Constant Coefficients B 19 MIN
3/4 OR 1/2 INCH VIDEO CASSETTE
See series title for descriptive statement.
From The Calculus Of Differential Equations Series.
Prod-MIOT Dist-MIOT

Solving The Quadratic Equation, Pt 1 C 45 MIN
2 INCH VIDEOTAPE
See series title for descriptive statement.
From The Fundamentals Of Mathematics (2nd Ed.) Unit III - Linear And Quadratic Functions Series.
Prod-CHITVC Dist-GPITVL

Solving The Quadratic Equation, Pt 2 C 45 MIN
2 INCH VIDEOTAPE
See series title for descriptive statement.
From The Fundamentals Of Mathematics (2nd Ed.) Unit III - Linear And Quadratic Functions Series.
Prod-CHITVC Dist-GPITVL

Solving Travel Problems C 22 MIN
16MM FILM OPTICAL SOUND I-H
Describes how handicapped passengers can respond to such typical travel problems as being late, missing the train or bus, being lost and getting hassled. Includes who to ask for help and the importance of being alert and staying calm.
Prod-PARPRO Dist-PARPRO

Solving Verbal Problems In Mathematics C 21 MIN
16MM FILM OPTICAL SOUND
Shows effective ways to promote verbal problem solving skills. Intersperses examples of teachers and pupils in action, using various problem solving techniques with examples of actual work that results from the use of multiple approaches.
From The Project On Interpreting Mathematics Education Research Series.
LC NO. 74-705661
Prod-USOE Dist-USNAC 1970

Solzhenitsyn's Children Are Making A Lot Of Noise In Paris C 88 MIN
16MM FILM, 3/4 OR 1/2 IN VIDEO C A
Looks at the New Philosophers, former European leftist activists whose thinking has been radically changed by Alexander Solzhenitsyn. Debates whether they will now influence the electorate decisively.
Prod-NFBC Dist-NFBC 1978

Soma Touch C 12 MIN
16MM FILM, 3/4 OR 1/2 IN VIDEO C A
Shows a dancer and artist share his masturbatory experience to orgasm and relaxing with good feeling.
Prod-NATSF Dist-MMRC

Somalia C 26 MIN
16MM FILM OPTICAL SOUND J-C A
Describes the geographical features of Ethiopia and tells about the customs, manners, morals, religions and vocations of the people living there.
LC NO. 72-701204
Prod-AVED Dist-AVED Prodn-FISC 1968

Somalia C 28 MIN
3/4 INCH VIDEOTAPE
Interviews a Somalian ambassador the United Nations. Discusses the refugee problem in Somalia. Hosted by Marilyn Perry. Includes a film clip.
From The International Byline Series.
Prod-PERRYM Dist-PERRYM

Somatic Consequences Of Emotional Starvation In Infants B 30 MIN
16MM FILM OPTICAL SOUND C T
Compares children raised in families with those in a foundling home. Illustrates that the emotional deprivation of the institutionalized children results in bodily retardation and other ill effects.
From The Film Studies Of The Psychoanalytic Research Project On Problems In Infancy Series.
Prod-SPITZ Dist-NYU 1949

Somatization - Possible Sexual Etiology C 30 MIN
3/4 OR 1/2 INCH VIDEO CASSETTE PRO
Shows patients presenting vague physical complaints whose underlying cause may be sex-related. Illustrates physicians' approaches to uncovering the interpersonal and sexual problems which may be presented as physical symptoms. Includes a thorough physical examination and appropriate tests by the physician in their treatment plan, and how the final diagnosis is arrived at through a process of elimination. Illustrates several common physical symptoms which may mask a sexual concern.
Prod-HSCIC Dist-HSCIC

Somatoform And Dissociative Disorders C 70 MIN
3/4 OR 1/2 INCH VIDEO CASSETTE PRO
Explains possible causes, symptoms, and treatment of the somatoform disorders.
From The Psychiatry Learning System, Pt 2 - Disorders Series.
Prod-HSCIC Dist-HSCIC 1982

Some African Diseases C 14 MIN
16MM FILM, 3/4 OR 1/2 IN VIDEO
Discusses symptoms and treatment of seven African tropical diseases.
Prod-UCEMC Dist-UCEMC

Some African Tropical Diseases C 15 MIN
16MM FILM OPTICAL SOUND
Depicts patients from various parts of Africa exhibiting signs and symptoms of schistosomiasis mansoni, yaws, African sleeping sickness, leprosy, kala azar and kawashlorkor. Presents diagrammatic representations of the epidemiology or etiology of each disease.
LC NO. FIA56-1101
Prod-MARJOM Dist-UCLA 1956

Some Afrikaners B 14 MIN
16MM FILM OPTICAL SOUND H-C A
Examines the white South African's ties to the land, his covenant with God and his determined persistence. Emphasizes the rural foundations of the Afrikaner. Based on the book entitled Some Afrikaners. Photographed by David Goldblatt.
LC NO. 76-703921
Prod-BFPS Dist-BFPS 1976

Some American Feminists C 56 MIN
16MM FILM, 3/4 OR 1/2 IN VIDEO H-C A
Explores the women's movements for equal rights by interviewing such feminists as Ti-Grace Atkinson, Rita Mae Brown, Betty Friedan, Margo Jefferson, Lila Karp and Kate Millett.
Prod-NFBC Dist-MOKIN 1980

Some Analytical Tools C 45 MIN
3/4 OR 1/2 INCH VIDEO CASSETTE
Describes some of the analytic tools used in the study of economics.
From The Economic Perspectives Series.
Prod-MDCPB Dist-MDCPB

Some Are More Equal Than Others B 40 MIN
16MM FILM, 3/4 OR 1/2 IN VIDEO H-C A
Considers the legal treatment of ethnic minorities, focusing on an inequitable bail system and discriminatory practices in jury selection.
Prod-CBSNEW Dist-CAROUF

Some Basic Differences In Newborn Infants During The Lying-In Period B 23 MIN
16MM FILM SILENT C T
Presents actual records of children from moment of birth to show the difference in activity and reactions to presentation, removal and restoration of objects of gratification. Emphasizes the importance in the child's total development and its mother's emotional adjustment to it.
From The Film Studies On Integrated Development Series.
Prod-FRIWOL Dist-NYU 1944

Some Basic Signs For Communicating With Deaf Patients C 10 MIN
3/4 OR 1/2 INCH VIDEO CASSETTE PRO
Presents short language course for nurses and doctors to learn simple medical sign to communicate with patients. Partially signed.
Prod-GALCO Dist-GALCO 1980

Some Beginnings Of Social Psychiatry B 14 MIN
16MM FILM OPTICAL SOUND PRO
Dr Erich Lindemann, professor emeritus of Harvard Medical School, lectures on community psychiatry. He describes the development of the field and names the persons who influenced his professional concern with predicament studies.
LC NO. FI68-252
Prod-HMS Dist-HMS Prodn-MASON 1966

Some Behavior Characteristics Of A Human And A Chimpanzee Infant In The Same Environment B 19 MIN
16MM FILM SILENT C T
Compares the general behavior of a normal human infant between the ages of 10 and 14.5 months with the be havior of a chimpanzee companion between the ages of 7.5 months and 12 months, both develop in typical human civilized surroundings. Illustrates six phases of behavioral development--upright walking, affectionate behavior toward adult, strength, indoor and outriding vehicles.
From The Ape And Child Series. Part 1
Prod-PSUPCR Dist-PSUPCR 1932

Some Blends Of S C 15 MIN
3/4 INCH VIDEO CASSETTE P
Explores various consonant blends of s, including SP, SPL, ST, SN, SL, SW and SM.
From The New Talking Shop Series.
Prod-BSPTV Dist-GPITVL 1978

Some Call It Greed C 51 MIN
16MM FILM, 3/4 OR 1/2 IN VIDEO J-C A
Describes the contributions of men such as J P Morgan, Andrew Carnegie, J Swift, Henry Ford and Alfred Sloan, whose drive for profit helped to make the United States the most productive economy in the world.
Prod-FORBES Dist-LCOA 1980

Some Call It Software C 10 MIN
16MM FILM OPTICAL SOUND
Shows how people assemble the instructions which enable computers to function and to help solve problems. Illustrates traffic control by computer.
LC NO. 72-700598
Prod-IBUSMA Dist-MTP 1972

Some Children Need Special Care C 14 MIN
3/4 OR 1/2 INCH VIDEO CASSETTE PRO
Gives helpful suggestions for assisting the handicapped child to develop and maintain good oral health habits.
Prod-AMDA Dist-AMDA 1979

Some Don't C 8 MIN
16MM FILM OPTICAL SOUND H-C A
Presents a subjective documentary film exemplifying man's desperate craving for female sensuality.
Prod-CFS Dist-CFS 1967

Some Examples Of Hypnotic Behavior B 11 MIN
16MM FILM SILENT C T
An experiment to demonstrate the affects of hypnosis on behavior induces illusions and hallucinations. Tests of depth of trance show that painful stimuli are ignored. Examples of regression, with tests, are shown and may be compared with the behavior of a normal child. Sensory selection and agnosia writing are illustrated along with immediate post-hypnotic disorientation and gradual reorientation.
Prod-PSUPCR Dist-PSUPCR 1946

Some Flowers Of The Narcissus - Frank Lloyd Wright C 22 MIN
16MM FILM OPTICAL SOUND C
Pictures four churches designed by Frank Lloyd Wright from 1906 to 1961, showing his prolific imagination, innovations, changing forms and constant daring.
LC NO. FIA67-1148
Prod-MARTNG Dist-RADIM 1967

Some Friendly Insects C 5 MIN
16MM FILM, 3/4 OR 1/2 IN VIDEO P-I
Explores through up-close photography the characteristics of several harmless insects.
From The Wonder Walks Series.
Prod-EBEC Dist-EBEC 1971

Some Functional Problems Of The Hemiplegic Patient C 11 MIN
16MM FILM MAGNETIC SOUND PRO
Explains the problems of the hemiplegic patient in carrying out daily activities like coming to a sitting position, transferring from wheelchair to bed, moving from wheelchair to toilet, going from chair to tub and dressing.
LC NO. 72-700642
Prod-KRI Dist-KRI 1965

Some General Principles Of Biliary Tract Surgery C 28 MIN
16MM FILM OPTICAL SOUND PRO
Demonstrates some anatomical features of the extrahepatic biliary tract and some technical aspects of surgeries of the gallbladder and bile ducts.
Prod-ACYDGD Dist-ACY 1961

Some General Reactions Of A Human And A Chimpanzee Infant After 6 Months In The Same... B 17 MIN
16MM FILM SILENT C T
Compares the non-experimental behavior of a human infant, age 16 to 19 months and a chimpanzee, age 13.5 to 16.5 months, after six months in the same environment. Shows nine comparisons, upright walking, reaction to colored picture book, difference in climbing ability, eating with spoon, drinking from glass, beginning cooperative play, pointing to parts of the body, imitation of scribbling of experimenter and affectionate behavior toward each other.
From The Ape And Child Series. Part 4
Prod-PSUPCR Dist-PSUPCR 1932

Some Justice C 60 MIN
16MM FILM, 3/4 OR 1/2 IN VIDEO C A
Explains that Germanicus' death has so roused Rome that not even the arranged suicide of Piso can take popular pressure off Tiberius.
From The I, Claudius Series. Number 6
Prod-BBCTV Dist-FI 1977

Some Like It Cold C 11 MIN
16MM FILM, 3/4 OR 1/2 IN VIDEO P
Uses boys and girls and amusing animal characters tasting hot and cold foods and examining hot and cold weather as a framework for understanding new word concepts, including eat, drink, hot, cold, good, best and open.
From The Reading And Word Play Series.
Prod-PEDF Dist-AIMS 1976

Some Like It Hot C 121 MIN
16MM FILM OPTICAL SOUND
Stars Jack Lemmon and Tony Curtis as a pair of musicians on the run from the mob. Tells how they dress as women and join an all-girl band. Directed by Billy Wilder.
Prod-UNKNWN Dist-UAE 1959

Some Misconceptions About Language, Pt 1 C 30 MIN
3/4 OR 1/2 INCH VIDEO CASSETTE C
See series title for descriptive statement.
From The Language And Meaning Series.
Prod-WUSFTV Dist-GPITVL 1983

Some Misconceptions About Language, Pt 2 C 30 MIN
3/4 OR 1/2 INCH VIDEO CASSETTE C
See series title for descriptive statement.
From The Language And Meaning Series.
Prod-WUSFTV Dist-GPITVL 1983

Some Observations Concerning The Phenomenology Of Oral Behavior In Small Infants B 20 MIN
16MM FILM SILENT C T
A documentation of variations in oral behavior in a group of infants under 24 weeks of age. Shows that mouth movements depend on neuromuscular maturation, different oral patterns and personal modifications.
From The Infant Psychology Series.
Prod-MENF Dist-NYU Prodn-ESCLEI 1951

Some Of My Best Friends Are Bottomless Dancers C 18 MIN
16MM FILM OPTICAL SOUND C A
Presents a cinema-verite study of Roman Balladine, the ex-choreographer for the Follies Bergere.
Prod-UWFKD Dist-UWFKD

Some Of Our Schoolmates Are Blind C 20 MIN
16MM FILM OPTICAL SOUND T
Describes the education of blind sighted children in a public elementary school in Temple City, California, pointing out how the blind child becomes identified with his peers and with the total school program. Shows the blind children in regular classroom work, on the playground and in sessions where special teachers meet special curriculum needs, such as the teaching of Braille.
LC NO. FIA65-1226
Prod-AFB Dist-AFB 1960

Some Of The Presidents' Men C 59 MIN
3/4 OR 1/2 INCH VIDEO CASSETTE
Features four former White House Press Secretaries giving their versions of the major events and decisions made by the Presidents they served. Participants include Pierre Salinger, George Reedy, Ron Ziegler and Ron Nessen.
Prod-KCTSTV Dist-PBS 1978

Some Of The Things That Go On Out There C 30 MIN
3/4 OR 1/2 INCH VIDEO CASSETTE H-C A
Focuses on adolescence, the time of experimentation, tension, growing and changing. Explores the range of parent-youth relationships.
Prod-PEREHR Dist-MMRC

Some Of These Days C 60 MIN
3/4 OR 1/2 INCH VIDEO CASSETTE
Profiles four women grappling with the process of aging in America. Uses the device of cross-cuttting between their present lives and their memories.
Prod-MEDIPR Dist-MEDIPR 1980

Some Of Your Best Friends C 40 MIN
16MM FILM OPTICAL SOUND
Documents the Gay Liberation Movement. Contains interviews with articulate gay civil rights leaders with various parades and demonstrations in protest of gays. Presents the case for homosexuality as an alternate life style.
LC NO. 72-702423
Prod-USC Dist-USC 1972

Some Of Your Bits Ain't Nice C 11 MIN
16MM FILM - VIDEO, ALL FORMATS J-H A
Presents an animated program about two teenagers that takes a humorous approach to the need to keep hands, hair, teeth, feet, body and clothes clean.
Prod-PEREN Dist-PEREN

Some Other Things To Think About C 28 MIN
3/4 OR 1/2 INCH VIDEO CASSETTE
Discusses the use of media aids in making effective business-related speeches.
From The Business Of Effective Speaking Series.
Prod-KYTV Dist-KYTV

Some Other Time C 27 MIN
16MM FILM OPTICAL SOUND
Depicts the effects of multiple sclerosis on youth, from the initial stages of depression through gradual emotional rehabilitation to that hopeful time when each day is lived for itself. Tells the story of Rob Paterson who has just learned that he has multiple sclerosis and how he learns to cope with MS with the help of Sarah, an MS volunteer.
Prod-MSCAN Dist-NMSS 1974

Some People Just Call It The Lake C 15 MIN
16MM FILM, 3/4 OR 1/2 IN VIDEO
Looks at the contrast in landscape surrounding Lake Mead and the Hoover Dam. Shows how wildlife, cacti and brilliant flowers thrive throughout the Lake Mead area. Highlights the Mojave desert and the tributaries of the Colorado River.
Prod-USNPS Dist-USNAC 1981

Some People Need Special Care C 14 MIN
16MM FILM OPTICAL SOUND A
Emphasizes the assistance the handicapped need to do for them what they may not be able to do for themselves, especially in the area of oral health. Shows both daily personal care and periodic professional treatment occurring in a center for developmentally disabled children.
Prod-AMDA Dist-MTP

Some Personal Learnings About Interpersonal Relationships B 33 MIN
16MM FILM, 3/4 OR 1/2 IN VIDEO H-C A S

Dr Carl R Rogers, founder of client-centered therapy, discusses the 'MYSTERIOUS BUSINESS OF RELATING WITH OTHER HUMAN BEINGS.' He contrasts real communication with superficial and unmeaningful communication.
From The Management Development Series.
Prod-UCLA Dist-UCEMC Prodn-UCLA 1966

Some Principles Of Non-Grading And Team Teaching B 60 MIN
16MM FILM OPTICAL SOUND T
Features Mrs Madeline Hunter, principal of the University Elementary School, responding to the questions and discussing the two most pervasive aspects of the laboratory schoolteam teaching and nongrading.
Prod-UCLA Dist-UCLA 1965

Some Problems C 15 MIN
16MM FILM MAGNETIC SOUND K-C A S
See series title for descriptive statement.
From The PANCOM Beginning Total Communication Program For Hearing Parents Of... Series. Level 2
LC NO. 77-700504
Prod-CSDE Dist-JOYCE Prodn-CSFDF 1977

Some Problems - Associated With Blasting B 60 MIN
3/4 OR 1/2 INCH VIDEO CASSETTE
See series title for descriptive statement.
From The Explosives And Their Use In Mining And Construction Series. Pt 8
Prod-UAZMIC Dist-UAZMIC 1977

Some Questions About Food Storage C 17 MIN
16MM FILM OPTICAL SOUND
Shows the school lunch program managers and workers, the important 'DOS-AND-DON'TS' involved in efficient transportation, store-room layout and proper conditions for dry, cool and freezer types of storage.
Prod-NYSED Dist-NYSED Prodn-SYRCU

Some R-Controlled Vowel Sounds C 20 MIN
3/4 OR 1/2 INCH VIDEO CASSETTE J-H
See series title for descriptive statement.
From The Getting The Word Series. Unit III
Prod-SCETV Dist-AITECH 1974

Some Secrets Should Be Told C 10 MIN
16MM FILM, 3/4 OR 1/2 IN VIDEO K-I
Introduces young children to child sexual abuse, focusing on Susan Linn and her puppets. Communicates the difference between good and bad touching and how to seek help if abused.
Prod-NWDIMF Dist-NWDIMF

Some Secrets Should Be Told C 12 MIN
16MM FILM, 3/4 OR 1/2 IN VIDEO P-I
Uses puppets to portray what child abuse is and distinguish it from normal love and affection. Shows the various people available to help children deal with the problem of child abuse and encourages children to express their feelings and concerns about the sexual abuse issue.
LC NO. 83-706379
Prod-FAMINF Dist-MTI

Some Serious Supervising C 30 MIN
3/4 OR 1/2 INCH VIDEO CASSETTE
See series title for descriptive statement.
From The Effective Supervision Series.
Prod-ERF Dist-DELTAK

Some Simulators C 29 MIN
2 INCH VIDEOTAPE
See series title for descriptive statement.
From The Interface Series.
Prod-KCET Dist-PUBTEL

Some Small Part Of Each Of Us B 30 MIN
16MM FILM OPTICAL SOUND
Presents a reading in observance of the first anniversary of the assassination of John F Kennedy. Includes photographs and speeches of the late President and excerpts from poems and essays written in tribute.
LC NO. FIA65-1102
Prod-JTS Dist-NAAJS Prodn-NBC 1965

Some Suprises B 15 MIN
2 INCH VIDEOTAPE P
See series title for descriptive statement.
From The Sounds Like Magic Series.
Prod-MOEBA Dist-GPITVL Prodn-KYNETV

Some Thoughts On Winter Flying C 21 MIN
3/4 OR 1/2 INCH VIDEO CASSETTE A
Shows experienced aviators in Alaska, bush pilots, air taxi operators and private pilots relating safety precautions for cold weather flying. Covers proper winter pre-flighting, airframe icing, ELT operations, ski flying, survival gear, fueling and 'white-out' conditions.
Prod-FAAFL Dist-AVIMA

Some Thoughts On Winter Flying C 21 MIN
16MM FILM, 3/4 OR 1/2 IN VIDEO
Discusses the hazards and safety precautions associated with cold weather flying. Covers proper winter pre-flighting, air-frame icing, ELT operations, ski flying, survival gear, fueling and the whiteout condition.
LC NO. 81-707209
Prod-USFAA Dist-USNAC 1975

Some To Demonstrate, Some To Destroy C 23 MIN
16MM FILM OPTICAL SOUND H-C A
Reviews the events of moratorium weekend, Nov 15, 1969, and illustrates police preparation and actions in dealing with demonstrators for peace in Vietnam.
LC NO. 77-705668
Prod-WMPD Dist-IACP Prodn-AVS 1970

Some Unsolved Problems In Geometry C 20 MIN
16MM FILM OPTICAL SOUND C
Presents several unsolved geometry problems and shows the solutions for some similar problems. Provides a brief history of the unsolved problems.
LC NO. 72-710646
Prod-MAA Dist-MLA 1970

Somebody Cares C 14 MIN
16MM FILM OPTICAL SOUND A
Tells how an unloved, unwanted young boy is sent to Yellowstone Boys Ranch in Montana, where he finds a home, a school and a sense of direction.
LC NO. 79-700943
Prod-YBR Dist-MARTC Prodn-MARTC 1979

Somebody Stole My Bike C 20 MIN
16MM FILM, 3/4 OR 1/2 IN VIDEO P-J
Presents preventive measures and techniques for protection against bicycle thieves.
Prod-DAVP Dist-AIMS 1972

Somebody Told Me C 24 MIN
16MM FILM, 3/4 OR 1/2 IN VIDEO A
Presents a case history of the installation of a new computer system in an office, and tells what was done to allay the fears of the office staff over the change, and how care was taken to provide the most comfortable and least stressful environment for equipment and staff.
Prod-MILLBK Dist-IFB

Somebody Waiting C 24 MIN
16MM FILM, 3/4 OR 1/2 IN VIDEO H-C A
Examines hospitalized children with severe cerebral dysfunction who are among the most physically, emotionally and mentally handicapped in society and are totally dependent on hospital staff. Shows how these 'HOPELESS CASES' can be helped by environmental stimulation and therapeutic handling and how their response to improved care improves the morale of the staff so that all concerned benefit.
Prod-UCSF Dist-UCEMC 1972

Someday C 11 MIN
16MM FILM OPTICAL SOUND
Depicts a utopian ski experience in Aspen, in Vail and in the Canadian Rockies. Shows a helicopter depositing ski enthusiasts on high slopes.
Prod-COLIM Dist-COLIM

Someday C 9 MIN
16MM FILM, 3/4 OR 1/2 IN VIDEO K
Presents four simple trip ideas. Depicts the supermarket, sailboat ride, zoo and a baseball game in an unusually imaginative way.
Prod-SF Dist-SF 1967

Someday I'll Be Big C 13 MIN
16MM FILM, 3/4 OR 1/2 IN VIDEO K-P
Shows caterpillar eggs about to hatch, with one asking Who Am I? What Am I? Illustrates the two themes with song and dance and ends with new born caterpillars saying 'You'll see, someday I'll be big.'
From The Growing Up With Sandy Offenheim Series.
LC NO. 82-707059
Prod-PLAYTM Dist-BCNFL 1982

Someone Cares C 24 MIN
16MM FILM OPTICAL SOUND K-I
Presents two stories designed to show that the Bible is God's word to his people. Tells of a boy who moves to the country from the city and is sad when his city friend breaks a promise to write. Relates what happens when he meets a Christian neighbor who explains that God never breaks his promise. Describes how a lion teaches a dragon that the Bible contains messages from God.
From The Good Time Growing Show Series. Show 1
Prod-WHTLIN Dist-WHTLIN

Someone Else's Crisis C 25 MIN
16MM FILM, 3/4 OR 1/2 IN VIDEO
Presents five vignettes representing situations a policeman might encounter such as a distressed child, a burglary, an armed robbery, a purse snatching and a rape. Shows the victims before and after their encounter with the police in order to train law enforcement officials to treat victims with empathy and sensitivity.
Prod-MTROLA Dist-MTI Prodn-FILMM 1975

Someone Has To Make It Happen - A Conversation With C Jackson Grayson, Jr C 22 MIN
16MM FILM OPTICAL SOUND
Presents C Jackson Grayson Jr, a director of the U S Price Commission. Discusses inflation and the role of the Federal government in a question and answer format with a group of housewives and professional women.
LC NO. 76-703438
Prod-USOPA Dist-USNA 1972

Someone I Once Knew C 30 MIN
16MM FILM, 3/4 OR 1/2 IN VIDEO H-C A
Looks at Alzheimer's Disease, a progressive mental deterioration which will affect one-sixth of the Americans who live to the age of 65. Offers case studies which reveal the painful changes that victims and their families endure.
LC NO. 83-707196
Prod-METROM Dist-MTI 1983

Someone Is Dying, Who Cares C 30 MIN
3/4 OR 1/2 INCH VIDEO CASSETTE PRO
Studies the feelings and attitudes of health-care team members in their ineteration with a dying patient. Shows interviews with each member conducted by a social worker shortly after the death.
Prod-UARIZ Dist-UARIZ

Someone Like You X 13 MIN
16MM FILM OPTICAL SOUND H-C A
Demonstrates the wide variety of administrative jobs in Girl Scouting, the many different kinds of people needed to fill them and the opportunities in this country and abroad. Shows scenes of Girl Scouting in action.
LC NO. FIA66-622
Prod-GSUSA Dist-VISION Prodn-VISION 1966

Someone New C 4 MIN
16MM FILM, 3/4 OR 1/2 IN VIDEO J-H
Uses animation to present the story of a boy who feels that someone seems to be missing from his house. Shows how he finally realizes that the missing someone is his old self because he has grown and changed. Based on the book Someone New by Charlotte Zolotow.
From The Wrong Way Kid Series.
LC NO. 83-707026
Prod-BOSUST Dist-CF 1983

Someone Special C 28 MIN
16MM FILM OPTICAL SOUND
Shows how a blind youth gains self-confidence and is aided in adjustment after spending his vacation at the Beacon Lodge Camp for the Blind.
LC NO. 73-702203
Prod-GE Dist-GE 1973

Someone Special C 15 MIN
16MM FILM, 3/4 OR 1/2 IN VIDEO I
Introduces David who has a crush on his teacher, Miss Simpson, and dreams that she is in love with him. Depicts his hurt when he realizes that she doesn't place him above the others, but cares for all of her students equally. Explains that crushes are a normal part of growth and psychological development.
From The Inside-Out Series.
LC NO. 73-702449
Prod-NITC Dist-AITECH 1973

Someone To Listen C 30 MIN
3/4 INCH VIDEOTAPE J A
Looks at the work of the Offender Aid and Restoration project in Charlottesville, Virginia, which attempts to provide hope, dignity and job opportunities to prisoners.
Prod-ABCVID Dist-ECUFLM 1979

Someone Who Cares C 11 MIN
16MM FILM OPTICAL SOUND
Depicts the rehabilitation of stroke victims.
LC NO. 74-706248
Prod-USSRS Dist-USNAC 1969

Someone You Know Drinks Too Much C 29 MIN
3/4 OR 1/2 INCH VIDEO CASSETTE
Discusses alcohol and alcoholism in America.
From The Here's To Your Health Series.
Prod-KERA Dist-PBS

Someone's In The Kitchen With Jaime (Captioned) C 25 MIN
16MM FILM, 3/4 OR 1/2 IN VIDEO J-H A
Illustrates how everyone needs home economics skills. Pictures a high school baseball team taking a home economics course.
Prod-LCOA Dist-LCOA Prodn-SPRBRE 1981

Someone's In The Kitchen With Jamie C 25 MIN
16MM FILM, 3/4 OR 1/2 IN VIDEO J-C A
Tells the story of a young high school baseball star who saves his mother's teaching job by getting his teammates to enroll in her home economics class. Recounts the pressure which the coach applies to the young man because of his unmanly pursuits.
Prod-LCOA Dist-LCOA Prodn-SPRBRE 1981

Somersault C 5 MIN
3/4 INCH VIDEO CASSETTE
Shows the New Mexican landscape as seen by a camera and mirrored globe somersaulting around the artist.
From The South-Western Landscapes Series.
Prod-EAI Dist-EAI

Somerset And You - What A Winning Combination C 15 MIN
16MM FILM OPTICAL SOUND
Dramatizes the importance of advertising, sales promotion and packaging. Shows a company spokesman who assumes the role of a liquor distributor salesman for a day.
LC NO. 78-701132
Prod-SMRSTI Dist-SMRSTI Prodn-DOMALB 1978

Something About Movies C 25 MIN
16MM FILM, 3/4 OR 1/2 IN VIDEO I-H
Introduces the art of filmmaking.
Prod-MOKIN Dist-MOKIN

Something About Photography C 9 MIN
16MM FILM, 3/4 OR 1/2 IN VIDEO
Shows the importance of the creative side of still photography. Records pointers and insights of Charles Eames on individual choices and opportunities that one has in the making of each photograph.
Prod-EAMES Dist-PFP 1976

Something Besides Rice C 28 MIN
16MM FILM OPTICAL SOUND
Shows that images we may associate with the word -missionary- need to begin changing as the nature of Christian mission itself changes around the world. Explains that mission today is being transformed into a world-wide sharing of skills and witness by Christians of many lands. Features three missionaries of this new global village who tell their personal stories of new forms of mission in medicine, educa tion, evangelism and social action.
Prod-TRAFCO Dist-ECUFLM

Something Besides Rice C 28 MIN
16MM FILM OPTICAL SOUND
Describes actual church missionary efforts in Nepal, Japan and the United States.
LC NO. 74-700114
Prod-UMCBM Dist-UMCBM 1973

Something Borrowed B 20 MIN
16MM FILM OPTICAL SOUND
Tells how a young woman must decide between maintaining her family ties by living near home, or following her husband to New York.
LC NO. 79-701295
Prod-USC Dist-USC 1979

Something Concrete C 26 MIN
16MM FILM, 3/4 OR 1/2 IN VIDEO IND
Illustrates concrete mix, the formwork and the delivery of the concrete after the formwork is ready. Animated sequences explain hydrostatic pressure. Safety precautions are given and both small and large projects are shown.
Prod-CSAO Dist-IFB

Something Different C 15 MIN
16MM FILM OPTICAL SOUND
Focuses on the new research approaches being used to find methods of ameliorating the effects of cerebral palsy.
LC NO. 77-702145
Prod-UCPA Dist-UCPA 1976

Something Extra C 30 MIN
3/4 OR 1/2 INCH VIDEO CASSETTE H A
Portrays a typing crisis in the office and compares the different responses of two workers, one who wastes no time, thinks ahead, communicates clearly, uses the phone effectively and takes clear messages to avoid interrupting her boss, and one who panics, complains, chats on the phone, leaves it unattended, takes inadequate messages and offends an important visitor.
From The Desk Set II Series
Prod-ERESI Dist-AITECH

Something Extra C 30 MIN
3/4 OR 1/2 INCH VIDEO CASSETTE
See series title for descriptive statement.
From The Desk Set II Series.
Prod-ERF Dist-DELTAK

Something For A Rainy Day C 18 MIN
16MM FILM OPTICAL SOUND
Explores a variety of methods for saving money.
From The Consumer Game Series.
LC NO. 74-70122
Prod-OECA Dist-OECA 1972

Something For Everyone C 28 MIN
16MM FILM, 3/4 OR 1/2 IN VIDEO H-C A
Explains that the basic unit of a Chinese People's Commune is the production team. Introduces the leader of one of these teams and illustrates the entire communal process.
From The Human Face Of China Series.
Prod-FLMAUS Dist-LCOA 1979

Something For Nothing C 30 MIN
3/4 OR 1/2 INCH VIDEO CASSETTE I-J
Discusses decision-making through the story of a shifty film producer that could cost Powerhouse its city license.
From The Powerhouse Series.
LC NO. 83-707183
Prod-EFCVA Dist-GA 1982

Something In The Air C 15 MIN
3/4 OR 1/2 INCH VIDEO CASSETTE I
Surveys the causes and the development of air pollution.
From The Matter And Motion Series. Module Blue
Prod-WHROTV Dist-AITECH 1973

Something More For Christmas C 18 MIN
16MM FILM OPTICAL SOUND
Tells the story of a Christmas tree. Shows the tree as it is grown on a farm by a young girl and follows it to the inner city, where it is bought and decorated by a group of children who want to surprise their mother.
LC NO. 79-701449
Prod-NCTA Dist-SOP Prodn-SOP 1979

Something Nobody Else Has - The Story Of Turtle Trapping In Louisiana C 29 MIN
3/4 OR 1/2 INCH VIDEO CASSETTE J-C A
Examines the plight of alligator snapping turtles, trapped and made into soup.
Prod-BULFRG Dist-BULFRG

Something Of The Danger That Exists C 59 MIN
3/4 OR 1/2 INCH VIDEO CASSETTE
Discusses the pharmacological aspects of alcohol and other drugs. Defines alcoholism as a disease and answers questions.
Prod-ICA Dist-USNPS

Something Queer At The Library C 10 MIN
16MM FILM, 3/4 OR 1/2 IN VIDEO K-I
Tells about two children whose discovery of mutilated library books strangely links up with a dog show in which they have entered their dog. Based on the book Something Queer At The Library by Elizabeth Levy.
From The Contemporary Children's Literature Series.
Prod-BOSUST Dist-CF 1978

Something Short Of Paradise C 91 MIN
16MM FILM OPTICAL SOUND
Describes the on-again, off-again relationship between a theater operator (David Steinberg) and a magazine reporter (Susan Sarandon).
Prod-AIP Dist-SWANK

Something Special - A Navy Career C 14 MIN
16MM FILM OPTICAL SOUND
Deals with careers in the U S Navy. Describes the opportunities in vocational and technical fields open only to high school graduates. Urges students to stay in school.
LC NO. 74-706581
Prod-USN Dist-USNAC 1970

Something To Build On C 22 MIN
16MM FILM OPTICAL SOUND
Presents the plight of farmworkers who are strapped with low income and no available credit and are unable to obtain decent housing. Depicts various housing programs which Rural America, Inc, is sponsoring to try to ease their plight.
LC NO. 79-701057
Prod-RURAM Dist-VICTFL Prodn-VICTFL 1979

Something To Die For C 35 MIN
16MM FILM OPTICAL SOUND
Tells the story of two Chinese high school students, and their desperate search for truth. Through a newly converted Indian youth, they come to a personal knowledge of Jesus Christ.
Prod-YOUTH Dist-GF 1959

Something To Do C 20 MIN
3/4 OR 1/2 INCH VIDEO CASSETTE I
Presents dramatizations of literary works that deal with personal interests and their contributions to growth and development.
From The Readers' Cube Series.
Prod-MDDE Dist-AITECH 1977

Something To Do With Safety Reps C 24 MIN
16MM FILM, 3/4 OR 1/2 IN VIDEO
Presents a fictionalized case study of two newly-trained safety representatives at a factory in England where the appointment of safety representatives is now mandatory. Compares the attitudes of the representatives toward their jobs.
Prod-MILLBK Dist-IFB

Something To Eat C 15 MIN
3/4 INCH VIDEO CASSETTE K-P
Offers an adaptation of the folktale Something To Eat.
From The I Can Read Series.
Prod-WCETTV Dist-GPITVL 1977

Something To Live For C 49 MIN
16MM FILM OPTICAL SOUND R
Explores the experiences of a Chinese-American girl in Hong Kong where she meets a young refugee from mainland China who is devoted to Christianity.
Prod-GF Dist-GF

Something To Work For C 30 MIN
16MM FILM, 3/4 OR 1/2 IN VIDEO PRO
Focuses on the problem of motivation from the management point of view. Reveals what happens when demands are high, when communication is open and when people are given support and encouragement in reaching common goals.
LC NO. FIA66-624
Prod-RTBL Dist-RTBL 1966

Something To Work For (Danish) C 30 MIN
16MM FILM, 3/4 OR 1/2 IN VIDEO PRO
Focuses on the problem of motivation from the management point of view. Reveals what happens when demands are high, when communication is open, and when people are given support and encouragement in reaching common goals.
Prod-RTBL Dist-RTBL 1966

Something To Work For (Dutch) C 30 MIN
16MM FILM, 3/4 OR 1/2 IN VIDEO PRO
Focuses on the problem of motivation from the management point of view. Reveals what happens when demands are high, when communication is open, and when people are given support and encouragement in reaching common goals.
Prod-RTBL Dist-RTBL 1966

Something To Work For (French) C 30 MIN
16MM FILM, 3/4 OR 1/2 IN VIDEO PRO
Focuses on the problem of motivation from the management point of view. Reveals what happens when demands are high, when communication is open, and when people are given support and encouragement in reaching common goals.
Prod-RTBL Dist-RTBL 1966

Something To Work For (German) C 30 MIN
16MM FILM, 3/4 OR 1/2 IN VIDEO PRO
Focuses on the problem of motivation from the management point of view. Reveals what happens when demands are high, when communication is open, and when people are given support and encouragement in reaching common goals.
Prod-RTBL Dist-RTBL 1966

Something To Work For (Japanese) C 30 MIN
16MM FILM, 3/4 OR 1/2 IN VIDEO PRO
Focuses on the problem of motivation from the management point of view. Reveals what happens when demands are high, when communication is open, and when people are given support and encouragement in reaching common goals.
Prod-RTBL Dist-RTBL 1966

Something To Work For (Norwegian) C 30 MIN
16MM FILM, 3/4 OR 1/2 IN VIDEO PRO
Focuses on the problem of motivation from the management point of view. Reveals what happens when demands are high, when communication is open, and when people are given support and encouragement in reaching common goals.
Prod-RTBL Dist-RTBL 1966

Something To Work For (Portuguese) C 30 MIN
16MM FILM, 3/4 OR 1/2 IN VIDEO PRO
Focuses on the problem of motivation from the management point of view. Reveals what happens when demands are high, when communication is open, and when people are given support and encouragement in reaching common goals.
Prod-RTBL Dist-RTBL 1966

Something To Work For (Spanish) X 30 MIN
16MM FILM, 3/4 OR 1/2 IN VIDEO PRO
Focuses on the problem of motivation from the management point of view. Reveals what happens when demands are high, when communication is open and when people are given support and encouragement in reaching common goals.
LC NO. FIA66-624
Prod-RTBL Dist-RTBL 1966

Something To Work For (Swedish) C 30 MIN
16MM FILM, 3/4 OR 1/2 IN VIDEO PRO
Focuses on the problem of motivation from the management point of view. Reveals what happens when demands are high, when communication is open, and when people are given support and encouragement in reaching common goals.
Prod-RTBL Dist-RTBL 1966

Something Ventured C 30 MIN
3/4 OR 1/2 INCH VIDEO CASSETTE I-J
Describes how Bobby's impulsiveness gets him involved with jewel thieves.
From The Powerhouse Series.
LC NO. 83-707184
Prod-EFCVA Dist-GA 1982

Something Wicked This Way Comes C 29 MIN
16MM FILM, 3/4 OR 1/2 IN VIDEO I-H
Reveals that when a stranger known as Mr Dark brings his traveling carnival to a small town, the task of saving family and friends from its destructive clutches falls on the unlikely shoulders of the town librarian. Based on the novel SOMETHING WICKED THIS WAY COMES by Ray Bradbury.
From The Film As Literature, Series 5 Series.
Prod-WDEMCO Dist-WDEMCO 1983

Something Worthwhile C 15 MIN
16MM FILM OPTICAL SOUND
Describes methods of burn prevention and emergency first aid for burns, and presents an example of a cooperative community event designed to call public attention to the importance of fire safety.
LC NO. 79-701490
Prod-MLIC Dist-MTP Prodn-CORASS 1979

Something's Happening To Tom C 15 MIN
16MM FILM OPTICAL SOUND PRO
Presents a case history of a depressive, including his symptoms, diagnosis, therapy and eventual recovery.
LC NO. 81-700491
Prod-CIBA Dist-MTP Prodn-TELTRO 1981

Something's Missing C 8 MIN
16MM FILM OPTICAL SOUND P
See series title for descriptive statement.
From The Mathematics For Elementary School Students - Whole Numbers Series.
LC NO. 73-701839
Prod-DAVFMS Dist-DAVFMS 1974

Sometime Samaritan, The C 50 MIN
16MM FILM OPTICAL SOUND
Features correspondent Michael Maclear investigating the fate of refugees who fled Vietnam to find a new life in Canada. Looks into Canada's erratic refugee policy.
LC NO. 77-702525
Prod-CTV Dist-CTV 1976

Sometimes A Great Notion C 113 MIN
16MM FILM OPTICAL SOUND
Focuses on an Oregon logging family. Stars Paul Newman and Henry Fonda.
Prod-UPCI Dist-TWYMAN 1971

Sometimes A Great Notion C
1/2 IN VIDEO CASSETTE BETA/VHS
Presents Ken Kesey's story about the life of a modern-day lumberjack's family in Oregon. Stars Henry Fonda, Paul Newman and Lee Remick.
Prod-GA Dist-GA

Sometimes I Look At My Life C 79 MIN
16MM FILM, 3/4 OR 1/2 IN VIDEO A
Portrays the film and musical career of Harry Belafonte. Includes his friendship with Paul Robeson, plus scenes of Belafonte performing in Cuba. English language version.
Prod-CUBAFI Dist-CNEMAG 1982

Sometimes I Wonder C 30 MIN
16MM FILM, 3/4 OR 1/2 IN VIDEO P-I A
Tells the story of two children faced with the birth of a new brother who run away from home to their grandmother's ranch. Features the birth of a new colt. Looks at life, death, love and family bonds.
Prod-MEDVEN Dist-MTI

Sometimes I Wonder Who I Am B 5 MIN
16MM FILM OPTICAL SOUND H
Tells about a young woman's struggle to decide whether she is a wife, a mother, a lover, or something else.
LC NO. 76-700262
Prod-BRNDNL Dist-NEWDAY 1970

Sometimes It's OK To Tattle C 12 MIN
16MM FILM, 3/4 OR 1/2 IN VIDEO P-I
Employs puppets to emphasize the community resources available to assist children if they are victims of child abuse.
Prod-FAMINF Dist-MTI

Sometimes It's Okay To Tattle C 12 MIN
16MM FILM, 3/4 OR 1/2 IN VIDEO K-I
Helps children identify and cope with general child abuse, featuring Susan Linn and her puppets. A companion piece to the film Some Secrets Should Be Told.
Prod-NWDIMF Dist-NWDIMF

Sometimes It's Turkey, Sometimes It's Feathers C 14 MIN
3/4 OR 1/2 INCH VIDEO CASSETTE P
See series title for descriptive statement.
From The Magic Pages Series.
Prod-KLVXTV Dist-AITECH 1976

Sometimes Sad But Mostly Glad C 10 MIN
3/4 OR 1/2 INCH VIDEO CASSETTE K-P
Focuses on the ability to recognize feelings in others.
From The Book, Look And Listen Series.
Prod-MDDE Dist-AITECH 1977

Sometimes Vowel, A B 15 MIN
2 INCH VIDEOTAPE P
See series title for descriptive statement.
From The Listen And Say - Vowels Series.
Prod-GPITVL Dist-GPITVL

Somewhere Before X 27 MIN
16MM FILM, 3/4 OR 1/2 IN VIDEO H-C A
Tells the story of a young unmarried girl who is rushed to the hospital in labor and deserted by the father of her child. Explains how her despair slowly begins to kill her unborn child. Stars Cindy Williams, Ron Howard and Mariette Hartley.
From The Insight Series.
Prod-PAULST Dist-PAULST

Somewhere Between X 50 MIN
3/4 OR 1/2 INCH VIDEO CASSETTE
Unfolds the controversy surrounding laws which discriminate against Indian women against the background of the personal experiences of five Indian women. Reveals the alienation of these women when they are forced to live apart from their communities because of the change of their legal status as Indians.
Prod-HYPMG Dist-CANFDW

Somewhere To Go C 40 MIN
16MM FILM OPTICAL SOUND
Presents a study taped over a period of six months at meetings of a group of Down's Syndrome children and their parents who were part of a hospital research project studying the children's health and development.
Prod-CHNMC Dist-EDC 1978

Sommerfeld Effect, The B 32 MIN
3/4 OR 1/2 INCH VIDEO CASSETTE
See series title for descriptive statement.
From The Nonlinear Vibrations Series.
Prod-MIOT Dist-MIOT

Sommerfuglen Onsker Tillykke (Happy Birthday From A Butterfly C 29 MIN
16MM FILM OPTICAL SOUND
A Danish language film. Presents a fairy tale of a child's birthday.
Prod-STATNS Dist-STATNS 1968

Son Of Lono C 11 MIN
16MM FILM OPTICAL SOUND J-C
Portrays the adventures of Captain Cook's cabin boy in 1779 Hawaii.
Prod-CINEPC Dist-CINEPC

Son Of Monte Cristo, The B 102 MIN
16MM FILM OPTICAL SOUND
Stars Louis Hayward as the son of the Count of Monte Cristo, foiling a scheme to take over the duchy of Lichtenberg.
Prod-UAA Dist-KITPAR 1940

Son Of Oil C 15 MIN
3/4 OR 1/2 INCH VIDEO CASSETTE
Presents a political conversation where one thing leads to another.
Prod-KITCHN Dist-KITCHN

Son Of Oil C 16 MIN
3/4 OR 1/2 INCH VIDEO CASSETTE
Records a tale of violence and capitalism in America woven with the artist's style.
Prod-EAI Dist-EAI

Son Of The Ocean C 28 MIN
16MM FILM, 3/4 OR 1/2 IN VIDEO H-C A
Follows a riverboat journey on the Yangtze River. Shows some of China's most beautiful, fertile and underdeveloped regions as well as some of its poorest and most populous regions.
From The Human Face Of China Series.
Prod-FLMAUS Dist-LCOA 1979

Son Of The Sheik B 27 MIN
16MM FILM OPTICAL SOUND
Presents the 1926 production of 'SON OF THE SHEIK,' a typical adventure of the golden age of movies. Stars Rudolph Valentino.
From The History Of The Motion Picture Series.
Prod-SF Dist-KILLIS 1960

Son Of The Sheik B 72 MIN
16MM FILM SILENT
Presents a Rudolph Valentino romance, where he plays a dual role of father and son.
Prod-UAA Dist-KITPAR 1926

Son Of The Sheik B 62 MIN
1/2 IN VIDEO CASSETTE (BETA)
Stars Rudolph Valentino as Ahmed, a desert sheik who wants to seek revenge after a dancing girl betrays him. Tells how he learns of her innocence and goes after the band of desert renegades who exploited her.
Prod-UNKNWN Dist-BHAWK 1926

Son Of The Sheik, The B 68 MIN
16MM FILM SILENT
Tells the story of Ahmed, a desert sheik who believes himself betrayed by a dancing girl, whereupon he abducts her and exacts his own form of revenge. Stars Rudolph Valentino and Vilma Banky. Directed by George Fitzmaurice.
Prod-UNKNWN Dist-KILLIS 1926

Son Of... C 15 MIN
2 INCH VIDEOTAPE
See series title for descriptive statement.
From The Umbrella Series.
Prod-KETCTV Dist-PUBTEL

Son Pantalon C 10 MIN
3/4 OR 1/2 INCH VIDEO CASSETTE
Focuses on clothing and possessive adjectives.
From The Salut - French Language Lessons Series.
Prod-BCNFL Dist-BCNFL 1984

Son Worshipers, The C 30 MIN
16MM FILM OPTICAL SOUND
Portrays the new American phenomenon of kids 'Turned On' for Jesus.
Prod-GF Dist-GF Prodn-YOUTH 1972

Sonata For Pen, Brush And Ruler C 11 MIN
16MM FILM OPTICAL SOUND
Expresses the use of color and image and the geometric-visceral patterns of the traditional direct-drawn film.
Prod-SPINLB Dist-FMCOOP 1968

Sonata In A Flat, Opus 110 C 59 MIN
3/4 INCH VIDEO CASSETTE
See series title for descriptive statement.
From The Beethoven - The Last Sonatas Series.
Prod-KQEDTV Dist-PUBTEL

Sonata In C Minor, Opus 111 C 59 MIN
3/4 INCH VIDEO CASSETTE
See series title for descriptive statement.
From The Beethoven - The Last Sonatas Series.
Prod-KQEDTV Dist-PUBTEL

Sonata In E Flat, Opus 109 C 58 MIN
3/4 INCH VIDEO CASSETTE
See series title for descriptive statement.
From The Beethoven - The Last Sonatas Series.
Prod-KQEDTV Dist-PUBTEL

Sonata-Allegro Forms, The - Stability Versus Instability, I B 45 MIN
2 INCH VIDEOTAPE C
See series title for descriptive statement.
From The General Humanities Series. Unit 3 - The Auditory Arts
Prod-CHITVC Dist-GPITVL Prodn-WTTWTV

Sonata-Allegro Forms, The - Stability Versus Instability, II B 45 MIN
2 INCH VIDEOTAPE C
See series title for descriptive statement.
From The General Humanities Series. Unit 3 - The Auditory Arts
Prod-CHITVC Dist-GPITVL Prodn-WTTWTV

Sonauto C 9 MIN
16MM FILM OPTICAL SOUND
Presents an experimental film without narration in which highway lines and roadside curbs move in time to original music. Includes captions.
LC NO. 77-700313
Prod-CANFDC Dist-CANFDC 1976

Song Accompaniment, Pt 1 C 29 MIN
2 INCH VIDEOTAPE
See series title for descriptive statement.
From The Playing The Guitar II Series.
Prod-KCET Dist-PUBTEL

Song Accompaniment, Pt 2 C 29 MIN
2 INCH VIDEOTAPE
See series title for descriptive statement.
From The Playing The Guitar II Series.
Prod-KCET Dist-PUBTEL

Song And Dance Routines C 30 MIN
3/4 OR 1/2 INCH VIDEO CASSETTE
Provides lessons in sign language on various song and dance routines.
From The Signing With Cindy Series.
Prod-KUHTTV Dist-MDCPB

Song At Twilight - An Essay On Aging C 59 MIN
3/4 OR 1/2 INCH VIDEO CASSETTE
Presents a documentary obout aging which explores the social, political, physical and economic problems of older people.
Prod-KOCETV Dist-PBS 1977

Song Bag-A Series
K-P
Includes 32 15-minute music lessons given by folk singer Tony Saletan. Invites children to hear and learn a variety of songs selected from the best of our folk tradition, and encourages children to participate in rhythmic movement, creativity, careful listening, expressive singing and the playing of simple instruments.
Prod-WESTEL Dist-WESTEL

Song Dog C
16MM FILM OPTICAL SOUND
Documents the life cycle of the coyote in Yellowstone National Park. Features a coyote pack in an environment where large mammals are abundant and human influence is minimal.
Prod-TRAILF Dist-TRAILF

Song Dog C 27 MIN
1/2 IN VIDEO CASSETTE BETA/VHS A
Describes life cycle of coyotes in Yellowstone National Park, including rearing of young, social behavior, hunting prey and communications. Relates coyotes to an environment consisting of large mammals.
LC NO. 84-707245
Prod-LANDTF Dist-LANDTF 1984

Song For Dead Warriors, A C 25 MIN
16MM FILM OPTICAL SOUND
Deals with the people and events surrounding the occupation of Wounded Knee by members of the American Indian Movement in 1973.
Prod-NEWTIM Dist-NEWTIM

Song For My Sister B 45 MIN
16MM FILM OPTICAL SOUND
Features the realistic portrayal of a teenager and her brother in their wanderings through New York City.
Prod-NYU Dist-NYU

Song For Prince Charlie, A C 18 MIN
16MM FILM, 3/4 OR 1/2 IN VIDEO I-H
Presents the story of the Stuart Rising in 1745 in Scotland. Documents the Scot's traditional use of song for expression of their national sentiments and to present stories.
Prod-SF Dist-SF 1973

Song Is Love, The C 54 MIN
16MM FILM OPTICAL SOUND
Various scenes picture Peter Yarrow, Paul Stookey and Mary Travers as individual people and also show how they relate to the singing group of Peter, Paul and Mary.
LC NO. 74-702867
Prod-MILPRO Dist-MILPRO 1970

Song Of Beauty, A C 12 MIN
16MM FILM, 3/4 OR 1/2 IN VIDEO P-I
Takes the viewer on a voyage with a group of elementary school students as they encounter beauty in nature, in each other and finally in themselves.
From The Bloomin' Human Series.
Prod-PAULST Dist-MEDIAG 1975

Song Of Light C 45 MIN
16MM FILM OPTICAL SOUND
Gives hope of recovery to crippled children by showing the actual life of the workers and children at the Fukushima Crippled Children's Home in Japan. Depicts the necessary education that is needed while children are being rehabilitated.
Prod-ISWELC Dist-ISWELC

Song Of Molasses C 23 MIN
16MM FILM, 3/4 OR 1/2 IN VIDEO I-H
Presents a re-creation of some of the personal issues and decisions that American colonists were forced to confront as their concerns increasingly diverged from the interests of England. Focuses on Job Smith, a ship's captain and distillery owner, who becomes caught in the middle of the new, rigid enforcement of the molasses tax.
From The Decades Of Decision - The American Revolution News.
LC NO. 80-706346
Prod-NGS Dist-NGS 1975

Song Of Myself, Pt 1 C 30 MIN
2 INCH VIDEOTAPE J-H
See series title for descriptive statement.
From The From Franklin To Frost - Walt Whitman Series.
Prod-MPATI Dist-GPITVL

Song Of Myself, Pt 2 C 30 MIN
2 INCH VIDEOTAPE J-H
See series title for descriptive statement.
From The From Franklin To Frost - Walt Whitman Series.
Prod-MPATI Dist-GPITVL

Song Of Senegal C 27 MIN
16MM FILM OPTICAL SOUND
Offers an overall view of the country of Senegal.
LC NO. 80-701454
Prod-MCDO Dist-MCDO 1980

Song Of Senegal (French) C 27 MIN
16MM FILM OPTICAL SOUND
Offers an overall view of the country of Senegal.
Prod-MCDO Dist-MCDO 1980

Song Of Songs, The C 10 MIN
16MM FILM OPTICAL SOUND
Uses the poetry from the Old Testament book Song of Solomon as dialog for a contemporary dramatic presentation.
LC NO. 75-700160
Prod-MARTC Dist-MARTC 1974

Song Of The Canary C 58 MIN
16MM FILM - 3/4 IN VIDEO H-C A
Focuses on the health hazards faced by employees of the textile and petrochemical industries.
LC NO. 79-706912
Prod-MANTEC Dist-NEWDAY 1979

Song Of The Earth, The - Jean Lurcat C 17 MIN
16MM FILM OPTICAL SOUND C
Describes the last tapestry made by the French artist Jean Lurcat, pointing out the themes of man's precarious mastery over nature and the opposition of evil and good. Pictures the artist at work and shows various aspects of his daily life.
LC NO. FIA67-1142
Prod-MRCNTN Dist-RADIM 1967

Song Of The Lark, The B 30 MIN
16MM FILM OPTICAL SOUND H-C A

Dramatizes the life of the first Baron Edmond de Rothschild, who contributed to the development of a viable economy in Palestine. (Kinescope)
From The Eternal Light Series.
LC NO. 76-700965
Prod-JTS Dist-NAAJS 1967

Song Of The North C
3/4 OR 1/2 INCH VIDEO CASSETTE
Focuses on Alaska as spring, summer and fall run together in a single three-month season. Shows some of the wildlife that thrive in that environment.
Prod-NWLDPR Dist-NWLDPR

Song Of The Paddle C 41 MIN
16MM FILM - 3/4 IN VIDEO J-C A
Follows a family canoeing across the waterways of Canada.
LC NO. 79-706322
Prod-NFBC Dist-NFBC 1979

Song Of The Prairie C 19 MIN
16MM FILM, 3/4 OR 1/2 IN VIDEO
Uses puppets to parody American westerns, specifically John Ford's film Stagecoach.
Prod-CON Dist-TEXFLM 1951

Song Of The Punjab B 19 MIN
16MM FILM OPTICAL SOUND I-C A
Presents the story of a Punjabi soldier returning home, getting married and then leaving home to rejoin his regiment. Features folk songs to tell the story, as sung on various occasions.
Prod-INDIA Dist-NEDINF

Song Of The Sandy Mooring C 24 MIN
16MM FILM - 3/4 IN VIDEO
Presents nature scenes of national parks in the United States. Issued in 1971 as a motion picture.
LC NO. 79-706160
Prod-USNPS Dist-USNAC 1979

Song Of The Snows C 12 MIN
16MM FILM OPTICAL SOUND I-C A
Shows pictures of the Himalayas, which span the entire northern frontiers of India for 1600 miles. Portrays the majestic heights of the Himalayan peaks and depicts how snow is transformed into glaciers, which give birth to such rivers as the Ganga, Yamuna, Brahmaputra and Kosi, the arteries which sustain life in the Indian plains.
Prod-INDIA Dist-NEDINF

Song Of The Wolves - A Profile Of Wildlife Sculpture C 45 MIN
16MM FILM OPTICAL SOUND A
Shows wildlife artist Wally Shoop as he creates two life-sized bronze sculptures of wolves. Describes the lost wax casting process and the artist's efforts to educate the general public concerning the plight of wild animals.
LC NO. 82-700159
Prod-BORMAS Dist-BORMAS 1982

Song Recital C 29 MIN
2 INCH VIDEOTAPE
See series title for descriptive statement.
From The Playing The Guitar II Series.
Prod-KCET Dist-PUBTEL

Song Remains The Same, The C 136 MIN
16MM FILM OPTICAL SOUND
Depicts the 1973 Madison Square Garden appearance by the rock group Led Zeppelin.
Prod-WB Dist-SWANK

Song Sampler - Review C 15 MIN
3/4 OR 1/2 INCH VIDEO CASSETTE P
Reviews the songs presented in the Song Sampler Series.
From The Song Sampler Series.
LC NO. 81-707070
Prod-JCITV Dist-GPITVL 1981

Song Sampler—A Series
P
Discusses the joys of singing and describes the basics of rhythm and notation. Focuses on American folk music.
Prod-JCITV Dist-GPITVL 1979

American Indian Music, Pt 1 15 MIN
American Indian Music, Pt 2 15 MIN
Animal Songs, Pt 1 15 MIN
Animal Songs, Pt 2 15 MIN
Ballads, Pt 1 15 MIN
Ballads, Pt 2 15 MIN
Cowboy Music, Pt 1 15 MIN
Cowboy Music, Pt 2 15 MIN
Dialog Songs, Pt 1 15 MIN
Dialog Songs, Pt 2 15 MIN
Favorite Folk Songs, Pt 1 15 MIN
Favorite Folk Songs, Pt 2 15 MIN
February Songs, Pt 1 15 MIN
February Songs, Pt 2 15 MIN
Fun And Nonsense, Pt 1 15 MIN
Fun And Nonsense, Pt 2 15 MIN
Game Songs, Pt 1 15 MIN
Game Songs, Pt 2 15 MIN
Holiday Music, Pt 1 15 MIN
Holiday Music, Pt 2 15 MIN
More About Rhythm, Pt 1 15 MIN
More About Rhythm, Pt 2 15 MIN
Mountain Songs, Pt 1 15 MIN
Mountain Songs, Pt 2 15 MIN
Railroad Songs, Pt 1 15 MIN
Railroad Songs, Pt 2 15 MIN
Review 15 MIN
Rhythms, Pt 1 15 MIN
Rhythms, Pt 2 15 MIN
Rounds, Pt 1 15 MIN
Rounds, Pt 2 15 MIN
Sing Along 15 MIN
Solo-Chorus Songs, Pt 1 15 MIN
Solo-Chorus Songs, Pt 2 15 MIN
Spirituals, Pt 1 15 MIN
Spirituals, Pt 2 15 MIN

Song Writer—A Series

Features Jerry H Bilik of the University of Michigan School of Music, a famous composer and arranger, songs.
Prod-UMITV Dist-UMITV 1977

Making A Melody 029 MIN
Making Arrangements 029 MIN
Post-Natal Care Of A Song 029 MIN
That Good Old Harmony 029 MIN
Words And Music 029 MIN

Songbook, The C 30 MIN
3/4 OR 1/2 INCH VIDEO CASSETTE I
Dramatizes contemporary Franco-American life in New England. Focuses on prejudice.
From The Franco File Series.
Prod-WENHTV Dist-GPITVL

Songs Alive C
16MM FILM, 3/4 OR 1/2 IN VIDEO
Uses traditional songs from the English-speaking world as a focus for language learning, at an intermediate level.
Prod-NORTNJ Dist-NORTNJ

Songs And Symphony C 29 MIN
3/4 INCH VIDEO CASSETTE
Demonstrates the interesting differences between composing songs and symphonies.
From The Music Shop Series.
Prod-UMITV Dist-UMITV 1974

Songs And Tales Of Yesteryear C 25 MIN
16MM FILM OPTICAL SOUND
Presents old songs and stories, sung and told by the early Canadian prairie pioneers.
LC NO. 76-701056
Prod-FIARTS Dist-CANFDC 1974

Songs For A Garden C 14 MIN
3/4 OR 1/2 INCH VIDEO CASSETTE P
See series title for descriptive statement.
From The Strawberry Square Series.
Prod-NEITV Dist-AITECH 1982

Songs From Papua New Guinea C 20 MIN
16MM FILM, 3/4 OR 1/2 IN VIDEO
Features 13 selections of tribal music from Papua, New Guinea.
Prod-UCEMC Dist-UCEMC

Songs From The Soul - The Negro Spiritual C 29 MIN
3/4 INCH VIDEO CASSETTE
Presents a recital of Negro spirituals conducted by Dr Eva Jessye and sung by a small choir of university students.
From The Song Writer Series.
Prod-UMITV Dist-UMITV 1977

Songs Of A Distant Jungle C 20 MIN
16MM FILM, 3/4 OR 1/2 IN VIDEO
Follows an American musician to Papua, New Guinea. Celebrates the universality of music.
Prod-UCEMC Dist-UCEMC

Songs Of Bengal B 11 MIN
16MM FILM OPTICAL SOUND I-C A
Captures the rhythm and pulse of life in a riverside village of Bengal, where songs form part of everyday life. Introduces the fisherman's song and the 'BAUL'S' song, along with the shepherd's flute music.
Prod-INDIA Dist-NEDINF

Songs Of Christmas And Hanukkah I C 14 MIN
3/4 OR 1/2 INCH VIDEO CASSETTE P-I
Presents some Christmas and Hanukkah songs.
From The Music And Me Series.
Prod-WDCNTV Dist-AITECH 1979

Songs Of Christmas And Hanukkah II C 15 MIN
3/4 OR 1/2 INCH VIDEO CASSETTE P-I
Presents some Christmas and Hanukkah songs.
From The Music And Me Series.
Prod-WDCNTV Dist-AITECH 1979

Songs Of Halloween C 15 MIN
3/4 OR 1/2 INCH VIDEO CASSETTE P-I
Presents some Halloween songs.
From The Music And Me Series.
Prod-WDCNTV Dist-AITECH 1979

Songs Of Innocence C 11 MIN
3/4 OR 1/2 INCH VIDEO CASSETTE
Evokes the fleetingness of childhood.
From The Four Songs Series.
Prod-EAI Dist-EAI

Songs Of Maharashtra, Pt 1 B 9 MIN
16MM FILM OPTICAL SOUND H-C A
Compiles the folk songs of Maharashtra, the occasions at which they are sung and their significance in the social life of the people.
Prod-INDIA Dist-NEDINF

Songs Of Maharashtra, Pt 2 B 13 MIN
16MM FILM OPTICAL SOUND H-C A
Compiles the folk songs of Maharashtra, the occasions at which they are sung and their significance in the social life of the people.
Prod-INDIA Dist-NEDINF

Songs Of My Hunter Heart - Laguna Songs And Poems C 34 MIN
3/4 OR 1/2 INCH VIDEO CASSETTE
Continues the oral tradition of the Laguna pueblo life by incorporating contemporary themes into work which retains Pueblo reverence for the spoken word.
From The Words And Place Series.
Prod-CWATER Dist-CWATER

Songs Of Thanksgiving C 15 MIN
3/4 OR 1/2 INCH VIDEO CASSETTE P-I
Presents some Thanksgiving songs.
From The Music And Me Series.
Prod-WDCNTV Dist-AITECH 1979

Songs Of The '80s C 17 MIN
3/4 OR 1/2 INCH VIDEO CASSETTE
Prod-EAI Dist-EAI

Songs Of The Auvergne B 20 MIN
16MM FILM OPTICAL SOUND
Pictures French village life and the countryside. Includes the singing of ancient provincial songs performed by Phyllis Curtin and members of the Boston Symphony Orchestra.
Prod-MORM Dist-RFL 1955

Songs Of The Labor Movement C 30 MIN
16MM FILM OPTICAL SOUND
Features Joe Glazer singing many of the labor songs that are heard at union meetings and conventions across America. Explains how these songs were born out of the bitter struggle to organize unions and issues which sparked long-term strikes.
Prod-UMICH Dist-AFLCIO 1961

Songs Of The West C 6 MIN
16MM FILM OPTICAL SOUND
Uses pictures and songs to trace the early history of the farming pioneers that settled on the Canadian prairies.
LC NO. 76-703083
Prod-FIARTS Dist-FIARTS 1974

Sonia Malkine C 52 MIN
3/4 OR 1/2 INCH VIDEO CASSETTE
Presents Sonia Malkine specializing in songs from France. She sings a French rendition of 'Where Have All the Flowers Gone?'
From The Rainbow Quest Series.
Prod-SEEGER Dist-CWATER

Sonia Malkine On Campus—A Series

Presents French folk singer, Sonia Malkine, on her visits to five Pennsylvania campuses. Focuses on Sonia, who sings and talks to students in both indoor and outdoor settings.
Prod-WITFTV Dist-PUBTEL

Dickinson College - Guest Michael Cooney,
Dickinson College - Guest Michael Cooney, 29 MIN
Franklin And Marshall College - Guest Billy 29 MIN
Franklin And Marshall College - Guest Billy 29 MIN
Lebanon Valley College - Guest Dan Smith, 29 MIN
Lebanon Valley College - Guest Dan Smith, 29 MIN
Millersville State College - Guest Frank 29 MIN
Millersville State College - Guest Frank 29 MIN
Shippensburg State College - Guest Brook 29 MIN
Shippensburg State College - Guest Brook 29 MIN

Sonic Boom - Thunder From The Blue Skies C 14 MIN
3/4 INCH VIDEO CASSETTE
Describes the phenomena of shock waves which produce sonic booms. Discusses the national security needs for military aircraft to make super-sonic practice runs over metropolitan areas. Shows how minimum altitude restrictions, scientific research and redesign of aircraft are working to reduce intensity of sonic booms.
Prod-USNAC Dist-USNAC 1972

Sonic Boom And You C 10 MIN
3/4 INCH VIDEO CASSETTE
Describes the sonic boom, the result of an aircraft flying faster than the speed of sounds, its cause and some of its effects.
Prod-USNAC Dist-USNAC 1972

Sonic Boom, The - Sound Waves Through Air C 7 MIN
16MM FILM, 3/4 OR 1/2 IN VIDEO I-H
Examines sound waves created by an airplane traveling at subsonic and supersonic speeds. Explains what causes a sonic boom.
Prod-IFFB Dist-CF 1984

Sonntag Morgen B 11 MIN
16MM FILM SILENT J-C A
Presents candid shots of people's faces moving about, expressing the human experience which has shaped them.
Prod-UWFKD Dist-UWFKD

Sonny Rollins C 37 MIN
16MM FILM - 1/2 IN VIDEO
Features a performance by Sonny Rollins live at Loren.
Prod-RHPSDY Dist-RHPSDY

Sonny Rollins Live C 36 MIN
16MM FILM, 3/4 OR 1/2 IN VIDEO
Presents a live performance by jazz tenor saxophonist Sonny Rollins, supported by Bob Cranshaw on bass, Walter Davis, Jr, on piano, Masuo on guitar and David Lee on drums.
LC NO. 79-706813
Prod-TCBREL Dist-TIMLIF 1979

Sonny Terry - Shoutin' The Blues C 6 MIN
3/4 INCH VIDEO CASSETTE J-C A
Focuses on blues harmonica player Sonny Terry.
LC NO. 80-707165
Prod-AGINP Dist-LAWREN 1976

Sonny Terry - Shoutin' The Blues (2nd Ed) C 6 MIN
16MM FILM OPTICAL SOUND J-C A
Offers a performance by blues harmonica player Sonny Terry.
LC NO. 80-701140
Prod-AGINP Dist-LAWREN 1976

Sonny Terry And Brownie McGhee C 52 MIN
3/4 OR 1/2 INCH VIDEO CASSETTE
Features Sonny Terry, the blind harmonica player and Brownie McGhee on guitar as they trade songs with Pete Seeger.
From The Rainbow Quest Series.
Prod-SEEGER Dist-CWATER

Sonny's Lucky Dream (How To Chase Decay Away) C 14 MIN
16MM FILM OPTICAL SOUND K-P
Illustrates the basic dental health rules, using puppets to dramatize the experiences of a little boy who eats too many sweets, is attacked by the villain decay, and is rescued by the dental health fairy.
LC NO. FIA68-2413
Prod-OHIOSU Dist-OSUMPD 1967

Sonrisas—A Series
I-H
Features bilingual programs portraying everyday problems experienced by children of various Hispanic cultures. Depicts the adventures of a group of children in an urban community center.
Prod-KRLNTV Dist-MDCPB 1979

A Comer 030 MIN
All In Its Proper Time 030 MIN
Artful Dodger, The 030 MIN
Bad Company 030 MIN
Beautiful People 030 MIN
Champ, The 030 MIN
Chance, A 030 MIN
Choice, The 030 MIN
Derecho De Estar 030 MIN
El Curro 030 MIN
Entendimiento 030 MIN
Face The Music 030 MIN
Finder's Keepers 030 MIN
Getting It Together / Tods Juntos 030 MIN
Girl Like That, A 030 MIN
Horse Of Pancho Villa, The 030 MIN
Job Worth Doing, A 030 MIN
La Quinceanera 030 MIN
La Sorpresa 030 MIN
Lagrimas De Apache 030 MIN
Magician, The 030 MIN
Misplaced Goals 030 MIN
My Friend Freddy 030 MIN
Need To Touch, The 030 MIN
Now And Forever 030 MIN
Organization 030 MIN
Oye Depiertate 030 MIN
Pachanga / Camp Out 030 MIN
Place To Be Yourself, A 030 MIN
Problem With Exhaustion 030 MIN
Return, The 030 MIN
Rich Dummy, The 030 MIN
Right Role, The 030 MIN
Room For Us 030 MIN
Sour Grapes 030 MIN
Tomorrow's Leaders 030 MIN
White Dominoes 030 MIN
Winners, The 030 MIN
You Bet Your Burger 030 MIN

Sons And Daughters / Drugs And Booze C 28 MIN
3/4 OR 1/2 INCH VIDEO CASSETTE
Describes what parents can do to understand children's use of alcohol and other drugs. Offers practical advice to parents whose children have already begun to use drugs.
Prod-ROGRSG Dist-ROGRSG

Sons Of Haji Omar C 58 MIN
3/4 OR 1/2 INCH VIDEO CASSETTE
Documents the annual migration, led by the son of a wealthy landowner in northeastern Afghanistan, from the spring lambing camp near Col to the bazaar city of Narin into the rich summer grazing pastures of the Hindu Kush. Chronicles the family and social customs, the religious life and the economic realities of a preindustrial market economy.
Prod-NFBC Dist-PSU

Sons Of The Anzacs 1939-1945 B 79 MIN
16MM FILM OPTICAL SOUND H-C A
Shows the campaigns in which Australians fought in World War II, with special reference to such battles as Tobruk and the Kokoda Trail.
LC NO. 74-709259
Prod-ANAIB Dist-AUIS 1968

Sons Of The Desert B 66 MIN
16MM FILM OPTICAL SOUND
Explains how Laurel and Hardy trick their wives into letting them attend a fraternal convention.
Prod-ROACH Dist-BHAWK 1933

Sons Of The Moon C 25 MIN
16MM FILM, 3/4 OR 1/2 IN VIDEO
Shows that the moon is a key symbol in the cosmology of the Ngas of Nigeria. Traces the moon's influence on the Ngas' work and thought during a single growing season.
Prod-UCEMC Dist-UCEMC

Sony AVC-3260 (Black And White Video Camera) C 7 MIN
3/4 OR 1/2 INCH VIDEO CASSETTE
See series title for descriptive statement.
From The Audio-Visual Skills Modules Series.
Prod-MDCC Dist-MDCC

Sony SLO-320 (Beta Video Recorder) C 6 MIN
3/4 OR 1/2 INCH VIDEO CASSETTE
See series title for descriptive statement.
From The Audio-Visual Skills Modules Series.
Prod-MDCC Dist-MDCC

Sony VO-2610 (U-matic Video Recorder) C 7 MIN
3/4 OR 1/2 INCH VIDEO CASSETTE
See series title for descriptive statement.
From The Audio-Visual Skills Modules Series.
Prod-MDCC Dist-MDCC

Sony 19 Inch Trinitron (Color Television Recorder C 6 MIN
3/4 OR 1/2 INCH VIDEO CASSETTE
See series title for descriptive statement.
From The Audio-Visual Skills Modules Series.
Prod-MDCC Dist-MDCC

Soon There Will Be No More Me C 10 MIN
16MM FILM, 3/4 OR 1/2 IN VIDEO H-C A
Tells the story of a 19-year-old mother who is dying.
Prod-ALSKOG Dist-CF 1972

Sooner The Better, The C 27 MIN
16MM FILM OPTICAL SOUND
Shows how nonsexist education is applied to preschool teaching.
From The Non-Sexist Early Education Films Series.
LC NO. 78-700383
Prod-WAA Dist-THIRD Prodn-SIMONJ 1977

Sooner The Better, The, Pt 1 C 14 MIN
3/4 OR 1/2 INCH VIDEO CASSETTE I
Focuses on physical assessment.
From The Conrad Series.
Prod-SCETV Dist-AITECH 1977

Sooner The Better, The, Pt 2 C 14 MIN
3/4 OR 1/2 INCH VIDEO CASSETTE I
Explores resources for health care.
From The Conrad Series.
Prod-SCETV Dist-AITECH 1977

Soopergoop C 13 MIN
16MM FILM, 3/4 OR 1/2 IN VIDEO P-I
Uses an animated story, about an actor and an advertising man and their deceptive television commercial for a cereal, to present the problem of false advertising and the need for concern about buying habits.
Prod-CF Dist-CF 1976

Soopergoop (Spanish) C 13 MIN
16MM FILM, 3/4 OR 1/2 IN VIDEO P-I
Uses animation to tell a story about two characters who concoct a TV commercial for a sweet cereal. Reveals the selling techniques and commercialism of television.
Prod-CF Dist-CF 1976

Sophia, Wisdom 3 - The Cliffs B 64 MIN
3/4 OR 1/2 INCH VIDEO CASSETTE
Documents the Ontological/Hysteric Theatre.
Prod-KITCHN Dist-KITCHN

Sophisticated Investing C 60 MIN
3/4 OR 1/2 INCH VIDEO CASSETTE
Presents Dr Mary Elizabeth Schlayer talking with moderator Susan Wright about sophisticated investing for women.
From The How To Be A Financially Secure Woman Series.
Prod-KUHTTV Dist-KUHTTV

Sophisticated Vamp C 4 MIN
16MM FILM OPTICAL SOUND J-C
Creates pure color forms which parade across the screen, zooming, then slowly undulating to the accompanying music of a vamp.
Prod-FAYMAN Dist-CFS

Sophocle's Oedipus Tyrannus C 60 MIN
3/4 OR 1/2 INCH VIDEO CASSETTE C
See series title for descriptive statement.
From The Drama - Play, Performance, Perception Series. Module 3
Prod-MDCC Dist-MDCC

Sorcerer C 121 MIN
16MM FILM OPTICAL SOUND
Dramatizes a suicidal mission in which a truckload of nitro must be driven through a South American jungle. Directed by William Friedkin.
Prod-UPCI Dist-SWANK

Sorcerer Of Sounds - The Claude Debussy Story X 30 MIN
2 INCH VIDEOTAPE P-I
Presents a performance of three pieces by Debussy including Pagodas, Violes and Reflections In The Water. Includes a choreographic interpretation of Debussy's Sonata For Flute, Harp and Viola which illustrates the affinity of French painting and music. Features Debussy's interpretation of a prelude from Bach's Well-Tempered Clavier. (Broadcast quality)
From The Masters Of Our Musical Heritage Series. No. 6
Prod-KTCATV Dist-GPITVL

Sorcerer's Apprentice, The C 10 MIN
16MM FILM, 3/4 OR 1/2 IN VIDEO
Presents Mickey Mouse as a sorcerer's apprentice who gives life to inanimate objects to the music of Paul Dukas. Taken from the full-length motion picture Fantasia.
Prod-DISNEY Dist-WDEMCO 1980

Sorcerer's Apprentice, The C 14 MIN
16MM FILM, 3/4 OR 1/2 IN VIDEO P-I
Tells the tale of the sorcerer's apprentice who enchants a broom to carry water for him. Shows how the sorcerer returns in time to prevent a disaster and how the apprentice learns a lesson.
Prod-CORF Dist-CORF 1971

Sorcerer's Apprentice, The C 14 MIN
16MM FILM, 3/4 OR 1/2 IN VIDEO P-I
Presents a musical picture story presenting Lisl Weil as she sketches with bright pastels the story of Paul Dukas' composition. As the music unfolds, Miss Weil interprets the adventures of the sorcerer, his helper and the demonic brooms.
Prod-WWS Dist-WWS 1964

Sorcerer's Apprentice, The C 27 MIN
16MM FILM, 3/4 OR 1/2 IN VIDEO P-J
Tells the story of Spellbinder the Sorcerer, who mistakenly hires a supposedly ignorant boy who uses the sorcerer's own magic to defeat him.
Prod-ROAESO Dist-PFP 1980

Sorcerer's Apprentice, The (French) C 26 MIN
16MM FILM, 3/4 OR 1/2 IN VIDEO P-I
A French language version of the film, The Sorcerer's Apprentice. Relates the tale of young Hans, apprentice to Spellbinder the Sorcerer, whose ability to read the Book of Magic becomes his secret weapon against the Sorcerer's evil powers, and who defeats his wicked master in a duel of magic.
Prod-ROAESO Dist-PFP

Sorcerer's Apprentice, The (Spanish) C 26 MIN
16MM FILM, 3/4 OR 1/2 IN VIDEO P-I
A Spanish language version of the film, The Sorcerer's Apprentice. Relates the tale of young Hans, apprentice to Spellbinder the Sorcerer, whose ability to read the Book of Magic becomes his secret weapon against the Sorcerer's evil powers, and who defeats his wicked master in a duel of magic.
Prod-ROAESO Dist-PFP

Sorcerers, Spells, Suspense C 20 MIN
3/4 OR 1/2 INCH VIDEO CASSETTE I
Presents dramatizations of literary works that deal with ghosts, witches and eerie settings.
From The Readers' Cube Series.
Prod-MDDE Dist-AITECH 1977

Sorcerers, The C 87 MIN
16MM FILM OPTICAL SOUND C A
Stars Boris Karloff, Susan George and Catherine Lacey. Tells the story of a professor who conducts a successful experiment to dominate a young man by mesmeric techniques, only to have the scheme run amuck.
Prod-CINEWO Dist-CINEWO 1967

Sore Throat C 10 MIN
3/4 OR 1/2 INCH VIDEO CASSETTE
Instructs the patient or family about sore throat, including causes, symptoms, control and treatment.
From The Take Care Of Yourself Series.
Prod-UARIZ Dist-UARIZ

Soren Kierkegaard C 57 MIN
16MM FILM, 3/4 OR 1/2 IN VIDEO
Deals with the life and thought of Soren Kierkegaard. Explains how his outlook on life was affected by his physical state and upbringing. Tells how he was drawn to a life of introspection and came to conclude that the only way to know God was to suffer and be scorned and rejected by men. Written and narrated by Malcolm Muggeridge.
From The Third Testament Series.
LC NO. 79-707923
Prod-CANBC Dist-TIMLIF Prodn-RAYTAF 1976

Sorianos, The C 9 MIN
16MM FILM, 3/4 OR 1/2 IN VIDEO H-C A
Focuses on a couple with 16 children. Stresses the togetherness and sharing in a large family.
From The American Family - An Endangered Species Series.
Prod-NBC Dist-FI 1979

Sorrow C 27 MIN
16MM FILM, 3/4 OR 1/2 IN VIDEO
Tells the Hungarian story of two brothers who are left identical sums of money, but one loses his fortune because of the efforts of Sorrow. Reveals that when the poor brother finally gets rid of Sorrow, he becomes wealthy. Shows the other brother releasing Sorrow in the hopes that he will once more make his brother poor, but that Sorrow instead attacks him, punishing him for his envy.
From The Storybook International Series.
Prod-JOU Dist-JOU 1982

Sorrow And The Pity, The B 260 MIN
16MM FILM OPTICAL SOUND H-C A
Examines the occupation of France by the Germans during World War II using reminiscences of individuals and officials involved in the events at the time. Concentrates on the themes of collaboration and resistance.
LC NO. 76-702631
Prod-NPSSRT Dist-CINEMV 1972

Sorrow And The Pity, The B
3/4 OR 1/2 INCH VIDEO CASSETTE
Documents the German occupation of France during World War II.
Prod-IHF Dist-IHF

Sorrows Of Gin, The C 60 MIN
16MM FILM, 3/4 OR 1/2 IN VIDEO H-C A
Centers on an eight-year-old girl's search for a sense of family amid the sophisticated and detached social whirl of her parents' lives. Stars Edward Herrman and Sigourney Weaver. Based on the short story The Sorrows Of Gin by John Cheever.
From The Cheever Short Stories Series.
LC NO. 81-707247
Prod-WNETTV Dist-FI 1979

Sorry, No Vacancy C 27 MIN
16MM FILM OPTICAL SOUND H-C A

A shortened version of the 52 minute film Sorry, No Vacancy. Illustrates the urgent conflict confronting the world between uncontrolled population growth and man's merciless consumption of the planet's dwindling resources.
LC NO. 76-703639
Prod-WILHIT Dist-MALIBU 1974

Sorry, No Vacancy C 52 MIN
16MM FILM OPTICAL SOUND H-C A
Studies the population growth with respect to food production, resource consumption, economic impact and ecological consequence.
LC NO. 73-701721
Prod-WILHIT Dist-WILHIT 1973

Sorter, The C 14 MIN
16MM FILM, 3/4 OR 1/2 IN VIDEO H-C A
Introduces the functioning of the parts of the sorter. Conducts a sorting operation to demonstrate the machine's capacity to read punched cards and to sort alphabetically. Shows how vast amounts of random data can be grouped and organized.
Prod-SF Dist-SF 1968

Sorting Casualties For Treatment And Evacuation C 5 MIN
3/4 OR 1/2 INCH VIDEO CASSETTE PRO
Illustrates procedures for proper sorting (triage) of casualties. Includes steps for determining the type of wound and condition of the patient in order to classify patients for evacuation.
From The EMT Video - Group One Series.
LC NO. 84-706986
Prod-USA Dist-USNAC 1983

Sorting Out Sorting C 30 MIN
16MM FILM, 3/4 OR 1/2 IN VIDEO
Employs computer animation to demonstrate nine computer sorting techniques grouped into insertion sorts, exchange sorts and selection sorts. Compares the efficiency of each sort.
Prod-UTORMC Dist-UTORMC

Sorting Things B 15 MIN
2 INCH VIDEOTAPE I
Discusses the organization and classification of materials.
From The Let's Explore Science Series.
Prod-GPITVL Dist-GPITVL

Sorting Things B 15 MIN
2 INCH VIDEOTAPE I
Studies the organization and classification of materials. (Broadcast quality)
From The Let's Explore Science Series. No. 2
Prod-POPS Dist-GPITVL Prodn-KOAPTV

SOS C 10 MIN
16MM FILM, 3/4 OR 1/2 IN VIDEO
Uses animation to follow the journey of a tenacious SOS signal as it searches the world for someone willing to save an endangered vessel.
Prod-KRATKY Dist-PHENIX 1979

SOS Soap Suds C 3 MIN
3/4 OR 1/2 INCH VIDEO CASSETTE
Shows a classic live television commercial with Durwood Kirby and Garry Moore.
Prod-BROOKC Dist-BROOKC

SOS, An C 5 MIN
3/4 OR 1/2 INCH VIDEO CASSETTE J-H
Shows the correct use of the words 'Past' and 'Passed' and 'Loose' and 'Lose'.
From The Write On, Set 2 Series.
Prod-CTI Dist-CTI

Soto C 15 MIN
16MM FILM, 3/4 OR 1/2 IN VIDEO J-C A
Provides a retrospective of the work of the Venezuelan artist Jesus Raphael Soto.
LC NO. 82-707011
Prod-OOAS Dist-MOMALA 1972

Soto (Spanish) C 15 MIN
16MM FILM, 3/4 OR 1/2 IN VIDEO J-C A
Provides a retrospective review of the work of the Venezuelan artist Jesus Raphael Soto.
Prod-OOAS Dist-MOMALA 1972

Soudain Le Paradis B 13 MIN
16MM FILM OPTICAL SOUND I-H
See series title for descriptive statement.
From The Les Francais Chez Vous Series. Set II, Lesson 25
LC NO. 77-704478
Prod-PEREN Dist-CHLTN 1967

Soul C 30 MIN
3/4 OR 1/2 INCH VIDEO CASSETTE J-H
Looks at the contributions of soul singer Stevie Wonder.
From The From Jumpstreet Series.
Prod-WETATV Dist-GPITVL 1979

Soul City C 2 MIN
16MM FILM OPTICAL SOUND
Uses a hand-tinted animation technique in a sequence of the punk rock group Fleshtones performing the song Soul City.
LC NO. 79-701058
Prod-JONESM Dist-AFA 1979

Soul Of Christmas, The C 58 MIN
3/4 OR 1/2 INCH VIDEO CASSETTE J A
Looks at Christmas Eve service at the Second Christian Church of the Christian Church (Disciples of Christ) in Indianapolis. Shows the diversity of the music and worship experiences of a fast-growing congregation. Shows the excitement and spontaneity of a black worship experience in the United States within the context of a mainstream Protestant denomination.
Prod-ABCNEW Dist-ECUFLM 1981

Soul To Soul C 29 MIN
3/4 INCH VIDEO CASSETTE
Examines the origins of soul music and its important relationship to blues and jazz.
From The Music Shop Series.
Prod-UMITV Dist-UMITV 1974

Souls C 7 MIN
16MM FILM OPTICAL SOUND
Describes an elderly shoe repair proprietor, his philosophy and some of his clients.
LC NO. 76-701482
Prod-CONCOL Dist-CONCOL 1975

Sound B 30 MIN
2 INCH VIDEOTAPE J
See series title for descriptive statement.
From The Investigating The World Of Science, Unit 1 - Matter And Energy Series.
Prod-MPATI Dist-GPITVL

Sound - A First Film C 10 MIN
16MM FILM, 3/4 OR 1/2 IN VIDEO P-I
LC NO. 84-707082
Prod-BARJA Dist-PHENIX 1983

Sound / Noise - Towards A Quieter Environment C 20 MIN
16MM FILM, 3/4 OR 1/2 IN VIDEO
Discusses the effects of noise on human health and behavior. Suggests some facilities and structures which could be designed for a quieter world.
Prod-DOCUA Dist-CNEMAG

Sound About C 11 MIN
16MM FILM, 3/4 OR 1/2 IN VIDEO P
Provides discovery experiences for students in their science study of concepts in sound.
Prod-AIMS Dist-AIMS 1969

Sound About (Spanish) C 11 MIN
16MM FILM, 3/4 OR 1/2 IN VIDEO P-I
Provides discovery experiences in science study of the concepts in sound. Follows two boys and their dog as they walk along a beach and learn about vibrations, pitch and echos.
Prod-CAHILL Dist-AIMS 1967

Sound And Advanced Graphics Capabilities C
3/4 OR 1/2 INCH VIDEO CASSETTE
Explains how to use Professional Authoring Software System (PASS) sound, advanced graphics and video interface facilities to enhance lessons. Introduces the concept of character sets and shows how to use the character set editor.
From The Authoring In PASS Series.
Prod-DELTAK Dist-DELTAK

Sound And Communications B 20 MIN
2 INCH VIDEOTAPE I
See series title for descriptive statement.
From The Science Room Series.
Prod-MCETV Dist-GPITVL Prodn-WVIZTV

Sound And Hearing C 14 MIN
3/4 OR 1/2 INCH VIDEO CASSETTE
Explains in detail how noise can damage the ears. Discusses decibels and sound intensity. Presents principles of hearing protection.
Prod-MEDFAC Dist-MEDFAC 1977

Sound And Hearing C 15 MIN
3/4 OR 1/2 INCH VIDEO CASSETTE P-I
Discusses sound and hearing.
From The Why Series.
Prod-WDCNTV Dist-AITECH 1976

Sound And How It Travels X 11 MIN
16MM FILM, 3/4 OR 1/2 IN VIDEO P
Defines sound and shows that it is caused by vibrations which must travel from their source through a sound medium to be heard. Demonstrates the difference between one sound and another, and reveals some of the important uses of sound.
Prod-EBF Dist-EBEC 1963

Sound And How It Travels (Spanish) C 11 MIN
16MM FILM, 3/4 OR 1/2 IN VIDEO P
Defines sound and shows that it is caused by vibrations. Reveals that vibrations must travel from their source through a sound medium in order to be heard.
Prod-EBEC Dist-EBEC

Sound And Its Effects C 22 MIN
3/4 OR 1/2 INCH VIDEO CASSETTE IND
Begins by defining sound, how it is produced, how it travels and how it is received by a detector. Uses animation to explain wave propagation through various media. Shows air-to-air photography to discuss match numbers and speed of sound. Photography illustrates formation of shock waves in transonic and supersonic flight.
From The Mathematics And Physics Series.
Prod-AVIMA Dist-AVIMA 1980

Sound And Movement C 17 MIN
16MM FILM OPTICAL SOUND J-C A
Illustrates movement improvisations accompanied by sounds of voice, hands and feet and a variety of conventional and unconventional instruments.
Prod-METT Dist-METT 1957

Sound And Movement C 30 MIN
3/4 OR 1/2 INCH VIDEO CASSETTE H-C A
Introduces paralinguistics, the sound of the voice, and kinesics, body movements, as nonverbal communication.
From The Principles of Human Communication Series.
Prod-UMINN Dist-GPITVL 1983

Sound And Moving Pictures C 25 MIN
16MM FILM, 3/4 OR 1/2 IN VIDEO J-C A
Discusses computer animation and art and the use of voice synthesizers.
From The Computer Programme Series. Episode 6
Prod-BBCTV Dist-FI 1982

Sound And The Painter B 6 MIN
16MM FILM OPTICAL SOUND C T
an experimental presentation of paintings with jazz accompaniment. Attempts to catch the visual mood in sound.
Prod-NYU Dist-NYU 1962

Sound And The Story C 26 MIN
16MM FILM OPTICAL SOUND
Demonstrates the production of a high-fidelity record of Tchaikovsky's 'ROMEO AND JULIET' performed by the Boston Symphony Orchestra, directed by Charles Munch.
Prod-RCA Dist-RCA 1956

Sound Application For Video C 30 MIN
3/4 OR 1/2 INCH VIDEO CASSETTE
Demonstrates audio recording equipment and use of sound effects and music tracks. Explains how sound alters mood.
From The Video - A Practical Guide...and More Series.
Prod-VIPUB Dist-VIPUB

Sound Approach, A C 13 MIN
16MM FILM OPTICAL SOUND
Deals with the impact of aviation noise on individuals and communities located near airports. Examines actions being taken by the aviation industry to reduce noise levels.
LC NO. 79-700028
Prod-USFAA Dist-USNAC 1978

Sound Around C 29 MIN
2 INCH VIDEOTAPE
See series title for descriptive statement.
From The Observing Eye Series.
Prod-WGBHTV Dist-PUBTEL

Sound Collector, The C 12 MIN
16MM FILM, 3/4 OR 1/2 IN VIDEO
Presents the story of six-year old Leonard who collects sounds and transforms them into imaginative adventure stories.
LC NO. 83-706633
Prod-NFBC Dist-NFBC 1982

Sound Discrimination Capacity Of The Hearing Impaired C 25 MIN
16MM FILM, 3/4 OR 1/2 IN VIDEO
Describes research conducted at Gallaudet College to explore the discrimination capacity of persons with moderate to severe sensoryneural deafness.
LC NO. 80-707414
Prod-USBEH Dist-USNAC 1980

Sound Film, A C 15 MIN
16MM FILM OPTICAL SOUND
Presents an experiment in layered sound, time and movement within and without the frame.
LC NO. 77-702648
Prod-CANFDC Dist-CANFDC 1976

Sound In The Sea C 30 MIN
3/4 OR 1/2 INCH VIDEO CASSETTE
Focuses on sound waves in the sea. Explains active and passive sonar and the uses of each. Discusses the shadow zone and the deep sound channel. Compares and contrasts the sound produced by sperm whales and humpback whales.
From The Oceanus - The Marine Environment Series. Lesson 22
Prod-SCCON Dist-CDTEL

Sound Is Found All Around C 15 MIN
3/4 INCH VIDEO CASSETTE P
See series title for descriptive statement.
From The I Need To Read Series.
Prod-WCETTV Dist-GPITVL 1975

Sound Level Meter Verification And Data Recording C 9 MIN
1/2 IN VIDEO CASSETTE BETA/VHS
Discusses noise measurement.
Prod-RMI Dist-RMI

Sound Level Meter Verification And Handling C 14 MIN
1/2 IN VIDEO CASSETTE BETA/VHS
Discusses noise measurement.
Prod-RMI Dist-RMI

Sound Motion Picture About Decibels, A C 18 MIN
16MM FILM OPTICAL SOUND
Uses simple experiments to illustrate why some sounds please and others annoy.
Prod-GM Dist-GM

Sound Motion Picture About Decibels, A C 25 MIN
3/4 OR 1/2 INCH VIDEO CASSETTE
Illustrates why some sounds please while others annoy. Investigates industrial and vehicular pollution and reveals some of the research being conducted in these areas.
Prod-HBS Dist-IVCH

Sound Of Dolphins, A C 22 MIN
16MM FILM, 3/4 OR 1/2 IN VIDEO I-C A
A Shortened version of A Sound Of Dolphins. Documents Jacques Cousteau's investigation of the social behavior and vocal communication of two dolphins caught in the waters off the coast of Spain.
From The Undersea World Of Jacques Cousteau Series.
Prod-METROM Dist-CF 1977

Sound Of Dolphins, A C 52 MIN
16MM FILM, 3/4 OR 1/2 IN VIDEO I-C A

Observes the communication system of dolphins. Shows experiments conducted in an ocean enclosure where the whistle/click conversations between a male and a female dolphin are recorded.
From The Undersea World Of Jacques Cousteau Series.
Prod-METROM Dist-CF 1977

Sound Of Flesh, The B 11 MIN
16MM FILM OPTICAL SOUND C A
Presents a satire on modern mores in our society.
Prod-CFS Dist-CFS 1968

Sound Of Miles Davis, The B 28 MIN
16MM FILM OPTICAL SOUND
Tells the story of Miles Davis. Features music written by Miles Davis and includes performances by Dave Brubeck, Gil Evans, Ahmad Jamal and the Miles Davis Sextet.
LC NO. FI68-654
Prod-CBSF Dist-CBSF 1959

Sound Of Music C 29 MIN
2 INCH VIDEOTAPE
See series title for descriptive statement.
From The Observing Eye Series.
Prod-WGBHTV Dist-PUBTEL

Sound Of My Own Name, The C 29 MIN
16MM FILM OPTICAL SOUND T
Shows how the opportunities of adult education can meet the challenge of providing adults with new educational experiences. Examines the problems faced by educationally deprived adult learners and discusses the solutions available through adult education.
LC NO. 75-702488
Prod-USOE Dist-USNAC Prodn-VISION 1974

Sound Of Rushing Water, The C 42 MIN
16MM FILM, 3/4 OR 1/2 IN VIDEO
Documents the efforts of the Shuar people of South America to resist the armed might of the Inca and Spanish empires. Tells of their efforts to maintain their cultural identity and traditions in the face of colonizing influences and pressures for social integration from Latin American republics.
Prod-CNEMAG Dist-CNEMAG

Sound Of Silence C 29 MIN
16MM FILM OPTICAL SOUND
Advocates the preservation of nature while providing a historical account of the Mississippi lands. Reveals what can happen to the land when people begin careless development.
LC NO. 80-700414
Prod-MAETEL Dist-MAETEL 1979

Sound Of Sound, The C 16 MIN
16MM FILM OPTICAL SOUND
Focuses on industrial noise and its insidious attack on hearing. Industrial workers speak candidly of their occupational deafness in an attempt to motivate industrial employees to wear proper hearing protecttion.
LC NO. 74-711499
Prod-AMOPT Dist-AMOPT 1970

Sound Of Sounds, The C 15 MIN
16MM FILM OPTICAL SOUND K-I
Follows Fingermouse and Flash as they collect noises on a tape-recorder to use in a story.
From The Fingermouse, Yoffy And Friends Series.
LC NO. 73-700436
Prod-BBCTV Dist-VEDO 1972

Sound Of Sunshine, Sound Of Rain C
16MM FILM, 3/4 OR 1/2 IN VIDEO P-I
Looks into the life of a blind, seven-year-old black boy and his intimate world of sounds and touch. Shows how his view of the world is affected by his handicap, his poverty and his race. Shows him on his treasured trips to the park, to the grocery store and into his child's world of sound images.
LC NO. 84-706032
Prod-HALEDA Dist-FLMFR 1983

Sound Of Thanksgiving, A B 30 MIN
16MM FILM OPTICAL SOUND
Features the New York Pro Musica, a group of eleven vocal and instrumental virtuosi. Depicts the use of a variety of rare instruments which provide a musical background for thanksgiving prayers. (Kinescope)
Prod-JTS Dist-NAAJS Prodn-NBCTV 1960

Sound Of Water, The C 20 MIN
3/4 OR 1/2 INCH VIDEO CASSETTE
Presents three prehistoric cultures of the American Southwest, namely the Anasazi, Hohokam and Sinagua. Spans a period of time between 300 BC to AD 1300.
LC NO. 83-706981
Prod-FLNPLN Dist-UARIZ Prodn-UARIZ 1983

Sound Of Words, The B 15 MIN
2 INCH VIDEOTAPE K-P
See series title for descriptive statement.
From The Magic Of Words Series.
Prod-GWTVAI Dist-GPITVL Prodn-WETATV

Sound Or Unsound C 57 MIN
16MM FILM, 3/4 OR 1/2 IN VIDEO H-C A
Looks at the births of folk, rock and electronic music, which were aided by the long-playing record, the transistor radio and television. Includes the sounds of a Duke Ellington medley, Bing Crosby's crooning, steel drums, Elvis Presley's rock and roll, Bob Dylan's Blowin' In The Wind and punk rock. Gives an account of the additional musical contributions of Faure, Britten, Gagnon, Bartok and Scriabin.
From The Music Of Man Series.
Prod-CANBC Dist-TIMLIF 1981

Sound Perception Method, The C 39 MIN
16MM FILM OPTICAL SOUND
Surveys the methods of instruction used at the Institute Voor Doven, Sint Michielsgestel, the Netherlands from home visit through integrated secondary school.
From The International Education Of The Hearing Impaired Child Series.
LC NO. 74-705667
Prod-USBEH Dist-USNAC 1970

Sound Solution, A C 13 MIN
3/4 OR 1/2 INCH VIDEO CASSETTE A
Stresses that people must share problem of abating noise from aircraft. Covers part of Federal Aviation regulations to show Federal Aviation Administration (FAA) responsibility in this area.
Prod-FAAFL Dist-AVIMA

Sound Waves And Stars - The Doppler Effect C 12 MIN
16MM FILM, 3/4 OR 1/2 IN VIDEO I-C A
Explains the Doppler effect, that sound travels in waves, that the waves ahead of a moving source increase in frequency and that the frequency of waves behind such a source decreases. Shows how scientists use the Doppler effect to learn about the universe.
Prod-FA Dist-PHENIX 1964

Sound Waves And Stars - The Doppler Effect (Spanish) C 12 MIN
16MM FILM, 3/4 OR 1/2 IN VIDEO I-C
Explains the Doppler effect, that sound travels in waves, that the waves ahead of a moving source increase in frequency and that the frequency of waves behind such a source decreases. Shows how scientists use the Doppler effect to learn about the universe.
Prod-FA Dist-PHENIX 1964

Sound Waves And Stars - The Doppler Effect (Dutch) C 12 MIN
16MM FILM, 3/4 OR 1/2 IN VIDEO I-C A
Explains the Doppler effect, that sound travels in waves, that the waves ahead of a moving source increase in frequency and that the frequency of waves behind such a source decreases. Shows how scientists use the Doppler effect to learn about the universe.
Prod-FA Dist-PHENIX 1964

Sound Waves In Air B 35 MIN
16MM FILM OPTICAL SOUND H-C
Investigates wave characteristics of sound transmission with large scale equipment, using frequencies up to 5000 cycles. Experiments in reflection, diffraction, interference and refraction are supplemented by ripple-tank analogies.
From The PSSC Physics Films Series.
Prod-PSSC Dist-MLA 1961

Soundaround C 30 MIN
16MM FILM, 3/4 OR 1/2 IN VIDEO H-C A
Explores various aspects of the human sound environment. Visits U V Muscio, president of Muzak, whose stimulus programming is contrasted with the experimental music of Obie-winning composer Elizabeth Swados. Looks at the impact of the telephone and discusses the demographic marketing theories of radio programming.
From The Media Probes Series.
Prod-LAYLEM Dist-TIMLIF 1980

Sounder C 15 MIN
3/4 OR 1/2 INCH VIDEO CASSETTE I
Presents passages from William Armstrong's story about a Southern black family and their hunting dog.
From The Storybound Series.
Prod-CTI Dist-CTI

Soundies B 60 MIN
3/4 OR 1/2 INCH VIDEO CASSETTE
Presents 'soundies' made for special juke boxes in the 1940s. Includes the Nat King Cole trio and Gene Krupa with Anita O'Day.
Prod-ADVCAS Dist-ADVCAS

Sounding Brass C 15 MIN
3/4 OR 1/2 INCH VIDEO CASSETTE P-I
Observes the assembly of a trombone at the King Instrument Company.
From The Explorers Unlimited Series.
Prod-WVIZTV Dist-AITECH 1971

Sounding For Urethral Strictures C 25 MIN
3/4 OR 1/2 INCH VIDEO CASSETTE PRO
See series title for descriptive statement.
From The Urology Series.
Prod-MSU Dist-MSU

Soundings C 19 MIN
3/4 OR 1/2 INCH VIDEO CASSETTE
See series title for descriptive statement.
From The Gary Hill, Part 3 Series.
Prod-EAI Dist-EAI

Sounds C 11 MIN
16MM FILM OPTICAL SOUND P-I
Presents a multiplicity of common sounds to develop and sharpen language and listening skills through awareness of environmental sounds.
LC NO. 75-713638
Prod-FILMSM Dist-FILMSM 1971

Sounds B 20 MIN
16MM FILM OPTICAL SOUND C A
See series title for descriptive statement.
From The All That I Am Series.
Prod-MPATI Dist-NWUFLM

Sounds C 10 MIN
2 INCH VIDEOTAPE
See series title for descriptive statement.
From The Janaki Series.
Prod-WGBHTV Dist-PUBTEL

Sounds C 15 MIN
2 INCH VIDEOTAPE K
Distinguishes different kinds of objects by the sounds they make.
From The Let's Go Sciencing, Unit I - Matter Series.
Prod-DETPS Dist-GPITVL

Sounds C 15 MIN
3/4 INCH VIDEO CASSETTE K-P
Features two mimes imitating the sounds of people and cities. Shows them responding dramatically to environmental sounds.
From The Adventures Of Milo And Maisie Series.
Prod-KRLNTV Dist-GPITVL 1977

Sounds Abound C 15 MIN
3/4 OR 1/2 INCH VIDEO CASSETTE P
See series title for descriptive statement.
From The Strawberry Square II - Take Time Series.
Prod-NEITV Dist-AITECH 1984

Sounds And How They Travel C 11 MIN
16MM FILM OPTICAL SOUND I-H
Presents the mechanics involved in the transmission, reflection and absorption of sound in air. Uses animation to convey invisible phenomena such as the compression and expansion and the special vibrating movement of air molecules and the formation of echoes.
LC NO. FIA66-134
Prod-ACA Dist-ACA 1965

Sounds and The Skills, The C 30 MIN
3/4 OR 1/2 INCH VIDEO CASSETTE
Outlines and describes the actor's task in interpreting Shakespeare's words. Features Ronald Watkins, Shakespearean actor and director.
From The Actor And Shakespeare Series.
Prod-NETCHE Dist-NETCHE 1971

Sounds Around Us C 15 MIN
3/4 OR 1/2 INCH VIDEO CASSETTE I
Investigates the origin of sound and how it is received by the human ear.
From The Matter And Motion Series. Module Blue
Prod-WHROTV Dist-AITECH 1973

Sounds Explored C 30 MIN
3/4 OR 1/2 INCH VIDEO CASSETTE C
See series title for descriptive statement.
From The In Our Own Image Series.
Prod-DALCCD Dist-DALCCD

Sounds Good B 27 MIN
16MM FILM OPTICAL SOUND
Demonstrates various microphones and sound mixes and illustrates the importance of sound perspective. Explains some of the difficulties encountered in achieving good sound quality in a television studio.
From The CETO Television Training Films Series.
Prod-CETO Dist-GPITVL

Sounds In The Silent Deep C 27 MIN
16MM FILM, 3/4 OR 1/2 IN VIDEO J-C
Studies animal behavior in order to demonstrate the importance of sound to underwater life. Discusses the importance of sound in everyday life.
Prod-MIS Dist-MIS 1972

Sounds Interesting C 25 MIN
16MM FILM, 3/4 OR 1/2 IN VIDEO H-C A
Studies how it is possible to generate music with a microcomputer. Introduces Dave Ellis, whose band uses a micro to create music and is provided total freedom to form every aspect of sound. Discusses computer languages and shows a program that works solely on human voice instructions.
From The Making The Most Of The Micro Series. Episode 7
Prod-BBCTV Dist-FI 1983

Sounds Like Magic—A Series
P
Points out the importance of having the ability to properly express and to communicate thoughts, feelings and desires to others. Presents stories, poetry and records for speech stimulation and shows how to develop physical dexterity through exercise. (Broadcast quality)
Prod-MOEBA Dist-GPITVL Prodn-KYNETV

Be Calm, Be Careful	15 MIN
Brownie And The Gremlin	15 MIN
Clues Of The Flying Fairies	15 MIN
Dreamland	15 MIN
Fairies, Fun And Fancy	15 MIN
Freddie, The Cricket	15 MIN
Further Dreamland Adventures	15 MIN
Ghosts And Goblins	15 MIN
I Choose Chocolate	15 MIN
Jars Of Jelly And Jam	15 MIN
Let's Listen	15 MIN
Magic Brew Of L-L-L-L, The	15 MIN
Magic Brew Of R-R-R-R, The	15 MIN
Magic Brew Of S-S-S-S, The	15 MIN
Magic Endings	15 MIN
Mother Gooseland	15 MIN
Off On A Magic Carpet	15 MIN
Our Glittering Playmates	15 MIN
Our Magic Brew	15 MIN
Our Magic Bubble Pop	15 MIN
Our Speech Rainbow	15 MIN
Princely Troll, The	15 MIN

Rabbits, Rabbits And More Rabbits 15 MIN
Singing With The Leprechauns 15 MIN
Sky Snoopers 15 MIN
Slinky And Blinky, The Gnomes 15 MIN
Some Suprises 15 MIN
Surprise - Sparkling Stars 15 MIN
There's Magic In Good Speech 15 MIN
Tricks We Can Do 15 MIN

Sounds Of Anger, Echoes Of Fear C 54 MIN
16MM FILM - 3/4 IN VIDEO PRO
Shows a traumatic situation involving a difficult, abrasive patient and how a clinical nurse, using analysis and techniques of intervention, helps the patient and staff develop insights and solutions.
LC NO. 77-702471
Prod-AJN Dist-AJN Prodn-CATTN 1977

Sounds Of Christmas - Songs Performed By The M D Anderson Choir C 42 MIN
3/4 INCH VIDEO CASSETTE
Presents Christmas music performed for the patients at the University of Texas M D Anderson Hospital.
Prod-UTAHTI Dist-UTAHTI

Sounds Of Christmas - Songs Performed By The M D Anderson Choir C 60 MIN
3/4 INCH VIDEO CASSETTE
Presents Christmas music performed for the patients at the University of Texas M D Anderson Hospital.
Prod-UTAHTI Dist-UTAHTI

Sounds Of Christmas, The C 29 MIN
3/4 OR 1/2 INCH VIDEO CASSETTE
Combines traditional Christmas songs performed by the Madrigal Singers of McGavock High School in Nashville, Tennessee with a ballet-and-puppet version of 'The Nutcracker' by the Dance Academy of South Hendersonville and the Tom Tichenor puppets.
Prod-WDCNTV Dist-PBS 1976

Sounds Of Cicada B 29 MIN
3/4 INCH VIDEO CASSETTE
Explores the important role the cicada plays in nature's cycle. Filmed on location in the singing creature's natural habitat.
Prod-UMITV Dist-UMITV 1971

Sounds Of Freedom C 29 MIN
16MM FILM OPTICAL SOUND H-C
Combines travelogue, consumer education and the economics of the food business in one entertaining and informative documentary. Shows Bob Richards, twice Olympic pole vault champion, on a sight-seeing trip in Europe. Includes the European 'FREEDOM BELL' which rings everyday. Leads to facts and conclusions of significance to all Americans.
Prod-GEMILL Dist-NINEFC

Sounds Of Hope - The Cochlear Implant C 50 MIN
3/4 OR 1/2 INCH VIDEO CASSETTE PRO
Presents the concepts of evaluation, placement and rehabilitative measures in the use of the single electrode cochlear implant.
Prod-HOUSEI Dist-HOUSEI

Sounds Of IE, EI - Syllabication Review, Careers Club C 20 MIN
3/4 OR 1/2 INCH VIDEO CASSETTE J-H
See series title for descriptive statement.
From The Getting The Word Series. Unit IV
Prod-SCETV Dist-AITECH 1974

Sounds Of Language, The B 32 MIN
16MM FILM OPTICAL SOUND H T
Explains various language sound systems--intonation patterns, rhythms, stresses and sounds. Points out that a problem in learning a second language is the tendency to carry over sound patterns of one's native speech. Shows a Spanish class for English speakers.
From The Principles And Methods Of Teaching A Second Language Series.
Prod-MLAA Dist-IU Prodn-RAY 1962

Sounds Of Love C 58 MIN
3/4 OR 1/2 INCH VIDEO CASSETTE
Presents Dr Leo Buscaglia sharing his inspiring philosophy of interpersonal communication and intimacy. Taped before a live audience at Harvard University's Sanders Theater.
Prod-PBS Dist-PBS

Sounds Of Love, The C 30 MIN
16MM FILM OPTICAL SOUND R
Probes the experiences of three well-known Christian women. Examines the lives of Maria Von Trapp, Corrie Ten Boom and Dale Evans.
Prod-GF Dist-GF

Sounds Of Myself C 15 MIN
16MM FILM, 3/4 OR 1/2 IN VIDEO K-P
Invites classroom children to discover sounds that their own bodies can make. Explores sounds that tell a story.
From The Ripples Series.
LC NO. 73-702152
Prod-NITC Dist-AITECH 1970

Sounds Of Nature C 16 MIN
16MM FILM OPTICAL SOUND
Features the use of natural sounds in conjunction with photography. Introduces Dan Gibson, a pioneer in this area who illustrates how such recordings are made and his technique of using blinds to capture wildlife on film.
Prod-AVEXP Dist-AVEXP 1971

Sounds Of Nature C 26 MIN
16MM FILM OPTICAL SOUND
Illustrates the ease with which even young children can record bird calls and other sounds of nature with the aid of a cassette recorder and a sound parabola.
LC NO. 76-702057
Prod-GIB Dist-KEGPL 1975

Sounds Of Nature C 26 MIN
16MM FILM OPTICAL SOUND I-C A
Shows many varieties of bird and animal life in Canada and the ease with which they can be recorded with the use of proper equipment.
From The Audubon Wildlife Theatre Series.
LC NO. 73-703222
Prod-KEGPL Dist-AVEXP 1973

Sounds Of Silence C 26 MIN
16MM FILM OPTICAL SOUND
Depicts the thrill and elation of skiing British Columbia's sky-high slopes. Explains that experts 'SHOP FOR CHALLENGES' by helicopter while the ordinary skier finds pleasure enough where chair-lifts and tows are handy.
Prod-NFBC Dist-CTFL 1972

Sounds Of Success C 30 MIN
3/4 OR 1/2 INCH VIDEO CASSETTE
See series title for descriptive statement.
From The Your Speaking Image - When Women Talk Business Series.
Prod-WHATV Dist-DELTAK

Sounds Of The Cello C 29 MIN
3/4 INCH VIDEO CASSETTE
Introduces the cello by examining its construction, place in the string family, range and musical qualities. Features Jerome Jelinek, University of Michigan music professor and cellist, as he performs Gabriel Faure's 'Elegy.'
Prod-UMITV Dist-UMITV 1974

Sounds Of The City C 30 MIN
3/4 OR 1/2 INCH VIDEO CASSETTE C
See series title for descriptive statement.
From The In Our Own Image Series.
Prod-DALCCD Dist-DALCCD

Sounds Of The Normal Heart, The C 17 MIN
16MM FILM OPTICAL SOUND
Demonstrates in a variety of ways the actual phenomena which create the four heart sounds. For first-year medical students.
LC NO. FIA65-427
Prod-WSU Dist-WSU 1964

Sounds Of The Normal Heart, The (French) C 17 MIN
16MM FILM OPTICAL SOUND
Demonstrates in a variety of ways the actual phenomena which create the four heart sounds. For first-year medical students.
Prod-WSU Dist-WSU 1964

Sounds Of The Normal Heart, The (German) C 17 MIN
16MM FILM OPTICAL SOUND
Demonstrates in a variety of ways the actual phenomena which create the four heart sounds. For first-year medical students.
Prod-WSU Dist-WSU 1964

Sounds Of The Normal Heart, The (Italian) C 17 MIN
16MM FILM OPTICAL SOUND
Demonstrates in a variety of ways the actual phenomena which create the four heart sounds. For first-year medical students.
Prod-WSU Dist-WSU 1964

Sounds Of The Normal Heart, The (Spanish) C 17 MIN
16MM FILM OPTICAL SOUND
Demonstrates in a variety of ways the actual phenomena which create the four heart sounds. For first-year medical students.
Prod-WSU Dist-WSU 1964

Sounds On The Sea C 28 MIN
16MM FILM OPTICAL SOUND
Explains that many of the sounds of the sea originate in marine life. Demonstrates how the sounds are analyzed, why the sounds are studied and how they can confuse the sonar operator.
LC NO. 74-705668
Prod-USN Dist-USNAC 1970

Sounds They Make—A Series
C T
Develops awareness of the less familiar aspects of the harp, trumpet and electronic synthesizer. Looks at the role of music in therapy and offers students a realistic look at the career opportunities in this field. Designed to supplement musical education curricula.
Prod-OHUTC Dist-OHUTC

Electronic Music 030 MIN
Music In Therapy 030 MIN
Trumpet Music Of The Baroque 030 MIN
Writing For The Modern Harp 030 MIN

Sounds To Say—A Series
P
Deals with the recognition of speech sounds in a four-unit course. Studies consonants, vowels, homophones and applied phonics.
Prod-TTOIC Dist-GPITVL Prodn-WGBHTV

Soundtrack B 10 MIN
16MM FILM OPTICAL SOUND
Shows how sound and image are conceived together as a unit in the artist's mind and built together frame by frame using the same manual recording process for each.
Prod-SPINLB Dist-FMCOOP 1969

Soup And Me C 24 MIN
16MM FILM, 3/4 OR 1/2 IN VIDEO
Features the adventures and misadventures of two boys growing up in a small town in Vermont. Based on the books Soup and Soup And Me by Robert Newton Peck. Originally shown on the television series ABC Weekend Specials.
LC NO. 79-707135
Prod-ABCTV Dist-MTI Prodn-ABCCIR 1977

Soup For President C 24 MIN
16MM FILM, 3/4 OR 1/2 IN VIDEO
Describes the loyalty of two best friends during election time at school. Based on the book Soup For President by Robert Peck. Originally shown on the television series ABC Weekend Specials.
LC NO. 79-707137
Prod-ABCTV Dist-MTI Prodn-ABCCIR 1979

Soup Of The Day Show, The C 30 MIN
3/4 OR 1/2 INCH VIDEO CASSETTE
Presents basically crazy cooks Larry Bly and Laban Johnson who offer recipes, cooking and shopping tips.
From The Cookin' Cheap Series.
Prod-WBRATV Dist-MDCPB

Soup Preparation C 15 MIN
16MM FILM, 3/4 OR 1/2 IN VIDEO
Demonstrates how to prepare various types of soups.
From The Professional Food Preparation And Service Series.
Prod-NEM Dist-NEM 1981

Soup Stone, The C 15 MIN
16MM FILM, 3/4 OR 1/2 IN VIDEO P-I
Relates the old French folk tale about the encounter between two itinerant peddlers and a village of gullible peasants who have hidden all their food. Tells how the peddlers get the villagers to share their food.
From The Timeless Tales Series.
Prod-LUF Dist-LUF 1983

Soup To Nuts—A Series
J-H
Shows how good nutrition and wise food choices can change one's life.
Prod-GSDE Dist-AITECH 1980

Balancing Act, The 015 MIN
Breaking The Fast 015 MIN
Chews For Yourself 015 MIN
Don't Weight Around 015 MIN
Foodstuff 015 MIN
Little Bit Of Everything, A 015 MIN
Shopping Sense - Self-Defense 015 MIN
There's No Magic 015 MIN
Tip The Scales In Your Favor 015 MIN
Today, Tomorrow, Forever 015 MIN

Soupa Avgolemono And Pilaf C 25 MIN
3/4 OR 1/2 INCH VIDEO CASSETTE PRO
Demonstrates the preparation of avgolemono soup and pilaf, two Middle Eastern dishes. The soup contains lemon juice, eggs and a chicken and rice broth.
Prod-CULINA Dist-CULINA

Soupe Du Jour C 29 MIN
2 INCH VIDEOTAPE
A French language videotape. Features Julia Child of Haute Cuisine au Vin demonstrating how to prepare soupe du jour. With captions.
From The French Chef (French) Series.
Prod-WGBHTV Dist-PUBTEL

Soupman C 25 MIN
16MM FILM, 3/4 OR 1/2 IN VIDEO I-H
Tells how a tough 14-year-old boy breaks into an old woman's house in order to steal her TV, but ends up making friends with her. Explains how he realizes the error of his previous ways and takes to the street to peddle hot soup and sandwiches to old people.
From The Reflections Series.
LC NO. 81-707268
Prod-PAULST Dist-MEDIAG 1980

Soups C
3/4 INCH VIDEO CASSETTE H A
Describes soup as a creative dish to make, even for the novice cook. Demonstrates basic methods for making meat and chicken stocks.
From The Matter Of Taste Series. Lesson 17
Prod-COAST Dist-CDTEL

Soups And Salads C 29 MIN
2 INCH VIDEOTAPE
Features gourmet-humorist Justin Wilson showing ways to prepare soups and salads with various ingredients.
From The Cookin' Cajun Series.
Prod-MAETEL Dist-PUBTEL

Soups, Sauces And Gravies C 24 MIN
16MM FILM OPTICAL SOUND
Shows basic skills and techniques used in the preparation of soups, sauces and gravies.
LC NO. 74-706582
Prod-USN Dist-USNAC 1970

Sour Dough C 3 MIN
16MM FILM - 3/4 IN VIDEO
Demonstrates two methods of making sour dough. Explains that the easiest way is to take a bit of ordinary yeast bread dough and put it to rest in a crock for a few days. Shows how to make sour dough from scratch by combining water, yeast and flour which, when stored in a crock for a few days, will also become sour dough. Clarifies that either of these added to ordinary bread dough will yield sour dough bread.
From The Beatrice Trum Hunter's Natural Foods Series.
Prod-PBS Dist-PUBTEL Prodn-WGBH 1974

Sour Grapes C 30 MIN
3/4 OR 1/2 INCH VIDEO CASSETTE P-I
See series title for descriptive statement.
From The Sonrisas Series.
Prod-KRLNTV Dist-MDCPB

Source Of Faith C 27 MIN
16MM FILM, 3/4 OR 1/2 IN VIDEO J-C A
Looks at the sights of Israel, focusing on its importance as the source of the Christian faith and depicting sites significant to the Judaic and Islamic religions.
Prod-MACMFL Dist-FI 1980

Source Of Power To Contract C 31 MIN
3/4 INCH VIDEO CASSETTE
Explains the legal basis of the authority of federal government contracting officers.
From The Basic Procurement Course Series.
LC NO. 80-706739
Prod-USGSFC Dist-USNAC Prodn-ADSAV 1978

Source Of Soul, The C 30 MIN
3/4 OR 1/2 INCH VIDEO CASSETTE J-H
Analyzes the source of soul music by presenting the music of Chuck Brown and the Soul Searchers and Michael Babtunde Olatunji.
From The From Jumpstreet Series.
Prod-WETATV Dist-GPITVL 1979

Source Rocks C 24 MIN
3/4 OR 1/2 INCH VIDEO CASSETTE IND
See series title for descriptive statement.
From The Basic And Petroleum Geology For Non-Geologists - Hydrocarbons And...-Series.
Prod-PHILLP Dist-GPCV

Source Rocks, Generation, Migration, And Accumulation C 33 MIN
3/4 OR 1/2 INCH VIDEO CASSETTE IND
See series title for descriptive statement.
From The Petroleum Geology Series.
Prod-GPCV Dist-GPCV

Sources - A Matter Of Trust C 29 MIN
3/4 OR 1/2 INCH VIDEO CASSETTE
Looks at the use of confidential sources in the wake of the Janet Cooke Pulitzer Prize fiasco in the Washington Post and the explosion of press self-examination that followed.
From The Inside Story Series.
Prod-PBS Dist-PBS 1981

Sources Of Air Pollution C 5 MIN
3/4 INCH VIDEO CASSETTE
Discusses the relationship between our modern technological way of life and air pollution. Cites the principle sources of air pollution.
Prod-USNAC Dist-USNAC 1972

Sources Of Capital C 11 MIN
16MM FILM OPTICAL SOUND
Explains methods by which a firm can most economically generate additional sources of capital for either on going business or expansion.
From The Running Your Own Business Series.
Prod-EFD Dist-EFD

Sources Of Capital C 30 MIN
3/4 INCH VIDEO CASSETTE
See series title for descriptive statement.
From The It's Everybody's Business Series. Unit 3, Financing A Business
Prod-DALCCD Dist-DALCCD

Sources Of Conflict C 12 MIN
2 INCH VIDEOTAPE C A
Features a humanistic psychologist who, by analysis and examples, discusses sources of internal conflict.
From The Interpersonal Competence, Unit 01 - The Self Series.
Prod-MVNE Dist-TELSTR 1973

Sources Of Dance C 15 MIN
16MM FILM, 3/4 OR 1/2 IN VIDEO J-C
Deals with origins of ideas for composition and the exploration of those ideas by extending them into studies for choreography.
From The Dance Experience - Training And Composing Series.
Prod-ATHI Dist-ATHI 1984

Sources Of Electrical Energy C 30 MIN
3/4 OR 1/2 INCH VIDEO CASSETTE IND
Covers sources of electrical energy including chemical reaction, electromagnetic induction, heat, light and pressure. Explains difference between primary and secondary cell and outlines transformer and generator action.
From The Basic Electricity, DC Series.
Prod-AVIMA Dist-AVIMA

Sources Of Energy C 15 MIN
2 INCH VIDEOTAPE P
Shows different forms of energy that can be used to set an object in motion or to alter its motion.
From The Science Is Searching Series.
Prod-DETPS Dist-GPITVL

Sources Of Foreign Material C 20 MIN
3/4 OR 1/2 INCH VIDEO CASSETTE
Discusses actual observations of frequently overlooked sources of foreign materials that can get into food, relating to maintenance activities, with emphasis on participation and cooperation, recognizing and reacting.
From The Food Safety And Plant Maintenance Series.
Prod-PLAID Dist-PLAID

Sources Of Funds C 30 MIN
3/4 OR 1/2 INCH VIDEO CASSETTE IND
Describes common sources of funds to finance investment projects. Shows examination of financial statement of a corporation as example problem.
From The Engineering Economy Series.
Prod-COLOSU Dist-COLOSU

Sources Of Ideas For Drawing C 29 MIN
3/4 INCH VIDEO CASSETTE C A
Suggests where to look for new sketching ideas. Explains the value of researching ideas for drawing.
From The Sketching Techniques Series. Lesson 25
Prod-COAST Dist-CDTEL

Sources Of Income C 30 MIN
3/4 OR 1/2 INCH VIDEO CASSETTE
Discusses sources, adequacy, and methods of increasing retirement income. Presented by Edwin Carey and Wilton Heyliger, Howard University School of Business and Public Administration.
From The How People Age 50 And Up Can Plan For A More Successful Retirement Series.
Prod-RCOMTV Dist-SYLWAT

Sources Of Information C 29 MIN
3/4 OR 1/2 INCH VIDEO CASSETTE
Presents an exploration of where and how people get information about sex and a discussion of the implications of those sources. Features Milton Diamond, Ph D, a biologist at the University of Hawaii, distinguishing between fact and fiction in sexual information and talking about direct and indirect sources.
From The Human Sexuality Series.
Prod-KHETTV Dist-PBS

Sources Of Law C 19 MIN
3/4 OR 1/2 INCH VIDEO CASSETTE H
Takes a historical look at our legal system, tracing the roots of law from the Code of Hammurabi to the American Bill of Rights.
From The Ways Of The Law Series.
Prod-SCITV Dist-GPITVL 1980

Sources Of Understanding X 30 MIN
2 INCH VIDEOTAPE I
Features host John Rugg briefly surveying the introduction of European and Asian cultures to this continent and the historically influential role that American Indian groups have had upon the development of the country. Explains the who, why, how and what of the telecourse. (Broadcast quality)
From The Cultural Understandings Series. No. 1
Prod-DENVPS Dist-GPITVL Prodn-KRMATV

Sourwood Mountain Dulcimers C 28 MIN
16MM FILM - 3/4 IN VIDEO
Shows master of the dulcimer, ID Stamper pass on his skill to a young man, John McCutcheon.
Prod-APPAL Dist-APPAL 1976

Sous Un Jour Nouveau C 13 MIN
16MM FILM OPTICAL SOUND K-P
A French language version of the motion picture New Look. Provides an explanation of family relations.
From The Family Relations (French) Series.
LC NO. 76-700140
Prod-MORLAT Dist-MORLAT 1974

South Africa C 28 MIN
3/4 INCH VIDEOTAPE
Interviews the Consul General of South Africa and the Counsellor of the South African Mission to the United Nations. Includes a film clip. Hosted by Marilyn Perry.
From The International Byline Series.
Prod-PERRYM Dist-PERRYM

South Africa (International Byline) C 28 MIN
3/4 INCH VIDEOTAPE
Interviews Mr David Steward, Counselor of the Permanent Mission of South Africa to the United Nations and Mr Carl Frank Noffke, Information Counselor of the Embassy of South Africa to the United States. Includes films on 'Zulu' and on Namibia.
From The International Byline Series.
Prod-PERRYM Dist-PERRYM

South Africa - The Riot That Won't Stop C 59 MIN
3/4 OR 1/2 INCH VIDEO CASSETTE
Examines the lives of blacks and whites in South Africa as they face political and racial unrest. Discusses the sharpening lines of conflict and how individuals are dealing with the pressure.
Prod-WGBHTV Dist-PBS 1978

South Africa - The White Laager C 59 MIN
16MM FILM, 3/4 OR 1/2 IN VIDEO I-C A
Explores the history of the Afrikaners from the arrival of the Dutch in 1652 to South Africa's adoption of the apartheid system.
Prod-WGBHTV Dist-LCOA 1978

South Africa And Apartheid C 29 MIN
2 INCH VIDEOTAPE
See series title for descriptive statement.
From The Course Of Our Times II Series.
Prod-WGBHTV Dist-PUBTEL

South Africa Belongs To Us C 35 MIN
16MM FILM OPTICAL SOUND
Portrays the lives of five typical South African women who convey the economic and emotional burdens borne by black women under apartheid.
Prod-CANWRL Dist-CANWRL 1981

South Africa Belongs To Us C 55 MIN
16MM FILM OPTICAL SOUND
Portrays the lives of five typical South African women who convey the economic and emotional burdens borne by black women under apartheid.
Prod-CANWRL Dist-CANWRL 1981

South Africa Belongs To Us C 57 MIN
16MM FILM, 3/4 OR 1/2 IN VIDEO
Views the devastating impact of apartheid on black women and the black family in South Africa. Looks at the life of a domestic servant in a white household, at the experiences in an illegal black shantytown and at a nurse at one of the few family planning clinics in Soweto.
Prod-AUCHWE Dist-ICARUS 1980

South Africa Wildlife C 15 MIN
3/4 OR 1/2 INCH VIDEO CASSETTE
Tells how wildlife in South Africa is endangered by man and discusses an approach to solving this problem.
Prod-UPI Dist-JOU

South African Essay, Pt 1, Fruit Of Fear B 59 MIN
16MM FILM, 3/4 OR 1/2 IN VIDEO H-C A
Reports on the South African dual standards of living from the lavish white sections to the black ghettos. Interviews such people as Nobel Peace Prize winner Chief Albert Luthuli, Frank Waring and author Alan Paton as to their attitudes toward this condition.
From The Changing World Series.
Prod-NET Dist-IU 1965

South African Essay, Pt 2, One Nation, Two Nationalisms B 59 MIN
16MM FILM, 3/4 OR 1/2 IN VIDEO H-C A
Examines the political machinery with which apartheid is enforced. Interviews white and black South Africans. Focusses on the power of the White Nationalist Party.
From The Changing World Series.
Prod-NET Dist-IU 1965

South African Farm, A C 51 MIN
16MM FILM, 3/4 OR 1/2 IN VIDEO
Presents a portrait of life in South Africa by South African filmmaker Paul Laufer. Shows the farm of Laufer's godfather, a Czech emigre. Interviews Black workers on the farm.
Prod-DOCEDR Dist-DOCEDR

South African Frontier B 14 MIN
16MM FILM OPTICAL SOUND J-C A
Presents a travelogue showing South African countryside and the colorful inhabitants.
Prod-SMUSA Dist-SMUSA

South African Mosaic C 19 MIN
16MM FILM OPTICAL SOUND J-C A
Describes the origin of South Africa's peoples and shows many aspects of their lives. Includes exotic Indian and Malayan religious ceremonies and dances.
Prod-SMUSA Dist-SMUSA

South America - A Trilogy--A Series
16MM FILM, 3/4 OR 1/2 IN VIDEO J-H
Shows that Bolivian tin miners, Brazilian city dwellers and Peruvian peasants share common economic and social problems in countries on our nearest neighboring continent, South America. Current conditions in these developing countries are made significant in three films.
Prod-THAMES Dist-MEDIAG 1979

Bolivia - The Tin Mountain 027 MIN
Brazil - Children Of The Miracle 027 MIN
Peru - The Revolution That Never Was 027 MIN

South America - Cartagena, A Colonial City C 17 MIN
16MM FILM, 3/4 OR 1/2 IN VIDEO I-H
Presents a typical day in the life of a young boy in Cartagena, Columbia. Shows aspects of life unique to South America plus the similarities of a boy's life in a small city anywhere.
Prod-EVANSA Dist-PHENIX 1969

South America - Estancia In Argentina C 21 MIN
16MM FILM, 3/4 OR 1/2 IN VIDEO I-H
Explores agricultural life in contemporary Argentina, showing the estancias (large ranches) on the fertile pampas. Tells how these huge ranches, although modern in some respects, resemble the feudal estates of the Middle Ages in which the wealthy owner feeds, clothes and shelters his workers and their families, most of whom spend their entire lives on the estancia.
Prod-EVANSA Dist-PHENIX 1969

South America - Indians Of The Andes C 21 MIN
16MM FILM, 3/4 OR 1/2 IN VIDEO J-H
Portrays the primitive way of life of an Inca boy and his family in an isolated Peruvian village in the Andes mountains.
Prod-EVANSA Dist-PHENIX 1969

South America - Land Of Many Faces C 15 MIN
16MM FILM, 3/4 OR 1/2 IN VIDEO I-J
Examines the contrasting characteristics of the nations and cultures of South America. Shows how the geography of South America includes high mountains, jungles and temperate regions.
From The South America Films Series.
Prod-MGHT Dist-MGHT 1975

South America - Life In The City C 10 MIN
16MM FILM, 3/4 OR 1/2 IN VIDEO I-H
Portrays the contrasts of progress and poverty, and old and new that exist in the South American cities of Rio De Janeiro and Sao Paulo in Brazil, Buenos Aires, Argentina, Caracas, Venezuela, Santiago, Chile; and Lima, Peru.
Prod-EVANSA Dist-PHENIX 1971

South America - Market Day C 10 MIN
16MM FILM, 3/4 OR 1/2 IN VIDEO I-J

Depicts market day in South America as an exciting, important and colorful event. Allows students to draw many conclusions about economic and social life in South American villages.
Prod-EVANSA Dist-PHENIX 1971

South America - Overview C 17 MIN
16MM FILM, 3/4 OR 1/2 IN VIDEO I-H
Explains that South America's move toward a modern society has been slow. Describes the change in the air.
From The Latin American Series - A Focus On People Series.
Prod-CLAIB Dist-SF 1972

South America - The Widening Gap C 15 MIN
16MM FILM, 3/4 OR 1/2 IN VIDEO I-J
Examines the widening gap between the rich and the poor in South America and shows how population growth could outstrip South America's resources and its ability to develop these resources.
From The South America Films Series.
Prod-MGHT Dist-MGHT 1975

South America Today C 25 MIN
16MM FILM, 3/4 OR 1/2 IN VIDEO J-C A
Illustrates the great diversity of racial and ethnic backgrounds in a continent of 200 million people. Points out South America's geographic and historical dimensions, its natural and cultural environment to consider in analyzing problems facing its peoples in the late twentieth century.
Prod-BRYAN Dist-IFF 1973

South America, History And Heritage C 17 MIN
16MM FILM, 3/4 OR 1/2 IN VIDEO I-H
Presents the history of South America from the 15th century to the 1970's. Deals with Inca civilization, the impact of colonial rule and the struggle for political and economic independence.
Prod-NEMESA Dist-PHENIX 1978

South America, Land And People C 21 MIN
16MM FILM, 3/4 OR 1/2 IN VIDEO I-H
Presents a geographical and cultural tour of South America, including the resources and economics of its major geographical regions. Presents important cities and historical sites.
Prod-NEMESA Dist-PHENIX 1978

South American Instruments, Pt 1 C 17 MIN
3/4 OR 1/2 INCH VIDEO CASSETTE
See series title for descriptive statement.
From The Musical Instruments Series.
Prod-WWVUTV Dist-GPITVL

South American Instruments, Pt 2 C 19 MIN
3/4 OR 1/2 INCH VIDEO CASSETTE
See series title for descriptive statement.
From The Musical Instruments Series.
Prod-WWVUTV Dist-GPITVL

South Americans In Cordoba C 13 MIN
3/4 OR 1/2 INCH VIDEO CASSETTE I-C A
Shows artists represented at the Cordoba Biennial in Argentina.
LC NO. 82-707001
Prod-MOMALA Dist-MOMALA

South Americans In Cordoba (Spanish) C 13 MIN
16MM FILM OPTICAL SOUND J-C
Introduces artists represented at the 1967 Cordoba Biennial in Argentina.
Prod-OOAS Dist-MOMALA 1966

South Atlantic Region, The C 15 MIN
16MM FILM, 3/4 OR 1/2 IN VIDEO J
Examines the people, industry, economy and landscape of the South Atlantic region of the United States.
From The U S Geography Series.
Prod-MGHT Dist-MGHT 1976

South Brazil C 19 MIN
16MM FILM, 3/4 OR 1/2 IN VIDEO I-H
Depicts the area between Rio De Janeiro, Santos and Sao Paulo, the center of developed wealth and population of Brazil, the largest country on the continent of South America. Shows how Brazil is now well into a period of unprecedented economic growth which has not affected most of the people and has been achieved only at the expense of some personal and institutional liberties.
From The Latin American Series - Focus On People Series.
Prod-CLAIB Dist-SF 1972

South By Northwest—A Series

Traces the importance of Black participation in the settling and development of the Pacific Northwest from 1788 to 1900 through a series of docu-dramas.
Prod-KWSU Dist-GPITVL 1977

Homesteaders	30 MIN
Montana, Pt 1	30 MIN
Montana, Pt 2	30 MIN
Roslyn Migration, The	30 MIN
York	30 MIN

South Central Region, The C 15 MIN
16MM FILM, 3/4 OR 1/2 IN VIDEO J
Examines the people, industry, economy and landscape of the South Central region of the United States.
From The U S Geography Series.
Prod-MGHT Dist-MGHT 1976

South Dakota Gold Miners C 20 MIN
3/4 OR 1/2 INCH VIDEO CASSETTE
Depicts problems of South Dakota gold miners, focusing on the famous Hearst empire mine, the Homestake Gold Mine. Considers working conditions, lung diseases, loss of pensions and a strike.
Prod-DCTVC Dist-DCTVC

South From Valdez C 21 MIN
16MM FILM OPTICAL SOUND
Documents a a single voyage of a large crude-oil carrier from the port of Valdez to the refinery in San Francisco.
LC NO. 80-700387
Prod-EXXON Dist-MTP Prodn-MFCFP 1980

South Of The Clouds C 35 MIN
16MM FILM OPTICAL SOUND J A
Reveals the gradual and complete transformation of Najila, a high caste Moslem, through her participation in the democratic life of a Christian college in Beirut, Lebanon.
Prod-YALEDV Dist-YALEDV

South Of Waldeyers C 20 MIN
16MM FILM OPTICAL SOUND PRO
Dr J A Hutch presents a study of the physiology of micturition. Includes an examination of the embryological origin of anatomical structures involved in pathological conditions and the rationale for their medical or surgical correction. For physicians and medical students.
LC NO. FIA68-823
Prod-EATONL Dist-EATONL Prodn-AVCORP 1968

South Pacific - End Of Eden (Spanish) C 58 MIN
16MM FILM, 3/4 OR 1/2 IN VIDEO
Deals with the life of New Guinea tribesmen, who are still living in the Stone Age, descendants of the H M S Bounty's mutineers, Gaugin's Tahiti and radioactive atolls. Includes a commentary by James Michener.
Prod-READER Dist-PFP

South Pacific, The - End Of Eden C 27 MIN
16MM FILM, 3/4 OR 1/2 IN VIDEO J-C A
A shortened version of the motion picture The South Pacific - End Of Eden. Follows James Michener as he examines the impact of 20th century life on the cultures of the Pacific Islands, including Easter Island, Tahiti, Pitcairn Island and the Stone Age tribes of the Solomon Islands and New Guinea.
From The James Michener's World Series.
Prod-READER Dist-PFP 1978

South Pacific, The - End Of Eden C 59 MIN
16MM FILM, 3/4 OR 1/2 IN VIDEO J-C A
Considers whether Pacific cultures will survive the impact of 20th century life. Visits Easter Island, Tahiti, Pitcairn Island and the Stone Age tribes of the Solomon Islands and New Guinea. Features American author James Michener.
From The James Michener's World Series.
Prod-READER Dist-PFP 1978

South Viet Nam - The Forgotten War B 9 MIN
16MM FILM OPTICAL SOUND
In 1954 French Indo-china was crumbling, and communists infiltrated into Hanoi to set up the new satellite country of North Viet Nam. America sent equipment and instructors to train the army of South viet Nam.
Prod-HEARST Dist-HEARST 1963

South Viet Nam - Tinderbox In Asia B 5 MIN
16MM FILM OPTICAL SOUND
Traces the birth and growth of the current crisis in Viet Nam.
From The Screen News Digest Series. Vol 4, Issue 9
Prod-HEARST Dist-HEARST 1962

South Vietnam - The People Of Saigon C 17 MIN
16MM FILM OPTICAL SOUND J-C A
Explains the effects that war has had on South VietNam. Shows the city of Saigon and describes the life of the people.
LC NO. 76-701205
Prod-BAILYL Dist-AVED 1969

South-East Nuba, The C 60 MIN
16MM FILM, 3/4 OR 1/2 IN VIDEO J-C A
Analyzes the Nuba who live in a very remote part of Africa near the center of the Sudan. Shows that they have their own flamboyant culture which includes body painting and the sport of bracelet fighting.
From The Worlds Apart Series.
Prod-BBCTV Dist-FI 1982

South-Western Landscapes—A Series

Presents art videos using mechanical and electronic devices to physically explore the New Mexican landscape. By Steina.
Prod-EAI Dist-EAI

Low Ride	003 MIN
Photographic Memory	005 MIN
Rest	003 MIN
Sky High	003 MIN
Somersault	005 MIN

South, The C 12 MIN
16MM FILM, 3/4 OR 1/2 IN VIDEO I-H
Presents a study of the people who make the South a distinct cultural and geographic entity within the whole of America today. Describes the history and geography of the South.
Prod-PARACO Dist-AIMS 1973

South, The C 24 MIN
16MM FILM, 3/4 OR 1/2 IN VIDEO I-H
Presents a study of the people who make the South a distinct cultural and geographic entity within the whole of America. Describes the history and geography of the South.
Prod-PARACO Dist-AIMS 1973

South, The C 30 MIN
16MM FILM, 3/4 OR 1/2 IN VIDEO I-C
Edited from the motion picture These States. Shows the role of the Southern states in the American Revolution, focusing on the battlefields, buildings and cultural riches which each state has in honor of its participation. Features Colonial Williamsburg, Monticello and the College of William and Mary.
Prod-BCTOS Dist-FI 1975

South, The C 30 MIN
2 INCH VIDEOTAPE
Depicts the 'stereotype' version of the ante-bellum South and contrasts it with the institution of slavery.
From The American History I Series.
Prod-DENVPS Dist-GPITVL

South, The (French) C 12 MIN
16MM FILM, 3/4 OR 1/2 IN VIDEO I-H
Presents a study of the poeple who make the South a distinct cultural and geographic entity within the whole of America today. Describes the history and geography of the South.
Prod-PARACO Dist-AIMS 1973

South, The (French) C 24 MIN
16MM FILM, 3/4 OR 1/2 IN VIDEO I-H
Presents a study of the people who make the South a distinct cultural and geographic entity within the whole of America. Describes the history and geography of the South.
Prod-PARACO Dist-AIMS 1973

South, The (German) C 12 MIN
16MM FILM, 3/4 OR 1/2 IN VIDEO I-H
Presents a study of the poeple who make the South a distinct cultural and geographic entity within the whole of America today. Describes the history and geography of the South.
Prod-PARACO Dist-AIMS 1973

South, The (German) C 24 MIN
16MM FILM, 3/4 OR 1/2 IN VIDEO I-H
Presents a study of the people who make the South a distinct cultural and geographic entity within the whole of America. Describes the history and geography of the South.
Prod-PARACO Dist-AIMS 1973

South, The (Italian) C 12 MIN
16MM FILM, 3/4 OR 1/2 IN VIDEO I-H
Presents a study of the poeple who make the South a distinct cultural and geographic entity within the whole of America today. Describes the history and geography of the South.
Prod-PARACO Dist-AIMS 1973

South, The (Italian) C 24 MIN
16MM FILM, 3/4 OR 1/2 IN VIDEO I-H
Presents a study of the people who make the South a distinct cultural and geographic entity within the whole of America. Describes the history and geography of the South.
Prod-PARACO Dist-AIMS 1973

South, The (Japanese) C 12 MIN
16MM FILM, 3/4 OR 1/2 IN VIDEO I-H
Presents a study of the poeple who make the South a distinct cultural and geographic entity within the whole of America today. Describes the history and geography of the South.
Prod-PARACO Dist-AIMS 1973

South, The (Japanese) C 24 MIN
16MM FILM, 3/4 OR 1/2 IN VIDEO I-H
Presents a study of the people who make the South a distinct cultural and geographic entity within the whole of America. Describes the history and geography of the South.
Prod-PARACO Dist-AIMS 1973

South, The (Portuguese) C 12 MIN
16MM FILM, 3/4 OR 1/2 IN VIDEO I-H
Presents a study of the poeple who make the South a distinct cultural and geographic entity within the whole of America today. Describes the history and geography of the South.
Prod-PARACO Dist-AIMS 1973

South, The (Portuguese) C 24 MIN
16MM FILM, 3/4 OR 1/2 IN VIDEO I-H
Presents a study of the people who make the South a distinct cultural and geographic entity within the whole of America. Describes the history and geography of the South.
Prod-PARACO Dist-AIMS 1973

South, The (Spanish) C 12 MIN
16MM FILM, 3/4 OR 1/2 IN VIDEO I-H
Presents a study of the poeple who make the South a distinct cultural and geographic entity within the whole of America today. Describes the history and geography of the South.
Prod-PARACO Dist-AIMS 1973

South, The (Spanish) C 24 MIN
16MM FILM, 3/4 OR 1/2 IN VIDEO I-H
Presents a study of the people who make the South a distinct cultural and geographic entity within the whole of America. Describes the history and geography of the South.
Prod-PARACO Dist-AIMS 1973

South, The - Health And Hunger B 23 MIN
16MM FILM OPTICAL SOUND H-C A
Discusses inadequate nutrition, lack of water, and too few medical facilites-problems which affect both the physical and mental development of southern blacks. Interviews the only black obstetrician in Mississippi and a midwife.
LC NO. 78-707229
Prod-NETRC Dist-IU 1969

Southeast Asia - A Culture History C 16 MIN
16MM FILM, 3/4 OR 1/2 IN VIDEO H-C A
Explains the cultures of Viet Nam, Laos, Cambodia and Thailand which are a blend of the indigenous tribal traditions with the high culture of Hindu-Buddhist India. Discusses how former centers of empire stand today as a testimony to the endurance of Buddhist and Brahman idea systems in Southeast Asia.
Prod-SIGMA Dist-FILCOM 1969

Southeast Asia - Burma And Thailand C 14 MIN
16MM FILM, 3/4 OR 1/2 IN VIDEO I-H
Shows differences and similarities between Burma and Thailand geographically, industrially, in the ways of life of the people and in their ethnic make-up.

From The Southeast Asia Series.
Prod-CORF Dist-CORF 1973

Southeast Asia - Lands And Peoples (2nd Ed) C 14 MIN
16MM FILM, 3/4 OR 1/2 IN VIDEO I-H
Examines the cultural, physical and economic geography of the countries of Southeast Asia. Shows how the people through their emergence from colonial status to independent nations, have used their lands to produce such products as rubber, oil, tin, teak and rice.
From The Southeast Asia Series.
Prod-CORF Dist-CORF 1976

Southeast Asia - Vietnam, Cambodia, Laos C 22 MIN
16MM FILM, 3/4 OR 1/2 IN VIDEO I-H
Points out that although the people of North and South Vietnam, Cambodia and Laos have much in common, there are differences in human use of the land. Gives a geographic overview and points out political and cultural factors that prevail there.
From The Southeast Asia Series.
Prod-CORF Dist-CORF 1973

Southeast Asia Geography C 21 MIN
16MM FILM, 3/4 OR 1/2 IN VIDEO I-H
Examines the geographic and climatic characteristics of Burma, Laos, Thailand, Cambodia and Malaya. Pictures the raw materials ans the surplus foods that make these nations politically important. Comments on Singapore's strategic postition and explores the changing role of the Western powers in Southeast Asia.
Prod-EVANSA Dist-PHENIX 1967

Southeast Asia Report - Cambodia, Vietnam, China—A Series

Depicts the tragedies of the war torn Cambodians in the aftermath of the Vietnam War. Portrays their efforts to rebuild their country in the midst of widespread death, destruction and starvation.
Prod-DCTVC Dist-DCTVC

Southeast Asia Report - Cambodia, Vietnam,
Southeast Asia Report - Cambodia, Vietnam, 030 MIN

Southeast Asia Report - Cambodia, Vietnam, China, Pt 1 C 30 MIN
3/4 OR 1/2 INCH VIDEO CASSETTE
Examines the first border conflicts between Vietnam and Cambodia, including footage from the border and an analysis of the situation by journalists, scholars, and United States State Department officials.
From The Southeast Asia Report - Cambodia, Vietnam, China Series.
Prod-DCTVC Dist-DCTVC

Southeast Asia Report - Cambodia, Vietnam, China, Pt 2 C 30 MIN
3/4 OR 1/2 INCH VIDEO CASSETTE
Covers the China-Vietnam War and the Vietnamese occupation of Cambodia and the carnage left by the Pol Pot regime.
From The Southeast Asia Report - Cambodia, Vietnam, China Series.
Prod-DCTVC Dist-DCTVC

Southeast Asia—A Series
16MM FILM, 3/4 OR 1/2 IN VIDEO I-H
Describes the resources and economic systems of Malaysia, Singapore, Vietnam, Cambodia, Laos, Burma and Thailand.
Prod-CORF Dist-CORF

Southeast Asia - Burma And Thailand 14 MIN
Southeast Asia - Lands And Peoples (2nd Ed) 14 MIN
Southeast Asia - Malaysia And Singapore 14 MIN
Southeast Asia - Vietnam, Cambodia, Laos 22 MIN

Southern Africa C 27 MIN
16MM FILM, 3/4 OR 1/2 IN VIDEO J-C A
Studies the emergence of black nationalism in South Africa during the 1970's. Describes internal problems, labor disputes, riots, and civil wars.
From The Seventies Series.
Prod-UPI Dist-JOU 1980

Southern Black Children C 27 MIN
16MM FILM OPTICAL SOUND H-C T
Presents children's vivid, dramatic play and traditional folk games photographed in Houston and the surrounding countryside. Shows cultural entities such as music, dancing, intricate hand clapping improvisations, call and response and circle games. Brings out the warm, easy interaction between old and young, boys and girls and children of different ages.
From The Play And Cultural Continuity Series. Part 2
Prod-CFDC Dist-CFDC 1977

Southern Cross Crusade B 50 MIN
16MM FILM OPTICAL SOUND
Shows the Billy Graham Team's Crusade in Australia and New Zealand.
Prod-GRAHAM Dist-WWPI 1959

Southern Germany, Pt 2 C 40 MIN
16MM FILM OPTICAL SOUND H-C A
Focuses on a variety of scenes as viewed and described by an American traveler.
Prod-WSTGLC Dist-WSTGLC

Southern Highlands - America's Pictureland C 28 MIN
16MM FILM OPTICAL SOUND
Covers both natural and man-made attractions in the southern Appalachian mountains. Includes views of the world's largest underground lake, Lookout Mountain, hang-gliding on Grandfather Mountain and Biltmore House in Asheville.
Prod-EKC Dist-EKC 1980

Southern Mountain Ranges, The, Pt 3 C 25 MIN
16MM FILM OPTICAL SOUND H-C A
Discusses each German region's lifestyles, economy, problems and opportunities for the future. Provides some unusual helicopter views of Germany's geography.
Prod-WSTGLC Dist-WSTGLC

Southern Star C 105 MIN
16MM FILM OPTICAL SOUND
Offers a spoof on jungle adventures. Stars George Segal, Ursula Andress and Orson Welles.
Prod-CPC Dist-TWYMAN 1969

Southern Symphony C 21 MIN
16MM FILM OPTICAL SOUND J-C A
Emphasizes the variety of cultures of South African peoples. Describes the cultural contributions of various national groups.
Prod-SMUSA Dist-SMUSA

Southern Voices C 58 MIN
3/4 INCH VIDEO CASSETTE
Documents the creation of Southern Voices, an avant-garde orchestral piece by Doris Hayes. Rehearsals and the final performance are shown, also interviews with Southerners. Taped by George Stoney.
Prod-EAI Dist-EAI

Southern 500, The C 28 MIN
16MM FILM, 3/4 OR 1/2 IN VIDEO I-C
Tells the history of the Southern 500 auto race and some of the racers who have won it, including Bobby Allison, Buddy Baker, Richard Petty, Cale Yarborough and David Pearson.
Prod-SF Dist-SF 1978

Southerner, The B 91 MIN
16MM FILM OPTICAL SOUND
Tells the story of a young man who decides to strike out on his own, leaving a safe job to grow cotton on a derelict farm. Stars Zachary Scott, Betty Field and Beulah Bondi. Directed by Jean Renoir.
Prod-UNKNWN Dist-REELIM 1945

Southland Empire C 28 MIN
16MM FILM OPTICAL SOUND
Highlights Southern California today. Shows missions, celebrations, sports, industry and scenic attractions blended in a fast-moving film enhanced with original music composed for the picture.
Prod-UPR Dist-PCF

Southward C 19 MIN
16MM FILM OPTICAL SOUND
Features The Australian Sydney Hobart Yacht Race as it was filmed aboard several of the competing yachts. Records the journey to Tasmania.
LC NO. 80-700925
Prod-TASCOR Dist-TASCOR 1976

Southwest Asia - Nations Of Complexity C 25 MIN
16MM FILM, 3/4 OR 1/2 IN VIDEO I-H A
Analyzes the changes in Turkey, Afghanistan, Iran and Pakistan and views the effects of poverty and religion.
From The Faces Of Man Series.
Prod-SCRESC Dist-MTI 1981

Southwest Conference Football Highlights 1972 C 29 MIN
16MM FILM OPTICAL SOUND J-C A
Shows highlights from the 1972 Southwest Conference football season, including portions of 12 regular season games. Includes the Texas victory over Alabama in the Cotton Bowl and the fifth annual presentation of the Kern Tipps Award to Robert Papelka of Southern Methodist University.
Prod-EXXON Dist-EXXON 1973

Southwest Indian Arts And Crafts C 13 MIN
16MM FILM, 3/4 OR 1/2 IN VIDEO P-I
Shows the southwestern Indians' artistry in Navajo rugs, San Ildefonso and Acomo pottery, Hopi and Zuni jewelry, Kachina dolls and Pima and Papago baskets.
Prod-CORF Dist-CORF 1973

Southwest Indians Of Early America C 14 MIN
16MM FILM, 3/4 OR 1/2 IN VIDEO I-J
Tells how the early Indians of the southwest met their needs through division of labor and use of natural resources. Shows dwellings and remains of the ancestors of the Hopi, Pima and Papago Indians that prospered a thousand years ago.
Prod-CORF Dist-CORF 1973

Southwest, The C 17 MIN
16MM FILM, 3/4 OR 1/2 IN VIDEO J
Examines the people, industry, economy and landscape of the Southwest region of the United States.
From The U S Geography Series.
Prod-MGHT Dist-MGHT 1976

Southwest, The C 25 MIN
16MM FILM, 3/4 OR 1/2 IN VIDEO I-J
Visits the Southwestern states of Texas, Oklahoma, Arizona and New Mexico which comprise an area with an international border, a rich ethnic mix and a bright future.
From The United States Geography Series.
Prod-NGS Dist-NGS 1983

Souvenir B 10 MIN
16MM FILM SILENT H-C A
Tells the story of a young photographer who becomes emotionally involved with his attractive model.
Prod-UWFKD Dist-UWFKD

Souvenirs C 15 MIN
16MM FILM OPTICAL SOUND
Highlights the workmanship of the Russian artisan. Includes a shopping trip, where even the ordinary shops sell extraordinary wares.
Prod-MTP Dist-MTP

Souvenirs From Kerala B 10 MIN
16MM FILM OPTICAL SOUND H-C A
Reveals the skill and ingenuity of the artisans of Kerala in the many handicrafts, which answer both aesthetic and functional needs. Explains how things of beauty are created out of waste materials.
Prod-INDIA Dist-NEDINF

Souvenirs From Sweden C 27 MIN
16MM FILM OPTICAL SOUND
Shows inanimate souvenirs from Lapland and Sweden springing to life to tell about Swedish culture, economy and people and to show the scenic splendors of Sweden. Presents views of sailing in the Archipelago, of the Orrefors Glass Works in the province of Smaland of the Vasa Ski Race in Mora, of Darlina and of the Nobel Festival in Stockholm.
LC NO. FIA66-1393
Prod-SWEDIN Dist-SWNTO 1960

Sovereign Self, The - Right To Live, Right To Die C 60 MIN
3/4 OR 1/2 INCH VIDEO CASSETTE
Discusses how personal freedoms and privacy are balanced against state intervention and societal rights in a presentation which touches on abortion, Baby Doe cases and the right to die.
From The Constitution - That Delicate Balance Series.
Prod-WTTWTV Dist-FI 1984

Soviet Army, The C 60 MIN
3/4 OR 1/2 INCH VIDEO CASSETTE
Looks behind the iron curtain at the modern armed forces of the Soviet Union. Exemplifies Soviet military training and deceptive Communist propaganda techniques.
Prod-IHF Dist-IHF

Soviet Boy C 16 MIN
16MM FILM, 3/4 OR 1/2 IN VIDEO P-J
Depicts the life and experiences of a Soviet boy today in Armenia, USSR.
Prod-ATLAP Dist-ATLAP

Soviet Central Asia C 25 MIN
3/4 OR 1/2 INCH VIDEO CASSETTE H-C A
Looks at Soviet Central Asia, a part of the USSR which is home for 40 to 50 million Moslems.
Prod-UPI Dist-JOU

Soviet Dissidents In Exile C 28 MIN
3/4 INCH VIDEO CASSETTE
Interviews five men who challenged the Soviet regime and were exiled. Discusses the problems of adjusting to a new country.
Prod-ADL Dist-ADL

Soviet Estonia C 20 MIN
3/4 OR 1/2 INCH VIDEO CASSETTE
Reviews the social and economic development of Soviet Estonia, one of the 15 constituent republics of the Soviet Union, and its achievements in industry, science and culture.
Prod-IHF Dist-IHF

Soviet Family, A C 23 MIN
3/4 OR 1/2 INCH VIDEO CASSETTE J-C A
Shows the daily life and concerns of a Moscow family, not of dissidents or of government figures or the army, but of a family. Reveals a way of life that has much in common with that of families elsewhere, but that also has been shaped by the Soviet system.
Prod-IFF Dist-IFF

Soviet Jews - A Culture In Peril B 27 MIN
16MM FILM OPTICAL SOUND
Presents Stuart Novins, former Moscow Bureau Chief and traces the 2000-year history of the Jewish people in what is now the USSR. Examines the lingering antiSemitism within the Soviet Union and proves the causes of the conflict between socialism and Judaism. Explores the extent of Jewish identity permitted by Soviet authorities and the reason why so many Jews continue their battle for emigration to Israel.
Prod-ADL Dist-ADL

Soviet Latvia C 20 MIN
3/4 OR 1/2 INCH VIDEO CASSETTE
Portrays Soviet Latvia, one of the 15 equal republics of the USSR. Focuses on the nation's capital, Riga, and its national traditions.
Prod-IHF Dist-IHF

Soviet Medicine B 30 MIN
16MM FILM, 3/4 OR 1/2 IN VIDEO H-C
Shows the emphasis on the health of Soviet citizen and the differences and similarities between Soviet and United States medical practices.
Prod-NET Dist-IU 1970

Soviet Paradise, The (German) B 14 MIN
3/4 OR 1/2 INCH VIDEO CASSETTE
Witnesses World War II's greatest land battles. Observes first-hand, life in Russia after 20 years of Soviet rule. Represents its citizenry as starving children, youthful gangs, cowed laborers and wretched peasants barely existing in dilapidated collective farms or in overcrowded city slums.
Prod-IHF Dist-IHF

Soviet People Are With Vietnam/Soviet People Support Vietnam B 60 MIN
3/4 OR 1/2 INCH VIDEO CASSETTE
Deals with Soviet material support given to the Vietnamese during the Vietnam war.
Prod-IHF Dist-IHF

Soviet Russia After Sputnik C 29 MIN
2 INCH VIDEOTAPE
See series title for descriptive statement.
From The Course Of Our Times II Series.
Prod-WGBHTV Dist-PUBTEL

Soviet School Children C 11 MIN
16MM FILM, 3/4 OR 1/2 IN VIDEO I-J T
Follows the school day of two Russian schoolgirls, one in the first grade and one in the fifth grade. Focuses on the subjects they study and the political youth groups they may join. Demonstrates how the Communist Party uses education to promote the party program.
Prod-BAILEY Dist-PHENIX 1968

Soviet Style—A Series
16MM FILM, 3/4 OR 1/2 IN VIDEO J-C A
Looks at the characteristics of the Russian economy, agriculture, politics, education and music.
Prod-JOU Dist-JOU 1982

Farming - Soviet Style	027 MIN
People's Music, A - Soviet Style	023 MIN
Politics - Soviet Style	027 MIN
School's In - Soviet Style	027 MIN
Working - Soviet Style	027 MIN

Soviet Turkmenistan C 20 MIN
3/4 OR 1/2 INCH VIDEO CASSETTE
Reviews the social and economic development of Soviet Turkmenistan and its achievements in industry, construction, oil and gas extraction, cotton growing, livestock raising, science and culture.
Prod-IHF Dist-IHF

Soviet Union - Civil War And Allied Intervention B 17 MIN
16MM FILM, 3/4 OR 1/2 IN VIDEO H-C
Discusses Russia's Civil War and looks at the Allies' intervention, which ended by the mid-1920's.
From The World War I Series.
Prod-CBSTV Dist-FI 1967

Soviet Union - Epic Land C 29 MIN
16MM FILM, 3/4 OR 1/2 IN VIDEO J-H
Emphasizes the size, political structure and potential of the Soviet Union and explores the cities and industry of European Russia.
Prod-EBEC Dist-EBEC 1971

Soviet Union - Foreign Politics And Brezhnev C 28 MIN
3/4 OR 1/2 INCH VIDEO CASSETTE H-C A
On the occasion of Leonid Brezhnev's death, after ruling the Soviet Union for 18 years, takes a look at his foreign policies which influenced every country in the world. Looks at the future foreign policy of his successor, Yuri Andropov.
Prod-JOU Dist-JOU

Soviet Union After Khrushchev, The C 29 MIN
2 INCH VIDEOTAPE
See series title for descriptive statement.
From The Course Of Our Times III Series.
Prod-WGBHTV Dist-PUBTEL

Soviet Union Is Our Home, The/Rude Awakening B 30 MIN
3/4 OR 1/2 INCH VIDEO CASSETTE
Documents the life of Jewish people in the Soviet Union and tells of Soviet Jews who had settled in Israel but returned to a better life in the USSR.
Prod-IHF Dist-IHF

Soviet Union, The - A New Look C 25 MIN
16MM FILM, 3/4 OR 1/2 IN VIDEO J-C A
Demonstrates the vastness and diversity of the Soviet Union's geography, variety of its citizens, and wide range of climate, customs, dress and background. Shows kindergartens, schools and universities, artists at work, a ballet school, tractor factory, new housing construction, a family spending an evening at home in Moscow, and a glimpse of women's roles in the Soviet Union.
Prod-IFF Dist-IFF 1978

Soviet Union, The - A Riddle Wrapped In A Mystery C 30 MIN
3/4 INCH VIDEO CASSETTE
See series title for descriptive statement.
From The Of Earth And Man Series.
Prod-MDCPB Dist-MDCPB

Soviet Union, The - A Student's Life X 21 MIN
16MM FILM, 3/4 OR 1/2 IN VIDEO I-H
Presents the structure of Soviet education, including early schooling, vocational schools, rigidity and difficulty of higher education and the background to the development of their type of education. Explains the social and recreational life of students as well as the importance of the school-state relationship.
Prod-EBEC Dist-EBEC 1972

Soviet Union, The - Faces Of Today C 26 MIN
16MM FILM, 3/4 OR 1/2 IN VIDEO I-H
Presents individuals from diverse segments of Soviet society to call attention to the size and regional variety of the Soviet Union and their ways of life. Features a member of a farm co-operative in European Russia, a professional in Tiblisi on the Turkish border, an engineer in Leningrad and a student in Siberia.
Prod-EBEC Dist-EBEC 1972

Soviet Union, The - Land Of The Peasant C 30 MIN
3/4 INCH VIDEO CASSETTE
See series title for descriptive statement.
From The Of Earth And Man Series.
Prod-MDCPB Dist-MDCPB

Soviet Union, The - Past And Present C 21 MIN
16MM FILM, 3/4 OR 1/2 IN VIDEO I-H
Traces Russia's history from Ivan the Terrible to the present, and focuses on current efforts to increase industrial output and improve living conditions.
Prod-CORF Dist-CORF 1970

Soviet Union, The - Temples Of Industry C 30 MIN
3/4 INCH VIDEO CASSETTE
See series title for descriptive statement.
From The Of Earth And Man Series.
Prod-MDCPB Dist-MDCPB

Soviet-Finnish War Of 1939-40 C 66 MIN
16MM FILM MAGNETIC SOUND C
Examines the origins and course of the war between Finland and the Soviet Union in 1939 and 1940. Emphasizes the role of the Red army and pays special attention to European reaction to the war.
From The British Universities Historical Studies In Film Series.
LC NO. 75-703311
Prod-IUHFC Dist-KRAUS 1975

Sow Seeds/Trust The Promise—A Series
J A
Contains segments for directing persons as they develop new skills in planning and leading camps and retreats. Features several experts, nationally recognized in theology, education and outdoor skills.
Prod-UMCOM Dist-ECUFLM

Community And Self Understanding	030 MIN
Outdoor Skills	030 MIN
Planning And Resourcing	030 MIN
Theology And Faith Development	030 MIN

Soweto B 16 MIN
16MM FILM OPTICAL SOUND H-C A
Looks at the people of Soweto, or South Western Townships, a Bantu suburb of Johannesburg in South Africa. Shows their homes, their environment and examines the restrictive laws which govern their lives.
LC NO. 76-703922
Prod-BFPS Dist-BFPS 1976

Soybeans C 3 MIN
16MM FILM - 3/4 IN VIDEO
Shows some of the many uses of the soybean, including being baked in a casserole and toasted as nibbles. Explains that soy grits and soy flour are used in baked goods and soy oil is good for a salad dressing. Points out that fermented soybean products include tamari, which is like Worchestershire sauce and mise, a soy paste for soup stock and casseroles. Demonstrates how to make tofu, a cheese made from soy flour.
From The Beatrice Trum Hunter's Natural Foods Series.
Prod-PBS Dist-PUBTEL Prodn-WGBH 1974

Soybeans - The Magic Beanstalk C 12 MIN
16MM FILM, 3/4 OR 1/2 IN VIDEO I-J
Shows how science and agriculture worked together to transform the soybean plant into a beanstalk almost magical in its usefulness.
Prod-CENTRO Dist-CORF

Soyez Un Professionel C 14 MIN
16MM FILM, 3/4 OR 1/2 IN VIDEO J-H A
A French-language version of the motion picture Be A Pro. Explains that professional players use the best equipment to protect themselves from injury when playing. Discusses such techniques as applied to automobile driving and machine work.
Prod-CHET Dist-IFB 1966

Soyuz/Apollo Link-up C 20 MIN
3/4 OR 1/2 INCH VIDEO CASSETTE
Tells the story of the first 'international flight of manned spaceships' which took place during the month of June, 1975. Shows Soviet and American astronauts in various stages of preparation.
Prod-IHF Dist-IHF

Space C 10 MIN
16MM FILM, 3/4 OR 1/2 IN VIDEO I-H A
Uses familiar objects and situations to show how we perceive space and how the artist utilizes it. Shows how space is defined and shaped by the objects which exist within it or enclose it.
From The Art Of Seeing Series.
Prod-AFA Dist-FI Prodn-ACI 1970

Space C 15 MIN
3/4 OR 1/2 INCH VIDEO CASSETTE K-J
See series title for descriptive statement.
From The Arts Express Series.
Prod-KYTV Dist-KYTV 1983

Space - Life Out There C 22 MIN
16MM FILM, 3/4 OR 1/2 IN VIDEO
Discusses the possibility of intelligent life on other planets. Features the views of Carl Sagan, author and exobiologist.
Prod-DOCUA Dist-CNEMAG

Space - The New Ocean C 10 MIN
16MM FILM OPTICAL SOUND
Explains U S military space research and development activities in relation to overall space exploration, featuring current and future space and missile programs of the U S Air Force.
LC NO. 75-703758
Prod-USAF Dist-USNAC 1971

Space - The New Perspective - Orbital Photography C 21 MIN
16MM FILM OPTICAL SOUND
Presents Mr Richard Underwood of the NASA Johnson Space Center, Phototechnology Division, discussing what space photography of Earth reveals to the scientist.
Prod-NASA Dist-NASA

Space Age - Dr Goddard To Project Gemini B 18 MIN
16MM FILM OPTICAL SOUND
Records the sights and sounds of the Space Age from the pioneering work of Robert Goddard to the cosmic conquests of Project Gemini.
From The Screen News Digest Series. Vol 7, Issue 9
Prod-HEARST Dist-HEARST 1965

Space Age Railroad C 18 MIN
16MM FILM OPTICAL SOUND
Tells the story of high speed test track, a research and development facility at Holloman AFB, New Mexico. Highlights advancements since the first track run in 1950. Illustrates monorail runs and explains principal braking systems. Explains the physical layout of areas and different experiments.
LC NO. 74-705669
Prod-USAF Dist-USNAC 1969

Space Age, The C 15 MIN
3/4 OR 1/2 INCH VIDEO CASSETTE I
See series title for descriptive statement.
From The Discovering Series. Unit 5 - Space
Prod-WDCNTV Dist-AITECH 1978

Space And The Atom C 27 MIN
16MM FILM OPTICAL SOUND PRO
Reports on many of the successes of nuclear energy in space, such as the SNAP generators. Delineates the joint efforts of the U S Atomic Energy Commission and the National Aeronautics and Space Administration to develop a nuclear rocket engine and depicts the future role of nuclear energy in space exploration.
LC NO. 70-714177
Prod-ANL Dist-USERD 1971

Space And Touch C 30 MIN
3/4 OR 1/2 INCH VIDEO CASSETTE H-C A
Explains the two nonverbal components, proxemics spatial relationships, and haptics - touching behaviors. Demonstrates the variables of communication and meaning associated with these two human behaviors.
From The Principles Of Human Communication Series.
Prod-UMINN Dist-GPITVL 1983

Space Between The Teeth, The C 9 MIN
3/4 OR 1/2 INCH VIDEO CASSETTE
Comments on man's feeling of entrapment in the man-made environment.
From The Four Songs Series.
Prod-EAI Dist-EAI

Space Child C 28 MIN
16MM FILM OPTICAL SOUND
Focuses on Paul Van Hoydonck and his conceptual sculpture.
LC NO. 77-702649
Prod-CANFDC Dist-CANFDC 1972

Space Communications C 19 MIN
16MM FILM OPTICAL SOUND
Uses animation to highlight the basic communications principles and techniques relating to space. Explains the behavior of electromagnetic waves and discusses factors, such as distance, payloads and telemetry.
LC NO. FIE61-122
Prod-USAF Dist-USNAC 1960

Space Connection, The C 10 MIN
16MM FILM OPTICAL SOUND
Describes a digital communication system which employs satellites to provide extremely wide bandwidth connections anywhere in the United States.
LC NO. 80-701455
Prod-SATBS Dist-FLECKG Prodn-FLECKG 1980

Space Down To Earth C 28 MIN
3/4 INCH VIDEO CASSETTE
Shows how Earth-orbiting satellites are serving mankind in the 1970's and discusses prospects for the next decade. Covers Earth resources surveys, measurement of pollution levels, long-range weather forecasts and improvement of navigation and communication. Issued in 1970 as a motion picture.
From The Space In The 70's Series.
LC NO. 79-706680
Prod-NASA Dist-USNAC 1979

Space Driving Tactics (2nd Ed) C 14 MIN
16MM FILM, 3/4 OR 1/2 IN VIDEO J-C A
Demonstrates the importance of keeping a safe distance from other vehicles on the highway and shows how to determine what distance is safe for various driving conditions.
LC NO. 81-706558
Prod-CAHILL Dist-AIMS 1980

Space Duet Of Gumdrop And Spider, The - Apollo 9 C 28 MIN
16MM FILM OPTICAL SOUND
Presents a view of the Apollo 9 astronauts before, during and after their earth orbital mission. Concentrates on the launching, rendezvous and docking of the command module (Gumdrop), lunar module (Spider) and the return and recovery of the crew.
Prod-NASA Dist-NASA

Space Eaters, The C 20 MIN
16MM FILM OPTICAL SOUND I
Presents the criteria for a transportation system and discusses the automobile in relationship to the criteria.
From The Inherit The Earth Series.
Prod-KQEDTV Dist-GPITVL

Space Expectations B 27 MIN
16MM FILM OPTICAL SOUND

Looks at the varied viewpoints of America's space program from a cross section of the general public.
Prod-NASA Dist-NASA 1973

Space Expectations (2nd Ed) C 27 MIN
16MM FILM OPTICAL SOUND
Examines varied viewpoints from a cross section of the general public concerning America's space program.
LC NO. 74-706523
Prod-NASA Dist-USNAC 1973

Space Experiments - Skylab C 15 MIN
3/4 OR 1/2 INCH VIDEO CASSETTE I
See series title for descriptive statement.
From The Discovering Series. Unit 5 - Space
Prod-WDCNTV Dist-AITECH 1978

Space Exploration C 15 MIN
3/4 INCH VIDEO CASSETTE I
Explains and illustrates the fundamental laws of inertia.
From The Search For Science (2nd Ed.) Unit II - Space Series.
Prod-WVIZTV Dist-GPITVL

Space Exploration - A Team Effort C 24 MIN
16MM FILM, 3/4 OR 1/2 IN VIDEO I-H
Introduces the contributions of scientists, engineers and technicians involved in the space program and who make it possible. Follows an astronaut through various training procedures and learning sessions. Reveals present methods of training and future plans.
From The World Of Work Series.
Prod-EBEC Dist-EBEC 1972

Space Filling Curves C 26 MIN
16MM FILM, 3/4 OR 1/2 IN VIDEO C
Features examples of space-filling curves, using computer animation.
From The Topology Series.
LC NO. 81-706240
Prod-EDC Dist-IFB 1975

Space Flight Around The Earth, A (German) C 12 MIN
16MM FILM, 3/4 OR 1/2 IN VIDEO P
Features the flights of John Glenn and Ed White. Pictures the earth as viewed from space.
Prod-DF Dist-CF

Space Flight Around The Earth, A (2nd Ed) C 12 MIN
16MM FILM, 3/4 OR 1/2 IN VIDEO P
Shows the appearance of the earth from space. Pictures the planet's roundness, oceans, land and atmosphere. Explains what causes night and day. Shows astronauts Glenn and White on their historic flights.
Prod-DF Dist-CF 1965

Space For Head And Hands C 20 MIN
3/4 OR 1/2 INCH VIDEO CASSETTE
Presents collaboration of Michael Tilson Thomas and video artist Ron Hays in an improvisation.
Prod-EAI Dist-EAI

Space For Man C 120 MIN
3/4 OR 1/2 INCH VIDEO CASSETTE
Combines the skills and facilities of some 20 nations for a critical look at how space technology has benefited man in the past and what it can do in the future.
Prod-NPACT Dist-PBS 1975

Space For The Mentally Retarded C 22 MIN
16MM FILM OPTICAL SOUND
Shows existing programs and facilities for the mentally retarded and points out remaining needs and how they might be met. Discusses the importance of a team approach in the provision of services to the mentally retarded.
Prod-USD Dist-USD 1968

Space For Women C 28 MIN
16MM FILM, 3/4 OR 1/2 IN VIDEO H-C A
Interviews women employed in NASA's space transportation programs and shows the variety of positions that they hold, ranging from electrical engineer, aerial photography analyst and safety specialist to astronaut mission specialist. Notes how the women obtained their training and qualified for their positions.
LC NO. 81-707192
Prod-NASA Dist-USNAC 1981

Space In The 70's - Aeronautics C 28 MIN
16MM FILM OPTICAL SOUND
Shows the problems of aeronautical flight and flight operations. Includes pictures of short haul aircrafts.
LC NO. 70-710249
Prod-NASA Dist-USNAC 1971

Space In The 70's - Challenge And Promise C 27 MIN
16MM FILM OPTICAL SOUND
Presents an updated overview of the content of space in the 70's series.
From The Space In The 70's Series.
LC NO. 74-705672
Prod-NASA Dist-USNAC 1973

Space In The 70's - Exploration Of The Planets C 25 MIN
16MM FILM OPTICAL SOUND
Summarizes the principal features of the planets and presents the various missions planned for their exploration during the decade of the 1970's.
From The Space In The 70's Series.
LC NO. 77-713562
Prod-NASA Dist-USNAC 1971

Space In The 70's - Man In Space - The Second Decade C 28 MIN
16MM FILM OPTICAL SOUND
Includes a brief history of where we stand now and views proposed future manned space flight programs. Presents mission activities and reasons behind extended Apollo lunar missions in 1971 and 1972, the first experimental space station called Skylab and the space shuttle later in the decade.
Prod-NASA Dist-USNAC 1971

Space In The 70's - Space Down To Earth C 28 MIN
16MM FILM OPTICAL SOUND I-C A
Shows how earth-orbiting satellites are serving mankind and what can be expected during the next decade. Includes earth resources surveys, measurements of pollution levels, long-range weather forecasts, precise earth measurements and improved navigation and communications.
From The Space In The 70's Series.
LC NO. 79-710645
Prod-NASA Dist-NASA 1970

Space In The 70's - The Knowledge Bank C 25 MIN
16MM FILM OPTICAL SOUND
Presents the idea that research results are deposits to be accumulated and later drawn upon - with the payoff frequently beyond even the range of science fiction. Takes a broad look at physics and astronomy research performed in the laboratory of space.
From The Space In The 70's Series.
LC NO. 76-713168
Prod-NASA Dist-USNAC 1971

Space In The 70's—A Series

Discusses U S space research and programs of the 1970's.
Prod-NASA Dist-USNAC 1979

Aeronautics	028 MIN
Challenge And Promise	027 MIN
Exploration Of The Planets	025 MIN
Knowledge Bank, The	025 MIN
Man In Space, The Second Decade	028 MIN
Space Down To Earth	028 MIN

Space Medicine B 29 MIN
3/4 INCH VIDEO CASSETTE
Discusses the medical progress and problems of sending a human being into space, the requirements of a space suit and life support equipment. Takes a look at the medical program for manned space flight.
Prod-USNAC Dist-USNAC 1972

Space Medicine - Serving Mankind C 14 MIN
3/4 OR 1/2 INCH VIDEO CASSETTE
Tells how technologies developed to safely facilitate man's exploration of space are now being used to prolong life and eradicate disease here on earth.
Prod-KINGFT Dist-KINGFT

Space Navigation C 21 MIN
16MM FILM OPTICAL SOUND J-H A
Illustrates with animation and live-action photography the equipment, techniques and mathematics of space navigation between the earth and moon and between the earth and other planets.
LC NO. FIE67-120
Prod-NASA Dist-NASA 1967

Space Neighbors C 15 MIN
3/4 OR 1/2 INCH VIDEO CASSETTE P-I
Discusses earth's space neighbors.
From The Why Series.
Prod-WDCNTV Dist-AITECH 1976

Space Orbits C 18 MIN
16MM FILM OPTICAL SOUND
Uses animation to present basic facts of orbital patterns and the forces which produce them. Tells how these projects follow natural laws formulated by Sir Isaac Newton.
LC NO. FIE61-123
Prod-USAF Dist-USNAC 1960

Space Patrol (1951,1953) C 60 MIN
3/4 OR 1/2 INCH VIDEO CASSETTE
Presents episodes from the 1951 space series with Commander Cory.
Prod-IHF Dist-IHF

Space Patrol (1953) C
3/4 OR 1/2 INCH VIDEO CASSETTE
Presents Commander Cory with high adventure in the vast regions of space from the 1953 space series.
Prod-IHF Dist-IHF

Space Planning C 30 MIN
2 INCH VIDEOTAPE C A
Explains the basic concepts of furniture arrangement. Defines the general goal of space planning.
From The Designing Home Interiors Series. Unit 12
Prod-COAST Dist-CDTEL Prodn-RSCCD

Space Project C 15 MIN
16MM FILM OPTICAL SOUND
Shows how drug stores become cluttered and disorganized because of the increase in products and promotion items in the same amount of space. Demonstrates ways in which pharmacists can make the best use of their available floor and display space.
LC NO. FIA67-1839
Prod-JAJ Dist-JAJ Prodn-STRAUS 1965

Space Rendezvous C 25 MIN
16MM FILM OPTICAL SOUND
Clarifies the principles and limitations of orbital maneuvering in outer space. Focuses primarily on coplanar orbits but also delineates the complexities of noncoplanar orbits for comparison. Points out the problems involved in transferring a vehicle from one orbit to another for rendezvous with another vehicle.
LC NO. 74-706251
Prod-USAF Dist-USNAC 1964

Space Research And You - Your Home And Environment C 15 MIN
16MM FILM, 3/4 OR 1/2 IN VIDEO
Illustrates spacecraft studies of Earth for inventory of resources and detection of pollution. Shows advanced technologies for acquiring energy from the sun and wind, sewage treatment facilities and energy-saving household devices.
From The Space Research And You Series.
Prod-NASA Dist-USNAC

Space Research And You - Your Transportation C 15 MIN
16MM FILM, 3/4 OR 1/2 IN VIDEO
Examines computer simulation teaching tools for training ships' crews, vertical takeoff and landing planes, electric cars, streamlining trucks, aircraft improvement and the space shuttle.
From The Space Research And You Series.
Prod-NASA Dist-USNAC

Space Research And You—A Series

Shows how the technology developed to explore planets and monitor the well-being of astronauts in space has led to advances in medicine, transportation and the environment.
Prod-NASA Dist-USNAC

Space Research And You - Your Home And	
Space Research And You - Your Transportation	015 MIN
Space Research And Your Health	015 MIN

Space Research And Your Health C 15 MIN
16MM FILM, 3/4 OR 1/2 IN VIDEO
Shows how NASA research has led to improved medical tools and new health practices. Shows miniaturized spacecraft components adapted into implantable devices for treatment of heart disease and diabetes, computer technology for medical diagnosis and communications systems for rural health care.
From The Space Research And You Series.
Prod-NASA Dist-USNAC

Space Salvage C 30 MIN
16MM FILM, 3/4 OR 1/2 IN VIDEO H-C A
Chronicles Lloyd's of London's plan to recover two satellites lost in space that it had insured.
From The Enterprise Series.
Prod-MTI Dist-MTI

Space Science - An Introduction (2nd Ed) C 14 MIN
16MM FILM, 3/4 OR 1/2 IN VIDEO I-J
Presents an introduction to the vocabulary and scientific principles of space travel. Uses animation and a specially designed model to show why some vehicles stay in orbit while others can travel through space.
From The Space Science Series.
Prod-CORF Dist-CORF 1977

Space Science - Comets, Meteors And Planetoids C 11 MIN
16MM FILM, 3/4 OR 1/2 IN VIDEO I-H
Shows how the spectroscope, radio and optical telescopes are used to provide information about the origin of comets, meteors and planetoids. Special effects show the meteor shower of 1833, the approach of Halley's comet and the movements of planetoids.
From The Space Science Series.
Prod-CORF Dist-CORF 1963

Space Science - Exploring The Moon C 16 MIN
16MM FILM, 3/4 OR 1/2 IN VIDEO J-C
Illustrates the 400-year-long story of lunar exploration, using ancient maps, photographs and motion pictures, including those taken by the first men on the moon.
From The Space Science Series.
Prod-CORF Dist-CORF 1969

Space Science - Galaxies And The Universe C 14 MIN
16MM FILM, 3/4 OR 1/2 IN VIDEO J-C
Describes the three types of galaxies. Shows the two types of star populations and quasars and illustrates the three most prominent theories of expansion.
From The Space Science Series.
Prod-CORF Dist-CORF 1969

Space Science - Studying The Stars C 13 MIN
16MM FILM, 3/4 OR 1/2 IN VIDEO I-H
Shows how optical and radio telescopes can measure the energy-radiation of stars and how distance to the stars can be found by the parallax method and by comparing their brightness or magnitude. Presents methods used to keep track of star movements, and how the star's light gives clues to its heat, composition, movement and size.
From The Space Science Series.
Prod-CORF Dist-CORF 1967

Space Science - The Planets C 16 MIN
16MM FILM, 3/4 OR 1/2 IN VIDEO I-H
Uses telescopic pictures, animation and special effects to survey the nine planets and their satellites. Discusses temperature and atmosphere of the planets, their periods of rotation and revolution, and their distance from the sun. Shows how instruments launched into space aid scientists in their study.
From The Space Science Series.
Prod-CORF Dist-CORF 1963

Space Science For Beginners C 11 MIN
16MM FILM, 3/4 OR 1/2 IN VIDEO P
Presents simple demonstrations with a balloon and a model rocket to illustrate the kind of action-reaction forces needed to travel away from the pull of the earth.
Prod-CORF Dist-CORF 1969

Space Science—A Series
16MM FILM, 3/4 OR 1/2 IN VIDEO I-J
Surveys major aspects of the space sciences, describing the moon, the planets, comets and meteors, the Sun, the stars and the galaxies.
Prod-CORF Dist-CORF

Space Science - An Introduction (2nd Ed) 14 MIN
Space Science - Comets, Meteors And Planetoids 11 MIN
Space Science - Exploring The Moon 16 MIN
Space Science - Galaxies And The Universe 14 MIN
Space Science - Studying The Stars 13 MIN
Space Science - The Planets 16 MIN
Space Science - The Sun As A Star 14 MIN

Space Shuttle C 15 MIN
16MM FILM, 3/4 OR 1/2 IN VIDEO
Describes the reusable space shuttle and its capabilities for replacing the expendable launch vehicle. Presents animated sequences illustrating a typical flight mission and the proposed use of the shuttle. Issued in 1975 as a motion picture.
LC NO. 80-707163
Prod-NASA Dist-USNAC 1980

Space Shuttle - A Remarkable Flying Machine C 30 MIN
16MM FILM OPTICAL SOUND
Describes in detail the first space shuttle flight. Shows the lift-off, in-flight activities and landing at Dryden Flight Research Center, California.
LC NO. 81-701641
Prod-NASA Dist-USNAC 1981

Space Shuttle - A Remarkable Flying Machine C 30 MIN
3/4 OR 1/2 INCH VIDEO CASSETTE
Tells the story of the development and first flight of the space shuttle Columbia.
Prod-IHF Dist-IHF

Space Shuttle - Mission To The Future C 27 MIN
16MM FILM, 3/4 OR 1/2 IN VIDEO
Documents the importance of the space shuttle to America and the world. Shows shuttle tests, the training of astronauts and space specialists at work. Includes brief comments on space exploration by novelists James Michener and Isaac Asimov.
LC NO. 81-707193
Prod-NASA Dist-USNAC 1981

Space Shuttle - Overview, May 1980 C 28 MIN
16MM FILM, 3/4 OR 1/2 IN VIDEO
Looks at the status of the space shuttle in mid-1980.
From The Space Shuttle Profile Series.
LC NO. 81-706323
Prod-NASA Dist-USNAC 1980

Space Shuttle - Platform To The Stars C 14 MIN
3/4 OR 1/2 INCH VIDEO CASSETTE
Focuses on the Space Shuttle and its role in America's continuing efforts to enlarge, or push back the horizons of space.
Prod-KINGFT Dist-KINGFT

Space Shuttle - The Orbiter C 14 MIN
16MM FILM, 3/4 OR 1/2 IN VIDEO
Explains the space transportation system in general, including the main components, the Orbiter, external tank and solid rocket boosters. Describes the size configuration and internal design of the Orbiter and the multitude of systems such as propulsion, thermal protection and computer.
From The Space Shuttle Profile Series.
Prod-NASA Dist-USNAC 1981

Space Shuttle Communications C 8 MIN
16MM FILM, 3/4 OR 1/2 IN VIDEO
Explains the vast communications and tracking support shuttle operations, including the tracking and data relay satellite systems to be used for payloads, the NASA communication network, domestic satellites and the deep space network for interplanetary missions.
From The Space Shuttle Profile Series.
Prod-NASA Dist-USNAC 1981

Space Shuttle Economics C 6 MIN
16MM FILM, 3/4 OR 1/2 IN VIDEO
Explains the economic advantages of the space shuttle system by pointing out the reusability of elements such as the solid rocket boosters and the orbiter. Discusses the financial gain from transporting satellites into space and the 'Gateway Special' program.
From The Space Shuttle Profile Series.
Prod-NASA Dist-USNAC

Space Shuttle Extra-Vehicular Activity C 12 MIN
16MM FILM, 3/4 OR 1/2 IN VIDEO
Explains the tools, tethers, space suits, life support systems and maneuvering units of extravehicular activity tasks that are planned for shuttle operations.
From The Space Shuttle Profile Series.
Prod-NASA Dist-USNAC 1981

Space Shuttle Ground Support C 8 MIN
16MM FILM, 3/4 OR 1/2 IN VIDEO
Outlines the role of the key facilities for shuttle operations. Discusses particular installations and their individual responsibilities with regard to the space shuttle program.
From The Space Shuttle Profile Series.
Prod-NASA Dist-USNAC 1981

Space Shuttle Missions And Payloads C 14 MIN
16MM FILM, 3/4 OR 1/2 IN VIDEO
Explains different kinds of missions and payloads that are planned for the space shuttle including placing, servicing and retrieving satellites in space, with a brief explanation of the purpose of these satellites. Looks at the multi-mission modular spacecraft, Long Duration Exposure Facility, space probes and Spacelab.
From The Space Shuttle Profile Series.
Prod-NASA Dist-USNAC 1981

Space Shuttle Overview 1980 C 30 MIN
3/4 OR 1/2 INCH VIDEO CASSETTE
Discusses the space shuttle.
From The History Of Space Travel Series.
Prod-NASAC Dist-MDCPB

Space Shuttle Profile—A Series
3/4 OR 1/2 INCH VIDEO CASSETTE
Discusses aspects of the space shuttle.
Prod-NASA Dist-USNAC

Space Shuttle - Overview, May 1980 028 MIN
Space Shuttle - The Orbiter 014 MIN
Space Shuttle Communications 008 MIN
Space Shuttle Economics 009 MIN
Space Shuttle Extra Vehicular Activity 012 MIN
Space Shuttle Ground Support 008 MIN
Space Shuttle Missions And Payloads 014 MIN
Space Shuttle Propulsion 012 MIN
Space Shuttle Spacelab 012 MIN
STS-1 Launch Aborts 005 MIN

Space Shuttle Propulsion C 12 MIN
16MM FILM, 3/4 OR 1/2 IN VIDEO
Explains the key propulsion systems, their use for shuttle operations and how they differ from past expendable systems. Looks at the reusable solid rocket boosters, the external tank, the main propulsion system, the reaction control system and the orbital maneuvering subsystem.
From The Space Shuttle Profile Series.
Prod-NASA Dist-USNAC 1981

Space Shuttle Spacelab C 12 MIN
16MM FILM, 3/4 OR 1/2 IN VIDEO
Describes the Spacelab Program, including information about the European Space Agency, the scientific expectations of Spacelab and the eight different Spacelab configurations.
From The Space Shuttle Profile Series.
Prod-NASA Dist-USNAC 1981

Space Shuttle, The C 4 MIN
16MM FILM OPTICAL SOUND
Gives the rationale for a reusable space launching vehicle for scientific experimentation. Describes a typical shuttle mission from launch to landing at Kennedy Space Center, Florida.
LC NO. 75-703074
Prod-NASA Dist-USNAC 1973

Space Shuttle, The C 14 MIN
3/4 OR 1/2 INCH VIDEO CASSETTE
Provides information on the U S Space Shuttle, emphasizing the importance of its success from a military and civilian perspective.
Prod-UPI Dist-JOU

Space Spraying Of Insecticides (Spanish) C 11 MIN
16MM FILM OPTICAL SOUND
Demonstrates techniques of space spraying for insect control over large areas and shows various types of modern power-spraying equipment.
LC NO. 74-705673
Prod-NMAC Dist-USNAC 1961

Space Spraying Of Insecticides (2nd Ed) C 11 MIN
16MM FILM OPTICAL SOUND
Demonstrates techniques of space spraying for insect control over large areas and shows various types of modern power-spraying equipment.
LC NO. FIE61-21
Prod-USPHS Dist-USNAC 1961

Space Suit C 5 MIN
3/4 INCH VIDEO CASSETTE
Describes the space suit worn on the Apollo missions. Issued in 1969 as a motion picture.
From The Apollo Digest Series.
LC NO. 79-706994
Prod-NASA Dist-USNAC 1979

Space Technology C 15 MIN
3/4 OR 1/2 INCH VIDEO CASSETTE I
See series title for descriptive statement.
From The Discovering Series. Unit 5 - Space
Prod-WDCNTV Dist-AITECH 1978

Space To Grow, A B 32 MIN
3/4 INCH VIDEO CASSETTE
Concentrates on the aims and techniques used by the upward bound program to motivate and rectify the academic disabilities of talented poor youngsters.
Prod-USNAC Dist-USNAC 1972

Space Trace C 11 MIN
16MM FILM OPTICAL SOUND
Uses experimental techniques to show an earthbound dancer spinning into outer space by means of a NASA rocket and ice dancing.
LC NO. 80-701379
Prod-ALLPI Dist-ALLPI 1980

Space Travel B 45 MIN
2 INCH VIDEOTAPE C
See series title for descriptive statement.
From The Physical Science Series. Unit 4 - Motion, Work And Energy
Prod-CHITVC Dist-GPITVL Prodn-WTTWTV

Space, Inc C 30 MIN
3/4 OR 1/2 INCH VIDEO CASSETTE
Looks at a new breed of entreprenuers who see space as the next frontier for private enterprise. Points out that space exploration so far has been a strictly government-financed operation.
From The Innovation Series.
Prod-WNETTV Dist-WNETTV 1983

Space, Time And Albert Einstein C 29 MIN
16MM FILM, 3/4 OR 1/2 IN VIDEO H-C
Discusses Einstein's Special Theory of Relativity. Includes archival footage of Einstein explaining aspects of his theory.
From The Dimensions In Science, Series 2 Series.
Prod-OECA Dist-FI 1979

Spaceborne C 14 MIN
16MM FILM, 3/4 OR 1/2 IN VIDEO
Presents a selection of film footage taken during the manned moon flights.
Prod-LAWHS Dist-PFP 1977

Spacecoast USA C 15 MIN
16MM FILM OPTICAL SOUND
Presents Florida's Cocoa Beach, a noted vacation spot and headquarters for the nation's space program.
Prod-FLADC Dist-FLADC

Spacecraft For Apollo C 6 MIN
16MM FILM - 3/4 IN VIDEO
Shows the command, service and lunar landing modules of the Apollo spacecraft. Issued in 1969 as a motion picture.
From The Apollo Digest Series.
LC NO. 79-706993
Prod-NASA Dist-USNAC 1979

Spacecraft System Design—A Series
PRO
Consists of 14 two-and-one-half-hour lectures on 41 video cassettes. Covers important design aspects of the space shuttle from inception to completion, and is presented by design engineering staff, Space Systems Group, Rockwell International.
Prod-USCITV Dist-AMCEE

Mission Support 420 MIN
Orbiter Assembly And Operation 420 MIN
Orbiter Configuration And Design 420 MIN
Preliminary Design 420 MIN
System Elements 420 MIN

Spacecraft Technology—A Series
PRO
Covers in 26 hours on 26 cassettes the principal fundamentals in space technology to date. Identifies main subject headings as introduction, with circular orbits and space environment, Satellite orbits, elliptical, with position calculation, electric power with solar eclipses, solar radiation and solar cells, power budget with bus regulation and batteries. Continues with spacecraft attitude control, thermal considerations, structure, testing, telemetry, tracking and command, station keeping and earth station pointing, reliability and communications subsystems.
Prod-USCITV Dist-AMCEE

Spaced Out Sports C 15 MIN
3/4 OR 1/2 INCH VIDEO CASSETTE A
Offers a look at the world of twentieth-century competitive sports from the supposed point of view of a future civilization. Provides light humor.
Prod-SFTI Dist-SFTI

Spaceflight—A Series

Explores the historical, political and technological events of the space race, and offers a complete, chronological and comprehensive study of the Earth's manned space program. Uses previously classified N A S A and government footage and information and rare footage from the Russian space program.
Prod-PBS Dist-PBS

One Giant Leap 060 MIN
Territory Ahead, The 060 MIN
Thunder In The Skies 060 MIN
Wings Of Mercury, The 060 MIN

Spacelab - The Manned Space Laboratory C 9 MIN
16MM FILM OPTICAL SOUND
Presents an animated conception of the European Space Agency's Spacelab and its projected functions. Shows how the Spacelab will have an integration center in the United States which will be open to worldwide input. Explains that the lab will carry equipment and researchers who will perform experiments sent in by scientists all over the world.
LC NO. 75-702874
Prod-EURSPA Dist-USNAC Prodn-LESFS

Spaces C 15 MIN
3/4 INCH VIDEO CASSETTE K-P
Shows mimes and children in various spaces, including their personal spaces, urban and natural spaces, and imaginative spaces.
From The Adventures Of Milo And Maisie Series.
Prod-KRLNTV Dist-GPITVL 1977

Spaces C 30 MIN
3/4 OR 1/2 INCH VIDEO CASSETTE I-J
Features a Black psychophysiologist and an Hispanic astronaut at work. Also shows high schoolers designing an experiment to be carried on a space shuttle flight and Anasazi Indians developing a solar calendar.
From The Spaces Series.
Prod-WETATV Dist-GPITVL 1983

Spaces Between People C 18 MIN
16MM FILM, 3/4 OR 1/2 IN VIDEO J-C A
Tells the story of a rookie teacher in England who abandons the traditional curriculum approach in order to attempt contact at the human level because he is faced with a class of rejects

from other schools. Points out that small successes are achieved, but much distance remains between teacher and student.
From The Searching For Values - A Film Anthology Series.
Prod-LCOA Dist-LCOA 1972

Spaces To Live In C 20 MIN
16MM FILM, 3/4 OR 1/2 IN VIDEO
Considers the organization and characteristics of planned spaces for community living. Studies the functional and aesthetic problems in the design of spaces for living.
From The Images And Things Series.
LC NO. 73-702112
Prod-NITC Dist-AITECH 1971

Spaces—A Series
I-J
Introduces people and careers in science and technology. Features successful Asian, Black, Hispanic or Native American scientists, engineers and students.
Prod-WETATV Dist-GPITVL 1983

Body, The	030 MIN
Communications	030 MIN
Computers	030 MIN
Ecology	030 MIN
Energy	030 MIN
Spaces	030 MIN

Spaceship Skylab - Wings Of Discovery C 9 MIN
16MM FILM OPTICAL SOUND
Examines the successes and failures of the Skylab program. Shows how man's ingenuity on the ground and in space helped save the Skylab mission and examines the many experiments made aboard the orbiting laboratory.
LC NO. 75-700584
Prod-NASA Dist-USNAC 1974

Spain C 29 MIN
2 INCH VIDEOTAPE
Features home economist Joan Hood presenting a culinary tour of specialty dishes from around the world. Shows the preparation of Spanish dishes ranging from peasant cookery to continental cuisine.
From The International Cookbook Series.
Prod-WMVSTV Dist-PUBTEL

Spain - A Catalonian Menu C 28 MIN
16MM FILM, 3/4 OR 1/2 IN VIDEO J-C A
Introduces the Spanish countryside and describes various Spanish delicacies.
From The World Of Cooking Series.
Prod-SCRESC Dist-MTI 1979

Spain - A Journey With Washington Irving C 25 MIN
16MM FILM, 3/4 OR 1/2 IN VIDEO H-C A
Presents a journey through Spain guided by Washington Irving's diary of the 1820's. Depicts the Festival of San Fermin in Pamplona, Holy Week festivities in Madrid and the richness of Spanish painting in the Prado Museum. Visits San Lucar and Barcelona.
LC NO. 80-706336
Prod-NGS Dist-NGS 1973

Spain - The Land And The Legend C 26 MIN
16MM FILM, 3/4 OR 1/2 IN VIDEO
A shortened version of the motion picture Spain - The Land And The Legend. Features author James Michener in an exploration of the history, culture, folklore and art of Spain.
From The James Michener's World Series.
Prod-READER Dist-PFP

Spain - The Land And The Legend C 58 MIN
16MM FILM, 3/4 OR 1/2 IN VIDEO
Features author James Michener in an exploration of the history, culture, folklore and art of Spain.
From The James Michener's World Series.
Prod-READER Dist-PFP 1978

Spain - The Land And The Legend (Spanish) C 58 MIN
16MM FILM, 3/4 OR 1/2 IN VIDEO
Presents a portrait of the Spanish countryside and character. Explores Spanish history and conveys a sense of the forces that have shaped Spain over the centuries. Includes a commentary by James Michener.
Prod-READER Dist-PFP

Spain - Years Of Revolution C 60 MIN
16MM FILM OPTICAL SOUND
Provides a history of the Spanish Civil War.
Prod-OHC Dist-HRC

Spain, The Years Of Revolution C 60 MIN
3/4 OR 1/2 INCH VIDEO CASSETTE
Traces the turbulent events in Spain from 1902 through the death of Generalissimo Francisco Franco in 1975.
Prod-IVCH Dist-IVCH

Spalding Gray's Map Of L A C 28 MIN
3/4 OR 1/2 INCH VIDEO CASSETTE
Intercuts reminiscing about seminal automobile influences with a narrative about arriving in Los Angeles. Presented by Bruce and Norman Yonemoto.
Prod-ARTINC Dist-ARTINC

Spalding Gray's Map Of LA C 28 MIN
3/4 INCH VIDEO CASSETTE
Presents Bruce and Norman Yonemoto's tape of Spalding Gray's trip to LA and the memories evoked there of cars he knew in his youth and the tragi-comic events that took place around them.
Prod-EAI Dist-EAI

Span Gas Calibration Of Direct Reading Instruments C 5 MIN
1/2 IN VIDEO CASSETTE BETA/VHS
Discusses calibration and analysis of gases.
Prod-RMI Dist-RMI

Span Of Attention, The B 17 MIN
16MM FILM OPTICAL SOUND P-C
Presents a laboratory test of attention, which projects varying numbers of dots at brief intervals, allowing time after each trial for the student to write down his estimate of the number of dots shown.
LC NO. 79-713856
Prod-NSF Dist-PSUPCR 1967

Spaniernes Spanien (The Spain Of The Spaniards) B 15 MIN
16MM FILM OPTICAL SOUND
A Danish language film. Points out the responsibility of the free democracies for the development in the Spain of Franco today, comparing the Spain of the tourists with that of the Spaniards.
Prod-STATNS Dist-STATNS 1966

Spanish Armada, The C 32 MIN
16MM FILM, 3/4 OR 1/2 IN VIDEO J-C A
Considers the 16th century conflict between England, weak from civil war, and Spain, powerful by the wealth of Mexico and Peru. Shows how the conflict culminated in the dispatch of the Armada to invade England.
Prod-NBCTV Dist-MGHT 1967

Spanish Civil War, The C 55 MIN
16MM FILM MAGNETIC SOUND C
Examines the origins and causes of the Spanish Civil War and the impact of the war on the people of Spain and on the people of Europe and the United States.
From The British Universities Historical Studies In Film Series.
LC NO. 75-703309
Prod-IUHFC Dist-KRAUS 1975

Spanish Civil War, The C 26 MIN
16MM FILM, 3/4 OR 1/2 IN VIDEO H-C
Examines the Spanish Civil War and points out that the inadequate response of the great democratic powers heightened the contempt of the Axis powers for the democratic world.
From The Between The Wars Series.
Prod-LNDBRG Dist-FI 1978

Spanish Civil War, The C 29 MIN
2 INCH VIDEOTAPE
See series title for descriptive statement.
From The Course Of Our Times I Series.
Prod-WGBHTV Dist-PUBTEL

Spanish Colonies C 30 MIN
2 INCH VIDEOTAPE
Examines the society of Europe immediately prior to the Age of Discovery, and compares with the great changes which took place around 1500.
From The American History I Series.
Prod-DENVPS Dist-GPITVL

Spanish Community Life X 15 MIN
16MM FILM, 3/4 OR 1/2 IN VIDEO I-H
Portrays life and customs of a typical Spanish pueblo. Illustrates ways in which Spain's modernization program is breaking down the old type of self-sufficient village.
Prod-GUM Dist-PHENIX 1961

Spanish Conquest Of The New World, The C 11 MIN
16MM FILM, 3/4 OR 1/2 IN VIDEO I-H
Depicts the various Spanish explorations from New Mexico to Peru under Cortez, Pizarro, Balboa, De Soto and others.
Prod-CORF Dist-CORF 1954

Spanish Explorers, The X 14 MIN
16MM FILM, 3/4 OR 1/2 IN VIDEO I-H
Uses live action photography, paintings and animation to depict the discovery of America through the eyes of Spanish explorers. Discusses Spain's reasons for exploration and shows the conquests of Cortez, Pizarro and others in the New World.
From The Age Of Exploration Series.
Prod-EBF Dist-EBEC 1965

Spanish Explorers, The (Spanish) C 15 MIN
16MM FILM, 3/4 OR 1/2 IN VIDEO I-H
Shows the discovery of America through the eyes of Spanish explorers. Explains why Europeans were anxious to find an ocean route to Asia.
Prod-EBEC Dist-EBEC

Spanish For Health Professionals—A Series
PRO
Enables hospital personnel to communicate in basic, simple phrases with patients who speak Spanish only.
Prod-HSCIC Dist-HSCIC

Donde Esta La Sala De Emergencia (Where Is	
Siga Las Instrucciones (Follow The Directions	020 MIN
Venga A Ayudarla (I Come To Help You)	020 MIN

Spanish For Latin America - Headstart (Spanish)—A Series

Presents instruction in Latin American Spanish.
Prod-USFSI Dist-USNAC

Cultural Orientation Tape For Panama (Spanish)	023 MIN
Spanish For Latin America - Headstart, Module	150 MIN
Spanish For Latin America - Headstart, Module	200 MIN
Spanish For Latin America - Headstart, Module	181 MIN
Spanish For Latin America - Headstart, Module	095 MIN

Spanish For Latin America - Headstart, Module 1 - Getting To Know You (Spanish) C 150 MIN
3/4 OR 1/2 INCH VIDEO CASSETTE
Presents a two-cassette set of Latin American Spanish instruction.
From The Spanish For Latin America - Headstart (Spanish) Series.
Prod-USFSI Dist-USNAC

Spanish For Latin America - Headstart, Module 2 - Getting Around (Spanish) C 200 MIN
3/4 OR 1/2 INCH VIDEO CASSETTE
Presents a two-cassette set of Latin American Spanish instruction.
From The Spanish For Latin America - Headstart (Spanish) Series.
Prod-USFSI Dist-USNAC

Spanish For Latin America - Headstart, Module 3 - Shopping (Spanish) C 181 MIN
3/4 OR 1/2 INCH VIDEO CASSETTE
Presents a two-cassette set of Latin American Spanish instruction.
From The Spanish For Latin America - Headstart (Spanish) Series.
Prod-USFSI Dist-USNAC

Spanish For Latin America - Headstart, Module 4 - At The Restaurant (Spanish) C 95 MIN
3/4 OR 1/2 INCH VIDEO CASSETTE
Presents a two-cassette set of Latin American Spanish instruction.
From The Spanish For Latin America - Headstart (Spanish) Series.
Prod-USFSI Dist-USNAC

Spanish For You--A Series C 30 MIN
16MM FILM OPTICAL SOUND I
Demonstrates the audio-lingual method of teaching Spanish, using films, records or tapes, role-playing, a variety of drills and objective tests.
Prod-LINGUA Dist-MLA Prodn-SCOTTG 1965

Atracciones De La Ciudad De Mexico - The	
Atracciones De La Ciudad De Mexico - The	15 MIN
De Compras - Shopping, Film A	15 MIN
De Compras - Shopping, Film B	15 MIN
El Cohete - The Rocket, Film A	15 MIN
El Cohete - The Rocket, Film B	15 MIN
El Cumpleanos - The Birthday Party, Film A	15 MIN
El Cumpleanos - The Birthday Party, Film B	15 MIN
El Parque De Diversiones - The Amusement Park	15 MIN
El Parque De Diversiones - The Amusement Park	15 MIN
El Partido De Beisbol - The Baseball Game,	15 MIN
El Partido De Beisbol - The Baseball Game,	15 MIN
El Rancho - The Ranch, Film A	15 MIN
El Rancho - The Ranch, Film B	15 MIN
El Restaurante - The Restaurant, Film A	15 MIN
El Restaurante - The Restaurant, Film B	15 MIN
El Ultimo Dia De Clases - The Last Day Of	15 MIN
El Ultimo Dia De Clases - The Last Day Of	15 MIN
El Zoologico - The Zoo, Film A	15 MIN
El Zoologico - The Zoo, Film B	15 MIN
En La Playa - At The Beach, Film A	15 MIN
En La Playa - At The Beach, Film B	15 MIN
La Entrevista - The Interview, Film A	15 MIN
La Entrevista - The Interview, Film B	15 MIN
La Llamada Telefonica - The Telephone Call,	15 MIN
La Llamada Telefonica - The Telephone Call,	15 MIN
Las Actividades - The Activities, Film A	15 MIN
Las Actividades - The Activities, Film B	15 MIN
Parque De Diversiones, El - The Amusement	15 MIN
Parque De Diversiones, El - The Amusement	15 MIN
Spanish For You - Test, Units 1 Through 7	15 MIN
Spanish For You - Test, Units 8 Through 14	15 MIN

Spanish Gallery, A C 29 MIN
2 INCH VIDEOTAPE
See series title for descriptive statement.
From The Museum Open House Series.
Prod-WGBHTV Dist-PUBTEL

Spanish Gypsies B 11 MIN
16MM FILM OPTICAL SOUND H-C
Shows Spanish gypsies holding a family festival in a grotto in Granada. Juan Salido and a group of artists perform a series of exciting flamenco folk dances and songs.
Prod-BRAU Dist-RADIM 1948

Spanish In The Southwest, The C 14 MIN
16MM FILM, 3/4 OR 1/2 IN VIDEO I-H
Describes Spain's exploration and conquest in the southwestern United States during the 16th century. Shows the role of the Catholic missions in the exchange of skills and traditions between Indians and Spaniards. Discusses how 300 years of Indian-Spanish culture has influenced American life.
From The Growth Of America's West Series.
Prod-CAPFLM Dist-PHENIX 1979

Spanish Influences In The United States (2nd Ed) C 14 MIN
16MM FILM, 3/4 OR 1/2 IN VIDEO I-J
Shows different ways in which the United States has been influenced by its Spanish heritage, such as language, home furnishings, architecture, place names, community development and life styles.
Prod-CORF Dist-CORF 1972

Spanish Language—A Series
16MM FILM, 3/4 OR 1/2 IN VIDEO H-C A
Introduces important cities and regions in Spain.
Prod-IFB Dist-IFB

Aragon Y Navarra	016 MIN
Barcelona	018 MIN
Castilla La Nueva	016 MIN
Castilla La Vieja	016 MIN
El Pais Vasco	016 MIN
Madrid - Capital De Espana	018 MIN

Sevilla 016 MIN

Spanish Lesson, No. 1 B 30 MIN
16MM FILM OPTICAL SOUND T
Shows how a master teacher of Spanish works with a group of nine-year-olds.
Prod-UCLA Dist-UCLA 1965

Spanish Newsreel—A Series

Prod-TWCF Dist-TWCF

Cuba Walks Out 7 MIN
Glenn Welcome 6 MIN
Plane Crash 8 MIN
Pope - New Cardinals 8 MIN

Spanish Smootheners C 30 MIN
2 INCH VIDEOTAPE T
See series title for descriptive statement.
From The Solutions In Communications Series.
Prod-SCCOE Dist-SCCOE

Spanish Sounds, The (Los Sonidos) C 30 MIN
3/4 INCH VIDEO CASSETTE H-C
See series title for descriptive statement.
From The Telespanol Uno Series.
Prod-WUSFTV Dist-GPITVL 1979

Spanish-American War, The C 30 MIN
3/4 OR 1/2 INCH VIDEO CASSETTE C
Discusses the Spanish American War, its aftermath and the Senate debate on the role of the U S in world affairs.
America - The Second Century Series.
Prod-DALCCD Dist-DALCCD

Spanish-American War, The C 30 MIN
2 INCH VIDEOTAPE
Concerns the events which caused the United States to abandon its traditional isolationism.
From The American History II Series.
Prod-KRMATV Dist-GPITVL

Spanky B 20 MIN
16MM FILM OPTICAL SOUND
Tells how Spanky causes trouble for big brother Breezy, who's trying to land a part in the Gang's barn play. Shows how the play turns into an egg-throwing free-for-all and Breezy proves remarkably resourceful at finding shields while still performing. A Little Rascals film.
Prod-ROACH Dist-BHAWK 1932

Spanning Vectors B 27 MIN
3/4 OR 1/2 INCH VIDEO CASSETTE
See series title for descriptive statement.
From The Calculus Of Linear Algebra Series.
Prod-MIOT Dist-MIOT

Spare The Rod C 30 MIN
16MM FILM - 3/4 IN VIDEO
Explains that discipline is often needed to teach children how to take care of themselves and live in a world with other people. Enumerates some of the different disciplinary techniques available to parents.
From The Footsteps Series.
LC NO. 79-707632
Prod-USOE Dist-USNAC 1978

Spare The Rod - Discipline C 23 MIN
16MM FILM - VIDEO, ALL FORMATS
Shows why discipline is necessary for young children. Presents a variety of disciplinary techniques for parents and guidelines for using them.
From The Footsteps Series.
Prod-PEREN Dist-PEREN

Spares Provisioning At A Desired Assurance Level, Optimization Of Spares Kits And... C 60 MIN
3/4 OR 1/2 INCH VIDEO CASSETTE C
Discusses spares provisioning at a desired assurance level, optimization of spares kits and reliability and availability of maintained systems. Presented by Dimitri Kececioglu, Professor of Aerospace and Mechanical Engineering, University of Arizona.
From The Maintainability, Operational Availability And Preventive Maintenance Of...Series. Pt 4
Prod-UAZMIC Dist-UAZMIC

Spark Of Life, A C 24 MIN
16MM FILM OPTICAL SOUND H-C A R
Investigates the origins of life, the nature of the soul and transmigration of the soul. Compares and contrasts ancient Indian interpretations of these questions as found in the Bhagavad-gita with those of modern science. Based on the book Bhagavad-gita As It Is by A C Bhaktivendanta Swami Prabhupada.
LC NO. 77-702976
Prod-ISKCON Dist-BHAKTI 1977

Spark Plug Service C 4 MIN
16MM FILM OPTICAL SOUND
Shows the steps to be followed when removing, cleaning, gapping and replacing spark plugs.
LC NO. FI68-254
Prod-RAYBAR Dist-RAYBAR 1966

Spark Plug Story C 15 MIN
16MM FILM OPTICAL SOUND
Presents the procedures involved in the manufacturing of spark plugs and their testing.
Prod-GM Dist-GM

Spark Plug, The C 21 MIN
16MM FILM OPTICAL SOUND
Uses macrophotography, time-lapse, animation and live-action photography in discussing the history, function, complex construction and design of spark plugs and their importance to the efficient operation of internal combustion engines. Explains trends toward improved emission control and fuel economy.
LC NO. 76-702674
Prod-CHSPC Dist-CHSPC Prodn-PORTA 1976

Spark Plug, The (Finnish) C 21 MIN
16MM FILM OPTICAL SOUND
Uses macrophotography, time-lapse, animation and live-action photography in discussing the history, function, complex construction and design of spark plugs and their importance to the efficient operation of internal combustion engines. Explains trends toward improved emission control and fuel economy.
LC NO. 76-702674
Prod-CHSPC Dist-CHSPC Prodn-PORTA

Spark Plug, The (Italian) C 21 MIN
16MM FILM OPTICAL SOUND
Uses macrophotography, time-lapse, animation and live-action photography in discussing the history, function, complex construction and design of spark plugs and their importance to the efficient operation of internal combustion engines. Explains trends toward improved emission control and fuel economy.
LC NO. 76-702674
Prod-CHSPC Dist-CHSPC Prodn-PORTA

Spark Plug, The (Spanish) C 21 MIN
16MM FILM OPTICAL SOUND
Uses macrophotography, time-lapse, animation and live-action photography in discussing the history, function, complex construction and design of spark plugs and their importance to the efficient operation of internal combustion engines. Explains trends toward improved emission control and fuel economy.
LC NO. 76-702674
Prod-CHSPC Dist-CHSPC Prodn-PORTA

Spark Plug, The (Swedish) C 21 MIN
16MM FILM OPTICAL SOUND
Uses macrophotography, time-lapse, animation and live-action photography in discussing the history, function, complex construction and design of spark plugs and their importance to the efficient operation of internal combustion engines. Explains trends toward improved emission control and fuel economy.
LC NO. 76-702674
Prod-CHSPC Dist-CHSPC Prodn-PORTA

Spark, The C 29 MIN
16MM FILM OPTICAL SOUND I A
Presents an ethnographic study of the Hasidic communities in New York. Depicts religious service, community activities, traditional services, a farbrengen or meeting called by the head rabbi and a Hasidic wedding ceremony and celebration. Uses paintings to portray the history of the movement.
LC NO. 75-702901
Prod-VANGU Dist-VANGU 1975

Sparkling Clearwater C 15 MIN
16MM FILM OPTICAL SOUND
Explores the variety of entertainment and recreation available in Clearwater, Florida.
Prod-FLADC Dist-FLADC

Sparky Vs The Snat C 8 MIN
16MM FILM, 3/4 OR 1/2 IN VIDEO I
Presents an animated program in which Sparky, the fire dog, and his niece and nephew produce a musical about fire protection, while the Snat, promoter of carelessness with fire, tries to ruin the show.
Prod-NFPA Dist-NFPA Prodn-ARIOLI 1979

Sparky, The Colt C 10 MIN
16MM FILM, 3/4 OR 1/2 IN VIDEO P-I
Presents the story of a wobbly little colt who learns to trot across the fields and finally makes friends with his little master.
Prod-CORF Dist-CORF 1950

Sparrow Family, The C 3 MIN
16MM FILM OPTICAL SOUND P-I
Discusses the family of birds known as sparrows.
From The Of All Things Series.
Prod-BAILYL Dist-AVED

Sparrows B 84 MIN
16MM FILM SILENT
Tells the story of a group of orphans who are kept in virtual slavery by the wicked Farmer Grimes, who runs a baby farm for the county. Shows that life would be unbearable if it weren't for plucky Mary with her protective pitchfork and her unshakable belief that God's eye is always on His sparrows. Stars Mary Pickford. Directed by William Beaudine.
Prod-UNKNWN Dist-KILLIS 1926

Spartree C 15 MIN
16MM FILM, 3/4 OR 1/2 IN VIDEO J-C A
Documents the work of the highrigger, a daredevil master lumberjack who risks life and limb to climb alone to the top of a towering Douglas fir.
LC NO. 80-706824
Prod-MERPI Dist-CORF 1980

Spasticity - A Review Of Treatment With Dantrolene Sodium C 20 MIN
16MM FILM OPTICAL SOUND PRO
Presents objective and subjective improvements in spastic patients treated with Dantrolene Sodium. Shows a Vietnam veteran with spinal cord injury and two multiple sclerosis patients discussing and illustrating their individual responses to Dantrolene Sodium.
LC NO. 75-702336
Prod-EATONL Dist-EATONL 1974

Spatial Learning And The Hippocampus C 24 MIN
16MM FILM, 3/4 OR 1/2 IN VIDEO
Uses documentary evidence from laboratory experiments to show that animals form cognitive maps of their environments as a means of developing their remarkable spatial capabilities. Shows how the equivalent of a set of mental maps may be used by animals as the basis of long-term memory.
Prod-OPENU Dist-MEDIAG Prodn-BBCTV 1982

Spatial Learning In The Preschool Years B 22 MIN
3/4 OR 1/2 INCH VIDEO CASSETTE PRO
Views a 'preoperational' child's understanding of three-dimensional space, such as the look, feel and positioning of objects. Shows gain of understanding through exploration and manipulation of objects and suggests appropriate classroom materials and experiences. Deals with spatial understanding in infancy.
Prod-HSERF Dist-HSERF

Spatial Relationships C 40 MIN
16MM FILM OPTICAL SOUND
Depicts stages in early cognitive development in accordance with Piaget's definitions. Reflects the developmental changes concerning the capacity to adapt to and comprehend properties of physical space from subjective space within the child's visually perceived range of movement to the stage of 'MENTAL REPRESENTATION.'
From The Aecom Scales Of Motorsensori Development Series.
Prod-VASSAR Dist-NYU

Spaulding-Richardson Composite Operation For Uterine Prolapse And Allied Conditions C 25 MIN
16MM FILM OPTICAL SOUND PRO
Portrays an operation for marked degrees of uterine prolapse. Shows that the operation overcomes some of the disadvantages of the Manchester Operation and yet retains some of its virtues.
Prod-ACYDGD Dist-ACY 1954

Spawning In An African Mouthbreeding Fish C 16 MIN
16MM FILM OPTICAL SOUND H-C A
Shows identification characteristics of male and female tilapia macrocephala, including courtship behavior and construction of nest. Describes how the male takes the eggs of the female into his mouth and stores them in an oral pouch where they are hatched. Uses closeups to show eggs and later embryos in the male's mouth. Shows the young released and at several stages of development.
LC NO. 70-708679
Prod-AMNH Dist-PSUPCR 1967

Speak Easy C
16MM FILM, 3/4 OR 1/2 IN VIDEO
Aims to teach everyday conversational language through a combination of mime, video and a variety of classroom activities.
Prod-NORTNJ Dist-NORTNJ

Speak The Language Of Success - A Handbook For Communication Skills C 30 MIN
3/4 OR 1/2 INCH VIDEO CASSETTE
Provides techniques in gaining communication skills. Includes remembering names, listening skills, keeping messages brief, and controlling silence. Presented by Ellen Phillips, Director, Speech and Dramatic Arts, Fairfax County Public Schools, Virginia.
Prod-RCOMTV Dist-SYLWAT

Speak Up C 14 MIN
16MM FILM, 3/4 OR 1/2 IN VIDEO P
Shows how speaking shares ideas directly with another person and demonstrates how different ways of speaking can affect the message spoken.
From The Serendipity Series.
Prod-MGHT Dist-MGHT 1976

Speak Up - Skills Of Oral Communication C
3/4 OR 1/2 INCH VIDEO CASSETTE H
Teaches the basic rules of speaking and dramatizes the four purposes of oral communication - narration, description, persuasion and argumentation.
Prod-CHUMAN Dist-GA

Speak Up On Television C 30 MIN
16MM FILM, 3/4 OR 1/2 IN VIDEO
Provides training in television communication. Includes handling news interviews, press conferences, talk shows and other television presentations.
From The Speak Up With Confidence Series.
Prod-NEM Dist-NEM

Speak Up Please B 15 MIN
2 INCH VIDEOTAPE K-P
See series title for descriptive statement.
From The Magic Of Words Series.
Prod-GWTVAI Dist-GPITVL Prodn-WETATV

Speak Up With Confidence C 30 MIN
16MM FILM, 3/4 OR 1/2 IN VIDEO
Provides instruction in public speaking for beginning and experienced speakers. Offers techniques for overcoming obstacles to effective presentations.
From The Speak Up With Confidence Series.
Prod-NEM Dist-NEM

Speak Up With Confidence—A Series

Consists of a training course in public speaking. Features Dinah Shore and Jack Valenti. Based on Valenti's book Speak Up With Confidence.
Prod-NEM Dist-NEM

Speak Up On Television 030 MIN
Speak Up With Confidence 030 MIN
Speak Up With Style 030 MIN

Speak Up With Style C 30 MIN
16MM FILM, 3/4 OR 1/2 IN VIDEO

Shows how to prepare and deliver a successful speech. Covers elements of style which produce clarity of content and audience rapport.
From The Speak Up With Confidence Series.
Prod-NEM Dist-NEM

Speak Up, Andrew C 18 MIN
16MM FILM, 3/4 OR 1/2 IN VIDEO I-J
Discusses the importance of developing good speaking skills through the story of a young boy who must make a speech on the subject.
LC NO. 81-707578
Prod-CF Dist-CF 1981

Speaker Of The House - The Legislative Process X 21 MIN
16MM FILM, 3/4 OR 1/2 IN VIDEO I-H
Examines responsibilities and activities of the speaker of a typical state assembly during the course of a legislative day. Speaker is shown fulfilling his double role as politician and lawmaker.
Prod-JOU Dist-JOU 1964

Speaker, The - A Film About Freedom C 42 MIN
16MM FILM OPTICAL SOUND H-C A
Presents a story concerning the First Amendment rights of a controversial university professor to speak at a high school.
LC NO. 77-700848
Prod-ALA Dist-ALA Prodn-VA 1977

Speakers With Cerebral Palsy C 25 MIN
16MM FILM OPTICAL SOUND
Illustrates variations in respiratory, laryngeal and articulatory functioning exhibited by individuals with cerebral palsy. Emphasizes the difficulty of describing fully the speech physiology problems of these individuals and in relating specific deviations in the functioning of the speech mechanism to specific speech deficits. Highlights the results of recent research.
From The Physiological Aspects Of Speech Series.
LC NO. FIA67-103
Prod-UIOWA Dist-UIOWA 1966

Speakers With Cleft Palates C 30 MIN
16MM FILM OPTICAL SOUND C
Uses X-ray photography to show the physiological characteristics of the speech of those with cleft palates. Depicts the effect on speech of deviations in the functioning of the velopharyngeal mechanism.
From The Physiological Aspects Of Speech Series.
Prod-UIOWA Dist-UIOWA 1964

Speaking Again - Options For The Laryngectomee, Pt 1 C 25 MIN
3/4 OR 1/2 INCH VIDEO CASSETTE
Presents communication alternatives for people who have lost their vocal cords or larynx.
Prod-BU Dist-BU

Speaking Again - Options For The Laryngectomee, Pt 2 C 25 MIN
3/4 OR 1/2 INCH VIDEO CASSETTE
Presents techniques for training laryngectomized individuals to use esophageal speech.
Prod-BU Dist-BU

Speaking Effectively C 30 MIN
3/4 OR 1/2 INCH VIDEO CASSETTE A
Shows how to keep control of a conversation when one is the initiator in the action. Presents hosts Richard Benjamin and Paula Prentiss advising on ways to get verbal and non-verbal feedback and emphasizing the importance of closing a communication.
From The Communication Skills For Managers Series.
Prod-TIMLIF Dist-TIMLIF 1981

Speaking Effectively - To One Or One Thousand C 21 MIN
16MM FILM, 3/4 OR 1/2 IN VIDEO H-C A
Offers keys for organizing and delivering conversational remarks and rehearsed speeches. Emphasizes body language, vocal quality, intonation, and the words themselves.
Prod-SUNSET Dist-CRMP 1980

Speaking Effectively, To One Or One Thousand (Spanish) C 21 MIN
16MM FILM, 3/4 OR 1/2 IN VIDEO H-C A
Shows that public speaking need not be painful and gives keys for improving communication skills. Explains that the intention of each spoken communication must be clear from the start.
Prod-SUNSET Dist-MGHT

Speaking For Business C 26 MIN
16MM FILM OPTICAL SOUND H-C A
Shows how the Chamber of Commerce of the United States is speaking for business and providing a dynamic leadership force for its nearly 200,000 members.
Prod-CCUS Dist-CCUS 1977

Speaking For Myself C 29 MIN
16MM FILM OPTICAL SOUND
Presents interviews with five developmentally handicapped adults, who challenge their interviewers' notions of what it means to be retarded.
LC NO. 80-701265
Prod-CCVA Dist-CCVA 1980

Speaking For Ourselves - The Challenge Of Being Deaf C 26 MIN
16MM FILM OPTICAL SOUND
Shows the challenge, complexity and intensity of the learning experience at the Lexington School for the Deaf, New York.
LC NO. 77-701454
Prod-LSFTD Dist-CFDC Prodn-TOGGFI 1977

Speaking For The Listener C 14 MIN
3/4 OR 1/2 INCH VIDEO CASSETTE
Emphasizes the advantages of being able to communicate face-to-face and the four major factors involved in planning a speech.
From The Effective Speaking Series.
Prod-RESEM Dist-RESEM

Speaking From Experience C 18 MIN
3/4 OR 1/2 INCH VIDEO CASSETTE IND
Explores human error in job-related accidents. Narrated by Pat Summerall.
Prod-FLMEDS Dist-FLMEDS

Speaking Of Explosions C 15 MIN
16MM FILM OPTICAL SOUND
Cites the hazards of unauthorized entry into armament test areas. Explains the dangers of duds and tells what action to take should certain pieces be found. Shows how ordnance drops are planned for practice and testing.
LC NO. 74-706253
Prod-USAF Dist-USNAC 1969

Speaking Of Harvey C 9 MIN
16MM FILM, 3/4 OR 1/2 IN VIDEO J-C A
Addresses the issue of animal experimentation in the world of science. Recommends special regard for the comfort of laboratory animals and stresses the need for all researchers to remain sensitized to the taking of laboratory life.
LC NO. 83-706941
Prod-FRIEDL Dist-PFP

Speaking Of Israel C 28 MIN
16MM FILM OPTICAL SOUND I-C A
Portrays Israel, as seen through the eyes of its inhabitants. Explores Tel Aviv, Haifa and the Negev Desert. Deals with archaelogy, science and the cultural life of Israel.
LC NO. 72-702955
Prod-ALDEN Dist-ALDEN 1969

Speaking Of Love C 54 MIN
3/4 OR 1/2 INCH VIDEO CASSETTE
See series title for descriptive statement.
From The Leo Buscaglia Series.
Prod-PBS Dist-DELTAK

Speaking Of Love C 60 MIN
3/4 INCH VIDEO CASSETTE A
Presents Dr Leo Buscaglia sharing his thoughts on the 'limitless concept' of love and the human potential for giving.
LC NO. 81-707486
Prod-KVIETV Dist-PBS 1981

Speaking Of Men C 20 MIN
16MM FILM OPTICAL SOUND H-C A
Presents three women who discuss their attitudes about men, their relationships with men and the importance of men in their lives.
LC NO. 78-701530
Prod-GROHER Dist-POLYMR 1977

Speaking Of Weather C 8 MIN
16MM FILM, 3/4 OR 1/2 IN VIDEO K-P
Introduces the phenomena of rain, snow, lightning, thunder and other meteorological mysteries. Explains how the sun, water and air converge to create daily and seasonal weather patterns.
Prod-WDEMCO Dist-WDEMCO 1982

Speaking Shakespearean Verse C 50 MIN
3/4 OR 1/2 INCH VIDEO CASSETTE
Presents members of the Royal Shakespeare Company who give a workshop on styles of speaking Shakespearean Verse, discuss approaches to the problem of speaking verse in drama and show how the RSC works on a text in rehearsal.
Prod-FOTH Dist-FOTH 1984

Speaking The Language C 15 MIN
16MM FILM, 3/4 OR 1/2 IN VIDEO
Demonstrates how the user communicates with a computer using a program language called BASIC.
From The Adventure Of The Mind Series.
Prod-IITC Dist-IU 1980

Speaking Without Words C 60 MIN
3/4 OR 1/2 INCH VIDEO CASSETTE J-C A
Examines the non-verbal ways human beings and other creatures communicate. Discusses the evolutionary history of animal communication. Looks at art, mathematics, roadside architecture and the story that bones can tell.
From The Smithsonian World Series.
Prod-WETATV Dist-WETATV Prodn-SMITHS

Spearhead At Juniper Gardens B 38 MIN
16MM FILM OPTICAL SOUND C A
Explains that the Juniper Gardens children's project is a program of research conducted in a deprived area of northeast Kansas City, Kansas. Shows how reinforcement principles are used to develop the language of preschoolers and to motivate slow-learning grade school children. Stresses community cooperation.
LC NO. 72-701017
Prod-UKANBC Dist-UKANS 1968

Special - Cyprus C 28 MIN
3/4 INCH VIDEOTAPE
Presents an interview with the president of Cyprus, Mr S Kyprianou. Focuses on political questions. Hosted by Marilyn Perry.
From The Marilyn's Manhatten Series.
Prod-PERRYM Dist-PERRYM

Special Analytical Tools C 10 MIN
3/4 OR 1/2 INCH VIDEO CASSETTE
See series title for descriptive statement.
From The Finance For Nonfinancial Managers Series.
Prod-DELTAK Dist-DELTAK

Special Cases C 13 MIN
16MM FILM, 3/4 OR 1/2 IN VIDEO H-C A
Depicts modern techniques that can assure safe childbirth even when complications arise. Discusses special cases, such as pregnancies of very young or old mothers, late or painful deliveries, breech births, premature deliveries and delivery by midwives.
From The Pregnancy And Childbirth Series.
Prod-DALHSU Dist-IFB Prodn-CRAF 1977

Special Cases (Captioned) C 13 MIN
16MM FILM, 3/4 OR 1/2 IN VIDEO H-C A
Depicts modern techniques that can assure safe childbirth even when complications arise. Discusses special cases, such as pregnancies of very young or very old mothers, late or painful deliveries, breech births, premature deliveries and delivery by midwives.
From The Pregnancy And Childbirth Series.
Prod-DALHSU Dist-IFB Prodn-CRAF 1977

Special Challenge Shots, The C 14 MIN
16MM FILM - 3/4 IN VIDEO H-C A
Explains how the design of a golf course and natural forces of weather test a golf player's skill. Demonstrates sand recovery techniques and setup and swing adjustments for uphill, downhill and sidehill situations, along with techniques for coping with headwinds and crosswinds.
From The Modern Golf Instruction In Motion Pictures Series. Unit 4
LC NO. 76-703595
Prod-NGF Dist-NGF Prodn-GOLF 1974

Special Children - Blind, Deaf, Physically Handicapped C 11 MIN
16MM FILM OPTICAL SOUND P-I
Shows a class discussion about handicapped children which was precipitated by a boy who saw a girl conversing with her parents in sign language.
Prod-ECC Dist-ECI 1977

Special Children Special Needs C 22 MIN
16MM FILM OPTICAL SOUND T
Presents a comprehensive approach to educating young, multi-handicapped children. Documents infants, preschoolers and outdoor learning environments, stressing the importance of providing experiences according to individual strengths and handicaps.
LC NO. 76-700932
Prod-NYUMC Dist-CFDC 1973

Special Children, Special Needs C 22 MIN
16MM FILM OPTICAL SOUND C A
Documents three adapted learning environments for multi-handicapped children that offer learning experiences based on individual strengths and weaknesses.
Prod-NYU Dist-NYU

Special Conditions C 25 MIN
16MM FILM OPTICAL SOUND H
Presents prepared decisions for responding successfully to conditions of fog, ice, rain, snow and darkness.
From The To Get From Here To There Series.
Prod-PROART Dist-PROART

Special Court At Christian Island, The C 9 MIN
16MM FILM OPTICAL SOUND
Concerns legal justice for Indian juveniles.
LC NO. 76-703085
Prod-CANFDC Dist-CANFDC 1975

Special Cycles C 15 MIN
3/4 OR 1/2 INCH VIDEO CASSETTE PRO
See series title for descriptive statement.
From The Numerical Control/Computer Numerical Control, Part 2 - Advanced Programming Series.
Prod-ICSINT Dist-ICSINT

Special Cycles C 17 MIN
3/4 OR 1/2 INCH VIDEO CASSETTE IND
Includes how to program a face mill operation, a rectangular pocket and a mill boring cycle.
From The Numerical Control/Computerized Numerical Control - Advanced Programming Series. Module 2
Prod-LEIKID Dist-LEIKID

Special Delivery C 7 MIN
16MM FILM - 3/4 IN VIDEO
Presents an animated comedy about a couple whose quiet existence is disrupted when the mailman falls on their icy steps.
LC NO. 79-706913
Prod-NFBC Dist-NFBC 1979

Special Delivery C 20 MIN
3/4 OR 1/2 INCH VIDEO CASSETTE
Takes a look at some of the new technology and some of the problems and hard decisions faced by parents and doctors in the pre- and post-natal care of infants.
Prod-WCCOTV Dist-WCCOTV 1982

Special Delivery—A Series
3/4 OR 1/2 INCH VIDEO CASSETTE P-I
Describes the abilities of mainstreamed, handicapped students, focusing on the similarities between nonhandicapped and handicapped students.
Prod-WNVT Dist-LAWREN 1979

Able Disabled, The	019 MIN
Blind Participate, The	020 MIN
Colin And Ricky	009 MIN
Common Show, The	028 MIN
Deaf Communicate	015 MIN
Positive Show, The	028 MIN
Reinforcement Show,, The	028 MIN
Special Show, The	028 MIN

Why Show, The 028 MIN

Special Education Curriculum Design - A Multisensory Approach—A Series
16MM FILM, 3/4 OR 1/2 IN VIDEO T
Discusses ways of mainstreaming handicapped children into regular art, life science and lab science classes.
Prod-MGHT Dist-MGHT Prodn-HADDOR 1979

Fulfillment Of Human Potenial 018 MIN
Mainstreaming Techniques - Life Science And Art 012 MIN
Special Education Techniques - Lab Science 024 MIN

Special Education For The Handicapped - Like You, Like Me C 20 MIN
16MM FILM, 3/4 OR 1/2 IN VIDEO T
Presents an introduction to the film series Like You, Like Me. Discusses the status of special education, stresses the importance of in-service training and continuing education, and outlines the development of innovative educational materials.
From The Like You, Like Me Series.
Prod-EBEC Dist-EBEC 1977

Special Education Techniques - Lab Science And Art C 24 MIN
16MM FILM, 3/4 OR 1/2 IN VIDEO T
Shows the design, adaptation, teaching strategies and implementation of laboratory science and art activities for elementary-level blind children and science activities for intermediate-level and gifted blind children.
From The Special Education Curriculum Design - A Multisensory Approach Series.
LC NO. 80-706559
Prod-MGHT Dist-MGHT Prodn-HADDOR 1979

Special Education—A Series

Focuses on different areas of special education.
Prod-DAVFMS Dist-DAVFMS

Lily - A Story About A Girl Like Me 014 MIN
Specific Learning Disabilities - Evaluation 028 MIN
Specific Learning Disabilities - Remedial 031 MIN
Specific Learning Disabilities In The Classroom 023 MIN

Special Effect, A C 14 MIN
16MM FILM OPTICAL SOUND
Tells the story of the wife of a film director who thinks her husband's special effects are inadequate. Shows how her husband and the film crew try to change her mind by trying the special effects on her.
LC NO. 80-700389
Prod-RICRUB Dist-RICRUB 1978

Special Effects C 14 MIN
16MM FILM, 3/4 OR 1/2 IN VIDEO
Demonstrates the how-to of most common special effects, including rainstorms, snow, fog, bullet holes, flaming arrows, and fire.
Prod-PFP Dist-PFP

Special Effects C 58 MIN
3/4 OR 1/2 INCH VIDEO CASSETTE
Shows how movie special effects are created.
Prod-UCEMC Dist-UCEMC

Special Effects In Sketches C 29 MIN
3/4 INCH VIDEO CASSETTE C A
Focuses on how to depict the more intangible objects that are not solid, such as fire and smoke. Points out some of the drawing and art elements used in sketching special effects.
From The Sketching Techniques Series. Lesson 22
Prod-COAST Dist-CDTEL

Special Equipment Rescues C 9 MIN
16MM FILM - 3/4 IN VIDEO I-C A
Shows how to rescue an unconscious scuba diver on the bottom and how to make use of the paddleboard, surfboard, rescue tube, torpedo buoy and rescue lines.
From The Lifesaving And Water Safety Series.
Prod-AMRC Dist-AMRC 1975

Special Examining Techniques For Children C 10 MIN
3/4 OR 1/2 INCH VIDEO CASSETTE PRO
Emphasizes techniques for reassuring, assessing, and examining uncooperative children. Demonstrates exam techniques for preschoolers.
Prod-HSCIC Dist-HSCIC 1980

Special Eye Care For Burns C 11 MIN
16MM FILM, 3/4 OR 1/2 IN VIDEO
Demonstrates the special eye care of patients suffering second and third degree burns of the face to prevent eye infection and corneal laceration.
LC NO. 81-706329
Prod-USA Dist-USNAC 1969

Special Friendship, A C 13 MIN
16MM FILM, 3/4 OR 1/2 IN VIDEO
Illustrates the unique relationship and bond between people and their pets. Emphasizes the need for training and proper care of pets.
LC NO. 83-706646
Prod-KLUCLA Dist-FLMFR 1983

Special Gift, A C 47 MIN
16MM FILM, 3/4 OR 1/2 IN VIDEO I-H A
Tells a story about a 14-year-old boy who can't decide if he should yield to his father's insistence to give up his ballet training and concentrate on the acceptable 'male' sport of basketball or if he should disobey his dad and risk ridicule and ostracism at school by admitting his commitment to dance.
From The Teenage Years Series.
LC NO. 79-708012
Prod-TAHSEM Dist-TIMLIF 1979

Special Goodwill Letters B 45 MIN
2 INCH VIDEOTAPE C
See series title for descriptive statement.
From The Business Writing Series. Unit I - Neutral Good-News Messages
Prod-CHITVC Dist-GPITVL Prodn-WTTWTV

Special Homecoming, The C 29 MIN
3/4 OR 1/2 INCH VIDEO CASSETTE H-C A
Points out that not all babies are healthy and normal at birth and that a family must adjust to the idea and the reality of a distressed infant.
From The Tomorrow's Families Series.
LC NO. 81-706908
Prod-MSDOE Dist-AITECH 1980

Special Interaction II B 15 MIN
2 INCH VIDEOTAPE P
See series title for descriptive statement.
From The Just Wondering Series.
Prod-EOPS Dist-GPITVL Prodn-KOACTV

Special Interactions - Magnets B 15 MIN
2 INCH VIDEOTAPE P
See series title for descriptive statement.
From The Just Wondering Series.
Prod-EOPS Dist-GPITVL Prodn-KOACTV

Special Issues In Using Analgesics C 30 MIN
3/4 OR 1/2 INCH VIDEO CASSETTE
Explores specific approaches for administering analgesics to patients with acute pain, chronic benign pain, a combination of acute and chronic pain, and cancer-related pain. Stresses nurse's role in these procedures.
Prod-HOSSN Dist-AJN

Special Kind Of Care, A C 14 MIN
16MM FILM OPTICAL SOUND
Explains how Cancer Care, InC, stands by with counseling, guidance and funds when a family member is struck down by cancer. Shows how all members of a family benefited from the assistance of a case worker.
LC NO. 77-702875
Prod-CANC Dist-HF Prodn-HF 1968

Special Kind Of Matter, A C 28 MIN
16MM FILM OPTICAL SOUND
Scientists involved in the medical finding discuss the discovery of prostaglandin, a family of natural substances crucial to many physiologic functions.
LC NO. 74-703248
Prod-UPJOHN Dist-UPJOHN 1974

Special Kind Of Matter, A C 30 MIN
3/4 OR 1/2 INCH VIDEO CASSETTE
Dramatizes the perseverance that helped doctors and researchers discover, isolate and develop a family of new substances that come from the human body.
Prod-IVCH Dist-IVCH

Special Kind Of Matter, A (French) C 28 MIN
16MM FILM OPTICAL SOUND
Scientists involved in the medical finding discuss the discovery of prostaglandin, a family of natural substances crucial to many physiologic functions.
LC NO. 74-703248
Prod-UPJOHN Dist-UPJOHN 1974

Special Kind Of Matter, A (German) C 28 MIN
16MM FILM OPTICAL SOUND
Scientists involved in the medical finding discuss the discovery of prostaglandin, a family of natural substances crucial to many physiologic functions.
LC NO. 74-703248
Prod-UPJOHN Dist-UPJOHN 1974

Special Kind Of Matter, A (Spanish) C 28 MIN
16MM FILM OPTICAL SOUND
Scientists involved in the medical finding discuss the discovery of prostaglandin, a family of natural substances crucial to many physiologic functions.
LC NO. 74-703248
Prod-UPJOHN Dist-UPJOHN 1974

Special Kind Of Morning, A C 28 MIN
16MM FILM OPTICAL SOUND K-I A
Follows two little girls on a trip to the zoo at daybreak, and shows the wonder of being alone with only the animals and their keepers and of sharing these experiences with each other.
From The What's New Series.
LC NO. 76-706114
Prod-KETCTV Dist-IU 1970

Special Kind Of Mother, A B 15 MIN
3/4 OR 1/2 INCH VIDEO CASSETTE PRO
Interactions between mother and baby emphasize mother's ability to understand, interpret and act upon child's needs. Comments on how the mother thought the baby felt in response to her actions.
Prod-HSERF Dist-HSERF

Special Magic Of Herself The Elf, The C 24 MIN
16MM FILM, 3/4 OR 1/2 IN VIDEO K-I
Presents an animated film about the adventures of Herself the elf and a madcap band of tiny elves whose magical powers help them protect the workings of nature.
Prod-PERSPF Dist-CORF 1984

Special Needs Learner Characteristics C 30 MIN
3/4 OR 1/2 INCH VIDEO CASSETTE
Identifies special needs learner characteristics of handicapped and disadvantaged learners.
From The Mainstreaming Secondary Special Vocational Needs Student Series.
Prod-PUAVC Dist-PUAVC

Special Needs Students In The Classroom C 30 MIN
3/4 OR 1/2 INCH VIDEO CASSETTE
Illustrates the range of problem students, from those with learning and behavioral problems to the medically and emotionally needy. Subject specialists discuss goals and strategies which the teacher can apply in actual classroom situations.
From The Teaching Students With Special Needs Series.
LC NO. 82-706691
Prod-MSITV Dist-PBS 1981

Special Olympics C 13 MIN
16MM FILM OPTICAL SOUND
Follows the activities of participants and volunteer workers at the California Special Olympics for the mentally handicapped.
From The Ara's Sports World Series.
LC NO. 78-701326
Prod-GOLDNH Dist-VIACOM 1977

Special Olympics, The C 15 MIN
16MM FILM, 3/4 OR 1/2 IN VIDEO H-C A
Captures the spirit of courage, determination and enthusiasm involved in the Special Olympics for the mentally retarded. Follows a group of athletes from the time their plane touches down at Los Angeles International Airport to the final jubilation of the victory celebration.
Prod-MEDIAG Dist-MEDIAG 1976

Special Paragraphs - Conclusions And Transitions C 30 MIN
3/4 OR 1/2 INCH VIDEO CASSETTE C
See series title for descriptive statement.
From The Writing For A Reason Series.
Prod-DALCCD Dist-DALCCD

Special Paragraphs - Introductions C 30 MIN
3/4 OR 1/2 INCH VIDEO CASSETTE C
See series title for descriptive statement.
From The Writing For A Reason Series.
Prod-DALCCD Dist-DALCCD

Special People - Library Service To Nursing Home Residents C 15 MIN
3/4 OR 1/2 INCH VIDEO CASSETTE
Discusses some of the emotional reactions that nursing home employees and library staff may experience while serving nursing home residents. Describes the kinds of services, programs and materials used at a particular convalescent center.
Prod-ANARCL Dist-LVN

Special Periodical Index C 6 MIN
3/4 OR 1/2 INCH VIDEO CASSETTE
Shows how to locate articles in professional journals by such periodical indexes such as the Social Science Index.
From The Library Skills Tapes Series.
Prod-MDCC Dist-MDCC

Special Place, A C 11 MIN
3/4 OR 1/2 INCH VIDEO CASSETTE C A
Shows two women who relate primarily to men sexually while they share an intense sexual and emotional relationship with each other.
Prod-NATSF Dist-MMRC

Special Problems B 30 MIN
16MM FILM OPTICAL SOUND
Discusses techniques useful in problem cases that commonly confront the supervisor. Relates techniques for supervising people stationed at long distances and outlines the job of the part-time supervisor.
From The Success In Supervision Series.
LC NO. 74-706254
Prod-WETATV Dist-USNAC 1965

Special Problems In The Management Of Peptic Ulcer C 40 MIN
16MM FILM OPTICAL SOUND PRO
Authorities discuss solutions to difficult diagnostic and therapeutic conditions, including esophageal ulcer, postbulbar ulcer, jejunal ulcer and pyloric obstruction and hemorrhage.
Prod-WFC Dist-WYLAB 1952

Special Procedures In IV Therapy - Part 3 C 19 MIN
3/4 OR 1/2 INCH VIDEO CASSETTE PRO
Illustrates two special procedures in IV therapy, the heparin lock and the teflon stylet.
From The Parenteral Therapy Series.
Prod-HSCIC Dist-HSCIC 1982

Special Products And Factoring B 31 MIN
16MM FILM OPTICAL SOUND H
Defines factoring. Shows how the form of a binomial is obtained by multiplying two generalized linear factors and then used to find the binomial factors. Describes the factor theorem for polynomials.
From The Intermediate Algebra Series.
Prod-CALVIN Dist-MLA Prodn-UNIVFI 1959

Special Purpose Semiconductors C 17 MIN
16MM FILM, 3/4 OR 1/2 IN VIDEO IND
Covers four of more important special purpose semiconductors. Explains construction and characteristics of the SCR.
From The Introduction To Solid State Electronics Series. Chapter 7
LC NO. 80-707265
Prod-TAT Dist-TAT

Special Purpose Semiconductors (Spanish) C 17 MIN
3/4 OR 1/2 INCH VIDEO CASSETTE IND
Covers four of more important special purpose semiconductors. Explains construction and characteristics of the SCR.
From The Introduction To Solid State Electronics (Spanish) Series. Chapter 7
Prod-TAT Dist-TAT

Special Purpose Tubes - Remote Cutoff And Beam Power Tubes B 18 MIN
16MM FILM OPTICAL SOUND
Discusses the distinguishing characteristics, operation, and advantages of remote cutoff tubes. Compares remote and sharp cutoff tubes and discusses the operation of a sharp cutoff tube. Discusses beam power tube construction and how the beam forming plates overcome the disadvantage of secondary emission. (Kinescope)
LC NO. 74-705677
Prod-USAF Dist-USNAC

Special Reference Materials C 7 MIN
3/4 OR 1/2 INCH VIDEO CASSETTE
Examines special reference books such as the Reader's Advisor, Bartlett's Familiar Quotations and the Nation and Florida Status.
From The Library Skills Tapes Series.
Prod-MDCC Dist-MDCC

Special Report C 17 MIN
16MM FILM OPTICAL SOUND
A scathing satire of the news coverage of the murder of a topless go-go dancer, Candy Parabola.
LC NO. 71-711502
Prod-USC Dist-USC 1970

Special Report To Stockholders C 7 MIN
16MM FILM OPTICAL SOUND
Presents an animated film of General Mills' 1951-1952 Annual Report and explains the company policy of reinvesting earnings in the business.
Prod-GEMILL Dist-GEMILL

Special Requests And Persuasive Claims B 45 MIN
2 INCH VIDEOTAPE C
See series title for descriptive statement.
From The Business Writing Series. Unit III - Persuasive Messages
Prod-CHITVC Dist-GPITVL Prodn-WTTWTV

Special Show, The C 28 MIN
16MM FILM - 3/4 IN VIDEO P-I
Illustrates difficulties faced daily by people with handicaps, viewed from their perspective.
From The Special Delivery Series.
LC NO. 79-706883
Prod-WNVTTV Dist-LAWREN 1979

Special Sounds C 15 MIN
3/4 INCH VIDEO CASSETTE P
Studies words in which x is pronounced ks and in which SQ is pronounced SKW.
From The New Talking Shop Series.
Prod-BSPTV Dist-GPITVL 1978

Special Steering And Sailing Rules B 14 MIN
16MM FILM OPTICAL SOUND
Gives the steering and sailing rules governing a steam vessel under way and a sailing fishing vessel. Defines 'PRIVILEGE' and 'BURDEN.'
LC NO. FIE52-956
Prod-USN Dist-USNAC 1943

Special Time For Parents And Children, A C 15 MIN
16MM FILM, 3/4 OR 1/2 IN VIDEO A
Shows how parents can have fun with their children while improving the quality of their life together through a very special bonding.
Prod-JOWA Dist-PEREN

Special Tour C 15 MIN
16MM FILM, 3/4 OR 1/2 IN VIDEO J-C A
Presents social and political issues through a science fiction story which dramatizes man's interactions with an authoritative computer.
LC NO. 77-701114
Prod-BURPT Dist-PFP 1973

Special Trade, A C 17 MIN
16MM FILM, 3/4 OR 1/2 IN VIDEO K-I
Presents a story about a friendship between a young girl and an older man. Tells how, as a baby, the young girl is taken for outings and taught to walk by her friend. Explains how one day the man returns home from the hospital in a wheelchair and it is the young girl's turn to take her friend for walks. Based on the book A Special Trade by Sally Whitman.
Prod-BARR Dist-BARR 1979

Special Treatment C 30 MIN
3/4 OR 1/2 INCH VIDEO CASSETTE C A
See series title for descriptive statement.
From The Loosening The Grip Series.
Prod-UMA Dist-GPITVL 1980

Special Universe Of Walter Krolik, The C 25 MIN
16MM FILM OPTICAL SOUND
Describes a family man who has TB. Examines the complex relationships between patient and medical and paramedical staff, with special emphasis on nurses.
Prod-NTBA Dist-AMLUNG 1966

Special Use Of Valuation - How And When To Use It C 51 MIN
3/4 OR 1/2 INCH VIDEO CASSETTE PRO
Covers the topic of special use valuation with particular emphasis on farmlands. Explains the cash value formula and alternative methods of valuation.
From The Postmortem Tax Planning After ERTA Series.
Prod-ABACPE Dist-ABACPE

Specialization C 15 MIN
3/4 OR 1/2 INCH VIDEO CASSETTE P
Uses the format of a television program to explain that specialization is an important aspect of production and that it often leads to more efficient production of goods and services. Demonstrates that there are both advantages and disadvantages to specialized tasks and jobs.
From The Pennywise Series. No. 6
LC NO. 82-706008
Prod-MAETEL Dist-GPITVL 1980

Specialized Centrifugal Pumps C 60 MIN
3/4 OR 1/2 INCH VIDEO CASSETTE IND
Features standardized end suction and vertical pumps.
From The Mechanical Equipment Maintenance Series.
Prod-ITCORP Dist-ITCORP

Specialized Centrifugal Pumps (Spanish) C 60 MIN
3/4 OR 1/2 INCH VIDEO CASSETTE IND
Features standardized end suction and vertical pumps.
From The Mechanical Equipment Maintenance (Spanish) Series.
Prod-ITCORP Dist-ITCORP

Specialized Nondestructive Testing Methods C 55 MIN
3/4 OR 1/2 INCH VIDEO CASSETTE PRO
Gives an overview of testing methods, including visual thermal, acoustical imaging and acoustic emission.
From The Fundamentals Of Nondestructive Testing Series.
Prod-AMCEE Dist-AMCEE

Specialties C 29 MIN
3/4 OR 1/2 INCH VIDEO CASSETTE
Presents coach Billy Hunter, players Mark Belanger and Don Baylor and Oriole manager Earl Weaver explaining base running, stealing, sliding and individual aspects of baseball and offering comments on winning attitudes and desire.
From The Basically Baseball Series.
Prod-MDCPB Dist-MDCPB

Specialty Strokes C 30 MIN
16MM FILM, 3/4 OR 1/2 IN VIDEO H-C A
See series title for descriptive statement.
From The Tennis Anyone Series.
LC NO. 79-706889
Prod-BATA Dist-TIMLIF 1979

Species And Evolution C 24 MIN
16MM FILM, 3/4 OR 1/2 IN VIDEO
Defines operationally what evolutionalists mean when they use the term species. Proposes that the variability of climate and terrain of places like Hawaii is one reason for the diversity of species in a locale.
Prod-OPENU Dist-MEDIAG Prodn-BBCTV 1982

Specific Gravity Separator C 3 MIN
16MM FILM OPTICAL SOUND H-C A
Uses both animation and live action to illustrate the stratifying action of a vibrating slanted deck combined with air, the uphill movement of heavy seeds and the migration of lighter seeds toward the lower end of the deck.
From The Principles Of Seed Processing Series.
LC NO. 77-701162
Prod-EVERSL Dist-IOWA Prodn-IOWA 1975

Specific Is Terrific, The (2nd Ed) C 9 MIN
16MM FILM, 3/4 OR 1/2 IN VIDEO I-C A
Points out that writing general statements does not make a very good impression. Stresses using nouns, verbs, adjectives and adverbs in a specific way to attract the interest of the reader.
From The Effective Writing Series.
Prod-CENTRO Dist-CORF 1983

Specific Learning Disabilities C 30 MIN
3/4 OR 1/2 INCH VIDEO CASSETTE T
Presents an overview of the basic psychological processes including reception, association and expression and describes how disabilities in any one process may affect learning. Considers ways of accommodating an individual's unique learning style. Concludes with an interview with two young adults who share their experiences as disabled students.
From The Promises To Keep Series. Module 3
Prod-VPISU Dist-LUF 1979

Specific Learning Disabilities - Evaluation C 28 MIN
16MM FILM OPTICAL SOUND T
Follows two learning-disabled children through a series of evaluative tasks to determine their learning strengths and weaknesses in order to give teachers a practical understanding of evaluative techniques.
LC NO. 75-704162
Prod-MHCF Dist-DAVFMS 1975

Specific Learning Disabilities - Evaluation C 28 MIN
3/4 OR 1/2 INCH VIDEO CASSETTE
Deals with the diagnosis and treatment of children with normal IQs who cannot learn in traditional ways.
From The Special Education Series.
Prod-DAVFMS Dist-DAVFMS

Specific Learning Disabilities - Remedial Programming C 31 MIN
16MM FILM OPTICAL SOUND T
Presents and discusses remedial techniques and procedures which teachers can use in the classroom. Describes how information gained through evaluation and observation can be translated into appropriate individualized remedial planning.
LC NO. 75-704163
Prod-MHCF Dist-DAVFMS 1975

Specific Learning Disabilities - Remedial Programming C 31 MIN
3/4 OR 1/2 INCH VIDEO CASSETTE
Deals with the diagnosis and treatment of children with normal IQs who cannot learn in traditional ways.
From The Special Education Series.
Prod-DAVFMS Dist-DAVFMS

Specific Learning Disabilities In The Classroom C 23 MIN
16MM FILM OPTICAL SOUND A
Defines and documents the most common types of specific learning disabilities. Presents a language learning hierarchy, illustrated by film footage, to show how and why learning disabilities impair academic development. Discusses resources outside of the school which can offer evaluative and remedial help.
LC NO. 75-703615
Prod-DAVFMS Dist-DAVFMS 1975

Specific Learning Disabilities In The Classroom C 23 MIN
3/4 OR 1/2 INCH VIDEO CASSETTE
Deals with the diagnosis and treatment of children with normal IQs who cannot learn in traditional ways.
From The Special Education Series.
Prod-DAVFMS Dist-DAVFMS

Specification Review, The - Meeting The User C 16 MIN
3/4 INCH VIDEO CASSETTE C
See series title for descriptive statement.
From The Principles Of Specification Design Series. Module 2
LC NO. 80-706740
Prod-BRA Dist-BRA 1980

Specifications And Equipment Details C
3/4 OR 1/2 INCH VIDEO CASSETTE IND
See series title for descriptive statement.
From The Drafting - Process Piping Drafting Series.
Prod-GPCV Dist-GPCV

Specifications And Tolerances C 32 MIN
3/4 OR 1/2 INCH VIDEO CASSETTE
Describes procedures to establish sspecifications and tolerances utilizing the statistical data available from quality control records.
From The Quality Control Series.
Prod-MIOT Dist-MIOT

Specified Perils C 29 MIN
3/4 INCH VIDEO CASSETTE
Discusses methods of maximizing the after-tax dollars for personal life insurance beneficiaries.
From The Life, Death And Taxes Series.
Prod-UMITV Dist-UMITV 1977

Spectacular Canyons C 17 MIN
16MM FILM, 3/4 OR 1/2 IN VIDEO J-H
Visits several spectacular canyons to investigate how they were formed. Deals with how different rocks contribute to canyon formation and the effects of erosion, uplift and plate tectonics. Discusses the Earth's geological history and speculates on what the Earth's future might be.
From The Natural Phenomena Series.
Prod-JOU Dist-JOU 1982

Spectral Analysis Of The Amniotic Fluid In Hemolytic Disease Of The Newborn B 22 MIN
16MM FILM OPTICAL SOUND PRO
Discusses amniocentesis, its indications and hazards.
From The Clinical Pathology Series.
Prod-NMAC Dist-USNAC 1972

Spectral Properties Of Soils C 30 MIN
3/4 OR 1/2 INCH VIDEO CASSETTE
Describes an experiment in which chemical and physical studies of 500 soils revealed that spectral properties of soils are related to the organic matter and other variables.
From The Introduction To Quantitative Analysis Of Remote Sensing Data Series.
Prod-PUAVC Dist-PUAVC

Spectrometric Oil Analysis Program C 19 MIN
3/4 OR 1/2 INCH VIDEO CASSETTE
Depicts the program for testing engine oil for metal traces from worn parts to predict potential engine trouble.
LC NO. 84-706487
Prod-USA Dist-USNAC 1983

Spectrophotometric Analysis C 15 MIN
3/4 OR 1/2 INCH VIDEO CASSETTE
Examines the nature of light, color and spectra. Illustrates the components and use of a calibrated spectrophotometer.
From The General Chemistry Laboratory Techniques Series.
Prod-UCEMC Dist-UCEMC

Spectrophotometric Study Of Complex Ions B 15 MIN
16MM FILM OPTICAL SOUND
Develops a procedure for using the spectrophotometer and illustrates a method for finding the formula of a complex ion, iron thiocyanate.
From The Experimental General Chemistry Series.
Prod-MLA Dist-MLA 1970

Spectroscopy C 13 MIN
16MM FILM OPTICAL SOUND
Introduces the student to the phenomena by which light is produced when an electrical discharge is passed through gases in an evacuated tube and other experiments.
From The Experimental General Chemistry Series.
Prod-MLA Dist-MLA

Spectroscopy C 9 MIN
3/4 INCH VIDEO CASSETTE
Demonstrates the concepts of color, absorption and emission. Introduces the properties of light, wavelength and frequency. Discusses the Balmer series.
From The Chemistry Videotape Series.
Prod-UMITV Dist-UMITV

Spectroscopy B 30 MIN
2 INCH VIDEOTAPE J
See series title for descriptive statement.
From The Investigating The World Of Science, Unit 1 - Matter And Energy Series.
Prod-MPATI Dist-GPITVL

Specula - Nasal And Vaginal C 14 MIN
3/4 INCH VIDEO CASSETTE PRO
Demonstrates various types of nasal and vaginal specula and discusses their special features. Describes measures for providing safety and comfort for the patient and includes suggestions for care, maintenance, and part replacement.
From The Instruments Of Physical Assessment Series.
LC NO. 80-707628
Prod-SUNYSB Dist-LIP 1980

Speculating And Spreading In Financial Futures C 30 MIN
3/4 OR 1/2 INCH VIDEO CASSETTE C A
Discusses trading on the financial futures market. Features Nancy Johnson and Carla Jane Eyre.
From The Commodities – The Professional Trader Series.
Prod-VIPUB Dist-VIPUB

Speculation Phase, The C 60 MIN
3/4 OR 1/2 INCH VIDEO CASSETTE IND
See series title for descriptive statement.
From The Value Engineering Series.
Prod-NCSU Dist-AMCEE

Speech - Upper Grade Level C 19 MIN
16MM FILM, 3/4 OR 1/2 IN VIDEO
Demonstrates a speech program for the hearing impaired at the upper grade levels. Presents lessons on definitions, adjectives and adverbs, and idiomatic expressions.
LC NO. 80-707428
Prod-USBEH Dist-USNAC

Speech And Language Disorders C 30 MIN
3/4 OR 1/2 INCH VIDEO CASSETTE T
Demonstrates normal communication development and selected disorders which may be exhibited in the classroom. Discusses how each disorder might be treated and how the regular classroom teacher can support corrective efforts.
From The Promises To Keep Series. Module 8
Prod-VPISU Dist-LUF 1979

Speech And Telephone B 15 MIN
2 INCH VIDEOTAPE P
See series title for descriptive statement.
From The Language Corner Series.
Prod-CVETVC Dist-GPITVL Prodn-WCVETV

Speech Indicator C 5 MIN
16MM FILM SILENT H-C A S
Describes the speech indicator in American sign language, telling what it is and how to use it. Signed for the deaf by Herb Larson, who relates a personal experience of what happened when he first used the device at home.
LC NO. 76-701704
Prod-JOYCE Dist-JOYCE 1975

Speech Instruction With A Deaf-Blind Pupil, No. 1 B 6 MIN
16MM FILM OPTICAL SOUND T
Depicts tactile lip reading and demonstrates the effort required by the pupil to grasp this technique.
Prod-CAMPF Dist-CAMPF 1968

Speech Lesson B 15 MIN
2 INCH VIDEOTAPE P
See series title for descriptive statement.
From The Language Corner Series.
Prod-CVETVC Dist-GPITVL Prodn-WCVETV

Speech Preparation B 13 MIN
16MM FILM OPTICAL SOUND H-C A
Presents the basic steps in preparing a speech.
Prod-CBF Dist-AVED 1958

Speech Reading B 28 MIN
16MM FILM - 3/4 IN VIDEO
Describes how persons with a hearing loss can learn, by careful interpretation of lip movements, to 'see' what people are saying. Shows how vowel and consonant sounds are formed by the mouth.
Prod-USNAC Dist-USNAC 1972

Speech Reading Materials–A Series
A
Provides skills in the speech reading process for both the hearing and the hearing-impaired person.
Prod-RMI Dist-RMI

Blade - Alveolars	010 MIN
Blade - Prepalatals	010 MIN
Conversational Skill Tape, Pt I	010 MIN
Conversational Skill Tape, Pt II	010 MIN
Horizontal Vowels And Semi-Vowels	010 MIN
Introduction To Bilabials	010 MIN
Lingua - Alveolars	010 MIN
Rounded Vowels And Labio-Dentals	010 MIN
Velars And Glottals	010 MIN
Vertical Vowels And Lingua-Dentals	010 MIN

Speech Rehabilitation Of The Laryngectomized Patient C 120 MIN
3/4 OR 1/2 INCH VIDEO CASSETTE
Revies normal aspects of anatomy and physiology as related to the acquisition of esophageal speech. Describes total laryngectomy surgery and the requisites for acquiring esophageal voice.
Prod-PUAVC Dist-PUAVC

Speech Science Applied To Clinical Management C 120 MIN
3/4 OR 1/2 INCH VIDEO CASSETTE
Reviews the role of speech science and the impact it has on clinical management. Presents some of the advances in instrumentation which can be applied to diagnosis and management.
Prod-PUAVC Dist-PUAVC

Speech Techniques B 11 MIN
16MM FILM OPTICAL SOUND J-H
Discusses the importance of good speech techniques in military instruction and illustrates techniques to be used, including looking at and talking directly to the the audience, attention to one's diction, exercising care in the use of mannerisms and speaking slowly enough to be understood.
From The Military Instruction Series.
LC NO. FIE56-247
Prod-USA Dist-USNAC 1956

Speech Understanding Using Hearsay C 45 MIN
3/4 OR 1/2 INCH VIDEO CASSETTE PRO
Covers interexpert communication, the role of knowledge on many levels, analysis, islands of reliability, and an illustration.
From The Artificial Intelligence - Pt 2, Expert Systems Series.
Prod-MIOT Dist-MIOT

Speech Understanding Using Hearsay II C 61 MIN
3/4 OR 1/2 INCH VIDEO CASSETTE C
See series title for descriptive statement.
From The Artificial Intelligence, Pt II - Expert Systems Series.
Prod-MIOT Dist-AMCEE

Speech, Music And Graphics C 18 MIN
3/4 OR 1/2 INCH VIDEO CASSETTE J-C A
Examines various types of functions which computers can perform such as data plotting, graphic displays and programmed speech.
From The Little Computers - See How They Run Series.
LC NO. 81-706871
Prod-ELDATA Dist-GPITVL 1980

Speech, The C 5 MIN
3/4 OR 1/2 INCH VIDEO CASSETTE
Demonstrates that when politics meet mass media, the result is the 'ultimate victory of form over content.'
Prod-EAI Dist-EAI

Speech, The - Doug Hall C 7 MIN
3/4 INCH VIDEO CASSETTE A
Prod-AFA Dist-AFA 1982

Speeches Of FDR–A Series

Presents three speeches by Franklin Delano Roosevelt.
Prod-NA Dist-USNAC

Speeches Of FDR, The - Address At Chautauqua,	
Speeches Of FDR, The - Navy And Total Defense	026 MIN
Speeches Of FDR, The - State Of The Union	042 MIN

Speeches Of FDR, The - Address At Chautauqua, New York, August 14, 1936 B 29 MIN
16MM FILM, 3/4 OR 1/2 IN VIDEO
Presents FDR's first address on foreign policy. He notes the tendency to hostile aggression growing in the world, details the areas in which the U S promoted good will and peace and repeats his inaugural statement about the Good-Neighbor Policy.
From The Speeches Of FDR Series.
Prod-NA Dist-USNAC

Speeches Of FDR, The - Navy And Total Defense Day Address, October 27, 1941 B 26 MIN
16MM FILM, 3/4 OR 1/2 IN VIDEO
Presents a speech made by FDR after an American ship was fired upon by Nazi submarines, and the USS Kearny was attacked by a German U-boat and eleven lives were lost.
From The Speeches Of FDR Series.
Prod-NA Dist-USNAC

Speeches Of FDR, The - State Of The Union Message, January 6, 1942 B 42 MIN
16MM FILM, 3/4 OR 1/2 IN VIDEO
Presents the State of the Union address by FDR one month after Pearl Harbor. He outlines the steps and sacrifices to be made in order to achieve victory in World War II and gives a history of the Axis powers and their conquests in the 1930's.
From The Speeches Of FDR Series.
Prod-NA Dist-USNAC

Speed C 30 MIN
3/4 OR 1/2 INCH VIDEO CASSETTE
See series title for descriptive statement.
From The Infinity Factory Series.
Prod-EDFCEN Dist-MDCPB

Speed And Explosion C 49 MIN
3/4 OR 1/2 INCH VIDEO CASSETTE
Shows how to build speed, power and performance for any sport. Teaches training techniques for increasing speed in short distances. Uses the program developed by Bob Ward, conditioning coach of the Dallas Cowboys.
Prod-ATHI Dist-ATHI

Speed And Graphs C 30 MIN
3/4 OR 1/2 INCH VIDEO CASSETTE
See series title for descriptive statement.
From The Infinity Factory Series.
Prod-EDFCEN Dist-MDCPB

Speed And Heat C 30 MIN
16MM FILM OPTICAL SOUND
Describes the problems which will be encountered by the supersonic transport of tomorrow and explains how research is helping to solve problems in construction, propulsion and the protection of the passengers by developing a whole new technology as well as a new plane.
LC NO. FIA65-617
Prod-NAA Dist-RCKWL 1964

Speed Drop B 5 MIN
16MM FILM OPTICAL SOUND
Demonstrates how load equalizer is added to the governor to control speed and how the power piston and piston and speeder spring function.
LC NO. FIE52-1084
Prod-USN Dist-USNAC 1948

Speed Learning–A Series
J-H
Provides simple techniques for improving reading skills and at the same time increasing enjoyment and reading.
Prod-LEARNI Dist-AITECH 1982

Active Mind	027 MIN
Art Of Reading, The	029 MIN
Competition With Yourself, A	027 MIN
Four On The Floor	028 MIN
Getting It All Together	028 MIN
It's All Right To Be Wrong	028 MIN
Pay-Off, The	027 MIN
Rapid Reading	029 MIN
Surveying For Hidden Treasure	027 MIN

Speed Of A Pulse In A Stretched Rope, The B 8 MIN
16MM FILM OPTICAL SOUND C
Shows how the speed of the propagation of a pulse along a stretched rope may be measured with a stop clock triggered by a photoelectric cell.
Prod-PUAVC Dist-PUAVC 1961

Speed Of Chemical Changes And Molecular Collision C 14 MIN
16MM FILM, 3/4 OR 1/2 IN VIDEO I-C A
Demonstrates an experiment which shows that chemical reactions can occur at different speeds. Presents a mechanical model of a reaction. Uses the model to formulate hypotheses concerning the factors that influence the speed of chemical change.
Prod-IWANMI Dist-PHENIX 1968

Speed Of Light B 21 MIN
16MM FILM OPTICAL SOUND H-C
Shows Dr Siebert of MIT measuring the speed of light in air at night, using a spark-gap, a photocell, parabolic mirrors and an oscilloscope. Later, shows him studying the speed of light in air and water in his laboratory using a high speed rotation mirror.
From The PSSC Physics Films Series.
Prod-PSSC Dist-MLA 1960

Speed Of Light C 30 MIN
16MM FILM OPTICAL SOUND H-C A
Presents a pre-Kennedy-assassination period film in which a California mother and daughter face paranoia-evoking circumstances in the American Midwest.
LC NO. 81-700399
Prod-HANVAN Dist-HANVAN 1980

Speed Of Light, The - Measurement And Applications B 14 MIN
16MM FILM, 3/4 OR 1/2 IN VIDEO J-C
Shows how Galileo, Fizeau, Roemer and Michelson contributed to the measurement of the speed of light and indicates some of the most important applications of this constant today. Michelson's famed experiment is shown in animation.
Prod-EBF Dist-EBEC 1955

Speed Of Living, The B 20 MIN
16MM FILM OPTICAL SOUND H-C A
Examines the symptoms of hyperthyroidism. Describes the tests, medical therapy and surgery that was performed on a woman patient.
From The Doctors At Work Series.
LC NO. FIA65-1362
Prod-CMA Dist-LAWREN Prodn-LAWREN 1962

Speed Reading C
1/2 IN VIDEO CASSETTE (VHS)
Presents a complete home video course in speed reading.
Prod-KARLVI Dist-KARLVI

Speed Reading - The Computer Course C
3/4 OR 1/2 INCH VIDEO CASSETTE
Teaches the user to read faster and more efficiently while providing a complete understanding of the theory and basics of speed reading. Includes three diskettes and a complete training manual containing instructional material and practice readings.
Prod-BBP Dist-DELTAK

Speed Reading In One Lesson C 11 MIN
16MM FILM OPTICAL SOUND I-C A
Shows that rapid reading is a skill that can easily be mastered at home or in the classroom. Provides step-by-step instruction for increasing reading speed.
LC NO. 75-701531
Prod-FFORIN Dist-FFORIN 1974

Speed Reading–A Series
16MM FILM, 3/4 OR 1/2 IN VIDEO H-C A
Presents a speed reading system, reinforced by reading exercises. Focuses on the art of skimming, acquiring better study habits and enlarging vocabulary.
LC NO. 79-707471
Prod-TIMLIF Dist-TIMLIF 1979

Speed-A-Way X 11 MIN
16MM FILM OPTICAL SOUND J-C T
Demonstrates the game, speed-a-way–a combination of soccer, basketball, speedball, field ball and hockey-in which the player is allowed to run with the ball.
Prod-LAR Dist-LAR 1952

Speed, INC C 27 MIN
16MM FILM OPTICAL SOUND J-C A

Highlights the 1966 professional football season, featuring team and individual performances of the Dallas Cowboys.
LC NO. FIA68-1440
Prod-NFL Dist-NFL 1967

Speeding C 21 MIN
16MM FILM, 3/4 OR 1/2 IN VIDEO H-C A
Consists of dramatized interviews with police officers and with motorists who have been ticketed for speeding, in which both sides express their thoughts on speeding violations.
Prod-BLOCK Dist-DIRECT 1978

Speedscene, The - The Problem Of Amphetamine Abuse C 17 MIN
16MM FILM, 3/4 OR 1/2 IN VIDEO H-C A
Offers graphic evidence against the use of amphetamines in any form other than for medical reasons.
Prod-MEDIC Dist-PHENIX 1969

Speedscene, The - The Problem Of Amphetamine Abuse (French) C 17 MIN
16MM FILM, 3/4 OR 1/2 IN VIDEO H-C A
Offers graphic evidence against the use of amphetamines in any form other than for medical reasons.
Prod-MEDIC Dist-PHENIX 1969

Speedscene, The - The Problem Of Amphetamine Abuse (German) C 17 MIN
16MM FILM, 3/4 OR 1/2 IN VIDEO H-C A
Offers graphic evidence against the use of amphetamines in any form other than for medical reasons.
Prod-MEDIC Dist-PHENIX 1969

Speedscene, The - The Problem Of Amphetamine Abuse (Portuguese) C 17 MIN
16MM FILM, 3/4 OR 1/2 IN VIDEO H-C A
Offers graphic evidence against the use of amphetamines in any form other than for medical reasons.
Prod-MEDIC Dist-PHENIX 1969

Speedscene, The - The Problem Of Amphetamine Abuse (Spanish) C 17 MIN
16MM FILM, 3/4 OR 1/2 IN VIDEO H-C A
Offers graphic evidence against the use of amphetamines in any form other than for medical reasons.
Prod-MEDIC Dist-PHENIX 1969

Speedway Through The Years B 30 MIN
16MM FILM OPTICAL SOUND
Shows 50 years of progress at Indianapolis.
Prod-SFI Dist-SFI

Speedway 79 Power Fuel C 1 MIN
3/4 OR 1/2 INCH VIDEO CASSETTE
Shows a classic animated television commercial with a jingle.
Prod-BROOKC Dist-BROOKC

Speedy B 72 MIN
16MM FILM, 3/4 OR 1/2 IN VIDEO
Tells how a hero comes to the rescue when his girlfriend's grandfather's horsecar is stolen by a gang. Stars Harold Lloyd. Issued in 1928 as a silent motion picture.
From The Harold Lloyd Series.
LC NO. 79-707470
Prod-LLOYDH Dist-TIMLIF 1976

Speedy Alka-Seltzer C 1 MIN
3/4 OR 1/2 INCH VIDEO CASSETTE
Shows a classic television commercial.
Prod-BROOKC Dist-BROOKC

Speedy Samurai, The C 13 MIN
16MM FILM OPTICAL SOUND
Describes Kanagawa with its many attractive resorts and its tourist industry.
Prod-UNIJAP Dist-UNIJAP 1970

Spell It Right C 20 MIN
2 INCH VIDEOTAPE P
See series title for descriptive statement.
From The Learning Our Language, Unit 2 - Dictionary Skills Series.
Prod-MPATI Dist-GPITVL

Spellbound (Razor Sequence) B 10 MIN
16MM FILM OPTICAL SOUND J-C A
Presents an excerpt from the 1945 motion picture Spellbound. Depicts an amnesiac wandering through a house carrying a razor. Directed by Alfred Hitchcock.
From The Film Study Extracts Series.
Prod-UNKNWN Dist-FI

Spelling C 30 MIN
3/4 OR 1/2 INCH VIDEO CASSETTE T
Provides an appreciation of the importance of spelling in academic success. Gives awareness of causes of spelling errors among handicapped children.
From The Stretch Subject Matter Materials For Teaching Handicapped Children Series.
Prod-HUBDSC Dist-HUBDSC

Spelling C 30 MIN
3/4 OR 1/2 INCH VIDEO CASSETTE T S
Shows strategies for mainstreaming eligible exceptional children. Presents a magician demonstrating some techniques of evaluating a child's spelling skills, of planning individualized remediate weaknesses and of increasing interest in spelling proficiency.
From The Project STRETCH (Strategies To Train Regular Educators To Teach Children With...) Series. Module 10
LC NO. 80-706646
Prod-METCO Dist-HUBDSC 1980

Spelling - An Introductory Film C 14 MIN
16MM FILM, 3/4 OR 1/2 IN VIDEO P
Describes how spelling and writing began, how spelling is a skill common to both reading and writing, how spelling is based on sounds, how letters in the alphabet stand for sounds, how there are more sounds than letters in the alphabet and how to listen for individual sounds in words.
From The Spelling Skills Series. No. 1
Prod-GLDWER Dist-JOU 1976

Spelling - Visualization, The Key To Spelling Success C 30 MIN
16MM FILM OPTICAL SOUND T
Demonstrates some techniques of evaluating a child's spelling skills, of planning individualized instruction to remediate weakness, and of increasing interest in spelling proficiency.
From The Project STRETCH Series. Module 10
LC NO. 80-700617
Prod-METCO Dist-HUBDSC Prodn-GAEDTN 1980

Spelling Complex Sounds C 13 MIN
16MM FILM, 3/4 OR 1/2 IN VIDEO P
Discusses consonant clusters and how to separate the sounds encountered in them, reviews the alphabet and its sounds, explores vowel sounds and the fact that there are different ways of spelling the long vowel sounds in words and, finally, introduces the dictionary as a spelling tool aid.
From The Spelling Skills Series. No. 3
Prod-GLDWER Dist-JOU 1976

Spelling Dragon, The C 16 MIN
16MM FILM, 3/4 OR 1/2 IN VIDEO P-I
Presents the Spelling Dragon who teaches a basic method for spelling any word, while entertaining with a story of knights and maidens in distress. Animated.
Prod-CHRSTD Dist-PHENIX 1982

Spelling Exercises With The Alphabet C 19 MIN
16MM FILM, 3/4 OR 1/2 IN VIDEO P-I
Starts with a brief review of the idea that the letters in our alphabet are symbols that stand for the sounds in words. Takes a trip through the alphabet step-by-step, illustrating the sound or sounds of each letter.
From The Spelling Skills Series. No. 4
Prod-GLDWER Dist-JOU 1977

Spelling Is Easy (2nd Ed) C 11 MIN
16MM FILM, 3/4 OR 1/2 IN VIDEO I-J
Presents the five rules for good spelling--hear, see, repeat, write and check the work.
Prod-CORF Dist-CORF 1968

Spelling Medical Terminology C 18 MIN
3/4 OR 1/2 INCH VIDEO CASSETTE PRO
Emphasizes the spelling of medical terminology. Analyzes the term's component parts, then links these components together using fundamental spelling rules.
From The Medical Terminology Series.
Prod-HSCIC Dist-HSCIC

Spelling Plural Nouns C 13 MIN
16MM FILM, 3/4 OR 1/2 IN VIDEO P
Deals with changing the singular form of a noun to the plural from.
From The Spelling Skills Series.
Prod-GLDWER Dist-JOU 1978

Spelling Secrets--A Series
P
Introduces a phonics approach to spelling and takes the expected, or most common spellings of English sounds, and teaches them in sequential order. Teaches spelling generalizations applicable to thousands of words and the student is led to look at words with discrimination to see if the word agrees or deviates from the expected spelling. Includes 16, 15-minute spelling lessons.
Prod-WESTEL Dist-WESTEL

Spelling Simple Sounds C 13 MIN
16MM FILM, 3/4 OR 1/2 IN VIDEO P
Reviews the alphabet as the base of our language, explores words as a sequence of sounds, distinguishes among the first, second and final sounds in short words, presents the idea of capital letters and introduces the capitalization of proper names.
From The Spelling Skills Series. No. 2
Prod-GLDWER Dist-JOU 1976

Spelling Skills--A Series
16MM FILM, 3/4 OR 1/2 IN VIDEO P
Prod-GLDWER Dist-JOU 1976

Spelling - An Introductory Film	014 MIN
Spelling Complex Sounds	013 MIN
Spelling Exercises With The Alphabet	019 MIN
Spelling Plural Nouns	013 MIN
Spelling Simple Sounds	013 MIN
Spelling Verbs	014 MIN

Spelling Verbs C 14 MIN
16MM FILM, 3/4 OR 1/2 IN VIDEO P-I
Details the use and the corresponding spelling of verbs.
From The Spelling Skills Series.
Prod-GLDWER Dist-JOU 1978

Spelman Story, The C 28 MIN
16MM FILM OPTICAL SOUND H-C A
A view of Spelman College as revealed as four graduates and students of today discuss the various facets of college life.
LC NO. 71-702580
Prod-SPEC Dist-CAMPF Prodn-CAMPF 1969

Spence Bay C 14 MIN
16MM FILM OPTICAL SOUND
Takes a look at the life of native peoples 250 miles north of the Canadian Arctic Circle as seen by 15 high school students from Toronto.
From The Journal Series.
LC NO. 77-702863
Prod-FIARTS Dist-CANFDC 1976

Spencers, The C 12 MIN
16MM FILM OPTICAL SOUND
Profiles a family's feelings, concerns, fears and hopes as it comes to terms with the impending death of 34-year-old Sandy Spencer.
From The Begin With Goodbye Series.
LC NO. 79-700284
Prod-UMCOM Dist-MMM 1979

Spencers, The C
3/4 OR 1/2 INCH VIDEO CASSETTE A
Looks at the Spencer family after the mother is diagnosed as having terminal cancer. Shows that after the inevitable feelings of anger, fear and self pity begin to subside, the family began to set goals. Discusses how vacations and holidays took on a special meaning as the Spencers learn to cherish each day they spent together.
From The Portraits Of Goodbye Series.
Prod-UMCOM Dist-ECUFLM 1980

Spend It All C 30 MIN
16MM FILM OPTICAL SOUND
Presents the history, dances, leisure, people and places of Louisiana's Cajun country.
From The Les Blank's Blues And Cajun Film Series
LC NO. 74-702671
Prod-FLOWER Dist-FLOWER 1974

Spend It All C 41 MIN
16MM FILM - 3/4 IN VIDEO
Presents the history, dances, leisure, people and places of Louisiana's Cajun country. Shows the Cajun people in various social and cultural activities. Issued in 1971 as a motion picture.
LC NO. 79-707412
Prod-FLOWER Dist-FLOWER 1979

Spend, Spend C 11 MIN
16MM FILM, 3/4 OR 1/2 IN VIDEO P-I
Explains that the retail purchaser is a universal victim, as witnessed in the story of a young boy who buys a scale model sports car which soon falls apart.
Prod-KINGSP Dist-PHENIX 1971

Spending Money X 15 MIN
16MM FILM OPTICAL SOUND P-I R
Tells the story about two children who learn there are right and wrong ways of obtaining and spending money.
From The Our Children Series.
Prod-FAMF Dist-FAMF

Spending Plan, A C 14 MIN
2 INCH VIDEOTAPE
Discusses how to spend money wisely and how to set up a budget.
From The Living Better II Series
Prod-MAETEL Dist-PUBTEL

Spent Reactor Fuel Storage In Granite C 13 MIN
16MM FILM OPTICAL SOUND
Documents the Lawrence Livermore Laboratory experimental program for storing spent nuclear fuel in an underground granite rock mass.
LC NO. 80-701561
Prod-LIVER Dist-LIVER 1980

Sperm Maturation In The Male Reproductive Tract - Development Of Motility X 14 MIN
16MM FILM, 3/4 OR 1/2 IN VIDEO
Shows the gradual attainment of motility as spermatozoa pass from the seminiferous tubules through the ductuli efferentes, the epididymis and finally enter the ductus deferens.
Prod-GABLHA Dist-UWASHP 1968

Sperry New Holland 1975 Agri-Newsreel C 27 MIN
16MM FILM OPTICAL SOUND
Presents a variety of events of interest to farmers, including reports on a farm in Chicago's zoo, news of a harvest of seaweed in New Hampshire and a report on research on animal feeding in Vermont.
LC NO. 75-700086
Prod-SPRYNH Dist-SRCNHD 1975

Sperry New Holland 1975 Agri-Newsreel (French) C 27 MIN
16MM FILM OPTICAL SOUND
Presents a variety of events of interest to farmers, including reports on a farm in Chicago's zoo, news of a harvest of seaweed in New Hampshire and a report on research on animal feeding in Vermont.
LC NO. 75-700086
Prod-SPRYNH Dist-SRCNHD 1975

Sperry Rand - Report To The Employees, 1976 C 13 MIN
16MM FILM OPTICAL SOUND
Presents a message to the employees of the Sperry Rand Corporation from the Chief Executive Officer of the company describing the operations of the firm in 1976.
LC NO. 76-702892
Prod-SRCNHD Dist-SRCNHD Prodn-CRABRO 1976

Sperry Rand - Report To The Employees, 1976 (Flemish) C 13 MIN
16MM FILM OPTICAL SOUND
Presents a message to the employees of the Sperry Rand Corporation from the Chief Executive Officer of the company describing the operations of the firm in 1976.
LC NO. 76-702892
Prod-SRCNHD Dist-SRCNHD Prodn-CRABRO 1976

Sperry Rand - Report To The Employees, 1976 (French) C 13 MIN
16MM FILM OPTICAL SOUND

Presents a message to the employees of the Sperry Rand Corporation from the Chief Executive Officer of the company describing the operations of the firm in 1976.
LC NO. 76-702892
Prod-SRCNHD Dist-SRCNHD Prodn-CRABRO 1976

Sperry Rand - Report To The Employees, 1976 (German) C 13 MIN
16MM FILM OPTICAL SOUND
Presents a message to the employees of the Sperry Rand Corporation from the Chief Executive Officer of the company describing the operations of the firm in 1976.
LC NO. 76-702892
Prod-SRCNHD Dist-SRCNHD Prodn-CRABRO 1976

Sperry Rand - Report To The Employees, 1976 (Italian) C 13 MIN
16MM FILM OPTICAL SOUND
Presents a message to the employees of the Sperry Rand Corporation from the Chief Executive Officer of the company describing the operations of the firm in 1976.
LC NO. 76-702892
Prod-SRCNHD Dist-SRCNHD Prodn-CRABRO 1976

Sperry Rand - Report To The Employees, 1976 (Portuguese) C 13 MIN
16MM FILM OPTICAL SOUND
Presents a message to the employees of the Sperry Rand Corporation from the Chief Executive Officer of the company describing the operations of the firm in 1976.
LC NO. 76-702892
Prod-SRCNHD Dist-SRCNHD Prodn-CRABRO 1976

Sperry Rand - Report To The Employees, 1976 (Spanish) C 13 MIN
16MM FILM OPTICAL SOUND
Presents a message to the employees of the Sperry Rand Corporation from the Chief Executive Officer of the company describing the operations of the firm in 1976.
LC NO. 76-702892
Prod-SRCNHD Dist-SRCNHD Prodn-CRABRO 1976

Spetzler Lumbar Peritoneal Shunt System C 13 MIN
3/4 OR 1/2 INCH VIDEO CASSETTE PRO
Shows the Spetzler lumbar peritoneal shunt system.
Prod-WFP Dist-WFP

SPFX - The Making Of The Empire Strikes Back C 52 MIN
16MM FILM, 3/4 OR 1/2 IN VIDEO H-C A
Discusses the art of creating film illusions. Focuses primarily on the special effects achieved in The Empire Strikes Back and offers segments from other milestone films in the realm of effects. Narrated by Mark Hamill.
Prod-GUSC Dist-FI 1980

Sphere Eversions C 8 MIN
16MM FILM, 3/4 OR 1/2 IN VIDEO
See series title for descriptive statement.
From The Topology Short Films Series.
LC NO. 81-706246
Prod-NSF Dist-IFB 1979

Spheres C 8 MIN
16MM FILM, 3/4 OR 1/2 IN VIDEO P-C A
An animated film in which a ball dances to the music of Bach.
Prod-NFBC Dist-IFB 1969

Spheres We See And Use C 9 MIN
16MM FILM, 3/4 OR 1/2 IN VIDEO P-I
Gives a clear definition of a sphere and explains that we can use spheres to help us move things and to give strength to things we build. Shows how spheres hold the most volume for a given surface area of any shape known.
Prod-BOUNDY Dist-PHENIX 1971

Spheres We See And Use (Spanish) C 9 MIN
16MM FILM, 3/4 OR 1/2 IN VIDEO P-I
Gives a clear definition of a sphere and explains that we can use spheres to help us move things and to give strength to things we build. Shows how spheres hold the most volume for a given surface area of any shape known.
Prod-BOUNDY Dist-PHENIX 1971

Spherical Space, No. 1 C 5 MIN
16MM FILM OPTICAL SOUND
Presents a metaphor of the change of perspective from the 19th century railroad man to the 21st century space-man.
Prod-VANBKS Dist-VANBKS

Sphero, The Reluctant Snowball C 15 MIN
3/4 OR 1/2 INCH VIDEO CASSETTE P
See series title for descriptive statement.
From The Magic Pages Series.
Prod-KLVXTV Dist-AITECH 1976

Sphincterotomy For Stenosis Of The Sphincter Of Oddi C 29 MIN
16MM FILM OPTICAL SOUND PRO
Presents Doctors Warren H Cole, W H Harridge and S S Roberts who believe there is a definite indication for cutting the sphincter of oddi when stenosis is encountered and shows three cases exemplifying this syndrome.
Prod-ACYDGD Dist-ACY 1962

Spice Of Life—A Series
J A
Highlights the role of herbs and spices as essential cooking ingredients in the cooking of all nations. Travels the world to show preparation of a variety of foods.
Prod-BLCKRD Dist-BCNFL

Allspice - One Spice	026 MIN
Chilies - A Dash Of Daring	026 MIN
Cinnamon - The Elegant Addition	026 MIN
Cloves - Nature's Little Nails	026 MIN
Curry Around The World	026 MIN
Garlic's Pungent Presence	026 MIN
Herbs - Aromatic Influences	026 MIN
Mustard - The Spice Of Nations	026 MIN
Nutmeg - Nature's Perfect Package	026 MIN
Pepper - The Master Spice	026 MIN
Peppercorns - Fresh Ground Flavor	026 MIN
Saffron - Autumn Gold	026 MIN
Spices Of India	026 MIN

Spice Of Life, The C 5 MIN
3/4 OR 1/2 INCH VIDEO CASSETTE J-H
Shows how to achieve variety in word order in writing.
From The Write On, Set 1 Series.
Prod-CTI Dist-CTI

Spice Of Life, The C 15 MIN
16MM FILM, 3/4 OR 1/2 IN VIDEO A
Tells of an elderly man who has lost all interest in eating and preparing meals since his wife died. Tells how his interest is rekindled after a conversation with his sister about the value of good nutrition.
Prod-NDC Dist-NDC 1983

Spices Of India, The C 26 MIN
3/4 OR 1/2 INCH VIDEO CASSETTE J A
Unveils India's talent in mixing spices such as turmeric, fenugreek, coriander, cumin, cardaman, pepper and chili. Illustrates an assortment of dishes.
From The Spice Of Life Series.
Prod-BLCKRD Dist-BCNFL 1985

Spider C 3 MIN
16MM FILM OPTICAL SOUND
Shows a closeup of a large, exotic spider spinning its web.
LC NO. 76-702058
Prod-BCPEMC Dist-BCPEMC 1975

Spider C 3 MIN
16MM FILM, 3/4 OR 1/2 IN VIDEO P-I
Shows the intricate details of web weaving. May be used in conjunction with Charlotte's Web.
From The Nature's Sights And Sounds Series.
Prod-MASLKS Dist-BCNFL 1984

Spider C 7 MIN
16MM FILM, 3/4 OR 1/2 IN VIDEO J-H A
Introduces Spider, a small wiry man who scales hamburgers onto grills, chops onions with the rapidity of machine gun fire and whisks dishes off the counter while recalling his career as a boxer.
Prod-FI Dist-TEXFLM 1975

Spider - Its Life And Web C 25 MIN
16MM FILM OPTICAL SOUND
Explains that the life of any spider is closely related to its web. Illustrates the features of a spider's body and shows how the life of the spider is centered around its web.
Prod-TOEI Dist-UNIJAP 1970

Spider And The Frenchman, The C 26 MIN
16MM FILM OPTICAL SOUND
Features skiing champions Spider Sabich and Jean-Claude Killy in a 40,000 dollar duel on identical parallel race courses.
Prod-BARP Dist-FFORIN

Spider Engineers C 16 MIN
16MM FILM, 3/4 OR 1/2 IN VIDEO P-J
The spider is shown to be an engineer of great skill and versatility. There are an estimated 100,000 species of spiders. In this study four typical species are considered—the orb weaver, the bolas spider, the diving spider, the trapdoor spider.
Prod-MIS Dist-MIS 1956

Spider Takes A Trip, The C 9 MIN
16MM FILM, 3/4 OR 1/2 IN VIDEO K-I
Uses a story about the adventures of a spider to develop skills in answering questions and predicting sentence endings.
From The Primary Language Development Series.
Prod-PEDF Dist-AIMS 1975

Spider Will Kill You, The C 30 MIN
16MM FILM OPTICAL SOUND
Depicts a story about a blind man who falls in love with a mannequin.
LC NO. 75-703034
Prod-DGAM Dist-DGAM 1974

Spider, The C 18 MIN
16MM FILM, 3/4 OR 1/2 IN VIDEO
Follows the lives of various species of spiders, pointing out varied and unusual behavior patterns. Edited from the television program Wild, Wild World Of Animals.
From The Wild, Wild World Of Animals Series.
LC NO. 79-707915
Prod-TIMLIF Dist-TIMLIF 1976

Spider's Strategem, The (Italian) C 97 MIN
16MM FILM OPTICAL SOUND
Takes place in a sleepy Italian village where a young man arrives to investigate the murder of his father, a local anti-Fascist hero assassinated 30 years before in a box at the opera house. Directed by Bernardo Bertolucci.
Prod-NYFLMS Dist-NYFLMS 1970

Spiderelephant C 8 MIN
16MM FILM, 3/4 OR 1/2 IN VIDEO J-C A
Shows a fantastic fable about a confused animal, half-elephant, half-spider, who questions whether time is moving forward or backward.
Prod-UWFKD Dist-TEXFLM

Spiders (2nd Ed) B 11 MIN
16MM FILM, 3/4 OR 1/2 IN VIDEO I-H
Illustrates the distinctive characteristics and habits of spiders, including the spinning of webs and the trapping of insects. Some of the types shown are the marbled spider, the black widow and the tarantula.
Prod-EBF Dist-EBEC 1956

Spiders - Aggression And Mating C 17 MIN
16MM FILM, 3/4 OR 1/2 IN VIDEO
Features the aggressive characteristics of the spider, showing how several kinds of webs are used to trap and kill prey. Illustrates the need of male and female to suspend normal aggressive behavior in order to mate.
From The Bio-Science Series.
LC NO. 80-706308
Prod-NGS Dist-NGS 1974

Spiders - Backyard Science (2nd Ed) C 13 MIN
16MM FILM, 3/4 OR 1/2 IN VIDEO P-I
Shows parts of a spider's body and explains how spiders function. Describes how spiders spin their webs and how they trap the insects and other small animals on which they feed. Illustrates the spider's life cycle and discusses the ways in which spiders contribute to our environment.
Prod-BEAN Dist-PHENIX 1978

Spielwaren Aus Nurnberg C 5 MIN
16MM FILM, 3/4 OR 1/2 IN VIDEO H-C A
A German-language version of the motion picture Toys From Nuremberg. Shows the toy-producing center of Nuremberg where some operations are still carried out by hand.
From The European Studies - Germany (German) Series.
Prod-MFAFRG Dist-IFB Prodn-BAYER 1973

Spies Among Us, The C 52 MIN
3/4 OR 1/2 INCH VIDEO CASSETTE H-C A
Explores the extent and danger of Soviet bloc spy activities in the U S. Covers the entire range of Soviet intelligence gathering operations and explains how U S counterintelligence is dealing with the situation. Highlights the problem of the illegal transfer of technical equipment and microcircuitry information arranged by the KGB.
Prod-NBCNEW Dist-FI 1981

Spies In The Wires C 48 MIN
3/4 OR 1/2 INCH VIDEO CASSETTE H-C A
Portrays the increasingly computerized operation of world banks, businesses, government defense systems and citizens' everyday lives. Discusses how large computers can be broken into, and preventive efforts to preserve privacy.
LC NO. 85-700905
Prod-BBCTV Dist-FI 1984

Spies, Nazis, And Reporters C 29 MIN
3/4 INCH VIDEO CASSETTE
Discusses editorials and other issues of investigative reporting. Analyzes the 'new' women's page.
From The City Desk Series.
Prod-UMITV Dist-UMITV 1976

Spike - A Montana Horseman C 12 MIN
16MM FILM, 3/4 OR 1/2 IN VIDEO J-H
Presents a portrait of Spike Van Cleve, a Montana horsebreeder whose lifestyle is based on values of hard work, commitment, loyalty, respect for horses and family continuity.
Prod-VARDIR Dist-LCOA 1977

Spike, The - Epilepsy C 50 MIN
16MM FILM, 3/4 OR 1/2 IN VIDEO C A
Offers information on epilepsy. Presents interviews with epileptics discussing their problems and pleading for understanding.
LC NO. 82-706961
Prod-BBCTV Dist-FI 1981

Spill Recovery - Navy Techniques For Oil Spill Containment And Removal In Harbors C 25 MIN
16MM FILM OPTICAL SOUND C A
Describes in-port oil spills control, reporting procedures and clean-up operations.
LC NO. 77-700086
Prod-USN Dist-USNAC 1975

Spilled Milk C 5 MIN
16MM FILM SILENT P-H S
Presents Louie J Fant Jr, relating in American sign language for the deaf an incident from his childhood involving a jar of milk and a set of instructions that he failed to follow concerning its disposal.
LC NO. 76-701705
Prod-JOYCE Dist-JOYCE 1975

Spin Out C 17 MIN
3/4 OR 1/2 INCH VIDEO CASSETTE
Prod-EAI Dist-EAI

Spin Out, Pt 1 C 17 MIN
3/4 OR 1/2 INCH VIDEO CASSETTE
Explores the domination of the imagination.
Prod-KITCHN Dist-KITCHN

Spinal Cord And Its Relations C 14 MIN
16MM FILM, 3/4 OR 1/2 IN VIDEO PRO
Examines the spinal cord and muscles of the back.
From The Cine-Prosector Series.
Prod-AVCORP Dist-TEF

Spinal Cord Injuries C 39 MIN
3/4 INCH VIDEO CASSETTE PRO
Informs insurance personnel of the effects of spinal cord injuries. Discusses basic anatomy and physiology of the spinal cord, and the relationship of the spinal cord to the brain. Includes discussion of practical problems of daily activity.
Prod-STFAIN Dist-RICHGO

Spinal Cord Injuries - Functional Expectations As Related To Level Of Injury C 25 MIN
16MM FILM OPTICAL SOUND
Demonstrates the degree of independence that the average patient can attain after injury at various neurological levels. Tells how this independence is accomplished through a program of strengthening the remaining active muscles and going through appropriate training.
Prod-RLAH Dist-RLAH

Spinal Muscular Atrophies C 39 MIN
3/4 INCH VIDEO CASSETTE PRO
Presents Dr Theodore L Munsat discussing spinal muscular atrophies.
From The Intensive Course In Neuromuscular Diseases Series.
LC NO. 76-706103
Prod-NINDIS Dist-USNAC 1974

Spine Flex C 10 MIN
2 INCH VIDEOTAPE
See series title for descriptive statement.
From The Janaki Series.
Prod-WGBHTV Dist-PUBTEL

Spinet Making In Colonial America C 54 MIN
16MM FILM OPTICAL SOUND
Shows the stages involved in making a spinet, using the tools and methods of 18th century Williamsburg, Virginia.
LC NO. 77-700005
Prod-CWMS Dist-CWMS 1976

Spinning B 15 MIN
16MM FILM OPTICAL SOUND
Presents an experimental film showing a man spinning from various angles.
LC NO. 77-702650
Prod-CANFDC Dist-CANFDC 1976

Spinning Memories - Oella C 25 MIN
3/4 OR 1/2 INCH VIDEO CASSETTE
Features interviews with residents of Oella, a small town on the banks of Maryland's Patapsco River.
Prod-BCPL Dist-LVN

Spinning Stories—A Series
P
Features storyteller-host Bob Callahan sharing his changing moods and many interests, including music, art, literature, outdoor activities and crafts.
Prod-MDDE Dist-AITECH 1977

Bubbles And Beanstalks	15 MIN
Do Something	15 MIN
Giggles And Grins	15 MIN
I Can, I Can	15 MIN
It's My Own	15 MIN
Look Around You	15 MIN
Look It Up	15 MIN
Making Moods	15 MIN
My Feelings	15 MIN
Once There Was	15 MIN
Reading On, And On	15 MIN
Tell A Tale	15 MIN
That's Me	15 MIN
What To Do	15 MIN
What's So Different	15 MIN

Spinnolio C 10 MIN
16MM FILM, 3/4 OR 1/2 IN VIDEO J-C A
Focuses on communication and human relationships through the satirical story of Spinnolio, who grows up, gets a job, retires and is carried off by motorcycle gangs and garbagemen to be used for diverse purposes, despite his wooden lifelessness.
Prod-NFBC Dist-NFBC 1978

Spiral Separator C 3 MIN
16MM FILM OPTICAL SOUND H-C A
Shows how descending concentric spiral channels are used to separate seeds based on their rolling velocity. Demonstrates separation of a typical mixture of good and split soybean seeds.
From The Principles Of Seed Processing Series.
LC NO. 77-701158
Prod-EVERSL Dist-IOWA Prodn-IOWA 1975

Spires / Ballots Report C 15 MIN
16MM FILM, 3/4 OR 1/2 IN VIDEO J-C A
Views man's previous attempts to solve the frustrating problem of information storage and retrieval while the narrator reports on two Stanford University research projects designed to computerize library systems, Stanford public information retrieval system and bibliographic automation of large library operations using time sharing. Produced by students of Stanford University's School of Communication.
Prod-STNFRD Dist-UCEMC 1970

Spirit Bay—A Series
I-J
Presents stories set on an Ojibway Indian reservation in Canada. Provides insight into the culture and character of Indian people. Shows children bridging the gap between ancient customs and the modern world.
Prod-TFW Dist-BCNFL

Blueberry Bicycle, The	028 MIN
Circle Of Life, The	028 MIN
Dancing Feathers	028 MIN
Pride Of Spirit Bay, The	028 MIN
Rabbit Goes Fishing	028 MIN
Rabbit Pulls His Weight	028 MIN
Time To Be Brave, A	028 MIN

Spirit Catcher - The Art Of Betye Saar C 28 MIN
16MM FILM, 3/4 OR 1/2 IN VIDEO H-C A
Profiles the life and work of assemblage artist Betye Saar. Shows how her fascination with the mystical and the unknown merges with her social concerns as a black American.
From The Originals - Women In Art Series.
LC NO. 80-706119
Prod-WNETTV Dist-FI 1978

Spirit Is Willing, The C 15 MIN
3/4 OR 1/2 INCH VIDEO CASSETTE I
See series title for descriptive statement.
From The Best Of Cover To Cover 2 Series.
Prod-WETATV Dist-WETATV

Spirit Of '76 C 28 MIN
16MM FILM OPTICAL SOUND I-C A
Tells the story of the air force's minuteman missile and its vital place in America's defense arsenal. Relives the saga of the first minuteman through the eyes of a young air force officer who takes a vital part in the firing and flight of today's minuteman, which is capable of delivering a war head on target more than 6000 miles away.
Prod-NAA Dist-RCKWL

Spirit Of Allensworth, The C 29 MIN
3/4 OR 1/2 INCH VIDEO CASSETTE I-C A
Offers a portrait of the life of Allen Allensworth, a former slave who attained the rank of lieutenant colonel in the US Army. Focuses on the town which he founded for Black Americans in California.
LC NO. 81-707290
Prod-KTEHTV Dist-KTEHTV 1980

Spirit Of America C 29 MIN
16MM FILM OPTICAL SOUND A
Traces Greg Breedlove's quest for the world land-speed record. Outlines his years of frustration and sacrifice in developing his jet car. Culminates with his 407.45 mph record run on the Bonneville Salt Flats in Utah.
Prod-GTARC Dist-GTARC

Spirit Of America - Volunteers C 26 MIN
16MM FILM, 3/4 OR 1/2 IN VIDEO A
Describes the story of volunteerism in America and includes scenes of some of the most disastrous fires in American history as well as the contributions of some of America's famous individuals.
Prod-NFPA Dist-NFPA Prodn-LAWDET 1983

Spirit Of America With Charles Kuralt, Pt 01 - Vermont, New Hampshire, Massachusetts, Maine C 18 MIN
16MM FILM, 3/4 OR 1/2 IN VIDEO I-H A
Presents a segment from the CBS television program On The Road in which news correspondent Charles Kuralt journeys to Vermont, New Hampshire, Massachusetts and Maine for a bi-centennial look at our nation's history.
Prod-CBSNEW Dist-PHENIX 1976

Spirit Of America With Charles Kuralt, Pt 02 - Rhode Island, Connecticut, New Jersey,... C 18 MIN
16MM FILM, 3/4 OR 1/2 IN VIDEO I-H A
Presents a segment from the CBS television program On The Road in which news correspondent Charles Kuralt journeys to Rhode Island, Connecticut, New Jersey and New York to seek out places, people and events that contributed to the development of America.
Prod-CBSNEW Dist-PHENIX 1976

Spirit Of America With Charles Kuralt, Pt 03 - Pennsylvania, Delaware, Maryland C 13 MIN
16MM FILM, 3/4 OR 1/2 IN VIDEO I-H A
Presents a segment from the CBS television program On The Road in which news correspondent Charles Kuralt journeys to Pennsylvania, Delaware and Maryland to seek out places, people and events that contributed to the development of America.
Prod-CBSNEW Dist-PHENIX 1976

Spirit Of America With Charles Kuralt, Pt 04 - Tennessee, Arkansas, Kentucky, West Virginia C 18 MIN
16MM FILM, 3/4 OR 1/2 IN VIDEO I-H A
Presents a segment from the CBS television program On The Road in which news correspondent Charles Kuralt journeys to Tennessee, Arkansas, Kentucky and West Virgina to seek out places, people and events that contributed to the development of America.
Prod-CBSNEW Dist-PHENIX 1976

Spirit Of America With Charles Kuralt, Pt 05 - Virginia, North Carolina, South Carolina,... C 18 MIN
16MM FILM, 3/4 OR 1/2 IN VIDEO I-H A
Presents a segment from the CBS television program On The Road in which news correspondent Charles Kuralt journeys to Virgina, North Carolina, South Carolina and Georgia to seek out places, people and events that contributed to the development of America.
Prod-CBSNEW Dist-PHENIX 1976

Spirit Of America With Charles Kuralt, Pt 06 - Florida, Alabama, Mississippi, Louisianna C 17 MIN
16MM FILM, 3/4 OR 1/2 IN VIDEO I-H A
Presents a segment from the CBS television program On The Road in which news correspondent Charles Kuralt journeys to Florida, Alabama, Louisianna and Mississippi to seek out places, people and events that contributed to the development of America.
Prod-CBSNEW Dist-PHENIX 1976

Spirit Of America With Charles Kuralt, Pt 07 - Texas, Oklahoma, Kansas, Nebraska C 19 MIN
16MM FILM, 3/4 OR 1/2 IN VIDEO I-H A
Presents a segment from the CBS television program On The Road in which news correspondent Charles Kuralt journeys to Texas, Oklahoma, Kansas and Nebraska to seek out places, people and events that contributed to the development of America.
Prod-CBSNEW Dist-PHENIX 1976

Spirit Of America With Charles Kuralt, Pt 08 - Minnesota, Iowa, Wisconsin, Missouri C 19 MIN
16MM FILM, 3/4 OR 1/2 IN VIDEO I-H A
Presents a segment from the CBS television program On The Road in which news correspondent Charles Kuralt journeys to Minnesota, Iowa, Wisconsin and Missouri to seek out places, people and events that contributed to the development of America.
Prod-CBSNEW Dist-PHENIX 1976

Spirit Of America With Charles Kuralt, Pt 09 - Michigan, Ohio, Indiana, Illinois C 18 MIN
16MM FILM, 3/4 OR 1/2 IN VIDEO I-H A
Presents a segment from the CBS television program On The Road in which news correspondent Charles Kuralt journeys to Michigan, Ohio, Illinois and Indiana to seek out places, people and events that contributed to the development of America.
Prod-CBSNEW Dist-PHENIX 1976

Spirit Of America With Charles Kuralt, Pt 10 - Montana, South Dakota, North Dakota, Wyoming C 17 MIN
16MM FILM, 3/4 OR 1/2 IN VIDEO I-H A
Presents a segment from the CBS television program On The Road in which news correspondent Charles Kuralt journeys to Montana, South Dakota, North Dakota and Wyoming to seek out places, people and events that contributed to the development of America.
Prod-CBSNEW Dist-PHENIX 1976

Spirit Of America With Charles Kuralt, Pt 11 - Colorado, New Mexico, Arizona C 12 MIN
16MM FILM, 3/4 OR 1/2 IN VIDEO I-H A
Presents a segment from the CBS television program On The Road in which news correspondent Charles Kuralt journeys to Montana, Colorado, New Mexico and Arizona to seek out places, people and events that contributed to the development of America.
Prod-CBSNEW Dist-PHENIX 1976

Spirit Of America With Charles Kuralt, Pt 12 - Washington, Oregon, Idaho, Alaska C 18 MIN
16MM FILM, 3/4 OR 1/2 IN VIDEO I-H A
Presents a segment from the CBS television program On The Road in which news correspondent Charles Kuralt journeys to Washington, Alaska, Oregon and Idaho to seek out places, people and events that contributed to the development of America.
Prod-CBSNEW Dist-PHENIX 1976

Spirit Of America With Charles Kuralt, Pt 13 - Nevada, Utah, California, Hawaii C 17 MIN
16MM FILM, 3/4 OR 1/2 IN VIDEO I-H A
Presents a segment from the CBS television program On The Road in which news correspondent Charles Kuralt journeys to California, Hawaii, Utah and Nevada to seek out places, people and events that contributed to the development of America.
Prod-CBSNEW Dist-PHENIX 1976

Spirit Of America With Charles Kuralt, Pt 14 - The Declaration Of Independence C 9 MIN
16MM FILM, 3/4 OR 1/2 IN VIDEO I-H A
Presents a segment from the CBS television program On The Road in which news correspondent Charles Kuralt journeys to Philadelphia to visit Independence Hall, where the determination of the Founding Fathers to declare independence from Great Britain was debated and decided.
Prod-CBSNEW Dist-PHENIX 1976

Spirit Of Bonaire, The C 13 MIN
16MM FILM OPTICAL SOUND
Shows how people on the small Caribbean island of Bonaire in the Netherlands Antilles have promoted tourism while maintaining their natural resources and wildlife.
LC NO. 80-701559
Prod-BONTB Dist-MORTNJ Prodn-MORTNJ 1980

Spirit Of Bonaire, The (German) C 13 MIN
16MM FILM OPTICAL SOUND
Shows how people on the small Caribbean island of Bonaire in the Netherlands Antilles have promoted tourism while maintaining their natural resources and wildlife.
LC NO. 80-701559
Prod-BONTB Dist-MORTNJ Prodn-MORTNJ 1980

Spirit Of Ethnography B 19 MIN
16MM FILM OPTICAL SOUND C
Takes a humorous look at the field of cultural anthropology. Chronicles the field research of a fictitious ethnographer embarking on his first field experience.
LC NO. 74-703643
Prod-PUAVC Dist-PSUPCR 1974

Spirit Of Freedom C 29 MIN
16MM FILM OPTICAL SOUND
Presents a patriotic panorama of America by the U S Navy Band.
LC NO. 74-706583
Prod-USN Dist-USNAC 1968

Spirit Of Lightning Snake C 14 MIN
16MM FILM OPTICAL SOUND P-J A
Shows how a young boy's search for Indian petrographs leads him to discover the legend of the Lightning Snake as danced for him by a Nootka Indian chief.
LC NO. 76-701920
Prod-INLEAS Dist-INLEAS 1975

Spirit Of Punxsutawney, The, Pt 1 B 29 MIN
16MM FILM OPTICAL SOUND H-C A
Documents the day-to-day routine of the staff of a small town

Pennsylvania newspaper called The Spirit. Illustrates the interaction between the editorial staff and the town's residents in order to present the newspaper as a sensitive institution that reacts to the needs of its rural community.
LC NO. 77-700949
Prod-WPSXTV Dist-PSU 1976

Spirit Of Punxsutawney, The, Pt 2 B 30 MIN
16MM FILM OPTICAL SOUND H-C A
Documents the day-to-day routine of the staff of a small town Pennsylvania newspaper called The Spirit. Illustrates the interaction between the editorial staff and the town's residents in order to present the newspaper as a sensitive institution that reacts to the needs of its rural community.
LC NO. 77-700949
Prod-WPSXTV Dist-PSU 1976

Spirit Of Rhythms And Blues, The B 30 MIN
16MM FILM OPTICAL SOUND H-C A
Larry Neal acts as moderator as A B Spellman and Julius Lester discuss the ethos of black America in the 1950's and comment on the influence of the wars on black culture as revealed in music, dance and radio programming.
From The Black History, Section 22 - The Cultural Scene Series.
LC NO. 79-704118
Prod-WCBSTV Dist-HRAW 1969

Spirit Of Romanticism, The C 29 MIN
16MM FILM, 3/4 OR 1/2 IN VIDEO H-C
Presents dramatizations that bring to life key events and personalities of the Romantic movement (1789-1838) in literature, music and art. Includes Carlyle describing the French Revolution, Delacroix painting Liberty Leading The People and Shelley as a young rebel and as a friend to Byron.
From The Humanities - Philosophy And Political Thought Series.
Prod-EBEC Dist-EBEC Prodn-BARNES

Spirit Of Rome, The X 29 MIN
16MM FILM, 3/4 OR 1/2 IN VIDEO H-C
Uses scenes from Shakespeare's Julius Caesar and George Bernard Shaw's Caesar and Cleopatra to depict the tremendous spectacle of ancient Rome. Filmed in Rome and London.
From The Humanities - The Heritage Of The Humanities Series.
Prod-EBF Dist-EBEC 1964

Spirit Of Rome, The (Spanish) C 29 MIN
16MM FILM, 3/4 OR 1/2 IN VIDEO H-C
Uses scenes from Shakespeare's Julius Caesar and George Bernard Shaw's Caesar and Cleopatra to depict the tremendous spectacle of ancient Rome. Filmed in Rome and London.
Prod-EBF Dist-EBEC

Spirit Of Stone C 25 MIN
16MM FILM, 3/4 OR 1/2 IN VIDEO H-C A
Shows how ancient art carvings are analyzed by anthropologists, art experts and other scientists in order to determine the full history and significance of these carvings and other artifacts.
Prod-EFD Dist-JOU 1974

Spirit Of The Dance, The B 21 MIN
16MM FILM OPTICAL SOUND
Depicts the classical dance and the many facets of the professional activity of a ballerina as illustrated in the life of Nina Vyroubva, star of the Paris Opera Ballet, who performs with other members of the ballet. Highlights the exacting disciplines which this art demands. Includes practice at the barre, executing new positions and rehearsals behind the scenes and on stage with ceaseless work towards perfection.
LC NO. FIA65-1038
Prod-DELOUD Dist-RADIM 1965

Spirit Of The Hunt C 29 MIN
3/4 OR 1/2 INCH VIDEO CASSETTE H-C A
Focusing on the material and spiritual importance of the buffalo to Native American life, gives an historic overview including the coming of the horse, arrival of the white man, and the subsequent destruction of the great herds.
Prod-HOWET Dist-CEPRO

Spirit Of The Pueblos - Kachina C 15 MIN
16MM FILM OPTICAL SOUND I-J
Discusses the historical, religious and cultural significance of kachina dolls, which are used as messenger spirits in the tribal rituals of American Southwest Indians.
LC NO. 78-700514
Prod-EDDIM Dist-EDDIM 1978

Spirit Of The Renaissance C 31 MIN
16MM FILM, 3/4 OR 1/2 IN VIDEO H-C
Explores the intellectual and artistic climate of Florence during the 14th and 15th centuries using scenes from the daily life of a contemporary Florentine. Discusses the lives of Petrach, Alberti and Leonardo da Vinci to illustrate the several facets of the Renaissance that made it so unique. Reflects on whether the spirit of an age ever dies.
From The Humanities - Philosophy And Political Thought Series.
Prod-EBEC Dist-EBEC 1971

Spirit Of The Renaissance (Spanish) C 31 MIN
16MM FILM, 3/4 OR 1/2 IN VIDEO H-C
Explores the intellectual and artistic climate of Florence during the 14th and 15th centuries using scenes from the daily life of a contemporary Florentine. Discusses the life of Petrach, Alberti and Leonardo da Vinci to illustrate the several facets of the Renaissance that made it so unique. Reflects on whether the spirit of an age ever dies.
Prod-EBEC Dist-EBEC 1971

Spirit Of The Tree, The C 12 MIN
16MM FILM OPTICAL SOUND P-C A
Describes the production of a Bible from the planting of a tree through the making of the paper to printing and binding.
LC NO. FIA68-826
Prod-ABS Dist-ABS 1967

Spirit Of The White Mountains C 13 MIN
16MM FILM OPTICAL SOUND I-J
Presents pioneering activities of the White Mountain Apaches. Describes their present day activities-farming, cattle raising, recreation and business meetings. Shows many areas that attract visitors to this part of Arizona.
Prod-DAGP Dist-MLA 1959

Spirit Of The Wind C 10 MIN
16MM FILM, 3/4 OR 1/2 IN VIDEO J-C A
A shortened version of the motion picture Spirit Of The Wind. Deals with sailboat racing on inland lakes, emphasizing the spirit of wind, water, competition and friendship. Discusses the emotional attachment sailors have for the sport, the mental preparation for the race and the physical rigors necessary to win.
Prod-TFW Dist-MCFI 1975

Spirit Of The Wind C 26 MIN
16MM FILM, 3/4 OR 1/2 IN VIDEO J-C A
Deals with sailboat racing on inland lakes, emphasizing the spirit of wind, water, competition and friendship. Discusses the emotional attachment sailors have for the sport, the mental preparation for the race and the physical rigors necessary to win.
Prod-TFW Dist-MCFI 1975

Spirit Of The Wind C 30 MIN
3/4 INCH VIDEO CASSETTE
Discusses the place of the horse in Indian life and culture.
From The Real People Series.
Prod-KSPSTV Dist-GPITVL 1976

Spirit Of Victory, The C 10 MIN
16MM FILM OPTICAL SOUND
Shows a re-creation of the last great Revolutionary War battle at Yorktown, Virginia, in 1781. Narrated by Charlton Heston.
Prod-USA Dist-MTP

Spirit Possession Of Alejandro Mamani, The C 27 MIN
16MM FILM OPTICAL SOUND H-C A
Presents an elderly Bolivian man nearing the end of his life who believes himself possessed by evil spirits. Reveals his personal tragedy as well as the universal confrontation with the unknown, old age and death.
From The Faces Of Change - Bolivia Series.
Prod-AUFS Dist-FLMLIB 1974

Spirit World Of Tidikawa, The C 50 MIN
3/4 INCH VIDEO CASSETTE
Short version of the documentary Tidikawa And Friends, which explores the daily lives of the Bedamini of Papua, New Guinea. Includes English narration throughout. Filmed in 1971.
Prod-BBCTV Dist-DOCEDR

Spirits Of America C 19 MIN
16MM FILM, 3/4 OR 1/2 IN VIDEO
Deals with issues, attitudes and standards of American drinking patterns and the historical and cultural aspects associated with them.
From The Decisions And Drinking Series.
LC NO. 80-707338
Prod-NIAAA Dist-USNAC 1978

Spiritual Aspects Of Patient Care, Pt 1 B 30 MIN
16MM FILM OPTICAL SOUND PRO
Presents a panel which includes a rabbi, a Catholic priest, a Protestant minister and a nurse who respond to questions relative to traditional ministrations and other spiritual needs of patients.
From The Directions For Education In Nursing Via Technology Series. Lesson 32
LC NO. 74-701805
Prod-DENT Dist-WSU 1974

Spiritual Aspects Of Patient Care, Pt 2 B 30 MIN
16MM FILM OPTICAL SOUND PRO
Presents a panel which includes a rabbi, a Catholic priest, a Protestant minister and a nurse who respond to questions relative to traditional ministrations and other spiritual needs of patients.
From The Directions For Education In Nursing Via Technology Series. Lesson 33
LC NO. 74-701806
Prod-DENT Dist-WSU 1974

Spiritual Frontier, The C 27 MIN
16MM FILM OPTICAL SOUND H-C A R
Describes the New Vrindaban farm community in West Virginia as an attempt at creating a model Krishna consciousness society.
LC NO. 77-702977
Prod-ISKCON Dist-BHAKTI 1976

Spiritual Ordering, A - The Metal Arts Of Africa C 20 MIN
3/4 OR 1/2 INCH VIDEO CASSETTE C A
Introduces major objects from Western and Central Africa illustrating how African artists have utilized a rich repertory of sacred gestures and frozen them in metal. Traces important themes such as the equestrian figure and zoomorphic representations of the snake.
LC NO. 84-706390
Prod-AFRAMI Dist-IU 1983

Spirituals, Pt 1 C 15 MIN
3/4 OR 1/2 INCH VIDEO CASSETTE P
Describes the characteristics of spirituals and shows how to recognize the ABA form. Explains the terms pentatonic and shows how to create an introduction and accompaniment for a song. Presents the songs All Night All Day, Get On Board and Michael Row The Boat Ashore.
From The Song Sampler Series.
LC NO. 81-707036
Prod-JCITV Dist-GPITVL 1981

Spirituals, Pt 2 C 15 MIN
3/4 OR 1/2 INCH VIDEO CASSETTE P
Describes the characteristics of spirituals and shows how to recognize the ABA form. Explains the terms pentatonic and shows how to create an introduction and accompaniment for a song. Presents the songs All Night All Day, Get On Board and Michael Row The Boat Ashore.
From The Song Sampler Series.
LC NO. 81-707036
Prod-JCITV Dist-GPITVL 1981

Spiro Malas C 29 MIN
2 INCH VIDEOTAPE
Presents exchanges and arguments between the dean of American theatre critics, Elliot Norton, and Spiro Malas.
From The Elliot Norton Reviews II Series.
Prod-WGBHTV Dist-PUBTEL

Spirometry - Early Detection Of Chronic Pulmonary Disease C 25 MIN
3/4 OR 1/2 INCH VIDEO CASSETTE PRO
Illustrates the functioning of the normal respiratory system, as well as what happens when ventilation is impaired, by means of animation. Details the office procedures whereby a doctor may evaluate typical patients with respiratory complaints.
Prod-WFP Dist-WFP

Spirometry - The Early Detection Of Chronic Obstructive Pulmonary Disease C 25 MIN
16MM FILM OPTICAL SOUND PRO
Illustrates the functioning of the normal respiratory system and shows what happens when ventilation is impaired.
LC NO. 79-702582
Prod-NTBA Dist-AMLUNG Prodn-WFP 1968

Spirometry - The Three Elements Of Effective Testing C 15 MIN
3/4 OR 1/2 INCH VIDEO CASSETTE A
Illustrates proper spirometer testing procedures. Discusses machine preparation, subject preparation, testing execution and test result validation.
Prod-USPHS Dist-USNAC 1980

SPLASH C 12 MIN
16MM FILM, 3/4 OR 1/2 IN VIDEO P
Uses animation in a story about water droplets to demonstrate the water cycle, the importance of water in urban living and the impact of pollution on this precious natural resource.
LC NO. 81-707585
Prod-NFBC Dist-CRMP 1982

Splash - Science And Swimming C 16 MIN
16MM FILM, 3/4 OR 1/2 IN VIDEO I-J
Features a puppet professor raising a number of questions involving swimming, floating, sinking, and the behavior of various objects in water.
From The Elementary Physical Science Series.
Prod-CENTRO Dist-CORF

Splenectomy C 21 MIN
3/4 OR 1/2 INCH VIDEO CASSETTE PRO
Describes the splenectomy.
Prod-WFP Dist-WFP Prodn-UKANMC

Splenectomy For Massive Splenomegaly C 19 MIN
3/4 OR 1/2 INCH VIDEO CASSETTE PRO
Demonstrates a splenectomy technique that minimizes complications, including pancreatitis, bleeding, infections, and splenic laceration. Traces the surgery of a patient with massive splenomegaly due to hairy-cell leukemia.
Prod-UARIZ Dist-UARIZ

Splenectomy In The Treatment Of Hypersplenism C 21 MIN
16MM FILM OPTICAL SOUND PRO
Demonstrates the technique of splenectomy.
Prod-ACYDGD Dist-ACY 1955

Splenectomy With Thoraco-Abdominal Incision C 20 MIN
16MM FILM OPTICAL SOUND PRO
Explains that a complete exposure of the operative field with a precise control of the vascular supply and minimal subsequent tissue necrosis are fundamental technical requirements for splenectomy with thoraco-abdominal incision.
Prod-ACYDGD Dist-ACY 1958

Splenorenal Anastomosis For Portal Hypertension C 19 MIN
16MM FILM OPTICAL SOUND PRO
Describes operation for relief of cirrhosis of the liver by anastomosing the renal vein to the splenic vein (relief of elevated pressure in the portal system.)
Prod-ACYDGD Dist-ACY 1950

Splenorenal Shunt For Portal Hypertension C 27 MIN
16MM FILM OPTICAL SOUND PRO
Presents the technique of three types of shunts, an end-to-side portacaval shunt for bleeding esophageal varices, a side-to-side portacaval shunt for intractable ascites and an end-to-side splenorenal shunt for bleeding esophageal varices.
Prod-ACYDGD Dist-ACY 1960

Splices And Terminations 5 KV - 20 KV C 60 MIN
3/4 OR 1/2 INCH VIDEO CASSETTE IND
See series title for descriptive statement.
From The Electrical Maintenance Training, Module E - Electrical Connection Series.
Prod-LEIKID Dist-LEIKID

Splicing A Wooden Spar C 21 MIN
16MM FILM - 3/4 IN VIDEO IND
Describes how to cut a scarf joint on a spar, how to finish a scarf face by hand, and how to glue and assemble a scarf joint. Explains how to make, glue and assemble reinforcement plates and how to trim a spar to shape and size. Issued in 1945 as a motion picture.
From The Aircraft Work - Aircraft Maintenance Series.
LC NO. 79-706795
Prod-USOE Dist-USNAC Prodn-HANDY 1979

Splinting - Open Fracture C 11 MIN
3/4 OR 1/2 INCH VIDEO CASSETTE PRO
Shows the steps to be followed in treating an open fracture on the battlefield, using Army-issue splints, cravats, and pressure dressings.
From The EMT Video - Group Two Series.
LC NO. 84-706490
Prod-USA Dist-USNAC 1983

Splinting - The Basswood Splint To The Forearm C 6 MIN
3/4 OR 1/2 INCH VIDEO CASSETTE PRO
Demonstrates the application of a basswood splint to immobolize a fractured forearm, including the sequence of steps for treating fractures.
From The EMT Video - Group Two Series.
LC NO. 84-706488
Prod-USA Dist-USNAC 1983

Splinting - The Dislocated Or Fractured Elbow C 6 MIN
3/4 OR 1/2 INCH VIDEO CASSETTE PRO
Shows the application of a wireladder splint for elbow fractures and explains splinting principles.
From The EMT Video - Group Two Series.
LC NO. 84-706489
Prod-USA Dist-USNAC 1983

Split Brain B 13 MIN
16MM FILM OPTICAL SOUND H-C A
Explains the revolutionary split-brain operation, performed at the California Institute of Technology, in which the two hemispheres of the brain are separated surgically along the corpus callosum. Demonstrates devices developed to test split-brain subjects to provide insight into the functioning of the brain.
Prod-NET Dist-IU 1964

Split Brain And Conscious Experience, The C 17 MIN
16MM FILM, 3/4 OR 1/2 IN VIDEO C
Presents a study of patients whose brains have been surgically separated in an attempt to control severe epilepsy. Shows surgery as well as experiments conducted on these patients.
Prod-CONCPT Dist-MTI 1977

Split Cherry Tree C 25 MIN
16MM FILM, 3/4 OR 1/2 IN VIDEO I-C A
Reveals that a father gains insight into the importance of education when he goes to his son's school to protest the boy's punishment for damaging a cherry tree during a class biology trip. Based on the short story Split Cherry Tree by Jesse Stuart.
From The LCA Short Story Library Series.
LC NO. 82-706848
Prod-LCOA Dist-LCOA Prodn-SNDRSJ 1982

Split Second C 28 MIN
16MM FILM OPTICAL SOUND
Looks at the world of drag racing with Jim Thompson as he sets a national speed record in the Modified Eliminator category.
Prod-FTARC Dist-FTARC

Split Second Fastening C
16MM FILM OPTICAL SOUND IND
Illustrates and explains the Nelson stud welding process, and gives a brief history of its inception during World War II.
Prod-NSW Dist-NSW

Split Second Safety - A Guide For Electrical Hazard Safety C 11 MIN
16MM FILM, 3/4 OR 1/2 IN VIDEO
Uses live action and animation to demonstrate the hazards and results of electrical line-to-ground fault problems. C F Dalziel explains electric circuiting and body resistance to electric current and presents safety precautions.
Prod-PASSEY Dist-FILCOM 1968

Split Second, The C 11 MIN
16MM FILM - 3/4 IN VIDEO
Presents a tour of a plant to show situations and conduct that lead to accidents. Presents accident victims and the wives of others who cannot understand how the accident happened or why.
Prod-BNA Dist-BNA

Split-Phase Motor - Rewinding B 28 MIN
16MM FILM - 3/4 IN VIDEO
Explains how to test a split-phase motor for electrical and mechanical faults. Demonstrates how to dismantle, strip and rewind the stator, form and install skein windings, lace, dip, and bake the stator, and assemble, lubricate and test the motor. Issued in 1945 as a motion picture.
From The Electrical Work - Motor Maintenance And Repair Series. Number 3
LC NO. 79-707706
Prod-USOE Dist-USNAC Prodn-CALVCO 1979

Split-Phase Motor Principles B 17 MIN
16MM FILM - 3/4 IN VIDEO IND
Shows construction of the stator and rotor of a machine, compares winding in the two-phase stator with split-phase stator, describes the effects of winding resistances and inductive reactances, and illustrates the use of the capacitor to produce phase displacement. Issued in 1945 as a motion picture.
From The Electrical Work - Electrical Machinery Series. No. 4
LC NO. 78-706134
Prod-USOE Dist-USNAC Prodn-RAYBEL 1978

Split-Phase Motor Principles (Spanish) B 17 MIN
16MM FILM OPTICAL SOUND
Shows construction of stator and rotor, comparison of winding in two-phase stator with split-phase stator, effects of winding resistances and inductive reactances, and use of capacitor to produce phase displacement.
From The Electrical Work Series. Electrical Machinery, No. 4
LC NO. 74-705685
Prod-USOE Dist-USNAC 1945

Splitting The Transference - Group Treatment And Psychopharmacology C 15 MIN
3/4 OR 1/2 INCH VIDEO CASSETTE
Presents Dr Harold F Searles belief about the use of psychopharmacological medications with borderline patients in analytic treatment. Shares his opinions about the impact of drugs, group and family therapy upon the transference.
From The Treatment Of The Borderline Patient Series.
Prod-HEMUL Dist-HEMUL

Spoiled Priest, The C 60 MIN
3/4 OR 1/2 INCH VIDEO CASSETTE C
Traces the conflict between rigid moral restraints and the lure of the sensual world in this dramatization of a Fitzgerald story.
From The World Of F Scott Fitzgerald Series.
Prod-DALCCD Dist-DALCCD

Spokane River, The C 24 MIN
16MM FILM OPTICAL SOUND I-C A
Traces the Spokane River from its source at Lake Coeur D'alene, Idaho, to its confluence with the mighty Columbia River. Points out historic and geographic highlights.
LC NO. 73-701096
Prod-PRYOR Dist-NWFLMP 1970

Spoken Language Disabilities C 30 MIN
3/4 OR 1/2 INCH VIDEO CASSETTE C A
Describes disorders of auditory reception, auditory expressive, and inner language.
From The Characteristics Of Learning Disabilities Series.
Prod-WCVETV Dist-FI 1976

Spokey The Clown And His Magic Bike C 15 MIN
16MM FILM OPTICAL SOUND P-I
Illustrates common bicycle safety problems by showing the correct way to ride safely. Tells a story about a clown who loans his talking bicycle to a boy who then learns that the best driver is a safe driver.
LC NO. 73-701351
Prod-SCREEI Dist-SCREEI 1973

Spondylolisthesis C 8 MIN
16MM FILM OPTICAL SOUND H-C
Pictures Dr Ben Wiltberger's operation for spinal fusion in spondylolisthesis of the spine.
Prod-OSUMPD Dist-OSUMPD 1961

Sponge - Treasure From The Sea C 14 MIN
16MM FILM OPTICAL SOUND
Shows the biology and uses of natural sponge. Depicts the 'SILENT' sponge auction, blessing of the waters and the dive for the golden cross.
LC NO. FIE64-203
Prod-USBCF Dist-USNOAA 1961

Sponge - Treasure From The Sea C 14 MIN
3/4 OR 1/2 INCH VIDEO CASSETTE
Describes the natural sponge industry of Tarpon Springs, Florida. Discusses the biology and uses of natural sponge. Issued as a motion picture in 1961.
LC NO. 80-707619
Prod-USBSFW Dist-USNAC 1980

Sponge Divers B 10 MIN
16MM FILM OPTICAL SOUND
Tells of the sponge industry of Florida. Emphasizes that the industry symbolizes opportunity for those who engage in it and also presents some hazards.
From The Land Of Opportunity Series.
Prod-REP Dist-REP 1950

Sponges And Coelenterates - Porous And Sac-Like Animals C 11 MIN
16MM FILM, 3/4 OR 1/2 IN VIDEO J-C
Studies the life cycles of sponges and coelenterates, the simplest multicellular animals. Describes the cell specialization, sexual and asexual reproduction and other characteristics of sponges, jellyfish, sea anemones, corals and hydras.
From The Major Phyla Series.
Prod-CORF Dist-CORF 1962

Spongeware C 30 MIN
3/4 INCH VIDEO CASSETTE
See series title for descriptive statement.
From The Antiques Series.
Prod-NHMNET Dist-PUBTEL

Spontaneous Combustion C 2 MIN
3/4 OR 1/2 INCH VIDEO CASSETTE H-C A
Presents comedy by the Brave New Workshop of the Twin Cities.
Prod-BRVNP Dist-UCV

Spook Spoofing B 22 MIN
16MM FILM OPTICAL SOUND
Tells how Farina uses his 'mumbo-jumbo' charm to protect him in a fight with Toughy. A Little Rascals film.
Prod-ROACH Dist-BHAWK 1928

Spooks B 8 MIN
16MM FILM OPTICAL SOUND
Describes Flip the Frog's adventures in a haunted house populated by a skeleton dancer, skeleton musicians, and a skeleton dog.
Prod-UNKNWN Dist-BHAWK 1930

Spooks, Cowboys, Gooks And Grunts C 50 MIN
16MM FILM OPTICAL SOUND
Shows correspondent Michael Maclear examining, in a two-part presentation, the fate of American soldiers who used terror and brutality to attempt to win the war in Vietnam, only to become victims of their own excesses. Notes the rejection, frustration and alienation of these men who, both as victims and scapegoats of the war, were unable to adjust to civilian life.
LC NO. 77-702526
Prod-CTV Dist-CTV 1976

Spooky Boo's And Room Noodles C 7 MIN
16MM FILM, 3/4 OR 1/2 IN VIDEO K-I
Deals with children's fear of the dark. Shows nighttime monsters and demons scurrying for cover when a child exerts power over them by invoking a simple rhyme.
Prod-PAJON Dist-CF 1977

Spoon River Anthology C 21 MIN
16MM FILM, 3/4 OR 1/2 IN VIDEO J-C A
Illustrates selections from Edgar Lee Master's Spoon River Anthology.
Prod-BFA Dist-PHENIX Prodn-SMITG 1976

Spoonful Of Lovin'—A Series
H-C A
Demonstrates how day care providers can improve their skills.
Prod-KRMATV Dist-AITECH 1981

Good Measure Of Safety, A	027 MIN
Gourmet Guide To Family Home Day Care, A	025 MIN
Natural Ingredients Development Of The	022 MIN
Recipe For Happy Children, A	026 MIN
Starting From Scratch - Birth To Three Years	029 MIN

Spor I Lyngen (Traces In The Heather) B 25 MIN
16MM FILM OPTICAL SOUND
A Danish language film. Attempts to perpetuate the Jutland Moorland peasant's background by telling the history of the Moors.
Prod-STATNS Dist-STATNS 1962

Sport Of Orienteering C 24 MIN
16MM FILM, 3/4 OR 1/2 IN VIDEO J-H A
Swedish youngsters follow a map over rough terrain, using a compass to find their way. Tells how to use a compass.
Prod-IFB Dist-IFB 1948

Sporting Chance, A C 25 MIN
16MM FILM OPTICAL SOUND J-H
Explains why girls should actively participate in sports and physical activities.
LC NO. 80-701574
Prod-TASCOR Dist-TASCOR 1980

Sporting Chance, A C 16 MIN
3/4 OR 1/2 INCH VIDEO CASSETTE
Reports on a successful health and sport center which offers the disabled a new lease on life. Shows handicapped people skiing, swimming, horseriding, shooting, and even dogsledding.
Prod-UPI Dist-JOU

Sporting Start, A B 11 MIN
16MM FILM OPTICAL SOUND H-C A
Highlights the activities of the National Institute of Sports in Patiala, India, set up by the government to train coaches from different parts of the country in all types of games and sports.
Prod-INDIA Dist-NEDINF

Sports C 20 MIN
3/4 OR 1/2 INCH VIDEO CASSETTE J-H
See series title for descriptive statement.
From The Contract Series.
Prod-KYTV Dist-AITECH 1977

Sports C 30 MIN
3/4 OR 1/2 INCH VIDEO CASSETTE C
Discusses ways in which sports reflect the values, biases and structure of American society.
From The Focus On Society Series.
Prod-DALCCD Dist-DALCCD

Sports C 30 MIN
3/4 OR 1/2 INCH VIDEO CASSETTE H-C A
Presents Lawrence Solow and Sharon Neumann Solow introducing American Sign Language used by the hearing-impaired. Emphasizes signs that have to do with sports.
From The Say It With Sign Series. Part 16
Prod-KNBCTV Dist-FI 1982

Sports - Power Basics—A Series
A
Assists the viewer in learning the basics in four sports, baseball, basketball, football and soccer. Includes step-by-step instruction.
Prod-RMI Dist-RMI

Power Basics Of Baseball
Power Basics Of Basketball
Power Basics Of Football
Power Basics Of Soccer

Sports - What's The Score C 29 MIN
3/4 INCH VIDEO CASSETTE
Discusses the value and harm of sports in American life. Explores women's attitudes toward sports.
From The Woman Series.
Prod-WNEDTV Dist-PUBTEL

Sports Action And Health C 22 MIN
16MM FILM, 3/4 OR 1/2 IN VIDEO J-C A
Uses footage of sports stars and sports action to discuss participation in sports and the concept of fitness as a total lifestyle, including good nutrition, exercise, sleep and avoidance of cigarettes, alcohol and drugs. Gives advice on warming up and down, doing conditioning exercises and taking care of injuries.
Prod-SIDRIS Dist-AIMS 1976

Sports Action And Health (Arabic) C 22 MIN
16MM FILM, 3/4 OR 1/2 IN VIDEO J-C A
Uses footage of sports stars and sports action to discuss participation in sports and the concept of fitness as a total lifestyle, including good nutrition, exercise, sleep and avoidance of cigarettes, alcohol and drugs. Gives advice on warming up and down, doing conditioning exercises and taking care of injuries.
Prod-SIDRIS Dist-AIMS 1976

Sports And Business C 29 MIN
16MM FILM OPTICAL SOUND
States that Americans are preoccupied with being number one. Shows that a sense of self-worth does not come from being number one and suggests that Christianity offers an alternative perception regarding self-worth.
From The We're Number One Series.
LC NO. 79-701399
Prod-AMERLC Dist-AMERLC 1978

Sports Bloopers II C 23 MIN
16MM FILM OPTICAL SOUND
Presents a variety of sports-oriented antics and pratfalls.
Prod-COORS Dist-MTP

Sports Car Racing C 3 MIN
16MM FILM OPTICAL SOUND P-I
Discusses sports car racing.
From The Of All Things Series.
Prod-BAILYL Dist-AVED

Sports Cartoon, The C 15 MIN
2 INCH VIDEOTAPE
See series title for descriptive statement.
From The Charlie's Pad Series.
Prod-WSIU Dist-PUBTEL

Sports Fishing C 3 MIN
16MM FILM OPTICAL SOUND P-I
Discusses sports fishing.
From The Of All Things Series.
Prod-BAILYL Dist-AVED

Sports For Elementary (Spanish)—A Series
16MM FILM, 3/4 OR 1/2 IN VIDEO I-J
Emphasizes basic skills and practice drills for favorite American sports.
Prod-CINEDU Dist-AIMS

Playing Basketball (Spanish) 13 MIN
Playing Softball (Spanish) 11 MIN
Playing Touch Football (Spanish) 12 MIN

Sports For Elementary—A Series
16MM FILM, 3/4 OR 1/2 IN VIDEO I-J
Emphasizes basic skills and practice drills for favorite American sports.
Prod-CINEDU Dist-AIMS

Playing Basketball 013 MIN
Playing Softball 011 MIN
Playing Touch Football 012 MIN

Sports For Life C 22 MIN
16MM FILM, 3/4 OR 1/2 IN VIDEO J-C A
Shows how different people in different walks of life are active in sports as a way to look and feel better in their daily lives.
Prod-BARR Dist-BARR 1976

Sports for Life (Captioned) C 22 MIN
16MM FILM - VIDEO, ALL FORMATS J-C A
Discusses the various benefits of participating in sports.
Prod-BARR Dist-BARR

Sports In America—A Series
16MM FILM, 3/4 OR 1/2 IN VIDEO J-C A
Presents James Michener as he examines the past, present and future of amateur and professional sports. Focuses on black athletes, women athletes and children who participate in sports.
Prod-EMLEN Dist-PFP

Black Athlete, The 058 MIN
Children And Sports 058 MIN
Women In Sports 058 MIN

Sports Influence On Dance Performance C 30 MIN
3/4 OR 1/2 INCH VIDEO CASSETTE
See series title for descriptive statement.
From The Athleticism In Dance Series.
Prod-ARCVID Dist-ARCVID

Sports Injuries C 29 MIN
3/4 OR 1/2 INCH VIDEO CASSETTE
Explains how to exercise and get into shape without being injured. Includes an on-location visit to the San Francisco 49ers.
From The Here's To Your Health Series.
Prod-KERA Dist-PBS

Sports Injuries And The Liability Of The Coach C 21 MIN
3/4 OR 1/2 INCH VIDEO CASSETTE T
Cites specific examples of liability situations and discusses how coaches can avoid negligence suits through an effective injury control program that addresses conditioning, skill development, performance, supervision and facilities.
From The Sports Medicine Series.
Prod-UNIDIM Dist-EBEC 1982

Sports Injuries Today C 8 MIN
3/4 OR 1/2 INCH VIDEO CASSETTE
Prepares the coach to recognize common sports injuries and understand the mechanism of injury. Emphasizes immediate on-site care that can be given by the coach and reviews a safe first aid technique.
From The Sports Medicine For Coaches Series.
Prod-UWASH Dist-UWASH

Sports Journal—A Series

Prod-FIARTS Dist-FIARTS 1975

Duel, The - Fencing 14 MIN
How's That Cricket 14 MIN
Serpent River Paddlers 14 MIN

Sports Legends—A Series
I-J
Prod-COUNFI Dist-COUNFI

Bob Petit 20 MIN
Eddie Arcaro 20 MIN
Elgin Baylor 20 MIN
Frank Gifford 20 MIN
Gale Sayers 20 MIN
Hugh Mac Elhenny 20 MIN
Jesse Owens 20 MIN
Joe Di Maggio (The Yankee Clipper) 20 MIN
Lenny Moore 20 MIN
Mickey Mantle 20 MIN
Paul Hornung 20 MIN
Red Auerbach 20 MIN
Roger Ward 20 MIN
Roy Campanella 20 MIN
Sam Snead 20 MIN

Sports Marketing - New Professionals At Cable News Network C 30 MIN
3/4 OR 1/2 INCH VIDEO CASSETTE
Discusses the $70 million gamble to create a financially viable alternative to the three broadcast networks for professional sports.
From The Contemporary Issues In Marketing Series.
Prod-CANTOR Dist-IVCH

Sports Medicine C 12 MIN
16MM FILM OPTICAL SOUND
Discusses medicines commonly used in sports.
From The Coaching Development Programme Series. No. 6
LC NO. 76-701058
Prod-SARBOO Dist-SARBOO Prodn-SVL 1974

Sports Medicine C 28 MIN
16MM FILM OPTICAL SOUND H-C A
Illustrates the use of scientific training methods to improve performances in sports. Focuses on weight training, interval training, fitness testing and treatment of injuries.
From The A Man And His Sport Series.
LC NO. 73-709319
Prod-ANAIB Dist-AUIS 1970

Sports Medicine C 30 MIN
3/4 OR 1/2 INCH VIDEO CASSETTE
Discusses sports medicine.
From The Lifelines Series.
Prod-UGATV Dist-MDCPB

Sports Medicine For Coaches—A Series

Reviews what coaches can do to make school sports programs safe for the athletes and more satisfying and rewarding for the coach. Each unit must be purchased with an accompaying slide show.
Prod-UWASH Dist-UWASH

First Step, The - Handling The Life 007 ..
Fueling The Body For Sports 009 MIN
Introduction To The Series 006 MIN
New Woman Athlete, The 009 MIN
Overuse Injuries - Too Much, Too Fast, Too Soon 010 MIN
Pathway To A Winning Season 008 MIN
Sports Injuries Today 008 MIN

Sports Medicine—A Series
16MM FILM, 3/4 OR 1/2 IN VIDEO T
Features practical demonstration and guidance on the diagnosis, treatment and prevention of sports injuries as well as pretraining and training practices that effectively minimize injuries.
Prod-UNIDIM Dist-EBEC 1982

Care And Prevention Of Heat Injury 022 MIN
Conditioning The Athlete To Prevent Sports 026 MIN
Drug Problems In Sports 024 MIN
Emergency Treatment Of Acute Knee Injuries 028 MIN
Eye Injuries Among Athletes 023 MIN
Inter-School Athletic Injury - Emergency Care 025 MIN
Introduction To Sports Medicine 026 MIN
Minimal Expectations For Health Supervision 019 MIN
Nutritional Consideration For The Athlete 024 MIN
Overuse Syndrome Of The Lower Extremity 027 MIN
Prevention And Field Management Of Head And 023 MIN
Prevention And Treatment Of Ankle Injuries 020 MIN
Prevention And Treatment Of Foot Injuries 025 MIN
Proper Dressing Of The Football Player 022 MIN
Psychology Of Sports 025 MIN
Sports Injuries And The Liability Of The Coach 021 MIN

Sports Medicine—A Series

Presents a series on sports medicine. Includes information on pre-participation physical examination and examination and treatment of injured athletes and runners.
Prod-VTRI Dist-VTRI

Field Evaluation And Care Of The Injured
Injuries To Runners
Phsyical Examination Of The Injured Athlete
Pre-Participation Physical Examination Of The

Sports Odyssey C 25 MIN
16MM FILM, 3/4 OR 1/2 IN VIDEO
Offers an action-packed sports spectacular featuring ski jumping, surfing, hang gliding, water skiing, skateboarding, and comedy.
Prod-MCFI Dist-MCFI

Sports Omnibus B 30 MIN
16MM FILM OPTICAL SOUND
Shows Globetrotters, rodeo, roller derby, Sam Snead and Rams-Bears.
Prod-SFI Dist-SFI

Sports Oriented Signs, Verbs And Personal Pronouns C 30 MIN
3/4 OR 1/2 INCH VIDEO CASSETTE
Provides sign language dealing with sports including verbs and personal pronouns.
From The Signing With Cindy Series.
Prod-KUHTTV Dist-MDCPB

Sports Photography of Robert Riger, The C
3/4 OR 1/2 INCH VIDEO CASSETTE
Explores the work of sports photographer and filmmaker Robert Riger. Presents footage from his films, an interview and insights into how he has fulfilled his goals.
Prod-SILVRP Dist-GA

Sports Profile C 29 MIN
16MM FILM, 3/4 OR 1/2 IN VIDEO I-C A
Focuses on Artie Wilson, a celebrity in the Negro Baseball League, as he tours his old Birmingham neighborhood and reminisces. Reenactments highlight his childhood and career. Looks at the life and career of Alice Coachman, a black Olympic Gold Medal high jumper and sprinter.
From The Were You There? Series.
LC NO. 83-706601
Prod-NGUZO Dist-BCNFL 1982

Sports Round-Up B 30 MIN
16MM FILM OPTICAL SOUND
Presents the best of events in four showings.
Prod-SFI Dist-SFI

Sports Safety C 22 MIN
16MM FILM, 3/4 OR 1/2 IN VIDEO I-H
Points out that some sports accidents involving a youngster may cause serious problems throughout his or her life. Features famous sports figures who explain what can be done to prevent injuries in such sports as baseball, basketball, football and soccer.
Prod-HANDEL Dist-HANDEL 1983

Sports Scholarships, Pt I - Advantages C 25 MIN
3/4 OR 1/2 INCH VIDEO CASSETTE J-C A
Interviews Joe Paterno, athletic director at Penn State University, and Eric Zemper, research coordinator at the National Collegiate Athletic Association, on the advantages of sports scholarships.
Prod-SIRS Dist-SIRS

Sports Scholarships, Pt II - Disadvantages C 25 MIN
3/4 OR 1/2 INCH VIDEO CASSETTE J-C A
Continues discussions with Joe Paterno and Eric Zemper on sports scholarships, this time touching on the disadvantages.
Prod-SIRS Dist-SIRS

Sports Show C 24 MIN
3/4 OR 1/2 INCH VIDEO CASSETTE
Features a high school tennis player whose goal is to win Wimbledon. Shows weight control programs for young people, handicapped horseback riding, how roller skates are made and activities of the Argonauts scuba diving club.
Prod-WCCOTV Dist-WCCOTV 1982

Sports Suite, A C 8 MIN
16MM FILM, 3/4 OR 1/2 IN VIDEO I-C A
Shows the excitement of participation in sports activities. Presents four vignettes, accompanied by classical music, in which youthful participants demonstrate the exuberance and joy they find in physical education and team sports, including gymnastics, volleyball, swimming and soccer.
LC NO. 77-701115
Prod-LIBERP Dist-PFP 1977

Sports That Set The Styles, The C 28 MIN
16MM FILM OPTICAL SOUND
Examines the history of women in sports. Shows how the nature of different sports influenced what the women players wore and how the clothes worn on the golf course, tennis court and beach eventually found their way into the home and into society.
Prod-SEARS Dist-MTP

Sports Thrills B
16MM FILM OPTICAL SOUND
Shows highlights from hockey, basketball, boxing and track.
Prod-SFI Dist-SFI

Sports Year '61 B 30 MIN
16MM FILM OPTICAL SOUND
Presents highlights from the Kentucky Derby, World Series, NFL, NHL, track and boxing.
Prod-SFI Dist-SFI

Sports Year 1969 C 25 MIN
16MM FILM OPTICAL SOUND
Pinpoints key sports happenings in 1969, such as the Triple Crown races, major events in baseball, football, track, boxing and tennis and other highlights in competitive sports. Narrated by Red Barber.
LC NO. 70-712878
Prod-UPITN Dist-SFI 1971

Sports Year 1970 C 25 MIN
16MM FILM OPTICAL SOUND
Highlights the key sports happenings of 1970, including events in football, baseball, boxing, golf and other sports. Narrated by Lindsay Nelson.
LC NO. 76-712877
Prod-UPITN Dist-SFI 1971

Sports-Oriented Signs, Verbs And Personal Pronouns C
3/4 OR 1/2 INCH VIDEO CASSETTE A
Opens with Cindy and troupe of male dancers performing 'Main Event.' Brings sign language into everyday word usage, including a bout with boxer Sugar Ray Leonard to demonstrate the manual sign for boxing.
From The Signing With Cindy Series.
Prod-GPCV Dist-GPCV

Sports, Society, And Self C 15 MIN
3/4 OR 1/2 INCH VIDEO CASSETTE I
Reveals that games are played and watched in every culture. Shows that the Tarahumara are excellent endurance runners, that physical training is important to the Japanese and that Africa's Baoule people enjoy a fast-paced game of mental skill called Aweie.
From The Across Cultures Series.
Prod-POSIMP Dist-AITECH Prodn-WETN 1983

Sportsmanlike Driving—A Series
C A
Points out the constantly increasing need to provide learning experiences in the proper operation of a motor vehicle. Presents illustrative concepts with demonstrations of the most widely-accepted techniques and principles of safe driving. (Broadcast quality)
Prod-AAAFTS Dist-GPITVL Prodn-SCETV

Advanced Driving	30 MIN
Alcohol And Drugs Versus Safe Driving	30 MIN
Attitude And Behavior Of A Good Driver	30 MIN
Basic Maneuvers, Pt 1 - Turning And Backing	30 MIN
Basic Maneuvers, Pt 2 - Hill Starts And Parking	30 MIN
Buying And Insuring Your Car	30 MIN
Driver's Permit Or Operator's License	30 MIN
Driving As Your Job	30 MIN
Driving In Cities And Towns	30 MIN
Driving In The Country	30 MIN
Driving On Freeways	30 MIN
Driving Under Adverse Conditions	30 MIN
Eyes Of The Driver, The	30 MIN
Fundamental Driving Techniques, Pt 1 -	30 MIN
Fundamental Driving Techniques, Pt 2 -	30 MIN
Getting Ready To Drive	30 MIN
How The Automobile Runs	30 MIN
Map Reading And Trip Planning	30 MIN
Motor Vehicle Laws	30 MIN
Night Driving And Seeing	30 MIN
Physical Fitness And Traffic Safety	30 MIN
Reaction, Braking And Stopping Distances	30 MIN
Skids And Skidding	30 MIN
Taking Care Of Your Car	30 MIN
Time To Live, A	30 MIN
Traffic - Present And Future Needs	30 MIN
Traffic Law Observance And Enforcement	30 MIN
Traffic Laws Made By Man	30 MIN
Traffic Laws Made By Nature	30 MIN
Traffic Safety, Vehicle Design And Equipment	30 MIN

Sportswear Special, The C 29 MIN
2 INCH VIDEOTAPE
See series title for descriptive statement.
From The Designing Women Series.
Prod-WKYCTV Dist-PUBTEL

Sportsworld—A Series

Presents various aspects of sports.
Prod-NBC Dist-NBC

Grow High On Love 23 MIN

Spot Prevention (Measles) C 14 MIN
3/4 INCH VIDEO CASSETTE K-I
Presents humorous illustrations of the chase and capture of the measles 'germ' and his 'conversion' to protective vaccine. Uses animation for the purpose of promoting immunization against measles in children.
Prod-USNAC Dist-USNAC 1972

Spot Welder Demonstration C 21 MIN
1/2 IN VIDEO CASSETTE BETA/VHS IND
Explains the basic operating procedure for a rocker arm foot operated floor model spot welder.
Prod-RMI Dist-RMI

Spot Welding B 20 MIN
16MM FILM, 3/4 OR 1/2 IN VIDEO
Shows how to spot weld parts of an access cover, set up the machine, remove and install electrodes, set pressure, current and time controls, test the setup and clean the electrode tips.
From The Aircraft Work Series. Assembling And Riveting, No. 9
Prod-USOE Dist-USNAC Prodn-TRADEF 1945

Spotlight On Deaf Artists C 33 MIN
3/4 OR 1/2 INCH VIDEO CASSETTE A
Narrates a tour of the exhibit of art works by deaf artists on display at Gallaudet College. Presents such artists as Goya, Washburn, Tilden, et al. Signed.
Prod-GALCO Dist-GALCO 1981

Spotlight On Negri Sembilan B 16 MIN
16MM FILM OPTICAL SOUND
Reviews the work done in rural development in Negri Sembilan, Malaysia, showing the opening of new land for settlement and cultivation of rubber, coconut, oil palms and other crops and some of the projects for the future.
Prod-FILEM Dist-PMFMUN 1961

Spotlight On Pahang B 18 MIN
16MM FILM OPTICAL SOUND
Discusses Pahang, Malaysia and its development. Shows how problems peculiar to this vast, largely unexplored state have been tackled to bring new life and hope to the fishermen and farmers who make up the bulk of its population.
Prod-FILEM Dist-PMFMUN 1961

Spotty C 15 MIN
3/4 OR 1/2 INCH VIDEO CASSETTE P
Presents the children's story Spotty by Margaret Rey.
From The Picture Book Park Series. Red Module
Prod-WVIZTV Dist-AITECH 1974

Spotty - Story Of A Fawn C 11 MIN
16MM FILM, 3/4 OR 1/2 IN VIDEO P-I
Presents the adventures of a wild fawn filmed against the authentic background of the north woods.
Prod-CORF Dist-CORF 1950

Spotty The Fawn In Winter C 11 MIN
16MM FILM, 3/4 OR 1/2 IN VIDEO P-I
Follows a fawn as he faces his first winter and shows how a girl helps him to survive.
Prod-CORF Dist-CORF 1958

Spray It On C 29 MIN
3/4 INCH VIDEO CASSETTE
Demonstrates the use of a spray gun to make pictures.
From The Artist At Work Series.
Prod-UMITV Dist-UMITV 1973

Spray Paint Defects - Their Cause And Cure—A Series
IND
Explains how spray processes work and how 33 common defects arise. Discusses how production parameters influence defects. Helps equip enrollees to prevent and solve spray paint problems. Notes how more than 90 defects are cross-indexed. Uses classroom format to videotape ten 25 to 45 minute lectures.
Prod-GMIEMI Dist-AMCEE

Tape 1
Tape 10
Tape 2
Tape 3
Tape 4
Tape 5
Tape 6
Tape 7
Tape 8
Tape 9

Spraying Equipment And Procedures, Pt 1 - Residual Spraying C 9 MIN
16MM FILM OPTICAL SOUND
Explains the meaning of residual spraying for fly control, the necessity for this type of spraying, and the methods of using hand and power spraying equipment.
From The Community Fly Control Series.
LC NO. FIE53-199
Prod-USPHS Dist-USNAC 1951

Spraying Equipment And Procedures, Pt 1 - Residual Spraying (French) C 9 MIN
16MM FILM OPTICAL SOUND
Explains the meaning of residual spraying for fly control, the necessity for this type of spraying and the methods of using hand and power spraying equipment.
From The Community Fly Control Series.
LC NO. FIE53-199
Prod-USPHS Dist-NMAC 1951

Spread Of Typhus, The B 2 MIN
16MM FILM, 3/4 OR 1/2 IN VIDEO H-C A
Shows close-up views of the louse and explains how it transmits typhus.
From The Microbiology Teaching Series.
Prod-UCEMC Dist-UCEMC 1961

Spread Out Or Squeeze In C 20 MIN
16MM FILM OPTICAL SOUND I
Discusses the effect that man as an environmental factor is having upon himself. Points out that our rapid increase in population is resulting in overpopulation with the accompanying problems of famine, disease and pollution. Explains that an increase in population density also means an increase in the amount of contacts for man to deal with, and consequently more stimuli, both negative and positive, for his nervous system to cope with.
From The Inherit The Earth Series.
Prod-KQEDTV Dist-GPITVL

Spread Spectrum—A Series
PRO
Serves as introduction to spread-spectrum concept and its applications, providing research-level understanding of several systems aspects. Emphasizes simple but rigorous formulation for analytical and computational techniques.
Prod-UMAEEE Dist-AMCEE

Spreading C 30 MIN
3/4 OR 1/2 INCH VIDEO CASSETTE C A
Presents Sherman Levine and trader John Carter explaining and discussing the procedures and characteristics of spread trading.
From The Commodities – The Professional Trader Series.
Prod-VIPUB Dist-VIPUB

Spreading - Surface Films Of Insoluble Monolayers B 51 MIN
3/4 OR 1/2 INCH VIDEO CASSETTE PRO
See series title for descriptive statement.
From The Colloid And Surface Chemistry - Surface Chemistry Series.
Prod-MIOT Dist-MIOT

Spreading Oceans C 24 MIN
16MM FILM, 3/4 OR 1/2 IN VIDEO C A
Explores continental drift, the opening of oceans and the movement of tectonic plates. Uses animation to show undersea structures such as transformed faults and plate boundaries as well as the dynamics of ocean-ocean and continent-continent collisions.
Prod-BBCTV Dist-MEDIAG 1981

Spreading, Surface Films Of Insoluble Monolayers C 51 MIN
3/4 OR 1/2 INCH VIDEO CASSETTE
See series title for descriptive statement.
From The Colloid And Surface Chemistry - Surface Chemistry Series.
Prod-KALMIA Dist-KALMIA

Sprechen Sie Deutsch C 15 MIN
16MM FILM, 3/4 OR 1/2 IN VIDEO
See series title for descriptive statement.
From The Guten Tag Series. Part 1
Prod-BAYER Dist-IFB 1968

Sprigs And Twigs C 15 MIN
16MM FILM OPTICAL SOUND K-I
Follows Fingermouse and Flash on a mission to collect spigs and twigs.
From The Fingermouse, Yoffy And Friends Series.
LC NO. 73-700437
Prod-BBCTV Dist-VEDO 1972

Spring C 9 MIN
16MM FILM, 3/4 OR 1/2 IN VIDEO I-C A
Records the beauty of the earth as it changes from winter to spring, while a young girl asks her father questions about the seasons.
Prod-PFP Dist-PFP 1973

Spring C 11 MIN
16MM FILM, 3/4 OR 1/2 IN VIDEO P-I
Depicts the beauty of spring and shows the exuberance of children playing in the sunshine.
From The Seasons Series.
LC NO. 80-707704
Prod-CENTRO Dist-CORF 1980

Spring C 15 MIN
3/4 INCH VIDEO CASSETTE P
See series title for descriptive statement.
From The Celebrate Series.
Prod-KUONTV Dist-GPITVL 1978

Spring C 16 MIN
16MM FILM, 3/4 OR 1/2 IN VIDEO P-I
Looks at the activities and changes common to the spring season such as birds returning from their wintering grounds and ice and snow beginning to melt. Shows the farmer plowing and sowing his fields while animals awaken from hibernation.
From The Four Seasons Series.
Prod-NGS Dist-NGS 1983

Spring - Nature's Sights And Sounds C 14 MIN
16MM FILM, 3/4 OR 1/2 IN VIDEO K-I
Celebrates the coming of spring in the forest as seen through the rebirth of wild plants and flowers, but principally through the birth of small animals. Shows frogs, woodchucks, honey bees, rabbits, foxes, raccoons, turtles, snakes, fish, snails, crayfish and a host of birds.
From The Nature's Sights And Sound Series.
Prod-MASLKS Dist-BCNFL 1983

Spring - Six Interpretations C 14 MIN
16MM FILM, 3/4 OR 1/2 IN VIDEO I-H
Uses interpretations of spring to explore methods through which ideas, feelings and perceptions are communicated.
Prod-BARR Dist-BARR 1975

Spring And Summer C 14 MIN
2 INCH VIDEOTAPE
Features nature photographer Jim Bones celebrating the beauty of spring and summer.
From The Images And Memories Series.
Prod-KERA Dist-PUBTEL

Spring Brings Changes (2nd Ed) C 11 MIN
16MM FILM, 3/4 OR 1/2 IN VIDEO K-I
Presents examples of plants and animals growing, budding, flowering, emerging and reproducing with the coming of spring.
Prod-CF Dist-CF 1976

Spring Cleaning C 30 MIN
3/4 OR 1/2 INCH VIDEO CASSETTE
See series title for descriptive statement.
From The Que Pasa, U S A Series.
Prod-WPBTTV Dist-MDCPB

Spring Comes To The City C 10 MIN
16MM FILM, 3/4 OR 1/2 IN VIDEO P
Shows a boy named Danny discovering the effect of spring's arrival in the city, such as animals reappearing, gardens being planted, streets being repaired and swings in the park.
From The Seasons In The City Series.
Prod-CORF Dist-CORF

Spring Comes To The Forest C 11 MIN
16MM FILM, 3/4 OR 1/2 IN VIDEO P-I
Shows, in a light, charming manner, the sequence of change in the plant and animal life of the forest during the spring months.
From The Seasons Series.
Prod-CORF Dist-CORF 1972

Spring Comes To The Pond C 11 MIN
16MM FILM, 3/4 OR 1/2 IN VIDEO P-I
Shows how the gradual changes in a pond affect living things

from the end of winter to the beginning of summer. Includes extreme close-ups and photomicrography to show protozoa and other minute forms of life found in a pond.
From The Seasons Series.
Prod-CORF Dist-CORF

Spring Harvest C 13 MIN
16MM FILM OPTICAL SOUND I-C A
Explores the process of creating maple syrup from maple sap in Vermont.
LC NO. 76-701635
Prod-GMCW Dist-GMCW 1976

Spring Impressions B 9 MIN
16MM FILM, 3/4 OR 1/2 IN VIDEO
Follows the progress of a little girl in spring through a field where the grass is almost as tall as she is, to a stream where she captures a frog to keep the rabbits in her basket company and to the birch woods where she finds forest wildflowers.
Prod-MORLAT Dist-SF

Spring In Iceland C 21 MIN
16MM FILM OPTICAL SOUND C A
Provides a vivid contrast between hot springs and volcanoes and the great glaciers which sit on top of volcanoes. Shows the varied bird and animal life of Iceland which can best be seen in the spring.
Prod-WSTGLC Dist-WSTGLC

Spring In Japan C 20 MIN
16MM FILM OPTICAL SOUND H-C A
Depicts spring in Japan while touring Japanese gardens, spring festivals, Mount Fuji and feudal castles.
LC NO. 77-702438
Prod-JNTA Dist-JNTA 1972

Spring In Nature C 17 MIN
16MM FILM, 3/4 OR 1/2 IN VIDEO P-I
Looks at life in the natural landscape during spring.
From The Seasons In Nature Series.
Prod-FLMFR Dist-FLMFR

Spring In The City X 11 MIN
16MM FILM, 3/4 OR 1/2 IN VIDEO P-I
Discusses the changes in nature in the spring and shows some of the activities of children and adults in the city during the spring season.
From The Language Arts - Creative Expression Series.
Prod-EBEC Dist-EBEC 1969

Spring In The Woods C 15 MIN
16MM FILM, 3/4 OR 1/2 IN VIDEO I-H
Shows the early signs of life in the woods during the spring. Describes how the environment of the woods supports each form of life that lives there.
From The Place To Live Series.
Prod-GRATV Dist-JOU

Spring Is A Season X 11 MIN
16MM FILM, 3/4 OR 1/2 IN VIDEO P-J
A young boy describes the signs of spring that he sees in the fields around his home. He records his discoveries on a calendar and notes the new plant growth, the change in the weather and the baby animals.
Prod-ALTSUL Dist-JOU 1961

Spring Is An Adventure C 11 MIN
16MM FILM, 3/4 OR 1/2 IN VIDEO P
Presents scenes typical of the arrival of spring, such as flowers blooming, robin's eggs hatching, searching for baby turtles and tadpoles in a stream, and planting a garden.
Prod-CORF Dist-CORF

Spring Is Here C 15 MIN
3/4 OR 1/2 INCH VIDEO CASSETTE K-P
Looks at all the signs of spring as well as the textures, sizes and shapes of spring.
From The Pass It On Series.
Prod-WKNOTV Dist-GPITVL 1983

Spring Is Here (Captioned) C 10 MIN
16MM FILM, 3/4 OR 1/2 IN VIDEO P
Examines animal and human life during the spring. Shows a group of school children preparing and planting a vegetable garden. Captioned for the hearing impaired.
Prod-BERLET Dist-IFB 1967

Spring Is Here (2nd Ed) C 11 MIN
16MM FILM, 3/4 OR 1/2 IN VIDEO P
Examines human and animal life during the spring. Shows a group school children preparing and planting a vegetable garden.
From The Seasons (2nd Ed) Series.
LC NO. 80-706439
Prod-IFB Dist-IFB Prodn-BERLET 1979

Spring Lawn Care C 30 MIN
1/2 IN VIDEO CASSETTE BETA/VHS
Discusses spring lawn care including raking, fertilizing, weed control and tuning up the lawn mower. Gives tips on planting parsnips and strawberries.
From The Victory Garden Series.
Prod-WGBHTV Dist-MTI

Spring Marsh C 26 MIN
16MM FILM OPTICAL SOUND I-C A
Uses wildlife scenes filmed in Michigan to stress the importance of the marsh as a refuge for many kinds of wildlife, and as a vital part of wildlife ecology.
From The Audubon Wildlife Theatre Series.
LC NO. 72-701737
Prod-KEGPL Dist-AVEXP 1971

Spring Migration C 16 MIN
16MM FILM OPTICAL SOUND I-C A
Portrays the migratory flights of sand hill cranes and Canadian geese.
LC NO. 75-703974
Prod-NOVACK Dist-RADIM 1975

Spring Nature Hike C 10 MIN
16MM FILM OPTICAL SOUND P-I
Stimulates student interest in the real world of nature. Follows two children as they discover the many new flowers and animals of springtime in the woods near their home. Points out that even city dwellers can enjoy and appreciate nature if they take the time to observe the happenings around them.
Prod-SF Dist-SF 1967

Spring Show C 24 MIN
3/4 OR 1/2 INCH VIDEO CASSETTE
Shows the skills and knowledge of a 14-year-old champion polo player, the training of police dogs, the art of becoming a cheerleader and some Scottish dancing.
Prod-WCCOTV Dist-WCCOTV 1981

Spring Tunes C 10 MIN
16MM FILM, 3/4 OR 1/2 IN VIDEO J-C
Presents an animated dramatization in which an egoist tries to destroy a small boy and his fiddle in order to stop the symphony of life.
Prod-ZAGREB Dist-IFB 1970

Spring Winding On The Lathe C
3/4 OR 1/2 INCH VIDEO CASSETTE
See series title for descriptive statement.
From The Intermediate Engine Lathe Operation Series.
Prod-VTRI Dist-VTRI

Spring Winding On The Lathe C 15 MIN
3/4 OR 1/2 INCH VIDEO CASSETTE IND
See series title for descriptive statement.
From The Machining And The Operation Of Machine Tools, Module 3 - Intermediate Engine Lathe Series.
Prod-LEIKID Dist-LEIKID

Spring Winding On The Lathe (Spanish) C
3/4 OR 1/2 INCH VIDEO CASSETTE
See series title for descriptive statement.
From The Intermediate Engine Lathe Operation (Spanish) Series.
Prod-VTRI Dist-VTRI

Spring-Cleaning The House And Chimney C 8 MIN
16MM FILM OPTICAL SOUND K-P
Follows Crystal and her friends as they decide to undertake spring-cleaning of the house and chimney.
From The Crystal Tipps And Alistair Series.
LC NO. 73-700458
Prod-BBCTV Dist-VEDO 1972

Springboard X 34 MIN
16MM FILM OPTICAL SOUND
Shows the Christian perspective being demonstrated by champion athletes who attend the FCA conference making a profound impression on a young baseball pitcher.
From The F C A Sports Film Series.
Prod-FELLCA Dist-WWPI 1960

Springman And The SS C 16 MIN
16MM FILM, 3/4 OR 1/2 IN VIDEO J-H A
Presents an animated story about a chimney sweep who discovers the power of a spring taken from an old love seat and uses it to annoy the SS troops who are occupying Czechoslovakia. Highlights the potential of the individual in the midst of an oppressive society.
LC NO. 81-706879
Prod-TRNKAJ Dist-PHENIX 1973

Springtime C 14 MIN
16MM FILM OPTICAL SOUND I-C A
Presents impressions of the arrival of spring in Ontario. Shows sugaring-off parties, trilliums blooming, fishermen fishing, children playing in a park and other signs of spring in country and city.
LC NO. 73-700553
Prod-CTFL Dist-CTFL 1972

Sprinklers C 15 MIN
3/4 OR 1/2 INCH VIDEO CASSETTE PRO
Explains the operation of water sprinkler systems including motor alarms, tapping into sprinkler systems for water supply and opening and closing sprinkler systems.
Prod-IFSTA Dist-IFSTA

Sprint Freestyle - Men C 15 MIN
16MM FILM, 3/4 OR 1/2 IN VIDEO J-C
Demonstrates entering through a spot during the start, placement of hands during freestyle catch and stroke mechanics including elbow recovery, shoulder rotation and kicking styles.
From The Swim Training - Men Series.
Prod-ATHI Dist-ATHI 1981

Sprint Races C 4 MIN
16MM FILM SILENT
Presents male athletes competing in sprint races, including Lewis, Smith, Leonard, Sanford, Floyd, Riddick, D Evans, Darden, Mennea, Wells, Quarrie, Wiley, Zuliani and Cameron.
Prod-TRACKN Dist-TRACKN 1982

Sprint Races (Women) C 4 MIN
16MM FILM SILENT
Shows female athletes competing in sprint races, including Hoyte, Gohr, Kondratyeva, Ashford, Bolden, Ottey, Griffith, Kratochvilova and Koch.
Prod-TRACKN Dist-TRACKN 1982

Sprint Techniques C 4 MIN
16MM FILM SILENT
Demonstrates various sprint techniques by such sprinters as Lewis, Sanford, Philips, Floyd, Calvin, Smith, Lattany, Glance, Wiley, Tabron and Panzo.
Prod-TRACKN Dist-TRACKN 1982

Sprint Techniques (Women) C 4 MIN
16MM FILM SILENT
Demonstrates sprint techniques used by various female athletes, including Ashford, Nedd, Kratochvilova, Brown, Ashford, Griffith, Ottey and Bacoul.
Prod-TRACKN Dist-TRACKN 1982

Sprint, The C 13 MIN
16MM FILM, 3/4 OR 1/2 IN VIDEO H-C A
Demonstrates performance and training in the sprint. Includes views of an actual competition.
From The Athletics Series.
LC NO. 80-706587
Prod-GSAVL Dist-IU 1980

Sprinter, The B 11 MIN
16MM FILM OPTICAL SOUND J-H
Describes effective techniques of starting, attaining maxmum speeds quickly, and running at maximum efficinarrated by Ed Temple of Tennessee A and I University.
Prod-BORDEN Dist-COCA

Sprints, Hurdles And Relays C 48 MIN
1/2 IN VIDEO CASSETTE BETA/VHS
See series title for descriptive statement.
From The Women's Track And Field Series.
Prod-MOHOMV Dist-MOHOMV

Sprints, Hurdles And Relays C 48 MIN
1/2 IN VIDEO CASSETTE BETA/VHS A
Deals with three events, sprints, hurdles and relays, requiring the use of sprinting techniques. Includes drills to develop sprinters, hurdlers and relay runners.
Prod-RMI Dist-RMI

Spriometry - The Early Detection Of Chronic Obstructive Pulmonary Disease C 25 MIN
16MM FILM OPTICAL SOUND
Uses animation to illustrate the functioning of the normal respiratory system and to show what happens when ventilation is impaired. Demonstrates the procedures whereby a doctor, in his office, may evaluate typical patients with respiratory complaints.
LC NO. 79-702582
Prod-NTBA Dist-AMLUNG Prodn-WFP 1968

Sprout Wings And Fly C 30 MIN
16MM FILM, 3/4 OR 1/2 IN VIDEO J-C A
Profiles old-timer fiddler Tommy Jarrell, his music, friends and family in rural North Carolina.
LC NO. 83-706781
Prod-FLOWER Dist-FLOWER Prodn-BLNKL 1983

Sprouts C 4 MIN
16MM FILM OPTICAL SOUND
See series title for descriptive statement.
From The Beatrice Trum Hunter's Natural Foods Series.
Prod-PUBTEL Dist-PBS 1974

Sprouts C 4 MIN
2 INCH VIDEOTAPE
Demonstrates how to sprout mung beans, fenugreek, sunflower seeds, alfalfa and soybeans. Suggests using sprouts instead of lettuce in sandwiches, for garnishing soups or casseroles or for salads.
From The Beatrice Trum Hunter's Natural Foods Series.
Prod-WGBH Dist-PUBTEL

Spruce Bog, The C 23 MIN
16MM FILM, 3/4 OR 1/2 IN VIDEO J-C
Describes the conditions under which a spruce bog is formed, with details of the plant types found at successive stages of development, from open water to mature forest. Uses time-lapse photography to show the growth and decay of vegetation.
Prod-NFBC Dist-NFBC 1958

Spruce House B 29 MIN
16MM FILM OPTICAL SOUND H-C A
Explains that the theory followed by Spruce House is that a patient's behavior is the result of the responses, by other people, to past behavior. Shows that normal behavior must then be rewarded and neurotic behavior ignored if behavior modification is to take place.
From The To Save Tomorrow Series.
Prod-NET Dist-IU

Sprucin' Up B 17 MIN
16MM FILM OPTICAL SOUND
Shows what happens when Spanky and Alfalfa vie for the same girl. A Little Rascals film.
Prod-ROACH Dist-BHAWK 1935

Spunky The Snowman C 7 MIN
16MM FILM, 3/4 OR 1/2 IN VIDEO
A story cartoon depicting Spunky the Snowman's visit to Santa.
Prod-FLEET Dist-FI 1957

Spur Dikes C 14 MIN
16MM FILM OPTICAL SOUND
Depicts the theory, laboratory research and practical application of spur dikes to control scour at bridge abutments in flood conditions. Explains the work of public roads departments in several states to establish a standard method of reducing damage and cost of maintenance at bridge locations.
LC NO. 74-705689
Prod-USDTFH Dist-USNAC 1965

Sputter Deposition - An Overview C 35 MIN
3/4 OR 1/2 INCH VIDEO CASSETTE IND

Describes variation of yield of neutral species as a function of kinetic energy of the input ion. Says yield from the target following ion impact is the fundamental basis of sputter deposition techniques, whether in magnetron, plasma or ion-beam schemes.
From The Plasma Sputtering, Deposition And Growth Of Microelectronic Films For VLSI Series.
Prod-COLOSU Dist-COLOSU

Sputum Specimens - Collection And Preparation C 18 MIN
3/4 OR 1/2 INCH VIDEO CASSETTE PRO
See series title for descriptive statement.
From The Cytotechnology Techniques Series.
Prod-WFP Dist-WFP

Spy By Marriage, A C
16MM FILM OPTICAL SOUND
Features Mrs Wolfgang Lotz, wife of one of Israel's most effective spies, who tells how she shared her husband's three-year espionage assignment in Cairo until they were caught and sent to prison.
From The Dateline Israel, 1973 Series.
Prod-ADL Dist-ADL

Spy, The C 22 MIN
16MM FILM OPTICAL SOUND P-I
Presents an adventure set in the time of the Saxons which tells how Robin is tricked into rescuing a youth and taking him back to the secret camp, not realizing that the youth has agreed with the Baron to spy on the outlaws.
From The Unbroken Arrow Series.
Prod-LUF Dist-LUF 1977

Spyfluen (The Bluebottle) B 13 MIN
16MM FILM SILENT
Describes the anatomy of the bluebottle, its egg-laying and development. Portrays the useful functions of the bluebottle in nature. Includes Danish subtitles.
Prod-STATNS Dist-STATNS 1950

Spying Out The Course B 30 MIN
2 INCH VIDEOTAPE
See series title for descriptive statement.
From The Program Development In The Kindergarten Series.
Prod-GPITVL Dist-GPITVL

Spying The Spy B 10 MIN
16MM FILM SILENT
Presents a story based on the American spy fever during World War I.
Prod-SPCTRA Dist-STRFLS 1917

SQL/DS And Relational Data Base Systems—A Series

Explains the advantages and disadvantages of IBM's SQL/DS and how it meets the objectives of data base organization. Answers important questions about relational data base in general and SQL/DS in particular.
Prod-DELTAK Dist-DELTAK

Basic Facilities Of SQL/DS 030 MIN
Management Implications Of SQL/DS 030 MIN
Relational Data Base 030 MIN

Square And Rectangular Duct End Cap Layout (Drive And Slip) C 9 MIN
1/2 IN VIDEO CASSETTE BETA/VHS IND
See series title for descriptive statement.
From The Metal Fabrication - Duct End Cap Layout Series.
Prod-RMI Dist-RMI

Square And Rectangular Duct End Cap Layout (Slip Pocket) C 10 MIN
1/2 IN VIDEO CASSETTE BETA/VHS IND
See series title for descriptive statement.
From The Metal Fabrication - Duct End Cap Layout Series.
Prod-RMI Dist-RMI

Square Butt Aluminum C 5 MIN
1/2 IN VIDEO CASSETTE BETA/VHS IND
See series title for descriptive statement.
From The Welding Training (Comprehensive) — Oxy-Acetylene Welding Series.
Prod-RMI Dist-RMI

Square Butt A1 C 2 MIN
1/2 IN VIDEO CASSETTE BETA/VHS IND
See series title for descriptive statement.
From The Welding Training (Comprehensive) - Tungsten Inert Gas (T I G) Welding Series.
Prod-RMI Dist-RMI

Square Butt Backhand C 7 MIN
1/2 IN VIDEO CASSETTE BETA/VHS IND
See series title for descriptive statement.
From The Welding Training (Comprehensive) — Oxy-Acetylene Welding Series.
Prod-RMI Dist-RMI

Square Butt Bronze C 6 MIN
1/2 IN VIDEO CASSETTE BETA/VHS IND
See series title for descriptive statement.
From The Welding Training (Comprehensive) — Oxy-Acetylene Welding Series.
Prod-RMI Dist-RMI

Square Butt Horizontal C 6 MIN
1/2 IN VIDEO CASSETTE BETA/VHS IND
See series title for descriptive statement.
From The Welding Training (Comprehensive) — Oxy-Acetylene Welding Series.
Prod-RMI Dist-RMI

Square Butt Joint C 2 MIN
1/2 IN VIDEO CASSETTE BETA/VHS IND
See series title for descriptive statement.
From The Welding Training (Comprehensive) - Metal Inert Gas (M I G) Welding Series.
Prod-RMI Dist-RMI

Square Butt Joint Aluminum With Fixture C 4 MIN
1/2 IN VIDEO CASSETTE BETA/VHS IND
See series title for descriptive statement.
From The Welding Training (Comprehensive) - Tungsten Inert Gas (T I G) Welding Series.
Prod-RMI Dist-RMI

Square Butt Joint Filler Rod C 6 MIN
1/2 IN VIDEO CASSETTE BETA/VHS IND
See series title for descriptive statement.
From The Welding Training (Comprehensive) — Oxy-Acetylene Welding Series.
Prod-RMI Dist-RMI

Square Butt Joint Flat C 2 MIN
1/2 IN VIDEO CASSETTE BETA/VHS IND
See series title for descriptive statement.
From The Welding Training (Comprehensive) - Metal Inert Gas (M I G) Welding Series.
Prod-RMI Dist-RMI

Square Butt Joint Flat (Aluminum) C 2 MIN
1/2 IN VIDEO CASSETTE BETA/VHS IND
See series title for descriptive statement.
From The Welding Training (Comprehensive) - Metal Inert Gas (M I G) Welding Series.
Prod-RMI Dist-RMI

Square Butt Joint Single-Pass C 6 MIN
1/2 IN VIDEO CASSETTE BETA/VHS IND
See series title for descriptive statement.
From The Welding Training (Comprehensive) - Basic Shielded Metal Arc Welding Series.
Prod-RMI Dist-RMI

Square Butt Joint Stainless C 4 MIN
1/2 IN VIDEO CASSETTE BETA/VHS IND
See series title for descriptive statement.
From The Welding Training (Comprehensive) - Tungsten Inert Gas (T I G) Welding Series.
Prod-RMI Dist-RMI

Square Butt Joint Stainless Vertical-Up C 2 MIN
1/2 IN VIDEO CASSETTE BETA/VHS IND
See series title for descriptive statement.
From The Welding Training (Comprehensive) - Tungsten Inert Gas (T I G) Welding Series.
Prod-RMI Dist-RMI

Square Butt Joints C 15 MIN
3/4 OR 1/2 INCH VIDEO CASSETTE IND
See series title for descriptive statement.
From The Arc Welding Training Series.
Prod-AVIMA Dist-AVIMA

Square Butt Silver Braze C 4 MIN
1/2 IN VIDEO CASSETTE BETA/VHS IND
See series title for descriptive statement.
From The Welding Training (Comprehensive) — Oxy-Acetylene Welding Series.
Prod-RMI Dist-RMI

Square Butt Stainless With Fixture C 4 MIN
1/2 IN VIDEO CASSETTE BETA/VHS IND
See series title for descriptive statement.
From The Welding Training (Comprehensive) - Tungsten Inert Gas (T I G) Welding Series.
Prod-RMI Dist-RMI

Square Butt Vertical-Up C 6 MIN
1/2 IN VIDEO CASSETTE BETA/VHS IND
See series title for descriptive statement.
From The Welding Training (Comprehensive) — Oxy-Acetylene Welding Series.
Prod-RMI Dist-RMI

Square Circle B 17 MIN
16MM FILM OPTICAL SOUND
Presents an 'OVER 30' hippie, who functions in the square world as a planner and architect and in his personal world as a member of the 'TURNED ON' generation.
Prod-UPENN Dist-UPENN 1968

Square Dance Video Workshop C 60 MIN
3/4 OR 1/2 INCH VIDEO CASSETTE J-C A
Shows a square dance caller instructing eight student dancers as they demonstrate forty rudimentary calls.
Prod-WALCHJ Dist-WALCHJ

Square Dancing Fundamentals, Pt 1 C 19 MIN
16MM FILM, 3/4 OR 1/2 IN VIDEO J-C A
Teaches the first 22 fundamental square dance movements, emphasizing good styling.
Prod-ASSOCF Dist-AIMS 1974

Square Dancing Fundamentals, Pt 2 C 17 MIN
16MM FILM, 3/4 OR 1/2 IN VIDEO I-C A
Teaches the last 13 of the fundamental square dance movements, emphasizing the shuffle step, styling and smooth execution of figures.
Prod-ASSOCF Dist-AIMS 1974

Square Heel And Throat Elbow Layout C 29 MIN
1/2 IN VIDEO CASSETTE BETA/VHS IND
Presents the way the square heel and throat elbow layout should be laid out, including the seam allowances.
Prod-RMI Dist-RMI

Square Or Rectangular Transition - Bottom Up, Double Offset, All Sides Slanting C 30 MIN
1/2 IN VIDEO CASSETTE BETA/VHS IND
See series title for descriptive statement.
From The Transition 'Top Up' Or 'Bottom Up' Or Top Down Or Bottom Down Series.
Prod-RMI Dist-RMI

Square Or Rectangular Transition - Equal Taper, Same Size Openings C 9 MIN
1/2 IN VIDEO CASSETTE BETA/VHS IND
Shows the full scale pattern layout working from a one-view working drawing or shop sketch. Discusses the process of triangulation. Deals with openings that are the same size, but which change from a horizontal to a vertical position.
Prod-RMI Dist-RMI

Square Or Rectangular Transition - Equal Taper, Different Size Openings C 18 MIN
1/2 IN VIDEO CASSETTE BETA/VHS IND
Shows the full scale pattern layout working from a shop sketch or one-view working drawing. Discusses the application of triangulation, and emphasizes the seam dimensions to determine whether or not the patterns are laid out accurately.
Prod-RMI Dist-RMI

Square Or Rectangular Transition - Flat On Top Or Bottom, Offset, Different Openings C 18 MIN
1/2 IN VIDEO CASSETTE BETA/VHS IND
Shows the full scale pattern development, working from a shop sketch or one-view working drawing. Emphasizes the application of flat top or bottom.
Prod-RMI Dist-RMI

Square Or Rectangular Transition - Three Straight Sides C 7 MIN
1/2 IN VIDEO CASSETTE BETA/VHS IND
Shows the use of a shop sketch to illustrate the most simple of transitional fittings, and develops full size patterns, using the best method. Discusses alternative methods.
Prod-RMI Dist-RMI

Square Or Rectangular Transition - Top Up, Double Offset, All Sides Slanting C 43 MIN
1/2 IN VIDEO CASSETTE BETA/VHS IND
See series title for descriptive statement.
From The Transition 'Top Up' Or 'Bottom Up' Or Top Down Or Bottom Down Series.
Prod-RMI Dist-RMI

Square Or Rectangular Transition - Two Straight Sides (Different Size Openings) C 14 MIN
1/2 IN VIDEO CASSETTE BETA/VHS IND
Illustrates the full scale pattern layout, working from a shop sketch or one-view working drawing. Shows the best seaming method.
Prod-RMI Dist-RMI

Square Or Rectangular Transition - Two Straight Sides (Same Size Openings) C 21 MIN
1/2 IN VIDEO CASSETTE BETA/VHS IND
Illustrates the pattern layout full scale, working from a shop sketch or one-view working drawing, and shows the best seaming method. Discusses some alternative methods.
Prod-RMI Dist-RMI

Square Pegs, Round Holes C 8 MIN
16MM FILM, 3/4 OR 1/2 IN VIDEO I-H
Tells how a young cube finds it impossible to fit into the niches society requires. Describes how he finally digs his own hole and discovers his own unique way of life.
Prod-FLMFR Dist-FLMFR

Square Throat Curved Heel Elbow Layout C 8 MIN
1/2 IN VIDEO CASSETTE BETA/VHS IND
Illustrates the correct way to lay out the cheek patterns for the square throat curved heel elbow, without choking the cheek off.
Prod-RMI Dist-RMI

Square To Round - Offset One-Way Openings Not Parallel C 28 MIN
1/2 IN VIDEO CASSETTE BETA/VHS IND
See series title for descriptive statement.
From The Metal Fabrication - Square To Round Layout Series.
Prod-RMI Dist-RMI

Square To Round Transition - Offset One-Way C 32 MIN
1/2 IN VIDEO CASSETTE BETA/VHS IND
See series title for descriptive statement.
From The Metal Fabrication - Square To Round Layout Series.
Prod-RMI Dist-RMI

Square Wave Characteristics B 16 MIN
16MM FILM, 3/4 OR 1/2 IN VIDEO
Compares audio and video wave forms. Discusses frequency composition and characteristics, and time base relationships of square waves in terms of wide band pass requirements.
Prod-USAF Dist-USNAC 1983

Square, The C 29 MIN
16MM FILM OPTICAL SOUND
Portrays a serious and idealistic youth in a middle class college setting, pressured into conformity by his peers and in employment interviews.
Prod-CAROUF Dist-CCNY

Squaregame Video C 27 MIN
3/4 INCH VIDEO CASSETTE
Presents dance choreographed by Merce Cunningham.
Prod-CUNDAN Dist-CUNDAN

Squares C 2 MIN
16MM FILM OPTICAL SOUND

Presents the development of color cell processes.
Prod-PFP Dist-CFS 1934

Squares And Triangles C 20 MIN
2 INCH VIDEOTAPE P
See series title for descriptive statement.
From The Mathemagic, Unit III - Geometry Series.
Prod-WMULTV Dist-GPITVL

Squares Are Not Bad C 6 MIN
16MM FILM, 3/4 OR 1/2 IN VIDEO P
Presents a story showing geometric shapes overcoming their prejudices toward one another, and together making more elaborate shapes.
From The Golden Book Storytime Series.
Prod-MTI Dist-MTI 1977

Squaring A Block C 39 MIN
1/2 IN VIDEO CASSETTE BETA/VHS IND
See series title for descriptive statement.
From The Machine Shop - Milling Machine Series.
Prod-RMI Dist-RMI

Squash—A Series
16MM FILM, 3/4 OR 1/2 IN VIDEO H-C A
Looks at squash, the oldest indoor racket sport, covering the key points of movement, position, wrist action, footwork and tactics.
Prod-ATHI Dist-ATHI 1979

Fundamentals Of Squash - Basic Shots And
Fundamentals Of Squash - Grip/Forehand/ 010 MIN
Fundamentals Of Squash - Serves/Returns/ 010 MIN

Squashed Show, The C 30 MIN
3/4 OR 1/2 INCH VIDEO CASSETTE
Presents basically crazy cooks Larry Bly and Laban Johnson who offer recipes, cooking and shopping tips.
From The Cookin' Cheap Series.
Prod-WBRATV Dist-MDCPB

Squatters - The Other Philadelphia Story C 27 MIN
16MM FILM, 3/4 OR 1/2 IN VIDEO J-C A
Tells of the movement of poor people who live in or squat abandoned buildings in order to get places to live and to change housing policy locally and nationally. Centers on the story of a group in Philadelphia.
LC NO. 84-706368
Prod-KOPPEC Dist-CNEMAG 1984

Squeak The Squirrel X 10 MIN
16MM FILM, 3/4 OR 1/2 IN VIDEO P-I
Illustrates how an animal can learn to find food that is hidden from view or out of reach.
Prod-CW Dist-CF Prodn-BECK 1951

Squeak The Squirrel (Captioned) X 10 MIN
16MM FILM, 3/4 OR 1/2 IN VIDEO P-I
Illustrates how an animal can learn to find food that is hidden from view or out of reach.
Prod-CW Dist-CF Prodn-BECK 1951

Squeaky And His Playmates C 5 MIN
16MM FILM OPTICAL SOUND K-P
Squeaky, a squirrel, helps Otto the auto impress that one should always 'PLAY AWAY FROM TRAFFIC.'
From The Otto The Auto Series
Prod-AAAFTS Dist-AAAFTS 1959

Squeaky Clean, Pt 1 C 14 MIN
3/4 OR 1/2 INCH VIDEO CASSETTE I
Discusses personal hygiene.
From The Conrad Series.
Prod-SCETV Dist-AITECH 1977

Squeaky Clean, Pt 2 C 14 MIN
3/4 OR 1/2 INCH VIDEO CASSETTE I
Examines the structure and function of the skin and discusses acne.
From The Conrad Series.
Prod-SCETV Dist-AITECH 1977

Squeeze Cementing C 30 MIN
3/4 OR 1/2 INCH VIDEO CASSETTE IND
Tells what squeeze cementing is, how it is used and what equipment is necessary. Explores some of the misconceptions about squeezing.
Prod-UTEXPE Dist-UTEXPE 1977

Squeeze Riveting - Stationary And Portable Riveters B 15 MIN
16MM FILM OPTICAL SOUND
Explains how to select correct rivet sets for stationary and portable squeezers, and shows how to set up and use the stationary squeezer and the portable squeezer.
From The Aircraft Work Series.
LC NO. FIE52-278
Prod-USOE Dist-USNAC

Squeeze Technique, The C 10 MIN
16MM FILM, 3/4 OR 1/2 IN VIDEO C A
Demonstrates the technique first introduced in 'Premature Ejaculation.' Gives background information and explains the basic technique and two stages of therapy.
Prod-NATSF Dist-MMRC

Squiggles C 15 MIN
3/4 OR 1/2 INCH VIDEO CASSETTE P
See series title for descriptive statement.
From The Let's Draw Series.
Prod-OCPS Dist-AITECH Prodn-KOKHTV 1976

Squires Of San Quentin C 30 MIN
16MM FILM, 3/4 OR 1/2 IN VIDEO A
Deals with the workshops for adolescent delinquent boys sponsored by the inmates of San Quentin Prison. Uses cinema verite footage to capture group meetings where conversation centers on a comparison of the youths' and convicts' actions in order to encourage the boys to become more introspective.
Prod-MITCHG Dist-MTI 1978

Squirrel On My Shoulder C 25 MIN
16MM FILM, 3/4 OR 1/2 IN VIDEO
Tells the story of a squirrel who was raised in the household of naturalist-filmmaker John Paling.
LC NO. 80-706913
Prod-BBCTV Dist-FI 1980

Squirrel-Cage Rotor Principles B 10 MIN
16MM FILM - 3/4 IN VIDEO IND
Deals with laws of magnetism and induced e.m.f., electron flow in squirrel-cage rotor setting up magnetic poles which create torque, and construction of squirrel-cage rotors. Issued in 1945 as a motion picture.
From The Electrical Work - Electrical Machinery Series.
LC NO. 78-706139
Prod-USOE Dist-USNAC Prodn-RAYBEL 1978

Squirrels Are Up, Squirrels Are Down - Adverbials Of Place C 10 MIN
16MM FILM, 3/4 OR 1/2 IN VIDEO P-I
Presents both orally and visually words selected from commonly used vocabulary lists for primary readers. Engages rhyme and music to create patterns that aid in retention of the words.
From The Reading Motivation Series.
Prod-BFA Dist-PHENIX 1972

Sredni Vashtar C 16 MIN
16MM FILM, 3/4 OR 1/2 IN VIDEO J-C A
Presents an adaptation of the short story Sredni Vashtar by Saki about a young boy who seeks escape from his cruel guardian and turns to his pet ferret, Sredni Vashtar, whom he believes to be endowed with magical powers.
LC NO. 81-706018
Prod-WHITS Dist-CRMP 1979

Sri Gurudev Answers Questions C 45 MIN
3/4 OR 1/2 INCH VIDEO CASSETTE
Answers questions on truth, satsang and health.
From The Camp Saginaw Retreat Series.
Prod-IYOGA Dist-IYOGA

Sri Gurudev Chanting C 60 MIN
3/4 OR 1/2 INCH VIDEO CASSETTE
Answers questions on pregnancy, sex and meditation.
From The Camp Saginaw Retreat Series.
Prod-IYOGA Dist-IYOGA

Sri Gurudev Discusses The Retreat C 60 MIN
3/4 OR 1/2 INCH VIDEO CASSETTE
Presents Sri Gurudev discussing the importance of discipline, relating stories of God, Adam and nonattachment.
From The Camp Saginaw Retreat Series.
Prod-IYOGA Dist-IYOGA

Sri Gurudev Speaks On Buddhahood C 60 MIN
3/4 OR 1/2 INCH VIDEO CASSETTE
Presents Sri Gurudev discussing Buddhahood and answering question on the spirituality of women, the nature of the mind and recognizing a true teacher.
From The Camp Saginaw Retreat Series.
Prod-IYOGA Dist-IYOGA

Sri Gurudev Speaks On Divine Mother C 20 MIN
3/4 OR 1/2 INCH VIDEO CASSETTE
Presents Sri Gurudev speaking on the aspect of the Divine Mother in all of us.
From The Camp Saginaw Retreat Series.
Prod-IYOGA Dist-IYOGA

Sri Gurudev Speaks On Ramana Maharshi C 60 MIN
3/4 OR 1/2 INCH VIDEO CASSETTE
Answers questions on pure love, child rearing and the ego.
From The Camp Saginaw Retreat Series.
Prod-IYOGA Dist-IYOGA

Sri Gurudev, His Early Life C 120 MIN
3/4 OR 1/2 INCH VIDEO CASSETTE
Presents Sri Gurudev answering questions and telling about his early life.
Prod-IYOGA Dist-IYOGA

Sri Lanka - Jewel Of The Orient C 24 MIN
16MM FILM, 3/4 OR 1/2 IN VIDEO J-C A
Discusses Sri Lanka, a tropical island located near the southern tip of India. Shows the people engaged in gem mining, pottery production, fishing, handcrafting of tortoiseshell jewelry, rice and tea farming, cinnamon processing and the carving of various wooden masks and artifacts. Includes sequences on the Hindu fire-walking ceremonies and the Buddhist pageant, Parahera, which involves torch light parades of decorated elephants.
Prod-CFDLD Dist-CORF 1977

Sri Lanka - Second Thoughts In The Third World C 29 MIN
3/4 OR 1/2 INCH VIDEO CASSETTE
Discusses government and economics in Sri Lanka, which has moved away from nationalized farming, bureaucracy and socialism. Explains how a new government was elected in 1977 which emphasizes economic and political liberty. Hosted by Ben Wattenberg.
From The Ben Wattenberg's 1980 Series.
Prod-WETATV Dist-PBS

Sri Swami Chidananda C 120 MIN
3/4 OR 1/2 INCH VIDEO CASSETTE
Presents Sri Swami Satchidananda introducing Sri Swami Chidananda, president of the Divine Life Society.
Prod-IYOGA Dist-IYOGA

SSW Test, The - A Measure Of Central Auditory Dysfunction C 20 MIN
16MM FILM OPTICAL SOUND PRO
Shows the use of the ssw test (dichotic speech test) as it relates to diagnosing site of lesion in three brain damaged aphasiac patients.
LC NO. 73-703118
Prod-MEMEC Dist-MEMEC 1970

St Albans - An Ethnic Programme C 20 MIN
16MM FILM OPTICAL SOUND
Presents the St Albans East Primary School in Melbourne, Australia, which has an enrollment of 800 pupils, 80% from non-English speaking backgrounds. Shows how the school runs an imaginative program in ethnic languages and cultures which involves parents, teachers and the community.
LC NO. 80-700837
Prod-CANCAE Dist-TASCOR 1978

St Augustine - The Oldest City C 14 MIN
16MM FILM, 3/4 OR 1/2 IN VIDEO I-H
Presents a field trip through the United States' oldest city, St Augustine in Florida.
From The Re-discovering America Series.
Prod-COP Dist-AIMS 1973

St Augustine, City Of The Centuries C 15 MIN
16MM FILM OPTICAL SOUND
Features St Augustine, the oldest city in Florida.
Prod-FLADC Dist-FLADC

St Croix - Reflections C 13 MIN
16MM FILM, 3/4 OR 1/2 IN VIDEO J A
Discusses the river's history, resources and changing uses while meeting old Northwest traders, trappers, explorers and mountain men.
Prod-USNPS Dist-USNAC 1985

St Joan C 60 MIN
3/4 OR 1/2 INCH VIDEO CASSETTE H-C A
Explores methods of character development. Uses the play St Joan as an example.
From The Drama - Play, Performance, Perception Series. Dramatis Personae
Prod-BBCTV Dist-FI 1978

St Lawrence Seaway - Pathway To The Atlantic C 15 MIN
16MM FILM, 3/4 OR 1/2 IN VIDEO I-J A
Contrasts the forest industries, fishing trade and handicrafts business with the heavy commercial industries along the St Lawrence River. Tells how fur and lumber are found in abundance, and how cod, halibut, lobster and many other kinds of fish are caught by the millions. Explains why the source of water power provides the greatest prosperity to the area's most important industry, paper manufacturing.
Prod-EVANSA Dist-PHENIX 1969

St Lawrence University C 5 MIN
16MM FILM OPTICAL SOUND J-H A
Depicts St Lawrence University, a small, co-ed university of 2000 students located in rural Canton, New York. Explains that St Lawrence has a January inter-term for independent study.
Prod-CAMPF Dist-CAMPF

St Louis C 25 MIN
16MM FILM OPTICAL SOUND
Tours the city of St Louis, Missouri, emphasizing its historic heritage.
LC NO. 79-700400
Prod-CHROMH Dist-CHROMH 1978

St Louis Blues B 20 MIN
16MM FILM OPTICAL SOUND
Features the only film in which the singer, Bessie Smith, ever appeared.
Prod-SPCTRA Dist-STRFLS 1929

St Louis Blues B 17 MIN
16MM FILM, 3/4 OR 1/2 IN VIDEO A
Presents the only film appearance of jazz singer Bessie Smith.
Prod-CNEMAG Dist-CNEMAG 1929

St Mary's Bridge Test C 9 MIN
16MM FILM OPTICAL SOUND
Describes the vibration frequency and live load tests conducted on the St Mary's Bridge, located at St Mary's, West Virginia, a sister bridge to the Point Pleasant Bridge, which collapsed in December 1967.
LC NO. 74-705692
Prod-USDTFH Dist-USNAC 1970

St Matthews Is My Home C 14 MIN
3/4 OR 1/2 INCH VIDEO CASSETTE P
Shows Joe narrating scenes from his life near a small rural town. Describes his family's involvement with the farm.
From The Under The Blue Umbrella Series.
Prod-SCETV Dist-AITECH 1977

St Patrick's Day C 15 MIN
3/4 INCH VIDEO CASSETTE P
See series title for descriptive statement.
From The Celebrate Series.
Prod-KUONTV Dist-GPITVL 1978

St Patrick's Day C 15 MIN
3/4 INCH VIDEO CASSETTE
See series title for descriptive statement.
From The Holiday Series.
Prod-WTVITV Dist-MDCPB

St Peter's People On The Move B 29 MIN
16MM FILM OPTICAL SOUND
Explores the feelings of the people and clergy of a metropolitan

church congregation, who are rich in heritage but unafraid of experimentation, as they move from their old church to a new area of the city.
LC NO. 74-700373
Prod-LUTHER Dist-LUTHER 1973

St Peters, Rome C 3 MIN
16MM FILM OPTICAL SOUND P-I
Discusses St Peters Cathedral in Rome, Italy.
From The Of All Things Series.
Prod-BAILYL Dist-AVED

St Valentine's Day C 15 MIN
3/4 INCH VIDEO CASSETTE
See series title for descriptive statement.
From The Holiday Series.
Prod-WTVITV Dist-MDCPB

St Valentine's Day Massacre C 12 MIN
16MM FILM OPTICAL SOUND H-C A
Presents an excerpt from the motion picture St Valentine's Day Massacre, issued in 1967. Features a dramatization of the feud between the gangs of Al Capone and Bugs Moran which resulted in the St Valentine's Day massacre in Chicago in 1929. Exemplifies the gangster film genre.
From The American Film Genre - The Gangster Film Series.
LC NO. 77-701140
Prod-TWCF Dist-FI 1975

St Vincent - The Island, The Dream, The Man C 14 MIN
16MM FILM OPTICAL SOUND
Explores St Vincent Island off Florida in the Gulf of Mexico.
Prod-FLADC Dist-FLADC

Stabilization Policy - Are We Still In Control C 30 MIN
3/4 OR 1/2 INCH VIDEO CASSETTE C
See series title for descriptive statement.
From The Economics USA Series.
Prod-WEFA Dist-ANNCPB

Stabilizing Soft Sites C 9 MIN
16MM FILM OPTICAL SOUND IND
Demonstrates how wet clay building sites can be cheaply and effectively stabilized by the addition of hydrated lime before building operations begin. Points out that initial stabilization reduces expensive delays caused by bogged vehicles and the unpleasant conditions that prevail on a clay building site in winter.
LC NO. FIA65-1078
Prod-CSIROA Dist-CSIROA 1963

Stable And Safe C 20 MIN
16MM FILM OPTICAL SOUND
Reveals what frequently happens when pilots inadvertently fly marginal or IFR weather and lost their visual reference, becoming dangerously disoriented. Describes the different types of stability augmentation systems available for use in general aviation aircraft to assist pilots in maintaining control.
LC NO. 74-705693
Prod-FAAFL Dist-USFAA 1969

Stack Architecture, Subroutines C 45 MIN
3/4 OR 1/2 INCH VIDEO CASSETTE IND
See series title for descriptive statement.
From The Microprocessors - Fundamental Concepts And Applications Series.
Prod-ICSINT Dist-ICSINT

Stack Environment (S-Machine), The C 50 MIN
3/4 OR 1/2 INCH VIDEO CASSETTE
Discusses identifier collision as motivation for a stack structured environment, definition of the S-machine and control trees in computer languages.
From The Computer Languages - Pt 1 Series.
Prod-MIOT Dist-MIOT

Stacking And Firing C 11 MIN
16MM FILM, 3/4 OR 1/2 IN VIDEO H-C A
Demonstrates the correct stacking of both green and glazed pottery in a small kiln. Shows each step in firing the pieces.
Prod-IU Dist-IU 1949

Stacking The Deck C 30 MIN
16MM FILM - 3/4 IN VIDEO
Explains how individuals develop either self-confidence or self-doubt and how they learn whether or not they are competent and possess basic coping skills. Suggests how to increase confidence in children.
From The Footsteps Series.
LC NO. 79-707634
Prod-USOE Dist-USNAC 1978

Staff Communication C 15 MIN
16MM FILM OPTICAL SOUND
Defines communication, stressing the role of empathy. Illustrates the problems, faults and misunderstandings of speaker and listener in the communication process and shows how to overcome obstacles to effective communication.
From The Developing Skills In Communications Series.
LC NO. 74-712969
Prod-TRNAID Dist-TRNAID 1969

Staff Development C 30 MIN
3/4 OR 1/2 INCH VIDEO CASSETTE
See series title for descriptive statement.
From The Recruiting And Developing The D P Professional Series.
Prod-DELTAK Dist-DELTAK

Staff Development And Training C 8 MIN
3/4 INCH VIDEO CASSETTE
Orients supervisory personnel to examination of organizational environment, learning needs assessment and identification of training resources.
From The Child Welfare Learning Laboratory Materials Series.
Prod-UMITV Dist-UMITV

Staff Development--A Series
PRO
Presents training in the area of patient family teaching, by providing a quick orientation to the characteristics and needs of each age group. Demonstrates communication skills and dramatic play techniques to assist children in dealing with their feelings about their hospital experience.
Prod-CFDC Dist-CFDC

Needle Play
Preparing A Child For A Renal Transplant
Preparing A Child For An Appendectomy
Preparing A Child For Anesthesia, OR,
Preparing A Child For Herniorrhaphy
Teaching A Child About Leukemia
Teaching A Child About Nephrosis

Staff Meetings That Work For You C 19 MIN
3/4 OR 1/2 INCH VIDEO CASSETTE
See series title for descriptive statement.
From The Personal Time Management Series.
Prod-TELSTR Dist-DELTAK

Staffing C 30 MIN
3/4 OR 1/2 INCH VIDEO CASSETTE C A
Discusses the importance of staffing to the success of the organization. Gives an in-depth case study at Reader's Digest headquarters in New York that reveals the anatomy of the staffing process at a major corporation.
From The Business Of Management Series. Lesson 13
Prod-SCCON Dist-SCCON

Staffing - Developing The Employee C
3/4 OR 1/2 INCH VIDEO CASSETTE
Discusses the manager's role in the induction of employees and the importance of this process to the employee's success.
From The Principles Of Management Series.
Prod-RMI Dist-RMI

Staffing - Matching People To Jobs C
3/4 OR 1/2 INCH VIDEO CASSETTE
Explains the relationship between organizing and staffing. Relates the importance of job analysis, job descriptions, and job specifications in the staffing process.
From The Principles Of Management Series.
Prod-RMI Dist-RMI

Staffing For Strength C 25 MIN
16MM FILM - 3/4 IN VIDEO IND
Defines the effective organization as one that can make common people achieve uncommon performance. The effective executive makes big demands on his subordinates but enables them to rise to meet these demands.
From The Effective Executive Series.
Prod-BNA Dist-BNA 1968

Staffing Skills C 45 MIN
3/4 OR 1/2 INCH VIDEO CASSETTE IND
Covers sources of personnel, methods of recruitment, cost of employment, proven interviewing techniques, orienting new employees, performance appraisals, incentives and continuing training.
From The Basic Management Skills For Engineers And Scientists Series.
Prod-USCITV Dist-AMCEE

Staffing The Executive Branch C 30 MIN
3/4 OR 1/2 INCH VIDEO CASSETTE C
Explains the selection of the President's Cabinet and major advisors and the roles they play in the executive office.
From The American Government 2 Series.
Prod-DALCCD Dist-DALCCD

Stage Door B 92 MIN
1/2 IN VIDEO CASSETTE (BETA)
Depicts the disappointments and successes of the women living in a theatrical boarding house. Stars Katharine Hepburn, Ginger Rogers, Lucille Ball and Eve Arden.
Prod-UNKNWN Dist-BHAWK 1937

Stage Fright (2nd Ed) C 13 MIN
16MM FILM, 3/4 OR 1/2 IN VIDEO H-C A
Focuses on the problem of stage fright and offers techniques for coping with this fear.
From The Art Of Communication Series.
LC NO. 79-701660
Prod-CENTRO Dist-CORF 1979

Staged Reconstruction Of A Severely Burned Hand C 20 MIN
16MM FILM OPTICAL SOUND PRO
Demonstrates procedures for correcting severe burn deformities in the hands of children. Emphasizes the value of early repeated operations.
LC NO. 75-702316
Prod-EATONL Dist-EATONL 1970

Stagedoor Canteen B 132 MIN
16MM FILM OPTICAL SOUND
Tells how a soldier falls in love with a canteen worker.
Prod-UAA Dist-KITPAR 1932

Stagedoor Canteen B 132 MIN
3/4 INCH VIDEO CASSETTE
Tells how three soldiers meet three girls at the Hollywood Canteen. Stars Tallulah Bankhead, Ray Bolger, Helen Hayes, Katherine Hepburn, Paul Muni, George Raft, Harpo Marx, and other stars and Big Bands.
Prod-UNKNWN Dist-VIDIM 1943

Stages - Houseman Directs Lear C 54 MIN
16MM FILM, 3/4 OR 1/2 IN VIDEO H-C A
Studies the staging of Shakespeare's play King Lear by actor/director John Houseman and his nationally-acclaimed Acting Company.
Prod-POPEA Dist-TEXFLM 1982

Stages Of Instruction, The - Application, Examination And Review Or Critique B 20 MIN
16MM FILM OPTICAL SOUND
Explains the importance of learning by doing, of giving examinations to improve learning and to measure the effectiveness of teaching.
From The Military Instruction Series.
LC NO. FIE56-245
Prod-USA Dist-USNAC 1956

Stages Of Instruction, The - Preparation B 12 MIN
16MM FILM OPTICAL SOUND
Discusses the importance of estimating the instructional situation and checking all arrangements to insure no slip up in the classroom.
From The Military Instruction Series.
LC NO. FIE56-243
Prod-USA Dist-USNAC 1956

Stages Of Instruction, The - Presentation B 12 MIN
16MM FILM OPTICAL SOUND
Explains the elements of presentation in military instruction and the lecture, conference and demonstration methods of explanation.
From The Military Instruction Series.
LC NO. FIE56-244
Prod-USA Dist-USNAC 1956

Stagflation - Why Couldn't We Beat It C 30 MIN
3/4 OR 1/2 INCH VIDEO CASSETTE C
See series title for descriptive statement.
From The Economics USA Series.
Prod-WEFA Dist-ANNCPB

Staggerlee B 55 MIN
16MM FILM OPTICAL SOUND
Presents the famous interview with jailed Panther leader Bobby Seale broadcasted nationally on N E T. Describes Bobby's experiences in jail, his life before he was a Panther, his reasons for becoming a revolutionary and the goals of the revolution.
Prod-SFN Dist-SFN

Staging Laparotomy For Hodgkin's Disease C 17 MIN
3/4 OR 1/2 INCH VIDEO CASSETTE PRO
Uses close-up videography to demonstrate the steps of a staging laparotomy.
Prod-UARIZ Dist-UARIZ

Staging Of Lung Cancer C 19 MIN
3/4 INCH VIDEO CASSETTE
Explains the classification of lung cancer into different stages. Discusses when, how and why cancer patients are grouped according to their stage of cancer.
Prod-UTAHTI Dist-UTAHTI

Staging The Advanced Cardiac Life Support Providers' Course C 30 MIN
16MM FILM - 3/4 IN VIDEO PRO
Provides visual orientation to the logistics of staging the advanced cardiac life support providers' course developed by the American Heart Association.
LC NO. 78-706113
Prod-NMAC Dist-USNAC 1978

Stain Gauge Transducer C 9 MIN
3/4 OR 1/2 INCH VIDEO CASSETTE PRO
Describes preparation of the pressure monitoring device including basic principles of the 3-way stopcock, flushing the transducer system assembly and bedside setup prior to the connection to arterial and venous lines.
Prod-UWASH Dist-UWASH

Stained Glass C 15 MIN
16MM FILM - 3/4 IN VIDEO
Traces the historical development of stained glass from the 12th century to the present. Depicts the creation of a stained glass window from the artist's sketches to the finished product.
LC NO. 70-707849
Prod-CROANC Dist-SKYE 1979

Stained Glass C 24 MIN
3/4 OR 1/2 INCH VIDEO CASSETTE J-H
Visits two famous glassmaking studios to examine step-by- step how various forms of stained glass are created. Shows techniques for creating a pattern, cutting the glass, and fitting the lead for a stained glass window.
Prod-CEPRO Dist-CEPRO

Stained Glass - A Photographic Essay C 8 MIN
16MM FILM, 3/4 OR 1/2 IN VIDEO I-C A
Shows a young craftsman expressing his love for beauty as he makes a stained glass work of art. Without narration.
Prod-SMALLY Dist-PHENIX 1970

Stained Glass - Painting With Light C 20 MIN
16MM FILM, 3/4 OR 1/2 IN VIDEO J-C A
Examines the work of artists and master craftsmen as they design and build glass windows and lamp shades. Explores both traditional and contemporary examples of stained glass construction.
Prod-BARR Dist-BARR 1974

Stained Glass Craft C 30 MIN
3/4 OR 1/2 INCH VIDEO CASSETTE H A
Discusses the materials used in stained glass work and demonstrates techniques and processes from the designing of the pattern to soldering the cames.
From The Arts And Crafts Series.
LC NO. 81-706991
Prod-GPITVL Dist-GPITVL 1981

Stained Glass Screens C 9 MIN
16MM FILM OPTICAL SOUND H-C A
Shows the stained glass screens executed by Australian painter Leonard French for the New National library in Canberra.
LC NO. 79-709228
Prod-ANAIB Dist-AUIS 1969

Stained Glass Windows C 32 MIN
16MM FILM OPTICAL SOUND H-C A
Presents complete instructions for making stained glass windows. Includes leaded and faceted glass.
LC NO. 72-701099
Prod-PISCES Dist-PISCES 1972

Staining Blood Films For Detection Of Malaria Parasites C 8 MIN
16MM FILM OPTICAL SOUND
Explains steps in staining blood films with giemsa stain to demonstrate maximum detail of blood parasites. Shows good and poor preparations and discusses errors.
LC NO. 74-705695
Prod-USPHS Dist-USNAC 1967

Staining Techniques C 32 MIN
3/4 OR 1/2 INCH VIDEO CASSETTE
Demonstrates how to stain bacterial cells for microscopic observation, using smears made from both broth and agar slant culture. Introduces the different types of dyes and the chemical reaction involved in the staining process in addition to coverage of the theoretical bases and procedures for performing the Gram stain, Zieh/-Neelsen acid-fast stain and Schaeffer-Fulton endaspore stain.
Prod-AMSM Dist-AVMM

Stairways To The Mayan Gods C 28 MIN
16MM FILM, 3/4 OR 1/2 IN VIDEO H-C A
Explores mythology and cities of ancient Mayan Mexico and Central America.
Prod-HP Dist-HP 1973

Staking Out The Oceans, A New Age In Marine Explorations X 14 MIN
16MM FILM OPTICAL SOUND I-C A
Examines a new age of exploration in claiming the resources in and under the sea.
From The Screen News Digest Series. Vol 17, Issue 5
Prod-HEARST Dist-HEARST 1975

Stalemate B 29 MIN
16MM FILM OPTICAL SOUND C
See series title for descriptive statement.
From The Mediation - Catalyst To Collective Bargaining Series.
Prod-KOACTV Dist-IU 1964

Stalemate C 30 MIN
16MM FILM OPTICAL SOUND J-C A
Tells the story of Jeffrey Harbor who, in obtaining his champion chess status, has lost connection with everyday life and shows how he becomes reconnected.
LC NO. 82-700268
Prod-WLCHCT Dist-WLCHCT 1982

Stalemate C 20 MIN
3/4 OR 1/2 INCH VIDEO CASSETTE
Looks at the beginning of World War I and the disillusionment it caused for both sides.
From The History In Action Series.
Prod-FOTH Dist-FOTH 1984

Stalin - Man And Image C 24 MIN
16MM FILM, 3/4 OR 1/2 IN VIDEO H-C A
Reveals Stalin's power of controlling the media and the importance of creating appropriate myths about the past.
From The Leaders Of The 20th Century - Portraits Of Power Series.
Prod-NIELSE Dist-LCOA 1979

Stalin - Man And Image (Spanish) C 24 MIN
16MM FILM, 3/4 OR 1/2 IN VIDEO H-C A
Documents Stalin's despotic control over the media, secret police and the army.
Prod-NIELSE Dist-LCOA 1979

Stalin - The Power Of Fear C 24 MIN
16MM FILM, 3/4 OR 1/2 IN VIDEO H-C A
Shows how Stalin used fear to forge his workers' new world.
From The Leaders Of The 20th Century - Portraits Of Power Series.
Prod-NIELSE Dist-LCOA 1979

Stalin - The Power Of Fear (Spanish) C 24 MIN
16MM FILM, 3/4 OR 1/2 IN VIDEO H-C A
Focuses on big brother Stalin as he tries to forge for his workers a brave new world.
Prod-NIELSE Dist-LCOA 1979

Stalin And Russian History (1879-1927) B 29 MIN
16MM FILM, 3/4 OR 1/2 IN VIDEO H-C A
Looks at Russian history between 1879 and 1927, focusing on the life of Joseph Stalin.
From The World Leaders Series.
Prod-CFDLD Dist-CORF

Stalin And Russian History (1928-1953) B 31 MIN
16MM FILM, 3/4 OR 1/2 IN VIDEO H-C A
Tells how Joseph Stalin ruled Russia with terror as his weapon. Examines his foreign policy, the 1932 pact with Hitler, the great battles of World War II, and the conferences of Teheran, Yalta and Potsdam.
From The World Leaders Series.
Prod-CFDLD Dist-CORF

Stalin And The Modernization Of Russia C 20 MIN
16MM FILM, 3/4 OR 1/2 IN VIDEO H-C A
Discusses Stalin's rise to power in Russia. Describes his five-year plans to modernize Russia, including massive industrial expansion and collectivization of agriculture. Tells how Stalin's purges, especially of the Red Army, may have weakened the country, making it vulnerable to the Nazis.
From The Twentieth Century History Series.
Prod-BBCTV Dist-FI 1981

Stalingrad C 60 MIN
16MM FILM OPTICAL SOUND H-C A
From The World At War Series.
LC NO. 76-701778
Prod-THAMES Dist-USCAN 1975

Stalingrad - June 9 1942-1943 C 52 MIN
16MM FILM, 3/4 OR 1/2 IN VIDEO H-C A
Describes how the Russian industrial city of Stalingrad became a symbol of Russia's desperate and stubborn resistance against Hitler's armies until Germany was defeated and Stalingrad was virtually destroyed. It was a psychological turning point in the war.
From The World At War Series.
Prod-THAMES Dist-MEDIAG 1973

Stalking Immortality C 58 MIN
16MM FILM OPTICAL SOUND
Explores various aspects of aging with emphasis on research to extend life expectancy and ways to live a longer, healthier life.
LC NO. 79-700285
Prod-JANEP Dist-JANEP 1979

Stalking Immortality, Pt 1 - What You Can Do To Prolong Life C 20 MIN
16MM FILM, 3/4 OR 1/2 IN VIDEO H-C
Studies the vital role played by regular exercise, diet, and vitamins in extending the span of life. Considers the significance of social factors such as second careers, community health services, and active social participation by the elderly.
LC NO. 81-706986
Prod-JANEP Dist-MTI 1980

Stalking Immortality, Pt 2 - What Medical Science Is Doing To Prolong Life C 20 MIN
16MM FILM, 3/4 OR 1/2 IN VIDEO H-C
Describes medical research aimed at prolonging life.
LC NO. 81-706986
Prod-JANEP Dist-MTI 1980

Stalking Seal On The Spring Ice, Pt 1 C 25 MIN
16MM FILM OPTICAL SOUND J-C
Portrays the traditional Eskimo life of the Netsilik Eskimos. Shows a family on the shore of Pelly Bay in May and June. Shows how seal are hunted and how the man and his wife skin the seals.
From The Netsilik Eskimos Series.
LC NO. 79-706940
Prod-NFBC Dist-EDC 1967

Stalking Seal On The Spring Ice, Pt 2 C 34 MIN
16MM FILM OPTICAL SOUND J-C
Portrays the traditional Eskimo life of the Netsilik Eskimos. Shows a family on the shore of Pelly Bay in May and June. Shows how seals are hunted and how the man and his wife skin the seals.
From The Netsilik Eskimos Series.
LC NO. 79-706940
Prod-NFBC Dist-EDC 1967

Stalling For Safety C 18 MIN
16MM FILM, 3/4 OR 1/2 IN VIDEO
Reviews the principles of aerodynamics and shows how stalls and spins occur. Demonstrates the warning signs of an approaching stall and points out the recovery actions that the pilot can take.
Prod-USFAA Dist-USNAC 1975

Stallions Of Distinction C 28 MIN
1/2 IN VIDEO CASSETTE BETA/VHS
Presents the 1983 All Arabian Show at the Griffith Park Equestrian Center.
Prod-MHRSMP Dist-EQVDL

Stallions Of Industry C 23 MIN
16MM FILM OPTICAL SOUND
Depicts comedically the political intrigues and conflicting ego trips of people working in a commercial photography studio, showing how their difficulties extend to the advertising agency and the clients.
LC NO. 79-700402
Prod-KANE Dist-KANE 1979

Stamen C 15 MIN
16MM FILM OPTICAL SOUND
Presents a sensitive interpretation of a male homosexual relationship. Describes how two young men meet in the city and work out living together. Indicates the warmth of their relationship and their pleasure in one another.
Prod-MMRC Dist-MMRC

Stamp Collecting And More Blacks On U S Stamps C 29 MIN
3/4 OR 1/2 INCH VIDEO CASSETTE
Prod-RCOMTV Dist-SYLWAT 1984

Stamp Is Born, A B 14 MIN
16MM FILM OPTICAL SOUND I-C
Illustrates the creation of postage stamps in Israel. Stamps mirror life in Israel—shown are stamps with pictures of archaeological sites, landscapes and historical landmarks.
Prod-ADL Dist-ADL

Stamp Of Approval, The C 21 MIN
3/4 INCH VIDEO CASSETTE
Explores the art of metal stamping from the caveman's early discovery to modern metal treatment. Discusses the continuous research to find newer and better methods of stamping.
Prod-UMITV Dist-UMITV 1975

Stamp Out Hog Cholera (Spanish) C 22 MIN
16MM FILM OPTICAL SOUND
Shows the impact of this disease on a hog producer who gambled with hog cholera and lost. Tells farmers what needs to be done to eradicate hog cholera, and how and why it should be done.
LC NO. 74-705697
Prod-USDA Dist-USNAC 1963

Stampede Fever C 27 MIN
16MM FILM OPTICAL SOUND
A review of the various events in the annual rodeo held at Calgary. Includes scenes of the parade, the chuckwagon race, the riding and roping in the corral, and the amusements on the midway.
LC NO. 75-705260
Prod-CTFL Dist-CTFL 1969

Stamps - A Nation's Calling Cards C 19 MIN
16MM FILM, 3/4 OR 1/2 IN VIDEO
Presents various historical postage stamps emphasizing the craftsmanship of the artist and engraver.
Prod-USPOST Dist-USNAC

Stan's Secret C 30 MIN
3/4 OR 1/2 INCH VIDEO CASSETTE I-J
Focuses on a summer camper's diabetes and explains the effects of sugar on the body.
From The High Feather Series. Pt 3
LC NO. 83-706049
Prod-NYSED Dist-GPITVL 1982

Stand Tall C 30 MIN
3/4 INCH VIDEO CASSETTE I-J
Focuses on the struggle of Asian-Americans against racism and oppression.
From The Pacific Bridges Series.
Prod-EDFCEN Dist-GPITVL 1978

Stand Ups C 20 MIN
16MM FILM, 3/4 OR 1/2 IN VIDEO
Contrasts the lives of three aspiring comedians as they share their hopes, inspirations and sometimes overwhelming frustrations. Views the performers pursuing recreational interests and working out new routines in their homes.
Prod-ASDA Dist-PHENIX 1978

Stand-Alone Micro, The C 25 MIN
3/4 OR 1/2 INCH VIDEO CASSETTE H-C A
Host Ian McNaught Davis examines stand-alone word processors and microcomputers likely to be used by individuals or offices with no previous computing knowledge. Emphasizes the need for reliable software knowledge.
From The Electronic Office Series.
LC NO. 85-700734
Prod-BBCTV Dist-FI 1984

Standard Cartoon Cliches C 15 MIN
2 INCH VIDEOTAPE
See series title for descriptive statement.
From The Charlie's Pad Series.
Prod-WSIU Dist-PUBTEL

Standard Clinical Oral Surgery Instruments C 13 MIN
3/4 INCH VIDEO CASSETTE PRO
Describes the use of oral surgery instruments and illustrates their placement on a tray.
LC NO. 79-706757
Prod-USCAR Dist-USNAC 1978

Standard First Aid Multi-Media Set, Pt 1 C 25 MIN
16MM FILM OPTICAL SOUND H-C A
Presents vignettes designed to set the stage for first aid, to pose questions on critical aspects of accidents and to carry implicit accident prevention messages. Demonstrates major topics involving basic first aid skills.
Prod-AMRC Dist-AMRC 1970

Standard First Aid Multi-Media Set, Pt 2 C 20 MIN
16MM FILM OPTICAL SOUND H-C A
Presents vignettes designed to set the stage for first aid, to pose questions on critical aspects of accidents and to carry implicit accident prevention messages. Demonstrates major topics involving basic first aid skills.
Prod-AMRC Dist-AMRC 1970

Standard First Aid Multi-Media Set, Pt 3 C 20 MIN
16MM FILM OPTICAL SOUND H-C A
Presents vignettes designed to set the stage for first aid, to pose questions on critical aspects of accidents and to carry implicit accident prevention messages. Demonstrates major topics involving basic first aid skills.
Prod-AMRC Dist-AMRC 1970

Standard First Aid Multi-Media Set, Pt 4 C 30 MIN
16MM FILM OPTICAL SOUND H-C A
Presents vignettes designed to set the stage for first aid, to pose questions on critical aspects of accidents and to carry implicit accident prevention messages. Demonstrates major topics involving basic first aid skills.
Prod-AMRC Dist-AMRC 1970

Standard Food Portions C 15 MIN
16MM FILM - 3/4 IN VIDEO IND
Defines a standard food portion and tells why this standard is used and how it is controlled.
From The Food Service Employee Series.
Prod-COPI Dist-COPI 1969

Standard Operating Procedures C 16 MIN
16MM FILM - 3/4 IN VIDEO
Tells how setting up and using standard operating procedures for every operation promotes safety, sets work performance standards, curbs bad work habits and improves morale, as well as

productivity. Discusses how to set up standard operating procedures, who should be involved, what to take into account and the supervisors' roles.
Prod-ALLIED Dist-BNA

Standard Penalty Forms I C 60 MIN
3/4 OR 1/2 INCH VIDEO CASSETTE
See series title for descriptive statement.
From The Engineering Design Optimization II Series. Pt 21
Prod-UAZMIC Dist-UAZMIC

Standard Penalty Forms II C 60 MIN
3/4 OR 1/2 INCH VIDEO CASSETTE
See series title for descriptive statement.
From The Engineering Design Optimization II Series. Pt 22
Prod-UAZMIC Dist-UAZMIC

Standard Plate Count Of Pasteurized And Raw Milk/Preparation And Analysis Of Yogurt 1... C 41 MIN
3/4 OR 1/2 INCH VIDEO CASSETTE
Includes three presentations titled Standard Plate Count Of Pasteurized And Raw Milk, Preparation And Analysis Of Yogurt and Pipetting in one tape numbered 6208. Covers the standard technique for determining viable bacterial populations in both pasteurized and raw milk samples. Covers identification of general sources of milk contamination and which diseases can be transmitted to man by drinking contaminated milk. serial dilution, plating and growth of yogurt bacteria as well as an examination of some distinctive cellular characteristics.
Prod-AMSM Dist-AVMM

Standard Steels C 12 MIN
3/4 OR 1/2 INCH VIDEO CASSETTE
Covers carbon in steel, steel classification, steel color codes, spark test for identifying steels, forms of steel, hot-rolled sheet steel and other types steel.
From The Working With Metals In The Plant Series.
Prod-TPCTRA Dist-TPCTRA

Standard Techniques Of Factoring B 29 MIN
16MM FILM OPTICAL SOUND H
Shows how to simplify by factoring in forms which are quadratic perfect square, sum of two cubes, quadratic not-perfect-square and difference of two cubes.
From The Advanced Algebra Series.
Prod-CALVIN Dist-MLA Prodn-UNIVFI 1960

Standard Units And Linear Measurement B 15 MIN
2 INCH VIDEOTAPE P
See series title for descriptive statement.
From The Just Wondering Series.
Prod-EOPS Dist-GPITVL Prodn-KOACTV

Standardization - Engineering Planning C 14 MIN
16MM FILM OPTICAL SOUND
Shows an analysis of the type of engineering and technical work which is necessary on a planned basis to achieve standardization objectives in large and complicated technical areas.
LC NO. FIE60-359
Prod-USN Dist-USNAC 1959

Standardized Practices For Conducting And Interpreting Cement Bond Logs C 78 MIN
3/4 OR 1/2 INCH VIDEO CASSETTE IND
Details the theory and practice of modern cement bond logging techniques. Shows an example of interpreting a log by means of a new quantitative technique.
Prod-FENECO Dist-UTEXPE

Standardized Test, The - An Educational Tool C 22 MIN
16MM FILM, 3/4 OR 1/2 IN VIDEO C T
Examines the criteria used to select an appropriate test, the importance of maintaining standard procedure in test administration and the value of the standardized test.
Prod-CALVIN Dist-IFB 1961

Standards And Appraisal - Aids To Control C 20 MIN
3/4 OR 1/2 INCH VIDEO CASSETTE
Introduces supervisors to the types of performance standards, how they are developed and how to apply the latest techniques in appraising performance against established standards.
From The Supervisory Management Course, Pt 1 Series. Unit 5
Prod-AMA Dist-AMA

Standards And Appraisals - Aid To Control C 24 MIN
3/4 OR 1/2 INCH VIDEO CASSETTE
Analyzes a relationship where the supervisor is not doing the job of 'subordinate developing'. Shows how the use of performance standards and appraisal techniques can correct the problem.
Prod-AMA Dist-AMA

Standards For Excellence C 29 MIN
16MM FILM OPTICAL SOUND A
Demonstrates the impact of standards and measurements on American society from the time of Thomas Jefferson through the 20th century. Cites important contributions which the National Bureau of Standards has made to scientific measurement.
LC NO. 77-700476
Prod-USNBS Dist-USNAC Prodn-SCREEN 1976

Standards For Survival C 18 MIN
16MM FILM, 3/4 OR 1/2 IN VIDEO
Illustrates how the ten standard firefighting orders and thirteen situations that shout 'watch out' can mean life or death in a wildfire.
Prod-FILCOM Dist-FILCOM

Standards Of Cleanliness C 17 MIN
16MM FILM - 3/4 IN VIDEO IND
Discusses the importance of cleanliness in food service, diseases caused by uncleanliness and standards of health set by government agencies.
From The Food Service Employee Series.
Prod-COPI Dist-COPI 1969

Standards Of Performance C 26 MIN
2 INCH VIDEOTAPE A
Features James L Hayes, president of the American Management Associations, describing the value of performance standards and the various kinds of standards that can be used.
From The How To Improve Managerial Performance - The AMA Performance Standards Program Series.
LC NO. 75-704234
Prod-AMA Dist-AMA 1974

Standards Of Performance C 120 MIN
3/4 OR 1/2 INCH VIDEO CASSETTE
Describes the value of performance standards in the public sector. Discusses various types of standards that can be used effectively and how staff members can formulate meaningful standards.
From The AMA's Program For Performance Appraisal Series.
Prod-AMA Dist-AMA

Standards Of Performance And Appraisal C
3/4 OR 1/2 INCH VIDEO CASSETTE
Spells out standards of performance and appraisal relationships in a practical, working formula. Teaches how to appraise subordinates' performances.
From The Essentials Of Management Series. Unit V.
Prod-AMA Dist-AMA

Standards, Styles And Keys C 30 MIN
3/4 OR 1/2 INCH VIDEO CASSETTE C
See series title for descriptive statement.
From The Language And Meaning Series.
Prod-WUSFTV Dist-GPITVL 1983

Standby, Load-Sharing, Multimode Function, Switch, And Bayesian Reliability, Spares... B 60 MIN
3/4 OR 1/2 INCH VIDEO CASSETTE
Discusses standby, load-sharing, multimode function, switch and bayesian reliability, spares provisioning and reliability optimization.
From The Reliability Engineering Principles And Benefits With Applications Series. Pt 4.
Prod-UAZMIC Dist-UAZMIC

Standing And Ground Maneuvering B 5 MIN
16MM FILM OPTICAL SOUND
Demonstrates standing and ground maneuvers used in judo for getting into position to control and to hold or lock a combative-trained attacker.
From The Combative Measures - Judo Series.
LC NO. 75-700844
Prod-USAF Dist-USNAC 1955

Standing Tall, Looking Good C 20 MIN
16MM FILM OPTICAL SOUND
Looks at the various aspects of a soldier's life, including basic training, teamwork, obstacle courses, challenges, inspections, confidence, graduation and advance training.
Prod-USA Dist-MTP 1982

Standing Waves And The Principle Of Superposition C 11 MIN
16MM FILM, 3/4 OR 1/2 IN VIDEO H-C
Introduces, defines and illustrates standing waves and the principle of superposition. Demonstrates what happens when waves meet and how a standing wave is formed by the superposition of identical traveling waves in opposite directions.
Prod-EBEC Dist-EBEC 1971

Standing Waves And The Principle Of Superposition (Spanish) C 11 MIN
16MM FILM, 3/4 OR 1/2 IN VIDEO H-C
Explains the formation and characteristics of Standing Waves, a physics principle basic to the understanding of the behavior of matter. Shows how Standing Waves are produced by the superposition of two identical wave patterns traveling in opposite directions. Extends the principle to an explanation of atomic structure.
Prod-EBEC Dist-EBEC

Standing Waves On Transmission Lines B 23 MIN
3/4 INCH VIDEO CASSETTE
Uses animated diagrams, laboratory demonstrations and analogies to explain causes, results and prevention of standing waves in radio high frequency transmission lines. Issued in 1945 as a motion picture.
From The Radio Technician Training Series.
LC NO. 78-706303
Prod-USN Dist-USNAC Prodn-LNS 1978

Stanford Chorale - Il Festino C 27 MIN
2 INCH VIDEOTAPE
Features the Stanford Chorale performing the Renaissance madrigal comedy, Il Festino, by Adriano Banchieri. Composed in 1908, the madrigals are intended to be sung before supper on Holy Thursday.
From The Synergism - Variatims In Music Series.
Prod-KQEDTV Dist-PUBTEL

Stanislavsky - Maker Of The Modern Theatre C 28 MIN
16MM FILM, 3/4 OR 1/2 IN VIDEO H-C A
Portrays the life, the times, and the ideas of a theatrical innovator, Constantine Stanislavsky, father of 'METHOD' acting and the founder of the Moscow Art Theater.
Prod-MANTLH Dist-FOTH 1972

Stanley William Hayter - The Artist As Teacher B 12 MIN
16MM FILM OPTICAL SOUND
A documentary film which presents a brief history of printmaking and covers a visit by Stanley William Hayter to the Ohio State University school of art. Hayter demonstrates the techniques he uses to etch, ink and print intaglio plates, commenting on his methods as he works and discussing printmaking and art in general.
LC NO. 72-711505
Prod-OSUMPD Dist-OSUMPD 1970

Stapedectomy C
3/4 OR 1/2 INCH VIDEO CASSETTE
Shows how a frozen stapes causes hearing loss. Shows how the stapes are surgically replaced. Details the operation and post-op recovery.
Prod-MIFE Dist-MIFE

Stapedectomy - Causes Of Failure C 54 MIN
3/4 OR 1/2 INCH VIDEO CASSETTE PRO
Shows the technical and anatomical problems encountered in stapes surgery and their solutions.
Prod-HOUSEI Dist-HOUSEI

Stapedectomy - IRP And TORP C 59 MIN
3/4 OR 1/2 INCH VIDEO CASSETTE PRO
Shows the use of a wire from the malleus handle (IRP) and the use of a total ossicular replacement prothesis (TORP) in primary stapedectomy procedures, necessitated by incus problems (short, necrotic, dislocated), idiopathic malleus head fixation, or oval window exposure problems.
Prod-HOUSEI Dist-HOUSEI

Stapedectomy - Prefabricated Wire Loop And Gelfoam Technique C 14 MIN
16MM FILM, 3/4 OR 1/2 IN VIDEO PRO
Shows stapedectomy with prefabricated wire loop and gelfoam technique.
Prod-EAR Dist-HOUSEI

Stapedectomy - 1980 C 59 MIN
3/4 OR 1/2 INCH VIDEO CASSETTE PRO
Demonstrates the use of both fascia and perichondrium in stapedectomy.
Prod-HOUSEI Dist-HOUSEI

Stapedectomy In The Fenestrated Ear C 23 MIN
16MM FILM, 3/4 OR 1/2 IN VIDEO PRO
Shows the anatomy and surgical technique of stapedectomy in the fenestrated ear. From the original film.
Prod-EAR Dist-HOUSEI

Stapedectomy, Prefabricated Wire Loop And Gelfoam Technique C 14 MIN
16MM FILM OPTICAL SOUND PRO
Depicts a new surgical technique for the correction of hearing loss due to otosclerosis. Explains that this method has been used successfully in over 3,000 cases of otosclerosis.
Prod-EAR Dist-EAR

Stapes Surgery When The Incus Is Absent C 28 MIN
3/4 OR 1/2 INCH VIDEO CASSETTE PRO
Discusses stapes surgery when the incus is absent.
Prod-HOUSEI Dist-HOUSEI

Staple Yarn Processing Machines C
3/4 OR 1/2 INCH VIDEO CASSETTE
See series title for descriptive statement.
From The ITMA 1983 Review Series.
Prod-NCSU Dist-NCSU

Star Birth In Our Galaxy C 30 MIN
3/4 OR 1/2 INCH VIDEO CASSETTE
Explores those known areas of the universe where stars are being born and dying, and points out that the sun is expected to live for 'only' five billion more years.
From The Astronomy Series.
Prod-NETCHE Dist-NETCHE 1973

Star Class, The C 28 MIN
16MM FILM, 3/4 OR 1/2 IN VIDEO
Reviews the history of the Star Class of sail boat from its development through the 1981 World Competition at Marblehead.
Prod-OFFSHR Dist-OFFSHR 1981

Star Clusters C 8 MIN
16MM FILM OPTICAL SOUND H-C A
Uses computer animation to examine two open star clusters, the Pleiades and the Hyades, and two globular clusters in the constellation Hercules.
From The Explorations In Space And Time Series.
LC NO. 75-703984
Prod-HMC Dist-HMC 1974

Star Is Born, A C 154 MIN
16MM FILM OPTICAL SOUND
Portrays two rock-music superstars, one rapidly on the rise and the other on the long spiral down. Stars Barbra Streisand and Kris Kristofferson.
Prod-WB Dist-SWANK

Star Is Grown, A C 30 MIN
1/2 IN VIDEO CASSETTE BETA/VHS
Discusses planting fall crops. Features Chef Marian preparing a garden staple for a special dish.
From The Victory Garden Series.
Prod-WGBHTV Dist-MTI

Star Of Bethlehem C 13 MIN
16MM FILM OPTICAL SOUND P-C A
Presents the story of Christmas based on the Gospels. Opens with the holy family traveling to Bethlehem and closes with the wise men bearing rich gifts. Includes a fascinating interpretation of the story of the wise men and how they may have reached Bethlehem.
Prod-CAFM Dist-CAFM

Star Of Bethlehem (1700 - 1750) C 12 MIN
16MM FILM OPTICAL SOUND

Presents tiny Baroque figurines depicting Christ's Nativity and reflecting the simple awe and piety of the Southern Italian peasants of the 18th century.
Prod-ROLAND Dist-ROLAND

Star Salesman C 17 MIN
16MM FILM, 3/4 OR 1/2 IN VIDEO J
Uses a story about a store where stars are sold to describe the variety of stars that exists in the universe and to promote the study of astronomy.
From The Universe And I Series.
LC NO. 80-706487
Prod-KYTV Dist-AITECH 1977

Star Seekers, The C 10 MIN
16MM FILM, 3/4 OR 1/2 IN VIDEO I-H A
Uses animation to show different theories of the universe from Greek to modern times. Theories include Babylonian, Copernican, Pythagorean, Kantian and current interpretations.
Prod-FINA Dist-SF Prodn-WILSON 1966

Star Spangled Banner C 5 MIN
16MM FILM OPTICAL SOUND H-C A
Explores the nature of war. Features music by 'The Grass Roots.'
Prod-PFP Dist-VIEWFI 1972

Star Spangled Banner I C 2 MIN
16MM FILM OPTICAL SOUND J-C A
Looks at America at its best and at it worst.
Prod-MCLAOG Dist-SLFP

Star Spangled Banner, The C 11 MIN
16MM FILM, 3/4 OR 1/2 IN VIDEO K-I
Instructs young students in the words, music and importance of our National anthem. Provides a better understanding of the 'STAR SPANGLED BANNER.'
From The Singing America's Songs Series.
Prod-EVANSA Dist-AIMS 1971

Star Spangled Salesman C 20 MIN
16MM FILM OPTICAL SOUND
Presents a savings bonds canvasser training film starring Howie Morris, Milton Berle, Carol Burnett and Jack Webb.
Prod-USSBD Dist-USSBD

Star Trek - The Motion Picture C 130 MIN
16MM FILM, 3/4 OR 1/2 IN VIDEO
Tells how the refurbished USS Enterprise soars off to solve the mystery of a powerful alien force.
Prod-PARACO Dist-FI 1979

Star Trek Episode - Amok Time C 55 MIN
16MM FILM OPTICAL SOUND
Presents a Star Trek episode in which the Enterprise goes to the planet Vulcan because Spock must mate or die.
Prod-NBCTV Dist-NAFVC 1979

Star Trek Episode - Cat's Paw C 55 MIN
16MM FILM OPTICAL SOUND
Presents a Star Trek episode in which the crew of the Enterprise, pitted against a witch and a warlock, continue their odyssey after Kirk vanquished these evil creatures.
Prod-NBCTV Dist-NAFVC 1979

Star Trek Episode - City On The Edge Of Forever C 52 MIN
16MM FILM OPTICAL SOUND
Presents a Star Trek episode in which Kirk travels through time when he has foreknowledge that Hitler will win World War II unless a girl dies in a 1939 traffic accident.
Prod-NBCTV Dist-NAFVC 1977

Star Trek Episode - Miri C 52 MIN
16MM FILM OPTICAL SOUND
Tells how the crew of the Enterprise lands on a planet where the only survivors of a killer virus are children. Describes what happens when one of the children falls in love with Kirk and she and the others begin harassing the Enterprise crew.
Prod-NBCTV Dist-REELIM

Star Trek Episode - Shore Leave C 52 MIN
16MM FILM OPTICAL SOUND
Describes the adventures of the Enterprise crew as they take shore leave on a bizarre planet.
Prod-NBCTV Dist-NAFVC

Star Trek Episode - Space Seed C 55 MIN
16MM FILM OPTICAL SOUND
Presents a Star Trek episode in which warlike, though genetically perfect, barbarians, placed in suspended animation and exiled to float through the voids of space, again threaten peace and civilization until the Enterprise intervenes. Stars Ricardo Montalban.
Prod-NBCTV Dist-NAFVC 1977

Star Trek Episode - The Trouble With Tribbles C 55 MIN
16MM FILM OPTICAL SOUND
Presents a Star Trek episode in which the Enterprise crew meet Tribbles, furry animals who love everybody and whom everybody loves. Tells how the death of the Tribbles uncovers the real problem, a threat to grain stores under Kirk's protection.
Prod-NBCTV Dist-NAFVC 1977

Star Wars - Fact Or Fiction C 28 MIN
3/4 OR 1/2 INCH VIDEO CASSETTE J-C
Debates such questions as whether the USSR started the arms race in space with the only antisatellite ready for deployment, whether an ABM can make nuclear weapons obsolete and whether space-defenses on both sides guarantee peace. Includes interviews with such officials as Admiral Eugene J Carroll, Jr, former commander of the aircraft carrier Midway and Dr Robert Bowman, Director of the Institute for Space and Security studies.
From The Issues In The News Series.
Prod-FUNPC Dist-CNEMAG 1984

Star-Crossed Love C 20 MIN
16MM FILM, 3/4 OR 1/2 IN VIDEO
Describes William Shakespeare's play Romeo And Juliet and the response it received in London in the 1590's.
From The World Of William Shakespeare Series.
LC NO. 80-706328
Prod-NGS Dist-NGS 1978

Star-Spangled Banner C 7 MIN
16MM FILM, 3/4 OR 1/2 IN VIDEO K-P
Combines illustrations inspired by the words of The Star-Spangled Banner with a performance of the music by the West Point Cadet Glee Club.
Prod-SCHNDL Dist-WWS 1975

Starfish C 8 MIN
16MM FILM, 3/4 OR 1/2 IN VIDEO I-C A
Describes this familiar creature of the tidepools and reefs and its strange ways.
Prod-ACI Dist-AIMS 1972

Starfish's Realm, The C 14 MIN
16MM FILM OPTICAL SOUND
Highlights the rhythmic natural movements achieved by various sea animals as they react to different species of starfish in their natural environment. Includes the true life drama of the events that may occur when a crab and an octopus meet.
Prod-WHTCAP Dist-RARIG 1971

Starjawzs Two B 5 MIN
3/4 OR 1/2 INCH VIDEO CASSETTE C A
Shows jumbled and humorous visions of the masturbatory fantasies of a young man enjoying the privacy of his bathroom.
Prod-MMRC Dist-MMRC

Starlife C 20 MIN
16MM FILM, 3/4 OR 1/2 IN VIDEO H-C A
Traces the long evolution of a star from its birth in the depths of a black nebula to its final extinction. Explains the process of nucleo-synthesis, red giants, 'bursters,' the warping of space-time, and the mysterious 'black hole.'
Prod-NFBC Dist-CF 1985

Starlore - Ancient American Sky Myths C 7 MIN
16MM FILM, 3/4 OR 1/2 IN VIDEO
Presents five animated legends about stars taken from Eskimo, Pawnee, Aztec, Inca and Brazilian Indian mythology. Includes the art styles and music characteristic of each culture.
LC NO. 83-706748
Prod-MUAMIN Dist-PFP Prodn-HUBLEY 1982

Starman In November C 25 MIN
16MM FILM OPTICAL SOUND
Features Albert Fisher, a young cartoonist from the Midwest, who comes to Los Angeles to live with his relatives and sell his cartoons. Explains that on the way to the bus depot, he is picked up by two girls who take him to the commune in which they live. Shows Albert in the commune, imagining himself as one of his cartoon creations, namely Starman.
LC NO. 75-700482
Prod-USC Dist-USC 1975

Starpahc C 28 MIN
16MM FILM, 3/4 OR 1/2 IN VIDEO
Illustrates the operations of the Health Delivery System by following the stages of health care administered to an Indian patient on the Arizona Papago Reservation. Explains the functions of Starpahc, combined NASA and United States Indian Health Service program, and describes the use of satellites in its medical communications system. Issued in 1976 as a motion picture.
LC NO. 80-707250
Prod-NASA Dist-USNAC 1980

Starry Messenger, The C 52 MIN
16MM FILM, 3/4 OR 1/2 IN VIDEO J-C A
Presents the story of man's early study of astronomy. Traces the origins of the scientific revolution through the conflict between fact and religious dogma, culminating in the trial of Galileo.
From The Ascent Of Man Series. No. 6
LC NO. 79-707221
Prod-BBCTV Dist-TIMLIF 1973

Starry Messenger, The (Spanish) C 52 MIN
16MM FILM OPTICAL SOUND H-C A
Presents the story of man's early study of astronomy. Traces the origins of the scientific revolution through the conflict between fact and religious dogma, culminating in the trial of Galileo.
From The Ascent Of Man Series. No. 6
LC NO. 74-702259
Prod-BBCTV Dist-TIMLIF 1973

Stars - A First Film C 13 MIN
16MM FILM, 3/4 OR 1/2 IN VIDEO P-I
Points out that people have tried to understand the stars since ancient times. Explains how studying the Sun, constellations, colors of stars, distances of stars from Earth and composition of stars has increased understanding of the entire galaxy.
Prod-AFAI Dist-PHENIX 1978

Stars - The Nuclear Furnace C 29 MIN
3/4 INCH VIDEO CASSETTE C A
Describes processes which maintain equilibrium within normal main sequence stars. Outlines theoretical process by which interstellar gas and dust gravitationally condense.
From The Project Universe - Astronomy Series. Lesson 23
Prod-COAST Dist-CDTEL Prodn-SCCON

Stars And Heroes C 20 MIN
16MM FILM, 3/4 OR 1/2 IN VIDEO
Shows the diverse ways art has been used to glorify and idolize gods, legendary figures and champions. Considers the nature of heroes and why a person is elevated to a place of honor and distinction.
From The Images And Things Series.
LC NO. 73-702113
Prod-NITC Dist-AITECH 1971

Stars And Stripes C 3 MIN
16MM FILM, 3/4 OR 1/2 IN VIDEO P-C T
Artist Norman McLaren draws directly upon film with ordinary pen and ink, creating stars and stripes which perform acrobatics to John Phillip Sousa's music.
Prod-NFBC Dist-IFB Prodn-MCLN 1950

Stars And Stripes B 15 MIN
2 INCH VIDEOTAPE P
See series title for descriptive statement.
From The Children's Literature Series. No. 19
Prod-NCET Dist-GPITVL Prodn-KUONTV

Stars And Stripes Forever C 14 MIN
3/4 OR 1/2 INCH VIDEO CASSETTE P-I
See series title for descriptive statement.
From The Ready, Sing Series.
Prod-ARKETV Dist-AITECH 1979

Stars At Night, The C 11 MIN
16MM FILM, 3/4 OR 1/2 IN VIDEO P
Explains why the stars cannot be seen by day, why they seem to move across the sky during the night, and why different constellations can be seen at different times of the year. Shows familiar constellations, including Orion the hunter and the Big and Little Dippers, as well as the planet Mars and the Milky Way galaxy.
Prod-CORF Dist-CORF 1967

Stars Over Broadway B 89 MIN
16MM FILM OPTICAL SOUND J-C A
Stars James Melton, Jane Froman and Pat O'Brien. Presents musical numbers created and staged by Busby Berkeley, including Broadway Cinderella, Don't Let Me Down, At Your Service Madame, September In The Rain and Carry Me Back To The Lone Prairie.
Prod-WB Dist-UAE 1935

Stars, Pt 1 C 9 MIN
16MM FILM, 3/4 OR 1/2 IN VIDEO K-I
Discusses the twinkling of stars, the North Star, and the constellations of the Big and Little Dippers and Cassiopeia.
From The Basic Facts About The Earth, Sun, Moon And Stars Series.
Prod-MORLAT Dist-SF 1967

Stars, Pt 2 C 8 MIN
16MM FILM, 3/4 OR 1/2 IN VIDEO K-P
Discusses the constellation Orion, the Milky Way, star charts and a constellarium.
From The Basic Facts About The Earth, Sun, Moon And Stars Series.
Prod-MORLAT Dist-SF 1967

Stars, The C 10 MIN
16MM FILM, 3/4 OR 1/2 IN VIDEO I-J
Follows the curriculum in elementary school astronomy as developed by the Illinois project of the National Science Foundation. Combines live photography, animation and special effects to investigate some basic concepts about the stars.
From The Astronomy Series.
Prod-HABER Dist-MGHT Prodn-HABER 1971

Starstruck C 30 MIN
16MM FILM, 3/4 OR 1/2 IN VIDEO J-H
An edited version of the motion picture Starstruck. Describes the decision 16-year-old Alicia must make, either to follow her wishes and become a singer or follow her mother's practical example and become a bookkeeper.
LC NO. 82-706578
Prod-HGATE Dist-LCOA 1981

Starstruck C 46 MIN
16MM FILM, 3/4 OR 1/2 IN VIDEO J-H
Describes the decision 16-year-old Alicia must make, either to follow her wishes and become a singer or follow her mother's practical example and become a bookkeeper.
LC NO. 82-706577
Prod-HGATE Dist-LCOA 1981

Start At Confusion C 20 MIN
3/4 OR 1/2 INCH VIDEO CASSETTE PRO
Defines confusion and discusses the application of reality orientation as a method of regaining memory, dignity and independence. Creates an illusion of confusion for the learner to develop greater understanding of the importance of time, place and identity in carrying out daily living activities. Emphasizes the interdependence of people necessary in maintaining a sense of reality.
LC NO. 79-720267
Prod-TRAINX Dist-TRAINX

Start By Loving C 29 MIN
16MM FILM, 3/4 OR 1/2 IN VIDEO H-C A
Focuses on a mother who cannot accept the differences between her sighted and her blind child. Concludes with the mother and her two children gaining a greater appreciation for one another through the help and insights of others.
From The Giving Birth And Independence Series.
Prod-JRLLL Dist-LAWREN 1981

Start Decorating With Color And Pattern C 20 MIN
3/4 OR 1/2 INCH VIDEO CASSETTE A
Tells about the basics of good interior design and decorating, and is aimed at young adults.
Prod-KAROL Dist-KAROL

Start Here - Adventure Into Science--A Series
I-H
Escorts students on a tour through the world of science, teaching

firsthand about the fantastic powers of air, light, gravity, inertia and more. Illustrates key principles of basic science, places key discoveries in historical context.
Prod-VIDART Dist-LANDMK 1983

Air At Work 025 MIN
Amazing Magnet 025 MIN
Build Your Own Machines 025 MIN
Electric Universe, The 025 MIN
Fantastic Power Of Air 025 MIN
Invisible Force 025 MIN
Jumping Molecules! 025 MIN
Liquid Show, The 025 MIN
Make A Noise! 025 MIN
Mix A Material 025 MIN
Quick As Light 025 MIN
Stop And Go 025 MIN

Start Of A Lifetime, The C 28 MIN
16MM FILM, 3/4 OR 1/2 IN VIDEO J A
Records the first fourteen months in the life of a child. Highlights nine developmental stages and illustrates the role of experience in developing physical, mental, social, emotional and creative abilities. Reveals a child's drive to learn about the world. Based on latest research.
Prod-BCNFL Dist-BCNFL 1985

Start Of A Lifetime, The (French) C 28 MIN
16MM FILM, 3/4 OR 1/2 IN VIDEO J A
The French language version of the film and videorecording The Start Of A Lifetime.
Prod-BCNFL Dist-BCNFL 1985

Start Of A War, The C 15 MIN
3/4 OR 1/2 INCH VIDEO CASSETTE P
Gives a fictionalized account of what life was like on the eve of the Revolutionary War.
From The Stories Of America Series.
Prod-OHSDE Dist-AITECH Prodn-WVIZTV 1976

Start Of Something Special, The C 12 MIN
16MM FILM OPTICAL SOUND
Explains the academic nature and benefits of the Naval Junior Officer Training Program as an elective science in secondary schools.
LC NO. 74-705699
Prod-USN Dist-USNAC 1972

Start Sleeves C 29 MIN
2 INCH VIDEOTAPE
See series title for descriptive statement.
From The Busy Knitter II Series.
Prod-WMVSTV Dist-PUBTEL

Start The Revolution Without Me C 98 MIN
16MM FILM OPTICAL SOUND
Stars Gene Wilder and Donald Sutherland playing dual roles as two sets of twins mixed at birth. Tells how they become involved in the French Revolution.
Prod-WB Dist-TWYMAN 1970

Start To Finish - Effective Discharge Planning C 19 MIN
3/4 OR 1/2 INCH VIDEO CASSETTE PRO
Describes the role of the Home Care Coordinator in discharge planning. Demonstrates how the Home Care Coordinator works with the patient and family, other health professionals and community agencies to help the patient make the transition from hospital to home care.
Prod-UMICHM Dist-UMICHM 1979

Start Up C 17 MIN
16MM FILM, 3/4 OR 1/2 IN VIDEO A
Emphasizes what pilots and their aircraft need, after a long layoff in winter, to prepare for spring flights.
Prod-FAAFL Dist-AVIMA

Start With The World B 30 MIN
16MM FILM OPTICAL SOUND H-C A
Presents a Hasidic legend in dramatic form and explores aspects of Martin Buber's philosophy.
From The Eternal Light Series.
LC NO. 70-700966
Prod-JTS Dist-NAAJS 1967

Start-Up C 30 MIN
16MM FILM, 3/4 OR 1/2 IN VIDEO C A
Tells of the difficulties of starting a business as background to the story of John De Lorean, a former General Motors employee who started a company capable of competing with automobile industry giants.
From The Enterprise Series.
LC NO. 81-707547
Prod-WGBHTV Dist-LCOA Prodn-DORSOL 1981

Starter Inspection And Overhaul C 33 MIN
3/4 OR 1/2 INCH VIDEO CASSETTE IND
Shows how to disassemble a starter motor with a solenoid switch and overrunning clutch drive. Discusses component testing and adjustment for installation on the vehicle.
From The Automechanics Series.
Prod-LEIKID Dist-LEIKID

Starting C 15 MIN
2 INCH VIDEOTAPE K
Describes how motion needs a push or a pull to get started.
From The Let's Go Sciencing, Unit II - Energy Series.
Prod-DETPS Dist-GPITVL

Starting A Business—A Series
16MM FILM, 3/4 OR 1/2 IN VIDEO H-C A
Examines basics of new venture creation, research, understanding dynamics of business entrepreneurship, basic economic theory applications, and motivates goal setting and achievement.
Prod-SOMFIL Dist-BCNFL 1982

Are You An Entrepreneur? 018 MIN
Do You Need A Business Plan? 021 MIN
How Can You Survive Business Crises? 021 MIN
How Do You Buy A Business? 021 MIN
How Do You Buy A Franchise? 021 MIN
How Much Capital Will You Need? 017 MIN
How Will You Find Capital? 021 MIN
How Will You Penetrate Your Market? 016 MIN
What Should Your Business Plan Contain? 022 MIN
What Will Your New Venture Demand? 020 MIN
What's The Best Business For You? 016 MIN
Who Will Help You Start Your Venture? 020 MIN
Who Will Your Customers Be? 018 MIN

Starting An Exercise Program C
3/4 OR 1/2 INCH VIDEO CASSETTE
Discusses benefits of aerobic exercises to improve cardiovascular fitness. Demonstrates how 3 different individuals begin and successfully continue an aerobic program.
Prod-MIFE Dist-MIFE

Starting An Exercise Program (Spanish) C
3/4 OR 1/2 INCH VIDEO CASSETTE
Discusses benefits of aerobic exercises to improve cardiovascular fitness. Demonstrates how 3 different individuals begin and successfully continue an aerobic exercise program.
Prod-MIFE Dist-MIFE

Starting An Intravenous Infusion C 21 MIN
3/4 OR 1/2 INCH VIDEO CASSETTE PRO
Illustrates proper methods for preparing and positioning IV equipment, selecting and cleaning the infusion site, applying a tourniquet, and inserting the needle into the vein. Demonstrates method for assembling the plasma protein kit so that the solution will flow freely after the clamp is released.
From The EMT Videos - Group Three Series.
Prod-USA Dist-USNAC 1983

Starting An IV C 10 MIN
3/4 OR 1/2 INCH VIDEO CASSETTE PRO
Shows technique used in starting intravenous therapy.
Prod-HSCIC Dist-HSCIC 1977

Starting And Stopping Sounds C 20 MIN
2 INCH VIDEOTAPE P
See series title for descriptive statement.
From The Learning Our Language, Unit IV - Speaking And Spelling Series.
Prod-MPATI Dist-GPITVL

Starting Circuit Testing C 18 MIN
3/4 OR 1/2 INCH VIDEO CASSETTE IND
Shows procedure for checking starter current draw. Covers free running tests.
From The Automechanics Series.
Prod-LEIKID Dist-LEIKID

Starting English Early C 30 MIN
16MM FILM OPTICAL SOUND T
Demonstrates techniques of teaching English as a second language to children of elementary school age.
LC NO. FIA68-232
Prod-UCLA Dist-UCLA Prodn-UCLAA 1967

Starting From Scratch C 29 MIN
2 INCH VIDEOTAPE
See series title for descriptive statement.
From The Making Things Grow III Series.
Prod-WGBHTV Dist-PUBTEL

Starting From Scratch - Birth To Three Years C 29 MIN
3/4 OR 1/2 INCH VIDEO CASSETTE H-C A
Presents journalist Reynalda Muse highlighting the mental, physical, social and emotional changes in children from birth to three years. Discusses the changing needs of children as they struggle for more independence and illustrates right and wrong methods of toilet training.
From The Spoonful Of Lovin' Series. No. 2
LC NO. 82-707398
Prod-KRMATV Dist-AITECH 1981

Starting Intravenous Infusions - Part 2 C 17 MIN
3/4 OR 1/2 INCH VIDEO CASSETTE PRO
Demonstrates the proper procedure for starting an intravenous (IV) infusion.
From The Parenteral Therapy Series.
Prod-HSCIC Dist-HSCIC 1981

Starting Nursery School - Patterns Of Beginning B 23 MIN
16MM FILM OPTICAL SOUND C T
Presents an approach to reducing the anxiety of children when starting nursery school, based on gradual acquaintance with the nursery school and longer periods away from mother.
From The Studies Of Normal Personality Development Series.
Prod-NYU Dist-NYU 1959

Starting School C 14 MIN
16MM FILM, 3/4 OR 1/2 IN VIDEO K-P
Shows the activities of one day in kindergarten class. Includes such lessons as recognition, cooking and communication.
Prod-EBEC Dist-EBEC 1973

Starting Small C 30 MIN
1/2 IN VIDEO CASSETTE BETA/VHS
Looks at investment clubs. Discusses getting financial aid to start a small business. Defines some economic concepts.
From The On The Money Series.
Prod-WGBHTV Dist-MTI

Starting The System C 13 MIN
3/4 OR 1/2 INCH VIDEO CASSETTE
See series title for descriptive statement.
From The Practical M B O Series.
Prod-DELTAK Dist-DELTAK

Starting To Dive B 10 MIN
16MM FILM, 3/4 OR 1/2 IN VIDEO I-H
Demonstrates basic elements and practices in diving. Shows exercises in preparation of more advanced dives, such as the somersault, back dive, arm stand dive and twist jump. Uses slow motion underwater photography.
Prod-BHA Dist-IFB 1965

Starting To Print C 29 MIN
3/4 OR 1/2 INCH VIDEO CASSETTE
Shows the steps necessary before printing enlargements after the negatives are ready.
From The Photo Show Series.
Prod-WGBHTV Dist-PBS 1981

Starting To Read—A Series
16MM FILM, 3/4 OR 1/2 IN VIDEO P
Prod-ACI Dist-AIMS 1971

County Fair 7 MIN
Ducks 8 MIN
In, Out, Up, Down, Over, Under, Upside Down 8 MIN
One Turkey, Two Turkey 6 MIN
Picnic 8 MIN
Playground 7 MIN
Rain 6 MIN
Safety As We Play 7 MIN
Sun 8 MIN
Wheel Is Round, A 8 MIN
Wind 8 MIN
Z Is For Zoo 8 MIN

Starting To Swim B 18 MIN
16MM FILM, 3/4 OR 1/2 IN VIDEO I-H
Explains sanitary measures and pool safety. Considers breathing, gliding, floating, elementary diving and other movements in the water.
Prod-BHA Dist-IFB 1965

Starting To Work Together C 20 MIN
3/4 OR 1/2 INCH VIDEO CASSETTE
Describes positive and disfunctional roles often played by members of a group, including standard setter, mediator, dominator and aggressor when starting to work together for action.
From The Working Together For Action Series.
Prod-SYRCU Dist-UWISC 1976

Starting Tomorrow C 29 MIN
16MM FILM, 3/4 OR 1/2 IN VIDEO C
Presents a thought-provoking mix of practical suggestions, workable classroom approaches, helpful tips and a few startling ideas that every teacher can use to improve human relations and school discipline. Features interviews with such therapists as William Glasser, Thomas Gordon and others.
From The Human Relations And School Discipline Series.
Prod-MFFD Dist-FI

Starting Tomorrow—A Series
T
Illustrates teaching styles and techniques which can be used at the elementary school level.
Prod-EALING Dist-WALKED

Cycles Of Life 25 MIN
Developing The Vocabulary 25 MIN
Discoveries In Three Dimension 30 MIN
Experiments In Color
Language Of Maps, The 30 MIN
Lesson Doesn't End, A 30 MIN
Matter Of Air, The 30 MIN
New Approaches To Individualizing The Math Text
New Approaches To Reading 30 MIN
New Approaches To Social Studies
New Approaches To Spelling 30 MIN
Planning The Story 30 MIN
Reproduction And Birth 25 MIN
School's Environment, The 30 MIN
Steps To Mature Reading 30 MIN
Widening World Of Books, The 30 MIN

Starting Up C 30 MIN
16MM FILM, 3/4 OR 1/2 IN VIDEO C A
See series title for descriptive statement.
From The Case Studies In Small Business Series.
Prod-UMA Dist-GPITVL 1979

Starting Vegetables Indoor C 29 MIN
3/4 OR 1/2 INCH VIDEO CASSETTE
See series title for descriptive statement.
From The Crockett's Victory Garden Series.
Prod-WGBHTV Dist-KINGFT

Starting With The Student C 91 MIN
3/4 OR 1/2 INCH VIDEO CASSETTE C T
Uses role playing and examples to teach agency field instructors how to prepare for the arrival of practicum students, to deal with initial student anxiety and to help the students setle in quickly.
From The Core Skills For Field Instructors Series. Program 1
Prod-MCGILU Dist-MCGILU 1983

Starting Your Project C 15 MIN
3/4 INCH VIDEO CASSETTE J-C A
See series title for descriptive statement.
From The Why Knot Series.
Prod-KETCTV Dist-GPITVL 1977

Starts, Turns And Progressive Drills C 23 MIN
16MM FILM, 3/4 OR 1/2 IN VIDEO
Demonstrates starts, turns and drills for individual swim strokes and conditioning exercises.
From The Swimming Series. No. 3
Prod-ATHI Dist-ATHI 1977

Starts, Turns And Tempo C 15 MIN
16MM FILM, 3/4 OR 1/2 IN VIDEO J-C
Presents University of Alabama head coach Don Gambril discussing stroke tempo, starts and turns.
From The Swim Training - Men Series.
Prod-ATHI Dist-ATHI 1981

Starwatchers Of Kitt Peak, The C 18 MIN
3/4 OR 1/2 INCH VIDEO CASSETTE
Presents the dramatic birth, growth and death of a single star as seen through the world's most powerful solar telescope, highlighted in this film about men and women astronomers at work.
Prod-KINGFT Dist-KINGFT

State Constitutions C 29 MIN
3/4 INCH VIDEO CASSETTE
Uses the constitutions of Texas, Illinois and California to illustrate the process of state constitutional change. Includes interviews with governors, judges and members of state legislatures who discuss issues involving lawmaking, court structuring and budgeting.
From The American Government Series.
LC NO. 79-706332
Prod-DALCCD Dist-DALCCD 1979

State Government - Resurgence Of Power C 21 MIN
16MM FILM, 3/4 OR 1/2 IN VIDEO J-H
Outlines the changing concepts and roles of State government in the United States. Shows how new leaders with fresh ideas have come forth and are willing to take responsibility for meeting the social and economic needs of the states.
Prod-EBEC Dist-EBEC 1976

State Lakes For Fishermen C 17 MIN
16MM FILM OPTICAL SOUND
Tennessee Charlie presents scenic views on fishing trips on ten lakes owned and managed by the Tennessee Game and Fish Commission. On these lakes the fisherman has no other recreational interference.
Prod-TGAFC Dist-TGAFC

State Lawmakers, The C 28 MIN
16MM FILM OPTICAL SOUND J-C A
Documents an actual legislative session during which a bill is introduced and drafted to allow voters the right to decide whether or not the voting age should be lowered from 21 to 18 years.
LC NO. 73-700024
Prod-SCREEI Dist-SCREEI 1971

State Legislature C 22 MIN
16MM FILM OPTICAL SOUND J-C A
Illustrates the work of the state legislature by tracing the progress of a bill. Shows how a bill originates, is passed through the legislature and is signed by the governor. Includes a sequence showing the law being tested in the State Supreme Court.
Prod-ACA Dist-ACA 1948

State Legislatures C 29 MIN
16MM FILM OPTICAL SOUND
Dramatizes the day-to-day work of a state legislator as he experiences the frustrations and achievements of his daily responsibilities. Discusses the workings of the legislative process, the mechanics of developing and passing a bill and the effect of this work on the lawmaker's personal life.
LC NO. 77-700577
Prod-NCSLS Dist-NCSLS Prodn-GUG 1976

State Legislatures C 30 MIN
3/4 OR 1/2 INCH VIDEO CASSETTE C
Compares the Texas and California state legislatures as classic examples of state government. Illustrates the relative power between the executive and legislative branches in each state and the way they differ.
From The American Government 2 Series.
Prod-DALCCD Dist-DALCCD

State Libraries - Materials, Manpower, Money C 20 MIN
3/4 INCH VIDEO CASSETTE T
Gives an overview of what services a typical state library can offer to other libraries in the state, such as special collections and services.
From The Access Series.
LC NO. 76-706262
Prod-UDEN Dist-USNAC 1976

State Machine, The - Definition Of Input And Output Signals C 30 MIN
3/4 OR 1/2 INCH VIDEO CASSETTE IND
Introduces concept of a state machine, which serves as a description for any digital system. Tells about timing, based on a clock for the state machine. Develops notation to design input and output signals.
From The Microprocessors For Monitoring And Control Series.
Prod-COLOSU Dist-COLOSU

State Of Apartheid, The - South Africa C 13 MIN
3/4 OR 1/2 INCH VIDEO CASSETTE H-C A
Discusses apartheid in South Africa.
Prod-UPI Dist-JOU

State Of English, The C 30 MIN
3/4 OR 1/2 INCH VIDEO CASSETTE
See series title for descriptive statement.
From The Language - Thinking, Writing, Communicating Series.
Prod-MDCPB Dist-MDCPB

State Of Hawaii, The C 29 MIN
16MM FILM OPTICAL SOUND I-C A
Illustrates the operation of the state government of the state of Hawaii.
Prod-CINEPC Dist-CINEPC

State Of Seizure C 25 MIN
3/4 OR 1/2 INCH VIDEO CASSETTE
Shows that epileptics can suffer as much from social rejection as they do from epilepsy itself. Has actress-singer Ketty Lester and other epileptics helping to explore their unique problems and their progress.
Prod-TRAINX Dist-TRAINX

State Of The Art Of Sex Education, Therapy And Counseling, The C 60 MIN
3/4 OR 1/2 INCH VIDEO CASSETTE
Presents the view of the eminent pioneering educator, Mary Calderone, MD, on the impact of changing sex values and practices on individuals and family life. Makes a plea for openness and truth to replace ignorance concerning human sexuality.
Prod-HEMUL Dist-HEMUL

State Of The City C 29 MIN
16MM FILM OPTICAL SOUND
Documents the consolidation of the government of Jacksonville, Florida.
Prod-FLADC Dist-FLADC

State Of The English - How Legitimate Is Black English C 60 MIN
3/4 OR 1/2 INCH VIDEO CASSETTE
Features critic John Simon, linguists J L Dillard and James Sledd, and Dr Geneva Smitherman joining Dick Cavett in a debate over the legitimacy of Black English as opposed to standard English.
From The Dick Cavett Show Series.
Prod-WNETTV Dist-WNETTV 1979

State Of The English - Usage And Abusage C 30 MIN
3/4 OR 1/2 INCH VIDEO CASSETTE
Presents linguists, critics and host Dick Cavett discussing linguistic purity and standardization versus linguistic pluralism.
From The Dick Cavett Show Series.
Prod-WNETTV Dist-WNETTV 1979

State Of The Nation C 20 MIN
2 INCH VIDEOTAPE J-H
Looks at the state of the nation today and projects what might lie ahead.
From The American System Series.
Prod-WCVETV Dist-GPITVL

State Of The Union B 5 MIN
16MM FILM OPTICAL SOUND
Replays President Kennedy's State of the Union Address of 1962.
From The Screen News Digest Series. Vol 4, Issue 7
Prod-HEARST Dist-HEARST 1962

State Of The Union, The - Viet Nam Report 1966 B 14 MIN
16MM FILM OPTICAL SOUND J-C A
Presents the report by President Johnson to the nation on the war in Vietnam.
From The Screen News Digest Series. Vol 8, Issue 7
LC NO. 73-700506
Prod-HEARST Dist-HEARST 1966

State Of The Unions, The C 60 MIN
3/4 INCH VIDEO CASSETTE H-C A
Presents Ben Wattenberg defending labor unions by arguing they have helped make America the most productive country in the world.
From The In Search Of The Real America Series.
Prod-WGBHTV Dist-KINGFT 1977

State Of The World Report C 15 MIN
3/4 OR 1/2 INCH VIDEO CASSETTE I-J
Illustrates the opportunities and responsibilities of individuals to participate in politics and government.
From The It's All Up To You Series.
Prod-COOPED Dist-AITECH Prodn-WHATV 1978

State Political Organization And Legislative Procedures B 20 MIN
16MM FILM OPTICAL SOUND H A
Dr Gary Brazier, assistant professor of government, Boston College, describes the important process of making and passing legislation at the state level.
From The Government And Public Affairs Films Series.
Prod-RSC Dist-MLA 1960

State Political Organization And Legislative Procedures - Dr Gary Brazier B 20 MIN
16MM FILM OPTICAL SOUND H-C
See series title for descriptive statement.
From The Building Political Leadership Series.
Prod-RSC Dist-MLA 1960

State Qualification Programs For Energy Auditors C 45 MIN
3/4 OR 1/2 INCH VIDEO CASSETTE PRO
Describes the impact of federal grants provided through the National Energy Act and the Department of Energy's two-phase program to assist the states in setting up their own technical assistance programs and energy conservation projects. Explores training and qualification requirements for state energy auditors as well.
From The Energy Auditing And Conservation Series.
LC NO. 81-706435
Prod-AMCEE Dist-AMCEE 1979

State Structure And Bodies Of People's Government In The USSR, The C 20 MIN
3/4 OR 1/2 INCH VIDEO CASSETTE
Explains the basic structure of the USSR as a federation of Union and autonomous republics, equal and sovereign, in which State power is concentrated in soviets, or councils. Focuses on the activities of the Supreme Soviets of the Turkmenian Soviet Socialist Republic and the Autonomous Republic of Abkhazia. Shows local government operation in the Vasileostrousky District Soviet in Leningrad. Includes episodes from Moscow, Leningrad, Ashkabad, Sukhumi and Leontyevo in Kalinin.
Prod-IHF Dist-IHF

State University In The South, A C 17 MIN
16MM FILM OPTICAL SOUND J-H A
Notes that while universities in the South are not so large as some of the Midwestern and western state universities, state institutions still require more independence and initiative than smaller, more cohesive schools. Shows how geography influences life-style and campus atmosphere at Louisiana State University.
From The College Selection Film Series.
LC NO. 76-713109
Prod-VISEDC Dist-VISEDC 1971

State Visit Of The President Of The Republic Of Germany To Malaysia B 15 MIN
16MM FILM OPTICAL SOUND
Records the state visit of President Leubke and Frau Luebke of the Republic of Germany to Malaysia. Shows the president and his official entourage of 15 visiting Parliament House, the National Operation Room, the University of Malaya and Museum Negara.
Prod-FILEM Dist-PMFMUN 1967

State Visit To Australia By Their Imperial Majesties, The Shahanshah Aryamehr And The... C 30 MIN
16MM FILM OPTICAL SOUND J-C A
Documents the visit to Australia in 1974 of the Shahanshah Aryamehr and Shahbanou of Iran. Shows them during official functions while in Australia and also in less formal moments during their visit.
LC NO. 76-700573
Prod-FLMAUS Dist-AUIS 1976

States Of Matter, The C 18 MIN
16MM FILM, 3/4 OR 1/2 IN VIDEO H-C A
Explains the four divisions of matter - liquids, solids, gases and plasma. Points out that the division between these states may in the future prove to be less important than the unity that exists between them.
From The Physical Science Film Series.
Prod-CRMP Dist-CRMP 1973

States Of Mind C 60 MIN
3/4 OR 1/2 INCH VIDEO CASSETTE C A
Discusses today's science of the brain and looks to its future in medicine, artificial intelligence and understanding the mind.
From The Brain, Mind And Behavior Series.
Prod-WNETTV Dist-FI

Statewide Educational Computing Network, A - The Minnesota Educational Computing... C 23 MIN
3/4 OR 1/2 INCH VIDEO CASSETTE J-C A
Complete title is Statewide Educational Computing Network, A - The Minnesota Educational Computing Consortium (MECC). Provides information on MECC, an organization created by four public educational systems in Minnesota to coordinate and provide computer services to students, teachers and educational administrators.
From The New Technology In Education Series.
Prod-USDOE Dist-USNAC 1983

Static C 3 MIN
3/4 OR 1/2 INCH VIDEO CASSETTE
Researches rudimentary goals in an overlapped construction of doubt, desire, anxiety and intent.
From The Still Life Series.
Prod-EAI Dist-EAI

Static And Current Electricity C 16 MIN
16MM FILM, 3/4 OR 1/2 IN VIDEO I-H
Uses carefully performed animated experiments and demonstrations to produce a clear understanding of the causes, effects and application of static charges and their relation to an electric current and a complete circuit.
From The Physical Science Series.
Prod-CORF Dist-CORF 1985

Static Electricity C 15 MIN
3/4 OR 1/2 INCH VIDEO CASSETTE P-I
Discusses static electricity.
From The Why Series.
Prod-WDCNTV Dist-AITECH 1976

Statics B 150 MIN
3/4 OR 1/2 INCH VIDEO CASSETTE PRO
See series title for descriptive statement.
From The Professional Engineer's Exam Refresher Course Series.
Prod-UMICE Dist-AMCEE

Statics C 180 MIN
3/4 OR 1/2 INCH VIDEO CASSETTE PRO
Comes in three one-hour tapes, forces moments, resultants, concurrent and non-concurrent, coplaner and non-coplaner systems, controids and equilibrium-free body diagrams.
From The Professional Engineer Review Series.
Prod-UILU Dist-AMCEE

Statics—A Series
C
Uses classroom format to videotape one one-hour and one 1 1/2 hour lectures per week for 13 weeks and 39 cassettes. Introduces principles of mechanics, equilibrium of particles and rigid bodies, construction of 'free-body' diagrams, analysis of two and three dimensional systems subjected to concentrated and distributed loads. Covers calculation of internal forces in trusses and beams, frames and machine elements.
Prod-USCCE Dist-AMCEE

Stating A Hypothesis B 15 MIN
2 INCH VIDEOTAPE P
See series title for descriptive statement.
From The Just Inquisitive Series. No. 19
Prod-EOPS Dist-GPITVL Prodn-KOACTV

Stating Your Purpose B 55 MIN
3/4 OR 1/2 INCH VIDEO CASSETTE IND
See series title for descriptive statement.
From The Technical And Professional Writing For Industry, Government And Business Series.
Prod-UMICE Dist-AMCEE

Station Master B 28 MIN
16MM FILM OPTICAL SOUND H-C A
Presents a drama set in the Ukraine during the 1919 Revolution. Tells the story of an old railway station master who becomes a victim of circumstances when an ammunition train has been delayed because the control switches have not been set.
Prod-UWFKD Dist-UWFKD

Station, Gait And Cerebellar Function C
3/4 OR 1/2 INCH VIDEO CASSETTE
See series title for descriptive statement.
From The Physical Assessment - Neurologic System Series.
Prod-CONMED Dist-CONMED

Stationmaster's Wife, The (German) C 111 MIN
16MM FILM OPTICAL SOUND
Tells about a petty civil servant enslaved, and ultimately undone,by his lust for his sensuous wife. Shows the underlying political forces at work in pre-war Germany. Includes English subtitles.
Prod-TLECUL Dist-TLECUL

Stations Of The Elevated C 45 MIN
3/4 INCH VIDEO CASSETTE J-C A
Studies the graffiti-covered subway trains of New York City. Develops a contrast between the illegal vandalism of graffiti and the legal vandalism of commercial bill boards.
Prod-FIRS Dist-FIRS

Statistical Analysis—A Series
C A
No information available.
Prod-UIDEEO Dist-UIDEEO

Statistical Averages - Expectation Of A Random Variable B 19 MIN
3/4 OR 1/2 INCH VIDEO CASSETTE PRO
Introduces the fundamental concept of expectation.
From The Probability And Random Processes - Statistical Averages Series.
Prod-MIOT Dist-MIOT

Statistical Design Of Experiments, The C 20 MIN
16MM FILM, 3/4 OR 1/2 IN VIDEO
Explains the concepts involved in the statistical design of scientific experiments. Issued as a motion picture in 1960.
LC NO. 80-707585
Prod-USN Dist-USNAC 1980

Statistical Graphs And Measures B 45 MIN
2 INCH VIDEOTAPE H-C
See series title for descriptive statement.
From The Fundamentals Of Mathematics Series. Unit 10 Statistics
Prod-CHITVC Dist-GPITVL Prodn-WTTWTV

Statistical Independence B 19 MIN
3/4 OR 1/2 INCH VIDEO CASSETTE PRO
Defines the fundamental concept of statistical independence.
From The Probability And Random Processes - Elementary Probability Theory Series.
Prod-MIOT Dist-MIOT

Statistical Independence And Memory B
16MM FILM OPTICAL SOUND
Summarizes the rules of probability and illustrates how one of these rules is used by psychologists to distinguish between short- and long-term memory.
Prod-OPENU Dist-OPENU

Statistical Methods For Research Workers—A Series
C A
Focuses on biometrical principles to analyze and interpret research problems. Designed to create an awareness of quantitative methods used in data analysis and design of experiments. Contains 43 one-hour videotapes.
Prod-UIDEEO Dist-UIDEEO

Statistical Quality Control - Process Control B 12 MIN
16MM FILM OPTICAL SOUND
Illustrates the statistical method involved in process control as a means for obtaining better products for the government at a cheaper price.
LC NO. FIE52-1254
Prod-USN Dist-USNAC 1951

Statistical Sampling - A Management Tool C 26 MIN
16MM FILM OPTICAL SOUND
Endeavors to bring about the understanding, acceptance and the use of statistical sampling as a management tool.
LC NO. 74-705700
Prod-USGSA Dist-USNAC 1968

Statistically-Independent Random Variables B 25 MIN
3/4 OR 1/2 INCH VIDEO CASSETTE PRO
Defines statistical independence in terms of probability distribution functions. Illustrates the concept with the derivation of a marginal density function. Introduces the idea of utility.
From The Probability And Random Processes - Random Variables Series.
Prod-MIOT Dist-MIOT

Statistics - Analyzing Data C 15 MIN
3/4 OR 1/2 INCH VIDEO CASSETTE I
Shows children analyzing their own data. Emphasizes the importance of asking questions to determine the validity of statistical information, concerning the source of the information, the size of the sample and how accurately the data are portrayed.
From The Math Works Series.
Prod-AITECH Dist-AITECH

Statistics - Collecting Data C 15 MIN
3/4 OR 1/2 INCH VIDEO CASSETTE I
Shows how data can help people make decisions and why it is important to think carefully about how to collect them. Considers determining what data are needed and deciding about the sample, the method of collecting data and the delineation and allocation of tasks.
From The Math Works Series.
Prod-AITECH Dist-AITECH

Statistics - Sampling C 15 MIN
3/4 OR 1/2 INCH VIDEO CASSETTE I
Gives examples of when to query an entire population, when to sample and what to consider when selecting a sample in statistics.
From The Math Works Series.
Prod-AITECH Dist-AITECH

Statistics And Graphs, Pt 1 C 20 MIN
3/4 INCH VIDEO CASSETTE H-C
Focuses on the types of statistics and graphs.
From The Mainly Math Series.
Prod-WCVETV Dist-GPITVL 1977

Statistics And Graphs, Pt 2 C 20 MIN
3/4 INCH VIDEO CASSETTE H-C
Shows how to organize and construct understandable graphs.
From The Mainly Math Series.
Prod-WCVETV Dist-GPITVL 1977

Statistics And Probability, Pt 1 B
16MM FILM OPTICAL SOUND
Introduces the concepts of statistics and probability.
Prod-OPENU Dist-OPENU

Statistics And Probability, Pt 2 B
16MM FILM OPTICAL SOUND
Follows the axiomatic approach to probability, stressing the direct link between the physical independence of two events and the definition of statistical independence.
Prod-OPENU Dist-OPENU

Statistics And Probability, Pt 3 B
16MM FILM OPTICAL SOUND
Examines sampling distributions and introduces the concept of a random variable.
Prod-OPENU Dist-OPENU

Statistics At A Glance C 26 MIN
16MM FILM, 3/4 OR 1/2 IN VIDEO
Introduces descriptive statistics and illustrates the widespread use of statistics in our daily activities. Covers frequency distribution, normal and skewed distributions, measures of central tendency variability, percentiles and correlation.
Prod-WILEYJ Dist-MEDIAG 1972

Statistics For Managers—A Series
IND
Discusses immediately useful statistical topics. Shows statistical methods to cut costs through sampling procedures. Tells how, for example, profits can be improved by analyzing sales figures and by reducing number of defective items produced. Provides an evaluation tool to help target problem areas in sales and production and substantiate advertising claims.
Prod-COLOSU Dist-COLOSU

Gathering Info - Sample Statistics
Goodness Of Fit
Graph Is Worth One Thousand Words, A
Normal Distribution
One-Sample Testing - Product Evaluation
Probability
Probability Distributions
Regression Analysis
Testing Multiple Means - AOV
Testing Proportions
Time-Series Analysis
Two-Sample Inference
Who Needs Statistics?

Statistics For Technicians—A Series
IND
Demonstrates real-world applications of statistical methodology to help get competitive position. Includes basic understanding of experimental design and process control concepts.
Prod-COLOSU Dist-COLOSU

Choosing And Evaluating Sample Information 020 MIN
Concepts Of Experimental Design 020 MIN
Decision Making From Samples 020 MIN
Estimation And Sample Size 020 MIN
Gathering And Interpreting Data 020 MIN
Percent Defectives For Small Samples 020 MIN
Process Control 020 MIN
Shutdown Rules For Variability And The Mean 020 MIN
Using The Normal Distribution 020 MIN

Statistics Of Polymer Coil Conformations - Viscosity Of Polymer Solutions B 40 MIN
3/4 OR 1/2 INCH VIDEO CASSETTE
See series title for descriptive statement.
From The Colloids And Surface Chemistry - Lyophilic Colloids Series.
Prod-MIOT Dist-MIOT

Statistics Of Polymer Coil Conformations, Viscosity Of Polymer Solutions C 40 MIN
3/4 OR 1/2 INCH VIDEO CASSETTE
See series title for descriptive statement.
From The Colloid And Surface Chemistry - Lyophilic Colloids Series.
Prod-KALMIA Dist-KALMIA

Statue Of Liberty, Body Of Iron, Soul Of Fire C 27 MIN
16MM FILM OPTICAL SOUND
Traces the history of the Statue of Liberty, from the sculptor's conception to its completion, and describes American's changing attitudes towards the meaning of the statue.
LC NO. 74-702890
Prod-AMEXCO Dist-WSTGLC Prodn-WSTGLF 1974

Statue Of Liberty, The C 11 MIN
16MM FILM, 3/4 OR 1/2 IN VIDEO J-C A
Shows the planning, construction and assembling of the Statue of Liberty in New York Harbor.
Prod-SWAIN Dist-MCFI 1977

Statue Of Liberty, The C 14 MIN
16MM FILM, 3/4 OR 1/2 IN VIDEO P-H
A history teacher and his son visit the Statue of Liberty and learn the history and meaning of the monument in New York harbor.
From The Americana Series. No. 2
Prod-HANDEL Dist-HANDEL 1966

Statue, The C 86 MIN
16MM FILM OPTICAL SOUND C A
Shows a college professor who is embarrassed when his sculptress wife makes a nude statue of him. Stars David Niven, John Cleese and Robert Vaughn.
Prod-CINERM Dist-TIMLIF 1970

Status - Key To Understanding The Customer's Frame Of Reference C
3/4 OR 1/2 INCH VIDEO CASSETTE
Shows sales people how to recognize and interpret status symbols to understand a customer's frame of reference.
From The Strategies For Successful Selling Series. Module 4
Prod-AMA Dist-AMA

Status Epilepticus C 20 MIN
3/4 OR 1/2 INCH VIDEO CASSETTE
Discusses status epilepticus, including identification, establishment of vital functions, examination, diagnosis and evaluation of drug usage.
From The Pediatric Emergency Management Series.
Prod-VTRI Dist-VTRI

Status Of Women, The - Strategy For Change C 30 MIN
16MM FILM OPTICAL SOUND
Provides an account of a conference sponsored by the National Action Committee on the Status of Women.
LC NO. 77-702652
Prod-ARMMOI Dist-CANFDC 1972

Staunch Tin Soldier, The C 27 MIN
16MM FILM, 3/4 OR 1/2 IN VIDEO P
Narrates the story of the toy soldier with only one leg. Follows the little soldier as he falls out a window, is eaten by a fish and finally returns to his first home.
Prod-EBEC Dist-EBEC Prodn-JOSHUA 1971

Stay Healthy C 15 MIN
2 INCH VIDEOTAPE
Establishes the concept of preventive medicine.
From The Let's Build A City Series.
Prod-WVIZTV Dist-GPITVL

Stay In School C 11 MIN
16MM FILM OPTICAL SOUND
Depicts teenagers who are deciding whether to get jobs or to continue their education.
Prod-CAMPF Dist-CAMPF

Stay With Me B 28 MIN
3/4 OR 1/2 INCH VIDEO CASSETTE H-C A
Tells the story of nurse, activist and lesbian, Karen Clark, whose campaign for state representative from Minneapolis created unprecedented conditions between tenants, senior citizens, gays and lesbians.
LC NO. 82-707308
Prod-UCV Dist-UCV 1982

Staying Alive C 23 MIN
16MM FILM, 3/4 OR 1/2 IN VIDEO
Helps employees develop essential safety habits and attitudes necessary for accident prevention both in the shop and out on construction sites.
Prod-KENNC Dist-MTI

Staying Alive - Decisions About Drinking And Driving C
3/4 OR 1/2 INCH VIDEO CASSETTE J-H
Tells the story of three teens who die in a wreck after a night of drinking. Shows how drinking attacks the body systems crucial to safe driving. Explores efforts that have prevented drunk driving and saved lives.
Prod-GA Dist-GA

Staying Here C 30 MIN
3/4 INCH VIDEO CASSETTE I-J
Discusses the lifestyles and the meaning of particular social institutions.
From The Pacific Bridges Series.
Prod-EDFCEN Dist-GPITVL 1978

Staying In Character C 20 MIN
16MM FILM OPTICAL SOUND
Presents advertising man Maxwell Arnold looking at the Jack Daniel's advertising credibility in terms of image and brand po-

sition. Compares the Jack Daniel's campaign with other campaigns of long duration and illustrates how consistency in character is the most valuable equity in Jack Daniel's advertising.
Prod-DANDIS Dist-MTP

Staying On The Safeside C 19 MIN
16MM FILM, 3/4 OR 1/2 IN VIDEO I-J
Presents The Wizard of No who helps a 13-year-old girl learn to say no and to guard against dangerous strangers.
From The Anti-Victimization Series.
Prod-MTI Dist-MTI

Staying Straight C
16MM FILM, 3/4 OR 1/2 IN VIDEO P-I
Demonstrates the physical, emotional and legal consequences of alcohol and drug abuse. Explores ways to say 'no' to peers when confronted with drugs.
Prod-NORWIN Dist-FLMFR 1984

Staying Well C 27 MIN
16MM FILM OPTICAL SOUND
Features people who tell how practical rules regarding diet, exercise and stress reduction helped them reach new levels of wellness.
Prod-NABSP Dist-NABSP

Staying Well With Harv And Marv C 13 MIN
16MM FILM, 3/4 OR 1/2 IN VIDEO P
Discusses the importance of good health habits, including proper exercise, sufficient rest, good nutrition, tooth care, personal hygiene and resolvement of emotional concerns.
LC NO. 83-706242
Prod-HIGGIN Dist-HIGGIN 1983

Staystitching And Directional Stitching C 3 MIN
16MM FILM SILENT J-C A
Defines the meaning of the terms grain, with the grain and against the grain. Illustrates the use, placement and direction of staystitching and shows how to determine the desirable direction for machine stitching.
From The Clothing Construction Techniques Series.
LC NO. 77-701176
Prod-IOWA Dist-IOWASP 1976

STD Bus, The C 60 MIN
3/4 OR 1/2 INCH VIDEO CASSETTE C
See series title for descriptive statement.
From The Microcomputer Bus Structures Series.
Prod-NEU Dist-AMCEE

Ste Genevieve - A French Legacy C 27 MIN
16MM FILM - 3/4 IN VIDEO
Presents a documentary on Ste Genevieve, Missouri, a small French town on the Mississippi, marked by a prosperous and advanced civilization in the early 1700'S. Illustrates that it is now a national historic site, yet the community retains its legacy from the past.
From The Synergism - Cities And Towns Series.
Prod-KETCTV Dist-PUBTEL

Steadfast Tin Soldier C 14 MIN
16MM FILM OPTICAL SOUND K-I
Hans Christian Andersen's well-known fairy story is dramatized with bright colored dolls and a delightful musical score.
Prod-CAP Dist-TEXFLM 1955

Steady As She Goes C 27 MIN
16MM FILM, 3/4 OR 1/2 IN VIDEO
Focuses on John Fulfit, a 70-year-old retired Canadian who indulges his childhood yearning to go to the sea by crafting rigged ships in bottles. Shows him working at his craft as he sings chanteys and philosophically converses with the camera. Employs archival stills to compare his work to actual vessel construction.
LC NO. 82-707032
Prod-NFBC Dist-NFBC 1982

Steady Rain, A C 25 MIN
16MM FILM OPTICAL SOUND
Tells how an eight-year-old boy witnesses a murder while looking through a window and comes to grips with the stormy events of his family's life.
LC NO. 80-700220
Prod-MLP Dist-MLP 1979

Steady State Availability Applications, Availability Improvement Considerations,... B 60 MIN
3/4 OR 1/2 INCH VIDEO CASSETTE
Treats steady state availability applications, availability improvement considerations, maintainability-cost considerations, and cost benefits from the implementation of reliability and maintainability engineering.
From The Maintainability, Operational Availability And Preventive Maintenance Of...Series. Pt 5
Prod-UAZMIC Dist-UAZMIC 1981

Steady State LQG Problem - Continuous-Time Case, The C 68 MIN
3/4 OR 1/2 INCH VIDEO CASSETTE PRO
See series title for descriptive statement.
From The Modern Control Theory - Stochastic Control Series.
Prod-MIOT Dist-MIOT

Steady State Power Flow 1 C
3/4 OR 1/2 INCH VIDEO CASSETTE IND
Includes power demand and supply, synchronism, phase angle limits, load transfer and per unit examples.
From The Electric Power System Operation Series. Tape 6
Prod-LEIKID Dist-LEIKID

Steady State Power Flow 2 C
3/4 OR 1/2 INCH VIDEO CASSETTE IND
Covers division of power flow, load flow examples, base case, effect of outages and distribution factors.
From The Electric Power System Operation Series. Tape 7
Prod-LEIKID Dist-LEIKID

Steady State Theory Computer Programs-Helicopter Example C 57 MIN
3/4 OR 1/2 INCH VIDEO CASSETTE PRO
See series title for descriptive statement.
From The Modern Control Theory - Stochastic Control Series.
Prod-MIOT Dist-MIOT

Steady State Voltage Control C
3/4 OR 1/2 INCH VIDEO CASSETTE IND
Includes voltage control by generators, control by transformers, distribution system voltage, transmission system voltage and case studies.
From The Electric Power System Operation Series. Tape 8
Prod-LEIKID Dist-LEIKID

Steady-State Kalman Filter - Discrete-Time Case C 43 MIN
3/4 OR 1/2 INCH VIDEO CASSETTE PRO
See series title for descriptive statement.
From The Modern Control Theory - Stochastic Estimation Series.
Prod-MIOT Dist-MIOT

Steady-State Kalman-Bucy Filter - Continuous-Time Case C 48 MIN
3/4 OR 1/2 INCH VIDEO CASSETTE PRO
See series title for descriptive statement.
From The Modern Control Theory - Stochastic Estimation Series.
Prod-MIOT Dist-MIOT

Steady-State Linear Regulator Problem For Constant Disturbances, The C 70 MIN
3/4 OR 1/2 INCH VIDEO CASSETTE PRO
See series title for descriptive statement.
From The Modern Control Theory - Deterministic Optimal Linear Feedback Series.
Prod-MIOT Dist-MIOT

Steady-State Linear-Quadratic Problem With Deterministic Disturbances C 41 MIN
3/4 OR 1/2 INCH VIDEO CASSETTE PRO
See series title for descriptive statement.
From The Modern Control Theory - Deterministic Optimal Linear Feedback Series.
Prod-MIOT Dist-MIOT

Steady-State Linear-Quadratic Problem, The - Continuous-Time Case C 51 MIN
3/4 OR 1/2 INCH VIDEO CASSETTE PRO
See series title for descriptive statement.
From The Modern Control Theory - Deterministic Optimal Linear Feedback Series.
Prod-MIOT Dist-MIOT

Steady-State Linear-Quadratic Problem, The - Discrete Time Case C 38 MIN
3/4 OR 1/2 INCH VIDEO CASSETTE PRO
See series title for descriptive statement.
From The Modern Control Theory - Deterministic Optimal Linear Feedback Series.
Prod-MIOT Dist-MIOT

Stealing C 12 MIN
16MM FILM, 3/4 OR 1/2 IN VIDEO I-J
Presents principles of honesty through the story of Johnny, a newspaper boy. Focuses on the moral issues which affect one's decision to steal.
From The Moral Decision Making Series.
Prod-MORLAT Dist-AIMS 1971

Steam C 5 MIN
16MM FILM OPTICAL SOUND
Examines the history and action of steam engines.
LC NO. 74-702768
Prod-SUNDEW Dist-CANFDC 1973

Steam And Gas Safety Valves C 60 MIN
3/4 OR 1/2 INCH VIDEO CASSETTE IND
See series title for descriptive statement.
From The Mechanical Equipment Maintenance, Module 14 - Relief Valves Series.
Prod-LEIKID Dist-LEIKID

Steam And Water Recovery And Effluent Treatment C
3/4 OR 1/2 INCH VIDEO CASSETTE IND
Demonstrates the typical white water loop throughout the mill. Reviews the changes in consistency that take place in the loop. Discusses heat recovery systems. Looks at the treatment and pollution control of effluent discharges from the process.
From The Pulp And Paper Training - Thermo-Mechanical Pulping Series.
Prod-LEIKID Dist-LEIKID

Steam Cooking Equipment C 20 MIN
1/2 IN VIDEO CASSETTE BETA/VHS
Provides operation and safety tips on using two standard steam cookers, a Vischer jet cooker and a steam jacketed kettle.
Prod-RMI Dist-RMI

Steam Engine And Turbine, The B 20 MIN
2 INCH VIDEOTAPE I
See series title for descriptive statement.
From The Science Room Series.
Prod-MCETV Dist-GPITVL Prodn-WVIZTV

Steam Engine Comes To The Farm, The C 15 MIN
16MM FILM, 3/4 OR 1/2 IN VIDEO I
Shows the inner workings of a steam engine and shows how it was used to power dozens of machines that planted, cultivated and harvested crops.
From The American Scrapbook Series.
Prod-WVIZTV Dist-GPITVL 1977

Steam Shovel C 7 MIN
16MM FILM OPTICAL SOUND
Studies the mysterious, comic and beautiful aspects of mechanical works of man. Features a 1920 2-B Eire steam shovel, a supporting cast of Model T's and curious onlookers.
LC NO. 75-703119
Prod-KOESTR Dist-KOESTR 1975

Steam Sterilization C 25 MIN
3/4 INCH VIDEO CASSETTE PRO
Discusses and demonstrates the procedures involved in the steam sterilization of medical instruments and supplies. Covers steam penetration, air pockets, temperature monitoring, and cleaning of sterilizers.
LC NO. 79-707311
Prod-USVA Dist-USNAC 1977

Steam Train Passes, A C 21 MIN
16MM FILM OPTICAL SOUND H-C A
Recreates the era of steam locomotion in Australia.
LC NO. 75-704207
Prod-FLMAUS Dist-AUIS 1974

Steam Traps - Operation And Maintenance C 18 MIN
3/4 OR 1/2 INCH VIDEO CASSETTE
Trains operating and maintenance personnel to identify and correct malfunctioning steam traps. Gives an inside view of steam traps in actual operation, as well as a descriptive walk-through of testing procedures and corrective actions.
Prod-AHOA Dist-AHOA 1980

Steam Turbine Operation C 60 MIN
3/4 OR 1/2 INCH VIDEO CASSETTE IND
Identifies the major parts of the steam turbine. Describes how an impulse steam turbine operates. Covers periodic operational check and reading temperature and pressure gauges.
From The Equipment Operation Training Program Series.
Prod-LEIKID Dist-LEIKID

Steam Turbine Operations C 60 MIN
3/4 OR 1/2 INCH VIDEO CASSETTE IND
Identifies the major parts of a steam turbine and tells how it operates. Highlights performing periodic operational checks.
From The Equipment Operation Training Program Series.
Prod-ITCORP Dist-ITCORP

Steamboat C 11 MIN
16MM FILM, 3/4 OR 1/2 IN VIDEO K-I
Presents a nonverbal exploration of the Delta Queen steamboat, the oldest overnight paddle wheeler on the Mississippi River, presented from a child's viewpoint. Records the actual sound of the boat's operations, combined with steam piano and river songs.
Prod-LSP Dist-LRF 1976

Steamboat - I Like It Here C 20 MIN
16MM FILM OPTICAL SOUND
Describes the friendliness, warmth and fun of Steamboat Ski Area, a resort in Steamboat Springs, Colorado.
LC NO. 80-701486
Prod-STEAMB Dist-STEAMB Prodn-GRIAKW 1980

Steamboat Bill C 11 MIN
16MM FILM, 3/4 OR 1/2 IN VIDEO I
Describes the exploits of Steamboat Bill, the famous riverboat captain.
From The American Folklore Series.
Prod-HRAW Dist-PHENIX 1971

Steamboat Bill Jr B 71 MIN
16MM FILM SILENT
Tells the story of riverboat owner Steamboat Bill who must battle his rival JJ King for control of the river's shipping lanes. Relates Bill's initial excitement when his son comes to visit him, anticipating an ally in the battle. Shows what happens when Junior turns out to be a moustachioed, ukelele-playing shrimp in college clothes. Stars Buster Keaton. Directed by Charles F Reisner.
Prod-FOXFC Dist-KILLIS 1928

Steamboat On The River C 18 MIN
16MM FILM, 3/4 OR 1/2 IN VIDEO I-C A
Describes the use of steamboats through history.
Prod-IFB Dist-IFB 1965

Steamboat Willie B 8 MIN
16MM FILM, 3/4 OR 1/2 IN VIDEO K-H
Presents Mickey Mouse as a crew member on a riverboat captained by Big Bad Pete. Features Minnie Mouse as another passenger who joins Mickey as he uses various props as musical instruments.
From The Mickey Mouse - The Early Years Series.
Prod-DISNEY Dist-WDEMCO 1978

Steamfitting - Cast Iron Boiler Assembly C 13 MIN
16MM FILM, 3/4 OR 1/2 IN VIDEO H-C A
Shows a two-man operation in boiler assembly. Discusses layout of section, base level and square, preparing push-nipples and locations, graphite and methods to ensure an even pull-up all around.
Prod-SF Dist-SF 1969

Steamfitting - Making A Welded Y-Joint C 13 MIN
16MM FILM, 3/4 OR 1/2 IN VIDEO H-C A
Explains how to make a welded Y-joint, including quartering, laying on template or marking pipe and branch, mitre and radial cutting with oxyacetylene torch, pre-heating, alignment and welding.
Prod-SF Dist-SF 1969

Steamfitting - Pipe Bending Techniques C 13 MIN
16MM FILM, 3/4 OR 1/2 IN VIDEO J A

Discusses pipe bending techniques, including measurement allowances, hydraulic bending equipment and bending operations. Covers heat bend, heating methods, heated areas and various applications.
Prod-SF Dist-SF 1969

Steel - Pretty, Design, Nice C 8 MIN
16MM FILM OPTICAL SOUND
Presents a free form look at steel in a myriad of applications - in art, in construction and in the home.
LC NO. 79-705671
Prod-AIAS Dist-AIAS Prodn-TTP 1969

Steel - The Metal Giant C 20 MIN
16MM FILM OPTICAL SOUND
Follows the steel-making process starting with the mining of taconite, limestone and coal, and proceding to the blast furnace and the casting, shaping and rolling of molten steel.
Prod-AIAS Dist-MTP

Steel - The Metal Giant C 12 MIN
16MM FILM, 3/4 OR 1/2 IN VIDEO I-J
Shows how steel is made.
LC NO. 81-707381
Prod-CENTEF Dist-CORF 1981

Steel And America - A New Look C 29 MIN
16MM FILM, 3/4 OR 1/2 IN VIDEO I-H
Donald Duck, as an old-time iron master, sword maker and scientist, dramatizes the story of steel from prehistoric times to the present. The theme of the partnership of America and steel is presented.
Prod-DISNEY Dist-WDEMCO

Steel And America - A New Look (Danish) C 29 MIN
16MM FILM, 3/4 OR 1/2 IN VIDEO I-H
Dramatizes the story of steel from prehistoric times to the present. Hosted by Donald Duck.
Prod-WDEMCO Dist-WDEMCO

Steel And America - A New Look (Spanish) C 29 MIN
16MM FILM, 3/4 OR 1/2 IN VIDEO I-H
Dramatizes the story of steel from prehistoric times to the present. Hosted by Donald Duck.
Prod-WDEMCO Dist-WDEMCO

Steel And America - A New Look (Swedish) C 29 MIN
16MM FILM, 3/4 OR 1/2 IN VIDEO I-H
Dramatizes the story of steel from prehistoric times to the present. Hosted by Donald Duck.
Prod-WDEMCO Dist-WDEMCO

Steel Drum Band C 29 MIN
3/4 INCH VIDEO CASSETTE
Covers the story of the conversion of the common oil drum into a sophisticated musical instrument. Features the Trinidad Tripoli Steel Drum Band.
Prod-UMITV Dist-UMITV 1976

Steel From Inland C 28 MIN
16MM FILM OPTICAL SOUND
Shows how iron ore, coal and limestone become steel at Inland Steel Company's Indiana Harbor Works at East Chicago, Indiana. Offers a close look at some of the new production and environmental technology that has changed the complexion of steelmaking.
Prod-INLSTL Dist-MTP 1982

Steel In Space C 30 MIN
3/4 OR 1/2 INCH VIDEO CASSETTE
Shows the shop fabrication and erection of the 600-foot tower with revolving restaurant, containing 3,700 tons of structural steel, for the Space Needle located at the Seattle World's Fair.
Prod-PACARF Dist-MPS

Steel Industry C 3 MIN
16MM FILM OPTICAL SOUND P-I
Discusses the steel industry.
From The Of All Things Series.
Prod-BAILYL Dist-AVED

Steel Lives Here C 15 MIN
16MM FILM OPTICAL SOUND IND
Illustrates designs and uses of steel for use in the building of homes.
LC NO. FIA68-120
Prod-AIAS Dist-AIAS Prodn-BASFRD 1968

Steel Making—A Series
IND
Describes a variety of operator tasks, and outlines the operation and maintenance procedures for specific machines related to the steel making process. Discusses safety practices.
Prod-LEIKID Dist-LEIKID

Back Care Basics	008 MIN
Ball Mill Forge	005 MIN
Blast Furnace Gas Hazards	007 MIN
Bloom And Billet Mill - Personal Safety	007 MIN
Coke Oven Sideman	006 MIN
Coke Ovens Door Machine	008 MIN
Continuous Wire Drawing Machine	010 MIN
Drop Forge Die Set Up	013 MIN
Fire Extinguishers - The First Minute Counts	010 MIN
Five Stand Scrap Man, The	013 MIN
Follow That Slab	008 MIN
Fowl Deed	008 MIN
General Safety - Steel Making	006 MIN
Guidesetting	014 MIN
Hand Traps	010 MIN
Hoist Safety	007 MIN
Hot Shear Laborer, The	006 MIN
It Only Takes A Minute (Rolling Mill)	006 MIN
Lift Truck Safety	012 MIN
Operating The Pendant Crane	007 MIN
Operation Of An Oxy-Fuel Gas Heating Torch	014 MIN
Rod Mill Trimmers	005 MIN
Roll Threading Setup Procedures	014 MIN
Safe Handling Of Oxy Fuel Gas Heating	014 MIN
Safety	006 MIN
Scarfing Safely	007 MIN
Shipping Hooker, The	008 MIN
Strapping Machine Operator (Rod Mill)	010 MIN
Strapping Machine Troubleshooting (Rod Mill)	008 MIN
Torch Safety	013 MIN
Working With Chains	005 MIN
Working With Lead	014 MIN

Steel On The Rouge C 19 MIN
16MM FILM, 3/4 OR 1/2 IN VIDEO J-C A
Shows the processes involved in making steel.
Prod-FMCMP Dist-FORDFL 1968

Steel Plus B 40 MIN
16MM FILM OPTICAL SOUND C
Shows the conversion of steel from the open hearth furnace into sheets and thence into tinplate by the hot-dipping process.
Prod-BFI Dist-HEFL 1952

Steel Rule (Spanish) B 14 MIN
16MM FILM, 3/4 OR 1/2 IN VIDEO
Discusses the variations found in steel rules, the types of scales found on them and their proper usage. Shows the procedure for transferring measurements by means of calipers and dividers.
From The Machine Shop Work Series.
Prod-USOE Dist-USNAC 1941

Steel Rule, The B 14 MIN
16MM FILM - 3/4 IN VIDEO
Shows how to read steel rules, use flexible hook and rule type gages, lay out holes with a combination square and scribe them with a divider. Demonstrates the use of inside and outside calipers to transfer dimensions to and from steel rules. Issued in 1941 as a motion picture.
From The Machine Shop Work - Precision Measurement Series. No. 1
LC NO. 79-707078
Prod-USOE Dist-USNAC Prodn-LNS 1979

Steel Town B 17 MIN
16MM FILM, 3/4 OR 1/2 IN VIDEO
Shows the steel mills, blast furnaces and lives of the steelworkers in Youngstown, Ohio. Issued in 1944 as a motion picture.
From The American Scene Series. No. 4
LC NO. 79-706480
Prod-USOWI Dist-USNAC 1979

Steelcase Unitrol C 6 MIN
16MM FILM OPTICAL SOUND
Shows the internal working components and operation of a swivel-tilt control mechanism for office chairs.
LC NO. 80-700221
Prod-STEEL Dist-STEEL Prodn-NEWCOM 1979

Steelhead River C 13 MIN
16MM FILM OPTICAL SOUND J-C A
Pictures the Steelhead River inhabited by the steelhead trout. Provides a preview of the kind of sport fishermen can expect when they visit Vancouver Island.
LC NO. 73-700896
Prod-NFBC Dist-CTFL 1968

Steelmakers C 28 MIN
16MM FILM OPTICAL SOUND
Offers a picture of the Bethlehem Steel Corporation, based on comments by its employees.
LC NO. 77-701455
Prod-BSC Dist-MTP Prodn-VISION 1976

Steelyard Blues C 92 MIN
16MM FILM OPTICAL SOUND
Tells how a bunch of social misfits escape to a utopian society.
Prod-WB Dist-TWYMAN 1973

Steep And Thorny Path, A C 30 MIN
3/4 OR 1/2 INCH VIDEO CASSETTE
Introduces the viewer to the definition of 'less developed country.' Explores the many problems encountered when such a country seeks growth.
From The Money Puzzle - The World Of Macroeconomics Series. Module 13
Prod-MDCC Dist-MDCC

Steepest Descent Method, The C 45 MIN
3/4 OR 1/2 INCH VIDEO CASSETTE PRO
Describes the simple digital computer algorithm to solve deterministic optimal control problems. Comes as package of two videotapes.
From The Modern Control Theory - Deterministic Optimal Control Series.
Prod-MIOT Dist-MIOT

Steer Clear C 20 MIN
3/4 OR 1/2 INCH VIDEO CASSETTE
Addresses the issues of chemically impaired driving. Demonstrates the effects of alcohol and marijuana on driving skills.
Prod-WHITEG Dist-WHITEG

Steer Wrestling Clinic C 30 MIN
1/2 IN VIDEO CASSETTE BETA/VHS
Demonstrates moves involved in steer wrestling.
From The Western Training Series.
Prod-EQVDL Dist-EQVDL

Steer Wrestling Techniques C 30 MIN
1/2 IN VIDEO CASSETTE BETA/VHS
Illustrates methods of winning steer wrestling.
From The Western Training Series.
Prod-EQVDL Dist-EQVDL

Steering Clear Of Lemons C 16 MIN
16MM FILM OPTICAL SOUND
Presents a consumer education film, providing information on product evaluation, buying, product safety and the role of Government, as seen through seven specific reports on diet foods, fair trade laws, stereos, pain relievers, 10-speed bikes, grade labeling of beef and aerosols.
From The Consumer Reports Series.
LC NO. 75-703537
Prod-CU Dist-CU 1975

Steering, Wheels, Front And Rear Axles B 19 MIN
16MM FILM OPTICAL SOUND
Discusses how to check for play in the steering wheel and the front end assembly, correct wheel runout, make a toe-in test and test springs, axles and overall backlash.
LC NO. FIE52-362
Prod-USOE Dist-USNAC 1945

Steffan The Violinmaker C 25 MIN
16MM FILM, 3/4 OR 1/2 IN VIDEO I-J A
Introduces Steffan, a West German boy who is carrying on a family tradition and becoming a violinmaker. Shows the gluing, oiling and toning process necessary to making a violin.
From The World Cultures And Youth Series.
LC NO. 80-706675
Prod-SUNRIS Dist-CORF 1980

Steichen - A Century In Photography C 60 MIN
3/4 OR 1/2 INCH VIDEO CASSETTE
Profiles the life and work of the late Edward Steichen one of the foremost photographers in the history of the art.
Prod-WXXITV Dist-PBS 1980

Steina Vasulka - Bad C 2 MIN
3/4 OR 1/2 INCH VIDEO CASSETTE
Involves the subjective framing of space.
Prod-ARTINC Dist-ARTINC

Steina Vasulka - Cantaloup C 28 MIN
3/4 OR 1/2 INCH VIDEO CASSETTE
Involves the subjective framing of space.
Prod-ARTINC Dist-ARTINC

Steina Vasulka - Let It Be B 4 MIN
3/4 OR 1/2 INCH VIDEO CASSETTE
Involves the subjective framing of space.
Prod-ARTINC Dist-ARTINC

Steina Vasulka - Selected Treecuts C 9 MIN
3/4 OR 1/2 INCH VIDEO CASSETTE
Involves the subjective framing of space.
Prod-ARTINC Dist-ARTINC

Steina Vasulka - Summer Salt C 18 MIN
3/4 OR 1/2 INCH VIDEO CASSETTE
Deals with the subjective framing of space.
Prod-ARTINC Dist-ARTINC

Steina Vasulka - Urban Episodes C 9 MIN
3/4 OR 1/2 INCH VIDEO CASSETTE
Involves the subjective framing of space.
Prod-ARTINC Dist-ARTINC

Steinberg (Born 1914) B 14 MIN
16MM FILM OPTICAL SOUND
Presents cartoonist Steinbeck's clever, nervous, mocking line as the camera jumps and circles around his witty drawings that so precisely lay bare all our solemn lunacies.
Prod-ROLAND Dist-ROLAND

Steinitz Style, The C 30 MIN
2 INCH VIDEOTAPE
See series title for descriptive statement.
From The Koltanowski On Chess Series.
Prod-KQEDTV Dist-PUBTEL

Stem Is Gone, The C 29 MIN
2 INCH VIDEOTAPE
See series title for descriptive statement.
From The Skiing Series.
Prod-KTCATV Dist-PUBTEL

Stensen's Duct - Key To Parotidectomy C 32 MIN
16MM FILM OPTICAL SOUND PRO
Depicts embryologic and anatomic information significant for parotidectomy. Presents four cases illustrating techniques of dissection and hemostasis. Stresses Stensen's duct as the easiest surgical approach to the parotid and the facial nerve.
Prod-ACYDGD Dist-ACY 1962

Step A Little Higher C 18 MIN
16MM FILM, 3/4 OR 1/2 IN VIDEO H-C A
Depicts the problems facing a functional illiterate as portrayed in the experiences and feelings of two men who never learned to read well. Shows how the adult reading center of the library aided these men.
Prod-CLEVPL Dist-FEIL Prodn-FEIL 1966

Step Aside, Step Down C 20 MIN
16MM FILM, 3/4 OR 1/2 IN VIDEO
Reports on the problems of aging in America, such as income, housing, nutrition and transportation. Shows successful private and government programs aimed at solving them.
LC NO. 81-706342
Prod-USSRS Dist-USNAC 1971

Step Behind—A Series

Demonstrates behavior modification and shows parents of the retarded how to practice behavior modification in the home.
Prod-HALLFM Dist-HALLFM

Ask Just For Little Things 20 MIN
Genesis 25 MIN
I'll Promise You A Tomorrow 20 MIN

Step By Step C 15 MIN
16MM FILM OPTICAL SOUND H-C A
Presents an alternative approach to educating handicapped children through integrating the child into normal classroom activities and through respect for individual differences.
LC NO. 78-701448
Prod-NYCBED Dist-CFDC Prodn-CFDC 1978

Step By Step C 11 MIN
16MM FILM, 3/4 OR 1/2 IN VIDEO
Reviews the place of children in different cultures. Recalls the barbarous treatment of children by early civilizations and looks at the basic rights of children.
LC NO. 79-706831
Prod-HUBLEY Dist-PFP 1979

Step By Step C 30 MIN
3/4 INCH VIDEO CASSETTE C
Tells how the Leichardt Council proposes to rebuild a park, allowing the community to be involved from design to completion, and to use previously unemployed people from the area to build it.
LC NO. 81-706501
Prod-SYDUN Dist-TASCOR 1980

Step By Step (Spanish) C 15 MIN
16MM FILM OPTICAL SOUND
Presents a Spanish language version of the film Step By Step, which presents an alternative approach to educating handicapped children through integrating the child into normal classroom activities and through respect for individual differences.
Prod-NYCBED Dist-CFDC

Step Family C 13 MIN
16MM FILM, 3/4 OR 1/2 IN VIDEO I-C A
Examines the impact of remarriage on both children and adults. Uses the case study of a fictional family to show the problems faced in accepting new parents and siblings.
From The Family Life - Transitions In Marriage Series.
LC NO. 81-707286
Prod-GORKER Dist-CORF 1981

Step Forward, A C 22 MIN
16MM FILM OPTICAL SOUND
Explains that roofmate is one of the Dow cost-reducing installation construction materials. Describes the benefits, production and application of this foam product.
Prod-DCC Dist-DCC

Step From The Shadows, A C 28 MIN
16MM FILM OPTICAL SOUND H-C
Stimulates interest and understanding of alcohol and other drug abuse problems.
Prod-LYNVIL Dist-NINEFC

Step In The Right Direction, A C 10 MIN
16MM FILM OPTICAL SOUND J-C A
Presents a ten-mile walk by 3,000 people to illustrate how people can become motivated to act on the world hunger situation.
LC NO. 78-701471
Prod-CROP Dist-CROP Prodn-FRMA 1978

Step In The Right Direction, A C 15 MIN
3/4 OR 1/2 INCH VIDEO CASSETTE
Discusses the importance of merchandise control procedures and techniques.
From The Small Business Administration Series.
Prod-IVCH Dist-IVCH

Step In Time, A C 29 MIN
3/4 OR 1/2 INCH VIDEO CASSETTE I A
Provides information for young persons on making responsible decisions about drinking.
Prod-SUTHRB Dist-SUTHRB

Step Into Space C 11 MIN
3/4 INCH VIDEO CASSETTE
Describes the training activities which all astronauts must experience, followed by more specialized training for a particular mission.
Prod-NASA Dist-NASA 1972

Step Method In Planning Development B 30 MIN
2 INCH VIDEOTAPE J-H
Teaches techniques of going step by step from a suspenseful beginning to a satisfactory conclusion. (Broadcast quality)
From The English Composition Series. Narration
Prod-GRETVO Dist-GPITVL Prodn-KUHTTV

Step Parenting C 20 MIN
16MM FILM OPTICAL SOUND A
Defines problems that occur in remarriage when children are involved. Educates general public about issues pertinent to step-parenting and to adults and children going through the experience.
Prod-AACD Dist-AACD 1974

Step Right Up C 7 MIN
16MM FILM OPTICAL SOUND
Presents an animated story in which a carnival barker reinforces the importance of a contributor's fair share gift, showing how the gift has helped others.
LC NO. 80-701560
Prod-UWAMER Dist-UWAMER Prodn-AUDVIS 1980

Step Right Up C 19 MIN
16MM FILM, 3/4 OR 1/2 IN VIDEO J-C A
Illustrates possible hazards and improper procedures when using ladders.
Prod-FILCOM Dist-FILCOM 1977

Step Style C 30 MIN
16MM FILM, 3/4 OR 1/2 IN VIDEO
Demonstrates dance step styles used throughout the world.
From The Movement Style And Culture Series.
Prod-CHORP Dist-UCEMC 1980

Step To Tomorrow, A C 13 MIN
3/4 OR 1/2 INCH VIDEO CASSETTE H-C
Introduces issues and adjustments new students will be forced to deal with on campus. Examines the fears and misconceptions students bring to college. Suggests ways of adapting to a new environment.
From The Developing Your Study Skills Series.
Prod-UWO Dist-BCNFL 1985

Step Too Slow, A C 25 MIN
16MM FILM, 3/4 OR 1/2 IN VIDEO J-C A
Reveals that when he is cut from the team, Bill Cameron wallows in self-pity. Shows him evaluating his life with the help of Judge Reinhold.
From The Reflections Series.
Prod-PAULST Dist-MEDIAG

Step-By-Step Process, The C 6 MIN
3/4 OR 1/2 INCH VIDEO CASSETTE
See series title for descriptive statement.
From The Practical M B O Series.
Prod-DELTAK Dist-DELTAK

Stephanie Takes Her Medicine C 9 MIN
3/4 OR 1/2 INCH VIDEO CASSETTE C A
Focuses on a hospital encounter in which a student nurse enters a playroom and tries in vain to give an unfamiliar liquid to a five-year-old girl.
From The Emotional Factors Affecting Children And Parents In The Hospital Series.
LC NO. 81-707457
Prod-LRF Dist-LRF 1979

Stephen Crane C 22 MIN
16MM FILM, 3/4 OR 1/2 IN VIDEO J-C A
Portrays American author Stephen Crane telling the story of his life and discussing his major works, including THE RED BADGE OF COURAGE.
From The Authors Series.
Prod-ALTPRO Dist-JOU 1978

Stephen Crane - The Blue Hotel B 30 MIN
2 INCH VIDEOTAPE J-H
From The Franklin To Frost Series.
Prod-GPITVL Dist-GPITVL

Stephen Crane - The Bride Comes To Yellow Sky B 30 MIN
2 INCH VIDEOTAPE J-H
From The Franklin To Frost Series.
Prod-GPITVL Dist-GPITVL

Stephen Crane - The Red Badge Of Courage, Pt 1 B 30 MIN
2 INCH VIDEOTAPE J-H
From The Franklin To Frost Series.
Prod-GPITVL Dist-GPITVL

Stephen Crane - The Red Badge Of Courage, Pt 2 B 30 MIN
2 INCH VIDEOTAPE J-H
From The Franklin To Frost Series.
Prod-GPITVL Dist-GPITVL

Stephen Crane's Three Miraculous Soldiers C 18 MIN
16MM FILM, 3/4 OR 1/2 IN VIDEO J-C A
Views the Civil War through the eyes of a young girl who is forced to see the humanity of both sides of a war when she encounters both Confederate and Union soldiers.
Prod-BFA Dist-PHENIX Prodn-SELLGB 1976

Stephen Edlich C 30 MIN
3/4 INCH VIDEO CASSETTE
Features sculptor-painter Stephen Edlich who discusses his collage paintings. Describes materials used.
From The Art Show Series.
Prod-UMITV Dist-UMITV

Stephen Foster And His Songs C 17 MIN
16MM FILM, 3/4 OR 1/2 IN VIDEO J-C A
Traces Stephen Foster's life, the highlights and the disappointments. Provides the historical background for the creation of his best known songs.
Prod-CORF Dist-CORF 1960

Stephen Foster's Footprints In Dream And Song C 15 MIN
16MM FILM OPTICAL SOUND
Presents the biography of Stephen Foster, composer of Florida's state song, Way Down Upon The Suwannee River.
Prod-FLADC Dist-FLADC

Stephens Family, the C 52 MIN
3/4 OR 1/2 INCH VIDEO CASSETTE A
Looks at an Iowa farm family as it experiences the staggering costs of land and equipment and a government policy which seems to be interfering in the family business. Shows that, although all six children want to stay on the farm, there is not enough land to divide among them and frustrations are beginning to be felt by those who realize that the land will never be theirs.
From The Six American Families Series.
Prod-GROUPW Dist-ECUFLM Prodn-UCHC 1976

Stephenses Of Iowa, The C 58 MIN
16MM FILM, 3/4 OR 1/2 IN VIDEO H-C A
Looks at a third-generation farm family whose good life is threatened by the staggering costs of land and equipment.
From The Six American Families Series.
Prod-GROUPW Dist-CAROUF

Stepparent Family, The C
1/2 IN VIDEO CASSETTE (VHS)
Looks at the complications of the stepparent family. Covers areas such as new siblings and differing blood ties.
From The Daddy Doesn't Live Here Anymore - The Single-Parent Family Series.
Prod-IBIS Dist-IBIS

Stepparent, The B 29 MIN
3/4 INCH VIDEO CASSETTE
Views the contemporary stepfamily with understanding in an effort to reverse society's stereotype of the 'cruel stepparent.'
Prod-UMITV Dist-UMITV 1971

Stepparenting C 25 MIN
3/4 OR 1/2 INCH VIDEO CASSETTE
Discusses feeling insecure, conflicts over child rearing practices and confusion as to who has authority over the child in remarriage situations.
Prod-POLYMR Dist-POLYMR

Stepparenting - New Families, Old Ties C 25 MIN
16MM FILM OPTICAL SOUND H-C A
Focuses on problems of being a stepparent and ways in which families deal with them.
LC NO. 77-701852
Prod-FELTHM Dist-POLYMR 1977

Stepparenting Issues C 20 MIN
16MM FILM, 3/4 OR 1/2 IN VIDEO A
Presents 13 vignettes illustrating common situations faced by stepparents including no time alone for the new couple, disagreements over having additional children, conflicts over childrearing, testing of authority, exploitation or nonacceptance of the new relationship by children and sibling rivalry.
Prod-MTI Dist-MTI

Steppe In Winter B 13 MIN
16MM FILM OPTICAL SOUND P-I
Shows how in the chilling cold of the steppe land of southeastern Europe, men, women, horses, dogs, cattle and sheep endure the long winter. Explains that the way of life of these people is influenced but not dominated by wind, cold and snow. Without narration.
LC NO. FIA67-1434
Prod-SF Dist-SF 1966

Stepping Into Rhythm—A Series
K-P
Prod-WVIZTV Dist-AITECH

Autumn Leaves Now Are Falling 014 MIN
Beautiful Home, Sweet Home 014 MIN
Black And Gold 014 MIN
Bowl Full Of Cricket, A 014 MIN
Circle Story, A 014 MIN
City Rhythms 014 MIN
Country Road 015 MIN
Gerald McBoing, Boing 015 MIN
Gracious Blessing 015 MIN
Happy New Year 014 MIN
Harpsichord The 014 MIN
Hear The Bells Ringing 014 MIN
Hello Ev'rybody 014 MIN
Hold On 015 MIN
I Like To Sing 014 MIN
Magic Vine, The 015 MIN
Major Or Minor 014 MIN
Merry Christmas 014 MIN
Moon Is Coming Out, The 014 MIN
My Twenty Pennies 014 MIN
Note Machine, The 014 MIN
Nothing But Sing 015 MIN
Of Thee I Sing 015 MIN
Oh, I Saw A Fox 014 MIN
Para Diddle 014 MIN
Percussion Family 014 MIN
Things To Do 014 MIN
Violin, The 014 MIN
Walkin' Blues 015 MIN
Winter Is 015 MIN

Stepping Out - The DeBolts Grow Up C 52 MIN
16MM FILM, 3/4 OR 1/2 IN VIDEO I-C A
Presents a view of the DeBolt family, with its twenty children, some of which are severely handicapped, who are now living at colleges and earning their own living. Tells how they have benefitted greatly from a loving family life.
LC NO. 81-707615
Prod-DAVIPR Dist-PFP Prodn-ELLOCO 1981

Stepping Stones B 10 MIN
16MM FILM OPTICAL SOUND S
Introduces the techniques used for teaching specific lip-reading skills and offers suggestions for the selection of a specific lip-reading word.
From The Parent Education - Information Films Series.
Prod-TC Dist-TC

Stepping Stones In Space B 14 MIN
16MM FILM OPTICAL SOUND I-C A
Presents a chronicle of the conquest of space from the pioneering flights of Dr Robert Hutchings Goodard in 1926 to the lunar landing of Apollo 17 in December, 1972.
From The Screen News Digest Series. Vol 15, Issue 5
LC NO. 73-701271
Prod-HEARST Dist-HEARST 1972

Stepping Stones To The Stars - The Air Force Museum C 27 MIN
16MM FILM OPTICAL SOUND

Describes the origin, purpose and contents of the Air Force Museum. Shows how old aircraft are restored, how the museum furnishes data on many subjects and how the museum's resources are made available to everybody on a nonprofit basis.
LC NO. 78-701848
Prod-USAF Dist-USNAC 1973

Steps C 2 MIN
16MM FILM OPTICAL SOUND
Uses graphics and optical effects as an opening and a tail for old films that still show the old PPG logo and the old name of the company (Pittsburgh Plate Glass.)
LC NO. 70-702588
Prod-PPG Dist-PPGC Prodn-TORCEL 1969

Steps In Teaching - And What Happens When You Miss One B 13 MIN
16MM FILM OPTICAL SOUND T
A shortened version, without commentary, of the film Steps In Teaching - And What Happens When You Miss One. Presents a highly skilled teacher working with inner-city children who are learning to tell time and to record that time in numerals.
From The Individualizing In A Group Series.
Prod-SPF Dist-SPF

Steps In Teaching - And What Happens When You Miss One B 30 MIN
16MM FILM OPTICAL SOUND T
Presents a highly skilled teacher working with inner-city children who are learning to tell time and to record that time in numerals.
From The Individualizing In A Group Series.
Prod-SPF Dist-SPF

Steps To Mature Reading B 30 MIN
16MM FILM OPTICAL SOUND T
Illustrates methods for improving reading ability.
From The Starting Tomorrow Series. Unit 3 - Individualizing Your Reading Program
LC NO. 75-714209
Prod-EALING Dist-WALKED Prodn-MIFE 1967

Steps To Recovery - Rehabilitation Of The Patient With Pulmonary Tuberculosis B 30 MIN
16MM FILM OPTICAL SOUND
Depicts the medical treatment and rehabilitation of tubercular patients as viewed through the eyes of two military patients hospitalized at Fitzsimons Army Hospital in Denver.
LC NO. FIE61-37
Prod-USA Dist-USNAC 1961

Steps Toward Maturity And Health C 10 MIN
16MM FILM, 3/4 OR 1/2 IN VIDEO P-I
Uses animation to show that as the body matures, responsibility for caring for it passes from nature, to parents and finally to the individual himself. Examines social, mental and physical health.
From The Triangle Of Health Series.
Prod-DISNEY Dist-WDEMCO 1968

Steps Toward Maturity And Health (Arabic) C 10 MIN
16MM FILM, 3/4 OR 1/2 IN VIDEO I-H
Traces maturation processes from prebirth through adolescence. Emphasizes accepting responsibility for oneself.
From The Triangle Of Health (Arabic) Series.
Prod-WDEMCO Dist-WDEMCO 1968

Steps Toward Maturity And Health (French) C 10 MIN
16MM FILM, 3/4 OR 1/2 IN VIDEO I-H
Traces maturation processes from prebirth through adolescence. Emphasizes accepting responsibility for oneself.
From The Triangle Of Health (French) Series.
Prod-WDEMCO Dist-WDEMCO 1968

Steps Toward Maturity And Health (German) C 10 MIN
16MM FILM, 3/4 OR 1/2 IN VIDEO I-H
Traces maturation processes from prebirth through adolescence. Emphasizes accepting responsibility for oneself.
From The Triangle Of Health (German) Series.
Prod-WDEMCO Dist-WDEMCO 1968

Steps Toward Maturity And Health (Hungarian) C 10 MIN
16MM FILM, 3/4 OR 1/2 IN VIDEO I-H
Traces maturation processes from prebirth through adolescence. Emphasizes accepting responsibility for oneself.
From The Triangle Of Health (Hungarian) Series.
Prod-WDEMCO Dist-WDEMCO 1968

Steps Toward Maturity And Health (Spanish) C 10 MIN
16MM FILM, 3/4 OR 1/2 IN VIDEO I-H
Traces maturation processes from prebirth through adolescence. Emphasizes accepting responsibility for oneself.
From The Triangle Of Health (Spanish) Series.
Prod-WDEMCO Dist-WDEMCO 1968

Steps Toward Maturity And Health (Swedish) C 10 MIN
16MM FILM, 3/4 OR 1/2 IN VIDEO I-H
Traces maturation processes from prebirth through adolescence. Emphasizes accepting responsibility for oneself.
From The Triangle Of Health (Swedish) Series.
Prod-WDEMCO Dist-WDEMCO 1968

Stereoscopics C 30 MIN
3/4 INCH VIDEO CASSETTE
See series title for descriptive statement.
From The Antiques Series.
Prod-NHMNET Dist-PUBTEL

Stereotactic Procedures For Parkinson's Disease C 25 MIN
16MM FILM OPTICAL SOUND PRO
Explains that it is now generally recognized that localized surgery within the basal ganglia can alleviate tremor and rigidity in better than 90 percent of cases of Parkinson's disease. Emphasizes that it is of paramount importance to use a precise technique, so as to avoid surrounding structures. Illustrates the beneficial effect of stereotactic procedures.
Prod-ACYDGD Dist-ACY 1963

Stereotyped Motor Mechanisms - The Extrapyramidal System C 18 MIN
16MM FILM, 3/4 OR 1/2 IN VIDEO PRO
See series title for descriptive statement.
From The Anatomical Basis Of Brain Function Series.
Prod-AVCORP Dist-TEF

Stereotyping - Sex C 30 MIN
3/4 OR 1/2 INCH VIDEO CASSETTE A
Points out how sex role stereotyping can inhibit personal growth and suggests how people overcome the limitations imposed by it, particularly among women.
From The Take Charge Series.
LC NO. 81-706070
Prod-USC Dist-USC 1979

Stereotyping People C 15 MIN
16MM FILM, 3/4 OR 1/2 IN VIDEO I
Tells how Lisa classifies her grandmother as an 'invalid old person' and treats her accordingly, until Mom helps Lisa realize the thoughtlessness of stereotyping people.
From The Thinkabout Series. Classifying
LC NO. 81-706123
Prod-ACCESS Dist-AITECH 1979

Steric Stabilization, Sensitized Flocculation C 41 MIN
3/4 OR 1/2 INCH VIDEO CASSETTE
See series title for descriptive statement.
From The Colloid And Surface Chemistry - Lyophobic Colloids Series.
Prod-KALMIA Dist-KALMIA

Steric Stabilization, Sensitized Flocculation B 41 MIN
3/4 OR 1/2 INCH VIDEO CASSETTE
See series title for descriptive statement.
From The Colloid And Surface Chemistry - Lyophobic Colloids Series.
Prod-MIOT Dist-MIOT

Sterile Supply Quality Assurance Control C 60 MIN
3/4 INCH VIDEO CASSETTE
Discusses procedures for quality control, monitoring and bacteriological control of medical supplies and equipment.
LC NO. 79-707312
Prod-USVA Dist-USNAC 1978

Sterile Technique C 16 MIN
3/4 OR 1/2 INCH VIDEO CASSETTE PRO
Demonstrates proper maneuvering in the sterile field, showing steam and gas sterilization, sterile gloving, skin prepping and the handling of sterile bundles and packages.
From The Basic Clinical Skills Series.
Prod-HSCIC Dist-HSCIC 1984

Sterile Technique For Tracheotomy Suctioning C 16 MIN
3/4 INCH VIDEO CASSETTE PRO
Demonstrates sterile tracheotomy suctioning procedures using a model with a cuffed tube.
LC NO. 80-706510
Prod-VAHSL Dist-USNAC 1978

Sterile Techniques For Oral Surgery And Periodontal Surgery Procedures C 19 MIN
1/2 IN VIDEO CASSETTE BETA/VHS PRO
Prod-RMI Dist-RMI

Sterilization And Consent C 29 MIN
3/4 INCH VIDEO CASSETTE
Discusses abuse in sterilization cases and describes a suit brought by ten women who were coercively sterilized.
From The Woman Series.
Prod-WNEDTV Dist-PUBTEL

Sterilization By Laparoscopy - General Anesthesia C
3/4 OR 1/2 INCH VIDEO CASSETTE
Presents a woman's experience before, during and after undergoing sterilization by laparoscopy using a general anesthetic.
Prod-MIFE Dist-MIFE

Sterilization By Laparoscopy - General Anesthesia (Spanish) C
3/4 OR 1/2 INCH VIDEO CASSETTE
Presents a woman's experience before, during and after undergoing sterilization by laparoscopy using general anesthetic.
Prod-MIFE Dist-MIFE

Sterilization By Laparoscopy - Local Anesthesia C
3/4 OR 1/2 INCH VIDEO CASSETTE
Presents the sterilization procedure by laparoscopy using a local anesthesia.
Prod-MIFE Dist-MIFE

Sterilization By Laparoscopy - Local Anesthesia (Spanish) C
3/4 OR 1/2 INCH VIDEO CASSETTE
Presents the sterilization procedure by laparoscopy using a local anesthesia.
Prod-MIFE Dist-MIFE

Sterilization By Laparoscopy - Local Anesthesia (Arabic) C
3/4 OR 1/2 INCH VIDEO CASSETTE
Presents the sterilization procedure by laparoscopy using a local anesthesia.
Prod-MIFE Dist-MIFE

Sterilization Monitoring Series C 35 MIN
3/4 INCH VIDEO CASSETTE PRO
Describes sterilization monitoring with emphasis on chemical and biological monitoring, and how to keep sterilization records.
Prod-MMAMC Dist-MMAMC

Sterilization Of The Female B 23 MIN
16MM FILM OPTICAL SOUND H-C A
Presents various aspects of the sterilization of the female explaining on which individuals it could be performed, how the operation should be done and what post-operative care should be taken.
Prod-INDIA Dist-NEDINF

Sterilization Problems And Techniques C 29 MIN
16MM FILM OPTICAL SOUND
Discusses various aspects of sterilization in hospital practice.
LC NO. 74-706255
Prod-USPHS Dist-USNAC 1963

Sterilization Procedures For The Medical Office C 29 MIN
16MM FILM OPTICAL SOUND PRO
Demonstrates procedures for the sterilization of instruments and supplies in the medical office. Defines standards for the cleaning and wrapping of materials, the length of exposure to sterilizing agents and the storage of sterile goods. Deals primarily with sterilization in a steam autoclave, but also covers the use of chemical germicides and ethylene oxide gas for certain applications.
Prod-WYETH Dist-WYLAB 1962

Sterilization Record Keeping C 6 MIN
3/4 INCH VIDEO CASSETTE PRO
Illustrates the hospital's need for sterilization records. Outlines components of a complete record keeping program and discusses their proper use. Depicts ways of coding information on load record labels and gives suggested applications for these labels. Illustrates completion of a load record form.
Prod-MMAMC Dist-MMAMC

Sterilizing Oral Surgery Instruments C 9 MIN
3/4 INCH VIDEO CASSETTE
Demonstrates a step-by-step procedure for sterilizing oral surgery instruments, explaining the importance of each step.
From The Oral Surgery Clinic Routine Series. Part 1
LC NO. 79-706762
Prod-MUSC Dist-USNAC 1978

Sterling Education Of Craftsmanship, A C 11 MIN
16MM FILM OPTICAL SOUND
Show the features of a Singer 16mm projector and emphasizes the quality of Singer Education Systems.
LC NO. 81-700436
Prod-SVE Dist-SVE 1981

Stern-Gerlach Experiment, The B 26 MIN
16MM FILM OPTICAL SOUND
Illustrates the Stern-gerlach experiment which demonstrates that a well collimated beam of cesium atoms is split into two distinct beams when it passes through a non-uniform magnetic field. Compares this result with what might be expected if different types of atoms and a uniform magnetic field were tested.
From The College Physics Film Program Series.
LC NO. FIA68-1443
Prod-EDS Dist-MLA 1967

Stethoscope C 15 MIN
3/4 INCH VIDEO CASSETTE PRO
Shows the wide variety of stethoscopes and explains each part of the instrument. Demonstrates correct usage and storage.
From The Instruments Of Physical Assessment Series.
LC NO. 80-707627
Prod-SUNYSB Dist-LIP 1980

Steve Addiss And Bill Crofut With Phan Duy C 52 MIN
3/4 OR 1/2 INCH VIDEO CASSETTE
Explores the Vietnamese musical tradition. Features Steve Addiss and Bill Crofut who have traveled in the Far East and Vietnamese musician Phan Duy.
From The Rainbow Quest Series.
Prod-SEEGER Dist-CWATER

Steve And Kathy And Al C 15 MIN
3/4 OR 1/2 INCH VIDEO CASSETTE P
Features the Thibodeau family of Five Islands, Maine.
From The Other Families, Other Friends Series. Blue Module - Maine
Prod-WVIZTV Dist-AITECH 1971

Steve Fagin - Virtual Play, The Double Direct Monkey Wrench In Black's Machinery C 80 MIN
3/4 OR 1/2 INCH VIDEO CASSETTE
Combines psychoanalytic theories, biographical snippets, Sybergian expositions and calculated Child's play.
Prod-ARTINC Dist-ARTINC

Stevedore's Song C 14 MIN
3/4 OR 1/2 INCH VIDEO CASSETTE P-I
See series title for descriptive statement.
From The Ready, Sing Series.
Prod-ARKETV Dist-AITECH 1979

Stevengraphs C 30 MIN
3/4 INCH VIDEO CASSETTE
See series title for descriptive statement.
From The Antiques Series.
Prod-NHMNET Dist-PUBTEL

Stevenson Palfi - Piano Players Rarely Ever Play Together C 76 MIN
3/4 OR 1/2 INCH VIDEO CASSETTE
Documents three generations of New Orleans pianists who strongly influenced each other's music.
Prod-ARTINC Dist-ARTINC

Stewardess C 21 MIN
16MM FILM OPTICAL SOUND
Takes a look at a day in the life of two stewardessess.
LC NO. 75-704339
Prod-CONCOL Dist-CONCOL 1973

Stewardship Of Abilities B 15 MIN
16MM FILM OPTICAL SOUND H-C A
Presents an important personal challenge for adults and young alike by exploring questions such as - are we making proper use of God-given abilities, are we living at our fullest for him, what can we do personally to spread the Gospel.
From The Discussion Series.
LC NO. 72-701676
Prod-CONCOR Dist-CPH 1963

Stick Puppets, Hand Puppets And Papier Mache Puppet Heads C 15 MIN
3/4 INCH VIDEO CASSETTE
See series title for descriptive statement.
From The Look And A Closer Look Series.
Prod-WCVETV Dist-GPITVL

Stick-Slip C 43 MIN
3/4 OR 1/2 INCH VIDEO CASSETTE
Discusses the relaxation and harmonic forms of frictional oscillations and how they arise. Teaches conditions for stick-slip and their relation to material properties.
From The Tribology 1 - Friction, Wear, And Lubrication Series.
Prod-MIOT Dist-MIOT

Sticks And Stones C 14 MIN
16MM FILM OPTICAL SOUND K-I
Shows how Yoffy sends Fingermouse to the beach to collect a variety of stones and then how Enoch helps him by building a cart out of sticks for carrying them.
From The Fingermouse, Yoffy And Friends Series.
LC NO. 73-700433
Prod-BBCTV Dist-VEDO 1972

Sticks And Stones Will Build A House C 30 MIN
2 INCH VIDEOTAPE
Traces the development of the Indian as a builder.
From The Indian Arts Series.
Prod-KUEDTV Dist-PUBTEL

Sticky My Fingers, Fleet My Feet C 23 MIN
16MM FILM OPTICAL SOUND
Shows a group of Madison Avenue touch football buffs who are beaten by a teenage boy and begin to feel their age.
LC NO. 74-707384
Prod-AMERFI Dist-TIMLIF Prodn-HANCKJ 1970

Still And Empty Center, The C 30 MIN
3/4 OR 1/2 INCH VIDEO CASSETTE C
See series title for descriptive statement.
From The Art Of Being Human Series. Module 7
Prod-MDCC Dist-MDCC

Still Going Places B 40 MIN
16MM FILM OPTICAL SOUND
Shows how patients who have incurred cardiovascular accidents can be physically, socially and economically rehabilitated, with the help of all of the medical disciplines.
Prod-STONEY Dist-PFI 1955

Still Got Life To Go C 30 MIN
16MM FILM OPTICAL SOUND
Shows inmates, prison officials and parole officers in Oklahoma City behind prison walls and in streets and alleys as they point out some of the causes of recidivism in the Oklahoma correctional system and the need for a meaningful rehabilitation program for first offenders.
LC NO. 74-715455
Prod-WKYTV Dist-WKYTV 1971

Still Life C 20 MIN
3/4 OR 1/2 INCH VIDEO CASSETTE
Explores the future territory of drama through interplay of language, music, visuals and structure.
Prod-KITCHN Dist-KITCHN

Still Life C 29 MIN
3/4 INCH VIDEO CASSETTE
See series title for descriptive statement.
From The Magic Of Oil Painting Series.
Prod-KOCETV Dist-PUBTEL

Still Life And Landscape - Basic Simple Shapes C 20 MIN
3/4 INCH VIDEO CASSETTE J-C
Shows how to draw basic simple shapes.
From The Basic Drawing Series.
LC NO. 79-706381
Prod-EDDIM Dist-EDDIM 1979

Still Life And Landscape - Complex Basic Shapes, Still Life C 20 MIN
3/4 INCH VIDEO CASSETTE J-C
Shows how to draw complex basic shapes and still life.
From The Basic Drawing Series.
LC NO. 79-706382
Prod-EDDIM Dist-EDDIM 1979

Still Life And Landscape - Irregular Shapes, Still Life C 20 MIN
3/4 INCH VIDEO CASSETTE J-C
Shows how to draw irregular shapes and still life.
From The Basic Drawing Series.
LC NO. 79-706383
Prod-EDDIM Dist-EDDIM 1979

Still Life And Landscape - Landscape With Perspective C 20 MIN
3/4 INCH VIDEO CASSETTE J-C
Shows how to draw a landscape with perspective.
From The Basic Drawing Series.
LC NO. 79-706387
Prod-EDDIM Dist-EDDIM 1979

Still Life And Landscape - Light And Shade, Basic Form, Still Life C 20 MIN
3/4 INCH VIDEO CASSETTE J-C
Shows how to draw light and shade, basic form, and still life.
From The Basic Drawing Series.
LC NO. 79-706384
Prod-EDDIM Dist-EDDIM 1979

Still Life And Landscape - Light And Shade, Drapery Problems C 20 MIN
3/4 INCH VIDEO CASSETTE J-C
Shows how to draw light and shade, and discusses drapery problems.
From The Basic Drawing Series.
LC NO. 79-706385
Prod-EDDIM Dist-EDDIM 1979

Still Life And Landscape - Perspective, Still Life, One And Two Point C 20 MIN
3/4 INCH VIDEO CASSETTE J-C
Demonstrates how to draw one- and two-point perspective and still life.
From The Basic Drawing Series.
LC NO. 79-706386
Prod-EDDIM Dist-EDDIM 1979

Still Life And Landscape - Review Complex Detail Drawings C 20 MIN
3/4 INCH VIDEO CASSETTE J-C
Presents a review of complex detail drawings.
From The Basic Drawing Series.
LC NO. 79-706388
Prod-EDDIM Dist-EDDIM 1979

Still Life—A Series

Presents six short works exploring the future territory of drama.
Prod-EAI Dist-EAI

Black And White 002 MIN
Dialogue 003 MIN
Don't Ask 001 MIN
Episode 004 MIN
Static 003 MIN
Thrown Stones 002 MIN

Still More Signs You Already Know C 30 MIN
3/4 OR 1/2 INCH VIDEO CASSETTE H-C A
Presents Lawrence Solow and Sharon Neumann Solow introducing American Sign Language used by the hearing-impaired. Emphasizes signs that resemble gestures already used by many people in spoken conversation.
From The Say It With Sign Series. Part 3
Prod-KNBCTV Dist-FI 1982

Still Pictures In ETV B 27 MIN
16MM FILM OPTICAL SOUND
Shows some criteria for a good still picture, such as shape, composition and grey scale. Presents an example combining good photography, music and camera work in an artistic whole.
From The CETO Television Training Films Series.
Prod-CETO Dist-GPITVL

Still Waters C 14 MIN
16MM FILM, 3/4 OR 1/2 IN VIDEO I-H
Observes birth, survival and death in a still pond. Combines music and photography to dramatize the difficult struggle for life in the pond.
Prod-CON Dist-TEXFLM 1968

Still Waters C 59 MIN
16MM FILM, 3/4 OR 1/2 IN VIDEO H-C A
Uses specially developed photographic techniques to capture animal life in and around a fresh water pond over a period of a year. Shows microscopic life, insects, amphibians, reptiles, fish, birds and mammals.
From The Nova Series.
Prod-WGBHTV Dist-TIMLIF 1978

Still-Life Sketches C 29 MIN
3/4 INCH VIDEO CASSETTE C A
Explains 'still life' as a reference. Shows steps used in drawing a still life. Emphasizes the importance of being able to draw independently from the still life by sketching several different kinds of a particular object.
From The Sketching Techniques Series. Lesson 13
Prod-COAST Dist-CDTEL

Stillbirth C 20 MIN
3/4 INCH VIDEO CASSETTE H-C A
Offers a portrait of a woman who was the mother of a stillborn child.
Prod-CHERIO Dist-GPITVL 1979

Stillbirth, Miscarriage, And Beyond - Healing Through Shared Experience C 29 MIN
16MM FILM, 3/4 OR 1/2 IN VIDEO A
Examines the experience of miscarriage and stillbirth. Intends to help viewers who have experienced either to express their feelings in a therapeutic manner. Emphasizes the opportunity for the professional audience to gain insight.
Prod-FAIRGH Dist-FAIRGH

Stillwater Runs Deep C 24 MIN
3/4 OR 1/2 INCH VIDEO CASSETTE
Shows how Stillwater Prison has begun a swing toward increased security measures and a decrease in treatment programs after two decades of liberal prison reform.
Prod-WCCOTV Dist-WCCOTV 1977

Stillwell Road B 49 MIN
3/4 OR 1/2 INCH VIDEO CASSETTE
Documents the Signal Corps activity on the China-Burma front, scene of one of the great victories of World War II.
Prod-IHF Dist-IHF

Stillwell Road, The B 51 MIN
16MM FILM, 3/4 OR 1/2 IN VIDEO
Presents a documentary record of the construction of a supply road through the mountains and jungles of Burma in World War II. Issued in 1949 as a motion picture.
From The Campaign Reports Series.
LC NO. 79-706702
Prod-USWD Dist-USNAC 1979

Stilt Dancers Of Long Bow Village C 27 MIN
16MM FILM, 3/4 OR 1/2 IN VIDEO A
Looks at a stilt-dancing festival in rural China which blends the color and action of the festival with scenes of peasants enjoying themselves and reminiscences about the ban on stilt dancing during the Cultural Revolution.
LC NO. 81-707224
Prod-GORDR Dist-FI 1980

Stimulants C 5 MIN
3/4 OR 1/2 INCH VIDEO CASSETTE
Describes the effects of stimulants on the nervous system. Issued in 1971 as a motion picture.
From The Single Concept Drug Film Series.
LC NO. 80-706849
Prod-NIMH Dist-USNAC 1980

Stimulants C 10 MIN
16MM FILM, 3/4 OR 1/2 IN VIDEO H A
Discusses the characteristics of stimulants. Identifies the signs of use and abuse, the pharmacological and behavioral effects, and the shortand long-term dangers.
From The Drug Information Series.
LC NO. 84-706156
Prod-MITCHG Dist-MTI 1983

Stimulation And Modeling Techniques C 54 MIN
3/4 OR 1/2 INCH VIDEO CASSETTE
Presents a review of simulation and modeling techniques (useful for digital, analog and hybrid computers). Illustrates the applicability of simulation and modeling.
From The Systems Engineering And Systems Management Series.
Prod-MIOT Dist-MIOT

Stimuli Releasing Sexual Behavior Of Domestic Turkeys C 19 MIN
16MM FILM SILENT C
Shows that the mating activity of turkeys is a stereotyped pattern of behavior, in which each responds to successive cues from its mate. Points out that in normal mating behavior, the male responds with a strutting display to the presence of females, the female crouches, male mounts, female elevates head, male makes cloacal contact, female extrudes oviduct, male inseminates. Through examples, demonstrates that the head is more important than the body in eliciting sexual behavior.
Prod-PSUPCR Dist-PSUPCR 1958

Stimuli Which Reduce Turnover B 29 MIN
16MM FILM OPTICAL SOUND
See series title for descriptive statement.
From The Controlling Turnover And Absenteeism Series.
LC NO. 76-703321
Prod-EDSD Dist-EDSD

Stimulus World Of The Infant C 9 MIN
16MM FILM OPTICAL SOUND
Depicts the stimulation of high-risk infants to detect retardation and to help minimize the possibility of developing disability at a later age.
LC NO. 72-702016
Prod-UKANBC Dist-UKANS 1971

Sting, The C 129 MIN
16MM FILM OPTICAL SOUND
Describes a colossal con game staged by two grifters in 1930's Chicago. Stars Paul Newman and Robert Redford.
Prod-UPCI Dist-TWYMAN 1973

Stinging-Celled Animals - Coelenterates C 17 MIN
16MM FILM, 3/4 OR 1/2 IN VIDEO H
Describes the characteristics of the phylum coelenterata, showing the body plan and processes. Examples of fresh and salt water coelenterates are shown.
From The Biology Series. Unit 7 - Animal Classification And Physiology
Prod-EBF Dist-EBEC 1962

Stinging-Celled Animals - Coelenterates (Spanish) C 17 MIN
16MM FILM, 3/4 OR 1/2 IN VIDEO H
Describes the phylum Coelenterata, including fresh and salt water examples. Shows the typical coelenterate body plan and provides examples of three classes of coelenterates.
From The Biology (Spanish) Series. Unit 7 - Animal Classification And Physiology
Prod-EBEC Dist-EBEC

Stirling Engine Brought Up To Date, The C 18 MIN
16MM FILM, 3/4 OR 1/2 IN VIDEO H-C A
Explains that a highly efficient engine has been developed from the original hot-air engine invented by Robert Stirling. Illustrates the function of cylinder, piston and the displacer.
Prod-PHILIS Dist-MGHT 1968

Stirring Of Politics, The C 30 MIN
16MM FILM OPTICAL SOUND R
Looks at the stresses the religious movement has caused within the youth culture. Analyses the nature and shortcomings of the

Jesus Movement and reveals some of the commercial aspects of the new religious fervor.
From The Devout Young Series.
Prod-OSSHE Dist-OSSHE

Stitchery C 15 MIN
16MM FILM, 3/4 OR 1/2 IN VIDEO J-C A
Explores the decorative and expressive possibilities of stitchery as an art form. Illustrates basic procedures which may be adapted to classroom use.
From The Rediscovery - Art Media Series.
Prod-ACI Dist-AIMS 1969

Stitchery (French) C 14 MIN
16MM FILM, 3/4 OR 1/2 IN VIDEO I-C A
Encompasses the techniques of embroidery, needlepoint and applique and demonstrates the basic procedures involved in each of these activities.
From The Rediscovery - Art Media (French) Series.
Prod-ACI Dist-AIMS 1969

Stitchery (Spanish) C 14 MIN
16MM FILM, 3/4 OR 1/2 IN VIDEO I-C A
Encompasses the techniques of embroidery, needlepoint and applique and demonstrates the basic procedures involved in each of these activities.
From The Rediscovery - Art Media (Spanish) Series.
Prod-ACI Dist-AIMS 1969

Stitching And Weaving C 20 MIN
2 INCH VIDEOTAPE I
Helps students learn various techniques in combining threads and fabrics.
From The Creating Art, Pt 2 - Learning To Create Art Forms Series.
Prod-GPITVL Dist-GPITVL

Stochastic Control C 50 MIN
3/4 OR 1/2 INCH VIDEO CASSETTE PRO
See series title for descriptive statement.
From The Modern Control Theory Series. Pt V
Prod-MIOT Dist-AMCEE

Stochastic Estimation C 50 MIN
3/4 OR 1/2 INCH VIDEO CASSETTE PRO
See series title for descriptive statement.
From The Modern Control Theory Series. Pt IV
Prod-MIOT Dist-AMCEE

Stochastic Matrices C 30 MIN
3/4 INCH VIDEO CASSETTE C
See series title for descriptive statement.
From The Introduction To Mathematics Series.
Prod-MDCPB Dist-MDCPB

Stock - Look And Listen C 20 MIN
3/4 INCH VIDEO CASSETTE J-H
Introduces the New York and American Stock Exchanges.
From The Dollar Data Series.
LC NO. 81-707386
Prod-WHROTV Dist-GPITVL 1974

Stock Market C 15 MIN
3/4 OR 1/2 INCH VIDEO CASSETTE I
Presents a cast of three ten-year-old children interacting with adults to demonstrate various economic concepts relating to the stock market.
From The Money Matters Series. Pt 6
LC NO. 83-706017
Prod-KEDTTV Dist-GPITVL 1982

Stock Market, The C 30 MIN
3/4 OR 1/2 INCH VIDEO CASSETTE C A
Discusses the advantages and disadvantages of stock ownership as a form of investing. Shows the stock market in operation. Defines several stock market terms.
From The Personal Finance Series. Lesson 17
Prod-SCCON Dist-CDTEL

Stock Preparation C 20 MIN
1/2 IN VIDEO CASSETTE BETA/VHS
Discusses how to prepare light and dark stock and how to obtain maximum flavor and nutrition in each.
Prod-RMI Dist-RMI

Stock Preparation Equipment C
3/4 OR 1/2 INCH VIDEO CASSETTE IND
Includes stock chests and papers, jordans and refiners and cleaners and screens used in paper stock preparation.
From The Pulp And Paper Training, Module 3 - Papermaking Series.
Prod-LEIKID Dist-LEIKID

Stock Strategies For Individuals C 25 MIN
3/4 OR 1/2 INCH VIDEO CASSETTE
Reveals ten surprising guidelines for stock buying. Discusses discount brokers, tax advantages of utilities and some little-known investment options.
From The Your Money Matters Series.
Prod-SKOKIE Dist-FILMID

Stockhausen, The Percussion, And Tristan Fry C 26 MIN
16MM FILM, 3/4 OR 1/2 IN VIDEO J-C A
Tells how twentieth-century composer Stockhausen is well-known for his electronic music in which the traditional percussion instrument variables of pitch, vibration, frequency and volume are controlled electronically. Features professional musician Tristan Fry demonstrating some of Stockhausen's music.
From The Musical Triangle Series.
Prod-THAMES Dist-MEDIAG 1975

Stockholm - The Most, Well, Almost C 22 MIN
16MM FILM OPTICAL SOUND C A
Describes the city of Stockholm, known for its perfection, neatness, urbanity and style.
Prod-WSTGLC Dist-WSTGLC

Stocking Up C 28 MIN
16MM FILM, 3/4 OR 1/2 IN VIDEO J-C A
Presents a young couple who demonstrate various methods for preserving home produce, emphasizing low energy techniques such as drying and storing food in a root cellar. Includes a demonstration of freezing and canning techniques and explains the pros and cons of each method in terms of nutrition and expense.
Prod-RPFD Dist-BULFRG 1982

Stocks C 10 MIN
3/4 OR 1/2 INCH VIDEO CASSETTE PRO
Shows how to make, cool and store the four basic stocks, brown, white or neutral, chicken and fish.
Prod-CULINA Dist-CULINA

Stocks In Action C 30 MIN
16MM FILM OPTICAL SOUND
Presents the spills and thrills of the circuit.
Prod-SFI Dist-SFI

Stocky Mariano C 5 MIN
3/4 OR 1/2 INCH VIDEO CASSETTE J-H
Teaches the use of strong verbs in writing.
From The Write On, Set 1 Series.
Prod-CTI Dist-CTI

Stockyards - End Of An Era C 59 MIN
16MM FILM - 3/4 IN VIDEO
Traces the 100-year history of the Chicago Stockyards which have always set the price for cattle until their recent closing.
Prod-WTTWTV Dist-PUBTEL 1973

Stolen Child C 8 MIN
16MM FILM, 3/4 OR 1/2 IN VIDEO K-P
Tells how a young girl and her animal friends hunt down the neighborhood scoundrel who stole her baby and baby carriage.
Prod-KRATKY Dist-PHENIX 1974

Stolen Children C 15 MIN
3/4 OR 1/2 INCH VIDEO CASSETTE H-C A
Explores the plight of children who are kidnapped by their own parents during custody battles. Documents the nine-year battle of a Canadian woman to regain custody of her two boys taken by her husband to Ireland.
Prod-CANBC Dist-JOU

Stolen For Love C 22 MIN
3/4 OR 1/2 INCH VIDEO CASSETTE
Deals with the subject of children kidnapped by a parent as a result of child custody or visitation disputes. Addresses concerns about child kidnapping laws, victimized parents, psychological and sometimes physical harm to the child. Includes case studies and talks with abductors.
Prod-WCCOTV Dist-WCCOTV

Stolen Necklace, The C 8 MIN
16MM FILM, 3/4 OR 1/2 IN VIDEO P-I
An adaptation of a tale from India, written and illustrated by Anne Rockwell, about a pearl necklace which is stolen from a princess by a monkey.
From The Children's Storybook Theater Series.
Prod-CLAIB Dist-AIMS 1971

Stolen Painting C 11 MIN
16MM FILM, 3/4 OR 1/2 IN VIDEO
Features Spunky Lucius who discovers that his wife and her portrait have been kidnapped by the ruthless criminal, Dr Guard. Tells how Lucius finally succeeds in rescuing his wife, and together they flee to an amusement park. Without narration.
LC NO. 81-706887
Prod-KRATKY Dist-PHENIX 1979

Stomach Formula, The C 60 MIN
1/2 IN VIDEO CASSETTE (VHS)
Presents Richard Simmons demonstrating an exercise formula to firm the stomach on a daily basis.
Prod-KARLVI Dist-KARLVI

Stomach Story, The C 15 MIN
16MM FILM, 3/4 OR 1/2 IN VIDEO K-I
Presents the Magnificent Body Model, a lifesize fanciful body replica, that conducts a tour of the human body. Features puppets representing the heart, lungs, stomach, liver and intestines. Shows how excitement, worry, over-eating, motion and germs can upset the stomach.
From The Healthwise Series.
LC NO. 83-707059
Prod-CORF Dist-CORF 1982

Stone Age Americans C 21 MIN
16MM FILM, 3/4 OR 1/2 IN VIDEO I-H
Presents a study of the Indians of the Mesa Verde in Colorado, who disappeared after 13 centuries of development. Examines the cliff dwellings and artifacts discovered in the Soda Canyon of Mesa Verde.
Prod-ABCNEW Dist-IFB Prodn-WILSND 1970

Stone Forest C 17 MIN
16MM FILM - 3/4 IN VIDEO
Illustrates the stages of petrification. Uses time lapse photography to depict the formation of crystals and the process by which fallen trees turn to stone.
LC NO. 79-706107
Prod-USNPS Dist-USNAC 1974

Stone In The River C 60 MIN
16MM FILM OPTICAL SOUND
Features the concept of behavior control and its implications and considers the way the penal system catches and twists its participants. Uses a dramatic structure.
Prod-NBCTV Dist-CCNCC

Stone Knapping In Modern Turkey B 12 MIN
16MM FILM OPTICAL SOUND C
Reveals techniques used by modern Turkish flint thieves to obtain blades from a piece of flint. Shows the method of applying direct percussion to the nucleus to strike a blade and the use of flint blades in threshing sledges by the local farmers.
LC NO. 75-700200
Prod-PSU Dist-PSUPCR 1974

Stone Mountain Carving B 29 MIN
16MM FILM OPTICAL SOUND I-H
Presents an in-progress report on the carving of Stone Mountain in Georgia. Discusses the modern methods used by the workers, and the mathematical planning that they employ in carving the huge Confederate memorial honoring Davis, Lee and Jackson.
LC NO. FIA68-3074
Prod-NET Dist-IU 1968

Stone Soup X 11 MIN
16MM FILM, 3/4 OR 1/2 IN VIDEO K-P
An iconographic film using the drawings from the book of the same title and narrated by the author, Marcia Brown. Relates the familiar story of soldiers who trick the reluctant villagers into feeding them.
Prod-WWS Dist-WWS 1955

Stone Soup, The C 12 MIN
3/4 OR 1/2 INCH VIDEO CASSETTE P
See series title for descriptive statement.
From The Magic Pages Series.
Prod-KLVXTV Dist-AITECH 1976

Stone Symposium C 30 MIN
3/4 INCH VIDEO CASSETTE
Presents three internationally renowned sculptors discussing their art and lives - Joan Gambioli, Anna-Maria Kubach-Wilmsen and Olga Janic.
Prod-WMENIF Dist-WMENIF

Stone Whistle, The C 29 MIN
16MM FILM OPTICAL SOUND
Features John Forsythe starring in a story about the human need to be remembered. Deals with the religious significance of monuments and includes a visit to Vermont's famous granite quarries.
Prod-BGA Dist-MTP

Stonecutter, The C 6 MIN
16MM FILM, 3/4 OR 1/2 IN VIDEO K-J
Uses animation to tell an ancient Japanese tale of envy and greed--the story of Tasaka, the stonecutter, who is granted his wishes to become a prince, the sun, a cloud and, finally, a gigantic mountain.
Prod-MDERMG Dist-WWS 1965

Stoned - An Anti-Drug Film C 30 MIN
16MM FILM, 3/4 OR 1/2 IN VIDEO J-H A
A shortened version of the motion picture Stoned - An Anti-Drug Film. Shows how adolescents searching for an identity often turn to drugs to bolster their self-doubts.
From The Learning To Be Human Series.
Prod-HGATE Dist-LCOA 1980

Stoned - An Anti-Drug Film C 46 MIN
16MM FILM, 3/4 OR 1/2 IN VIDEO J-H
Introduces Jack Melon, a shy teenager who turns to marijuana to become noticed by his friends and family. Shows that after a near-accident while stoned, he realizes that he must be himself.
Prod-HGATE Dist-LCOA 1980

Stoned - An Anti-Drug Film (Captioned) C 30 MIN
16MM FILM, 3/4 OR 1/2 IN VIDEO J-H A
Deals with the adolescent need for a positive self-image and friends who support it. Portrays a shy teenager who uses marijuana in order to feel popular. Edited.
Prod-HGATE Dist-LCOA 1981

Stoned - An Anti-Drug Film (Captioned) C 46 MIN
16MM FILM, 3/4 OR 1/2 IN VIDEO J-H A
Deals with the adolescent need for a positive self-image and friends who support it. Portrays a shy teenager who uses marijuana in order to feel popular. Full version.
Prod-HGATE Dist-LCOA 1981

Stonehenge C 16 MIN
16MM FILM, 3/4 OR 1/2 IN VIDEO I-C A
Looks at the archaeological research which has attempted to discover the significance of Stonehenge, the most celebrated megalithic structure in England. Speculates on how the stones were brought to the site and erected.
Prod-LUF Dist-LUF 1980

Stonehenge - Mystery In The Plain C 24 MIN
16MM FILM, 3/4 OR 1/2 IN VIDEO I A
Captures the myths and legends of Stonehenge. Explores the mystery of its origins.
Prod-VORFLM Dist-EBEC 1980

Stones In The Urinary Tract C 8 MIN
3/4 OR 1/2 INCH VIDEO CASSETTE
Uses illustrations and graphics to explain to the patient what causes symptoms and where stones in the urinary tract may occur. Describes what the patient can do to improve the condition.
From The Take Care Of Yourself Series.
Prod-UARIZ Dist-UARIZ

Stones Of Amiens, The B 29 MIN
16MM FILM OPTICAL SOUND J-C A

Shows how the Notre Dame Cathedral in Amiens, France, is a symbol of the unity of thirteenth century Christianity and Gothic art. Includes John Ruskin's poetic description of the cathedral and the words of such scholars as St Thomas Acquinas.
From The Legacy Series.
LC NO. 73-707200
Prod-NET Dist-IU 1965

Stones Of Eden C 25 MIN
16MM FILM, 3/4 OR 1/2 IN VIDEO A
Portrays a year in the life of a farmer and his family in the mountains of Central Afghanistan. Discusses problems common to most farmers in the developing world.
Prod-CNEMAG Dist-CNEMAG 1966

Stonewall Jackson's Way B 27 MIN
16MM FILM OPTICAL SOUND I-H A
Reveals the character of Stonewall Jackson and his influence on the men who fought in his command. Traces his military career from his training of troops in 1861 until his death at Chancellorsville in 1863.
Prod-VADE Dist-VADE 1963

Stonewall Joe B 29 MIN
3/4 OR 1/2 INCH VIDEO CASSETTE
Portrays Joe Robertson, grandnephew of Grandma Moses. Displays the dying New England craft of dry-laid stonewall building and the traditions of folk art and Scots-Irish music.
Prod-KITCHN Dist-KITCHN

Stoneware C 28 MIN
2 INCH VIDEOTAPE
Features Mrs Peterson describing certain ceramic processes for her classroom at the University of Southern California. Demonstrates how to work with stoneware.
From The Wheels, Kilns And Clay Series.
Prod-USC Dist-PUBTEL

Stoney Knows How C 30 MIN
16MM FILM, 3/4 OR 1/2 IN VIDEO
Interviews the late Leonard St Clair, a paraplegic dwarf, a carnival sword swallower as a child and a tattoo artist since 1928.
Prod-FLOWER Dist-FLOWER 1982

Stop C 11 MIN
16MM FILM, 3/4 OR 1/2 IN VIDEO H-C A
Records and elaborates on the satirical messages of hundreds of caricaturists from all over the world who urge man to find an end to such world problems as pollution, overpopulation, drug abuse, war and murder.
Prod-VARDFM Dist-IFB 1977

Stop - Police C 14 MIN
16MM FILM, 3/4 OR 1/2 IN VIDEO
Looks at when a police officer should use deadly force. Analyzes the high level of skill development and training that help make up an officer's decision to use deadly force and the incredible pressures on each officer to make the right decision every time. Narrated by Harry Reasoner and originally shown on the CBS program 60 Minutes.
Prod-CBSNEW Dist-MTI

Stop A Fire Before It Starts C 10 MIN
16MM FILM, 3/4 OR 1/2 IN VIDEO J-C A
Explains the basic ingredients of fire and shows how everyday materials can become explosive in the presence of sparks, cigarettes and other ignited materials. Demonstrates typical on-the-job locations where hazardous fire situations are encountered.
Prod-NSC Dist-JOU 1975

Stop And Go C 25 MIN
16MM FILM, 3/4 OR 1/2 IN VIDEO I-H
Illustrates experiments to show how objects behave when subjected to inertia, action and reaction, both on Earth and in outer space.
From The Start Here - Adventure Into Science Series.
Prod-VIDART Dist-LANDMK 1983

Stop And Go, Pt 1 C 11 MIN
3/4 OR 1/2 INCH VIDEO CASSETTE
Includes procedures in interrupted partner stimulation therapy. The female demonstrates interrupted manual stimulation, interrupted stimulation with lubricants, and interrupted oral stimulation.
From The EDCOA Sexual Counseling Series.
Prod-MMRC Dist-MMRC

Stop And Go, Pt 2 C 10 MIN
3/4 OR 1/2 INCH VIDEO CASSETTE
Demonstrates the proper procedure for female-above penile insertion, intravaginal sensory appreciation and interrupted thrusting by the female.
From The EDCOA Sexual Counseling Series.
Prod-MMRC Dist-MMRC

Stop Driving Us Crazy C 10 MIN
16MM FILM OPTICAL SOUND H A
Rusty, a visitor from outer space who looks like a car, cannot communicate with people, only with cars. He says that people's words of love and respect are forgotten when driving and asks viewers what they intend to do about it.
Prod-MCSC Dist-ECUFLM

Stop Drunk Driving - A Call To Action C 18 MIN
3/4 OR 1/2 INCH VIDEO CASSETTE J A
Strives to raise public awareness about drunk driving. Discusses what can be done to curtail drinking and driving.
Prod-AMINS Dist-SUTHRB

Stop Drunken Driving - A Call To Action C 15 MIN
3/4 INCH VIDEO CASSETTE
Illustrates the disastrous results that can take place when people drink and drive. Urges action against this problem.
Prod-AMINS Dist-MTP

Stop In The Marshland B 31 MIN
16MM FILM OPTICAL SOUND A
Portrays the character of a brakeman of a freight train in the middle of Nordic marshland. Follows the brakeman as he incurs the wrath of his co-workers when he decides to stay behind.
LC NO. 73-702754
Prod-NLC Dist-NLC 1973

Stop Motion Miracles B 6 MIN
16MM FILM OPTICAL SOUND
A 1953 Screen News Digest excerpt shows the development of plant life and the motion picture techniques which speed up the growth of flowers, as cactus, hibiscus, and daffodils, and root development of beans, and cancerous growth of cells.
From The News Magazine Of The Screen Series. Vol 4, No. 1
Prod-PATHE Dist-HEARST 1953

Stop Or Go - An Experiment In Genetics C 29 MIN
16MM FILM OPTICAL SOUND H-C A
Documents an experiment which analyzes the genetic code of a mutant virus. Shows geneticists at Rockefeller University as they separate mutant viruses from non-mutants, grow new generations of mutants, extract mutant genetic material and test this material for its ability to manufacture a certain protein.
From The Spectrum Series.
LC NO. FIA68-2299
Prod-NET Dist-IU 1968

Stop Press C 15 MIN
16MM FILM, 3/4 OR 1/2 IN VIDEO I-J
Presents a musical about punctuation, featuring a song-and-dance man as the period, an English tart as the comma, a mime clown as the question mark and sing-ing-and-dancing twins as the quotation marks.
Prod-THAMES Dist-MEDIAG 1983

Stop Procrastinating - Act Now C 23 MIN
16MM FILM - VIDEO, ALL FORMATS
Explores reasons for procrastination and provides methods for overcoming the habit.
Prod-CALLFM Dist-BARR

Stop Rats Forever C 15 MIN
16MM FILM OPTICAL SOUND
Deals with the problems rats cause for farmers every year. Uses scenes of live wild rats killing chickens, starting fires, and spreading diseases that cut into farmer's profits. Explains how to get rid of them.
Prod-VENARD Dist-VENARD

Stop Rubella C 14 MIN
16MM FILM OPTICAL SOUND
Explains the dangers of the disease rubella and shows how mothers and their unborn children can be protected from it. This film can be used as part of an immunization program or with parents of handicapped children.
LC NO. 74-705703
Prod-USPHS Dist-USNAC 1969

Stop Ruining America's Past B 22 MIN
16MM FILM OPTICAL SOUND H-C A
Documents the campaign to save archeological sites in Illinois from destruction by urban and industrial expansion. Explains the significance of the sites. Shows archeologists and students during an emergency midwinter dig.
From The Public Broadcast Laboratory Series.
LC NO. FIA68-1943
Prod-NET Dist-IU 1968

Stop Smoking B 30 MIN
3/4 OR 1/2 INCH VIDEO CASSETTE
Gives subliminal suggestions to help one to stop smoking.
Prod-ADVCAS Dist-ADVCAS

Stop Smoking With Alf Fowles C 60 MIN
1/2 IN VIDEO CASSETTE BETA/VHS
Presents a program for smokers who want to quit. Combines deep relaxation with visual messages directed at the subconscious.
Prod-MOHOMV Dist-MOHOMV

Stop That Fire C 12 MIN
16MM FILM, 3/4 OR 1/2 IN VIDEO A
Gives examples of various types of fires, how they start, and how to extinguish them. Safety devices such as sprinkler systems and fire extinguishers are explained, and the need for prevention measures and proper emergency training is stressed.
Prod-IFB Dist-IFB

Stop The World - Maggie Wants To Get Off C 30 MIN
16MM FILM, 3/4 OR 1/2 IN VIDEO J-H A
Reveals that when she presumes that she is responsible for her parents' divorce, Maggie angrily runs out into traffic and is struck by a car. Shows that during her recovery, her family, friends and teacher help her realize she wasn't responsible for the break-up.
From The Moving Right Along Series.
Prod-WQED Dist-MTI 1983

Stop-And-Frisk Doctrine, The C 50 MIN
3/4 OR 1/2 INCH VIDEO CASSETTE PRO
Discusses the stop-and-frisk doctrine, its application and exceptions. Discusses reasonableness of police action in hot pursuit and the plain view doctrine.
From The Criminal Procedure And The Trial Advocate Series.
Prod-ABACPE Dist-ABACPE

Stop, Look And Laugh B 78 MIN
16MM FILM OPTICAL SOUND I-C
Presents the three stooges popping up in the stories Paul Winchell tells Jerry Mahoney and Knucklehead Smith in the course of a day.
Prod-CPC Dist-TWYMAN 1960

Stop, Look And Think (2nd Ed) C 11 MIN
16MM FILM, 3/4 OR 1/2 IN VIDEO K-P
Shows how to cross streets safely. Uses animation and live action to demonstrate driver reaction time, braking distance of automobiles and stopping distance of children when walking versus running.
Prod-CAHILL Dist-AIMS 1978

Stopover, The B 14 MIN
16MM FILM, 3/4 OR 1/2 IN VIDEO J-C A
Depicts a traveler at a stopover in a bus terminal who demonstrates the possibility of living gourmet style while traveling by Greyhound bus.
Prod-STEINP Dist-PHENIX 1975

Stopping C 15 MIN
2 INCH VIDEOTAPE K
Shows that a force is required to stop the motion of an object or to change the direction of a moving object.
From The Let's Go Sciencing, Unit II - Energy Series.
Prod-DETPS Dist-GPITVL

Stopping Foodservice Waste (Rev Ed) C
16MM FILM, 3/4 OR 1/2 IN VIDEO
Dramatizes ways to avoid wasteful practices and save money in all food service operations. Shows waste caused by discarding perfectly good food, ignoring portion control and being wasteful in the handling and storing of food, dishware and utensils.
From The Professional Food Preparation And Service Programs Series.
Prod-NEM Dist-NEM 1983

Stopping History C 57 MIN
3/4 OR 1/2 INCH VIDEO CASSETTE H-C A
Provokes viewers to confront the question of nuclear war and to consider their role in impeding nuclear devastation.
LC NO. 84-707811
Prod-KQEDTV Dist-ADAIR 1984

Stopping Time C 30 MIN
3/4 OR 1/2 INCH VIDEO CASSETTE
Explores the relationship between photography and art, how it usurps paintings' function of documenting history and causes painters to seek out the reality beneath the surface of things and people.
From The Eye To Eye Series.
Prod-WGBHTV Dist-EAI Prodn-MOFAB

Storage And Handling Of Combustibles C 60 MIN
3/4 OR 1/2 INCH VIDEO CASSETTE IND
See series title for descriptive statement.
From The Industrial Fire Hazard Recognition And Control Series.
Prod-NCSU Dist-AMCEE

Storage Classes C
3/4 OR 1/2 INCH VIDEO CASSETTE
Explains the position of storage class specifier to the type specifier in a declaration statement. Illustrates the scope, life, implicit and explicit initialization values which a storage class may assume. Describes the characteristics of the automatic, register, external and static storage classes and identifies the reasons for selecting a particular storage class for an identifier.
From The 'C' Language Programming Series.
Prod-COMTEG Dist-COMTEG

Store, The C 118 MIN
16MM FILM, 3/4 OR 1/2 IN VIDEO
Portrays the main Nieman-Marcus store and corporate headquarters in Dallas. Includes sequences on the selection, presentation, marketing, pricing, advertising and selling of a vast array of consumer products. Shows internal management and organizational aspects of a large corporation.
Prod-WISEF Dist-ZIPRAH

Stored Product Pests C
3/4 OR 1/2 INCH VIDEO CASSETTE
See series title for descriptive statement.
From The Pest Control Technology Correspondence Course Series.
Prod-PUAVC Dist-PUAVC

Storefront X 40 MIN
16MM FILM - 3/4 IN VIDEO
Describes the training and role of non-professional aides in a neighborhood Storefront Center. Depicts the anger and frustrations of ghetto life in the South Bronx, New York, New York.
Prod-USOEO Dist-USNAC 1972

Storehouse Of Minerals C 15 MIN
3/4 OR 1/2 INCH VIDEO CASSETTE I
Presents John Rugg visiting several Rocky Mountain mining sites, discussing surface and underground operations. Shows an open-pit molybdenum mine, milling, tailing ponds and land reclamation. Highlights early gold and silver booms through dramatic vignettes showing the roles played by Horace Greeley and H A W Taylor.
From The American Legacy Series. Program 11
LC NO. 83-706668
Prod-KRMATV Dist-AITECH 1983

Stories C 14 MIN
16MM FILM, 3/4 OR 1/2 IN VIDEO K-I
Shows children working with a teacher and making up a round-robin collaborative story, formulating characters, illustrating how they get ideas for stories and how settings can add to stories and talking about the importance of beginnings and endings.
From The Joy Of Writing Series.
Prod-CF Dist-CF 1977

Stories For A New View - The Earth's Plants, Pt 1 B 15 MIN
2 INCH VIDEOTAPE P

Explains that living things are specially adapted to a certain environment and tells how the classification of living things is based on the characteristics held in common within the group.
From The Science Is Everywhere Series. No. 31
Prod-DETPS Dist-GPITVL

Stories For A New View - The Earth's Plants, Pt 2 B 15 MIN
2 INCH VIDEOTAPE P
Explains that living things are specially adapted to a certain environment and tells how the classification of living things is based on the characteristics held in common within the group.
From The Science Is Everywhere Series. No. 32
Prod-DETPS Dist-GPITVL

Stories In Clay C 6 MIN
16MM FILM, 3/4 OR 1/2 IN VIDEO P-I
Shows children working with clay and creating clay figures, followed by animated sequences featuring the figures.
Prod-ACI Dist-AIMS 1972

Stories In Paper C 9 MIN
16MM FILM, 3/4 OR 1/2 IN VIDEO P-I
Uses live-action segments, followed by animation, to demonstrate how paper puppets can be utilized to act out a story. Introduces a young girl who makes a movable figure out of paper and, as she works, explains how she makes the figure so that she can move it in telling a story.
Prod-ACI Dist-AIMS 1972

Stories In Picture B 15 MIN
2 INCH VIDEOTAPE K-P
Discusses the art of cartooning. (Broadcast quality)
From The Magic Of Words Series.
Prod-GWTVAI Dist-GPITVL Prodn-WETATV

Stories In String C 8 MIN
16MM FILM, 3/4 OR 1/2 IN VIDEO P-I
Uses live action and animated sequences to introduce a technique of making string figures.
Prod-ACI Dist-AIMS 1972

Stories In The News C 15 MIN
3/4 OR 1/2 INCH VIDEO CASSETTE P
Combines looking, listening, talking, writing and reading to help establish the link between oral and written language. Presents a feature newspaper story from the Long Beach, California Independent Press Telegram.
From The I Want To Read Series.
Prod-LACOS Dist-GPITVL 1976

Stories Of America—A Series
P
Introduces American history from Columbus to Theodore Roosevelt through the medium of storytelling. Explains that some of the stories are purely fictional and are intended to relate the lifestyle of a period, while others are based on factual events and real people. Features storyteller Ann Mc Gregor.
Prod-OHSDE Dist-AITECH Prodn-WVIZTV 1976

America Is Named 15 MIN
Annie Oakley 15 MIN
Ben Franklin 15 MIN
California Gold Rush, The 15 MIN
Children Of The Mayflower 15 MIN
Clara Barton 15 MIN
Daniel Boone 15 MIN
Davy Crockett 15 MIN
Discover America 15 MIN
Father Is President 15 MIN
First Cars, The 15 MIN
George Washington 15 MIN
Gretchen Goes West 15 MIN
Growers, The 15 MIN
Indian Summer 15 MIN
John Billington And Squanto 15 MIN
Lewis And Clark 15 MIN
Little Yellow Fur 15 MIN
Martin And Abraham Lincoln 15 MIN
Needles And Bread 15 MIN
New Amsterdam 15 MIN
Oregon Trail 15 MIN
Our Country's Birthday 15 MIN
Pecos Bill 15 MIN
Pocahontas 15 MIN
Pony Express, The 15 MIN
Robert Fulton 15 MIN
Runaway Slave 15 MIN
Start Of A War, The 15 MIN
Tom Edison 15 MIN
Transcontinental Railroad, The 15 MIN
Underground Railroad, The 15 MIN

Stories Of Stories C 20 MIN
3/4 OR 1/2 INCH VIDEO CASSETTE P
Describes the origins of storytelling, presenting the stories Feather Toes and How Anansi The Spider Stole The Sky God's Stories.
From The Folk Book Series.
Prod-UWISC Dist-AITECH 1980

Stories Of Tuktu - A Children's Adventure Series—A Series
16MM FILM, 3/4 OR 1/2 IN VIDEO K-J
Follows Tuktu, an Eskimo boy, in authentic Arctic adventures. Edited from documentary film footage of the life of the Netsilik Eskimos before acculturation by the white man's ways.
Prod-NFBC Dist-FI 1969

Tuktu And His Animal Friends 14 MIN
Tuktu And His Eskimo Dogs 14 MIN
Tuktu And His Nice New Clothes 14 MIN
Tuktu And The Big Kayak 14 MIN
Tuktu And The Big Seal 14 MIN
Tuktu And The Caribou Hunt 14 MIN
Tuktu And The Clever Hands 14 MIN
Tuktu And The Indoor Games 14 MIN
Tuktu And The Magic Bow 14 MIN
Tuktu And The Magic Spear 14 MIN
Tuktu And The Snow Palace 14 MIN
Tuktu And The Ten Thousand Fishes 14 MIN
Tuktu And The Trials Of Strength 14 MIN

Stories Should Be Shared C 15 MIN
16MM FILM OPTICAL SOUND C T
As part of their reading enrichment program, elementary school children act out stories they have read.
Prod-WSU Dist-WSU 1958

Stories, Myths, Ironies And Songs C 70 MIN
3/4 OR 1/2 INCH VIDEO CASSETTE
Presents 21 segments relating the author's experiences and ideas about our culture, ethics and myths.
Prod-KITCHN Dist-KITCHN

Stories, Stories, Stories C 10 MIN
3/4 OR 1/2 INCH VIDEO CASSETTE K-P
Helps children to develop a sense of personal accomplishment regarding their ability to read or interpret sounds, pictures and stories.
From The Book, Look And Listen Series.
Prod-MDDE Dist-AITECH 1977

Storing Information C 30 MIN
3/4 OR 1/2 INCH VIDEO CASSETTE A
Examines the computer as a tool for the storage and retrieval of information. Demonstrates how to move information from computer to disk or how to use the computer as a filing system.
From The Bits And Bytes Series. Pt 4
Prod-TVOTAR Dist-TIMLIF 1984

Storing, Retrieving, Printing And Advanced Features C
3/4 OR 1/2 INCH VIDEO CASSETTE
Explains how to store a MultiPlan worksheet, retrieve a worksheet and print a worksheet in part or whole, or copy it onto a diskette. Describes advanced features of MultiPlan, including storing, iteration, window creation and linking worksheets.
From The Using MultiPlan Series.
Prod-COMTEG Dist-COMTEG

Storm C 29 MIN
16MM FILM, 3/4 OR 1/2 IN VIDEO
Documents the flooding that resulted from Tropical Storm Agnes. Focuses on the Wyoming Valley in Pennsylvania, where Wilkes-Barre and other towns safely evacuated 80,000 people when the Susquehanna River reached a crest of 40 feet.
Prod-USFDAA Dist-USNAC 1974

Storm Boy C 33 MIN
3/4 OR 1/2 INCH VIDEO CASSETTE I-J
A shortened version of the motion picture Storm Boy. Shows how a boy learns about life from an adopted pelican, an aborigine and his own father.
From The Learning To Be Human Series.
Prod-SAFC Dist-LCOA

Storm Boy C 90 MIN
16MM FILM, 3/4 OR 1/2 IN VIDEO
Details the idyllic existence of Storm Boy, his father and his pet pelican on an isolated portion of South Australia. Shows that when the pelican is shot, Storm Boy is prompted to choose between his current lifestyle and rejoining society.
Prod-UNKNWN Dist-LCOA 1976

Storm Of Strangers—A Series
16MM FILM, 3/4 OR 1/2 IN VIDEO
Tells the story of the mass movement of immigrants from Ireland, Italy, China and Israel to America.
Prod-MACMFL Dist-FI 1974

Irish, The 30 MIN
Italian American 26 MIN
Jewish American 26 MIN
Jung Sai - Chinese American 29 MIN

Storm Over Asia B 70 MIN
3/4 OR 1/2 INCH VIDEO CASSETTE
Offers a film directed by P I Podovkin.
Prod-IHF Dist-IHF

Storm Over The Supreme Court, Pt 1 - 1790-1932 B 21 MIN
16MM FILM, 3/4 OR 1/2 IN VIDEO J-C A
Traces the development of the Supreme Court as a strong force in American government.
Prod-CBSNEW Dist-CAROUF

Storm Over The Supreme Court, Pt 2 - 1932-1963 B 32 MIN
16MM FILM, 3/4 OR 1/2 IN VIDEO J-C A
Looks at events in the Supreme Court from the era of Franklin Roosevelt until 1963.
Prod-CBSNEW Dist-CAROUF

Storm Signal C
16MM FILM, 3/4 OR 1/2 IN VIDEO
Shows how the lives of a young married couple disintegrate as they battle heroin addiction.
Prod-DREWAS Dist-DIRECT 1966

Storm Water Management - Detention Storage And Ordinances Relat ing To Flood...—A Series
C
Focuses on planning aspects of storm water management including detention facilities, cost allocaton methods, erosion and sediment control and related ordinances and regulations. Includes eight hours of lectures on eight tapes. Segment III of the course Storm Water Management.
Prod-GATECH Dist-AMCEE

Storm Water Management - Hydrologic Design And Hydrologic Design Of Inlets...—A Series
C
Covers engineering aspects of storm water management including commonly used hydrologic methods as well as conventional and improved inlet and culvert design concepts. Includes 10 tapes of one hour each. Segment I of the course Storm Water Management.
Prod-GATECH Dist-AMCEE

Storm Water Management - Microcomputers And Hydrologic Analysis—A Series
C
Demonstates how to use Apple or IBM microcomputers in conducting hydrologic studies. Includes two hours of instruction on how to modify the progress to meet local needs. Segment II of the course Storm Water Management.
Prod-GATECH Dist-AMCEE

Storm Water Management, Part 1 - Hydrologic Design And Hydraulic Design Of Inlets—A Series
PRO
Covers in ten hours of classroom format lectures the engineering aspects of storm water management including hydrologic methods as well as conventional and improved inlet and culvert design concepts.
Prod-GATECH Dist-AMCEE

Storm Water Management, Part 2 Microcomputers And Hydrologic...—A Series
PRO
Demonstrates how to use Apple or IBM microcomputers in conducting hydrologic studies. Uses classroom format in video taping two hours of lectures, and shows how to modify the program to fit local needs.
Prod-GATECH Dist-AMCEE

Storm Water Management, Part 3 - Detention Storage And Ordinances...Control—A Series
PRO
Uses classroom format to videotape eight one hour lectures. Focuses on planning aspects of storm water management including detention facilities, cost allocation methods, erosion and sediment control and related ordinances nad regulations.
Prod-GATECH Dist-AMCEE

Storm, A Strife, A C 28 MIN
16MM FILM OPTICAL SOUND H-C A
Deals with the relationship between emotional well-being and physical health. Tells the story of Trish, who aggravates an illness worrying about family problems and is able to be helped only after her doctor and her minister get together.
Prod-AMEDA Dist-AMEDA

Storm, The C 15 MIN
1/2 IN VIDEO CASSETTE BETA/VHS I-J
Describes how the Mimi is caught in a storm and disabled while tracking a tagged whale. Includes a trip to the top of New Hampshire's Mount Washington, where meteorologists study what is sometimes labeled 'the worst weather in the world'.
From The Voyage Of The Mimi Series.
Prod-HRAW Dist-HRAW

Storms - An Introduction C 14 MIN
16MM FILM, 3/4 OR 1/2 IN VIDEO I-J
Offers examples of thunderstorms, hurricanes, tornadoes and blizzards and describes the weather patterns that generate them.
Prod-BEAN Dist-PHENIX 1981

Storms - The Restless Atmosphere C 22 MIN
16MM FILM, 3/4 OR 1/2 IN VIDEO I-H
Describes the atmospheric condition which creates thunderstorms, tornadoes and hurricanes. Shows how stresses built up in atmospheric heat and circulation are dissipated.
From The Earth Science Program Series.
Prod-EBEC Dist-EBEC 1974

Stormwater Pollution Control - A New Technology C 29 MIN
16MM FILM OPTICAL SOUND
Describes techniques being developed to solve the problem of handling the overflow of raw sewage from storm sewage systems that occurs after heavy rains.
LC NO. 74-706585
Prod-USEPA Dist-USNAC 1974

Stormy The Thoroughbred C 46 MIN
16MM FILM, 3/4 OR 1/2 IN VIDEO
Presents the story of Stormy, a little horse who didn't belong.
From The Animal Featurettes, Set 1 Series.
Prod-DISNEY Dist-WDEMCO 1967

Story About Feelings, A C 10 MIN
3/4 OR 1/2 INCH VIDEO CASSETTE K-I A
Discusses alcoholism and other drug dependencies as designed for and narrated by 5 to 8 year old children. Contains animation based on children's drawings as well as live classroom scenes. Treats chemical dependency as an unpleasant illness rather than something making a person bad.
Prod-JOHNIN Dist-EDMI 1981

Story About Ping, The B 10 MIN
16MM FILM, 3/4 OR 1/2 IN VIDEO K-P
An iconographic motion picture based on the children's book of the same title by Flack and Wiese.
Prod-WWS Dist-WWS 1957

Story By The Teacher B 15 MIN
2 INCH VIDEOTAPE P

See series title for descriptive statement.
From The Language Corner Series.
Prod-CVETVC Dist-GPITVL Prodn-WCVETV

Story Elements C 15 MIN
3/4 OR 1/2 INCH VIDEO CASSETTE J-H
Shows a ninth-grade class studying television involved in such diverse projects as a documentary on interesting after school jobs, situation comedies, commercials and political commercials for school office candidates.
From The Tuned-In Series. Lesson 7
Prod-WNETTV Dist-FI 1982

Story Into Film - Clark's The Portable Phonograph C 10 MIN
16MM FILM, 3/4 OR 1/2 IN VIDEO J-C A
Presents a commentary by producer/director John Barnes on Walter Van Tilburg Clark's The Portable Phonograph in which he discusses the process and problems of translating the short story to a filmed dramatization.
From The Humanities - Short Story Showcase Series.
Prod-EBEC Dist-EBEC 1977

Story Line C 15 MIN
3/4 OR 1/2 INCH VIDEO CASSETTE P
Combines looking, listening, talking, writing and reading to help establish the link between oral and written language. Presents the story The Fox And The Stork by Dr Jose Antonio Elgorriaga.
From The I Want To Read Series.
Prod-LACOS Dist-GPITVL 1976

Story Maker C 15 MIN
3/4 OR 1/2 INCH VIDEO CASSETTE P
See series title for descriptive statement.
From The Word Shop Series.
Prod-WETATV Dist-WETATV

Story Of 'Dance In America,' The C 30 MIN
3/4 OR 1/2 INCH VIDEO CASSETTE
See series title for descriptive statement.
From The Dance On Television And Film Series.
Prod-ARCVID Dist-ARCVID

Story Of '91,' The C 30 MIN
16MM FILM OPTICAL SOUND
Portrays the function of the local union and its close relationship to members on and off the job. Reflects the history of their union and its hard-won benefits at a special meeting.
Prod-ILGWU Dist-AFLCIO 1963

Story Of A Book (2nd Ed) C 16 MIN
16MM FILM, 3/4 OR 1/2 IN VIDEO I-J
Tells how author Marguerite Henry conceives and writes a book. Discusses where ideas come from, research in the library and on location, writing and rewriting, creating the illustrations, planning the dummy, and printing.
Prod-PPIPER Dist-CF 1980

Story Of A Check, The (2nd Ed) C 11 MIN
16MM FILM, 3/4 OR 1/2 IN VIDEO I-J
Illustrates how the checking system works, from writing individual checks to the process by which banks handle millions of dollars in checks every day.
Prod-WILETS Dist-BARR 1981

Story Of A Communist, The C 70 MIN
3/4 OR 1/2 INCH VIDEO CASSETTE
Presents a biography of Leonid Ilyich Brezhnev, General Secretary of the CPSU Central Committee and Chairman of the Presidium of the Supreme Soviet of the USSR.
Prod-IHF Dist-IHF

Story Of A Congressman, The B 25 MIN
16MM FILM OPTICAL SOUND I-H A
Follows the activities of a congressman during his reelection campaign. Discussions between the incumbent and his opponent emphasize that the strength of a free government lies with an intelligent voting public.
LC NO. FIA66-1304
Prod-WOLPER Dist-SF 1965

Story Of A Craftsman, The C 21 MIN
16MM FILM OPTICAL SOUND
Follows the work of Dominic Callicchio, an expert metal craftsman, as he makes a trumpet from a raw piece of brass. Shows how his skills are thriving in an increasing technological age.
LC NO. 76-700427
Prod-TAPDEM Dist-MALIBU 1975

Story Of A Dam C 17 MIN
16MM FILM OPTICAL SOUND J-C
Follows the building of the Hoover Dam Reservoir at Columbus, Ohio, over a period of three years.
Prod-OSUMPD Dist-OSUMPD 1955

Story Of A Dancer, The B 26 MIN
16MM FILM OPTICAL SOUND
Presents an original ballet which portrays the dance career of Melanie Alexander from her days as a beginner to her debut as a prima ballerina.
LC NO. FI67-4
Prod-WOLPER Dist-SF 1963

Story Of A Hospital Fire C 27 MIN
16MM FILM, 3/4 OR 1/2 IN VIDEO
Shows a hospital fire, describing what can happen when health care personnel aren't trained in basic emergency fire procedures. Based on an actual hospital fire in Sweden.
Prod-MINERV Dist-FILCOM

Story Of A Love Affair (Italian) B 102 MIN
16MM FILM OPTICAL SOUND
Features the debut of Michelangelo Antonioni as a director. Relates the story of a grubby private detective, a glamorous femme fatale and a pair of lovers conniving to bump off an unwanted spouse.
Prod-NYFLMS Dist-NYFLMS 1950

Story Of A Newspaperman, The B 25 MIN
16MM FILM OPTICAL SOUND I-H A
Shows some of the problems faced by a small town newspaperman, who must report world and local news to his readers and must also solicit advertising and take an editorial stand on matters raised by public officials.
LC NO. FIA66-1306
Prod-WOLPER Dist-SF 1963

Story Of A Peace Pipe (Ceremonial Pipes) C 16 MIN
16MM FILM OPTICAL SOUND
Discusses a fine specimen of historic and prehistoric pipes from the University of Oklahoma museum. Shows the making of an altar to Wah-kon-tah, the center of the universe, the here and the everywhere. Explains the significance of the pipe as a symbol of communion and a pledge of honor and trust.
Prod-UOKLA Dist-UOKLA

Story Of A Policeman, The B 25 MIN
16MM FILM OPTICAL SOUND I-H A
Reveals how Police Chief Edward Allan strengthened the police force in Santa Ana, California, a city which prior to 1955 had one of the highest unsolved crime rates in the United States.
LC NO. FI67-2
Prod-WOLPER Dist-SF 1962

Story Of A Prisoner, The B 26 MIN
16MM FILM OPTICAL SOUND H
Follows a day in the San Ouentin prison life of inmate Jim Britt. Shows his work and school routine and includes a visit from his wife and interview with his parole board. A group therapy session brings out the story of his wasted youth and the drug addiction that led to the criminal acts which put him behind bars. Demonstrates how the penal system gives a weak man the opportunity to mature into a responsible member of society.
LC NO. FI66-2
Prod-WOLPER Dist-SF 1962

Story Of A Songwriter, The B 27 MIN
16MM FILM OPTICAL SOUND
Portrays the life of songwriter Sammy Cahn as he relaxes with his famous show-business friends and as he works on his newest project, a nightclub routine for singer-dancer Juliet Prowse.
LC NO. FI67-21
Prod-WOLPER Dist-SF 1963

Story Of A Spark Plug B 34 MIN
16MM FILM OPTICAL SOUND
Shows the manufacture, operation and care of the spark plug.
Prod-USDIBM Dist-USDIBM 1942

Story Of A Storm C 29 MIN
16MM FILM OPTICAL SOUND
Describes how the Navy Weather Service helps Navy and cargo ships to avoid adverse weather conditions.
LC NO. 74-706586
Prod-USN Dist-USNAC 1972

Story Of A Story B 20 MIN
16MM FILM OPTICAL SOUND
Examines how a newspaper operates by following a simple story, the daily weather report, from the time it first comes into the newspaper office over the teletype, through writing, editing, typesetting composition and printing, until it bocomes part of a newspaper on the way to the newsstand.
Prod-UPENN Dist-UPENN 1961

Story Of A Violin, The B 5 MIN
16MM FILM OPTICAL SOUND
Follows violin maker Gaggini as he creates a handmade Stradivarius violin. Shows how each step is done without haste and carried out with tender care.
From The Screen News Digest Series. Vol 3, Issue 4
Prod-HEARST Dist-HEARST 1960

Story Of A Writer, The B 25 MIN
16MM FILM, 3/4 OR 1/2 IN VIDEO I-H A
Science fiction writer Ray Bradbury shows how he conceives, ponders and produces such tales as 'MARTIAN CHRONICLES,' 'DANDELION WINE,' and 'FAHRENHEIT 451.'
Prod-WOLPER Dist-SF 1963

Story Of Alaska's Sawmills, The C 30 MIN
16MM FILM OPTICAL SOUND
Presents an historical documentary of Alaska's timber industry, focusing on the development and operations of Alaska's sawmills from 1850 to the present. Uses historical photographs to show early Russian sawmills before Alaska was purchased by the United States. Explores changing markets and the drive to attract pulp companies in order to stabilize Southeast Alaska's fluctuating, seasonal economy.
Prod-AKLOGA Dist-AKLOGA

Story Of An Air Force Base, The B 10 MIN
16MM FILM OPTICAL SOUND
Portrays air pioneers and aviation history as General Thomas D White narrates events linking Bolling Air Force Base to growth and development of the USAF.
LC NO. FIE63-273
Prod-USAF Dist-USNAC 1962

Story Of An Artist, The B 26 MIN
16MM FILM, 3/4 OR 1/2 IN VIDEO
Portrays artist Ed Keinholz at work as he searches through junkyards, thrift stores and manikin factories to find the raw materials to create sculptures reflective of modern life.
Prod-WOLPER Dist-SF 1962

Story Of Anna O, The B 19 MIN
16MM FILM OPTICAL SOUND J-C A
Dramatizes the case history of Anna O, who caused Sigmund Freud to develop his theory on the origins of hysteria and the of psychoanalysis.
LC NO. 82-700533
Prod-FLOWER Dist-FLOWER 1979

Story Of Arc Welding, A C 24 MIN
16MM FILM OPTICAL SOUND
Explains the advantages of arc welding and shows how it is done. Depicts its uses in industry, on the farm and for the repair of military equipment.
Prod-USDIBM Dist-USDIBM 1945

Story Of Art, The - The Thing Made C 30 MIN
2 INCH VIDEOTAPE J-H
See series title for descriptive statement.
From The From Franklin To Frost - Narrative Fiction Series.
Prod-MPATI Dist-GPITVL

Story Of Camp Century, The - City Under The Ice C 32 MIN
16MM FILM OPTICAL SOUND
A nontechnical account of the planning and constuction of camp century, a nuclear-powered U S Army Arctic Research Laboratory buried below the Greenland ice cap. Describes the planning, installation, testing and operation of the nuclear power plant which provides electricity and space heating.
LC NO. FIE64-179
Prod-USA Dist-USNAC 1961

Story Of Carl Gustav Jung—A Series
16MM FILM, 3/4 OR 1/2 IN VIDEO
Discusses the life and thoughts of Carl Gustav Jung. Includes footage of Jung on safari in Africa, as well as a group of early family photographs.
Prod-BBCTV Dist-FI

In Search Of The Soul 30 MIN
Mystery That Heals, The 30 MIN
Sixty-Seven Thousand Dreams 30 MIN

Story Of Cerro-Bolivar, The C 14 MIN
16MM FILM OPTICAL SOUND H-C A
Revised edition of Iron Ore From Cerro-Bolivar. Tells the story of the discovery of the iron ore mine called Cerro-Bolivar in 1947, the initial planning, clearing of jungles, dredging rivers, construction of docks, railroads, bridges, ore loading facilities, power and water plants and the completed communities.
Prod-HANDY Dist-USSC 1954

Story Of Chaim Rumkowski And The Jews Of Lodz, The B 55 MIN
16MM FILM, 3/4 OR 1/2 IN VIDEO
Presents the story of Chaim Rumkowski, who was appointed by the Nazis as the Chairman of the Lodz Jewish Council and who was responsible for establishing a vast bureaucracy to administer all social services within the ghetto. Tells how Rumkowski attempted to turn the Lodz ghetto into an industrial center that would become indispensable to the German war effort, thus enabling the Jews of Lodz to survive the war. Depicts the conditions of daily life, the gradual disintegration of the ghetto and the deportations to death camps.
LC NO. 83-706912
Prod-CNEMAG Dist-CNEMAG 1983

Story Of Christmas, The C 8 MIN
16MM FILM, 3/4 OR 1/2 IN VIDEO I-H
Uses medieval settings, music and animation, in order to present a version of the Christmas story.
Prod-NFBC Dist-FI 1976

Story Of Christopher Columbus X 17 MIN
16MM FILM, 3/4 OR 1/2 IN VIDEO I-J
Re-enacts the events leading to the discovery of America by Columbus. Portrays Columbus' life from boyhood to the time when he landed on the tiny island of San Salvador on October 12, 1492.
Prod-EMERFC Dist-EBEC 1948

Story Of Cinderella, The X 7 MIN
16MM FILM, 3/4 OR 1/2 IN VIDEO K-I
Presents the fairy tale of Cinderella as seen and interpreted in water color and crayon drawings by fifth grade children. Provides narration by the children.
Prod-NFBC Dist-NFBC 1958

Story Of Copper, A C 33 MIN
16MM FILM OPTICAL SOUND
Tells the story of the mining and manufacture of copper from the crude ore to the finished product.
Prod-USDIBM Dist-USDIBM 1951

Story Of Copper, The C 14 MIN
16MM FILM OPTICAL SOUND
Shows the production of copper from open cut mining operations, crushing, flotation and smelting to final electrolysis.
LC NO. 80-700926
Prod-TASCOR Dist-TASCOR 1965

Story Of Croesus C 30 MIN
3/4 INCH VIDEO CASSETTE
Discusses how Croesus, the wealthiest man in the world, sought immortality through continuation of his bloodline and reputation and lost both.
From The Herodotus - Father Of History Series.
Prod-UMITV Dist-UMITV 1980

Story Of Danny, The B 30 MIN
2 INCH VIDEOTAPE T
Dr Dreikurs demonstrates a method of analyzing a written report of a child's behavior. Adler used this method to train people in increasing their sensitivity and diagnostic ability. (Broadcast quality)

From The Dynamics Of Classroom Behavior Series.
Prod-VTETV Dist-GPITVL Prodn-WETKTV

Story Of David, The C 16 MIN
16MM FILM OPTICAL SOUND C
Presents an interview with David, a small boy born without a larnyx who has taught himself to speak. The interviewer, Dr Lawrence Pratt, gives an explanation of this extraordinary phenomenon.
Prod-WSU Dist-WSU 1958

Story Of Debbie, The B 25 MIN
16MM FILM OPTICAL SOUND I-C A
Debbie, who has lived with relatives and in foster homes and institution for 11 years, is shown at the children's Baptist home in Los Angeles as she attempts to adjust to life while awaiting a reunion with her family and a return to a more normal life.
From The Family Life Education And Human Growth Series.
LC NO. FIA66-1182
Prod-WOLPER Dist-SF 1963

Story Of Dentistry, The C 20 MIN
16MM FILM OPTICAL SOUND
Using historical photographs, the history of dentistry is traced from ancient Egypt to the present. Scenes of USC'S School of Dentistry depict modern dental practices.
LC NO. 75-703234
Prod-USC Dist-USC 1964

Story Of Discovery, A - Why Plants Bend Toward Light X 13 MIN
16MM FILM, 3/4 OR 1/2 IN VIDEO I
Illustrates the experimental process by duplicating the experiments performed by Darwin and later scientists to explain why plants bend toward light.
From The Basic Life Science Series. World Of Green Plants
Prod-EBF Dist-EBEC 1966

Story Of Discovery, A - Why Plants Bend Toward Light (Spanish) C 13 MIN
16MM FILM, 3/4 OR 1/2 IN VIDEO I
Replicates experiments performed by Darwin and later scientists to illustrate an historical approach to experimentation.
Prod-EBEC Dist-EBEC

Story Of Electricity, The - The Greeks To Franklin C 14 MIN
16MM FILM, 3/4 OR 1/2 IN VIDEO I-J
Traces the key advances in man's knowledge of electricity from the early Greek's electron, or amber, to Benjamin Franklin's single-fluid theory. Illustrates the ideas, methods and inventions of William Gilbert, Stephen Gray, Francis Hauksbee, Pieter Van Musschenbroek and Benjamin Franklin.
Prod-CORF Dist-CORF 1968

Story Of Eric, The C 34 MIN
16MM FILM, 3/4 OR 1/2 IN VIDEO
Follows a couple through Lamaze classes, their extra weeks of waiting and finally to labor and delivery in a conventional delivery room.
Prod-ASPPO Dist-CENTRE 1972

Story Of Esther, The C 50 MIN
16MM FILM, 3/4 OR 1/2 IN VIDEO I-C A
Reveals how Queen Esther of Persia, who is secretly a Hebrew, discovers a plot to seize the King's throne. Shows how she tricks one of the plotters into revealing the plot before the King. Stars Victoria Principal and Michael Ansara.
From The Greatest Heroes Of The Bible Series.
Prod-LUF Dist-LUF 1979

Story Of Floating Weeds, A B 89 MIN
16MM FILM SILENT
Concerns a down-at-the-heels acting troupe that reaches the end of the line in a remote mountain town. Explores the relationships between the members of the troupe as they begin to go their separate ways. A Japanese production.
Prod-NYFLMS Dist-NYFLMS 1934

Story Of Gasoline, The (2nd Ed) B 23 MIN
16MM FILM OPTICAL SOUND
Traces the story of gasoline from crude oil to finished product and explains in simple terms the complex structural patterns of petroleum molecules making up the fuel that propels millions of automobiles, farm equipment, airplanes and other internal combustion engines.
Prod-USDIBM Dist-USDIBM 1958

Story Of Good King Huemac, The C 21 MIN
16MM FILM, 3/4 OR 1/2 IN VIDEO P-I
Tells how underworld creatures conspire to bring evil into the happy Toltec kingdom by poisoning the king.
LC NO. 80-706007
Prod-FICHTR Dist-TEXFLM 1979

Story Of Hawaii, The B 5 MIN
16MM FILM OPTICAL SOUND
Presents a 1952 Screen News Digest Film excerpt showing a brief pre-statehood Hawaii. Gives a general introduction, although the information is somewhat dated.
From The News Magazine Of The Screen Series. Vol 2, No. 6
Prod-PATHE Dist-HEARST 1952

Story Of John Henry, The C 15 MIN
3/4 INCH VIDEO CASSETTE P
Retells the American legend of John Henry.
From The Magic Carpet Series.
Prod-SDCSS Dist-GPITVL 1977

Story Of Kigtak B 22 MIN
16MM FILM OPTICAL SOUND T
A teacher-training film in which Don Koeller of Davis School, Newton Massachusetts, uses 16mm kinescope film in teaching his fifth grade children.
LC NO. 79-702590
Prod-EDS Dist-EDC 1968

Story Of King Midas, The X 11 MIN
16MM FILM, 3/4 OR 1/2 IN VIDEO P-I
Presents the classic story book tale of the king with the golden touch, who learns that greed can bring unhappiness.
Prod-HARRY Dist-PHENIX 1954

Story Of L Sharkey, The C 22 MIN
16MM FILM OPTICAL SOUND H-C A
Describes how a young journalist in a small town latches on to a story of an old hermit who hasn't been seen for more than 40 years. Tells how the story could mean a big break for the journalist, but the townspeople don't want him to disturb the hermit.
LC NO. 81-701144
Prod-USC Dist-USC 1981

Story Of Lili Marlene, The B 22 MIN
3/4 OR 1/2 INCH VIDEO CASSETTE
Documents the famous World War II song 'Lili Marlene', with historical footage.
Prod-IHF Dist-IHF

Story Of Lubricating Oil, The C 22 MIN
16MM FILM OPTICAL SOUND
Explains in animation how lubricating oil is produced and processed to meet the needs of modern machinery.
Prod-USDIBM Dist-USDIBM 1949

Story Of Luggage, The - From Caveman To Spaceman C 20 MIN
16MM FILM OPTICAL SOUND
Shows how the story of luggage is also the story of man and his need to travel. Traces the history of luggage as it has been made and used by the Stone Age cave dwellers, Pharaoh, the Greeks, the Romans, through the Renaissance, the New World colonists, the American Indians, the Western Pioneers to the present Jet Age. Narrated by Astronaut Scott Carrenter.
Prod-SAMCOR Dist-CROSSC

Story Of Measuring Time - Hours, Minutes, Seconds (2nd Ed) C 12 MIN
16MM FILM, 3/4 OR 1/2 IN VIDEO I
Uses animation to trace the history of time-keeping.
Prod-CORF Dist-CORF

Story Of Menhaden, The C 20 MIN
16MM FILM OPTICAL SOUND
Explains methods of catching and processing menhaden. Shows how the fish is used for such products as cosmetics, paint, linoleum and animal foods.
Prod-USBCF Dist-USNOAA Prodn-SUN 1951

Story Of Molly Pitcher, The C 15 MIN
16MM FILM, 3/4 OR 1/2 IN VIDEO P
Retells the legend of Molly Pitcher, American heroine of the Revolutionary War.
From The Magic Carpet Series.
Prod-SDCSS Dist-GPITVL 1979

Story Of Naval Aviation, The (2nd Ed) B 27 MIN
16MM FILM, 3/4 OR 1/2 IN VIDEO
Traces the development of U S Naval Aviation from its earliest days to its modern day role as the primary striking weapon of the fleet. Depicts the first trans-Atlantic flight and the first U S carrier landing.
LC NO. 81-706654
Prod-USN Dist-USNAC 1961

Story Of Nickel Refining B 22 MIN
16MM FILM OPTICAL SOUND
Shows steps in nickel refining, including the pouring and casting of nickel, a method of recovering nickel from the furnace slag and the preparation of a black nickel oxide virtually free of sulfur.
Prod-USDIBM Dist-USDIBM Prodn-INICKL 1950

Story Of Oak Ridge Operations, The C 28 MIN
16MM FILM OPTICAL SOUND J-C A
Covers the major activities of the Atomic Energy Commission Oak Ridge operations office, which supports programs of national defense and the peaceful applications of atomic energy. Portrays the gaseous diff1sion plant production of enriched uranium for fueling nuclear power plants, research activities and the use of radiation to diagnose and treat disease.
LC NO. 72-700020
Prod-ORNLAB Dist-USERD 1972

Story Of Old Glory, The C 12 MIN
3/4 OR 1/2 INCH VIDEO CASSETTE
Traces the history of the American flag. Issued as a motion picture in 1968.
LC NO. 80-707746
Prod-USMC Dist-USNAC 1980

Story Of Our Money System C 11 MIN
16MM FILM, 3/4 OR 1/2 IN VIDEO I-J
Explains how the unified money system came about.
Prod-CORF Dist-CORF

Story Of Our New Baby, The C 11 MIN
16MM FILM, 3/4 OR 1/2 IN VIDEO P-I
Shows a pregnant woman explaining to her daughter how a baby develops inside the mother. Describes the family's preparations and adjustments concerning the birth of the baby.
Prod-CORF Dist-CORF 1971

Story Of Our Number System C 11 MIN
16MM FILM, 3/4 OR 1/2 IN VIDEO I-H
Traces the historical development of numbers from the counting systems of the Babylonian Empire, the Mayan civilization, and Rome.
Prod-CORF Dist-CORF

Story Of Outdoor Advertising C 13 MIN
16MM FILM OPTICAL SOUND
Demonstrates the effectiveness of outdoor advertising on today's consumers. Points out that the automobile, the connecting link between household and market lace, had become the recognized basis for determining the market.
Prod-GOUTAD Dist-CCNY

Story Of People, The C 15 MIN
2 INCH VIDEOTAPE I
Presents a pictorial biography of Kennedy.
From The Images Series.
Prod-CVETVC Dist-GPITVL

Story Of Power C 3 MIN
16MM FILM OPTICAL SOUND P-I
Tells the story of power.
From The Of All Things Series.
Prod-BAILYL Dist-AVED

Story Of Prehistoric Man, The C 11 MIN
16MM FILM, 3/4 OR 1/2 IN VIDEO I-H
Describes the life, appearance, habitat and achievements of prehistoric man. Bases the description on artifacts, cave paintings and skeletal remains. Indicates the Old and New Stone Ages, and shows the geographical areas in which prehistoric man lived.
Prod-CORF Dist-CORF 1953

Story Of Radiation, The—A Series
J-C A
Outlines known facts about radiation and discusses basic questions such as what it is, how it affects the body and how its risks can be assessed.
Prod-EDMI Dist-EDMI 1982

Radiation - Can We Control It?	015 MIN
Radiation - Can We Use It?	015 MIN
Radiation - Does It Affect Us?	015 MIN
Radiation - Is It Safe?	015 MIN
Radiation - What Does It Do?	015 MIN
Radiation - What Effect Does It Have?	015 MIN
Radiation - What Is It Made Of?	015 MIN
Radiation - What Is It?	015 MIN
Radiation - Where Do We Go From Here?	015 MIN
Radiation - Where Is It?	015 MIN

Story Of Rebild, The C 19 MIN
16MM FILM OPTICAL SOUND
Presents the Danish-American Fourth of July celebration at Rebild.
Prod-RDCG Dist-AUDPLN

Story Of Renal Calculi, The C 32 MIN
16MM FILM OPTICAL SOUND PRO
Describes the various etiologic factors associated with the formation of renal calculi and the phases of preoperative investigation that are essential to establishing the underlying causative factor in each individual patient. Outlines the surgical removal of stones by pelviolithotomy, nephrolithotomy and by resection of lower pole of kidney.
Prod-ACYDGD Dist-ACY 1957

Story Of Rocky Mountain Spotted Fever, The C 29 MIN
16MM FILM OPTICAL SOUND
Shows the tick life-cycle, rodent poisoning, cattle dipping and tick parasite and liveration. Demonstrates the discovery of the yolk sac vaccine and the advent of the therapeutic antibiotics.
LC NO. 74-705705
Prod-NMAC Dist-USNAC 1969

Story Of Soil, The C 15 MIN
16MM FILM OPTICAL SOUND
Shows a farmer who explains the origin of soil and its importance in conservation.
LC NO. 79-700286
Prod-THUPRO Dist-ECI 1978

Story Of Solo, The C 20 MIN
16MM FILM, 3/4 OR 1/2 IN VIDEO I-J
Presents a study of the social structure and behavior of a pack of wild dogs, particularly of the relationship of a pup named Solo to the pack and the pack leader.
Prod-FI Dist-FI 1974

Story Of Stamps, The C 10 MIN
16MM FILM OPTICAL SOUND
Re-creates Israel's history through stamps.
Prod-ALDEN Dist-ALDEN

Story Of Susan McKellar, The - Cystic Fibrosis C 20 MIN
16MM FILM, 3/4 OR 1/2 IN VIDEO
Shows how Susan McKellar has maintained a marriage and career as a nurse although she has suffered from cystic fibrosis all her life. Discusses the disease and how she adapts to its treatment.
LC NO. 83-706584
Prod-CANBC Dist-FLMLIB

Story Of The Aztecs, The C 19 MIN
16MM FILM, 3/4 OR 1/2 IN VIDEO
Presents the accomplishments of the Aztecs, showing ruins of the Aztec empire. Points out their relationship to the Mexican people.
From The Mexican Heritage Series.
Prod-STEXMF Dist-FI 1976

Story Of The Bells X 10 MIN
16MM FILM OPTICAL SOUND
Examines the unique tone characteristics of a carribon bell in terms of the fundamental and the overtones. Emphasizes the need for arrangements and compositions for carribon.
Prod-IOWA Dist-IOWA

Story Of The Blood Stream (2nd Ed) C 24 MIN
16MM FILM, 3/4 OR 1/2 IN VIDEO J-C
Shows how the circulatory system supplies each cell of the human body with fuel, with oxygen to burn the fuel and how it carries off the waste products. Studies in detail the red cell, white cell and capillaries. Reveals the aortic and mitral valves of a human heart. Refers to a computer the determination of the optimum shape for a red cell as it relates to its respiratory function.
Prod-MIS Dist-MIS 1968

Story Of The Cat, The C 15 MIN
16MM FILM, 3/4 OR 1/2 IN VIDEO
Offers the story of a cat who leads an exciting life until he begins to grow old. Reveals that he spends his old age remembering what it was like to be young.
LC NO. 83-706710
Prod-HELNEG Dist-IFB 1983

Story Of The Earth Satellite, The B 5 MIN
16MM FILM OPTICAL SOUND
Presents a 1957 Screen News Digest film excerpt which shows through animation, a man-made moon to return information, about the size and shape of the earth, and the density of the atmosphere back to earth by radio.
From The News Magazine Of The Screen Series. Vol 7, No. 10
Prod-PATHE Dist-HEARST 1957

Story Of The Great Lakes B 28 MIN
16MM FILM OPTICAL SOUND
Portrays the economic importance of the Great Lakes in the transportation of iron ore, coal and grain, and the uses of the U S Coast Guard on this waterway.
LC NO. FIE54-95
Prod-USCG Dist-USNAC 1954

Story Of The Great Lakes B 25 MIN
3/4 INCH VIDEO CASSETTE
Discusses the overall economic significance of the Great Lakes and the important role played by the Coast Guard. Features the cyclic changes in physical features and transportation function of the Great Lakes during the changing seasons.
Prod-USNAC Dist-USNAC 1972

Story Of The Great Rivers C 28 MIN
16MM FILM OPTICAL SOUND
Uses animated maps and live footage to show the early days of the Mississippi, Missouri and Ohio Rivers, the advent of the coast guard on those rivers and their early duties.
LC NO. FIE63-241
Prod-USGS Dist-USNAC 1961

Story Of The Horn, The C 29 MIN
3/4 INCH VIDEO CASSETTE
Looks at the history of the French horn. Tours one of the most extensive private collections of horns in the United States.
Prod-UMITV Dist-UMITV 1975

Story Of The Military Aircraft Storage And Disposition, The - Desert Bonanza C 16 MIN
16MM FILM OPTICAL SOUND
Depicts the mission of the Military Aircraft Storage and Disposition Center at Davis-Monthan Air Force Base in Arizona. Shows how aircraft no longer needed in active inventory are processed for storage and reclamation of parts.
LC NO. 74-706260
Prod-USAF Dist-USNAC 1966

Story Of The NLRB, The C 23 MIN
16MM FILM OPTICAL SOUND
Presents workers in a textile plant in New Jersey who decide to form a union. Explains that when their employers don't recognize them, they familiarize themselves with the functioning of the National Labor Relations Board, region 2.
Prod-RUTGER Dist-AFLCIO 1955

Story Of The Prodigal Son B 22 MIN
16MM FILM OPTICAL SOUND P-C A
Explains God's loving forgiveness of repented wrong. Presents a parable about a younger son who takes his inheritance, squanders it in a far country and is reduced to feeding swine. Tells how he returns home repentant and is received by a forgiving father.
Prod-CAFM Dist-CAFM

Story Of The Serials B 27 MIN
16MM FILM OPTICAL SOUND H-C
Shows the development of the cliff-hangers of silent days, from 1914 with Pearl White's 'THE PERILS OF PAULINE' to 1929 with the advent of sound in motion pictures. Parallels the reign of serial queens with woman's struggle for social and political equality.
From The History Of The Motion Picture Series.
Prod-SF Dist-KILLIS 1960

Story Of The Soviet Constitution, The C 30 MIN
3/4 OR 1/2 INCH VIDEO CASSETTE
Reviews the political system of the USSR, focusing on the Soviet Constitution.
Prod-IHF Dist-IHF

Story Of The Space Age, The - A Special Report B 19 MIN
16MM FILM OPTICAL SOUND
Traces Space-Age progress, exploring the pioneering genius of Robert Hutchings Goodard to the present work of Project Gemini.
From The Screen News Digest Series. Vol 7, Issue 9
LC NO. FIA68-2100
Prod-HEARST Dist-HEARST 1965

Story Of The Star Spangled Banner, The C 10 MIN
16MM FILM OPTICAL SOUND H-C A S
Tells the story of the Star-Spangled Banner in American sign language. Filmed at locations where Francis Scott Key wrote this national anthem. Signed by Louie J Fant, Jr.
LC NO. 76-701097
Prod-JOYCE Dist-JOYCE 1976

Story Of The Unknown Soldier - How They Signed The Kellogg-Briand Pact And Ended... B 12 MIN
16MM FILM, 3/4 OR 1/2 IN VIDEO H-C A
Focuses on the idealistic signing of the Kellog-Brian pact, aimed at making war illegal. Includes footage of the nations of the world as they armed themselves for yet another confrontation.
LC NO. 80-706697
Prod-STORCH Dist-IFB 1932

Story Of The 747 C 28 MIN
16MM FILM OPTICAL SOUND
Tells the story of the Boeing 747 airplane from the point of view of the people and civilizations whose lives it touches.
LC NO. 77-702291
Prod-BOEING Dist-WELBIT Prodn-WELBIT 1977

Story Of Walter, The C 9 MIN
16MM FILM - 3/4 IN VIDEO H-C A
Features research being done on feline leukemia by former Leukemia Society of America scholars. Notes that researchers have isolated a leukemia virus in cats and are now working on perfection of a vaccine which can prevent feline leukemia. Concludes that information from these efforts could be vital to developing a vaccine to prevent leukemia in humans.
LC NO. 83-706830
Prod-METROM Dist-LEUSA Prodn-HMS 1981

Story Of Weights And Measures (2nd Ed) C 11 MIN
16MM FILM, 3/4 OR 1/2 IN VIDEO J
Uses animation to trace the history of measurement. Shows the many advantages of the metric system.
Prod-CORF Dist-CORF

Story Of Wine, Pt 1, The C 90 MIN
1/2 IN VIDEO CASSETTE BETA/VHS A
Features history of wine, and two types of wine Clarets and Aperitifs. Narrated by Baron Philippe De Rothschild.
Prod-LCOA Dist-LCOA

Story Of Wine, Pt 2, The C 90 MIN
1/2 IN VIDEO CASSETTE BETA/VHS A
Features story of cognac, wine tasting and popularity of wine. Narrated by Baron Philippe De Rothschild.
Prod-LCOA Dist-LCOA

Story Of Zachary Zween C 13 MIN
16MM FILM, 3/4 OR 1/2 IN VIDEO K-I
Presents a schoolboy who is always last suddenly finding himself 'FIRST' when he gets lost in the big city.
Prod-SF Dist-SF 1972

Story Playing C 15 MIN
3/4 OR 1/2 INCH VIDEO CASSETTE P
See series title for descriptive statement.
From The Word Shop Series.
Prod-WETATV Dist-WETATV

Story Problems C 15 MIN
3/4 INCH VIDEO CASSETTE P
Explains how to write a solution to story problems using addition and regrouping.
From The Studio M Series.
Prod-WCETTV Dist-GPITVL 1979

Story Problems With The Four Operations C 15 MIN
3/4 INCH VIDEO CASSETTE P
Gives a story problem to explain when to add, subtract, multiply or divide.
From The Studio M Series.
Prod-WCETTV Dist-GPITVL 1979

Story Problems, Pt 1 C 15 MIN
3/4 INCH VIDEO CASSETTE P
Tells how to decide to add or subtract when given a word problem.
From The Measure Up Series.
Prod-WCETTV Dist-GPITVL 1977

Story Problems, Pt 2 C 15 MIN
3/4 INCH VIDEO CASSETTE P
Shows how to solve a word problem.
From The Measure Up Series.
Prod-WCETTV Dist-GPITVL 1977

Story Starters C 15 MIN
2 INCH VIDEOTAPE P
Provides an enrichment program in the communitive arts area by the art of story telling.
From The Word Magic (2nd Ed) Series.
Prod-CVETVC Dist-GPITVL

Story Tellers Of The Canterbury Tales, The C 17 MIN
16MM FILM OPTICAL SOUND
Gives excerpts from the General Prologue and the Canon's Yeoman's prologue of Chaucer's Canterbury tales. Narration is in Middle English.
LC NO. FIA55-271
Prod-USC Dist-USC 1953

Story Telling C 15 MIN
3/4 OR 1/2 INCH VIDEO CASSETTE P
See series title for descriptive statement.
From The Word Shop Series.
Prod-WETATV Dist-WETATV

Story Telling C 17 MIN
3/4 OR 1/2 INCH VIDEO CASSETTE
Illustrates how story telling can be used as a teaching aid in developing speech and language capabilities in hearing-impaired individuals.
LC NO. 80-707429
Prod-USBEH Dist-USNAC 1980

Story Time C 5 MIN
16MM FILM OPTICAL SOUND J-C A
Shows a student carrying out an activity she has planned ahead of time which is reading a story to the children. Depicts roles helpers play in their setting, and the particular interaction that takes place during story time.
From The Exploring Childhood Series.
LC NO. 76-701897
Prod-EDC Dist-EDC Prodn-FRIEDJ 1975

Story Time C 30 MIN
3/4 OR 1/2 INCH VIDEO CASSETTE K-P
See series title for descriptive statement.
From The Villa Alegre Series.
Prod-BCTV Dist-MDCPB

Story Time Is Fun B 15 MIN
2 INCH VIDEOTAPE P
Discusses reading as a good way to enjoy oneself. Explains that books provide experiences that otherwise would not be available. (Broadcast quality)
From The Around The Corner Series. No. 33
Prod-FWCETV Dist-GPITVL Prodn-WEDUTV

Story Turn Around C 15 MIN
3/4 INCH VIDEO CASSETTE K-P
Features an adaptation of the English folktale The Old Woman And Her Pig.
From The I Can Read Series.
Prod-WCETTV Dist-GPITVL 1977

Story-Telling B 17 MIN
16MM FILM OPTICAL SOUND
Demonstrates, through the story Jack and the Beanstalk, how story telling can be used as an effective teaching aid in speech and language development of the hearing impaired.
LC NO. 74-705708
Prod-USA Dist-USNAC

Story, A Story, A C 10 MIN
16MM FILM, 3/4 OR 1/2 IN VIDEO K-P
Tells the story of how long ago there were no stories on earth for children to hear and that all stories belonged to Nyame, the sky god. Explains that Anase, the spider man, wanted to buy some of these stories, so he spun a web up to the sky and went to bargain with the sky god. Uses narration and woodcuts capturing the flavor of African language, customs and lifestyles to show how Anase paid the price.
Prod-WWS Dist-WWS 1973

Storybook International—A Series
16MM FILM, 3/4 OR 1/2 IN VIDEO
Presents children's stories from countries around the world.
Prod-JOU Dist-JOU 1982

Cap O'Rushes 027 MIN
Clever Manka 027 MIN
Emperor And The Abbot, The 027 MIN
Five Loaves, The 027 MIN
Foolish Brother, The 027 MIN
Forbidden Door, The 027 MIN
Grief Of Pi-Kari, The 027 MIN
Haunted Pastures, The 027 MIN
Hinemoa 027 MIN
Island Of Drums, The 027 MIN
Morwen Of The Woodlands 027 MIN
Moses And The Lime Kiln 027 MIN
Nikorima 027 MIN
Pedlar's Dream, The 027 MIN
Priest Know-All, The 027 MIN
Riches Or Happiness 027 MIN
Russian And The Tartar, The 027 MIN
Simpleton Peter 027 MIN
Soldier Who Didn't Wash, The 027 MIN
Sorrow 027 MIN
Straw Hat, The 027 MIN
Twelve Months, The 027 MIN
Well Of The World's End, The 027 MIN
Widow's Lazy Daughter, The 027 MIN

Storybound—A Series
I
Presents passages from books for young people. Encourages students to read the books themselves to find out the endings.
Prod-CTI Dist-CTI

Bridge To Terebitha 015 MIN
Call It Courage 015 MIN
Escape From Warsaw 015 MIN
Ghosts I Have Been 015 MIN
Island Of The Blue Dolphins 015 MIN
It's Not The End Of The World 015 MIN
Konrad 015 MIN
Lizard Music 015 MIN
Mojo And The Russians 015 MIN
Pilot Down, Presumed Dead 015 MIN
Pinballs, The 015 MIN
Pinch 015 MIN
Sounder 015 MIN
Tuck Everlasting 015 MIN
Witch Of Blackbird Pond, The 015 MIN
Wrinkle In Time, A 015 MIN

Storymaker C 14 MIN
16MM FILM, 3/4 OR 1/2 IN VIDEO I-J
Presents a documentary through which viewers experience the fervor, depression and elation involved in the creation of a children's book. Features authorillustator Don Freeman as he makes preliminary sketches and talks about the source of a story idea.
Prod-CF Dist-CF 1972

Storyteller, The C 30 MIN
16MM FILM OPTICAL SOUND
Portrays a gentlemen recounting a love story to a group of prostitutes in a bordello. Reveals eventually that the story is really about the gentleman and his relationship with a beautiful young girl.
LC NO. 79-700287
Prod-CHESLE Dist-CHESLE 1978

Storytellers, The C 15 MIN
2 INCH VIDEOTAPE J-H
Describes people whose careers involve translating dreams, events, attitudes, ambitions and all the elements of human joy and sorrow into experiences that others can share through poetry, novels, drama, satire and short stories.
From The Work Is For Real Series.
Prod-STETVC Dist-GPITVL

Storytelling C 30 MIN
1/2 IN VIDEO CASSETTE BETA/VHS K-I
See series title for descriptive statement.
From The Jump Over The Moon - Sharing Literature With Young Children Series.
Prod-HRAW Dist-HRAW

Storytelling - A Beginning C 15 MIN
3/4 OR 1/2 INCH VIDEO CASSETTE
Stresses that storytellers are people of all ages and backgrounds. Shows how storytellers begin to learn a new story.
Prod-CCPL Dist-LVN

Storytelling - Art And Tradition C 90 MIN
3/4 OR 1/2 INCH VIDEO CASSETTE A
Introduces the custom, craft and experience of storytelling. Includes origins and development, material selection, learning, training and techniques. Includes public library experiences. Presented by Teresa Toscano.
LC NO. 82-707986
Prod-TVR Dist-CATHLA

Storytelling In America C 58 MIN
3/4 OR 1/2 INCH VIDEO CASSETTE J-C A
Presents an engaging look at the traditional art of storytelling and its modern practitioners. Filmed at the tenth National Storytelling Festival at Jonesborough, Tennessee.
LC NO. 84-707093
Prod-NAPPS Dist-NSRC

Storytelling Time B 20 MIN
2 INCH VIDEOTAPE P
Gives some standards for good storytelling. (Broadcast quality)
From The Language Lane Series. Lesson 17
Prod-CVETVC Dist-GPITVL Prodn-WCVETV

Storytime—A Series
K-P
Presents storyteller Jean Beasley offering her interpretations of various children's stories.
Prod-WCETTV Dist-GPITVL 1976

Alexander And The Wind-Up Mouse 15 MIN
Animal's Christmas, The 15 MIN
Blind Men And The Elephant, The 15 MIN
Elephant's Child, The 15 MIN
Emperor's New Clothes, The 15 MIN
Favorite Poems 15 MIN
Fire Bringer, The 15 MIN
Gertie, The Duck 15 MIN
Gunniwolf, The 15 MIN
How To Scare A Lion 15 MIN
Ice 15 MIN
King Midas 15 MIN
Little Red Fire Engine, The 15 MIN
Little Red Lighthouse, The - The Great Gray 15 MIN
Man Who Kept House, The 15 MIN
Monkey And The Crocodile, The 15 MIN
Most Remarkable Cat, The 15 MIN
Mr Willoughby's Christmas 15 MIN
Nail Soup 15 MIN
Nice Little Ugly Witch, The 15 MIN
Raccoons Are For Loving 15 MIN
Randy's Thanksgiving 15 MIN
Secret Seller, The 15 MIN
Shoemaker And The Elves, The 15 MIN
Snail And The Caterpillar, The 15 MIN
Sultan's Bath, The 15 MIN
Susan's Valentine Surprise 15 MIN
Sylvester And The Magic Pebble 15 MIN
Tale Of The Name Of The Tree, The 15 MIN
Three Billy Goats Gruff, The 15 MIN
Tikki Tiki Tembo 15 MIN
Whirly Bird 15 MIN

Stowaway, Pt 1 - Disease And Personal Hygiene B 17 MIN
16MM FILM OPTICAL SOUND
Depicts obvious and obscure ways in which disease is spread by food-handling personnel.
LC NO. FIE52-1520
Prod-USA Dist-USNAC 1948

Stowaway, Pt 2 - Balley Sanitation B 17 MIN
16MM FILM OPTICAL SOUND
Shows sanitary measures for use in all food service organizations to prevent spread of disease.
LC NO. FIE52-1521
Prod-USA Dist-USNAC 1948

Stowaway, The C 23 MIN
16MM FILM, 3/4 OR 1/2 IN VIDEO P-I
Presents a contemporary story, based on the fairy tale Pinocchio, about a young Italian stowaway who encounters the lovable baker Gepetto and a dancing striped Pizza Man who leads him on the path to truth.
From The Unicorn Tales Series.
LC NO. 80-706519
Prod-MGHT Dist-MGHT Prodn-DENOIA 1980

Strabismus C
3/4 OR 1/2 INCH VIDEO CASSETTE
Reviews the nature of both congenital and acquired Strabismus and the threat of Amblyopia. Depicts the underlying problem in the brain's eye control center and how this results in turned eyes and two-dimensional sight. Explains how treatment can be a long term process of patching, glasses, and surgery. Presents surgery along with risks and recovery. Emphasizes early treatment.
Prod-MIFE Dist-MIFE

Strabismus C 8 MIN
3/4 OR 1/2 INCH VIDEO CASSETTE
Discusses the nature of strabismus and related problems. Stresses the importance of early and appropriate treatment.
Prod-TRAINX Dist-TRAINX

Strabismus C 9 MIN
3/4 OR 1/2 INCH VIDEO CASSETTE
Explains the eye condition strabismus. Stresses the need for early and vigorous treatment.
Prod-MEDFAC Dist-MEDFAC 1974

Strabismus (Rev Ed) C 17 MIN
16MM FILM, 3/4 OR 1/2 IN VIDEO PRO
Discusses strabismus in children and describes the goals for successful treatment, the suitable age for eyedrops and ointments, eyeglasses and modern surgery.
Prod-PRORE Dist-PRORE

Strabismus (Spanish) C 17 MIN
16MM FILM, 3/4 OR 1/2 IN VIDEO PRO
Discusses strabismus in children and describes the goals for successful treatment, the suitable age for eyedrops and ointments, eyeglasses and modern surgery.
Prod-PRORE Dist-PRORE

Strabismus And Amblyopia C 15 MIN
3/4 OR 1/2 INCH VIDEO CASSETTE PRO
Discusses the physiologic procedures of how the retina perceives an image and how both eyes work to produce a binocular image (fusion), deviations in the optical system which inhibit tests used to diagnose these deviations and appropriate management.
Prod-UMICHM Dist-UMICHM 1976

Strabismus Surgery C 11 MIN
3/4 OR 1/2 INCH VIDEO CASSETTE PRO
Demonstrates a simple and effective approach to operating on ocular muscles.
Prod-HSCIC Dist-HSCIC 1984

Straddle And Surface Milling To Close Tolerances B 27 MIN
16MM FILM, 3/4 OR 1/2 IN VIDEO
Demonstrates how to make surface- and straddle-milling cutter setups, to surface-mill four sides of a workpiece and to machine a workpiece to a T shape by straddle-milling.
From The Machine Shop Work - Operations On The Milling Machine Series. No. 2
Prod-USOE Dist-USNAC Prodn-CARFI 1941

Straddle Milling B 17 MIN
16MM FILM, 3/4 OR 1/2 IN VIDEO
Demonstrates how to use an indexing fixture for production milling operations, space cutters on an arbor for straddle milling and mill parallel bosses on connecting rods.
From The Machine Shop Work - Operations On The Milling Machine Series. No. 3
Prod-USOE Dist-USNAC 1941

Straight Allowance Application On Transitions C 28 MIN
1/2 IN VIDEO CASSETTE BETA/VHS IND
Discusses the reason for using a straight allowance when developing patterns for transitions which permits faster assembly of fittings and duct work when doing installations.
Prod-RMI Dist-RMI

Straight And Round C 15 MIN
16MM FILM OPTICAL SOUND K-I
Follows Yoffy as he searches for round and straight objects in order to tell a story about two countries, one in which everything is curved and one in which everything is straight.
From The Fingermouse, Yoffy And Friends Series.
LC NO. 73-700441
Prod-BBCTV Dist-VEDO 1972

Straight Jacket C 8 MIN
3/4 INCH VIDEO CASSETTE
Looks at the 'Feminization' of an adult female who models herself, in terms of make-up and postures, on images of women in fashion and movie magazines. Focuses on an active subject against a background of photographs.
From The Student Workshop Videotapes Series.
Prod-WMENIF Dist-WMENIF

Straight Line Kinematics B 34 MIN
16MM FILM OPTICAL SOUND H-C
Explains the concepts of distance, speed, acceleration and time. Uses measuring equipment in a test car to illustrate the concepts.
From The PSSC Physics Films Series.
Prod-PSSC Dist-MLA 1960

Straight On Till Morning C 21 MIN
16MM FILM OPTICAL SOUND
Tells how a sensitive eight-year-old girl attempts to come to terms with the death of her divorced father by creating a fantasy involving Peter Pan to explain his disappearance.
LC NO. 79-700288
Prod-ROPELT Dist-ROPELT 1978

Straight Talk C 15 MIN
16MM FILM OPTICAL SOUND H A
Examines General Motors Institute, an accredited degree-granting engineering college.
Prod-GM Dist-GM

Straight Talk About Drugs C 16 MIN
3/4 OR 1/2 INCH VIDEO CASSETTE J A
Focuses on the widespread nature of drug abuse and how it affects persons of all ethnic origins, income or education.
Prod-SUTHRB Dist-SUTHRB

Straight Talk About Drugs - Psychedelics, PCP And Dangerous Combinations C 39 MIN
3/4 OR 1/2 INCH VIDEO CASSETTE J-H
Identifies drugs classed as psychedelics including LSD, mescaline, psilocybin and PCP. Discusses the reasons why people use these drugs, including their effects and legal implications. Describes the dangers of combining drugs and driving under the influence of drugs.
From The Straight Talk About Drugs Series.
LC NO. 82-706873
Prod-GA Dist-GA 1982

Straight Talk About Drugs - Stimulants And Narcotics C 50 MIN
3/4 OR 1/2 INCH VIDEO CASSETTE J-H
Identifies stimulants and drugs and discusses the dangers and effects of their use. Explores some of the common reasons that people use drugs and describes programs that help rehabilitate the narcotic addict.
From The Straight Talk About Drugs Series.
LC NO. 82-706872
Prod-GA Dist-GA 1982

Straight Talk About Drugs - Tranquilizers And Sedatives C 40 MIN
3/4 OR 1/2 INCH VIDEO CASSETTE J-H
Explores the use of tranquilizers and sedatives, including their dangers and effects. Gives an overview of drug use and explains the differences between drug use and misuse.
From The Straight Talk About Drugs Series.
LC NO. 82-706871
Prod-GA Dist-GA 1982

Straight Talk About Drugs—A Series
J-H
Discusses the use and abuse of such drugs as tranquilizers, sedatives, stimulants, psychedelics and PCP.
Prod-GA Dist-GA 1982

Straight Talk About Drugs - Psychedelics, PCP
Straight Talk About Drugs - Stimulants And 050 MIN
Straight Talk About Drugs - Tranquilizers And 040 MIN

Straight Talk On Eye Safety C 12 MIN
16MM FILM - 3/4 IN VIDEO
Features two veteran campaigners against blinding eye accident in industry, Bill Frank, blinded in a shop accident and James O'Neil, authority on eye safety. Describes the consequences of eye accidents to the wife and children of the victim. Encourages 100 per cent eye protection in shop, home and school.
Prod-HF Dist-HF 1972

Straight Thinking For Stress Management C 32 MIN
3/4 OR 1/2 INCH VIDEO CASSETTE
See series title for descriptive statement.
From The Practical Stress Management With Dr Barry Alberstein Series.
Prod-DELTAK Dist-DELTAK

Straight Time C 107 MIN
16MM FILM OPTICAL SOUND
Focuses on a man who is paroled after six years in jail but who eventually returns to a life of crime. Stars Dustin Hoffman.
Prod-WB Dist-SWANK

Straight Turning Between Centers C
3/4 OR 1/2 INCH VIDEO CASSETTE
See series title for descriptive statement.
From The Basic Engine Lathe Series.
Prod-VTRI Dist-VTRI

Straight Turning Between Centers C 15 MIN
3/4 OR 1/2 INCH VIDEO CASSETTE
See series title for descriptive statement.
From The Machine Technology I - Basic Machine Technology Series.
Prod-CAMB Dist-CAMB

Straight Turning Between Centers C 15 MIN
3/4 OR 1/2 INCH VIDEO CASSETTE IND
See series title for descriptive statement.
From The Machining And The operation Of Machine Tools, Module 2 - Engine Lathe Series.
Prod-LEIKID Dist-LEIKID

Straight Turning Between Centers (Spanish) C
3/4 OR 1/2 INCH VIDEO CASSETTE
See series title for descriptive statement.
From The Basic Engine Lathe (Spanish) Series.
Prod-VTRI Dist-VTRI

Straight Turning Between Centers On The Lathe C 18 MIN
16MM FILM, 3/4 OR 1/2 IN VIDEO J-C A
Demonstrates the straight turning between centers operation on the lathe.
From The Metal Shop - Safety And Operations Series.
Prod-EPRI Dist-AIMS Prodn-EPRI 1970

Straight Turning Between Centers On The Lathe (Arabic) C 18 MIN
16MM FILM, 3/4 OR 1/2 IN VIDEO J-C A

Demonstrates the straight turning between centers operation on the lathe.
From The Metal Shop - Safety And Operations Series.
Prod-EPRI Dist-AIMS Prodn-EPRI 1970

Straight Turning Between Centers On The Lathe (Spanish) C 18 MIN
16MM FILM, 3/4 OR 1/2 IN VIDEO J-C A
Demonstrates the straight turning between centers operation on the lathe.
From The Metal Shop - Safety And Operations Series.
Prod-EPRI Dist-AIMS Prodn-EPRI 1970

Straight Turning Work Of Two Diameters C
3/4 OR 1/2 INCH VIDEO CASSETTE
See series title for descriptive statement.
From The Basic Engine Lathe Series.
Prod-VTRI Dist-VTRI

Straight Turning Work Of Two Diameters C 15 MIN
3/4 OR 1/2 INCH VIDEO CASSETTE
See series title for descriptive statement.
From The Machine Technology I - Basic Machine Technology Series.
Prod-CAMB Dist-CAMB

Straight Turning Work Of Two Diameters C 15 MIN
3/4 OR 1/2 INCH VIDEO CASSETTE IND
See series title for descriptive statement.
From The Machining And The Operation Of Machine Tools, Module 2 - Engine Lathe Series.
Prod-LEIKID Dist-LEIKID

Straight Turning Work Of Two Diameters (Spanish) C
3/4 OR 1/2 INCH VIDEO CASSETTE
See series title for descriptive statement.
From The Basic Engine Lathe (Spanish) Series.
Prod-VTRI Dist-VTRI

Straight Up And Away C 15 MIN
16MM FILM OPTICAL SOUND
Depicts opportunities for helicopter pilots offered by the Marine Corps.
LC NO. 74-706587
Prod-USN Dist-USNAC 1970

Straight-Hole Drilling Practices C 29 MIN
3/4 OR 1/2 INCH VIDEO CASSETTE IND
Covers the principles of straight-hole drilling. Focuses on the well-drilling industry.
Prod-UTEXPE Dist-UTEXPE 1964

Straight-Line Ripsaw, The C 48 MIN
3/4 OR 1/2 INCH VIDEO CASSETTE IND
Shows all steps of the power fed ripsaw operation. Emphasizes high wood yield.
From The Furniture Manufacturing Series.
Prod-LEIKID Dist-LEIKID

Straightforward Communication C 19 MIN
3/4 OR 1/2 INCH VIDEO CASSETTE
See series title for descriptive statement.
From The Leadership Link - Fundamentals Of Effective Supervision Series.
Prod-CHSH Dist-DELTAK

Strained Knot, The - Crises In Marriage C 30 MIN
3/4 OR 1/2 INCH VIDEO CASSETTE C A
Discusses how emotional instability in one or both partners can seriously affect the marriage. Examines the disillusionment and unrealistic expectations that may be created by financial difficulties, having and rearing children, illness or death and parental meddling.
From The Family Portrait - A Study Of Contemporary Lifestyles Series. Lesson 20
Prod-SCCON Dist-CDTEL

Strainers, Filters, And Traps C 60 MIN
3/4 OR 1/2 INCH VIDEO CASSETTE IND
See series title for descriptive statement.
From The Mechanical Equipment Maintenance, Module 7 - Piping Series.
Prod-LEIKID Dist-LEIKID

Straining, Stretching, Dividing - Division, Three-Digit Dividend, Two-Digit Divisor C 15 MIN
3/4 OR 1/2 INCH VIDEO CASSETTE I
Tells how Alice's desire to lose weight creates situations in which she divides by a two-digit divisor. Explains the sequence necessary to find a quotient when using a calculator.
From The Figure Out Series.
Prod-MAETEL Dist-AITECH 1982

Strains, Sprains, Dislocations And Fractures C 30 MIN
3/4 OR 1/2 INCH VIDEO CASSETTE
Deals with injuries requiring specific types of bandages and splints until a doctor can set the break.
From The First Aid In The Classroom Series.
Prod-NETCHE Dist-NETCHE 1973

Straits Detroit (The Detroit River) C 33 MIN
16MM FILM OPTICAL SOUND
Presents a view of the cultural, economic and scientific importance of the Detroit River and the influence the river has had on the history of the region through which it flows.
LC NO. 72-702182
Prod-WSU Dist-WSU 1972

Stranden (The Seashore) C 22 MIN
16MM FILM OPTICAL SOUND
Presents different types of seashores, showing bird life, a bathing beach, fishermen starting directly from flat beach and flocks of birds above the sea. Includes music and sound effects.
Prod-STATNS Dist-STATNS 1962

Strandskade - Haematopus Ostralegus (Oyster Catcher) C 5 MIN
16MM FILM OPTICAL SOUND
Presents a description of the oyster catcher in its natural surroundings, accompanied by sound effects.
Prod-STATNS Dist-STATNS 1965

Strange And Unusual Animals - Adaptation To Environment C 10 MIN
16MM FILM, 3/4 OR 1/2 IN VIDEO I-C A
Studies several animals including the elephant, the ostrich, the cassowary, the bat, the sloth, the leaf frog, the aardvark, the giant anteater, the echidna, the kangaroo, the duck-billed platypus and the koala bear and discusses man's place in nature.
Prod-LATHAM Dist-AIMS 1974

Strange Bird C 10 MIN
16MM FILM, 3/4 OR 1/2 IN VIDEO P-I
Presents the animated story of a bird which hatches in an alarm clock. Shows that after some moments of frustration, the mother bird learns that there is a place in the bird world for an alarm clock.
LC NO. 80-707241
Prod-ZAGREB Dist-IFB 1975

Strange Case Of Mr Finch, The C 16 MIN
16MM FILM, 3/4 OR 1/2 IN VIDEO P-I
Discusses the importance of effective listening skills.
LC NO. 83-706342
Prod-EBERHT Dist-FLMFR 1983

Strange Case Of The Cosmic Rays, The C 59 MIN
16MM FILM - 3/4 IN VIDEO H
Probes the mysteries of cosmic rays. Discusses their characteristics, behavior and the work of scientists in their search for more knowledge of matter and energy.
From The Bell System Science Series.
Prod-ATAT Dist-WAVE Prodn-CAPRA 1957

Strange Case Of The English Language, The X 48 MIN
16MM FILM, 3/4 OR 1/2 IN VIDEO H-C A
Explains that a great way to learn about the idiosyncrasies of the English language, as it is spoken and written, is to study film clips of noted public figures. CBS's Harry Reasoner comments on John F Kennedy, Everett Dirksen, Billy Graham and many others. Points up the stylistic quirks and overuse of pet phrases. Features interviews with various language experts.
Prod-CBSTV Dist-PHENIX 1968

Strange Creature - The Echidna C 14 MIN
3/4 OR 1/2 INCH VIDEO CASSETTE P-C A
Reveals that only two animals lay eggs like reptiles but suckle their young like mammals, and both live in Australia. Describes the echidna, or spiny ant-eater as one of these strange creatures (the other is the platypus). Shows on film, recorded for the first time, the young hatching from its egg and being carried in its mother's pouch. Notes how the echidna lives by tearing open ant nests and licking up the ants with its sticky tongue.
Prod-EDMI Dist-EDMI 1971

Strange Creatures Of The Night C 52 MIN
16MM FILM, 3/4 OR 1/2 IN VIDEO
Uses night-vision camera devices in presenting studies of bats, owls, hyenas and sightless cave-dwelling fish during their nighttime activities.
LC NO. 80-706366
Prod-NGS Dist-NGS 1973

Strange Fruit C 33 MIN
16MM FILM, 3/4 OR 1/2 IN VIDEO H-C A
Tells the story of Henry Brown, a Black painter who faces the ugliness of racism while trying to exercise his freedom to vote. Based on the book Strange Fruit by Lillian Smith.
Prod-AMERFI Dist-LCOA Prodn-PINSKR 1979

Strange Occurrence At Elm View Library C 18 MIN
16MM FILM, 3/4 OR 1/2 IN VIDEO I-J
Shows a girl encountering the ghost of Ben Franklin, who teaches her the proper way to do library research. Demonstrates the use of the card catalog and the Reader's Guide to Periodicals.
LC NO. 83-707144
Prod-EBERT Dist-FLMFR 1983

Strange Partners (Symbiosis In The Sea) C 12 MIN
16MM FILM OPTICAL SOUND
Portrays the relationship of marine animals. Includes scenes of small fish riding on the backs of larger fish, a pearlfish living within a sea cucumber, neon gobies cleaning parasites off of large fish and microscopic scenes of parasites in gills.
LC NO. 73-702421
Prod-REELA Dist-MIAMIS 1968

Strange Sleep C 59 MIN
16MM FILM, 3/4 OR 1/2 IN VIDEO H-C A
Traces the history of the development of anesthesia.
From The Nova Series.
LC NO. 79-707229
Prod-WGBHTV Dist-TIMLIF 1976

Strange Story Of The Frog Who Became A Prince, The C 12 MIN
3/4 INCH VIDEO CASSETTE P
Describes a frog who becomes a prince against his wishes. Depicts his attempts to restore himself to froghood.
From The Desire To Read Series.
Prod-XEROX Dist-GA Prodn-BOSUST 1972

Strange Story Of The Frog Who Became A Prince C 12 MIN
16MM FILM, 3/4 OR 1/2 IN VIDEO P
Points out that being just exactly what you are is the nicest thing of all through the story of a frog who is changed into a prince by a snap-happy witch.
From The Desire To Read Series.
Prod-XEROX Dist-GA Prodn-BOSUST 1972

Strange Undersea Life B 9 MIN
16MM FILM OPTICAL SOUND
Presents excerpts from 1955 and 1956 Screen News Difilms which show San Francisco's Steinhart Aquarium's vast and varied marine families--yellow-tails, dugongs, turkey fish, mata-mata turtle and other strange marine life. Features other marine creatures as well as Waikiki's Aquarium, the showcase of tropical fish.
From The News Magazine Of The Screen Series. Vol 6, No. 10
Prod-PATHE Dist-HEARST 1956

Stranger At Green Knowe, A C 15 MIN
3/4 OR 1/2 INCH VIDEO CASSETTE I
See series title for descriptive statement.
From The Best Of Cover To Cover 2 Series.
Prod-WETATV Dist-WETATV

Stranger From Kahiki C 11 MIN
16MM FILM OPTICAL SOUND
Tells the legend of the origin of the ti leaf plant.
Prod-CINEPC Dist-CINEPC 1975

Stranger In Blue, The C 20 MIN
3/4 INCH VIDEO CASSETTE I
Explains that rules must be enforced and respected if they are to be effective.
From The Children And The Law (Intermediate) Series.
Prod-KTCATV Dist-GPITVL

Stranger In His Own Country C 30 MIN
16MM FILM OPTICAL SOUND
Depicts hostels and sheltered workshops at Slough, England. Demonstrates that severely mentally handicapped children can acquire social and vocational skills when given appropriate care and training and many can undertake ordinary jobs in the open community.
Prod-YORKU Dist-YORKU

Stranger Than Science Fiction C 17 MIN
16MM FILM, 3/4 OR 1/2 IN VIDEO J-C A
Edited version of the 1969 motion picture of the same title. Shows some of the scientific achievements of today which were depicted in the science fiction literature of the past.
From The Twenty-First Century Series.
Prod-CBSNEW Dist-MGHT 1975

Stranger Than Science Fiction C 27 MIN
16MM FILM, 3/4 OR 1/2 IN VIDEO J-H
Shows some scientific achievements of today which were depicted in the science fiction literature of the past.
From The 21st Century Series.
Prod-CBSNEW Dist-MGHT 1969

Stranger, The C 13 MIN
3/4 OR 1/2 INCH VIDEO CASSETTE P
See series title for descriptive statement.
From The Strawberry Square Series.
Prod-NEITV Dist-AITECH 1982

Stranger, The B 95 MIN
3/4 OR 1/2 INCH VIDEO CASSETTE
Tells about a Nazi war criminal about to marry an unsuspecting woman. Stars Orson wells.
Prod-ADVCAS Dist-ADVCAS

Strangers C 14 MIN
16MM FILM, 3/4 OR 1/2 IN VIDEO S
Uses a TV game show format to show how to act with strangers in public.
From The Good Life Series.
LC NO. 81-706181
Prod-DUDLYN Dist-HUBDSC 1981

Strangers C 14 MIN
3/4 OR 1/2 INCH VIDEO CASSETTE S
Demonstrates how to react with strangers in public places. Uses mentally handicapped actors.
From The Good Life Series.
Prod-HUBDSC Dist-HUBDSC

Strangers - The Story Of A Mother And Daughter C 96 MIN
3/4 OR 1/2 INCH VIDEO CASSETTE H-C A
Portrays the reunion of an embittered mother who reunites with her daughter after a 20-year estrangement. Shows that although the reunion starts off shakily, the mother eventually lowers her defenses and both enjoy a happy summer. Stars Bette Davis and Gena Rowlands.
Prod-TIMLIF Dist-TIMLIF 1982

Strangers And Kin C 58 MIN
3/4 INCH VIDEO CASSETTE
Relates the history of images and stereotypes of mountain people and the conflict between modernization and tradition. Juxtaposes Hollywood film clips, network television shows, dramatic sketches and interviews with contemporary Appalachians.
Prod-APPAL Dist-APPAL

Strangers At The Door C 28 MIN
16MM FILM, 3/4 OR 1/2 IN VIDEO I-H
Tells how an immigrant family is split apart at the immigration clearance center in 1907 Quebec. Shows how their dreams of a bright future are destroyed.
From The Adventures In History Series.
LC NO. 82-706169
Prod-NFBC Dist-FI 1978

Strangers In The Homeland C 60 MIN
16MM FILM OPTICAL SOUND
Shows a fictional family examining their decisions in pre-Revolutionary War times, in the South of the 1940s and during the Vietnam War.
Prod-NBCTV Dist-CCNCC

Strangers We Meet C 10 MIN
16MM FILM, 3/4 OR 1/2 IN VIDEO P-I
Deals with child molestation prevention. Teaches safety rules to be followed whenever any unknown person speaks to a child.
Prod-DAVP Dist-AIMS 1977

Strangest Secret, The C
1/2 IN VIDEO CASSETTE BETA/VHS
Presents a program for developing positive attitudes and setting and achieving goals. Discusses topics such as time management, human relations and self-achievement.
Prod-NIGCON Dist-NIGCON

Strangleholds On The Therapist - Failure To Leave The Office, Phone Calls And Panic... C 16 MIN
3/4 OR 1/2 INCH VIDEO CASSETTE
Reveals clinical details of difficult and interpersonally controlling emotions of borderline patients. Discusses how to handle these reactions.
From The Treatment Of The Borderline Patient Series.
Prod-HEMUL Dist-HEMUL

Strangulated Femoral Hernia C 12 MIN
16MM FILM OPTICAL SOUND PRO
Shows the varied pathology of strangulated femoral hernia, including Richter's type of hernia with minimal vascular changes, strangulation of bowel which shows remarkable improvement after release of constriction, strangulation of bowel which is obviously gangrenous and Richter's type hernia with small bowel obstruction.
Prod-ACYDGD Dist-ACY 1958

Strangulated Obstruction Of The Intestine C 22 MIN
16MM FILM OPTICAL SOUND PRO
Shows differences in the known or suspected lethal factors between short, medium and long-loop strangulations of the intestine by means of operative findings in patients, animated drawings and microscopic studies.
Prod-ACYDGD Dist-ACY 1960

Strapping Machine Operator (Rod Mill) C 8 MIN
3/4 OR 1/2 INCH VIDEO CASSETTE IND
Illustrates the duties of the operator of an automatic strapping machine dispenser and seal magazine.
From The Steel Making Series.
Prod-LEIKID Dist-LEIKID

Strapping Machine Troubleshooting (Rod Mill) C 10 MIN
3/4 OR 1/2 INCH VIDEO CASSETTE IND
Shows how to correct strapping machine problems and get the machine back on line quickly and safely.
From The Steel Making Series.
Prod-LEIKID Dist-LEIKID

Straps And Transportation Bridles B 15 MIN
16MM FILM OPTICAL SOUND
Shows how to attach straps and bridles to various types of draughts, and how to use dunnage properly.
LC NO. FIE52-1587
Prod-USA Dist-USNAC 1949

Strat C 26 MIN
16MM FILM OPTICAL SOUND J-C A
A cinema verte portrait of Stratford Sherman, showing how he goes about trying to institute change at his exclusive eastern preparatory school. Includes scenes of him at home and on his European summer vacation.
From The Jason Films Portrait Series.
LC NO. 76-705673
Prod-JASON Dist-JASON 1970

Strata - The Earth's Changing Crust C 11 MIN
16MM FILM, 3/4 OR 1/2 IN VIDEO I-C A
Presents a study of strata, or rock layers, found in many parts of the earth. Points out faulted strata which indicate changes in the earth's crust.
Prod-FA Dist-PHENIX Prodn-IWANMI 1966

Strategic Framework And Fallacies C 45 MIN
3/4 OR 1/2 INCH VIDEO CASSETTE IND
Discusses planning hierarchies, criteria for success, screening requirements, two case histories, fallacy of optimized R and D spending and a practical product example.
From The New Product Development Series.
Prod-AMCEE Dist-AMCEE

Strategic Impact Of Information Technology—A Series

Teaches the strategic impact of information technology, what these impacts are and how they can be managed. No. 71-0XX
Prod-DELTAK Dist-DELTAK

Impact On Business Operations, The	030 MIN
Impact On Office And Home, The	030 MIN
Managing Information Technology	030 MIN

Strategic Impact Of Technology C 44 MIN
3/4 OR 1/2 INCH VIDEO CASSETTE
Lectures on product categories, intelligent product marketing considerations and the advantages of microprocessor-based products.
From The Management Of Microprocessor Technology Series.
Prod-MIOT Dist-MIOT

Strategic Impact Of Technology C 45 MIN
3/4 OR 1/2 INCH VIDEO CASSETTE IND
See series title for descriptive statement.
From The Management Of Microprocessor Technology Series.
Prod-ICSINT Dist-ICSINT

Strategic Planning, William S Birnbaum C
3/4 OR 1/2 INCH VIDEO CASSETTE PRO
See series title for descriptive statement.
From The Management Skills Series.
Prod-AMCEE Dist-AMCEE

Strategic Selling - A Thinking Person's Guide—A Series
16MM FILM, 3/4 OR 1/2 IN VIDEO A
Presents selling skills for professional salesmen as well as occupations which are not usually associated with selling, such as bankers, computer specialists and other professionals.
Prod-TIMLIF Dist-TIMLIF 1984

Customized Closing	060 MIN
Overcoming Resistance	060 MIN
Understanding Buyer Behavior	060 MIN

Strategic Trust - The Making Of Nuclear Free Palau C 58 MIN
16MM FILM, 3/4 OR 1/2 IN VIDEO H-C A
Tells the story of Palau, a tiny Micronesian republic which, despite economic and political pressure from the U S, has adopted the world's first nuclear free constitution. Raises the question of whether local citizens have the right to decide if nuclear weapons will be deployed on their soil.
Prod-CNEMAG Dist-CNEMAG

Strategies C 15 MIN
3/4 INCH VIDEO CASSETTE I
Tells how to find solutions to mathematical games and puzzles.
From The Math - No Mystery Series.
Prod-WCETTV Dist-GPITVL 1977

Strategies C 30 MIN
3/4 OR 1/2 INCH VIDEO CASSETTE
Deals with strategies for the selection and design of computer security safeguards with special emphasis on the role of corporate management in initiating and sustaining an effective security effort.
From The Corporate Computer Security Strategy Series.
Prod-DELTAK Dist-DELTAK

Strategies And Plans C 45 MIN
3/4 OR 1/2 INCH VIDEO CASSETTE
Gives users an understanding of how a data strategy is derived from an analysis of the organization and operations of the business entity and how they can work effectively with the analysts in planning the data base.
From The Data Analysis For End Users Series.
Prod-DELTAK Dist-DELTAK

Strategies And Tactics C
16MM FILM - 3/4 IN VIDEO A
Discusses strategy and tactics and negotiations, including the 'when' strategy, forebearance, surprise, fait accompli, withdrawal, reversal, limits, feinting, participation, association, crossroads, random sample and bracketing.
From The Art Of Negotiating Series. Module 4
Prod-BNA Dist-BNA 1983

Strategies And Tactics And Counters (With Life Illustrations) C 41 MIN
3/4 OR 1/2 INCH VIDEO CASSETTE
See series title for descriptive statement.
From The Art Of Negotiating Series.
Prod-DELTAK Dist-DELTAK

Strategies For A Comprehension-Centered Reading Program C 29 MIN
3/4 OR 1/2 INCH VIDEO CASSETTE T
See series title for descriptive statement.
From The Reading Comprehension Series.
Prod-IU Dist-HNEDBK

Strategies For Language Learning C
3/4 OR 1/2 INCH VIDEO CASSETTE T
Shows teachers that students are natural readers due to linguistic capabilities. Illustrates learning methods through literature, poetry, music and personal experience.
From The Increasing Children's Motivation To Read And Write Series.
Prod-EPCO Dist-EDCORP

Strategies For Leadership - Collaboration C 30 MIN
3/4 OR 1/2 INCH VIDEO CASSETTE
Focuses on the need for collaboration with other health workers, clients and families to obtain the best possible health care for clients. Uses vignettes to demonstrate how every person involved in a collaboration can make a unique contribution.
From The Dimensions Of Leadership In Nursing Series.
Prod-AJN Dist-AJN

Strategies For Leadership - Conflict Management C 30 MIN
16MM FILM - 3/4 IN VIDEO PRO
Discusses conflict management, using three nursing situations which illustrate stages of conflict management and problems that arise at each stage. Emphasizes that knowledge of how to manage the conflict process allows both conflict and change to be more positive and productive.
From The Dimensions Of Leadership In Nursing Series.
LC NO. 77-702476
Prod-AJN Dist-AJN Prodn-CATTN 1977

Strategies For Leadership - Confrontation C 30 MIN
16MM FILM - 3/4 IN VIDEO PRO
Explores confrontation as a valuable and positive dimension of leadership. Explores the development of different kinds of confrontation and attitudes toward the process, showing specific strategies that can be used to make confrontation an effective element of leadership.
From The Dimensions Of Leadership In Nursing Series.
LC NO. 77-702475
Prod-AJN Dist-AJN Prodn-CATTN 1977

Strategies For Leadership - Problem Solving C 30 MIN
16MM FILM - 3/4 IN VIDEO PRO
Analyzes problem solving, using two nursing situations that involve application of steps in the problem-solving process. Covers defining a problem, collecting relevant data, canvassing alternatives, implementing action and evaluating results.
From The Dimensions Of Leadership In Nursing Series.
LC NO. 77-702474
Prod-AJN Dist-AJN Prodn-CATTN 1977

Strategies For Learning - Teaching In The Preschool Classroom With Handicapped And... C 20 MIN
3/4 OR 1/2 INCH VIDEO CASSETTE
Demonstrates that mainstreaming at the beginning level can be an effective way to assure equal education for both handicapped and nonhandicapped children. Presents an innovative classroom emphasizing the use of appropriate teaching strategies in order to promote children's from each other, from their teacher, and from exploring their environment.
Prod-UNEBO Dist-UNEBO

Strategies For Solving Word Problems In Algebra - Basic Operations And Formula Problems C
3/4 OR 1/2 INCH VIDEO CASSETTE H
Gives a basic approach for solving word problems such as weight and age, electricity, leverage, temperature and distance-rate-time problems.
Prod-GA Dist-GA

Strategies For Solving Word Problems In Algebra - Basic Operations C 34 MIN
3/4 OR 1/2 INCH VIDEO CASSETTE
Uses simple age problems as examples to introduce a five-step strategy for solving algebraic word problems.
LC NO. 81-706690
Prod-CHUMAN Dist-GA 1981

Strategies For Solving Word Problems In Algebra - Formula Problems C 32 MIN
3/4 OR 1/2 INCH VIDEO CASSETTE
Uses simple age problems as examples to introduce a five-step strategy for solving algebraic word problems. Discusses time-rate-distance problems and includes examples of overtaking and interception.
LC NO. 81-706691
Prod-CHUMAN Dist-GA 1981

Strategies For Successful Selling—A Series

Focuses on the behavioral selling skills that spell the critical difference in today's marketplace.
Prod-AMA Dist-AMA

Belief System For Success In Selling, A
Professional Nature Of Selling, The
Psychological Make-Up Of A Customer, The
Psychology Of Persuasion, The
Self-Image Concepts In Selling, The
Status - Key To Understanding The Customer's Temperament And Personality In Selling

Strategies In College Teaching—A Series
16MM FILM, 3/4 OR 1/2 IN VIDEO T
Prod-IU Dist-IU 1977

Effective Grouping Techniques	24 MIN
Leading Discussions, Whole Class	49 MIN
Media In The Classroom	48 MIN
Observing Teaching	50 MIN

Strategies Of Effective Teaching—A Series
T
Offers basic strategies for getting students' attention, motivating them, leading them to think more deeply, and increasing their classroom participation.
Prod-PCSB Dist-AITECH 1980

Application To The Classroom	029 MIN
Applied Observation And Analysis Techniques	029 MIN
Attention, Curiosity, And Motivation	029 MIN
Demonstration Lessons	059 MIN
Increasing Student Participation	023 MIN
Individual Teaching Styles	029 MIN
Integration Of Teaching Strategies	026 MIN
Overview - Teaching Operations And	029 MIN
Questioning Techniques And Probing	029 MIN

Strategy And Tactics C 30 MIN
3/4 OR 1/2 INCH VIDEO CASSETTE H-C A
See series title for descriptive statement.
From The Tennis Anyone Series.
LC NO. 79-706889
Prod-BATA Dist-TIMLIF 1979

Strategy And Tactics In Negotiations C 50 MIN
3/4 OR 1/2 INCH VIDEO CASSETTE PRO
Suggests ways to deal with negotiation practices, including threats, promises, ambiguities and mediation.
From The Negotiation Lectures Series.
Prod-NITA Dist-ABACPE

Strategy For Productive Behavior B 20 MIN
16MM FILM - 3/4 IN VIDEO IND
Tells how managers can effectively motivate employees
From The Motivation And Productivity Series.
Prod-BNA Dist-BNA 1969

Strategy For Singles, Doubles, Cut-Throat C 10 MIN
16MM FILM, 3/4 OR 1/2 IN VIDEO I-C A
Focuses on the strategy for singles, doubles and cut-throat in racquetball.
From The Racquetball Series. No. 4
LC NO. 81-706055
Prod-ATHI Dist-ATHI 1979

Strategy For Survival - Behavioral Ecology Of The Monarch Butterfly C 30 MIN
16MM FILM OPTICAL SOUND H-C
Offers a look at the nature of the behavioral and ecological interactions characteristic of life and focuses on the migratory and mating behaviors of the monarch butterfly.
LC NO. 77-701273
Prod-HANOVR Dist-HAR 1977

Strategy For Winning C 20 MIN
16MM FILM, 3/4 OR 1/2 IN VIDEO
Focuses on the process of gaining acceptance and support for new ideas in an organization. Shows a young manager overcoming obstacles such as disappointment, adamant opposition and politics, as he plots a winning course for himself and his organization.
From The Professional Management Program Series.
Prod-NEM Dist-NEM 1977

Strategy For Winning (Spanish) C 20 MIN
16MM FILM, 3/4 OR 1/2 IN VIDEO
Stresses the importance of positive attitude, persistence and sensitivity to the opinions of others in gaining acceptance of new ideas.
From The Communications And Selling Program (Spanish) Series.
Prod-NEM Dist-NEM

Strategy Of The Achiever C 27 MIN
16MM FILM OPTICAL SOUND
Presents a story about a yacht skipper and his crew who win first place in an ocean race by putting into action a systematic plan for achievement.
LC NO. 78-701449
Prod-VANTCO Dist-VANTCO 1977

Strategy Shots C 15 MIN
16MM FILM OPTICAL SOUND
Features Ilie Nastase explaining and demonstrating various strategy shots in tennis, including the lob, the overhead and the drop shot.
From The Tennis The Nasty Way Series.
LC NO. 76-703087
Prod-SLANJ Dist-MARMO 1975

Stratford Shakespeare Knew, The C 17 MIN
16MM FILM OPTICAL SOUND J-C
Presents a photographic study of Shakespeare's Stratford properties - his home, Hathaway Cottage, Arden House, Trinity Chruch, new house and the English countryside.
LC NO. 70-713539
Prod-PERFET Dist-PERFET 1971

Stratified Flow C 26 MIN
16MM FILM, 3/4 OR 1/2 IN VIDEO H-C
Analyzes stratified fluid systems through experiments showing that density variations help make possible forces that can generate internal waves, inhibit turbulent diffusion, or create strong velocity gradients and jets. Depicts applications in nature ranging from open-channel flows of water to atmospheric waves in the lee of mountain ranges.
From The Fluid Mechanics Series.
Prod-NCFMF Dist-EBEC 1969

Stravinsky B 58 MIN
16MM FILM OPTICAL SOUND
Presents the composer, Igor Stravinsky, at home in California, conducting a rehearsal, holding a press conference, and discussing creativity with Balanchine and his own work with Rolf Lieberman. By Richard Leacock and Rolf Lieberman.
Prod-PENNAS Dist-PENNAS

Stravinsky B 43 MIN
16MM FILM, 3/4 OR 1/2 IN VIDEO J-C A
Offers a portrait of composer Igor Stravinsky. Shows him conducting, being honored by the Pope, visiting fellow artists, and working with choreographer George Balanchine.
Prod-CBSNEW Dist-CAROUF

Straw Hat, The C 27 MIN
16MM FILM, 3/4 OR 1/2 IN VIDEO
Presents the German story of a peasant who is tricked by merchants when selling his house. Shows him retaliating and tricking the merchants with a clever plan involving a straw hat.
From The Storybook International Series.
Prod-JOU Dist-JOU 1982

Strawberry Shortcake In Big Apple City C 24 MIN
16MM FILM OPTICAL SOUND K-I
Uses animation to present a story about Strawberry Shortcake, who becomes a finalist in a baking contest and flies to Big Apple City for the televised bake-off. Describes the troubles Strawberry encounters when the other finalist, Peculiar Purple Pieman, tries to keep her from taking part in the finals. Shows how truth, justice and Strawberry's delicious shortcake recipe triumph and the Purple Pieman earns a well-deserved fate.
Prod-CORF Dist-CORF 1982

Strawberry Square II - Take Time—A Series
P
Uses music stories to explore different musical styles and sounds.
Prod-NEITV Dist-AITECH 1984

Beginning, The	015 MIN
Can You Remember	015 MIN
Country Critters	015 MIN
Farm Sense	015 MIN
Festival	015 MIN
Orion	015 MIN
Put-Together	015 MIN
Rhythm And Blues	015 MIN
Ricky	015 MIN
Sculpting On The Square	015 MIN
Shake It Up - Gospel	015 MIN
Sounds Abound	015 MIN
Take Time	015 MIN
Web, The	015 MIN
Word Play	015 MIN

Strawberry Square—A Series
P
Uses stories to introduce musical concepts like melody, harmony and tempo.
Prod-NEITV Dist-AITECH 1982

Balloons	015 MIN
Breakfast Rolls By	014 MIN
Circles, Squares, Triangles, And Things	015 MIN
Curing The Grumpies	015 MIN
Day For Trees, A	015 MIN
Finale	015 MIN
Finish The Job Key	014 MIN
Fizzles And Fuzzies	013 MIN
Fly Away	015 MIN
Friends	014 MIN
Getting Acquainted	014 MIN
Gift For Skipper, A	013 MIN
Goodbye, Mr Jingle	015 MIN
I Like Me	014 MIN
It's Halloween	015 MIN
Jingle Gets The News	015 MIN
Keeping Fit	012 MIN
Let A Song Be A Friend	015 MIN
Let's Be Flexible	015 MIN
Little By Little	014 MIN
New Day, A	014 MIN
On Stage	015 MIN
Pet Shop, The	015 MIN
Rainy Day, A	014 MIN
Remembering	015 MIN
Skipper Gets A Piano	015 MIN
Songs For A Garden	014 MIN
Stranger, The	013 MIN
Tell Me A Story	014 MIN
Thanksgiving	015 MIN
This Land Is Your Land	014 MIN
Trip To The Forest, A	015 MIN
We Can Do It Too	015 MIN

Stray, The C 14 MIN
16MM FILM OPTICAL SOUND P-H
A dramatization about a young child who got lost while visiting the zoo with a group of twelve children, and the celebration which took place when the boy was found.
From The Parable Series.
LC NO. 71-713243
Prod-FRACOC Dist-FRACOC 1971

Stream C 15 MIN
16MM FILM, 3/4 OR 1/2 IN VIDEO I-H
Describes how a businessman on a holiday in the country begins to sail his model boat. Depicts the man's search for his boat after it slips away and sails through pollutants.
Prod-COMICO Dist-AIMS 1969

Stream Community, A C 15 MIN
3/4 OR 1/2 INCH VIDEO CASSETTE P-I
Discusses the living things found in a stream.
From The Why Series.
Prod-WDCNTV Dist-AITECH 1976

Stream Deposits C 37 MIN
3/4 OR 1/2 INCH VIDEO CASSETTE IND
See series title for descriptive statement.
From The Basic And Petroleum Geology For Non-Geologists - Landforms Series.
Prod-PHILLP Dist-GPCV

Stream Environment, A C 9 MIN
16MM FILM, 3/4 OR 1/2 IN VIDEO P-I
Explores a stream that begins high in the mountains and slowly grows from the melting snow. Points out that as the stream grows, the variety of life that lives along the stream grows too. Explains that plants are nourished by the water and in turn provides food and shelter for birds, mammals and insects.
Prod-BARR Dist-BARR 1972

Stream Environment, A (Spanish) C 9 MIN
16MM FILM - VIDEO, ALL FORMATS K-I
Explores a stream, from its source high in the mountains. Shows the many forms of life both above and below the surface that depend on the water.
Prod-BARR Dist-BARR

Stream Fish Management C 11 MIN
16MM FILM OPTICAL SOUND
Traces the steps taken in managing the natural fishing streams of Tennessee to improve fishing.
Prod-TGAFC Dist-TGAFC

Stream Flow Processes C 38 MIN
3/4 OR 1/2 INCH VIDEO CASSETTE IND
See series title for descriptive statement.
From The Basic And Petroleum Geology For Non-Geologists - Landforms Series.
Prod-PHILLP Dist-GPCV

Stream, The C 15 MIN
16MM FILM, 3/4 OR 1/2 IN VIDEO I-H
Examines the two basic types of stream environments and describes the life forms especially adapted to both environments.
From The Living Science Series.
Prod-IFB Dist-IFB 1962

Stream, The (Captioned) C 15 MIN
16MM FILM, 3/4 OR 1/2 IN VIDEO I-H
Examines the two basic types of stream environments and describes the life forms especially adapted to both environments. Captioned for the hearing-impaired.
From The Living Science Series.
Prod-IFB Dist-IFB 1962

Streams B 6 MIN
16MM FILM OPTICAL SOUND
Shows a dance by Robert Cohan concerned with a quiet meditation on one's many selves, the discovery of a quiet credo at the center of one's being.
Prod-FFRONT Dist-EDC 1961

Street Angel B 102 MIN
16MM FILM SILENT
Tells the story of the love between Angelo and Gino, a poor painter who has her pose for a Madonna portrait. Reveals that when she runs afoul of the law and is sent to prison, Gino grows despondent and loses all interest in his work. Shows that when she is released, they are reunited and she convinces him she is still worthy of having posed for a Madonna. Stars Janet Gaynor and Charles Farrell. Directed by Frank Borzage.
Prod-FOXFC Dist-KILLIS 1928

Street Corner Stories B 80 MIN
16MM FILM OPTICAL SOUND
Documents mornings with a group of men who congregate at a corner store each day to socialize before they go to work. Portrays the black story-telling tradition, the spoken blues milieu and black street culture.
Prod-BLKFMF Dist-BLKFMF

Street Crime - What To Do C 20 MIN
16MM FILM, 3/4 OR 1/2 IN VIDEO
Emphasizes the importance of common sense when riding on buses and trains or returning to a parked car. Provides some good tips on self-defense in situations threatening personal safety.
Prod-RIPOL Dist-MTI

Street Drugs - Just The Facts C 25 MIN
3/4 OR 1/2 INCH VIDEO CASSETTE
Investigates the world of street drugs and details the physiological effects of LSD, speed, barbiturates, marijuana, heroin and alcohol.
Prod-TRAINX Dist-TRAINX

Street Drugs And Medicine Chests C 29 MIN
3/4 OR 1/2 INCH VIDEO CASSETTE
Looks at substance abuse, what it is, how it works and how it can be beaten.
From The Here's To Your Health Series.
Prod-KERA Dist-PBS

Street Freaks C 4 MIN
16MM FILM, 3/4 OR 1/2 IN VIDEO J-C A
Offers an animated view of New York City street life, featuring a young street musician who finds the competition too stiff until he joins in the live-and-let-live attitude of the other street people.
Prod-CANEJ Dist-PHENIX 1978

Street Furniture C 20 MIN
16MM FILM, 3/4 OR 1/2 IN VIDEO
Considers the function and appearance of streets and the objects along them. Looks at streets as a reflection of the people who use them and as a source of imagery for artists.
From The Images And Things Series.
LC NO. 73-702114
Prod-NITC Dist-AITECH 1971

Street Gangs - Challenge For Law Enforcement C 20 MIN
16MM FILM, 3/4 OR 1/2 IN VIDEO A
Presents interviews with gang members in order to provide police officers with a look at the structure and workings of a street gang and the attitudes of its members.
Prod-CAHILL Dist-AIMS 1978

Street Musique C 9 MIN
16MM FILM, 3/4 OR 1/2 IN VIDEO J-H A
Records artist Ryan Larkin's reactions to the performance of a group of street musicians.
Prod-NFBC Dist-NFBC 1973

Street Safety And Car Theft C 30 MIN
3/4 OR 1/2 INCH VIDEO CASSETTE
Discusses street safety and ways of preventing car theft.
From The Burglar-Proofing Series.
Prod-MDCPB Dist-MDCPB

Street Scene B 28 MIN
16MM FILM OPTICAL SOUND
Explains how the misbeliefs and terror of a white college girl bring death at the hands of the police to a non-political middle class blackman.
LC NO. 75-703235
Prod-USC Dist-USC 1972

Street Scene B 80 MIN
16MM FILM OPTICAL SOUND
Focuses on a young girl whose life is torn apart when her father discovers her mother with another man. Stars Sylvia Sidney, William Collier, Jr, and Estelle Taylor. Based on the play Street Scene by Elmer Rice.
Prod-UNKNWN Dist-REELIM 1931

Street Talk C 8 MIN
16MM FILM, 3/4 OR 1/2 IN VIDEO P
Uses a puppet to tell how to interpret various pedestrian street signs and markings. Illustrates four major types of pedestrian accidents.
Prod-GOLDCF Dist-AIMS 1976

Street Vibrato B 13 MIN
16MM FILM OPTICAL SOUND

Explores the thoughts and feelings of an aspiring classical violinist who plays on the street corners of New York City. Contrasts the musician's views on the value of playing in the streets with those of his peers who believe that it is detrimental to his career.
LC NO. 79-701388
Prod-MSAL Dist-MSAL 1979

Street-Meat-Meet C 15 MIN
16MM FILM OPTICAL SOUND
Documents circumnavigating and compiling images and scenes of New York City.
Prod-VANBKS Dist-VANBKS

Street, The C 10 MIN
16MM FILM, 3/4 OR 1/2 IN VIDEO J-C A
Based on a selection from the novel THE STREET. Tells the story of the slow death of a grandmother, making a statement about family interaction with the aged.
Prod-NFBC Dist-NFBC 1976

Streetcar Named Desire, A B 122 MIN
16MM FILM OPTICAL SOUND
Provides a filmed adaptation of the play A Streetcar Named Desire. Stars Marlon Brando and Vivien Leigh.
Prod-UAA Dist-UAE 1951

Streetproofing C 28 MIN
3/4 OR 1/2 INCH VIDEO CASSETTE
Uses short vignettes to illustrate some of the inherent hazards in the environment. Provides the 'know how' to avoid dangerous situations and to have fun safely.
From The Youth Lifeskills Series.
Prod-SCCL Dist-HMDI

Streets Belong To The People, The B 5 MIN
16MM FILM OPTICAL SOUND
Shows a battle between Haight street people and the San Francisco tractical squad. The soundtrack consists of contemporary rock.
Prod-SFN Dist-SFN 1967

Streets Of Greenwood B 20 MIN
16MM FILM OPTICAL SOUND
Documents the civil rights struggle in Greenwood, Mississippi in 1963, while the Student Non-Violent Co-Ordinating Committee was registering black voters.
Prod-NEWTIM Dist-NEWTIM

Streets Of Saigon, The C 28 MIN
16MM FILM, 3/4 OR 1/2 IN VIDEO J-H
Indicates that in the last ten years the population of Saigon has grown ten times. Tells that American soldiers once came looking for girls and marijuana, but now they are rarely seen and the only reminder of them is the babies they have left behind. Depicts these children, many orphaned and homeless, who have been forced to make a living in the streets.
Prod-NFBC Dist-FI 1973

Strega Nonna C 9 MIN
16MM FILM, 3/4 OR 1/2 IN VIDEO K-P
Presents an Italian folktale about a wise old woman with a magic pasta pot, who leaves her helper alone with the pot. Depicts the disaster that ensues when the helper tries to show the townspeople how the pot works. Based on the book Strega Nonna by Tomie de Paola.
Prod-WWS Dist-WWS 1978

Strength And Deformation Of Solids—A Series
IND
Prod-NSF Dist-PSU

Concepts Of Dislocations 7 MIN
Deformation Of Crystalline Materials, Pt 1 5 MIN
Deformation Of Crystalline Materials, Pt 2 7 MIN
Introduction To Strengthening Materials 6 MIN

Strength In The West C 20 MIN
16MM FILM OPTICAL SOUND C
Presents a general survey of modern steel production, including open-cast mining, blast furnace, steel furnaces, milling operations and making steel pipes.
Prod-KAISER Dist-HEFL 1952

Strength Of Materials C 180 MIN
3/4 OR 1/2 INCH VIDEO CASSETTE PRO
Covers in three one-hour tapes, axial bending and terminal stresses, maximum normal and maximum shearing stresses, and deformations.
From The Professional Engineer Review Series.
Prod-UILU Dist-AMCEE

Strength Through Struggle - A Chronicle Of Labor Organization In Ohio C 25 MIN
16MM FILM OPTICAL SOUND
Tells the story of labor organization in Ohio.
Prod-OHC Dist-HRC

Strength Through Weakness C 30 MIN
2 INCH VIDEOTAPE
See series title for descriptive statement.
From The Koltanowski On Chess Series.
Prod-KQEDTV Dist-PUBTEL

Strengthening Organizational Relationships X 30 MIN
16MM FILM OPTICAL SOUND C T
Teaches the nursing instructor various principles, tools and methods of teaching. Stresses the importance of developing organizational teamwork involving effective communication and influence, decentralized and coordinated decision-making and high performance goals and high motivation.
From The Teaching Role Series.
LC NO. 73-703327
Prod-MVNE Dist-TELSTR 1968

Strengths And Weaknesses - College Students With Learning Disabilities C 26 MIN
16MM FILM, 3/4 OR 1/2 IN VIDEO H-C A
Explores the situation of the learning disabled student in the college environment. Compares four students' perceptions of their problems with current professional opinions and examines the role of assessment, coping behavior and remediation as factors in a successful college experience.
LC NO. 82-707064
Prod-IOWA Dist-LAWREN 1981

Stress B 11 MIN
16MM FILM, 3/4 OR 1/2 IN VIDEO C A
Dr Hans Selye of the University of Montreal explains his theory of the nature of stress as a general alarm reaction through the pituitary and adrenal glands, set off by disease, injury or mental pressure.
Prod-NFBC Dist-NFBC 1956

Stress C 14 MIN
3/4 OR 1/2 INCH VIDEO CASSETTE
Identifies and defines stress and its effects on the body. Tells how to recognize it in its early stages and how to avoid or reduce it.
Prod-HP Dist-HP

Stress C 15 MIN
3/4 OR 1/2 INCH VIDEO CASSETTE
Teaches how to manage the tension and pressures of everyday living.
Prod-AHOA Dist-AHOA

Stress C 16 MIN
16MM FILM, 3/4 OR 1/2 IN VIDEO J-C A
Examines the concept of stress in conjunction with a variety of people and lifestyles. Monitors the activities of a businessman equipped with a device which monitors his body's stress reactions.
From The World Of Health Series.
Prod-INFORP Dist-SF 1975

Stress C 16 MIN
16MM FILM, 3/4 OR 1/2 IN VIDEO A
Presents the causes, effects and origins of stress. Provides ways to avoid and identify stress and dramatizes ways of controlling it.
Prod-PRORE Dist-PRORE

Stress C 29 MIN
3/4 INCH VIDEO CASSETTE C A
Shows that all motivation is based on stress. Describes roles of autonomic nervous system and adrenal glands in stress. Offers suggestions on ways to withstand stress.
From The Understanding Human Behavior - An Introduction To Psychology Series. Lesson 14
Prod-COAST Dist-CDTEL

Stress C 30 MIN
3/4 OR 1/2 INCH VIDEO CASSETTE PRO
Focuses on the many factors that cause stress and investigates ways that people are successfully coping with it. Examines the fine balance of pressure and relaxation needed to provide a vigorous, stimulating and healthy pattern of life. Includes the tape entitled Back To Square One.
Prod-CTVC Dist-GPITVL 1981

Stress - A Personal Challenge C 30 MIN
16MM FILM, 3/4 OR 1/2 IN VIDEO H-C
Suggests how to avoid the destructive effects of the stress response.
LC NO. 80-707526
Prod-SLUMC Dist-MTI 1980

Stress - Distress C 21 MIN
16MM FILM, 3/4 OR 1/2 IN VIDEO H-C A
Discusses stress, pointing out that when stress turns to distress, it can make people sick. Describes the prevalent stressors, the consequences of stress, and novel methods that help to prevent, cope and release stress. Demonstrates home-grown methods as well as scientific treatments which include meditation and biofeedback.
Prod-HANDEL Dist-HANDEL 1982

Stress - Is Your Lifestyle Killing You C 29 MIN
3/4 OR 1/2 INCH VIDEO CASSETTE
Deals with stress and how to control it.
From The Here's To Your Health Series.
Prod-KERA Dist-PBS

Stress - It's Just What You Think C 19 MIN
16MM FILM, 3/4 OR 1/2 IN VIDEO I-H
Uses interviews with teen-agers to help young people understand how to cope with stress. Shows ways of removing or reducing stress by changing the situation or oneself and by learning to relax.
From The Health - Body And Mind Series.
Prod-BARR Dist-BARR 1982

Stress - Learning How To Handle It C 23 MIN
16MM FILM, 3/4 OR 1/2 IN VIDEO J-H
Discusses causes of stress and how our bodies react to it. Provides workable solutions for dealing with it. Focuses on self-help group of teenagers as they learn to recognize and handle stress in their lives.
Prod-SAIF Dist-AIMS 1984

Stress - The Management Challenge C 15 MIN
3/4 OR 1/2 INCH VIDEO CASSETTE
Gives step-by-step instructions on developing a management style that turns unavoidable workplace stress into a positive force.
Prod-WHITEG Dist-WHITEG

Stress - You Can Live With It C 26 MIN
16MM FILM, 3/4 OR 1/2 IN VIDEO

Uses case histories to show the negative effects that stressful lifestyles, attitudes and behaviors can have on a person's health. Shows that stress can cause heart attacks, increased cholesterol levels and other chronic ailments.
LC NO. 83-706716
Prod-MITCHG Dist-MTI

Stress And Coping C 21 MIN
2 INCH VIDEOTAPE C A
Features a humanistic psychologist who, by analysis and examples, discusses how to cope with stress.
From The Interpersonal Competence, Unit 07 - Stress Series.
Prod-MVNE Dist-TELSTR 1973

Stress And Emotion C 60 MIN
3/4 OR 1/2 INCH VIDEO CASSETTE C A
Discusses pain, anxiety and behavior.
From The Brain, Mind And Behavior Series.
Prod-WNETTV Dist-FI

Stress And How To Live With It C 29 MIN
3/4 OR 1/2 INCH VIDEO CASSETTE
Prod-RCOMTV Dist-SYLWAT 1982

Stress And How To Manage It C 29 MIN
3/4 OR 1/2 INCH VIDEO CASSETTE
Prod-RCOMTV Dist-SYLWAT 1984

Stress And Relaxation C 26 MIN
3/4 OR 1/2 INCH VIDEO CASSETTE
Provides a step-by-step guide to stress identification and relaxation therapy.
Prod-ARFO Dist-ARFO 1981

Stress And Strain C 20 MIN
3/4 OR 1/2 INCH VIDEO CASSETTE H-C A
See series title for descriptive statement.
From The Engineering Crafts Series.
Prod-BBCTV Dist-FI 1981

Stress And The Adaptation Syndrome C 35 MIN
16MM FILM OPTICAL SOUND
Depicts the effects of various physical and psychiatric stresses and the mechanisms by which animals effect adaptation. Reveals Dr Hans Selye's contribution to the understanding of the inter-relationship between stress and disease.
Prod-SHNKRN Dist-PFI 1956

Stress And The Child C 10 MIN
16MM FILM, 3/4 OR 1/2 IN VIDEO A
Explores the real stresses children face as they grow from infancy to puberty. Reveals that the time is difficult for parents as they must oftentime stand by helplessly. Offers suggested methods for parents to use in coping with these problems.
From The Prepared Childbirth And Parenting Series.
Prod-JOU Dist-JOU 1982

Stress And The Hot Reactor C 23 MIN
16MM FILM OPTICAL SOUND PRO
Demonstrates the relationship of stress to cardiovascular disease. Features Dr Robert Eliot at the University of Nebraska Simulation Laboratory.
Prod-GEIGY Dist-GEIGY

Stress And The New Family C 29 MIN
3/4 OR 1/2 INCH VIDEO CASSETTE H-C A
Describes how individuals and families develop ways of coping with the tensions which occur when a new child is added to the family.
From the Tomorrow's Families Series.
LC NO. 81-706921
Prod-MSDOE Dist-AITECH 1980

Stress And The Office - Introduction C 12 MIN
3/4 OR 1/2 INCH VIDEO CASSETTE
See series title for descriptive statement.
From The Stress And The Office Series.
Prod-VIDEOC Dist-DELTAK

Stress And The Office - Week One, Seated Exercises C 54 MIN
3/4 OR 1/2 INCH VIDEO CASSETTE
See series title for descriptive statement.
From The Stress And The Office Series.
Prod-VIDEOC Dist-DELTAK

Stress And The Office - Week Three, Floor Exercises C 48 MIN
3/4 OR 1/2 INCH VIDEO CASSETTE
See series title for descriptive statement.
From The Stress And The Office Series.
Prod-VIDEOC Dist-DELTAK

Stress And The Office - Week Two, Standing Exercises C 51 MIN
3/4 OR 1/2 INCH VIDEO CASSETTE
See series title for descriptive statement.
From The Stress And The Office Series.
Prod-VIDEOC Dist-DELTAK

Stress And The Office—A Series

Provides a program to help anyone who works in an office environment to achieve physical fitness. Includes a participant's guide.
Prod-VIDEOC Dist-DELTAK

Stress And The Office - Introduction 012 MIN
Stress And The Office - Week One, Seated 054 MIN
Stress And The Office - Week Three, Floor 048 MIN
Stress And The Office - Week Two, Standing 051 MIN

Stress And Wellness—A Series
16MM FILM, 3/4 OR 1/2 IN VIDEO

Discusses the importance of stress management, exercise and nutrition in maintaining good health.
Prod-MTI Dist-MTI

Lifesavers - Fitness And Nutrition 020 MIN
Stress - You Can Live With It 026 MIN

Stress And You—A Series
16MM FILM, 3/4 OR 1/2 IN VIDEO H-C A
Offers suggestions on means to cope with stress.
Prod-MAWBYN Dist-AMEDFL Prodn-AMEDFL 1978

Learning To Cope 14 MIN
Relaxation Techniques 11 MIN
Stress, Health And You 18 MIN

Stress Corrosion Of Mg Base Alloys B 18 MIN
16MM FILM OPTICAL SOUND J-C
Shows how corrosion is controlled by the metallurgy of the alloy—intergranular or transgranular.
Prod-OSUMPD Dist-OSUMPD 1952

Stress Corrosion Of Stainless Steel B 13 MIN
16MM FILM OPTICAL SOUND J-C
Uses time lapse photography and photomicrography to show the rapid accumulation of corrosion products which may play a role in the mechanism of stress corrosion cracking in austenitic stainless steel in chloride solutions.
LC NO. FIA66-21
Prod-OSUMPD Dist-OSUMPD 1959

Stress In Critical Care Nursing Practice C 26 MIN
3/4 INCH VIDEO CASSETTE PRO
Presents an analysis of aspects of critical care nursing that lead to undesirable stressors affecting patients, nurses and families. Highlights intervention techniques that will reduce these stress factors.
From The Stress In Critical Illness Series. Module 4
LC NO. 80-707624
Prod-BRA Dist-BRA 1980

Stress In Critical Illness—A Series
PRO
Describes the physical manifestations of stress and shows how nurses can relieve stress in their patients and in themselves.
Prod-BRA Dist-BRA 1980

Family Stress In Critical Illness 022 MIN
Physiologic Manifestations Of Stress 024 MIN
Psychologic Stress In Critical Illness 026 MIN
Stress In Critical Care Nursing Practice 026 MIN

Stress In The Foster Family C 30 MIN
3/4 OR 1/2 INCH VIDEO CASSETTE
Presents a professional stress management consultant and foster parents discussing the particular stresses created by the foster care situation and ways to deal effectively with them.
From The Home Is Where The Care Is Series. Module 7
Prod-MTI Dist-MTI 1984

Stress In The Later Years C 24 MIN
16MM FILM, 3/4 OR 1/2 IN VIDEO C A
Gives an understanding of how the special stresses of older people, such as loss, loneliness and retirement, can cause physical disorders. Introduces relaxation and other techniques, and offers suggestions for enjoying social activities.
From The Be Well - The Later Years Series.
LC NO. 83-706449
Prod-CF Dist-CF 1983

Stress Intelligence - An Approach To Stress Management—A Series

Presents a three-part seminar by Dr Eugene Jennings on the nature and effects of stress, and the steps to take to avoid stress. Includes a short text that can be used for review and reference during and after completion of the series.
Prod-DELTAK Dist-DELTAK

Avoiding Stress - The Future Manager 030 MIN
Effects Of Stress, The - The Shortfall 030 MIN
Understanding Stress - The Marginal Manager 030 MIN

Stress Management C 11 MIN
16MM FILM, 3/4 OR 1/2 IN VIDEO PRO
Describes the effects of stress on correctional officers. Offers techniques to handle stress and identifies ineffective methods of dealing with stress, including abuse of alcohol or other drugs, overeating and withdrawal. Presents a program for stress management that includes exercise, talking about problems, developing outside interests and taking time to be alone.
From The Correctional Officers Series.
Prod-AIMS Dist-AIMS 1981

Stress Management C 17 MIN
16MM FILM, 3/4 OR 1/2 IN VIDEO PRO
Describes the symptoms of stress and various methods of dealing with it.
From The Survival Of The Fittest Series.
Prod-PRORE Dist-PRORE

Stress Management C 17 MIN
3/4 OR 1/2 INCH VIDEO CASSETTE
Delivers valuable insights into the control of stress, including a number of systems that allow stress to be understood in its true state - as a subjective thing, unique to each individual.
From The Survival Of The Fittest Series.
Prod-SCCL Dist-HMDI

Stress Management - A Positive Strategy—A Series
16MM FILM, 3/4 OR 1/2 IN VIDEO A
Uses interviews, interspersed with dramatic sequences and the views of recognized authorities, to show managers how to cope stress.
LC NO. 82-706501
Prod-TIMLIF Dist-TIMLIF 1982

Becoming Aware 030 MIN
Looking Ahead 030 MIN
Managing Yourself 030 MIN
Solving Problems 030 MIN
Taking Stocks 030 MIN

Stress Management - Coping With Stress C 30 MIN
3/4 OR 1/2 INCH VIDEO CASSETTE
Demonstrates the program for dealing with stress. Demonstrates techniques for rational reevaluation, coping self-statements, and other relaxation techniques.
Prod-IRL Dist-IRL

Stress Management - The Rational-Emotive Approach C 30 MIN
3/4 OR 1/2 INCH VIDEO CASSETTE
Outlines the rational-emotive approach to stress management. Shows a group of participants doing exercises to reduce stress.
Prod-IRL Dist-IRL

Stress Management - Wedding Daze C 23 MIN
16MM FILM, 3/4 OR 1/2 IN VIDEO H-C A
Provides insights into the sources of stress as well as its effects. Presents techniques and strategies for coping with stress. Uses a case study that involves a wedding.
Prod-AIMS Dist-AIMS

Stress Management System—A Series
16MM FILM, 3/4 OR 1/2 IN VIDEO A
Discusses how stress can be recognized and controlled.
Prod-MTI Dist-MTI 1983

Introduction To Stress 012 MIN
Lifesavers - Fitness And Nutrition 021 MIN
Long-Term Stress Management 015 MIN
Trauma Stress Management 012 MIN

Stress Mess, The C 25 MIN
16MM FILM, 3/4 OR 1/2 IN VIDEO J-C A
Follows a fictitious family through a stress-filled day. Addresses many of the problems that cause stress and shows how to manage and identify stress in daily living.
Prod-BARR Dist-BARR 1982

Stress Of Separation C 16 MIN
16MM FILM, 3/4 OR 1/2 IN VIDEO C A
Shows that children have the most difficulty coping with separation between the ages of seven months and three years. Visits a day-care center and shows the behavior of children after their parents have left.
From The Under Fives Series.
Prod-GRATV Dist-FLMLIB 1982

Stress Relief - The Heimlich Method C 16 MIN
16MM FILM, 3/4 OR 1/2 IN VIDEO H-C A
Presents Dr Henry Heimlich who discusses the causes of stress, the symptoms or early warning signs, strategies for cooling off a stressful situation, and strategies for changing attitudes that allow stress to rule.
Prod-AIMS Dist-AIMS 1983

Stress Relief Techniques C
1/2 IN VIDEO CASSETTE BETA/VHS
See series title for descriptive statement.
From The R M I Stress Management Series Series.
Prod-RMI Dist-RMI

Stress Training For Police—A Series
PRO
Discusses primary feelings encountered by police officers under conditions of stress, such as fear, anger and psychic pain.
Prod-IACP Dist-FMD Prodn-RUBINR 1970

Fear And Anxiety 10 MIN
Feeling Good 9 MIN
Humiliation And Anger 10 MIN

Stress Training For Teachers—A Series
T
Discusses feelings of humiliation, anger and fear and compassion towards students on the part of teachers.
Prod-NYSED Dist-FMD 1974

Black Is The Color 17 MIN
Crossing The Line 16 MIN
Crunch, The 16 MIN

Stress—A Series

Presents a series on stress by Dr Kenneth Greenspar and Dr Milton M Berger.
Prod-HEMUL Dist-HEMUL

Hypertension - The Relaxation Response As
Stress-Related Disorders And Their Management 060 MIN

Stress-Related Disorders And Their Management Through Biofeedback And Relaxation Training C 60 MIN
3/4 OR 1/2 INCH VIDEO CASSETTE
Features Dr Kenneth Greenspan discussing and demonstrating to Dr Milton Berger some biofeedback and relaxation techniques to relieve patients with migraine headaches and phobic anxiety, as well as integrating these with psychodynamic and pharmacological treatments.
From The Stress Series.
Prod-HEMUL Dist-HEMUL

Stress, Health And You C 18 MIN
3/4 OR 1/2 INCH VIDEO CASSETTE C A
Presents Dr Hand Selye and Richard Rahe explaining how a person's health is modified by stressful events and discussing different individuals' responses to it. Offers suggestions on avoiding stress and introduces methods of meditation, biofeedback and relaxation therapy.
LC NO. 80-706914
Prod-AMEDFL Dist-TIMLIF

Stress, Health And You C 18 MIN
16MM FILM, 3/4 OR 1/2 IN VIDEO H-C A
Focuses on the causes and effects of stress and shows how dramatic changes affect the human body.
From The Stress And You Series.
Prod-MAWBYN Dist-AMEDFL Prodn-AMEDFL 1978

Stress, Tension, And The Relaxation Response C 20 MIN
3/4 OR 1/2 INCH VIDEO CASSETTE
Identifies causes of and physiological responses to stress and explains how stress can lead to high blood pressure. Describes the relaxation response and discusses its importance in counteracting effects of stress and helping to reduce blood pressure.
LC NO. 77-730596
Prod-TRAINX Dist-TRAINX

Stress, The Time Bomb Within C
3/4 OR 1/2 INCH VIDEO CASSETTE J-H
Shows how to help teens recognize stress and handle it. Identifies common causes of stress and outlines methods for breaking patterns of tension.
Prod-AVNA Dist-GA

Stress, With Dr Roy Martin C 55 MIN
3/4 INCH VIDEO CASSETTE
Discusses the origin of stress and what we can do about eliminating or overcoming stressful situations.
Prod-UTAHTI Dist-UTAHTI

Stresses In Elastic Masses, Pt 2 B 60 MIN
3/4 OR 1/2 INCH VIDEO CASSETTE
See series title for descriptive statement.
From The Bases For Several Pavement Design Methods Series. Pt 3
Prod-UAZMIC Dist-UAZMIC 1977

Stresses To Elastic Masses, Pt 1 B 60 MIN
3/4 OR 1/2 INCH VIDEO CASSETTE
See series title for descriptive statement.
From The Bases For Several Pavement Design Methods Series. Pt 2
Prod-UAZMIC Dist-UAZMIC 1977

Stretch A Rubber Band And Learn Geometry C 30 MIN
2 INCH VIDEOTAPE
Introduces the student to some of the metric and non-metric properties of geometry through the use of the geoboard. Covers line segments, triangles, quadrilaterals, parallel line segments and perpendicular line segments.
From The Devices In Their Hands - Math In Their Minds Series.
Prod-GPITVL Dist-GPITVL

Stretch Concepts For Teaching Handicapped Children—A Series
T
Includes concepts for teaching handicapped students in regular classrooms. Can be applied to all children in varied educational settings.
Prod-HUBDSC Dist-HUBDSC

Assessment 030 MIN
Grouping And Special Students 030 MIN
Label The Behavior 030 MIN
Learning Styles 030 MIN
Mainstreaming 030 MIN
Peer Tutoring 030 MIN
Value Clarification 030 MIN

Stretch Of Imagination, A C 27 MIN
16MM FILM OPTICAL SOUND
Describes how scientists discovered a process of converting petroleum hydrocarbons into a new family of synthetic rubbers, including natsyn, the molecular duplicate of natural tree-grown rubber and tufsyn, a synthetic rubber which, when combined with other synthetic or natural rubbers, provides a tough and abrasion-resistant compound.
LC NO. FIE65-35
Prod-GTARC Dist-GTARC 1964

Stretch Of Imagination, The - The Synthetic Duplication Of Natural Rubber C 27 MIN
16MM FILM OPTICAL SOUND I-C
Shows how scientists have created various synthetics having certain properties of natural rubber. Describes their supreme achievement of 1962, polyisoprene, composed of man-made molecules which duplicate those found in the latex of the rubber tree.
LC NO. FIA64-161
Prod-GTARC Dist-USDIBM 1964

Stretch Strategies For Teaching Handicapped Children—A Series
T
Includes concepts for teaching handicapped children in regular classrooms. Can be applied to all children in varied educational settings.
Prod-HUBDSC Dist-HUBDSC

Behavior Modification 030 MIN
Classroom Management 030 MIN
Individualized Instruction 030 MIN
Learning Centers 030 MIN
Parent Counseling 030 MIN

Questioning Skills 030 MIN
Simulation 030 MIN

Stretch Subject Matter Materials For Teaching Handicapped Children—A Series
T
Includes concepts for teaching handicapped students in regular classrooms. Can be applied to all children in varied educational settings. Covers several teaching areas.
Prod-HUBDSC Dist-HUBDSC

Art And The Exceptional Student 030 MIN
Career Education 030 MIN
Language Experience Approach 030 MIN
Mathematics And The Special Student 030 MIN
Reading In The Content Area 030 MIN
Spelling 030 MIN

Stretcher Transport C 16 MIN
16MM FILM - 3/4 IN VIDEO H-C A
Demonstrates standard procedures for the safe utilization of stretchers.
From The Nurse's Aide, Orderly And Attendant Series.
Prod-COPI Dist-COPI 1969

Stretching And Mobilization For The Parkinson Patient C 7 MIN
16MM FILM OPTICAL SOUND
Demonstrates stretching and mobilization techniques for use with Parkinson patients.
LC NO. 74-705710
Prod-USPHS Dist-USNAC 1967

Stretching Mobile Home Heating Dollars C 50 MIN
3/4 OR 1/2 INCH VIDEO CASSETTE C A
Describes typical mobile home construction methods and shows where added insulation and materials could save heating money. Gives cost analysis of input materials and resulting dollar savings.
LC NO. 83-707106
Prod-CUETV Dist-CUNIV 1983

Stretching Out C 3 MIN
16MM FILM OPTICAL SOUND I-C
Presents a cartoon film dealing with mind expansion.
Prod-CFS Dist-CFS 1968

Stretching Soft Ears C 47 MIN
3/4 INCH VIDEO CASSETTE
Features the music of Charles Ives (1874-1954) as presented by jazz musician Paul Winter. Includes a birthday tribute in the family backyard, concert preparations, performance and historical narrative in Ives' own voice.
Prod-DOCEDR Dist-DOCEDR

Strictly On Your Own C 29 MIN
16MM FILM OPTICAL SOUND
Describes life as a woman recruit in the U S Marine Corps.
LC NO. 74-706589
Prod-USN Dist-USNAC 1971

Strictly Speaking C 31 MIN
16MM FILM, 3/4 OR 1/2 IN VIDEO
Argues for specific and concrete expression, pointing out that clarity of speech results in improved effectiveness. Based on the books A Civil Tongue and Strictly Speaking by Edwin Newman.
Prod-CCCD Dist-CCCD 1979

Strider - A Film C 29 MIN
16MM FILM OPTICAL SOUND
Depicts campus life and classroom scenes of NROTC midshipmen. Describes the advantages of the NROTC college scholarship program, which leads to a degree as well as a career as a Naval or Marine Corps officer.
LC NO. 74-705711
Prod-USN Dist-USNAC 1970

Strider's House B 23 MIN
16MM FILM OPTICAL SOUND
Depicts a fictitious novelist named Strider Park, who realizes as he lies near death that he must resolve certain neglected parts of his life before he goes.
LC NO. 81-700322
Prod-USC Dist-USC 1980

Strike B 78 MIN
3/4 OR 1/2 INCH VIDEO CASSETTE
Addresses the suppression of a 1912 factory workers' strike in Russia.
Prod-IHF Dist-IHF

Strike Back At Strokes C 25 MIN
3/4 OR 1/2 INCH VIDEO CASSETTE
Notes that the third largest cause of death in the United States is stroke. Shows what a stroke is and how it may be prevented. Demonstrates newest techniques for rehabilitating stroke patients, including a Neuromuscular Asist Device which enables many paralyzed patients to walk. Depicts several stroke victims telling how this affliction has affected their lives.
Prod-TRAINX Dist-TRAINX

Strike City C 30 MIN
16MM FILM OPTICAL SOUND
Shows the plantation workers in Mississippi in 1967, going on strike against the exploitation of the plantation system and their decision to form their own collective. Explains how after much effort they obtain permanent housing.
Prod-DOJGRI Dist-NEWSR 1967

Strike City B 30 MIN
16MM FILM OPTICAL SOUND
Shows how the Mississippi plantation workers on strike formed their own collective and how they finally withdrew the pressure from Mississippi's senators.
From The Black Liberation Series.
Prod-SFN Dist-SFN 1967

Strike Command C 29 MIN
16MM FILM OPTICAL SOUND
Shows the fighting potential of the U S Strike Command, a joint command which includes fighting men of the Army, Navy and Air Force.
From The Big Picture Series.
LC NO. 74-706263
Prod-USA Dist-USNAC 1965

Strike Hard, Strike Home B 26 MIN
16MM FILM OPTICAL SOUND
Documentary footage shows the allied invasion of Sicily July 10, 1943, the collapse of the Mussolini regime two weeks later, the surrender of Italy in September by Marshal Badoglio and the meeting between Churchill and Roosevelt in Washington. Based on the book 'THE SECOND WORLD WAR,' by Winston S Churchill.
From The Winston Churchill - The Valiant Years Series. No. 13
LC NO. FI67-2114
Prod-ABCTV Dist-SG 1961

Strikes - Protesting To Gain Power As Well As Economic Advantage C 15 MIN
16MM FILM OPTICAL SOUND
Examines labor protest against management by contrasting the relatively uncomplicated issues of the 1902 United Mine Workers effort to raise their pay. Promotes an understanding of basic sociological concepts.
Prod-INTEXT Dist-REAF

Striking C 15 MIN
3/4 OR 1/2 INCH VIDEO CASSETTE T
Explains how to teach primary students to strike with a racket and about the face of the implement, lever length, striking a stationary and a moving ball.
From The Leaps And Bounds Series. No. 16
Prod-HSDE Dist-AITECH 1984

Striking A Balance C 30 MIN
16MM FILM - 3/4 IN VIDEO J-C A
States that man has used DDT to improve his public health and to increase his agricultural yields. Explains that DDT today isn't as useful as it once was because of the ability of insects to develop resistance. Features a dialogue between a Nobel Prize winner, Norman Borlaug and the Father of the Green Revolution, David Brower.
From The Man Builds - Man Destroys Series.
Prod-UN Dist-GPITVL 1972

Striking Against Objects C 3 MIN
16MM FILM, 3/4 OR 1/2 IN VIDEO IND
Depicts ways in which workers may injure themselves in striking-against-objects accidents by showing what happens to an office worker when she trips up steps, drops papers into a fan, falls over boxes and slips on the floor.
From The Accident Prevention Series.
Prod-IAPA Dist-IFB 1972

Striking Against Objects (Spanish) C 3 MIN
16MM FILM, 3/4 OR 1/2 IN VIDEO IND
Depicts ways in which workers may injure themselves in striking-against-objects accidents by showing what happens to an office worker when she trips up steps, drops papers into a fan, falls over boxes and slips on the floor.
From The Accident Prevention (Spanish) Series.
Prod-IAPA Dist-IFB 1972

Striking An Arc, Restarting The Arc And Running A Continuous Bead In The Flat (Spanish) C
3/4 OR 1/2 INCH VIDEO CASSETTE
See series title for descriptive statement.
From The Shielded Metal Arc Welding (Spanish) Series.
Prod-VTRI Dist-VTRI

Striking An Arc, Restarting The Arc And Running A Continuous Bead In The Flat Position C 15 MIN
3/4 OR 1/2 INCH VIDEO CASSETTE IND
See series title for descriptive statement.
From The Welding - Shielded Metal-Arc Welding Series.
Prod-ICSINT Dist-ICSINT

Striking Arcs With E-6010 Cellulose Electrodes C 13 MIN
3/4 OR 1/2 INCH VIDEO CASSETTE IND
See series title for descriptive statement.
From The Electric Arc Welding Series. Chapter 3
Prod-TAT Dist-TAT

Striking Arcs With E-7018 Low Hydrogen Electrodes C 13 MIN
3/4 OR 1/2 INCH VIDEO CASSETTE IND
See series title for descriptive statement.
From The Electric Arc Welding Series. Chapter 4
Prod-TAT Dist-TAT

Strindberg's The Ghost Sonata C 60 MIN
3/4 OR 1/2 INCH VIDEO CASSETTE C
See series title for descriptive statement.
From The Drama - Play, Performance, Perception Series. Module 2
Prod-MDCC Dist-MDCC

String - Knotting And Weaving C 10 MIN
16MM FILM, 3/4 OR 1/2 IN VIDEO J-C A
Offers an introduction to creative weaving, knotting and macrame.
Prod-FLMFR Dist-FLMFR

String Family, The C 15 MIN
3/4 OR 1/2 INCH VIDEO CASSETTE P
Teaches recognition of string musical instruments.
From The Music Machine Series.
Prod-GPITVL Dist-GPITVL

String Family, The C 15 MIN
3/4 OR 1/2 INCH VIDEO CASSETTE P-I
Discusses the string family of instruments.
From The Music And Me Series.
Prod-WDCNTV Dist-AITECH 1979

String Processing B
16MM FILM OPTICAL SOUND
Deals with the construction of algorithms for processing strings.
Prod-OPENU Dist-OPENU

String Quartet C 47 MIN
16MM FILM OPTICAL SOUND H-C A
Presents the Debussy Quartet in G Minor as played by the Carl Pini String Quartet. Studies the four players as they talk about their lives and careers and their dedication to chamber music.
LC NO. 73-702266
Prod-ANAIB Dist-AUIS 1972

String, The C 19 MIN
16MM FILM OPTICAL SOUND K-C A
A fantasy about a magic ball of twine which, because it cannot be cut, winds in and out of the lives and property of the townspeople who are lifted out of themselves and made more sensitive to one another.
LC NO. 72-700403
Prod-FILMC Dist-MMA 1970

Stringbean, The B 17 MIN
16MM FILM, 3/4 OR 1/2 IN VIDEO I-C A
Tells of a woman who raises a bean plant in a can outside her window until it grows too big and she transplants it amidst some ornamental shrubbery. Reveals that when gardeners uproot the plant believing it to be a weed, the woman starts the process from scratch.
Prod-JANUS Dist-TEXFLM 1964

Stringer - Portrait Of A Newsreel Cameraman C 28 MIN
16MM FILM, 3/4 OR 1/2 IN VIDEO H A
Describes the career of Mike Gittinger, a freelance cameraman for the major newsreels between 1928 and 1940. Tells how he filmed the news when he could, and created the news when he couldn't.
Prod-FORMM Dist-FI 1979

Stringer Bead C 7 MIN
1/2 IN VIDEO CASSETTE BETA/VHS IND
See series title for descriptive statement.
From The Welding Training (Comprehensive) --- Oxy-Acetylene Welding Series.
Prod-RMI Dist-RMI

Stringer Beads C 15 MIN
3/4 OR 1/2 INCH VIDEO CASSETTE IND
See series title for descriptive statement.
From The Arc Welding Training Series.
Prod-AVIMA Dist-AVIMA

Stringer Beads With E-6010 C 13 MIN
3/4 OR 1/2 INCH VIDEO CASSETTE IND
See series title for descriptive statement.
From The Electric Arc Welding Series. Chapter 5
Prod-TAT Dist-TAT

Stringer Beads With E-7018 C 13 MIN
3/4 OR 1/2 INCH VIDEO CASSETTE IND
See series title for descriptive statement.
From The Electric Arc Welding Series. Chapter 6
Prod-TAT Dist-TAT

Stringing Along C 15 MIN
16MM FILM OPTICAL SOUND K-I
Follows Yoffy and his friends as they collect various kinds of string.
From The Fingermouse, Yoffy And Friends Series.
LC NO. 73-700439
Prod-BBCTV Dist-VEDO 1972

Strings And Things C 25 MIN
16MM FILM, 3/4 OR 1/2 IN VIDEO J-C A
Looks at the way a computer can handle words and presents some of the principles involved in managing a large program.
From The Making The Most Of The Micro Series. Episode 3
Prod-BBCTV Dist-FI 1983

Strip Mined Lands Can Be Reclaimed C 20 MIN
16MM FILM OPTICAL SOUND
Demonstrates the restoration of land following coal strip mining operations.
LC NO. 80-701175
Prod-TVA Dist-USNAC 1974

Strip Mining - Energy, Environment And Economics C 50 MIN
3/4 INCH VIDEO CASSETTE
Details the beginnings, growth and consequences of strip mining, the long term environmental effects, and the need for jobs created by strip mining.
Prod-APPAL Dist-APPAL 1979

Strip Mining In Appalachia B 29 MIN
16MM FILM - 3/4 IN VIDEO J-H A
Views the destruction left in the wake of strip mining with reports from coal mining company executives as well as interviews with people whose lands have been victims of this operation.
Prod-APPAL Dist-APPAL 1973

Stripe Removal By High Temperature Burning With Excess Oxygen C 10 MIN
16MM FILM OPTICAL SOUND

Demonstrates the removal of the painted lines on road surfaces by a method of burning.
LC NO. 80-701085
Prod-USFHAD Dist-USNAC 1980

Striped Ice Cream C 15 MIN
3/4 OR 1/2 INCH VIDEO CASSETTE I
Tells of a girl who wants striped ice cream for her eighth birthday party. From the story by Joan Lexau.
From The Book Bird Series.
Prod-CTI Dist-CTI

Stripmining - Energy, Environment And Economics C 50 MIN
16MM FILM OPTICAL SOUND H A
Discusses the origin and growth of strip mining, and the consequences of this type of mining for the Appalachian region.
LC NO. 80-700960
Prod-APPAL Dist-APPAL 1979

Striptease C 1 MIN
16MM FILM OPTICAL SOUND
Depicts an apparent striptease which turns out to be something entirely different.
Prod-ZAGREB Dist-VIEWFI 1970

Strobe Ode C
3/4 OR 1/2 INCH VIDEO CASSETTE
From The Two Programs By Stan Vanderbeek Series.
Prod-EAI Dist-EAI

Stroke B 18 MIN
16MM FILM OPTICAL SOUND H-C A
Follows the progress of a stroke patient through diagnostic tests, physical therapy and excercises. Explains the nature of various types of brain damage and the treatment indicated.
From The Doctors At Work Series.
LC NO. FIA65-1363
Prod-CMA Dist-LAWREN Prodn-LAWREN 1961

Stroke C 17 MIN
3/4 INCH VIDEOTAPE
Interviews stroke patients and a family member of a stroke patient. Discusses the major types of strokes and details many of the cognitive and social consequences. Provides information about various therapies the stroke patient is likely to need.
Prod-UNDMC Dist-UNDMC

Stroke C 19 MIN
3/4 OR 1/2 INCH VIDEO CASSETTE PRO
Describes the clinical course of a stroke. Relates pathology to signs and symptoms. Explains rehabilitation. Stresses need for physical therapy and emotional support.
Prod-MEDFAC Dist-MEDFAC 1979

Stroke C 30 MIN
3/4 OR 1/2 INCH VIDEO CASSETTE
Tells that stroke is the third largest killer in America, but only one in six stroke victims actually die. Each year one millions Americans are crippled by this disease. Looks at causes and treatments of stroke, featuring neurologist Dr Roger Rosenberg.
From The Here's To Your Health Series.
Prod-KERA Dist-PBS 1979

Stroke C 30 MIN
3/4 OR 1/2 INCH VIDEO CASSETTE
See series title for descriptive statement.
From The Here's To Your Health Series.
Prod-PBS Dist-DELTAK

Stroke C 60 MIN
3/4 OR 1/2 INCH VIDEO CASSETTE
Discusses the three kinds of stroke, the warning symptoms and how a stroke affects the central nervous system. Describes rehabilitation and new diagnostic techniques using brain scans.
From The Medicine For The Layman Series.
LC NO. 84-706512
Prod-NIH Dist-USNAC 1983

Stroke - A Program For The Family C 16 MIN
3/4 OR 1/2 INCH VIDEO CASSETTE
Discusses and describes stroke, and its possible causes and the highly individual symptoms that may occur all for the victim's family. Describes treatment that he may receive, and the roles of various health care proffesionals who may be involved in patient care. Concludes by outlining the important considerations in helping the patient to adjust on his/her return home.
LC NO. 83-730050
Prod-TRAINX Dist-TRAINX

Stroke - Focus On Feelings C 23 MIN
3/4 INCH VIDEO CASSETTE
Explores the emotional effects of stroke on individuals and their families. Shows people who have had strokes and family members talking about coping with anger, depression and loss. Demonstrates that one still has choices in life and can regain a sense of self-worth and a quality of living.
Prod-ORACLE Dist-ORACLE

Stroke - Focus On Independence B 25 MIN
2 INCH VIDEOTAPE PRO
Demonstrates how to help the stroke patient become self-sufficient by teaching them rehabilitative techniques of self-exercise, feeding procedures and knowledge of their illness. Stresses the task of the rehabilitative nurse in handling the patient's depression and how she can give counseling to both the patient and the family.
Prod-AJN Dist-AJN 1967

Stroke - What Exactly Is A Stroke? C 30 MIN
3/4 OR 1/2 INCH VIDEO CASSETTE C T
Answers the question of what can be done to minimize the risk of being stricken by stroke and how to ease the anguish of those who have suffered a stroke. Explores the 'cardio-vascular accidents' we call stroke.
From The Here's To Your Health Series.
Prod-DALCCD Dist-DALCCD

Stroke Awareness And Prevention C
3/4 OR 1/2 INCH VIDEO CASSETTE
Explains how people often experience temporary symptoms similar to a stroke. Warns not to ignore them in order to avoid a stroke.
Prod-MIFE Dist-MIFE

Stroke Awareness And Prevention (Arabic) C
3/4 OR 1/2 INCH VIDEO CASSETTE
Explains how people often experience temporary symptoms similar to a stroke. Warns not to ignore them in order to avoid a stroke.
Prod-MIFE Dist-MIFE

Stroke Awareness And Prevention (Spanish) C
3/4 OR 1/2 INCH VIDEO CASSETTE
Explains how people often experience temporary symptoms similar to a stroke. Warns not to ignore them in order to avoid a stroke.
Prod-MIFE Dist-MIFE

Stroke Management Decisions C 67 MIN
3/4 INCH VIDEO CASSETTE PRO
Shows factors influencing the decision to perform lumbar puncture and anticoagulation therapy in the stroke patient. Examines the recommendation for arteriography for the stroke patient and factors influencing the decision to refer the patient for surgical treatment. Discusses prevention of stroke and supportive care of the stroke patient.
LC NO. 76-706104
Prod-WARMP Dist-USNAC 1970

Stroke Management Decisions, Pt 1 C 22 MIN
3/4 OR 1/2 INCH VIDEO CASSETTE
Identifies factors influencing the decision to perform lumbar puncture and to use anticoagulation therapy on the stroke patient.
Prod-WARMP Dist-USNAC

Stroke Management Decisions, Pt 2 C 23 MIN
3/4 OR 1/2 INCH VIDEO CASSETTE
Discusses factors influencing the decision to recommend arteriography or surgery for the stroke patient.
Prod-WARMP Dist-USNAC

Stroke Management Decisions, Pt 3 C 22 MIN
3/4 OR 1/2 INCH VIDEO CASSETTE
Discusses prevention and supportive care in dealing with the stroke patient or potential stroke patient. Shows film clips of patient interviews to illustrate points of clinical importance.
Prod-WARMP Dist-USNAC

Stroke Of The Pen, A B 16 MIN
16MM FILM, 3/4 OR 1/2 IN VIDEO I-C A
Presents a study of presidential decision-making. Concentrates on President Kennedy's decision to sign an executive order desegregating housing. Chronicles the deliberations and delays which turn a simple 'stroke of the pen' into something more complex.
LC NO. 75-703002
Prod-KENJML Dist-PFP Prodn-ENVIC 1975

Stroke Patient, The C 30 MIN
3/4 OR 1/2 INCH VIDEO CASSETTE
Presents a nurse's home visit to a 45-year-old stroke victim. Explores patient's family history. Evaluates patient's range of motion and ability to get in and out of bed. Reviews discharge treatment plan, diet and rehabilitative activity.
From The Simulated Home Visits Series.
Prod-UTEXN Dist-AJN

Stroke Rehabilitation C 69 MIN
3/4 INCH VIDEO CASSETTE PRO
Deals with means of determining the learning ability of the stroke patient so that retraining can be planned. Demonstrates the initial and intermediate phases of retraining patients for independence in self-care activities. Describes techniques for reestablishing ambulation and below-the-waist dressing skills and explains the reasons for speech therapy.
LC NO. 76-706105
Prod-WARMP Dist-USNAC 1970

Stroke Story C 30 MIN
16MM FILM OPTICAL SOUND
Looks at the lives of three stroke victims and their families. Explores the problems faced by these families as they help a family member recover from a stroke.
LC NO. 80-700308
Prod-RICHGO Dist-RICHGO Prodn-SHANDA 1979

Stroke, A - Recovering Together C 24 MIN
3/4 OR 1/2 INCH VIDEO CASSETTE
Describes why strokes occur, shows the predominant forms of aphasia and reviews coping and communication skills for use with stroke victims. Includes comments from a spouse group and profiles of stroke victims demonstrating various levels of recovery.
Prod-VAMCSL Dist-USNAC

Strokes C 28 MIN
16MM FILM OPTICAL SOUND H-C A
Explains how we can be less afraid to ask for and accept recognition and love.
From The Learning To Live Series.
Prod-TRAFCO Dist-ECUFLM 1974

Strokes C 11 MIN
16MM FILM, 3/4 OR 1/2 IN VIDEO H-C A
Details diseases of the arteries and how strokes can result. Explains the process of recovery and the need for rehabilitation. Urges prevention by proper diet, exercise and stress reduction.
From The Cardiovascular Disease Series.
LC NO. 83-706645
Prod-CF Dist-CF 1983

Strong Feelings C 15 MIN
16MM FILM, 3/4 OR 1/2 IN VIDEO I
Presents a sequence of zany dreams, in which Edgar discovers how love, fright, embarrassment, confusion and disappointment can affect the body.
From The Inside-Out Series.
LC NO. 73-702450
Prod-NITC Dist-AITECH 1973

Strong Kids, Safe Kids C
1/2 IN VIDEO CASSETTE BETA/VHS
Presents Henry Winkler and other TV personalities telling children how to avoid situations and actions that can lead to abuse or abduction.
Prod-GA Dist-GA

Strong Man, The B 78 MIN
16MM FILM SILENT J-C A
Presents a Harry Langdon feature directed by Frank Capra.
Prod-MGM Dist-TWYMAN 1926

Stronger, The C 18 MIN
16MM FILM, 3/4 OR 1/2 IN VIDEO H-C A
Portrays an encounter between two actresses in a cafe and the effect that this meeting has on the two women.
Prod-BURF Dist-PHENIX Prodn-YOUNGP 1970

Strongest Man In The World, The C 29 MIN
3/4 OR 1/2 INCH VIDEO CASSETTE P-C A
Recounts the success story of Mike Swistum, featured as the strongest man in the world with the 1923 Ringling Brothers, Barnum, and Bailey Circus. Features Swistum speaking in English and Ukrainian, the language of his Manitoba, Canada, hometown.
Prod-KINOF Dist-KINFIL 1981

Strongest Man, The C 20 MIN
16MM FILM, 3/4 OR 1/2 IN VIDEO P-I S
Reveals that when Billy fails to make the all-star baseball team, he becomes angry and blames his father, a paraplegic who is unable to practice with him. Shows his father explaining that his handicap is something he cannot change and that they must both learn to accept it.
Prod-JNSNR Dist-BARR 1982

Stroszek C 108 MIN
16MM FILM OPTICAL SOUND
Tells how three Berlin misfits travel to Wisconsin and find a bleak Eldorado of TV, football, CB radio and mobile homesteading. Directed by Werner Herzog. In German and English, with English subtitles.
Prod-UNKNWN Dist-NYFLMS 1977

Stroszek C 110 MIN
16MM FILM OPTICAL SOUND
A German language film with English subtitles. Presents Werner Herzog's film of ex-convict Bruno Strosvek, who offers refuge to a battered prostitute, Eva, and who later travels to the United States with her and a friend, Clemens. Continues as Eva becomes disillusioned, deserts Bruno and leaves for Canada, and concludes after a robbery in which Clemens is apprehended, with Bruno escaping and enigmatically vanishing.
Prod-WSTGLC Dist-WSTGLC 1977

Struck C 29 MIN
2 INCH VIDEOTAPE
See series title for descriptive statement.
From The Our Street Series.
Prod-MDCPB Dist-PUBTEL

Structural Abnormalities Of Human Autosomes B 30 MIN
16MM FILM OPTICAL SOUND PRO
Discusses the mammalian chromosome and various rearrangements produced by abnormal disruption and rejoining. Explains that sometimes these abnormalities are inherited and at other times they are produced De Novo. Demonstrates the karotypes and syndromes found in 4p-, 5p- and 18q syndromes.
From The Clinical Pathology Series.
Prod-NMAC Dist-USNAC 1970

Structural Analysis–A Series
PRO
Uses classroom format to videotape one one-hour and one 1 1/2 hour lecture per week for 13 weeks and 39 cassettes. Shows use of classical methods of analysis, least work, conjugate beam, column analogy and virtual work methods to solve statically indeterminate problems. Introduces Newmark's techniques for approximate solutions for beam moments, shears and deflections. Tells how these techniques are used to solve stability problems for buckling models and to find eigenvalues and eigenvectors in the dynamic analysis of beams.
Prod-USCCE Dist-AMCEE

Structural Collapse C
3/4 OR 1/2 INCH VIDEO CASSETTE
Details procedures during fire fighting operations that enhance this lesson on structural collapse. Points out the principle causes of building collapse and illustrates ways fire fighters can recognize deficiencies in certain types of building construction.
From The Safety Series.
Prod-NFPA Dist-NFPA 1981

Structural Coupling C 60 MIN
3/4 OR 1/2 INCH VIDEO CASSETTE A
Presents biologist Humberto Maturana discussing structural coupling.
From The Biology Of Cognition And Language Series. Program 5
Prod-UCEMC Dist-UCEMC

Structural Examination - Gross Motion Testing C 14 MIN
3/4 OR 1/2 INCH VIDEO CASSETTE PRO
Describes movements in relation to the orientation planes of the body. Details the techniques of motion testing. Tests symmetry of the range of motion and the degree of resistance to motion. Elaborates the palpatory criteria with graphics.
From The Osteopathic Examination And Manipulation Series.
Prod-MSU Dist-MSU

Structural Examination - Initial Screen C 14 MIN
3/4 OR 1/2 INCH VIDEO CASSETTE PRO
Shows how diagnosis of the musculoskeletal problem begins with a screening examination of the entire body in order to narrow down the attention of the examiner to any major dysfunction centering within a particular region. Demonstrates procedures. Examines symmetries of structure, tissue and motion.
From The Osteopathic Examination And Manipulation Series.
Prod-MSU Dist-MSU

Structural Examination - Local Scan C 18 MIN
3/4 OR 1/2 INCH VIDEO CASSETTE PRO
Examines the scan in detail. Demonstrates procedures for testing function segment-to-segment throughout costal, shoulder and spinal regions.
From The Osteopathic Examination And Manipulation Series.
Prod-MSU Dist-MSU

Structural Examination - Spinal Segmental Definition C
3/4 OR 1/2 INCH VIDEO CASSETTE PRO
Gives a brief review of the initial structural examination tests that detect the presence and location of dysfunction in the spinal system. Demonstrates tests that provide segmental definition in each spinal region. Illustrates how this diagnostic information becomes immediately useful in restoring motion function.
From The Osteopathic Examination And Manipulation Series.
Prod-MSU Dist-MSU

Structural Fire Attack C 21 MIN
16MM FILM OPTICAL SOUND PRO
Relates fire spread history to actual fire extension in structures. Covers preplanning for structural fires and techniques of confining and extinguishing fires.
LC NO. 78-700578
Prod-FIREF Dist-COURTR 1978

Structural Fires B 31 MIN
16MM FILM OPTICAL SOUND PRO
Shows how a variety of fires are extinguished with a minimum of water damage. Depicts all types of engine companies in action at scenes of actual fires.
Prod-LAFIRE Dist-LAFIRE

Structural Foundations C 180 MIN
3/4 OR 1/2 INCH VIDEO CASSETTE PRO
Discusses artificial heat extractors, the Long pile, the Balch tube, Rice system, and 'aerospace spin off' and the like.
From The Arctic Engineering Series.
Prod-UAKEN Dist-AMCEE

Structural Geology C 30 MIN
3/4 OR 1/2 INCH VIDEO CASSETTE C
Points out several structurally interesting features of earth. Explains the training of astronauts to become scientific observers and photographers.
From The Earth, Sea And Sky Series.
Prod-DALCCD Dist-DALCCD

Structural Geology - Faults C 33 MIN
3/4 OR 1/2 INCH VIDEO CASSETTE IND
See series title for descriptive statement.
From The Basic And Petroleum Geology For Non-Geologists - Structural...--Series.
Prod-PHILLP Dist-GPCV

Structural Geology - Folds C 25 MIN
3/4 OR 1/2 INCH VIDEO CASSETTE IND
See series title for descriptive statement.
From The Basic And Petroleum Geology For Non-Geologists - Structural...--Series.
Prod-PHILLP Dist-GPCV

Structural Homologies And Co-Evolution C 20 MIN
3/4 OR 1/2 INCH VIDEO CASSETTE
Examines the similarities of structure between different species and co-evolutionary relationships. Emphasizes the similarities of structure between a lizard's leg, a bat's wing, a human arm, a sheep's leg and a porpoise's paddle.
From The Evolution Series.
Prod-FOTH Dist-FOTH 1984

Structure And Function Of Hemoglobin, The C 25 MIN
16MM FILM, 3/4 OR 1/2 IN VIDEO
Uses computer-generated anaglyphic photography of ball-and-stick models of a hemoglobin molecule to explain the biochemical mechanism by which hemoglobin binds and releases oxygen. Illustrates the roles of several of the individual aminoacid residues by building the molecule stage by stage.
Prod-OPENU Dist-MEDIAG Prodn-BBCTV 1981

Structure And Physiology Of The Avian Egg C 15 MIN
16MM FILM, 3/4 OR 1/2 IN VIDEO
Illustrates the enormous variety of shapes and colors of bird eggs. Examines their structure.
From The Aspects Of Animal Behavior Series.
Prod-UCLA Dist-UCEMC

Structure Fires B 31 MIN
16MM FILM, 3/4 OR 1/2 IN VIDEO H-C A
Demonstrates methods of putting out fires with a minimum of water damage. Shows all types of engine companies fighting dwelling, mercantile, warehouse, factory, theater, basement and attic fires. Explains fire-fighting strategy.
Prod-LACFD Dist-FILCOM 1951

Structure In Stories C 15 MIN
3/4 OR 1/2 INCH VIDEO CASSETTE P
See series title for descriptive statement.
From The Word Shop Series.
Prod-WETATV Dist-WETATV

Structure Of A Computer, The B
16MM FILM OPTICAL SOUND
Introduces computing and tells how a computer can be used as an aid to problem solving.
Prod-OPENU Dist-OPENU

Structure Of Assemblers C 50 MIN
3/4 OR 1/2 INCH VIDEO CASSETTE
Discusses the translation process, how A(M) works, 1 vs 2 passes and space-time tradeoffs in computer languages.
From The Computer Languages - Pt 1 Series.
Prod-MIOT Dist-MIOT

Structure Of Gardens, The C 15 MIN
16MM FILM OPTICAL SOUND I-C A
Views demonstration gardens in California public parks which can serve as sources of inspiration to homeowners. Includes comments by landscape architects and garden attendants.
Prod-CRA Dist-CRA

Structure Of Lysozyme, The C 24 MIN
16MM FILM, 3/4 OR 1/2 IN VIDEO
Describes methods used to establish the molecular structure of the enzyme lysozyme, unique in molecular biology as the first enzyme for which both a catalytic mechanism and a detailed molecular structure had been developed.
Prod-OPENU Dist-MEDIAG Prodn-BBCTV 1978

Structure Of Minerals, Pt 1 B 27 MIN
16MM FILM OPTICAL SOUND C A
Demonstrating the law of constancy of interfacial angles, outlines crystal systems using length and angular relationships of axes and symmetry planes. Employs X-ray equipment, picture of a path of X-rays through a mineral and an example of an X-ray diffraction pattern to explain internal structure and symmetry.
Prod-UTEX Dist-UTEX 1960

Structure Of Minerals, Pt 2 B 26 MIN
16MM FILM OPTICAL SOUND C A
Describes the silicon-oxygen tetrahedron and follows its assembly into chains and sheets to form minerals of Bowen's reaction series. Describes the latter to show major mineral types.
Prod-UTEX Dist-UTEX 1960

Structure Of Protein, The C 16 MIN
16MM FILM, 3/4 OR 1/2 IN VIDEO J-H
Traces the development of proteins including the building of amino acids, polypeptides, protein molecules and the message DNA which is transferred to RNA to act as a template for the construction of proteins.
Prod-LEVER Dist-PHENIX 1970

Structure Of Proteins B 10 MIN
16MM FILM SILENT C
Presents a detailed study of the structures of myoglobin and lysozyme.
From The Molecular Biology Films Series.
LC NO. 73-709327
Prod-ERCMIT Dist-EDC 1970

Structure Of Successful Programs C 60 MIN
3/4 OR 1/2 INCH VIDEO CASSETTE IND
See series title for descriptive statement.
From The Quality Circle Concepts Series.
Prod-NCSU Dist-AMCEE

Structure Of Systems, The, Pt 1 B
16MM FILM OPTICAL SOUND
Analyzes a mathematical model whose state is defined by a finite number of time dependent qualities.
Prod-OPENU Dist-OPENU

Structure Of Systems, The, Pt 2 B
16MM FILM OPTICAL SOUND
Analyzes physical systems whose state is determined by a finite number of variables. Focuses on an electrical system.
Prod-OPENU Dist-OPENU

Structure Of The Earth B 27 MIN
16MM FILM OPTICAL SOUND C A
Illustrates that the continental platform and ocean floors dominate the surface of the earth. Summarizes Pratt and Airy's hypotheses of isostasy and garners evidence from seismographs on the interior of the earth. Illustrates the difference between 'P' and 'S' STRUCTURE OF A CONTINENT.
Prod-UTEX Dist-UTEX 1960

Structure Within The Image C 30 MIN
3/4 OR 1/2 INCH VIDEO CASSETTE
See series title for descriptive statement.
From The Photographic Vision - All About Photography Series.
Prod-COAST Dist-CDTEL

Structured Design Examples C 55 MIN
3/4 OR 1/2 INCH VIDEO CASSETTE PRO
Covers the full-adder (FA) and its NAND gate realization. Gives alternative FA designs. Deals with alternative state machines.
From The Introduction To VLSI Series.
Prod-MIOT Dist-MIOT

Structured Interviews With Young Children C 49 MIN
3/4 OR 1/2 INCH VIDEO CASSETTE
Presents interviews with young children which facilitate the needs of all family members. Points out that setting limits, sharing information, communication boundaries and handling change represent four important goals.
Prod-WRAMC Dist-UWISC 1979

Structured Program Design—A Series

Prod-EDTRCS Dist-EDTRCS

Managing A Structured Programming Project 015 MIN

Structured Programming And Software Maintenance C 30 MIN
3/4 OR 1/2 INCH VIDEO CASSETTE IND
Introduces structured programming and illustrates with diagrams and examples. Emphasizes relationship of techniques to reduced software-development and maintenance costs in the software life cycle.
From The Micros For Managers - Software Series
Prod-COLOSU Dist-COLOSU

Structured Settlements C 180 MIN
3/4 OR 1/2 INCH VIDEO CASSETTE PRO
Presents the advantages and disadvantages of structured settlements in tort liability claims from the perspective of the plaintiff, the defendent, their respective counsels and the insurer.
Prod-ALIABA Dist-ALIABA

Structured Techniques - A Software Development Series B 10 MIN
3/4 OR 1/2 INCH VIDEO CASSETTE C
Uses classroom format to videotape ten one-hour lectures. Introduces structured techniques and includes improving software life cycle and quality, relationships and compatibilities among the various structured techniques and management considerations for effective utilization.
Prod-ILIOT Dist-AMCEE

Structured Techniques - An Overview—A Series

Provides a familiarity with the collection of methodologies, techniques and tools that are commonly referred to as structured techniques and an awareness of how these techniques can be used to combat many software problems and help meet the growing demands for more and better quality software.
Prod-DELTAK Dist-DELTAK

Introduction To Structured Techniques 030 MIN
Management View Of Structured Techniques, A 030 MIN
Relationships Among Structured Techniques 030 MIN

Structured Vs Unstructured Approaches C 20 MIN
3/4 INCH VIDEO CASSETTE PRO
Presents a panel discussion of formal and informal approaches to executive development using examples from the public and private sectors. Features participants from the United States Civil Service Commission, the Social Security Administration and the Martin Marietta Corporation, who point out the need for organizations to consciously plan for executive development.
From The Executive Development And Training Issues - Government And Industry Series. Part 1
LC NO. 77-700634
Prod-USCSC Dist-USNAC 1976

Structures C 24 MIN
16MM FILM, 3/4 OR 1/2 IN VIDEO
Analyzes engineering structures by explaining their components and structural failure by means of demonstrations and a case study. Explains the main types of structural components and studies the actual case of a new power line tower design.
Prod-OPENU Dist-MEDIAG Prodn-BBCTV 1981

Structures C 30 MIN
2 INCH VIDEOTAPE
See series title for descriptive statement.
From The Trains, Tracks And Trestles Series.
Prod-WMVSTV Dist-PUBTEL

Structures - Foundations C 180 MIN
3/4 OR 1/2 INCH VIDEO CASSETTE PRO
Covers, in three one-hour tapes, structural members and components, foundations, retaining wall and dams.
From The Professional Engineer Review Series.
Prod-UILU Dist-AMCEE

Structures And Unions C
3/4 OR 1/2 INCH VIDEO CASSETTE
Defines and describes a structure, detailing the types of members which a structure may contain. Describes the syntax for defining, declaring and initializing a structure.
From The 'C' Language Programming Series.
Prod-COMTEG Dist-COMTEG

Structuring Single Attribute Utility Functions C 48 MIN
3/4 OR 1/2 INCH VIDEO CASSETTE
See series title for descriptive statement.
From The Decision Analysis Series.
Prod-MIOT Dist-MIOT

Structuring The Environment And Managing Behavior Of The Physically Handicapped Child C 14 MIN
3/4 INCH VIDEOTAPE
Covers basic methods used in behavior modification program for children. Discusses positive reinforcement, limit setting, establishing routines, negative reinforcement, time-out, modeling, charting, parental consistency and punishment as communication.
Prod-UNDMC Dist-UNDMC

Structuring The Learning Environment C
3/4 OR 1/2 INCH VIDEO CASSETTE S
Gives the concepts of normalization, the ten-point plan for increasing desirable behavior, why inappropriate behaviors occur, how to handle disruptive students.
From The Effective Behavioral Programming Series.
Prod-RESPRC Dist-RESPRC

Structuring The Topic C
3/4 OR 1/2 INCH VIDEO CASSETTE C
Explains why an audience needs clear structured writing by showing 'How-To' strategies to plan and organize the writing.
From The Write Course - An Introduction To College Composition Series.
Prod-DALCCD Dist-DALCCD

Structuring The Topic C 30 MIN
3/4 OR 1/2 INCH VIDEO CASSETTE C A
Explains why an audience needs clearly structured writing by showing 'how-to' strategies to plan and organize writing.
From The Write Course - An Introduction To College Composition Series.
LC NO. 85-700977
Prod-FI Dist-FI 1984

Struggle - The Highest Form Of Education B 30 MIN
16MM FILM OPTICAL SOUND H-C
James Campbell traces the efforts of black communities in the North to achieve community control of local schools from 1849 to the present. He describes the current conflict regarding public school systems, the roles played by various personalities and their accomplishments.
From The Black Heritage, Section 21 - Protest And Rebellion In The North Series.
LC NO. 77-704112
Prod-WCBSTV Dist-HRAW 1969

Struggle And The Triumph, The C 25 MIN
16MM FILM - 3/4 IN VIDEO I-C A
Provides a look at the Olympic games and at the work of the U S Olympic Committee.
LC NO. 81-706236
Prod-TAUPR Dist-USOC Prodn-USOC 1980

Struggle At Sea B 26 MIN
16MM FILM OPTICAL SOUND
Using documentary footage shows the results of the Nazi U-boat campaign against British shipping and Churchill's response to this peril in the battle of the Atlantic. Pictures the sinking of the German battleship Bismarck and the United States announcement of a new aid policy towards Britain. Based on the book 'THE SECOND WORLD WAR,' by Winston S Churchill.
From The Winston Churchill - The Valiant Years Series. No. 7
LC NO. FI67-2115
Prod-ABCTV Dist-SG 1961

Struggle For Los Trabajos C 35 MIN
16MM FILM, 3/4 OR 1/2 IN VIDEO H-C A
Explains the investigation and conciliation processes that result when a complaint of job discrimination is filed with the Equal Employment Opportunity Commission.
Prod-USEEOC Dist-GREAVW 1975

Struggle For Objectivity, The B 30 MIN
2 INCH VIDEOTAPE PRO
Helps nursing students understand the importance of objectivity in accepting others and in developing their skills in treating patients.
From The Mental Health Concepts For Nursing, Unit 3 - Acceptance Of Others Series.
LC NO. 73-702644
Prod-GPITVL Dist-GPITVL 1971

Struggle For Power C 30 MIN
3/4 OR 1/2 INCH VIDEO CASSETTE
Reports on the many directions in the complex struggle to supplement the dwindling petroleum-based fuels with alternative sources.
Prod-IVCH Dist-IVCH

Struggle For Vicksburg, The C 19 MIN
16MM FILM, 3/4 OR 1/2 IN VIDEO J-C A
Explains the importance of Vicksburg in the Civil War and relates the human story of the Union and Confederate soldiers involved in the struggle.
Prod-CENTRO Dist-CORF

Struggle In Birmingham, The C 58 MIN
1/2 IN VIDEO CASSETTE BETA/VHS
Presents a portrait of Jesse Jackson, activist minister turned presidential contender. Follows Reverend Jackson and his operatives as they try to gain the support of both mainstream political leaders and the disenfranchised. Portrays the dilemma of established black leaders who must choose between support of Jackson and the front-running party candidates.
From The Frontline Series.
Prod-DOCCON Dist-PBS

Struggle Of Coon Branch Mountain, The B 13 MIN
16MM FILM - 3/4 IN VIDEO H A
Relates the struggle of a small West Virginia community for better roads and schools.
Prod-APPAL Dist-APPAL 1973

Strychnine In The Soup C 30 MIN
3/4 OR 1/2 INCH VIDEO CASSETTE C A
Presents an adaptation of the short story Strychnine In The Soup by P G Wodehouse.
From The Wodehouse Playhouse Series.
Prod-BBCTV Dist-TIMLIF 1980

Strychnine Toxicosis In The Dog C 11 MIN
16MM FILM OPTICAL SOUND C
Follows two dogs receiving different levels of strychnine through clinical signs and includes treatment with sodium pentobarbital and activated charcoal.
LC NO. 83-700622
Prod-IOWA Dist-IOWA 1983

STS-1 Launch Aborts C 5 MIN
16MM FILM, 3/4 OR 1/2 IN VIDEO
Depicts launch abort modes for the STS mission, including once-around-abort and the use of the Northrup strip in New Mexico if Edwards Air Force Base in California is unusable or the orbiter must re-enter on an orbit that makes the Northrup a safer alternative to Edwards.
From The Space Shuttle Profile Series.
Prod-NASA Dist-USNAC 1981

Stuart Hodes, Liz Thompson And Brann Wry C 30 MIN
3/4 OR 1/2 INCH VIDEO CASSETTE
See series title for descriptive statement.
From The Second Time Around - Career Options For Dancers Series.
Prod-ARCVID Dist-ARCVID

Stuart Hodes, Liz Thompson And Brann Wry C 30 MIN
3/4 OR 1/2 INCH VIDEO CASSETTE
See series title for descriptive statement.
From The Eye On Dance - Second Time Around, Career Options For Dancers Series.
Prod-ARTRES Dist-ARTRES

Stuart Little C 52 MIN
16MM FILM, 3/4 OR 1/2 IN VIDEO K-P
Tells the story of a boy, born five inches tall and weighing five ounces, with ears, whiskers and tail like those of a mouse. Follows him in his adventures, including a sailboat race across a lake in New York's Central Park, a rescue from a trash boat and a northbound trip in search of Margalo, a bird who has flown away from New York City because of a threatening note.
Prod-NBC Dist-MGHT 1968

Stuart Little, Pt 1 C 20 MIN
16MM FILM, 3/4 OR 1/2 IN VIDEO K-P
Tells the story of a boy, born five inches tall and weighing five ounces, with ears, whiskers and tail like those of a mouse. Because of his size, many adventures befall him - a sailboat race across a lake in New York's Central Park, a rescue from a trash boat and a northbound trip in search of Margalo, a bird who has flown away from New York City because of a threatening note.
Prod-NBC Dist-MGHT 1968

Stuart Little, Pt 2 C 32 MIN
16MM FILM, 3/4 OR 1/2 IN VIDEO K-P
Tells the story of a boy, born five inches tall and weighing five ounces, with ears, whiskers and tail like those of a mouse. Because of his size, many adventures befall him - a sailboat race across a lake in New York's Central Park, a rescue from a trash boat and a northbound trip in search of Margalo, a bird who has flown away from New York City because of a threatening note.
Prod-NBC Dist-MGHT 1968

Stuarts Restored, The C 60 MIN
16MM FILM, 3/4 OR 1/2 IN VIDEO H-C A
Tells how the later Stuarts were responsible for Newmarket, Royal Ascot, Chelsea Pensioners, and the Crown Jewels. Discusses their patronage of architect Christopher Wren.
From The Royal Heritage Series.
Prod-BBCTV Dist-FI 1977

Stuck On Cactus C 29 MIN
3/4 INCH VIDEO CASSETTE
Examines the Christmas cactus and lesser known varieties.
From The House Botanist Series.
Prod-UMITV Dist-UMITV 1978

Stuckgut C 90 MIN
16MM FILM OPTICAL SOUND
A German language film with English subtitles. Tells the story of a 49-year-old truck driver who loses his license because of drunken driving. Details his unsuccessful search for employment as he discovers his age is a disadvantage. He does not give up, and with the help of friends, finds a steady job.
Prod-WSTGLC Dist-WSTGLC 1981

Stud Farm, The (Hungarian) C 100 MIN
16MM FILM OPTICAL SOUND
Focuses on the workers at a Hungarian horse-breeding farm during the early 1950's. Directed by Andras Kovacs. With English subtitles.
Prod-UNKNWN Dist-NYFLMS 1978

Student And The Client, The C 67 MIN
3/4 OR 1/2 INCH VIDEO CASSETTE C T
Focuses on how a field instructor can help the practicum student develop the skills for 'tuning in' to the client, responding directly to indirect client clues and contracting with the client.
From The Core Skills For Field Instructors Series. Program 2
LC NO. 83-706439
Prod-MCGILU Dist-MCGILU 1983

Student And Variable Modular Scheduling, The C 23 MIN
16MM FILM OPTICAL SOUND H-C A
Shows appropriate student behavior in small group discussions, large group presentations and unscheduled time activities. Examines the possible pitfalls for the student in a variable modular schedule. Relates these experiences to non-school situations and varied learning opportunities.
LC NO. 78-710819
Prod-EDUC Dist-EDUC 1970

Student As Interviewer, The C 53 MIN
3/4 OR 1/2 INCH VIDEO CASSETTE T
Shows how interviewing is learned and used by students as they keep journals and write papers.
From The Process-Centered Composition Series.
LC NO. 79-706301
Prod-IU Dist-IU 1977

Student As Teacher, The C 28 MIN
16MM FILM OPTICAL SOUND T
Discusses student roles in the educational process, emphasizing the involvement of students in teaching capacities.
Prod-EDUC Dist-EDUC

Student Involvement Program For Developing Values, A C 29 MIN
3/4 OR 1/2 INCH VIDEO CASSETTE T
Features students, teachers, administrators and members of the Bergenfield, New Jersey Public School System and community who show how values clarification, student involvement in a variety of projects and interaction with community groups all contribute to student self-esteem and the welfare of the community.
From The Successful Teaching Practices Series.
Prod-UNIDIM Dist-EBEC 1982

Student Reflections On Social Work Field Training - Reflections On Preparation For... C 59 MIN
3/4 OR 1/2 INCH VIDEO CASSETTE
Consists of instructors and a group of graduate students from the Walter Reed Army Medical Center discussing their definition of social work and their reasons for entering the social work profession. Discusses the differences between social work and other mental health service delivery professions.
Prod-WRAMC Dist-UWISC 1979

Student Reflections On Social Work Field Training - Reflections On Social Work... C 59 MIN
3/4 OR 1/2 INCH VIDEO CASSETTE
Continues the discussion between instructors and graduate students from Walter Reed Army Medical Center on social work supervision. Illustrates the importance of social work supervisors having a good self-understanding so they do not hide in a role play.
Prod-WRAMC Dist-UWISC 1979

Student Self-Concept And Standards C 27 MIN
3/4 OR 1/2 INCH VIDEO CASSETTE T
Introduces teacher Joe Michel who demonstrates how he contributes to student self-concept through such teaching techniques as establishing and maintaining high standards, encouraging inquisitive learning, individualizing through small group tasks and humanistic teaching.
From The Successful Teaching Practices Series.
Prod-UNIDIM Dist-EBEC 1982

Student Services In Higher Education C 33 MIN
3/4 OR 1/2 INCH VIDEO CASSETTE A
Presents a panel discussion on higher education counseling issues. Increasing their client base and use of outreach programs helps counselors to improve services. Effective for in-service training programs and for students near completion of their curricula. A user's guide is included.
Prod-AACD Dist-AACD 1984

Student To Staff Nurse - Bridging The Gap C 120 MIN
3/4 OR 1/2 INCH VIDEO CASSETTE
Describes a preceptorship program designed to help bridge the gap between the nursing student role and the new staff nurse role. Discusses college-hospital collaboration and joint planning, the structure of the program, the roles of participants, the evaluation process and implications of the model for nursing.
Prod-OHCO Dist-AJN

Student Workshop Videotapes—A Series

Presents videotapes produced from student workshops.
Prod-WMENIF Dist-WMENIF

Art For Whom	008 MIN
Straight Jacket	008 MIN
Sur/Face	013 MIN

Student-Directed Curriculum - An Alternative Educational Approach C 21 MIN
16MM FILM OPTICAL SOUND H-C A
Focuses on the perception of inner-city students on how education can satisfy their concerns. Shows the strategies taken by the institute for the advancement of urban education in identifying the problems at an inner city high school and in setting up a pilot program that incorporated all the elements of an alternative educational approach.
LC NO. 72-701995
Prod-EDUC Dist-EDUC 1971

Student, The C 29 MIN
2 INCH VIDEOTAPE
See series title for descriptive statement.
From The Discover Flying - Just Like A Bird Series.
Prod-WKYCTV Dist-PUBTEL

Student's Guide To IIS Coursewriter, A C
3/4 OR 1/2 INCH VIDEO CASSETTE
Portrays the steps used by a student signing on to the coursewriter authoring course and illustrates the various keywords that are used to request information or to switch topics.
From The Authoring In IIS Coursewriter Series.
Prod-DELTAK Dist-DELTAK

Student's Impact On The Agency System, The C 44 MIN
3/4 OR 1/2 INCH VIDEO CASSETTE C T
Focuses on how to help students deal with questions and concerns about agency policy and procedures which emerge during the course of the school year. Discusses ways in which field instructors can help students assess their role in the system, develop formal and informal means for influencing policy or procedures and communicate effectively with other staff.
From The Core Skills For Field Instructors Series. Program 4
LC NO. 83-706441
Prod-MCGILU Dist-MCGILU 1983

Students As Their Own Editors C 40 MIN
3/4 OR 1/2 INCH VIDEO CASSETTE T
Presents a system of teaching students how to edit their own and other's work.
From The Process-Centered Composition Series.
LC NO. 79-706300
Prod-IU Dist-IU 1977

Students Evaluate Their Own Generalizations B 22 MIN
16MM FILM OPTICAL SOUND P-I
Shows a teaching strategy for developing children's thinking.
Prod-AWPC Dist-AWPC 1968

Students Track The Space Age B 6 MIN
16MM FILM OPTICAL SOUND J A
Presents a group of students who have collected, repaired and modernized more than a million dollars in surplus and obsolete military tracking equipment and who can evesdrop on actual exchanges between the Cape Kennedy control center and American astronauts in orbit.
From The Screen News Digest Series. Vol 6, Issue 7
LC NO. FIA68-2078
Prod-HEARST Dist-HEARST 1964

Studies In Bacteriology, Pt 2, Motility B 4 MIN
16MM FILM SILENT
Uses cinephotomicrography to show the motility of monotrichous, amphitrichous and peritrichous bacteria.
LC NO. FIE63-633
Prod-USPHS Dist-USNAC 1953

Studies In Bacteriology, Pt 3, Cell Division B 4 MIN
16MM FILM SILENT
Uses cinephotomicrography to show the process of cell division of spherical and rod-shaped bacteria.
LC NO. FIE53-664
Prod-USPHS Dist-USNAC 1953

Studies In Interviewing—A Series

Demonstrates in four different versions of two different interview situations how interviewers' skills and attitudes affect the interviewee and determine the success of the interview. Designed specifically for training social workers, but useful in many fields that require effective interviewing. Sponsored by the California State Department of Social Welfare. To be used with guides supplied with films.
Prod-USC Dist-USC 1965

Aid To Families With Dependent Children
Unmarried Mother Interview - Peters - Browning 68 MIN

Studies In Meteorology C 15 MIN
16MM FILM OPTICAL SOUND C
Presents the efforts to decrease the destructive wind velocity of hurricanes, examine physics of clouds and regulate snow and hail formation.
From The Science In Action Series.
Prod-ALLFP Dist-COUNFI

Studies In Movement Design B 10 MIN
16MM FILM OPTICAL SOUND
Shows Barbara Mettler teaching a group of boys and girls at the Creative Dance Center in 1966.
From The Creative Dance For Children Series.
Prod-METT Dist-METT 1977

Studies Of Normal Personality Development—A Series
C
Presents studies on normal childhood personality development.
Prod-NYU Dist-NYU

Abby's First Two Years - A Backward Look 030 MIN
And Then Ice Cream 011 MIN
Ballons - Aggression And Destruction Games 017 MIN
Finger Painting 022 MIN
Frustration Play Techniques 035 MIN
Incitement To Reading 037 MIN
Learning Is Searching - A Third Grade Studies 030 MIN
Long Time To Grow, Pt 1 - Two- And 037 MIN
Long Time To Grow, Pt 2 - Four- And Five-Year 037 MIN
Long Time To Grow, Pt 3 - Six-, Seven- And 030 MIN
Meeting Emotional Needs In Childhood 033 MIN
Pay Attention - Problems Of Hard Of 027 MIN
Starting Nursery School - Patterns Of 023 MIN
This Is Robert - A Study Of Personality 080 MIN
Understanding Children's Play 011 MIN
When Should Grownups Help 014 MIN
When Should Grownups Stop Fights 015 MIN

Studio M—A Series
P
Discusses aspects of mathematics.
Prod-WCETTV Dist-GPITVL 1979

Addition And Subtraction Facts Of 13 And 14 15 MIN
Addition And Subtraction Facts Of 15 And 16 15 MIN
Addition And Subtraction Facts Of 17 And 18 15 MIN
Addition And Subtraction Facts Through 11 And 15 MIN
Addition With 2-3 Digit Numbers 15 MIN
Compare And Order Numbers 15 MIN
Division, Pt 1 15 MIN
Division, Pt 2 15 MIN
Estimating Time To The Nearest One-Minute 15 MIN
Estimation 15 MIN
Fractions, Pt 1 - Studio M 15 MIN
Fractions, Pt 2 - Studio M 15 MIN
Geometry - Three-Dimensional Shapes 15 MIN
Geometry - Two-Dimensional Shapes 15 MIN
Greater Than, Less Than 15 MIN
Linear Measurement 15 MIN
Liquid Volume 15 MIN
Money, Pt 1 15 MIN
Money, Pt 2 15 MIN
Multiplication, Pt 1 15 MIN
Multiplication, Pt 2 15 MIN
Numeration To 999 15 MIN
Odd And Even 15 MIN
Review Of Previews - 31 Lessons 15 MIN
Story Problems 15 MIN
Story Problems With The Four Operations 15 MIN
Subtraction - Two-Digit Regrouping 15 MIN
Subtraction Regrouping - Story Problems 15 MIN
Symmetry 15 MIN
Time - Five Minutes 15 MIN
Values Of Digits 15 MIN
Weight 15 MIN

Studio, The C 30 MIN
3/4 OR 1/2 INCH VIDEO CASSETTE
See series title for descriptive statement.
From The Photographic Vision - All About Photography Series.
Prod-COAST Dist-CDTEL

Studmill Story, The C 15 MIN
16MM FILM, 3/4 OR 1/2 IN VIDEO
Looks at the operations and economic importance of studmills, which convert logs into 2x4 studs that frame the buildings and homes of America. Traces the operations of a typical mill, following harvested logs from the woodyard through bucking, canting, rough sawing, drying, planing, grading, trimming and packing for shipment to customers.
From The Forest Resources Films Series.
Prod-REGIS Dist-GPITVL

Studs Terkel's Chicago C 25 MIN
16MM FILM, 3/4 OR 1/2 IN VIDEO H-C A
Presents author and television personality Studs Terkel on a tour of the city of Chicago.
From The Cities Series.
Prod-NIELSE Dist-LCOA Prodn-MCGREE 1980

Study From Life C 32 MIN
16MM FILM OPTICAL SOUND
Explains why and illustrates how live animals are used in medical research. Demonstrates the value of animals in VA'S Research Program. Stresses the humane procedures employed by VA researchers in handling animals.
Prod-USVA Dist-USVA 1963

Study From Life, Pt 1, Laboratory Animals In Laboratory Research C 32 MIN
16MM FILM OPTICAL SOUND
Depicts the personal responsibility of the researcher in the care and use of laboratory animals in medical research. Tells of the development of the artificial heart pacemaker. For hospital personnel and associated community groups.
From The Animal Care Series.
LC NO. FIE65-96
Prod-USVA Dist-USNAC Prodn-USPHS 1963

Study In A And Vibrato Technique C 29 MIN
2 INCH VIDEOTAPE
See series title for descriptive statement.
From The Playing The Guitar II Series.
Prod-KCET Dist-PUBTEL

Study In Choreography For Camera, A C 4 MIN
16MM FILM OPTICAL SOUND
Presents an experiment in film-dance.
Prod-GROVE Dist-GROVE

Study In Color B 28 MIN
16MM FILM OPTICAL SOUND H-C A
Two players, a white man who wears a negro mask and a negro who wears a white mask, discuss the racial problem in separate soliloquies.
From The Study In Color Series.
LC NO. FIA65-1640
Prod-WMSBTV Dist-ADL 1964

Study In Color—A Series

Prod-WMSBTV Dist-ADL

Boy - An Experience In The Search For Identity 12 MIN
Job, The 29 MIN
Study In Color 29 MIN

Study In Development, A C 10 MIN
16MM FILM OPTICAL SOUND
Covers a seminar on development held in Kuala Lumpur. Shows participants in the seminar, who came from various Asian countries, touring some development projects in Malaysia to observe hand development implementation in the country.
Prod-FILEM Dist-PMFMUN 1970

Study In Human Development - Pt 1, Six To Thirty Weeks B 19 MIN
16MM FILM SILENT C T
Shows the reactions of a boy to objects at ages of six, 12, 17, 21, 25 and 30 weeks. Demonstrates supine, prone and sitting postures at 21 weeks, rolling from back to stomach and early patterns of crawling and feeding. Depicts the development of manipulation, the response to soundmaking objects and improvements in postural and locomotor activities at ages between 25 and 30 weeks.
Prod-PSUPCR Dist-PSUPCR 1946

Study In Human Development - Pt 2, Forty-Two Weeks To Fifteen Months B 17 MIN
16MM FILM SILENT C T
Pictures a child's development at 42 weeks, 12 and 15 months of age. Emphasizes gross motor development and perceptual-manipulatory reactions to objects including a cup, spoon, bell, hoop, ball and mirror. Shows that child pulls up, stands, crawls, mounts stairs and exhibits walking readiness. At age one tests are given for fine manipulation, imitation and stair climbing. The development of motor skills is further demonstrated at 15 months and interaction with another child is described.
Prod-PSUPCR Dist-PSUPCR 1946

Study In Human Development - Pt 3, Nineteen Months To Two Years And Eight Months B 19 MIN
16MM FILM SILENT C T
Emphasizes the child's continued gross and fine development and the beginnings of cooperative play. Shows, at 19 months, imitating building a block tower, drinking by holding a glass with both hands, throwing a ball, exhibiting handedness and playing non-cooperatively. At two years, the boy walks up stairs but hesitates in descending, marks on paper without making patterns but still plays individualistically. At 32 months, the child plays more cooperatively and uses a wide variety of toys and play equipment.
Prod-PSUPCR Dist-PSUPCR 1946

Study In Human Development - Pt 4, Three Years To Five Years B 18 MIN
16MM FILM SILENT C T
Demonstrates the child's development of skill in drawing and typical motor coordination at three years. Depicts the improvement in coordination, ability in drawing and rudimentary musical skill. Performance tests for intelligence are applied at four years.
Prod-PSUPCR Dist-PSUPCR 1948

Study In Maternal Attitudes, A B 30 MIN
16MM FILM OPTICAL SOUND
Describes a project whose purpose is to make the study and treatment of the emotional life of children and mothers an integral part of pediatrics and child health supervision.
Prod-NYU Dist-NYU

Study In Wet C 7 MIN
16MM FILM, 3/4 OR 1/2 IN VIDEO H A
Uses water as a disciplined instrument to create a musical event and relates it to spectacular film scenes.
Prod-GROENG Dist-AIMS 1966

Study Is Not A Dirty Word C 10 MIN
3/4 OR 1/2 INCH VIDEO CASSETTE H-C A
Presents a guide to developing effective study techniques. Includes notetaking and improving memory and motivation.
Prod-SEVDIM Dist-SEVDIM

Study Makes The Grade C 15 MIN
16MM FILM - VIDEO, ALL FORMATS K-J
Presents a Fat Albert cartoon focusing on learning how to study and showing that cheaters end up losing.
From The Fat Albert And The Cosby Kids IV Series.
Prod-BARR Dist-BARR Prodn-FLMTON

Study Of Crystals, A C 17 MIN
16MM FILM, 3/4 OR 1/2 IN VIDEO H A
Shows the crystallization of many compounds through microphotography. Illustrates fusion methods in chemical research by Dr Walter Mc Crone whose studies in crystallography and microscopy are internationally known.
Prod-JOU Dist-JOU 1961

Study Of Drawings, The C 24 MIN
16MM FILM, 3/4 OR 1/2 IN VIDEO
Reviews a selection of the finest drawings by Italian artists of the Renaissance in a variety of media including pen, metalpoint, chalk, brush and ink. Explains that drawings are an important tool used by 16th century artists to record preliminary ideas and allow investigation of the structure and form of objects before painting and carving them.
Prod-OPENU Dist-MEDIAG Prodn-BBCTV 1981

Study Of Equivalent And Nonequivalent Stimuli In The Rat B 18 MIN
16MM FILM SILENT C T
Shows animals which are trained, using the Lashley jumping technique, to respond to the smaller of two black circular areas in a gray background. Depicts the animals being tested to determine the preferences for patterns which differ partially from the original stimuli, in order to discover the attributes of the original pattern which determined the animal's choices. Illustrates Kluever's concept of equivalent stimuli and its relation to the study of perception and transfer of training animals.
Prod-PSUPCR Dist-PSUPCR 1937

Study Of Grain Growth In Berylium Oxide Using A New Transmitted Light Hot Stage C 16 MIN
16MM FILM OPTICAL SOUND
Depicts the design and operation of a new hot stage used with a polarizing microscope and transmitted light. Examines time-dependent reactions and structural changes in transparent crystalline materials at temperatures as high as 2,000 oC in vacuum.
LC NO. FIE56-212
Prod-USAEC Dist-USNAC

Study Of Rocks C 49 MIN
3/4 OR 1/2 INCH VIDEO CASSETTE IND
See series title for descriptive statement.
From The Basic And Petroleum Geology For Non-geologists - Fundamentals And...-Series.
Prod-PHILLP Dist-GPCV

Study Of The USSR, A B 30 MIN
16MM FILM OPTICAL SOUND
Explores the Soviet Union in depth tracing its history, expansion, culture, philosophy and advancement in science and education.
Prod-USDD Dist-USNAC

Study Of Things Which Influence Behavior B 29 MIN
16MM FILM OPTICAL SOUND
See series title for descriptive statement.
From The Controlling Turnover And Absenteeism Series.
LC NO. 76-703321
Prod-EDSD Dist-EDSD

Study Of Twins, Pt 1 B 17 MIN
16MM FILM SILENT C
Presents the growth and development of identical twin boys. Deals primarily with responses to everyday, informal situations

and stresses the differences between the developing twins. Illustrates motor growth at 14, 22, 28 and 40 weeks, especially the differences in rate of development among various parts of the body. Emphasizes the cephalocaudal pattern.
Prod-PSUPCR Dist-PSUPCR 1947

Study Of Twins, Pt 2 B 17 MIN
16MM FILM SILENT C
Shows identical twins at 12, 15, 18 and 21 months. Demonstrates the getting up, standing and walking stages. Shows the amount of independent and cooperative play.
Prod-PSUPCR Dist-PSUPCR 1947

Study Of Twins, Pt 3 B 18 MIN
16MM FILM SILENT C
Records the behavior of identical twins at 24, 28 and 32 months. Shows amicable but independent play and the rapidity of development of motor skills and of larger muscles.
Prod-PSUPCR Dist-PSUPCR 1949

Study Of Twins, Pt 4 B 19 MIN
16MM FILM SILENT C
Records the behavior of identical twins at three, four and five years. Illustrates increasingly cooperative play and improved muscular coordination. Shows ultimate self-sufficiency in such activities as eating, washing teeth and playing.
Prod-PSUPCR Dist-PSUPCR 1951

Study Of Variation, A - Making A Histogram B 15 MIN
2 INCH VIDEOTAPE P
See series title for descriptive statement.
From The Just Wondering Series.
Prod-EOPS Dist-GPITVL Prodn-KOACTV

Study Of Young Children's Strength (Push, Pull, Twist And Squeeze) C 15 MIN
16MM FILM OPTICAL SOUND H-C A
Depicts research methods and equipment used by bureau scientists in determining what forces children are capable of exerting when pushing, pulling, twisting and squeezing.
LC NO. 74-700155
Prod-USNBOS Dist-USNBOS 1973

Study Schedules That Really Work C 30 MIN
3/4 OR 1/2 INCH VIDEO CASSETTE
Shows how to analyze study needs and set up a personalized schedule. Demonstrates how to stay on schedule.
From The Better Learning Habit Series.
Prod-TELSTR Dist-DELTAK

Study Skills - Note Taking And Outlining C
16MM FILM, 3/4 OR 1/2 IN VIDEO I
Shows how to take the main ideas from various sources of information and write them in note form. Describes how to organize these notes in outline form and demonstrates why this can be useful, not only in evaluating the importance of information but also in aiding to turn it into a clear and concise report.
Prod-HIGGIN Dist-HIGGIN 1984

Study Skills - Organize It C
16MM FILM, 3/4 OR 1/2 IN VIDEO I
Demonstrates the concepts of organization, from basic everyday examples to those needed in classwork. Shows how organizing one's work, in its preparation as well as in its presentation, will yield a better product and simplify the process.
Prod-HIGGIN Dist-HIGGIN 1984

Study Skills - Researching And Writing A Report C
16MM FILM, 3/4 OR 1/2 IN VIDEO I
Describes how, with the help of a cleverly programmed robot, the necessary steps in creating a report and the reasons why they are important, can be accomplished. Shows how to select a topic, research and gather information, organize notes and write a report in a clear form.
Prod-HIGGIN Dist-HIGGIN 1984

Study Skills - Take That Test C
16MM FILM, 3/4 OR 1/2 IN VIDEO I
Discusses how to develop good study habits, learn to follow and understand directions, intelligently answer multiple choice, true-false and essay questions, plan one's time in relation to the test and appropriately respond if stumped.
LC NO. 84-706227
Prod-HIGGIN Dist-HIGGIN 1984

Study Skills—A Series
I
Stresses the value of good study skills for high school work, college and everyday activities.
Prod-WCVETV Dist-GPITVL 1979

Gathering Information 20 MIN
Library Media Center, The 20 MIN
Locating Information 20 MIN
Organizing Information 20 MIN
Preparation For Study 20 MIN
Recall And Testing 20 MIN

Study Skills, The C 30 MIN
2 INCH VIDEOTAPE T
Examines four areas in the study skills phase of instruction, locating information, organizing data, understanding and evaluating and retention of pertinent material.
From The Child Reads Series.
Prod-WENHTV Dist-GPITVL

Study Strategies - Notes C 13 MIN
16MM FILM, 3/4 OR 1/2 IN VIDEO J-C
Offers suggestions for improving notetaking skills, including the advantages of the two column format and the use of note cards.
From The Study Strategies Series.
Prod-CORF Dist-CORF

Study Strategies - Tests C 11 MIN
16MM FILM, 3/4 OR 1/2 IN VIDEO J-C
Shows how to prepare psychologically, emotionally, physically and mentally for taking tests. Stresses proper preparation, handling tension, setting up a plan of attack and dealing with both objective and subjective questions.
From The Study Strategies Series.
Prod-CORF Dist-CORF

Study Strategies—A Series
16MM FILM, 3/4 OR 1/2 IN VIDEO J-C
Discusses how to prepare for tests, how to take useful notes and how to complete school assignments successfully.
Prod-CORF Dist-CORF

Study Strategies - Assignments 15 MIN
Study Strategies - Notes 13 MIN
Study Strategies - Tests 11 MIN

Study Tips C 13 MIN
3/4 OR 1/2 INCH VIDEO CASSETTE H-C A
Emphasizes a positive attitude toward study and more effective study techniques.
Prod-SEVDIM Dist-SEVDIM

Studying - A Way To Learn C
16MM FILM - VIDEO, ALL FORMATS J-H
Teaches children the importance of good study habits.
Prod-SAIF Dist-BARR

Studying Chemical Interactions C 17 MIN
16MM FILM, 3/4 OR 1/2 IN VIDEO I-H
Reviews the difference between a physical and a chemical change. Defines atoms, molecules, elements and compounds. Illustrates three basic chemical interactions, combination, decomposition and replacement. Introduces simple chemical formulas and equations and discusses laboratory safety.
From The Scientific Investigation Series.
Prod-GLDWER Dist-JOU 1978

Studying Children C 30 MIN
3/4 INCH VIDEO CASSETTE
Shows how the developmental psychologies approach their subject and discusses the ethics of conducting research with children.
From The Growing Years Series.
Prod-COAST Dist-CDTEL

Studying Electricity C 16 MIN
16MM FILM, 3/4 OR 1/2 IN VIDEO I-H
Shows ways electricity can be produced using materials available at home or school. Investigates the relationship between electricity and magnetism and how that relationship is used to produce alternating current. Demonstrates the difference between direct and alternating current.
From The Scientific Investigation Series.
Prod-GLDWER Dist-JOU 1978

Studying Electricity (Spanish) C 16 MIN
16MM FILM, 3/4 OR 1/2 IN VIDEO I-H
Shows ways electricity can be produced using materials available at home or school. Investigates the relationship between electricity and magnetism and how the relationship is used to produce alternating current. Demonstrates the difference between direct and alternating current.
From The Scientific Investigation Series.
Prod-GLDWER Dist-JOU 1976

Studying Fluid Behavior C 17 MIN
16MM FILM, 3/4 OR 1/2 IN VIDEO I-H
Demonstrates the behavior of fluids. Illustrates that fluids will flow in solids, liquids and gases if given somewhere to go.
From The Scientific Investigation Series.
Prod-GLDWER Dist-JOU 1979

Studying Fluid Behavior (Captioned) C 17 MIN
16MM FILM, 3/4 OR 1/2 IN VIDEO I-H
Demonstrates the behavior of fluids. Illustrates that fluids will flow in solids, liquids and gases if given somewhere to go.
From The Scientific Investigation Series.
Prod-GLDWER Dist-JOU 1979

Studying Gravitation And Mass C 16 MIN
16MM FILM, 3/4 OR 1/2 IN VIDEO I-J
Explores the concept of gravity, the effect of distance and mass and the differentiation between mass and weight.
From The Scientific Investigation Series.
Prod-GLDWER Dist-JOU 1977

Studying Heat And Its Behavior C 17 MIN
16MM FILM, 3/4 OR 1/2 IN VIDEO I-H
Investigates what heat is, what cold is, how heat relates to the three states of matter, and sources of heat, such as combustion, electricity, friction, agitation and chemical action. Studies the behavior of heat and its relationship to light.
From The Scientific Investigation Series.
Prod-GLDWER Dist-JOU 1978

Studying The Behavior Of Light C 16 MIN
16MM FILM, 3/4 OR 1/2 IN VIDEO I-J
Uses everyday materials to study the wavelike action of light and determine the spectra of several different light sources. Presents practical scientific uses for these observed phenomena.
From The Scientific Investigation Series.
Prod-GLDWER Dist-JOU 1977

Studying The Big Cats Of Africa C 15 MIN
16MM FILM OPTICAL SOUND C
Presents the new scientific studies on the big cats of Africa including the lion, leopard and cheetah. Encompasses population surveys of leopards, observations of the social lives of lions and predator/prey measurements of cheetahs.
From The Science In Action Series.
Prod-ALLFP Dist-COUNFI

Stuff We Throw Away, The C 22 MIN
16MM FILM OPTICAL SOUND J A
Shows innovative demonstration grants and research activities being developed by the Bureau of Solid Waste Management of the federal government in association with local communities.
LC NO. 75-714059
Prod-USEPA Dist-FINLYS 1970

Stunde Null B 108 MIN
16MM FILM OPTICAL SOUND
A German language film with English subtitles. Relates the events following July 1, 1945, the end of the war in Europe. The Americans are forced to withdraw from Leipzig and leave the territory to the Russians in accordance with the Jalta agreement. Deals with the hopes and fears of the people of Leipzig.
Prod-WSTGLC Dist-WSTGLC 1976

Stuntman C 30 MIN
1/2 IN VIDEO CASSETTE BETA/VHS
Deals with the life and work of Conrad Palmisano, age 34, a Hollywood stuntman, who is one of the two hundred active, working stuntmen. He appears in the film Heart Like A Wheel.
From The American Professionals Series.
Prod-WTBS Dist-RMI

Stuntman, The C 11 MIN
16MM FILM, 3/4 OR 1/2 IN VIDEO
Documents a day in the life of a stunt man as Greg Anderson reveals the work he does. Shows how certain stunts are performed and tells why he decided to work in films as a stunt man.
Prod-PFP Dist-PFP 1973

Stunts C 7 MIN
16MM FILM, 3/4 OR 1/2 IN VIDEO J-C A
Reveals the variety of brave and remarkable stunts performed by stunt people. Emphasizes the daring of these highly paid, professional, thrill-seeking athletes.
LC NO. 84-706807
Prod-PHENIX Dist-PHENIX 1983

Sturcturing Communication C 30 MIN
3/4 OR 1/2 INCH VIDEO CASSETTE C A
Covers the appropriateness of communication. Examines what time and location are best and what pressures, personalities, preconceptions and/or unconscious motivations are present.
From The Family Portrait - A Study Of Contemporary Lifestyles Series. Lesson 16
Prod-SCCON Dist-CDTEL

Stuttering B 29 MIN
16MM FILM OPTICAL SOUND C T
Presents a TV program sponsored by the Council of adult Stutterers, showing stutterers discussing the nature of stuttering, its problems, and control.
Prod-CAMPF Dist-CAMPF

Stuttering And Two-Factor Behavior C 109 MIN
3/4 OR 1/2 INCH VIDEO CASSETTE
Offers Brutten and Shoemaker's two-factor theory of stuttering and examples of terms frequently used in the treatment of extinguishing Factor one conditioning.
Prod-PUAVC Dist-PUAVC

Stuttering Therapy - A Human Approach C 119 MIN
3/4 OR 1/2 INCH VIDEO CASSETTE
Discusses the goals of avoidance and reduction therapy, and defines the stuttering problem and its historical background.
Prod-PUAVC Dist-PUAVC

Stuttering Therapy - Broad Spectrum Behavior Modification C 95 MIN
3/4 OR 1/2 INCH VIDEO CASSETTE
Focuses on learning and conditioning principles as applied to stuttering therapy. Gives attention to transfer procedures.
Prod-PUAVC Dist-PUAVC

Stuttering Therapy And Operant Conditioning C 116 MIN
3/4 OR 1/2 INCH VIDEO CASSETTE
Considers the relationship between traditional therapy and those involving operant principles.
Prod-PUAVC Dist-PUAVC

Style C
3/4 OR 1/2 INCH VIDEO CASSETTE C
Examines achieving an individual style appropriate to the writing situation using voice, tone and point of view.
From The Write Course - An Introduction To College Composition Series.
Prod-DALCCD Dist-DALCCD

Style C 30 MIN
3/4 OR 1/2 INCH VIDEO CASSETTE C
See series title for descriptive statement.
From The Writing For A Reason Series.
Prod-DALCCD Dist-DALCCD

Style C 30 MIN
3/4 OR 1/2 INCH VIDEO CASSETTE C A
Discusses achieving an individual style appropriate to the writing situation using voice, tone and point of view.
From The Write Course - An Introduction To College Composition Series.
Prod-FI Dist-FI 1984

Style - The Man And His Work C 45 MIN
16MM FILM OPTICAL SOUND H-C A
Presents a comparative analysis of the traits of style from the Medieval Italian schools through the works of such artists as Rubens, Rembrandt, Picasso and Braque.
From The Man And His Art Series.
Prod-WTTWTV Dist-GPITVL

Style And Design In Slovak Furniture (1250 - 1900) C 13 MIN
16MM FILM OPTICAL SOUND
Studies Slovak furniture from a simple carved Gothic chest still strong with folk art to richly inlaid four-poster beds that seem like ships of sleep, to spindle-legged tables almost too refined to bear.
Prod-ROLAND Dist-ROLAND

Style In Band Performance B 29 MIN
2 INCH VIDEOTAPE
See series title for descriptive statement.
From The American Band Goes Symphonic Series.
Prod-WGTV Dist-PUBTEL

Style Of Champions C 19 MIN
16MM FILM OPTICAL SOUND H-C A
John Konrads, former Australian Olympic swimming champion looks at and talks about swimming in Australia. Examines training methods while slow motion and underwater photography is used to show various swimming styles.
LC NO. 78-709320
Prod-ANAIB Dist-AUIS 1970

Styles C 15 MIN
3/4 OR 1/2 INCH VIDEO CASSETTE P
Demonstrates varying characteristics of musical sounds.
From The Music Machine Series.
Prod-GPITVL Dist-GPITVL

Styles C 22 MIN
16MM FILM, 3/4 OR 1/2 IN VIDEO J-C
Points out that suburban life has given young people many choices. Explains that they can follow their parents' example, rebel, or try and find their own path. Presents three young people who communicate their feelings and goals.
Prod-WOMBAT Dist-WOMBAT

Styles In Song Accompaniment C 29 MIN
2 INCH VIDEOTAPE
See series title for descriptive statement.
From The Playing The Guitar I Series.
Prod-KCET Dist-PUBTEL

Styles Of Communication C 15 MIN
16MM FILM, 3/4 OR 1/2 IN VIDEO I
Tells how three young people learn to adjust their language to the situation. Explains that a polite, specific complaint is more effective than angry accusations.
From The Thinkabout Series. Communicating Effectively
LC NO. 81-706124
Prod-EDFCEN Dist-AITECH 1979

Styles Of Leadership C 18 MIN
3/4 OR 1/2 INCH VIDEO CASSETTE
Looks at the common traits of leaders and gives a definition of leadership.
From The Leadership Series. Module 2
Prod-RESEM Dist-RESEM

Styles Of Leadership C 30 MIN
3/4 OR 1/2 INCH VIDEO CASSETTE C A
Focuses on a number of questions that must be answered in order to understand leadership. Includes what makes an effective leader in today's complex world and how good leaders deal with people they lead. Explores several different styles of leadership such as autocratic, participative and laissez-faire.
From The Business Of Management Series. Lesson 16
Prod-SCCON Dist-SCCON

Styles Of Leadership (2nd Ed) C 26 MIN
16MM FILM, 3/4 OR 1/2 IN VIDEO
Uses a common business problem to illustrate four management leadership styles.
Prod-RTBL Dist-RTBL 1980

Styles Of Leadership (2nd Ed) (Dutch) C 26 MIN
16MM FILM, 3/4 OR 1/2 IN VIDEO
Uses a common business problem to illustrate four management leadership styles.
Prod-RTBL Dist-RTBL 1980

Styles Of Leadership (2nd Ed) (French) C 26 MIN
16MM FILM, 3/4 OR 1/2 IN VIDEO
Uses a common business problem to illustrate four management leadership styles.
Prod-RTBL Dist-RTBL 1980

Styles Of Leadership (2nd Ed) (German) C 26 MIN
16MM FILM, 3/4 OR 1/2 IN VIDEO
Uses a common business problem to illustrate four management leadership styles.
Prod-RTBL Dist-RTBL 1980

Styles Of Leadership (2nd Ed) (Japanese) C 26 MIN
16MM FILM, 3/4 OR 1/2 IN VIDEO
Uses a common business problem to illustrate four management leadership styles.
Prod-RTBL Dist-RTBL 1980

Styles Of Leadership (2nd Ed) (Norwegian) C 26 MIN
16MM FILM, 3/4 OR 1/2 IN VIDEO
Uses a common business problem to illustrate four management leadership styles.
Prod-RTBL Dist-RTBL 1980

Styles Of Leadership (2nd Ed) (Spanish) C 26 MIN
16MM FILM, 3/4 OR 1/2 IN VIDEO
Uses a common business problem to illustrate four management leadership styles.
Prod-RTBL Dist-RTBL 1980

Styles Of Leadership (2nd Ed) (Swedish) C 26 MIN
16MM FILM, 3/4 OR 1/2 IN VIDEO
Uses a common business problem to illustrate four management leadership styles.
Prod-RTBL Dist-RTBL 1980

Styles Of Leadership - Theory H B 50 MIN
3/4 OR 1/2 INCH VIDEO CASSETTE
Dramatizes the reason for changing the style of leadership to better fit the situation and needs of different subordinate groups.
Prod-IVCH Dist-IVCH

Styles Of Sketching C 29 MIN
3/4 INCH VIDEO CASSETTE C A
Shows examples of contrasting styles and explains how a style is formed. Focuses on guest artist and cartoonist Tom Shannon as he demonstrates his particular drawing style.
From The Sketching Techniques Series. Lesson 21
Prod-COAST Dist-CDTEL

Styles That Made A Splash, The C 20 MIN
16MM FILM OPTICAL SOUND
Shows the many transformations of female bathing costumes in America. Traces the evolution of styles and the battles that women waged in quest of a simple, functional suit.
LC NO. 77-702417
Prod-SEARS Dist-MTP Prodn-DELMRK 1977

Styling For Magazines And TV C
3/4 OR 1/2 INCH VIDEO CASSETTE
Shows a versatile haircut that provides three hairstyles which range from the everyday to the theatrical.
Prod-MPCEDP Dist-MPCEDP 1984

Styling For The Total Look C
3/4 OR 1/2 INCH VIDEO CASSETTE
Shows how a different hairstyle can make a person look thinner, taller and lovelier.
Prod-MPCEDP Dist-MPCEDP 1984

Stylization And Fantasy C 30 MIN
3/4 OR 1/2 INCH VIDEO CASSETTE
Describes how stylization and fantasy in make-up suspend reality and create something new, in this case, the hare from The Tortoise And The Hare. Deals with costume, which plays an important role as well.
From The Actor's Face As A Canvas Series.
Prod-NETCHE Dist-NETCHE 1973

Stylized Realism C 30 MIN
3/4 OR 1/2 INCH VIDEO CASSETTE
Describes a more intense form of make-up which should be carefully matched with the style and purposes of the play. Involves leaving areas of light and shadow in definite patterns, rather than fusing them.
From The Actor's Face As A Canvas Series.
Prod-NETCHE Dist-NETCHE 1973

Styx B 11 MIN
16MM FILM OPTICAL SOUND
Presents an impressionistic view of a subway.
LC NO. 76-702614
Prod-KRAWZJ Dist-KRAWZJ 1976

Su Casa Esta En Orden C 18 MIN
16MM FILM, 3/4 OR 1/2 IN VIDEO
A Spanish-language version of the motion picture Your House In Order. Shows how industrial accidents can be the results of poor housekeeping and sloppiness. Uses the examples of a reckless forklift operator, a careless maintenance man, two workers unloading pipe without looking, a lathe operator who doesn't clean up the scrap and other workers leaving tools and trucks in dangerous places.
LC NO. 83-706814
Prod-MILLBK Dist-IFB

Sub-Costal Approach To The Kidney C 15 MIN
16MM FILM OPTICAL SOUND
Depicts the anatomical structure encountered in the approaches to the kidney through the sub-costal incision. Emphasizes the anatomical difference between this approach and other types of incisions.
From The Anatomy Of The Flank Series.
Prod-EATONL Dist-EATONL 1971

Sub-Igloo C 20 MIN
16MM FILM, 3/4 OR 1/2 IN VIDEO H
Reports on a scientific expedition that put a plastic bubble on the floor of the Arctic Ocean to serve as a workshop and rest station for scientists working below the Arctic ice.
Prod-NFBC Dist-IFB 1973

Sub-Routines C 18 MIN
3/4 OR 1/2 INCH VIDEO CASSETTE IND
Includes several aspects of a subroutine such as definition, executing and writing.
From The Numerical Control/Computerized Numerical Control - Advanced Programming Series. Module 2
Prod-LEIKID Dist-LEIKID

Subarachnoid Endolymphatic Shunt For Meniere's Disease C 13 MIN
16MM FILM OPTICAL SOUND PRO
Depicts a new concept in the surgical treatment of Meniere's disease. Explains that the fluid of the endolymphatic is shunted into the subarachnoid space to equalize the pressure of the two systems.
Prod-EAR Dist-EAR

Subarctic Cross-Country Mobility, Pt 2 - Summer Operations B 11 MIN
16MM FILM OPTICAL SOUND
Illustrates and compares summer and winter aspects of subarctic terrain and shows how various routes are traversed in this area through scenes of a platoon journey through the forest, over the tundra and finally through muskeg.
LC NO. FIE56-212
Prod-USA Dist-USNAC 1956

Subatomic Babies C 8 MIN
3/4 OR 1/2 INCH VIDEO CASSETTE
Prod-EAI Dist-EAI

Subatomic Babies C 8 MIN
3/4 OR 1/2 INCH VIDEO CASSETTE
Deals with technological destruction.
Prod-KITCHN Dist-KITCHN

Subclavian Catheterization C 11 MIN
3/4 OR 1/2 INCH VIDEO CASSETTE PRO
Reviews essential equipment and illustrates the step-by-step analysis of the technique as well as demonstrating the actual procedure on two trauma victims. Indications, cautions and confirmation of placement are also included.
Prod-UWASH Dist-UWASH

Subconscious Sales Power B 30 MIN
3/4 OR 1/2 INCH VIDEO CASSETTE
Provides subliminal suggestions for sales power.
Prod-ADVCAS Dist-ADVCAS

Subcutaneous And Intramuscular Injections B 30 MIN
16MM FILM OPTICAL SOUND PRO
Demonstrates procedures and techniques for preparing and administering subcutaneous injections and intramuscular injections.
From The Directions For Education In Nursing Via Technology Series. Lesson 17
LC NO. 74-701792
Prod-DENT Dist-WSU 1974

Subcutaneous Injections C 8 MIN
1/2 IN VIDEO CASSETTE BETA/VHS
Describes how to administer subcutaneous injections.
Prod-RMI Dist-RMI

Subdiaphragmatic Abscess C 15 MIN
16MM FILM OPTICAL SOUND PRO
Depicts the common site for such abscesses and the surgical approach for draining two of them in different subphrenic spaces.
Prod-ACYDGD Dist-ACY 1954

Subgingival Curettage C 16 MIN
16MM FILM - 3/4 IN VIDEO PRO
Demonstrates subgingival curettage and root planing of periodontically involved teeth. Explains the rationale for these therapeutic procedures.
LC NO. 77-706190
Prod-USVA Dist-USNAC 1972

Subject - Narcotics X 21 MIN
16MM FILM OPTICAL SOUND PRO
Presents detailed information on how narcotics are used, how they can be identified, and how they affect the addict. (Restricted from the general public and from all youth groups)
Prod-ANLAM Dist-NEFA Prodn-SANDRS 1952

Subject Headings Classification B 60 MIN
3/4 OR 1/2 INCH VIDEO CASSETTE
See series title for descriptive statement.
From The Library Organization Series. Pt 5
Prod-UAZMIC Dist-UAZMIC 1977

Subject Is Flowers, The C 29 MIN
3/4 INCH VIDEO CASSETTE
Explores the geometry of flowers using pastels.
From The Artist At Work Series.
Prod-UMITV Dist-UMITV 1973

Subject Was Taxes, The B 16 MIN
16MM FILM, 3/4 OR 1/2 IN VIDEO H-C A
Traces the history of taxes and shows how taxes are used.
LC NO. 81-706304
Prod-USIRS Dist-USNAC 1980

Subliminal Perception C 29 MIN
3/4 INCH VIDEO CASSETTE C A
Discusses difficulties of attempts to conduct scientific research in areas of parapsychology. Distinguishes between various kinds of perception.
From The Understanding Human Behavior - An Introduction To Psychology Series. Lesson 11
Prod-COAST Dist-CDTEL

Submandibular Triangle C 14 MIN
16MM FILM - 3/4 IN VIDEO PRO
Uses dissection and drawings to demonstrate the boundaries and structures of the submandibular triangle.
From The Anatomy Of The Head And Neck Series.
LC NO. 78-706253
Prod-USVA Dist-USNAC Prodn-VADTC 1978

Submarine B 93 MIN
16MM FILM SILENT
Relates how a deep-sea diver interrupts his honeymoon to try and unearth a sunken wreck. Shows what happens when he returns home to find his wife in the arms of his best friend, and describes his dilemma when his friend is trapped in a submarine. Directed by Frank Capra.
Prod-CPC Dist-KITPAR 1928

Submarine, The, Pt 3 - Diving And Surfacing B 12 MIN
16MM FILM OPTICAL SOUND
Discusses methods used by a submarine in submerging and explains positive, negative and neutral buoyancy. Presents an evaluation of surfacing.
LC NO. FIE56-333
Prod-USN Dist-USNAC 1955

Submarine, The, Pt 4 - Operating Submerged B 18 MIN
16MM FILM OPTICAL SOUND

Shows the operation of a submarine while submerged, including the use of special ballast tanks, trim tanks and submarine speed of contract depths. Describes the snorkel system and the operation of snorkeling.
LC NO. FIE66-334
Prod-USN Dist-USNAC 1955

Submarines, The C 28 MIN
16MM FILM OPTICAL SOUND
Shows the specialized skills, duties and responsibilities which keep U S Navy submarines prepared to battle other submarines.
LC NO. 74-706267
Prod-USN Dist-USNAC 1967

Submental Triangle, The C 8 MIN
16MM FILM OPTICAL SOUND
Demonstrates the boundaries of the submental triangle in this dissection and uses drawings for clarification.
From The Anatomy Of The Head And Neck Series.
LC NO. 74-705718
Prod-USVA Dist-USNAC Prodn-LUSD 1967

Submental Triangle, The C 15 MIN
3/4 INCH VIDEO CASSETTE PRO
Presents drawings and dissection showing the boundaries and relationship of the submental triangle. Issued in 1967 as a motion picture.
LC NO. 78-706201
Prod-USVA Dist-USNAC Prodn-DTC 1978

Submerged Arc Welding C 15 MIN
3/4 OR 1/2 INCH VIDEO CASSETTE IND
See series title for descriptive statement.
From The Welding - MIG And TIG Welding Series.
Prod-ICSINT Dist-ICSINT

Submerged Arc Welding (Spanish) C
3/4 OR 1/2 INCH VIDEO CASSETTE
See series title for descriptive statement.
From The MIG And TIG Welding (Spanish) Series.
Prod-VTRI Dist-VTRI

Suboccipital Region, The C 8 MIN
16MM FILM, 3/4 OR 1/2 IN VIDEO C A
Demonstrates the dissection of the suboccipital region.
From The Guides To Dissection Series.
Prod-UCLA Dist-TEF

Suboptimal Nonlinear Filtering Algorithm-Discrete-Time C 87 MIN
3/4 OR 1/2 INCH VIDEO CASSETTE PRO
See series title for descriptive statement.
From The Modern Control Theory - Stochastic Estimation Series.
Prod-MIOT Dist-MIOT

Subphrenic Abscess C 19 MIN
16MM FILM OPTICAL SOUND PRO
Attempts to simplify the complex and confusing anatomy and pathology of the subphrenic spaces. Shows the treatment of right and left sided abscess based upon the concept of the anatomy presented.
Prod-ACYDGD Dist-ACY 1962

Subroutine, PRINT USING C 60 MIN
3/4 OR 1/2 INCH VIDEO CASSETTE
See series title for descriptive statement.
From The Introduction To BASIC Series. Lecture 13
Prod-UIDEEO Dist-UIDEEO

Subroutines C 15 MIN
3/4 OR 1/2 INCH VIDEO CASSETTE PRO
See series title for descriptive statement.
From The Numerical Control/Computer Numerical Control, Part 2 - Advanced Programming Series.
Prod-ICSINT Dist-ICSINT

Subroutines / Program Construction C 30 MIN
3/4 OR 1/2 INCH VIDEO CASSETTE J-C A
Discusses the use of top-down design to implement block structure. Shows how the 'gosub' statement can be used to access the subroutine. Explains 'gosub, return' statements, internal subroutines within the main program, the 'end' statement and 'rem' statements. Examines program output in terms of sequence, repetition, alternation or conditional flow, and logical groups. Deals with the use of planning grids for formulating subroutines and for determining call line numbers for the subroutines.
From The Programming For Microcomputers Series. Unit 11 And 12
LC NO. 83-707129
Prod-IU Dist-IU 1983

Subroutines And Functions C 22 MIN
3/4 OR 1/2 INCH VIDEO CASSETTE H-C A
Explains how to build modular programs using subroutines. Demonstrates how to use the functions built into the BASIC language.
From The Basic Power Series.
Prod-VANGU Dist-UCEMC

Subscripted Variables C 60 MIN
3/4 OR 1/2 INCH VIDEO CASSETTE
See series title for descriptive statement.
From The Introduction To BASIC Series. Lecture 9
Prod-UIDEEO Dist-UIDEEO

Subscripted Variables And Arrays C 22 MIN
3/4 OR 1/2 INCH VIDEO CASSETTE H-C A
Introduces dimensioned variables. Shows how to design a 'bubble sort' routine.
From The Basic Power Series.
Prod-VANGU Dist-UCEMC

Subsets C 20 MIN
2 INCH VIDEOTAPE P
See series title for descriptive statement.
From The Mathemagic, Unit I - Place Value Series.
Prod-WMULTV Dist-GPITVL

Subsistence Level C 10 MIN
16MM FILM, 3/4 OR 1/2 IN VIDEO
Explains the problems of subsistence economies. Discusses the movement from a subsistence economy to a modern industrial state.
From The Foundations Of Wealth Series.
Prod-FOTH Dist-FOTH

Substance Abuse - A Management Intervention Program C 17 MIN
16MM FILM, 3/4 OR 1/2 IN VIDEO C A
Discusses the cost of firing an employee who's addicted to alcohol or other drugs. Outlines a program of managerial intervention that will help the decision maker restore the employee to full productivity.
LC NO. 83-706390
Prod-AIMS Dist-AIMS 1983

Substance Abuse - Alcoholism And Drug Dependence, Pts 1-3 C 125 MIN
3/4 OR 1/2 INCH VIDEO CASSETTE PRO
Discusses the progressive nature of alcoholism and drug dependence, including diagnosis and treatment. Includes a lengthy question and answer session.
Prod-USVA Dist-USNAC

Substance Use Disorders C
3/4 OR 1/2 INCH VIDEO CASSETTE PRO
Identifies the diagnostic criteria for substance use disorders. Covers the nine categories of abused substances, the clinical picture produced by intoxication, and withdrawal syndromes associated with them.
From The Psychiatry Learning System, Pt 2 - Disorders Series.
Prod-HSCIC Dist-HSCIC 1982

Substantive Criminal Law - Happy Here C 19 MIN
3/4 OR 1/2 INCH VIDEO CASSETTE H
Using mime sequences, this lesson examines criminal law concepts such as crimes against the person. Includes a stark black-and-white interview with a prisoner.
From The Ways Of The Law Series.
Prod-SCITV Dist-GPITVL 1980

Substantive Law - Consent To Treatment C 51 MIN
3/4 OR 1/2 INCH VIDEO CASSETTE PRO
Examines different types of consent, problems involving consent, timeliness of consent and the common-knowledge doctrine in preparation of a medical malpractice case.
From The Preparing And Trying A Medical Malpractice Case Series.
Prod-ABACPE Dist-ABACPE

Substantive Law - Vicarious Liability And Hospital Records C 99 MIN
3/4 OR 1/2 INCH VIDEO CASSETTE PRO
Discusses vicarious liability of both the physician and the hospital and defenses in medical malpractice cases. Examines various hospital records and the liability of those creating or maintaining the records.
From The Preparing And Trying A Medical Malpractice Case Series.
Prod-ABACPE Dist-ABACPE

Substantive Law Of The Physician-Patient Relationship C 50 MIN
3/4 OR 1/2 INCH VIDEO CASSETTE PRO
Examines the legal basis for the relationship between patient and physician.
From The Preparing And Trying A Medical Malpractice Case Series.
Prod-ABACPE Dist-ABACPE

Substrate Injection Of Electrons, Miscellaneous Topics, And Matching B 75 MIN
3/4 OR 1/2 INCH VIDEO CASSETTE
See series title for descriptive statement.
From The Analog IC Layout Design Considerations Series. Pt 4
Prod-UAZMIC Dist-UAZMIC

Substructure Analysis And Design—A Series
PRO
Uses classroom format to videotape one one-hour and one 1 1/2 hour lecture weekly for 13 weeks and 39 cassettes. Reviews fundamentals of soil mechanics, subsurface exploration procedures, sampling techniques and field tests. Covers bearing capacity applications to shallow foundations, calculations of earth pressures under loaded areas and consolidation and elastic settlement calculation methods. Discusses beams on elastic foundations, lateral earth pressure, earth retaining structures and deep foundations.
Prod-USCCE Dist-AMCEE

Subsurface Fluid Flow Mechanics C 59 MIN
3/4 OR 1/2 INCH VIDEO CASSETTE IND
See series title for descriptive statement.
From The Basic And Petroleum Geology For Non-Geologists - Landforms II Series.
Prod-PHILLP Dist-GPCV

Subsurface Fluids C 43 MIN
3/4 OR 1/2 INCH VIDEO CASSETTE IND
See series title for descriptive statement.
From The Basic Geology Series.
Prod-GPCV Dist-GPCV

Subsurface Investigation - The Reason Why C 28 MIN
16MM FILM, 3/4 OR 1/2 IN VIDEO
Explains how proper soil and topographic studies are important for highway planning in order to identify potential problems which might increase maintenance costs later.
Prod-CDT Dist-USNAC 1978

Subsurface Mapping C 27 MIN
3/4 OR 1/2 INCH VIDEO CASSETTE IND
See series title for descriptive statement.
From The Basic And Petroleum Geology For Non-Geologists - Sedimentary Rocks Series.
Prod-PHILLP Dist-GPCV

Subsystems And Variables - The Whirly Bird System C 20 MIN
3/4 INCH VIDEO CASSETTE T
Depicts a way of correlating the science lesson with career education. Introduces the concepts of variables and controlling variables and shows classroom scenes of children solving problems and making inferences.
From The Science In The Elementary School - Physical Science Series.
Prod-UWKY Dist-GPITVL 1979

Subterranean Termites C
3/4 OR 1/2 INCH VIDEO CASSETTE
See series title for descriptive statement.
From The Pest Control Technology Correspondence Course Series.
Prod-PUAVC Dist-PUAVC

Subtle Influences Of Product Advertisement B 30 MIN
3/4 OR 1/2 INCH VIDEO CASSETTE
Discusses the use of fear and sex 'sells' in advertising and uses illustrative posters and media ads as examples. Points out the subtle inclusion of sexual imagery in subliminal advertising.
Prod-UWISC Dist-UWISC 1977

Subtotal Gastrectomy For Duodenal Ulcer Perforating Into The Pancreas C 29 MIN
16MM FILM OPTICAL SOUND PRO
Illustrates a technique which has proved safe for handling the difficult duodenal ulcer without jeopardizing the integrity of the pancreas or bile duct, and yet fulfilling the physiologic obligations of an adequate gastric resection for peptic ulcer diathesis.
Prod-ACYDGD Dist-ACY 1951

Subtotal Pancreatectomy For Adenoma Of Islet Of Langerhans C 15 MIN
16MM FILM OPTICAL SOUND PRO
Demonstrates the technique employed in the resection of the distal portion of the pancreas for a large islet cell tumor. Describes the various methods of approaching the pancreas.
Prod-ACYDGD Dist-ACY 1954

Subtotal Parotidectomy C 27 MIN
3/4 OR 1/2 INCH VIDEO CASSETTE
See series title for descriptive statement.
From The Head And Neck Series.
Prod-SVL Dist-SVL

Subtotal Parotidectomy For Inflammatory Disease C 26 MIN
3/4 OR 1/2 INCH VIDEO CASSETTE
See series title for descriptive statement.
From The Head And Neck Series.
Prod-SVL Dist-SVL

Subtotal Thyroidectomy C 17 MIN
3/4 OR 1/2 INCH VIDEO CASSETTE
See series title for descriptive statement.
From The Head And Neck Series.
Prod-SVL Dist-SVL

Subtracting C 9 MIN
16MM FILM, 3/4 OR 1/2 IN VIDEO P
Features a magician who makes snowflakes appear, stay, or disappear in order to illustrate that subtraction is a way of counting backward. Shows the meaning of subtract, less, minus and equal signs.
From The Basic Math Series.
Prod-BFA Dist-PHENIX 1979

Subtracting Expanded Numerals C 20 MIN
2 INCH VIDEOTAPE P
See series title for descriptive statement.
From The Mathemagic, Unit V - Addition And Subtraction series.
Prod-WMULTV Dist-GPITVL

Subtracting Fractions C 9 MIN
3/4 INCH VIDEO CASSETTE
See series title for descriptive statement.
From The Basic Math Skills Series. Subtracting Fractions
Prod-TELSTR Dist-TELSTR

Subtracting In Column Form C 20 MIN
2 INCH VIDEOTAPE P
See series title for descriptive statement.
From The Mathemagic, Unit V - Addition And Subtraction series.
Prod-WMULTV Dist-GPITVL

Subtracting Like Mixed Numbers C 10 MIN
3/4 INCH VIDEO CASSETTE
See series title for descriptive statement.
From The Basic Math Skills Series. Subtracting Fractions
Prod-TELSTR Dist-TELSTR

Subtracting Unlike Mixed Numbers C 8 MIN
3/4 INCH VIDEO CASSETTE
See series title for descriptive statement.
From The Basic Math Skills Series. Subtracting Fractions
Prod-TELSTR Dist-TELSTR

Subtraction C 13 MIN
16MM FILM, 3/4 OR 1/2 IN VIDEO P
Shows how subtraction is related to addition and focuses on the various properties of subtraction. Tells how to use the subtraction algorithm in subtracting one two-digit number from another.
From The Beginning Mathematics Series.
Prod-JOU Dist-JOU

Subtraction C 15 MIN
3/4 INCH VIDEO CASSETTE I
Discusses subtraction when renaming is needed. Explains how to check a subtraction problem by addition.
From The Math - No Mystery Series.
Prod-WCETTV Dist-GPITVL 1977

Subtraction (Spanish) C 14 MIN
16MM FILM, 3/4 OR 1/2 IN VIDEO P
Shows how subtraction is related to addition and discusses the subtraction algorithm.
From The Beginning Mathematics Series.
Prod-GLDWER Dist-JOU 1973

Subtraction (3rd Ed) C 12 MIN
16MM FILM, 3/4 OR 1/2 IN VIDEO P
Uses animation to teach subtraction.
From The Math For Beginners (3rd Ed) Series.
Prod-CORF Dist-CORF

Subtraction - Sums To Six C 15 MIN
3/4 INCH VIDEO CASSETTE P
Demonstrates how to write a subtraction fact with 'minus' and 'equal' symbols.
From The Measure Up Series.
Prod-WCETTV Dist-GPITVL 1977

Subtraction - Sums To Ten, Pt 1 C 15 MIN
3/4 INCH VIDEO CASSETTE P
Explains how to write subtraction facts to a sum of ten.
From The Measure Up Series.
Prod-WCETTV Dist-GPITVL 1977

Subtraction - Sums To Ten, Pt 2 C 15 MIN
3/4 INCH VIDEO CASSETTE P
Shows comparison of two numbers and the subsequent writing of the corresponding subtraction fact.
From The Measure Up Series.
Prod-WCETTV Dist-GPITVL 1977

Subtraction - Two-Digit Regrouping C 15 MIN
3/4 INCH VIDEO CASSETTE P
Tells how to regroup one ten as ten ones.
From The Studio M Series.
Prod-WCETTV Dist-GPITVL 1979

Subtraction - 1, Using The Cuisenaire Rods C 8 MIN
16MM FILM OPTICAL SOUND P-I
Presents the use of the cuisenaire rods as an aid to the learning of subtraction in the classroom for students and teachers.
Prod-MMP Dist-MMP 1962

Subtraction - 2, Using The Cuisenaire Rods C 9 MIN
16MM FILM OPTICAL SOUND P-I
Presents the use of the cuisenaire rods as an aid to the learning of subtraction in the classroom for students and teachers.
Prod-MMP Dist-MMP 1964

Subtraction Facts C 16 MIN
3/4 OR 1/2 INCH VIDEO CASSETTE P
Presents basic subtraction facts.
From The Math Cycle Series.
Prod-WDCNTV Dist-GPITVL 1983

Subtraction Gang, The - Subtraction, Pt 1 C 14 MIN
3/4 OR 1/2 INCH VIDEO CASSETTE P
Uses an Old West fantasy to provide practice in subtraction.
From The Math Country Series.
Prod-KYTV Dist-AITECH 1979

Subtraction Of Tens And Ones C 15 MIN
3/4 INCH VIDEO CASSETTE P
Introduces two-place subtraction problems that do not require regrouping.
From The Math Factory, Module IV - Problem Solving Series.
Prod-MAETEL Dist-GPITVL 1973

Subtraction Of Whole Numbers - Mathematics, Grade 5 B 20 MIN
2 INCH VIDEOTAPE I
See series title for descriptive statement.
From The Mathematics, Grade 5 Series.
Prod-DENVPS Dist-GPITVL Prodn-KRMATV

Subtraction Regrouping - Story Problems C 15 MIN
3/4 INCH VIDEO CASSETTE P
Shows how to use subtraction to solve word problems.
From The Studio M Series.
Prod-WCETTV Dist-GPITVL 1979

Subtraction Squadron - Subtraction, Pt 3 C 14 MIN
3/4 OR 1/2 INCH VIDEO CASSETTE P
Tells how Estill skywrites a subtraction problem and Lionel runs out of gas.
From The Math Country Series.
Prod-KYTV Dist-AITECH 1979

Subtraction Using Expanded Notation C 20 MIN
2 INCH VIDEOTAPE P
See series title for descriptive statement.
From The Mathemagic, Unit II - Addition And Subtraction Series.
Prod-WMULTV Dist-GPITVL

Subtraction, Division And Mixed Numbers C 12 MIN
16MM FILM, 3/4 OR 1/2 IN VIDEO
Presents an animated story dealing with the subtraction and division of fractions and the manipulation of mixed numbers.
From The Mathematics - An Animated Approach To Fractions Series. Part 3
Prod-FI Dist-FI

Subtractor, The - Subtraction, Pt 2 C 14 MIN
3/4 OR 1/2 INCH VIDEO CASSETTE P
Tells how Lionel hires a 'deficiency' expert who illustrates the need for practical thinking about subtraction.
From The Math Country Series.
Prod-KYTV Dist-AITECH 1979

Suburban Strategies - Dayton Malling, LA, Century City C 17 MIN
3/4 OR 1/2 INCH VIDEO CASSETTE
Contrasts typical images from a suburban shopping mall. Depicts four interrelated natural and artificial environments in Los Angeles.
Prod-KITCHN Dist-KITCHN

Suburban Wall C 50 MIN
16MM FILM OPTICAL SOUND J-H
Explores the factors responsible for the deteriorating housing situation in suburban America. Points out that of the 60 million housing units in this country, 11 million are either substandard, overcrowded, or both. Examines restrictive zoning requirements, the flight of jobs to the suburbs without housing for the jobholders and inequities of the property-tax structure.
Prod-WBCPRO Dist-WBCPRO 1971

Subvalvular Aortic Stenosis C 6 MIN
16MM FILM OPTICAL SOUND PRO
Uses animated sequences at normal and reduced speeds in order to show the events taking place in a single cardiac cycle. Demonstrates the generation of the mitral component of the first sound, the ejection systolic murmur and the aortic component of the second sound.
From The Physiological And Clinical Aspects of Cardiac Auscultation Series.
LC NO. 76-700954
Prod-MEDIC Dist-LIP 1976

Subversion C 27 MIN
2 INCH VIDEOTAPE
Documents life in the detention camps in the western United States, where thousands of Japanese-Americans were incarcerated during World War II.
From The Synergism - In Today's World Series.
Prod-KQEDTV Dist-PUBTEL 1971

Subversive C 58 MIN
3/4 OR 1/2 INCH VIDEO CASSETTE H-C A
Biography of Terry Petters, a Seattle, Washington pariah turned hero. Follows fifty years of his colorful and complicated life.
Prod-UCV Dist-UCV

Subway B 4 MIN
16MM FILM OPTICAL SOUND
Portrays on man's experience on a cold speeding subway where all the characters are mere shadows. Demonstrates the animity of man in a large society.
LC NO. 75-700483
Prod-USC Dist-USC 1975

Success - The Marva Collins Approach C 28 MIN
16MM FILM, 3/4 OR 1/2 IN VIDEO T
Presents a documentary on the teaching methods used by Marva Collins in her West Side Preparatory School in Chicago where phonics, classical literature and a sincere love of children are emphasized.
From The Dealing With Social Problems In The Classroom Series.
Prod-BELLDA Dist-FI 1981

Success Image—A Series
A
Shows women how to project a professional business image in the work place, how a consistent business look gives the impression the woman is serious about her job and career. Tells how to make a wardrobe work and demonstrates the impacts of color, clothing, organization and accessories. Features Vicki Keltner, author, publisher, consultant and successful businesswoman.
Prod-GPCV Dist-GPCV

Economics Of Your Success Image, The
Finishing Touch, The
Suits, Symbols And Success

Success In Supervision—A Series

Presents basic supervisory and administrative techniques which lead to improved production and better relationships with people.
Prod-WETATV Dist-USNAC

Basic Principles Of Supervision, Pt 1 30 MIN
Basic Principles Of Supervision, Pt 2 30 MIN
Basic Principles Of Supervision, Pt 3 30 MIN
Communications - Talking And Listening 30 MIN
Communications - Writing And Reading 30 MIN
Motivation 30 MIN
Orgnization 30 MIN
Participation 30 MIN
Planning, Scheduling, Organizing Work And 30 MIN
Special Problems 30 MIN
Training 30 MIN
Working With People 30 MIN

Success In The Job Market—A Series
H
Explains how high school students can prepare for the world of work.
Prod-KUONTV Dist-GPITVL 1980

Behind Closed Doors 15 MIN
Company, The 15 MIN
Let Me Count The Ways I Know Me 15 MIN
Loving Me Is Loving You 15 MIN
Search, The 15 MIN
Working At The Car Wash Blues 15 MIN

Success Or Failure - It's Up To You C 15 MIN
3/4 OR 1/2 INCH VIDEO CASSETTE A
Features baseball Hall of Famer Harmon Killebrew, along with baseball star Rod Carew, emphasizing the importance of confronting situations where failure is possible, rather than dodging them. Offers advice on pulling out of dry spells.
Prod-SFTI Dist-SFTI

Success Oriented Schools C
3/4 OR 1/2 INCH VIDEO CASSETTE T
Presents a process that the educational planner can follow to problem solve and make decisions. Helps develop a system that develops a successful environment for students.
From The School Inservice Videotape Series.
Prod-TERRAS Dist-SLOSSF

Success Story C 15 MIN
16MM FILM, 3/4 OR 1/2 IN VIDEO I-J
Explores the various ways to define success and emphasizes the implications of one's own definition of the concept.
From The Bread And Butterflies Series.
LC NO. 74-703182
Prod-AITV Dist-AITECH Prodn-WNVT 1973

Success Story - How Insects Survive C 28 MIN
16MM FILM, 3/4 OR 1/2 IN VIDEO J-C A
Shows how insects have adapted successfully to a variety of environments and how they are capable of utilizing almost every available food form. Explains how their astonishing defense capabilities have evolved through instinctive behavior and physical adaptations.
Prod-EBEC Dist-EBEC

Success With Indoor Plants C 57 MIN
1/2 IN VIDEO CASSETTE BETA/VHS
Shows how to care for indoor plants. Demonstrates starting new plants and potting and repotting. Includes proper ways to water and prune and methods of controlling insects and disease.
From The Lawn And Garden Series.
Prod-MOHOMV Dist-MOHOMV

Success World C 22 MIN
3/4 OR 1/2 INCH VIDEO CASSETTE I A
Features Art Linkletter as he comments on successful entrepreneurs.
Prod-SUTHRB Dist-SUTHRB

Success, Needs And Interests C 30 MIN
3/4 OR 1/2 INCH VIDEO CASSETTE T
Tells how to take into account the success, needs and interests of adult basic education students.
From The Basic Education - Teaching The Adult Series.
Prod-MDDE Dist-MDCPB

Success, The AMA Course For Office Employees - Course Overview C 5 MIN
2 INCH VIDEOTAPE
Presents an instructional program for office employees. Explains the SUCCESS course.
From The SUCCESS, The AMA Course For Office Employees Series.
Prod-AMA Dist-AMA

Success, The AMA Course For Office Employees—A Series

Prod-AMA Dist-AMA 1972

Getting Completed Staff Work From Others 008 MIN
Give Change A Chance 008 MIN
How To Follow Through On An Assignment 008 MIN
Invitation And The Plan 006 MIN
Manager's Job Responsibilities, The 003 MIN
Manager's Operating Realities 008 MIN
Success, The AMA Course For Office 005 MIN
They're Always Changing Things 006 MIN
Three Managerial Styles 013 MIN
While You were Out 009 MIN
Why Communication Goes Wrong 009 MIN

Successful Breastfeeding - Right From The Start C 24 MIN
3/4 OR 1/2 INCH VIDEO CASSETTE C A
Aims at helping new mothers overcome the minor difficulties associated with breastfeeding. Presents the advantages of breastfeeding, technique and scheduling routines, as well as the possible difficulties.
Prod-UCOLO Dist-TEF

Successful Cold Call Selling C
16MM FILM, 3/4 OR 1/2 IN VIDEO
Helps salespeople overcome call reluctance, turn resistance into interest and identify the buying authority.
Prod-BNA Dist-BNA

Successful Delegation C 15 MIN
16MM FILM, 3/4 OR 1/2 IN VIDEO
Illustrates that managers can actually enhance their position, and their value to the company, by giving subordinates the authority to act independently. Helps them understand that managers who don't delegate are not earning their salaries because they are too busy with routine work to do the organizing, planning and decision making they're paid to do.
Prod-EFM Dist-EFM

Successful Duck Hunting C 44 MIN
1/2 IN VIDEO CASSETTE BETA/VHS

Demonstrates duck hunting. Covers such areas as duck calls, decoy setting and selecting a blind. Shows what works best in various ponds and marshes.
Prod-MOHOMV Dist-MOHOMV

Successful Fire Service Leadership C
3/4 OR 1/2 INCH VIDEO CASSETTE
See series title for descriptive statement.
From The Fire Away Series.
Prod-NFPA Dist-NFPA

Successful Manager, The C 10 MIN
3/4 OR 1/2 INCH VIDEO CASSETTE
Defines who managers are, what they do, what is expected of them and what the attributes of a successful managers are.
From The Management of Work Series. Module 1
Prod-RESEM Dist-RESEM

Successful Parenting C 30 MIN
3/4 OR 1/2 INCH VIDEO CASSETTE C A
Explores interaction between the couple and the child, child development and disciplinary approaches in parenting.
From The Family Portrait - A Study Of Contemporary Lifestyles Series. Lesson 26
Prod-SCCON Dist-CDTEL

Successful Persuasion - A New Approach To Selling C 14 MIN
16MM FILM, 3/4 OR 1/2 IN VIDEO J-C A
Concentrates on the buy-sell relationship. Looks behind what people say to what they might actually mean. Illustrates both successful and unsuccessful attempts at persuasion.
From The Communications And Selling Program Series.
Prod-NEM Dist-NEM 1975

Successful Persuasion - A New Approach To Selling (Spanish) C 14 MIN
16MM FILM, 3/4 OR 1/2 IN VIDEO
Teaches the dynamics of the persuasion transaction using everyday situations. Stresses the importance of listening and feedback in two-way communications.
From The Communications And Selling Program (Spanish) Series.
Prod-NEM Dist-NEM

Successful Speaker B 10 MIN
16MM FILM OPTICAL SOUND I-C A
Explains that success in speech depends on enthusiasm and spontaneity, directness, communicative posture, control of nervous tension, movement and gesture, and vocal variety.
Prod-UNEBR Dist-UNEBR

Successful Supervision C
3/4 INCH VIDEOTAPE C A
Teaches supervisory skills to trainees. Explains how to work successfully and confidently with subordinates, how to handle differences, praise workers, correct worker performance and prioritize, analyze, delegate and follow up on work.
Prod-OSDVTE Dist-OSDVTE

Successful Teaching Practices—A Series
16MM FILM, 3/4 OR 1/2 IN VIDEO T
Provides methods teachers may use to motivate students, work with the gifted and maintain discipline.
Prod-UNIDIM Dist-EBEC 1982

Classroom Management - The Student's Role	027 MIN
Creating A Positive Classroom Atmosphere	019 MIN
Developing Leadership Skills	027 MIN
Free To Teach - Unchaining Teachers	026 MIN
Gifted Program In Action, A	027 MIN
Giftedness In All Children, The	027 MIN
Individualizing Instruction Through	025 MIN
Innovative Teaching For Student Motivation	019 MIN
Motivation In The Classroom	027 MIN
Politics Of Working Together In A Gifted And	028 MIN
Positive Discipline In The Classroom	028 MIN
Reading In The Content Area	026 MIN
Student Involvement Program For Developing	029 MIN
Student Self-Concept And Standards	027 MIN
Teacher's Prescription For Reducing	023 MIN
Teaching Is An Attitude	027 MIN

Successful Termination C
3/4 OR 1/2 INCH VIDEO CASSETTE
Demonstrates the delicate process of terminating employees.
Prod-DBMI Dist-DBMI

Successfully Defending Against The Pass C
3/4 OR 1/2 INCH VIDEO CASSETTE T
Features Defense Coach Jerry Sandusky directing demonstrations of techniques and drills used in teaching various types of pass coverage, pass rush, intercepting and recovering fumbles.
From The Joe Paterno - Coaching Winning Football Series.
Prod-UNIDIM Dist-EBEC 1982

Succession - From Sand Dune To Forest X 16 MIN
16MM FILM, 3/4 OR 1/2 IN VIDEO H
Illustrates the process and general principles of ecological succession by which an area slowly and continuously changes until it becomes a stable natural community. Photographed in the Lake Michigan dunes.
From The Biology Series. Unit 1 - Ecology
Prod-EBF Dist-EBEC 1960

Succession - From Sand Dune To Forest (Spanish) C 16 MIN
16MM FILM, 3/4 OR 1/2 IN VIDEO H
Outlines the principles of ecological succession, the process by which an area changes until it becomes a stable natural community.
From The Biology (Spanish) Series. Unit 1 - Ecology
Prod-EBEC Dist-EBEC

Succession On Lava C 14 MIN
16MM FILM, 3/4 OR 1/2 IN VIDEO J-H
Photographs the many stages of succession that exist at different locations in Hawaii at the site of volcanic eruptions. Includes scenes of destruction due to lava flows and pumice, dramatizing how swiftly the surrounding area becomes hostile to all forms of life. Shows how each new form of life that strives for survival further modifies the environment and eventually re-establishes a complex web of life.
From The Biology Series. Unit 1 - Ecology
Prod-EBEC Dist-EBEC 1970

Succession On Lava (Spanish) C 14 MIN
16MM FILM, 3/4 OR 1/2 IN VIDEO J-H
Photographs the many stages of succession that exist at different locations in Hawaii at the site of volcanic eruptions. Includes scenes of destruction due to lava flows and pumice, dramatizing how swiftly the surrounding area becomes hostile to all forms of life. Shows how each new form of life that strives for survival further modifies the environment and eventually re-establishes a complex web of life.
From The Biology Series. Unit 1 - Ecology
Prod-EBEC Dist-EBEC 1970

Succoth C 15 MIN
16MM FILM OPTICAL SOUND
Shows how the Festival of Succoth is celebrated in Israel.
Prod-ALDEN Dist-ALDEN

Succulents C 29 MIN
3/4 INCH VIDEO CASSETTE
Shows how to divide, transplant and display succulents.
From The House Botanist Series.
Prod-UMITV Dist-UMITV 1978

Succulents, The C 30 MIN
2 INCH VIDEOTAPE
Features Thalassa Cruso discussing different aspects of gardening. Shows how to care for succulents.
From The Making Things Grow I Series.
Prod-WGBHTV Dist-PUBTEL

Sucessful Strategies For Manufacturing Management—A Series

Examines how to plan and design a strategy to deploy the new systems of manufacturing technology. Includes a discussion of the critical factors of success, factors that transcend industry, nationality, culture and company size. Examines recent history, the present situation and trends for the future.
Prod-DELTAK Dist-DELTAK

Developing An Effective Manufacturing Strategy	030 MIN
Profile Of A Willing Competitor	030 MIN
Winners And Losers - A Worldwide Survey	030 MIN

Such A Beautiful Day C 15 MIN
16MM FILM, 3/4 OR 1/2 IN VIDEO
Explores the relationship between alcohol and highway safety.
LC NO. 80-706835
Prod-USHTSA Dist-USNAC 1975

Such A Place C 28 MIN
2 INCH VIDEOTAPE
Presents a documentary in cinema verite style about very old people in a nursing home. Focuses on the people who live there, the daily routines, from the distribution of mail to visits to the home's beauty parlor.
From The Synergism - In Today's World Series.
Prod-JSRI Dist-PUBTEL

Sucker Rod Failures - Causes And Prevention C 25 MIN
3/4 OR 1/2 INCH VIDEO CASSETTE IND
Discusses methods and techniques of reducing sucker rod failures.
Prod-UTEXPE Dist-UTEXPE 1975

Sucking Doctor B 45 MIN
16MM FILM OPTICAL SOUND
Presents, in its entirety, the second and final night of a curing ceremony held by the Kashia group of the southwestern Pomo Indians. Shows how on the first night (may 31, 1963,) while the Shaman was in a hypnotic trance, the patient's pain was located and the germs removed from his body. Includes how the Shaman effected this by means of the spiritual instrument she possesses in her throat, and finally, the pain removed, in the form of a quartz crystal.
Prod-HEICK Dist-UCEMC 1964

Sucking Wounds Of The Chest C 12 MIN
16MM FILM OPTICAL SOUND
Demonstrates five important steps in prompt and proper treatment for a sucking chest wound by means of a simulated casualty on the battlefront.
LC NO. FIE54-288
Prod-USN Dist-USNAC 1953

Suction Biopsy Of The Gastrointestinal Mucosa C 16 MIN
16MM FILM OPTICAL SOUND
Shows how suction biopsy tubes are passed under fluoroscopic control. Illustrates techniques for passing the pylorus as well as the necessity for taking small bowel biopsies near the duodenojejunal junction. Depicts the use of the suction biopsy tube in the esophagus, stomach and rectum. Features the detail of handling the biopsy to minimize trauma and to assure perfect orientation. Explains that if the biopsies are not handled atraumatically and if they are not perfectly oriented, then subsequent processing of interpretable biopsies will be impossible.
LC NO. 74-705719
Prod-USPHS Dist-USNAC 1967

Suction Tip Placement C 8 MIN
16MM FILM - 3/4 IN VIDEO
Demonstrates how to position a suction tip an all areas of the mouth for oral evacuation.
Prod-SAIT Dist-SAIT 1973

Suctioning The Patient With A Tracheotomy C 16 MIN
16MM FILM, 3/4 OR 1/2 IN VIDEO PRO
Demonstrates the aseptic technique for suctioning a patient with a mannekin and a real patient. Covers reasons for suctioning, supplies and equipment needed, patient preparation, positions, disposal of used materials and recording essential information.
Prod-PRORE Dist-PRORE

Sudden Changes - Post Hysterectomy Syndrome C 29 MIN
16MM FILM, 3/4 OR 1/2 IN VIDEO A
Concentrates on both the physical and emotional sides of this common but sometimes controversial surgical procedure. Explores hysterectomy from the point of view of doctors, medical researcherauthors and women's rights activists. Suggests discussion of alternatives by women facing hysterectomy.
Prod-CNEMAG Dist-CNEMAG 1985

Sudden Emergencies B 5 MIN
16MM FILM OPTICAL SOUND J
Stresses the importance of knowing how to react to sudden emergencies encountered in driving.
From The Driver Education Series.
LC NO. FIA66-1007
Prod-AMROIL Dist-AMROIL 1964

Sudden Infant Death Syndrome C 4 MIN
16MM FILM - 3/4 IN VIDEO C A
Explains that Sudden Infant Death Syndrome (SIDS) takes the lives of about 8,000 infants each year in the United States. Discusses methods of prediction and prevention. Deals with the grief of SIDS parents.
From The Sudden Infant Death Syndrome Series.
LC NO. 79-706265
Prod-USHSA Dist-USNAC Prodn-NOWAKA 1979

Sudden Infant Death Syndrome - After Our Baby Died C 26 MIN
16MM FILM OPTICAL SOUND
Communicates the nature and intensity of parents who have lost children to Sudden Infant Death Syndrome.
Prod-USHHS Dist-TOGGFI 1975

Sudden Infant Death Syndrome—A Series

Discusses various aspects of Sudden Infant Death Syndrome, including methods of prediction and prevention, how to deal with the grief of the parents and how to handle distress calls by parents.
Prod-USHSA Dist-USNAC Prodn-NOWAKA 1979

After Our Baby Died	20 MIN
Call For Help, A	19 MIN
Sudden Infant Death Syndrome	4 MIN
You Are Not Alone	

Sudden Natural Death B 25 MIN
16MM FILM - 3/4 IN VIDEO PRO
Discusses aspects of sudden natural death, with emphasis on the most common cause - occlusive coronary artery disease.
From The Clinical Pathology - Forensic Medicine Outlines Series.
LC NO. 76-706240
Prod-NMAC Dist-USNAC 1970

Sudden Unexpected Natural Death C 39 MIN
3/4 INCH VIDEO CASSETTE PRO
Presents several cases of individuals who were presumed healthy, but died within 24 hours of the onset of symptoms. Discusses sudden natural deaths causes by various heart diseases, central nervous disorders and respiratory dysfunction.
From The Forensic Medicine Teaching Programs Series. No. 6
LC NO. 78-706056
Prod-NMAC Dist-USNAC Prodn-NYUCM 1978

Sudden Wealth Of The Poor People Of Kombach (German) B 94 MIN
16MM FILM OPTICAL SOUND
Suggests that superstition and religion, public school teaching and a paternalizing concept of justice make poor people into simpletons who are taught to laugh at their own misfortunes. Follows a true story about seven peasants who, in 1821, robbed a tax collector's wagon and were subsequently caught, tried and executed for their crime.
Prod-NYFLMS Dist-NYFLMS 1971

Suddenly And Without Warning C 6 MIN
16MM FILM OPTICAL SOUND
Stresses safety in boating and shows how boating accidents can happen.
LC NO. 75-700588
Prod-USCG Dist-USNAC 1971

Suddenly, Last Summer B 114 MIN
16MM FILM OPTICAL SOUND C A
Stars Elizabeth Taylor as a beautiful patient of a neuro-surgeon, played by Montgomery Clift. Describes her on the brink of insanity after witnessing the violent death of her young male cousin.
Prod-CPC Dist-TIMLIF

Sue And Sandra C 6 MIN
16MM FILM, 3/4 OR 1/2 IN VIDEO I
See series title for descriptive statement.
From The Being Friends Series.
Prod-USDHEW Dist-USNAC

Sue's Leg - Remembering The Thirties / Twyla Tharp And Dancers C 60 MIN
16MM FILM, 3/4 OR 1/2 IN VIDEO H-C A

Presents choreographer Twyla Tharp and her dance company performing her creation, entitled Sue's Legs, to the music of the late jazz artist Fats Waller.
From The Dance In America Series.
Prod-WNETTV Dist-IU 1977

Suez C 14 MIN
16MM FILM OPTICAL SOUND I-H
Shows the skillful navigation by specially trained pilots through the Suez Canal. Offers helpful background for the issues and problems connected with the Suez Canal today.
Prod-IFF Dist-IFF 1956

Suez Canal B 13 MIN
3/4 OR 1/2 INCH VIDEO CASSETTE
Examines the history of the Suez Canal since its opening in 1869 and looks at the crucial role it has played in the Middle East.
Prod-KINGFT Dist-KINGFT

Suez Canal - Politics Of Control C 16 MIN
3/4 OR 1/2 INCH VIDEO CASSETTE H-C A
Examines the incident in 1956 when President Nassar of Egypt nationalized the Suez Canal. Investigates its role in the Middle East and international politics since that time.
Prod-JOU Dist-JOU

Suffer Little Children B 10 MIN
16MM FILM OPTICAL SOUND
Depicts young children in an institution for the mentally retarded. Raises the questions of how and why they were institutionalized and what has become of them. Shows equally disabled children who live at home and attend a nursery school in their own community.
Prod-CMHRF Dist-CMHRF

Suffer The Children C 16 MIN
16MM FILM, 3/4 OR 1/2 IN VIDEO H-C A
Presents children sharing their anguish at having to deal with alcholic parents. Explains that children of alcoholics often grow up to be introverted and friendless.
Prod-CBSNEW Dist-CAROUF

Sufferin' Until Suffrage C 3 MIN
3/4 OR 1/2 INCH VIDEO CASSETTE I
Examines women's struggle to vote, showing suffragettes like Susan B Anthony march in demonstrations, carry signs and spark passage of the 19th amendment.
From The America Rock Series.
Prod-ABCTV Dist-GA Prodn-SCOROC 1976

Suffragists After A Century C 16 MIN
16MM FILM OPTICAL SOUND
Focuses on ten Canadian women in a discussion of the status of the women's movement in Canada.
LC NO. 77-702656
Prod-OFWTA Dist-MARMO 1975

Sugar C
3/4 INCH VIDEO CASSETTE H A
Shows how to make chocolate truffles with praline filling. Illustrates basic principles of sugar cookery.
From The Matter Of Taste Series. Lesson 18
Prod-COAST Dist-CDTEL

Sugar And Spice And All Is Not Nice C 19 MIN
16MM FILM, 3/4 OR 1/2 IN VIDEO H-C A
Interviews actual rape victims. Points out the need for self defense and a change in social and cultural attitudes.
Prod-LCOA Dist-LCOA 1985

Sugar Beet, The - How Sweet It Is C 13 MIN
16MM FILM, 3/4 OR 1/2 IN VIDEO P-J
Shows the special machines crawling over fields, planting, spraying, weeding and harvesting sugar beets. Demonstrates how inside the plant, giant washing wheels clean and carry the beets to be sliced, diced and boiled. Concludes with huge centrifuges whirling the juice from the syrup, leaving fine white crystals ready for drying, sifting and packaging.
Prod-BORTF Dist-BCNFL 1983

Sugar Bowl Classic B 14 MIN
16MM FILM OPTICAL SOUND
Shows the highlights of the football game between the Naval Academy and the University of Mississippi in the Sugar Bowl at New Orleans, Louisiana, on January 1, 1955.
Prod-USA Dist-USNAC

Sugar Campaign C 15 MIN
3/4 OR 1/2 INCH VIDEO CASSETTE P-I
Inspects the complex operation of producing sugar from sugar beets.
From The Explorers Unlimited Series.
Prod-WVIZTV Dist-AITECH 1971

Sugar Cane C 11 MIN
16MM FILM, 3/4 OR 1/2 IN VIDEO J-H A
Looks at the communal life of the workers on the island of Negros in the Philippines as they harvest the sugar cane fields. Shows that the process from harvest to raw sugar crystals takes only 24 hours.
Prod-LUF Dist-LUF 1979

Sugar Cereal Imitation Orange Breakfast, The C 8 MIN
16MM FILM, 3/4 OR 1/2 IN VIDEO I-C A
Shows how advertising can sell the sugar-frosted breakfast cereals even though they may be bad for the teeth and low in nutrition. Examines various orange juice products, discussing water, sugar, chemicals and other additives.
Prod-WNETTV Dist-BNCHMK 1972

Sugar Country C 27 MIN
16MM FILM OPTICAL SOUND I-H
Depicts the entire operations of the sugar industry from planting cane to packages on the grocery shelf. Discusses labor and environmental problems facing the industry. Shows how the industry is solving these problems.
Prod-FLADC Dist-FLADC 1973

Sugar Film, The C 27 MIN
16MM FILM, 3/4 OR 1/2 IN VIDEO I-C A
A shortened version of the motion picture The Sugar Film. Discusses the harm sugar does, such as increasing the chance of heart disease, contributing 15-20 percent of a person's total caloric intake and producing a craving for more sugar.
LC NO. 81-706390
Prod-LISNDO Dist-PFP 1980

Sugar Film, The C 28 MIN
3/4 OR 1/2 INCH VIDEO CASSETTE
Points out that the average American consumes 129 pounds of sugar per year, compared with only four pounds 200 years ago. Examines the effects of this enormous dietary change on the physical and mental health of Americans.
Prod-LACFU Dist-IA

Sugar Film, The C 57 MIN
16MM FILM, 3/4 OR 1/2 IN VIDEO I-C A
Discusses the harm sugar does, such as increasing the chance of heart disease, contributing 15-20 percent of a person's total caloric intake and producing a craving for more sugar.
Prod-LISNDO Dist-PFP 1980

Sugar From Beets C 5 MIN
16MM FILM, 3/4 OR 1/2 IN VIDEO
Describes the processes involved in obtaining sugar from beets.
From The European Studies - Germany Series. Part 12
Prod-BAYER Dist-IFB 1973

Sugar In Egypt C 13 MIN
16MM FILM, 3/4 OR 1/2 IN VIDEO P-C
Shows the steps in the productoon of sugar, explains why progress is slow in using modern harvesting methods and tells why sugar has become a major Egyptian product.
From The Man And His World Series.
Prod-FI Dist-FI 1969

Sugar Is Not Enough C 14 MIN
16MM FILM, 3/4 OR 1/2 IN VIDEO I-J
Depicts the difficult work day of a fourteen-year old son of sugar cane farmers in Ecuador, as head of the family because his father works far away, coming home only occasionally. Shows a never-ending series of tasks, including cutting, crushing and refining the sugar cane as a cash crop for family support, going to school in a nearby town, and helping his mother with younger siblings as well as hunting and fishing.
From The Just One Child Series.
Prod-REYEXP Dist-BCNFL 1983

Sugar Mill, The (Captioned) C 10 MIN
16MM FILM, 3/4 OR 1/2 IN VIDEO A
Discusses the methods of sugar production in the Brazilian Northeast and the character of the mills and the life around them. Portuguese dialog with English subtitles.
Prod-CNEMAG Dist-CNEMAG

Sugar Mountain Blues C 28 MIN
3/4 INCH VIDEO CASSETTE
Shows diabetic young people monitoring their own blood glucose levels and taking part in vigorous activity, including a mountain climbing weekend. Features mountain scenery.
Prod-BIODYN Dist-MTP

Sugar Ray Leonard C 11 MIN
3/4 INCH VIDEO CASSETTE
Features Sugar Ray Leonard describing the information services available at the library. Focuses on career changes and possibilities.
Prod-MDPL Dist-LVN

Sugar Sullivan, Al Minns And Jane Goldberg C 30 MIN
3/4 OR 1/2 INCH VIDEO CASSETTE
See series title for descriptive statement.
From The Eye On Dance - Third World Dance, Tracing Roots Series.
Prod-ARTRES Dist-ARTRES

Sugarbush C 15 MIN
3/4 OR 1/2 INCH VIDEO CASSETTE P-I
Pictures a sugarbush to observe the old-fashioned method of making maple syrup.
From The Explorers Unlimited Series.
Prod-WVIZTV Dist-AITECH 1971

Suggestion Box B 9 MIN
16MM FILM OPTICAL SOUND
Describes how war plant workers in 1944 were encouraged to submit suggestions and how some of these suggestions, when put into practice, resulted in saving of time, labor and materials.
Prod-USOE Dist-USNAC 1945

Suggestion System In Japan C 30 MIN
3/4 OR 1/2 INCH VIDEO CASSETTE A
See series title for descriptive statement.
From The Business Nippon Series.
LC NO. 85-702164
Prod-JAPCTV Dist-EBEC 1984

Suggestion System In Japanese Corporations C 30 MIN
3/4 OR 1/2 INCH VIDEO CASSETTE A
See series title for descriptive statement.
From The Business Nippon Series.
LC NO. 85-702163
Prod-JAPCTV Dist-EBEC 1984

Suggestions About Correcting And Criticizing People B 29 MIN
16MM FILM OPTICAL SOUND
See series title for descriptive statement.
From The Controlling Turnover And Absenteeism Series.
LC NO. 76-703321
Prod-EDSD Dist-EDSD

Suggestive Selling For Waiters And Waitresses (Rev Ed) C
16MM FILM, 3/4 OR 1/2 IN VIDEO
Demonstrates basic principles of suggestive selling and menu merchandising. Distinguishes the unimaginative order-taker from the profit-producing salesperson with special emphasis on the art of suggestive selling. Discusses the importance of the serving staff's understanding the psychology of the customer and having a thorough knowledge of menu items.
From The Professional Food Preparation And Service Programs Series.
Prod-NEM Dist-NEM 1983

Suggestopedia, A Science Of Learning B 30 MIN
3/4 OR 1/2 INCH VIDEO CASSETTE
Demonstrates the USSR version of psychological teaching methods known as Suggestopedia which enables students to learn a foreign language in as little time as a month.
Prod-EAI Dist-EAI

Suho And The White Horse C 10 MIN
16MM FILM, 3/4 OR 1/2 IN VIDEO K-I
Retells the Mongolian legend about a poor shepherd whose devotion to his horse resulted in the creation of the traditional horse-headed fiddle of the Mongolian steppes. Based on the book Suho And The White Horse by Yuzo Otsuka.
Prod-WWS Dist-WWS Prodn-SCHNDL 1982

Suicidal Patient, The C
3/4 OR 1/2 INCH VIDEO CASSETTE
Shows how proper evaluation and management of suicidal patients may ultimately prevent self-imposed death. Provides techniques necessary for dealing with this crisis.
From The Crisis Intervention Series.
Prod-VTRI Dist-VTRI

Suicidal Patient, The C 20 MIN
3/4 OR 1/2 INCH VIDEO CASSETTE PRO
Teaches effective inter-activity with the suicidal patient so that assessment of lethality and appropriate disposition can be achieved. Covers common factors precipitating suicidal behavior, interview guidelines and follow-up care.
From The Medical Crisis Intervention Series.
Prod-LEIKID Dist-LEIKID

Suicide C 17 MIN
3/4 OR 1/2 INCH VIDEO CASSETTE PRO
Explores attempted suicide, an emotional event and a challenge to nursing care. Reveals circumstances commonly observed among depressed persons who become suicidal and the events that may precede their suicide attempts.
LC NO. 77-730531
Prod-TRAINX Dist-TRAINX

Suicide C 30 MIN
3/4 OR 1/2 INCH VIDEO CASSETTE H-C A
Dramatizes the investigations of the staff of a high school newspaper. Focuses on suicide.
From The New Voice Series.
Prod-WGBHTV Dist-GPITVL

Suicide - But Jack Was A Good Driver C 15 MIN
16MM FILM, 3/4 OR 1/2 IN VIDEO I-H
Presents two boys exploring the subject of suicide because of their fear that their friend may have tried to take his own life.
From The Conflict And Awareness Series.
Prod-CRMP Dist-CRMP 1974

Suicide - Causes And Prevention—A Series

Examines the social and psychological causes of suicide. Argues that most suicide can be prevented.
Prod-IBIS Dist-IBIS

Causes
Prevention

Suicide - It Doesn't Have To Happen C 20 MIN
16MM FILM, 3/4 OR 1/2 IN VIDEO H-C
Presents a dramatization, based on case histories, about a high school teacher who helps a suicidal student.
Prod-BFA Dist-PHENIX Prodn-CHUTEP 1976

Suicide - Teenage Crisis C 10 MIN
16MM FILM, 3/4 OR 1/2 IN VIDEO
Explores the problem of teenage suicide and describes a variety of school and community programs that can saved troubled lives through counseling. Originally shown on the CBS television program 30 Minutes.
LC NO. 81-706015
Prod-CBSNEW Dist-CRMP 1981

Suicide - The Unheard Cry B 45 MIN
16MM FILM, 3/4 OR 1/2 IN VIDEO
Presents an analysis of suicidal personalities and their behavior patterns as may be encountered in military life. Emphasizes the assistance that can be offered to prevent suicide attempts.
LC NO. 82-707208
Prod-USA Dist-USNAC 1969

Suicide - The Warning Signs C 24 MIN
16MM FILM, 3/4 OR 1/2 IN VIDEO J-C A
Presents a dramatization about three teenagers who exhibit some of the most common warning signs of suicide.
Prod-CENTRO Dist-CORF 1982

Suicide - The Will To Die C 60 MIN
16MM FILM OPTICAL SOUND
Examines the psychological and emotional context of suicide. In-

troduces a woman who attempted to take her life, reveals what drove her to the act and explains how she learned to make a successful adjustment to life.
Prod-NABSP Dist-NABSP

Suicide At 17 C 18 MIN
16MM FILM - 3/4 IN VIDEO H-C A
Documents the suicide of one teenager, showing how it affected his parents and friends.
Prod-EISBGI Dist-LAWREN 1977

Suicide Clinic - A Cry For Help B 28 MIN
16MM FILM, 3/4 OR 1/2 IN VIDEO
Examines what may lie behind a suicide attempt. Points out that suicides cross all socioeconomic levels and that these persons are not necessarily less stable emotionally. Shows how suicide clinics can help people who are contemplating suicide.
LC NO. 80-707100
Prod-NET Dist-IU 1971

Suicide For Glory B 27 MIN
16MM FILM, 3/4 OR 1/2 IN VIDEO J-H
Shows highlights of the Battle for Okinawa.
From The Victory At Sea Series.
Prod-NBCTV Dist-LUF

Suicide Intervention C 30 MIN
16MM FILM - 3/4 IN VIDEO PRO
Examines the nurse's potential in suicide intervention. Uses two case studies of varying lethal risk to point up assessment and therapeutic possibilities. Discusses preventive tactics, including the use of the suicide hotline.
LC NO. 76-701627
Prod-AJN Dist-AJN Prodn-WGNCP 1976

Suicide Prevention - The Physician's Role B 20 MIN
16MM FILM OPTICAL SOUND
Presents an analysis of suicidal clues. Explains that in the United States in 1966, suicide ranked among the first ten causes of death—third highest in the age group 15-25. Dramatizes, in five case histories, early clues to suicide and their proper management.
LC NO. FIA67-624
Prod-ROCHEL Dist-AMEDA Prodn-VISPRJ 1967

Suicide Prevention Center Of Los Angeles B 19 MIN
16MM FILM OPTICAL SOUND
Presents a documentary report showing the research which led to the establishment of the Suicide Prevention Center of Los Angeles. Includes a description of how the center functions and lists some of its purposes and goals. Emphasizes the increasing seriousness of the problem of suicide, the number ten killer in the U S. Produced with an animated camera technique which uses still photographs and a spontaneous narration by the co-directors of the center.
LC NO. 75-703236
Prod-USPHS Dist-USC 1962

Suicide Prevention In Hospitals B 30 MIN
16MM FILM, 3/4 OR 1/2 IN VIDEO
Shows how hospital personnel can anticipate and prevent suicide attempts. Based on 12 years of research by the VA's unit for the study of unpredicted death.
Prod-USVA Dist-USNAC

Suitable For Framing B 26 MIN
16MM FILM OPTICAL SOUND
Looks at a mystery love triangle set in a film noir milieu.
LC NO. 79-700734
Prod-GDG Dist-GDG 1979

Suite Fantaisiste C 9 MIN
3/4 OR 1/2 INCH VIDEO CASSETTE
Presents a look at 18th century life as seen through dance poetry and the 'fan language' of the time. Performed by the New York Baroque Dance Company, with Celia Ipiotis and Jeff Bush.
From The Videodance Project, Vol 1 Series.
Prod-ARCVID Dist-ARCVID

Suite Fantaisiste C 9 MIN
3/4 OR 1/2 INCH VIDEO CASSETTE
Looks at 18th century life seen through dance, poetry and the 'fan language' of the time. Features musical performers Sandra Miller, James Richmond and Sarah Cunningham.
From The Videodance Project - Volume One Series.
Prod-ARTRES Dist-ARTRES

Suite Of Berber Dances B 10 MIN
16MM FILM OPTICAL SOUND
Presents a study of three folk dances of the berbers of Morocco. Includes a dance by a group of men providing their own music, a war dance from the foothills of the Atlas Mountains and a fiery 'GEUDRA' by a nomad girl of the western Sahara.
Prod-CENCM Dist-RADIM 1963

Suite Of Faces B 11 MIN
16MM FILM OPTICAL SOUND
Reviews the faces from French art in 13th century stone, 16th century oils and wood-cuts and engravings of all periods, surviving today in the people of France.
Prod-FILIM Dist-RADIM

Suite 212 C 30 MIN
3/4 OR 1/2 INCH VIDEO CASSETTE
Includes some of Nam June Paik's early works spiced by his special brand of multi-national humor.
Prod-EAI Dist-EAI

Suits, Symbols And Success C
3/4 OR 1/2 INCH VIDEO CASSETTE A
Examines the suit as a symbol, explaining the importance of color, the best fabrics and styles for busines wear, the basic business looks, importance of attitude, and the need for consistency in a business wardrobe.
From The Success Image Series.
Prod-GPCV Dist-GPCV

Sukarno And The Emergence Of Indonesia C 29 MIN
2 INCH VIDEOTAPE
See series title for descriptive statement.
From The Course Of Our Times II Series.
Prod-WGBHTV Dist-PUBTEL

Sulfonamides And Penicillins C 30 MIN
16MM FILM OPTICAL SOUND C
See series title for descriptive statement.
From The Pharmacology Series.
LC NO. 73-703355
Prod-MVNE Dist-TELSTR 1971

Sulfur And Its Compounds (2nd Ed) C 14 MIN
16MM FILM, 3/4 OR 1/2 IN VIDEO H-C
Demonstrates the chemical and physical properties of sulfur, including the formation of its allotropic forms. Describes the Frasch process, and emphasizes the importance of sulfur in modern industry, medicine and agriculture.
Prod-CORF Dist-CORF 1962

Sullivan's Travels B 91 MIN
16MM FILM OPTICAL SOUND
Tells how Hollywood director John L Sullivan, dissatisfied with his moneymaking escapist entertainments, dons a tramp's garb and sets forth to see how the other half lives. Directed by Preston Sturges.
Prod-UPCI Dist-TWYMAN

Sulmet Sulfamethazine In The Treatment Of Livestock Disease C 35 MIN
16MM FILM OPTICAL SOUND H-C A
Explains that special attention is given to the major infectious diseases of horses, swine, sheep, beef cattle and dairy cattle. Describes the use of the wonderworking sulfa drug, sulmet sulfamethazine, and shows the results of treatment by those drugs.
Prod-TF Dist-LEDR 1949

Sulphur B 21 MIN
16MM FILM OPTICAL SOUND C
Shows the mining of sulfur by the Frasch process and its uses both in the elemental form and after conversion of sulfuric acid.
Prod-TEXGS Dist-HEFL 1953

Sultan's Bath, The C 15 MIN
3/4 INCH VIDEO CASSETTE K-P
See series title for descriptive statement.
From The Storytime Series.
Prod-WCETTV Dist-GPITVL 1976

Sum And Difference C 15 MIN
3/4 INCH VIDEO CASSETTE I
Discusses addends and sums and shows how to find missing parts.
From The Math - No Mystery Series.
Prod-WCETTV Dist-GPITVL 1977

Sum And Product Of Roots Of Quadratic Equation, Pt 1 C 45 MIN
2 INCH VIDEOTAPE
See series title for descriptive statement.
From The Fundamentals Of Mathematics (2nd Ed.) Unit III - Linear And Quadratic Functions Series.
Prod-CHITVC Dist-GPITVL

Sum And Product Of Roots Of Quadratic Equation, Pt 2 C 45 MIN
2 INCH VIDEOTAPE
See series title for descriptive statement.
From The Fundamentals Of Mathematics (2nd Ed.) Unit III - Linear And Quadratic Functions Series.
Prod-CHITVC Dist-GPITVL

Summarizing C 15 MIN
16MM FILM, 3/4 OR 1/2 IN VIDEO I
Tells how a paraplegic man works up a good resume and lands a job at a sporting goods store.
From The Thinkabout Series. Reshaping Information
LC NO. 81-706125
Prod-KERA Dist-AITECH 1979

Summary B 29 MIN
16MM FILM OPTICAL SOUND
See series title for descriptive statement.
From The Controlling Turnover And Absenteeism Series.
LC NO. 76-703321
Prod-EDSD Dist-EDSD

Summary C 30 MIN
3/4 OR 1/2 INCH VIDEO CASSETTE IND
Summarizes previous 19 lectures. Presents series of stages for introduction of software engineering techniques into an organization.
From The Software Engineering - A First Course Series.
Prod-COLOSU Dist-COLOSU

Summary C 30 MIN
3/4 OR 1/2 INCH VIDEO CASSETTE
Discusses simple adjustments and checks on the power train system and reviews all of the material in the course.
From The Keep It Running Series.
Prod-NETCHE Dist-NETCHE 1982

Summary And Posttest C 50 MIN
3/4 OR 1/2 INCH VIDEO CASSETTE IND
See series title for descriptive statement.
From The Task Analysis And Job Instructor Training Series.
Prod-NCSU Dist-AMCEE

Summary And Review Of Sketching Techniques C 29 MIN
3/4 INCH VIDEO CASSETTE C A
Reviews important aspects of sketching. Reemphasizes drawing as a vehicle for the visual communication of ideas.
From The Sketching Techniques Series. Lesson 30
Prod-COAST Dist-CDTEL

Summary Court-Martial, The B 45 MIN
16MM FILM OPTICAL SOUND
Presents four typical cases which may be tried in a summary court-martial. Illustrates conditions which prompt a recommendation for trial, relationship of the summary court officer to the accused and the procedure followed in trial, conviction and sentencing.
LC NO. FIE54-374
Prod-USA Dist-USNAC 1954

Summary Of Earth Science C 30 MIN
3/4 OR 1/2 INCH VIDEO CASSETTE C
Completes the geologic history of the USA from 200 million years ago to the present. Provides a summary of the 30 half-hour lessons in the Earth, Sea and Sky Series.
From The Earth, Sea And Sky Series.
Prod-DALCCD Dist-DALCCD

Summary Of The Course C 30 MIN
3/4 INCH VIDEO CASSETTE C
See series title for descriptive statement.
From The Introduction To Mathematics Series.
Prod-MDCPB Dist-MDCPB

Summation B 34 MIN
16MM FILM OPTICAL SOUND C
Deals with various aspects of a criminal lawsuit involving a liquor store robbery case. Includes extracts of the summation by each counsel, the retirement by the jury for deliberation, and the verdict.
From The Criminal Law Series. No. 12
LC NO. 70-714044
Prod-RPATLF Dist-RPATLF 1968

Summations And Notation C
3/4 INCH VIDEO CASSETTE
See series title for descriptive statement.
From The Calculus Series.
Prod-MDDE Dist-MDCPB

Summer C 11 MIN
16MM FILM, 3/4 OR 1/2 IN VIDEO P-I
Shows children enjoying various summer activities.
From The Seasons Series.
LC NO. 80-707705
Prod-CENTRO Dist-CORF 1980

Summer C 15 MIN
3/4 INCH VIDEO CASSETTE P
See series title for descriptive statement.
From The Celebrate Series.
Prod-KUONTV Dist-GPITVL 1978

Summer C 15 MIN
16MM FILM, 3/4 OR 1/2 IN VIDEO P-I
Looks at the activities and changes common to the summer season such as crops developing in the fields and the forest turning green with new growth. Shows bees collecting pollen and nectar, birds feeding their young and a caterpillar becoming a beautiful butterfly.
From The Four Seasons Series.
Prod-NGS Dist-NGS 1983

Summer - Nature's Sights And Sounds C 14 MIN
16MM FILM, 3/4 OR 1/2 IN VIDEO P-I
Shows the effect of the warm sun on wildlife areas from the far northern tundra to the southern forests.
From The Nature's Sights And Sounds Series.
Prod-MASLKS Dist-BCNFL 1984

Summer - 1966 B 20 MIN
16MM FILM OPTICAL SOUND
Documents significant events of the summer of 1966, such as the flights of Geminis 9 and 10 and Surveyor, de Gaulle's visit to Russia, the work of archaeologists in Bolivia, and the rebuilding of South Vietnam.
From The Screen News Digest Series. Vol 9, Issue 1
Prod-HEARST Dist-HEARST 1966

Summer Adventure C 19 MIN
16MM FILM OPTICAL SOUND
Tells the story of the Summer Adventure program at the High Country Inn of Winter Park, Colorado, a vacation program which offers challenges in the Colorado outdoors.
LC NO. 77-702147
Prod-HIGHCI Dist-LANGED Prodn-LANGED 1977

Summer Camp C 13 MIN
16MM FILM, 3/4 OR 1/2 IN VIDEO P-I
Describes the gang's adventures at summer camp.
From The Learning Values With Fat Albert Series.
Prod-FLMTON Dist-CRMP 1977

Summer Children, The B 44 MIN
16MM FILM OPTICAL SOUND T
A study of the education of disadvantaged children. Examines an experimental program at a university laboratory school where four teachers carried out a language arts program with a group of four-to eightyear-olds from a depressed area. Shows classroom incidents as they actually occurred, explaining how children and teachers learned from each other.
LC NO. FIA67-625
Prod-FAE Dist-UCLA Prodn-SPF 1965

Summer Decision X 30 MIN
16MM FILM OPTICAL SOUND I-H T R
Tells the story of a high school graduate who is torn between going to college in the fall or having a surfing vacation in Hawaii. Shows that he attends a summer church camp where he learns the importance of faith.

LC NO. FIA66-1336
Prod-FAMF Dist-FAMF 1966

Summer Dreams C 3 MIN
3/4 OR 1/2 INCH VIDEO CASSETTE
Presents a whimsical flow of memories from childhood using the process of rotoscoping live-action images.
Prod-MEDIPR Dist-MEDIPR 1979

Summer Hanging Plants C 29 MIN
2 INCH VIDEOTAPE
Features Thalassa Cruso discussing different aspects of gardening. Explains how to grow and care for geraniums.
From The Making Things Grow III Series.
Prod-WGBHTV Dist-PUBTEL

Summer Harvest X 29 MIN
16MM FILM OPTICAL SOUND J T
Sam Levenson narrates the story of Wichita, Kansas, where youngsters voluntarily go to summer school for enrichment and credit.
Prod-NEA Dist-NEA 1962

Summer Ice C 23 MIN
3/4 OR 1/2 INCH VIDEO CASSETTE
Visits the seventh continent, Antarctica where Adelie penguins breed by the millions on the summer ice. Follows the nesting and breeding procedures until it's time to return to deep ocean for the winter.
Prod-NWLDPR Dist-NWLDPR

Summer In Nature C 14 MIN
16MM FILM, 3/4 OR 1/2 IN VIDEO P-I
Looks at life in the natural landscape during summer.
From The Seasons In Nature Series.
Prod-FLMFR Dist-FLMFR

Summer In The Parks C 15 MIN
16MM FILM OPTICAL SOUND
Portrays the summer in the parks project. Shows children from the Washington, DC, metropolitan area as they are involved in the varied activities of the program.
LC NO. 78-707385
Prod-USNPS Dist-USNPS 1969

Summer In The Parks, 1968 C 19 MIN
3/4 INCH VIDEO CASSETTE
Shows the U S National Park Service's Summer in the Parks program and depicts the reactions of participating children in the metropolitan Washington, DC, area. Issued in 1969 as a motion picture.
LC NO. 79-706161
Prod-USNPS Dist-USNAC 1979

Summer Incident C 27 MIN
16MM FILM OPTICAL SOUND
Uses the Lebanon crisis to emphasize the importance of being able to react quickly to continuous world crises and small war situations. Shows the important role played by the navy and marine corps in supporting the foreign policy of the United States. Features the sixth fleet.
Prod-USN Dist-USNAC 1959

Summer Is An Adventure C 11 MIN
16MM FILM, 3/4 OR 1/2 IN VIDEO P
Shows typical summertime activities, such as having fun at the beach, walking in the woods and enjoying long, warm days.
Prod-CORF Dist-CORF

Summer Is Here (Captioned) C 10 MIN
16MM FILM, 3/4 OR 1/2 IN VIDEO P
Captures the hot weather fun of camping, swimmming and the Fourth of July. Describes animal life during the summer. Captioned for the hearing impaired.
Prod-BERLET Dist-IFB 1967

Summer Is Here (2nd Ed) C 11 MIN
16MM FILM, 3/4 OR 1/2 IN VIDEO P
Captures the hot weather fun of camping, swimming and the Fourth of July. Describes animal activities during the summer.
From The Seasons (2nd Ed) Series.
LC NO. 80-706440
Prod-IFB Dist-IFB Prodn-BERLET 1979

Summer Journal, Unit 1 - You Are What You Feel—A Series
J
Stresses building a good self-image and acquiring the ability to deal with positive and negative emotions.
Prod-WNINTV Dist-GPITVL

Do You Have Esp 30 MIN
Focus On Overcoming Fears 30 MIN
How Do You Feel About Animals 30 MIN
How Do You Feel About Superstition 30 MIN
How Does Astrology Explain Human Personality 30 MIN
Locate Yourself In Space And Time 30 MIN
Probing Ones' Feelings About Superstition 30 MIN
What Makes A Man Masculine 30 MIN
What Makes A Woman Feminine 30 MIN
What Will I Be Next 30 MIN
Who Am I 30 MIN

Summer Journal, Unit 2 - You Are What You Can Do—A Series
J
Emphasizes the importance of developing vocabulary, comprehension, speed and study skills.
Prod-WNINTV Dist-GPITVL

Explain The Mysterious Events 30 MIN
Explore Slang And Figurative Language 30 MIN
Focus On Career Choices 30 MIN
Focus On Driver Education 30 MIN
How Do The Bill Of Rights Affect You 30 MIN
Improve Oral Reading Skills 30 MIN
Improve Your Reading Skills With O R E 30 MIN
Scan Reading Materials 30 MIN
What Are The Classifications Of Races Of 30 MIN
What Do You Know About Computers 30 MIN

Summer Journal, Unit 3 - You Are What You Say —A Series
J
Deals with creative writing.
Prod-WNINTV Dist-GPITVL

Express Your Feelings Through Haiku 30 MIN
Focus On Writing Stories 30 MIN

Summer Journal, Unit 4 - You Are What You Think—A Series
J
Deals with forming opinions.
Prod-WNINTV Dist-GPITVL

Decisions, Decision, Decisions 30 MIN
Explore The Choices Socrates Had To Make 30 MIN
Focus On Conflict 30 MIN
Getting The Most Out Of The Newspaper 30 MIN
Sharpen Your Thinking 30 MIN
What Is Your Attitude Toward Justice 30 MIN

Summer Journal, Unit 5 - You Are What Others See In You—A Series
J
Deals with social relationships, especially as they are related to making friends and getting along with one's family.
Prod-WNINTV Dist-GPITVL

Developing A Love For Horses 30 MIN
Evaluate Yourself 30 MIN
Focus On Conflict Between Generations 30 MIN
Focus On Devotion 30 MIN
Focus On The Entire Family 30 MIN
I Have A Dream 30 MIN
Reflect On Your Grandparents 30 MIN
Review 'The Great Search' 30 MIN
Tune In On Yourself 30 MIN
What Music Are You Like 30 MIN
What The World Needs Now Is Somebody To Listen 30 MIN
Who Do I Portray To Others 30 MIN

Summer Landscape C 29 MIN
3/4 INCH VIDEO CASSETTE
See series title for descriptive statement.
From The Magic Of Oil Painting Series.
Prod-KOCETV Dist-PUBTEL

Summer Magic C 109 MIN
16MM FILM OPTICAL SOUND
Presents the story of a widow who gives up her home in Boston and brings her three children to a small sleepy village in Maine. Discusses the almost immediate pandemonium and hilarity which ensues.
Prod-DISNEY Dist-TWYMAN 1967

Summer Movements In The Arctic B 15 MIN
16MM FILM OPTICAL SOUND
Describes the terrain of arctic and subarctic regions, the difficulties of moving men and supplies and problems of camping and survival.
LC NO. FIE55-199
Prod-USA Dist-USNAC 1950

Summer Of '42 C 102 MIN
16MM FILM OPTICAL SOUND
Describes a young boy's coming of age in a small New England community in 1942.
Prod-WB Dist-TWYMAN 1971

Summer Of '63 C 20 MIN
16MM FILM, 3/4 OR 1/2 IN VIDEO J-H
Dramatizes how VD touched three of the four main characters in this film and explores the VD problem of yesterday and the VD epidemic of today.
Prod-DAVP Dist-AIMS 1974

Summer Of '72, The C 8 MIN
16MM FILM OPTICAL SOUND
Examines the Rapid City flash flood and Tropical Storm Agnes, the worst natural disasters in America's history. Relates what happened as told by those who lived through it.
Prod-AMRC Dist-AMRC 1972

Summer Of Decision - Central America C 52 MIN
3/4 OR 1/2 INCH VIDEO CASSETTE H-C A
Guides through the labyrinth of Central America. Reveals a Reagan administration, sure of its investments in Central America while depicting a cautious American public reluctant to participate in yet another guerilla war fought on foreign soil.
Prod-NBCNEW Dist-FI

Summer Of Judgment - The Impeachment Hearings C 60 MIN
3/4 OR 1/2 INCH VIDEO CASSETTE H-C A
Tells the story of the Articles Of Impeachment being drafted by the House Judiciary Committee. Contains footage of the original committee debates as well as interviews of many of the participants ten years later.
Prod-WETATV Dist-WETATV

Summer Of Judgment - The Watergate Hearings C 114 MIN
3/4 OR 1/2 INCH VIDEO CASSETTE H-C A
Distills the six months of Watergate hearings. Introduces members of the senate investigating committee and the Nixon aides whose testimonies are heard. Presents personal recollections of participants' thoughts and feelings as events were unfolding. Includes archival stills which are periodically montaged with the interviews. Provdes a contemporary perspective on the impact of Watergate.
LC NO. 83-707474
Prod-WETATV Dist-WETATV 1983

Summer Of My German Soldier C 98 MIN
16MM FILM, 3/4 OR 1/2 IN VIDEO J-C A
Tells the story of Patty Bergen, a Jewish girl who is treated as an outsider by her neighbors in Jenkinsville. Shows how she forms a friendship with a German POW being held there during World War II. Stars Kristy McNichol and Bruce Davidson.
Prod-HGATE Dist-LCOA 1978

Summer Of My German Soldier (Captioned) C 98 MIN
16MM FILM, 3/4 OR 1/2 IN VIDEO P-C A
Tells the story of a young Jewish girl who befriends and gives shelter to a German prisoner-of-war. Based on the novel by Bette Greene.
Prod-HGATE Dist-LCOA 1978

Summer Of The Swans, The C 15 MIN
3/4 OR 1/2 INCH VIDEO CASSETTE I
See series title for descriptive statement.
From The Best Of Cover To Cover 2 Series.
Prod-WETATV Dist-WETATV

Summer Quest C 1 MIN
3/4 INCH VIDEO CASSETTE
Encourages the use of the public library in the summer.
Prod-MDPL Dist-LVN

Summer Salads C 30 MIN
3/4 OR 1/2 INCH VIDEO CASSETTE H-C
Tells how to buy, mix and fix salads.
From The French Chef Series.
Prod-WGBH Dist-KINGFT

Summer Salt C 19 MIN
3/4 OR 1/2 INCH VIDEO CASSETTE
Prod-EAI Dist-EAI

Summer Solstice C 48 MIN
16MM FILM, 3/4 OR 1/2 IN VIDEO H-C A
Looks at a couple whose marriage has lasted 50 years. Joins them on a visit to the beach where they met and fell in love and where they recount the joyous moments and the losses in their marriage.
LC NO. 83-706994
Prod-WCVBTV Dist-MTI 1983

Summer Songs C 15 MIN
3/4 OR 1/2 INCH VIDEO CASSETTE P
Presents singing games for summer vacation.
From The Music Machine Series.
Prod-GPITVL Dist-GPITVL

Summer Sports (Summer Fun) C 3 MIN
16MM FILM OPTICAL SOUND P-I
Discusses sports and fun activities for summer.
From The Of All Things Series.
Prod-BAILYL Dist-AVED

Summer Switch C 31 MIN
16MM FILM, 3/4 OR 1/2 IN VIDEO I-H
Tells story of a father and son who trade places, as the father goes to summer camp and the son goes to Hollywood. Edited version.
Prod-HGATE Dist-LCOA 1985

Summer Switch C 46 MIN
16MM FILM, 3/4 OR 1/2 IN VIDEO I-H
Tells story of a father and son who trade places, as the father goes to summer camp and the son goes to Hollywood. Full version.
Prod-HGATE Dist-LCOA 1985

Summer Vegetables C 30 MIN
1/2 IN VIDEO CASSETTE BETA/VHS
Presents a bumper crop of summer vegetables. Surveys the thriving perennial garden. Checks the progress of a fruit orchard.
From The Victory Garden Series.
Prod-WGBHTV Dist-MTI

Summer 68 C 60 MIN
16MM FILM OPTICAL SOUND
Focuses on draft resistance in Boston in an attempt to define the nature of commitment to the 'MOVEMENT' against a backdrop of the summer's activity.
Prod-FRUDOU Dist-NEWSR 1968

Summer, 1966 - A Nation Builds Under Fire B 4 MIN
16MM FILM OPTICAL SOUND J-C A
Studies the struggle of South Vietnam to defend her freedom and to build her future.
From The Screen News Digest Series. Vol 9, Issue 1
LC NO. 72-700282
Prod-HEARST Dist-HEARST 1966

Summer, 1966 - Conquest In Space B 4 MIN
16MM FILM OPTICAL SOUND J-C A
A review of space achievements by the United States in the summer of 1966. Includes scenes of the walk around the world by astronaut Eugene Cernan, the lunar photographs made by Surveyor, and the docking in space of Agena 10 and Gemini 10.
From The Screen News Digest Series. Vol 9, Issue 1
LC NO. 70-700279
Prod-HEARST Dist-HEARST 1966

Summer, 1966 - Mission To Moscow B 5 MIN
16MM FILM OPTICAL SOUND J-C A

A view of life in Moscow, and a report on the visit of Charles de Gaulle to the Russian capital.
From The Screen News Digest Series. Vol 9, Issue 1
LC NO. 79-700281
Prod-HEARST Dist-HEARST 1966

Summer, 1966 - Pilgrimage Into The Past B 4 MIN
16MM FILM OPTICAL SOUND J-C
Shows scenes of an archeological expedition to the land of the Tiwanakus in Bolivia.
From The Screen News Digest Series. Vol 9, Issue 1
LC NO. 75-700280
Prod-HEARST Dist-HEARST 1966

Summer's On C 29 MIN
3/4 INCH VIDEO CASSETTE
Discusses the plentiful supply of edible plants found in the wilds in the summer.
From The Edible Wild Plants Series.
Prod-UMITV Dist-UMITV 1978

Summerhill C 28 MIN
16MM FILM, 3/4 OR 1/2 IN VIDEO J-C A
Visits England's progressive school, Summerhill, founded by Alexander Neill forty-five years ago to prove that students can make decisions about their studies without lessening the quality of their education.
Prod-NFBC Dist-NFBC Prodn-NFBC 1967

Summering House Plants C 29 MIN
2 INCH VIDEOTAPE
See series title for descriptive statement.
From The Making Things Grow III Series.
Prod-WGBHTV Dist-PUBTEL

Summerplay C 16 MIN
16MM FILM OPTICAL SOUND J-C A
Follows several divergent characters at a public beach as they interact with one another. Presents a moving expression of growth, maturity and group pressures.
Prod-COUNTR Dist-COUNTR 1972

Summertime - Wintertime C 4 MIN
16MM FILM OPTICAL SOUND P-I
Presents a collage of winter and summer activities with numerous ideas for comparison, discussion and language development.
From The Mini Movies - Springboard For Learning - Unit 1, Who Are We Series.
LC NO. 76-703088
Prod-MORLAT Dist-MORLAT 1975

Summit C 12 MIN
16MM FILM OPTICAL SOUND
Presents world leaders at the crossroads.
Prod-VANBKS Dist-VANBKS 1963

Summons For The Queen (Zatykac Na Kralovnu) (Czech) B 110 MIN
3/4 OR 1/2 INCH VIDEO CASSETTE
Tells the story of a carefree woman living beyond her means who is summoned for questioning by the Czech police, but in the meantime is found raped and murdered, leading to the discovery of a black-market network. Directed by Dusan Klein. With English subtitles.
Prod-IHF Dist-IHF

Sums And Differences B 10 MIN
3/4 OR 1/2 INCH VIDEO CASSETTE
See series title for descriptive statement.
From The Gary Hill, Part 2 Series.
Prod-EAI Dist-EAI

Sums Up To Six C 15 MIN
3/4 INCH VIDEO CASSETTE P
Shows how, if given a model, a student can write an addition fact with 'plus' and 'minus' symbols.
From The Measure Up Series.
Prod-WCETTV Dist-GPITVL 1977

Sun C 8 MIN
16MM FILM, 3/4 OR 1/2 IN VIDEO K-P
Teaches a sight vocabulary with beautiful photographic settings and folk-song sound track.
From The Starting To Read Series.
Prod-ACI Dist-AIMS 1970

Sun C 15 MIN
3/4 OR 1/2 INCH VIDEO CASSETTE P
Shows Pocus comparing the brightness of sunny days in winter and summer, and contrasts seasonal temperatures. Presents Hocus studying the factors that affect temperature with a little help from Myrtle and animation.
From The Let Me See Series. No. 4
Prod-WETN Dist-AITECH Prodn-STSU 1982

Sun And Other Stars, The B 20 MIN
2 INCH VIDEOTAPE I
See series title for descriptive statement.
From The Science Room Series.
Prod-MCETV Dist-GPITVL Prodn-WVIZTV

Sun And The Earth, The C 15 MIN
3/4 OR 1/2 INCH VIDEO CASSETTE P-I
Discusses the sun and the earth.
From The Why Series.
Prod-WDCNTV Dist-AITECH 1976

Sun And The Wind, The B 41 MIN
16MM FILM OPTICAL SOUND
A dramatization of the Aesop fable the Sun and the Wind in which a man realizes his close association with nature after he has unsuccessfully competed with natural forces.
LC NO. 71-711510
Prod-EARTH Dist-CANCIN 1971

Sun Brushed C 14 MIN
16MM FILM, 3/4 OR 1/2 IN VIDEO C A
Shows a young California couple making love on an outdoor deck overlooking the beach at Big Sur. Discusses such techniques as oral sex and rotating thrust.
Prod-NATSF Dist-MMRC 1974

Sun Causes, Earth Phenomena C 13 MIN
16MM FILM OPTICAL SOUND
Demonstrates how activities on the surface of the sun can cause Earth communication breakdowns, navigation systems failures and power blackouts, as well as affecting the weather and biosphere.
Prod-ALLFP Dist-NSTA 1978

Sun Children C 14 MIN
3/4 OR 1/2 INCH VIDEO CASSETTE C A
Shows a couple on their way to a secluded beach in Big Sur. Demonstrates a variety of sexual acts with its emphasis on mutual oral activity.
Prod-NATSF Dist-MMRC

Sun Country C 18 MIN
16MM FILM OPTICAL SOUND C A
Describes the 'SUN COUNTRY' as beginning at Miami and Miami beach, Florida and ending in the Bahamas and the out-islands. Depicts the land and water sports there and its unspoiled natural beauty. Points out that it is for those escapists who want sights, sounds and things to do that are out of the ordinary.
Prod-MCDO Dist-MCDO 1968

Sun Dagger, The C 28 MIN
16MM FILM, 3/4 OR 1/2 IN VIDEO J-C A
An edited version on the motion picture The Sun Dagger. Tells the story of the discovery in New Mexico of the Sun, an early Indian artifact which marks the extreme positions of both the sun and the moon. Narrated by Robert Redford.
LC NO. 83-706286
Prod-SLSTCE Dist-BULFRG 1983

Sun Dagger, The C 59 MIN
16MM FILM, 3/4 OR 1/2 IN VIDEO J-C A
Tells the story of the discovery in New Mexico of the Sun, an early Indian artifact which marks the extreme positions of both the sun and the moon. Narrated by Robert Redford.
LC NO. 83-706287
Prod-SLSTCE Dist-BULFRG 1983

Sun Dried Foods C 29 MIN
16MM FILM, 3/4 OR 1/2 IN VIDEO H-C A
Focuses on traditional methods of harvesting, preserving and using fruits, vegetables, herbs and meats. Shows a Mexican-American family as they go about the daily routines of an active farm that epitomizes the 'small is beautiful' approach.
Prod-SELFR Dist-BULFRG 1980

Sun Is Alive And Well In Miami, The C 14 MIN
16MM FILM OPTICAL SOUND
Presents the wide range of activities and sports in Miami, the sun and fun capital of the world.
Prod-MIMET Dist-MIMET

Sun Is Red, The C 13 MIN
16MM FILM OPTICAL SOUND
Investigates the problem of pollution and the individual's role in combating it. Uses animation and real film.
Prod-RDCG Dist-AUDPLN

Sun King, - Louis XIV And Versailles C 45 MIN
2 INCH VIDEOTAPE
See series title for descriptive statement.
From The Humanities Series. Unit I - Persons, Places And Events
Prod-WTTWTV Dist-GPITVL

Sun King, The B 29 MIN
16MM FILM, 3/4 OR 1/2 IN VIDEO J-C A
Examines the power and ritual of monarchy by focusing on King Louis XIV. Provides quotes from the French king and shows scenes of the Versailles palace.
From The Legacy Series.
LC NO. 80-707070
Prod-NET Dist-IU 1965

Sun Movie C 10 MIN
16MM FILM OPTICAL SOUND
Presents an animated film showing the Sun passing and a lone person.
LC NO. 77-702659
Prod-CANFDC Dist-CANFDC 1973

Sun Power C 13 MIN
16MM FILM, 3/4 OR 1/2 IN VIDEO I-J
Uses animation to present the sun telling its own story and explaining how its energy is transferred to life on earth.
LC NO. 81-706632
Prod-SHIRE Dist-BARR 1982

Sun Power For Farms C 12 MIN
16MM FILM - 3/4 IN VIDEO J-H A
Presents developments in the use of solar energy in agriculture.
LC NO. 79-706190
Prod-USDA Dist-USNAC 1979

Sun Ra - A Joyful Noise C 60 MIN
16MM FILM, 3/4 OR 1/2 IN VIDEO
Profiles Sun Ra, probably the most flamboyant and eccentric composer in jazz, as he expounds on his music and the world he sees around him.
Prod-MUGGE Dist-DIRECT 1980

Sun Seekers, The - A Surf Odyssey C 27 MIN
16MM FILM OPTICAL SOUND
Communicates the Gospel of Christ by telling about individuals whose lives were changed. Shows the beauty of God's creation, focusing on big-wave surfing.
LC NO. 74-700377
Prod-OUTRCH Dist-OUTRCH 1973

Sun Song - The Mosaic Art Of John De Groot C 26 MIN
16MM FILM OPTICAL SOUND
Examines the work of artist John de Groot as he prepares a large mosaic for downtown Fort Lauderdale, Florida. Traces his years of study and his development of tile murals.
LC NO. 75-700484
Prod-LYON Dist-LYON 1975

Sun Symbol In Art, The C 15 MIN
16MM FILM, 3/4 OR 1/2 IN VIDEO I-J
Shows the response of man to the sun through its significance in a number of works of art ranging from early Egyptian times through modern contemporary artists working in many kinds of media. Shows fourth grade students creating their own sun symbols. Emphasizes the sun as a source of inspiration to the artist.
Prod-BURN Dist-PHENIX 1968

Sun Watchers, The C 30 MIN
16MM FILM, 3/4 OR 1/2 IN VIDEO I-H
Studies the sun's normal and unusual activities as seen from the world's major solar observatories.
From The World We Live In Series.
Prod-TIMELI Dist-MGHT 1968

Sun Will Rise, The C 35 MIN
16MM FILM, 3/4 OR 1/2 IN VIDEO
Tells the story of young members of the African National Congress, sentenced to death or to life imprisonment in South Africa for their activities to end apartheid. Tells the story through the eyes of these young Nationalists and reflects the parents' growing awareness of their children's commitment and sacrifices.
Prod-IDAF Dist-ICARUS 1983

Sun-Maid - The World's Favorite Raisin C 21 MIN
16MM FILM OPTICAL SOUND
Details the history of the Sun-Maid company and the care given to their raisins. Shows how the Sun-Maid raisin girl became one of the world's most recognized trademarks. Presents the various stages of stemming, grading and washing raisins.
Prod-SUNMAD Dist-MTP

Sun, Run And Fun B 15 MIN
2 INCH VIDEOTAPE P
See series title for descriptive statement.
From The Children's Literature Series. No. 30
Prod-NCET Dist-GPITVL Prodn-KUONTV

Sun, Stars And Planets, The B 45 MIN
2 INCH VIDEOTAPE C
See series title for descriptive statement.
From The Physical Science Series. Unit 3 - Astronomy
Prod-CHITVC Dist-GPITVL Prodn-WTTWTV

Sun, The C 15 MIN
16MM FILM OPTICAL SOUND I-C A
Explores the sun's cultural, philosophical and scientific significance to mankind throughout the ages, including the present and future.
Prod-HAPLV Dist-DANPRO 1974

Sun, The C 9 MIN
16MM FILM, 3/4 OR 1/2 IN VIDEO K-I
Tells what the sun is and what its role is in animal and plant life, light and heat energy.
From The Science Series.
Prod-MORLAT Dist-SF 1967

Sun, The C 11 MIN
16MM FILM, 3/4 OR 1/2 IN VIDEO I-J
Follows the curriculum for elementary school astronomy as developed by the Illinois Project. Combines live photography, animation and special effects to investigate some basic concepts about the Sun.
From The Astronomy Series.
Prod-MGHBLA Dist-MGHT Prodn-HABER 1971

Sun, The - Earth's Star C 20 MIN
16MM FILM, 3/4 OR 1/2 IN VIDEO J-C A
Discusses the sun and the impact of its radiation on Earth, including the vital role it plays in photosynthesis and the production of food for mankind. Considers various scientific theories regarding the effects on Earth of sunspot activity and solar flares.
LC NO. 80-706298
Prod-NGS Dist-NGS 1980

Sun, The - Its Power And Promise C 24 MIN
16MM FILM, 3/4 OR 1/2 IN VIDEO I-J
Shows how man has paid tribute to the sun throughout history. Examines the sun's role in the creation of familiar energy sources such as food, wind, petroleum, coal and natural gas. Points out the need for the new and cleaner sources of energy. Evaluates the potential of alternative energy sources such as nuclear energy and geothermal energy. Takes a close look at the source of solar energy, the sun itself. Surveys the present and potential uses of solar energy.
From The Wide World Of Adventure Series.
Prod-AVATLI Dist-EBEC 1977

Sun, The - Power For Our Solar System C 38 MIN
3/4 OR 1/2 INCH VIDEO CASSETTE J-C
Examines the most important aspects of the sun's nature and functioning by explaining its chemical composition and physical structure. Describes the effect of the sun's energy upon Earth and explains the greenhouse effect. Takes a look at those questions about the sun which still remain unanswered.
LC NO. 81-706758
Prod-SCIMAN Dist-GA 1982

Sun, The - Prominences And Flares C
3/4 OR 1/2 INCH VIDEO CASSETTE
Depicts scenes of solar prominences and flares. Shows the relationship between flares and sunspots.
From The Experiments In Space Series.
Prod-EDMEC Dist-EDMEC

Sun, Wind And Wood C 25 MIN
16MM FILM, 3/4 OR 1/2 IN VIDEO J-C A
Shows how some people are using more solar and wind energy and relying less on non-renewable energy. Looks at a 'bio-shelter' home, a house heated by solar power, and a house powered by a windmill.
Prod-NFBC Dist-BNCHMK 1980

Sun's Energy, The C 17 MIN
16MM FILM OPTICAL SOUND I-H
Explains why the sun's energy utilized directly or indirectly is the basis of all life on earth. Shows practical ways in which the sun's energy is being used and how it may be used in the future.
LC NO. FIA60-685
Prod-ACA Dist-ACA 1960

Sun's Gonna Shine, The C 10 MIN
16MM FILM - 3/4 IN VIDEO J-C A
Captures the music and early life of blues singer Lightnin' Hopkins. Visits Hopkins' hometown of Centerville, Texas, where the singer re-creates his decision at the age of eight to stop chopping cotton and sing for his living.
LC NO. 79-707413
Prod-FLOWER Dist-FLOWER 1979

Sunbelt City - Phoenix, Arizona C 20 MIN
16MM FILM, 3/4 OR 1/2 IN VIDEO H-C A
Shows that the city of Phoenix, Arizona is booming with new industry, a new population and, perhaps most importantly, new money. Speculates on the continued attractiveness of a city with such high costs in public services, water, utilities and energy.
From The America In Transition Series.
Prod-BBCTV Dist-FI 1983

Sunbuilders C 20 MIN
16MM FILM, 3/4 OR 1/2 IN VIDEO
Explains the basic concepts of passive solar energy design, showing examples of how these concepts are being transformed into reality by architects, builders and other solar advocates.
LC NO. 81-706429
Prod-USDOE Dist-USNAC Prodn-KIRNHA 1979

Sunday And Monday In Silence C 52 MIN
16MM FILM, 3/4 OR 1/2 IN VIDEO C A
Documents the complications of coping successfully with deafness in the family on both a normal weekday and during the weekend. Describes one family in which normal parents raise two children who were born deaf and another family in which all the family's members are deaf except for one girl with normal hearing.
Prod-THAMES Dist-MEDIAG 1973

Sunday Between Wars C 41 MIN
16MM FILM OPTICAL SOUND
Presents a fictional dialogue between a contemporary woman and Walt Whitman concerning accomplishments and failures in the United States between 1865 and 1917.
LC NO. 79-700290
Prod-MADDOW Dist-MADDOW 1979

Sunday Dinner C 12 MIN
16MM FILM, 3/4 OR 1/2 IN VIDEO J-C A
Tells the story of how an elderly lady and a local junkman collect food, wine and other necessities to make their Sunday dinner cozy and homelike.
Prod-LINSAL Dist-PHENIX 1976

Sunday In Peking C 19 MIN
16MM FILM, 3/4 OR 1/2 IN VIDEO H-C A
Contrasts the new culture of China with the old in the city of Peking.
Prod-ARGOS Dist-TEXFLM 1968

Sunday Lark B 12 MIN
16MM FILM, 3/4 OR 1/2 IN VIDEO I-C A
Pictures a six-year-old girl who wanders into New York's Wall Street on a Sunday afternoon, showing her interest in the staple guns, electric pencil sharpeners, various IBM computers and other office paraphernalia in a huge empty office in a skyscraper.
Prod-CRSCND Dist-MGHT 1963

Sunday Morning B 15 MIN
16MM FILM OPTICAL SOUND
Explores religious feeling and the grandeur and oppressive power of the concept of God. Opens with a sequence showing nature existing as beautiful and pure, and then focuses on the actions of a small girl as she prepares for church.
Prod-UPENN Dist-UPENN 1964

Sunday Morning Dance B 5 MIN
16MM FILM OPTICAL SOUND
Compares studio dance and performance dance.
LC NO. 76-701483
Prod-YORKU Dist-YORKU 1975

Sunday Night Show C 30 MIN
3/4 OR 1/2 INCH VIDEO CASSETTE
Presents basically crazy cooks Larry Bly and Laban Johnson who offer recipes, cooking and shopping tips.
From The Cookin' Cheap Series.
Prod-WBRATV Dist-MDCPB

Sunday Night Supper C 29 MIN
3/4 OR 1/2 INCH VIDEO CASSETTE
See series title for descriptive statement.
From The Julia Child And Company Series.
Prod-WGBHTV Dist-PBS

Sunday Picnic B 11 MIN
16MM FILM OPTICAL SOUND H-C A
Portrays the essence of the generation gap by showing various people who are upset by a young man who flirts with a young girl in their midst. Focuses on the confrontation of the young and the old, which ends in a mutual sense of alienation.
LC NO. 72-700402
Prod-ZAGREB Dist-MMA 1970

Sunflowers - More Than A Pretty Face C 13 MIN
16MM FILM, 3/4 OR 1/2 IN VIDEO P-J
Begins with spring seeding, then blossoms into fields of brilliant yellow as the sunflower plants mature and become ready for harvest. Shows the processing plant where the seeds become golden oil ready for salads and cooking.
Prod-BORTF Dist-BCNFL 1983

Sunken Fleet, The B 11 MIN
16MM FILM OPTICAL SOUND
Explains the feats by skilled deep-sea divers whose work makes possible the refloating of a sunken merchant vessel.
Prod-FILIM Dist-RADIM

Sunken Treasure C 21 MIN
16MM FILM, 3/4 OR 1/2 IN VIDEO I-C
A shortened version of Sunken Treasure. Shows Jacques Cousteau and his crew exploring the site of a wreck believed to be the command ship of the 1641 New World armada. Shows the crew as they test underwater archeological salvaging techniques.
From The Undersea World Of Jacques Cousteau Series.
Prod-METROM Dist-CF 1970

Sunken Treasure C 52 MIN
16MM FILM, 3/4 OR 1/2 IN VIDEO
Explores the site of a wreck believed to be the command ship of the 1641 New World Armada.
From The Undersea World Of Jacques Cousteau Series.
Prod-METROM Dist-CF 1972

Sunken Wrecks C 22 MIN
16MM FILM OPTICAL SOUND
Explores the depths of Key West where the ocean's great ecosystem has absorbed wreckage of centuries-old Spanish galleons up to World War II fighter aircraft. Shows that these vessels now shelter snapper, amberjack, cobia and a myriad of other species of fish.
Prod-BRNSWK Dist-KAROL

Sunlight - A First Film C 9 MIN
16MM FILM, 3/4 OR 1/2 IN VIDEO P-I
Tells how every day the sun brings light and life to the earth. Describes how sunlight brings out the color of things around us, brings us warmth and gives us shadows and changing seasons. Points out that all life on earth needs sunlight.
Prod-NELLES Dist-PHENIX 1971

Sunlight And Shadow In Painting C 11 MIN
16MM FILM, 3/4 OR 1/2 IN VIDEO I-H A
Shows the effects created by light and dark areas on an artist's subject, and how he uses light and simulates shadows with color, line and shading in his painting.
Prod-STOKSF Dist-PHENIX 1968

Sunlit Chariot, The C 30 MIN
3/4 OR 1/2 INCH VIDEO CASSETTE C
See series title for descriptive statement.
From The Art Of Being Human Series. Module 13
Prod-MDCC Dist-MDCC

Sunlit Night's Land Cruise B 15 MIN
16MM FILM OPTICAL SOUND
Portrays an eight day trip by a modern train from southern Sweden to above the Arctic Circle.
Prod-ASI Dist-AUDPLN

Sunny Day, A C 5 MIN
16MM FILM OPTICAL SOUND K-I
Portrays an insect community in puppet animation. Shows how human beings appear and cause the community problems and dangers, which the insects cope with.
From The Adventures In The High Grass Series.
LC NO. 74-702124
Prod-MMA Dist-MMA 1972

Sunny Side Of Life C 56 MIN
16MM FILM - 1/2 IN VIDEO
Documents the Carter family and their music at the Carter Family Fold in southwestern Virginia. Features interviews, dancing and performances by members of the Carter family and other musicians. Includes a visual essay on traditional life and work in the region and the place music holds in it.
Prod-APPAL Dist-APPAL

Sunnyside Up C 7 MIN
16MM FILM OPTICAL SOUND I-C A
Uses a variety of visual techniques to present trees, signs, buildings, designs and windows reflected in water. Includes more somber scenes of the effect pollution could have on the environment.
Prod-NYFLMS Dist-NYFLMS

Sunrise B 110 MIN
16MM FILM SILENT
Shows how a vacationing lady from the city engages the interest of a young farmer and enslaves him. Reveals what happens when she persuades him to murder his wife, sell his farm and join her in the city. Details the many reasons why the plot does not go as planned. Stars George O'Brien and Janet Gaynor. Directed by F W Murnau.
Prod-FOXFC Dist-KILLIS 1927

Sunriver C 26 MIN
16MM FILM OPTICAL SOUND
Shows the planner and the architect of Sunriver, a vacation-home community on the Deschutes River in central Oregon which is designed to function without automobiles. Discusses the probability of the site's becoming a year-round recreation area.
LC NO. 72-700169
Prod-SUNRVP Dist-GROENG 1971

Sunset C 29 MIN
3/4 INCH VIDEO CASSETTE
See series title for descriptive statement.
From The Magic Of Oil Painting Series.
Prod-KOCETV Dist-PUBTEL

Sunset Crater, Arizona C 5 MIN
16MM FILM - 3/4 IN VIDEO
Explains and re-creates the geological phenomena that resulted in Sunset Crater in Arizona's Sunset Crater National Monument.
LC NO. 79-708128
Prod-USNPS Dist-USNAC 1979

Sunset Division - 41st Infantry Division B 13 MIN
16MM FILM, 3/4 OR 1/2 IN VIDEO H A
Presents the film record of the 41st (Sunset) Infantry Division's role in the Pacific during World War II.
Prod-USA Dist-USNAC 1950

Sunshine B 29 MIN
2 INCH VIDEOTAPE K-P
See series title for descriptive statement.
From The Children's Fair Series.
Prod-WMVSTV Dist-PUBTEL

Sunshine Showplace C 14 MIN
16MM FILM OPTICAL SOUND I-C
Tours five major attractions of the city of St Petersburg in Florida.
LC NO. FIA67-628
Prod-FDC Dist-FDC 1966

Sunshine State Of Florida, The C 16 MIN
16MM FILM OPTICAL SOUND K-C A
Examines the sunshine state of Florida, America's year round vacationland.
Prod-BECKLY Dist-BECKLY

Sunshine's On The Way C 30 MIN
16MM FILM, 3/4 OR 1/2 IN VIDEO J-H
A shortened version of the motion picture Sunshine's On The Way. Tells the story of a teenaged assistant at a retirement home who persuades the newest arrival, a jazz trombonist she idolizes, to help the other musicians there to improve their band enough to get a job on the Tonight Show.
Prod-HGATE Dist-LCOA 1980

Sunshine's On The Way C 47 MIN
16MM FILM, 3/4 OR 1/2 IN VIDEO J-H
Tells the story of a teenaged assistant at a retirement home who persuades the newest arrival, a jazz trombonist she idolizes, to help the other musicians there to improve their band enough to get a job on the Tonight Show.
Prod-HGATE Dist-LCOA 1980

Sunshine's On The Way (Captioned) C 30 MIN
16MM FILM, 3/4 OR 1/2 IN VIDEO J-H A
Tells the story of a young girl who persuades a jazz trombonist to help her get a band of senior citizens into good shape. Edited version.
Prod-HGATE Dist-LCOA 1981

Sunshine's On The Way (Captioned) C 47 MIN
16MM FILM, 3/4 OR 1/2 IN VIDEO J-H A
Tells of a teenage girl working at a retirement home who gets a jazz trombonist to help her organize a senior citizen band. Full version.
Prod-HGATE Dist-LCOA 1981

Sunspot Mystery, The - Sun-Weather Connection C 30 MIN
16MM FILM, 3/4 OR 1/2 IN VIDEO H-C A
Covers research done on predicting the Sun's effect on weather, including the discovery of a 22-year drought cycle, solar winds, coronal holes and effects on the ozone layer. Explains research ranging from an analysis of tree rings to solar experiments in Skylab.
From The Nova Series.
LC NO. 79-707253
Prod-WGBHTV Dist-TIMLIF 1977

Sunspot Mystery, The - Sunspots Explained C 31 MIN
16MM FILM, 3/4 OR 1/2 IN VIDEO H-C A
Explores how the Sun's changes affect the Earth. Interweaves 20th century research on aurorae, solar constants, sunspot cycles and tree ring analysis with historical scientific records.
From The Nova Series.
LC NO. 79-707254
Prod-WGBHTV Dist-TIMLIF 1977

Sunstone C 3 MIN
3/4 OR 1/2 INCH VIDEO CASSETTE
Presents the ultimate high-tech program which is synthesized from eight months of work on a digital computer.
Prod-EAI Dist-EAI

Super Bear - The Grizzly C 23 MIN
3/4 OR 1/2 INCH VIDEO CASSETTE K-C A
Introduces the grizzly against the backdrop of Alaska and Yellowstone. Shows a mother grizzly caring for her young.
Prod-NWLDPR Dist-NWLDPR

Super Bowl XI C 20 MIN
16MM FILM OPTICAL SOUND
Presents the story of the 1977 World Championship of pro football.

LC NO. 77-701456
Prod-NFL Dist-NFL 1977

Super Bugs C 14 MIN
3/4 OR 1/2 INCH VIDEO CASSETTE P-I
See series title for descriptive statement.
From The Young At Art Series.
Prod-WSKJTV Dist-AITECH 1980

Super Celsius C 3 MIN
3/4 OR 1/2 INCH VIDEO CASSETTE P-I
Introduces animated superhero Super Celsius, who masquerades as a mild-mannered TV weatherman in order to explain the Celsius temperature scale.
From The Metric Marvels Series.
Prod-NBCTV Dist-GA 1978

Super Chaperone C 30 MIN
3/4 OR 1/2 INCH VIDEO CASSETTE
See series title for descriptive statement.
From The Que Pasa, U S A Series.
Prod-WPBTTV Dist-MDCPB

Super Marketing At The Supermarket C 29 MIN
3/4 OR 1/2 INCH VIDEO CASSETTE H-C A
Deals with techniques supermarkets use to encourage shoppers to buy. Provides an inside look at store layout and displays, games, gimmicks, ad promotions, package design and pricing technique.
From The Be A Better Shopper Series. Program 11
LC NO. 81-707311
Prod-CUETV Dist-CUNIV 1978

Super Realists C 15 MIN
3/4 OR 1/2 INCH VIDEO CASSETTE P-I
See series title for descriptive statement.
From The Young At Art Series.
Prod-WSKJTV Dist-AITECH 1980

Super Sunday - Laughter And Legend C 27 MIN
16MM FILM OPTICAL SOUND
Presents the comedy highlights from the first 13 Super Bowl games.
Prod-ANHBUS Dist-MTP

Super-Artist, Andy Warhol C 22 MIN
16MM FILM OPTICAL SOUND H-C A
A visit with super-artist, Andy Warhol, showing him at work, reviews his views on pop art and presents examples of his work.
LC NO. FIA67-1277
Prod-TORBTB Dist-GROVE 1967

Super-Human Flights Of Submoronic Fancies C 12 MIN
3/4 OR 1/2 INCH VIDEO CASSETTE
Weaves a progression of thoughts on morality and ethics in the modern world.
Prod-EAI Dist-EAI

Super-Vision—A Series
IND
Targets on-the-job people problems, and shows supervisors the different choices possible in handling these problems. Includes a participant's workbook and a leader's guide.
Prod-VCI Dist-DELTAK 1977

Acting The OK Way 034 MIN
Games Are Not Fun 036 MIN
Good Strokes Make Happier Folks 034 MIN
Time Has Come, The 030 MIN
Using The Five You's 037 MIN
When The Unexpected Happens 036 MIN
Who In Me To Who In You 026 MIN
Your Behavior Affects Results 027 MIN

Super-Volt Radiation B 50 MIN
16MM FILM OPTICAL SOUND PRO
Shows the use of high voltage X-rays, cobalt radiation and linear accelerators in the treatment of breast and lung cancers, Hodgkin's disease and other types of cancer.
Prod-CMA Dist-LAWREN

Superb Lyrebird C 10 MIN
16MM FILM OPTICAL SOUND J-H
Presents without spoken commentary, views of the primitive lyrebird and scientific record of the territorial calls of the bird.
LC NO. FIA65-1080
Prod-CSIROA Dist-CSIROA 1963

Supercharging And Fuel Injection B 20 MIN
16MM FILM - 3/4 IN VIDEO
Discusses the supercharging and fuel injection systems used on army vehicles to provide increased horsepower for engines without increasing the size of the engine. Discusses the purpose, components and functions of the supercharging and fuel injection system. Issued in 1956 as a motion picture.
LC NO. 79-707543
Prod-USA Dist-USNAC 1979

Superconducting Magnet For Fusion Research, A C 22 MIN
16MM FILM OPTICAL SOUND C A
Describes the thirteen-ton superconducting magnet now in experimental use at the Lawrence Radiation Laboratory at the University of California at Livermore. Shows how the magnet is used in a supercool environment to confine hydrogen plasma in an attempt to produce controlled fusion energy on earth.
LC NO. 72-702145
Prod-USAEC Dist-USERD 1972

Superconducting Magnets C 13 MIN
16MM FILM OPTICAL SOUND H-C A
Describes the basic design problems of superconducting magnets. Includes pictures of the Argonne National Laboratory's 67,000 Gauss magnet during fabrication and testing.
LC NO. FIE67-135
Prod-ANL Dist-USERD 1966

Superconductors C 24 MIN
16MM FILM, 3/4 OR 1/2 IN VIDEO
Introduces the phenomenon of electrical superconductivity. Shows how superconductors can help clean up pollution, facilitate brain surgery, provide power through special generators, and solve the rapid transit problem with the magnaplane.
Prod-DOCUA Dist-CNEMAG

Superconductors - Tomorrow's Energy Breakthrough Is Here C 21 MIN
16MM FILM OPTICAL SOUND J-C A
Discusses superconductors and future prospects for their application in brain and cancer surgery, for cleaning up pollution in air and water, for providing power and for use in solving rapid transit problems.
LC NO. 76-701714
Prod-DOCUA Dist-CNEMAG

Superconductors - Tomorrow's Energy Breakthrough Is Here C 20 MIN
16MM FILM, 3/4 OR 1/2 IN VIDEO J-C A
Explains what superconductors are and how they work. Shows how they may clean up pollution in air and water, make possible operations deep in the brain, provide power through special generators and solve rapid transit problems with the magneplane, which runs on tracks and can go 100 miles per hour.
From The Coping With Tomorrow Series.
Prod-DOCUA Dist-AIMS 1975

Superficial Back, The C 10 MIN
16MM FILM, 3/4 OR 1/2 IN VIDEO C A
Focuses on the back region. Demonstrates the dissection of the superficial back.
From The Guides To Dissection Series.
Prod-UCLA Dist-TEF

Superfluous Citizen, The C 28 MIN
3/4 OR 1/2 INCH VIDEO CASSETTE
See series title for descriptive statement.
From The All About Welfare Series.
Prod-WITFTV Dist-PBS

Supergrandpa C 20 MIN
16MM FILM OPTICAL SOUND I-C A
Presents in American sign language the story of Gastaf Hakansson and the bicycle race that he won in Sweden in 1951. Signed by Howard Busby.
LC NO. 76-701099
Prod-JOYCE Dist-JOYCE 1975

Superimposition B 15 MIN
16MM FILM OPTICAL SOUND
Includes similies of a slippery television tube gesticulating, breaking and supplying a long view of multiple images.
Prod-VANBKS Dist-VANBKS 1968

Superimposition B 30 MIN
16MM FILM OPTICAL SOUND
Explains the engineering principles involved in superimposition. Demonstrates the various methods of insuring proper line-up of one camera picture with another and surveys some of the most commonly found examples of superimposition.
From The CETO Television Training Films Series.
Prod-CETO Dist-GPITVL

Superjock C 16 MIN
16MM FILM, 3/4 OR 1/2 IN VIDEO J-C A
Shows how an overweight, middle-aged man and his overweight son learn that improper diet, heavy smoking and lack of exercise greatly diminish one's sense of well-being and seriously endanger one's life.
From The Physical Fitness Series.
Prod-ALTSUL Dist-JOU 1978

Superjock Scales Down C 15 MIN
16MM FILM, 3/4 OR 1/2 IN VIDEO J-C A
Tells how Superjock loses 45 pounds and makes major modifications to his life style. Stresses the importance of continued exercise and regular dieting.
From The Physical Fitness Series.
Prod-ALTSUL Dist-JOU 1980

Superlative Horse, The C 36 MIN
16MM FILM, 3/4 OR 1/2 IN VIDEO P-H A
Tells a tale from ancient China which proves that people should not judge things, animals or even other people by their outward appearances, but by their inner qualities. Based on the folk tale The Superlative Horse by Jean Merrill.
Prod-NYSED Dist-PHENIX Prodn-FURRER 1975

Superliners, The - Twilight Of An Era C 59 MIN
16MM FILM, 3/4 OR 1/2 IN VIDEO
Takes a nostalgic look at the luxury liners such as the Normandie, Titanic, Queen Mary, Queen Elizabeth and the Queen Elizabeth 2, which plied the North Atlantic in the first half of the twentieth century.
LC NO. 80-706356
Prod-NGS Dist-NGS 1980

Superman C 142 MIN
16MM FILM OPTICAL SOUND
Stars Christopher Reeve as Superman, the Man of Steel who disguises himself as mild-mannered Clark Kent. Features Margot Kidder, Marlon Brando and Gene Hackman.
Prod-WB Dist-SWANK

Superman And The Bride C 40 MIN
16MM FILM, 3/4 OR 1/2 IN VIDEO J-C A
Shows how stereotyped images of men and women are perpetuated by messages in the mass media because the phenomenon benefits them financially. Stereotypes are broken when women are portrayed as active, confident and self-reliant, dispelling the myth that all men are Supermen and all women are brides.
Prod-THAMES Dist-MEDIAG 1977

Supermarket (2nd Ed) C 14 MIN
16MM FILM, 3/4 OR 1/2 IN VIDEO P
Takes a behind-the-scenes look at the running of a supermarket. Features the store manager, who explains what kind of skills and how much work is involved. Shows delivery men, butchers, produce people, stockmen and bookkeepers.
LC NO. 83-706800
Prod-HIGGIN Dist-HIGGIN 1984

Supermarket - Ten Cent Store C 29 MIN
2 INCH VIDEOTAPE
See series title for descriptive statement.
From The Making Things Grow III Series.
Prod-WGBHTV Dist-PUBTEL

Supermarket Botany C 15 MIN
3/4 OR 1/2 INCH VIDEO CASSETTE
Discusses the principle parts of plants, using common supermarket fruits and vegetables as examples. Describes the structure and role of plants in many familiar items.
Prod-CBSC Dist-CBSC

Supermarket Dollar C 14 MIN
2 INCH VIDEOTAPE
See series title for descriptive statement.
From The Living Better I Series.
Prod-MAETEL Dist-PUBTEL

Supermarket, The - A Great American Invention C 28 MIN
16MM FILM OPTICAL SOUND
Show changes in goods and services provided by the supermarket as a result of advanced technology and the changing social needs of Americans.
LC NO. 80-701622
Prod-FMI Dist-MTP Prodn-CRANDL 1980

Supermarket, The Mammoth Mousetrap C
3/4 OR 1/2 INCH VIDEO CASSETTE
Discusses how changes in food shopping habits can effect weight control. Encourages expression of feeling about the problems involved in shopping for food while one is trying to lose weight.
Prod-DIETF Dist-KORSCR Prodn-MUTRAP

Supermarkets C 30 MIN
3/4 OR 1/2 INCH VIDEO CASSETTE
Presents tips on using supermarkets.
From The Consumer Survival Series. Shopping
Prod-MDCPB Dist-MDCPB

Supermarkets / Orthodontics / Condominiums C
3/4 OR 1/2 INCH VIDEO CASSETTE
Discusses various aspects of supermarkets, orthodontics and condominiums.
From The Consumer Survival Series.
Prod-MDCPB Dist-MDCPB

Supermemory—A Series

Reveals how to develop a dynamic memory quickly and easily by association.
Prod-CSU Dist-AMCEE

Supermemory, Pt 01 060 MIN
Supermemory, Pt 02 060 MIN
Supermemory, Pt 03 060 MIN
Supermemory, Pt 04 060 MIN
Supermemory, Pt 05 060 MIN
Supermemory, Pt 06 060 MIN
Supermemory, Pt 07 060 MIN
Supermemory, Pt 08 060 MIN
Supermemory, Pt 09 060 MIN
Supermemory, Pt 10 060 MIN

Supermemory, Pt 01 C 60 MIN
3/4 OR 1/2 INCH VIDEO CASSETTE
Presents the goals of the Supermemory series and tells how to remember numbers.
From The Supermemory Series.
Prod-CSU Dist-AMCEE

Supermemory, Pt 02 C 60 MIN
3/4 OR 1/2 INCH VIDEO CASSETTE
Tells how to recall long lists of facts.
From The Supermemory Series.
Prod-CSU Dist-AMCEE

Supermemory, Pt 03 C 60 MIN
3/4 OR 1/2 INCH VIDEO CASSETTE
Explains the association technique, its practical application and value. Shows how to recall long lists of facts, concepts and ideas and how to recall familiar information.
From The Supermemory Series.
Prod-CSU Dist-AMCEE

Supermemory, Pt 04 C 60 MIN
3/4 OR 1/2 INCH VIDEO CASSETTE
Tells how to remember names and faces.
From The Supermemory Series.
Prod-CSU Dist-AMCEE

Supermemory, Pt 05 C 60 MIN
3/4 OR 1/2 INCH VIDEO CASSETTE
Illustrates how to accurately and speedily remember facts from reading. Includes examples of professional, personal and academic reading material.
From The Supermemory Series.
Prod-CSU Dist-AMCEE

Supermemory, Pt 06 C 60 MIN
3/4 OR 1/2 INCH VIDEO CASSETTE
Shows how to master numbers, including telephone numbers, appointments and schedules, formulas and equations.
From The Supermemory Series.
Prod-CSU Dist-AMCEE

Supermemory, Pt 07 C 60 MIN
3/4 OR 1/2 INCH VIDEO CASSETTE
Shows how to improve concentration and how to eliminate absentmindedness.
From The Supermemory Series.
Prod-CSU Dist-AMCEE

Supermemory, Pt 08 C 60 MIN
3/4 OR 1/2 INCH VIDEO CASSETTE
Shows how to spell perfectly, how to instantly recall complicated mathematics, diagrams and locations. Includes how to take better notes during lectures and meetings.
From The Supermemory Series.
Prod-CSU Dist-AMCEE

Supermemory, Pt 09 C 60 MIN
3/4 OR 1/2 INCH VIDEO CASSETTE
Shows how to remember jokes, anecdotes and quotations for quotations for speeches, presentations and meetings.
From The Supermemory Series.
Prod-CSU Dist-AMCEE

Supermemory, Pt 10 C 60 MIN
3/4 OR 1/2 INCH VIDEO CASSETTE
Tells how to learn vocabularies, terms and definitions in seconds, and how to learn a foreign language in half the time. Summarizes accomplishments, objectives and goals of the Supermemory series.
From The Supermemory Series.
Prod-CSU Dist-AMCEE

Supermouse C 8 MIN
16MM FILM, 3/4 OR 1/2 IN VIDEO P-I
Presents an animated film featuring a day in the life of Supermouse, who lives the perfect existence, until he wakes up and finds out it is only a dream.
Prod-KRATKY Dist-PHENIX

Supernovas And Pulsars C 29 MIN
3/4 INCH VIDEO CASSETTE C A
Contrasts nova with supernova. Describes and illustrates current theories of conditions leading to the supernova event. Discusses properties of the neutron star.
From The Project Universe - Astronomy Series. Lesson 25
Prod-COAST Dist-CDTEL Prodn-SCCON

Superport C 13 MIN
3/4 OR 1/2 INCH VIDEO CASSETTE
Goes on a musical voyage to scenic Bantry, Ireland, where super-tankers are blending with the environment in the struggle for energy.
Prod-HBS Dist-IVCH

Superpower Diplomacy - Should The U S Reject Detente As Its Strategy In Dealing... C 59 MIN
3/4 INCH VIDEO CASSETTE
Presents a debate on whether or not the United States should reject detente as its strategy when dealing with the Soviet Union. Features Elmo Zumwalt and Lincoln P Bloomfield.
From The Advocates Series.
Prod-WGBHTV Dist-PUBTEL

Supersonic Laboratory C 16 MIN
16MM FILM OPTICAL SOUND
Discusses past and present facilities of the supersonic test tract at the Naval Weapons Center in China Lake, California.
LC NO. 74-706590
Prod-USN Dist-USNAC 1971

Supersonic Thunderbirds C 14 MIN
16MM FILM OPTICAL SOUND
Visits the Supersonic Thunderbirds jet aerobats in their homes. Shows how they live during their offduty time. Includes scenes of the men in action.
LC NO. FIE63-116
Prod-USDD Dist-USNAC 1959

Superstar C 30 MIN
3/4 OR 1/2 INCH VIDEO CASSETTE H-C A
Presents a story centering on the member of a musical band. Uses the story to try to reduce the minority isolation of Mexican-American students by showing the teenager as an individual, as a member of a unique cultural group and as a member of a larger complex society.
From The La Esquina (English) Series.
Prod-SWEDL Dist-GPITVL 1976

Superstar Sports Tapes—A Series

Presents tapes that discuss the fundamentals of water skiing. Includes rules, technique and equipment.
Prod-TRASS Dist-TRASS

Barefoot Skiing	120 MIN
Beginning And Intermediate Skiing	045 MIN
Jumping	085 MIN
Overall Skiing	030 MIN
Slalom	080 MIN
Trick Skiing	105 MIN
Waterskiing For Kids	030 MIN

Superstitions C 29 MIN
2 INCH VIDEOTAPE
Features Shirley Winston, psychic author and lecturer, joining Dr Puryear in an examination of modern day superstitions and their origins.
From The Who Is Man Series.
Prod-WHROTV Dist-PUBTEL

Supervised Clinical Sexology C
3/4 OR 1/2 INCH VIDEO CASSETTE PRO
See series title for descriptive statement.
From The Independent Study In Human Sexuality Series.
Prod-MMRC Dist-MMRC

Supervising And People Problems C 21 MIN
16MM FILM, 3/4 OR 1/2 IN VIDEO A
Focuses on skills needed by managers who must deal with employees' personal problems that affect work performances. Uses both dramatized episodes and lectures.
From The Supervising For Results Series.
Prod-INCC Dist-PHENIX 1982

Supervising And The Organization C 21 MIN
16MM FILM, 3/4 OR 1/2 IN VIDEO A
Deals with the importance of good supervision to an organization.
From The Supervising For Results Series.
Prod-INCC Dist-PHENIX 1982

Supervising For Productivity C 18 MIN
16MM FILM, 3/4 OR 1/2 IN VIDEO A
Demonstrates how good supervision can aid productivity.
From The Supervising For Results Series.
Prod-INCC Dist-PHENIX 1982

Supervising For Results—A Series
16MM FILM, 3/4 OR 1/2 IN VIDEO A
Deals with various aspects of supervision.
Prod-INCC Dist-PHENIX 1982

Supervising And People Problems	021 MIN
Supervising And The Organization	021 MIN
Supervising For Productivity	018 MIN
Supervisory Communication Skills	021 MIN

Supervising For Safety—A Series

Deals with the foreman as a leader and supervisor of people. Stresses that human relations and foremanemployee relations are often important in accident causation.
Prod-NSC Dist-NSC

Call 'EM ON THE CARPET	10 MIN
Fragile, Handle Feelings With Care	10 MIN
It's An Order	10 MIN

Supervising The Disadvantaged—A Series

Seeks to develop an awareness in managers and supervisors of some of the problems they'll face in working with the disadvantaged. Discusses techniques for interviewing, training, resolving conflict and motivation.
Prod-RESEM Dist-RESEM

General Problems In Supervising The	
Interviewing The Disadvantaged	011 MIN
Motivating The Disadvantaged	010 MIN
Resolving Interpersonal Conflicts	011 MIN
Training The Disadvantaged	011 MIN

Supervising Women Workers B 11 MIN
16MM FILM - 3/4 IN VIDEO
Shows a plant manager telling his foreman what to expect from women workers. Issued in 1944 as a motion picture.
From The Problems In Supervision Series.
LC NO. 79-706450
Prod-USOE Dist-USNAC Prodn-KER 1979

Supervising Workers On The Job B 10 MIN
16MM FILM - 3/4 IN VIDEO
Illustrates good and poor methods of supervision, including the necessity of obtaining the confidence of workers and the dangers of actions which indicate snooping. Issued in 1944 as a motion picture.
From The Problems In Supervision Series.
LC NO. 79-706452
Prod-USOE Dist-USNAC Prodn-CARFI 1979

Supervising Workers On The Job (Spanish) B 10 MIN
16MM FILM OPTICAL SOUND
Dramatizes incidents illustrating good and poor methods of supervision, including the necessity for obtaining -snoopervising.-
From The Problems In Supervision Series.
LC NO. FIE62-83
Prod-USOE Dist-USNAC 1944

Supervision B 28 MIN
16MM FILM OPTICAL SOUND PRO
Presents a record of an actual supervisory interview illustrating the consultee-centered reduction of theme interference method of consultation as taught by Gerald Caplan, MD, laboratory of community psychiatry, Harvard Medical School.
Prod-HMS Dist-HMS 1964

Supervision C 8 MIN
16MM FILM, 3/4 OR 1/2 IN VIDEO
Examines the role of the supervisor in risk control and demonstrates that effective supervision reduces accidents.
From The Safety And You Series.
Prod-FILCOM Dist-FILCOM

Supervision De Los Obreros En Su Trabajo B 10 MIN
3/4 INCH VIDEO CASSETTE
A Spanish language videocassette. Uses dramatized incidents to illustrate good and poor methods of supervision, discussing the importance of obtaining the confidence of workers and describing the dangers of 'snoopervising'. Issued in 1959 as a motion picture.
LC NO. 79-706681
Prod-USOE Dist-USNAC 1979

Supervision In Vocational Rehabilitation Counseling C 50 MIN
16MM FILM OPTICAL SOUND C T
Helps counseling students, counselors, administrators and supervisors identify the essential interpersonal aspects of the supervisory process in vocational rehabilitation counseling.
LC NO. 73-702922
Prod-CFDC Dist-CFDC 1966

Supervision Prescription C 30 MIN
3/4 OR 1/2 INCH VIDEO CASSETTE A
Deals with supervision techniques in the health care industry. Uses story format showing a new head nurse who learns fundamentals of management.
Prod-AMEDIA Dist-AMEDIA

Supervisor And OJT—A Series

Deals with the supervisor's responsibility for on-the-job training (OJT) and presents the basic three-step process for teaching specific skills or procedures. Offers guidelines for task analysis, writing training objectives and evaluating training.
Prod-RESEM Dist-RESEM

Analyzing For Training	012 MIN
Following Up On Training	009 MIN
How To Do On-The-Job Training	012 MIN
Preparing Training Objectives	012 MIN
Training For Upward Mobility	016 MIN

Supervisor As A Classroom Instructor—A Series

Provides some elementary teaching theory, practical help for writing objectives, classroom teaching techniques and evaluation of training sessions for supervisors who conduct classroom training sessions.
From The Supervisor And OJT Series.
Prod-RESEM Dist-RESEM

Communications And Learning Process	011 MIN
Effective Teaching Techniques	012 MIN
Evaluation And Follow-Up	012 MIN
Helping The Learner Learn	010 MIN
Preplanning And Objectives	011 MIN
Teaching-Learning Process, The	011 MIN

Supervisor As A Communicator, The C 12 MIN
3/4 OR 1/2 INCH VIDEO CASSETTE
Shows how the supervisor is in a unique position as a communicator because he/she must communicate both up and down the organizational ladder. Shows how to develop essential techniques for communicating effectively in both directions.
From The Effective Communicating Skills Series.
Prod-RESEM Dist-RESEM

Supervisor As A Leader, The B 27 MIN
3/4 INCH VIDEO CASSETTE
Illustrates poor supervisory practices. Issued in 1944 as a motion picture.
From The Problems In Supervision Series.
LC NO. 79-706453
Prod-USOE Dist-USNAC Prodn-CARFI 1979

Supervisor As An Educator, The C 12 MIN
16MM FILM - 3/4 IN VIDEO
Shows supervisors how to plan, present, evaluate and follow up on safety instructions to their people and keep them safety conscious.
Prod-ALLIED Dist-BNA

Supervisor, The C 15 MIN
16MM FILM OPTICAL SOUND
Observes a foreman at a gas plant and his methods of supervision in a hazardous environment.
From The H2S Training Series.
LC NO. 77-700318
Prod-AWCB Dist-FLMWST Prodn-FLMWST 1977

Supervisor, The C 20 MIN
3/4 OR 1/2 INCH VIDEO CASSETTE
Concentrates on supervision on hazardous environments. Shows a supervisor's effectiveness by his intelligent behavior and his ways of relating to the people about him.
From The Hydrogen Sulphide Safety Series,
Prod-FLMWST Dist-FLMWST

Supervisor, The - Motivating Through Insight C 12 MIN
16MM FILM, 3/4 OR 1/2 IN VIDEO PRO
Shows techniques of employee motivation. Explains that in order to motivate people to do their work well, the supervisor must develop insight into human emotions, his own as well as those of the employees.
From The Professional Management Program Series.
LC NO. 74-700227
Prod-NEM Dist-NEM 1971

Supervisor's Role In Food Distribution—A Series

Covers the supervisor's role in meeting the requirements of laws governing holding, shipping and receiving foods.
Prod-PLAID Dist-PLAID

Compliance With Food Law	021 MIN
Involving Hourly Personnel	016 MIN
Pest Management And Programs	014 MIN
Pesticides And Pest Management	026 MIN
Recognition Of Defects	024 MIN

Supervisor's Role In Hiring New Employees, The C 20 MIN
3/4 OR 1/2 INCH VIDEO CASSETTE
Explains how to reduce chances for error in selecting and placing new employees. Dramatizes real-life situations so supervisors can understand why and where difficulties arise.
Prod-BBP Dist-BBP

Supervisor's Role In Increasing Productivity, The C 20 MIN
3/4 OR 1/2 INCH VIDEO CASSETTE
Dramatizes the strategies that successful supervisors use to insure high rates of production.
Prod-BBP Dist-BBP

Supervisor's Role In Preventing Employee Pilferage And Theft, The C 20 MIN
3/4 OR 1/2 INCH VIDEO CASSETTE
Shows supervisors that their attitude can encourage or discourage employee pilferage rates.
Prod-BBP Dist-BBP

Supervisor's Role In Preventing Grievances And Arbitration, The C 20 MIN
3/4 OR 1/2 INCH VIDEO CASSETTE
Reveals through real-life dramatizations how four common supervisory mistakes magnify minor disputes into heated confrontations. Shows how to correct these mistakes.
Prod-BBP Dist-BBP

Supervisor's Role In Quality Control, The C 20 MIN
3/4 OR 1/2 INCH VIDEO CASSETTE
Shows supervisors what they must do to get top-grade quality consistently.
Prod-BBP Dist-BBP

Supervisor's Role In Security, The C 20 MIN
3/4 OR 1/2 INCH VIDEO CASSETTE
Provides supervisors with practical techniques they can use to discourage thieves from breaking into the company.
Prod-BBP Dist-BBP

Supervisor's Role In Simplifying Work Procedures, The C 20 MIN
3/4 OR 1/2 INCH VIDEO CASSETTE
Presents five sequences modeled on real-life situations in a typical plant where supervisors and managers analyze procedures to find hidden problems, uncover weak links and develop a more productive work force.
Prod-BBP Dist-BBP

Supervisor's Role In Training New Employees, The C 20 MIN
3/4 OR 1/2 INCH VIDEO CASSETTE
Stresses the necessity of getting new employees off to the right start.
Prod-BBP Dist-BBP

Supervisor's Safety Meeting, The C
16MM FILM - 3/4 IN VIDEO A
Shows how to plan, conduct and participate in meetings to establish safety policies and procedures.
Prod-BNA Dist-BNA 1983

Supervisors And Arbitration, The C 20 MIN
3/4 OR 1/2 INCH VIDEO CASSETTE
Reveals through actual documented grievance cases the five leading reasons why disciplinary penalties are very often reversed at arbitration.
Prod-BBP Dist-BBP

Supervisors And Interpersonal Relations–A Series

Examines the supervisor's role in managing attitudes and interpersonal relations, within the work group. Includes suggestions for determining causes of conflict and some ways it may be reduced or eliminated.
Prod-RESEM Dist-RESEM

General Problems Of Interpersonal Conflict 011 MIN
Improving Attitudes Toward Subordinates 014 MIN
Improving Attitudes Toward Supervision 012 MIN
Improving Relations Between Peers 012 MIN
Reducing Conflict In The Organization 014 MIN

Supervisory Communication Skills C 21 MIN
16MM FILM, 3/4 OR 1/2 IN VIDEO A
Focuses on the skills supervisors need in order to communicate beneficially with their employees, their fellow managers and their superiors. Uses both dramatized episodes and lectures.
From The Supervising For Results Series.
Prod-INCC Dist-PHENIX 1982

Supervisory Development For Law Enforcement–A Series
16MM FILM, 3/4 OR 1/2 IN VIDEO
Employs open-ended vignettes to show how police supervisory personnel should handle leadership and discipline problems.
Prod-HAR Dist-MTI

Discipline 020 MIN
Leadership 018 MIN

Supervisory Error C 12 MIN
16MM FILM - 3/4 IN VIDEO
Points out that the chain of responsibility for safety is company-wide, ranging from training workers properly and overseeing their work to buying equipment on the basis of quality, not price.
Prod-ALLIED Dist-BNA

Supervisory Grid, The C 25 MIN
16MM FILM - 3/4 IN VIDEO
Uses individual vignettes showing effective and ineffective styles of supervision. Discusses the leadership process, awareness of personal leadership styles and self-development. Based on the book The Grid For Supervisory Effectiveness by Robert R Blake and Jane Srygley Moutoun.
LC NO. 77-700004
Prod-BNA Dist-BNA 1976

Supervisory Leadership–A Series
IND
Emphasizes basic human relations, tasks and skills in supervisory leadership.
LC NO. 72-703320
Prod-EDSD Dist-EDSD

Attitudes Of People 29 MIN
Basic Skills Of Effective Leadership 29 MIN
Fundamental Duties Of The Supervisor 29 MIN
Group Participation 29 MIN
I Pattern Of Behavior, The 29 MIN
Improving Skills Of Communication 29 MIN
Improving Skills Of Listening 29 MIN
Levels Of Human Need 29 MIN

Supervisory Liability, Management Responsibility And Accountability C 24 MIN
16MM FILM, 3/4 OR 1/2 IN VIDEO
Stresses the identification and reduction of risks in minimizing areas of responsibility for which police supervisory personnel may be held civilly liable.
From The Police Civil Liability Series. Part 5
Prod-HAR Dist-MTI Prodn-BAY 1979

Supervisory Management Course, Pt 1 (French) C 8 MIN
3/4 OR 1/2 INCH VIDEO CASSETTE
Presents an inclusive course in the principles and applications of professional management, featuring techniques for team-building and setting objectives.
Prod-AMA Dist-AMA

Supervisory Management Course, Pt 1 (Spanish) C 8 MIN
3/4 OR 1/2 INCH VIDEO CASSETTE
Presents an inclusive course in the principles and applications of professional management, featuring techniques for team-building and setting objectives.
Prod-AMA Dist-AMA

Supervisory Management Course, Pt 1–A Series

Helps people make the critical transition from worker to supervisor. Attacks the seven key management areas in which supervisors are tested most vigorously including planning, organization, control, setting standards of performance, communication, motivation and decision-making.
Prod-AMA Dist-AMA

Communications 020 MIN
Controlling - Keeping Plans On Target 020 MIN
Decision-Making 020 MIN
Motivation - The Test Of Leadership 020 MIN
Nature Of Management, The 020 MIN
Organizing - Structuring The Work Of The Plan 020 MIN
Planning - The Future's First Step 020 MIN
Standards And Appraisal - Aids To Control 020 MIN

Supervisory Management Course, Pt 2–A Series

Offers a comprehensive course covering the basics for all pre-supervisory personnel and line and staff supervisors who want a solid grounding in people skills.
Prod-AMA Dist-AMA

Supervisory Responsibility C 22 MIN
3/4 OR 1/2 INCH VIDEO CASSETTE
Explores the concept of food protection, coupled with the ability to see and recognize problems common to food processing plants from the point of view of the supervisor.
From The Food Plant Supervisor - Understanding And Performing Inplant Food Safety Insp Series.
Prod-PLAID Dist-PLAID

Supervisory Training (Industrial)–A Series
16MM FILM, 3/4 OR 1/2 IN VIDEO A
Deals with various aspects of supervision in an industrial setting.
Prod-CRMP Dist-CRMP 1983

Assessing Employee Performance (Industry)
Coaching For Improved Performance (Industry)
Dealing With Employee Complaints (Industry)
Dealing With Employee Conflicts (Industry)
Dealing With Employee Response To Controls
Delegating Effectively (Industry)
Fundamental Skills Of Communicating With
Fundamental Skills Of Managing People
Getting Employee Commitment To The Plan
Giving Orders And Instructions (Industry)
Implementing Change (Industry)
Improving Employee Work Habits (Industry)
Terminating An Employee (Industry)
Training The Trainer
Using Positive Discipline (Industry)

Supervisory Training - Office–A Series
16MM FILM, 3/4 OR 1/2 IN VIDEO A
Discusses various aspects of office supervision.
Prod-CRMP Dist-CRMP 1983

Assessing Employee Performance (Office)
Coaching For Improved Performance (Office)
Dealing With Employee Complaints (Office)
Dealing With Employee Conflicts (Office)
Dealing With Employee Response To Controls
Delegating Effectively (Office)
Fundamental Skills Of Communicating With
Fundamental Skills Of Managing People (Office)
Getting Employee Commitment To The Plan
Giving Orders And Instructions (Office)
Implementing Change (Office)
Improving Employee Work Habits (Office)
Terminating An Employee (Office)
Training The Trainer
Using Positive Discipline (Office)

Supervisory Training–A Series

Motivates metal mine supervisory personnel to stress safety in all facets of the mining process.
LC NO. 74-705723
Prod-USBM Dist-USNAC 1969

Man And His Habits 13 MIN
Man's Shortcomings 13 MIN
Motivation - A Means To Accident Prevention 10 MIN
Safety Consciousness 10 MIN

Superwelder C 16 MIN
16MM FILM, 3/4 OR 1/2 IN VIDEO
Shows welding processes and applications in maintenance shop settings. Emphasizes basic measures for protecting the body and equipping the work area. Demonstrates how to handle special circumstances or unsafe conditions.
Prod-ERF Dist-MTI

Superwelder, The C 16 MIN
3/4 OR 1/2 INCH VIDEO CASSETTE
Features welding and cutting operations with detailed guide to safety precautions before, during and after welding.
Prod-EDRF Dist-EDRF

Supplemental Foods C 13 MIN
3/4 OR 1/2 INCH VIDEO CASSETTE J-H A
Teaches how to recognize when babies are ready for more than just milk, and what kinds of food to include.
From The Nutrition For The Newborn Series. Pt III
Prod-POAPLE Dist-POAPLE

Supplementing Direct Experiences B 30 MIN
2 INCH VIDEOTAPE
Shows the science teacher how to select reference materials which enable children to acquire and develop skills of obtaining valid information from sources other than direct experience.
From The Science In Your Classroom Series.
Prod-WENHTV Dist-GPITVL

Supply C 19 MIN
16MM FILM, 3/4 OR 1/2 IN VIDEO H A
Shows how the amount of goods produced and supplied responds to market price and how anticipated sales, selling prices, costs and profits guide a potential producer.
From The People On Market Street Series.
Prod-FNDREE Dist-WDEMCO Prodn-KAHNT 1977

Supply C 30 MIN
3/4 OR 1/2 INCH VIDEO CASSETTE T
Presents Dr Willard M Kniep of Arizona State University instructing teachers in the strategies and skills of teaching children economics and consumer education concepts. Focuses on the topic of supply by explaining it and then demonstrating specific approaches that teachers can use in their classrooms.
From The Economics Exchange Series. Program 3
LC NO. 82-706415
Prod-KAETTV Dist-GPITVL 1981

Supply And Demand C 14 MIN
16MM FILM, 3/4 OR 1/2 IN VIDEO J-H
Defines the economic forces of supply and demand, and shows how they influence prices and the types of goods and amounts that are produced. Points out that producers and consumers communicate with each other through these forces, with the result that an equilibrium price is set, but seldom maintained for a long time.
Prod-GREENF Dist-PHENIX 1980

Supply And Demand - Price And The Consumer C 10 MIN
16MM FILM, 3/4 OR 1/2 IN VIDEO
Introduces the law of supply and demand. Compares markets in which prices are fixed to markets in which prices change in response to demand and supply.
From The Foundations Of Wealth Series.
Prod-FOTH Dist-FOTH

Supply And Demand - Price And The Producer C 10 MIN
16MM FILM, 3/4 OR 1/2 IN VIDEO
Shows how supply and demand affect price. Discusses how producers react to changing prices.
From The Foundations Of Wealth Series.
Prod-FOTH Dist-FOTH

Supply And Demand - What Sets The Price C 30 MIN
3/4 OR 1/2 INCH VIDEO CASSETTE C
See series title for descriptive statement.
From The Economics USA Series.
Prod-WEFA Dist-ANNCPB

Supply Lines C 20 MIN
3/4 INCH VIDEO CASSETTE I
Emphasizes the importance of truck, rail and air freight in keeping a city supplied with the needs of a population. Looks at the significance of water, gas and electric lines.
From The Exploring Our Nation Series.
Prod-KRMATV Dist-GPITVL 1975

Supply Manager's Dilemma, The C 19 MIN
16MM FILM, 3/4 OR 1/2 IN VIDEO
Describes the influence of order costs, holding costs and shortages in determining supply management policy.
Prod-USN Dist-USNAC 1960

Supply Schedule For Wumpets, A C 10 MIN
16MM FILM, 3/4 OR 1/2 IN VIDEO H-C

Distills the principles of economists such as Adam Smith, David Ricardo and Alfred Marshall. Defines the law of supply and shows the effect of a change in the quantity supplied and a change in supply.
From The Economics Series.
Prod-MEDIAG Dist-MEDIAG 1981

Support During Labor C 20 MIN
16MM FILM OPTICAL SOUND PRO
Shows techniques of giving emotional and physical support throughout normal labor with particular attention to positions that increase comfort.
Prod-UMISS Dist-UMISS 1959

Support Motion C 60 MIN
3/4 OR 1/2 INCH VIDEO CASSETTE C
Gives a wind example and earthquake example of support motion.
From The Fundamentals Of Dynamic Analysis For Structural Design Series.
Prod-USCCE Dist-AMCEE

Support Your Child In School C 1 MIN
16MM FILM OPTICAL SOUND A
Stresses the importance of parental involvement in children's school activities.
LC NO. 75-701991
Prod-LEECC Dist-LEECC 1975

Support Your Local Poet C 27 MIN
3/4 INCH VIDEO CASSETTE H-C A
Deals with the life and work of 25-year-old poet and rock journalist Steve Turner.
Prod-CHERIO Dist-GPITVL

Supporting A Candidate C 15 MIN
3/4 OR 1/2 INCH VIDEO CASSETTE H
Shows how individual citizens can work on behalf of a political candidate.
From The By The People Series.
Prod-CTI Dist-CTI

Supporting Ongoing Operations C 45 MIN
3/4 OR 1/2 INCH VIDEO CASSETTE
Stresses that the information system user must remain involved after the system is implemented and that data accuracy and system evaluation are two major concerns of the user at this phase of the system life cycle.
From The User Responsibilities In Information Management Series.
Prod-DELTAK Dist-DELTAK

Supportive Care C 28 MIN
16MM FILM - 3/4 IN VIDEO PRO
Demonstrates nursing care for the neurologically disabled patient designed to restore a normal range of joint motion, intact skin, adequate weight and skin turgor, adequate sleep and rest and normal fecal elimination.
From The Neurologically Disabled Patient, Pt 1 - Nursing During The Acute Stage Series.
LC NO. 77-700604
Prod-AJN Dist-AJN Prodn-TVPC 1977

Supportive Care Measures - Granulocyte And Platelet Transfusions C 20 MIN
3/4 INCH VIDEO CASSETTE
Discusses blood component replacement factors.
Prod-UTAHTI Dist-UTAHTI

Supportive Coaching C 30 MIN
3/4 OR 1/2 INCH VIDEO CASSETTE
Distinguishes between 'boss' and 'manager.' Covers the steps essential for achievement and relates them to the manager's task of stimulating accomplishment by his people.
From The Performance Reviews That Build Commitment Series. Session 5
Prod-PRODEV Dist-DELTAK

Suppose That All Animals And All Plants Are Represented By The Branches Of A Tree - The... C 52 MIN
16MM FILM, 3/4 OR 1/2 IN VIDEO H-C A
Speculates that animals and plants are represented by the branches of a tree, the tree of life. Reveals how Charles Darwin gets more clues on evolution from the Galapagos Island, returns to England after a five-year voyage and settles down to a life of science.
From The Voyages Of Charles Darwin Series.
Prod-BBCTV Dist-TIMLIF 1980

Suppose That All Animals And All Plants Are Represented By Branches Of A Tree, A Tree Of... C 52 MIN
1/2 IN VIDEO CASSETTE (VHS)
Complete title reads Suppose That All Animals And All Plants Are Represented By Branches Of A Tree, A Tree Of Life. Tells about the H M S Beagle returning to England and Darwin settling into his science career.
From The Voyage Of Charles Darwin Series.
Prod-OHC Dist-HRC

Suppose There Were Only People C 15 MIN
3/4 OR 1/2 INCH VIDEO CASSETTE K-P
Shows that human beings depend on other living things.
From The Dragons, Wagons And Wax, Set 1 Series.
Prod-CTI Dist-CTI

Suppression Of Food Intake By Experimental Obesity B 18 MIN
16MM FILM OPTICAL SOUND
Shows the surgical preparation of a rat for an experiment to determine whether action of the hypothalmus controls obesity. Explains the rationale behind the psychological experiment, and shows the surgery on the rat in detail.
Prod-UPENN Dist-UPENN 1961

Supraomohyoid Neck Dissection C 13 MIN
16MM FILM OPTICAL SOUND PRO
Demonstrates a supraomohyoid neck dissection following surgery of the lip. Shows the anatomical structures in detail as the entire supraomohyoid lymphatics are removed, together with the sub-maxillary gland.
Prod-ACYDGD Dist-ACY 1950

Supraperiosteal And Incisive Injections, The C 20 MIN
16MM FILM OPTICAL SOUND
Demonstrates for dentists and dental students the local anesthetic injections frequently used in the dental profession. Shows osteological considerations and dissection material on the cadaver, and presents examples of techniques used on patients.
LC NO. 72-700485
Prod-LOMA Dist-LOMA 1970

Suprapubic Vesico-Urethral Suspension For Stress Incontinence C 18 MIN
16MM FILM OPTICAL SOUND PRO
Explains that suprapubic vesico-urethral suspension for correction of urinary stress incontinence in women has proven to be a valuable operation. Presents the technique of Dr Victor F Marshall.
Prod-ACYDGD Dist-ACY 1969

Supravalvular Aortic Stenosis C 7 MIN
16MM FILM OPTICAL SOUND PRO
Uses animated sequences at normal and reduced speeds in order to show the events taking place in a single cardiac cycle. Demonstrates the generation of the fourth sound, the mitral component of the first sound, the ejection systolic murmur and the aortic component of the second sound.
From The Physiological And Clinical Aspects Of Cardiac Auscultation Series.
LC NO. 76-700953
Prod-MEDIC Dist-LIP 1976

Supravalvular Aortic Stenosis - Extented Aortoplasty C 10 MIN
16MM FILM OPTICAL SOUND
Describes a surgical procedure for the repair of supravalvular aortic stenosis. Compares the traditional approach to this technique and demonstrates the latter procedure on a patient.
LC NO. 77-700418
Prod-UI Dist-UIOWA 1976

Supreme Court - Influences Of Personalities C 30 MIN
3/4 OR 1/2 INCH VIDEO CASSETTE C
Studies the Marshall, Taney and Warren Supreme Courts. Demonstrates the ways the prejudices and persuasions, the ideals and ideology of the judges shape the judicial progress of the nation.
From The American Government 2 Series.
Prod-DALCCD Dist-DALCCD

Supreme Court And Society C 29 MIN
16MM FILM OPTICAL SOUND J-H
Shows how the Supreme Court as a policy-making body directly affects the legal, social and political realities of the nation. Illustrates with cases from the Dred Scott decision of 1857 to the obscenity cases of the 1960's.
From The Government Story Series. No. 40
LC NO. 70-707202
Prod-WEBC Dist-WESTLC 1968

Supreme Court Decisions That Changed The Nation—A Series
H
Combines photographs, video sequences and period art to illustrate the impact these Supreme Court decisions have had on our concept of justice.
Prod-GA Dist-GA

Brown Vs Board Of Education
Dred Scott Decision, The
Gideon Vs Wainwright And Miranda Vs Arizona
Marbury Vs Madison
McCulloch Vs Maryland
Plessy Vs Ferguson

Supreme Court, The C 23 MIN
16MM FILM OPTICAL SOUND
Examines the role of the Supreme Court in guaranteeing justice. Highlights cases and decisions dealing with freedom of religion and the rights of the accused. Explains how a President is overruled and an Act of Congress is declared unconstitutional.
LC NO. 75-701208
Prod-USDD Dist-USNAC 1970

Supreme Court, The C 20 MIN
2 INCH VIDEOTAPE J-H
Views the Supreme Court from its beginning to today. Highlights many of the major decisions rendered by the court that have had an effect on this nation's development.
From The American System Series.
Prod-WCVETV Dist-GPITVL

Supreme Court, The C 30 MIN
16MM FILM, 3/4 OR 1/2 IN VIDEO J-C A
Discusses the history and operation of the U S Supreme Court. Includes observations by Chief Justice Warren Burger and Justice Lewis F Powell, Jr.
Prod-WCVETV Dist-GPITVL 1978

Sur Faces C 59 MIN
3/4 OR 1/2 INCH VIDEO CASSETTE
Features eight performers portraying aspects of man-woman encounters in a collage of various forms of historic dramatic styles.
Prod-EAI Dist-EAI

Sur La Tour Eiffel (On The Eiffel Tower) C 15 MIN
16MM FILM OPTICAL SOUND H
A French language film. Presents a tour of Eiffel Tower taken by Caroline, Victor and Elisabeth, who encounters a youth named Jacques, who becomes friends with the girls and a bore to Victor.
From The Toute La Bande Series. No. 7
LC NO. 71-715481
Prod-SCHMAG Dist-SCHMAG 1970

Sur Le Pont D'Avignon C 6 MIN
16MM FILM, 3/4 OR 1/2 IN VIDEO
Uses puppets to act out a French folk song.
Prod-NFBC Dist-IFB 1953

Sur Le Toit C 13 MIN
16MM FILM OPTICAL SOUND J A
From The En Francais, Set 2 Series.
Prod-PEREN Dist-CHLTN 1969

Sur/Face C 13 MIN
3/4 INCH VIDEO CASSETTE
Explores the nature of masks and of identity constructed upon appearances or variations of one's appearance.
From The Student Workshop Videotapes Series.
Prod-WMENIF Dist-WMENIF

Suramericanos En Cordoba C 13 MIN
16MM FILM OPTICAL SOUND H-C A
Focuses on the artists represented at the 1967 Cordoba Biennial in Argentina.
LC NO. 75-700288
Prod-OOAS Dist-PAN 1970

Sure Defense, The C 25 MIN
16MM FILM OPTICAL SOUND
Presents a panorama of scenic Washington, DC, including the White House, the capitol, the Lincoln Memorial and cherry blossoms along the tidal basin. Depicts a special meeting in the Pentagon where Billy Graham delivers a stirring message.
Prod-WWP Dist-NINEFC

Sure, I Can Dance C 25 MIN
16MM FILM OPTICAL SOUND I-C A
Proceeds from the assumption that anyone can dance and presents professional performers demonstrating exercises designed to teach the novice the basic movements of modern dance.
LC NO. 76-703994
Prod-HAIJUS Dist-RADIM 1976

Surefootin' C 17 MIN
16MM FILM OPTICAL SOUND
Discusses skateboard safety, including how to fall, skateboard maintenance and skateboard techniques.
LC NO. 78-701510
Prod-IDQ Dist-MTP Prodn-MARGOI 1978

Surface C 10 MIN
16MM FILM OPTICAL SOUND
Depicts a study of the abstract patterns of color and motion reflected in the surface of water.
LC NO. 76-703260
Prod-QUAF Dist-CANFDC 1975

Surface And Subsurface Mapping C 45 MIN
3/4 OR 1/2 INCH VIDEO CASSETTE IND
See series title for descriptive statement.
From The Basic Geology Series.
Prod-GPCV Dist-GPCV

Surface And Volume Measurement B 15 MIN
2 INCH VIDEOTAPE P
See series title for descriptive statement.
From The Just Wondering Series.
Prod-EOPS Dist-GPITVL Prodn-KOACTV

Surface Blasting In Metal And Nonmetal Mines C 18 MIN
16MM FILM, 3/4 OR 1/2 IN VIDEO IND
Shows some of the most common hazards encountered in surface blasting operations and emphasizes the need for greater safety precautions in the use of explosives.
Prod-USDL Dist-USNAC

Surface Blasting, Pt 1 B 60 MIN
3/4 OR 1/2 INCH VIDEO CASSETTE
See series title for descriptive statement.
From The Explosives And Their Use In Mining And Construction Series. Pt 5
Prod-UAZMIC Dist-UAZMIC 1977

Surface Blasting, Pt 2 B 60 MIN
3/4 OR 1/2 INCH VIDEO CASSETTE
See series title for descriptive statement.
From The Explosives And Their Use In Mining And Construction Series. Pt 6
Prod-UAZMIC Dist-UAZMIC 1977

Surface Damage C 25 MIN
3/4 OR 1/2 INCH VIDEO CASSETTE H-C A
Examines differences between veneered and solid furniture. Shows how to repair damage to solid surfaces with stopper, filler and wax, how veneers are made, relaying veneer, stringing and banding and inlay motifs.
From The Better Than New Series.
Prod-BBCTV Dist-FI

Surface Energy Effects C 43 MIN
3/4 OR 1/2 INCH VIDEO CASSETTE
Discusses the Leadmedium interface in magnetic recording applications.
From The Tribology 2 - Advances In Friction, Wear, And Lubrication Series.
Prod-MIOT Dist-MIOT

Surface Fatigue Wear C 37 MIN
3/4 OR 1/2 INCH VIDEO CASSETTE

Teaches the mechanism of surface fatigue wear and the laws governing it.
From The Tribology 1 - Friction, Wear, And Lubrication Series.
Prod-MIOT Dist-MIOT

Surface Finishing - You Can't Live Without It C 15 MIN
16MM FILM OPTICAL SOUND
Looks at the surface finishing industry and its role in America's progress and in providing jobs. Includes footage of the space shuttle Columbia and looks at the role surface finishing played in its construction.
Prod-MTP Dist-MTP

Surface Grinder No. 1 - Mounting Work On A Magnetic Chuck C 16 MIN
1/2 IN VIDEO CASSETTE BETA/VHS IND
Introduces permanent and electro-magnetic chucks, and demonstrates safe methods of mounting work of different shapes and sizes. Stresses safe setup with the workpiece well supported.
From The Machine Shop - Surface Grinder Series.
Prod-RMI Dist-RMI

Surface Grinder No. 2 - Mounting And Dressing The Wheel C 10 MIN
1/2 IN VIDEO CASSETTE BETA/VHS IND
Explains how to test a wheel for cracks and the proper mounting procedure. Emphasizes correct positioning of a diamond dresser for truing the wheel.
From The Machine Shop - Surface Grinder Series.
Prod-RMI Dist-RMI

Surface Grinder No. 3 - Grinding Flat Surfaces C 14 MIN
1/2 IN VIDEO CASSETTE BETA/VHS IND
Describes the proper way to mount the workpiece and how to touch off and traverse grind a flat surface. Stresses care in 'stoning' and cleaning the magnetic chuck and workpiece.
From The Machine Shop - Surface Grinder Series.
Prod-RMI Dist-RMI

Surface Grinder No. 4 - Squaring Up A Block C 18 MIN
1/2 IN VIDEO CASSETTE BETA/VHS IND
Covers the proper sequence for grinding all six surfaces of a block, using an angle plate. Emphasizes the importance of precise squareness of adjoining surfaces.
From The Machine Shop - Surface Grinder Series.
Prod-RMI Dist-RMI

Surface Grinder No. 5 - Grinding To Remove Warp C 19 MIN
1/2 IN VIDEO CASSETTE BETA/VHS IND
Explains how to grind work that is bowed by shimming. Includes use of dial indicator to determine amount of bow.
From The Machine Shop - Surface Grinder Series.
Prod-RMI Dist-RMI

Surface Grinder No. 6 - Grinding A Vertical Surface C 16 MIN
1/2 IN VIDEO CASSETTE BETA/VHS IND
Discusses applications for 'Side wheel' grinding, and explains how to relieve the side of the wheel and the technique for grinding a vertical surface to maximum accuracy.
From The Machine Shop - Surface Grinder Series.
Prod-RMI Dist-RMI

Surface Grinder No. 7 - Grinding A 90 Degree 'V' C 25 MIN
1/2 IN VIDEO CASSETTE BETA/VHS IND
Demonstrates the setup of a magnetic sine plate to grind a 90 degree 'V'. Includes use of a table of sine bar constants and method of selecting and 'wringing' gage blocks together. Stresses grinding techniques that result in maximum accuracy.
From The Machine Shop - Surface Grinder Series.
Prod-RMI Dist-RMI

Surface Grinder No. 8 - Surface Grinding Problems C 12 MIN
1/2 IN VIDEO CASSETTE BETA/VHS IND
Identifies common surface grinding problems which show up as poor surface finish on the workpiece. Covers basic points in selecting, mounting and dressing the grinding wheel.
From The Machine Shop - Surface Grinder Series.
Prod-RMI Dist-RMI

Surface Hardening C 50 MIN
3/4 OR 1/2 INCH VIDEO CASSETTE PRO
Deals with surface hardening. Studies carburizing, carbonitriding and nitriding.
From The Heat Treatment - Metallurgy And Application Series.
Prod-AMCEE Dist-AMCEE

Surface Lures And Buzz Baits C 30 MIN
16MM FILM OPTICAL SOUND
Explains how to use surface lures and buzz baits.
Prod-GLNLAU Dist-GLNLAU 1982

Surface Of The Earth C 11 MIN
16MM FILM OPTICAL SOUND P-I A
Shows the process of rock formation and discusses the effect of water and wind on the earth, and causes and effects of glaciers, hot springs, earthquakes and volcanoes. Describes how mountains rise from the earth and are slowly worn away, and how caves and caverns are formed.
Prod-AVED Dist-AVED 1959

Surface Potentials - Structure Of The Electric Double Layer B 54 MIN
3/4 OR 1/2 INCH VIDEO CASSETTE PRO
See series title for descriptive statement.
From The Colloid And Surface Chemistry - Surface Chemistry Series.
Prod-MIOT Dist-MIOT

Surface Potentials, Structure Of The Electric Double Layer C 54 MIN
3/4 OR 1/2 INCH VIDEO CASSETTE
See series title for descriptive statement.
From The Colloid And Surface Chemistry - Surface Chemistry Series.
Prod-KALMIA Dist-KALMIA

Surface Sampling For Microorganisms - Swab Method C 5 MIN
16MM FILM - 3/4 IN VIDEO
Shows techniques and procedures of surface sampling for bacteria in hospitals, using the swab and template. Shows reasons for surface sampling, techniques of sampling on flat and irregular surfaces, processing of swabs and rinse liquids, counting microbial colonies, and interpretation of results. Issued in 1965 as a motion picture.
LC NO. 78-706108
Prod-USPHS Dist-USNAC Prodn-NMAC 1978

Surface Sampling For Microorganisms - Rodac Method C 8 MIN
16MM FILM - 3/4 IN VIDEO
Shows techniques and procedures of surface sampling for bacteria in hospitals, using the Rodac plate. Gives reasons for surface sampling, directions for preparation of the agar sampling plates, a description of random and geo-grid sampling methods and directions for counting and reporting colonies. Issued in 1965 as a motion picture.
LC NO. 78-706107
Prod-USPHS Dist-USNAC Prodn-NMAC 1978

Surface Tension And Surface Energies C 40 MIN
3/4 OR 1/2 INCH VIDEO CASSETTE
See series title for descriptive statement.
From The Colloid And Surface Chemistry - Surface Chemistry Series.
Prod-KALMIA Dist-KALMIA

Surface Tension And Surface Energies B 40 MIN
3/4 OR 1/2 INCH VIDEO CASSETTE PRO
See series title for descriptive statement.
From The Colloid And Surface Chemistry - Surface Chemistry Series.
Prod-MIOT Dist-MIOT

Surface Tension And Surface Structure Of Solids B 52 MIN
3/4 OR 1/2 INCH VIDEO CASSETTE PRO
See series title for descriptive statement.
From The Colloid And Surface Chemistry - Surface Chemistry Series.
Prod-MIOT Dist-MIOT

Surface Tension And Surface Structure Of Solids C 52 MIN
3/4 OR 1/2 INCH VIDEO CASSETTE
See series title for descriptive statement.
From The Colloid And Surface Chemistry - Surface Chemistry Series.
Prod-KALMIA Dist-KALMIA

Surface Tension In Fluid Mechanics C 29 MIN
16MM FILM, 3/4 OR 1/2 IN VIDEO H-C
Illustrates effects of surface tension in experiments including soap film intersections, break-up of jets and sheets into droplets, capillary action, wetting and non-wetting droplets, generation and motion of bubbles, and chemical and electric effects.
From The Fluid Mechanics Series.
Prod-NCFMF Dist-EBEC 1966

Surfboards, Skateboards And Big Big Waves C 10 MIN
16MM FILM OPTICAL SOUND
Pictures the famous surfing spots of Ala Moana, Anaheim and Waimea Bay and features acrobatics of the world's best skate-boarders.
LC NO. 70-708684
Prod-GROENG Dist-AMEDFL 1969

Surfclubbing C 3 MIN
3/4 OR 1/2 INCH VIDEO CASSETTE
Deals with a psychedelic day at the beach for people who usually go out at night. By Emily Armstrong and Pat Ivers.
Prod-KITCHN Dist-KITCHN

Surgery / Employment / Insurance C
3/4 OR 1/2 INCH VIDEO CASSETTE
Presents tips on arranging surgery, employment and insurance.
From The Consumer Survival Series.
Prod-MDCPB Dist-MDCPB

Surgery And Radiation C 23 MIN
3/4 INCH VIDEO CASSETTE PRO
See series title for descriptive statement.
From The Cancer Series. Module 3
LC NO. 81-707090
Prod-BRA Dist-BRA 1981

Surgery For Advanced Cancer Of Pelvic Viscera C 35 MIN
16MM FILM OPTICAL SOUND PRO
Illustrates certain features of the technique of radical pelvic surgery for cancer. Emphasizes total pelvic exenteration for recurrent cancer of the cervix. Shows modifications of the operation for limited lesions and for advanced cancer of the rectum and rectosigmoid.
Prod-ACYDGD Dist-ACY 1961

Surgery For Massive Hemorrhage From Gastroduodenal Ulcer C 32 MIN
16MM FILM OPTICAL SOUND PRO
Discusses the problems of diagnosis and surgical technique by illustrating gastric resection on two elderly patients, one with penetrating posterior wall duodenal ulcer and one with gastric ulcer. Covers clinical data of a five-year study of the management of severely bleeding gastroduodenal ulcer.
Prod-ACYDGD Dist-ACY 1952

Surgery For Multiple Stones In The Kidney Pelvis And Calyces C 17 MIN
16MM FILM OPTICAL SOUND
Illustrates surgery for multiple stones in the kidney pelvis and calyces. Includes demonstration of surgical technique on a fresh human autopsy kidney along with artists' illustrations. Shows exposure provided for easy access to fragmented or multiple stones in the renal pelvis and calyces.
LC NO. 75-702251
Prod-EATONL Dist-EATONL 1972

Surgery For Vesicular Ureteral Reflux C 57 MIN
16MM FILM OPTICAL SOUND
Demonstrates various surgical techniques of extra-vesicular surgery for reflux and shows the similarities, differences and indications for each technique. Includes a panel discussion by different surgeons.
From The Visits In Urology Series.
LC NO. 79-701326
Prod-EATONL Dist-EATONL Prodn-AEGIS 1979

Surgery Of Cancer Of The Colon C 24 MIN
16MM FILM OPTICAL SOUND PRO
Shows that there is some leeway in choosing the proper operation for cancer of the colon. Illustrates cancer of the colon located in different portions and the method by which it is handled under different circumstances.
Prod-ACYDGD Dist-ACY 1960

Surgery Of Decubitus Ulcer - Wire Button Technique C 20 MIN
16MM FILM OPTICAL SOUND
Shows the technique of closures of sacral, troachanteric and ischial decubitus ulcers.
Prod-USVA Dist-USVA 1962

Surgery Of Male Genital Lymphadema C 13 MIN
3/4 OR 1/2 INCH VIDEO CASSETTE PRO
Describes in detail a surgical treatment for treating genital lymphadema, a grotesque disease which affects especially those in equatorial latitudes.
Prod-WFP Dist-WFP

Surgery Of Primary Aldosteronism, The C 23 MIN
16MM FILM OPTICAL SOUND PRO
Presents Richard H Egdahl, MD, who discusses the methods of diagnosis and localization preoperatively of aldosterone-secreting tumors. Demonstrates the techniques of both the anterior and posterior approaches to the adrenals, and gives reasons for the author's preference for the posterior approach, if the side of the tumor has been determined pre-operatively.
Prod-ACYDGD Dist-ACY 1968

Surgery Of Subcutaneous Tumors In Parakeets C 11 MIN
16MM FILM OPTICAL SOUND PRO
Illustrates the different types of tumors observed in the parakeet. Discusses the technique for weighing the birds, emphasizing its importance with relation to the anesthesia.
Prod-NYZS Dist-AMVMA

Surgery Of The Adrenal Glands C 19 MIN
16MM FILM OPTICAL SOUND PRO
Presents Dr Victor Richards who demonstrates the surgical exposures of the adrenal glands, the two main approaches, a retroperitoneal subdiaphragmatic approach and a transabdominal approach.
Prod-ACYDGD Dist-ACY 1956

Surgery Of The Carpal Tunnel C 29 MIN
3/4 OR 1/2 INCH VIDEO CASSETTE PRO
Outlines important anatomical landmarks, covers symptoms and diagnosis, details surgical procedure and its hazards and describes postoperative care of the carpal tunnel patient.
Prod-HSCIC Dist-HSCIC 1984

Surgery Of The Horseshoe Kidney C 24 MIN
16MM FILM OPTICAL SOUND
Presents three patients exhibiting variations of the horseshoe kidney to illustrate a technique in accomplishing the two major surgical objectives of correction of various pathological processes and conservation of a maximal amount of functioning renal tissue. Features aortograms and post-operative intravenous pyelograms which illustrate pre-operative pathology and post-operative function.
LC NO. 75-702298
Prod-EATONL Dist-EATONL 1966

Surgery Of The Parotid Gland - As Aided By Differential Staining C 14 MIN
3/4 OR 1/2 INCH VIDEO CASSETTE PRO
Shows surgery of the parotid gland as aided by differential staining.
Prod-WFP Dist-WFP Prodn-UKANMC

Surgery Of The Pituitary C 30 MIN
16MM FILM OPTICAL SOUND PRO
Shows an acromegalic patient before, during and after cryphypophyaectomy. Uses live action and animation to demonstrate pre- and post-operative symptoms and appearance.
LC NO. FIA68-235
Prod-PFI Dist-UCLAA Prodn-UCLAA 1967

Surgery Of The Prostate Gland C 16 MIN
16MM FILM, 3/4 OR 1/2 IN VIDEO A
Examines how benign prostatic hypertrophy occurs and how it differs from cancer. Reviews trans-urethral resection, open prostatectomy, and the effects of genito-urinary function. Gives guidelines for post-operative care.
Prod-PRORE Dist-PRORE

Surgery Of The Prostate Gland (Spanish) C 16 MIN
16MM FILM, 3/4 OR 1/2 IN VIDEO PRO

Discusses benign prostatic hypertrophy and how it differs from cancer. Explains the surgical procedure and presents guidelines for post-operative care.
Prod-PRORE Dist-PRORE

Surgery Of Upper Urinary Tract Stone Disease C 39 MIN
16MM FILM OPTICAL SOUND PRO
Presents Dr Joseph J Kaufman interviewing Professor Jose Marie Gil-Vernet of the University of Barcelona, Spain, who discusses his approaches to upper tract stone disease. Discusses various techniques of treatment.
From The Visits In Urology Series.
LC NO. 78-701379
Prod-EATONL Dist-EATONL Prodn-AEGIS 1978

Surgery Without Ligature C 13 MIN
16MM FILM OPTICAL SOUND PRO
Describes and demonstrates a new type of hemostatic clip.
Prod-UCLA Dist-UCLA 1968

Surgery, Anesthesia And Chronic Obstructive Lung Disease C 16 MIN
3/4 OR 1/2 INCH VIDEO CASSETTE PRO
Discusses determination of patients predisposed to respiratory complications through an appropriate history and physical exam. Emphasizes utilizing these findings and information to prepare these patients for surgery and anesthesia.
Prod-UMICHM Dist-UMICHM 1975

Surgical Anatomy Of Inguinal Region C 29 MIN
16MM FILM OPTICAL SOUND PRO
Reveals a dissection of the inguinal area on a fresh cadaver specimen, as encountered in hernia repair. Demonstrates Cooper's ligament.
Prod-ACYDGD Dist-ACY 1950

Surgical Anatomy Of The Anterior Abdominal Wall C 17 MIN
16MM FILM OPTICAL SOUND PRO
Presents cadaver dissection and abdominal anatomy from a surgeon's point of view. Shows the location of the four major incisions and follows the dissection, layer by layer, giving special attention to muscles and the rectus sheath. For surgeons, residents and first year anatomy students.
LC NO. 74-702597
Prod-EATONL Dist-EATONL Prodn-AVCORP 1969

Surgical Anatomy Of The Female Pelvis C 10 MIN
16MM FILM OPTICAL SOUND PRO
Demonstrates the surgical anatomy of the female pelvis.
Prod-SQUIBB Dist-SQUIBB

Surgical Anatomy Of The Female Perineum C 25 MIN
16MM FILM OPTICAL SOUND PRO
Uses fresh cadaver material to illustrate the anatomy of the female perineum.
Prod-ACYDGD Dist-ACY 1952

Surgical Anatomy Of The Female Perineum C 27 MIN
16MM FILM OPTICAL SOUND PRO
Shows a systematic cadaver dissection of the female perineum, including the vaginal vault.
Prod-LOMAM Dist-LOMAM

Surgical Anatomy Of The Human Kidney And Its Applications C 25 MIN
16MM FILM OPTICAL SOUND
Uses art, animation and corrosion casts of the kidney to demonstrate its surgical anatomy. Emphasizes the arterial distribution within the kidney.
LC NO. 79-701327
Prod-EATONL Dist-EATONL Prodn-AEGIS 1979

Surgical Anatomy Of The Lateral Neck C 10 MIN
16MM FILM OPTICAL SOUND PRO
Demonstrates the anatomy encountered during surgical procedures in the lateral neck through the dissection of a cadaver and medical artwork.
Prod-SQUIBB Dist-SQUIBB

Surgical Anatomy Of The Lateral Neck C 25 MIN
16MM FILM OPTICAL SOUND PRO
Demonstrates the important structures of the lateral neck by cadaver dissection.
Prod-ACYDGD Dist-ACY 1954

Surgical Anatomy Of The Male Perineum C 20 MIN
16MM FILM OPTICAL SOUND PRO
Shows a systematic dissection of the male perineum with particular emphasis on the perineal approach to the prostate.
Prod-LOMAM Dist-LOMAM

Surgical Anatomy Of The Parotid Area C 18 MIN
16MM FILM OPTICAL SOUND PRO
Presents an anatomical study of the parotid gland and facial nerve, using fresh cadaver material for demonstration. Shows the anatomy of this area with particular reference to nerves, blood and vessels and other structures encountered in removal of the parotid gland.
Prod-ACYDGD Dist-ACY 1953

Surgical Anatomy Of The Pulmonary Hilum - Left Lung C 20 MIN
16MM FILM OPTICAL SOUND
Companion to the film 'SURGICAL ANATOMY OF THE PULMONARY HILUM - RIGHT LUNG.' Uses sequences from six different surgical procedures and animated sequences to illustrate the various points of reference which must be recognized in order that lung tissue excision may be accomplished with maximum salvage of healthy tissue.
Prod-UWASHM Dist-PFI 1960

Surgical Anatomy Of The Pulmonary Hilum - Right Lung C 20 MIN
16MM FILM OPTICAL SOUND
Companion to the film 'SURGICAL ANATOMY OF THE PULMONARY HILUM - LEFT LUNG.' Illustrates the various points of reference which must be recognized in order that lung tissue excision may be accomplished with maximum salvage of healthy tissue. Presents animated sequences and sequences demonstrating six different surgical procedures.
Prod-UWASHM Dist-PFI 1960

Surgical Anatomy Of The Pulmonary Hilum-Right Lung C 24 MIN
3/4 OR 1/2 INCH VIDEO CASSETTE PRO
Presents the surgical anatomy of the pulmonary hilum, specifically the right lung.
Prod-WFP Dist-WFP Prodn-UKANMC

Surgical Anatomy Of The Pulmonary Hilum-Left Lung C 29 MIN
3/4 OR 1/2 INCH VIDEO CASSETTE PRO
Presents the surgical anatomy of the pulmonary himum, specifically the left lung.
Prod-WFP Dist-WFP Prodn-UKANMC

Surgical Anatomy Of The Thyroid Gland C 18 MIN
16MM FILM OPTICAL SOUND PRO
Shows an anatomical dissection of a fresh cadaver. Emphasizes the arterial supply and the relation of the recurrent laryngeal nerve.
Prod-ACYDGD Dist-ACY 1954

Surgical Approach To Parotid Tumors, The C 21 MIN
16MM FILM OPTICAL SOUND PRO
Illustrates the surgical approach to parotid resection utilizing peripheral identification of the facial nerve. Discusses the anatomy, technique and indications.
Prod-ACYDGD Dist-ACY 1967

Surgical Approaches To The Ankle C 32 MIN
3/4 OR 1/2 INCH VIDEO CASSETTE PRO
See series title for descriptive statement.
From The Surgical Approaches Series.
Prod-WFP Dist-WFP

Surgical Approaches To The Ankle Joint C 32 MIN
16MM FILM OPTICAL SOUND
Shows the anatomy of the dorsolateral and medical aspects of the ankle joint. Shows operations employing approaches to the dorsal, lateral, medial and posterior aspects of the joint.
LC NO. FIE63-106
Prod-USVA Dist-USVA 1952

Surgical Approaches To The Bones Of The Foot C 32 MIN
16MM FILM OPTICAL SOUND
Shows the anatomy of the dorsolateral and medical aspects of the foot. Discusses operations employing approaches to the dorsal, dorsolateral and plantar aspects and an approach for bunionectomy.
LC NO. FIE53-107
Prod-USVA Dist-USVA 1952

Surgical Approaches To The Bones Of The Wrist C 34 MIN
16MM FILM OPTICAL SOUND
Shows the anatomy of the volar, dorsal and ulnar aspects of the wrist. Presents operations employing approaches to the volar, radio-volar, ulnar and dorsal aspects.
LC NO. FIE53-108
Prod-USVA Dist-USVA 1952

Surgical Approaches To The Elbow C 38 MIN
3/4 OR 1/2 INCH VIDEO CASSETTE PRO
See series title for descriptive statement.
From The Surgical Approaches Series.
Prod-WFP Dist-WFP

Surgical Approaches To The Elbow Joint C 39 MIN
16MM FILM OPTICAL SOUND
Shows the anatomy of the anterior and the posterior aspects of the joint. Presents operations employing approaches to the anterolateral, lateral, medial and posterior aspects of the joint.
LC NO. FIE53-109
Prod-USVA Dist-USVA 1950

Surgical Approaches To The Foot C 32 MIN
3/4 OR 1/2 INCH VIDEO CASSETTE PRO
See series title for descriptive statement.
From The Surgical Approaches Series.
Prod-WFP Dist-WFP

Surgical Approaches To The Hip C 36 MIN
3/4 OR 1/2 INCH VIDEO CASSETTE PRO
See series title for descriptive statement.
From The Surgical Approaches Series.
Prod-WFP Dist-WFP

Surgical Approaches To The Hip Joint C 36 MIN
16MM FILM OPTICAL SOUND
Shows the anatomy of the anterior and posterior aspects of the hip joint. Presents operations employing approaches to the anterolateral, straight lateral and posterolateral aspects of the joint.
LC NO. FIE52-2215
Prod-USVA Dist-USVA 1951

Surgical Approaches To The Knee C 36 MIN
3/4 OR 1/2 INCH VIDEO CASSETTE PRO
See series title for descriptive statement.
From The Surgical Approaches Series.
Prod-WFP Dist-WFP

Surgical Approaches To The Knee Joint C 37 MIN
16MM FILM OPTICAL SOUND
Shows the anatomy of the anterior and posterior aspects of the knee joint. Presents operations employing approaches to the anterior and posterior aspects and to the medial and lateral semilunar cartilages.
LC NO. FIE53-110
Prod-USVA Dist-USVA 1951

Surgical Approaches To The Scapulohumeral Joint C 36 MIN
16MM FILM OPTICAL SOUND
Emphasizes the anatomy of each aspect of a joint in approaching that joint surgically. Depicts the bones, ligaments, muscles, tendons and neurovascular structures with which the surgeon must deal in various approaches to the shoulder joint. Shows actual surgical operations utilizing anterior, posterior and muscle splitting incisions with emphasis always on the anatomy of the region.
LC NO. FIE53-111
Prod-USVA Dist-USVA 1949

Surgical Approaches To The Scapulohumeral Joint C 36 MIN
3/4 OR 1/2 INCH VIDEO CASSETTE PRO
See series title for descriptive statement.
From The Surgical Approaches Series.
Prod-WFP Dist-WFP

Surgical Approaches To The Spine And Sacroiliac C 28 MIN
3/4 OR 1/2 INCH VIDEO CASSETTE PRO
See series title for descriptive statement.
From The Surgical Approaches Series.
Prod-WFP Dist-WFP

Surgical Approaches To The Spine And Sacroiliac C 28 MIN
16MM FILM OPTICAL SOUND
Shows the anatomy of the posterior aspect of the sacroiliac, the anterior and posterior aspects of the region of the spine with emphasis on the lumbar area. Demonstrates approaches to the sacroiliac and the retroperitoneal space.
LC NO. FIE53-112
Prod-USVA Dist-USVA 1952

Surgical Approaches To The Sternoclavicular And Acromioclavicular Joints C 17 MIN
16MM FILM OPTICAL SOUND
Shows the anatomy of the anterior aspect of the two joints as an operation approaching each joint.
LC NO. FIE53-110
Prod-USVA Dist-USVA 1952

Surgical Approaches To The Sternoclavicular And Acromioclavicular Joint C 16 MIN
3/4 OR 1/2 INCH VIDEO CASSETTE PRO
See series title for descriptive statement.
From The Surgical Approaches Series.
Prod-WFP Dist-WFP

Surgical Approaches To The Wrist C 33 MIN
3/4 OR 1/2 INCH VIDEO CASSETTE PRO
See series title for descriptive statement.
From The Surgical Approaches Series.
Prod-WFP Dist-WFP

Surgical Approaches—A Series
PRO
Demonstrates operative procedure approaches to the joints of the body. Uses animated diagrams to clarify the structures and steps of each operation.
Prod-WFP Dist-WFP

Surgical Approaches To The Ankle	032 MIN
Surgical Approaches To The Elbow	038 MIN
Surgical Approaches To The Foot	032 MIN
Surgical Approaches To The Hip	036 MIN
Surgical Approaches To The Knee	036 MIN
Surgical Approaches To The Scapulohumeral Joint	036 MIN
Surgical Approaches To The Spine And	028 MIN
Surgical Approaches To The Sternoclavicular	016 MIN
Surgical Approaches To The Wrist	033 MIN

Surgical Asepsis B 23 MIN
16MM FILM OPTICAL SOUND PRO
Discusses methods of sterilization giving advantages and disadvantages. Demonstrates rules of procedure when opening sterile packages, adding sterile equipment and one method of putting on a pair of sterile gloves.
From The Directions For Education In Nursing Via Technology Series. Lesson 15
LC NO. 74-701789
Prod-DENT Dist-WSU 1974

Surgical Care Of The Injured Hand C 29 MIN
16MM FILM OPTICAL SOUND PRO
Depicts the reconstruction of the flexor and extensor mechanisms in the hand as pertains to specific injuries which are narrated.
Prod-ACYDGD Dist-ACY 1965

Surgical Complications - Thoracic, Biliary Pancreatic, Alimentary C 35 MIN
16MM FILM OPTICAL SOUND PRO
Shows operative management of thoracic duct fistula, common duct stricture, pancreatic pseudocyst, postgastrectomy malnutrition by conversion of Billroth II anastomosis to Billroth I, enterovaginal fistula and pelvic abscess drained through the rectum.
Prod-ACYDGD Dist-ACY 1967

Surgical Consideration In The Treatment Of Cerebral Arterial Insufficiency C 38 MIN
3/4 OR 1/2 INCH VIDEO CASSETTE PRO
Shows how patients can be helped by surgical correction of extracranial occlusive lesions which cause cerebral arterial in-

sufficiency. Demonstrates preoperative techniques for determining the site of the occlusion or area of narrowing in the artery.
Prod-PRIMED Dist-PRIMED

Surgical Consideration Of Cerebral Arterial Insufficiency C 30 MIN
16MM FILM OPTICAL SOUND
Discusses the surgical treatment of extracranial occlusive disease causing cerebral arterial insuffiency. Presents four cases illustrating the various lesions and techniques employed in the treatment of this disease, using both bypass graft and endarterectomy.
LC NO. DIA66-63
Prod-EATON Dist-EATON Prodn-AVCORP 1961

Surgical Consideration Of Occlusive Disease Of The Abdominal Aorta, Iliac, Femoral Arteries C 30 MIN
16MM FILM OPTICAL SOUND
Discusses surgical consideration of occlusive disease of the abdominal aorta, iliac and femoral arteries. Demonstrates in detail the operative techniques as applied to patients. Includes statistics compiled from a study of patients with occlusions.
LC NO. FIA66-64
Prod-EATON Dist-EATON Prodn-AVCORP 1961

Surgical Correction Of Ankyloglossia C 5 MIN
16MM FILM - 3/4 IN VIDEO PRO
Shows how an unusually short fibrous lingual frenum is severed to permit a normal range of mobility of the tongue. Demonstrates the care taken to avoid the submaxillary duct and to create adequate space in the ventral surface where the extrinsic musculature is attached.
LC NO. 78-706010
Prod-USVA Dist-USNAC 1977

Surgical Correction Of Aortic Stenosis, The C 28 MIN
16MM FILM OPTICAL SOUND PRO
Presents the transventricular approach in the surgical treatment of aortic stenosis. Gives indications for aortic commissurotomy.
Prod-ACYDGD Dist-ACY 1953

Surgical Correction Of Blepharoptosis C 15 MIN
16MM FILM OPTICAL SOUND
Demonstrates the technique of making the incisions, isolating the levator, determining the extent of resection and proper placing of sutures through the various layers of the eyelid on the correction of certain cases of blepharoptosis.
LC NO. FIA66-896
Prod-ACYDGD Dist-ACY 1962

Surgical Correction Of Congenital Deformities C 120 MIN
3/4 OR 1/2 INCH VIDEO CASSETTE PRO
Demonstrates Dr Dieter Buck-Gramcko's special technique for treatment of some of the frequently encountered congenital anomalies of the hand. Presents a demonstration of an original technique of pollicization for congenital absence of the thumb.
Prod-ASSH Dist-ASSH

Surgical Correction Of Hydronephrosis, Pt 1 - Non-Dismembering Procedures—A Series

Prod-EATONL Dist-EATONL 1968

Classical Foley Y-Plasty In A Horseshoe Kidney 15 MIN
Modified Davis Intubated Ureterotomy 15 MIN
Non-Dismembering Procedures 20 MIN
Vertical Flap Ureteropelvioplasty 20 MIN

Surgical Correction Of Hydronephrosis, Pt 2 - Dismembering Procedures—A Series

Prod-EATONL Dist-EATONL 1968

Cuff Re-Implantation Procedure 15 MIN
Dismembered Foly Y-Plasty, The 15 MIN
Dismembering Procedures 15 MIN
Pelvic Cuff Reimplantation Of The Ureter 15 MIN
Uretero-Ureteral Anastamosis 20 MIN

Surgical Correction Of Hydronephrosis, Pt 3 - Procedures Common To Most...—A Series

Prod-EATONL Dist-EATONL 1972

Procedures Common To Most Pyeloplasties, Pt 1 15 MIN
Procedures Common To Most Pyeloplasties, Pt 2 15 MIN
Procedures Common To Most Pyeloplasties, Pt 3 15 MIN

Surgical Correction Of Hypertelorism C 9 MIN
16MM FILM OPTICAL SOUND
Describes the correction of extreme cases of hypertelorism by revision of the bony framework and adjustment of the contour of the overlying soft tissues. Shows the surgical technique used on the second side after healing of the first side has been accomplished.
LC NO. FIA66-897
Prod-ACYDGD Dist-ACY 1962

Surgical Correction Of Tetralogy Of Fallot C 12 MIN
3/4 OR 1/2 INCH VIDEO CASSETTE PRO
Shows diagnostic studies which delineate this congenital cardiovascular abnormality and discusses the values of various techniques. Demonstrates surgical reconstruction with closure of the ventricular septal defect and elimination of pulmonary stenosis. Presents drawings which illustrate the various progressive steps in this operation.
Prod-PRIMED Dist-PRIMED

Surgical Creation Of A Sensitive Thumb C 20 MIN
16MM FILM OPTICAL SOUND
Presents a detailed demonstration of Dr Johnson's technique in creating a sensitive thumb for a two-anda-half-year-old child with a congenital absence of the distal two-thirds of the left hand. Shows the utility and durability of the reconstructed digit.
LC NO. FIA66-65
Prod-EATON Dist-EATON Prodn-AVCORP 1962

Surgical Drains C 11 MIN
3/4 OR 1/2 INCH VIDEO CASSETTE PRO
Illustrates how different drains are used and shows how to change surgical drain dressings.
From The Basic Clinical Skills Series.
Prod-HSCIC Dist-HSCIC 1984

Surgical Dressings C 7 MIN
3/4 OR 1/2 INCH VIDEO CASSETTE PRO
Discusses the dry, nonadherent, sealed, moist and medicated types of dressings and tells how to determine which to use.
From The Basic Clinical Skills Series.
Prod-HSCIC Dist-HSCIC 1984

Surgical Elimination Of Periodontal Pockets C 13 MIN
16MM FILM - 3/4 IN VIDEO PRO
Explains procedures involved in surgical elimination of periodontal pockets for a patient with overall horizontal bone loss, interproximal bone craters and deep interproximal pockets. Demonstrates flap design, tissue removal, planing of exposed root surfaces, bone recontouring and flap readaptation.
LC NO. 79-706491
Prod-USVA Dist-USNAC Prodn-VADTC 1977

Surgical Endodontics C 20 MIN
16MM FILM OPTICAL SOUND PRO
Demonstrates curettage and root resection. Explains the process of periotic reaction and the techniques and precautions that should be taken when surgery is necessary.
LC NO. 78-701242
Prod-USN Dist-USNAC 1964

Surgical Endodontics C 15 MIN
16MM FILM - 3/4 IN VIDEO PRO
Describes the process of periapical inflammatory reaction. Demonstrates the surgical corrective procedures of curettage and root resection. Issued in 1964 as a motion picture.
LC NO. 78-706131
Prod-USN Dist-USNAC 1978

Surgical Excision Of Mandibular Tori C 10 MIN
16MM FILM, 3/4 OR 1/2 IN VIDEO
Demonstrates an accepted technique for the surgical procedure for the removal of a torus, which is indicated when it interferes with speech or a prosthetic appliance.
Prod-VADTC Dist-USNAC 1972

Surgical Excision Of Maxillary Torus C 10 MIN
16MM FILM OPTICAL SOUND PRO
Describes the indication for the surgical removal of a maxillary torus and demonstrates an accepted technique for this procedure.
LC NO. 74-706408
Prod-USVA Dist-USNAC 1972

Surgical Excision Of Oral Leukoplakia C 6 MIN
16MM FILM, 3/4 OR 1/2 IN VIDEO
Demonstrates the surgical removal of leukoplakia in the oral cavity utilizing a stripping technique. Presents microscopic findings.
Prod-VADTC Dist-AMDA 1969

Surgical Excison Of Maxillary Torus C 10 MIN
3/4 INCH VIDEO CASSETTE PRO
Describes the indications for the surgical removal of a maxillary torus and demonstrates a technique for this procedure. Issued in 1972 as a motion picture.
LC NO. 78-706011
Prod-USVA Dist-USNAC 1977

Surgical Exploration For Obscure Massive Upper Gastrointestinal Hemorrhage C 29 MIN
16MM FILM OPTICAL SOUND PRO
Depicts certain steps in operative technique which should be taken before restoring 'BLIND GASTRECTOMY' for severe upper gastrointestinal hemorrhage. Explains that this method has significantly reduced the need for 'BLIND GASTRECTOMY' with its intrinsic risk of overlooking a surgically correctable source of bleeding.
Prod-ACYDGD Dist-ACY 1956

Surgical Grand Rounds C 90 MIN
3/4 INCH VIDEO CASSETTE PRO
Shows grand rounds at the University of Washington Department of Surgery. Shows physicians discussing lung metastases in a 60-year-old male with a brain tumor. Deals with operative and postoperative aspects of a 37-year-old male with persistent recurrence of polyps. Focuses on postoperative aspects of lung metastases in a brain tumor patient and discusses carcinoma aspects of a patient with obstructive jaundice.
LC NO. 76-706107
Prod-WARMP Dist-USNAC 1971

Surgical Implant Of The Lost Mandibular Condyle With A Stainless Steel Mesh... C 8 MIN
16MM FILM OPTICAL SOUND
Points out that failure to reduce and immobilize the fractured mandibular condyle frequently results in poor articulation of the teeth, open bit or inability to open the mouth. Shows the use of a prothestic implant for correction of these complications.
LC NO. 74-705725
Prod-USVA Dist-USNAC 1970

Surgical Implant Replacement Of The Fractured Displaced Condyle C 8 MIN
16MM FILM OPTICAL SOUND PRO
Points out that failure to reduce and immobilize the fractured mandibular condyle may cause poor articulation of the teeth, open bite or inability to open the mouth. Demonstrates the use of prosthetic implant for correction of these complications.
LC NO. 74-706410
Prod-USVA Dist-USNAC 1968

Surgical Implant Replacement Of The Lost Mandibular Condyle With A Stainlesss Steel... C 7 MIN
3/4 OR 1/2 INCH VIDEO CASSETTE
Shows the use of a prosthetic implant for correcting poor articulation of the teeth, open bite or inability to open mouth caused by the failure to reduce and immobilize the fractured mandibular condyle.
Prod-VADTC Dist-AMDA 1970

Surgical Implantation Of An Inflatable Penile Prosthesis C 20 MIN
16MM FILM OPTICAL SOUND PRO
Demonstrates the inflatable penile prosthesis.
LC NO. 80-701417
Prod-EATONL Dist-EATONL Prodn-AEGIS 1980

Surgical Interview, The C 13 MIN
3/4 INCH VIDEO CASSETTE PRO
Discusses a patient interview conducted by a surgeon. Explains that this case is difficult because of the physical and psychological problems of the patient.
From The Patient Interview - Science Or Art Series.
Prod-PRIMED Dist-PRIMED

Surgical Management Of An Axillary Burn Web C 12 MIN
16MM FILM OPTICAL SOUND
Portrays an axilla webbing resulting from a thermal injury on the trunk and arm of a five-year-old child. Illustrates the correction which is carried out through normal tissue and can be performed earlier than most contractures.
LC NO. 75-702318
Prod-EATONL Dist-EATONL 1967

Surgical Management Of Calcific Pancreatitis C 22 MIN
16MM FILM OPTICAL SOUND PRO
Presents the concept that in calcific pancreatitis the calcareous material is intraductal. Includes the surgical procedure employed in three illustrative cases together with roentgenologic demonstration of the calcific disease, pathologic specimens and the results of preoperative and postoperative blood lipid studies.
Prod-ACYDGD Dist-ACY 1955

Surgical Management Of Crohn's Disease C 30 MIN
3/4 OR 1/2 INCH VIDEO CASSETTE
Reviews surgical aspects of Crohn's disease. Discusses the indications for surgery and the types of operations performed.
Prod-ROWLAB Dist-ROWLAB

Surgical Management Of Eyelid Burns C 10 MIN
16MM FILM OPTICAL SOUND
Demonstrates the use of large, free, full-thickness skin grafts in the correction of eyelid contractures resulting from thermal injuries. Stresses the principles of contracture release and correction with skin grafts. Discusses the essentials of post-operative management and shows long term results.
LC NO. 75-702317
Prod-EATONL Dist-EATONL 1967

Surgical Management Of Primary Hyperthyroidism C 21 MIN
16MM FILM OPTICAL SOUND PRO
Demonstrates the technique of subtotal thyroidectomy for primary hyperthyroidism devised by Dr Frank H Lahey. Emphasizes placing a low collar incision and elevation of the upper flap.
Prod-ACYDGD Dist-ACY 1950

Surgical Management Of Visceral Arterial Occlusion C 30 MIN
16MM FILM OPTICAL SOUND PRO
Shows that the two most important abdominal vascular syndromes, renal vascular hypertension and abdominal angina, may both be produced by the same mechanism, extrinsic compression by the crus of the diaphragm or intrinsic occlusion of the major visceral vessels.
Prod-ACYDGD Dist-ACY 1968

Surgical Nursing Care Of The Eye Patient C 22 MIN
16MM FILM OPTICAL SOUND
Describes the role of the eye nurse in a hospital and as assistant to the opthalmic surgeon. Discusses the training and abilities which are required for the eye nurse in the surgical nursing care of the eye patient.
LC NO. FIA66-899
Prod-ACYDGD Dist-ACY 1963

Surgical Preparation Of The Dog For The Physiology Laboratory C 21 MIN
16MM FILM OPTICAL SOUND C
Demonstrates the preliminary surgical procedures used to prepare the dog for general laboratory work, including administration of an anesthetic and tracheal and arterial cannulation.
Prod-WSU Dist-WSU 1959

Surgical Problems In Ulcerative Colitis C 26 MIN
16MM FILM OPTICAL SOUND PRO
Presents certain phases of ulcerative colitis by means of selected X-ray films and by slides of specimens, with special emphasis on the risk of cancer in longstanding cases.
Prod-ACYDGD Dist-ACY 1956

Surgical Procedure For Dog Experiments C 25 MIN
3/4 OR 1/2 INCH VIDEO CASSETTE PRO
Demonstrates techniques used to prepare a dog for various physiological experiments.
Prod-HSCIC Dist-HSCIC 1981

Surgical Procedure In The Penetrating Duodenal Ulcer With Massive Uncontrollable... C 25 MIN
16MM FILM OPTICAL SOUND PRO
Explains that 421 cases of massive hemorrhage from peptic ulcer have been observed on the fourth surgical division of Bellevue Hospital since 1928. Points out that the cases of uncontrollable hemorrhage in this series represent only 14 percent of the total, including those being operated upon as emergency or dying under conservative management.
Prod-ACYDGD Dist-ACY 1956

Surgical Procedures - An Integral Part Of General Practice C 180 MIN
3/4 INCH VIDEO CASSETTE PRO
Demonstrates oral surgical procedures that are normally done by general practitioners in their offices. Shows removal of an impacted tooth, a dental cyst and a torus palatinus. Demonstrates a biopsy procedure and multiple extractions with insertion of an immediate denture. Discusses time-tested surgical principles.
LC NO. 76-706164
Prod-USDH Dist-USNAC 1976

Surgical Recognition And Management Of Valvular Heart Disease, Pt 3 C 28 MIN
3/4 INCH VIDEO CASSETTE PRO
Discusses surgical management of mitral and aortic stenosis and regurgitation.
LC NO. 76-706108
Prod-WARMP Dist-USNAC 1969

Surgical Reduction Of The Maxillary Tuberosity C 13 MIN
3/4 OR 1/2 INCH VIDEO CASSETTE
Demonstrates a recommended surgical procedure for reduction of the maxillary tuberosity, considered by some prosthodonists to be a neglected factor in the construction of dentures.
Prod-VADTC Dist-AMDA 1969

Surgical Rehabilitation Of The Adult Cardiac C 33 MIN
16MM FILM OPTICAL SOUND PRO
Presents the techniques of several common corrective cardiac operations. Emphasizes the selection of adult patients for surgery from the standpoint of expected rehabilitation.
Prod-ACYDGD Dist-ACY 1965

Surgical Rehabilitation Of The Atrophied Mandible In Preparation For Denture Prosthesis C 25 MIN
16MM FILM OPTICAL SOUND
Explains that the atrophic mandible usually presents great difficulty of a satisfactory full denture prosthesis. Presents a technique, developed by Professor Hugo Obwegeser of the University of Zurich, Switzerland, which makes the patient's remaining mandibular bone available as a denture base. Shows an actual case from start to finish.
LC NO. 75-702330
Prod-EATONL Dist-EATONL 1968

Surgical Removal Of Impacted Mandibular Third Molar C 6 MIN
16MM FILM - 3/4 IN VIDEO PRO
Demonstrates a technique for the surgical removal of a mesio-angular impacted mandibular third molar. Shows controlled sectioning of the tooth utilizing a bur and elevator. Issued in 1968 as a motion picture.
LC NO. 78-706013
Prod-USVA Dist-USNAC 1977

Surgical Removal Of Impacted Maxillary Third Molar C 5 MIN
16MM FILM - 3/4 IN VIDEO PRO
Demonstrates the surgical removal of a distoangular maxillary third molar impaction. Issued in 1968 as a motion picture.
LC NO. 78-706012
Prod-USVA Dist-USNAC 1977

Surgical Removal Of Lesions In Pulmonary Tuberculosis C 2 MIN
16MM FILM, 3/4 OR 1/2 IN VIDEO PRO
Reproduces a roentgenogram of the chest of a patient with a persistent chronic lesion of tuberculosis. Shows how portions of the right lung are removed and how the tuberculous nodule is removed and cut open to expose the caseous material.
Prod-UCEMC Dist-UCEMC 1961

Surgical Removal Of Mesio-Angular Impacted Third Molar C 4 MIN
16MM FILM OPTICAL SOUND PRO
Shows how a mesio-angular impacted lower third molar is surgically removed without sectioning. Emphasizes the importance of obtaining adequate surgical exposure and following prescribed surgical techniques.
LC NO. 75-701329
Prod-USVA Dist-USNAC 1974

Surgical Removal Of Mesioangular Impacted Lower Third Molar C 4 MIN
3/4 OR 1/2 INCH VIDEO CASSETTE
Emphasizes the importance of obtaining adequate surgical exposure and following prescribed surgical techniques in a clinical demonstration.
Prod-VADTC Dist-AMDA 1973

Surgical Removal Of Vertically Impacted Upper And Lower Third Molars C 5 MIN
16MM FILM, 3/4 OR 1/2 IN VIDEO PRO
Describes the removal of vertically impacted upper and lower third molars. Shows the incision and how access to the upper third molar is gained.
LC NO. 80-706792
Prod-USVA Dist-USNAC Prodn-VADTC 1980

Surgical Repair Of Complete Uterine Prolapse C 29 MIN
16MM FILM OPTICAL SOUND PRO
Shows that vaginal hysterectomy (Heaney technique) precedes the anterior and posterior vaginal repair in a 60-year-old multiparous woman with third degree prosthedentia. Includes the surgical repair of the prolapsed bladder and rectal walls.
Prod-ACYDGD Dist-ACY 1952

Surgical Repair Of Direct Inguinal Hernia With Rectus Sheath Graft C 20 MIN
3/4 OR 1/2 INCH VIDEO CASSETTE PRO
Prod-PRIMED Dist-PRIMED

Surgical Repair Of Facial Lacerations For Optimum Cosmetic Results C 20 MIN
16MM FILM OPTICAL SOUND
Provides a detailed demonstration of a technique of repair designed to secure optimum cosmetic results for facial lacerations resulting from automobile accidents. Illustrates the use of instruments, sutures and local anesthesia for debridement and subcutaneous and cutaneous closures.
Prod-EATONL Dist-EATONL 1957

Surgical Repair Of Hydronephrosis C 23 MIN
16MM FILM OPTICAL SOUND
Uses preoperative X-rays, medical illustrations and postoperative excretory urograms to illustrate the principles of Dr Hamm's operative technique in two patients with a solitary left kidney with serious hydronephrosis and renal stones. Describes modifications of the V-Y plasty and emphasizes the rationale of eliminating splints and nephrostomy tubes.
LC NO. FIA66-66
Prod-EATON Dist-EATON Prodn-AVCORP 1965

Surgical Repair Of Hypospadias, The C 25 MIN
16MM FILM OPTICAL SOUND
Shows in detail the surgical techniques of repairing hypospadias as demonstrated in operations performed on two patients.
LC NO. FIA66-67
Prod-EATON Dist-EATON Prodn-AVCORP 1961

Surgical Repair Of Peyronie's Disease With Dermis Graft C 14 MIN
16MM FILM OPTICAL SOUND
Shows how to repair Peyronie's disease by resecting the plaque and covering the defect in the tunica albuginea with a graft of dermis obtained from the skin of the abdomen. Demonstrates the pathology of Peyronie's disease and depicts a surgical procedure using the above technique.
LC NO. 75-702248
Prod-EATONL Dist-EATONL 1973

Surgical Repair Of The Adult Cleft Palate C 19 MIN
3/4 OR 1/2 INCH VIDEO CASSETTE PRO
Details an unusual case history in which surgery is performed to correct a cleft palate in an adult.
Prod-WFP Dist-WFP

Surgical Replacement Of The Mandible With Stainless Steel Mesh C 16 MIN
16MM FILM, 3/4 OR 1/2 IN VIDEO
Demonstrates the surgical replacement of large segments of the mandible using cast stainless steel mesh. Proves that this prosthesis is capable of restoring both esthetics and function.
Prod-VADTC Dist-AMDA 1970

Surgical Restoration Of Voice Following Total Laryngectomy C 120 MIN
3/4 OR 1/2 INCH VIDEO CASSETTE
Brief discussion of the historical perspectives of the surgical restoration of voice following total laryngectomy.
Prod-PUAVC Dist-PUAVC

Surgical Separation Of Conjoined Twins - Three Case Studies C 30 MIN
3/4 OR 1/2 INCH VIDEO CASSETTE PRO
Acquaints surgeons, nurses, anesthesiologists, pediatricians, operating room personnel, and medical students with examples of three complex surgical operations for separation of conjoined twins.
Prod-HSCIC Dist-HSCIC 1984

Surgical Skin Prep, The C 14 MIN
3/4 OR 1/2 INCH VIDEO CASSETTE PRO
Discusses the surgical skin prep.
Prod-WFP Dist-WFP

Surgical Skin Preparation C 13 MIN
3/4 OR 1/2 INCH VIDEO CASSETTE C A
Discusses and demonstrates the three phases of surgical skin preparation which minimize the potential of bacterial contamination in a surgical wound.
Prod-UTEXN Dist-TEF

Surgical Technique For Correction Of Complete Urinary Incontinence C 15 MIN
16MM FILM OPTICAL SOUND PRO
Presents a detailed demonstration of a surgical technique successfully applied for correction of postprostatectomy total urinary incontinence. Uses animation and art work to clarify various steps in the procedure.
LC NO. 75-702246
Prod-EATONL Dist-EATONL 1973

Surgical Technique For Multiplex Total Knee Replacement C 32 MIN
3/4 OR 1/2 INCH VIDEO CASSETTE PRO
See series title for descriptive statement.
From The Prothesis Films Series.
Prod-WFP Dist-WFP

Surgical Techniques In Intrathoracic Respiratory Diseases B 38 MIN
16MM FILM OPTICAL SOUND PRO
Presents the unilateral surgical opening of the thoracic cavity with emphasis on dissection, ligation and closure.
Prod-AMVMA Dist-AMVMA

Surgical Techniques Of The Several Types Of Skin Graft C 33 MIN
16MM FILM OPTICAL SOUND PRO
Presents the technique of application of thick-split grafts and whole-thickness grafts of skin. Demonstrates the use of dermatape and the cutting of skin grafts by the dermatome, the electro-dermatome and by hand.
Prod-ACYDGD Dist-ACY 1952

Surgical Techniques, Incisions, And Closures C 30 MIN
16MM FILM OPTICAL SOUND
Demonstrates correct techniques for performing a surgical incision, closing the wound with sutures and dressing the wound.
LC NO. 80-700393
Prod-NOEJM Dist-COM 1979

Surgical Treatment For Ankylosis Of The Temporomandibular Joint C 10 MIN
16MM FILM, 3/4 OR 1/2 IN VIDEO
Demonstrates a surgical corrective procedure using a tyconium prosthesis constructed to the measurements of the English penny.
Prod-VADTC Dist-AMDA 1970

Surgical Treatment For Varicose Veins B 20 MIN
16MM FILM OPTICAL SOUND H-C A
Examines the causes of varicose veins and the recommended surgery for the condition. Shows the stripling procedure which is involved in vascular surgery. Emphasizes the danger in neglecting a severe condition.
From The Doctors At Work Series.
LC NO. FIA65-1364
Prod-CMA Dist-LAWREN Prodn-LAWREN 1961

Surgical Treatment Of Atrial Septal Defects C 20 MIN
16MM FILM OPTICAL SOUND PRO
Presents case studies illustrating several types of atrial septal defects and the technical problems each presents in surgical repair.
Prod-SQUIBB Dist-SQUIBB

Surgical Treatment Of Benign Breast Diseases C 35 MIN
16MM FILM OPTICAL SOUND PRO
Shows the techniques for diagnosis and treatment, combined with the least deformity, in patients with fibro-adenoma, cystic disease, ectasia, intraductal papilloma, recurring sub and para areolar abscesses.
Prod-ACYDGD Dist-ACY 1969

Surgical Treatment Of Bronchogenic Carcinoma C 29 MIN
16MM FILM OPTICAL SOUND PRO
Points out that for the surgical treatment of bronchogenic carcinoma, radical pneumonectomy probably offers the best prognosis to the patients. Emphasizes that in selected cases, however, lobectomy with mediastinal lymphadenectomy should be the elected procedure.
Prod-ACYDGD Dist-ACY 1957

Surgical Treatment Of Direct Hernia C 31 MIN
16MM FILM OPTICAL SOUND PRO
Outlines the surgical treatment of direct hernia, emphasizing a major point. Demonstrates that the operation for direct hernia should be a radical one, including steps that may not be necessary for all simpler and direct hernias.
Prod-ACYDGD Dist-ACY 1956

Surgical Treatment Of Diverticulitis C 20 MIN
16MM FILM OPTICAL SOUND PRO
Explains that the mortality rate for the surgical treatment of diverticulitis is low but that the morbidity remains high. Emphasizes that it can only be reduced if surgeons will operate upon selected patients with diverticulitis before they develop a complication of their disease.
Prod-ACYDGD Dist-ACY 1961

Surgical Treatment Of Diverticulitis Of The Sigmoid C 33 MIN
16MM FILM OPTICAL SOUND PRO
Considers the various stages of pathology along with the indications for surgery and the type of surgical operation needed for diverticulitis of the sigmoid.
Prod-ACYDGD Dist-ACY 1953

Surgical Treatment Of Gastric Ulcer C 25 MIN
16MM FILM OPTICAL SOUND PRO
Depicts the surgical treatment of a fifty-year-old woman with a giant gastric ulcer. Demonstrates the sequential technical maneuvers in performing a conservative subtotal gastrectomy with a Billroth II type anastomosis.
Prod-ACYDGD Dist-ACY 1962

Surgical Treatment Of Gastric Ulcer C 27 MIN
16MM FILM OPTICAL SOUND PRO
Describes the surgical management of an 80 year old woman with a gastric ulcer recurring despite intensive medical management. Shows that the operative procdure consists of a partial gastrectomy and Billroth I reconstruction.
Prod-ACYDGD Dist-ACY 1968

Surgical Treatment Of Hyperparathyroidism C 25 MIN
16MM FILM OPTICAL SOUND PRO
Illustrates some of the technical problems involved in the surgical care of hyperparathyroidism.
Prod-ACYDGD Dist-ACY 1964

Surgical Treatment Of Incontinence In The Male (Silicone Gel Prosthesis Technique) C 14 MIN
16MM FILM OPTICAL SOUND
Presents an operation for treatment of incontinence in the male

based on the principle of compressing the bulbous urethra with a soft implantable silicone gel prosthesis, anchored by dacron straps placed around the crura for initial fixation. Uses medical illustrations to show the anatomy involved.
LC NO. 75-702284
Prod-EATONL Dist-EATONL 1973

Surgical Treatment Of Machine Induced Genital Trauma C 13 MIN
16MM FILM OPTICAL SOUND PRO
Demonstrates the manner in which rural avulsion genital injuries occur and the surgical technique utilized in the management of the denuded penile shaft and testis.
LC NO. 75-702230
Prod-EATONL Dist-EATONL 1974

Surgical Treatment Of Megacolon C 21 MIN
16MM FILM OPTICAL SOUND PRO
Demonstrates the technique of resection of the aganglionic segment. Discusses problems related to a preliminary transverse colostomy.
Prod-ACYDGD Dist-ACY 1965

Surgical Treatment Of Priapism C 14 MIN
16MM FILM OPTICAL SOUND
Demonstrates Dr Chester C Winter's technique for the anastomosis of the saphenous vein to the corpus cavernosum in a 21-year-old patient who was seen five days after he experienced a second episode of idiopathic priapism. Follows the patient for a period of five months following surgery.
LC NO. 75-702296
Prod-EATONL Dist-EATONL 1965

Surgical Treatment Of Prolapse Of The Rectum C 31 MIN
16MM FILM OPTICAL SOUND PRO
Shows the surgical treatment of true prolapse of the rectum by a one-stage operation with a perineal approach. Explains that the procedure is based upon the concept that true rectal prolapse is essentially a sliding hernia of the cul-de-sac through a defect in the pelvic diaphragm.
Prod-ACYDGD Dist-ACY 1957

Surgical Treatment Of Renal Injury C 20 MIN
16MM FILM OPTICAL SOUND
Presents a plan of surgical management which has evolved in the treatment of renal injury from experience with the management of over 100 patients with penetrating renal injury. Shows that certain parts of this plan have been expanded and incorporated into the surgical management of renal neoplasm and calculous disease.
From The Surgical Treatment Of Genito-Urinary Trauma Series.
LC NO. 75-702271
Prod-EATONL Dist-EATONL 1969

Surgical Treatment Of Renovascular Hypertension C 30 MIN
16MM FILM OPTICAL SOUND
Deals with the surgical treatment of renovascular hypertension. Demonstrates diagnostic procedures, including renography, the Howard test and a surgical technique used successfully in 1,400 consecutive aortograms. Demonstrates the details of the surgical procedures in several patients.
LC NO. FIA66-556
Prod-EATON Dist-EATON 1961

Surgical Treatment Of Small Bowel Obstruction Resulting From Occlusion Of The... C 15 MIN
16MM FILM OPTICAL SOUND PRO
Explains that partial intestinal obstruction has been caused by stenosis of the small bowel, secondary to healed infarction and is treated by segmental resection with end-to-end anastomosis.
Prod-ACYDGD Dist-ACY 1964

Surgical Treatment Of The Tetralogy Of Fallot C 32 MIN
16MM FILM OPTICAL SOUND PRO
Demonstrates the creation of an artificial ductus arteriosis in the surgical treatment of tetralogy of fallot.
Prod-ACYDGD Dist-ACY 1953

Surgical Treatment Of Ureteral Trauma C 15 MIN
16MM FILM OPTICAL SOUND
Presents a new technique developed by Drs C Eugene Carlton Jr and Russell Scott Jr for the primary watertight repair of ureteral injury. Points out that this technique of watertight non-intubated repair has markedly reduced the incidence of ureteral stricture formation.
From The Surgical Treatment Of Genito-Urinary Trauma Series.
LC NO. 75-702272
Prod-EATONL Dist-EATONL 1970

Surgical Treatment Of Urethral Trauma C 15 MIN
16MM FILM OPTICAL SOUND
Points out that the incidence of urethral stricture following significant urethral trauma is extremely high. Shows how Drs C Eugene Carlton Jr and Russell Scott Jr have employed early surgical debridement and primary watertight repair in the treatment of significant urethral trauma and have found that the incidence of structure formation has been virtually eliminated. Illustrates the technique of the primary surgical repair of the injured urethra.
Prod-EATONL Dist-EATONL 1970

Surgical Treatment Of Varicose Veins, The C 24 MIN
16MM FILM OPTICAL SOUND PRO
Demonstrates the ligation of the long and short saphenous veins at their junction with the deep venous system together with stripping of these segments and supplemented with individual ligation of perforators.
Prod-ACYDGD Dist-ACY 1955

Surgical Treatment Of Ventricular Septal Defect - Technique And Results In 292 Cases C 20 MIN
16MM FILM OPTICAL SOUND PRO
Examines the surgical treatment of ventricular septal defects in which cardiopulmonary bypass was used.
Prod-SQUIBB Dist-SQUIBB

Surgical Wound Infections C 16 MIN
3/4 OR 1/2 INCH VIDEO CASSETTE PRO
Covers the classification of surgical infections and the etiologic agents involved in nosocomial surgical wound infections. Identifies factors that might predispose patients to surgical wound infections.
From The Hospital Infection Control - Infection Control For Medical Practitioners Series.
Prod-HSCIC Dist-HSCIC

Surgical-Orthodontic Correction Of Maxillary Protrusions C 22 MIN
16MM FILM OPTICAL SOUND
Depicts the evaluation and treatment of a patient with severe malocclusion, emphasizing the coordinated efforts of the involved dental specialists.
LC NO. 70-715308
Prod-MAYO Dist-MAYO 1970

Surprise - Sparkling Stars B 15 MIN
2 INCH VIDEOTAPE P
See series title for descriptive statement.
From The Sounds Like Magic Series.
Prod-MOEBA Dist-GPITVL Prodn-KYNETV

Surprise For Otto, A C 4 MIN
16MM FILM OPTICAL SOUND K-I
Considers if the green traffic light always means 'go.'
From The Otto The Auto Series.
Prod-AAAFTS Dist-AAAFTS 1971

Surprise, The C 15 MIN
3/4 OR 1/2 INCH VIDEO CASSETTE K-P
Shows how properties of matter are used to describe and compare materials.
From The Dragons, Wagons And Wax, Set 1 Series.
Prod-CTI Dist-CTI

Surprises Of Failure Can Lead To The Secrets Of Success, The C 28 MIN
16MM FILM OPTICAL SOUND
Presents 27 people who have known disappointment and failure but who went on to become successful.
From The You Can Do It - If Series.
LC NO. 81-700092
Prod-VANDER Dist-VANDER 1980

Surprising Amsterdam C 28 MIN
16MM FILM OPTICAL SOUND
Illustrates the diversity of life, history and entertainment in Amsterdam, as a means of encouraging travelers to that city.
LC NO. 72-700032
Prod-KLMRDA Dist-KLMRDA 1971

Surreal Cartoon Situations C 15 MIN
2 INCH VIDEOTAPE
See series title for descriptive statement.
From The Charlie's Pad Series.
Prod-WSIU Dist-PUBTEL

Surreal Estate C 10 MIN
16MM FILM OPTICAL SOUND
Relates the story of a man who encounters a house for sale which has doorways, rooms, stairways, restaurants and museums which appear and disappear. Reveals that after several adventures, he makes his way out and is greeted by a peculiar realtor.
LC NO. 78-700312
Prod-SLVRMN Dist-SLVRMN 1977

Surrealism C 7 MIN
16MM FILM, 3/4 OR 1/2 IN VIDEO J-C
Explains the modern art style of surrealism which extracts things from their usual settings and places them in unnatural surroundings. Points out how surrealistic symbols provide a quality of mystery and intrigue.
From The Understanding Modern Art Series.
Prod-THIEB Dist-PHENIX 1961

Surrealism C 24 MIN
16MM FILM, 3/4 OR 1/2 IN VIDEO H-C A
Studies the mysterious faces of surrealism in the works of such artists as Ernst, Klee, Miro, Tanguy, Magritte and Dali. Points out the 'INTENTIONAL ABSURDITY,' the fantasies and the dreams which mark this movement.
Prod-IFB Dist-IFB

Surrealism - Inner Space C 29 MIN
2 INCH VIDEOTAPE
See series title for descriptive statement.
From The Museum Open House Series.
Prod-WGBHTV Dist-PUBTEL

Surrealism - Seekers Of The Dream C 29 MIN
2 INCH VIDEOTAPE
See series title for descriptive statement.
From The Museum Open House Series.
Prod-WGBHTV Dist-PUBTEL

Surrealism And Dada C 18 MIN
16MM FILM, 3/4 OR 1/2 IN VIDEO H-C
Illustrates the history of surrealism and dada in the twentieth century art through the work of painters such as Dali, Ernst, Miro and Klee.
Prod-TEXFLM Dist-TEXFLM

Surrender At Appomattox C 52 MIN
16MM FILM OPTICAL SOUND J-H
Shows how America's Civil War ended when two great generals, Robert E Lee and Ulysses S Grant, met to make peace and reunite a nation.
Prod-WOLPER Dist-FI 1974

Surrender At Appomattox C 15 MIN
3/4 OR 1/2 INCH VIDEO CASSETTE
Uses archival stills, original illustrations and quotes from eyewitnesses to relive the surrender of the Confederacy at Appomattox Courthouse in Virginia.
LC NO. 84-706417
Prod-USNPS Dist-USNAC 1982

Surrender At Appomattox, Pt 1 - The Union Triumphant (1863-1865) C 26 MIN
16MM FILM OPTICAL SOUND J-H
Shows how America's Civil War ended when two great generals, Robert E Lee and Ulysses S Grant, met to make peace and reunite a nation.
Prod-WOLPER Dist-FI 1974

Surrender At Appomattox, Pt 2 - Appomattox Court House (1865) C 26 MIN
16MM FILM OPTICAL SOUND J-H
Shows how America's Civil War ended when two great generals, Robert E Lee and Ulysses S Grant, met to make peace and reunite a nation.
Prod-WOLPER Dist-FI 1974

Surrender At Fort Donelson C 5 MIN
16MM FILM - 3/4 IN VIDEO
Re-creates the night of February 15, 1862, when Confederate Generals Floyd, Pillow and Buckner struggled to decide whether their cold and weary troops could cut through the reinforced Union lines surrounding Fort Donelson or whether they would have to surrender.
LC NO. 79-708080
Prod-USNPS Dist-USNAC 1979

Surrounded - Peer Group Membership C 15 MIN
16MM FILM, 3/4 OR 1/2 IN VIDEO J-H
Describes Kelly's struggle to decide whether or not to tell her friends that she has epilepsy.
From The On The Level Series.
LC NO. 81-706932
Prod-EDFCEN Dist-AITECH 1980

Surrounded By Life C 30 MIN
3/4 OR 1/2 INCH VIDEO CASSETTE
See series title for descriptive statement.
From The Rebop Series.
Prod-WGBHTV Dist-MDCPB

Surveillance - Bruce Charlesworth C 21 MIN
3/4 INCH VIDEO CASSETTE C A
Prod-AFA Dist-AFA 1981

Surveillance - Who's Watching B 60 MIN
16MM FILM, 3/4 OR 1/2 IN VIDEO
Presents an on-the-scene investigation of political surveillance and harassment of individuals with a major focus upon the activities of the Chicago Police Department's 'RED SQUAD.' Features interviews with persons who have been affected by surveillance, government officials and former FBI agents. Examines the dissemination of information about private citizens by the FBI, city police departments and other agencies.
LC NO. 80-707101
Prod-IU Dist-IU 1973

Survey Of Children's Speech Disorders, A C 29 MIN
16MM FILM OPTICAL SOUND C
Illustrates how children with problems of hearing, cleft palate, cerebral palsy, articulation and stuttering learn to use and understand speech.
Prod-UIOWA Dist-UIOWA 1961

Survey Of English Literature I—A Series

Examines English literature from Beowulf to Henry Fielding, keyed to the Norton Anthology of English Literature.
Prod-MDCPB Dist-MDCPB

Adam Unparadised - Book IX Of Paradise Lost	
Age Of Gold, The - The Battle Of Maldon And	045 MIN
Ancient Poets And Modern Ladies - The Rape Of	045 MIN
Chaucer's World - General Prologue,	045 MIN
Cut Is The Branch - Christopher Marlowe's Dr	045 MIN
Dream Of Man, The - The Renaissance In England	045 MIN
End Of An Era - Beowulf	045 MIN
Escape Into Reality - Pre-Romantic Poetry -	045 MIN
Fortunate Fall - Paradoxical Results Of	045 MIN
Growing Up In Eastcheap - Shakespeare's Henry	045 MIN
Hero And Villain - The Role Of Satan In	045 MIN
Horse Sense About Houyhnhnms - The Fourth	045 MIN
Long Voyage Home, The - Donne's Religious	045 MIN
Love Conquers All - Love, Human, Divine,	045 MIN
Love Story - Donne's Love Poetry	045 MIN
Madness And Method - The Play Within The	045 MIN
Man In The Ironic Mask, The - Jonathan	045 MIN
Miller's Tale	045 MIN
Name Of The Age, The - James Boswell And	045 MIN
New And Novel - The Development Of The Novel	045 MIN
Ourselves To Know - Alexander Pope's Essay On	045 MIN
Pardoner's Secret	045 MIN
Plump Jack - Shakespeare's Henry IV - Prince	045 MIN
Poet And Hero - Milton's Paradise Lost - The	045 MIN
Questions Of Hamlet - Why Did Hamlet Delay	045 MIN
Theatre Of The Mind - John Donne's	045 MIN
Through The Looking Glass - Introduction -	045 MIN
Virtue Rewarded - Henry Fielding's Joseph	045 MIN
Woe That Is In Marriage - The Wife Of Bath	045 MIN

Yorick's Skull - Gallows Humour In Hamlet 045 MIN

Survey Of Multiattribute Utility Theory C 53 MIN
3/4 OR 1/2 INCH VIDEO CASSETTE
See series title for descriptive statement.
From The Decision Analysis Series.
Prod-MIOT Dist-MIOT

Survey Of Office Automation Applications C 45 MIN
3/4 OR 1/2 INCH VIDEO CASSETTE
Provides descriptions of the objectives, implementation strategies and results of office automation applications in a cross section of organizations.
From The Management Strategies For Office Automation Series.
Prod-DELTAK Dist-DELTAK

Survey Of Refuse Disposal Methods, A C 10 MIN
16MM FILM OPTICAL SOUND
Demonstrates advantages and disadvantages of types of refuse disposal ranging from open dumps and dumping in oceans and rivers to scientifically engineered metropolitan incineration and sanitary landfills.
LC NO. FIE60-79
Prod-USPHS Dist-USNAC 1959

Survey Of The Primates C 38 MIN
16MM FILM OPTICAL SOUND H-C
Presents nine of the eleven families which comprise the order of primates and uses forty-nine different primate forms to represent those families. Attempts to encourage respect for non-human primates as unique and valuable forms of life that must be protected from forces which threaten their extinction.
LC NO. 76-710734
Prod-APPLE Dist-PHM 1970

Survey, The C 20 MIN
16MM FILM, 3/4 OR 1/2 IN VIDEO
Demonstrates techniques used in conducting a problem-oriented archaeological survey. Follows a survey team as it moves through the Skagit River Delta in Washington State. Presents processes of surface collecting, measurement and recording.
Prod-SF Dist-SF

Surveying A Casualty C 9 MIN
3/4 OR 1/2 INCH VIDEO CASSETTE PRO
Portrays the process of determining the severity of a victim's wounds, and prioritizing and providing appropriate treatment.
From The EMT Video - Group One Series.
LC NO. 84-706492
Prod-USA Dist-USNAC 1983

Surveying For Hidden Treasure C 26 MIN
3/4 OR 1/2 INCH VIDEO CASSETTE
See series title for descriptive statement.
From The Art Of Reading/Speed Learning Series.
Prod-LEARNI Dist-DELTAK

Surveying For Hidden Treasure C 27 MIN
3/4 OR 1/2 INCH VIDEO CASSETTE J-H
Shows how to scrutinize a book for hidden meanings. Reveals that the title, front matter, first page and illustrations can reveals a lot to the person who knows what to look for.
From The Speed Learning Series.
Prod-LEARNI Dist-AITECH 1982

Surveying For Hidden Treasure C 30 MIN
3/4 OR 1/2 INCH VIDEO CASSETTE
Discusses surveying as a major step in sharpening purpose for reading and provides an overview of the material that has to be read to help students decide what reading skills to use in dealing with that reading.
From The Speed Learning Video Series. Show 7
Prod-LEARNI Dist-LEARNI

Surveying The Stars C 29 MIN
3/4 INCH VIDEO CASSETTE C A
Focuses on methods of determining distances to stars and movement of stars in relation to solar system. Describes use of blink comparator and Doppler effect.
From The Project Universe - Astronomy Series. Lesson 16
Prod-COAST Dist-CDTEL Prodn-SCCON

Survie C 17 MIN
16MM FILM OPTICAL SOUND
A French language film. Shows the need for motorcycle safety instruction and some of the teaching methods used in existing motorcycle training courses.
LC NO. 77-702660
Prod-CANHSC Dist-CANHSC Prodn-CRAF 1976

Survival C 17 MIN
16MM FILM OPTICAL SOUND
Shows the need for motorcycle safety instruction and some of the teaching methods used in existing motorcycle training courses.
LC NO. 77-702660
Prod-CANHSC Dist-CANHSC Prodn-CRAF 1976

Survival C 18 MIN
16MM FILM OPTICAL SOUND J-C A
Demonstrates the use of satellite communications systems in predicting and coping with natural disasters.
LC NO. 77-700779
Prod-NASA Dist-USNAC 1976

Survival B 30 MIN
16MM FILM OPTICAL SOUND PRO
Discusses man's use of judgment in protecting and maintaining the essential elements of his environment for survival.
From The Public Health Science - Bioenvironmental Health Series.
Prod-KUHTTV Dist-GPITVL

Survival C 10 MIN
16MM FILM, 3/4 OR 1/2 IN VIDEO IND
Describes a new life craft that is now used on many ships, tankers and off-shore oil and gas rigs. Explains the features of this 28-man survival capsule, revealing that it is unsinkable, impact resistant, radar reflective and fireproof.
Prod-IFB Dist-IFB 1975

Survival C 16 MIN
16MM FILM, 3/4 OR 1/2 IN VIDEO J-H A
Demonstrates the training program developed by the Motorcycle Safety Council to provide both safe riding strategies for bikers and basic information about motorcycle maintenance.
Prod-NFBC Dist-MEDIAG 1985

Survival C 20 MIN
3/4 OR 1/2 INCH VIDEO CASSETTE J-C A
Discusses various aspects of survival safety.
From The Safety Sense Series. Pt. 12
Prod-WCVETV Dist-GPITVL 1981

Survival C 28 MIN
3/4 OR 1/2 INCH VIDEO CASSETTE H-C A
Tells how pollution, population and the depletion of non-renewable resources concern countries of all sizes.
Prod-UPI Dist-JOU

Survival B 30 MIN
2 INCH VIDEOTAPE PRO
Discusses man's use of judgment in protecting and maintaining the essential elements of his environment for survival. (Broadcast quality)
From The Public Health Science Series. Unit V - Introduction To Bioenvironmental Health
Prod-TEXWU Dist-GPITVL Prodn-KUHTTV

Survival After High School C 17 MIN
16MM FILM, 3/4 OR 1/2 IN VIDEO J-H
Demonstrates common problems associated with such things as dealing with landlord, paying bills and balancing a checkbook. Shows students who are living on their own for the first time how to handle these everyday problems.
LC NO. 81-707266
Prod-CENTRO Dist-CORF 1981

Survival And Advancement C 30 MIN
3/4 OR 1/2 INCH VIDEO CASSETTE C A
Discusses the issue of how to survive and advance within an organization.
From The Business Of Management Series. Lesson 24
Prod-SCCON Dist-SCCON

Survival And Evasion In Southeast Asia-Short-Term Evasion C 21 MIN
3/4 OR 1/2 INCH VIDEO CASSETTE
Trains U S pilots on what to do if shot down over enemy territory.
Prod-IHF Dist-IHF

Survival And The Senses C 25 MIN
16MM FILM, 3/4 OR 1/2 IN VIDEO H-C A
Uses observations, experiments and animation to show how sense organs make animals aware of their environments and determine their behavior. Points out that there are animal senses which man cannot equal.
From The Behavior And Survival Series.
Prod-MGHT Dist-MGHT 1973

Survival Factor, The - Defense Mechanisms In The Sea C 12 MIN
16MM FILM OPTICAL SOUND J-C A
Covers in broad terms the defense mechanisms of sea creatures in deep water in the Benthic environment.
From The Living World Of The Sea Series.
LC NO. 72-702644
Prod-REELA Dist-MIAMIS 1969

Survival For Sportsmen C 11 MIN
16MM FILM OPTICAL SOUND
Demonstrates water safety for sportsmen, showing what to do when a boat tips over.
Prod-AREDC Dist-AMRC 1972

Survival In The Animal World C 11 MIN
16MM FILM, 3/4 OR 1/2 IN VIDEO I-J
Observes a variety of animal life to show that the different species have developed physical traits and instincts that help them to survive.
Prod-WER Dist-JOU 1971

Survival In The Sahel C 15 MIN
16MM FILM OPTICAL SOUND
Shows the effects of the drought on humans, animals and environment in Central and West Africa and Ethiopia. Stresses the massive relief effort mounted by the United States Government, other nations and private agencies and individuals. Emphasizes the role of the U S Agency for International Development in helping to increase food production and to improve nutrition, health, transportation, reforestation and water supply.
LC NO. 75-702875
Prod-USAID Dist-USNAC 1975

Survival In The Sea C 30 MIN
16MM FILM, 3/4 OR 1/2 IN VIDEO J-H
Studies the struggle for survival among sea creatures and explains some of the reasons why fish have become adapted through natural selection.
From The World We Live In Series.
Prod-TIMELI Dist-MGHT 1968

Survival In The Wilderness-A Series
3/4 OR 1/2 INCH VIDEO CASSETTE I-H A
Prod-MORLAT Dist-SF

Artificial Respiration 010 MIN
Bush First Aid, Pt 1 010 MIN
Bush First Aid, Pt 2 010 MIN
Distress Signals, Pt 1 010 MIN
Distress Signals, Pt 2 010 MIN
Dressing Fish 010 MIN
Drownproofing 010 MIN
Fire Making And Shelters 010 MIN
Fundamental Canoeing 010 MIN
Proper Summer Bush Clothing 010 MIN
Survival Kit, The, Pt 1 010 MIN
Survival Kit, The, Pt 2 010 MIN
Use And Care Of Axes And Knives 010 MIN
Using A Compass 010 MIN

Survival In The Winter Storm C 27 MIN
16MM FILM - 3/4 IN VIDEO
Deals with dangers inherent in winter weather, giving advice on how to prepare for severe weather conditions. Explains the meaning of specific forecasts and points out the necessity for emergency planning by local governments. Issued in 1974 as a motion picture.
LC NO. 80-707129
Prod-USFDAA Dist-USNAC Prodn-BAY 1980

Survival Kit, The, Pt 1 C 10 MIN
16MM FILM, 3/4 OR 1/2 IN VIDEO I-H
Shows a survival kit which is contained in a box six inches long by four inches wide and two inches deep. Details the items in the survival kit and explains how they are designed to combat the seven enemies of survival.
From The Survival In The Wilderness Series.
Prod-MORLAT Dist-SF 1967

Survival Kit, The, Pt 2 C 10 MIN
16MM FILM, 3/4 OR 1/2 IN VIDEO I-H
Explains that the seven enemies of survival are fear, pain, cold, thirst, hunger, fatigue and loneliness. Shows how two girls, who despite a serious accident in witch they lost everything except their survival kit, are abot to make themselves comfortable in a short space of time and take positive action to ensure that their rescue is effected.
From The Survival In The Wilderness Series.
Prod-MORLAT Dist-SF 1967

Survival Of Sontheary Sou, The C 53 MIN
3/4 INCH VIDEOTAPE
Documents the story of a Cambodian refugee in America, and the atrocities in Cambodia of the Khmer Rouge. Intended for relevant secondary school programs and university courses, mental health professionals and religions and community groups. In two parts of 30 minutes and 23 minutes.
Prod-BARND Dist-BARND

Survival Of Spaceship Earth C 60 MIN
16MM FILM OPTICAL SOUND
Presents a devastating environmental statement, a shocking brutal look at some of the world today which may become most of the world tomorrow.
LC NO. 73-701359
Prod-WB Dist-WB 1972

Survival Of The Black College C 29 MIN
3/4 INCH VIDEO CASSETTE
Discusses the problems facing black colleges today.
From The Like It Is Series.
Prod-OHC Dist-HRC

Survival Of The Fittest C 15 MIN
3/4 OR 1/2 INCH VIDEO CASSETTE I
As Grandpa and Caroline fish in the creek, Caroline wonders what happened to the Swensons who used to live there. Grandpa tells her that they left long ago and tells her the story of the Survival of the Fittest during pioneer days.
From The We Are One Series.
Prod-NEITV Dist-GPITVL 1983

Survival Of The Fittest C 52 MIN
16MM FILM, 3/4 OR 1/2 IN VIDEO
Covers quarter horse conformation and the relation of form to function.
Prod-AQHORS Dist-AQHORS 1978

Survival Of The Fittest C 60 MIN
3/4 OR 1/2 INCH VIDEO CASSETTE J-H A
Uses slow-motion photography to show how a horse's conformation helps or hinders the ability to perform and how it affects health.
Prod-CUETV Dist-CUNIV

Survival Of The Fittest (Spanish) C 52 MIN
16MM FILM, 3/4 OR 1/2 IN VIDEO
Covers quarter horse conformation and the relation of form to function.
Prod-AQHORS Dist-AQHORS 1978

Survival Of The Fittest-A Series
PRO
Discusses health promotion programs and provides the latest information on cardiovascular health, stress, nutrition, exercise and diet.
Prod-PRORE Dist-PRORE

Employee Fitness - Fact Or Fantasy 024 MIN
Fitness Formula, The 027 MIN
Health Fitness Professionals, The 018 MIN
Heart Disease - Prevention And Rehabilitation 017 MIN
Stress Management 017 MIN
Wellness In The Workplace 024 MIN

Survival Of The Fittest-A Series

Discusses the needs of the growth industry that has arisen from the fitness boom and the health promotion marketplace. Helps to understand the importance of preventive measures avail-

able to persons suffering from heart disease or stress related problems.
Prod-SCCL Dist-HMDI

Employee Fitness - Fact Or Fantasy 024 MIN
Fitness Formula, The 027 MIN
Health Fitness Professionals, The 018 MIN
Heart Disease - Prevention And Rehabilitation 017 MIN
Stress Management 017 MIN
Wellness Is The Workplace 024 MIN

Survival Of The Kit Fox - A Conservation Case Study C 15 MIN
16MM FILM, 3/4 OR 1/2 IN VIDEO I-H
Observes the kit fox, a small prairie animal, throughout one full year. Shows her in each of the four seasons building her den, raising her young and hunting for food. Studies methods of wildlife conservation.
Prod-ALTSUL Dist-JOU 1967

Survival Of The Species, The C 55 MIN
16MM FILM, 3/4 OR 1/2 IN VIDEO H-C A
Examines the crucial behavior patterns, including aggression, which has made man the type of species he is. Looks at new evidence that suggests the human animal will survive.
From The Making Of Mankind Series.
Prod-BBCTV Dist-TIMLIF 1982

Survival Run C 12 MIN
16MM FILM, 3/4 OR 1/2 IN VIDEO
Documents the efforts of Harry Cordellos, a blind marathon runner, as he competes in the Dipsea Race.
Prod-MAGUSF Dist-PFP 1979

Survival Shooting Techniques C 35 MIN
16MM FILM, 3/4 OR 1/2 IN VIDEO
Presents state-of-the-art techniques for survival shooting with a revolver, automatic and shotgun. Includes patterns of encounter instinct shooting, disarming techniques, shooting behind natural cover, shooting in low light level conditions and reloading under fire.
Prod-MTI Dist-MTI 1979

Survival Skills C 30 MIN
3/4 OR 1/2 INCH VIDEO CASSETTE
Takes a look at the range of competencies that comprise survival skills and ways. Tells how curriculum can introduce some of these skills, such as understanding want ads, locating community resources and learning about health care and personal finances.
From The Teaching Students With Special Needs Series.
Prod-MSITV Dist-PBS 1981

Survival Skills - Organizing And Maintaining A Home C
3/4 OR 1/2 INCH VIDEO CASSETTE J-H A
Teaches home management. Gives information on organizing living quarters, and management, upkeep and simple repair of the home. Includes decor development and cleaning.
Prod-EDUACT Dist-EDUACT

Survival Skills For The Classroom Teacher—A Series
16MM FILM, 3/4 OR 1/2 IN VIDEO T
Looks at the real everyday problems facing the modern teacher including teacher stress, questioning techniques, sexism, stereotyping and multi-cultural education.
Prod-MFFD Dist-FI

Assertive Discipline In The Classroom 029 MIN
Coping With Teacher Stress 029 MIN
Dare To Discipline 029 MIN
Glasser On Discipline 028 MIN
Multi-Cultural Education - A Teaching Style 029 MIN
New Approaches To Big Problems 029 MIN
Questions For Thinking 028 MIN
Sexism, Stereotyping And Hidden Values 029 MIN
Starting Tomorrow 029 MIN
Ten Steps To Discipline 029 MIN
Who, What And Why Of Authority, The 029 MIN
Working In The Integrated Classroom 029 MIN

Survival Stresses C 30 MIN
16MM FILM, 3/4 OR 1/2 IN VIDEO
Discusses major physiological stresses that may be encountered by persons facing a survival situation in the Arctic, in the desert, in the tropics and on water.
Prod-USAF Dist-USNAC 1961

Survival Swimming C 7 MIN
16MM FILM - 3/4 IN VIDEO
Shows floating and treading techniques usable after falling into water with clothes on.
From The Lifesaving And Water Safety Series.
Prod-AMRC Dist-AMRC 1975

Survival Swimming B 14 MIN
16MM FILM, 3/4 OR 1/2 IN VIDEO J-C
Demonstrates skills of survival swimming, including floating, side and breast strokes and treading water. Illustrates cases where underwater swimming may be necessary and describes how to jump. Discusses the correct use of a tow line or rope ladder, correct ways of getting into and out of the water, and the use of clothing for support.
From The Learning To Swim Series.
Prod-BHA Dist-IFB Prodn-IFB 1965

Survival Swimming - To Save A Life C 15 MIN
16MM FILM, 3/4 OR 1/2 IN VIDEO J-C A
Depicts typical water emergency situations and common sense precautions which can prevent danger. Illustrates swimming with full clothing, clothing inflation techniques and flotation methods by which an individual can survive until a rescue is completed.
From The To Save A Life Series.
Prod-EBEC Dist-EBEC 1977

Survival Tactics C 22 MIN
16MM FILM, 3/4 OR 1/2 IN VIDEO
Deals with the problem of extremist attacks. Describes self-defense tactics for the police officer whenever he encounters situations of extreme and unexpected danger. Explores fighting techniques necessary for survival in a sudden, desperate physical attack. Features attackers wielding knives, homemade flame throwers, bottled acid and other sinister weapons.
Prod-WORON Dist-MTI

Survival Under The Sun, Pt 1 C 30 MIN
3/4 OR 1/2 INCH VIDEO CASSETTE J-H
Shows the conversion of sunshine into electricity using silicone cells like those which cover a 17-foot high satellite 'launched' right in Professor George Porter's lecture hall.
From The Natural History Of A Sunbeam Series.
Prod-KINGFT Dist-KINGFT

Survival Under The Sun, Pt 2 C 30 MIN
3/4 OR 1/2 INCH VIDEO CASSETTE J-H
Discusses the science of photobiology and experimental attempts to imitate the energy-producing action of plants in the laboratory.
From The Natural History Of A Sunbeam Series.
Prod-KINGFT Dist-KINGFT

Survivers, The (Captioned) C 130 MIN
16MM FILM, 3/4 OR 1/2 IN VIDEO A
Portrays a family of aristocratic origin in Cuba which decides to stay on after the 1959 revolution, isolating themselves in their mansion with their servants until they end in cannibalism. Spanish dialog with English subtitles.
Prod-CNEMAG Dist-CNEMAG 1978

Surviving A Presentation C 22 MIN
3/4 OR 1/2 INCH VIDEO CASSETTE
Breaks down a presentation into easy to understand components so facts don't get lost in the delivery. Says after completing the program, trainers will be able to design an introduction, prepare a statement of purpose and develop main ideas. Explores elements crucial to successful delivery.
Prod-GPCV Dist-GPCV

Surviving Hostage Situations C 45 MIN
16MM FILM, 3/4 OR 1/2 IN VIDEO
Provides a case history of the kidnapping of a company executive. Analyzes the kidnapping process and the various phases undergone by kidnappers, victims and third parties such as the family, the company and law enforcement. Shows how the victim can cope with every phase.
Prod-MTI Dist-MTI

Surviving Hostage Situations (Spanish) C 25 MIN
16MM FILM, 3/4 OR 1/2 IN VIDEO
Develops the concept of the kidnap process and examines the types of events and behaviors that occur in each phase involving the terrorists, the victims and third parties.
Prod-WORON Dist-MTI

Surviving Lifestyle Drugs C 45 MIN
1/2 IN VIDEO CASSETTE (VHS) I-C A
Discusses the most widely used drugs in America caffeine, nicotine, over-the-counter drugs, Valium, alcohol and marijuana. Assesses their nature, effects and risks, and weighs potential benefits against possible harm.
LC NO. 85-703936
Prod-HRMC Dist-HRMC

Surviving Lifestyle Drugs—A Series

Deals with the nature, effects and risks of commonly used lifestyle drugs.
Prod-IBIS Dist-IBIS

Alcohol And Marijuana
Caffeine And Nicotine
Over-The-Counter Drugs And Valium

Surviving The Cold C 12 MIN
16MM FILM, 3/4 OR 1/2 IN VIDEO I-H A
Explores hibernation, migration and other methods used by various animals to survive cold winter weather.
From The Many Worlds Of Nature Series.
Prod-SCRESC Dist-MTI

Survivor B 30 MIN
3/4 OR 1/2 INCH VIDEO CASSETTE
Presents the memories, stories and experiences, past and present, of Henry Martinson, a 97-year-old one-time farmer, labor organizer, Socialist Party official, writer, editor, poet and Labor Commissioner of North Dakota.
Prod-NFPS Dist-NFPS

Survivor Of The Holocaust, A C 29 MIN
3/4 OR 1/2 INCH VIDEO CASSETTE
Presents the story of one man's survival in the Nazi work and death camps during World War II. Like so many others in the concentration camps, the memories of that experience will affect him today.
From The Tom Cottle Show Series.
Prod-WGBHTV Dist-PBS 1981

Survivors C 58 MIN
16MM FILM - 3/4 IN VIDEO J-C A
Examines the profound physical, emotional and financial hardships which characterize the lives of over 1000 socially neglected Japanese-Americans who were trapped in Japan during the war and suffered the tragedy of the atomic blasts.
Prod-FIRS Dist-FIRS

Survivors, The B 5 MIN
16MM FILM OPTICAL SOUND
Presents a dramatic confrontation between the last man and woman left on earth after an atomic war. Shows that the woman has lost faith in humanity and sees no hope for any possible future generation.
LC NO. 75-703237
Prod-USC Dist-USC 1967

Survol De La Provence C 7 MIN
16MM FILM, 3/4 OR 1/2 IN VIDEO H-C A
A French language videocassette. Presents an overview of Provence, discussing its literary and historical past.
From The Chroniques De France Series.
LC NO. 81-706550
Prod-ADPF Dist-IFB 1980

Susan B 5 MIN
16MM FILM OPTICAL SOUND
Demonstrates a classroom behavior counseling problem involving a quiet and withdrawn nine-year-old girl who becomes erratic and destructive when she is brought to school against her will by an insistent mother. Shows how the child is classified as mentally retarded and how she makes no friends among her peers.
LC NO. 76-703891
Prod-HURRO Dist-USNAC Prodn-CONALF 1971

Susan C 16 MIN
16MM FILM, 3/4 OR 1/2 IN VIDEO C A
Demonstrates a number of masturbatory techniques for women.
Prod-NATSF Dist-MMRC

Susan After The Sugar Harvest C 27 MIN
16MM FILM OPTICAL SOUND J-C A
Explains that Susan was disillusioned with life until she signed up to go to Cuba to help with the sugar harvest. Points out that she experienced a sense of profound closeness to her fellow workers as they labored together in the fields, cutting down sugar cane, sweating under the hot sun, working for a common purpose, with everyone sharing his joys, his food and his few possessions without considering himself to be better than the rest.
LC NO. 72-702844
Prod-ROBINP Dist-RADIM 1971

Susan And David C 28 MIN
3/4 OR 1/2 INCH VIDEO CASSETTE
Shows a deeply caring couple in a celebration of unrepressed playful, nourishing sexuality. Reveals their feelings about making this film.
From The Mutuality Series.
Prod-MMRC Dist-MMRC

Susan And Mrs Stanton C 20 MIN
3/4 INCH VIDEO CASSETTE I
Offers information on Susan B Anthony and Elizabeth Cady Stanton.
From The Truly American Series.
Prod-WVIZTV Dist-GPITVL 1979

Susan Meiselas On Nicaragua C 30 MIN
3/4 OR 1/2 INCH VIDEO CASSETTE
Features photojournalist Susan Meiselas discussing her work in Central America. Focuses on her photographs of Nicaragua which chronicle the Central American struggle as she describes her experiences in Nicaragua and discusses the role of the American press as witness.
From The Fronteras Series.
Prod-KPBS Dist-KPBS

Susan Mogul - Comedy As A Back Up B 10 MIN
3/4 OR 1/2 INCH VIDEO CASSETTE
Shows Susan Mogul preparing for failure at her art career.
Prod-ARTINC Dist-ARTINC

Susan Mogul - Dressing Up B 7 MIN
3/4 OR 1/2 INCH VIDEO CASSETTE
Reveals the prices of garments.
Prod-ARTINC Dist-ARTINC

Susan Mogul - Last Jew In America C 9 MIN
3/4 OR 1/2 INCH VIDEO CASSETTE
Presents a lecture on Jewish schooling. Exposes certain entertainers.
Prod-ARTINC Dist-ARTINC

Susan Mogul - Take Off B 10 MIN
3/4 OR 1/2 INCH VIDEO CASSETTE
Presents a parody of Vito Acconci's Undertone. Discusses the history of a vibrator.
Prod-ARTINC Dist-ARTINC

Susan Mogul - Waiting At The Soda Fountain C 24 MIN
3/4 OR 1/2 INCH VIDEO CASSETTE
Tells about women's working process and men's authority to designate talent and control women's economic destiny.
Prod-ARTINC Dist-ARTINC

Susan Peterson, Artist-Potter C 28 MIN
2 INCH VIDEOTAPE
Features Mrs Peterson describing certain ceramic processes for her classroom at the University of Southern California.
From The Wheels, Kilns And Clay Series.
Prod-USC Dist-PUBTEL

Susan Rogers - Good Grief C 22 MIN
3/4 OR 1/2 INCH VIDEO CASSETTE
Features a comedy about a young woman artist who dies, then returns home for a nostalgic look at her 'perfect' past.
Prod-ARTINC Dist-ARTINC

Susan Starr B 54 MIN
16MM FILM, 3/4 OR 1/2 IN VIDEO C A
Follows three days in the life of Susan Starr, competitor in the finals of Dimitri Mitropoulos international piano competition.

Shows her during the competition at the Metropolitan Opera House, backstage as her rivals perform and onstage as she performs.
Prod-DREW Dist-DIRECT 1970

Susan's Image C 15 MIN
3/4 OR 1/2 INCH VIDEO CASSETTE J-C A
Explores how one's self image affects the decision-making process. Interviews young television stars and recovering drug and alcohol addicts.
From The Chemical People Educational Modules Series.
Prod-MTI Dist-MTI

Susan's Valentine Surprise C 15 MIN
3/4 INCH VIDEO CASSETTE K-P
See series title for descriptive statement.
From The Storytime Series.
Prod-WCETTV Dist-GPITVL 1976

Susceptibility Testing C 11 MIN
16MM FILM OPTICAL SOUND PRO
Describes the most commonly used antibiotic sensitivity tests, including the Kirby-Bauer or agar diffusion test, the tube dilution method and the agar dilution method.
Prod-ACYLLD Dist-LEDR 1974

Susie, The Little Blue Coupe C 8 MIN
16MM FILM, 3/4 OR 1/2 IN VIDEO P-I
A story of the odyssey of Susie, a little coupe, from showroom, used-car lot and junkyard to her restoration as a hot rod.
Prod-DISNEY Dist-WDEMCO 1971

Suspects And Witnesses, Pt 4 - Use Of The Polygraph In Investigations B 26 MIN
16MM FILM OPTICAL SOUND PRO
Presents a pre-test interview with suspect, test examination procedure, analysis of polygraph indications and post-test interrogation of suspect.
LC NO. 74-705733
Prod-USA Dist-USNAC 1967

Suspended Monorail In Japan C 24 MIN
16MM FILM OPTICAL SOUND
Explains that a suspended monorail system, seven kilometers in length, has been constructed in the fast growing Shonan-Enoshima residential area near Tokyo. Points out that this is the world's first monorail for practical purposes using the suspended type system, built to cope with the ever-increasing demand for commuter transportation in the vicinity. Shows how the project has been pushed forward without interfering with the everyday traffic and life of the people, and emphasizes safety of the monorail system.
Prod-UNIJAP Dist-UNIJAP

Suspense And Mystery B 20 MIN
2 INCH VIDEOTAPE I
Introduces the suspense and mystery story at a child's level of interest. (Broadcast quality)
From The Quest For The Best Series.
Prod-DENVPS Dist-GPITVL

Suspension C 9 MIN
16MM FILM OPTICAL SOUND
Presents an interpretation of a state of suspension through visual effects, dance, movement and sound.
LC NO. 77-702661
Prod-HUNNL Dist-CANFDC 1974

Suspension Bridge, The C 26 MIN
16MM FILM OPTICAL SOUND J-C A
Shows the many phases of suspension bridge construction with the skill of the bridgemen working hundreds of feet up with perfect precision and accuracy.
Prod-USSC Dist-USSC 1955

Suspension Test C 30 MIN
1/2 IN VIDEO CASSETTE BETA/VHS
Shows how to test a car's suspension for cracks. Discusses choosing the right bolt. Looks at tire gauges. Features a Peugot station wagon.
From The Last Chance Garage Series.
Prod-WGBHTV Dist-MTI

Suspicious Client, The C 30 MIN
16MM FILM - 3/4 IN VIDEO PRO
Presents course instructors Grayce Sills and Doreen James Wise discussing the development of the suspicious client's pattern of behavior, as well as nursing activities aimed at establishing a trust relationship between the nurse and client. Presents brief sketches of nurse-client interactions illustrating the suspicious person's behavior and the responses of the nurse.
LC NO. 77-700134
Prod-AJN Dist-AJN Prodn-WGNCP 1977

Suspicious Patient, The B 44 MIN
16MM FILM OPTICAL SOUND PRO
Discusses the communicational value of the suspicious patient's behavior with regard to his need for and capacity to profit from a therapeutic relationship.
From The Nursing In Psychiatry Series.
LC NO. 70-703439
Prod-VDONUR Dist-AJN Prodn-WTTWTV 1968

Sutton Hoo Ship Burial, The C 25 MIN
16MM FILM, 3/4 OR 1/2 IN VIDEO
Provides a day-to-day account of the 1939 discovery and excavation of a ship buried at the site of Sutton Hoo in Sussex 1,300 years ago.
Prod-UTORMC Dist-UTORMC 1972

Suture And Staple Removal C 11 MIN
3/4 OR 1/2 INCH VIDEO CASSETTE PRO
Demostrates the removal of running stitches, interrupted stitches and staples.
From The Basic Clinical Skills Series.
Prod-HSCIC Dist-HSCIC 1984

Sutures And Suture Books C 4 MIN
1/2 IN VIDEO CASSETTE BETA/VHS
Explains how to prepare sutures, suture books and how to pass sutures.
Prod-RMI Dist-RMI

Sutures, Needles And Skin Closure Materials C 21 MIN
16MM FILM, 3/4 OR 1/2 IN VIDEO PRO
Introduces the types, uses and preparation of sutures, needles and skin closure materials.
Prod-CWRU Dist-FEIL 1971

Suwannee Adventure C 14 MIN
16MM FILM OPTICAL SOUND
Presents a canoe trip down the historic Suwannee River through north Florida to the Gulf of Mexico.
Prod-FLADC Dist-FLADC

Suzhou C 28 MIN
16MM FILM, 3/4 OR 1/2 IN VIDEO J-C A
Explores the Chinese urban experience, past and present. Focuses on the historical sites, scenery and culture in Suzhou, China, and observes the activities of its modern residents.
From The Cities In China Series.
LC NO. 82-706431
Prod-YUNGLI Dist-UCEMC 1981

Suzy's Test / Max's Story / Mrs Mulch's Story C 15 MIN
3/4 OR 1/2 INCH VIDEO CASSETTE P
Presents stories presented by Muppet-like Clyde Frog presenting stories emphasizing positive self-images, feelings of optimism and self-confidence.
From The Clyde Frog Show Series.
Prod-MAETEL Dist-GPITVL 1977

Suzy's War C 24 MIN
3/4 OR 1/2 INCH VIDEO CASSETTE
Relates the story of a ghetto child who fights back against the fear and violence that rules her street in an attempt to make her neighborhood a better place to live.
From The Young People's Specials Series.
Prod-MULTPP Dist-MULTPP

Svea-Newport Incident, The B 3 MIN
16MM FILM OPTICAL SOUND
Shows the collision of the SVEA and the Newport and describes the causes of the accident.
LC NO. FIE52-950
Prod-USN Dist-USNAC 1943

Sven Nykvist C 26 MIN
16MM FILM, 3/4 OR 1/2 IN VIDEO J-C A
Explores the life and work of cinematographer Sven Nykvist. Emphasizes his style of lighting and sense of humanity by showing film clips from key Bergman-Nykvist productions.
Prod-VISPUB Dist-TEXFLM 1974

Svengali B 45 MIN
16MM FILM SILENT
Features John Barrymore as Svengali, a man who tries to shape and remold his female subject, Trilby.
From The Movies - Our Modern Art Series.
Prod-SPCTRA Dist-STRFLS 1933

Svengali B 80 MIN
16MM FILM OPTICAL SOUND
Stars John Barrymore, Marian Marsh and Donald Crisp in Du Maurier's story about Svengali's hypnotic powers over the girl who calls herself Trilby.
Prod-WB Dist-KITPAR 1931

Svengali B 44 MIN
16MM FILM, 3/4 OR 1/2 IN VIDEO I A
Features John Barrymore in the immortal story of Svengali's 'MANUFACTURED' love. Presents an aging music teacher who weaves a spell to capture the affection of the beautiful young Trilby - a spell that is unbroken even in death.
Prod-SF Dist-SF 1971

Swaco Super Choke C 20 MIN
3/4 OR 1/2 INCH VIDEO CASSETTE IND
Introduces the remote-controlled, adjustable choke made by Dresser Swaco. Looks at the special advantages of its design and function in general well-killing procedures.
Prod-UTEXPE Dist-UTEXPE 1981

Swaco Vacuum Degasser C 19 MIN
3/4 OR 1/2 INCH VIDEO CASSETTE IND
Covers the purpose, operation, installation and maintenance of the Dresser Swaco vacuum tank degasser.
Prod-UTEXPE Dist-UTEXPE 1980

Swag B 26 MIN
16MM FILM OPTICAL SOUND
A drama about a tough boy from the city streets who is temporarily lured away from his usual haunts by the attractions of an older woman.
LC NO. 75-700326
Prod-POSTMN Dist-POSTMN 1974

Swaging Cable Terminals B 12 MIN
16MM FILM OPTICAL SOUND
Depicts how to measure and mark the cable accurately, set up the swaging machine, check the terminal after swaging and remove, clean and reassemble the parts of the machine.
LC NO. FIE52-267
Prod-USOE Dist-USNAC 1944

Swallows C 3 MIN
16MM FILM OPTICAL SOUND P-I
Discusses the birds known as swallows.
From The Of All Things Series.
Prod-BAILYL Dist-AVED

Swami Chidananda C 60 MIN
3/4 OR 1/2 INCH VIDEO CASSETTE
Introduces Swami Chidananda giving a talk about divine origins, divine path and ultimate goal.
Prod-IYOGA Dist-IYOGA

Swami's Children B 50 MIN
3/4 OR 1/2 INCH VIDEO CASSETTE
Documents the dynamic and positive results people receive through their practice of Yoga.
Prod-CBSF Dist-IYOGA Prodn-WNETTV

Swamp And Mr Harkins, The C 16 MIN
16MM FILM OPTICAL SOUND I-C A
Introduces an old trapper who recalls past years when he hunted alligators and lived off the wildlife in the wilderness swamps of the Atchafalaya River in Louisiana. Reveals that his problems now are caused by a dam built 20 years ago which has changed the river so much that floods a foot or more deep come into his house. States that he is too old to get a job, can't afford the city and doesn't want to depend on his children, so he tenaciously struggles to stay in his lifelong home.
Prod-SPRAGE Dist-ADAMSF 1980

Swamp Critters C 26 MIN
16MM FILM, 3/4 OR 1/2 IN VIDEO
Depicts North America's southern swamps. Shows amazing and amusing wild creatures.
Prod-STOUFP Dist-STOUFP 1982

Swamp Ecosystem, A C 25 MIN
16MM FILM, 3/4 OR 1/2 IN VIDEO J-C A
Looks at the ecosystem of the largest freshwater swamp in North America, the Okefenokee Swamp. Views its inhabitants, such as alligators and giant carnivorous pitcher plants.
LC NO. 83-706732
Prod-NGS Dist-NGS 1983

Swamp Things C 23 MIN
3/4 OR 1/2 INCH VIDEO CASSETTE
Explores the mysterious waters of the Everglades. Shows underneath the surface and a host of creatures who have adapted to a world that rises and falls from season to season.
Prod-NWLDPR Dist-NWLDPR

Swampdwellers, The B 40 MIN
16MM FILM, 3/4 OR 1/2 IN VIDEO J-H A
Features a young African who returns to his village and discovers that he has grown too sophisticated to accept his parent's beliefs. Tells how, disillusioned also by urban life, he is caught between two conflicting cultures, unable to identify with either.
LC NO. 81-706888
Prod-SOYNKA Dist-PHENIX 1973

Swan Ganz Cathete - The Internal Jugular Approach C 22 MIN
3/4 OR 1/2 INCH VIDEO CASSETTE PRO
Describes the technique for inserting a catheter through the jugular vein and heart into the pulmonary artery to monitor hemo-dynamic parameters.
Prod-WFP Dist-WFP

Swan Song, The C 25 MIN
16MM FILM, 3/4 OR 1/2 IN VIDEO J-C A
Shows an old actor on a deserted stage drunkenly reflecting on his life. Adapted from a short story by Anton Chekhov.
Prod-CINREP Dist-CAROUF

Swan Songs C 14 MIN
3/4 OR 1/2 INCH VIDEO CASSETTE
Prod-EAI Dist-EAI

Swan-Ganz Pacing TD Catheter C 12 MIN
3/4 OR 1/2 INCH VIDEO CASSETTE PRO
Shows Swan-Ganz pacing TD catheter.
Prod-WFP Dist-WFP

Swan, The C
3/4 OR 1/2 INCH VIDEO CASSETTE
See series title for descriptive statement.
From The Ice Carving Series.
Prod-CULINA Dist-CULINA

Swarming Hordes, The C 58 MIN
3/4 OR 1/2 INCH VIDEO CASSETTE J-C A
Describes how successfully insects have developed through eons of evolution. Shows examples of moulting, metamorphosis, camouflage and social cooperation as seen in termite colonies, beehives and among army ants.
From The Life On Earth Series. Program 4
LC NO. 82-706676
Prod-BBCTV Dist-FI 1981

Swarming In Honey Bees C 8 MIN
16MM FILM, 3/4 OR 1/2 IN VIDEO
Shows views of honey bees swarming about the captive queen bee, describing how and why they periodically swarm and discussing what scientists are learning through research about the swarming of bees.
Prod-NYSCAG Dist-CUNIV 1964

Swashbucklers, The B 28 MIN
16MM FILM OPTICAL SOUND
A history of adventure films with colorful heroes from the early silents to the present. Scenes from the mark of Zorro, Sea Hawk, and the Charge of the Light Brigade are shown as well as clips of such stars as Doublas Fairbanks Sr and Errol Flynn.
From The Hollywood And The Stars Series.
LC NO. 76-702001
Prod-WOLPER Dist-WOLPER 1964

Swb C 11 MIN
16MM FILM OPTICAL SOUND C A
A French language film. Tells the story of a modern photographer who searches for a girl to replace his lost model. Includes English subtitles.
Prod-UWFKD Dist-UWFKD

Sweat And Cheers C 15 MIN
3/4 INCH VIDEO CASSETTE P-I
Presents a lesson on sports.
From The Can You Imagine Series.
Prod-WVIZTV Dist-GPITVL

Sweat And Steel C 16 MIN
16MM FILM OPTICAL SOUND H-C A
Introduces the sport of bodybuilding, showing scenes of different bodybuilders going through their workouts at Gold's Gym. Traces the progress of one amateur as he prepares for and competes in a bodybuilding contest.
LC NO. 78-701622
Prod-USC Dist-USC 1978

Sweat Of The Sun, The C 52 MIN
16MM FILM, 3/4 OR 1/2 IN VIDEO H-C A
Explores the Pre-Columbian Indian civilizations of Central and South America in which native craftsmen fashioned gold into works of art. Shows Aztec and Inca sites while describing the lives of the people who occupied them and examines the treasures that remain, now housed in museums throughout the world.
From The Tribal Eye Series.
LC NO. 79-707114
Prod-BBCTV Dist-TIMLIF 1976

Sweat Testing For Cystic Fibrosis Of The Pancreas C 10 MIN
3/4 OR 1/2 INCH VIDEO CASSETTE PRO
Demonstrates the pilocarpine iontophoretic method of performing a sweat test for cystic fibrosis of the pancreas.
Prod-HSCIC Dist-HSCIC 1981

Sweater, The - A Childhood Recollection By Roch Carrier C 10 MIN
16MM FILM, 3/4 OR 1/2 IN VIDEO I-C A
Presents Roch Carrier recalling a painful incident of having his favorite hockey sweater, which was like those worn by the Montreal Canadiens, mistakenly replaced by a sweater like those of their archrivals.
LC NO. 82-706191
Prod-NFBC Dist-NFBC Prodn-CANVER 1981

Sweden C 15 MIN
16MM FILM, 3/4 OR 1/2 IN VIDEO I-J A
Emphasizes the social and economic geography of Sweden, observing the abundant natural resources and the adaptation of the people to climate and physical features. Shows how forest products, tourism, agriculture and shipbuilding help give this nation an excellent export market.
Prod-LUF Dist-LUF 1979

Sweden C 22 MIN
16MM FILM, 3/4 OR 1/2 IN VIDEO J-H
Shows how Swedes in different provinces lives and work. Looks at the political system of Sweden.
From The Modern Europe Series.
Prod-JOU Dist-JOU

Sweden C 29 MIN
2 INCH VIDEOTAPE
Features home economist Joan Hood presenting a culinary tour of specialty dishes from around the world. Shows the preparation of Swedish dishes ranging from peasant cookery to continental cuisine.
From The International Cookbook Series.
Prod-WMVSTV Dist-PUBTEL

Sweden - Vikings Now Style C 28 MIN
16MM FILM, 3/4 OR 1/2 IN VIDEO P-C A
Relates the history of Sweden to its oceanbound geography. Compares the old and new Stockholm, and its industries. Discusses the sources of income and the benefits of the modern welfare state. Includes views of Lappland, the university town of Uppsala, the Hanseatic town of Visby and the world-famous Milles gardens with its sculptures by Carl Milles.
Prod-HANDEL Dist-HANDEL 1969

Sweden - Waiting For Spring C 58 MIN
3/4 INCH VIDEO CASSETTE
Presents a portrait of Sweden as the paramount example of the ultimate success of social engineering. Tells how the Swedes have achieved a degree of social justice and equality unmatched anywhere as a result of their collective decision that the individual should sacrifice for the benefit of the group. Questions whether the next generation of Swedes will be willing to continue this policy.
From The World Series.
LC NO. 79-708092
Prod-WGBHTV Dist-PBS 1979

Sweden And Lovely C 10 MIN
16MM FILM OPTICAL SOUND
Presents the young as well as the old in Sweden.
Prod-SWNTO Dist-SWNTO 1967

Sweden Film Shorts, Pt 1 - Sweden's Sunny Arctic C 5 MIN
16MM FILM OPTICAL SOUND
Portrays Sweden's Lappland, a delightful northern playground with plenty of opportunity for sightseeing, fishing and skiing.
Prod-SWNTO Dist-SWNTO

Sweden Film Shorts, Pt 3 - Sweden's Chateaux Country C 5 MIN
16MM FILM OPTICAL SOUND
Portrays Sweden's chateaux country.
Prod-SWNTO Dist-SWNTO

Sweden Film Shorts, Pt 4 - Sweden's Island Capital C 5 MIN
16MM FILM OPTICAL SOUND
Portrays Stockholm, including a visit to the remains of the warship 'VASA.'
Prod-SWNTO Dist-SWNTO

Sweden Folm Shorts, Pt 2 - Midsummer In Sweden's Dalarna C 5 MIN
16MM FILM OPTICAL SOUND
Features Rattvik and Leksand with the original music of Dalarna and all the richness of the Dalecarlia fiddles.
Prod-SWNTO Dist-SWNTO

Sweden In World Affairs B 30 MIN
16MM FILM OPTICAL SOUND
Discusses Sweden's position as a neutral but not neutralist nation.
From The Face Of Sweden Series.
Prod-SIS Dist-SIS 1963

Sweden's Forest Heritage C 18 MIN
16MM FILM OPTICAL SOUND
Illustrates modern forestry in Sweden, showing timber and the transportation and treatment of the wood.
Prod-ASI Dist-AUDPLN

Swedenborg, The Man Who Had To Know C 28 MIN
16MM FILM OPTICAL SOUND
Dramatizes key events in the life of Emanuel Swedenborg, including his breakthroughs in anatomy and brain research, his discovery of endocrine glands, his invention of an aircraft, and his assistance in founding the sciences of crystallography and metallurgy. Explores his religious and philosophical beliefs.
LC NO. 80-700077
Prod-SWEDF Dist-MTP 1978

Swedes In America B 16 MIN
3/4 INCH VIDEO CASSETTE
Features Ingrid Bergman telling of the lives and contributions of Swedes in America, particularly the Swedish-American families in Minnesota. Contains a portrayal of Carl Sandburg.
From The American Scene Series. No. 1
LC NO. 79-706697
Prod-USOWI Dist-USNAC 1979

Swedish Cinema Classica B 40 MIN
16MM FILM OPTICAL SOUND
Presents sequences from original films to portray the great period of Swedish silent cinema, the epoch of Victor Sjostrom and Mauritz Stiller.
Prod-SIS Dist-SIS

Swedish Couple Discuss Swedish Social Structures, A, Pt I B 6 MIN
3/4 OR 1/2 INCH VIDEO CASSETTE
Discusses the family in Sweden with a Swedish couple, who characterize it as 'small, weak and often dissolving.' Reviews the family, noting demographic data, the divorce rate and the roles of both parents in the labor force and the family.
Prod-UWISC Dist-UWISC 1975

Swedish Couple Discuss Swedish Social Structures, A, Pt II B 40 MIN
3/4 OR 1/2 INCH VIDEO CASSETTE
Continues a discussion with a Swedish couple on the place of the Swedish woman in the labor force, marital relation- ships and children and daycare.
Prod-UWISC Dist-UWISC 1975

Swedish Peasant Paintings C 13 MIN
16MM FILM OPTICAL SOUND
Presents peasant paintings from the province of Dalarna.
Prod-ASI Dist-AUDPLN

Swedish Summer Day C 20 MIN
16MM FILM OPTICAL SOUND
Portrays nature and animal life in the scenic summer surroundings of the Swedish countryside.
Prod-MTP Dist-SIS 1959

Sweet And Sour C 29 MIN
2 INCH VIDEOTAPE
Features Joyce Chen showing how to adapt Chinese recipes so that they can be prepared in the American kitchen and still retain the authentic flavor. Demonstrates how to prepare sweet and sour sauce.
From The Joyce Chen Cooks Series.
Prod-WGBHTV Dist-PUBTEL

Sweet Betsy From Pike C 15 MIN
3/4 OR 1/2 INCH VIDEO CASSETTE P-I
See series title for descriptive statement.
From The Ready, Sing Series.
Prod-ARKETV Dist-AITECH 1979

Sweet Dreams B 13 MIN
3/4 OR 1/2 INCH VIDEO CASSETTE C A
Combines erotic fantasy with one woman's masturbation pattern. Explains that her sexual orientation does not rule out male-inclusive fantasy.
Prod-NATSF Dist-MMRC

Sweet England's Pride C 90 MIN
16MM FILM, 3/4 OR 1/2 IN VIDEO
Portrays the last years of the reign of Queen Elizabeth I, focusing on her romance with the Earl of Essex and his execution when he attempted to raise a rebellion against her.
From The Elizabeth R Series. No. 6
LC NO. 77-701553
Prod-BBCTV Dist-FI 1976

Sweet Fresh Water C 55 MIN
16MM FILM, 3/4 OR 1/2 IN VIDEO H-C A
Follows the Amazon River from its source in the Peruvian Andes to its huge coastal delta in Brazil. Shows how great waterfalls such as the Angel Falls in Venezuela and Iguassu in Brazil shape the landscape.
From The Living Planet Series. Pt 8
Prod-BBCTV Dist-TIMLIF 1984

Sweet Honey In The Rock C 60 MIN
3/4 OR 1/2 INCH VIDEO CASSETTE
Prod-RCOMTV Dist-SYLWAT 1980

Sweet Lavender B 10 MIN
16MM FILM OPTICAL SOUND
Examines withdrawal and desertion, the inability to find a positive, fruitful relationship to one's society. Centers on an old woman who sells lavender sachets on a busy city street.
Prod-UPENN Dist-UPENN 1965

Sweet Light C 10 MIN
3/4 OR 1/2 INCH VIDEO CASSETTE
See series title for descriptive statement.
From The Memory Surfaces And Mental Prayers Series.
Prod-EAI Dist-EAI

Sweet Return B 8 MIN
16MM FILM OPTICAL SOUND
A study of racial consciousness as portrayed in a traditional gun duel, photographed in a turn-of-the-century setting, in which the antagonists, a noble black man and a beautiful white youth are pitted against each other by their domineering female seconds.
LC NO. 71-702599
Prod-USC Dist-USC 1968

Sweet Sixteen And Pregnant C 28 MIN
16MM FILM, 3/4 OR 1/2 IN VIDEO J-H
Tells the stories of five teenaged girls who wrestled with the problems and pressures of pregnancy.
Prod-BELLDA Dist-MTI

Sweet Sixteen And Pregnant C 29 MIN
16MM FILM, 3/4 OR 1/2 IN VIDEO T
Tells the story of five young girls, ages 13 through 17, each of whom had to deal with an unexpected pregnancy. Reveals the reality of teenage pregnancy through young women who have experienced first-hand the sadness, abandonment, anger and frustration that so often follow the discovery that one is expecting a child.
From The Dealing With Social Problems In The Classroom Series.
Prod-MFFD Dist-FI 1983

Sweet Smell Of Freedom, The C 27 MIN
16MM FILM OPTICAL SOUND
Describes new methods in prison rehabilitation used at the D C men's reformatory, Lorton, Virginia. Shows staff problems and relates aspects of the life of prison inmates. Includes interviews with inmates and officials.
LC NO. FIA68-551
Prod-WMALTV Dist-WMALTV 1967

Sweet Smell Of Success, The C 24 MIN
16MM FILM, 3/4 OR 1/2 IN VIDEO
Demonstrates the spectroscopic technique employed by organic chemists in a professional analysis laboratory for molecular identification.
Prod-OPENU Dist-MEDIAG Prodn-BBCTV 1982

Sweet Sounds C 28 MIN
16MM FILM, 3/4 OR 1/2 IN VIDEO
Explores methods of teaching music to young children.
Prod-MIPR Dist-TEXFLM 1977

Sweet Verticality C 30 MIN
3/4 OR 1/2 INCH VIDEO CASSETTE
Pays hommage to New York City. Presents verse by Joe Ribar as images move graphically over the city-scapes.
Prod-EAI Dist-EAI

Sweetheart Of The Rodeo C 24 MIN
16MM FILM OPTICAL SOUND
Features Dee Watt, the British Columbia champion of barrel racing.
LC NO. 76-703809
Prod-BCDA Dist-BCDA 1975

Sweets Of Japan C 26 MIN
16MM FILM OPTICAL SOUND
Traces the beginning of a distinctive confectionery in Japan that is scarcely known outside the country.
Prod-UNIJAP Dist-UNIJAP 1965

Sweetwater C 30 MIN
16MM FILM, 3/4 OR 1/2 IN VIDEO I-H A
Reveals how barriers can be surmounted when we drop our defenses and admit to human need.
Prod-LCOA Dist-LCOA 1985

Sweetwater Junction C 38 MIN
16MM FILM, 3/4 OR 1/2 IN VIDEO J-H A
Presents a documentary on the annual Rattlesnake Round-Up held in Sweetwater, Texas, which includes milking venom from rattlesnakes and an unusual pageant featuring women from the Sweetwater area.
LC NO. 81-706641
Prod-SLUIZR Dist-PHENIX 1980

Swifty C 30 MIN
3/4 OR 1/2 INCH VIDEO CASSETTE I-J
Focuses on sensible weight loss and gives tips on self-image, diet, exercise and teamwork.
From The High Feather Series. Pt 2

LC NO. 83-706048
Prod-NYSED Dist-GPITVL 1982

Swim And Stay Fit X 5 MIN
16MM FILM OPTICAL SOUND
Emphasizes that swimming is one of the best ways to achieve physical fitness. Shows people of all ages, even the disabled, having fun as they improve their swimming skills.
Prod-SLACC Dist-AMRC 1964

Swim Meet C 15 MIN
16MM FILM OPTICAL SOUND
Explains the duties of the officials at swimming meets as seen by leading United States' coaches. Shows events at the National AAU women's swimming meet in May, 1965.
LC NO. FIA66-539
Prod-GROENG Dist-GROENG 1965

Swim Training - Men—A Series
16MM FILM, 3/4 OR 1/2 IN VIDEO J-C
Demonstrates how men can perform such swimming strokes as the backstroke, the butterfly and the breaststroke.
Prod-ATHI Dist-ATHI 1981

Backstroke - Men 015 MIN
Backstroke Strokes, Drills, Starts And Turns 015 MIN
Breaststroke - Men 015 MIN
Breaststroke Strokes, Drills, Starts And Turns 015 MIN
Butterfly - Men 015 MIN
Butterfly Strokes, Drills, Starts And Turns 015 MIN
Distance Freestyle - Men 015 MIN
Freestyle Strokes, Drills, Starts And Turns 015 MIN
Sprint Freestyle - Men 015 MIN
Starts, Turns And Tempo 015 MIN

Swim Training - Women—A Series
16MM FILM, 3/4 OR 1/2 IN VIDEO J-C
Demonstrates how women swimmers can properly execute the backstroke, butterfly and breaststroke.
Prod-ATHI Dist-ATHI 1981

Backstroke - Women 015 MIN
Breaststroke - Women 015 MIN
Butterfly - Women 015 MIN
Freestyle - Women 015 MIN

Swimmer C 23 MIN
16MM FILM OPTICAL SOUND
Shows the construction of a unique and powerful sculpture by artist Don Seiler.
LC NO. 75-700087
Prod-KANE Dist-KANE 1974

Swimmer C 26 MIN
16MM FILM OPTICAL SOUND J-C A
Shows how two Australian swimming champions, Karen Moras and Diana Rickard, live and train.
From The Man And His Sport Series.
LC NO. 72-701522
Prod-ANAIB Dist-AUIS 1972

Swimming B 13 MIN
16MM FILM OPTICAL SOUND
Jim Gray demonstrates difference between old and new methods of swim instruction, especially for parents faced with challenge of teaching children to swim.
Prod-SFI Dist-SFI

Swimming And Diving Today C 17 MIN
16MM FILM OPTICAL SOUND J-C A
Uses slow motion, stop action and instant replay to clarify rule interpretations for interscholastic swimming. Describes the rules and correct officiating procedures for the benefit of competitive swimmers and divers, coaches, officials and spectators.
LC NO. 74-703505
Prod-NFSHSA Dist-OSFS 1974

Swimming For Survival B 18 MIN
16MM FILM - 3/4 IN VIDEO
Shows basic swimming skills and stresses their importance as lifesaving techniques in emergency situations. Issued in 1954 as a motion picture.
LC NO. 79-706004
Prod-USN Dist-USNAC 1978

Swimming Pool, The C 7 MIN
16MM FILM, 3/4 OR 1/2 IN VIDEO I-J A
Uses animation to show how a man's new swimming pool becomes a magnet for trespassing children, sailboats, a spaceship, a thirsty elephant and a ten-car pileup.
Prod-BOZETO Dist-TEXFLM 1977

Swimming Rescues C 8 MIN
16MM FILM - 3/4 IN VIDEO
Reviews fundamental swimming skills for lifesaving training. Demonstrates various entries, stroke adaptations, approaches, carries and tired-swimmer assists.
From The Lifesaving And Water Safety Series.
Prod-AMRC Dist-AMRC 1975

Swimming Skills And Drills - Back Crawl, Breaststroke And Turns C 39 MIN
1/2 IN VIDEO CASSETTE BETA/VHS A
Breaks down the two strokes into progressive steps for coaching or teaching, and demonstrates proper arm and leg action, breathing and turns. Includes a variety of drills swimmers can use to develop these techniques. Uses underwater photography in regular speed, slow motion and stop frames to demonstrate how each stroke should be performed and how to go about developing the strokes through practice drills. Features swimming coach Dick Hannula and world class swimmers.
Prod-RMI Dist-RMI

Swimming Skills And Drills - Crawl And Butterfly C 41 MIN
1/2 IN VIDEO CASSETTE BETA/VHS A
Breaks down the crawl and butterfly strokes into progressive steps to be used in teaching, and demonstrates the proper techniques for the arm actions, leg kicks and breathing. Demonstrates numerous drills to be used in developing these techniques. Includes extensive use of underwater photography in regular speed, slow motion and stop frame, showing how each stroke should be performed through practice drills. Features swimming coach Dick Hannula and elite-class swimmers.
Prod-RMI Dist-RMI

Swimming—A Series
16MM FILM, 3/4 OR 1/2 IN VIDEO
Demonstrates various swimming techniques and strokes.
Prod-ATHI Dist-ATHI 1977

Breast Stroke And Butterfly Technique 20 MIN
Freestyle Stroke And Backstroke Techniques 22 MIN
Starts, Turns And Progressive Drills 23 MIN

Swimming, Scuba Diving And Fishing At The Seashore C 8 MIN
16MM FILM OPTICAL SOUND K-P
Follows Crystal and her friends as they spend a pleasant holiday at the seashore, where they swim, dive, play in the sand, explore underwater and go fishing.
From The Crystal Tipps And Alistair Series.
LC NO. 73-700450
Prod-BBCTV Dist-VEDO 1972

Swimmy C 6 MIN
16MM FILM OPTICAL SOUND K-I
An animated film which tells the story of Swimmy, a small fish who, having escaped the jaws of the great gray tuna, discovers the marvelous underwater world of strange caverns, luminous fish and flowers that open at a touch.
LC NO. 75-705157
Prod-CONNF Dist-CONNF 1969

Swine Flu Caper, The C 22 MIN
16MM FILM, 3/4 OR 1/2 IN VIDEO
Portrays Dr Anthony Morris, a virologist with the National Institute of Health and the Food and Drug Administration, who was fired after objecting to the swine flu vaccine.
Prod-NEWTIM Dist-NEWTIM

Swineherd, The C 13 MIN
16MM FILM, 3/4 OR 1/2 IN VIDEO K-P
Presents an animated adaptation of Hans Christian Andersen's tale The Swineherd, as illustrated by Bjorn Wiinblad. Tells about a princess who scorns the love of a prince until he disguises himself as a swineherd.
LC NO. 75-701093
Prod-NORDV Dist-WWS Prodn-KRATKY 1975

Swing Bass C 29 MIN
3/4 INCH VIDEO CASSETTE H A
Reviews scales and chords in A-flat major and E-flat major. Introduces swing bass, one of the most common of accompaniment patterns, and arpeggios.
From The Beginning Piano - An Adult Approach Series. Lesson 25
Prod-COAST Dist-CDTEL

Swing Of Things, The C 29 MIN
2 INCH VIDEOTAPE
See series title for descriptive statement.
From The Observing Eye Series.
Prod-WGBHTV Dist-PUBTEL

Swing That Swung Back, The C 6 MIN
16MM FILM OPTICAL SOUND A
Discusses playground safety equipment using animation and a plot involving two stereotypic detectives investigating an accident.
LC NO. 76-704012
Prod-CPSAFC Dist-USNAC Prodn-CAS 1976

Swinging Quanta C 9 MIN
16MM FILM, 3/4 OR 1/2 IN VIDEO C
Presents a visualization of solutions for the quantum harmonic oscillator. Displays Eigen-functions and combines them to construct a Gaussian packet having a time-dependent probability amplitude of a classic nature.
LC NO. 83-706690
Prod-BREGMN Dist-IFB

Swinging Rhythm C 29 MIN
3/4 INCH VIDEO CASSETTE H A
Discusses swinging rhythm, or the unequal division of the beat used universally in many musical forms, including jazz, musical theater, and commercial music. Begins two new pieces.
From The Beginning Piano - An Adult Approach Series. Lesson 21
Prod-COAST Dist-CDTEL

Swish - Science And Curveballs and Gliders C 20 MIN
16MM FILM, 3/4 OR 1/2 IN VIDEO I-J
Features a puppet professor investigating the concepts of air pressure, lift, airfoil design, streamlines, fluid flow, Bernoulli's Paradox, and even spit balls.
From The Elementary Physical Science Series.
Prod-CENTRO Dist-CORF

Swiss Family Robinson C 27 MIN
16MM FILM, 3/4 OR 1/2 IN VIDEO J-H
Presents an excerpt from the film Swiss Family Robinson. Stars John Mills and James MacArthur. Based on the novel SWISS FAMILY ROBINSON by Johann Wyss.
From The Film As Literature, Series 1 Series.
Prod-DISNEY Dist-WDEMCO Prodn-WDEMCO

Swiss Graffiti C 6 MIN
16MM FILM, 3/4 OR 1/2 IN VIDEO
Presents a story based on the premise that the primitive graffiti telling the story of the creation and found on walls throughout the world uses symbols of masculine supremacy. Tells how one day Eve gets tired of her role and the symbols change.
Prod-VEUREN Dist-PHENIX 1977

Swiss Miss B 73 MIN
16MM FILM OPTICAL SOUND I-C
Features Laurel and Hardy as mousetrap salesmen in Switzerland and one of their demonstrations in a luxury hotel which backfires. Shows how the boys end up in the kitchen where, for every dish they break, they must put in one more day of duty.
From The Laurel And Hardy Festival Series.
Prod-BHAWK Dist-BHAWK 1938

Switch On The Sun (2nd Ed) C 15 MIN
3/4 INCH VIDEO CASSETTE I-H
Presents sources of power that are being exhausted by energy consumption rates. Explains various methods of solar energy conversion and shows how this source of power is being used in homes and manufacturing plants.
LC NO. 77-703421
Prod-XEROXF Dist-GA 1977

Switchboard C 28 MIN
3/4 INCH VIDEO CASSETTE
Presents a group of former drug users who are now working on a drug hotline program. Discusses drug supply and demand, drug-related experiences, and the value of open communication.
From The Are You Listening Series.
LC NO. 80-707153
Prod-STURTM Dist-STURTM 1972

Switched-On Kitchen, The C 30 MIN
3/4 OR 1/2 INCH VIDEO CASSETTE J-H A
Presents Graham Kerr offering a potpourri of ideas on poaching, baking and breading fish.
Prod-CUETV Dist-CUNIV 1975

Switchgear, Tape 1 - Introduction, Bus Apparatus, Interrupting Devices, Air... C 60 MIN
3/4 OR 1/2 INCH VIDEO CASSETTE IND
See series title for descriptive statement.
From The Electrical Equipment Maintenance Series. Module 4
LC NO. 80-706013
Prod-ITCORP Dist-ITCORP 1980

Switchgear, Tape 2 - Current Carrying Devices, Racking Systems, Testing... C 60 MIN
3/4 OR 1/2 INCH VIDEO CASSETTE IND
See series title for descriptive statement.
From The Electrical Equipment Maintenance Series. Module 4
LC NO. 80-706014
Prod-ITCORP Dist-ITCORP 1980

Switching C 45 MIN
3/4 OR 1/2 INCH VIDEO CASSETTE C
Includes network topology, star, true, bus and distributed, fully connected, ring, comibinations, switching techniques and comparisons, physical and virtual circuit switching, message switching, broadcasting, and control functions, routing and flow control.
From The Telecommunications And The Computer Series.
LC NO. 81-707502
Prod-AMCEE Dist-AMCEE 1981

Switching C 51 MIN
3/4 OR 1/2 INCH VIDEO CASSETTE
Discusses switching techniques and comparisons.
From The Telecommunications And The Computer Series.
Prod-MIOT Dist-MIOT

Switching And Finite Automata Theory—A Series
C A
Covers finite-state automata, functional decomposition, threshold logic and several sequential circuit designs. Contains 35 one-hour videotapes.
Prod-UIDEEO Dist-UIDEEO

Switching And Isolating Devices C
3/4 OR 1/2 INCH VIDEO CASSETTE IND
Looks at the various types of switching devices which are installed to interrupt current flow or isolate circuits. Shows how these devices work. Includes circuit breakers, arc suppressing devices and maintenance considerations.
From The Distribution System Operation Series. Topic 7
Prod-LEIKID Dist-LEIKID

Switching On C 57 MIN
3/4 OR 1/2 INCH VIDEO CASSETTE C A
Surveys the silicon-chip industry and shows how the computer is revolutionizing the ways in which people live and learn. Includes examples of architects, doctors and composers who are applying computers to do their research and work.
LC NO. 82-706229
Prod-CANBC Dist-FLMLIB 1981

Switzerland C 19 MIN
16MM FILM, 3/4 OR 1/2 IN VIDEO I-H
Looks at the people, geography, industries and history of Switzerland.
From The Modern Europe Series.
Prod-JOU Dist-JOU

Switzerland C 29 MIN
3/4 OR 1/2 INCH VIDEO CASSETTE
Features home economist Joan Hood presenting a culinary tour of specialty dishes from around the world. Shows the preparation of Swiss dishes ranging from peasant cookery to continental cuisine.
From The International Cookbook Series.
Prod-WMVSTV Dist-PUBTEL

Switzerland C 33 MIN
16MM FILM, 3/4 OR 1/2 IN VIDEO I-C A
Shows life in Switzerland, including farming, skiing, celebrations and traditions.
Prod-DISNEY Dist-WDEMCO 1959

Switzerland - Life In A Mountain Village X 14 MIN
16MM FILM, 3/4 OR 1/2 IN VIDEO P-I
Pictures the way of life in the Swiss village of Evolene. Shows the activities of one village family. Describes their home life, recreation, farm work including the pasturing of the cows and cheese-making, and school work. Depicts the beautiful, yet rugged, geography of rural Switzerland.
Prod-EBF Dist-EBEC 1963

Switzerland - Life In A Mountain Village (Spanish) C 14 MIN
16MM FILM, 3/4 OR 1/2 IN VIDEO P-I
Depicts the rugged geography of rural Switzerland and features the way of life in a small Swiss village. Shows the home life, recreation, farm work and other traditional activities of the villagers.
Prod-EBEC Dist-EBEC

Switzerland Today C 17 MIN
16MM FILM, 3/4 OR 1/2 IN VIDEO I-C A
Looks at modern Switzerland, emphasizing the urbanization of a population traditionally skilled in manipulative abilities and the adaptation of industry to the necessity of importing almost all raw materials. Shows the resultant changes in agriculture and the highly organized tourist industry.
Prod-LUF Dist-LUF 1980

Switzerland, Yugoslavia, Iceland, California, Connecticut, Tunisia C 27 MIN
16MM FILM OPTICAL SOUND P-I
Describes the lives of children in Switzerland, Iceland, California, Connecticut and Tunisia. Relates a Yugoslavian folk tale about a czar who has the ears of a goat.
From The Big Blue Marble - Children Around The World Series. Program A
LC NO. 76-700639
Prod-ALVEN Dist-VITT 1975

Swivel Bar Transfer For Quadriplegia C 11 MIN
3/4 INCH VIDEO CASSETTE PRO
Shows a physical therapist preparing the swivel bar and hi-lo bed for giving minimal assistance to a quadriplegic patient during transfer from wheelchair to bed. Presents the equipment needed and its proper assembly for use. Includes a demonstration of the safety precautions necessary to prevent equipment failure or possibly injury to the patient.
From The Wheelchair Transfers Series.
Prod-PRIMED Dist-PRIMED

Swivel Bar Transfer For Quadriplegia, Pt 1 C 12 MIN
16MM FILM OPTICAL SOUND PRO
Presents a physical therapist and a quadriplegic patient demonstrating the swivel bar transfer technique.
Prod-CINEMP Dist-RLAH

Swivels, Blocks, Rotaries C 25 MIN
16MM FILM, 3/4 OR 1/2 IN VIDEO IND
See series title for descriptive statement.
From The You Need To Know Series.
Prod-UTEXPE Dist-UTEXPE

SWLA C 8 MIN
16MM FILM OPTICAL SOUND I-C A
Presents a semi-abstract interpretation of an Industrial area in southwest Los Angeles, using special optical effects.
Prod-CFS Dist-CFS 1971

Swoosh Away The Glop C 29 MIN
2 INCH VIDEOTAPE
See series title for descriptive statement.
From The Tin Lady Series.
Prod-NJPBA Dist-PUBTEL

Sword And The Flute, The C 24 MIN
16MM FILM OPTICAL SOUND J-C A
Uses Indian music and Moghul and Rajput miniature paintings in presenting four facets in the thinking of India--the courtly conqueror Emperor Akbar, the saintly life of the Yogin and the respect shown the true ascetic, the spiritual meaning of romantic love between man and woman and the adored divine bridegroom, which is one of the symbols as represented by the Lord Krishna.
LC NO. FIA59-522
Prod-IVORYJ Dist-RADIM 1959

Sword Of Gideon, The C 12 MIN
16MM FILM OPTICAL SOUND
A dramatization of the account in the Bible telling how Gideon became convinced of the strength of the Lord.
From The Tales From The Great Book Series.
LC NO. 73-713502
Prod-GDLP Dist-HALCOM 1971

SX-70 C 11 MIN
16MM FILM, 3/4 OR 1/2 IN VIDEO
Documents the invention, technology and potential of the SX-70 photographic system developed by Edwin Land.
Prod-POLARD Dist-PFP Prodn-EAMES 1973

Sybil C
1/2 IN VIDEO CASSETTE BETA/VHS
Presents the true story of a woman who developed 16 separate personalities, starring Sally Field.
Prod-GA Dist-GA

Sybil's Plight - A Family's Adjustment To Chronic Illness B 21 MIN
3/4 OR 1/2 INCH VIDEO CASSETTE
Demonstrates the problems of a family in its adjustment to chronic catastrophic illness. Shows edited segments of actual family interviews. Demonstrates the effect of genetic implications on parent-child relationships.
Prod-PSU Dist-PSU

Sydney Harbour Bridge C 13 MIN
16MM FILM OPTICAL SOUND
Presents a panoramic view of Sydney Harbour Bridge popularized in many tourist postcards.
LC NO. 80-700882
Prod-WINKLP Dist-TASCOR 1978

Sydney Opera House, The C 12 MIN
16MM FILM, 3/4 OR 1/2 IN VIDEO
Presents an aesthetic and factual study of the Sydney Opera House, including comments on its architect, design, politics, costs and building time.
Prod-RNBWP Dist-TEXFLM 1976

Sydney Opera House, 1972 C 9 MIN
16MM FILM OPTICAL SOUND J-C A
Presents a progress report on the Sydney opera house, showing final stages of construction.
LC NO. 73-702485
Prod-FLMAUS Dist-AUIS 1973

Sykes C 13 MIN
16MM FILM, 3/4 OR 1/2 IN VIDEO J-C A
Describes the experiences of Dierdre Walsh, a VISTA volunteer in the ghettos of Chicago and Erie, Pennsylvania. Portrays the life of Sykes, a proud pensionner who lives in Chicago, capturing his life style in a positive statement.
Prod-PERSPF Dist-CORF 1974

Sylvan Sewer, A C 25 MIN
16MM FILM OPTICAL SOUND
Explains that the 33 miles of Washington, D C's Rock Creek is more than a recreational stream flowing through Rock Creek Park. Reveals the stream as a vital element in the Maryland-District of Columbia watershed. Follows a group of college students as they explore sources of pollution and the environmental dangers involved.
From The Perspective Series.
LC NO. 73-700770
Prod-WRCTV Dist-WRCTV 1972

Sylvester C 6 MIN
16MM FILM, 3/4 OR 1/2 IN VIDEO P
Tells the story of Sylvester, a mouse who loves music. Tells how Sylvester becomes the world's first guitar playing mouse.
From The Golden Book Storytime Series.
Prod-WPES Dist-MTI

Sylvester And The Magic Pebble C 15 MIN
3/4 INCH VIDEO CASSETTE K-P
See series title for descriptive statement.
From The Storytime Series.
Prod-WCETTV Dist-GPITVL 1976

Sylvester And The Magic Pebble C 15 MIN
3/4 OR 1/2 INCH VIDEO CASSETTE P
Presents the children's story Sylvester And The Magic Pebble by William Steig. Includes the poem How Many'Ers' Are You by Marcie Hans.
From The Picture Book Park Series. Blue Module
Prod-WVIZTV Dist-AITECH 1974

Sylvia Gelber - An Interview C 28 MIN
3/4 INCH VIDEO CASSETTE
Presents Sylvia Gelber, Director of the Women's Bureau of Labour Canada, discussing the position of women in the labour force.
Prod-WMENIF Dist-WMENIF

Sylvia Nolan And Paul Moore C 30 MIN
3/4 OR 1/2 INCH VIDEO CASSETTE
Looks at creativity behind the scenes of a dance production. Features 'Esoterica' with Diana Byers. Hosted by Celia Ipiotis.
From The Eye On Dance - Behind The Scenes Series.
Prod-ARTRES Dist-ARTRES

Symbiosis C 4 MIN
16MM FILM, 3/4 OR 1/2 IN VIDEO J-C A
Uses animation to tell the story of an island that runs away from home to avoid destruction by the 'occasionals' who visit it on weekends. Shows how the island searches the world for a more suitable home, but finding none returns home to a prodigal's welcome.
LC NO. 80-706556
Prod-COXDA Dist-IFB 1977

Symbiosis C 10 MIN
16MM FILM, 3/4 OR 1/2 IN VIDEO J-H
Points out the many examples in nature of organisms living together in mutual dependence. Gives insights into the relationship called symbiosis.
Prod-BFA Dist-PHENIX 1973

Symbiosis (Swedish) C 10 MIN
16MM FILM, 3/4 OR 1/2 IN VIDEO J-H
Points out the many examples in nature of organisms living together in mutual dependence. Gives insights into the relationship called symbiosis.
Prod-BFA Dist-PHENIX 1973

Symbiosis - Mutualism, Parasitism, Commensalism, Pt 1 X 20 MIN
2 INCH VIDEOTAPE I
See series title for descriptive statement.
From The Process And Proof Series. No. 30
Prod-MCETV Dist-GPITVL Prodn-WVIZTV

Symbiosis - Mutualism, Parasitism, Commensalism, Pt 2 X 20 MIN
2 INCH VIDEOTAPE I
See series title for descriptive statement.
From The Process And Proof Series. No. 31
Prod-MCETV Dist-GPITVL Prodn-WVIZTV

Symbol Boy C 5 MIN
16MM FILM, 3/4 OR 1/2 IN VIDEO C A
Uses animated drawings in order to introduce the basic vocabulary of Blissymbols. Shows how the Bliss system can be useful in helping the verbally handicapped communicate.
Prod-NFBC Dist-BNCHMK 1976

Symbolic Programming - Assembler Language B 45 MIN
2 INCH VIDEOTAPE
See series title for descriptive statement.
From The Data Processing, Unit 3 - Instructing The Computer Series.
Prod-GPITVL Dist-GPITVL

Symbolic Programming Languages C 30 MIN
3/4 INCH VIDEO CASSETTE H A
Explores the evolution and detailed construction of a typical Symbolic Assembly Program. Discusses the advantages of this mode of programming.
From The Computing For Every Man Series.
Prod-NYSED Dist-NYSED 1973

Symbolism In Literature C 15 MIN
16MM FILM, 3/4 OR 1/2 IN VIDEO J-C
Uses the UPA cartoon version of Poe's 'TELL-TALE HEART' to develop concepts of literary symbolism.
Prod-SIGMA Dist-FILCOM 1966

Symbols C 15 MIN
16MM FILM, 3/4 OR 1/2 IN VIDEO I
Tells how Lee receives cards with mysterious symbols on them and cracks the code to discover that she has a secret admirer.
From The Thinkabout Series. Reshaping Information
LC NO. 81-706126
Prod-EDFCEN Dist-AITECH 1979

Symbols And Components B 33 MIN
16MM FILM - 3/4 IN VIDEO
Illustrates a practical electrical circuit, using symbols to represent the electrical components and measuring instruments. Explains electrical grounds, fuses and switches. Issued in 1965 as a motion picture.
LC NO. 80-707258
Prod-USAF Dist-USNAC 1980

Symbols Of Expression B 26 MIN
16MM FILM SILENT C T
Extends the theme of unity of personality (expressive behavior). attempts to demonstrate that an individual's drawings, 'DOODLINGS,' art productions, dance forms, signatures or written productions embody the 'KEY SYMBOL' of personality. Demonstrates with children, college students and shows signatures and musical manuscripts of Bach, Beethoven and Mozart.
Prod-PSUPCR Dist-PSUPCR 1952

Symbols On Schematics C 12 MIN
3/4 OR 1/2 INCH VIDEO CASSETTE
Features common features of schematics, differences, use and understanding symbols.
From The Reading Schematics And Symbols Series.
Prod-TPCTRA Dist-TPCTRA

Symbols On Schematics (Spanish) C 12 MIN
3/4 OR 1/2 INCH VIDEO CASSETTE
Features common features of schematics, differences, use and understanding symbols.
From The Reading Schematics And Symbols Series.
Prod-TPCTRA Dist-TPCTRA

Symbols, Equations And The Computer C 23 MIN
16MM FILM, 3/4 OR 1/2 IN VIDEO
Describes the symbols and equations needed to find the answer to the shape of the famous Golden Section. Shows where the symbols come from and explores iteration methods to find the answers.
Prod-OPENU Dist-MEDIAG Prodn-BBCTV 1979

Symbols, Part 1 C 16 MIN
3/4 OR 1/2 INCH VIDEO CASSETTE IND
Introduces eight geometric symbols and uses them in simple drawings. Include flatness, straightness, squareness, parallelism, angularity, symmetry, profile of a line and profile of a surface.
From The Geometric Dimensioning And Tolerancing Series.
Prod-GMIEMI Dist-AMCEE

Symbols, Part 2 C 20 MIN
3/4 OR 1/2 INCH VIDEO CASSETTE IND
Introduces four more geometric symbols including roundness, concentricity, cylindricity and runabout. Presents a brief history of Time Position as well.
From The Geometric Dimensioning And Tolerancing Series.
Prod-GMIEMI Dist-AMCEE

Symmetrical Components--A Series
C A
Includes a review of basics, shunt faults, series faults, sequence impedances, symmetry changes, simultaneous faults and computer solutions. Contains 43 fifty-minute videotapes.
Prod-UIDEEO Dist-UIDEEO

Symmetries Of The Cube C 14 MIN
16MM FILM, 3/4 OR 1/2 IN VIDEO H-C
Exhibits symmetries of the square as products of reflections. Studies the octahedral group via reflections.
From The Geometry Series.
Prod-UMINN Dist-IFB 1971

Symmetry C 11 MIN
16MM FILM, 3/4 OR 1/2 IN VIDEO J A

Use animated semi-abstract figures to depict and define symmetry. Examines a controlled progression of simple to complex symmetries and points out that symmetries obey strict mathematical principles.
LC NO. 83-706686
Prod-STGT Dist-IFB 1982

Symmetry B 15 MIN
2 INCH VIDEOTAPE P
See series title for descriptive statement.
From The Just Curious Series. No. 3
Prod-EOPS Dist-GPITVL Prodn-KOACTV

Symmetry C 15 MIN
3/4 OR 1/2 INCH VIDEO CASSETTE I-J
Shows how to draw a design to represent symmetry about one line, two perpendicular lines and a point.
From The Math Matters Series. Blue Module
Prod-STETVC Dist-AITECH Prodn-KLRNTV 1975

Symmetry C 15 MIN
3/4 INCH VIDEO CASSETTE P
Shows how to determine symmetry with respect to a line.
From The Studio M Series.
Prod-WCETTV Dist-GPITVL 1979

Symmetry - A First Film C 14 MIN
16MM FILM, 3/4 OR 1/2 IN VIDEO P-J
Uses attractive visuals of both ordinary and exotic objects to illustrate mirror symmetry, radial symmetry and rhythm.
LC NO. 84-706808
Prod-BFA Dist-PHENIX 1983

Symmetry And Shapes - Mirror Image C 20 MIN
16MM FILM, 3/4 OR 1/2 IN VIDEO I-J
Discusses aspects of symmetry and shapes.
From The Mathscore One Series.
Prod-BBCTV Dist-FI

Symmetry And Shapes - S For Shapes C 20 MIN
16MM FILM, 3/4 OR 1/2 IN VIDEO I
Discusses aspects of symmetry and shapes.
From The Mathscore Two Series.
Prod-BBCTV Dist-FI

Symmetry In Physical Law B 57 MIN
16MM FILM - 3/4 IN VIDEO
Covers the symmetries of physical phenomena. Covers translations in space and time, rotations in space, the consequence of relative motion and the interconnections of space and time.
From The Feynman Lectures - The Character Of Physical Law Series.
Prod-BBCTV Dist-EDC 1965

Sympathomimetic Blocking Agents, Ganglionic Blocking Agents And Anti-Hypertensive Agents C 30 MIN
16MM FILM OPTICAL SOUND C
See series title for descriptive statement.
From The Pharmacology Series.
LC NO. 73-703340
Prod-MVNE Dist-TELSTR 1971

Sympathomimetics B 30 MIN
16MM FILM OPTICAL SOUND C
Reviews the anatomy and physiology of the autonomic nervous system. Shows effects of various sympathomimetic drugs caused by their action of stimulating sympathetic nerve activity.
From The Pharmacology Series.
LC NO. 73-703339
Prod-MVNE Dist-TELSTR 1971

Sympathy For The Devil (1 Plus 1) C 110 MIN
16MM FILM OPTICAL SOUND H-C A
Presents Jean-Luc Godard's, Sympathy For The Devil (1 Plus 1) with the accompaniment of the Rolling Stones. Touches on the issues of black power, rape, murder, fascism, acid, pornography, sex and brutality.
Prod-NLC Dist-NLC

Symphonic Cello Soli C 30 MIN
3/4 OR 1/2 INCH VIDEO CASSETTE J-H A
See series title for descriptive statement.
From The Cello Sounds Of Today Series.
Prod-IU Dist-IU 1984

Symphonie Diagonale B 7 MIN
16MM FILM SILENT
Features hieroglyphic forms moving along an invisible diagonal in a work by Viking Eggeling, recognized by fellow artists as a 'lucid thinker and creator'. Produced 1921-25.
Prod-STARRC Dist-STARRC

Symphonie Einer Weltstadt B 79 MIN
16MM FILM OPTICAL SOUND H-C
A German language film. Views the people, industry and recreation of pre-war Berlin against a background of symphonic music.
LC NO. 79-712386
Prod-LAFRGL Dist-TRANSW 1970

Symphonie Einer Weltstadt - Berlin Wie Es War B 79 MIN
16MM FILM, 3/4 OR 1/2 IN VIDEO H-C A
A German language film. Presents glimpses of the Berlin of the 1930's.
Prod-IFB Dist-IFB 1939

Symphonie Pastorale B 105 MIN
16MM FILM OPTICAL SOUND
Features the story of a girl, blind and orphaned, who is adopted by the village minister. Shows how as time goes by, the minister's affection grows into love.
Prod-CON Dist-TRANSW 1964

Symphonie Realiste B 13 MIN
16MM FILM OPTICAL SOUND I-H
See series title for descriptive statement.
From The Les Francais Chez Vous Series. Set I, Lesson 13
LC NO. 70-704479
Prod-PEREN Dist-CHLTN 1967

Symphony Across The Land B 50 MIN
16MM FILM OPTICAL SOUND H A
Explains the role of music in the U S and features leading symphony orchestras from various states as they perform music by American composers.
LC NO. FIE63-52
Prod-USIS Dist-USIS 1959

Symphony In Black B 9 MIN
16MM FILM OPTICAL SOUND
Features Louis Armstrong and Billie Holiday in a musical short.
Prod-SPCTRA Dist-STRFLS 1935

Symphony In Steel C 14 MIN
16MM FILM OPTICAL SOUND
Describes an air trip to the West Indies at carnival time. Views the islands and their inhabitants, documenting the hand-crafting of a steel orchestra from discarded oil barrels. Presents the November, 1966, visit of a steel band to Barbados for Independence Week celebrations.
LC NO. FIA68-832
Prod-PANWA Dist-PANWA Prodn-ENOS 1967

Symphony In The Mountains (German) B 75 MIN
3/4 OR 1/2 INCH VIDEO CASSETTE
Presents a romance about a public-school teacher who teaches singing and skiing instead of the regular curriculum against the advice of his superiors and falls in love with the sister of one of his students. Features songs by the Vienna Boys Choir. With English subtitles.
Prod-IHF Dist-IHF

Symphony No. 1 C 60 MIN
3/4 INCH VIDEO CASSETTE
Presents the Detroit Symphony Orchestra, under the direction of Antal Dorati, performing Beethoven's Symphony No. 1. Features the conductor discussing the symphony with E G Marshall.
From The Beethoven Festival Series.
Prod-WTVSTV Dist-PUBTEL

Symphony No. 2 C 60 MIN
3/4 INCH VIDEO CASSETTE
Presents the Detroit Symphony Orchestra, under the direction of Antal Dorati, performing Beethoven's Symphony No. 2. Features the conductor discussing the symphony with E G Marshall.
From The Beethoven Festival Series.
Prod-WTVSTV Dist-PUBTEL

Symphony No. 3 C 60 MIN
3/4 INCH VIDEO CASSETTE
Presents the Detroit Symphony Orchestra, under the direction of Antal Dorati, performing Beethoven's Symphony No. 3. Features the conductor discussing the symphony with E G Marshall.
From The Beethoven Festival Series.
Prod-WTVSTV Dist-PUBTEL

Symphony No. 4 C 60 MIN
3/4 INCH VIDEO CASSETTE
Presents the Detroit Symphony Orchestra, under the direction of Antal Dorati, performing Beethoven's Symphony No. 4. Features the conductor discussing the symphony with E G Marshall.
From The Beethoven Festival Series.
Prod-WTVSTV Dist-PUBTEL

Symphony No. 5 C 60 MIN
3/4 INCH VIDEO CASSETTE H-C A
Presents narrator E.G. Marshall and conductor Antal Dorati discussing Beethoven's Fifth Symphony. Includes a performance of the work by the Detroit Symphony Orchestra.
From The Beethoven Festival Series.
LC NO. 79-708047
Prod-WTVSTV Dist-PUBTEL 1979

Symphony No. 6 C 60 MIN
3/4 INCH VIDEO CASSETTE
Presents the Detroit Symphony Orchestra, under the direction of Antal Dorati, performing Beethoven's Symphony No. 6. Features the conductor discussing the symphony with E G Marshall.
From The Beethoven Festival Series.
Prod-WTVSTV Dist-PUBTEL

Symphony No. 7 C 60 MIN
3/4 INCH VIDEO CASSETTE
Presents the Detroit Symphony Orchestra, under the direction of Antal Dorati, performing Beethoven's Symphony No. 7. Features the conductor discussing the symphony with E G Marshall.
From The Beethoven Festival Series.
Prod-WTVSTV Dist-PUBTEL

Symphony No. 8 C 60 MIN
3/4 INCH VIDEO CASSETTE
Presents the Detroit Symphony Orchestra, under the direction of Antal Dorati, performing Beethoven's Symphony No. 8. Features the conductor discussing the symphony with E G Marshall.
From The Beethoven Festival Series.
Prod-WTVSTV Dist-PUBTEL

Symphony No. 9 C 60 MIN
3/4 INCH VIDEO CASSETTE
Presents the Detroit Symphony Orchestra, under the direction of Antal Dorati, performing Beethoven's Symphony No. 9. Features the conductor discussing the symphony with E G Marshall.
From The Beethoven Festival Series.
Prod-WTVSTV Dist-PUBTEL

Symphony Of A World City - Berlin As It Was B 79 MIN
16MM FILM, 3/4 OR 1/2 IN VIDEO H-C A
An English language version of the 1939 film Symphonie Einer Weltstadt - Berlin Wie Es War. Presents glimpses of the Berlin of the 1930's.
LC NO. 80-706720
Prod-IFB Dist-IFB 1977

Symphony On Ice C 10 MIN
16MM FILM OPTICAL SOUND
Features the game of hockey, a sport which requires split-second decisions from each player who must travel down the ice at speeds in excess of 50 miles per hour. Explains the gear used by the players and the techniques of playing well.
Prod-FILMSM Dist-FILMSM

Symphony Orchestra, The (2nd Ed) X 14 MIN
16MM FILM, 3/4 OR 1/2 IN VIDEO I-H
Shows how the orchestra developed from an ensemble of five string players to the symphonic organization. Uses excerpts from works by Dvorak, Mozart, Bach, Wagner and Berlioz, to demonstrate the contribution of each major development in the orchestra.
Prod-EBF Dist-EBEC 1956

Symphony Orchestra, The (2nd Ed) (Spanish) C 14 MIN
16MM FILM, 3/4 OR 1/2 IN VIDEO I-H
Traces the development of the orchestra from an ensemble of five string players to a large symphonic organization. Uses examples from the musical masterworks of three centuries to demonstrate the contribution of each major development in the orchestra. Features the Vienna Symphony Orchestra.
Prod-EBEC Dist-EBEC

Symphony Sound With Henry Lewis And The Royal Philharmonic, The C 27 MIN
16MM FILM, 3/4 OR 1/2 IN VIDEO H-C A
Henry Lewis discusses the unique characteristics of the Symphony orchestra and describes the instruments and their particular roles within the symphony.
Prod-IQFILM Dist-LCOA Prodn-SAUDEK 1970

Symposium Of Popular Songs C 16 MIN
16MM FILM, 3/4 OR 1/2 IN VIDEO P-H
Takes a look at various forms of popular songs and how they have changed with the passage of time.
Prod-DISNEY Dist-WDEMCO Prodn-WDEMCO 1962

Symptom As Expression Of Anxiety, The B 44 MIN
16MM FILM OPTICAL SOUND PRO
Explains how the nurse utilizes concepts of anxiety and psychodynamics to understand a patient's behavior and implement her understanding to plan nursing interventions.
From The Nursing In Psychiatry Series.
LC NO. 75-703440
Prod-VDONUR Dist-AJN Prodn-WTTWTV 1968

Symptomatic Postgastrectomy Patient, The C 22 MIN
16MM FILM OPTICAL SOUND
Presents fiberscopic photographs of postoperative complications of the stomach.
LC NO. 74-705734
Prod-NMAC Dist-USNAC 1969

Symptoms And Treatment Of Marine Injuries C 18 MIN
3/4 OR 1/2 INCH VIDEO CASSETTE PRO
Demonstrates how to diagnose and treat eight kinds of injuries from marine life.
Prod-HSCIC Dist-HSCIC 1977

Symptoms In Schizophrenia B 18 MIN
16MM FILM SILENT C A
Demonstrates various symptoms in schizophrenia, such as social apathy, delusions, hallucinations, hebephrenic reactions, cerea flexibilitas, rigidity, motor stereotypes, posturing and echopraxia in typical cases. For medical and allied groups.
Prod-PSUPCR Dist-PSUPCR 1938

Symptoms Of Coronary Heart Disease C
3/4 OR 1/2 INCH VIDEO CASSETTE
Discusses symptoms of coronary heart disease.
Prod-MEDFAC Dist-MEDFAC

Symptoms Of Sobriety C 45 MIN
16MM FILM OPTICAL SOUND
Describes the signs of recovery from alcoholism and the symptoms of ideal sobriety.
Prod-FMARTN Dist-KELLYP

Synchro Systems B 28 MIN
3/4 INCH VIDEO CASSETTE
Explains how a synchro generator controls the movement of a synchro motor and shows the electrical transfer of angular motion between two remote points. Demonstrates the operation of a control transformer and a differential synchro generator and tells how to use a control transformer as a receiver and a differential synchro generator when putting correction into the signal of the circuit. Issued in 1944 as a motion picture.
From The Radio Technician Training Series.
LC NO. 78-706304
Prod-USN Dist-USNAC Prodn-HOLMES 1978

Synchro Systems, Pt 2 B 13 MIN
16MM FILM, 3/4 OR 1/2 IN VIDEO
Shows the operation of a control transformer and a differential synchro generator. Explains how to use a control transformer as a receiver and a differential synchro generator when putting corrections into the signal of the circuit.

From The Radio Technician Training Series.
Prod-USN Dist-USNAC Prodn-HOLMES 1948

Synchromy C 8 MIN
16MM FILM, 3/4 OR 1/2 IN VIDEO P-J A
Uses moving colors to create a visual conception of music. Presents various patterns and frequencies, which represent musical shapes from a corresponding soundtrack.
Prod-NFBC Dist-NFBC 1972

Synchronized Swimming B 17 MIN
16MM FILM, 3/4 OR 1/2 IN VIDEO J-C
Introduces synchronized swimming. Shows basic skills required for strokes, summersaults, rotation and figure work. Underwater photography describes various movements.
Prod-BHA Dist-IFB 1968

Synchronous Combined Protocolectomy For Mucosal Ulcerative Colitis C 46 MIN
3/4 OR 1/2 INCH VIDEO CASSETTE
See series title for descriptive statement.
From The Gastrointestinal Series.
Prod-SVL Dist-SVL

Synchronous Combined Resection Of The Rectum C 32 MIN
16MM FILM OPTICAL SOUND PRO
Shows details of a two-team abdomino-perineal resection of the rectum for carcinoma, using a simple technique of positioning the legs on mayo high stands.
Prod-ACYDGD Dist-ACY 1969

Synchronous Machines - Electromechanical Dynamics B 33 MIN
3/4 INCH VIDEOTAPE
Focuses on electromagnetic fields and forces as they interact with moving and deformable media.
Prod-NCEEF Dist-EDC

Synchros B 25 MIN
16MM FILM, 3/4 OR 1/2 IN VIDEO H A
Describes the construction, operation, and electrical characteristics of a synchro device, emphasizing the voltage induced into the stator with the rotor at various positions. Defines such terms as electrical balance, correspondence, friction and torque.
Prod-USNAC Dist-USNAC 1984

Synchroscope B 38 MIN
16MM FILM OPTICAL SOUND
Shows the block diagram of the vertical and horizontal channels of a typical synchroscope and traces a signal through both channels. Uses the Tektronix 502A oscilloscope to demonstrate how the various controls affect signal presentation. (Kinescope)
LC NO. 74-705735
Prod-USAF Dist-USNAC

Synchrotron C 15 MIN
16MM FILM OPTICAL SOUND H-C A
Uses live action and animation to discuss the components and operation of the Cambridge electron accelerator, a high energy physics research laboratory operated by Harvard and the Massachusetts Institute of Technology. Includes scenes of scientists performing experiments to test old and new theories regarding the basic nature of matter.
LC NO. 75-700729
Prod-HPP Dist-USERD 1968

Syndactylism - Surgical Management C 25 MIN
3/4 OR 1/2 INCH VIDEO CASSETTE PRO
Discusses incidence and classification of syndactylism of the hand. Demonstrates three different operations, along with follow-ups to show end result.
Prod-ASSH Dist-ASSH

Syndromes C
3/4 OR 1/2 INCH VIDEO CASSETTE
Presents five syndromes attributable to sexually transmitted disease. Presents signs and symptoms and treatment for each disease.
From The Sexually Transmitted Diseases Series.
Prod-CONMED Dist-CONMED

Synectics And Group Investigation C 30 MIN
3/4 OR 1/2 INCH VIDEO CASSETTE
Demonstrates one aspect of synectics, a strategy for developing and improving creative problem solving ability. Describes synectics activities which enhance the problem-solving capacity and creative thinking processes of the individual student, with the teacher acting as the facilitator. Presents a second model in which the teacher and her students are involved in a group investigation of the concept of communication through social inquiry, which is a more structured model than the synectics model.
From The Classroom Teaching Models Series.
Prod-NETCHE Dist-NETCHE 1979

Synergism - Cities And Towns—A Series

Prod-PUBTEL Dist-PUBTEL

Five Days In Moorefield 28 MIN
Promise City 29 MIN
Ste Genevieve - A French Legacy 27 MIN
This City Is Milwaukee 27 MIN

Synergism - Command Performance—A Series

Prod-PUBTEL Dist-PUBTEL

American Highlands, The 58 MIN
Budaya - The Performing Arts 59 MIN
Dance - Africa 62 MIN
O Say Can You Sing 60 MIN
Rochester Philharmonic Orchestra, The 60 MIN

Synergism - Encore—A Series

Prod-PUBTEL Dist-PUBTEL

Art Of Bunraku, The 29 MIN
Dances Of Greece 29 MIN
Fantasy In Mime 29 MIN
Gallery Of Children, A 29 MIN
Mr Smith And Other Nonsense 29 MIN
Music Of Japan, The - Koto Music 29 MIN

Synergism - Gallimaufry—A Series

Prod-PUBTEL Dist-PUBTEL

Fence Around The Amish (Award Series 1967) 29 MIN
Gold Was Where You Found It (Award Series 1966) 29 MIN
I'll Get There Soon's I Can (Award Series 1966) 28 MIN
Only Yesterday (Award Series 1965) 29 MIN
Secrets Of A Brook (Award Series 1967) 30 MIN

Synergism - In Today's World—A Series

Examines some of today's problems including, old age, race relations, inflation, poverty, welfare and foster homes, death and disease.
Prod-PUBTEL Dist-PUBTEL

Bill Cosby On Prejudice 29 MIN
Chicano 28 MIN
Inflation 27 MIN
Low View From A Dark Shadow 29 MIN
Mark Waters Story, The 29 MIN
Marshes Of 'Two' Street, The 29 MIN
Questions 29 MIN
Subversion 27 MIN
Such A Place 28 MIN
Underground Film 29 MIN
Until I Die 29 MIN
Watts Tower Theatre Workshop 28 MIN

Synergism - Profiles, People—A Series

Offers individual portraits and intimate glimpses of people who have left the mark of their creative personalities upon their communities and in some cases upon the world.
Prod-PUBTEL Dist-PUBTEL

Art Of Luigi Lucioni, The 29 MIN
Artist Of Savitiria, The 29 MIN
Brandywine Tradition, The 26 MIN
Bryan Beavers - A Moving Portrait 29 MIN
Degrazia 29 MIN
In Pursuit Of Discovery - The Memoirs Of Jane Kennedy - To Be Free 28 MIN
27 MIN
Mr Thoreau Takes A Trip - A Week On The 27 MIN
Transitions - Conversations With Wendell 30 MIN
Woman As Painter 29 MIN

Synergism - The Challenge Of Sports—A Series

Presents a rodeo circuit, mountain climbing, soaring and the annual races to the top of Pikes Peak.
Prod-PUBTEL Dist-PUBTEL

Ascent 30 MIN
Racing On Thin Air 29 MIN
Soaring Over The Rockies 30 MIN
This Is Rodeo 29 MIN

Synergism - Variations In Music—A Series

Highlights three aspects of musical performance exploring the influence of the Christian church upon music and in particular upon jazz, a Renaissance madrigal comedy written in 1608 and a look at the innovative instruments of a highly unorthodox musician.
Prod-PUBTEL Dist-PUBTEL

Come Blow Your Horn 29 MIN
Music Of Harry Partch, The 30 MIN
Stanford Chorale - Il Festino 27 MIN

Syngerism - Troubled Humanity—A Series

Explores some of society's problems including, drugs, alcoholism, juvenile detention and bussing.
Prod-PUBTEL Dist-PUBTEL

Drugs In The Tenderloin 52 MIN
No Gun Towers, No Fences 59 MIN
Tiger By The Tail 58 MIN
With All Deliberate Speed 59 MIN

Synonyms B 15 MIN
2 INCH VIDEOTAPE P
See series title for descriptive statement.
From The Language Corner Series.
Prod-CVETVC Dist-GPITVL Prodn-WCVETV

Synoptiscope, The - How To Use It C 20 MIN
3/4 OR 1/2 INCH VIDEO CASSETTE PRO
Teaches students how to use the synoptiscope for testing simultaneous perception, fusion, stereopsis, retinal correspondence, and cardinal position of gaze.
Prod-HSCIC Dist-HSCIC 1981

Syntactic And Semantic Development C 136 MIN
3/4 OR 1/2 INCH VIDEO CASSETTE
Addresses three basic questions regarding the nature of early semantic and syntactic development in communication.
From The Meeting The Communications Needs Of The Severely/Profoundly Handicapped 1980 Series.
Prod-PUAVC Dist-PUAVC

Synthesis C 30 MIN
3/4 OR 1/2 INCH VIDEO CASSETTE
Presents three works by Stephen Beck, an electronic artist, which demonstrate his virtuosity and his artistic range.
Prod-EAI Dist-EAI

Synthesis Approach To Reading, A C 30 MIN
3/4 OR 1/2 INCH VIDEO CASSETTE T
Discusses a synthesis approach to reading in children with special needs.
From The Teaching Children With Special Needs Series.
Prod-MDDE Dist-MDCPB

Synthesis Of An Organic Compound C 22 MIN
16MM FILM OPTICAL SOUND H
Shows the synthesis of 2-butanone, a ketone, from 2butanol, an alcohol, as an example of a common type of organic synthesis. Cites three basic steps in the process—synthesis, purification and identification.
From The CHEM Study Films Series.
Prod-CHEMS Dist-MLA 1962

Synthesis Of Neuroanatomy, Pt 1 C 18 MIN
16MM FILM, 3/4 OR 1/2 IN VIDEO PRO
See series title for descriptive statement.
From The Anatomical Basis Of Brain Function Series.
Prod-AVCORP Dist-TEF

Synthesis Of Neuroanatomy, Pt 2 C 18 MIN
16MM FILM, 3/4 OR 1/2 IN VIDEO PRO
See series title for descriptive statement.
From The Anatomical Basis Of Brain Function Series.
Prod-AVCORP Dist-TEF

Synthesis Of The Failure Governing Stress And Strength Distributions Including Monte Carlo... B 60 MIN
3/4 OR 1/2 INCH VIDEO CASSETTE C
Treats synthesis of the failure governing stress and strength distributions including Monte Carlo simulation. Narrated by Dimitri Kececioglu, Professor of Aerospace and Mechanical Engineering at the University of Arizona.
From The Mechanical Component Reliability Prediction, Probabilistic Design For Reliability...Series. Pt 2
Prod-UAZMIC Dist-UAZMIC

Synthesis—A Series

Explores the scientific and technical aspects of hotly debated public policy issues of national interest and the particular concern of Western states.
Prod-KPBS Dist-KPBS

Alaska Oil - America's Pipe Dream? 030 MIN
Arctic's TV Generation, The 030 MIN
Closing The Learning Gap 030 MIN
Coal - Solution Or Pollution? 030 MIN
Creation Vs Evolution - Battle In The Classroom 060 MIN
Defusing Cancer's Time Bomb 030 MIN
Grand Canyon - Who Needs It? 030 MIN
Here Today, Here Tomorrow, Radioactive Wastes 030 MIN
Looking For Aquarius - California's Quest 030 MIN
Mt St Helens - Why They Died 030 MIN
Nisei - Legacy 030 MIN
President's Scientist - A Conversation With 030 MIN

Synthetic Sapphire B 7 MIN
16MM FILM OPTICAL SOUND C
Examines the manufacture of synthetic sapphire from alumina and gives some examples of its uses.
Prod-BFI Dist-HEFL 1946

Syphay Family, The C 29 MIN
3/4 OR 1/2 INCH VIDEO CASSETTE
Traces the lineage of the Syphay's, one of Virginia's oldest black families, to the owner of the Arlington Plantation.
Prod-RCOMTV Dist-SYLWAT 1985

Syphilis B 14 MIN
16MM FILM OPTICAL SOUND PRO
Covers the diagnosis of early, latent and late syphilis.
Prod-USPHS Dist-NMAC 1941

Syphilis C 15 MIN
3/4 OR 1/2 INCH VIDEO CASSETTE
Presents a detailed explanation of the nature of syphilis. Discusses diagnosis. Stresses early and appropriate treatment.
Prod-MEDFAC Dist-MEDFAC 1973

Syphilitic Venereal Disease C 25 MIN
16MM FILM OPTICAL SOUND PRO
Organizes and clarifies for the physician the stages and types of syphilis with correct diagnosis and treatment discussed.
Prod-SQUIBB Dist-SQUIBB 1954

Syphilitic Venereal Disease (2nd Ed) C 19 MIN
16MM FILM OPTICAL SOUND PRO
Examines the types and stages of syphilis, explaining the course of the disease in terms of the pathologic processes initiated by the infecting Treponema pallidum organism. Illustrates the variety of symptoms by clinical material, to the end that correct diagnosis may by made and proper treatment given.
Prod-SQUIBB Dist-SQUIBB

Syracuse, A University Perspective C 19 MIN
16MM FILM OPTICAL SOUND
Features students and faculty members at Syracuse University commenting on the nature of the institution and its academic

and extracurricular opportunities. Explores the diversity of the large university experience and attempts to help high school students in choosing a college.
LC NO. 79-701389
Prod-CAMPF Dist-CAMPF 1978

Syrian Arab Republic C 28 MIN
3/4 INCH VIDEOTAPE
Interviews Ambassador Hammoud El-Choufi, permanent representative to the United Nations, on Syria today and the advancement the country has made in the last few years. Includes a film clip on Syria's industrialization.
From The International Byline Series.
Prod-PERRYM Dist-PERRYM

Systamodules C 13 MIN
16MM FILM OPTICAL SOUND
Shows a new concept in hospital pharmacy patient care, based on a system of unique modular environments. Traces these modules through their conception, documentation, design and application.
LC NO. 77-700420
Prod-FISHSC Dist-FISHSC 1976

System Analysis - Design C 30 MIN
3/4 OR 1/2 INCH VIDEO CASSETTE H-C A
Presents the process of designing a system and the role of the system analyst.
From The Making It Count Series.
LC NO. 80-707573
Prod-BCSC Dist-BCSC 1980

System Analysis - Development And Implementation C 30 MIN
3/4 OR 1/2 INCH VIDEO CASSETTE H-C A
Shows the development and implementation phases of a system. Discusses the skills required of programmers and their role in system development.
From The Making It Count Series.
LC NO. 80-707574
Prod-BCSC Dist-BCSC 1980

System Analysis - Problem Definition C 30 MIN
3/4 OR 1/2 INCH VIDEO CASSETTE H-C A
Shows how information systems are developed, starting with user requirements and proceeding through the phases of system design. Outlines the process and examines the first two steps, problem definition and project analysis. Describes the role of the system analyst. Covers techniques of investigation, analysis of information, and planning and control methods.
From The Making It Count Series.
LC NO. 80-707572
Prod-BCSC Dist-BCSC 1980

System Analysis, Pt I C 50 MIN
3/4 OR 1/2 INCH VIDEO CASSETTE PRO
See series title for descriptive statement.
From The Modern Control Theory Series. Pt I
Prod-MIOT Dist-AMCEE

System And Machine Design C 43 MIN
3/4 OR 1/2 INCH VIDEO CASSETTE IND
Tells how to approach a noise control problem, solutions to common noise sources, motors, fans, gears, vibrators and pneumatic tools.
From The Industrial Noise Control, Part I - Fundamentals Series.
LC NO. 81-707500
Prod-AMCEE Dist-AMCEE 1981

System Classification B 27 MIN
3/4 OR 1/2 INCH VIDEO CASSETTE PRO
Provides an investigation of the classification of systems according to their input-output properties.
From The Probability And Random Processes - Linear Systems Series.
Prod-MIOT Dist-MIOT

System Configuration B 60 MIN
3/4 OR 1/2 INCH VIDEO CASSETTE
See series title for descriptive statement.
From The Understanding Microprocessors Series. Pt 11
Prod-UAZMIC Dist-UAZMIC 1979

System Descriptions B 22 MIN
3/4 OR 1/2 INCH VIDEO CASSETTE PRO
Introduces the basic concept of a single-input single-output system, and presents a number of examples and special cases including the important class of of linear systems.
From The Probability And Random Processes - Linear Systems Series.
Prod-MIOT Dist-MIOT

System Design - The Beginning C 45 MIN
3/4 OR 1/2 INCH VIDEO CASSETTE PRO
Defines four generalized project management systems. Deals with asking the right design questions.
From The Advanced Project Management Series.
Prod-AMCEE Dist-AMCEE

System Elements B 420 MIN
3/4 OR 1/2 INCH VIDEO CASSETTE PRO
Discusses main system elements of the space shuttle, including main engines, external tank, solid rocket booster and orbiter.
From The Spacecraft System Design Series.
Prod-USCITV Dist-AMCEE

System Error Budget, The C 41 MIN
3/4 OR 1/2 INCH VIDEO CASSETTE
Illustrates the application of system error analysis to practical systems. Establishes system error budgets based on an analysis of these systems.
From The Systems Engineering And Systems Management Series.
Prod-MIOT Dist-MIOT

System For Overdenture Retention C 14 MIN
3/4 OR 1/2 INCH VIDEO CASSETTE
Describes the use of the zest anchor system which consists of a metallic sleeve and nylon post, one of the stud attachments available commercially which can be utilized to enhance the retention of complete removable overdentures.
Prod-VADTC Dist-AMDA 1981

System For Overdenture Retention, A C 14 MIN
16MM FILM, 3/4 OR 1/2 IN VIDEO PRO
Details the clinical and laboratory steps involved in the fabrication of overdentures, utilizing attachments. Describes indications and contraindications.
Prod-VADTC Dist-USNAC

System Functions B 35 MIN
3/4 OR 1/2 INCH VIDEO CASSETTE PRO
Describes some techniques for measuring system functions (impulse response and frequency response), and also considers the analysis of linear systems characterized by differential equations, or the cascade of several linear systems.
From The Probability And Random Processes - Linear Systems Series.
Prod-MIOT Dist-MIOT

System In Solution, A C 20 MIN
3/4 INCH VIDEO CASSETTE T
Shows how teachers can introduce the concept of systems by using an aluminum-copper chloride interaction experiment. Uses classroom scenes to illustrate problem solving.
From The Science In The Elementary School - Physical Science Series.
Prod-UWKY Dist-GPITVL 1979

System Is Based On 10, The C 20 MIN
3/4 INCH VIDEO CASSETTE J-C A
Emphasizes decimal prefixes and points out that the decimal system uses 10 and multiples of 10 as bases.
From The Metric System Series.
Prod-MAETEL Dist-GPITVL 1975

System Of Gross Examination In The Eye Laboratory C 20 MIN
16MM FILM OPTICAL SOUND PRO
Uses live action, animated drawings and still photos to demonstrate the step-by-step process of gross examination.
LC NO. FIA68-236
Prod-UCLA Dist-UCLAA 1967

System Of Integers, The, Pt 1 C 45 MIN
2 INCH VIDEOTAPE
See series title for descriptive statement.
From The Fundamentals Of Mathematics (2nd Ed.) Unit I - Number Theory Series.
Prod-CHITVC Dist-GPITVL

System Of Integers, The, Pt 2 C 45 MIN
2 INCH VIDEOTAPE
See series title for descriptive statement.
From The Fundamentals Of Mathematics (2nd Ed.) Unit I - Number Theory Series.
Prod-CHITVC Dist-GPITVL

System Operating Manual C
3/4 OR 1/2 INCH VIDEO CASSETTE IND
Covers system interties, operation coordination, generator control, interchange, reliability generation capacity, transmission, maintenance coordination, system disturbances and communications.
From The Electric Power System Operation Series. Tape 20
Prod-LEIKID Dist-LEIKID

System Operation Checks C 60 MIN
3/4 OR 1/2 INCH VIDEO CASSETTE IND
Explains general system check, checking refrigerant charge, leak testing, maintaining lubrication level and start-up procedures.
From The Air Conditioning And Refrigeration-- Training Series.
Prod-ITCORP Dist-ITCORP

System Protection And Relaying--A Series

Focuses on such topics as system applications of lightning and other surge protective systems. Contains 40 fifty-minute videotape lectures.
Prod-UIDEEO Dist-UIDEEO

System Redundancy And Failure Detection Requirements C 36 MIN
3/4 OR 1/2 INCH VIDEO CASSETTE
Discusses the need for redundancy to improve system reliability. Analyzes grouping and alternative failure, detection techniques for redundancy.
From The Systems Engineering And Systems Management Series.
Prod-MIOT Dist-MIOT

System Reliability, Maintainability And Availability C 41 MIN
3/4 OR 1/2 INCH VIDEO CASSETTE
Presents definitions and terminology used in the fields of reliability, maintainability and availability. analyzes the basic foundations of a system reliability program. Presents methods for improving maintainability.
From The Systems Engineering And Systems Management Series.
Prod-MIOT Dist-MIOT

System Testing Techniques C 46 MIN
3/4 OR 1/2 INCH VIDEO CASSETTE
Presents the basic foundations of system test. Illustrates an example for testing a large naval shipyard system.
From The Systems Engineering And Systems Management Series.
Prod-MIOT Dist-MIOT

System 12 C 20 MIN
16MM FILM OPTICAL SOUND
Explains the function of System 12 components by visiting the various sites in Europe and America where they were developed or are produced. Introduces the actual people involved who explain this digital switching system.
LC NO. 82-700191
Prod-ITTEM Dist-BLUMAR Prodn-BLUMAR 1981

System, The C 14 MIN
16MM FILM OPTICAL SOUND
Looks at the American economic system through the eyes of high school students.
Prod-EXXON Dist-MTP 1982

Systematic Approach To Organizing An Energy Audit, A C 45 MIN
3/4 OR 1/2 INCH VIDEO CASSETTE PRO
Shows Mr Susemichel discussing how energy resources management fits into management of the total facility, and describes practical plant alterations that save money and can be used in figuring the plant's payback analysis. Also talks about the impact and necessity of energy audits and the importance of the team approach in resource management.
From The Energy Auditing And Conservation Series.
LC NO. 81-706444
Prod-AMCEE Dist-AMCEE 1979

Systematic Jury Selection Techniques - A Lecture By Hans Zeisel C 32 MIN
3/4 OR 1/2 INCH VIDEO CASSETTE PRO
Attacks the mystique of jury selection as Hans Zeisel describes his research and experimentation in the federal courts. Stresses the importance of assembling facts and tangible information during voir dire and questions methods that emphasize surveying demographic information or observing body language.
Prod-ABACPE Dist-ABACPE

Systematic Periodontal Examination And Charting C 16 MIN
3/4 OR 1/2 INCH VIDEO CASSETTE PRO
Presents a method for the examination of the periodontally involved dentition and offers a format for the eliciting and recording of diagnostic data.
Prod-VADTC Dist-USNAC 1982

Systematic Procedures And Numerical Example C 38 MIN
3/4 OR 1/2 INCH VIDEO CASSETTE PRO
See series title for descriptive statement.
From The Modern Control Theory - Stochastic Control Series.
Prod-MIOT Dist-MIOT

Systematic Program Design Model For Therapeutic Recreation, A C 30 MIN
3/4 OR 1/2 INCH VIDEO CASSETTE PRO
Provides guidelines for systematically developing a therapeutic recreation program. Includes information on needs assessment, program development and evaluation.
LC NO. 80-707596
Prod-VAMCMM Dist-USNAC 1980

Systemic Disease And The Eye, Pt 1 C 12 MIN
3/4 OR 1/2 INCH VIDEO CASSETTE PRO
Discusses the pathogenesis and related ocular findings for congenital and acquired syphilis, tuberculosis, systemic viral infections (herpes simplex, varicella-zoster, rubella), systemic fungal infections (candidiasis, histoplasmosis), toxoplasmosis, Reiter's syndrome, sarcoidosis and connective tissue disorders (systemic lupus erythematosus).
Prod-UMICHM Dist-UMICHM 1976

Systemic Disease And The Eye, Pt 2 C 13 MIN
3/4 OR 1/2 INCH VIDEO CASSETTE PRO
Considers the relationship of ocular findings to seven systemic diseases. Presents detailed descriptions of the physician in diagnosing these disease entities.
Prod-UMICHM Dist-UMICHM 1976

Systemic Disease And The Eye, Pt 3 C 15 MIN
3/4 OR 1/2 INCH VIDEO CASSETTE PRO
Describes ocular defects which are transmitted genetically. Discusses examples of genetic disorders which involve the eye.
Prod-UMICHM Dist-UMICHM 1976

Systemic Disease And The Eye, Pt 4 C 15 MIN
3/4 OR 1/2 INCH VIDEO CASSETTE PRO
Discusses cardiovascular disorders which result in changes in blood vessels within the eye. Describes ocular findings in arteriosclerosis, atherosclerosis and early advanced hypertension. Presents drugs used to treat systemic diseases which cause ocular change.
Prod-UMICHM Dist-UMICHM 1976

Systemic Lupus Erythematosus (SLE) - It Means Some Changes C 26 MIN
3/4 OR 1/2 INCH VIDEO CASSETTE
Provides an insight into patients with systemic lupus erythematosus (SLE). Discusses their reactions to the diagnosis, symptoms, medications and the emotional impact of illness on themselves and their families.
Prod-UMICHM Dist-UMICHM 1981

Systems Analysis B
16MM FILM OPTICAL SOUND
Deals with three key ideas in systems analysis.
Prod-OPENU Dist-OPENU

Systems Analysis - Means-Ends Diagnosis B 29 MIN
16MM FILM OPTICAL SOUND IND
See series title for descriptive statement.
From The Quantitative Approaches To Decision Making Series.
LC NO. 74-703326
Prod-EDSD Dist-EDSD 1969

Systems And Sub-Systems B 15 MIN
2 INCH VIDEOTAPE P
See series title for descriptive statement.
From The Just Wondering Series.
Prod-EOPS Dist-GPITVL Prodn-KOACTV

Systems And Sub-Systems In Experiments B 15 MIN
2 INCH VIDEOTAPE P
See series title for descriptive statement.
From The Just Wondering Series.
Prod-EOPS Dist-GPITVL Prodn-KOACTV

Systems Approach To Social Worker Practices B 30 MIN
3/4 OR 1/2 INCH VIDEO CASSETTE
Answers questions about how the systems approach to social work practices, coupled with other programs, helps the social worker deal with many elements in a practice situation.
Prod-VRL Dist-UWISC

Systems Development - A Case Study C
16MM FILM - 3/4 IN VIDEO H-C A
Shows how the Salz Tannery considered a computer by using such methods as a feasibility study, requirements definition, evaluation, selection and system design.
From The Computers At Work - Concepts And Applications Series. Module 6
Prod-BNA Dist-BNA 1983

Systems Development - A Case Study C
3/4 OR 1/2 INCH VIDEO CASSETTE
Discusses the importance of the systems development process for businesses considering investing in computer information systems and discusses in sequence the steps in the system development process.
From The Computers At Work Series.
Prod-COMTEG Dist-COMTEG

Systems Engineering And Systems Management-A Series

Provides the concepts, methodology and procedure necessary to engineer and manage a large system from inception through system test and evaluation.
Prod-MIOT Dist-MIOT

Introduction To Systems Management Techniques 037 MIN
Management Control Of System Schedule And Cost 055 MIN
Performance 041 MIN
Scope Of Systems Engineering Problem 053 MIN
Stimulation And Modeling Techniques 054 MIN
System Error Budget, The 041 MIN
System Redundancy And Failure Detection 036 MIN
System Reliability, Maintainability And 041 MIN
System Testing Techniques 046 MIN
Systems Management Strategies 055 MIN

Systems For Precise Observations For Teachers-A Series

Prod-USOE Dist-USNAC 1970

Devices For Self-Help Task Performance 018 MIN
Problems In Academic Task Performance 006 MIN
Problems In Self-Help Task Performance 007 MIN

Systems In Experiments B 15 MIN
2 INCH VIDEOTAPE P
See series title for descriptive statement.
From The Just Wondering Series.
Prod-EOPS Dist-GPITVL Prodn-KOACTV

Systems Management Strategies C 55 MIN
3/4 OR 1/2 INCH VIDEO CASSETTE
Analyzes alternative systems management strategies. Stresses the importance of effective communication concepts in systems management.
From The Systems Engineering And Systems Management Series.
Prod-MIOT Dist-MIOT

Systems Network Architecture C 45 MIN
3/4 OR 1/2 INCH VIDEO CASSETTE
Presents the IBM terminology that is used to describe the various parts of the System Network Architecture (SNA) network. Presents examples of actual IBM hardware implementations, including the new IBM 8100 series.
From The Network Architectures - A Communications Revolution Series.
Prod-DELTAK Dist-DELTAK

Systems Of Differential Equations B
16MM FILM OPTICAL SOUND
Proves that the general solution of the system of equations (for zero initial velocities) is an arbitrary combination of the three 'normal mode solutions.'
Prod-OPENU Dist-OPENU

Systems Of Linear Equations, Pt 1 C 30 MIN
3/4 INCH VIDEO CASSETTE C
See series title for descriptive statement.
From The Introduction To Mathematics Series.
Prod-MDCPB Dist-MDCPB

Systems Of Linear Equations, Pt 2 C 30 MIN
3/4 INCH VIDEO CASSETTE C
See series title for descriptive statement.
From The Introduction To Mathematics Series.
Prod-MDCPB Dist-MDCPB

Systems Of Linear Functions C 45 MIN
2 INCH VIDEOTAPE
See series title for descriptive statement.
From The Fundamentals Of Mathematics (2nd Ed.) Unit III - Linear And Quadratic Functions Series.
Prod-CHITVC Dist-GPITVL

Systems, Pt 1 C 36 MIN
3/4 OR 1/2 INCH VIDEO CASSETTE PRO
Describes loop and complete interconnect systems. Discusses shared memory and global bus multiprocessors.
From The Introduction To Distributed Processor Communication Architecture Series.
Prod-AMCEE Dist-AMCEE

Systems, Pt 1 C 39 MIN
3/4 OR 1/2 INCH VIDEO CASSETTE
Discusses loop systems, complete interconnect systems, shared memory multiprocessors and global bus multiprocessors.
From The Distributed Processor Communication Architecture Series.
Prod-MIOT Dist-MIOT

Systems, Pt 2 C 36 MIN
3/4 OR 1/2 INCH VIDEO CASSETTE PRO
Covers various systems, including remote access networks. Deals with applications.
From The Introduction To Distributed Processor Communication Architecture Series.
Prod-AMCEE Dist-AMCEE

Systems, Pt 2 C 42 MIN
3/4 OR 1/2 INCH VIDEO CASSETTE
Discusses remote access networks, central control loop systems, central control bus systems, regular network and structured systems.
From The Distributed Processor Communication Architecture Series.
Prod-MIOT Dist-MIOT

Syzygy C 27 MIN
16MM FILM OPTICAL SOUND
An introduction to contemporary problems of society and the role of the church, as stimulated by a group discussion of a three-part film dealing with war, cities and people.
LC NO. 71-702600
Prod-CCNCC Dist-CCNCC Prodn-STEEGP 1969

Szechuan And Northern Dishes C 60 MIN
3/4 OR 1/2 INCH VIDEO CASSETTE J A
Demonstrates how to create basic dishes from Szechwan Province and northern China. Includes slicing technique, rice cookery and advanced skills. Features Chef Rhonda Yee preparing twelve dishes, including Mongolian beef and sweet and sour Shanghai.
Prod-CINAS Dist-CINAS 1982

T

T A For Teachers C 30 MIN
3/4 OR 1/2 INCH VIDEO CASSETTE T
See series title for descriptive statement.
From The Dealing In Discipline Series.
Prod-UKY Dist-GPITVL 1980

T And E C 15 MIN
3/4 INCH VIDEO CASSETTE P
From The Writing Time Series.
Prod-WHROTV Dist-GPITVL

T And F C 15 MIN
3/4 INCH VIDEO CASSETTE P
From The Writing Time Series.
Prod-WHROTV Dist-GPITVL

T As In Transportation C 15 MIN
16MM FILM OPTICAL SOUND
Shows how the Southern Pacific Transportation Company handles a container shipment from the time it arrives at a West Coast port until it reaches its final destination. Uses animation to explain concepts such as minibridge and land bridge.
LC NO. 78-701473
Prod-SPTC Dist-SPTC 1977

T As In Transportation (Spanish) C 15 MIN
16MM FILM OPTICAL SOUND
Shows how the Southern Pacific Transportation Company handles a container shipment from the time it arrives at a West Coast port until it reaches its final destination. Uses animation to explain concepts such as minibridge and land bridge.
LC NO. 78-701473
Prod-SPTC Dist-SPTC 1977

T Distribution, The B
16MM FILM OPTICAL SOUND
Discusses the problem of making inferences about a population when only small samples are available.
Prod-OPENU Dist-OPENU

T E T In High School C 29 MIN
16MM FILM, 3/4 OR 1/2 IN VIDEO
Presents Dr Thomas Gordon explaining how the concepts of teacher effectiveness training apply at the the secondary level. Includes Dr Gordon's associate, Noel Burch, demonstrating the 'no lose' method of resolving conflicts.
From The Dealing With Classroom Problems Series.
Prod-MFFD Dist-FI 1975

T H White - THE ONCE AND FUTURE KING C 26 MIN
2 INCH VIDEOTAPE
Presents readings from THE ONCE AND FUTURE KING by T H White.
From The One To One Series.
Prod-WETATV Dist-PUBTEL

T Is For Tumbleweed C 18 MIN
16MM FILM, 3/4 OR 1/2 IN VIDEO K A
Portrays the racing, creeping, leaping travels of a tumbleweed and the encounters it has with people, animals and things. Stimulates creative writing.
Prod-PFP Dist-PFP 1956

T Joint C 12 MIN
1/2 IN VIDEO CASSETTE BETA/VHS IND
See series title for descriptive statement.
From The Welding Training (Comprehensive) - Basic Shielded Metal Arc Welding Series.
Prod-RMI Dist-RMI

T Joint - Multi-Pass Weave C 6 MIN
1/2 IN VIDEO CASSETTE BETA/VHS IND
See series title for descriptive statement.
From The Welding Training (Comprehensive) - Basic Shielded Metal Arc Welding Series.
Prod-RMI Dist-RMI

T Joint - 3-Pass Stringer C 7 MIN
1/2 IN VIDEO CASSETTE BETA/VHS IND
See series title for descriptive statement.
From The Welding Training (Comprehensive) - Basic Shielded Metal Arc Welding Series.
Prod-RMI Dist-RMI

T Joint Aluminum Braze C 5 MIN
1/2 IN VIDEO CASSETTE BETA/VHS IND
See series title for descriptive statement.
From The Welding Training (Comprehensive) — Oxy-Acetylene Welding Series.
Prod-RMI Dist-RMI

T Minus Two Hours C 17 MIN
16MM FILM OPTICAL SOUND IND
Reviews the nationwide research and development facilitates of the Thiokol Chemical Corporation. Illustrates the techniques and tools used by the various divisions to develop rocket engines. Comments upon the role of rockets in defense and civilian safety.
LC NO. FIA67-2340
Prod-THIOKL Dist-THIOKL Prodn-FILMEN 1960

T R Country C 14 MIN
16MM FILM OPTICAL SOUND
Uses the words of Theodore Roosevelt as narrative in showing the Badlands of North Dakota in both winter and summer as Roosevelt saw them. Includes numerous wildlife scenes.
LC NO. 80-701938
Prod-USNPS Dist-USNAC 1980

T R S 80 Model IV C 24 MIN
1/2 IN VIDEO CASSETTE BETA/VHS
See series title for descriptive statement.
From The Computer Education / Programming / Operations Series.
Prod-RMI Dist-RMI

T S Eliot - Selected Poetry C 29 MIN
2 INCH VIDEOTAPE
Presents the poetry of T S Eliot.
From The One To One Series.
Prod-WETATV Dist-PUBTEL

T Sound, The - The Tiniest Tick C 15 MIN
2 INCH VIDEOTAPE P
Introduces some of the consonant sounds met in early reading. Identifies the written letter with the spoken sound.
From The Listen And Say Series.
Prod-MPATI Dist-GPITVL

T U R-A Teaching Film C 20 MIN
16MM FILM OPTICAL SOUND
Demonstrates the usefulness of the motion picture for teaching the processes involved in a transurethral prostatectomy. Includes an introduction to key points using medical illustrations and endoscopic photography
LC NO. FIA67-636
Prod-EATONL Dist-EATONL Prodn-AVCORP 1966

T V - The Anonymous Teacher C 15 MIN
3/4 OR 1/2 INCH VIDEO CASSETTE A
Probes the effect of television viewing on children. Discusses parental concern with regard to violence, commercial advertising and sexual and racial stereotyping. Narrated by Dr Robert M Liebert.
Prod-UMCOM Dist-ECUFLM 1976

T-Cells And The Major Histocompatibility Complex C 24 MIN
16MM FILM, 3/4 OR 1/2 IN VIDEO
Provides insights into the role of the major histocompatibility complex molecules in the T-cell recognition and regulation which biochemists expect to provide some of the missing clues to future research about immunology. Examines relationships between T-cells and the MHC antigens.
Prod-OPENU Dist-MEDIAG Prodn-BBCTV 1978

T-Joint Fillet Weld Ten-Gauge Steel Demonstration C 5 MIN
1/2 IN VIDEO CASSETTE BETA/VHS IND
Shows the recommended technique for making a fillet weld on ten-gauge material.
Prod-RMI Dist-RMI

T-Joint 20-Gauge To 10-Gauge Steel Demonstration C 4 MIN
1/2 IN VIDEO CASSETTE BETA/VHS IND
Outlines the technique used to weld a thin piece of metal to a heavier piece of metal.
Prod-RMI Dist-RMI

T-Joint, Lap Joint, And Outside Corner Welds All Positions Using Electric Arc C 15 MIN
3/4 OR 1/2 INCH VIDEO CASSETTE
See series title for descriptive statement.
From The Welding II - Basic Shielded Metal Arc Welding series.
Prod-CAMB Dist-CAMB

T-Joint, Lap Joint, Outside Corner - All Positions (MIG) Welding C 15 MIN
3/4 OR 1/2 INCH VIDEO CASSETTE
See series title for descriptive statement.
From The Welding III - TIG and MIG (Industry) Welding series.
Prod-CAMB Dist-CAMB

T-Joint, Lap Joint, Outside Corner Joint In Flat Position (Spanish) C
3/4 OR 1/2 INCH VIDEO CASSETTE
See series title for descriptive statement.
From The Shielded Metal Arc Welding (Spanish) Series.
Prod-VTRI Dist-VTRI

T-Joint, Lap Joint, Outside Corner Joint In An Overhead Position (Spanish) C
3/4 OR 1/2 INCH VIDEO CASSETTE
See series title for descriptive statement.
From The Shielded Metal Arc Welding (Spanish) Series.
Prod-VTRI Dist-VTRI

T-Joint, Lap Joint, Outside Corner Joint In An Overhead Position C 15 MIN
3/4 OR 1/2 INCH VIDEO CASSETTE IND
See series title for descriptive statement.
From The Welding - Shielded Metal-Arc Welding Series.
Prod-ICSINT Dist-ICSINT

T-Joint, Lap Joint, Outside Corner Joint In A Horizontal Position With SMAW (Spanish) C
3/4 OR 1/2 INCH VIDEO CASSETTE
See series title for descriptive statement.
From The Shielded Metal Arc Welding (Spanish) Series.
Prod-VTRI Dist-VTRI

T-Joint, Lap Joint, Outside Corner Joint In A Horizontal Position With SMAW C 15 MIN
3/4 OR 1/2 INCH VIDEO CASSETTE IND
See series title for descriptive statement.
From The Welding - Shielded Metal-Arc Welding Series.
Prod-ICSINT Dist-ICSINT

T-Joint, Lap Joint, Outside Corner Joint In A Vertical Up Position With SMAW (Spanish) C
3/4 OR 1/2 INCH VIDEO CASSETTE
See series title for descriptive statement.
From The Shielded Metal Arc Welding (Spanish) Series.
Prod-VTRI Dist-VTRI

T-Joint, Lap Joint, Outside Corner Joint In A Vertical Up Position With SMAW C 15 MIN
3/4 OR 1/2 INCH VIDEO CASSETTE IND
See series title for descriptive statement.
From The Welding - Shielded Metal-Arc Welding Series.
Prod-ICSINT Dist-ICSINT

T-Joint, Lap Joint, Outside Corner, Joint In Flat Position C 15 MIN
3/4 OR 1/2 INCH VIDEO CASSETTE IND
See series title for descriptive statement.
From The Welding - Shielded Metal-Arc Welding Series.
Prod-ICSINT Dist-ICSINT

T'Ai Chi Ch'uan B 8 MIN
16MM FILM, 3/4 OR 1/2 IN VIDEO
Analyzes the aesthetic and spiritual values of the traditional form of spiritual and physical exercise in China called T'ai Chi Ch'uan. Filmed in Taiwan.
Prod-DAVT Dist-DAVT 1969

T'ai Chi Ch'uan—A Series

Presents T'ai Chi Ch'uan, a sport which originated several hundred years ago in China. Features Marshall Ho'O, professor of Chinese history at the California Institute of the Arts, instructing the fundamentals of T'ai Chi performance and history.
Prod-KCET Dist-PUBTEL

T'ai Chi Ch'uan, Program 01 29 MIN
T'ai Chi Ch'uan, Program 02 29 MIN
T'ai Chi Ch'uan, Program 03 29 MIN
T'ai Chi Ch'uan, Program 04 29 MIN
T'ai Chi Ch'uan, Program 05 29 MIN
T'ai Chi Ch'uan, Program 06 29 MIN
T'ai Chi Ch'uan, Program 07 29 MIN
T'ai Chi Ch'uan, Program 08 29 MIN
T'ai Chi Ch'uan, Program 09 29 MIN
T'ai Chi Ch'uan, Program 10 29 MIN
T'ai Chi Ch'uan, Program 11 29 MIN
T'ai Chi Ch'uan, Program 12 29 MIN
T'ai Chi Ch'uan, Program 13 29 MIN
T'ai Chi Ch'uan, Program 14 29 MIN
T'ai Chi Ch'uan, Program 15 29 MIN
T'ai Chi Ch'uan, Program 16 29 MIN
T'ai Chi Ch'uan, Program 17 29 MIN
T'ai Chi Ch'uan, Program 18 29 MIN
T'ai Chi Ch'uan, Program 19 29 MIN
T'ai Chi Ch'uan, Program 20 29 MIN
T'ai Chi Ch'uan, Program 21 29 MIN
T'ai Chi Ch'uan, Program 22 29 MIN
T'ai Chi Ch'uan, Program 23 29 MIN
T'ai Chi Ch'uan, Program 24 29 MIN
T'ai Chi Ch'uan, Program 25 29 MIN
T'ai Chi Ch'uan, Program 26 29 MIN

T'ai Chi Ch'uan, Program 01 C 29 MIN
2 INCH VIDEOTAPE
See series title for descriptive statement.
From The T'ai Chi Ch'uan Series.
Prod-KCET Dist-PUBTEL

T'ai Chi Ch'uan, Program 02 C 29 MIN
2 INCH VIDEOTAPE
See series title for descriptive statement.
From The T'ai Chi Ch'uan Series.
Prod-KCET Dist-PUBTEL

T'ai Chi Ch'uan, Program 03 C 29 MIN
2 INCH VIDEOTAPE
See series title for descriptive statement.
From The T'ai Chi Ch'uan Series.
Prod-KCET Dist-PUBTEL

T'ai Chi Ch'uan, Program 04 C 29 MIN
2 INCH VIDEOTAPE
See series title for descriptive statement.
From The T'ai Chi Ch'uan Series.
Prod-KCET Dist-PUBTEL

T'ai Chi Ch'uan, Program 05 C 29 MIN
2 INCH VIDEOTAPE
See series title for descriptive statement.
From The T'ai Chi Ch'uan Series.
Prod-KCET Dist-PUBTEL

T'ai Chi Ch'uan, Program 06 C 29 MIN
2 INCH VIDEOTAPE
See series title for descriptive statement.
From The T'ai Chi Ch'uan Series.
Prod-KCET Dist-PUBTEL

T'ai Chi Ch'uan, Program 07 C 29 MIN
2 INCH VIDEOTAPE
See series title for descriptive statement.
From The T'ai Chi Ch'uan Series.
Prod-KCET Dist-PUBTEL

T'ai Chi Ch'uan, Program 08 C 29 MIN
2 INCH VIDEOTAPE
See series title for descriptive statement.
From The T'ai Chi Ch'uan Series.
Prod-KCET Dist-PUBTEL

T'ai Chi Ch'uan, Program 09 C 29 MIN
2 INCH VIDEOTAPE
See series title for descriptive statement.
From The T'ai Chi Ch'uan Series.
Prod-KCET Dist-PUBTEL

T'ai Chi Ch'uan, Program 10 C 29 MIN
2 INCH VIDEOTAPE
See series title for descriptive statement.
From The T'ai Chi Ch'uan Series.
Prod-KCET Dist-PUBTEL

T'ai Chi Ch'uan, Program 11 C 29 MIN
2 INCH VIDEOTAPE
See series title for descriptive statement.
From The T'ai Chi Ch'uan Series.
Prod-KCET Dist-PUBTEL

T'ai Chi Ch'uan, Program 12 C 29 MIN
2 INCH VIDEOTAPE
See series title for descriptive statement.
From The T'ai Chi Ch'uan Series.
Prod-KCET Dist-PUBTEL

T'ai Chi Ch'uan, Program 13 C 29 MIN
2 INCH VIDEOTAPE
See series title for descriptive statement.
From The T'ai Chi Ch'uan Series.
Prod-KCET Dist-PUBTEL

T'ai Chi Ch'uan, Program 14 C 29 MIN
2 INCH VIDEOTAPE
See series title for descriptive statement.
From The T'ai Chi Ch'uan Series.
Prod-KCET Dist-PUBTEL

T'ai Chi Ch'uan, Program 15 C 29 MIN
2 INCH VIDEOTAPE
See series title for descriptive statement.
From The T'ai Chi Ch'uan Series.
Prod-KCET Dist-PUBTEL

T'ai Chi Ch'uan, Program 16 C 29 MIN
2 INCH VIDEOTAPE
See series title for descriptive statement.
From The T'ai Chi Ch'uan Series.
Prod-KCET Dist-PUBTEL

T'ai Chi Ch'uan, Program 17 C 29 MIN
2 INCH VIDEOTAPE
See series title for descriptive statement.
From The T'ai Chi Ch'uan Series.
Prod-KCET Dist-PUBTEL

T'ai Chi Ch'uan, Program 18 C 29 MIN
2 INCH VIDEOTAPE
See series title for descriptive statement.
From The T'ai Chi Ch'uan Series.
Prod-KCET Dist-PUBTEL

T'ai Chi Ch'uan, Program 19 C 29 MIN
2 INCH VIDEOTAPE
See series title for descriptive statement.
From The T'ai Chi Ch'uan Series.
Prod-KCET Dist-PUBTEL

T'ai Chi Ch'uan, Program 20 C 29 MIN
2 INCH VIDEOTAPE
See series title for descriptive statement.
From The T'ai Chi Ch'uan Series.
Prod-KCET Dist-PUBTEL

T'ai Chi Ch'uan, Program 21 C 29 MIN
2 INCH VIDEOTAPE
See series title for descriptive statement.
From The T'ai Chi Ch'uan Series.
Prod-KCET Dist-PUBTEL

T'ai Chi Ch'uan, Program 22 C 29 MIN
2 INCH VIDEOTAPE
See series title for descriptive statement.
From The T'ai Chi Ch'uan Series.
Prod-KCET Dist-PUBTEL

T'ai Chi Ch'uan, Program 23 C 29 MIN
2 INCH VIDEOTAPE
See series title for descriptive statement.
From The T'ai Chi Ch'uan Series.
Prod-KCET Dist-PUBTEL

T'ai Chi Ch'uan, Program 24 C 29 MIN
2 INCH VIDEOTAPE
See series title for descriptive statement.
From The T'ai Chi Ch'uan Series.
Prod-KCET Dist-PUBTEL

T'ai Chi Ch'uan, Program 25 C 29 MIN
2 INCH VIDEOTAPE
See series title for descriptive statement.
From The T'ai Chi Ch'uan Series.
Prod-KCET Dist-PUBTEL

T'ai Chi Ch'uan, Program 26 C 29 MIN
2 INCH VIDEOTAPE
See series title for descriptive statement.
From The T'ai Chi Ch'uan Series.
Prod-KCET Dist-PUBTEL

Tablatoons C 5 MIN
16MM FILM OPTICAL SOUND
Presents a visual interpretation of Indian drum pieces using scratching and bleaching of film emulsion and rotoscoped spinning bodies in a succession of light and dark flashes.
LC NO. 76-703090
Prod-SHERCL Dist-CANFDC 1975

Table Looms C 16 MIN
3/4 OR 1/2 INCH VIDEO CASSETTE H-C
Introduces the parts of the table loom and tells how the weaver must become fully acquainted with its operation. Notes special attention given to preparing the warp and loading it in the loom. Shows how a beautiful shoulder bag is produced and the steps in finishing it off.
Prod-EDMI Dist-EDMI 1976

Table Manners C 16 MIN
16MM FILM, 3/4 OR 1/2 IN VIDEO S
Uses a TV game show format to demonstrate appropriate table manners.
From The Good Life Series.
LC NO. 81-706180
Prod-DUDLYN Dist-HUBDSC 1981

Table Representation Of The Next State Function And Outputs - Class-0 Machines,... C 30 MIN
3/4 OR 1/2 INCH VIDEO CASSETTE IND
Introduces use of a table to represent next state and output that is used directly for microprocessor implementation. Shows how digital design systems are broken up into machine classes to aid in design formulation.
From The Microprocessors For Monitoring And Control Series.
Prod-COLOSU Dist-COLOSU

Table Settings C 8 MIN
16MM FILM, 3/4 OR 1/2 IN VIDEO IND
Shows tables being set for breakfast, lunch and dinner and explains why correct procedures make for smooth service and add to the guests' enjoyment.
From The Professional Food Preparation And Service Program Series.
Prod-NEM Dist-NEM 1969

Table Settings (Spanish) C 8 MIN
16MM FILM, 3/4 OR 1/2 IN VIDEO
Shows tables being set for breakfast, lunch and dinner and explains why correct procedures make for smooth service and add to the guests' enjoyment.
From The Professional Food Preparation And Service Program (Spanish) Series.
Prod-NEM Dist-NEM 1969

Table Talk C 13 MIN
3/4 OR 1/2 INCH VIDEO CASSETTE
Explores 'food messages.' Shows how family, friends and culture influence choice of foods. Points out how foods and the way people eat affect them.
Prod-AMRC Dist-AMRC

Table Treatment C 41 MIN
3/4 OR 1/2 INCH VIDEO CASSETTE
See series title for descriptive statement.
From The Proprioceptive Neuromuscular Facilitation Series.
Prod-UMDSM Dist-UMDSM

Tableau Vivant C 11 MIN
16MM FILM, 3/4 OR 1/2 IN VIDEO P-I
Reveals that when Boy is called upon to entertain a child he is babysitting, he makes a crude motion picture machine in a stream. Illustrates the principle of motion pictures and simplifies the phenomenon of persistence of vision, on which the concept of motion pictures is based.
From The Inventive Child Series.
Prod-POLSKI Dist-EBEC 1983

Tableaux D'Une Exposition B 10 MIN
16MM FILM OPTICAL SOUND
Illustrates a Moussorgsky tone poem with episodes from the composer's childhood in Russia and Alexander Alexeieff's memories of his own childhood there, using two pinboards, a

small one that revolves and a stable one behind it. Introduced in English by Alexeieff.
Prod-STARRC Dist-STARRC 1972

Tableros Para Demostracion Y Exhibicion C 15 MIN
16MM FILM, 3/4 OR 1/2 IN VIDEO J A
A Spanish-language version of the motion picture Display And Presentation Boards. Provides a compact, practical and up-to-date look at display and presentation boards which can be used in a variety of teaching and learning situations. Explores the nature and potential of six different display and presentation boards - felt, hook and loop, magnetic, peg, electric and combination.
Prod-IFB Dist-IFB 1971

Tables Of Trigonometric Ratios B 29 MIN
16MM FILM OPTICAL SOUND H
Describes the format and range of conventional trigonometric tables. Shows the compression of the tables resulting from the recognition of the inverse relations. Illustrates the use of the tables.
From The Trigonometry Series.
Prod-CALVIN Dist-MLA Prodn-UNIVFI 1959

Tableside Cooking - Entrees C
3/4 OR 1/2 INCH VIDEO CASSETTE
See series title for descriptive statement.
From The Tableside Series.
Prod-CULINA Dist-CULINA

Tableside Cooking - Flaming Coffees C
3/4 OR 1/2 INCH VIDEO CASSETTE
See series title for descriptive statement.
From The Tableside Series.
Prod-CULINA Dist-CULINA

Tableside Cooking - Flaming Desserts C
3/4 OR 1/2 INCH VIDEO CASSETTE
See series title for descriptive statement.
From The Tableside Series.
Prod-CULINA Dist-CULINA

Tableside Fruit Carving C
3/4 OR 1/2 INCH VIDEO CASSETTE
See series title for descriptive statement.
From The Tableside Series.
Prod-CULINA Dist-CULINA

Tableside—A Series

Prod-CULINA Dist-CULINA

Route Du Champagne
Selecting And Handling Glassware
Tableside Cooking - Entrees
Tableside Cooking - Flaming Coffees
Tableside Cooking - Flaming Desserts
Tableside Fruit Carving

Tabu B 86 MIN
16MM FILM SILENT
A silent motion picture with German and English subtitles. Shows a lost paradise, with the actors portraying the natives of Tahiti.
Prod-WSTGLC Dist-WSTGLC 1930

Tabular Representation Of Function C 45 MIN
2 INCH VIDEOTAPE
See series title for descriptive statement.
From The Fundamentals Of Mathematics (2nd Ed.) Unit II - Relations And Functions Series.
Prod-CHITVC Dist-GPITVL

TAC In Action B 15 MIN
16MM FILM OPTICAL SOUND
Describes TAC'S capabilities in aerial firepower, reconnaissance, guerrilla warfare and assault airlifts. Reviews TAC'S role in the Cuban crisis and in Vietnam coin operations.
LC NO. 74-706269
Prod-USAF Dist-USNAC 1964

Tachyarrhythmias C 19 MIN
3/4 OR 1/2 INCH VIDEO CASSETTE
Discusses tachyarrhythmias, diagnosis and treatment.
From The Emergency Management - The First 30 Minutes, Vol II Series.
Prod-VTRI Dist-VTRI

Tackling Textbooks C 10 MIN
3/4 OR 1/2 INCH VIDEO CASSETTE H-C
Centers around a student having difficulty keeping up with assigned reading. Shows students how to analyze reading habits in order to develop proper reading techniques. Presents the SQ4R technique.
From The Developing Your Study Skills Series.
Prod-UWO Dist-BCNFL 1985

Tackling The Demons C 18 MIN
3/4 OR 1/2 INCH VIDEO CASSETTE
See series title for descriptive statement.
From The Better Spelling Series. Lesson 4B
Prod-TELSTR Dist-DELTAK

Tacoma Narrows Bridge Collapse W-4 C 35MIN
16MM FILM OPTICAL SOUND J-C A
Pictures the large amplitude resonance vibration of the bridge, nodal lines of the surface of the roadway and the total collapse.
From The Single-Concept Films In Physics Series.
Prod-OSUMPD Dist-OSUMPD 1963

Tactical Air Power C 20 MIN
16MM FILM, 3/4 OR 1/2 IN VIDEO
Demonstrates the latest striking power capabilities of the Tactical Air Command and discusses its importance.
LC NO. 81-707727
Prod-USAF Dist-USNAC 1967

Tactical Bomber In All-Weather Operations B 11 MIN
16MM FILM OPTICAL SOUND
Demonstrates the uses and operations of the tactical bomber and the need for close coordination of air, land and sea forces in modern warfare.
LC NO. FIE58-277
Prod-USAF Dist-USNAC 1957

Tactics For Doubles Play C 9 MIN
16MM FILM, 3/4 OR 1/2 IN VIDEO H-C A
Emphasizes the importance of the first serve and how to take command at the net in tennis.
From The Tennis Tactics Series.
Prod-ATHI Dist-ATHI 1980

Tactics For Ground Strokes C 9 MIN
16MM FILM, 3/4 OR 1/2 IN VIDEO H-C A
Demonstrates the grip, the proper stance and follow through for forehand and backhand ground strokes in tennis.
From The Tennis Tactics Series.
Prod-ATHI Dist-ATHI 1980

Tactics For Return Of Service C 9 MIN
16MM FILM, 3/4 OR 1/2 IN VIDEO H-C A
Shows how to return a tennis serve down the line, cross court and hit to the server's feet.
From The Tennis Tactics Series.
Prod-ATHI Dist-ATHI 1980

Tactics For Singles Play C 9 MIN
16MM FILM, 3/4 OR 1/2 IN VIDEO H-C A
Covers the proper use of geometry in determining shot placement in tennis.
From The Tennis Tactics Series.
Prod-ATHI Dist-ATHI 1980

Tactics For Specialty Shots C 9 MIN
16MM FILM, 3/4 OR 1/2 IN VIDEO H-C A
Illustrates the use of volleys, overheads, lobs and drop shots in tennis.
From The Tennis Tactics Series.
Prod-ATHI Dist-ATHI 1980

Tactics For The Serve C 9 MIN
16MM FILM, 3/4 OR 1/2 IN VIDEO H-C A
Demonstrates how to use the slice, spin serve and the cannon ball in tennis.
From The Tennis Tactics Series.
Prod-ATHI Dist-ATHI 1980

Tactics Of Pressure C 25 MIN
16MM FILM, 3/4 OR 1/2 IN VIDEO A
Presents a lecture by Chester L Karrass describing various pressure tactics used in negotiations. Tells how to apply pressure and gives defenses against pressure.
From The Negotiating Successfully Series. Part 4
LC NO. 79-707431
Prod-TIMLIF Dist-TIMLIF 1975

Tad, The Frog C 11 MIN
16MM FILM, 3/4 OR 1/2 IN VIDEO P
Shows the growth stages of a frog, including the egg and tadpole periods. Explains how frogs breathe, eat and live. Also instills ideas of pet care and conservation of wild life.
Prod-CORF Dist-CORF 1965

Tadpoles And Frogs C 12 MIN
16MM FILM, 3/4 OR 1/2 IN VIDEO P-I
Follows the transformation of a tadpole into a frog and shows how it begins to swim, grow and develop hindlimbs and forelimbs.
LC NO. 80-706248
Prod-NGS Dist-NGS 1979

Taffy C 30 MIN
3/4 OR 1/2 INCH VIDEO CASSETTE I-J
Tells how a young girl gets a job at a sugar shack during maple sugar time. Describes the history and methods of the maple sugar industry.
Prod-CANBC Dist-JOU

Taffy And The Jungle Hunter C 87 MIN
16MM FILM OPTICAL SOUND I-J
Tells of a hunter who captures wild animals for zoos. Shows how he takes his little son and the boy's widowed governess on one of his expeditions.
Prod-CINEWO Dist-CINEWO 1965

Taffy's Imagination (Fear Of The Dark) C 12 MIN
16MM FILM, 3/4 OR 1/2 IN VIDEO K-P
Uses a puppet story to present realistic explanations of imagined fantasies so that darkness can be faced with confidence. Explains that Taffy is afraid of the dark until her puppet friends, Butch and Coslo, teach her their night game. Shows how she discovers that things she saw and heard were created in her imagination.
From The Forest Town Fables Series.
Prod-CORF Dist-CORF 1974

Tag Der Freiheit - Unsere Wehrmacht B 21 MIN
3/4 OR 1/2 INCH VIDEO CASSETTE
Depicts a mock battle staged by German troops during the colorful ceremonies at Nuremburg on German Armed Forces Day 1935. Pays special tribute to the Germany Army.
Prod-IHF Dist-IHF

Tag Der Idioten C 110 MIN
16MM FILM OPTICAL SOUND A
A German language film with English subtitles. Studies a young woman's slow descent into madness. She feels isolated because she proves to be too mad for the outside world and too normal to be institutionalized. Ends when her destructive powers overtake body and mind.
Prod-WSTGLC Dist-WSTGLC 1981

Tagging Australian Salmon C 11 MIN
16MM FILM OPTICAL SOUND A
Deals with the techniques used by the Commonwealth Scientific and Industrial Research Organization (CSIRO) division of fisheries and oceanography in tagging juvenile and mature Australian salmon. Points out the importance in the current population study of the return of tags from all tagged fish caught.
LC NO. FIA65-1081
Prod-CSIROA Dist-CSIROA 1964

Tahere Tikitiki - The Making Of A Maori Canoe C 40 MIN
16MM FILM, 3/4 OR 1/2 IN VIDEO J A
Portrays the making of a Maori canoe, showing all the traditions from the felling of the trees to the final launching. Interweaves the process of building with its significance to Maori culture and the changing of the seasons.
Prod-NFUNZ Dist-NWDIMF

Tahiti Seaventure C 14 MIN
16MM FILM OPTICAL SOUND C A
Presents scenes of a voyage through six remote islands in French Polynesia, pointing out that the islands are among the last of a vanishing South Sea paradise.
LC NO. 78-713451
Prod-MCDO Dist-MCDO 1971

Tahtonka - Plains Indians Buffalo Culture C 30 MIN
16MM FILM, 3/4 OR 1/2 IN VIDEO I-C A
Relates the history of the Plains Indians and their buffalo culture from the pre-horse period to the time of the mountain men, the hide hunters and the decimation of the mighty herds. Reviews the ghost dance craze and the massacre of Wounded Knee.
Prod-PSLI Dist-AIMS Prodn-NAUMAN 1966

Tailgating - How Close Is Too Close C 11 MIN
16MM FILM, 3/4 OR 1/2 IN VIDEO J-C A
Shows, through the use of animation, the hazards of tailgating and a simple method to avoid it. Discusses the development of tailgating situations and procedures for correcting them.
Prod-CAHILL Dist-AIMS 1976

Tailgating - How Close Is Too Close (Spanish) C 11 MIN
16MM FILM, 3/4 OR 1/2 IN VIDEO J-C A
Shows, through the use of animation, the hazards of tailgating and a simple method to avoid it. Discusses the development of tailgating situations and procedures for correcting them.
Prod-CAHILL Dist-AIMS 1976

Tailor And The Weaver, The C 20 MIN
3/4 INCH VIDEO CASSETTE I
Presents an Appalachian folktale revolving around the superstition, trickery and greed that strain the friendship between two families.
From The Wonderama Of The Arts Series.
Prod-WBRATV Dist-GPITVL 1979

Tailoring, Pt 2 - Finishing The Simple Coat C 29 MIN
2 INCH VIDEOTAPE
See series title for descriptive statement.
From The Designing Women Series.
Prod-WKYCTV Dist-PUBTEL

Tailoring, Pt 3 - Making A Simple Suit C 29 MIN
2 INCH VIDEOTAPE
See series title for descriptive statement.
From The Designing Women Series.
Prod-WKYCTV Dist-PUBTEL

Tailoring, Pt 4 - Finishing The Simple Suit C 29 MIN
2 INCH VIDEOTAPE
See series title for descriptive statement.
From The Designing Women Series.
Prod-WKYCTV Dist-PUBTEL

Tailspin C 30 MIN
3/4 OR 1/2 INCH VIDEO CASSETTE C A
Presents the story of the Braniff Airline bankruptcy, showing how the chief executive officer tried desperately to restructure the billion-dollar company's operations in a few short months. Illustrates the high level of competition in the airline industry.
From The Enterprise II Series.
LC NO. 83-706197
Prod-WGBHTV Dist-LCOA 1983

Tailwater Trout C 11 MIN
16MM FILM OPTICAL SOUND
Introduces a new sport to Tennessee fishermen - trout fishing in the tailwaters of the Great Lakes of the South. Tells of the growth of rainbow trout in the cold waters below storage reservoir dams.
Prod-TGAFC Dist-TGAFC

Taiwan (Formosa) - Blueprint For Development C 20 MIN
3/4 INCH VIDEO CASSETTE H-C
See series title for descriptive statement.
From The Geography For The '70's Series.
Prod-KLRNTV Dist-GPITVL

Taiwan - Silk And Strings C 18 MIN
16MM FILM, 3/4 OR 1/2 IN VIDEO J-C A
Presents traditional aspects of Taiwanese culture. Contrasts the simple life, costumes and arts and crafts of the original natives of Taiwan with the culture of the Chinese. Focuses on the traditions of China as they are retained on Taiwan, including the cultivation of the arts, music and calligraphy.
Prod-CFDLD Dist-CORF 1977

Taiwan, Nevada, France, England, Guatemala C 27 MIN
16MM FILM OPTICAL SOUND P-I
Describes aspects of life in Taiwan, Nevada, England and Guatemala. Presents a French folk tale about a bridge inspector who makes an agreement with the devil.
From The Big Blue Marble - Children Around The World Series. Program B

LC NO. 76-700640
Prod-ALVEN Dist-VITT 1975

Taj Mahal C 14 MIN
16MM FILM OPTICAL SOUND H-C A
Shows the beauty of Taj Mahal, dedicated by Shah Jehan to Mumtaz Mahal. Features the marble changing color and mood every hour, the gardens, the red sandstone gateway and the white slabs inlaid with floral and calligraphic designs.
Prod-INDIA Dist-NEDINF

Taj Mahal - That's All C 29 MIN
3/4 OR 1/2 INCH VIDEO CASSETTE
Discusses the impact of black music on America and the western world.
From The Interface Series.
Prod-WETATV Dist-PBS

Taj Mahal, The C 29 MIN
16MM FILM, 3/4 OR 1/2 IN VIDEO J-C
Reveals that India's Taj Mahal stands as a timeless memorial to 17th-century emperor's love for his lost queen.
LC NO. 84-706030
Prod-GTARC Dist-EBEC 1981

Tajimoltik (Five Days Without Name) C 30 MIN
3/4 INCH VIDEO CASSETTE
Describes the five remaining days of the Mayan calendar which counts only 360 days. Features the celebrations which combine elements in Spanish Catholicism and traditional rituals and cargo fiestas.
Prod-OKEXNO Dist-DOCEDR

Take 'Er Down B 13 MIN
16MM FILM OPTICAL SOUND
Presents a history of the development of submarines in the U S Navy from 1900 to 1954. Includes scenes of the USS Nautilus, the first nuclear-powered vessel.
Prod-USN Dist-USNAC 1954

Take 'Er down / The Nuclear Navy / The Submarines C 69 MIN
3/4 OR 1/2 INCH VIDEO CASSETTE
Tells the history of the development of submarines in the U S Navy from 1900 to the USS Nautilus in 1954 (in black and white). Presents a documentary on the Navy's development of nuclear power and its application in long-range submarines. Focuses on the specialized skills and responsibilities that keep U S Navy submarines ready for battle.
Prod-IHF Dist-IHF

Take A Can Of Salmon C 14 MIN
16MM FILM OPTICAL SOUND P-C
Tells how a can of salmon can be made into many different meals. Visits six typical American cities and demonstrates the preparation of a favorite recipe of each city.
LC NO. FIE64-204
Prod-USBCF Dist-USNOAA 1960

Take A Chance - Learn Probability C 30 MIN
2 INCH VIDEOTAPE
Demonstrates to the student a relatively new but important topic of elementary mathematics probability. Presents concepts such as ratio and the meaning of fractional numbers.
From The Devices In Their Hands - Math In Their Minds Series.
Prod-GPITVL Dist-GPITVL

Take A Deep Breath C 15 MIN
3/4 OR 1/2 INCH VIDEO CASSETTE P
Uses a burning candle to demonstrate the body's need for air. Discusses how air gets in and out of the body. (Broadcast quality)
From The All About You Series.
Prod-NITC Dist-AITECH Prodn-TTOIC 1975

Take A Giant Step C 6 MIN
16MM FILM OPTICAL SOUND IND
Presents Hank, the new supervisor, who finds that paperwork goes with management. Shows how, as he flounders in administrative details or ignores what he considers petty details, he loses the respect of his employees.
From The Human Side Of Supervision Series.
LC NO. 73-701929
Prod-VOAERO Dist-VOAERO 1972

Take A Good Look C 15 MIN
16MM FILM, 3/4 OR 1/2 IN VIDEO
Follows a young girl as she uses a magnifying glass to examine many things in her backyard.
From The Ripples Series.
LC NO. 73-702155
Prod-NITC Dist-AITECH

Take A Good Look 1959 ABC C
3/4 OR 1/2 INCH VIDEO CASSETTE
Shows Ernie Kovaks hosting an unusual show with Hans Conried, Cesar Romero and Edie Adams.
Prod-IHF Dist-IHF

Take A Guess - Estimation And Problem Solving B 20 MIN
3/4 INCH VIDEO CASSETTE P
See series title for descriptive statement.
From The Let's Figure It Out Series.
Prod-WNYETV Dist-NYSED 1968

Take A Little Pride C 10 MIN
16MM FILM - 3/4 IN VIDEO P-I
Shows elementary students planning and participating in projects to beautify and improve their schools.
Prod-PARKRD Dist-LAWREN

Take A Look At Yourself C 16 MIN
16MM FILM OPTICAL SOUND I-J
Deals with the need for laws and the necessity for upholding them. Discusses the growing antagonism toward the man who wears the police uniform and suggests that the man in uniform is an individual whose motives, aside from earning a livelihood, may very well be altruistic. Features Bill, a highly sensitive boy antagonistic toward authority, who finally realizes his own helplessness and his need for the protection society has provided for him after his bike is stolen.
From The Human Values Series.
LC NO. 74-712725
Prod-MENKNS Dist-MALIBU 1970

Take A Poetry Break C 30 MIN
3/4 OR 1/2 INCH VIDEO CASSETTE
Presents librarian/educator Dr Caroline Feller Bauer who demonstrates the traditional methods for developing interest in poems, and utilizes a variety of media, such as posters, costumes, puppets, magic tricks and simple props to enhance her presentation.
Prod-ALA Dist-PBS

Take A Sample B
16MM FILM OPTICAL SOUND
Shows how a random sample of only 1,000 people from a total population of 50 million allows one to estimate the proportion one is looking for.
Prod-OPENU Dist-OPENU

Take A Stand C 25 MIN
16MM FILM OPTICAL SOUND A
Documents how a victim-advocate program can help elderly people fight back through the court system when they are the victim of violent crime.
LC NO. 82-700786
Prod-TNF Dist-FLMLIB 1982

Take Care C 30 MIN
3/4 OR 1/2 INCH VIDEO CASSETTE A
Discusses customer relations. Includes suggestions on first impressions, dealing with irate customers and telephone techniques. Uses a fictionalized story.
Prod-AMEDIA Dist-AMEDIA

Take Care Of Your Teeth C 4 MIN
16MM FILM, 3/4 OR 1/2 IN VIDEO K-I
Features Fumble and the dentist, who explain that crunching an apple or munching a carrot will do if brushing is not possible.
From The Most Important Person - Health And Your Body Series.
Prod-EBEC Dist-EBEC

Take Care Of YourseIF—A Series

Provides basic information for patients to educate them on individual medical problems.
Prod-UARIZ Dist-UARIZ

Angina Pectoris 009 MIN
Colds And Flu 009 MIN
Gout 011 MIN
High Blood Pressure 007 MIN
Hyperthyroidism 010 MIN
Hypothyroidism 008 MIN
Infectious Mononucleosis 008 MIN
Iron Deficiency Anemia 008 MIN
Middle Ear Infection 008 MIN
Monilial Vaginitis 007 MIN
Postmenopausal Vaginitis 007 MIN
Sore Throat 010 MIN
Stones In The Urinary Tract 008 MIN
Trichomonal Vaginitis 009 MIN
Urinary Tract Infections 007 MIN

Take Charge! - Your Skill In Reading C 36 MIN
3/4 OR 1/2 INCH VIDEO CASSETTE A
Encourages those individuals who have the ability, but choose not to read, to hone their reading skills.
LC NO. 83-706122
Prod-CFLA Dist-CFLA 1982

Take Command C 30 MIN
16MM FILM, 3/4 OR 1/2 IN VIDEO
Features astronaut Walter Schirra, Jr in a story to inspire, encourage and stimulate salesmen to overcome every obstacle and surmount every difficulty to reach goals set for them.
Prod-DARTNL Dist-DARTNL

Take Fewer Steps - Layout Studies C 14 MIN
16MM FILM, 3/4 OR 1/2 IN VIDEO
Describes layout studies, focusing on their purpose, use, preparation and application. Discusses how to prepare a layout chart and how to use it to determine distances traveled by people or materials.
LC NO. 82-706142
Prod-USA Dist-USNAC 1973

Take It Easy C 9 MIN
16MM FILM OPTICAL SOUND
Shows farmers the advantage of new round baling equipment made by Sperry New Holland.
LC NO. 74-703230
Prod-SPRYNH Dist-SRCNHD Prodn-FILMFI 1974

Take It Easy And Live C 27 MIN
16MM FILM OPTICAL SOUND C A
Revised edition of 'TAKE IT EASY.' Features a housewife, who is a cardiac patient. Demonstrates easy solutions to housework problems and discusses benefits of the work saving programs conducted by Wayne State University and the Heart Association.
Prod-WSU Dist-WSU 1954

Take It From A Champion C 26 MIN
16MM FILM OPTICAL SOUND J-C A
Presents professional race drivers demonstrating driving safety habits on the track, including the 1956 Indianapolis and Darlington '500' Nascar's Daytona Beach race.
Prod-DYN Dist-CHSPC 1956

Take It From Here (Captioned) C 25 MIN
16MM FILM OPTICAL SOUND PRO
Explains a step by step approach to setting up a continuing education program for deaf adults.
Prod-GALCO Dist-GALCO 1977

Take It From The Beginning C 15 MIN
3/4 OR 1/2 INCH VIDEO CASSETTE T
Uses the adventures of a pirate and his three friends to explore the many facets of language arts. Focuses on initial sounds and demonstrates their use in oral and written expression.
From The Hidden Treasures Series. No. 3
LC NO. 82-706527
Prod-WCVETV Dist-GPITVL 1980

Take It From The Pros C 16 MIN
16MM FILM OPTICAL SOUND
Strives to influence portable grinder operators to practice safety measures when mounting grinding wheels and handling portable grinders. Demonstrates safety practices in handling portable grinders.
LC NO. 72-701078
Prod-IRC Dist-WSTGLC 1971

Take It To Heart - Stress, Hypertension, And Heart Disease C 30 MIN
3/4 OR 1/2 INCH VIDEO CASSETTE
Covers the dangers of stressful American lifestyles. Discusses the burden that everyday stress places upon the heart and considers ways of coping with stressful situations.
Prod-FAIRGH Dist-FAIRGH

Take Joy C 11 MIN
16MM FILM OPTICAL SOUND P-I
Points out that the body and its systems help a person to enjoy life and that it is necessary to take care of these systems.
LC NO. 74-702891
Prod-AMCS Dist-AMCS Prodn-GITTFI 1973

Take Me Back To Crested Butte C 14 MIN
16MM FILM OPTICAL SOUND
Shows the ambience of Crested Butte, Colorado, which makes it unique among American ski resorts.
LC NO. 79-701532
Prod-CREBUT Dist-CREBUT Prodn-MARGOI 1979

Take Me To Your Leader C 25 MIN
3/4 OR 1/2 INCH VIDEO CASSETTE
Visits with Wisconsin and Minnesota residents who have seen UFO's, and with scientists who say there is more to the sightings than meets the eye.
Prod-WCCOTV Dist-WCCOTV 1976

Take Me Up To The Ballgame C 25 MIN
16MM FILM, 3/4 OR 1/2 IN VIDEO
Depicts ragtag baseball team of rabbit, cow and cat playing intergalactic champions from outer space. Shows how, in animation, earth team turns tables on cheating spacers.
Prod-NELVNA Dist-BCNFL 1983

Take My Arm C 15 MIN
16MM FILM OPTICAL SOUND J-C A
Shows the staff and trainees of the Texas Center For The Blind and how they describe the purpose, methods and accomplishments of the Center's adult blind rehabilitation program.
LC NO. 77-701858
Prod-CASTOP Dist-TEXCFB 1977

Take Nothing For Granted C 19 MIN
16MM FILM, 3/4 OR 1/2 IN VIDEO IND
Shows how Harry Sparks, the guardian angel of electrical workers, almost loses an electrician whose only mistake was assuming the power was off when he started repair work.
Prod-IAPA Dist-IFB 1975

Take Off C 10 MIN
16MM FILM OPTICAL SOUND I-C A
Presents a series of vignettes on skiing. Creative use of the camera and background music are used to create a visual poem on the pleasures of the sport. Without narration.
Prod-SUMMIT Dist-VIEWFI 1970

Take Off For Opportunities C 11 MIN
16MM FILM OPTICAL SOUND
Looks at the careers of an air frame and power mechanic, an avionics technician and an aeronautical engineer.
Prod-GEAVMA Dist-MTP

Take One C 120 MIN
1/2 IN VIDEO CASSETTE BETA/VHS
Presents a compilation of films and video programs from Appalshop on mountain life and music. Includes major portions of four films, including Sourwood Mountain Dulcimer and Ramsey Trade Fair, as well as excerpts from the Headwaters television series. Includes performances by Nimrod Workman, I D Stamper and many others.
Prod-APPAL Dist-APPAL

Take One With You B 26 MIN
16MM FILM OPTICAL SOUND
Presents documentary footage showing the British preparations for a German invasion after the fall of France and the inception of the lend-lease program after Churchill's appeals for assistance to Roosevelt. Based on the book 'THE SECOND WORLD WAR,' by Winston S Churchill.
From The Winston Churchill - The Valiant Years Series.
LC NO. FI67-2116
Prod-ABC Dist-SG 1961

Take Tea And See C 1 MIN
3/4 OR 1/2 INCH VIDEO CASSETTE
Shows a classic television commercial.
Prod-BROOKC Dist-BROOKC

Take Ten For Safety—A Series
16MM FILM, 3/4 OR 1/2 IN VIDEO IND
Presents essential safety habits and attitudes for accident prevention in industrial situations.
Prod-OLINC Dist-MTI

Basic Personal Protective Equipment	008 MIN
Decision For Safety	006 MIN
Elevated Areas	009 MIN
Guarding	007 MIN
Hazardous Area Identification	009 MIN
Hot Work	009 MIN
Lock-Out	008 MIN
Moment For Decision	008 MIN
Portable Ladders	008 MIN
Vessel Entry	012 MIN

Take That First Step X 28 MIN
16MM FILM OPTICAL SOUND J-C T
Tells how a retarded boy and a college student meet by accident, and how the student is influenced to enter the field of special education. Provides information about the problems and challenges of special education.
LC NO. 71-713897
Prod-SREB Dist-NMAC 1967

Take The Chair C 28 MIN
16MM FILM - 3/4 IN VIDEO
Presents methods, actions and techniques to improve the ability to conduct or participate effectively in a meeting.
Prod-BNA Dist-BNA

Take The First Step C 30 MIN
2 INCH VIDEOTAPE C A
Highlights the points for a prospective buyer or renter to look for in a new home.
From The Designing Home Interiors Series. Unit 7
Prod-COAST Dist-CDTEL Prodn-RSCCD

Take The Plunge C 30 MIN
1/2 IN VIDEO CASSETTE BETA/VHS
Explores an underwater garden. Gives hiking tips. Presents campsite drinking toasts.
From The Great Outdoors Series.
Prod-WGBHTV Dist-MTI

Take The Time C 18 MIN
16MM FILM OPTICAL SOUND
Shows the various guidelines a woman must follow to stay physically fit. Discusses the importance of getting and staying in shape and the nutritious foods that are needed to fuel the body.
Prod-CRAISN Dist-MTP

Take This Woman C 25 MIN
3/4 INCH VIDEO CASSETTE
Surveys lack of equal educational and occupational opportunities for women. Concludes that women, who make up half the population of the United States, are not being used to their full potential.
Prod-ADL Dist-ADL

Take Time C 15 MIN
3/4 OR 1/2 INCH VIDEO CASSETTE P
See series title for descriptive statement.
From The Strawberry Square II - Take Time Series.
Prod-NEITV Dist-AITECH 1984

Take Time To Live B 12 MIN
16MM FILM OPTICAL SOUND
Tells how hurrying on the job often causes accidents. Suggests allowing a little extra time each day to insure safety.
Prod-NSC Dist-NSC

Take Two From The Sea C 28 MIN
16MM FILM OPTICAL SOUND I-H
Examines the exploits of the diving expeditions for marine life under the sea.
Prod-USDC Dist-USNOAA

Take Two, They're Small C 14 MIN
16MM FILM, 3/4 OR 1/2 IN VIDEO P-I
Relates how the gang takes action against a shoplifter.
From The Learning Values With Fat Albert Series.
Prod-FLMTON Dist-CRMP 1977

Take Your Choice - Substitution C 15 MIN
3/4 OR 1/2 INCH VIDEO CASSETTE J-H
Explains that because business is slow at Dougherty's store, the family must make a variety of substitutions to get by. Deals with making substitutions due to economic necessity.
From The Give And Take Series. Pt 11
LC NO. 83-706378
Prod-AITV Dist-AITECH 1982

Take 5—A Series

Prod-MARHLL Dist-MARHLL

Face Value	010 MIN

Take-Off C 30 MIN
16MM FILM, 3/4 OR 1/2 IN VIDEO H-C A
Describes the race to develop a small, fuel-efficient plane to capture the corporate airplane market.
From The Enterprise Series.
Prod-MTI Dist-MTI

Take-Off And Landings C 29 MIN
2 INCH VIDEOTAPE
See series title for descriptive statement.
From The Discover Flying - Just Like A Bird Series.
Prod-WKYCTV Dist-PUBTEL

Take-Out Doubles C 30 MIN
3/4 OR 1/2 INCH VIDEO CASSETTE A
See series title for descriptive statement.
From The Play Bridge Series.
Prod-KYTV Dist-KYTV 1983

Take'Er Down B 13 MIN
16MM FILM OPTICAL SOUND
Presents a history of the development of submarines in the U S Navy from 1900 to 1954. Includes scenes of the USS Nautilus, the first nuclear-powered vessel.
LC NO. FIE54-403
Prod-USN Dist-USNAC 1954

Takeaway Babies, The C 25 MIN
16MM FILM OPTICAL SOUND
Presents correspondent Michael Maclear reporting on international child adoption practices. Notes that countries of the Third World have lenient regulations permitting the adoption of their children.
LC NO. 77-702527
Prod-CTV Dist-CTV 1976

Takedown Techniques C 22 MIN
16MM FILM, 3/4 OR 1/2 IN VIDEO
Demonstrates takedowns in the sport of wrestling. Includes basic arm drags and fireman's carries.
From The Wrestling Series. No. 2
Prod-ATHI Dist-ATHI 1976

Taken For Granted C 15 MIN
16MM FILM, 3/4 OR 1/2 IN VIDEO
Deals with elevator safety. Discusses what to do if an elevator stalls, what to do in case of fire, when to push the stop button and safe ways to ride an escalator.
Prod-KLEINW Dist-KLEINW

Takeoffs And Landings C 12 MIN
3/4 OR 1/2 INCH VIDEO CASSETTE A
Highlights proper safety techniques and procedures while taking off and landing light aircraft under potentially hazardous conditions. Includes three subtitled four-minute segments on Short Field, Soft Field and Crosswind operations.
Prod-FAAFL Dist-AVIMA

Takeoffs And Landings C 13 MIN
16MM FILM, 3/4 OR 1/2 IN VIDEO
Highlights the proper safety techniques and procedures to employ while taking off and landing light aircraft under potentially hazardous conditions, including a short field, a soft field and crosswinds.
Prod-USFAA Dist-USNAC 1975

Takeover C 90 MIN
16MM FILM OPTICAL SOUND
Documents the bitter political confrontation between the Australian Federal government and the Aurukun Aboriginal Reserve against the government of the state of Queensland over bauxite deposits on the reserve.
Prod-AUSIAS Dist-UCEMC 1981

Taking A Chance C 30 MIN
3/4 OR 1/2 INCH VIDEO CASSETTE J-H
Presents a fictional story of a talented teenager and two friends who are running a television station while the owner is recovering from an illness. Reviews adjective phrases in a story dealing with two youthful reporters' interviews with a young convict. Shows that good writing skills are necessary in real-life experiences.
From The Edit Point Series. Pt 5
LC NO. 83-706437
Prod-MAETEL Dist-GPITVL 1983

Taking A DeltaVision Course C 30 MIN
3/4 OR 1/2 INCH VIDEO CASSETTE
Explains how to take a multimedia skills course. Defines multimedia training and introduces the basic architecture used to design a DELTAK skills course. Discusses the purpose and benefits of the courseware.
From The Using DELTAK Courses Series.
Prod-DELTAK Dist-DELTAK

Taking A Trip Through Visicalc C 38 MIN
3/4 OR 1/2 INCH VIDEO CASSETTE
Features computer expert Barbara McMullen offering a young friend elementary instruction in microcomputer programming, use of the Keyboard and the Apple II power pack. Demonstrates how to maintain a mailing list.
Prod-STURTM Dist-STURTM 1982

Taking Action C 15 MIN
3/4 OR 1/2 INCH VIDEO CASSETTE
Shows How members of a group working together learn to identify their objectives, identify people in decision-making roles, develop their case through research and outreach and finally, develop tactics.
From The Working Together For Action Series.
Prod-SYRCU Dist-UWISC 1976

Taking Aim C 30 MIN
3/4 OR 1/2 INCH VIDEO CASSETTE
See series title for descriptive statement.
From The Rebop Series.
Prod-WGBHTV Dist-MDCPB

Taking America's Measure C 15 MIN
3/4 OR 1/2 INCH VIDEO CASSETTE
Reports on the National Bureau of Standards and its pursuit of discoveries in the basics of measurement.
From The Screen News Digest Series.
Prod-HEARST Dist-HEARST

Taking And Defending Depositions C 202 MIN
3/4 OR 1/2 INCH VIDEO CASSETTE PRO
Teaches the fundamental skills and techniques involved in preparing for and taking and defending depositions.
Prod-ABACPE Dist-ABACPE

Taking Back Detroit C 55 MIN
16MM FILM, 3/4 OR 1/2 IN VIDEO A
Presents Detroit City Councilman Kenneth V Cockrel and Recorder's Court Judge Justin Ravitz promoting their shared Marxist approaches for conquering Detroit's debilitating poverty.
Prod-ICARUS Dist-ICARUS 1981

Taking Blood Pressure C 10 MIN
3/4 OR 1/2 INCH VIDEO CASSETTE
Explains blood pressure and how it is measured. Describes technique of using a sphygmomanometer step by step.
Prod-MEDFAC Dist-MEDFAC 1981

Taking Blood Pressure Readings C 20 MIN
3/4 OR 1/2 INCH VIDEO CASSETTE PRO
Explains basic terms of blood pressure reading, such as blood pressure, systolic, and diastolic, and demonstrates the reading of an aneroid manometer. Shows a procedure for taking blood pressure, including blood pressure reading trials.
From The Blood Pressure Series.
LC NO. 79-706007
Prod-IU Dist-IU 1978

Taking Body Measurements C 4 MIN
16MM FILM SILENT J-C A
Illustrates taking essential body measurements used in selecting and altering a pattern. Includes measuring upper and lower body and measuring upper arm circumference, arm length and wrist circumference.
LC NO. 77-701163
Prod-IOWA Dist-IOWA 1976

Taking Care C 15 MIN
3/4 OR 1/2 INCH VIDEO CASSETTE J
Tells the story of a boy who gets a job at a bike shop and learns about the basics of bicycle maintenance and repair.
From The It's Your Turn Series.
Prod-WETN Dist-AITECH 1977

Taking Care Of Business C 15 MIN
16MM FILM, 3/4 OR 1/2 IN VIDEO I
Shows the concepts of responsibility and self-control through the story of David, the eldest of four children, who has a great many household tasks because both his parents work.
From The Bread And Butterflies Series.
LC NO. 74-703180
Prod-AITV Dist-AITECH Prodn-KETCTV 1973

Taking Care Of The Engine C 30 MIN
3/4 OR 1/2 INCH VIDEO CASSETTE
Identifies the parts of an internal-combustion engine, describes the way a four-stroke power cycle internal-combustion engine works and performs a compression check, including recording and interpreting the results.
From The Keep It Running Series.
Prod-NETCHE Dist-NETCHE 1982

Taking Care Of Your Body C 18 MIN
3/4 OR 1/2 INCH VIDEO CASSETTE
Notes that since diabetics are more prone to infection, a daily routine of careful examination of skin, teeth, feet and legs is very important. Stresses early recognition and treatment of cuts, bruises, and injuries as essential to good diabetic care.
LC NO. 83-730079
Prod-TRAINX Dist-TRAINX

Taking Care Of Your Body (Spanish) C 18 MIN
3/4 OR 1/2 INCH VIDEO CASSETTE
Notes that since diabetics are more prone to infection, a daily routine of careful examination of skin, teeth, feet and legs is very important. Stresses early recognition and treatment of cuts, bruises, and injuries as essential to good diabetic care.
LC NO. 83-730079
Prod-TRAINX Dist-TRAINX

Taking Care Of Your Car C 20 MIN
3/4 OR 1/2 INCH VIDEO CASSETTE
Deals with preventive maintenance and car inspections which can be done by the driver in little time.
Prod-BUMPA Dist-BUMPA

Taking Care Of Your Car B 30 MIN
16MM FILM - 3/4 IN VIDEO C A
See series title for descriptive statement.
From The Sportsmanlike Driving Series. Refresher Course
Prod-AAAFTS Dist-GPITVL Prodn-SCETV

Taking Care Of Your School Building C 15 MIN
16MM FILM, 3/4 OR 1/2 IN VIDEO P-I
Uses a talking school building to show that students play an important role in the care of school buildings. Points out the many ways in which floors, walls, fixtures and furniture are damaged or abused. Reveals that increased maintenance and replacement costs mean less money to buy new materials and equipment.
From The School Citizenship Series.
LC NO. 79-707213
Prod-CENTRO Dist-CORF 1979

Taking Chances C 22 MIN
16MM FILM, 3/4 OR 1/2 IN VIDEO J-H
Follows the romantic relationship between Kathy and Leigh, interspersing their story with discussion among other teenagers expressing feelings and concerns about their sexual coming-of-age. Stresses communciation and explores some of the reasons that underlie the non-use of birth control among sexually active teenagers.
Prod-MOBIUS Dist-CF 1979

Taking Disciplinary Action C 10 MIN
3/4 OR 1/2 INCH VIDEO CASSETTE
Provides steps to take when reprimanding an employee. Describes how to encourage change and avoid termination proceedings.
From The Management In Action Series.
Prod-MTI Dist-MTI

Taking Inside Measurements C 9 MIN
16MM FILM, 3/4 OR 1/2 IN VIDEO J-C A
See series title for descriptive statement.
From The Power Mechanics Series.
Prod-THIOKL Dist-CAROUF

Taking It In Stride - Positive Approaches To Stress Management C 22 MIN
16MM FILM, 3/4 OR 1/2 IN VIDEO A
Tells how individuals can manage stress and take responsibility for the way they feel. Identifies stressful situations and investigates the interrelationship of health and habits. Offers suggestions for coping with stress, such as various methods of relaxation, doing fewer things better and adapting to a workable load of responsibilities.
LC NO. 82-706464
Prod-SPEF Dist-SPEF 1981

Taking Off C 30 MIN
16MM FILM, 3/4 OR 1/2 IN VIDEO C A
See series title for descriptive statement.
From The Case Studies In Small Business Series.
Prod-UMA Dist-GPITVL 1979

Taking On Tomorrow C 29 MIN
16MM FILM, 3/4 OR 1/2 IN VIDEO
Discusses the mainstreaming of handicapped students in postsecondary vocational education programs.
LC NO. 81-706788
Prod-USDED Dist-USNAC 1981

Taking Our Bodies Back - The Women's Health Movement C 30 MIN
16MM FILM, 3/4 OR 1/2 IN VIDEO
Explores ten critical areas of the women's health movement from the revolutionary concept of self-help to the issue of informed surgical consent. Documents a growing movement of women to regain control of their bodies. Shows women becoming aware of their rights in dealing with the medical industry.
Prod-CMBRD Dist-CMBRD 1974

Taking Ownership C 29 MIN
3/4 OR 1/2 INCH VIDEO CASSETTE T
Discusses helping children develop a functional view of learning and re-value reading and writing. Stresses not reducing literacy to a set of rules.
From The Authoring Cycle - Read Better, Write Better, Reason Better Series.
Prod-IU Dist-HNEDBK

Taking Stock C 15 MIN
3/4 OR 1/2 INCH VIDEO CASSETTE H A
Concerns the financial problems of four characters with the two older friends having a disappointing exchange, one teenager complaining about deductions from her first paycheck and the other being chided for not finding work.
From The Old Enough To Care Series.
Prod-ETVCON Dist-AITECH

Taking Stock C 30 MIN
1/2 IN VIDEO CASSETTE BETA/VHS
Surveys various stock strategies. Discusses inheritance taxes and insurance. Makes predictions about the nation's job market.
From The On The Money Series.
Prod-WGBHTV Dist-MTI

Taking Stocks C 30 MIN
3/4 OR 1/2 INCH VIDEO CASSETTE A
Explains how individuals can develop an awareness of stress in their lives and how they can learn to recognize the first signs of trouble. Examines the relationship between people's responses to stress and their health, as well as their ability to function efficiently as executives.
From The Stress Management - A Positive Strategy Series. Pt 2
LC NO. 82-706501
Prod-TIMLIF Dist-TIMLIF 1982

Taking The Helm C 15 MIN
3/4 INCH VIDEO CASSETTE J-C A
Describes how steer and dock a small boat.
From The Afloat And Aboat Series.
Prod-MDDE Dist-GPITVL 1979

Taking The Initiative—A Series

Trains employees to expect more of themselves, initiate productive action and ideas, and become more sensitive to their manager's needs. Challenges managers to be more effective.
Prod-BNA Dist-BNA

How To Ask For Clarification Or Help 009 MIN
How To Express Your Concern About A Situation 007 MIN
How To Participate In A Performance Appraisal 011 MIN
How To Present A New Or Better Idea 006 MIN
How To Take The Initiative In Planning, 008 MIN

Taking The Patient's Temperature C 8 MIN
3/4 OR 1/2 INCH VIDEO CASSETTE PRO
Describes the oral and the rectal thermometer and states the average readings and average times required to gain accurate readings for both types of thermometers. Demonstrates the proper methods of inserting both. Emphasizes the importance of cleaning the thermometer before and after it is used and of washing the hands before and after the thermometer is handled.
LC NO. 77-731353
Prod-TRAINX Dist-TRAINX

Taking The Patient's Temperature (Spanish) C 8 MIN
3/4 OR 1/2 INCH VIDEO CASSETTE PRO
Describes the oral and rectal thermometer and states the average readings and average times required to gain accurate readings for both types of thermometers. Demonstrates the proper methods of inserting both. Emphasizes the importance of cleaning the thermometer before and after it is used and of washing the hands before and after the thermometer is handled.
LC NO. 77-731353
Prod-TRAINX Dist-TRAINX

Taking The Pledge C 1 MIN
3/4 OR 1/2 INCH VIDEO CASSETTE
Focuses on group of high school girls who agree to quit smoking. As they shake hands on the deal, announcer says the girls have made a pact to win happier, healthier lives, and asks 'why don't you make a pact and be a winner, too?' Uses TV spot format.
Prod-AMCS Dist-AMCS 1979

Taking The Static Out Of Statistics B 57 MIN
3/4 OR 1/2 INCH VIDEO CASSETTE
Presents beginning concepts in statistics.
Prod-BU Dist-BU

Taking Time C 30 MIN
3/4 OR 1/2 INCH VIDEO CASSETTE
Talks about the artifacts men have made when they fashion time into things.
From The Eye To Eye Series.
Prod-WGBHTV Dist-EAI Prodn-MOFAB

Taking Time To Feel—A Series
C A
Deals with emotional aspects of human sexuality in a three part series. Depicts a man and a woman enjoying the world around them and taking genuine pleasure in being together
Prod-MMRC Dist-MMRC

Taking Time to Feel, Pt 1 008 MIN
Taking Time to Feel, Pt 2 008 MIN
Taking Time to Feel, Pt 3 010 MIN

Taking Time to Feel, Pt 1 C 8 MIN
3/4 OR 1/2 INCH VIDEO CASSETTE C A
Depicts a man and a woman ejoying the world around them, and themselves, making it vividly clear that being in touch with one's own sexuality helps to feel fulfillment with a partner.
From The Taking Time To Feel Series.
Prod-MMRC Dist-MMRC

Taking Time To Feel, Pt 2 C 8 MIN
3/4 OR 1/2 INCH VIDEO CASSETTE C A
Depicts a man and a woman ejoying the world around them, and themselves, making it vividly clear that being in touch with one's own sexuality helps to feel fulfillment with a partner.
From The Taking Time To Feel Series.
Prod-MMRC Dist-MMRC

Taking Time To Feel, Pt 3 C 10 MIN
3/4 OR 1/2 INCH VIDEO CASSETTE C A
Shows a couple, married fourteen years, taking genuine pleasure in being together.
From The Taking Time To Feel Series.
Prod-MMRC Dist-MMRC

Tal Farlow B 2 MIN
16MM FILM OPTICAL SOUND
Presents Len Lye's last scratch film, completed by his assistant, Steven Jones. Features white lines that 'dance' and 'sway' to a jazz guitar solo by Tal Farlow.
Prod-STARRC Dist-STARRC 1980

Tala C 8 MIN
16MM FILM OPTICAL SOUND
Views a crack in the ice, following it through a complex series of variations and repetitions in color distortions and superimposition.
LC NO. 77-702663
Prod-CANCOU Dist-CANFDC Prodn-STONEH 1976

Tale Of 'O', A C 27 MIN
16MM FILM, 3/4 OR 1/2 IN VIDEO
Tells the story of what happens to any new or different kind of person in a group, and how to manage that situation. Parallels the real-life experience of women and minorities and depersonalizes the situation to allow others to identify with the victim of tokenism.
Prod-GOODMI Dist-GOODMI

Tale Of A Hare Or We're All Different Somewhere, The C 45 MIN
16MM FILM OPTICAL SOUND I-C A
Describes what cleft lips and palates are and what it's like to have one or the other.
Prod-UPITTS Dist-UPITTS 1977

Tale Of A TV Mouse, A C 14 MIN
16MM FILM, 3/4 OR 1/2 IN VIDEO P
Tells the story of a puppet mouse named Lucille whose entire life revolves around the television. Shows how it affects her life and what finally happens to convince her to break the TV habit.
Prod-PUPPET Dist-FILCOM 1979

Tale Of Bhutan, A C 27 MIN
16MM FILM, 3/4 OR 1/2 IN VIDEO K-I
Presents a pantomime which tells how technology gradually initiates change in the traditional kingdom of Bhutan, a small independent state in the eastern Himalayas.
LC NO. 80-707724
Prod-UNICEF Dist-CAROUF 1980

Tale Of Five Cities, A - Tax Revolt Pennsylvania Style C 26 MIN
3/4 OR 1/2 INCH VIDEO CASSETTE
Details a system pioneered by five Pennsylvania cities to gain more revenue from property taxes in a way that is less burdensome to most home owners and progressive businesses. Covers systems implemented in Scranton, Harrisburg, McKeesport, Pittsburgh and New Castle.
Prod-CPUBD Dist-CPUBD

Tale Of Four Wishes, A C 42 MIN
16MM FILM, 3/4 OR 1/2 IN VIDEO K-I
Relates the story of Jane who finds herself trapped in family conflicts until Skeeter offers advice based on the books Hug Me by Pattie Stren, The Man Who Had No Dream by Adelaide Holl, The Silver Pony by Lynd Ward and Jane, Wishing by Toby Tobias.
LC NO. 81-707556
Prod-BOSUST Dist-CF 1981

Tale Of Heike, The C 27 MIN
16MM FILM OPTICAL SOUND
A Japanese language film. Presents the historical facts and Buddhist concept of understanding by depicting the rise and fall of the Heike and Genji clans. Portrays the powers of the Heike clan, the rise of the Genji and the defeat and fall of the Heike, ending with prayers for an everlasting peace in the Buddhist paradise.
Prod-GAKKEN Dist-UNIJAP 1969

Tale Of King Midas, The C 18 MIN
16MM FILM, 3/4 OR 1/2 IN VIDEO P-I
Tells a tale about a god who grants a wish to a mortal, King Midas, who asks that everything he touches turn to gold. Explains how he soon discovers the consequences of his wish and asks that the god remove it.
Prod-EBEC Dist-EBEC 1974

Tale Of King Midas, The (Spanish) C 18 MIN
16MM FILM, 3/4 OR 1/2 IN VIDEO P-I
Tells the Greek legend of King Midas, explaining how he gets into trouble with the gods.
Prod-EBEC Dist-EBEC

Tale Of One City C 15 MIN
16MM FILM OPTICAL SOUND J-C A
Portrays the unhappy plight of ordinary people who live in cities where planning has not taken their needs into account. Points out the pressures on City Hall by vested interests to compromise the best interests of citizens.
LC NO. 78-701233
Prod-FLMAUS Dist-AUIS 1976

Tale Of Rumpelstiltskin C 21 MIN
16MM FILM, 3/4 OR 1/2 IN VIDEO P-I
Presents an adaptation of the story of Rumpelstiltskin.
Prod-EBEC Dist-EBEC 1974

Tale Of Rumplestiltskin (Captioned) C 21 MIN
16MM FILM, 3/4 OR 1/2 IN VIDEO P-I
Presents an adaptation of the story of Rumplestiltskin.
Prod-EBEC Dist-EBEC 1974

Tale Of The Cold Smoke C 24 MIN
16MM FILM OPTICAL SOUND
Tells a tall tale about how Montana's Bridger Bowl originally got its powder snow and shows the pleasures and challenges of recreational skiing.
LC NO. 78-701572
Prod-BRIBOW Dist-BRIBOW Prodn-WAF 1978

Tale Of The Ground Hog's Shadow, A C 11 MIN
16MM FILM, 3/4 OR 1/2 IN VIDEO P-I
Tells the legend of the ground hog through an adventure of a raccoon searching for news of coming spring.
Prod-CORF Dist-CORF 1955

Tale Of The Gypsy Robe, The C 30 MIN
3/4 OR 1/2 INCH VIDEO CASSETTE
See series title for descriptive statement.
From The Broadway Series.
Prod-ARCVID Dist-ARCVID

Tale Of The Name Of The Tree, The C 15 MIN
3/4 INCH VIDEO CASSETTE K-P
See series title for descriptive statement.
From The Storytime Series.
Prod-WCETTV Dist-GPITVL 1976

Tale Of The Ugly Duckling C 8 MIN
16MM FILM, 3/4 OR 1/2 IN VIDEO P
Tells the story of the Ugly Duckling who, rejected, not belonging to the group, has to live in an alien environment and go through many unhappy experiences before finding his own kind.
From The Halas And Batchelor Fairy Tale Series.
Prod-HALAS Dist-EBEC 1969

Tale Of The Ugly Duckling (Spanish) C 8 MIN
16MM FILM, 3/4 OR 1/2 IN VIDEO P
Tells the story of the Ugly Duckling, who, rejected and not belonging to the group, has to live in an alien environment and go through many unhappy experiences before finding his own kind.
Prod-HALAS Dist-EBEC 1969

Tale Of Three Churches C 25 MIN
16MM FILM OPTICAL SOUND C A
Shows how inflation prevented three overseas congregations from purchasing land and building churches. Explains how each of their dilemmas was solved.
Prod-CBFMS Dist-CBFMS

Tale Of Three Cities, A C 28 MIN
16MM FILM, 3/4 OR 1/2 IN VIDEO J-H

Visits three different cities on three different continents in three different stages of development. Views their different approaches to the same problems. Discusses the population growth and the added stresses that will place on the world's cities. Visits Djakarta, Indonesia, Caracas, Venezuela and Stockholm, Sweden.
Prod-JOU Dist-JOU 1974

Tale Of Till, A C 11 MIN
16MM FILM, 3/4 OR 1/2 IN VIDEO
Introduces Till Eulenspeigel and his place in German literature. Presents an outdoor puppet show of one of Till's stories.
Prod-FLMFR Dist-FLMFR

Tale Of Two Cities B 12 MIN
16MM FILM, 3/4 OR 1/2 IN VIDEO
Documents the effects of the bombing on Hiroshima and Nagasaki. Issued in 1942 as a motion picture.
LC NO. 80-706778
Prod-USWD Dist-USNAC 1980

Tale Of Two Cities, A B 44 MIN
16MM FILM OPTICAL SOUND I-H
Re-enacts Dickens' tale of heroism, devotion and tragedy against the background of the French Revolution. Stars Ronald Colman as Sydney Carton.
LC NO. FIA52-4978
Prod-PMI Dist-FI 1935

Tale Of Two Cities, A B 70 MIN
16MM FILM SILENT
Shows how unrequited love leads to a brave sacrifice by a French aristocrat who is the exact double of a man loved by the woman he adores. Stars William Farnum and Jewel Carmen. Directed by Frank Lloyd.
Prod-FOXFC Dist-KILLIS 1917

Tale Of Two Cities, A B 117 MIN
16MM FILM OPTICAL SOUND
Tells the classic story of Sydney Carton, a disillusioned lawyer whose life is brightened by love for Lucie Manette, a member of the French revolutionaries. Reveals his sacrifice for her, as he exchanges places with her husband and goes to the guillotine. Features Dirk Bogarde and Dorothy Tutin. Directed by Ralph Thomas. Based on the novel A TALE OF TWO CITIES by Charles Dickens.
Prod-RANK Dist-LCOA 1958

Tale Of Two Critters, A C 48 MIN
16MM FILM, 3/4 OR 1/2 IN VIDEO I-H
Tells how a baby raccoon and a bear cub, separated from their families, find themselves unlikely companions on an adventure-filled trek in the Pacific Northwest.
From The Animal Featurettes, Set 3 Series.
Prod-DISNEY Dist-WDEMCO 1977

Tale Of Two Leopards, A C 23 MIN
3/4 OR 1/2 INCH VIDEO CASSETTE
Focuses on the leopard in southern Kenya where they still live in large numbers. Relates their dilemma with the Masai tribesmen.
Prod-NWLDPR Dist-NWLDPR

Tale Of Two Neighbors C 15 MIN
3/4 OR 1/2 INCH VIDEO CASSETTE P
Compares two neighbors.
From The Neighborhoods Series.
Prod-NEITV Dist-GPITVL 1981

Tale Of Two Rivers, A C 40 MIN
16MM FILM, 3/4 OR 1/2 IN VIDEO H-C A
Shows the significance to the study of human development of the valleys of the Dordogne and Vezere rivers in France. Includes scenes of modern life in the Dordogne and then explores the area's importance in the study of history. Discusses the significance of various archeological sites and examines the concern of present-day inhabitants for preserving their Languedocian customs and language. The narration is edited from interviews with archeologists, historians and art historians.
Prod-SMITCB Dist-UCEMC 1974

Tale Of Urashima Taro, The C 15 MIN
3/4 OR 1/2 INCH VIDEO CASSETTE P-I
Tells the Japanese tale of how Taro spends three days with a beautiful princess deep in the sea but, when he returns to his village, hundreds of years seem to have passed.
From The Sixteen Tales Series.
Prod-KLCSTV Dist-AITECH

Taleb And His Lamb C 16 MIN
16MM FILM, 3/4 OR 1/2 IN VIDEO I
Presents a Bedouin tale about a shepherd boy who watches over his father's small flock and learns to love one of the lambs. Reveals the values of the Bedouin culture.
Prod-BARR Dist-BARR 1975

Taleb And His Lamb (Captioned) C 16 MIN
16MM FILM - VIDEO, ALL FORMATS K-J
Tells a Bedouin folk tale about a shepherd boy and a lamb.
Prod-BARR Dist-BARR

Talent For America C 28 MIN
16MM FILM OPTICAL SOUND
Features the music, dance and performances of three young members of Affiliate Artists, an organization for young performing artists who aim at refining their own talents and creating new audiences for the arts.
LC NO. 79-701487
Prod-SEARS Dist-MTP Prodn-UIP 1978

Talent For America C 30 MIN
16MM FILM OPTICAL SOUND
Presents an overview of the Affiliate Artists program and tells how the organization sends talented performers to rural communities.
LC NO. 78-701499
Prod-DREWAS Dist-DREWAS 1978

Talent For Disaster C 16 MIN
16MM FILM, 3/4 OR 1/2 IN VIDEO J-C
Presents a fire boss in a fire camp explaining the tremendous effort and costs involved in fighting a wildfire. Stresses the importance of fire safety awareness.
Prod-PUBSF Dist-FILCOM

Talent For Life, A - Jews Of The Italian Renaissance C 58 MIN
16MM FILM OPTICAL SOUND
Focuses on the Jewish experience during the Italian Renaissance. Traces the history of Jews in Italy from their origins as Roman slaves to their life in the ghettos of Venice. Originally broadcast on the television program The Eternal Light.
LC NO. 80-700287
Prod-NBC Dist-NBC 1979

Talent For Tony, A C 13 MIN
16MM FILM OPTICAL SOUND K-P
Explains that when five-year-old Tony is asked by his artist-father to make some drawings, his fear of failure gets in the way. Shows how he discovers that the one talent to be treasured is belief in himself.
From The Parables Series.
LC NO. 72-703206
Prod-FRACOC Dist-FRACOC 1971

Talent Search C 60 MIN
1/2 IN VIDEO CASSETTE BETA/VHS
Presents a variety of tests to help determine an athlete's best track and field event.
From The Women's Track And Field Series.
Prod-MOHOMV Dist-MOHOMV

Talent Search C 60 MIN
1/2 IN VIDEO CASSETTE BETA/VHS A
Gives track coaches and athletes a variety of tests which will help determine each potential athlete's best event. Features Dr Ken Foreman.
Prod-RMI Dist-RMI

Talent Show Today C 10 MIN
3/4 OR 1/2 INCH VIDEO CASSETTE K-P
Focuses on an awareness of individual talents and physical skills.
From The Book, Look And Listen Series.
Prod-MDDE Dist-AITECH 1977

Tales From Other Worlds C 60 MIN
16MM FILM, 3/4 OR 1/2 IN VIDEO C A
Presents, through footage shot in space and special effects, a look at the star of Jupiter, the volcano of Io and the full surface of Venus through acid rain clouds. Discusses the yet undiscovered Death Star which may have killed the dinosaurs and millions of other species.
From The Planet Earth Series.
Prod-ANNCPB Dist-FI

Tales From The Vienna Woods C 12 MIN
16MM FILM OPTICAL SOUND
Presents a collage about courtship, love and marriage based on the letters of Sigmund Freud and journals of the period.
LC NO. 76-700158
Prod-MCGILU Dist-MCGILU 1974

Tales Of Hiawatha C 19 MIN
16MM FILM, 3/4 OR 1/2 IN VIDEO P-H
A puppet film adapted from Henry Wadsworth Longfellow's epic, 'THE SONG OF HIAWATHA.' Combines sections of the poem with narration to relate the Indian legend.
Prod-SF Dist-SF Prodn-BERMIS 1967

Tales Of Hoffmann, The (French) C 160 MIN
3/4 OR 1/2 INCH VIDEO CASSETTE A
Portrays three strange love affairs, one with a doll, another with a glittering courtesan, the third with an ambitious but fragile singer in Offenbach's musical, The Tales Of Hoffman.
Prod-EDDIM Dist-EDDIM

Tales Of Hoffnung–A Series
16MM FILM, 3/4 OR 1/2 IN VIDEO
Presents stories based on the cartoons of Gerald Hoffnung.
Prod-HALAS Dist-PHENIX 1981

Birds, Bees And Storks	006 MIN
Hoffnung Maestro, The	008 MIN
Hoffnung Music Academy, The	008 MIN
Hoffnung Symphony Orchestra, The	008 MIN
Hoffnung Vacuum Cleaner, The	008 MIN
Professor Ya-Ya's Memoirs	008 MIN

Tales Of New Jersey C 25 MIN
16MM FILM OPTICAL SOUND
Tells legends and folklore of New Jersey set to a background of original music and lyrics.
LC NO. 76-701405
Prod-NJBTC Dist-NJBTC Prodn-MURPHO 1976

Tales Of Olga Da Polga, The C 15 MIN
3/4 OR 1/2 INCH VIDEO CASSETTE P
See series title for descriptive statement.
From The Best Of Cover To Cover 1 Series.
Prod-WETATV Dist-WETATV

Tales Of Pluto–A Series
16MM FILM, 3/4 OR 1/2 IN VIDEO
Presents animated stories featuring Pluto the dog.
Prod-DISNEY Dist-WDEMCO

Dog Watch	008 MIN
Pluto's Surprise Package	008 MIN
Wonder Dog	008 MIN

Tales Of Terror C 90 MIN
16MM FILM OPTICAL SOUND J-C A
Stars Vincent Price and Basil Rathbone in three of Edgar Allan Poe's most chilling tales, utilizing all the gripping psychological terror elements which have made his works memorable. Includes The Black Cat, Morella and The Facts In The Case Of M Valdemar.
Prod-AIP Dist-TIMLIF 1962

Tales Of The Muscogee C
3/4 OR 1/2 INCH VIDEO CASSETTE
Portrays the rich history and folklore of the Creek Indians. Examines three folktales in terms of legend, myth and fable.
Prod-CEPRO Dist-CEPRO

Tales Of The Muscogee C 15 MIN
3/4 OR 1/2 INCH VIDEO CASSETTE I-H
Introduces the rich world of Creek Indian folklore as a form of entertainment and moral teaching for children.
Prod-CEPRO Dist-CEPRO

Tales Of The Snow Monkey C 23 MIN
3/4 OR 1/2 INCH VIDEO CASSETTE K-C A
Tells the story of the amazingly smart and ever-adaptable Japanese snow monkey which has managed to adapt to conditions that have killed off most of Japan's other wildlife species.
Prod-NWLDPR Dist-NWLDPR

Tales Of Tomorrow - Our Elders C 22 MIN
16MM FILM, 3/4 OR 1/2 IN VIDEO
Contrasts the lifestyles of several elderly people with handicapping conditions. Shows one couple in which the husband has heart trouble and the wife has Alzheimer's disease moving into a home for the aged while another woman insists on living independently at 80, though wheelchair bound.
LC NO. 84-706139
Prod-MARTNB Dist-FLMLIB 1982

Tales Of Washington Irving C 45 MIN
16MM FILM OPTICAL SOUND
Uses animation to bring some of Washington Irving's favorite places and people back to life. Includes the stories of Ichabod Crane and Rip Van Winkle.
Prod-API Dist-TWYMAN

Tales Tall And Otherwise B 29 MIN
3/4 INCH VIDEO CASSETTE
Discusses the persistence of tales such as Paul Bunyan and Brer Rabbit. Features a professional storyteller.
From The Folklore - U S A Series.
Prod-UMITV Dist-UMITV 1967

Tales The People Tell In China / Favorite Fairy Tales Told In Japan C 15 MIN
3/4 OR 1/2 INCH VIDEO CASSETTE P
See series title for descriptive statement.
From The Best Of Cover To Cover 1 Series.
Prod-WETATV Dist-WETATV

Tales Your Grandpa Heard C 20 MIN
2 INCH VIDEOTAPE P-I
See series title for descriptive statement.
From The Learning Our Language, Unit V - Exploring With Books Series.
Prod-MPATI Dist-GPITVL

Taliesin East C 11 MIN
16MM FILM OPTICAL SOUND C A
Depicts the home of American architect Frank Lloyd Wright, near Madison, Wisconsin.
LC NO. FIA52-665
Prod-DAVISJ Dist-RADIM 1951

Taliesin West C 11 MIN
16MM FILM OPTICAL SOUND C A
Uses a film record to describe the desert house of Frank Lloyd Wright and a brief narration, written by Wright himself. Explains some of his ideas about the relationship between modern art and nature.
LC NO. FIA52-664
Prod-DAVISJ Dist-RADIM 1951

Talisman - Barra C 37 MIN
2 INCH VIDEOTAPE
Describes the restoration of a Scottish castle, the ancestral home of the clan Mac Neil.
Prod-VTETV Dist-PUBTEL

Talk - Don't Fight C 15 MIN
16MM FILM - VIDEO, ALL FORMATS K-J
Teaches that fighting and revenge lead only to death, when little Fernando is caught in a crossfire between rival gangs.
From The Fat Albert And The Cosby Kids IV Series.
Prod-BARR Dist-BARR Prodn-FLMTON

Talk Of The Town, The B 118 MIN
16MM FILM OPTICAL SOUND
Tells how Cary Grant finds refuge in the summer cottage of a celebrated jurist when he is falsely accused of arson. Follows Jean Arthur's attempts to get the jurist to defend Grant in a new trial. Directed by George Stevens.
Prod-CPC Dist-TIMLIF 1942

Talk To Everyone C 15 MIN
2 INCH VIDEOTAPE
Describes what mass communication is and how it is used.
From The Let's Build A City Series.
Prod-WVIZTV Dist-GPITVL

Talk To Me C 15 MIN
2 INCH VIDEOTAPE
Establishes a realization of the need for communication, particularly person-to-person communication.
From The Let's Build A City Series.
Prod-WVIZTV Dist-GPITVL

Talk To Me - A Visit With Mr Carpenter C 8 MIN
16MM FILM OPTICAL SOUND J-C A
Presents a statement on growing old, featuring present and past experiences of Authur H Carpenter, an 85-year-old man who was a singer, an architect and an artist, including his concern for the future.
LC NO. 76-701175
Prod-TATANA Dist-ARTCOP 1974

Talk To The Animals C 10 MIN
16MM FILM OPTICAL SOUND P-I
An excerpt from the motion picture Doctor Dolittle. Shows Doctor Dolittle receiving lessons in animal language from Polynesia the Parrot. Introduces communication methods and nonverbal communication or body language. Based on the story Doctor Dolittle by Hugh Lofting.
From The Peppermint Stick Selection Series.
LC NO. 76-701278
Prod-FI Dist-FI 1978

Talk To The Animals C 14 MIN
16MM FILM, 3/4 OR 1/2 IN VIDEO A
Shows scientists communicating with apes by teaching them sign language and through the use of a talking typewriter or computer. Points out that these communication methods can be used to help teach language to the mentally retarded and to brain-damaged children.
Prod-CBSTV Dist-MGHT 1978

Talk, Listen, And Learn C 35 MIN
16MM FILM, 3/4 OR 1/2 IN VIDEO
Presents actual situations in which young people discuss issues such as alcohol, drugs and sexual behavior in order to demonstrate techniques for leading small group discussions.
LC NO. 80-706842
Prod-JOB Dist-USNAC 1980

Talk, Talk, Talk B 10 MIN
16MM FILM OPTICAL SOUND S
Shows the beginning of lip-reading and how an awareness of lip movements can be developed and utilized for the development of lip-reading skills.
From The Parent Education - Information Films Series.
Prod-TC Dist-TC

Talk, Talk, Talk C 15 MIN
3/4 OR 1/2 INCH VIDEO CASSETTE P
Points out that most animals can't learn to talk with words because they lack the nerve network in the brain that makes human speech possible.
From The All About You Series.
Prod-WGBHTV Dist-AITECH Prodn-TTOIC 1975

Talking C 4 MIN
16MM FILM OPTICAL SOUND P-I
Deals with an extended concept of talking by presenting nonword responses as a form of communication.
From The Mini Movies - Springboard For Learning - Unit 1, Who Are We Series.
LC NO. 76-703091
Prod-MORLAT Dist-MORLAT 1975

Talking About Beliefs B 14 MIN
16MM FILM OPTICAL SOUND I-H T
Shows students in a fifth-grade class in Newton, Massachusetts, discussing Eskimo beliefs, and in the process examining their own.
From The Classroom As A Learning Community Series.
LC NO. 76-714106
Prod-EDC Dist-EDC 1971

Talking About Breastfeeding C 17 MIN
16MM FILM OPTICAL SOUND H-C A
Affirms the values of breastfeeding as the simplest, safest and most nutritious way to feed an infant and helps allay common fears. Features a number of nursing mothers who have overcome medical problems and social pressures to breastfeed speaking of their experiences.
LC NO. 74-703684
Prod-POLYMR Dist-POLYMR 1971

Talking About Deafness C 30 MIN
3/4 OR 1/2 INCH VIDEO CASSETTE
Discusses various aspects of deafness.
From The Signing With Cindy Series.
Prod-KUHTTV Dist-MDCPB

Talking About Old People B 19 MIN
16MM FILM OPTICAL SOUND I-H T
Shows a classroom situation in which the students have read 'THE KIGTAK STORY' and are discussing the problem that the Netsilik Eskimos have in taking care of their old people.
From The Classroom As A Learning Community Series.
LC NO. 72-714105
Prod-EDC Dist-EDC 1971

Talking About Pots C 25 MIN
3/4 OR 1/2 INCH VIDEO CASSETTE H-C A
Features a discussion among a potter, a member of the Crafts Advisory Council, a gallery owner and a collector which centers on appreciation of individual pieces of work by contemporary potters. Shows potters at work.
From The Craft Of The Potter Series.
Prod-BBCTV Dist-FI

Talking And Listening C 11 MIN
16MM FILM, 3/4 OR 1/2 IN VIDEO P-I
Provides some ways to talk and listen that will help in learning and understanding.
Prod-CORF Dist-CORF 1968

Talking Back C
3/4 OR 1/2 INCH VIDEO CASSETTE
Shows how to take positive steps to impact the low back pain problem.
Prod-VISUCP Dist-VISUCP

Talking Car, The C 17 MIN
16MM FILM OPTICAL SOUND
Uses a dramatized incident in which a car comes to life in the dream of a small boy to teach the See And Be Seen rules of traffic safety.
LC NO. 72-705680
Prod-AAAFTS Dist-AAAFTS Prodn-HIGGIN 1969

Talking Crime C 30 MIN
3/4 OR 1/2 INCH VIDEO CASSETTE
Answers some common questions about crime. Takes a look at the homicide rate and examines the role of the news.
Prod-NOVID Dist-NOVID

Talking Hands C 20 MIN
16MM FILM OPTICAL SOUND I-C
Gives a basic introduction to the universal sign language of the American Indian. A storyteller recounts the battle of the Washita in hand talk.
From The Plains Indians Culture Series.
Prod-UOKLA Dist-UOKLA 1954

Talking Hands B 15 MIN
2 INCH VIDEOTAPE K-P
Explores several ideas for using puppets in skits. (Broadcast quality)
From The Magic Of Words Series.
Prod-GWTVAI Dist-GPITVL Prodn-WETATV

Talking It Over C 20 MIN
16MM FILM, 3/4 OR 1/2 IN VIDEO T
Features educators, tutors and students in adult literacy discussing the special physiological, psychological, cultural and educational needs of the adult learner. Notes that knowledge of these needs helps the tutor decide what objectives, strategies and materials should be used with the individual learner.
From The Literacy Instructor Training Series.
LC NO. 80-706064
Prod-IU Dist-IU 1978

Talking Machine, The - From Tinfoil To LP C 13 MIN
16MM FILM, 3/4 OR 1/2 IN VIDEO J-C
Presents an account of the history of sound recording from tinfoil to the LP. Commemorates the 100th anniversary of the invention of the phonograph.
From The Screen News Digest Series. Volume 20 Issue 3
Prod-HEARST Dist-HEARST

Talking Mailbox, The C 20 MIN
2 INCH VIDEOTAPE P
See series title for descriptive statement.
From The Learning Our Language, Unit III - Creative Writing Series.
Prod-MPATI Dist-GPITVL

Talking Nicaragua C 39 MIN
1/2 IN VIDEO CASSETTE BETA/VHS
Recounts the highlights of Nicaragua's history since the days of Sandino, through dramatic presentations by actors Susan Sarandon, Edward Herrmann, and others, who recreate the stories of present day Nicaraguans, victims of attacks launched by counterrevolutionary forces along the border with Honduras.
Prod-ICARUS Dist-ICARUS

Talking Of Safety C 24 MIN
16MM FILM, 3/4 OR 1/2 IN VIDEO A
Deals with the effectiveness of safety committee meetings. Shows how a newly-appointed safety supervisor at a brick and manufacturing plant in England makes his committee work more effectively while promoting clearly-defined objectives.
LC NO. 81-707628
Prod-MILLBK Dist-IFB 1980

Talking On Paper C 40 MIN
3/4 OR 1/2 INCH VIDEO CASSETTE
See series title for descriptive statement.
From The Effective Writing Series.
Prod-TWAIN Dist-DELTAK

Talking Ourselves Into Trouble B 29 MIN
16MM FILM OPTICAL SOUND C A
Discusses general semantics and how undifferentiated reactions to words lead to lack of communication. Develops the idea that language determines limits of a person's world.
From The Language In Action Series.
Prod-NET Dist-IU Prodn-KQEDTV

Talking Out Conflict C 15 MIN
3/4 OR 1/2 INCH VIDEO CASSETTE
Stresses that managers must deal with conflicts or they will only become worse. Points out that the keys to conflict resolution are a positive attitude and an effort to be honest and open with everyone involved.
Prod-EFM Dist-EFM

Talking Parcel, The C 40 MIN
16MM FILM, 3/4 OR 1/2 IN VIDEO I A
Presents characters and incidents based on ancient myths which come to life in full animation with voices by British personalities and incidental music by a rock composer.
Prod-THAMES Dist-MEDIAG 1978

Talking Plant, The C 54 MIN
3/4 OR 1/2 INCH VIDEO CASSETTE I-H A
Teaches parts of a plant and their functions to stimulate an interest in growing plants and to explain how to use plants in the environment.
Prod-CUETV Dist-CUNIV 1975

Talking Round The World C 15 MIN
16MM FILM, 3/4 OR 1/2 IN VIDEO
Follows American children as they visit the homes of children from Ghana, India and Japan. Shows the similarities and differences in their lives.

From The Ripples Series.
LC NO. 73-702156
Prod-NITC Dist-AITECH

Talking Shop C 23 MIN
16MM FILM OPTICAL SOUND
Presents Hazardous Harry, a bungling hero who shows how not to use hand tools. Shows how injuries can be avoided.
Prod-MTP Dist-MTP

Talking To A Machine C 25 MIN
16MM FILM, 3/4 OR 1/2 IN VIDEO J-C A
Discusses computer languages, comparing BASIC with English and describing holed cards that once programmed a steam organ.
From The Computer Programme Series. Episode 3
Prod-BBCTV Dist-FI 1982

Talking Turtle C 48 MIN
16MM FILM, 3/4 OR 1/2 IN VIDEO C A
Discusses the uses and potential of Lugo, a new computer language developed to meet the need for computers to enrich the range of experience for children. Adapted from the Nova series.
Prod-BBCTV Dist-MEDIAG Prodn-OPENU 1984

Talking Turtle C 57 MIN
16MM FILM, 3/4 OR 1/2 IN VIDEO H-C A
Looks at computers in the classroom through the eyes of MIT's Seymour Papert, inventor of the computer language LOGO and father of the Turtle, a computerized robot that crawls on the floor and communicates in a versatile language even five-year-olds can learn.
From The Nova Series.
Prod-WGBHTV Dist-TIMLIF 1984

Talking With Pictures C 37 MIN
3/4 OR 1/2 INCH VIDEO CASSETTE
Focuses on three types of visuals which can greatly enhance presentations of ideas, plans, products and results to audiences large and small. Demonstrates the flipchart, the 35mm slide and the overhead transparency. Shows how to design effective visuals and most effective way to use each type.
Prod-MELROS Dist-VISUCP

Talking With Thoreau C 29 MIN
16MM FILM, 3/4 OR 1/2 IN VIDEO H-C
Uses a science fiction device of time-travel to present the thoughts of Henry David Thoreau. Stages a visit between Thoreau and four present-day distinguished personages, set in his cabin at Walden Pond.
From The Humanities - Philosophy And Political Thought Series.
Prod-EBEC Dist-EBEC 1975

Talking With Young Children About Death C 28 MIN
3/4 OR 1/2 INCH VIDEO CASSETTE
Reveals how adults can help children understand death and cope with sadness.
Prod-FAMCOM Dist-FAMCOM

Tall Blue Money Three, The C 25 MIN
16MM FILM OPTICAL SOUND
Portrays the story of how by adopting a new concept in farm management, a 400 acre farm with one concrete silo and one feedlot accomodating 100 head of cattle, grew to 1,200 acres, with 10 harvestores and 4 feedlots where 1,500 to 2,000 head of beef are finished each year.
Prod-VENARD Dist-VENARD

Tall Buildings C 5 MIN
16MM FILM, 3/4 OR 1/2 IN VIDEO I-H
Tells how the great shift in urban population has necessitated the increasing development of tall buildings. Stresses the importance of developing tall structures which will be ultilitarian, safe and functional for the occupants.
Prod-NSF Dist-AMEDFL 1975

Tall Dilemma C 21 MIN
16MM FILM, 3/4 OR 1/2 IN VIDEO
Presents the conditions and reasons why firefighters must expect an unusually severe occupant life loss during a serious high rise building fire and discusses what fire departments, building management and occupants can do to prevent it.
Prod-AREASX Dist-FILCOM 1974

Tall Ships C 16 MIN
16MM FILM OPTICAL SOUND
Focuses on the Coast Guard training ship Eagle.
Prod-OFFSHR Dist-OFFSHR

Tall Ships Are Coming, The C 28 MIN
16MM FILM OPTICAL SOUND
Shows crews training and sailing in European waters during the summer of 1975 as preparation for Operation Sail 1976. Views the celebration of the 700th birthday of the city of Amsterdam and a sailing spectacle in London called the London Festival of Sail.
LC NO. 76-700716
Prod-DREWAS Dist-DREWAS 1975

Tall Spinster Of Gimel, The B 30 MIN
16MM FILM OPTICAL SOUND
A folk tale about the trials and tribulations of a six foot spinster who wants a husband and seeks the help of village leaders on the matter.
LC NO. FIA64-1118
Prod-JTS Dist-NAAJS Prodn-NBC 1959

Tall Stacks C 16 MIN
16MM FILM OPTICAL SOUND PRO
Reports on the five-year study on the effects of large power plants on the gaseous and particulate concentrations at various elevations and distances from selected tall stacks installations.

LC NO. 74-705737
Prod-USEPA Dist-USNAC 1972

Tall T, The C 80 MIN
16MM FILM OPTICAL SOUND
Stars Randolph Scott as a man who encounters a vicious gang of killers.
Prod-CPC Dist-KITPAR 1956

Tall Tales C 15 MIN
3/4 OR 1/2 INCH VIDEO CASSETTE P
See series title for descriptive statement.
From The Word Shop Series.
Prod-WETATV Dist-WETATV

Tall Tales And Folklore C 20 MIN
3/4 OR 1/2 INCH VIDEO CASSETTE H-C A
Presents yarns spun around the stove in a country stove, including stories of Paul Bunyan, Pecos Bill and some Black American tales, among others.
From The American Literature Series.
LC NO. 83-706257
Prod-AUBU Dist-AITECH 1983

Tall Tales And True C 30 MIN
16MM FILM OPTICAL SOUND
A documentary film showing the floats, bands and festivities of the floral festival and parade held in Pasadena, California, on New Year's Day, 1960.
LC NO. FIA66-857
Prod-TRA Dist-TRA Prodn-WMSTER 1960

Tall Tina C 15 MIN
3/4 INCH VIDEO CASSETTE P
Presents the children's story Tall Tina by Muriel Stanek.
From The Tilson's Book Shop Series.
Prod-WVIZTV Dist-GPITVL 1975

Tall Top Tree House C 15 MIN
3/4 OR 1/2 INCH VIDEO CASSETTE P
Presents Dr Allhart, who runs the animal clinic at Tall Top Tree House, discussing different classes or groups of animals.
From The Dr Allhart And Patience Series.
LC NO. 81-707534
Prod-JCITV Dist-GPITVL 1979

Tallador, The - The Story Of Tampico Fibre C 12 MIN
16MM FILM OPTICAL SOUND P-C
Shows how Tampico fiber is picked from plants in Mexico and then processed into the material that is used for making quality brushes.
LC NO. 75-700013
Prod-MDFC Dist-MIFE 1971

Tallahassee C 15 MIN
16MM FILM OPTICAL SOUND
Presents a musical tour of Tallahassee, the state capital of Florida.
Prod-FLADC Dist-FLADC

Talley Beatty, Norma Miller C 30 MIN
3/4 OR 1/2 INCH VIDEO CASSETTE
Discusses how popular dance came to the stage. Features Miki Giffune on dance styles in clubs. Hosted by Celia Ipiotis.
From The Eye On Dance - Popular Culture And Dance Series.
Prod-ARTRES Dist-ARTRES

Talmage Farlow C 58 MIN
16MM FILM - 1/2 IN VIDEO
Deals with the music and personality of jazz musician Talmage Farlow. Includes Farlow rehearsing with Tommy Flanagan and Red Mitchell.
Prod-RHPSDY Dist-RHPSDY 1980

Talons C 22 MIN
16MM FILM, 3/4 OR 1/2 IN VIDEO I-H
Surveys a variety of birds of prey all sharing features of hooked, tearing beaks, keen eyesight, and taloned feet. Points out how such birds have suffered badly at man's hands, through ignorance, neglect, shooting and the like. Shows the kestrel, hen harrier, red kite, buzzard, goshawk, sparrow hawk, peregine falcon, golden eagle, osprey and short eared, barn and tawny owls.
From the RSPB Collection Series.
Prod-RSFPB Dist-BCNFL 1982

Tam Lin C 15 MIN
16MM FILM, 3/4 OR 1/2 IN VIDEO J-C
Combines animation with live action to tell the story of a young princess who must rescue the knight, Tam Lin, from an evil abductress.
LC NO. 83-706621
Prod-KORM Dist-PHENIX 1983

Tamales C 15 MIN
3/4 OR 1/2 INCH VIDEO CASSETTE PRO
Demonstrates the preparation of tamales - corn dough spread over corn husks, filled, and steamed.
Prod-CULINA Dist-CULINA

Tambor Diego C 5 MIN
16MM FILM, 3/4 OR 1/2 IN VIDEO K-P
A Spanish-language version of the motion picture Drummer Hoff. Offers an adaptation of a folk verse about the building of a cannon.
Prod-WWS Dist-WWS 1969

Tame Or Wild C 15 MIN
3/4 INCH VIDEO CASSETTE P
Explains the relationships between man and animals. Includes affectionate pets, such as dogs and cats, pets that must be kept confined, such as rabbits and parakeets and animals who have developed a dependence on man, such as mice.
From The Tell Me What You See Series.
Prod-WVIZTV Dist-GPITVL

Tame The Wind C 28 MIN
16MM FILM, 3/4 OR 1/2 IN VIDEO J-C
Discusses the growing science of weather modification and shows how its techniques are being used today to make rain, suppress hail and lightning and clear fog.
Prod-UN Dist-JOU 1974

Tamer Of Wild Horses C 8 MIN
16MM FILM, 3/4 OR 1/2 IN VIDEO
The tamer has found a metal monster looking very much like a horse. When he tries to move the creature, it turns into a mechanized monster threatening to destroy everything. Yet, when the right lever is pulled, the technical miracle spreads its wings and enables the man to fly into space.
Prod-ZAGREB Dist-TEXFLM

Taming Of The Shrew, The C 122 MIN
16MM FILM OPTICAL SOUND
Stars Richard Burton as Petruchio and Elizabeth Taylor as the shrewish Kate. Based on Shakespeare's comedy The Taming Of The Shrew.
Prod-CPC Dist-TIMLIF 1967

Taming Of The Shrew, The C 13 MIN
16MM FILM, 3/4 OR 1/2 IN VIDEO H-C A
An excerpt from the play of the same title. Presents Act I, Scene 2 as Hortensio tells his friend Petruchio of Katharine and Act II, Scene 1 in which Petruchio meets Katharine.
From The Shakespeare Series.
Prod-IFB Dist-IFB 1974

Taming Of The Shrew, The C 120 MIN
3/4 OR 1/2 INCH VIDEO CASSETTE
Presents the American Conservatory Theater's interpretation of William Shakespeare's The Taming Of The Shrew. Tells the story of a young man's raucous campaign to gain the hand of the uncooperative woman he has decided to marry for her dowry.
Prod-WNETTV Dist-WNETTV

Taming Of The Shrew, The C 127 MIN
3/4 OR 1/2 INCH VIDEO CASSETTE H-C A
Presents William Shakespeare's play The Taming Of The Shrew which is a comic confrontation between the sexes.
From The Shakespeare Plays Series.
LC NO. 81-706562
Prod-BBCTV Dist-TIMLIF

Taming Of The Shrew, The - Katherina - The Shrew Type Plus B 45 MIN
2 INCH VIDEOTAPE C
See series title for descriptive statement.
From The Shakespeare Series.
Prod-CHITVC Dist-GPITVL Prodn-WTTWTV

Taming Of The Shrew, The - Unbalance Of Plots B 45 MIN
2 INCH VIDEOTAPE C
See series title for descriptive statement.
From The Shakespeare Series.
Prod-CHITVC Dist-GPITVL Prodn-WTTWTV

Taming The Wild C 15 MIN
16MM FILM OPTICAL SOUND
Presents Michigan wildlife, including cock pheasant turned mother, black bass fed by man and wolf pup in civilized setting.
Prod-SFI Dist-SFI

Tammy X 40 MIN
16MM FILM OPTICAL SOUND P-C A
Explains that Tammy, a lovable, lonely little girl, is involved in a serious accident, but that through the efforts of her pastor and the family doctor her life is spared to witness for Christ in her own home.
LC NO. FIA55-979
Prod-CONCOR Dist-CPH 1953

Tammy The Toad C 11 MIN
16MM FILM, 3/4 OR 1/2 IN VIDEO P-I
A story about Tammy, a child toad, who decides to leave home in order to achieve rightful appreciation. An adaptation of the parable of the prodigal son.
Prod-LEAR Dist-PHENIX 1970

Tangential And Normal Vectors B 28 MIN
3/4 OR 1/2 INCH VIDEO CASSETTE
See series title for descriptive statement.
From The Calculus Of Several Variables - Vector--Calculus Series.
Prod-MIOT Dist-MIOT

Tangled Hearts C 30 MIN
3/4 OR 1/2 INCH VIDEO CASSETTE C A
Presents an adaptation of the short story Tangled Hearts by P G Wodehouse.
From The Wodehouse Playhouse Series.
Prod-BBCTV Dist-TIMLIF 1980

Tangled Webs C 29 MIN
16MM FILM, 3/4 OR 1/2 IN VIDEO A
Focuses on problem behavior in children and how to handle it through the dramatization of a situation in the fictional Tristero family, in which Ann Marie struggles to understand why her young son Paul is constantly lying. Includes a brief introduction and commentary by real-life families and child development experts.
From The Footsteps Series.
LC NO. 80-707204
Prod-USDED Dist-USNAC Prodn-EDFCEN 1980

Tangled World—A Series
J A
Presents documentaries on the social problems of our time.
Prod-YALEDV Dist-YALEDV

Affluent Society, The 28 MIN
International Affairs 28 MIN
Self-Understanding 28 MIN
Sex And The Family 28 MIN

Tango C 8 MIN
16MM FILM, 3/4 OR 1/2 IN VIDEO C A
Offers a metaphoric picture of human fate illustrated by the experiences of many people appearing on the screen at the same time but oblivious to each other.
Prod-POLSKI Dist-IFEX 1983

Tango Tangles B 10 MIN
16MM FILM SILENT
Tells the story of two men who are smitten with the same hat check girl at a dance. Stars Charlie Chaplin and Fatty Arbuckle.
Prod-KEYFC Dist-BHAWK 1914

Tangram C 3 MIN
16MM FILM, 3/4 OR 1/2 IN VIDEO
Uses animation to show the endless design possibilities of tangrams, ancient Chinese puzzles consisting of seven pieces.
Prod-SLASOR Dist-PFP

Tank Calibration C 32 MIN
3/4 OR 1/2 INCH VIDEO CASSETTE IND
Explains current API recommendations for strapping cylindrical upright tanks that contain petroleum or petroleum products.
Prod-UTEXPE Dist-UTEXPE

Tank Platoon In Fire And Movement C 26 MIN
16MM FILM OPTICAL SOUND
Demonstrates basic techniques of mass movement and of fire and movement operations, with emphasis on the platoon leader's responsibilities. Deals with factors that the platoon leader must consider when making decisions under combat conditions.
LC NO. 80-701843
Prod-USA Dist-USNAC 1980

Tanka C 9 MIN
16MM FILM OPTICAL SOUND
Portrays a vision of the peaceful and wrathful gods, derived from the Tibetan Book Of The Dead and photographed from Tibetan paintings in major American collections.
LC NO. 76-703160
Prod-LEBRUD Dist-CFS 1976

Tanker Safety Depends On You C 13 MIN
16MM FILM, 3/4 OR 1/2 IN VIDEO
Shows the explosion and fire of the Sensenina in Los Angeles Harbor. Explores the causes of tanker fires and explosions and stresses safety in elimination of all ignition sources.
Prod-USCG Dist-USNAC

Tankers - The Ocean's Pipeline C 26 MIN
3/4 OR 1/2 INCH VIDEO CASSETTE
Follows several supertankers and their crews along international routes, documents life at sea for the men of Chevron Shipping Company.
LC NO. 83-706984
Prod-CIM Dist-MTP 1983

Tanks, But No Thanks - Measuring Volume C 14 MIN
3/4 OR 1/2 INCH VIDEO CASSETTE P
Describes why Lionel is forced to admit that his eyes have fooled him.
From The Math Country Series.
Prod-KYTV Dist-AITECH 1979

Tanner 19 Procedure For Afferent Loop Syndrome C 23 MIN
3/4 OR 1/2 INCH VIDEO CASSETTE
See series title for descriptive statement.
From The Gastrointestinal Series.
Prod-SVL Dist-SVL

Tanya The Puppeteer C 25 MIN
16MM FILM, 3/4 OR 1/2 IN VIDEO J-C A
Introduces a Russian girl and shows her efforts to master the art of puppeteering.
From The World Cultures And Youth Series.
Prod-SUNRIS Dist-CORF 1981

Tanzania - The Quiet Revolution B 60 MIN
16MM FILM, 3/4 OR 1/2 IN VIDEO H-C A
Depicts the geography and peoples of Tanzania. Reveals problems of poverty, illiteracy and racism. President Nyerere explains his policy of nonalignment.
From The Changing World Series. No. 11
Prod-NET Dist-IU Prodn-WGBHTV 1964

Taoism C 15 MIN
16MM FILM OPTICAL SOUND H-C A
Studies the principles of Taoist philosophy and describes its effects on traditional Chinese thinking.
LC NO. 81-700282
Prod-HP Dist-HP 1981

Taoism C 22 MIN
3/4 OR 1/2 INCH VIDEO CASSETTE
Looks at Taoist philosophy in contemporary China.
Prod-HP Dist-HP

Taoism - A Question Of Balance C 52 MIN
16MM FILM, 3/4 OR 1/2 IN VIDEO H-C A
Examines the different types of religious beliefs that make up the spiritual life of Taiwan, including a Confucian respect for the past, the cosmic pattern of the Tao that manifests itself through oracles and the worship of local gods who dispense justice and favors.
From The Long Search Series. No. 11
LC NO. 79-707801
Prod-BBCTV Dist-TIMLIF 1978

Tap And Die Threading On The Lathe C
3/4 OR 1/2 INCH VIDEO CASSETTE
See series title for descriptive statement.
From The Intermediate Engine Lathe Operation Series.
Prod-VTRI Dist-VTRI

Tap And Die Threading On The Lathe C 15 MIN
3/4 OR 1/2 INCH VIDEO CASSETTE
See series title for descriptive statement.
From The Machine Technology III - Intermediate Engine Lathe Series.
Prod-CAMB Dist-CAMB

Tap And Die Threading On The Lathe C 15 MIN
3/4 OR 1/2 INCH VIDEO CASSETTE IND
See series title for descriptive statement.
From The Machining And The Operation Of Machine Tools, Module 3 - Intermediate Engine Lathe Series.
Prod-LEIKID Dist-LEIKID

Tap And Die Threading On The Lathe (Spanish) C
3/4 OR 1/2 INCH VIDEO CASSETTE
See series title for descriptive statement.
From The Intermediate Engine Lathe Operation (Spanish) Series.
Prod-VTRI Dist-VTRI

Tap Collar Closed Corners Fabrication C 9 MIN
1/2 IN VIDEO CASSETTE BETA/VHS IND
See series title for descriptive statement.
From The Metal Fabrication - Tap Collar Type Of Fittings Series.
Prod-RMI Dist-RMI

Tap Collar Open Corners Fabrication C 13 MIN
1/2 IN VIDEO CASSETTE BETA/VHS IND
See series title for descriptive statement.
From The Metal Fabrication - Tap Collar Type Of Fittings Series.
Prod-RMI Dist-RMI

Tap Dance Kid, The C 33 MIN
16MM FILM, 3/4 OR 1/2 IN VIDEO I-H
A shortened version of the motion picture The Tap Dance Kid. Shows how a father objects to his 8-year-old boy's desire to become a dancer until the boy's sister intervenes on behalf of children's rights and takes the boy to an audition.
Prod-LCOA Dist-LCOA 1978

Tap Dance Kid, The C 49 MIN
16MM FILM, 3/4 OR 1/2 IN VIDEO I-H
Shows how a father objects to his 8-year-old boy's desire to become a dancer until the boy's sister intervenes on behalf of children's rights and takes the boy to an audition.
Prod-LCOA Dist-LCOA 1978

Tap Dance Kid, The (Captioned) C 33 MIN
16MM FILM, 3/4 OR 1/2 IN VIDEO P-J A
Tells about an eight-year-old boy who dreams of being on Broadway a tap dancer, and the opposition he encounters from his father. Edited.
Prod-LCOA Dist-LCOA 1979

Tap Dance Kid, The (Captioned) C 49 MIN
16MM FILM, 3/4 OR 1/2 IN VIDEO P-J A
Tells about an eight-year-old boy who dreams of being on Broadway a tap dancer, and the opposition he encounters from his father. Full length version.
Prod-LCOA Dist-LCOA 1979

Tap Dance Kid, The (French) C 33 MIN
16MM FILM, 3/4 OR 1/2 IN VIDEO P-J A
Tells about an eight-year-old boy who dreams of being on Broadway as a tap dancer, and the opposition he encounters from his father.Edited version.
Prod-LCOA Dist-LCOA 1979

Tap Dance Kid, The (French) C 49 MIN
16MM FILM, 3/4 OR 1/2 IN VIDEO P-J A
Tells about an eight-year-old boy who dreams of being on Broadway a tap dancer, and the opposition he encounters from his father. Full length.
Prod-LCOA Dist-LCOA 1979

Tap Dance Kid, The (Spanish) C 33 MIN
16MM FILM, 3/4 OR 1/2 IN VIDEO P-J A
Tells the story of an eight-year-old boy who dreams of being on Broadway as a tap dancer, and the opposition he encounters from his father. Edited version.
Prod-LCOA Dist-LCOA 1979

Tap Dance Kid, The (Spanish) C 49 MIN
16MM FILM, 3/4 OR 1/2 IN VIDEO P-J A
Relates the story of an eight-year-old boy who dreams of being on Broadway as a tap dancer, and the opposition of his father. Spanish, French, and captioned versions. Unedited version.
Prod-LCOA Dist-LCOA 1979

Tape For Sam, A C 15 MIN
3/4 INCH VIDEO CASSETTE PRO
Dr. Hugh Leichtman shows how an audiotape is a practical tool for helping disturbed children. As director of Wediko Children's Services, he prepares an audiotape for a child's use after he leaves their summer camp. Shows how it is a lasting reminder of the interest and concern of those who worked with him over the summer, helping the child to focus on themes of personal therapy and growth.
LC NO. 82-706742
Prod-MASON Dist-DOCUFL 1981

Tape Kit Windshield Installation With Exposed Wipers C 28 MIN
1/2 IN VIDEO CASSETTE BETA/VHS
Deals with auto body repair. Describes the installation process from wire cut-out to pinch welt primer to tape installation.
Prod-RMI Dist-RMI

Tape 1 C
3/4 OR 1/2 INCH VIDEO CASSETTE IND
Covers paint composition.
From The Spray Paint Defects - Their Cause And Cure Series.
Prod-GMIEMI Dist-AMCEE

Tape 10 C
3/4 OR 1/2 INCH VIDEO CASSETTE IND
Covers crazing, fading, loss of gloss, peeling, poor hiding power and yellowing.
From The Spray Paint Defects - Their Cause And Cure Series.
Prod-GMIEMI Dist-AMCEE

Tape 2 C
3/4 OR 1/2 INCH VIDEO CASSETTE IND
Covers paint properties.
From The Spray Paint Defects - Their Cause And Cure Series.
Prod-GMIEMI Dist-AMCEE

Tape 3 C
3/4 OR 1/2 INCH VIDEO CASSETTE IND
Covers conventional air spray.
From The Spray Paint Defects - Their Cause And Cure Series.
Prod-GMIEMI Dist-AMCEE

Tape 4 C
3/4 OR 1/2 INCH VIDEO CASSETTE IND
Discusses airless, electrostatic and high speed rotary spray.
From The Spray Paint Defects - Their Cause And Cure Series.
Prod-GMIEMI Dist-AMCEE

Tape 5 C
3/4 OR 1/2 INCH VIDEO CASSETTE IND
Covers orange peel, sagging, cobwebbing, dry spray and low gloss.
From The Spray Paint Defects - Their Cause And Cure Series.
Prod-GMIEMI Dist-AMCEE

Tape 6 C
3/4 OR 1/2 INCH VIDEO CASSETTE IND
Illustrates bubbles, popping, fatty edges, striping and solvent washing.
From The Spray Paint Defects - Their Cause And Cure Series.
Prod-GMIEMI Dist-AMCEE

Tape 7 C
3/4 OR 1/2 INCH VIDEO CASSETTE IND
Covers fish eyes, blushing, mottle, wrinkling and water spotting.
From The Spray Paint Defects - Their Cause And Cure Series.
Prod-GMIEMI Dist-AMCEE

Tape 8 C
3/4 OR 1/2 INCH VIDEO CASSETTE IND
Talks about bleeding, color mis-match, oven fouling, seedy paint, blooming and over-spray cratering.
From The Spray Paint Defects - Their Cause And Cure Series.
Prod-GMIEMI Dist-AMCEE

Tape 9 C
3/4 OR 1/2 INCH VIDEO CASSETTE IND
Covers blisters, bronzing, chalking, chipping, corrosion and cracking.
From The Spray Paint Defects - Their Cause And
Prod-GMIEMI Dist-AMCEE

Taper Key Installation And Removal C 14 MIN
16MM FILM, 3/4 OR 1/2 IN VIDEO IND
Shows how to measure the keyway for correct size and taper, how the key is machined and how to fit the key for the best results. Demonstrates three different ways of removing a stubborn key.
Prod-MOKIN Dist-MOKIN

Taper Key, Installation And Removal C 14 MIN
3/4 OR 1/2 INCH VIDEO CASSETTE IND
Shows how to measure the keyway for correct size and taper, how the key is machined and how to fit the key for the best results. Demonstrates three different ways of removing a stubborn key.
From The Marshall Maintenance Training Programs Series. Tape 10
Prod-LEIKID Dist-LEIKID

Taper Turning C 14 MIN
16MM FILM, 3/4 OR 1/2 IN VIDEO IND
Shows operation, application and limitations of the compound slide, taper turning attachment, form tools, free hand turning, profile turning attachment and offset tailstock.
From The Vocational Skillfilms - Machine Shop Skills Series.
Prod-RTBL Dist-RTBL 1982

Taper Turning (Spanish) C
16MM FILM, 3/4 OR 1/2 IN VIDEO A
Portrays operation, application and limitations of the compound slide, taper turning attachment, form tools, free hand turning, profile turning attachment and offset tailstock.
From The Vocational Skillfilms - Machine Shop Skills Series.
Prod-RTBL Dist-RTBL

Taper Turning On A Lathe C 15 MIN
3/4 OR 1/2 INCH VIDEO CASSETTE
See series title for descriptive statement.
From The Machine Technology I - Basic Machine Technology Series.
Prod-CAMB Dist-CAMB

Taper Turning On A Lathe C 15 MIN
3/4 OR 1/2 INCH VIDEO CASSETTE IND
See series title for descriptive statement.
From The Machining And The Operation Of Machine Tools, Module 2 - Engine Lathe Series.
Prod-LEIKID Dist-LEIKID

Taper Turning On The Lathe C
3/4 OR 1/2 INCH VIDEO CASSETTE
See series title for descriptive statement.
From The Basic Engine Lathe Series.
Prod-VTRI Dist-VTRI

Taper Turning On The Lathe (Spanish) C
3/4 OR 1/2 INCH VIDEO CASSETTE
See series title for descriptive statement.
From The Basic Engine Lathe (Spanish) Series.
Prod-VTRI Dist-VTRI

Tapestry C 25 MIN
3/4 OR 1/2 INCH VIDEO CASSETTE J-C A
Portrays some of the work of the Edinburgh Tapestry Company. Presents the work of Fiona Mathison and Archie Brennan. Includes Coptic and Peruvian work from the Royal Scottish Museum.
From The Craft Of The Weaver Series.
Prod-BBCTV Dist-FI 1983

Tapir Distribution C 15 MIN
16MM FILM - 3/4 IN VIDEO
Shows how a Yanamamo headman uses the gift of tapir meat to reinforce an alliance with his in-laws.
Prod-DOCEDR Dist-DOCEDR

Tapping The Source C 18 MIN
16MM FILM OPTICAL SOUND
Traces the history of the Sun's role as a primary energy source. Includes interviews which reveal how solar power is used in providing energy for home use.
LC NO. 78-701511
Prod-LILC Dist-LILC Prodn-GLYNG 1978

Tapping Threads On The Engine Lathe C 22 MIN
1/2 IN VIDEO CASSETTE BETA/VHS IND
See series title for descriptive statement.
From The Machine Shop - Engine Lathe Series.
Prod-RMI Dist-RMI

Tar Baby B 18 MIN
16MM FILM OPTICAL SOUND
Shows the dynamics at work when three inner-city residents encounter each other and find their lives altered by that encounter.
LC NO. 76-701407
Prod-UMD Dist-UMD Prodn-ROBINE 1975

Tar Pit, The - Death Trap Of The Ages C 20 MIN
2 INCH VIDEOTAPE I
See series title for descriptive statement.
From The Exploring With Science, Unit XII - Prehistory series.
Prod-MPATI Dist-GPITVL

Tar Sands - Future Fuel C 27 MIN
16MM FILM OPTICAL SOUND
Considers the practicality of the United States' development of tar sands deposits. Asks if the deposits are needed to supplement and thereby conserve conventional fuels.
From The Energy Sources - A New Beginning Series.
Prod-UCOLO Dist-UCOLO

Tara, The Stonecutter C 8 MIN
16MM FILM, 3/4 OR 1/2 IN VIDEO I-C A
Presents the Japanese folktale of Tara, the stonecutter.
Prod-AIMS Dist-AIMS 1962

Tara, The Stonecutter (Spanish) C 8 MIN
16MM FILM, 3/4 OR 1/2 IN VIDEO K-I
A Japanese folktale of a poor stonecutter who desires to be emperor, the sun, the mountain and finally himself once again.
Prod-CAHILL Dist-AIMS 1955

Tara's Mulch Garden C 21 MIN
16MM FILM, 3/4 OR 1/2 IN VIDEO J-C A
Explains that vegetable gardening through the use of mulch is a low-cost way of feeding one's family, using a minimum of tools and no chemical fertilizers or pesticides.
Prod-NFBC Dist-WOMBAT

Tarahumara, The C 30 MIN
16MM FILM OPTICAL SOUND J-H A
Offers one a unique insight into the workings of the Tarahumara Indians of Mexico. Shows the famous runners of Tarahumara.
LC NO. 85-703553
Prod-BYU Dist-EBEC 1983

Tarahumara, The C 15 MIN
3/4 OR 1/2 INCH VIDEO CASSETTE I
Introduces the Tarahumara Indians of Mexico, an independent, hardworking people who live and farm in the mountain valleys and canyons. Shows that their isolation helps insure stability and so they ask little of and extend little to the world beyond their mountains.
From The Across Cultures Series.
Prod-POSIMP Dist-AITECH Prodn-WETN 1983

Taram - A Minangkabau Village C 22 MIN
16MM FILM OPTICAL SOUND H-C A
Examines the matrilineal social structure of a Minangkabau village in Indonesia.
From The Asian Neighbors - Indonesia Series.
LC NO. 75-703587
Prod-FLMAUS Dist-AVIS 1975

Target - For Antares C 16 MIN
16MM FILM OPTICAL SOUND
Uses micro-cinematography and animation to describe the fabrication of microscopic targets, which are used to generate energy through laser-fusion techniques.
LC NO. 78-700313
Prod-LASL Dist-LASL 1978

Target - Quackery B 12 MIN
3/4 OR 1/2 INCH VIDEO CASSETTE
Discusses the first efforts to combat quack medicine in the treatment of arthritis. Includes footage from hearings held by the U S Senate in 1962.
Prod-WSTGLC Dist-WSTGLC

Target - Tokyo C 30 MIN
3/4 OR 1/2 INCH VIDEO CASSETTE H-C A
See series title for descriptive statement.
From The World War II - GI Diary Series.
Prod-TIMLIF Dist-TIMLIF 1980

Target Five C 48 MIN
3/4 OR 1/2 INCH VIDEO CASSETTE
Demonstrates four manipulative response forms demonstrated by a family situation. Describes the three essential qualities of an actualizing relationship.
Prod-PSYCHD Dist-PSYCHD

Target Five, Pt 1 C 26 MIN
16MM FILM OPTICAL SOUND C A
Features psychologist Virginia Satir as she demonstrates the four manipulative response forms in cooperation with Everett L Shostron.
LC NO. 74-703169
Prod-PSYCHF Dist-PSYCHD 1969

Target Five, Pt 2 C 22 MIN
16MM FILM OPTICAL SOUND C A
Provides a description of the three essential qualities of an actualizing relationship, hearing and listening, understanding and mutual meaning.
LC NO. 74-703169
Prod-PSYCHF Dist-PSYCHD 1969

Target For Antares C 17 MIN
16MM FILM OPTICAL SOUND J-C A
Describes the construction of microscopic fuel targets for use with high power lasers to create fusion energy.
LC NO. 78-700313
Prod-LASL Dist-LASL 1978

Target For Terror C 18 MIN
16MM FILM OPTICAL SOUND
Uses a fictionalized burglary incident in order to show how to install security improvements in homes.
LC NO. 75-700088
Prod-WEIFAL Dist-WEIFAL Prodn-CHENRB 1974

Target For Today B 92 MIN
3/4 OR 1/2 INCH VIDEO CASSETTE
Presents a detailed account of the operations of a bombing mission by the U S 8th Air Force from planning to execution. Features actual 8th Air Force personnel on location.
Prod-IHF Dist-IHF

Target For Tonight B 50 MIN
3/4 OR 1/2 INCH VIDEO CASSETTE
Views a single action of war, involving a Wellington bomber whose crew are ordered to Germany to destroy oil-storage tanks at Kiel during World War II.
Prod-IHF Dist-IHF

Target Markets C 30 MIN
3/4 OR 1/2 INCH VIDEO CASSETTE
Explains 'market segmentation,' demographic factors which can be used for segmentation. Addresses psychographics and their relationship to the segmentation process.
From The Marketing Perspectives Series.
Prod-MATC Dist-WFVTAE

Target Moon (2nd Ed) C 24 MIN
16MM FILM, 3/4 OR 1/2 IN VIDEO I-C A
Presents a study of American and Russian attempts to reach the moon that emphasizes the physics and reasons for the effort. Reviews man's age-old striving to go to the moon, indicating how scientific curiosity and national rivalries have spurred it on. Focuses on the Apollo project.
From The Man Into Space - The Story Of Rockets And Space Science Series.
Prod-ACI Dist-AIMS 1974

Target Nevada C 14 MIN
16MM FILM, 3/4 OR 1/2 IN VIDEO
Tells the story of the USAF support to the Atomic Energy Commission in atomic testing. Shows all phases of preparation, detonation and aftereffects of a nuclear test.
Prod-USDD Dist-USNAC

Target Nicaragua - 1983 C 40 MIN
16MM FILM, 3/4 OR 1/2 IN VIDEO
Reports on a covert war carried out by the CIA against the Sandinista government of Nicaragua.
Prod-STDC Dist-NEWTIM

Target Suribachi B 27 MIN
16MM FILM, 3/4 OR 1/2 IN VIDEO J-H
Shows the Battle for Iwo Jima during World War II.
From The Victory At Sea Series.
Prod-NBCTV Dist-LUF

Target Suribachi - Iwo Jima B 30 MIN
16MM FILM OPTICAL SOUND I-C
Depicts the battle for Iwo Jima, the most concentrated naval bombardment of World War II. Explains that Iwo Jima provided an indispensable air base for the Allies.
From The Victory At Sea Series.
Prod-GRACUR Dist-GRACUR

Target Tokyo B 22 MIN
16MM FILM, 3/4 OR 1/2 IN VIDEO
Follows the training of a B-29 crew from the training center at Grand Island, NE, to a mission over Tokyo in World War II.
Prod-USAF Dist-USNAC

Target Tooth Decay X 11 MIN
16MM FILM OPTICAL SOUND
Stresses the place of modern dental care, including the sodium fluoride treatment, in the community health program.
Prod-UOKLA Dist-UOKLA

Target Within Range - The Key Role Of The USAF Navigator C 19 MIN
16MM FILM OPTICAL SOUND
Depicts the diversified mission of the USAF navigator who works around the clock and around the world to keep America's defensive and offensive power effectively poised.
Prod-USDD Dist-USNAC 1960

Target Zone, The - Aiming For Whole Body Fitness C 30 MIN
16MM FILM, 3/4 OR 1/2 IN VIDEO A
Explains how to design an optimum, aerobic conditioning program.
LC NO. 84-706503
Prod-LISNDO Dist-PFP 1984

Target 100 Per Cent Plus C 18 MIN
16MM FILM OPTICAL SOUND
Presents information on how diet and nutrition affect cystic fibrosis and how good nutrition practiced in family home diets can help with energy and growth needs.
LC NO. 80-700222
Prod-JAJ Dist-RNBWP Prodn-RNBWP 1979

Targets C 19 MIN
16MM FILM, 3/4 OR 1/2 IN VIDEO J-C
Emphasizes that teenagers do not have to be alone when dealing with such personal problems as molestation, domestic violence, alcoholism or peer pressure.
From The Anti-Victimization Series.
Prod-MTI Dist-MTI

Tarjetas De Seguridad B 18 MIN
16MM FILM, 3/4 OR 1/2 IN VIDEO J-C A
A Spanish-language version of the motion picture It's In The Cards. Illustrates the importance of obeying rules of safety rather than depending on luck.
Prod-ABPPCO Dist-IFB Prodn-CRAF 1963

Tarnished Badge C 24 MIN
16MM FILM, 3/4 OR 1/2 IN VIDEO
Details the downfall of an experienced sergeant who succumbs to the temptations of corruption. Looks at the consequences of the sergeant's act to his self-esteem, financial security, family, fellow officers and department.
Prod-WORON Dist-MTI

Tarpon C 22 MIN
16MM FILM OPTICAL SOUND
Looks at the behavior of tarpon and highlights the mysterious occurrance known as daisy chaining.
Prod-BRNSWK Dist-KAROL

Tartes Aux Fruits C 29 MIN
2 INCH VIDEOTAPE
A French language videotape. Features Julia Child of Haute Cuisine au Vin demonstrating how to prepare tartes aux fruits. With captions.
From The French Chef (French) Series.
Prod-WGBHTV Dist-PUBTEL

Tartuffe (German) B 71 MIN
16MM FILM SILENT
A silent motion picture with German subtitles. Tells the story of Tartuffe, loosely based on Moliere's classical work of the same name.
Prod-WSTGLC Dist-WSTGLC

Tarzan Of The Apes B 66 MIN
16MM FILM SILENT
Tells how an English infant is lost in the jungle and emerges as a brawny hero. Stars Elmo Lincoln.
Prod-UNKNWN Dist-KITPAR 1918

Task - Theory, Structure And Application B 45 MIN
16MM FILM OPTICAL SOUND
Demonstrates the cycle of action of the task from the signal for attention through reinforced performance, applying it to pre-reading and pre-arithmetic tasks.
Prod-ADL Dist-ADL

Task Analysis - An Aid To Planning And Teaching C 50 MIN
3/4 OR 1/2 INCH VIDEO CASSETTE IND
See series title for descriptive statement.
From The Task Analysis And Job Instructor Training Series.
Prod-NCSU Dist-AMCEE

Task Analysis And Job Instructor Training–A Series
IND
Notes that use of task analysis is a proven instructional approach, that benefits of well trained employees include higher job satisfaction, greater self-confidence, higher productivity, fewer mistakes and accidents, less rework and lost time, better quality products and more satisfied customers. Assists participants in using task analysis as an aid to planning, teaching, applying and evaluating instruction.
Prod-NCSU Dist-AMCEE

Developing A Course Of Study Using Task
Developing Lesson Plans 050 MIN
Evaluation 050 MIN
Instructional Aids And Devices 050 MIN
Introduction 050 MIN
Principles Of Learning 050 MIN
Summary And Posttest 050 MIN
Task Analysis - An Aid To Planning And Teaching 050 MIN
Teaching Techniques 050 MIN
Writing Instructional Objectives Using Task 050 MIN

Task Centered Approach, Initial Phase B 60 MIN
3/4 OR 1/2 INCH VIDEO CASSETTE
Demonstrates 'initial screening' interview techniques. Illustrates the task oriented techniques to reduce the client's anxiety.
Prod-UCHI Dist-UCHI 1975

Task Centered Casework, Pt I C 60 MIN
3/4 OR 1/2 INCH VIDEO CASSETTE
Consists of two role play sessions with a client and therapist. Provides suggestions for improving study habits of college students having problems with school.
Prod-UWASH Dist-UWISC

Task Centered Casework, Pt II C 50 MIN
3/4 OR 1/2 INCH VIDEO CASSETTE
Presents two role play sessions between a therapist and client, who is not sure she wants to complete her pregnancy.
Prod-UWASH Dist-UWISC

Task Centered Interviews With A Phobic Client B 30 MIN
3/4 OR 1/2 INCH VIDEO CASSETTE
Consists of several short interviews with a phobic client who is afraid to go outside alone. Shows how the client progresses by following exercises prescribed by therapist.
Prod-UCHI Dist-UWISC 1976

Task Descriptions/Task Analysis C
3/4 OR 1/2 INCH VIDEO CASSETTE T
See series title for descriptive statement.
From The Learning System Design Series. Unit 3
Prod-MSU Dist-MSU

Task Force South - The Battle For The Falklands C 120 MIN
3/4 OR 1/2 INCH VIDEO CASSETTE H-C A
Reveals the background which led to Britain's battle for the Falkland Islands, Britain's biggest and bloodiest military operation since World War II.
Prod-BBCTV Dist-FI 1982

Task Of The Teacher C 43 MIN
16MM FILM OPTICAL SOUND T
Illustrates and analyzes the qualities, talents, skills and techniques necessary for teachers in informal English schools. Shows children through age 12 in eight schools. Depicts buildings with modern open-plans and older structures in both suburban and urban settings. Describes team teaching, resource centers, individual and group studies and work with children of mixed abilities.
LC NO. 73-703424
Prod-STOCKC Dist-AGAPR 1973

Task-Centered Family Contracting Session With Jim Goetz B 30 MIN
3/4 OR 1/2 INCH VIDEO CASSETTE
Presents a contracting session with a marital couple in which the social worker explores potential target problems, arrives at an agreement on priority problems and beginning task work is developed.
Prod-UWISC Dist-UWISC 1979

Task-Centered Treatment With A Marital Couple C 60 MIN
3/4 OR 1/2 INCH VIDEO CASSETTE
Presents a task-centered session with a marital couple. Develops tasks in an attempt to interrupt and change the identified cycle. Includes narration, charts of main points and a discussion by Prof Rooney.
Prod-UWISC Dist-UWISC 1980

Tasks Of Teaching, Pt 1 C 30 MIN
3/4 OR 1/2 INCH VIDEO CASSETTE T
See series title for descriptive statement.
From The Protocol Materials In Teacher Education - The Process Of Teaching, Pt 1 Series.
Prod-MSU Dist-MSU

Tasks Of Teaching, Pt 2 C 20 MIN
3/4 OR 1/2 INCH VIDEO CASSETTE T
See series title for descriptive statement.
From The Protocol Materials In Teacher Education - The Process Of Teaching, Pt 1 Series.
Prod-MSU Dist-MSU

Tasmania, Australia C 18 MIN
16MM FILM OPTICAL SOUND
Describes the business potential and personal satisfaction that can be achieved by migrants establishing themselves in Tasmania.
LC NO. 80-801575
Prod-TASCOR Dist-TASCOR 1980

Tasmanian Forests - Where And Why C 7 MIN
16MM FILM OPTICAL SOUND
Features a variety of Tasmanian forests and explains why particular types of forests may be found in particular areas.
LC NO. 80-700927
Prod-TASCOR Dist-TASCOR 1976

Tasmanian Military Tattoo C 28 MIN
16MM FILM OPTICAL SOUND
Presents a record of Tasmania's first Tattoo which was modeled on the Edinburgh Tattoo.
LC NO. 80-700928
Prod-TASCOR Dist-TASCOR 1976

Tassili N'ajjer - Prehistoric Rock Paintings Of The Sahara (Neolithic-2000 BC) C 16 MIN
16MM FILM OPTICAL SOUND
Presents prehistoric rock paintings of the Sahara Desert from the Neolithic period to 2000 BC.
Prod-ROLAND Dist-ROLAND

Taste Of China—A Series
16MM FILM, 3/4 OR 1/2 IN VIDEO J-C A
Presents Kenneth Lo, a foremost authority on Chinese food, assisted by gourmet personality Vincent Price and well-known Chinese chefs preparing a complete Chinese meal in each program of this series.
Prod-THAMES Dist-MEDIAG 1983

Taste Of China—A Series
16MM FILM, 3/4 OR 1/2 IN VIDEO J-C A
Shows various regions of China and the cuisines which are typical of the area.
LC NO. 84-707744
Prod-UCEMC Dist-UCEMC 1984

Family Table, The 029 MIN
Food For Body And Spirit 029 MIN
Masters Of The Wok 029 MIN
Water Farmers 029 MIN

Taste Of China, Pt 1 - Rice C 38 MIN
3/4 OR 1/2 INCH VIDEO CASSETTE J-C A
Presents Kenneth Lo, a foremost authority on Chinese food, assisted by gourmet personality Vincent Price and well-known Chinese chefs preparing and serving a complete Chinese meal.
From The Taste Of China Series.
Prod-THAMES Dist-MEDIAG 1983

Taste Of China, Pt 2 - Noodles C 38 MIN
3/4 OR 1/2 INCH VIDEO CASSETTE J-C A
Presents Kenneth Lo, a foremost authority on Chinese food, assisted by gourmet personality Vincent Price and well-known Chinese chefs preparing and serving a complete Chinese meal.
From The Taste Of China Series.
Prod-THAMES Dist-MEDIAG 1983

Taste Of China, Pt 3 - Meal And Fish C 38 MIN
3/4 OR 1/2 INCH VIDEO CASSETTE J-C A
Presents Kenneth Lo, a foremost authority on Chinese food, assisted by gourmet personality Vincent Price and well-known Chinese chefs preparing and serving a complete Chinese meal.
From The Taste Of China Series.
Prod-THAMES Dist-MEDIAG 1983

Taste Of China, Pt 4 - Chicken And Duck C 38 MIN
3/4 OR 1/2 INCH VIDEO CASSETTE J-C A
Presents Kenneth Lo, a foremost authority on Chinese food, assisted by gourmet personality Vincent Price and well-known Chinese chefs preparing and serving a complete Chinese meal.
From The Taste Of China Series.
Prod-THAMES Dist-MEDIAG 1983

Taste Of China, Pt 5 - Buffet Of Chinese Food C 38 MIN
3/4 OR 1/2 INCH VIDEO CASSETTE J-C A
Presents Kenneth Lo, a foremost authority on Chinese food, assisted by gourmet personality Vincent Price and well-known Chinese chefs preparing and serving a complete Chinese meal.
From The Taste Of China Series.
Prod-THAMES Dist-MEDIAG 1983

Taste Of Nutrition, A C 10 MIN
16MM FILM OPTICAL SOUND
Illustrates the importance of nutrition workshops. Shows that teaching nutrition can be fun.
LC NO. 75-701933
Prod-INMILK Dist-VIP Prodn-INST 1974

Taste Of Paradise, A C 26 MIN
16MM FILM OPTICAL SOUND
Tells the history of the pineapple and how it is planted, cultivated and harvested in Hawaii. Highlights the discovery of pineapple by Columbus, its introduction to the western world and the development of the Hawaiian pineapple.
Prod-PINEH Dist-MTP 1982

Taste, Smell, Hearing C 29 MIN
3/4 INCH VIDEO CASSETTE C A
Compares senses of taste, smell, and hearing. Describes functions and physiology of these senses with special attention to hearing. Shows footage of sound waves.
From The Understanding Human Behavior - An Introduction To Psychology Series. Lesson 7
Prod-COAST Dist-CDTEL

Tasteful Romance C 6 MIN
16MM FILM OPTICAL SOUND
Uses animation to create comedy, romance and adventure around a boy-meets-girl theme in a fantasy candyland inhabited by two walking lip characters.
LC NO. 79-700291
Prod-COLCLI Dist-COLCLI 1978

Tastes C 15 MIN
2 INCH VIDEOTAPE K
Identifies many kinds of matter by a characteristic taste.
From The Let's Go Sciencing, Unit I - Matter Series.
Prod-DETPS Dist-GPITVL

Tasting C 4 MIN
16MM FILM, 3/4 OR 1/2 IN VIDEO K-I
Presents Fumble's monkey pointing out the different areas of the tongue as the children try out sweet, salty and sour tastes.
From The Most Important Person - Senses Series.
Prod-EBEC Dist-EBEC

Tasting And Smelling B 20 MIN
16MM FILM OPTICAL SOUND C A
See series title for descriptive statement.
From The All That I Am Series.
Prod-MPATI Dist-NWUFLM

Tasting Party C 4 MIN
16MM FILM, 3/4 OR 1/2 IN VIDEO K-I
Views Fumble, bird and the children enjoying blueberry blintzes, tacos, ravioli and stuffed peppers.
From The Most Important Person - Nutrition Series.
Prod-EBEC Dist-EBEC 1972

Tatara - An Old Iron Making Process Of Japan C 30 MIN
16MM FILM OPTICAL SOUND
Explains that the word 'TATARA' was recorded as early as the eighth century, referring to the traditional process of making iron and steel from iron sand with charcoal. Advocates that this process still produces excellent iron and steel.
Prod-IWANMI Dist-UNIJAP 1970

Tatting, Hairpin Lace And Broomstick Lace C 52 MIN
1/2 IN VIDEO CASSETTE BETA/VHS
Explains how to tat with heavy or fine cord and string. Describes the proper way to thread a shuttle and how to make a shawl, blanket and belt.
Prod-RMI Dist-RMI

Tatting, Hairpine Lace And Broomstick Lace C 52 MIN
1/2 IN VIDEO CASSETTE BETA/VHS
Shows how to tat with heavy or fine cord and string. Demonstrates the proper way to thread a shuttle. Shows how to make a shawl, blanket and belt.
From The Crafts And Decorating Series.
Prod-MOHOMV Dist-MOHOMV

Tattoo C 26 MIN
16MM FILM OPTICAL SOUND
Explores reasons for the popularity of tattoos and examines the American subculture associated with tattooing and heavily tattooed people.
LC NO. 79-700292
Prod-DECDER Dist-DECDER 1979

Tattooed Man, The C 35 MIN
16MM FILM OPTICAL SOUND
Presents an underground art film about the children of the water and the tattooed man.
Prod-IMPACT Dist-IMPACT

Tattooed Tears C 85 MIN
16MM FILM, 3/4 OR 1/2 IN VIDEO H-C A
Looks inside a California youth detention center and training school. Captures the oppressive daily routine and encounters between inmates and their guardians. Raises questions about the presumed goal of rehabilitation or the system's ability to cause any real change in such alienated young men.
Prod-CF Dist-CF 1978

Tatyana Mamonova, Russian Feminist C 60 MIN
3/4 INCH VIDEO CASSETTE
Introduces Tatyana Mamonova, Russian Feminist on her visit to Canada. She answers questions about her life and the condition of women in the Soviet Union.
Prod-AMELIA Dist-WMENIF

Taurus-Gulf Trade Incident, The B 3 MIN
16MM FILM OPTICAL SOUND
Describes the collision of the gulf trade and the Taurus and the causes of the accident.
LC NO. FIE52-946
Prod-USN Dist-USNAC 1944

Tauu - En Atoll I Stillehavet (Tauu - An Atoll In The Pacific) C 32 MIN
16MM FILM OPTICAL SOUND
A Danish langauge film. Portrays the daily life of the population on Tauu, a Pacific atoll. Shows how different articles are manufactured for local use.
Prod-STATNS Dist-STATNS 1967

Tauw C 27 MIN
16MM FILM OPTICAL SOUND
A study of the new generation in Africa as evidenced in the life of 20-year-old Tauw. Demonstrates the young man's hopes and frustrations, the gap between his life style and that of his parents and his struggle with the realities of life in a developing nation. Filmed in Dakar.
LC NO. 77-711517
Prod-CCNCC Dist-CCNCC 1970

Tavern Celebration, A C 15 MIN
16MM FILM, 3/4 OR 1/2 IN VIDEO
See series title for descriptive statement.
From The Rudolf Nureyev's Film Of Don Quixote Series.
Prod-WRO Dist-SF Prodn-IARTS 1978

Tawny Scrawny Lion C 6 MIN
16MM FILM, 3/4 OR 1/2 IN VIDEO P
Relates the story of how a scrawny, irritable lion learns how to be healthy and happy from a rabbit.
From The Golden Book Storytime Films Series.
Prod-MTI Dist-MTI 1977

Tawny Scrawny Lion C 7 MIN
16MM FILM, 3/4 OR 1/2 IN VIDEO K-P
Presents a story about how a proud, fat, little rabbit helps his animal friends by outwitting a hungry, tawny, scrawny lion. Shows that through the things he does, the little rabbit not only makes a friend of the lion but he also finds a way to satisfy the lion's hunger. Emphasizes that it is not one's size that is important but rather it is the quality of thinking and doing that counts.
Prod-WPES Dist-BARR 1974

Tax Aspects Of Divorce With Professor Frank E A Sander, Pt 1 C 52 MIN
3/4 OR 1/2 INCH VIDEO CASSETTE PRO
Examines income, estate and gift tax problems arising from marriage dissolution or separation, including alimony and separate maintenance, child support, transfers of property and use of alimony trusts.
From The NPI Video CLE Series. Vol 6
LC NO. 80-706567
Prod-NPRI Dist-NPRI 1978

Tax Aspects Of Divorce With Professor Frank E A Sander, Pt 2 C 52 MIN
3/4 OR 1/2 INCH VIDEO CASSETTE PRO
Examines income, estate and gift tax problems arising from marriage dissolution or separation, including alimony and separate maintenance, child support, transfers of property and use of alimony trusts.
From The NPI Video CLE Series. Vol 6
LC NO. 80-706567
Prod-NPRI Dist-NPRI 1978

Tax Aspects Of Divorce With Professor Frank E A Sander, Pt 3 C 53 MIN
3/4 OR 1/2 INCH VIDEO CASSETTE PRO
Examines income, estate and gift tax problems arising from marriage dissolution or separation, including alimony and separate maintenance, child support, transfers of property and use of alimony trusts.
From The NPI Video CLE Series. Vol 6
LC NO. 80-706567
Prod-NPRI Dist-NPRI 1978

Tax Aspects Of Divorce With Professor Frank E A Sander, Pt 4 C 53 MIN
3/4 OR 1/2 INCH VIDEO CASSETTE PRO
Examines income, estate and gift tax problems arising from marriage dissolution or separation, including alimony and separate maintenance, child support, transfers of property and use of alimony trusts.
From The NPI Video CLE Series. Vol 6
LC NO. 80-706567
Prod-NPRI Dist-NPRI 1978

Tax Reform Act Of 1984 - Overview C 30 MIN
3/4 OR 1/2 INCH VIDEO CASSETTE PRO
See series title for descriptive statement.
From The Tax Reform Act Of 1984 Series.
Prod-ALIABA Dist-ALIABA

Tax Reform Act Of 1984—A Series
PRO
Presents questions on the Tax Reform Act of 1984 with answers by the individuals from government who developed the legislation.
Prod-ALIABA Dist-ALIABA

Accounting, Deferred Payments, Time Value Of
Corporate Provisions - Subchapter C 030 MIN
Domestic Relations 030 MIN
Foreign Tax 030 MIN
Fringe Benefits And Cafeteria Plans 030 MIN
Government And Tax-Exempt Entity Leasing 030 MIN
IDB's 030 MIN
Insurance 030 MIN
Partnerships 030 MIN
Provisions Affecting Qualified Plans 030 MIN
Tax Reform Act Of 1984 - Overview 030 MIN
Tax Shelters 030 MIN
VEBA's 030 MIN

Tax Shelters C 30 MIN
3/4 OR 1/2 INCH VIDEO CASSETTE PRO
Presents questions on tax shelters as affected by the Tax Reform Act of 1984 with answers by the individuals from government who developed the legislation.
From The Tax Reform Act Of 1984 Series.
Prod-ALIABA Dist-ALIABA

Tax-Saving Strategies C 30 MIN
3/4 OR 1/2 INCH VIDEO CASSETTE C A
Presents some of the more common strategies that can be used to minimize the amount of federal income tax that must be paid. Includes tax exempt and tax-deferred income, income splitting and tax shelters. Explores procedures for filing tax returns and surviving an audit.
From The Personal Finance Series. Lesson 26
Prod-SCCON Dist-CDTEL

Taxation C 11 MIN
16MM FILM OPTICAL SOUND
Shows that with proper planning and record keeping, a businessman can avoid paying more taxes that the law intends.
From The Running Your Own Business Series.
Prod-EFD Dist-EFD

Taxation - What And When C 30 MIN
3/4 OR 1/2 INCH VIDEO CASSETTE
Presents a comprehensive look at the wide variety of taxes from estate tax to tax on capital gains. Also looks at tax exclusions and deductibles, required taxes and post-mortem tax planning.
From The This Is My Will Series.
Prod-WMHTTV Dist-PBS 1983

Taxation And Public Policy C 30 MIN
3/4 OR 1/2 INCH VIDEO CASSETTE C
Discusses taxation and public policy.
From The Accounting Series. Pt 9
Prod-UMA Dist-GPITVL 1980

Taxation Without Representation C 16 MIN
16MM FILM, 3/4 OR 1/2 IN VIDEO I-J
Explains how the years of peace and prosperity ended with the levying of the Sugar and Stamp Acts and later the Townshend Acts.
From The American History - Birth Of A Nation Series.
Prod-AIMS Dist-AIMS 1967

Taxes - Who Needs Them C 25 MIN
16MM FILM, 3/4 OR 1/2 IN VIDEO I-C A
Enumerates some of the taxes the average citizen has to pay,

such as taxes on income, property, sales and excise taxes on certain items. Points out the many services that are financed by taxes, such as the police, courts, fire departments, health services and others.
Prod-HANDEL Dist-HANDEL 1974

Taxes - Why We Have Them C 14 MIN
16MM FILM, 3/4 OR 1/2 IN VIDEO
Explains why taxes have increased during the history of the United States. Describes the kinds of taxes collected by the three levels of government. Defines progressive and regressive taxes and the advantages and disadvantages of each and classifies some criteria needed to balance taxes and services.
Prod-GREENF Dist-PHENIX 1978

Taxes, Taxes C 27 MIN
16MM FILM, 3/4 OR 1/2 IN VIDEO
Discusses the U S tax system including who pays, how much and the possibilities of reform.
Prod-SCHLP Dist-RBFLM 1978

Taxi C 58 MIN
3/4 OR 1/2 INCH VIDEO CASSETTE A
Interviews drivers, fleet owners and dispatchers and pairs their comments with images revealing cab school students unable to pinpoint major streets and locations and cabbies dealing with assorted colorful customers.
LC NO. 84-707118
Prod-HAMMOA Dist-NFBC 1983

Taxi Driver C 112 MIN
16MM FILM OPTICAL SOUND
Focuses on a New York cab driver who becomes compulsively involved with the city's 'night people.' Directed by Martin Scorcese.
Prod-CPC Dist-SWANK

Taxonomy C 45 MIN
3/4 OR 1/2 INCH VIDEO CASSETTE C
Deals with the ways species are classified.
From The Biology I Series.
Prod-MDCPB Dist-MDCPB

Taxonomy - How Living Organisms Differ C
3/4 OR 1/2 INCH VIDEO CASSETTE H
Introduces the principles of taxonomy and explains Linnaeus' system of classification of related groups. Examines different types of organisms and explains why scientists research fossils, genes, anatomy and physiology in their efforts to determine how organisms should be classified.
Prod-GA Dist-GA

Taxwise Giving C 29 MIN
3/4 OR 1/2 INCH VIDEO CASSETTE
Presents tax attorney Conrad Teitell and narrator Carter Randall discussing the ways in which the tax laws can be used to maximize the benefits of giving for both the donor and the recipient.
LC NO. 82-707042
Prod-KVIETV Dist-PBS 1982

Taylor Approximations B
16MM FILM OPTICAL SOUND
Deals with Taylor approximations, Taylor's theorem, and the three different forms of remainder of the Taylor polynomial.
Prod-OPENU Dist-OPENU

Taylor Polynomials C 24 MIN
16MM FILM, 3/4 OR 1/2 IN VIDEO
Discusses Taylor polynomials.
Prod-OPENU Dist-MEDIAG Prodn-BBCTV 1979

Taylor Series B
16MM FILM OPTICAL SOUND
Deals with the convergence of general complex power series and the definition of the circle of convergence. Asks whether the function defined by a convergent power series is analytic. Describes the result of analytic continuation which guarantees uniqueness when a real power series is extended to include complex variables.
Prod-OPENU Dist-OPENU

Tch, Tch, Tch, What A Way To Build A Railroad C 10 MIN
16MM FILM OPTICAL SOUND
Follows the steps in building a railroad from planning to completion, covering engineering, machines and machinists. Includes animation and split-screen optical effects.
LC NO. 70-712854
Prod-SPRRC Dist-FILCOM 1969

Tchaikovsky And The Russians C 26 MIN
16MM FILM, 3/4 OR 1/2 IN VIDEO H-C A
Tells how a new form of classical choreography resulted from the fusion in Russia of French and Italian traditions. Presents the grand pas de deux from Sleeping Beauty and from The Bluebird.
From The Ballet For All Series.
Prod-THAMES Dist-MEDIAG 1978

Tchaikovsky Competition - Violin And Piano, Victoria Mullora Et Al C 90 MIN
3/4 OR 1/2 INCH VIDEO CASSETTE
Prod-MSTVIS Dist-MSTVIS

Tchigorin Vs Mackenzie C 13 MIN
16MM FILM OPTICAL SOUND
Presents a chess game in which a rook sacrifice leads to an interesting artistic finish.
From The Check And Mate Series.
LC NO. 74-701259
Prod-OECA Dist-OECA 1972

Tchou Tchou C 15 MIN
16MM FILM, 3/4 OR 1/2 IN VIDEO P-J
Uses building blocks to tell a story about a peaceful place in which children can play until it turns into a realm of danger because of the appearance of a dragon. Tells how the children outwit and tame the dragon.
Prod-NFBC Dist-EBEC 1972

Tea For Elsa B 10 MIN
16MM FILM OPTICAL SOUND J-C A
Contrasts the tense excitement of a museum robbery with the monotonous routine of a chairwoman to make a powerful statement about apathy and non-involvement.
Prod-COUNTR Dist-COUNTR 1972

Tea Jar Bake, A C 20 MIN
3/4 OR 1/2 INCH VIDEO CASSETTE PRO
Demonstrates baking shrimp, chicken and mushrooms in a tea jar, and filling colored and salted clamshells with other delicacies. The whole is served among miniature colored flames.
From The Japanese Cuisine Series.
Prod-CULINA Dist-CULINA

Teach A Child To Talk C 15 MIN
16MM FILM OPTICAL SOUND A
Follows the development of normal speech and language from birth to 3 years with suggestions for parents.
LC NO. 76-700270
Prod-DEVLSC Dist-CEBCO

Teach For Transfer, Pt 1 C 21 MIN
16MM FILM, 3/4 OR 1/2 IN VIDEO
Discusses and illustrates the main factors which facilitate and those which prevent the transfer of pupils' learning to new situations.
Prod-SPF Dist-SPF

Teach For Transfer, Pt 2 C 20 MIN
16MM FILM, 3/4 OR 1/2 IN VIDEO
Discusses and illustrates the main factors which facilitate and those which prevent the transfer of pupils' learning to new situations.
Prod-SPF Dist-SPF

Teach Me C 10 MIN
16MM FILM OPTICAL SOUND C T
Presents a report of the practical side of a unique special education center now in its third year. Shows that the Warren Development Center has gained the reputation of an intricate combination course of work where Maryland's school systems can attempt to close the breach between the need and supply of teachers trained to work with special problem children.
Prod-HALLFM Dist-HALLFM

Teach Me C 20 MIN
16MM FILM OPTICAL SOUND J-C T
Excerpted from the 1967 feature length film 'UP THE DOWN STAIRCASE' directed by Mike Nichols. A beginning teacher discovers that the rewards of motivating disadvantaged students outweigh environmental handicaps.
LC NO. FIA68-2500
Prod-TFC Dist-IU Prodn-WB 1968

Teach Me How I Can Do It Myself C 29 MIN
16MM FILM, 3/4 OR 1/2 IN VIDEO C A
A documentary account of the philosophy and practices of the Montessori method of elementary education. Presents scenes of children at a Montessori kindergarten and at a public elementary Montessori school in The Netherlands. Explains that the Montessori method is a total way of life that involves the child, the parents and the teachers.
Prod-STNEON Dist-IFB 1971

Teach Me To Dance C 28 MIN
16MM FILM, 3/4 OR 1/2 IN VIDEO I-H
Shows how a young Ukrainian immigrant is assigned a school recitation which sends her into despair, since she has difficulty with English. Describes her relationship with a friend who helps her overcome her problem.
From The Adventures In History Series.
Prod-NFBC Dist-FI 1978

Teach More Faster, Pt 1 B 29 MIN
16MM FILM OPTICAL SOUND C T
Shows how to apply psychological principles in planning material to be taught. Demonstrates the most effective way to sequence lessons, the importance of making material meaningful, how some material can be taught faster and the effect of previously learned material.
LC NO. 82-701103
Prod-SPF Dist-SPF 1970

Teach More Faster, Pt 2 B 29 MIN
16MM FILM OPTICAL SOUND C T
Deals with psychological principles that eliminate the need for a great deal of practice. Reviews importance of motivation, meaning, vividness and sequence of material. Discusses overt and covert participation of the learner, clarifies the influence of positive and negative transfer and shows how the reinforcement theory is related to cognitive learning as well as behavior.
LC NO. 82-701103
Prod-SPF Dist-SPF 1970

Teach More Faster, Pt 3 B 29 MIN
16MM FILM OPTICAL SOUND C T
Describes the three essential elements of planned practice--how much to practice, how long to practice and how often to practice. Reviews the principles of learning taught in the entire series.
LC NO. 82-701103
Prod-SPF Dist-SPF 1970

Teach Safety C 15 MIN
16MM FILM, 3/4 OR 1/2 IN VIDEO
Stresses the importance of the supervisor's responsibility for teaching minors the correct, safe and efficient methods of performing their jobs.
From The Foremanship Training Series.
LC NO. 82-706283
Prod-USBM Dist-USNAC 1968

Teach Your Horse To Bow For Easy Mounting C 17 MIN
1/2 IN VIDEO CASSETTE BETA/VHS
Shows how to teach a horse to bow for easy mounting.
Prod-MHRSMP Dist-EQVDL

Teacher C 15 MIN
3/4 OR 1/2 INCH VIDEO CASSETTE I
Explains the qualifications and personal qualities required for a successful career as a teacher.
From The Career Awareness Series.
Prod-KLVXTV Dist-GPITVL 1973

Teacher And Peer Attitudes C 30 MIN
3/4 OR 1/2 INCH VIDEO CASSETTE
Presents consultants discussing the complexities of teacher attitudes toward students and how to manage student attitudes.
From The Teaching Students With Special Needs Series.
Prod-MSITV Dist-PBS 1981

Teacher And Technology, The X 49 MIN
16MM FILM OPTICAL SOUND T
Presents a series of pictorially documented programs which illustrate some of the ways in which technology is being used to meet the dual problems of masses of students and the need for individualized instruction.
From The Communication Theory And The New Educational Media Series.
LC NO. FIA68-833
Prod-USOE Dist-USNAC 1967

Teacher As A Storyteller C 20 MIN
16MM FILM OPTICAL SOUND
Bill Martin reads poetry, tells stories, and engages children in oral reponses to what they have heard. He shows how he believes language is learned through the ear, not the eye. He also discusses three levels of language - home rooted, public and life lifting.
From The Sound Of Language Series.
LC NO. FIA-640
Prod-OHIOSU Dist-OSUMPD 1967

Teacher As Club Leader, The C 25 MIN
16MM FILM OPTICAL SOUND
Discusses the role of the teacher in the Academic Club Method developed at the Kingsbury Center Lab School.
From The Learning For A Lifetime - The Academic Club Method Series. Part 5
Prod-KINGS Dist-KINGS

Teacher Attitude I C 30 MIN
3/4 OR 1/2 INCH VIDEO CASSETTE T
Discusses the importance of teacher attitude when dealing with children with special needs.
From The Teaching Children With Special Needs Series.
Prod-MDDE Dist-MDCPB

Teacher Attitude II C 30 MIN
3/4 OR 1/2 INCH VIDEO CASSETTE T
Discusses the importance of teacher attitude when dealing with children with special needs.
From The Teaching Children With Special Needs Series.
Prod-MDDE Dist-MDCPB

Teacher Decision Making B 26 MIN
16MM FILM OPTICAL SOUND C R
Discusses daily teaching decisions which are identified and grouped in three categories--academic content, behavior of the learner and behavior of the teacher. Presents the relationship of these decisions to the most recent research in learning so that teachers can increase their efficiency and effectiveness in the classsroom.
From The Translating Theory Into Classroom Practice Series.
Prod-SPF Dist-SPF 1967

Teacher Effectiveness Training C 29 MIN
16MM FILM, 3/4 OR 1/2 IN VIDEO
Outlines the methods created and developed by Dr Thomas Gordon, originator of Teacher Effectiveness Training, a system of techniques now widely used by teachers in building more effective classroom relationships. Illustrates and explains the concepts of 'ACTIVE LISTENING,' "I" messages' and the 'NO-LOSE METHOD' for resolving conflicts.
From The Human Relations And School Discipline Series.
Prod-MFFD Dist-FI

Teacher For Dona Ines, A C 30 MIN
3/4 OR 1/2 INCH VIDEO CASSETTE
See series title for descriptive statement.
From The Mundo Real Series.
Prod-CPT Dist-MDCPB

Teacher In Reflection, A X 11 MIN
16MM FILM, 3/4 OR 1/2 IN VIDEO T
Demonstrates how class meetings can be used by grade school teachers to work out students' personal and classroom problems.
From The One To Grow On Series.
LC NO. 80-706191
Prod-NIMH Dist-USNAC Prodn-UCLA 1979

Teacher Stress, Pt 1 C 20 MIN
3/4 OR 1/2 INCH VIDEO CASSETTE T
Explains various ways in which stress affects productivity as educators.
From The On And About Instruction Series.
Prod-VADE Dist-GPITVL 1983

Teacher Stress, Pt 2 C 29 MIN
3/4 OR 1/2 INCH VIDEO CASSETTE T
Gives various techniques that both groups and individuals can use to relieve stress situations.

From The On And About Instruction Series.
Prod-VADE Dist-GPITVL 1983

Teacher Support C 15 MIN
16MM FILM OPTICAL SOUND
Shows how the emotionally handicapped student at the League School for seriously disturbed children is afforded the full range of clinical treatment and therapy through an elaborate teacher support system.
From The League School For Seriously Disturbed Children Series.
LC NO. 75-702438
Prod-USBEH Dist-USNAC Prodn-AIRLIE 1973

Teacher To Teacher On Individualization, Pt 1 - How To Get An Individual Started C 26 MIN
16MM FILM OPTICAL SOUND C T
Emphasizes the steps that need to be taken by the classroom teacher to individualize instruction.
Prod-SPF Dist-SPF 1969

Teacher To Teacher On Individualization, Pt 2 - How To Get An Individual Started, Further... C 26 MIN
16MM FILM OPTICAL SOUND C T
Provides the viewer with specific illustration of individualization and shows how the teacher analyzes each situation.
Prod-SPF Dist-SPF 1969

Teacher Training Experiences And Issues C 47 MIN
3/4 OR 1/2 INCH VIDEO CASSETTE J-C A
Presents experiences and issues in training teachers for computer use in the classroom and discusses Computer Using Educators (CUE), a teachers' organization for computer education.
From The New Technology In Education Series.
Prod-USDOE Dist-USNAC 1983

Teacher Variable, The - An Interview With Vera Milz C 29 MIN
3/4 OR 1/2 INCH VIDEO CASSETTE T
See series title for descriptive statement.
From The Reading Comprehension Series.
Prod-IU Dist-HNEDBK

Teacher-Directed Television Instruction B 28 MIN
3/4 INCH VIDEO CASSETTE
Demonstrates a television facility which frees university and school faculties from some of the restrictions inherent in traditional television presentations, permitting push-button control of the medium.
Prod-USNAC Dist-USNAC 1972

Teacher-Made Tests C 11 MIN
3/4 OR 1/2 INCH VIDEO CASSETTE T
Explains how to prepare relevant and effective teacher-made tests.
From The Tests Series.
Prod-WTVITV Dist-AITECH 1980

Teacher-Student Interaction Analysis C 18 MIN
3/4 OR 1/2 INCH VIDEO CASSETTE PRO
Helps clinical and classroom instructors in allied health, nursing, and medicine to understand more fully their role in the teaching-learning process and how to improve it. Covers instructor's behavior when working with a student, a process for objectively analyzing that behavior, and the establishment of goals for promoting more desirable teacher behavior.
Prod-HSCIC Dist-HSCIC

Teacher/Pupil Interactions C 30 MIN
3/4 OR 1/2 INCH VIDEO CASSETTE T
Looks at teacher/pupil interactions in an educational setting.
From The Interaction - Human Concerns In The Schools Series.
Prod-MDDE Dist-MDCPB

Teacher, Lester Bit Me C 9 MIN
16MM FILM, 3/4 OR 1/2 IN VIDEO C
Uses animation to tell about a preschool day when everything goes wrong. Exaggerates typical crises that arise when working with young children, providing a basis for discussion on how to handle the problems.
LC NO. 80-706445
Prod-EDC Dist-IFB 1978

Teacher, Take Us Orienteering C 14 MIN
16MM FILM, 3/4 OR 1/2 IN VIDEO I-H
Shows a group of school children becoming acquainted with the sport of orienteering, which requires participants to use a map and compass to check in at various control points and be the first to finish a pre-defined course.
LC NO. 83-706713
Prod-OFA Dist-IFB 1982

Teacher, The (Inservice) C 15 MIN
3/4 OR 1/2 INCH VIDEO CASSETTE T
Deals with organizing and implementing the investigative experience for science fairs.
From The Sci-Fair Series.
Prod-MAETEL Dist-GPITVL

Teacher, The - A Community Helper X 10 MIN
16MM FILM OPTICAL SOUND P A
Describes a typical day in the life of a primary school teacher. Shows her as she plans the lesson, teaches, confers with a parent, attends the university and performs other duties as a mother, homemaker and responsible member of the community.
LC NO. FIA67-1908
Prod-SIGMA Dist-FILCOM 1967

Teacher's Aides - A New Opportunity B 21 MIN
16MM FILM, 3/4 OR 1/2 IN VIDEO T S R
Depicts the training of para-professional teacher's aides for pre-schools.
Prod-USOEO Dist-USNAC

Teacher's Beau B 19 MIN
16MM FILM OPTICAL SOUND
Tells how the Gang tries to discourage their teacher from marrying, fearing what the 'new' teacher might be like. A Little Rascals film.
Prod-ROACH Dist-BHAWK 1935

Teacher's Prescription For Reducing Vandalism, A C 23 MIN
16MM FILM, 3/4 OR 1/2 IN VIDEO T
Reveals how art teacher Gary Obermayer and his students at Seward Junior High School have transformed an old, ugly building into a cheerful place through creative expression. Shows how this has altered the attitude of all students and reduced vandalism.
From The Successful Teaching Practices Series.
Prod-UNIDIM Dist-EBEC 1982

Teachers C 13 MIN
16MM FILM OPTICAL SOUND C T
Satirizes four types of teachers in order to show that the teacher is the most important audio-visual 'AID' in the classroom.
Prod-DAWSON Dist-FRAF 1958

Teachers Ask C 30 MIN
3/4 OR 1/2 INCH VIDEO CASSETTE T
Contains an overview of the Creative Dramatics series and its philosophy. Answers questions most commonly asked by teachers during creative dramatics workshops.
From The Creative Dramatics (Teacher) Series.
Prod-NEWITV Dist-AITECH 1977

Teachers, Friends And Roller Skaters C 22 MIN
16MM FILM OPTICAL SOUND
Follows the progress of one young couple as they learn to roller skate, showing their initial awkwardness and gradual development into proficient skaters. Offers demonstrations and explanations of basic roller skating techniques.
Prod-MTP Dist-MTP

Teachers, Gardeners, Paths And Shadows C 28 MIN
16MM FILM OPTICAL SOUND C A
Presents a conversation with Paul Kurtz, retired Superintendent of Schools for Blair County, Pennsylvania, talking to Marlowe Froke about his educational philosophies and his love for gardening.
LC NO. 76-703733
Prod-WPSXTV Dist-PSU 1976

Teachers, Parents And Children - Growth Through Cooperation C 17 MIN
3/4 OR 1/2 INCH VIDEO CASSETTE
See series title for descriptive statement.
From The Early Childhood Development Series.
Prod-DAVFMS Dist-DAVFMS

Teachers, Parents, Children C 17 MIN
16MM FILM OPTICAL SOUND J-C A
Explains how to construct alliances between families and teachers to ease a child's entrance into school.
Prod-DAVFMS Dist-DAVFMS 1974

Teachers' Meeting C 30 MIN
16MM FILM, 3/4 OR 1/2 IN VIDEO C T
Longer version of the videocassette A Faculty Feeling. Portrays a faculty meeting in which the teachers of a school discuss whether they are a collection of isolated individuals under one roof or a united faculty whose members work together. Focuses on the professional responsibilities of the teacher.
From The Heart Of Teaching Series.
LC NO. 80-706431
Prod-AITV Dist-AITECH Prodn-KETCTV 1976

Teaching C 30 MIN
3/4 OR 1/2 INCH VIDEO CASSETTE
Deals with the teaching of black literature, which, for a white teacher is often difficult, with a great temptation to alter the language and experience of the black writer. Emphasizes accuracy as being essential for an understanding of the black experience.
From The Black Literature Series.
Prod-NETCHE Dist-NETCHE 1971

Teaching A Child About Leukemia C
3/4 INCH VIDEO CASSETTE PRO
Shows how to teach children about leukemia. Treats pre-teaching conference with parent, family reaction to illness, understanding of diagnostic tests, symptoms of illness and use of visual aids.
From The Staff Development Series.
Prod-CFDC Dist-CFDC

Teaching A Child About Nephrosis C
3/4 INCH VIDEO CASSETTE PRO
Presents a situation where a child with nephrosis is unprepared for hospitalization and refuses to cooperate. Discusses feelings about hospitalization, understanding of the illness, use of body outline to present anatomy and physiology, and use of equipment for explanation.
From The Staff Development Series.
Prod-CFDC Dist-CFDC

Teaching A Language Structure By The Australian Situational Method, Pt 1 B 15 MIN
16MM FILM OPTICAL SOUND C T
Explains the teaching of English as a foreign language.
LC NO. 73-702486
Prod-FLMAUS Dist-AUIS 1973

Teaching A Language Structure By The Australian Situational Method, Pt 2 B 15 MIN
16MM FILM OPTICAL SOUND C T
Explains the teaching of English as a foreign language.
LC NO. 73-702486
Prod-FLMAUS Dist-AUIS 1973

Teaching About Physics And Society B 30 MIN
16MM FILM OPTICAL SOUND C A
Two of the Project Physics directors and two teachers discuss the importance of having students become aware of the impact of science, especially physics, on social concepts and actions and explain the role of the Project Physics classroom in developing these concepts.
From The Harvard Project Physics Teacher Briefings Series. No. 7
LC NO. 79-709149
Prod-HPP Dist-HRAW 1969

Teaching Adults C 29 MIN
16MM FILM OPTICAL SOUND
See series title for descriptive statement.
From The Teaching Series.
Prod-BROADM Dist-BROADM 1977

Teaching And Learning - Grades 1-2 C 17 MIN
16MM FILM, 3/4 OR 1/2 IN VIDEO T
Demonstrates teacher preparation, interaction between pupils, teachers and materials and the selection of appropriate learning experiences in light of the session objectives.
Prod-GENEVA Dist-AIMS 1971

Teaching And Learning - Grades 3-4 C 21 MIN
16MM FILM, 3/4 OR 1/2 IN VIDEO T
Provides an opportunity to observe team teaching, the interaction process and the opening, developing and concluding of a unit of study.
Prod-GENEVA Dist-AIMS 1971

Teaching And Learning - Grades 5-6 C 21 MIN
16MM FILM, 3/4 OR 1/2 IN VIDEO T
Shows children building a time ladder to gain a concept of long past events in history and preparing their own dramatization of the events leading to the revolt after Soloman's death. Features teachers holding a critique session afterward to analyze their own successes and failures in the unit.
Prod-GENEVA Dist-AIMS 1971

Teaching And Learning - Grades 7-8 C 22 MIN
16MM FILM, 3/4 OR 1/2 IN VIDEO T
Uses the inquiry approach with junior high level students, as they try to understand the social concerns involved in the period of Amos. Covers the unit from introduction to conclusion and shows two teachers working cooperatively, student-teacher interaction and student-to-student interaction.
Prod-GENEVA Dist-AIMS 1971

Teaching And Testing For Results C 30 MIN
3/4 OR 1/2 INCH VIDEO CASSETTE T
Presents a working example of an approach to adaptive education to increase effectiveness and efficiency in instruction.
From The On And About Instruction Series.
Prod-VADE Dist-GPITVL 1983

Teaching Babies, Creepers And Toddlers At Church C 29 MIN
16MM FILM OPTICAL SOUND
See series title for descriptive statement.
From The Teaching Series.
Prod-BROADM Dist-BROADM 1977

Teaching Basic Concepts B 52 MIN
16MM FILM OPTICAL SOUND
Presents explanation of techniques which enables teachers to teach concepts precisely, to teach children individually and as a group and an introduction to the 'TASK,' a basic teaching unit.
Prod-ADL Dist-ADL

Teaching Basic Reading C 30 MIN
3/4 OR 1/2 INCH VIDEO CASSETTE T
Explains how to teach basic reading to adult basic education students.
From The Basic Education - Teaching The Adult Series.
Prod-MDDE Dist-MDCPB

Teaching Basic Skills With Film C 90 MIN
3/4 OR 1/2 INCH VIDEO CASSETTE T
Presents a workshop session offering suggestions for effective and creative teaching with film.
LC NO. 80-707451
Prod-LCOA Dist-LCOA 1980

Teaching Breast Self-Examination - Baseline C 24 MIN
3/4 OR 1/2 INCH VIDEO CASSETTE
Presents incorporation of Breast Health Education Protocol into history/physical exam.
From The Focus On Cancer - Prevention And Early Detection Series.
Prod-UWASH Dist-UWASH

Teaching Breast Self-Examination - Office Visit C 22 MIN
3/4 OR 1/2 INCH VIDEO CASSETTE
Demonstrates use of Breast Health Education Protocol to teach health education.
From The Focus On Cancer - Prevention And Early Detection Series.
Prod-UWASH Dist-UWASH

Teaching By Guided Discussion B 21 MIN
16MM FILM OPTICAL SOUND
Presents an air university academic course instructor conducting a seminar in teaching psychology.
LC NO. FIE58-279
Prod-USAF Dist-USNAC 1957

Teaching Children Poison Prevention C 14 MIN
16MM FILM OPTICAL SOUND
Informs children and their parents of potential poison hazards contained in the medicine cabinet.
LC NO. 76-703161
Prod-PD Dist-MTP Prodn-FJMGWP 1976

Teaching Children Self-Control C 26 MIN
16MM FILM OPTICAL SOUND T
Demonstrates problem-solving techniques for dealing with defiant and assaultive classroom behavior. Illustrates the methods of an experienced teacher as she joins her children in their struggle to acquire impulse control and self-mastery.
LC NO. 79-701119
Prod-PSW Dist-NYU 1978

Teaching Children To Read—A Series
16MM FILM, 3/4 OR 1/2 IN VIDEO T
Deals with various aspects of teaching children to read.
Prod-MFFD Dist-FI

Building On What Children Know 029 MIN
Developing Effective Reading Materials 030 MIN
Helping The Reluctant Reader 029 MIN
Human Behavior And Reading 029 MIN
Organizing The Reading Environment 029 MIN
Planning For Change 029 MIN
Reading As A Part Of Life 029 MIN
Role Of Phonics, The 029 MIN
Thinking, Writing And Reading 029 MIN
Using Human Resources 029 MIN
Ways Of Assessing Reading Progress 029 MIN
What About Reading Systems 029 MIN

Teaching Children With Special Needs - Preview C 30 MIN
3/4 OR 1/2 INCH VIDEO CASSETTE T
Offers a preview of the Teaching Children With Special Needs Series.
From The Teaching Children With Special Needs Series.
Prod-MDDE Dist-MDCPB

Teaching Children With Special Needs - Review C 30 MIN
3/4 OR 1/2 INCH VIDEO CASSETTE T
Reviews the main points of the Teaching Children With Special Needs Series.
From The Teaching Children With Special Needs Series.
Prod-MDDE Dist-MDCPB

Teaching Children With Special Needs—A Series
T
Discusses the observation, identification and management of children with special needs.
Prod-MDDE Dist-MDCPB

Analytic Approach To Reading, An 030 MIN
Behavior Problems I 030 MIN
Behavior Problems II 030 MIN
Informal Assessment Of Reading 030 MIN
Learning Styles 030 MIN
Mathematical Problems I 030 MIN
Mathematical Problems II 030 MIN
Observation Of Behavior 030 MIN
Oral Expressive Language 030 MIN
Oral Receptive Language 030 MIN
Referral Process, The 030 MIN
Synthesis Approach To Reading, A 030 MIN
Teacher Attitude I 030 MIN
Teacher Attitude II 030 MIN
Teaching Children With Special Needs - Preview 030 MIN
Teaching Children With Special Needs - Review 030 MIN

Teaching Crutch Walking B 13 MIN
16MM FILM OPTICAL SOUND A
Explains how to teach the patient to walk in a walker, and how to learn the various methods of crutch walking--two-point, four-point and swinging. Shows how to sit, rise and climb stairs and discusses the safety factors involved in crutch walking.
LC NO. FIE52-411
Prod-USOE Dist-USNAC 1945

Teaching Crutch Walking C 9 MIN
3/4 OR 1/2 INCH VIDEO CASSETTE PRO
Shows how to fit a patient with crutches and how to instruct a patient in walking, sitting, and climbing stairs with them. Demonstrates guarding against a fall, the four-point gait, the three-point gait, the swing-through gait, and the proper method of negotiating stairs without rails.
Prod-HSCIC Dist-HSCIC

Teaching Early Reading—A Series
T
Consists of six programs on teaching reading as an integrated language process. Deals with strategies in the instructional process allowing for a variety of methods of reading instruction. Shows how to work with individual student differences.
Prod-CTI Dist-CTI

How Can I Help Them - Effective Instruction 030 MIN
How Do They Understand-Comprehension 030 MIN
What Do They Do - Word Recognition 030 MIN
When Are They Ready - Reading Readiness 030 MIN
Where Do They Come From - Language Development 030 MIN
Where Do They Go From Here - Motivating The 030 MIN

Teaching English Conversation B 23 MIN
3/4 INCH VIDEO CASSETTE T
Presents the hearing and speaking method of teaching English as a foreign language. Issued in 1963 as a motion picture.
LC NO. 78-706150
Prod-USIA Dist-USNAC Prodn-CRAV 1978

Teaching English Grammar B 19 MIN
3/4 INCH VIDEO CASSETTE T
Shows how the drill method is used in teaching English grammar through structural pattern practice. Gives examples of both simple and complex patterns. Issued in 1960 as a motion picture.
LC NO. 78-706151
Prod-USIA Dist-USNAC Prodn-ALLEY 1978

Teaching English In Kindergarten - ESL C 14 MIN
16MM FILM OPTICAL SOUND T
Shows a bilingual kindergarten with an ESL (English as a second language) orientation, attended by children who speak predominantly Spanish.
From The JAB Reading Series.
LC NO. 75-703880
Prod-JBFL Dist-JBFL 1973

Teaching English In Kindergarten - ESL (Spanish) C 14 MIN
16MM FILM OPTICAL SOUND T
Uses an English as a second language approach, ESL, and examines a day in the life of kindergarten students who are bilingual and who speak Spanish in the home. Demonstrates how the class can be conducted in English.
Prod-JBFL Dist-JBFL

Teaching English Pronunciation B 20 MIN
3/4 INCH VIDEO CASSETTE T
Shows how to teach correct pronunciation, how to direct students in practicing correct pronunciation and how to help students recognize and overcome errors. Issued in 1963 as a motion picture.
LC NO. 78-706153
Prod-USIA Dist-USNAC 1978

Teaching English Speech B 17 MIN
3/4 INCH VIDEO CASSETTE T
Introduces a teacher-training program which emphasizes the aural-oral approach to teaching English. Issued in 1964 as a motion picture.
LC NO. 78-706154
Prod-USIA Dist-USNAC 1978

Teaching For Retention C 30 MIN
3/4 OR 1/2 INCH VIDEO CASSETTE
Provides a summary of principles of learning. Identifies and illustrates five critical principles of learning which have the power to increase retention of what has been learned.
From The Aide-ing In Education Series.
Prod-SPF Dist-SPF

Teaching Fours And Fives At Church C 29 MIN
16MM FILM OPTICAL SOUND
See series title for descriptive statement.
From The Teaching Series.
Prod-BROADM Dist-BROADM 1977

Teaching History, Geography And Civics C 27 MIN
16MM FILM OPTICAL SOUND
Shows the Academic Club Method at the Kingsbury Center Lab School where study of the social development of man is achieved through clubs organized around six periods of history.
From The Learning For A Lifetime - The Academic Club Method Series. Part 4
Prod-KINGS Dist-KINGS

Teaching Infants And Toddlers—A Series
H-C A
Demonstrates how infants and toddlers learn through the senses of feeling, seeing and hearing. Shows the youngsters general reactions to parental stimuli.
Prod-BGSU Dist-GPITVL 1978

Fifteen To Twenty Months 013 MIN
Four To Five Months 009 MIN
Nine To Eleven Months 011 MIN
One To Three Months 009 MIN
Six To Eight Months 010 MIN
Twelve To Fourteen Months 012 MIN
Twenty-One To Twenty-Nine Months 013 MIN

Teaching Interpersonal Skills To Health Professionals, Program 1, Overview C 15 MIN
3/4 OR 1/2 INCH VIDEO CASSETTE T
Presents a brief overview of the Interpersonal Skills Programs to help potential users determine if the series is appropriate to their needs.
Prod-NMAC Dist-USNAC

Teaching Interpersonal Skills To Health Professionals C 100 MIN
3/4 INCH VIDEO CASSETTE T
Presents an overview of the interpersonal skills program. Discusses elements in preparing for instruction, shows how to explain the instructional intensions, demonstrates skills to be learned, reviews effective and ineffective feedback and documents and critiques practice experiences.
LC NO. 79-706871
Prod-NMAC Dist-USNAC 1978

Teaching Interpersonal Skills To Health Professionals, Programs 2-7 C 85 MIN
3/4 OR 1/2 INCH VIDEO CASSETTE T
Discusses the importance of advance planning in preparing for instruction, demonstrating skills to be learned, providing practice opportunities, documenting and critiquing practice experiences, making video recordings and other key elements used in teaching interpersonal skills.
Prod-NMAC Dist-USNAC

Teaching Is An Attitude C 27 MIN
16MM FILM, 3/4 OR 1/2 IN VIDEO T
Features teacher John Robinson showing how innate attitudes can be used in areas of student classroom behavior, racial issues, values clarification and the cooperative learning process.
From The Successful Teaching Practices Series.
Prod-UNIDIM Dist-EBEC 1982

Teaching Johnny To Swim (2nd Ed) C 15 MIN
16MM FILM OPTICAL SOUND
Shows that children can be taught to swim by utilizing the Red Cross booklet Teaching Johnny To Swim. Shows a young boy and his sister learning swimming, diving and lifesaving techniques from their parents.
Prod-MLIC Dist-AMRC Prodn-AMRC 1973

Teaching Learning Process, The C 25 MIN
3/4 OR 1/2 INCH VIDEO CASSETTE
Explains the basics of the teaching/learning process and defines the roles of both the teacher and the learner in patient education. Discusses the components of the teaching/learning process, including assessment, formulation of objectives, motivation and reinforcement, establishment of the learning environment, learning activities and evaluation.
From The How To Of Patient Education Series.
Prod-FAIRGH Dist-FAIRGH

Teaching Machines C 30 MIN
3/4 OR 1/2 INCH VIDEO CASSETTE T
Discusses the use of teaching machines with adult basic education students.
From The Basic Education - Teaching The Adult Series.
Prod-MDDE Dist-MDCPB

Teaching Machines And Programmed Learning B 29 MIN
3/4 INCH VIDEO CASSETTE
Presents three discussions concerning programmed learning. Includes B F Skinner explaining the theory of programmed learning, Arthur Lumsdaine describing a variety of teaching machines and programmed materials and Robert Glaser discussing the implication of such machines and materials for education.
Prod-USNAC Dist-USNAC 1972

Teaching Machines And Sidney Pressey B 12 MIN
16MM FILM OPTICAL SOUND J-C
Introduces Sidney Pressey, emeritus professor at Ohio State University, and the teaching machine he invented in 1925. Comments on forms of programmed instruction and concludes with a prediction by Pressey about the relation of automated instruction to the teacher.
From The Communication Theory And The New Educational Media Series.
LC NO. 74-705748
Prod-USOE Dist-USNAC 1966

Teaching Mathematics - Basic Level C 30 MIN
3/4 OR 1/2 INCH VIDEO CASSETTE T
Shows how to teach basic level mathematics to adult basic education students.
From The Basic Education - Teaching The Adult Series.
Prod-MDDE Dist-MDCPB

Teaching Middle And Younger Children C 29 MIN
16MM FILM OPTICAL SOUND
See series title for descriptive statement.
From The Teaching Series.
Prod-BROADM Dist-BROADM 1977

Teaching Observed C
16MM FILM, 3/4 OR 1/2 IN VIDEO
Shows six teachers from different countries in Africa and Asia at work in their own environment teaching English.
Prod-NORTNJ Dist-NORTNJ

Teaching Older Children C 29 MIN
16MM FILM OPTICAL SOUND
See series title for descriptive statement.
From The Teaching Series.
Prod-BROADM Dist-BROADM 1977

Teaching Patients - Three Vignettes C 19 MIN
3/4 OR 1/2 INCH VIDEO CASSETTE PRO
Consists of three 5-minute, unrehearsed patient education vignettes characteristic of typical interactions. Discusses the teaching of patients.
Prod-UMICHM Dist-UMICHM 1981

Teaching Programs In Child Development—A Series
PRO
Trains health-care professionals in the assessment of children with developmental problems.
Prod-UARIZ Dist-UARIZ

Case Studies In Child Development-David 031 MIN
End Is My Beginning, The - An 040 MIN
Handicapped Child - Issues In 025 MIN

Teaching Reading Comprehension C 30 MIN
3/4 OR 1/2 INCH VIDEO CASSETTE T
Explains how to teach reading comprehension to adult basic education students.
From The Basic Education - Teaching The Adult Series.
Prod-MDDE Dist-MDCPB

Teaching Reading To Spanish Speakers C 14 MIN
16MM FILM OPTICAL SOUND T
Reports on an experiment to begin reading instruction in both English and Spanish for Spanish-speaking children in kindergarten.
From The JAB Reading Series.
LC NO. 75-703879
Prod-JBFL Dist-JBFL 1973

Teaching Reading To Spanish Speakers (Spanish) C 14 MIN
16MM FILM OPTICAL SOUND T
Presents a teaching experiment that introduces reading to Spanish-speaking kindergarteners in their native language. Shows how the experimental program functions and teacher attitudes toward the program.
Prod-JBFL Dist-JBFL

Teaching Role Of Nursing Supervisors C 12 MIN
3/4 OR 1/2 INCH VIDEO CASSETTE
Focuses on how the nursing supervisor provides ongoing instruction to nurses. Includes 12 half-hour lessons.
Prod-TELSTR Dist-TELSTR

Teaching Role—A Series
C T
Gives teachers without a formal education background the skills and concepts required to improve their teaching. Presents techniques for communicating objectives to faculty and students, for performance review and supportive evaluation in dealing with student attitudes.
Prod-MVNE Dist-TELSTR 1968

Creative Problem Solving 30 MIN
Essential Methods Of The Teaching-Learning 30 MIN
Essential Methods Of The Teaching-Learning 30 MIN
Evaluation Of Student Performance 30 MIN
Faculty Self-Development 30 MIN
Formulation Of Objectives, The 30 MIN
How People Learn 30 MIN
How To Motivate The Student 30 MIN
Instructor Skills In Supportive Evaluation 30 MIN
Role Of The Instructor 30 MIN
Strengthening Organizational Relationships 30 MIN
Understanding And Dealing With Student 30 MIN

Teaching Safety On The Job X 10 MIN
16MM FILM OPTICAL SOUND
Shows how to make the instruction understood, checking and follow-up. Shows how to build safety into job training.
From The Human Factors In Safety Series.
Prod-NSC Dist-NSC

Teaching Self-examination Of The Breasts C 20 MIN
3/4 OR 1/2 INCH VIDEO CASSETTE PRO
Includes both a demonstration of the techniques which a health professional may use in teaching self-examinations of the breasts and a demonstration of a woman doing a complete self-examination of the breasts. Discusses specific areas where metastases commonly occur and the characteristics of a breast mass which should be reported.
Prod-UMICHM Dist-UMICHM 1975

Teaching Sign Language To The Chimpanzee, Washoe B 48 MIN
16MM FILM OPTICAL SOUND H-C A
Documents Project Washoe, in which two-way communication was established with a chimpanzee by means of the sign language of the American deaf, Ameslan. Illustrates the range of Washoe's vocabulary, including signs for objects, proper names and actions and the development of sentence-like sequences of signs.
LC NO. 74-702783
Prod-UNEV Dist-PSUPCR 1973

Teaching Social And Leisure Skills To Youth With Autism C 35 MIN
3/4 OR 1/2 INCH VIDEO CASSETTE C A
Documents the activities of five autistic students, illustrating their problems relating socially, using leisure time and coping in the community. Outlines skill objectives which deal with feelings, touching, communication, leisure and other social activities.
LC NO. 84-706391
Prod-IU Dist-IU 1983

Teaching Strategies For The Development Of Auditory Verbal Communication—A Series

Demonstrates teaching strategies for development of auditory-verbal communication. Portrays children aged 13 months to six years with severe to profound hearing impairments attending the Acoupedic Program at Porter Memorial Hospital in Denver, Co. Describes teaching strategies used, audiograms, and brief case histories for each child.
Prod-BELLAG Dist-BELLAG 1981

Auditory Discrimination, Feedback And--k 060 MIN
Auditory Attention, Localization And Vocal Play 060 MIN
Development Of Auditory Memory Span And 060 MIN
Development Of Symdic Language - Auditory 060 MIN
Preparation For Mainstreaming 060 MIN

Teaching Students With Special Needs—A Series

Presents a variety of instructional techniques and strategies which can help educators recognize and identify students' emotional, physical and learning disabilities.
Prod-MSITV Dist-PBS 1981

Behavior Problems In The Classroom 030 MIN
Career And Vocational Education 030 MIN
Development Characteristics Of Adolescents 030 MIN
Employability And The World Of Work 030 MIN
Instruction In Mathematics 030 MIN
Instruction In Reading 030 MIN
Instruction In Social Studies And Science 030 MIN
Instruction In Written Expression 030 MIN
Management Of Classroom Environment 030 MIN
Medical Problems 030 MIN
Parent Conferencing 030 MIN
Special Needs Students In The Classroom 030 MIN
Survival Skills 030 MIN
Teacher And Peer Attitudes 030 MIN
Team Approach, The 030 MIN

Teaching Styles C 29 MIN
3/4 OR 1/2 INCH VIDEO CASSETTE T
Shows the importance of incorporating a variety of materials and methods into one's personal teaching style.
From The On And About Instruction Series.
Prod-VADE Dist-GPITVL 1983

Teaching Styles, 1 B 30 MIN
16MM FILM OPTICAL SOUND T
A teacher in a small rural school in Maine shows films of his community, of the modified multi-media system in use in his classroom and of his students engaged in several activities. Other teachers discuss his teaching style with him.
From The Harvard Project Physics Teacher Briefing Series. No. 8
LC NO. 72-709131
Prod-WGBH Dist-HRAW 1969

Teaching Styles, 2 B 30 MIN
16MM FILM OPTICAL SOUND T
A teacher in a suburban California town shows films of his students doing group research, working in laboratory activities and choosing what classroom activity to engage in from many available options. A panel discusses with the teacher the advantages and limitations of his teaching style.
From The Harvard Project Physics Teacher Briefings Series. No. 9
LC NO. 76-709132
Prod-HPP Dist-HRAW 1969

Teaching Styles, 3 B 30 MIN
16MM FILM OPTICAL SOUND T
A teacher in a conventional Massachusetts school shows films of his fairly conventional classroom approach which offers students a diversity of activities, including laboratory work. A panel discusses the teacher's style of teaching.
From The Harvard Project Physics Teacher Briefings, No. 10 Series.
LC NO. 70-709133
Prod-WGBH Dist-HRAW 1969

Teaching Techniques C 50 MIN
3/4 OR 1/2 INCH VIDEO CASSETTE IND
Covers behavioral objectives, factors that influence learning, teaching methods and teaching on the job.
From The Training The Trainer Series.
Prod-LEIKID Dist-LEIKID

Teaching Techniques C 50 MIN
3/4 OR 1/2 INCH VIDEO CASSETTE IND
See series title for descriptive statement.
From The Task Analysis And Job Instructor Training Series.
Prod-NCSU Dist-AMCEE

Teaching The Child Who Is Retarded C 20 MIN
16MM FILM OPTICAL SOUND
Depicts classroom situations for retarded children at the University of South Dakota summer school program. Illustrates various methods of teaching retarded children.
Prod-USD Dist-USD

Teaching The Severely Handicapped C 14 MIN
16MM FILM OPTICAL SOUND T S
Visits classrooms where special equipment and systematic instruction are used to help severely handicapped children achieve their potential.
From The Exceptional Learners Series.
LC NO. 79-700714
Prod-MERILC Dist-MERILC 1978

Teaching The Slow Learner—A Series
C
Demonstrates successful techniques for using nonbook materials to teach the slow learner.
Prod-HRAW Dist-HRAW

Teaching To Develop Independent Learners, Pt 1 - 4-8 Years C 29 MIN
3/4 OR 1/2 INCH VIDEO CASSETTE
Describes the educational and emotional values achieved by teaching students to become independent learners and stresses the importance of the teacher's skill in attaining that goal.
Prod-SPF Dist-SPF

Teaching To Develop Independent Learners, Pt 2 - 4-8 Year Olds C 29 MIN
3/4 OR 1/2 INCH VIDEO CASSETTE
Follows same group of students from Part 1 two months later. Relationships on the teaching-learning process which make an increasing degree of independence possible are identified.
Prod-SPF Dist-SPF

Teaching To Develop Independent Learners, Pt 3 - 4-8 Year Olds C 29 MIN
3/4 OR 1/2 INCH VIDEO CASSETTE
Observes the same group of students from Part 2 five months later. Summarizes the skills which must be taught in order to foster independent learning and suggests many practical techniques for use in the classroom.
Prod-SPF Dist-SPF

Teaching To Develop Independent Learners, Pt 4 - 9-13 Year Olds C 29 MIN
3/4 OR 1/2 INCH VIDEO CASSETTE
Reviews the values inherent in helping students become independent learners and introduces a list of skills which must be acquired before that objective can be attained.
Prod-SPF Dist-SPF

Teaching To Objectives, Pt 1 C 30 MIN
3/4 OR 1/2 INCH VIDEO CASSETTE T
Divides the classification of instructional objectives into three categories - informational, conceptual and procedural.
From The On And About Instruction Series.
Prod-VADE Dist-GPITVL 1983

Teaching To Objectives, Pt 2 C 30 MIN
3/4 OR 1/2 INCH VIDEO CASSETTE T
Divides the classification of instructional objectives into three categories - informational, conceptual and procedural.
From The On And About Instruction Series.
Prod-VADE Dist-GPITVL 1983

Teaching Tomorrow C 12 MIN
16MM FILM OPTICAL SOUND P-I T
Shows a primary school classroom in rural Kenya, where African children learn science in new ways by using local materials and modern methods. A teacher training film.
LC NO. 74-712804
Prod-EDC Dist-EDC 1970

Teaching Transurethral Surgery Using A Cow's Udder C 15 MIN
16MM FILM OPTICAL SOUND PRO
Uses a cow's udder, which simulates in many respects the obstructed human bladder to indicate the technique of transurethral surgery.
LC NO. FIA66-22
Prod-OSUMPD Dist-OSUMPD 1964

Teaching Word Recognition C 30 MIN
3/4 OR 1/2 INCH VIDEO CASSETTE T
Explains how to teach word recognition to adult basic education students.
From The Basic Education - Teaching The Adult Series.
Prod-MDDE Dist-MDCPB

Teaching Writing C 30 MIN
3/4 OR 1/2 INCH VIDEO CASSETTE T
Demonstrates how to teach writing to adult basic education students.
From The Basic Education - Teaching The Adult Series.
Prod-MDDE Dist-MDCPB

Teaching Writing - A Process Approach—A Series

Presents theories and practices to assist teaching professionals in the instruction of writing.
Prod-MSITV Dist-PBS 1982

Diagnosis 029 MIN
Evaluation 029 MIN
Organizing A Year's Program 029 MIN
Prewriting, Pt 1 029 MIN
Prewriting, Pt 2 029 MIN
Rewriting - Proofreading 029 MIN
Rewriting - Revising 029 MIN
Writing 029 MIN
Writing Process, The - An Overview 029 MIN

Teaching Writing - The Process C 28 MIN
16MM FILM, 3/4 OR 1/2 IN VIDEO T
Presents authors and teachers sharing the writing exercises which they initiate to prompt written expression from their students' life experiences and imaginations. Observes the application of these writing procedures in fourth grade through high school classes.
From The Dealing With Social Problems In The Classroom Series.
LC NO. 82-706668
Prod-MFFD Dist-FI 1982

Teaching Young Adults C 29 MIN
16MM FILM OPTICAL SOUND
See series title for descriptive statement.
From The Teaching Series.
Prod-BROADM Dist-BROADM 1977

Teaching your First Class C 30 MIN
3/4 OR 1/2 INCH VIDEO CASSETTE T
Discusses preparing for a first class and keeping the lesson on track.
From The Training The Trainer Series.
Prod-ITCORP Dist-ITCORP

Teaching Your Wings To Fly C 19 MIN
16MM FILM, 3/4 OR 1/2 IN VIDEO K-P
Deals with the importance of movement, using the mind and body as one to help a child reach his or her full potential. Shows children involved in activities such as the clapping orchestra, invisible strings, train engineers, and trees and hammocks.
LC NO. 78-701762
Prod-BARAL Dist-FLMFR 1978

Teaching Your Wings To Fly C 19 MIN
3/4 INCH VIDEO CASSETTE
Demonstrates how preschool and elementary children can be taught body control, coordination, creativity, self-discipline and self-esteem through body movement and imaginative games.
Prod-LAWREN Dist-LAWREN

Teaching Your Wings To Fly - Learning Through Movement C 19 MIN
16MM FILM - 3/4 IN VIDEO T
Presents dance instructor Anne Lief Barlin demonstrating how to teach young children movement activities designed to enhance body control, self-esteem, spacial awareness, coordination, relationships with others, and relaxation.
LC NO. 78-701762
Prod-BARAL Dist-LAWREN 1978

Teaching Youth C 29 MIN
16MM FILM OPTICAL SOUND
See series title for descriptive statement.
From The Teaching Series.
Prod-BROADM Dist-BROADM 1977

Teaching—A Series

Analyzes the dynamics involved in the teaching-learning process.
Prod-BROADM Dist-BROADM 1977

Teaching Adults 029 MIN
Teaching Babies, Creepers And Toddlers 029 MIN
Teaching Fours And Fives At Church 029 MIN
Teaching Middle And Younger Children 029 MIN

Teaching Older Children 029 MIN
Teaching Young Adults 029 MIN
Teaching Youth 029 MIN

Teaching-Learning Process, The C 11 MIN
3/4 OR 1/2 INCH VIDEO CASSETTE
Looks at the basic elements of the teaching-learning process, including the teacher, the learner, the subject matter and the environment in which the learning takes place.
From The Supervisor As A Classroom Instructor Series. Module 1
Prod-RESEM Dist-RESEM

Tealia C 10 MIN
16MM FILM, 3/4 OR 1/2 IN VIDEO
Gives a presentation of an original ballet choreographed and performed by dancers of the San Francisco Ballet.
Prod-ROARP Dist-PHENIX 1977

Team Approach To Patient Management, A C 20 MIN
3/4 OR 1/2 INCH VIDEO CASSETTE PRO
Discusses the health care team as it applies to the treatment of people with diabetes. Emphasizes the facts that quality care is based on each team member performing his defined role, the agreement of each member in the team philosophy of treatment, and the effectiveness of the team leader.
From The Life With Diabetes Series.
LC NO. 81-707065
Prod-UMICH Dist-UMICH 1980

Team Approach To Patient Management, A C 20 MIN
3/4 OR 1/2 INCH VIDEO CASSETTE PRO
Presents a discussion of the health care team as it applies to the treatment of people with diabetes.
Prod-UMICHM Dist-UMICHM 1980

Team Approach, The C 30 MIN
3/4 OR 1/2 INCH VIDEO CASSETTE
Presents a discussion of student interdisciplinary action and its composition and usefulness in considering problems recommending solutions.
From The Teaching Students With Special Needs Series.
Prod-MSITV Dist-PBS 1981

Team Building C 15 MIN
16MM FILM OPTICAL SOUND
Shows a mock classroom session of instruction on team building for hospital employees.
From The ICARE Training Series.
LC NO. 75-704050
Prod-BHME Dist-USNAC Prodn-ARHERF 1975

Team Building C 18 MIN
16MM FILM, 3/4 OR 1/2 IN VIDEO C A
Outlines necessary steps to follow and describes common pitfalls to avoid in order to change a group of people into an effective team.
LC NO. 82-707361
Prod-CRMP Dist-CRMP 1982

Team Building C 30 MIN
16MM FILM - 3/4 IN VIDEO IND
Sheldon Davis of TRW INC, systems group, describes how an organization goes about introducing team building and discusses its purposes.
From The Effective Organization Series.
Prod-BNA Dist-BNA 1971

Team Building (Spanish) C 18 MIN
16MM FILM, 3/4 OR 1/2 IN VIDEO C A
Outlines necessary steps to follow and describes common pitfalls to avoid in order to change a group of people into an effective team.
Prod-CRMP Dist-CRMP 1982

Team Building For Administrative Support Staff—A Series

Designed to improve communicaition interaction, commitment and productivity for administrative and managerial support staff.
Prod-AMA Dist-AMA

Developing On-The-Job Communication Skills
Making The Most Of On-The-Job Changes
Using Managerial Techniques On The Job
Working Effectively With Different Managerial
Working With Others

Team Conferences B 30 MIN
16MM FILM OPTICAL SOUND C A
Presents and identifies communication elements in a team conference to observe and analyze specific communication skills in problem solving groups.
From The Nursing - R Plus M Equals C, Relationship Plus Meaning Equals Communication Series.
LC NO. 74-700212
Prod-NTCN Dist-NTCN 1971

Team Leader's Module C 26 MIN
3/4 INCH VIDEO CASSETTE
Summarizes the rationale for the employee training program within the Veterans Administration Medical Administration Service.
LC NO. 79-707306
Prod-USVA Dist-USNAC 1978

Team Of Two, A C 30 MIN
16MM FILM, 3/4 OR 1/2 IN VIDEO
Shows how managers and their secretaries might work together as a more productive team.
Prod-CCCD Dist-CCCD

Team Planning In The Cognitively Oriented Curriculum B 18 MIN
3/4 OR 1/2 INCH VIDEO CASSETTE PRO
Shows two preschool teachers at important points of the school day, planning activities, sharing observations of children and evaluating the effectiveness of planned activities.
Prod-HSERF Dist-HSERF

Team Roping C 26 MIN
16MM FILM, 3/4 OR 1/2 IN VIDEO
Deals with team roping including techniques and pointers on the selection and use of rope, and the training and selection of team roping horses.
Prod-AQHORS Dist-AQHORS 1978

Team Roping Clinic C 30 MIN
1/2 IN VIDEO CASSETTE BETA/VHS
Demonstrates how to win team roping.
From The Western Training Series.
Prod-EQVDL Dist-EQVDL

Team Show, A C 30 MIN
3/4 OR 1/2 INCH VIDEO CASSETTE P-I
Features three musical teams, including a 14-piece string orchestra, a group of eight violinists, and The Haydn Trio. Points out that while it is important to be able to play solo, it is also very important and great fun to learn to play with others. Presents Heiichiro Ohyama, principal viola of the Los Angeles Philharmonic Orchestra. Hosted by Florence Henderson.
From The Musical Encounter Series.
Prod-KLCSTV Dist-GPITVL 1983

Team Spirit C 18 MIN
16MM FILM OPTICAL SOUND
Depicts joint American and Korean military operations in the Pacific.
LC NO. 78-701900
Prod-USDDI Dist-USNAC 1978

Team That Hustles, The - The Inside Story Of Your Bones And Muscles C 15 MIN
3/4 OR 1/2 INCH VIDEO CASSETTE P-I
Presents Slim Goodbody and a friendly skeleton who chat about bones and their structure. Shows different types of bones, joints, and muscles, and how they work together. Stresses good food and exercise.
From The Inside Story With Slim Goodbody Series.
Prod-UWISC Dist-AITECH 1981

Team Work For A Controlled Environment C 24 MIN
16MM FILM OPTICAL SOUND
Stresses the importance of healthful living and working conditions at Air Force installations and shows how a successful preventive-medicine program is dependent upon the continuing joint efforts of the various activities concerned.
LC NO. FIE59-232
Prod-USAF Dist-USNAC 1958

Team-Work C 11 MIN
16MM FILM, 3/4 OR 1/2 IN VIDEO
Offers a nonverbal parable from the People's Republic of China about three monks and their development of a cooperative system of collecting water from a spring at the foot of the mountain.
Prod-FLMFR Dist-FLMFR 1982

Team, The C 29 MIN
16MM FILM OPTICAL SOUND
Documents the work and scope of Magen David Adom, Israel's Red Cross service.
Prod-YANIV Dist-ALDEN

Teamwork C
3/4 OR 1/2 INCH VIDEO CASSETTE
Emphasizes communication and participation by quality circle members. Stresses reacting to ideas rather than to the person presenting them.
From The Implementing Quality Circles Series.
Prod-BNA Dist-BNA

Teamwork C 8 MIN
3/4 OR 1/2 INCH VIDEO CASSETTE A
Shows how commitment to a team can make the difference between success and failure in sports and business. Narrated by Jack Whitaker.
Prod-SFTI Dist-SFTI

Teamwork - A Film From The People's Republic Of China C 11 MIN
16MM FILM, 3/4 OR 1/2 IN VIDEO H-C A
Uses a story about three feuding monks, who must replenish their temple's water, in order to demonstrate the importance of teamwork. Shows how the monks develop a new and ingenious method for sharing the task. Designed to illustrate the dynamics of groups and how these dynamics affect group performance.
LC NO. 83-706002
Prod-SAFS Dist-SALENG 1982

Teamwork - An Introduction To Group Dynamics C 24 MIN
16MM FILM, 3/4 OR 1/2 IN VIDEO C A
Presents the film Teamwork, a short animated film from China, after which Dr Frank Wagner analyzes the film, indicating the six sources of conflict illustrated.
LC NO. 84-706177
Prod-SALENG Dist-SALENG 1984

Teamwork And Concluding Remarks C 45 MIN
3/4 OR 1/2 INCH VIDEO CASSETTE IND
Covers corporate annual planning, phases of new product development, integrating activities of disparate departments, organizational options, reducing organizational conflict, requirement of objective reviews and concentrating resources for pay off and summary.
From The New Product Development Series.
Prod-AMCEE Dist-AMCEE

Teamwork And Leadership C 29 MIN
2 INCH VIDEOTAPE C A
Features a humanistic psychologist who, by analysis and examples, discusses teamwork and leadership.
From The Interpersonal Competence, Unit 08 - Groups Series.
Prod-MVNE Dist-TELSTR 1973

Teamwork For Safety X 10 MIN
16MM FILM OPTICAL SOUND
Illustrates making a group of people feel like part of a team and function like one. Shows how team effort helps prevent accidents.
From The Human Factors In Safety Series.
Prod-NSC Dist-NSC

Teamwork In Action C 30 MIN
16MM FILM OPTICAL SOUND
Presents the story of an industrial accident in Ontario, Canada, and tells how it is handled under the workmen's compensation law of the province of Ontario.
Prod-ISWELC Dist-AFLCIO 1958

Teamwork In Action C 33 MIN
16MM FILM OPTICAL SOUND
Tells what happens to an Ontario workman and his family when he is disabled by an industrial accident. Shows the roles of various members of the team with whom the victim comes into contact as a result of his accident.
Prod-ISWELC Dist-ISWELC

Teamwork On The Nevada Range C 18 MIN
16MM FILM OPTICAL SOUND
Tells the story of rural development through the combined efforts of government agencies and Nevada ranchers.
LC NO. FIE63-217
Prod-USDA Dist-USNAC 1963

Teamwork On The Potomac C 29 MIN
16MM FILM OPTICAL SOUND
A story about pollution in the Potomac River. Shows the river at its worst and describes the difficult climb toward restoration. Discusses pollution and waste-disposal methods. Explores water-management problems in detail.
LC NO. FIA66-790
Prod-FINLYS Dist-FINLYS 1965

Teamworking C 13 MIN
16MM FILM, 3/4 OR 1/2 IN VIDEO J-C A
Observes the creative efforts of three teams, a group of ecologically-minded architects, a crew of Ford automobile design engineers and talented members of a ballet company.
Prod-WILANH Dist-PHENIX

Teapots C 28 MIN
2 INCH VIDEOTAPE
Features Mrs Peterson describing certain ceramic processes for her classroom at the University of Southern California. Includes a demonstration with teapots.
From The Wheels, Kilns And Clay Series.
Prod-USC Dist-PUBTEL

Tear Gas And Self-Defense C 14 MIN
16MM FILM, 3/4 OR 1/2 IN VIDEO H-C A
Presents tear gas as an effective and safe self-defense weapon, but one that is controlled by law. Describes the effect of the gas on the criminal and shows how to use the cannisters. Distinguishes between legal and illegal use, stressing that tear gas should be used only to allow the user to escape.
Prod-AIMS Dist-AIMS 1981

Teasing And Being Teased C 22 MIN
16MM FILM, 3/4 OR 1/2 IN VIDEO K-P S
Presents Mr Rogers presenting segments on how teasing can make people feel bad. Discusses growing up with a physical handicap and being teased in order to help develop an appreciation of other people's differences.
From The I Am, I Can, I Will, Level II Series.
LC NO. 80-706549
Prod-FAMCOM Dist-HUBDSC 1979

Teasing, Breeding And Semen Collection In The Horse C 25 MIN
1/2 IN VIDEO CASSETTE BETA/VHS
Gives examples of estrus in mares. Tells how to wash a horse's penis. Discusses condoms and artificial vaginas for semen collection.
Prod-UMINN Dist-EQVDL

Tech Island C 14 MIN
3/4 INCH VIDEO CASSETTE
Profiles four Long Island engineers and their work.
Prod-WSTGLC Dist-WSTGLC

Technical And Professional Writing For Industry, Government And Business—A Series
IND
Trains participants to write reports of the sort required of practicing engineers and managers in industry, government and business. Emphasizes the needs of complex audiences and will improve student's ability to analyze audiences, state problems, design reports, prepare visual aids, and write and edit memos, reports and articles.
Prod-UMICE Dist-AMCEE

Analyzing Your Audience 055 MIN
Arranging The Discussion - Persuasive And 055 MIN
Designing The Basic Structure 055 MIN
Editing 055 MIN
Editing - Plain English 055 MIN
Handling Length And Complexity 055 MIN
High Frequency Errors 055 MIN
Planning Layout And Graphics 055 MIN
Preparing And Evaluating Reports Systematically 055 MIN

Stating Your Purpose 055 MIN
Tricks Of The Trade 055 MIN
Writing And Editing 055 MIN

Technical Bias - A Current Disease C 53 MIN
3/4 OR 1/2 INCH VIDEO CASSETTE
Expresses a professor's view on a major chemical company's 'failure' to apply the marketing concept.
From The Introduction To Marketing, A Lecture Series.
Prod-IVCH Dist-IVCH

Technical Bias And The Better Mousetrap C 53 MIN
3/4 OR 1/2 INCH VIDEO CASSETTE
Shows one attempt to capitalize on Emerson's advice, with disastrous results. Debunks the 'myth of the better mousetrap' and gives new insights into the philosophy of the marketing concept.
From The Introduction To Marketing, A Lecture Series.
Prod-IVCH Dist-IVCH

Technical Considerations In Hemipelvectomy C 16 MIN
16MM FILM OPTICAL SOUND PRO
Demonstrates a tumor of the upper femur for which hemipelvectomy is indicated. Shows the case of a 60 year old woman with a chondrosarcoma of the left pubis with details of the operative procedures.
Prod-ACYDGD Dist-ACY 1955

Technical Data Management And Documentation B 42 MIN
16MM FILM OPTICAL SOUND
Presents a panel discussion on the status of the Department of Defense management program. Discusses program weaknesses, problems and improvement possibilities.
LC NO. 74-706272
Prod-USAF Dist-USNAC 1965

Technical Procedures For Diagnosis And Therapy In Children C 27 MIN
16MM FILM OPTICAL SOUND PRO
Gives step-by-step procedures for femoral venipuncture, internal jugular puncture, lumbar puncture, subdural tap, gastric lavage, scalp venipuncture and cutdown.
LC NO. 74-705752
Prod-USN Dist-USNAC 1965

Technical Proposal Evaluation C 19 MIN
3/4 OR 1/2 INCH VIDEO CASSETTE
Describes the methodology of evaluating technical proposals.
LC NO. 80-706762
Prod-USDL Dist-USNAC 1978

Technical Side Of Production, The C 30 MIN
3/4 OR 1/2 INCH VIDEO CASSETTE
See series title for descriptive statement.
From The Behind The Scenes Series.
Prod-ARCVID Dist-ARCVID

Technical Side Of TV, The C 12 MIN
16MM FILM, 3/4 OR 1/2 IN VIDEO I-J
Describes the technical aspects of producing a television program.
From The Getting The Most Out Of TV Series.
LC NO. 81-706057
Prod-TAPPRO Dist-MTI 1981

Technical Studies—A Series
16MM FILM, 3/4 OR 1/2 IN VIDEO H-C A
Illustrates the practical application of concepts in materials and engineering science.
Prod-BBCTV Dist-FI 1981

Die And Investment Casting 025 MIN
Engineering Design 025 MIN
Forging 025 MIN
Heat Treatment 025 MIN
Manufacturing With Plastics 025 MIN
Micro-Electronics 025 MIN
Pressworking 025 MIN
Properties Of Plastics 025 MIN
Rolling 025 MIN
Sand Casting 025 MIN

Technical Venture Strategies C 49 MIN
3/4 OR 1/2 INCH VIDEO CASSETTE
Discusses entrepreneurial alternatives, investments in small companies, joint ventures and new venture spin-offs, internal venture generation and directions for enhancing new venture results.
From The Management Of Technological Innovation Series.
Prod-MIOT Dist-MIOT

Technical Writing C 150 MIN
3/4 OR 1/2 INCH VIDEO CASSETTE
Teaches how to convey technical material with specific audiences in mind. Reveals how to develop an organizational approach to technical writing that communicates effectively.
Prod-AMCHEM Dist-AMCHEM

Technical Writing Techniques C 15 MIN
3/4 OR 1/2 INCH VIDEO CASSETTE
See series title for descriptive statement.
From The Technical Writing Series.
Prod-DELTAK Dist-DELTAK Prodn-TRESA

Technical Writing—A Series

Covers the basic skills and techniques of technical writing.
Prod-DELTAK Dist-DELTAK Prodn-TRESA

Applied Technical Writing 015 MIN
Efficient Technical Writing 015 MIN
Technical Writing Techniques 015 MIN

Technical/Manufacturing Cluster 1 C 20 MIN
3/4 OR 1/2 INCH VIDEO CASSETTE
Discusses the requirements and duties for such jobs as welder, drafter, sheet metal worker and instrumentation technician.
From The Vocational Visions Series.
Prod-GA Dist-GA

Technical/Manufacturing Cluster 2 C 25 MIN
3/4 OR 1/2 INCH VIDEO CASSETTE
Discusses the requirements and duties for such jobs as computer programmer, engineering technician, fluid power technologist, avionics technician and parts merchandiser.
From The Vocational Visions Series.
Prod-GA Dist-GA

Technicians Of Tomorrow C 20 MIN
16MM FILM OPTICAL SOUND
Describes the training of specialists—the engineering technicians in two-year technical colleges—and points out the increasing need for them in American industry.
Prod-SGF Dist-USOE 1966

Technique B 29 MIN
16MM FILM, 3/4 OR 1/2 IN VIDEO H-C A
Illustrates from the collection of Ansel Adams the use of light, filters, exposure, magnification and interpretation. Demonstrates the use of these techniques to achieve given effects.
From The Photography - The Incisive Art Series.
LC NO. 80-707013
Prod-NET Dist-IU Prodn-KQEDTV 1962

Technique For Making A Slide Culture C 18 MIN
3/4 INCH VIDEO CASSETTE
Demonstrates step-by-step mycological techniques used to identify a fungal culture.
LC NO. 80-706766
Prod-CFDISC Dist-USNAC 1979

Technique For Propelling Standard Wheelchair By Hemiplegic Patient C 8 MIN
16MM FILM OPTICAL SOUND
Demonstrates the manner in which a hemiplegic can be taught to use a wheelchair.
LC NO. 74-705753
Prod-USPHS Dist-USNAC 1966

Technique Of Brain Surgery Of The Cat With Observations On Vestibular Disfunction... B 15 MIN
16MM FILM OPTICAL SOUND C
Describes surgical operation on a cat to section the eighth cranial nerve and shows the many classical symptoms of vestibular disfunction.
Prod-NESMKA Dist-PSUPCR 1939

Technique Of Clinical Electromyography C 17 MIN
16MM FILM OPTICAL SOUND PRO
Demonstrates the use of the electromyograph and shows procedures employed in the use of the electrode needle. Illustrates the impulses caused from muscular contractions.
Prod-LOMAM Dist-LOMAM

Technique Of Fresh-Frozen Section Histochemistry As Applied To Muscle Biopsies C 15 MIN
3/4 INCH VIDEO CASSETTE PRO
Presents Dr Guy Cunningham lecturing on the technique of fresh-frozen section histochemistry as applied to muscle biopsies.
From The Intensive Course In Neuromuscular Diseases Series.
LC NO. 76-706109
Prod-NINDIS Dist-USNAC 1974

Technique Of Intra-Articular And Peri-Articular Injection C 20 MIN
16MM FILM OPTICAL SOUND PRO
Uses animation and live action to show Dr Edward Boland's technique of injecting the most commonly-affected sites. Shows where the needle penetrates, and discusses contraindications and necessary precautions.
From The Upjohn Vanguard Of Medicine Series.
LC NO. 79-703007
Prod-UPJOHN Dist-UPJOHN Prodn-WFP 1969

Technique Of Intra-Articular And Peri-Articular Injection, The C 20 MIN
3/4 OR 1/2 INCH VIDEO CASSETTE PRO
Describes the technique for correct injection of the principle joints in the body by means of actual demonstration and anatomical drawings.
Prod-WFP Dist-WFP

Technique Of Intracellular Perfusion Of Squid Giant Axon, The C 10 MIN
16MM FILM OPTICAL SOUND
Demonstrates the introduction of perfusion fluid into the inlet and outlet cannulas of the axon by means of the micromanipulator.
LC NO. 74-706274
Prod-NIMH Dist-USNAC 1969

Technique Of Menisectomy, The C 20 MIN
16MM FILM, 3/4 OR 1/2 IN VIDEO PRO
Shows the principles involved in different menisectomy techniques, such as exposure through skin incision, preservation of idle structures, retention and evaluation of posterior horn and excision of the posterior portion.
Prod-WRAIR Dist-USNAC

Technique Of Platelet Transfusion - Om-1284 C 22 MIN
16MM FILM OPTICAL SOUND PRO
Demonstrates a medical technique that is substantially reducing leukemia deaths due to hemorrhaging. Demonstrates the method of obtaining blood platelets by plasmapheresis.
Prod-NIH Dist-USNAC 1966

Technique Of Radical Cystectomy, The C 42 MIN
16MM FILM OPTICAL SOUND PRO
Demonstrates a systemic and meticulous approach to radical cystectomy with en bloc pelvic lymph node dissection.
LC NO. 75-702233
Prod-EATONL Dist-EATONL 1974

Technique Of Total Hip Replacement, A C 25 MIN
16MM FILM, 3/4 OR 1/2 IN VIDEO PRO
Introduces the Charnley technique of total hip replacement.
Prod-CMA Dist-LAWREN

Techniques C
3/4 OR 1/2 INCH VIDEO CASSETTE
Describes the technical aspects of working in various media and presents examples of works by artists who have excelled in the various techniques.
From The Metropolitan Museum Seminars In Art Series.
Prod-GA Dist-GA

Techniques C 30 MIN
3/4 OR 1/2 INCH VIDEO CASSETTE
Provides an overview of the basic security controls that can be applied to computer systems. Discusses security controls in terms of physical controls, logical controls, administrative controls and legal/social controls.
From The Corporate Computer Security Strategy Series.
Prod-DELTAK Dist-DELTAK

Techniques C 40 MIN
3/4 OR 1/2 INCH VIDEO CASSETTE
Highlights creative teaching methods to begin productive discussionS. Focuses on church youth group training.
From The Active Learning For Youth Series.
Prod-UMCOM Dist-ECUFLM

Techniques - Titration Of An Acid With A Base C 8 MIN
16MM FILM, 3/4 OR 1/2 IN VIDEO H-C
Details the procedures for titration involving addition of a sodium hydroxide solution of known concentration to a solution that contains an unknown quantity of acid by means of a buret.
Prod-CENTRO Dist-CORF

Techniques - Use Of Volumetric Glassware C 8 MIN
16MM FILM, 3/4 OR 1/2 IN VIDEO H-C
Explains the techniques for using volumetric glassware found in chemistry laboratories.
Prod-CENTRO Dist-CORF

Techniques And Applications Of Infrared B 120 MIN
16MM FILM OPTICAL SOUND IND
Introduces the theory of infrared radiation absorption and demonstrates techniques of sample handling and the uses of various instruments.
LC NO. 79-701626
Prod-AMCHEM Dist-AMCHEM 1976

Techniques And Practices For Equipment Operators C 60 MIN
3/4 OR 1/2 INCH VIDEO CASSETTE IND
States basic safety practices and relates them to specific plant safety regulations and procedures. Provides guidelines for responding to problems. Identifies guidelines for monitoring operations and for making changes to equipment.
From The Equipment Operation Training Program Series.
Prod-ITCORP Dist-ITCORP

Techniques For Detection Of Viruses In Blood Destined For Transfusion B 30 MIN
3/4 INCH VIDEO CASSETTE PRO
Describes and evaluates the agar gel diffusion and high voltage immunoelectro-osmophoresis (IEOP) tests for the detection of the SH antigen.
From The Clinical Pathology Series.
LC NO. 76-706110
Prod-NMAC Dist-USNAC 1970

Techniques For Handling Difficult People And Listening To Yourself C 16 MIN
3/4 OR 1/2 INCH VIDEO CASSETTE
See series title for descriptive statement.
From The Listening - The Forgotten Skill Series.
Prod-DELTAK Dist-DELTAK

Techniques For Security And Privacy In Computer Systems—A Series
16MM FILM, 3/4 OR 1/2 IN VIDEO A
Discusses techniques for security and privacy in computer systems. Hosted by Professor Lance J Hoffman.
Prod-UCEMC Dist-UCEMC

Authentication Methods In Computer Systems
Authorization And Logging In Computer Systems
Modern Encryption Techniques

Techniques For Supporting The Laboring Woman C 34 MIN
3/4 OR 1/2 INCH VIDEO CASSETTE PRO
Outlines guidelines for nurse's role in helping the woman in labor to relax, minimize her discomfort, and stay in control.
Prod-HSCIC Dist-HSCIC 1982

Techniques In Hanging Wallpaper C 21 MIN
16MM FILM, 3/4 OR 1/2 IN VIDEO J-C A
Illustrates basic equipment needed for hanging wallpaper. Tells how to remove the old paper and how to measure, cut and apply the new wallpaper.
From The Home Repairs Series.
LC NO. 81-706036
Prod-CENTRO Dist-CORF 1981

Techniques Of Army News Photography, The B 27 MIN
16MM FILM OPTICAL SOUND
Shows experts in photojournalism who design and illustrate es-

sentials of superior news photography, covering still and motion picture techniques.
LC NO. FIE64-24
Prod-USA Dist-USNAC 1963

Techniques Of Artificial Respiration C 11 MIN
16MM FILM OPTICAL SOUND
Deals with mouth-to-mouth resuscitation. Based on materials contained in the Standard First Aid Multimedia series.
Prod-AMRC Dist-AMRC 1973

Techniques Of Artificial Respiration (Spanish) C 11 MIN
16MM FILM OPTICAL SOUND
Deals with mouth-to-mouth resuscitation. Based on material contained in the Standard First Aid Multimedia series.
Prod-AMRC Dist-AMRC 1973

Techniques Of Ball Handling C 20 MIN
16MM FILM, 3/4 OR 1/2 IN VIDEO I-C A
Explains the fundamentals of basketball by focusing on ball handling, the seven basic passes, dribbling and drills.
From The Basketball Series. No. 1
Prod-ATHI Dist-ATHI 1976

Techniques Of Bone Marrow Aspiration C 8 MIN
3/4 INCH VIDEO CASSETTE
Gives the indications for performing bone marrow aspiration and biopsy. Demonstrates the two-needle technique for performing the aspiration, then the biopsy.
Prod-UTAHTI Dist-UTAHTI

Techniques Of Cell Assembly B 6 MIN
16MM FILM OPTICAL SOUND PRO
Examines the procedures of taking the nucleus, the cytoplasm and the cell membrane from different amoebas and combining them to form new amoeba-like organisms.
Prod-SQUIBB Dist-SQUIBB

Techniques Of Decision Making C 28 MIN
16MM FILM OPTICAL SOUND A
Presents practical methods for making decisions and applying them to typical on-the-job situations.
From The You In Public Service Series.
LC NO. 77-700969
Prod-USOE Dist-USNAC 1977

Techniques Of Defense C 20 MIN
16MM FILM, 3/4 OR 1/2 IN VIDEO I-C A
Explains the fundamentals of basketball by focusing on techniques of defense.
From The Basketball Series. No. 4
Prod-ATHI Dist-ATHI 1976

Techniques Of Defensive Driving–A Series
I-H A
Teaches the skills and techniques of defensive driving.
Prod-NSC Dist-NSC

Car Ahead, The 11 MIN
Car Behind, The 8 MIN
Crossroads Crash, The 8 MIN
Driving Expressways 11 MIN
Head-On Crash, The 10 MIN
Mystery Crash, The 8 MIN
Passing And Being Passed 10 MIN
Who's To Blame 10 MIN

Techniques of Drownproofing C 20 MIN
3/4 OR 1/2 INCH VIDEO CASSETTE
Teaches the exact techniques for survival in water as they are taught to trainees assigned to the United States Navy Underwater Survivor's School.
Prod-PRIMED Dist-PRIMED

Techniques Of Endometrial Biopsy C 12 MIN
3/4 INCH VIDEO CASSETTE
Demonstrates the instruments and techniques of the endometrial biopsy. Describes the cytologic examination of the biopsied tissue.
Prod-UTAHTI Dist-UTAHTI

Techniques Of Exhaled-Air Artificial Respiration B 12 MIN
16MM FILM OPTICAL SOUND
Shows how to administer mouth-to-mouth artificial respiration.
LC NO. FIE60-121
Prod-USAF Dist-USNAC 1959

Techniques Of Flying C 29 MIN
2 INCH VIDEOTAPE
See series title for descriptive statement.
From The Discover Flying - Just Like A Bird Series.
Prod-WKYCTV Dist-PUBTEL

Techniques Of Implanting The Port-a-Cath For Hepatic Artery Access C 8 MIN
3/4 INCH VIDEO CASSETTE
Illustrates the technique of inserting an implantible drug-delivery device known as a port-a-cath.
Prod-UTAHTI Dist-UTAHTI

Techniques Of Microvascular Anastomosis C 45 MIN
3/4 OR 1/2 INCH VIDEO CASSETTE PRO
Outlines and illustrates in detail how to perform microvascular anastomosis.
Prod-HSCIC Dist-HSCIC 1984

Techniques Of Non-Verbal Psychological Testing C 20 MIN
16MM FILM, 3/4 OR 1/2 IN VIDEO C A
Depicts psychological evaluation of children who cannot be examined by the usual intelligence tests because of very young age, physical handicaps or foreign culture. Shows use of non-verbal techniques such as Gesell development scales, Leiter international performance scale, parts of the Merrill-Palmer scale and Peabody vocabulary test.
Prod-ROSSCJ Dist-IFB 1965

Techniques Of Offense C 20 MIN
16MM FILM, 3/4 OR 1/2 IN VIDEO I-C A
Explains the fundamentals of basketball by focusing on the offensive game.
From The Basketball Series. No. 3
Prod-ATHI Dist-ATHI 1976

Techniques Of Paper Sculpture C 10 MIN
16MM FILM OPTICAL SOUND I-C A
Techniques of paper sculpturing are demonstrated and varied uses of this medium from party favors to lifesize figures for drapery displays are illustrated. (Also known as 'PAPER SCULPTURE')
Prod-ALLMOR Dist-AVED 1958

Techniques Of Parenteral Injection C 22 MIN
16MM FILM OPTICAL SOUND PRO
Focuses on the techniques involved in giving medications by injection and includes the four most common methods of parenteral injection, the intramuscular injection, the subcutaneous, the intradermal and the intravenous.
Prod-BECDIC Dist-SCITIF 1970

Techniques Of Physical Diagnosis - A Visual Approach–A Series

Demonstrates the physical examination in fine detail. Examines the head, neck, heart, thorax and abdomen.
Prod-MEDMDS Dist-MEDMDS

Abdomen, The 022 MIN
Head And Neck, The, PtA 017 MIN
Head And Neck, The, PtB 020 MIN
Heart, The 017 MIN
Thorax And Lungs, The 022 MIN

Techniques Of Shooting C 19 MIN
16MM FILM, 3/4 OR 1/2 IN VIDEO I-C A
Explains the fundamentals of basketball by focusing on the shooting game and a series of drills designed to improve offensive play.
From The Basketball Series. No. 2
Prod-ATHI Dist-ATHI 1976

Techniques Of Speech Correction C 8 MIN
16MM FILM, 3/4 OR 1/2 IN VIDEO
Shows a group of primary, intermediate and senior high school students who are involved in language development and speech correction.
LC NO. 80-707430
Prod-USBEH Dist-USNAC 1980

Techniques Of Thyroid Surgery C 29 MIN
16MM FILM OPTICAL SOUND PRO
Shows techniques of operations for cancers of the thyroid, multinodular goiters, solitary nodules and intrathoracic goiters. Shows the diagnosis and treatment of thyroiditis.
Prod-ACYDGD Dist-ACY 1955

Techniques Of Titration C 13 MIN
16MM FILM, 3/4 OR 1/2 IN VIDEO J-H A
Shows the preparation of a buret for titration and the correct techniques for performing simple acid-base titrations. Follows the steps outlined for cleaning, filling and preparing for titration.
From The Basic Laboratory Techniques In Chemistry Series.
Prod-LUF Dist-LUF 1981

Techniques Of Working With Addicts C 50 MIN
16MM FILM OPTICAL SOUND
Uses a series of simulated counseling sessions to describe behavior patterns of drug addicts and to depict counseling methods used to deal with them.
From The Films And Tapes For Drug Abuse Treatment Personnel Series.
LC NO. 73-703451
Prod-NIMH Dist-NIMH Prodn-UMIAMI 1973

Technological Man C 25 MIN
16MM FILM OPTICAL SOUND J-C A
Compares biological adaptation with technological invention and points out the differences in the rates of change. Looks at social factors contributing to the development of western technology. Argues the pros and cons of modern technology.
From The Science Of Life Series.
LC NO. 81-700850
Prod-CRIPSE Dist-WARDS 1981

Technologies For The Information Age C 210 MIN
3/4 OR 1/2 INCH VIDEO CASSETTE PRO
Discusses approaches to modern communications research. Describes original contributions in software, hardware, systems design and engineering.
Prod-AMCEE Dist-AMCEE

Technology C 45 MIN
3/4 OR 1/2 INCH VIDEO CASSETTE
Discusses some of the most powerful of the new information technologies, including video conferencing, communications satellites, computer networks, computer manufacturer influences and common carrier contributions.
From The Corporate Network Strategy Series.
Prod-DELTAK Dist-DELTAK

Technology - Catastrophe Or Commitment C 20 MIN
16MM FILM, 3/4 OR 1/2 IN VIDEO
Questions the idea that advanced technology offers the ultimate solution to all of society's problems, pointing out that some solutions kill even as they cure. Examines the dilemma of increasing industrialization and dwindling natural resources.
Prod-DOCUA Dist-CNEMAG

Technology And Reading Instruction C 30 MIN
2 INCH VIDEOTAPE T
Focuses on a number of innovations in methods and materials for classroom use.
From The Child Reads Series.
Prod-WENHTV Dist-GPITVL

Technology And The Disabled C 30 MIN
3/4 OR 1/2 INCH VIDEO CASSETTE
Discusses technology that may eventually allow the crippled to walk or the blind to see.
From The Innovation Series.
Prod-WNETTV Dist-WNETTV 1983

Technology And Values - The Energy Connection C 19 MIN
16MM FILM, 3/4 OR 1/2 IN VIDEO J-C A
Describes the world energy crisis and its affect on the environment. Discusses the need for conserving the existing supply of fossil fuel and for developing alternative energy sources.
Prod-AMSFLM Dist-BARR 1979

Technology At Your Fingertips C 20 MIN
16MM FILM OPTICAL SOUND
Describes how private firms have made practical use of NASA technology, including the technical information retrieval services made available through the agency's technology utilization program.
LC NO. 76-702701
Prod-NASA Dist-USNAC 1970

Technology For Spacecraft Design, A C 12 MIN
16MM FILM OPTICAL SOUND J-C
Shows technology being developed to enable scientists and engineers to design and build a flyable regenerative life support system for manned space missions of months or years.
From The Living In Space Series. Part 3
Prod-NASA Dist-NASA 1966

Technology For Spacecraft, A - Living In Space, Pt 2 C 12 MIN
16MM FILM OPTICAL SOUND
Shows the features that must be incorporated into a spacecraft intended for long duration manned space flight and the technology that is being developed to solve the numerous problems.
Prod-NASA Dist-NASA

Technology In Education C 28 MIN
16MM FILM OPTICAL SOUND T
Educational technology as a useful ally in the education.
From The Innovations In Education Series.
Prod-EDUC Dist-EDUC

Technology Utilization C 30 MIN
16MM FILM OPTICAL SOUND
Describes how private firms have made practical use of NASA technology, including the technical information retrieval services made available through the agency's technology utilization program.
LC NO. 76-702702
Prod-NASA Dist-USNAC 1970

Technology/Transformation - Wonder Woman C 7 MIN
3/4 OR 1/2 INCH VIDEO CASSETTE
See series title for descriptive statement.
From The Short Works By Dana Birnbaum Series.
Prod-EAI Dist-EAI

Technology, Innovation, And Industrial Development–A Series

Details how policies and programs for technological innovation in U S Industry can contribute to continued renewal of a dynamic economy.
Prod-MIOT Dist-MIOT

Dynamic View Of The Economy, A 051 MIN
Dynamic View Of The Firm, A 051 MIN
Dynamics Of An Economy 033 MIN
Dynamics Of Change In The Automobile Industry 071 MIN
Dynamics Of Change In The Electronics Industry 052 MIN
Dynamics Of Change In The Industrial Gas 037 MIN
Dynamics Of Change In The Textile Industry 053 MIN
Effects Of Change On Productivity And Labor 037 MIN
Importance Of Technology And Innovation, The 043 MIN
Innovative Dynamism And International Trade 056 MIN
Policies And Programs Of Other Governments 034 MIN
Possible Programs And Policies Of The U S 027 MIN
R And D And Innovation 045 MIN
Regulation And Innovation 051 MIN
Venturing - Old And New Firms 054 MIN
Views Of The Council On Economic Development 018 MIN

Technology, Transformation - Wonder Woman C 7 MIN
3/4 OR 1/2 INCH VIDEO CASSETTE
Presents a stutter-step progression of those moments of transformation within the television show Wonder Woman.
Prod-KITCHN Dist-KITCHN

Technology's Heartbeat C 30 MIN
3/4 OR 1/2 INCH VIDEO CASSETTE C
See series title for descriptive statement.
From The Time's Harvest - Exploring The Future Series.
Prod-MDCPB Dist-MDCPB

Ted Baryluk's Grocery B 10 MIN
3/4 OR 1/2 INCH VIDEO CASSETTE J-C A
Looks at Canadian Ted Baryluk's beliefs and background as he ponders retirement and the futile hope that his daughter will take over his grocery store.
LC NO. 83-707256
Prod-SCOTTM Dist-NFBC 1983

Ted Turner And The News War C 30 MIN
16MM FILM, 3/4 OR 1/2 IN VIDEO H-C A
Describes a winner-take-all contest between Cable News Network and ABC Group W's Satellite News Channel.
From The Enterprise Series.
Prod-MTI Dist-MTI

Ted Turner And The News War C 30 MIN
3/4 OR 1/2 INCH VIDEO CASSETTE H-C A
Discusses the battle between Ted Turner and his Cable News Network and ABC-Group W's Satellite News Channel. Tells how millions of viewers and hundreds of millions of dollars are at stake.
From The Enterprise III Series.
Prod-WGBHTV Dist-KINGFT

Ted Williams And The Atlantic Salmon C 28 MIN
16MM FILM OPTICAL SOUND
Shows sportsman Ted Williams as he attempts to catch Atlantic salmon on the Miramichi River in Canada.
LC NO. 75-702664
Prod-SEARS Dist-MTP Prodn-TELAIR 1974

Teddy C 17 MIN
3/4 OR 1/2 INCH VIDEO CASSETTE
Describes the experiences of a black teenager, focusing on his views of the system and showing his relationship with the church. Issued in 1971 as a motion picture.
From The Social Seminar Series.
LC NO. 80-707358
Prod-NIMH Dist-USNAC 1980

Teddy C 27 MIN
16MM FILM, 3/4 OR 1/2 IN VIDEO H-C A
Portrays a young man with a facial disfigurement who has not been out of the house in 25 years. Shows what happens when a friend convinces him that true beauty comes from within. Stars June Lockhart and Bud Cort.
From The Insight Series.
Prod-PAULST Dist-PAULST

Teddy At The Throttle B 20 MIN
16MM FILM OPTICAL SOUND I A
Features Gloria Swanson, Wallace Berry and Bobby Vernon in the 1916 Sennet Commedy, 'TEDDY AT THE THROTTLE.' Presents a typical 'VILLAIN-SWEETHEART-HERO' triangle, including automobile chases and close calls with speeding trains.
LC NO. 79-711886
Prod-MSENP Dist-BHAWK 1916

Teddy Bear's Balloon Trip, The C 14 MIN
16MM FILM, 3/4 OR 1/2 IN VIDEO P
Provides a background for language arts activities such as story-telling, creative dramatics and reading. Features a trip across Europe to Asia as a German girl sends her teddy bear by balloon with a gift for Chinese children.
Prod-CORF Dist-CORF 1970

Teddy Dibble - Selected Works 1985, The Man Who Made Faces, New Findings In Medical... C 4 MIN
3/4 OR 1/2 INCH VIDEO CASSETTE
Complete title reads Teddy Dibble - Selected Works 1985, The Man Who Made Faces, New Findings In Medical Science, what A Difference A Day Makes, The Moustache. Presents comedy hijinks.
Prod-ARTINC Dist-ARTINC

Teddy Dibble - The KCPT Tapes, If Looks Could Kill, The Sound Of Music, The Sound Of... C 10 MIN
3/4 OR 1/2 INCH VIDEO CASSETTE
Complete title reads Teddy Dibble - The KCPT Tapes, IF Looks Could Kill, The sound Of Music, The Sound Of Defiance, Practice Makes Perfect, A Scar-y Story. Makes fun of everything from medical ettiquette to prevalent truisms.
Prod-ARTINC Dist-ARTINC

Teddy Roosevelt - The Right Man At The Right Time C 28 MIN
16MM FILM, 3/4 OR 1/2 IN VIDEO J-C A
Explains that America was in severe crisis when Theodore Roosevelt came to the presidency in 1901. Shows how the power of big business was virtually unchecked by the government and that organized labor was still relatively weak. Features Roosevelt, known as the great Trust-Buster, who later changed his views to favor both business and labor.
Prod-LCOA Dist-LCOA 1974

Teddy Roosevelt - The Right Man At The Right Time (Spanish) C 28 MIN
16MM FILM, 3/4 OR 1/2 IN VIDEO J-C A
Traces key events of Teddy Roosevelt's administration, highlighting his leadership in breaking trusts, forcing arbitrations and instigating social and economic reforms.
Prod-LCOA Dist-LCOA 1974

Teeming Life Within The Sea, The B 7 MIN
16MM FILM OPTICAL SOUND
Presents a 1956 Screen News Digest film excerpt showing how microphotography captures on film the living animals in the salt water world near the Massachusetts coast. Shows specimens collected from the sea under the microscope's magnification.
From The News Magazine Of The Screen Series. Vol 7, No. 4
Prod-PATHE Dist-HEARST 1956

Teen Crime C 25 MIN
3/4 OR 1/2 INCH VIDEO CASSETTE J-C A
Discusses crime prevention, creative rehabilitation and the types of young adults who get into trouble and why.
Prod-SIRS Dist-SIRS

Teen Menstruation C
3/4 OR 1/2 INCH VIDEO CASSETTE
Addresses the two major menstrual problems encountered by teenagers, irregularity and late onset. Covers other helpful information on menstruation.
Prod-MIFE Dist-MIFE

Teen Mother - A Story Of Coping C 24 MIN
16MM FILM, 3/4 OR 1/2 IN VIDEO J-H
Provides insight into the reality of a teenage mother's life. Explores such issues as child care, housing, finance, education and social life.
Prod-MOBIUS Dist-CF 1981

Teen Rights C 25 MIN
3/4 OR 1/2 INCH VIDEO CASSETTE J-C A
Discusses the Youth Policy Institute, a unique organization founded by the late Robert F Kennedy Memorial where young adults monitor and publish reports on all litigation that affects the lives of American youth.
Prod-SIRS Dist-SIRS

Teen Runaways, Pt II - Effects And Solutions C 25 MIN
3/4 OR 1/2 INCH VIDEO CASSETTE J-C A
Continues the discussion about runaway teenagers.
Prod-SIRS Dist-SIRS

Teen Runaways, Pt I - Causes And Effects C 25 MIN
3/4 OR 1/2 INCH VIDEO CASSETTE J-C A
Interviews Rev Leonard Scheider, director of emergency shelter in New York City and Father Bruce Ritter, founder and director of 'Under 21/Convenant House' in New York City on the subject of runaway teenagers.
Prod-SIRS Dist-SIRS

Teen Scene C 38 MIN
16MM FILM OPTICAL SOUND
Provides birth control information for teenagers and their parents.
LC NO. 72-702343
Prod-PPFA Dist-PPFA 1972

Teen Sexuality - What's Right For You C 29 MIN
16MM FILM, 3/4 OR 1/2 IN VIDEO J-H
Presents teenagers discussing such topics as masturbation, pornography, homosexuality and venereal disease with a pair of doctors.
Prod-UUAMC Dist-PEREN

Teen Suicide - Who, Why And How You Can Prevent It C
3/4 OR 1/2 INCH VIDEO CASSETTE J-H
Tells which teens are most likely to attempt suicide and why. Shows how to recognize critical signs and where and how to seek help.
Prod-GA Dist-GA

Teen Times - Neither Fish Nor Fowl C 29 MIN
3/4 OR 1/2 INCH VIDEO CASSETTE T
See series title for descriptive statement.
From The Coping With Kids Series.
Prod-MFFD Dist-FI

Teen Times - Neither Fish Nor Fowl C 30 MIN
3/4 OR 1/2 INCH VIDEO CASSETTE
Discusses techniques for coping with the challenging period of development known as the teen years. Looks at the time between the dependence of the child and the autonomy of the adult as being difficult years for both parent and child.
From The Coping With Kids Series.
Prod-OHUTC Dist-OHUTC

Teen Tutor B 38 MIN
16MM FILM OPTICAL SOUND
Shows the operation of the Teen Tutor Program, in which seventh-grade boys and girls study child development, tutor kindergarten children and work in an integrated curriculum toward self-knowledge and social development. Portrays a Teen Tutor with his teachers and his classmates as he struggles with feelings about himself, his parents and younger children .
LC NO. 70-705682
Prod-SOUCS Dist-OSUMPD Prodn-OSUPD 1969

Teen-Age Mother, The C 26 MIN
3/4 OR 1/2 INCH VIDEO CASSETTE
Addresses the complex issue of adolescent mothers who discover that the adult world of single parenting at age 16 is not attractive.
Prod-WCCOTV Dist-WCCOTV 1981

Teen-age Weight Control C 16 MIN
3/4 OR 1/2 INCH VIDEO CASSETTE
Focuses on proper nutrition for teenagers. Discusses weight control. Stresses problems of snacking and junk foods.
Prod-MEDFAC Dist-MEDFAC 1981

Teen-Age Whiz Kids C 11 MIN
16MM FILM, 3/4 OR 1/2 IN VIDEO I-C A
Focuses on two exceptionally bright young teenagers who are accelerating their studies in a special program at the University of Washington. Shows the teenagers in college courses and with college classmates, while the remarks of their parents and a university administrator voice some of the cautions with which they approach this acceleration of academics. Originally shown on the CBS program 30 Minutes.
Prod-CBSNEW Dist-MOKIN 1981

Teenage Addiction - Alcohol And Drugs C 30 MIN
3/4 OR 1/2 INCH VIDEO CASSETTE
Tells the story of the nation's chemically dependent teenagers, focusing on eight recovering, addicted teenagers from the Twin Cities.
Prod-WCCOTV Dist-WCCOTV 1981

Teenage Blues - Coping With Depression C
3/4 OR 1/2 INCH VIDEO CASSETTE J-C
Introduces students to the concept of depression, some common causes and symptoms, where and how to get help. Suggests self-help methods for alleviating mild depression while cautioning that some severe cases require outside assistance. Includes teacher's guide.
Prod-SUNCOM Dist-SUNCOM

Teenage Challenge B 30 MIN
16MM FILM OPTICAL SOUND J-H T R
Portrays how a school essay contest is the basis for an examination of the problem of how a Christian teenager can seek God's will and still be popular.
From The Teenage Film Series.
LC NO. FIA67-1924
Prod-FAMF Dist-FAMF 1958

Teenage Christmas X 30 MIN
16MM FILM OPTICAL SOUND J-H T R
Points out how a group of teenagers, caught in the pressures of a commercial Christmas season, realize the true meaning of Christmas as they tell the story of the coming of Christ to two small children.
From The Teenage Film Series.
LC NO. FIA67-1923
Prod-FAMF Dist-FAMF 1959

Teenage Code B 30 MIN
16MM FILM OPTICAL SOUND J-H T R
Dramatizes a situation in which a Christian boy must choose between conflicting ideas about cheating.
From The Teenage Film Series.
LC NO. FIA67-1922
Prod-FAMF Dist-FAMF 1958

Teenage Conflict B 30 MIN
16MM FILM OPTICAL SOUND J-H T R
Describes how a boy and his sister, who have rejected the Christian faith for new scientific concepts, are shown by a scientist the relationship between the scientific approach and Christian concepts.
From The Teenage Film Series.
LC NO. FIA67-1921
Prod-FAMF Dist-FAMF 1959

Teenage Crusade B 30 MIN
16MM FILM OPTICAL SOUND J-H T R
Portrays two boys involved in planning a visitation crusade with their youth group. Tells how their plans to bring other youths to church were almost wrecked by a rough crowd. Shows how they meet the problem with sincerity and friendliness and accomplish their goal.
From The Teenage Series.
LC NO. FIA67-1920
Prod-FAMF Dist-FAMF 1960

Teenage Drinking - A National Crisis C 32 MIN
16MM FILM, 3/4 OR 1/2 IN VIDEO J-C A
Presents four young people who discuss graphically why teenage drinking is a national problem. Offers advice on how to recognize a drinking problem, how young people can handle friends who urge them to drink and how parents can help youngsters who are struggling with alcohol abuse.
Prod-ABCTV Dist-MTI 1982

Teenage Drinking - Hey, How About Another One C 15 MIN
16MM FILM, 3/4 OR 1/2 IN VIDEO J-H
Shows two high school students deciding that alcohol will help them relax for an exam.
From The Conflict And Awareness Series.
Prod-CRMP Dist-CRMP 1975

Teenage Dropouts - Wasted Wealth C 60 MIN
3/4 OR 1/2 INCH VIDEO CASSETTE I-C A
Documents the problems of teenage dropouts. Includes discussions with parents, teachers, police and judges. Looks at some alternative educational programs.
Prod-WETATV Dist-WETATV

Teenage Entrepreneurs, Pt I - Teenagers Learning About Entrepreneurship C 25 MIN
3/4 OR 1/2 INCH VIDEO CASSETTE J-C A
Focuses on teenage entrepreneurs who own their own businesses. Profiles four student businesses and discusses regulating competition on campus.
Prod-SIRS Dist-SIRS

Teenage Entrepreneurs, Pt II - Teenagers Design Programs For Home Computers C 25 MIN
3/4 OR 1/2 INCH VIDEO CASSETTE J-C A
Illustrates the increasing popularity among teenagers of designing computer programs and becoming involved in computer-related businesses.
Prod-SIRS Dist-SIRS

Teenage Father C 30 MIN
16MM FILM OPTICAL SOUND J-C A
Looks at teenage parenthood from the points of view of the unmarried father, the mother, peers, and both sets of parents.
LC NO. 79-701017
Prod-CHSCA Dist-CHSCA Prodn-NEWVIS 1978

Teenage Girls C 58 MIN
3/4 OR 1/2 INCH VIDEO CASSETTE A
Focuses on three lower-class urban families in which the relationships among family members are marred by constant strife.
LC NO. 81-707244
Prod-CCABC Dist-CCABC 1980

Teenage Homosexuality C 11 MIN
16MM FILM, 3/4 OR 1/2 IN VIDEO J-C A
Presents five gay teenagers describing their lifestyles. Interviews a psychiatrist who works with gay teenagers and offers the opinions of a mother of a gay teenager. Originally shown on the CBS television series 30 Minutes.

LC NO. 80-707728
Prod-CBSNEW Dist-CAROUF 1980

Teenage Idols, Pt 1 B 26 MIN
16MM FILM OPTICAL SOUND
Presents stars popular with teenagers since World War II, including singers Frank Sinatra, Elvis Presley, Pat Boone and Ricky Nelson, disc jockey Dick Clark, and actors James Dean, Marlon Brando and Sandra Dee.
From The Hollywood And The Stars Series.
LC NO. FI68-269
Prod-WOLPER Dist-WOLPER 1964

Teenage Idols, Pt 2 B 26 MIN
16MM FILM OPTICAL SOUND
Discusses the career of teenage idol, Fabian, and discusses the publicity prior to his appearance, his rise to stardom, his loneliness and decision to buy out his contract in order to attempt an acting career.
From The Hollywood And The Stars Series.
LC NO. FI68-270
Prod-WOLPER Dist-WOLPER 1964

Teenage Immigrants C 25 MIN
3/4 OR 1/2 INCH VIDEO CASSETTE J-C A
Illustrates how teenage immigrants have the burden of coming to terms with where their home is.
Prod-SIRS Dist-SIRS

Teenage Loyalty B 30 MIN
16MM FILM OPTICAL SOUND J-H T R
Dramatizes circumstances that make a high school leader realize that her first loyalty should be to Christ.
From The Teenage Film Series.
LC NO. FIA67-1919
Prod-FAMF Dist-FAMF 1959

Teenage Marriage C 25 MIN
3/4 OR 1/2 INCH VIDEO CASSETTE J-C A
Presents a 'family living' course in which young couples are paired and taught to deal with wedding plans, insurance, apartment seeking, finance and emotional trauma.
Prod-SIRS Dist-SIRS

Teenage Mother - A Broken Dream C 15 MIN
16MM FILM, 3/4 OR 1/2 IN VIDEO J-C A
Examines the life of a 15-year-old unwed mother.
Prod-CBSNEW Dist-CAROUF

Teenage Parents C 10 MIN
16MM FILM, 3/4 OR 1/2 IN VIDEO J-H
Documents the lifestyles of two teenaged married couples who are discovering what it is like to assume the responsibilities of marriage and parenthood while still teenagers.
LC NO. 81-706013
Prod-CBSNEW Dist-CRMP 1981

Teenage Pregnancy C 14 MIN
16MM FILM, 3/4 OR 1/2 IN VIDEO J-C A
Shows that a teenage daughter's pregnancy brings emotional and psychological upheaval to the entire family.
From The Family Life Education And Human Growth Series.
Prod-SF Dist-SF 1970

Teenage Pregnancy C 29 MIN
3/4 INCH VIDEO CASSETTE
Examines the implications of teenage pregnancy.
From The Woman Series.
Prod-WNEDTV Dist-PUBTEL

Teenage Pregnancy - An American Crisis C 55 MIN
3/4 INCH VIDEO CASSETTE
Looks at the increasing number of teenage pregnancies, the sexual attitudes of young people, and the roles that parents, peers, church, school and society play in sex education.
Prod-OHC Dist-HRC

Teenage Pregnancy - No Easy Answers C 22 MIN
16MM FILM, 3/4 OR 1/2 IN VIDEO J-H
Looks at a 15-year-old girl who learns that she is pregnant and must choose among abortion, adoption, single parenting or marriage.
Prod-SHIRE Dist-BARR 1980

Teenage Pregnancy Experience, The C 26 MIN
16MM FILM - 3/4 IN VIDEO I-C A
Follows two school-age mothers through pregnancy, labor and birth. Shows them caring for their young infants.
From The Parenting Experience Series.
LC NO. 81-706053
Prod-COURTR Dist-PARPIC 1981

Teenage Revolution B 52 MIN
16MM FILM OPTICAL SOUND
Studies American teenagers and their activities, their economic power, their idols and their social life. Deals with the teenage scientist, the dropout and many other facets of teenage life.
LC NO. FIA66-652
Prod-FI Dist-WOLPER Prodn-WOLPER 1965

Teenage Romance B 30 MIN
16MM FILM OPTICAL SOUND J-H T R
Discusses teenage dating and the problems and adjustments of going steady.
From The Teenage Film Series.
LC NO. FIA67-1917
Prod-FAMF Dist-FAMF 1959

Teenage Sexuality And Contraception C 13 MIN
16MM FILM - 3/4 IN VIDEO J-H
Enumerates contraceptive methods available with and without a prescription. Describes procedures for their proper use and discusses the advantages, disadvantages and failure rate of each.

LC NO. 79-707947
Prod-MIFE Dist-MIFE 1979

Teenage Shoplifting C 10 MIN
16MM FILM, 3/4 OR 1/2 IN VIDEO J-H
Focuses on a community where store owners and parents are working to curb shoplifting.
LC NO. 81-706014
Prod-CBSNEW Dist-CRMP 1981

Teenage Suicide C 16 MIN
16MM FILM, 3/4 OR 1/2 IN VIDEO A
Examines the reasons for the number of teenage suicides. Interviews parents, professional authorities and emotionally disturbed youths.
Prod-CBSNEW Dist-MTI 1979

Teenage Suicide C 25 MIN
3/4 OR 1/2 INCH VIDEO CASSETTE J-C A
Explores the growing problem of teenage suicide in America. Shows how organizations such as the National Suicide Hotline in Denver have been formed to help young adults overcome serious depression.
Prod-SIRS Dist-SIRS

Teenage Suicide C 60 MIN
16MM FILM, 3/4 OR 1/2 IN VIDEO H-C A
Explores the lives and deaths of four American teenagers. States that every day in America, 18 young people commit suicide. Narrated by Timothy Hutton.
Prod-LNDBRG Dist-FI 1981

Teenage Suicide - Is Anyone Listening C 22 MIN
16MM FILM, 3/4 OR 1/2 IN VIDEO J-H
Explores the mounting problem of severe depression in adolescence. Tells the stories of a 16-year-old boy and a 14-year-old girl who have attempted suicide.
Prod-BARR Dist-BARR 1980

Teenage Suicide - The Ultimate Dropout C 29 MIN
3/4 OR 1/2 INCH VIDEO CASSETTE
Offers advice by psychiatrists and social workers to families facing a potential suicide crisis.
Prod-KAETTV Dist-PBS 1980

Teenage Testament B 30 MIN
16MM FILM OPTICAL SOUND J-H T R
Presents how a teenage boy with active Christian convictions reacts to a situation in which his faith is seriously tested.
From The Teenage Film Series.
LC NO. FIA67-1916
Prod-FAMF Dist-FAMF 1959

Teenage Turn-On - Drinking And Drugs C 38 MIN
16MM FILM, 3/4 OR 1/2 IN VIDEO J-H
Presents addicted teenagers telling their stories. Visits a drug treatment center and a half-way house.
Prod-ABCNEW Dist-CRMP 1977

Teenage Witness B 30 MIN
16MM FILM OPTICAL SOUND J-H T R
Tells the experiences of a boy who, despite unhappy school and home situations, continues to share his Christian faith.
From The Teenage Film Series.
LC NO. FIA67-1915
Prod-FAMF Dist-FAMF 1958

Teenage Years—A Series
16MM FILM, 3/4 OR 1/2 IN VIDEO
Prod-TIMLIF Dist-TIMLIF 1976

Amazing Cosmic Awareness Of Duffy Moon, The	32 MIN
Blind Sunday	31 MIN
Bridge Of Adam Rush, The	47 MIN
Escape Of A One-Ton Pet, The	41 MIN
Follow The North Star	47 MIN
Gaucho	47 MIN
Heartbreak Winner	47 MIN
Hewitt's Just Different	47 MIN
Home Run For Love, A	47 MIN
Home To Stay	47 MIN
Horrible Honchos, The	31 MIN
I Don't Know Who I Am	30 MIN
It's A Mile From Here To Glory	47 MIN
Me And Dad's New Wife	33 MIN
Mighty Moose And The Quarterback Kid	31 MIN
Mom And Dad Can't Hear Me	47 MIN
My Mom's Having A Baby	47 MIN
New York City, Too Far From Tampa Blues	47 MIN
P J And The President's Son	47 MIN
Rocking Chair Rebellion, The	30 MIN
Rookie Of The Year	47 MIN
Sara's Summer Of The Swans	33 MIN
Secret Life Of T K Dearing, The	47 MIN
Special Gift, A	47 MIN
Tell Me My Name	52 MIN
Terrible Secret, The	47 MIN
What Are Friends For	47 MIN
Which Mother Is Mine	47 MIN

Teenage Years, The C 56 MIN
3/4 INCH VIDEO CASSETTE
Reveals the stories of two disabled adults and their parents as they look back on how they coped with the special problems they faced as teenagers. Covers such topics as sexuality, self-esteem and school relationships.
Prod-ESST Dist-ESST 1983

Teenager Pregnancy C 25 MIN
3/4 OR 1/2 INCH VIDEO CASSETTE J-C A
Examines the problem of teenage pregnancy from the perspective of education and the difficult process of decision making.
Prod-SIRS Dist-SIRS

Teenager's Choice B 30 MIN
16MM FILM OPTICAL SOUND J-H T R
Uses a dramatization about two teenagers who, on a dare from friends, decide to elope, to explain that marriage is not an escape or a situation to be taken lightly, but that it is a God-given relationship.
From The Teenage Film Series.
LC NO. FIA67-1914
Prod-FAMF Dist-FAMF 1959

Teenager's Underground Guide To Understanding Parents, A C 25 MIN
16MM FILM, 3/4 OR 1/2 IN VIDEO J-C A
Provides information which helps teens understand how parents feel about chemical abuse and how to make life easier for everyone.
Prod-WQED Dist-MTI

Teenagers - How To Get And Keep A Job C
16MM FILM, 3/4 OR 1/2 IN VIDEO
Explores the importance of a positive attitude, promptness, honesty and good customer relations.
Prod-HIGGIN Dist-HIGGIN

Teenagers Of The World—A Series
I-J
Examines the lives of young people in Yemen, Cuba, India and Ethiopia.
Prod-UNICEF Dist-GPITVL 1978

Cuba	30 MIN
Ethiopia	30 MIN
India - Teenagers Of The World	30 MIN
Yemen	30 MIN

Teenagers Talk - Getting Through Adolescence C 12 MIN
16MM FILM, 3/4 OR 1/2 IN VIDEO J-H
Uses animation to present problems of adolescence. Discusses relationships with parents and friends and decisions about freedom, sex and drugs. Describes this as a time for finding one's identity.
Prod-WEISSM Dist-PHENIX 1975

Teenagers' Parents B 30 MIN
16MM FILM OPTICAL SOUND J-H T R
Presents a teenage discussion on parents as people and disciplinarians. Shows the reactions of the parents when they hear a tape recording of the discussion.
From The Teenage Film Series.
LC NO. FIA67-1918
Prod-FAMF Dist-FAMF 1959

Teens And Teeth - The Orthodontic Years C 15 MIN
16MM FILM OPTICAL SOUND J-C A
Presents teens discussing braces worn on teeth and the views of two orthodontists.
Prod-AAORTH Dist-AAORTH 1982

Teens And Teeth - The Orthodontic Years C 14 MIN
3/4 INCH VIDEO CASSETTE
Discusses questions concerning orthodontics that often arise during the teen years. Presents teachers, teenagers and orthodontists addressing these concerns.
Prod-AAORTH Dist-MTP

Teens Having Babies C 20 MIN
3/4 OR 1/2 INCH VIDEO CASSETTE I-H
Offers teenage mothers-to-be an opportunity to become acquainted with childbirth. Shows adolescent girls talking with nurses, physicians and social workers, who clearly explain the procedures for prenatal visits as they use or describe essential medical instruments. Enumerates the indications of labor and cesarean delivery and shows an actual childbirth.
LC NO. 83-707044
Prod-POLYMR Dist-POLYMR 1983

Teens Who Choose Life - The Suicidal Crisis C
3/4 OR 1/2 INCH VIDEO CASSETTE J-C
Explores the dynamics of teen suicide, using the moving stories of three teenagers who attempted suicide and survived. Emphasizes strategies to cope with stress and depression. Demonstrates that the first step is to choose life. Includes teacher's guide.
Prod-SUNCOM Dist-SUNCOM

Teeny-Tiny And The Witch-Woman C 14 MIN
16MM FILM, 3/4 OR 1/2 IN VIDEO K-I
Presents a Turkish folktale about three brothers who, despite their mother's warnings, go into the forest to play and encounter the witch-woman who eats little children.
LC NO. 80-706211
Prod-WWS Dist-WWS 1980

Teeth - People Are Smarter Than Germs C 10 MIN
16MM FILM OPTICAL SOUND
Demonstrates how people who are taking care of their teeth are also looking after their health.
From The Health Series.
LC NO. 75-704341
Prod-MORLAT Dist-MORLAT 1974

Teeth - Some Facts To Chew On C 14 MIN
16MM FILM, 3/4 OR 1/2 IN VIDEO I-J
Illustrates the location and function of incisors, cuspids, bicuspids and molars. Uses animation to show the components of teeth and to demonstrate how plaque can result in tooth decay. Provides information on the proper care of teeth.
LC NO. 81-707327
Prod-CENTRO Dist-CORF 1981

Teeth Are For Chewing C 11 MIN
16MM FILM, 3/4 OR 1/2 IN VIDEO I
Reviews normal tooth development in human beings and studies

the process of replacement of primary teeth. Demonstrates proper tooth care and explores the many varieties of teeth found in the animal kingdom.
Prod-DISNEY Dist-WDEMCO 1971

Teeth Are For Chewing (Arabic) C 11 MIN
16MM FILM, 3/4 OR 1/2 IN VIDEO P
Explains the functions, development and care of teeth.
Prod-WDEMCO Dist-WDEMCO 1971

Teeth Are For Chewing (French) C 11 MIN
16MM FILM, 3/4 OR 1/2 IN VIDEO P
Explains the functions, development and care of teeth.
Prod-WDEMCO Dist-WDEMCO 1971

Teeth Are For Chewing (Hungarian) C 11 MIN
16MM FILM, 3/4 OR 1/2 IN VIDEO P
Explains the functions, development and care of teeth.
Prod-WDEMCO Dist-WDEMCO 1971

Teeth Are For Chewing (Thai) C 11 MIN
16MM FILM, 3/4 OR 1/2 IN VIDEO P
Explains the functions, development and care of teeth.
Prod-WDEMCO Dist-WDEMCO 1971

Teeth Are For Keeping C 15 MIN
16MM FILM, 3/4 OR 1/2 IN VIDEO I-J
Teaches important lessons about preventing dental disease as two 10-year-old boys take refuge from a pursuer in the neighborhood dental clinic.
Prod-AMDA Dist-AMDA 1972

Teeth Are Good Things To Have C 13 MIN
16MM FILM OPTICAL SOUND P-J A
Portrays the necessity of a personal, in-home program of preventive hygiene.
Prod-JAJ Dist-JAJ 1973

Teeth Are To Keep C 11 MIN
16MM FILM, 3/4 OR 1/2 IN VIDEO P-I
Animated drawings show the four essentials of good teeth care–eat proper food, avoid sweets, brush teeth after each meal and visit the dentist twice a year.
Prod-NFBC Dist-NFBC 1950

Teeth White - Teeth Bright C 10 MIN
16MM FILM, 3/4 OR 1/2 IN VIDEO P-I
Shows a young boy caring for his teeth and emphasizes the importance of brushing correctly, drinking milk, eating the right foods and having regular check-ups.
Prod-MORLAT Dist-SF 1965

Teeth, The C 12 MIN
16MM FILM, 3/4 OR 1/2 IN VIDEO J-H
See series title for descriptive statement.
From The Exploring The Body Series.
Prod-IFFB Dist-FI 1972

Tehching Hsieh - One Year Performance, Time Clock Piece C 7 MIN
3/4 OR 1/2 INCH VIDEO CASSETTE
Represents the time of labor and life in images of spinning clock hands and growing hair.
Prod-ARTINC Dist-ARTINC

Teine Samoa - A Girl Of Samoa C 26 MIN
16MM FILM, 3/4 OR 1/2 IN VIDEO J-H
Views life in a village in Western Samoa through the eyes of a young educated girl who is faced with the choice of either remaining with her family or seeking a life further afield. Examines her role in the traditional family structure, her daily duties, moments of relaxation and the tensions brought about when the outside world appears to offer opportunities of a new and different life.
From The Girl Of Series.
Prod-JOU Dist-JOU 1982

Tejst - Cepphus Grylle (Black Guillemot) C 4 MIN
16MM FILM OPTICAL SOUND
Presents a description of the black quillemot in its natural surroundings, accompanied by music and sound effects.
Prod-STATNS Dist-STATNS 1965

Tekenfilm C 3 MIN
16MM FILM, 3/4 OR 1/2 IN VIDEO
Uses animation to show how a figure drawn in pencil prances and frolics on the drawing board until he is threatened by an eraser.
LC NO. 79-707950
Prod-REUSN Dist-IFB 1977

Telecommunications C 28 MIN
3/4 OR 1/2 INCH VIDEO CASSETTE T
See series title for descriptive statement.
From The Next Steps With Computers In The Classroom Series.
Prod-PBS Dist-PBS

Telecommunications C 30 MIN
3/4 OR 1/2 INCH VIDEO CASSETTE
Demonstrates how communications satellites work, and what new programming is under development.
From The Innovation Series.
Prod-WNETTV Dist-WNETTV 1983

Telecommunications - An Overview C
3/4 OR 1/2 INCH VIDEO CASSETTE
Presents the concepts and specific information on the use of remote telecommunications systems. Covers modems, communications, software, videotex, teletext and local area netwoks. From J A M Video Training.
Prod-DSIM Dist-DSIM

Telecommunications And The Computer–A Series
C

Provides introduction to such topics as terminal interfaces, multiplexing, switching techniques, error control, computer networks, data base distribution systems, security in data communications and the management of computer networks. Features Dr Ira W Cotton, Senior Associate with Booz, Allen and Hamilton management consulting firm in Bethesda, Maryland, and adjunct associate professor at George Washington University.
LC NO. 81-707502
Prod-AMCEE Dist-AMCEE 1981

Computer Networks	045 MIN
Data Base Distribution	045 MIN
Error Control	045 MIN
Introduction To Data Communication	045 MIN
Link Control Procedures	045 MIN
Management Of Data Communications	045 MIN
Multiplexing	045 MIN
Network Architecture	045 MIN
Security In Data Communications	045 MIN
Signalling And Modulation	045 MIN
Switching	045 MIN
Terminal Equipment And Interfaces	045 MIN

Telecommunications And The Computer–A Series

Provides an introduction to such topics as terminal interfaces, multiplexing, switching techniques, error control, computer networks, data base distribution systems, security in data communications and the management of computer networks.
Prod-MIOT Dist-MIOT

Computer NetworkS	060 MIN
Data Base Distribution	051 MIN
Error Control	043 MIN
Introduction To Data Communication	035 MIN
Link Control Procedures	056 MIN
Management Of Data Communications	042 MIN
Multiplexing	044 MIN
Network Architecture	048 MIN
Security In Data Communications	046 MIN
Signaling And Modulation	030 MIN
Switching	051 MIN
Terminal Equipment And Interfaces	049 MIN

Telegraph Line C 3 MIN
3/4 OR 1/2 INCH VIDEO CASSETTE I
Features the human nervous system and shows how it functions as the body's communications system.
From The Science Rock Series.
Prod-ABCTV Dist-GA

Telemarketing For Better Business Results–A Series

Develops telemarketing skills, using the telephone as an effective selling tool. Covers product/service and competition knowledge, handling objections, planning and time management, developing prospects, making product recommendations, opening the call, identifying and developing customer needs and closing. Includes a workbook.
Prod-COMTEL Dist-DELTAK

Handling Customer Objections	009 MIN
Handling Incoming Calls	012 MIN
Identifying And Developing Customer Needs	016 MIN
Making Product Recommendations And Closing	015 MIN
Opening A Telemarketing Call	014 MIN
Product And Competitive Knowledge	009 MIN
Prospecting And Planning	007 MIN

Telemetry In Emergency Care C 30 MIN
3/4 OR 1/2 INCH VIDEO CASSETTE
Explores the mobile intensive care program of Northwest Community Hospital in Arlington Heights, Illinois, and gives behind-the-scene details of how to start and operate a life-saving, two-way radio-telemetry communications network.
Prod-TEACHM Dist-TEACHM

Teleological And Cosmological Arguments C 25 MIN
3/4 OR 1/2 INCH VIDEO CASSETTE C
See series title for descriptive statement.
From The Introduction To Philosophy Series.
Prod-UDEL Dist-UDEL

Telephone Concept C 6 MIN
3/4 OR 1/2 INCH VIDEO CASSETTE I-H A
Uses archival photographs and drawings that depict Alexander Graham Bell's telephone concept.
Prod-CRAF Dist-NFBC 1981

Telephone Creek C
3/4 OR 1/2 INCH VIDEO CASSETTE
Prod-FO Dist-FO

Telephone Film, The B 7 MIN
16MM FILM OPTICAL SOUND
Presents a humorous compilation of telephone scenes from old movies.
LC NO. 74-703020
Prod-BFC Dist-CANFDC 1973

Telephone For Help X 9 MIN
16MM FILM, 3/4 OR 1/2 IN VIDEO P-I
Shows three situations in which children call the police, the firemen and the telephone operator for help. Explains that giving information clearly and precisely helps rescuers.
Prod-RBNETT Dist-PHENIX 1968

Telephone Interviewing C 16 MIN
3/4 OR 1/2 INCH VIDEO CASSETTE
Shows quality of casework by telephone by using proper procedures and interviewing skills.
Prod-AMRC Dist-AMRC 1978

Telephone Lineman C 15 MIN
16MM FILM, 3/4 OR 1/2 IN VIDEO I
From The Career Awareness Series.
Prod-KLVXTV Dist-GPITVL

Telephone Manners C 10 MIN
16MM FILM, 3/4 OR 1/2 IN VIDEO J-C A
Presents basic training for every person who must use the telephone in business. Includes tips on courtesy when answering the phone, taking messages, transferring and placing a call. Gives special attention to warmth and friendliness, its importance and what it means to the person who receives it. Stresses the fact that the voice on the phone is the voice of the business or organization it represents.
From The Professional Hospitality Program Series.
LC NO. 74-700225
Prod-NEM Dist-NEM 1973

Telephone Manners (Spanish) C 10 MIN
16MM FILM, 3/4 OR 1/2 IN VIDEO
Discusses telephone courtesy as a vital element in both internal and external communications in any organization. Demonstrates important steps in placing and answering a phone call.
From The Communications And Selling Program (Spanish) Series.
Prod-NEM Dist-NEM

Telephone Manners 2 (Rev Ed) C 11 MIN
16MM FILM, 3/4 OR 1/2 IN VIDEO
Demonstrates courteous and effective use of the telephone in business.
From The Customer Service, Courtesy And Selling Programs Series.
Prod-NEM Dist-NEM

Telephone Manners 2 (Rev Ed) (Spanish) C 11 MIN
16MM FILM, 3/4 OR 1/2 IN VIDEO
Demonstrates courteous and effective use of the telephone in business.
From The Customer Service, Courtesy And Selling Programs (Spanish) Series.
Prod-NEM Dist-NEM

Telephone Operator C 15 MIN
16MM FILM, 3/4 OR 1/2 IN VIDEO I
From The Career Awareness Series.
Prod-KLVXTV Dist-GPITVL

Telephone, The - Tool Or Tyrant C 23 MIN
16MM FILM, 3/4 OR 1/2 IN VIDEO A
Explains how to use the telephone efficiently in an office setting.
Prod-CCCD Dist-CCCD 1983

Telephones C 30 MIN
3/4 OR 1/2 INCH VIDEO CASSETTE
Presents tips on the care of telephones.
From The Consumer Survival Series. Homes
Prod-MDCPB Dist-MDCPB

Telephoning By TTY C 7 MIN
16MM FILM SILENT J-C A S
Records in American sign language a conversation between a deaf husband and wife on using the TTY (teletypewriter) more efficiently, he for his social work and she for her women's club activities. Signed for the deaf by Mr and Mrs Kyle Workman.
LC NO. 76-701706
Prod-JOYCE Dist-JOYCE 1975

Teleprocessing And Time Sharing Systems B 45 MIN
2 INCH VIDEOTAPE
See series title for descriptive statement.
From The Data Processing, Unit 4 - Applications And Career Opportunities Series.
Prod-GPITVL Dist-GPITVL

Teleprocessing Systems C
16MM FILM - 3/4 IN VIDEO H-C A
Defines teleprocessing and gives examples of it. Goes into teleprocessing hardware and programs, data and data protection, procedures and people.
From The Computers At Work - Concepts And Applications Series. Module 9
Prod-BNA Dist-BNA 1983

Teleprocessing Systems C
3/4 OR 1/2 INCH VIDEO CASSETTE
Explains the difference between a business computer system and a business teleprocessing system and illustrates the basic types of hardware associated with teleprocessing systems.
From The Computers At Work Series.
Prod-COMTEG Dist-COMTEG

Telescope, The C 8 MIN
16MM FILM, 3/4 OR 1/2 IN VIDEO I-C A
Presents an animated allegory about a young girl who loves to gaze at the stars and discovers that her imagination is as powerful as her cardboard telescope in making the stars and planets come close.
Prod-EBEC Dist-EBEC Prodn-AESOP 1977

Telescope, The B 20 MIN
2 INCH VIDEOTAPE I
See series title for descriptive statement.
From The Science Room Series.
Prod-MCETV Dist-GPITVL Prodn-WVIZTV

Telescopes (French) C 15 MIN
3/4 OR 1/2 INCH VIDEO CASSETTE H-C A
Visits a hilltop overlooking the countryside and the Observatory of Saint-Michel-de-Provence.
From The En Francais Series. Part 2 - Temporal Relationships, Logical Relationships
Prod-MOFAFR Dist-AITECH 1970

Telespanol Uno—A Series H-C
Offers an introduction to the Spanish language.
Prod-WUSFTV Dist-GPITVL 1979

Adjectives, The (Los Adjetivos) 30 MIN
Basic Sentences (Las Oraciones) 30 MIN
Commands, The (Los Imperativos) 30 MIN
Demonstratives, The (Los Demonstrivos) 30 MIN
Direct Object Pronoun (Complemento Directo 30 MIN
Indirect Object Pronoun (Complemento 30 MIN
Possessives, The (Los Posesivos) 30 MIN
Reflexives, The (Los Refexivos) 30 MIN
Ser / Estar 30 MIN
Spanish Sounds, The (Los Sonidos) 30 MIN

TeleTapes C 28 MIN
3/4 OR 1/2 INCH VIDEO CASSETTE
Looks at TV and everyday life. Explores the content and time structure of broadcast TV. Includes three parts, 'Teletricks - TV Environment,' 'TeleGames - And Now, the News,' and 'TelePuzzles - TV Movies.'
Prod-EAI Dist-EAI

Teletherapy And Brachytherapy C 18 MIN
16MM FILM OPTICAL SOUND
Shows the diagnostic and therapeutic uses of such radioisotopes as CP-60, CS-137, EU-152-154, I-131 and Y-90 in teletherapy and brachytherapy by using machines that aim a high-energy beam at a tumor or by using implants of radioactive materials in the form of needles, beads, sterile tubing or seeds.
LC NO. FIE63-192
Prod-USAEC Dist-USNAC 1958

Television C 15 MIN
3/4 OR 1/2 INCH VIDEO CASSETTE J-H
Offers scenes before and during the telecasting of The Phil Donahue Show.
From The Media Machine Series.
Prod-WVIZTV Dist-GPITVL 1975

Television B 20 MIN
2 INCH VIDEOTAPE I
See series title for descriptive statement.
From The Science Room Series.
Prod-MCETV Dist-GPITVL Prodn-WVIZTV

Television - A Political Machine B 14 MIN
16MM FILM OPTICAL SOUND H-C A
Discusses how politics has been affected by the use of television, as evidenced in the 1968 Indiana presidential primary.
From The Public Broadcast Laboratory Series.
LC NO. FIA68-3075
Prod-NET Dist-IU 1968

Television - Behind The Scenes C 23 MIN
16MM FILM, 3/4 OR 1/2 IN VIDEO I-H
Provides a behind-the-scenes look at the filming of a network television show. Explores the job responsibilities of the production staff and stars.
From The Wide World Of Adventure Series.
Prod-AVATLI Dist-EBEC

Television - Line By Line C 11 MIN
16MM FILM, 3/4 OR 1/2 IN VIDEO H-C
Uses animation to explain the principles of television.
Prod-IFB Dist-IFB 1970

Television - Testing The Future C 11 MIN
3/4 OR 1/2 INCH VIDEO CASSETTE
Explores experiments in television broadcasting in three different locales where television is used to deliver services to the elderly, as a training tool for firefighters and as an aid in teaching English, spelling and arithmetic.
LC NO. 81-707114
Prod-NSF Dist-USNAC Prodn-MEDFO 1979

Television - The Electric Art C 30 MIN
3/4 OR 1/2 INCH VIDEO CASSETTE C
See series title for descriptive statement.
G81 From The Art Of Being Human Series. Module 9
Prod-MDCC Dist-MDCC

Television And Politics C 25 MIN
16MM FILM, 3/4 OR 1/2 IN VIDEO J-C A
Outlines the history of political television commercials, beginning in 1948. Examines many campaign commercials that use Madison Avenue techniques to package and sell politicians. Newsman Mike Wallace questions politicians and political consultants who plan and produce the candidates' commercials.
Prod-CBSTV Dist-PHENIX 1971

Television Delivers People C 6 MIN
3/4 OR 1/2 INCH VIDEO CASSETTE
Focuses on broadcasting as corporate monopoly and imperialism. Uses irony.
Prod-KITCHN Dist-KITCHN

Television Explosion, The C 57 MIN
3/4 OR 1/2 INCH VIDEO CASSETTE H-C A
Explains that, of all the technical innovations of the past, none has pervaded people's daily lives so much as television. Looks at the new technologies that are creating a second television revolution which could well transform people's lives again.
From The Nova Series.
LC NO. 83-706192
Prod-WGBHTV Dist-TIMLIF 1982

Television In The Classroom C
3/4 INCH VIDEO CASSETTE T
Describes how to use television in the classroom, showing a variety of teachers, environments and techniques.
From The Visual Learning Series. Session 3
Prod-NYSED Dist-NYSED

Television Land C 12 MIN
16MM FILM, 3/4 OR 1/2 IN VIDEO
Takes a look at television in the 1950's and 60's, including news documentaries, commercials, series and specials. Includes the Arthur Godfrey Show, What's My Line, This Is Your Life, the Milton Berle Show, Your Shows Of Shows and others.
Prod-BRAVC Dist-PFP

Television News C 15 MIN
3/4 OR 1/2 INCH VIDEO CASSETTE J-H
Shows two ninth-graders accompanying a television reporter on a a day of news reporting. Reveals that a lot of information gathered during the day is edited out by the time the stories get on the air.
From The Tuned-In Series. Lesson 3
Prod-WNETTV Dist-FI 1982

Television News C 15 MIN
3/4 OR 1/2 INCH VIDEO CASSETTE J-H
Follows a reporter in the preparation of a story for a television news program.
From The Media Machine Series.
Prod-WVIZTV Dist-GPITVL 1975

Television Newsman, The C 28 MIN
16MM FILM, 3/4 OR 1/2 IN VIDEO J-C A
Traces the workings of a television news operation and the job of a TV field reporter. Spotlights Bill Redeker of television station KABC in Los Angeles.
Prod-BRAVC Dist-PFP 1975

Television Perspective, The C 30 MIN
3/4 OR 1/2 INCH VIDEO CASSETTE
Introduces the technical aspects of ITV utilizations.
From The ITV Utilization Series.
Prod-NETCHE Dist-NETCHE 1970

Television Picture And Those Who Make It, The C 24 MIN
16MM FILM, 3/4 OR 1/2 IN VIDEO H-C A
Surveys the realities and excitement of working in television production, from advertising to news.
Prod-BARLOW Dist-PHENIX 1980

Television Serves Its Community C 15 MIN
16MM FILM, 3/4 OR 1/2 IN VIDEO I-H
Shows how television programs are prepared for transmission to the homes of a community. Follows three programs as they are planned, rehearsed and televised. Shows the use of live cameras, film, magnetic tape and remote pick-ups from trucks and helicopters.
Prod-GOLD Dist-PHENIX 1960

Television Studio, The C 15 MIN
3/4 OR 1/2 INCH VIDEO CASSETTE J-H
Accompanies a ninth-grade class as it tours a television studio and gets a demonstration of the equipment. Shows an editor selecting video segments for the news and reveals that television news must be brief and is therefore often incomplete.
From The Tuned-In Series. Lesson 2
Prod-WNETTV Dist-FI 1982

Television Techniques For Teachers C 24 MIN
16MM FILM OPTICAL SOUND T
Examines what happens when a teacher suddenly finds himself with a television set in his classroom and is faced with the problems of scheduling, review of programs, ordering materials and working the televised lessons into his daily lesson plans. Recognizes difficulties associated with the introduction of instructional television into classrooms and attempts to provide some practical answers that might be implemented in any classroom anywhere in the country.
Prod-GPITVL Dist-GPITVL

Television, A Teaching Assistance, Presenting Patterns Of Inter-Institutional And ... B 28 MIN
3/4 INCH VIDEO CASSETTE
Presents examples of patterns of inter-institutional and inter-regional teaching on television in selected areas of the United States, including the educational advantages to both staff and students of cooperative uses of television in college teaching.
Prod-USNAC Dist-USNAC 1972

TeleVisions—A Series
Presents four light music pieces produced with broadcast quality
Prod-WTV Dist-EAI

Aquarelles 008 MIN
Koan 003 MIN
Tempest 005 MIN
Voyage 008 MIN

TELL - Techniques In Early Language Learning C 17 MIN
3/4 OR 1/2 INCH VIDEO CASSETTE C
Describes a developmental pre-school language curriculum based on environmental assistance that attempted to stimulate, increase and improve the expressive aspects of two-year-old children's language functioning.
Prod-AIMS Dist-AIMS 1971

Tell A Tale C 15 MIN
3/4 OR 1/2 INCH VIDEO CASSETTE P
Demonstrates the use of art, music and drama as forms of storytelling.
From The Spinning Stories Series.
Prod-MDDE Dist-AITECH 1977

Tell Me A Story C 14 MIN
3/4 OR 1/2 INCH VIDEO CASSETTE P
See series title for descriptive statement.
From The Strawberry Square Series.
Prod-NEITV Dist-AITECH 1982

Tell Me A Story B 15 MIN
2 INCH VIDEOTAPE P
Encourages students to use crayons to tell a story about their own family and what their mother or father does during the day.
From The Art Corner Series.
Prod-CVETVC Dist-GPITVL Prodn-WCVETV

Tell Me About Yourself C 27 MIN
16MM FILM, 3/4 OR 1/2 IN VIDEO A
Presents the entire interview process, emphasizing the thought processes of the interviewer as she attempts to achieve her interview objectives.
Prod-RTBL Dist-RTBL 1976

Tell Me About Yourself (Dutch) C 27 MIN
16MM FILM, 3/4 OR 1/2 IN VIDEO A
Presents the entire interview process, emphasizing the thought processes of the interviewer as she attempts to achieve her interview objectives.
Prod-RTBL Dist-RTBL 1976

Tell Me About Yourself (Japanese) C 27 MIN
16MM FILM, 3/4 OR 1/2 IN VIDEO A
Presents the entire interview process, emphasizing the thought processes of the interviewer as she attempts to achieve her interview objectives.
Prod-RTBL Dist-RTBL 1976

Tell Me About Yourself (Norwegian) C 27 MIN
16MM FILM, 3/4 OR 1/2 IN VIDEO A
Presents the entire interview process, emphasizing the thought processes of the interviewer as she attempts to achieve her interview objectives.
Prod-RTBL Dist-RTBL 1976

Tell Me About Yourself (Spanish) C 27 MIN
16MM FILM, 3/4 OR 1/2 IN VIDEO A
Presents the entire interview process, emphasizing the thought processes of the interviewer as she attempts to achieve her interview objectives.
Prod-RTBL Dist-RTBL 1976

Tell Me About Yourself (Swedish) C 27 MIN
16MM FILM, 3/4 OR 1/2 IN VIDEO A
Presents the entire interview process, emphasizing the thought processes of the interviewer as she attempts to achieve her interview objectives.
Prod-RTBL Dist-RTBL 1976

Tell Me All About It - What Makes A Friend So Special C 9 MIN
16MM FILM, 3/4 OR 1/2 IN VIDEO P
Relates incidents involving children and their friends, and what their friendships mean to them. Encourages written and oral expressions among young students.
From The Read On Series.
Prod-ACI Dist-AIMS 1971

Tell Me How - Exposition C 15 MIN
2 INCH VIDEOTAPE J
Emphasizes clarity as the key to exposition.
From The From Me To You...In Writing, Pt 1 Series
Prod-DELE Dist-GPITVL

Tell Me My Name C 52 MIN
16MM FILM, 3/4 OR 1/2 IN VIDEO I-H A
Tells the story of a girl, given up at birth for adoption, who tracks down and confronts her natural mother hoping for immediate recognition, welcome and love. Based on the book Tell Me My Name by Mary Carter.
From The Teenage Years Series.
LC NO. 80-706921
Prod-SUSSK Dist-TIMLIF 1979

Tell Me What You See—A Series P
Prod-WVIZTV Dist-GPITVL

All Kinds Of Animals 15 MIN
Animals With Mobile Homes 15 MIN
Are Legs Really Necessary 15 MIN
Cats, The 15 MIN
Coral Life 15 MIN
Do All Birds Fly 15 MIN
Looking Back 15 MIN
Other Clawed Animals 15 MIN
Primates 15 MIN
Sea Life That Doesn't Crawl 15 MIN
Tame Or Wild 15 MIN
What Can Birds Do 15 MIN

Tell Me Who I Am C 29 MIN
3/4 INCH VIDEO CASSETTE
Investigates the dilemma resulting from recent attempts to provide relevant and useful educational opportunities to an ethnically diverse population in Canada's northland. Raises the question of social change vs indigenous culture. Also available in two-inch quad and one-inch videotape.
From The North Of 60 Degrees - Destiny Uncertain Series.
Prod-TVOTAR Dist-NAMPBC

Tell Me Who You Are C 15 MIN
3/4 OR 1/2 INCH VIDEO CASSETTE I-J
Promotes a recognition and acceptance of other world views.
From The It's All Up To You Series.
Prod-COOPED Dist-AITECH Prodn-WHATV 1978

Tell My Wife I Won't Be Home For Dinner C 32 MIN
16MM FILM, 3/4 OR 1/2 IN VIDEO H-C A
Presents three humorous exaggerations of time mismanagement. Contends that effective use of time is measured by results, not by the number of hours spent on a job.
Prod-MTLTD Dist-MTI 1980

Tell Them About Us C 28 MIN
16MM FILM OPTICAL SOUND
Describes the prevocational program at Aneth Community School in Aneth, Utah, which was begun in 1965 with Title I funds. Shows how the school helps Navajo teenagers obtain training in a variety of vocational skills.
LC NO. 77-700063
Prod-USBIA Dist-BAILYL Prodn-BAILYL 1976

Tell Them I'm A Mermaid C 23 MIN
3/4 OR 1/2 INCH VIDEO CASSETTE
Presents seven women with disabilities in a musical theatre piece. Reveals their memories and aspirations, their joys and sorrows, expressed candidly and without bitterness.
Prod-TAPEME Dist-EMBASY Prodn-EMBASY

Tell Us A Story B 15 MIN
2 INCH VIDEOTAPE K-P
Activates creative thinking through development of an interesting story. (Broadcast quality)
From The Magic Of Words Series.
Prod-GWTVAI Dist-GPITVL Prodn-WETATV

Tell Us How You Feel C 4 MIN
16MM FILM, 3/4 OR 1/2 IN VIDEO K-I
Stresses the importance of communicating feelings. Explains the need to tell a shoe salesman if a shoe doesn't fit.
From The Most Important Person - Health And Your Body Series.
Prod-EBEC Dist-EBEC 1972

Tell-Tale Heart By Edgar Allan Poe, The C 15 MIN
16MM FILM, 3/4 OR 1/2 IN VIDEO J-C A
Presents a tale of terror about an imagined or actual murder and the very real guilt and its consequences experienced by the murderer. Based on the short story The Tell-Tale Heart by Edgar Allan Poe.
From The Short Story Series.
LC NO. 83-706129
Prod-IITC Dist-IU 1982

Tell-Tale Heart, The B 20 MIN
16MM FILM OPTICAL SOUND J-C
Presents Edgar Allen Poe's story of the apprentice who killed his master and then was driven to confession by what he thought was the sound of the dead man's beating heart.
LC NO. FIA52-4355
Prod-MGM Dist-FI 1953

Tell-Tale Heart, The B 23 MIN
16MM FILM OPTICAL SOUND I-H
From his cell, a madman relates how he committed murder, revealing an obsessed and guilt-ridden mind.
LC NO. FI68-656
Prod-CBSF Dist-CBSF 1959

Tell-Tale Heart, The C 8 MIN
16MM FILM, 3/4 OR 1/2 IN VIDEO J-H
Presents an animated version of Edgar Allen Poe's short story The Tell-Tale Heart, with James Mason as the narrative voice of the killer. Shows how a man's guilt becomes his undoing.
Prod-BOSUST Dist-LCOA 1969

Tell-Tale Heart, The B 25 MIN
16MM FILM, 3/4 OR 1/2 IN VIDEO J-C A
Presents an adaptation of the Edgar Allen Poe story, 'THE TELL-TALE HEART,' a study in psychological suspense and terror.
LC NO. 82-706592
Prod-AMERFI Dist-CF 1974

Tellico Trout C 11 MIN
16MM FILM OPTICAL SOUND
Shows the mountain-stream trout fishing country of Southeast Tennessee. Studies how trout which have been reared in game and fish commission hatcheries, adapt to the streams where they are released.
Prod-TGAFC Dist-TGAFC

Telling A Story B 15 MIN
2 INCH VIDEOTAPE P
See series title for descriptive statement.
From The Language Corner Series.
Prod-CVETVC Dist-GPITVL Prodn-WCVETV

Telling By Touch B 15 MIN
2 INCH VIDEOTAPE P
See series title for descriptive statement.
From The Just Wondering Series.
Prod-EOPS Dist-GPITVL Prodn-KOACTV

Telling Stories To Children C 27 MIN
3/4 INCH VIDEO CASSETTE
Presents the essentials of story telling techniques through observation of two experienced story tellers and the development of skill in a young librarian. Indicates the integration of art and music with folk and fairy tales.
Prod-UMITV Dist-UMITV 1959

Telling The Parents—A Series
PRO
Discusses professional behavior in helping parents of newborn babies with birth defects.
Prod-SWBCC Dist-UWISC Prodn-UEUWIS 1977

Bennetts, The	2 MIN
Dr Voss And Mrs Mc Gill	2 MIN
How Do You Tell The Parents	15 MIN
Jean	21 MIN
Schuster Family, The	2 MIN
Sympathy	2 MIN

Telling Time C 11 MIN
16MM FILM, 3/4 OR 1/2 IN VIDEO P
Presents a musician who uses magic tricks to explain how to read time in hours, half hours and quarter hours.
From The Basic Math Series.
Prod-SYKES Dist-PHENIX 1980

Telling Time C 20 MIN
2 INCH VIDEOTAPE P
See series title for descriptive statement.
From The Mathemagic, Unit VI - Measurement Series.
Prod-WMULTV Dist-GPITVL

Telling Time With Count Clock C 15 MIN
16MM FILM, 3/4 OR 1/2 IN VIDEO P
Introduces Count Clock who teaches two children how to tell time.
LC NO. 83-706201
Prod-HIGGIN Dist-HIGGIN 1983

Tembo - The Baby Elephant C 10 MIN
16MM FILM, 3/4 OR 1/2 IN VIDEO P-I
Tells about the habits of an elephant family in Africa. Shows other animals that live close to the elephants.
Prod-BARR Dist-BARR 1968

Tembo - The Baby Elephant (Captioned) C 10 MIN
16MM FILM - VIDEO, ALL FORMATS K-I
Tells the story of a baby African elephant, his dependence on his mother and the herd, and shows some of the other animals who share his natural home.
Prod-BARR Dist-BARR

Temores C 8 MIN
16MM FILM OPTICAL SOUND P
Uses live-action and animation to show how making an acquaintance with a frightening thing or person can help to overcome fear of it.
From The Project Bilingual Series.
LC NO. 75-703540
Prod-SANISD Dist-SUTHLA Prodn-SUTHLA 1975

Tempera As Watercolor C 15 MIN
3/4 OR 1/2 INCH VIDEO CASSETTE P-I
Discusses the use of tempera as watercolor.
From The Young At Art Series.
Prod-WSKJTV Dist-AITECH 1980

Temperament And Personality In Selling C
3/4 OR 1/2 INCH VIDEO CASSETTE
Teaches sales people to recognize basic characteristics of temperament and personalities and how to deal with them in selling.
From The Strategies For Successful Selling Series. Module 5
Prod-AMA Dist-AMA

Temperate Deciduous Forest, The X 17 MIN
16MM FILM, 3/4 OR 1/2 IN VIDEO H
Illustrates the complex network of plant and animal relationships that make up the temperate deciduous forest community. Photomicrography, time-lapse and live photography are used to show the adaptations of deciduous plants and animals to seasonal changes.
From The Biology Series. Unit 2 - Ecosystems
Prod-EBF Dist-EBEC 1962

Temperate Deciduous Forest, The (Spanish) C 17 MIN
16MM FILM, 3/4 OR 1/2 IN VIDEO H
Reveals the complex network of plant and animal relationships in the temperate deciduous forest community. Shows typical forest inhabitants in each season of the year.
From The Biology (Spanish) Series. Unit 2 - Ecosystems
Prod-EBEC Dist-EBEC

Temperature B 22 MIN
16MM FILM OPTICAL SOUND H
Shows how 'ENERGY LEVEL,' or temperature, can be determined by measuring a function of the kinetic energy of the molecules of a gas. Introduces the constant volume gas thermometer. Defines the Celsius (centigrade) scale of temperature.
From The Heat Series.
Prod-CETO Dist-GPITVL

Temperature C 20 MIN
3/4 INCH VIDEO CASSETTE I
Gives information on the history of Celsius measurement and tells how to convert from Fahrenheit to Celsius.
From The Metric Marmalade Series.
Prod-WCVETV Dist-GPITVL 1979

Temperature C 25 MIN
3/4 OR 1/2 INCH VIDEO CASSETTE
Explains the origin and usage of a Celsius thermometer. Presents common Celsius temperatures to use as reference points.
From The Metric Education Video Tapes For Pre And Inservice Teachers (K-8) Series.
Prod-PUAVC Dist-PUAVC

Temperature - Thermometer C 20 MIN
2 INCH VIDEOTAPE I
See series title for descriptive statement.
From The Exploring With Science, Unit IV - Air Series.
Prod-MPATI Dist-GPITVL

Temperature And Review C 30 MIN
3/4 INCH VIDEO CASSETTE T
Examines the Celsius scale of temperature measurement. Presents classroom activities in which children learn about this measurement system.
From The Measure For Measure Series.
Prod-UWISCM Dist-GPITVL 1979

Temperature And Wind C 8 MIN
16MM FILM, 3/4 OR 1/2 IN VIDEO I-J
Defines weather as the condition of the atmosphere which surrounds the Earth. Shows how weather reports are made by observing and measuring air temperature, movement, moisture and pressure.
From The Weather - Air In Action Series.
Prod-CAHILL Dist-AIMS 1965

Temperature Control Devices C 14 MIN
16MM FILM, 3/4 OR 1/2 IN VIDEO H-C
Discusses thermometers and their function in relation to a modern air conditioning complex, transducers and transmitters, thermometer location, central control panels, meters and recorders.
Prod-SF Dist-SF 1970

Temperature Control System C 29 MIN
3/4 INCH VIDEO CASSETTE C
Discusses temperature control components, including intrinsic and extrinsic factors. Describes their functions and problems and emphasizes the heat exchanger, the thermostatic missing valve, water supply problems and calibration of thermometers.
From The Radiographic Processing Series. Pt 9
LC NO. 77-706078
Prod-USVA Dist-USNAC 1975

Temperature Regulation C 13 MIN
16MM FILM, 3/4 OR 1/2 IN VIDEO H-C
Discusses the regulation of body temperature. Illustrates the systems involved in cooling the body and explains the control systems. Describes the relevant sensory receptors in the skin and around the hypothalamus. Emphasizes variation in heat loss connected to ambient temperature.
LC NO. 80-706180
Prod-IFFB Dist-IFB 1979

Temperature Waves W-1 C 3 MIN
16MM FILM SILENT J-C
Thermometers are inserted in holes in a brass rod to show a wave front as one end of the rod is cycled in temperature.
From The Single-Concept Films In Physics Series.
Prod-OSUMPD Dist-OSUMPD 1963

Temperature, Energy And Thermal Equilibrium C 3 MIN
16MM FILM OPTICAL SOUND H-C A
Introduces temperature as a measure of kinetic energy. Uses spikes corresponding to speeds of particles and a meter displaying average kinetic energy to indicate gas 'TEMPERATURE.'
From The Kinetic Theory By Computer Animation Series.
LC NO. 73-703242
Prod-KALMIA Dist-KALMIA 1973

Temperature, Pressure And Fluids, Pt 1 Gases C 30 MIN
3/4 OR 1/2 INCH VIDEO CASSETTE IND
Covers laws of physics relating to gases. Sketches Boyle's Law's, Charles' Law's, and Gay Lusac's help in developing absolute temperature scales. Shows laboratory experiments to explain temperature and pressure effects on gases.
From The Mathematics And Physics Series.
Prod-AVIMA Dist-AVIMA 1980

Temperature, Pressure And Fluids, Pt 2 Liquids C 16 MIN
3/4 OR 1/2 INCH VIDEO CASSETTE IND
Introduces fluid dynamics. Uses animation to show relationship between forces, area and pressure of confined liquids.
From The Mathematics And Physics Series.
Prod-AVIMA Dist-AVIMA 1980

Temperature, Pulse And Respiration C 14 MIN
3/4 OR 1/2 INCH VIDEO CASSETTE J-C A
An instructional film on cardinal symptoms and TPR equipment, oral and rectal thermometers, reading care of thermometers, taking temperatures and taking a pulse and respirations.
Prod-SF Dist-SF 1969

Temperature, Pulse And Respiration - Theory B 27 MIN
16MM FILM OPTICAL SOUND PRO
Uses animation to show the physiology of temperature, pulse and respiration and their interrelation.
From The Directions For Education In Nursing Via Technology Series. Lesson 8
LC NO. 74-701781
Prod-DENT Dist-WSU 1974

Temperature, Pulse, Respiration B 15 MIN
16MM FILM OPTICAL SOUND J-H
Demonstrates how to take the pulse, temperature and respiration. Explains how to accomplish it methodically and points out the locations where the pulse beat may be found.
Prod-MLA Dist-MLA Prodn-USN 1943

Tempering Of Steel C 50 MIN
3/4 OR 1/2 INCH VIDEO CASSETTE PRO
Explores methods of obtaining strength, hardness, ductility and toughness in steel.
From The Heat Treatment - Metallurgy And Application Series.
Prod-AMCEE Dist-AMCEE

Tempest B 27 MIN
16MM FILM OPTICAL SOUND H-C
Presents the 1928 production of 'TEMPEST,' a colorful romance with Russian Revolution background. Stars John Barrymore. Directed by Sam Taylor.
From The History Of The Motion Picture Series.
Prod-SF Dist-KILLIS 1960

Tempest B 102 MIN
16MM FILM SILENT
Tells the story of an enlisted sergeant of the dragoons in the Imperial Army of the Czar Nicholas the second and a stunning princess, daughter of a general. Stars John Barrymore and Camilla Horn. Directed by Sam Taylor.
Prod-UNKNWN Dist-KILLIS 1928

Tempest C 5 MIN
3/4 OR 1/2 INCH VIDEO CASSETTE

Evokes the feeling of a summer storm with a shower of complex motion graphics set to music featuring the hammer dulcimer.
From The TeleVisions Series.
Prod-WTV Dist-EAI

Tempest And Summary, The - The Poetic Drama - Poet And Playwright B 45 MIN
2 INCH VIDEOTAPE C
See series title for descriptive statement.
From The Shakespeare Series.
Prod-CHITVC Dist-GPITVL Prodn-WTTWTV

Tempest, The C 14 MIN
16MM FILM, 3/4 OR 1/2 IN VIDEO H-C
See series title for descriptive statement.
From The Shakespeare Series.
Prod-IFB Dist-IFB 1974

Tempest, The C 30 MIN
3/4 OR 1/2 INCH VIDEO CASSETTE J-C A
Presents an adaptation of the Shakespearean play The Tempest, a romantic drama of the timeless struggle to create an ordered society and the cost that this entails. Includes the plays A Midsummer Night's Dream, King Lear and As You Like It on the same tape.
From The Shakespeare In Perspective Series.
LC NO. 84-707155
Prod-FI Dist-FI 1984

Tempest, The C 76 MIN
3/4 OR 1/2 INCH VIDEO CASSETTE
Offers a production of Shakespeare's play The Tempest starring Maurice Evans, Richard Burton, Tom Poston and Lee Remick.
Prod-FOTH Dist-FOTH 1984

Tempest, The C 126 MIN
16MM FILM, 3/4 OR 1/2 IN VIDEO H-C A
Dramatizes Shakespeare's The Tempest. Serves as an introduction to Elizabethan theater, as a companion to reading the play, or, by itself, as a teaching tool.
Prod-BARDPR Dist-EBEC 1983

Tempest, The C 150 MIN
3/4 OR 1/2 INCH VIDEO CASSETTE
Presents Shakespeare's play The Tempest, which revolves around an enchanted island, an exiled duke, young lovers and a framework of conspiracy as they affect dramatic and emotional romances.
From The Shakespeare Plays Series.
LC NO. 79-707319
Prod-BBCTV Dist-TIMLIF 1980

Tempest, The - Shakespeare's Unique Observance Of The Unities B 45 MIN
2 INCH VIDEOTAPE C
See series title for descriptive statement.
From The Shakespeare Series.
Prod-CHITVC Dist-GPITVL Prodn-WTTWTV

Temple Of Apollo At Bassae C 16 MIN
16MM FILM, 3/4 OR 1/2 IN VIDEO
Explores the temple near Bassae, a small Greek village southwest of Athens. Explains that the structure with its Doric columns was created by the designer of the Parthenon, Ictinus.
Prod-MCBRID Dist-IFB 1974

Temple Of Apollo At Bassae (Greek) C 16 MIN
16MM FILM, 3/4 OR 1/2 IN VIDEO H-C
Visits a temple created by Ictinus, designer of the Parthenon, lost to modern man until rediscovered in 1765.
Prod-IFB Dist-IFB

Temple Of Twenty Pagodas, The C 21 MIN
16MM FILM, 3/4 OR 1/2 IN VIDEO J-C A
Views the daily life of a Buddhist Monastery and the village which it serves in northern Thailand.
Prod-FLMAUS Dist-SF 1973

Temple Priests And Civil Servants C 25 MIN
16MM FILM, 3/4 OR 1/2 IN VIDEO
Examines such subjects as the relationship between pharaoh, gods, priests and common people in ancient Egypt.
From The Ancient Lives Series.
Prod-FOTH Dist-FOTH

Temple, The C 30 MIN
16MM FILM OPTICAL SOUND R
Captures the essence of modern Israel. Focuses on efforts made by Israelis to learn the ancient rites of temple worship by digging among the rocks of their native land.
Prod-GF Dist-GF

Temples Of Tomorrow B 12 MIN
16MM FILM OPTICAL SOUND H-C A
Surveys the hydro-electric projects in India, which the late Jawaharlal Nehru described as 'TEMPLES OF TOMORROW.' Discusses projects which are transforming the lives of the people.
Prod-INDIA Dist-NEDINF

Tempo C 29 MIN
3/4 INCH VIDEO CASSETTE H A
Reviews A-major scale. Introduces the principal tempo indications found in music notation.
From The Beginning Piano - An Adult Approach Series. Lesson 14
Prod-COAST Dist-CDTEL

Tempo - Australia In The Seventies C 24 MIN
16MM FILM OPTICAL SOUND H-C A
Emphasizes the great potential for growth and development in Australia in the 1970's.
LC NO. 72-702254
Prod-ANAIB Dist-SF 1972

Tempo And Dynamics C 15 MIN
3/4 OR 1/2 INCH VIDEO CASSETTE P-I
Discusses tempo and dynamics in music.
From The Music And Me Series.
Prod-WDCNTV Dist-AITECH 1979

Temporal And Infratemporal Regions, The C 15 MIN
3/4 OR 1/2 INCH VIDEO CASSETTE C A
Describes the boundaries, demonstrates the bones and identifies the bony regions of the temporal and infratemporal areas of the skull.
From The Skull Anatomy Series.
Prod-UTXHSA Dist-TEF

Temporal Bone From Above, The - The Mid-Cranial Fossa Approach C 29 MIN
16MM FILM OPTICAL SOUND PRO
Demonstrates in detail the surgical anatomy of the temporal bone from above. Serves as a teaching aid for those interested in learning to approach the contents of the temporal bone and posterior fossa through the mid-cranial fossa. Demonstrates the anatomy of this area as a surgeon would encounter it and then correlates the anatomical points demonstrated with practical surgical uses of the approach.
Prod-EAR Dist-EAR

Temporal Mandibular Joint Eminectomy C 19 MIN
16MM FILM OPTICAL SOUND
Shows pre-operative live action films and radiographs of the patient's distress, following through with surgery and a description of the patient's post-operative relief.
LC NO. 77-705684
Prod-OSUMPD Dist-OSUMPD 1969

Temporal Parameters Of Auditory Stimulus Response Control C 10 MIN
16MM FILM OPTICAL SOUND C A
Demonstrates a test which presents signals in random or alternating order with nonaudible control periods. Illustrates accident safeguards and their effect on test results and subject behavior.
LC NO. 78-701611
Prod-UKANS Dist-UKANS 1974

Temporalis Muscle Transfer For Lagophthalmos C 18 MIN
3/4 OR 1/2 INCH VIDEO CASSETTE PRO
Presents temporalis muscle transfer for lagophthalmos.
Prod-WFP Dist-WFP Prodn-UKANMC

Temporary Admission C 27 MIN
16MM FILM, 3/4 OR 1/2 IN VIDEO
Looks at the contemporary situation of immigrant laborers. Traces the history of the great waves of immigration and explores the social, economic and legal aspects of immigration.
From The Five Billion People Series.
Prod-LEFSP Dist-CNEMAG

Temporary Grounding For De-Energized Maintenance C
3/4 OR 1/2 INCH VIDEO CASSETTE IND
Demonstrates procedures for grounding an overhead distribution line on a tangent structure, a vertical running corner and a vertical deadend.
From The Live Line Maintenance Series.
Prod-LEIKID Dist-LEIKID

Temporary Plastic Bridges C 19 MIN
16MM FILM OPTICAL SOUND
Gives a clinical demonstration of the construction of a temporary plastic bridge of four teeth.
LC NO. 74-705758
Prod-USA Dist-USNAC 1964

Temporary Restoration Of A Class II Mesio-Occlusal Cavity Preparation With Zinc... C 10 MIN
16MM FILM - 3/4 IN VIDEO PRO
Demonstrates placing a mechanical retainer and matrix band, placing and contouring the zinc-oxide and eugenol materials and adjusting occlusion in a manikin. Shows four-handed procedures.
From The Restoration Of Cavity Preparation With Amalgam And Tooth-Colored Materials Series. Module 11a
LC NO. 76-706195
Prod-USBHRD Dist-USNAC Prodn-NMAC 1974

Temporary Support Structures C 21 MIN
16MM FILM, 3/4 OR 1/2 IN VIDEO
Shows the errors and omissions which cause a temporary support structure to collapse. Stresses the need for sound design of framework, good choice of equipment and materials, and ample financial support. Covers operations from a simple propping system support to large and complex support structures for major engineering projects.
Prod-NFBTE Dist-IFB

Temporomandibular Joint C 10 MIN
16MM FILM OPTICAL SOUND PRO
Demonstrates the anatomy and function of the temporomandibular joint by means of dissection and artists' illustrations.
From The Anatomy Of The Head And Neck Series.
LC NO. 73-702968
Prod-USVA Dist-USNAC Prodn-LUSD 1969

Temporomandibular Joint Arthroplasty - Intracapsular C 13 MIN
16MM FILM, 3/4 OR 1/2 IN VIDEO PRO
Describes and demonstrates the surgical procedures of a temporomandibular joint arthroplasty and evaluates postoperative results.
LC NO. 81-706371
Prod-VADTC Dist-USNAC 1981

Temporomandibular Joint, The C 8 MIN
3/4 INCH VIDEO CASSETTE PRO
Demonstrates the anatomy and function of the temporomandibular joint.
From The Anatomy Of The Head And Neck Series.
LC NO. 78-706254
Prod-USVA Dist-USNAC Prodn-VADTC 1978

Temptation Of Power, The C 43 MIN
16MM FILM, 3/4 OR 1/2 IN VIDEO H-C A
Probes the reasons for widespread discontent among Iran's population during the rule of the Shah. Focuses on elements such as poverty, the roles of the military and police, the demolition of ancient buildings and villages, the erosion of the traditional way of life, land reform, and rapid westernization.
Prod-ICARUS Dist-ICARUS 1979

Temptation Of Red Yisroel, The B 30 MIN
16MM FILM OPTICAL SOUND H-C A
Presents a fantasy drawn from Hasidic legend, in which the story moves from the Polish town of Bialystok to the Heavenly Court. Portrays such characters as a bevy of cantankerous angels, a magnanimous pickpocket and an unworldly rabbi and his wife. (Kinescope)
From The Eternal Light Series.
LC NO. 73-700975
Prod-JTS Dist-NAAJS 1968

Tempting Of Eve B 7 MIN
16MM FILM OPTICAL SOUND
Presents an animated version of the story of Adam and Eve.
LC NO. 75-704343
Prod-CCAAT Dist-CCAAT 1974

Ten Billion Dollar Rip-Off, The C 22 MIN
16MM FILM, 3/4 OR 1/2 IN VIDEO J-C A
Dramatizes the story of a young girl who steals from her employer and the tragic consequences of her actions. Shows five key rules developed by security experts to help employees curb theft and avoid trouble themselves.
Prod-GIFL Dist-MTI 1983

Ten Commandments Of Cross-Examination, The C 60 MIN
3/4 OR 1/2 INCH VIDEO CASSETTE PRO
Describes qualities of an effective cross-examiner and a method for recognizing a persuasive argument. Outlines Irving Younger's ten commandments of cross-examination.
Prod-ABACPE Dist-ABACPE

Ten Commandments Of Gun Safety C 12 MIN
16MM FILM, 3/4 OR 1/2 IN VIDEO I-C A
Fundamentals of gun handling and behavior when hunting.
Prod-MORLAT Dist-SF 1967

Ten Commandments, The C 50 MIN
16MM FILM, 3/4 OR 1/2 IN VIDEO I-C A
Tells the story of how Moses leads his people out of Egypt and brings them to Mt Sinai where he receives the Ten Commandments, while the Israelites fall into sin, drinking and feasting. Stars John Marley and Kristoffer Tabori.
From The Greatest Heroes Of The Bible Series.
Prod-LUF Dist-LUF 1979

Ten Days In Calcutta C
16MM FILM OPTICAL SOUND
Portrays Mrinal Sen, one of India's most famous directors.
Prod-TLECUL Dist-TLECUL

Ten Days Per Man C 26 MIN
16MM FILM OPTICAL SOUND
Discusses today's highway problems.
Prod-GM Dist-GM

Ten Days That Shook The World B 75 MIN
3/4 OR 1/2 INCH VIDEO CASSETTE
Recreates the historic events of the Bolshevik Revolution in many of the actual locations. Based on John Reed's book of the same title.
Prod-IHF Dist-IHF

Ten Factors C 30 MIN
3/4 OR 1/2 INCH VIDEO CASSETTE
Presents ten factors that help make a good listener. Discusses the differences between good and poor listeners.
From The Effective Listening Series. Tape 3
Prod-TELSTR Dist-TELSTR

Ten Factors Of Good Listening C 30 MIN
3/4 OR 1/2 INCH VIDEO CASSETTE
Gives ten differences between good and poor listeners. Includes a drama showing a communication breakdown and the listening failures that caused it.
Prod-TELSTR Dist-DELTAK

Ten For Gold C 28 MIN
3/4 OR 1/2 INCH VIDEO CASSETTE A
Tells the story of Bruce Jenner's triumph in the 1976 Olympic decathalon. Emphasizes how he motivated himself to come back from defeat to reach new heights.
Prod-SFTI Dist-SFTI

Ten From Your Show Of Shows B 92 MIN
16MM FILM OPTICAL SOUND
Presents an anthology of skits from the early 50's television comedy Your Show Of Shows. Stars Sid Caesar, Imogene Coca and Carl Reiner.
Prod-WB Dist-TWYMAN 1972

Ten Little Engines C 8 MIN
16MM FILM OPTICAL SOUND H-C A
Pictures automobile drivers violating the rules of the road and causing accidents as a result of driving too fast for conditions, improper passing and drinking.

LC NO. FIA68-246
Prod-AETNA Dist-AETNA Prodn-AETNA 1967

Ten Little Indians - Beginning Subtraction Concepts C 11 MIN
16MM FILM, 3/4 OR 1/2 IN VIDEO P
An animated film employs the nursery rhyme as an aid in understanding subtraction concepts. Shows subtraction as the inverse of addition, explains the meaning of 'take away', 'how many more are needed' and 'the difference'.
Prod-CORF Dist-CORF 1965

Ten Long Minutes X 13 MIN
16MM FILM OPTICAL SOUND
Illustrates the story of a worker whose wife and children are on vacation and who may have been in an accident. Provides a memorable lesson in off-job safety.
Prod-NSC Dist-NSC

Ten Minutes Of Protection C 8 MIN
16MM FILM OPTICAL SOUND IND
Describes a variety of fire tests conducted on lightweight steel roof supports. Shows how tests evaluated the insulating materials which are applied to steel joints in order to provide them with ten minutes of fire protection.
LC NO. 77-703347
Prod-USGSA Dist-USNAC Prodn-ILIOT 1977

Ten Occupational Fields - How Do I Explore Them C
3/4 OR 1/2 INCH VIDEO CASSETTE
Explores ten occupational fields and describes specific jobs in depth according to a set of specific criteria for analyzing jobs.
From The Employability Skills Series.
Prod-ILCS Dist-CAMB

Ten Seconds That Shook The World B 50 MIN
16MM FILM, 3/4 OR 1/2 IN VIDEO J-C
Portrays the joint efforts of the United States and Great Britain which produced the atomic bomb that brought the war in the Pacific to an end. Shows how peaceful uses of atomic energy can help to create a new and better world.
Prod-PMI Dist-FI 1963

Ten Shots In A Boarding House B 3 MIN
16MM FILM OPTICAL SOUND
Deals with the mystery of a boarding house by presenting ten shots of scenes there.
LC NO. 77-702667
Prod-CANFDC Dist-CANFDC 1976

Ten Steps To Discipline C 29 MIN
3/4 OR 1/2 INCH VIDEO CASSETTE T
Presents ten steps for disciplining in the classroom.
From The Survival Skills For The Classroom Teacher Series.
Prod-MFFD Dist-FI

Ten Tahun Herdeka B 24 MIN
16MM FILM OPTICAL SOUND
Shows the celebrations of ten years of independence in Malaysia.
Prod-FILEM Dist-PMFMUN 1967

Ten Takes Flight C 14 MIN
16MM FILM OPTICAL SOUND C A
Presents the final minutes just prior to and including the first flight of the DC-10. Features scenes of construction and rollout of the aircraft.
Prod-MCDO Dist-MCDO 1970

Ten The Magic Number C 13 MIN
16MM FILM, 3/4 OR 1/2 IN VIDEO I-C A
Presents an animated story about a man who finds out about metric measurement in a time-travel voyage to the future. Shows how the differences between the metric and English systems cause him many problems.
Prod-CAMETR Dist-NFBC 1975

Ten Times Empty (Greece) C 21 MIN
16MM FILM, 3/4 OR 1/2 IN VIDEO J-C A
Features an eleven-year-old boy from the Greek island of Simi describing how the one-time shipping center is losing its population due to pollution and over-fishing.
From The Village Life Series.
Prod-JPFLM Dist-JOU Prodn-TAW 1977

Ten Ugly Pounds C 29 MIN
2 INCH VIDEOTAPE
See series title for descriptive statement.
From The Maggie And The Beautiful Machine - Eating Series.
Prod-WGBHTV Dist-PUBTEL

Ten Ways To Tell If You're In Love C 29 MIN
16MM FILM, 3/4 OR 1/2 IN VIDEO H-C A
Presents Rev Jack F Paul offering advice and guidance to an audience of college students on the subject of forming lasting relationships. Discusses 10 practical guidelines for helping young people, especially women, decide if they are really in love and emphasizes the importance of moral values for establishing a lasting marriage.
LC NO. 81-707010
Prod-BANHST Dist-PHENIX 1980

Ten Who Dared C 92 MIN
16MM FILM OPTICAL SOUND
Presents ten rugged adventurers who undertake a perilous journey from which only six will return. Features the story of Major Powell's first daring conquest of the Colorado River in 1869.
Prod-DISNEY Dist-TWYMAN 1963

Ten Who Dared—A Series
16MM FILM, 3/4 OR 1/2 IN VIDEO
Dramatizes the journeys of ten explorers from different countries who traveled to world frontiers. Portrays their search for and discoveries of land, routes and civilizations.
Prod-BBCTV Dist-TIMLIF 1976

Alexander Von Humboldt 52 MIN
Burke And Wills 52 MIN
Captain James Cook 52 MIN
Charles Doughty 52 MIN
Christopher Columbus 52 MIN
Francisco Pizarro 52 MIN
Henry Morton Stanley 52 MIN
Jedediah Smith 52 MIN
Mary Kingsley 52 MIN
Roald Amundsen 52 MIN

Ten Years After B 52 MIN
16MM FILM OPTICAL SOUND
Uses the tenth-year reunion of the filmmaker's high school class as a backdrop and examines the lives of six individuals from the Class of '65, the changes they have undergone and the realities they now face.
LC NO. 77-702153
Prod-TEMPLU Dist-TEMPLU Prodn-BARBA 1977

Ten Years Of The Berlin Wall C 19 MIN
3/4 OR 1/2 INCH VIDEO CASSETTE H-C A
Documents the building of the Berlin Wall and the East-West relationships during the ten-year period following it.
Prod-UPI Dist-JOU

Ten Years To Tomorrow C 25 MIN
16MM FILM OPTICAL SOUND
Points out the value of the communication satellite network. Shows how in Quito, Ecuador, an international team under the guidance of COMSAT connects another seven million people to the worldwide communication satellite network.
LC NO. 73-700785
Prod-COMSAC Dist-GUG 1973

Ten-8 C 39 MIN
16MM FILM OPTICAL SOUND
Depicts the duties performed by Tennessee game and fish officers and the equipment which aids them in enforcement. Includes a footrace to catch two deer poachers who are apprehended with the aid of a radio equipped plane and cars.
Prod-TGAFC Dist-TGAFC

Tenants' Act, The B 5 MIN
16MM FILM OPTICAL SOUND
Deals with the issue of women's liberation in the context of the class struggle.
LC NO. 74-702769
Prod-REDTRK Dist-CANFDC 1973

Tencan, The - Grouping And Regrouping C 14 MIN
3/4 OR 1/2 INCH VIDEO CASSETTE P
Describes Martha's discovery of how place value is related to regrouping.
From The Math Country Series.
Prod-KYTV Dist-AITECH 1979

Tender Balance, A C 17 MIN
16MM FILM, 3/4 OR 1/2 IN VIDEO J-C A
Discusses the problem of communication between teenagers and their parents. Shows a young man talking to his parents about hisgirlfriend and his sister's struggle to avoid her father's protectiveness. Intended to trigger discussion among students.
Prod-PALLP Dist-FI

Tender Game C 6 MIN
16MM FILM, 3/4 OR 1/2 IN VIDEO J-H
Presents an exercise in the free association of popular music and popular images to the tune of 'Tenderly' sung by Ella Fitzgerald and played by the Oscar Peterson Trio.
Prod-HUBLEY Dist-TEXFLM 1976

Tender Mansion, The C 17 MIN
16MM FILM OPTICAL SOUND J-H
Discusses the cause and effects of environmental pollution, exploring the consequences of many commonly suggested solutions. Encourages the adoption of a meaningful ecological awareness by all citizens and the application of that awareness in their daily lives.
Prod-DRPEP Dist-DRPEP

Tender Tale Of Cinderella Penguin, The C 10 MIN
16MM FILM, 3/4 OR 1/2 IN VIDEO
Presents an animated story, without words and set to a wide variety of musical selections, which spoofs the traditional tale of Cinderella, with penguins playing the story's characters.
LC NO. 82-706612
Prod-NFBC Dist-NFBC Prodn-PRLMNJ 1981

Tendon Injuries C 26 MIN
16MM FILM OPTICAL SOUND PRO
Presents a brief demonstration of the healing process of tendons to illustrate the principles underlying tendon suturing. Depicts the details of the operative technic of the insertion of a tendon graft into a digit.
Prod-ACYDGD Dist-ACY 1953

Tendon Transfers In The Quadriplegic Hand C 60 MIN
3/4 OR 1/2 INCH VIDEO CASSETTE PRO
Presents Professor Eric Moberg, MD's lecture on the study of surgical techniques and treatment of the quadriplegic upper extremity.
Prod-ASSH Dist-ASSH

Tenement, The B 40 MIN
3/4 INCH VIDEO CASSETTE
Portrays nine black families in a Chicago ghetto in 1967. Focuses on the impact of poverty on black Americans. Originally broadcast as a CBS Reports documentary.
Prod-CBSNEW Dist-ADL 1967

Tenn-Tom - A New Waterway For America C 28 MIN
16MM FILM OPTICAL SOUND
Tours the Tennessee-Tombigbee Waterway, a 234-mile waterway which joins two of the busiest navigation systems in the Southeast.
Prod-USAE Dist-MTP

Tennant Creek In Passing C 7 MIN
16MM FILM OPTICAL SOUND J-C A
Presents impressions of life in Tennant Creek, a small town in the Australian outback.
LC NO. 75-702392
Prod-FLMAUS Dist-AUIS 1974

Tenneco - Night And Day C 17 MIN
16MM FILM OPTICAL SOUND
Traces the global operations of Tenneco, Inc. Shows how Tenneco balances strong energy production and exploration operations with a variety of consumer and industrial businesses.
Prod-FENECO Dist-MTP

Tennessee Birdwalk C 6 MIN
3/4 INCH VIDEO CASSETTE P
Features bald birds, birds flying north in the winter, and other aviary improbabilities.
Prod-NBCTV Dist-GA

Tennessee River - Conservation And Power C 14 MIN
16MM FILM, 3/4 OR 1/2 IN VIDEO I-H
Discusses the Tennesse Valley Program which has proved that man can alter his environment to his advantage and correct past ecological mistakes. Tells how the development of this area by the Federal government has resulted in benefits to both the people living in the area and to those beyond the valley. Points out that the quality of life in the area has been greatly affected by the wise use of this river resource.
Prod-EVANSA Dist-PHENIX 1971

Tennessee Valley, The C 15 MIN
3/4 OR 1/2 INCH VIDEO CASSETTE I
Presents John Rugg reviewing the history of the Tennessee Valley through scenes of the British at Fort Loudon, early pioneers at Rocky Mount, a flatboat trip down the river and the slow deterioration of the valley's resources. Gives a first-hand look at how the Tennessee Valley Authority helped reclaim the region.
From The American Legacy Series. Program 5
LC NO. 83-706662
Prod-KRMATV Dist-AITECH 1983

Tennessee Williams - Theater In Process C 29 MIN
16MM FILM, 3/4 OR 1/2 IN VIDEO H-C A
Goes behind the scenes for a glimpse at the creation of Tennessee William's The Red Devil Battery Sign. Shows how the play progresses from first rehearsals through opening performances.
From The Humanities - The Drama Series.
Prod-SIGNET Dist-EBEC

Tennessee's Partner By Bret Harte C 15 MIN
16MM FILM, 3/4 OR 1/2 IN VIDEO J-C A
Tells a story of genuine love and friendship between two men whose characters and appearances belie their sentimental hearts. Based on the short story Tennessee's Partner by Bret Harte.
From The Short Story Series.
LC NO. 83-706140
Prod-IITC Dist-IU 1978

Tennis - Basic Tactics For Doubles C 13 MIN
16MM FILM, 3/4 OR 1/2 IN VIDEO J-C A
Demonstrates doubles tactics through strategic court positions, service net approach, return of serve, lobbing, poaching, net play and other fundamentals.
From The Tennis Series.
Prod-BFA Dist-PHENIX 1968

Tennis - Basic Tactics For Doubles (Spanish) C 13 MIN
16MM FILM, 3/4 OR 1/2 IN VIDEO J-C A
Demonstrates doubles tactics through strategic court positions, service net approach, return of serve, lobbing, poaching, net play and other fundamentals.
From The Tennis Series.
Prod-BFA Dist-PHENIX 1968

Tennis - Basic Tactics For Singles C 13 MIN
16MM FILM, 3/4 OR 1/2 IN VIDEO J-H A
Explains that the basic strategy for beginners is to keep the ball in play. Shows that once that is mastered, placing the ball where opponents least expect it is good strategy, since a running shot is considerably harder to make. The basic stroke fundamentals are followed by the correct positions, the changing of shot directions, the ways to take advantage of an opponent's weaknesses and ways to regain position.
From The Tennis Series.
Prod-BFA Dist-PHENIX 1968

Tennis - Basic Tactics For Singles (Spanish) C 13 MIN
16MM FILM, 3/4 OR 1/2 IN VIDEO J-H A
Explains that the basic strategy for beginners is to keep the ball in play. Shows that once that is mastered, placing the ball where opponents least expect it is good strategy, since a running shot is considerably harder to make. The basic stroke fundamentals are followed by the correct positions, the changing of shot directions, the ways to take advantage of an opponent's weaknesses and ways to regain position.
From The Tennis Series.
Prod-BFA Dist-PHENIX 1968

Tennis - Tut Bartzen B 13 MIN
16MM FILM OPTICAL SOUND
Shows Davis cup star and national clay courts champ demonstrating how to serve, play the net and how to stroke forehand and backhand.
Prod-SFI Dist-SFI

Tennis Anyone - Introduction C 30 MIN
3/4 OR 1/2 INCH VIDEO CASSETTE H-C A

See series title for descriptive statement.
From The Tennis Anyone Series.
LC NO. 79-706889
Prod-BATA Dist-TIMLIF 1979

Tennis Anyone—A Series
16MM FILM, 3/4 OR 1/2 IN VIDEO H-C A
Presents Dennis Van der Meer, director of the Tennis America training camp at Lake Tahoe and winner of the U S Lawn Tennis Association's 'Outstanding Educator' award, designing a program of tennis instruction.
LC NO. 79-706889
Prod-BATA Dist-TIMLIF 1979

Backhand, The 30 MIN
Forehand, The 30 MIN
Serve, The 30 MIN
Specialty Strokes 30 MIN
Strategy And Tactics 30 MIN
Tennis Anyone - Introduction 30 MIN

Tennis Everyone C 15 MIN
16MM FILM OPTICAL SOUND
Examines Florida's tennis facilities and presents hints to improve your game.
Prod-FLADC Dist-FLADC

Tennis Everyone C 26 MIN
3/4 OR 1/2 INCH VIDEO CASSETTE
Explores the growth and popularity of this sport with plenty of action.
Prod-KAROL Dist-KAROL

Tennis Grips And Strokes X 11 MIN
16MM FILM, 3/4 OR 1/2 IN VIDEO J-C A
Uses slow-motion, hold frames and identification titles to demonstrate in detail tennis fundamentals, such as forehand and backhand grips and drives, backhand volley, serves and the overhead smash.
Prod-SLACK Dist-PHENIX 1966

Tennis Lesson, The C 9 MIN
16MM FILM, 3/4 OR 1/2 IN VIDEO C A
Focuses on the brief, passionate encounter between an attractive housewife and a tennis ball machine.
Prod-KARGL Dist-PHENIX 1977

Tennis Match, The C 15 MIN
16MM FILM, 3/4 OR 1/2 IN VIDEO H-C A
Shows how four man are reduced to squabbling infants during a doubles tennis match.
Prod-KARGL Dist-PHENIX 1978

Tennis Mothers C 14 MIN
16MM FILM, 3/4 OR 1/2 IN VIDEO J-C A
Presents a typical day in the life of a 12-year-old girl and her mother, who is determined that her daughter is going to be a champion tennis star.
Prod-CBSNEW Dist-CAROUF

Tennis Philosophy And The Forehand Stroke C 29 MIN
3/4 OR 1/2 INCH VIDEO CASSETTE
See series title for descriptive statement.
From The Vic Braden's Tennis For The Future Series.
Prod-WGBHTV Dist-PBS 1981

Tennis Racquet C 7 MIN
16MM FILM, 3/4 OR 1/2 IN VIDEO P-J
Features Goofy as the scorekeeper in a slapstick version of the traditionally polite game of tennis.
From The Goofy Over Sports Series.
Prod-DISNEY Dist-WDEMCO 1977

Tennis Racquet (Spanish) C 7 MIN
16MM FILM, 3/4 OR 1/2 IN VIDEO I-H
Presents Goofy on the tennis courts.
From The Goofy Over Sports (Spanish) Series.
Prod-WDEMCO Dist-WDEMCO 1977

Tennis Tactics—A Series
16MM FILM, 3/4 OR 1/2 IN VIDEO H-C A
Emphasizes the tactical aspects of the game of tennis.
Prod-ATHI Dist-ATHI 1980

Importance Of Practice, The 009 MIN
Tactics For Doubles Play 009 MIN
Tactics For Ground Strokes 009 MIN
Tactics For Return Of Service 009 MIN
Tactics For Singles Play 009 MIN
Tactics For Specialty Shots 009 MIN
Tactics For The Serve 009 MIN

Tennis The Nasty Way—A Series
16MM FILM, 3/4 OR 1/2 IN VIDEO
Prod-SLANJ Dist-AIMS 1975

Tennis With Ilie Nastase - Backhand 013 MIN
Tennis With Ilie Nastase - Forehand 012 MIN
Tennis With Ilie Nastase - Serve And Volley 013 MIN
Tennis With Ilie Nastase - Strategy Shots 010 MIN

Tennis With Ilie Nastase - Backhand C 13 MIN
16MM FILM, 3/4 OR 1/2 IN VIDEO J-C A
Presents Ilie Nastase explaining the different backhand grips. Reviews the stroke and shows that the swing and follow-through is similar to the forehand.
From The Tennis The Nasty Way Series.
Prod-SF Dist-AIMS Prodn-SLANJ 1975

Tennis With Ilie Nastase - Forehand C 12 MIN
16MM FILM, 3/4 OR 1/2 IN VIDEO J-C A
Presents Ilie Nastase demonstrating the fundamentals of the forehand and the importance of watching the ball and keeping the knees flexed. Shows the backswing. Explains and reviews basic strokes and variations, how to hit flat, topspin and slice forehands and when to use each most effectively.
From The Tennis The Nasty Way Series.
Prod-SF Dist-AIMS Prodn-SLANJ 1975

Tennis With Ilie Nastase - Serve And Volley C 13 MIN
16MM FILM, 3/4 OR 1/2 IN VIDEO J-C A
Explains that a service is broken down into three increasing component parts. Shows slow motion shots of increasing the power in the serve by snapping the wrist and straightening the body at the moment of impact. Demonstrates putting spin on the ball. Discusses and demonstrates three important elements of the volley.
From The Tennis The Nasty Way Series.
Prod-SF Dist-AIMS 1975

Tennis With Ilie Nastase - Strategy Shots C 10 MIN
16MM FILM, 3/4 OR 1/2 IN VIDEO J-C A
Considers three storkes, the overhead, the lob and the drop shot. Shows the similarity between the overhead and service, offensive and defensive lobs and demonstrates the drop shot.
From The Tennis The Nasty Way Series.
Prod-SF Dist-AIMS Prodn-SLANJ 1975

Tennis With Stan Smith C 60 MIN
1/2 IN VIDEO CASSETTE BETA/VHS
Presents neuromuscular training using Stan Smith as the model for an improved tennis game. Includes four audiocassettes and personal training guide.
Prod-SYBVIS Dist-SYBVIS

Tennis—A Series
16MM FILM, 3/4 OR 1/2 IN VIDEO J-C A
Prod-ATHI Dist-ATHI 1976

Applying Forehand And Backhand Strokes 20 MIN
Forehand And Backhand Strokes 23 MIN
Net Play 21 MIN
Serve, The 20 MIN

Tennis—A Series
16MM FILM, 3/4 OR 1/2 IN VIDEO J-C A
Prod-BFA Dist-PHENIX 1968

Introduction To Tennis 14 MIN
Tennis - Basic Tactics For Doubles 13 MIN
Tennis - Basic Tactics For Singles 13 MIN

Tension And Relaxation B 13 MIN
16MM FILM OPTICAL SOUND
Shows Barbara Mettler teaching a group of boys and girls at the Creative Dance Center in 1966.
From The Creative Dance For Children Series.
Prod-METT Dist-METT 1977

Tension Application On Rear-End Collision, Ford Hardtop C 19 MIN
1/2 IN VIDEO CASSETTE BETA/VHS
Deals with auto body repair.
Prod-RMI Dist-RMI

Tension Hook Up And Accessories C 8 MIN
1/2 IN VIDEO CASSETTE BETA/VHS
Deals with auto body repair. Demonstrates pull hook up and hardware on damages.
Prod-RMI Dist-RMI

Tension Testing B 21 MIN
16MM FILM - 3/4 IN VIDEO
Shows how a hydraulic tension-testing machine operates and how to prepare the machine and a specimen for testing. Describes how to conduct the test to determine the specimen's elastic limit, yield point and ultimate strength. Issued in 1944 as a motion picture.
From The Engineering Series.
LC NO. 79-706442
Prod-USOE Dist-USNAC Prodn-AUDIO 1979

Tension, Worry And Ulcers C 50 MIN
16MM FILM OPTICAL SOUND PRO
Shows the diagnosis and management of duodenal ulcers and the removal of a major portion of a patient's stomach in a corrective procedure to prevent recurrence of persistent ulcers.
Prod-CMA Dist-LAWREN

Tent Flaps And Flapjacks C 26 MIN
16MM FILM OPTICAL SOUND
Portrays the recreational opportunities in the national forests in the northcentral states.
LC NO. FIE63-218
Prod-USDA Dist-USNAC 1962

Tent Is Not Enough, A B 14 MIN
16MM FILM OPTICAL SOUND H-C A
Observes World Refugee Year. Traces the road traveled by millions of people who were uprooted by wars and religious persecution over the past two decades. Focuses on the Arab countries and Israel where an acute refugee problem remains unsolved.
Prod-ADL Dist-ADL

Tentacles C 96 MIN
16MM FILM OPTICAL SOUND H A
Describes a giant octopus that leaves its victims as skeletons washed up on a California beach. Stars Shelley Winters, John Huston and Henry Fonda.
Prod-ECE Dist-TIMLIF 1982

Tenth International Games For The Deaf C 40 MIN
16MM FILM OPTICAL SOUND
Shows the strength and skill of deaf contestants participating in an Olympic sports spectacle.
LC NO. FIA66-670
Prod-MONUMT Dist-MONUMT 1965

Tenth Month, The C 123 MIN
3/4 OR 1/2 INCH VIDEO CASSETTE H-C A
Tells the story of a female journalist who finds herself single, middle-aged and pregnant. Shows how she rebuffs family pressure to get rid of the baby, rents a cheap flat in a rough New York neighborhood and begins an ever hopeful vigil for the birth of the child. Stars Carol Burnett.
Prod-TIMLIF Dist-TIMLIF 1982

Tents, Gear And Horseback Tour C 30 MIN
1/2 IN VIDEO CASSETTE BETA/VHS
Introduces a tentmaker. Discusses choosing a campsite and gear. Features a Los Angeles urban wilderness and a horseback tour.
From The Great Outdoors Series.
Prod-WGBHTV Dist-MTI

Tepoztlan C 30 MIN
16MM FILM, 3/4 OR 1/2 IN VIDEO C A
Documents traditional lifeways in Tepoztlan including daily activities of the people, the cultivation of maize, planting, harvesting and grinding.
Prod-GRISWD Dist-PHENIX 1970

Tepoztlan In Transition C 20 MIN
16MM FILM, 3/4 OR 1/2 IN VIDEO C
Tells how the village of Tepoztlan emerges from its traditional isolation through mechanization which brings modern methods of irrigation and cultivation and a new type of employer-employee relationship as skilled labor develops in the village.
Prod-HRAW Dist-PHENIX 1970

Tepozton C 11 MIN
16MM FILM, 3/4 OR 1/2 IN VIDEO I-J
Presents a Mexican legend of the mischevous boy who is half Aztec God and half human.
From The American Folklore Series.
Prod-HRAW Dist-PHENIX 1971

Tepozton, The Magic Boy From The Mountains C 15 MIN
3/4 OR 1/2 INCH VIDEO CASSETTE P-I
Tells Mexican tale of Tepozton who offers to take his old father's place as a sacrifice to the giant, finds a way to conquer the giant and become king.
From The Sixteen Tales Series.
Prod-KLCSTV Dist-AITECH

Teresa Venerdi (Captioned) B 90 MIN
16MM FILM, 3/4 OR 1/2 IN VIDEO A
Portrays the story of a young girl in an orphanage in this romantic comedy with social overtones. Italian dialog with English subtitles.
Prod-CNEMAG Dist-CNEMAG 1941

Terex 33-15 C 11 MIN
16MM FILM OPTICAL SOUND
Demonstrates the largest diesel electric hauler built and designed in Canada.
LC NO. 75-703437
Prod-GMCAN Dist-GMCAN Prodn-EDITC 1973

Tereza (Czech) B 91 MIN
3/4 OR 1/2 INCH VIDEO CASSETTE
Tells of a female police officer who solves a complicated murder. Based on motifs from the novel by Anna Sedlmaye Rovia. Directed by Pavel Blumenfeld and starring Jirina Suorcova. With English subtitles.
Prod-IHF Dist-IHF

Terminal Equipment And Interfaces C 45 MIN
3/4 OR 1/2 INCH VIDEO CASSETTE C
Cover user-terminal functions such as input, output, communications parameters, including simplex, duplex, synchrony and signalling, terminal interfaces current loop, parallel, RS-232 and subsets RS-449, /.21, terminal intelligence and operating terminals.
From The Telecommunications And The Computer Series.
LC NO. 81-707502
Prod-AMCEE Dist-AMCEE 1981

Terminal Equipment And Interfaces C 49 MIN
3/4 OR 1/2 INCH VIDEO CASSETTE
See series title for descriptive statement.
From The Telecommunications And The Computer Series.
Prod-MIOT Dist-MIOT

Terminal Illness—A Series

Six videotapes devoted to the feelings and experiences of Dr Gary Leinbach who was dying of cancer. Reveals the specific problem areas in his terminal care which are universal. Relates his experiences, fears and reactions which are common to one facing impending death.
Prod-UWASHP Dist-UWASHP

Grieving Process, The 025 MIN
Grieving Process, The 1 045 MIN
Interviews With The Patient 015 MIN
Pain Management 037 MIN
Religion And The Clergy 035 MIN
Role Of The Physician, The 044 MIN

Terminal On My Desk, A - The Impact Of Data Processing In The Office C 29 MIN
3/4 OR 1/2 INCH VIDEO CASSETTE C A
Presents case studies of two large firms in England and Paris which demonstrate how the new technology is revolutionizing working conditions. Focuses on the need for involving individual workers in the process of implementing change.
From The Re-Making Of Work Series.
Prod-BLCKBY Dist-EBEC 1983

Terminal Self C 9 MIN
16MM FILM OPTICAL SOUND

An experimental film in which a photograph of the head of a girl is reproduced in pink vapors which change to multiple images that flutter in circular motion and finally converge into a single expression, that of the death mask.
LC NO. 72-700681
Prod-WHIT Dist-UWFKD 1971

Terminating An Employee (Industry) C
16MM FILM, 3/4 OR 1/2 IN VIDEO A
Shows how to terminate an employee in industrial setting.
From The Supervisory Training (Industry) Series.
Prod-CRMP Dist-CRMP 1983

Terminating An Employee (Office) C
16MM FILM, 3/4 OR 1/2 IN VIDEO A
Shows how to terminate an employee in an office setting.
From The Supervisory Training (Office) Series.
Prod-CRMP Dist-CRMP 1983

Termination Of Cardiac Arrhythmias C 11 MIN
3/4 INCH VIDEO CASSETTE PRO
Discusses the use of electrical energy for external defibrillization of the heart.
From The Cardiopulmonary Resuscitation Series.
Prod-PRIMED Dist-PRIMED

Termination Of Parental Rights C 59 MIN
3/4 OR 1/2 INCH VIDEO CASSETTE
Discusses procedural requirements for termination of parental legal rights.
From The Legal Training For Children Welfare Workers Series. Pt IV
Prod-UWISC Dist-UWISC 1975

Termination Phase, The C 22 MIN
3/4 OR 1/2 INCH VIDEO CASSETTE
Presents the final segment in the series as a young woman shows marked improvement in her situation during the course of her session. Indicates that her placement in a temporary shelter has had a beneficial effect and she displays an awareness of her past child abuse.
From The Social Work Interviewing Series.
Prod-UCALG Dist-UWISC 1978

Termination, Pt 8 C 50 MIN
3/4 OR 1/2 INCH VIDEO CASSETTE
Discusses the feelings of members of a relational growth group as group termination draws near. Explores feelings of withdrawal.
From The Relationship Growth Group Series.
Prod-WRAMC Dist-UWISC 1979

Terminaton In The Task-Centered Approach B 60 MIN
3/4 OR 1/2 INCH VIDEO CASSETTE
Uses the task-centered approach to demonstrate the steps in termination. Interviews a practitioner who works with the elderly about issues in termination with this population sub-group.
Prod-UWISC Dist-UWISC 1980

Terminus B 26 MIN
16MM FILM OPTICAL SOUND I-C A
Candidly studies, without narration, London's Waterloo Station. The fragmented sound score--jazz, half-heard dialogue and signal box noises--underscores the fragmentary nature of the peoples' experiences in a railroad station. Portrays the life cycle of the termite, types of termites and how science copes with the problems created by these insects.
LC NO. FIA65-1122
Prod-BTF Dist-SF 1964

Termites - Architects Of The Underground C 9 MIN
16MM FILM, 3/4 OR 1/2 IN VIDEO I-J
Explains that termites have been among the most elusive animals for study with their antipathy to light, their underground nests and their sensitivity to sound and movement, making them difficult subjects.
From The Real World Of Insects Series.
Prod-LCOA Dist-LCOA 1973

Termites - Architects Of The Underground (Captioned) C 9 MIN
16MM FILM, 3/4 OR 1/2 IN VIDEO P-C A
Presents an interesting study of termites, including their sensitivity to light, alien sound and movement.
From The Real World Of Insects Series.
Prod-PEGASO Dist-LCOA 1973

Termites - Architects Of The Underground (Spanish) C 9 MIN
16MM FILM, 3/4 OR 1/2 IN VIDEO P-C A
Presents an interesting study of termites, including their sensitivity to light, alien sound and movement.
From The Real World Of Insects Series.
Prod-PEGASO Dist-LCOA 1973

Termites And Telescopes C 58 MIN
16MM FILM OPTICAL SOUND
Presents Dr Philip Morrison providing a commentary on the nature of civilization.
From The Nova Series.
Prod-WGBHTV Dist-KINGFT

Termites And Telescopes C 58 MIN
3/4 INCH VIDEO CASSETTE
Presents commentary on the nature of civilization by Dr Phillip Morrison, Institute Professor and Professor of Physics at the Massachusetts Institute of Technology. Discusses the rise of civilization and the differences between animals, which adapt in sometimes astonishing ways to their environment, and man, who has shaped diverse environments to suit himself.
From The Nova Series.
Prod-BBCTV Dist-PBS 1980

Terms Of Endearment C
1/2 IN VIDEO CASSETTE BETA/VHS
Chronicles a mother and daughter's difficult relationship. Stars Shirley MacLaine, Debra Winger and Jack Nicholson.
Prod-GA Dist-GA

Ternary Diagrams Derived From Binaries C 6 MIN
16MM FILM OPTICAL SOUND C
Depicts the relationship of phase diagrams to real cases of materials technology. Uses computer animation to show the construction of a ternary system from three binary systems. Explains the projection of the upper curved surfaces onto the base of the solid model. Demonstrates that the projection contains information about composition, primary phase fields and temperature in a given ternary system.
From The Phase Equilibria Series.
LC NO. 78-700705
Prod-NSF Dist-PSU Prodn-MSRL 1976

Ternary Phase Diagram C 7 MIN
16MM FILM OPTICAL SOUND
Depicts the development of a new and rapid technique for preparation of ternary phase diagrams required in the search for useful alloys. Shows techniques for determining ternary phase alloy diagrams that make it possible to circumvent a previously tedious, time consuming and costly research procedure.
LC NO. 74-705761
Prod-USAEC Dist-USNAC 1965

Terra - Our World--A Series
I-J
Introduces environmental issues, including food, energy and pollution.
Prod-MSDOE Dist-AITECH 1980

Energy	020 MIN
Energy Alternatives	020 MIN
Environments	020 MIN
Food And People	020 MIN
Food In The Environment	020 MIN
Future, The	020 MIN
Non-Renewable Resources	020 MIN
Places Where People Live	020 MIN
Quality Of Life	020 MIN
Renewable Resources	020 MIN

Terra Degli Dea Madre C 16 MIN
3/4 INCH VIDEO CASSETTE
Presents a continuation of the project by Marina Abramovic and Ulay begun in City of Angels, to explore time and place in relation to a culture and its people. Taped in Sicily, this study in contrasts reveals the affinity of the people for their environment.
Prod-EAI Dist-EAI

Terra Maria C 23 MIN
16MM FILM OPTICAL SOUND J-H
Presents the complete story of ancient St Mary's City, the first capital of Maryland.
Prod-SHUGA Dist-SHUGA 1973

Terra Sancta - A Film Of Israel C 31 MIN
16MM FILM, 3/4 OR 1/2 IN VIDEO H-C
Shows an Israeli citizen pausing to look at his country and its 4000 years of history, as well as the modern cities which are the heart of Israel's vitality. Introduces the people of Israel, those who have come to find a new life and those who were born there.
Prod-IFB Dist-IFB 1969

Terradynamics C 21 MIN
16MM FILM OPTICAL SOUND H-C A
Explains that the Earth penetration program at Sandia Laboratories is concerned with determining the nature and composition of sub-surface soil using earth-penetrating, ballistic vehicles. Shows early experimentation, the evolution of the program, the delivery techniques and design of several penetration vehicles, plus a typical recovery operation and post-recovery analysis. Discusses the unique soil-motion studies conducted by the Terradynamics Division of Sandia.
LC NO. FIE68-96
Prod-USAEC Dist-USERD Prodn-SANDIA 1968

Terrain Investigation Techniques C 16 MIN
16MM FILM OPTICAL SOUND
Describes preliminary engineering problems involved in choosing the best location for a new highway. Presents four techniques used to analyze terrain--photo investigation, seismic refraction, electrical resistivity and confirmation borings.
LC NO. FIA68-838
Prod-OHIOSU Dist-OSUMPD Prodn-OSUMPD 1967

Terrains B 30 MIN
3/4 OR 1/2 INCH VIDEO CASSETTE
Presents three nude studies by Jeff Bush.
Prod-ARCVID Dist-ARCVID

Terrains C 30 MIN
3/4 OR 1/2 INCH VIDEO CASSETTE
Presents three nude studies by Jeff Bush. Shows the video screen becoming a window upon image composition which shifts in response to contrasting contours.
Prod-ARTRES Dist-ARTRES 1978

Terrarium, The - Classroom Science C 12 MIN
16MM FILM, 3/4 OR 1/2 IN VIDEO P-I
Explains that a terrarium is a small copy of part of the out-of-doors. Shows how to build two types of terraria--a copy of an area where there is moss and sufficient water to sustain it and a copy of a desert area. Shows the kinds of plants and animals which can live in each terrarium.
Prod-BEAN Dist-PHENIX 1967

Terrariums C 29 MIN
3/4 OR 1/2 INCH VIDEO CASSETTE
See series title for descriptive statement.
From The Crockett's Victory Garden Series.
Prod-WGBHTV Dist-KINGFT

Terre D'Alsace C 12 MIN
16MM FILM OPTICAL SOUND H
A French language film. Explores Strasbourg and provides a close-up of a hard-working family of farmers.
From The Aspects De France Series.
Prod-WSU Dist-MLA Prodn-BORGLM 1966

Terre Sans Pain (Land Without Bread) B 31 MIN
3/4 INCH VIDEO CASSETTE
Features the Hurdanos villages of the Extremadura region of Western Spain. Describes, in a surrealist style, the plight of people living on poor land and their neglect by the central government between 1922 and 1932, when the film was originally made.
Prod-BUNUEL Dist-DOCEDR 1975

Terremoto C 28 MIN
16MM FILM - 3/4 IN VIDEO
Shows how volunteers from all over the world helped the survivors of a destructive earthquake in Guatemala. Not available to school audiences.
Prod-SALVA Dist-MTP

Terrestrial Magnetism X 20 MIN
2 INCH VIDEOTAPE I
See series title for descriptive statement.
From The Process And Proof Series. No. 4
Prod-MCETV Dist-GPITVL Prodn-WVIZTV

Terrible News, The C 25 MIN
16MM FILM OPTICAL SOUND
Points out that the production of concentrated energy at fossil fuel plants generates concentrated wastes which alter the balance of the natural energy system. Focuses on Montana, offering examples of the tangible effects of industrial operations on their immediate surroundings.
LC NO. 73-702382
Prod-BITROT Dist-BITROT 1972

Terrible Secret, The C 47 MIN
16MM FILM, 3/4 OR 1/2 IN VIDEO
Deals with the experiences of two teenagers when one becomes involved in a hit-and-run accident and the other cheats in order to win a tennis scholarship. Based on the book Haunted Summer by Hope Dahle Jordan. Originally shown on the television series ABC Afterschool Specials.
From The Teenage Years Series.
LC NO. 79-706739
Prod-WILSND Dist-TIMLIF 1979

Terrible Tiles, The C 15 MIN
3/4 OR 1/2 INCH VIDEO CASSETTE K-P
Shows how objects can be classified by a given property.
From The Dragons, Wagons And Wax, Set 1 Series.
Prod-CTI Dist-CTI

Terrible Tuesday C 23 MIN
16MM FILM, 3/4 OR 1/2 IN VIDEO J A
Portrays the devastating tornado which struck Wichita Falls, Texas in 1979. Reports the impressions of survivors, records the city's annual disaster drill, and features tornado footage. Discusses how to survive a tornado.
Prod-NOAA Dist-USNAC 1984

Terrible Two's And Trusting Three's C 22 MIN
16MM FILM, 3/4 OR 1/2 IN VIDEO H-C A
Views two- and three-year-old children in order to show how their behaviors and abilities develop.
Prod-NFBC Dist-CRMP 1951

Terribly Strange Bed, A C 24 MIN
16MM FILM, 3/4 OR 1/2 IN VIDEO I-C
Tells a story about an organized band of criminals who operate a gambling house in the slums of Paris and their sinister method of reclaiming their losses and disposing of the winners. Televised on CBS in the Orson Wells Great Mystery Series.
From The Orson Welles Great Mysteries Series.
Prod-ANGLIA Dist-EBEC 1975

Terrines And Pates (French) C 29 MIN
2 INCH VIDEOTAPE
Features Julia Child of Haute Cuisine au Vin demonstrating how to prepare pates. With captions.
From The French Chef (French) Series.
Prod-WGBHTV Dist-PUBTEL

Territory Ahead, The C 60 MIN
3/4 OR 1/2 INCH VIDEO CASSETTE
Studies current and future directions in space, including the unveiling of the first reusable space vehicle, the space shuttle, the first woman in space, Sally Ride, the rapid commercialization of space, the 'Star Wars' scenario and the growing militarization of space. Ends with an eye to the future, including N A S A's unmanned planetary program, and explores the possibilities of space stations, colonies, and traveling on to the stars.
From The Spaceflight Series.
Prod-PBS Dist-PBS

Territory And Space C 30 MIN
3/4 OR 1/2 INCH VIDEO CASSETTE C
See series title for descriptive statement.
From The Art Of Being Human Series. Module 7
Prod-MDCC Dist-MDCC

Territory In Conflict C 28 MIN
3/4 OR 1/2 INCH VIDEO CASSETTE
Portrays the conflict between the people of a small Colorado mountain town and a huge corporation intent on mining one of the largest molybdenum deposits in the world.
Prod-CEPRO Dist-CEPRO

Terror - To Confront Or Concede C 52 MIN
3/4 OR 1/2 INCH VIDEO CASSETTE C A
Examines the question of whether nations should submit to terroristic blackmail. Includes interviews with Canadian and South American terrorists who discuss their political ambitions and terrorist tactics.
LC NO. 79-707357
Prod-BBCTV Dist-FI 1978

Terror By Night B 60 MIN
1/2 IN VIDEO CASSETTE (BETA)
Tells how Holmes and Watson are hired to protect a huge diamond on a train trip to Scotland. Stars Basil Rathbone and Nigel Bruce.
Prod-UNKNWN Dist-VIDIM 1946

Terror Of Anaphylaxis, The C 14 MIN
3/4 OR 1/2 INCH VIDEO CASSETTE PRO
Describes the early and late signs and symptoms of an anaphylactic reaction. Differentiates airway obstruction due to bronchospasm from that due to upper airway obstruction. Details the proper treatment and lists the precautions which minimize the risk of a serious anaphylactic reaction.
Prod-UMICHM Dist-UMICHM 1974

Terrorism - The World At Bay C 119 MIN
3/4 OR 1/2 INCH VIDEO CASSETTE
Presents an investigation of the causes and effects of worldwide terrorism on people, governments, diplomacy and political decision-making.
Prod-WHYY Dist-PBS 1978

Tesselations C 20 MIN
3/4 OR 1/2 INCH VIDEO CASSETTE H
Presents teachers Beth McKenna and David Edmonds investigating many aspects of tesselations including regular, semiregular and demiregular, as well as Islamic mosaics. Views transformational geometry by presenting Escher's tesselations and showing how to create them.
From The Shapes Of Geometry Series. Pt 4
LC NO. 82-707390
Prod-WVIZTV Dist-GPITVL 1982

Tesselations And Area - A Cover Up C 20 MIN
16MM FILM, 3/4 OR 1/2 IN VIDEO I-J
Discusses aspects of tesselations and area.
From The Mathscore One Series.
Prod-BBCTV Dist-FI

Tesselations And Area - Space Count C 20 MIN
16MM FILM, 3/4 OR 1/2 IN VIDEO I
Discusses aspects of tesselations and area.
From The Mathscore Two Series.
Prod-BBCTV Dist-FI

Test And Maintenance Equipment C 60 MIN
3/4 OR 1/2 INCH VIDEO CASSETTE IND
Covers gauge manifolds, temperature sensors, leak detection devices, vacuum pumps and suction line filter dryers.
From The Air Conditioning And Refrigeration-- Training Series.
Prod-ITCORP Dist-ITCORP

Test Can Teach, A C 10 MIN
16MM FILM, 3/4 OR 1/2 IN VIDEO I-H
Demonstrates that a returned teacher-graded test can be a useful educational tool and can be helpful in improving future test performance. Suggests specific techniques that will enable the student to review and to react to the returned test paper.
Prod-ALTSUL Dist-JOU 1968

Test For The West B 27 MIN
16MM FILM OPTICAL SOUND
Traces the history of Germany from a prosperous center of European culture in the 1920's through the Hitler Era and the post-war period. Discusses current foreign policy regarding Berlin.
Prod-CHRNOS Dist-AFLCIO 1962

Test Instruments, Pt 1 - Multimeters, Basic Circuits, Movements C 60 MIN
3/4 OR 1/2 INCH VIDEO CASSETTE IND
See series title for descriptive statement.
From The Electrical Maintenance Basics Series.
Prod-ITCORP Dist-ITCORP

Test Instruments, Pt 1 - Multimeters, Basic-Circuits, Movements (Spanish) C 60 MIN
3/4 OR 1/2 INCH VIDEO CASSETTE IND
See series title for descriptive statement.
From The Electrical Maintenance Basics (Spanish) Series.
Prod-ITCORP Dist-ITCORP

Test Instruments, Pt 2 - Multimeter Use C 60 MIN
3/4 OR 1/2 INCH VIDEO CASSETTE IND
See series title for descriptive statement.
From The Electrical Maintenance Basics Series.
Prod-ITCORP Dist-ITCORP

Test Instruments, Pt 2 - Multimeter Use-(Spanish) C 60 MIN
3/4 OR 1/2 INCH VIDEO CASSETTE IND
See series title for descriptive statement.
From The Electrical Maintenance Basics (Spanish) Series.
Prod-ITCORP Dist-ITCORP

Test Instruments, Pt 3 - Megohmmeters, Voltage Testers, Clamp-On Ammeters C 60 MIN
3/4 OR 1/2 INCH VIDEO CASSETTE IND
See series title for descriptive statement.
From The Electrical Maintenance Basics Series.
Prod-ITCORP Dist-ITCORP

Test Instruments, Pt 3 - Megohmmeters, - Voltage Testers, Clamp-On Ammeters (Spanish) C 60 MIN
3/4 OR 1/2 INCH VIDEO CASSETTE IND
See series title for descriptive statement.
From The Electrical Maintenance Basics (Spanish) Series.
Prod-ITCORP Dist-ITCORP

Test Instruments, Pt 4 - Miscellaneous, Bridges, Phase Rotation, Phase Sequence,... C 60 MIN
3/4 OR 1/2 INCH VIDEO CASSETTE IND
Complete title reads Test Instruments, Pt 4 Miscellaneous, Bridges, Phase Rotation, Phase Sequence, Variable Current Tester. Provides instruction in mechanical maintenance.
From The Electrical Maintenance Basics Series.
Prod-ITCORP Dist-ITCORP

Test Instruments, Pt 4 - Miscellaneous, - Bridges, Phase Rotation, Phase Sequence,... C 60 MIN
3/4 OR 1/2 INCH VIDEO CASSETTE IND
Complete title reads Test Instruments, Pt 4 Miscellaneous, Bridges, Phase Rotation, Phase Sequence, Variable Current Tester (Spanish). Provides instruction in electrical maintenance.
From The Electrical Maintenance Basics (Spanish) Series.
Prod-ITCORP Dist-ITCORP

Test Of Standard Written English C 120 MIN
3/4 OR 1/2 INCH VIDEO CASSETTE
See series title for descriptive statement.
From The SAT Exam Preparation Series.
Prod-KRLSOF Dist-KRLSOF 1985

Test Of Violence, A C 20 MIN
16MM FILM OPTICAL SOUND H-C A
Presents a view of violence in contemporary society as visualized in the paintings of noted Spanish artist Juan Genoves.
Prod-UWFKD Dist-UWFKD

Test Preparation—A Series
16MM FILM, 3/4 OR 1/2 IN VIDEO I-H
Presents information on how to prepare for tests. Includes strategies for taking college entrance exams and discusses test-taking skills which students should acquire prior to high school.
Prod-BOBROW Dist-CF 1982

Be Prepared For The A C T 030 MIN
Be Prepared For The S A T And The P S A T 030 MIN
Don't Be Afraid, It's Only A Test 016 MIN

Test Taking C 20 MIN
3/4 OR 1/2 INCH VIDEO CASSETTE H A
Shows how to develop strategies to study for and take exams. Tells how to analyze test results.
From The Art Of Learning Series.
Prod-WCVETV Dist-GPITVL 1984

Test Tubes In The Sea C 6 MIN
16MM FILM, 3/4 OR 1/2 IN VIDEO J-C A
Focuses on an international team of scientists as they measure pollutants in the sea in an attempt to find out how much pollution the ocean can absorb.
Prod-NSF Dist-AMEDFL 1975

Test Your Suggestability C 8 MIN
16MM FILM OPTICAL SOUND H-C
Demonstrates when and how to suggest related items and multiple quantities in making a sale. Shows how to determine what to suggest, how to make the suggestion specific, time the suggestion appropriately and explain additional purchase benefits to the customer.
From The Professional Selling Practices Series 2 Series.
LC NO. 77-702356
Prod-SAUM Dist-SAUM Prodn-CALPRO 1968

Test-Taking Skills - Effective Study Techniques C
3/4 OR 1/2 INCH VIDEO CASSETTE H
Reviews skills that help students prepare for objective and essay test questions.
Prod-GA Dist-GA

Test-Taking Skills - How To Succeed On Standardized Examinations C 37 MIN
3/4 OR 1/2 INCH VIDEO CASSETTE
Shows how to relieve anxieties when taking standardized tests by preparing and becoming familiar with the types of questions on the test. Reviews mathematics problems, reading, antonyms, sentence completions, analogies and standard written English.
LC NO. 81-706695
Prod-CHUMAN Dist-GA 1981

Test-Tube Babies - A Daughter For Judy C 57 MIN
16MM FILM, 3/4 OR 1/2 IN VIDEO H-C A
Looks at the intriguing science which has made it possible to conceive human babies outside the womb. Discusses the disturbing social issues it raises.
From The Nova Series.
LC NO. 83-706031
Prod-WGBHTV Dist-TIMLIF 1982

Test, Pt 1 C 29 MIN
2 INCH VIDEOTAPE
See series title for descriptive statement.
From The Maggie And The Beautiful Machine - General Shape-up Series.
Prod-WGBHTV Dist-PUBTEL

Test, Pt 2 C 29 MIN
2 INCH VIDEOTAPE
See series title for descriptive statement.
From The Maggie And The Beautiful Machine - General Shape-up Series.
Prod-WGBHTV Dist-PUBTEL

Test, The C 11 MIN
3/4 OR 1/2 INCH VIDEO CASSETTE T
Emphasizes the importance of helping students learn how to take standardized achievement tests. Gives tips for reducing trauma experienced by teachers and students on test day.
From The Tests Series.
Prod-WTVITV Dist-AITECH 1980

Testament C
1/2 IN VIDEO CASSETTE BETA/VHS
Tells the story of a mother of three who struggles to keep her family together after a nuclear attack. Stars Jane Alexander and William Devane.
Prod-GA Dist-GA

Testicular Autotransplantation After Laparoscopic Localization C 11 MIN
3/4 OR 1/2 INCH VIDEO CASSETTE PRO
Covers laparoscopy used to localize the nonpalpable testes in a one-year-old male and subsequent testicular autotransplantation performed to correct the high position of the child's testes and the short card.
Prod-HSCIC Dist-HSCIC 1984

Testicular Self Examination C 8 MIN
3/4 INCH VIDEO CASSETTE
Explains the importance of testicular self-examination and demonstrates the procedure.
Prod-UTAHTI Dist-UTAHTI

Testicular Torsion C 15 MIN
16MM FILM OPTICAL SOUND
Uses art and animation to depict the fetal development of the testicle. Presents a comparison of normal and abnormal testis, illustrating various abnormalities, all exhibiting testicular torsion. Points out that early diagnosis and treatment is the only means of preserving the testicle prone to torsion.
LC NO. 75-702287
Prod-EATONL Dist-EATONL 1972

Testifying In Court C 9 MIN
16MM FILM OPTICAL SOUND H-C A
Helps police officers become acquainted with procedures for testifying in court. Discusses pretrial preparation, demeanor outside the courtroom and proper behavior on the witness stand.
LC NO. 75-701985
Prod-MCCRNE Dist-MCCRNE 1975

Testing C 60 MIN
3/4 OR 1/2 INCH VIDEO CASSETTE IND
Explains various types of inspections and tests. Compares destructive and non-destructive tests. Covers tensile, bend torsion, impact and vibration, ultrasonic, dye penetrant and eddy current.
From The Quality Assurance Series.
Prod-LEIKID Dist-LEIKID

Testing - None Of The Above C 33 MIN
16MM FILM OPTICAL SOUND C A
Presents a school counselor as she looks at several aspects of standardized tests. Examines the effect of test scores on teacher expectations, the scarcity concept of education, and the validity of test items.
LC NO. 78-701450
Prod-UWISC Dist-UWISC 1978

Testing - What's It All About? C
3/4 OR 1/2 INCH VIDEO CASSETTE A
Provides information to parents about testing experiences children undergo during their elementary and secondary schooling.
From The Vital Link Series.
Prod-EDCC Dist-EDCC

Testing An Adult Male Aphasic Patient C 20 MIN
16MM FILM OPTICAL SOUND PRO
Ronald S Krug Administers the Halstead-Wepman Aphasia Screening Test as adapted by Reitan to a 55-year-old male with a malignant tumor in the posterior portion of the left cerebral hemisphere in order to evaluate the types and extent of the symbolic or aphasic disturbances present.
From The Psychological Evaluation Of Patients With Cerebral Dysfunction Series.
LC NO. 72-700634
Prod-UOKLA Dist-UOKLA 1966

Testing And Individual Therapy For Aphasia C 28 MIN
3/4 OR 1/2 INCH VIDEO CASSETTE PRO
Shows tests for determining the nature and extent of an individual's aphasia. Follows retraining of aphasics from each category (motor, sensory and formulation).
From The Aphasia Series.
Prod-WFP Dist-WFP

Testing And Observing Liquids B 15 MIN
2 INCH VIDEOTAPE P
See series title for descriptive statement.
From The Just Inquisitive Series. No. 5
Prod-EOPS Dist-GPITVL Prodn-KOACTV

Testing Apollo C 5 MIN
3/4 INCH VIDEO CASSETTE
Illustrates the testing programs for the saturn and Apollo spacecrafts. Shows testing sequences in the vehicle-assembly building and on the launch pad. Issued in 1969 as a motion picture.
From The Apollo Digest Series.
LC NO. 79-706995
Prod-NASA Dist-USNAC 1979

Testing Children With Multiple Handicaps B 30 MIN
16MM FILM OPTICAL SOUND S
Demonstrates the educational evaluation of preschool children with single and multiple handicaps. Illustrates the function of the multi-disciplinary team.
Prod-UCPA Dist-UCPA

Testing Equipment And Approaches C 29 MIN
2 INCH VIDEOTAPE
Features Dr Puryear and his guest Elmer Green (director of research on voluntary control, the Menninger Foundation) who discuss and demonstrate contemporary methods and modern sophisticated equipment developed for more precise measurement of ESP and related phenomena.
From The Who Is Man Series.
Prod-WHROTV Dist-PUBTEL

Testing Generator Output C 4 MIN
16MM FILM OPTICAL SOUND
Points out the use of the tachometer and the proper reading of the ampmeter and voltmeter.
LC NO. FI68-275
Prod-RAYBAR Dist-RAYBAR 1966

Testing Headlight Aim C 4 MIN
16MM FILM OPTICAL SOUND
Shows steps taken before adjusting headlight aim. Demonstrates the method of fixing the meter bulb, points out different parts and shows how to align the headlights.
LC NO. FI68-276
Prod-RAYBAR Dist-RAYBAR 1966

Testing Irradiated Steel C 16 MIN
16MM FILM OPTICAL SOUND
Shows the performance of crack arrest tests on steel specimens after they have been irradiated. Includes shots of the actual irradiation and the remote handling techniques made necessary by the radioactivity of the specimens.
Prod-UKAEA Dist-UKAEA 1964

Testing Multiple Means - AOV C
3/4 OR 1/2 INCH VIDEO CASSETTE IND
Defines this testing as a way of making comparisons of two or more products. Discusses Completely Randomized and Randomized Block Design. Illustrates use of the LSD test to determine which means are different.
From The Statistics For Managers Series.
Prod-COLOSU Dist-COLOSU

Testing Multiply Handicapped Children B 30 MIN
16MM FILM OPTICAL SOUND
Illustrates techniques for evaluating children with multiple disabilities. Shows case studies of three children--one with a severe cerebral palsy condition and a related speech problem, another with severe visual and auditory impairments and a third who is hyperactive-distractible with mental retardation. Emphasizes the importance of the examiner being adaptible and flexible.
LC NO. FIA67-1280
Prod-UCPA Dist-UCPA Prodn-NWSUSA 1963

Testing Objectives C 30 MIN
3/4 OR 1/2 INCH VIDEO CASSETTE T
See series title for descriptive statement.
From The Eager To Learn Series.
Prod-KTEHTV Dist-KTEHTV

Testing Of Antimicrobial Agents/Coagulase And Antibody Reactions C 29 MIN
3/4 OR 1/2 INCH VIDEO CASSETTE
Includes two presentations on one tape number 6206. Presents basic techniques employing filter paper discs to determine antimicrobial effectiveness of disinfectants/antiseptics and antibiotics/sulfonamides.. Identifies land measures zones of inhibition and considers factors influencing the size of such zones.
Prod-AMSM Dist-AVMM

Testing Process, The C 35 MIN
3/4 INCH VIDEO CASSETTE C A
See series title for descriptive statement.
From The Software Management For Small Computers Series.
LC NO. 81-706201
Prod-AMCEE Dist-AMCEE 1980

Testing Proportions C
3/4 OR 1/2 INCH VIDEO CASSETTE IND
Defines as a formalized to decision making involving go/no-go data. Uses normal approximation to test oneand two-sample proportions, while the chi-square is used to test one or more proportions.
From The Statistics For Managers Series.
Prod-COLOSU Dist-COLOSU

Testing The Multiply Handicapped Children, Millicent B 30 MIN
16MM FILM OPTICAL SOUND
Depicts the testing of Millicent, age four and one-half who is hyperactive, distractable and mentally retarded.
Prod-UCPA Dist-UCPA

Testing, Symbolic Execution And Formal Verification C 30 MIN
3/4 OR 1/2 INCH VIDEO CASSETTE IND
Concludes discussion of current issues in program-testing. Covers symbolic execution and relationship of testing to formal verification.
From The Software Engineering - A First Course Series.
Prod-COLOSU Dist-COLOSU

Testing, Tension And Competition C 25 MIN
3/4 OR 1/2 INCH VIDEO CASSETTE J-C A
Interviews Dr Slack and Dr Porter of Beth Israel Hospital in Boston about their criticism of the emphasis placed on standardized testing in high school. Discusses their belief that the Scholastic Aptitude Test in particular provokes anxiety and that the results often leave a negative mark on a student's self-esteem.
Prod-SIRS Dist-SIRS

Testport C 29 MIN
16MM FILM OPTICAL SOUND
Describes the mission and services of the Naval Air Test Center in Patuxent River, Maryland.
LC NO. 74-706593
Prod-USN Dist-USNAC 1971

Tests And Stress C 12 MIN
3/4 OR 1/2 INCH VIDEO CASSETTE H A
Reveals that Susan, Alan and Lucy are all nervous about the typing test. Explains that Susan doesn't listen or ask for instructions, Alan arrives late and is tired, hungry and hostile while Lucy has practiced at home, listens carefully, asks questions and does well.
From The Making It Work Series.
Prod-ERF Dist-AITECH 1983

Tests For Qualitative Data (Proportions) C 30 MIN
3/4 OR 1/2 INCH VIDEO CASSETTE IND
Uses normal and Chi-Square tests for determining if goals are met (a specific proportion defective) or for comparison of several production lines or procedures.
From The Engineering Statistics Series.
Prod-COLOSU Dist-COLOSU

Tests Of Hypotheses B 30 MIN
16MM FILM OPTICAL SOUND PRO
Presents the testing of hypotheses by the use of a test statistic 'THE Z SCORE' and probability theory. Features the normal curve as the frame of reference which has previously been used for estimating characteristics of a population from a sample.
From The Public Health Science - Biostatistics Series.
Prod-KUHTTV Dist-GPITVL

Tests Of Hypotheses B 30 MIN
2 INCH VIDEOTAPE PRO
See series title for descriptive statement.
From The Public Health Science Series. Unit II - Introduction To Biostatistics
Prod-TEXWU Dist-GPITVL Prodn-KUHTTV

Tests—A Series
T
Explains what teachers should expect of tests and suggests how to get the most out of test data, so that valuable instruction time can be returned to the classroom.
Prod-WTVITV Dist-AITECH 1980

Know The Score 011 MIN
Teacher-Made Tests 011 MIN
Test, The 011 MIN
Tests, Tests, Tests 011 MIN

Tests, Tests, Tests C 11 MIN
3/4 OR 1/2 INCH VIDEO CASSETTE T
Explains the purpose of tests and looks at the differences among the various types of tests.
From The Tests Series.
Prod-WTVITV Dist-AITECH 1980

Tet, 1968 C 60 MIN
3/4 OR 1/2 INCH VIDEO CASSETTE H-C A
Shows that one of the big turning points in the war in Vietnam came when the Americans thought they were winning but were actually in a stalemate. Reveals that on the Tet holiday, attacks came in areas the U S thought to be secure, including Saigon. States that the defeats caused second thoughts in Washington that eventually resulted in President Johnson's decision to call a partial bombing halt.
From The Vietnam - A Television History Series. Episode 7
Prod-WGBHTV Dist-FI 1983

Tetanus Prophylaxis And Management C 25 MIN
16MM FILM OPTICAL SOUND PRO
Explains that tetanus is a dire, but completely preventable disease. Depicts aspects of tetanus treatment and prevention.
Prod-ACYDGD Dist-ACY 1965

Tetralogy Of Fallot C 30 MIN
16MM FILM OPTICAL SOUND PRO
Presents a review of the embryonic development of the heart and examines the Blalock-Taussig and Potts-Smith surgical procedures for correcting Tetralogy of Fallot.
Prod-SQUIBB Dist-SQUIBB

Tex C 26 MIN
16MM FILM, 3/4 OR 1/2 IN VIDEO J-H
Offers an abbreviated version of the motion picture Tex about the coming of age of a 15-year-old boy in rural Oklahoma who must deal with family conflicts, peer pressure, emotional instability, and experimentation with sex and drugs. Based on the novel TEX by S E Hinton.
From The Film As Literature, Series 4 Series.
Prod-WDEMCO Dist-WDEMCO 1982

Texas C
3/4 OR 1/2 INCH VIDEO CASSETTE
Presents five segments about the state of Texas, a vast and sprawling land that brings to mind images of cowboys, wide open spaces, oil rigs, millionaires and the magic of myth and legend.
From The Portrait Of America Series.
Prod-TBS Dist-TBS

Texas - The Economic Geography Of The Coastal Plains Region C 30 MIN
16MM FILM OPTICAL SOUND J-C A
Discusses the economic geography of the coastal plains of Texas. Reveals how this area is divided into various regions, each of which has its own unique economic characteristic.
Prod-ACA Dist-ACA 1974

Texas - The Economic Geography Of The Great Plains And Mountains And Basins Regions C 26 MIN
16MM FILM OPTICAL SOUND J-C A
Discusses the economic geography of the great plains, mountains and basins regions of Texas. Reveals how each area has its own unique economic characteristic.
Prod-ACA Dist-ACA 1974

Texas - The Economic Geography Of The North Central Plains Region C 23 MIN
16MM FILM OPTICAL SOUND J-C A
Discusses the economic geography of the north central plains region of Texas. Reveals how this region is divided into sub-areas, each of which has its own unique economic characteristics.
Prod-ACA Dist-ACA 1974

Texas And Its Natural Resources C 27 MIN
16MM FILM OPTICAL SOUND
Describes the magnitude of Texas mineral and energy resources. Also discusses agriculture, cattle and sheep raising, transportation facilities, and climate. Made in co-operation with the Texas Gulf Sulphur Co.
Prod-USDIBM Dist-USDIBM Prodn-JAMIE 1955

Texas History - Anglo-American Settlement To Pre-Civil War Period C 27 MIN
16MM FILM OPTICAL SOUND J-C A
Describes the triumphs and trials leading to the Anglo-American settlement of Texas before the Civil War. Includes an account of the efforts of Moses and Stephen Austin and the events leading to the storming of the Alamo.
Prod-ACA Dist-ACA 1974

Texas History - From Prehistoric Times To Anglo-American Settlement C 23 MIN
16MM FILM OPTICAL SOUND J-C A
Describes Texas history from prehistoric times to the times of Anglo-American settlement.
Prod-ACA Dist-ACA 1974

Texas History - The Civil War Period To Modern Texas C 22 MIN
16MM FILM OPTICAL SOUND J-C A
Covers the history of Texas from the Civil War period to modern times.
Prod-ACA Dist-ACA 1974

Texas Wiretap Law, The C 15 MIN
3/4 INCH VIDEO CASSETTE H-C A
Explains Texas' 1981 wiretap law that allows state law enforcement officers to tap phones to determine drug-related offenses. Interviews with an undercover narcotics agent and an attorney provide comparisons of this law with those in other states. Discusses privacy and surveillance techniques.
LC NO. 82-707074
Prod-SWINS Dist-SWINS 1981

Texas, Virgin Islands, Holland C 27 MIN
16MM FILM OPTICAL SOUND P-I
Portrays a minicycle contest in Texas, a salt pond in the Virgin Islands and a circus school in Holland. Relates a folk tale from Bulgaria about a spoiled girl.
From The Big Blue Marble - Children Around The World Series. Program O
LC NO. 76-700627
Prod-ALVEN Dist-VITT 1975

Text Editor, Part I C 30 MIN
3/4 OR 1/2 INCH VIDEO CASSETTE IND
Explains editor command line, addressing, search capability, and editor commands - ed, p, a, i, c, u, and q.
From The UNIX Series.
Prod-COLOSU Dist-COLOSU

Text Editor, Part II C 30 MIN
3/4 OR 1/2 INCH VIDEO CASSETTE IND
Goes into file backup, file recovery, and editor commands - d, s, m, t, j, w, e, f, and r.
From The UNIX Series.
Prod-COLOSU Dist-COLOSU

Textile Art C 15 MIN
3/4 OR 1/2 INCH VIDEO CASSETTE P-I
Discusses textile art.
From The Young At Art Series.
Prod-WSKJTV Dist-AITECH 1980

Textile Design—A Series
16MM FILM, 3/4 OR 1/2 IN VIDEO I-C A
Introduces the most important aspects of textile design.
Prod-PARACO Dist-AIMS

Batik 10 MIN
Tie Dye 15 MIN
Weaving With Looms You Can Make 16 MIN
With Fabric And Thread 15 MIN

Textile Industry C 3 MIN
16MM FILM OPTICAL SOUND P-I
Discusses the textile industry.
From The Of All Things Series.
Prod-BAILYL Dist-AVED

Textile Printing C 29 MIN
2 INCH VIDEOTAPE
See series title for descriptive statement.
From The Exploring The Crafts - Silk Screen Printing Series.
Prod-NHN Dist-PUBTEL

Textile Testing Using The Instron C 22 MIN
3/4 OR 1/2 INCH VIDEO CASSETTE C A
Offers basic examples of textile testing using the Instron to execute ASTM standard test procedures. Includes four test procedures, tensile properties of fabrics, tear strength of woven fabrics, tensile properties of fibers and compression testing of carpets.
From The Measuring The Performance Of Textiles - Textile Testing Series. No. 2

LC NO. 81-707150
Prod-CUETV Dist-CUNIV 1981

Textiles C 29 MIN
3/4 INCH VIDEO CASSETTE
Presents Navajo weavers Martha Began and Lillian Dineyazhe using wool and cotton yarns to create rugs, blankets and wall hangings. Hopi fabric designer Manfred Susunkewa uses ancient and modern tribal designs for silkscreening. Also available in two-inch quad and one-inch videocassette.
From The Indian Arts At The Phoenix Heard Museum Series.
Prod-KAETTV Dist-NAMPBC

Textiles And Ornamental Arts Of India C 12 MIN
16MM FILM, 3/4 OR 1/2 IN VIDEO H-C A
Records an exhibition of East Indian arts and crafts shown by the museum of modern art in New York in 1955. Motion is created by using the metric-cutting film technique.
Prod-EAMES Dist-EBEC 1955

Texts Generate Other Texts C 30 MIN
3/4 OR 1/2 INCH VIDEO CASSETTE H-C A
See series title for descriptive statement.
From The Introduction To Technical And Business Communication Series.
Prod-UMINN Dist-GPITVL 1983

Texture C 15 MIN
3/4 OR 1/2 INCH VIDEO CASSETTE K-J
See series title for descriptive statement.
From The Arts Express Series.
Prod-KYTV Dist-KYTV 1983

Textures C 15 MIN
2 INCH VIDEOTAPE K
Describes the various textures of materials by the senses of sight and touch.
From The Let's Go Sciencing, Unit I - Matter Series.
Prod-DETPS Dist-GPITVL

Textures C 15 MIN
3/4 INCH VIDEO CASSETTE K-P
Shows children exploring textures in nature, playing matching games and watching the creation of a ceramic pot. Points out that foods have different textures. Introduces texture games.
From The Adventures Of Milo And Maisie Series.
Prod-KRLNTV Dist-GPITVL 1977

Textures And Shapes C 15 MIN
3/4 INCH VIDEO CASSETTE P
Explores the texture and shapes of objects with the purpose of stimulating young children to use their tactile and visual perceptions in the creation of graphic designs and compositions. Introduces basic geometric shapes and shows their texture through rubbings, which children can make and use to create their own designs.
From The Is The Sky Always Blue Series.
LC NO. 80-706688
Prod-WDCNTV Dist-GPITVL 1979

Textures Of The Great Lakes C 6 MIN
16MM FILM OPTICAL SOUND J-C
Presents an artistic interpretation of the textural qualities of the waters, beaches, dunes and woods of the Great Lakes region. Synchronizes visual images with harp accompaniment.
From The Creative Motivational Series.
LC NO. FIA66-769
Prod-LOH Dist-LOH 1966

Texturing Clay C 28 MIN
2 INCH VIDEOTAPE
Features Mrs Peterson describing certain ceramic processes for her classroom at the University of Southern California. Demonstrates how to texture clay.
From The Wheels, Kilns And Clay Series.
Prod-USC Dist-PUBTEL

TH Sounds, The C 15 MIN
3/4 INCH VIDEO CASSETTE
Focuses on the two types of TH sounds, one voiceless and the other voiced.
From The New Talking Shop Series.
Prod-BSPTV Dist-GPITVL 1978

Thai Images Of The Buddha X 14 MIN
16MM FILM OPTICAL SOUND H-C A
Uses ancient statuary from the arts of Thailand exhibit to show the transformation of the Buddha image from that of revered teacher to that of a supreme diety. Discusses the historical course of Buddhism.
From The Arts Of The Orient Series.
Prod-IU Dist-IU 1963

Thailand C 13 MIN
16MM FILM OPTICAL SOUND
Shows the hundreds of canals which crisscross the countryside of Thailand and run through the city of Bangkok carrying 80 percent of the bustling internal traffic.
From The New Horizons Series.
Prod-TWCF Dist-PANWA

Thailand C 28 MIN
3/4 INCH VIDEOTAPE
Interviews Ambassador Birabhongse Kasemri, permanent representative of Thailand to the United Nations. Discusses the people and attractions of Thailand. Includes two film clips of Thailand.
From The International Byline Series.
Prod-PERRYM Dist-PERRYM

Thailand C 29 MIN
3/4 INCH VIDEO CASSETTE
Focuses on Thailand, describing the assistance offered by members of the U S Army. Issued in 1963 as a motion picture.
From The Big Picture Series.
LC NO. 79-706682
Prod-USA Dist-USNAC 1979

Thailand C 30 MIN
3/4 INCH VIDEO CASSETTE I-J
Profiles Montry, a fisher boy in a quiet village in Thailand.
From The Families Of The World Series.
Prod-UNICEF Dist-GPITVL 1974

Thailand - Ally Under Fire B 20 MIN
16MM FILM OPTICAL SOUND
Discusses various aspects of Thailand, such as its history, economy, agriculture, aid from the United States and commitment in Vietnam.
From The Screen News Digest Series. Vol 9, Issue 7
Prod-HEARST Dist-HEARST 1967

Thailand - Bicentennial C 27 MIN
3/4 OR 1/2 INCH VIDEO CASSETTE H-C A
Presents Thailand celebrating the bicentennial of its Royal Family - the Chakri dynasty. Examines the history of the dynasty as well as the social, political and economic problems facing contemporary Thailand.
Prod-JOU Dist-JOU

Thailand - Goodbye To The Small And Magic Dragon C 30 MIN
16MM FILM OPTICAL SOUND I-C
Presents Thailand as a place on the other side of the Earth where there exists a kind of timeless, oriental Oz filled with magnificent temples and fabled palaces where jeweled elephants once fought with ancient heroes and lovely women danced.
From The Human Dimension Series.
LC NO. 76-713866
Prod-GRACUR Dist-GRACUR 1971

Thailand - Land Of Freedom C 28 MIN
16MM FILM, 3/4 OR 1/2 IN VIDEO H-C
Presents a travelogue about Thailand, covering its various regions, industries, cities, flowers, animals, accommodations, food and religion.
Prod-POLNIS Dist-IFB

Thailand - Land Of Smiles C 27 MIN
16MM FILM, 3/4 OR 1/2 IN VIDEO J-C A
Presents traditional aspects of the culture of Thailand. Discusses the geography, emphasizing the importance of water for travel and agriculture. Shows dances, festivals, handicrafts and the influence of religion on Thailand's culture.
Prod-CFDLD Dist-CORF 1977

Thailand - Life Along The Khlongs C 22 MIN
16MM FILM, 3/4 OR 1/2 IN VIDEO
Looks at the life of a family who lives along the canals or Khlongs of Thailand. Views the family's morning swim, their trip to a floating market, their water school bus and their water festival.
Prod-HANDEL Dist-HANDEL 1983

Thailand Today C 16 MIN
16MM FILM, 3/4 OR 1/2 IN VIDEO J-H
Describes traditions and life styles in Thailand.
From The People And Places In Asia Series.
LC NO. 81-706490
Prod-WOVIEN Dist-IFB 1980

Thailand Today (Swedish) C 16 MIN
16MM FILM, 3/4 OR 1/2 IN VIDEO J-H
Describes traditions and life styles in Thailand.
Prod-WOVIEN Dist-IFB 1980

Thames, The C 59 MIN
16MM FILM, 3/4 OR 1/2 IN VIDEO I-C A
Looks at the Thames River and its history. Highlights its inspiration for writers, its tradition of amusements, and focus of studies, celebration and affection for the English people. Reports the results of an extensive cleanup program that is restoring the river to new vitality.
LC NO. 82-707109
Prod-NGS Dist-NGS 1982

Thanatopsis B 6 MIN
16MM FILM OPTICAL SOUND
Presents a somber study of the ornamented steps, windows, doors and elaborately designed railings and trimmings of an old deserted house about to be demolished.
LC NO. 75-703239
Prod-USC Dist-USC 1965

Thanh C 9 MIN
16MM FILM OPTICAL SOUND I-H
Introduces Pham Thanh, a 15-year-old refugee from Vietnam who tells his classmates of the tragedy of seeing American soldiers destroy his village and kill his mother, father and grandmother. Relates his daily struggle to deal with the loneliness, fear and depression that have been part of his life since he was airlifted out of Vietnam.
From The Rebop Series.
LC NO. 79-700477
Prod-WGBHTV Dist-IU 1979

Thank God And The Revolution C 50 MIN
16MM FILM, 3/4 OR 1/2 IN VIDEO H-C A
Focuses on the role of organized religion in the Nicaraguan guerrilla movement. Shows members of the Roman Catholic clergy serving as government officials and various Nicaraguans as they testify to the inspirational and unifying force of Christianity in the revolutionary struggle and reforms in Nicaragua.
LC NO. 82-706411
Prod-TERCIN Dist-ICARUS 1981

Thank God, It's Friday C 26 MIN
16MM FILM, 3/4 OR 1/2 IN VIDEO C A
Reveals that as managers develop their own potential, a company also develops and benefits. Uses the examples of two brothers working for two different companies to show the different paths self-development may take. Deals with identifying personal goals, planning to achieve these goals, monitoring achievement and reassessing goals as necessary.
Prod-MILLBK Dist-IFB

Thank Heaven C 3 MIN
16MM FILM OPTICAL SOUND H-C A
Uses animation to tell of a new recruit from earth who makes some very surprising discoveries about God's plumbing.
Prod-UWFKD Dist-UWFKD

Thank You B 15 MIN
2 INCH VIDEOTAPE P
See series title for descriptive statement.
From The Children's Literature Series. No. 8
Prod-NCET Dist-GPITVL Prodn-KUONTV

Thank You M'am C 12 MIN
16MM FILM, 3/4 OR 1/2 IN VIDEO I-H
Presents an adaptation of the short story Thank You M'am by Langston Hughes about an older Black woman who makes a Black youth pay the consequences for trying to steal her pocketbook.
Prod-SUGERA Dist-PHENIX 1976

Thank You, M'am / A Father Like That C 30 MIN
1/2 IN VIDEO CASSETTE BETA/VHS
Presents an adaptation of a short story by Langston Hughes about a boy who tries to steal a purse. Tells the story of a boy who has never met his father, based on the book by Charlotte Zolotow.
Prod-BFA Dist-BFA

Thanks A'Plenty Boss—A Series
16MM FILM, 3/4 OR 1/2 IN VIDEO
Prod-RTBL Dist-RTBL 1973

Correct Way Of Correcting, The 22 MIN
Rewards Of Rewarding, The 24 MIN

Thanks For The Dinner C 10 MIN
3/4 INCH VIDEO CASSETTE
Tells about a man who, because of neglect, must have all of his teeth extracted. Shows how he adjusts to dentures and is instructed in taking proper care of them. Issued in 1969 as a motion picture.
LC NO. 78-706244
Prod-USVA Dist-USNAC Prodn-VADTC 1978

Thanks For The Memory C 14 MIN
3/4 OR 1/2 INCH VIDEO CASSETTE
See series title for descriptive statement.
From The Funny Business Series.
Prod-LCOA Dist-DELTAK

Thanks For The Memory C 24 MIN
16MM FILM, 3/4 OR 1/2 IN VIDEO A
Demonstrates techniques for memory improvement.
Prod-SEVDIM Dist-SEVDIM

Thanks For The One Time C 45 MIN
16MM FILM, 3/4 OR 1/2 IN VIDEO J-H A
Presents the story of an alcoholic physician who can't bring himself to admit that he has a drinking problem. Illustrates the techniques of intervention in order to help the alcoholic take the first step toward help.
LC NO. 81-706000
Prod-SHANDA Dist-LCOA 1981

Thanks To You C 13 MIN
16MM FILM OPTICAL SOUND
Tells the story of Sharon, a child inflicted with cystic fibrosis and gives brief glimpses of others helped by United Fund contributions.
LC NO. 77-700422
Prod-UFCMD Dist-CPTCO Prodn-CPTCO 1976

Thanksgiving C 5 MIN
16MM FILM OPTICAL SOUND
Presents a story about a plucked and ready-to-cook turkey that suddenly drops off the stove and attempts to escape.
LC NO. 75-703438
Prod-CANFDC Dist-CANFDC 1974

Thanksgiving C 15 MIN
3/4 OR 1/2 INCH VIDEO CASSETTE P
Explores musical phrasing. Uses a Thanksgiving theme.
From The Music Machine Series.
Prod-GPITVL Dist-GPITVL

Thanksgiving C 15 MIN
3/4 INCH VIDEO CASSETTE P
See series title for descriptive statement.
From The Celebrate Series.
Prod-KUONTV Dist-GPITVL 1978

Thanksgiving C 15 MIN
3/4 OR 1/2 INCH VIDEO CASSETTE P
See series title for descriptive statement.
From The Strawberry Square Series.
Prod-NEITV Dist-AITECH 1982

Thanksgiving C 15 MIN
3/4 OR 1/2 INCH VIDEO CASSETTE I-J
Demonstrates how to develop an illustration by arranging people, settings and costumes.
From The Draw Man Series.
Prod-OCPS Dist-AITECH 1975

Thanksgiving C 15 MIN
3/4 INCH VIDEO CASSETTE
See series title for descriptive statement.

From The Holiday Series.
Prod-WTVITV Dist-MDCPB

Thanksgiving (Let's Draw) C 15 MIN
3/4 OR 1/2 INCH VIDEO CASSETTE P
See series title for descriptive statement.
From The Let's Draw Series.
Prod-OCPS Dist-AITECH Prodn-KOKHTV 1976

Thanksgiving - The Pilgrims C 14 MIN
2 INCH VIDEOTAPE
See series title for descriptive statement.
From The Muffinland - Holiday Specials Series.
Prod-WGTV Dist-PUBTEL

Thanksgiving - The Things I Like Best C 14 MIN
2 INCH VIDEOTAPE
See series title for descriptive statement.
From The Muffinland - Holiday Specials Series.
Prod-WGTV Dist-PUBTEL

Thanksgiving Dinner C
1/2 IN VIDEO CASSETTE BETA/VHS
Demonstrates Thanksgiving recipes such as baked turkey, dressings, vegetables and pies.
From The Video Cooking Library Series.
Prod-KARTES Dist-KARTES

Thanksgiving In Peshawar C 17 MIN
3/4 OR 1/2 INCH VIDEO CASSETTE
Presents a documentary by Kirk Douglas on his visit to Afghan refugee camps near Peshawar, Pakistan. Reviews the history of Afghanistan and discusses the Soviet invasion, emphasizing the plight of the refugees.
LC NO. 84-706401
Prod-USIA Dist-USNAC 1983

Thanos And Despina (Greek) B 96 MIN
16MM FILM OPTICAL SOUND C A
Shows the battle between the sexes, classes and generations in contemporary Greece. With English subtitles.
Prod-GROVE Dist-GROVE

That All May Be One C 28 MIN
16MM FILM OPTICAL SOUND R
Presents a collage of pictures, songs and poetry suggesting a way of seeing the world in terms of a Christian mission.
Prod-UCCAND Dist-CCNCC

That All May Learn B 19 MIN
16MM FILM OPTICAL SOUND
The evils of illiteracy are demonstrated in this story of exploitation of a Mexican farmer and his family.
Prod-UN Dist-UN

That Certain Thing B 70 MIN
16MM FILM SILENT
Tells how a rich boy is disinherited when he marries the girl who works in a cigar store. Shows what happens when the young couple launches their own thriving business and causes the boy's father to reconsider. Directed by Frank Capra.
Prod-CPC Dist-KITPAR 1928

That Fabulous Face X 4 MIN
16MM FILM OPTICAL SOUND I-C A
An art film which presents a series of black and white photographs of a Negro woman using dramatic movements to music by Chopin and then converts the photographs with special graphic effects and color painting-in techniques.
LC NO. 78-714215
Prod-ZINNJ Dist-ZINNJ 1971

That Feeling Of Falling C 9 MIN
16MM FILM, 3/4 OR 1/2 IN VIDEO
Discusses product improvements that can prevent stairway falls, glass door accidents and bathtub slips and falls. Suggests handrails on stairs, handgrips on bathroom walls and slip-resistant surfaces on stairways.
Prod-CPSAFC Dist-USNAC 1976

That Good Old Harmony C 29 MIN
3/4 INCH VIDEO CASSETTE
Shows how harmony fits into song writing.
From The Song Writer Series.
Prod-UMITV Dist-UMITV 1977

That It May Never Die - A Record Of The Chattooga River C 28 MIN
16MM FILM OPTICAL SOUND I-C
Presents the story of one of the last free flowing unpolluted rivers in the southeastern United States and explains how it is being preserved in its natural state.
Prod-GCCED Dist-GCCED 1972

That Job Interview C 16 MIN
3/4 INCH VIDEO CASSETTE
Provides information on how military personnel should conduct themselves during civilian job interviews.
From The Career Job Opportunity Series.
LC NO. 76-706168
Prod-USDLMA Dist-USNAC 1976

That Long Night In '43 B 110 MIN
16MM FILM, 3/4 OR 1/2 IN VIDEO A
Presents a wartime tale of a Fascist massacre of partisans. English dubbed version.
Prod-CNEMAG Dist-CNEMAG 1960

That Makes Two Of Us C 44 MIN
3/4 OR 1/2 INCH VIDEO CASSETTE A
Presents story of relationship of two deaf people, one from an oral background and the other from a sign language background. Signed.
Prod-GALCO Dist-GALCO 1982

That March Incident B 4 MIN
16MM FILM OPTICAL SOUND
Illustrates the nuclear power plant accident at Three Mile Island in Pennsylvania and the effect it had on the area's inhabitants.
LC NO. 80-701267
Prod-VINBKS Dist-TEMPLU 1980

That One Good Spirit - An Indian Christmas Story C 16 MIN
3/4 INCH VIDEO CASSETTE K
Presents the clay-animated tale of a young Ute Indian boy who has a special experience on Christmas Eve, a visit from an Indian Santa Claus. Also available in two-inch quad and one-inch videotape.
Prod-UTEAVD Dist-NAMPBC

That Others May Live - The Mission Of The Air Rescue Service C 22 MIN
16MM FILM OPTICAL SOUND
Points out the ability and dedication of the Air Rescue Service (ARS) in saving imperiled civilians. Explains how ARS, with its top-flight capsule recovery teams, is geared to the space age.
LC NO. FIE63-325
Prod-USDD Dist-USNAC 1963

That Our Children Will Not Die C 60 MIN
16MM FILM - 3/4 IN VIDEO
Examines three primary health care systems in Nigeria, West Africa. Explains that malnutrition, infection, fever, diarrhea and coughs are preventable problems that can be cured by non-professionals.
Prod-FDF Dist-DOCEDR Prodn-CHOPRA

That The Deaf May Speak C 42 MIN
16MM FILM OPTICAL SOUND
Studies the problems of the deaf child. Describes the parents' reaction when they learn their child is deaf. Traces the training and development of a deaf child from nursery school to the eighth grade.
Prod-LSFTD Dist-CFDC Prodn-CFDC 1951

That The Last Be The Best C 28 MIN
16MM FILM OPTICAL SOUND
Reports on initiatives of the Conference on Aging and shows film clips of President Nixon as he addresses the final session on December 2, 1971.
LC NO. 74-705768
Prod-USSRS Dist-USNAC 1971

That These Things Shall Not Be Forgotten C 30 MIN
3/4 INCH VIDEO CASSETTE
Discusses Herodotus' view that while facts are important, what they tell about human behavior is more important.
From The Herodotus - Father Of History Series.
Prod-UMITV Dist-UMITV 1980

That They May Learn C 30 MIN
16MM FILM OPTICAL SOUND T
Uses examples from Navajo Indian schools to show how Title I funds are to be used in assisting students from low income families to reach the educational goals established for them.
LC NO. 75-702929
Prod-USBIA Dist-AVED Prodn-BAILYL 1975

That Uncertain Paradise C 57 MIN
16MM FILM OPTICAL SOUND H-C A
Examines conditions in the United States Trust Territory of the Pacific Islands, or Micronesia. Explores the native cultures of the islands, describes the history of the area and discusses its governmental system, its political future and its relationship with the United States.
LC NO. 74-703250
Prod-WGTV Dist-WGTV 1974

That Uncertain Paradise, Pt 1 C 29 MIN
16MM FILM OPTICAL SOUND H-C A
Examines conditions in the United States Trust Territory of the Pacific Islands, or Micronesia. Explores the native cultures of the islands, describes the history of the area and discusses its governmental system, its political future and its relationship with the United States.
LC NO. 74-703250
Prod-WGTV Dist-WGTV 1973

That Uncertain Paradise, Pt 2 C 29 MIN
16MM FILM OPTICAL SOUND H-C A
Examines conditions in the United States Trust Territory of the Pacific Islands, or Micronesia. Explores the native cultures of the islands, describes the history of the area and discusses its governmental system, its political future and its relationship with the United States.
LC NO. 74-703250
Prod-WGTV Dist-WGTV 1973

That War In Korea C 79 MIN
16MM FILM, 3/4 OR 1/2 IN VIDEO J-C
Uses newsreel footage to present an overview of the Korean conflict, the first unified international action against aggression. Commentary by Richard Boone.
Prod-NBCTV Dist-FI 1966

That We May Serve C 28 MIN
16MM FILM OPTICAL SOUND
Presents the story of the supply service of the Department of medicine and surgery of the VA. Discusses its program of quality control so that thousands of professional and support personnel may better serve their veterans.
Prod-USVA Dist-USVA 1960

That Yuckie Feeling C 15 MIN
3/4 INCH VIDEO CASSETTE P
Features Frank experiencing the feeling of pain. Stresses the importance of requesting help when necessary. Discusses the importance of securing proper drugs and medicines from doctors.

From The Think Fine - Feel Fine Series.
Prod-KTCATV Dist-GPITVL

That's A Good Question—A Series
I
Presents a discussion on race and prejudice and the general aspects of human relations.
Prod-KGEDTV Dist-GPITVL

How Does Prejudice Come Out	30 MIN
What Does It Mean To Be A Black American	30 MIN
What Does It Mean To Be A Chinese American	30 MIN
What Does It Mean To Be A Japanese American	30 MIN
What Does It Mean To Be A Native American	30 MIN
What Does Race Mean	30 MIN
What Is A Minority Group, Pt I	30 MIN
What Is A Minority Group, Pt II	30 MIN
What Is La Raza	30 MIN
Why Are People Prejudiced	30 MIN
Why Ask Me	30 MIN
Why Can't People Get Along And How Can A	30 MIN

That's All We Need C 16 MIN
16MM FILM OPTICAL SOUND I-J
Presents the 'six and a half' gang who decide to erect an old hut as headquarters for an 'adventure playground' on some local wasteland without anticipating the confusion in store with the demolition gang and the police.
From The Magnificent 6 And 1/2 Series.
Prod-CHILDF Dist-LUF 1972

That's Bluegrass C 56 MIN
16MM FILM OPTICAL SOUND I-C A
Examines Bluegrass Music as a unique form of American music and culture. Interviews musicians who made contributions to the growth of this musical form and shows them performing the songs that made them famous.
LC NO. 79-700459
Prod-MNTFLM Dist-MNTFLM 1979

That's Business—A Series

Discusses aspects of accounting and finance.
Prod-WELSHJ Dist-OWNMAN 1978

Accounting Process, The	27 MIN
Accounts Receivable	34 MIN
Balance Sheet, The	21 MIN
Cash Flow Forecasting	30 MIN
Financing Growth	34 MIN
Profit Forecasting	30 MIN

That's Incredible, New Orleans! C 15 MIN
3/4 OR 1/2 INCH VIDEO CASSETTE
Uses the familiar format of television's 'That's Incredible' show to take a look at the variety of ways parents can get involved in their kids' education.
Prod-NOVID Dist-NOVID

That's It, Forget It C 5 MIN
3/4 INCH VIDEO CASSETTE
Presents a study of music video as a way of life for four southern California teenagers, by Branda Miller.
Prod-EAI Dist-EAI

That's Life—A Series

Presents Dr Morris Tiktin, a family therapist, who works with the Playbox Players, a Portland repertory group, illustrating the do's and don'ts in dealing with people.
Prod-KOAPTV Dist-PUBTEL

Great Debate, The	29 MIN
Great Expectations	29 MIN
Is Anybody Listening	29 MIN
It's OK To Be Angry	29 MIN
Kids Are People, Too	29 MIN
Lost And Found	29 MIN
Make Up Your Mind	29 MIN
New Life, A	29 MIN
So You Live By Yourself	29 MIN
Turn Yourself On	29 MIN
Who Am I	29 MIN
You Are Not Alone	29 MIN
Zest For Living, A	29 MIN

That's Marilyn C 28 MIN
3/4 OR 1/2 INCH VIDEO CASSETTE
Illustrates the anger and resentment within a family disrupted by alcohol. Provides an understanding of some of the sufferings of thousands of young people.
Prod-ARFO Dist-ARFO

That's Me C 9 MIN
16MM FILM OPTICAL SOUND K
Encourages a child to take a look at himself and the world around him. Allows him to identify with the grown-up world and everyday activities.
From The Amazing Life Game Theater Series.
LC NO. 72-701742
Prod-HMC Dist-HMC 1971

That's Me C 15 MIN
3/4 OR 1/2 INCH VIDEO CASSETTE P
Explores through literature the process of developing self-awareness.
From The Spinning Stories Series.
Prod-MDDE Dist-AITECH 1977

That's Mine C 15 MIN
16MM FILM OPTICAL SOUND K-P
Uses games, dramatizations and candid camera interviews with children to explain the concepts of individual ownership, responsibilities of group ownership and causes and solutions of conflict over possessions.

LC NO. 76-703640
Prod-TAPDEM Dist-MALIBU 1976

That's My Bike C 12 MIN
16MM FILM, 3/4 OR 1/2 IN VIDEO I
Tells the story of Lawrence, an industrious teenager who is tempted by a friend to move some stolen merchandise, but refuses. Shows him finding an honest way to make money, even after his bike is stolen.
From The Learning Laws - Respect For Yourself, Others And The Law Series.
Prod-WDEMCO Dist-WDEMCO 1982

That's My Name - Don't Wear It Out C 26 MIN
16MM FILM, 3/4 OR 1/2 IN VIDEO P-C A
Tells the story of troublesome but sensitive adolescent who befriends a deaf youngster. Shows how both boys mature from this relationship, the older boy becoming less wary of involvement and the younger boy learning to push beyond the limitations of this handicap.
Prod-OECA Dist-LCOA 1976

That's My Name - Don't Wear It Out (Captioned) C 26 MIN
16MM FILM, 3/4 OR 1/2 IN VIDEO P-H A
Tells the story of a troublesome adolescent who befriends a deaf youngster.
Prod-OECA Dist-LCOA 1977

That's My Name - Don't Wear It Out (Spanish) C 26 MIN
16MM FILM, 3/4 OR 1/2 IN VIDEO P-H A
Tells the story of a troublesome adolescent who befriends a deaf youngster.
Prod-OECA Dist-LCOA 1977

That's Nice C 3 MIN
16MM FILM OPTICAL SOUND I-C A
Presents a sensitive cinepoem of a merry-go-round ride, emphasizing the abstract imagery latent there.
Prod-CFS Dist-CFS 1968

That's No Tomato C 30 MIN
3/4 OR 1/2 INCH VIDEO CASSETTE
See series title for descriptive statement.
From The Creativity With Bill Moyers Series.
Prod-PBS Dist-DELTAK

That's No Tomato, That's A Work Of Art C 29 MIN
3/4 OR 1/2 INCH VIDEO CASSETTE H-C A
States that the tomato is one of America's favorite vegetables, with the average American consuming 50 pounds or more each year. Tells how a great deal of creative effort is still being poured into producing more profitable and valuable tomatoes.
From The Creativity With Bill Moyers Series.
Prod-CORPEL Dist-PBS 1982

That's Not Me They're Talking About C 30 MIN
3/4 INCH VIDEO CASSETTE
Looks at the presentation of women in TV, movies, advertising, music, fashion and the visual arts, decodes, the images and examines the connections between them and women's lives. Discusses the problems created by these images along with suggestions for improving the portrayal of women in the media.
Prod-WMENIF Dist-WMENIF

That's Not My Job C 26 MIN
16MM FILM, 3/4 OR 1/2 IN VIDEO PRO
Discusses the importance of training each employee of a large organization to understand his role and his relationship to other employees. Demonstrates that cooperative effort contributes to the end product or service of the group.
LC NO. FIA67-645
Prod-RTBL Dist-RTBL 1967

That's Not My Job (Captioned) C 26 MIN
16MM FILM, 3/4 OR 1/2 IN VIDEO
Discusses the importance of training each employee of a large organization to understand his role and his relationship to other employees. Demonstrates that cooperative effort contributes to the end product or service of the group.
Prod-RTBL Dist-RTBL 1967

That's Not My Job (Dutch) C 26 MIN
16MM FILM, 3/4 OR 1/2 IN VIDEO PRO
Discusses the importance of training each employee of a large organization to understand his role and his relationship to other employees. Demonstrates that cooperative effort contributes to the end product or service of the group.
Prod-RTBL Dist-RTBL 1967

That's Not My Job (Japanese) C 26 MIN
16MM FILM, 3/4 OR 1/2 IN VIDEO PRO
Discusses the importance of training each employee of a large organization to understand his role and his relationship to other employees. Demonstrates that cooperative effort contributes to the end product or service of the group.
Prod-RTBL Dist-RTBL 1967

That's Not My Job (Norwegian) C 26 MIN
16MM FILM, 3/4 OR 1/2 IN VIDEO PRO
Discusses the importance of training each employee of a large organization to understand his role and his relationship to other employees. Demonstrates that cooperative effort contributes to the end product or service of the group.
Prod-RTBL Dist-RTBL 1967

That's Not My Job (Swedish) C 26 MIN
16MM FILM, 3/4 OR 1/2 IN VIDEO PRO
Discusses the importance of training each employee of a large organization to understand his role and his relationship to other employees. Demonstrates that cooperative effort contributes to the end product or service of the group.
Prod-RTBL Dist-RTBL 1967

That's Our Baby C 13 MIN
16MM FILM, 3/4 OR 1/2 IN VIDEO H-C A
Presents prepared childbirth - exercise, breathing, nutrition, participation of father.
Prod-AGINP Dist-AGINP

That's Our Baby C 22 MIN
16MM FILM, 3/4 OR 1/2 IN VIDEO H-C A
Uses the example of the filmmaker, his wife and their first child to demonstrate the techniques of Lamaze training in childbirth.
Prod-LAWREN Dist-LAWREN Prodn-AGINSJ 1975

That's Rich - And A Little About Long Distance C 28 MIN
16MM FILM OPTICAL SOUND
Features entertainer Rich Little doing a series of impersonations to demonstrate how zero-plus and one-plus long distance telephone calls are made.
LC NO. 70-713389
Prod-SWBELL Dist-SWBELL 1971

That's Right Edie C 15 MIN
3/4 OR 1/2 INCH VIDEO CASSETTE P
Presents the children's story That's Right, Edie by Johanna Johnston.
From The Picture Book Park Series. Blue Module
Prod-WVIZTV Dist-AITECH 1974

That's Stealing C 17 MIN
16MM FILM, 3/4 OR 1/2 IN VIDEO P-I
Presents the story of two girls in sixth grade and how one of them develops the bad habit of stealing. Shows how the girls deal with the problem.
Prod-EBERHT Dist-FLMFR 1984

That's The Rule! C 30 MIN
3/4 OR 1/2 INCH VIDEO CASSETTE
Presents a practical and effective way to help supervisors enforce safety rules without employee resentment and rebellion.
Prod-EDRF Dist-EDRF

That's What It's All About C 29 MIN
16MM FILM OPTICAL SOUND
Depicts all aspects of the Regional Intervention Program for unmanageable children, from initial intake through the various behavior modification modules to the child's return to a normal public school within the community.
From The Regional Intervention Program Series.
LC NO. 75-702439
Prod-USBEH Dist-USNAC 1973

That's What Living's About C 18 MIN
16MM FILM, 3/4 OR 1/2 IN VIDEO J-C A
Presents a philosophical look at leisure, what it means and how it affects our lives now and in the furture. Explores uses and misuses of leisure. Illustrates broad concepts of leisure and recreation, showing balance between work and leisure. Shows a variey of community resources to help develop leisure values and skills and discover interests.
Prod-UCEMC Dist-UCEMC 1973

That's What We're Here For C 32 MIN
16MM FILM OPTICAL SOUND
Depicts all phases of Veterans Administration hospital dentistry, including the various residency programs, graduate training and continuing education. Features Veterans Administration dental personnel at six major hospitals throughout the United States.
LC NO. 76-702719
Prod-USVA Dist-USNAC Prodn-VADTC 1975

Thatching C 15 MIN
16MM FILM, 3/4 OR 1/2 IN VIDEO I-C A
Details the process of thatching a cottage, using the techniques of the New England colonists.
Prod-PLIMOT Dist-IFB 1970

The Comic Book Kids 2 C 60 MIN
3/4 OR 1/2 INCH VIDEO CASSETTE P-I
Presents people of the future, Carrie and Skeets, and Bigfoot, the legendary ape-man of the Pacific Northwest. Includes Time Tables, a science fiction story.
Prod-CNVID Dist-KTVID 1981

The Great Director - Unknown Chaplin C 52 MIN
16MM FILM, 3/4 OR 1/2 IN VIDEO H-C A
Presents interviews with family and associates of Charlie Chaplin to add insight to extracts from feature films made by the comic between 1918 and 1931.
Prod-THAMES Dist-MEDIAG 1983

The Vital Moment C 30 MIN
3/4 OR 1/2 INCH VIDEO CASSETTE H-C A
Explains importance of precision and timing in action photography using examples from wrestling, white-water canoeing and a motorcycle stunt team.
From The What A Picture - The Complete Photography Course By John Hedgecoe Series. Program 2
Prod-THREMI Dist-FI

Thea C 27 MIN
16MM FILM, 3/4 OR 1/2 IN VIDEO H-C A
Describes how a male chauvinist mathematician meets a fascinating woman who turns out to be the feminine side of God. Stars Julie Sommars, Jess Walton and Alan Feinstein.
From The Insight Series.
Prod-PAULST Dist-PAULST

Thea C 27 MIN
3/4 OR 1/2 INCH VIDEO CASSETTE J A
Dramatizes the story of a male chauvinist who learns about the feminine side of God and himself.
Prod-SUTHRB Dist-SUTHRB

Theater B 20 MIN
16MM FILM OPTICAL SOUND C A
An English and Finnish language motion picture. Presents an impressionist documentary of the Finnish National Theatre's production of Beckett's Waiting For Godot. Delves beneath the surface of acting, lighting, set and costume design to study the interrelationships among these basic elements of theater.
Prod-SRKTJ Dist-MOMA 1957

Theater Fur Kinder C 5 MIN
16MM FILM, 3/4 OR 1/2 IN VIDEO H-C A
A German-language version of the motion picture Junior Theatre (Children's Theatre.) Shows children as both spectators and participants in the theater as they help to produce plays.
From The European Studies - Germany (German) Series.
Prod-MFAFRG Dist-IFB Prodn-BAYER 1973

Theater In Shakespeare's Time, The C 14 MIN
16MM FILM, 3/4 OR 1/2 IN VIDEO J-C A
Visualizes the many facets and traditions of the Elizabethan Theater and the unique characteristics of the stage within the context of the society of Shakespeare's time. Explains that Shakespeare wrote his plays for the stage on which they were performed, for the actors and for an audience which represented a cross-section of the citizens of London.
Prod-BFA Dist-PHENIX 1973

Theater Of The Night - The Science Of Sleep And Dreams--A Series

Explores the stages of sleep, sleep disorders and research on dreams. Interviews leading researchers in the study of sleep and dreams.
Prod-IBIS Dist-IBIS

Probing The Mysteries Of Sleep
Things That Go Wrong In The Night
World Of Dreams, The

Theater Of The Night - The Science Of Sleep And Dreams C 45 MIN
1/2 IN VIDEO CASSETTE (VHS) J-C A
Visits sleep labs and describes the most current research on sleep and dreams. Details sleep stages and causes and treatments of sleep disorders.
LC NO. 85-703878
Prod-HRMC Dist-HRMC

Theatre - Why Criticize? C 29 MIN
3/4 INCH VIDEO CASSETTE
Debates the validity of criticism, who should criticize and how they should criticize.
From The Off Stage Series.
Prod-UMITV Dist-UMITV 1975

Theatre And Your Community C 20 MIN
16MM FILM OPTICAL SOUND
Outlines the history of community theater in America, and shows the steps in organizing such a theater. Includes scenes from various productions of a number of community theaters.
LC NO. 79-705060
Prod-UMISS Dist-UMISS 1969

Theatre Arts C 15 MIN
16MM FILM OPTICAL SOUND
Takes a look at the theater arts program at Confederation College, Ontario.
LC NO. 75-704344
Prod-CONCOL Dist-CONCOL 1974

Theatre At Work, The C 30 MIN
3/4 OR 1/2 INCH VIDEO CASSETTE C
See series title for descriptive statement.
From The In Our Own Image Series.
Prod-DALCCD Dist-DALCCD

Theatre D'Enfants (Les Marionnettes) C 7 MIN
16MM FILM, 3/4 OR 1/2 IN VIDEO H-C A
A French language videocassette. Shows a marionette theater in France.
From The Chroniques De France Series.
LC NO. 81-706553
Prod-ADPF Dist-IFB 1980

Theatre For Children - Designing The Setting C 27 MIN
16MM FILM OPTICAL SOUND
Emphasizes the importance of scenic elements for the child audience. Demonstrates the designer's approach, script requirements, style, form, facility and stock pieces. Shows the designer in production with plans, paint, props and lights.
Prod-HALLJL Dist-USC 1975

Theatre Fundamentals - Backstage, Is It Safe C 21 MIN
16MM FILM, 3/4 OR 1/2 IN VIDEO C A
Examines the issue of stage safety through the comments of technical directors and theater safety experts interspersed with documentary footage of practices backstage. Uses original footage of Buster Keaton with appropriate music by theater organist Dennis James.
Prod-IU Dist-IU 1983

Theatre Fundamentals - Breath Of Performance C 14 MIN
16MM FILM, 3/4 OR 1/2 IN VIDEO H-C A
Demonstrates the proper blend of speech and body training which leads to effective use of the voice in theater. Shows theater students performing exercises designed to develop a sense of proper body alignment, foster efficient breathing, and refine coordination of movement.
Prod-IU Dist-IU 1980

Theatre Fundamentals - Costumes On Stage C 26 MIN
16MM FILM, 3/4 OR 1/2 IN VIDEO H-C A
Illustrates the step-by-step creation of costumes for a theatrical-

production. Begins with pre-production conferences, and demonstrates costume research, design, cutting, assembling, and fitting.
Prod-IU Dist-IU 1985

Theatre Fundamentals - Stage Lighting C 16 MIN
16MM FILM, 3/4 OR 1/2 IN VIDEO H-C A
Demonstrates four properties of light and shows their functions in stage lighting.
Prod-IU Dist-IU 1981

Theatre In The Streets C 59 MIN
2 INCH VIDEOTAPE
Presents the Philadelphia Street Theatre which consists of a truckful of actors coming into the community to entertain.
From The Festivals Of Pennsylvania Series.
Prod-WHYY Dist-PUBTEL

Theatre Of China C 29 MIN
3/4 INCH VIDEO CASSETTE
Examines Chinese Theatre, from the classical to the contemporary. Discusses proletariat drama.
From The Off Stage Series.
Prod-UMITV Dist-UMITV 1975

Theatre Of Etienne Decroux, The B 23 MIN
16MM FILM OPTICAL SOUND
Documents the efforts of Etienne Decroux to establish mime as an art in its own right in an autonomous branch of theatre.
Prod-FILIM Dist-RADIM

Theatre Of Social Problems, The - Ibsen, Hedda Gabler C 45 MIN
16MM FILM, 3/4 OR 1/2 IN VIDEO H-C A
Presents an abridged version of Ibsen's play, Hedda Gabler, the story of a woman's tormented search for self-fulfillment in a world dominated by men.
From The History Of The Drama Series.
LC NO. 76-700971
Prod-FOTH Dist-FOTH 1976

Theatre Of The Absurd - Pirandello, Six Characters In Search Of An Author C 52 MIN
16MM FILM, 3/4 OR 1/2 IN VIDEO J-C A
Presents an adaptation in English of Pirandello's play, Six Characters In Search Of An Author, in which six characters seek to exchange their fixed, frozen form in art for the uncertainty of life.
From The History Of The Drama Series.
LC NO. 76-703608
Prod-FOTH Dist-FOTH 1976

Theatre Of The Mind - John Donne's Metaphysical Style C 45 MIN
3/4 OR 1/2 INCH VIDEO CASSETTE
Analyzes John Donne's metaphysical style.
From The Survey Of English Literature I Series.
Prod-MDCPB Dist-MDCPB

Theatre, Opera, The Concert Stage C 30 MIN
3/4 OR 1/2 INCH VIDEO CASSETTE C
Discusses black trends in the theatre, opera and the concert stage.
From The Afro-American Perspectives Series.
Prod-MDDE Dist-MDCPB

Theatre, The - One Of The Humanities C 30 MIN
16MM FILM, 3/4 OR 1/2 IN VIDEO H-C
Considers the three main elements of any play and considers their interrelationship. Examines the play itself, the actors and the audience.
From The Humanities - The Drama Series.
Prod-EBF Dist-EBEC 1959

Theatrical Cartooning C 15 MIN
2 INCH VIDEOTAPE
See series title for descriptive statement.
From The Charlie's Pad Series.
Prod-WSIU Dist-PUBTEL

Theatrical Makeup - Painting Old Age C 28 MIN
3/4 OR 1/2 INCH VIDEO CASSETTE
Shows how to paint sags, hollows and wrinkles on a face to create the illusion of old age.
Prod-UCEMC Dist-UCEMC

Theatrical Makeup - Projecting The Actor's Features C 28 MIN
3/4 OR 1/2 INCH VIDEO CASSETTE
Introduces theatrical makeup-greasepaint, pancake and cream sticks. Shows how to apply each for straight and for corrective makeup.
Prod-UCEMC Dist-UCEMC

Theatrical Makeup - Special Effects C 28 MIN
3/4 OR 1/2 INCH VIDEO CASSETTE
Illustrates techniques of makeup special effects such as building a mustache or beard and creating wounds or bruises.
Prod-UCEMC Dist-UCEMC

Theft Of Fire, The C 15 MIN
3/4 OR 1/2 INCH VIDEO CASSETTE K-P
See series title for descriptive statement.
From The Gather Round Series.
Prod-CTI Dist-CTI

Theft, The C 25 MIN
16MM FILM, 3/4 OR 1/2 IN VIDEO I-J
Presents a story about a jobless youngster who agrees to go along with an older boy on a burglary and about the anxiety he faces afterwards.
Prod-KLINGL Dist-LRF 1975

Theft, The X 27 MIN
16MM FILM, 3/4 OR 1/2 IN VIDEO J-C A
Examines a couple's struggle for a more open and trusting relationship. Tells what happens when a midnight thief breaks into their house and forces them to reexamine their marriage. Stars Larry Pressman, Sharon Farrell and Lou Antonio.
From The Insight Series.
Prod-PAULST Dist-PAULST

Their Best Teacher - PhDs Learn From Mr Boy C 10 MIN
16MM FILM, 3/4 OR 1/2 IN VIDEO C A
Presents two professors in special education who tell how they have learned from their mentally retarded son.
LC NO. 83-707156
Prod-CBSNEW Dist-LAWREN 1983

Their Finest Hour C 27 MIN
3/4 INCH VIDEO CASSETTE
Relates five incidents in which lives were actually saved by people who remembered what Red Cross had taught them in first aid, cardiopulmonary resuscitation (CPR) or water safety courses.
Prod-AMRC Dist-AMRC 1979

Their Finest Paragraph C 5 MIN
3/4 OR 1/2 INCH VIDEO CASSETTE J-H
Deals with emphasis in writing. See also the title The Rocking Horse Writer.
From The Write On, Set 2 Series.
Prod-CTI Dist-CTI

Their First Teachers B 15 MIN
16MM FILM OPTICAL SOUND C T
Deals with the relationships between parents and children. Shows the effects of parental understanding on the personal adjustment and maturation of children.
Prod-CCNY Dist-PSUPCR 1956

Their Game Was Golf C 28 MIN
16MM FILM OPTICAL SOUND
Presents St Lucie, Florida, as a favorite site for the Ladies Professional Golf Association tournaments.
Prod-FLADC Dist-FLADC

Their Own Brand C 30 MIN
16MM FILM, 3/4 OR 1/2 IN VIDEO C A
See series title for descriptive statement.
From The Case Studies In Small Business Series.
Prod-UMA Dist-GPITVL 1979

Their Right To Belong B 15 MIN
16MM FILM OPTICAL SOUND
Shows a sheltered workshop program including special special training classes for the trainable mentally retarded.
Prod-OARC Dist-OARC

Their Royal Highnesses Princess Margrethe And Prince Henrik Visit Canada C 12 MIN
16MM FILM OPTICAL SOUND
Follows the royal couple on their official visit to Canada in September 1967.
Prod-RDCG Dist-AUDPLN

Theirs Is The Kingdom C 5 MIN
16MM FILM OPTICAL SOUND J-C A
Features two high school boys, attempting to solve the problems of poverty in a Mexican border town, cause a near riot because of their insensitivity. Depicts that they re-examine their motives and return to try again.
From The Beatitude Series.
LC NO. 72-700775
Prod-FRACOC Dist-FRACOC 1972

Them Not-So-Dry Bones C 3 MIN
3/4 OR 1/2 INCH VIDEO CASSETTE P-I
Uses animation to discuss the topic of human anatomy.
From The Science Rock Series.
Prod-ABCTV Dist-GA 1979

Them People C 43 MIN
16MM FILM OPTICAL SOUND J-C A
Shows the operation of urban welfare systems as exemplified by systems in Cleveland, which are supposed to help the poor, but instead work to their detriment. Describes efforts by various church and civic groups to change these systems.
LC NO. 70-705685
Prod-UMCBM Dist-UMCBM 1970

Them Thar' Hills B 21 MIN
16MM FILM OPTICAL SOUND
Describes how Laurel and Hardy rent a trailer and move into a campground just vacated by moonshiners.
Prod-ROACH Dist-BHAWK 1934

Theme And Variations C 58 MIN
3/4 OR 1/2 INCH VIDEO CASSETTE J-C A
Describes some of the diverse specializations which mammals have evolved to obtain food, to move, to navigate and, in some instances, to communicate.
From The Life On Earth Series. Program 10
LC NO. 82-706682
Prod-BBCTV Dist-FI 1981

Theme And Voice In Poetry C 30 MIN
3/4 OR 1/2 INCH VIDEO CASSETTE C
See series title for descriptive statement.
From The Communicating Through Literature Series.
Prod-DALCCD Dist-DALCCD

Theme Song B 30 MIN
3/4 OR 1/2 INCH VIDEO CASSETTE
Deals with the direct address of the viewer by the performer. Explores the intimacy of the television viewing situation.
Prod-KITCHN Dist-KITCHN

Themes - The Day When Nothing Made Sense C 10 MIN
16MM FILM, 3/4 OR 1/2 IN VIDEO I-H
Illustrates the need for logical order by showing how a teenage boy struggles through a day in which nothing follows in a logical sequence. Demonstrates the need for organization in writing themes.
From The Sentences And Paragraphs Series.
LC NO. 81-706042
Prod-CENTRO Dist-CORF 1981

Themes And Moods C 30 MIN
2 INCH VIDEOTAPE C A
Shows the design principle of harmony as the key to establishing the theme or mood of a room. Discusses formal and informal themes.
From The Designing Home Interiors Series. Unit 5
Prod-COAST Dist-CDTEL Prodn-RSCCD

Themes In Fiction C 30 MIN
3/4 OR 1/2 INCH VIDEO CASSETTE C
See series title for descriptive statement.
From The Communicating Through Literature Series.
Prod-DALCCD Dist-DALCCD

Then And Now C 30 MIN
3/4 INCH VIDEO CASSETTE I-J
Highlights and summarizes the Pacific Bridges series, which deals with Asian-American culture.
From The Pacific Bridges Series.
Prod-EDFCEN Dist-GPITVL 1978

Then One Year (Rev Ed) C 20 MIN
16MM FILM, 3/4 OR 1/2 IN VIDEO I-J
Discusses the primary and secondary changes at adolescence in boys and girls.
LC NO. 84-706729
Prod-CF Dist-CF 1984

Then One Year (Spanish) C 19 MIN
16MM FILM, 3/4 OR 1/2 IN VIDEO I-J
Uses animation to discuss primary and secondary changes at adolescence in boys and girls.
Prod-CF Dist-CF 1972

Then What Happened C 20 MIN
2 INCH VIDEOTAPE P
See series title for descriptive statement.
From The Learning Our Language, Unit 1 - Listening Skills Series.
Prod-MPATI Dist-GPITVL

Thenow C 14 MIN
16MM FILM OPTICAL SOUND
Presents a single Black girl moving through a dream of her past lives, when she was Black and when she was White, when her lovers were Black and when her lovers were White. Shows interracial couples together at play and in sexual intercourse. Describes thenow as a liberation of the habit of labels in interracial understanding, a deeper understanding of our common flow of life, our common ties as people working out Our destinations.
Prod-MMRC Dist-MMRC

Theodolite, The C 13 MIN
3/4 OR 1/2 INCH VIDEO CASSETTE IND
Teaches how to set up the theodolite and center it over a point. Emphasizes the method for reading horizontals as well as angles and double checking these readings.
From The Marshall Maintenance Training Programs Series. Tape 42
Prod-LEIKID Dist-LEIKID

Theodore Bikel And Rashid Hussain C 52 MIN
3/4 OR 1/2 INCH VIDEO CASSETTE
Presents Israeli and Arabic music and poetry in their original language and in translation. Features Pete Seeger on banjo and Theodore Bikel on guitar.
From The Rainbow Quest Series.
Prod-SEEGER Dist-CWATER

Theodore Gericault (Spanish) C 26 MIN
16MM FILM, 3/4 OR 1/2 IN VIDEO H-C A
See series title for descriptive statement.
From The Romantic Vs Classic Art (Spanish) Series.
Prod-VPSL Dist-PFP

Theodore M Hesburgh, Education, Religion, Pt 1 C 29 MIN
3/4 OR 1/2 INCH VIDEO CASSETTE A
See series title for descriptive statement.
From The Quest For Peace Series.
Prod-AACD Dist-AACD 1984

Theodore M Hesburgh, Education, Religion, Pt 2 C 29 MIN
3/4 OR 1/2 INCH VIDEO CASSETTE A
See series title for descriptive statement.
From The Quest For Peace Series.
Prod-AACD Dist-AACD 1984

Theodore Roosevelt B 20 MIN
2 INCH VIDEOTAPE I
See series title for descriptive statement.
From The Americans All Series.
Prod-DENVPS Dist-GPITVL Prodn-KRMATV

Theodore Roosevelt - American B 27 MIN
16MM FILM, 3/4 OR 1/2 IN VIDEO
Presents the highlights of Roosevelt's life, from his boyhood out West through his role in national and international affairs. Particular emphasis is given to the development of his political career.
Prod-USDD Dist-USNAC 1958

Theodore Roosevelt - Cowboy In The White House C 29 MIN
16MM FILM, 3/4 OR 1/2 IN VIDEO J-C A

Traces the life and career of Theodore Roosevelt.
From The Nobel Prizewinners Series.
Prod-CFDLD Dist-CORF

Theodore Roosevelt - He Who Has Planted Will Preserve C 28 MIN
3/4 OR 1/2 INCH VIDEO CASSETTE
Presents a portrait of Theodore Roosevelt, the 26th President of the United States, who was an ardent conservationist long before it became fashionable.
From The Naturalists Series.
Prod-KRMATV Dist-PBS 1973

Theodore Roosevelt's Sagamore Hill C 25 MIN
16MM FILM OPTICAL SOUND
Presents E G Marshall who conducts a tour of Sagamore Hill, the home of Theodore Roosevelt, at Cove Neck, New York. Reveals the personal and public history of President Roosevelt and gives insight into his character.
From The American Life Style Series.
LC NO. 73-700491
Prod-BASFIN Dist-SHOWCO 1972

Theodore Roosevelt's Sagamore Hill C 23 MIN
16MM FILM, 3/4 OR 1/2 IN VIDEO J-C A
Tours the summer home of Theodore Roosevelt on Long Island. Shows how the home, Sagamore Hill, is testimony to Roosevelt's energy and to the rich and happy life he shared there with his wife and six children.
From The American Lifestyle - U S Presidents Series.
Prod-COMCO Dist-AIMS 1975

Theology And Faith Development C 30 MIN
3/4 OR 1/2 INCH VIDEO CASSETTE J A
Discusses experimental Bible study and planning Bible study. Examines theologizing models and theologizing with music. Features Walter Wink and Charles McCullough.
From The Sow Seeds/Trust The Promise Series.
Prod-UMCOM Dist-ECUFLM

Theology And The Kingdom Of God C
3/4 OR 1/2 INCH VIDEO CASSETTE A
Features a presentation by Marjorie Hewit Suchocki, professor of theology and director of the Doctor of Ministry program at Pittsburg Theological Seminary.
Prod-WHSPRO Dist-ECUFLM 1983

Theonie - Arni Me Kolokithakia (Lamb With A Little Zucchini) C 15 MIN
2 INCH VIDEOTAPE
Shows Theonie preparing kolokithakia and arni which are prepared separately and combined before baking. Tells the difference between spring lamb, yearling lamb and mutton.
From The Theonie Series.
Prod-WGBHTV Dist-PUBTEL

Theonie - Baklavas C 15 MIN
2 INCH VIDEOTAPE
Shows Theonie making baklavas, the sweet of a thousand layers made with walnuts, spices and many layers of phillo, a paper-thin pastry sheet. Demonstrates the process of clarifying butter, the Greek way of peeling an orange or lemon so the entire rind peels off in a single strip and how to crush walnuts with a wooden mortar and pestle so that there are pieces as well as powdered walnuts for the filling.
From The Theonie Series.
Prod-WGBHTV Dist-PUBTEL

Theonie - Dolmathes (Stuffed Grape Leaves) C 15 MIN
2 INCH VIDEOTAPE
Shows how to make stuffed grape leaves. Explains that the stuffing is a basic meat sauce with pine nuts, dill weed and rice.
From The Theonie Series.
Prod-WGBHTV Dist-PUBTEL

Theonie - Fasoulakia Fresca (Fresh Green Beans) C 15 MIN
2 INCH VIDEOTAPE
Demonstrates three ways to prepare fresh green beans.
From The Theonie Series.
Prod-WGBHTV Dist-PUBTEL

Theonie - Garithes Me Fetta (Shrimp Baked With Fetta Cheese) C 14 MIN
2 INCH VIDEOTAPE
Demonstrates how to peel and devein fresh shrimp. Shows that after preparing the sauce with olive oil, onions, tomatoes, parsley, garlic, wine, salt and pepper, Theonie sears the shrimp and soueezes lemon juice over them. Explains that the ingredients are assembled in layers in the baking dish and cooked for a short time in a very hot oven.
From The Theonie Series.
Prod-WGBHTV Dist-PUBTEL

Theonie - Ghighes Me Arni (Giant Beans With Lamb) C 14 MIN
2 INCH VIDEOTAPE
Shows how to prepare the shoulder chops, browning them in hot olive oil before adding onion, celery, tomato paste, salt and pepper, cumin, water and pre-soaked beans. Gives instructions for the cooking, draining and chilling of beans combined with onion, celery and tomato paste and dressed as a salad with latholemono, an olive oil, lemon and garlic dressing.
From The Theonie Series.
Prod-WGBHTV Dist-PUBTEL

Theonie - Hilopittas (Noodles) C 15 MIN
2 INCH VIDEOTAPE
Shows how to make hilopittas. Suggests serving the noodles with butter, butter and kephalotiri or Parmesan cheese, or with a combination of honey, cinnamon and crushed sesame seeds.
From The Theonie Series.
Prod-WGBHTV Dist-PUBTEL

Theonie - Lahano Dolmathes (Cabbage Leaves Stuffed With Pork) C 14 MIN
2 INCH VIDEOTAPE
Demonstrates how to select a good head of cabbage, how to core it and steam it to make the leaves pliable for stuffing. Shows how to make the stuffing for lahano dolmathes by combining rice, scallions, dill weed, egg, tomato paste, salt and pepper. Explains that a saucepan is lined with some of the outer cabbage leaves to prevent the stuffed leaves from scorching, then the rolled leaves are layered and olive oil and chicken broth is poured over them.
From The Theonie Series.
Prod-WGBHTV Dist-PUBTEL

Theonie - Melopitta Nissiotiki (Island Honey And Cheese Pie) C 15 MIN
2 INCH VIDEOTAPE
Demonstrates the preparation of honey cheese pie. Shows how to make the filling by mixing sugar and ricotta cheese, honey, slightly-beaten eggs and grated lemon rind.
From The Theonie Series.
Prod-WGBHTV Dist-PUBTEL

Theonie - Moussaka (Eggplant) C 15 MIN
2 INCH VIDEOTAPE
Shows how to select an eggplant and prepare Moussaka.
From The Theonie Series.
Prod-WGBHTV Dist-PUBTEL

Theonie - Ornitha Kokkinisti (Pot-Roasted Chicken) C 15 MIN
2 INCH VIDEOTAPE
Shows how to prepare chicken for stuffing. Explains how to make the stuffing using chicken liver, olive oil, scallions, ground beef, rice, tomato paste, pine nuts, thyme, parsley, salt and pepper. Outlines the rest of the cooking procedures necessary in making pot-roasted chicken.
From The Theonie Series.
Prod-WGBHTV Dist-PUBTEL

Theonie - Pastitsion (Baked Spaghetti And Meat Sauce) C 15 MIN
2 INCH VIDEOTAPE
Shows how to cook pastitsion made with ground lamb, olive oil, onion, tomato sauce, crushed garlic, parsley, thyme, salt, pepper and wine. Explains how to layer the meat sauce and spaghetti in a crumbed baking pan and gives instructions for making a white sauce to top the dish.
From The Theonie Series.
Prod-WGBHTV Dist-PUBTEL

Theonie - Phinikia (Spiced Bars In Lemon Syrup) C 14 MIN
2 INCH VIDEOTAPE
Shows how to combine ground walnuts, sugar, cinnamon and egg to make phinikia, a Greek Christmas cookie.
From The Theonie Series.
Prod-WGBHTV Dist-PUBTEL

Theonie - Portokalli Glyko (Orange Sweets) C 14 MIN
2 INCH VIDEOTAPE
Shows how to select medium-sized naval oranges for candied orange peel. Explains how to cut the skin in six sections and remove the peels. Features the skins being formed into tight rolls which are cooked in syrup.
From The Theonie Series.
Prod-WGBHTV Dist-PUBTEL

Theonie - Psari Plaki And Horiatiki Salata (Baked Fish And Peasant Salad) C 15 MIN
2 INCH VIDEOTAPE
Shows how to make psari plaki. Suggests using scup, bluefish, snapper, striped bass or any delicately flavored fish and tells how to see if the fish is fresh. Prepares a peasant salad with Greek olives and crumbled feta cheese with a vinegar, garlic and olive dressing.
From The Theonie Series.
Prod-WGBHTV Dist-PUBTEL

Theonie - Psaria Nissiotika (Island Fish Soup) C 15 MIN
2 INCH VIDEOTAPE
Suggests using perch for making fish soup, since it is the closest fish to the scorpios. Shows how to bone the fish, saving the fillets to add later to the soup. Shows Theonie combining the fish bones, tomato, potato, onion, parsley, olive oil, white wine and water, cooking the stock, straining it through a fine sieve, mashing the vegetables and adding the fillets.
From The Theonie Series.
Prod-WGBHTV Dist-PUBTEL

Theonie - Ravanie (Walnut Cake) C 15 MIN
2 INCH VIDEOTAPE
Shows how to make ravanie. Explains that the secret of a successful cake is the rapid and thorough combining of the dry and wet ingredients. Stresses that since the cake contains no baking powder to make it rise, the egg whites must not be allowed to collapse in mixing.
From The Theonie Series.
Prod-WGBHTV Dist-PUBTEL

Theonie - Salates Kalorkerines (Summer Salads) C 14 MIN
2 INCH VIDEOTAPE
Shows how to select a cucumber and also how to prepare a yogurt and cucumber salad and eggplant salad sauce.
From The Theonie Series.
Prod-WGBHTV Dist-PUBTEL

Theonie - Souppa Avgolemono (Egg Lemon Soup) C 14 MIN
2 INCH VIDEOTAPE
Shows how egg and lemon are combined to make avgolemono sauce which crowns many Greek dishes. Presents Theonie making souppa avgolemono.
From The Theonie Series.
Prod-WGBHTV Dist-PUBTEL

Theonie - Souppes Hymoniatikes (Winter Soups) C 14 MIN
2 INCH VIDEOTAPE
Prepares souppa fakki made with lentils, onion, celery, minced garlic, tomato paste and olive oil. Demonstrates the preparation of another favorite Greek soup, lahaniki souppa, or winter vegetable soup.
From The Theonie Series.
Prod-WGBHTV Dist-PUBTEL

Theonie - Spanikopitta (Spinach Pie) C 15 MIN
2 INCH VIDEOTAPE
Demonstrates the kneading and rolling of the pie crust for spanikopitta and the preparation of the filling of spinach, scallions, onion and dill.
From The Theonie Series.
Prod-WGBHTV Dist-PUBTEL

Theonie - Stiffato (Beef Stew) C 14 MIN
2 INCH VIDEOTAPE
Shows that staffato is cooked with onions, wine and herbs during the winter months in Greece. Presents several different cuts of chuck beef which could be used in preparing this stew. Shows how to trim and cut walnut-sized chunks of meat which are then browned in hot olive oil.
From The Theonie Series.
Prod-WGBHTV Dist-PUBTEL

Theonie - Tarama And Tahi (Appetizers With Tarama And Tahi) C 15 MIN
2 INCH VIDEOTAPE
Shows that the secret of making tarama is crushing the eggs with pestle and wooden bowl and using wet, stale bread to cut the saltiness. Explains how to make the basic tahi sauce and a variation of it with crushed chick peas.
From The Theonie Series.
Prod-WGBHTV Dist-PUBTEL

Theonie - Tiropittes (Cheese Triangles) C 15 MIN
2 INCH VIDEOTAPE
Shows how to make tiropittes, a combination of feta and mizithra cheese, eggs, parsley and white pepper. Demonstrates another variation of cheese pastry, tirotrigonas or cheese pie.
From The Theonie Series.
Prod-WGBHTV Dist-PUBTEL

Theonie - Youvetsi (Lamb With Orzo) C 15 MIN
2 INCH VIDEOTAPE
Demonstrates how to bone a leg of lamb and how to make the little barley, or kritharaki pasta, by pinching off bits of dough and rolling them between the fingers to form little seed-shaped bits.
From The Theonie Series.
Prod-WGBHTV Dist-PUBTEL

Theonie - Zouzoukakia (Meatball Sausages In Wine Sauce) C 14 MIN
2 INCH VIDEOTAPE
Shows how to make the Greek dish zouzoukakia using ground meat mixed with damp stale bread bits, eggs, garlic, parsley, grated cheese, ground cumin, salt and pepper. Prepares the wine sauce with tomato sauce, garlic, red wine, olive oil and pepper.
From The Theonie Series.
Prod-WGBHTV Dist-PUBTEL

Theonie—A Series

Describes how to create traditional Greek foods.
Prod-WGBHTV Dist-PUBTEL

Theonie - Arni Me Kolokithakia (Lamb With A	15 MIN
Theonie - Baklavas	15 MIN
Theonie - Dolmathes (Stuffed Grape Leaves)	15 MIN
Theonie - Fasoulakia Fresca (Fresh Green Beans)	15 MIN
Theonie - Garithes Me Fetta (Shrimp Baked	14 MIN
Theonie - Ghighes Me Arni (Giant Beans With	14 MIN
Theonie - Hilopittas (Noodles)	15 MIN
Theonie - Lahano Dolmathes (Cabbage Leaves	14 MIN
Theonie - Melopitta Nissiotiki (Island Honey	15 MIN
Theonie - Moussaka (Eggplant)	15 MIN
Theonie - Ornitha Kokkinisti (Pot-Roasted	15 MIN
Theonie - Pastitsion (Baked Spaghetti And	15 MIN
Theonie - Phinikia (Spiced Bars In Lemon Syrup)	14 MIN
Theonie - Portokalli Glyko (Orange Sweets)	14 MIN
Theonie - Psari Plaki And Horiatiki Salata	15 MIN
Theonie - Psaria Nissiotika (Island Fish Soup)	15 MIN
Theonie - Ravanie (Walnut Cake)	15 MIN
Theonie - Salates Kalorkerines (Summer Salads)	14 MIN
Theonie - Souppa Avgolemono (Egg Lemon Soup)	14 MIN
Theonie - Souppes Hymoniatikes (Winter Soups)	14 MIN
Theonie - Spanikopitta (Spinach Pie)	15 MIN
Theonie - Stiffato (Beef Stew)	14 MIN
Theonie - Tarama And Tahi (Appetizers With	15 MIN
Theonie - Tiropittes (Cheese Triangles)	15 MIN
Theonie - Youvetsi (Lamb With Orzo)	15 MIN
Theonie - Zouzoukakia (Meatball Sausages In	14 MIN

Theorem Of The Mean, The C 10 MIN
16MM FILM OPTICAL SOUND
States the theorem of the mean and how it is derived from Rolle's theorem. Develops the intermediate function to which Rolle's theorem is applied.
From The MAA Calculus Series.
Prod-MAA Dist-MLA

Theorem Of The Mean, The C 28 MIN
16MM FILM OPTICAL SOUND H-C
Derives the theorem of the mean from Rolle's theorem. Gives particular attention to developing the intermediate function to

which Rolle's theorem is applied. An animated film narrated by Felix P Welch.
From The Maa Calculus Series.
LC NO. FIA68-2216
Prod-MAA Dist-MLA 1967

Theorem Proving B 18 MIN
3/4 OR 1/2 INCH VIDEO CASSETTE PRO
Introduces lecture on theorem proving.
From The Probability And Random Processes - Elementary Probability Theory Series.
Prod-MIOT Dist-MIOT

Theories Of Evolution C 45 MIN
3/4 OR 1/2 INCH VIDEO CASSETTE C
Presents various theories of evolution.
From The Biology I Series.
Prod-MDCPB Dist-MDCPB

Theories On The Origin Of Life X 14 MIN
16MM FILM, 3/4 OR 1/2 IN VIDEO H-C
Discusses four theories which explain the origin of life.
From The Biology Series. Unit 10 - Evolution
Prod-EBEC Dist-EBEC 1969

Theory C 18 MIN
16MM FILM - 3/4 IN VIDEO I-J
Points out that in scientific investigation, theories explain and set in motion other processes of problem solving.
From The Search For Solutions Series.
LC NO. 80-706246
Prod-PLYBCK Dist-KAROL 1979

Theory And Design Of Plates—A Series
PRO
Uses classroom format to videotape one one-hour and one 1 1/2 hour lecture per week for 13 weeks and 39 tapes. Covers development of plate bending theory, application to circular plates, rectangular plates and other geometrical forms. Goes into finite difference techniques for solutions, large deflections, orthotropic plates and thermal stresses in plates.
Prod-USCCE Dist-AMCEE

Theory And Layout C 15 MIN
1/2 IN VIDEO CASSETTE BETA/VHS IND
Deals with square and rectangular duct layout. Illustrates the various methods of making a straight piece of duct work, and discusses seaming techniques.
Prod-RMI Dist-RMI

Theory And Practice Of Fire Extinguishment C 60 MIN
3/4 OR 1/2 INCH VIDEO CASSETTE IND
See series title for descriptive statement.
From The Industrial Fire Hazard Recognition And Control Series.
Prod-NCSU Dist-AMCEE

Theory And Testing Of Lead Acid Batteries C 30 MIN
3/4 OR 1/2 INCH VIDEO CASSETTE IND
Illustrates storage battery as portable electric energy. Shows primary and secondary cell and theory of operation of the most popular secondary cell the lead acid battery. Tells how to service and maintain this battery and discusses safety procedures and servicing equipment.
From The Basic Electricity, DC Series.
Prod-AVIMA Dist-AVIMA

Theory And Testing Of Nickel-Cadmium Batteries C 30 MIN
3/4 OR 1/2 INCH VIDEO CASSETTE IND
Covers theory of operation and the special construction and servicing equipment necessary for nickel-cadmium batteries. Pays special attention to safety precautions and need for a special service area.
From The Basic Electricity, DC Series.
Prod-AVIMA Dist-AVIMA

Theory Into Practice C 29 MIN
16MM FILM, 3/4 OR 1/2 IN VIDEO
Documents individualized instruction as practiced at University Elementary School on the campus of UCLA, with commentary by Dr Madeline Hunter, principal of the school and creator of the program. Includes sequences filmed at an inner-city school where the theories and techniques are being field-tested.
From The Human Relations And School Discipline Series.
Prod-MFFD Dist-FI

Theory Of Debye And Huckel - Effect Of The Ionic Atmospheres On Activities / Energy,... C 46 MIN
3/4 OR 1/2 INCH VIDEO CASSETTE
Discusses the theory of Debye and Huckel, effect of the ionic atmospheres on activities, energy, free energy of ionic atmospheres, osmotic coefficient, activity coefficient, application of Debye and Huckel theory to osmotic coefficients and to the heat of dilution, application of Debye and Huckel theory to activity coefficients, solubility of sparingly soluble salts, dissociation constants of weak acids and kinetics of reaction.
From The Electrochemistry, Pt II - Thermodynamics Of Electrolytic Solutions Series.
Prod-MIOT Dist-MIOT

Theory Of Debye And Huckel, Effect Of The Ionic Atmospheres On Activities, Energy... C 46 MIN
3/4 OR 1/2 INCH VIDEO CASSETTE
Discusses the theory of Debye and Huckel, effect of the ionic atmospheres on activities, energy, applications, solubility of sparingly soluble salts, dissociation constants of weak acids and kinetics of reaction.
From The Electrochemistry Series.
Prod-KALMIA Dist-KALMIA

Theory Of Electrophoresis C 29 MIN
3/4 OR 1/2 INCH VIDEO CASSETTE
See series title for descriptive statement.
From The Colloid And Surface Chemistry - Electrokinetics And Membrane...Series.
Prod-KALMIA Dist-KALMIA

Theory Of Electrophoresis B 29 MIN
3/4 OR 1/2 INCH VIDEO CASSETTE
See series title for descriptive statement.
From The Colloids And Surface Chemistry Electrokinetics And Membrane...-Series.
Prod-MIOT Dist-MIOT

Theory Of Equations And Synthetic Division B 29 MIN
16MM FILM OPTICAL SOUND H
Uses the technique of plotting by completing the square to graph a variety of parabolas, displaced from their axes in various ways. Shows use of synthetic division to test for roots of cubic equations.
From The Advanced Algebra Series.
Prod-CALVIN Dist-MLA Prodn-UNIVFI 1960

Theory Of Evolution C 29 MIN
3/4 INCH VIDEO CASSETTE C A
Discusses Charles Darwin and development of theory of evolution. Shows films of Gallapogos Islands where Darwin formulated his theory. Covers five parts of the theory.
From The Introducing Biology Series. Program 34
Prod-COAST Dist-CDTEL

Theory Of Helicopter Flight, The C 22 MIN
16MM FILM - 3/4 IN VIDEO
Describes how the helicopter obtains lift, directional stability and control. Shows the use of helicopters in war and peace. Issued in 1969 as a motion picture.
LC NO. 79-708129
Prod-USN Dist-USNAC 1979

Theory Of Language Translation—A Series
C
Covers formal translation of programming languages, program syntax and semantics, finite state grammars and recognizers. Shows context free passing techniques such as recursive descent, precedence, LL (K), LR (K) and SLR (K). Discusses machine independent code improvement and generation and syntax directed translation schema.
Prod-UMD Dist-AMCEE

Theory Of Limits, Pt 1 - Limits Of Sequences B 34 MIN
16MM FILM OPTICAL SOUND H-C
Professor E J Mc Shane, with the aid of animation, defines the limit of a sequence using the concept of an advanced set.
From The Mathematics Today Series.
LC NO. FIA66-1270
Prod-MAA Dist-MLA 1963

Theory Of Limits, Pt 2 - Limits Of Functions And Limit Processes B 38 MIN
16MM FILM OPTICAL SOUND H-C
Professor E J Mc Shane applies the method of advanced sets to the definition of a limit of a real valued function and to the definition of an integral.
From The Mathematics Today Series.
LC NO. FIA66-1270
Prod-MAA Dist-MLA 1963

Theory Of Limits, Pt 3 B 13 MIN
16MM FILM OPTICAL SOUND H-C
Professor E J Mc Shane applies the method 'ADVANCED SETS' to cauchy convergence.
From The Mathematics Today Series.
LC NO. FIA66-1270
Prod-MAA Dist-MLA 1963

Theory Of Magnetism - Molecular C 20 MIN
2 INCH VIDEOTAPE I
See series title for descriptive statement.
From The Exploring With Science, Unit VII - Magnetism Series.
Prod-MPATI Dist-GPITVL

Theory Of Management Development C 28 MIN
16MM FILM, 3/4 OR 1/2 IN VIDEO
Lectures on some of the assumptions upon which management development theory is based. Proposes that people have a 'theory bin' containing value systems, predispositions, assumptions, hunches and expectations.
From The Management Development Series.
Prod-UCLA Dist-UCEMC

Theory Of Optical Waveguides C 34 MIN
3/4 OR 1/2 INCH VIDEO CASSETTE C
Presents a comparison of geometric or 'ray optic' approach to wavelength theory with the electromagnetic field or 'physical optic' approach. Discusses theoretical derivation of the mode profiles and cutoff conditions for planar waveguides.
From The Integrated Optics Series.
Prod-UDEL Dist-UDEL

Theory Of Processing C 29 MIN
3/4 INCH VIDEO CASSETTE C
Reviews formation of latent image and development of visable image, developer oxidation, relationship of time and temperature to development, calculation of film development time in a processor, standard processing or cycle time and standard radiographic processing.
From The Radiographic Processing Series. Pt 2
LC NO. 77-706071
Prod-USVA Dist-USNAC 1975

Theory Of Programming Languages—A Series
PRO
Uses classroom format to videotape two 75-minute lectures weekly for 14 weeks and 56 cassettes. Covers syntactic and models of programming languages, finite state processors and their application to lexical analysis, context free languages LR(k), precedence languages as models of programming languages, extensions to context free grammars such as property grammars, inherited and synthesized attributes, van Wijngaarden grammars (Algo 68), abstract syntax, the Vienna definition language, graph models and Translator writing systems.
Prod-UMD Dist-AMCEE

Theory Of Relativity - An Introduction C 20 MIN
16MM FILM, 3/4 OR 1/2 IN VIDEO H-C
Depicts everyday examples of the relativity of motion, then postulates the unchanging velocity of light. Deduces the time-dilation formula and applies it to atomic clocks, atmospheric mesons, and daily experience.
LC NO. 81-706487
Prod-IFB Dist-IFB 1981

Theory Of The Lead-Acid Storage Battery B 25 MIN
16MM FILM OPTICAL SOUND
Shows in detail, by use of animation, how chemical energy is converted into electrical energy to produce electromotive force.
LC NO. FIE60-215
Prod-USN Dist-USNAC 1959

Theory On Concept Formation B 30 MIN
16MM FILM OPTICAL SOUND P-H
Shows Dr Anthony Mc Naughton lecturing on children developing satisfactory understanding through wide experience.
Prod-AWPC Dist-AWPC 1968

Theory Vs Practice - Bennis On Leadership C 30 MIN
3/4 INCH VIDEO CASSETTE
Features an interview with Dr Warren Bennis, former president of the University of Cincinnati. Deals with qualities necessary for leadership and problems that face leaders.
From The Decision Makers Series.
Prod-OHC Dist-HRC

Theory X And Theory Y - Two Sets Of Assumptions In Management C 10 MIN
16MM FILM, 3/4 OR 1/2 IN VIDEO
Features John Morse of the Harvard Business School who discusses the managerial theories of management specialist douglas Mc Gregor.
Prod-SALENG Dist-SALENG 1974

Theory X And Theory Y - Work Of Douglas Mc Gregor, Pt 1 - Description C 25 MIN
16MM FILM - 3/4 IN VIDEO IND
Describes the findings of Douglas Mc Gregor concerning his theory X and theory Y, two basic sets of assumptions about human nature which characterize management style.
From The Motivation And Productivity Series.
Prod-BNA Dist-BNA Prodn-QUEST 1969

Theory X And Theory Y - Work Of Douglas Mc Gregor, Pt 2 - Application C 25 MIN
16MM FILM - 3/4 IN VIDEO IND
Shows the resulting limited gains in production where theory X management style is practiced and explains how and why theory Y management style will influence more effective employee behavior.
From The Motivation And Productivity Series.
Prod-BNA Dist-BNA Prodn-QUEST 1969

Therapeutic Activity For Perceptual-Motor Dysfunction Through Use Of A Scooter B 15 MIN
16MM FILM OPTICAL SOUND
Shows a variety of tasks, all using a scooter and designed to provide specific types of sensory input to enchance sensitory integration and the ability to motor plan.
LC NO. 74-700851
Prod-USC Dist-USC 1969

Therapeutic Community, The C 28 MIN
16MM FILM OPTICAL SOUND
The model therapeutic community at a Michigan State Hospital is described by staff, administrators and patients. Presents the strains and stresses, pleasures and rewards involved in the attempt of the hospital community to duplicate life outside the hospital.
LC NO. 74-705686
Prod-UMITV Dist-UMICH 1969

Therapeutic Exercise - Orthopedics B 28 MIN
16MM FILM OPTICAL SOUND
Demonstrates therapeutic exercises suitable in the management of orthopedic cases.
LC NO. FIE52-1726
Prod-USA Dist-USNAC 1950

Therapeutic Exercise Equipment With Pulleys B 30 MIN
3/4 OR 1/2 INCH VIDEO CASSETTE
Demonstrates various therapeutic exercise equipment used with patients that have muscular weakness. Explains the concept of mechanical advantage in relation to fixed and movable pulleys. Includes demonstrations of different wall weights, the elgin table and various springs and slings for therapeutic exercise.
Prod-UWASH Dist-UWASH

Therapeutic Injection Of The Stifle Ligaments In The Horse B 21 MIN
16MM FILM OPTICAL SOUND PRO
Discusses various lameness involving the stifle joint and ligaments around the stifle joint. Uses schematic drawings to give a clear picture of the anatomy of the joint. (Kinescope)
Prod-AMVMA Dist-AMVMA

Therapeutic Interaction With A Schizophrenic Patient B 10 MIN
3/4 OR 1/2 INCH VIDEO CASSETTE
Simulates nurse-patient interaction in the setting of an inpatient treatment environment where the patient displays schizophrenic behaviors.
Prod-UWASHP Dist-UWASHP

Therapeutic Intervention In Assaultive Behavior C 19 MIN
3/4 OR 1/2 INCH VIDEO CASSETTE PRO
Discusses three elements in the intervention of assaultive behavior - verbal intervention, defense skills and physical intervention. Intended for VA nurses and mental health care personnel.
Prod-VAMCNY Dist-USNAC 1984

Therapeutic Relationships—A Series

Demonstrates results of planned, rather than unplanned, intervention in therapeutic relationships. Helps assess client needs, plan therapeutic interactions, implement those plans and evaluate the results.
Prod-AJN Dist-AJN

Clarifying Relationships 041 MIN
Creative Listening 042 MIN
Therapeutic Silence 030 MIN

Therapeutic Silence C 30 MIN
3/4 OR 1/2 INCH VIDEO CASSETTE
Illustrates how a skillful, understanding nurse helps improve the outlook of a severely depressed adolescent who has been hospitalized following a suicide attempt.
From The Therapeutic Relationships Series.
Prod-AJN Dist-AJN

Therapeutic Techniques For Hispanic, Black And American Indian Clients, Pt I C 60 MIN
3/4 OR 1/2 INCH VIDEO CASSETTE
Discusses therapeutic techniques in working with Hispanic, Black and American Indian clients. Points out historical, cultural and social factors which are relevant in assessing client problems.
Prod-UWISC Dist-UWISC 1981

Therapeutic Techniques For Hispanic, Black, And American Indian Clients, Pt II C 30 MIN
3/4 OR 1/2 INCH VIDEO CASSETTE
Continues the discussions on working with minority clients.
Prod-UWISC Dist-UWISC 1981

Therapeutic Techniques, Pt I- Interpretations, Silence And How Silence Is... C 30 MIN
3/4 OR 1/2 INCH VIDEO CASSETTE
Emphasizes the need of the therapist's sensitivity to the patient's skill in coercing the therapist into making too many early interpretations.
From The Treatment Of The Borderline Patient Series.
Prod-HEMUL Dist-HEMUL

Therapeutic Techniques, Pt II - 'Good Mothering' C 15 MIN
3/4 OR 1/2 INCH VIDEO CASSETTE
Discusses the non-constructive value of certain kinds of supper and so-called 'good mothering' in the treatment of borderline patients who become guilty at their inability to be equally feeling or caring.
From The Treatment Of The Borderline Patient Series.
Prod-HEMUL Dist-HEMUL

Therapeutic Techniques, Pt III - Between Therapist And Patient - Communications,... C 24 MIN
3/4 OR 1/2 INCH VIDEO CASSETTE
Stresses the value of the therapist communicating free-associations, fears and other feelings and inner subjective data which occur during a session with a therapist.
From The Treatment Of The Borderline Patient Series.
Prod-HEMUL Dist-HEMUL

Therapeutic Touch, The - Healing In The New Age C 35 MIN
16MM FILM, 3/4 OR 1/2 IN VIDEO
Shows paranormal healing detailing Dr Dolores Krieger's hemoglobin research and 'the therapeutic touch'.
Prod-HP Dist-HP

Therapeutic Use Of Self B 30 MIN
2 INCH VIDEOTAPE PRO
Helps nursing students understand how a therapeutic use of self can improve their abilities in treating patients.
From The Mental Health Concepts For Nursing, Unit 4 - The Nurse - Patient Relationship Series.
LC NO. 73-702651
Prod-GPITVL Dist-GPITVL 1971

Therapeutic Use Of Toys B 28 MIN
3/4 OR 1/2 INCH VIDEO CASSETTE
Demonstrates the use of toys to elicit a specific motor response such as prone extension, supine flexion, postural support with push pattern, finger and wrist extension and grasp with wrist stabilization.
Prod-BU Dist-BU

Therapeutic Vocal Cord Injection - A Seventeen Year Overview C 25 MIN
3/4 OR 1/2 INCH VIDEO CASSETTE PRO
Gives a history and summary of vocal cord injection for therapeutic purposes. Includes a demonstration of the technique and its results.
Prod-USVA Dist-USNAC 1981

Therapeutic Vs Non-Therapeutic Communication C 20 MIN
3/4 OR 1/2 INCH VIDEO CASSETTE PRO
Uses six scenes of two versions each. Uses both non-therapeutic and therapeutic modalities.
Prod-HSCIC Dist-HSCIC 1978

Therapeutically Radiated Breast C 29 MIN
3/4 INCH VIDEO CASSETTE
Speaks about the advantages of radiation therapy over surgery.
Prod-UTAHTI Dist-UTAHTI

Therapist(s) - Couple Communication C 55 MIN
3/4 OR 1/2 INCH VIDEO CASSETTE
Reveals the 'what and how' of communication between married co-therapists and four couples in a program which focuses on reinforcement rather than on discounting for more functional marriages.
From The Family Communication Series.
Prod-HEMUL Dist-HEMUL

Therapist(s) - Family Communication C 60 MIN
3/4 OR 1/2 INCH VIDEO CASSETTE
Reveals how therapists communicate openly and directly with a family to establish a working alliance, minimize scapegoating, disqualifications, vindictiveness and guilt provoking, while increasing objectivity and responsibility in the parents for the children as well as themselves.
From The Family Communication Series.
Prod-HEMUL Dist-HEMUL

Therapy - What Do You Want Me To Say C 15 MIN
16MM FILM, 3/4 OR 1/2 IN VIDEO J-H
Describes the stigmas and benefits of therapy, showing a high school girl who has been pressured into seeing a psychologist.
From The Conflict And Awareness Series.
Prod-CRMP Dist-CRMP 1975

Therapy Can Be Fun - A Look At Sensory Integrative Activities C
3/4 OR 1/2 INCH VIDEO CASSETTE
Presents an introduction to the use of sensory integrative treatment activities and demonstrates a variety of activities that may be used. Addresses areas of sensory integration including tactile, vestibular, proprioception, equilibrium vestibular-bilateral integration and motor planning.
Prod-UWASH Dist-UWASH

Therapy In Motion C 13 MIN
16MM FILM, 3/4 OR 1/2 IN VIDEO
Demonstrates how arthritis sufferers can help themselves to feel better. Emphasizes the importance of establishing a daily routine that balances rest with proper exercise.
Prod-MINIP Dist-MTI 1980

Therapy Of Prayer, The B 30 MIN
16MM FILM OPTICAL SOUND
Depicts emotional difficulty encountered by the parents of a boy who stutters. Shows the mother enrolled in a prayer therapy treatment course at the University of Redlands where she discovers the true cause of the son's affliction.
Prod-GUIDAS Dist-WWPI 1959

Therayattam B 18 MIN
16MM FILM OPTICAL SOUND
Presents a documentary on one of the oldest forms of organized dance worship of North Malabar in South India, performed in the courtyard of the village shrine in honor of the heroes of legend, faith or family.
Prod-JOHN Dist-RADIM

There Ain't No Flies On Us C 28 MIN
3/4 INCH VIDEO CASSETTE
Illustrates camping and recreational activities and facilities for physically handicapped youngsters as seen from their viewpoint with their thoughts, ideas and feelings expressed.
Prod-ESST Dist-ESST 1978

There Are Choices C 18 MIN
16MM FILM OPTICAL SOUND
Tells the story of how former world champion cowboy Jim Shoulders became a small businessman. Juxtaposes his story with that of Blue Bell, an American corporation which makes Wrangler jeans.
LC NO. 78-701133
Prod-BLUBEL Dist-WSTGLC Prodn-HOLBEA 1978

There Are Many Ways To Go C 15 MIN
16MM FILM, 3/4 OR 1/2 IN VIDEO I
Shows how three young ice-skaters prepare for a competition by using a problem-solving guide.
From The Thinkabout Series. Classifying
LC NO. 81-706127
Prod-EDFCEN Dist-AITECH 1979

There Are No Clowns C
3/4 OR 1/2 INCH VIDEO CASSETTE IND
Features Glenn Ford in a dramatic demonstration of the power of carbon dioxide and nitrogen in well servicing operations. Discusses proper bleed back procedures and safe work practices.
Prod-GPCV Dist-GPCV

There Are No Clowns (French) C
3/4 OR 1/2 INCH VIDEO CASSETTE IND
Features Glenn Ford in a dramatic demonstration of the power of carbon dioxide and nitrogen in well servicing operations. Discusses proper bleed back procedures and safe work practices.
Prod-GPCV Dist-GPCV

There Are Ways To Remember C 14 MIN
16MM FILM, 3/4 OR 1/2 IN VIDEO I
Tells how Cindy's instructor gives her advice on remembering.
From The Thinkabout Series. Collecting Information
LC NO. 81-706130
Prod-OECA Dist-AITECH 1979

There Are Yachts At The Bottom Of My Garden C 10 MIN
16MM FILM, 3/4 OR 1/2 IN VIDEO J-C A
Shows sailing on Sydney Harbor, Australia, where a great number of boat owners have harbor-front homes and there are literally yachts at the bottom of the garden.
Prod-ANAIB Dist-JOU Prodn-FLMAUS 1974

There But For Fortune C 60 MIN
16MM FILM - 3/4 IN VIDEO J-C A
Chronicles the Latin American concert tour taken by Joan Baez which was impeded by government intimidation due to her public position as a humanitarian activist. Paints a stirring portrait of human suffering and details one woman's efforts to add a measure of concern to an inhumane situation.
Prod-FIRS Dist-FIRS

There Comes A Time C 30 MIN
16MM FILM - 3/4 IN VIDEO
Discusses some of the things parents need in order to do a good job raising their children. Enumerates resources that are available to help meet these needs, and suggests ways in which parents can go about finding the help they need.
From The Footsteps Series.
LC NO. 79-707635
Prod-USOE Dist-USNAC 1978

There Go I C 26 MIN
16MM FILM OPTICAL SOUND H-C A
Dramatizes a successful manager's view of the barriers facing the disabled worker. Discusses job modifications, workplace accomodations and the sensitive relations with coworkers.
LC NO. 81-701029
Prod-MALIBU Dist-MALIBU Prodn-MENKNS 1981

There Goes The Bride C 29 MIN
2 INCH VIDEOTAPE
See series title for descriptive statement.
From The Our Street Series.
Prod-MDCPB Dist-PUBTEL

There Goes The Neighbourhood C 13 MIN
16MM FILM OPTICAL SOUND
Poses possible solutions to housing problems as a reaction to the rising demolition of neighborhoods in Montreal. Focuses on the St Louis district in downtown Montreal.
LC NO. 76-703331
Prod-CANFDC Dist-CANFDC 1975

There Is A Law Against It C 8 MIN
16MM FILM, 3/4 OR 1/2 IN VIDEO J-C A
Introduces familiar consumer problems, including garnishment of wages, unauthorized auto repair work, payment demanded for a debt already paid, and high pressure door-to-door salesmen. Dramatizes how California consumer laws protect the consumer in each case.
Prod-FLMFR Dist-FLMFR

There Is A Law Against It (Spanish) C 8 MIN
16MM FILM, 3/4 OR 1/2 IN VIDEO J-C A
Introduces familiar consumer problems, including garnishment of wages, unauthorized auto repair work, payment demanded for a debt already paid, and high pressure door-to-door salesmen. Dramatizes how California consumer laws protect the consumer in each case.
Prod-FLMFR Dist-FLMFR

There Is A Place Called Sesame Place C 12 MIN
3/4 INCH VIDEO CASSETTE
Depicts Sesame Place, an innovative park where families with children aged 3 to 13 play and learn together. Features computer games, a TV studio and active outdoor play equipment.
Prod-ANHBUS Dist-MTP

There Is A Road C 1 MIN
3/4 OR 1/2 INCH VIDEO CASSETTE
Employs TV spot format and voice-over technique to stress need for volunteers to drive cancer patients to and from treatment along 'The Road To Recovery.'
Prod-AMCS Dist-AMCS 1982

There Is A Way (2nd Ed) C 27 MIN
16MM FILM, 3/4 OR 1/2 IN VIDEO
Portrays life of F-105 pilots who fight the air war in Southeast Asia daily. Pictures their hazardous missions against determined enemy in the North, while pilots and crews tell about the job they are doing and why.
LC NO. 81-706529
Prod-USAF Dist-USNAC 1967

There Is No 'Nothing' Job C 15 MIN
2 INCH VIDEOTAPE J-H
Discusses the proper attitude toward work, no matter what type of job is involved.
From The Work Is For Real Series.
Prod-STETVC Dist-GPITVL

There Is No One Like Me B 20 MIN
16MM FILM OPTICAL SOUND C A
See series title for descriptive statement.
From The All That I Am Series.
Prod-MPATI Dist-NWUFLM

There Must Be A Catch C 12 MIN
16MM FILM, 3/4 OR 1/2 IN VIDEO
Presents a job interview in order to depict the effect of an inept and insensitive interviewer, from the point of view of youth who deserve a better reception and an employer who desperately needs employees. Issued in 1968 as a motion picture.
From The Career Job Opportunities Series.
LC NO. 79-707864
Prod-USBES Dist-USNAC Prodn-CMC 1979

There Ought'a Be A Law C 25 MIN
16MM FILM OPTICAL SOUND
Looks at the litter problem and workable solutions to it. Studies Bottle Bill legislation and two viable alternatives, Resource Recovery and the Clean Community System.
Prod-AIAS Dist-MTP

There They Go C 25 MIN
16MM FILM OPTICAL SOUND A

Goes behind the scenes to show how fine race horses are developed. Visits famous trainers and jockeys at thoroughbred farms and race track stables. Hosted by Jack Kramer.
Prod-HLYWDT Dist-HLYWDT

There Was A Crooked Man C 20 MIN
3/4 OR 1/2 INCH VIDEO CASSETTE P-I
Introduces the woodwind family.
From The USS Rhythm Series.
Prod-ARKETV Dist-AITECH 1977

There Was An Old Woman C 14 MIN
3/4 OR 1/2 INCH VIDEO CASSETTE P-I
See series title for descriptive statement.
From The Ready, Sing Series.
Prod-ARKETV Dist-AITECH 1979

There Will Be A Slight Delay C 30 MIN
3/4 OR 1/2 INCH VIDEO CASSETTE
Looks at the congestion in transportation that the ever-increasing flow of people and goods has created. Argues for an integrated plan to save lives and reduce costs of delays.
Prod-IVCH Dist-IVCH

There's A Message For You C 15 MIN
3/4 OR 1/2 INCH VIDEO CASSETTE J
Uses a dramatic approach to reading and understanding expository texts. Focuses on techniques that get the author's purpose and message across, previewing techniques and clues to textbook messages.
From The Reading For A Reason Series. No. 3
LC NO. 83-706574
Prod-WETN Dist-AITECH Prodn-GBCTP 1983

There's A Motor In Me—A Series
K-P
Includes 15, 15-minute language arts lessons. Teaches children to improve their speech performance and to help them with the language development process. Aims at creating an awareness of articulation errors.
Prod-WESTEL Dist-WESTEL

There's Always A Question C 8 MIN
16MM FILM OPTICAL SOUND
Tells a story about two unseen beings who observe the function of the Earth, the development of life forms there and man's evolution to the present-day energy crisis. Designed to raise questions about alternative energy sources.
LC NO. 75-700353
Prod-SCE Dist-SCE 1974

There's Always A Risk C 15 MIN
16MM FILM, 3/4 OR 1/2 IN VIDEO I
Tells how the passengers of a crashed plane begin to hike for help while two boys pick up their emergency message.
From The Thinkabout Series. Solving Problems
LC NO. 81-706128
Prod-KOCETV Dist-AITECH 1979

There's Always Fishing C 16 MIN
16MM FILM OPTICAL SOUND
Tennessee Charlie tells the story of year-round fishing for sauger, walleye and bass. The catfish derby below Pickwick Dam, and the excitement of fishing for stripes and smallmouth bass are pictured.
Prod-TGAFC Dist-TGAFC

There's Magic In Good Speech B 15 MIN
2 INCH VIDEOTAPE P
See series title for descriptive statement.
From The Sounds Like Magic Series.
Prod-MOEBA Dist-GPITVL Prodn-KYNETV

There's More To Life (Captioned) C 25 MIN
16MM FILM OPTICAL SOUND S
Encourages participation in continuing education courses. Shows deaf people involved in a variety of continuing education classes.
Prod-GALCO Dist-GALCO 1977

There's More To Me Than What You See C 29 MIN
16MM FILM OPTICAL SOUND H-C A
Depicts the experiences of three disabled persons, their attitudes about themselves and the attitudes of others toward them. Focuses on the barriers society has erected against the disabled and the daily challenges that they must face.
LC NO. 82-700189
Prod-AMERLC Dist-APH 1981

There's No Business Like Big Business C 30 MIN
3/4 INCH VIDEO CASSETTE H-C A
Presents Ben J Wattenberg, author of The Real America, arguing that the American corporation provides more people with more necessities and luxuries than any system the world has ever seen and that bigness, by itself, is no vice.
From The In Search Of The Real America Series.
Prod-WGBHTV Dist-KINGFT 1977

There's No Business Like Show Business C 15 MIN
3/4 OR 1/2 INCH VIDEO CASSETTE J-H
Explores the motion picture industry. Interviews people involved in making movies.
From The Movies, Movies Series.
Prod-CTI Dist-CTI

There's No Excuse - Using Safe Operating Procedures C
16MM FILM - 3/4 IN VIDEO A
Stresses that good safety procedures are the first line of defense in accident prevention.
Prod-BNA Dist-BNA 1983

There's No Magic C 15 MIN
3/4 OR 1/2 INCH VIDEO CASSETTE J-H
Explains that wise decisions about food affect physical, mental and emotional development. Shows how Lee learns that she doesn't need a stable to look and feel better.
From The Soup To Nuts Series.
Prod-GSDE Dist-AITECH 1980

There's No Place Like Home C 15 MIN
16MM FILM OPTICAL SOUND
Recounts how Senior Companions help elderly citizens maintain their independence and continue to live in their own homes. Shows the volunteers helping with shopping, light housework and heavier chores.
Prod-ACTON Dist-MTP

There's Nobody Else Like You C 14 MIN
16MM FILM, 3/4 OR 1/2 IN VIDEO P-I
Reveals that it is both natural and desirable that people have different appearances, interests and skills. Documents a trip to the zoo, a classroom discussion and a recreation of a school recess. Uses the events of the day and the words of children to show that everyone is truly an individual.
Prod-FILMSW Dist-FLMFR 1973

There's Nobody Else Like You (Spanish) C 14 MIN
16MM FILM, 3/4 OR 1/2 IN VIDEO P-I
Reveals that it is both natural and desirable that people have different appearances, interests and skills. Documents a trip to the zoo, a classroom discussion and a recreation of a school recess. Uses the events of the day and the words of children to show that everyone is truly an individual.
Prod-FILMSW Dist-FLMFR 1973

There's Nothing Magical About Nuclear Power C 24 MIN
16MM FILM OPTICAL SOUND
Uses various photographic tricks in presenting a tour of a nuclear power plant. Explains nuclear powered electric generation.
LC NO. 77-702155
Prod-BGECO Dist-BGECO 1977

There's Plenty Of Gold C 30 MIN
3/4 OR 1/2 INCH VIDEO CASSETTE
Examines some of the newest successes in mineral exploration. Shows that world mineral requirements can be met by modern technology, responsible people and international cooperation.
Prod-IVCH Dist-IVCH

There's Something About A Story C 27 MIN
16MM FILM OPTICAL SOUND P
Uses the comments of storytellers and sequences from storytelling situations to show the value of storytelling with children 6 through 12 years of age. Discusses where to find stories and the basic tehcniques for preparing and presenting them.
LC NO. 71-704569
Prod-PULIDO Dist-CONNF Prodn-CONNF 1969

There's The Land - Have You Seen It C 30 MIN
16MM FILM OPTICAL SOUND J-H A
Visits the fabled land of the Yukon and Alaska following the main routes of entry--sea, rail and air. Shows what visitors discover when they travel the White Pass and Yukon route to the famed Eldorado of other days.
LC NO. 70-700898
Prod-NFBC Dist-CTFL 1967

There's The Rub C 8 MIN
16MM FILM OPTICAL SOUND
Focuses on the massage parlors of Toronto, Canada, and the attitudes of the people who operate them, work in them, patronize them or want to have them closed down.
LC NO. 77-702668
Prod-CANFDC Dist-CANFDC

There's Trouble Underfoot C 15 MIN
16MM FILM, 3/4 OR 1/2 IN VIDEO J-C A
Presents techniques for cleaning carpets, including shampoo, steam and dry cleaning. Shows how to establish a daily vacuuming regimen.
Prod-KLEINW Dist-KLEINW

Thermal Environment Of The Neonate (2nd Ed) C 14 MIN
3/4 OR 1/2 INCH VIDEO CASSETTE PRO
Discusses the modalities of heat loss, the infants' metabolic responses to heat loss or gain, the effect of birth weight on thermoregulation, thermal stress in low birth weight infants and the prevention of cold stress.
Prod-UMICHM Dist-UMICHM 1983

Thermal Equilibrium B 15 MIN
2 INCH VIDEOTAPE P
See series title for descriptive statement.
From The Just Curious Series. No. 25
Prod-EOPS Dist-GPITVL Prodn-KOACTV

Thermal Interactions B 15 MIN
2 INCH VIDEOTAPE P
See series title for descriptive statement.
From The Just Wondering Series.
Prod-EOPS Dist-GPITVL Prodn-KOACTV

Thermal Interactions - Just Curious C 15 MIN
2 INCH VIDEOTAPE P
See series title for descriptive statement.
From The Just Curious Series. No. 24
Prod-EOPS Dist-GPITVL Prodn-KOACTV

Thermal Metal Refining C 35 MIN
3/4 INCH VIDEO CASSETTE C A
See series title for descriptive statement.
From The Elements Of Metallurgy Series.
LC NO. 81-706194
Prod-AMCEE Dist-AMCEE 1980

Thermal Metal Refining C 45 MIN
3/4 OR 1/2 INCH VIDEO CASSETTE PRO
See series title for descriptive statement.
From The Elements Of Metallurgy Series.
Prod-ICSINT Dist-ICSINT

Thermal Separation C 60 MIN
3/4 OR 1/2 INCH VIDEO CASSETTE IND
Goes into evaporation and condensation, vapor pressures and boiling points of liquids, distillation, fractional distillation, continuous rectification and fractionation of petroleum.
From The Chemistry Training Series.
Prod-ITCORP Dist-ITCORP

Thermal Storage Systems C 60 MIN
3/4 OR 1/2 INCH VIDEO CASSETTE IND
Presents a lecture dealing with how energy is stored in various solar systems, the characteristics of these systems and their input, delivered load and storage capabilities.
From the Solar Energy - Fundamentals And Applications Series.
LC NO. 81-706413
Prod-USCCE Dist-AMCEE 1977

Thermal Wilderness, The C 29 MIN
16MM FILM OPTICAL SOUND I-C A
Follows the fortunes of a backpacking party through two days of a heat wave. Demonstrates pacing, exposure avoidance and water and salt intake. Emphasizes prevention of heat disorders but demonstrates identification and early treatment of salt depletion, dehydration and incipient heat stroke.
LC NO. 76-702108
Prod-SAFECO Dist-LAWJ Prodn-LAWJ 1975

Thermodynamics B 150 MIN
3/4 OR 1/2 INCH VIDEO CASSETTE PRO
See series title for descriptive statement.
From The Professional Engineer's Exam Refresher Course Series.
Prod-UMICE Dist-AMCEE

Thermodynamics C 180 MIN
3/4 OR 1/2 INCH VIDEO CASSETTE PRO
Covers, in three one-hour tapes, ideal gases and the gas laws, properties of gases to pressure, volume, temperature and internal energy, changes of state, the first and second laws of thermodynamics, heat transfer, conductor and convection, thermal conducting, coefficient of heat transfer and film coefficients.
From The Professional Engineer Review Series.
Prod-UILU Dist-AMCEE

Thermodynamics And Vacancies C 30 MIN
3/4 OR 1/2 INCH VIDEO CASSETTE PRO
Emphasizes Gibbs free energy and its minimization as the basis for understanding phase transformations.
From The Elements Of Physical Metallurgy Series.
Prod-AMCEE Dist-AMCEE

Thermodynamics Of Electrochemical Corrosion 2 - Stability (Pourbaix) Diagrams C 51 MIN
3/4 OR 1/2 INCH VIDEO CASSETTE
Tells how stability (Pourbaix) diagrams are the electrochemical equivalent of metallurgical phase diagrams and shows, in a compact form, phase stability as a function of electrode potential and solution ph.
From The Corrosion Engineering Series.
Prod-MIOT Dist-MIOT

Thermodynamics Of Electrochemical Corrosion 3 - Application Of Stability Diagrams C 52 MIN
3/4 OR 1/2 INCH VIDEO CASSETTE
Considers the corrosion of iron in terms of important anodic (metal dissolution, passivation, etc) and cathodic (proton and oxygen reduction) partial processes with the aid of stability diagrams. Illustrates the utility of such diagrams in terms of corrosion control.
From The Corrosion Engineering Series.
Prod-MIOT Dist-MIOT

Thermodynamics Of Electrochemical Corrosion 1 - The Nernst Equation C 58 MIN
3/4 OR 1/2 INCH VIDEO CASSETTE
Develops a measure of the relative tendency of metals to corrode. Illustrates the fundamental thermodynamic expression relating single electrode potentials to the effective concentration of species in solution, the Nernst equation.
From The Corrosion Engineering Series.
Prod-MIOT Dist-MIOT

Thermodynamics Of Electrochemical Corrosion - The Nernst Equation C 58 MIN
3/4 OR 1/2 INCH VIDEO CASSETTE PRO
See series title for descriptive statement.
From The Corrosion Engineering Series.
Prod-GPCV Dist-GPCV

Thermodynamics Of Electrochemical Corrosion - Stability (Pourbaix) Diagrams C 51 MIN
3/4 OR 1/2 INCH VIDEO CASSETTE PRO
See series title for descriptive statement.
From The Corrosion Engineering Series.
Prod-GPCV Dist-GPCV

Thermodynamics Of Electrochemical Corrosion - Application Of Stability Diagrams C 52 MIN
3/4 OR 1/2 INCH VIDEO CASSETTE PRO
See series title for descriptive statement.
From The Corrosion Engineering Series.
Prod-GPCV Dist-GPCV

Thermodynamics Of fluid Interfaces C 48 MIN
3/4 OR 1/2 INCH VIDEO CASSETTE
See series title for descriptive statement.
From The Colloid And Surface Chemistry - Surface Chemistry Series.
Prod-KALMIA Dist-KALMIA

Thermodynamics Of Fluid Interfaces B 48 MIN
3/4 OR 1/2 INCH VIDEO CASSETTE PRO
See series title for descriptive statement.
From The Colloid And Surface Chemistry - Surface Chemistry Series.
Prod-MIOT Dist-MIOT

Thermodynamics Of Polymer Solutions/Osmotic Pressure B 52 MIN
3/4 OR 1/2 INCH VIDEO CASSETTE
See series title for descriptive statement.
From The Colloids And Surface Chemistry - Lyophilic Colloids Series.
Prod-MIOT Dist-MIOT

Thermodynamics Of Polymer Solutions, Osmotic Pressure C 52 MIN
3/4 OR 1/2 INCH VIDEO CASSETTE
See series title for descriptive statement.
From The Colloid And Surface Chemistry - Lyophilic Colloids Series.
Prod-KALMIA Dist-KALMIA

Thermography C 28 MIN
2 INCH VIDEOTAPE
See series title for descriptive statement.
From The Interface Series.
Prod-KCET Dist-PUBTEL

Thermometers B 22 MIN
16MM FILM OPTICAL SOUND H
Shows how other properties, less fundamental than the pressure of a gas, are used to measure temperature. Points out that these include liquid in glass thermometers, the clinical thermometer and thermometers which depend on the expansion of a bimetal strip of thermoelectric effects.
From The Heat Series.
Prod-CETO Dist-GPITVL

Thermometers C 15 MIN
2 INCH VIDEOTAPE P
Demonstrates changes in heat energy and how it can be measured by a thermometer.
From The Science Is Searching Series.
Prod-DETPS Dist-GPITVL

Thermometers - How They Help Us C 9 MIN
16MM FILM OPTICAL SOUND P-I
Illustrates the basic principle that liquids expand when heated and contract when cooled. Shows a thermometer being built and used and explains the different sorts of liquids used in thermometers.
LC NO. FIA65-1107
Prod-SIGMA Dist-FILCOM 1964

Thermometers - The Hot And Cold Of It C
16MM FILM, 3/4 OR 1/2 IN VIDEO
Shows how a thermometer works. Covers a variety of thermometers and their purposes.
Prod-HIGGIN Dist-HIGGIN

Thermometers And How They Work C 10 MIN
16MM FILM, 3/4 OR 1/2 IN VIDEO P
Demonstrates thermometers made with liquids, those made with gases and those made with solids. Explains expansion and contraction of materials. Shows how thermometers are used in various occupations.
Prod-EBF Dist-EBEC 1963

Thermometers And How They Work (Spanish) C 11 MIN
16MM FILM, 3/4 OR 1/2 IN VIDEO P
Explores the three basic types of thermometers and uses simple demonstrations to show how each type works.
Prod-EBEC Dist-EBEC

Thermoplastics C 13 MIN
16MM FILM, 3/4 OR 1/2 IN VIDEO J-C A
A thermoplastic project--forming, shaping, finishing and joining.
From The Plastics And Fiber Glass Series.
Prod-MORLAT Dist-SF 1967

These Are Our Children C 20 MIN
16MM FILM OPTICAL SOUND PRO
Shows the education and training of cerebral palsied children at the Eastern New York Orthopedic Hospital School.
Prod-UCPA Dist-UCPA 1951

These Are Our Forests C 14 MIN
16MM FILM OPTICAL SOUND
Examines the role of timber in the Southwestern United States, where wood is often the primary energy source for cooking and heating. Describes various types of woodburning stoves and the different kinds of timber they burn.
LC NO. 79-700828
Prod-USFS Dist-USNAC Prodn-USDA 1979

These Are The Days C 20 MIN
16MM FILM, 3/4 OR 1/2 IN VIDEO J-C A
Addresses fears and aging sterotypes creatively and directly. Shows intergenerational relationships which blossom through a common interest, breaks down age barriers and erects a positive view of growing older.
Prod-CLNTCR Dist-FILMID

These Honored Dead - Civil War, Pt 2 - (1863-1865) X 24 MIN
16MM FILM OPTICAL SOUND I-C A
Presents highlights of the final Civil War years, such as the battle of Gettysburg, the fall of Vicksburg, the industrial might of the North, King Cotton, Appomattox and the assassination of President Lincoln.
From The Exploring - The Story Of America, Set 2 Series.
LC NO. FIA68-1058
Prod-NBCTV Dist-GRACUR 1968

These Items On Sale C 20 MIN
16MM FILM OPTICAL SOUND
A study of the reaction of three women who meet at the funeral of their old, beloved teacher.
LC NO. 73-713387
Prod-GCCED Dist-GCCED 1971

These People - Focus On Community Care For The Mentally Disabled C 29 MIN
16MM FILM, 3/4 OR 1/2 IN VIDEO A
Portrays Wilkes-Barre, Pennsysylvania, to examine the issues involved in providing alternative treatment of mentally disabled individuals in small community care facilities. Includes a segment of a public forum on the subject, in which mental patients, community leaders, neighbors, legislators and mental patients express their views and reactions to the issues.
LC NO. 79-708053
Prod-HORIHS Dist-PEREN 1979

These People Are Working C 28 MIN
3/4 OR 1/2 INCH VIDEO CASSETTE
Presents actor James Stacy, who lost an arm and leg in an accident several years ago, hosting this documentary about remarkable people who have achieved successful careers in spite of physical and mental handicaps.
Prod-KAETTV Dist-PBS 1979

These Special People C 16 MIN
16MM FILM, 3/4 OR 1/2 IN VIDEO
Explores the work of electronics technicians in the Federal Aviation Administration. Tells how they install, operate and maintain the nation's complex airway facilities network.
Prod-USFAA Dist-USNAC Prodn-IMAGA 1979

These Stones Remain C 27 MIN
16MM FILM OPTICAL SOUND
Depicts Irish stone carving from the earliest times to the 12th century, shown in its natural surroundings along with many locations in the west of Ireland.
Prod-CONSUI Dist-CONSUI

These Things Are Ours C 26 MIN
16MM FILM OPTICAL SOUND
Uses a walk through a wilderness area of the Midwestern United States during each of the four seasons to examine a profusion of plants and animals and the destruction caused by insecticides and man-made hazards.
From The Audubon Wildlife Theatre Series.
LC NO. 78-710208
Prod-KEGPL Dist-AVEXP 1970

These Too Are Our Children C 40 MIN
16MM FILM OPTICAL SOUND
Demonstrates methods of working with mentally retarded and physically handicapped persons, as practiced by the Boulder County Board of Developmental Disabilities in Colorado.
Prod-UCOLO Dist-UCOLO

These Were The Maya C 19 MIN
16MM FILM, 3/4 OR 1/2 IN VIDEO
Focuses on the Yucatan Peninsula, the site of the Mayan ruins of Chichen Itza, Uxmal, Dzibilchaltun and Tulum. Features the Mayas who populate the cities of the Yucatan and shows architecture and industry along with the old customs.
From The Mexican Heritage Series.
Prod-STEXMF Dist-FI 1976

Theseus And The Minotaur C 21 MIN
16MM FILM, 3/4 OR 1/2 IN VIDEO
Presents the Greek myth about Theseus and his encounter with the Minotaur.
Prod-KINGSP Dist-PHENIX 1970

Theseus And The Minotaur - A Greek Folk Tale C 5 MIN
16MM FILM, 3/4 OR 1/2 IN VIDEO P-I
Presents the story of Theseus, a young prince of Athens, who was a great warrior even as a boy. Explains how he outwitted Minos, the cruel King of Crete, and slew Minotaur, the monster.
Prod-PIC Dist-LUF 1972

They C 16 MIN
16MM FILM, 3/4 OR 1/2 IN VIDEO
Uses symbolism to examine the human society in microcosm. Suggests some alternatives to the status quo.
Prod-PHENIX Dist-CORF

They (Spanish) C 16 MIN
16MM FILM, 3/4 OR 1/2 IN VIDEO
Uses symbolism to examine the human society in microcosm. Suggests some alternatives to the status quo.
Prod-PHENIX Dist-CORF

They All Can Work C 28 MIN
16MM FILM, 3/4 OR 1/2 IN VIDEO H-C A
Looks at the employees of the Natural Recovery Systems, who are all physically and mentally handicapped. Shows them on and off the job, learning new skills and generally relaxing among themselves in the company cafeteria.
Prod-NFBC Dist-NFBC 1977

They All Learn C 28 MIN
16MM FILM OPTICAL SOUND
Explores the remaking of twelve schools in a poor rural Southern district, from a traditional, self contained arrangement to a more informal, continuous, child-centered program. This project was intended to eliminate deficiencies and improve achievement in one of the poorest and most underfunded counties in the United States.
Prod-PROMET Dist-PROMET

They Also Learn B 14 MIN
16MM FILM OPTICAL SOUND
Discusses the program of a residential school for both educable and trainable children at the University of South Dakota. Depicts teacher training, psychological diagnosis and staff evaluation procedures in a summer school.
Prod-USD Dist-USD

They Appreciate You More C 16 MIN
16MM FILM, 3/4 OR 1/2 IN VIDEO H-C A
Looks at a family in which both adults work and share in the household responsibilities.
From The Working Mother Series.
Prod-NFBC Dist-NFBC 1974

They Are Their Own Gifts C 52 MIN
16MM FILM OPTICAL SOUND C A
Uses documentary photographs and interviews to present the lives and contributions of poetess Muriel Rukeyser, portrait artist Alice Neel and choreographer Anna Sokolow. Includes commentary by the artists.
LC NO. 78-702046
Prod-RHOMUR Dist-RHOMUR 1978

They Call Him Ah Kung C 24 MIN
16MM FILM OPTICAL SOUND
Profiles Ah Kung, a Taiwanese schoolboy who will inherit the family farm but may leave it in favor of industry and an urban lifestyle. Explains that this is faced by many of his fellow schoolmates and that it affects Taiwan's ability to feed its population properly.
From The Faces Of Change - Taiwan Series.
Prod-AUFS Dist-WHEELK

They Call It Pro Football C 27 MIN
16MM FILM OPTICAL SOUND
Describes the violence and excitement in professional football today and its effect on players, coaches and spectators.
LC NO. FIA68-372
Prod-AMEXCO Dist-NFL 1967

They Call It Wildcat C 32 MIN
16MM FILM OPTICAL SOUND J-C A
Shows the efforts of the Vera Institute of Justice, through its creation of the Wildcat Services Corporation. Explains how the institute helps drug addicts and criminal offenders find work in New York City.
LC NO. 75-702966
Prod-FDF Dist-KAROL Prodn-STONEY 1975

They Call Me Names C 22 MIN
16MM FILM, 3/4 OR 1/2 IN VIDEO H-C A S
Portrays the lives of mentally different young people and explores how they perceive a world in which they are told often and in many ways that they are retarded.
Prod-EFFEX Dist-PHENIX 1972

They Call The Wind Energy C 29 MIN
3/4 INCH VIDEO CASSETTE
Traces the history of the use of wind as an energy source and examines the concept and details of wind generation.
LC NO. 79-707935
Prod-UMICH Dist-UMICH 1979

They Called Me Stupid C 20 MIN
3/4 OR 1/2 INCH VIDEO CASSETTE H-C A
Focuses on dyslexia, the perceptual disorder which impairs the individual's ability to receive and communicate information accurately.
Prod-CANBC Dist-JOU

They Called The Island Long C 22 MIN
16MM FILM OPTICAL SOUND I-C A
Explores Long Island and the activities of its resi dents, in all its seasons, at work and at play. Learning and putting knowledge to use.
LC NO. FIA68-840
Prod-LILC Dist-LILC Prodn-AERLOG 1967

They Came To Race C 30 MIN
16MM FILM OPTICAL SOUND
Tells the story of men and machines in record-breaking competition at Indy in 1965 and final exciting outcome as Jim Clark comes in.
Prod-SFI Dist-SFI

They Came To Stay C 12 MIN
16MM FILM OPTICAL SOUND
Examines the effects of terrorism on the lives of Israelis in border development towns, focusing on Kiryat Shemona and Ma 'Alot. Shows what must be done to maintain these towns as viable parts of Israeli society.
Prod-UJA Dist-ALDEN

They Came To Stay C 29 MIN
3/4 INCH VIDEO CASSETTE
Features the region once governed by the Hudson's Bay Company. Follows the growth of the fur trade and the whaling industry, the role of the federal government, and the changes brought by industry and government. Also available in two-inch quad and one-inch videotape.
From The North Of 60 Degrees - Destiny Uncertain Series.
Prod-TVOTAR Dist-NAMPBC

They Can Be Helped C 22 MIN
16MM FILM, 3/4 OR 1/2 IN VIDEO H-C A
Shows the methods used to help four severely handicapped children at the National Children's Home in England. Studies the children's progress over a period of six months.
LC NO. 81-707639
Prod-NACHH Dist-IFB Prodn-BADDH 1981

They Can Do It B 34 MIN
16MM FILM OPTICAL SOUND T
Visits the classroom of Lovie Glenn with her 26 underprivildged children. Emphasizes the task of teaching the child in such a way as to provide learning and experiences for his education.

The child must not only learn specific subjects, but must be taught how to learn in an educational framework.
LC NO. 75-707939
Prod-EDS Dist-EDC 1968

They Can Do It B 53 MIN
16MM FILM OPTICAL SOUND T
Deals with 26 first graders in the Pastorius Public School in Philadelphia who have never been in school before. Starts with the second day of school, following the class on five visits throughout the year.
From The Early Childhood Education Study Of Education Development Center Series.
LC NO. 75-707939
Prod-EDS Dist-EDC 1969

They Change Their Tune C 20 MIN
2 INCH VIDEOTAPE P
See series title for descriptive statement.
From The Learning Our Language, Unit 2 - Dictionary Skills Series.
Prod-MPATI Dist-GPITVL

They Clear The Way C 29 MIN
16MM FILM OPTICAL SOUND
Describes U S Army engineers whose job it is to build bridges, airfields and roads in Vietnam in order to bring mobility to combat forces.
From The Big Picture Series.
LC NO. 74-706277
Prod-USA Dist-USNAC 1967

They Do Recover C 22 MIN
16MM FILM, 3/4 OR 1/2 IN VIDEO J A
Features Dinah Shore as she discusses the affects of alcohol with Shecky Greene, Doc Severinsen and Ralph Waite.
Prod-SUTHRB Dist-SUTHRB

They Don't Build Them Like They Used To C 22 MIN
16MM FILM OPTICAL SOUND
Juxtaposes the use of building materials and techniques of the 1970's with the work of yesteryear.
LC NO. 77-702669
Prod-HUDAC Dist-INCC 1975

They Go Boom B 21 MIN
16MM FILM OPTICAL SOUND
Tells what happens when Oliver Hardy comes down with a roaring cold and Stan Laurel plays doctor.
Prod-ROACH Dist-BHAWK 1929

They Grow In Silence C 120 MIN
3/4 INCH VIDEO CASSETTE
Focuses on the social and emotional implications of hearing impairment. Presents parents of deaf children talking about their feelings of guilt and helplessness, as well as their special pride in their children's achievements. Features deaf teenagers revealing their own feelings.
Prod-MDCPB Dist-MDCPB

They Hailed A Steamboat Anyplace B 30 MIN
16MM FILM OPTICAL SOUND P-H
Recreates the period from 1840 to 1918 in Oregon's Williamette Valley, when the river was the main route of travel and trade.
Prod-PCCOL Dist-PCCOL 1973

They Hailed A Steamboat Anyplace B 28 MIN
3/4 OR 1/2 INCH VIDEO CASSETTE
Features four oldtimers recalling the days when steamboats went up and down the Willamette River in Oregon. Uses still photography, old documentary footage and period music.
Prod-MEDIPR Dist-MEDIPR 1974

They Harness Nature B 20 MIN
16MM FILM OPTICAL SOUND
Describes the work done by the Drainage and Irrigation Department of Malaysia together with the farmers to create new productive areas.
Prod-FILEM Dist-PMFMUN 1958

They Knew They Were Pilgrims C 12 MIN
16MM FILM OPTICAL SOUND
A documentary narrative, which traces the Pilgrim adventure from its origins in Babworth, England, to the arrival of the Pilgrims at Plymouth in New England
LC NO. 72-701077
Prod-PLIMOT Dist-PLIMOT 1971

They Know What They Want C 8 MIN
16MM FILM OPTICAL SOUND H-C
Encourages sales people to interpret customer requests in terms of available stock. Demonstrates effective techniques for presenting and selling appropriate substitute merchandise.
From The Professional Selling Practices Series 2 Series.
LC NO. 77-702354
Prod-SAUM Dist-SAUM Prodn-CALPRO 1968

They Laid It On The Line C 29 MIN
2 INCH VIDEOTAPE
Presents people who have risked their jobs and reputations to help fight pollution.
From The Turning Points Series.
Prod-WVIZTV Dist-PUBTEL

They Live By Water C 26 MIN
16MM FILM OPTICAL SOUND P-C A
Shows the world of an ordinary pond including the hydra, a multi-armed creature, a tiger that lives under water and a scorpion that looks like a dead twig.
From The Audubon Wildlife Theatre Series.
LC NO. 74-709409
Prod-KEGPL Dist-AVEXP 1969

They Made Me A Criminal B 92 MIN
3/4 INCH VIDEO CASSETTE
Stars John Garfield as a boxing champion who becomes a fugitive on the run.
Prod-UNKNWN Dist-VIDIM 1939

They Made Our Country Great C 20 MIN
2 INCH VIDEOTAPE P-I
See series title for descriptive statement.
From The Learning Our Language, Unit V - Exploring With Books Series.
Prod-MPATI Dist-GPITVL

They Met At The Fair B 17 MIN
16MM FILM OPTICAL SOUND
Views the United Packing House Workers of America picket lines of 1948 when the National Guard troops, company thugs and local police helped herd scabs through the lines. Shows funeral scenes of three workers killed in their efforts to raise their standard of living.
Prod-UPWA Dist-AFLCIO 1948

They Never Told Me C
3/4 OR 1/2 INCH VIDEO CASSETTE IND
Looks at what a union can and cannot do for employees, at potential risks involved in unionization such as loss of access to management, loss of right to bargain individually, negative objects of strikes and increased production costs, loss of income because of union dues and possible loss of jobs.
From The Meeting The Union Challenge Series.
Prod-GPCV Dist-GPCV

They Promised To Take Our Land C 26 MIN
16MM FILM, 3/4 OR 1/2 IN VIDEO
Looks at the exploitation of Indian resources during the 19th and 20th centuries.
From The Native Americans Series.
Prod-BBCTV Dist-CNEMAG

They Served, We Remember And Honor C 20 MIN
16MM FILM OPTICAL SOUND
Shows Memorial Day services at Arlington National Cemetery in 1979, including the placing of wreaths at the Tomb of the Unknowns and at a plaque honoring Vietnam veterans. Shows the ceremony entitled No Greater Love, which was presented by children of servicemen killed, disabled or missing in action during the Vietnamese conflict.
LC NO. 80-700768
Prod-USVA Dist-USNAC 1979

They Shall See C 5 MIN
16MM FILM OPTICAL SOUND J-C A
Presents the wonder of the everyday world around us as seen through the human eye.
LC NO. 73-701881
Prod-FRACOC Dist-FRACOC 1972

They Shouldn't Call Iceland, Iceland C 28 MIN
16MM FILM OPTICAL SOUND
Presents a travelog on Iceland.
LC NO. 77-700423
Prod-ICETB Dist-ICETB Prodn-FILMAU 1976

They Shouldn't Call Iceland, Iceland C 28 MIN
16MM FILM OPTICAL SOUND C A
Provides an introduction to Iceland, including a brief trip to Greenland revealing the eerie and crystal beauty of the iceflows and icebergs, and a visit to the volcanic island of Heimaey.
Prod-WSTGLC Dist-WSTGLC

They Shouldn't Call Iceland, Iceland (Norwegian) C 28 MIN
16MM FILM OPTICAL SOUND
Presents a travelog on Iceland.
LC NO. 77-700423
Prod-ICETB Dist-ICETB Prodn-FILMAU 1976

They Shouldn't Call Iceland, Iceland (French) C 28 MIN
16MM FILM OPTICAL SOUND
Presents a travelog on Iceland.
LC NO. 77-700423
Prod-ICETB Dist-ICETB Prodn-FILMAU 1976

They Shouldn't Call Iceland, Iceland (German) C 28 MIN
16MM FILM OPTICAL SOUND
Presents a travelog on Iceland.
LC NO. 77-700423
Prod-ICETB Dist-ICETB Prodn-FILMAU 1976

They Shouldn't Call Iceland, Iceland (Spanish) C 28 MIN
16MM FILM OPTICAL SOUND
Presents a travelog on Iceland.
LC NO. 77-700423
Prod-ICETB Dist-ICETB Prodn-FILMAU 1976

They Sing Of A Heaven C 16 MIN
16MM FILM OPTICAL SOUND
Documents sacred harp singing, a 200-year-old traditon of religious singing which survives today in the rural South.
LC NO. 72-702179
Prod-UMISS Dist-UMISS 1972

They Steamed To Glory C 22 MIN
16MM FILM, 3/4 OR 1/2 IN VIDEO I-C A
Describes the history of the steam engine in the United States from 1931 to 1960.
Prod-IFB Dist-IFB 1962

They Used To Call 'Em Trailers C 16 MIN
16MM FILM OPTICAL SOUND
Uses on-location interviews to offer varying points of view regarding trailer park living. Attempts to dispel the notion that trailer living is undesirable.
LC NO. 79-701018
Prod-DEANZA Dist-JEFFIL Prodn-JEFFIL 1978

They Went That-A-Way B 26 MIN
16MM FILM OPTICAL SOUND
Explores the Western movie from 'THE GREAT TRAIN ROBBERY' made in the early 1900's to 'HOW THE WEST WAS WON' made in 1963. Includes scenes which feature William S Hart, Tom Mix, John Wayne, Gary Cooper, Roy Rogers and Gene Autry.
LC NO. FI68-309
Prod-WOLPER Dist-WOLPER 1963

They Went That-A-Way And That-A-Way C 106 MIN
16MM FILM OPTICAL SOUND
Tells how two bumbling deputies are planted inside a federal prison to track down stolen government bonds. Stars Tim Conway.
Prod-UNKNWN Dist-TWYMAN 1978

They Were Cars C 11 MIN
16MM FILM, 3/4 OR 1/2 IN VIDEO P-J
Presents a musical tour of an auto wrecking yard which teaches action verb concepts while supplying material for independent observations about obsolescence and reliability.
From The Reading Vocabulary Series.
Prod-KINGSP Dist-PHENIX 1971

They Were First B 10 MIN
16MM FILM OPTICAL SOUND
A 1954 screen news digest excerpt recalls the history of powered flight from the Wright brothers days to super-sonic jets. Shows plane factories of World War I period, mail first flown by air, the Bill Mitchell demonstration of air power, Lindbergh, Amelia Earhart and World War II precision bombing.
From The News Magazine Of The Screen Series. Vol 4, No. 9
Prod-PATHE Dist-HEARST 1954

They Who Serve C 32 MIN
16MM FILM OPTICAL SOUND
Presents impressive displays of Jewish ritual objects, crafted in Europe from the 14th to 19th centuries.
Prod-ADL Dist-ADL

They Will See Flowers B 4 MIN
16MM FILM OPTICAL SOUND
Presents slow-motion sequences from a New York demonstration protesting the treatment of Jews in the USSR combined with still sequences of photographs of Jews who have been trapped behind the Iron Curtain. Points out the determination of brave people who struggle to be free.
Prod-ADL Dist-ADL

They Won't Forget B 94 MIN
16MM FILM OPTICAL SOUND
Explores the murder of a Southern high school girl. Tells how an innocent Northern teacher is accused, unleashing a crazed and vengeful mob determined to see the murderer hang. Stars Lana Turner and Claude Rains. Directed by Mervyn LeRoy.
Prod-UAA Dist-UAE

They Worry About Me C 14 MIN
3/4 OR 1/2 INCH VIDEO CASSETTE J-C A
See series title for descriptive statement.
From The Poetry Alive Series.
Prod-CMSS Dist-AITECH 1978

They're Always Changing Things C 6 MIN
2 INCH VIDEOTAPE
Presents an instructional course for office employees. Offers a case study which identifies and evaluates the ways in which people react to change. Discusses the merits of each type of reaction.
From The SUCCESS, The AMA Course For Office Employees Series.
LC NO. 75-704211
Prod-AMA Dist-AMA 1972

They're Out To Get You C 13 MIN
16MM FILM OPTICAL SOUND
A dramatization about two cellmates, one a professional shoplifter, who form a shoplifting team and plot their future crimes against retail store operators. Designed to motivate small retailers to take preventive measures that will limit shoplifting in their stores.
LC NO. 70-705012
Prod-USSBA Dist-USSBA Prodn-BARTNF 1969

They're Out To Get You C 13 MIN
3/4 INCH VIDEO CASSETTE
Presents a dramatization about two cellmates, one a professional shoplifter, who form a shoplifting team and plot their future crimes against retail store operators. Discusses preventive measures for small retailers that will limit shoplifting in their stores. Issued in 1969 as a motion picture.
LC NO. 80-706682
Prod-USSBA Dist-USNAC Prodn-BARTNF 1980

They're Out To Get You C 14 MIN
3/4 OR 1/2 INCH VIDEO CASSETTE
Portrays a jailed professional shoplifter who is making plans to resume his trade when released. Points out preventive measures store owners should take.
From The Small Business Administration Series.
Prod-IVCH Dist-IVCH

They're Your Kids C 19 MIN
16MM FILM, 3/4 OR 1/2 IN VIDEO
Compares the boredom of students in traditional schools and the enthusiasm of students in participatory education programs. Gives a hopeful view of the possibilities of secondary education.
Prod-UCEMC Dist-UCEMC

They're Your People B 29 MIN
16MM FILM OPTICAL SOUND H-C A
Shows how to aid short-term patients and help local communities develop their own mental health facilities.

From The To Save Tomorrow Series.
Prod-NET Dist-IU 1971

They've Killed President Lincoln C 52 MIN
16MM FILM OPTICAL SOUND I-C A
Uses authentic still pictures to recreate the events and intrigue leading up to the assassination of President Lincoln and the bizarre aftermath. Emphasizes the futility of political assassinations and explains that while a great public leader can be murdered, his ideas often live on to inspire succeeding generations.
LC NO. 79-712185
Prod-QUO Dist-FI 1971

Thicker Than Water B 22 MIN
16MM FILM OPTICAL SOUND
Tells the story of a man who has a bill to pay and makes the mistake of asking a friend to take the money to the store for him. Stars Stan Laurel and Oliver Hardy.
Prod-ROACH Dist-TWYMAN 1935

Thief And The Hangman, The B 30 MIN
16MM FILM OPTICAL SOUND
Explores the question, 'WHO MAY ADMINISTER JUSTICE' in the style of a morality fable. Deals with the time of moral man in an immoral society and shows that all men sin.
LC NO. FIA64-1138
Prod-JTS Dist-NAAJS Prodn-NBC 1953

Thief In The Night (SIDS) C 25 MIN
3/4 OR 1/2 INCH VIDEO CASSETTE
Profiles four families who have lost their children to Sudden Infant Death Syndrom (SIDS). Shows how to deal with the guilt, fear and ignorance.
Prod-TRAINX Dist-TRAINX

Thief In The Soil C 10 MIN
16MM FILM OPTICAL SOUND
Explains the danger of underground soil destruction and suggests fumigation as a solution to the problem.
Prod-DCC Dist-DCC

Thief Of Bagdad B 27 MIN
16MM FILM OPTICAL SOUND H-C
Presents 'THIEF OF BAGDAD,' showing Douglas Fairbanks as he battles monsters and mongol hordes led by a renegade who has designs on a princess.
From The History Of The Motion Picture Series.
Prod-SF Dist-KILLIS 1960

Thief Of Bagdad, The B 140 MIN
16MM FILM SILENT
Presents an Arabian night fantasy about Ahmed, a notorious thief who reforms when he falls in love with the Princess. Recounts that in order to prove himself worthy, he has to undergo a series of adventures. Stars Douglas Fairbanks, Sr. Directed by Raoul Walsh.
Prod-UNKNWN Dist-KILLIS 1924

Thief Tax, The C 20 MIN
3/4 OR 1/2 INCH VIDEO CASSETTE IND
Points out that the theft of tools, equipment and crude oil costs everybody money - the company, the consumer and the employee. Shows how field operators and supervisors can help prevent this costly problem.
Prod-TEXACO Dist-UTEXPE

Thigh And Gluteal Region - Unit 23 C 27 MIN
3/4 OR 1/2 INCH VIDEO CASSETTE PRO
Discusses the anterior aspect of the thigh, including the anterior and medial compartments and their innervation and vascular supply, the gluteal region and the posterior compartment of the thigh.
From The Gross Anatomy Prosection Demonstration Series.
Prod-HSCIC Dist-HSCIC

Thighs And Whispers - A Look At Lingerie C 45 MIN
1/2 IN VIDEO CASSETTE (VHS)
Looks at the lingerie women have chosen from the 1880s to modern days.
Prod-KARLVI Dist-KARLVI

Thin Dime, A C 10 MIN
16MM FILM SILENT C
Presents a surrealistic study of a beautiful woman with an artificial leg.
Prod-PIKE Dist-CFS

Thin Edge Of The Bay C 22 MIN
16MM FILM, 3/4 OR 1/2 IN VIDEO
Uses San Francisco Bay as a focus to study the economic and political conflicts over shrinking environmental resources in urban areas. Highlights the complex factors involved in all environmental and land-use decision-making.
Prod-LANDYR Dist-UCEMC 1980

Thin Edge—A Series
16MM FILM, 3/4 OR 1/2 IN VIDEO H-C A
Prod-EDUCBC Dist-IU

Aggression - The Explosive Emotion 59 MIN
Anxiety - The Endless Crisis 59 MIN
Depression - The Shadowed Valley 59 MIN
Guilt - The Psychic Censor 59 MIN
Sexuality - The Human Heritage 59 MIN

Thin Edge—A Series

Discusses the principal troubles that cause or lead to less-than-satisfactory and normal mental health. Includes, in the five-part series, depression, aggression, guilt, anxiety and sexuality.
Prod-TRAINX Dist-TRAINX

Aggression - The Explosive Emotion 060 MIN
Anxiety - The Endless Crisis 060 MIN
Depression - The Shadowed Valley 060 MIN
Guilt - The Psychic Censor 060 MIN
Sexuality - The Human Heritage 060 MIN

Thin Hyper Shell, The C 27 MIN
16MM FILM OPTICAL SOUND
Describes the erection of a hyperbolic paraboloid roof at Purdue University under an advanced concept of construction.
Prod-DCC Dist-DCC

Thin Layer Chromatography C 10 MIN
3/4 OR 1/2 INCH VIDEO CASSETTE C A
Shows how to separate a mixture of strongly colored dyes by using a silica gel TLC plate and a widemouthed bottle as a developing chamber.
From The Chemistry - Master/Apprentice Series. Program 203
LC NO. 82-706054
Prod-CUETV Dist-CUNIV 1981

Thin Layer Chromatography C 13 MIN
3/4 OR 1/2 INCH VIDEO CASSETTE
Emphasizes the similarities in the principles of thin layer and column chromatography. Considers choosing a stationary phase and solvent.
From The Organic Chemistry Laboratory Techniques Series.
Prod-UCLA Dist-UCEMC

Thin Red Line, The B 99 MIN
16MM FILM OPTICAL SOUND C A
Tells of a soldier on Guadalcanal who constantly and compulsively risks his life in combat to smother his fear of becoming a coward and of his ironic friendship with a sergeant who masks his every human feeling with a cold, impersonal attitude.
Prod-CINEWO Dist-CINEWO 1964

Thin-Shelled Concrete Roofs C 7 MIN
3/4 OR 1/2 INCH VIDEO CASSETTE
Develops the concept of Gauss-Curvature as a basis for the classification of thin shells into developable, synclastic and anticlastic surfaces.
Prod-UAZMIC Dist-UAZMIC

Things A Teacher Sees, The C 19 MIN
16MM FILM, 3/4 OR 1/2 IN VIDEO C T
Stresses the value of teacher observation for detecting physical and emotional health problems of pupils.
Prod-UOKLA Dist-IFB 1964

Things Are Different Now C 15 MIN
16MM FILM, 3/4 OR 1/2 IN VIDEO
Focuses on a Black 12-year-old boy and his perception of the recent divorce of his parents.
From The Reflections Series.
LC NO. 79-706605
Prod-PAULST Dist-MEDIAG 1978

Things Aren't What They Used To Be C 12 MIN
16MM FILM OPTICAL SOUND
Pictures the problems of the elderly pedestrian and follows some elderly pedestrians as they try to handle today's traffic complexities. Explains rules for safe walking.
Prod-AAAFTS Dist-AAAFTS 1975

Things Begin To Change On Planet Purple C 28 MIN
16MM FILM, 3/4 OR 1/2 IN VIDEO K-P
Presents Mr Rogers talking and singing about new things and new ideas being exciting. Tells how Purple Panda stays in the neighborhood while Paul and Paula return and introduce changes to make everyone different. Reveals that the planet is renamed Planet Purple Fairchilde in honor of Lady Elaine.
From The Purple Adventures Of Lady Elaine Fairchilde Series. Program 5
LC NO. 80-706562
Prod-FAMCOM Dist-HUBDSC 1979

Things Change - Solids, Liquids, Gases X 10 MIN
16MM FILM, 3/4 OR 1/2 IN VIDEO P
Explains how to identify solids, liquids and gases, and shows how matter can change from one state to another in different environments and temperatures.
Prod-EBEC Dist-EBEC 1969

Things In Motion C 15 MIN
3/4 OR 1/2 INCH VIDEO CASSETTE I
Shows that we increase our use of fuels as we explore space.
From The L-Four Series.
Prod-CTI Dist-CTI

Things Of Beauty C 29 MIN
3/4 INCH VIDEO CASSETTE
Explores why artists paint still lifes and how viewers react to them.
From The Creation Of Art Series.
Prod-UMITV Dist-UMITV 1975

Things Of Value C 14 MIN
2 INCH VIDEOTAPE
Gives background information about old bottles, depression glass, barbed wire, fruit jars and wire insulators. Explains that by knowing what objects are in demand by collectors, the home viewer can gain satisfaction from owning them, or he can get fair prices by selling them.
From The Living Better II Series.
Prod-MAETEL Dist-PUBTEL

Things That Go Bump - In Your G I Tract C 29 MIN
3/4 OR 1/2 INCH VIDEO CASSETTE
Examines the digestive system and efforts to treat and prevent ulcers.
From The Here's To Your Health Series.
Prod-KERA Dist-PBS

Things That Go Wrong In The Night C
1/2 IN VIDEO CASSETTE (VHS)
Examines causes and treatments of sleep disorders. Explores circadian sleep rhythms and dramatizes an experiment of a researcher's months in a dark cave.
From The Theater Of The Night - The Science Of Sleep And Dreams Series.
Prod-IBIS Dist-IBIS

Things To Come C 3 MIN
16MM FILM OPTICAL SOUND I-C A
Presents an abstract film exercise.
Prod-CFS Dist-CFS 1954

Things To Come C 26 MIN
16MM FILM, 3/4 OR 1/2 IN VIDEO J-C A
Looks at computer technology and its effects on society, focusing on agriculture and information processing.
From The Computer Programme Series. Episode 10
LC NO. 82-707088
Prod-BBCTV Dist-FI 1982

Things To Do C 14 MIN
3/4 OR 1/2 INCH VIDEO CASSETTE P
Introduces high and low tones and distinguishes them from low and soft sounds.
From The Stepping Into Rhythm Series.
Prod-WVIZTV Dist-AITECH

Things To Do When You Visit The Zoo C 15 MIN
16MM FILM, 3/4 OR 1/2 IN VIDEO K-I
Follows a group of children on a visit to the zoo in order to explain concepts about the animal world and to examine some of its individual members, including the elephant, the giraffe, the lion, the monkey and the snake. Stresses rules of conduct and safety and explains reasons for maintaining a zoo.
Prod-JOU Dist-JOU 1967

Things To Use C 20 MIN
16MM FILM, 3/4 OR 1/2 IN VIDEO
Focuses on manufactured objects used for daily tasks in homes, offices and industry. Examines the qualities of form in these objects in relation to their functions and the preferences of their users.
From The Images And Things Series.
LC NO. 73-702115
Prod-NITC Dist-AITECH

Things Worth Keeping C 30 MIN
16MM FILM - 3/4 IN VIDEO J-C A
Indicates Europe's, Asia's and America's special problems and solutions to the questions of who is to decide what is worth saving, how those objects will be used and finally what the link is between preservation of heritage and the physical and spiritual environment.
From The Man Builds - Man Destroys Series.
Prod-UN Dist-GPITVL

Things Worth Saving C 14 MIN
16MM FILM OPTICAL SOUND
Explores the potential of large-scale resource recovery from America's growing volume of municipal solid waste, trash and garbage. Shows that future systems will separate valuable resources for recycling and use as fuel for heat and electrical systems.
Prod-FINLYS Dist-FINLYS 1972

Things You Should Know About Your Financial Institution C 25 MIN
3/4 OR 1/2 INCH VIDEO CASSETTE
Discusses money market, super now accounts and what deregulation means to the average customer.
From The Your Money Matters Series.
Prod-FILMID Dist-FILMID

Things, Ideas, People C 15 MIN
16MM FILM, 3/4 OR 1/2 IN VIDEO I
Shows the broad number of work options open to students and the similarities and differences among work roles.
From The Bread And Butterflies Series.
LC NO. 74-703186
Prod-AITV Dist-AITECH Prodn-WNVT 1973

Think C 6 MIN
16MM FILM OPTICAL SOUND
Discusses the problems of pollution and ecology.
LC NO. 75-704345
Prod-CONCOL Dist-CONCOL 1974

Think About Your Back C
16MM FILM - 3/4 IN VIDEO A
Alerts workers to the painful reality of back injuries and demonstrates how they can protect themselves against such injuries.
Prod-BNA Dist-BNA 1983

Think Ahead C 15 MIN
3/4 OR 1/2 INCH VIDEO CASSETTE P
Describes Molly's anger when she is told by her brother that she is too young to go with them to the hobby shop. Explains that when she storms into the library, Sam helps her think of the possible consequences of the revenge she's planning and she decides on another approach with good results.
From The Out And About Series.
Prod-STSU Dist-AITECH Prodn-WETN 1984

Think Fine - Feel Fine—A Series
P
Prod-KTCATV Dist-GPITVL

Bottles, Jars, Tubes And Boxes 15 MIN
Happy Package, The 15 MIN
Piece That Wouldn't Fit 15 MIN
Sad Balloon, The 15 MIN
That Yuckle Feeling 15 MIN

What Goes Aaaaakkkkk 15 MIN

Think Food C 20 MIN
16MM FILM OPTICAL SOUND H
Shows young people being trained for jobs in the retail food industry.
From The Career Guidance Series.
Prod-KRMATV Dist-GPITVL

Think Like A Mountain C 28 MIN
16MM FILM - 3/4 IN VIDEO
Deals with rare and endangered species of wildlife and the U S Forest Service's concern with protecting them. Interviews mountain men, cowboys, wolf trappers and a hermit on the desert who recall the changes they have witnessed in the land and its wildlife.
Prod-USDA Dist-USNAC 1972

Think Metric C 10 MIN
16MM FILM OPTICAL SOUND I
Uses animated characters to demonstrate metric measurement of length, liquid volume and mass.
LC NO. 75-701532
Prod-FFORIN Dist-FFORIN 1974

Think Metric (2nd Ed) C 14 MIN
16MM FILM, 3/4 OR 1/2 IN VIDEO I-J
The second edition of The Metric System. Demonstrates measuring and weighing with metric units. Features televised coverage of The Metric Games to introduce the metric system.
From The Let's Measure Series.
Prod-CORF Dist-CORF

Think Metric–A Series
16MM FILM, 3/4 OR 1/2 IN VIDEO P-I
Introduces the concept of measuring with metric units.
Prod-BARR Dist-BARR

Measure Length - Think Metric 009 MIN
Measure Volume - Think Metric 009 MIN
Measure Weight - Think Metric 009 MIN

Think Nutrition - Consuming Interest C 26 MIN
16MM FILM OPTICAL SOUND
Takes a tour of a typical U S supermarket and suggests how to get the best food buys.
Prod-LOMA Dist-LOMA

Think Nutrition - Eating Without Meat C 26 MIN
16MM FILM OPTICAL SOUND
Discusses the advantages of a vegetarian diet.
Prod-LOMA Dist-LOMA

Think Nutrition - Meals Without Meat C 26 MIN
16MM FILM OPTICAL SOUND
Tells why a vegetarian diet is preferable to a meat diet. Offers a history of vegetarian diet at Loma Linda Medical Center. Outlines the four basic food groups and shows how the vegetarian diet can be a balanced diet.
Prod-LOMA Dist-LOMA

Think Nutrition - Overweight C 25 MIN
16MM FILM OPTICAL SOUND
Explores the basic causes of overweight, emphasizing the need for balanced diet and plenty of exercise. Compares the caloric levels of various foods and discusses different types of exercise.
Prod-LOMA Dist-LOMA

Think Nutrition - Vitamins C 22 MIN
16MM FILM OPTICAL SOUND
Discusses the use of vitamins, pointing out that taking excessive vitamin supplements can be harmful. Shows how a balanced vitamin intake can be derived from a balanced diet.
Prod-LOMA Dist-LOMA

Think Positive C 20 MIN
16MM FILM, 3/4 OR 1/2 IN VIDEO A
Discusses the importance of attitude to a successful career in selling.
Prod-SANDYC Dist-RTBL

Think Tall (Captioned) C 10 MIN
16MM FILM, 3/4 OR 1/2 IN VIDEO P
A revised edition of the 1957 film Beginning Good Posture Habits. Shows the results of standing, walking and sitting tall. Views several people and observes different walking postures. Teaches posture exercises.
Prod-CORF Dist-CORF 1975

Think Tall - Sell Up To Quality C 8 MIN
16MM FILM OPTICAL SOUND H-C
Encourages a positive, professional point of view in selecting and presenting quality merchandise. Shows how to trade through emphasis on quality instead of price.
From The Professional Selling Practices Series 2 Series.
LC NO. 77-702357
Prod-SAUM Dist-SAUM Prodn-CALPRO 1968

Think Tanks - Prophets Of The Future C 20 MIN
16MM FILM, 3/4 OR 1/2 IN VIDEO
Looks at the work of the Hudson Institute of New York, a think tank which evaluates the prospects of mankind, advises major corporations and government agencies, and seeks out solutions for energy problems and poverty.
Prod-DOCUA Dist-CNEMAG

Think Twice - The Persuasion Game C 19 MIN
16MM FILM, 3/4 OR 1/2 IN VIDEO J-C
Presents vignettes which dramatize ways in which the power of persuasion is used to influence the public.
Prod-CF Dist-CF 1978

Think Twice - They're Confusing You C 19 MIN
16MM FILM, 3/4 OR 1/2 IN VIDEO J-C
Illustrates kinds of faulty or misleading information, such as oversimplification, distortion of facts and logical fallacies.
Prod-CF Dist-CF 1978

Think Win C 30 MIN
16MM FILM, 3/4 OR 1/2 IN VIDEO PRO
Features star football player and salesman, George Blanda, relates his philosophy and personal experiences in football and sales to inspire the sales training and motivation of others.
Prod-TAKTEN Dist-DARTNL 1971

Thinkabout–A Series
I
Emphasizes the importance of reasoning skills.
Prod-PRODRS Dist-AITECH 1980

Approximating 015 MIN
Bigger Picture, The 015 MIN
Blockbusting 015 MIN
Brainstorming 015 MIN
But, What Does It Mean 015 MIN
Calm Your Jitters 015 MIN
Checking Conclusions 015 MIN
Classifying Information 015 MIN
Classifying Objects 015 MIN
Communication Patterns 015 MIN
Cultural Patterns 015 MIN
Design A Language 015 MIN
Drawing Conclusions 015 MIN
Estimating 015 MIN
Find Your Guide 015 MIN
Get Ahead With Goals 015 MIN
Hanging In There 015 MIN
How Do You Change Them 015 MIN
Make A Deal With Yourself 015 MIN
Make A Present For The Future 015 MIN
Make Something New 015 MIN
Making A Presentation 015 MIN
Making It Come Alive 015 MIN
Making Your Point 015 MIN
Maps And Models 015 MIN
Matter Of Time, A 015 MIN
Meaning Is More Than Words 015 MIN
More Than You Think 015 MIN
Nature's Patterns 015 MIN
One Step At A Time 015 MIN
One Thing Leads To Another 015 MIN
People Patterns 015 MIN
Persuasive Techniques 015 MIN
Plan A City Of The Future 015 MIN
Plan Ahead 015 MIN
Planning A Presentation 015 MIN
Point Of View 015 MIN
Practice For Success 015 MIN
Remember The Audience 015 MIN
Search For The Unknown 015 MIN
Should I Believe It 015 MIN
Stereotyping People 015 MIN
Styles Of Communication 015 MIN
Summarizing 015 MIN
Symbols 015 MIN
There Are Many Ways To Go 015 MIN
There Are Ways To Remember 015 MIN
There's Always A Risk 015 MIN
Using Estimating And Approximating 015 MIN
What Are They 015 MIN
What Do I Know 015 MIN
What Should I Do 015 MIN
What's Enough 015 MIN
What's Important 015 MIN
What's The Meaning 015 MIN
Where Are You Coming From 015 MIN
Where Do You Find Them 015 MIN
Where Should I Go 015 MIN
Why Bother 015 MIN
You Can Remember 015 MIN

Thinkabout–A Series
I
Focuses on 13 general thinking skills and demonstrates problem-solving techniques.
Prod-AITV Dist-AITECH 1979

Approximating 015 MIN
Bigger Picture, The 015 MIN
Blockbusting 015 MIN
Brainstorming 015 MIN
But, What Does It Mean 015 MIN
Calm Your Jitters 015 MIN
Checking Conclusions 015 MIN
Classifying Information 015 MIN
Classifying Objects 015 MIN
Communication Patterns 015 MIN
Cultural Patterns 015 MIN
Design A Language 015 MIN
Drawing Conclusions 014 MIN
Estimating 015 MIN
Find Your Guide 015 MIN
Get Ahead With Goals 015 MIN
Hanging In There 015 MIN
How Do You Change Them 015 MIN
Make A Deal With Yourself 015 MIN
Make A Present For The Future 015 MIN
Make Something New 014 MIN
Making A Presentation 015 MIN
Making It Come Alive 015 MIN
Making Your Point 016 MIN
Maps And Models 015 MIN
Matter Of Time, A 015 MIN
Meaning Is More Than Words 014 MIN
More Than You Think 015 MIN
Nature's Patterns 015 MIN
One Step At A Time 015 MIN
One Thing Leads To Another 014 MIN
People Patterns 015 MIN
Persuasive Techniques 014 MIN
Plan A City Of The Future 015 MIN
Plan Ahead 014 MIN
Planning A Presentation 015 MIN
Point Of View 015 MIN
Practice For Success 014 MIN
Remember The Audience 014 MIN
Search For The Unknown 015 MIN
Should I Believe It 015 MIN
Stereotyping People 014 MIN
Styles Of Communication 015 MIN
Summarizing 015 MIN
Symbols 014 MIN
There Are Many Ways To Go 015 MIN
There Are Ways To Remember 014 MIN
There's Always A Risk 015 MIN
Using Estimating And Approximating 015 MIN
Ways To Remember 015 MIN
What Are They 014 MIN
What Do I Know 015 MIN
What Should I Do 015 MIN
What's Enough 015 MIN
What's Important 015 MIN
What's The Meaning 014 MIN
Where Are You Coming From 014 MIN
Where Did You Find Them 015 MIN
Where Should I Go 015 MIN
Why Bother 015 MIN

Thinking About Drinking (2nd Ed) C 17 MIN
16MM FILM, 3/4 OR 1/2 IN VIDEO J
Presents basic information about alcoholic beverages and the effects of alcohol on the human nervous system and behavior. Provides scientific findings on the dangers of mixing alcohol and drugs and the effects of alcohol on the human fetus.
Prod-HIGGIN Dist-HIGGIN 1981

Thinking About Hands - Laboratory C 12 MIN
16MM FILM, 3/4 OR 1/2 IN VIDEO
Illustrates how normally safe tasks in the laboratory can become hazardous because of inattention to routine, poor position, improper tools, lack of protective equipment or failure to follow procedure. Analyzes incidents according to primary cause and other contributing factors.
Prod-OLINC Dist-MTI

Thinking About Hands - Manufacturing C 12 MIN
16MM FILM, 3/4 OR 1/2 IN VIDEO
Illustrates how normally safe tasks in manufacturing can become hazardous because of inattention to routine, poor position, improper tools, lack of protective equipment or failure to follow procedure. Analyzes incidents according to primary cause and other contributing factors.
Prod-OLINC Dist-MTI

Thinking About Rocks C 15 MIN
3/4 OR 1/2 INCH VIDEO CASSETTE I
Looks at the way rocks are broken down by the forces of nature.
From The Matter And Motion Series. Module Red
Prod-WHROTV Dist-AITECH 1973

Thinking Ahead C 30 MIN
3/4 INCH VIDEO CASSETTE
See series title for descriptive statement.
From The Ounce Of Prevention Series.
Prod-CFDC Dist-CFDC

Thinking And Reasoning In Preschool Children B 23 MIN
3/4 OR 1/2 INCH VIDEO CASSETTE PRO
Takes an overview of important concepts and reasoning abilities that children develop during the 'preoperational' period. Shows how preschool children's understanding of the world affects their behavior and problem-solving methods.
Prod-HSERF Dist-HSERF

Thinking Big B 15 MIN
2 INCH VIDEOTAPE P
See series title for descriptive statement.
From The Children's Literature Series. No. 14
Prod-NCET Dist-GPITVL Prodn-KUONTV

Thinking In Action–A Series
16MM FILM, 3/4 OR 1/2 IN VIDEO A
Shows how to improve productive thinking in a business environment. Features Dr Edward DeBono.
Prod-BBCTV Dist-FI 1983

Action, Planning And Implementation 013 MIN
Creativity, Design And Innovation 013 MIN
Decision, Choice And Evaluation 013 MIN
Improvement, Review And Productivity 013 MIN
People, Communication And Negotiation 013 MIN
Problems, Crises And Opportunities 013 MIN

Thinking In Sets C 11 MIN
16MM FILM OPTICAL SOUND I-H
Shows how to think in sets and explains their relation. Introduces the idea of things being naturally grouped together by their likenesses or their position. Instills a feeling for the relations between groups of numbers, such as 3, 6, 15, 33 and 87 belonging together as a result of their divisibility by 3. Describes the relations between geometric figures, such as line segments.
From The Pathways To Modern Math Series.
LC NO. FIA64-1445
Prod-GE Dist-GE

Thinking In The Future Tense C 28 MIN
3/4 OR 1/2 INCH VIDEO CASSETTE A
Centers around an ecumenical conference with futurist Dr Edward Lindaman who examines the shape of things to come. Includes genetic engineering, communication technology, sharing of natural resources and pollution. Intended to stimu-

late discussion of how our Christian belief can and should affect our response to the future.
Prod-DCCMS Dist-ECUFLM 1981

Thinking It Through C 23 MIN
16MM FILM, 3/4 OR 1/2 IN VIDEO C A
Presents a checklist for management problem solving, including identifying the problem, gathering facts, identifying alternatives, evaluating and selecting alternatives, implementing the decision and evaluating the decision.
Prod-PILSBY Dist-RTBL 1978

Thinking It Through (Dutch) C 23 MIN
16MM FILM, 3/4 OR 1/2 IN VIDEO C A
Presents a checklist for management problem solving, including identifying the problem, gathering facts, identifying alternatives, evaluating and selecting alternatives, implementing the decision and evaluating the decision.
Prod-PILSBY Dist-RTBL 1978

Thinking It Through (Swedish) C 23 MIN
16MM FILM, 3/4 OR 1/2 IN VIDEO C A
Presents a checklist for management problem solving, including identifying the problem, gathering facts, identifying alternatives, evaluating and selecting alternatives, implementing the decision and evaluating the decision.
Prod-PILSBY Dist-RTBL 1978

Thinking Machine, The C 25 MIN
16MM FILM, 3/4 OR 1/2 IN VIDEO J-C A
Reveals how computers are almost taught to think so that they can perform tasks ranging from playing games to performing medical diagnosis.
From The Computer Programme Series. Episode 8
Prod-BBCTV Dist-FI 1982

Thinking Made Visible C 70 MIN
16MM FILM OPTICAL SOUND
Presents two lectures by Dr George D Linton, who explains the importance of proper writing in communicating to others.
From The What Is Good Writing Series.
LC NO. 76-702720
Prod-USFAA Dist-USNAC Prodn-NAVALP 1964

Thinking Of Others C 4 MIN
16MM FILM, 3/4 OR 1/2 IN VIDEO K-I
Portrays Nancy's feelings, as she realizes that being selfish is no fun since you end up being alone.
From The Most Important Person - Getting Along With Others Series.
Prod-EBEC Dist-EBEC 1972

Thinking Skills - Introduction To Critical Thinking C 68 MIN
1/2 IN VIDEO CASSETTE (VHS) J-C A
Presents thinking as a skill which can be improved. Illustrates successful learning techniques, distinguishes inductive from deductive reasoning, and tells how to improve insight and imagination.
LC NO. 85-703
Prod-HRMC Dist-HRMC

Thinking The Clearing As A Step To A New Beginning C 120 MIN
3/4 OR 1/2 INCH VIDEO CASSETTE A
See series title for descriptive statement.
From The Beyond Philosophy - The Thought Of Martin Heidegger Series. Program 12
Prod-UCEMC Dist-UCEMC

Thinking Through Safety - The Job Safety And Health Analysis C
16MM FILM - 3/4 IN VIDEO A
Illustrates how to gather information, write job safety and health analyses and set up procedures to perform jobs safely.
Prod-BNA Dist-BNA 1983

Thinking Twice C 30 MIN
16MM FILM OPTICAL SOUND
Shows an American family coming to grips with the arms race and nuclear war. Views the past, present and future consequences of nuclear war.
Prod-SKYE Dist-SKYE 1981

Thinking, Writing And Reading C 29 MIN
16MM FILM, 3/4 OR 1/2 IN VIDEO T
Examines the total-language approach to learning, emphasizing the thinking-writing-reading continuum.
From The Teaching Children To Read Series.
Prod-MFFD Dist-FI 1975

Thinner Usage By Temperature Range C 10 MIN
1/2 IN VIDEO CASSETTE BETA/VHS
Deals with auto body repair. Gives the usual temperature breaks for thinness, using Dupont and Ditzler thinners as examples.
Prod-RMI Dist-RMI

Thinnest Slice, The B 21 MIN
16MM FILM OPTICAL SOUND
Tissue is sliced to 1/500,000th of an inch on a microtome by Dr Daniel Pease in a technique which he and Dr Richard Baker developed in the U S C laboratories.
LC NO. FIA52-176
Prod-USC Dist-USC 1949

Third - Teaching Basic Mathematics Skills—A Series

Presents six educators and their views on the teaching of mathematics.
Prod-EDCPUB Dist-EDCPUB

Carol Dodd Thornton
Frank K Lester
Phares O'Daffer
Ross Taylor
Shirley A Hill
Zalman P Usiskin

Third Attribute, The B 30 MIN
16MM FILM OPTICAL SOUND
Relates the story of an arrogant young scholar who becomes embittered after a crippling illness. Tells how the target of his bitterness is his servant, who tries to teach him justice, mercy and humility.
Prod-JTS Dist-NAAJS Prodn-NBCTV 1953

Third Avenue C 60 MIN
3/4 INCH VIDEO CASSETTE A
Presents a look at the seamy side of urban life by focusing on six people who live or work along New York's Third Avenue.
LC NO. 80-706227
Prod-DCTVC Dist-DCTVC 1979

Third Avenue El C 11 MIN
16MM FILM, 3/4 OR 1/2 IN VIDEO J-C
Presents a study of New York's now departed railway, the Third Avenue El, coordinated with the music of Haydn and the artistry of the late Wanda Landowska on the harpsichord. Depicts a poetic and nostalgic train ride through old New York.
Prod-DAVC Dist-AIMS 1957

Third Coast, The C 55 MIN
16MM FILM OPTICAL SOUND
Examines life in Houston, Texas, as rapid growth, booming economy, the oil industry, and the Bible Belt meet the western frontier in the 1980's.
From The World Exchange Series.
LC NO. 81-700502
Prod-VIDVER Dist-DIRECT 1981

Third Cod War, The C 17 MIN
3/4 OR 1/2 INCH VIDEO CASSETTE H-C A
Describes a dispute between the United Kingdom and Iceland which centered on the extent of territorial waters and fishing rights.
Prod-UPI Dist-JOU

Third Dimension, The C 25 MIN
2 INCH VIDEOTAPE I
Shows sculpture in wood, soap and salvage.
From The Art For Every Day Series.
Prod-CVETVC Dist-GPITVL

Third Front, The B 50 MIN
16MM FILM OPTICAL SOUND
Presents the British Broadcasting Corporation's Centenary Year salute to the Red Cross. Includes footage from national societies and film made at the Secretariat of the League and the International Committee of the Red Cross.
Prod-BBCTV Dist-AMRC 1963

Third Generation, The (German) C 111 MIN
16MM FILM OPTICAL SOUND
Follows a band of German urban guerrillas, created by a computer tycoon who knows that terrorism sells surveillance devices. Directed by Rainer Werner Fassbinder. With English subtitles.
Prod-UNKNWN Dist-NYFLMS 1979

Third Grade Science B 11 MIN
16MM FILM OPTICAL SOUND C T
Discusses various uses of programmed instruction in teaching third grade science.
From The Programmed Instruction - The Teacher's Role Series.
LC NO. 74-705776
Prod-USOE Dist-USNAC 1966

Third Grade Science (Spanish) B 11 MIN
16MM FILM OPTICAL SOUND
Stimulates teacher discussion of the various uses of programmed instruction in teaching third grade science.
From The Programmed Instruction - The Teachers Role (Spanish) Series.
LC NO. 74-705777
Prod-USOE Dist-USNAC 1966

Third Grade Science (Spanish) B 11 MIN
16MM FILM - 3/4 IN VIDEO T
Discusses various uses of programmed instruction in teaching third grade science. Issued in 1966 as a motion picture.
From The Programmed Instruction - The Teacher's Role (Spanish) Series.
LC NO. 79-707565
Prod-USOE Dist-USNAC 1979

Third Lantern For The Third Century, The C 28 MIN
16MM FILM OPTICAL SOUND
Shows the April 1975 ceremony in the Old North Church in Boston commemorating the 200th anniversary of Paul Revere's ride. Includes an address by President Ford.
LC NO. 75-704437
Prod-USARBA Dist-USNAC Prodn-WBZTV 1975

Third Millenium, The C 95 MIN
16MM FILM, 3/4 OR 1/2 IN VIDEO
Examines the people, the ecology and the fate of the Amazon basin. Chronicles Senator Evandro Carreira's political campaign tour by boat through a remote jungle between Brazil, Columbia and Peru where he meets with his constituency, the Indian population of the region.
Prod-STOPFM Dist-CNEMAG

Third Pollution, The C 23 MIN
16MM FILM OPTICAL SOUND I-C A
Portrays America's solid waste problem and its relation to air pollution and water contamination. Outlines alternatives for community action, including procedures for obtaining federal or state assistance.
LC NO. FIA67-652
Prod-FINLYS Dist-FINLYS 1966

Third R - Teaching Basic Mathematics Skills—A Series
T
Presents practical, classroom-tested ideas for teaching strategies related to major skill areas in mathematics.
Prod-EPCO Dist-EDCORP

Calculators And Computers In The School Math
Developing Computational Skills
Geometry And Measurement In A Balanced Math
Overview Of School Mathematics In The 80's, An
Problem-Solving 1 - The Basic Skill
Using Math In Everyday Situations

Third Tape C 5 MIN
3/4 OR 1/2 INCH VIDEO CASSETTE
Shows a man trying to abstract himself using age old methods reminiscent of German expressionism, cubism and surrealism.
From The Four Short Tapes Series.
Prod-EAI Dist-EAI

Third Team On The Field, The - Umpiring Baseball C 17 MIN
16MM FILM, 3/4 OR 1/2 IN VIDEO H-C A
Explains the individual responsibilities of the plate and base umpire, with special emphasis on the two-person system. Shows how the two umpires can get into postion to make the right call anywhere.
Prod-NCAA Dist-ATHI 1982

Third Temple, The C 17 MIN
16MM FILM OPTICAL SOUND
Portrays modern Israel marching forward in the wake of the persecuted wandering Jew.
Prod-ALDEN Dist-ALDEN

Third Testament—A Series
16MM FILM, 3/4 OR 1/2 IN VIDEO
Prod-NIELSE Dist-TIMLIF 1974

Blaise Pascal	057 MIN
Dietrich Bonhoeffer	057 MIN
Leo Tolstoy	057 MIN
Saint Augustine	057 MIN
Soren Kierkegaard	057 MIN
William Blake	057 MIN

Third Times Luck, Dan Spock C 20 MIN
16MM FILM OPTICAL SOUND I-C A
See series title for descriptive statement.
From The Cellar Door Cine Mites Series.
LC NO. 74-701552
Prod-CELLAR Dist-CELLAR 1972

Third Trimester, The C 29 MIN
3/4 OR 1/2 INCH VIDEO CASSETTE H-C A
Shows how the fetus grows during the third trimester of pregnancy and how the parents prepare for the birth, often in childbirth classes.
From The Tomorrow's Families Series.
LC NO. 81-706901
Prod-MSDOE Dist-AITECH 1980

Third Wave—A Series

Takes you into the fantastic civilization of tomorrow that is bursting into life today. Presents the problems and challenges of moving toward a third-wave society, and includes an interview with Alvin Toffler at the end of each program, in which he discusses the changes corporate management can expect and the steps to be taken as the world moves from a second-wave industrial society to a third-wave society. Adapted from the PBS special and based on Alvin Toffler's book, The Third Wave.
Prod-TRIWVE Dist-DELTAK

Changing Business Environment, The	030 MIN
Management Faces The Waves Of Change	030 MIN
Managing The Transition	030 MIN
New Age Of Diversity, The	030 MIN
Tomorrow's Tools	030 MIN

Third Wind C 15 MIN
3/4 OR 1/2 INCH VIDEO CASSETTE H A
Shows a disappointed high school athlete looking for an alternative, an old widow proving herself capable of practical tasks and a teenager facing the loss of his longtime girlfriend.
From The Old Enough To Care Series.
Prod-ETVCON Dist-AITECH

Third World And The U S National Interest, The B 27 MIN
16MM FILM OPTICAL SOUND
Roger G Mastrude interviews Frank M Coffin, who explores in depth and detail the political and philosophical justifications for United States economic assistance to the 'THIRD WORLD.'
LC NO. FIE65-22
Prod-USAID Dist-USNAC 1964

Third World Dance - Beyond The White Stream—A Series

Presents programs from the New York City Cable TV series Eye On Dance. Discusses black and other ethnic dance forms.
Prod-ARCVID Dist-ARCVID

Defining Black Dance	030 MIN
Ethnic Dance And How Those Of Other Cultures	030 MIN
Historical Perspectives On Black Dancers In	030 MIN
Toward A Broader Understanding Of Ethnic Dance	030 MIN

Third World Dance - Tracing Roots—A Series

Presents programs from the New York City Cable TV series Eye On Dance. Discusses ethnic dance, its performers, origins and infuence.
Prod-ARCVID Dist-ARCVID

Black Ballet In America 030 MIN
Legendary Women In Dance - Syvilla Fort And 030 MIN
Origins And Influences Of Ethnic Dance 030 MIN
Rhythm's The Name Of The Game 030 MIN

Third World News Coverage C 30 MIN
3/4 OR 1/2 INCH VIDEO CASSETTE
Discusses alleged deficiencies in the way Western news media cover Third World issues. Features host Daniel Schorr and several international leaders in print and broadcast communications.
From The Issues In World Communications, 1979 Series.
Prod-OHUTC Dist-OHUTC

Third World, The - An Introduction C 21 MIN
16MM FILM, 3/4 OR 1/2 IN VIDEO J-C A
Presents an introduction to the concept of the Third World. States that most Third World nations were once colonies of First World nations and still depend on their ex-rulers for much of their trade and military assistance. Discusses the problems, the solutions and the future of a huge part of our world.
LC NO. 84-707084
Prod-BFA Dist-PHENIX 1983

Third World, The - Nonalignment As National Policy C 17 MIN
16MM FILM, 3/4 OR 1/2 IN VIDEO J-H
Defines the growing power of the so-called non-aligned nations, who are increasingly using their natural resources for diplomatic-economic purposes.
Prod-HEARST Dist-HEARST 1972

Thirds C 20 MIN
2 INCH VIDEOTAPE P
See series title for descriptive statement.
From The Mathemagic, Unit IV - Fractions Series.
Prod-WMULTV Dist-GPITVL

Thirdstring C 15 MIN
16MM FILM OPTICAL SOUND
Shows how a young boy suffers from a domineering sister and a mother who has failed to understand her son. Explains how he seeks escape in fantasies but his sister is determined to rid him of the 'EVIL SPIRIT' which possesses him.
LC NO. 72-702434
Prod-USC Dist-USC 1972

Thirteen Minutes To Wait C 51 MIN
3/4 INCH VIDEO CASSETTE
Shows Toronto's Steve Podborski waiting 13 minutes to find out his World Cup downhill ski racing rival beat him by 28/100ths of a second. Explains how he went on to become ranked best in the world.
Prod-LAURON Dist-LAURON

Thirteenth Chamber Of The Copper Prince, The C 9 MIN
16MM FILM, 3/4 OR 1/2 IN VIDEO I-C A
Tells the story of a corpulent, meat-eating prince who falls in love with a beautiful vegetarian princess. Because the prince wants to marry the princess, he tells her he has become a vegetarian, but in the 13th chamber the prince has hidden stores of meat. Describes what happens when the princess finds out about the prince's secret hoard.
LC NO. 84-707085
Prod-KRATKY Dist-PHENIX 1983

Thirteenth Floor, The C 9 MIN
16MM FILM, 3/4 OR 1/2 IN VIDEO A
Looks at the causes of classic office accidents such as falls, run-ins with office machines and small fires.
LC NO. 84-706662
Prod-EUSA Dist-IFB

Thirty Days Beneath The Sea C 15 MIN
16MM FILM OPTICAL SOUND
Shows the drifting voyage of the Ben Franklin submersible under the Gulf Stream and how the new knowlege is derived from the cruise to the addition of the understanding of the oceans.
LC NO. 74-705778
Prod-USN Dist-USNAC 1971

Thirty Demons C 30 MIN
2 INCH VIDEOTAPE T
See series title for descriptive statement.
From The Solutions In Communications Series.
Prod-SCCOE Dist-SCCOE

Thirty Pieces Of Silver X 15 MIN
16MM FILM OPTICAL SOUND J-H A
Mary anoints Jesus' head and feet in the house of Simon in Bethany. Judas speaks scornfully of this waste and Jesus rebukes him. Judas makes his way to the chief priests to bargain with them to betray Jesus for thirty pieces of silver.
From The Living Bible Series.
Prod-FAMF Dist-FAMF

Thirty Second Dream, The C 15 MIN
16MM FILM OPTICAL SOUND J-C A
Presents a montage of television commercials, pointing out the messages conveyed by their portrayal of family life, intimacy, vitality and success.
LC NO. 78-701078
Prod-LABRSE Dist-MMM 1977

Thirty Second Spots C 15 MIN
3/4 OR 1/2 INCH VIDEO CASSETTE
Prod-EAI Dist-EAI

Thirty Second Spots - TV Commercials For Artists C 15 MIN
3/4 OR 1/2 INCH VIDEO CASSETTE
Makes miniature statements with economy of time in mind.
Prod-KITCHN Dist-KITCHN

Thirty Three B
16MM FILM OPTICAL SOUND
Illustrates some of the abstract ideas of Galois theory by using the television studio floor to represent a collection of numbers in the complex field C and constructing physical objects to take on the role of mathematical entities.
Prod-OPENU Dist-OPENU

Thirty Years Of Fun B 85 MIN
16MM FILM, 3/4 OR 1/2 IN VIDEO
Offers a history of the silent movie era and shows some of the events of that era, captured on newsreel film.
Prod-YNGSNR Dist-CAROUF

Thirty-Five Mm Photography Basic Part 1 C 80 MIN
3/4 OR 1/2 INCH VIDEO CASSETTE J-C A
Shows the beginner or casual user of 35mm cameras the use of the controls and such materials as films, flash units, tripods, winders and lenses. Tells how to choose additional equipment. Signed for the deaf.
LC NO. 83-706444
Prod-MEMREP Dist-MEMREP 1983

Thirty-Five-C, 45-C Tractor Shovels C 16 MIN
16MM FILM OPTICAL SOUND
Shows common applications for two tractor shovels produced by Clark Equipment Company and provides specifications which are important to potential purchasers.
LC NO. 78-701575
Prod-CLARK Dist-PILOT Prodn-PILOT 1978

Thirty-Four Years After Hitler C 19 MIN
16MM FILM, 3/4 OR 1/2 IN VIDEO
Reports on the ways the Hitler legacy lives on in Germany and is supported through an American operation in Lincoln, Nebraska. Tells of neo-Nazi groups in Germany in the 1970's that have been known to destroy Jewish cemeteries, paint swastikas on the streets and distribute anti-Semitic propaganda. Originally shown on the television program 60 Minutes.
LC NO. 79-706430
Prod-CBSNEW Dist-CAROUF 1979

Thirty-Nine, Single And Pregnant C 18 MIN
16MM FILM, 3/4 OR 1/2 IN VIDEO A
Tells about Jane Davis, who decided to carry through her pregnancy and become a single parent. Shows the difficulties she faced in being separated from her child, forfeiting jobs, seeking a larger place to live, and raising him without a father and on a limited budget.
LC NO. 82-706982
Prod-WYNNC Dist-FLMLIB 1982

Thirty-Second Infantry Division B 18 MIN
16MM FILM, 3/4 OR 1/2 IN VIDEO
Traces the history of U S Army's 32nd Infantry Division through the Civil War, Spanish-American War, Mexican Border Campaign, World War I and World War II.
Prod-USA Dist-USNAC 1954

Thirty-Second President, The C 55 MIN
3/4 OR 1/2 INCH VIDEO CASSETTE
Examines the role of advertising in politics in the 20th century, featuring an interview with the late Rosser Reeves, an advertising executive who worked on early political television advertising for Dwight D Eisenhower. Includes a discussion with media whiz Tony Schwartz about how electoral politics have changed with the increased use of television advertising. Hosted by Bill Moyers.
From The Walk Through The 20th Century With Bill Moyers Series.
Prod-CORPEL Dist-PBS

Thirty-Six B 30 MIN
16MM FILM OPTICAL SOUND
Re-tells an old European legend that in every generation there are thirty-six secret Tzaddikim, or saints, simple men unmarked by any distinction.
LC NO. FIA64-1136
Prod-JTS Dist-NAAJS Prodn-NBC 1957

Thirty-Sixth Infantry Division B 21 MIN
16MM FILM, 3/4 OR 1/2 IN VIDEO H A
Presents the 36th Infantry Division's part in the battles at Salerno, San Pietro, Cassino, Anzio and Germany.
Prod-USA Dist-USNAC 1953

Thirty-Three Men C 30 MIN
16MM FILM OPTICAL SOUND
A picture story of Rodger Ward's second win at Indianapolis in 1962.
Prod-SFI Dist-SFI

Thirukkal—A Series

Presents Sri Gurudev discussing the Thirukkural by Saint Thiruvalluvar. Includes praise of God, excellence of rain, greatness of ascetics and assertion of the strength of virtue.
Prod-IYOGA Dist-IYOGA

This Bloody, Blundering Business B 30 MIN
16MM FILM, 3/4 OR 1/2 IN VIDEO A
Discusses the history of American intervention in the Philippines following the Spanish American War.
Prod-CNEMAG Dist-CNEMAG 1978

This Britain - Heritage Of The Sea C 52 MIN
16MM FILM, 3/4 OR 1/2 IN VIDEO
Looks at the traditional British heritage of the sea as reflected in the lives of the country's people. Shows the lives and work of fishermen in the Hebrides, the day-to-day activities of an apprentice lighterman on the Thames and the traditions of the feudal ruler of the Isle of Sark.
LC NO. 80-706385
Prod-NGS Dist-NGS 1975

This Business Of Numbers C 20 MIN
16MM FILM OPTICAL SOUND
Gives a completely animated study of arithmetic from cavemen to the present day. Includes man's need for numbers for counting and use in the modern data processing system.
Prod-UNIVAC Dist-UNIVAC 1969

This Business Of Turkeys C 17 MIN
16MM FILM OPTICAL SOUND I-C
Surveys the history of turkeys and turkey growing. Studies the development of the bird from egg to maturity. Indicates the best methods of turkey raising.
Prod-OSUMPD Dist-OSUMPD 1957

This Cat Can Play Anything C 28 MIN
3/4 OR 1/2 INCH VIDEO CASSETTE
Features Emmanuel 'Manny' Sayles, one of New Orleans' greatest banjo and guitar jazzmen, in this documentary which aired nationally on PBS. Traces the historical and musical milestones in Sayles' life while visiting the places where he evolved into a working musician.
Prod-NOVID Dist-NOVID

This Child Is Rated X C 54 MIN
16MM FILM, 3/4 OR 1/2 IN VIDEO I A
Examines the inequities of juvenile justice and abuse of children's rights in America. Focuses on two types of children—the child who committed a child's crime and the child who has committed a very serious crime.
Prod-NBC Dist-FI 1971

This City Is Milwaukee C 27 MIN
2 INCH VIDEOTAPE
Points out the many works of art which combine to make the 'look' of the city complete. Portrays its parks, large office buildings, churches and public buildings which possess qualities of distinction and aestheticism.
Prod-WHATV Dist-PUBTEL

This Country Called Deutschland C 27 MIN
16MM FILM OPTICAL SOUND
Presents a visual portrait of Germany through the eyes of a young German woman who receives a letter from friends overseas announcing their impending arrival. Includes the Kurfurstendamm in Berlin, Hamburg's 'Reeperbahn', the Munich 'Oktoberfest,' and museums, cathedrals, romantic castles and medieval towns.
Prod-WSTGLC Dist-WSTGLC

This Dog Is Real C 15 MIN
16MM FILM, 3/4 OR 1/2 IN VIDEO
Tells the story of a little girl whose family buys a dog. Shows how the animal is selected and focuses on the responsibilities of each family member in caring for it. Highlights the services of the veterinarian and obedience trainer.
Prod-KLEINW Dist-KLEINW 1978

This England C 26 MIN
16MM FILM OPTICAL SOUND I A
Demonstrates how wildlife wilderness areas have been preserved in modern, industrialized England.
From The Audubon Wildlife Theatre Series.
LC NO. 72-701987
Prod-KEGPL Dist-AVEXP 1970

This Film Has No Title B 5 MIN
16MM FILM OPTICAL SOUND
Presents a visual mood piece of a young girl rediscovering the shape and textures of the world. Shows how the young Caucasian girl is brought face to face with a young Negro girl on the other side of a fence, exchanging glances and going in opposite directions.
LC NO. 75-703240
Prod-USC Dist-USC 1965

This Film Is About Rape C 30 MIN
16MM FILM, 3/4 OR 1/2 IN VIDEO
Offers suggestions for reducing vulnerability to rape and for responding both physically and psychologically should an attack occur. Presents various methods for dealing with the rape problem including assertiveness training, self-defense classes and rape crisis hotlines.
Prod-MTI Dist-MTI

This For That C 15 MIN
3/4 INCH VIDEO CASSETTE P
Features the children's story This For That by Ann Clark.
From The Tilson's Book Shop Series.
Prod-WVIZTV Dist-GPITVL 1975

This Guy Denenberg C 29 MIN
2 INCH VIDEOTAPE
Looks at Herbert Denenberg, a relatively unknown professor from the Wharton School of Finance, who was sworn in on January, 1971 as Insurance Commissioner for the Commonwealth of Pennsylvania and whose name three months later was practically a household word throughout the state. Explains Denenberg's conflicts with the State Medical Society.
From The Turning Points Series.
Prod-WQED Dist-PUBTEL

This Is A Cooperative C 28 MIN
16MM FILM, 3/4 OR 1/2 IN VIDEO J-C
Host Lorne Greene discusses the role of consumer cooperatives in urban and rural society, showing the activities of a health cooperative, a housing cooperative, a credit union and a farm family.
Prod-CLUSA Dist-JOU Prodn-ALTSUL 1967

This Is A Football C 28 MIN
16MM FILM OPTICAL SOUND
A study of the football, its effect on the game and the men who play it. Includes scenes from games played by the teams in the National Football League.
From The NFL Action Series.
LC NO. 77-702615
Prod-NFL Dist-NFL 1967

This Is A Laboratory School B 29 MIN
16MM FILM OPTICAL SOUND T
Shows the role of the laboratory school in education. Includes views of social studies, art, mathematics and science classes with comments by the children and teachers.
LC NO. FIA65-475
Prod-UCLA Dist-UCLA Prodn-SPF 1964

This Is A Recorded Message C 10 MIN
16MM FILM, 3/4 OR 1/2 IN VIDEO J-C
Includes cut-out color ads projected in fragmented, rapid succession representing the barrage of advertising that assails the individual almost from the time he enters the world and evinces the reality hidden behind the false images.
Prod-NFBC Dist-NFBC 1973

This Is Advertising C 27 MIN
16MM FILM OPTICAL SOUND
Explains the vital role of advertising to salesmen, dealers, employees and community groups.
Prod-ANA Dist-CCNY

This Is An Emergency C 25 MIN
3/4 OR 1/2 INCH VIDEO CASSETTE
Gives a patient's eye view of an emergency, from treatment on the scene by a fire department paramedic squad through an ambulance ride and concluding with the treatment in the emergency room, complete with life-restoring measures.
Prod-TRAINX Dist-TRAINX

This Is An Emergency C 29 MIN
16MM FILM, 3/4 OR 1/2 IN VIDEO H-C A
Points out that industry consumes half of North America's energy. Shows how factories in Sweden conserve energy and how Canadian factories are trying to do the same.
Prod-NFBC Dist-NFBC 1980

This Is Ben Shahn C 17 MIN
16MM FILM, 3/4 OR 1/2 IN VIDEO J-C A
Ben Shahn discusses his personal philosophy and how it is reflected in his paintings. He discusses some of his works and the impulses and events which prompted their creation.
Prod-CBSTV Dist-PHENIX 1968

This Is Betty Crocker C 23 MIN
16MM FILM OPTICAL SOUND H-C
Pictures the seven kitchens of the world at General Mills, INC, to show the many employees at work through a day of developing and testing products and recipes for packages and cookbooks, preparing food for photography and answering Betty Crocker's mail. Contains close-ups of beautiful foods and time-saving techniques which homemakers can adapt to their own cooking needs.
Prod-GEMILL Dist-NINEFC

This Is Boeing C 13 MIN
16MM FILM OPTICAL SOUND
Traces the history of Boeing's involvement in air travel and looks ahead to its activities in space. Describes employment opportunities for graduating engineers and scientists.
LC NO. 79-701060
Prod-BOEING Dist-CORPOR Prodn-CORPOR 1979

This Is British Nuclear Fuels Limited C 23 MIN
16MM FILM OPTICAL SOUND
Features the process of uranium fuel manufacturing at British Nuclear Fuels Limited plant at Springfields. Shows their enrichment plant at Capenhurst and their processing and plutonium fuel manufacturing plants at Windscale. Shows that BNFL provides a comprehensive nuclear fuel service to reactor operators throughout the world.
Prod-UKAEA Dist-UKAEA 1971

This Is Camping C 18 MIN
16MM FILM, 3/4 OR 1/2 IN VIDEO I-C A
Presents a look at organized camping and the many facilities and activities offered campers. Shows how the campers learn cooperation, conservation and ecology through their involvement with nature and each other.
LC NO. 80-707102
Prod-IU Dist-IU 1972

This Is Canada - Columbia Icefields In The Canadian Rockies C 5 MIN
16MM FILM OPTICAL SOUND
Follows an automobile ride over the Columbia Glacier in the Canadian Rockies and shows views of other attractions in Jasper National Park.
LC NO. FIA67-32
Prod-CNR Dist-CTFL 1966

This Is Edward R Murrow B 44 MIN
16MM FILM, 3/4 OR 1/2 IN VIDEO H-C A
Highlights the career of journalist/commentator Edward R Murrow, including excerpts from many of his most famous broadcasts.
Prod-CBSNEW Dist-CAROUF

This Is Edward Steichen B 27 MIN
16MM FILM, 3/4 OR 1/2 IN VIDEO J-C A
Profiles Edward Steichen, who elevated portrait photography to an art.
Prod-WCBSTV Dist-CAROUF

This Is Fraud C 9 MIN
16MM FILM, 3/4 OR 1/2 IN VIDEO J-C A
Illustrates the old 'bait and switch' technique and the methods of a crafty door-to-door salesman.
From The Consumer Education Series.
Prod-FLMFR Dist-FLMFR 1972

This Is Fraud (Captioned Version) C 9 MIN
16MM FILM, 3/4 OR 1/2 IN VIDEO J-C A
Illustrates the old 'bait and switch' technique and the methods of a crafty door-to-door salesman.
From The Consumer Education Series.
Prod-FLMFR Dist-FLMFR 1972

This Is Fraud (Spanish) C 8 MIN
16MM FILM, 3/4 OR 1/2 IN VIDEO J-C A
Shows three consumers who have been swindled by using 'bait and switch' techniques, by using dishonest techniques to make a product seem to perform better and by having promises made which were not included in a written contract. Describes the methods of recourse which each consumer has available.
Prod-FLMFR Dist-FLMFR 1973

This Is Frederica C 25 MIN
16MM FILM - 3/4 IN VIDEO
Re-creates scenes of town life in the early 18th century village of Fort Frederica on Saint Simon's Island, Georgia. Relates the importance of the fort as a buffer against Spanish expansion from the south.
LC NO. 79-706162
Prod-USNPS Dist-USNAC 1979

This Is Guatemala C 24 MIN
16MM FILM OPTICAL SOUND I-C A
Features a tour of Guatemala, showing areas where various stages of the culture and history of Central America are still visible.
LC NO. 77-701859
Prod-CASTOP Dist-CASTOP 1975

This Is Ham Radio C 15 MIN
16MM FILM, 3/4 OR 1/2 IN VIDEO I-C A
Shows the various activities of ham radio operations, including rigging an antenna, talking with nearby ham operators, using mobile equipment, participating in club field days and contacting other hams all over the world. Gives basic information about the hobby and the skills and knowledge the hobby develops.
Prod-FLMFR Dist-FLMFR

This Is Harness Racing C 15 MIN
16MM FILM, 3/4 OR 1/2 IN VIDEO J-C A
Focuses on the sport of harness racing. Shows those who train, drive and look after the horses. Explains the difference between a pacer and a trotter and uses slow motion techniques to describe each gait.
Prod-LANGED Dist-MCFI 1975

This Is Hawaii C 14 MIN
16MM FILM OPTICAL SOUND I-C
Presents Hawaii industrially and socially through visits to schools, churches, factories and tourists attractions.
LC NO. FIA61-805
Prod-CLI Dist-CLI 1961

This Is Hawaii C 28 MIN
16MM FILM OPTICAL SOUND
Features Don Ho, singing star, as he tours the Hawaiian Islands. Captures the beauty, color and splendor of this little corner of the world through background music of Hawaiian songs.
LC NO. 73-711524
Prod-UAL Dist-MTP 1971

This Is Hope Enterprises:025MVSTNFLD C 25 MIN
16MM FILM, 3/4 OR 1/2 IN VIDEO C A
Portrays a model human service agency meeting the challenge of the Right-to-Education mandate and the conversion of large state institutions to locally run programs.
Prod-STNFLD Dist-STNFLD

This Is Livestock Pooling C 5 MIN
16MM FILM OPTICAL SOUND
Shows the selling of livestock through auction marketing pooling. Explains the advantages of marketing livestock by this method.
LC NO. 74-705780
Prod-USDA Dist-USNAC 1964

This Is Mack C 17 MIN
16MM FILM OPTICAL SOUND
Surveys the history and accomplishments of the firm Mack Trucks and takes a look at Mack's power, facilities and service capabilities today.
LC NO. 75-700486
Prod-MACKT Dist-MACKT Prodn-HARDAS 1974

This Is Magnesium B 15 MIN
16MM FILM OPTICAL SOUND
Depicts the unlimited resources, methods of extraction and countless uses of magnesium, which is obtained from sea water.
Prod-USDIBM Dist-USDIBM Prodn-DCC 1952

This Is Marina City C 18 MIN
16MM FILM OPTICAL SOUND
Describes the planning, building and use of twin circular towers at one edge of Chicago's central business district.
Prod-PRTLND Dist-PRTLND 1966

This Is Marshall McLuhan - The Medium Is The Massage C 53 MIN
16MM FILM, 3/4 OR 1/2 IN VIDEO H-C A
Presents Marshall McLuhan's ideas about the manner in which all media of communication shape and alter society. Concentrates on the electronic media and instruments which speed up life, process information, and shape sensibilities.
Prod-NBC Dist-CRMP 1967

This Is Me C 4 MIN
16MM FILM, 3/4 OR 1/2 IN VIDEO K-I
Depicts Fumble's dissatisfaction when he decides that his painting is not perfect. Follows, as a friend reminds him that what matters is that he tried and that 'IT'S AN ORIGINAL.'
From The Most Important Person - Creative Expression Series.
Prod-EBEC Dist-EBEC 1972

This Is Mexico C 27 MIN
16MM FILM OPTICAL SOUND I-C A
Shows modern Mexico and how successive civilizations, arts and cultures--Mayan, Toltec and Spanish--have left their marks in city, town and countryside. Depicts progress in industry, education and recreation.
Prod-BARONA Dist-AVED 1963

This Is Mission, USA B 10 MIN
16MM FILM OPTICAL SOUND
Presents a kaleidoscopic view of the variety of ministries and needs of the Baptist missions in the United States. Includes a short narration taken from the book 'SEE HOW LOVE WORKS,' by Walker L Knight and Don Rutledge.
LC NO. 73-702060
Prod-BHMB Dist-BHMB 1972

This Is My Friend C 10 MIN
16MM FILM, 3/4 OR 1/2 IN VIDEO P-I
Presents a visual poem of friendship involving a boy and a girl.
Prod-KINGSP Dist-PHENIX

This Is My Grandmother B 15 MIN
16MM FILM OPTICAL SOUND
Portrays 80-year-old Gertrude Day. Shows how the widow of 20 years relives memories with family and friends.
LC NO. 77-702671
Prod-CANFDC Dist-CANFDC 1976

This Is My Home--A Series
P-I
Provides students with an understanding of how communities function and how they differ. Shows how location affects life and industry. Features children and their families from five different communities in northwestern Canada. Shows similarities and differences in family life.
Prod-BCNFL Dist-BCNFL

Historic Fort Town, A - Fort St James	014 MIN
Island Below The Sea, An - Westham Island	014 MIN
Mining Community, A - Kimberley	014 MIN
Rocky Mountain Town, A - Revelstoke	014 MIN
Seacoast Port City, A - Port Of Vancouver	014 MIN

This Is My Life C 20 MIN
2 INCH VIDEOTAPE P
See series title for descriptive statement.
From The Learning Our Language, Unit III - Creative Writing Series.
Prod-MPATI Dist-GPITVL

This Is My Own - The Rockwell Kent Collection C 44 MIN
16MM FILM OPTICAL SOUND
Examines the complexity of the work of artist Rockwell Kent as seen in collections of his work at his former home, at SUNY College, and in the Soviet Union.
LC NO. 80-700396
Prod-SUNY Dist-SUNY 1979

This Is My Son C 60 MIN
16MM FILM OPTICAL SOUND
Reveals the pain of a widower and his new wife whose first son is afflicted with Down's Syndrome.
Prod-NBCTV Dist-CCNCC

This Is My Will--A Series

Presents a series on financial planning that helps you realize options you have for planning and managing your estate.
Prod-WMHTTV Dist-PBS 1983

How To Go About It	030 MIN
Taxation - What And When	030 MIN
Why	030 MIN

This Is New Jersey C 30 MIN
16MM FILM OPTICAL SOUND
The state of New Jersy--Its history, character, people, beauty, industry, agriculture and recreational areas.
Prod-NJBTC Dist-NJBTC 1958

This Is New York C 12 MIN
16MM FILM, 3/4 OR 1/2 IN VIDEO P-I
An iconographic motion picture, using original illustrations from the children's book by Miroslav Sasek, about a young French boy's visit to New York City and his witty and informative reactions.
Prod-WWS Dist-WWS 1962

This Is Noel Coward C 60 MIN
16MM FILM OPTICAL SOUND J-C A
Documents the life of British playwright and humorist, Noel Coward. Includes an interview with Coward, filmed shortly before his death and intercut with biographical photographs, scenes from stage and film productions of his work and interviews with close acquaintances. Narrated by Sir John Gielgud.
Prod-CANTOR Dist-CANTOR

This Is Not A Museum C 13 MIN
3/4 OR 1/2 INCH VIDEO CASSETTE
Comments humorously on the intellectualization of modern art. Makes visual references to the work of such artists as Picasso, Rousseau, Goya, Magritte and Oldenburg. Uses animation.
Prod-HAUGSE Dist-MEDIPR 1974

This Is Our Farm C 11 MIN
16MM FILM OPTICAL SOUND
Shows a unique children's farm in Israel.
Prod-ALDEN Dist-ALDEN

This Is Philosophy C 27 MIN
16MM FILM OPTICAL SOUND H-C A
Introduces high school students to the field of philosophy. Shows the possibilities for study in philosophy and examines the contribution of philosophy to the solution and clarification of issues and problems.
LC NO. 74-702393
Prod-FLMAUS Dist-AUIS 1974

This Is Robert (2nd Ed) C 45 MIN
16MM FILM OPTICAL SOUND
Presents a longitundinal study tracing the growth of Robert, an agressive but appealing child, from nursery school at two to the public school at seven.
From The Studies Of Normal Personality Development Series.
Prod-VASSAR Dist-NYU

This Is Rockwell C 22 MIN
16MM FILM OPTICAL SOUND
Tours several of Rockwell International's facilities and shows the kinds of products Rockwell makes.
LC NO. 74-700379
Prod-RCKWL Dist-RCKWL 1974

This Is Rodeo C 30 MIN
2 INCH VIDEOTAPE
Captures the excitement of the Western rodeo from bulldogging to chuck wagon racing.
From The Synergism - The Challenge Of Sports Series.
Prod-KRMATV Dist-PUBTEL

This Is Sailing - First Essential Skills C 19 MIN
16MM FILM OPTICAL SOUND J-C A
Presents the first essential skills in sailing. Covers sailing terms, points of sail, force vectors, tacking, jibbing, sail trim, hull balance, picking up a mooring and landing at a dock and on the bench.
LC NO. 74-703810
Prod-SAIL Dist-SAIL 1974

This Is Sailing - Introduction To A Boat C 19 MIN
16MM FILM OPTICAL SOUND J-C A
Presents an introduction to a sailboat. Discusses the important parts of a boat, the mainsail draft, stepping the mast, hoisting sail, launching from shore and dock, steering and getting underway.
LC NO. 74-703809
Prod-SAIL Dist-SAIL 1974

This Is Sailing - More Advanced Techniques C 19 MIN
16MM FILM OPTICAL SOUND J-C A
Depicts advanced techniques in sailing, including spinnaker gear, hoisting, trimming, jibbing and lowering the spinnaker, spilling wind, reefing and shortening sail in heavy weather, capsize recover, planing and trapeze.
LC NO. 74-703811
Prod-SAIL Dist-SAIL

This Is Sea World C 9 MIN
16MM FILM OPTICAL SOUND
Presents Sea World, Florida's largest marine life park.
Prod-FLADC Dist-FLADC

This Is TB B 10 MIN
16MM FILM OPTICAL SOUND I-C A
Outlines the cause, spread and prevention of tuberculosis.
Prod-NTBA Dist-AMLUNG 1946

This Is The Home Of Mrs Levant Graham B 15 MIN
16MM FILM, 3/4 OR 1/2 IN VIDEO H-C A
Focuses on a Washington, D C, mother in a Black ghetto and her large, loose-knit family.
Prod-PFP Dist-PFP 1970

This Is The John Birch Society - An Invitation To Membership B 115 MIN
16MM FILM OPTICAL SOUND A
Presents G Edward Griffin, author and active member of the John Birch Society, who lectures on the purposes, organizational structure and plan of action of the John Birch Society.
LC NO. 73-700815
Prod-AMMED Dist-AMMED 1970

This Is The Life C 15 MIN
3/4 OR 1/2 INCH VIDEO CASSETTE K-P
Examines human movement, growth, eating, breathing and reproduction.
From The Dragons, Wagons And Wax, Set 2 Series.
Prod-CTI Dist-CTI

This Is The Life—A Series

Prod-LUTTEL Dist-LUTTEL

Elm Street Divided	029 MIN
Hunger Next Door, The	029 MIN
Only Hooked A Little	029 MIN
Project Compassion	029 MIN
Sins Of The Father	029 MIN

This Is The Truth C 5 MIN
3/4 OR 1/2 INCH VIDEO CASSETTE
Focuses on political manipulation through mass media.
Prod-EAI Dist-EAI

This Is The United Nations C 15 MIN
16MM FILM, 3/4 OR 1/2 IN VIDEO J-C
Describes the basic structure and major functions of the United Nations.
Prod-UN Dist-BARR 1977

This Is The Way We Go To School C 28 MIN
16MM FILM OPTICAL SOUND
Presents three separate and distinct models of teaching techniques - the first based on the BereiterEngelmann direct teaching method, the second stressing emotional and social development and the third concentrating on cognitive learning devised from the work of Piaget.
Prod-ADL Dist-ADL

This Is Volleyball C 30 MIN
16MM FILM OPTICAL SOUND H-C A
Presents an overview of individual skills and basic team tactics in volleyball from the 1976 Olympics.
Prod-CVA Dist-CVA 1977

This Is Volleyball C
3/4 OR 1/2 INCH VIDEO CASSETTE
Presents a technical narrative that discusses the sport of volleyball.
Prod-CVA Dist-CVA

This Is Where It All Began C 24 MIN
16MM FILM OPTICAL SOUND
Tells the history of Christianity in the Holy Land.
Prod-ALDEN Dist-ALDEN

This Is William Brose Productions, Incorporated C 4 MIN
16MM FILM OPTICAL SOUND
Uses clips from films of William Brose Productions to demonstrate the firm's image-building potential for prospective clients. Documents the firm's day-to-day activities, emphasizing the creative process.
LC NO. 76-703165
Prod-BROSEB Dist-BROSEB Prodn-CUTPRO 1975

This Is You C
3/4 OR 1/2 INCH VIDEO CASSETTE J-H
Focuses on students' real problems and presents solutions. Includes teenage pregnancy. Discusses love and the elements of successful relationships.
Prod-EDUACT Dist-EDUACT

This Is You (Arabic)—A Series
P
Discusses the function and needs of the human body. Features animation.
Prod-WDEMCO Dist-WDEMCO

You And Your Ears (Arabic)	008 MIN
You And Your Eyes (Arabic)	008 MIN
You And Your Five Senses (Arabic)	008 MIN
You And Your Food (Arabic)	008 MIN
You And Your Sense Of Smell And Taste (Arabic)	008 MIN
You And Your Sense Of Touch (Arabic)	008 MIN
You, The Human Animal (Arabic)	008 MIN
You, The Living Machine (Arabic)	008 MIN

This Is You (Dutch)—A Series
P
Discusses the function and needs of the human body. Features animation.
Prod-WDEMCO Dist-WDEMCO

You And Your Ears (Dutch)	008 MIN
You And Your Eyes (Dutch)	008 MIN
You And Your Food (Dutch)	008 MIN

This Is You (French)—A Series
P
Discusses the function and needs of the human body. Features animation.
Prod-WDEMCO Dist-WDEMCO

You And Your Ears (French)	008 MIN
You And Your Eyes (French)	008 MIN
You And Your Five Senses (French)	008 MIN
You And Your Food (French)	008 MIN
You And Your Sense Of Touch (French)	008 MIN
You, The Human Animal (French)	008 MIN
You, The Living Machine (French)	008 MIN

This Is You (Spanish)—A Series
P
Discusses the function and needs of the human body. Features animation.
Prod-WDEMCO Dist-WDEMCO

You And Your Ears (Spanish)	008 MIN
You And Your Eyes (Spanish)	008 MIN
You And Your Five Senses (Spanish)	008 MIN
You And Your Food (Spanish)	008 MIN
You, The Human Animal (Spanish)	008 MIN

This Is You (Thai)—A Series
P
Discusses the function and needs of the human body. Features animation.
Prod-WDEMCO Dist-WDEMCO

You And Your Ears (Thai)	008 MIN
You And Your Eyes (Thai)	008 MIN
You And Your Food (Thai)	008 MIN

This Is You—A Series
16MM FILM, 3/4 OR 1/2 IN VIDEO K-I
Explains the functions and structure of various parts of the human body.
Prod-DISNEY Dist-WDEMCO

You - And Your Ears	008 MIN
You - And Your Eyes	008 MIN
You - And Your Five Senses	008 MIN
You - And Your Food	008 MIN
You - And Your Sense Of Smell And Taste	008 MIN
You - And Your Sense Of Touch	008 MIN
You - The Human Animal	008 MIN
You - The Living Machine	008 MIN

This Is Your Museum Speaking C 14 MIN
16MM FILM, 3/4 OR 1/2 IN VIDEO I-J
Tells how a night watchman learns more about the museum during one amazing night.
LC NO. 81-707524
Prod-NFBC Dist-FI 1980

This Isn't Wonderland C 57 MIN
3/4 OR 1/2 INCH VIDEO CASSETTE
Attempts to identify the cultural factors that generate women's role dilemmas, and the madness which can result. Explores a woman's attempts to deal with severe depression. Discusses other women's confrontation with madness.
Prod-WMENIF Dist-WMENIF

This Land C 15 MIN
16MM FILM OPTICAL SOUND
Describes a land settlement project in Kenya as seen by a Peace Corps volunteer working as a land settlement officer, pointing out the transition between old and new in Kenya.
LC NO. FIE67-141
Prod-USPC Dist-USNAC Prodn-FREUND 1966

This Land C 17 MIN
16MM FILM OPTICAL SOUND I-C A
Highpoints the history of the United States, from its Beginnings through to the Civil War. Shows places in U S National Parks where historical events occurred.
LC NO. FIE67-80
Prod-NEWSPX Dist-USNAC 1967

This Land C 17 MIN
3/4 INCH VIDEO CASSETTE
Highlights the natural resources, variety, grandeur and significance of America's national parks. Issued in 1967 as a motion picture.
LC NO. 79-706164
Prod-USNPS Dist-USNAC 1979

This Land Is C 58 MIN
16MM FILM OPTICAL SOUND
Traces the history and character of the southern Illinois region, utilizing folk stories and contemporary witticisms.
LC NO. 70-705690
Prod-SILLU Dist-SIUFP Prodn-SIUFP 1969

This Land Is Your Land C 14 MIN
3/4 OR 1/2 INCH VIDEO CASSETTE P
See series title for descriptive statement.
From The Strawberry Square Series.
Prod-NEITV Dist-AITECH 1982

This Little Penny Went To Market - Money C 14 MIN
3/4 OR 1/2 INCH VIDEO CASSETTE P
Shows Jerry learning about money and finding out how to count his change after a purchase.
From The Math Country Series.
Prod-KYTV Dist-AITECH 1979

This Man Must Die (French) C 115 MIN
16MM FILM OPTICAL SOUND C A
Tells the story of a grief-stricken father who sets out to find the killer of his son and to gain revenge in a small village on the French coast. Includes English subtitles.
Prod-CINEWO Dist-CINEWO 1970

This Matter Of Motivation C 28 MIN
16MM FILM, 3/4 OR 1/2 IN VIDEO IND
Introduces a series of case-study films designed to help managers and supervisors handle employee problems effectively. Discusses the effectiveness of behavioral science motivational techniques, focusing on the theories of Dr Federick Herzberg. Describes how to apply these techniques to personnel problems.
From The This Matter Of Motivation Series.
Prod-CTRACT Dist-DARTNL Prodn-CALVIN 1971

This Matter Of Motivation—A Series
16MM FILM, 3/4 OR 1/2 IN VIDEO IND
Presents behavioral science films based on the principles developed by Dr Frederick Herzberg of case Western Reserve University, who many believe is the preeminent authority in employee motivation. Covers specific personnel problems.
Prod-CTRACT Dist-DARTNL Prodn-CALVIN 1969

Among The Missing	9 MIN
Ball Of Fire	4 MIN
Gilded Lily, The	5 MIN
Harry's Hangover	5 MIN
Indispensible Miss Spencer, The	5 MIN
Nice Guy, The	4 MIN
Pacesetter, The	6 MIN
People Will Talk	4 MIN
Perfect Job For Jim, The	4 MIN
Puzzle, The	6 MIN
Roadblock, The	6 MIN
Shades Of Black And White	5 MIN
This Matter Of Motivation - The Basic	28 MIN

This Most Gallant Gentleman C 10 MIN
16MM FILM OPTICAL SOUND
Describes the life of Roger Casement, using the 1965 state funeral as background.
Prod-CONSUI Dist-CONSUI

This My Life C 23 MIN
16MM FILM OPTICAL SOUND
Explores the opportunities for service in the physical therapy field.
Prod-LOMA Dist-LOMA

This New Frontier C 27 MIN
16MM FILM OPTICAL SOUND
Portrays the length and breadth of Israel, from military-agricultural settlements on the Golan Heights to the beaches of Eilat and from Jerusalem's holy shrines to cosmopolitan Tel Aviv.
Prod-ADL Dist-ADL

This Old House - Ranch-Style House—A Series

Presents host Bob Vila as he introduces a plan to restore a 1950's ranch-style tract house badly in need of more space.
Prod-WGBHTV Dist-PBS 1981

This Old House - Ranch-Style House, Pt 01 029 MIN
This Old House - Ranch-Style House, Pt 02 029 MIN
This Old House - Ranch-Style House, Pt 03 029 MIN
This Old House - Ranch-Style House, Pt 04 029 MIN
This Old House - Ranch-Style House, Pt 05 029 MIN
This Old House - Ranch-Style House, Pt 06 029 MIN
This Old House - Ranch-Style House, Pt 07 029 MIN
This Old House - Ranch-Style House, Pt 08 029 MIN
This Old House - Ranch-Style House, Pt 09 029 MIN
This Old House - Ranch-Style House, Pt 10 029 MIN
This Old House - Ranch-Style House, Pt 11 029 MIN
This Old House - Ranch-Style House, Pt 12 029 MIN
This Old House - Ranch-Style House, Pt 13 029 MIN

This Old House - Ranch-Style House, Pt 01 C 29 MIN
3/4 OR 1/2 INCH VIDEO CASSETTE
See series title for descriptive statement.
From The This Old House - Ranch Style House Series.
Prod-WGBHTV Dist-PBS 1981

This Old House - Ranch-Style House, Pt 02 C 29 MIN
3/4 OR 1/2 INCH VIDEO CASSETTE
Shows how to pour the footings for the breezeway/greenhouse between the house and the garage. Gives the house a high-tech energy audit, complete with on-the-spot computer print-out and recommendations for cost-effective solutions to specific energy problems.
From The This Old House - Ranch Style House Series.
Prod-WGBHTV Dist-PBS 1981

This Old House - Ranch-Style House, Pt 03 C 29 MIN
3/4 OR 1/2 INCH VIDEO CASSETTE
Presents host Bob Vila assessing the efficiency of the house's heating plant. Carpenter Norm Abram builds the framing for the breezeway/greenhouse and replaces windows. In the house Bob Vila steams off the old wallpaper.
From The This Old House - Ranch Style House Series.
Prod-WGBHTV Dist-PBS 1981

This Old House - Ranch-Style House, Pt 04 C 29 MIN
3/4 OR 1/2 INCH VIDEO CASSETTE
Presents host Bob Vila discussing plans for installing a wood burning stove in the Family Room. Carpenter Norm Abram roughs in the new bath off the Master Bedroom, then goes outside to check the condition of the roof.
From The This Old House - Ranch Style House Series.
Prod-WGBHTV Dist-PBS 1981

This Old House - Ranch-Style House, Pt 05 C 29 MIN
3/4 OR 1/2 INCH VIDEO CASSETTE
Shows how to waterproof a basement and install a woodstove and free-standing chimney. Norm Abram puts in the new windows and doors.
From The This Old House - Ranch Style House Series.
Prod-WGBHTV Dist-PBS 1981

This Old House - Ranch-Style House, Pt 06 C 29 MIN
3/4 OR 1/2 INCH VIDEO CASSETTE
Shows Bob Vila helping to install the shower in the new Master Bathroom. Bob and carpenter Norm Abram show how to construct your own kitchen cabinets.
From The This Old House - Ranch Style House Series.
Prod-WGBHTV Dist-PBS 1981

This Old House - Ranch-Style House, Pt 07 C 29 MIN
3/4 OR 1/2 INCH VIDEO CASSETTE
Shows Bob Vila and carpenter Norm Abram tearing down the old wood panelling in the basement wreck room. Upstairs shows how to install the kitchen counter tops and decorate the Master Bath.
From The This Old House - Ranch Style House Series.
Prod-WGBHTV Dist-PBS 1981

This Old House - Ranch-Style House, Pt 08 C 29 MIN
3/4 OR 1/2 INCH VIDEO CASSETTE
Shows how to wire the new breezeway addition and how to put insulation in the garage-turned-Family Room.
From The This Old House - Ranch Style House Series.
Prod-WGBHTV Dist-PBS 1981

This Old House - Ranch-Style House, Pt 09 C 29 MIN
3/4 OR 1/2 INCH VIDEO CASSETTE
Carpenter Norm Abram shows the right way to dry wall a new room, including tips on taping and sanding.
From The This Old House - Ranch Style House Series.
Prod-WGBHTV Dist-PBS 1981

This Old House - Ranch-Style House, Pt 10 C 29 MIN
3/4 OR 1/2 INCH VIDEO CASSETTE
Bob Vila shows how to trim the windows and doors. Gives time-saving tips on preparing and painting interior walls.
From The This Old House - Ranch Style House Series.
Prod-WGBHTV Dist-PBS 1981

This Old House - Ranch-Style House, Pt 11 C 29 MIN
3/4 OR 1/2 INCH VIDEO CASSETTE
Shows Bob Vila installing new appliances in the kitchen. Carpenter Norm Abram builds a new rear Deck/Patio. Indoors Bob shows professional secrets for mistake-proof wallpapering.
From The This Old House - Ranch Style House Series.
Prod-WGBHTV Dist-PBS 1981

This Old House - Ranch-Style House, Pt 12 C 29 MIN
3/4 OR 1/2 INCH VIDEO CASSETTE
Bob Vila gives some pointers on laying a no-wax floor. Discusses the finishing touches of the house renovation and landscaping.
From The This Old House - Ranch Style House Series.
Prod-WGBHTV Dist-PBS 1981

This Old House - Ranch-Style House, Pt 13 C 29 MIN
3/4 OR 1/2 INCH VIDEO CASSETTE
Takes a tour of the former 50's style ranch house now renovated to an energy-efficient home for the 80's.
From The This Old House - Ranch Style House Series.
Prod-WGBHTV Dist-PBS 1981

This Old House - The Bigelow House—A Series

Presents designer and builder Bob Vila as he follows the renovation of the Bigelow House, offering step-by-step expert advice, practical tips and enthusiastic encouragement to do-it-yourselfers of all levels.
Prod-WGBHTV Dist-PBS 1981

This Old House - The Bigelow House, Pt 01 029 MIN
This Old House - The Bigelow House, Pt 02 029 MIN
This Old House - The Bigelow House, Pt 03 029 MIN
This Old House - The Bigelow House, Pt 04 029 MIN
This Old House - The Bigelow House, Pt 05 029 MIN
This Old House - The Bigelow House, Pt 06 029 MIN
This Old House - The Bigelow House, Pt 07 029 MIN
This Old House - The Bigelow House, Pt 08 029 MIN
This Old House - The Bigelow House, Pt 09 029 MIN
This Old House - The Bigelow House, Pt 10 029 MIN
This Old House - The Bigelow House, Pt 11 029 MIN
This Old House - The Bigelow House, Pt 12 029 MIN
This Old House - The Bigelow House, Pt 13 029 MIN
This Old House - The Bigelow House, Pt 14 029 MIN
This Old House - The Bigelow House, Pt 15 029 MIN
This Old House - The Bigelow House, Pt 16 029 MIN
This Old House - The Bigelow House, Pt 17 029 MIN
This Old House - The Bigelow House, Pt 18 029 MIN
This Old House - The Bigelow House, Pt 19 029 MIN
This Old House - The Bigelow House, Pt 20 029 MIN
This Old House - The Bigelow House, Pt 21 029 MIN
This Old House - The Bigelow House, Pt 22 029 MIN
This Old House - The Bigelow House, Pt 23 029 MIN
This Old House - The Bigelow House, Pt 24 029 MIN
This Old House - The Bigelow House, Pt 25 029 MIN
This Old House - The Bigelow House, Pt 26 029 MIN
This Old House - The Bigelow House, Pt 27 029 MIN

This Old House - The Bigelow House, Pt 01 C 29 MIN
3/4 OR 1/2 INCH VIDEO CASSETTE
Presents host Bob Vila as he introduces the Bigelow House, a rambling 19th-century hilltop home in Newton, Massachusetts, designed by noted Victorian architect H H Richardson. The plan is to convert the abandoned structure into five modern condominium units while preserving its architectural integrity.
From The This Old House - The Bigelow House Series.
Prod-WGBHTV Dist-PBS 1981

This Old House - The Bigelow House, Pt 03 C 29 MIN
3/4 OR 1/2 INCH VIDEO CASSETTE
After demolition is nearly complete, host Bob Vila shows some of the problems he's uncovered, including extensive damage from carpenter ants, vandals and rot.
From The This Old House - The Bigelow House Series.
Prod-WGBHTV Dist-PBS 1981

This Old House - The Bigelow House, Pt 04 C 29 MIN
3/4 OR 1/2 INCH VIDEO CASSETTE
Presents Bob Vila discussing some of the key decisions to be made about condominium sales. Plans are made to install woodburning stoves in the Icehouse and Woodshed units.
From The This Old House - The Bigelow House Series.
Prod-WGBHTV Dist-PBS 1981

This Old House - The Bigelow House, Pt 05 C 29 MIN
3/4 OR 1/2 INCH VIDEO CASSETTE
Carpenter Norm Abram shows us how to pour a concrete wall and Tom Wirth, a landscape architect, discusses the lay of the land.
From The This Old House - The Bigelow House Series.
Prod-WGBHTV Dist-PBS 1981

This Old House - The Bigelow House, Pt 06 C 29 MIN
3/4 OR 1/2 INCH VIDEO CASSETTE
Shows an exterminator giving the house a top-to-bottom bug check. Professor John Coolidge talks about the architect of the Bigelow House, H H Richardson, considered the foremost Victorian architect of the 19th century.
From The This Old House - The Bigelow House Series.
Prod-WGBHTV Dist-PBS 1981

This Old House - The Bigelow House, Pt 07 C 29 MIN
3/4 OR 1/2 INCH VIDEO CASSETTE
Presents Bob Vila discussing plans for a new historically compatible five-car garage. The electrician begins wiring and a solar energy expert recommends the best location for a solar collector.
From The This Old House - The Bigelow House Series.
Prod-WGBHTV Dist-PBS 1981

This Old House - The Bigelow House, Pt 08 C 29 MIN
3/4 OR 1/2 INCH VIDEO CASSETTE
Presents host Bob Vila and chief carpenter Norm Abram as they give a progress report on the house. Tells how to winterize the energy-guzzling summer home with insulation and fireplace fix-ups.
From The This Old House - The Bigelow House Series.
Prod-WGBHTV Dist-PBS 1981

This Old House - The Bigelow House, Pt 09 C 29 MIN
3/4 OR 1/2 INCH VIDEO CASSETTE
Bob Vila shows an efficient aesthetic European version of a radiator. Shows Norm Abram installing new windows and a lighting expert makes some illuminating recommendations.
From The This Old House - The Bigelow House Series.
Prod-WGBHTV Dist-PBS 1981

This Old House - The Bigelow House, Pt 10 C 29 MIN
3/4 OR 1/2 INCH VIDEO CASSETTE
Shows the South roof getting an ice shield and cedar shingles and the living room wall getting a layer of energy-saving polystyrene board. Also the grounds get a facelifting.
From The This Old House - The Bigelow House Series.
Prod-WGBHTV Dist-PBS 1981

This Old House - The Bigelow House, Pt 11 C 29 MIN
3/4 OR 1/2 INCH VIDEO CASSETTE
Presents Bob Vila looking at the wiring needs in the Barn unit. Demonstrates lathing and plastering and talks about choosing tiles for the foyer in the Main House.
From The This Old House - The Bigelow House Series.
Prod-WGBHTV Dist-PBS 1981

This Old House - The Bigelow House, Pt 12 C 29 MIN
3/4 OR 1/2 INCH VIDEO CASSETTE
Shingling is completed on the south side of the Bungalow and the lights are in place in the Main House. Tile setter Charlie English shows how to trim tiles.
From The This Old House - The Bigelow House Series.
Prod-WGBHTV Dist-PBS 1981

This Old House - The Bigelow House, Pt 13 C 29 MIN
3/4 OR 1/2 INCH VIDEO CASSETTE
Discusses the best tiles for the Master Bath, how the electrical work is progressing and what type of cabinets should be used in the kitchen of the Main House.
From The This Old House - The Bigelow House Series.
Prod-WGBHTV Dist-PBS 1981

This Old House - The Bigelow House, Pt 14 C 29 MIN
3/4 OR 1/2 INCH VIDEO CASSETTE
Shows some tough shingling jobs on the turret and rooftop Belvediere. Includes how to install a skylight, hook up a toilet and discusses water service for the house.
From The This Old House - The Bigelow House Series.
Prod-WGBHTV Dist-PBS 1981

This Old House - The Bigelow House, Pt 15 C 29 MIN
3/4 OR 1/2 INCH VIDEO CASSETTE
Shows the crawlspace in the Barn getting a concrete floor and the Main House gets a parquet floor. Also shows tile grouting.
From The This Old House - The Bigelow House Series.
Prod-WGBHTV Dist-PBS 1981

This Old House - The Bigelow House, Pt 16 C 29 MIN
3/4 OR 1/2 INCH VIDEO CASSETTE
Shows Bob Vila sizing up the tree cutting and clearing job outside the Ice House unit. In the Barn, he discusses the wood beam framing and in the Main House, looks at the stairway.
From The This Old House - The Bigelow House Series.
Prod-WGBHTV Dist-PBS 1981

This Old House - The Bigelow House, Pt 17 C 29 MIN
3/4 OR 1/2 INCH VIDEO CASSETTE
Presents Bob Vila reviewing plans for the interior of the Barn unit. In the Main House he decides that some of the floors will have to go. The plumber installs the Powder Room sink.
From The This Old House - The Bigelow House Series.
Prod-WGBHTV Dist-PBS 1981

This Old House - The Bigelow House, Pt 18 C 29 MIN
3/4 OR 1/2 INCH VIDEO CASSETTE
Shows Bob Vila touring the Barn and giving more thought to the hardwood floors in the Main House. Shows how to select locks and hardware for the antique doors.
From The This Old House - The Bigelow House Series.
Prod-WGBHTV Dist-PBS 1981

This Old House - The Bigelow House, Pt 19 C 29 MIN
3/4 OR 1/2 INCH VIDEO CASSETTE
Presents carpenter Norm Abram installing the unusual floor-to-ceiling triple hung windows, while Charlie, the finish carpenter, sets in window casings and kitchen cabinets.
From The This Old House - The Bigelow House Series.
Prod-WGBHTV Dist-PBS 1981

This Old House - The Bigelow House, Pt 2 C 29 MIN
3/4 OR 1/2 INCH VIDEO CASSETTE
Presents Bob Vila discussing plans for renovating the Barn unit - insulating, demolition and replacing broken windows.
From The This Old House - The Bigelow House Series.
Prod-WGBHTV Dist-PBS 1981

This Old House - The Bigelow House, Pt 20 C 29 MIN
3/4 OR 1/2 INCH VIDEO CASSETTE
Shows the kitchen in the Main House getting a ceramic tile floor. The south facade gets a glass sunbath, the Barn gets a heating/cooling fan and the fireplace gets a new stone face.
From The This Old House - The Bigelow House Series.
Prod-WGBHTV Dist-PBS 1981

This Old House - The Bigelow House, Pt 21 C 29 MIN
3/4 OR 1/2 INCH VIDEO CASSETTE
Shows the old metal garages coming down and Barn lighting being installed. In the Main House, air conditioning and kitchen window casings are installed.
From The This Old House - The Bigelow House Series.
Prod-WGBHTV Dist-PBS 1981

This Old House - The Bigelow House, Pt 22 C 29 MIN
3/4 OR 1/2 INCH VIDEO CASSETTE
Plans are made for a new garage. Norm Abram discusses the stairway in the Barn and at the Main House a downdraft stove is installed and the sunbath gets a copper roof.

From The This Old House - The Bigelow House Series.
Prod-WGBHTV Dist-PBS 1981

This Old House - The Bigelow House, Pt 23 C 29 MIN
3/4 OR 1/2 INCH VIDEO CASSETTE
Bob Vila inspects the custom-made hardwood spiral staircase in the Barn and takes us on a tour of the factory where it was made. Looks at the repairs on the fireplace tiles in the Main House.
From The This Old House - The Bigelow House Series.
Prod-WGBHTV Dist-PBS 1981

This Old House - The Bigelow House, Pt 24 C 29 MIN
3/4 OR 1/2 INCH VIDEO CASSETTE
Shows Bob Vila inspecting the custom-built kitchen cabinets in the Barn and checks the plastering work upstairs. Landscape architect Tom Wirth gives a lesson in brick paving and takes us on a tour of a granite quarry.
From The This Old House - The Bigelow House Series.
Prod-WGBHTV Dist-PBS 1981

This Old House - The Bigelow House, Pt 25 C 29 MIN
3/4 OR 1/2 INCH VIDEO CASSETTE
Shows the white cedar shingling going up in the Barn greenhouse and inside the Barn, Bob Vila oversees installation of a heat pump, then he helps apply the exterior stain to the Main House.
From The This Old House - The Bigelow House Series.
Prod-WGBHTV Dist-PBS 1981

This Old House - The Bigelow House, Pt 26 C 29 MIN
3/4 OR 1/2 INCH VIDEO CASSETTE
Bob Vila takes a stroll around the grounds and shows that the landscaping is well underway. There has been great progress at the Ice House and Woodshed and the Barn is nearly completed.
From The This Old House - The Bigelow House Series.
Prod-WGBHTV Dist-PBS 1981

This Old House - The Bigelow House, Pt 27 C 60 MIN
3/4 OR 1/2 INCH VIDEO CASSETTE
Presents host Bob Vila taking a grand tour of the newly renovated Bigelow House.
From The This Old House - The Bigelow House Series.
Prod-WGBHTV Dist-PBS 1981

This Old House, Pt 1 - The Dorchester—A Series

Demonstrates the home remodeling process step by step. Features the transformation of a dilapidated house into a Victorian home.
Prod-WGBHTV Dist-MTI

Ceiling And Renovation 030 MIN
Closer Look, A 030 MIN
Finishing Touches 030 MIN
First Impression 030 MIN
Flooring And Masonry 030 MIN
Heating And Insulation 030 MIN
History Preserved 030 MIN
Landscape Design 030 MIN
Paint Stripping Hints 030 MIN
Parquet And Tile Floors 030 MIN
Plasterers, Roofers, Carpenters 030 MIN
Question Of Heating, The 030 MIN
Unforeseen Problems 030 MIN

This Old House, Pt 2 - Suburban '50s—A Series

Demonstrates the home remodeling process step by step. Features the transformation of a ranch-style tract house.
Prod-WGBHTV Dist-MTI

Counter Top Installation 030 MIN
Dry Wall 030 MIN
Energy Audit 030 MIN
Framing And Addition 030 MIN
Grand Tour 030 MIN
Master Bathroom 030 MIN
Mistake-Proof Wallpapering 030 MIN
No-Wax Floors 030 MIN
Proposal For Expansion 030 MIN
Roof Check 030 MIN
Trimming And Painting 030 MIN
Waterproofing The Basement 030 MIN
Wiring And Insulation 030 MIN

This One For Dad C 18 MIN
16MM FILM, 3/4 OR 1/2 IN VIDEO J-C R
Addresses the acceptance of death with a story about a boy who idolized his father and had to face the reality of his father's death.
From The Reflections Series.
Prod-PAULST Dist-PAULST 1978

This Other Eden C 60 MIN
16MM FILM OPTICAL SOUND
Traces the history of England, emphasizing the role of religion. Includes scenes of Stonehenge, the sanctuary at Glastonbury, the fortress of Maiden Castle, and Bamburg Castle.
LC NO. 80-700288
Prod-NBC Dist-NBC 1979

This Our India C 9 MIN
16MM FILM OPTICAL SOUND H-C A
Presents the basic geographic and economic facts about India. Uses animated maps and diagrams to show how the people of India are striving to achieve a fuller and better life.
Prod-INDIA Dist-NEDINF

This Question Of Violence B 59 MIN
16MM FILM OPTICAL SOUND H-C A
Reports on the historical, social and psychological factors which underline violence in modern life. Presents a discussion by psychiatrists of the problem of agression. Traces the history of violence in the United States, emphasizing that periods of dramatic social change have most often been associated with outbreaks of violence. Examines the responsibilities of the mass media with respect to violence.
LC NO. FIA68-3077
Prod-NET Dist-IU 1968

This Side Is Good C 18 MIN
16MM FILM, 3/4 OR 1/2 IN VIDEO
Focuses on 72-year-old Sidney Keller six years after a severe stroke left him paralyzed on his right side and moderately aphasic. Shows his activities of daily living, his day-to-day struggles and adjustments, his interactions with family and friends and his volunteer work as a messenger at a Veterans Administration Hospital.
Prod-FLMLIB Dist-FLMLIB 1983

This Side Of Eden C 25 MIN
16MM FILM, 3/4 OR 1/2 IN VIDEO H-C A
Tells how Adam and Eve, guilt-stricken over Eden and appalled at Cain's murder of Abel, become alienated from each other. Describes how God intervenes. Stars Ed Asner, Carol Burnett and Walter Matthau.
Prod-PAULST Dist-MEDIAG

This Thing Called Change C 9 MIN
16MM FILM, 3/4 OR 1/2 IN VIDEO IND
Suggests that new realities are here and the comfortable past will never return.
Prod-CCCD Dist-CCCD

This Time On My Own C 33 MIN
16MM FILM, 3/4 OR 1/2 IN VIDEO J-C
Tells the story of Kim Williams, a promising teenage swimmer whose discovery that she has epilepsy forces her into a dramatic re-evaluation of her future. Reveals that her coach, teachers, family and friends begin to treat her differently. Explains how Steve Connors, a new boy in school, helps her overcome the attitude of those people who assume that epilepsy has to be a disability.
LC NO. 84-706730
Prod-CANBC Dist-CF 1984

This Time Sweden C 25 MIN
16MM FILM OPTICAL SOUND
Features Sweden away from the large cities, the country itself with the people who are hospitable and proud to show the visitor their modern country.
Prod-SWNTO Dist-SWNTO

This Tiny World C 15 MIN
16MM FILM, 3/4 OR 1/2 IN VIDEO
Reveals the life which is found in a group of oldfashioned toys.
Prod-PHENIX Dist-PHENIX 1973

This Trembling Earth C 22 MIN
3/4 OR 1/2 INCH VIDEO CASSETTE J-H
See series title for descriptive statement.
From The Phenomenal World Series.
Prod-EBEC Dist-EBEC 1983

This Was The Beginning—A Series
16MM FILM, 3/4 OR 1/2 IN VIDEO J-C
Groups vertebrates and invertebrates according to common characteristics and evolutionary sequence.
Prod-NFBC Dist-IFB

This Was The Beginning, Pt 1 - The
This Was The Beginning, Pt 2 - The 011 MIN

This Was The Beginning, Pt 1 - The Invertebrates C 13 MIN
16MM FILM, 3/4 OR 1/2 IN VIDEO J-C
Presents the first invertebrates which appeared in the oceans, including algae, sponges, coelenterates, worms, mollusks, arthropods and echinoderms.
From The This Was The Beginning Series.
Prod-NFBC Dist-IFB 1982

This Was The Beginning, Pt 2 - The Vertebrates C 11 MIN
16MM FILM, 3/4 OR 1/2 IN VIDEO J-C
Considers the classification of vertebrates, including cartilaginous fish, bony fish, amphibians, reptiles, birds and mammals. Highlights physical characteristics, environmental adaptations and reproductive behaviors which differentiate the groupings. Shows that man is a remarkable primate set apart by his brain and hand.
From The This Was The Beginning Series.
Prod-NFBC Dist-IFB 1982

This Way To Heaven B 30 MIN
16MM FILM OPTICAL SOUND I-C A
A story about a young boy who asks his sunday school superintendent about the way to heaven.
LC NO. 72-701661
Prod-CONCOR Dist-CPH 1956

This Way To Safety C 10 MIN
16MM FILM OPTICAL SOUND
Depicts a pharmacist and his assistant who present examples of how people knowingly or unknowingly misuse medicines designed to relieve mental and physical distress.
From The Drugs And Medicine Series.
LC NO. 76-702571
Prod-MORLAT Dist-MORLAT 1975

This Way To The White House B 13 MIN
16MM FILM OPTICAL SOUND J-H
Shows the making of a President. Depicts the color and excitement of the American electoral process of nomination, election and inauguration.
From The Screen News Digest Series. Vol 15, Issue 6
LC NO. 73-701272
Prod-HEARST Dist-HEARST 1973

This World Is Not For Children C 54 MIN
16MM FILM OPTICAL SOUND H-C A
Concerns children everywhere as victims of superstition, ignorance and the indifference of the privileged. Shows children in scenes from Peru, Africa, Columbia, Thailand, Japan and India, who are overworked, socially rejected, exploited and have short life expectancies. Narrated by Peter Ustinov. Made In England.
LC NO. 76-701399
Prod-PRICER Dist-MMA 1975

This Year, Next Year, Sometime B 19 MIN
16MM FILM OPTICAL SOUND C T
Describes the work of Dr Joshua Bierer, who extended the day-hospital concept to treatment of emotionally disturbed children. Depicts the center's facilities and the basic idea behind it.
Prod-CASH Dist-NYU 1962

This Year's Hero C 12 MIN
16MM FILM OPTICAL SOUND
Demonstrates the economic, social and physical hardships that can affect family life when excessive drinking is a problem.
LC NO. 77-702673
Prod-ODH Dist-ODH Prodn-CRAF 1975

Thomas Alva Edison - The Wizard Of Menlo Park C 25 MIN
16MM FILM, 3/4 OR 1/2 IN VIDEO I-C A
Discusses the life of Thomas Alva Edison. Tells how he created the phonograph, the incandescent light bulb, the electric railroad, the motion picture projector and the storage battery.
From The Americana Series.
Prod-HANDEL Dist-HANDEL 1982

Thomas And The Fiscal Fighters C 30 MIN
3/4 OR 1/2 INCH VIDEO CASSETTE
Differentiates between the two main types of discretionary fiscal policies - increased government expeditures or decreased taxes.
From The Money Puzzle - The World Of Macroeconomics Series. Module 9
Prod-MDCC Dist-MDCC

Thomas Corwin B 51 MIN
16MM FILM, 3/4 OR 1/2 IN VIDEO I-H
Dramatizes the opposition of Senator Thomas Corwin to the Mexican War. Shows how he ignored public opinion in his refusal to support military appropriations. Based on book Profiles In Courage by John F Kennedy.
From The Profiles In Courage Series.
LC NO. 83-706546
Prod-SAUDEK Dist-SSSSV 1965

Thomas E Dewey B 26 MIN
16MM FILM, 3/4 OR 1/2 IN VIDEO I-C A
Uses rare actuality footage to portray the personal life and history-making deeds of Thomas E Dewey.
From The Biography Series.
Prod-WOLPER Dist-SF 1963

Thomas Edison B 7 MIN
16MM FILM OPTICAL SOUND
Presents a 1955 Screen News Digest excerpt illustrating many of the results of Thomas Edison's inventive genius. Portrays his laboratory as he left it. Shows his first phonography which still works, the incandescent light, motion picture photography and other Edison legacies.
From The News Magazine Of The Screen Series. Vol 3 No. 6
Prod-PATHE Dist-HEARST 1953

Thomas Edison B 20 MIN
2 INCH VIDEOTAPE I
See series title for descriptive statement.
From The Americans All Series.
Prod-DENVPS Dist-GPITVL Prodn-KRMATV

Thomas Edison - Let There Be Light B 15 MIN
1/2 IN VIDEO CASSETTE BETA/VHS
Dramatizes the life of Thomas Edison, inventor of the phonograph, the motion picture camera and the incandescent lamp.
Prod-STAR Dist-STAR

Thomas Edison - Lightning Slinger C 51 MIN
16MM FILM, 3/4 OR 1/2 IN VIDEO I-H
Recreates the turning point in the life of young Thomas Edison, focusing on the hardships he overcame to become one of the world's greatest inventors.
From The Great Americans Series.
Prod-LUF Dist-LUF 1979

Thomas Edison's Glenmont C 23 MIN
16MM FILM, 3/4 OR 1/2 IN VIDEO I-C A
Presents a guided tour of the residence of Thomas Edison, Glenmont. Describes the life and inventions of Edison.
From The American Lifestyle - Industrialists And Inventors Series.
Prod-COMCO Dist-AIMS 1978

Thomas Hardy's Wessex C 30 MIN
3/4 INCH VIDEO CASSETTE H-C A
Presents a dramatized presentation of the poetry of Thomas Hardy, filmed in the southwest corner of England.
From The Anyone For Tennyson Series.
Prod-NETCHE Dist-GPITVL

Thomas Hart Benton B 51 MIN
16MM FILM, 3/4 OR 1/2 IN VIDEO I-H
Dramatizes the role of Missouri Senator Thomas Hart Benton in opposing the extension of slavery into California and prevent-

ing Missouri from seceding from the Union. Analyzes interpretations of the Constitution that led the country into a civil war. Based on book Profiles In Courage by John F Kennedy.
From The Profiles In Courage Series.
LC NO. 83-706547
Prod-SAUDEK Dist-SSSSV 1964

Thomas Hart Benton's 'The Sources Of Country Music' C 27 MIN
16MM FILM, 3/4 OR 1/2 IN VIDEO
Documents from inception to completion the final work of the American muralist, Thomas Hart Benton.
Prod-KAWVAL Dist-KAWVAL

Thomas Jefferson C 13 MIN
16MM FILM, 3/4 OR 1/2 IN VIDEO I-J
Outlines the achievements and career of Thomas Jefferson.
From The Great Americans Series.
Prod-EBEC Dist-EBEC 1980

Thomas Jefferson B 20 MIN
3/4 OR 1/2 INCH VIDEO CASSETTE I
See series title for descriptive statement.
From The Americans All Series.
Prod-DENVPS Dist-GPITVL Prodn-KRMATV

Thomas Jefferson C 26 MIN
3/4 OR 1/2 INCH VIDEO CASSETTE I-C A
See series title for descriptive statement.
From The American Presidents Series.
Prod-DAVCO Dist-GPITVL

Thomas Jefferson C 26 MIN
16MM FILM, 3/4 OR 1/2 IN VIDEO I-H
Portrays the life of Thomas Jefferson, who was the author of the Declaration of Independence and later became President of the United States. Shows how he almost single-handedly built the foundation for democracy in America.
From The American Presidents Series.
Prod-JOU Dist-JOU 1978

Thomas Jefferson C 28 MIN
16MM FILM, 3/4 OR 1/2 IN VIDEO P-C
Shows Jefferson's self-written epitaph stating that he was the father of the University of Virginia, and the author of the Declaration of Independence and the Virginia Statute for Religious Freedom. Discusses the many other accomplishments of Jefferson and the riddle of why he chose to mention only these three. Describes Jefferson's contributions to science and agriculture and his love for the arts.
From The Americana Series. No. 3
Prod-HANDEL Dist-HANDEL 1967

Thomas Jefferson - Man From Monticello C 14 MIN
16MM FILM OPTICAL SOUND
Offers a tour of Monticello and the University of Virginia in an exploration of the architectural ideas of Thomas Jefferson. Shows how these ideas included the use of brick and other materials.
LC NO. 76-700431
Prod-BRICKI Dist-BRICKI Prodn-KAUFMH 1975

Thomas Jefferson's Monticello C 24 MIN
16MM FILM, 3/4 OR 1/2 IN VIDEO J-C A
Tours Jefferson's spacious home in Virginia. Shows how Monticello reflects Jefferson's life style.
From The American Lifestyle - U S Presidents Series.
Prod-COMCO Dist-AIMS 1975

Thomas Paine C 14 MIN
16MM FILM, 3/4 OR 1/2 IN VIDEO J-H
Presents the life of Thomas Paine and his major writings on democracy and individual rights. Shows the influence Paine had on the course of events leading up to the American Revolution.
Prod-EBEC Dist-EBEC 1975

Thomas Paine B 20 MIN
2 INCH VIDEOTAPE I
See series title for descriptive statement.
From The Americans All Series.
Prod-DENVPS Dist-GPITVL Prodn-KRMATV

Thomas The Imposter (French) B 94 MIN
16MM FILM OPTICAL SOUND
Tells how an ambiguous young man plays with fiction and reality in the great theatre of World War I. Directed by Georges Franju. With English subtitles.
Prod-UNKNWN Dist-NYFLMS 1965

Thomas, Aged Two Years And Four Months - In Foster Care For Ten Days C 38 MIN
16MM FILM OPTICAL SOUND
Depicts Thomas, a well-developed, manly and confident boy, who joins a foster family while his mother is giving birth. Shows that throughout his stay he conducts himself competently, using the foster relationships adequately while retaining a clear memory of his mother and the certainty of reunion.
From The Young Children In Brief Separation Series.
Prod-VASSAR Dist-NYU

Thonk - Science And Hitting A Ball C 20 MIN
16MM FILM, 3/4 OR 1/2 IN VIDEO I-J
Investigates scientific principles involved in favorite sports, including tennis, golf and baseball.
From The Elementary Physical Science Series.
Prod-CENTRO Dist-CORF

Thor Heyerdahl's Incredible Voyage C 25 MIN
3/4 OR 1/2 INCH VIDEO CASSETTE
Describes Thor Heyerdahl's journey on the RA-2 from North Africa to the West Indies, which was designed to prove a link between the Egyptian and Mexican cultures.
Prod-UPI Dist-JOU

Thoracentesis C 9 MIN
3/4 OR 1/2 INCH VIDEO CASSETTE PRO
See series title for descriptive statement.
From The Medical Skills Films Series.
Prod-WFP Dist-WFP

Thoracentesis C 23 MIN
3/4 OR 1/2 INCH VIDEO CASSETTE PRO
Describes situations in which thoracentesis is used and presents the information needed to perform the procedure successfully.
Prod-HSCIC Dist-HSCIC 1977

Thoracic Cage, Pt 1 - True Ribs C 14 MIN
3/4 OR 1/2 INCH VIDEO CASSETTE PRO
Demonstrates basic rib movements of the true ribs during respiration. Shows how to test rib function for signs of disturbances in both the inhalation and exhalation phase. Demonstrates articulatory and muscle energy manipulative procedures.
From The Osteopathic Examination And Manipulation Series.
Prod-MSU Dist-MSU

Thoracic Mediastinum, The C 18 MIN
16MM FILM, 3/4 OR 1/2 IN VIDEO PRO
Outlines the boundaries of the mediastinum within the thoracic cavity.
From The Cine-Prosector Series.
Prod-AVCORP Dist-TEF

Thoracic Outlet Syndrome C 22 MIN
16MM FILM OPTICAL SOUND PRO
Reviews the anatomy, symptomatology and physical examination of thoracic outlet syndrome. Demonstrates the surgical treatment using the axillary approach for first rib resection.
Prod-ACYDGD Dist-ACY 1970

Thoracic Region, Pt 1 C 14 MIN
3/4 OR 1/2 INCH VIDEO CASSETTE PRO
Focuses on manipulative procedures and diagnosis in the upper thoracic region. Explains the principle of a direct technique. Shows three types of direct procedures in detail.
From The Osteopathic Examination And Manipulation Series.
Prod-MSU Dist-MSU

Thoracic Region, Pt 2 C 12 MIN
3/4 OR 1/2 INCH VIDEO CASSETTE PRO
Demonstrates examination and manipulative techniques for the thoracic spine with the patient seated astride the table. Emphasizes localization of operator forces and careful monitoring of the segmental dysfunction. Presents three types of direct technique.
From The Osteopathic Examination And Manipulation Series.
Prod-MSU Dist-MSU

Thoracic Spine, The C 19 MIN
3/4 OR 1/2 INCH VIDEO CASSETTE
Gives seven manipulative techniques for the treatment of the thoracic spine.
From The Cyriax On Orthopaedic Medicine Series.
Prod-VTRI Dist-VTRI

Thoracic—A Series

Presents a series on thoracic surgery.
Prod-SVL Dist-SVL

Axillary Thoractomy, Apical Pleurectomy And Gastric Cardioplasty 029 MIN
Gastroplasty And Hiatus Hernia Repair 045 MIN
Pectus Excavatum 029 MIN
Right Lower Lobectomy 018 MIN
Right Upper Lobectomy 039 MIN
Thoracotomy For Benign Mesenchymoma Of The 019 MIN
Trans-Cervical Thymectomy 017 MIN

Thoraco-Abdominal Approach To The Kidney C 14 MIN
16MM FILM OPTICAL SOUND
Shows that the thoraco-abdominal incision provides excellent exposure for renal surgery, particularly in cases of superior pole or large renal tumors. Describes the anatomy encountered in this approach including views of an actual operation.
From The Anatomy Of The Flank Series.
Prod-EATONL Dist-EATONL 1970

Thoraco-Abdominal Nephrectomy C 26 MIN
16MM FILM OPTICAL SOUND PRO
Demonstrates the removal of kidney tumors through the abdominothoracic approach. Explains that the excellent exposure obtained reduces trauma to the growth, permits early occlusion of the vascular pedicle and allows complete removal of the neoplasm with the adjacent tissue and lymph nodes.
Prod-ACYDGD Dist-ACY 1954

Thoracoabdominal Retroperitoneal Lymph Node Dissection, The C 25 MIN
16MM FILM OPTICAL SOUND
Explains that radical retroperitoneal lymph node dissection is an effective and proven way of curing patients with non-seminomanous testis tumors. Demonstrates the thoracoabdominal approach to retroperitoneal lymph node dissection, including both the right and left side approach, first in a patient without metastatic disease and then in a patient with extensive left retroperitoneal metastases.
LC NO. 75-702245
Prod-EATONL Dist-EATONL 1973

Thoracotomy For Benign Mesenchymoma Of The Mediastinum C 19 MIN
3/4 OR 1/2 INCH VIDEO CASSETTE
See series title for descriptive statement.
From The Thoracic Series.
Prod-SVL Dist-SVL

Thorax And Lungs C 30 MIN
3/4 OR 1/2 INCH VIDEO CASSETTE PRO
Views a physical assessment by a nurse practitioner of the thorax and lungs of a live patient.
From The Health Assessment Series.
Prod-BRA Dist-BRA

Thorax And Lungs C 30 MIN
3/4 OR 1/2 INCH VIDEO CASSETTE PRO
See series title for descriptive statement.
From The Health Assessment Series. Module 4
Prod-MDCC Dist-MDCC

Thorax And Lungs (2nd Ed) C 18 MIN
16MM FILM - 3/4 IN VIDEO PRO
Demonstrates the physical examination of the thorax and lungs, showing necessary procedures, manipulations, pacing, positions and patient-examiner interactions.
From The Visual Guide To Physical Examination (2nd Ed) Series.
LC NO. 81-707477
Prod-LIP Dist-LIP Prodn-JACSTO 1981

Thorax And Lungs, The C 22 MIN
3/4 OR 1/2 INCH VIDEO CASSETTE
Reviews the techniques of thoracic inspection, palpation, percussion and auscultation. Examines the trachea and rib excursion. Concludes with a review of auscultation maneuvers used to accentuate abnormal breath sounds.
From The Techniques of Physical Diagnosis - A Visual Approach Series.
Prod-MEDMDS Dist-MEDMDS

Thoreau's Maine Woods C 20 MIN
16MM FILM OPTICAL SOUND I-C
Re-traces the routes of Henry David Thoreau's trips through the Maine woods in the mid-19th century. Narrated by Richard Wilbur. Based on selections from The Maine Woods by Henry David Thoreau.
From The America's Wildlife Heritage Series.
LC NO. 79-700090
Prod-FENWCK Dist-FENWCK 1978

Thoreau's Maine Woods C 21 MIN
16MM FILM, 3/4 OR 1/2 IN VIDEO J-C A
Shows two canoeists retracing Henry David Thoreau's trips through the Maine woods. Presents selections from Thoreau's writings.
Prod-FENWCK Dist-FI 1978

Thorne Family Film X 85 MIN
3/4 OR 1/2 INCH VIDEO CASSETTE
Traces the story of the descendants of Jonathan C and Margaretta Williams Thorne, who came to Umatilla County, Oregon, in the 1880s to become farmers. Focuses on their values and on the challenge from mechanization.
Prod-MEDIPR Dist-MEDIPR 1977

Thornton Wilder B 24 MIN
16MM FILM, 3/4 OR 1/2 IN VIDEO J-C A
Examines the life and work of Thronton Wilder. Presents the humanist, the scholar and the dramatic innovator behind the facade of the popular playwright-novelist.
From The Films For The Humanities Series.
Prod-MANTLH Dist-FOTH 1967

Thornton Wilder's Our Town C
3/4 OR 1/2 INCH VIDEO CASSETTE
Prod-MSTVIS Dist-MSTVIS

Thoroughbred Affair B 14 MIN
16MM FILM OPTICAL SOUND
Presents a high-society horse show on the Main Line in Philadelphia which provides an opportunity for some oblique commentary on the American social system.
LC NO. 73-700619
Prod-TEMPLU Dist-TEMPLU 1971

Thoroughbred Heroes C 55 MIN
1/2 IN VIDEO CASSETTE BETA/VHS
Highlights 25 years of thoroughbred history. Includes races and training scenes.
Prod-EQVDL Dist-EQVDL

Thoroughbred Racing And The Calder Concept C 13 MIN
16MM FILM OPTICAL SOUND
Traces the development of a synthetic racing surface designed to reduce injuries to jockeys and horses.
LC NO. 77-702293
Prod-CALDRC Dist-TELAIR Prodn-TELAIR 1977

Thoroughbreds C 14 MIN
16MM FILM, 3/4 OR 1/2 IN VIDEO P-I
Shows the various stages of development of thoroughbred racehorses and explains how they are bred, trained and raced.
Prod-MEDLIM Dist-LUF 1979

Thoroughbreds C 29 MIN
2 INCH VIDEOTAPE
See series title for descriptive statement.
From The Maggie And The Beautiful Machine - Eating Series.
Prod-WGBHTV Dist-PUBTEL

Thoroughly Modern Millicent C 14 MIN
16MM FILM, 3/4 OR 1/2 IN VIDEO J-C A
Shows the dawn-to-past-dusk day of U S Congresswoman Millicent Fenwick, documenting the energy and dedication with which she serves her New Jersey constituents. Includes some family and archival photographs. Originally shown on the CBS program 60 Minutes.
Prod-CBSNEW Dist-MOKIN 1981

Thoroughly Modern Molly C 14 MIN
16MM FILM OPTICAL SOUND
Depicts various jobs, duty stations and training of modern women marines.

LC NO. 74-706595
Prod-USN Dist-USNAC 1968

Those Bad Dude Laundry Germs C 8 MIN
3/4 OR 1/2 INCH VIDEO CASSETTE
Designed to train laundry personnel in hospitals and other institutions where preventing disease transmission is of paramount importance. Illustrates growth and transmission of germs, demonstrates correct hand washing, and provides six basic rules to prevent infection.
Prod-HSCIC Dist-HSCIC

Those Calloways C 131 MIN
16MM FILM OPTICAL SOUND I-C
Stars Brian Keith, Vera Miles and Walter Brennan. Portrays a family of rural Vermont establishing a permanent lake sanctuary for the great geese flocks who migrate south through their New England town each year.
Prod-DISNEY Dist-UAE 1964

Those Crazy Canucks C 47 MIN
3/4 INCH VIDEO CASSETTE
Features Canada's outstanding downhill ski team as it competes in one of the most dynamic and dangerous sports in the world.
Prod-LAURON Dist-LAURON

Those First Years C 17 MIN
16MM FILM, 3/4 OR 1/2 IN VIDEO
Explores the first years of human development, showing that investigation and exploration, development of coordination, compliance and role modeling are typical features of this age level.
From The Behaviorally Speaking Series.
LC NO. 79-706179
Prod-NMAC Dist-USNAC 1979

Those Flying Canucks C 53 MIN
3/4 INCH VIDEO CASSETTE
Highlights two talented young men who train and work together while competing against each other and the world for ski jumping sumpremacy.
Prod-LAURON Dist-LAURON

Those Four Cozy Walls B 52 MIN
16MM FILM OPTICAL SOUND
Discusses the mission of the church in the world of today.
LC NO. 79-702610
Prod-UMCH Dist-UMCH 1968

Those Good Ol' Days C 26 MIN
16MM FILM OPTICAL SOUND I-C A
Shows conflict between landowners and the increasing number of hunters. Two farmers find that a farm can produce crops and wildlife.
Prod-TGAFC Dist-TGAFC 1961

Those Good Old Golden Rule Days C 15 MIN
3/4 OR 1/2 INCH VIDEO CASSETTE I
Features Grandpa singing a song from his schooldays about the presidents of the United States. He tells Caroline about the schools in the pioneer days.
From The We Are One Series.
Prod-NEITV Dist-GPITVL 1983

Those Incredible Diving Machines C 23 MIN
16MM FILM, 3/4 OR 1/2 IN VIDEO
A shortened version of Those Incredible Diving Machines. Traces the history of attempts to improve techniques and equipment to explore or exploit the riches of the sea. Describes future possibilities in this area.
From The Undersea World Of Jacques Cousteau Series.
Prod-METROM Dist-CF 1970

Those Incredible Diving Machines C 52 MIN
16MM FILM, 3/4 OR 1/2 IN VIDEO
Traces attempts to probe the ocean's depths from Alexander the Great's glass diving barrel to the development of the aqualungs and mini-subs of the 1970's.
From The Undersea World Of Jacques Cousteau Series.
Prod-METROM Dist-CF 1971

Those Mail Order Millions C 10 MIN
16MM FILM, 3/4 OR 1/2 IN VIDEO I-H A
Shows how to avoid misleading and fraudulent mail order practices.
From The Consumer Fraud Series.
Prod-PART Dist-PFP 1976

Those People Can't Do It C 21 MIN
3/4 OR 1/2 INCH VIDEO CASSETTE
See series title for descriptive statement.
From The Sex And Disability Series. Pt 2
Prod-MLLRE Dist-AJN

Those People Can't Have Kids C 22 MIN
3/4 OR 1/2 INCH VIDEO CASSETTE
See series title for descriptive statement.
From The Sex And Disability Series. Pt 4
Prod-MLLRE Dist-AJN

Those People Don't Enjoy It C 23 MIN
3/4 OR 1/2 INCH VIDEO CASSETTE
See series title for descriptive statement.
From The Sex And Disability Series. Pt 3
Prod-MLLRE Dist-AJN

Those People Don't Want It C 13 MIN
3/4 OR 1/2 INCH VIDEO CASSETTE
See series title for descriptive statement.
From The Sex And Disability Series. Pt 1
Prod-MLLRE Dist-AJN

Those Vital First Minutes C 22 MIN
16MM FILM OPTICAL SOUND
Dramatizes an accident involving hazardous materials in transit and then shows the cooperation of police, truck drivers, shippers and government in keeping the accident under control and protecting all those involved.
LC NO. 76-702677
Prod-DUPONT Dist-DUPONT Prodn-HANDY 1976

Those Were The Days X 22 MIN
16MM FILM, 3/4 OR 1/2 IN VIDEO K-P
A motion picture scrapbook of people and things in America from 1910 through 1950. Incudes scenes of an early barber shop, a blacksmith shop, an old turkey farm, a barnstorming airplane of the 1920's, a threshing machine, steam trains and cowboys. Shows people picking cotton, pitching hay onto a wagon and stacking hay.
Prod-FO Dist-FO 1972

Those Who Care C 14 MIN
16MM FILM OPTICAL SOUND
Illustrates the wide range of services provided by the volunteers of the Red Cross in the Chicago area.
Prod-AREDC Dist-AMRC

Those Who Go B 33 MIN
16MM FILM OPTICAL SOUND
Presents a statement about the world based on Georg Trakl's poem Offenbarung Und Untergang.
LC NO. 79-700293
Prod-POORI Dist-POORI 1979

Those Who Know Choose Gleaner Combines C 15 MIN
16MM FILM OPTICAL SOUND
Shows the Gleaner Combines as seen by qualified observers.
Prod-ALLISC Dist-IDEALF

Those Who Mourn C 5 MIN
16MM FILM OPTICAL SOUND H A
Describes a young wife's struggles to overcome grief at the loss of her husband and her growth through suffering.
From The Beatitude Series.
LC NO. 72-700776
Prod-FRACOC Dist-FRACOC 1972

Those Who Sing Together C 28 MIN
16MM FILM, 3/4 OR 1/2 IN VIDEO J-H
Introduces Indian culture through songs, dances and mythology reflecting the cycle of life from birth to death. Compares the instruments and songs of the Plains Indians with those from the Pacific Northwest.
Prod-DEVGCF Dist-MGHT 1978

Those Who Stay Behind C 16 MIN
16MM FILM OPTICAL SOUND
Shows the problems of the isolated and disadvantaged rural family and emphasizes those problems that face a family having an afflicted child.
LC NO. 74-705785
Prod-USSRS Dist-USNAC 1969

Thou Shalt Teach Them Diligently B 30 MIN
16MM FILM OPTICAL SOUND
Explains some of the religious observances in a Jewish home - Mezuzah, Tefillin, Siddur and Birkat Hamazon. (Kinescope)
Prod-JTS Dist-NAAJS Prodn-NBCTV 1951

Though I Walk Through The Valley C 29 MIN
16MM FILM, 3/4 OR 1/2 IN VIDEO
A dramatization about a terminal cancer patient, showing how, by means of his Christian faith, he was able to face death without fear.
Prod-GF Dist-PFP 1972

Though I Walk Through The Valley (German) C 30 MIN
16MM FILM, 3/4 OR 1/2 IN VIDEO J-C A
Presents a powerful statement on death and religious faith, which documents the last months of terminal cancer patient, Tony Brouwer, in a straightforward, unsentimental style. Includes the comments and reactions of Brouwer and his family.
Prod-GF Dist-PFP

Though The Earth Be Moved - The Alaskan Earthquake B 45 MIN
16MM FILM, 3/4 OR 1/2 IN VIDEO
Shows the Good Friday earthquake of 1964 which struck Alaska, causing death, damage and leaving cities helpless in the wave of shock, fire and seismic sea waves.
LC NO. 76-706222
Prod-USOCD Dist-USNAC Prodn-AUDIO 1965

Thought Dreams C
16MM FILM OPTICAL SOUND
Presents an experimental film based on a game of hide and seek by Barbar Linkevitch.
Prod-CANCIN Dist-CANCIN

Thought For Food C 20 MIN
3/4 INCH VIDEO CASSETTE J-H
Features a teen-ager illustrating how to make the most of the food dollar.
From The Dollar Data Series.
LC NO. 81-707360
Prod-WHROTV Dist-GPITVL 1974

Thought For Food - The World Food Conference Of 1976 C 28 MIN
16MM FILM OPTICAL SOUND
Documents the 1976 World Food Conference. Describes the gravity of the food situation in the 1970's, presents issues related to production, distribution and consumption of food, identifies available solutions and considers the possible consequences of inaction.
LC NO. 77-700581
Prod-WFDI Dist-IOWA Prodn-IOWA 1977

Thought Processes - Conscious And Subconscious C 30 MIN
3/4 OR 1/2 INCH VIDEO CASSETTE
See series title for descriptive statement.
From The Personal Development And Professional Growth - Mike McCaffrey's Focus Seminar Series.
Prod-DELTAK Dist-DELTAK

Thought You'd Never Ask C 12 MIN
16MM FILM OPTICAL SOUND
Focuses on a salesman as he presents his company's advertising and packaging program to distributor salesmen.
LC NO. 78-700222
Prod-SMRSTI Dist-SMRSTI 1977

Thoughts On Fox Hunting C 29 MIN
16MM FILM, 3/4 OR 1/2 IN VIDEO J-C A
Follows two fox hunts and shows how hounds are trained. Based on the book Thoughts On Hunting by Peter Beckford.
Prod-DAVT Dist-DAVT 1979

Thoughts On Fox Hunting C 30 MIN
16MM FILM - VIDEO, ALL FORMATS A
Illustrates the art of an American huntsman in Virginia engaged in traditional English-style fox hunting. Based on Lord Peter Beckford's 1781 classic 'Thoughts On Hunting.'
From The American Traditional Culture Series.
Prod-DAVT Dist-DAVT

Thoughts On The Run C 9 MIN
16MM FILM, 3/4 OR 1/2 IN VIDEO A
Discusses how jogging has impacted the lifestyles of millions of Americans. Presents Dr George Sheehan offering his thoughts on the importance of physical fitness in building the complete person.
Prod-SPORP Dist-MTI 1979

Thoughts, Words And Promises C
3/4 OR 1/2 INCH VIDEO CASSETTE T
Presents a variety of methods to stimulate children's desire to read and write. Illustrates strategies to help teachers guide students from single words to paragraphs.
From The Increasing Children's Motivation To Read And Write Series.
Prod-EPCO Dist-EDCORP

Thousand And One Naughts, A C 8 MIN
16MM FILM OPTICAL SOUND P
See series title for descriptive statement.
From The Mathematics For Elementary School Students - Whole Numbers Series.
LC NO. 73-701849
Prod-DAVFMS Dist-DAVFMS 1974

Thousand And One Years Ago, A - Inca Art Of Peru (400 - 1000 A D) C 12 MIN
16MM FILM OPTICAL SOUND
Presents Inca art of Peru dating from 400 to 1000 A D, showing scenes of war, daily life, demons and vivid animals. Shows that the whole range of Inca life and death is preserved in these artifacts of a lost culture in clay, stone, wood and paper-thin gold.
Prod-ROLAND Dist-ROLAND

Thousand Days, A - A Tribute To John F Kennedy B 22 MIN
16MM FILM OPTICAL SOUND
Uses the words of John Fitzgerald Kennedy, drawn from his speeches, his press conferences and his interviews to describe the goals which he had set for himself as President and the future he had envisioned for himself and his country. Surveys the accomplishment of Kennedy as President of the United States.
LC NO. FIA65-476
Prod-WOLPER Dist-WOLPER 1964

Thousand Days, The / Sicily - Key To Victory B 40 MIN
3/4 OR 1/2 INCH VIDEO CASSETTE
Presents Canada's preparations to become the 'machine shop of the empire' during the first thousand days of World War II, including the expansion of its army and air force and the construction of a tank factory and machine-gun factory. Records the achievements of Canada's First Division in the Sicilian campaign of June 1943, where British, American and Canadian forces were combined for the first time in a large military operation.
Prod-IHF Dist-IHF

Thousand Flowers Will Suddenly Blossom, A C 25 MIN
16MM FILM OPTICAL SOUND I-C A
Explains that thousands of spectators fill the slopes of the natural amphitheater at kibbutz Dahlia, to watch the annual folk dance festival. Shows different ethnic groups displaying their national costumes through their traditional folk dances.
LC NO. 72-702954
Prod-YEHU Dist-ALDEN 1970

Thousand Suns, A C 9 MIN
16MM FILM, 3/4 OR 1/2 IN VIDEO
Shows how people in the United States have used energy capabilities to create luxuries never dreamed possible, but have also created a throw-away society where little of value endures. Emphasizes the importance of creating values that last, such as self-respect and respect for all other living things.
Prod-BARR Dist-BARR 1974

Thousand Victories, A C 17 MIN
16MM FILM OPTICAL SOUND
Documents the daily life of young Michael Radcliff, born without hands, as he adapts to the use of his surgically-separated forearm bones.
LC NO. 75-701736
Prod-WRAMC Dist-USNAC 1973

Thousand Words, A C 29 MIN
2 INCH VIDEOTAPE

See series title for descriptive statement.
From The Museum Open House Series.
Prod-WGBHTV Dist-PUBTEL

Thousand Years Of Gujarat B 20 MIN
16MM FILM OPTICAL SOUND H-C A
Presents the rich heritage of Gujarat dating back more than a thousand years and shows historical temples, fortresses, gateways, mosques and minarets scattered all over the state.
Prod-INDIA Dist-NEDINF

Thousands Watch C 7 MIN
3/4 OR 1/2 INCH VIDEO CASSETTE
Presented by Dan Reeves and Jon L Hilton.
Prod-ARTINC Dist-ARTINC

Thousands Watch C 7 MIN
3/4 OR 1/2 INCH VIDEO CASSETTE
Prod-EAI Dist-EAI

Thread Of Hope, A C 19 MIN
16MM FILM OPTICAL SOUND
Presents a dramatized case study of the application of a cancer treatment teachnique. Shows the process of hyperthermic perfusion in which the patient's extremity is isolated, the blood in the area is heated and artificially circulated and drugs are injected into the bloodstream.
LC NO. 77-701837
Prod-STEHLN Dist-MFCFP Prodn-MFCFP 1977

Thread Of Life, The C 55 MIN
16MM FILM - 3/4 IN VIDEO J-H
Shows the development of the science of genetics, beginning with the cross-pollination experiments by Gregor Mendel through the study of genes, chromosomes and DNA in the 1950's.
From The Bell System Science Series.
Prod-ATAT Dist-WAVE 1960

Thread, The C 11 MIN
16MM FILM OPTICAL SOUND
Presents a dramatization based on a true story of the death of an old seamstress.
LC NO. 76-701377
Prod-SFRASU Dist-SFRASU 1973

Threading Taps And Dies, Pt 7 B 15 MIN
16MM FILM OPTICAL SOUND
Shows sequences and close-ups of the operations involved in tapping and threading as the worker views them in performance of the task. Explains the uses of taper, plug and bottoming taps and shows die adjustments for obtaining the desired fit of threads to tapped holes.
LC NO. FIE58-8
Prod-USN Dist-USNAC 1954

Threads C 110 MIN
16MM FILM, 3/4 OR 1/2 IN VIDEO C A
Gives an account of what might happen during and after a nuclear attack on Britain, based on scientific, medical, agricultural and psychological research. Covers a time span from a month before to 13 years after the war and relates events through the experiences of two families, one working-class and one middle-class. Portrays the breakdown of the supporting threads of a technologically advanced society.
Prod-BBCTV Dist-FI Prodn-WESWTV

Threat - Car Bomb C 20 MIN
16MM FILM OPTICAL SOUND
Demonstrates the effects of various explosive devices on a standard automobile. Explains how to protect a vehicle and how to conduct a cursory vehicle search, stressing reliance on professional ordnance technicians.
LC NO. 77-702294
Prod-MCCRNE Dist-MCCRNE 1977

Threatened Paradise C 30 MIN
2 INCH VIDEOTAPE
Explains that people are the cause of environmental decay in Florida. Features fishermen who discuss the industrial threat to Florida's fish supply. Narrated by Cliff Robertson.
Prod-WPBTTV Dist-PUBTEL

Threatening Sky, The B 40 MIN
16MM FILM OPTICAL SOUND
Presents a sober, well documented assessment of the bombing of North Vietnam, including the destruction of civilian areas, crops and factories. Shows the reactions and defense measures taken by the population. Introduction by Bertrand Russell.
Prod-VDR Dist-SFN 1967

Threats C 30 MIN
3/4 OR 1/2 INCH VIDEO CASSETTE
Deals with threats to which computer systems are potentially vulnerable and describes the various types of threats, relating them to the concepts of computer security, accuracy and privacy.
From The Corporate Computer Security Strategy Series.
Prod-DELTAK Dist-DELTAK

Three B 8 MIN
16MM FILM OPTICAL SOUND I-C
Records the imaginery love triangle of a frustrated introvert.
Prod-JORDAL Dist-CFS

Three A'S, Three B'S And One C B 48 MIN
16MM FILM OPTICAL SOUND T
An unrehearsed teacher-training film in which David Page demonstrates methods of presenting material as he teaches one of the University of Illinois arithmetic project topics to a class of fifth-graders. The class uncovers several of the surprising things that happen with number line rules.
From The University Of Illinois Arithmetic Project Series.
LC NO. 74-702617
Prod-EDS Dist-AGAPR 1969

Three Against The World C 25 MIN
3/4 INCH VIDEO CASSETTE
Focuses on ski racing and the racer, illustrating that success is largely determined by the excellence of the equipment and the best technical strategy.
Prod-LAURON Dist-LAURON

Three American Guns C 35 MIN
16MM FILM, 3/4 OR 1/2 IN VIDEO H-C A
Introduces three people who purchased guns for protection and used them. Re-enacts the events using most of the real participants.
Prod-BELLDA Dist-MTI 1983

Three Appeals C 60 MIN
3/4 OR 1/2 INCH VIDEO CASSETTE
Examines the state appeals process, focusing on three cases presented to the New York State Court of Appeals. Includes the oral arguments, interviews with the defendants, the plaintiffs and their attorneys, and commentary by Professor Charles Nesson, Associate Dean at Harvard Law School. Concludes with the decisions in each case, an explanation of how they were reached, and what they mean for the parties involved.
Prod-WNETTV Dist-WNETTV

Three Appendectomies C 30 MIN
3/4 OR 1/2 INCH VIDEO CASSETTE
See series title for descriptive statement.
From The Pediatric Series.
Prod-SVL Dist-SVL

Three Approaches To Group Therapy, Pt 1 C 38 MIN
16MM FILM - 3/4 IN VIDEO H-C A
Presents Dr Everett L Shostrom discussing his theories as presented in his book, ACTUALIZING THERAPY.
LC NO. 75-701108
Prod-PSYCHD Dist-PSYCHD 1974

Three Approaches To Group Therapy, Pt 2 C 40 MIN
16MM FILM - 3/4 IN VIDEO H-C A
Presents Dr Albert Ellis demonstrating his techniques of rational-emotive therapy as presented in his book, REASON AND EMOTION IN PSYCHOTHERAPY.
LC NO. 75-701112
Prod-PSYCHD Dist-PSYCHD 1974

Three Approaches To Group Therapy, Pt 3 C 38 MIN
16MM FILM - 3/4 IN VIDEO H-C A
Presents Dr Harold Greenwald using the type of therapy presented in his book, DECISION THERAPY.
LC NO. 75-701113
Prod-PSYCHD Dist-PSYCHD 1974

Three Approaches To Psychotherapy II—A Series

Presents three approaches to psychotherapy from three experts in the field.
Prod-PSYCHD Dist-PSYCHD

Actualizing Therapy 048 MIN
Client-centered Therapy 048 MIN
Multimodel Behavior Therapy 048 MIN

Three Approaches To Psychotherapy, No. 1 - Dr Carl Rogers X 48 MIN
16MM FILM OPTICAL SOUND C T
Describes client-centered therapy as practiced by Dr Carl Rogers. Shows his interview with patient Gloria and gives a summation of the effectiveness of the interview. Correlated with the textbook 'THERAPEUTIC PSYCHOLOGY' by L Brammer and E Shastrom.
LC NO. FIA66-1379
Prod-PSYCHF Dist-PSYCHD 1965

Three Approaches To Psychotherapy, No. 2 - Dr Frederick Perls X 32 MIN
16MM FILM OPTICAL SOUND C T
Describes the Gestalt therapy as practiced by Dr Frederick Perls. Shows his interview with patient Gloria and gives a summation of the effectiveness of the interview. Correlated with the textbook 'THERAPEUTIC PSYCHOLOGY' by L Brammer and E Shastrom.
LC NO. FIA66-1380
Prod-PSYCHF Dist-PSYCHD 1965

Three Approaches To Psychotherapy, No. 3 - Dr Albert Ellis X 42 MIN
16MM FILM OPTICAL SOUND C T
Describes rational-emotive psycho-therapy as practiced by Dr Albert Ellis. Shows his interview with patient Gloria and gives a summation of the effectiveness of the interview. Includes an evaluation by Gloria of her therapy with doctors Carl Rogers, Frederick Perls and Albert Ellis. Correlated with the textbook 'THERAPEUTIC PSYCHOLOGY' by L Brammer and E Shastrom.
LC NO. FIA66-1381
Prod-PSYCHF Dist-PSYCHD 1965

Three Axis Linear Milling C 15 MIN
3/4 OR 1/2 INCH VIDEO CASSETTE PRO
See series title for descriptive statement.
From The Numerical Control/Computer Numerical Control, Pt 1 - Fundamentals Series.
Prod-ICSINT Dist-ICSINT

Three Bad Men B 92 MIN
16MM FILM SILENT
Presents the story of three outlaws who join a girl on the Western trail and decide to protect her after her father is killed by a rival gang. Stars George O'Brien and Lou Tellegen. Directed by Lou Ford.
Prod-FOXFC Dist-KILLIS 1926

Three Barleycorns Equal An Inch C 15 MIN
3/4 INCH VIDEO CASSETTE J-C A
Examines the need for measurement and traces the development of some customary units of measurement. Points out the logic of the metric system.
From The Measure To Measure Series.
Prod-WCVETV Dist-GPITVL 1975

Three Billion Years Of Life - The C 70 MIN
3/4 OR 1/2 INCH VIDEO CASSETTE J-C
Traces organic evolution from the origins of life to the appearance of Homo sapiens. Discusses the Paleozoic, Mesozoic and Cenozoic Eras.
LC NO. 84-707111
Prod-SCIMAN Dist-SCIMAN 1976

Three Billion Years Of Life - The Drama Of Evolution
3/4 OR 1/2 INCH VIDEO CASSETTE C
Follows the chronology of organic evolution through three billion years, from the origins of life to the appearance of Homo sapiens.
Prod-SCIMAN Dist-GA

Three Billy Goats Gruff, The C 15 MIN
16MM FILM, 3/4 OR 1/2 IN VIDEO P
Tells the story of the Three Billy Goats Gruff.
From The Magic Carpet Series.
Prod-SDCSS Dist-GPITVL 1977

Three Billy Goats Gruff, The C 15 MIN
3/4 INCH VIDEO CASSETTE K-P
See series title for descriptive statement.
From The Storytime Series.
Prod-WCETTV Dist-GPITVL 1976

Three Black Writers B 30 MIN
16MM FILM OPTICAL SOUND H-C A
Larry Neal acts as moderator as Addison Gayle, Toni Cade and Charlie L Russell discuss the change in Black culture since the 1950's as revealed in the writings of Ralph Ellison, James Baldwin and Richard Wright.
From The Black History, Section 22 - The Cultural Scene Series.
LC NO. 72-704119
Prod-WCBSTV Dist-HRAW 1969

Three Brothers In Haiti C 17 MIN
16MM FILM, 3/4 OR 1/2 IN VIDEO P-C
Describes farm life in Haiti and explains government attempts to improve farming methods.
From The Man And His World Series.
Prod-FI Dist-FI 1969

Three Brothers, Playing A Broken Tune - Crescendos And Climaxes C 11 MIN
3/4 OR 1/2 INCH VIDEO CASSETTE
Reflects upon childhood innocence. Confronts a basic contradiction between representation and reality.
Prod-KITCHN Dist-KITCHN

Three Brothers, The - An African Folk Tale C 7 MIN
16MM FILM, 3/4 OR 1/2 IN VIDEO P-I
Tells of three brothers who go on a journey because the one who brings back the most extraordinary gift will win the hand of the prettiest girl in the village.
From The Folk Tales From Around The World Series.
Prod-ADPF Dist-SF 1980

Three By Martha Graham, Pt 1 - Cortege Of Eagles C 38 MIN
16MM FILM, 3/4 OR 1/2 IN VIDEO
Presents Cortege Of Eagles as performed by the Martha Graham Dancers.
Prod-PFP Dist-PFP 1969

Three By Martha Graham, Pt 2 - Acrobats Of God C 22 MIN
16MM FILM, 3/4 OR 1/2 IN VIDEO
Presents Acrobats Of God as performed by the Martha Graham Dancers.
Prod-PFP Dist-PFP 1969

Three By Martha Graham, Pt 3 - Seraphic Dialog C 25 MIN
16MM FILM, 3/4 OR 1/2 IN VIDEO
Presents Seraphic Dialog as performed by the Martha Graham Dancers.
Prod-PFP Dist-PFP 1969

Three By The Sea C 30 MIN
3/4 OR 1/2 INCH VIDEO CASSETTE P
Relates that as LeVar Burton strolls on the beach reading Three By The Sea, he learns that stories can be created out of the sea, the sand, the air and imagination.
From The Reading Rainbow Series. No. 12
Prod-WNEDTV Dist-GPITVL 1982

Three Cheers On A June Day C 14 MIN
16MM FILM OPTICAL SOUND
Shows June Week and graduation at the Naval Academy at Annapolis, Maryland.
LC NO. 74-705439
Prod-USN Dist-USNAC 1968

Three Chimes C 9 MIN
3/4 OR 1/2 INCH VIDEO CASSETTE J A
Recreates the story of Peter's betrayal of Christ. Uses an unusual photographic technique and a modern setting.
Prod-UMCOM Dist-ECUFLM

Three Cognitive Skills - Middle Childhood C 20 MIN
16MM FILM, 3/4 OR 1/2 IN VIDEO H-C A
Shows that a variety of factors can affect the development of a child's reading, memory and creativity skills.

From The Growing Years (CRMP) Series.
Prod-COAST Dist-CRMP 1978

Three Commemorative Stamps C 5 MIN
16MM FILM OPTICAL SOUND
Presents three short vignettes about three well-known commemorative stamps.
LC NO. 74-703243
Prod-USPOST Dist-USPOST Prodn-WWFI 1974

Three Dances From Cholla-Do, Korea C 23 MIN
16MM FILM, 3/4 OR 1/2 IN VIDEO
Presents three different types of dance from the Cholla region of South Korea, performed by professional dancers.
Prod-UWASH Dist-UWASHP

Three Day Gold C 70 MIN
1/2 IN VIDEO CASSETTE BETA/VHS
Features the U S Three-Day Team's preparation and the 1976 Olympic Three-Day Equestrian Event in Quebec.
Prod-USCTA Dist-EQVDL

Three Days In Szczecin C
16MM FILM OPTICAL SOUND H-C A
Re-creates a confrontation between striking Polish dock-workers and the head of the Polish Communist Party. Based on tape recordings kept by Polish workers.
From The World Series.
Prod-GRATV Dist-GRATV 1977

Three Days In The County Jail C 19 MIN
16MM FILM, 3/4 OR 1/2 IN VIDEO I-C
Dramatizes the life and daily routine of a large county jail. Illustrates methods and programs of rehabilitation. Presents the story through the eyes of a young man who was arrested for drunk driving and hit-and-run.
From The Under The Law, Pt 2 Series.
Prod-USNEI Dist-WDEMCO 1975

Three Days On A River In A Red Canoe C 30 MIN
3/4 OR 1/2 INCH VIDEO CASSETTE P
Presents the story Three Days On A River In A Red Canoe. Shows Levar Burton encountering fun and exciting challenges as he goes camping with a group of enthusiastic young friends.
From The Reading Rainbow Series. No. 9
Prod-WNEDTV Dist-GPITVL 1982

Three Days Respite C 15 MIN
16MM FILM, 3/4 OR 1/2 IN VIDEO H-C A
Explores the joy and release of carnival time in a town in the northeast of Brazil.
Prod-SLUIZR Dist-PHENIX 1974

Three Decades Of Donald Duck—A Series
16MM FILM, 3/4 OR 1/2 IN VIDEO
Presents Donald Duck cartoons.
Prod-DISNEY Dist-WDEMCO

Donald's Nephew 008 MIN
Fire Chief 008 MIN
Up A Tree 008 MIN

Three Dimensional Discipline C
16MM FILM, 3/4 OR 1/2 IN VIDEO T
Discusses classroom discipline techniques.
From The Dealing With Social Problems In The Classroom Series.
Prod-MFFD Dist-FI 1983

Three Dimensional Vectors B 26 MIN
3/4 OR 1/2 INCH VIDEO CASSETTE
See series title for descriptive statement.
From The Calculus Of Several Variables - Vector--Arithmetic Series.
Prod-MIOT Dist-MIOT

Three Directions In Australian Pop Music C 11 MIN
16MM FILM OPTICAL SOUND J-C A
Presents three contrasting styles of performance illustrating some of the latest developments in the Australian pop music scene.
LC NO. 73-702488
Prod-FLMAUS Dist-AUIS 1973

Three Domestics B 36 MIN
3/4 INCH VIDEO CASSETTE
Shows Pittsburgh police interviewing in three domestic situations, specifically arrest on assault and battery, removing a belligerent husband, and jailing a drunken father.
From The Pittsburgh Police Series.
Prod-DOCEDR Dist-DOCEDR Prodn-MSHLLJ

Three E's C 29 MIN
16MM FILM OPTICAL SOUND I-C A
Reviews the interrelationship between the three E's, energy, economics and environment. Describes the problems that have arisen in each area and presents some possible solutions. Explains some possibilities, as well as actual accomplishments, in the application of technology to our environmental problems.
Prod-EXXON Dist-EXXON 1973

Three Excerpts From A Group Dance Improvisation C 31 MIN
3/4 OR 1/2 INCH VIDEO CASSETTE
Shows three excerpts from a group dance improvisation.
Prod-METT Dist-METT

Three Faces Of Iceland C 25 MIN
16MM FILM OPTICAL SOUND C A
Traces the history of Iceland in words and images through the centuries, and uses the celebration of eleven hundred years of settlement in 1974 as a springboard. Describes Icelandic history from Viking days to modern times.
Prod-WSTGLC Dist-WSTGLC

Three Faces Of Stanley C 10 MIN
16MM FILM OPTICAL SOUND H-C A
Presents an animated cartoon with a humorous approach to some of the fears that Stanley has of the 'procto' examination. Outlines the value of the exam in detecting early cases of cancer of the colon and rectum.
Prod-AMCS Dist-AMCS

Three Facets Of Adventure C 28 MIN
16MM FILM OPTICAL SOUND C A
Examines the scenic attractions, social background and other items of interest to tourists and students in Holland, Italy and Israel.
LC NO. FIA66-868
Prod-DACKLM Dist-MCDO 1965

Three Families C 30 MIN
3/4 OR 1/2 INCH VIDEO CASSETTE H-C A
See series title for descriptive statement.
From The Japan - The Changing Tradition Series.
Prod-UMA Dist-GPITVL 1978

Three Families Of Jerusalem C 24 MIN
16MM FILM, 3/4 OR 1/2 IN VIDEO
Presents interviews with three families of the Jewish, Christian and Islamic religions to study how these families are vehicles for transmitting religion and microcosms of communities that are defined in part by their religions.
Prod-OPENU Dist-MEDIAG Prodn-BBCTV 1979

Three Fools, The C 9 MIN
16MM FILM, 3/4 OR 1/2 IN VIDEO P
Describes the odd and humorous behavior of three heroes shown trying to hatch eggs, shifting a tree to lie under its shade and building a bridge.
Prod-SF Dist-SF 1972

Three For The City C 15 MIN
16MM FILM OPTICAL SOUND
Documents the initial tests and demonstrations of three innovative buses of radical design and engineering, collectively named Transbus.
LC NO. 78-700821
Prod-USUMTA Dist-USNAC 1978

Three For The Road—A Series
16MM FILM, 3/4 OR 1/2 IN VIDEO H-C A
Discusses safe driving techniques, informs about the effects of alcohol and discourages the mixing of drinking and driving.
Prod-OMTC Dist-IFB

Alcohol You, The 025 MIN
No Thanks, I'm Driving 016 MIN
Power Under Control 022 MIN

Three Fox Fables B 11 MIN
16MM FILM, 3/4 OR 1/2 IN VIDEO P-I
Uses real-life photography to portray three Aesop fables, the Fox and the Grapes, the Fox and the Crow and the Fox and the Stork.
Prod-EBF Dist-EBEC 1948

Three Fox Fables (Spanish) B 11 MIN
16MM FILM, 3/4 OR 1/2 IN VIDEO P-I
Presents Aesop's fables The Fox And The Grapes, The Fox And The Crow and The Fox And The Storm. Uses real animals to re-enact the tales.
Prod-EBEC Dist-EBEC

Three Generations C 27 MIN
16MM FILM OPTICAL SOUND
Tells of the many steps required to manufacture the quality farm equipment needed to enable today's farmers to increase the productivity of their land and at the same time maintain its capabilities to produce equal abundance for their children and grandchildren.
Prod-NIFE Dist-VENARD

Three Generations Of Javanese Women C 29 MIN
3/4 INCH VIDEO CASSETTE J-C
Presents a group of Javanese women talking about sex roles, family life, village society and family planning. Describes the changes that have taken place in their lives as a result of using contraception.
From The Are You Listening Series.
LC NO. 80-707406
Prod-STURTM Dist-STURTM 1980

Three Gifts C 16 MIN
16MM FILM, 3/4 OR 1/2 IN VIDEO K-P
Features a puppet presentation of a fairy tale where two greedy characters try to steal the three magic gifts.
Prod-CZECFM Dist-PHENIX 1974

Three Golden Hairs C 13 MIN
16MM FILM, 3/4 OR 1/2 IN VIDEO K-I
Uses animation to tell the story of the girl who needs three golden hairs from the chin of the devil in order to win her prince and kingdom. Based on the fairy tale Der Teufel Mit Den Drei Goldenen Haaren by the Brothers Grimm.
From The Grimm's Fairy Tales Series.
Prod-BOSUST Dist-CF 1977

Three Golden Hairs (Spanish) C 13 MIN
16MM FILM, 3/4 OR 1/2 IN VIDEO P-J
Shows how a queen's greed causes her defeat.
From The Grimm's Fairy Tale (Spanish) Series.
Prod-BOSUST Dist-CF

Three Guesses C 29 MIN
16MM FILM, 3/4 OR 1/2 IN VIDEO H-C A
Studies Miss Jackie Burroughs of Toronto, representing the many roles that she, as one individual, assumes in the course of one day. Explains that she is, at the same time, actress, mother, daughter, woman and estranged wife.
Prod-NFBC Dist-PHENIX 1973

Three Herding Societies - Lapp, Quechua, Masai C 13 MIN
16MM FILM, 3/4 OR 1/2 IN VIDEO P-J
Examines three herding societies, showing that the three different cultures share many common elements due to their focus on herding. Looks at Lapps herding reindeer in northern Finland, Quechuas herding alpacas and llamas in Peru, and Masais herding cattle in the Great Rift Valley of Equatorial Africa in Kenya.
Prod-CORF Dist-CORF 1981

Three Heroes C 22 MIN
16MM FILM OPTICAL SOUND I-H A
Presents three Carnegie Medal winners and the heroic deeds that entitled them to this award. Features each hero relating how he saved the life of another human being.
LC NO. 73-702729
Prod-WGBHTV Dist-IU 1973

Three Horsemen C 55 MIN
16MM FILM OPTICAL SOUND
Offers an ethnographic documentary about three generations of aboriginal stockmen, aged 75, 46 and 13, who are trying to establish an all-Aboriginal cattle station on Cape York peninsula in Australia's northern Queensland.
Prod-AUSIAS Dist-UCEMC 1983

Three Hundred And Four Bushel Challenge C 15 MIN
16MM FILM OPTICAL SOUND
Presents the 1974 national Future Farmers of America (FFA) Crop Production Proficiency challenge winner Kenny Little of Louisiana and describes the cultural practices responsible for increased corn yields.
Prod-FUNKBS Dist-VENARD

Three Husbands C 43 MIN
3/4 OR 1/2 INCH VIDEO CASSETTE PRO
Shows three husbands, 34-52 years old, discussing their feelings about their wives' breast cancers. Includes effects of the illness on marriage and children, sexual functioning, reactons to mastectomy, perspectives about medical treatment, concerns about the future and ways husbands support thier wives emotionally.
Prod-UMICHM Dist-UMICHM 1982

Three In A Round B 7 MIN
16MM FILM OPTICAL SOUND
Presents a dance short in which two or more roles are performed simultaneously by the same person, appearing sometimes as a mirror image, sometimes moving in counterpoint to himself. Provides a series of dance patterns embracing techniques from popular ballet, modern dance and jazz.
Prod-WEAVRR Dist-RADIM

Three Is A Magic Number C 4 MIN
3/4 OR 1/2 INCH VIDEO CASSETTE P-I
Uses songs and cartoons to explore the mathematical possibilities of the number three.
From The Multiplication Rock Series.
Prod-ABCTV Dist-GA 1974

Three Island Women C 17 MIN
16MM FILM OPTICAL SOUND
Introduces a young woman, a middle-aged woman and an old woman who all agree that life on a small Chinese island in Hong Kong waters is better for them now than in the past. Shows them participating fully in the island's decision-making and economic life, while sharing with men the rigors of manual labor.
From The Faces Of Change - China Coast Series.
Prod-AUFS Dist-WHEELK

Three Key Controls C 29 MIN
3/4 OR 1/2 INCH VIDEO CASSETTE
Shows camera control, how to use the aperture, the shutter speed and the focus.
From The Photo Show Series.
Prod-WGBHTV Dist-PBS 1981

Three Key Questions In Coronary Disease B 90 MIN
16MM FILM OPTICAL SOUND PRO
Presents a panel of doctors discussing and debating the value and role of surgery, dietary fat and anticoagulant therapy in heart disease. Shows Dr Charles P Bailey of the Hahnemann Medical College performing an inverse endarterectomy.
Prod-UPJOHN Dist-UPJOHN

Three Letter Word For Love, A C 27 MIN
16MM FILM, 3/4 OR 1/2 IN VIDEO
Features a discussion between young minority men and women who voice their feelings, thoughts, misconceptions and fantasies about sex.
Prod-DOCUA Dist-CNEMAG

Three Little Kittens (2nd Ed) X 10 MIN
16MM FILM, 3/4 OR 1/2 IN VIDEO P
Traces the development of three kittens from birth until they are taken from their mother. Studies the characteristics and habits of cats and kittens.
Prod-EBF Dist-EBEC 1953

Three Little Pigs C 8 MIN
16MM FILM, 3/4 OR 1/2 IN VIDEO K-I
Tells the story of the Three Little Pigs.
Prod-DISNEY Dist-WDEMCO 1956

Three Little Pigs, The C 15 MIN
16MM FILM OPTICAL SOUND
Tells the story of the three little pigs and how they leave home and Ma Hog to gain their independence. Discusses how each of the little pigs deal with adversity.
Prod-BROADM Dist-BROADM 1976

Three Little Pigs, The (French) C 9 MIN
16MM FILM, 3/4 OR 1/2 IN VIDEO P

Teaches the importance of budgeting time for work and play.
Prod-WDEMCO Dist-WDEMCO 1956

Three Little Pigs, The - Background For Reading And Expression C 10 MIN
16MM FILM, 3/4 OR 1/2 IN VIDEO P
Uses real animals to retell the story of the Three Little Pigs.
Prod-CORF Dist-CORF 1956

Three Little Rabbits C 6 MIN
16MM FILM, 3/4 OR 1/2 IN VIDEO P-I
Presents an animated fable which tells how a joke turns into panic for several creatures of the forest and a hapless hunter.
Prod-HUNGFM Dist-LCOA 1974

Three Little Rabbits (Spanish) C 6 MIN
16MM FILM, 3/4 OR 1/2 IN VIDEO P-I
Tells the story of a magpie who overhears three little rabbits planning to change their menu from carrots to fox meat.
Prod-HUNGFM Dist-LCOA 1974

Three Little Wizards - An Adventure In Color C 7 MIN
16MM FILM, 3/4 OR 1/2 IN VIDEO P-I
The story of three wizards, red, yellow and blue, who discover that colors - and people, too - are at their best when in harmony.
Prod-VIKING Dist-SF 1966

Three Lives C 70 MIN
16MM FILM OPTICAL SOUND
Brings together without pretense or parallel, the lives of three women, Mallory Millett-Jones, Lillian Shreve, a reflective middle-aged woman and Robin Mide, a 'LIBERATED WOMAN.'
Prod-WLIBCC Dist-IMPACT 1970

Three Lives - Counseling The Terminally Ill C 57 MIN
3/4 OR 1/2 INCH VIDEO CASSETTE
Exposes the problems and concerns faced by the counselor of the dying and a moving portrait of three women who face their deaths with dignity and courage.
Prod-PELICN Dist-PELICN

Three Managerial Styles C 13 MIN
2 INCH VIDEOTAPE
Presents an instructional course for office employees. Portrays three different managerial styles. Shows the difference of each style as it is applied to the same managerial situation.
From The SUCCESS, The AMA Course For Office Employees Series.
LC NO. 75-704210
Prod-AMA Dist-AMA 1972

Three Meals A Day, Plus C 28 MIN
3/4 OR 1/2 INCH VIDEO CASSETTE J-H A
See series title for descriptive statement.
From The Food For Youth Series.
Prod-CUETV Dist-CUNIV 1975

Three Meals A Day, Plus C 29 MIN
16MM FILM, 3/4 OR 1/2 IN VIDEO
Emphasizes that although lunch is only one of a child's three or more meals a day, it may be the only nutritionally balanced meal he has all day. Points out the importance of proper food served at breakfast and dinner and makes suggestions for adding nutritious snacks to daily food intake.
From The Food For Youth Series.
LC NO. 81-706397
Prod-USFNS Dist-USNAC Prodn-WGBH 1981

Three Men In A Tub B 10 MIN
16MM FILM OPTICAL SOUND
Depicts a boat race between Alfalfa and Waldo which becomes a contest for Darla's affections. A Little Rascals film.
Prod-ROACH Dist-BHAWK 1938

Three Methods Of Facing Work To Length C
3/4 OR 1/2 INCH VIDEO CASSETTE
See series title for descriptive statement.
From The Basic Engine Lathe Series.
Prod-VTRI Dist-VTRI

Three Methods Of Facing Work To Length C 15 MIN
3/4 OR 1/2 INCH VIDEO CASSETTE
See series title for descriptive statement.
From The Machine Technology I - Basic Machine Technology Series.
Prod-CAMB Dist-CAMB

Three Methods Of Facing Work To Length C 15 MIN
3/4 OR 1/2 INCH VIDEO CASSETTE IND
See series title for descriptive statement.
From The Machining And The Operation Of Machine Tools, Module 2 - Engine Lathe Series.
Prod-LEIKID Dist-LEIKID

Three Methods Of Facing Work To Length (Spanish) C
3/4 OR 1/2 INCH VIDEO CASSETTE
See series title for descriptive statement.
From The Basic Engine Lathe (Spanish) Series.
Prod-VTRI Dist-VTRI

Three Miles High C 50 MIN
16MM FILM, 3/4 OR 1/2 IN VIDEO J-C A
Presents reporter Miles Kingston who begins a trip from Cuzco, Peru on the highest railway in the world, across the Andes mountains to La Paz, Bolivia. Observes all types of South American scenery, including the lost Inca city of Machu Pichu.
From The Great Railways Journeys Of The World Series.
LC NO. 82-706722
Prod-BBCTV Dist-FI 1981

Three Minute Warning C 15 MIN
16MM FILM, 3/4 OR 1/2 IN VIDEO
Presents television commentator Martin Agronsky who discusses smoke detectors. Covers the various kinds of smoke detectors and their installation in the home.
Prod-KLEINW Dist-KLEINW 1978

Three Minutes To Live C 33 MIN
16MM FILM OPTICAL SOUND
Stresses safety consciousness of workers and the use of modern safety techniques. As Death observes and narrates, Hydrogen Sulphide Gas attempts to become one of Death's foremost agents. Includes animation.
LC NO. 75-700009
Prod-FLMWST Dist-FLMWST 1974

Three Minutes To Live C
3/4 OR 1/2 INCH VIDEO CASSETTE
Pits hydrogen sulphide and death against human intelligence. Uses a plot in which 'Death' is personified as a black-cloaked motorcyclist and hydrogen sulphide as an invisible vicious killer, represented by a hidden voice.
From The Hydrogen Sulphide Safety Series.
Prod-FLMWST Dist-FLMWST

Three Modes Of Visualization For The Larynx C 7 MIN
3/4 OR 1/2 INCH VIDEO CASSETTE PRO
Demonstrates three methods to visualize the larnyx and surrounding anatomical landmarks.
Prod-HSCIC Dist-HSCIC 1984

Three Moods B 8 MIN
16MM FILM OPTICAL SOUND
Presents later visions based on Moussorgsky's music, with slow-moving shadows on a sleepless night, an accelerated passage of drawings and sketches moving across the screen and a third mood of conflict between material goods and artistic aims. Produced by Alexander Alexeieff and Claire Parker.
Prod-STARRC Dist-STARRC 1980

Three Movers C 26 MIN
16MM FILM, 3/4 OR 1/2 IN VIDEO H-C A
Shows what happens to a traffic law violator after receiving three moving violations in Illinois. Dramatizes common moving traffic violations and explains the technology used to apprehend drivers.
LC NO. 81-706156
Prod-IFB Dist-IFB 1980

Three Musketeers With Mr Magoo, The C 52 MIN
16MM FILM OPTICAL SOUND P-I
Prod-FI Dist-FI

Three New Orleans C 18 MIN
16MM FILM OPTICAL SOUND
Depicts a dramatic story based on the premise that man has the power to control his future, which tells about a house in New Orleans, Louisiana, covering its past, present and future.
LC NO. 75-703295
Prod-UNORL Dist-UNORL 1975

Three New York Painters C 29 MIN
3/4 INCH VIDEO CASSETTE
Focuses on three young painters living in the Soho section of New York City.
From The Art Show Series.
Prod-UMITV Dist-UMITV

Three Of Us, The B 30 MIN
16MM FILM OPTICAL SOUND
Presents a documentary about the filmmaker's parents, focusing on their lives, marriage and relationship to their son, who reveals details of his life previously unknown to them.
LC NO. 77-702676
Prod-ROWBR Dist-CANFDC 1976

Three Paths - Hinduism, Buddhism, And Taoism C 18 MIN
16MM FILM, 3/4 OR 1/2 IN VIDEO J-C A
Examines Hinduism, Buddhism and Taoism and the worshippers of each religion.
LC NO. 82-706477
Prod-HP Dist-HP 1981

Three Phases Of A Therapeutic Relationship, The C 17 MIN
3/4 INCH VIDEO CASSETTE PRO
Uses a simulation of an actual clinical case in which a nurse performed therapy for seven months to demonstrate the initiation, working and termination phases of a therapeutic relationship.
LC NO. 79-707736
Prod-UMICHM Dist-UMMCML Prodn-UMISU 1975

Three Pirates C 19 MIN
3/4 OR 1/2 INCH VIDEO CASSETTE P-I
Compares even and uneven rhythms in music.
From The USS Rhythm Series.
Prod-ARKETV Dist-AITECH 1977

Three Poems B 10 MIN
16MM FILM OPTICAL SOUND
Presents three poems, the first a literal look at the bathroom sink, tub and toilet, the second a peaceful winter in Toronto, the third a short pan of Yonge Street.
LC NO. 77-702675
Prod-CANFDC Dist-CANFDC 1975

Three R's For Healthy Smiles C 15 MIN
16MM FILM OPTICAL SOUND
A puppet film exhorting the importance of good health habits in the care of teeth.
LC NO. FIA64-246
Prod-USC Dist-USC

Three R's, The C 15 MIN
3/4 OR 1/2 INCH VIDEO CASSETTE I
Illustrates the concepts of rhythm and simple metrical patterns in poetry.
From The Tyger, Tyger Burning Bright Series.
Prod-CTI Dist-CTI

Three Robbers, The C 6 MIN
16MM FILM, 3/4 OR 1/2 IN VIDEO K-P
Explains that three fierce robbers terrify the countryside until they meet a little girl named Tiffany. Points out that under Tiffany's golden charm the robbers turn their gold to good use and all ends happily.
Prod-WWS Dist-WWS 1972

Three Short Tapes By Barbara Buckner—A Series

Presents three short tapes by Barbara Buckner, video artist.
Prod-EAI Dist-EAI

Heads 006 MIN
Hearts 012 MIN
Milennia 006 MIN

Three Short Tapes—A Series

Presents three short videotapes by video artist Peter Campus.
Prod-EAI Dist-EAI

R-G-B 011 MIN
Set of Coincidence 013 MIN
Three Transitions 005 MIN

Three Sisters, The C 60 MIN
3/4 OR 1/2 INCH VIDEO CASSETTE H-C A
Develops an appreciation of the playwright's craft in shaping the elements of plot, theme and character. Uses the play The Three Sisters as an example.
From The Drama - Play, Performance, Perception Series. Playwrights And Plotting
Prod-BBCTV Dist-FI 1978

Three Sisters, The C 135 MIN
16MM FILM, 3/4 OR 1/2 IN VIDEO
Presents Anton Chekhov's play The Three Sisters, featuring Janet Suzman.
From The Classic Theatre Series.
LC NO. 79-706930
Prod-BBCTV Dist-FI 1976

Three Songs By Leadbelly C 8 MIN
16MM FILM OPTICAL SOUND J-C A
Shows Huddie Ledbetter in 1945 singing three of his best known folk songs.
LC NO. 75-701089
Prod-SEEGER Dist-RADIM 1975

Three Stone Blades C 16 MIN
16MM FILM, 3/4 OR 1/2 IN VIDEO I-H
Dramatizes an Eskimo legend about a widow and her selfish sister-in-law.
Prod-IFB Dist-IFB 1971

Three Stone Blades (Captioned) C 16 MIN
16MM FILM, 3/4 OR 1/2 IN VIDEO I-H
Dramatizes an Eskimo legend about a widow and her selfish sister-in-law.
Prod-IFB Dist-IFB 1971

Three Stooges Film Festival, The - Vol 1 B 80 MIN
3/4 OR 1/2 INCH VIDEO CASSETTE
Stars the Three Stooges in four short slapstick comedies - Disorder In The Court, Brideless Groom, Sing A Song of Six Pants and Malice In The Palace.
Prod-ADVCAS Dist-ADVCAS

Three Story Suite C 30 MIN
3/4 OR 1/2 INCH VIDEO CASSETTE
Presents a trio of folktales performed by storyteller Laura Simms. Uses video effects to make visual the magic of these myths.
From The Doris Chase Concepts Series.
Prod-CHASED Dist-CHASED

Three Styles Of Marital Conflict C 14 MIN
16MM FILM, 3/4 OR 1/2 IN VIDEO
Features true-to-life vignettes depicting three common types of marital conflict.
Prod-RESPRC Dist-RESPRC

Three The Hard Way C 92 MIN
16MM FILM OPTICAL SOUND H-C A
Features Jim Brown as star and Gordon Parks, Jr as director in a study of the problems of three black business executives who are forced into a struggle with a secret racist organization.
Prod-CINEWO Dist-CINEWO 1974

Three Thirty-Six B 3 MIN
16MM FILM OPTICAL SOUND
Shows a campus guard finding a suicide victim hanging in a storeroom.
LC NO. 76-701437
Prod-SFRASU Dist-SFRASU 1975

Three Times Tables C 25 MIN
3/4 OR 1/2 INCH VIDEO CASSETTE H-C A
Demonstrates frame drop-leaf and pedestal tables in visits to a variety of old houses. Gives tips on repairing each type.
From The Better Than New Series.
Prod-BBCTV Dist-FI

Three Times Three C 14 MIN
16MM FILM - 3/4 IN VIDEO
Discusses factors which contribute to small business success, such as the ability of the owner, an understanding of financial matters and the effective use of management techniques.
LC NO. 79-707550
Prod-USSBA Dist-USNAC 1979

Three Times Three C 15 MIN
3/4 OR 1/2 INCH VIDEO CASSETTE
Dramatizes nine keys to small business success such as personal ability, use of assistance and information, insurance, regulation and taxes, business opportunity, sources of capital, records, financial factors, organization and planning.
From The Small Business Administration Series.
Prod-IVCH Dist-IVCH

Three To Get Ready C 25 MIN
3/4 OR 1/2 INCH VIDEO CASSETTE
Presents a filmed history of a group of children taken at various times during their first three years. Shows their mental and physical development, then a nursery school teacher tells and demonstrates how to prepare the unpredictable and sometimes assertive three-year-old for nursery school.
Prod-TRAINX Dist-TRAINX

Three To Go B 90 MIN
16MM FILM OPTICAL SOUND H-C A
Presents three stories, entitled Michael, Judy and Toula, which portray some of the problems of modern youth.
LC NO. 75-713559
Prod-ANAIB Dist-AUIS 1971

Three To Go, Pt 1 - Michael B 31 MIN
16MM FILM OPTICAL SOUND H-C A
Shows how a young man is caught between the opposing pulls of a conventional middle-class family and his pad-dwelling, pot-smoking friends.
Prod-ANAIB Dist-AUIS 1971

Three To Go, Pt 2 - Judy B 30 MIN
16MM FILM OPTICAL SOUND H-C A
Presents the story of a young middle-class girl, in a country town, wanting to leave for the big city against the wishes of parents and boyfriends.
Prod-ANAIB Dist-AUIS 1971

Three To Go, Pt 3 - Toula B 30 MIN
16MM FILM OPTICAL SOUND H-C A
Presents Toula, a Greek girl, whose family has been in Australia four years. Explains how she and her brother must reconcile the Greek and Australian way of life.
Prod-ANAIB Dist-AUIS 1971

Three To Make Ready C 30 MIN
16MM FILM OPTICAL SOUND A
Illustrates the three areas of child assistance provided by the Kansas Children's Service League--aid for unwed mothers, care and placement of children and emergency care for abandoned or deserted children.
LC NO. FIA68-841
Prod-KCSL Dist-UKANS Prodn-CENTRO 1967

Three Track C 18 MIN
16MM FILM, 3/4 OR 1/2 IN VIDEO J-C A
Looks at a ski school for pupils with learning disabilities. Shows the pupils being taught by volunteer instructors from the Canadian Ski Alliance.
Prod-NFBC Dist-NFBC 1979

Three Transitions C 5 MIN
3/4 OR 1/2 INCH VIDEO CASSETTE
Presents a performer who steps through himself in a two- fold, three-dimensional space.
From The Three Short Tapes Series.
Prod-EAI Dist-EAI

Three Types Of Oxy-Acetylene Flames, The Neutral, Oxidizing, Carburizing C 15 MIN
3/4 OR 1/2 INCH VIDEO CASSETTE
See series title for descriptive statement.
From The Welding I - Basic Oxy-Acetylene Welding Series.
Prod-CAMB Dist-CAMB

Three Types Of Oxy-Acetylene Flames, The Neutral, Oxidizing, Carburizing C 15 MIN
3/4 OR 1/2 INCH VIDEO CASSETTE IND
See series title for descriptive statement.
From The Welding - Oxy-Acetylene Welding Series.
Prod-ICSINT Dist-ICSINT

Three Types Of Oxy-Acetylene Flames, The - Neutral, Oxidizing, Carburizing (Spanish) C
3/4 OR 1/2 INCH VIDEO CASSETTE
See series title for descriptive statement.
From The Oxy-Acetylene Welding (Spanish) Series.
Prod-VTRI Dist-VTRI

Three Valleys Of Saint Lucia, The C 60 MIN
3/4 OR 1/2 INCH VIDEO CASSETTE
Deals with the work of an international team of doctors and scientists who have turned the lush Caribbean island of Saint Lucia into a lifesized laboratory to study the most effective means of controlling the spread of schistosomiasis, a human parasitic disease.
From The Quest For The Killers Series.
Prod-PBS Dist-PBS

Three Wheeled Fairytale C 20 MIN
16MM FILM OPTICAL SOUND
Presents a modern musical fairytale about a little girl and a meter maid who go out to find the world together.
LC NO. 70-713386
Prod-USC Dist-USC 1972

Three Wise Boys X 30 MIN
16MM FILM OPTICAL SOUND P-H T R
Tells a story about three boys who are brought face to face with meaning of Christmas when a destitute young couple and their sick baby take up temporary quarters in an abandoned farm house down the road.
Prod-FAMF Dist-FAMF

Three Women Alone C 49 MIN
16MM FILM OPTICAL SOUND
Presents socio-economic profiles of three women pioneering their newly emerging role of women without men in today's society.
LC NO. 74-702518
Prod-RKOTV Dist-SSC 1974

Three Works By Ian Hugo--A Series

Presents works by filmmaker Ian Hugo.
Prod-EAI Dist-EAI

Aphrodisiac II	006 MIN
Levitation	006 MIN
Transcending	015 MIN

Three Worlds Of Bali, The C 59 MIN
16MM FILM OPTICAL SOUND A
Features anthropologist Steve Lansing who explores the Indonesian, temple-based civilization of Bali which is coming to terms with the technological West. Shows how the Balinese religion unites and involves the people at every level of society.
LC NO. 82-700763
Prod-PBA Dist-DOCEDR Prodn-ABRMSE 1981

Three Worlds Of Bali, The C 59 MIN
3/4 OR 1/2 INCH VIDEO CASSETTE A
Features anthropologist Steve Lansing who explores the Indonesian, temple-based civilization of Bali which is coming to terms with the technological West. Shows how the Balinese religion unites and involves the people at every level of society.
Prod-PBA Dist-PBS Prodn-ABRMSE 1981

Three Worlds Of Childhood C 29 MIN
16MM FILM - 3/4 IN VIDEO H-C A
Presents Dr Urie Bronfenbrenner examining how children are raised in the Soviet Union, China and the United States. Offers suggestions for improving the American system of child rearing.
LC NO. 81-707366
Prod-CUNIV Dist-CUNIV 1975

Three Worlds Of Gulliver, The C 100 MIN
16MM FILM OPTICAL SOUND I-C
Stars Kerwin Mathews as the real-size Gulliver, traveling through the fabulous nation of beings only six to seven inches high, and then to Brobdingnag, the land of 40-foot giants.
Prod-CPC Dist-TIMLIF 1960

Three Years Of Adolf Hitler B
3/4 OR 1/2 INCH VIDEO CASSETTE
Shows scenes of Hitler's speeches and colorful rallies in an effort to mold the image of the Fuehrer in the eyes of the average German citizen.
From The Pre-War German Featurettes Series.
Prod-IHF Dist-IHF

Three 19th Century Watercolorists C 30 MIN
3/4 INCH VIDEO CASSETTE
See series title for descriptive statement.
From The Antiques Series.
Prod-NHMNET Dist-PUBTEL

Three-Axis Linear Milling C 18 MIN
3/4 OR 1/2 INCH VIDEO CASSETTE IND
Covers a compound angle, the dimensions of compound angle and 3-axis milling.
From The Numerical Control/Computerized Numerical Control, Module 1 - Fundamentals Series.
Prod-LEIKID Dist-LEIKID

Three-D Collage C 30 MIN
3/4 OR 1/2 INCH VIDEO CASSETTE
Shows how to transform a medium-sized mirror into a showpiece as Erica adds a latticework trim of ribbons, stuffed strawberries and three-dimensional leaves. Shows how to embroider jewelry boxes and make artificial flowers with pipe cleaners and brushed wool stitch.
From The Erica Series.
Prod-WGBHTV Dist-KINGFT

Three-D Defense...Self Defense For Women C 7 MIN
3/4 OR 1/2 INCH VIDEO CASSETTE
Instructs women of all ages in delaying, discouraging and disabling tactics to be used in a variety of threatening or potentially dangerous situations.
Prod-AFFVID Dist-AFFVID

Three-Dimensional Graphics C
3/4 OR 1/2 INCH VIDEO CASSETTE A
Surveys the most advanced applications available.
From The All About Computer Graphics Series.
Prod-EDDIM Dist-EDDIM

Three-Foot Squaring Shear Operation C 12 MIN
1/2 IN VIDEO CASSETTE BETA/VHS IND
Illustrates the operation of a three-foot squaring shear that has been converted from a manual to a hydraulic operation.
Prod-RMI Dist-RMI

Three-Headed Dragon, The C 25 MIN
3/4 OR 1/2 INCH VIDEO CASSETTE J A
Exposes the three-folder barrier to recovery from alcoholism, drinking, thinking, and feeling.
Prod-SUTHRB Dist-SUTHRB

Three-Hundred Feet To The Moon C 22 MIN
16MM FILM OPTICAL SOUND
Shows the history and development of the Lunar Landing Training Vehicle from its conception through the various design stages and tests to the present configuration.
Prod-NASA Dist-NASA

Three-Hundred-And-Four Bushel Challenge, The C 16 MIN
16MM FILM OPTICAL SOUND
Describes the 304 bushel challenge which originated in the 304-bushel yield produced by a 16-year-old Mississippi boy. Includes the cultural practices responsible for the increased corn yields of national winners. Second in a series.
Prod-FUNKBS Dist-VENARD

Three-M Brand Oil Sorbent C 18 MIN
16MM FILM OPTICAL SOUND
Explains what oil sorbents are and shows how to store, use and dispose of oil wastes.
LC NO. 76-702305
Prod-MMAMC Dist-MMAMC 1976

Three-M Toolbox For Imagineering C 18 MIN
16MM FILM OPTICAL SOUND
Pictures a wide and largely unrelated group of products manufactured by 3M Company Industrial Specialties Division. Uses two mimes who appear with a toolbox and demonstrate an assortment of products used for cushioning, reinforcing, joining and protecting.
LC NO. 75-700323
Prod-MMAMC Dist-MMAMC Prodn-TRMBLE 1974

Three-Phase Circuits, Motors, Transformers C 60 MIN
3/4 OR 1/2 INCH VIDEO CASSETTE IND
See series title for descriptive statement.
From The Electrical Maintenance Training, Module A - AC And DC Theory Series.
Prod-LEIKID Dist-LEIKID

Three-Phase Motor, Pt 1 - Preparing To Rewind B 17 MIN
16MM FILM - 3/4 IN VIDEO
Explains how to interpret and record nameplate data of a three-phase motor. Demonstrates how to identify the line and finish leads, remove coil and determine coil span, and use a coil winding machine. Issued in 1945 as a motion picture.
From The Electrical Work - Motor Maintenance And Repair Series. Number 4
LC NO. 79-707707
Prod-USOE Dist-USNAC Prodn-CALVCO 1979

Three-Phase Motor, Pt 2 - Rewinding B 17 MIN
16MM FILM - 3/4 IN VIDEO
Demonstrates techniques for rewinding a three-phase motor, explaining how to insert mush coils, separators, and insulation, make a delta connection, and fold, trim and wedge slot insulation around windings. Issued in 1945 as a motion picture.
From The Electrical Work - Motor Maintenance And Repair Series. Number 5
LC NO. 79-707708
Prod-USOE Dist-USNAC Prodn-CALVCO 1979

Three-Pipe Problem, A C 28 MIN
16MM FILM OPTICAL SOUND C A
Describes an approach to problem solving and decision making based on an actual case study from the files of social psychologist Charles Kepner and sociologist Benjamin Tregoe.
LC NO. 72-701859
Prod-VOAERO Dist-VOAERO 1972

Three-Point Contact, The C 7 MIN
16MM FILM, 3/4 OR 1/2 IN VIDEO IND
Demonstrates safe ways of mounting and dismounting heavy construction equipment. Discusses other hazards and recommends modifications to improve hand and foot holds. Gives tips for safe operation.
Prod-CSAO Dist-IFB

Three-Ring Government C 3 MIN
3/4 OR 1/2 INCH VIDEO CASSETTE P-I
Uses animation and rock music in examining the government by comparing its three branches to a three-ring circus.
From The America Rock Series.
Prod-ABCTV Dist-GA Prodn-SCOROC 1977

Three-State Bus Concepts C 55 MIN
3/4 OR 1/2 INCH VIDEO CASSETTE PRO
See series title for descriptive statement.
From The Digital Electronics Series.
Prod-MIOT Dist-MIOT

Three-Ten To Yuma B 92 MIN
16MM FILM OPTICAL SOUND
Shows how Western conventions are reversed with the heroic virtues portrayed in the character of the villain. The film pits Van Heflin's all-too-fallible dirt farmer against Glenn Ford's outlaw, whom Heflin has been hired to guard until the three-ten can take him away.
Prod-CON Dist-TIMLIF 1957

Three-Two-One Contact Space - What's It Like Out There C
3/4 OR 1/2 INCH VIDEO CASSETTE
Presents a visit to NASA's high-tech facilities as astronauts prepare for a space flight. Includes an interview with Sally Ride and views of the planets, with a discussion on the possibility of extraterrestrial life.
Prod-CTELWO Dist-GA

Three-Wire Handshake C 30 MIN
3/4 OR 1/2 INCH VIDEO CASSETTE IND
Shows how two or more asynchronous devices can communicate over same set of wires. Describes three-wire handshake flowchart by using a logic timing diagram.
From The IEEE 488 Bus Series.
Prod-COLOSU Dist-COLOSU

Three-Wire Service Entrance B 24 MIN
16MM FILM - 3/4 IN VIDEO
Shows how to mount and connect an outdoor meter connection

box, mount and connect a service control box, ground a three-wire service entrance installation and install a concentric service entrance cable.
From The Electrical Work - Wiring Series. No. 5
LC NO. 79-707492
Prod-USOE Dist-USNAC Prodn-RAYBEL 1979

Three-2-1 Contact - Food And Fuel–A Series

A set of three videocassettes which travels to New York's Bronx Zoo, to a bakery and to a corn farm to investigate the delicate balance between food consumption and energy needs. Discusses caloric values and how a person's level of activity should determine what and how much they eat.
Prod-CTELWO Dist-GA 1984

Three-2-1 Contact - Forces And Motion–A Series

Demonstrates the forces at work in such things as an awesome avalanche, a careening roller-coaster ride and in a rising balloon. Explains the reasons why pulleys and levers make lifting easier.
Prod-CTELWO Dist-GA 1984

Three-2-1 Contact - The Five Senses–A Series

A set of two videocassettes which explores the five senses. Explains why certain animals have developed particularly keen senses and how sounds can be created, transmitted and reproduced electronically. Looks at the reflex responses of newborn babies.
Prod-CTELWO Dist-GA 1984

Three-2-1 Contact - Water - Medium For Life–A Series

A set of three videocassettes which travels around the earth to learn how and why the water cycle is integral to life on earth. Explores the unique requirements of wetlands life at the Okefenokee Swamp and how plants and animals in the desert survive in low-water environments.
Prod-CTELWO Dist-GA 1984

Three's A Crowd B 65 MIN
16MM FILM SILENT J-C A
Stars Harry Langdon in a story about an unmarried tenement boy who works long hours for a wagon owner, lives alone and dreams of having a wife and family.
Prod-MGM Dist-TWYMAN 1927

Threshing Wheat B 9 MIN
16MM FILM OPTICAL SOUND P-C A
Shows the Tajik farmers threshing the wheat, as they drive their oxen to pull a wooden sledge over the grain in order to separate the grain from the husks.
From The Mountain Peoples Of Central Asia Series.
LC NO. 73-702412
Prod-IFF Dist-IFF 1972

Threshing Wheat (Tajik) B 9 MIN
3/4 OR 1/2 INCH VIDEO CASSETTE
See series title for descriptive statement.
From The Mountain Peoples Of Central Asia (Afghanistan) Series.
Prod-IFF Dist-IFF

Threshold C 27 MIN
16MM FILM OPTICAL SOUND
Illustrates the relationship between research and medical care. Shows the broad scope of modern research-based anesthesiology - surgery, respiratory and intensive care units for the critically ill and the diagnosis and treatment of persistent pain.
LC NO. 74-705788
Prod-USDHEW Dist-USNAC 1969

Threshold C 25 MIN
16MM FILM, 3/4 OR 1/2 IN VIDEO H-C A
Presents a lyrical fantasy on the meanings of life and death.
Prod-LEVINS Dist-PFP 1970

Threshold - The Blue Angels Experience C 89 MIN
16MM FILM OPTICAL SOUND PRO
Captures the excitement of special peak experiences encountered in the flight, with the Blue Angels Jet Aerobatic Airshow. Puts viewers in the cockpit of a 1600 mile per hour F-4 Phantom, flying through violent buffeting jet streams in 8-G formation aerobatics.
Prod-ASVS Dist-ASVS

Threshold Of Liberty, The C 52 MIN
16MM FILM, 3/4 OR 1/2 IN VIDEO C A
Discusses the impact of surrealism and shows examples of art and architecture produced by this movement, including the Ideal Temple built in rural France, the Watts Towers, and paintings by Miro, Dali, Magritte and others.
From The Shock Of The New Series.
LC NO. 80-706954
Prod-BBCTV Dist-TIMLIF 1980

Threshold, The C 28 MIN
16MM FILM OPTICAL SOUND C A
A behind-the-scenes look at some unusual Spanish industries, both ancient and modern. Demonstrates how air cargo is contributing to the industrial progress of Spain.
LC NO. 70-713504
Prod-MCDO Dist-MCDO 1971

Thrombectomy For Ileofemoral And Axillary Vein Thrombosis C 25 MIN
16MM FILM OPTICAL SOUND PRO
Shows how venous thrombosis in the early stages is properly treated by anticoagulants. Demonstrates two procedures, one for iliofemoral thrombosis and one for axillary vein thrombosis.
Prod-ACYDGD Dist-ACY 1964

Thrombin Clotting Time / Fibrinogen Assay C 13 MIN
3/4 OR 1/2 INCH VIDEO CASSETTE
Describes the use of thrombin clotting time as a tool for monitoring heparin therapy and a simple, rapid assay for clottable fibrinogens. Demonstrates selected blood coagulation methods.
From The Blood Coagulation Laboratory Techniques Series.
LC NO. 79-707606
Prod-UMICH Dist-UMICH 1977

Throne Of Blood (First Meeting With The Spirit) C 12 MIN
16MM FILM OPTICAL SOUND
Presents the story of Washizu and Miki who are on their way home from battle when they get lost in a labyrinthine forest where they meet a spirit who prophesies Washizu's ascendancy and the succession by Miki's son. Designed to create images of symbolic meaning which give visual expression to the themes and motifs of Shakespeare's Macbeth without retaining any of the original text.
From The Film Study Extracts Series.
Prod-UNKNWN Dist-FI

Throne Of Blood (Japanese) B 105 MIN
3/4 OR 1/2 INCH VIDEO CASSETTE
Presents an adaptation of Shakespeare's Macbeth set in 16th century Japan during the Sengoku civil wars. Stars Toshiro Mifune. Directed by Akira Kurosawa. With English subtitles.
Prod-IHF Dist-IHF

Through Adam's Eyes B 13 MIN
16MM FILM OPTICAL SOUND
Presents a portrait of a 7-year-old boy who underwent dramatic facial reconstructive surgery.
LC NO. 78-701576
Prod-SAGETB Dist-TEMPLU 1978

Through Animal Eyes C 50 MIN
3/4 OR 1/2 INCH VIDEO CASSETTE H-C A
Attempts to visualize the natural world through various animal eyes, using special video techniques and cameras. Presents images as seen by a chameleon's eyes moving in two directions at once, a night hunting animal seeking prey in the dark and the compound eyes of shrimps, crabs and insects with their multi-faceted view.
Prod-WNETTV Dist-FI Prodn-BBCTV

Through Conflict To Negotiation B 47 MIN
16MM FILM, 3/4 OR 1/2 IN VIDEO
Shows what occurs when a community action group in Rochester, New York, confronts the largest employer in the community on the issue of corporate responsibility and employment of minority groups.
From The Organizing For Power - The Alinsky Approach Series.
Prod-NFBC Dist-FI 1970

Through Different Eyes C 15 MIN
16MM FILM OPTICAL SOUND H-C A
Features retarded children in a day-training program receiving specialized training for their handicaps. Emphasizes need of retarded children for training and highlights the areas in which training must be applied. Examines social needs of the children as well as the impact a retarded child has on the rest of the family.
LC NO. 79-709689
Prod-PECKM Dist-PCHENT 1970

Through Gates Of Splendor C 36 MIN
16MM FILM OPTICAL SOUND
Tells the story of five young missionaries killed by the savage Aucas in Ecuador, much of this film was taken on the beach by the men themselves shortly before they were killed. Narrated by Betty Elliott--who with her small daughter went to live among the savages who killed her husband.
Prod-YOUTH Dist-GF

Through Heaven's Gate C 30 MIN
3/4 INCH VIDEO CASSETTE
Dramatizes the encounter between a black man and a white man in the subterranean depths of the New York transit system.
Prod-BLKFMF Dist-BLKFMF

Through Joy And Beyond, The Life Of C S Lewis, Pt 1 - The Formative Years C 52 MIN
16MM FILM OPTICAL SOUND H-C A
Documents the life, works and times of author C S Lewis.
LC NO. 79-700593
Prod-LRDKNG Dist-YOUTH 1979

Through Joy And Beyond, The Life Of C S Lewis, Pt 2 - The Informed Years C 52 MIN
16MM FILM OPTICAL SOUND H-C A
Documents the life, works and times of author C S Lewis.
LC NO. 79-700593
Prod-LRDKNG Dist-YOUTH 1979

Through Joy And Beyond, The Life Of C S Lewis, Pt 3 - Jack Remembered C 54 MIN
16MM FILM OPTICAL SOUND H-C A
Documents the life, works and times of author C S Lewis.
LC NO. 79-700593
Prod-LRDKNG Dist-YOUTH 1979

Through Media C 36 MIN
3/4 OR 1/2 INCH VIDEO CASSETTE
Introduces the novice or experienced media person to the numerous uses of readily available media tools. Focuses on church youth group training.
From The Active Learning For Youth Series.
Prod-UMCOM Dist-ECUFLM

Through My Eyes (Kilkenny) C 31 MIN
16MM FILM OPTICAL SOUND T
Illustrates the open plan school technique at the primary school level using the example of Kilkenny Primary School in Kilkenny, South Australia.
From The Through My Eyes Series.
LC NO. 75-702394
Prod-FLMAUS Dist-AUIS 1974

Through My Eyes (Stradbroke) C 26 MIN
16MM FILM OPTICAL SOUND T
Examines the operation of an open plan school system at the infants school level using the example of Stradbroke Infants School in Stradbroke, South Australia.
From The Through My Eyes Series.
LC NO. 75-702395
Prod-FLMAUS Dist-AUIS 1974

Through Simulation Games C 47 MIN
3/4 OR 1/2 INCH VIDEO CASSETTE
Describes the value of simulation games. Illustrates this method of learning which church youth groups can play.
From The Active Learning For Youth Series.
Prod-UMCOM Dist-ECUFLM

Through The Genetic Maze–A Series

Examines the field of Bioethics, focusing on the human and social implications posed by this genetic technology.
Prod-PSU Dist-PBS 1982

Beautiful Baby Boy, But, A 058 MIN
Fifty/Fifty Chance, A 058 MIN
To Build Our Future 058 MIN
Two-Edged Sword 058 MIN
We Can Decide 058 MIN

Through The Lens C 30 MIN
3/4 OR 1/2 INCH VIDEO CASSETTE C
See series title for descriptive statement.
From The In Our Own Image Series.
Prod-DALCCD Dist-DALCCD

Through The Looking Glass C 10 MIN
16MM FILM OPTICAL SOUND
Presents new abstract forms by applying principles of distortion to familiar forms and principles of nature.
Prod-DAVISJ Dist-RADIM

Through The Looking Glass - Introduction - Caedmon's Hymm C 45 MIN
3/4 OR 1/2 INCH VIDEO CASSETTE
Introduces English literature by analyzing the content of Caedmon's Hymm.
From The Survey Of English Literature I Series.
Prod-MDCPB Dist-MDCPB

Through The Looking Glass Darkly C 51 MIN
16MM FILM OPTICAL SOUND
Presents a historical documentary on the black man in Oklahoma.
From The Spectrum Series.
LC NO. 74-700380
Prod-WKYTV Dist-WKYTV 1973

Through The Magic Mirror C 12 MIN
16MM FILM OPTICAL SOUND
Presents a series of vignettes about the dental future of infants in which all adult roles, except that of the dentist, are played by children.
LC NO. 74-700511
Prod-ASODFC Dist-ASODFC 1973

Through The Mask - Oceanography C 25 MIN
3/4 OR 1/2 INCH VIDEO CASSETTE
Takes the viewers to underwater worlds ranging from a Paris pond to a Red Sea reef.
Prod-DAVFMS Dist-DAVFMS

Through The Mill Once More C 30 MIN
16MM FILM - 3/4 IN VIDEO J-C A
Explains that today even the United States has run out of frontiers and the realization has come that our resources are limited and we must try to keep what exists. Examines present waste and future possibilities, focusing on the rapid development of recycling technology. Shows a variety of research projects and plants using by-products of other industries.
From The Man Builds - Man Destroys Series.
Prod-UN Dist-GPITVL

Through The Northwest Passage C 28 MIN
16MM FILM OPTICAL SOUND
Documents the well-publicized voyage of the S S Manhattan, through the Northwest Passage to Alaska's north slope. Explains that as a practical one for shipping crude oil to eastern markets, the ship was a floating laboratory of oceanographers and geologists.
Prod-HUMBLE Dist-MTP

Through The Pages–A Series
P
Incorporates drama, illustrations, on-location action and colorful settings to bring alive selected stories.
Prod-WVIZTV Dist-GPITVL 1982

Anansi, The Spider Man 015 MIN
Family Secrets - Five Very Important Stories 015 MIN
Great Pete Penny, The 015 MIN
How I Hunted The Little Fellows 015 MIN
Jabberwocky / The Ice Cream Cone Coot And 015 MIN
Jumanji 015 MIN
Lafcadio, The Lion Who Shot Back 015 MIN
Mummies Made In Egypt 015 MIN
Poetry 015 MIN
What's The Big Idea, Ben Franklin 015 MIN

Through The Safety Net C 58 MIN
1/2 IN VIDEO CASSETTE BETA/VHS
Originally shown as Work Is Who Decides Disability. Discusses the Social Security Administration's review of more than 775,000 disability pension cases and its disqualification of 40 percent of them from receiving benefits. Questions the basis for making the decisions and the people responsible for making these decisions.
From The Frontline Series.
Prod-DOCCON Dist-PBS

Through The Spring C 29 MIN
3/4 INCH VIDEO CASSETTE
Discusses eight unusual edible wild plants. Shows where to find them.
From The Edible Wild Plants Series.
Prod-UMITV Dist-UMITV 1978

Through Young People's Eyes C 29 MIN
16MM FILM, 3/4 OR 1/2 IN VIDEO J-C A
Looks at the daily lives of black and hispanic teenagers, primarily girls. Uses candid interviews to explore the advantages and disadvantages of adolescence in a poor urban neighborhood.
LC NO. 84-707125
Prod-RMMB Dist-CNEMAG 1983

Throw Me A Rainbow C 12 MIN
16MM FILM OPTICAL SOUND
Relates the story of some elderly women who love to paint and how they are affected by the appearance of noted art collector Joseph Hirshhorn.
Prod-CELLAR Dist-CELLAR

Throwing C 11 MIN
16MM FILM, 3/4 OR 1/2 IN VIDEO
Demonstrates the shaping of various clay pieces on a potter's wheel, showing each step in making a bowl and special steps in completing a low, flat plate and pitcher.
From The Craftsmanship In Clay Series.
Prod-IU Dist-IU 1950

Throwing C 25 MIN
3/4 OR 1/2 INCH VIDEO CASSETTE H-C A
Demonstrates different types of pottery wheels - hand, kick and power - and how to throw different clay bodies on the wheel. Shows stoneware being prepared and thrown and porcelain being thrown in a variety of shapes.
From The Craft Of The Potter Series.
Prod-BBCTV Dist-FI

Throwing Events, The - Men C 21 MIN
16MM FILM, 3/4 OR 1/2 IN VIDEO J-C
Emphasizes correct form and technique for the discus, shot and javelin. Provides drills and coaching points.
From The LeRoy Walker Track And Field - Men Series.
Prod-ATHI Dist-ATHI 1976

Throwing Events, The - Women C 20 MIN
16MM FILM, 3/4 OR 1/2 IN VIDEO J-C
Presents the discus, shot and javelin events showing correct form, technique and recommended drills. Shows key points to help the competitor reach the highest performance levels.
From The LeRoy Walker Track And Field - Women Series.
Prod-ATHI Dist-ATHI 1976

Throwing On The Run B 11 MIN
16MM FILM OPTICAL SOUND J-H
Features coach John Mc Kay of the University of Southern California who discusses the football technique of throwing on the run.
Prod-BOR Dist-COCA

Throwing Pitchers, Pulling Handles C 28 MIN
2 INCH VIDEOTAPE
Features Mrs Peterson describing certain ceramic processes for her classroom at the University of Southern California. Demonstrates how to throw pitchers and pull handles.
From The Wheels, Kilns And Clay Series.
Prod-USC Dist-PUBTEL

Throwing, Pt 1 C 29 MIN
2 INCH VIDEOTAPE
Features Mrs Vivika Heino introducing and demonstrating basic techniques in throwing.
From The Exploring The Crafts - Pottery Series.
Prod-WENHTV Dist-PUBTEL

Throwing, Pt 2 C 29 MIN
2 INCH VIDEOTAPE
Features Mrs Vivika Heino introducing and demonstrating basic techniques in throwing.
From The Exploring The Crafts - Pottery Series.
Prod-WENHTV Dist-PUBTEL

Thrown Stones C 2 MIN
3/4 OR 1/2 INCH VIDEO CASSETTE
Shows tapes of editing to highlight and to allow the vagueness of reality to overcome the barrier of perfect lives.
From The Still Life Series.
Prod-EAI Dist-EAI

Thru The Eyes Of A Child C 30 MIN
16MM FILM OPTICAL SOUND
Shows the floats, bands and horses of the Rose Parade held in Pasadena, California, on New Years Day, 1971.
LC NO. 73-700799
Prod-TRA Dist-TRA 1971

Thru The Mirror C 8 MIN
16MM FILM, 3/4 OR 1/2 IN VIDEO K-H
Presents Mickey Mouse in an adaptation of the book Through The Looking Glass by Lewis Carroll. Tells how Mickey falls asleep and dreams that he steps through the mirror into a world where furniture comes to life and where he has to do battle with a pack of cards.
From The Mickey Mouse - The Early Years Series.
Prod-DISNEY Dist-WDEMCO 1978

Thrufeed Grinding A Straight Pin, Pt 1 B 29 MIN
16MM FILM, 3/4 OR 1/2 IN VIDEO
Explains the principle of centerless grinding and describes the basic elements of the centerless grinding machine. Shows how to set up the machine and true the grinding and regulating wheels.
From The Machine Shop Work - Operations On The Centerless Grinding Machine Series. No. 1
Prod-USOE Dist-USNAC Prodn-RAYBEL 1944

Thrufeed Grinding A Straight Pin, Pt 2 B 28 MIN
16MM FILM, 3/4 OR 1/2 IN VIDEO
Shows how to balance the grinding wheel, position work for grinding, adjust work guides, take a trial grind, eliminate taper in the grinding wheel, use a crown cam to dress the grinding wheel and check the workpieces.
From The Machine Shop Work - Operations On The Centerless Grinding Machine Series. No. 2
Prod-USOE Dist-USNAC Prodn-RAYBEL 1944

Thumb Nail Sketches C 29 MIN
3/4 INCH VIDEO CASSETTE
Focuses on arranging and rearranging one's picture.
From The Artist At Work Series.
Prod-UMITV Dist-UMITV 1973

Thumb Reconstruction By Fifth Digit Transportation C 20 MIN
16MM FILM OPTICAL SOUND
Discusses three methods of thumb reconstruction. Illustrates digit migration on neurovascular pedicles in four subjects exhibiting various results of series trauma. Shows surgically, graphically and with follow-up demonstration the provision of a hand with a reconstructed thumb.
LC NO. FIA66-68
Prod-EATONL Dist-EATONL Prodn-AVCORP 1964

Thumb Reconstruction By Toe Transfer C 15 MIN
16MM FILM OPTICAL SOUND
Illustrates the successful transplantation of the second toe to the residual head of the proximal phalanx. Pictures the seven-year follow-up which shows excelent growth of the distal phalanges and shaft.
LC NO. FIA66-69
Prod-EATONL Dist-EATONL Prodn-AVCORP 1960

Thumbelina B 10 MIN
16MM FILM OPTICAL SOUND K-I
Presents the fairy tale Thumbelina in animated silhouette form. Based on the live shadow plays Lotte Reiniger produced for BBC Television.
From The Lotte Reiniger's Animated Fairy Tales Series.
Prod-PRIMP Dist-MOMA 1955

Thumbelina C 9 MIN
16MM FILM, 3/4 OR 1/2 IN VIDEO P-I
Presents the Hans Christian Andersen story of Thumbelina, about a tiny girl who encounters many unusual experiences before she finds the home where she really belongs.
From The Classic Tales Retold Series.
Prod-BFA Dist-PHENIX 1977

Thumbelina C 16 MIN
16MM FILM, 3/4 OR 1/2 IN VIDEO K-P
Explains how a miniature girl escapes marriage to an ugly toad and a mole by flying to a faraway country on the back of a dove. Relates how she meets a king who is just her size.
Prod-CORF Dist-CORF 1981

Thumbelina (Captioned) C 16 MIN
16MM FILM, 3/4 OR 1/2 IN VIDEO K-P
Explains how a miniature girl escapes marriage to an ugly toad and a mole by flying to a faraway country on the back of a dove. Relates how she meets a king who is just her size.
Prod-CORF Dist-CORF 1981

Thumbnail Sketch, The C 29 MIN
3/4 INCH VIDEO CASSETTE C A
Teaches how to think with a pencil. Shows how to jot down the main idea of a sketch with the greatest economy of time.
From The Sketching Techniques Series. Lesson 5
Prod-COAST Dist-CDTEL

Thumbs Down - Hitchhiking C 17 MIN
16MM FILM, 3/4 OR 1/2 IN VIDEO
Points out the dangers of hitchhiking by presenting dramatizations and offering interviews with real victims of hitchhiking-related crimes.
Prod-FLMFR Dist-FLMFR

Thunder In Munich B 28 MIN
16MM FILM, 3/4 OR 1/2 IN VIDEO J-C A
Tells the true story of a German Jesuit priest who preaches against anti-Semitism during the Nazi regime and is sent to a concentration camp. Stars Robert Lansing.
From The Insight Series.
Prod-PAULST Dist-PAULST

Thunder In The Skies C 52 MIN
16MM FILM, 3/4 OR 1/2 IN VIDEO
Details the changes in construction and energy usage which occurred when the climate of Europe changed dramatically in the 13th century. Shows how the scarcity of firewood contributed to the invention of the steam engine, which was the predecessor of gasoline-powered engines.
From The Connections Series. No. 6
LC NO. 79-706745
Prod-BBCTV Dist-TIMLIF 1979

Thunder In The Skies C 60 MIN
3/4 OR 1/2 INCH VIDEO CASSETTE
Traces the early history of man's adventures in space, including the career of inventor Robert Goddard, the early development of the rocket as a weapon of war in Germany, pilot Chuck Yeager's breaking the sound barrier, the launching of the Soviet satellite, Sputnik 1. Details the challenge to America's technical excellence, the formation of N A S A, and the selection of the Mercury astronauts.
From The Spaceflight Series.
Prod-PBS Dist-PBS

Thunder Mountain C
3/4 OR 1/2 INCH VIDEO CASSETTE
Prod-FO Dist-FO

Thunder Out Of China B 20 MIN
3/4 OR 1/2 INCH VIDEO CASSETTE
Documents the Japanese-Chinese war that predicted America's entry into the Pacific war.
Prod-IHF Dist-IHF

Thunderbird (2nd Ed) B 23 MIN
16MM FILM OPTICAL SOUND J A
Retells the Indian legend of the thunderbird on Mount Olympus and pictures the lore of the Indians of Northwest. Shows how Indians hew a sea-going canoe from a cedar log. Includes views of sea lions, of seagull hatching and of a traditional hunt from an open canoe.
LC NO. FIA68-2355
Prod-RARIG Dist-RARIG 1963

Thunderbirds, The C 6 MIN
16MM FILM OPTICAL SOUND I-H A
Shows historical highlights of the U S Air Force Thunderbirds in action, without narration.
LC NO. 77-700967
Prod-USAF Dist-USNAC 1975

Thunderbirds, The / Supersonic Thunderbirds / Crossover C 35 MIN
3/4 OR 1/2 INCH VIDEO CASSETTE
Presents the Thunderbirds flying various aircraft from the 4-84G through the 44-E. Shows the jet aerobats flying Super Sabres in power climbs, cloverleaf turns, loops, 360-degree turns and the 'bomb burst.' Presents a documentary of the Thunderbirds on a goodwill tour of South America giving aerial demonstrations.
Prod-IHF Dist-IHF

Thunderbolt C 43 MIN
16MM FILM - 3/4 IN VIDEO
Tells about the 57th Fighter Group which participated in Operation Strangle in Italy in 1944 while flying the P-47 Thunderbolt fighter-bomber from bases in Corsica. Issued in 1946 as a motion picture.
LC NO. 79-706474
Prod-USAF Dist-USNAC 1979

Thunderbolt C 45 MIN
3/4 OR 1/2 INCH VIDEO CASSETTE
Relates the activities of the 57th Fighter Group during 'Operation Strangle' which destroyed vital supply routes deep behind German lines. Introduced by James Stewart and narrated by Lloyd Bridges.
Prod-IHF Dist-IHF

Thunderbolts, The - Ramrod To Emden B 33 MIN
16MM FILM, 3/4 OR 1/2 IN VIDEO
Shows the planning for an escort of P-47 airplanes to accompany a bombing mission over Emden, German, during World War II. Includes combat scenes showing fighters downing German planes and shows the pilots being debriefed after the mission.
LC NO. 82-706707
Prod-USAF Dist-USNAC 1943

Thunderstorm, The C 9 MIN
16MM FILM, 3/4 OR 1/2 IN VIDEO P-I
Tells a story about a boy who, during a search for his lost dog, discovers the interdependence of all living things in nature.
Prod-LCOA Dist-LCOA 1969

Thunderstorm, The C 29 MIN
2 INCH VIDEOTAPE
Features meteorologist Frank Sechrish introducing the largest thunderstorm model ever made and illustrating where all the rain, hail and tornadoes come from.
From The Weather Series.
Prod-WHATV Dist-PUBTEL

Thursday Auction C 20 MIN
16MM FILM OPTICAL SOUND
Presents a documentary about the old Kitchener stockyards.
LC NO. 76-701379
Prod-CCAAT Dist-CCAAT 1975

Thursday's Child Has Far To Go C 43 MIN
3/4 INCH VIDEO CASSETTE
Describes the reactions of three mothers on finding out their children are physically disabled. Reveals their difficult experiences with the medical profession in dealing with their situations.
Prod-ESST Dist-ESST 1981

Thursday's Children C 28 MIN
16MM FILM OPTICAL SOUND T S
Visits a special school which helps children with learning disabilities related to emotional problems overcome such problems. Features four pre-school children and ways their emotional problems are recognized and dealt with by the school staff.
LC NO. 72-708248
Prod-KETCTV Dist-KETCTV 1970

Thy Sins Are Forgiven X 15 MIN
16MM FILM OPTICAL SOUND J-H T R
Jesus is teaching on the roof of a house in Capernaum when four friends carry a sick man up to Him. Jesus says to the man,

'THY SINS ARE FORGIVEN,' and heals him. Later Jesus calls Matthew to 'FOLLOW ME.' the Pharisees question Jesus about fasting and He replies with three parables.
From The Living Bible Series.
Prod-FAMF Dist-FAMF

Thy Will Be Done C 25 MIN
16MM FILM OPTICAL SOUND
Presents correspondent Michael Maclear examining the issue of capital punishment and considering pros and cons of the debate.
LC NO. 77-702530
Prod-CTV Dist-CTV 1976

Thy Will Be Done C 90 MIN
3/4 OR 1/2 INCH VIDEO CASSETTE
Features an investigation of mind control as related to religious cults.
Prod-WCCOTV Dist-WCCOTV 1980

Thyration Sawtooth Generator B 25 MIN
16MM FILM OPTICAL SOUND
Shows an electron beam moving across the face of an oscilloscope and points out that the thyration saw-tooth generator produces the waveshapes required to move the electron beam. Gives a detailed analysis of the circuit operation and constructs a time amplitude graph of the sawtooth waves, explaining its physical and electrical length. (Kinescope)
LC NO. 74-705506
Prod-USAF Dist-USNAC

Thyristors And Optoelectronics C 60 MIN
1 INCH VIDEOTAPE IND
Describes representative applications, operating principles and key specifications of devices in both thyristors and optoelectronics, SCR, TRIAC, photodiode, phototransistor and light-emitting diode.
From The Understanding Semiconductors Course Outline Series. No. 09
Prod-TXINLC Dist-TXINLC

Thyroglossal Duct Cyst Resection C 12 MIN
3/4 OR 1/2 INCH VIDEO CASSETTE
See series title for descriptive statement.
From The Head And Neck Series.
Prod-SVL Dist-SVL

Thyroid And Antithyroid Drugs B 30 MIN
16MM FILM OPTICAL SOUND C
Reviews the synthesis of the thyroid hormones and explains what an underproduction or an overproduction of these hormones will produce. Illustrates how antithyroid drugs interfere with the action of the thyroid gland.
From The Pharmacology Series.
LC NO. 73-703353
Prod-MVNE Dist-TELSTR 1971

Thyroid Area, The C 6 MIN
16MM FILM - 3/4 IN VIDEO PRO
Demonstrates the dissection of deeper structures of the thyroid area, noting practical surgical applications. Reviews diagrammatically the entire pretracheal area.
From The Anatomy Of The Head And Neck Series.
LC NO. 78-706255
Prod-USVA Dist-USNAC Prodn-VADTC 1978

Thyroid Cancer C 22 MIN
16MM FILM OPTICAL SOUND PRO
Presents a dramatic narrative between a resident doctor and a specialist who answers questions regarding thyroid cancer. Uses animation, live action photography of actual cases, X-rays, surgery and radioactive isotope therapy to illustrate points in the narrative.
LC NO. 74-706127
Prod-AEGIS Dist-AMCS 1969

Thyroid Cancer - Diagnosis And Treatment C 20 MIN
16MM FILM OPTICAL SOUND PRO
Demonstrates diagnostic procedures used for thyroid gland tumors including palpation, radioactive isotope scans, radiography and biopsy. Presents patterns of metastasis, and surgical approaches to management ranging from radical to conservative with rationale for each.
Prod-AMCS Dist-AMCS 1969

Thyroid Gland, The C 30 MIN
3/4 OR 1/2 INCH VIDEO CASSETTE
Discusses the role of the thyroid gland and the malfunctions that can occur. Looks at symptoms of thyroid diseases. Covers medical and surgical corrections.
Prod-UILCCC Dist-AL

Thyroid Physiology And Disease - Hyperthyroidism And Thyroiditis B 55 MIN
16MM FILM OPTICAL SOUND PRO
Reviews the classification of hyperthyroidism. Includes a discussion of Graves' disease, its pathogenesis, clinical manifestation and treatment.
From The Clinical Pathology Series.
Prod-NMAC Dist-USNAC 1970

Thyroid Physiology And Disease - Hypothyroidism B 49 MIN
16MM FILM OPTICAL SOUND PRO
Discusses the classifications of hypothyroidism, reviews the types of cretinism due to inborn errors in metabolism and gives clinical manifestations of hypothyroidism.
From The Clinical Pathology Series.
Prod-NMAC Dist-USNAC 1970

Thyroid Physiology And Disease - Normal Physiology And Diagnostic Tests, Pt 1 B 33 MIN
16MM FILM OPTICAL SOUND PRO
Discusses the normal anatomy and physiology of the thyroid as related to clinical problems.
From The Clinical Pathology Series.
Prod-NMAC Dist-USNAC 1970

Thyroid Physiology And Disease - Normal Physiology And Diagnostic Tests, Pt 2 B 33 MIN
16MM FILM OPTICAL SOUND PRO
Discusses the normal anatomy and physiology of the thyroid as related to clinical problems.
From The Clinical Pathology Series.
Prod-NMAC Dist-USNAC 1970

Thyroid Physiology And Disease - Thyroid Nodules And Cancer B 34 MIN
16MM FILM OPTICAL SOUND PRO
Discusses the varieties of thyroid cancer, the management of the thyroid nodule and attempts to formulate a rational approach to the problem.
From The Clinical Pathology Series.
Prod-NMAC Dist-USNAC 1970

Thyroid Today C 30 MIN
16MM FILM OPTICAL SOUND
Discusses thyroid disease and therapy.
LC NO. 76-701065
Prod-BAXLAB Dist-BAXLAB 1974

Thyroid Uptake And Scan C
3/4 OR 1/2 INCH VIDEO CASSETTE
See series title for descriptive statement.
From The X-Ray Procedures In Layman's Terms Series.
Prod-FAIRGH Dist-FAIRGH

Thyroidectomy - A Half Century Of Experience C 30 MIN
16MM FILM OPTICAL SOUND PRO
Demonstrates the Lahey clinic technique of thyroidectomy, originally developed by Dr Frank H Lahey. Explains that an adequate incision, high mobilization of the skin flap, and the routine division of the strip muscle, make possible the actual visualization of every important structure encountered in a thyroidectomy.
Prod-ACYDGD Dist-ACY 1963

Thyroidectomy - A Safe Operation C 24 MIN
16MM FILM OPTICAL SOUND PRO
Emphasizes techniques that have made thyroidectomy a safe procedure. Presents scenes from operations done for four different pathological conditions to show positioning, anesthesia, exposure, hemostasis, avoidance of injury to vital structures and closures.
Prod-ACYDGD Dist-ACY 1960

Thyroidectomy For Papillary Carcinoma Of Thyroid With Cervical Metastases C 18 MIN
16MM FILM OPTICAL SOUND PRO
Shows the complete removal of one lobe and isthmus of the thyroid involved by papillary carcinoma. Demonstrates resection of the regional lymph nodes, care being taken to preserve the recurrent laryngeal nerve.
Prod-ACYDGD Dist-ACY 1951

Ti-Grace Atkinson - Radical Activist/ Political Theorist C 28 MIN
3/4 INCH VIDEO CASSETTE
Features Ti-Grace Atkinson talking on feminism and class, socialist feminism, and the role of men in the women's movement. Suggests a few 'mechanisms for survival,' and describes marriage and motherhood as anti-feminist institutions.
Prod-WMENIF Dist-WMENIF

Ti-Jean Goes Lumbering C 16 MIN
16MM FILM, 3/4 OR 1/2 IN VIDEO P-I
Presents a French-Canadian folk tale about a mysterious stranger who behaves like a young Paul Bunyan.
Prod-NFBC Dist-IFB 1953

Ti-Jean Goes Lumbering (Captioned) C 16 MIN
16MM FILM, 3/4 OR 1/2 IN VIDEO P-I
Presents a French-Canadian folktale about the fantastic exploits of a mysterious little boy who one day rides into a winter logging camp on a big white horse. Shows that his exploits dwarf those of even the hardiest lumberjack as he fells lumber, cuts, carries and plies heavy logs, and comes out the victor in every contest. Portrays typical life in a Canadian logging camp.
Prod-NFBC Dist-IFB 1953

Ti-Jean Lenador C 16 MIN
16MM FILM, 3/4 OR 1/2 IN VIDEO P-I
A Spanish language version of Ti-Jean Goes Lumbering. Presents a French-Canadian folk tale about a mysterious stranger who behaves like a young Paul Bunyan.
Prod-NFBC Dist-IFB 1953

TI-99/4A Home Computer C
3/4 OR 1/2 INCH VIDEO CASSETTE
Presents basic operation procedures for the TI-99/4A Home Computer.
From The Basic Computer Operations Series.
Prod-LIBFSC Dist-LIBFSC

Tiberias - Land Of The Emperors C 14 MIN
16MM FILM OPTICAL SOUND
Points out that the ancient town of Tiberias on the Sea of Galilee was built by Herod as a tribute to the Roman emperor Tiberius. Points out its historic and religious significance, the natural beauty of its surroundings and boating, water skiing and cultural activities.
Prod-ALDEN Dist-ALDEN

Tibet - A Buddhist Trilogy—A Series
16MM FILM, 3/4 OR 1/2 IN VIDEO
Looks at the Tibetan Buddhist religion, culture and politics using scenes of rituals and daily life never before seen by outsiders.
Prod-COLLAS Dist-UCEMC

Fields Of The Senses, The 050 MIN
Prophecy, A 054 MIN
Radiating The Fruit Of Truth 129 MIN

Tibetan Medicine - A Buddhist Approach To Healing C 35 MIN
16MM FILM, 3/4 OR 1/2 IN VIDEO
Presents Tibetan approaches to medicine which treats the patient rather than the disease. Calls the 'poisons' of ignorance, passion and aggression the cause of disease. Shows acupuncture and moxabustion.
Prod-HP Dist-HP

Tibetan Traders (Rev Ed) C 22 MIN
16MM FILM - 3/4 IN VIDEO J-C
Shows the exciting life, the beliefs and the epic journey of semi-nomadic traders dwelling in one of the strategic mountain passes between Communist China and India.
Prod-ATLAP Dist-ATLAP 1968

TIC - Index To Energy C 6 MIN
16MM FILM OPTICAL SOUND A
Visits the Technical Information Center at the Department of Energy in Oakridge, Tennessee. Focuses on the Center's computerized capability to gather, abstract and catalog technical reports and scientific papers at the rate of one million per year.
LC NO. 77-703416
Prod-USERD Dist-USNAC 1977

Tic Toc Time Clock C 11 MIN
16MM FILM, 3/4 OR 1/2 IN VIDEO P-I
Uses a group of students forming a living clock under the direction of a coach in order to show how to tell time and read a clock.
Prod-BFA Dist-PHENIX Prodn-JACOBL 1976

Ticket To Sydney C 10 MIN
16MM FILM OPTICAL SOUND J-C A
Presents a portrait of life in Sydney, Australia's largest city, as commuters hurry to arrive at work on time.
LC NO. 72-702253
Prod-ANAIB Dist-AUIS 1972

Ticket To Utopia C 29 MIN
3/4 INCH VIDEO CASSETTE
Features actors, folk singers and artists giving a video tour of some of man's most beautiful visions of utopia. Focuses on why these visions persist.
Prod-UMITV Dist-UMITV 1975

Tickle Me C 90 MIN
16MM FILM OPTICAL SOUND C A
Stars Elvis Presley and Julie Adams in a story about a 'BEAUTY FARM' out West where the girls spend daddy's money rolling off excess pounds and smoothing out wrinkles.
Prod-CINEWO Dist-CINEWO 1965

Ticks And Tick-Borne Diseases C 19 MIN
16MM FILM OPTICAL SOUND
Discusses ticks, their importance in transmitting diseases, their biology and their control.
LC NO. FIE61-46
Prod-USPHS Dist-USNAC 1960

Ticks And Tick-Borne Diseases (Spanish) C 19 MIN
16MM FILM OPTICAL SOUND
Discusses ticks and their importance in transmitting diseases, the biology of ticks and how to control them.
LC NO. 74-705791
Prod-NMAC Dist-USNAC 1960

Ticonderoga - A Classic Under Sail C 13 MIN
16MM FILM OPTICAL SOUND
Documents the history, launching and racing records of the classic sailboat Ticonderoga.
LC NO. 77-700583
Prod-PICNIC Dist-PICNIC 1977

Tidal Flat And Its Ecosystem C 20 MIN
16MM FILM, 3/4 OR 1/2 IN VIDEO J-C A
Discusses the organisms that flourish in tidal flats and explains the food chains that exist in these areas.
LC NO. 80-706295
Prod-NGS Dist-NGS 1979

Tide Commercial C 1 MIN
3/4 OR 1/2 INCH VIDEO CASSETTE
Shows a classic television commercial.
Prod-BROOKC Dist-BROOKC

Tidelands - Where Sea And Land Meet C 13 MIN
16MM FILM OPTICAL SOUND I-C A
Describes saltwater tidelands through the use of time-lapse photography during a 12-hour period.
LC NO. 77-701863
Prod-SAMSHL Dist-HLSPRO 1977

Tidepool - A Miracle Where Sea Meets Land C 11 MIN
16MM FILM OPTICAL SOUND I-J
Examines the variety of plants and animals which live in a tidepool.
LC NO. 74-703050
Prod-CROCHI Dist-AVED 1974

Tides Of The Ocean - What They Are And How The Sun And Moon Cause Them C 17 MIN
16MM FILM OPTICAL SOUND J-C
Uses animation to explain the causes of ocean tides, showing the effect of centrifugal force and the gravitational attraction of the sun and the moon on the waters. Discusses the uses of the ocean tides and points out that the activities of man must be planned to fit the rhythm of the tides.
LC NO. FIA64-47
Prod-ACA Dist-ACA 1964

Tidewater To Piedmont C 15 MIN
3/4 OR 1/2 INCH VIDEO CASSETTE I
Shows that tobacco is very important in Virginia's tidewater area while cotton and the textile industry is important on the Piedmont. Discusses George Washington Carver and the development of peanut farming.
From The American Legacy Series. Program 4
Prod-KRMATV Dist-AITECH 1983

Tidikawa And Friends C 82 MIN
3/4 INCH VIDEO CASSETTE
Long version of the documentary, The Spirit World Of Tidikawa. Focuses on a spirit medium of the Bedamini of Papua, New Guinea. Includes English narration at the beginning only.
Prod-BBCTV Dist-DOCEDR

Tie Dye C 16 MIN
16MM FILM, 3/4 OR 1/2 IN VIDEO J-C A
Demonstrates the techniques and design elements of tie dyeing in step-by-step procedures. Suggests possibilities for exploration and experimentation and shows a number of finished tie-dyed fabrics.
From The Textile Design Series.
Prod-TETKOW Dist-AIMS 1974

Tied To The Sea C 14 MIN
16MM FILM OPTICAL SOUND
Describes various forms of water recreation in the peaceful waters of the bays and inlets between British Columbia and Vancouver Island. Includes schooner racing, the bathtub regatta, salmon fishing, water skiing and seafood cookouts.
Prod-CTFL Dist-CTFL

Ties That Bind, The C 27 MIN
3/4 OR 1/2 INCH VIDEO CASSETTE A
Describes and illustrates the evolving process of parents' attachment to their baby during pregnancy, delivery and the first weeks of the child's life.
LC NO. 81-707012
Prod-POLYMR Dist-POLYMR

TIG Structural And Pipe Welding C 60 MIN
3/4 OR 1/2 INCH VIDEO CASSETTE IND
Goes into structural aspects, carbon steel pipe, stainless steel pipe, combination of TIG and 'stick.'
From The Welding Training Series.
Prod-ITCORP Dist-ITCORP

Tiger And The Rabbit, The C 15 MIN
3/4 OR 1/2 INCH VIDEO CASSETTE P-I
Tells a story from Puerto Rico and Africa of a rabbit outsmarting a tiger three times.
From The Sixteen Tales Series.
Prod-KLCSTV Dist-AITECH

Tiger At The Gate C 20 MIN
3/4 OR 1/2 INCH VIDEO CASSETTE
Analyzes the underpinnings of Hitler's appeal and his rise to power.
From The History In Action Series.
Prod-FOTH Dist-FOTH 1984

Tiger By The Tail C 35 MIN
16MM FILM OPTICAL SOUND H-C A
Describes some aspects of alcoholism - its causes, problems and a method of treatment - using the experiences of an actual alcoholic.
LC NO. 77-715307
Prod-UARIZ Dist-IU 1971

Tiger By The Tail C 58 MIN
2 INCH VIDEOTAPE
Presents a documentary study of the causes, problems and treatment of alcoholism. Features two actual alcoholics. Explores the work of Dr Richard L Reilly and his staff of the Tucson General Hospital Detoxification, Rehabilitation and Research Center. Interviews experts in the field of alcoholism and depicts the actual experiences of alcoholics.
From The Syngerism - Troubled Humanity Series.
Prod-KUATTV Dist-PUBTEL

Tiger In The House C 14 MIN
16MM FILM, 3/4 OR 1/2 IN VIDEO I-J
Stresses the need for fire warning devices in the home. Details operation, placement, maintenance, costs and limitations of detectors.
From The Fire Survival Series.
Prod-AREASX Dist-FILCOM

Tiger Rag C 3 MIN
16MM FILM OPTICAL SOUND P-H
Shows a stylized cartoon adaptation of the Les PaulMary Ford recording of 'TIGER RAG.'
Prod-SAXOND Dist-CFS

Tiger's Nest, The C 25 MIN
16MM FILM, 3/4 OR 1/2 IN VIDEO
Demonstrates how Buddhism has shaped the history of Bhutan, focusing on 'The Tiger's Nest,' where it is said the demons standing in the way of the spread of Buddhism were conquered.
From The Land Of The Dragon Series.
Prod-NOMDFI Dist-LANDMK

Tight Lines North C 32 MIN
16MM FILM OPTICAL SOUND
Presents Red Fisher fishing the waters of northern Manitoba for brook trout.
Prod-BRNSWK Dist-KAROL

Tight Packers And Loose Packers C 57 MIN
16MM FILM, 3/4 OR 1/2 IN VIDEO
Examines the conflicts between the abolitionists and those with vested interests in the slave trade during the late 18th century.
From The Fight Against Slavery Series. No. 4
LC NO. 79-707667
Prod-BBCTV Dist-TIMLIF 1977

Tight Times C 30 MIN
3/4 OR 1/2 INCH VIDEO CASSETTE P
Presents LeVar Burton introducing the book Tight Times and showing his friends how to have a great time without spending a dime, including checking out the public library.
From The Reading Rainbow Series. No. 1
Prod-WNEDTV Dist-GPITVL 1982

Tighten The Drums - Self-Decoration Among The Enga C 58 MIN
3/4 INCH VIDEO CASSETTE
Shows the visual language of body decoration performed by the Enga people of Papua, New Guinea. Filmed by Chris Owen.
Prod-IPANGS Dist-DOCEDR

Tighten Your Belts, Bite The Bullet C 48 MIN
16MM FILM, 3/4 OR 1/2 IN VIDEO A
Uses animation, archival photography and on-site photography to show how New York City and Cleveland grappled with their financial woes. Reveals that while New York City sought solvency through financial arrangements with its banks, Cleveland refused to have its largest bank buy it out of default. Points out that cities, not financial institutions, should have control of their governments.
LC NO. 82-706297
Prod-CCFG Dist-ICARUS Prodn-MIGALU 1981

Tightrope C 30 MIN
16MM FILM - 3/4 IN VIDEO
Demonstrates how attitudes toward child rearing have changed over the past 50 years and how children are affected by extreme approaches. Emphasizes that in parenting moderation is the best policy.
From The Footsteps Series.
LC NO. 79-707636
Prod-USOE Dist-USNAC 1978

Tightrope Walkers, The C 30 MIN
3/4 OR 1/2 INCH VIDEO CASSETTE
Focuses on the complexities of the exchange rate. Includes the meaning of the 'balance of trade' and the 'balance of payments.'
From The Money Puzzle - The World Of Macroeconomics Series. Module 15
Prod-MDCC Dist-MDCC

Tigris Expedition, The C 59 MIN
16MM FILM, 3/4 OR 1/2 IN VIDEO
Follows explorer Thor Heyerdahl and his crew as they sail their bardi reed boat, the Tigris, over routes believed to have been followed by Sumerian traders 5,000 years ago. Examines Heyerdahl's motivations for risking his life in the search for knowledge and adventure.
LC NO. 80-706395
Prod-NGS Dist-NGS 1979

Tijerina B 30 MIN
16MM FILM, 3/4 OR 1/2 IN VIDEO J-C A
Records the fiery speech by Reies Lopez Tijerina, the charismatic spokesman for many of the Southwest's Mexican-American citizens. Presents Tijerina as he tells the people to return to the communal Spanish pueblo system, the need for radical improvement in education and economic opportunity for Mexican-Americans and for a unification of 'HISPANO' citizens against 'ANGLO' power structures.
Prod-UCLA Dist-UCEMC 1969

Tikal C 5 MIN
16MM FILM OPTICAL SOUND
Shows the Mayan ruins of Tikal in Guatemala.
LC NO. 76-703332
Prod-SUMHIL Dist-SUMHIL 1974

Tikal C 23 MIN
16MM FILM OPTICAL SOUND H-C A
Presents an introduction to Mayan civilization through the architecture of Tikal in Guatemala.
LC NO. 78-700711
Prod-HEIDK Dist-PSUPCR Prodn-HEIDK 1977

Tikki Tiki Tembo C 15 MIN
3/4 INCH VIDEO CASSETTE K-P
See series title for descriptive statement.
From The Storytime Series.
Prod-WCETTV Dist-GPITVL 1976

Tikki Tikki Tembo C 9 MIN
16MM FILM, 3/4 OR 1/2 IN VIDEO K-P
Uses the pictures and text of the book of the same title, retold by Arlene Mosel and illustrated by Blair Lent. Shows why parents today give their children short names.
Prod-SCHNDL Dist-WWS 1974

Til There Was You C 9 MIN
16MM FILM OPTICAL SOUND
Focuses on four mentally retarded individuals who have learned to cope with their handicaps and to function successfully in society.
LC NO. 78-700223
Prod-UWAMER Dist-UWAMER Prodn-FORIP 1977

Tiles Teach Mathematics C 30 MIN
2 INCH VIDEOTAPE
Presents a brief review of the basic concepts of sets. Reviews these concepts through the use of concrete objects.
From The Devices In Their Hands - Math In Their Minds Series.
Prod-GPITVL Dist-GPITVL

Till The Butcher Cuts Him Down C 53 MIN
16MM FILM - 1/2 IN VIDEO
Documents the music and life of New Orleans jazz trumpeter Kid Punch Miller.
Prod-RHPSDY Dist-RHPSDY 1971

Till The Clouds Roll By C 137 MIN
16MM FILM OPTICAL SOUND
Presents a fictionalized version of the life of songwriter Jerome Kern. Stars Robert Walker, Judy Garland, and Van Heflin.
Prod-MGM Dist-REELIM 1946

Tillerman, The C 15 MIN
16MM FILM, 3/4 OR 1/2 IN VIDEO H-C A
Presents the story of the tillerman or the back seat driver on a fire apparatus. Describes the tillerman's duties and gives instructions on negotiating all types of corners.
Prod-LACFD Dist-FILCOM 1958

Tillie, The Unhappy Hippopotamus C 12 MIN
16MM FILM, 3/4 OR 1/2 IN VIDEO P-I
Tells the tale of a hippopotamus who lives a happy life until she overhears a man describe hippos as 'ugly, thick-skinned grunters.' Shows her search to try and become beautiful and the lesson she finally learns.
Prod-TRNKAJ Dist-LCOA 1979

Tillie, The Unhappy Hippopotamus (Captioned) C 12 MIN
16MM FILM, 3/4 OR 1/2 IN VIDEO P-I
Tells the story of Tillie the hippo, who requests to be changed into a butterfly, a fish and a bird.
Prod-TRNKAJ Dist-LCOA 1979

Tillie's Punctured Romance B 73 MIN
16MM FILM SILENT
Tells the outrageous story of the city slicker who marries country maiden Tillie for her inheritance, which he intends to share with his former sweetheart. Describes what happens when Tillie discovers the conspiracy. Stars Charlie Chaplin and Marie Dressler. Directed by Mack Sennett.
Prod-UNKNWN Dist-KILLIS 1914

Tillie's Punctured Romance B 77 MIN
1/2 IN VIDEO CASSETTE (BETA)
Tells how an innocent, if somewhat gigantic, country girl is led astray in the big city. Stars Charlie Chaplin and Marie Dressler. Includes a one-reeler called Those Love Pangs.
Prod-UNKNWN Dist-VIDIM 1914

Tilson's Book Shop—A Series
P
Presents various children's stories.
Prod-WVIZTV Dist-GPITVL 1975

Amelia Bedelia	15 MIN
Bargain For Frances, A	15 MIN
Be Nice To Josephine	15 MIN
Bear Who Saw The Spring, The	15 MIN
Berenstain Bears, The	15 MIN
Bremen Town Musicians, The	15 MIN
Cheerful Quiet, The / Too Much Noise	15 MIN
Dog Who Thought He Was A Boy, The	15 MIN
Elizabeth / The Winter Cat	15 MIN
Even The Devil Is Afraid Of A Shrew / A Penny	15 MIN
Fastest Quitter In Town, The	15 MIN
Fir Tree, The	15 MIN
Frog And Toad Are Friends / Some Frogs Have	15 MIN
Gary And The Very Terrible Monster / The	15 MIN
Grandpa's Farm	15 MIN
Hansel And Gretel	15 MIN
Ira Sleeps Over / An Anteater Named Arthur	15 MIN
Jennifer And Josephine	15 MIN
Leopold, The See-Through Crumbpicker	15 MIN
Man Named Lincoln, A	15 MIN
Mommies / Are You My Mother / The Way Mothers	15 MIN
Mr Egbert Nosh / The Biggest House In The World	15 MIN
Petunia	15 MIN
Puss In Boots	15 MIN
Skyful Of Dragons, A / Soo Ling Finds A Way	15 MIN
Smart Bear	15 MIN
Tall Tina	15 MIN
This For That	15 MIN
Trouble With Spider, The / Spiders Are Spinners	15 MIN
What's The Matter With Carruthers	15 MIN
When Shoes Eat Socks	15 MIN
Witchy Broom, The	15 MIN

Tilt C 19 MIN
16MM FILM, 3/4 OR 1/2 IN VIDEO J-C A
Explains that in the first decade of development of the Information and Public Affairs Department of the World Bank, 1960 to 1970, much was learned from the successes and failures in seeking to change the quality of life in the poorer parts of the globe.
Prod-NFBC Dist-MGHT 1973

Tilting Pad, Oil Film, Trust Bearings C 60 MIN
3/4 OR 1/2 INCH VIDEO CASSETTE IND
See series title for descriptive statement.
From The Mechanical Equipment Maintenance, Module 4 - Bearings And Lubrication Series.
Prod-LEIKID Dist-LEIKID

Tim - His Sensory-Motor Development C 31 MIN
16MM FILM, 3/4 OR 1/2 IN VIDEO PRO
Shows Dr Clair Kopp as she records the pattern of growth of an infant in a study based on the work of Jean Piaget. Examines new evidence that the origins of intelligence develop in the sensory-motor period, the time from birth to about two years of age.
Prod-UCLA Dist-MTI 1974

Tim Miller, Pooh Kaye And Ishmael Houston-Jones C 30 MIN
3/4 OR 1/2 INCH VIDEO CASSETTE

See series title for descriptive statement.
From The Experimentalists Series.
Prod-ARCVID Dist-ARCVID

Tim Miller, Pooh Kaye And Ishmael Houston-Jones C 30 MIN
3/4 OR 1/2 INCH VIDEO CASSETTE
See series title for descriptive statement.
From The Eye On Dance - The Experimentalists Series.
Prod-ARTRES Dist-ARTRES

Timber - EAC In Canada C 23 MIN
16MM FILM OPTICAL SOUND
Shows what man has done with the one-million acre TAHSIS forest area on Vancouver Island.
Prod-RDCG Dist-AUDPLN

Timber And Totem Poles C 11 MIN
16MM FILM OPTICAL SOUND
Shows the timber resources of the Tongass National Forest in southeast Alaska and explains the meaning of the totem poles of the Indians.
LC NO. 74-705806
Prod-USDA Dist-USNAC 1949

Timber In Finland C 15 MIN
16MM FILM, 3/4 OR 1/2 IN VIDEO P-C
Shows how natural highways of lakes and rivers are used to carry pulp to the paper mills. Discusses reconstruction efforts to reclaim bottom land for the use of forestry and safeguards employed to avoid the exhausting of natural resocuces.
From The Man And His World Series.
Prod-FI Dist-FI 1969

Timber Today And Tomorrow C 20 MIN
16MM FILM OPTICAL SOUND
Shows how by scientific forestry, grazing lands are protected, erosion is prevented and wild life is preserved.
Prod-CALVIN Dist-CALVIN 1953

Timber Town C 13 MIN
16MM FILM OPTICAL SOUND J-C A
Explains that the logging industry provides the livelihood of a small town nestled in the hardwood forests of the southwestern corner of Australia. Views the life of the townspeople and the operations of the logging industry - timber getting, re-forestation and control of brush fires.
LC NO. 73-702489
Prod-FLMAUS Dist-AUIS 1973

Timberlane, A Sculpture Garden C 17 MIN
16MM FILM OPTICAL SOUND
Presents a history of the sculpture garden at Timberlane, the Wurtzburger family estate in Pikesville, Maryland. Includes a look at the sculptures by 20th century artists.
LC NO. 78-701634
Prod-PSU Dist-PSU 1978

Timberline C 16 MIN
16MM FILM, 3/4 OR 1/2 IN VIDEO I-H
Illustrates the mixture of flora and fauna that flourishes at the ill-defined zone above which trees will not grow, but tundra life teems.
From The Mountain Habitat Series.
Prod-KARVF Dist-BCNFL 1982

Timbromania C 29 MIN
16MM FILM OPTICAL SOUND J-C A
Surveys the history of stamp collecting as a craze that began in the late 1860's and has evolved into dedicated collecting and serious research.
LC NO. 79-701754
Prod-PSU Dist-PSU 1979

Time C 14 MIN
16MM FILM, 3/4 OR 1/2 IN VIDEO P-I
Teaches that time is another form of measurement which is determined by different standards according to different needs.
From The Science Processes Series.
Prod-MGHT Dist-MGHT 1970

Time C 20 MIN
2 INCH VIDEOTAPE P
See series title for descriptive statement.
From The Mathemagic, Unit VI - Measurement Series.
Prod-WMULTV Dist-GPITVL

Time - Five Minutes C 15 MIN
3/4 INCH VIDEO CASSETTE P
Tells how to estimate and tell the time to the nearest five minutes on different types of clocks.
From The Studio M Series.
Prod-WCETTV Dist-GPITVL 1979

Time - Measurement And Meaning C 26 MIN
16MM FILM, 3/4 OR 1/2 IN VIDEO H-C
Examines concepts of time dilation, the entropy principle and astronomical time, the relation of subjective and external time, and the definition of a second. Shows scientific timepieces such as an atomic clock and a water clock, as well as a brief glimpse of a cyclotron.
Prod-EBEC Dist-EBEC 1974

Time After Time C 122 MIN
16MM FILM OPTICAL SOUND
Tells how H G Wells travels forward in time in order to catch Jack the Ripper. Describes Wells' adventures in 1979 San Francisco. Stars Malcolm McDowell and Mary Steenburgen.
Prod-WB Dist-SWANK

Time After Time C 15 MIN
16MM FILM, 3/4 OR 1/2 IN VIDEO P
Introduces the concept of time, what it is and how it is measured. Explains the human body clock and the inner biological clock possessed by every living thing. Describe how the sun and moon are used to measure days, months, seasons and years.
LC NO. 84-706222
Prod-SHIRE Dist-BARR 1983

Time And A Place, A C 9 MIN
16MM FILM, 3/4 OR 1/2 IN VIDEO K-P
Tells the story of a young bug named Bucky who hates school and wants to spend his time playing. Shows how he runs away only to realize that he belongs at home.
Prod-BARR Dist-BARR 1978

Time And Clocks B 28 MIN
16MM FILM OPTICAL SOUND H-C
Discusses concepts of time measurement and shows various devices used to measure and record time intervals. Points out that the accuracy of a clock can be judged only by comparison with another clock.
From The PSSC Physics Films Series.
Prod-PSSC Dist-MLA 1958

Time And Direction C 7 MIN
16MM FILM, 3/4 OR 1/2 IN VIDEO K-I
Explores sundials and compasses as indicators of time and direction, and discusses where the sun rises and sets.
From The Science Series.
Prod-MORLAT Dist-SF 1967

Time And Light C 60 MIN
3/4 OR 1/2 INCH VIDEO CASSETTE J-C A
Explores time measured by the evolution of the sea urchin and the changes in bamboo. Tours a collection of time pieces. Visits the birthplace of our present-day calendar. Examines 19th-century artist Thomas Moran's use of light to portray earth's timetable in the Grand Canyon.
From The Smithsonian World Series.
Prod-WETATV Dist-WETATV Prodn-SMITHS

Time And Motion C 30 MIN
3/4 OR 1/2 INCH VIDEO CASSETTE
See series title for descriptive statement.
From The Photographic Vision - All About Photography Series.
Prod-COAST Dist-CDTEL

Time And Place C 17 MIN
16MM FILM OPTICAL SOUND H-C A
Presents an impressionistic study of Australia's living environment, including architecture and urban development.
Prod-ANAIB Dist-AUIS 1971

Time And Place For Everything, A C 15 MIN
16MM FILM, 3/4 OR 1/2 IN VIDEO A
Shows how planning can expedite getting a job done, by an example from the construction industry. An on-site examination reveals much better results could be obtained through planning deliveries, scheduling operations and using a flow chart.
Prod-CSAO Dist-IFB

Time And Seasons / Documentary - Miss Deaf Texas C 30 MIN
3/4 OR 1/2 INCH VIDEO CASSETTE
Provides sign language dealing with time and seasons. Includes a documentary on Miss Deaf Texas.
From The Signing With Cindy Series.
Prod-KUHTTV Dist-MDCPB

Time And Seasons Plus A Documentary - Miss Deaf Texas C
3/4 OR 1/2 INCH VIDEO CASSETTE A
Shows Cindy Cochran entering the dream world of 'Fame,' looks at signs relating to time and the seasons, and visits Miss Deaf Texas to look at how handicaps do not have to inhibit behavior.
From The Signing With Cindy Series.
Prod-GPCV Dist-GPCV

Time And Suzie Thompson B 20 MIN
16MM FILM OPTICAL SOUND H-C A
Presents the case of a young housewife who delays medical attention after detecting a lump in her breast. Surveys various courses of treatment including biopsy, frozen section and mastectomy.
From The Doctors At Work Series.
LC NO. FIA65-1365
Prod-CMA Dist-LAWREN Prodn-LAWREN 1963

Time And Temperature C 30 MIN
3/4 OR 1/2 INCH VIDEO CASSETTE
See series title for descriptive statement.
From The Infinity Factory Series.
Prod-EDFCEN Dist-MDCPB

Time And Terri Adams B 16 MIN
16MM FILM OPTICAL SOUND H-C A
A hysterectomy is performed after a malignant cystic growth is found in an ovary of a mother of four children.
LC NO. FIA65-1356
Prod-CMA Dist-LAWREN Prodn-LAWREN 1963

Time And Territory Management C
3/4 OR 1/2 INCH VIDEO CASSETTE
Helps sellers to develop plans and strategies of account territory coverage. Includes such topics as selling versus managing accounts, time wasters and savers, sales forecasting game plan, call frequency and time apportionment.
From The Making Of A Salesman Series. Session 8
Prod-PRODEV Dist-PRODEV

Time And Two Women C 18 MIN
16MM FILM OPTICAL SOUND H-C S
Dr Joe V Meigs, consulting visiting gynecologist to the Vincent Memorial Hospital at the Massachusetts General Hospital, Boston, explains how cancer of the uterus can be detected in the earliest stages through cell examination - 'PAP' test - as part of annual health checkups.
Prod-AMCS Dist-AMCS 1957

Time And Two Women (Spanish) C 18 MIN
16MM FILM OPTICAL SOUND H-C S
Dr Joe V Meigs, consulting visiting gynecologist to the Vincent Memorial Hospital at the Massachusetts General Hospital, Boston, explains how cancer of the uterus can be detected in the earliest stages through cell examination - 'PAP' test - as part of annual health checkups.
Prod-AMCS Dist-AMCS 1957

Time Bomb C 35 MIN
3/4 OR 1/2 INCH VIDEO CASSETTE
Tells the story of a computer department overtaken by a series of disasters because security systems were not developed or enforced. Highlights such areas as program change controls, back-up, user checks, documentation, management of key staff and physical security.
Prod-MELROS Dist-VISUCP

Time Bomb At Fifty Fathoms C 20 MIN
16MM FILM, 3/4 OR 1/2 IN VIDEO I-H A
Documents the efforts of a Provincial Magistrate in Otranto, Italy, to avert an ecological disaster off the coast of his town.
From The Cousteau Odyssey, Series 2 Series.
Prod-COUSTS Dist-WDEMCO 1979

Time Bomb In The River C 24 MIN
16MM FILM OPTICAL SOUND
Documents the search, recovery and salvage of four huge tanks of dangerous liquid chlorine from the Mississippi River near Natchez, Mississippi. Covers the emergency planning of several agencies to protect the health and welfare of 80 thousand residents in a radius of 30 miles of the sunken barge.
LC NO. 74-705794
Prod-USAE Dist-USNAC 1963

Time Bomb Within, The C 14 MIN
16MM FILM, 3/4 OR 1/2 IN VIDEO H-C A
Tells how uncontrolled stress is a significant factor in absenteeism and loss of efficiency. Outlines major health consequences of unrelieved stress and suggests ways to lessen its effects.
From The Managing Stress Series.
Prod-CENTRO Dist-CORF 1984

Time Capsule Of Electrical Progress C 3 MIN
16MM FILM OPTICAL SOUND
Discusses major developments in the history of electricity from Thomas Edison to the moon flights.
LC NO. 78-706128
Prod-GE Dist-STEEGP 1969

Time Changes The Land - A Geologic Study C 23 MIN
16MM FILM, 3/4 OR 1/2 IN VIDEO J-H A
Pictures the land formations in Zion and Bryce Canyons and explains their development. Studies the geological and ecological aspects of the region.
Prod-HOE Dist-MCFI

Time Changes The Land - A Geologic Study (Captioned) C 23 MIN
16MM FILM, 3/4 OR 1/2 IN VIDEO J-H A
Pictures the land formations in Zion and Bryce Canyons and explains their development. Studies the geological and ecological aspects of the region.
Prod-HOE Dist-MCFI

Time Dilation - An Experiment With Mu-Mesons B 36 MIN
16MM FILM OPTICAL SOUND H A
Depicts an experiment at Massachusetts Institute of Technology and on top of Mt Washington, New Hampshire, using radioactive decay of cosmic ray mu-mesons to show the dilation of time. Features David H Frisch, Mit, and James H Smith, University of Illinois.
From The PSSC College Physics Films Series.
LC NO. FIA67-5925
Prod-PSSC Dist-MLA 1966

Time Exposure - William Henry Jackson, Picture Maker Of The Old West C 28 MIN
16MM FILM - 3/4 IN VIDEO H-C A
Focuses on the life of artist and photographer William Henry Jackson and depicts his photographic documentation of the American West during the late 19th century.
LC NO. 80-706408
Prod-CRYSP Dist-CRYSP 1979

Time Flies C 15 MIN
16MM FILM OPTICAL SOUND P-I
Presents Our Gang on a map-reading exercise and tells how they become completely lost. Shows how they take the advice of a seafarer and end up creating havoc through lanes, hedges, restaurants, shops and even a deep freeze plant.
Prod-CHILDF Dist-LUF 1972

Time Flies C 25 MIN
16MM FILM OPTICAL SOUND H A
Traces the history of commercial air service in Europe. Includes scenes of the first 'flying boat,' an early catapult launch for planes and the first airmail service between Europe and the Americas. Narrated by Frank Blair.
Prod-WSTGLC Dist-WSTGLC

Time For Action B 15 MIN
16MM FILM OPTICAL SOUND
Deals with three phases of the program of the General Federation of Woman's Clubs--the Community Inprovement Program, the seminars on leadership training held in various U S cities, and the emphasis on Western hemispheric solidarity.
Prod-UOKLA Dist-UOKLA

Time For Building, A B 60 MIN
16MM FILM OPTICAL SOUND
Presents highly charged discussions from various parts of the country including a Negro group in Mississippi.
Prod-LUTHER Dist-LUTHER

Time For Caring C 41 MIN
3/4 OR 1/2 INCH VIDEO CASSETTE
Presents an in-depth look at the role of the volunteer in hospice care. Focuses on quality of life rather than on dying. Shows how the skills and talents of volunteers are incorporated into the program.
Prod-NFBC Dist-AJN

Time For Caring C 42 MIN
16MM FILM, 3/4 OR 1/2 IN VIDEO
Presents the experiences and resourcefulness of volunteers working on a palliative care team.
LC NO. 83-707159
Prod-NFBC Dist-NFBC 1982

Time For Caring, A - The School's Response To The Sexually Abused Child C 28 MIN
3/4 INCH VIDEO CASSETTE C A
Discusses behavioral signs which should alert teachers and other staff members to the possibility of sexual abuse of children.
Prod-PRFLM Dist-LAWREN

Time For Caring, A - The School's Response To The Sexually Abused Child C 28 MIN
16MM FILM - 3/4 IN VIDEO
Explains what steps can be taken by schools to protect a sexually abused child from further abuse.
From The Sexual Abuse Of Children Series.
LC NO. 79-706192
Prod-BAKRSR Dist-LAWREN Prodn-PROFPR 1979

Time For Change, A C 15 MIN
16MM FILM OPTICAL SOUND
Follows the political campaign of a black candidate for the office of mayor and shows his frustrations in terms of unregistered voters and the political machine.
LC NO. 77-711533
Prod-ROPE Dist-ROPE 1970

Time For Change, A - The Calculus C 25 MIN
16MM FILM OPTICAL SOUND
Tells how the first half of the 17th century saw the origins of calculus in the work of many mathematicians dotted around Europe.
Prod-OPENU Dist-GPITVL

Time For Clocks C 11 MIN
16MM FILM, 3/4 OR 1/2 IN VIDEO P
Shows two children learning the importance of time in their daily lives. Introduces time-telling techniques.
Prod-EH Dist-EBEC

Time For Decision C 28 MIN
3/4 OR 1/2 INCH VIDEO CASSETTE J A
Tells the story of a housewife whose attorney husband is an alcoholic.
Prod-SUTHRB Dist-SUTHRB

Time For Decision (Spanish) C 28 MIN
3/4 OR 1/2 INCH VIDEO CASSETTE J A
Tells the story of a housewife whose attorney husband is an alcoholic.
Prod-SUTHRB Dist-SUTHRB

Time For Decision, A C 16 MIN
16MM FILM OPTICAL SOUND A
Uses animation to illustrate the history and hazards of cigarette smoking. Designed for presentation to community leaders.
LC NO. FIA67-656
Prod-AMCS Dist-AMCS Prodn-HANBAR 1966

Time For Decision, A C 29 MIN
16MM FILM, 3/4 OR 1/2 IN VIDEO H-C A
Shows the problem of the compulsive drinker and how his family can find guidance in attaining a normal life, even though the alcoholic may continue drinking.
Prod-AIMS Dist-AIMS 1967

Time For Decision, A C 29 MIN
3/4 OR 1/2 INCH VIDEO CASSETTE
Presents a story of a compulsive drinker and how his family finds help through the public and private resources available in the community.
Prod-LACFU Dist-IA

Time For Decision, A (Spanish) C 29 MIN
16MM FILM, 3/4 OR 1/2 IN VIDEO H-C A
Presents the story of a lawyer who becomes a compulsive drinker.
Prod-LAC Dist-AIMS 1969

Time For English, Beginning Level--A Series C 30 MIN
2 INCH VIDEOTAPE A
Presents lessons for teaching English as a second language.
Prod-GPITVL Dist-GPITVL

Time For English, Intermediate Level--A Series C 30 MIN
2 INCH VIDEOTAPE A
Presents lessons for teaching English as a second language.
Prod-GPITVL Dist-GPITVL

Time For Every Season, A C 30 MIN
16MM FILM OPTICAL SOUND
Summarizes Dr Everett L Shostrom's Actualizing Therapy, which uses the idea that man's nature consists of four major polarities - anger, love, strength and weakness, analogous to winter, summer, spring and fall.
Prod-PSYCHD Dist-PSYCHD

Time For Georgia, A B 15 MIN
16MM FILM OPTICAL SOUND H-C A
A documentary film which describes the pathology of Georgia, a three-year-old girl with infantile autism. Portrays the value and urgency of placing autistic children in a pre-school nursery school for seriously disturbed children.
LC NO. 78-711422
Prod-PSW Dist-NYU 1971

Time For Living C 20 MIN
16MM FILM OPTICAL SOUND
Portrays the summer resort program of young life, a non-sectarian Christian organization, for high school students at seven resorts and ranches in Colorado.
LC NO. 72-700595
Prod-YLC Dist-YLC 1972

Time For Living, A C 12 MIN
16MM FILM OPTICAL SOUND
Discusses courses and training programs for those over age 50 to learn how to retire.
LC NO. 75-703616
Prod-UCONN Dist-UCONN Prodn-RIEBR 1975

Time For Myself C 30 MIN
3/4 OR 1/2 INCH VIDEO CASSETTE J-H
Points out that part of becoming mature is accepting different realities like sickness and aging - how to live with the inevitable and how to deal with personal conflicts and needs without deserting others in the process.
From The Y E S Inc Series.
Prod-KCET Dist-GPITVL 1983

Time For Rain, A C 8 MIN
16MM FILM, 3/4 OR 1/2 IN VIDEO P-I
Follows a young boy on a walk through an urban environment during a rain shower to show the effects brought about by the rain.
From The Wonder Walks Series.
Prod-EBEC Dist-EBEC 1971

Time For Sun, A C 6 MIN
16MM FILM, 3/4 OR 1/2 IN VIDEO P-I
Shows effects of the sun on plants, animals and a variety of materials.
From The Wonder Walks Series.
Prod-EBEC Dist-EBEC 1971

Time For Survival C 25 MIN
16MM FILM, 3/4 OR 1/2 IN VIDEO
Shows the role of natural diversity in maintaining environmental stability and discusses the importance of all species. Shows how some of man's activities simplify the environment and thereby go against nature's direction.
Prod-NAS Dist-PHENIX 1979

Time For Talent, A X 29 MIN
16MM FILM OPTICAL SOUND T
Explores three school programs for the gifted student.
Prod-NEA Dist-NEA 1961

Time For Winning, A C 23 MIN
16MM FILM OPTICAL SOUND
Focuses around the address delivered by Fran Tarkenton at the Scholarship Award Banquet in Chattanooga, Tennesse, for the Fellowship of Christian Athletes.
Prod-FELLCA Dist-FELLCA

Time For Witches, A C 15 MIN
3/4 OR 1/2 INCH VIDEO CASSETTE P
Combines looking, listening, talking, writing and reading to help establish the link between oral and written language. Presents the story Spooky Story by Bill Martin, Jr.
From The I Want To Read Series.
Prod-LACOS Dist-GPITVL 1976

Time For Work And Time For Play C 15 MIN
16MM FILM OPTICAL SOUND
Deals with Denmark as an industrial nation. Shows its development from an agricultural nation to an industrial one.
Prod-RDCG Dist-AUDPLN

Time Form Color C 18 MIN
16MM FILM OPTICAL SOUND
Records the fossilization of trees, plants, shells, driftwood and debris from distant ships blended with their original colors, textures and dimensions.
Prod-FILIM Dist-RADIM

Time Game, The C 14 MIN
16MM FILM, 3/4 OR 1/2 IN VIDEO IND
Teaches time management using the analogy of a card game in which the stakes are managerial success and the chips are segments of time. Suggests keeping time log, and ways of controlling crises and establishing priorities.
From The Professional Management Program Series.
Prod-NEM Dist-NEM 1975

Time Game, The (Spanish) C 14 MIN
16MM FILM, 3/4 OR 1/2 IN VIDEO
Deals with time management in business.
From The Professional Management Program (Spanish) Series.
Prod-NEM Dist-NEM

Time Has Come, The C 22 MIN
16MM FILM OPTICAL SOUND A
Explores the elements of a non-sexist home environment and deals with influences outside the home, such as television and school.
From The Non-Sexist Early Education Films Series.
LC NO. 78-700385
Prod-WAA Dist-THIRD Prodn-SIMONJ 1977

Time Has Come, The C 30 MIN
3/4 OR 1/2 INCH VIDEO CASSETTE IND
Covers the on-the-job interpersonal communications that affect productivity.
From The Super-Vision Series.
LC NO. 79-706778
Prod-VCI Dist-DELTAK 1977

Time I C 30 MIN
3/4 OR 1/2 INCH VIDEO CASSETTE H-C A
Presents Lawrence Solow and Sharon Neumann Solow introducing American Sign Language used by the hearing-impaired. Emphasizes signs that have to do with time.
From The Say It With Sign Series. Part 11
Prod-KNBCTV Dist-FI 1982

Time II C 30 MIN
3/4 OR 1/2 INCH VIDEO CASSETTE H-C A
Presents Lawrence Solow and Sharon Neumann Solow introducing American Sign Language used by the hearing-impaired. Emphasizes signs that have to do with time.
From The Say It With Sign Series. Part 12
Prod-KNBCTV Dist-FI 1982

Time III C 30 MIN
3/4 OR 1/2 INCH VIDEO CASSETTE H-C A
Presents Lawrence Solow and Sharon Neumann Solow introducing American Sign Language used by the hearing-impaired. Emphasizes signs that have to do with time.
From The Say It With Sign Series. Part 13
Prod-KNBCTV Dist-FI 1982

Time Integration Methods And Applications B 60 MIN
3/4 OR 1/2 INCH VIDEO CASSETTE
See series title for descriptive statement.
From The Heat Transfer Analysis By Finite Element Methods Series.
Prod-UAZMIC Dist-UAZMIC 1979

Time Is C 30 MIN
16MM FILM, 3/4 OR 1/2 IN VIDEO
Presents the major historical developments of the concept of time.
Prod-MGHT Dist-MGHT 1964

Time Is For Taking C 23 MIN
16MM FILM OPTICAL SOUND
Gives insight into the world of the retarded child through everyday situations involving children at a residential camp for the retarded. Shows how problems develop and are solved by skillful counselors.
LC NO. FIA65-478
Prod-FINLYS Dist-FINLYS 1964

Time Is Money C 30 MIN
16MM FILM, 3/4 OR 1/2 IN VIDEO
Presents techniques in time management for salespeople. Points out that salespeople sell more when they make better use of their time, but that most salespeople waste 80 percent of their time. Stars Burgess Meredith and Ron Masak.
Prod-CCCD Dist-CCCD

Time Is Out Of Joint, The C 20 MIN
16MM FILM, 3/4 OR 1/2 IN VIDEO
Explores the reasons why William Shakespeare chose a medieval setting for his play Hamlet, with emphasis on the political and social situation in England at the time.
From The World Of William Shakespeare Series.
LC NO. 80-706325
Prod-NGS Dist-NGS 1978

Time Lag B
3/4 OR 1/2 INCH VIDEO CASSETTE
Pictures a drawing, rehearsal space acting out a new America. Uses street-theatrical language.
From The Red Tapes Series.
Prod-KITCHN Dist-KITCHN

Time Line C 10 MIN
16MM FILM, 3/4 OR 1/2 IN VIDEO P-I
Shows a small child unrolling a large roll of cloth which is a time line and walking through time, from era to era, watching the changing geological state of the Earth and its varying patterns of plant and animal population.
Prod-FLMFR Dist-FLMFR

Time Line - Managing The Moment For Safety, The C 13 MIN
3/4 OR 1/2 INCH VIDEO CASSETTE H-C A
Looks at how accidents can happen when people lose control of the present because their minds are on the past or the future.
Prod-ATBELL Dist-MTI

Time Machine C 45 MIN
16MM FILM, 3/4 OR 1/2 IN VIDEO J-C A
Describes the adventures of a scientist who invents a machine that can travel back and forth through time. Based on the story The Time Machine by H G Wells.
From The Classic Stories Series.
Prod-LUF Dist-LUF 1979

Time Machine C 105 MIN
16MM FILM, 3/4 OR 1/2 IN VIDEO J-C A
Presents the story of a scientist who invents a machine which allows him to travel back and forth through time. Based on the story The Time Machine by H G Wells.
Prod-LUF Dist-LUF 1979

Time Machine, The C 29 MIN
16MM FILM, 3/4 OR 1/2 IN VIDEO H-C
Focuses on the work of Fermilab, one of the largest laboratories of physics in the world. Shows how scientists use the tools of high-energy physics to peel away layer after layer of the innermost structure of matter.
From The Dimensions In Science, Series 2 Series.
Prod-OECA Dist-FI 1979

Time Machine, The - A Novel By H G Wells C 15 MIN
16MM FILM, 3/4 OR 1/2 IN VIDEO J-C A
Presents a fictional trip from Victorian England to a society of the future. Based on the novel THE TIME MACHINE by H G Wells.
From The Novel Series.

LC NO. 83-706267
Prod-IITC Dist-IU 1982

Time Management C 30 MIN
3/4 OR 1/2 INCH VIDEO CASSETTE
See series title for descriptive statement.
From The Management For Engineers Series.
Prod-UKY Dist-SME

Time Management - A Practical Approach—A Series

Offers practical tips for changing behavior, attitudes and physical environment to gain more control over how time is spent. Includes a unique game based on William Oncken's techniques for time management.
Prod-PACPL Dist-DELTAK Prodn-ONCKEW

Avoiding Time Traps
Getting Things Done
Planning Your Time

Time Management - A Second Chance C 22 MIN
16MM FILM, 3/4 OR 1/2 IN VIDEO C A
Summarizes principles and practices of time management proven effective for faculty and staff in colleges and universities.
Prod-IU Dist-IU 1984

Time Management For Managers And Professionals—A Series

Teaches a strategy for time management, which will enable participants to maximize the contribution they make to the organization. Includes a student text and workbook, a discussion leader's guide and a Train-the-Trainer session. Features Bill Oncken.
Prod-DELTAK Dist-DELTAK Prodn-ONCKEW

Collecting Subordinate-Imposed Time - The
Controlling Boss-Imposed Time 030 MIN
Controlling System-Imposed Time - Making The 020 MIN
Freedom And Leverage 024 MIN
Getting Rid Of Subordinate-Imposed Time - The 025 MIN
Managing Your Molecule 015 MIN
Molecule Of Management, The 022 MIN
Time Management Problem - Peers 020 MIN
Time Management Problem - Subordinates 012 MIN
Time Management Problem - The Boss 020 MIN
Using Time Management 019 MIN
Vocational Time Vs Management Time 020 MIN

Time Management For Managers—A Series
16MM FILM, 3/4 OR 1/2 IN VIDEO A
Explains how managers can avoid common problems and use their time more effectively. Covers such topics as decision-making, delegating, scheduling and managing interruptions. Hosted by Christopher Reeve.
Prod-TIMLIF Dist-TIMLIF 1981

Decision-Making 030 MIN
Delegating 030 MIN
Managing Interruptions 030 MIN
Managing Time - Professional And Personal 030 MIN
Principles Of Time Management 030 MIN
Scheduling 030 MIN

Time Management For Managing Stress C 27 MIN
3/4 OR 1/2 INCH VIDEO CASSETTE
See series title for descriptive statement.
From The Practical Stress Management With Dr Barry Alberstein Series.
Prod-DELTAK Dist-DELTAK

Time Management For Supervisors C 14 MIN
16MM FILM, 3/4 OR 1/2 IN VIDEO
Provides supervisors with specific practical time management techniques that can be used immediately, shows them the advantages of written daily plans in keeping their schedules on target and how to take control of their employees' time.
Prod-EFM Dist-EFM

Time Management Problem - Peers C 20 MIN
3/4 OR 1/2 INCH VIDEO CASSETTE
See series title for descriptive statement.
From The Time Management For Managers And Professionals Series.
Prod-DELTAK Dist-DELTAK Prodn-ONCKEW

Time Management Problem - Subordinates C 12 MIN
3/4 OR 1/2 INCH VIDEO CASSETTE
See series title for descriptive statement.
From The Time Management For Managers And Professionals Series.
Prod-DELTAK Dist-DELTAK Prodn-ONCKEW

Time Management Problem - The Boss C 20 MIN
3/4 OR 1/2 INCH VIDEO CASSETTE
See series title for descriptive statement.
From The Time Management For Managers And Professionals Series.
Prod-DELTAK Dist-DELTAK Prodn-ONCKEW

Time Management, E Byron Chew C
3/4 OR 1/2 INCH VIDEO CASSETTE PRO
See series title for descriptive statement.
From The Management Skills Series.
Prod-AMCEE Dist-AMCEE

Time Of Apollo, The C 28 MIN
16MM FILM - 3/4 IN VIDEO
Presents President John F Kennedy stating in 1961 that America should commit itself to achieving the goal, before this decade is out, of landing a man on the moon and returning him safely to Earth. Issued in 1975 as a motion picture.
LC NO. 79-708020
Prod-NASA Dist-USNAC Prodn-IMAGA 1979

Time Of Challenge, A C 27 MIN
16MM FILM OPTICAL SOUND
Commemorates the 100th anniversary of the AFL-CIO and organized labor, portraying the struggle of working men and women for fair wages, decent working conditions and economic security. Features various union leaders.
Prod-AFLCIO Dist-MTP

Time Of Changes, A C 15 MIN
16MM FILM, 3/4 OR 1/2 IN VIDEO I-J
Shows how technological changes can affect career decisions. Explains that technology has made some working roles obsolete, but has created others.
From The Whatcha Gonna Do Series.
Prod-NVETA Dist-EBEC

Time Of Hope, A C 14 MIN
16MM FILM OPTICAL SOUND
Depicts efforts of the U S Agency for International Development in producing measle vaccines and conducting mass immunization programs in new African nations. Shows American, French and African teams at work.
LC NO. FIA66-664
Prod-MESHDO Dist-MESHDO Prodn-VISION 1965

Time Of Life B 18 MIN
16MM FILM OPTICAL SOUND H-C A
Discusses the nature and symptoms of the menopause and describes satisfactory ways of meeting the psychological and physiological problems of this period.
From The Doctors At Work Series.
LC NO. FIA65-1367
Prod-CMA Dist-LAWREN Prodn-LAWREN 1962

Time Of Our Lives, The C 12 MIN
3/4 OR 1/2 INCH VIDEO CASSETTE
Stresses the necessity of good planning if work is to fit into time available and introduces the key elements of good time management.
From The Management of Time Series. Module 1
Prod-RESEM Dist-RESEM

Time Of Our Lives, The C 27 MIN
1 INCH VIDEOTAPE
Stresses the importance of keeping fit and specific ways to do it. Endorsed by the President of the United States in connection with his physical fitness program.
Prod-AMDAS Dist-MTP

Time Of The Cree C 26 MIN
16MM FILM OPTICAL SOUND
Investigates the way of life and the past of a Cree family whose ancestors have inhabited Manitoba's Boreal Forest for 6,000 years.
LC NO. 77-702677
Prod-SINROD Dist-CANFDC 1974

Time Of The Grizzly C 26 MIN
16MM FILM, 3/4 OR 1/2 IN VIDEO
Examines the grizzly bear's life cycle and our attitudes toward this wild animal.
Prod-STOUFP Dist-STOUFP

Time Of The Horn B 7 MIN
16MM FILM, 3/4 OR 1/2 IN VIDEO P-C A
A small negro boy retrieves a discarded trumpet and loses himself in a jazz fantasy of his own imagining. Musical background is a Duke Ellington composition interpreted by Jonah Jones. No narration is used.
Prod-JOU Dist-JOU Prodn-MERRTT 1965

Time Of The Jackal C 50 MIN
16MM FILM OPTICAL SOUND
Examines the phenomenon of terrorism and its implications for society.
From The Window On The World Series.
LC NO. 77-702828
Prod-CTV Dist-CTV 1976

Time Of The Jackals C 51 MIN
16MM FILM, 3/4 OR 1/2 IN VIDEO H-C A
Recreates the 1975 terrorist assauult on OPEC headquarters in Vienna. Illustrates graphically the modus operandi of the terrorist group and profiles their leader. Considers the general question of political conspiracy and international terrorism.
Prod-CTV Dist-FI 1976

Time Of The Locust B 12 MIN
16MM FILM, 3/4 OR 1/2 IN VIDEO
Uses footage shot by American, Japanese, and Vietnamese cameramen, revealing the agonies of the war in South Vietnam.
Prod-AMFS Dist-CNEMAG 1966

Time Of The Saviour C 24 MIN
16MM FILM OPTICAL SOUND
Deals with Guru Maharj Ji and his movement, focusing on the main figures of the movement. Raises questions about financing, authenticity of teaching and sentimental exploitation of followers.
LC NO. 74-700251
Prod-PACE Dist-PACE 1973

Time Of The West C 36 MIN
3/4 INCH VIDEO CASSETTE
Pictures the paths of early European explorers of the West. Uses photographs, paintings and filmed sequences to show views of the Oregon Trail, the Lewis and Clark route to the Pacific, the California gold country and the Santa Fe Trail. Issued in 1966 as a motion picture.
LC NO. 79-706165
Prod-USNPS Dist-USNAC Prodn-GUG 1979

Time Of Their Lives, The B 29 MIN
16MM FILM OPTICAL SOUND T
Presents one morning in the lives of 24 5-year-olds in kindergarten.
Prod-NEA Dist-NEA 1962

Time Of Waking, A C 30 MIN
16MM FILM OPTICAL SOUND I-C
Says that in the life of every boy there is a time when his future leaps before him and he begins to sense a certain order. Presents a mirror for the human spirit through the ages and explains that if we are to understand ourselves we must try to understand history.
From The Human Dimension Series.
Prod-GRACUR Dist-GRACUR

Time Of Wonder C 13 MIN
16MM FILM, 3/4 OR 1/2 IN VIDEO K-P
Uses watercolor illustrations from the children's picture book of the same name by Robert Mc Closkey. Shows the wonders of nature on an island in Maine.
Prod-WWS Dist-WWS 1961

Time Of Your Life C 15 MIN
16MM FILM OPTICAL SOUND
Features Panama City, on Florida's Miracle Strip.
Prod-FLADC Dist-FLADC

Time Of Your Life, The C 17 MIN
16MM FILM OPTICAL SOUND
A promotional film which encourages the prospective buyer to plan for the future by investing in mutual funds.
LC NO. 72-701786
Prod-OPMC Dist-OPMC 1971

Time Of Your Life, The C 28 MIN
16MM FILM, 3/4 OR 1/2 IN VIDEO
Offers insights into the need for time management and suggests techniques for managing time so that more work can be accomplished with less effort.
Prod-CCCD Dist-CCCD 1974

Time On Your Hands C 12 MIN
3/4 OR 1/2 INCH VIDEO CASSETTE
Revolves around a student's inability to schedule his time and the obvious consequences. Illustrates the importance of time management and provides suggestions for developing a system of monitoring and evaluating specific goals.
From The Developing Your Study Skills Series.
Prod-BCNFL Dist-BCNFL 1985

Time Out (Graffiti) (Spanish) C 10 MIN
16MM FILM, 3/4 OR 1/2 IN VIDEO P-H
Tells the story of five youngsters tempted to write graffiti, one who is bored, one who is pressured by peers, one who is having trouble at home and school, one who is an average neighborhood kid and one who is new and wants to fit in. Deals with basic truths about graffiti, that it is a crime and can cause trouble for the writer, the family and the community and can be avoided by a simple mental formula.
Prod-KLUCLA Dist-FLMFR

Time Out - Graffiti C 10 MIN
16MM FILM, 3/4 OR 1/2 IN VIDEO I-H
Presents various arguments against graffiti-writing which are climaxed by the realistic arrest, trial and conviction of a young graffitist.
LC NO. 82-707299
Prod-KLUCLA Dist-FLMFR 1982

Time Out For Life C 10 MIN
16MM FILM OPTICAL SOUND H-C A
Dramatizes the life of a young mother who was persuaded to have a pap test. Shows that as a result of the test, uterine cancer was detected and subsequently removed.
Prod-AMCS Dist-AMCS

Time Out For Man C 28 MIN
16MM FILM OPTICAL SOUND
Shows the visits of a team of humanists in the national humanities series in a small South Dakota town.
LC NO. 72-702435
Prod-WWNFF Dist-WWNFF Prodn-CINEMK 1972

Time Out For Trouble B 22 MIN
16MM FILM, 3/4 OR 1/2 IN VIDEO H-C A
Illustrates the most common accidents causing serious injury in the home and explains that mental attitudes are the real cause of the trouble. Suggests a course of action to eliminate such injuries.
Prod-IFB Dist-IFB 1962

Time Out—A Series

Looks at the phenomenon of battered wives.
Prod-ODNP Dist-ODNP 1981

Deck The Halls 018 MIN
Shifting Gears 012 MIN
Up The Creek 015 MIN

Time Piece C 8 MIN
16MM FILM, 3/4 OR 1/2 IN VIDEO J A
Combines comedy and serious comment to show one man's life in today's urban 'rat race.' Portrays the hero, a typical young executive, as he is hospitalized and his daily tasks flash before his eyes, alternating between realism and wild dreams. Suggests modern man's helplessness in his complex world.
Prod-MUPPTS Dist-MGHT 1966

Time Structures C 28 MIN
16MM FILM OPTICAL SOUND H-C A
Suggests that how we use our time affects the priorities in our lives. Reveals how we can gain control or direction of our use of time.

From The Learning To Live Series.
Prod-TRAFCO Dist-ECUFLM 1974

Time Structures C 30 MIN
3/4 OR 1/2 INCH VIDEO CASSETTE A
Discusses how the use of our time affects the priorities in our lives. Examines how we can gain control of direction in our use of time. Uses transactional analysis to discuss the issues.
From The Learning To Live Series.
Prod-UMCOM Dist-ECUFLM 1974

Time Study Rating B 10 MIN
16MM FILM, 3/4 OR 1/2 IN VIDEO
Presents an operator working at different rates. Allows viewers to judge the operator's rate of activity. Used in training time study personnel.
Prod-UCEMC Dist-UCEMC

Time Table C 8 MIN
16MM FILM, 3/4 OR 1/2 IN VIDEO J-C A
Offers an animated comment on air travel. Shows a man discovering Icarus-like wings and attempting to fly. Depicts the same man making a frustrating and dangerous jet flight.
Prod-ZAGREB Dist-IFB 1980

Time To Be Brave, A C 30 MIN
3/4 OR 1/2 INCH VIDEO CASSETTE I-J
Tells the story of a young Indian girl who is afraid of trains, the only link between the wilderness and outside world, because her sick mother left on the train and did not return, and her brother entrained for school. Explains how her father teaches her to hunt and track and survive under adversity. Proves she can conquer fear when her father is hurt and she must flag down the train for much needed help.
From The Spirit Bay Series.
Prod-TFW Dist-BCNFL

Time To Begin B 14 MIN
16MM FILM OPTICAL SOUND
Demonstrates the benefits of learning music through a unique method of group piano teaching. Traces, in beginners' piano classes, each step in the development of basic musical concepts and skills.
LC NO. 76-706130
Prod-SMUSA Dist-SMUSA Prodn-JHNSTN 1969

Time To Care C 18 MIN
3/4 INCH VIDEO CASSETTE H-C A
Tells how a group of churches in Bushey, England, have organized to offer help to people in need.
Prod-CHERIO Dist-GPITVL 1977

Time To Come Home C 24 MIN
3/4 OR 1/2 INCH VIDEO CASSETTE
Shows how three families lived and cared for their terminally ill children, with home care made possible by the support of nursing services.
Prod-UMINN Dist-AJN

Time To Dance--A Series
16MM FILM, 3/4 OR 1/2 IN VIDEO C A
Prod-NET Dist-IU Prodn-WGBHTV 1960

Choreographer At Work, A	29 MIN
Classical Ballet	29 MIN
Dance - A Reflection Of Our Times	29 MIN
Ethnic Dance - Round Trip To Trinidad	29 MIN
Great Performance In Dance	29 MIN
Invention In Dance	29 MIN
Language Of Dance, The	29 MIN
Modern Ballet	29 MIN
Time To Dance, A	29 MIN

Time To Dance, A B 29 MIN
16MM FILM, 3/4 OR 1/2 IN VIDEO C A
Discusses and illustrates the three major forms of dance--ethnic, ballet and modern. Shows two performances of European ethnic dances and examples of a 17th century court dance, classical ballet and dance satire to introduce forms of the modern dance. (Kinescope)
From The Time To Dance Series.
LC NO. 80-707035
Prod-NET Dist-IU Prodn-WGBHTV 1960

Time To Die, A C 49 MIN
16MM FILM, 3/4 OR 1/2 IN VIDEO
Follows the lives of three people courageously facing death from terminal illness. Focuses on the support groups of an organization called Omega, which was formed to help people deal with the fears and burdens of impending death and to help ease the bereavement of the surviving spouses.
From The Death And Dying Series.
LC NO. 83-707101
Prod-CBSNEW Dist-MTI 1983

Time To Grow C 28 MIN
16MM FILM OPTICAL SOUND H-C A
Shows an innovative idea in elementary education, the pre-first grade class. Explains that these classes are based on the idea that many children need maturing before they are ready for the demanding work of first grade. Portrays testing and two classes of pre-first grade in action.
Prod-CAMPF Dist-CAMPF

Time To Grow, A C 17 MIN
16MM FILM OPTICAL SOUND
Shows Sperry Corporation employees at work, speaking about the challenges and opportunities their jobs present, especially in relation to personal and corporate growth objectives.
LC NO. 82-700196
Prod-SRCNHD Dist-SRCNHD Prodn-HOLDEN 1981

Time To Grow, A (Dutch) C 17 MIN
16MM FILM OPTICAL SOUND
Shows Sperry Corporation employees at work, speaking about the challenges and opportunities their jobs present, especially in relation to personal and corporate growth objectives.
Prod-SRCNHD Dist-SRCNHD Prodn-HOLDEN 1981

Time To Grow, A (French) C 17 MIN
16MM FILM OPTICAL SOUND
Shows Sperry Corporation employees at work, speaking about the challenges and opportunities their jobs present, especially in relation to personal and corporate growth objectives.
Prod-SRCNHD Dist-SRCNHD Prodn-HOLDEN 1981

Time To Grow, A (German) C 17 MIN
16MM FILM OPTICAL SOUND
Shows Sperry Corporation employees at work, speaking about the challenges and opportunities their jobs present, especially in relation to personal and corporate growth objectives.
Prod-SRCNHD Dist-SRCNHD Prodn-HOLDEN 1981

Time To Grow, A (Italian) C 17 MIN
16MM FILM OPTICAL SOUND
Shows Sperry Corporation employees at work, speaking about the challenges and opportunities their jobs present, especially in relation to personal and corporate growth objectives.
Prod-SRCNHD Dist-SRCNHD Prodn-HOLDEN 1981

Time To Grow, A (Portuguese) C 17 MIN
16MM FILM OPTICAL SOUND
Shows Sperry Corporation employees at work, speaking about the challenges and opportunities their jobs present, especially in relation to personal and corporate growth objectives.
Prod-SRCNHD Dist-SRCNHD Prodn-HOLDEN 1981

Time To Grow, A (Spanish) C 17 MIN
16MM FILM OPTICAL SOUND
Shows Sperry Corporation employees at work, speaking about the challenges and opportunities their jobs present, especially in relation to personal and corporate growth objectives.
Prod-SRCNHD Dist-SRCNHD Prodn-HOLDEN 1981

Time To Laugh, A C 15 MIN
2 INCH VIDEOTAPE I
Introduces different forms of drama. Emphasizes comedy.
From The Images Series.
Prod-CVETVC Dist-GPITVL

Time To Learn, A - Reality Orientation In The Nursing Home C 28 MIN
3/4 INCH VIDEO CASSETTE
Emphasizes the implementation process of reality orientation in three nursing home settings. Illustrates staff training in the facilities using various teaching techniques and demonstrates methods of implementing reality orientation. Issued in 1973 as a motion picture.
LC NO. 78-706260
Prod-VAHT Dist-USNAC 1978

Time To Leave - A Time To Return C 22 MIN
16MM FILM OPTICAL SOUND H-C A
Tells the story of political upheavals punctuated by missionary evacuations and re-entries in the country of Zaire.
Prod-CBFMS Dist-CBFMS

Time To Live, A B 30 MIN
16MM FILM OPTICAL SOUND A
Tells the story of a professor, after witnessing a nuclear test explosion, who questions his Pastor about the future of mankind. The Pastor discusses the hope of the Christian for the future.
LC NO. FIA65-1616
Prod-CPH Dist-CPH 1964

Time To Live, A C 29 MIN
3/4 INCH VIDEO CASSETTE
Focuses on the introduction of technology in the area of health care.
From The On To Tomorrow Series.
Prod-UMITV Dist-UMITV 1976

Time To Live, A C 29 MIN
2 INCH VIDEOTAPE
Examines the phenomenon of growing old in a youth-oriented society.
From The Turning Points Series.
Prod-WPBTTV Dist-PUBTEL

Time To Live, A B 30 MIN
16MM FILM - 3/4 IN VIDEO C A
See series title for descriptive statement.
From The Sportsmanlike Driving Series. Refresher Course
Prod-AAAFTS Dist-GPITVL Prodn-SCETV

Time To Live, A C 50 MIN
3/4 OR 1/2 INCH VIDEO CASSETTE
See series title for descriptive statement.
From The Leo Buscaglia Series.
Prod-PBS Dist-DELTAK

Time To Live, A C 55 MIN
3/4 OR 1/2 INCH VIDEO CASSETTE
Presents a documentary of the Ninth Annual Communist Youth Festival held in Sofia, Bulgaria in 1968. Attacks the Vietnam War and stresses solidarity, world peace and freedom. Opens with a parade with groups from Europe, China, Japan, Vietnam, Africa and South America. Features songs, ethnic dances, native costumes and a carnival. Portrays deserters from the U S armed forces criticizing America.
Prod-IHF Dist-IHF

Time To Live, A - With Leo Buscaglia C 50 MIN
3/4 OR 1/2 INCH VIDEO CASSETTE
Before a throng of California picnickers, Leo Buscaglia delivers a secular sermon on the importance and uses of time. He urges listeners to value the present moment and grow through learning, listening, giving, loving and fun.
LC NO. 82-707324
Prod-KVIETV Dist-PBS 1982

Time To Plant, A C 30 MIN
16MM FILM OPTICAL SOUND H-C A
Uses a dramatization about a doctor who begins practice in a small community and helps others discard their prejudices, in order to show that a person is not prejudiced if he adheres to his Christian convictions.
LC NO. 73-715495
Prod-CONCOR Dist-CPH 1969

Time To Pretend C 15 MIN
3/4 OR 1/2 INCH VIDEO CASSETTE P
Combines looking, listening, talking, writing and reading to help establish the link between oral and written language. Presents the story The Cat Who Thought He Was A Tiger by Polly Cameron.
From The I Want To Read Series.
Prod-LACOS Dist-GPITVL 1976

Time To Rejoice, A C 14 MIN
16MM FILM OPTICAL SOUND
Explores the difficult and day-to-day problems of absorbing new immigrants from the Soviet Union into Israeli society.
Prod-UJA Dist-ALDEN

Time To Remember, A C 19 MIN
16MM FILM OPTICAL SOUND J-C A
Uses graphic scenes to convey the horror of the Holocaust.
Prod-NJWB Dist-NJWB 1980

Time To Remember, A B 20 MIN
16MM FILM, 3/4 OR 1/2 IN VIDEO
Provides scenes of Jewish life in Eastern Europe before World War II and provides a moving oral history of the holocaust from the perspective of four survivors.
Prod-CNEMAG Dist-CNEMAG

Time To Run C 97 MIN
16MM FILM OPTICAL SOUND R
Presents Christian answers to problems of alienation, loneliness, and frustration that divide families.
LC NO. 75-702383
Prod-WWPI Dist-WWPI 1973

Time To Speak, A X 30 MIN
16MM FILM OPTICAL SOUND J-H T R
A story of a man who works faithfully at his job and his Christian living. Although some people feel that he overdoes it in matters of religion, he continues to put his Christian testimony into action as well as into words.
LC NO. FIA67-1913
Prod-FAMF Dist-FAMF 1966

Time To Stop Is Now, The C 5 MIN
16MM FILM OPTICAL SOUND H-C
Emphasizes that the time to stop cigarette smoking is now. Explains that the body shows determination to repair itself if given the chance.
Prod-AMCS Dist-AMCS

Time To Tell Time C
16MM FILM, 3/4 OR 1/2 IN VIDEO P
Depicts how Everett the cuckoo bird is taught to tell time by Clarence, the kindly old household cat. Discusses the concepts of years, months, days, hours, minutes and seconds.
Prod-ARMUND Dist-BARR 1983

Time To Understand, A C 20 MIN
3/4 OR 1/2 INCH VIDEO CASSETTE
Presents a series of vignettes documenting a survey of a VA medical center, conducted by representatives of the Joint Commission on Accreditation of Hospitals.
LC NO. 80-706133
Prod-USVA Dist-USNAC 1978

Time Together C 14 MIN
16MM FILM OPTICAL SOUND K-P
Tells a story about a boy who wants his father to love him but whose father is too busy to show that he cares.
From The Family Relations Series.
LC NO. 74-703452
Prod-MORLAT Dist-MORLAT 1974

Time Trap, The C 28 MIN
3/4 OR 1/2 INCH VIDEO CASSETTE A
Focuses on proper use of time in business and industry. Identifies and provides solutions for several time wasters. Uses story format. Based on books by Dr R Alec Mackenzie.
Prod-AMEDIA Dist-AMEDIA

Time Traveler's Guide To Energy, The C 27 MIN
16MM FILM, 3/4 OR 1/2 IN VIDEO I-J
Examines the historical persistence of human ingenuity related to energy. Presents various energy sources and their means of production and suggests career possibilities in the field of energy.
Prod-EPCOT Dist-EPCOT 1983

Time Traveler's Guide To Energy, The C 27 MIN
16MM FILM, 3/4 OR 1/2 IN VIDEO I-J
Traces the historical persistence of human ingenuity in harnessing various sources of energy, including coal, wind, naturagas, solar and nuclear power.
Prod-WDEMCO Dist-WDEMCO

Time Values C 29 MIN
3/4 INCH VIDEO CASSETTE H A
Reviews scale forms and earlier pieces. Presents new pieces. Introduces concepts of time values and rhythm.
From The Beginning Piano - An Adult Approach Series. Lesson 4
Prod-COAST Dist-CDTEL

Time Will Be, The C 3 MIN
16MM FILM OPTICAL SOUND
Stresses that the crises of pollution and dimishing fuel supplies are only now beginning to make an impression on the public. Presents a view of what the rapidly multiplying auto population and the subsequent pollution may someday result in.
Prod-SLFP Dist-SLFP

Time Zero C 11 MIN
16MM FILM OPTICAL SOUND
Depicts parallels between the interactive process of art and the use of instant photography as a responsive medium.
LC NO. 80-701456
Prod-POLARD Dist-POLARD Prodn-FLECKG 1980

Time-Lapse Studies Of Glacier Flow B 14 MIN
16MM FILM SILENT
Offers a time-lapse study of glacier motions including material collected over several years from Pacific Northwest glaciers by the University of Washington and the U S Geological Survey. Illustrates the flow of glacier ice over an icefall during periods of three to four months.
Prod-LACHAP Dist-UWASHP 1973

Time-Ordered Sequences B 15 MIN
2 INCH VIDEOTAPE P
See series title for descriptive statement.
From The Just Inquisitive Series. No. 15
Prod-EOPS Dist-GPITVL Prodn-KOACTV

Time-Out For Basketball C
3/4 OR 1/2 INCH VIDEO CASSETTE
Contains many interesting graphics and teaching aids which give a better comprehension of the rules of high school basketball.
LC NO. 83-706826
Prod-NFSHSA Dist-NFSHSA

Time-Rite Indicator C 10 MIN
3/4 OR 1/2 INCH VIDEO CASSETTE IND
Covers basic construction of the Time-Rite Piston Position Indicator, nomenclature, assembly and installation into the cylinder. Shows how to use the Time-Rite to locate the piston firing position.
From The Aviation Technician Training Program Series.
Prod-AVIMA Dist-AVIMA 1980

Time-Series Analysis C
3/4 OR 1/2 INCH VIDEO CASSETTE IND
Says this analysis amounts to understanding the effects of seasonal, cyclical, and trend factors to make forecasts. Covers traditional smoothing and decomposition techniques in detail.
From The Statistics For Managers Series.
Prod-COLOSU Dist-COLOSU

Time, Lines, And Events (2nd Ed) C 15 MIN
16MM FILM, 3/4 OR 1/2 IN VIDEO I-J
Uses animation to present a visualization of time as a system for measuring events. Shows how to make a timeline and discusses the vastness of geologic time.
LC NO. 82-706591
Prod-DF Dist-CF 1980

Time, Pt 1 C 15 MIN
3/4 INCH VIDEO CASSETTE P
Shows how to use the hour hand on the clock.
From The Measure Up Series.
Prod-WCETTV Dist-GPITVL 1977

Time, Pt 2 C 15 MIN
3/4 INCH VIDEO CASSETTE P
Shows how to read multiples of five minutes on a clock.
From The Measure Up Series.
Prod-WCETTV Dist-GPITVL 1977

Time, The Most Precious Resource C 30 MIN
3/4 OR 1/2 INCH VIDEO CASSETTE
Discusses how we use our time and influence others to use theirs. Explores the opportunities for leadership in dealing with the intra- and inter-personal factors. Shows the relationship between the need for recognition and time structure.
From The Organizational Transactions Series.
Prod-PRODEV Dist-PRODEV

Time's Harvest - Exploring The Future—A Series
C
Introduces the underlying philosophies and major issues in the field of future studies. Draws upon and introduces the works of several major writers in the field and examines the methodologies and techniques used by those involved in future research.
Prod-MDCPB Dist-MDCPB

Becoming An American 030 MIN
Coming Transformation, The 030 MIN
Computer Comes Home, The 030 MIN
Inheriting The Earth 030 MIN
Planning For Tomorrow 030 MIN
Question Of Growth, A 030 MIN
Running Out Of Water 030 MIN
Technology's Heartbeat 030 MIN

Time's Lost Children C 29 MIN
2 INCH VIDEOTAPE
Explores the world of the autistic child from the perspective of parents, teachers and doctors. Examines the traits of autism, often obscured until a seemingly normal child reaches the age of two or three and describes the effects of autism on the children's families.
Prod-KPBS Dist-PUBTEL

Timekeeper, The C 22 MIN
16MM FILM OPTICAL SOUND
Presents an account of man's early record in Minnesota, using today's timepieces as a point of reference. Depicts activities of the Minnesota Historical Society in recording today's events for tomorrow.
LC NO. 75-700312
Prod-MINHS Dist-MINHS Prodn-TCR 1974

Timeless Tahiti C 14 MIN
16MM FILM OPTICAL SOUND
Attempts to capture the romance of French Polynesia by showing the islands of Tahiti, Moorea, Bora Bora, Raiatea and Rangiroa.
LC NO. 78-700669
Prod-UTA Dist-MCDO Prodn-MCDO 1978

Timeless Tales—A Series
P-I
Presents lively fairy tales.
Prod-WESFAL Dist-LUF

Emperor's New Clothes, The 015 MIN
Fir Tree, The 013 MIN
Rumplestiltskin 015 MIN
Soup Stone, The 015 MIN

Timeless Temiar C 55 MIN
16MM FILM OPTICAL SOUND
Portrays the life cycle of the nomads. Describes their communal way of living, extended families, beliefs and rudimentary divisions of labor. Includes chants instrumental music and dances of the nomads.
LC NO. FIA64-1385
Prod-MALAYF Dist-PMFMUN 1956

Timepiece C 10 MIN
16MM FILM OPTICAL SOUND
Tells the story of a young executive caught up in the urban rat race. Shows how a typical day flashes before his eyes during a recuperative stay in the hospital. Concludes with a frantic, surrealistic chase sequence that is half-comedy and half-nightmare.
Prod-HENASS Dist-FLMLIB

Times Square Show C 7 MIN
3/4 OR 1/2 INCH VIDEO CASSETTE
Documents the June 1980 show in which the Downtown Art/Fashion/Street scene and some uptown affiliates met in order to give this decade a right start.
Prod-KITCHN Dist-KITCHN

Times 3 B 6 MIN
16MM FILM OPTICAL SOUND
Points out that life is an ongoing process and each person is a thousand selves blending and fading from one to the other.
LC NO. 76-701382
Prod-SFRASU Dist-SFRASU 1973

Times, The - They Are A'changing C 20 MIN
3/4 INCH VIDEO CASSETTE J-H
Utilizes films and cartoons to illustrate changes in food, clothing, housing, transportation, advertising, consumer awareness and consumer legislation.
From The Dollar Data Series.
LC NO. 81-707355
Prod-WHROTV Dist-GPITVL 1974

Timing An Engine C 4 MIN
16MM FILM OPTICAL SOUND
Shows the timing of an engine with the use of a timing list and includes the hook up and adjustment of the distributor.
LC NO. FI68-280
Prod-RAYBAR Dist-RAYBAR 1966

Timing Belts And Flat Belts C 28 MIN
3/4 OR 1/2 INCH VIDEO CASSETTE IND
Focuses on timing belts and includes a short discussion of flat belts. Explains belt construction and compares types.
Prod-TAT Dist-TAT

Timing Events B 15 MIN
2 INCH VIDEOTAPE P
See series title for descriptive statement.
From The Just Curious Series. No. 23
Prod-EOPS Dist-GPITVL Prodn-KOACTV

Timing Examples C 30 MIN
3/4 OR 1/2 INCH VIDEO CASSETTE
Uses two detailed examples to show how to deal with timing design problems of both asynchronous and synchronous systems.
From The Digital Sub-Systems Series.
Prod-TXINLC Dist-TXINLC

Timon Of Athens C 128 MIN
3/4 OR 1/2 INCH VIDEO CASSETTE H-C A
Presents William Shakespeare's play Timon Of Athens which details the transformation of a noble Athenian from a reckless spendthrift to a mad misanthrope.
From The Shakespeare Plays Series.
LC NO. 82-707354
Prod-BBCTV Dist-TIMLIF 1981

Timothy The Turtle X 5 MIN
16MM FILM OPTICAL SOUND K-P
The importance of watching for turning cars is not realized. Otto the Auto teams up with Timothy the Turtle to impress that this rule is very important.
From The Otto The Auto Series.
Prod-AAAFTS Dist-AAAFTS 1959

Timpani Techniques C 20 MIN
16MM FILM, 3/4 OR 1/2 IN VIDEO J-C
Describes kettle drums of four sizes. Discusses plastic heads versus calf, stick selection, French and German grips, instructions on fourth and fifth tuning, the tuning range, the correct position at the drum, strikes, proper beating area, dampening and muting, sticking, sustained roll and roll ending. Includes demonstrations by Donald Kiss.
From The Musical Instruments Series.
Prod-CROWB Dist-MCFI Prodn-FLMMKR 1969

Tin Lady—A Series
Features Gen Ventrone of Harlingen, New Jersey instructing in the early American folk art of stencilling on wood and tin.
Prod-NJPBA Dist-PUBTEL

Copying, Cuttin' And Cussin' 28 MIN
Final Touch, The 28 MIN
Getting It All Together 28 MIN
Now You're An Artist 29 MIN
Shading, Strokes And Striping 29 MIN
Swoosh Away The Glop 29 MIN

Tin Mining C 10 MIN
16MM FILM, 3/4 OR 1/2 IN VIDEO J-H A
Explores Malaysia, which is the world's leading producer of tin and has been mining it for 500 years. Shows how gravel pumps and dredging are used to mine the metal. Views the communal lives of the workers who live in company housing.
Prod-LUF Dist-LUF 1979

Tin Pan Fire Drill C 15 MIN
16MM FILM OPTICAL SOUND
Shows school fire drill and young boy who is interested in trying the drill idea at home. Firemen come to his home to make plans with the family for a safe exit, including a tin pan alarm.
Prod-PUBSF Dist-FILCOM

Tina, Come Back C
3/4 OR 1/2 INCH VIDEO CASSETTE
See series title for descriptive statement.
From The Fragments from Willoughby's Video Performances - Pt I Series.
Prod-EAI Dist-EAI

Tina's Tea Party B 29 MIN
2 INCH VIDEOTAPE K-P
See series title for descriptive statement.
From The Children's Fair Series.
Prod-WMVSTV Dist-PUBTEL

Tinder Box, The C 8 MIN
16MM FILM OPTICAL SOUND K-I
An animated cartoon. Tells the story of a soldier who acquires a magic tinder box with which he can command a great dog who fulfills his every wish.
From The Language Arts Series.
LC NO. FIA68-1044
Prod-NBC Dist-GRACUR 1968

Tinder Box, The C 25 MIN
16MM FILM, 3/4 OR 1/2 IN VIDEO
Presents a live-action adaptation of Hans Christian Andersen's fairy tale 'THE TINDER BOX,' the story about a soldier who wins the princess with the help of the dogs that guard the magic tinder box.
Prod-EBEC Dist-EBEC 1971

Tinga Layo C 14 MIN
3/4 OR 1/2 INCH VIDEO CASSETTE P-I
See series title for descriptive statement.
From The Ready, Sing Series.
Prod-ARKETV Dist-AITECH 1979

Tinikling - The Bamboo Dance C 17 MIN
16MM FILM OPTICAL SOUND I-C
Shows adaptation of popular Philippine folk dance into a modern physical education activity.
From The Physical Fitness Series.
LC NO. FIA68-2553
Prod-MMP Dist-MMP 1967

Tinning And Solder Wiping B 26 MIN
16MM FILM - 3/4 IN VIDEO IND
Demonstrates techniques for cleaning copper tubing for tinning, applying flux to copper, and tinning copper tubing by hand and by dipping. Issued in 1944 as a motion picture.
From The Shipbuilding Skills - Coppersmithing Series. Number 4
LC NO. 79-707987
Prod-USOE Dist-USNAC Prodn-RCM 1979

Tinnitus - Patient Management C 55 MIN
3/4 OR 1/2 INCH VIDEO CASSETTE PRO
Presents a round table discussion on tinnitus and various methods of management of the patient with this complaint. Discusses the use of hearing aids, tinnitus maskers, and biofeedback treatment.
Prod-HOUSEI Dist-HOUSEI

Tinnitus - Treatment With Biofeedback C 56 MIN
3/4 OR 1/2 INCH VIDEO CASSETTE PRO
Discusses tinnitus and the use of biofeedback in its treatment.
Prod-HOUSEI Dist-HOUSEI

Tinnitus Masking C 37 MIN
3/4 OR 1/2 INCH VIDEO CASSETTE PRO
Discusses the indications for a tinnitus masker in various types of cases. Presented by Dr J Vernon, authority on tinnitus masking.
Prod-HOUSEI Dist-HOUSEI

Tinplate C 27 MIN
16MM FILM OPTICAL SOUND
Traces the history of tinplate and contrasts the slow hand methods used in medieval Europe with more modern methods. Shows how raw materials are converted into thin sheet steel, and tinplating by two processes—hot dip and electrolytic.
Prod-USDIBM Dist-USDIBM Prodn-ATLAS 1949

Tinseltown And The Big Apple C 24 MIN
16MM FILM, 3/4 OR 1/2 IN VIDEO
Gives a child-eye-view of the nation's two largest cities, New York and Los Angeles.
From The Young People's Specials Series.
Prod-MULTPP Dist-MULTPP

Tinsmithing C 29 MIN
2 INCH VIDEOTAPE
See series title for descriptive statement.
From The Commonwealth Series.
Prod-WITFTV Dist-PUBTEL

Tint Retouch (3) C
3/4 OR 1/2 INCH VIDEO CASSETTE
Examines factors determing the need for a retouch, examining hair for formula change and methods of matching the regrowth to the ends. Analyzes protective measure for the client's safety. Details the bottle method of application with correct subsectioning, application of color and timing factors. Demonstrates 'soap capping,' correct removal and styling techniques.
Prod-MPCEDP Dist-MPCEDP 1984

Tintoretto B 29 MIN
3/4 INCH VIDEO CASSETTE
Examines the innovations of Tintoretto's painting techniques. Discusses how he anticipated both the Baroque and the Mannerist styles and influenced later painters.
From The Meet The Masters Series.
Prod-UMITV Dist-UMITV 1966

Tintypes B 11 MIN
16MM FILM OPTICAL SOUND
Presents the pictorial beauty of the tintype pictures of the 1800's accompanied by the fragmentary comments of the youth of today.
Prod-FINLYS Dist-FINLYS

Tinwork Of Northern New Mexico C 14 MIN
16MM FILM, 3/4 OR 1/2 IN VIDEO
Portrays Emilio and Senaida Romero, artisans who carry on the centuries old Hispanic tradition of tinwork.
Prod-BLUSKY Dist-ONEWST

Tiny B 19 MIN
16MM FILM OPTICAL SOUND
Uses animation to tell a story about a growing dinosaur.
LC NO. 76-701383
Prod-CONCRU Dist-CONCRU 1975

Tip The Scales In Your Favor C 15 MIN
3/4 OR 1/2 INCH VIDEO CASSETTE J-H
Tells how Linda and Bones, who are unhappy about their weight for opposite reasons, learn to choose appropriate patterns of eating and exercise.
From The Soup To Nuts Series.
Prod-GSDE Dist-AITECH 1980

Tippecanoe And Lyndon Too C 24 MIN
16MM FILM, 3/4 OR 1/2 IN VIDEO I-H
Demonstrates the changes in presidentail election campaigns since Washington.
From The Smithsonian Series.
Prod-NBCTV Dist-MGHT 1966

Tippecanoe And Tyler Too B 12 MIN
16MM FILM OPTICAL SOUND I-H A
Focuses on the presidential campaign of 1840. Traces the careers of President William Henry Harrison and President John Tyler from their youth to their terms in the White House. Reveals their political growth and achievements.
Prod-VADE Dist-VADE 1960

Tipping The Scales C 55 MIN
16MM FILM, 3/4 OR 1/2 IN VIDEO H-C A
Discusses the problems of overweight and underweight. Shows how the body stores and uses food, with regard to metabolism, fat cell storage and appetite regulation. Describes research being done on the effects of prenatal diet and childhood eating patterns and examines some drastic measures that are needed by the extremely overweight. Provides information on anorexia nervosa, investigating the psychological pattern that leads to this sometimes fatal condition.
From The Nature Of Things Series.
LC NO. 82-707329
Prod-CANBC Dist-FLMLIB 1982

Tips For Fuel Savers C 15 MIN
16MM FILM OPTICAL SOUND
Deals with the continuing need for fuel-efficient driving, and presents ten tested and proven tips.
From The Driving To Survive Series.
Prod-BUMPA Dist-BUMPA

Tips For The Beginning French Horn Player C 37 MIN
1/2 IN VIDEO CASSETTE BETA/VHS
Provides instruction in learning to play the French horn.
Prod-MOHOMV Dist-MOHOMV

Tips From The Pros C 30 MIN
1/2 IN VIDEO CASSETTE BETA/VHS
Talks about soil preparation, crop varieties and harvesting.
From The Victory Garden Series.
Prod-WGBHTV Dist-MTI

Tips From Top Pros - Grip B 13 MIN
16MM FILM OPTICAL SOUND
From The Tips From Top Pros Series. No. 4
Prod-SFI Dist-SFI

Tips From Top Pros - How To Handle Each Club B 13 MIN
16MM FILM OPTICAL SOUND
From The Tips From Top Pros Series. No. 1
Prod-SFI Dist-SFI

Tips From Top Pros - Long Irons B 13 MIN
16MM FILM OPTICAL SOUND
From The Tips From Top Pros Series. No. 3
Prod-SFI Dist-SFI

Tips From Top Pros - Trouble Lies B 13 MIN
16MM FILM OPTICAL SOUND
From The Tips From Top Pros Series. No. 2
Prod-SFI Dist-SFI

Tips From Top Pros—A Series

Shows the winning technique and style of the pros as demonstrated by Jimmy Demaret.
Prod-SFI Dist-SFI

Tips From Top Pros - Grip 13 MIN
Tips From Top Pros - How To Handle Each Club 13 MIN
Tips From Top Pros - Long Irons 13 MIN
Tips From Top Pros - Trouble Lies 13 MIN

Tire Changing And Right Of Way C 14 MIN
16MM FILM, 3/4 OR 1/2 IN VIDEO H
Shows the proper way to change a tire. Covers parking the car in a safe place, the use of emergency flashers and flares, and the dangers involved in tire changing. Discusses the issue of right of way in different situations.
Prod-SF Dist-SF 1974

Tire Wise C 15 MIN
16MM FILM, 3/4 OR 1/2 IN VIDEO H-C A
Presents what to know when buying and using a set of automobile tires. Explains how tires are manufactured and the differences between the three main types of tires. Tells how to get maximum tire mileage and driving safety. Examines details on skids, chains, changing a tire, hydroplaning and other aspects of tire use, care and behavior.
Prod-CAHILL Dist-AIMS 1976

Tires C 11 MIN
16MM FILM OPTICAL SOUND I-C A
Observes tire sculptor William Weisz as he recycles discarded tires into dragons, elephants and other creative shapes and structures.
LC NO. 77-702873
Prod-YANIVY Dist-IFF 1977

Tires C 11 MIN
3/4 OR 1/2 INCH VIDEO CASSETTE
Shows how something as ordinary as a rubber tire can become a playground or an art form after wear precludes vehicle use. Demonstrates how tire sculpture became an innovative, community-constructed playground created entirely from tires. Reveals every facet of the design process beginning with the original manufacture of tires accompanied by music as enthusiastic children play on the tire structures.
Prod-IFF Dist-IFF

Tires And Wheels C 5 MIN
16MM FILM, 3/4 OR 1/2 IN VIDEO H-C A
Shows how to check tire pressure, wear and damage, tread depth, valves, spoke tension and wheel bearings on a motorcycle. Includes methods for changing tires and verifying speedometer drive and drive chain connections.
From The Basic Motorcycle Maintenance Series.
LC NO. 81-706496
Prod-PACEST Dist-IFB 1980

Tiropetes, Spanakopetes And Bourach Bi Lahmeh C 32 MIN
3/4 OR 1/2 INCH VIDEO CASSETTE PRO
Demonstrates three ways to use phyllo dough, in the creation of cheese pies, spinach pies and meat pies.
Prod-CULINA Dist-CULINA

Tisser De La Laine C 6 MIN
16MM FILM, 3/4 OR 1/2 IN VIDEO I-H
Describes techniques in building a simple loom out of an old broom and a few pieces of wood.
Prod-CRAF Dist-IFB Prodn-CRAF 1957

Tissot - A Passionate Odyssey C 28 MIN
16MM FILM OPTICAL SOUND R
Depicts Victorian artist, Jean-Jacques Tissot's art, combined with animation, to present the story of Easter.
Prod-UCCAND Dist-UCCAND

Tissue Culture Approach In Studying Normal And Diseased Muscles C 39 MIN
3/4 INCH VIDEO CASSETTE
Uses illustrative slides to present an approach to studying normal and diseased muscles.
LC NO. 76-706111
Prod-NINDIS Dist-USNAC 1974

Tissue Culture Of Normal And Abnormal Human Muscles C 45 MIN
3/4 INCH VIDEO CASSETTE PRO
Presents Dr Robert I Roelofs lecturing on tissue culture of normal and abnormal human muscles.
From The Intensive Course In Neuromuscular Diseases Series.
LC NO. 76-706112
Prod-NINDIS Dist-USNAC 1974

Tissues C 29 MIN
3/4 INCH VIDEO CASSETTE C A
Describes characteristics and functions of the four types of tissues found in multicellular animals. Gives examples of different types of tissues including those in the leaf of a plant and in a blood vessel.
From The Introducing Biology Series. Program 6
Prod-COAST Dist-CDTEL

Tissues Of The Human Body C 16 MIN
16MM FILM, 3/4 OR 1/2 IN VIDEO J-H
A detailed explanation of the various types of tissues found in the body. Tissues of skin, muscle, tendons, nerves and blood are discussed. Utilizes animation techniques as well as live photography.
Prod-CF Dist-CF 1963

Tit For Tat B 19 MIN
16MM FILM OPTICAL SOUND
Tells how Laurel and Hardy open an electrical shop and decide to make friends with the delicatessen owner next store, who wants to have nothing to do with them.
Prod-ROACH Dist-BHAWK 1935

Titan 5 C 30 MIN
16MM FILM OPTICAL SOUND H-C A R
A fictional account of an astronaut who, confused about the purpose of his life and the moon mission, questions his beliefs. Introduces a close friend who is an unbeliver and a missionary who is recently from the seminary cause the man to realize his responsibility and to renew his faith in God's will.
LC NO. 72-701667
Prod-CONCOR Dist-CPH 1966

Titanic B 14 MIN
16MM FILM SILENT
Uses a composite of motion picture sequences to depict the sinking of the Titanic in 1912.
LC NO. 74-713146
Prod-BHAWK Dist-BHAWK 1960

Titanic In A Tub - The Golden Age Of Toy Boats C 28 MIN
16MM FILM OPTICAL SOUND J-C A
Looks at the golden age of toy boats, featuring a bathtub re-creation of the sinking of the Titanic. Uses archival stills and footage to show their full-scale counterparts from the 1890's to the 1930's. Narrated by Rex Harrison.
LC NO. 82-700316
Prod-SEVSEA Dist-DIRECT 1982

Titicut Follies C 89 MIN
16MM FILM, 3/4 OR 1/2 IN VIDEO
Depicts life behind the walls of an institution for the criminal insane. Shows society's treatment of these citizens.
Prod-WISEF Dist-ZIPRAH

Title Drive C 20 MIN
16MM FILM OPTICAL SOUND
Describes the role of Evinrude Motors in boat racing. Shows Cesare Scotti's drive for the World Outboard Championship at Lake Havasu, Arizona. Discusses the two major European marathons, the six hours of Paris and the six hours of Berlin, as well as the Gold Coast Marathon in Miami and the Lake Elsinore Marathon in California.
LC NO. 70-706131
Prod-OMCEMD Dist-SS Prodn-PEAW 1970

Title IX - Fair Play In The Schools C 29 MIN
3/4 INCH VIDEO CASSETTE
Focuses on the ramifications of Title IX of the Education Amendments of 1972, which prohibits sex discrimination in school athletics and other programs receiving federal assistance.
From The Woman Series.
Prod-WNEDTV Dist-PUBTEL

Title Withdrawn C 50 MIN
3/4 OR 1/2 INCH VIDEO CASSETTE
Illustrates the song Night Sport from the performance process Automatic Writing. Deals with the architecture of self-description.
Prod-KITCHN Dist-KITCHN

Titles Available C 5 MIN
3/4 OR 1/2 INCH VIDEO CASSETTE C A
Shows a man reading 250 titles of pornography books with slang words and great expression.
Prod-NATSF Dist-MMRC

Tito - Power Of Resistance C 24 MIN
16MM FILM, 3/4 OR 1/2 IN VIDEO H-C A
Documents how Yugoslavian President Tito used resistance to achieve power and then used that power to change the course of history. Narrated by Henry Fonda.
From The Leaders Of The 20th Century - Portraits Of Power Series.
Prod-NIELSE Dist-LCOA 1980

Tito And The Balkan Tinderbox C 29 MIN
2 INCH VIDEOTAPE
See series title for descriptive statement.
From The Course Of Our Times I Series.
Prod-WGBHTV Dist-PUBTEL

Tito And The Strategy Of Non-Alignment C 29 MIN
2 INCH VIDEOTAPE
See series title for descriptive statement.
From The Course Of Our Times III Series.
Prod-WGBHTV Dist-PUBTEL

Tito Profile C 25 MIN
3/4 OR 1/2 INCH VIDEO CASSETTE H-C A
Chronicles the rise to power of Yugoslavian leader Tito. Tells how he left his nation a legacy of freedom and prosperity unknown to any other Marxist nation.
Prod-UPI Dist-JOU

Tito Visits Moscow (Russian) B 30 MIN
3/4 OR 1/2 INCH VIDEO CASSETTE
Presents the 1956 Moscow visit of Josip Broz Tito, Communist president of Yugoslavia, in three Soviet newsreels. Includes a synchronous-sound Russian-language speech by Tito. With English subtitles.
Prod-IHF Dist-IHF

Titration I C 10 MIN
3/4 OR 1/2 INCH VIDEO CASSETTE C A
Demonstrates how a sample of acid is titrated with base, using a buret, first performing a rough titration to approximately locate the endpoint, then accurately determining the endpoint.
From The Chemistry - Master/Apprentice Series. Program 3
LC NO. 82-706037
Prod-CUETV Dist-CUNIV 1981

Titration II C 13 MIN
3/4 OR 1/2 INCH VIDEO CASSETTE C A
Shows how a sample of acid is titrated with base using a buret. Explains many of the accepted procedures in volumetric titrations, demonstrating the fine points such as splitting drops by rapid rotation of the stopcock.
From The Chemistry - Master/Apprentice Series. Program 101
LC NO. 82-706048
Prod-CUETV Dist-CUNIV 1981

Titus Andronicus C 120 MIN
3/4 OR 1/2 INCH VIDEO CASSETTE H-C A
Presents William Shakespeare's tragedy Titus Andronicus which draws on mythology for the rape and mutilation of Lavinia and for the banquet at which Tamora is served the flesh of her sons.
From The Shakespeare Plays Series.
Prod-BBCTV Dist-TIMLIF 1984

Tivoli C 10 MIN
16MM FILM OPTICAL SOUND
Shows people of all ages enjoying the rides, music, games, playgrounds, food and fun at Tivoli Gardens in Copenhagen, Denmark.
LC NO. 74-711535
Prod-COMCO Dist-COMCO 1970

Tivoli Rhythms C 10 MIN
16MM FILM OPTICAL SOUND
Presents the Tivoli Gardens from morning until night.
Prod-RDCG Dist-AUDPLN

Tjurunga (2nd Ed) C 19 MIN
16MM FILM OPTICAL SOUND I-C A
Views the trees and wild flowers of Central Australia, tribal elders in a ceremony, fire making, cooking of emus and witchery grubs and aboriginal children at play.
LC NO. 73-702490
Prod-FLMAUS Dist-AUIS 1973

TMJ Prosthesis Implant - A Surgical Treatment For Temporomandibular Disease C 19 MIN
3/4 OR 1/2 INCH VIDEO CASSETTE PRO
Demonstrates how properly diagnosed patients with TMJ disease may have many of their symptoms relieved by surgical restoration of the temporomandibular joint by means of a metal implant.
Prod-WFP Dist-WFP

TMP Equipment C
3/4 OR 1/2 INCH VIDEO CASSETTE IND
Demonstrates thermo-mechanical process. Gives examples of equipment used. Includes types of steaming vessels, feeders, refiners and various equipment layouts.
From The Pulp And Paper Training - Thermo-Mechanical Pulping Series.
Prod-LEIKID Dist-LEIKID

TMX - A Tandem Mirror Nuclear Fusion Experiment C 18 MIN
16MM FILM OPTICAL SOUND
Uses animation to show one of the significant advances in plasma physics, the tandem mirror concept. Shows the assembly of a research facility and a typical experimental run in this nuclear fusion project conducted for the U S Department of Energy.
LC NO. 80-701562
Prod-LIVER Dist-LIVER 1980

TNRC Presents - Health And Self--A Series
J-H
Presents members of the Twelfth Night Repertory Company who use humor, satire, music, dance and drama to help focus attention on attitudes regarding alcohol, drugs, environmental pollution, smoking, friendship, exercise and prejudice.
Prod-KLCSTV Dist-AITECH 1984

American Heartbeat 015 MIN
Choices 015 MIN
Friend A Day, A 015 MIN
Great American Smoke Out, The 015 MIN
High And Dry 015 MIN
Name That Label 015 MIN
Out Of The Blue 015 MIN

TNT Teens 'n Theatre C 28 MIN
3/4 OR 1/2 INCH VIDEO CASSETTE J-C A
Traces the development of a group of San Francisco multi-ethnic teenagers from audition-line hopefuls to a full-fledged peer education, family life theater company. Highlights issues of sexual stereo-types, peer pressure and peer support.
Prod-UCSFLT Dist-MMRC

To A Babysitter (2nd Ed) C 17 MIN
16MM FILM, 3/4 OR 1/2 IN VIDEO J-C A
Follows a girl through an evening of baby sitting. Emphasizes what she must do to be a satisfactory 'substitute' parent. Shows employer's obligations.
Prod-HIGGIN Dist-HIGGIN 1974

To A Different Drum C 20 MIN
16MM FILM, 3/4 OR 1/2 IN VIDEO J-H
Presents Henry David Thoreau, the naturalist and author, and Deborah Sampson, who fought in the American Revolution as a 'male' soldier, as examples of persons who have found themselves at odds with a society that has insisted on conformity.
From The Matter Of Fact Series.
LC NO. 74-703209
Prod-NITC Dist-AITECH Prodn-WETATV 1973

To A Good, Long Life C 20 MIN
16MM FILM, 3/4 OR 1/2 IN VIDEO J-C A
Focuses on three elderly people who are leading vigorous, interesting lives. Reveals some of the difficulties that each has gone beyond in learning to live creatively rather than merely coping.
Prod-BFA Dist-PHENIX Prodn-JANOFF 1976

To A New Land C 30 MIN
3/4 INCH VIDEO CASSETTE I-J
Explains how some of the first Asian-Americans arrived in the United States.
From The Pacific Bridges Series.
Prod-EDFCEN Dist-GPITVL 1978

To Age Is Human--A Series
H A
Prod-WPSXTV Dist-PSU

Faces Of 'A' Wing, The 58 MIN
Final, Proud Days Of Elsie Wurster, The 58 MIN

To Alter Human Behavior - Without Mind Control C 20 MIN
16MM FILM, 3/4 OR 1/2 IN VIDEO
Investigates aspects of behavior modification.
Prod-DOCUA Dist-CNEMAG

To Be A Bedouin C 15 MIN
3/4 OR 1/2 INCH VIDEO CASSETTE I
Shows the Bedouin way of life.
From The Encounter In The Desert Series.
Prod-CTI Dist-CTI

To Be A Clown C 24 MIN
16MM FILM, 3/4 OR 1/2 IN VIDEO J-C A
Shows the steps one must take in order to be a clown. Presents an eight-week workshop at Ottawa's National Arts Center in Canada, where students dance in baggy pants, juggle, walk tightropes, practice gags and experiment with masks and makeup.
Prod-SALZP Dist-AIMS 1975

To Be A Doctor B 30 MIN
16MM FILM OPTICAL SOUND H-C
An overview of the life of a doctor--his training, his work and his interest in community affairs.
From The Doctors At Work Series.
LC NO. FIA65-1368
Prod-CMA Dist-LAWREN Prodn-LAWREN 1961

To Be A Doctor C 52 MIN
16MM FILM, 3/4 OR 1/2 IN VIDEO H-C A
Explores the world of medical students and interns, focusing on their difficulties and ethical dilemmas. Narrated by Tom Brokaw.
Prod-NBC Dist-FI 1980

To Be A Friend C 14 MIN
16MM FILM OPTICAL SOUND J-H
Describes friendships experienced by youth.
From The Circle Of Life Series.
LC NO. 73-700928
Prod-BBF Dist-BBF 1973

To Be A Man C 14 MIN
16MM FILM OPTICAL SOUND J-H
A verite soundtrack of live interviews forms the basis for a study of boyhood, personhood, masculinity, anti-stereotypes, sexuality and idealism. Includes impressionistic visuals.
From The Circle Of Life Series.
LC NO. 78-705695
Prod-BBF Dist-BBF 1970

To Be A Man C 58 MIN
16MM FILM OPTICAL SOUND
Studies the American male's historical and traditional role in society. Profiles men's changing status and values through interviews with several prominent men and women.
LC NO. 78-700225
Prod-BLACKW Dist-BLACKW 1977

To Be A Man C 44 MIN
16MM FILM, 3/4 OR 1/2 IN VIDEO
Questions the traditional masculine roles, showing men who have tried to shake off the old male stereotypes.
Prod-PERSPF Dist-CORF

To Be A Parent C 15 MIN
16MM FILM OPTICAL SOUND
Examines young people as they look at their parents, parents as they look at themselves and grandparents as they look back on both.
From The Circle Of Life Series.
LC NO. 73-701411
Prod-BBF Dist-BBF 1972

To Be A Person C 19 MIN
16MM FILM OPTICAL SOUND
Deals with the identity, self-awareness and personality of an individual.
From The Circle Of Life Series.
LC NO. 73-701412
Prod-BBF Dist-BBF 1972

To Be A Winner, Back Your Winners C 17 MIN
3/4 OR 1/2 INCH VIDEO CASSETTE
Attempts to convince managers that they must downplay functional tasks and concentrate on people in order to be really effective as managers. Illustrates that the three most important jobs they do are to communicate expectations, inspect results and provide feedback. Helps trainees get maximum return on their efforts by showing them where to put 80 percent of their time.
Prod-EFM Dist-EFM

To Be A Woman C 14 MIN
16MM FILM OPTICAL SOUND J-H
A verite soundtrack of live interviews forms the basis for a study of girlhood, personhood, femininity, anti-stereotypes, sexuality and idealism. Includes impressionistic visuals.
From The Circle Of Life Series.
LC NO. 74-705694
Prod-BBF Dist-BBF 1970

To Be A Woman-Soldier C 50 MIN
16MM FILM OPTICAL SOUND J-C A
Analyzes the types of tasks performed by women in the Israeli armed forces and how they are striving to perform jobs other than clerical, answering phones and delivering mail.
Prod-NJWB Dist-NJWB 1981

To Be Afraid C 14 MIN
16MM FILM OPTICAL SOUND
Suggests that repressed and unspoken fears exert a powerful inhibiting force on the development of human potential. Traces several kinds of fear and seeks the root causes.
From The Circle Of Life Series.
Prod-BBF Dist-BBF

To Be Afraid C 15 MIN
16MM FILM OPTICAL SOUND J-H
Focuses on different categories of fear, including fear of physical things, fear of failure, fear of rejection and fear of the future.
From The Inner Circle Series.
LC NO. 79-701070
Prod-BBF Dist-BBF 1975

To Be Alone C 15 MIN
16MM FILM OPTICAL SOUND
Explores the human aspects of loneliness. Shows how loneliness can be a source for refreshment and creativity and also a source of pain if caused by inner conflict or by an alienating society.
From The Inner Circle Series.
LC NO. 75-702666
Prod-BBF Dist-BBF 1975

To Be An Ingenor C 29 MIN
3/4 INCH VIDEO CASSETTE
Gives a perspective on engineering. Includes the ideas of ingenuity at work and technological substitution as characteristics of today.
From The Future Without Shock Series.
Prod-UMITV Dist-UMITV 1976

To Be Aware Of Death C 15 MIN
16MM FILM OPTICAL SOUND
Presents young people taking a look at death and gives observations and personal insights from their experiences with death in their families, school and neighborhood.
LC NO. 74-703269
Prod-BBF Dist-BBF 1974

To Be Continued C 14 MIN
16MM FILM OPTICAL SOUND
Deals with disappointment, loss, setback, hurt, failure and personal catastrophes. Explains that life must somehow go on in spite of these blows. Suggests that the purpose of life is to get on with it, that life is meant to be continued.
From The Circle Of Life Series.
Prod-BBF Dist-BBF

To Be Growing Older C 14 MIN
16MM FILM OPTICAL SOUND
Points out that miracle drugs have prolonged our life span and added to our life problems. Explains that children must face the challenge of aging parents and seek for a truly human response.
From The Circle Of Life Series.
LC NO. 73-701413
Prod-BBF Dist-BBF 1972

To Be In Love C 14 MIN
16MM FILM OPTICAL SOUND J-H A
Points out what Aristotle, Ovid, Jesus, Mohammed, Chaucer, Shakespeare and Disraeli thought about love to trigger response to and discussion of love.
From The Circle Of Life Series.
Prod-BBF Dist-BBF 1971

To Be Married C 14 MIN
16MM FILM OPTICAL SOUND H-C A
Opens up for discussion such areas of marriage as communication, signs of affection, wedding day, types of wedding ceremonies, divorce, building together, living together and friends in marriage.
From The Circle Of Life Series.
LC NO. 73-700532
Prod-BBF Dist-BBF 1971

To Be Somebody C 29 MIN
16MM FILM OPTICAL SOUND H-C
Records the progress of a young Mexican-American woman going out into the unfamiliar world of the Anglo in search of employment. Shows how, after several unsuccessful attempts to find work, she receives help from a counselor in a local training program for youth.
Prod-ATLAP Dist-ATLAP 1974

To Be Somebody C 35 MIN
3/4 INCH VIDEO CASSETTE H-C A

Depicts the progress of a young Mexican woman as she faces the prospects of searching for a job in the unfamiliar world of the Anglo.
Prod-ATLAP Dist-ATLAP 1971

To Be The Best C 25 MIN
3/4 INCH VIDEO CASSETTE
A condensed version of the film The Best Downhill Racer. Dramatizes the story of downhill ski racing star Steve Podborski who became the first non-European male to capture downhill racing's highest honor.
Prod-LAURON Dist-LAURON

To Be The Best (French) C 25 MIN
3/4 INCH VIDEO CASSETTE
A condensed version of the film The Best Downhill Racer. Dramatizes the story of downhill ski racing star Steve Podborski who became the first non-European male to capture downhill racing's highest honor.
Prod-LAURON Dist-LAURON

To Be The Best (German) C 25 MIN
3/4 INCH VIDEO CASSETTE
A condensed version of the film The Best Downhill Racer. Dramatizes the story of downhill ski racing star Steve Podborski who became the first non-European male to capture downhill racing's highest honor.
Prod-LAURON Dist-LAURON

To Be True To Yourself C 15 MIN
16MM FILM OPTICAL SOUND J-H
Looks at a person's identity as part of the maturing process. Points out that a sense of identity and worth comes, in part, from being true to oneself.
From The Inner Circle Series.
LC NO. 79-701071
Prod-BBF Dist-BBF 1976

To Be Young, Gifted And Black C 90 MIN
16MM FILM, 3/4 OR 1/2 IN VIDEO H-C A
Presents a play depicting the life and works of the late black playwright, Lorraine Hasberry. Portrays her struggles, from her first visit to the South, to the streets of Harlem. Stars Ruby Dee, Al Freeman, Claudia Mc Neil, Barbara Barrie and Lauren Jones.
Prod-NET Dist-IU 1972

To Be 30 C 13 MIN
16MM FILM, 3/4 OR 1/2 IN VIDEO I-H
Produced in commemoration of the U N's 30th anniversary, the film presents a capsulization of the organization's history as interpreted by a fictional U N employee who is also celebrating his 30th birthday. Discusses some major international problems and assesses the U N's strengths and weaknesses in dealing with these problems. Features music of the British rock group Pink Floyd.
Prod-UN Dist-SF 1976

To Bear Witness C 41 MIN
16MM FILM, 3/4 OR 1/2 IN VIDEO H-C A
Documents the liberation of Nazi concentration camps. Includes first person accounts, historical footage and still photographs, and speeches from the first International Liberators Conference.
Prod-USHMC Dist-BFA 1984

To Bear Witness C 42 MIN
3/4 OR 1/2 INCH VIDEO CASSETTE
Uses the framework of the National Liberators Conference to recount the liberation of the Nazi Death Camps. Includes interviews with survivors and with liberators from some of the 14 armies, on rare historic footage.
Prod-USNAC Dist-USNAC 1983

To Bottle The Sun C 5 MIN
16MM FILM OPTICAL SOUND I-H
Explores the possibility of fusion power reactors as an alternative way of satisfying our future expanding energy needs with coal, gas and oil in limited supply.
LC NO. 73-701364
Prod-NSF Dist-AMEDFL 1973

To Breathe Or Not To Breathe - A Test On Lungs And Smoking C 23 MIN
3/4 OR 1/2 INCH VIDEO CASSETTE H-C A
Offers a quiz which tests knowledge of the lungs, breathing, and smoking.
Prod-WNBCTV Dist-CAROUF

To Breathe, To Breathe, To Live C 15 MIN
16MM FILM OPTICAL SOUND C A
Demonstrates the diagnostic differences between high and low respiratory obstructive syndromes in young children with acute infectious disease.
LC NO. 75-701742
Prod-CARNA Dist-BANDER Prodn-FLAGG 1968

To Breathe, To Brethe, To live C 13 MIN
3/4 OR 1/2 INCH VIDEO CASSETTE PRO
Details the diagnosis of high and low respiratory obstructive diseases in children.
Prod-BANDER Dist-BANDER

To Bridge The Gap B 31 MIN
16MM FILM OPTICAL SOUND
Portrays a study tour of Scandinavian and English facilities for the mentally retarded.
Prod-COUKLA Dist-WCCOTV 1967

To Brooklyn With Love C 23 MIN
16MM FILM OPTICAL SOUND
Presents a tour of the cultural institutions in Brooklyn, New York.
LC NO. 78-700226
Prod-BAILYB Dist-BEMPS 1977

To Brooklyn With Love C 25 MIN
3/4 OR 1/2 INCH VIDEO CASSETTE
Presents a visual tour of the cultural institutions in Brooklyn, including the Brooklyn Academy of Music, the oldest performing arts center in America, and the Brooklyn Public Library, over three million volumes strong and still growing.
Prod-IVCH Dist-IVCH

To Build Gigantic Ships C 29 MIN
16MM FILM OPTICAL SOUND
Introduces an outline of the research activities, manufacturing facilities and engineering techniques for building the largest ship of the time 'VERGEFUS' at a Nagasaki shipyard.
Prod-UNIJAP Dist-UNIJAP 1968

To Build Our Future C 58 MIN
3/4 OR 1/2 INCH VIDEO CASSETTE
Takes a look at the meaning of the word eugenics showing how current genetic research represents continuum.
From The Through The Genetic Maze Series.
Prod-PSU Dist-PBS 1982

To Buy Or Not To Buy C 20 MIN
3/4 OR 1/2 INCH VIDEO CASSETTE I-J
Uses common situations to explain the concept of market demand. Shows how factors such as price affect demand and how advertising increases the buying market.
From The Trade-Offs Series.
LC NO. 80-707342
Prod-AITV Dist-AITECH Prodn-EDFCEN 1978

To Buy Or Not To Buy C 20 MIN
3/4 INCH VIDEO CASSETTE J-H
Shows shopping situations in order to examine the different facets of comparative shopping and to illustrate the importance of informed decision making before buying.
From The Dollar Data Series.
LC NO. 81-707351
Prod-WHROTV Dist-GPITVL 1974

To Buy Or Not To Buy - Buyers And Market Demand C 20 MIN
16MM FILM OPTICAL SOUND I-J
Shows how factors such as price affect demand and how advertising increases the buying market.
From The Trade-Offs Series. No. 10
LC NO. 79-701475
Prod-EDFCEN Dist-AITECH 1978

To Call Ducks C 15 MIN
16MM FILM OPTICAL SOUND
Don Ansley, Tennessee Duck-Calling Champion, demonstrates the proper techniques in blowing a duck call and illustrates when to use a particular call, depending on the action of the ducks being called.
Prod-TGAFC Dist-TGAFC

To Capture The Power Of Sun And Tide C 24 MIN
16MM FILM, 3/4 OR 1/2 IN VIDEO
Focuses on the sun and the moon as our oldest inexhaustible and non-polluting sources of energy. Illustrates applications of solar energy and experiments to harness tidal power, a by-product of the moon's gravitational pull.
Prod-DOCUA Dist-CNEMAG 1973

To Care - America's Voluntary Spirit C
16MM FILM, 3/4 OR 1/2 IN VIDEO
Offers a tribute to the people and organizations who perform the volunteer and charity work needed in America.
Prod-FI Dist-FI

To Care For Them C 28 MIN
16MM FILM - 3/4 IN VIDEO
Discusses aspects of nursing.
LC NO. 78-706146
Prod-USVA Dist-USNAC Prodn-USVA 1978

To Catch A Dream C 27 MIN
16MM FILM OPTICAL SOUND C A
Visits the castles and historical monuments of Spain and views the resorts of Mallorca and the countrysides of the Canary Islands.
Prod-MCDO Dist-MCDO 1963

To Catch A Meal - Feeding In The Sea C 13 MIN
16MM FILM OPTICAL SOUND
Discusses the variety of marine feeding techniques in the planktonic, nektonic and benthic regions.
LC NO. 71-705696
Prod-REELA Dist-MIAMIS 1969

To Catch A Porpoise C 29 MIN
16MM FILM OPTICAL SOUND
Follows a collecting crew from the Miami seaquarium as they go on a trip to catch porpoises. Includes underwater scenes which depict the man-against-thesea aspect of capturing three of these animals. Shows the return of the porpoises at the seaquarium where they are trained to take part in the show at the new York world's fair.
LC NO. FIA65-497
Prod-MIAMIS Dist-MIAMIS Prodn-REELA 1964

To Change The Picture C 12 MIN
16MM FILM OPTICAL SOUND
Presents youths from kindergarten through university and discusses the areas of increased support that the United Jewish Appeal must give to the youth of Israel in light of the Yom Kippur War.
Prod-UJA Dist-ALDEN

To Choose A Camera C 29 MIN
3/4 OR 1/2 INCH VIDEO CASSETTE
Introduces a variety of cameras, how they came to exist and how they are used.
From The Photo Show Series.
Prod-WGBHTV Dist-PBS 1981

To Choose The Sea C 14 MIN
16MM FILM OPTICAL SOUND
Presents high school senior John Rodgers as he faces the decision of which college and career to choose. Tells how he decides on the Coast Guard Academy and is shown in classrooms, labs, off-duty activities and summer cruises aboard the sailing ship Eagle. Shows John in several assignments--shipboard duty, aviation and postgraduate work.
LC NO. 75-700880
Prod-USCG Dist-USNAC 1965

To Climb A Mountain C 15 MIN
16MM FILM, 3/4 OR 1/2 IN VIDEO I-C A
Shows how blindness is a handicap that can be overcome. Presents a story about a young man and woman and a group of their friends who successfully climb a mountain. Explores their feelings about their accomplishment as blind people and examines the attitudes of society about blindness.
Prod-BFA Dist-PHENIX 1975

To Climb A Mountain C 25 MIN
16MM FILM, 3/4 OR 1/2 IN VIDEO J-C A
Relates the trouble that Steve has when he sells his car to help a black family. Shows the importance of unselfish love. Stars Emilio Estevez
From The Reflections Series.
Prod-PAULST Dist-MEDIAG

To Communicate Is The Beginning C 30 MIN
16MM FILM OPTICAL SOUND
Illustrates the dramatic growth of communications in the United States and shows key people involved in its history and process. Emphasizes the role of the Bell System in this history.
LC NO. 76-701408
Prod-SANDIA Dist-SANDIA Prodn-KRASAG 1976

To Cook A Duck C 10 MIN
16MM FILM - 3/4 IN VIDEO J-C A
Follows the game bird from the time it is harvested until it is ready to eat. Discusses the field dressing and processing of waterfowl.
LC NO. 80-707561
Prod-WESTWN Dist-WESTWN 1977

To Defeat The Doomsday Doctrine - The World Isn't Running Out Of Everything Quite... C 20 MIN
16MM FILM, 3/4 OR 1/2 IN VIDEO
Explains that too much pessimism about the environment can be as damaging as too much optimism, since doomsday attitudes can breed inaction and turn justifiable fear into a self-fulfilling prophecy.
Prod-DOCUA Dist-CNEMAG

To Die Today B 50 MIN
16MM FILM, 3/4 OR 1/2 IN VIDEO H-C A
Focuses on Dr Elizabeth Kubler Ross, whose work has called attention to the 'CRISIS OF DYING.' Presents her theory of the five emotional stages through which patients pass and interviews a young patient with Hodgkins disease who seems to have reached an acceptance of his condition.
Prod-CANBC Dist-FLMLIB 1972

To Die With Dignity - To Live With Grief C 29 MIN
3/4 INCH VIDEO CASSETTE
Focuses on coping with death and living with grief after the loss of a loved one. Interviews a terminally ill leukemia patient, a physician who works with the terminally ill and others including relatives, counselors and patients.
Prod-UMITV Dist-UMITV 1978

To Die, To Live - The Survivors Of Hiroshima C 63 MIN
16MM FILM, 3/4 OR 1/2 IN VIDEO H-C A
Presents the thoughts and feelings of survivors of the atomic bomb blast at Hiroshima, including their guilt at being alive when others are dead and their worries about the still-remaining dangers of radiation.
Prod-BBCTV Dist-FI 1982

To Discover A New Psychic Force C 20 MIN
16MM FILM, 3/4 OR 1/2 IN VIDEO
Looks at psychokinesis, the mind's power to alter the outside world directly, without muscular contact. Discusses experiments in prophecy and in psychic healing.
Prod-DOCUA Dist-CNEMAG

To Discover Our Body's Time Clock - Anticipate The Rhythm Of Your Ecstasy And... C 20 MIN
16MM FILM, 3/4 OR 1/2 IN VIDEO
Looks at the rise and fall of human energy patterns, or biorhythms, and shows how knowledge of these patterns can enrich life.
Prod-DOCUA Dist-CNEMAG

To Do Battle In The Land C 27 MIN
16MM FILM, 3/4 OR 1/2 IN VIDEO J A
Portrays conditions in the North and South that led to abolitionist John Brown's raid on the Federal Arsenal at Harper's Ferry, Virginia, in 1859. Uses archival photographs. Portrays Brown's involvement during the 1855 Kansas slavery skirmishes.
Prod-USNPS Dist-USNAC 1985

To Eliminate All Unreasonable Risk C 15 MIN
16MM FILM OPTICAL SOUND
Uses a narrative centered around a Bogart type character in order to explain the identity and purpose of the Consumer Product Safety Commission.
LC NO. 75-700091
Prod-CPSAFC Dist-CPSAFC Prodn-CAS 1974

To Escape, To Return - The Church, Refugees And Development C 21 MIN
16MM FILM OPTICAL SOUND R
Documents the church's role in helping refugees in Tanzania and Bangladesh gain self-sufficiency and self-respect. Records natives' progress in agriculture, education, home construction, medical care and hygiene and vocational training.
Prod-UCCAND Dist-UCCAND

To Expect To Die - A Film About Living C 59 MIN
3/4 OR 1/2 INCH VIDEO CASSETTE
Presents an account of a dying man's last months of life as he faced death from cancer.
Prod-KQEDTV Dist-PBS 1977

To Fall Or Not To Fall C 9 MIN
16MM FILM OPTICAL SOUND A
Shows man, from the caveman to the modern industrial worker, falling down on things, from things and over things. Points out that injuries and deaths from falls can be avoided by wearing proper footwear, avoiding unsafe actions and conditions, practicing good housekeeping and using common sense.
LC NO. FIA67-660
Prod-AETNA Dist-AETNA 1966

To Fill A Need C 27 MIN
16MM FILM, 3/4 OR 1/2 IN VIDEO
Dramatizes how computers serving as job banks provide faster, better service for both jobless applicants and employers. Issued in 1971 as a motion picture.
From The Career Job Opportunity Series.
LC NO. 79-706032
Prod-USDLMA Dist-USNAC 1978

To Find A Friend C 15 MIN
16MM FILM OPTICAL SOUND
Shows what can be accomplished when people of different generations draw together in friendship.
From The Growing Up - Growing Older Series
Prod-SEARSF Dist-MTP 1982

To Find A Market C 19 MIN
16MM FILM OPTICAL SOUND
Documents the grain marketing exchange in which farmers, operators of terminal elevators, the Minneapolis Grain Exchange, and the American public take part.
LC NO. 79-700294
Prod-MGE Dist-BOYD Prodn-VIBFI 1979

To Find A Way B 34 MIN
16MM FILM OPTICAL SOUND C A
Follows a teacher education program given by Lowell State College in Massachusetts, based on the workshop process in order to initiate and involve future teachers in open education.
LC NO. 75-701395
Prod-EDC Dist-EDC 1971

To Find Answers C 29 MIN
16MM FILM, 3/4 OR 1/2 IN VIDEO
Presents Mary Switzer, administrator of the Social and Rehabilitation Service, and Dr Howard Rusk, director of the Institute of Rehabilitation Medicine at New York University Medical Center, discussing research for the handicapped.
From The To Live Again Series.
LC NO. 80-706860
Prod-USSRS Dist-USNAC 1980

To Find Our Life - The Peyote Hunt Of Huichol's Mexico C 65 MIN
16MM FILM OPTICAL SOUND C T
Follows a group of Indians on their ritual journey to obtain peyote in the high desert country. Shows ritual eating of peyote and subsequent trance.
Prod-UCLA Dist-UCLA 1969

To Find The Baruya Story C 64 MIN
16MM FILM, 3/4 OR 1/2 IN VIDEO
Documents the Baruya of New Guinea.
Prod-DOCEDR Dist-DOCEDR

To Fly C 27 MIN
16MM FILM OPTICAL SOUND
Shows how Americans moved westward across the continental United States and developed transportation as they went. Explains how this trend culminated in the achievement of flight and the venture into space.
LC NO. 76-702901
Prod-CONOCO Dist-CONOCO Prodn-THOMP 1976

To Forget Venice (Italian) C 108 MIN
16MM FILM OPTICAL SOUND
Explores the lives of five people who gather at a country house. Addresses aging, homosexuality, love and death. Includes English subtitles.
Prod-TLECUL Dist-TLECUL

To Forgive A Thief B 30 MIN
16MM FILM OPTICAL SOUND J-C A
Portrays a small group of Christians who set out to share their faith with four delinquent boys. Includes adventures leading from the jail cell of a delinquent youth to a surfing party, a daring motorcycle ride across the hills, a mysterious chain of roberies, an enraged neighborhood and ends in a quiet cemetary. Examines the meaning of forgiveness.
Prod-CAFM Dist-CAFM

To Form A More Perfect Union C 31 MIN
16MM FILM, 3/4 OR 1/2 IN VIDEO
Recreates the way in which the United States Constitution was ratified, showing how Samuel Adams and Governor John Hancock proposed amendments which were accepted by the Federalists.
From The Decades Of Decision - The American Revolution Series.
LC NO. 80-706352
Prod-NGS Dist-NGS 1975

To Free Their Minds C 34 MIN
16MM FILM, 3/4 OR 1/2 IN VIDEO T
Discusses the methods by which a teacher trained to teach a homogeneous racial group of children adjusts to the demands of an integrated classroom.
Prod-GREAVW Dist-GREAVW 1974

To Get From Here To There—A Series

H

Prod-PROART Dist-PROART

City Driving	34 MIN
Driver, The	31 MIN
Driving Like A Pro	31 MIN
Expect The Unexpected	32 MIN
Expressway Driving	30 MIN
Handling Emergencies	23 MIN
It Takes More Than Cars	23 MIN
It's A Moving World	23 MIN
Jungle On Wheels	22 MIN
Look At The Equipment, A	26 MIN
Rural Driving	35 MIN
Signs Of Life	27 MIN
Special Conditions	25 MIN
Where Do We Go From Here	33 MIN
World Outside, The	34 MIN

To Go On The Floor B 13 MIN
16MM FILM OPTICAL SOUND
Examines the confusion and frustration of the first months in the life of a student nurse, when she is forced to work with graphics and mock-ups, and never sees a real patient. Ends with the frightening and challenging day when she gets her cap and 'GOES ON THE FLOOR.'
Prod-UPENN Dist-UPENN 1966

To Have A Friend, Be A Friend C 9 MIN
16MM FILM, 3/4 OR 1/2 IN VIDEO K-P
Uses a story about animals on a make-believe island to illustrate a principle of friendship.
Prod-SAIF Dist-BARR 1977

To Have And Not To Hold - Helping Parents Of Premies Cope C 21 MIN
3/4 OR 1/2 INCH VIDEO CASSETTE
Contains a series of interviews with parents of premature babies. Gives valuable information to parents to help them understand and accept the experience of the Neonatal Intensive Care Unit.
Prod-POLYMR Dist-POLYMR

To Hear Your Banjo Play B 16 MIN
16MM FILM, 3/4 OR 1/2 IN VIDEO I-C
Presents the origin of the banjo, the development of southern folk music and its influence upon Americans. Pete Seeger plays his banjo and narrates the story.
Prod-LERNER Dist-FI Prodn-VAND 1947

To Help A Child C 22 MIN
16MM FILM OPTICAL SOUND
Reports on a comprehensive preventive dentistry demonstration program involving over 20,000 school children in ten cities in the United States.
LC NO. 79-701451
Prod-RWJF Dist-KAROL Prodn-GITTFI 1979

To Help Man Find His Way C 30 MIN
16MM FILM OPTICAL SOUND
Portrays the functions and services of the U S Environmental Science Services Administration's coast and geodetic survey pertaining to geodesy, geomagnetism, seismology, cartography, photogrammetry, hydrography and oceanography.
Prod-USNOAA Dist-USNOAA 1964

To Help Them Learn C 21 MIN
16MM FILM, 3/4 OR 1/2 IN VIDEO T
Examines the role of audiovisual media in modern education. Shows the use of media for captivating children's attention, offering a variety of approaches to learning and stimulating students through meaningful experiences.
Prod-AECT Dist-CF 1977

To Help Themselves C 28 MIN
16MM FILM OPTICAL SOUND J-C A
Shows that rapid and radical social change must keep pace with basic human needs. Shows the Camp Evans Project, aided by C R O P food-for-work. Explains that Camp Evans is a novel experiment, begun by Manila lawyer Alphonso Felix, to resettle one and one-half million slum dwellers in a self-contained rural setting.
LC NO. 73-703388
Prod-CROP Dist-CROP 1972

To Humanize Our Police - No More TV-Image Cops C 20 MIN
16MM FILM, 3/4 OR 1/2 IN VIDEO
Investigates the reality behind the paramilitary, pursuit-car image of the police portrayed by television and feature films. Suggests how the police role can be revamped in order to humanize the police and turn the cop on the beat into an accomplished public servant.
Prod-DOCUA Dist-CNEMAG

To Humanize The Assembly Line - Freeing Us From Dull, Boring Work C 20 MIN
16MM FILM, 3/4 OR 1/2 IN VIDEO
Visits the Volvo plant in Sweden to investigate an attempt to make work more meaningful and satisfying.
Prod-DOCUA Dist-CNEMAG

To Imitate The Sun C 33 MIN
16MM FILM OPTICAL SOUND H-C A
Covers controlled thermonuclear research over two decades. Includes the philosophy of two-X-two, Scylla IV, scyllac, astron, stellerators and tokamaks.
LC NO. 76-714165
Prod-USAEC Dist-USERD 1971

To Kayak C 33 MIN
16MM FILM, 3/4 OR 1/2 IN VIDEO
Covers Kayaking's many aspects, including equipment, safety practices, how to get started, cruising, racing, and various strokes and maneuvers.
Prod-DICEP Dist-BODFIL 1975

To Keep A Heritage Alive C 30 MIN
3/4 OR 1/2 INCH VIDEO CASSETTE
Shows how the Oneida Indians work to preserve their heritage by educating their children.
From The Forest Spirits Series.
Prod-NEWIST Dist-GPITVL

To Keep It, You Have To Give It Away C 60 MIN
16MM FILM - 3/4 IN VIDEO P A
Explores a wide variety of approaches to drug abuse rehabilitation, including detoxification units, methadone maintenance, the live-in therapeutic community, the out-patient facility and the religious-based community. Provides insight into the feelings, problems and aspirations of the addict and reveals common philosophies about rehabilitation through interviews with staff members of various facilities, addicts and ex-addicts.
From The Turned On Crisis Series.
Prod-WQED Dist-GPITVL

To Keep Our Liberty C 23 MIN
16MM FILM, 3/4 OR 1/2 IN VIDEO
Describes critical issues and events connected with the decision of the Colonies to declare independence from Great Britain. Covers the period from 1763 to 1775. Issued in 1974 as a motion picture.
LC NO. 78-706132
Prod-USNPS Dist-USNAC Prodn-KAMCO 1978

To Kill A Mockingbird B 110 MIN
16MM FILM OPTICAL SOUND I-H
Concerns a trial lawyer in a southern town who defends a falsely accused black man. Stars Gregory Peck.
Prod-UPCI Dist-SWANK

To Kill The Future C 16 MIN
16MM FILM, 3/4 OR 1/2 IN VIDEO J-C A
Describes the fight for tougher drunk driving laws and penalties. Encourages closer parent-teenager communication.
Prod-NBCNEW Dist-MTI

To Know The Sound Of The World C 21 MIN
16MM FILM OPTICAL SOUND
Focuses on patients at the Boys Town Institute for Communication Disorders in Children. Shows examples of communication disorders and tells how the institute's team approach provides services to handicapped children and their parents.
LC NO. 79-700326
Prod-FFBH Dist-CPF Prodn-CPF 1978

To Labrador For Brook Trout C 13 MIN
16MM FILM OPTICAL SOUND
Shows experienced fisherman Lee Wulff and his wife as they compete for trout in the streams of Labrador.
LC NO. FIA68-1574
Prod-CTFL Dist-CTFL 1967

To Last A Lifetime C 16 MIN
3/4 OR 1/2 INCH VIDEO CASSETTE IND
Examines methods to prevent industrial accidents. Focuses on back injuries. Investigates the relationship of the worker's mental attitude and protection for the back.
Prod-FLMEDS Dist-FLMEDS

To Lead C 5 MIN
16MM FILM, 3/4 OR 1/2 IN VIDEO I-H
Uses animation to present the story of a group of birds that sing harmoniously until interrupted by a crow. Tells how the birds try to eliminate the crow but find a more workable solution in making the crow their conductor.
Prod-FILBUL Dist-PHENIX 1982

To Live Again C 25 MIN
16MM FILM - 3/4 IN VIDEO J-C A
Explores a new concept in treatment of alcoholism through a conventional hospital program combined with a special Outward Bound Program. Explores how a holistic approach strengthens personal development, interpersonal effectiveness, environmental awareness and redefines personal values.
Prod-DURNCD Dist-CRYSP

To Live Again—A Series

Presents case studies of people who have been rehabilitated in one way or another.
Prod-USSRS Dist-USNAC 1980

After The Accident	029 MIN
Alcohol	029 MIN
Black Curtain, The	028 MIN
Drugs	029 MIN
Glass Wall, The	029 MIN
Great Expectations	029 MIN
Last Chance, The	029 MIN
New Start, A	029 MIN
To Find Answers	029 MIN
When There's A Will	029 MIN

To Live And Breathe C 12 MIN
16MM FILM OPTICAL SOUND
Identifies the leading causes of air pollution and tells how they

affect the environment. Focuses on the thoughts and actions of people concerned about air pollution and explains what can be done by individuals or as members of the community to combat the problem.
LC NO. 72-702436
Prod-AETNA Dist-AETNA 1971

To Live And Move According To Your Nature Is Called Love B 29 MIN
16MM FILM OPTICAL SOUND H-C A
Shows attempts to organize residents to cope with community problems. Explains that on the belief that social problems contribute to mental illness, these problems must be identified and solutions seen before real in-roads to mental health can begin.
From The To Save Tomorrow Series.
Prod-NET Dist-IU

To Live In Darkness B 13 MIN
16MM FILM OPTICAL SOUND
Portrays three men who lost their eyesight because of carelessness.
LC NO. FIE54-228
Prod-MOGULS Dist-USNAC 1947

To Live In Freedom C 54 MIN
16MM FILM OPTICAL SOUND
Presents a critique of the Israeli reality, analyzes the Israeli and Palestinian class structure, and contains material filmed on the West Bank.
Prod-ICARUS Dist-ICARUS 1975

To Live On C 26 MIN
16MM FILM OPTICAL SOUND H-C A
Shows how a group of physically handicapped people worked and fought their way back to lead productive, independent lives.
Prod-HESS Dist-FLMLIB

To Live On Earth C 15 MIN
16MM FILM OPTICAL SOUND
Explains the implementation of a natural resources curriculum designed to instill a sense of environmental awareness in elementary school students.
Prod-NILLU Dist-NILLU 1970

To Live On The Land C 24 MIN
16MM FILM OPTICAL SOUND I-C
Discusses adaptation to the stresses of life on land, including the development of lungs, kidneys, temperature control and internal fertilization. Shows how such animals as lung fish, hermit crabs, mud skippers and salt water frogs have adapted to two different environments.
From The Animal Secrets 1967 Series.
LC NO. FIA68-1032
Prod-NBC Dist-GRACUR 1967

To Live Together B 34 MIN
16MM FILM OPTICAL SOUND H-C A
Shows the difficulties encountered and the experiences shared by children at an interracial summer camp. Concludes that to learn democracy, children must have a chance to live it.
Prod-ADL Dist-ADL

To Live Until You Die C 57 MIN
16MM FILM, 3/4 OR 1/2 IN VIDEO H-C A
Presents an intimate portrait of Dr Elizabeth Kubler-Ross and her work with the dying.
From The Nova Series.
Prod-WGBHTV Dist-TIMLIF 1982

To Live With Dignity C 29 MIN
16MM FILM OPTICAL SOUND
Examines a three-month action research project at Ypsilanti State Hospital in which 20 very disoriented people received group therapy.
LC NO. 73-701120
Prod-UMITV Dist-UMICH 1972

To Live With Herds B 70 MIN
16MM FILM, 3/4 OR 1/2 IN VIDEO
Demonstrates the effects of nation-building in pre-Amin Uganda on the semi-nomadic, pastoral Jie. Looks at life in a traditional Jie homestead during a harsh dry season.
Prod-MCDGAL Dist-UCEMC 1974

To Love C 25 MIN
16MM FILM, 3/4 OR 1/2 IN VIDEO J-C A
Tells how love between two people survives even in a mechanized, work-oriented world.
Prod-WOMBAT Dist-WOMBAT

To Make A Buche (French) C 29 MIN
2 INCH VIDEOTAPE
Features Julia Child of Haute Cuisine au Vin demonstrating how to prepare a buche. With captions.
From The French Chef (French) Series.
Prod-WGBHTV Dist-PUBTEL

To Make A Dance C 15 MIN
16MM FILM, 3/4 OR 1/2 IN VIDEO
Shows a professional dancer performing a dance that she has created. Demonstrates her experiments with different ways to clap, turn and skip.
From The Ripples Series.
LC NO. 73-702157
Prod-NITC Dist-AITECH

To Make Man Immune From Disease C 20 MIN
16MM FILM, 3/4 OR 1/2 IN VIDEO
Explores research into the human immune system.
Prod-DOCUA Dist-CNEMAG

To Make Man Into Superman C 20 MIN
16MM FILM, 3/4 OR 1/2 IN VIDEO
Interviews Professor Robert Ettinger, an exponent of the cryonic movement which will freeze people into a state of suspended animation in which they could remain until they could be cured of their diseases.
Prod-DOCUA Dist-CNEMAG

To Make The Balance B 33 MIN
16MM FILM, 3/4 OR 1/2 IN VIDEO H-C A
Observes procedures used in a bi-lingual Spanish-Zapotec town in Mexico for the settlement of disputes in the town court. Features five cases portraying settlement of family, neighborhood and inter-village disputes.
Prod-NALA Dist-UCEMC Prodn-UCB 1970

To Make The Most Of Today C 14 MIN
16MM FILM OPTICAL SOUND
Explains the physical, economic, social and emotional problems of multiple sclerosis patients and their families. Concentrates on those services which are provided by an MS chapter, including transportation assistance, special equipment in the home, job counseling and placement and coordination of social services such as the Visiting Nurse Service.
Prod-VISION Dist-NMSS 1974

To Market, To Market C 30 MIN
3/4 OR 1/2 INCH VIDEO CASSETTE H-C A
Shows the importance of the resume and job interview through the portrayal of a 40-year-old unemployed man who is trying to organize his job search in some logical way. Uses a dream sequence to show how he learns to develop a proper resume and sharpen his interviewing skills.
From The Come Alive Series. No. 5
LC NO. 82-706072
Prod-UAKRON Dist-GPITVL 1981

To Measure The Earth C 30 MIN
3/4 INCH VIDEO CASSETTE
Explains the geometry of Eratosthenes and the difficulty of transferring a globe to flat paper. Discusses the history and methodology of surveying. Demonstrates surveying equipment.
From The Maps - Horizons To Knowledge Series.
Prod-UMITV Dist-UMITV 1980

To Meet The Challenge C 19 MIN
16MM FILM OPTICAL SOUND
Points out many new and unique manufacturing techniques applied in the foundry industry.
Prod-GM Dist-GM

To Open A Closed Door C 15 MIN
16MM FILM OPTICAL SOUND
Highlights two aspects of a social worker's involvement in a child abuse case, the initial interview with suspected abusive family members and testifying as an expert witness in court.
From The Child Abuse And Neglect Series.
LC NO. 78-701589
Prod-UKANS Dist-UKANS Prodn-UKANS 1977

To Orbit And Back C 14 MIN
16MM FILM OPTICAL SOUND I-C A
Describes a space shuttle mission of the mid-1970's. Depicts a shuttle booster and orbiter being launched, the orbiter's rendezvous and docking with an earth orbiting space station and the orbiter's return to a runway landing on the earth.
Prod-NAA Dist-RCKWL

To Planet Earth With Love C 30 MIN
16MM FILM OPTICAL SOUND R
Tells of the many jobs and short-term positions open to men and women willing to serve the Christian community. Explores the spiritual needs and opportunities in a changing world and how they must be met.
Prod-GF Dist-GF

To Predict And Control Earthquakes C 20 MIN
16MM FILM, 3/4 OR 1/2 IN VIDEO
Investigates scientists' efforts to understand and predict earthquakes. Discusses the concept of continental drift and examines the San Andreas Fault.
Prod-DOCUA Dist-CNEMAG

To Prepare A Child C 23 MIN
16MM FILM OPTICAL SOUND
Uses the experiences of three children and their families to stress the importance of preparing a child emotionally for a hospitalization experience.
LC NO. 76-700434
Prod-CHNMC Dist-CHNMC Prodn-PAPPVA 1975

To Preserve, To Resist, To Protect C 22 MIN
16MM FILM - 3/4 IN VIDEO
Shows 200 years of coastal defense as seen through the changes evident at Fort Moultrie, South Carolina.
LC NO. 79-706166
Prod-USNPS Dist-USNAC 1979

To Reach The Dawn C 48 MIN
16MM FILM OPTICAL SOUND J-H
Tells the story of R S Reynolds Sr and his founding of the Reynolds Metals Company. Documents the events in his life from the turn of the century through world War II.
LC NO. 76-702320
Prod-REYMC Dist-REYMC 1967

To Remember Or To Forget (Russian) C 100 MIN
16MM FILM OPTICAL SOUND C A
A Russian language film with English subtitles. Relates that against her doctor's orders, a contemporary Soviet woman decides to have a baby in hopes that it will improve relations with her husband. Shows that when the newborn baby dies, she adopts an abandoned baby and experiences an unusual twist of fate.
LC NO. 83-700203
Prod-RIGAFS Dist-IFEX Prodn-SOVEXP 1982

To Roast A Turkey (French) C 29 MIN
2 INCH VIDEOTAPE
Features Julia Child of Haute Cuisine au Vin demonstrating how to roast a turkey. With captions.
From The French Chef (French) Series.
Prod-WGBHTV Dist-PUBTEL

To Run C 11 MIN
16MM FILM OPTICAL SOUND J-C A
Studies a cross-country ski racer, revealing the training and determination required for this demanding sport. Shows the skier in training and in competition.
LC NO. 73-702261
Prod-ANAIB Dist-AUIS 1971

To Save A Life C 14 MIN
3/4 OR 1/2 INCH VIDEO CASSETTE
Demonstrates an emergency method for non-instrument rated airplane pilots to use when they have by accident become caught in weather without ground reference of any kind. Discusses the 'one-hundred and eighty degree turn procedure.' Shows how an air traffic controller can 'talk' a pilot out of the weather.
Prod-AOPA Dist-FO Prodn-FO

To Save A Life - Trauma Centers C 20 MIN
16MM FILM, 3/4 OR 1/2 IN VIDEO H-C
Describes the concept of trauma centers and analyzes some of the difficult social policy issues it poses.
Prod-ABCNEW Dist-MTI 1980

To Save A Life—A Series
16MM FILM, 3/4 OR 1/2 IN VIDEO J-C A
Prod-EBEC Dist-EBEC 1977

Burns - Emergency Procedures	015 MIN
Choking - To Save A Life	012 MIN
CPR - To Save A Life (2nd Ed)	014 MIN
Poisons - Emergency Procedures	015 MIN
Survival Swimming - To Save A Life	015 MIN

To Save A Species C 15 MIN
16MM FILM OPTICAL SOUND C
Details several projects now underway to protect threatened North American species. Examines an intensive ecological study of the endangered prairie pronghorn of the American Northwest.
From The Science In Action Series.
Prod-ALLFP Dist-COUNFI

To Save Our Environment - Conservation C 13 MIN
16MM FILM, 3/4 OR 1/2 IN VIDEO I-H
Presents a high school student who gives his view of the environment, and discusses how to implement those measures which would conserve human resources, clean air, and pure water.
Prod-ALTSUL Dist-JOU 1971

To Save The Amazon's Green Hell C 20 MIN
16MM FILM, 3/4 OR 1/2 IN VIDEO
Describes the shrinkage of the Amazon River and its rain forest and looks at efforts to save this region.
Prod-DOCUA Dist-CNEMAG

To Save Tomorrow—A Series
16MM FILM, 3/4 OR 1/2 IN VIDEO H-C A
Reviews various rehabilitation approaches to mental illness by hospitals, half-way houses and the local community.
Prod-NET Dist-IU

Fountain House	29 MIN
Horizon House	29 MIN
Operation Reentry	30 MIN
Spruce House	29 MIN
They're Your People	29 MIN
To Live And Move According To Your Nature Is	29 MIN
Wellmet House	30 MIN

To Say I Am C 30 MIN
16MM FILM - 3/4 IN VIDEO
Focuses on children who cannot use their speech mechanism and have limited bodily movement because of several handicaps. Tells how they are learning to use non-oral communications to 'speak.'
LC NO. 80-707162
Prod-KOCETV Dist-LAWREN 1980

To Search For America C 17 MIN
16MM FILM, 3/4 OR 1/2 IN VIDEO J-C A
Searches into the romantic American past and into the superreal present for an answer to the question, 'WHY ARE WE THE WAY WE ARE TODAY.' Employs various film techniques. Introduces E G Marshall as narrator.
Prod-PFP Dist-PFP 1973

To Secure These Rights C 22 MIN
16MM FILM OPTICAL SOUND
Examines the sentiments of average Virginians of 1775. Reveals their concerns and explains why they supported their leaders so strongly during the American Revolution.
LC NO. 76-703470
Prod-VIRGDE Dist-VADE Prodn-VADE 1976

To See Again - Corneal Transplant B 37 MIN
16MM FILM OPTICAL SOUND PRO
Presents patients before and after they have have their sight restored through corneal transplant. Provides a step-by-step view of the surgical procedure used.
Prod-CMA Dist-LAWREN

To See Another Day C 17 MIN
16MM FILM, 3/4 OR 1/2 IN VIDEO A
Points out the obvious hazards in an industrial setting, then reveals the not-so-obvious hazards in an office. Dramatized scenes show trips and falls, injury from sharp instruments,

electrical equipment, fire, improper lifting techniques, and other problems caused by haste and thoughtlessness.
Prod-MILLBK Dist-IFB

To See Clearly C 9 MIN
3/4 OR 1/2 INCH VIDEO CASSETTE PRO
Describes the surgical procedure, Radial Keratotomy, to correct myopia.
Prod-WFP Dist-WFP

To See Or Not To See C 15 MIN
2 INCH VIDEOTAPE J
Stresses the necessity of creating pictures in the imagination of the reader.
From The From Me To You...In Writing, Pt 2 Series.
Prod-DELE Dist-GPITVL

To See Ourselves X 13 MIN
16MM FILM OPTICAL SOUND H-C A
Shows how Jim Morrow learns to see himself from the other man's point of view. Through the magic of camera he is allowed to see himself as others see him.
LC NO. 72-702438
Prod-AETNA Dist-AETNA 1972

To Seek, To Teach, To Heal C 29 MIN
16MM FILM OPTICAL SOUND
Focuses on the way the nation's network of medical centers, medical research institutions and medical schools can mobilize and bring man's newest knowledge into life-saving use through a dramatization about a young boy's fight for life.
LC NO. 74-705799
Prod-USNIH Dist-USNAC

To Sell Or Not To Sell C 20 MIN
3/4 OR 1/2 INCH VIDEO CASSETTE
Explains the concept of market supply and shows how factors such as production costs and market demand affect supply of a given product.
From The Trade-Offs Series.
LC NO. 79-707343
Prod-EDFCEN Dist-AITECH 1978

To Sell Or Not To Sell - Sellers And Market Supply C 20 MIN
16MM FILM OPTICAL SOUND I-J
Points out how factors such as production costs and market demand affect the supply of a given product. Tells how Cathy weighs the costs and benefits of making wooden trays for Mrs Guthrie's gift shop against those of gardening for neighbors.
From The Trade-Offs Series. No. 11
LC NO. 79-701476
Prod-EDFCEN Dist-AITECH 1978

To Serve All, Pt 1 C 30 MIN
16MM FILM OPTICAL SOUND PRO
Presents interviews with each of the living past presidents of the American College of Surgeons. Describes important events that took place during the administration of each of these past presidents.
Prod-ACYDGD Dist-ACY 1963

To Serve All, Pt 2 C 35 MIN
16MM FILM OPTICAL SOUND PRO
Presents interviews with past presidents of the American College of Surgeons.
Prod-ACYDGD Dist-ACY 1970

To Share A Vision C 29 MIN
3/4 OR 1/2 INCH VIDEO CASSETTE H-C A
By documenting the life of a poet who is going blind and presenting positive portraits of several blind persons, helps sighted people to look beyond the handicap and see the blind as potential associates, friends, and lovers.
LC NO. 82-707090
Prod-WADSWB Dist-WADSWB 1982

To Shoot Or Not To Shoot C 18 MIN
3/4 OR 1/2 INCH VIDEO CASSETTE H-C A
Discusses the dilemma police face when deciding whether or not to shoot. Hosted by NBC News' Lloyd Dobyns, who took part in a unique course being offered in Miami to help train and advise cops in dealing with these situations.
Prod-NBCNEW Dist-FI 1983

To Sing Our Own Song C 50 MIN
16MM FILM, 3/4 OR 1/2 IN VIDEO J-C A
Presents Jose Diokno, a man who is active in the anti-Marcos movement in the Philippines. Argues that he sees a rich and selfish elite benefiting from the wealth of his land while the poor become more and more convinced that change can come only through violence. Criticizes the United States for supporting a repressive regime.
Prod-BBCTV Dist-FI 1982

To Sir, With Love C 105 MIN
16MM FILM OPTICAL SOUND
Tells the story of a teacher who gets his first job in a tough London slum school. Stars Sidney Poitier.
Prod-CPC Dist-TIMLIF 1967

To Sleep - Perchance To Dream B 30 MIN
16MM FILM, 3/4 OR 1/2 IN VIDEO H-C A
Documents several experiments to determine the relationship of dreams to stomach secretions, the amount of time infants spend dreaming, and the effect of depriving a subject of his dreams. Filmed at the sleep laboratory at UCLA.
From The Spectrum Series.
LC NO. 80-707104
Prod-NET Dist-IU 1967

To Solve The ESP Mystery C 20 MIN
16MM FILM, 3/4 OR 1/2 IN VIDEO
Shows experiments in extra-sensory perception, precognition, and telepathy.
Prod-DOCUA Dist-CNEMAG

To Sorrow C 5 MIN
3/4 INCH VIDEO CASSETTE
Presents a modern tone poem inspired by the poetry of Thomas Hardy, by Kit Fitzgerald.
Prod-EAI Dist-EAI

To Speak Again C 16 MIN
16MM FILM OPTICAL SOUND H-C A
Provides insight to the laryngectomy patient and his family.
Prod-AMCS Dist-AMCS

To Speak Or Not To Speak C 11 MIN
16MM FILM, 3/4 OR 1/2 IN VIDEO J-C
Uses an animated film to demonstrate that people who lack knowledge of their political affairs are ripe for manipulation or takeover by special interests or by totalitarian governments. Without narration.
Prod-SERVA Dist-IFB 1972

To Speak With Friends B 29 MIN
16MM FILM - 3/4 IN VIDEO
Illustrates instructional practices in elementary and secondary schools using language laboratories, television, motion pictures, recordings, slides and other special audio-visual facilities to help students in understanding and speaking foreign languages.
Prod-USOE Dist-USNAC Prodn-NEA 1972

To Stem The Black Tide B 14 MIN
16MM FILM OPTICAL SOUND
Shows the U S Coast Guard's role in the detection, location and prevention of oil spills and pollution. Features technology and manpower being employed in handling oil spills and pollution.
LC NO. 76-703892
Prod-USCG Dist-USNAC 1976

To Stuff A Cabbage (French) C 29 MIN
2 INCH VIDEOTAPE
Features Julia Child of Haute Cuisine au Vin demonstrating how to stuff a cabbage. With captions.
From The French Chef (French) Series.
Prod-WGBHTV Dist-PUBTEL

To Stuff A Sausage (French) C 29 MIN
2 INCH VIDEOTAPE
Features Julia Child of Haute Cuisine au Vin demonstrating how to stuff a sausage. With captions.
From The French Chef (French) Series.
Prod-WGBHTV Dist-PUBTEL

To Take A Hand C 17 MIN
16MM FILM OPTICAL SOUND
Follows a young nurse in a specialized cancer hospital through her period of adjustment, her change in attitudes and concepts, her realization that cancer can be cured, that there is hope and that she as an individual nurse can contribute to helping every cancer patient.
LC NO. 75-711538
Prod-UTAHTI Dist-UTAHTI 1970

To Take A Hand C 20 MIN
16MM FILM OPTICAL SOUND
Portrays a young nurse in a specialized cancer hospital as she experiences a period of adjustment and change in pre-conceived attitudes, ultimately gaining not only an awareness that there is hope for the cancer patient but also that, by becoming sincerely involved with the patient, she as an individual nurse can make a vital contribution.
Prod-AMCS Dist-AMCS 1972

To Taste Victory C 18 MIN
16MM FILM OPTICAL SOUND
Shows the activities of the Special Olympic training program for retarded children. Includes participation of retarded boys from the Parsons State Hospital and Training Center at Parsons, Kansas.
LC NO. 72-702015
Prod-UKANBC Dist-PSHTCA 1970

To Tell A Tale C 15 MIN
2 INCH VIDEOTAPE J
Shows three methods of emphasizing what you want in a story and discusses the importance of variety in a story.
From The From Me To You...In Writing, Pt 1 Series
Prod-DELE Dist-GPITVL

To The Edge Of Outer Space C 12 MIN
16MM FILM OPTICAL SOUND
Shows man's flight in the X-15 aircraft.
Prod-THIOKL Dist-THIOKL 1959

To The Edge Of The Universe C 23 MIN
16MM FILM, 3/4 OR 1/2 IN VIDEO H-C
Describes the construction and use of a radio telescope to measure a specific quasar. Shows basic concepts as the size of the universe, light years as a means of measuring astronomical distances, the doppler shift to determine direction of movement, the need for careful observation and measurement in scientific research and some of the methods of astronomers.
Prod-NFBC Dist-NFBC 1970

To The Gates Of Japan B 50 MIN
3/4 OR 1/2 INCH VIDEO CASSETTE
Explains Japanese strategy in the Pacific war. Shows good action scenes on the Solomon islands and Marianas. Shows excellent aircraft carrier footage.
Prod-IHF Dist-IHF

To The Honey Tree C 12 MIN
16MM FILM, 3/4 OR 1/2 IN VIDEO I
Shows a children's trip through a wooded area where they discover the tooth of an unknown animal and the habits of honey bees.
Prod-SF Dist-SF 1973

To The People Of The World (Captioned) C 21 MIN
16MM FILM, 3/4 OR 1/2 IN VIDEO A
Discusses human rights and the conditions of political prisoners in Chile since the military coup in 1973. Spanish dialog with English subtitles.
Prod-MARGIB Dist-CNEMAG 1975

To The Pond C 13 MIN
16MM FILM, 3/4 OR 1/2 IN VIDEO I
Presents scenes of children on their way to a pond where they discover how to make flour from cattail, find fresh herbs, carve apples, make scale prints and paint with natural dyes.
Prod-SF Dist-SF 1973

To The Prairies C 28 MIN
16MM FILM OPTICAL SOUND
Presents impressions of the immigration to the Canadian West.
From The Canadian Mosiac Series.
LC NO. 74-701279
Prod-OECA Dist-OECA 1972

To The Shores Of Iwo Jima C 19 MIN
16MM FILM, 3/4 OR 1/2 IN VIDEO
A documentary account of the American invasion of Iwo Jima. Shows ship bombardment, rocket fire, air bombing, the use of flame throwers and scenes of individual and group combat.
Prod-USN Dist-USNAC

To The Waterfall C 13 MIN
16MM FILM, 3/4 OR 1/2 IN VIDEO I
Shows scenes of children on their way to a waterfall where they learn how Indians used mud, berries and feathers to decorate themselves.
Prod-SF Dist-SF 1973

To The Wild Country—A Series

Prod-CANBC Dist-KEGPL Prodn-KEGPL 1974

Great Canadian Southwest, The	55 MIN
Great Gulf, The - The Saint Lawrence	55 MIN
Land Of The Big Ice	55 MIN
Wild Corners Of The Great Lakes	55 MIN
Wild Lens In Algonquin, A	55 MIN

To Think Of Dying C 58 MIN
3/4 OR 1/2 INCH VIDEO CASSETTE
Presents a frank conversation about death between two people dealing with it, Orville Kelly, a terminal cancer patient and Lynn Caine who wrote the best-selling book 'Widow'.
Prod-KTCATV Dist-PBS 1974

To Tommy With Love C 22 MIN
16MM FILM OPTICAL SOUND
Depicts a family where the father is constantly away on business trips, and shows how the Cub Scout program brings the family closer together.
Prod-BSA Dist-BSA 1982

To Touch A Dream C 3 MIN
16MM FILM, 3/4 OR 1/2 IN VIDEO J-H A
Shows a young girl realizing her fantasy of dancing.
Prod-RITWAX Dist-MTOLP 1984

To Touch Today C 24 MIN
3/4 OR 1/2 INCH VIDEO CASSETTE PRO
Sensitizes viewers to the feelings and experiences that bereaved parents must face. Explains purpose and value of the support group, SHARE.
Prod-HSCIC Dist-HSCIC 1984

To Touch Within, An Erotic Massage C 14 MIN
3/4 OR 1/2 INCH VIDEO CASSETTE C A
Focuses on a man's caring energy in a massage of long, slow and intensely erotic strokes for his female partner.
Prod-NATSF Dist-MMRC

To Train And Protect C 15 MIN
16MM FILM OPTICAL SOUND
Shows five segments of Arctic survival training, including the water survival training, the research vessel thunderbolt training, the helicopter simulator program and pilot screening. Insures the safety and protection of Air Force flying personnel and emphasizes proficiency, safety and savings.
LC NO. 75-700591
Prod-USAF Dist-USNAC 1974

To Try Again - And Succeed C 8 MIN
16MM FILM, 3/4 OR 1/2 IN VIDEO J-C A
Presents an animated eagle who is afraid to fly but yearns to soar. Explains that with the help of someone who cares, he finally succeeds.
LC NO. 82-706597
Prod-BOSUST Dist-CF 1980

To Try Again And Succeed (Norwegian) C 8 MIN
16MM FILM, 3/4 OR 1/2 IN VIDEO I-C A
Portrays the little eagle who fears flying, learns self-confidence and finally succeeds.
Prod-BOSUST Dist-CF

To Walk In Faith C 30 MIN
16MM FILM OPTICAL SOUND H A
Three years ago Olympic trainee Doug North had an accident that ended his skiing career. He returns to college to earn his diploma. Crippled, Doug is led back to a meaningful Christian life through the effort of a campus Pastor and the genuine concern of a coed.
LC NO. FIA68-1495
Prod-CONCOR Dist-CPH 1968

To Walk On The Moon C 17 MIN
16MM FILM OPTICAL SOUND I-C A
Summarizes the Apollo program from its beginning in 1961

through the historic moon walk of astronauts Armstrong and Aldrin in July, 1969. Includes motion picture and still photographs taken during the Apollo Seven, Eight, Nine, Ten and 11 flights.
Prod-NAA Dist-RCKWL

To Win At All Costs C 50 MIN
1/2 IN VIDEO CASSETTE BETA/VHS
Presents an overview of the history of the America's Cup.
Prod-GRANBN Dist-OFFSHR

To Win At All Costs - The Story Of The America's Cup C 56 MIN
1/2 IN VIDEO CASSETTE BETA/VHS
Tells the story of the America Cup races from 1851 to 1983, when Australia brought an end to one of the longest winning streaks in history.
Prod-MYSTIC Dist-MYSTIC 1983

To Work C 27 MIN
16MM FILM, 3/4 OR 1/2 IN VIDEO
Examines work as seen from a historical perspective and as it is in the modern world. Questions the present mode of work by setting it within a critical and historical context.
From The Five Billion People Series.
Prod-LEFSP Dist-CNEMAG

To Work With The Forest C 14 MIN
16MM FILM OPTICAL SOUND
Tells of the work of professional foresters.
Prod-SAFO Dist-SAFO

To Your Credit C 18 MIN
16MM FILM OPTICAL SOUND
Dramatizes in documentary style the money and credit problems that many real-life families are facing.
Prod-GEMILL Dist-GEMILL

To Your Good Health (Captioned) C 30 MIN
16MM FILM OPTICAL SOUND S
Presents typical health care situations to help hearing-impaired people become better consumers of health care services.
Prod-GALCO Dist-GALCO

To Your Heart's Content - Positive Approaches To Fitness C 26 MIN
16MM FILM OPTICAL SOUND A
Promotes cardiovascular fitness by offering advice from a cardiologist, an exercise physiologist and a world champion cyclist who suggests a gradual but steady inauguration of an exercise regime. Introduces such people as 86-year-old Hulda Crooks, who relishes mountain climbing.
LC NO. 83-700502
Prod-SPEF Dist-SPEF 1982

Toad A Trois C 3 MIN
3/4 OR 1/2 INCH VIDEO CASSETTE C A
Presents three beanbag toads engaging in animated sexual activity
Prod-MMRC Dist-MMRC

Toads - Some Are, Some Aren't C 8 MIN
16MM FILM, 3/4 OR 1/2 IN VIDEO K-I
Stimulates an awareness of the differences between two animals, the toad and the horned toad, which are called by the same name but which, on looking closer, show many different characteristics.
Prod-COLLRD Dist-BARR 1976

Toads - Some Are, Some Aren't (Spanish) C 8 MIN
16MM FILM - VIDEO, ALL FORMATS K-I
Shows the difference between a true toad and a horned lizard. Uses two 'talking' animals, Warty Bliggens and Cactus Clyde.
Prod-COLLRD Dist-BARR

Toast C 12 MIN
16MM FILM, 3/4 OR 1/2 IN VIDEO
Focuses on the excessive use of fossil fuels in the preparation and marketing of food. Traces the production and distribution of a loaf of bread from oil wellhead to end use. Illustrates the concept of net energy profit.
LC NO. 82-707181
Prod-BULFRG Dist-BULFRG 1977

Tobacco C 3 MIN
16MM FILM OPTICAL SOUND P-I
Discusses the tobacco industry.
From The Of All Things Series.
Prod-BAILYL Dist-AVED

Tobacco C 5 MIN
3/4 INCH VIDEO CASSETTE
Discusses the quantity of tobacco sold in the United States and the connection between smoking and respiratory damage. Issued in 1971 as a motion picture.
From The Single Concept Drug Film Series.
LC NO. 80-706850
Prod-NIMH Dist-USNAC 1980

Tobacco - The Complete Story C 30 MIN
3/4 OR 1/2 INCH VIDEO CASSETTE
Takes a new look at tobacco and provides an objective overview on smoking and its impact on social and economic life.
Prod-ARFO Dist-ARFO 1981

Tobacco - The Idiot's Delight (2nd Ed) C 19 MIN
16MM FILM OPTICAL SOUND J-C
Uses a series of satirical vignettes to show how social pressures influence young people to accept smoking. Shows cases of tobacco addiction and points out possible adverse physical effects of tobacco.
LC NO. 76-703181
Prod-MTVTM Dist-MTVTM 1976

Tobacco Fantasy C 2 MIN
16MM FILM, 3/4 OR 1/2 IN VIDEO
Presents tobacco fragments which come to life in sweeping pictorial images of a great toreador's encounter with a celebrated bull.
Prod-ANIMAF Dist-IFEX 1983

Tobacco Problem, The - What Do You Think C 17 MIN
16MM FILM, 3/4 OR 1/2 IN VIDEO J-H
Points out the dangers of smoking by presenting interviews and demonstrations by laboratory scientists and doctors. Emphasizes the reasons why people smoke, showing particularly how our culture influences smoking. Tells how people feel about their own habit and that of others.
From The What Do You Think Series.
Prod-EBEC Dist-EBEC 1971

Tobias On The Evolution Of Man C 18 MIN
16MM FILM, 3/4 OR 1/2 IN VIDEO
Summarizes Phillip Tobias' contributions to paleoanthropology in the field and in the laboratory. Presents Tobias discussing the evolution of man, considering various hominid species and their relationship to Homo sapiens.
LC NO. 80-706331
Prod-NGS Dist-NGS 1975

Tobruk To Tarakan B 30 MIN
16MM FILM OPTICAL SOUND H-C A
Examines the Australian Army in World War II.
Prod-ANAIB Dist-AUIS 1965

Toccata For Toy Trains C 14 MIN
16MM FILM, 3/4 OR 1/2 IN VIDEO K-C A
Shows toy trains as they journey from roundhouse and yards, into stations and out, through countryside and village, and on to their destination. All characters, architecture and objects with which the sets are built are toys, most of them made a number of years ago.
Prod-EAMES Dist-PFP 1957

Today And Tomorrow C 28 MIN
16MM FILM OPTICAL SOUND
Shows VA youth volunteers in both career explorations and indirect patient service assignments.
LC NO. 74-705802
Prod-USVA Dist-USNAC 1973

Today And Tomorrow C 60 MIN
3/4 OR 1/2 INCH VIDEO CASSETTE J-C A
Presents flutist James Galway discussing how modern music is more difficult to understand or assess. Includes example of the music of Lennon and McCartney, Copland and Stravinsky.
From The James Galway's Music In Time Series.
Prod-POLTEL Dist-FOTH 1982

Today For Tomorrow C 15 MIN
16MM FILM OPTICAL SOUND
Explains that keeping aviation's mushrooming growth on safety's centerline is faa's most important job. Summarizes faa's major research and development projects and the outstanding personnel and unique testing and simulation facilities that enable NAFEC to create or re-create any kind of flight situation, all in the name of safety.
LC NO. 74-705803
Prod-FAAFL Dist-USFAA 1969

Today I Am A Man, I Think C 22 MIN
16MM FILM OPTICAL SOUND
Tells how a young boy approaching his bar mitzvah questions its traditions and meaning as his parents try to turn it into a Hollywood party.
LC NO. 80-700489
Prod-USC Dist-USC 1980

Today The Information Explosion, Tomorrow C 16 MIN
16MM FILM, 3/4 OR 1/2 IN VIDEO J-C A
Examines the vastness of media and its effect on daily life. Explains that since the invention of the printing press, the availability of information has expanded rapidly.
Prod-CORF Dist-CORF 1977

Today, Tomorrow, Forever C 15 MIN
3/4 OR 1/2 INCH VIDEO CASSETTE J-H
Points out that it's up to each individual to decide whether or not to age in a healthy way. Explains that changes in body and lifestyle require new food choices throughout life.
From The Soup To Nuts Series.
Prod-GSDE Dist-AITECH 1980

Today's Army Is An Education C 18 MIN
16MM FILM OPTICAL SOUND
Shows the many opportunities available for higher education in the U S Army including apprenticeship programs, tuition assistance, ROTC, scholarships, resident medical programs, appointments to West Point and other programs leading to college degrees.
Prod-USA Dist-MTP

Today's Broadway Gypsies C 30 MIN
3/4 OR 1/2 INCH VIDEO CASSETTE
See series title for descriptive statement.
From The Broadway Dance Series.
Prod-ARCVID Dist-ARCVID

Today's Children C 28 MIN
16MM FILM OPTICAL SOUND C T
Describes the model Early Childhood Program, a program funded under Title III, Elementary and Secondary Act of 1965, as amended. Shows effective ways of introducing young children to the wide world of learning. Portrays children engaged in individualized activities in the areas of language skills, reading and mathematical concepts.
Prod-HALLFM Dist-HALLFM

Today's Computers, What They Are, How They Work C
3/4 OR 1/2 INCH VIDEO CASSETTE J-H
Indroduces the different kinds of computers - main frame, mini and micro computers. Shows and describes the functions of computer hardware.
From The Computer Literacy And Understanding Series.
Prod-EDUACT Dist-EDUACT

Today's Culture - Options After High School C 17 MIN
16MM FILM, 3/4 OR 1/2 IN VIDEO H
Presents interviews with various people in order to show the wide range of opportunities now open to high school graduates.
Prod-CORF Dist-CORF 1976

Today's Family - Adjusting To Change C
3/4 OR 1/2 INCH VIDEO CASSETTE A
Looks at how family members are coping with change.
From The Vital Link Series.
Prod-EDCC Dist-EDCC

Today's Family - Adjusting To Change C 28 MIN
3/4 OR 1/2 INCH VIDEO CASSETTE
Looks at the new variety of family styles - from those in which both parents work or where there's only parent to those with a step-parent or only one child. Considers the current status of the traditional two-parent, father-supported family.
Prod-GA Dist-GA

Today's Guidelines For Pork C
16MM FILM OPTICAL SOUND
Presents illustrations of pork quality and evaluates live animals and carcasses. Includes a discussion of loin eye, marbling, length and backfat to make No 1-2-3-4 hogs. Finishes with scenes of the national barrow show.
Prod-NPPC Dist-VENARD

Today's History—A Series
16MM FILM, 3/4 OR 1/2 IN VIDEO H-C
Presents excerpts from important events in the twentieth century.
Prod-JOU Dist-JOU 1984

Inflation - Who Wins 026 MIN
Invisible History 026 MIN
Oil Age, The 026 MIN
Poland 026 MIN
Utopias 026 MIN
Whatever Happened To Marx 026 MIN
Why War 026 MIN
Why Work 026 MIN
Women And Society 026 MIN

Today's Newspaper C 22 MIN
16MM FILM, 3/4 OR 1/2 IN VIDEO H-C
Tells exactly what goes on in the production of a daily periodical. Covers editorials, advertising, photography, art, composition, printing and circulation.
Prod-COP Dist-AIMS 1972

Today's Newspaper (Spanish) C 22 MIN
16MM FILM, 3/4 OR 1/2 IN VIDEO H-C
Looks at the production process of a daily periodical, covering editorial, circulation and the future of the journalism profession.
Prod-COP Dist-AIMS 1972

Today's Veterinarian C 23 MIN
16MM FILM OPTICAL SOUND
Looks at the duties of the modern veterinarian, including small animal care, public health, agriculture and zoo medicine. Accompanies veterinarians as they make their daily rounds seeing to the health of their animal charges.
Prod-AMVMA Dist-MTP

Todd - Growing Up In Appalachia C 14 MIN
16MM FILM, 3/4 OR 1/2 IN VIDEO P-J
Tells the story of Todd, a boy from an Appalachian family of very limited means, who finds a purse full of food stamps. Reveals Todd's character by the decision he makes when he sees the owner's name and address in the purse.
From The Many Americans Series.
Prod-ENGLE Dist-LCOA 1971

Todd - Growing Up In Appalachia (Captioned) C 12 MIN
16MM FILM, 3/4 OR 1/2 IN VIDEO I-J A
Tells the story of poverty and the temptations that come with it.
Prod-LCOA Dist-LCOA 1970

Toddler C 40 MIN
3/4 OR 1/2 INCH VIDEO CASSETTE
Demonstrates significant spheres of development, including physical, cognitive and psychosocial. Stresses accident prevention.
From The Infancy Through Adolescence Series.
Prod-WSUN Dist-AJN

Toddler Management C 19 MIN
16MM FILM OPTICAL SOUND
Explains how mothers are taught to modify unacceptable behavior in their preschool children through a program run entirely by mothers who are nonprofessional in the clinical sense, but who have been through the program themselves and are now using their experiences to help others.
From The Regional Intervention Program Series.
LC NO. 75-702440
Prod-USBEH Dist-USNAC Prodn-AIRLIE 1973

Toddler, The - Origins Of Independence B 44 MIN
16MM FILM OPTICAL SOUND
Discusses the toddler and his need to become more independent with regard to his motor and social skills.
From The Man - His Growth And Development, Birth Through Adolescence Series.
LC NO. 75-703692
Prod-VDONUR Dist-AJN Prodn-WTTWTV 1967

Toddler's Hours Of Hazard, The C 14 MIN
16MM FILM OPTICAL SOUND H-C A
Examines the problem of home accidents which involve the very young and suggests ways in which the annual toll of deaths and injuries can be reduced. Depicts a day in the life of an average American family and shows how minor irritations can breed accidents.
LC NO. FIA66-659
Prod-AETNA Dist-AETNA 1965

Todolos Del Mundo C 30 MIN
3/4 OR 1/2 INCH VIDEO CASSETTE K-P
See series title for descriptive statement.
From The Villa Alegre Series.
Prod-BCTV Dist-MDCPB

Todos Santos Cuchumatan C 29 MIN
16MM FILM - 3/4 IN VIDEO
Profiles the plight of the Mam Indians of the Cuchumatan highlands in Guatemala. Explains how Guatemala is run by and for the Ladinos, people of mixed European and Indian ancestry who make up almost half of the population, while the rest are Indians who have been isolated geographically until roads were cut into the mountains for cheap labor on cotton farms. Reveals the detrimental changes in the Indian traditions and lifestyle. In Indian and Spanish with English voice-over.
Prod-KCET Dist-KCET

Todos Santos Cuchumatan - Report From A Guatemalan Village C 41 MIN
16MM FILM, 3/4 OR 1/2 IN VIDEO
Offers an intimate portrait of everyday life in one Mam Indian village called Todos Santos Cuchumatan, nestled in a valley of the Cuchumatanes mountains of Guatemala at an altitude of nearly 9,000 feet above sea level. Documents the annual sequence of harvest, the elaborate fiesta of Todos Santos and the mass seasonal migration out of the mountain village to work in the cotton plantations of Guatemala's hot and humid lowlands.
Prod-CARREO Dist-ICARUS

Toe To Hand Transfer For Thumb Reconstruction C 14 MIN
3/4 OR 1/2 INCH VIDEO CASSETTE PRO
Discusses the technique of reconstructing a thumb by free toe transfer. Describes and shows preoperative planning, operative technique and long term results. Assumes microsurgery technical expertise.
Prod-ASSH Dist-ASSH

Toes Tell C 6 MIN
16MM FILM, 3/4 OR 1/2 IN VIDEO K-I
A barefoot girl steps on and feels many textures with her toes.
From The Magic Moments Series.
Prod-EBEC Dist-EBEC 1969

Together C 37 MIN
16MM FILM OPTICAL SOUND
Examines the explosive structural changes going on in the entire Swedish society which is leaving a very definite mark on Swedish consumer cooperation.
Prod-ASI Dist-AUDPLN 1964

Together C 52 MIN
3/4 OR 1/2 INCH VIDEO CASSETTE
See series title for descriptive statement.
From The Leo Buscaglia Series.
Prod-PBS Dist-DELTAK

Together Alone C 30 MIN
16MM FILM, 3/4 OR 1/2 IN VIDEO A
Looks at three couples through various stages of their attempt to conquer infertility. Looks at some of the causes of sterility, several tests administered to both partners, the characteristics patients seek in trusted physicians and some treatments undergone to ameliorate the chances of conception.
LC NO. 83-706202
Prod-PEREN Dist-PEREN 1981

Together For Children C 6 MIN
16MM FILM, 3/4 OR 1/2 IN VIDEO
Provides an animated look at racial prejudice and the development of tolerance and harmony.
LC NO. 82-706021
Prod-UNICEF Dist-PHENIX Prodn-HALAS 1981

Together They Learn C 28 MIN
3/4 OR 1/2 INCH VIDEO CASSETTE
Presents a program for elementary school children who are retarded or emotionally handicapped. Includes math, reading and science. Emphasizes social interaction between the retarded children and other classmates.
From The Integration Of Children With Special Needs In A Regular Classroom Series.
Prod-LPS Dist-AITECH Prodn-WGBHTV 1975

Together With Leo Buscaglia C 52 MIN
3/4 OR 1/2 INCH VIDEO CASSETTE
Presents Dr Leo Buscaglia discussing the concept of how togetherness and sharing leads to fulfillment in loving relationships.
Prod-KVIETV Dist-PBS 1952

Together With Love C 30 MIN
3/4 OR 1/2 INCH VIDEO CASSETTE
Follows a couple's preparation for childbirth from classes through the birth experience.
Prod-CENTRE Dist-CENTRE

Together, Pt 1 - The Early Years C 33 MIN
16MM FILM OPTICAL SOUND
Features psychologists Fred S Keller and B F Skinner who discuss their undergraduate experiences, their associations with such notable contemporaries as Boring and Dallenbach and their first attempts to teach a new science.
LC NO. 74-700002
Prod-APPLE Dist-PHM 1973

Together, Pt 2 - 1930 To Tomorrow C 28 MIN
16MM FILM OPTICAL SOUND
Features psychologists Fred S Keller and B F Skinner who discuss the growth of modern psychology and its future direction.
LC NO. 74-700003
Prod-APPLE Dist-PHM 1973

Together, Sweetly C 15 MIN
16MM FILM OPTICAL SOUND C A
A short version of the film How To Make A Woman. Reveals the anatomy of a typical marriage in which a wife gives up her identity to please and serve her husband. Shows what can happen in such a relationship as seen from a feminist point of view.
LC NO. 76-703918
Prod-POLYMR Dist-POLYMR 1973

Together, With Love C 29 MIN
16MM FILM OPTICAL SOUND A
Tells the stories of two couples and their experiences at the time of their baby's birth with the prepared childbirth process.
LC NO. 82-700136
Prod-CENTRE Dist-CENTRE 1981

Togetherness C 15 MIN
3/4 OR 1/2 INCH VIDEO CASSETTE K-P
Shows that living things must depend on other living things for survival.
From The Dragons, Wagons And Wax, Set 1 Series.
Prod-CTI Dist-CTI

Toilet Training C 52 MIN
3/4 OR 1/2 INCH VIDEO CASSETTE S
Presents for retarded persons, the most salient points of toilet training program developed by Dr. Richard M. Foxx and Dr. Nathan H. Azrin.
Prod-RESPRC Dist-RESPRC

Toilette C 7 MIN
16MM FILM, 3/4 OR 1/2 IN VIDEO H-C A
Uses clay animation to show an insecure woman who keeps trying to change her image.
Prod-FREMNJ Dist-TEXFLM 1977

Toine C 15 MIN
16MM FILM, 3/4 OR 1/2 IN VIDEO H-C A
Tells how a brutish husband in a provincial town is domesticated by his wife and mother. Based on the work of Guy de Maupassant.
Prod-JANUS Dist-FI 1979

Token Economy - Behaviorism Applied C 23 MIN
16MM FILM, 3/4 OR 1/2 IN VIDEO H-C A
Psychologist B F Skinner outlines his theories on the treatment of the mentally ill, criminals and retardates, showing the successful application of these theories in a mental health facility.
Prod-CRMP Dist-CRMP 1972

Token Gesture, A C 8 MIN
16MM FILM, 3/4 OR 1/2 IN VIDEO H-C A
Presents a satiric portrayal of the stereotypes that are applied to the sexes. Examines the historical development of these attitudes, starting at birth and continuing through adulthood.
Prod-NFBC Dist-MGHT 1977

Token System For Behavior Modification, A C 10 MIN
16MM FILM OPTICAL SOUND
Demonstrates the use of a token economy in a behavioral reinforcement education program to teach moderately and severly retarded girls self-help and occupational skills.
LC NO. 72-702014
Prod-UKANBC Dist-PSHTCA 1971

Tokens Of Love X 15 MIN
16MM FILM OPTICAL SOUND P-I R
Tells a story which teaches Christian attitudes of cooperation and sharing in everyday home chores. Shows how three children learn to have more appreciation and affection for their parents.
From The Our Children Series.
Prod-FAMF Dist-FAMF

Tokyo Breaks The Quake Barrier - The Kasumigaseki High-Rise Building Project, Pt 1 C 27 MIN
16MM FILM OPTICAL SOUND
Explains that Japan is a volcanic land and every year there are numerous earthquakes, most of them minor, but so frequent that until now high buildings have been impractical. Points out that today, however, with improved building methods a 36 story building has been constructed in Tokyo. Shows how such a structure is made not only practical but safe.
Prod-UNIJAP Dist-UNIJAP 1966

Tokyo Crusade C 28 MIN
16MM FILM OPTICAL SOUND
Points out that Japan is primarily a Buddhist country and Christians are an extreme minority. Depicts the overwhelming response to the Billy Graham crusade in Tokyo. Features a personal word of witness from English 'POP' star Cliff Richard and former baseball star, Bobby Richardson, as well as an address by Billy Graham.
Prod-WWP Dist-NINEFC

Tokyo In Tennessee C 16 MIN
16MM FILM, 3/4 OR 1/2 IN VIDEO J-C A
Shows how Nissan Motors of Japan is opening a 69-acre automotive plant in Smyrna, Tennessee, and hoping to teach American workers the Japanese work ethic of 'master your equipment, love your fellow worker.' Offers the remarks of a core of Smyrna plant workers who were trained in Japan and who are optimistic about the undertaking. Includes the comments of United Auto Workers President Douglas Fraser who voices skepticism. Originally shown on the CBS television program 60 Minutes.
LC NO. 83-706581
Prod-CBSNEW Dist-CAROUF 1983

Tokyo Industrial Worker C 17 MIN
16MM FILM, 3/4 OR 1/2 IN VIDEO P-C
Shows a metropolitan area in Tokyo with old customs and new western customs side by side. Shows the transition of an industrial worker from a modern factory to his Japanese cultural home.
From The Man And His World Series.
Prod-FI Dist-FI 1969

Tokyo Move Skywards - The Kasumigaseki High-Rise Building Project, Pt 2 C 35 MIN
16MM FILM OPTICAL SOUND
Shows the first high-rise building construction in Japan from its beginning to the completion of erecting the steel frame. Points out that the steel framework is an embodiment of the essence of Japanese architecture at the world's highest level.
Prod-UNIJAP Dist-UNIJAP 1967

Tokyo Story (Japanese) B 134 MIN
16MM FILM OPTICAL SOUND
Explores the potential violence found in a Japanese family and looks at the sad and necessary differences between generations of the same family.
Prod-NYFLMS Dist-NYFLMS 1953

Tokyo, In Old Times And Today C 25 MIN
16MM FILM OPTICAL SOUND
Catches phases of Tokyo in olden times and today, introducing important paintings, cultural inheritances and actual landscapes. Describes history, culture and living of the castle town of Edo (Tokyo.)
Prod-TOEI Dist-UNIJAP 1971

Tokyo's Giant Landmark - The Kasumigaseki High-Rise Building Project C 42 MIN
16MM FILM OPTICAL SOUND
Points out that the Kasumigaseki-Mitsui building was until recently the tallest in all Asia. Shows the various techniques by which it was made, the labor and imagination which went into its construction and its successful completion. Emphasizes that in an earthquake prone land, in a city where much of the land is reclaimed, its construction posed many difficult and unusual construction problems.
Prod-UNIJAP Dist-UNIJAP 1968

Tokyo's New National Museum Of Modern Art C 18 MIN
16MM FILM OPTICAL SOUND
Explains that the National Museum of Modern Art at Tokyo was born in the Kitanomaru Park of the Imperial Palace. Records the construction process, explains some examples of Japanese art works exhibited at this museum and mentions its function as a quiet retreat for the people of Tokyo.
Prod-UNIJAP Dist-UNIJAP 1969

Toll Gate, The B 59 MIN
16MM FILM SILENT
Introduces Black Deering, an Old West outlaw who risks capture and his life to rescue a drowning child and to warn an outlying post of Indian uprisings. Stars William S Hart and Anna Q Nilsson. Directed by Lambert Hillyer.
Prod-UNKNWN Dist-KILLIS 1920

Toll Gate, The B 71 MIN
16MM FILM OPTICAL SOUND
Western melodrama. Outlaw 'BLACK' Deering escapes after being captured during a train robbery, finds and kills the man who betrayed him, and finally wins the respect and admiration of the sheriff by deliberately casting away his freedom in defense of a young woman and her child.
LC NO. FI68-442
Prod-HARW Dist-BHAWK 1920

Toller C 52 MIN
16MM FILM OPTICAL SOUND
Presents a portrait of Canadian figure skater and artist Toller Cranston. Uses special effects to compare his paintings with his skating style.
LC NO. 77-702680
Prod-NORNDA Dist-VIP 1976

Toller C 26 MIN
16MM FILM, 3/4 OR 1/2 IN VIDEO J-C A
Captures the grace and genius of Canadian skater Toller Cranston, who has also brought his talents to the world of painting.
Prod-INST Dist-WOMBAT

Toller Cranston - Imagery And Ice C 9 MIN
16MM FILM OPTICAL SOUND
Presents an interview with Canadian ice skating champion Toller Cranston in which he discusses both his skating and his painting.
LC NO. 77-702681
Prod-CANBC Dist-INCC Prodn-BASSTJ 1973

Toltec Mystery, The C 26 MIN
16MM FILM OPTICAL SOUND I-C A
Explores the mysterious fact that, while the Mayan people exist today, the Toltecs are completely extinct. Reveals clear-cut evidences in the ancient city of Chichen Itza of the infiltration of the Mayan culture by that of the Toltecs.
LC NO. FIA66-1400
Prod-HENSON Dist-AVED 1966

Tom C 19 MIN
3/4 INCH VIDEO CASSETTE
Tells about the values and attitudes of a 26-year-old man who is a heavy user of drugs. Questions what drugs offer him and examines his feelings about alternate routes to heightened awareness. Issued in 1971 as a motion picture.

From The Social Seminar Series.
LC NO. 80-707359
Prod-NIMH Dist-USNAC 1980

Tom And Virl Osmond C 15 MIN
16MM FILM, 3/4 OR 1/2 IN VIDEO I-H S
Profiles Tom and Virl Osmond, who are both hard of hearing. Shows how the brothers are an integral part of the Osmond family of performers in spite of their hearing problem.
From The Truly Exceptional People Series.
Prod-WDEMCO Dist-WDEMCO 1979

Tom Braidwood C
3/4 OR 1/2 INCH VIDEO CASSETTE
Portrays Tom Braidwood, British Columbian filmmaker with interviews and film clips.
From The Filmmakers' Showcase Series.
Prod-CANFDW Dist-CANFDW

Tom Brydon C
3/4 OR 1/2 INCH VIDEO CASSETTE
Portrays Tom Brydon, British Columbian filmmaker with interviews and film clips.
From The Filmmakers' Showcase Series.
Prod-CANFDW Dist-CANFDW

Tom Cat's Meow C 13 MIN
16MM FILM, 3/4 OR 1/2 IN VIDEO P-J
Uses animation and puppets in an adaptation of a classic Czechoslovakian fairytale about a little girl whose mistreatment by her stepmother and stepsister brings rewards from the tomcat she has befriended. Made in Czechoslovakia.
Prod-SFSP Dist-PHENIX 1976

Tom Cottle Show—A Series

Presents psychologist Dr Tom Cottle talking with people who have lived through and adjusted to a variety of crises.
Prod-WGBHTV Dist-PBS 1981

Being Well 029 MIN
Birthright 029 MIN
Marriage Story, A 029 MIN
Michael's Story 029 MIN
Survivor Of The Holocaust 029 MIN

Tom Edison C 15 MIN
3/4 OR 1/2 INCH VIDEO CASSETTE P
Spans Thomas Edison's life from his first failing experiment at four to his many adult successes.
From The Stories Of America Series.
Prod-OHSDE Dist-AITECH Prodn-WVIZTV 1976

Tom Harper Story, The C 13 MIN
16MM FILM OPTICAL SOUND
Tells how a young man pulled himself through the rigors of cancer.
LC NO. 79-700327
Prod-AMCS Dist-AMCS Prodn-TAPPRO 1978

Tom Horn C 98 MIN
16MM FILM OPTICAL SOUND
Stars Steve McQueen as a gunfighter who lives by his own code of honor.
Prod-WB Dist-SWANK

Tom Jones C 127 MIN
16MM FILM OPTICAL SOUND
Presents an adaptation of Henry Fielding's novel TOM JONES, following the adventures of a country lad who leaves home to explore the world. Stars Albert Finney and Susannah York. Directed by Tony Richardson.
Prod-UNKNWN Dist-UAE 1963

Tom Jones C 14 MIN
3/4 OR 1/2 INCH VIDEO CASSETTE PRO
Shows Tom Jones, American medical illustrator, demonstrating and talking about his techniques to a group of students at the University Of California at Los Angeles (UCLA).
Prod-WFP Dist-WFP

Tom Lehrer Sings Pollution C 3 MIN
16MM FILM OPTICAL SOUND
Presents a musical satire on the effects of air and water pollution.
LC NO. FIE68-23
Prod-USPHS Dist-USPHS Prodn-ASTRAF 1967

Tom Magee, Man Of Iron C 30 MIN
3/4 OR 1/2 INCH VIDEO CASSETTE I A
Shows the rigorous training that enabled Canadian Tom Magers to become the youngest super heavyweight world power lifting champion in 1982. Documents Magee's competition performance in Munich, Germany.
Prod-MOBIUS Dist-MOBIUS 1983

Tom Paxton, The Clancy Brothers And Tommy Makem C 52 MIN
3/4 OR 1/2 INCH VIDEO CASSETTE
Presents the Clancy Brothers and Tommy Makem from Ireland singing traditional and contemporary Irish songs.
From The Rainbow Quest Series.
Prod-SEEGER Dist-CWATER

Tom Thumb C 10 MIN
16MM FILM, 3/4 OR 1/2 IN VIDEO K-I
Presents an animated adaptation of the classic fairy tale about tiny Tom Thumb, who is able to overcome dangerous obstacles despite his size.
From The Grimm's Fairy Tales Series.
Prod-BOSUST Dist-CF 1978

Tom Thumb (Spanish) C 10 MIN
16MM FILM, 3/4 OR 1/2 IN VIDEO P-J
Depicts the adventures of Tom Thumb. Shows that avarice is punished.
From The Grimm's Fairy Tale (Spanish) Series.
Prod-BOSUST Dist-CF

Tom Thumb In King Arthur's Court C 20 MIN
16MM FILM, 3/4 OR 1/2 IN VIDEO K-I
Traces the life of Tom Thumb from his birth in the heart of a rose to the day he is made a Knight of the Round Table. Demonstrates that valor is not a matter of size but of spirit.
Prod-CORF Dist-CORF 1963

Tom's New House C 15 MIN
3/4 OR 1/2 INCH VIDEO CASSETTE K-P
Shows how wedges and screws work.
From The Dragons, Wagons And Wax, Set 1 Series.
Prod-CTI Dist-CTI

Tomato Salad Plates C 4 MIN
3/4 OR 1/2 INCH VIDEO CASSETTE PRO
Shows how to make tomato poinsettias stuffed with a filling and arranged on a bed of lettuce with thin-sliced cucumber and boiled egg quarters. Contains tips on the preparation of lettuce and peeling tomatoes.
Prod-CULINA Dist-CULINA

Tomatoes C 10 MIN
16MM FILM, 3/4 OR 1/2 IN VIDEO P-I
Shows how a bountiful tomato crop which they cannot personally eat prompts Boy and Grandpa to use the principle of the screw and lever to invent a press to squeeze out the juice. Demonstrates the interrelationship between machines and food preparation and preservation.
From The Inventive Child Series.
Prod-POLSKI Dist-EBEC 1983

Tomatoes - From Seed To Table C 11 MIN
16MM FILM, 3/4 OR 1/2 IN VIDEO P-I
Discusses the raising and processing of tomatoes.
Prod-FILMSW Dist-FLMFR

Tomi Ungerer, Storyteller C 21 MIN
16MM FILM, 3/4 OR 1/2 IN VIDEO
Interviews author and illustrator of children's books Tomi Ungerer. Discussses his thoughts and feelings about his work, his world and his personal life. Includes scenes from the motion pictures The Three Robber, The Beast Of Monsieur Racine and Moon Man.
Prod-WWS Dist-WWS 1981

Tommie, Suzie And The Cardboard Box C 15 MIN
16MM FILM OPTICAL SOUND P-I
Uses three stories about a young boy and girl and their cardboard box to illustrate story structure.
From The Creative Writing Skills Series.
LC NO. 74-703611
Prod-MORLAT Dist-MORLAT 1973

Tommy C 18 MIN
16MM FILM OPTICAL SOUND
Presents a shortened version of the rock opera Tommy about a deaf, dumb and blind youth and his parents' attempt to cure him. Stars Roger Daltry, Ann-Margret and Jack Nicholson.
Prod-WGBHTV Dist-TIMLIF 1982

Tommy Cat C 8 MIN
16MM FILM, 3/4 OR 1/2 IN VIDEO K-P
Presents a story which has two alternate endings. Considers the implications and meanings of each ending.
From The Tommy, Tubby, Tuffy Series.
Prod-MORLAT Dist-LUF 1974

Tommy Tricycle X 5 MIN
16MM FILM OPTICAL SOUND P-I
Presents Otto the Auto who demonstrates through the help of his friends tricycle safety rules.
From The Otto The Auto Series.
Prod-AAAFTS Dist-AAAFTS

Tommy, Suzie And The Cardboard Box C 15 MIN
16MM FILM, 3/4 OR 1/2 IN VIDEO I-J
Portrays the cardboard box as one of the earliest means of make-believe for a child. Stimulates creative imagination to produce stories and plays of a student's very own.
From The Creative Writing Series.
Prod-MORLAT Dist-AIMS 1971

Tommy, Tubby, Tuffy—A Series
16MM FILM, 3/4 OR 1/2 IN VIDEO P
Presents three stories dealing with a cat, a bunny and a puppy.
Prod-LUF Dist-LUF 1979

Tommy Cat 009 MIN
Tubby Bunny 012 MIN
Tuffy Puppy 009 MIN

Tommy's First Car C 11 MIN
16MM FILM, 3/4 OR 1/2 IN VIDEO J-C A
Shows how Tommy learns how to make an intelligent decision about buying a used car as his father tells him where to look for clues that can indicate the car's condition and possible necessary repairs or replacements.
From The Consumer Education Series.
Prod-LEARN Dist-FLMFR 1972

Tommy's First Car (Captioned Version) C 11 MIN
16MM FILM, 3/4 OR 1/2 IN VIDEO J-C A
Shows how Tommy learns how to make an intelligent decision about buying a used car as his father tells him where to look for clues that can indicate the car's condition and possible necessary repairs or replacements.
From The Consumer Education Series.
Prod-LEARN Dist-FLMFR 1972

Tommy's First Car (Spanish) C 11 MIN
16MM FILM, 3/4 OR 1/2 IN VIDEO J-C A
Describes how to go about buying a used car. Shows where to look for clues regarding the car's condition and possible necessary repairs and how to road test a car. Explains the importance of having a mechanic examine the car before buying it.
Prod-LEARN Dist-FLMFR 1972

Tomorrow Again B 16 MIN
16MM FILM OPTICAL SOUND J-C A
A fictional story, presented in the form of a documentary, about a sweet, old lady who lives in a shabby hotel for senior citizens. Pictures the psychological problems which develop because of her loneliness and isolation.
LC NO. 72-701541
Prod-PFP Dist-VIEWFI 1972

Tomorrow And Yesterday - Modern Technology And Ancient Culture C 28 MIN
16MM FILM, 3/4 OR 1/2 IN VIDEO H-C A
Looks at the daily events in the life of the Kimuras, a modern Japanese family headed by a design engineer in a large construction company.
From The Human Face Of Japan Series.
LC NO. 82-707154
Prod-FLMAUS Dist-LCOA 1982

Tomorrow Begins Yesterday C 29 MIN
16MM FILM OPTICAL SOUND
Describes a program in industrial arts for children on the seventh-grade level. Presents the background, rationale and application of the program, and depicts the educational processes as well as some of the projected outcomes.
LC NO. 77-711541
Prod-UMD Dist-UMD 1970

Tomorrow Came Much Later - A Journey Of Conscience C 58 MIN
16MM FILM, 3/4 OR 1/2 IN VIDEO J-C A
Recounts a journey by a high school class, their teacher and a survivor of the Holocaust. Includes visits to Warsaw, Auschwitz and the Majdanek and Mauthausen concentration camps and an interview with famed Nazi-hunter Simon Wiesenthal.
LC NO. 81-707498
Prod-WVIZTV Dist-CORF 1981

Tomorrow Comes Early C 25 MIN
16MM FILM OPTICAL SOUND
Provides an opportunity for adults to discuss the psychological and spiritual problems of growing older, from the Christian perspective by presenting the story of Paul Butram, a middle-aged college professor who is forced to come to grips with his own advancing maturity. Depicts the depth of his personal search for meaning and self-affirmation.
Prod-FAMF Dist-FAMF

Tomorrow I'll Be There C 11 MIN
16MM FILM, 3/4 OR 1/2 IN VIDEO K-P
Shows a youngster offering new reflections on his ideas about life and growing up as he writes in his diary, and songs and dance illustrate his ideas.
From The Growing Up With Sandy Offenheim Series.
LC NO. 82-707059
Prod-PLAYTM Dist-BCNFL 1982

Tomorrow Is Here C 12 MIN
16MM FILM OPTICAL SOUND
Takes a look at the activities of insulation contractors.
LC NO. 76-700202
Prod-NICA Dist-NICA Prodn-AVS 1975

Tomorrow Is Maybe C 59 MIN
2 INCH VIDEOTAPE
See series title for descriptive statement.
From The Environment - Today And Tomorrow Series.
Prod-KRMATV Dist-PUBTEL

Tomorrow Is Today C 21 MIN
16MM FILM OPTICAL SOUND
Tells about the programs and services of the National Holstein Association from production testing, classification and sire summaries to procedures at the National Office in Brattleboro, Vermont and the Genetic Evaluation and Management Service and International Marketing Service of HFS, Inc.
Prod-HFAA Dist-HFAA

Tomorrow Is Too Late B 16 MIN
16MM FILM OPTICAL SOUND H-C A
A medical examination produces X-ray evidence of a lung lesion and biopsy shows a malignancy. Shows the surgical procedure for a lung cancer operation—from the removal of the ribs and excision of the upper right lobe to closure of the bronchus.
From The Doctors At Work Series.
LC NO. FIA65-1369
Prod-CMA Dist-LAWREN Prodn-LAWREN 1961

Tomorrow Mind C 22 MIN
16MM FILM OPTICAL SOUND
Looks at the research projects carried out by the General Motors Research Laboratories.
LC NO. 80-701315
Prod-GM Dist-GM Prodn-CENTRO 1980

Tomorrow Mind (German) C 22 MIN
16MM FILM OPTICAL SOUND
Looks at the research projects carried out by the General Motors Research Laboratories.
LC NO. 80-701315
Prod-GM Dist-GM Prodn-CENTRO 1980

Tomorrow Mind (Japanese) C 22 MIN
16MM FILM OPTICAL SOUND
Looks at the research projects carried out by the General Motors Research Laboratories.
LC NO. 80-701315
Prod-GM Dist-GM Prodn-CENTRO 1980

Tomorrow Mind (Spanish) C 22 MIN
16MM FILM OPTICAL SOUND
Looks at the research projects carried out by the General Motors Research Laboratories.
LC NO. 80-701315
Prod-GM Dist-GM Prodn-CENTRO 1980

Tomorrow Will Not Wait - Air, Water And Land Conservation C 13 MIN
16MM FILM OPTICAL SOUND
Cites people for befouling the air, water and soil and shows attempts by the Air Force to do something to stop pollution where possible.
LC NO. 74-705805
Prod-USAF Dist-USNAC 1970

Tomorrow/Today–A Series
J-C A
Uses a magazine format to explain new scientific research and technological innovations and their implications for the future.
Prod-KTEHTV Dist-KTEHTV

Tomorrow/Today, No. 01 029 MIN
Tomorrow/Today, No. 02 029 MIN
Tomorrow/Today, No. 03 029 MIN
Tomorrow/Today, No. 04 029 MIN
Tomorrow/Today, No. 05 029 MIN
Tomorrow/Today, No. 06 029 MIN
Tomorrow/Today, No. 07 029 MIN
Tomorrow/Today, No. 08 029 MIN
Tomorrow/Today, No. 09 029 MIN
Tomorrow/Today, No. 10 029 MIN
Tomorrow/Today, No. 11 029 MIN
Tomorrow/Today, No. 12 029 MIN
Tomorrow/Today, No. 13 029 MIN

Tomorrow/Today, No. 01 C 29 MIN
3/4 OR 1/2 INCH VIDEO CASSETTE J-C A
Segments concern ultrasonic imaging used in medicine, history of microelectronics, genetic engineering patents and comments of biologist Paul Ehrlich on the need for better public understanding of science.
From The Tomorrow/Today Series.
Prod-KTEHTV Dist-KTEHTV 1981

Tomorrow/Today, No. 02 C 29 MIN
3/4 OR 1/2 INCH VIDEO CASSETTE J-C A
Segments include non-chemical pest control, space shuttle, food additives as a possible cause of hyperactivity, Feingold Diet and Stewart Brand discussing space colonies.
From The Tomorrow/Today Series.
Prod-KTEHTV Dist-KTEHTV 1981

Tomorrow/Today, No. 03 C 29 MIN
3/4 OR 1/2 INCH VIDEO CASSETTE J-C A
Segments include Itelsat-V, the Metcalf Site archeological dig, safety hazards in electronic industries and Third World countries being exploited by earth resources satellites.
From The Tomorrow/Today Series.
Prod-KTEHTV Dist-KTEHTV 1981

Tomorrow/Today, No. 04 C 29 MIN
3/4 OR 1/2 INCH VIDEO CASSETTE J-C A
Segments feature Stanford Linear Accelerator Center and the search for sub-atomic 'quarks,' Northern Elephant Seals' recovery from near extinction, computer crime and comments of Linus Pauling.
From The Tomorrow/Today, Series.
Prod-KTEHTV Dist-KTEHTV 1981

Tomorrow/Today, No. 05 C 29 MIN
3/4 OR 1/2 INCH VIDEO CASSETTE J-C A
Segments cover experimental NASA aircraft Tiltrotor XV-15 and Quiet Shorthand Research Aircraft, photovoltaic solar energy and spinal rehabilitation methods.
From The Tomorrow/Today Series.
Prod-KTEHTV Dist-KTEHTV 1981

Tomorrow/Today, No. 06 C 29 MIN
3/4 OR 1/2 INCH VIDEO CASSETTE J-C A
Segments include Lick Observatory's search for the birth of the universe lasers used in eye surgery, welding and fusion power, recycling toxic chemicals, think tanks and self-fulfilling prophecies.
From The Tomorrow/Today Series.
Prod-KTEHTV Dist-KTEHTV 1981

Tomorrow/Today, No. 07 C 29 MIN
3/4 OR 1/2 INCH VIDEO CASSETTE J-C A
Segments include USGS efforts to predict earthquakes, independent inventors, and medical costs.
From The Tomorrow/Today Series.
Prod-KTEHTV Dist-KTEHTV 1981

Tomorrow/Today, No. 08 C 29 MIN
3/4 OR 1/2 INCH VIDEO CASSETTE J-C A
Contains segments concerning computers learning to speak and listen (speech recognition and synthesis circuits), ethanol and methanol, and a summary of Voyager missions to Saturn and Jupiter.
From The Tomorrow/Today Series.
Prod-KTEHTV Dist-KTEHTV 1981

Tomorrow/Today, No. 09 C 29 MIN
3/4 OR 1/2 INCH VIDEO CASSETTE J-C A
Features alternatives to shots and pills such as transdermal disc and time-release devices for drug delivery, computers in the classroom, and the defense factor in Bay Area electronics industries.
From The Tomorrow/Today Series.
Prod-KTEHTV Dist-KTEHTV 1981

Tomorrow/Today, No. 10 C 28 MIN
3/4 OR 1/2 INCH VIDEO CASSETTE J-C A
Features CAD/CAM computer design and manufacture, biofeedback, and Japanese semiconductor manufacturers competing for US markets.
From The Tomorrow/Today Series.
Prod-KTEHTV Dist-KTEHTV 1981

Tomorrow/Today, No. 11 C 29 MIN
3/4 OR 1/2 INCH VIDEO CASSETTE
Shows artificial intelligence in PUFF computer programs which diagnoses lung diseases, San Francisco's Exploratorium which is a hands-on science/technology museum, earthquake effects and preparedness.
From The Tomorrow/Today Series.
Prod-KTEHTV Dist-KTEHTV 1981

Tomorrow/Today, No. 12 C 29 MIN
3/4 OR 1/2 INCH VIDEO CASSETTE J-C A
Feature SP Communications competing with the Bell System for toll service, Christen Eagle Kitbuilt aerobatic biplane, and Interferon linked to Downs Syndrome.
From The Tomorrow/Today Series.
Prod-KTEHTV Dist-KTEHTV 1981

Tomorrow/Today, No. 13 C 29 MIN
3/4 OR 1/2 INCH VIDEO CASSETTE J A
Includes safety of oral contraceptives, the MFTF-B fusion experiment at Lawrence Livermore Labs, and a portrait of electronic music pioneer Bernie Krause.
From The Tomorrow/Today Series.
Prod-KTEHTV Dist-KTEHTV 1981

Tomorrow, Megalopolis C 20 MIN
3/4 INCH VIDEO CASSETTE I
Investigates the elements of a megalopolis and the need for young people to understand the problems of the future and the plans to solve them.
From The Exploring Our Nation Series.
Prod-KRMATV Dist-GPITVL 1975

Tomorrow's Beef Today C 45 MIN
16MM FILM OPTICAL SOUND
Shows how artificial insemination, blood-typing, electronic computed performance and progeny records, ultrasonic loin eye measurements, pelvic measurements and tenderness beef tests are used at the Litton Charolais Ranch.
Prod-VENARD Dist-VENARD 1967

Tomorrow's Canberra C 35 MIN
16MM FILM OPTICAL SOUND H-C A
Shows how Canberra, Australia's national capital, is being developed from a design by Chicago architect Walter Burley Griffin.
LC NO. 73-702491
Prod-FLMAUS Dist-AUIS 1973

Tomorrow's Child C 52 MIN
16MM FILM OPTICAL SOUND C A
Describes the experiments being done with frozen embryos to produce a test tube baby at the Queen Victoria Medical Centre in Melbourne, Australia by the Monash University Medical Team. Discusses the ethical aspects of the experiments.
Prod-NOMDFI Dist-LANDMK 1982

Tomorrow's Child C 48 MIN
3/4 OR 1/2 INCH VIDEO CASSETTE
Presents the story behind the latest advances in test-tube baby techniques, revealing the human and scientific aspects in embryo transfers.
Prod-NOMDFI Dist-LANDMK Prodn-KPG

Tomorrow's Children B 55 MIN
16MM FILM OPTICAL SOUND
Tells how a young woman about to get married finds herself under pressure from townspeople, who consider her a derelict and insist that she be sterilized so that she won't have any unacceptable children. Directed by Bryan Foy, Jr.
Prod-UNKNWN Dist-REELIM 1934

Tomorrow's Children (Rev Ed) C 17 MIN
16MM FILM - VIDEO, ALL FORMATS J-C A
Deals with the issue of population growth. Shows the problem of overpopulation and the need for birth control.
Prod-MAYERH Dist-PEREN

Tomorrow's Children (Rev Ed) (Spanish) C 17 MIN
16MM FILM - VIDEO, ALL FORMATS J-C A
Deals with the issue of population growth. Shows the problem of overpopulation and the need for birth control.
Prod-MAYERH Dist-PEREN

Tomorrow's Customers C 34 MIN
16MM FILM - 3/4 IN VIDEO IND
Discusses the importance of innovative marketing as a means of reaching tomorrow's customers. Examines how consumerism and environmental awareness affect the market place.
From The Managing Discontinuity Series.
Prod-BNA Dist-BNA

Tomorrow's Drivers B 10 MIN
16MM FILM OPTICAL SOUND
Records what one city is doing to solve the problem of tomorrow's (and today's) drivers, narrated by James Stewart.
Prod-GM Dist-GM

Tomorrow's Energy Today C 33 MIN
16MM FILM, 3/4 OR 1/2 IN VIDEO J-C A
Describes a number of successful attempts to obtain energy from renewable sources. Shows how alternative energy sources can be combined with conventional fossil fuels and established energy systems and how dependency on fossil fuels can be alleviated by adopting unconventional ways to use them.
Prod-NFBC Dist-NFBC 1981

Tomorrow's Families–A Series
H-C A
Uses the stories of a group of young adults to illustrate the physical, emotional, and economic aspects of childhood. Narrated by Greg Morris.
Prod-MSDOE Dist-AITECH 1980

Caring For The Infant 029 MIN
Decision For Nonparenthood, The 029 MIN
Decision For Parenthood, The 029 MIN
Economic Factors In The Parenthood Decision 029 MIN
Emotional Development Of The Infant 029 MIN
Family Adapts, The 029 MIN
First Trimester, The 029 MIN
First Year In Review, The 029 MIN
Help For Families 029 MIN
Infant's Hospital Experience, The 029 MIN
Intellectual Development Of The Infant 029 MIN
Labor And Delivery 029 MIN
Medical Care During Pregnancy 029 MIN
New Family Homecoming, The 029 MIN
Newborn, The 029 MIN
Parents' Hospital Experience, The 029 MIN
Physical Development Of The Infant 029 MIN
Physical Factors In The Parenthood Decision 029 MIN
Pregnancy Occurs 029 MIN
Preparation For Homecoming 029 MIN
Role Of Others, The 029 MIN
Role Of The Father, The 029 MIN
Role Of The Mother, The 029 MIN
Second Trimester, The 029 MIN
Self-Awareness And The Prospective Parent 029 MIN
Social Development Of The Infant 029 MIN
Social Factors In The Parenthood Decision 029 MIN
Special Homecoming, The 029 MIN
Stress And The New Family 029 MIN
Third Trimester, The 029 MIN

Tomorrow's Leaders C 30 MIN
3/4 OR 1/2 INCH VIDEO CASSETTE P-I
See series title for descriptive statement.
From The Sonrisas Series.
Prod-KRLNTV Dist-MDCPB

Tomorrow's Leaders C 30 MIN
3/4 INCH VIDEO CASSETTE
Shows a high school drama group performing in a series of dramatizations of their own creation on the topic of sexism, along with role reversal techniques.
Prod-WMENIF Dist-WMENIF

Tomorrow's Newspaper B 11 MIN
16MM FILM OPTICAL SOUND J-C A
Portrays the oppressive day-by-day life of a small newspaper boy as he is shaped prematurely into an adult by the sordid events in the world which he cannot understand.
LC NO. 72-700401
Prod-ZAGREB Dist-MMA 1971

Tomorrow's Oil Today C 16 MIN
16MM FILM, 3/4 OR 1/2 IN VIDEO
Describes the role of the Bartlesville Energy Technology Center and the U S Department of Energy in the development of enhanced oirecovery and improved drilling technology. Includes animation.
Prod-USDOE Dist-USNAC 1983

Tomorrow's People C 17 MIN
16MM FILM - 3/4 IN VIDEO
Presents mountain music, accompanied by a visual essay on Appalachian people and places.
Prod-APPAL Dist-APPAL

Tomorrow's Power - Today C 6 MIN
16MM FILM OPTICAL SOUND
Introduces the fundamentals of atomic power. Describes the advantages of nuclear power and considers how it is used to generate electricity.
LC NO. FIE66-150
Prod-USAEC Dist-USNAC Prodn-ANL 1964

Tomorrow's Quake C 16 MIN
16MM FILM, 3/4 OR 1/2 IN VIDEO
Explores the feasibility of earthquake prediction. Uses live action and animation to explain continental drift, dilatency, plate tectonics, earthquake waves and seismic velocity changes.
Prod-HALLL Dist-AMEDFL 1977

Tomorrow's Scientists At Argonne C 14 MIN
3/4 INCH VIDEO CASSETTE
Shows the winners of the USAEC Special Award at the Argonne National Laboratory during their nuclear research orientation week. Includes highlights of science projects, scenes of research and development facilities at Argonne and a discussion of the challenges that await young scientists.
Prod-USNAC Dist-USNAC 1972

Tomorrow's Television - Get What You Like Or Like What You Get B 62 MIN
16MM FILM OPTICAL SOUND H-C
Shows how the competitive struggle between various segments of the communication industry inhibits and influences what is shown on television.
LC NO. 70-706848
Prod-NET Dist-IU 1970

Tomorrow's Tools C 30 MIN
3/4 OR 1/2 INCH VIDEO CASSETTE
See series title for descriptive statement.
From The Third Wave Series.
Prod-TRIWVE Dist-DELTAK

Tomorrow's World C 24 MIN
16MM FILM - VIDEO, ALL FORMATS J-C A
Shows how Mexico, Algeria and Thailand are working to control the rate of population growth.
Prod-UN Dist-PEREN

Tomorrow's Yesterday C 29 MIN
16MM FILM OPTICAL SOUND I-C A
Presents a documentary on Amerian Indians, as they were, as they are, and as they hope to be, emphasizing the positive things they are doing to improve their circumstances and prepare themselves to live in a modern world.
LC NO. 73-700090
Prod-BYU Dist-BYU 1972

Tomorrow's Yesterday C 30 MIN
3/4 INCH VIDEO CASSETTE
Shows how the Pueblo people adapt to the challenges of modern civilization while maintaining their identity and culture. Also available in two-inch quad and one-inch videotape.
Prod-KBYU Dist-NAMPBC

Tomten, The C 8 MIN
16MM FILM, 3/4 OR 1/2 IN VIDEO K-P
Reveals that at a lonely old farmhouse on a crisp winter night everyone is sleeping except old Tomten, the troll. Shows that Tomten goes about comforting the animals in his silent language. Based on the book The Tomten by Astrid Lindgren.
Prod-WWS Dist-WWS Prodn-SCHNDL 1982

Tone Color C 10 MIN
16MM FILM OPTICAL SOUND K-P
Presents an explanation of various tone colors in music.
Prod-CEMREL Dist-VIP 1974

Tone Color C 15 MIN
3/4 OR 1/2 INCH VIDEO CASSETTE P
Discusses the basics of sound recognition.
From The Music Machine Series.
Prod-INDIPS Dist-GPITVL 1981

Tone Production, Vibrato And Dynamics C 29 MIN
2 INCH VIDEOTAPE
See series title for descriptive statement.
From The Playing The Guitar I Series.
Prod-KCET Dist-PUBTEL

Tone Tales C 10 MIN
3/4 OR 1/2 INCH VIDEO CASSETTE K-P
Focuses on the ability to associate stories and characters with orchestral music and single instruments.
From The Book, Look And Listen Series.
Prod-MDDE Dist-AITECH 1977

Tonga Royal (Tonga) C 20 MIN
16MM FILM, 3/4 OR 1/2 IN VIDEO J-C A
Views the Pacific island kingdom of Tonga. Shows the natural beauty, the people and the ceremonies of the island.
From The Village Life Series.
Prod-JPFLM Dist-JOU Prodn-TAW 1977

Tongpan B 63 MIN
16MM FILM OPTICAL SOUND H-C
A Thai language film with English subtitles. Uses the story of a poverty-stricken farmer in Northeast Thailand to depict political conditions there in the mid-1970's. Tells how the farmer loses his land when a hydroelectric dam cuts off his water supply, forcing him to support his family with menial jobs. Shows how his life drastically changes when he meets a student who involves him in a seminar to discuss the possibility of another hydroelectric project.
LC NO. 79-701023
Prod-ISANFG Dist-ISANFG 1979

Tongue, Teeth, Jaws And Lips B 20 MIN
2 INCH VIDEOTAPE P
Presents reasons for speaking distinctly and well. (Broadcast quality)
From The Language Lane Series. Lesson 4
Prod-CVETVC Dist-GPITVL Prodn-WCVETV

Tongues C 20 MIN
3/4 OR 1/2 INCH VIDEO CASSETTE
Prod-EAI Dist-EAI

Tongues Of Fire C 28 MIN
16MM FILM OPTICAL SOUND J-C A
Presents the story of a Hawaiian woman who defies pagan superstition of her people and reaffirms faith of the natives and a young missionary couple. Interprets Christianity as a faith that has hope at its base.
Prod-CAFM Dist-CAFM

Tongues Of Men, Pt 1 - Disaster At Babel C 58 MIN
16MM FILM - 3/4 IN VIDEO
Examines how and why so many languages came about. Explores Noam Chomsky's 'universalist' approach to language, which suggests that language has universal components which far outweigh the differences between tongues.
From The Nova Series.
Prod-BBCTV Dist-PBS 1977

Tongues Of Men, Pt 2 - A World Language C 58 MIN
16MM FILM - 3/4 IN VIDEO
Investigates the attempts man has made to cope with the confusion caused by the use of many languages. Points out that in the past Latin and French have been bids for a universal language, but have been superceded by idiomatic American-English, which is used by over two-fifths of the human race and has become the obligatory second language of the world.
From The Nova Series.
Prod-BBCTV Dist-PBS 1977

Toni Morrison C 28 MIN
16MM FILM, 3/4 OR 1/2 IN VIDEO
Describes the life and work of black author Toni Morrison.
From The Writer In America Series.
Prod-PERSPF Dist-CORF

Tonio Kroger B 88 MIN
16MM FILM OPTICAL SOUND
Depicts a writer-hero's feelings as he travels to southern Italy to visit the homeland of his mother.
Prod-CON Dist-TRANSW 1965

Tonometry C 9 MIN
16MM FILM OPTICAL SOUND
Shows step-by-step procedures of using a Schiotz tonometer to measure intraocular pressure. Discusses basic components of the Schiotz tonometer.
From The Medical Skills Library Series.
LC NO. 74-702523
Prod-AMCP Dist-SUTHLA Prodn-MEDEX 1974

Tonometry C 16 MIN
16MM FILM OPTICAL SOUND PRO
Depicts two methods of conducting glaucoma tests, using the Schiotz tenometer and using an electronic tonographer. Explains the effects of pressure on eye functions, stresses the importance of sterilizing equipment and shows how to calibrate instruments and record test results.
LC NO. 78-700892
Prod-USA Dist-USNAC 1977

Tonometry C 9 MIN
3/4 OR 1/2 INCH VIDEO CASSETTE PRO
See series title for descriptive statement.
From The Medical Skills Films Series.
Prod-WFP Dist-WFP

Tonsillectomy B 16 MIN
16MM FILM OPTICAL SOUND H-C A
A doctor explains the necessity for the removal of a child's adenoids and tonsils. Describes the emotional preparation of the child for hospitalization. Follows the doctor as he performs the operation.
LC NO. FIA65-1370
Prod-CMA Dist-LAWREN Prodn-LAWREN 1961

Tonsillectomy And Adenoidectomy C
3/4 OR 1/2 INCH VIDEO CASSETTE
Explains what the tonsils and adenoids are, what they do and under what conditions it is advisable to remove either one or both. Describes the surgical procedures.
Prod-MIFE Dist-MIFE

Tonsillectomy And Adenoidectomy (Arabic) C
3/4 OR 1/2 INCH VIDEO CASSETTE
Explains what the tonsils and adenoids are, what they do and under what conditions it is advisable to remove either one or both. Describes the surgical procedures.
Prod-MIFE Dist-MIFE

Tonsils And Adenoids C 9 MIN
16MM FILM, 3/4 OR 1/2 IN VIDEO A
Informs parents about the anatomy and function of children's tonsils and adenoids, reasons for surgery, and telling children about surgery. Reviews hospital and home care and the parent's role in reassuring the child.
Prod-PRORE Dist-PRORE

Tony And The Election C 6 MIN
16MM FILM, 3/4 OR 1/2 IN VIDEO I
See series title for descriptive statement.
From The Being Friends Series.
Prod-USDHEW Dist-USNAC

Tony Bennett C 58 MIN
3/4 OR 1/2 INCH VIDEO CASSETTE
See series title for descriptive statement.
From The Evening At Pops Series.
Prod-WGBHTV Dist-PBS 1978

Tony Fontane Story, The C 80 MIN
16MM FILM OPTICAL SOUND
Tells the story of Tony Fontane, a singer. Discusses the role of Christ in his life.
Prod-YOUTH Dist-GF

Tony Oursler - Evol C 28 MIN
3/4 OR 1/2 INCH VIDEO CASSETTE
Features primitive psychoanalytic 'bad boy' actings.
Prod-CAT Dist-ARTINC

Tony Oursler - Son Of Oil C 18 MIN
3/4 OR 1/2 INCH VIDEO CASSETTE
Contains primitive psychoanalytic 'bad boy' actings.
Prod-ARTINC Dist-ARTINC

Tony Oursler - The Weak Bullet C 14 MIN
3/4 OR 1/2 INCH VIDEO CASSETTE
Presents an expressionistic reverie. Incorporates phantasmagoric sets.
Prod-ARTINC Dist-ARTINC

Tony Westman C
3/4 OR 1/2 INCH VIDEO CASSETTE
Portrays Tony Westman, British Columbian filmmaker with interviews and film clips.
From The Filmmakers' Showcase Series.
Prod-CANFDW Dist-CANFDW

Too Far, Too Fast C 20 MIN
16MM FILM, 3/4 OR 1/2 IN VIDEO J-C
Visits a new development in the town of Oita, a scheme designed to attract industries to areas away from the overcrowded East Coast of Japan. Discusses the environmental problems created by the development. Examines the future of Japan and asks if the system will be able to adjust to the probably inevitable task of slowing things down.
From The Japan - The Crowded Islands Series.
Prod-BBCTV Dist-FI 1982

Too Few...Too Far...To Matter C 12 MIN
16MM FILM OPTICAL SOUND
Depicts the problems of rural health delivery systems in Montana, New Mexico and South Dakota. Explains the contrast between rural and urban health delivery systems, especially as it relates to services for developmental disabilities.
LC NO. 78-701617
Prod-USDDIS Dist-USNAC Prodn-FINTO 1978

Too Good To Miss - Suggestions For Summer Reading B 20 MIN
2 INCH VIDEOTAPE I
Mentions the books that children themselves pick as the best. (Broadcast quality)
From The Quest For The Best Series.
Prod-DENVPS Dist-GPITVL Prodn-KRMATV

Too Late For Questions C 20 MIN
3/4 OR 1/2 INCH VIDEO CASSETTE IND
Describes survival equipment and its use upon abandonment of a marine tanker vessel. Details lifeboats and rafts and the gear found on them.
Prod-TEXACO Dist-UTEXPE

Too Late To Wait C 28 MIN
16MM FILM OPTICAL SOUND J-C A
Features an unrehearsed rap session with a group of black students and closes with an explanation of how anyone can know Christ personally.
LC NO. 73-701572
Prod-CCFC Dist-CCFC 1972

Too Many Bozos C 6 MIN
16MM FILM, 3/4 OR 1/2 IN VIDEO P
Tells the story of a boy who tries out several kinds of pets before he finds just the right one.
From The Golden Book Storytime Series.
Prod-MTI Dist-MTI 1977

Too Many Elephants C 25 MIN
16MM FILM, 3/4 OR 1/2 IN VIDEO H-C A
Features scientists who investigate the migrations and feeding habits of elephants in the Serengeti area. Examines questions of behavior and ecology.
From The Behavior And Survival Series.
Prod-MGHT Dist-MGHT 1973

Too Many Geeziks - Problem Solving And Predicting Patterns C 14 MIN
3/4 OR 1/2 INCH VIDEO CASSETTE P
Describes a package containing rapidly reproducing creatures in order to discuss techniques of problem solving.
From The Math Country Series.
Prod-KYTV Dist-AITECH 1979

Too Many People C 8 MIN
16MM FILM, 3/4 OR 1/2 IN VIDEO P-J
Describes the problem of population growth in terms that a child can understand. Depicts the results of overpopulation in traffic, litter and pollution. Illustrates zero population growth as the answer.
From The Caring About Our Community Series.
Prod-GORKER Dist-AIMS 1973

Too Much Month Left At The End Of The Money C 20 MIN
3/4 INCH VIDEO CASSETTE J-H
Presents a dramatization of a family with money problems, illustrating how a lack of planning affects the economical and emotional well-being of a family.
From The Dollar Data Series.
LC NO. 81-707353
Prod-WHROTV Dist-GPITVL 1974

Too Much Noise C 15 MIN
3/4 OR 1/2 INCH VIDEO CASSETTE K-P
Introduces an old man who is beleaguered by the normal noises of his daily life. Tells what happens when a wise man advises him to get noisy animals such as a cow, a hen, a dog and finally a cat.
From The Words And Pictures Series.
Prod-FI Dist-FI

Too Much Of A Good Thing C 13 MIN
16MM FILM, 3/4 OR 1/2 IN VIDEO I
Shows how different TV viewing habits have enormous consequences for people throughout their lives.
From The Learning Laws - Respect For Yourself, Others And The Law Series.
Prod-WDEMCO Dist-WDEMCO 1982

Too Much Off The Top C 6 MIN
16MM FILM, 3/4 OR 1/2 IN VIDEO K-I
Tells how Paddington Bear takes a job in a barber shop. Based on chapter six of the book Paddington At Work by Michael Bond.
From The Paddington Bear, Series 1 Series.
LC NO. 80-707228
Prod-BONDM Dist-FLMFR Prodn-FILMF 1977

Too Much, Too Little C 25 MIN
3/4 OR 1/2 INCH VIDEO CASSETTE H-C
Traces the history of the U S monetary and banking system and the events that led Congress to establish the Federal Reserve System designed to regulate the balance between too much and too little. Makes clear how the money supply affects the national economy with engravings, photographs, newsreel footage and dramatizations. Includes story of two modern teenagers involved in buying and selling a car.
Prod-FRBS Dist-AITECH

Too Proud To Beg C 29 MIN
2 INCH VIDEOTAPE
See series title for descriptive statement.

From The Our Street Series.
Prod-MDCPB Dist-PUBTEL

Too Splendid To Lose C 29 MIN
16MM FILM, 3/4 OR 1/2 IN VIDEO
Illustrates the architectural and structural restoration of the California State Capitol.
Prod-UCEMC Dist-UCEMC

Too Tough To Care C 18 MIN
16MM FILM, 3/4 OR 1/2 IN VIDEO I-J
Delivers an anti-smoking message by telling about the Finster Tobacco Company who must find an advertising theme they can use to hook kids on smoking and combat all this talk about lung cancer, heart disease and respiratory illness.
Prod-PARKRD Dist-LAWREN

Too Young To Burn C 26 MIN
16MM FILM OPTICAL SOUND
Focuses on how to teach children about fire and emphasizes the necessity of pre-school education, protection and discipline by parents.
Prod-LAFIRE Dist-LAFIRE

Too Young To Say C 15 MIN
16MM FILM OPTICAL SOUND
Demonstrates the use of the audiometer as a means of determining the threshold of hearing for the very young child.
LC NO. FIA56-1238
Prod-USC Dist-USC 1955

Tool Bound Behavior C 20 MIN
3/4 INCH VIDEO CASSETTE PRO
Presents tool behavior as the first of five components of skill development within an apprenticeship model of occupational behavior. Defines all five components and applies them to the teaching-learning process. Narrated by Cynthia Heard.
Prod-AOTA Dist-AOTA 1977

Tool Box I, The C 30 MIN
3/4 OR 1/2 INCH VIDEO CASSETTE
Discusses various tools used in home repair.
From The You Can Fixit Series.
Prod-WRJATV Dist-MDCPB

Tool Box II, The C 30 MIN
3/4 OR 1/2 INCH VIDEO CASSETTE
Discusses various tools used in home repair.
From The You Can Fixit Series.
Prod-WRJATV Dist-MDCPB

Tool Movie, The C 12 MIN
16MM FILM, 3/4 OR 1/2 IN VIDEO P-I
Presents a humorous history of the evolution of tools from the days of the caveman to the 1970's.
Prod-JACOBL Dist-AIMS Prodn-JACOBL 1976

Tool Sharpening C 12 MIN
3/4 OR 1/2 INCH VIDEO CASSETTE
Covers the reasons for sharpening tools and various methods such as whetstones, using a bench grinder and othe sharpening methods.
From The Using Portable Power Tool Series.
Prod-TPCTRA Dist-TPCTRA

Tool Sharpening (Spanish) C 12 MIN
3/4 OR 1/2 INCH VIDEO CASSETTE
Covers the reasons for sharpening tools and various methods such as whetstones, using a bench grinder and other sharpening methods.
From The Using Portable Power Tools Series.
Prod-TPCTRA Dist-TPCTRA

Tool Users, The C 14 MIN
16MM FILM, 3/4 OR 1/2 IN VIDEO I-H
Shows how animals are tool users with examples of the weaver ant constructing his home, the finch pecking for food and the chimpanzee assembling and using a simple tool.
From The Animal Behavior Series.
LC NO. 80-706273
Prod-NGS Dist-NGS 1975

Tool Using C 23 MIN
16MM FILM, 3/4 OR 1/2 IN VIDEO H-C A
Shows how the adult male chimpanzee makes and uses tools and how the young prepare for these tasks in the way they play with objects, learning through observation and imitation. Includes views of chimpanzees using sticks and stones as weapons against baboons.
From The Jane Goodall - Studies Of The Chimpanzee Series.
LC NO. 80-706275
Prod-NGS Dist-NGS 1976

Toolbox Ballet C 8 MIN
3/4 INCH VIDEO CASSETTE P
Shows various tools performing a ballet in which each tool's individual dance mimics its function.
Prod-NBCTV Dist-GA

Toolmaker's Art, The C 19 MIN
16MM FILM OPTICAL SOUND J-C A
Shows how the tool, die and machining industry works and presents the professionals who make it run. Features an explanation of the career opportunities open to young people.
Prod-NATTDP Dist-MTP

Toolmaker's Vise (Advanced) C
3/4 OR 1/2 INCH VIDEO CASSETTE
See series title for descriptive statement.
From The Blueprint Reading Series.
Prod-VTRI Dist-VTRI

Toolmaker's Vise (Advanced) (Spanish) C
3/4 OR 1/2 INCH VIDEO CASSETTE
See series title for descriptive statement.
From The Blueprint Reading (Spanish) Series.
Prod-VTRI Dist-VTRI

Tools C 6 MIN
16MM FILM, 3/4 OR 1/2 IN VIDEO
Illustrates that the use of sophisticated tools requires special safety precautions.
From The Safety And You Series.
Prod-FILCOM Dist-FILCOM

Tools For Research C 40 MIN
16MM FILM, 3/4 OR 1/2 IN VIDEO
Raises the curtain on the research industry and its treatment of animals. Looks at who suffers and who profits. Attempts to interview researchers who were reluctant to talk on the topic of research treatment of animals.
Prod-LIBANI Dist-BULFRG 1983

Tools For Sketching C 29 MIN
3/4 INCH VIDEO CASSETTE C A
Discusses some common tools used in sketching. Explains advantages of some tools over others. Includes use of color and variety of media.
From The Sketching Techniques Series. Lesson 23
Prod-COAST Dist-CDTEL

Tools For The Beginning Carpenter C 60 MIN
1/2 IN VIDEO CASSETTE BETA/VHS IND
Explains the basic tools needed for the beginning carpenter's tool box, including striking tools, measuring tools, cutting tools, fastening tools and miscellaneous specialty tools.
Prod-RMI Dist-RMI

Tools Of Ethnomusicology B 27 MIN
16MM FILM OPTICAL SOUND PRO
Features a television program of non-western music.
Prod-UCLA Dist-UCLA

Tools Of Ignorance C 26 MIN
16MM FILM OPTICAL SOUND I-C A
Presents Johnny Bench discussing his job as All-Star catcher of the Cincinnati Reds and clarifies how the 'MEN BEHIND THE PLATE' have stepped into the limelight in recent years, overcoming the stigma of the 'TOOLS OF IGNORANCE,' an expression referring to the specialized gear worn by catchers.
LC NO. 72-702514
Prod-SFI Dist-SFI 1972

Tools Of Job Hunting C 30 MIN
3/4 OR 1/2 INCH VIDEO CASSETTE H-C A
Emphasizes the things the job seeker should know, have and do before wading into the job market.
From The Kirby Stanat On Jobs Series.
Prod-SUMITP Dist-GPITVL 1983

Tools Of The Trade C 30 MIN
3/4 INCH VIDEO CASSETTE
See series title for descriptive statement.
From The Woodcarver's Workshop Series.
Prod-WOSUTV Dist-PUBTEL

Tools Of Writing C 30 MIN
3/4 OR 1/2 INCH VIDEO CASSETTE A
Focuses on teaching effective writing to office workers. Emphasizes the importance of being clear, correct, concise and complete. Hosted by Cicely Tyson.
From The Writing For Work Series. Pt 1
LC NO. 81-706735
Prod-TIMLIF Dist-TIMLIF 1981

Tools That Shaped America C
16MM FILM OPTICAL SOUND
Sketches the early history of the most basic tools, focusing on the grinding wheel. Discusses new types of grinding wheels and safety measures.
Prod-CINE Dist-GWI

Toot, Whistle, Plunk And Boom C 10 MIN
16MM FILM, 3/4 OR 1/2 IN VIDEO I-H A
Animated cartoons show origin and development of the four classes of musical instruments in a modern symphony--horns, woodwinds, strings and percussion.
Prod-DISNEY Dist-WDEMCO 1959

Tooth Truth With Harv And Marv C 11 MIN
16MM FILM, 3/4 OR 1/2 IN VIDEO P
Show Harv and Marv as they visit a dentist's office and listen as Debbie and Jimmy learn the correct way to brush and floss their teeth and its importance to their future health.
Prod-HIGGIN Dist-HIGGIN 1976

Toothbrushing - The Bass Method (Rev Ed) C 9 MIN
3/4 OR 1/2 INCH VIDEO CASSETTE
Describes the Bass toothbrushing technique, emphasizing effective removal of bacterial plaque through frequent toothbrushing. Demonstrates the technique on both a typodont and in the mouth of a patient. Shows changes in brush position and grip needed to reach all tooth surfaces.
Prod-USVA Dist-USNAC 1981

Toothbrushing - The Circular Scrub Method (Rev Ed) C 7 MIN
3/4 OR 1/2 INCH VIDEO CASSETTE
Demonstrates effective removal of bacterial plaque through proper toothbrushing. Describes the circular scrub method using a soft multi-tufted toothbrush. Emphasizes changes in brush position and grip necessary for adequate cleaning of the various tooth surfaces.
Prod-USVA Dist-USNAC 1981

Toothbrushing With Charlie Brown C 5 MIN
16MM FILM, 3/4 OR 1/2 IN VIDEO
Features Charlie Brown teaching Linus and Snoopy how to brush their teeth properly.
Prod-AMDA Dist-AMDA 1978

Toothpaste Millionaire, The C 15 MIN
3/4 OR 1/2 INCH VIDEO CASSETTE I
Tells a story about moneymaking that shows toothpaste sales is big business. From the book by Jean Merrill.
From The Book Bird Series.
Prod-CTI Dist-CTI

Toothpicks C 4 MIN
16MM FILM OPTICAL SOUND P-I
Shows the many uses of the toothpick, from hors d'oeuvres to sculptures.
From The Mini Movies - Springboard For Learning - Unit 2, What Do We Series.
LC NO. 76-703095
Prod-MORLAT Dist-MORLAT 1975

Toots Thielman C 58 MIN
3/4 OR 1/2 INCH VIDEO CASSETTE
See series title for descriptive statement.
From The Evening At Pops Series.
Prod-WGBHTV Dist-PBS 1978

Top And Bottom Of Our Nation, The B 6 MIN
16MM FILM OPTICAL SOUND
Presents a 1956 Screen News Digest film excerpt showing how Death Valley is below sea level and the High Sierras surrounding it which are the lowest and highest points in the U S. Portrays the once important a post era includes Mt Whitney and other picturesque crops.
From The News Magazine Of The Screen Series. Vol 6 No. 6
Prod-PATHE Dist-HEARST 1956

Top Axe C 24 MIN
16MM FILM OPTICAL SOUND
Presents an account of the world's chopping and sawing championships.
LC NO. 80-700929
Prod-TASCOR Dist-TASCOR 1974

Top End C 16 MIN
16MM FILM OPTICAL SOUND H-C A
Studies four people who either own their own farms or work on the land in Australia's northern territory.
LC NO. 73-709832
Prod-ANAIB Dist-AUIS 1970

Top Of Europe B 22 MIN
16MM FILM OPTICAL SOUND
Illustrates the life of the lapps on the north cape of Sweden.
Prod-ASI Dist-AUDPLN

Top Of The Line C 30 MIN
3/4 OR 1/2 INCH VIDEO CASSETTE J-H
Helps young people learn to 'pay their dues' in order to achieve their aspirations. States that in addition to dreaming big dreams and getting excited about a bright future, one must also perform seemingly mundane but necessary tasks in a capable, committed and conscientious manner.
From The Y E S Inc Series.
Prod-KCET Dist-GPITVL 1983

Top Of The World - Taiga, Tundra And Ice Cap (Captioned) C 20 MIN
16MM FILM, 3/4 OR 1/2 IN VIDEO I-H
Explores the remote areas of Canada, Siberia and Alaska. Shows how early inhabitants adapted to isolation and ponders effects of pollution and pipelines.
Prod-LCOA Dist-LCOA 1972

Top Of The World, The - Taiga, Tundra And Ice Cap C 19 MIN
16MM FILM, 3/4 OR 1/2 IN VIDEO I-C A
Shows the geographical characteristics and types of natural life to be found in the world's three northern-most regions, Canada, Siberia and Alaska. Suggests what the consequences might be should man seek to exploit the area's resources without sufficient concern for land and the balance of nature.
From The Comparative Cultures And Geography Series.
Prod-LCOA Dist-LCOA 1972

Top Priority C 10 MIN
16MM FILM, 3/4 OR 1/2 IN VIDEO H-C A
Relates a family's joy when a long-awaited truck carrying irrigation equipment for their dying farm is finally seen approaching on the horizon. Shows their bitter disappointment when it turns out to be an Army truck delivering missiles. Examines the dilemma of man's basic needs being neglected while huge sums of money are earmarked for war.
LC NO. 83-706683
Prod-NFBC Dist-EBEC 1982

Topanga, Liberty And Mulholland Fires C 20 MIN
16MM FILM OPTICAL SOUND
Shows footage of various fires in the Malibu area in Southern California in 1958. Without narration.
Prod-LAFIRE Dist-LAFIRE

Topeka Is A People Place C 26 MIN
16MM FILM OPTICAL SOUND
Uses pictures, sound effects, music and occasional words to show various aspects that make Topeka, Kansas an enjoyable city in which to live.
LC NO. 74-711543
Prod-SWBELL Dist-SWBELL 1970

Topic Sentence B 30 MIN
2 INCH VIDEOTAPE J-H
Introduces expository writing and shows the value of the topic sentence. (Broadcast quality)
From The English Composition Series. Exposition
Prod-GRETVO Dist-GPITVL Prodn-KUHTTV

Topical Anesthesia For Endoscopic Examination Of The Upper And Lower Airways C 16 MIN
3/4 OR 1/2 INCH VIDEO CASSETTE PRO

Demonstrates the administration of topical anesthesia for an endoscopic examination by either the transnasal or transoral route. Emphasizes the material used, sequence of administration and precautions observed when using lidocaine.
Prod-USVA Dist-USNAC

Topical Fluorides For Caries Prevention C 10 MIN
16MM FILM OPTICAL SOUND PRO
Presents a story from bench to field of topical fluorides in caries prevention. Emphasizes fluoride mouth rinse and economy when used.
LC NO. 77-700088
Prod-NMAC Dist-USNAC 1975

Topical Fluorides For Caries Prevention C 10 MIN
3/4 INCH VIDEO CASSETTE
Discusses topical fluorides in caries prevention. Emphasizes fluoride mouth rinse and shows self-application by school children. Includes laboratory techniques and experiments used in the development of available agents and gives the results of studies of such agents.
LC NO. 78-706046
Prod-NIDR Dist-USNAC 1978

Topographic Anatomy Of Articular Sites, Pt 1 - General And Axial C 20 MIN
16MM FILM, 3/4 OR 1/2 IN VIDEO C A
See series title for descriptive statement.
From The Skeletal And Topographic Anatomy Series.
Prod-UTEXMH Dist-TEF

Topographic Anatomy Of Articular Sites, Pt 2 - Appendicular (Upper Extremity) C 19 MIN
16MM FILM, 3/4 OR 1/2 IN VIDEO C A
See series title for descriptive statement.
From The Skeletal And Topographic Anatomy Series.
Prod-UTEXMH Dist-TEF

Topographic Anatomy Of Articular Sites, Pt 3 - Appendicular (Lower Extremity) C 20 MIN
16MM FILM, 3/4 OR 1/2 IN VIDEO C A
See series title for descriptive statement.
From The Skeletal And Topographic Anatomy Series.
Prod-UTEXMH Dist-TEF

Topographic Anatomy Of The Abdomen C 18 MIN
16MM FILM, 3/4 OR 1/2 IN VIDEO C A
See series title for descriptive statement.
From The Skeletal And Topographic Anatomy Series.
Prod-UTEXMH Dist-TEF

Topographic Anatomy Of The Back C 20 MIN
16MM FILM, 3/4 OR 1/2 IN VIDEO C A
See series title for descriptive statement.
From The Skeletal And Topographic Anatomy Series.
Prod-UTEXMH Dist-TEF

Topographic Anatomy Of The Head And Neck, Pt 1 - The Neck C 17 MIN
16MM FILM, 3/4 OR 1/2 IN VIDEO C A
See series title for descriptive statement.
From The Skeletal And Topographic Anatomy Series.
Prod-UTEXMH Dist-TEF

Topographic Anatomy Of The Head And Neck, Pt 2 - The Face C 12 MIN
16MM FILM, 3/4 OR 1/2 IN VIDEO C A
See series title for descriptive statement.
From The Skeletal And Topographic Anatomy Series.
Prod-UTEXMH Dist-TEF

Topographic Anatomy Of The Head And Neck, Pt 3 - The Cranium C 20 MIN
16MM FILM, 3/4 OR 1/2 IN VIDEO C A
See series title for descriptive statement.
From The Skeletal And Topographic Anatomy Series.
Prod-UTEXMH Dist-TEF

Topographic Anatomy Of The Head And Neck, Pt 4 - The Oral Cavity C 19 MIN
16MM FILM, 3/4 OR 1/2 IN VIDEO C A
See series title for descriptive statement.
From The Skeletal And Topographic Anatomy Series.
Prod-UTEXMH Dist-TEF

Topographic Anatomy Of The Lower Extremity, Pt 1 - Femoral, Gluteal And Popliteal Regions C 17 MIN
16MM FILM, 3/4 OR 1/2 IN VIDEO C A
See series title for descriptive statement.
From The Skeletal And Topographic Anatomy Series.
Prod-UTEXMH Dist-TEF

Topographic Anatomy Of The Lower Extremity, Pt 2 - Knee, Leg, Ankle And Foot C 18 MIN
16MM FILM, 3/4 OR 1/2 IN VIDEO C A
See series title for descriptive statement.
From The Skeletal And Topographic Anatomy Series.
Prod-UTEXMH Dist-TEF

Topographic Anatomy Of The Pelvis, Perineum And Inguinal Regions C 18 MIN
16MM FILM, 3/4 OR 1/2 IN VIDEO C A
See series title for descriptive statement.
From The Skeletal And Topographic Anatomy Series.
Prod-UTEXMH Dist-TEF

Topographic Anatomy Of The Thorax, Pt 1 - External Features C 19 MIN
16MM FILM, 3/4 OR 1/2 IN VIDEO C A
See series title for descriptive statement.
From The Skeletal And Topographic Anatomy Series.
Prod-UTEXMH Dist-TEF

Topographic Anatomy Of The Thorax, Pt 2 - Internal Features C 19 MIN
16MM FILM, 3/4 OR 1/2 IN VIDEO C A
See series title for descriptive statement.
From The Skeletal And Topographic Anatomy Series.
Prod-UTEXMH Dist-TEF

Topographic Anatomy Of The Upper And Lower Extremities - Nerve Injury C 22 MIN
16MM FILM, 3/4 OR 1/2 IN VIDEO C A
See series title for descriptive statement.
From The Skeletal And Topographic Anatomy Series.
Prod-UTEXMH Dist-TEF

Topographic Anatomy Of The Upper Extremity, Shoulder, Axilla, Arm And Elbow C 15 MIN
16MM FILM, 3/4 OR 1/2 IN VIDEO C A
See series title for descriptive statement.
From The Skeletal And Topographic Anatomy Series.
Prod-UTEXMH Dist-TEF

Topographic Anatomy Of The Upper Extremity, Part 2 - Forearm, Wrist And Hand C 15 MIN
16MM FILM, 3/4 OR 1/2 IN VIDEO C A
See series title for descriptive statement.
From The Skeletal And Topographic Anatomy Series.
Prod-UTEXMH Dist-TEF

Topographic And Geological Maps C 51 MIN
3/4 OR 1/2 INCH VIDEO CASSETTE IND
See series title for descriptive statement.
From The Basic And Petroleum Geology For Non-Geologists - Structural...-Series.
Prod-PHILLP Dist-GPCV

Topographic Features, Pt 1 C 15 MIN
3/4 INCH VIDEO CASSETTE P-I
Presents several topographic features such as river, delta, mouth and sea and gives practice in locating these features on a map.
From The B B's Cover The Globe Series.
Prod-MAETEL Dist-GPITVL

Topographic Features, Pt 2 C 15 MIN
3/4 INCH VIDEO CASSETTE P-I
Presents several topographic features such as strait, canal, isthmus, peninsula and island and gives practice in locating these features on a map.
From The B B's Cover The Globe Series.
Prod-MAETEL Dist-GPITVL

Topology B
16MM FILM OPTICAL SOUND
Shows that by considering more general forms of transformation one can extend the congruence classes of Euclidean geometry to much wider equivalence classes.
Prod-OPENU Dist-OPENU

Topology B 30 MIN
16MM FILM OPTICAL SOUND H A
Professor Raoul Bott introduces topology with contrasting notions of geometrical equivalence. Professor Marston Morse, with the aid of models and charts, describes the basic ideas of topological critical point theory.
From The MAA Individual Lecturers Series.
Prod-MAA Dist-MLA 1966

Topology - Some Historical Concepts C 22 MIN
16MM FILM OPTICAL SOUND
Uses diagrammatic animation in a presentation of some qualitative concepts of topology, including transformations, Jordan curve theorem, existence solutions and fixed points.
LC NO. 74-700696
Prod-CLI Dist-CLI 1974

Topology - Summary B
16MM FILM OPTICAL SOUND
Summarizes topological concepts, giving particular emphasis to the Brouwer fixed point theorem.
Prod-OPENU Dist-OPENU

Topology I C 20 MIN
3/4 OR 1/2 INCH VIDEO CASSETTE H
Presents Beth McKenna and David Edmonds discussing 'rubber sheet geometry' and illustrating basic terms and definitions such as topological transformations and equivalent figures. Investigates some of the properties of the Moebius strip.
From The Shapes Of Geometry Series. Pt 1
LC NO. 82-707387
Prod-WVIZTV Dist-GPITVL 1982

Topology II C 20 MIN
3/4 OR 1/2 INCH VIDEO CASSETTE H
Presents Beth McKenna and David Edmonds discussing the Klein bottle, Leonhard Euler and the Koenigsburg Bridge problem. Deals with the topics of networks and Euler's theorem and the application of the theorem to the Platonic solids.
From The Shapes Of Geometry Series. Pt 2
LC NO. 82-707388
Prod-WVIZTV Dist-GPITVL 1982

Topology Short Films—A Series
16MM FILM, 3/4 OR 1/2 IN VIDEO
Uses computer animation to illustrate the concept of limit and space-filling curves, sphere eversions, and other topological theories.
Prod-NSF Dist-IFB 1979

Butterfly Catastrophe, The 005 MIN
Limit Curves And Curves Of Infinite Length 014 MIN
Limit Surfaces And Space Filling Curves 011 MIN
Sierpinski's Curve Fills Space 005 MIN
Sphere Eversions 008 MIN
Zooms On Self-Similar Figures 008 MIN

Topology With Raoul Bott And Marston Morse B 30 MIN
16MM FILM OPTICAL SOUND
Presents a discussion on topology with Raoul Bott and Marston Morse. Professor Bott uses models, charts and other devices to introduce the subject of topology. Professor Morse describes the basic ideas of topological critical point theory. John Mackenzie moderates.
From The Mathematics Today Series.
LC NO. FIA66-1279
Prod-WNEDTV Dist-MLA Prodn-MACKNZ 1966

Topology—A Series
16MM FILM, 3/4 OR 1/2 IN VIDEO C
Discusses aspects of topology.
Prod-EDC Dist-IFB

Regular Homotopies In The Plane, Pt 1 014 MIN
Regular Homotopies In The Plane, Pt 2 019 MIN
Space Filling Curves 026 MIN
Turning A Sphere Inside Out 023 MIN

Topology, Pt 1 B
16MM FILM OPTICAL SOUND
Offers an introduction to topology. Gives the four properties of a general distance function, or metric.
Prod-OPENU Dist-OPENU

Topology, Pt 2 - Continuity B
16MM FILM OPTICAL SOUND
Investigates the continuity of a specific function.
Prod-OPENU Dist-OPENU

Topology, Pt 3 - Topological Spaces B
16MM FILM OPTICAL SOUND
Introduces the notion of a topological space and uses the framework of topological spaces to study continuous functions.
Prod-OPENU Dist-OPENU

Topology, Pt 4 - Closure B
16MM FILM OPTICAL SOUND
Introduces the concept of a closed set in a topological space. Presents a construction for the closure of an arbitrary set in a space and relates the ideas of closure and continuity to each other.
Prod-OPENU Dist-OPENU

Topology, Pt 5 - Induced Topologies B
16MM FILM OPTICAL SOUND
Considers a problem in topology involving the creation of a continuous map.
Prod-OPENU Dist-OPENU

Topping Off The CN Tower C 30 MIN
3/4 OR 1/2 INCH VIDEO CASSETTE
Illustrates the topping of the Canadian National Tower. Shows how the final 32 feet of the mast were put in place by helicopter, an unparalleled 'high wire' act.
Prod-AISC Dist-MPS

Tops C 8 MIN
16MM FILM, 3/4 OR 1/2 IN VIDEO J-C
Reveals how tops are wound or prepared, how they are launched, how they spin, whirl and wobble and how they die.
From The Eames Film Collection Series.
Prod-EAMES Dist-EBEC 1973

Topsoil And Vegetation C 9 MIN
16MM FILM, 3/4 OR 1/2 IN VIDEO J-C A
Shows how topsoil is formed. Stresses that cultivable land is in short supply in the world and that the land needs to be treated more carefully.
Prod-NORSK Dist-AIMS 1977

Topsy Turvy House C 11 MIN
16MM FILM, 3/4 OR 1/2 IN VIDEO P
Presents a set of key words, a narration in rhyme and a series of activities in a topsy turvy house.
Prod-CORF Dist-CORF 1974

Tora Tora Tora C 144 MIN
1/2 IN VIDEO CASSETTE (BETA)
Chronicles the bombing of Pearl Harbor from both the American and Japanese points of view. Stars Martin Balsam, E G Marshall and James Whitmore.
Prod-UNKNWN Dist-BHAWK 1970

Torch And The Torso, The - Miguel Berrocal B 14 MIN
16MM FILM OPTICAL SOUND
Pictures the work of Spanish sculptor Miguel Berrocal. Shows him in his studio where he makes metal figures, using a panoply of elements and tools to produce extra ordinary forms which may be disassembled and re-assembled. Filmed in Spain.
LC NO. FIA66-1368
Prod-ENGLEJ Dist-RADIM 1966

Torch Is Lit, The B 26 MIN
16MM FILM OPTICAL SOUND
Describes British losses in Libya and Egyptusing documentary footage. Shows scenes of the fall of Tobruk, Churchill's meeting with Roosevelt in June 1942, and the allied landings in Algeria, November 8, 1942. Based on the book 'THE SECOND WORLD WAR,' by Winston S Churchill.
From The Winston Churchill - The Valiant Years Series. No. 11
LC NO. FI67-2117
Prod-ABCTV Dist-SG 1961

Torch Safety C 13 MIN
3/4 OR 1/2 INCH VIDEO CASSETTE IND
Presents the safety procedures and equipment required for the safe operation of a torch.
From The Steel Making Series.
Prod-LEIKID Dist-LEIKID

Torch Welding B 17 MIN
16MM FILM OPTICAL SOUND
Shows how to make a good torch weld and gives examples of torch welding aluminum forgings. Pictures castings and aluminum sheet and plate.
From The How To Weld Aluminum Series.
Prod-USDIBM Dist-USDIBM 1946

Tordon - A Global Solution To A Global Problem C 18 MIN
16MM FILM OPTICAL SOUND
Shows the use of tordon to rid croplands and pasturelands of weeds and shrubs.
Prod-DCC Dist-DCC

Torment Of Joan Of Arc, The C 22 MIN
16MM FILM, 3/4 OR 1/2 IN VIDEO I-H
Shows turbulent France during the 15th century and a young peasant girl, Joan of Arc, who is on trial for heresy and treason. Explains that by refusing to deny the charges against her, Joan faces the penalty of being burned at the stake.
From The You Are There Series.
Prod-CBSTV Dist-PHENIX 1972

Tornado C 14 MIN
16MM FILM, 3/4 OR 1/2 IN VIDEO J-H T
Shows the nearly tragic event of a tornado that traps three young people. Presents the tornado's devastation of a nearby town.
From The Your Chance To Live Series.
Prod-USDCPA Dist-MTI 1972

Tornado C 15 MIN
3/4 INCH VIDEO CASSETTE
Tells the story of a typical midwestern city that lies in the path of a destructive tornado. Includes scenes of a tornado in action and describes protective preparations. Shows weather conditions which generate tornadoes, as well as ESSA - Weather Bureau methods of charting conditions and issuing warning to the public.
LC NO. 76-706180
Prod-USESSA Dist-USNAC Prodn-ASTRAF 1968

Tornado - A Spotter's Guide C 16 MIN
16MM FILM, 3/4 OR 1/2 IN VIDEO A
Explains methods of visually detecting and reporting severe storms and tornadoes.
LC NO. 82-706705
Prod-USNWS Dist-USNAC 1977

Tornado Below C 15 MIN
3/4 OR 1/2 INCH VIDEO CASSETTE
Offers an explanation of the most dreaded of weather phenomena, the tornado. Shows how weather satellites combine in man's efforts to reduce casualties during a tornado alert.
From The LANDSAT Series.
Prod-IVCH Dist-IVCH

Tornado Below C 15 MIN
16MM FILM - 3/4 IN VIDEO
Explains how tornadoes are formed, gives their characteristics and tells of the destruction they cause. Relates this information to work being done in the laboratory to better understand the tornado and stresses the importance of information from early warning weather satellites.
From The Rediscovery Series.
LC NO. 77-706147
Prod-NASA Dist-USNAC 1977

Tornado Disaster Action C 4 MIN
16MM FILM OPTICAL SOUND
Uses animation to illustrate the steps that can be taken to protect lives and property in areas under official tornado warning.
Prod-AMRC Dist-AMRC 1968

Tornadoes C 29 MIN
2 INCH VIDEOTAPE
Features meteorologist Frank Sechrist showing where the tornado forms in the cumulonimbus cloud and illustrating the anatomy of the tornado. Explains the difference between tornadoes, water spouts and sand storms and describes the conditions necessary for a tornado to develop.
From The Weather Series.
Prod-WHATV Dist-PUBTEL

Toronto - The Queen City C 14 MIN
16MM FILM OPTICAL SOUND
Surveys the city of Toronto and its tourist attractions.
LC NO. FIA68-1230
Prod-MORLAT Dist-MORLAT 1968

Torques And Gyroscopes C 30 MIN
16MM FILM, 3/4 OR 1/2 IN VIDEO C A
Explains why a spinning top doesn't topple, how a torque acts on a spinning object causing the angular momentum to change but the object only processes.
From The Mechanical Universe Series.
Prod-ANNCPB Dist-FI

Torquing C 11 MIN
3/4 OR 1/2 INCH VIDEO CASSETTE IND
Demonstrates the utilization of torque in tightening threaded fasteners with emphasis on the use of washers and proper lubrication. Uses animation.
From The Marshall Maintenance Training Programs Series. Tape 34
Prod-LEIKID Dist-LEIKID

Torquing C 11 MIN
16MM FILM, 3/4 OR 1/2 IN VIDEO IND
Demonstrates the utilization of torque in tightening threaded fasteners with emphasis on the use of washers and proper lubrication. Shows three methods of torquing and the recommended procedures for installing flanges or manway covers.
Prod-MOKIN Dist-MOKIN

Torrential Rains C 27 MIN
16MM FILM OPTICAL SOUND
A Japanese language film. Explains that ruins of a legendary town Kusado-Sengen-Cho were found in the Ashida River bed in the western part of Fukuyama city. Points out that torrential rains destroyed this town several hundred years ago and that now the factors causing torrential rains are being studied with the help of today's science and technology and it may soon be possible to forecast such downpours.
Prod-UNIJAP Dist-UNIJAP 1969

Torres-Garcia And The Universal Constructivism (Spanish) C 30 MIN
3/4 OR 1/2 INCH VIDEO CASSETTE J-C A
Discusses the life and works of Uruguayan painter Joaquin Torres Garcia.
Prod-MOMALA Dist-MOMALA

Torres-Garcia And The Universal Constructivism C 30 MIN
16MM FILM, 3/4 OR 1/2 IN VIDEO J-C A
Discusses the life and works of Uruguayan painter Joaquin Torres Garcia.
LC NO. 82-707026
Prod-OOAS Dist-MOMALA

Torres-Garcia Y El Constructuvismo Universal C 30 MIN
16MM FILM OPTICAL SOUND
A Spanish version of Torres-Garcia And The Universal Constructivism. Discusses the life and works of Uruguayan painter Joaquin Torres-Garcia.
LC NO. 75-700627
Prod-OOAS Dist-MOMALA 1975

Tort Law C 29 MIN
2 INCH VIDEOTAPE H-C A
Focuses on tort law, the laws that deals with personal injury of all kinds. Shows a skit by the Ace Trucking Company, which brings up the question of fault in an accident, prompting a discussion of whether or not the idea of fault is a valid basis for settling such cases.
From The Just Generation Series.
Prod-WITFTV Dist-PUBTEL 1972

Tortillas And Tacos C 18 MIN
3/4 OR 1/2 INCH VIDEO CASSETTE PRO
Shows how to make tortillas and use them in preparing tacos.
Prod-CULINA Dist-CULINA

Tortoise And The Hare C 15 MIN
16MM FILM OPTICAL SOUND
Features Grady Nutt giving a blow-by-blow account of the Identiapolis, which is the result of Harry Turtle challenging the boastful Jacques Rabbit to a race. Using tactics and patience Harry crosses the finish line first and proves that he too is worth something.
Prod-BROADM Dist-BROADM 1976

Tortoise And The Hare C 9 MIN
16MM FILM, 3/4 OR 1/2 IN VIDEO P-I
A cartoon telling the story of the persistent tortoise who wins a race with the over-confident hare.
Prod-DISNEY Dist-WDEMCO 1954

Tortoise And The Hare, The (French) C 8 MIN
16MM FILM, 3/4 OR 1/2 IN VIDEO P
Illustrates the qualities of modesty and perseverance.
Prod-WDEMCO Dist-WDEMCO 1954

Torts - You As A Victim C 29 MIN
3/4 INCH VIDEO CASSETTE C A
Examines principles and applications of tort law that protect victims of injurious acts. Defines a tort. Enumerates freedoms or inherent rights of all individuals.
From The You And The Law Series. Lesson 8
Prod-COAST Dist-CDTEL Prodn-SADCC

Torts - You As Accused C 29 MIN
3/4 INCH VIDEO CASSETTE C A
Defines defenses available to a person accused of torts. Discusses how insurance can provide protection from financial loss for someone accused of wrongdoing.
From The You And The Law Series. Lesson 9
Prod-COAST Dist-CDTEL Prodn-SADCC

Torture Of Mothers, The C 60 MIN
16MM FILM OPTICAL SOUND
Presents a documentary re-creation of the case known as the Harlem Six from the Harlem riot in the summer of 1964. Shows the inability of the mothers of the six to deal with the criminal justice system. Includes original tape recordings of the mothers' statements. Based on the book by Truman Nelson.
Prod-BLKFMF Dist-BLKFMF

Toscanini - The Maestro C 60 MIN
3/4 OR 1/2 INCH VIDEO CASSETTE
Presents a musical portrait of Toscanini. Includes tapes of television performances and home movies. Examines the extent of his influence in music.
Prod-ROPE Dist-FOTH

Total Anomalies Pulmonary Venous Drainage C 15 MIN
16MM FILM OPTICAL SOUND
Demonstrates a method of complete repair of total anomalous pulmonary venous drainage. Shows step by step an operation performed on an eight-year-boy who had exertional dyspnea, cyanosis, clubbing of the nails and the typical mediastinal configuaration.
LC NO. FIA66-70
Prod-EATONL Dist-EATONL Prodn-AVCORP 1961

Total Back Care, Phase I C 15 MIN
3/4 INCH VIDEO CASSETTE A
Examines how and why lower back pain occurs.
Prod-KRI Dist-KRI

Total Back Care, Phase II C 40 MIN
3/4 INCH VIDEO CASSETTE A
Provides guidelines for care and use of the back. Includes discussion of exercise, diet and proper body mechanics.
Prod-KRI Dist-KRI

Total Body Massage C 10 MIN
2 INCH VIDEOTAPE
See series title for descriptive statement.
From The Janaki Series.
Prod-WGBHTV Dist-PUBTEL

Total Colectomy C 27 MIN
16MM FILM OPTICAL SOUND
Shows the isolation of the distal ileum, the performance of an anal ileostomy, the excision of the two proximal stomata and the re-establishment of ileal continuity by anastomosis as an optional procedure if warranted by nutritional state and sphincter control.
Prod-USVA Dist-USVA 1957

Total Colectomy For Ulcerative Colitis In Corticosteroid Treated Patients C 25 MIN
16MM FILM OPTICAL SOUND PRO
Illustrates one stage total colectomy with combined abdominoperineal resection for ulcerative colitis in a corticosteroid treated patient.
Prod-ACYDGD Dist-ACY 1961

Total Coliform Determination In Drinking Water, Membrane Filtration Technique... C 9 MIN
1/2 IN VIDEO CASSETTE BETA/VHS
Complete title is Total Coliform Determination In Drinking Water, Membrane Filtration Technique, Sample Collection. Discusses water purification, drinking water, and sample collection in water analysis.
Prod-RMI Dist-RMI

Total Coliform Determination In Drinking Water - Membrane Filtration Technique... C 4 MIN
1/2 IN VIDEO CASSETTE BETA/VHS
Complete title is Total Coliform Determination In Drinking Water, Membrane Filtration Technique Introduction. Discusses water purification and drinking water, and provides an introduction to water analysis.
Prod-RMI Dist-RMI

Total Coliform Determination In Drinking Water, Membrane Filtration Technique... C 10 MIN
1/2 IN VIDEO CASSETTE BETA/VHS
Complete title is Total Coliform Determination In Drinking Water, Membrane Filtration Technique - Sample Dilution. Discusses water purification, water analysis and drinking water.
Prod-RMI Dist-RMI

Total Coliform Determination In Drinking Water - M F Technique - Membrane Filtration... C 21 MIN
1/2 IN VIDEO CASSETTE BETA/VHS
Complete title is Total Coliform Determination In Drinking Water - M F Technique - Membrane Filtration Procedure. Discusses water purification, water reuse, and water and wastewater technology.
Prod-RMI Dist-RMI

Total Communication C 15 MIN
16MM FILM OPTICAL SOUND C A
Explains and demonstrates total communication. Shows a preschool class of deaf children and interviews parents of young deaf children.
From The Western Maryland College Series.
LC NO. 74-706283
Prod-WMARYC Dist-USNAC 1973

Total Environment Range, The C 22 MIN
16MM FILM OPTICAL SOUND
Describes the mission and capabilities of the U S Navy's Pacific Missile Range Facility, Hawaiian area.
LC NO. 75-701738
Prod-USN Dist-USNAC 1973

Total Fitness In 30 Minutes A Week C 30 MIN
16MM FILM, 3/4 OR 1/2 IN VIDEO H-C A
Demonstrates how to develop a personal fitness program, regardless of age, weight, sex, occupation or physical condition. Explains why exercise is essential to fitness. Based on the book Total Fitness In 30 Minutes A Week by Laurence E Morehouse.
Prod-PFP Dist-PFP 1976

Total Fitness In 30 Minutes A Week (Spanish) C 30 MIN
16MM FILM, 3/4 OR 1/2 IN VIDEO A
A Spanish language version of the film, Total Fitness In 30 Minutes A Week. Deals with pulse rate exercises for personal fitness. Based on the book by Dr Lawrence Morehouse, who designed the physical conditioning program for N A S A's Skylab astronauts.
Prod-PFP Dist-PFP

Total Gastrectomy In Ulcerogenic Tumor Of The Pancreas C 29 MIN
16MM FILM OPTICAL SOUND PRO
Presents a female patient harboring a malignant ulcerogenic tumor of the pancreas with intractable diarrhea of at least 10 years duration. Includes the effects on small bowel motility and their pertinent steps of total gastrectomy with an end to side esophagojejunostomy and jejuno-jejunostomy.
Prod-ACYDGD Dist-ACY 1963

Total Gastrectomy Using The Abdominothoracic Approach C 39 MIN
16MM FILM OPTICAL SOUND PRO
Explains that from the technical point of view, total gastrectomy performed through the ordinary abdominal incision may be exceedingly difficult. Demonstrates the superiority of the abdominothoracic approach.
Prod-ACYDGD Dist-ACY 1955

Total Gastrectomy With Jejunal Interposition C 23 MIN
16MM FILM OPTICAL SOUND PRO
Presents a method whereby a segment of the proximal jejunum is employed to replace the stomach and reestablish continuity between the esophagus and duodenum. Demonstrates total gastrectomy performed in the treatment of malignant gastric neoplasms and accompanied by splenectomy and excision of the omentum.
Prod-ACYDGD Dist-ACY 1960

Total Health C 60 MIN
3/4 OR 1/2 INCH VIDEO CASSETTE J A
Gives a comprehensive look at a new form of medical practice called 'holistic medicine'. Looks at holistic centers across the nation where the body, mind and spirit are taken into consideration as religion and medicine combine to comfort both the young and the old.
Prod-NBCNEW Dist-ECUFLM 1980

Total Hip Joint Replacement C
3/4 OR 1/2 INCH VIDEO CASSETTE
Shows how the hip joint can degenerate to the point where total replacement is necessary. Describes the surgical procedures and therapy required along with the results that can be expected.
Prod-MIFE Dist-MIFE

Total Hip Joint Replacement (Arabic) C
3/4 OR 1/2 INCH VIDEO CASSETTE
Shows how the hip joint can degenerate to the point where total replacement is necessary. Describes the surgical procedures and therapy required along with the results that can be expected.
Prod-MIFE Dist-MIFE

Total Hip Joint Replacement (Spanish) C
3/4 OR 1/2 INCH VIDEO CASSETTE
Shows how the hip joint can degenerate to the point where total replacement is necessary. Describes the surgical procedures and therapy required along with the results that can be expected.
Prod-MIFE Dist-MIFE

Total Hip Prostheses C 48 MIN
3/4 OR 1/2 INCH VIDEO CASSETTE
Three parts dealing with total hip prostheses including pre-operation planning, surgical techniques and special techniques and complications.
Prod-SPRVER Dist-SPRVER

Total Hip Prosthesis C 34 MIN
16MM FILM OPTICAL SOUND
Shows the anatomical and mechanical design of binding-type total hip prosthesis made of titanium alloy. Explains that the prosthesis is combined of three parts.
Prod-UNIJAP Dist-UNIJAP 1971

Total Hip Replacement C 16 MIN
16MM FILM, 3/4 OR 1/2 IN VIDEO A
Explains how the new joint works and provides an understanding of the purpose and expected results of the procedure. Gives a representation of the usual hospital and therapy experience as well as instructions for post-operative care.
Prod-PRORE Dist-PRORE

Total Laryngectomy C 12 MIN
16MM FILM SILENT PRO
Explains the reasons for performing a total laryngectomy and considers the anesthesia used for this operation.
Prod-LOMAM Dist-LOMAM

Total Laryngectomy C 17 MIN
16MM FILM OPTICAL SOUND PRO
Explains that the operation of total laryngectomy is used for cancer of the intrinsic larynx, or true vocal cord, too advanced for treatment by radiation therapy or by a lesser surgical procedure.
Prod-ACYDGD Dist-ACY 1963

Total Look, The C 22 MIN
16MM FILM OPTICAL SOUND
Points out that many years ago, ceilings were recognized as one of the most important dimensions of interior design. Explains that now, through the design and development of modern materials, unique styling and simplified installation techniques, ceilings are once again being used to produce a total look in home decoration. Describes the new ceiling materials and shows how they can be used to add the comfort of sound conditioning, modern decoration, and trouble-free ceilings to new as well as older homes.
Prod-ACOC Dist-ACOC

Total Ovariectomy And Adrenalectomy C 17 MIN
16MM FILM OPTICAL SOUND PRO
Presents Dr Willard H Persons who points out that certain metastases from mammary cancer remain hormone dependent, and are benefited by castration. Advises that total ovariectomy and adrenalectomy should be restricted to women who have advanced carcinomatosis, subsequent to breast cancer, and who have failed to respond to all other known methods of treatment. Shows the more important technical aspects of adrena lectomy.
Prod-ACYDGD Dist-ACY 1959

Total Parenteral Nutrition - An Overview C 13 MIN
3/4 OR 1/2 INCH VIDEO CASSETTE PRO
Defines total parenteral nutrition (TPN) and presents the goals of TPN therapy and its primary indications.
LC NO. 80-730658
Prod-TRAINX Dist-TRAINX

Total Parenteral Nutrition - Nursing Care The Administration Set C 12 MIN
3/4 OR 1/2 INCH VIDEO CASSETTE PRO
Demonstrates the actions of the nurse in changing the dressing for the patient receiving total parenteral nutrition. Emphasizes aseptic technique.
LC NO. 80-730658
Prod-TRAINX Dist-TRAINX

Total Parenteral Nutrition - Nursing Care - 1 The Protocol C 10 MIN
3/4 OR 1/2 INCH VIDEO CASSETTE PRO
Explains the ongoing nursing care for the patient who is receiving total parenteral nutrition (TPN) therapy. Demonstrates nursing care performed every hour, including checking the rate of the infusion, checking the IV tubing and the dressing and observing the patient's behavior.
LC NO. 80-730658
Prod-TRAINX Dist-TRAINX

Total Parenteral Nutrition - Preparing The Patient C 11 MIN
3/4 OR 1/2 INCH VIDEO CASSETTE PRO
Demonstrates ways in which the nurse teaches the patient about total parenteral nutrition (TPN) therapy. Illustrates examples of typical patient concerns about TPN.
LC NO. 80-730658
Prod-TRAINX Dist-TRAINX

Total Parenteral Nutrition, Part Two Complications of TPN C 29 MIN
3/4 OR 1/2 INCH VIDEO CASSETTE PRO
Discusses the technical, metabolic and septic complications of total parenteral nutrition. Identifies signs and symptoms of the most common complications. Describes preventive steps and initial treatment and recommends equipment and supplies which can decrease the incidence of complications. Provides a thorough overview of possible problems and their solutions for the physician with primary responsibility for the monitoring and care of patients receiving parenteral nutrition.
Prod-UMICHM Dist-UMICHM 1982

Total Parenteral Nutrition, Pt 1 C 21 MIN
3/4 OR 1/2 INCH VIDEO CASSETTE PRO
Provides an introduction and overview of total parenteral nutrition (TPN) as a method of either primary or supportive therapy for adult patients. Discusses nutritional requirements during disease, specific indications for TPN therapy, catheter insertion and care. Provides specific information regarding TPN solutions and their administration.
Prod-UMICHM Dist-UMICHM 1980

Total Parotidectomy C 22 MIN
3/4 OR 1/2 INCH VIDEO CASSETTE
See series title for descriptive statement.
From The Head And Neck Series.
Prod-SVL Dist-SVL

Total Physical Fitness For Men C 43 MIN
1/2 IN VIDEO CASSETTE BETA/VHS A
Presents a series of exercises that will lead to cardiovascular fitness, flexibility and strength.
Prod-RMI Dist-RMI

Total Quality Control C 30 MIN
3/4 OR 1/2 INCH VIDEO CASSETTE A
See series title for descriptive statement.
From The Business Nippon Series.
LC NO. 85-702165
Prod-JAPCTV Dist-EBEC 1984

Total Rehabilitation Of A Bilateral High Upper Extremity Amputee C 30 MIN
16MM FILM OPTICAL SOUND
Shows how a bilateral double high-arm amputee can be restored to functional capacity.
Prod-USVA Dist-USVA 1959

Total Self Defense C
1/2 IN VIDEO CASSETTE (VHS)
Presents a three part program on self defense including home protection, personal safety and basic martial arts.
Prod-KARLVI Dist-KARLVI

Total Solids And Volatile Solids Determination In Wastewater C 10 MIN
1/2 IN VIDEO CASSETTE BETA/VHS
Discusses sewage, sludge, water and wastewater technology.
Prod-RMI Dist-RMI

Total Surgical Decompression Of Late Intestinal Obstruction C 29 MIN
16MM FILM OPTICAL SOUND PRO
Explains that in late obstruction of the small intestine, complete surgical decompression of the distended atonic gut from treitz' ligament to point of obstruction is essential to recovery. Illustrates a facile method to accomplish this.
Prod-ACYDGD Dist-ACY 1964

Total Thyroidectomy And Neck Dissection For Thyroid Cancer C 24 MIN
16MM FILM OPTICAL SOUND PRO
Depicts a method of evaluation and the surgical treatment of well differentiated carcinoma of the thyroid in a child with bilateral lob involvement, cervical lymphnode metastases and tracheal invasion.
Prod-ACYDGD Dist-ACY 1968

Total Transsacral Prostatectomy C 25 MIN
16MM FILM OPTICAL SOUND
Presents a technique for the transsacral approach to the prostate in two patients. Defines the improved exposure of the prostate, the lower posterior bladder, the seminal vesicles, the retrovesical ureters and the prosimal urethra. Stresses visualization of the lower rectum and treatment of associated rectal, urethral or vesical fistulae seen in association with anal atresia.
LC NO. 75-702308
Prod-EATONL Dist-EATONL 1966

Total War B 26 MIN
16MM FILM, 3/4 OR 1/2 IN VIDEO H-C A
Surveys the destructive elements of war as seen by the civilians who faced the brunt of Hitler's 'WAR OF TERROR.' Shows how war touches all of humanity and that total victory by blitzkrieg, as envisaged by Hitler, did nothing more than to wreck havoc and destruction on all involved.
Prod-NFBC Dist-LCOA Prodn-JACKS 1969

Total Wrist Joint Replacement C 15 MIN
3/4 OR 1/2 INCH VIDEO CASSETTE
Demonstrates surgical techniques, results and possible complications in total wrist joint replacement.
Prod-SPRVER Dist-SPRVER

Totalitarian Temptation, The C 30 MIN
3/4 INCH VIDEO CASSETTE H-C A
Presents a discussion between Ben J Wattenberg and author Jean Francois Revel on the question of whether democracy is doomed, pointing out that European voters have moved to the left while capitalism has become a dirty word.
From The In Search Of The Real America Series.
Prod-WGBHTV Dist-KINGFT 1977

Totem Pole C 27 MIN
16MM FILM, 3/4 OR 1/2 IN VIDEO J-C A
Describes the development of the seven types of totem poles and house posts. Discusses each in terms of a social system and mythology that stresses kinship, rank and ostentatious display of wealth. Shows the ancient method of felling a large cedar tree and erecting a pole. Mungo Martin, a famous carver and chief of the Kwakiutl, carves a totem pole.
From The American Indian Series.
Prod-UCEMC Dist-UCEMC 1963

Totems C 14 MIN
16MM FILM OPTICAL SOUND
Offers an interesting but dated look at Northwest Coast Indian art. Donated from the Louis Huber Collection.
Prod-OREGHS Dist-OREGHS

Tots / Air Fare / Utilities C
3/4 OR 1/2 INCH VIDEO CASSETTE
Presents tips on child care, air travel and utilities.
From The Consumer Survival Series.
Prod-MDCPB Dist-MDCPB

Tots / OTC Drugs / Banks C
3/4 OR 1/2 INCH VIDEO CASSETTE
Presents tips on caring for children, over-the-counter drugs and banks.
From The Consumer Survival Series.
Prod-MDCPB Dist-MDCPB

Touch C 32 MIN
16MM FILM, 3/4 OR 1/2 IN VIDEO P-I A
Teaches children to recognize good touch and bad touch. Based on a play created by the Illusion Theater Company in conjunction with sexual abuse prevention experts.
Prod-MEDVEN Dist-MTI

Touch And Feel C 15 MIN
3/4 OR 1/2 INCH VIDEO CASSETTE P
Explains that everything has texture and shows examples. Discusses how man and nature change the texture of things and how artists use line, shape, color and pattern to simulate texture or sometimes use real texture in their works.
From The Primary Art Series.
Prod-WETATV Dist-AITECH

Touch Clay, A Ceramic Experience B 30 MIN
16MM FILM OPTICAL SOUND J-C A
Depicts natural objects that typify the things which inspire ceramist Dik Schwanke. Shows Schwanke working in his studio and pictures some of his pottery and sculpture. Accompanied by music by the 'SHAGS.'
From The Creative Person Series.
Prod-NET Dist-IU 1967

Touch Football - The Game Of Action C 10 MIN
16MM FILM, 3/4 OR 1/2 IN VIDEO J-C
Illustrates the rules and skill elements of touch football through the game action of a group of high school athletes. Reveals the safety tactics and vigorous participation required in the sport. Depicts techniques for good passing, receiving and punting.
Prod-TFBCH Dist-AIMS 1972

Touch Football - The Game Of Action (Spanish) C 10 MIN
16MM FILM, 3/4 OR 1/2 IN VIDEO J-C
Shows high school athletes as they demonstrate techniques for good passing, receiving and punting as well as a variety of fast motion drills for the game of touch football.
Prod-TFBCH Dist-AIMS 1972

Touch Of Finland, A C 28 MIN
16MM FILM OPTICAL SOUND
Pictures the beauty of Finland.
LC NO. 79-700329
Prod-FNTO Dist-FNTO Prodn-FILMAU 1978

Touch Of Finland, A C 28 MIN
16MM FILM OPTICAL SOUND C A
Focuses on the natural and man-made attractions of Finland. Covers the scenic lake district, Finland's Summer Festivals, and many of Finland's product designs and shopping values.
Prod-WSTGLC Dist-WSTGLC

Touch Of Gold, A C 28 MIN
16MM FILM OPTICAL SOUND
Tells the story of gold jewelry through the ages with historic re-enactments showing its use in the court of kings, as treasure acquired by the Conquistadores and its high-style uses in today's world of fashion.
Prod-MTP Dist-MTP

Touch Of Hands, A C 27 MIN
16MM FILM, 3/4 OR 1/2 IN VIDEO
Follows the activities of an artist-teacher and a class of special education students in a rural elementary school as they prepare a puppet show.
Prod-FRICEC Dist-STNFLD Prodn-UPITTS 1978

Touch Of Humor, A C 20 MIN
3/4 OR 1/2 INCH VIDEO CASSETTE I
Presents dramatizations of literary works that deal with humor as a mode of perceiving. Discusses the underlying seriousness of some humor.
From The Readers' Cube Series.
Prod-MDDE Dist-AITECH 1977

Touch Of Legend C 50 MIN
16MM FILM OPTICAL SOUND
Presents a musical re-creation of the Trail of '98 featuring Ian and Sylvia Tyson. Shows how they follow the original Klondike Gold Rush route from Skagway, Alaska, to the Yukon Territory.
LC NO. 76-700160
Prod-CHET Dist-CHET 1974

Touch Of Love, A C 18 MIN
16MM FILM OPTICAL SOUND
Describes the Foster Grandparent Program.
LC NO. 80-701489
Prod-ACTON Dist-ACTON Prodn-TFVSIX 1980

Touch Of Magic, A C 5 MIN
16MM FILM OPTICAL SOUND
Presents the Orange Bird exhibit at Disney World, Florida.
Prod-FLADC Dist-FLADC

Touch Of Murder, A C 60 MIN
16MM FILM, 3/4 OR 1/2 IN VIDEO C A
Tells how Claudius' grandmother Livia poisons Augustus' heir Marcellus.
From The I, Claudius Series. Number 1
Prod-BBCTV Dist-FI 1977

Touch Of Paris, A C 20 MIN
3/4 OR 1/2 INCH VIDEO CASSETTE J-C A
Shows Paris, including its cafes, flower carts and markets and bakeries. Watches a bouillabaisse in the making and demonstrates how to make a light, fluffy omelet. Views artists at work in Montmartre and visits the Louvre and the Eiffel Tower.
LC NO. 82-706787
Prod-AWSS Dist-AWSS 1981

Touch Of Royalty - Roberto Clemente (Spanish) C 26 MIN
16MM FILM OPTICAL SOUND I-C A
Presents a remembrance of Roberto Clemente, an all-star baseball player.
LC NO. 74-700469
Prod-WWF Dist-SFI 1973

Touch Of Royalty, A C 26 MIN
16MM FILM OPTICAL SOUND J-C A
Recounts Roberto Clemente's brilliant career as a right fielder for the Pittsburgh Pirates, including anecdotes given by teammates, sports writers and Clemente's wife, Vera.
LC NO. 74-700468
Prod-WWF Dist-SFI 1973

Touch Of Royalty, A (Spanish) C 26 MIN
16MM FILM OPTICAL SOUND J-C A
Recounts Roberto Clemente's brillant career as a right fielder for the Pittsburgh Pirates, including anecdotes given by teammates, sports writers and Clemente's wife, Vera.
LC NO. 74-700468
Prod-WWF Dist-SFI 1973

Touch Of Royalty, A - Roberto Clemente C 26 MIN
16MM FILM OPTICAL SOUND I-C A
Presents a remembrance of Roberto Clemente, an all-star baseball player.
LC NO. 74-700469
Prod-WWF Dist-SFI 1973

Touch Of Sensitivity C 50 MIN
16MM FILM, 3/4 OR 1/2 IN VIDEO H-C A
Focuses on the sense of touch, showing how touch deprivation can lead to serious emotional and physical problems. Discusses the benefits of touch therapy.
Prod-BBCTV Dist-FI 1981

Touch Of Summer, A C 28 MIN
16MM FILM OPTICAL SOUND
Presents the impressions of American teenagers after traveling the length and breadth of the country of Israel.
Prod-ALDEN Dist-ALDEN

Touch The Earth C 17 MIN
16MM FILM OPTICAL SOUND
Depicts the activities of three teenage curators at the Dayton Museum of Natural History. Includes interviews with the three in which they talk about their work and about the value of nature study in general.
LC NO. 78-700316
Prod-DAYMU Dist-DAYMU Prodn-HANKJS 1978

Touch The Earth C
3/4 OR 1/2 INCH VIDEO CASSETTE
Provides a portrait of Native American existence. Tells the story of the Indians' loss of their way of life. Utilizes photographs of Edward S Curtis.
Prod-CEPRO Dist-CEPRO

Touch, The C 122 MIN
3/4 OR 1/2 INCH VIDEO CASSETTE
Presents a drama in three acts about a deaf-blind man living on his own for the first time. Adapted from Butterflies Are Free by Leonard Gershe. On three tapes, one act each. Signed.
Prod-HMTD Dist-GALCO Prodn-GALCO 1977

Touchdown B 10 MIN
16MM FILM OPTICAL SOUND
Studies the control tower of a modern airport contrasted with the public waiting rooms in the same airport. Explains the tension one might have expected in the tower is evident in the 'RELAXED' public spaces.
Prod-UPENN Dist-UPENN 1971

Touchdown C 27 MIN
16MM FILM OPTICAL SOUND
Tells how a college football player becomes paralyzed in a household accident. Follows the young man as he learns to cope with his disability and explores his changing relationship with his father who is unable to accept it.
LC NO. 79-701393
Prod-RICHGO Dist-RICHGO Prodn-CRASCO 1979

Touchdowns And Horses - Goles Y Caballos C 6 MIN
16MM FILM, 3/4 OR 1/2 IN VIDEO P-I
Presents a follow-up for the park field trip.
From The Bilingual Film Series, Module 5 - Summerfun Series.
Prod-BRNTNO Dist-CAROUF 1973

Touches C
3/4 OR 1/2 INCH VIDEO CASSETTE T
Discusses positive as well as problematic touches and encourages youngsters to confide in school personnel. Explains techniques for conducting satisfactory discussions with individual students and reporting suspected cases of abuse to proper authorities.
Prod-GA Dist-GA 1984

Touching C 4 MIN
16MM FILM OPTICAL SOUND P-I
Examines various textures encountered by children as they explore nature.
From The Mini Movies - Springboard For Learning - Unit 1, Who Are We Series.
LC NO. 76-703096
Prod-MORLAT Dist-MORLAT 1975

Touching C 14 MIN
16MM FILM OPTICAL SOUND
A young soldier on a one-day pass reaches out in desperation, finally finding an old friend, some genuine warmth and a temporary reprive from his Vietnam memories.
LC NO. 78-711544
Prod-USC Dist-USC 1970

Touching C 17 MIN
16MM FILM OPTICAL SOUND
Portrays a male who has a C-6 spinal cord injury. Explains that he was injured seven years ago and has been with his partner for three years. Stresses that oral sexuality is the primary means of sexual expression open to persons with this type of lesion.
Prod-MMRC Dist-MMRC

Touching B 20 MIN
16MM FILM OPTICAL SOUND C A
See series title for descriptive statement.
From The All That I Am Series.
Prod-MPATI Dist-NWUFLM

Touching C 4 MIN
16MM FILM, 3/4 OR 1/2 IN VIDEO K-I
Depicts the land of touch, where Judy meets some varied personalities - soft, sharp, rough, smooth and slippery.
From The Most Important Person - Senses Series.
Prod-EBEC Dist-EBEC 1973

Touching C 16 MIN
3/4 OR 1/2 INCH VIDEO CASSETTE C A
Shows a male paraplegic and his partner of the last three years. Emphasizes oral sexuality as the primary means of sexual expression and pleasuring open to persons with this type of injury.
Prod-NATSF Dist-MMRC

Touching C 35 MIN
16MM FILM - 3/4 IN VIDEO
Features Dr Ashley Montagu discussing the key concepts of his book Touching. Illustrates the importance of early tactile experiences and the use of touching in encounter therapy.
LC NO. 78-700319
Prod-PSYCHF Dist-PSYCHD 1975

Touching Problem, The C 8 MIN
16MM FILM, 3/4 OR 1/2 IN VIDEO A
Looks at how adults can help children deal with sexual abuse by presenting the case history of a young girl's molestation by a male relative.
Prod-KVOSTV Dist-MTI 1982

Touching The World C 15 MIN
16MM FILM, 3/4 OR 1/2 IN VIDEO
Examines and explores, with a group of children, the different 'FEELS' of things. Shows how the children experiment with such things as crinkly and corrugated paper, big balloons, rope, water, a nylon parachute and live bugs.
From The Ripples Series.
LC NO. 73-702158
Prod-NITC Dist-AITECH

Tough Defense - It'll Keep You In The Game C 56 MIN
1/2 IN VIDEO CASSETTE BETA/VHS
Demonstrates defensive play in men's basketball. Deals with both man-for-man and zone defensive strategy.
From The Men's Basketball Basics Series.
Prod-MOHOMV Dist-MOHOMV

Tough Love C 30 MIN
16MM FILM OPTICAL SOUND R
Presents a story about love and faith behind prison walls.
Prod-OUTRCH Dist-OUTRCH

Tough Old Gut C 60 MIN
16MM FILM OPTICAL SOUND H-C A
From The World At War Series.
LC NO. 76-701778
Prod-THAMES Dist-USCAN 1975

Tough Old Gut - Italy, November 1942- June 1944 C 52 MIN
16MM FILM, 3/4 OR 1/2 IN VIDEO H-C A
States that Sicily was not the soft underbelly of the Mediterranean that Churchill imagined it to be. Shows that it was more like a tough old gut, but once the Anglo-American advance began to turn the tide it resulted in the conquest of the Axis forces between November 1942 and June 1944.
From The World At War Series.
Prod-THAMES Dist-MEDIAG 1973

Tough Shots C 29 MIN
3/4 OR 1/2 INCH VIDEO CASSETTE
Discusses picture taking problems and how to solve them. Includes how to shoot in rain and snow, how to take self-portraits and candid picture taking without being obvious.
From The Photo Show Series.
Prod-WGBHTV Dist-PBS 1981

Tough Winter, A B 21 MIN
16MM FILM OPTICAL SOUND
Presents a Little Rascals film featuring black comedian Stepin Fetchit.
Prod-ROACH Dist-BHAWK 1930

Tough-Minded Management—A Series
16MM FILM - 3/4 IN VIDEO IND
Prod-BNA Dist-BNA 1969

Fully Functioning Individual, The	25 MIN
Fully Functioning Organization	25 MIN
Fully Functioning Society, The	25 MIN
Man In The Mirror, The	25 MIN
Management By Example	25 MIN

Tough, Pretty Or Smart - A Portrait Of The Patoka Valley Boys C 29 MIN
16MM FILM, 3/4 OR 1/2 IN VIDEO I A
Portrays old-time string band whose members span three generations. Presents and enhances old-time music in documentary form.
Prod-KANLEW Dist-KANLEW 1981

Toughest Barrier, The C 15 MIN
16MM FILM, 3/4 OR 1/2 IN VIDEO J-C A
Presents a warm and personal encounter with four handicapped adults and shows how they live and respond to various social attitudes which bar them from job opportunities, marriage, and normal social and sexual relations.
LC NO. 81-707488
Prod-IOWA Dist-CORF 1981

Toughest Game In Town B 79 MIN
16MM FILM OPTICAL SOUND A
Presents suggestions for social workers and community organizers regarding the struggles of a people's corporation. Shows how poor Chicanos of Santa Fe, New Mexico, come to grips with the powers that control their lives.
LC NO. 73-703226
Prod-BALLIS Dist-BALLIS

Toughest Job You'll Ever Love, The C 10 MIN
16MM FILM OPTICAL SOUND
A shortened version of the motion picture The Toughest Job You'll Ever Love. Shows Peace Corps Volunteers in Nepal, Columbia and Nigeria as they describe their experiences and explain what their service in the Peace Corps has meant to them.
LC NO. 79-701707
Prod-ACTON Dist-USNAC 1978

Toughest Job You'll Ever Love, The C 25 MIN
16MM FILM OPTICAL SOUND
Shows Peace Corps volunteers in Nepal, Colombia and Nigeria as they describe their experiences and explain what their service in the Peace Corps has meant to them.
LC NO. 79-701708
Prod-ACTON Dist-USNAC 1978

Toughest Target, The C 30 MIN
3/4 OR 1/2 INCH VIDEO CASSETTE H-C A
See series title for descriptive statement.
From The World War II - GI Diary Series.
Prod-TIMLIF Dist-TIMLIF 1980

Toujours En Retard Nicolas B 13 MIN
16MM FILM OPTICAL SOUND J-H
See series title for descriptive statement.
From The En France Avec Nicolas Series. Set I, Lesson 8
LC NO. 72-704502
Prod-PEREN Dist-CHLTN 1968

Toujours En Retard Nicolas, Student Exercises C 8 MIN
16MM FILM OPTICAL SOUND J-H
See series title for descriptive statement.
From The En France Avec Nicolas Series. Set II, Lesson 8
LC NO. 76-704503
Prod-PEREN Dist-CHLTN 1968

Toula (The Water Spirit) C 80 MIN
3/4 INCH VIDEO CASSETTE
Tells of drought in the West African Sahel, an ecological belt between the savannah grasslands and the Sahara Desert. Features Hansa and Songhay farmers and Fulani nomads. Filmed in 1972. Recounts the Nigerian mythic legend of Toula, the Water spirit, using a contemporary setting.
Prod-FDF Dist-DOCEDR Prodn-CHOPRA

Toulin's Model Of Argument C 16 MIN
3/4 OR 1/2 INCH VIDEO CASSETTE H-C A
Teaches the basic components of an argument as well as the differences between an argument and an assertion. Covers the material used in composition, speech, communication and debate classes.
From The Communication Series.
Prod-MSU Dist-MSU

Toulouse C 7 MIN
16MM FILM, 3/4 OR 1/2 IN VIDEO H-C A
A French language videocassette. Presents Toulouse as a city of education and aviation.
From The Chroniques De France Series.
LC NO. 81-706549
Prod-ADPF Dist-IFB 1980

Toulouse-Lautrec B 29 MIN
3/4 INCH VIDEO CASSETTE
Examines the techniques Toulouse-Lautrec used as a commercial artist, illustrator and painter to capture the humanity of Bohemian life in Paris.
From The Meet The Masters Series.
Prod-UMITV Dist-UMITV 1966

Toulouse-Lautrec (1864 - 1901) C 15 MIN
16MM FILM OPTICAL SOUND
Presents paintings of Toulouse-Lautrec, whose only weapon against self-mockery was a sharp eye for the degradations and harsh beauty of lives seemingly more glamorous than his own.
Prod-ROLAND Dist-ROLAND

Tour En L'Air (English) C 50 MIN
16MM FILM, 3/4 OR 1/2 IN VIDEO J-C A
Presents Canadian ballet dancers David and Anna Marie Holmes discussing the discipline of their art, the strains of living and working in the same ventures. Includes footage of the dancers in rehearsal and in performance around the world.
Prod-NFBC Dist-NFBC 1974

Tour Louisiana Travel—A Series

Prod-LATPA Dist-RAMSEY Prodn-RAMSEY 1978

Louisiana's Fabled Plantations 28 MIN

Tour Of The Jack Daniel Distillery, A C 18 MIN
16MM FILM - 3/4 IN VIDEO
Interweaves the history of the Jack Daniel Distillery with that of Lynchburg, Tennessee. Explains the four stages of whiskey production.
Prod-DANDIS Dist-MTP

Tour Of The Plant, A C 22 MIN
16MM FILM OPTICAL SOUND
Shows how Johnson Outboards designs, tests and manufactures its outboard motors.
LC NO. 78-700318
Prod-JOHOUT Dist-SS Prodn-GROENG 1978

Tour Of The Prado, A C
1/2 IN VIDEO CASSETTE BETA/VHS
Presents a tour of the Prado in Madrid, spotlighting works by Titian, El Greco, Velasquez, Goya and Murillo.
Prod-GA Dist-GA

Tour Of The Thomas H Ince Studios B 30 MIN
16MM FILM SILENT I-C A
Presents a tour of the Thomas H Ince Studios, featuring glimpses of famous stars of the early silent period, including Louise Glaum, Lloyd Huges, Lewis Stone and House Peters. Carries subtitles.
LC NO. 75-703861
Prod-FIRSTN Dist-BHAWK 1922

Tour Of The Vatican Museums, A C
1/2 IN VIDEO CASSETTE BETA/VHS
Views the riches of the Vatican, from Michelangelo's Sistine Chapel to paintings by Raphael, Martini, Lorenzetti and others.
Prod-GA Dist-GA

Tourette Syndrome - The Sudden Intruder C 46 MIN
16MM FILM OPTICAL SOUND
Documents the experiences of six individuals suffering from the primary and secondary effects of Tourette syndrome. Uses animation to describe the breakdown of motor control that results and the brain mechanisms that are affected.
LC NO. 78-701329
Prod-UCLA Dist-UCLA 1978

Touring On Two Wheels C 20 MIN
3/4 OR 1/2 INCH VIDEO CASSETTE J-C A
Discusses bicycle trips as a practical alternative to motor-powered excursions. Shows touring bikes, camping gear and packing tips. Includes information on tire changes, broken spokes, derailleurs and brake adjustments, along with the use of campgrounds vs the semiwilderness and rules of the road.
LC NO. 82-706788
Prod-AWSS Dist-AWSS 1981

Touring Paris—A Series
H-C A
Helps advanced students of French develop proficiency in communicating with native speakers. Demonstrates different practical activities.
Prod-THAMES Dist-MEDIAG 1984

Arriving In Paris 020 MIN
Camping In France 020 MIN
Exploring Paris 020 MIN
French Restaurants 020 MIN
Parisian Sights And Shops 020 MIN

Touring Red China - Teenage Impressions C 9 MIN
16MM FILM, 3/4 OR 1/2 IN VIDEO I-H
Shows a group of Connecticut high school students on a tour of the People's Republic of China. Presents the reactions of the students to the Chinese culture.
Prod-CBSNEW Dist-MOKIN 1979

Touristen In Heidelberg C 5 MIN
16MM FILM, 3/4 OR 1/2 IN VIDEO H-C A
A German-language version of the motion picture Tourists In Heidelberg. Delineates the history and tourist attractions of Germany's oldest university city, Heidelberg.
From The European Studies - Germany (German) Series.
Prod-MFAFRG Dist-IFB Prodn-BAYER 1973

Tourists In Heidelberg C 5 MIN
16MM FILM, 3/4 OR 1/2 IN VIDEO
Delineates history and tourist attractions in Heidelberg, Germany's oldest university city.
From The European Studies - Germany Series. Part 20
Prod-BAYER Dist-IFB 1973

Tourmaline - Maine's Mountain Treasure C 13 MIN
16MM FILM OPTICAL SOUND
Examines the recent discovery of a large pocket of the gem tourmaline by an amateur rockhound on Plumbago Mountain, Maine.
LC NO. 74-700384
Prod-FOURNR Dist-UME 1974

Tourne Potatoes C 5 MIN
3/4 OR 1/2 INCH VIDEO CASSETTE PRO
Shows how to carve potatoes into the shapes needed for noisette, rissole, fondante and chateau.
Prod-CULINA Dist-CULINA

Tout Ecartille C 6 MIN
16MM FILM, 3/4 OR 1/2 IN VIDEO J-C A
Uses rapid, twirling, flashing images to create a poetic film allegory. Centers around a faceless man wearing a flowing, black magician's cape as he laughingly creates havoc wherever he visits.
Prod-NFBC Dist-NFBC 1976

Tout Va Bien C 95 MIN
16MM FILM OPTICAL SOUND
A French language film. Tells the story of a serious filmmaker, played by Yves Montand, who has lapsed into the easy money world of television commericals. Focuses also on Jane Fonda as an American reporter who makes a decision to quit establishment journalism.
Prod-NYFLMS Dist-NYFLMS 1972

Toute La Bande - Episode 01 - Arrivee D'Elisabeth C 15 MIN
16MM FILM OPTICAL SOUND I-H
Tells the story of Elisabeth from Orlay, who missed her hosts, the Ermonts, at the airport of Daker due to the ermonts' late start and heavy traffic. Concludes with the happy get together of the guest and the host's entire family.
Prod-SCHMAG Dist-SCHMAG 1970

Toute La Bande - Episode 02 - Jeudi C 15 MIN
16MM FILM OPTICAL SOUND I-H
Explains that Elisabeth has chosen the carnations for Mrs Ermont's present through the suggestion of Mrs Ermont's son, Victor, who also received a record as a gift for his help.
Prod-SCHMAG Dist-SCHMAG 1970

Toute La Bande - Episode 03 - Depart En Vacances C 15 MIN
16MM FILM OPTICAL SOUND I-H
Follows the Ermonts to their vacation in Brittany. Includes a picnic near a river bank and the little fishing port where the Ermont's have their little summer home.
Prod-SCHMAG Dist-SCHMAG 1970

Toute La Bande - Episode 04 - Vacances En Bretagne C 15 MIN
16MM FILM OPTICAL SOUND I-H
Presents the Ermonts, their children, Caroline and Victor and their friends spending their wonderful vacation in Brittany. Includes window shopping, eating at the cafe and boat rides.
Prod-SCHMAG Dist-SCHMAG 1970

Toute La Bande - Episode 05 - Aventure En Mer C 15 MIN
16MM FILM OPTICAL SOUND I-H
Tells the adventure of Victor's and Jean-Louis' motorboat ride and how they returned safely with the help of a fisherman's family.
Prod-SCHMAG Dist-SCHMAG 1970

Toute La Bande - Episode 06 - La Rentree C 15 MIN
16MM FILM OPTICAL SOUND I-H
Tells the adventure of Caroline's and Victor's trip to a shop to buy their school supplies which brought Caroline's teacher's reprimands for wearing make-up.
Prod-SCHMAG Dist-SCHMAG 1970

Toute La Bande - Episode 07 - Sur La Tour Eiffel C 15 MIN
16MM FILM OPTICAL SOUND I-H
Presents a tour of the Eiffel Tower taken by Caroline, Victor and Elisabeth, who encounter a youth named Jacques, who becomes friends with the girls and a bore to Victor.
Prod-SCHMAG Dist-SCHMAG 1970

Toute La Bande - Episode 08 - Feu Vert C 15 MIN
16MM FILM OPTICAL SOUND I-H
Tells of the adventure of Caroline and Anne's motorbike ride to the Bois de Boulogne to meet Jacques, who was Caroline's boy friend, but soon got attracted to Anne.
Prod-SCHMAG Dist-SCHMAG 1970

Toute La Bande - Episode 09 - Bricolage C 15 MIN
16MM FILM OPTICAL SOUND I-H
Depicts how, through a visit to Caroline's and Victor's Uncle Paul to ask for his help, Jacques' intelligent interest in Uncle Paul's puttering activities results in the uncle treating him as a member of the family.
Prod-SCHMAG Dist-SCHMAG 1970

Toute La Bande - Episode 10 - A Versailles C 15 MIN
16MM FILM OPTICAL SOUND I-H
Presents a tour around Versailles taken by Caroline and Elisabeth. Includes the great ornamental fountains, gardens and Marie Antoinette's model farm.
Prod-SCHMAG Dist-SCHMAG 1970

Toute La Bande - Episode 11 - Panne D'Essence C 15 MIN
16MM FILM OPTICAL SOUND I-H
Features Victor, who took his father's car to the movie without his father's consent and is punished by having to spend his own money to fill up the tank and wash the car instead of watching his favorite soccer team on television.
Prod-SCHMAG Dist-SCHMAG 1970

Toute La Bande - Episode 12 - Le Vieux Paris C 15 MIN
16MM FILM OPTICAL SOUND I-H
Presents the adventures of Caroline, Elisabeth and Jacques as they travel through the Ile de la Cite and the Palace des vosges.
Prod-SCHMAG Dist-SCHMAG 1970

Toute La Bande - Episode 13 - Bon Anniversaire C 15 MIN
16MM FILM OPTICAL SOUND I-H
Describes how Victor uses his birthday gift of cash from his father to treat all his friends to an evening at a discotheque, which turns out to be a combination of birthday party, reunion and farewell—for the next day the Ermonts and Elisabeth are going to the south of France.
Prod-SCHMAG Dist-SCHMAG 1970

TOW Modifications And Maintenance Lessons Learned C 12 MIN
3/4 OR 1/2 INCH VIDEO CASSETTE
Illustrates modifications to the TOW weapon, showing both the old and newly-modified components, such as the launch tube, sight reticle light control, and changes affecting radio interference and missile simulation rounds. Emphasizes precautions to be observed by TOW crew members for boresighting and transporting the optical sight.
LC NO. 81-706252
Prod-USA Dist-USNAC 1981

Toward A Broader Understanding Of Ethnic Dance C 30 MIN
3/4 OR 1/2 INCH VIDEO CASSETTE
See series title for descriptive statement.
From The Third World Dance - Beyond The White Stream Series.
Prod-ARCVID Dist-ARCVID

Toward A Caring Community C 28 MIN
16MM FILM, 3/4 OR 1/2 IN VIDEO
Explores community attitudes toward mental patients by showing highlights of a workshop in which a cross section of New Jersey residents tackles the issues and problems of community care. Includes a historical review of attitudes toward the mentally ill and their treatment, a summary of the work of Dorothea Dix and commentary by an articulate representative of mental patients.
Prod-NJDHS Dist-UCEMC 1980

Toward A More Common Language C 27 MIN
16MM FILM OPTICAL SOUND
Presents a general overview of state education agencies, their growth, responsibilities, relationships to other state agencies, organization, functions and problems and the State Education Agency Handbook VII.
LC NO. 74-705807
Prod-USOE Dist-USNAC 1973

Toward A New Day - 1965-1980 C 58 MIN
16MM FILM, 3/4 OR 1/2 IN VIDEO J-C A
See series title for descriptive statement.
From The I Remember Harlem Series. Part 4
LC NO. 82-706644
Prod-MILESW Dist-FOTH 1981

Toward An Integrated Personality B 30 MIN
2 INCH VIDEOTAPE PRO
Helps nursing students understand how the development of an integrated personality can help their abilities in treating patients.
From The Mental Health Concepts For Nursing, Unit 1 - Self-Understanding Series.
LC NO. 73-702636
Prod-GPITVL Dist-GPITVL 1971

Toward Careers In Agriculture C 21 MIN
16MM FILM OPTICAL SOUND
Delineates the importance of agriculture to primarily industrial states like Connecticut. Shows ways students train for jobs in modern agriculture through vocational agriculture programs in specialized high school curricula.
Prod-SGF Dist-USOE 1967

Toward Freedom - 1940-1965 C 58 MIN
16MM FILM, 3/4 OR 1/2 IN VIDEO J-C A
See series title for descriptive statement.
From The I Remember Harlem Series. Part 3
LC NO. 82-706644
Prod-MILESW Dist-FOTH 1981

Toward Full Integration C 29 MIN
16MM FILM OPTICAL SOUND
Describes efforts by the U S Navy to upgrade civilian minority

group employees. Documents the double dilemma that confronted the navy - making supervisors aware of their responsibility for motivating advancement through training and convincing employees that training for advancement is offered in good faith.
LC NO. 74-705808
Prod-ADL Dist-ADL

Toward Immortality C 27 MIN
16MM FILM, 3/4 OR 1/2 IN VIDEO A
Focuses on studies in California and Texas proving that undernutrition without malnutrition, increasing food value while paring calories, not only prolongs the life of laboratory mammals, but also improves their health. Notes that nutritional adjustments teamed with regular exercise are one means of stalling the aging process. Compares the southeast U S with a comparable area in the northern Midwest where the soil and water are richer in minerals and trace elements. Visits laboratories, interviews researchers and looks at the aging. Suplements MTI's Stalking Immortality.
Prod-MTI Dist-MTI

Toward Immortality C 50 MIN
16MM FILM, 3/4 OR 1/2 IN VIDEO H-C A
Discusses the explosion of information that has begun to reveal why people die and how they can remain young.
Prod-GANNET Dist-MTI 1983

Toward Price-Based Reimbursement C
3/4 OR 1/2 INCH VIDEO CASSETTE
Illustrates important reimbursement implications of medical care pricing. Shows the department-by-department roller coaster of margins within an institution.
From The Revenues, Rates And Reimbursements Series.
Prod-TEACHM Dist-TEACHM

Toward The Gilded Age - Inventions And Big Business - 1876-1898 X 24 MIN
16MM FILM OPTICAL SOUND I-C A
Discusses important aspects of the late 19th century, including conservation, the end of the frontier, big business and inventions, such as the phonograph, electric light bulbs, the electric elevator and the telephone. Covers men such as Vanderbilt, Carnegie, Rockefeller and Roosevelt.
From The Exploring - The Story Of America, Set 2 Series.
LC NO. FIA68-1061
Prod-NBCTV Dist-GRACUR 1966

Toward The Global Family C 20 MIN
16MM FILM, 3/4 OR 1/2 IN VIDEO H-C A
Addresses the impact of technology on business, industry, finance, the military and global relations.
From The Communications Revolution Series.
Prod-NVIDC Dist-MTI

Toward The Least Restrictive Environment C 27 MIN
16MM FILM OPTICAL SOUND
Presents teachers' views on the placement of handicapped students into classes with the nonhandicapped. Features one student expressing his feelings regarding attendance at a high school as compared with special school.
Prod-PDPI Dist-PDPI 1979

Toward The Sun C 28 MIN
16MM FILM OPTICAL SOUND H-C A
Looks at some of the research into tapping and storing the sun's energy for use in heating homes and providing power for industry. Visits a project in Nebraska where solar power is used in an irrigation scheme which delivers a thousand gallons a minute. Shows the Tower Power in Mexico which uses thousands of mirrors to concentrate the sun's rays so that they are able to burn through two-inch steel plates.
Prod-CANBC Dist-FI

Toward The Unexplored C 26 MIN
16MM FILM, 3/4 OR 1/2 IN VIDEO
Traces the history of Edwards Air Force Base, California, as an air proving ground and research center since the early days of aviation and documents experiments in rocketry.
LC NO. 81-706655
Prod-USAF Dist-USNAC 1967

Toward 2001 C 22 MIN
16MM FILM OPTICAL SOUND
Presents experts from business, government and the academic community, who express their views about the electrical power needs of the United States and the options available to the electrical utility industry.
LC NO. 78-700399
Prod-CONTR Dist-CONTR Prodn-FILMA 1977

Towards A Better Society B 12 MIN
16MM FILM OPTICAL SOUND H-C A
Presents the heart of a small Indian village built around a family facing the problem of social customs which are barriers to education and progress. Shows the change from old orthodox ways to new ones, which are paving the way to a better nation.
Prod-INDIA Dist-NEDINF

Towards A Modern Europe C 30 MIN
16MM FILM, 3/4 OR 1/2 IN VIDEO H-C
Discusses the Renaissance and the Reformation. Focuses on the exploration of the world and aspects of Dutch and French history.
From The Outline History Of Europe Series.
LC NO. 79-708118
Prod-POLNIS Dist-IFB 1975

Towards A New Community I - The Search For Alternatives C 29 MIN
2 INCH VIDEOTAPE
See series title for descriptive statement.
From The Black Experience Series.
Prod-WTTWTV Dist-PUBTEL

Towards A New Community II - The Experience Of Blackness C 29 MIN
2 INCH VIDEOTAPE
See series title for descriptive statement.
From The Black Experience Series.
Prod-WTTWTV Dist-PUBTEL

Towards Acceptance, The Journey Of A Soul C 42 MIN
3/4 INCH VIDEO CASSETTE PRO
Presents a series of three interviews with the mother of a child with spina bifida who would not benefit from surgery. Paints a positive picture as mother describes the reactions within her family.
Prod-ESST Dist-ESST 1981

Towards An Understanding Of Pain C 16 MIN
16MM FILM OPTICAL SOUND PRO
Provides an overall review of current concepts of pain perception and their neurophysiological foundations.
Prod-GEIGY Dist-GEIGY

Towards Visual Learning C
3/4 INCH VIDEO CASSETTE T
Defines the impact of television on society and comments on the implications of instructional television for education.
From The Visual Learning Series. Session 1
Prod-NYSED Dist-NYSED

Tower Of Babel C 51 MIN
16MM FILM, 3/4 OR 1/2 IN VIDEO I-C A
Reveals that Amathar's original plan to build a tower to enable people to walk into the heavens and be with God is corrupted as he insists that his likeness be placed on the tower. Shows that because of Amathar's vanity God destroys the tower and gives people different languages. Stars Vince Edwards and Richard Basehart.
From The Greatest Heroes Of The Bible Series.
Prod-LUF Dist-LUF 1979

Tower Of Fire C 20 MIN
16MM FILM OPTICAL SOUND P-I
Presents an adventure set in the time of the Saxons which tells how the Baron is building a watchtower which will overlook the forest and reveal the outlaws' movements. Describes how Robin is determined to destroy the tower.
From The Unbroken Arrow Series.
Prod-LUF Dist-LUF 1977

Tower Of Washington, The C 21 MIN
16MM FILM OPTICAL SOUND J-C A
Describes the construction of the Gloria in excelsis tower at the Washington Cathedral. Tells about the bells which were cast in England, pictures their installation and shows the ringing of the bells and carillon on the day of the dedication. Includes excerpts from Chief Justice Earl Warren's dedication message.
LC NO. FIA65-490
Prod-NCATHA Dist-NCATHA Prodn-CAPFL 1964

Towers Without Infernos C 15 MIN
16MM FILM OPTICAL SOUND C
Tells how today's highrise buildings pose unique problems to those involved in fire prevention, fire protection and fire suppression. Shows some of the latest methods and techniques developed to prevent and control future highrise fires.
From The Science In Action Series.
Prod-ALLFP Dist-COUNFI

Towers, The C 13 MIN
16MM FILM OPTICAL SOUND P-I
Shows the building of the Watts Towers by an Italian immigrant, Simon Rodia.
Prod-HALE Dist-CFS 1965

Town Against TB C 30 MIN
16MM FILM OPTICAL SOUND
Discusses the planning, execution and results of a pilot community tuberculin testing program conducted in 1963 in Toms River, New Jersey. Presents a blueprint which can be followed by medical, health and civic groups in all communities planning disease detection and immunization programs.
Prod-ACYLLD Dist-LEDR 1964

Town Blody Hall C 88 MIN
16MM FILM, 3/4 OR 1/2 IN VIDEO
Features Norman Mailer vs Germaine Greer in the Great Debate on Women's Liberation at Town Hall, New York City in 1971. Other participants include Jill Johnston, Diana Trilling, Elizabeth Hartwick and Anatole Broyard. By Chris Hegdus and D A Pennebaker.
Prod-PENNAS Dist-PENNAS

Town Hall—A Series

Presents a series of discussions about public issues and political affairs with notable personalities in Kentucky.
Prod-EASTKU Dist-EASTKU

Town In Old Mexico, A C 10 MIN
16MM FILM OPTICAL SOUND
Depicts 17th century architecture and beautiful gardens in the villages of Puebla, Oribaza and Fortin de las Floras.
LC NO. FIA52-675
Prod-UWF Dist-USOIAA 1944

Town Mouse And The Country Mouse, The C 6 MIN
16MM FILM, 3/4 OR 1/2 IN VIDEO P
Presents an Aesop's fable about a field mouse who visits an elegant house mouse. Shows that although the house mouse has a more luxurious lifestyle, it is also more dangerous because there is a cat stalking him at all times.
Prod-NFBC Dist-BNCHMK 1981

Town Neighborhood - A General Description C 15 MIN
3/4 OR 1/2 INCH VIDEO CASSETTE P
Offers a general description of a town neighborhood.
From The Neighborhoods Series.
Prod-NEITV Dist-GPITVL 1981

Town Neighborhood - Good Neighbors Help Each Other C 15 MIN
3/4 OR 1/2 INCH VIDEO CASSETTE P
Explains how good neighbors help each other in towns.
From The Neighborhoods Series.
Prod-NEITV Dist-GPITVL 1981

Town That Never Was, The C 20 MIN
16MM FILM OPTICAL SOUND
Recounts the history of Los Alamos, New Mexico, and the creation of the Los Alamos Scientific Laboratory in the 1940's.
LC NO. 81-700291
Prod-LASL Dist-LASL 1980

Town That Washes Its Water, A C 13 MIN
16MM FILM, 3/4 OR 1/2 IN VIDEO I-C A
Reports on a pioneer reclamation program that is turning sewage water into a valuable community asset.
From The Screen News Digest Series. Vol 13, Issue 1
Prod-HEARST Dist-HEARST 1970

Town, The C 13 MIN
16MM FILM, 3/4 OR 1/2 IN VIDEO
Shows life in Madison, Indiana, focusing on the social and civil life of the people. Issued in 1944 as a motion picture.
LC NO. 79-706477
Prod-USOWI Dist-USNAC 1979

Towser And Goblin Gobble (Curiosity) C 5 MIN
16MM FILM, 3/4 OR 1/2 IN VIDEO
Tells a story of Towser using a clever ploy to escape from Goblin Gobble.
From The Towser Series.
Prod-JOU Dist-JOU

Towser And Sadie's Birthday (Imagination) C 5 MIN
16MM FILM, 3/4 OR 1/2 IN VIDEO
Tells a story about wanting to give a friend a present.
From The Towser Series.
Prod-JOU Dist-JOU

Towser And Sadie's Robot (Modern Conveniences) C 5 MIN
16MM FILM, 3/4 OR 1/2 IN VIDEO
Shows the cat Towser being commanded by a robot.
From The Towser Series.
Prod-JOU Dist-JOU

Towser And The Alien Invader (Strategy) C 5 MIN
16MM FILM, 3/4 OR 1/2 IN VIDEO
Shows the cat Towser saving the king from an alien from the planet Nice.
From The Towser Series.
Prod-JOU Dist-JOU

Towser And The Black Hole (Listening To Sound Advice) C 5 MIN
16MM FILM, 3/4 OR 1/2 IN VIDEO
Shows the cat Towser lured to a Black Hole even though he was warned against entering it.
From The Towser Series.
Prod-JOU Dist-JOU

Towser And The Black Knight (Courage) C 5 MIN
16MM FILM, 3/4 OR 1/2 IN VIDEO
Shows the cat Towser bravely challenging the Black Knight.
From The Towser Series.
Prod-JOU Dist-JOU

Towser And The Conjuror (Confidence) C 5 MIN
16MM FILM, 3/4 OR 1/2 IN VIDEO
Shows Towser restoring a magician's ability to perform by having faith in him.
From The Towser Series.
Prod-JOU Dist-JOU

Towser And The Dentist (Quackery) C 5 MIN
16MM FILM, 3/4 OR 1/2 IN VIDEO
Tells of Towser's friends offering cures for his toothache. Shows the importance of good dental care.
From The Towser Series.
Prod-JOU Dist-JOU

Towser And The Dinner Party (Deception) C 5 MIN
16MM FILM, 3/4 OR 1/2 IN VIDEO
Tells of Towser hiring a caterer to prepare a feast, when he'd promised to cook it himself.
From The Towser Series.
Prod-JOU Dist-JOU

Towser And The Dragon (Giftgiving) C 5 MIN
16MM FILM, 3/4 OR 1/2 IN VIDEO
Tells of the cat Towser trying to give away what he believes to be a useless dragon.
From The Towser Series.
Prod-JOU Dist-JOU

Towser And The Flight (Faith) C 5 MIN
16MM FILM, 3/4 OR 1/2 IN VIDEO
Shows the cat Towser being able to fly like a bird as long as he believes in his ability to fly.
From The Towser Series.
Prod-JOU Dist-JOU

Towser And The Funny Face (Punishments) C 5 MIN
16MM FILM, 3/4 OR 1/2 IN VIDEO
Shows Towser being punished by the wind for making funny faces and startling people.
From The Towser Series.
Prod-JOU Dist-JOU

Towser And The Haunted House (Fear) C 5 MIN
16MM FILM, 3/4 OR 1/2 IN VIDEO
Shows Towser boasting that he's not afraid of a haunted house.
From The Towser Series.
Prod-JOU Dist-JOU

Towser And The Holiday (Adventure) C 5 MIN
16MM FILM, 3/4 OR 1/2 IN VIDEO
Tells of Towser taking a camping trip to cure his boredom.
From The Towser Series.
Prod-JOU Dist-JOU

Towser And The Lion (Bravery) C 5 MIN
16MM FILM, 3/4 OR 1/2 IN VIDEO
Shows the cat Towser going after a lion.
From The Towser Series.
Prod-JOU Dist-JOU

Towser And The Magic Apple (Happiness) C 5 MIN
16MM FILM, 3/4 OR 1/2 IN VIDEO
Tells of a magic apple which is supposed to give happiness.
From The Towser Series.
Prod-JOU Dist-JOU

Towser And The Nosey Parker (Behavior) C 5 MIN
16MM FILM, 3/4 OR 1/2 IN VIDEO
Shows a creature who sniffs everything and causes a commotion.
From The Towser Series.
Prod-JOU Dist-JOU

Towser And The Secret (Ambition) C 5 MIN
16MM FILM, 3/4 OR 1/2 IN VIDEO
Tells of Towser trying to find out a butterfly's secret.
From The Towser Series.
Prod-JOU Dist-JOU

Towser And The Slight Accident (Love) C 5 MIN
16MM FILM, 3/4 OR 1/2 IN VIDEO
Tells of Towser trying science and magic to help his sore foot and finding help in an unexpected source.
From The Towser Series.
Prod-JOU Dist-JOU

Towser And The Smile Machine (Appearances Can Be Deceiving) C 5 MIN
16MM FILM, 3/4 OR 1/2 IN VIDEO
Tells of Towser visiting a doctor to get help with his smile.
From The Towser Series.
Prod-JOU Dist-JOU

Towser And The Snow Man (Illusion) C 5 MIN
16MM FILM, 3/4 OR 1/2 IN VIDEO
Tells of Towser making a snowman in the shape of a wizard.
From The Towser Series.
Prod-JOU Dist-JOU

Towser And The Space Shot (Judgment) C 5 MIN
16MM FILM, 3/4 OR 1/2 IN VIDEO
Tells of Towser showing good sense in declining to travel on a spacecraft going to the moon.
From The Towser Series.
Prod-JOU Dist-JOU

Towser And The Terrible Thing (Problem Solving) C 5 MIN
16MM FILM, 3/4 OR 1/2 IN VIDEO
Shows Towser devising an ingeneous solution to a terrible problem.
From The Towser Series.
Prod-JOU Dist-JOU

Towser And The Water Rats (Bargaining) C 5 MIN
16MM FILM, 3/4 OR 1/2 IN VIDEO
Tells a story of two water rats who want to buy Towser's house.
From The Towser Series.
Prod-JOU Dist-JOU

Towser And The Wizard (Trickery) C 5 MIN
16MM FILM, 3/4 OR 1/2 IN VIDEO
Tells of a wizard who pretends to lose his powers in order to take a holiday.
From The Towser Series.
Prod-JOU Dist-JOU

Towser And Uncle Bosco (Practical Jokes) C 5 MIN
16MM FILM, 3/4 OR 1/2 IN VIDEO
Tells of a practical joker who learns the error of his ways.
From The Towser Series.
Prod-JOU Dist-JOU

Towser—A Series

Consists of animated programs about the cat Towser and his friends. Uses simple story lines to present a variety of lessons.
Prod-JOU Dist-JOU

Towser And Goblin Gobble (Curiosity)	005 MIN
Towser And Sadie's Birthday (Imagination)	005 MIN
Towser And Sadie's Robot (Modern Conveniences)	005 MIN
Towser And The Alien Invader (Strategy)	005 MIN
Towser And The Black Hole (Listening To Sound	005 MIN
Towser And The Black Knight (Courage)	005 MIN
Towser And The Conjuror (Confidence)	005 MIN
Towser And The Dentist (Quackery)	005 MIN
Towser And The Dinner Party (Deception)	005 MIN
Towser And The Dragon (Giftgiving)	005 MIN
Towser And The Flight (Faith)	005 MIN
Towser And The Funny Face (Punishments)	005 MIN
Towser And The Haunted House (Fear)	005 MIN
Towser And The Holiday (Adventure)	005 MIN
Towser And The Lion (Bravery)	005 MIN
Towser And The Magic Apple (Happiness)	005 MIN
Towser And The Nosey Parker (Behavior)	005 MIN
Towser And The Secret (Ambition)	005 MIN
Towser And The Slight Accident (Love)	005 MIN
Towser And The Smile Machine (Appearances Can	005 MIN
Towser And The Snow Man (Illusion)	005 MIN
Towser And The Space Shot (Judgment)	005 MIN
Towser And The Terrible Thing (Problem Solving)	005 MIN
Towser And The Water Rats (Bargaining)	005 MIN
Towser And The Wizard (Trickery)	005 MIN
Towser And Uncle Bosco (Practical Jokes)	005 MIN

Toxic Hazards In Industry C 23 MIN
16MM FILM, 3/4 OR 1/2 IN VIDEO IND
Discusses the hazards of such toxic substances as silica, asbestos, lead, unrefined mineral oils, carbon dioxide, benzene and trichloroethylene. Deals with absorption routes and how the hazards may be kept within safe limits.
Prod-MILLBK Dist-IFB

Toxic Waste In America C 25 MIN
3/4 OR 1/2 INCH VIDEO CASSETTE
Examines how people's lives have been destroyed when they became victims of toxic wastes at Woodstock, New York. Depicts the residents of Seymour, Indiana, as they stop a toxic waste dump in their community. Reviews the story of Hugh Kaufman, an official with the Environmental Protection Agency (EPA) who blew the whistle on EPA corruption which was resulting in lay law enforcement.
Prod-DCTVC Dist-DCTVC

Toxicological Review - Charles Kokoski, PHD C 29 MIN
3/4 INCH VIDEO CASSETTE PRO
Examines the link between additives and the microbiological contamination of food, malnutrition and environmental contamination.
From The Food And Nutrition Seminars For Health Professionals Series.
LC NO. 78-706167
Prod-USFDA Dist-USNAC 1976

Toxigenicity Test Of C Diphteriae C 13 MIN
16MM FILM OPTICAL SOUND
Explains procedures of the in-vitro test and animal tests for the detection of toxigenic strains of corynebacterium diphtheriae. Shows preparation of materials and interpretation of results of the tests.
LC NO. FIE63-111
Prod-USPHS Dist-USNAC 1962

Toy That Grew Up II—A Series

Presents a review of the early days of the silver screen. Recreates silent films with informative commentary and authentic background music.
Prod-WTTWTV Dist-PUBTEL

Bells, The	76 MIN
Cops, Comics And Girls, Pt 1	54 MIN
Cops, Comics And Girls, Pt 2	59 MIN
Films Of Ben Turpin, The	64 MIN
Foolish Wives	91 MIN
Heart Of Texas Ryan, The	64 MIN
Judith Of Bethulia	61 MIN
Mad Whirl, The	71 MIN
Magic Movies Of Georges Malies, The	56 MIN
Mickey	61 MIN
Serials, The, Pt 1	64 MIN
Serials, The, Pt 2	64 MIN
Shamrock And The Rose, The	68 MIN

Toying With Reality C 27 MIN
3/4 OR 1/2 INCH VIDEO CASSETTE C
Deals with how the right kinds of playthings can simulate growth and development in children and points out that too often toy selection is left to big business and the pressures of Santa Claus.
From The Learning Through Play - Programs Series. Program 3
Prod-UTORMC Dist-UTORMC 1976

Toying With Reality C 28 MIN
3/4 OR 1/2 INCH VIDEO CASSETTE H-C A
Depicts children playing with clay, blocks, a piano bench, a guinea pig and other items. Discusses the restrictive messages conveyed in many expensive toys.
From The Learning Through Play Series.
Prod-UTORMC Dist-UTORMC 1980

Toylandia C 30 MIN
3/4 OR 1/2 INCH VIDEO CASSETTE K-P
See series title for descriptive statement.
From The Villa Alegre Series.
Prod-BCTV Dist-MDCPB

Toys C 7 MIN
16MM FILM, 3/4 OR 1/2 IN VIDEO H-C A
Examines the possible effects of modern war toys on children in a fantasy about a deadly battle fought by war toys in a Christmas store window.
Prod-NFBC Dist-MGHT 1966

Toys C 30 MIN
3/4 OR 1/2 INCH VIDEO CASSETTE
Presents guests who are experts in their respective fields who share tips on collecting and caring for antique toys.
From The Antique Shop Series.
Prod-WVPTTV Dist-MDCPB

Toys And Games For Five Years And Older C 14 MIN
2 INCH VIDEOTAPE
See series title for descriptive statement.
From The Living Better I Series.
Prod-MAETEL Dist-PUBTEL

Toys And Games For Preschoolers C 14 MIN
2 INCH VIDEOTAPE
See series title for descriptive statement.
From The Living Better I Series.
Prod-MAETEL Dist-PUBTEL

Toys For Children C 29 MIN
3/4 OR 1/2 INCH VIDEO CASSETTE
Suggests how parents can steer their children towards toys that are free of racist and sexist stereotypes.
From The Woman Series.
Prod-WNEDTV Dist-PBS

Toys From Nuremberg C 5 MIN
16MM FILM, 3/4 OR 1/2 IN VIDEO H-C A
Shows the toy-producing center of Nuremberg where some operations are still carried out by hand.
From The European Studies - Germany Series.
Prod-MFAFRG Dist-IFB Prodn-BAYER 1973

Toys-R-Us (Regional Marketing And Synergism) C 30 MIN
3/4 OR 1/2 INCH VIDEO CASSETTE
See series title for descriptive statement.
From The Contemporary Issues In Marketing Series.
Prod-CANTOR Dist-IVCH

TR And His Times C 58 MIN
3/4 OR 1/2 INCH VIDEO CASSETTE
Presents a portrait of Theodore Roosevelt and his America.
From The Walk Through The 20th Century With Bill Moyers Series.
LC NO. 84-706735
Prod-CORPEL Dist-PBS 1983

TR Country C 14 MIN
3/4 OR 1/2 INCH VIDEO CASSETTE
Uses the words of Theodore Roosevelt as narrative in showing the Badlands of North Dakota.
LC NO. 80-707709
Prod-USNPS Dist-USNAC 1980

Trabago C 30 MIN
3/4 OR 1/2 INCH VIDEO CASSETTE K-P
See series title for descriptive statement.
From The Villa Alegre Series.
Prod-BCTV Dist-MDCPB

Trabajando Con Proporciones C 12 MIN
16MM FILM, 3/4 OR 1/2 IN VIDEO H
A Spanish language version of the videocassette Proportion At Work. Introduces ratio and proportion as practical tools for solving problems by indirect measurement.
Prod-IFB Dist-IFB 1960

Trace And Breakpoint C 30 MIN
3/4 OR 1/2 INCH VIDEO CASSETTE IND
Explains SHIFT and ROTATE instructions while using TUTOR commands. Shows differences in trace (T) and breakpoint (BR) commands.
From The Hands-On With The 68000 Series.
Prod-COLOSU Dist-COLOSU

Trace Of Blood, A B 13 MIN
16MM FILM OPTICAL SOUND H-C A
Describes the treatment of a bladder cancer after a physician discovers traces of blood in a patients urine. Shows details of the surgical procedure for a bladder resection.
From The Doctors At Work Series.
LC NO. FIA65-1374
Prod-CMA Dist-LAWREN Prodn-LAWREN 1962

Tracer-Flo Movie C 10 MIN
16MM FILM OPTICAL SOUND C
Shows the state of the art of the tracer-flo process. Illustrates the tracer-flo process leak tests, microelectronic hybrids, semiconductors and integrated circuits by forcing Krypton 85 into the packages and then running them through a counting station to detect emissions.
LC NO. 76-701100
Prod-JOYCE Dist-JOYCE 1975

Tracheal Triangle, The C 8 MIN
16MM FILM - 3/4 IN VIDEO PRO
Uses an anterior neck dissection to illustrate the boundaries and major structures of the tracheal triangle.
From The Anatomy Of The Head And Neck Series.
LC NO. 78-706256
Prod-USVA Dist-USNAC Prodn-VADTC 1978

Tracheobronchial Collapse In Bronchitis C 17 MIN
16MM FILM OPTICAL SOUND
Demonstrates the relationship between the degree of tracheobronchial collapse and the extent of pulmonary disease, as well as showing that it is related to a 'VICIOUS CYCLE OF CHRONIC BRONCHITIS.'
Prod-USVA Dist-USVA 1962

Tracheostomy C 9 MIN
3/4 OR 1/2 INCH VIDEO CASSETTE PRO
See series title for descriptive statement.
From The Medical Skills Films Series.
Prod-WFP Dist-WFP

Tracheostomy C 11 MIN
3/4 OR 1/2 INCH VIDEO CASSETTE
See series title for descriptive statement.
From The Head And Neck Series.
Prod-SVL Dist-SVL

Tracheostomy And Mechanical Ventilation C 20 MIN
16MM FILM OPTICAL SOUND PRO
Demonstrates the technique of mechanical support of ventilation including tracheostomy, respirators, blood gases, tracheal toilet, antibiotics and alternating tracheostomy cuff pressure site.
Prod-ACYDGD Dist-ACY 1968

Tracheostomy Care C 25 MIN
16MM FILM OPTICAL SOUND PRO
Presents a description and demonstration of current techniques for deciding indication for tracheostomy, operative technique, choice of cannulae and postoperative nursing care.
Prod-ACYDGD Dist-ACY 1971

Tracheotomy And Cricothyrotomy C 23 MIN
16MM FILM OPTICAL SOUND
Companion to the film 'EMERGENCY AIRWAY.' Compares emergency methods for relieving obstructions in the upper and lower airways of dogs. Shows improvised devices, with stress on their hazards and crudity.
Prod-PFI Dist-PFI 1960

Tracheotomy And Cricothyrotomy C 27 MIN
3/4 OR 1/2 INCH VIDEO CASSETTE PRO
Describes tracheotomy and cricothyrotomy.
Prod-WFP Dist-WFP Prodn-UKANMC

Tracing The Roots Of Dance With Hanya Holm C 30 MIN
3/4 OR 1/2 INCH VIDEO CASSETTE
See series title for descriptive statement.
From The Shaping Today With Yesterday Series.
Prod-ARCVID Dist-ARCVID

Tracing With Ink B 32 MIN
16MM FILM OPTICAL SOUND C A
Demonstrates tracing on cloth. Shows procedures for handling the ink bottle and for filling, adjusting, using, cleaning and sharpening pens.
Prod-PUAVC Dist-PUAVC 1957

Track And Field - Conditioning The 400 Meter Runner And Intermediate Hurdler C 20 MIN
16MM FILM, 3/4 OR 1/2 IN VIDEO J-C
Explains special conditioning approaches for the 400 meter runner and intermediate hurdler. Breaks down each approach into elements of strength, flexibility, endurance and speed.
From The Coach Bill Dillinger Track And Field Series.
Prod-ATHI Dist-ATHI 1981

Track And Field - Discus Technique C 20 MIN
16MM FILM, 3/4 OR 1/2 IN VIDEO J-C
Observes each phase of the discus throwing motion and shows drills for mastering each.
From The Coach Bill Dillinger Track And Field Series.
Prod-ATHI Dist-ATHI 1981

Track And Field - Distance Conditioning C 20 MIN
16MM FILM, 3/4 OR 1/2 IN VIDEO J-C
Illustrates Coach Bill Dillinger's guidelines and drills for competitive distance running.
From The Coach Bill Dillinger Track And Field Series.
Prod-ATHI Dist-ATHI 1981

Track And Field - Distance Technique C 20 MIN
16MM FILM, 3/4 OR 1/2 IN VIDEO J-C
Details aspects of top running form. Explains when to lay back and when to make a move.
From The Coach Bill Dillinger Track And Field Series.
Prod-ATHI Dist-ATHI 1981

Track And Field - Hammer Techniques C 20 MIN
16MM FILM, 3/4 OR 1/2 IN VIDEO J-C
Takes the beginner, novice and expert through the fundamentals and advanced techniques of the hammer throw.
From The Coach Bill Dillinger Track And Field Series.
Prod-ATHI Dist-ATHI 1981

Track And Field - High Jump C 20 MIN
16MM FILM, 3/4 OR 1/2 IN VIDEO J-C
Presents Denis Whitby taking viewers through all jump events outlining areas for improvement.
From The Coach Bill Dillinger Track And Field Series.
Prod-ATHI Dist-ATHI 1981

Track And Field - Hurdle Techniques C 20 MIN
16MM FILM, 3/4 OR 1/2 IN VIDEO J-C
Demonstrates the proper form for high and intermediate hurdles as well as over and between hurdles.
From The Coach Bill Dillinger Track And Field Series.
Prod-ATHI Dist-ATHI 1981

Track And Field - Javelin Techniques C 20 MIN
16MM FILM, 3/4 OR 1/2 IN VIDEO J-C
Demonstrates the javelin throw and presents hints and drills to help gain proficiency.
From The Coach Bill Dillinger Track And Field Series.
Prod-ATHI Dist-ATHI 1981

Track And Field - Jump Conditioning C 20 MIN
16MM FILM, 3/4 OR 1/2 IN VIDEO J-C
Addresses how to develop explosiveness as well as other aspects of the long, triple and high jump.
From The Coach Bill Dillinger Track And Field Series.
Prod-ATHI Dist-ATHI 1981

Track And Field - Pole Vault Conditioning C 20 MIN
16MM FILM, 3/4 OR 1/2 IN VIDEO J-C
Shows how the pole vault combines sprinter speed, shot-putter strength and acrobatic ability.
From The Coach Bill Dillinger Track And Field Series.
Prod-ATHI Dist-ATHI 1981

Track And Field - Pole Vault Technique C 20 MIN
16MM FILM, 3/4 OR 1/2 IN VIDEO J-C
Presents all the aspects of pole vaulting using special technical effects.
From The Coach Bill Dillinger Track And Field Series.
Prod-ATHI Dist-ATHI 1981

Track And Field - Relay Techniques C 20 MIN
16MM FILM, 3/4 OR 1/2 IN VIDEO J-C
Outlines the phases of the 400-meter and mile relays showing the desirability of certain methods of exchanging the baton.
From The Coach Bill Dillinger Track And Field Series.
Prod-ATHI Dist-ATHI 1981

Track And Field - Shot Put Technique C 20 MIN
16MM FILM, 3/4 OR 1/2 IN VIDEO J-C
Illustrates the latest developments in shot-put techniques as exhibited by world class athletes.
From The Coach Bill Dillinger Track And Field Series.
Prod-ATHI Dist-ATHI 1981

Track And Field - Sprint Conditioning C 20 MIN
16MM FILM, 3/4 OR 1/2 IN VIDEO J-C
Demonstrates that conditioning for the 100 and 200 meters and high hurdles is divided into strength, flexibility and endurance. Includes special drills to improve performance.
From The Coach Bill Dillinger Track And Field Series.
Prod-ATHI Dist-ATHI 1981

Track And Field - Sprint Techniques C 20 MIN
16MM FILM, 3/4 OR 1/2 IN VIDEO J-C
Shows how to develop leg speed, stride length and arm action in sprints. Covers block clearance, race patterns and drills to improve ability.
From The Coach Bill Dillinger Track And Field Series.
Prod-ATHI Dist-ATHI 1981

Track And Field - Triple Jump, Long Jump Techniques C 20 MIN
16MM FILM, 3/4 OR 1/2 IN VIDEO J-C
Demonstrates how the long jump and triple jump are similar in technique. Details jump phases and specialty drills.
From The Coach Bill Dillinger Track And Field Series.
Prod-ATHI Dist-ATHI 1981

Track And Field - Weight Events Conditioning C 20 MIN
16MM FILM, 3/4 OR 1/2 IN VIDEO J-C
Emphasizes developing strength and channeling it into throwing action. Demonstrates proper weight lifting techniques.
From The Coach Bill Dillinger Track And Field Series.
Prod-ATHI Dist-ATHI 1981

Track And Field - Women—A Series
16MM FILM, 3/4 OR 1/2 IN VIDEO J-C
Presents Dr Ken Foreman discussing various aspects of women's track and field events.
Prod-ATHI Dist-ATHI 1981

Women's Track And Field - Conditioning 033 MIN
Women's Track And Field - Sprints, Hurdles 048 MIN
Women's Track And Field - Talent Search 060 MIN

Track And Field For Boys And Girls - Field Events C 16 MIN
16MM FILM, 3/4 OR 1/2 IN VIDEO I-H
Analyses five popular field events for boys and girls, defining terms and establishing correct techniques for each. Uses slow motion and freeze-frame photography to demonstrate the correct techniques for the high jump, pole vault, long jump, triple jump and shot put.
Prod-ASSOCF Dist-AIMS 1976

Track And Field For Boys And Girls - Field Events (Arabic) C 16 MIN
16MM FILM, 3/4 OR 1/2 IN VIDEO I-H
Analyses five popular field events for boys and girls, defining terms and establishing correct techniques for each. Uses slow motion and freeze-frame photography to demonstrate the correct techniques for the high jump, pole vault, long jump, triple jump and shot put.
Prod-ASSOCF Dist-AIMS 1976

Track And Field For Boys And Girls - Running Events C 17 MIN
16MM FILM, 3/4 OR 1/2 IN VIDEO I-H
Uses slow-motion and freeze frames in demonstrating the fundamentals of starting and running sprints, distance races, hurdles and relays.
Prod-ASSOCF Dist-AIMS 1976

Track And Field Skills C 16 MIN
16MM FILM OPTICAL SOUND J-H
Presents an introduction to the high jump, broad or long jump, pole vault and shot put. Uses slow motion and frozen action to describe techniques. Depicts track and field event winners of the 1964 Olympics.
Prod-SLFP Dist-SLFP 1966

Track And Field Today C 28 MIN
16MM FILM OPTICAL SOUND J-C
This film takes a totally new analytic view of this whole area of athletic competition in the interests of participants, officials, coaches and spectators. Shows in fascinating close-up detail the basics of winning and record-setting performance—by the rules.
LC NO. 75-713516
Prod-OSFS Dist-OSFS Prodn-CALPRO 1971

Track Of The Consolidated Health Record C 35 MIN
3/4 INCH VIDEO CASSETTE
Traces the flow of consolidated health records through a typical Veterans Administration health care facility.
LC NO. 79-707307
Prod-USVA Dist-USNAC 1978

Track Stars - The Unseen Heroes Of Movie Sound C 8 MIN
16MM FILM, 3/4 OR 1/2 IN VIDEO J-C A
Takes a behind-the-scenes look at the people who work at a motion picture sound studio and how they provide sound effects for movies and TV.
Prod-FIARTS Dist-LCOA 1979

Track Two C 90 MIN
16MM FILM - 3/4 IN VIDEO C A
Focuses on the notorious 1981 bathhouse raids that galvanized divergent gay interests into a powerful political force. Documents Toronto torn apart by bigotry and violence.
Prod-FIRS Dist-FIRS

Track 13 B 24 MIN
16MM FILM OPTICAL SOUND J-C A
Features famous people who bear witness to the power of God in their own lives. Includes redcap Ralston Young of Reader's Digest fame, ex-Communist Grace Lumkin, trial lawyer John Tabor and ex-Air Force Colonel John Robie.
Prod-CAFM Dist-CAFM

Track, No. 1 - Wes Santee B 13 MIN
16MM FILM OPTICAL SOUND
Olympic star miler shows how to run the mile and tells what it takes to run a 4-minute mile. Includes information on how to train, and get into condition for competition.
Prod-SFI Dist-SFI

Track, No. 2 B 13 MIN
16MM FILM OPTICAL SOUND
Presents tips from top college track men, including Bob Derrick, the record holder of 60 yard indoor hurdles and Hendrix Kruger, South African pole vaulter. Covers most of the track events, including shot put, discus, pole vault, broad jump and hurdles.
Prod-SFI Dist-SFI

Tracker C 12 MIN
16MM FILM OPTICAL SOUND
Demonstrates the peacetime role of an eastern air squadron of the Canadian Armed Forces in maintaining daily surveillance of ocean areas adjacent to the Canadian coastline and of the eastern Arctic.
LC NO. 76-701388
Prod-CDND Dist-CDND Prodn-NFBC 1974

Tracking In The Desert C 15 MIN
3/4 OR 1/2 INCH VIDEO CASSETTE I
Shows the life of Bedouin nomads, and encounters with a snake, scorpion and rabbit.
From The Encounter In The Desert Series.
Prod-CTI Dist-CTI

Tracking The North American Mountain Lion C 23 MIN
16MM FILM, 3/4 OR 1/2 IN VIDEO H-C A
Studies the American mountain lion in the Idaho Primitive Area. Discusses the predatory habits and other characteristics of these animals.
LC NO. 80-706302
Prod-NGS Dist-NGS 1976

Tracking The Supertrains C 57 MIN
3/4 OR 1/2 INCH VIDEO CASSETTE H-C A
Discusses a joint Japanese-American project to put the Japanese 'bullet' train in service between Los Angeles and San Diego. Considers the developments in train system design that are making high-speed travel possible.
From The Nova Series.
Prod-WGBHTV Dist-TIMLIF 1982

Tracks Of The Iron Horse C 28 MIN
16MM FILM OPTICAL SOUND I-C A
Tells of the building of the first transcontinental railroad and of the part it played in developing the American West.
Prod-UPR Dist-PCF

Traction—A Series

Presents a series on the principles of traction, application of traction and nursing care for the patient in traction.
Prod-FAIRGH Dist-FAIRGH

Application Of Traction 030 MIN
Nursing Care For The Patient In Traction 030 MIN
Principles Of Traction 020 MIN

Tractors C 24 MIN
3/4 OR 1/2 INCH VIDEO CASSETTE
Covers the various options available for lifting a tractor off victim after a tractor overturn. Describes the many factors that can hinder rescue.
From The Agricultural Accidents And Rescue Series.
Prod-PSU Dist-PSU

Trade C 10 MIN
16MM FILM, 3/4 OR 1/2 IN VIDEO P-I
Describes the complete trade cycle by tracing the route tomatoes take from grower to consumer, in the simplest possible terms. Provides an introduction to the economic cycle and the determination of prices.
From The Economics For The Elementary Series.
Prod-EVANSA Dist-AIMS 1971

Trade And Economics C 30 MIN
3/4 INCH VIDEO CASSETTE
Discusses methods by which China is trying to modernize her economy. Looks at problems associated with international business dealings with China.
From The China After Mao Series.
Prod-UMITV Dist-UMITV 1980

Trade Show Selling—A Series

Tells how to maximize sales opportunities at trade show exhibition booths. Points out special techniques in which few sales persons are trained. Covers concepts of critical path, network analysis and project management.
Prod-VIDART Dist-VISUCP

How Not To Exhibit Yourself 030 MIN

It'll Be OK On The Day 028 MIN

Trade Unions C 43 MIN
16MM FILM OPTICAL SOUND H-C A
Reports on the everyday activities of a trade unionist, and explains the historic development of trade unionism in Germany.
Prod-WSTGLC Dist-WSTGLC

Trade Unions - Putting You In The Picture C 12 MIN
16MM FILM OPTICAL SOUND
Shows the historical development of trade unions in Australia and explains their basic functions. Stresses the importance of migrant workers becoming more involved in union activities.
LC NO. 80-700845
Prod-NSWF Dist-TASCOR 1978

Trade-Offs And Future Trends C 30 MIN
3/4 OR 1/2 INCH VIDEO CASSETTE IND
Contrasts project implementations via random logic or microprocessors, with emphasis on software development costs. Explores high-level language versus assembly-language trade-offs. Concludes with future trends affecting software development.
From The Micros For Managers - Software Series.
Prod-COLOSU Dist-COLOSU

Trade-Offs Between Optical Source Types C 50 MIN
3/4 OR 1/2 INCH VIDEO CASSETTE PRO
Discusses of the trade-off between the various optical source types and which type is used in which circumstances.
From The Optical Fiber Communications Series.
Prod-NCSU Dist-AMCEE

Trade-Offs—A Series

Shows children engaging in simple business activities in order to point out basic economic concepts.
Prod-EDFCEN Dist-AITECH 1978

About Trade-Offs 012 MIN
At What Price 020 MIN
Choice 020 MIN
Does It Pay 020 MIN
Give And Take 020 MIN
Helping Out 020 MIN
How Could That Happen 020 MIN
Innocent Bystanders 020 MIN
Learning And Earning 020 MIN
Less And More 020 MIN
Malcolm Decides 020 MIN
Phil Saunders On Trade-Offs 025 MIN
To Buy Or Not To Buy 020 MIN
To Sell Or Not To Sell 020 MIN
We Decide 020 MIN
Why Money 020 MIN
Working Together 020 MIN

Trademarks - The Name Game C 15 MIN
16MM FILM OPTICAL SOUND
Uses the Eric Bass Puppets to explain the basic concepts of trademarks and brand names, including their function, history, selection, clearance and protection.
Prod-MTP Dist-MTP

Trademarks - The Name Of The Game C 15 MIN
3/4 INCH VIDEO CASSETTE
Features the Eric Bass Puppets playing the parts of a trademark expert and two business partners with a new product. Uses humor to explain various aspects of trademarks, including their function, history, selection, clearance and protection.
Prod-USTRAD Dist-MTP

Trader Vic's Used Cars C 10 MIN
16MM FILM, 3/4 OR 1/2 IN VIDEO J-C
Presents a film portrait of Victor Snyder, a Southern California used car dealer. Portrays Trader Vic and talks frankly about his business and shares his secrets of success.
Prod-BRAVC Dist-EBEC 1976

Trading C 15 MIN
3/4 OR 1/2 INCH VIDEO CASSETTE P
Introduces the concept of trading, defines goods and services, and discusses barter and money as systems of exchange.
From The Common Cents Series.
Prod-KETCTV Dist-AITECH 1977

Trading C 57 MIN
16MM FILM, 3/4 OR 1/2 IN VIDEO H-C A
Illustrates changing attitudes toward business in China by looking at individual enterprises. Examines recent experiments with free enterprise, leading to critical questions about whether trade with the outside world can be encouraged without Western influences undermining traditional values.
From The Heart Of The Dragon Series. Pt 12
Prod-ASH Dist-TIMLIF 1984

Trading And Sharing With The World C 20 MIN
2 INCH VIDEOTAPE J-H
Looks at the trading relationship between America and other countries.
From The Our World Of Economics Series.
Prod-MPATI Dist-GPITVL

Trading The Sun C 20 MIN
16MM FILM, 3/4 OR 1/2 IN VIDEO J-H
Studies the importance of tourism to the economy of certain Caribbean islands, but also looks at the danger which outside patterns of behavior can have on local society.
From The One World Series.
Prod-BBCTV Dist-FI 1982

Tradition C 20 MIN
16MM FILM - 3/4 IN VIDEO
Presents a moonshiner and an IRS agent discussing the history of moonshining, the economic and traditional forces that motivate illegal whiskey making, laws and penalties.
Prod-APPAL Dist-APPAL 1973

Tradition And Contemporary Judaism - Maimonides - Torah And Philosophic...—A Series

Examines the relevance of Moses Maimonides, a 12th century rabbi, statesman and philosopher. Focuses on the Torah and the Philosophic Quest. Narrated by Rabbi David Hartman.
Prod-ADL Dist-ADL

Abraham, Moses And Maimonides 015 MIN
Athens And Jerusalem 015 MIN
Law Ethics And Love Of God 015 MIN
Philosophy Of Community 015 MIN

Tradition And Contemporary Judaism - Joy And Responsibility—A Series

Explores Judaism in terms of knowledge of science and psychology. Features Rabbi David Hartman in a series of four lectures.
Prod-ADL Dist-ADL

Faith In The Age Of Technology 028 MIN
Interdependence - God And Man 028 MIN
Israel And The Renewal Of Judaism 028 MIN
Religious Laws As The Source Of Joy 028 MIN

Tradition And Contemporary Judaism - Prayer And The Jewish People—A Series

Explores the role of prayer in the lives of Jewish people. Features Rabbi David Hartman.
Prod-ADL Dist-ADL

Amidah - An Encounter With God 015 MIN
Morning Prayers - A Celebration Of The Gift 015 MIN
Priesthood To People - Transfer of Prayer 015 MIN
Shema - An Affirmation Of Belief, Love And 015 MIN

Tradition In Music, A C 28 MIN
16MM FILM OPTICAL SOUND
Shows the U S Navy Band during rehearsals and recording sessions and shows the work involved in keeping the band in shape.
LC NO. 74-705812
Prod-USN Dist-USNAC 1969

Tradition Of Conscience, A C 27 MIN
16MM FILM OPTICAL SOUND
Pictures the operation of a major newspaper. Follows one day's editions of the St Louis post dispatch from the teletype machines to the street. Shows how the philosophy and historical background of the paper help shape the editing and reporting of today's events.
LC NO. FIA66-653
Prod-PULTZR Dist-GUG Prodn-GUG 1966

Tradition Of Service C 20 MIN
16MM FILM OPTICAL SOUND
Surveys the Chesapeake and Potomac Telephone Company's years of service from 1875 to 1975. Draws attention to the role of the company's employees in keeping the communication system working.
LC NO. 77-702160
Prod-CPTCO Dist-CPTCO Prodn-COMFLM 1977

Traditional And Religious Music C 60 MIN
3/4 INCH VIDEO CASSETTE
See series title for descriptive statement.
From The Grass Roots Series.
Prod-MDCPB Dist-MDCPB

Traditional Birthing - Maude Bryant C 19 MIN
3/4 OR 1/2 INCH VIDEO CASSETTE PRO
Conveys refreshing attitude towards using a midwife at birth of baby. Reflects on Maude Bryant who delivered over one hundred births in rural North Carolina.
Prod-HSCIC Dist-HSCIC 1984

Traditional Company, The C 24 MIN
16MM FILM, 3/4 OR 1/2 IN VIDEO H-C A
Presents a traditional firm which gives workers the option to become shareholders in order to promote greater worker interest in management. Industrial democracy is a possible solution to the management problems of industrial conflict and low productivity, including worker participation.
From The What About The Workers Series.
Prod-THAMES Dist-MEDIAG 1978

Traditional Handicrafts C 15 MIN
16MM FILM OPTICAL SOUND J A
Examines traditional Chinese handicrafts as the craftsmen perform curio carving, glass bottle painting, ivory carving, dollmaking and other crafts.
From The How Yukong Moved The Mountains Series.
LC NO. 80-700604
Prod-CAPI Dist-CINPER 1976

Traditional Upholstery C 25 MIN
3/4 OR 1/2 INCH VIDEO CASSETTE H-C A
Demonstrates the remaking of a dining room chair from the canvas webbing upwards.
From The Better Than New Series.
Prod-BBCTV Dist-FI

Traffic - Present And Future Needs B 30 MIN
16MM FILM - 3/4 IN VIDEO C A
See series title for descriptive statement.
From The Sportsmanlike Driving Series.
Prod-AAAFTS Dist-GPITVL Prodn-SCETV

Traffic Court C 14 MIN
16MM FILM, 3/4 OR 1/2 IN VIDEO J-C A
Observes traffic court procedures in order to familiarize the viewer with the consequences of traffic violations.
Prod-CAHILL Dist-AIMS 1972

Traffic Court (Captioned) C 14 MIN
16MM FILM, 3/4 OR 1/2 IN VIDEO J-C A
Observes traffic court procedures in order to familiarize the viewer with the consequences of traffic violations.
Prod-CAHILL Dist-AIMS 1972

Traffic Court (Spanish) C 14 MIN
16MM FILM, 3/4 OR 1/2 IN VIDEO J-C A
Observes traffic court procedures in order to familiarize the viewer with the consequences of traffic violations.
Prod-CAHILL Dist-AIMS 1972

Traffic Direction And Control C 20 MIN
16MM FILM, 3/4 OR 1/2 IN VIDEO
Presents a variety of traffic and pedestrian control situations including daytime, nighttime, inclement weather, traffic after major events and highway situations. Demonstrates the need for consistent traffic direction, hand signals and gestures, and correct use of the whistle, baton, flashlight, flares and reflectorized aids.
Prod-WORON Dist-MTI

Traffic In Souls B 50 MIN
16MM FILM SILENT
Takes a look at white slavery in New York during the early part of the 20th century.
Prod-UNKNWN Dist-REELIM 1913

Traffic Law Observance And Enforcement B 30 MIN
16MM FILM - 3/4 IN VIDEO C A
See series title for descriptive statement.
From The Sportsmanlike Driving Series. Refresher Course
Prod-AAAFTS Dist-GPITVL Prodn-SCETV

Traffic Laws C 20 MIN
3/4 OR 1/2 INCH VIDEO CASSETTE
Emphasizes laws of parking, speeding, right-of-way, car positioning and passing that are recommended by the Uniform Vehicle Code. Presents the general rules a driver must follow while operating a motor vehicle.
Prod-BUMPA Dist-BUMPA

Traffic Laws Made By Man B 30 MIN
16MM FILM - 3/4 IN VIDEO C A
See series title for descriptive statement.
From The Sportsmanlike Driving Series. Refresher Course
Prod-AAAFTS Dist-GPITVL Prodn-SCETV

Traffic Laws Made By Nature B 30 MIN
16MM FILM - 3/4 IN VIDEO C A
See series title for descriptive statement.
From The Sportsmanlike Driving Series. Refresher Course
Prod-AAAFTS Dist-GPITVL Prodn-SCETV

Traffic Or Transit C 30 MIN
16MM FILM - 3/4 IN VIDEO J-C A
Discusses that the need for subsidized urban transit is necessary but that most people still cling to the independence and the convenience of their own car. Looks at some of the wasteful aspects of using the automobile as a routine means of transportation as compared to rail and bus transit and shows examples of successful modern mass transit systems.
From The Man Builds - Man Destroys Series.
Prod-UN Dist-GPITVL

Traffic Safety C 28 MIN
3/4 OR 1/2 INCH VIDEO CASSETTE J A
Features actor Robert Horton as he discusses the Alcohol Safety Action Program.
Prod-SUTHRB Dist-SUTHRB

Traffic Safety Advanced Driving - The Greater Adventure C 26 MIN
16MM FILM OPTICAL SOUND
Dramatizes the relationship between traffic safety attitudes and society and points out the individual responsibilities to self and society.
LC NO. 74-705813
Prod-USAF Dist-USNAC 1969

Traffic Safety, Vehicle Design And Equipment B 30 MIN
16MM FILM - 3/4 IN VIDEO C A
See series title for descriptive statement.
From The Sportsmanlike Driving Series.
Prod-AAAFTS Dist-GPITVL Prodn-SCETV

Traffic Trials - Heaven Won't Wait C 19 MIN
16MM FILM, 3/4 OR 1/2 IN VIDEO J-C A
Tells how six drivers appear before a heavenly judge to review the driving errors that caused their deaths.
LC NO. 81-706718
Prod-CAHILL Dist-AIMS

Traffic Trigger Films—A Series
J-H
Presents open-ended traffic situations and discusses values, attitudes and decisions.
Prod-PROART Dist-PROART 1974

Behind The Wheel, Pt 1 8 MIN
Behind The Wheel, Pt 2 8 MIN
Driving While Intoxicated 28 MIN

Traffic Violation C 30 MIN
3/4 OR 1/2 INCH VIDEO CASSETTE H
Discusses the most frequent traffic violations which lead to accidents, such as speeding, drunk driving, tailgating, failure to yield the right of way, and mechanical defects of the car.

From The Behind The Wheel Series.
Prod-WCVETV Dist-GPITVL 1983

Traffic Watcher C 14 MIN
16MM FILM, 3/4 OR 1/2 IN VIDEO P-I
Depicts a day in the life of Captain Dan, traffic helicopter pilot in Washington, DC, emphasizing his participation in the elementary school traffic safety program.
Prod-WPLM Dist-EBEC 1972

Traffic World, The C 15 MIN
16MM FILM OPTICAL SOUND
Deals with the right-of-way laws, stressing the importance of giving the right-of-way rather than insisting on it.
From The Driving To Survive Series.
Prod-BUMPA Dist-BUMPA

Traffic World, The C 14 MIN
3/4 OR 1/2 INCH VIDEO CASSETTE
Explains the signs that control and the rules that regulate the traffic world.
Prod-PARPRO Dist-PARPRO

Tragada Bahavi - A Rural Theater Troupe Of Gujarat C 42 MIN
3/4 INCH VIDEO CASSETTE
Follows a troupe of Bhavai performers through the Indian countryside. Shows preparations and negotiations with village sponsors. Illustrates an evening of a miracle play, comic skits, dances, juggling and a romantic drama.
Prod-DOCEDR Dist-DOCEDR

Tragedy C 15 MIN
16MM FILM OPTICAL SOUND H-C
Shows how the play 'MACBETH' affects us as a tragedy. Presents how Macbeth, in the circumstances in which he lives and because of the decisions he has made, is led inevitably by a chain of cause and effect to suffering and death.
From The Art Of Shakespeare In Macbeth Series.
Prod-KINGSP Dist-HRAW

Tragedy Of Addiction, The - The Trip Back C 28 MIN
16MM FILM OPTICAL SOUND H-C A
Contains a film report of one of many lectures to high school students by Florrie Fisher, who lost 23 years of her life to drug addiction. Miss Fisher spares her audience none of the tragic, sordid details of a drug addict's life. Hers is a rare talent to communicate with young men and women - she tells it like it is.
Prod-UTEX Dist-AVON

Tragedy Of Antony And Cleopatra, The C 190 MIN
16MM FILM, 3/4 OR 1/2 IN VIDEO H-C A
Presents the story of Antony and Cleopatra. Shows Antony as a man born to rule but brought to ruin by his own lust. Depicts the complexities of the destructive and desired Cleopatra.
Prod-BARDPR Dist-EBEC 1983

Tragedy Of Black Suicide, The, Pt 1 C 29 MIN
3/4 OR 1/2 INCH VIDEO CASSETTE
Prod-RCOMTV Dist-SYLWAT 1981

Tragedy Of Black Suicide, The, Pt 2 C 29 MIN
3/4 OR 1/2 INCH VIDEO CASSETTE
Prod-RCOMTV Dist-SYLWAT 1981

Tragedy Of Hamlet, Prince Of Denmark, The B 45 MIN
16MM FILM SILENT C A
Presents the Gallaudet College Dramatics Club's performance of the Shakespeare classic. Signed.
Prod-GALCO Dist-GALCO 1958

Tragedy Of King Richard II, The C 172 MIN
16MM FILM, 3/4 OR 1/2 IN VIDEO H-C A
Based on The Chronicles by English historian Raphael Holinshed. Represents the first time Shakespeare explored the idea that character may determine fate. Presents the weak, self-centered King Richard II, who becomes so out of touch with reality that his only defense of his kingdon is the hope that God can save him.
Prod-BARDPR Dist-EBEC 1981

Tragedy Of Macbeth, The C 150 MIN
16MM FILM, 3/4 OR 1/2 IN VIDEO H-C A
Explores the moral and psychological effects of evil in the life of one man.
Prod-BARDPR Dist-EBEC 1981

Tragedy Of The Commons, The C 23 MIN
16MM FILM, 3/4 OR 1/2 IN VIDEO H
Presents four sequences all related to overpopulation. Stresses the need for man to regulate population before nature, through disease or some type of violence, regulates the size of the population for man.
Prod-KINGSP Dist-PHENIX 1971

Tragedy Of The Red Salmon C 24 MIN
16MM FILM, 3/4 OR 1/2 IN VIDEO I-C
A shortened version of Tragedy Of The Red Salmon. Shows Jacques Cousteau and his crew as they study the migration of the red sockeye salmon. Focuses on the salmon's journey from Fraser Lake in Alaska to the ocean and back again to the lake.
From The Undersea World Of Jacques Cousteau Series.
Prod-METROM Dist-CF 1975

Tragedy Of The Red Salmon C 60 MIN
16MM FILM, 3/4 OR 1/2 IN VIDEO
Presents Jacques Cousteau and his crew recording the arrival of the red salmon in Olga Bay. Shows the salmon's perilous rush upstream, pictures the circling courtship dance and the spawning rituals, as well as the fertilizing of the eggs in the nest. Raises the question of how much man should meddle with natural events he does not fully understand.
From The Undersea World Of Jacques Cousteau Series.
Prod-METROM Dist-CF 1970

Tragedy Of The Red Salmon, The (Spanish) C 24 MIN
16MM FILM, 3/4 OR 1/2 IN VIDEO
Documents the salmon's upstream migration to its spawning grounds in its home river, where eggs are laid and fertilized before the adults die.
From The Undersea World Of Jacques Cousteau Series.
Prod-METROM Dist-CF 1975

Tragedy Or Triumph C 28 MIN
16MM FILM, 3/4 OR 1/2 IN VIDEO J-C A
Explores the problems of hunger and food production in the modern world.
Prod-UN Dist-JOU 1975

Tragic Comic, The C 27 MIN
16MM FILM - 3/4 IN VIDEO
Depicts alcohol abuse by portraying an alcoholic comedian drinking his way through his television performance. Presents statistics on use of alcohol in this country.
Prod-SALVA Dist-MTP

Tragic Vision, The C 30 MIN
3/4 OR 1/2 INCH VIDEO CASSETTE C
See series title for descriptive statement.
From The Art Of Being Human Series. Module 8
Prod-MDCC Dist-MDCC

Tragicomedy Of Marriage, The B 10 MIN
16MM FILM OPTICAL SOUND A
Presents a spoof of experimental films that use sexual symbolism to excess. Deals with a husband, who wanted a wife for domestic reasons and who is afraid of sex, and a wife, who married for sex and hates housework.
Prod-PIKE Dist-CFS

Trail Horse, The C 22 MIN
16MM FILM, 3/4 OR 1/2 IN VIDEO
Discusses the trail horse events including basic and advanced training methods which demonstrate what makes a good trail horse. Shows the origination of obstacles used in the class, utilizing actual trail ride sequences.
Prod-AQHORS Dist-AQHORS

Trail North, The C 30 MIN
3/4 OR 1/2 INCH VIDEO CASSETTE
Provides a personal view of the history of Mexican immigration to the United States. Follows anthropologist Dr Robert Alvarez and his son as they recreate the journey of their ancestors. Narrated by Martin Sheen. Filmed in Baja, California.
Prod-KPBS Dist-KPBS

Trail Of Broken Treaties C 26 MIN
16MM FILM, 3/4 OR 1/2 IN VIDEO
Examines social problems faced by American Indians and focuses on the attempts of Indian leaders to improve the situation.
From The Native Americans Series.
Prod-BBCTV Dist-CNEMAG

Trail Of Tears C 20 MIN
16MM FILM, 3/4 OR 1/2 IN VIDEO J-H
Discusses the American Indian's struggle to maintain his identity and preserve his heritage. Focuses on the forced removal of the Cherokees from their homelands and their anguished exodus to the West along the trail of tears.
From The Matter Of Fact Series.
LC NO. 74-703207
Prod-NITC Dist-AITECH Prodn-WETATV 1973

Trail Of The Buffalo C 9 MIN
16MM FILM, 3/4 OR 1/2 IN VIDEO P-I
Describes and laments the passing of the huge buffalo that once roamed the prairies.
LC NO. 83-706587
Prod-JHNSTN Dist-EBEC 1983

Trail Of The Ice Age Blues C 29 MIN
16MM FILM, 3/4 OR 1/2 IN VIDEO J-C
Describes the Ice Age and its effects on the surface of the Earth. Considers the possibility of a new Ice Age.
From The Planet Of Man Series.
Prod-OECA Dist-FI 1976

Trail Of The Tarpon C 14 MIN
16MM FILM OPTICAL SOUND
Shows Dave Newell fishing for Florida tarpon at Marco Island, Cape Sable and the Everglades.
Prod-FLADC Dist-FLADC

Trail Ride C 20 MIN
16MM FILM OPTICAL SOUND I-J
Shows how city boys visiting at the Blood Indian Reserve in Alberta ride herd, help brand calves and spend the night in tepees with the Blood Indians who have gathered for a sun dance.
LC NO. FIA65-1854
Prod-NFBC Dist-SF 1964

Trailblazer C 20 MIN
3/4 INCH VIDEO CASSETTE
Tells the story of Trailblazer, the first major pipeline to tap the natural gas reserves of the Rocky Mountain Overthrust area. Describes the 800-mile system running from Whitney Canyon in Wyoming to Beatrice, Nebraska.
Prod-MIDCON Dist-MTP

Trailblazers Of Modern Dance C 60 MIN
16MM FILM, 3/4 OR 1/2 IN VIDEO
Reviews the history of modern dance in America from its beginnings in the early 1900s to the appearance of Martha Graham in the early 1930s. Includes rare film footage of Doris Humphrey, Ruth St Denis, Anna Pavlova and what is believed to be Isadora Duncan, along with reconstructed performances of Duncan's etudes, St Denis and Humphrey's Soaring and Ted Shawn's Polonaise.
From The Dance In America Series.
LC NO. 79-708056
Prod-WNETTV Dist-IU 1979

Trailing A River C 20 MIN
3/4 INCH VIDEO CASSETTE I
Shows a raft in the Colorado River from its source on the western slope of the Rockies to the Gulf of California.
From The Understanding Our World, Unit II - Geography We Should Know Series.
Prod-KRMATV Dist-GPITVL

Train Ride To Grandfathers C 3 MIN
16MM FILM SILENT I-H S
Presents Florian Caliguiri relating to the deaf in American sign language his childhood experiences traveling by train to visit his grandfather.
LC NO. 76-701707
Prod-JOYCE Dist-JOYCE 1975

Train Rolls On, The B 33 MIN
16MM FILM OPTICAL SOUND
Examines the work and career of Soviet filmmaker Alexander Medvedkin. Shows how Medvedkin moved camera crews into the interior of the Soviet Union in order to bring the cinema to the Russian masses.
LC NO. 75-702768
Prod-MARKC Dist-NYFLMS 1975

Training B 30 MIN
16MM FILM OPTICAL SOUND
Discusses the methods of determining how much money an organization can afford to put into training and reviews a number of ideas basic to success in training or teaching people.
From The Success In Supervision Series.
LC NO. 74-706286
Prod-WETATV Dist-USNAC 1965

Training C
1/2 IN VIDEO CASSETTE (VHS)
Explains training techniques for achieving and maintaining physical fitness.
From The Dynamics Of Fitness - The Body In Action Series.
Prod-IBIS Dist-IBIS

Training C 40 MIN
3/4 OR 1/2 INCH VIDEO CASSETTE
See series title for descriptive statement.
From The Effective Supervision Series.
Prod-ERF Dist-DELTAK

Training C 60 MIN
3/4 OR 1/2 INCH VIDEO CASSETTE IND
See series title for descriptive statement.
From The Quality Circle Concepts Series.
Prod-NCSU Dist-AMCEE

Training - A Major Responsibility C 10 MIN
3/4 OR 1/2 INCH VIDEO CASSETTE
Explains that training is an investment in time and that a supervisor's ability to get things done through others depends on the training others have received.
From The New Supervisor Series. Module 4
Prod-RESEM Dist-RESEM

Training Activity, The C 11 MIN
3/4 OR 1/2 INCH VIDEO CASSETTE
Deals with both the 'how to' and the 'why' of training with emphasis on actual practice rather than theory.
From The Pre-Supervisory Training Series. Module 3
Prod-RESEM Dist-RESEM

Training Aids B 23 MIN
16MM FILM OPTICAL SOUND
Describes the uses of simple and complex training aids including chalkboards, filmstrips, slides, transparencies, working models and motion pictures.
From The Military Instruction Series. No. 3
LC NO. FIE56-246
Prod-USA Dist-USNAC 1956

Training Aids B 23 MIN
3/4 INCH VIDEO CASSETTE
Discusses the types, characteristics and uses of simple and complex training aids, including chalkboards, filmstrips, slides, transparencies, working models and motion pictures.
Prod-USNAC Dist-USNAC 1972

Training Aids - Classroom Utilization B 15 MIN
16MM FILM OPTICAL SOUND
Shows how a good navy instructor uses audio-visual aids to encourage student participation in class.
LC NO. FIE52-1290
Prod-USN Dist-USNAC Prodn-DEFREN 1950

Training Aids - Selection And Planning B 16 MIN
16MM FILM OPTICAL SOUND
Shows how a navy instructor selects motion pictures, charts and models to fit into his lesson and how he checks the aids, equipment and classroom prior to use.
LC NO. FIE52-1289
Prod-USN Dist-USNAC Prodn-DEFREN 1951

Training Aids - Slides, Large Drawings And Transparencies C 18 MIN
16MM FILM OPTICAL SOUND
Explains the nature of the equipment and materials which are needed and the opportunities for preparing and using such training aids by naval instructors.
LC NO. FIE52-1973
Prod-USNAC Dist-USNAC 1951

Training At The Peking Circus C 16 MIN
16MM FILM OPTICAL SOUND J A
Provides a behind-the-scenes look at the Peking Circus, showing various performers rehearsing their acts. Concludes with an actual performance of the circus, showing the acts of the performers seen earlier in rehearsal.
From The How Yukong Moved The Mountains Series.
LC NO. 80-700639
Prod-CAPI Dist-CINPER 1979

Training Decisions In A Microteaching Clinic C 28 MIN
16MM FILM OPTICAL SOUND T
Discusses the various training procedures and issues which provide teachers with specific skills and wider range of instructional alternatives for their professional performance.
Prod-EDUC Dist-EDUC

Training Dogs The Woodhouse Way—A Series
16MM FILM, 3/4 OR 1/2 IN VIDEO H-C A
Presents Barbara Woodhouse's way of training dogs with love and firmness.
Prod-BBCTV Dist-FI 1982

Advance, Stand, Sit And Down, The 030 MIN
Come When Called 030 MIN
Down, The 030 MIN
Nervous Dogs 030 MIN
Problem Dogs 030 MIN
Puppies 030 MIN
Right Start, The 030 MIN
Show Handling 030 MIN
Sit And Stay 030 MIN
Walking To Heel 030 MIN

Training For Tracking C 15 MIN
16MM FILM, 3/4 OR 1/2 IN VIDEO
Illustrates a variety of techniques used to train dogs for tracking.
From The Dog Obedience Training Series.
Prod-KLEINW Dist-KLEINW 1974

Training For Upward Mobility C 16 MIN
3/4 OR 1/2 INCH VIDEO CASSETTE
Defines upward mobility and shows why it is important to organizations. Gives three practical advantages of moving people upward within the organization, and the major reasons for failure of upward mobility training and ways to overcome them.
From The Supervisor And OJT Series. Module 4
Prod-RESEM Dist-RESEM

Training Manager's Guide To IIS Coursewriter, A C
3/4 OR 1/2 INCH VIDEO CASSETTE
Provides a view of the steps involved in devising a plan for the numbering of students and the categorization of student records. Portrays the facilities that the various Interactive Instructional System (IIS) administrative commands provide for student registration and removal.
From The Authoring In IIS Coursewriter Series.
Prod-DELTAK Dist-DELTAK

Training Manikin, The C 10 MIN
16MM FILM, 3/4 OR 1/2 IN VIDEO H-C A
An instructor and his pupils demonstrate ways in which a manikin fabricated to resemble a human being may be used to train a class in exhaled air resuscitation and closed chest cardiac massage. Describes the care and maintenance of the manikin, as well as the hygienic precautions to be taken in order to safeguard users.
From The Emergency Resuscitation Series. No. 4
Prod-BRITAD Dist-IFB 1964

Training Manikin, The C 10 MIN
16MM FILM, 3/4 OR 1/2 IN VIDEO C A
Demonstrates how a manikin, carefully fabricated to resemble a human being, may be used to train a class in exhaled air resuscitation and closed cardiac massage.
From The Emergency Resuscitation Series.
Prod-UKMD Dist-IFB 1964

Training Memorandum, The C 12 MIN
16MM FILM, 3/4 OR 1/2 IN VIDEO H-C A
Discusses the benefits of training to change attitudes of resistance and indifference. Takes a skeptical supervisor through a series of experiences which motivate him to see training in a new light. Illustrates examples of modern training methods and philosophy.
From The Professional Management Program Series.
LC NO. 74-700230
Prod-NEM Dist-NEM 1973

Training Methods C 15 MIN
16MM FILM OPTICAL SOUND
Discusses training methods for various sports.
From The Coaching Development Programme Series. No. 9
LC NO. 76-701067
Prod-SARBOO Dist-SARBOO Prodn-SVL 1974

Training Module On Role Enactment In Children's Play—A Series
A
Prod-UPITTS Dist-CFDC Prodn-CFDC 1974

City Builders, The 29 MIN
Concept Instancing Of Role Enactment 13 MIN
Moat Monster, The 12 MIN
Role Enactment In Children's Play - A 29 MIN
What Happens When You Go To The Hospital 12 MIN

Training Program Design C
3/4 OR 1/2 INCH VIDEO CASSETTE
Uses a systematic approach to the design of a training program. Identifies each step to be performed.
Prod-XEROX Dist-DELTAK

Training Resources And Techniques C 25 MIN
16MM FILM OPTICAL SOUND PRO
Shows several training programs, facilities and procedures which vocational counselors employ in rehabilitation programs for retarded clients.
From The Counseling The Mentally Retarded Series. No. 3
LC NO. 72-702013
Prod-UKANBC Dist-NMAC 1968

Training Resources And Techniques C 28 MIN
3/4 OR 1/2 INCH VIDEO CASSETTE
Prod-PRIMED Dist-PRIMED

Training The Advocate C
3/4 OR 1/2 INCH VIDEO CASSETTE PRO
Designed as a basic trial skills training program. Includes trial demonstrations, critiques, interviews with the expert faculty and discussions of communications skills that can enhance an attorney's presentation in court.
Prod-ABACPE Dist-ABACPE

Training The Advocate—A Series
PRO
Integrates video presentations with written materials to take the attorney through every stage of the trial process. Includes demonstrations by skilled trial lawyers, an overview and post-trial discussion among the faculty.
Prod-AMBAR Dist-ABACPE

Closing Arguments - Pt 1 057 MIN
Closing Arguments - Pt 2 029 MIN
Cross Examination 055 MIN
Direct Examination 057 MIN
Expert Witness - Damages 058 MIN
Expert Witness - Liability 057 MIN
Introduction And Use Of Demonstrative 056 MIN
Jury Deliberation 043 MIN
Jury Selection 060 MIN
Laying The Foundation For Exhibits And 049 MIN
Opening Statements 059 MIN

Training The Disadvantaged C 11 MIN
3/4 OR 1/2 INCH VIDEO CASSETTE
Points out that the disadvantaged should be allowed to progress in meaningful tasks at a rate that will build up confidence and insure ultimate success on the job.
From The Supervising The Disadvantaged Series. Module 5
Prod-RESEM Dist-RESEM

Training The School Bus Driver C 26 MIN
16MM FILM - 3/4 IN VIDEO A
Examines the responsibilities of the school bus driver, emphasizing the exacting nature of his job. Looks at the rigorous driver training required for school bus work.
Prod-PARKRD Dist-LAWREN

Training The Trainer C
16MM FILM, 3/4 OR 1/2 IN VIDEO A
Shows how to prepare for the presentation of both the Supervisory Training (Office) series and the Supervisory Training (Industrial) series.
From The Supervisory Training (Office) Series.
Prod-CRMP Dist-CRMP 1983

Training The Trainer—A Series
T
Features teaching techniques. Presented by Dr Donald F Michalak. Includes participant manuals, facilitator's guide and overhead transparencies.
Prod-ITCORP Dist-ITCORP

Administering The Training Program 030 MIN
Developing And Using Lesson Plans 030 MIN
Developing And Writing Training Objectives 030 MIN
Elements Of Effective Training, The 030 MIN
Instructing To Facilitate Learning 030 MIN
Learning-How It Occurs 030 MIN
Measuring Instructional Effectiveness 030 MIN
Methods For Teaching Information 030 MIN
Methods For Teaching Skills 030 MIN
On-The-Job Training 030 MIN
Planning For Effective Training 030 MIN
Principles Of Visual Training 030 MIN
Teaching Your First Class 030 MIN
Using Visual Aids Effectively 030 MIN

Training The Trainer—A Series
IND
Teaches the learner or inexperienced trainer the principles of effective instruction. Shows how to determine trainee needs and levels, establish realistic performance objectives, design and manage training sessions and assess results of training situations.
Prod-LEIKID Dist-LEIKID

Administration And Evaluation 050 MIN
Presentation 050 MIN
Research And Preparation 050 MIN
Teaching Techniques 050 MIN

Training The Young Horse C 27 MIN
16MM FILM, 3/4 OR 1/2 IN VIDEO J-C A
Shows the step-by-step training of a young horse, from the handling and grooming of a foal through the introduction of complete tack and rider at age three to four years old. Covers leading, training on a lunge rein and in the basic paces, beginning jumping and the gradual addition of the tack. Emphasizes teaching the horse obedience, rhythm, and balance, with gradual introduction of the rider to the horse. Introduced by Princess Anne of Great Britain.
From The Riding Training Series.
Prod-BHORSE Dist-IU Prodn-GSAVL 1979

Training Tips C 25 MIN
16MM FILM, 3/4 OR 1/2 IN VIDEO H-C A
Presents a training aid for fire department officers.
Prod-LACFD Dist-FILCOM 1964

Training Your Dog C 60 MIN
1/2 IN VIDEO CASSETTE (BETA)
Offers information on dog training, explaining how to turn a squirming ball of fluff into a respectable canine citizen.
Prod-CINAS Dist-HOMET

Trains C 5 MIN
16MM FILM OPTICAL SOUND
Depicts a historical journey on Canada's last operating steam engine.
LC NO. 76-703814
Prod-YORKU Dist-YORKU 1976

Trains C 14 MIN
3/4 OR 1/2 INCH VIDEO CASSETTE P
Depicts Peggy after a train trip, describing the different cars on her train. Shows that the freight train she sees also has specialized cars.
From The Under The Yellow Balloon Series.
Prod-SCETV Dist-AITECH 1980

Trains C 15 MIN
16MM FILM, 3/4 OR 1/2 IN VIDEO I-H A
Presents a quick survey of railroads, past, present and future. Demonstrates influence of the railroad on our native American music. Portrays the excitement variety of railroad careers.
Prod-COMICO Dist-AIMS 1970

Trains - A First Film C 11 MIN
16MM FILM, 3/4 OR 1/2 IN VIDEO P-I
Shows passenger trains and freight trains, diesel engines and cars made for special purposes. Explains the jobs of the men who run the train. Shows how a train is made up in the railroad yard for its trip to the next city.
Prod-BEAN Dist-PHENIX 1969

Trains And More Trains - Trenes Y Mas Trenes C 11 MIN
16MM FILM, 3/4 OR 1/2 IN VIDEO P-I
Presents an introduction to freight and commuter trains via documentary footage. Discusses Amtrak, the 'train of the future.'
From The Bilingual Film Series, Module 4 - Transportation And Community Workers Series.
Prod-BRNTNO Dist-CAROUF 1973

Trains And Planes B 15 MIN
2 INCH VIDEOTAPE P-I
See series title for descriptive statement.
From The Our Changing Community Series.
Prod-VITA Dist-GPITVL 1967

Trains, Tracks And Trestles—A Series

Discusses model railroading, exploring basic track plans, the different types of equipment available, benchwork and wiring and the construction of scenery and structures.
Prod-WMVSTV Dist-PUBTEL

Bench Work And Wiring 30 MIN
Gauges 30 MIN
Scenery 30 MIN
Structures 30 MIN

Trainwatcher C 60 MIN
1/2 IN VIDEO CASSETTE BETA/VHS
Follows an Amtrak train ride to Seattle during the Winter of 1980. Shows an icy scene in Portland, Oregon, shots from the Chicago elevated train and early streetcars once used in southern California.
From The Trainwatcher Series.
Prod-DELUZ Dist-DELUZ

Trainwatcher Five C 60 MIN
1/2 IN VIDEO CASSETTE BETA/VHS
Focuses on a visit to the Sacramento Rail Museums by several well-known steam locomotives. Includes nearby scenery and Amtrak rail operations.
From The Trainwatcher Series.
Prod-DELUZ Dist-DELUZ 1981

Trainwatcher Four C 60 MIN
1/2 IN VIDEO CASSETTE BETA/VHS
Records freight operations on the Union Pacific and Southern Railway in California. Presents a walk through a classic U P Pullman car, a look at San Francisco's streetcars, and two well-known steam engines in the East.
From The Trainwatcher Series.
Prod-DELUZ Dist-DELUZ

Trainwatcher Six C 60 MIN
1/2 IN VIDEO CASSETTE BETA/VHS
Shows the new San Diego light rail transit, a rail exhibit at the Los Angeles Fair Grounds and the double-decked commuter trains operated by the Southern Pacific. Traces a train ride through the Yosemite region of California.
From The Trainwatcher Series.
Prod-DELUZ Dist-DELUZ 1982

Trainwatcher Three C 60 MIN
1/2 IN VIDEO CASSETTE BETA/VHS
Shows the operation of the Washington, DC Metro, that City's terminal, a run on the Southern Crescent and a run along with the Union Pacific's Northern No. 8444.
From The Trainwatcher Series.
Prod-DELUZ Dist-DELUZ

Trainwatcher Two C 60 MIN
1/2 IN VIDEO CASSETTE BETA/VHS
Features diesel freight operation on the Santa Fe, Southern Pacific, Union Pacific, Burlington Northern, and Denver and Rio Grande Western railroads. Visits the Sierra Railroad for old steam locomotives in action.

From The Trainwatcher Series.
Prod-DELUZ Dist-DELUZ

Trainwatcher—A Series

Shows vintage steam locomotives, both stationary and on runs, in various locations around the country. Features scenes of natural beauty.
Prod-DELUZ Dist-DELUZ

Trainwatcher	060 MIN
Trainwatcher Five	060 MIN
Trainwatcher Four	060 MIN
Trainwatcher Six	060 MIN
Trainwatcher Three	060 MIN
Trainwatcher Two	060 MIN

Traitor Within, The C 11 MIN
16MM FILM OPTICAL SOUND I-H
Shows how cancer progresses within the human body if nothing is done about it when the first danger signal is given. Describes the danger signals and explains what to do about them.
Prod-AMCS Dist-AMCS Prodn-SUTHP 1947

Traitor Within, The (Spanish) C 11 MIN
16MM FILM OPTICAL SOUND J-H T
Shows how cancer progresses within the human body if nothing is done about it when the first danger signal is given. A description of the danger signals and an explanation of what to do about them is presented.
Prod-AMCS Dist-AMCS Prodn-SUTHP 1947

Traitors, The (Captioned) C 109 MIN
16MM FILM, 3/4 OR 1/2 IN VIDEO A
Portrays the life of trade union leader Roberto Barrera of Argentina and his opposition by militant leftist workers in this survey of Argentine history from the overthrow of Peron in 1955 to his return in 1973. Spanish dialog with English subtitles.
Prod-TRIFCW Dist-CNEMAG 1973

Tramp Tramp Tramp B 65 MIN
16MM FILM SILENT J-C A
Stars Harry Langdon as one of the last small time hand-made shoe manufacturers who are being put out of business by their mechanized competitors.
Prod-MGM Dist-TWYMAN 1926

Tramp, The B 28 MIN
16MM FILM SILENT J-H
Portrays pathos and comedy in this first Chaplin classic. Shows Charlie as he rescues a girl from robbers, falls in love with her and gives her up when her fiancee arrives. Features Edna Purviance and Bud Jamison.
From The Essanay Period Of Chaplin Comedy Series.
LC NO. 72-711887
Prod-ENY Dist-BHAWK 1915

Trampoline Fundamentals C 11 MIN
16MM FILM, 3/4 OR 1/2 IN VIDEO J-C A
Features an instructor and a group of high school boys and girls demonstrating the basic fundamentals of trampolining.
Prod-BFA Dist-PHENIX 1961

Trance And Dance In Bali B 20 MIN
16MM FILM OPTICAL SOUND C T
Shows a Balinese ceremonial dance depicting the struggle between life and death. Describes how they accompany their ceremony with trance seizures and comic interludes.
From The Character Formation In Different Cultures Series.
Prod-MEAD Dist-NYU 1951

Tranquilizers, A New Idea In Animal Feeds B 15 MIN
16MM FILM OPTICAL SOUND
Describes the work that is done by the Pfizer experimental farms in improving the economic and nutritive value of animal feeds through the use of tranquilizers. Demonstrates that when tranquilizers are added to feed, the animal not only improves emotionally, but gains in weight with less food consumption than before.
LC NO. FI68-659
Prod-PFI Dist-PFI Prodn-STARIF 1958

Trans-Alpine Pipeline, The C 30 MIN
3/4 OR 1/2 INCH VIDEO CASSETTE
Shows men of many nationalities and an army of construction equipment building the TAL pipeline from Trieste, Italy, to Ingolstadt in Bavaria.
Prod-IVCH Dist-IVCH

Trans-Cervical Thymectomy C 17 MIN
3/4 OR 1/2 INCH VIDEO CASSETTE
See series title for descriptive statement.
From The Thoracic Series.
Prod-SVL Dist-SVL

Transabdominal Adrenalectomy For Encocrine Disease C 26 MIN
16MM FILM OPTICAL SOUND PRO
Presents Edwin H Ellison, MD and George J Hamwi, MD, who point out that the anterior transabdominal approach permits preliminary exposure, and careful inspection of all adrenal tissue through one incision, before deciding on the definite operative procedure. Examines the principles of abdominal exposure, with special emphasis on mobilisation permitting a bilateral total or subtotal adrenalectomy. Includes a demonstration.
Prod-ACYDGD Dist-ACY 1957

Transabdominal Bilateral Adrenalectomy And Ovariectomy C 18 MIN
16MM FILM OPTICAL SOUND PRO
Depicts a transabdominal approach to combined bilateral adrenalectomy and ovariectomy and describes its indications and advantages especially as related to disseminated mammary cancer.
Prod-ACYDGD Dist-ACY 1969

Transabdominal Bilateral Retroperitoneal Lymphadenectomy For Testis Tumors C 15 MIN
16MM FILM OPTICAL SOUND PRO
Shows the diagnostic procedures and the operative procedure for the treatment of testicular tumors, stage I and II, which are non-seminomatous. Gives the results of over 65 patients having at least a 3-year followup.
LC NO. 75-702240
Prod-EATONL Dist-EATONL 1974

Transabdominal Hysterectomy For Benign Disease C 29 MIN
16MM FILM OPTICAL SOUND PRO
Explains that benign disease of the uterus if frequently complicated by significant involvement of other structures and that the surgical management of these complications is perhaps best undertaken by a general surgeon.
Prod-ACYDGD Dist-ACY 1958

Transabdominal Vagotomy, One Layer Pyloroplasty, Tube Gastrostomy C 27 MIN
16MM FILM OPTICAL SOUND PRO
Shows techniques of vagotomy, utilizing traction on the stomach and upward retraction of the liver, one layer heineke-mikulicz pyloroplasty and tube gastrostomy.
Prod-ACYDGD Dist-ACY 1959

Transactional Analysis C 31 MIN
16MM FILM, 3/4 OR 1/2 IN VIDEO H-C A
Shows how transactional analysis is being used to expose non-productive games and psychologically stifling habits of people in authority. Tells how TA can improve human relations while aiding motivation.
Prod-CRMP Dist-CRMP 1975

Transactional Analysis - A Demonstration With Art C 25 MIN
16MM FILM OPTICAL SOUND A
Indicates what therapy to use in the case of a client who is violently expressing anger. Points out, in this case, that behind the anger is the game If-It-Weren't-For-You.
Prod-AACD Dist-AACD 1973

Transactional Analysis - A Demonstration With Pat C 36 MIN
16MM FILM OPTICAL SOUND A
Demonstrates TA concept of the victim-persecutor-rescuer triangle with a client who has a marital problem. Becomes clear that the game being played is If It Weren't For Her. Analyzes what transpires.
Prod-AACD Dist-AACD 1973

Transactional Analysis - A Demonstration With Elaine C 33 MIN
16MM FILM OPTICAL SOUND A
Demonstates the game Why-Don't-You and the game Yes, But. Analyzes the therapeutic process. Demonstrates TA with a young woman who is engaging in self-defeating behavior.
Prod-AACD Dist-AACD 1973

Transactional Analysis - Better Communications For Organizations C 26 MIN
16MM FILM, 3/4 OR 1/2 IN VIDEO
Explains how transactional analysis can be used to create a more productive corporate atmosphere.
From The Human Resources And Organizational Behavior Series.
Prod-DOCUA Dist-CNEMAG

Transactional Analysis For Educators C 50 MIN
3/4 OR 1/2 INCH VIDEO CASSETTE
Explains the theories behind transactional analysis and shows how this approach can be used to improve the educator's interpersonal relations with students and co-workers.
LC NO. 82-706451
Prod-AFSCD Dist-AFSCD 1979

Transactional Analysis—A Series
16MM FILM, 3/4 OR 1/2 IN VIDEO J-C
Prod-BFA Dist-PHENIX 1976

Meet Your Parent, Adult, Child	9 MIN
We're OK	9 MIN

Transactional Group Therapy With Muriel James C 32 MIN
3/4 INCH VIDEO CASSETTE
Dr Muriel James applies the principles of Transactional Analysis to group therapy. Demonstrates the power of an expert in the field.
Prod-PSYCHD Dist-PSYCHD

Transactions C 30 MIN
16MM FILM, 3/4 OR 1/2 IN VIDEO A
Uses transactional analysis to deal with human relationship in conflict. Looks at how three ego states are involved when two people relate (transact). Discusses how people's ego states 'hook' one another's.
From The Learning To Live Series.
Prod-TRAFCO Dist-ECUFLM 1974

Transactions - Letting Go And Taking Hold (Spanish) C 29 MIN
16MM FILM, 3/4 OR 1/2 IN VIDEO H-C A
Examines the transitional process that is involved when an employee has to adapt to a new job.
Prod-CRMP Dist-MGHT 1979

Transcending C 15 MIN
3/4 OR 1/2 INCH VIDEO CASSETTE
Presents a fantasized saga of a person whose two brain parts have become separated and the adventures and misadventures he experiences in attempting to bring his head together. Includes mime by Yass Hakoshima.
From The Three Works By Ian Hugo Series.
Prod-EAI Dist-EAI

Transcending Illness C 28 MIN
3/4 OR 1/2 INCH VIDEO CASSETTE
Presents a cancer patient talking about her disease and cure, beginning with her first knowledge of the operation, a mastectomy, her and her husband's reaction to the result, and the changes she made in her life to remain victorious over the cancer.
Prod-HP Dist-HP

Transcochlear Approach To The Skull Base C 30 MIN
3/4 OR 1/2 INCH VIDEO CASSETTE PRO
Demonstrates the approach to tumors of the skull base that arise medial to the internal auditory canal, or from the clivus. Involves a forward extension of the translabyrinthine opening, and the cochlea is removed with the facial nerve rerouted posteriorly. Shows that the forward limit of the dissection is the internal carotid artery.
Prod-HOUSEI Dist-HOUSEI

Transcochlear Removal Of Congenital Cholesteatoma C 56 MIN
3/4 OR 1/2 INCH VIDEO CASSETTE PRO
Presents a case history, a postoperative interview with the patient, and the procedure used in the removal of a large cholesteatoma using the transcochlear technique with microsurgical approach to lesion in the mastoid and inner ear.
Prod-HOUSEI Dist-HOUSEI

Transcontinental Railroad, The C 15 MIN
3/4 OR 1/2 INCH VIDEO CASSETTE P
Focuses on two Irish immigrants, father and son, who worked on the first transcontinental railroad.
From The Stories Of America Series.
Prod-OHSDE Dist-AITECH Prodn-WVIZTV 1976

Transcutaneous Electrical Nerve Stimulation C 28 MIN
3/4 OR 1/2 INCH VIDEO CASSETTE A
Discusses the benefits and advantages of TENS therapy, components of the TENS unit, use of controls and adjustments, application and care of electrodes, batteries and cautions.
Prod-VAMSLC Dist-USNAC 1984

Transduodenal Section Of The Sphincter Of Oddi For Pancreatitis C 24 MIN
16MM FILM OPTICAL SOUND PRO
Presents Henry Doubilet, MD and John H Mulholland, Md, showing the technique and etiology of sphincterotomy and operative cholangiography, in the treatment of recurrent acute pancreatitis.
Prod-ACYDGD Dist-ACY 1952

Transfer B 7 MIN
16MM FILM OPTICAL SOUND
Shows a poetic fantasy depicting a streetcar gliding through the streets of Toronto, its interior full of the memories of all those people who once grasped its rails.
LC NO. 76-703262
Prod-CANFDC Dist-CANFDC 1974

Transfer And Ambulation B 30 MIN
16MM FILM OPTICAL SOUND PRO
Demonstrates how to assist a patient to ambulate and how to transfer a patient from bed to stretcher and using hemiplegic and pivot techniques, from bed to wheelchair.
From The Directions For Education In Nursing Via Technology Series. Lesson 13
LC NO. 74-701787
Prod-DENT Dist-WSU 1974

Transfer From Bed To Wheelchair With Assistance C 7 MIN
16MM FILM - 3/4 IN VIDEO
Shows a procedure for transferring a hemiplegic patient from a low bed to a sitting position, to a standing position and to a wheelchair with the assistance of an attendant. Issued in 1965 as a motion picture.
LC NO. 77-706090
Prod-USPHS Dist-USNAC 1977

Transfer Molding - Molding A Part With Inserts B 10 MIN
16MM FILM OPTICAL SOUND
Explains how transfer molding differs from compression molding. Shows how to mold a part by the transfer method and coordinate steps of the molding cycle.
From The Plastics Series. No. 5
LC NO. FIE52-297
Prod-USOE Dist-USNAC Prodn-CARFI 1945

Transfer Of Power, The B 29 MIN
16MM FILM OPTICAL SOUND J-H
Explains how the office of the President of the United States changes hands and analyzes the problems involved in this change. Discusses the relative roles of both the outgoing and incoming presidents.
From The Government Story Series. No. 23
LC NO. 79-707207
Prod-WEBC Dist-WESTLC 1968

Transference And Countertransference C 30 MIN
3/4 OR 1/2 INCH VIDEO CASSETTE
Discusses the major use of transference-countertransference feelings and associations to improve and sustain the relationship while understanding and respecting the stage of therapeutic symbiosis in the working through process of borderline patients.
From The Treatment Of The Borderline Patient Series.
Prod-HEMUL Dist-HEMUL

Transference Numbers - Hittorf Method / Transference Numbers - Moving Boundary... C 54 MIN
3/4 OR 1/2 INCH VIDEO CASSETTE

Discusses transference numbers, Hittorf Method, numbers, moving boundary method in solutions of one binary electrolyte, transference numbers moving boundary with mixtures, complexes and 'true transference numbers.'
From The Electrochemistry, Pt I - Introduction Series.
Prod-MIOT Dist-MIOT

Transference Numbers-Hittorf Method, Moving Boundary Method In Solutions Of One Binary... C 54 MIN
3/4 OR 1/2 INCH VIDEO CASSETTE
Teaches transference numbers-Hittorf Method, moving boundary method in solutions of one binary electrolyte, moving boundary with mixtures, complexes and 'true transference numbers.'
From The Electrochemistry Series.
Prod-KALMIA Dist-KALMIA

Transferring From Wheelchair To Bed - Non-Affected Side Of Patient Next To Bed C 5 MIN
16MM FILM OPTICAL SOUND
Demonstrates a technique of transferring a patient from a wheelchair to a bed with his non-affected side next to the bed.
LC NO. 74-705814
Prod-USPHS Dist-USNAC 1966

Transferring From Wheelchair To Bed - Affected Side Of Patient Next To Bed C 5 MIN
16MM FILM - 3/4 IN VIDEO
Demonstrates the technique of transferring a patient from a wheelchair to a bed with his affected side next to his bed.
LC NO. 77-706091
Prod-USPHS Dist-USNAC 1966

Transferring From Wheelchair To Bed With Maximal Assistance C 4 MIN
16MM FILM OPTICAL SOUND
Demonstrates the safest and easiest way to transfer the patient who needs maximal assistance from wheelchair to bed.
LC NO. 74-705816
Prod-USPHS Dist-USNAC 1966

Transferring From Wheelchair To Bed-Affected Side Of Patient Next To Bed C 6 MIN
3/4 OR 1/2 INCH VIDEO CASSETTE
Explains with narration and close-up camera views the procedure that a patient uses to transfer himself from a wheelchair to a bed. Depicts locking wheelchair brakes, placement of feet and hands for standing, adjusting body position, raising from a sitting to a standing position and sitting down, and laying down and raising back up again to a sitting position in bed.
Prod-PRIMED Dist-PRIMED

Transferring Pattern Markings C 4 MIN
16MM FILM SILENT J-C A
Illustrates alternate methods for transferring pattern markings, including tracing wheel and carbon paper, tailor's tacks and pins. Shows how to transfer needed markings from the wrong side to the right side of the fabric.
From The Clothing Construction Techniques Series.
LC NO. 77-701170
Prod-IOWA Dist-IOWASP 1976

Transferring The Patient With Arthritis C 9 MIN
16MM FILM OPTICAL SOUND
Demonstrates the proper transfer of the patient with arthritis, a technique often neglected but which can contribute much to the comfort of the afflicted person.
LC NO. 74-705818
Prod-NMAC Dist-USNAC 1968

Transfers - A Key Rehabilitation C 13 MIN
3/4 OR 1/2 INCH VIDEO CASSETTE
Prod-UMDSM Dist-UMDSM

Transfiguration, The X 20 MIN
16MM FILM OPTICAL SOUND J-H T R
Jesus asks the disciples who men say that He is. Peter confesses that Jesus is the Christ. Six days later Jesus takes James, Peter and John to the mountain where He is transfigured before them. At the foot of the mountain Jesus heals an epileptic boy.
From The Living Bible Series.
Prod-FAMF Dist-FAMF

Transformation Methods/Introduction C 60 MIN
3/4 OR 1/2 INCH VIDEO CASSETTE
See series title for descriptive statement.
From The Engineering Design Optimization II Series. Pt 20
Prod-UAZMIC Dist-UAZMIC

Transformation Methods, Pt 1 B 60 MIN
3/4 OR 1/2 INCH VIDEO CASSETTE
See series title for descriptive statement.
From The Engineering Design Optimization I Series. Pt 19
Prod-UAZMIC Dist-UAZMIC

Transformation Methods, Pt 2 B 60 MIN
3/4 OR 1/2 INCH VIDEO CASSETTE
See series title for descriptive statement.
From The Engineering Design Optimization I Series. Pt 20
Prod-UAZMIC Dist-UAZMIC

Transformation Methods, Pt 3 B 60 MIN
3/4 OR 1/2 INCH VIDEO CASSETTE
See series title for descriptive statement.
From The Engineering Design Optimization I Series. Pt 21
Prod-UAZMIC Dist-UAZMIC

Transformation Methods, Pt 4 B 60 MIN
3/4 OR 1/2 INCH VIDEO CASSETTE
See series title for descriptive statement.
From The Engineering Design Optimization I Series. Pt 22
Prod-UAZMIC Dist-UAZMIC

Transformation Of Mabel Wells, The C 12 MIN
3/4 INCH VIDEO CASSETTE I-H
Tells how a cranky old lady learns that people really like her.
Prod-GA Dist-GA

Transformation Of Richard Nixon, The C 29 MIN
2 INCH VIDEOTAPE
See series title for descriptive statement.
From The Course Of Our Times III Series.
Prod-WGBHTV Dist-PUBTEL

Transformations And Matrices C 24 MIN
16MM FILM, 3/4 OR 1/2 IN VIDEO
Asks which types of transformations of the plane can be represented by matrices.
Prod-OPENU Dist-MEDIAG Prodn-BBCTV

Transformations In Steel C 30 MIN
3/4 OR 1/2 INCH VIDEO CASSETTE PRO
Presents thermal treatments which control the properties of steel.
From The Elements Of Physical Metallurgy Series.
Prod-AMCEE Dist-AMCEE

Transformers C
3/4 OR 1/2 INCH VIDEO CASSETTE IND
Covers the design, construction and application of those transformers used throughout the power distribution system. Includes types of transformers, single and three phase connections and maintenance considerations.
From The Distribution System Operation Series. Topic 6
Prod-LEIKID Dist-LEIKID

Transformers C
3/4 OR 1/2 INCH VIDEO CASSETTE
See series title for descriptive statement.
From The Basic AC Circuits Series.
Prod-VTRI Dist-VTRI

Transformers C 20 MIN
3/4 OR 1/2 INCH VIDEO CASSETTE
See series title for descriptive statement.
From The Basic AC Circuits, Laboratory--Sessions--A Series.
Prod-TXINLC Dist-TXINLC

Transformers C 30 MIN
16MM FILM, 3/4 OR 1/2 IN VIDEO
Defines transformer action, step-up and step-down, turns ratio and coefficient of coupling. Illustrates the relationship between the magnitude of voltage and current in a transformer. Issued in 1957 as a motion picture.
LC NO. 78-706203
Prod-USAF Dist-USNAC 1978

Transforming Sentences B 15 MIN
2 INCH VIDEOTAPE I
Describes how one sentence may be transformed into a semantically new sentence without altering the basic structure. Features selections such as The Potatoes' Dance by Vachel Lindsay and Advice To A Bird, Species Unknown by Georgie Starbuck Galbraith. (Broadcast quality)
From The Bill Martin Series. No. 4
Prod-BRITED Dist-GPITVL Prodn-KQEDTV

Transient C 24 MIN
16MM FILM OPTICAL SOUND
Deals with transient workers and their role on fruit-growing farms in South Okanagan, British Columbia.
LC NO. 76-703815
Prod-BCDA Dist-BCDA 1975

Transients In Power Systems--A Series
C A
Designed to assist in identification and familiarity with those phenomena which produce transient voltage phenomena on power systems. Presents 42 fifty-minute videotape lectures.
Prod-UIDEEO Dist-UIDEEO

Transistor Amplifier Principles - Classification And Coupling B 27 MIN
16MM FILM - 3/4 IN VIDEO
Explains the functions of voltage and current amplifiers. Illustrates the principles of several classes of bias levels and four types of couplings. Discusses frequency range. Issued in 1967 as a motion picture.
LC NO. 79-707751
Prod-USAF Dist-USNAC 1979

Transistor Amplifiers C 18 MIN
16MM FILM OPTICAL SOUND IND
Describes characteristics of the three basic transistor amplifier configurations and tells about some uses of the different amplifiers.
From The Solid State Electronics Series. Chapter 4
LC NO. 80-701538
Prod-TAT Dist-TAT 1980

Transistor Amplifiers C 17 MIN
3/4 OR 1/2 INCH VIDEO CASSETTE IND
Develops three basic transistor amplifier configurations. Defines basic electronic terminology.
From The Introduction To Solid State Electronics Series. Chapter 4
LC NO. 80-707262
Prod-TAT Dist-TAT

Transistor Amplifiers (Spanish) C 17 MIN
3/4 OR 1/2 INCH VIDEO CASSETTE IND
Develops three basic transistor amplifier configurations. Defines basic electronic terminology.
From The Introduction To Solid State Electronics (Spanish) Series. Chapter 4
Prod-TAT Dist-TAT

Transistor FM Detector B 35 MIN
16MM FILM, 3/4 OR 1/2 IN VIDEO
Discusses the characteristics of a symmetrical transistor and reviews the phase relationship of voltage and current in a transformer. Explains the operation of the FM detector at the center frequency of the input and at frequencies above and below the center frequency. (Kinescope)
Prod-USAF Dist-USNAC

Transistor FM Oscillator B 29 MIN
16MM FILM, 3/4 OR 1/2 IN VIDEO
Compares the transistor FM oscillator and the reactance tube modulator. Explains the operation of the circuit, how the depletion region is established and how it can be used as a variable capacitance under a changing reverse bias. Shows how the voltage variable capacitor can be used in conjunction with an oscillator to make up a transistor FM oscillator. (Kinescope)
Prod-USAF Dist-USNAC

Transistor Operations C
3/4 OR 1/2 INCH VIDEO CASSETTE
See series title for descriptive statement.
From The Digital Techniques Series.
Prod-HTHZEN Dist-HTHZEN

Transistor Operations C
3/4 OR 1/2 INCH VIDEO CASSETTE
See series title for descriptive statement.
From The Digital Techniques Video Training Course Series.
Prod-VTRI Dist-VTRI

Transistor Push-Pull Amplifier B 27 MIN
16MM FILM, 3/4 OR 1/2 IN VIDEO
Illustrates the principles and explains the advantages of the push-pull amplifier. Points out the functions and benefits of input transformer, discusses troubleshooting and explains two methods of achieving input.
Prod-USAF Dist-USNAC 1967

Transistor Push-Pull Amplifiers B 26 MIN
16MM FILM, 3/4 OR 1/2 IN VIDEO
Explains the operation of a push-pull amplifier and the effects of bias. Shows output waveshapes and compares classes as to fidelity, harmonics and efficiency. Discusses troubleshooting and compares two methods of obtaining inputs.
Prod-USAF Dist-USNAC

Transistor Stabilization B 19 MIN
16MM FILM, 3/4 OR 1/2 IN VIDEO
Shows how a change in ambient temperature affects transistor stabilization and discusses its effect on circuit output. Explains thermistor characteristics and stabilization. Explains the function of forward and reverse biased temperature stabilization diodes.
Prod-USAF Dist-USNAC

Transistor Structure And Technology C 38 MIN
16MM FILM OPTICAL SOUND C
Describes how the alloy junction transistor (PNP) is made, discusses the limitation of its speed and voltage characteristics and points out the characteristics of pnip and npnn types. Shows the fabrication of NPNN transistors. Includes a brief review of the power handling capability and heat dissipation.
From The Semiconductor Electronics Education Com- Mittee Films Series.
LC NO. 70-703368
Prod-BELLTL Dist-EDC 1967

Transistor Tetrodes And Field Effect Transistors B 14 MIN
16MM FILM, 3/4 OR 1/2 IN VIDEO
Introduces transistor tetrodes and discusses their fundamental characteristics and elements. Introduces the field effect transistor and covers its basic characteristics. (Kinescope)
Prod-USAF Dist-USNAC

Transistor Theory And Testing Silicon Controlled Rectifiers C 60 MIN
3/4 OR 1/2 INCH VIDEO CASSETTE IND
See series title for descriptive statement.
From The Electrical Maintenance Training, Module 7 - Solid-State Devices Series.
Prod-LEIKID Dist-LEIKID

Transistor Triode Characteristics B 26 MIN
16MM FILM, 3/4 OR 1/2 IN VIDEO
Illustrates how to draw load lines from characteristic curves for CE and CB configurations. Defines alpha and beta as they pertain to transistors. Shows how to solve for actual current gain, voltage gain and power gain for CB configuration, using characteristic curves and load lines. (Kinescope)
Prod-USAF Dist-USNAC

Transistor Triodes B 7 MIN
16MM FILM OPTICAL SOUND
Explains derivation of the word 'transistor.' Identifies the elements of a PNP and an NPN transistor, by using block diagrams and discusses a method of remembering P and N type materials and the relative size of the transistor element. (Kinescope)
LC NO. 74-705823
Prod-USAF Dist-USNAC

Transistor Triodes - Construction B 25 MIN
16MM FILM, 3/4 OR 1/2 IN VIDEO
Explains the construction and functions of triode transistors. Shows the differences between PNP and NPN transistors and describes how emitter, collector and base operate in each type.
Prod-USAF Dist-USNAC 1967

Transistor Triodes And Special Purpose Devices - Bias I B 27 MIN
16MM FILM, 3/4 OR 1/2 IN VIDEO
Discusses and illustrates forward and reverse bias of a PN junction and requires the student to draw a block diagram with forward bias and one with reverse bias. Shows how an NPN transistor is forward and reverse biased for efficient operation.

LC NO. 82-706699
Prod-USAF Dist-USNAC

Transistor Triodes And Special Purpose Devices - Bias II B 27 MIN
16MM FILM, 3/4 OR 1/2 IN VIDEO
Discusses the depletion area at the junctions of a transistor, followed by an explanation of the effect of forward and reverse biasing on the majority and minority carriers in both.
Prod-USAF Dist-USNAC

Transistor Triodes And Special Purpose Devices - Common-Base Configurations B 29 MIN
16MM FILM, 3/4 OR 1/2 IN VIDEO
Shows and discusses the schematic representation of a common-base transistor circuit, giving the identifying characteristics for a PNP and an NPN type. Explains the purpose of each component.
LC NO. 82-706698
Prod-USAF Dist-USNAC 1942

Transistor Triodes And Special Purpose Devices - Common-Collector Configuration B 16 MIN
16MM FILM, 3/4 OR 1/2 IN VIDEO
Provides information designed to enable the student to identify and state the purpose of various elements in NPN and PNP transistor common collector circuits.
LC NO. 82-706700
Prod-USAF Dist-USNAC

Transistor Triodes And Special Purpose Devices - Operation B 16 MIN
16MM FILM, 3/4 OR 1/2 IN VIDEO
Illustrates the three configurations of transistor circuits and traces the current flow. Explains the amount of current in each part of a transistor circuit and the effect of an increase in total current in a transistor circuit.
Prod-USAF Dist-USNAC

Transistorized Audio Amplifier B 22 MIN
16MM FILM, 3/4 OR 1/2 IN VIDEO
Explains the principles of the common base (in phase) and the common emitter (out of phase) audio amplifiers. Describes outlet characteristics and shows how to calculate voltage, power and current gain.
Prod-USAF Dist-USNAC 1967

Transistorized Hartley Oscillator B 40 MIN
16MM FILM, 3/4 OR 1/2 IN VIDEO
Discusses the transistorized version of both the series and Shunt Hartley oscillators. Compares the two, emphasizing circuit identification, purpose of each component, direct current paths, feedback paths and the effects of varying feedback.
LC NO. 82-706738
Prod-USAF Dist-USNAC 1965

Transistorized Regulated Power Supply B 24 MIN
16MM FILM - 3/4 IN VIDEO
Explains the advantages of a regulated supply, how regulation is accomplished using simplified schematics and the purpose of each control, as well as suggested operating procedure.
LC NO. 79-707709
Prod-USAF Dist-USNAC 1979

Transistors C 12 MIN
3/4 OR 1/2 INCH VIDEO CASSETTE
Defines transistors. Covers bipolar transistor operation, current gain, voltage and power gains.
From The Industrial Electronics-- Semiconductors Series.
Prod-TPCTRA Dist-TPCTRA

Transistors (Spanish) C 12 MIN
3/4 OR 1/2 INCH VIDEO CASSETTE
Defines transistors. Covers bipolar transistor operation, current gain, voltage and power gains.
From The Industrial Electronics - Semiconductors (Spanish) Series.
Prod-TPCTRA Dist-TPCTRA

Transistors - High Frequency Operations - Amplifiers And Oscillators B 14 MIN
16MM FILM, 3/4 OR 1/2 IN VIDEO
Describes how transistors operate in high frequency amplifiers and in oscillator circuits. Shows the influence of transit effects in the base. Explains collector capacitance and base resistance on high frequency performance.
LC NO. 82-706740
Prod-USN Dist-USNAC 1959

Transistors - How They Work, How They Are Made C 60 MIN
1 INCH VIDEOTAPE IND
Describes how the holes and free electrons in an N-P-N transistor enable it to switch and vary a large 'working' current in response to a small 'control' current. Illustrates the manufacturing techniques used for all semiconductor products.
From The Understanding Semiconductors Course Outline Series. No. 07
Prod-TXINLC Dist-TXINLC

Transistors - Low Frequency Amplifiers B 15 MIN
16MM FILM, 3/4 OR 1/2 IN VIDEO
Shows how transistors are used to amplify low frequencies in common base, emitter and collector circuits.
LC NO. 82-706739
Prod-USN Dist-USNAC Prodn-BRAY 1958

Transistors - Minority Carriers B 10 MIN
16MM FILM, 3/4 OR 1/2 IN VIDEO H-C A
Introduces the principle of minority carriers, shows how they produce a small reverse current under normal conditions and demonstrates the limitations imposed on transistor behavior by minority carriers when the transistor is heated or loaded.
LC NO. 82-706154
Prod-NF Dist-USNAC 1958

Transistors - P-N Junction Fundamentals B 11 MIN
16MM FILM, 3/4 OR 1/2 IN VIDEO
Explains the theory and mechanisms of semi-conductor diode and transistor action, and discusses the fundamental principles that apply to all transistors and junction rectifiers.
LC NO. 82-706155
Prod-USN Dist-USNAC Prodn-BRAY 1957

Transistors - Servicing Techniques B 14 MIN
16MM FILM, 3/4 OR 1/2 IN VIDEO H-C A
Discusses common types of transistor failures such as opens, shorts, high leakage current, low gain and problems in localizing them. Demonstrates, with overshoulder camera views, the special techniques that must be used with transistorized equipment.
Prod-NF Dist-USNAC 1960

Transistors - Switching B 13 MIN
16MM FILM OPTICAL SOUND H-C A
Shows examples of switching circuits in transistorized computers, explaining briefly the concept of digital computation and how transistors are used. Shows in more detail how a simple transistor switch works, with special attention to minority carrier storage in the base, showing how delaying effects of this storage are overcome.
LC NO. FIE60-56
Prod-NF Dist-USNAC 1959

Transistors - Switching B 14 MIN
3/4 INCH VIDEO CASSETTE
Provides examples of switching circuits in transistorized computers and explains briefly the concept of digital computation. Shows how transistors are used and how a simple transistor switch functions, illustrating ways in which the delaying effects of minority carrier storage are overcome. Issued in 1959 as a motion picture.
LC NO. 79-707699
Prod-USN Dist-USNAC 1979

Transistors - Triode Fundamentals B 11 MIN
16MM FILM, 3/4 OR 1/2 IN VIDEO
Shows that junction transistors, or triodes, consist of three sections with two P-N junctions separating them, and discusses the fundamentals of this arrangement as an amplifying device.
LC NO. 82-706153
Prod-USN Dist-USNAC Prodn-BRAY 1957

Transistors, Pt 1 - Introduction B 17 MIN
16MM FILM, 3/4 OR 1/2 IN VIDEO
Describes the construction, characteristics, operation and application of transistors.
LC NO. 79-707690
Prod-USA Dist-USNAC 1979

Transistors, Pt 2 - Semiconductors And Semiconductor Diodes B 27 MIN
16MM FILM, 3/4 OR 1/2 IN VIDEO
Illustrates the composition and properties of crystal diodes and describes semiconductor materials used in their manufacture.
LC NO. 79-707691
Prod-USA Dist-USNAC 1979

Transistors, Pt 3 - NPN Transistors B 23 MIN
16MM FILM, 3/4 OR 1/2 IN VIDEO
Describes the construction and properties of NPN transistors, showing how they function in basic transistor circuits. Explains how current flow and amplification are achieved.
LC NO. 79-707693
Prod-USA Dist-USNAC 1979

Transistors, Pt 4 - PNP Transistors B 26 MIN
16MM FILM, 3/4 OR 1/2 IN VIDEO
Describes the characteristics of PNP transistors and compares their capabilities and functioning to NPN transistors. Explains how currents flow through circuits.
LC NO. 79-707694
Prod-USA Dist-USNAC 1979

Transistors, Pt 5 - Transistor Amplifier And Oscillator Circuits B 30 MIN
16MM FILM, 3/4 OR 1/2 IN VIDEO
Explains and illustrates the feature and operations of tuned amplifier and oscillator circuits, including the Armstrong and Hartley types.
LC NO. 79-707695
Prod-USA Dist-USNAC 1979

Transistors, Pt 6 - Transistors In Pulse Applications B 39 MIN
16MM FILM, 3/4 OR 1/2 IN VIDEO
Discusses the use of transistors in pulse applications, focusing on the characteristics and applications of square sawtooth and spiked pulses. Explains how transistors form various types of multivibrators.
LC NO. 79-707696
Prod-USA Dist-USNAC 1979

Transistors, Pt 7 - Troubleshooting Transistor Circuits B 31 MIN
16MM FILM, 3/4 OR 1/2 IN VIDEO
Explains how to check, search, localize and isolate malfunctions in transistor circuits and points out various safety measures.
LC NO. 79-707697
Prod-USA Dist-USNAC 1979

Transistors, Pt 8 - Repairing Transistor Circuits B 28 MIN
16MM FILM, 3/4 OR 1/2 IN VIDEO
Demonstrates equipment and techniques for repairing soldered joints, cracks and delaminated conductors in circuits. Shows how to test circuits and how to remove and replace lead and flush-mounted circuit components.
LC NO. 79-707698
Prod-USA Dist-USNAC 1979

Transistors, Semiconductor Diodes, Half Wave Rectifiers C 17 MIN
3/4 OR 1/2 INCH VIDEO CASSETTE IND
Defines and explains transistor. Shows parts of a transistor. Includes beginning study of half wave rectification and its application.
From The Introduction To Solid State Electronic Series. Chapter 2
LC NO. 80-707260
Prod-TAT Dist-TAT

Transistors, Semiconductor Diodes, Half Wave Rectifiers (Spanish) C 17 MIN
3/4 OR 1/2 INCH VIDEO CASSETTE
From The Introduction To Solid State Electronic Series. Chapter 2
Prod-TAT Dist-TAT

Transistors, Semiconductor Diodes, Half-Wave Rectifiers C 16 MIN
16MM FILM OPTICAL SOUND IND
Describes transistors, semiconductors, diodes, and half-wave rectifiers and illustrates their use.
From The Solid State Electronics Series. Chapter 2
LC NO. 80-701536
Prod-TAT Dist-TAT 1980

Transit Options For Small Communities C 28 MIN
16MM FILM OPTICAL SOUND A
Focuses on four small communities and their efforts to solve their mass transportation problems.
LC NO. 78-700823
Prod-USUMTA Dist-USNAC 1976

Transit To Black B 13 MIN
16MM FILM OPTICAL SOUND C T
A 'MODERN ALLEGORY' depicting the loneliness of a middle-aged man.
Prod-NYU Dist-NYU 1962

Transition C 7 MIN
16MM FILM OPTICAL SOUND
Uses experimental techniques to allow dance movements and visual treatments to take their own course.
LC NO. 77-702685
Prod-HUNNL Dist-CANFDC 1975

Transition C 29 MIN
16MM FILM OPTICAL SOUND
Documents the culture of northwest Montana's Flathead Valley from Indian days to the 1970's. Emphasizes changing lifestyles that will affect the valley's future social, economic and cultural changes.
LC NO. 79-700405
Prod-FVCC Dist-FVCC 1979

Transition - Double Offset, One Elevation - Sides Of Openings Parallel C 28 MIN
1/2 IN VIDEO CASSETTE BETA/VHS IND
See series title for descriptive statement.
From The Exercise In Triangulating One-Piece Patterns Series.
Prod-RMI Dist-RMI

Transition - One Elevation, Sides Of Openings Parallel C 29 MIN
1/2 IN VIDEO CASSETTE BETA/VHS IND
See series title for descriptive statement.
From The Exercise In Triangulating One-Piece Patterns Series.
Prod-RMI Dist-RMI

Transition 'Top Up' Or 'Bottom Up' Or Top Down Or Bottom Down—A Series
IND
Demonstrates the full scale pattern development, working from a shop sketch or one-view drawing. Explains the application of the process of triangulation to develop the stretchout or true length of each of the four sides involved and how the seams may be 'chased around' once one of the sides is accurately developed.
Prod-RMI Dist-RMI

Square Or Rectangular Transition - Bottom Up,
Square Or Rectangular Transition - Top Up, 043 MIN

Transition Generation - A Third World Problem C 20 MIN
3/4 OR 1/2 INCH VIDEO CASSETTE J-C A
Points out the problems people the world over have in questioning traditional values while selecting only what is useful from western cultures. Highlights these problems by following three young people in their struggles to find a place in Afghanistan society. Shows an educated young man feeling out of place on return to his village, a son of a rich city man who cannot find a job and a liberated young woman who sees her place to be is in the home but does not wear a veil in public.
Prod-IFF Dist-IFF

Transition Trek C 5 MIN
3/4 OR 1/2 INCH VIDEO CASSETTE J-H
Demonstrates making transitions between paragraphs.
From The Write On, Set 2 Series.
Prod-CTI Dist-CTI

Transitional Elbow - Flat Top Or Bottom, Change Cheek C 28 MIN
1/2 IN VIDEO CASSETTE BETA/VHS IND
See series title for descriptive statement.
From The Metal Fabrication - Transitional Elbows Series.
Prod-RMI Dist-RMI

Transitional Elbow - Flat Top Or Bottom, Same Size Cheeks C 37 MIN
1/2 IN VIDEO CASSETTE BETA/VHS IND
See series title for descriptive statement.
From The Metal Fabrication - Transitional Elbows Series.
Prod-RMI Dist-RMI

Transitional S-Offset (Flat Top Or Bottom) C 22 MIN
1/2 IN VIDEO CASSETTE BETA/VHS IND
Illustrates the layout for a transitional S-offset, using a mechanical method and involving the process of triangulation for the slanting cheek stretchout.
Prod-RMI Dist-RMI

Transitional S-Offset (Top Or Bottom Up Or Down) C 19 MIN
1/2 IN VIDEO CASSETTE BETA/VHS IND
Explains the way the two cheeks are developed and the application of the stretchout of the cheeks to develop the wrappers for the throat or heel.
Prod-RMI Dist-RMI

Transitions C 28 MIN
16MM FILM, 3/4 OR 1/2 IN VIDEO I-C A
Introduces three disabled adults whose goal is to be as independent as they can. Points out that their spunk and persistence is aided by families, governmental service agencies, and private organizations.
LC NO. 81-707564
Prod-SEPT Dist-PEREN 1981

Transitions - Caught At Midlife--A Series

Looks at the state of life between the ages of 40 and 60. Discusses what happens during this period, who it affects and what can be done about it.
Prod-UMITV Dist-UMITV 1980

Aging Parents	030 MIN
Divorce	030 MIN
Empty Nest	030 MIN
Health And Mortality	030 MIN
Intimacy	030 MIN
Marriage	030 MIN
Parenting	030 MIN
Physical Changes	030 MIN
Widowhood	030 MIN
Work	030 MIN

Transitions - Conversations With Wendell Castle C 30 MIN
2 INCH VIDEOTAPE
See series title for descriptive statement.
From The Synergism - Profiles, People Series.
Prod-WXXITV Dist-PUBTEL

Transitions - Letting Go And Taking Hold C 29 MIN
16MM FILM, 3/4 OR 1/2 IN VIDEO H-C A
Examines the psychological and structural interrelationships that come into play during transitional phases in an organization.
Prod-CRMP Dist-CRMP 1979

Transitions--A Series
A
Focuses on changes that occur throughout one's life. Designed for adult experiential learners. Includes life transitions, learning and goal setting.
Prod-OHUTC Dist-OHUTC

Adults And Learning	028 MIN
Goals And Risk Taking	030 MIN
Introduction To Learning, An	029 MIN
Life Transitions	030 MIN

Translabyrinthine Approach - Removal Of Acoustic Neuroma C 22 MIN
16MM FILM OPTICAL SOUND PRO
Uses animation and live action to show the surgical approach for the actual removal of an acoustic tumor. Discusses the problems as the surgery progresses and demonstrates how the tumor is separated from important structures and removed.
LC NO. FIA65-491
Prod-EAR Dist-EAR Prodn-WFP 1964

Translabyrinthine Approach To The Internal Auditory Meatus And Posterior Fossa For Removal C 15 MIN
16MM FILM OPTICAL SOUND PRO
Depicts the translabyrinthine approach to the cerebellopontine angle for the removal of acoustic neuromas. Describes the method of saving the facial nerve function and of avoiding injury to the anterior inferior cerebello artery.
Prod-EAR Dist-EAR

Translating Theory Into Classroom Practices--A Series

Prod-SPF Dist-SPF 1967

Motivation Theory For Teachers	28 MIN
Reinforcement Theory For Teachers	28 MIN
Retention Theory For Teachers	28 MIN
Teacher Decision Making	26 MIN

Translations C 15 MIN
3/4 OR 1/2 INCH VIDEO CASSETTE PRO
See series title for descriptive statement.
From The Numerical Control/Computer Numerical Control, Part 2 - Advanced Programmming Series.
Prod-ICSINT Dist-ICSINT

Translations C 18 MIN
3/4 OR 1/2 INCH VIDEO CASSETTE IND
Discusses program requirements for translation, translating a program to a new location and translating to the first point of origin.
From The Numerical Control/Computerized Numerical Control - Advanced Programming Series. Module 2
Prod-LEIKID Dist-LEIKID

Translator Circuits C 30 MIN
3/4 OR 1/2 INCH VIDEO CASSETTE PRO
Discusses application of integrated circuits that provide interface between one logic system of ECL, TTL or MOS to another logic system of a different type which may be ECL, TTL or MOS.
From The Linear And Interface Circuits, Part II - Interface Integrated Circuits Series.
Prod-TXINLC Dist-TXINLC

Translator Design C 42 MIN
3/4 OR 1/2 INCH VIDEO CASSETTE PRO
Uses classroom format to videotape 42 one-hour lectures on 42 cassettes. Reveals a comprehensive study of computer compilers and how to construct them. Include as topics, basic organization of compilers and interpreters, fundamentals of formal language theory, lexical analysis and parsing techniques, syntax-directed translation, code generation, opitimization and error recovery.
Prod-UMAEEE Dist-AMCEE

Translucent B 5 MIN
3/4 INCH VIDEO CASSETTE
Presents video art created by playing off the presence of the TV monitor and exploring instant feedback.
From The James Byrne - Five Works 1974-79 Series.
Prod-EAI Dist-EAI

Transmagnifican Dambamuality B 8 MIN
16MM FILM OPTICAL SOUND
Portrays in slapstick manner a teenager's frenetic struggle for creative self-realization in the environment of a large family in a small apartment.
Prod-GRAYRK Dist-BLKFMF

Transmetatarsal Amputation C 25 MIN
16MM FILM OPTICAL SOUND PRO
Shows that the transmetatarsal amputation is a useful operation in some patients with ischemic lesions or diabetic gangrene of the toes. Discusses the indications for the transmetatarsal amputation and illustrates the step by step technique of the procedure.
Prod-ACYDGD Dist-ACY 1963

Transmission - The Pipeline Company C 19 MIN
3/4 OR 1/2 INCH VIDEO CASSETTE IND
Explains Gas transportation from the well to the distribution company. Covers pipeline construction, finance, legal requirements, gas control and operations.
From The Introduction To The Natural Gas Industry Series. Part 3
Prod-UTEXPE Dist-UTEXPE

Transmission Issues C 31 MIN
3/4 OR 1/2 INCH VIDEO CASSETTE
See series title for descriptive statement.
From The Distributed Processor Communication Architecture Series.
Prod-MIOT Dist-MIOT

Transmission Issues C 36 MIN
3/4 OR 1/2 INCH VIDEO CASSETTE PRO
Considers direction and overlap of signals. Discusses modulation techniques. Highlights data link protocols.
From The Introduction To Distributed Processor Communication Architecture Series.
Prod-AMCEE Dist-AMCEE

Transmission Issues C 40 MIN
3/4 INCH VIDEO CASSETTE C A
See series title for descriptive statement.
From The Distributed Processor Communication Architecture Series.
LC NO. 81-706193
Prod-AMCEE Dist-AMCEE 1979

Transmission Lines B 20 MIN
16MM FILM, 3/4 OR 1/2 IN VIDEO
Discusses the types of transmission lines, such as the open two-wire line, the twin lead line, the twisted pair, flexible coaxial cable and rigid coaxial cable. Explains the major kinds of losses occurring in transmission lines. (Kinescope)
Prod-USAF Dist-USNAC 1964

Transmission Of Information B 13 MIN
16MM FILM SILENT C T
Presents a test to discern the amount of information transmitted as a function of different stimulus dimensions. Shows students estimating width of diamonds, the variation in horizontal position of squares and the variation of the size of squares.
LC NO. 75-713855
Prod-NSF Dist-PSUPCR 1968

Transmission Security B 19 MIN
16MM FILM OPTICAL SOUND
Cautions radio operators against any action which might reveal a location or aid the enemy in any way. Points out the danger in sneaking out messages, sending unauthorized messages and cutting in.
LC NO. FIE52-1103
Prod-USN Dist-USNAC 1948

Transmission Techniques C 50 MIN
3/4 OR 1/2 INCH VIDEO CASSETTE PRO
Discusses asynchronous and synchronous transmission. Covers error detection and parity.
From The Fundamentals Of Data Communications Series.
Prod-AMCEE Dist-AMCEE

Transmission, Drive Shaft And Differential B 14 MIN
16MM FILM OPTICAL SOUND
Explains how to check the transmission gear shift mechanism, drive shaft and differential and test their running condition.
Prod-USOE Dist-USNAC

Transmitter CFAC C 26 MIN
16MM FILM OPTICAL SOUND
Shows what happens when a radio station decides to increase its broadcast power and relocate its transmitter site.
LC NO. 76-701068
Prod-SAIT Dist-SAIT 1974

Transnational Manager As Cultural Change Agents C
3/4 OR 1/2 INCH VIDEO CASSETTE IND
Explains how the corporate representative abroad should be open to personal change and what skills are necessary to bring about positive systems change.
From The Managing Cultural Differences Series.
Prod-GPCV Dist-GPCV

Transnational Managers As Intercultural Communicators C
3/4 OR 1/2 INCH VIDEO CASSETTE IND
Reviews concepts and challenges in cross-cultural communication and the interaction skills needed in a host culture, with an in-depth look at non-verbal communication.
From The Managing Cultural Differences Series.
Prod-GPCV Dist-GPCV

Transnationals, The C 28 MIN
16MM FILM, 3/4 OR 1/2 IN VIDEO J-C A
Looks at the activities of multinational corporations, questioning whether they have an excessive influence on national economies.
Prod-LUF Dist-LUF 1979

Transoral Introduction Of The Flexible Bronchoscope C 13 MIN
3/4 OR 1/2 INCH VIDEO CASSETTE PRO
Presents a systematic method for introducing the flexible bronchoscope. An oral endotracheal tube is used as an adjunct and helpful hints and actual endoscopic views are used to assist in its placement.
LC NO. 82-706314
Prod-VAMSLC Dist-USNAC 1982

Transorbital Lobotomy - Pt 1 B 12 MIN
16MM FILM OPTICAL SOUND PRO
Traces the history of transorbital lobotomy, which is a modification of the recognized technique for prefrontal lobotomy. A demonstration of surgical procedures on cadaver preparations is presented and cadaver and clinical brains displaying transorbital operation are investigated. Depicts in full detail a bilateral operation employing electroshock anesthesia. Showings restricted
Prod-PSUPCR Dist-PSUPCR 1949

Transorbital Lobotomy - Pt 2, Clinical Study Of A Catatonic B 9 MIN
16MM FILM OPTICAL SOUND C T
Follows a 19-year-old male catatonic before and after treatment by transorbital lobotomy. Shows that the patient largely lost his anxious, delusional and hallucinated symptoms after therapy and found employment as a musician and as a salesman. Depicts the operation and recovery in still photography. Concludes with a gross dissection of frontal lobes after death, 11 months post-operatively.
Prod-PSUPCR Dist-PSUPCR 1950

Transparency And Translucency X 20 MIN
2 INCH VIDEOTAPE I
See series title for descriptive statement.
From The Process And Proof Series. No. 15
Prod-MCETV Dist-GPITVL Prodn-WVIZTV

Transplant C 17 MIN
16MM FILM, 3/4 OR 1/2 IN VIDEO H-C A
Presents sequences on adopted children, migrant children in an alien culture and old people in a nursing home to illustrate how human beings, like plants, adjust to the shock of being transplanted.
Prod-GORKER Dist-AIMS 1974

Transplant C 97 MIN
3/4 OR 1/2 INCH VIDEO CASSETTE C A
Tells of a workaholic businessman who suffers two heart attacks, which severely damage his heart. Depicts his fear when he is faced with the prospect of a risky heart transplant to save his life. Stars Kevin Dobson and Melinda Dillon.
Prod-TIMLIF Dist-TIMLIF 1982

Transplant Experience, The C 50 MIN
16MM FILM, 3/4 OR 1/2 IN VIDEO H-C A
Documents a heart-transplant operation, including the rehabilitation process to help the patient's body accept the alien organ. Examines the ways in which a transplant affects the patient's life.
From The Nova Series.
LC NO. 79-707250
Prod-WGBHTV Dist-TIMLIF 1976

Transplant Surgery C 29 MIN
3/4 OR 1/2 INCH VIDEO CASSETTE
Discusses transplant surgery, examining the problems facing the surgeon in any transplant operation. Shows a surgeon performing a kidney transplant.
From The Daniel Foster, MD Series.
Prod-KERA Dist-PBS

Transplantation Of Sentiment C 11 MIN
16MM FILM OPTICAL SOUND C A
Shows the way in which society makes individuals conform to its demands by telling the story of a milkman who is attacked by his milk tank and, after he receives help from no one, begins to deliver bombs instead of milk.
LC NO. 72-700400
Prod-MMA Dist-MMA 1971

Transpo '72 C 28 MIN
16MM FILM OPTICAL SOUND

Highlights the activities at transpo '72 AND DESCRIBES THE EFFORTS OF THE FORD MOTOR COMPANY TO DEVELOP CLEANER, SAFER AUTOMOBILES.
LC NO. 73-701629
Prod-FMCMP Dist-FORDFL 1972

Transpo 72 C 11 MIN
16MM FILM OPTICAL SOUND
Shows events at Transpo '72, held at Dulles International Airport in May, 1972.
LC NO. 75-700701
Prod-USDTFH Dist-USNAC 1972

Transport And Session Protocols C 50 MIN
3/4 OR 1/2 INCH VIDEO CASSETTE PRO
Discusses transport services. Deals with the ISO family, network service and primitives.
From The Computer Communications - Protocols And Architectures, Pt 2 Series.
Prod-AMCEE Dist-AMCEE

Transport Coefficients - Conductivity C
3/4 OR 1/2 INCH VIDEO CASSETTE IND
States coefficients that describe mobility and conductivity are derived from the Boltzmann equation and compares to those previously obtained from the Langevin equation. Explains necessity for corrections to the simple Langevin calculation.
From The Plasma Process Technology Fundamentals Series.
Prod-COLOSU Dist-COLOSU

Transport Coefficients - Mobility And Diffusion C
3/4 OR 1/2 INCH VIDEO CASSETTE IND
Emphasizes comparison of mobility and diffusion fluxes. Compares Langevin equation results again with those derived from the Boltzmann equation. Discusses decreases in both electron and ion mobilities under high applied fields.
From The Plasma Process Technology Fundamentals Series.
Prod-COLOSU Dist-COLOSU

Transport Game C 10 MIN
16MM FILM OPTICAL SOUND
Illustrates Tasmania's transport system.
LC NO. 80-700930
Prod-TASCOR Dist-TASCOR 1978

Transport Phenomena In Solution, I - Conductance - Transference Numbers /... C 53 MIN
3/4 OR 1/2 INCH VIDEO CASSETTE
Discusses transport phenomena in solution, including conductance, transference numbers, electrophoresis and electrokinetic phenomena.
From The Electrochemistry, Pt IV - Transport Phenomena In Solutions Series.
Prod-MIOT Dist-MIOT

Transport Phenomena In Solution, II - Diffusion - Viscosity / Time Of Relaxation /... C 49 MIN
3/4 OR 1/2 INCH VIDEO CASSETTE
Discusses transport phenomena in solution, II, diffusion, viscosity, time of relaxation, non-aqueous solvents, ion pair formation, Walden's Rule and applications (especially titrations) of conductance.
From The Electrochemistry, Pt IV - Transport Phenomena In Solutions Series.
Prod-MIOT Dist-MIOT

Transport Phenomena In Solution, Pt 1 - Conductance, Transference Numbers,... C 53 MIN
3/4 OR 1/2 INCH VIDEO CASSETTE
Discusses transport phenomena in solution, Part 1 conductance, transference numbers, electrophoresis and electrokinetic phenomena.
From The Electrochemistry Series.
Prod-KALMIA Dist-KALMIA

Transport Phenomena In Solution, Pt 2 - Diffusion, Viscosity, Time Of Relaxation... C 49 MIN
3/4 OR 1/2 INCH VIDEO CASSETTE
Discusses transport phenomena in solution, Part 2 diffusion, viscosity, time of relaxation, non-aqueous solvents, ion pair formation, Walden's Rule and applications.
From The Electrochemistry Series.
Prod-KALMIA Dist-KALMIA

Transport System C 29 MIN
3/4 INCH VIDEO CASSETTE C
Shows how radiographic processing time is controlled in the processor by the transport system. Discusses the relationship between the transport system and the subsystems for handling and moving the film, including components, functions and problems.
From The Radiographic Processing Series. Pt 8
LC NO. 77-706077
Prod-USVA Dist-USNAC 1975

Transport Systems In Animals C 17 MIN
16MM FILM, 3/4 OR 1/2 IN VIDEO J-C
Explains that single-celled organisms transport materials by the streaming of cytoplasm and diffusion. Points out that the structure of hydra and planaria permit rapid exchange of gases, while larger animals have internal circulatory systems consisting of blood vessels and a pump or heart. Compares the heart structures and circulatory systems of various animals.
From The Animal Systems Series.
LC NO. 80-707018
Prod-IU Dist-IU 1971

Transportation C 6 MIN
16MM FILM, 3/4 OR 1/2 IN VIDEO K-I
See series title for descriptive statement.
From The Kingdom Of Could Be You Series.
Prod-EBEC Dist-EBEC 1974

Transportation C 30 MIN
3/4 INCH VIDEO CASSETTE
See series title for descriptive statement.
From The It's Everybody's Business Series. Unit 5, Operating A Business
Prod-DALCCD Dist-DALCCD

Transportation C 30 MIN
3/4 OR 1/2 INCH VIDEO CASSETTE C A
Deals with important factors the consumer should consider when purchasing and operating an automobile. Includes buying a new or used car, dealer versus individual financing plans and various types of automobile insurance coverage.
From The Personal Finance Series. Lesson 6
Prod-SCCON Dist-CDTEL

Transportation C 180 MIN
3/4 OR 1/2 INCH VIDEO CASSETTE PRO
Covers route locations, resource development and glaciers.
From The Arctic Engineering Series.
Prod-UAKEN Dist-AMCEE

Transportation (Rev Ed) C 8 MIN
3/4 OR 1/2 INCH VIDEO CASSETTE
Details proper handling and transporting casualties, stressing careful examination and correct treatment before movement of the injured is attempted. Displays several types of stretchers, including the army type, stokes navala model, stretcher boards and the Bureau of Mines utility splint. Covers the most effective methods of carrying a patient without a stretcher, including one-man, two-man, and three-man lift and carry.
From The First Aid (Rev Ed) Series.
Prod-USMESA Dist-USNAC 1981

Transportation - A Basic Need C 12 MIN
16MM FILM, 3/4 OR 1/2 IN VIDEO P-I
Shows how transportation affects people's lives and how various types of vehicles are used to move people and things within a community.
Prod-ODYSSP Dist-EBEC 1980

Transportation - A First Film On The Airport C 11 MIN
16MM FILM, 3/4 OR 1/2 IN VIDEO P-I
Examines the advantages and disadvantages derived by the community from a big city airport.
Prod-BEAN Dist-PHENIX 1972

Transportation - A First Film On The Airport (French) C 11 MIN
16MM FILM, 3/4 OR 1/2 IN VIDEO P-I
Examines the advantages and disadvantages derived by the community from a big city airport.
Prod-BEAN Dist-PHENIX 1972

Transportation - Barges C 15 MIN
16MM FILM OPTICAL SOUND K-J
Follows the progress of a cargo of corn from the farmer's field in Illinois to an ocean steamer at the port of New Orleans. Points out that along the way, this barge encounters a variety of river vessels, from towboats to ocean-going freighters, each one playing its part in the complex economic scheme of supply and demand.
Prod-COMICO Dist-COMICO

Transportation - Master Or Servant C 56 MIN
16MM FILM, 3/4 OR 1/2 IN VIDEO H-C
Debates whether society should continue to depend on the automobile or switch to public transportation methods.
Prod-SF Dist-SF 1973

Transportation - The Way Ahead C 8 MIN
16MM FILM - 3/4 IN VIDEO
Describes various Energy Research and Development Administration programs aimed at developing fuel sources for automobiles. Discusses research being conducted with methanol, isopropanol, denatured alcohol and other fuels not derived from petroleum.
LC NO. 79-706191
Prod-USERD Dist-USNAC 1979

Transportation And Communication In Underground Coal Mines C 9 MIN
16MM FILM, 3/4 OR 1/2 IN VIDEO
Shows accidents involving the transportation of men and materials in a mine, with follow-ups showing what the safe procedure should have been. Explains and demonstrates underground mine communications systems.
Prod-USDL Dist-USNAC

Transportation Around The World C 11 MIN
16MM FILM, 3/4 OR 1/2 IN VIDEO P-I
Relates geography in different places to forms of travel. Illustrates land, water and air transportation in such places as the Andes, the Arctic, Japan and the United States.
Prod-CORF Dist-CORF 1969

Transportation By Bus C 10 MIN
16MM FILM, 3/4 OR 1/2 IN VIDEO K-I
Two children go to the bus terminal where they buy tickets, check their baggage and board the bus. In the meantime the bus is being prepared for the journey.
From The Transportation Series.
Prod-FILMSW Dist-FLMFR 1968

Transportation By Freight Train C 10 MIN
16MM FILM, 3/4 OR 1/2 IN VIDEO P-I
Shows special kinds of freight cars carrying different things that are used in everyday life. Also shows the engineer, conductor, flagman, dispatcher and other railroad personnel and equipment needed.
From The Transportation Series.
Prod-FILMSW Dist-FLMFR 1968

Transportation By Freight Train (Captioned Version) C 10 MIN
16MM FILM, 3/4 OR 1/2 IN VIDEO P-I
Shows special kinds of freight cars carrying different things that are used in everyday life. Also shows the engineer, conductor, flagman, dispatcher and other railroad personnel and equipment needed.
From The Transportation Series.
Prod-FILMSW Dist-FLMFR 1968

Transportation by Helicopter C 11 MIN
16MM FILM, 3/4 OR 1/2 IN VIDEO K-I
Shows how helicopters fly straight up, sideways, in one place and backwards. Illustrates how they are used in construction for lifting and stringing cable, in agriculture for pest and disease control, in emergency search and rescue missions, in transportation of passengers and light cargo and in carrying men and equipment to and from remote locations.
From The Transportation Series.
Prod-FILMSW Dist-FLMFR 1968

Transportation By Helicopter (Captioned Version) C 11 MIN
16MM FILM, 3/4 OR 1/2 IN VIDEO K-I
Shows how helicopters fly straight up, sideways, in one place and backwards. Illustrates how they are used in construction for lifting and stringing cable, in agriculture for pest and disease control, in emergency search and rescue missions, in transportation of passengers and light cargo and in carrying men and equipment to and from remote locations.
From The Transportation Series.
Prod-FILMSW Dist-FLMFR 1968

Transportation By Inland Waterways C 10 MIN
16MM FILM, 3/4 OR 1/2 IN VIDEO P-I
Shows barges and boats of all kinds carrying people and cargo on lakes, rivers and canals. Animation illustrates how locks on inland waterways work. The functions of the coast guard patrolling inland waterways are shown.
From The Transportation Series.
Prod-FILMSW Dist-FLMFR 1968

Transportation In America - A History C 17 MIN
16MM FILM, 3/4 OR 1/2 IN VIDEO I-J
A revised edition of Transportation - Footpath To Air Lane. Discusses the history of transportation in the United States, emphasizing economic and social pressures. Shows the drastic changes brought about by steam and internal combustion engines and covers the space shuttle of the future and the need for conservation of resources.
Prod-CF Dist-CF 1983

Transportation In America's History C 19 MIN
16MM FILM, 3/4 OR 1/2 IN VIDEO P-J
Traces the development of rail, auto and air travel from the American Revolution to the present day. Shows how the need to move people and their goods faster and farther led to the invention and the continuing improvement of transportation.
LC NO. 84-700709
Prod-NORWIN Dist-FLMFR 1984

Transportation In Neighborhoods C 15 MIN
3/4 OR 1/2 INCH VIDEO CASSETTE P
Looks at transportation in neighborhoods.
From The Neighborhoods Series.
Prod-NEITV Dist-GPITVL 1981

Transportation Is Moving C 11 MIN
16MM FILM, 3/4 OR 1/2 IN VIDEO K-I
Features all modes of transportation with emphasis on moving people and goods. Stresses economics in fulfilling our daily needs.
From The Transportation Series.
Prod-FILMSW Dist-FLMFR 1970

Transportation Maintenance C 11 MIN
16MM FILM, 3/4 OR 1/2 IN VIDEO P-I
Shows mechanics demonstrating their skills to illustrate how effectively community transportation may function.
From The Transportation Series.
Prod-FILMSW Dist-FLMFR 1969

Transportation Of The Injured C 14 MIN
16MM FILM OPTICAL SOUND
Shows how to use materials to be found in disaster areas to improvise means of moving injured persons. Describes precautions to prevent further injuries. To be used with the course 'MEDICAL SELF-HELP TRAINING.'
From The Medical Self-Help Series.
LC NO. 74-705845
Prod-USDHEW Dist-USNAC Prodn-USOCD 1960

Transportation Of The Injured C 22 MIN
16MM FILM OPTICAL SOUND PRO
Explains that immediate care, safe and expeditious transportation of an injured person to a hospital is an important part of the overall management. Demonstrates recommended methods for a selected group of common injuries.
Prod-ACYDGD Dist-ACY 1956

Transportation Of The Injured C 15 MIN
3/4 INCH VIDEO CASSETTE PRO
Demonstrates methods for moving people from the scene of an injury to a hospital emergency room facility. Shows the three-man carry. Discusses specific types of injuries for immobilizing and positioning injured people prior to lifting and transporting. Gives special consideration to the person with a spinal cord injury.
From The Trauma Series.
Prod-PRIMED Dist-PRIMED

Transportation Of The Injured (Spanish) C 14 MIN
16MM FILM OPTICAL SOUND
Teaches the individual how to take care of his medical and health needs in time of disaster when medical assistance might not be readily available. Presents instructions on transportation of the injured.

From The Medical Self-Help Series.
LC NO. 75-702552
Prod-USPHS Dist-USNAC 1965

Transportation Of The Sick And Wounded B 27 MIN
16MM FILM OPTICAL SOUND
Deals with patient evacuation in the field by means of manual carries, animal carries and military vehicles and aircraft.
LC NO. 74-705846
Prod-USA Dist-USNAC 1964

Transportation Revolution, The - Story Of America's Growth (Captioned) C 19 MIN
16MM FILM, 3/4 OR 1/2 IN VIDEO I-J
Highlights the history-making steps in road, rail and air transportation.
Prod-SCNDRI Dist-LCOA 1970

Transportation Revolution, The - Story Of America's Growth C 21 MIN
16MM FILM, 3/4 OR 1/2 IN VIDEO I-J
Traces the development of transportation from the horse and buggy to the airplane, highlighting the important stages in the development of more rapid, comfortable and efficient means of travel in America. Covers today's problems of congestion and pollution that mobility has brought with it.
Prod-SCNDRI Dist-LCOA 1970

Transportation—A Series
16MM FILM, 3/4 OR 1/2 IN VIDEO P-I
Discusses different methods of transporting goods and people as well as the importance of transportation maintenance.
Prod-FILMSW Dist-FLMFR

Transportation By Bus	010 MIN
Transportation By Freight Train	010 MIN
Transportation By Helicopter	010 MIN
Transportation By Inland Waterways	010 MIN
Transportation Is Moving	011 MIN
Transportation Maintenance	011 MIN
Trucks And Truck Transportation	011 MIN

Transportation/Mechanical Cluster C 20 MIN
3/4 OR 1/2 INCH VIDEO CASSETTE
Discusses the requirements and duties for such jobs as auto mechanic, auto body worker, diesel mechanic and truck driver.
From The Vocational Visions Series.
Prod-GA Dist-GA

Transportation's Role In Disaster C 15 MIN
16MM FILM OPTICAL SOUND
Describes the contribution of the National Defense Transportation Association, which has provided transportation services during major disasters over the last two decades.
LC NO. 74-706288
Prod-USOCD Dist-USNAC 1972

Transporting And Placing Quality Concrete C 27 MIN
16MM FILM, 3/4 OR 1/2 IN VIDEO
A revised version of How To Transport, Place, Finish And Cure Quality Concrete. Demonstrates methods used for transporting concrete from the batch plant to the job and subsequent handling on the job site to convey, place and consolidate concrete into the forms. Emphasizes correct techniques for various types of structures and under varying conditions.
LC NO. 82-706083
Prod-PRTLND Dist-PRTLND 1976

Transporting And Refining C 12 MIN
3/4 OR 1/2 INCH VIDEO CASSETTE IND
Shows how hydrocarbons produced from the well are collected and transported by pipeline, truck and tanker. Inspects fractionating and cracking towers and other refining operations.
From The Overview Of The Petroleum Industry Series.
Prod-GPCV Dist-GPCV

Transporting Of A Casualty, The C 9 MIN
16MM FILM, 3/4 OR 1/2 IN VIDEO A
Describes casualty transportation methods which can be used by one person or by a team of two people. Provides information on the use of stretchers, special requirements for moving individuals with suspected spinal injuries and procedures for carrying an injured in a confined space.
From The First Aid Series.
LC NO. 81-707504
Prod-HBL Dist-IFB 1977

Transporting The Patient For Surgery C 18 MIN
16MM FILM OPTICAL SOUND PRO
Stresses basic operating room nursing principles as they apply to the transportation of the patient to and from the operating room.
Prod-ACYDGD Dist-ACY 1958

Transposition Of The Index Finger For Amputated Thumb C 12 MIN
16MM FILM OPTICAL SOUND PRO
Describes in detail the operative procedure for pollicization of the index finger.
Prod-ACYDGD Dist-ACY 1957

Transpubic Repair Of Membranous Urethral Strictures C 14 MIN
16MM FILM OPTICAL SOUND
Demonstrates the transpubic repair of membranous urethral strictures. Explains that the operation is only suitable for patients with traumatic strictures and should not be used for strictures due to previous gonorrheal infection.
LC NO. 75-702257
Prod-EATONL Dist-EATONL 1973

Transseptal Orchiopexy For Cryptorchidism C 12 MIN
16MM FILM OPTICAL SOUND
Dr H C Miller discusses three major surgical methods of correcting cryptorchidism in order to produce mature healthy sperm, to minimize trauma and to permit easier physical examination of the tests. Shows views of a typical transseptal operation and illustrates the technique used.
LC NO. FIA66-71
Prod-EATONL Dist-EATONL Prodn-AVCORP 1965

Transsexuals - I Want To Be Me C 22 MIN
3/4 OR 1/2 INCH VIDEO CASSETTE
Reports on people who feel trapped in the body of the wrong sex. Includes interviews with transsexuals before and after sex-change surgery. Describes how their dilemma affected them, their families and friends.
Prod-WCCOTV Dist-WCCOTV 1974

Transthoracic Partial Gastrectomy C 28 MIN
16MM FILM OPTICAL SOUND PRO
Shows intrathoracic esophageo-gastric anastomosis for carcinoma of the cardia.
Prod-ACYDGD Dist-ACY 1950

Transthoracic Repair Of Sliding Hiatal Hernia C 14 MIN
16MM FILM SILENT
Illustrates the mechanism and surgical repair of sliding hiatal hernia.
Prod-USVA Dist-USVA 1955

Transthoracic Repair Of Sliding Hiatus Hernia With Reflux Esophagitis By The Mark ... C 28 MIN
16MM FILM OPTICAL SOUND PRO
Presents the evaluation and repair of the herniated and incompetent gastroesophageal junction as developed by Belsey. Emphasizes the techniques important to achieve relief of symptoms and a low recurrence rate.
Prod-ACYDGD Dist-ACY 1970

Transuranium Elements C 23 MIN
16MM FILM OPTICAL SOUND H A
Features four chemists from Lawrence Radiation Laboratory who were involved in the actual discovery and identification of the transuranium elements.
From The CHEM Study Films Series.
Prod-CHEMS Dist-MLA 1962

Transuranium Elements, The B 58 MIN
16MM FILM OPTICAL SOUND
Dr Glenn T Seaborg describes the work leading to the discovery of all of the know transuranium elements, from element 93 through element 104. Discusses some practical applications of transuranium elements and the possibility of making newer, very heavy elements.
LC NO. FIE68-74
Prod-USAEC Dist-USERD 1968

Transurethral Prostatectomy - A Teaching Film C 20 MIN
16MM FILM OPTICAL SOUND
Demonstrates the usefulness of the motion picture for teaching the procedure of transurethral prostatectomy. Acquaints the beginner with key points always encountered during transurethral prostatectomy.
Prod-EATONL Dist-EATONL 1966

Transurethral Resection Of Bladder Neck Obstruction C 20 MIN
16MM FILM OPTICAL SOUND
Discusses the indications for the various surgical approaches to the prostate and demonstrates the required diagnostic procedures and equipment. Includes a demonstration of a technique for transurethral prostatectomy.
LC NO. 75-702310
Prod-EATONL Dist-EATONL 1966

Transurethral Resection Of Bladder Tumor C 20 MIN
16MM FILM OPTICAL SOUND
Demonstrates the rationale and technique of transurethral resection of the large B-one bladder cancer, including intravenous pyelography and a discussion of the required armamentarium.
LC NO. 75-702309
Prod-EATONL Dist-EATONL 1966

Transurethral Resection Of The Prostate (TURP) C 10 MIN
3/4 OR 1/2 INCH VIDEO CASSETTE
Helps the patient understand the closed prostate surgery technique using the resectoscope, pre-and post-procedures, the urinary catheter and necessary postoperative precautions.
Prod-TRAINX Dist-TRAINX

Transvesico-Capsular Prostatectomy - An Improved Technique C 20 MIN
16MM FILM OPTICAL SOUND
Demonstrates step-by-step the procedures followed in a prostatectomy using the transvesico-capsular technique. Combines the good features of both retropubic and suprapubic enucleation.
LC NO. FIA66-73
Prod-EATONL Dist-EATONL Prodn-AVCORP 1960

Transvestism And Transsexualism C 60 MIN
3/4 OR 1/2 INCH VIDEO CASSETTE
Discusses the causes, diagnosis and therapeutic management of transvestism and transsexualism, which are often erroneously linked to homosexuality. Presents evaluation factors important in differential diagnosis.
Prod-HEMUL Dist-HEMUL

Trap Of Hate C 30 MIN
16MM FILM OPTICAL SOUND J-C A
Gives an account of the separation of a young man and his girlfriend which is caused when her parents learn that the boy's cousin has been in prison.
LC NO. 72-701642
Prod-CONCOR Dist-CPH 1968

Trap Of Solid Gold, The B 51 MIN
16MM FILM, 3/4 OR 1/2 IN VIDEO H-C
Shows the consequences of living beyond one's means, as exemplified in problems of a young executive who is caught in a trap of living beyond his income because of the status games of his company.
Prod-ABCTV Dist-IFB Prodn-MARKB 1969

Trapdoor, The B 30 MIN
16MM FILM OPTICAL SOUND
Tells how Jewish settlers in Newport, Rhode Island, came to understand the American principle of religious freedom. Describes how, expecting bigotry and intolerance, a secret tunnel and trapdoor for escaping from pogroms were built into the synagogue but were discovered to be unnecessary. (Kinescope)
Prod-JTS Dist-NAAJS Prodn-NBCTV 1954

Trapezoidal Sweep Generator - TSTR B 33 MIN
16MM FILM OPTICAL SOUND
Shows how the transistor trapezoidal sweep generator can be identified. Explains the purpose of the circuit components and develops a step-by-step analysis of the circuit's operation. (Kinescope)
LC NO. 74-705848
Prod-USAF Dist-USNAC

Trapezoidal Sweep Generator - TV B 19 MIN
16MM FILM OPTICAL SOUND
Explains a typical radar indicator and television receiver, making specific reference to the type of deflection used in each system. Develops the required waveform necessary for electromagnetic deflection. (Kinescope)
LC NO. 74-705849
Prod-USAF Dist-USNAC

Trapped (Rescue Work) B 20 MIN
16MM FILM OPTICAL SOUND
Emphasizes the need for trained rescue workers and shows many of the risks, as well as the rewards, of rescue.
LC NO. FIE55-45
Prod-USDD Dist-USNAC 1962

Trapper Dan C 15 MIN
16MM FILM OPTICAL SOUND
Spoofs silent movie serials.
LC NO. 75-703441
Prod-SFRASU Dist-SFRASU 1974

Trapping Of Free Radicals At Low Temperatures C 14 MIN
16MM FILM OPTICAL SOUND J-C A
Describes the behavior of free radicals as highly reactive molecular fragments. Explains their importance in high-temperature reactions and rocket flames.
LC NO. FIE61-147
Prod-USNBOS Dist-USNAC 1960

Traps C 43 MIN
3/4 OR 1/2 INCH VIDEO CASSETTE IND
See series title for descriptive statement.
From The Petroleum Geology Series.
Prod-GPCV Dist-GPCV

Traps - Anticlines C 31 MIN
3/4 OR 1/2 INCH VIDEO CASSETTE IND
See series title for descriptive statement.
From The Basic And Petroleum Geology For Non-Geologists-Traps Series.
Prod-PHILLP Dist-GPCV

Traps - Faulting C 33 MIN
3/4 OR 1/2 INCH VIDEO CASSETTE IND
See series title for descriptive statement.
From The Basic And Petroleum Geology For Non-Geologists - Traps Series.
Prod-PHILLP Dist-GPCV

Traps - Salt Domes C 38 MIN
3/4 OR 1/2 INCH VIDEO CASSETTE IND
See series title for descriptive statement.
From The Basic And Petroleum Geology For Non-Geologists - Traps Series.
Prod-PHILLP Dist-GPCV

Traps - Stratigraphic C 44 MIN
3/4 OR 1/2 INCH VIDEO CASSETTE IND
See series title for descriptive statement.
From The Basic And Petroleum Geology For Non-Geologists - Traps Series.
Prod-PHILLP Dist-GPCV

Traps And Snares - Summer C 11 MIN
16MM FILM, 3/4 OR 1/2 IN VIDEO I-H
Shows the construction and operation of traps and snares that can be used to obtain food in an emergency in the wilderness. The instructor in this film is an expert Indian trapper who regularly uses the traps and snares shown.
Prod-SF Dist-SF 1968

Traps And Snares - Winter C 12 MIN
16MM FILM, 3/4 OR 1/2 IN VIDEO I-H
Explains that Indian hunters still use ancient methods to trap wild game in the winter wilderness. Shows, how any person lost in the woods can use the same technique to catch small game.
Prod-SF Dist-SF 1968

Tratamiento Del Traumatismo Toracico C 26 MIN
3/4 OR 1/2 INCH VIDEO CASSETTE PRO
A Spanish language version of Management of Toracic Trauma. Discusses the more common surgical thoracic emergencies in the categories of penetrating and non-penetrating trauma. Presents the pathophysiology of thoracic trauma, the evaluation of patients with chest trauma, the initiation of appropriate

therapy and some of the life-threatening injuries which may occur with little or no external evidence.
Prod-UMICHM Dist-UMICHM 1981

Trauer Um Einen Verlorenen Sohn C 103 MIN
16MM FILM OPTICAL SOUND
A German language film with English subtitles. Captures the pain and anguish of a family who follows their drug-addicted son through withdrawal, relapse, change to harder drugs and finally death.
Prod-WSTGLC Dist-WSTGLC

Trauma C 41 MIN
3/4 INCH VIDEO CASSETTE PRO
Discusses gunshot wounds, emphasizing those caused by hand guns or pistols.
From The Forensic Medicine Teaching Programs Series.
LC NO. 78-706058
Prod-NMAC Dist-USNAC Prodn-NYUCM 1978

Trauma C 43 MIN
3/4 OR 1/2 INCH VIDEO CASSETTE PRO
Focuses on commonly litigated injuries caused by vehicular and industrial accidents. Explains priorities in treating multiple trauma.
From The Attorneys' Guide To Medicine Series.
Prod-PBI Dist-ABACPE

Trauma - It's An Emergency C 25 MIN
3/4 OR 1/2 INCH VIDEO CASSETTE
Explores what is, and what isn't, being done for the 52 million Americans who are injured in accidents and violent crimes each year. Answers these questions by learning how they can prevent accidents and what they can do to save the lives of trauma victim.
From The Killers Series.
Prod-TRAINX Dist-TRAINX

Trauma And Shock C 17 MIN
16MM FILM, 3/4 OR 1/2 IN VIDEO J-C A
Dramatizes situations involving trauma and shock and shows how each victim should be treated.
From The Emergency First Aid Series.
Prod-MLIC Dist-JOU 1980

Trauma Care - A Life At Stake C 23 MIN
16MM FILM, 3/4 OR 1/2 IN VIDEO J-C A
Uses reenactments of actual situations to illustrate how trauma can happen, how improper emergency assistance might be administered and how proper emergency care should be rendered to the victim before taking him to the hospital.
Prod-CAHILL Dist-AIMS Prodn-RALMON 1977

Trauma Care - A Life At Stake (Arabic) C 23 MIN
16MM FILM, 3/4 OR 1/2 IN VIDEO J-C A
Uses reenactments of actual situations to illustrate how trauma can happen, how improper emergency assistance might be administered and how proper emergency care should be rendered to the victim before taking him to the hospital.
Prod-CAHILL Dist-AIMS Prodn-RALMON 1977

Trauma Care - A Life At Stake (Spanish) C 23 MIN
16MM FILM, 3/4 OR 1/2 IN VIDEO J-C A
Uses reenactments of actual situations to illustrate how trauma can happen, how improper emergency assistance might be administered and how proper emergency care should be rendered to the victim before taking him to the hospital.
Prod-CAHILL Dist-AIMS Prodn-RALMON 1977

Trauma Of Treatment, The - A Patient's First Experience In Physical Therapy C 15 MIN
16MM FILM OPTICAL SOUND PRO
Presents the story of a young man's first physical therapy experience after a motorcycle accident. Shows therapists evaluating and treating his brachial plexus injury with professional competence and outward warmth, but their failure to communicate effectively causes anxieties to build up.
LC NO. 73-706384
Prod-USC Dist-USC Prodn-USCSM 1970

Trauma Patient, The C 22 MIN
16MM FILM, 3/4 OR 1/2 IN VIDEO PRO
Demonstrates treatment for victims of traumatic injury. Utilizes typical victims to show steps involved in the assessment and stabilization of injuries. Describes anatomic and physiological defects produced by trauma and details the necessary clinical behavior.
LC NO. 77-701118
Prod-SCOTR Dist-PFP 1977

Trauma Stress Management C 12 MIN
16MM FILM, 3/4 OR 1/2 IN VIDEO A
Uses case histories to explore effective and ineffective techniques of stress management.
From The Stress Management System Series. Film 2
Prod-MTI Dist-MTI 1983

Traumatic And Chemical Asphyxiation, Pt 1 C 28 MIN
16MM FILM - 3/4 IN VIDEO PRO
Discusses natural and traumatic causes of asphyxiation. Includes strangulation, suffocation, drowning, inhalation of lethal gases, pressure on the chest, strangulation due to food swallowing, carbon monoxide poisoning, glue sniffing and anesthetic gases. Features Dr Milton Helpern, Chief Medical Examiner for the City of New York, presenting the material in all its medical-legal aspects.
From The Clinical Pathology - Forensic Medicine Outlines Series.
Prod-NMAC Dist-USNAC

Traumatic And Chemical Asphyxiation, Pt 2 B 28 MIN
16MM FILM OPTICAL SOUND PRO
Discusses natural and traumatic causes of asphyxiation, such as strangulation, suffocation, drowning, inhalation of suffocating gases, pressure on the chest, strangulation due to food swallowing, carbon monoxide poisoning, glue sniffing and anesthetic gases. (Kinescope)
From The Clinical Pathology - Forensic Medicine Outlines Series.
LC NO. 74-705851
Prod-NMAC Dist-USNAC 1970

Traumatic And Chemical Asphyxiation, Pt 2 C 27 MIN
3/4 INCH VIDEO CASSETTE PRO
Discusses natural and traumatic causes of asphyxiation. Includes strangulation, suffocation, drowning, inhalation of lethal gases, pressure on the chest, strangulation due to food swallowing, carbon monoxide poisoning, glue sniffing and anesthetic gases. Features Dr Milton Helpern, Chief Medical Examiner for the City of New York, presenting the material and its medical-legal aspects.
From The Forensic Medicine Series.
Prod-PRIMED Dist-PRIMED

Traumatic Aneurysm Of The Thoracic Aorta Resection And Direct Reanastomosis C 22 MIN
16MM FILM OPTICAL SOUND PRO
Introduces a new concept in the surgical management of traumatic aneurysm of the thoracic aorta. Shows that the aneurysm was resected with the aid of left atrialfemoral artery by-pass, and the aorta reanastomosed without interposition of a graft.
Prod-ACYDGD Dist-ACY 1960

Traumatic Hernia Of The Diaphragm C 25 MIN
16MM FILM OPTICAL SOUND PRO
Demonstrates various pathological and clinical problems which have resulted from traumatic injuries of the diaphragm.
Prod-ACYDGD Dist-ACY 1956

Traumatic Injuries C 156 MIN
3/4 INCH VIDEO CASSETTE PRO
Discusses traumatic injuries in terms of forensic pathology.
From The Forensic Medicine Teaching Programs Series. No. 7
LC NO. 78-706059
Prod-NMAC Dist-USNAC Prodn-NYUCM 1978

Traumatic Instability Of The Wrist C 40 MIN
3/4 OR 1/2 INCH VIDEO CASSETTE PRO
Presents anatomic considerations, biomechanical bases, and the diagnostic clues to collapse deformities and instabilities following intracarpel fractures, dislocations and sprains of the wrist. Shows Dr Ronald L Linscheid treating illustrative cases.
Prod-ASSH Dist-ASSH

Traumatic Oval Window Fistula C 49 MIN
3/4 OR 1/2 INCH VIDEO CASSETTE PRO
Discusses the controversial and misunderstood subject of oval window fistula.
Prod-HOUSEI Dist-HOUSEI

Traumatic Transection Of The Pancreas Complicated By Intervascular Hemolysis C 11 MIN
3/4 OR 1/2 INCH VIDEO CASSETTE PRO
Shows traumatic transection of the pancreas complicated by intervascular hemolysis.
Prod-WFP Dist-WFP Prodn-UKANMC

Travase Ulcer Care, Adjunctive Therapy C 15 MIN
16MM FILM OPTICAL SOUND
Discusses adjunctive therapy for a travase ulcer.
LC NO. 76-701069
Prod-BAXLAB Dist-BAXLAB 1974

Travel Barrier B 19 MIN
16MM FILM OPTICAL SOUND
Discusses the problems of the handicapped in using public transportation. Shows future plans to eliminate many of these problems and offers advice to the handicapped who use public facilities now.
LC NO. 75-700703
Prod-USDTFH Dist-USNAC 1970

Travel Movies - Travel Scandinavia C 28 MIN
16MM FILM OPTICAL SOUND
Travels through Norway, Denmark and Sweden and shows the world's largest cross-country ski race. Views the culture, industry and recreational facilities in the area.
Prod-EKC Dist-EKC 1977

Travel Tales In Flowers C 34 MIN
16MM FILM OPTICAL SOUND
Presents the Tournament of Roses held in Pasadena, California, on January 2, 1967. Includes views of the all-flower floats, bands and horses.
LC NO. FIA67-1210
Prod-TRA Dist-TRA 1967

Travel Time C 15 MIN
2 INCH VIDEOTAPE
Shows some kinds of transportation that are necessary to a city.
From The Let's Build A City Series.
Prod-WVIZTV Dist-GPITVL

Travelbug—A Series

Prod-SFI Dist-SFI

Grand Canyon, The 13 MIN
Land Of Mystery 13 MIN
Mountain Fun 13 MIN
Oregon Scenics 13 MIN

Traveler's Cheques - A Safer Way C 14 MIN
16MM FILM, 3/4 OR 1/2 IN VIDEO H-C A
Takes a behind-the-scenes look at the design, printing and safeguarding of traveler's checks.
Prod-KLEINW Dist-KLEINW 1981

Traveler's Tales C 30 MIN
3/4 INCH VIDEO CASSETTE
Features classicist Dr Theodore Buttrey showing Herodotus retelling outlandish stories without evaluation as to their credibility.
From The Herodotus - Father Of History Series.
Prod-UMITV Dist-UMITV 1980

Traveler's Tales C 60 MIN
16MM FILM, 3/4 OR 1/2 IN VIDEO J-C A
Shows scientists in the midst of conducting an exploratory mission to Jupiter, using the Voyager II spacecraft. Explains how data on the planet is transmitted and processed. Explores the nature of the Jovian system and contrasts 20th century space exploration with exploration in 17th century Holland. Based on the book Cosmos by Carl Sagan. Narrated by Carl Sagan.
From The Cosmos Series. Program 6
LC NO. 81-707203
Prod-KCET Dist-FI 1980

Travelers On The Wing C 24 MIN
16MM FILM OPTICAL SOUND I-C
Studies bird migration. Discusses several theories which explain how birds know their destination and the appropriate time to go.
From The Animal Secrets Series.
LC NO. FIA68-1030
Prod-NBC Dist-GRACUR 1967

Travelin' Shoes C 15 MIN
16MM FILM, 3/4 OR 1/2 IN VIDEO
Presents the Billups family's mixed feelings of joy, remorse and anticipation as they prepare to move to Washington, DC.
From The Inside-Out Series.
Prod-NITC Dist-AITECH

Traveling C 15 MIN
3/4 OR 1/2 INCH VIDEO CASSETTE P-I
Tells what to take along when you travel by car, bus or airplane and what precautions you should take to make such a trip safer.
From The Safer You Series.
Prod-WCVETV Dist-GPITVL 1984

Traveling Hopefully C 28 MIN
16MM FILM, 3/4 OR 1/2 IN VIDEO H-C A
Profiles Roger Baldwin, founder of the American Civil Liberties Union. Features Baldwin's conversations with Edward Kennedy, Arthur Schlesinger, Norman Lear and Gail Sheehy. Includes archive footage from the Scopes Trial, Klan marches and American Nazi demonstrations, all of which show the relevance of Baldwin's concerns.
Prod-FI Dist-FI 1981

Traveller From An Antique Land C 30 MIN
3/4 OR 1/2 INCH VIDEO CASSETTE
Explores and explains the Egyptians' meticulous attention to the preservation of the body after death. Includes a retinue of pathologists performing an autopsy to determine the origins of disease.
Prod-CANBC Dist-JOU

Travellin Round C 31 MIN
16MM FILM OPTICAL SOUND J-C A
Details the adventures of three young Australians as they travel around Australia by landrover and motorbike, starting from Sydney, they travel to the Great Barrier Reef, Darwin, Perth and Adelaide and on the return route, one of them detours to the island State of Tasmania.
LC NO. 76-701871
Prod-FLMAUS Dist-AUIS Prodn-FLMAUS 1974

Travelling Light C 30 MIN
3/4 OR 1/2 INCH VIDEO CASSETTE H-C A
Features the ideas demonstrated in the first seven programs being put into action in Egypt. Shows holiday photography and its memories, surprises, disappointments and triumphs.
From The What A Picture - The Complete Photography Course By John Hedgecoe Series. Program 8
Prod-THREMI Dist-FI

Travelling Together C 7 MIN
3/4 OR 1/2 INCH VIDEO CASSETTE K-P
Allows children a personal glimpse at a variety of people mover systems, including buses, boats, planes and trains.
From The Looking For Series.
Prod-FILMID Dist-FILMID

Travels C 30 MIN
3/4 OR 1/2 INCH VIDEO CASSETTE
Deals with trips to the United States, Spain and Israel.
Prod-KITCHN Dist-KITCHN

Travels - Five Works By Shalom Gorewitz—A Series

Presents five works by video artist Shalom Gorewitz which have been widely shown throughout the U S.
Prod-EAI Dist-EAI

Autumn Floods 006 MIN
Corandero, El 005 MIN
Delta Visions 005 MIN
Excavations 006 MIN
Measures of Volatility 006 MIN

Travels In The Combat Zone C 30 MIN
3/4 OR 1/2 INCH VIDEO CASSETTE
Reveals a woman's view of the harsh and beautiful realities of city living and her travels through the eternal combat zone of cities and men.
From The Doris Chase Concepts Series.
Prod-CHASED Dist-CHASED

Travels In Undiscovered Country C 27 MIN
3/4 OR 1/2 INCH VIDEO CASSETTE
Discloses the experiences of people who have clinically died and been resuscitated. Points out the growing controversy in medical and religious circles about the validity of these experiences.
Prod-WCCOTV Dist-WCCOTV 1977

Travels Of Timothy Trent, The C 10 MIN
16MM FILM, 3/4 OR 1/2 IN VIDEO
Explains that safety packaging is a valuable tool that offers an additional margin of safety from accidental poisoning. Issued in 1976 as a motion picture.
LC NO. 80-707131
Prod-USCPSC Dist-USNAC 1980

Tray Set-Up For Various Examinations C 12 MIN
1/2 IN VIDEO CASSETTE BETA/VHS
Explains how to set up for minor surgery, proctoscopic exams, and eye, ear, nose and throat exams.
Prod-RMI Dist-RMI

Treacherous Paradise C 23 MIN
3/4 OR 1/2 INCH VIDEO CASSETTE K-C A
Explores a coral reef in the Pacific Ocean, Truk Lagoon. Shows the once desolate lagoon, now a dazzling kaleidoscope of marine life.
Prod-NWLDPR Dist-NWLDPR

Tread Softly C 27 MIN
3/4 INCH VIDEOTAPE
Portrays the relationship between an older and a younger woman. Reveals the difficulties and differences in their ages as well as their different identities as lesbian woman.
Prod-WMEN Dist-WMEN

Tread Softly C 30 MIN
2 INCH VIDEOTAPE C A
Examines standard and custom-made soft floor coverings. Filmed at a carpet manufacturing company.
From The Designing Home Interiors Series. Unit 14
Prod-COAST Dist-CDTEL Prodn-RSCCD

Treadle And Bobbin C 9 MIN
16MM FILM OPTICAL SOUND P-C A
Records the precision and rhythmic movements of a foot pedal-driven sewing machine. Follows its floral motifs, ornate scroll work and cast-iron arabesques.
Prod-GALENT Dist-RADIM 1954

Treason Of Benedict Arnold C 22 MIN
16MM FILM, 3/4 OR 1/2 IN VIDEO I-H
Documents the intrigues surrounding Benedict Arnold's treason in aiding the British to capture West Point, and the effects of his actions upon the course of the Revolutionary War.
From The Your Are There Series.
Prod-CBSTV Dist-PHENIX 1972

Treasure C 59 MIN
16MM FILM, 3/4 OR 1/2 IN VIDEO
Documents the search for gold and silver from a sunken Spanish galleon off the Florida Keys.
LC NO. 80-706371
Prod-NGS Dist-NGS 1976

Treasure City C 15 MIN
16MM FILM OPTICAL SOUND
Explores the port city of Tampa, Florida.
Prod-FLADC Dist-FLADC

Treasure From The Sea C 4 MIN
16MM FILM, 3/4 OR 1/2 IN VIDEO C A
Offers a comedic adventure on the high seas in search of buried treasure.
Prod-GOLSH Dist-MTI 1982

Treasure Ho C 15 MIN
3/4 OR 1/2 INCH VIDEO CASSETTE K-P
Demonstrates use of the lever and the inclined plane.
From The Dragons, Wagons And Wax, Set 1 Series.
Prod-CTI Dist-CTI

Treasure Hunt C 20 MIN
16MM FILM OPTICAL SOUND P-I
Reveals that when a treasure hunt is organized, the Graham children and Alice the chimp compete enthusiastically. Shows that when some of their opponents compete unfairly, the chimp mates show that they can come up with some tricks of their own.
Prod-LUF Dist-LUF 1978

Treasure Hunt C 15 MIN
16MM FILM, 3/4 OR 1/2 IN VIDEO I
Explores the process of producing income and shows some of the different ways of participating in the economic system.
From The Bread And Butterflies Series.
LC NO. 74-703174
Prod-AITV Dist-AITECH Prodn-WNVT 1973

Treasure Hunt, A C 15 MIN
3/4 OR 1/2 INCH VIDEO CASSETTE P
Reveals that finalists in a community treasure hunt have trouble if they don't know the cardinal directions or right from left.
From The Under The Yellow Balloon Series.
Prod-SCETV Dist-AITECH 1980

Treasure Hunt, The (Teamwork) C 11 MIN
16MM FILM, 3/4 OR 1/2 IN VIDEO K-P
Shows how the puppet friends of forest town learn the value of working together when they choose teams and go on a treasure hunt.
From The Forest Town Fables Series.
Prod-CORF Dist-CORF 1974

Treasure In The Pyramid C 10 MIN
16MM FILM, 3/4 OR 1/2 IN VIDEO I-J
Uses puppets in order to tell an adventure story about an intrepid pair who foil the plans of a group of robbers seeking to take the treasure in a Mayan pyramid.
From The Deadly Scent Series.
Prod-SFSP Dist-PHENIX 1974

Treasure In The Sea, A - The Channel Islands National Park C 24 MIN
16MM FILM, 3/4 OR 1/2 IN VIDEO
Stresses the impact of man's presence on the fragile ecology of the Channel Islands off the coast of California. Encompasses their history, geology, biology and ethnology.
Prod-USNPS Dist-USNAC

Treasure Island C 15 MIN
16MM FILM OPTICAL SOUND
Presents the legendary Long John Silver, a venturesome pirate, exploring Treasure Island.
Prod-FLADC Dist-FLADC

Treasure Island C 40 MIN
16MM FILM OPTICAL SOUND J-H
Tells the story of the gallant young Jim Hawkins pitted against the nefarious John Silver. Describes the plot summary and vivid character studies of the many intriguing personalities in this Stevenson's classic.
Prod-FI Dist-FI

Treasure Island C 19 MIN
3/4 OR 1/2 INCH VIDEO CASSETTE
Explores the legend of Captain Kidd's great buried treasure in Nova Scotia, and describes the attempts to retrieve the booty.
Prod-CANBC Dist-JOU

Treasure Island C 22 MIN
16MM FILM, 3/4 OR 1/2 IN VIDEO I-H
Presents an animated version of the Stevenson classic, TREASURE ISLAND.
Prod-AIMS Dist-AIMS 1983

Treasure Island C 30 MIN
16MM FILM, 3/4 OR 1/2 IN VIDEO J-H
Presents an excerpt from the film Treasure Island which reveals how young Jim Hawkins gets involved in a search for buried pirate treasure along with the greedy Long John Silver. Based on the novel TREASURE ISLAND by Robert Louis Stevenson.
From The Films As Literature, Series 1 Series
Prod-DISNEY Dist-WDEMCO Prodn-WDEMCO

Treasure Island With Mr Magoo C 52 MIN
16MM FILM OPTICAL SOUND P-I
Prod-FI Dist-FI

Treasure Of The Grotoceans, The C 16 MIN
16MM FILM, 3/4 OR 1/2 IN VIDEO I-J A
Uses puppets to present an underwater fantasy about ecology and conservation. Shows two Grotoceans discovering all kinds of surprises awaiting them as they roam the sea in search of treasure.
Prod-NFBC Dist-NFBC 1980

Treasure Search, Pt 1 - Diamonds In The Surf C 28 MIN
3/4 OR 1/2 INCH VIDEO CASSETTE
Presents treasure hunters who use metal detectors to locate lost valuables in the shallow waters of Chesapeake Bay. Shows them recovering coins, jewelry and other collectibles and researching their value in books, newspaper and interviews. Explains how their hobby became and full-time occupation.
LC NO. 84-707119
Prod-CREVID Dist-CREVID 1983

Treasures In Snow C 7 MIN
16MM FILM, 3/4 OR 1/2 IN VIDEO I-J
Explains that snow is a storehouse for water, a source of power for generating electricity and a source of recreation. Presents the concepts of evaporation and condensation. Shows the symmetrical perfection of individual snowflakes.
Prod-MIS Dist-MIS 1955

Treasures Of Abu Simbel, The B 3 MIN
16MM FILM OPTICAL SOUND
Shows how the ancient statues and treasures of Abu Simbel in Egypt are threatened by the building of the Aswan Dam. Uses animation to describe the UNESCO plan to reassemble them on higher ground.
From The Screen News Digest Series. Vol 6, Issue 10
LC NO. FIA68-2083
Prod-HEARST Dist-HEARST 1964

Treasures Of Canned Salmon C 21 MIN
16MM FILM OPTICAL SOUND
Presents the story of canned salmon from the time it is caught through canning to use in soups, salads, main dishes and sandwiches.
Prod-MTP Dist-MTP

Treasures Of Germany C 28 MIN
16MM FILM OPTICAL SOUND C A
Explores the art and architecture of the Federal Republic of Germany, and traces Germany's cultural history using the masterworks of different historical periods. Explains how skilled German artisans have interpreted the Central European spirit down through the ages.
Prod-WSTGLC Dist-WSTGLC

Treasures Of King Tut, The C 15 MIN
16MM FILM OPTICAL SOUND I-C A
Surveys the art objects, gold and jewels found in King Tut's tomb.
LC NO. 78-700513
Prod-EDDIM Dist-EDDIM 1978

Treasures Of The Earth (2nd Ed) C 15 MIN
16MM FILM, 3/4 OR 1/2 IN VIDEO I-J
Describes the forces in the Earth's crust which cause deformations in rocks, thereby allowing concentration of minerals by various kinds of water action. Discusses coal formation and the accumulation of oil.
Prod-CF Dist-CF 1974

Treasures Of The Gulf C 50 MIN
3/4 OR 1/2 INCH VIDEO CASSETTE H-C A
Looks at how the Persian Gulf has maintained its ecological balance of marine life and vast oil fields but is now threatened with devastation as the war between Iran and Iraq heats up with attacks on the oil wells and tankers.
Prod-WNETTV Dist-FI

Treasures Of The Uffizi C 28 MIN
16MM FILM OPTICAL SOUND I-J
European art authority, Pietro Annigoni, comments on art works in the Uffizi, a one-time office building of Florence, Italy, used by the 15th century medici family who collected and preserved many paintings.
Prod-GALERY Dist-MLA 1965

Treasures Of Time - Oriental Art C 15 MIN
16MM FILM, 3/4 OR 1/2 IN VIDEO I-H
Shows how sculpture, miniature models, scrolls, paintings, pottery and furniture reveal the history and culture of the Orient.
Prod-HORPRO Dist-IFB 1964

Treasures Of Time - Painting C 15 MIN
16MM FILM, 3/4 OR 1/2 IN VIDEO I-H
Presents an historical survey of painting, with examples from prehistoric times to the 20th century.
Prod-HORPRO Dist-IFB 1964

Treasures Of Time - Sculpture C 15 MIN
16MM FILM, 3/4 OR 1/2 IN VIDEO I-H
Offers an elementary study of sculpture which relates the works in museums to everyday life.
Prod-HORPRO Dist-IFB 1964

Treasures Of Tuscany—A Series

Prod-WESTCB Dist-RADIM

Basilica Of San Lorenzo, The	24 MIN
Basilica Of Santa Croce, The	26 MIN
Cantoria Of Luca Della Robbia, The	15 MIN
Cathedral And Baptistry Of Florence, The	24 MIN
Davids Of Florence, The	13 MIN
Florentine Architecture Of The Renaissance	27 MIN
Siena	22 MIN

Treasures Of Tutankhamen, The - An Introduction To Ancient Egypt C
3/4 OR 1/2 INCH VIDEO CASSETTE
Relates the artifacts found in the tomb of Tutankhamen to the culture and religion of ancient Egypt. Photographs show the pieces as examples of the cultural wealth and artistic brilliance of ancient Egyptian society.
Prod-GA Dist-GA

Treasures Of Tutankhamum C 5 MIN
16MM FILM OPTICAL SOUND
Shows the beauty and splendor of treasures from King Tutankhamun's tomb. Studies gold and alabaster objects, masterpieces of inlaid jewelry and other artifacts designed to glorify the king or to accompany him in the afterworld.
Prod-USNGA Dist-USNGA

Treasures Of Tutankhamun C 29 MIN
3/4 OR 1/2 INCH VIDEO CASSETTE
Presents an essay on the traveling exhibits of artifacts unearthed from the tomb of King Tutankhamun, the young Egyptian ruler who died in 1325 BC.
Prod-WTTWTV Dist-PBS 1979

Treat Wood Right C 22 MIN
16MM FILM OPTICAL SOUND H-C A
Discusses the advantages of using treated wood to control decay and insect pests. Presents the problems of decay which begin from the moment the tree is cut and depicts the operations of the wood preserving industry. Emphasizes the use of the wood preservative, pentachlorophenol.
Prod-DCC Dist-DCC 1952

Treating Crude-Oil Emulsions C 27 MIN
16MM FILM, 3/4 OR 1/2 IN VIDEO IND
Covers the key points in the handling and treatment of crude-oil emulsions.
Prod-UTEXPE Dist-UTEXPE 1981

Treating Erectile Problems C 20 MIN
3/4 OR 1/2 INCH VIDEO CASSETTE C A
Part two of a two part series on erectile problems. Couple discusses anxiety related to sexual performance. Focuses on sexual fantasy and relaxation training.
Prod-MMRC Dist-MMRC

Treating Heart Attacks C 10 MIN
3/4 OR 1/2 INCH VIDEO CASSETTE H-C A
Describes how a portable monitor, originally created for the space program, is being used by paramedics treating heart attack victims.
Prod-UPI Dist-JOU

Treating Vaginismus C 19 MIN
3/4 OR 1/2 INCH VIDEO CASSETTE C A
Explains the condition vaginismus and describes its treatment through sex therapy.
LC NO. 84-707244
Prod-MMRC Dist-MMRC

Treatment C 30 MIN
3/4 OR 1/2 INCH VIDEO CASSETTE H-C A

See series title for descriptive statement.
From The Fundamentals Of Alcohol Problems Series.
Prod-UMINN Dist-GPITVL 1978

Treatment - New Teams C 10 MIN
3/4 OR 1/2 INCH VIDEO CASSETTE
Examines the use of paraprofessionals as a resource for the professional coming in contact with drug and drug-related programs. Issued in 1971 as a motion picture.
From The Professional Drug Films Series.
LC NO. 80-707347
Prod-NIMH Dist-USNAC 1980

Treatment Available To The Injured Dancer C 30 MIN
3/4 OR 1/2 INCH VIDEO CASSETTE
See series title for descriptive statement.
From The Dancers' Health Alert Series.
Prod-ARCVID Dist-ARCVID

Treatment By Married Co-Therapists Of A Couple Moving Toward Divorce C 60 MIN
3/4 OR 1/2 INCH VIDEO CASSETTE
Features a severely dysfunctional couple which is helped to gain understanding of their marriage from past to present and given supportive guidance as they move toward a separation. Shows special efforts by therapists to stop the parents from using the children as pawns and scapegoats.
From The Family And Group Therapy Series.
Prod-HEMUL Dist-HEMUL

Treatment For A Traumatic Amputation C 8 MIN
3/4 OR 1/2 INCH VIDEO CASSETTE PRO
Gives a detailed sequence of steps for caring for complete and partial amputations, including application of a tourniquet and pressure dressing.
From The EMT Video - Group One Series.
LC NO. 84-706495
Prod-USA Dist-USNAC 1979

Treatment For Alcoholics C 28 MIN
3/4 OR 1/2 INCH VIDEO CASSETTE J A
Focuses on alcohol treatment such as modalites and 'Significant Others.'
Prod-SUTHRB Dist-SUTHRB

Treatment For An Open Chest Wound C 6 MIN
3/4 OR 1/2 INCH VIDEO CASSETTE PRO
Shows treatment procedures for an open chest wound, including checking for other wounds, checking the airway, removing clothing and debris near the wound, sealing the wound, placing a sterile dressing over the material used to close a sucking wound, and applying and securing the bandage.
From The EMT Video - Group One Series.
LC NO. 84-706496
Prod-USA Dist-USNAC 1983

Treatment For Recurrent Traumatic Pterygium C 12 MIN
16MM FILM OPTICAL SOUND PRO
Illustrates two methods of treatment for recurrent traumatic pterygium, use of conjunctiva taken from the upper lid of the opposite eye and use of a mucous membrane graft.
Prod-ACYDGD Dist-ACY 1962

Treatment Is The Crisis, The - L-Dopa And Parkinson's Disease C 31 MIN
16MM FILM OPTICAL SOUND C A
Documents the effects of the drug L-dopa on elderly patients suffering from Parkinson's disease. Shows the progress of several patients with the individuals and their families explaining the effects of the disease and its treatment.
LC NO. 73-703367
Prod-TRNSIT Dist-TRNSIT 1972

Treatment Of Abdominal Penetrating Wounds In Civilian Practice C 33 MIN
16MM FILM OPTICAL SOUND PRO
Explains that few injuries require greater surgical skill and resourcefulness for successful management than penetrating abdominal wounds. Depicts the method of managing these serious injuries in civilian practice.
Prod-ACYDGD Dist-ACY 1961

Treatment Of Abdominal Trauma C 21 MIN
16MM FILM OPTICAL SOUND PRO
Shows the resuscitative and diagnostic approach in the management of patients with abdominal injury. Demonstrates diagnostic peritoneal lavage in patients with blunt abdominal injury. Shows operative findings in these patients.
Prod-ACYDGD Dist-ACY 1969

Treatment Of Acne C 20 MIN
3/4 OR 1/2 INCH VIDEO CASSETTE PRO
Reviews several varieties of acne with respect to age to onset, areas of the body affected, endocrine system involvement and internal and external factors that may affect the condition. Reviews the characteristics of the four grades of acne vulgaris. Identifies therapeutic management alternatives for each grade of acne vulgaris and for each of the other types of acne presented.
Prod-UMICHM Dist-UMICHM 1978

Treatment Of An Open Abdominal Wound C 6 MIN
3/4 OR 1/2 INCH VIDEO CASSETTE PRO
Shows treatment procedures for an open abdominal wound with exposed intestines, including removing restrictive clothing, and preparing, applying and securing a dressing to the wound.
From The EMT Video - Group One Series.
LC NO. 84-706497
Prod-USA Dist-USNAC 1983

Treatment Of Aneurysms Of The Peripheral Arteries C 11 MIN
16MM FILM OPTICAL SOUND
Discusses the treatment of arteriosclerotic and traumatic aneurysms of the femoral and popliteal arteries. Discusses two connected cases.
Prod-USVA Dist-USVA 1956

Treatment Of Carcinoma Of The Stomach In Elderly Patients C 28 MIN
16MM FILM OPTICAL SOUND PRO
Depicts the treatment of three patients with cancer of the stomach, 63, 69 and 75 years of age, who had advanced arteriosclerosis and coronary artery disease. Emphasizes preservation of adequate blood supply to the gastric remnant.
Prod-ACYDGD Dist-ACY 1962

Treatment Of Cardiac Arrhythmias By Drugs And Electricity, The B 85 MIN
16MM FILM OPTICAL SOUND PRO
Clarifies current usage of drugs and electrical devices for the control of cardiac arrhythmias.
From The Boston Medical Reports Series.
LC NO. 74-705855
Prod-NMAC Dist-NMAC 1968

Treatment Of Dysphonia, The C 18 MIN
3/4 OR 1/2 INCH VIDEO CASSETTE PRO
Demonstrates the use of silicone and teflon injections directly into a paralyzed vocal chord. Demonstrates usefulness of the method in the correction of dysphonia by before and after treatment voice recordings.
Prod-WFP Dist-WFP

Treatment Of Hansen's Disease C 17 MIN
3/4 INCH VIDEO CASSETTE PRO
Discusses management of uncomplicated Hansen's disease or leprosy. Outlines basic drug choices, treatment regimes, efficacy measurements, drug resistance problems and research efforts.
LC NO. 79-706706
Prod-USPHS Dist-USNAC 1977

Treatment Of Heat Injuries C 9 MIN
3/4 OR 1/2 INCH VIDEO CASSETTE PRO
Demonstrates procedures for identifying heat cramps, exhaustion, and stroke, with differentiation of symptoms for each and the emergency treatment to be given.
From The EMT Video - Group One Series.
LC NO. 84-706498
Prod-USA Dist-USNAC 1983

Treatment Of Infrabony Pocket With Three Osseous Walls C 14 MIN
16MM FILM OPTICAL SOUND
Demonstrates the surgical management of an infrabony pocket involving the maxillary premolar.
LC NO. 74-705856
Prod-USVA Dist-USNAC 1968

Treatment Of Infrabony Pocket With Three Osseous Walls C 14 MIN
3/4 OR 1/2 INCH VIDEO CASSETTE
Demonstrates the surgical management of an infrabony pocket involving the maxillary premolar. Shows how the periodontal ligament and bone marrow are used to provide two sources of repair tissue.
Prod-VADTC Dist-AMDA 1969

Treatment Of Mental Disorders B 20 MIN
16MM FILM SILENT C T
Shows various aspects of a hospital for psychotics, such as interviews of patients and procedures of physical examination when they are admitted, methods of forced feeding with patients who refuse to eat, continuous baths for calming down excited patients, hot boxes and lamps for heat therapy, use of sedatives and narcotics, use of insulin and metrazol therapy on schizophrenics and other types, fever therapy, occupational therapy and recreational management.
Prod-PSUPCR Dist-PSUPCR 1939

Treatment Of Pain, The C 30 MIN
3/4 OR 1/2 INCH VIDEO CASSETTE
Discusses the medical treatment of pain.
From The Lifelines Series.
Prod-UGATV Dist-MDCPB

Treatment Of Parkinsonism With Levodopa C 14 MIN
16MM FILM OPTICAL SOUND
Depicts the features of the disease of Parkinsonism and discusses the historical and biochemical impact and relevance of levodopa. Illustrates the side effects of dyskinesia and some other major side effects of the medication.
LC NO. 75-702333
Prod-EATONL Dist-EATONL 1971

Treatment Of Patients In Chronic Renal Failure C 24 MIN
16MM FILM OPTICAL SOUND PRO
Illustrates the treatment of patients with chronic renal insufficiency. Includes renal transplantation, institutional dialysis and home dialysis.
Prod-ACYDGD Dist-ACY 1968

Treatment Of Simple Head Injuries C 15 MIN
16MM FILM OPTICAL SOUND PRO
Emphasizes the meticulous care necessary in the examination and treatment of the simple head injury. Explains that proper early treatment of the simple head injury will prevent or anticipate the occurrence of serious results.
Prod-ACYDGD Dist-ACY 1954

Treatment Of Strabismus C 8 MIN
3/4 OR 1/2 INCH VIDEO CASSETTE
Reviews reasons for and principles of treatment of strabismus.
Prod-MEDFAC Dist-MEDFAC 1974

Treatment Of The Borderline Patient—A Series

Presents a series on the treatment of the borderline patient with Harold F Searles, MD, professor of psychiatry at Georgetown University School of Medicine.
Prod-HEMUL Dist-HEMUL

Cure, The - Playfulness And Other Signs Of	
Definition Of The Borderline Patient	027 MIN
Problems Of The Therapeutic Symbiosis	016 MIN
Selecting Patients For Treatment	015 MIN
Separation Anxiety And Wishes To Be Rid Of	015 MIN
Splitting The Transference - Group Treatment	015 MIN
Strangleholds On The Therapist Failure To	016 MIN
Therapeutic Techniques, Pt I-	030 MIN
Therapeutic Techniques, Pt II -'Good	015 MIN
Therapeutic Techniques, Pt III - Between	024 MIN
Transference And Countertransference	030 MIN
Word Order, The Pause And The Importance Of	015 MIN

Treatment Of The Mutilating Hand Injury C 60 MIN
3/4 OR 1/2 INCH VIDEO CASSETTE PRO
Presents a classification of the mutilating hand injuries with diagrams. Shows that photographs of representative cases taken before and after operation demonstrate unusual surgical technique.
Prod-ASSH Dist-ASSH

Treatment Urgent B 17 MIN
16MM FILM OPTICAL SOUND H-C A
A chronic condition of endometriosis is treated surgically with the removal of the uterus. Describes the doctor's method of handling the emotional reactions of the patient before the hysterectomy takes place and follows the doctor as he performs the surgery.
From The Doctors At Work Series.
LC NO. FIA65-1371
Prod-CMA Dist-LAWREN Prodn-LAWREN 1962

Tree And Shrub Planting C 12 MIN
16MM FILM, 3/4 OR 1/2 IN VIDEO I-C A
Points out that how you care for trees or shrubs at transplanting time will govern their future growth rate, appearance and general well-being. Discusses the types of material available to the home gardener. Shows methods for planting and care after planting.
From The Garden Methods Series.
Prod-PEREN Dist-PEREN

Tree Blossoms C 12 MIN
16MM FILM, 3/4 OR 1/2 IN VIDEO I-H A
Shows that trees can be flowering plants of great beauty.
From The Many Worlds Of Nature Series.
Prod-SCRESC Dist-MTI

Tree Community, A C 18 MIN
16MM FILM, 3/4 OR 1/2 IN VIDEO I-J
Describes how various plants and animals use a large oak tree as a source of food and shelter. Traces the growth of the tree and emphasizes the flow of energy from the Sun and the recycling of minerals from the Earth.
LC NO. 83-706698
Prod-SHMNKI Dist-IFB 1979

Tree Community, A (Captioned) C 18 MIN
16MM FILM, 3/4 OR 1/2 IN VIDEO
Presents an introduction to the ecological community consisting of a mature oak tree and the various animals and plants which use it as a source of food and shelter. Follows the growth cycle of the tree through the seasons and examines the flow of energy from the sun and the recycling of minerals from the soil.
Prod-SHMNKI Dist-IFB 1979

Tree Environment (1) C 50 MIN
3/4 OR 1/2 INCH VIDEO CASSETTE
Gives definition of T-machine in LISP, as a modification of the S-machine in computer languages.
From The Computer Languages - Pt 1 Series.
Prod-MIOT Dist-MIOT

Tree Environment (2) C 50 MIN
3/4 OR 1/2 INCH VIDEO CASSETTE
Lectures on upward FUNARG problem, as evaluated by the T-machine and sketch of equivalence proof for tree machine and normal order algorithm.
From The Computer Languages - Pt 1 Series.
Prod-MIOT Dist-MIOT

Tree Grading C 28 MIN
16MM FILM OPTICAL SOUND
Discusses the procedures of tree grading.
LC NO. 75-700704
Prod-USDA Dist-USNAC

Tree Improvement And Genetics C 26 MIN
16MM FILM, 3/4 OR 1/2 IN VIDEO H-C
Discusses the many aspects of growth and form considered in the improvement of the quality and growth of trees.
Prod-HARL Dist-IFB 1966

Tree Is A Living Thing, A X 11 MIN
16MM FILM, 3/4 OR 1/2 IN VIDEO P
Relates the story of a boy's discovery that a tree grows from a single seed. Teaches how and why the life-cycle of a tree changes through seasons. Illustrates how the age of a tree is determined and how a tree is fed through the process of photosynthesis.
Prod-NFBC Dist-EBEC 1964

Tree Is A Living Thing, A (Spanish) C 11 MIN
16MM FILM, 3/4 OR 1/2 IN VIDEO P
Shows how a tree's life cycle changes through the seasons, how a tree's age is determined and how a tree is nourished through photosynthesis.
Prod-EBEC Dist-EBEC

Tree Lives, The B 30 MIN
16MM FILM OPTICAL SOUND
Tells the story of Theodor Herzl, who, in his effort to secure Palestine as a homeland for the Jews, obtains an interview with the Kaiser in Palestine in the year 1898.
LC NO. FIA64-1181
Prod-JTS Dist-NAAJS Prodn-NBC 1961

Tree Of Life C 26 MIN
16MM FILM OPTICAL SOUND
A short version of the film Tree Of Life. Presents a lyrical exploration of the unique meaning of Jewishness in the land of Israel, past and present. Narrated by Lord Laurence Olivier.
Prod-UJA Dist-ALDEN

Tree Of Life C 52 MIN
16MM FILM OPTICAL SOUND
Explores the meaning of Jewishness as it is seen in Israel.
LC NO. 75-700487
Prod-UJA Dist-ALDEN 1974

Tree Of Life, The C 20 MIN
16MM FILM, 3/4 OR 1/2 IN VIDEO
Documents the Volador ritual as performed by the Totonac Indians of Mexico.
Prod-FLOWER Dist-FLOWER

Tree Of Thorns C 50 MIN
16MM FILM, 3/4 OR 1/2 IN VIDEO H-C A
Illustrates the delicate harmony of nature, focusing on the African acacia tree and showing how it is being threatened.
Prod-BBCTV Dist-FI 1981

Tree Of Truth, The - Relationship Between Addition And Subtraction C 9 MIN
16MM FILM, 3/4 OR 1/2 IN VIDEO P-I
Uses the story of a greedy king to point out that addition and subtraction are interrelated.
From The Math That Counts Series.
Prod-DAVFMS Dist-EBEC

Tree Of Wooden Clogs, The (Italian) C 185 MIN
16MM FILM OPTICAL SOUND
Describes incidents in the lives of four families sharecropping in Lombardy at the turn of the century. Directed by Ermanno Olmi. With English subtitles.
Prod-UNKNWN Dist-NYFLMS 1978

Tree Portraits C 21 MIN
16MM FILM, 3/4 OR 1/2 IN VIDEO J-H
Shows views of common trees of the United States and explains how to identify a tree by its leaves, flowers, fruits, seeds, twigs and bark.
Prod-HARL Dist-IFB 1967

Tree Power C 28 MIN
16MM FILM, 3/4 OR 1/2 IN VIDEO A
Offers information on converting to wood fuel as a major home energy source. Discusses equipment, costs and safety.
LC NO. 82-707182
Prod-NFBC Dist-BULFRG 1980

Tree Top Targets C 17 MIN
16MM FILM OPTICAL SOUND
Tennessee charlie discusses the various methods of squirrel hunting and the life history of the squirrel. Depicts still hunts, hunts with dogs and scenes of activities in the life of the squirrel.
Prod-TGAFC Dist-TGAFC

Tree, A Rock, A Cloud, A C 19 MIN
16MM FILM, 3/4 OR 1/2 IN VIDEO J-C A
Relates the meeting of a young newsboy and an old man at a restaurant where the old man explains his mysterious method for learning to love other people. Based on the short story A Tree, A Rock, A Cloud by Carson McCullers.
Prod-FLMPRS Dist-PHENIX 1980

Tree, The (2nd Ed) C 11 MIN
16MM FILM, 3/4 OR 1/2 IN VIDEO I-C A
Describes the beauty of trees and their importance to birds, insects, other plants, animals and people. Introduces the concept that living things depend on each other.
Prod-CF Dist-CF 1977

Tree, The (2nd Ed) (Captioned) C 11 MIN
16MM FILM, 3/4 OR 1/2 IN VIDEO I-C A
Describes the beauty of trees and their importance to birds, insects, other plants, animals and people. Introduces the concept that living things depend on each other.
Prod-CF Dist-CF 1977

Treehouse C 9 MIN
16MM FILM, 3/4 OR 1/2 IN VIDEO P-I
Questions whether or not man can live in the world without obliterating its beauty. Shows how a bulldozer operator strikes up a friendship with a young boy who has built a treehouse on the edge of a site the man has been assigned to clear. Ends with the driver unable to tell the boy why his tree, the last bit of greenery in a vast sea of tract homes, has to come down.
Prod-KINGSP Dist-PHENIX 1969

Trees C 14 MIN
3/4 OR 1/2 INCH VIDEO CASSETTE P
Shows how to draw trees.
From The Let's Draw Series.
Prod-KOKHTV Dist-AITECH 1976

Trees C 15 MIN
2 INCH VIDEOTAPE K
Illustrates trees as large green plants which produce seeds.
From The Let's Go Sciencing, Unit III - Life Series.
Prod-DETPS Dist-GPITVL

Trees C 15 MIN
3/4 OR 1/2 INCH VIDEO CASSETTE P-I
Discusses trees.
From The Why Series.
Prod-WDCNTV Dist-AITECH 1976

Trees C 30 MIN
3/4 OR 1/2 INCH VIDEO CASSETTE C A
Stresses that purchasing and planting a tree for the home garden is a major step. Discusses comparing the advantages and disadvantages of particular kinds of trees.
From The Home Gardener With John Lenanton Series. Lesson 17
Prod-COAST Dist-CDTEL

Trees - How To Know Them C 14 MIN
16MM FILM, 3/4 OR 1/2 IN VIDEO J-C A
Describes the identifying features of trees as they change through the seasons.
Prod-IFB Dist-IFB 1970

Trees - How We Identify Them C 11 MIN
16MM FILM, 3/4 OR 1/2 IN VIDEO I-J
Suggests ways for recognizing various kinds of trees through shape, bark, leaves and fruit. Explains the differences between deciduous trees and evergreens. Shows individual characteristics of several trees.
Prod-CORF Dist-CORF 1958

Trees - Our Plant Giants C 14 MIN
16MM FILM OPTICAL SOUND P-J
Discusses the growth of trees, shows various types of trees and explains how to tell the age of a tree. Describes the uses of trees.
From The Science In Our Space Age Series.
LC NO. FIA60-3065
Prod-ACA Dist-ACA 1960

Trees - Their Flowers And Seeds C 11 MIN
16MM FILM, 3/4 OR 1/2 IN VIDEO P-I
Shows a variety of tree flowers and their main parts, and explains how they produce fruits containing seeds for the next generation.
Prod-CORF Dist-CORF 1969

Trees - Their Importance To Man C 14 MIN
16MM FILM OPTICAL SOUND P-H
Depicts the many ways in which man benefits from the fruitless tree. Presents an overview of the importance of the tree to the development of America. Deals with conservation and manufacturing with emphasis on the practical use as well as the aesthetic value of trees.
Prod-AVED Dist-AVED 1969

Trees And Their Care C 29 MIN
16MM FILM, 3/4 OR 1/2 IN VIDEO H-C
Describes the principal phases in the care of shade trees, including transplanting, pruning, spraying, feeding, and methods of repairing storm damage.
Prod-OTT Dist-IFB 1964

Trees And Their Importance X 12 MIN
16MM FILM, 3/4 OR 1/2 IN VIDEO I
Emphasizes conservation, the importance of trees as a renewable resource and their role in water and soil conservation. Uses animation to show life processes of a tree and how trees contribute to man's welfare.
Prod-EBEC Dist-EBEC 1966

Trees For Arid Landscapes, A Video Dictionary C 2 MIN
3/4 OR 1/2 INCH VIDEO CASSETTE
Demonstrates the growth habits, performances, ornamental value and botanical features of 20 specially selected trees, proven arid land performers in landscapes receiving low rainfall accumulations.
Prod-UAZMIC Dist-UAZMIC

Trees In The Wind B 30 MIN
16MM FILM OPTICAL SOUND
Relates an episode from the life of Chaim Soutine, who at 17, despite the traditional Jewish hostility of his family to art, decided to become an artist. (Kinescope)
Prod-JTS Dist-NAAJS Prodn-NBCTV 1956

Trees, The Biggest And The Oldest Living Things C 19 MIN
16MM FILM, 3/4 OR 1/2 IN VIDEO J-H
Searches out some of the biggest and oldest trees to find out how they grow so big and what they tell us about man and his environment. Shows how information is gathered from trees and how that data is applied to other sciences.
From The Natural Phenomena Series.
Prod-JOU Dist-JOU 1982

Trees, The Endless Harvest C 9 MIN
16MM FILM, 3/4 OR 1/2 IN VIDEO
Shows the scientific harvesting and regeneration techniques the forest industry uses to help assure a continuing and growing supply of high-quality timber.
From The Forest Resources Films Series.
Prod-REGIS Dist-GPITVL

Trek To Totality C 28 MIN
16MM FILM OPTICAL SOUND
Uses historic photos, solar observatory footage and live expedition coverage in discussing the history of eclipse expeditions and solar physics. Examines the 1980 Los Alamos Scientific Lab Airborne expedition to Africa to see the 1980 solar eclipse.
LC NO. 80-701270
Prod-LASL Dist-LASL 1980

Trembling Cartoon Band C 20 MIN
16MM FILM OPTICAL SOUND K-I
Presents animated designs made out of cut-outs, mache, flip cards and stuffed cloth.
Prod-YELLOW Dist-YELLOW 1972

Trembling Earth, The B 30 MIN
16MM FILM OPTICAL SOUND J-C A
Explains earthquakes and the seismic studies of the Lamont Geological Observatory of Columbia University. Presents aerial views of two major faults and explains their relationship to earthquakes. Shows seismologists on an Alaskan expedition. Provides scenes of the 1964 Alaskan earthquake.
From The Spectrum Series.
LC NO. FIA68-1272
Prod-NET Dist-IU 1968

Trenching - A Grave Affair C 15 MIN
3/4 OR 1/2 INCH VIDEO CASSETTE
Covers basic trenching activities such as entering properly, sloping properly, dangerous horsing around with equipment and placing of equipment safely. Points out the responsibility of foreman and workers for safe working conditions.
From The Safety For Oilfield Contractors Series.
Prod-FLMWST Dist-FLMWST

Trends C 14 MIN
16MM FILM, 3/4 OR 1/2 IN VIDEO J-C A
Focuses on the rights and responsibilities of the individual in a free society.
Prod-NILCOM Dist-MCFI 1978

Trends C 27 MIN
16MM FILM, 3/4 OR 1/2 IN VIDEO J-C A
Examines developments in scientific and social affairs during the 1970's.
From The Seventies Series.
Prod-UPI Dist-JOU 1980

Trends C 30 MIN
3/4 OR 1/2 INCH VIDEO CASSETTE
Discusses individual differences, including handicapping conditions and explores what a handicap means for the student, the parent, the teacher and the school administrator. Provides historical perspective on the development of educational response to handicapped students and illustrates the current principles and procedural safeguards which have been incorporated into state and federal law (Education for All Handicapped Children Act).
From The Educational Alternatives For Handicapped Students Series.
Prod-NETCHE Dist-NETCHE 1977

Trends C 45 MIN
3/4 OR 1/2 INCH VIDEO CASSETTE
Explores the major trends that are leading towards the use of communications network architectures. Presents the layers that are used in network software and concentrates on the similarities between the different architectures.
From The Network Architectures - A Communications Revolution Series.
Prod-DELTAK Dist-DELTAK

Trends In Community Health Nursing C 17 MIN
3/4 OR 1/2 INCH VIDEO CASSETTE PRO
Highlights the major historical developments in public health and compares them with current trends in community health organizations through utilization of historical photographs. Provides comparisons relating to focus of services, number and type of personnel, functions of community health nurses and mortality rate changes from 1910-1970.
Prod-UMICHM Dist-UMICHM 1976

Trends In Maternal And Infant Care B 44 MIN
16MM FILM OPTICAL SOUND PRO
Discusses the development of the children's bureau, current infant and maternal mortality rates, both national and international and goals for the future.
From The Maternity Nursing Series.
LC NO. 71-703395
Prod-VDONUR Dist-AJN Prodn-WTTWTV 1966

Tres Mujeres C 29 MIN
3/4 OR 1/2 INCH VIDEO CASSETTE
Documents the lives of three generations of Puerto Rican women in New York. Focuses on the mother-daughter relationship and how it deeply touches all women.
From The Interface Series.
Prod-WETATV Dist-PBS

Tres Riches Heures De L'Afrique Romaine C 20 MIN
16MM FILM OPTICAL SOUND H-C A
Uses architectural remains, sculpture and mosaics to suggest what the Roman period in Africa may have been like. Emphasizes mosaics showing mythological scenes as well as scenes of everyday life.
Prod-FACSEA Dist-FACSEA

Tri-Continental (Cuba) C 10 MIN
16MM FILM OPTICAL SOUND
Depicts the spirit of the revolution in music and dance. Shows a short speech concluding the conference by Fidel of the 1966 cultural Congress of the peoples of Asia, Africa and Latin America held in Halana.
Prod-NEWSR Dist-NEWSR

Trial - The First Day B 90 MIN
16MM FILM, 3/4 OR 1/2 IN VIDEO H-C A
Discusses the trial of Lauren R Watson, a black man and known member of the Black Panther Party, who allegedly interfered with a police officer and resisted arrest. Tells how he and his lawyer doubted that he could receive a fair trial with an all-white middle-class jury. Discusses what is meant by a jury of one's peers.
From The Trial - The City And County Of Denver Vs Lauren R Watson Series.

LC NO. 80-707057
Prod-NET Dist-IU 1970

Trial - The Fourth And Final Day B 90 MIN
16MM FILM, 3/4 OR 1/2 IN VIDEO H-C A
Shows the final day of the trial where both sides rest their case after closing arguments and instructions are given to the jury, which then spends two hours deliberating on the verdict. Interviews the judge, the arresting officer, both attorneys and the defendant. Conducts interviews with the jury members after the verdict is returned and tries to determine why they voted as they did.
From The Trial - The City And County Of Denver Vs Lauren R Watson Series.
LC NO. 80-707060
Prod-NET Dist-IU 1970

Trial - The Second Day B 90 MIN
16MM FILM, 3/4 OR 1/2 IN VIDEO H-C A
Presents the prosecution's case against Lauren R Watson in the first day of the actual trial, including the examination and cross-examination of the arresting officer and a fellow patrolman, the only witnesses for the prosecution. Shows how the prosecution tries to prove that Watson resisted arrest and interfered with a police officer when he was apprehended for an alleged traffic violoation, whereas the defense attorney tries to show that Watson is innocent.
From The Trial - The City And County Of Denver Vs Lauren R Watson Series.
LC NO. 80-707058
Prod-NET Dist-IU 1970

Trial - The Third Day B 90 MIN
16MM FILM, 3/4 OR 1/2 IN VIDEO H-C A
Continues the trial with the prosecution resting its case and the defense making a motion for a judgement of acquittal and then presenting its witnesses. Tells how the interference charge is dropped for lack of evidence. Presents the defense trying to show that the defendant was being harassed and that he did not resist arrest. Uses post-trial interviews in stating that this trial has political as well as judicial significance and that class in justice must be eliminated.
From The Trial - The City And County Of Denver Vs Lauren R Watson Series.
LC NO. 80-707059
Prod-NET Dist-IU 1970

Trial And Death Of Socrates, The B 25 MIN
16MM FILM OPTICAL SOUND
Presents a drama. Before dying, Socrates defends his decision to live his philosophy and place the state above the individual. Depicts his trial at which he expostulates that the unexamined life is not worth living.
LC NO. FI68-660
Prod-CBSF Dist-CBSF 1960

Trial And Error C 18 MIN
16MM FILM - 3/4 IN VIDEO I-J
Explains that the process of trial and error is the basis of all scientific investigation and learning.
From The Search For Solutions Series.
LC NO. 80-706244
Prod-PLYBCK Dist-KAROL 1979

Trial Balance C 27 MIN
16MM FILM OPTICAL SOUND J-C
Uses animation to show the scientific achievements of nasa's space programs. Emphasizes the knowledge that has been gained from studies of upper atmosphere physics, solar physics and planetology.
LC NO. 74-705858
Prod-NASA Dist-NASA 1965

Trial Before Pilate X 15 MIN
16MM FILM OPTICAL SOUND J-H T R
Jesus is brought to pilate for judgment, but Pilate can find no fault with him and sends him to Herod. Jesus is retirmed to Pilate who turns him over to the mob to be crucified. The soldiers place a crown of thorns on his head as he is led away.
From The Living Bible Series.
Prod-FAMF Dist-FAMF

Trial By Fire X 28 MIN
16MM FILM, 3/4 OR 1/2 IN VIDEO J-C A
Relates the story of a combat pilot who decides not to bomb a village. Stars Bradford Dillman, Ricardo Montalban and Pippa Scott.
From The Insight Series.
Prod-PAULST Dist-PAULST

Trial By Fire (Spanish) X 28 MIN
16MM FILM, 3/4 OR 1/2 IN VIDEO J-C A
Relates the story of a combat pilot who decides not to bomb a village. Stars Bradford Dillman, Ricardo Montalban and Pippa Scott.
From The Insight Series.
Prod-PAULST Dist-PAULST

Trial Notebook - A Lecture By James J Brosnahan C 41 MIN
3/4 INCH VIDEO CASSETTE PRO
Present James J Brosnahan explaining the use of a trial notebook.
LC NO. 81-706219
Prod-ABACPE Dist-ABACPE 1979

Trial Of A Civil (Personal Injury) Case—A Series
PRO
Presents a personal injury case in which the plaintiff's spouse died of injuries sustained in a pedestrian-auto accident.
Prod-ABACPE Dist-ABACPE

Closing Arguments In A Personal Injury Case I 051 MIN
Closing Arguments In A Personal Injury Case II 030 MIN
Closing Arguments In A Personal Injury Case III 058 MIN
Comparative Cross-Examination Of An Economist 053 MIN
Direct And Comparative Cross-Examination Of 056 MIN
Direct Examination Of An Economist In A 030 MIN
Jury Selection In A Personal Injury Case - A 057 MIN

Trial Of A Civil Lawsuit—A Series
PRO
Features a mock trial of an actual products liability case involving defective farm equipment. Combines most of the elements missing in many litigation programs utilizing a lecture approach.
Prod-SBWI Dist-ABACPE

Closing Arguments 050 MIN
Direct And Cross-Examination Of Defendant 048 MIN
Direct And Cross-Examination Of Plaintiff 035 MIN
Direct And Cross-Examination Of Plaintiff's 040 MIN
Direct And Cross-Examination Of Plaintiff's1 052 MIN
Faculty Discussions With Jurors 016 MIN
Jury Deliberations 038 MIN
Plaintiff And Defendant Opening Statements 037 MIN

Trial Of A Criminal (Federal Narcotics) Case—A Series
PRO
Demonstrates a drug-related conspiracy case in which one witness has received immunity from prosecution. Follows the trial through selection of jury, direct and cross-examination of defendant and expert witness, and closing arguments.
Prod-ABACPE Dist-ABACPE

Closing Arguments In A Federal Narcotics Case 045 MIN
Comparative Cross-Examination Of A Government 027 MIN
Comparative Cross-Examination Of A Witness 050 MIN
Jury Selection In A Federal Narcotics Case - 058 MIN
Opening Statements In A Federal Narcotics Case 027 MIN

Trial Of A Criminal Case—A Series
PRO
Observes experienced criminal lawyers as they prepare and try a criminal case. Reveals strategies and techniques at each phase of the case. Observes a jury as it deliberates and shows jurors commenting on the effectiveness of the strategies and techniques used in the case.
Prod-SBWI Dist-ABACPE

Criminal Trial Series 431 MIN
Preliminary Hearing Of A Criminal Case 161 MIN

Trial Of An Antitrust Bid-Rigging Case—A Series
PRO
Presents the trial of a complex white collar criminal case. Provides strategies for criminal litigation as well as tips for dealing with juries, opposing counsel and expert and turncoat witnesses.
Prod-ABACPE Dist-ABACPE

Closing Arguments 076 MIN
Examination Of The Expert Witness, The 100 MIN
Examination Of The Government Witness, The 069 MIN

Trial Of An Antitrust Case—A Series
PRO
Shows litigation attorneys conducting a mock antitrust trial in a lawsuit brought by a terminated dealer against a national franchiser.
LC NO. 80-707194
Prod-ABACPE Dist-ABACPE 1977

Trial Of An Equal Employment Opportunity Case C
3/4 OR 1/2 INCH VIDEO CASSETTE PRO
Presents a simulated class-action employment discrimination case in which there has been a determination of liability. Focuses on the second stage of the proceedings where injunctive relief is formulated, back pay is litigated and attorneys' fees awarded.
Prod-ABACPE Dist-ABACPE

Trial Of An Extracontractural Damages Case C 24 MIN
3/4 OR 1/2 INCH VIDEO CASSETTE
Helps attorneys prepare to pursue or defend extracontractural damage claims. Provides guide to theories, strategies and techniques effective in trials.
Prod-ABACPE Dist-ABACPE

Trial Of Denton Cooley, The C 59 MIN
3/4 INCH VIDEO CASSETTE
Re-enacts the 1972 trial of Houston surgeon Dr Denton Cooley, who implanted, for the first time, a completely artificial heart in a human being. Explores the issues raised in this malpractice case, including what constitutes informed consent, how far a patient should trust a doctor to act in the patient's own best interest and how satisfactory are guidelines regulating human experiment.
From The Nova Series.
Prod-WGBHTV Dist-PBS 1978

Trial Of Leonard Peltier, The B 16 MIN
3/4 OR 1/2 INCH VIDEO CASSETTE H-C A
Reports on the US Government's murder case against American Indian Movement Leader Leonard Peltier which drew many sympathetic Native Americans who criticized the Federal Government, both on the reservations and with the proceedings of Peltier's case.
Prod-UCV Dist-UCV

Trial Of Susan B Anthony, The C 22 MIN
16MM FILM, 3/4 OR 1/2 IN VIDEO
Depicts the second day of legal proceedings in which Susan B Anthony is being procecuted for voting.
From The You Are There Series.
Prod-CBSTV Dist-PHENIX

Trial Of Uriel, The B 30 MIN
16MM FILM OPTICAL SOUND
States that wisdom and scholarship are precious although they are insufficient by themselves. Dramatizes the moral with the story of a humble water carrier who, in spite of discouragement from learned men, is able to enter heaven. (Kinescope)
Prod-JTS Dist-NAAJS Prodn-NBCTV 1959

Trial of Xavier Solorzano, The C 90 MIN
3/4 OR 1/2 INCH VIDEO CASSETTE
Follows the proceedings of a real-life trial condensing over 60 hours of trial footage into a 90-minute program. Narrated by Raymond Burr.
Prod-WTTWTV Dist-PBS 1979

Trial Presentation C 46 MIN
3/4 OR 1/2 INCH VIDEO CASSETTE PRO
See series title for descriptive statement.
From The James Jean Trial Advocacy Series.
Prod-ABACPE Dist-ABACPE

Trial Techniques - A Products Liability Case—A Series
PRO
Presents a trial in a products liability case based on facts borrowed from actual litigated cases. Offers testimony by actual experts in engineering and medicine. Follows each stage of the trial.
Prod-ABACPE Dist-ABACPE

Closing Statements In A Products Liability Case 108 MIN
Direct And Cross-Examination Of Defendant's 168 MIN
Direct And Cross-Examination Of Plaintiff And 157 MIN
Direct And Cross-Examination Of Plaintiff's 058 MIN
Direct And Cross-Examination Of Plaintiff's 145 MIN
Opening Statements In A Products Liability Case 060 MIN

Trial Techniques In A Custody Case C 74 MIN
3/4 OR 1/2 INCH VIDEO CASSETTE PRO
Demonstrates the direct and cross-examination of an expert witness in a custody case. Discusses the role of both direct and cross-examination and effective preparation of an expert witness for examination.
From The Preparing And Trying A Custody Case Series.
Prod-ABACPE Dist-ABACPE

Trial Techniques With Professor Irving Younger, Pt 1 C 52 MIN
3/4 OR 1/2 INCH VIDEO CASSETTE PRO
Presents Professor Irving Younger discussing elements, techniques and strategies for trial-winning conduct by lawyers, including jury selection, opening statement and summation.
From The NPI Video CLE Series. Vol 4
LC NO. 80-706565
Prod-NPRI Dist-NPRI 1979

Trial Techniques With Professor Irving Younger, Pt 2 C 52 MIN
3/4 OR 1/2 INCH VIDEO CASSETTE PRO
Presents Professor Irving Younger discussing elements, techniques and strategies for trial-winning conduct by lawyers, including jury selection, opening statement and summation.
From The NPI Video CLE Series. Vol 4
LC NO. 80-706565
Prod-NPRI Dist-NPRI 1979

Trial Techniques With Professor Irving Younger, Pt 3 C 52 MIN
3/4 OR 1/2 INCH VIDEO CASSETTE PRO
Presents Professor Irving Younger discussing elements, techniques and strategies for trial-winning conduct by lawyers, including jury selection, opening statement and summation.
From The NPI Video CLE Series. Vol 4
LC NO. 80-706565
Prod-NPRI Dist-NPRI 1979

Trial Techniques With Professor Irving Younger, Pt 4 C 52 MIN
3/4 OR 1/2 INCH VIDEO CASSETTE PRO
Presents Professor Irving Younger discussing elements, techniques and strategies for trial-winning conduct by lawyers, including jury selection, opening statement and summation.
From The NPI Video CLE Series. Vol 4
LC NO. 80-706565
Prod-NPRI Dist-NPRI 1979

Trial Techniques With Professor Irving Younger, Pt 5 C 53 MIN
3/4 OR 1/2 INCH VIDEO CASSETTE PRO
Presents Professor Irving Younger discussing elements, techniques and strategies for trial-winning conduct by lawyers, including jury selection, opening statement and summation.
From The NPI Video CLE Series. Vol 4
LC NO. 80-706565
Prod-NPRI Dist-NPRI 1979

Trial Techniques With Professor Irving Younger, Pt 6 C 53 MIN
3/4 OR 1/2 INCH VIDEO CASSETTE PRO
Presents Professor Irving Younger discussing elements, techniques and strategies for trial-winning conduct by lawyers, including jury selection, opening statement and summation.
From The NPI Video CLE Series. Vol 4
LC NO. 80-706565
Prod-NPRI Dist-NPRI 1979

Trial Techniques With Professor Irving Younger, Pt 7 C 53 MIN
3/4 OR 1/2 INCH VIDEO CASSETTE PRO
Presents Professor Irving Younger discussing elements, techniques and strategies for trial-winning conduct by lawyers, including jury selection, opening statement and summation.

From The NPI Video CLE Series. Vol 4
LC NO. 80-706565
Prod-NPRI Dist-NPRI 1979

Trial Techniques With Professor Irving Younger, Pt 8 C 53 MIN
3/4 OR 1/2 INCH VIDEO CASSETTE PRO
Presents Professor Irving Younger discussing elements, techniques and strategies for trial-winning conduct by lawyers, including jury selection, opening statement and summation.
From The NPI Video CLE Series. Vol 4
LC NO. 80-706565
Prod-NPRI Dist-NPRI 1979

Trials Of Alger Hiss, The C 165 MIN
16MM FILM, 3/4 OR 1/2 IN VIDEO
Documents the story of Alger Hiss, a State Department official who was accused in an espionage and perjury case which first brought then-Congressman Richard M Nixon to national prominence.
Prod-HISTOF Dist-DIRECT 1980

Trials Of Franz Kafka, The B 15 MIN
16MM FILM, 3/4 OR 1/2 IN VIDEO H-C A
Explores the 'TRIALS' of childhood, youth and tragic adulthood which Franz Kafka transformed into novels and stories. Helps in the understanding of modern man's anxiety and alienation.
Prod-MANTLH Dist-FOTH 1969

Trials Of Richard / Ability Grouping C 29 MIN
3/4 INCH VIDEO CASSETTE
Tells how a black student copes with life at a previously all-white school in Memphis, Tennessee. Explores how class assignments in an Evanston, Illinois, school, which are meant to separate students by academic ability, actually interfere with desegregation.
From The As We See It Series.
Prod-WTTWTV Dist-PUBTEL

Triangle And Anchor - Chelsea Porcelain From The Williamsburg Collection C 22 MIN
16MM FILM OPTICAL SOUND A
Traces the history of porcelain from China in the ninth century to Chelsea, England, in the mid-18th century. Discusses the various factory marks used on Chelsea porcelain and shows the development from simple white tableware to elaborately colored and gilded dishes and figurines.
LC NO. 78-701824
Prod-CWMS Dist-CWMS 1978

Triangle Factory Fire Scandal, The C
1/2 IN VIDEO CASSETTE BETA/VHS
Describes the events leading up to the 1911 fire in New York where 146 women lost their lives. Starring Stephanie Zimbalist.
Prod-GA Dist-GA

Triangle Fire Factory Scandal, The C 98 MIN
16MM FILM OPTICAL SOUND
Presents a story based on the sweatshop fire of March 14, 1911, in which 146 female garment workers perished. Highlights the conflict between organized labor and management and the struggle for better working conditions.
LC NO. 79-700372
Prod-LNDBRG Dist-LNDBRG 1979

Triangle Of Health (Arabic)—A Series
I-H
Shows how to balance physical, mental and social aspects of health.
Prod-WDEMCO Dist-WDEMCO

Physical Fitness And Good Health (Arabic) 010 MIN
Social Side Of Health, The (Arabic) 010 MIN
Steps Toward Maturity And Health (Arabic) 010 MIN
Understanding Stresses And Strains (Arabic) 010 MIN

Triangle Of Health (French)—A Series
I-H
Shows how to balance physical, mental and social aspects of health.
Prod-WDEMCO Dist-WDEMCO

Physical Fitness And Good Health (French) 010 MIN
Social Side Of Health, The (French) 010 MIN
Steps Toward Maturity And Health (French) 010 MIN
Understanding Stresses And Strains (French) 010 MIN

Triangle Of Health (German)—A Series
I-H
Shows how to balance physical, mental and social aspects of health.
Prod-WDEMCO Dist-WDEMCO

Physical Fitness And Good Health (German) 010 MIN
Social Side Of Health, The (German) 010 MIN
Steps Toward Maturity And Health (German) 010 MIN
Understanding Stresses And Strains (German) 010 MIN

Triangle Of Health (Hungarian)—A Series
I-H
Shows how to balance physical, mental and social aspects of health.
Prod-WDEMCO Dist-WDEMCO

Physical Fitness And Good Health (Hungarian) 010 MIN
Steps Toward Maturity And Health (Hungarian) 010 MIN
Understanding Stresses And Strains (Hungarian) 010 MIN

Triangle Of Health (Spanish)—A Series
I-H
Shows how to balance physical, mental and social aspects of health.
Prod-WDEMCO Dist-WDEMCO

Physical Fitness And Good Health (Spanish) 010 MIN
Social Side Of Health, The (Spanish) 010 MIN
Steps Toward Maturity And Health (Spanish) 010 MIN
Understanding Stresses And Strains (Spanish) 010 MIN

Triangle Of Health (Swedish)—A Series
I-H
Shows how to balance physical, mental and social aspects of health.
Prod-WDEMCO Dist-WDEMCO

Physical Fitness And Good Health (Swedish) 010 MIN
Steps Toward Maturity And Health (Swedish) 010 MIN
Understanding Stresses And Strains (Swedish) 010 MIN

Triangle Of Health—A Series
16MM FILM, 3/4 OR 1/2 IN VIDEO
Prod-UPJOHN Dist-WDEMCO

Physical Fitness And Good Health 10 MIN
Social Side Of Health 10 MIN
Steps Toward Maturity And Health 10 MIN
Understanding Stresses And Strains 10 MIN

Triangle—A Series
16MM FILM, 3/4 OR 1/2 IN VIDEO J-H
Uses animation to illustrate aspects of triangles.
Prod-IFB Dist-IFB

Congruent Triangles 007 MIN
Journey To The Center Of A Triangle 009 MIN
Similar Triangles 008 MIN
Trio For Three Angles 008 MIN

Triangles C 15 MIN
3/4 OR 1/2 INCH VIDEO CASSETTE I-J
Identifies and defines equilateral, isosceles, scalene and right triangles.
From The Math Matters Series. Blue Module
Prod-STETVC Dist-AITECH Prodn-KLRNTV 1975

Triangles - An Introduction C 10 MIN
16MM FILM, 3/4 OR 1/2 IN VIDEO P-I
Introduces the properties of the triangle, stressing the relationship between the size of the angles and the length of the opposite sides.
Prod-BOUNDY Dist-PHENIX Prodn-BOUNDY 1966

Triangles - Sides And Angles C 11 MIN
16MM FILM, 3/4 OR 1/2 IN VIDEO P-I
Demonstrates that the longest side of a triangle is opposite the largest angle, that the shortest side is opposite the smallest angle and that if two sides of a triangle are the same length, the angles opposite them will be the same size.
Prod-BOUNDY Dist-PHENIX 1966

Triangulos C 8 MIN
16MM FILM, 3/4 OR 1/2 IN VIDEO J-H
A Spanish language version of the videocassette Trio For Three Angles. Uses the movements of free-swinging angles, synchronized with music, to explain the relationships of the triangle's different components.
Prod-IFB Dist-IFB 1968

Tribal Carvings From New Guinea C 29 MIN
2 INCH VIDEOTAPE
See series title for descriptive statement.
From The Museum Open House Series.
Prod-WGBHTV Dist-PUBTEL

Tribal Eye—A Series
16MM FILM, 3/4 OR 1/2 IN VIDEO
Examines the traditions and lifestyles of various tribes around the world.
Prod-BBCTV Dist-TIMLIF 1976

Across The Frontiers 52 MIN
Behind The Mask 52 MIN
Crooked Beak Of Heaven, The 52 MIN
Kingdom Of Bronze 52 MIN
Man Blong Custom 52 MIN
Sweat Of The Sun, The 52 MIN
Woven Gardens 52 MIN

Tribal Government C 19 MIN
16MM FILM OPTICAL SOUND
Shows how effective tribal governments operate and what tribal members should expect from their government. Focuses on governmental processes and institutions, such as tribal councils, courts, and police.
LC NO. 80-700418
Prod-IDIL Dist-IDIL Prodn-CINNAP 1980

Tribal Groups Of Central India - The Chota Maria, The Bhils C 40 MIN
16MM FILM OPTICAL SOUND H-C A
Compares the daily lifestyles, ceremonial rites, and dance forms of the Chota Maria and Bhil tribes of central India.
From The Central India - Lifeways, Ceremony, Dance Series. No. 1
LC NO. 78-701749
Prod-ITHCOL Dist-ITHCOL 1978

Tribal Self-Determination, Government And Culture C 30 MIN
3/4 OR 1/2 INCH VIDEO CASSETTE
Looks at Fort Berthold, North Dakota, where three affiliated tribes of American Indians live. Examines the Tribal Council which consists of elected representatives from the tribes. Stresses their determination to develop their own standards and points out that they regard the running of the reservation as the same as running a state or business.
Prod-MINOND Dist-UWISC 1979

Tribe And The Professor, The C 44 MIN
3/4 OR 1/2 INCH VIDEO CASSETTE
Reconstructs the past of the Makah Indians past. Portrays their newly awakened awareness of their long and rich cultural heritage.
Prod-UWASHP Dist-UWASHP

Tribe And The Professor, The - Ozette Archaeology (Rev Ed) C 44 MIN
16MM FILM OPTICAL SOUND
Recounts the unearthing of a longhouse in Cape Alva, Washington, which had been used by Ozette Indians 500 years before. Illustrates the scientific processes involved in the restoration and preservation of more than 50,000 items found during the excavation including baskets, boxes, bowls, awls, harpoons, paddles and blankets.
Prod-KIRKRL Dist-UWASHP 1978

Tribe Of The Turquoise Waters C 13 MIN
16MM FILM OPTICAL SOUND H
Shows life in a small Indian village hidden in an almost inaccessible valley in a remote part of the Grand Canyon.
Prod-DAGP Dist-MLA 1952

Tribes Of The Eastern Plains B 30 MIN
16MM FILM OPTICAL SOUND J-C A
Describes the complicated political and social organizations of the Indian farming tribes and their profound religious beliefs. Traces their history from prehistoric times to the present.
From The Great Plains Trilogy, 2 Series. Nomad And Indians - Early Man On The Plains
Prod-KUONTV Dist-UNL 1954

Tribology C 30 MIN
3/4 OR 1/2 INCH VIDEO CASSETTE
Discusses the various topics that constitute the field of tribology and their interrelation.
From The Tribology 1 - Friction, Wear, And Lubrication Series.
Prod-MIOT Dist-MIOT

Tribology 1 - Friction, Wear, And Lubrication—A Series

Provides a solid basic understanding of triboloby, and the way it may be used to solve engineering problems.
Prod-MIOT Dist-MIOT

Abrasive Wear 041 MIN
Adhesive Particle Size 036 MIN
Adhesive Wear 043 MIN
Corrosive Wear 038 MIN
Friction 038 MIN
Lubrication (1) 043 MIN
Lubrication (2) 045 MIN
Stick-Slip 043 MIN
Surface Fatique Wear 037 MIN
Tribology 030 MIN
Troubleshooting 038 MIN
Wear 032 MIN

Tribology 2 - Advances In Friction, Wear, And Lubrication—A Series

Provides a basic understanding of tribology.
Prod-MIOT Dist-MIOT

Abrasive Wear And Erosion 049 MIN
Adhesive Wear 040 MIN
Experimental Techniques 041 MIN
Friction 042 MIN
Lubrication - The Automobile 044 MIN
Sliding Electric Contacts 048 MIN
Surface Energy Effects 043 MIN
Tribology 2 - Advances In Friction, Wear, And 039 MIN

Tribology 2 - Advances In Friction, Wear, And Lubrication - Introduction C 39 MIN
3/4 OR 1/2 INCH VIDEO CASSETTE
Discusses the economic importance of tribology, the literature of the past few years, fatigue theories of adhesive wear and their status and recent trends in research and development.
From The Tribology 2 - Advances In Friction, Wear, And Lubrication Series.
Prod-MIOT Dist-MIOT

Tribute To Africa C 13 MIN
16MM FILM OPTICAL SOUND
Uses a filmograph of Eliot Elisofon's photographs and live action to present a tribute to African art and culture. Portrays both the old and the new Africa.
LC NO. 75-703544
Prod-MAFA Dist-MAFA Prodn-LITWKS 1975

Tribute To Anonymous, A C 30 MIN
3/4 INCH VIDEO CASSETTE H-C A
Features Fred Gwynne and the First Poetry Quartet reading poems by anonymous poets.
From The Anyone For Tennyson Series.
Prod-NETCHE Dist-GPITVL

Tribute To Crop Proficiency C 9 MIN
16MM FILM OPTICAL SOUND
Presents the national winner of the Future Farmers of America (FFA) Crop Proficiency award, Vernon Rohrschreib.
Prod-FUNKBS Dist-VENARD

Tribute To John Cage, A C 60 MIN
3/4 OR 1/2 INCH VIDEO CASSETTE
Features John Cage, recreating his memorable piano performance at Woodstock. Includes Russell Connor's interview of composer Alvin Lucier.
Prod-EAI Dist-EAI

Tribute To Larry, A C 24 MIN
16MM FILM OPTICAL SOUND

Deals with the story of a woman whose need for the man in her life is so strong that nothing can destroy her desire to believe in him.
LC NO. 79-701243
Prod-STAN Dist-STAN 1979

Tribute To Malcolm X, A B 15 MIN
16MM FILM, 3/4 OR 1/2 IN VIDEO H-C A
Discusses the influence of Malcolm X upon the present black liberation movement. Includes an interview with his widow, Betty Shabbazz.
Prod-NETRC Dist-IU 1969

Tribute To Nam June Paik, A C 28 MIN
3/4 OR 1/2 INCH VIDEO CASSETTE
Assesses Nam June Paik, video artist, regarding his career and his impact on artists and others.
Prod-EAI Dist-EAI

Tribute To Nam June Paik, A C 28 MIN
3/4 OR 1/2 INCH VIDEO CASSETTE
Portrays a man who won't sit still. Reflects the philosophic and comic style of Nam June Paik.
Prod-KITCHN Dist-KITCHN

Tribute To Poland C 18 MIN
3/4 INCH VIDEO CASSETTE
Features Father Terrence Mulkerin, Catholic Relief Services Coordinator for Refugees and Disasters, explaining how Catholic Relief Services food shipments to Poland are distributed throughout the country with the help of local parishes.
Prod-CATHRS Dist-MTP

Tribute To President Herbert Clark Hoover, A B 11 MIN
16MM FILM OPTICAL SOUND
Highlights President Hoover's ability as an organizer and views his humanitarian work as a food administrator in World Wars I and II. Cites his contribution to government reorganization as secretary of commerce and as an elder statesman and advisor to presidents.
LC NO. 74-705859
Prod-USDD Dist-USNAC 1964

Trichomonal Vaginitis C 9 MIN
3/4 OR 1/2 INCH VIDEO CASSETTE
Focuses on the symptoms, medication and treatment for trichomonal vaginitis. Explains infection and the correct insertion of vaginal creams, tables and suppositories.
From The Take Care Of Yourself Series.
Prod-UARIZ Dist-UARIZ

Trick Or Treat C 8 MIN
16MM FILM, 3/4 OR 1/2 IN VIDEO
Presents a Haloween with Donald Duck to stress the idea that playing practical jokes can backfire and cause danger or injury to others.
Prod-DISNEY Dist-WDEMCO 1968

Trick Or Treat C 16 MIN
16MM FILM, 3/4 OR 1/2 IN VIDEO I-J
An open-end film about two boys who persuade two younger boys to pull a prank which results in a serious accident.
Prod-CF Dist-CF 1969

Trick Skiing C 105 MIN
3/4 OR 1/2 INCH VIDEO CASSETTE
Covers equipment, boats, training and advanced trick runs in trick water skiing. Presents over 50 different tricks. Stars Cory Pickos.
From The Superstar Sports Tapes Series.
Prod-TRASS Dist-TRASS

Tricks And Treasures B 15 MIN
2 INCH VIDEOTAPE P
See series title for descriptive statement.
From The Children's Literature Series. No. 9
Prod-NCET Dist-GPITVL Prodn-KUONTV

Tricks Of The Trade B 55 MIN
3/4 OR 1/2 INCH VIDEO CASSETTE IND
See series title for descriptive statement.
From The Technical And Professional Writing For Industry, Government And Business Series.
Prod-UMICE Dist-AMCEE

Tricks We Can Do B 15 MIN
2 INCH VIDEOTAPE P
See series title for descriptive statement.
From The Sounds Like Magic Series.
Prod-MOEBA Dist-GPITVL Prodn-KYNETV

Trickster Tales C 20 MIN
3/4 OR 1/2 INCH VIDEO CASSETTE P
Features folk tales centering around the trickster hero.
From The Folk Book Series.
LC NO. 80-707186
Prod-UWISC Dist-AITECH 1980

Tricky C 20 MIN
16MM FILM OPTICAL SOUND
Looks at a day in the life of Dick Thorton, a football player.
LC NO. 75-704348
Prod-CONCOL Dist-CONCOL 1973

Trier Und Frankfurt C 4 MIN
16MM FILM OPTICAL SOUND
From The Beginning German Films (German) Series.
Prod-MGHT Dist-CCNY

Trier, Roman Imperial City C 5 MIN
16MM FILM, 3/4 OR 1/2 IN VIDEO
Explains the development of Trier under nearly 500 years of ancient Roman rule.
From The European Studies - Germany Series. Part 17
Prod-BAYER Dist-IFB 1973

Trier, Romische Kaiserstadt C 5 MIN
16MM FILM, 3/4 OR 1/2 IN VIDEO H-C A
A German-language version of the motion picture Trier, Roman Imperial City. Explains the development of Trier under nearly 500 years of ancient Roman rule.
From The European Studies - Germany (German) Series.
Prod-MFAFRG Dist-IFB Prodn-BAYER 1973

Trifles C 21 MIN
16MM FILM, 3/4 OR 1/2 IN VIDEO J-C A
Tells how two women and three men attempt to solve the murder of a farmer. Based on the story Trifles by Susan Glaspell.
Prod-MORANM Dist-PHENIX 1979

Trifles C 22 MIN
3/4 OR 1/2 INCH VIDEO CASSETTE H-C
Narrates a low-key detective story based on Pulitzer Prize winning play by Susan Glaspell.
Prod-CEPRO Dist-CEPRO

Trig Functions And Derivatives C
3/4 INCH VIDEO CASSETTE
See series title for descriptive statement.
From The Calculus Series.
Prod-MDDE Dist-MDCPB

Trigger Effect, The C 52 MIN
16MM FILM, 3/4 OR 1/2 IN VIDEO
Explains how plowing, building, writing, taxation, and astronomy began in Egypt. Illustrates man's dependence on complex technological networks by reconstructing the New York City power blackout of 1965.
From The Connections Series. No. 1
LC NO. 79-706740
Prod-BBCTV Dist-TIMLIF 1979

Trigger Films On Aging C 14 MIN
16MM FILM OPTICAL SOUND
Presents a discussion film on problems of the aged. Features five vignettes, each establishing a problem situation in the life of an elderly person which builds to an emotional climax and abruptly ends.
LC NO. 70-715305
Prod-UMITV Dist-UMICH 1971

Trigger Foods C 7 MIN
16MM FILM, 3/4 OR 1/2 IN VIDEO A
Explains carbohydrates and their relationship to tooth decay. Describes how certain foods trigger the tooth decay process and the importance of avoiding those foods between meals. Presents suggestions for snacks that are not harmful to the teeth.
Prod-PRORE Dist-PRORE

Trigger Foods (Spanish) C 7 MIN
16MM FILM, 3/4 OR 1/2 IN VIDEO PRO
Explains carbohydrates and their relationship to tooth decay. Discusses how certain foods can trigger the decay process.
Prod-PRORE Dist-PRORE

Trigger Squeeze, M1 Rifle B 5 MIN
16MM FILM OPTICAL SOUND
Explains the correct method of squeezing the trigger of the MI rifle, including grasp of rifle, position of fingers, breathing, sight alignment and trigger squeeze.
LC NO. FIE55-362
Prod-USA Dist-USNAC 1955

Trigonal Ileal Anastomosis C 14 MIN
16MM FILM OPTICAL SOUND
Demonstrates a method of joining the urinary tract to the isolated ileal conduit which prevents reflux of loop urine to the kidneys. Shows that this is accomplished by performing an anastomosis between the intact unmobilized trigone and the isolated ileal conduit.
LC NO. 75-702253
Prod-EATONL Dist-EATONL 1973

Trigonometric Functions C 30 MIN
3/4 INCH VIDEO CASSETTE C
See series title for descriptive statement.
From The Introduction To Mathematics Series.
Prod-MDCPB Dist-MDCPB

Trigonometric Limits C
3/4 INCH VIDEO CASSETTE
See series title for descriptive statement.
From The Calculus Series.
Prod-MDDE Dist-MDCPB

Trigonometric Ratios As Periodic Functions B 28 MIN
16MM FILM OPTICAL SOUND H
Shows the use of trigonometric functions in problems involving conic sections and periodic motion. Describes the generation of a circle, ellipse, parabola and hyperbola using sections of a cone. Pictures the graph of a sine curve.
From The Trigonometry Series.
Prod-CALVIN Dist-MLA Prodn-UNIVFI 1959

Trigonometry C 12 MIN
3/4 OR 1/2 INCH VIDEO CASSETTE
Covers properties of triangles, trig functions, tables and inverse trig functions.
From The Using Mathematics In The Plant Series.
Prod-TPCTRA Dist-TPCTRA

Trigonometry C 15 MIN
3/4 OR 1/2 INCH VIDEO CASSETTE IND
See series title for descriptive statement.
From The Basic Shop Math Series.
Prod-ICSINT Dist-ICSINT

Trigonometry C 30 MIN
3/4 INCH VIDEO CASSETTE C
See series title for descriptive statement.
From The Introduction To Mathematics Series.
Prod-MDCPB Dist-MDCPB

Trigonometry (Spanish) C 12 MIN
3/4 OR 1/2 INCH VIDEO CASSETTE
Covers properties of triangles, trig functions, tables and inverse trig functions.
From The Using Mathematics In The Plant Series.
Prod-TPCTRA Dist-TPCTRA

Trigonometry And Shadows B 26 MIN
16MM FILM OPTICAL SOUND H
Reviews various applications of trigonometry, such as surveying, construction and navigation, and briefly describes the early history of trigonometry. Explains the significance of the ratio of lengths of the sides of a triangle and defines the sine of an angle.
From The Trigonometry Series.
Prod-CALVIN Dist-MLA Prodn-UNIVFI 1959

Trigonometry Measures The Earth B 28 MIN
16MM FILM OPTICAL SOUND H
Shows how Eratosthenes, in Ancient Greece, used trigonometry and shadows cast by the sun to measure the circumference and diameter of the earth to an accuracy of two percent. Describes a method of finding the distance to the moon by trigonometry.
From The Trigonometry Series.
Prod-CALVIN Dist-MLA Prodn-UNIVFI 1959

Trigonometry Of Large Angles B 30 MIN
16MM FILM OPTICAL SOUND H
Explains that definitions of trigonometric functions in terms of R, X and Y apply to any large angle if the sign of the function is identified. Proves that trigonometric identities work in all four quadrants. Shows the reduction of functions of negative angles to functions of equivalent positive angles.
From The Trigonometry Series.
Prod-CALVIN Dist-MLA Prodn-UNIVFI 1959

Trillion Dollars For Defense, A C 60 MIN
3/4 OR 1/2 INCH VIDEO CASSETTE H-C A
Visits an arms fair where manufacturers exhibit their latest high technology weapons systems. Suggests that the emphasis on such expensive and complex weapons detracts from a leaner, simpler and tougher armed forces.
Prod-WNETTV Dist-FI 1982

Trilogy C
16MM FILM OPTICAL SOUND
Presents a look at the nostalgia of the past, the middle road of the present and the horror of the future.
Prod-CANCIN Dist-CANCIN

Trilogy B 10 MIN
16MM FILM OPTICAL SOUND
Presents a visual expression of the complex love relationship between three people and the mental conflict it produces.
LC NO. 75-703245
Prod-USC Dist-USC 1969

Trim Foot Of Thrown Bowl C 28 MIN
2 INCH VIDEOTAPE
Features Mrs Peterson describing certain ceramic processes for her classroom at the University of Southern California. Demonstrates how to trim the foot of a thrown bowl.
From The Wheels, Kilns And Clay Series.
Prod-USC Dist-PUBTEL

Trimming And Making Cylinders C 29 MIN
2 INCH VIDEOTAPE
Features Mrs Vivika Heino introducing and demonstrating basic techniques in trimming and making cylinders.
From The Exploring The Crafts - Pottery Series.
Prod-WENHTV Dist-PUBTEL

Trimming And Painting C 30 MIN
1/2 IN VIDEO CASSETTE BETA/VHS
Provides a lesson on trimming windows and doors. Gives tips on preparing and painting interior walls.
From The This Old House, Pt 2 - Suburban '50s Series.
Prod-WGBHTV Dist-MTI

Trimming And Shoeing The Normal Horse Foot C 26 MIN
1/2 IN VIDEO CASSETTE BETA/VHS
Makes simple shoe and hoof maintenance. Covers the removing of clinches to filing.
Prod-COLOSU Dist-EQVDL

Trio C 10 MIN
16MM FILM, 3/4 OR 1/2 IN VIDEO H-C A
Offers an animated social satire showing how a man, a dog and a cat live together. Explains that the dog does all the work while the lazy cat profits from every situation.
Prod-ZAGREB Dist-IFB 1977

Trio - Easley Blackwood C 29 MIN
2 INCH VIDEOTAPE
Presents the music of the Easley Blackwood Trio.
From The Young Musical Artists Series.
Prod-WKARTV Dist-PUBTEL

Trio For Three Angles C 8 MIN
16MM FILM, 3/4 OR 1/2 IN VIDEO J-H
Uses the movements of free-swinging angles, synchronized with music, to explain the relationships of the triangle's different components.
From The Triangle Series.
Prod-IFB Dist-IFB 1968

Triode Limiters B 24 MIN
16MM FILM OPTICAL SOUND
Discusses how limiting is accomplished using a triode tube. Describes the characteristics and operation of the cut-off limiter,

the saturation limiter and the over-driver limiter and explains the effect on limiting when bias is changed. (Kinescope)
LC NO. 74-705861
Prod-USAF Dist-USNAC

Triode, The - Amplification B 14 MIN
16MM FILM OPTICAL SOUND
Discusses the diode and triode, electric fields, a triode amplifier circuit, amplification of DC voltage changes, alternating voltages, distortion, and amplication of audio frequency signals.
LC NO. FIE52-189
Prod-SCE Dist-USNAC 1945

Triode, The - Amplification B 14 MIN
3/4 INCH VIDEO CASSETTE
Explains the principles of the diode and triode, covering topics such as electric fields, amplifier circuits, amplification of the DC voltage changes, alternating voltages, distortion, and amplification of audio frequency signals. Issued in 1945 as a motion picture.
From The Engineering - Electronics Series. No. 3
LC NO. 79-706284
Prod-USOE Dist-USNAC Prodn-LNS 1979

Trip Into The Hole C
3/4 OR 1/2 INCH VIDEO CASSETTE IND
Shows that 'Making Hole' is what it's all about. Includes preparation for the trip in, getting the new bit ready, making up the first drill collar connection making up the rest of the collars, and two ways of making up the pipe, spinning chain and pipe spinner.
From The Working Offshore Series.
Prod-GPCV Dist-GPCV

Trip Out Of The Hole C
3/4 OR 1/2 INCH VIDEO CASSETTE IND
Details procedures for getting the drill pipe out of the hole. Includes preparing for wet pipe, safety prepara- tions, breaking out the kelly and a stand of pipe, a stand of collars and preparing the new bit.
From The Working Offshore Series.
Prod-GPCV Dist-GPCV

Trip Through Imagination, A C 15 MIN
2 INCH VIDEOTAPE P
Provides an enrichment program in the communitive arts area by using the world of make-believe.
From The Word Magic (2nd Ed) Series.
Prod-CVETVC Dist-GPITVL

Trip To Awareness - A Jain Pilgrimage To India C 30 MIN
3/4 OR 1/2 INCH VIDEO CASSETTE
Presents architecture and sculpture of India as well as the contemporary concepts of Jainism which include their recipe for self-realization, ahimsa or nonviolence and reverence for life.
Prod-HP Dist-HP

Trip To Awareness, A C 30 MIN
16MM FILM OPTICAL SOUND J-C A
Examines Jain temples in India in order to show the differences between Jainism and Buddhism and to show the Jain formula for self-realization.
LC NO. 76-702075
Prod-HP Dist-HP 1976

Trip To Modern China, A C 26 MIN
16MM FILM, 3/4 OR 1/2 IN VIDEO J-C A
Shows China from Peking to the fertile Yangtze River basin and on to the industrial-commercial city of Shang-Hai. Presents a comprehensive picture of the rural, communal and urban lives of the Chinese people. Considers both the benefits and the disadvantages of communism.
Prod-KINGSP Dist-PHENIX 1973

Trip To The Forest, A C 15 MIN
3/4 OR 1/2 INCH VIDEO CASSETTE P
See series title for descriptive statement.
From The Strawberry Square Series.
Prod-NEITV Dist-AITECH 1982

Trip To The Hospital, A C 15 MIN
3/4 OR 1/2 INCH VIDEO CASSETTE K-P
Observes what takes place in all areas of a hospital and tells why people have to go there.
From The Pass It On Series.
Prod-WKNOTV Dist-GPITVL 1983

Trip To The Moon B 9 MIN
16MM FILM OPTICAL SOUND H-C
Features an early film classic by France's George Melies, using trick photography in a film picturing travel in outer space. Includes scenes of dancers from the Theatre Du Chatelet and acrobats from the Folies-Bergere.
Prod-MELIES Dist-FCE

Trip To The Moon, A B 7 MIN
16MM FILM OPTICAL SOUND
Presents the most famous example of the early 'TRICK' photography used in films produced in 1904 by George Melies.
Prod-MELIES Dist-CFS

Trip To The Planets, A X 15 MIN
16MM FILM, 3/4 OR 1/2 IN VIDEO I-J
Provides an imaginary trip through space and an observation flight close to the surface of the moon. Explains the origin of the craters and 'SEAS,' and illustrates devices for measuring temperatures and the effects of gravity. Includes footage of the Russian lunar probe to the 'DARK' side of the moon.
Prod-EBF Dist-EBEC 1963

Trip To The Planets, A (Spanish) C 15 MIN
16MM FILM, 3/4 OR 1/2 IN VIDEO I-J
Illustrates an imaginary trip to the planets. Examines the structure, motion, size and imagined surface appearance of the planets. Explains how the Sun produces its enormous energy.
Prod-EBEC Dist-EBEC

Trip To The Top, The B 29 MIN
16MM FILM OPTICAL SOUND J-H
Explains how seniority leads to power and affects the working Congress and points out how committee chairmen, having attained their positions through seniority, may block legislation that the majority of congressmen and their constituents want.
From The Government Story Series. No. 11
LC NO. 72-707208
Prod-WEBC Dist-WESTLC 1968

Trip To The University, A C 14 MIN
2 INCH VIDEOTAPE
See series title for descriptive statement.
From The Muffinland Series.
Prod-WGTV Dist-PUBTEL

Trip To Where, A C 50 MIN
16MM FILM OPTICAL SOUND H-C A
Dramatizes the impact of drug use on the lives and careers of three youthful sailors. Explains about methedrine, barbiturates and alcohol and centers on the abuse of marijuana and LSD.
LC NO. 74-705863
Prod-USN Dist-USNAC 1968

Trip, The C 5 MIN
16MM FILM, 3/4 OR 1/2 IN VIDEO K-I
Tells the story of a young boy who is lonely in his new neighborhood until he converts a shoebox into a magic diorama and sees his old friends trick-or-treating. Based on the story The Trip by Ezra Jack Keats.
Prod-WWS Dist-WWS 1980

Tripes A La Mode (French) C 29 MIN
2 INCH VIDEOTAPE
A French language videotape. Features Julia Child of Haute Cuisine au Vin demonstrating how to prepare tripes a la mode. With captions.
From The French Chef (French) Series.
Prod-WGBHTV Dist-PUBTEL

Triple 'A' Agency, The - Anger, Advocacy, Action B 50 MIN
3/4 OR 1/2 INCH VIDEO CASSETTE
See series title for descriptive statement.
From The Social Responses To Aging Care And The Caring For Older People Series. Pt 6
Prod-UAZMIC Dist-UAZMIC 1976

Triple Amputee Steps Out, A C 14 MIN
16MM FILM OPTICAL SOUND
Illustrates specific instruction techniques to provide ambulation training for a triple amputee and shows the use of the Hosmer kee unit in the primvisional limb, balance, gait training and transfer activities.
Prod-USVA Dist-USVA 1963

Triple Jump C 4 MIN
16MM FILM SILENT
Provides examples of male athletes competing in the triple jump, including Banks, Zou, Oliveira, Valyukevich, Marlow, Mayfield, Bakosi, Benson and Agbebaku.
Prod-TRACKN Dist-TRACKN 1982

Triple Jump, The C 11 MIN
16MM FILM, 3/4 OR 1/2 IN VIDEO H-C A
Analyzes key movements in the triple jump. Discusses training for this event and includes scenes of an actual competition.
From The Athletics Series.
LC NO. 80-706588
Prod-GSAVL Dist-IU 1980

Tripping C 15 MIN
16MM FILM, 3/4 OR 1/2 IN VIDEO J-H S
Demonstrates techniques of 'turning on' without drugs.
From The Drug Films - Alternatives To Drugs Series.
Prod-FLMFR Dist-FLMFR 1970

Tripping On Two C 25 MIN
16MM FILM OPTICAL SOUND I-C A
Presents bicycle safety tips covering how to detect and avoid hazards, how to ride defensively, how to see and be seen and how to understand and obey the rules of the road.
Prod-PROART Dist-PROART

Triptych C 10 MIN
16MM FILM OPTICAL SOUND
Presents a visual adaptation of the dance Three Characters for a Passion Play. Portrays in Medieval imagery, the knowledge of inevitable betrayal, the act itself and the loneliness and self-acceptance following.
Prod-FRAF Dist-FRAF

Triumph And Defeat X 30 MIN
16MM FILM OPTICAL SOUND J-C A
Portrays Jesus' triumphal entry into jersusalem, and tells how he cleansed the Temple, celebrated his last supper and stood trials.
From The Living Christ Series.
Prod-CAFM Dist-ECUFLM

Triumph At Tokyo C 35 MIN
16MM FILM OPTICAL SOUND
Presents highlights from the 18th Olympiad in Tokyo, Japan. Features outstanding young men and women who tell the meaning that Jesus Christ has given to thier lives and to theis faith in the disciplined world of the athlete.
Prod-WWP Dist-NINEFC

Triumph In France B 26 MIN
16MM FILM OPTICAL SOUND
Describes with documentary footage the V-1 bombings of London, the allied landings in southern France, the allied breakthrough in Normandy and the liberation of Paris. Based on the book 'THE SECOND WORLD WAR,' by Winston S Churchill.
From The Winston Churchill - The Valiant Years Series. No. 20
LC NO. FI67-2118
Prod-ABCTV Dist-SG 1961

Triumph Of Modern Engineering, A - A Record Of The Tokyo Monorail Line C 24 MIN
16MM FILM OPTICAL SOUND
Explains that the monorail line was planned and constructed in order to relieve the congested traffic between Tokyo International Airport and the heart of the metropolis. Records the important sections of the line constructed by a Japanese construction company, applying the prefabricated tunnel methods, reverse circulation method, Dywidag method and others which require highly advanced techniques.
Prod-UNIJAP Dist-UNIJAP 1964

Triumph Of The Will B 50 MIN
16MM FILM OPTICAL SOUND
Presents the official record for the Sixth Nazi Party held at Nuremberg in September, 1934. Directed by Leni Riefenstahl.
Prod-RIEFSL Dist-REELIM 1934

Triumph Of The Will (German) B 110 MIN
16MM FILM, 3/4 OR 1/2 IN VIDEO
Documents the Nazi's Sixth Party Congress in 1934 in Nuremberg. Shows Hitler appearing as a savior, speeches by Goebbels, Goering, Himmler and Hess, the marching, pomp and pageantry. Directed by Leni Riefenstahl.
Prod-RIEFSL Dist-PHENIX 1936

Triumph Of The Will (German) B 120 MIN
3/4 OR 1/2 INCH VIDEO CASSETTE
Focuses on the 1934 Nazi Party congress. Expresses one individual's impression of the Hitler movement. Conveys the complete dominance of one man's personality over an entire nation.
Prod-IHF Dist-IHF

Triumph Of The Will (The Arrival Of Hitler) B 12 MIN
16MM FILM OPTICAL SOUND J-C A
Presents an excerpt from the 1935 documentary Triumph Of The Will. Depicts Hitler's arrival at the party rally in Nuremberg. Directed by Leni Riefenstahl.
From The Film Study Extracts Series.
Prod-RIEFSL Dist-FI

Triumphant X 17 MIN
16MM FILM OPTICAL SOUND J-H T R
Presents the story of Paul who preaches to all, even while a prisoner in Rome. Shows a mature triumphant Christian philosophy as demonstrated in the life of Paul.
Prod-BROADM Dist-FAMF 1957

Triumphant Symphony C 15 MIN
16MM FILM, 3/4 OR 1/2 IN VIDEO
Uses animation to depict the industrial revolution in the mid-19th century. Focuses on the economic crisis of 1873, which occurred when many small factories closed down and unemployment swelled.
From The History Book Series. Volume 5
Prod-STATNS Dist-CNEMAG

Trobriand Cricket - An Ingenious Response To Colonialism C 54 MIN
16MM FILM, 3/4 OR 1/2 IN VIDEO
Documents the modifications made by the residents of the Trobriand Islands in Papua, New Guinea to the traditional British game of cricket. Shows how the islanders have changed the game into an outlet for mock warfare, community interchange, tribal rivalry, sexual innuendo and a lot of riotous fun.
Prod-LEAKIL Dist-UCEMC 1976

Trobriand Islands - Kula And Cricket C 30 MIN
3/4 INCH VIDEO CASSETTE
See series title for descriptive statement.
From The Of Earth And Man Series.
Prod-MDCPB Dist-MDCPB

Trocar Decompression In Acute Small Bowel Obstruction C 21 MIN
16MM FILM OPTICAL SOUND
Uses illustrations and surgical photography to describe the technique for small bowel decompression with the trocar.
LC NO. FIA67-667
Prod-AVCORP Dist-AMCSUR 1966

Trogmoffy Reading Preparation—A Series
16MM FILM, 3/4 OR 1/2 IN VIDEO K-P
Demonstrates a number of techniques to develop decoding skills through the use of phonics and sight vocabulary. Introduces Trogmoffy, a large orange-furred, barrel-shaped creature from Saturn, who is intelligent but unable to speak in human terms.
Prod-KINGSP Dist-PHENIX 1971

Adventures Of Trogmoffy - Rescue On A 14 _
Adventures Of Trogmoffy - Timmy And Margaret 14 MIN

Troilus And Cressida C 190 MIN
3/4 OR 1/2 INCH VIDEO CASSETTE H-C A
Presents William Shakespeare's play Troilus And Cressida about two lovers who mock love.
From The Shakespeare Plays Series.
LC NO. 82-707357
Prod-BBCTV Dist-TIMLIF 1982

Troilus And Cressida - Shakespeare's Most 'Modern' Play - Tragi-Comedy Of Disillusionment B 45 MIN
2 INCH VIDEOTAPE C
See series title for descriptive statement.
From The Shakespeare Series.
Prod-CHITVC Dist-GPITVL Prodn-WTTWTV

Trois Themes B 8 MIN
16MM FILM OPTICAL SOUND

Presents later visions based on Moussorgsky's music, with slow-moving shadows on a sleepless night, an accelerated passage of drawings and sketches moving across the screen, and a third mood of conflict between material goods and artistic aims. Produced by Alexander Alexeieff and Claire Parker.
Prod-STARRC Dist-STARRC 1980

Troll Music, The C 15 MIN
3/4 OR 1/2 INCH VIDEO CASSETTE P
See series title for descriptive statement.
From The Magic Pages Series.
Prod-KLVXTV Dist-AITECH 1976

Troll Troop C 20 MIN
16MM FILM OPTICAL SOUND P-I
Presents cut-offs and flip cards.
Prod-YELLOW Dist-YELLOW 1973

Trolls And The Christmas Express, The C 25 MIN
16MM FILM, 3/4 OR 1/2 IN VIDEO
Describes what happens when six mischievous trolls try to ruin Christmas for all children, first by sabotaging Santa's toy production and then by keeping the reindeer up so that they are too tired to pull Santa's sleigh.
Prod-CORF Dist-CORF 1981

Trolls Of Norway C 15 MIN
16MM FILM OPTICAL SOUND P-I
Uses short narrated sequences to introduce trolls, a product of Norway's folklore.
Prod-MMP Dist-MMP

Tron C 24 MIN
16MM FILM, 3/4 OR 1/2 IN VIDEO J-H
Offers highlights from the motion picture Tron, which goes inside a computer where a real-life computer genius is pitted against electronic foes.
Prod-WDEMCO Dist-WDEMCO 1983

Troops, The C 58 MIN
3/4 OR 1/2 INCH VIDEO CASSETTE H-C A
Discusses the history of black military participation from World War II to Vietnam. Discusses President Truman's executive order of 1948 which suggested the end of segregation in the Armed Forces, and the achievement of full integration in the Vietnam War.
From The Different Drummer - Blacks In The Military Series.
LC NO. 85-700750
Prod-WNETTV Dist-FI 1983

Trope B 8 MIN
16MM FILM OPTICAL SOUND
A purposeless film which anyone can enjoy. An experimental approach in the treatment of four extremely conversational people at dinner. The film-maker combines time analysis with 'SMALL TALK' in an amusing treatment of a common situation. (A USC cinema student workshop production.)
Prod-USC Dist-USC 1965

Trophy Case, The C 26 MIN
16MM FILM OPTICAL SOUND J-C A
Tells a story about a father who gives his all so his son can do and be all the things that he couldn't be when he was young. Shows how the father suddenly has to face the fact that his son has other goals and abilities in his life.
LC NO. 80-700051
Prod-BYU Dist-BYU 1979

Trophy Elk C 15 MIN
16MM FILM OPTICAL SOUND
Shows hunters fashioning Indian game calls from native plant climaxed by downing king of the herd with a single arrow.
Prod-SFI Dist-SFI

Tropic Seacoast Survival C 23 MIN
16MM FILM OPTICAL SOUND
Explains the teaching procedures and techniques to be followed for survival along tropical seacoasts.
LC NO. 74-705864
Prod-USAF Dist-USNAC 1961

Tropic Seas, The C 30 MIN
3/4 OR 1/2 INCH VIDEO CASSETTE
Focuses on the waters of the tropic zones. Contrasts the biological and physiological properties of the tropical seas. Examines the coral animal and reef ecosystem.
From The Oceanus - The Marine Environment Series. Lesson 25
Prod-SCCON Dist-CDTEL

Tropical Africa C 29 MIN
16MM FILM OPTICAL SOUND I-C
Overall view of the tropical portion of the African continent. Shows geography, history, life in villages and cities, education, religion, industry and social changes.
LC NO. FIA66-1854
Prod-IFF Dist-IFF 1961

Tropical Botany Film–A Series
J-C
Prod-IOWA Dist-IOWA 1973

Flowering And Fruiting Of Papaya 3 MIN
Fruiting Of Cacao 2 MIN
Fruiting Of Coffee 3 MIN
Growth And Fruiting Of African Oil Palm 3 MIN
Growth And Fruiting Of Banana 5 MIN
Growth And Fruiting Of Pineapple 3 MIN

Tropical Circulation C 13 MIN
16MM FILM, 3/4 OR 1/2 IN VIDEO I-H
Uses animation to explain tropical weather patterns. Discusses global circulation of cold and warm air masses which bring about wet and dry seasons in the Tropics.
Prod-IFFB Dist-CF 1984

Tropical Climate - Hawaii C 30 MIN
1/2 IN VIDEO CASSETTE BETA/VHS
Describes Hawaii's year-round growing climate where Chinese, Japanese, Vietnamese and other Asian-style crops thrive.
From The Victory Garden Series.
Prod-WGBHTV Dist-MTI

Tropical Harvest C 17 MIN
16MM FILM, 3/4 OR 1/2 IN VIDEO I-H
Shows how a variety of plantation and natural crops of the tropics are grown. Describes the cultivation and processing of tea, coffee, rubber, cashew nuts, peppers and coconuts.
Prod-BHA Dist-IFB 1963

Tropical Jungle C 15 MIN
16MM FILM, 3/4 OR 1/2 IN VIDEO I-J
Depicts the sounds, sights and conditions found in a typical tropical jungle in Malaya. Includes examples of unusual plants and animals and shows a native making fires and hunting.
Prod-IFB Dist-IFB 1965

Tropical Rain Forest, The X 17 MIN
16MM FILM, 3/4 OR 1/2 IN VIDEO H
Defines the tropical rain forest and shows the principal characteristics and locations. Presents the way various forms of plant and animal life adapt and live together.
From The Biology Series. Unit 2 - Ecosystems
Prod-EBF Dist-EBEC 1962

Tropical Rain Forest, The (Spanish) C 17 MIN
16MM FILM, 3/4 OR 1/2 IN VIDEO H
Examines the rich variety of animal and plant life in the humid environment of the tropical rain forest. Shows the layered structure of vegetation and describes conditions of temperature and rainfall.
From The Biology (Spanish) Series. Unit 2 - Ecosystems
Prod-EBEC Dist-EBEC

Tropici (Italian) B 87 MIN
16MM FILM OPTICAL SOUND
An English subtitle version of the Italian language film. Tells of a poor Brazilian family who is forced to migrate to Sao Paulo in hopes of finding work. Describes encounters with the various people the family meets on its journey.
Prod-NYFLMS Dist-NYFLMS 1969

Tropici (Portuguese) B 87 MIN
16MM FILM OPTICAL SOUND
An English subtitle version of the Portuguese language film. Tells of a poor Brazilian family who is forced to migrate to Sao Paulo in hopes of finding work. Describes encounters with the various people the family meets on its journey.
Prod-NYFLMS Dist-NYFLMS 1969

Tropics, The - A Garden In Time C 11 MIN
16MM FILM OPTICAL SOUND
Shows the value of the tropics to mankind and explains the work being done by the Pacific Tropical Botanical Garden to preserve tropical plants through research, collection and education.
LC NO. 82-700271
Prod-PACTBG Dist-SUNSET Prodn-SUNSET 1981

Tropism, Pt 1 C 15 MIN
3/4 INCH VIDEO CASSETTE I
Explains tropism as a vital process of plants.
From The Search For Science (2nd Ed.) Unit VIII - Plants Series.
Prod-WVIZTV Dist-GPITVL

Tropism, Pt 2 C 15 MIN
3/4 INCH VIDEO CASSETTE I
Explains growth hormones and how they affect plant growth.
From The Search For Science (2nd Ed.) Unit VIII - Plants Series.
Prod-WVIZTV Dist-GPITVL

Trouble At Home - Learning To Cope C
3/4 OR 1/2 INCH VIDEO CASSETTE I-J
Aids in understanding and coping with the fear, anger and resentment which occurs in a troubled home. Dramatizes such family problems as divorce, alcoholism, and unemployment. Describes methods of recognizing and accepting feeling. Outlines coping process.
Prod-SUNCOM Dist-SUNCOM

Trouble At Number Thirty-Two / Paddington And The Christmas Shopping / Christmas C 17 MIN
16MM FILM, 3/4 OR 1/2 IN VIDEO K-I
Describes Paddington Bear's first encounter with snow. Tells how he goes Christmas shopping and enjoys his first Christmas with the Brown family. Based on chapters three, five and six of the book More About Paddington by Michael Bond.
From The Paddington Bear, Series 1 Series.
LC NO. 80-707229
Prod-BONDM Dist-FLMFR Prodn-FILMF 1977

Trouble At Tonti Station C 25 MIN
16MM FILM, 3/4 OR 1/2 IN VIDEO
Presents an actual account of civil defense teams in action. Shows how a train accident at Tonti Station in Illinois brought quick action from civil defense and volunteer forces in performing lifesaving and rescue missions.
Prod-USDCPA Dist-USNAC 1976

Trouble Down At Studleigh C 30 MIN
3/4 OR 1/2 INCH VIDEO CASSETTE C A
Presents an adaptation of the short story Trouble Down At Studleigh by P G Wodehouse.
From The Wodehouse Playhouse Series.
Prod-BBCTV Dist-TIMLIF 1980

Trouble For Lucy C 14 MIN
3/4 OR 1/2 INCH VIDEO CASSETTE P-I
Introduces the story of a young girl who travels with her family and puppy on the Oregon Trail in 1843. Shows that trouble comes when the girl leaves the wagon train in search of her puppy. Based on the book Trouble For Lucy by Carla Stevens.
From The Readit Series.
LC NO. 83-706832
Prod-POSIMP Dist-AITECH 1982

Trouble In Paradise B 86 MIN
16MM FILM OPTICAL SOUND
Features Herbert Marshall as the dashing Gaston Monescu, Miriam Hopkins as the Countess, and Kay Francis as the millionaress who takes them both under her wing. Directed by Ernst Lubitsch.
Prod-PARACO Dist-TWYMAN

Trouble In The Family B 90 MIN
16MM FILM OPTICAL SOUND H-C A
Shows how a therapist works with a family to get at the root of their problems. Dr Nathan W Ackerman, clinical professor of psychiatry at Columbia University, discusses family therapy with Harold Mayer.
From The America's Crises Series.
LC NO. FIA66-1125
Prod-NET Dist-IU 1965

Trouble In The Firehouse C 23 MIN
16MM FILM OPTICAL SOUND
Deals with a mayor's decision of a moratorium on new hiring. Poses the questions as to whether the manning table is 'mandatory' or merely a 'goal.'
Prod-AARA Dist-AARA

Trouble In The Ghetto C 25 MIN
16MM FILM OPTICAL SOUND
Examines the causes of the high rate of violent crime in Atlanta's ghetto.
LC NO. 74-702524
Prod-WAGATV Dist-WAGATV 1974

Trouble In Utopia C 52 MIN
16MM FILM, 3/4 OR 1/2 IN VIDEO C A
Describes the work of the German and Italian visionary architects. Tells how the Bauhaus and the functionalist faith started the worldwide spread of the glass-box style. Points out that the great myth of the architect as social legislator came to an end in the strange wasteland of Brasilia.
From The Shock Of The New Series.
LC NO. 80-706953
Prod-BBCTV Dist-TIMLIF 1980

Trouble On Fashion Avenue C 60 MIN
3/4 OR 1/2 INCH VIDEO CASSETTE J-C A
Investigates the economic problems of the New York City garment industry, focusing on sweatshop conditions, the state of trade unions, the impact of imports and the role of organized crime.
LC NO. 84-707173
Prod-TVGDAP Dist-CNEMAG 1982

Trouble Shooting Aids C 36 MIN
3/4 OR 1/2 INCH VIDEO CASSETTE PRO
Shows the difference between testing and debugging. Describes useful trouble shooting tools.
From The Software Management For Small Computers Series.
Prod-AMCEE Dist-AMCEE

Trouble Shooting Problems - Fuel Induction B 17 MIN
16MM FILM OPTICAL SOUND
Illustrates how to locate trouble within the fuel system and how to correct over-heating, round running at idling speed and failure to develop full power.
LC NO. FIE52-160
Prod-USOE Dist-USNAC 1945

Trouble Shooting Problems - Ignition B 19 MIN
16MM FILM OPTICAL SOUND
Demonstrates how to locate trouble within the ignition system when an engine fails to start, when it runs roughly and when it fails to develop full power.
LC NO. FIE52-250
Prod-USOE Dist-USNAC 1945

Trouble Shooting Problems - Mechanical And Lubrication B 10 MIN
16MM FILM OPTICAL SOUND
Shows how to check symptoms and locate causes of an airplane engine's running rough, of low oil pressure and of high oil temperature.
LC NO. FIE52-147
Prod-USOE Dist-USNAC 1945

Trouble Shooting Your Car B 12 MIN
16MM FILM OPTICAL SOUND H
Shows what a driver should do to locate and correct minor car troubles and how to recognize symptoms of impending trouble.
From The Automotive Operation And Maintenance Series. Automobile Operation, No. 5
LC NO. FIE52-348
Prod-USOE Dist-USNAC 1945

Trouble With Angels, The C 112 MIN
16MM FILM OPTICAL SOUND I-C
Stars Rosalind Russell as a Mother Superior who runs a convent school with considerable discipline and a sense of humor. Features Hayley Mills as a highspirited student determined to break every rule in the book just for the fun of it.
Prod-CPC Dist-TIMLIF 1966

Trouble With Charlie, The - An Introduction To Financial Counseling C 23 MIN
16MM FILM OPTICAL SOUND A
Presents financial counseling consultants James L Lee and

Charles J Pulvino demonstrating counseling skills for loan officers, using a typical customer named Charlie.
LC NO. 79-701810
Prod-EMCORP Dist-EMCORP 1979

Trouble With Ice, The C 10 MIN
16MM FILM, 3/4 OR 1/2 IN VIDEO I-H
Teaches various rescue techniques to be used when aiding a person who has fallen through the ice.
Prod-BSA Dist-AIMS 1971

Trouble With Life, The C 20 MIN
3/4 OR 1/2 INCH VIDEO CASSETTE I
Presents dramatizations of literary works that deal with conflict as part of the experiences of life.
From The Readers' Cube Series.
Prod-MDDE Dist-AITECH 1977

Trouble With Miss Switch, The C 48 MIN
16MM FILM, 3/4 OR 1/2 IN VIDEO I-J
Describes the events which ensue when Miss Switch, the best teacher at Pepperdine, is revealed as a witch. Based on the children's book The Trouble With Miss Switch. Originally shown on the television series ABC Weekend Specials.
LC NO. 80-707528
Prod-ABCTV Dist-MTI 1980

Trouble With Mother, The C 24 MIN
3/4 OR 1/2 INCH VIDEO CASSETTE
Looks at the story of a mother and daughter in conflict over the role of women in our changing society. Stars Sandy Dennis.
From The Young People's Specials Series.
Prod-MULTPP Dist-MULTPP

Trouble With Spider, The / Spiders Are Spinners C 15 MIN
3/4 INCH VIDEO CASSETTE P
Presents the children's stories The Trouble With Spider by Robert Kraus and Spiders Are Spinners by Ellsworth Rosen.
From The Tilson's Book Shop Series.
Prod-WVIZTV Dist-GPITVL 1975

Trouble With Strangers C 10 MIN
16MM FILM, 3/4 OR 1/2 IN VIDEO P
Communicates through a child's eyes the problem of molestation. Shows the police rescuing a little girl and explaining how to avoid most situations involving such a danger.
Prod-DAVP Dist-AIMS 1975

Trouble With The Law C 16 MIN
16MM FILM, 3/4 OR 1/2 IN VIDEO J-C A
Explains that a college student involved in an auto accident rejects the standard by which the court finds him guilty and decides that justice has not been served by the legal process.
From The Searching For Values - A Film Anthology Series.
Prod-LCOA Dist-LCOA 1972

Trouble With Tommy, The C 10 MIN
16MM FILM, 3/4 OR 1/2 IN VIDEO P-I
Presents a view of shoplifting from the child's viewpoint. Tells what happens when a child is encouraged to steal and is later caught.
Prod-CREATP Dist-MTI

Trouble With Trash, The C 30 MIN
3/4 OR 1/2 INCH VIDEO CASSETTE
Looks at the spiraling waste disposal problem. Explains modern sanitary landfill techniques.
Prod-IVCH Dist-IVCH

Trouble-Shooting An Electrocardiogram C 11 MIN
1/2 IN VIDEO CASSETTE BETA/VHS
Explains how to eliminate artifacts.
Prod-RMI Dist-RMI

Trouble-Shooting SCR Motor Controls C 29 MIN
3/4 OR 1/2 INCH VIDEO CASSETTE IND
Explains operation and repair of DC motor control systems. Provides opportunity to apply understanding of solid state electronics theory in a practical industrial context.
Prod-TAT Dist-TAT

Trouble-Shooting SCR Motor Controls (Spanish) C 29 MIN
3/4 OR 1/2 INCH VIDEO CASSETTE IND
Explains operation and repair of DC motor control systems. Provides opportunity to apply understanding of solid state electronics theory in a practical industrial context.
Prod-TAT Dist-TAT

Troubled Campers B 16 MIN
16MM FILM OPTICAL SOUND PRO
Uses a composite of several episodes of spontaneous behavior to show various emotionally disturbed boys during a summer at a therapeutic camp.
From The Wediko Series.
LC NO. 71-713199
Prod-MASON Dist-DOCUFL 1971

Troubled Campers B 18 MIN
3/4 OR 1/2 INCH VIDEO CASSETTE T
Designed to introduce some of the dimensions of emotional handicaps and to encourage discussion about prevention, treatment, rehabilitation and education, especially as related to emotionally disturbed children campers.
From The Wediko Series - Emotionally Disturbed-- Children At Camp Series.
Prod-DOCUFL Dist-DOCUFL

Troubled Cities, The B 60 MIN
16MM FILM OPTICAL SOUND H-C A
Examines the attempts being made to solve problems brought about by the urban population explosion.
From The America's Crises Series.
LC NO. FIA67-1843
Prod-NET Dist-IU 1966

Troubled Employee, The C 25 MIN
16MM FILM, 3/4 OR 1/2 IN VIDEO
Tells managers how to identify workers with personal problems and what to do to return them to productivity.
Prod-DARTNL Dist-ROGRSG

Troubled Neighbors - Cuba And The United States B 15 MIN
16MM FILM OPTICAL SOUND I-C A
Analyzes the changing nature of Cuban-American relations since Fidel Castro's seizure of power in 1959. Covers Castro's journey to power, nationalization of utility companies, the missile crisis and the significant differences which continue to exist between the two countries.
From The Screen News Digest Series. Vol 18, Issue 4
LC NO. 76-701849
Prod-HEARST Dist-HEARST 1975

Troubled Waters C 28 MIN
16MM FILM OPTICAL SOUND J-C
Describes pollution in the United States, using the example of the heavily populated and industrialized Ohio River Valley.
Prod-USSCPW Dist-USNAC 1966

Troubled Waters C 28 MIN
16MM FILM, 3/4 OR 1/2 IN VIDEO
Explores threats to California's coastal wildlife. Investigates oil exploration and drilling, water diversion, marshland filling and commercial waterfront developments.
Prod-UCEMC Dist-UCEMC

Troublemakers B 54 MIN
16MM FILM, 3/4 OR 1/2 IN VIDEO
Documents the roots of political turmoil in the Sixties. Portrays efforts of former Students For A Democratic Society (SDS), including Tom Hayden, to organize people in the black community of Newark, NJ to work for social change.
Prod-CNEMAG Dist-CNEMAG 1966

Troubles And Triumphs C 20 MIN
3/4 OR 1/2 INCH VIDEO CASSETTE I
Presents dramatizations of literary works that deal with the universal problems that people share.
From The Readers' Cube Series.
Prod-MDDE Dist-AITECH 1977

Troubles Going To Las Vegas C 4 MIN
16MM FILM SILENT J-C A
Relates in American sign language the catastrophe of a young deaf Chicano traveling to Las Vegas on vacation. Signed for the deaf by Ralph Gardenas.
LC NO. 76-701708
Prod-JOYCE Dist-JOYCE 1975

Troubles With 'S,' The - Initial 'S' C 30 MIN
2 INCH VIDEOTAPE T
See series title for descriptive statement.
From The Solutions In Communications Series.
Prod-SCCOE Dist-SCCOE

Troubles--A Series
16MM FILM, 3/4 OR 1/2 IN VIDEO H-C A
Discusses the context and the issues of the troubles between Northern Ireland and Britain which are the background for understanding the seemingly insoluble stalemate of the present day. Illuminates the central themes of the modern struggle from historical perspectives.
Prod-THAMES Dist-MEDIAG 1982

Troubles, The - Conquest 054 MIN
Troubles, The - Deadlock 054 MIN
Troubles, The - Intervention 054 MIN
Troubles, The - Partition 054 MIN
Troubles, The - Rebellion 054 MIN
Troubles, The - Rising 054 MIN

Troubles, The C 35 MIN
3/4 OR 1/2 INCH VIDEO CASSETTE
Examines the history and current issues of the 800-year-old conflict between Protestants and Catholics in Ireland.
Prod-WCCOTV Dist-WCCOTV 1981

Troubles, The - Conquest C 54 MIN
3/4 OR 1/2 INCH VIDEO CASSETTE H-C A
Uses eminent historians, nineteenth-century photographs, motion picture film from the early twentieth century and folk memories to trace Irish hisotry from the sixteenth century to the 1916 Easter Rising. Helps to explain what is happening today in Northern Ireland.
From The Troubles Series.
Prod-THAMES Dist-MEDIAG 1982

Troubles, The - Deadlock C 54 MIN
3/4 OR 1/2 INCH VIDEO CASSETTE H-C A
Presents the story of Bobby Sands, convicted member of the Irish Republican Army, who was serving a fourteen-year prison sentence for firearms charges when he was elected to Parliament. He was the thirteenth Irish nationalist to die from a hunger strike during the twentieth century as he protested his imprisonment on political grounds.
From The Troubles Series.
Prod-THAMES Dist-MEDIAG 1982

Troubles, The - Intervention C 54 MIN
3/4 OR 1/2 INCH VIDEO CASSETTE H-C A
Portrays the streets of Northern Ireland, occupied by the British Army, as they are normally. Shows the streets not erupting in smoke, but quiet, tense, and socially deprived in some areas.
From The Troubles Series.
Prod-THAMES Dist-MEDIAG 1982

Troubles, The - Partition C 54 MIN
3/4 OR 1/2 INCH VIDEO CASSETTE H-C A
Presents the history of Northern Ireland from 1920 to 1970, using newly-discovered archive film and eye-witness accounts. Features interviews with Glen Barr, who presents the loyalist perspective and Michael Farrell presenting the Republican viewpoint.
From The Troubles Series.
Prod-THAMES Dist-MEDIAG 1982

Troubles, The - Rebellion C 54 MIN
3/4 OR 1/2 INCH VIDEO CASSETTE H-C A
Details Bloody Sunday, January 30, 1972, which signalled the collapse of the Northern Ireland Parliament at Stormont and the beginning of direct rule by Britain. Covers the period beginning in 1966 that led up to this historic event.
From The Troubles Series.
Prod-THAMES Dist-MEDIAG 1982

Troubles, The - Rising C 54 MIN
3/4 OR 1/2 INCH VIDEO CASSETTE H-C A
Describes how the British left 26 counties when Ireland was partitioned in 1921. The struggle of Irish nationalists began in the nineteenth century in the British Parliament and culminated in the country of Northern Ireland.
From The Troubles Series.
Prod-THAMES Dist-MEDIAG 1982

Troubleshooting C
16MM FILM - 3/4 IN VIDEO IND
Explains troubleshooting of analog and digital control systems.
From The Instrumentation Maintenance Series.
Prod-ISA Dist-ISA

Troubleshooting C 38 MIN
3/4 OR 1/2 INCH VIDEO CASSETTE
Teaches a systematic procedure for troubleshooting, including determining the characteristics and function of the failed part.
From The Tribology 1 - Friction, Wear, And Lubrication Series.
Prod-MIOT Dist-MIOT

Troubleshooting C 60 MIN
3/4 OR 1/2 INCH VIDEO CASSETTE IND
See series title for descriptive statement.
From The Electrical Maintenance Training, Module 2 - Motors Series.
Prod-LEIKID Dist-LEIKID

Troubleshooting Amplifiers C 12 MIN
3/4 OR 1/2 INCH VIDEO CASSETTE
Covers the troubleshooting of single-stage amplifiers, troubleshooting using DC and AC analysis, a three-stage amplifier and other troubleshooting techniques.
From The Industrial Electronics - Amplifiers Series.
Prod-TPCTRA Dist-TPCTRA

Troubleshooting Centrifugal Pumps C 60 MIN
3/4 OR 1/2 INCH VIDEO CASSETTE
Covers troubleshooting centrifugal pumps. Outlines the conditions required for normal operation.
From The Troubleshooting Series.
Prod-ITCORP Dist-ITCORP

Troubleshooting Digital Sub-Systems C 30 MIN
3/4 OR 1/2 INCH VIDEO CASSETTE
Gives sound approach for troubleshooting either for system check-out or for maintenance. Shows tour of digital test equipment.
From The Digital Sub-Systems Series.
Prod-TXINLC Dist-TXINLC

Troubleshooting Electrical Circuits C 16 MIN
16MM FILM, 3/4 OR 1/2 IN VIDEO
Shows how to locate and repair shorted, grounded and open circuits.
Prod-USAF Dist-USNAC

Troubleshooting Field Device Malfunctions C 30 MIN
3/4 OR 1/2 INCH VIDEO CASSETTE
Deals with troubleshooting field device malfunctions. Stresses interpreting the program.
From The Programmable Controllers Series.
Prod-ITCORP Dist-ITCORP

Troubleshooting Logic System C 12 MIN
3/4 OR 1/2 INCH VIDEO CASSETTE
Shows how to recognize types of logic subassemblies, troubleshooting logic subassemblies and pin-pointing malfunctions using logic probes.
From The Industrial Electronics - Logic Circuits Series.
Prod-TPCTRA Dist-TPCTRA

Troubleshooting Logic Systems (Spanish) C 12 MIN
3/4 OR 1/2 INCH VIDEO CASSETTE
Shows how to recognize types of logic subassemblies, troubleshooting logic subassemblies and pin-pointing malfunctions using logic probes.
From The Industrial Electronics - Logic Circuits (Spanish) Series.
Prod-TPCTRA Dist-TPCTRA

Troubleshooting Oscillators And Multivibrators C 12 MIN
3/4 OR 1/2 INCH VIDEO CASSETTE
Shows how to remove load from a circuit, to locate the malfunctioning assembly, to repair oscillators and multivibrators.
From The Industrial Electronics - Oscillators And Multivibrators Series.
Prod-TPCTRA Dist-TPCTRA

Troubleshooting P C Malfunctions C 30 MIN
3/4 OR 1/2 INCH VIDEO CASSETTE
Deals with troubleshooting P C Malfunctions. Points to CPU, I O, and power supply problems.
From The Programmable Controllers Series.
Prod-ITCORP Dist-ITCORP

Troubleshooting Positive Displacement Pumps C 60 MIN
3/4 OR 1/2 INCH VIDEO CASSETTE
Examines troubleshooting positive displacement pumps. Includes performing operational checks on suction components, speed control components and packing.
From The Troubleshooting Series.
Prod-ITCORP Dist-ITCORP

Troubleshooting Power Supplies C 12 MIN
3/4 OR 1/2 INCH VIDEO CASSETTE
Covers general troubleshooting approach, preliminary checks, locating the faulty major section, signal tracing, troubleshooting the source, converter and regulator.
From The Industrial Electronics - Power Supplies Series.
Prod-TPCTRA Dist-TPCTRA

Troubleshooting Reciprocating Air Compressors C 60 MIN
3/4 OR 1/2 INCH VIDEO CASSETTE
Investigates troubleshooting reciprocating air compressors. Describes conditions required for normal operation. Discusses performing operational checks.
From The Troubleshooting Series.
Prod-ITCORP Dist-ITCORP

Troubleshooting Techniques C 12 MIN
3/4 OR 1/2 INCH VIDEO CASSETTE
Shows how to recognize normal operations and simple testing and observation. Covers routine and emergency repairs.
From The Developing Troubleshooting Skills Series.
Prod-TPCTRA Dist-TPCTRA

Troubleshooting Techniques C 30 MIN
3/4 OR 1/2 INCH VIDEO CASSETTE
Delineates troubleshooting techniques. Stresses developing a logical approach.
From The Programmable Controllers Series.
Prod-ITCORP Dist-ITCORP

Troubleshooting—A Series

Presents a skills training program, focusing on troubleshooting. Contains student workbooks, instructor's guides and overhead transparencies.
Prod-ITCORP Dist-ITCORP

Principles Of Mechanical Troubleshooting 060 MIN
Troubleshooting Centrifugal Pumps 060 MIN
Troubleshooting Positive Displacement Pumps 060 MIN
Troubleshooting Reciprocating Air Compressors 060 MIN

Troublesome Pronouns - Who And Whom C 11 MIN
1/2 IN VIDEO CASSETTE BETA/VHS
See series title for descriptive statement.
From The English And Speech Series.
Prod-RMI Dist-RMI

Troublesome Verbs - Lie And Lay, Sit And Set, Rise And Raise C 11 MIN
1/2 IN VIDEO CASSETTE BETA/VHS
See series title for descriptive statement.
From The English And Speech Series.
Prod-RMI Dist-RMI

Trousseau To Treasure, A C 29 MIN
2 INCH VIDEOTAPE
See series title for descriptive statement.
From The Designing Women Series.
Prod-WKYCTV Dist-PUBTEL

Trout Fishing In Tasmania C 19 MIN
16MM FILM OPTICAL SOUND
Presents a guide on where fish are to be found in Tasmania.
LC NO. 80-700931
Prod-TASCOR Dist-TASCOR 1976

Trout Stream In Winter, A C 19 MIN
16MM FILM OPTICAL SOUND C A
Studies the behavior of trout, including reproduction and spawning. Looks at the dangers posed to stream ecology by low snowfall in a high snowpack area and by formation of frazil and anchor ice.
LC NO. 80-701583
Prod-RBVH Dist-PSUPCR 1980

Trout That Stole The Rainbow, The C 8 MIN
16MM FILM OPTICAL SOUND
Tells how the world loses all color when a selfish trout cannot resist the beauty of the rainbow and steals it. As punishment, the sun paints the trout in rainbow colors that can be enjoyed by all but Trout.
Prod-NFBC Dist-NFBC 1982

Trout That Stole The Rainbow, The C 8 MIN
3/4 OR 1/2 INCH VIDEO CASSETTE
Tells how the world loses all color when a selfish trout cannot resist the beauty of the rainbow and steals it. As punishment, the sun paints the trout in rainbow colors that can be enjoyed by all but Trout.
Prod-NFBC Dist-GA 1982

Trout Transportation C
3/4 OR 1/2 INCH VIDEO CASSETTE
Prod-FO Dist-FO

Trout USA C 13 MIN
16MM FILM OPTICAL SOUND I-H A
A study of the trout industry, showing trout forming techniques, factory processing and preparation for market. Includes underwater photogrphy, showing net-building and spawning.
LC NO. 70-702881
Prod-USNOAA Dist-USNOAA 1968

Trout USA C 14 MIN
3/4 OR 1/2 INCH VIDEO CASSETTE
Studies the trout industry, discusses trout fishing as a sport, and tells how to prepare trout for the table.
LC NO. 80-797745
Prod-USBCF Dist-USNAC 1980

Troy-Patterson B 30 MIN
16MM FILM OPTICAL SOUND
From The IBC Championship Fights, Series 2 Series.
Prod-SFI Dist-SFI

Truce In Korea B 7 MIN
16MM FILM OPTICAL SOUND
Presents clips from 1953-54 Screen News Digest films on the Korean truce including the United Nations agreement, return of gi's and Korean reconstruction and the homecoming of other united Nation's troops and repatriation.
From The News Magazine Of The Screen Series. Vol 3, No. 10
Prod-PATHE Dist-HEARST 1954

Truce In The Forest C 38 MIN
16MM FILM OPTICAL SOUND
Tells the story of a German widow who extends her hospitality to both German and American soldiers on Christmas Eve, 1944.
LC NO. 78-700227
Prod-FAMF Dist-FAMF 1977

Truck Driver Named Gret, A C 11 MIN
16MM FILM, 3/4 OR 1/2 IN VIDEO
Profiles a 38-year-old wife, mother and delivery truck driver. Explores her motives and the varied attitudes of family members, storeowners and the people she encounters on the job. Explodes myths and stereotypes of women who choose non-traditional fields of work.
Prod-LEVKOF Dist-CAROUF

Truck Drivers Only (2nd Ed) C 15 MIN
16MM FILM, 3/4 OR 1/2 IN VIDEO PRO
Explains how professional drivers can set their own standard of ability and conduct while working.
Prod-OREIDA Dist-FO 1966

Truck Stop X 28 MIN
16MM FILM, 3/4 OR 1/2 IN VIDEO J-C A
Depicts a young waitress who has always refused to commit herself to a lasting relationship. Shows what happens when someone she really cares about abandons her. Stars John Astin, Deborah Winters and Tim Matheson.
From The Insight Series.
Prod-PAULST Dist-PAULST

Truck Stop (Spanish) X 28 MIN
16MM FILM, 3/4 OR 1/2 IN VIDEO J-C A
Depicts a young waitress who has always refused to commit herself to a lasting relationship. Shows what happens when someone she really cares about abandons her. Stars John Astin, Deborah Winters and Tim Matheson.
From The Insight Series.
Prod-PAULST Dist-PAULST

Truck Transport - On The Long Haul C 17 MIN
16MM FILM OPTICAL SOUND P-J
Shows a truck and trailer on the road from Los Angeles to Spokane, emphasizing the care and maintenance of the truck, rotation of drivers and scheduling.
LC NO. FIA55-715
Prod-ACA Dist-ACA 1954

Truck, Utility, 1/4-Ton M151A2 - Characteristics And Handling C 18 MIN
16MM FILM OPTICAL SOUND
Offers points in the operation of the M151A2 utility truck and demonstrates its different uses.
LC NO. 80-701086
Prod-USA Dist-USNAC 1971

Truckers For Christ C 17 MIN
16MM FILM OPTICAL SOUND
Shows a documentary about a Canadian-based missionary group of truckers headquartered in Waterloo, Ontario, who own and operate mobile chapels that travel the truckstops and terminals of North America in order to provide religious services for truckers.
LC NO. 76-703823
Prod-YORKU Dist-YORKU Prodn-DSBB 1976

Truckin' - The Road To Shreveport B 12 MIN
16MM FILM OPTICAL SOUND
Compares the comments and experiences of two truckers on a nonstop haul to Shreveport to those of another driver who hauled goods across the country in a horse and wagon more than a century ago.
LC NO. 75-702999
Prod-TEMPLU Dist-DEPRTF 1974

Trucks And Truck Transportation C 11 MIN
16MM FILM, 3/4 OR 1/2 IN VIDEO K-I
Shows how vans, flat-bed trucks and tankers bring goods to the businesses and individuals in a community.
From The Transportation Series.
Prod-FILMSW Dist-FLMFR Prodn-LILLYL 1968

Trucks In Our Neighborhood - A First Film X 12 MIN
16MM FILM, 3/4 OR 1/2 IN VIDEO P
Pictures the various trucks that might come to the neighborhood. Shows the trucks and the workers who drive them as they provide services, make deliveries and repairs and do the general work needed to keep a neighborhood running smoothly.
Prod-FA Dist-PHENIX 1967

Trudy Pitts C 30 MIN
2 INCH VIDEOTAPE
Presents the jazz music of Trudy Pitts. Features host Jim Rockwell interviewing the artist.
From The People In Jazz Series.
Prod-WTVSTV Dist-PUBTEL

True And False Prophecy—A Series
A
Features Dr James A Sanders, noted biblical scholar and theologian, as he discusses history, scripture and biblical tradition intermixed with his prophecy.
Prod-UMCOM Dist-ECUFLM 1982

Amos 030 MIN
Ezekiel And Another Isaiah 030 MIN
Hosea 030 MIN
Jesus 030 MIN
Micah And Isaiah 030 MIN

True Art Of Making Lasagna, The C 7 MIN
16MM FILM SILENT J-C A S
Presents two cooks discussing in American sign language the subject of making lasagna and gives their individual recipes for making it. Signed for the deaf by Carolyn Larson and Florian Caliguiri.
LC NO. 76-701709
Prod-JOYCE Dist-JOYCE 1975

True Blue C 30 MIN
16MM FILM - 3/4 IN VIDEO
Illustrates why children put so much into play. Tells what play means to them and what they learn from it. Shows what parents can do to encourage and support their children's play and how they too can benefit from this aspect of growth.
From The Footsteps Series.
LC NO. 79-707637
Prod-USOE Dist-USNAC 1978

True Cross Fire C 48 MIN
3/4 OR 1/2 INCH VIDEO CASSETTE
Presents a parody of docu-dramas that examines memory and information.
Prod-KITCHN Dist-KITCHN

True Glory B 85 MIN
16MM FILM, 3/4 OR 1/2 IN VIDEO
Depicts the World War II campaign in Europe from D-day to V-E day. Directed by Garson Kanin and Carol Reed. Issued in 1945 as a motion picture.
LC NO. 79-706287
Prod-JAFPC Dist-USNAC 1979

True Heart Susie B 87 MIN
16MM FILM SILENT
Tells how a plain girl sacrifices everything to send her love to college and how he pays her back by falling for a wicked city woman. Stars Lillian Gish. Directed by D W Griffith.
Prod-UNKNWN Dist-REELIM 1919

True Heart Susie B 87 MIN
1/2 IN VIDEO CASSETTE (BETA)
Shows how a country girl sacrifices her cow to send her true love to college, only to have him repay her kindness by falling in love with a wicked city woman. Stars Lillian Gish. Directed by D W Griffith.
Prod-GFITH Dist-VIDIM 1919

True Standard, A C 12 MIN
16MM FILM OPTICAL SOUND A
Shows how weights and measures are maintained at the international, national and state levels. Includes illustrations of careful testing procedures.
LC NO. FIE55-51
Prod-USNBOS Dist-USNBOS 1954

True Story About A Not-So-Famous Person, A C 57 MIN
16MM FILM OPTICAL SOUND A
Depicts the frustrations of an artist trying to market himself during the McCarthy Era of the 1950s. Illustrates the repercussions of the artist's situation through a dream set in the 1800s.
LC NO. 80-701528
Prod-WARNKE Dist-WARNKE 1980

True Values C 10 MIN
16MM FILM, 3/4 OR 1/2 IN VIDEO P-I
Helps children to look beyond the immediate situation, to understand the responsibility inherent in mutual trust. Raises the question of true values, faced with the opportunity to exploit the moment, to cheat a parent or a friend.
Prod-SF Dist-SF 1970

True You Attitude C 30 MIN
3/4 OR 1/2 INCH VIDEO CASSETTE
Looks at how to get the reader of a business letter to see the writer's viewpoint. Discusses what is real courtesy.
From The Better Business Letters Series. Lesson 5
Prod-TELSTR Dist-TELSTR

True-You Attitude C 30 MIN
3/4 OR 1/2 INCH VIDEO CASSETTE
See series title for descriptive statement.
From The Better Business Letters Series.
Prod-TELSTR Dist-DELTAK

Truing Balance Wheels B 14 MIN
16MM FILM OPTICAL SOUND
Shows how to recognize and correct a balance wheel which does not run true, including the use of calipers, bending the wheel, using a wrench and cleaning the balance wheel.
From The Light Mechanics Series.
Prod-USVA Dist-USVA 1949

Truly American—A Series
I
Offers biographical portraits of famous Americans.
Prod-WVIZTV Dist-GPITVL 1979

Albert Einstein	20 MIN
Amelia Earhart	20 MIN
Carl Sandburg	20 MIN
Dr Elizabeth And Teacher Mary	20 MIN
Dr Martin Luther King, Jr	20 MIN
Eleanor Roosevelt	20 MIN
Everyday Hero	20 MIN
General And Honest Abe, The	20 MIN
Girl In The Checkered Coat, The	20 MIN
Hannibal Boy	20 MIN
Harry Truman	20 MIN
Helen Keller	20 MIN
Hero Of San Juan Hill, The	20 MIN
I-Tan-Chan	20 MIN
Jackie Robinson	20 MIN
Jemmy And Dolley	20 MIN
Jesse Owens	20 MIN
Jim Thorpe	20 MIN
Jonas Salk	20 MIN
Langston Hughes	20 MIN
Louis Armstrong	20 MIN
Marian Anderson	20 MIN
Pioneer Of Labor	20 MIN
Ragtime King	20 MIN
Saga Of Monticello And Old Hickory, The	20 MIN
Slave Who Wouldn't Give Up, The	20 MIN
Susan And Mrs Stanton	20 MIN
Truth And Moses, The	20 MIN
Two Benjamins, The	20 MIN
Walt Disney	20 MIN
Whitney Young	20 MIN
Will Rogers	20 MIN

Truly Exceptional People–A Series
16MM FILM, 3/4 OR 1/2 IN VIDEO
Looks at several individuals who have overcome handicaps and achieved success.
Prod-WDEMCO Dist-WDEMCO

Carol Johnston	015 MIN
Dan Haley	011 MIN
Tom And Virl Osmond	015 MIN

Truly Exceptional, The - Carol Johnston (French) C 16 MIN
16MM FILM, 3/4 OR 1/2 IN VIDEO I-H
Features the story of Carol Johnston, born with one arm, who became a champion gymnast.
Prod-WDEMCO Dist-WDEMCO 1979

Truly Exceptional, The - Carol Johnston (Greek) C 16 MIN
16MM FILM, 3/4 OR 1/2 IN VIDEO I-H
Features the story of Carol Johnston, born with one arm, who became a champion gymnast.
Prod-WDEMCO Dist-WDEMCO 1979

Truman - A Self Portrait X 21 MIN
16MM FILM, 3/4 OR 1/2 IN VIDEO H A
Portrays the character of Harry S Truman. Presents historic footage and includes material from Truman's memoirs and public statements. Includes such historic events as VJ Day and the post-war era, the first nuclear weapons, the Berlin airlift, the Korean War and the MacArthur recall.
Prod-SMITHS Dist-USNAC 1984

Truman - Years Of Decision C 24 MIN
16MM FILM, 3/4 OR 1/2 IN VIDEO H-C A
States that the presidency of Harry Truman was marked by great events and great decisions. Originally shown on the Canadian television program Portraits Of Power.
From The Leaders Of The 20th Century - Portraits Of Power Series.
Prod-NIELSE Dist-LCOA 1980

Truman And Containment B 15 MIN
16MM FILM, 3/4 OR 1/2 IN VIDEO H-C A
Documents the growing tensions between the United States and the Soviet Union at the end of World War II. Identifies the origins of the Cold War and examines why the United States pursued a policy of containment in the post-war years.
From The American Foreign Policy Series.
Prod-EBEC Dist-EBEC 1981

Truman And The Atomic Bomb B 15 MIN
16MM FILM, 3/4 OR 1/2 IN VIDEO J-H
Discusses President Truman's decision to drop the first atom bomb on Japan.
From The Truman Years Series.
Prod-LCOA Dist-LCOA 1969

Truman And The Cold War B 16 MIN
16MM FILM, 3/4 OR 1/2 IN VIDEO J-H
Discusses Truman's role in aiding European countries whose freedom was imperiled by the Soviet Union.
From The Truman Years Series.
Prod-LCOA Dist-LCOA 1969

Truman And The Korean War B 18 MIN
16MM FILM, 3/4 OR 1/2 IN VIDEO J-H
Discusses the involvement of the United States with Korea, the role of Truman in bringing the issue to the United Nations, his dismissal of Mac Arthur, and his role in ending the fighting.
From The Truman Years Series.
Prod-LCOA Dist-LCOA 1969

Truman And The Uses Of Power B 18 MIN
16MM FILM, 3/4 OR 1/2 IN VIDEO J-H
Presents a survey of the key aspects of the domestic policies of Truman following World War II.
From The Truman Years Series.
Prod-LCOA Dist-LCOA 1969

Truman Capote's Trilogy C 99 MIN
16MM FILM OPTICAL SOUND H-C A
Presents three of Truman Capote's short stories, all of which share a common theme of loneliness. Features Maureen Stapleton, Geraldine Page and Martin Balsam.
Prod-AA Dist-CINEWO 1969

Truman Era, The C 29 MIN
2 INCH VIDEOTAPE
See series title for descriptive statement.
From The Course Of Our Times II Series.
Prod-WGBHTV Dist-PUBTEL

Truman Years–A Series
16MM FILM, 3/4 OR 1/2 IN VIDEO J-C A
Documents the important role President Harry Truman played in the ending of World War II, the execution of the Korean War and the expansion of presidential power.
Prod-LCOA Dist-LCOA

Truman And The Atomic Bomb	015 MIN
Truman And The Cold War	016 MIN
Truman And The Korean War	018 MIN
Truman And The Uses Of Power	018 MIN

Trumpet Music Of The Baroque C 30 MIN
3/4 OR 1/2 INCH VIDEO CASSETTE
Explains instrument construction and performance technique of the trumpet in the Baroque era. Defines and illustrates terms through the performance of works by Torelli, Purcell and other composers of the period. Gives an introduction to Baroque music.
From The Sounds They Make Series.
Prod-OHUTC Dist-OHUTC

Trumpit B 7 MIN
16MM FILM OPTICAL SOUND C A
Presents a dadaistic comedy about frustrated love.
Prod-CFS Dist-CFS 1954

Truncal Vagotomy And Antrectomy For Duodenal Ulcer C 33 MIN
3/4 OR 1/2 INCH VIDEO CASSETTE
See series title for descriptive statement.
From The Gastrointestinal Series.
Prod-SVL Dist-SVL

Truncal Vagotomy And Pyloroplasty For Obstructing Duodenal Ulcer C 31 MIN
3/4 OR 1/2 INCH VIDEO CASSETTE
See series title for descriptive statement.
From The Gastrointestinal Series.
Prod-SVL Dist-SVL

Truncated Cone - Radial Line Method, Openings Not Parallel C 19 MIN
1/2 IN VIDEO CASSETTE BETA/VHS IND
See series title for descriptive statement.
From The Metal Fabrication - Round Tapers Series.
Prod-RMI Dist-RMI

Trust C 2 MIN
16MM FILM OPTICAL SOUND I-H A R
Explores the belief that in increasing the ability to trust, people experience life more fully.
From The Meditation Series.
LC NO. 80-700746
Prod-IKONOG Dist-IKONOG 1975

Trust Brenda C 30 MIN
16MM FILM, 3/4 OR 1/2 IN VIDEO J-H A
Questions whether Brenda should follow her immigrant mother's traditional cultural values or assert her independence to gain her friends' acceptance. Reveals that her mother's accident helps them both realize that they each have needs that must be recognized.
From The Moving Right Along Series.
Prod-WQED Dist-MTI 1983

Trusts And Trust Busters C 25 MIN
16MM FILM, 3/4 OR 1/2 IN VIDEO J-C A
Focuses on the major events which precipitated reform and resulted in government regulations under Roosevelt against the all-powerful trusts.
From The American History Series.
Prod-CRMP Dist-CRMP 1968

Trut B 18 MIN
16MM FILM OPTICAL SOUND
A Swedish language film. Portrays the tyrant of the shore to be the Swedish sea hawk. Shows how it seizes and devours the eggs and chicks of other sea birds while they stand helpless.
Prod-SUC Dist-MOMA 1944

Truth C 60 MIN
3/4 OR 1/2 INCH VIDEO CASSETTE A
Presents Bill Moyers and a panel who discuss the concept of truth with Mortimer J Adler. Explores and weighs the different notions of objective and subjective truth. Examines the idea that a truth is true for all men everywhere and for all time.
From The Six Great Ideas Series.
LC NO. 83-706819
Prod-WNETTV Dist-FI 1982

Truth About Communism, The B 30 MIN
3/4 OR 1/2 INCH VIDEO CASSETTE
Features Ronald Reagan as host and narrator of a documentary about the communist threat to the free world with an introduction by Alexander Kerensky, the first premier of the provisional Russian Government in 1917. Traces the development of the Communist movement from birth, the Lenin years, its struggle for direction, the Stalin years (featuring a response by Trotsky attacking the Stalin purges) and the ascendancy of Nikita Khrushchev.
Prod-IHF Dist-IHF

Truth About George, The C 30 MIN
3/4 OR 1/2 INCH VIDEO CASSETTE C A
Presents an adaptation of the short story The Truth About George by P G Wodehouse.
From The Wodehouse Playhouse Series.
Prod-BBCTV Dist-TIMLIF 1980

Truth And Consequences C 20 MIN
16MM FILM - 3/4 IN VIDEO J
Presents a dialogue between Attorney Thomas Kerr and a group of junior high school students, in order to bring students a better understanding of the legal implications of using or abusing drugs. Covers the penalties for transporting, using and selling drugs, the constitutionality of search and seizure procedures and the adequacy of the juvenile court system.
From The Nobody But Yourself Series.
Prod-WQED Dist-GPITVL

Truth And Moses, The C 20 MIN
3/4 INCH VIDEO CASSETTE I
Describes the lives of Sojourner Truth and Harriet Tubman.
From The Truly American Series.
Prod-WVIZTV Dist-GPITVL 1979

Truth In Lending Simplification C
3/4 OR 1/2 INCH VIDEO CASSETTE PRO
Presents lecture by banking expert on truth in lending.
Prod-PROEDS Dist-PROEDS

Truth Of Fiction, The C 18 MIN
16MM FILM, 3/4 OR 1/2 IN VIDEO J-H
Presents an introduction to the study of fiction.
From The Humanities Series.
Prod-MGHT Dist-MGHT Prodn-JOSHUA 1971

Truth Telling In The Health Professions C 38 MIN
3/4 OR 1/2 INCH VIDEO CASSETTE PRO
Presents historical perspective of ethical dilemmas, dramatization of a case, and answers discussed within the framework of the professional code of ethics, the patient's right to know and the law.
Prod-BU Dist-BU

Truth Through Mass Individuation C 10 MIN
3/4 OR 1/2 INCH VIDEO CASSETTE
Explores man's environment.
From The Four Songs Series.
Prod-EAI Dist-EAI

Truth-Seeker - Sophocles C 45 MIN
2 INCH VIDEOTAPE
See series title for descriptive statement.
From The Humanities Series. Unit II - The World Of Myth And Legend
Prod-WTTWTV Dist-GPITVL

Truth, Justice And The American Way B 4 MIN
16MM FILM OPTICAL SOUND
A comedy in which, during a cops and robbers chase, an odd assortment of characters are revealed to be other than what they had first appeared to be. Superman to the rescue. (A USC cinema student workshop production.)
LC NO. 75-703246
Prod-USC Dist-USC 1963

Try A Little Tenderness C 60 MIN
3/4 OR 1/2 INCH VIDEO CASSETTE H-C A
Points out that common symptoms can have many possible causes. Traces the long methodical and often humorous route which leads to a final diagnosis. Based on the book The Body In Question by Jonathan Miller. Narrated by Jonathan Miller.
From The Body In Question Series. Program 2
LC NO. 81-706942
Prod-BBCTV Dist-FI 1979

Try For Touch B 18 MIN
16MM FILM OPTICAL SOUND
Analyzes the nature of violence as seen in a group of sunday rugby players in Central Park. Interweaves the players, their audience and their reactions to and comments on 'BODY CONTACT' and 'VIOLENCE' in a view of people's reaction to blood, hurt and aggression.
Prod-UPENN Dist-UPENN 1970

Try It, They'll Like It C 28 MIN
16MM FILM OPTICAL SOUND
Explains ways that parents can motivate their children. Stresses positive reinforcement of teachers' efforts.
From The You Can Do It - If Series.
LC NO. 81-700093
Prod-VANDER Dist-VANDER

Try It, You'll Like It C 29 MIN
3/4 OR 1/2 INCH VIDEO CASSETTE P-I
Tells the story of a ten-year-old Chinese American boy who learns ways to move between traditional and contemporary lifestyles.
From The Bean Sprouts Series.
Prod-CTPROJ Dist-GPITVL

Try It, You'll Like It C 30 MIN
3/4 OR 1/2 INCH VIDEO CASSETTE
See series title for descriptive statement.
From The Bean Sprouts Series.
Prod-CTPROJ Dist-MDCPB

Try Out C 15 MIN
16MM FILM, 3/4 OR 1/2 IN VIDEO I-J
Involves students in a variety of career-related activities, motivating them to consider how their own experiences can guide them in career choices.
From The Whatcha Gonna Do Series.
Prod-NVETA Dist-EBEC 1974

Try To See It My Way C 27 MIN
3/4 OR 1/2 INCH VIDEO CASSETTE
Shows what has been going wrong in the administrative routines in an office partnership.
From The Secretary And Management Relationship Series. No 1
Prod-VIDART Dist-VISUCP

Trying Again C 19 MIN
16MM FILM, 3/4 OR 1/2 IN VIDEO K-P S
Presents Mr Rogers talking to a man with a hip defect and uses puppets to explain that often people have to try and try again to do certain difficult things. Encourages people to do as much as they can by themselves, then ask for help.
From The I Am, I Can, I Will, Level II Series.
LC NO. 80-706550
Prod-FAMCOM Dist-HUBDSC 1979

Trying On Shoes And Boots To Get Ready For A Picnic C 8 MIN
16MM FILM OPTICAL SOUND K-P
Follows Crystal and Alistair as they try on many different styles of shoes and boots in preparation for a picnic with flutter and fancy.
From The Crystal Tipps And Alistair Series.
LC NO. 73-700456
Prod-BBCTV Dist-VEDO 1972

Trying Times (Making Decisions) C 15 MIN
16MM FILM, 3/4 OR 1/2 IN VIDEO J
Suggests ways of making self-enhancing decisions in the face of peer pressure. Discusses ways of increasing awareness of personal values and beliefs.
From The Self Incorporated Series.
LC NO. 75-703955
Prod-AITV Dist-AITECH Prodn-NVETA 1975

Trying Times - Crisis In Fertility C 33 MIN
16MM FILM, 3/4 OR 1/2 IN VIDEO
Relieves the sense of isolation felt by infertile couples and demonstrates the importance of empathetic care by professionals from the time of initial recognition of a problem through workup and treatment and consideration of alternatives, including adoption and donor insemination.
Prod-FANPRO Dist-FANPRO

Tryout Performances, Pt 1 B 29 MIN
16MM FILM OPTICAL SOUND IND
See series title for descriptive statement.
From The Job Instructor Training Series.
LC NO. 77-703324
Prod-EDSD Dist-EDSD

Tryout Performances, Pt 2 B 29 MIN
16MM FILM OPTICAL SOUND IND
See series title for descriptive statement.
From The Job Instructor Training Series.
LC NO. 77-703324
Prod-EDSD Dist-EDSD

TSCA 8C Recording/Reporting Requirements C 18 MIN
3/4 OR 1/2 INCH VIDEO CASSETTE A
Discusses requirements for the chemical industry in the reporting and retention of allegations of health effects and damage to the environment by a specific chemical.
Prod-USEPA Dist-USNAC 1983

Tsetse - The Fly That Would Be King C 28 MIN
16MM FILM OPTICAL SOUND
Looks at the impact of the tsetse fly on Africa and discusses some of the scientific research being done to alleviate this problem. Shows how the United States supports research that will benefit developing countries.
LC NO. 80-700944
Prod-USAID Dist-USNAC Prodn-COMCOR 1979

Tsetse - The Fly That Would Be King C 20 MIN
3/4 INCH VIDEO CASSETTE
Looks at the impact of the tsetse fly in Africa and examines some of the scientific research directed at eradicating this scourge. Discusses American support of research that will benefit developing countries. Issued in 1979 as a motion picture.
LC NO. 80-707249
Prod-USAID Dist-USNAC 1980

Tsetse Trap, The C 59 MIN
16MM FILM, 3/4 OR 1/2 IN VIDEO H-C A
Discusses the problem of the tsetse fly, which causes bovine sleeping sickness and destroys potential food supplies for millions of people. Points out that despite 30 years of effort aimed at controlling the insect, a 1,000-mile-wide belt of devastated lands across 35 African countries proves that no solution has been found.
From The Nova Series.
LC NO. 79-708142
Prod-WGBHTV Dist-TIMLIF 1978

Tsunami C 28 MIN
16MM FILM OPTICAL SOUND
Documents the phenomenon and potential dangers of seismic sea waves, frequently called 'TIDAL WAVES.' Explains preventive measures taken at the municipal level during a Tsunami emergency.
Prod-USNOAA Dist-USNOAA

TT-47UG Teletypewriter - General Principles And Operation B 16 MIN
16MM FILM OPTICAL SOUND
Explains how teletypewriters are used in the navy's communications system and demonstrates for the operator the basic principles of operation, use of the various function keys and correct procedures for setting up messages and securing the machine.
LC NO. FIE54-285
Prod-USN Dist-USNAC 1953

TT-47UG Teletypewriter - Installation And Performance Tests B 14 MIN
16MM FILM OPTICAL SOUND
Demonstrates the step-by-step procedure for unpacking, installation and assembly of the TT-47ug teletypewriter.
LC NO. FIE54-286
Prod-USN Dist-USNAC 1953

TT-47UG Teletypewriter - Preventive Maintenance B 6 MIN
16MM FILM OPTICAL SOUND
Explains the importance of frequent checks and stresses the preventive maintenance technique for the TT-47ug teletypwriter. Shows cleaning, oiling and minor adjusting of the machine.
LC NO. FIE54-287
Prod-USN Dist-USNAC 1953

TTL/ECL Logic Circuits C
3/4 OR 1/2 INCH VIDEO CASSETTE
See series title for descriptive statement.
From The Digital Techniques Video Training Course Series.
Prod-VTRI Dist-VTRI

TTL, ECL Logic Circuits C
3/4 OR 1/2 INCH VIDEO CASSETTE
See series title for descriptive statement.
From The Digital Techniques Series.
Prod-HTHZEN Dist-HTHZEN

TTY/Telephone C 30 MIN
3/4 OR 1/2 INCH VIDEO CASSETTE H-C A
Presents Lawrence Solow and Sharon Neumann Solow introducing American Sign Language used by the hearing-impaired. Emphasizes signs having to to do with TTY and the telephone.
From The Say It With Sign Series. Part 27
Prod-KNBCTV Dist-FI 1982

Tu Es Dans La Maison C 10 MIN
3/4 OR 1/2 INCH VIDEO CASSETTE
Focuses on home life and prepositions.
From The Salut - French Language Lessons Series.
Prod-BCNFL Dist-BCNFL 1984

Tuareg C 46 MIN
16MM FILM, 3/4 OR 1/2 IN VIDEO A
Documents the life of the Tauregs, a proud, nomadic people of Niger. Shows how a devastating drought has forced them to live in refugee camps, engage in manual labor, and accept aid from Catholic missionaries.
From The World Around Us Series.
LC NO. 79-708095
Prod-BBCTV Dist-ICARUS 1979

Tubal Ligation C
3/4 OR 1/2 INCH VIDEO CASSETTE
Describes the various permanent surgical procedures of terminating fertility. Depicts various techniques.
Prod-MIFE Dist-MIFE

Tubal Ligation C 58 MIN
3/4 OR 1/2 INCH VIDEO CASSETTE
Describes how tubal ligation prevents pregnancy.
LC NO. 78-730127
Prod-TRAINX Dist-TRAINX

Tubal Ligation (French) C
3/4 OR 1/2 INCH VIDEO CASSETTE
Describes the various permanent surgical procedures of terminating fertility. Depicts various techniques.
Prod-MIFE Dist-MIFE

Tubal Ligation (Spanish) C
3/4 OR 1/2 INCH VIDEO CASSETTE
Describes the various permanent surgical procedures of terminating fertility. Depicts various techniques.
Prod-MIFE Dist-MIFE

Tubal Ligation (Spanish) C 5 MIN
3/4 OR 1/2 INCH VIDEO CASSETTE
Describes how tubal ligation prevents pregnancy.
LC NO. 78-730127
Prod-TRAINX Dist-TRAINX

Tubal Ligation (2nd Ed) C 9 MIN
3/4 OR 1/2 INCH VIDEO CASSETTE
Presents the physiology of tubal ligation and explains how it prevents pregnancy.
Prod-MEDFAC Dist-MEDFAC 1975

Tubby Bunny C 12 MIN
16MM FILM, 3/4 OR 1/2 IN VIDEO P
Introduces Tubby, a thoughtless, greedy bunny who escapes from the rabbit hutch into a world of danger. Presents two alternatives regarding his fate.
From The Tommy, Tubby, Tuffy Series.
Prod-LUF Dist-LUF 1979

Tubby The Tuba C 9 MIN
16MM FILM OPTICAL SOUND P-J
Presents a cinematic adaptation of the children's story about a tuba who longs to play his own melody in the symphony orchestra.
Prod-PALG Dist-CFS

Tube And Eye, The X 30 MIN
3/4 OR 1/2 INCH VIDEO CASSETTE
Psychopharmacologist Peter Crown and videographer Bill Etra research the unnatural demands of perceptions which TV places on the videographer and viewer. Ends with a demonstration of how video can visualize the power of emotion.
Prod-EAI Dist-EAI

Tube And Shape Bending B 14 MIN
16MM FILM OPTICAL SOUND
Explains hand bending, bending by power machines, cold and hot bending of aluminum.
From The How To Form Aluminum Series.
LC NO. FIE52-635
Prod-USDIBM Dist-USDIBM 1944

Tube Bending By Hand B 15 MIN
16MM FILM OPTICAL SOUND
Explains why tubes must be bent for installation in airplanes. Demonstrates how to set up the tube bending machine for the job and how the various parts of the machine function.
LC NO. FIE52-20
Prod-USOE Dist-USNAC 1943

Tube Repair C 60 MIN
3/4 OR 1/2 INCH VIDEO CASSETTE IND
See series title for descriptive statement.
From The Mechanical Equipment Maintenance, Module 10 - Boiler And Boiler Equipment Series.
Prod-LEIKID Dist-LEIKID

Tube Tester Operation B 9 MIN
16MM FILM - 3/4 IN VIDEO
Shows how to use testers to check cathode emission and dynamic mutual conductance of tubes. Issued in 1944 as a motion picture.
From The Radio Technician Training Series.
LC NO. 78-706305
Prod-USN Dist-USNAC Prodn-HOLMES 1978

Tuberculin Skin Testing C 14 MIN
16MM FILM OPTICAL SOUND PRO
Provides a general description of tuberculosis, the time span in which it can occur and the organs of the body it may affect if left untreated.
LC NO. 77-700079
Prod-USN Dist-USNAC 1976

Tuberculosis C 10 MIN
16MM FILM, 3/4 OR 1/2 IN VIDEO
Explains the cause, symptoms and transmission of tuberculosis, and emphasizes that the disease is controllable and curable. Issued in 1946 as a motion picture.
From The Health For The Americas Series.
LC NO. 80-707387
Prod-USOIAA Dist-USNAC Prodn-DISNEY 1980

Tuberculosis - The Disease And Its Management C
3/4 OR 1/2 INCH VIDEO CASSETTE
Explains the cause and development of tuberculosis, the mode of transmission, the precautions necessary to prevent spread and the essential role of medication in treating the disease.
Prod-MIFE Dist-MIFE

Tuberculosis - The Disease And Its Management (Spanish) C
3/4 OR 1/2 INCH VIDEO CASSETTE
Explains the cause and development of tuberculosis, the mode of transmission, the precautions necessary to prevent spread and the essential role of medication in treating the disease.
Prod-MIFE Dist-MIFE

Tuberculosis - The Disease And Its Management (Arabic) C
3/4 OR 1/2 INCH VIDEO CASSETTE
Explains the cause and development of tuberculosis, the mode of transmission, the precautions necessary to prevent spread and essential role of medication in treating the disease.
Prod-MIFE Dist-MIFE

Tuberculosis And The Primary Care Physician C 17 MIN
3/4 OR 1/2 INCH VIDEO CASSETTE PRO
Reviews the pathogenesis of tuberculosis and provides guidelines to the primary care physician for prevention, treatment and management of the tuberculosis patient. Emphasizes particularly the circumstances under which the prevention or treatment of tuberculosis is indicated and the use of isoniazid in managing the tuberculosis patient.
Prod-UMICHM Dist-UMICHM 1980

Tuberculosis Laboratory Procedures - Fluorescent Staining And Ziehl-Neelsen Staining C 8 MIN
3/4 INCH VIDEO CASSETTE
Demonstrates two methods of detecting the presence of acid-fact organisms in sputum. Issued in 1965 as a motion picture.
LC NO. 78-706277
Prod-USPHS Dist-USNAC 1978

Tubex (Superscript R) Closed System Injections C 14 MIN
16MM FILM OPTICAL SOUND PRO
An in-service training film for nurses which demonstrates the step-by-step procedures for loading, administering and disposing of tubex sterile cartridgeinjections.
LC NO. 77-715453
Prod-WYETH Dist-WYLAB 1971

Tubing And Piping C 60 MIN
3/4 OR 1/2 INCH VIDEO CASSETTE IND
See series title for descriptive statement.
From The Mechanical Equipment Maintenance, Module 7 - Piping Series.
Prod-LEIKID Dist-LEIKID

Tubing Installations And Brazing C 60 MIN
3/4 OR 1/2 INCH VIDEO CASSETTE IND
See series title for descriptive statement.
From The Instrumentation Basics - Instrumentation Electrical And Mechanical Connections Series. Tape 4
Prod-ISA Dist-ISA

Tuck Everlasting C 15 MIN
3/4 OR 1/2 INCH VIDEO CASSETTE I

Presents passages from Natalie Babbitt's story about a spring that bestows eternal life.
From The Storybound Series.
Prod-CTI Dist-CTI

Tudors, The C 60 MIN
16MM FILM, 3/4 OR 1/2 IN VIDEO H-C A
Explores St James Palace, Hampton Court, and King's College Chapel at Cambridge, looking at the paintings and collections of each.
From The Royal Heritage Series.
Prod-BBCTV Dist-FI 1977

Tuesday Group, The C 14 MIN
16MM FILM, 3/4 OR 1/2 IN VIDEO PRO
Documents a group session of severely emotionally and physically deteriorated elderly persons. Illustrates therapeutic group work techniques.
Prod-FEIL Dist-FEIL

Tuesday, May 19th, 1981 C 12 MIN
16MM FILM OPTICAL SOUND
Describes five tragic accidents that may occur if safety regulations relating to chemical transportation are not observed.
LC NO. 78-700319
Prod-UCC Dist-UCC Prodn-GLYNG 1977

Tuffy Puppy C 9 MIN
16MM FILM, 3/4 OR 1/2 IN VIDEO P
Portrays what happens when Tuffy, a happy-go-lucky puppy, gets lost and cannot remember the instructions his mother gave him. Presents two alternatives regarding his fate.
From The Tommy, Tubby, Tuffy Series.
Prod-LUF Dist-LUF 1979

Tuffy, The Sea Teacher C 28 MIN
16MM FILM OPTICAL SOUND
Presents a study of dolphins and other sea animals. Shows the methods of catching, training and testing dolphins and presents the results of some of these tests.
LC NO. 74-706598
Prod-USN Dist-USNAC 1972

Tuffy, The Turtle C 11 MIN
16MM FILM, 3/4 OR 1/2 IN VIDEO P
Animals of the pond teased Tuffy, the turtle, because his shell made him slow and clumsy. A snail helps Tuffy realize that a hard shell can be very useful.
Prod-CORF Dist-CORF 1965

Tuft Of Flowers C 7 MIN
16MM FILM OPTICAL SOUND P-C
A cinepoem visually interpreting the poem 'TUFT OF FLOWERS' by Robert Frost.
Prod-CFS Dist-CFS

Tug Of War C 9 MIN
16MM FILM OPTICAL SOUND H-C A
Portrays South American Yanomamo Indian women and children playing tug-of-war.
From The Yanomamo Series.
Prod-DOCEDR Dist-DOCEDR 1975

Tug-Of War, Yanamamo C 9 MIN
3/4 INCH VIDEO CASSETTE
Shows the playful side of Yanamamo life during the rainy season when women and children play tug-of-war. Filmed by Timothy Asch and Napoleon Chagnon.
Prod-DOCEDR Dist-DOCEDR

Tug-Of-War, Bushmen C 6 MIN
3/4 INCH VIDEO CASSETTE
Shows boys of bushmen, Namibia, wrestling over a length of rubber hose.
From The San (Bushmen) Series.
Prod-DOCEDR Dist-DOCEDR Prodn-MRSHL

Tugboat Captain C 14 MIN
16MM FILM, 3/4 OR 1/2 IN VIDEO I-H
Presents the work of tugboats in New York Harbor. Studies the life of the captain of one of these boats.
From The World Of Work Series.
Prod-EBEC Dist-EBEC 1971

Tugboat Christina B 20 MIN
16MM FILM OPTICAL SOUND
Shows a day on the river in the life of a river tugboat, depicting the tugboat getting underway in the morning, working on the Delaware River, and returning to its berth in the evening. Portrays how each member of the crew contributes to the operation of the tugboat.
Prod-UPENN Dist-UPENN 1962

Tugboat Mickey C 8 MIN
16MM FILM, 3/4 OR 1/2 IN VIDEO
Depicts what happens when tugboat captain Mickey Mouse mistakes a radio drama episode for an actual sinking ship.
From The Gang's All Here Series.
Prod-DISNEY Dist-WDEMCO

Tukiki And His Search For A Merry Christmas C 25 MIN
16MM FILM, 3/4 OR 1/2 IN VIDEO K-I
Introduces Tukiki, an Eskimo boy who is bewildered by the meaning of a colorful Christmas card blown in on the wind. Shows him getting no response from his busy friends and finally turning to the Northwind who blows him around the world where he is introduced to many Christmas customs.
Prod-CORF Dist-CORF 1980

Tuktu And His Animal Friends C 14 MIN
16MM FILM, 3/4 OR 1/2 IN VIDEO K-J
Tells a story about Tuktu, a Netsilik Eskimo boy. Shows some of the smaller animals that live in the Arctic, including lemmings, weasels, ducks and kittiwakes. Describes some of the flowers of the Arctic.
From The Stories Of Tuktu - A Children's Adventure Series.
Prod-NFBC Dist-FI 1969

Tuktu And His Eskimo Dogs C 14 MIN
16MM FILM, 3/4 OR 1/2 IN VIDEO K-J
Tells a story about Tuktu, a Netsilik Eskimo boy. Shows how dogs are used by the Eskimo in winter and summer as pack animals and for hunting purposes.
From The Stories Of Tuktu - A Children's Adventure Series.
Prod-NFBC Dist-FI 1969

Tuktu And His Nice New Clothes C 14 MIN
16MM FILM, 3/4 OR 1/2 IN VIDEO K-J
Tells a story about Tuktu, a Netsilik Eskimo boy. Shows the cutting, stitching, and use of Arctic clothing, and points out the importance of sewing in an Eskimo household.
From The Stories Of Tuktu - A Children's Adventure Series.
Prod-NFBC Dist-FI 1969

Tuktu And The Big Kayak C 14 MIN
16MM FILM, 3/4 OR 1/2 IN VIDEO K-J
Tells a story about Tuktu, a Netsilik Eskimo boy. Shows the contruction of a kayak.
From The Stories Of Tuktu - A Children's Adventure Series.
Prod-NFBC Dist-FI 1969

Tuktu And The Big Seal C 14 MIN
16MM FILM, 3/4 OR 1/2 IN VIDEO K-J
Tells a story about Tuktu, a Netsilik Eskimo boy. Show how eskimos carry out a seal hunt.
From The Stories Of Tuktu - A Children's Adventure Series.
Prod-NFBC Dist-FI 1969

Tuktu And The Caribou Hunt C 14 MIN
16MM FILM, 3/4 OR 1/2 IN VIDEO K-J
Tells a story about Tuktu, a Netsilik Eskimo boy. Shows Eskimos hunting caribou from their kayaks when the animals cross the small lakes to reach new grazing ground.
From The Stories Of Tuktu - A Children's Adventure Series.
Prod-NFBC Dist-FI 1969

Tuktu And The Clever Hands C 14 MIN
16MM FILM, 3/4 OR 1/2 IN VIDEO K-J
Tells a story about Tuktu, a Netsilik Eskimo boy. Shows some of the things made by the Eskimos, and describes the use the Eskimos make of the few materials that are available in the harsh environment.
From The Stories Of Tuktu - A Children's Adventure Series.
Prod-NFBC Dist-FI 1969

Tuktu And The Indoor Games C 14 MIN
16MM FILM, 3/4 OR 1/2 IN VIDEO K-J
Tells a story about Tuktu, a Netsilik Eskimo boy. Describes some of the indoor games played by Eskimos.
From The Stories Of Tuktu - A Children's Adventure Series.
Prod-NFBC Dist-FI 1969

Tuktu And The Magic Bow C 14 MIN
16MM FILM, 3/4 OR 1/2 IN VIDEO K-J
Tells a story about Tuktu, a Netsilik Eskimo boy. Shows a bow being made, and Eskimos practicing their shooting skill, using snow men and snow bears as targets.
From The Stories Of Tuktu - A Children's Adventure Series.
Prod-NFBC Dist-FI 1969

Tuktu And The Magic Spear C 14 MIN
16MM FILM, 3/4 OR 1/2 IN VIDEO K-J
Tells a story about Tuktu, a Netsilik Eskimo boy. Shows how the Eskimos fish through the ice during the winter and how they fish in the summer.
From The Stories Of Tuktu - A Children's Adventure Series.
Prod-NFBC Dist-FI 1969

Tuktu And The Snow Palace C 14 MIN
16MM FILM, 3/4 OR 1/2 IN VIDEO K-J
Tells a story about Tuktu, a Netsilik Eskimo boy. Shows Eskimos traveling to a new hunting ground to build igloos, including a giant igloo where feasting, dancing and games are held.
From The Stories Of Tuktu - A Children's Adventure Series.
Prod-NFBC Dist-FI 1969

Tuktu And The Ten Thousand Fishes C 14 MIN
16MM FILM, 3/4 OR 1/2 IN VIDEO K-J
Tells a story about Tuktu, a Netsilik Eskimo boy. Shows eskimos spear fishing and making fire with the Eskimo fire drill.
From The Stories Of Tuktu - A Children's Adventure Series.
Prod-NFBC Dist-FI 1969

Tuktu And The Trials Of Strength C 14 MIN
16MM FILM, 3/4 OR 1/2 IN VIDEO K-J
Tells a story about Tuktu, a Netsilik Eskimo boy. Shows Eskimo hunters demonstrating and testing their strength in boxing, tug-of-war, and other strenuous activities. Includes scenes of the drum dance.
From The Stories Of Tuktu - A Children's Adventure Series.
Prod-NFBC Dist-FI 1969

Tula To Tulum C 27 MIN
16MM FILM OPTICAL SOUND
Features an interpretation of the archaeology of Mexico in the form of a trip.
Prod-NYU Dist-NYU

Tule C 34 MIN
3/4 OR 1/2 INCH VIDEO CASSETTE
Records the vanishing life style of the Cuna Indians on the islands of Ustupu off the Atlantic coast of Panama, makers of colorful molas.
Prod-EAI Dist-EAI

Tule Technology - Northern Paiute Uses Of Marsh Resources In Western Nevada C 42 MIN
3/4 OR 1/2 INCH VIDEO CASSETTE
Shows an Indian woman and members of her family constructing a duck egg bag, cattail house, duck decoy and tule boat from marsh resources in Western Nevada. Includes reminiscences of many aspects of traditional Paiute life that have disappeared. Narrated by the Indian woman's son and granddaughter.
Prod-PSU Dist-SIFP

Tulsa, Building A World Around You C 17 MIN
16MM FILM OPTICAL SOUND
Creates a montage of local scenery and events reflecting an atmosphere unique to Tulsa, Oklahoma.
LC NO. 79-701063
Prod-UTICA Dist-TULSAS Prodn-TULSAS 1979

Tumacacori C 14 MIN
16MM FILM - 3/4 IN VIDEO
Emphasizes that English was a foreign language in the American Southwest during the era of Spanish dominance. Offers a picture of life at a typical Spanish mission church.
LC NO. 79-706167
Prod-USNPS Dist-USNAC Prodn-KAETTV 1979

Tumacacori (Spanish) C 14 MIN
16MM FILM - 3/4 IN VIDEO
Emphasizes that English was a foreign language in the American Southwest during the era of Spanish dominance. Offers a picture of life at a typical Spanish mission church.
LC NO. 79-706167
Prod-USNPS Dist-USNAC Prodn-KAETTV 1979

Tumbles, Mumbles And Bumbles C 13 MIN
16MM FILM, 3/4 OR 1/2 IN VIDEO
Presents sports action which shows how everyone can learn from mistakes.
Prod-PFP Dist-PFP 1983

Tumbleweed C 14 MIN
16MM FILM, 3/4 OR 1/2 IN VIDEO
Follows a tumbleweed through the many encounters it has on the plains and in the cities of the Southwest.
Prod-ACI Dist-AIMS 1972

Tumbleweeds B 89 MIN
16MM FILM SILENT
Tells the story of the newly-opened Cherokee Strip of the Old West. Portrays Don Carver, who is mistaken for a sooner who supposedly sneaks over the boundary line to make a claim sooner than the official starting time set by the government. Shows what happens when he is imprisoned and later escapes. Stars William S Hart and Lucien Littlefield. Directed by King Baggott.
Prod-UNKNWN Dist-KILLIS 1925

Tumbling - Elementary For Boys And Girls C 13 MIN
16MM FILM, 3/4 OR 1/2 IN VIDEO P-I
Shows how tumbling can help a student develop body image, spatial awareness and symmetrical use of both sides of the body. Presents basic tumbling stunts in sequential manner for a beginning tumbling class.
Prod-AIMS Dist-AIMS 1973

Tumbling - Elementary For Boys And Girls (Spanish) C 13 MIN
16MM FILM, 3/4 OR 1/2 IN VIDEO P-I
Shows how tumbling can help a student develop body image, spatial awareness and symmetrical use of both sides of the body. Presents basic stumbling stunts in sequential manner for a beginning tumbling class.
Prod-AIMS Dist-AIMS 1973

Tumbling - Intermediate For Boys And Girls C 17 MIN
16MM FILM, 3/4 OR 1/2 IN VIDEO P-I
Explains that in tumbling, the small and large muscles of the body are used to build flexibility, agility and endurance. Shows how bilateral development, coordination, self-confidence and attention span can be improved through continued participation in a tumbling program. Presents stunts starting with the forward roll and building toward the handspring.
Prod-AIMS Dist-AIMS 1973

Tumbling - Intermediate For Boys And Girls (Spanish) C 17 MIN
16MM FILM, 3/4 OR 1/2 IN VIDEO P-I
Explains that in tumbling, the small and large muscles of the body are used to build flexibility, agility and endurance. Shows how bilateral development, coordination, self-confidence and attention span can be improved through continued participation in a tumbling program. Presents stunts starting with the forward roll and building toward the handspring.
Prod-AIMS Dist-AIMS 1973

Tumbling - Primary Skills C 9 MIN
16MM FILM, 3/4 OR 1/2 IN VIDEO P
Illustrates good form in the performance of basic tumbling skills which can be learned by the elementary student. Demonstrates the egg sit, egg roll, forward roll, backward roll, frog head stand and head stand. Emphasizes correct position of head, hands and feet and stresses safety procedures.
Prod-PART Dist-PHENIX 1970

Tumbling - The Basic Skills C 10 MIN
16MM FILM, 3/4 OR 1/2 IN VIDEO J-H
Depicts the total body coordination effort utilized in performing tumbling stunts. Shows six young gymnasts executing shoulder, forward and backward rolls, cartwheels and head, neck, fronthand and backhand springs.
Prod-OF Dist-AIMS 1974

Tumbling - The Forward Roll C 11 MIN
16MM FILM OPTICAL SOUND P-J
Explains the value of tumbling as a physical exercise activity. Shows how to perform the forward roll and demonstrates class activities using it.
LC NO. FIA67-55
Prod-MMP Dist-MMP 1966

Tumbling And Floor Exercise C 12 MIN
16MM FILM, 3/4 OR 1/2 IN VIDEO I-J
Demonstrates proper techniques in log rolls, shoulder rolls, forward and backward rolls, cartwheels, roundoffs, leg circles, head stands and other tumbling and floor exercises.
Prod-AIMS Dist-AIMS 1970

Tumbling And Floor Exercise (Arabic) C 12 MIN
16MM FILM, 3/4 OR 1/2 IN VIDEO I-C
Demonstrates proper techniques in various tumbling and floor exercise skills, from basic to intermediate difficulty.
Prod-ASSOCF Dist-AIMS Prodn-SADLO 1970

Tumbling And Floor Exercise (Spanish) C 12 MIN
16MM FILM, 3/4 OR 1/2 IN VIDEO I-C
Demonstrates proper techniques in various tumbling and floor exercise skills, from basic to intermediate difficulty.
Prod-ASSOCF Dist-AIMS Prodn-SADLO 1970

Tumbling For Cheerleaders C 25 MIN
3/4 OR 1/2 INCH VIDEO CASSETTE
See series title for descriptive statement.
From The Video For Cheerleading Series.
Prod-ATHI Dist-ATHI

Tumbling I C 15 MIN
3/4 OR 1/2 INCH VIDEO CASSETTE T
Demonstrates how to explain to primary students the basics of tumbling, including rolls, principles for efficient rolling, balancing and safety, tumbling as part of a sequence, rolling and balancing in a sequence.
From The Leaps And Bounds Series. No. 8
Prod-HSDE Dist-AITECH 1984

Tumbling II C 15 MIN
3/4 OR 1/2 INCH VIDEO CASSETTE T
Demonstrates how to explain to primary students the basics of tumbling, including warming up, rocking, back shoulder roll, backward roll, awareness of alignment, sequential movement of the spine and upside-down orientation.
From The Leaps And Bounds Series. No. 9
Prod-HSDE Dist-AITECH 1984

Tumbling 2 - Progression Of Skills C 11 MIN
16MM FILM OPTICAL SOUND I-H
Presents examples of training of elementary school children in performance of the backward roll, headstand, running handsprings, forward somersaults, backward handsprings, backward somersaults, cartwheels and roundoffs. Discusses how tumbling skills lend themselves to progressive development.
LC NO. 77-702997
Prod-MMP Dist-MMP 1968

Tumors Of The Eye, Current Outlook B 28 MIN
16MM FILM OPTICAL SOUND PRO
Discusses several approaches to the problem of management of tumors of the eye, as presented during a 1969 meeting of the American Radium Society at Philadelphia, Pennsylvania.
From The Cancer Management Series.
Prod-AMCRAD Dist-NMAC 1969

Tumors Of The Head And Neck C 73 MIN
3/4 INCH VIDEO CASSETTE PRO
Presents an anatomical review of the head and neck, outlines methods of examination and describes the various lesions which occur in this area. Discusses asymptomatic neck masses and considers cancer of the larynx.
LC NO. 76-706121
Prod-WARMP Dist-USNAC 1969

Tumors Of The Major Salivary Glands C 16 MIN
16MM FILM OPTICAL SOUND PRO
Illustrates the differential diagnosis and management of tumors of the major salivary glands - parotid, submaxillary and sublingual. Lists the relative incidence of the various neoplastic lesions of these glands.
Prod-AMCS Dist-AMCS 1967

Tun Razak The New Head Of Government B 11 MIN
16MM FILM OPTICAL SOUND
Records the transfer of leadership from Tunku Abdul Rahman to the new Prime Minister, Tun Abdul Razak. Covers the ceremonial swearing-in of Tun Razak and his cabinet.
Prod-FILEM Dist-PMFMUN 1970

Tuna Angling - The Art And Science Of Big Game Fishing C 26 MIN
16MM FILM OPTICAL SOUND
A world record holder fisherman demonstrates baiting and fighting a powerful tuna.
LC NO. FIA68-1575
Prod-CTFL Dist-CTFL 1967

Tune In On Yourself C 30 MIN
2 INCH VIDEOTAPE J
See series title for descriptive statement.
From The Summer Journal, Unit 5 - You Are What Others See In You Series.
Prod-WNINTV Dist-GPITVL

Tune-Up, Pt I C 30 MIN
3/4 OR 1/2 INCH VIDEO CASSETTE
Covers minor tune-ups on the ignition and fuel systems, identifies parts and discusses the need for periodic tune-ups.
From The Keep It Running Series.
Prod-NETCHE Dist-NETCHE 1982

Tune-Up, Pt II C 30 MIN
3/4 OR 1/2 INCH VIDEO CASSETTE
Explains how to use a vacuum gauge and perform spark plug and distributor inspections and service.
From The Keep It Running Series.
Prod-NETCHE Dist-NETCHE 1982

Tune-Up, Pt III C 30 MIN
3/4 OR 1/2 INCH VIDEO CASSETTE
Covers inspection and replacement of high-tension ignition wires and adjustment of points, ignition timing and carburetor.
From The Keep It Running Series.
Prod-NETCHE Dist-NETCHE 1982

Tuned Base Oscillator B 30 MIN
16MM FILM OPTICAL SOUND
Compares the tuned base oscillator circuit and the grid oscillator. Points out how each of the four requirements for oscillation is met in the tuned base oscillator. Explains the checks for oscillation and the symptoms that would occur for each component failure. (Kinescope)
LC NO. 74-705866
Prod-USAF Dist-USNAC

Tuned Centrifugal Pendulum B 24 MIN
3/4 OR 1/2 INCH VIDEO CASSETTE
See series title for descriptive statement.
From The Nonlinear Vibrations Series.
Prod-MIOT Dist-MIOT

Tuned Circuits B 28 MIN
16MM FILM OPTICAL SOUND
Explains the theories behind the electronics of tuned circuits and application of these theories to a practical radio receiver layout and a radio transmitter.
LC NO. FIE55-13
Prod-USA Dist-USNAC 1954

Tuned Plate Oscillator B 19 MIN
16MM FILM, 3/4 OR 1/2 IN VIDEO
Develops and explains the major differences between an RF and an audio oscillator. Shows the purpose of each component in the schematic diagram. Kinescope)
Prod-USAF Dist-USNAC 1965

Tuned-In—A Series
16MM FILM, 3/4 OR 1/2 IN VIDEO J-H
Tells the story of students in a ninth-grade language arts class who are learning about television. Shows how young people can become more alert and selective television viewers.
Prod-WNETTV Dist-FI 1982

Commercials	015 MIN
Critical Reviewing	015 MIN
Editing / Music / Special Effects	015 MIN
Interviewing	015 MIN
Program Types / Stereotyping	015 MIN
Story Elements	015 MIN
Television News	015 MIN
Television Studio	015 MIN
Viewing Habits	015 MIN
Writing Reviews	015 MIN

Tunes Of Language Intonation And Meaning, The C 30 MIN
3/4 OR 1/2 INCH VIDEO CASSETTE C
See series title for descriptive statement.
From The Language And Meaning Series.
Prod-WUSFTV Dist-GPITVL 1983

Tuning C 25 MIN
3/4 OR 1/2 INCH VIDEO CASSETTE J-C A
Explains types and gauge of guitar string and the problems of drum tuning, teaching that drum tuning is important for the authenticity of different styles.
From The Rockschool Series.
Prod-BBCTV Dist-FI

Tunis '77 C 30 MIN
16MM FILM OPTICAL SOUND
Documents the first World Youth Tournament in soccer for the Coca-Cola Cup.
LC NO. 78-700228
Prod-COCA Dist-COCA Prodn-OGHAR 1977

Tunis '77 (French) C 30 MIN
16MM FILM OPTICAL SOUND
Documents the first World Youth Tournament in soccer for the Coca-Cola Cup.
LC NO. 78-700228
Prod-COCA Dist-COCA Prodn-OGHAR 1977

Tunis '77 (German) C 30 MIN
16MM FILM OPTICAL SOUND
Documents the first World Youth Tournament in soccer for the Coca-Cola Cup.
LC NO. 78-700228
Prod-COCA Dist-COCA Prodn-OGHAR 1977

Tunis '77 (Spanish) C 30 MIN
16MM FILM OPTICAL SOUND
Documents the first World Youth Tournament in soccer for the Coca-Cola Cup.
LC NO. 78-700228
Prod-COCA Dist-COCA Prodn-OGHAR 1977

Tunnel Diode Amplifier B 18 MIN
16MM FILM, 3/4 OR 1/2 IN VIDEO
Identifies the tunnel diode as an amplifier when it is operated within the negative resistance portion of its characteristic operating curve.
Prod-USAF Dist-USNAC 1983

Tunnel, The C 25 MIN
16MM FILM, 3/4 OR 1/2 IN VIDEO J-C A
Shows how a young man becomes enmeshed in a maze of conflicting authorities and personalities after he becomes involved in violence in a school.
Prod-LRF Dist-LRF Prodn-DONMAC 1974

Tunnels Under Chicago C 16 MIN
16MM FILM, 3/4 OR 1/2 IN VIDEO
Explains the operations of the Robbins Company in designing, building and operating tunneling machines used in a sewer project in Chicago.
LC NO. 82-706094
Prod-ROBBNS Dist-AMMPCO Prodn-AMMPCO 1981

Tununeremiut - The People Of Tununak C 35 MIN
3/4 INCH VIDEO CASSETTE
Documents a series of episodes in the lives of the people of Tununak, on the southwestern coast of Alaska. Shows them evacuating the village because of a nuclear test at Amchitka, finding their way in bad weather and gathering for traditional story-dancing.
Prod-AKNATH Dist-DOCEDR

Tupamaros (Captioned) C 50 MIN
16MM FILM, 3/4 OR 1/2 IN VIDEO A
Portrays Uruguay's National Liberation Movement, its origins, reasons for the guerilla struggle, and special tactics it employs. Spanish dialog with English subtitles.
Prod-SBC Dist-CNEMAG 1972

Turandot C 120 MIN
3/4 OR 1/2 INCH VIDEO CASSETTE A
Presents a cruel Oriental princess who poses deadly riddles to those who love her, in Giacomo Puccini's opera, Turandot.
Prod-EDDIM Dist-EDDIM

Turbine C 11 MIN
16MM FILM, 3/4 OR 1/2 IN VIDEO P-I
Details that when Boy observes some natural occurrences that dramatize the power of wind and water, he creates devices to indicate wind direction and velocity, then experiments with ways to make waterpower turn the mill wheel he has invented. Demonstrates that water has weight and illustrates the principles of wind and water power.
From The Inventive Child Series.
Prod-POLSKI Dist-EBEC 1983

Turbines, Pt 1 C
3/4 OR 1/2 INCH VIDEO CASSETTE IND
Covers principles, construction, oil system and gland seal system of turbines.
From The Industrial Training, Module 4 - Power Production Series.
Prod-LEIKID Dist-LEIKID

Turbines, Pt 2 C
3/4 OR 1/2 INCH VIDEO CASSETTE IND
Covers several aspects of turbines including back-pressure turbines and control equipment.
From The Industrial Training, Module 4 - Power Production Series.
Prod-LEIKID Dist-LEIKID

Turbines, Pt 3 C
3/4 OR 1/2 INCH VIDEO CASSETTE IND
Discusses the steam system, protection gear, supervisory equipment and turbine operation.
From The Industrial Training, Module 4 - Power Production Series.
Prod-LEIKID Dist-LEIKID

Turboprop / Turboshaft Engines - Introduction C 13 MIN
16MM FILM OPTICAL SOUND
Outlines the theory of operation of turboprop and turboshaft engines with comparison to the turbojet engine. Shows testing and assembly of engine components in manufacture and the maintenance and operation of the engines.
LC NO. FIE60-57
Prod-USN Dist-USNAC 1959

Turbulence C 29 MIN
16MM FILM, 3/4 OR 1/2 IN VIDEO H-C
Illustrates aspects of turbulence, includes the effect of Reynolds number on inception and on turbulent flows increased pressure drop in pipe-flow, efficient mixing, turbulent transport of momentum and scalar properties, Reynolds stress and effects of buoyancy.
From The Fluid Mechanics Films Series.
Prod-NCFMF Dist-EBEC 1968

Turing Machines B
16MM FILM OPTICAL SOUND
Shows how a Turing machine will convert a unary to a ternary representation. Includes an analogy involving three rugby players with special jumpers and numbers on their backs.
Prod-OPENU Dist-OPENU

Turing Machines And Functions B
16MM FILM OPTICAL SOUND
Introduces the technique of arithmetization, which shows how to move just one step in a Turing machine using functions.
Prod-OPENU Dist-OPENU

Turing Machines And Post Systems C
16MM FILM OPTICAL SOUND
Analyzes the logic of structure and computational aspects of language, arriving at the basic ingredients of the post system-alphabet axiom and production. Shows post systems as equivalent to Turing machines.
Prod-OPENU Dist-OPENU

Turkana Conversations Trilogy—A Series
16MM FILM, 3/4 OR 1/2 IN VIDEO
Looks at the lives of the Turkana, seminomadic herders who live in the dry thorn country of northwestern Kenya. Presented in Turkana with English subtitles.
Prod-MCDGAL Dist-UCEMC

Lorang's Way (Turkana)	069 MIN
Wedding Camels, The (Turkana)	108 MIN
Wife Among Wives, A (Turkana)	072 MIN

Turkey C 13 MIN
16MM FILM OPTICAL SOUND
Presents Istanbul, a skyline of spires and minarets and mosques. Features the unusual - a lemonade vendor dispensing refreshment on the spot, samovars brewing tea and Turkish coffee.
From The New Horizons Series.
Prod-TWCF Dist-PANWA

Turkey C 27 MIN
3/4 OR 1/2 INCH VIDEO CASSETTE J-C A
Prod-IFF Dist-IFF

Turkey C 29 MIN
2 INCH VIDEOTAPE
Features home economist Joan Hood presenting a culinary tour of specialty dishes from around the world. Shows the preparation of Turkish dishes ranging from peasant cookery to continental cuisine.
From The International Cookbook Series.
Prod-WMVSTV Dist-PUBTEL

Turkey C 30 MIN
3/4 INCH VIDEO CASSETTE I-J
Shows the life of a family living in a suburb of Istanbul. Focuses on the changing status of women and the emphasis on education and health.
From The Families Of The World Series.
Prod-UNICEF Dist-GPITVL 1974

Turkey - Crossroads Of The Ancient World C 27 MIN
16MM FILM, 3/4 OR 1/2 IN VIDEO I-C A
Explains that ancient Turkey was the meeting point and the battleground for many different cultures, including the Hittites, the Assyrians, the Persians, the Greeks, the Romans, the Turks and the Mongols.
From The People And Places Of Antiquity Series.
Prod-CFDLD Dist-CORF

Turkey - Nation In Transition C 27 MIN
16MM FILM OPTICAL SOUND I-C
Summarizes Turkish history. Surveys modern Turkey from the days of Kemal Ataturk to the present. Describes the progress Turkey has made.
Prod-IFF Dist-IFF 1962

Turkey Shoot, The B 27 MIN
16MM FILM, 3/4 OR 1/2 IN VIDEO J-H
Looks at the conquest and development of the Mariana Islands during World War II.
From The Victory At Sea Series.
Prod-NBCTV Dist-LUF

Turkiye C 16 MIN
16MM FILM, 3/4 OR 1/2 IN VIDEO I-C A
Presents a panorama of historical and modern sights in Turkey, including monuments, classical ruins, castles and temples.
LC NO. 77-703269
Prod-TIO Dist-PFP Prodn-LFILMT 1977

Turmoil In Communist China - The Troubles Of Mao-Tse-Tung B 16 MIN
16MM FILM OPTICAL SOUND J-C A
Tells the story of Mao Tse-Tung and presents the history of China since the founding of the Chinese Communist Party in 1921.
From The Screen News Digest Series. Vol 9, Issue 10
LC NO. 73-700277
Prod-HEARST Dist-HEARST 1967

Turn A Handle, Flick A Switch (2nd Rev Ed) C 14 MIN
16MM FILM, 3/4 OR 1/2 IN VIDEO I-J
Uses animation and a simple experiment to explain where water, gas and electricity come from and how they get to homes. Stresses conservation of water and power.
LC NO. 83-706799
Prod-CF Dist-CF 1983

Turn Left At Charlotte C 21 MIN
16MM FILM OPTICAL SOUND
Features Richard Petty, the most successful race driver in NASCAR Grand National racing history, and his father Lee explaining the philosophy behind the Petty family racing effort. Includes films of Richard's crash at Darlington Raceway.
Prod-GTARC Dist-GTARC

Turn Of The Century C 24 MIN
16MM FILM OPTICAL SOUND
Explores the effects of the massive influx of immigrants at the turn of the century, what we learned from the invasion of Cuba and the feelings and attitudes reflected in American sports, politics and business.
Prod-INTEXT Dist-REAF

Turn Of The Century B 30 MIN
16MM FILM, 3/4 OR 1/2 IN VIDEO J-H
Pictures the European world and way of life which was destroyed when the first world war shook the world and shows the personalities and forces which led up to the war.
From The Twentieth Century Series.
Prod-CBSNEW Dist-MGHT 1960

Turn Of The Century - 20th Century America - 1898-1914 X 24 MIN
16MM FILM OPTICAL SOUND I-C A
Discusses the first automobile and airplane, the new immigration, Einstein's discovery of relativity and other highlights of the turn of the century, which saw America grow from a nation of farmers to a nation of factories and big cities, becoming a world power.
From The Exploring - The Story Of America, Set 2 Series.
LC NO. FIA68-1062
Prod-NBCTV Dist-GRACUR 1966

Turn Of The Century, The C 60 MIN
3/4 OR 1/2 INCH VIDEO CASSETTE J-C A
Presents flutist James Galway discussing how music became much more cosmopolitan around the turn of the century. Includes examples from The Mikado, Madame Butterfly, Strauss' Salome and Debussy's La Mer.
From The James Galway's Music In Time Series.
Prod-POLTEL Dist-FOTH 1982

Turn Off Pollution C 11 MIN
16MM FILM, 3/4 OR 1/2 IN VIDEO P
Stresses the importance of becoming involved in issues regarding pollution and taking steps to improve matters. Suggests steps elementary school children can take to curb the destruction of the environment.
Prod-EBEC Dist-EBEC 1971

Turn On, Light, Adjust Cutting Torch To A Neutral Flame, And Turn Off Oxyacetylene... C 8 MIN
1/2 INCH VIDEOTAPE C A
Complete title is Turn On, Light, Adjust Cutting Torch To A Neutral Flame, And Turn Off Oxyacetylene Cutting Equipment. Shows equipment and materials and demonstrates procedures for turning on, lighting, adjusting and turning off the cutting torch. Emphasizes safety and distinguishing among the three types of flames.
Prod-OSDVTE Dist-OSDVTE

Turn The Other Cheek X 15 MIN
16MM FILM OPTICAL SOUND P-I R
Tells the story about a misunderstanding between some children and their parents which provides a practical illustration of Jesus' teaching to 'TURN THE OTHER CHEEK.'
From The Our Children Series.
Prod-FAMF Dist-FAMF

Turn To Nature B 20 MIN
2 INCH VIDEOTAPE P-I
Deals with nature as an inspiration for artists. An awareness of the beauty in trees will be interpreted by children.
From The Art Adventures Series.
Prod-CVETVC Dist-GPITVL Prodn-WCVETV

Turn Toward Identity C 28 MIN
3/4 OR 1/2 INCH VIDEO CASSETTE PRO
Discusses the roles of patient, staff members and family in reestablishing the lost identity of a confused person. Describes specific techniques such as the use of clocks, calendars, personal possessions, sounds and colors. Emphasizes the importance of communicating expectations. Encourages the learner to have patience and perserverance when dealing with the confused individual and assurance that the rewards for patient as well as for the staff are well worth the wait.
LC NO. 79-720267
Prod-TRAINX Dist-TRAINX

Turn Yourself On C 29 MIN
2 INCH VIDEOTAPE
See series title for descriptive statement.
From The That's Life Series.
Prod-KOAPTV Dist-PUBTEL

Turn-Of-The-Century America C 14 MIN
16MM FILM OPTICAL SOUND
Examines a major exhibition of turn-of-the-century American art showing the period's pictorial arts. Discusses the rich complexity of forms, themes and techniques that reflect the diversity and vitality of the era.
LC NO. 79-700332
Prod-ENN Dist-KAROL 1978

Turnaround C 28 MIN
16MM FILM OPTICAL SOUND H-C A
Documents the causes, events and results of the Homestead Steel Strike of 1892, which pitted the Amalgamated Association Of Iron And Steel Workers against the combined forces of the Carnegie Steel Company of Pennsylvania and a private army of Pinkerton agents.
LC NO. 76-703734
Prod-WPSXTV Dist-PSU 1976

Turned On C 7 MIN
16MM FILM, 3/4 OR 1/2 IN VIDEO P-C A
Shows dune buggies, surfing, snowmobiles, skiing, sailing and other sports as activities which emphasize the coordination and capabilities of the human body.
Prod-PFP Dist-PFP 1969

Turned On Crisis—A Series
P A
Prod-WQED Dist-GPITVL

Because That's My Way	60 MIN
Concept, The	60 MIN
First Dimension - Information And Understanding	60 MIN
High Is Not Very Far Off The Ground	60 MIN
Say What We Feel, Not What We Ought To Say	60 MIN
Shade Of A Toothpick, The	60 MIN
To Keep It, You Have To Give It Away	60 MIN
Why Can't You Hear Through The Noise In Your	60 MIN

Turned Round To See C 11 MIN
16MM FILM OPTICAL SOUND H-C A
A dramatization about the experiences of a lonely and puzzled seventeen-year-old boy who wanders into a teenage discotheque. Expresses the fundamental belief that the revelation of Christ encompasses a revelation of self and that such a revelation leads an individual to reach out to others.
From The Revelation Series.
LC NO. 71-711553
Prod-FRACOC Dist-FRACOC 1970

Turner (1775 - 1851) C 12 MIN
16MM FILM OPTICAL SOUND
Presents paintings by Turner that dramatized nature.
Prod-ROLAND Dist-ROLAND

Turning C 20 MIN
3/4 OR 1/2 INCH VIDEO CASSETTE J-C
See series title for descriptive statement.
From The Math Topics - Trigonometry Series.
Prod-BBCTV Dist-FI

Turning A Cylinder Between Centers B 17 MIN
16MM FILM OPTICAL SOUND
Points out how to choose stock and mount it on a wood lathe for turning between centers. Demonstrates the use of a parting tool and skew chisel. Explains sand turning work.
From The Precision Wood Machining Series. Operations On The Wood Lathe.
LC NO. FIE52-44
Prod-USOE Dist-USNAC Prodn-PHOTOS 1944

Turning A Cylinder Between Centers And Turning Work On A Face Plate B 30 MIN
16MM FILM OPTICAL SOUND
Points out how to choose stock and mount it on a wood lathe for turning between centers. Demonstrates the use of a parting tool and skew chisel. Explains sand turning work. Shows the various types of face plates. Explains how to attach the stock to the face plate, how to true up the wood, how to scribe the work for inside turning, how to use round nose and diamond point chisels and how to smoothe the recess bottom.
From The Precision Wood Machining Series. Operations On The Wood Lathe.
Prod-USOE Dist-USNAC Prodn-PHOTOS 1944

Turning A Radius C
3/4 OR 1/2 INCH VIDEO CASSETTE
See series title for descriptive statement.
From The Basic Engine Lathe Series.
Prod-VTRI Dist-VTRI

Turning A Radius C 15 MIN
3/4 OR 1/2 INCH VIDEO CASSETTE
See series title for descriptive statement.
From The Machine Technology I - Basic Machine Technology Series.
Prod-CAMB Dist-CAMB

Turning A Radius C 15 MIN
3/4 OR 1/2 INCH VIDEO CASSETTE IND
See series title for descriptive statement.
From The Machining And The operation Of Machine Tools, Module 2 - Engine Lathe Series.
Prod-LEIKID Dist-LEIKID

Turning A Radius (Spanish) C
3/4 OR 1/2 INCH VIDEO CASSETTE
See series title for descriptive statement.
From The Basic Engine Lathe (Spanish) Series.
Prod-VTRI Dist-VTRI

Turning A Sphere Inside Out C 23 MIN
16MM FILM, 3/4 OR 1/2 IN VIDEO C
Discusses the problem of turning a sphere inside out by passing the surface through itself without making any holes or creases. Uses computer animation to reveal the continuous motion of the sphere.
From The Topology Series.
LC NO. 81-706241
Prod-EDC Dist-IFB 1976

Turning A Taper With The Tailstock Set Over B 17 MIN
16MM FILM - 3/4 IN VIDEO
Shows how to calculate tailstock offset for cutting tapers, how to offset the tailstock and how to turn a taper with the tailstock set over. Issued in 1942 as a motion picture.
From The Machine Shop Work - Operations On The Engine Lathe Series. No. 6
LC NO. 79-707090
Prod-USOE Dist-USNAC Prodn-WCSS 1979

Turning And Review C 29 MIN
3/4 OR 1/2 INCH VIDEO CASSETTE
Demonstrates the three most useful turns, the step, skating and the parallel turns, and gives a general review of all cross country skiing techniques.
From The Cross Country Ski School Series.
Prod-VTETV Dist-PBS 1981

Turning Around C 23 MIN
16MM FILM OPTICAL SOUND H-C A
Shows how efforts by residents, local banks, government and private foundations are helping to reverse the pattern of urban decline in Cincinnati.
LC NO. 75-702969
Prod-FDF Dist-KAROL 1975

Turning Between Centers C 18 MIN
3/4 OR 1/2 INCH VIDEO CASSETTE IND
Focuses on aligning machine centers, drilling center holes and mounting the workpiece. Gives methods for straight turning and for taper turning.
From The Introduction To Machine Technology, Module 2 Series.
Prod-LEIKID Dist-LEIKID

Turning Between Centers C 40 MIN
1/2 IN VIDEO CASSETTE BETA/VHS IND
See series title for descriptive statement.
From The Machine Shop - Engine Lathe Series.
Prod-RMI Dist-RMI

Turning Brass With Hand Graver, Pt 1 B 14 MIN
16MM FILM OPTICAL SOUND
Demonstrates how to use a graver in turning, facing and chamfering a brass dowel.
From The Light Mechanics Series.
Prod-USVA Dist-USVA 1949

Turning Brass With Hand Graver, Pt 2 B 11 MIN
16MM FILM OPTICAL SOUND
Demonstrates how to use a graver in reducing diameter of brass wire and in squaring the shoulder.
From The Light Mechanics Series.
Prod-USVA Dist-USVA 1949

Turning Decisions Into Programs C 15 MIN
3/4 OR 1/2 INCH VIDEO CASSETTE J-H
Explores the decisions made in developing radio and television programming to serve the needs of the audience.
From The Broadcasting Series.
Prod-CTI Dist-CTI

Turning Of The Tide B 26 MIN
16MM FILM OPTICAL SOUND
Uses documentary footage to describe the nightly bombing of German installations as the Allies began to achieve air supremacy and shows how the German U-boat menace was brought under control and how the stumbling blocks of Cassino and Anzio were overcome. Based on the book 'THE SECOND WORLD WAR,' by Winston S Churchill.
From The Winston Churchill - The Valiant Years Series. No. 16
LC NO. FI67-2119
Prod-ABCTV Dist-SG 1961

Turning Off - Drugs And Peer Pressure C
3/4 OR 1/2 INCH VIDEO CASSETTE J-H
Explores peer pressure as a motivating factor in drug involvement. Dramatizes how peer pressure works. Provides assertive techniques in role-playing situations to help cope with peer pressure.
Prod-SUNCOM Dist-SUNCOM

Turning On The Power C 20 MIN
3/4 OR 1/2 INCH VIDEO CASSETTE
See series title for descriptive statement.
From The Productivity / Quality Of Work Life Series.
Prod-GOODMI Dist-DELTAK

Turning Point B 24 MIN
16MM FILM OPTICAL SOUND H
Shows the tension of the days leading to the overthrow of the Nazi empire and the massive effort to soften the defenses of Hitler's 'FORTRESS EUROPE,' then sweeps into the agony and triumph on the beaches of Normandy.
Prod-REAF Dist-REAF 1969

Turning Point C 28 MIN
16MM FILM OPTICAL SOUND A
Summarizes the major issues of population, poverty, food, energy, and inflation which were discussed and debated at a special session of the United Nations general assembly held in 1974.
From The International Zone Series.
LC NO. 75-703638
Prod-UN Dist-UN 1974

Turning Point, The C 9 MIN
16MM FILM OPTICAL SOUND
Uses the example of a widowed factory worker with two small children in order to show the kinds of help available from United Way services.
LC NO. 74-700267
Prod-UWAMER Dist-UWAMER 1973

Turning Point, The C 24 MIN
16MM FILM OPTICAL SOUND
Discusses the care and cleanliness required for the production of small precision instrument ball bearings.
Prod-GM Dist-GM

Turning Point, The C 30 MIN
3/4 OR 1/2 INCH VIDEO CASSETTE
Discusses the new paradigms in physics and how they are leading to the reconceptualizing of other academic disciplines into a more holistic view of society and nature. Presented by Dr Fritjof Capra, author of The Turning Point.
From The Creating Alternative Futures Series.
Prod-BULFRG Dist-BULFRG

Turning Points C 19 MIN
16MM FILM OPTICAL SOUND H
Uses 'MACBETH' as an example of a skillfilly structured dramatic work. Explains the structure of a play and how the action moves from one turning point to another.
Prod-SINGER Dist-SVE 1968

Turning Points C 35 MIN
16MM FILM, 3/4 OR 1/2 IN VIDEO
Presents three women who have decided to pursue college and careers describing their daily lives and the impact of their decisions.
Prod-CCNY Dist-CORF 1979

Turning Points—A Series

Prod-PUBTEL Dist-PUBTEL

Cable Revolution, The	29 MIN
Crossroads - New Treatment For Alcoholics	29 MIN
Flower Under The Bridge, A	29 MIN
Free State Of Winston, The	29 MIN
Frozen Hopes In Milwaukee	28 MIN
Here I Am	29 MIN
Incident At Cass Lake	29 MIN
Is There A Bike In The Mix	29 MIN
Next Crisis, The - Death In The Mines	29 MIN
Nuclear Reactions	28 MIN
Patients Without Doctors	29 MIN
Pigs No More	29 MIN
Public Education - At Whose Expense	29 MIN
Rescue Of A River	29 MIN
They Laid It On The Line	29 MIN
This Guy Denenberg	29 MIN
Time To Live, A	29 MIN
Vanishing Towns	29 MIN
Walk The First Step	28 MIN
What's Really Comin' Down	29 MIN

Turning Taper Work B 12 MIN
16MM FILM OPTICAL SOUND H A
Explains centering cylindrical wood stock for spindle turning. Tells how and when to make clearance cuts. Shows how to establish the diameters of a taper, how to turn a single taper, how to establish diameters for turning two tapers from a single piece of material and how to turn them.
LC NO. FIE52-45
Prod-UWF Dist-USNAC 1944

Turning The Tide B 22 MIN
3/4 INCH VIDEO CASSETTE
Deals with military operations in Korea from August 10 to September 20, 1950.
From The Combat Bulletin Series. No. 102
LC NO. 79-706638
Prod-USA Dist-USNAC 1979

Turning To Giddings And Lewis C 21 MIN
16MM FILM OPTICAL SOUND
Demonstrates a numerically-controlled lathe manufactured by Giddings and Lewis Machine Tool Company.
LC NO. 80-700224
Prod-GIDLEW Dist-LOGPRO Prodn-LOGPRO 1979

Turning Work Held On A Fixture B 21 MIN
16MM FILM - 3/4 IN VIDEO
Shows how to drill a workpiece held in a lathe chuck. Demonstrates how to bore a tapered hole with a taper-turning attachment, how to check the accuracy of the hole and how to ream a tapered hole to finished size. Issued in 1941 as a motion picture.
From The Machine Shop Work - Operations On The Engine Lathe Series. No. 10
LC NO. 79-707091
Prod-USOE Dist-USNAC Prodn-ATLAS 1979

Turning Work Held On A Mandrel B 20 MIN
16MM FILM - 3/4 IN VIDEO
Describes the mandrel and its uses. Shows how to fit the mandrel into the workpiece, how to cut a bevel using the compound rest, how to calculate speed and feed and how to set the controls. Issued in 1943 as a motion picture.
From The Machine Shop Work - Operations On The Engine Lathe Series. No. 13
LC NO. 79-707092
Prod-USOE Dist-USNAC Prodn-ATLAS 1979

Turning Work Held On A Mandrel (Spanish) B 20 MIN
16MM FILM, 3/4 OR 1/2 IN VIDEO
Describes the uses of the mandrel. Shows how to fit a mandrel into the workpiece, how to cut a bevel, use the compound rest, how to calculate speed and feed and how to set the controls.
From The Machine Shop Work Series. Operations On The Engine Hathe, No. 10
Prod-USOE Dist-USNAC 1943

Turning Work In A Chuck B 15 MIN
16MM FILM OPTICAL SOUND
Explains how to mount work on a face plate, turn one face of the work, make a chuck for the opposite face and remove rechucked work from the chuck.
LC NO. FIE52-51
Prod-USOE Dist-USNAC 1944

Turning Work In A Chuck And Face Turning A Collar B 30 MIN
16MM FILM OPTICAL SOUND
Examines the various types of face plates. Describes how to attach stock to a face plate, and how to true up and scribe the work. Explains the use of a chuck in machine work. Points out how to use round nose and diamond point chisels.
From The Precision Wood Machining Series. Operations On The Wood Lathe.
Prod-USOE Dist-USNAC Prodn-PHOTOS 1944

Turning Work Of Two Diameters B 14 MIN
16MM FILM OPTICAL SOUND
Demonstrates the use of roughing, finishing, facing and radius tools.
From The Machine Shop Work Series.
LC NO. FIE51-515
Prod-USOE Dist-USNAC Prodn-HANDY 1941

Turning Work On A Face Plate B 15 MIN
16MM FILM OPTICAL SOUND
Shows the various types of face plates. Explains how to attach the stock to the face plate, how to true up the wood, how to scribe the work for inside turning, how to use the round nose chisel and diamond point chisel and how to smoothe the recess bottom.
From The Precision Wood Machining Series. Operations On The Wood Lathe.
LC NO. FIE52-50
Prod-USOE Dist-USNAC Prodn-PHOTOS 1944

Turning Work On Two Diameters B 14 MIN
16MM FILM, 3/4 OR 1/2 IN VIDEO
Shows how to use roughing, finishing, facing and radius tools. Demonstrates how to rough-turn and finish-turn a workpiece having two diameters, how to face a workpiece and how to machine a fillet. Issued in 1941 as a motion picture.
From The Machine Shop Work - Operations On The Engine Lathe Series. No. 2
LC NO. 79-707093
Prod-USOE Dist-USNAC Prodn-HANDY 1979

Turning Working Held On A Fixture (Spanish) B 21 MIN
16MM FILM OPTICAL SOUND
Shows how to mount an irregularly shaped casting that can't be held in a chuck. Explains mounting and centering this fixture on a lathe, selecting and mounting tools, turning, facing, boring, counterboring and ream surfaces of a valve bonnet.
From The Machine Shop Work Series. Operations On The Engine Hathe, No. 10
LC NO. FIE62-86
Prod-USOE Dist-USNAC 1944

Turnpike C 20 MIN
16MM FILM OPTICAL SOUND
Tells the story of the New Jersey Turnpike and its continuing expansion to accomodate the large numbers of cars, trucks and buses that use its multiple asphalt-paved road. Features the highway's up-to-date design concepts, construction materials and innovative road-building techniques.
Prod-AI Dist-AI

Turns And Turnabouts C 12 MIN
16MM FILM, 3/4 OR 1/2 IN VIDEO H
Shows how to adjust lane positions before a turn. Depicts how to make right and left turns from both two-way and one-way streets. Reveals the proper way of making a U-turn and Y-turn, and an alley or driveway turnabout.
Prod-SF Dist-SF 1974

Turret Lathe No. 1 - Familiarization C 17 MIN
1/2 IN VIDEO CASSETTE BETA/VHS IND
Introduces the controls and adjustments common to ram type turret lathes.
From The Machine Shop - Turret Lathe Series.
Prod-RMI Dist-RMI

Turret Lathe No. 2 - Drilling, Tapping, Knurling, Forming C 21 MIN
1/2 IN VIDEO CASSETTE BETA/VHS IND
Explains the sequence of operations for making a typical production part. Describes collet adjustment and the setting of turret and carriage stops. Includes an explanation of the releasing tap holder and knurling tool.
From The Machine Shop - Turret Lathe Series.
Prod-RMI Dist-RMI

Turret Lathe No. 3 - Plunge Forming And Self-Opening Die Setups C 12 MIN
1/2 IN VIDEO CASSETTE BETA/VHS IND
Demonstrates the use of the form tool to machine several diameters at once. Explains the set-up and use of the 'Geometric' type self-opening die head.
From The Machine Shop - Turret Lathe Series.
Prod-RMI Dist-RMI

Turret Lathe No. 4 - Bar Turner Setup And Adjustment C 18 MIN
1/2 IN VIDEO CASSETTE BETA/VHS IND
Explains the function of the bar turner in machining accurate diameters and demonstrates set-up and adjustment.
From The Machine Shop - Turret Lathe Series.
Prod-RMI Dist-RMI

Turret Lathe, The - An Introduction B 17 MIN
16MM FILM - 3/4 IN VIDEO
Discusses functions of the head, hexagon turret, square turret and bed. Shows how to determine the sequence of operations, how to take a multiple cut and how to combine cuts from the hexagon and square turrets. Issued in 1945 as a motion picture.
From The Machine Shop Work - Operations On The Turret Lathe Series. No. 1
LC NO. 79-706808
Prod-USOE Dist-USNAC Prodn-ESCAR 1979

Turtle C 22 MIN
16MM FILM, 3/4 OR 1/2 IN VIDEO P-I
Presents a marine biologist telling how he is helping to restore the numbers of endangered green turtles in Florida and a scientist who studies the habits of the California desert tortoise. Uses fable and song to tell of the docile nature of the turtle. Hosted by Hal Linden.
From The Animals, Animals, Animals Series.
Prod-ABCNEW Dist-MEDIAG 1977

Turtle People, The C 26 MIN
16MM FILM OPTICAL SOUND
Presents a case study of the ecological and cultural changes that result from so-called development. Shows the Miskito Indians of Eastern Nicaragua who have depended on the sea turtle for food in the past and are now hunting the turtles to sell for cash.
LC NO. 74-700505
Prod-BCFILM Dist-BCFILM 1973

Turtle Talk C 5 MIN
16MM FILM OPTICAL SOUND
Locates the luckiest turtle in the world at Silver Springs, Florida, where he describes his neighbors, friends and visitors.
Prod-FLADC Dist-FLADC

Turtle, The C 8 MIN
16MM FILM, 3/4 OR 1/2 IN VIDEO K-P
Presents the story of Little Dog and his friend Kitten, helping a mother hen and her chicks. Tells how when one of the chicks keeps wandering away, they block the entrance with a rock but she keeps running away. Explains that the reason for this is that the rock is really a turtle.
From The Little Dog Series.
Prod-ROMAF Dist-PHENIX

Turtle, The - Care Of A Pet C 8 MIN
16MM FILM, 3/4 OR 1/2 IN VIDEO K-I
Shows the living habits of a pet turtle and the various activities involved in taking care of it. Shows how to feed the turtle, the proper living environment for the turtle and its characteristics.
Prod-BEAN Dist-PHENIX Prodn-BEAN 1962

Turtle, The - Care Of A Pet (Spanish) C 8 MIN
16MM FILM, 3/4 OR 1/2 IN VIDEO K-I
Shows the living habits of a pet turtle and the various activities involved in taking care of it. Shows how to feed the turtle, the proper living environment for the turtle and its characteristics.
Prod-BEAN Dist-PHENIX Prodn-BEAN 1962

Turtles Everywhere C 15 MIN
3/4 OR 1/2 INCH VIDEO CASSETTE P
Combines looking, listening, talking, writing and reading to help establish the link between oral and written language. Presents the story Timothy Turtle by Alice Vaught Davis.
From The I Want To Read Series.
Prod-LACOS Dist-GPITVL 1976

Turumba C 94 MIN
3/4 OR 1/2 INCH VIDEO CASSETTE
Focuses on one family who traditionally made papier-mache animals to sell during the Turumba religious festival.
Prod-FLOWER Dist-FLOWER

Tuskegee Airmen's Story- 1941-1948—A Series

Prod-RCOMTV Dist-SYLWAT

Black Eagles, The - A Picture Story 020 MIN
Tuskegee Airmen's Story, Pt 1 029 MIN
Tuskegee Airmen's Story, Pt 2 029 MIN
Tuskegee Airmen's Story, Pt 3 029 MIN
Tuskegee Airmen's Story, Pt 4 029 MIN

Tuskegee Airmen's Story, Pt 1 C 29 MIN
3/4 OR 1/2 INCH VIDEO CASSETTE
From The Tuskegee Airmen's Story - 1941-1948 Series.
Prod-RCOMTV Dist-SYLWAT 1982

Tuskegee Airmen's Story, Pt 2 C 29 MIN
3/4 OR 1/2 INCH VIDEO CASSETTE
From The Tuskegee Airmen's Story - 1941-1948 Series.
Prod-RCOMTV Dist-SYLWAT 1982

Tuskegee Airmen's Story, Pt 3 C 29 MIN
3/4 OR 1/2 INCH VIDEO CASSETTE
From The Tuskegee Airmen's Story - 1941-1948 Series.
Prod-RCOMTV Dist-SYLWAT 1982

Tuskegee Airmen's Story, Pt 4 C 29 MIN
3/4 OR 1/2 INCH VIDEO CASSETTE
From The Tuskegee Airmen's Story - 1941-1948 Series.
Prod-RCOMTV Dist-SYLWAT 1982

Tut - The Boy King C 52 MIN
16MM FILM, 3/4 OR 1/2 IN VIDEO J-C
Offers a view of 55 of the treasures from the tomb of Tutankhamun, including parchesi-like games the ten-year-old Pharoah used, his diminuitive ebony and gold inlaid chair, statues and jewelry.
Prod-NBCTV Dist-FI 1977

Tut And Tuttle C 97 MIN
3/4 OR 1/2 INCH VIDEO CASSETTE
Tells what happens when a disgraced junior high school student is magically transported back to ancient Egypt and becomes involved in the kidnapping of King Tutankhamen. Stars Chris Barnes, Hans Conreid and Vic Tayback.
Prod-TIMLIF Dist-TIMLIF 1983

Tutankhamun - Life And Death—A Series
I-H
Re-enacts the discovery of the tomb of Tutankhamun.
Prod-KCPQTV Dist-AITECH 1979

Death 015 MIN
Life 015 MIN

Tutankhamun - The Immortal Pharaoh C 12 MIN
16MM FILM, 3/4 OR 1/2 IN VIDEO I-H A
Inspects the treasures from the tomb of King Tutankhamun. Describes the discovery of the tomb in 1922.
Prod-UHOU Dist-AIMS 1968

Tutankhamun Live Forever C 55 MIN
16MM FILM, 3/4 OR 1/2 IN VIDEO J-C A
Explores the treasures of Tutankhamun, Egypt's boy king, as viewed in his tomb. Displays 55 magnificent treasures with details on the people of Egypt, it's geography and its religion.
Prod-FORWOP Dist-IFEX 1983

Tutor, The C 30 MIN
3/4 OR 1/2 INCH VIDEO CASSETTE I
Dramatizes contemporary Franco-American life. Focuses on showing appreciation.
From The Franco File Series.
Prod-WENHTV Dist-GPITVL

Tutors Of Fernald, The B 35 MIN
16MM FILM OPTICAL SOUND C T
Shows the activities of a remedial school at the University of California at Los Angeles in which Black and white pupils with similar learning disabilities but from differing socio-economic backgrounds tutor each other as part of their special education program.
LC NO. 72-702443
Prod-UCLA Dist-SPF 1972

Tuxedo Junction C 23 MIN
3/4 OR 1/2 INCH VIDEO CASSETTE K-C A
Shows the Falkland Islands where 57 different species of birds live. Shows five species of penguins which make magic of the surrounding waters.
Prod-NWLDPR Dist-NWLDPR

TV Ads - Our Mini-Myths C 16 MIN
16MM FILM, 3/4 OR 1/2 IN VIDEO H-C A
Presents 11 Clio Award-winning television commercials grouped according to their persuasive intent.
LC NO. 77-703270
Prod-CESCFA Dist-PFP 1977

TV And Thee C 22 MIN
16MM FILM OPTICAL SOUND R
Considers the effect of television on family relationships and on an individual's relationship with God.
Prod-GF Dist-GF

TV Commercials B 3 MIN
16MM FILM OPTICAL SOUND
Presents two animated examples of commericals for early television. Includes Muntaz TV and an Oklahoma Gas Company sequence.
Prod-PFP Dist-CFS 1952

TV Commercials Winners Reel 1983 / International Film And TV Festival Of New York C 55 MIN
3/4 INCH VIDEO CASSETTE
Presents 1983's most creative and sales-effective television commercials, including a diversity of ideas and techniques representing a cross-section of current creative and marketing trends worldwide.
Prod-WSTGLC Dist-WSTGLC

TV Engineer C 15 MIN
16MM FILM, 3/4 OR 1/2 IN VIDEO I
From The Career Awareness Series.
Prod-KLVXTV Dist-GPITVL

TV For Better Or Worse C 29 MIN
3/4 OR 1/2 INCH VIDEO CASSETTE
Presents an examination of the future of television as a creative, ethically concerned medium. Features Norman Lear, Gene Roddenberry, Earl Hamner, William Link, Richard Levinson, James Brooks and actor Alan Alda.
Prod-WCVETV Dist-PBS 1977

TV Guide, A - Thinking About What We Watch C 17 MIN
16MM FILM, 3/4 OR 1/2 IN VIDEO I-J
Questions the reality and values presented on television. Includes segments from television shows and commercials.
Prod-CF Dist-CF 1978

TV In The Classroom C 20 MIN
2 INCH VIDEOTAPE T
Explains the unique function of instructional television. Illustrates how close-ups can enlarge images so that all students can get a good view of experiments, how certain experiments can be used on television that could not be performed in the average classroom, how 'supers' can clarify spelling of words and understanding of concepts, how the intimacy of television gives eye contact not possible in the tra ditional classroom and how visuals can be used to advantage. (Broadcast quality)
Prod-KNMETV Dist-GPITVL

TV Interview C 30 MIN
3/4 OR 1/2 INCH VIDEO CASSETTE
See series title for descriptive statement.
From The Que Pasa, U S A Series.
Prod-WPBTTV Dist-MDCPB

TV Interview (With S Vanderbeek) C 13 MIN
16MM FILM OPTICAL SOUND
Presents an electric-collage via video-tape of an interview with Stan Vanderbeek.
Prod-VANBKS Dist-VANBKS

TV Is For Learning C 15 MIN
3/4 OR 1/2 INCH VIDEO CASSETTE K-P
Discusses the different kinds of shows on TV and classifies real and make believe shows.
From The Pass It On Series.
Prod-WKNOTV Dist-GPITVL 1983

TV Kid, The C 15 MIN
3/4 OR 1/2 INCH VIDEO CASSETTE I
Tells of a lonely boy who gains a new understanding of himself and others after he is bitten by a rattlesnake. From the story by Betsy Byars.
From The Book Bird Series.
Prod-CTI Dist-CTI

TV News C 30 MIN
16MM FILM, 3/4 OR 1/2 IN VIDEO H-C A
Examines how the drive for ratings has led to some dazzling newsroom packages. Introduces news consultant Frank Magid who advises local news operations on how to put pizzazz into their newscasts. Visits Phoenix, where a jet helicopter is expanding the concept of live coverage and Los Angeles, where a third-place station is challenging the local news competitors in a rating war. Narrated by John Cameron Swayze.
From The Media Probes Series.
Prod-LAYLEM Dist-TIMLIF 1982

TV News - Behind The Scenes C 27 MIN
16MM FILM, 3/4 OR 1/2 IN VIDEO J-C A
Observes key members of New York's channel seven 'EYE WITNESS NEWS' teams as they assign, gather and produce the local news. Compares objective and subjective news analysis and reviews the standards for on-the-spot documentation of events.
From The World Of Work Series.
Prod-EBEC Dist-EBEC 1973

TV News - Measure Of The Medium C 16 MIN
16MM FILM, 3/4 OR 1/2 IN VIDEO I-H A
Demonstrates the complexities of broadcast journalism and portrays some of the factors that inhibit complete objective reporting.
Prod-SHANA Dist-PHENIX 1971

TV News Reporter C 15 MIN
16MM FILM, 3/4 OR 1/2 IN VIDEO I
From The Career Awareness Series.
Prod-KLVXTV Dist-GPITVL

TV On Trial C 119 MIN
3/4 OR 1/2 INCH VIDEO CASSETTE
Features a documentary of the trial of 15-year-old Ronny Zamora charged with the murder of his next door neighbor during an attempted robbery.
Prod-WPBTTV Dist-PBS 1978

TV Or Not TV C 15 MIN
16MM FILM, 3/4 OR 1/2 IN VIDEO P-J
Uses animation to tell a story about a boy who spends so much time watching television that he forgets about his friends and his commitments. Shows how he misses an opportunity to go to a rock concert and must watch it on TV instead.
From The Fat Albert And The Cosby Kids, Series II Series.
Prod-FLMTON Dist-BARR 1979

TV, Behind The Screen C 16 MIN
16MM FILM, 3/4 OR 1/2 IN VIDEO P-I
Demonstrates how television shows are created by writers, editors and film crews. Focuses on special effects and dramatic productions and introduces various television jobs.
Prod-CF Dist-CF 1978

TV, The Anonymous Teacher C 15 MIN
16MM FILM OPTICAL SOUND H-C A
Suggests that television has a strong influence on children. Interviews experts concerned about the effects of television upon children.
Prod-TRAFCO Dist-ECUFLM 1976

Tviggy C 13 MIN
16MM FILM OPTICAL SOUND J-C A
Tells about the dreams of a young girl to become a famous fashion model.
Prod-SF Dist-SF

Twain - Critical Theory C 30 MIN
2 INCH VIDEOTAPE J-H
See series title for descriptive statement.
From The From Franklin To Frost - Mark Twain Series.
Prod-MPATI Dist-GPITVL

Twas The Night Before Christmas C 25 MIN
16MM FILM, 3/4 OR 1/2 IN VIDEO
Presents an animated expansion of Clement Moore's poem. States that the poem is the climax of the original story about Santa with hurt feelings.
Prod-PERSPF Dist-CORF 1982

Twelfth Anniversary Celebration C 165 MIN
3/4 OR 1/2 INCH VIDEO CASSETTE
Celebrates the 12th Anniversary of Sri Gurudev's arrival in the United States. Recreates his arrival with a series of skits based on his biography.
Prod-IYOGA Dist-IYOGA

Twelfth Night C 124 MIN
3/4 OR 1/2 INCH VIDEO CASSETTE
Presents Shakespeare's play Twelfth Night, which describes the romantic infatuation of Orsino, the devoted loyalty of Viola, the selfless friendship of Antonio and the self-love of the ambitious steward Malvolio. Stars Alec McCowen, Trevor Peacock and Felicity Kendall.
From The Shakespeare Plays Series.
LC NO. 79-707320
Prod-BBCTV Dist-TIMLIF 1980

Twelfth Night - An Introduction C 23 MIN
16MM FILM, 3/4 OR 1/2 IN VIDEO J-C A
Presents scenes of Shakespeare's play Twelfth Night. Attempts to preserve the continuity of the comedy and suggests its prevailing mood and rhythm, the tone and manner of expression of the characters and an idea of Elizabethan costuming.
From The Shakespeare Series.
Prod-SEABEN Dist-PHENIX 1969

Twelfth Night - Blend Of Romance And Realism B 45 MIN
2 INCH VIDEOTAPE C
See series title for descriptive statement.
From The Shakespeare Series.
Prod-CHITVC Dist-GPITVL Prodn-WTTWTV

Twelfth Night - Complication Of Plot Successfully Handled B 45 MIN
2 INCH VIDEOTAPE C
See series title for descriptive statement.
From The Shakespeare Series.
Prod-CHITVC Dist-GPITVL Prodn-WTTWTV

Twelfth Rib Approach To The Kidney C 15 MIN
16MM FILM OPTICAL SOUND
Demonstrates surgical intervention. Uses medical illustrations and animation in conjunction with a complete operative procedure to deal with various types of renal pathology. Discusses all anatomical aspects.
From The Anatomy Of The Flank Series.
LC NO. 77-706141
Prod-EATONL Dist-EATON Prodn-AVCORP 1970

Twelve Angry Men B 95 MIN
16MM FILM OPTICAL SOUND
Depicts a jury room where the guilt or innocence of a ghetto youth is at stake. Stars Henry Fonda and Lee J Cobb. Directed by Sidney Lumet.
Prod-UAA Dist-UAE 1957

Twelve Authorities Evaluate Fluoride C 29 MIN
16MM FILM OPTICAL SOUND PRO

Presents a panel discussion composed of doctors and dentists evaluating the effective use of fluoride in the prevention of child tooth decay.
Prod-UPJOHN Dist-UPJOHN 1963

Twelve Days Of Christmas C 4 MIN
16MM FILM, 3/4 OR 1/2 IN VIDEO
Uses animation to present the song The Twelve Days Of Christmas accompanied by a school madrigal group.
Prod-INTERA Dist-FI 1977

Twelve Days of Christmas, The C 5 MIN
16MM FILM, 3/4 OR 1/2 IN VIDEO K-P
Presents the traditional song-accumulation of gifts given on the twelve days of Christmas.
Prod-WWS Dist-WWS 1972

Twelve Days Of Christmas, The C 7 MIN
16MM FILM, 3/4 OR 1/2 IN VIDEO P-I
Uses animation to illustrate the traditional Christmas song The Twelve Days Of Christmas.
Prod-UPA Dist-MCFI 1976

Twelve Decades Of Concrete In American Architecture—A Series

Presents the history of concrete construction from 1844 through the 1960's, in the United States.
Prod-PRTLND Dist-PRTLND

Architect's Material, The - 1960's 023 MIN
Long Years Of Experiment, The - 1844-1920 016 MIN
Material That Can Do Almost Anything, The 021 MIN
New Dimensions In Concrete - Through The 60's 016 MIN
Search For A New Architecture, The - 1920-1950 012 MIN

Twelve Gemini, The C 20 MIN
3/4 INCH VIDEO CASSETTE
Summarizes some of the scientific experiments performed aboard the long duration flights of the Gemini program. Includes highlights from each Gemini mission.
Prod-NASA Dist-NASA 1972

Twelve Like You C 25 MIN
16MM FILM, 3/4 OR 1/2 IN VIDEO
Presents a discussion of career opportunities for women by women. Asks each woman to analyze and appraise her own assets and liabilities, and helps her find answers to crucial career questions.
Prod-CCCD Dist-CCCD

Twelve Minutes A Day C 20 MIN
3/4 OR 1/2 INCH VIDEO CASSETTE
See series title for descriptive statement.
From The Productivity / Quality Of Work Life Series.
Prod-GOODMI Dist-DELTAK

Twelve Months, The C 27 MIN
16MM FILM, 3/4 OR 1/2 IN VIDEO
Presents a Hungarian tale of a girl who is sent out to do impossible tasks by her stepmother and stepsister. Shows how she is helped at these tasks by the twelve months of the year which she encounters. Reveals how the months freeze the stepmother and stepsister in a blizzard, freeing her to marry a farmer and find happiness.
From The Storybook International Series.
Prod-JOU Dist-JOU 1982

Twelve Months, The - A Czechoslovakian Fairy Tale C 11 MIN
16MM FILM, 3/4 OR 1/2 IN VIDEO K-P
Presents the Czechoslovakian fairy tale The Twelve Months. Shows how Marushka's ungrateful stepmother and jealous stepsister try to get rid of her by sending her out for violets, strawberries and apples in the middle of winter. Tells how she comes upon the spirits of the twelve months, who according to legend meet to plan the seasons. Describes how her stepmother and stepsister are lost when they try to find the spirits and Marushka begins a new life with a loving and generous family.
From The Favorite Fairy Tales And Fables Series.
Prod-CORF Dist-CORF 1980

Twelve O'Clock High B 34 MIN
3/4 OR 1/2 INCH VIDEO CASSETTE H-C A
Offers a perceptive psychological study of an Air Force commander and his efforts to rebuild a bomber squadron whose shattered morale threatens the effectiveness of their crucial missions. Stars Gregory Peck. An abridged version of the motion picture 12 O'Clock High.
Prod-TWCF Dist-FI 1949

Twelve Recent Advances In Reproductive Physiology B 29 MIN
16MM FILM OPTICAL SOUND C A
Discusses recent research in reproductive physiology, biochemistry, endocrinology, genetics and clinical pathology.
From The Nine To Get Ready Series.
Prod-KUONTV Dist-UNEBR 1965

Twelve Step Plan To Citizen CPR Training, A C 16 MIN
3/4 OR 1/2 INCH VIDEO CASSETTE
Lists the procedures that an organization can follow to implement a citizen cardiopulmonary resuscitation training program.
LC NO. 81-707110
Prod-NIH Dist-USNAC 1981

Twelve Steps, The C 45 MIN
16MM FILM, 3/4 OR 1/2 IN VIDEO
Discusses the Twelve Steps of Alcoholics Anonymous and what they mean to one man. Notes that this film is not endorsed by Alcoholics Anaonymous World Services, Inc, which does not endorse any outside enterprise.
Prod-FMARTN Dist-KELLYP

Twelve To Fourteen Months C 12 MIN
3/4 OR 1/2 INCH VIDEO CASSETTE H-C A
Shows how infants between the ages of twelve to fourteen months learn by seeing, hearing, imitation, spatial relationships, self-awareness, imagination, problem-solving and language.
From The Teaching Infants And Toddlers Series. Pt 5
Prod-BGSU Dist-GPITVL 1978

Twelve-Gauge, 4-Foot Box And Pan Apron Brake C 12 MIN
1/2 IN VIDEO CASSETTE BETA/VHS IND
Discusses the basic set-up and operation of a box and pan brake.
Prod-RMI Dist-RMI

Twelve-To-Fourteen Year Olds C 16 MIN
3/4 OR 1/2 INCH VIDEO CASSETTE J
Features three young people debunking myths about sexual assault or rape. Illustrates the safety rules for preventing sexual abuse with examples of assertiveness, trusting one's feelings and telling others of experiences. Demonstrates how to walk, answer the door or phone and make a scene.
From The Child Sexual Abuse - An Ounce Of Prevention Series.
Prod-PPCIN Dist-AITECH

Twenties, The C 25 MIN
16MM FILM, 3/4 OR 1/2 IN VIDEO J-C A
Traces the divisiveness and paradoxes of the 1920's, the boom in consumer capitalism, the issues dividing America, and the stock market crash.
From The American History Series.
Prod-CRMP Dist-CRMP 1969

Twenties, The C 58 MIN
3/4 OR 1/2 INCH VIDEO CASSETTE
Describes the 1920's as a decade in which old America was vanishing and a new urban nation was forming. Bill Moyers speaks with several Americans who lived through those years.
From The Walk Through The 20th Century With Bill Moyers Series.
Prod-CORPEL Dist-PBS 1982

Twentieth Century B 93 MIN
16MM FILM OPTICAL SOUND J-C A
Stars John Barrymore and Carole Lombard. Represents the height of Hollywood glamor during the Depression years of the thirties.
Prod-CPC Dist-TIMLIF 1934

Twentieth Century Art - A Break With Tradition C 20 MIN
16MM FILM OPTICAL SOUND J-C
Discusses how modern artists defied tradition in their search for new dimensions of expression. Shows how artists use novel styles and techniques to interpret the ever-changing face of twentieth century life.
From The History Through Art Series.
LC NO. FIA65-492
Prod-ALEF Dist-ALEF 1965

Twentieth Century Epidemic C 30 MIN
3/4 OR 1/2 INCH VIDEO CASSETTE
Portrays diseases of the heart and blood vessels as the epidemic of the twentieth century. Stresses prevention of cardiovascular diseases through reduction of such high-risk factors such as overweight, fat-saturated diets, underexercise and cigarette smoking.
Prod-PRIMED Dist-PRIMED

Twentieth Century History—A Series
16MM FILM, 3/4 OR 1/2 IN VIDEO H-C A
Illuminates the events and issues that have been critical in shaping modern world history. Uses archival footage, animated maps and illustrations to document actions that have reverberated around the world.
Prod-BBCTV Dist-FI 1981

Boom And Bust 020 MIN
Britain Alone 020 MIN
Cold War - Confrontation 020 MIN
Hitler's Germany 1933-1936 020 MIN
India - The Brightest Jewel 020 MIN
Israel And The Arab States 020 MIN
Make Germany Pay 020 MIN
Mr Kennedy And Mr Krushchev 020 MIN
One Man's Revolution - Mao Tse-Tung 020 MIN
Pearl Harbor to Hiroshima 020 MIN
Road To Berlin, The 020 MIN
Roosevelt And The New Deal 020 MIN
Stalin And The Modernization Of Russia 020 MIN
Why Appeasement 020 MIN

Twentieth Century Poetry 1 C 20 MIN
3/4 OR 1/2 INCH VIDEO CASSETTE H-C A
Presents performers interpreting familiar poems by popular 20th century poets, including Carl Sandburg, Robert Frost and Edna St Vincent Millay.
From The American Literature Series.
LC NO. 83-706206
Prod-AUBU Dist-AITECH 1983

Twentieth Century Poetry 2 C 20 MIN
3/4 OR 1/2 INCH VIDEO CASSETTE H-C A
Presents performers interpreting familiar poems by popular 20th century poets, including e e cummings, W H Auden and Theodore Roethke.
From The American Literature Series.
LC NO. 83-706207
Prod-AUBU Dist-AITECH 1983

Twentieth Century River C 29 MIN
16MM FILM OPTICAL SOUND
Describes how a plan for the Potomac River Basin is drafted, showing the engineers, scientists, conservationists and other specialists at work. Probes such problems as flood, drought, pollution, sedimentation, development of recreation areas and aquiring lands for parks.
LC NO. FIA66-789
Prod-FINLYS Dist-FINLYS Prodn-FF 1962

Twenty And Ten C 15 MIN
3/4 OR 1/2 INCH VIDEO CASSETTE P-I
Introduces the story about 20 school children who hide ten Jewish children from the Nazis occupying France during World War II. Shows that the children are safe only if the others can keep silent and not get caught taking them food at night. Based on the book Twenty And Ten by Claire Huchet Bishop.
From The Readit Series.
LC NO. 83-706831
Prod-POSIMP Dist-AITECH 1982

Twenty Eight - Forty Six C 29 MIN
3/4 OR 1/2 INCH VIDEO CASSETTE
Features a collection of five video compositions accompanied by a sound track of synthesized music. The abstract works use the video art technique developed by producer Willard Rosenquist and his colleagues at the National Center for Experiments in Television.
Prod-KCTSTV Dist-PBS 1978

Twenty First Annual World Eskimo Indian Olympics, The C 27 MIN
3/4 OR 1/2 INCH VIDEO CASSETTE H-C A
Excerpts participants' remarks at the 1982 World Eskimo Indian Olympics, observes their dedicated training and records the wholesome competition of the knuckle hop, greased pole walk, seal skinning contest and other events.
LC NO. 83-706859
Prod-BLUMBS Dist-BLUMBS 1983

Twenty Is Plenty C 23 MIN
3/4 INCH VIDEO CASSETTE A
Presents twenty suggestions from multiple-handicapped individuals on what persons beginning a career in rehabilitation should know, and gives a humorous look at special problems.
LC NO. 81-707317
Prod-UCPNYC Dist-UCPNYC 1981

Twenty Mile Limit C 12 MIN
16MM FILM OPTICAL SOUND
Discusses living toward the future and not in the past.
LC NO. 80-700270
Prod-HORNP Dist-HORNP 1980

Twenty Miles From Everything C 16 MIN
16MM FILM, 3/4 OR 1/2 IN VIDEO
Focuses on six rural transportation systems and the various methods of conveyance which are employed. Illustrates how the people who rely on the availability of such systems would be severely restricted in their activities without them.
Prod-USFHAD Dist-USNAC Prodn-NOWAKA 1979

Twenty Million Miles To Earth B 82 MIN
16MM FILM OPTICAL SOUND J-C A
Stars William Hopper and Joan Taylor. Shows a U S rocketship returning from Venus with a strange cargo from that planet. Introduces a miniature specimen of the Venus-beast which doubles in size every night to become a monster susceptible only to paralyzing electric shock.
Prod-CPC Dist-TWYMAN

Twenty Minutes C 16 MIN
3/4 OR 1/2 INCH VIDEO CASSETTE
Explores techniques for conducting a reference interview with a library patron.
Prod-BCPL Dist-LVN

Twenty Seconds A Day - Coping With Diabetes C 32 MIN
3/4 INCH VIDEO CASSETTE PRO
Presents interviews with a broad spectrum of diabetic patients to determine how they deal with their disease. Discusses diet regimen, scheduling, diabetic rebellion, feelings about death, long-term complications, patient education, compliance and scare tactics, the value of honesty, and the lack of sensitivity on the part of health professionals involved in caring for people with diabetes.
From The Life With Diabetes Series.
LC NO. 81-707066
Prod-UMICH Dist-UMICH 1980

Twenty Seven Hundred/7200 Variable Venturi Carburetor C 25 MIN
3/4 OR 1/2 INCH VIDEO CASSETTE
Discusses diagnosis, adjustment and operation of the Variable Venturi Carburetor. Provides propane enrichment idle mixture adjustment procedure. Contains modifications from 1977-82 as well as complete carburetor specifications.
Prod-FORDSP Dist-FORDSP

Twenty Six Times In A Row C 24 MIN
16MM FILM, 3/4 OR 1/2 IN VIDEO H-C A
Examines the strategies and techniques of marathon running and focuses on the winner of the 1976 Olympic Marathon.
Prod-NFBC Dist-FI 1980

Twenty Thousand Leagues Under The Sea C 27 MIN
16MM FILM, 3/4 OR 1/2 IN VIDEO
An edited version of the feature film 20,000 Leagues Under The Sea. Stars James Mason, Kirk Douglas, and Peter Lorre.
From The Films As Literature, Series 1 Series.
Prod-DISNEY Dist-WDEMCO

Twenty-Eight Degrees Above-Below C 10 MIN
16MM FILM, 3/4 OR 1/2 IN VIDEO H
Describes the MacInnis Expedition, which made a dive into the polar sea to test the ability of man and his equipment to function in that extremely hostile environment.
Prod-NFBC Dist-IFB 1974

Twenty-Eight Grams Of Prevention - Safety For Today's Laboratory C 24 MIN
16MM FILM, 3/4 OR 1/2 IN VIDEO
Helps laboratory workers understand the need for safety regulations in the laboratory. Explains the need for safety regulations, training and proper safety equipment and protective clothing. Uses dramatic re-enactments in order to show the consequences of carelessness.
Prod-FISHSC Dist-FILCOM 1975

Twenty-first Annual World Eskimo-Indian Olympics, The C 27 MIN
3/4 OR 1/2 INCH VIDEO CASSETTE
Documents feats of extraordinary skill and strength based on Eskimo-Indian traditions.
Prod-EAI Dist-EAI

Twenty-First Century—A Series
16MM FILM, 3/4 OR 1/2 IN VIDEO J-H A
Looks at such topics as the cities of the future, the first ten months of life, the food revolution, educational technology and robotics.
Prod-CBSNEW Dist-CRMP

Cities Of The Future	025 MIN
First Ten Months Of Life	054 MIN
Food Revolution	026 MIN
Four-Day Week	026 MIN
From Cradle To Classroom	052 MIN
Incredible Voyage	026 MIN
Miracle Of The Mind	026 MIN
Stranger Than Science Fiction	030 MIN
Weird World Of Robots	026 MIN

Twenty-First Century—A Series

Prod-UCC Dist-MTP

Atomic Medicine	30 MIN
Bats, Birds And Bionics	30 MIN
Computer Revolution, The, Pt 1	30 MIN
Computer Revolution, The, Pt 2	30 MIN
Four-Day Week, The	30 MIN
Laser, The - A Light Fantastic	30 MIN
Miracle Of The Mind	30 MIN

Twenty-Five Feet From The Face C 17 MIN
16MM FILM, 3/4 OR 1/2 IN VIDEO
Points out the leading causes of coal mine roof-fall accidents and outlines proper safety procedures for making a working place safe. Demonstrates various types of roof bolting equipment and roof control techniques. Emphasizes the workers learning and following the mine's approved roof-control plan, learning to recognize and properly evaluate roof conditions, and applying available roof control devices.
LC NO. 82-706933
Prod-USDL Dist-USNAC 1982

Twenty-Nine-Year-Old Men and Women Talk About Their Sexuality C 56 MIN
3/4 OR 1/2 INCH VIDEO CASSETTE
Explores the changing attitudes of society toward sexuality. Features two males and two females reviewing their sex education from 'playing doctor' as kids to attitudes, feelings, practices and problems related to the sexual revolution and the women's movement.
Prod-HEMUL Dist-HEMUL

Twenty-One Days Of Laura Wells, The C 21 MIN
16MM FILM OPTICAL SOUND
Traces the odyssey of a young woman from the onset of an illness through her treatment and recovery in order to demonstrate the costs involved.
LC NO. 79-701170
Prod-AETNA Dist-AETNA Prodn-VISION 1979

Twenty-One Dollars Or Twenty-One Days B 8 MIN
3/4 INCH VIDEO CASSETTE
Features a black man arrested for disorderly conduct and resisting arrest telling his story in night court.
From The Pittsburgh Police Series.
Prod-DOCEDR Dist-DOCEDR Prodn-MSHLLJ

Twenty-One Going On 70 C 29 MIN
16MM FILM OPTICAL SOUND R
Shows how a young man developed a new belief in Christ after working with elderly people.
Prod-OUTRCH Dist-OUTRCH

Twenty-One Hundred Year Old Tomb Excavated C 30 MIN
16MM FILM OPTICAL SOUND
Records the discovery of a 2,100-year-old tomb, recently unearthed in central China. Examines the body of a woman and the burial accessories recovered from the tomb.
Prod-GROVE Dist-GROVE 1975

Twenty-One To Twenty-Nine Months C 13 MIN
3/4 OR 1/2 INCH VIDEO CASSETTE H-C A
Shows how infants between the ages of 21 to 29 months learn through fine motor activities, gross motor activities, self-awareness, imagination, self-care, problem-solving and language.
From The Teaching Infants And Toddlers Series. Pt 7
Prod-BGSU Dist-GPITVL 1978

Twenty-Seventh Infantry Division B 20 MIN
16MM FILM, 3/4 OR 1/2 IN VIDEO H A
Presents the campaigns at Makin, Eniwetok, Saipan and Okinawa.
Prod-USA Dist-USNAC 1953

Twenty-Six Feet, One Point One Four Nine Nine For String Player C 42 MIN
3/4 OR 1/2 INCH VIDEO CASSETTE
Records a concert performed by cellist Charlotte Moorman and video artist Nam June Paik of the composition by John Cage.
From The Two Works By Judd Yalkut Series.
Prod-EAI Dist-EAI

Twenty-Six Model 21 Interpreting Card Punch B 35 MIN
16MM FILM OPTICAL SOUND IND
Shows the operation and servicing of the IBM 26 model 21 interpret/punch and sense unit.
LC NO. FI67-2025
Prod-IBUSMA Dist-IBUSMA 1963

Twenty-Six Times In A Row C 24 MIN
16MM FILM, 3/4 OR 1/2 IN VIDEO H A
Waldemar Cierpinski discusses his record-breaking performance in the Marathon at the XXI Olympic Games in Montreal and his feelings about running and athletic achievement.
Prod-NFBC Dist-FI

Twenty-Sixth Infantry Division B 16 MIN
16MM FILM, 3/4 OR 1/2 IN VIDEO H A
Presents scenes of the 26th Infantry Division combat operations in New Guinea, including actions at Maffin Bay, the amphibious landing at Sansapor to build an air base, and the assault landing at Lingayen Gulf, Luzon.
Prod-USA Dist-USNAC 1952

Twenty-Third Cease Fire, The C 52 MIN
16MM FILM OPTICAL SOUND
Relates the story of the brief interlude during the Lebanese civil war, the twenty-third cease fire, and describes life in war-torn Beirut.
Prod-ICARUS Dist-ICARUS

Twenty-Three - Twenty-Eight C 46 MIN
16MM FILM OPTICAL SOUND
Features a young factory worker presenting the importance of material and energy resources and the need for improved productivity and efficiency in industry.
LC NO. 75-703122
Prod-FTARC Dist-FTARC Prodn-HEN 1975

Twenty-Three Skidoo B 10 MIN
16MM FILM, 3/4 OR 1/2 IN VIDEO
Dramatizes the horror of the neutron bomb by showing a metropolis without a trace of human life, then focusing on a news teletype which has stopped halfway through its message reporting the explosion of the world's first neutron bomb.
Prod-NFBC Dist-NFBC 1964

Twenty, Cubed B 18 MIN
16MM FILM OPTICAL SOUND
Explores a variety of ways of seeing. Attempts, through both visual and sound close-ups, to portray the world as it seems when one experiences it 'UP CLOSE.' Describes a day in the life of a young man who gets up, shaves, examines his image, goes to work, meets a client in a go-go bar, attends a party, finds a girl and looks too closely at his world.
Prod-UPENN Dist-UPENN 1967

Twice A Day Everyday C 14 MIN
16MM FILM OPTICAL SOUND
Promotes the use of automated cattle feeding equipment by examining the history of farm mechanization and by showing examples of mechanization and automation in industry.
LC NO. 72-700166
Prod-VENARD Dist-VENARD 1971

Twice Amsterdam C 14 MIN
16MM FILM OPTICAL SOUND
Presents the development of a new urban area to include comfort, good design, reasonably priced housing with open spaces, gardens and recreation within walking distance.
Prod-DPWAM Dist-AFLCIO 1965

Twice Two B 21 MIN
16MM FILM OPTICAL SOUND
Features Laurel and Hardy as themselves and as their wives.
Prod-ROACH Dist-BHAWK 1933

Twice Upon A Time C 15 MIN
3/4 OR 1/2 INCH VIDEO CASSETTE P
See series title for descriptive statement.
From The Magic Pages Series.
Prod-KLVXTV Dist-AITECH 1976

Twice Upon A Time C 15 MIN
3/4 OR 1/2 INCH VIDEO CASSETTE
Centers on a controversial study at the University of Minnesota which involves twins separated at birth and their reunion as adults.
Prod-WCCOTV Dist-WCCOTV 1980

Twice Upon A Time Or Helping You Helps Me C 29 MIN
3/4 OR 1/2 INCH VIDEO CASSETTE T
See series title for descriptive statement.
From The Coping With Kids Series.
Prod-MFFD Dist-FI

Twice Upon A Time, Or Helping You Helps Me C 30 MIN
3/4 OR 1/2 INCH VIDEO CASSETTE
Introduces parent and teacher discussion groups as a means of learning how to cope with kids.
From The Coping With Kids Series.
Prod-OHUTC Dist-OHUTC

Twin Power Scraper C
16MM FILM OPTICAL SOUND
Shows the applications of the Twin Power Scraper in the earth moving job.
Prod-GM Dist-GM

Twinkle, Twinkle, Little Star C 29 MIN
3/4 INCH VIDEO CASSETTE
Focuses on what children learn when they take music lessons.
From The Music Shop Series.
Prod-UMITV Dist-UMITV 1974

Twins C 50 MIN
16MM FILM OPTICAL SOUND A
Tells how a pair of twins wake up to their 30th birthdays. Shows how one twin, a Chaplinesque bum, devises a plan to kill his brother while the other, a cop with a new bulletproof vest, becomes obsessed with his bowling ball.
LC NO. 80-701382
Prod-AHEARN Dist-AHEARN 1980

Twist Drill Procedure C 16 MIN
3/4 OR 1/2 INCH VIDEO CASSETTE PRO
Focuses on diagnostic and therapeutic applications of the procedure. Reviews equipment, anatomical landmarks and a step-by-step analysis of the technique. Demonstrates procedure on trauma victims with interacerebral hemorrhage and chronic subdural hematoma.
Prod-UWASH Dist-UWASH

Twist Drills, Pt 5 B 7 MIN
16MM FILM OPTICAL SOUND
Explains the size designation of twist drills, their cutting action and how they are used and sharpened.
LC NO. FIE58-6
Prod-USN Dist-USNAC 1954

Twisted Cross, The B 55 MIN
16MM FILM, 3/4 OR 1/2 IN VIDEO J-C A
Uses the story of Adolf Hitler and the Nazi movement to trace the rise and fall of a dictator. Includes scenes extracted from a captured German film.
From The Project 20 Series.
Prod-NBCTV Dist-MGHT 1958

Twister C 27 MIN
16MM FILM, 3/4 OR 1/2 IN VIDEO
Tells the story of how the city of Lubbock, Texas, responded when a tornado struck. Demonstrates the need for an emergency operating center to handle such disasters.
Prod-USDCPA Dist-USNAC 1973

Twitch, The C 13 MIN
16MM FILM, 3/4 OR 1/2 IN VIDEO I-C A
Tells a story about a cat who sets out to find Utopia but finds instead a kingdom of brutal conformists ruled by a king with a nervous twitch.
Prod-NFBC Dist-SF 1976

Two AM Feeding C 24 MIN
16MM FILM OPTICAL SOUND A
Documents the trials and tribulations of new parenthood through the observation of first-time mothers and fathers, and through stills and film footage of life in various homes. Covers such topics as breast-feeding, physical recovery, infant fussiness, sexuality, marital disagreements, role of the father, and single parenthood.
LC NO. 83-700118
Prod-NEWDAY Dist-NEWDAY 1983

Two American Audiences B 40 MIN
16MM FILM OPTICAL SOUND
Presents a discussion between Jean-Luc Godard and New York University students on filmmaking and politics, intercut with scenes from La Chinoise. By Mark Woodcock.
Prod-PENNAS Dist-PENNAS

Two Bagatelles C 3 MIN
16MM FILM, 3/4 OR 1/2 IN VIDEO
Combines two films, 'ON THE LAWN' and 'IN THE BACKYARD.' Shows animated live actors dancing to waltzes and marches.
Prod-NFBC Dist-IFB 1952

Two Baroque Churches In Germany C 11 MIN
16MM FILM, 3/4 OR 1/2 IN VIDEO J-C
Uses two churches, Vierzehnheiligen and Ottobeurer, as examples of mid-18th century German Baroque style.
Prod-EAMES Dist-PFP 1955

Two Become One C 10 MIN
16MM FILM OPTICAL SOUND P-J
Explains where sperm comes from, and how it reaches the egg. Uses live and animated photography to illustrate. Introduces the concept of female cycles and traces the changes in the uterus and the development of a fertilized egg in the female human.
From The Family Life And Sex Education Series.
Prod-SF Dist-SF 1968

Two Benjamins, The C 20 MIN
3/4 INCH VIDEO CASSETTE I
Discusses the lives of Benjamin Franklin and Benjamin Banneker.
From The Truly American Series.
Prod-WVIZTV Dist-GPITVL 1979

Two Black Churches C 21 MIN
16MM FILM - 3/4 IN VIDEO C A
Explores black religious expression, ranging from old-time religious baptisms in rural Mississippi to an urban sanctified service in New Haven, Connecticut.
Prod-SOFOLK Dist-SOFOLK

Two Bolts Of Lightning C 15 MIN
16MM FILM, 3/4 OR 1/2 IN VIDEO
Looks at the ancient sport of cutter and chariot racing, an approved American Quarter Horse Association event.
Prod-AQHORS Dist-AQHORS

Two Brains, The C 60 MIN
3/4 OR 1/2 INCH VIDEO CASSETTE C A
Discusses the cortical hemispheres, the relation of thought and language, and sex differences of the human brain.

From The Brain, Mind And Behavior Series.
Prod-WNETTV Dist-FI

Two Breaths To... C 7 MIN
16MM FILM - 3/4 IN VIDEO
Uses animation to dramatize the danger of working on oxygen-deficient areas. Describes procedures which are essential for the prevention of injuries or accidents in mining and construction work. Issued in 1979 as a motion picture.
LC NO. 80-707127
Prod-USDOE Dist-USNAC Prodn-HANBAR 1980

Two Brothers B 4 MIN
3/4 INCH VIDEO CASSETTE
Shows a family attempting to solve a dispute among themselves over a brother's damaged car, after the police have been called to intervene.
From The Pittsburgh Police Series.
Prod-DOCEDR Dist-DOCEDR Prodn-MSHLLJ

Two Brothers In Greece C 15 MIN
16MM FILM, 3/4 OR 1/2 IN VIDEO P-C
Looks at two Greek brothers, one who remains in the village of Peloponnesus to continue farming thus helping his brother financially as he goes to engineering school, while the other runs a tourist boat through the Greek Isles.
From The Man And His World Series.
Prod-FI Dist-FI 1969

Two By Forsyth—A Series

Presents adaptations of two stories by Frederick Forsyth.
Prod-FOTH Dist-FOTH 1984

Careful Man, A 026 MIN
Privilege 026 MIN

Two Castles B 3 MIN
16MM FILM OPTICAL SOUND
Emphasizes the aggression and futility of war by featuring a determined knight. Pictures the knight persisting in his attacks on another apparently untenanted castle across the valley. Shows that the harder he tries, the less fruit his actions bear. Illustrates the backfiring of his missiles damaging his own fortress.
Prod-JANUS Dist-VIEWFI 1963

Two Cents' Worth—A Series
P
Presents a series of social studies lessons.
Prod-WIEC Dist-AITECH Prodn-WHATV 1976

Buy, Buy, Buy - Economic Choice 015 MIN
Changes - Causality 015 MIN
Don't Feed The Animals - Law Enforcement 015 MIN
I Need Somebody - Interdependence 015 MIN
It Belongs To You And Me - Cultural Change 015 MIN
It's Not The Same - Change 015 MIN
Let's Get Together - Culture 015 MIN
Lost And Found - Spatial Relationships 015 MIN
Play Fair - Voluntary Compliance 015 MIN
We're In This Together - Scarcity And 015 MIN
What I Like - Spatial Interaction 015 MIN
Which Way - Mapping 015 MIN
Why Can't I - Laws 015 MIN
Work, Work, Work - Income 015 MIN
Your Choice - Decision-Making 015 MIN

Two Centuries Of Black American Art C 26 MIN
16MM FILM OPTICAL SOUND I-C
Traces the African influences in the first Black art in America, the widening range of work produced in the slave era, the early struggles for serious recognition in the 19th century and the cosmopolitan backgrounds and important work of modern Black American artists.
LC NO. 77-700588
Prod-PHILMO Dist-MTP 1976

Two Centuries Of Black American Art C 20 MIN
16MM FILM, 3/4 OR 1/2 IN VIDEO J-C A
Surveys black American art, tracing the African influences in early work, the widening range of work produced in the slave era, the early struggles for serious recognition in the 19th century and the important contributions of today's black American artists.
Prod-MOSCAR Dist-PFP

Two Centuries Of Service C 29 MIN
16MM FILM OPTICAL SOUND
Emphasizes people-to-people assistance programs, research, development, medical advances and humanitarian efforts which have led to many of the conveniences in the 20th century.
LC NO. 76-702735
Prod-USA Dist-USNAC 1975

Two Cheers For The CIA C 30 MIN
3/4 INCH VIDEO CASSETTE H-C A
Features a discussion between author Ben J Wattenberg, Thomas Karamessines, former head of all CIA clandestine activities, and Richard Helms, former director of the CIA.
From The In Search Of The Real America Series.
Prod-WGBHTV Dist-KINGFT 1977

Two Children - Contrasting Aspects Of Personality Development B 20 MIN
16MM FILM OPTICAL SOUND C T
Shows the different ways two children respond during the lying-in period, and the influence of activity type on development from birth to eight years.
From The Film Studies On Integrated Development Series.
Prod-FRIWOL Dist-NYU 1942

Two Cities - London And New York C 23 MIN
16MM FILM, 3/4 OR 1/2 IN VIDEO P-I
Presents a comparison of the quality of life and the approach to urban problems of two Western Englishspeaking international capitals - London and New York. Describes their differences in ethnic make-up, cultural traditions, physical layout, community organization, benefits and problems.
From The Comparative Cultures And Geography Series.
Prod-LCOA Dist-LCOA 1973

Two Cities - London And New York (Spanish) C 23 MIN
16MM FILM, 3/4 OR 1/2 IN VIDEO I-H
Investigates the texture of life in two metropolitan areas by inquiring whether their differences are due to various factors.
Prod-LCOA Dist-LCOA 1973

Two Communities C 30 MIN
16MM FILM OPTICAL SOUND R
Explores the devotion found in two traditional but disparate religious groups. Shows monks at the Mount Baldy Zen Center in California during an intensive week of meditation and shows life in an Episcopal monastery in San Francisco's Mission District.
From The Devout Young Series.
Prod-OSSHE Dist-OSSHE

Two Cops C 27 MIN
16MM FILM, 3/4 OR 1/2 IN VIDEO H-C A
Takes a look at two police officers on the job.
Prod-BRAVC Dist-MTI 1977

Two Deaths Of Adolph Hitler C 52 MIN
3/4 OR 1/2 INCH VIDEO CASSETTE H-C A
States that how Hitler ended his life is a matter surrounded by mystery even today. His German followers say he shot himself in the head with a pistol, a defeated leader's traditional, honorable way to avoid capture rather than with the coward's method, poison.
From The World At War Specials Series.
Prod-THAMES Dist-MEDIAG 1974

Two Deserts - Sahara And Sonora C 16 MIN
16MM FILM, 3/4 OR 1/2 IN VIDEO P-H
Shows how the Sahara Desert in Africa and the Sonora Desert in America are physically similar yet totally different. Includes what the deserts have in common and tells how factors of economics, religion, culture and technology make regions different.
From The Comparative Cultures And Geography Series.
Prod-LCOA Dist-LCOA 1971

Two Deserts - Sahara And Sonora (Captioned) C 17 MIN
16MM FILM, 3/4 OR 1/2 IN VIDEO I-H
Offers a comparison of Africa's Sahara and America's Sonora deserts. Shows how they are totally different in the ways their heat, aridness, and soil affect the lives of their inhabitants, despite their physical similarities.
Prod-LCOA Dist-LCOA 1971

Two Deserts - Sahara And Sonora (Spanish) C 17 MIN
16MM FILM, 3/4 OR 1/2 IN VIDEO I-H
Offers a comparison of Africa's Sahara and America's Sonora deserts. Shows how they are totally different in the ways their heat, aridness, and soil affect the lives of their inhabitants, despite their physical similarities.
Prod-LCOA Dist-LCOA 1971

Two Earner Family, The C 29 MIN
3/4 OR 1/2 INCH VIDEO CASSETTE
Focuses on the economic and sociological implications of women entering the work force in increasing numbers.
From The Woman Series.
Prod-WNEDTV Dist-PBS

Two Faces Of Group Leadership C 30 MIN
3/4 OR 1/2 INCH VIDEO CASSETTE
Makes it clear that group therapy is only as good as their leaders and leaders are only as good as their leadership skills.
Prod-PSYCHD Dist-PSYCHD

Two Factories - Japanese And American C 22 MIN
16MM FILM, 3/4 OR 1/2 IN VIDEO I-J
Compares the lives of the workers at the Sylvania Plant in Batavis, New York, with those at the MatsuShita electronics complex in Osaka, Japan. Points out the contrasts in the ways these two giant concerns relate to the people who work for them.
From The Comparative Cultures And Geography Series.
Prod-LCOA Dist-LCOA 1974

Two Factories - Japanese And American (Captioned) C 22 MIN
16MM FILM, 3/4 OR 1/2 IN VIDEO I-H
Examines two electronic firms - Sylvania and Matsushita. Looks at needs, interests and aspirations of employees and management.
Prod-LCOA Dist-LCOA 1974

Two Factories - Japanese And American (Spanish) C 22 MIN
16MM FILM, 3/4 OR 1/2 IN VIDEO I-H
Examines two electronic firms - Sylvania and Matsushita. Looks at the needs, interests and aspirations of employees and management.
Prod-LCOA Dist-LCOA 1974

Two Families C 30 MIN
3/4 OR 1/2 INCH VIDEO CASSETTE
See series title for descriptive statement.
From The Arabs And Israelis Series.
Prod-WGBHTV Dist-PBS

Two Families - African And American C 22 MIN
16MM FILM, 3/4 OR 1/2 IN VIDEO P-I
Shows how the family, the basic unit and essential strength of all societies, can vary dramatically in form, function and philosophy. Depicts two family structures, one in central West Africa and one in New York City, and explores what may account for their differences.
From The Comparative Cultures And Geography Series.
Prod-LCOA Dist-LCOA 1974

Two Families - African And American (Spanish) C 22 MIN
16MM FILM, 3/4 OR 1/2 IN VIDEO I-H
Presents a view of parents, work, games, treatment of older people, marriage, customs and education in two different locales - Central West Africa and New York City.
Prod-LCOA Dist-LCOA 1974

Two Farms - Hungary And Wisconsin C 22 MIN
16MM FILM, 3/4 OR 1/2 IN VIDEO P-I
Contrasts farm life in Wisconsin and southeastern Hungary following one family in each rural area through a daily routine. Features members of the families commenting on how their farms operate and what they find satisfying in their lives.
From The Comparative Cultures And Geography Series.
Prod-LCOA Dist-LCOA 1973

Two Farms - Hungary And Wisconsin (Spanish) C 22 MIN
16MM FILM, 3/4 OR 1/2 IN VIDEO I-H
Draws parallels between a collective farm in southeastern Hungary and a family-owned farm in central United States.
Prod-LCOA Dist-LCOA 1973

Two Feet To The Grave B 29 MIN
16MM FILM OPTICAL SOUND
Uses hidden cameras and cordless microphones to film jaywalking incidents in an attempt to bring public attention to a serious traffic safety problem. Violators are questioned about the reasons for their fatal attitude toward safety. Includes corrective recommendations.
LC NO. 79-711555
Prod-WCKTTV Dist-WCKTTV 1970

Two Feet Under The Roof B 5 MIN
16MM FILM OPTICAL SOUND
An experimental film which contrasts the visual qualities and texture of a New York City rooftop with the movements of a pair of legs in a confined apartment.
LC NO. 75-700490
Prod-CRAR Dist-CRAR 1975

Two For Fox, Two For Crow C 16 MIN
16MM FILM OPTICAL SOUND
Features Elanco products, presenting the case for continued use of pesticides and other agricultural chemicals. Discusses statistics on the huge increases in crop yields made possible by the widespread use of pesticides and on the crop and livestock losses that would occur if the use of all agriculture chemicals were stopped. Tours Elanco's research laboratory, showing the procedures for testing the safety and effectiveness of new chemical products.
Prod-LILLY Dist-MTP 1972

Two For Glory C 30 MIN
16MM FILM OPTICAL SOUND A
Tells how a frustrated young man, unsatisfied with his life, executes a desperate attempt to achieve fame and success.
LC NO. 81-700400
Prod-MIKAS Dist-MIKAS 1980

Two For The Show C 22 MIN
16MM FILM OPTICAL SOUND
Traces the two-year growing and production cycle of roses at the Jackson and Perkins Company Wasco, California fields, including planting, budding, cultivating, harvesting, grading, packing and shipping.
Prod-JACPER Dist-JACPER

Two For Tomorrow—A Series
P
Prod-BEOC Dist-GPITVL

Air 10 MIN
Astronomy 10 MIN
Heat 10 MIN
Magnets 10 MIN
Rocks 10 MIN
Seeds 10 MIN
Water 10 MIN
Weather 10 MIN

Two Gentlemen Of Verona C 137 MIN
3/4 OR 1/2 INCH VIDEO CASSETTE H-C A
Presents William Shakespeare's play Two Gentlemen Of Verona in which two good friends both find themselves in love with Silvia, daughter of the Duke of Milan, who has promised her to another.
From The Shakespeare Plays Series.
Prod-BBCTV Dist-TIMLIF 1984

Two Girls Called Eve C 18 MIN
16MM FILM, 3/4 OR 1/2 IN VIDEO I-C
Demonstrates the relationship of two young girls about the age of nine. Uses no narration to follow a summer seaside friendship which faces everyday challenges experienced by most children.
Prod-POLSKI Dist-MCFI 1973

Two Grasslands - Texas And Iran C 21 MIN
16MM FILM, 3/4 OR 1/2 IN VIDEO K-I
Features the Edwards Plateau in Texas and the steppes of Iran as grasslands similar in rainfall pattern and sparsity of vegetation. Uses dramatic photography and spontaneous comments by individuals in each area to reveal the interrelationship between land, technology and culture.
From The Comparative Cultures And Geography Series.
Prod-LCOA Dist-LCOA 1971

Two Grasslands - Texas And Iran (Spanish) C 21 MIN
16MM FILM, 3/4 OR 1/2 IN VIDEO I-H
Presents the many contrasts in national costume, music, living habits, foods and general philosophy of the people of the grasslands of Texas and Iran.
Prod-LCOA Dist-LCOA 1971

Two Great Crusades C
3/4 OR 1/2 INCH VIDEO CASSETTE
Prod-MSTVIS Dist-MSTVIS

Two Hearts - The Ludwig Van Beethoven Story X 30 MIN
2 INCH VIDEOTAPE P-I
Features a conversation in which Beethoven, Prince Lichnowsky, Ferdinand Ries and Johann Schuller discuss Beethoven's new Third Symphony and his reference to his hero, Napoleon. Presents excerpts from Prometheus Theme from Symphony no. 3 (Eroica,) Piano Sonata in F Minor (Appassionata) and Serenade in D Major for flute, violin and viola. (Broadcast quality)
From The Masters Of Our Musical Heritage Series. No. 3
Prod-KTCATV Dist-GPITVL

Two Hundred C 3 MIN
16MM FILM - 3/4 IN VIDEO H-C A
Explores the themes of historical and contemporary American culture.
LC NO. 77-706006
Prod-USIA Dist-USNAC 1975

Two Hundred Fifty Thousand Ways To Destroy A Child's Life Without Leaving Home C 15 MIN
16MM FILM, 3/4 OR 1/2 IN VIDEO J-C A
Shows how the accidental poisoning of infants and children can be avoided at each stage of their development.
Prod-CORHUM Dist-MCFI 1975

Two Hundred Miles C 29 MIN
16MM FILM, 3/4 OR 1/2 IN VIDEO
Presents five experts who discuss the Fisheries Conservation and Management Act of 1976, which extended the U S fishing jurisdiction to 200 miles off the coast.
LC NO. 80-707620
Prod-NOAA Dist-USNAC 1980

Two Hundred Ninety-Nine Foxtrot C 11 MIN
16MM FILM, 3/4 OR 1/2 IN VIDEO
Shows the last flyable B-29 superfortress as it flies from the Naval air facility at China Lake to the aircraft 'Boneyard' at Barstow, California.
LC NO. 81-706656
Prod-USN Dist-USNAC Prodn-USNPC 1977

Two Hundred Twenty Blues C 18 MIN
16MM FILM, 3/4 OR 1/2 IN VIDEO J-H
Questions the value of integration in a system that is run by whites. Tells the story of Sonny, a Black high school athlete who is looking forward to an athletic scholarship to sponsor his education in architecture and shows how Larry, a new black militant student, challenges Sonny's security in a white system. Describes how Sonny's integrated life is now torn between Black and white.
Prod-KINGSP Dist-PHENIX 1970

Two If By Sea B 27 MIN
16MM FILM, 3/4 OR 1/2 IN VIDEO J-H
Shows highlights of the Battles for Peleliu and Angour during World War II.
From The Victory At Sea Series.
Prod-NBCTV Dist-LUF

Two Is The Twice Of One C 20 MIN
3/4 INCH VIDEO CASSETTE J-H
Illustrates the expenses and some problems encountered by young people setting up their first home.
From The Dollar Data Series.
LC NO. 81-707423
Prod-WHROTV Dist-GPITVL 1974

Two Laws Of Algebra C 4 MIN
16MM FILM, 3/4 OR 1/2 IN VIDEO
Presents the associative and distributive processes in algebra by using animation to manipulate formulas.
Prod-EAMES Dist-PFP 1973

Two Lines Are Better Than One C 15 MIN
3/4 OR 1/2 INCH VIDEO CASSETTE I
Introduces rhyme and meter for writing poetry.
From The Tyger, Tyger Burning Bright Series.
Prod-CTI Dist-CTI

Two Little Frosts C 13 MIN
16MM FILM, 3/4 OR 1/2 IN VIDEO
Presents an animated story about two frost creatures who assume that an old peasant will be an easy target. Shows how, despite all their attempts, the experienced woodsman goes on about his work.
LC NO. 81-706880
Prod-TRNKAJ Dist-PHENIX 1973

Two Little Owls C 20 MIN
16MM FILM, 3/4 OR 1/2 IN VIDEO J-C A
Shows scientists climbing to a 55 foot high nest to band young owls. Follows the owls from the time they hatch as little white pullballs to the time they fledge. Depicts a uniquely different nocturnal bird that isn't often seen in the wild.
Prod-BERLET Dist-BERLET

Two Little Soldiers By Guy De Maupassant, The C 15 MIN
16MM FILM, 3/4 OR 1/2 IN VIDEO J-C A
Explores the consequences of friendship betrayed, emphasizing the despair which can occur when one partner directs excessive attention toward a third person whose friendship the two once shared. Based on the short story Two Little Soldiers By Guy de Maupassant.
From The Short Story Series.
LC NO. 83-706139
Prod-IITC Dist-IU 1982

Two Masks - One Face C 60 MIN
3/4 OR 1/2 INCH VIDEO CASSETTE H-C A
See series title for descriptive statement.
From The Art Of Being Human Series.
Prod-FI Dist-FI 1978

Two Men And A Wardrobe B 15 MIN
16MM FILM, 3/4 OR 1/2 IN VIDEO H-C A
Presents Polish film director Roman Polanski's fantasy-parable about two men who are denied the hospitality of a town because they carry a large wardrobe cabinet with them.
Prod-POLSKI Dist-TEXFLM 1957

Two Men And A Wardrobe / The Fat And The Lean B 35 MIN
3/4 OR 1/2 INCH VIDEO CASSETTE
Presents a fantasy-parable elucidating the problems of maintaining a private life in the world today, an example of absurdism without dialogue. Uses the relationship between a vulgar, filthy man and his browbeaten servant to attack government tyranny and absurdity, a parable told in terms of broad comedy. Directed by Roman Polanski.
Prod-IHF Dist-IHF

Two Minutes C 2 MIN
16MM FILM OPTICAL SOUND J-C
Presents the history of the state of Israel told vividly and dramatically in still photos.
Prod-STNIZ Dist-SLFP 1969

Two Minutes - The History Of Israel In Two Minutes C 3 MIN
16MM FILM OPTICAL SOUND I-C A
A kaleidoscopic, almost subliminal survey of the history of Israel from 1938-1971, using over 500 still photos.
Prod-CFS Dist-CFS

Two More Every Second C 30 MIN
3/4 OR 1/2 INCH VIDEO CASSETTE C A
See series title for descriptive statement.
From The Introduction To World Food Problems Series.
Prod-UMA Dist-GPITVL 1977

Two Mountainlands - Alps And Andes C 15 MIN
16MM FILM, 3/4 OR 1/2 IN VIDEO K-P
Shows how the Alps and the Andes Mountains are both similar and different through unrehearsed comments of people of each region and photography.
From The Comparative Cultures And Geography Series.
Prod-LCOA Dist-LCOA 1971

Two Mountainlands - Alps And Andes (Captioned) C 15 MIN
16MM FILM, 3/4 OR 1/2 IN VIDEO I-H
Compares two different lifestyles through unrehearsed comments of the people and searching photography of the Alps and the Andes
Prod-LCOA Dist-LCOA 1971

Two Mountainlands - Alps And Andes (Spanish) C 15 MIN
16MM FILM, 3/4 OR 1/2 IN VIDEO I-H
Compares two different lifestyles through unrehearsed comments of the people and searching photography of the Alps and the Andes
Prod-LCOA Dist-LCOA 1971

Two Names - Jose C 30 MIN
3/4 OR 1/2 INCH VIDEO CASSETTE
See series title for descriptive statement.
From The Rebop Series.
Prod-WGBHTV Dist-MDCPB

Two Of Hearts C 60 MIN
3/4 OR 1/2 INCH VIDEO CASSETTE J A
Presents the story of a young black girl in desperate need of a kidney transplant who learns upon meeting her long-absent mother that she is really bi-racial.
From The Rainbow Movie Of The Week Series.
Prod-RAINTV Dist-GPITVL 1981

Two Or Three Things I Know About Her (French) C 85 MIN
16MM FILM OPTICAL SOUND
Describes a Parisian housewife who turns part-time prostitute to make ends meet. Directed by Jean-Luc Godard. With English subtitles.
Prod-UNKNWN Dist-NYFLMS 1966

Two Original Open-Heart Operations C 25 MIN
16MM FILM OPTICAL SOUND PRO
Presents two open-heart operations. Shows the repair of a rupture at the base of the aorta into the left atrium and the removal of a billiard ball-sized myxomatous tumor from the left ventricle.
Prod-UPJOHN Dist-UPJOHN 1959

Two Plus Six Minus 1 C 18 MIN
16MM FILM OPTICAL SOUND
A revealing look into the lives of eight teenagers, two who meet their need for companionship, acceptance and peer recognition through wholesome fun and activities and six who depend upon alcoholic beverages for their kicks.
LC NO. 74-702898
Prod-MARTC Dist-MARTC 1973

Two Ports B
16MM FILM OPTICAL SOUND
Introduces two-port network theory.
Prod-OPENU Dist-OPENU

Two Profession Marriage, The C 29 MIN
3/4 OR 1/2 INCH VIDEO CASSETTE
Features a successful two-profession couple discussing their feelings about their situation and telling how other people react to it.
From The Woman Series.
Prod-WNEDTV Dist-PBS

Two Programs By Stan Vanderbeek–A Series

Presents programs by Stan Vanderbeek, about-garde video artist.
Prod-EAI Dist-EAI

Strobe Ode 008 MIN
Vanishing Point 010 MIN

Two Programs By William Roarty C 28 MIN
3/4 OR 1/2 INCH VIDEO CASSETTE
Presents two programs by William Roarty, painter and teacher.
Prod-EAI Dist-EAI

Two Puppet Shows C 9 MIN
16MM FILM, 3/4 OR 1/2 IN VIDEO P-J
Presents two mechanical puppet shows filmed at the IBM exhibit of the New York World's Fair, humorously explaining aspects of computer operation.
Prod-EAMES Dist-PFP 1965

Two Rescuer CPR C 15 MIN
16MM FILM, 3/4 OR 1/2 IN VIDEO H-C A
See series title for descriptive statement.
From The REACT - Review Of Emergency Aid And CPR Training Series.
Prod-MTI Dist-MTI

Two See C 15 MIN
16MM FILM OPTICAL SOUND
A montage of the various aspects of training guide dogs for the blind, showing a dog's development from the time it leaves the care of a young boy to its final training as a guide dog by the Pilot Dog Organization.
LC NO. 77-705704
Prod-PIDO Dist-OSUMPD Prodn-OSUPD 1969

Two Sleeping Lions X 5 MIN
16MM FILM OPTICAL SOUND K-P
Presents Otto, an animated automobile which is disturbed about the people who are crossing the street in mid-block. Shows how Otto the Auto makes use of caged circus lions to stress that no one should cross from between parked cars.
From The Otto The Auto Series.
Prod-AAAFTS Dist-AAAFTS 1957

Two Sons (Family Communications) C 15 MIN
16MM FILM, 3/4 OR 1/2 IN VIDEO J
Presents a family situation in which one son is cast as the good boy and one son as the bad boy. Discusses how to deal with this problem.
From The Self Incorporated Series.
LC NO. 75-703957
Prod-AITV Dist-AITECH Prodn-KETCTV 1975

Two Sounds Of OO - Ways To Break Words Into Syllables C 20 MIN
3/4 OR 1/2 INCH VIDEO CASSETTE J-H
See series title for descriptive statement.
From The Getting The Word Series. Unit IV
Prod-SCETV Dist-AITECH 1974

Two Steps At A Time B 8 MIN
16MM FILM OPTICAL SOUND
Studies a young woman whose rehabilitation from an accident which resulted in the loss of both legs and one arm is complicated by the addition of the role of mother to that of wife.
Prod-USC Dist-USC 1981

Two Steps To Safety B 10 MIN
16MM FILM OPTICAL SOUND
Discusses knowing yourself and your job as requisites to safety.
From The Personal Side Of Safety Series.
Prod-NSC Dist-NSC

Two Stories For Christmas C 30 MIN
16MM FILM OPTICAL SOUND K-P
Presents the stories of Christopher Mouse and When the Littlest Camel Knelt, done in cartoon art form.
Prod-YALEDV Dist-YALEDV

Two Tars B 30 MIN
16MM FILM SILENT I-C
Features two GOBS on shore leave, a rented Model T roadster, two girls, a traffic jam and a mile long string of now vintage automobiles in this comedy, starring Laurel and Hardy.
From The Laurel And Hardy Festival Series.
LC NO. 73-713145
Prod-ROACH Dist-BHAWK 1928

Two Thanksgiving Day Gentlemen By O Henry, The C 15 MIN
16MM FILM, 3/4 OR 1/2 IN VIDEO J-C A
Tells the story of a special Thanksgiving Day feast given each year by an old man tied to tradition for a seemingly less fortunate man. Based on the short story The Two Thanksgiving Day Gentlemen by O Henry.
From The Short Story Series.
LC NO. 83-706141
Prod-IITC Dist-IU 1982

Two Thousand Years In One Generation C 20 MIN
16MM FILM, 3/4 OR 1/2 IN VIDEO H-C A
Explores the impact of new technology on developing nations and responsibilities that come with it.

From The Communications Revolution Series.
Prod-NVIDC Dist-MTI

Two To Get Ready C 30 MIN
16MM FILM, 3/4 OR 1/2 IN VIDEO
Examines the various emotions which both parents experience during pregnancy, suggesting ways to resolve these feelings and prepare for the birth of the child and the role of a parent.
From The Footsteps Series.
Prod-USOE Dist-USNAC 1978

Two To Get Ready - Prenatal Preparation C 23 MIN
16MM FILM - VIDEO, ALL FORMATS
Deals with the ways parents-to-be prepare for the birth of a child. Focuses on psychological preparation.
From The Footsteps Series.
Prod-PEREN Dist-PEREN

Two Towns - Gubbio, Italy And Chillicothe, Ohio C 22 MIN
16MM FILM, 3/4 OR 1/2 IN VIDEO P-I
Explains that the towns of Gubbio in Italy and Chillicothe in southeastern Ohio are both agricultural centers of about 30 thousand people. Describes the different value systems based on historical, cultural and geographical considerations that have created different life styles. Shows scenes of daily routines.
From The Comparative Cultures And Geography Series.
Prod-LCOA Dist-LCOA 1973

Two Towns - Gubbio, Italy, And Chillicothe, Ohio (Spanish) C 22 MIN
16MM FILM, 3/4 OR 1/2 IN VIDEO I-H
Explores the ways in which Gubbio, Italy, and Chillicothe, Ohio, function as communities.
Prod-LCOA Dist-LCOA 1973

Two Traditions, The C 50 MIN
3/4 OR 1/2 INCH VIDEO CASSETTE
Explains how Shakespeare's heightened language and modern naturalistic expectations must be brought into balance if Shakespeare is to be meaningful. Deals with how to understand Shakespeare's texts, which were written 200 years before motivation and characterization entered the critical vocabulary.
From The Royal Shakespeare Company Series.
Prod-FOTH Dist-FOTH 1984

Two Wagons - Both Covered B 20 MIN
16MM FILM SILENT
Stars Will Rogers in a satire of a wagon train movie.
Prod-UNKNWN Dist-REELIM 1923

Two Witches C 1 MIN
3/4 OR 1/2 INCH VIDEO CASSETTE
Explains, in a television spot featuring two different witches, that we are what we eat.
Prod-KIDSCO Dist-KIDSCO

Two Words For One C 20 MIN
2 INCH VIDEOTAPE P
See series title for descriptive statement.
From The Learning Our Language, Unit 2 - Dictionary Skills Series.
Prod-MPATI Dist-GPITVL

Two Works By Jud Yalkut—A Series

Prod-EAI Dist-EAI

Chocolate Cello, The 030 MIN
Twenty-Six Feet, One Point One Four Nine Nine 042 MIN

Two Worlds C 30 MIN
3/4 INCH VIDEO CASSETTE
Discusses the condition of today's American Indian. Focuses on problems of integrating Indian into mainstream of American life.
Prod-KNBCTV Dist-ADL

Two Worlds Of Angelita, The C 73 MIN
3/4 INCH VIDEO CASSETTE I-C A
A spanish language videocassette with English subtitles. Relates the odyssey of a Puerto Rican family through the eyes of the nine-year-old daughter.
LC NO. 84-706138
Prod-FIRS Dist-FIRS 1983

Two Worlds Of Hong Kong, The C 24 MIN
16MM FILM, 3/4 OR 1/2 IN VIDEO J-C A
Explores the clash between the cultures of the East and the West as exemplified by the lives of two Hong Kong families. Shows how changing values can affect traditional lifestyles and strain strong family ties. Explores the street markets, the religious shrines and Hong Kong's busy harbor.
LC NO. 80-706318
Prod-NGS Dist-NGS 1979

Two Worlds To Remember C 40 MIN
16MM FILM, 3/4 OR 1/2 IN VIDEO H-C A
Presents two elderly women, a widowed actress and a divorcee, who share their transition from previously independent lives to a Jewish home for the aged. Follows them through the sensitive process of adjustment and their attempt to keep the two worlds of the past and present in balance.
Prod-JNSNP Dist-PHENIX 1978

Two Worlds, Twenty Years B 29 MIN
16MM FILM - 3/4 IN VIDEO
Contrasts the economic development of Belgium and Czechoslovakia in the post-World War II era. Issued in 1971 as a motion picture.
LC NO. 79-706683
Prod-NATO Dist-USNAC 1979

Two-Cycle Engine, The C 4 MIN
16MM FILM, 3/4 OR 1/2 IN VIDEO J-C A
See series title for descriptive statement.
From The Power Mechanics Series.
Prod-THIOKL Dist-CAROUF

Two-D And 3-Art C 15 MIN
3/4 INCH VIDEO CASSETTE P
See series title for descriptive statement.
From The Is The Sky Always Blue Series.
Prod-WDCNTV Dist-GPITVL 1979

Two-Dimensional Echocardiography C 9 MIN
3/4 OR 1/2 INCH VIDEO CASSETTE PRO
Demonstrates techniques for taking echocardiograms and outlines various uses for the tests. Covers three case studies.
Prod-HSCIC Dist-HSCIC Prodn-HSCIC 1984

Two-Dimensional Graphics C 17 MIN
3/4 OR 1/2 INCH VIDEO CASSETTE A
Examines the possibilities of flat graphics in business, industry and the professions. Discusses simulations, CAD/CAM interactive programing, animation and more.
From The All About Computer Graphics Series.
Prod-EDDIM Dist-EDDIM

Two-Edged Sword, A C 58 MIN
3/4 OR 1/2 INCH VIDEO CASSETTE
Focuses on Tay Sachs disease, a fatal genetic disease affecting infants causing them to lose their sight, hearing and other senses, as well as motor functions.
From The Through The Genetic Maze Series.
Prod-PSU Dist-PBS 1982

Two-Headed Dragon, The B 16 MIN
16MM FILM OPTICAL SOUND J-C A
Examines the struggle between Chiang Kai-Shek, leader of Nationalist China, and Mao Tse-Tung, leader of Communist China, for control of the country. Discusses the decision of the United Nations to seat the People's Republic of China and to expel the Nationalist Chinese government.
From The Screen News Digest Series. Vol 14, No. 3
LC NO. 72-702750
Prod-HEARST Dist-HEARST 1971

Two-Hundred One - Two-Hundred Three B 20 MIN
16MM FILM OPTICAL SOUND H-C A
Presents two occupants of neighboring hotel rooms, one an occidental male, the other an oriental female. Follows the private fantasies of each as they see the other in terms of the myths wrought by Hollywood movies.
LC NO. FIA68-373
Prod-SHAHK Dist-CFS 1970

Two-Legged Space Ship, The C 15 MIN
16MM FILM, 3/4 OR 1/2 IN VIDEO P-I
Presents a narcotics primer in which a group of elementary school students learn that they can do their part right now in stopping the pollution of the earth, the space ship of all mankind, by deciding not to pollute their own bodies and minds.
Prod-DAVP Dist-AIMS 1972

Two-Minute Drill, The C 17 MIN
16MM FILM OPTICAL SOUND
Presents Fran Tarkenton who explains how sales and support people can apply the time management techniques of a premiere quarterback. Uses football footage to stress that time is the most precious ally.
Prod-PROIC Dist-PROIC 1979

Two-Pencil Technique, The C 29 MIN
3/4 INCH VIDEO CASSETTE C A
Reviews elements of drawing and introduces the two pencil technique. Demonstrates use of color to give drawings a finished look.
From The Sketching Techniques Series. Lesson 2
Prod-COAST Dist-CDTEL

Two-Person Communication—A Series
16MM FILM - 3/4 IN VIDEO IND
Focuses on the communication and control skills of reporting, negotiating and counseling.
Prod-BNA Dist-BNA

Building A Working Team - Let's Get
Gathering Good Information - Get'em Up, Scout 026 MIN
Helping People Develop - Don't Tell Me 033 MIN
Maintaining The Organization - How Far 033 MIN
Seeking Understanding And Acceptance - Try 033 MIN

Two-Rescuer CPR C 9 MIN
3/4 OR 1/2 INCH VIDEO CASSETTE PRO
Explains three ways the procedures should be varied with two rescuers instead of one.
From The Cardiopulmonary Resuscitation Series.
Prod-HSCIC Dist-HSCIC 1984

Two-Sample Inference C
3/4 OR 1/2 INCH VIDEO CASSETTE IND
Describes two-sample inference as way of making fair comparisons between one's own products, or a comparison with your product and the competition. Discusses paired and unpaired sample designs. Covers how to use these designs and how to calculate the statistics.
From The Statistics For Managers Series.
Prod-COLOSU Dist-COLOSU

Two-Sample Tests For Quantitative Data C 30 MIN
3/4 OR 1/2 INCH VIDEO CASSETTE IND
Includes F test for comparing two variances as well as two-sample independent t and paired t tests. Says paired t is used to compare before and after results. Discusses comparison of results from two production lines for comparing independent samples. Emphasizes proper distinction and usage of non-independent and independent sampling.
From The Engineering Statistics Series.
Prod-COLOSU Dist-COLOSU

Two-Team Pelvic Exenteration C 33 MIN
16MM FILM OPTICAL SOUND PRO
Demonstrates total pelvic exenteration carried out by two surgical teams operating simultaneously through the perineum and abdomen. Includes positioning the patient, the pelvic lymph node dissection, the perineal dissection, the en bloc mobilization of the pelvic viscera and the construction of an ileal urinary conduit.
Prod-ACYDGD Dist-ACY 1959

Two-Tenths Percent Solution, The C 6 MIN
16MM FILM OPTICAL SOUND A
Describes the benefits and procedures for conducting fluoride mouth rinse programs in schools.
Prod-NIH Dist-MTP

Two-Wheeler C 17 MIN
16MM FILM - 3/4 IN VIDEO P-C A
Provides a penetrating view inside the world of bicycle racing. Experiences the color and excitement of the sport.
Prod-OAKCRK Dist-CRYSP

Two-Year-Old Goes To Hospital, A B 50 MIN
16MM FILM OPTICAL SOUND
Shows the behavior of a two-year-old during a stay of eight days in a hospital ward as part of a study of the effects of maternal deprivation.
Prod-NYU Dist-NYU

Two-Year-Old Goes to Hospital, A (Abridged Ed) B 30 MIN
16MM FILM OPTICAL SOUND
Features the abridged version of the film showing the behavior of a two-year-old during her eight day stay in a hospital ward as part of a study of the effects of maternal deprivation. Omits much of the research detail of the original to leave a pure narrative.
Prod-NYU Dist-NYU

Two, Three Fasten Your Ski C 17 MIN
16MM FILM, 3/4 OR 1/2 IN VIDEO I-C
Tells the story of three amputee patients at Children's Hospital in Denver who are enrolled in the hospital's rehabilitation Amputee Ski School.
Prod-OAKCRK Dist-PHENIX 1972

Two, Three, Fasten Your Ski C 18 MIN
3/4 INCH VIDEO CASSETTE P-C A
Portrays the exciting hospital rehabilitation program for amputee skiers. Outlines the learning process necessary for the amputee and the challenges from the skiers point of view.
Prod-LENATK Dist-CRYSP

TWU Tel C 19 MIN
3/4 INCH VIDEO CASSETTE
Discusses the issues of the strike of the employees of the Telecommunications Workers Union in British Columbia, 1981. Provides the public with some understanding of the working conditions in a modern day 'sweat shop'.
Prod-AMELIA Dist-WMENIF

Ty's Home-Made Band C 20 MIN
1/2 IN VIDEO CASSETTE BETA/VHS
Tells the story of a traveling minstrel teaching a boy how to make music from home-made instruments. Based on the book by Mildred Pitts Walter.
Prod-BFA Dist-BFA

Ty's Home-Made Band C 20 MIN
16MM FILM, 3/4 OR 1/2 IN VIDEO P-I
Tells how a traveling musician convinces a young boy that he can have his own band by using things found around the house, and with helpful parents and friends, he succeeds and entertains everyone with a concert, led by his musician friend.
LC NO. 84-706736
Prod-EVRGRN Dist-PHENIX 1983

Ty's One Man Band C 30 MIN
3/4 OR 1/2 INCH VIDEO CASSETTE P
Presents Lou Rawls narrating the story of a mysterious stranger who creates a one-man band out of odds and ends. Shows LeVar Burton discovering lots of different music and Ben Vereen dancing.
From The Reading Rainbow Series. No. 15
Prod-WNEDTV Dist-GPITVL 1982

Tyger, Tyger Burning Bright—A Series
I
Presents a program in creative writing. Uses drama, pantomime, film, music, poetry, prose and analogies to stimulate the creative writing experience. Includes writing exercises.
Prod-CTI Dist-CTI

Cement Your Thoughts 015 MIN
Each Teach 015 MIN
Every Word Counts 015 MIN
Frog's Back Is Like, A 015 MIN
Give Your Character Warts 015 MIN
It Isn't Easy To Be Simple 015 MIN
Limericks For Laughs 015 MIN
Making The Scene 015 MIN
Ordinary Can Be Extraordinary, The 015 MIN
Picture It With Words 015 MIN
Poetry Is Made By People 015 MIN
Repeat Yourself, Please 015 MIN
Reshape, Remake 015 MIN
Three R's, The 015 MIN
Two Lines Are Better Than One 015 MIN
Weave A Web Of Mystery 015 MIN

Tying The Knot B 26 MIN
16MM FILM OPTICAL SOUND

Uses documentary footage to describe Churchill's meeting with Roosevelt aboard the USS Quiney in Alexandria Harbor, the first crossing of the Rine at Remagen Bridge, British opposition to Eisenhower's plan to let the Russians enter Berlin and the death of Roosevelt. Based on the book 'THE SECOND WORLD WAR,' by Winston S Churchill
From The Winston Churchill—The Valiant Years Series. No. 24
LC NO. FI67-2120
Prod-ABCTV Dist-SG 1961

Tyner - Shared Parenting C 25 MIN
3/4 INCH VIDEO CASSETTE C A
Shows how a mother and father share the early rearing of their four-month-old child between themselves and an infant day-care center.
LC NO. 81-706226
Prod-CUETV Dist-CUNIV 1981

Type A Personality C 30 MIN
3/4 OR 1/2 INCH VIDEO CASSETTE
States that if you are a Type A personality you are more likely to suffer a heart attack than others.
From The Here's To Your Health Series.
LC NO. 82-706500
Prod-KERA Dist-PBS 1979

Type A Personality C 30 MIN
3/4 OR 1/2 INCH VIDEO CASSETTE
See series title for descriptive statement.
From The Here's To Your Health Series.
Prod-PBS Dist-DELTAK

Type A Personality And Heart Disease C 30 MIN
3/4 OR 1/2 INCH VIDEO CASSETTE C T
Discusses the Type A personality. Suggests ways of controlling such behavior to minimize its risk to health.
From The Here's To Your Health Series.
Prod-DALCCD Dist-DALCCD

Type Two Diabetes - A New Approach To Patient Management C 31 MIN
3/4 OR 1/2 INCH VIDEO CASSETTE PRO
Demonstrates changes in insulin secretion and in insulin resistance that lead to the development of Type II or ketosis-resistant diabetes mellitus. Illustrates the interrelationships among changes in insulin resistance, insulin secretion and blood glucose concentration. Presents a short-term therapeutic intervention that will enhance the chances of preserving part of the patients' endogenous glucose regulatory system and long-term blood sugar control.
Prod-UMICHM Dist-UMICHM 1983

Type Z - An Alternative Management Style C 95 MIN
3/4 OR 1/2 INCH VIDEO CASSETTE A
Presents William G Ouchi, professor at UCLA Graduate School of Management, explaining his Type Z theory of management. Describes the American and Japanese approaches to management, puts them in their cultural contexts and discusses how American companies could profitably borrow techniques from the Japanese.
Prod-CBSFOX Dist-CBSFOX

Types Of Adjustments For Auto Door Glass C 9 MIN
1/2 IN VIDEO CASSETTE BETA/VHS
Deals with auto body repair. Demonstrates components of mechanism and adjustment procedures.
Prod-RMI Dist-RMI

Types Of Controllers C 30 MIN
3/4 OR 1/2 INCH VIDEO CASSETTE
Shows in depth look at controller types from previous session design examples. Emphasizes hardware implementation.
From The Digital Sub-Systems Series.
Prod-TXINLC Dist-TXINLC

Types Of Floors C 11 MIN
16MM FILM - 3/4 IN VIDEO IND
Presents the types of floors commonly found in health care facilities, stressing the proper cleaning and maintenance of each type.
From The Housekeeping Personnel Series.
Prod-COPI Dist-COPI 1972

Types Of Maps C 20 MIN
3/4 INCH VIDEO CASSETTE I-J
Shows professionals talking about the use of maps in their work. Describes possible advancements and developments in mapmaking.
From The Map And Globe Skills Series.
Prod-WCVETV Dist-GPITVL 1979

Types Of Paint Finishes C 13 MIN
1/2 IN VIDEO CASSETTE BETA/VHS
Deals with auto body repair. Explains the difference between lacquers and enamels and the advantages and disadvantages of both. Discusses the characteristics of lacquers and enamels.
Prod-RMI Dist-RMI

Typewriter Techniques C 12 MIN
16MM FILM, 3/4 OR 1/2 IN VIDEO J-H
Analyzes the action of electric typing as compared to manual typing and then describes the manipulative parts of the manual machine—the function adn purpose of the space bar and the tabulator, setting the margin and responding to the bell. Closely analyzes the various functions of the back spacer, the carriage release, the line finder, the margin release and the variable button. Further demonstrations show the location of numbers and their operation.
Prod-SEF Dist-SF 1968

Typewriting, Unit 1 - Keyboard Control—A Series

Prod-GPITVL Dist-GPITVL

A S D F And J K L Keys 30 MIN
C M W Y V N Keys 30 MIN
E U G And Right Shift Keys 30 MIN
I O T Keys, Counting Errors 30 MIN
R H And Left Shift Keys 30 MIN
X P B Z Q Keys 30 MIN

Typewriting, Unit 2 - Skill Development—A Series

Prod-GPITVL Dist-GPITVL

Skill Drills - Paragraph Centering, Block
Skill Drills - Vertical And Horizontal 30 MIN

Typewriting, Unit 3 - Number Key Control—A Series

Prod-GPITVL Dist-GPITVL

One 2 3 4 5 6 7 8 9 0 Keys 30 MIN
One-Half, One-Fourth, 5 6 Keys, Centering 30 MIN

Typewriting, Unit 4 - Skill Development—A Series

Prod-GPITVL Dist-GPITVL

Selective Practice - Margin Bell 30 MIN
Selective Practice - Word Division, Pt 1 30 MIN
Selective Practice - Word Division, Pt 2 30 MIN

Typewriting, Unit 5 - Correspondence, Tabulations And Manuscripts—A Series

Prod-GPITVL Dist-GPITVL

Basic Open-Style Tables 30 MIN
Basic Report Forms 30 MIN
Blocked Business Letters 30 MIN
Blocked Personal Letters 30 MIN
Column-Headed Tables 30 MIN
Constructed Symbols, Enumerations 30 MIN
Review - Letter, Table Manuscript 30 MIN

Typewriting, Unit 6 - Skill Development—A Series

Prod-GPITVL Dist-GPITVL

Selective Practice - Centering On Line 30 MIN
Selective Practice - Corrections 30 MIN
Selective Practice - Insertions 30 MIN

Typewriting, Unit 7 - Postal Cards, Forms, Manuscripts—A Series

Prod-GPITVL Dist-GPITVL

Addressing Envelopes - Attention And Subject
Bound Manuscripts With Footnotes 30 MIN
Inter-Office Memorandum Forms 30 MIN
Invoice And Telegram Forms - Carbons 30 MIN
Plain And Fill-In Postal Cards 30 MIN
Review - Letters, Forms, Reports 30 MIN
Revision Marks, Unbound Reports, How To Erase 30 MIN

Typical Appearance And Behavior Of Newborns C 20 MIN
3/4 OR 1/2 INCH VIDEO CASSETTE H-C A
Gives parents basic information about the physical signs and behavior of newborns. Explains that some may seem unusual or abnormal, but are common.
Prod-UARIZ Dist-UARIZ

Typical Frame Damage C 6 MIN
1/2 IN VIDEO CASSETTE BETA/VHS
Deals with auto body repair. Discusses rear and front end damages, yield point by yield point.
Prod-RMI Dist-RMI

Typical Instrumentation Diagrams, Loop Diagrams C 60 MIN
3/4 OR 1/2 INCH VIDEO CASSETTE IND
See series title for descriptive statement.
From The Instrumentation Basics - Instrumentation Diagrams And Symbols Series. Tape 2
Prod-ISA Dist-ISA

Typing - Insurance—A Series

Prod-RMI Dist-RMI

Insurance Abstracting 007 MIN
Insurance Typewriting - Auto Insurance 012 MIN
Insurance Typewriting - Fire Insurance 007 MIN
Insurance Typewriting - Health Insurance 007 MIN
Insurance Typewriting - Homeowner's Insurance 011 MIN
Insurance Typewriting - Inland Marine Insurance 010 MIN
Insurance Typewriting - Introduction 004 MIN
Insurance Typewriting - Life Insurance 010 MIN

Typing - Legal—A Series

Prod-RMI Dist-RMI

Legal Typing - A Lawyer Defines A Good Legal
Legal Typing - Course Introduction 017 MIN

Typing - Medical—A Series

Prod-RMI Dist-RMI

Medical Assistant's Transcribing 006 MIN
Medical Transcribing 008 MIN
Medical Typing - Consultation Report 004 MIN
Medical Typing - Discharge Summary Or 006 MIN
Medical Typing - Electroencephalogram 006 MIN
Medical Typing - Filing Rules 010 MIN
Medical Typing - History And Physical 012 MIN
Medical Typing - Introduction 006 MIN
Medical Typing - Laboratory 017 MIN
Medical Typing - Medical Records 012 MIN
Medical Typing - Operative Report 004 MIN
Medical Typing - Radiology 016 MIN
Problem-Oriented Medical Record 004 MIN

Typing A Resume C 8 MIN
1/2 IN VIDEO CASSETTE BETA/VHS
Prod-RMI Dist-RMI

Typing Skills - Fields Of Typing C 14 MIN
16MM FILM, 3/4 OR 1/2 IN VIDEO H-C A
Offers pointers for student and working typists on how to improve efficiency and reduce wasted time in many kinds of typing jobs.
From The Typing Skills Series.
Prod-CORF Dist-CORF 1972

Typing Skills - Position And Keystroke C 11 MIN
16MM FILM, 3/4 OR 1/2 IN VIDEO H-C A
Uses slow-motion photography from a time and motion study to show the role keystroke has in good typing practices.
From The Typing Skills Series.
Prod-CORF Dist-CORF 1972

Typing Skills—A Series
16MM FILM, 3/4 OR 1/2 IN VIDEO H-C A
Explains the different kinds of typing skills and shows how typing can be used in various jobs and for personal needs.
Prod-CORF Dist-CORF

Typing Skills - Building Speed 011 MIN
Typing Skills - Daily Job Techniques 013 MIN
Typing Skills - Fields Of Typing 014 MIN
Typing Skills - Position And Keystroke 011 MIN

Typing Techniques C 12 MIN
16MM FILM, 3/4 OR 1/2 IN VIDEO I-H
Presents various typing techniques including correcting typographical errors on ordinary typing paper and on carbons, handling and insertion of carbon copies, insertion, lining up and typing envelopes in the single and multiple envelope systems and the re-alignment of an interrupted letter. Reveals important facets of electric typing in relation to the balancing force of the keys and impression indicator.
From The Business And Office Practices Series.
Prod-SF Dist-SF 1969

Tyrannus Nix C 12 MIN
16MM FILM OPTICAL SOUND H-C A
Presents a case against Richard Nixon, narrated by American poet Lawrence Ferlinghetti. Describes Nixon as a computerized man, a war machine who betrays the American dream.
Prod-NYFLMS Dist-NYFLMS

Tyranny Of Control, The C 60 MIN
16MM FILM, 3/4 OR 1/2 IN VIDEO H-C A
Presents case studies of both free and controlled societies which support Dr Milton Friedman's argument against protection of domestic industry. Offers a debate between Dr Friedman and others who both agree and disagree with his views.
From The Free To Choose Series.
Prod-EBEC Dist-EBEC 1983

Tyranny Of Control, The (Discussion) C 30 MIN
16MM FILM, 3/4 OR 1/2 IN VIDEO H-C A
Offers a debate between Dr Milton Friedman and others on government protection of domestic industry.
From The Free To Choose (Discussion) Series.
Prod-EBEC Dist-EBEC 1983

Tyranny Of Control, The (Documentary) C 30 MIN
16MM FILM, 3/4 OR 1/2 IN VIDEO H-C A
Presents case studies of both free and controlled societies which support Dr Milton Friedman's argument against protection of domestic industry.
From The Free To Choose (Documentary) Series.
Prod-EBEC Dist-EBEC 1983

Tyrone Guthrie B 30 MIN
16MM FILM OPTICAL SOUND H-C A
Presents theatrical director Tyrone Guthrie, his ideas and methods of working. Shows him at home in Ireland, conducting a rehearsal in New York and talking with students at an American college. Guthrie discusses his general philosophy toward the theater as a medium.
From The Creative Person Series.
Prod-NET Dist-IU Prodn-BBCTV 1967

Tzaddik C 30 MIN
3/4 OR 1/2 INCH VIDEO CASSETTE
Presents ballet by Eliot Feld starring Mr Feld. The ballet celebrates the joy and satisfaction which devout Hassidic Jews derive from the study of the Bible and the Talmud.
Prod-EAI Dist-EAI

U

U N At Work B 17 MIN
16MM FILM OPTICAL SOUND J-H A
Depicts the birth and workings of the International Children's Emergency Fund.
Prod-UN Dist-UN 1949

U N I Shear C 4 MIN
1/2 IN VIDEO CASSETTE BETA/VHS IND

Develops manipulative welding skills using industrial equipment, and demonstrates common types of weld joints used in welding fabrication and repair. Includes a student workbook.
Prod-RMI Dist-RMI

U N In Crisis - A Successor For U Thant B 17 MIN
16MM FILM OPTICAL SOUND J-C A
Traces the history of the United Nations, and discusses the office of the secretary general.
From The Screen News Digest Series. Vol 9, Issue 3
LC NO. 77-700278
Prod-HEARST Dist-HEARST 1966

U N Proceedings - Anti-Zionist Resolution C 15 MIN
16MM FILM OPTICAL SOUND
Presents a condensation of the United Nations proceedings on November 10, 1975, on the Anti-Zionist Resolution, including selections of Ambassador Herzog and Ambassador Moynihan's speeches.
Prod-UJA Dist-ALDEN

U N Vs The Mid-East, The C
16MM FILM OPTICAL SOUND
Features Israel's Foreign Minister, Ambassador Abba Eban, who talks about his country's first 25 years and reveals its attitude today toward the United Nations and the possibilities for peace in the Middle East.
From The Dateline Israel, 1973 Series.
Prod-ADL Dist-ADL

U S - Soviet Joint Space Mission C 15 MIN
16MM FILM OPTICAL SOUND
Presents a pictorial report on the events leading up to the historic Apollo-Soyuz mission.
LC NO. 76-700488
Prod-NASA Dist-USNAC 1976

U S Air Force C 15 MIN
3/4 OR 1/2 INCH VIDEO CASSETTE I
Explains the qualifications and personal qualities required for a successful career in the U S Air Force.
From The Career Awareness Series.
Prod-KLVXTV Dist-GPITVL 1973

U S Air Force Academy C 4 MIN
16MM FILM OPTICAL SOUND
Tours the U S Air Force Academy. Designed to instill employees of Sears, Roebuck and Company with pride in America.
From The Update Appliances Meetings Series.
LC NO. 75-703012
Prod-SEARS Dist-SRCIPP 1975

U S And China C 29 MIN
3/4 INCH VIDEO CASSETTE
Assesses the relationship between the United States and China.
From The Conversations With Allen Whiting Series.
Prod-UMITV Dist-UMITV 1979

U S Army Air Force Report B 50 MIN
3/4 OR 1/2 INCH VIDEO CASSETTE
Introduces the first Army Air Force report made to be shown to the public. Contains air-combat footage from all theaters of war taken from 1941 through 1944.
Prod-IHF Dist-IHF

U S Cavalry Horsemanship Training—A Series

Demonstrates basic horsemarship techniques.
Prod-USCAVM Dist-EQVDL

Horsemanship - Aids And Gaits 038 MIN
Horsemanship - Care Of The Animal In The Field 031 MIN
Horsemanship - How To Saddle And Bridle 022 MIN
Horsemanship - Jumping And Cross Country 032 MIN
Horsemanship - Mounting And Dismounting 030 MIN
Horsemanship - Suppling Exercises 016 MIN

U S Champions, Pt 1 C 29 MIN
2 INCH VIDEOTAPE
See series title for descriptive statement.
From The Grand Master Chess Series.
Prod-KQEDTV Dist-PUBTEL

U S Champions, Pt 2 C 29 MIN
2 INCH VIDEOTAPE
See series title for descriptive statement.
From The Grand Master Chess Series.
Prod-KQEDTV Dist-PUBTEL

U S China Relations C 30 MIN
3/4 INCH VIDEO CASSETTE
Reflects on transitions and motives upon which America's relationship with China is based.
From The China After Mao Series.
Prod-UMITV Dist-UMITV 1980

U S Chronicle—A Series

Prod-WVIATV Dist-WVIATV 1980

At The Gate Alone 029 MIN

U S Cities - Growth And Development C 19 MIN
16MM FILM, 3/4 OR 1/2 IN VIDEO J-H
Examines the forces that shape American cities and how they determine a city's future growth or decline.
LC NO. 84-706059
Prod-JAYD Dist-EBEC 1984

U S Geography—A Series
16MM FILM, 3/4 OR 1/2 IN VIDEO J
Depicts the geography and way of life in principal regions of the United States.
Prod-MGHT Dist-MGHT

Agricultural Midwest, The 15 MIN
Manufacturing Midwest, The 15 MIN
Middle Atlantic Region, The 15 MIN
New England 15 MIN
Pacific Northwest, The 18 MIN
South Atlantic Region, The 15 MIN
South Central Region, The 15 MIN
Southwest, The 15 MIN

U S Grant - I Remember Appomattox C 17 MIN
16MM FILM, 3/4 OR 1/2 IN VIDEO I-C A
Dramatizes Ulysses S Grant's reminisces about Lee's surrender at Appomattox, Civil War battles, his boyhood days, love of horses and his West Point years.
Prod-CORF Dist-CORF 1976

U S Is - People, The C 15 MIN
16MM FILM, 3/4 OR 1/2 IN VIDEO I-C A
Explores the variety of national origins, places, lifestyles and occupations of the people of the United States. Shows how these have changed since the nation's beginning and points out certain American traits and beliefs.
Prod-MLTES Dist-PHENIX 1979

U S Is, The - Resources C 14 MIN
16MM FILM, 3/4 OR 1/2 IN VIDEO I-C A
Surveys the United States reserves of natural resources and points out that a high productivity of raw materials, goods and energy results from the availability of these resources. Emphasizes the importance of using the remaining resources wisely.
Prod-MLTES Dist-PHENIX 1979

U S Is, The - Resources (Swedish) C 14 MIN
16MM FILM, 3/4 OR 1/2 IN VIDEO I-C A
Surveys the United States reserves of natural resources and points out that a high productivity of raw materials, goods and energy results from the availability of these resources. Emphasizes the importance of using the remaining resources wisely.
Prod-MLTES Dist-PHENIX 1979

U S Marine Corps Bicentennial Television Spot C 2 MIN
16MM FILM, 3/4 OR 1/2 IN VIDEO H-C A
Illustrates patriotic scenery with the American National Anthem played by the Marine Corps Band.
Prod-USMC Dist-USNAC 1976

U S Men's Championships C
3/4 OR 1/2 INCH VIDEO CASSETTE
Prod-MSTVIS Dist-MSTVIS

U S Naval Observatory C 18 MIN
16MM FILM OPTICAL SOUND
Shows how astronomers and mathematicians determine time, predict and publish the positions of the sun, moon, stars and planets for navigation and scientific purposes in addition to doing fundamental astronomical research.
LC NO. 74-705869
Prod-USN Dist-USNAC 1970

U S Naval Test Pilot School, The C 13 MIN
16MM FILM OPTICAL SOUND
Follows a test pilot through the school at the Patuxent River Naval Air Station, showing the school's academic and flying curricula.
LC NO. FIE63-57
Prod-USN Dist-USNAC 1959

U S Navy Armored Life Jacket B 7 MIN
16MM FILM OPTICAL SOUND
Demonstrates how a bullet-proof fabric material called Doran can be used to protect Navy personnel against small arms fire.
LC NO. FIE52-1272
Prod-USN Dist-USNAC 1945

U S Neutrality, 1914-1917 B 17 MIN
16MM FILM, 3/4 OR 1/2 IN VIDEO H-C
Describes American neutrality during World War I, explaining how events gradually forged a national consensus against Germany.
From The World War I Series.
Prod-CBSTV Dist-FI 1967

U S Office Of Personnel Management C 20 MIN
3/4 OR 1/2 INCH VIDEO CASSETTE C A
A revised version of the 1978 videotape Federal Civil Service. Explains application procedures for obtaining a job in the U S government. Discusses the Professional Administrative Career Examination, hiring policies, advancement opportunities, the locations of jobs, and the lifestyles of employees.
From The Clues To Career Opportunities For Liberal Arts Graduates Series.
LC NO. 80-706239
Prod-IU Dist-IU 1979

U S Open, The - Trevino At Merion C 30 MIN
16MM FILM OPTICAL SOUND J-C A
Presents highlights of the 1971 U S Open, held at the Merion Golf Course in Philadelphia.
LC NO. 72-703184
Prod-USGOLF Dist-SFI 1972

U S Presidential Elections 1928-1968—A Series
C
Highlights the problems, politics and issues of the day from the presidential election of Herbert Hoover in 1928 through the election of Richard Nixon in 1968.
Prod-KRAUS Dist-KRAUS Prodn-AMSLFM 1975

Presidential Campaign Of 1952 9 MIN
Presidential Campaign Of 1956 9 MIN
Presidential Election Of 1928 7 MIN
Presidential Election Of 1932 16 MIN
Presidential Election Of 1936 7 MIN
Presidential Election Of 1940 6 MIN
Presidential Election Of 1944 9 MIN
Presidential Election Of 1948 10 MIN
Presidential Election Of 1960 16 MIN
Presidential Election Of 1964 10 MIN
Presidential Election Of 1968 9 MIN

U S Regions - Contrasts Of Land And People C 26 MIN
16MM FILM, 3/4 OR 1/2 IN VIDEO I-H
Describes and illustrates traditional regions of the United States. Shows how regional differences result from a combination of differences in physical environment and human history.
Prod-EBEC Dist-EBEC 1986

U S Senator, The C 20 MIN
2 INCH VIDEOTAPE J-H
Discusses, through a series of interviews, what a senator is, what he does, and the challenges he faces.
From The American System Series.
Prod-WCVETV Dist-GPITVL

U S Social Classes C 30 MIN
3/4 OR 1/2 INCH VIDEO CASSETTE C
Discusses two social classes, their values, behavior patterns and activities.
From The Focus On Society Series.
Prod-DALCCD Dist-DALCCD

U S Specialty Cities - Manufacturing Cities C 26 MIN
16MM FILM OPTICAL SOUND H-C A
Identifies and examines cities in the United States which specialize in manufacturing. Considers the historic, geographic, economic and social factors surrounding these cities and takes a look at their future viability.
LC NO. 76-700295
Prod-IU Dist-IU 1975

U S Staff Report No. 1 B 30 MIN
3/4 OR 1/2 INCH VIDEO CASSETTE
Presents U S Staff Reports from July, 1944, including Monsoons In Burma and Armies Near Gothic Line.
Prod-IHF Dist-IHF

U S Staff Report No. 2 B 30 MIN
3/4 OR 1/2 INCH VIDEO CASSETTE
Presents U S Staff Reports from 1944 including Chinese Round Out Training In Yunan and Allies take Elba.
Prod-IHF Dist-IHF

U S Staff Report No. 3 B 30 MIN
3/4 OR 1/2 INCH VIDEO CASSETTE
Presents U S Staff Reports from Nov-Dec, 1944, including Japs Saipan Base and Activities in East China.
Prod-IHF Dist-IHF

U S Staff Report No. 4 B 30 MIN
3/4 OR 1/2 INCH VIDEO CASSETTE
Presents U S Staff Reports from 1944 including 5th Army Enters Pisa and Activities in Burma - Aircraft Evacuating Wounded.
Prod-IHF Dist-IHF

U S Sweat C 15 MIN
3/4 OR 1/2 INCH VIDEO CASSETTE
Presents a montage of American landscape as seen from an automobile. Intercuts alarming events, places and sounds that interpret what is seen.
Prod-KITCHN Dist-KITCHN

U S Sweat - Shalom Gorewitz C 15 MIN
3/4 INCH VIDEO CASSETTE A
Prod-AFA Dist-AFA 1982

U S Vs USSR - Who's Ahead C 28 MIN
16MM FILM, 3/4 OR 1/2 IN VIDEO J-C
Strives to answer the question of which of the superpowers is militarily strongest. Interviews such experts as former director of the CIA William Colby, Admiral Hyman Rickover, General Homer Boushey (USAF), former director of Missiles Development at Wright Patterson AFB, and General William Fairbourn (USMC), former director of Operations and Planning for the Joint Chiefs of Staff.
From The Issues In The News Series.
Prod-FUNPC Dist-CNEMAG 1984

U S War Department Report - July 1943 - The Battle Of Industry B 55 MIN
3/4 OR 1/2 INCH VIDEO CASSETTE
Illustrates, through captured Japanese and German footage, the importance of industrial production. Includes a complete film segment from a German newsreel showing the Mussolini rescue.
Prod-IHF Dist-IHF

U S Women's Championships C
3/4 OR 1/2 INCH VIDEO CASSETTE
Prod-MSTVIS Dist-MSTVIS

U S-Soviet Relations - Potsdam To Vietnam C 27 MIN
3/4 OR 1/2 INCH VIDEO CASSETTE H-C A
Provides background on the relationships existing between the United States and Russia from the close of World War II to 1972. Focuses on the Cold War, the Korean conflict, the introduction of detente, and Vietnam.
Prod-UPI Dist-JOU

U S-Soviet Space Mission, The C 26 MIN
3/4 OR 1/2 INCH VIDEO CASSETTE
Documents the American-Russian space linkup in 1975. Explains that this was an historic moment not only in space technology but in United States-Soviet relations.
Prod-UPI Dist-JOU

U S/Europe Economic Conflict C 25 MIN
3/4 OR 1/2 INCH VIDEO CASSETTE H-C A
Discusses the fact that as the international economy continues

to experience recession the relations between the United States and Europe have experienced stresses with respect to trade, import/export and licensing. Explores the political and diplomatic implications of these controversies.
Prod-JOU Dist-JOU

U.S. Culture C 30 MIN
3/4 OR 1/2 INCH VIDEO CASSETTE C
Studies pleasure as a value and its impact upon American life in areas such as economics, family and community.
From The Focus On Society Series.
Prod-DALCCD Dist-DALCCD

U-Boot Am Feind/Now It Can Be Told B 39 MIN
3/4 OR 1/2 INCH VIDEO CASSETTE
Documents life on board a U-boat in the North Atlantic during World War II.
Prod-IHF Dist-IHF

U-100 Insulin C 12 MIN
3/4 OR 1/2 INCH VIDEO CASSETTE
Describes the U-100 insulin. Points out the differences of U-100 from other strengths of insulin.
Prod-MEDFAC Dist-MEDFAC 1981

Ubu Roi C 60 MIN
3/4 OR 1/2 INCH VIDEO CASSETTE H-C A
Discusses stylization, avantgardism, black theatre and realism in drama. Uses the play Ubu Roi as an example.
From The Drama - Play, Performance, Perception Series. Conventions Of The Theatre
Prod-BBCTV Dist-FI 1978

Uddeholm - A World Industry B 31 MIN
16MM FILM OPTICAL SOUND
Features Prince Wilhelm who pays a visit to Uddeholm's factory in the province of Varmland.
Prod-ASI Dist-AUDPLN

UFO - Unrestrained Flying Objects C 14 MIN
16MM FILM OPTICAL SOUND H A
Argues for universal and constant use of automobile seat belts. Describes their proper use and adjustment.
LC NO. 73-701439
Prod-GM Dist-GM Prodn-HANDY 1968

UFO - Unrestrained Flying Objects (2nd Ed) C 15 MIN
16MM FILM OPTICAL SOUND
Features crash tests conducted at the General Motors proving grounds using instrumented dummies to shows what happens in automobile collisions when restraints are used and when they are not used. Shows the correct way to wear seat belts and discusses other types of passive restraints.
LC NO. 79-700456
Prod-GM Dist-GM Prodn-COMICO 1978

UFO, The C 5 MIN
3/4 OR 1/2 INCH VIDEO CASSETTE J-H
Deals with avoiding jargon in writing.
From The Write On, Set 1 Series.
Prod-CTI Dist-CTI

UF6 From British Nuclear Fuels Limited C 15 MIN
16MM FILM OPTICAL SOUND
Illustrates the large-scale facilities for the conversion of uranium ore concentrates to uranium hexafluoride at Springfields. Shows the complete process from the refining of uranium ore at the mine to the final transport of uranium hexafluoride to US-AEC plants for enrichment.
Prod-UKAEA Dist-UKAEA 1971

Uganda - Guerrilla Threat C 22 MIN
3/4 OR 1/2 INCH VIDEO CASSETTE H-C A
Tells how Uganda, after ousting Idi Amin, stuggles under the cloud of that rule as guerrilla fighters continue to attack. Examines the past, present and future of Uganda.
Prod-JOU Dist-JOU

Ugly Duckling, The C 20 MIN
16MM FILM OPTICAL SOUND
Depicts the Hans Christian Andersen story of a baby swan and how he grew up to be a beautiful bird in spite of many hardships.
Prod-UNIJAP Dist-UNIJAP 1969

Ugly Duckling, The C 8 MIN
16MM FILM, 3/4 OR 1/2 IN VIDEO P-I
A baby duckling is shunned by his family because of his ugliness. He is rejected by all other birds and animals until a mother swan adopts him as one of her own. An animated cartoon.
Prod-DISNEY Dist-WDEMCO 1955

Ugly Duckling, The C 8 MIN
16MM FILM, 3/4 OR 1/2 IN VIDEO P
Demonstrates the need to tolerate individual differences and to believe in oneself. An animated international version.
Prod-WDEMCO Dist-WDEMCO 1955

Ugly Duckling, The C 11 MIN
16MM FILM, 3/4 OR 1/2 IN VIDEO P-I
Hans Christian Anderson's famous fairy tale of the unwanted duckling who becomes a beautiful swan. Filmed in Europe.
Prod-CORF Dist-CORF 1953

Ugly Duckling, The X 11 MIN
16MM FILM, 3/4 OR 1/2 IN VIDEO P-I
Presents the familiar fairy tale by Hans Christian Andersen, The Ugly Duckling, using real animals.
Prod-EBF Dist-EBEC 1952

Ugly Duckling, The C 11 MIN
16MM FILM, 3/4 OR 1/2 IN VIDEO P-I
Uses animation to tell the story of a homely duckling which grows up to be a beautiful swan. Based on the story The Ugly Duckling by Hans Christian Andersen.
From The Classic Tales Retold Series.
Prod-GREATT Dist-PHENIX 1979

Ugly Duckling, The C 15 MIN
3/4 OR 1/2 INCH VIDEO CASSETTE K-P
See series title for descriptive statement.
From The Gather Round Series.
Prod-CTI Dist-CTI

Ugly Duckling, The C 15 MIN
16MM FILM, 3/4 OR 1/2 IN VIDEO K-P
Presents an adaptation of Hans Christian Andersen's fairy tale The Ugly Duckling, which tells how an ugly bird turns into a beautiful swan.
Prod-NORDV Dist-WWS Prodn-KRATKY 1976

Ugly Duckling, The B 15 MIN
2 INCH VIDEOTAPE K-P
See series title for descriptive statement.
From The Tell Me A Story Series.
Prod-WQED Dist-NCSCT

Ugly Duckling, The (Spanish) C 11 MIN
16MM FILM, 3/4 OR 1/2 IN VIDEO P-I
Presents the Spanish language version of the film and videorecording The Ugly Duckling.
Prod-EBF Dist-EBEC 1953

Ugly Duckling, The (2nd Ed) C 17 MIN
16MM FILM, 3/4 OR 1/2 IN VIDEO K-I
Uses animated puppets to present Hans Christian Andersen's tale The Ugly Duckling. Follows the duckling through his many ordeals and then shares his exultation when he finds that he has become a swan.
Prod-CORF Dist-CORF 1982

Ugly Little Boy, The C 26 MIN
16MM FILM, 3/4 OR 1/2 IN VIDEO J-C A
Presents the story by Isaac Asimov about a child brought back through time from the Neanderthal age by a group of scientists who ignore the human factor in their experiment.
From The Classics, Dark And Dangerous Series.
Prod-LCOA Dist-LCOA 1977

Ugly Little Boy, The (Captioned) C 26 MIN
16MM FILM, 3/4 OR 1/2 IN VIDEO P-C A
Tells the story of a nurse caring for a young man brought back from the Neanderthal Age. Based on Story by Isaac Azimov.
From The Classics Dark And Dangerous (Captioned) Series.
Prod-LCOA Dist-LCOA 1977

Ugly Little Boy, The (Spanish) C 26 MIN
16MM FILM, 3/4 OR 1/2 IN VIDEO P-C A
Tells the story of a nurse, and a child brought back from the Neanderthal Age. Based on a story by Isaac Asimov.
From The Classics Dark And Dangerous (Spanish) Series.
Prod-LCOA Dist-LCOA 1977

Uhh, Whoosh And Thud - Science In Throwing And Catching C 14 MIN
16MM FILM, 3/4 OR 1/2 IN VIDEO I-J
Presents a puppet professor posing problems about the flight of balls.
From The Elementary Physical Science Series.
Prod-CENTRO Dist-CORF

Ujima - Modupe And The Flood C 5 MIN
16MM FILM, 3/4 OR 1/2 IN VIDEO K-I
Illustrates how a farmer in West Africa notices a dam is about to burst and drown his neighbors in the valley below, and saves them by setting his own house on fire, and causing the villagers to rush up the hill to help him.
From The Nguzo Saba-Folklore For Children Series.
Prod-NGUZO Dist-BCNFL 1979

Ujjaini B 12 MIN
16MM FILM OPTICAL SOUND H-C A
Presents Ujjain, in Rajasthan, as a famous seat of learning in history. Discusses the Sanskirt poet Kalidas, who lived there, the famous observatory and the enlightened ruler, Vikramaditya.
Prod-INDIA Dist-NEDINF

Ukiyo-E Prints C 22 MIN
16MM FILM OPTICAL SOUND
Presents Ukiyo-e (pictures of the transient world) which reflect the life and sentiments of the commoners of the Edo period (17th-19th centuries.)
Prod-UNIJAP Dist-UNIJAP 1969

Ukraine C 29 MIN
2 INCH VIDEOTAPE
Features home economist Joan Hood presenting a culinary tour of specialty dishes from around the world. Shows the preparation of Ukrainian dishes ranging from peasant cookery to continental cuisine.
From The International Cookbook Series.
Prod-WMVSTV Dist-PUBTEL

Ula No Weo C 26 MIN
16MM FILM OPTICAL SOUND
Shows how to learn the hula.
Prod-CINEPC Dist-CINEPC 1964

Ulcer At Work B 26 MIN
16MM FILM, 3/4 OR 1/2 IN VIDEO A
Demonstrates how the peptic ulcer can create unhappiness and failure in man's working and personal life.
Prod-UOKLA Dist-IFB 1959

Ulcerative Colitis B 30 MIN
16MM FILM OPTICAL SOUND PRO
Examines the possible role of autoimmunity as a cause of ulcerative colitis. Reviews the use of immunosuppressive agents in its therapy. Presents details of the two main types of therapy corticosteroids and colectomy.
From The Boston Medical Reports Series.
LC NO. 74-705870
Prod-NMAC Dist-NMAC 1966

Ulcerative Colitis C
3/4 OR 1/2 INCH VIDEO CASSETTE
Differentiates between spastic colon, irritable bowel and ulcerative colitis. Details symptoms, treatment and possible surgery intervention where medication hasn't helped.
Prod-MIFE Dist-MIFE Prodn-NFIC

Ultimate Answer, The C 28 MIN
3/4 OR 1/2 INCH VIDEO CASSETTE J A
Features actor Hugh O'Brian who shares his experiences with Dr. Albert Schweitzer.
Prod-SUTHRB Dist-SUTHRB

Ultimate Challenge C 23 MIN
16MM FILM OPTICAL SOUND
Demonstrates how the B F Goodrich off-the-shelf street Radial T/A tires meet the challenge of the 14.1 mile race course at Nurburgring, Germany.
Prod-GC Dist-MTP

Ultimate Energy, The C 28 MIN
16MM FILM, 3/4 OR 1/2 IN VIDEO
Discusses the complex problems facing scientific researchers in their efforts to achieve fusion power. Outlines the theory of fusion power and describes experiments being conducted in the field. Includes interviews with physicists and visits to five fusion research laboratories.
LC NO. 79-706011
Prod-USERD Dist-USNAC 1976

Ultimate In Restorative Denistry With Peter K Thomas, The - How And Why This Is Achieved C 180 MIN
3/4 INCH VIDEO CASSETTE
Offers an unedited presentation by Peter K Thomas, DDS, Beverly Hills, California, demonstrating his advanced methods of cavity preparation, his favorite tissue displacement and impression techniques and the ultimate systems in centric bite registration and face bow transfer, as well as principles of his famous waxing techniques in the development of organic occlusion.
Prod-AMDA Dist-AMDA 1979

Ultimate Machine, The C 30 MIN
16MM FILM, 3/4 OR 1/2 IN VIDEO
Relates man's building of machines to his own interpretation of himself and his goals.
From The Life Around Us Series.
LC NO. 79-707841
Prod-TIMLIF Dist-TIMLIF 1971

Ultimate Machine, The (Spanish) C 30 MIN
16MM FILM OPTICAL SOUND
Traces the development of the computer and examines its uses in industry, science and education.
From The Life Around Us (Spanish) Series.
LC NO. 78-700059
Prod-TIMLIF Dist-TIMLIF 1971

Ultimate Mystery, The C 40 MIN
16MM FILM, 3/4 OR 1/2 IN VIDEO
Presents Apollo 14 astronaut Edgar D Mitchell's contention that there is a oneness to all living things. Purports to contain scientific data supporting claims of mystics through the ages.
Prod-HP Dist-HP

Ultimate Outpost, The C 29 MIN
3/4 OR 1/2 INCH VIDEO CASSETTE
Examines how Erik the Red discovered and settled the island of Greenland, how Leif the Lucky discovered the areas known as Labrador and North Newfoundland and how the Vikings colonized Iceland.
From The Vikings Series.
Prod-KTCATV Dist-PBS 1980

Ultimate Speed, The - An Exploration With High Energy Electrons B 38 MIN
16MM FILM OPTICAL SOUND H-C
Demonstrates the relationship between kinetic energy of electrons and their speed, using calorimetric means and time-of-flight techniques. Shows a result which agrees with the theory of special relativity. Features William Bertozzi of the Massachusetts Institute of Technology.
From The PSSC College Physics Films Series.
LC NO. FIA67-5924
Prod-PSSC Dist-MLA 1966

Ultimates, The C 29 MIN
2 INCH VIDEOTAPE
See series title for descriptive statement.
From The Our Street Series.
Prod-MDCPB Dist-PUBTEL

Ultra Sonic Method I C 10 MIN
3/4 OR 1/2 INCH VIDEO CASSETTE IND
Describes the theory, equipment and procedures involved in basic ultrasonic testing. Demonstrates actual thickness measurement and flaw detection tests.
Prod-HTAVTI Dist-MOKIN

Ultra Structure Of The Lower Motor Neurons And Muscle Fibers C 32 MIN
3/4 INCH VIDEO CASSETTE PRO
Presents Dr Jerry E Mendell lecturing on the ultra structure of the lower motor neurons and muscle fibers.
From The Intensive Course In Neuromuscular Diseases Series.
LC NO. 76-706123
Prod-NINDIS Dist-USNAC 1974

Ultracentrifuge C 51 MIN
3/4 OR 1/2 INCH VIDEO CASSETTE

See series title for descriptive statement.
From The Colloid And Surface Chemistry - Lyophilic Colloids Series.
Prod-KALMIA Dist-KALMIA

Ultracentrifuge, The B 51 MIN
3/4 OR 1/2 INCH VIDEO CASSETTE
See series title for descriptive statement.
From The Colloids And Surface Chemistry - Lyophilic Colloids Series.
Prod-MIOT Dist-MIOT

Ultrasonic Aspiration Biopsy Technique C 20 MIN
3/4 INCH VIDEO CASSETTE PRO
Deals with the use of ultrasound as an aid in the biopsy of tissues and the aspiration of fluid. Describes how the use of ultrasound aspiration biopsy transducer avoids the undesirable consequence of other methods, such as inadvertent penetration of normal structures.
From The Ultrasound In Diagnostic Medicine Series.
LC NO. 79-707580
Prod-NSF Dist-USNAC 1976

Ultrasonic Evaluation Of Cerebral Trauma C 20 MIN
3/4 INCH VIDEO CASSETTE
Deals with the findings of echoencephalography in trauma with particular reference to cerebral contusion, hematoma formation and traumatic communicating hydrocephalus.
From The Ultrasound In Diagnostic Medicine Series.
LC NO. 79-707581
Prod-NSF Dist-USNAC 1976

Ultrasonic Inspection C
3/4 OR 1/2 INCH VIDEO CASSETTE IND
Discusses advantages and limitations, criteria for successful inspection, test equipment, techniques, discontinuity measurement and identification, irrelevant indications, locating the discontinuity and evaluation of discontinuities.
From The Welding Inspection And Quality Control Series.
Prod-AMCEE Dist-AMCEE

Ultrasonic Testing Applications C 55 MIN
3/4 OR 1/2 INCH VIDEO CASSETTE PRO
Surveys ultrasonic testing applications. Provides calibration standards. Discusses advantages and limitations.
From The Fundamentals Of Nondestructive Testing Series.
Prod-AMCEE Dist-AMCEE

Ultrasonic Testing Fundamentals C 55 MIN
3/4 OR 1/2 INCH VIDEO CASSETTE PRO
Surveys the history and development of ultrasonic testing. Cites the principles of wave propagation. Describes equipment.
From The Fundamentals Of Nondestructive Testing Series.
Prod-AMCEE Dist-AMCEE

Ultrasonic Tomography Of The Eye And Orbit C 19 MIN
3/4 INCH VIDEO CASSETTE PRO
Demonstrates the immersion technique using kinetic horizonal and vertical scans to produce a B-scans in real time to assist in diagnosing eye and orbit abnormalities.
From The Ultrasound In Diagnostic Medicine Series.
LC NO. 79-708120
Prod-USVA Dist-USNAC 1979

Ultrasonography Of The Breast C 35 MIN
3/4 INCH VIDEO CASSETTE
Demonstrates how to use ultrasound equipment. Shows the results of effective and ineffective imagery.
Prod-UTAHTI Dist-UTAHTI

Ultrasound And The CT Scanner C 15 MIN
3/4 OR 1/2 INCH VIDEO CASSETTE
Presents some of the latest advances in radiology. Shows how ultrasound utilizes sound waves that bounce off internal structures.
From The X-Ray Procedures In Layman's Terms Series.
Prod-FAIRGH Dist-FAIRGH

Ultrasound In Diagnostic Medicine—A Series
PRO
Discusses the use of ultrasound in diagnostic medicine.
Prod-USVA Dist-USNAC

Doppler Ultrasonic Evaluation Of Peripheral
Retroperitoneal Ultrasonography 018 MIN
Ultrasonic Tomography Of The Eye And Orbit 019 MIN

Ultrasound In Obstetrics And Gynecology C 20 MIN
3/4 INCH VIDEO CASSETTE PRO
Discusses ultrasonography of the fetus. Considers number, location, normal and abnormal growth patterns, abnormalities of the fetus, the normal uterus and ovary, and findings related to contraceptive devices.
LC NO. 79-708004
Prod-NSF Dist-USNAC 1977

Ultrasound In Renal Stone Surgery C 15 MIN
3/4 OR 1/2 INCH VIDEO CASSETTE
Shows the surgical technique that allows intrarenal surgery without interruption of the renal arterial supply.
Prod-SPRVER Dist-SPRVER

Ultrasound Of The Breast C 11 MIN
3/4 INCH VIDEO CASSETTE
Discusses the use of ultrasound in the detection and diagnosis of breast disease.
Prod-UTAHTI Dist-UTAHTI

Ulysses B 140 MIN
16MM FILM, 3/4 OR 1/2 IN VIDEO H-C A
Presents an adaptation of James Joyce's novel Ulysses.
Prod-STRICK Dist-TEXFLM 1967

Umbra C 18 MIN
16MM FILM OPTICAL SOUND A
Uses experimental techniques to show how film can be used as a filter between the filmmaker and the environment.
LC NO. 80-701383
Prod-SEIB Dist-SEIB 1980

Umbrella—A Series

Features Ruth Garvey with ideas for tackling the little things in life.
Prod-KETCTV Dist-PUBTEL

Afghan, Caftan And Friends 15 MIN
Doo-Dads For Daddy 15 MIN
Everything Under One Lid 15 MIN
Guess What 15 MIN
How To Cheat At Bridge 15 MIN
Let's Think Fat 15 MIN
Liberated Tops 15 MIN
Little People Clothes 15 MIN
Manly Bacon, Unholey And Two-Minute Mousse 15 MIN
On The Seventh Day She Wore It 15 MIN
Open And Shut 15 MIN
Son Of... 15 MIN
Wrap It Up 15 MIN

Umealit - The Whale Hunter C 60 MIN
16MM FILM OPTICAL SOUND
Captures the work, danger, ceremony and cameraderie of an Eskimo whale hunter. Contrasts past and present practices of whaling and critiques the controversy surrounding the International Whaling Commission and the Eskimos of Barrow, Alaska.
From The Nova Series.
Prod-WGBHTV Dist-KINGFT 1979

Umealit - The Whale Hunters C 58 MIN
3/4 INCH VIDEO CASSETTE
Discusses the 'save the whales' movement from the viewpoint of the Eskimos, hunters of the bowhead whale for thousands of years, who still rely on hunting as a way of life and a means of survival. Explores questions of Native rights, the politics of international conservation, and the adequacy of biological research on the bowhead.
From The Nova Series.
LC NO. 80-707287
Prod-WGBHTV Dist-PBS 1980

Umoja - Tiger And The Big Wind C 8 MIN
16MM FILM, 3/4 OR 1/2 IN VIDEO K-I
Relates how, during a long summer drought, the only available food and water was guarded by a large tiger who refused to share with other jungle creatures. Solves problem by showing how Brer Rabbit devised a plan to outwit the tiger so that all small creatures working together need never be hungry again.
From The Nguzo Saba Folklore For Children Series.
Prod-NGUZO Dist-BCNFL 1979

UMP - The NAVAIR Way C 30 MIN
16MM FILM OPTICAL SOUND
Shows how the U S Naval Air Systems Command deals with a person who joins the Upward Mobility Program (UMP.)
LC NO. 75-700882
Prod-USN Dist-USNAC 1974

UMWA 1970 - A House Divided B 14 MIN
3/4 INCH VIDEO CASSETTE
Contrasts United Mine Worker of America president Tony Boyle's speech at a miner's rally with those of the anti-Boyle faction.
Prod-APPAL Dist-APPAL 1971

Un Amigo C 40 MIN
16MM FILM OPTICAL SOUND P-I
Prod-FI Dist-FI

Un Asunto De Familia B 31 MIN
16MM FILM, 3/4 OR 1/2 IN VIDEO C A
A Spanish language film. Presents a trained family caseworker who is helping a family to understand its behavior problems. Shows viewer the techniques of interviewing and how to assist people in solving their own problems.
Prod-FSAA Dist-IFB Prodn-MHFB 1966

Un Chien Andalou B 16 MIN
16MM FILM, 3/4 OR 1/2 IN VIDEO H-C A
Presents an early attempt at avant-garde filmmaking by Luis Buñuel and Salvador Dali.
Prod-PFP Dist-TEXFLM 1970

Un Grand Verrier B 20 MIN
16MM FILM OPTICAL SOUND
A French language film. Depicts the artist-artisan, Marinot, as he makes his original creations after hours in a glass factory. Uses little narration.
Prod-FACSEA Dist-FACSEA

Un Homme Tranquille B 7 MIN
16MM FILM OPTICAL SOUND I-C A
A French language film. The dialogue is exactly that of the humorous situation in the audio-visual lesson.
From The Voix Et Images De France Series.
Prod-PEREN Dist-CHLTN Prodn-CRDDF 1962

Un Hotel A Paris C 11 MIN
16MM FILM, 3/4 OR 1/2 IN VIDEO
See series title for descriptive statement.
From The Sejour En France Series.
Prod-SEABEN Dist-IFB 1970

Un Hypermarche C 19 MIN
16MM FILM, 3/4 OR 1/2 IN VIDEO H-C
Shows how to select and purchase goods, as well as asking directions, in a supermarket located outside the city of Angers. Describes the vast emporium which sells a huge variety of products and is an economical shopping place for both local residents and tourist.
From The La France Telle Qu'Elle Est Series.
Prod-THAMES Dist-MEDIAG 1977

UN Is For You, The C 14 MIN
16MM FILM, 3/4 OR 1/2 IN VIDEO P-I
Introduces the United Nations and its functions.
Prod-UN Dist-LCOA 1984

Un Petit Navire C 13 MIN
16MM FILM OPTICAL SOUND J A
From The En Francaise, Set 2 Series.
Prod-PEREN Dist-CHLTN 1969

Un Problema De Algebra B 11 MIN
16MM FILM OPTICAL SOUND J-C A
A Spanish language film. See series title for annotation.
From The Beginning Spanish Series. No. 1
Prod-CBF Dist-AVED 1960

Un Repas Chez Francis C 11 MIN
16MM FILM, 3/4 OR 1/2 IN VIDEO
See series title for descriptive statement.
From The Sejour En France Series.
Prod-SEABEN Dist-IFB 1970

Un Viaje A Mexico C 9 MIN
16MM FILM OPTICAL SOUND K-I
A Spanish language film. Views Tony and Tina on vacation in Mexico, where they see some of the variety and vitality of that nation and learn that Mexican Americans can be proud of their ethnic and linguistic ties with Mexico.
From The Project Bilingual Series.
LC NO. 74-700386
Prod-SANISD Dist-SUTHLA

Una Carta A Amy C 7 MIN
16MM FILM, 3/4 OR 1/2 IN VIDEO K-P
A Spanish-language version of the motion picture A Letter To Amy. Tells the story of Peter who is having a birthday party and although he has asked all his friends in person, he decides to write out one special invitation to a girl. Shows what happens before he reaches the mailbox, leaving him very mixed-up and worried about whether or not she will come to the party.
Prod-WWS Dist-WWS Prodn-SCHNDL 1970

Una Familia De Peces C 11 MIN
16MM FILM, 3/4 OR 1/2 IN VIDEO P-I
Spanish version of 'A FISH FAMILY.' Pictures the complete reproduction cycle of the blue acara fish. Includes the processes of preparing the nest, laying and fertilizing the eggs, incubation care, constructing the nursery, transporting hatchlings to nurseries and guarding the young. Emphasizes the close family relationship of the blue acaras.
Prod-MIS Dist-MIS

Una Vita In Scatola (A Life In A Tin) C 7 MIN
16MM FILM OPTICAL SOUND J-C
An animated film without dialog which presents life as man's conformity to a succession of social norms in the midst of people who do not care.
LC NO. 72-702041
Prod-BOZETO Dist-UWFKD 1972

Unaccustomed As They Are C 30 MIN
16MM FILM - 3/4 IN VIDEO IND
Presents Joe Powell, noted public speaker and management consultant, who shares his secrets for preparing and delivering a good, effective speech.
Prod-BNA Dist-BNA 1971

Unapproachable, The C
16MM FILM OPTICAL SOUND
Features an aging, reclusive star whose privacy is unexpectedly interrupted by a young admirer.
Prod-TLECUL Dist-TLECUL

Unbilical Hernia C 11 MIN
3/4 OR 1/2 INCH VIDEO CASSETTE
See series title for descriptive statement.
From The Hernia Series.
Prod-SVL Dist-SVL

Unbroken Arrow—A Series
16MM FILM, 3/4 OR 1/2 IN VIDEO P-I
Presents six adventures set in Britain during the time of the Saxons.
Prod-LUF Dist-LUF 1977

Captured 021 MIN
Crusaders, The 021 MIN
Fair Exchange 022 MIN
Red Plague, The 021 MIN
Spy, The 022 MIN
Tower Of Fire 020 MIN

Uncalculated Risk, The C 26 MIN
16MM FILM, 3/4 OR 1/2 IN VIDEO C A
Shows how to distinguish between guesswork and fact and how to minimize the risk of uncritical inferences. Describes how to recognize inference and observation.
LC NO. 73-700188
Prod-RTBL Dist-RTBL 1971

Uncalculated Risk, The (French) C 26 MIN
16MM FILM, 3/4 OR 1/2 IN VIDEO C A
Shows how to tell guesswork from fact, and how to minimize the risk of uncritical inferences. Describes how to distinguish inference from observation.
Prod-RTBL Dist-RTBL 1971

Uncensored Movies B 17 MIN
16MM FILM SILENT
Presents Will Rogers satirizing some of the famous stars and motion pictures of the 1920s including William S Hart, Tom Mix

The Covered Wagon, Way Down East, Rudolph Valentino in The Sheik and a risque Cecil B DeMille bedroom scene.
Prod-UNKNWN Dist-KILLIS 1923

Uncertainty And Time C 45 MIN
3/4 OR 1/2 INCH VIDEO CASSETTE PRO
Discusses individual style. Points to the differences among projects. Considers time.
From The Advanced Project Management Series.
Prod-AMCEE Dist-AMCEE

Unchained Goddess, The C 59 MIN
3/4 INCH VIDEO CASSETTE J-H
Discusses weather, explaining what it is, what causes it, and what scientists are doing to predict and control it. Includes scenes of hurricanes, tornadoes and lightning.
From The Bell System Science Series.
Prod-ATAT Dist-WAVE Prodn-CAPRA 1958

Uncle Ben C 27 MIN
16MM FILM OPTICAL SOUND
Tells the story of a man who is an alcoholic but who overcomes his problems and cares for his orphaned niece and nephews.
LC NO. 79-700333
Prod-BYU Dist-BYU 1978

Uncle David Macon Show, The C 58 MIN
3/4 OR 1/2 INCH VIDEO CASSETTE
Combines documentary technique and variety show format to examine the life and times of David Harrison Macon, a Tennessee banjo player who was one of America's most important folksingers.
Prod-EAI Dist-EAI

Uncle Homer, Big John And Mr Bass C 25 MIN
16MM FILM OPTICAL SOUND
Presents two fishermen illustrating favorite casting and bass fishing techniques using Zebco tackle under all conditions in all types of water.
Prod-BRNSWK Dist-KAROL

Uncle Homer, Big John Mister Bass C 24 MIN
16MM FILM OPTICAL SOUND
Features Homer Circle and John Powell offering their individual techniques in hooking and landing bass.
Prod-MERMAR Dist-TELEFM

Uncle Jack's Mimosa C 24 MIN
3/4 OR 1/2 INCH VIDEO CASSETTE H
Presents high school senior Jerry Malone discussing taxation and credit.
From The Dollar Scholar Series. Pt 10
LC NO. 82-707408
Prod-BCSBIT Dist-GPITVL 1982

Uncle Jim's Dairy Farm C 25 MIN
16MM FILM, 3/4 OR 1/2 IN VIDEO I-J
Shows a different way of looking at rural life. Features the story of a city boy on the farm. Shows a family that succeeds by striving together.
Prod-MTOLP Dist-MTOLP 1975

Uncle Jim's Dairy Farm - A Summer Visit With Aunt Helen And Uncle Jim C 22 MIN
16MM FILM OPTICAL SOUND
Tells of a boy named George who visits his cousin on a modern dairy farm. Shows him learning to care for calves, milk cows, manage the business, shop and prepare meals.
Prod-NDC Dist-NDC 1977

Uncle Miltie And The Whiz C 28 MIN
3/4 OR 1/2 INCH VIDEO CASSETTE
Features Fred Rogers visiting with two professional comedians, Milton Berle and Joe Restivo, a young man whose career is just beginning.
From The Old Friends - New Friends Series.
Prod-FAMCOM Dist-PBS 1981

Uncle Monty's Gone C 14 MIN
16MM FILM, 3/4 OR 1/2 IN VIDEO P-I
Explains how Undine must learn to cope with her grief when her Uncle Monty dies.
From The Learning Values With Fat Albert Series.
Prod-FLMTON Dist-CRMP 1977

Uncle Sam - The Man And The Legend C 23 MIN
16MM FILM OPTICAL SOUND
Recounts the life and work of Sam Wilson, an American merchant who became the model for America's Uncle Sam. Shows the towns and countryside in which he worked during the early 19th century.
LC NO. 76-700203
Prod-NAR Dist-NAR Prodn-USHJMA 1976

Uncle Sam Magoo C 28 MIN
16MM FILM, 3/4 OR 1/2 IN VIDEO P-J
A shortened version of the motion picture Uncle Sam Magoo. Uses cartoon character Mr Magoo to outline America's history from the founding of the New World to the landing on the moon.
Prod-UPA Dist-MCFI

Uncle Sam Magoo C 52 MIN
16MM FILM, 3/4 OR 1/2 IN VIDEO P-J
Uses cartoon character Mr Magoo to outline America's history from the founding of the New World to the landing on the moon.
Prod-UPA Dist-MCFI

Uncle Smiley And The Junkyard Playground C 13 MIN
16MM FILM, 3/4 OR 1/2 IN VIDEO P-I
Portrays Uncle Smiley and the children converting a junk-strewn lot into a delightful play area, imaginatively turning much of the junk to use.
From The Uncle Smiley Series.
Prod-GMEFL Dist-LCOA 1972

Uncle Smiley Follows The Seasons C 13 MIN
16MM FILM, 3/4 OR 1/2 IN VIDEO P-I
Depicts the fascinating rhythm of nature, with children as an inextricable part. Shows how all four seasons, that 'rotate like a ferris wheel,' are interrelated.
From The Uncle Smiley Series.
Prod-GMEFL Dist-LCOA 1972

Uncle Smiley Follows The Seasons (Captioned) C 14 MIN
16MM FILM, 3/4 OR 1/2 IN VIDEO P-I
Makes us aware of our environment by introducing the beauties of nature through the four seasons.
From The Uncle Smiley Series.
Prod-GMEFL Dist-LCOA 1972

Uncle Smiley Goes Camping C 16 MIN
16MM FILM, 3/4 OR 1/2 IN VIDEO K-P
Shows children how to protect their environment by keeping it clean and safe.
From The Uncle Smiley Series.
Prod-GMEFL Dist-LCOA 1972

Uncle Smiley Goes Planting C 15 MIN
16MM FILM, 3/4 OR 1/2 IN VIDEO P-I
Shows Uncle Smiley and children planting trees in an area ravaged by forest fire, utilizeing modern reforestation techniques.
From The Uncle Smiley Series.
Prod-GMEFL Dist-LCOA 1972

Uncle Smiley Goes Recycling C 13 MIN
16MM FILM, 3/4 OR 1/2 IN VIDEO K-P
Introduces the term 'RECYCLING' to children and provides information about different recycling possibilities.
From The Uncle Smiley Series.
Prod-GMEFL Dist-LCOA 1972

Uncle Smiley Goes To The Beach C 13 MIN
16MM FILM, 3/4 OR 1/2 IN VIDEO P-I
Shows Uncle Smiley and his group playing where land and sea meet. Emphasizes the possibilities for either use or misuse of public beaches.
From The Uncle Smiley Series.
Prod-GMEFL Dist-LCOA 1972

Uncle Smiley Goes Up The River C 11 MIN
16MM FILM, 3/4 OR 1/2 IN VIDEO P-I
Portrays Uncle Smiley and his group joining in an actual community-action program to clean up a river and its banks.
From The Uncle Smiley Series.
Prod-GMEFL Dist-LCOA 1972

Uncle Smiley—A Series
16MM FILM, 3/4 OR 1/2 IN VIDEO P-I
Features significant ecological concepts, combined with a humorous format and catchy songs. Presents Uncle Smiley, a rotund, cheerful fellow who leads a group of young friends on adventures that stress a closer understanding and appreciation of nature.
Prod-GMEFL Dist-LCOA 1972

Uncle Smiley And The Junkyard Playground	13 MIN
Uncle Smiley Follows The Seasons	13 MIN
Uncle Smiley Goes Camping	16 MIN
Uncle Smiley Goes Planting	15 MIN
Uncle Smiley Goes Recycling	13 MIN
Uncle Smiley Goes To The Beach	13 MIN
Uncle Smiley Goes Up The River	11 MIN

Uncle Vanya C 130 MIN
16MM FILM OPTICAL SOUND H-C A
Presents a film of the stage production of Chekhov's Uncle Vanya, as performed by the Chichester Festival Theatre, with Laurence Olivier as director.
LC NO. 74-701905
Prod-BRENT Dist-CANTOR 1973

Uncommon Images C 22 MIN
16MM FILM OPTICAL SOUND
Presents the work of black photographer James Van DerZee, who set up shop in Harlem at the beginning of the 20th century and for 60 years recorded the public and private life of the black community.
LC NO. 77-702162
Prod-WNBCTV Dist-FLMLIB Prodn-BARRON

Uncommon Journey, An C
1/2 IN VIDEO CASSETTE BETA/VHS
Deals with issues of leadership style, personality and group dynamics through the story of eight women who participated in a two-week wilderness experience.
From The Adult Years - Continuity And Change Series.
Prod-OHUTC Dist-OHUTC

Uncommon Man, An C 17 MIN
3/4 OR 1/2 INCH VIDEO CASSETTE
Illustrates an interview with former Governor James Longley of Maine, who is facing terminal cancer. Includes introduction and closing by Kirk Douglas and reveals a personal account of how one man dealt with life.
Prod-AMCS Dist-AMCS 1982

Uncommon Man, The C 20 MIN
16MM FILM OPTICAL SOUND
Presents a cinema verite and avant garde treatment of the modern large corporation's concern with science and society as its efforts in these areas relate to the future.
LC NO. 70-706142
Prod-MONSAN Dist-SMUSA Prodn-TECHST 1969

Uncommon Places - The Architecture Of Frank Lloyd Wright C 60 MIN
3/4 OR 1/2 INCH VIDEO CASSETTE J-C A
Deals with the work of Frank Lloyd Wright, the renowned architect, and notes the influence of nature's geometric forms upon his designs. Includes Wright's recorded remarks, the comments of current residents of Wright homes, and the reminiscences of Wright's apprentices and of his wife, Olgivanna.
Prod-WHATV Dist-PBS

Uncommonplace, The C 8 MIN
16MM FILM, 3/4 OR 1/2 IN VIDEO
Highlights the city of Norfolk, Virginia, including its festivals, museums and recreational attractions.
Prod-KLEINW Dist-KLEINW 1979

Unconquered C 15 MIN
16MM FILM OPTICAL SOUND
Examines the Seminole Indians of Florida.
Prod-FLADC Dist-FLADC

Unconscious Cultural Clashes—A Series
T
Presents six 30-minute programs designed to provide insight into the causes of misunderstanding between Mexican-Americans and Anglos.
Prod-KTEHTV Dist-SCCOE

Unconscious Cultural Clashes—A Series

Presents a background of cultural information and underlines areas where misunderstandings can and do occur.
Prod-SCCOE Dist-SCCOE

Customs	30 MIN
Education Vs Education	30 MIN
Grand Assumptions	30 MIN
Look Me In The Eye	30 MIN
Objective - Acculturation	30 MIN
Outlook	30 MIN

Unconscious Level (Section A), The C 25 MIN
3/4 OR 1/2 INCH VIDEO CASSETTE
See series title for descriptive statement.
From The Management By Responsibility Series.
Prod-TRAINS Dist-DELTAK

Unconscious Level (Section B), The C 33 MIN
3/4 OR 1/2 INCH VIDEO CASSETTE
See series title for descriptive statement.
From The Management By Responsibility Series.
Prod-TRAINS Dist-DELTAK

Unconventional Gas Resources C 29 MIN
16MM FILM, 3/4 OR 1/2 IN VIDEO
Provides an overview of Department Of Energy, industry, state and national lab activities in the recovery of unconventional gas. Shows coring operations, test wells, production enhancement and how they relate to methane from coalbeds, geopressured acquifiers, eastern gas shales and western gas sands.
LC NO. 81-706313
Prod-USDOE Dist-USNAC Prodn-DOSTEF 1980

Uncounted Enemy - Unproven Conspiracy C 29 MIN
3/4 OR 1/2 INCH VIDEO CASSETTE
Examines the 1982 CBS documentary, The Uncounted Enemy - A Vietnam Deception. Tells how it created great repercussions as it alleged that General William Westmoreland had been involved in a conspiracy to deceive both government leaders and the American public about enemy troop strength in Vietnam.
From The Inside Story Series.
Prod-PBS Dist-PBS 1981

Uncovering, Remedying And Reporting Antitrust Violations C 176 MIN
3/4 OR 1/2 INCH VIDEO CASSETTE PRO
Uncovers antitrust problem and discusses appropriate compliance action. Explores obligations to report violations. Provides criteria for a corporation's determination of need to seek outside counsel and shows the method by which to choose such counsel.
From The Preventive Antitrust - Corporate Compliance Program Series.
Prod-ABACPE Dist-ABACPE

Uncrating And Assembly Of The P-47 Thunderbolt Airplane / Dive Bombing B 60 MIN
3/4 OR 1/2 INCH VIDEO CASSETTE
Illustrates step-by-step assembling of the P-47 thunderbolt on the field without heavy lifting equipment. Depicts various dive-bombing techniques as Army Air Force training.
Prod-IHF Dist-IHF

Und Viel Zu Essen Nicht Vergessen C 15 MIN
16MM FILM, 3/4 OR 1/2 IN VIDEO
See series title for descriptive statement.
From The Guten Tag Series. Part 20
Prod-BAYER Dist-IFB 1968

Und Weit Und Breit Keine Tankstelle C 15 MIN
16MM FILM, 3/4 OR 1/2 IN VIDEO
See series title for descriptive statement.
From The Guten Tag Wie Geht's Series. Part 12
Prod-BAYER Dist-IFB 1973

Undebt, The C 5 MIN
3/4 OR 1/2 INCH VIDEO CASSETTE H-C A
Presents comedy by the Brave New World Workshop of the Twin Cities.
Prod-BRVNP Dist-UCV

Under Arrest C 15 MIN
16MM FILM, 3/4 OR 1/2 IN VIDEO J-C
Shows what happens when a young man, stopped by police because of his resemblance to a wanted murderer, resists arrest and assaults a police officer. Examines the rights and duties

of the police and the citizen and explains the incident from both points of view.
Prod-NELCO Dist-WDEMCO 1974

Under Fire C
1/2 IN VIDEO CASSETTE BETA/VHS
Tells the story of correspondents caught up in intrigue and violence during the 1979 overthrow of Somoza in Nicaragua. Stars Nick Nolte and Joanna Cassidy.
Prod-GA Dist-GA

Under Fives—A Series
3/4 OR 1/2 INCH VIDEO CASSETTE C A
Demonstrates that the feelings of children must be recognized and their needs met if they are to grow up emotionally healthy.
Prod-GRATV Dist-FLMLIB 1982

Pre-Verbal Communication 016 MIN
Stress Of Separation 016 MIN

Under High Skies C 28 MIN
16MM FILM OPTICAL SOUND H-C A
Describes Northern Germany and its trading towns, such as Bremen, Bremerhaven and Hamburg, whose close economic ties were forged with European and overseas partners. Presents three people and the circumstances peculiar to their lives - a fisherman from the North Sea coast, a coffee merchant in Hamburg and a farmer in East Frisia.
Prod-WSTGLC Dist-WSTGLC

Under New Management C 30 MIN
16MM FILM - 3/4 IN VIDEO J-C A
Shows the great Brazilian rain forest, the biggest unexplored land mass on earth and one of the world's important oxygen suppliers. Explains that Brazil regards this area as the key to new prosperity.
From The Man Builds - Man Destroys Series.
Prod-UN Dist-GPITVL

Under One Roof C 19 MIN
16MM FILM OPTICAL SOUND A
Explains the benefits of a hospital Triage Clinic for communities with little medical care.
Prod-FMSP Dist-FMSP 1977

Under One Roof C 16 MIN
3/4 OR 1/2 INCH VIDEO CASSETTE J A
Documents the workings of a comprehensive ambulatory care center where all health care services are under one roof.
Prod-SUTHRB Dist-SUTHRB

Under One Roof (Spanish) C 19 MIN
16MM FILM OPTICAL SOUND A
Explains the benefits of a hospital Triage Clinic for communities with little medical care.
Prod-FMSP Dist-FMSP 1977

Under Pressure B 31 MIN
3/4 INCH VIDEO CASSETTE
Shows the pressures under which members of a large city police department must work. Stresses the importance of handling any situation which may occur during a policeman's daily routine patrol.
Prod-USNAC Dist-USNAC 1972

Under Royal Patronage B 28 MIN
16MM FILM SILENT
A comedy about the clever ruse planned by a prince and his friend to avoid a state marriage.
LC NO. 77-713144
Prod-ENY Dist-BHAWK

Under Sail - Week 1 C 30 MIN
3/4 OR 1/2 INCH VIDEO CASSETTE H-C A
Presents host Robbie Doyle explaining what's on board for the next eight weeks and providing an introduction to the pleasures of sailing.
From The Under Sail Series.
Prod-KINGFT Dist-KINGFT

Under Sail - Week 2 C 30 MIN
3/4 OR 1/2 INCH VIDEO CASSETTE H-C A
Shows what is required to safely take off and return for a short sail in the harbor. Reviews the balance of forces involved in sailing and some of the tools sailors use to take advantage of those forces.
From The Under Sail Series.
Prod-KINGFT Dist-KINGFT

Under Sail - Week 3 C 30 MIN
3/4 OR 1/2 INCH VIDEO CASSETTE H-C A
Describes the guidelines by which sea persons conduct themselves and their vessels safely. Examines how the shape of sails and tools for sail-shaping affect the balance of forces at work on the water.
From The Under Sail Series.
Prod-KINGFT Dist-KINGFT

Under Sail - Week 5 C 30 MIN
3/4 OR 1/2 INCH VIDEO CASSETTE H-C A
Focuses on spinnakers, their theory, practice, care and handling.
From The Under Sail Series.
Prod-KINGFT Dist-KINGFT

Under Sail - Week 6 C 30 MIN
3/4 OR 1/2 INCH VIDEO CASSETTE H-C A
Tells, after motoring out of the marina, how to hoist a sail at sea. Discuses boardsailing and navigation.
From The Under Sail Series.
Prod-KINGFT Dist-KINGFT

Under Sail - Week 7 C 30 MIN
3/4 OR 1/2 INCH VIDEO CASSETTE H-C A
Discusses problem-solving, including what to do when someone falls overboard, when a line gets caught in the propeller and when a boat capsizes.
From The Under Sail Series.
Prod-KINGFT Dist-KINGFT

Under Sail - Week 8 C 30 MIN
3/4 OR 1/2 INCH VIDEO CASSETTE H-C A
Begins with a trip to a boat show, where viewers learn what to keep in mind when shopping for a boat. Travels to St Croix for a look at a sailing school and finally discusses how to go about chartering a sailboat in the Caribbean.
From The Under Sail Series.
Prod-KINGFT Dist-KINGFT

Under Sail - Work 4 C 30 MIN
3/4 OR 1/2 INCH VIDEO CASSETTE H-C A
Puts together all of the elements learned to this point in order to actually sail a course.
From The Under Sail Series.
Prod-KINGFT Dist-KINGFT

Under Sail—A Series
H-C A
Introduces the pleasure, beauty and sport of sailing.
Prod-KINGFT Dist-KINGFT

Under Sail - Week 1 030 MIN
Under Sail - Week 2 030 MIN
Under Sail - Week 3 030 MIN
Under Sail - Week 4 030 MIN
Under Sail - Week 5 030 MIN
Under Sail - Week 6 030 MIN
Under Sail - Week 7 030 MIN
Under Sail - Week 8 030 MIN

Under Sail—A Series

Discusses the background, skills and information required for sailing.
Prod-WGBHTV Dist-MTI

All Hands On Deck 030 MIN
Common Courtesy 030 MIN
Every Sailor's Dream 030 MIN
Full Speed Ahead 030 MIN
Man Overboard 030 MIN
On The Open Sea 030 MIN
Right On Course 030 MIN
Set Sail 030 MIN

Under The Bethlehem Star C 8 MIN
16MM FILM OPTICAL SOUND P-H T R
A village shepherd family taking care of their sheep in the hills go into Bethlehem and find Joseph and Mary and the new-born Infant Jesus in a stable. Later, wise men from the East follow the sign of the star to the house where the young Child is found and offer their gifts to him.
From The Christ, The Light Of The World Series.
Prod-FAMF Dist-FAMF

Under The Blue Umbrella—A Series
P
Uses various formats to discuss an individual's self-concept, differences among people, the functions of families, basic human needs, the world of work, money and its uses, maps and globes, and citizenship and government.
Prod-SCETV Dist-AITECH 1977

Alike But Different 014 MIN
Beat The Buzzer 014 MIN
Beth's New Shoes 014 MIN
Family Portraits 014 MIN
Grandmother's Coming 014 MIN
It's A Grand Old Flag 014 MIN
It's Payday 014 MIN
It's Time To Go To Work 014 MIN
New York's My Town 014 MIN
Questions And Answers - Globes 013 MIN
Questions And Answers - Maps 014 MIN
St Matthews Is My Home 014 MIN
Washington, DC - A Special City 014 MIN
Westville, 1850 014 MIN
What's Wrong 013 MIN
Yes, I Can 013 MIN

Under The Clouds Of War B 20 MIN
16MM FILM, 3/4 OR 1/2 IN VIDEO
Consists of film of military actions, including Mussolini's invasion of Ethiopia, Hitlers's invasion of Austria and the Spanish Civil War.
From The March Of Time Series.
LC NO. 79-707371
Prod-TIMLIF Dist-TIMLIF 1974

Under The Covers - American Quilts C 12 MIN
16MM FILM, 3/4 OR 1/2 IN VIDEO H
Focuses on the historical importance and homespun vitality of American quilts while showing different patterns, stitches, colors and shapes.
Prod-PFP Dist-PFP 1976

Under The Hood C 21 MIN
16MM FILM, 3/4 OR 1/2 IN VIDEO
Demonstrates how to service the automobile battery, the alternator belt, the air filter and windshield wipers.
Prod-ODECA Dist-BULFRG

Under The Hood C 35 MIN
16MM FILM, 3/4 OR 1/2 IN VIDEO
Demonstrates how to make regular inspections of tires, shock absorbers, the brake system and the exhaust system. Shows how to identify problems early and describe the problems accurately to a mechanic.
Prod-ODECA Dist-BULFRG

Under The Influence C 27 MIN
16MM FILM OPTICAL SOUND J-C
Documents the 1975 tests designed to discover exactly how impaired the average driver is at .10 percent blood alcohol concentration. Shows that the results, although often startling and humorous, carry tragic implications.
LC NO. 77-701382
Prod-NHTSA Dist-IA 1976

Under The Influence C 25 MIN
16MM FILM, 3/4 OR 1/2 IN VIDEO
Documents a test of driving proficiency at .10 blood/alcohol. Compares drivers' ability to negotiate a driving course sober and after five to six drinks.
Prod-USDTFH Dist-USNAC

Under The Influence C 26 MIN
16MM FILM, 3/4 OR 1/2 IN VIDEO J A
Shows what occurs when average drivers are under the influence of drugs or alcohol under controlled conditions and their subsequent physical impairment.
Prod-RAMFLM Dist-SUTHRB

Under The Influence C 27 MIN
3/4 OR 1/2 INCH VIDEO CASSETTE
Presents a documentary report on a test done to see how 36 average people could handle a car after drinking to the point of being legally drunk. Displays the driving impairment suffered by all of these people.
Prod-LACFU Dist-IA

Under The Law, Pt 1—A Series
16MM FILM, 3/4 OR 1/2 IN VIDEO J-C
Presents stories which illustrate the value of interpretation of individual circumstances in criminal legal procedure.
Prod-USNEI Dist-WDEMCO 1974

Arrest And Seize 17 MIN
Hitchhike, The 17 MIN
Muggers 15 MIN
Plea, The 15 MIN
Ripoff, The 15 MIN

Under The Law, Pt 2—A Series
16MM FILM, 3/4 OR 1/2 IN VIDEO I-C
Presents stories illustrating the value of individual interpretation of the circumstances in criminal legal procedure.
Prod-USNEI Dist-WDEMCO 1975

Bad Guys - Good Guys 25 MIN
Matter Of David J, The 16 MIN
Three Days In The County Jail 19 MIN
Vandals 17 MIN

Under The Men's Tree B 15 MIN
16MM FILM, 3/4 OR 1/2 IN VIDEO H-C A
Shows life in a Jie cattle camp in the Karamoja district of northern Uganda. Focuses on a group of men as they cut cowhide rope, tell stories and sleep.
Prod-MCDGAL Dist-UCEMC 1973

Under The Rainbow C 11 MIN
16MM FILM, 3/4 OR 1/2 IN VIDEO J-C
Tells about two people, each living in a world of his own, who must learn to appreciate one another's culture and ideals.
Prod-NFBC Dist-EBEC 1974

Under The Sky C 20 MIN
3/4 OR 1/2 INCH VIDEO CASSETTE I
Presents dramatizations of literary works that deal with the interdependence of people and nature.
From The Readers' Cube Series.
Prod-MDDE Dist-AITECH 1977

Under The Yellow Balloon—A Series
P
Presents stories on a variety of topics such as moving to a new city, family economics, adoption, different occupations, trains, planes and ships.
Prod-SCETV Dist-AITECH 1980

Buying A House 013 MIN
Daddy's Gone 014 MIN
Errands For Mama 014 MIN
Flying 014 MIN
I'm Adopted 014 MIN
It's My Job 014 MIN
Making A Newspaper 013 MIN
My New Home 014 MIN
Phone Isn't Working, The 014 MIN
Ships A'Sail 014 MIN
Trains 014 MIN
Treasure Hunt, A 015 MIN
We're Spending Too Much Money 012 MIN
What Should I Buy 014 MIN
Where Are We 014 MIN
Working In Washington 013 MIN

Under-Secretary General Of U N For The Office Of Press Information C 28 MIN
3/4 INCH VIDEOTAPE
Presents an interview with Under-Secretary-General of the United Nations for the Department of Press Information Genichi Akatani on the United Nations' place in the world. Hosted by Marilyn Perry.
From The Marilyn's Manhatten Series.
Prod-PERRYM Dist-PERRYM

Undercurrents C 12 MIN
16MM FILM, 3/4 OR 1/2 IN VIDEO J-C A
Presents impressions of the blue-green depths of the Mexican seas, showing fish swaying like orchestral members tuning up, crabs dancing and a giant manta ray waltzing with the camera.
Prod-PHENIX Dist-PHENIX 1973

Underglaze And Overglaze Decor C 28 MIN
2 INCH VIDEOTAPE
Features Mrs Peterson describing certain ceramic processes for her classroom at the University of Southern California. Illustrates underglaze and overglaze decor.
From The Wheels, Kilns And Clay Series.
Prod-USC Dist-PUBTEL

Undergraduate Medical Education C 78 MIN
3/4 INCH VIDEO CASSETTE
Presents a discussion on undergraduate medical education by Dr John A Cooper given at the Colloquium on the Bicentennial of Medicine in the United States. Based on the paper Undergraduate Medical Education by John A Cooper in the book Advances In American Medicine - Essays At The Bicentennial.
LC NO. 77-706034
Prod-NMAC Dist-USNAC 1976

Underground B 5 MIN
16MM FILM OPTICAL SOUND H-C A
Presents a cinematic examination of subway paranoia presented in a series of still photographs interspersed with scenes of a moving subway train.
Prod-UWFKD Dist-UWFKD

Underground C 88 MIN
16MM FILM - 3/4 IN VIDEO J-C A
Recreates the history of the political activism of the 1960's and 1970's and the Weather Underground Organization. Brings the era vividly to life by interweaving their personal political development with the significant events and personalities of that decade.
Prod-FIRS Dist-FIRS

Underground Blasting B 60 MIN
3/4 OR 1/2 INCH VIDEO CASSETTE
See series title for descriptive statement.
From The Explosives And Their Use In Mining And Construction Series. Pt 7
Prod-UAZMIC Dist-UAZMIC 1977

Underground Coal Mine Blasting C 19 MIN
16MM FILM OPTICAL SOUND
Points out the importance of using explosives as a kind of industrial force to remove coal from the Earth. Describes some of the more common hazards encountered when working with explosives, detonators and related equipment.
LC NO. 76-701543
Prod-USMESA Dist-USNAC 1975

Underground Film C 29 MIN
2 INCH VIDEOTAPE
Explores the phenomenon of the underground film movement. Follows Chick Strand as she films on location, edits in her studio garret and philosophizes on the art of fimmaking. Visits the office of Genesis Films in Los Angeles, a company formed by young filmmakers to distribute their films. Includes a visit to a midnight showing of underground films at the Unicorn Theatre in La Jollo.
From The Synergism - In Today's World Series.
Prod-KPBS Dist-PUBTEL

Underground Haulage Hazards C 12 MIN
16MM FILM, 3/4 OR 1/2 IN VIDEO IND
Presents an overview of factors that can contribute to accidents involving haulage vehicles in underground mines and shows methods of prevention.
Prod-USDL Dist-USNAC 1983

Underground Housing C 22 MIN
3/4 OR 1/2 INCH VIDEO CASSETTE
Visits several existing underground homes in Minnesota, a new trend in energy saving which saves up to 70 per cent in energy bills.
Prod-WCCOTV Dist-WCCOTV 1978

Underground Movie, The C 14 MIN
16MM FILM OPTICAL SOUND K-I
Introduces the basic composition of the Earth's interior by presenting an animated story about a journey through the center of of the Earth.
LC NO. 77-703381
Prod-NFBC Dist-BESTF 1972

Underground Nuclear Weapons Testing C 29 MIN
16MM FILM OPTICAL SOUND H-C
Shows how underground tests of nuclear weapons are planned and conducted at the Nevada test site in a manner designed to contain radioactivity within the ground and to comply with the limited Test Ban Treaty, while providing the diagnostic information needed. Explains various types of nuclear tests and the use of various test areas and their facilities.
LC NO. FIE67-133
Prod-NOO Dist-USNAC 1967

Underground Railroad, The C 15 MIN
3/4 OR 1/2 INCH VIDEO CASSETTE P
Focuses on the contribution of one young boy to the Underground Railroad.
From The Stories Of America Series.
Prod-OHSDE Dist-AITECH Prodn-WVIZTV 1976

Underground Waters C 19 MIN
16MM FILM OPTICAL SOUND
Portrays the water cycle, action of rainwater on rocks, caverns, underground streams and hot springs.
Prod-BELMNE Dist-BELMNE 1958

Underhand Throw And Catch C 15 MIN
3/4 OR 1/2 INCH VIDEO CASSETTE T
Explains how to teach primary students the underhand roll, how to catch a rolling ball, rolling at stationary and moving targets, the underhand self-toss, the throw for force and the throw for accuracy.

From The Leaps And Bounds Series. No. 12
Prod-HSDE Dist-AITECH 1984

Underlining And Stay Stitching C 29 MIN
2 INCH VIDEOTAPE
Features Mrs Ruth Hickman demonstrating how to underline and stay stitch.
From The Sewing Skills - Tailoring Series.
Prod-KRMATV Dist-PUBTEL

Underlining Techniques C 5 MIN
16MM FILM SILENT J-C A
Describes uses of underlinings and shows the attachme of the underlining fabric to the fashion fabric. Illustrates techniques of stitching darts and hemming when an underlining is used.
From The Clothing Construction Techniques Series.
LC NO. 77-701174
Prod-IOWA Dist-IOWASP 1976

Undermining The Great Depression C 25 MIN
3/4 OR 1/2 INCH VIDEO CASSETTE
Narrates the story of a small Oregon town's unique means of survival during the Great Depression, gold mining in their own backyards. Presents five oldtimers recalling stories of the period.
Prod-MEDIPR Dist-MEDIPR 1981

Underscan B 8 MIN
3/4 INCH VIDEO CASSETTE
Chronicles the daily events in the aging woman's life, including the gradual deterioration of both her body and her house. Creates a moving narrative about the process of growing old.
Prod-WMEN Dist-WMEN

Undersea Adventures Of Pickle And Bill, The C 24 MIN
3/4 OR 1/2 INCH VIDEO CASSETTE
Follows two teenagers on a zoological expedition to Jamaica.
From The Young People's Specials Series.
Prod-MULTPP Dist-MULTPP

Undersea Explorer C 14 MIN
16MM FILM OPTICAL SOUND
Tells about the operating techniques and features common to Navy and commercial submersibles. Shows methods used to avoid them.
LC NO. 74-705871
Prod-USN Dist-USNAC 1971

Undersea World Of Jacques Cousteau—A Series
16MM FILM, 3/4 OR 1/2 IN VIDEO I-C
Describes the oceanographic voyages and discoveries of Jacques Cousteau.
Prod-METROM Dist-CF

Beneath The Frozen World	023 MIN
Coral Jungle	023 MIN
Desert Whales	023 MIN
Dragons Of The Galapagos, The	023 MIN
Five Hundred Million Years Beneath The Sea	024 MIN
Flight Of The Penguins	025 MIN
Green Sea Turtle, The	022 MIN
Legend Of Lake Titicaca	022 MIN
Mysteries Of The Hidden Reefs	023 MIN
Night Of The Squid, The	022 MIN
Octopus, Octopus	022 MIN
Return Of The Sea Elephant	020 MIN
Sea Birds Of Isabela, The	023 MIN
Seals	022 MIN
Sharks	024 MIN
Singing Whales, The	024 MIN
Smile Of The Walrus, The	022 MIN
Sound Of Dolphins, A	022 MIN
Sunken Treasure	021 MIN
Those Incredible Diving Machines	023 MIN
Tragedy Of The Red Salmon	024 MIN
Unsinkable Sea Otter, The	025 MIN
Water Planet, The	019 MIN
Whales	022 MIN

Understanding C 57 MIN
16MM FILM, 3/4 OR 1/2 IN VIDEO H-C A
Reveals that modern Chinese scientists and technologists are trying to catch up after the disruptions of the Cultural Revolution. Shows that in today's China, modern science and ancient belief exist side by side.
From The Heart Of The Dragon Series. Pt 9
Prod-ASH Dist-TIMLIF 1984

Understanding Abstraction In Art C 20 MIN
3/4 INCH VIDEO CASSETTE
Explains aspects of abstract art, showing how technique influences style and pointing out the relationship between mood, color, and communication.
LC NO. 79-706379
Prod-EDDIM Dist-EDDIM 1979

Understanding Adolescence C 22 MIN
16MM FILM - VIDEO, ALL FORMATS
Features fresh insights into the complex social pressures that affect both adolescent and adult, to encourage increased empathy toward the pressures each face.
From The Youth Lifeskills Series.
Prod-SCCL Dist-PEREN

Understanding Aggression C 29 MIN
16MM FILM OPTICAL SOUND J-C A
Combines artwork depicting man's aggressive behavior throughout the centuries with live-action sequences in order to examine the problem of the possible destruction of mankind by means of man's own aggressive tendencies. Psychologist Roger Ulrich discusses his theories of aggression and demonstrates some of his findings with actual animal experiments that reveal various causes of aggression.

LC NO. 72-702515
Prod-APPLE Dist-PHM 1971

Understanding Alcohol Use And Abuse C 12 MIN
16MM FILM, 3/4 OR 1/2 IN VIDEO I-H
Discusses the physical, mental and social effects of alcohol. Describes the four stages of inebriation. Examines the various factors which may lead to the use and abuse of alcohol.
Prod-WDEMCO Dist-WDEMCO 1979

Understanding Alcohol Use And Abuse (French) C 12 MIN
16MM FILM, 3/4 OR 1/2 IN VIDEO I-H
Outlines the four stages of inebriation. Explores the reasons people drink.
Prod-WDEMCO Dist-WDEMCO 1979

Understanding Alcohol Use And Abuse (Thai) C 12 MIN
16MM FILM, 3/4 OR 1/2 IN VIDEO I-H
Outlines the four stages of inebriation. Explores the reasons people drink.
Prod-WDEMCO Dist-WDEMCO 1979

Understanding Allergies C
3/4 OR 1/2 INCH VIDEO CASSETTE
Discusses how allergies can take many forms, the action of histamines, the various diagnostic procedures available and the recommended management procedures including desensitization shots.
Prod-MIFE Dist-MIFE

Understanding Allergies (Arabic) C
3/4 OR 1/2 INCH VIDEO CASSETTE
Discusses how allergies can take many forms, the action of histamines, the various diagnostic procedures available and the recommended management procedures including desensitization shots.
Prod-MIFE Dist-MIFE

Understanding Allergies (Spanish) C
3/4 OR 1/2 INCH VIDEO CASSETTE
Discusses how allergies can take many forms, the action of histamines, the various diagnostic procedures available and the recommended management procedures including desensitization shots.
Prod-MIFE Dist-MIFE

Understanding And Dealing With Sexual Variations C
3/4 OR 1/2 INCH VIDEO CASSETTE PRO
See series title for descriptive statement.
From The Continuing Medical Education - Basic Sexology Series.
Prod-TIASHS Dist-MMRC

Understanding And Dealing With Student Attitudes And Behavior X 30 MIN
16MM FILM OPTICAL SOUND C T
Teaches the nursing instructor various principles, tools and methods of teaching. Deals with student attitudes, how they relate to behavior and tells how both can be changed.
From The Teaching Role Series.
LC NO. 73-703326
Prod-MVNE Dist-TELSTR 1968

Understanding And Overcoming Emotional Upset C
3/4 OR 1/2 INCH VIDEO CASSETTE
Shows how to change irrational self-talk and how to translate rational thinking into behavioral change.
Prod-IRL Dist-IRL

Understanding And Using Fractions C
3/4 OR 1/2 INCH VIDEO CASSETTE J
Uses real-life problems to demonstrate operations performed on fractions, from finding equivalent fractions to renaming improper fractions, and multiplication and division of fractions and mixed numbers.
Prod-GA Dist-GA

Understanding Angina Pectoris C 12 MIN
3/4 OR 1/2 INCH VIDEO CASSETTE
Describes angina pectoris, what it is and why it happens. Uses terse narration and full-color visuals to present the relationship between physical and emotional stress and angina.
LC NO. 77-730406
Prod-TRAINX Dist-TRAINX

Understanding Asthma (2nd Ed) C 14 MIN
3/4 OR 1/2 INCH VIDEO CASSETTE
Describes the clinical characteristics of asthma. Presents the physiological facts about asthma. Explains the role of allergy, emotion, and family history in asthma.
Prod-MEDFAC Dist-MEDFAC 1980

Understanding Babysitting C 11 MIN
16MM FILM, 3/4 OR 1/2 IN VIDEO J-C A
Shows how to seek and accept work as a babysitter in a business-like way, how to create a good first impression on a job and how to establish a trusting relationship with parents and children.
From The Babysitter Series. Unit 1
Prod-SOCOM Dist-FILCOM 1979

Understanding Barriers C
16MM FILM - 3/4 IN VIDEO A
Shows how to overcome barriers to successful negotiations, communicate effectively, learn how to listen, prepare through role playing, psychodrama, conferences, brainstorming and other methods.
From The Art Of Negotiating Series. Module 7
Prod-BNA Dist-BNA 1983

Understanding Behavior In Organizations - How I Feel Is What I Do C 26 MIN
16MM FILM, 3/4 OR 1/2 IN VIDEO

Demonstrates how a knowledge of human behavior can help in designing more effective organizations.
From The Human Resources And Organizational Behavior Series.
Prod-DOCUA Dist-CNEMAG

Understanding Blood Sugar C 21 MIN
16MM FILM, 3/4 OR 1/2 IN VIDEO A
Explains the body's use of sugar and the pathophysiology of diabetes. Describes how blood sugar acts during the course of a day. Includes information on causes, treatment and prevention of ketoacidosis and low blood sugar as well as guidelines for meals, exercise and insulin.
Prod-PRORE Dist-PRORE

Understanding Business Finance—A Series

Presents an overview of financial concepts to increase the 'botton line' and/or cash flow of the orgaization.
Prod-VIDART Dist-VISUCP

Balance Sheet Barrier, The	030 MIN
Control Of Working Capital, The	025 MIN
Cost, Profit And Break-Even	021 MIN
Depreciation And Inflation	018 MIN

Understanding Business Graphics—A Series

Explores the rapidly growing field of computer generated graphics with an emphasis on business use. Examines the advantages and potential applications of business graphics and the hardware and software resources now becoming available.
Prod-DELTAK Dist-DELTAK

Computer Graphics In Business	030 MIN
Graphics Applications	030 MIN
Graphics Systems	030 MIN

Understanding Buyer Behavior C 60 MIN
3/4 OR 1/2 INCH VIDEO CASSETTE A
Shows how to interpret a buyer's behavior, which invariably provides clues to the identification of his or her need. Emphasizes listening actively, observing nonverbal behavior, questioning effectively and paraphrasing effectively.
From The Strategic Selling - A Thinking Person's Guide Series. Pt 2
Prod-TIMLIF Dist-TIMLIF 1984

Understanding Chemotherapy C
3/4 OR 1/2 INCH VIDEO CASSETTE
Presents information essential to the new chemotherapy patient. Uses computer graphics and animation to describe how cancer grows within the body and how chemotherapy works in treating cancer cells.
Prod-GRANVW Dist-GRANVW

Understanding Children's Drawings B 11 MIN
16MM FILM OPTICAL SOUND J-C
Follows a child's progress from primitive scribblings, through a recognition of form and design, to the emergence of a story-telling picture.
Prod-BOXAVR Dist-RADIM 1949

Understanding Children's Play B 12 MIN
16MM FILM OPTICAL SOUND C T
Shows how adults can understand and help children through observation of their use of toys and play materials. A variety of materials made available in a nursery school room, including blocks, poster paints, crayons, clay, and watercolors are presented.
From The Studies Of Normal Personality – Development Series.
Prod-ZACHRY Dist-NYU 1948

Understanding Cities—A Series
16MM FILM, 3/4 OR 1/2 IN VIDEO H-C A
Explains the design and development of great European and American cities, providing historical background on the people and institutions who shaped these marvelous urban areas and thus helped shaped the course of history.
Prod-FI Dist-FI 1983

American Urban Experience, The	027 MIN
City Of The Future, The	027 MIN
John Nash And London	027 MIN
Paris - Living Space	027 MIN
Rome - Impact Of An Idea	027 MIN

Understanding Color - Color By Addition C 14 MIN
16MM FILM OPTICAL SOUND J-C
Explores principles governing addition of primary colors of light. Shows how white and various hues of colored light are made. Studies a color TV screen.
LC NO. FIA66-133
Prod-ACA Dist-ACA 1965

Understanding Composition In Art C 17 MIN
16MM FILM OPTICAL SOUND J-C A
Introduces a wide variety of paintings and sculpture, including many of the contemporary styles - hard edge abstracts, pop art, kinetic sculpture, shaped canvas and other. Stresses that composition is experiment and change, and discusses balance, positive and negative space, form, detail, texture and rhythm.
LC NO. 79-715408
Prod-ACA Dist-ACA 1971

Understanding Computers C
3/4 OR 1/2 INCH VIDEO CASSETTE
Describes in non-technical terms exactly what computers can and can't do. Shows why computers are more suitable for some applications than others. Emphasises the programmer's responsibility for efficient utilization of the computer.
From The Audio Visual Library Of Computer Education Series.
Prod-PRISPR Dist-PRISPR

Understanding Cultural Differences C
3/4 OR 1/2 INCH VIDEO CASSETTE IND
Examines concepts of culture in general and ways of analyzing a culture, providing a model with benchmarks or identifying characteristics of any culture.
From The Managing Cultural Differences Series.
Prod-GPCV Dist-GPCV

Understanding Data Base C 30 MIN
3/4 OR 1/2 INCH VIDEO CASSETTE
Provides an overview of data base technology and the jargon that describes it. Explains the basic terms and principles of data base technology and describes the end user's essential role in data base evolution.
From The End User's Guide To Data Base Series.
Prod-DELTAK Dist-DELTAK

Understanding Decimals C 13 MIN
3/4 INCH VIDEO CASSETTE
See series title for descriptive statement.
From The Basic Math Skills Series. Adding, Subtracting, Multiplying Decimals
Prod-TELSTR Dist-TELSTR

Understanding Diabetes C 35 MIN
16MM FILM OPTICAL SOUND PRO
Presents basic concepts of diabetes including clinical and public health aspects, epidemiological factors, modern concepts and methods of management, prevention of aceu problems and the early recognition of degenerative complications.
From The Diabetes Nursing Series.
LC NO. FIA67-5618
Prod-ANANLN Dist-AJN 1967

Understanding Diabetes—A Series

Points out that the key to a diabetic living a normal life is the patient's understanding of diabetes and willingness to take the action necessary to maintain health.
Prod-FAIRGH Dist-FAIRGH

Good Nutrition And The Diabetic	024 MIN
Insulin, Insulin Administration And	018 MIN
Personal Care Considerations Of The Diabetic	022 MIN
Roadmap To Control, The	017 MIN

Understanding Different Points Of View C 20 MIN
16MM FILM, 3/4 OR 1/2 IN VIDEO T
See series title for descriptive statement.
From The Discussing Controversial Issues Series.
Prod-FWLERD Dist-AITECH 1975

Understanding Dinnerware C 15 MIN
16MM FILM, 3/4 OR 1/2 IN VIDEO J-C A
Shows two little girls who startle their parents by shopping for their own fine china. Discusses stoneware, earthenware, porcelain and progressive china.
Prod-KLEINW Dist-KLEINW 1977

Understanding DP/OA Integration C 45 MIN
3/4 OR 1/2 INCH VIDEO CASSETTE
Looks at some of the successful systems that have integrated data processing functions with office automation to create total information management systems, the process by which integration was achieved and the important issue of human involvement in system integration.
From The Integrating DP And Office Automation Series.
Prod-DELTAK Dist-DELTAK

Understanding Figurative Language C 30 MIN
3/4 OR 1/2 INCH VIDEO CASSETTE
See series title for descriptive statement.
From The Prose Literature Series.
Prod-CAMB Dist-CAMB

Understanding For The Future X 30 MIN
2 INCH VIDEOTAPE I
Emphasizes some of the historical contributions made by ethnic groups and brings out the importance of the role that all groups play within the society today. Views young people and adults discussing problems affecting all people and offers suggestions for better understanding for the future. (Broadcast quality)
From The Cultural Understandings Series. No. 14
Prod-DENVPS Dist-GPITVL Prodn-KRMATV

Understanding Forms C 30 MIN
3/4 OR 1/2 INCH VIDEO CASSETTE
See series title for descriptive statement.
From The Practical Reading Series.
Prod-CAMB Dist-CAMB

Understanding Frustration And Its Effects B 29 MIN
16MM FILM OPTICAL SOUND
See series title for descriptive statement.
From The Controlling Turnover And Absenteeism Series.
LC NO. 76-703321
Prod-EDSD Dist-EDSD

Understanding Greenhouse Flammability C 18 MIN
16MM FILM OPTICAL SOUND
Describes a three-year research project done at Colorado State University using controlled burnings of an actual greenhouse covered with rigid and film plastics. Discusses types of covers and structures, employee safety, alarm systems and sprinkler systems.
Prod-COLOSU Dist-COLOSU 1977

Understanding Hidden Meanings In Conversation C
16MM FILM - 3/4 IN VIDEO A
Shows how conversations reveal more than is intended and demonstrates ear-opening methods and experiences. Describes meta-talk and gestures with attitudes and relationships.
From The Art Of Negotiating Series. Module 10
Prod-BNA Dist-BNA 1983

Understanding Hidden Meanings In Conversation (Meta-Talk) C 33 MIN
3/4 OR 1/2 INCH VIDEO CASSETTE
See series title for descriptive statement.
From The Art Of Negotiating Series.
Prod-DELTAK Dist-DELTAK

Understanding Human Behavior - An Introduction To Psychology—A Series
C A
Reinforces visually the concepts in the telecourse text. Gives viewer a better understanding of the classic experiments in psychology. Applies basic concepts of psychology to all age groups and to everyday situations.
Prod-COAST Dist-CDTEL

Abnormal Psychology	029 MIN
Altered States Of Consciousness	029 MIN
Applied Psychology	029 MIN
Brain, The	029 MIN
Cognitive Development	029 MIN
Conditioning	029 MIN
Consciousness And Sleep	029 MIN
Emotional Development	029 MIN
Functions Of The Brain	029 MIN
Genetic Psychology	029 MIN
Human Psychology	029 MIN
Interpersonal Attraction	029 MIN
Memory	029 MIN
Motivation And Hunger	029 MIN
Operant Conditioning	029 MIN
Pain And Hypnosis	029 MIN
Personality Tests	029 MIN
Personality Theory	029 MIN
Persuasion	029 MIN
Psychotherapy, Pt 1	029 MIN
Psychotherapy, Pt 2	029 MIN
Sensory Deprivation And Controlled Sensory	029 MIN
Sensory Psychology	029 MIN
Sexual Motivation	029 MIN
Social Groups	029 MIN
Stress	029 MIN
Subliminal Perception	029 MIN
Taste, Smell, Hearing	029 MIN
Vision	029 MIN
Visual Perception	029 MIN

Understanding Human Reproduction C
3/4 OR 1/2 INCH VIDEO CASSETTE J-H
Designed as a foundation for sex education. Gives students a thorough understanding of human reproduction. Describes human reproductive systems. Explains conception. Follows fetal development. Concludes with labor and delivery and the bonding of parents and child.
Prod-SUNCOM Dist-SUNCOM

Understanding Industrial Hygiene C 18 MIN
3/4 OR 1/2 INCH VIDEO CASSETTE IND
Introduces supervisors to industrial hygiene (IH)basics. Shows three ways toxic substances can enter the body, how to test worker's exposure and how to protect against radiation and other IH problems.
From The Foreman's Accident Prevention Series.
Prod-GPCV Dist-GPCV

Understanding Infant Behavior B 44 MIN
16MM FILM OPTICAL SOUND
Discusses the infant's behavior as a reaction to his basic needs. Describes the problems provoked by parental expectancy, demands and reactions regarding feeding procedures, masturbation, sleep and toilet training.
From The Man - His Growth And Development, Birth Through Adolescence Series.
LC NO. 79-703693
Prod-VDONUR Dist-AJN Prodn-WTTWTV 1967

Understanding Infertility C 10 MIN
16MM FILM, 3/4 OR 1/2 IN VIDEO PRO
Explains how a pregnancy occurs and how any dysfunction in the process may lead to infertility. Discusses causes and treatments for infertility for both men and women.
Prod-PRORE Dist-PRORE

Understanding Instructions C 11 MIN
16MM FILM, 3/4 OR 1/2 IN VIDEO I
Shows how a young boy in school follows instructions by asking questions, learning signs and symbols and by following steps carefully. Gives specific pointers for improving the ability to understand and follow instructions.
Prod-CORF Dist-CORF 1975

Understanding Labor C 11 MIN
16MM FILM, 3/4 OR 1/2 IN VIDEO
Describes what labor is, the stages of labor and how to recognize true labor from false labor.
From The Prepared Childbirth And Parenting Series.
Prod-JOU Dist-JOU 1979

Understanding Labor And Delivery C 21 MIN
16MM FILM, 3/4 OR 1/2 IN VIDEO
Highlights the importance of patient/physician discussion regarding options and contingencies on the medical procedures to be employed at the time of labor and childbirth. Provides background material for expectant mothers and fathers. Indicates how a father can provide support throughout labor and delivery and shows two actual childbirths.
Prod-AMCOG Dist-AMCOG

Understanding Law C
3/4 OR 1/2 INCH VIDEO CASSETTE J-H
Describes what happens when kids break the law. Discusses le-

gal responsibilities of parents, children and schools. Includes a complete court case of young people arrested for drug use.
Prod-EDUACT Dist-EDUACT

Understanding Lightning And Thunder C 20 MIN
16MM FILM OPTICAL SOUND J-H
Discusses the safety rules relating to lightning and thunder.
LC NO. 79-701647
Prod-REDDB Dist-ECI 1977

Understanding Microprocessors—A Series
C
Introduces the basics of microprocessors, a short course taught by Ron Bishop, system operations manager.
Prod-UAZMIC Dist-UAZMIC

Addressing Modes	060 MIN
Basic Electronics	060 MIN
Digital Arithmetic	060 MIN
Logic Elements	060 MIN
M-Sixty-Eight Hundred Hardware - ACIA, PIA	060 MIN
M-Sixty-Eight Hundred Hardware - MPU, RAM, ROM	060 MIN
Microcomputer Overview	060 MIN
Number Systems	060 MIN
Program Examples	060 MIN
Sixty-Eight Hundred Instruction Set, Pt 1	060 MIN
Sixty-Eight Hundred Instruction Set, Pt 2	060 MIN
System Configuration	060 MIN

Understanding Motivation C 28 MIN
16MM FILM - 3/4 IN VIDEO IND
Presents Dr Saul W Gellerman, executive research consultant at International Business Machines Corporation, who explains the individual needs of workers and how their motivation is a product of the kind of world they think they live in.
From The Motivation And Productivity Series.
Prod-BNA Dist-BNA 1967

Understanding Movies C 13 MIN
16MM FILM, 3/4 OR 1/2 IN VIDEO
Uses a film sequence to show how time speeds up, stretches or condenses according to the filmmaker's wishes.
Prod-NYT Dist-CORF

Understanding On-Line Systems C 20 MIN
3/4 OR 1/2 INCH VIDEO CASSETTE
Stresses the growing importance of end-user participation in the application development process, provides the user with a functional description of on-line systems and makes the distinction between on-line access to computing resources and traditional batch processing.
From The On-Line Systems Concepts For Users Series.
Prod-DELTAK Dist-DELTAK

Understanding Our Earth - Glaciers (2nd Ed) C 11 MIN
16MM FILM, 3/4 OR 1/2 IN VIDEO I-J
Presents glaciers from Alaska, the United States, Canada and Europe to show the different kinds and to explain how they are formed. Examines the formation of icebergs and the significance and impact of glaciers during the ice age. Shows evidences of glaciation in glacier lakes in the Rocky Mountains, soil in the Midwest, glacial drift in New England and the Matterhorn peak in the Swiss Alps.
From The Understanding Our Earth Series.
Prod-CORF Dist-CORF 1977

Understanding Our Earth - How Its Surface Changes (2nd Ed) C 12 MIN
16MM FILM, 3/4 OR 1/2 IN VIDEO I-J
Investigates the forces which cause changes in the earth's surface, such as wind, water, glaciers, rivers, volcanoes and human activities.
From The Understanding Our Earth Series.
Prod-CORF Dist-CORF 1977

Understanding Our Earth - Rocks And Minerals (2nd Ed) C 12 MIN
16MM FILM, 3/4 OR 1/2 IN VIDEO I-J
Describes the three classes of rocks, their formations and uses.
From The Understanding Our Earth Series.
Prod-CORF Dist-CORF 1977

Understanding Our Earth - Soil (2nd Ed) C 12 MIN
16MM FILM, 3/4 OR 1/2 IN VIDEO I-J
Explains the soil profile, which consists of topsoil, subsoil, mantle rock and bedrock. Presents a breakdown of the elements of soil and describes the process of soil making, whereby rocks are broken down by erosion and decaying matter changes into humus. Covers the types of soil throughout the United States and the importance of conservation.
From The Understanding Our Earth Series.
Prod-CORF Dist-CORF 1977

Understanding Our Earth—A Series
16MM FILM, 3/4 OR 1/2 IN VIDEO I-J
Prod-CORF Dist-CORF 1977

Understanding Our Earth - Glaciers (2nd Ed)	11 MIN
Understanding Our Earth - How Its Surface	12 MIN
Understanding Our Earth - Rocks And Minerals	12 MIN
Understanding Our Earth - Soil (2nd Ed)	11 MIN

Understanding Our World, Unit I - Tools We Use—A Series
I
Prod-KRMATV Dist-GPITVL

All Kinds Of Maps	20 MIN
Globes Are Useful	20 MIN
Modern Mapmakers	20 MIN
Reading A Map	20 MIN
World Streets And Avenues	20 MIN

Understanding Our World, Unit II - Geography We Should Know—A Series
I
Prod-KRMATV Dist-GPITVL

Islands Of Japan	20 MIN
Land Below The Sea	20 MIN
Life On The Great Plains	20 MIN
Mountainous Land	20 MIN
Oceans Surround Us	20 MIN
Trailing A River	20 MIN
What Is A Desert	20 MIN

Understanding Our World, Unit III - Living In Other Lands—A Series
I
Prod-KRMATV Dist-GPITVL

Australian Contrast	20 MIN
High In The Andes	20 MIN
Impressions In East Africa	20 MIN
Islands Of Japan	20 MIN
Land Below The Sea	20 MIN

Understanding Percent C 10 MIN
3/4 INCH VIDEO CASSETTE
See series title for descriptive statement.
From The Basic Math Skills Series. Per Cent
Prod-TELSTR Dist-TELSTR

Understanding Personal Interaction Styles C
3/4 OR 1/2 INCH VIDEO CASSETTE
See series title for descriptive statement.
From The Management Diagnostic Series.
Prod-THGHT Dist-DELTAK

Understanding Personality And Behavior C 23 MIN
3/4 OR 1/2 INCH VIDEO CASSETTE
Demonstrates how a better understanding of basic human needs can help supervisors deal successfully with troubled employees.
Prod-AMA Dist-AMA

Understanding Place Value C 15 MIN
3/4 OR 1/2 INCH VIDEO CASSETTE I
Explains that Kaylin learns the hard way how the place value of a number changes when another number is put to its right - she ends up with too many cookies and too many ads. Includes an animated segment in which Zero teaches Numberville about place value.
From The It Figures Series. No. 5
Prod-AITV Dist-AITECH Prodn-NJN 1982

Understanding Radiation Therapy C
3/4 OR 1/2 INCH VIDEO CASSETTE
Presents information essential to the new radiation therapy patient. Uses computer graphics and animation to describe how cancer grows within the body and how radiation therapy works in treating cancer cells.
Prod-GRANVW Dist-GRANVW

Understanding Relations B
16MM FILM OPTICAL SOUND
Illustrates general concepts of relation and equivalence relation.
Prod-OPENU Dist-OPENU

Understanding Remainders C 14 MIN
3/4 OR 1/2 INCH VIDEO CASSETTE I
Shows that Mary finds that what she and her friends do with remainders depends on the situation. Includes an animated segment in which Little Boy Blue meets the Big Bad Wolf and learns to think about remainders before sounding the alarm.
From The It Figures Series. No. 17
Prod-AITV Dist-AITECH Prodn-NJN 1982

Understanding Semiconductors Course Outline —A Series
IND
Concerns fundamental electronics technology. Begins with the end systems and works down through circuits to components and semiconductor theory.
Prod-TXINLC Dist-TXINLC

Basic Circuit Functions In The System	60 MIN
Digital Integrated Circuits	60 MIN
Diode Performance And Specifications	60 MIN
Diodes - What They Do And How They Work	60 MIN
How Circuits Make Decisions	60 MIN
Introduction To Integrated Circuits	60 MIN
Mos And Linear Integrated Circuits	60 MIN
P-N-P Transistor And Transistor Specifications	60 MIN
Relating Semiconductors To Systems	60 MIN
Thyristors And Optoelectronics	60 MIN
Transistors - How They Work, How They Are Made	60 MIN
What Electricity Does In Every Electric System	60 MIN

Understanding Sexuality C 30 MIN
16MM FILM, 3/4 OR 1/2 IN VIDEO H-C A
Suggests how parents can answer their children's questions about sex.
From The Look At Me Series.
Prod-WTTWTV Dist-FI 1980

Understanding Shakespeare - His Sources C 19 MIN
16MM FILM, 3/4 OR 1/2 IN VIDEO J-C
Presents excerpts from four plays of Shakespeare to show how he enhanced his sources with imagination, knowledge of human nature and command of language.
From The Shakespeare Series.
Prod-GATEEF Dist-CORF 1971

Understanding Shakespeare - His Stagecraft C 25 MIN
16MM FILM, 3/4 OR 1/2 IN VIDEO J-C
Uses stagings of episodes from four plays by Shakespeare to show how the theaters of Elizabethan England affected the way in which the plays were written.
From The Shakespeare Series.
Prod-GATEEF Dist-CORF 1971

Understanding Soccer Movie, The C 18 MIN
16MM FILM OPTICAL SOUND J-C A
Uses game action, planned action and animation to capture the excitement of soccer and to show the basic rules governing play.
LC NO. 76-700210
Prod-GRADYM Dist-FILMSM 1975

Understanding Software C 21 MIN
3/4 OR 1/2 INCH VIDEO CASSETTE C
Discusses types, applications and the choosing of software.
From The Business Computing - Cut Down To Size Series. Pt 4
Prod-ELDATA Dist-GPITVL 1980

Understanding Space And Time—A Series
16MM FILM, 3/4 OR 1/2 IN VIDEO
Charts the development of the understanding of the physical universe. Emphasizes the importance of the theory of relativity, showing it to be the central pillar of 20th-century physics and the framework for man's comprehension of such discoveries as pulsars, quasars and black holes.
Prod-BBCTV Dist-UCEMC 1980

As Surely As Columbus Saw America	028 MIN
At The Frontier	028 MIN
Conflict Brought To Light	028 MIN
E Equals MC Squared	028 MIN
Ground Control To Mr Galileo	028 MIN
Isolated Fact, An	028 MIN
Marking Time	028 MIN
Measuring Shadows - The Universe Today	028 MIN
Note Of Uncertainty, A - The Universe Tomorrow	028 MIN
Pushed To The Limit	028 MIN
Royal Road	028 MIN
Shades Of Black	028 MIN
Vanished Brilliance - The Universe Yesterday	028 MIN

Understanding Stress - The Marginal Manager C 30 MIN
3/4 OR 1/2 INCH VIDEO CASSETTE
See series title for descriptive statement.
From The Stress Intelligence - An Approach To Stress Management Series.
Prod-DELTAK Dist-DELTAK

Understanding Stresses And Strains C 10 MIN
16MM FILM, 3/4 OR 1/2 IN VIDEO I-J
Discusses the mental side of the health triangle, with emphasis on the pressures and worries of everyday life which can damage man's health.
From The Triangle Of Health Series.
Prod-DISNEY Dist-WDEMCO 1968

Understanding Stresses And Strains (Arabic) C 10 MIN
16MM FILM, 3/4 OR 1/2 IN VIDEO I-H
Shows what excessive worry can do to the mind and body. Suggests using common sense to minimize stresses and strains.
From The Triangle Of Health (Arabic) Series.
Prod-WDEMCO Dist-WDEMCO 1968

Understanding Stresses And Strains (French) C 10 MIN
16MM FILM, 3/4 OR 1/2 IN VIDEO I-H
Shows what excessive worry can do to the mind and body. Suggests using common sense to minimize stresses and strains.
From The Triangle Of Health (French) Series.
Prod-WDEMCO Dist-WDEMCO 1968

Understanding Stresses And Strains (German) C 10 MIN
16MM FILM, 3/4 OR 1/2 IN VIDEO I-H
Shows what excessive worry can do to the mind and body. Suggests using common sense to minimize stresses and strains.
From The Triangle Of Health (German) Series.
Prod-WDEMCO Dist-WDEMCO 1968

Understanding Stresses And Strains (Hungarian) C 10 MIN
16MM FILM, 3/4 OR 1/2 IN VIDEO I-H
Shows what excessive worry can do to the mind and body. Suggests using common sense to minimize stresses and strains.
From The Triangle Of Health (Hungarian) Series.
Prod-WDEMCO Dist-WDEMCO 1968

Understanding Stresses And Strains (Spanish) C 10 MIN
16MM FILM, 3/4 OR 1/2 IN VIDEO I-H
Shows what excessive worry can do to the mind and body. Suggests using common sense to minimize stresses and strains.
From The Triangle Of Health (Spanish) Series.
Prod-WDEMCO Dist-WDEMCO 1968

Understanding Stresses And Strains (Swedish) C 10 MIN
16MM FILM, 3/4 OR 1/2 IN VIDEO I-H
Shows what excessive worry can do to the mind and body. Suggests using common sense to minimize stresses and strains.
From The Triangle Of Health (Swedish) Series.
Prod-WDEMCO Dist-WDEMCO 1968

Understanding The American Economy C
1/2 IN VIDEO CASSETTE (VHS)
Discusses capitalism, the price system, GNP, inflation, business cycle, unemployment, corporations, public sector and private sector.
Prod-HRMC Dist-HRMC

Understanding The Assignment C 30 MIN
3/4 OR 1/2 INCH VIDEO CASSETTE H-C A
See series title for descriptive statement.
From The Introduction To Technical And Business Communication Series.
Prod-UMINN Dist-GPITVL 1983

Understanding The Atom, No. 01 - Alpha, Beta And Gamma B 44 MIN
16MM FILM - 3/4 IN VIDEO
Presents a lecture-demonstration by Dr Ralph T Overman, giving insight into the origin and nature of alpha, beta and gamma radiation. Discusses neutron absorption causing a state of unstable nuclei and the transformation of excess neutrons, returning the nuclei into a stable state. Shows that gamma radiation arises from a nuclear cooling process.
LC NO. 80-706614
Prod-USAEC Dist-USNAC Prodn-NYU 1980

Understanding The Atom, No. 02 - Nuclear Reactions B 29 MIN
16MM FILM OPTICAL SOUND
Discusses neutron capture processes, fission by neutrons, calculations involving activation of gold in a nuclear reaction and detection of minute quantities.
LC NO. FIE64-7
Prod-USAEC Dist-USERD

Understanding The Atom, No. 02 - Radiation And Matter B 44 MIN
3/4 INCH VIDEO CASSETTE
Presents a lecture-demonstration by Dr Ralph T Overman considering the interaction of radiation with matter and the development of various processes by which alpha, beta and gamma radiation give up energy to their surroundings.
Prod-USAEC Dist-USNAC 1972

Understanding The Atom, No. 03 - Properties Of Radiation B 30 MIN
16MM FILM OPTICAL SOUND H-C A
Discusses laws of radioactive decay, standard deviation in counts, energy distribution of alpha and beta - emitters, absorption curves, self-absorption and scattering.
Prod-USAEC Dist-USERD 1962

Understanding The Atom, No. 03 - Radiation Detection By Ionization B 30 MIN
3/4 INCH VIDEO CASSETTE
Presents a lecture-demonstration by Dr Ralph T Overman describing basic principles of ionization detectors. Gives brief descriptions of ionization chambers, proportional counters and Geiger counters. Discusses the resolving tome of a counter, as well as the various components of practical instruments, including amplifiers and scalers.
LC NO. 80-706619
Prod-USAEC Dist-USNAC Prodn-EDUCBC 1980

Understanding The Atom, No. 04 - Radiation And Matter B 44 MIN
16MM FILM OPTICAL SOUND H-C A
Considers the interaction of radiation with matter and develops the various processes by which alpha, beta and gamma radiation give up energy to their surroundings. Explains the relation between energy of a particle and the number of ion pairs formed. Discusses gamma and the four possibilities of gamma ray absorption.
LC NO. FIE64-3
Prod-USAEC Dist-USERD 1962

Understanding The Atom, No. 04 - Radiation Detection By Scintillation B 30 MIN
3/4 INCH VIDEO CASSETTE
Presents a lecture-demonstration by Dr Ralph T Overman reviewing gamma interaction with matter. Describes the scintillation process and the efficiency of the conversion of gamma radiation to visible light by the scintillator. Describes the operation of a photomultiplier tube, the principles behind a pulse-height analyzer and the use of solid-state radiation detectors.
LC NO. 80-706615
Prod-USAEC Dist-USNAC Prodn-EDUCBC 1980

Understanding The Atom, No. 05 - Properties Of Radiation B 30 MIN
3/4 INCH VIDEO CASSETTE
Presents a lecture-demonstration by Dr Ralph T Overman discussing general problems of radiation decay, standard deviations in experimental counts, the energy spectrum from alpha and beta emitters, the use of absorption curves to study energy distribution of beta radiation, as well as the problems of self-absorption, specific activity and backscattering of radiation.
Prod-USAEC Dist-USNAC 1972

Understanding The Atom, No. 05 - Radiation Detection By Ionization B 30 MIN
16MM FILM OPTICAL SOUND H-C A
Discusses principles of ionization detectors. Provides examples of suitable instruments and a detailed discussion of the geiger counter.
LC NO. FIE64-4
Prod-USAEC Dist-USERD 1962

Understanding The Atom, No. 06 - Nuclear Reactions B 30 MIN
3/4 INCH VIDEO CASSETTE
Presents a lecture-demonstration by Dr Ralph T Overman discussing some of the basic concepts of nuclear reaction, neutron capture processes, nuclear fission, examples of calculations used in nuclear reactions and the technique of activation analysis.
LC NO. 80-706620
Prod-USAEC Dist-USNAC Prodn-EDUCBC 1980

Understanding The Atom, No. 06 - Radiation Detection By Scintillation B 30 MIN
16MM FILM OPTICAL SOUND H-C A
Discusses the reaction of gamma-radiation with matter, the scintillation process, solid and liquid scintillator detection devices and the operation of a pulse-height analyzer.
LC NO. FIE64-5
Prod-USAEC Dist-USERD 1962

Understanding The Atom, No. 07 - Radiological Safety B 30 MIN
16MM FILM - 3/4 IN VIDEO
Examines the field of radiological safety or health physics and gives a basis for perspective on potential biological radiation damage. Considers background radiation, size of dosages and their varying effects. Describes distance, time of exposure and shielding as factors to be considered in controlling radiation hazards.
LC NO. 80-706618
Prod-USAEC Dist-USNAC Prodn-EDUCBC 1980

Understanding The Atom, No. 08 - Radioisotope Applications In Industry B 26 MIN
16MM FILM - 3/4 IN VIDEO
Presents a lecture-demonstration by Paul C Aebersold, director of isotope development, Atomic Energy Commission, discussing the various industrial uses of radioisotopes in tire plants, steel mills, in the petroleum and chemical industries and in food plants.
LC NO. 80-706617
Prod-USAEC Dist-USNAC Prodn-EDUCBC 1980

Understanding The Atom, No. 09 - Radioisotopes In Biology And Agriculture B 26 MIN
16MM FILM - 3/4 IN VIDEO
Discusses the applications of atomic energy in agriculture and biology. Shows how radioisotopic tracers are used in determining the structure and role of nucleic acids and other cellular components, including the specific structure of a proton. Includes examples of plant breeding projects, theories of aging, and other examples on the effect of radiation effects in living systems.
Prod-USAEC Dist-USNAC 1972

Understanding The Atom, No. 10 - Radioisotoper Applications In Medicine B 26 MIN
16MM FILM - 3/4 IN VIDEO
Traces the development of the use of radioisotopes and radiation in the field of medicine from the early work by Hervesy to the present. Includes studies of atherosclerosis, cobalt-labeled vitamin b-12, the use of iodine radioisotopes in determining thyroid physiology and pathology, the localization of brain tumors, determination of volume of body fluids and the measurement of red cell volume and life time. Discusses its use in treating disease, such as hyperthyroidism and cancer.
LC NO. 80-706616
Prod-USAEC Dist-USNAC Prodn-EDUCBC 1980

Understanding The Atom, No. 11 - The Atom In Physical Science B 26 MIN
16MM FILM - 3/4 IN VIDEO
Outlines the type of experiments used in the production of transuranium elements as described by Dr Glen T Seaborg, chairman, Atomic Energy Commission. Describes the various sources used in producing new elements and points out that elements not yet discovered will be characterized by very short half-lives, requiring electronic means of testing rather than chemical techniques.
LC NO. 80-706621
Prod-USAEC Dist-USNAC Prodn-EDUCBC 1980

Understanding The Basics C 34 MIN
3/4 OR 1/2 INCH VIDEO CASSETTE PRO
Gives a general overview of legal research, then focuses upon computer research. Provides demonstrations on Lexis and Westlaw systems.
From The Computers In Legal Research Series.
Prod-ABACPE Dist-ABACPE

Understanding The Business Of World And Stocks C 58 MIN
1/2 IN VIDEO CASSETTE BETA/VHS
Deals with common and preferred stocks. Provides an overview of business structure and practice, securities terminology and stockholder rights.
Prod-RMI Dist-RMI

Understanding The Business World And Stocks C 58 MIN
1/2 IN VIDEO CASSETTE BETA/VHS
Explains Common and preferred stocks. Discusses securities terminology. Provides an overview of business structure and practice.
From The Investing Series.
Prod-MOHOMV Dist-MOHOMV

Understanding The Cardiac Workup C 18 MIN
3/4 OR 1/2 INCH VIDEO CASSETTE
Explains what the cardiac workup is and discusses its role in preventing and minimizing heart problems. Describes electrocardiograms, blood tests and X-ray procedures that may be required during a cardiac workup.
LC NO. 77-730598
Prod-TRAINX Dist-TRAINX

Understanding The Deaf C 21 MIN
16MM FILM, 3/4 OR 1/2 IN VIDEO J-C A
Records instructional methods used with the deaf. Presents many of the obstacles which deaf children must overcome in their education.
Prod-PORTAM Dist-PEREN 1977

Understanding The Expectation Effect C 30 MIN
3/4 OR 1/2 INCH VIDEO CASSETTE T
Explains the expectation effect in an educational setting.
From The Interaction - Human Concerns In The Schools Series.
Prod-MDDE Dist-MDCPB

Understanding The Importance Of Electrical Systems C 35 MIN
3/4 INCH VIDEO CASSETTE C A
See series title for descriptive statement.
From The Energy Conservation In Industrial Plants Series.
LC NO. 81-706196
Prod-AMCEE Dist-AMCEE 1979

Understanding The Japanese C 30 MIN
16MM FILM OPTICAL SOUND
Describes how the Japanese view romance, love and marriage by interviewing six foreign residents of Japan.
Prod-MTP Dist-MTP

Understanding The Listening Process C 11 MIN
3/4 OR 1/2 INCH VIDEO CASSETTE
See series title for descriptive statement.
From The Listening - The Forgotten Skill Series.
Prod-DELTAK Dist-DELTAK

Understanding The Metric System C 8 MIN
16MM FILM OPTICAL SOUND J-C A
Shows the importance of understanding the metric system, particularly for laboratory work. Explains the metric system and how it is related to systems of ten.
From The Measurement Series.
LC NO. 78-700703
Prod-PSU Dist-PSU 1972

Understanding The Patient (Cultural Factors) B 30 MIN
2 INCH VIDEOTAPE PRO
Helps nursing students development an understanding of the variety of cultural factors which may impede acceptance and understanding of the patient.
From The Mental Health Concepts For Nursing, Unit 4 - The Nurse - Patient Relationship Series.
LC NO. 73-702650
Prod-GPITVL Dist-GPITVL 1971

Understanding The Pill C 9 MIN
16MM FILM, 3/4 OR 1/2 IN VIDEO A
Examines oral contraceptives and how they work. Gives directions for use, posible complications and limitations and signs and symptoms to be reported.
Prod-PRORE Dist-PRORE

Understanding The Science Behind Food Preservation C 15 MIN
16MM FILM, 3/4 OR 1/2 IN VIDEO C A
Explains the scientific reasons for bacterial growth causing spoilage in canned food.
Prod-CUETV Dist-CUNIV 1976

Understanding The Steps In The Normal Grieving Process C 90 MIN
3/4 OR 1/2 INCH VIDEO CASSETTE A
See series title for descriptive statement.
From The Growing Through Loss - A Howard Clinebell Resource Series. Session 2
Prod-UMCOM Dist-ECUFLM 1982

Understanding The Totality C 55 MIN
3/4 OR 1/2 INCH VIDEO CASSETTE
Presents Margaret Rood on understanding the totality of physical therapy.
Prod-UMDSM Dist-UMDSM

Understanding Topographic Maps C 14 MIN
16MM FILM, 3/4 OR 1/2 IN VIDEO J-H
Describes how a topographic map is made, demonstrates the meaning of contour lines and explains the uses of the topographic map.
Prod-WILEYJ Dist-MEDIAG 1970

Understanding Urine Testing C 30 MIN
16MM FILM, 3/4 OR 1/2 IN VIDEO A
Informs about glucose metabolism, ketone formation and renal thresholds. Shows types of urine test materials, which tests to use, when to test and exceptions to normal test routines. Describes equipment, procedures and results. Reviews storage and handling, and the effects of diet, medication and physical condition.
Prod-PRORE Dist-PRORE

Understanding Weather And Climate C
3/4 OR 1/2 INCH VIDEO CASSETTE H
Examines the major factors that affect weather, various types of weather phenomena, the vocabulary of weather observation and the instruments used to trace weather patterns.
Prod-GA Dist-GA

Understanding What We Value C 30 MIN
3/4 OR 1/2 INCH VIDEO CASSETTE T
Looks at the role of values in a school setting.
From The Interaction - Human Concerns In The Schools Series.
Prod-MDDE Dist-MDCPB

Understanding Your Anesthesia (Rev Ed) C 8 MIN
16MM FILM, 3/4 OR 1/2 IN VIDEO PRO
Describes anesthesiology as a medical specialty developed to control pain, and helps reduce the fear and apprehension associated with surgical experiences.
Prod-PRORE Dist-PRORE

Understanding Your Anesthesia (Spanish) C 8 MIN
16MM FILM, 3/4 OR 1/2 IN VIDEO PRO
Describes anesthesiology as a medical specialty developed to control pain, and helps reduce the fear and apprehension associated with surgical experiences.
Prod-PRORE Dist-PRORE

Understanding Your Safety Responsibility C 14 MIN
3/4 OR 1/2 INCH VIDEO CASSETTE IND
Gives seven rules to observe in order to attain the company's accident prevention goals while ensuring the safety of the entire work crew.
From The Foreman's Accident Prevention Series.
Prod-GPCV Dist-GPCV

Understudy, The C 26 MIN
16MM FILM OPTICAL SOUND
Tells the story of a tangled love relationship which spans 30 years.
LC NO. 76-701490
Prod-ONCA Dist-ONCA Prodn-DABRKF 1975

Undertow C 9 MIN
16MM FILM OPTICAL SOUND H-C
Features a symbolic fantasy of a young woman's conflict between sexual desires and religious training.
Prod-JORDAL Dist-CFS

Undertow And Count Me Gone C 20 MIN
3/4 OR 1/2 INCH VIDEO CASSETTE J-H
Presents UNDERTOW by Finn Haverold, set in Norway. Tells of a young boy's idolatry for an older boy who has stolen a sailboat. Narrates from COUNT ME GONE by Annable and Edgar Johnson, set in an American city. Describes how a boy becomes disillusioned after his brother uses him as a scapegoat to cover his own inadequacies. (Broadcast quality)
From The Matter Of Fiction Series. No. 12
Prod-WETATV Dist-AITECH

Underwater C 15 MIN
3/4 OR 1/2 INCH VIDEO CASSETTE P
See series title for descriptive statement.
From The Let's Draw Series.
Prod-OCPS Dist-AITECH Prodn-KOKHTV 1976

Underwater Flight Of The Tufted Puffin C 9 MIN
16MM FILM, 3/4 OR 1/2 IN VIDEO
Shows the surface and underwater locomotion of the tufted puffin, a marine bird that swims underwater by means of synchronous movements of partially flexed wings. Analyzes the development of thrust by the wings and the use of the feet, tail and bill for steering and maneuvering.
From The Aspects Of Animal Behavior Series.
Prod-UCLA Dist-UCEMC 1979

Underwater Louisbourg C 12 MIN
16MM FILM OPTICAL SOUND
Follows a group of divers as they explore shipwrecks in the harbor off the shore of the Louisbourg fortress in Nova Scotia.
LC NO. 75-703442
Prod-NSDTI Dist-NSDTI 1972

Underwater Sound - Basic Principles C 21 MIN
16MM FILM OPTICAL SOUND
Illustrates the basic principles of the behavior of sound under water. Shows the effects of absorption, scattering, bottom loss and sound refraction on sound transmissions in the sea.
LC NO. 74-705872
Prod-USN Dist-USNAC 1969

Undescended Testis C 15 MIN
3/4 OR 1/2 INCH VIDEO CASSETTE
See series title for descriptive statement.
From The Pediatric Series.
Prod-SVL Dist-SVL

Undetermined Coefficients B 29 MIN
3/4 OR 1/2 INCH VIDEO CASSETTE
See series title for descriptive statement.
From The Calculus Of Differential Equations Series.
Prod-MIOT Dist-MIOT

Undifferentiated Lump, The C 10 MIN
16MM FILM, 3/4 OR 1/2 IN VIDEO H-C A
Demonstrates the use of differential reinforcement to shape a student's verbal behavior.
Prod-STNFLD Dist-STNFLD

Undramatic Slave, The B 30 MIN
16MM FILM OPTICAL SOUND H-C A
Lerone Bennett describes the many undramatic but effective forms of resistance which were evidence of the day-to-day hostility of the slaves, and explains the solidarity of the movement which resulted in a legacy of rebellion.
From The Black History, Section 05 - Rebellion And Resistance Series.
LC NO. 79-704047
Prod-WCBSTV Dist-HRAW 1969

Une Femme Douce C 87 MIN
16MM FILM OPTICAL SOUND
A French language film. Uses a series of flashbacks to tell the story of a young wife who commits suicide. Follows her husband's reconstruction of the past as he sits by her bed.
Prod-NYFLMS Dist-NYFLMS 1969

Une Femme Douce C 87 MIN
16MM FILM OPTICAL SOUND
A French language film with English subtitles. Describes a young woman who marries an introspective pawnbroker and begins a mysterious process of oppression. Directed by Robert Bresson.
Prod-UNKNWN Dist-NYFLMS 1969

Une Journee Au Lycee C 16 MIN
16MM FILM, 3/4 OR 1/2 IN VIDEO
See series title for descriptive statement.
From The Lettres D'un Ami Francais Series.
Prod-SEABEN Dist-IFB 1962

Une Journee Dans Les Reserves Africaines C 23 MIN
16MM FILM OPTICAL SOUND I-C A
A French language film. Views African wildlife reservations.
Prod-FACSEA Dist-FACSEA

Une Nuit Sur Le Mont Chauve B 8 MIN
16MM FILM OPTICAL SOUND
Presents the first film made on the pinboard, an animation classic illustrating the music of Moussorgsky's tone poem, Night On Bald Mountain, and creates a fantasy world of witches, demons, and skeletons. By Alexander Alexeiff and Claire Parker.
Prod-STARRC Dist-STARRC 1933

Une Ombre Du Passe C 15 MIN
16MM FILM, 3/4 OR 1/2 IN VIDEO C A
See series title for descriptive statement.
From The La Maree Et Ses Secrets Series.
Prod-FI Dist-FI

Une Simple Histoire B 60 MIN
16MM FILM OPTICAL SOUND
A French language film. Focuses on a young woman who moves to Paris with her daughter to look for work and shelter. Finds her after nine days, without a job and without a home, until she moves in with an older woman.
Prod-NYFLMS Dist-NYFLMS 1957

Une Soiree Chez Les Carre C 10 MIN
16MM FILM, 3/4 OR 1/2 IN VIDEO J-C A
See series title for descriptive statement.
From The Les Aventures De Monsieur Carre Series.
LC NO. 81-706491
Prod-HALAS Dist-IFB 1978

Une Vile De Province C 19 MIN
16MM FILM, 3/4 OR 1/2 IN VIDEO H-C
Describes a visit to a small market town, purchasing hardware and medicine in shops whose description ends in '-erie' on the market square of the town of Bauge, located in the Loire Valley.
From The La France Telle Qu'Elle Est Series.
Prod-THAMES Dist-MEDIAG 1977

UNESCO C 28 MIN
3/4 INCH VIDEOTAPE
Interviews Mr Doudou Diene, director of UNESCO liason office at the United Nations in New York. Presents slides and film clips on UNESCO's achievements. Hosted by Marilyn Perry.
From The International Byline Series.
Prod-PERRYM Dist-PERRYM

UNESCO And The Press - Who Wants Control And Why? C 30 MIN
3/4 OR 1/2 INCH VIDEO CASSETTE
Focuses on the differences and proposed controls on international reporting. Discusses deficiencies in global news coverage and the impact the United Nations' 1979 McBride Commission findings have on journalistic license. Moderate by Elmer Lower.
From The Issues In World Communications, 1980 Series.
Prod-OHUTC Dist-OHUTC

Uneven Parallel Bars For Girls C 15 MIN
16MM FILM, 3/4 OR 1/2 IN VIDEO H-C
Demonstrates beginning, intermediate and advanced skills on the uneven parallel bars for girls. Portrays spotting techniques and combined movements in sequence.
Prod-AIMS Dist-AIMS 1971

Uneven Parallel Bars For Girls (Arabic) C 13 MIN
16MM FILM, 3/4 OR 1/2 IN VIDEO J-C
Demonstrates beginning, intermediate and advanced skills for girls on the uneven parallel bars.
Prod-AIMS Dist-AIMS 1971

Uneven Parallel Bars For Girls (Spanish) C 13 MIN
16MM FILM, 3/4 OR 1/2 IN VIDEO J-C
Demonstrates beginning, intermediate and advanced skills for girls on the uneven parallel bars.
Prod-AIMS Dist-AIMS 1971

Uneven Seesaw, The - Sexual Abuse Of Children C 20 MIN
3/4 OR 1/2 INCH VIDEO CASSETTE C A
Speaks to people who were victims of sexual abuse and incest as children. Discusses the roots of our public policies. Details the state's intervention in incest cases.
Prod-MMRC Dist-MMRC

Uneventful Day C 29 MIN
16MM FILM, 3/4 OR 1/2 IN VIDEO J-C
Looks at the process of geological weathering, depicting the physical and chemical forces that produce the variety and beauty of the Earth's georama.
From The Planet Of Man Series.
Prod-OECA Dist-FI 1976

Unexpected, The C 20 MIN
16MM FILM OPTICAL SOUND
Examines some of Xerox Corporation's television commercials and tells how they came to be. Describes the growth of Xerox as it relates to the television advertising medium.
LC NO. 75-703123
Prod-XEROX Dist-WSTGLC 1975

Unexpected, The C 53 MIN
16MM FILM, 3/4 OR 1/2 IN VIDEO H-C A
Relates what happens when a gold miner runs amok in his camp, killing two other miners. Depicts the informal trial which takes place, affording the Indian guides a chance to ponder the curious ways of white man's justice. Based on the short story The Unexpected by Jack London.
From The Jack London's Tales Of The Klondike Series.
LC NO. 84-706233
Prod-NORWK Dist-EBEC 1982

Unexplained Injury, An C 31 MIN
16MM FILM OPTICAL SOUND A
Looks at a case of child abuse, emphasizing the factors in the backgrounds of the parents which make them act this way.
Prod-UTORMC Dist-LAWREN

Unexplained Injury, An C 31 MIN
3/4 INCH VIDEO CASSETTE
Tells how a little boy's injuries are recognized by a school nurse as being related to child abuse.
Prod-UTORMC Dist-LAWREN 1980

Unfair Exchange C 27 MIN
16MM FILM, 3/4 OR 1/2 IN VIDEO
Investigates the economic relationship between developed and underdeveloped countries. Examines the situation in which underdeveloped countries export raw materials and import finished products, explaining the relationship between buyer and seller, and how prices are fixed on the international market.
From The Five Billion People Series.
Prod-LEFSP Dist-CNEMAG

Unfinished Business C 27 MIN
16MM FILM, 3/4 OR 1/2 IN VIDEO H-C A
Tells the story of Jim, whose relationship with his father improves dramatically after his father is hospitalized and Jim must care for him.
From The Insight Series.
Prod-PAULST Dist-PAULST

Unfinished Symphony C 15 MIN
16MM FILM OPTICAL SOUND
Presents an appeal for funds to protect endangered species around the world.
LC NO. 78-701577
Prod-WWF Dist-WWF Prodn-PHILMO 1978

Unfinished Task, The B 72 MIN
16MM FILM OPTICAL SOUND A
A story of the conflict which arises between a materialistic father and his spiritually minded son when the son follows his violation as a foreign missionary. Traces the father's realization of the importance and urgency of his son's calling.
LC NO. 72-701651
Prod-CONCOR Dist-CPH 1956

Unfolding B 17 MIN
16MM FILM, 3/4 OR 1/2 IN VIDEO C A
Focuses mainly on two couples. Suggests universal awareness, aloneness, fantasies, searching, touching, loving.
Prod-NATSF Dist-MMRC

Unfolding Infant Behavior B 44 MIN
16MM FILM OPTICAL SOUND
Discusses the innate potential of infants as seen through specific reflexive reactions, cephalo-caudal sequences and the parallel development of language and physiological reactions, such as crying, other sound productions and gestures.
From The Man - His Growth And Development, Birth Through Adolescence Series.
LC NO. 72-703694
Prod-VDONUR Dist-AJN Prodn-WTTWTV 1967

Unforeseen Problems C 30 MIN
1/2 IN VIDEO CASSETTE BETA/VHS
Uncovers some problems in a house about to be renovated, from the roof to the plumbing.
From The This Old House, Pt 1 - The Dorchester Series.
Prod-WGBHTV Dist-MTI

UNFPA C 28 MIN
3/4 INCH VIDEOTAPE
Interviews Mr Rafael M Salas, Executive Director of the United Nations Fund for Population Activities. Illustrates the goals and program activities of UNFPA through a film. Hosted by Marilyn Perry.
From The International Byline Series.
Prod-PERRYM Dist-PERRYM

Unfried Clams C 29 MIN
2 INCH VIDEOTAPE
See series title for descriptive statement.
From The Observing Eye Series.
Prod-WGBHTV Dist-PUBTEL

Unfriendly Flora And Fauna C 15 MIN
16MM FILM, 3/4 OR 1/2 IN VIDEO J-C A
Offers an overview of plants and animals that are harmful to humans, including jimsonweed, poison ivy and oak, nightshade, mushrooms, snakes, spiders, scorpion and wasps.
LC NO. 81-706039
Prod-CENTRO Dist-CORF 1980

Ung (Young) B 28 MIN
16MM FILM OPTICAL SOUND
A Danish language film. Presents a round table conference between youngsters. Discusses young people's attitude to the fear of the atomic bomb, modern requirements as regards education and specialization, choice of a career and the pleasure taken in one's work, young people's need for a place of their own and their view of sexual life.
Prod-STATNS Dist-STATNS 1965

UNICEF C 28 MIN
3/4 INCH VIDEOTAPE
Interviews H R H Prince Talal Bin Abdul Aziz Al Saud of Saudi Arabia as he discusses the United Nations Children's Fund and his activities as the Fund's special envoy. Includes a film clip on UNICEF.
From The International Byline Series.
Prod-PERRYM Dist-PERRYM

UNICEF Christmas Show C 28 MIN
3/4 INCH VIDEOTAPE
Features Celeste Holm as she brings a Christmas message at the beginning of the show. Interviews the Executive Director of UNICEF. Presents a film clip on children from different parts of the world.
From The International Byline Series.
Prod-PERRYM Dist-PERRYM

Unicorn C
1/2 IN VIDEO CASSETTE BETA/VHS
Deals with the unicorn.
Prod-EQVDL Dist-EQVDL

Unicorn - In The Island Of Magic C
1/2 IN VIDEO CASSETTE BETA/VHS
Deals with the Island of Magic and a unicorn.
Prod-EQVDL Dist-EQVDL

Unicorn Tales—A Series
16MM FILM, 3/4 OR 1/2 IN VIDEO P-J
Presents contemporary children's stories which are based on classic fairy tales.
Prod-MGHT Dist-MGHT Prodn-DENOIA 1980

Alex And The Wonderful Doowah Lamp	023 MIN
Big Apple Birthday	023 MIN
Carnival Circus	023 MIN
Magic Hat, The	023 MIN
Magic Pony Ride, The	023 MIN
Magnificent Major, The	023 MIN
Maltese Unicorn, The	023 MIN
Stowaway, The	023 MIN

Unicorn Tales, Pt 1 C
1/2 IN VIDEO CASSETTE BETA/VHS
Features unicorn tales.
Prod-EQVDL Dist-EQVDL

Unicorn Tales, Pt 2 C
1/2 IN VIDEO CASSETTE BETA/VHS
Tells tales about unicorns.
Prod-EQVDL Dist-EQVDL

Unicorn, The C 13 MIN
16MM FILM OPTICAL SOUND
Presents a view from aboard the Unicorn, one of the ships in the Operation Sail 1976 Parade of Sail from Greenwich, Connecticut, to Graves End Bay.
LC NO. 79-700735
Prod-MCGUST Dist-MCGUST 1976

Unicycle - Looking At My World C 15 MIN
16MM FILM, 3/4 OR 1/2 IN VIDEO I-H
Raises the question of establishing personal values and goals with an account of the thoughts a young man has about himself, older people and life in general, while riding his unicycle.
Prod-BARR Dist-BARR Prodn-BESSD 1976

Unicycle Race, The C 8 MIN
16MM FILM, 3/4 OR 1/2 IN VIDEO P-I
Presents an animated story about a unicycle race in which the good pair of legs triumphs over the dastardly plots of the evil red pair of legs.
Prod-SWARR Dist-LRF 1980

Unification Of A Double Uterus C 16 MIN
16MM FILM OPTICAL SOUND PRO
Presents a case of a double uterus. Describes the clinical problem history, laboratory findings and management. Illustrates the operative technique with the end results.
Prod-ACYDGD Dist-ACY 1969

Uniform Annual Cash Flow Method C 30 MIN
3/4 OR 1/2 INCH VIDEO CASSETTE IND
Introduces the evaluation method which converts all cash flows to a time adjusted equivalent annual amount. Illustrates economic evaluation of solar energy for residential heating as example problem.
From The Engineering Econony Series.
Prod-COLOSU Dist-COLOSU

Uniform Annual Cash Flow Method (Japanese) C 30 MIN
3/4 OR 1/2 INCH VIDEO CASSETTE IND
Introduces the evaluation method which converts all cash flows to a time adjusted equivalent annual amount. Illustrates economic evaluation of solar energy for residential heating as example problem.
From The Engineering Econony Series.
Prod-COLOSU Dist-COLOSU

Uniform Guidelines On Employee Selection Procedures C 48 MIN
3/4 OR 1/2 INCH VIDEO CASSETTE
Provides a general overview of the purpose and scope of the uniform guidelines on employee selection procedures. Contains a discussion of these guidelines by staff of the Office of Personnel Management.
LC NO. 79-707988
Prod-USOPMA Dist-USNAC Prodn-DEFCOM 1979

Unijunction Sawtooth Generator B 29 MIN
16MM FILM OPTICAL SOUND
Explains the physical and electrical operating characteristics of the unijunction transistor, and identifies the sawtooth generator circuit using a unijunction transistor, and explains the purpose of each component. (Kinescope)
LC NO. 74-705873
Prod-USAF Dist-USNAC

Unijunction Transistor And Tunnel Diode B 9 MIN
16MM FILM OPTICAL SOUND
Introduces the unijunction transistor and tunnel diode. Discusses their fundamental characteristics and identifies component parts. (Kinescope)
LC NO. 74-705874
Prod-USAF Dist-USNAC

Unilateral Hypertrophy Of Mandibular Condyle C 4 MIN
16MM FILM SILENT PRO
Examines unilateral hypertrophy of mandibular condyle, a condition with no known cause.
Prod-LOMAM Dist-LOMAM

Uninvited Guest, The C 23 MIN
16MM FILM, 3/4 OR 1/2 IN VIDEO
Presents the rules for fire prevention, control and escape as they apply to work areas, especially in hotels. Explains the fire prevention responsibilities of watchmen, maids, housekeepers, kitchen staff and management.
Prod-WALGRV Dist-IFB

Uninvited, The - The Homeless Of Phoenix C 28 MIN
16MM FILM, 3/4 OR 1/2 IN VIDEO
Examines the problems facing thousands of impoverished, homeless people who have settled in a tent-city in Phoenix, Arizona, the solutions to those problems posed by church, civic and government agencies, and the fear and hostility expressed by local businesses and residents.
Prod-ABCNEW Dist-TEXFLM

Union C 15 MIN
16MM FILM OPTICAL SOUND
Shows how the oil workers in Northern California struck and how they asked the students at San Francisco State and University of California to join the union in the struggle, January 1969.
Prod-NEWSR Dist-NEWSR 1969

Union C
3/4 OR 1/2 INCH VIDEO CASSETTE
Presents electronic artist Stephen Beck as he uses processes of unification at material and spiritual levels.
Prod-EAI Dist-EAI

Union Besieged, The (1861-1862) C 22 MIN
16MM FILM OPTICAL SOUND J-H
Presents Lincoln facing the tasks of hastily assembling a strong army and choosing a general, General Mc Clellan. Explains how hostility toward Lincoln and the ensuing battle of wills deeply affected the events of the early Civil War.
Prod-WOLPER Dist-FI 1974

Union Headquarters C 24 MIN
16MM FILM OPTICAL SOUND
Presents a member of the union and his wife as he visits the International Association of Machinists headquarters in Washington. Describes the various departments of the union, teaching about the services performed, the structure of the union and what happens to members' dues.
Prod-IAM Dist-AFLCIO 1963

Union Maids B 50 MIN
16MM FILM OPTICAL SOUND J-C A
Presents an adaptation of the book entitled RANK AND FILE by Alice Lynd about the American labor movement in the 1930's. Relates the personal experiences of three militant women who tried to organize laborers in Chicago in this period.
LC NO. 76-703655
Prod-RKLENP Dist-NEWDAY 1976

Union Of Disjoint Sets, Pt 1 C 20 MIN
2 INCH VIDEOTAPE P
See series title for descriptive statement.
From The Mathemagic, Unit II - Addition And Subtraction Series.
Prod-WMULTV Dist-GPITVL

Union Of Disjoint Sets, Pt 2 C 20 MIN
2 INCH VIDEOTAPE P
See series title for descriptive statement.
From The Mathemagic, Unit II - Addition And Subtraction Series.
Prod-WMULTV Dist-GPITVL

Union Pacific Steam C 60 MIN
1/2 IN VIDEO CASSETTE BETA/VHS
Chronicles a one-day Railfan Excursion consisting of a railroad trip from Denver to Laramie, Wyoming, and back, behind Union Pacific Engine No. 8444.
Prod-DELUZ Dist-DELUZ 1978

Union Steward And You, The C 15 MIN
16MM FILM, 3/4 OR 1/2 IN VIDEO
Shows the relationship between a first line supervisor and a union steward in solving problems.
LC NO. 81-706379
Prod-USN Dist-USNAC 1969

Union Theological Seminary C 18 MIN
16MM FILM OPTICAL SOUND
Presents an impressionistic montage about life and work at Union Theological Seminary.
LC NO. 74-700491
Prod-UTS Dist-UTS 1973

Union Triumphant, The (1863-1865) C 30 MIN
16MM FILM OPTICAL SOUND J-H
Presents the defeat and withdrawal at Gettysburg of General Robert E Lee's Confederate Army constituting the turning point of America's Civil War. Analyzes the war from a 19th-century civilian viewpoint, evaluating the desertions, riots and public disenchantment with an unwinnable war. Concludes with the collapse of the Confederacy.
Prod-WOLPER Dist-FI 1974

Union With A Future In The Industry Of The Future, The B 14 MIN
16MM FILM OPTICAL SOUND
Combines scenes from the 1962 Convention of the International Chemical Workers Union with industrial shots and a report on the wide range of services which the international union performs for its members.
Prod-ICHEMU Dist-AFLCIO 1963

Unions - Awareness And Organizing Tactics C
3/4 OR 1/2 INCH VIDEO CASSETTE IND
Shows how unions work to turn the work force against the company. Discusses union tactics, peer pressure, how unions infiltrate a company and gain access to personal data of employees, the business approach of unions and how they work to gain influence in the work place.
From The Meeting The Union Challenge Series.
Prod-GPCV Dist-GPCV

Unions - Strategies For Prevention C
3/4 OR 1/2 INCH VIDEO CASSETTE IND
Shows what can and cannot be done to defeat an organizing campaigns. Shows that supervisors must know the law, facts about company policies and benefit, and how to detect early signs of union activity.
From The Meeting The Union Challenge Series.
Prod-GPCV Dist-GPCV

Unique Beginnings C 30 MIN
16MM FILM, 3/4 OR 1/2 IN VIDEO A
Focuses on mothers and fathers who watch hopefully as doctors struggle to save their children's lives. Examines medical ethics and responsibilities, the quality of life, the rights of the disabled, familial love and the death of very young babies.
Prod-AMERFF Dist-PEREN 1982

Uniroyal World Junior Curling Championship, 1976 C 17 MIN
16MM FILM OPTICAL SOUND
Covers the 1976 Uniroyal World Junior Curling Championship held in Aviemore, Scotland.
LC NO. 77-702692
Prod-UNIRYL Dist-CHET Prodn-CHET 1976

Unisphere - Biggest World On Earth C 14 MIN
16MM FILM OPTICAL SOUND H-C A
Discusses concepts of design behind the unisphere of the U S Steel Corporation, and its construction at the New York World's Fair.
LC NO. FI67-45
Prod-USSC Dist-USSC 1964

Unit I - Review Of Basics C 12 MIN
3/4 OR 1/2 INCH VIDEO CASSETTE C
Covers electric circuits, basic mechanical relationships, time varying fields and basic machine concepts.
From The Electric Machinery Fundamentals Series.
Prod-UIDEEO Dist-AMCEE

Unit II - Energy Conversion Concepts C 12 MIN
3/4 OR 1/2 INCH VIDEO CASSETTE C
Covers generated voltage, transformers, force and torque production and rating and heating.
From The Electric Machinery Fundamentals Series.
Prod-UIDEEO Dist-AMCEE

Unit III - Synchronous Machine Basics C 12 MIN
3/4 OR 1/2 INCH VIDEO CASSETTE C
Includes steady state concepts, circuit model, power factor and power angle relationships as well as the salient rotor theory.
From The Electric Machinery Fundamentals Series.
Prod-UIDEEO Dist-AMCEE

Unit IV - Synchronous Generator Control And Protection C 12 MIN
3/4 OR 1/2 INCH VIDEO CASSETTE C
Contains information on normal operation, fault conditions, transient stability and protection.
From The Electric Machinery Fundamentals Series.
Prod-UIDEEO Dist-AMCEE

Unit Method - Pupil Centered, Pt 3, Wise B 48 MIN
16MM FILM OPTICAL SOUND C
An unrehearsed class session where the teacher does not know what subject the class will choose to study until the decision is made during the class period.
Prod-PSU Dist-PSU Prodn-PATRCK 1962

Unit Pricing C 15 MIN
3/4 OR 1/2 INCH VIDEO CASSETTE I-J
Shows how a robot housekeeper is sent to the factory for an adjustment in his circuitry which will equip him to do comparison shopping.
From The Math Matters Series. Green Module
Prod-KRLNTV Dist-AITECH 1975

Unit Record Applications B 45 MIN
2 INCH VIDEOTAPE
See series title for descriptive statement.
From The Data Processing, Unit 1 - Introduction To Data Processing Series.
Prod-GPITVL Dist-GPITVL

Unit Removal And Installation Of The Cylinder Power Assembly Of The General Motor's Series... C 35 MIN
16MM FILM - 3/4 IN VIDEO IND
Uses a General Motors' series 645 diesel engine to illustrate the step-by-step removal and installation of a cylinder power assembly on a diesel engine.
LC NO. 78-700006
Prod-VCI Dist-VCI 1974

Unit Removal And Installation Of The Cylinder Power Assembly Of The General... (Arabic) C 35 MIN
16MM FILM - 3/4 IN VIDEO IND
Uses a General Motors' series 645 diesel engine to illustrate the step-by-step removal and installation of a cylinder power assembly on a diesel engine.
LC NO. 78-700006
Prod-VCI Dist-VCI 1974

Unit Removal And Installation Of The Cylinder Power Assembly Of The General... (Chinese) C 35 MIN
16MM FILM - 3/4 IN VIDEO IND
Uses a General Motors' series 645 diesel engine to illustrate the step-by-step removal and installation of a cylinder power assembly on a diesel engine.
LC NO. 78-700006
Prod-VCI Dist-VCI 1974

Unit Removal And Installation Of The Cylinder Power Assembly Of The General... (Russian) C 35 MIN
16MM FILM - 3/4 IN VIDEO IND

Uses a General Motors' series 645 diesel engine to illustrate the step-by-step removal and installation of a cylinder power assembly on a diesel engine.
LC NO. 78-700006
Prod-VCI Dist-VCI 1974

Unit Removal And Installation Of The Cylinder Power Assembly Of The General... (Spanish) C 35 MIN
16MM FILM - 3/4 IN VIDEO IND
Uses a General Motors' series 645 diesel engine to illustrate the step-by-step removal and installation of a cylinder power assembly on a diesel engine.
LC NO. 78-700006
Prod-VCI Dist-VCI 1974

United Graphics Communication System C 8 MIN
3/4 OR 1/2 INCH VIDEO CASSETTE
Provides an overview of the Veterans Administration guidelines for a unified graphics communications system as developed by Malcolm Grear Designers.
LC NO. 80-707597
Prod-VAHSL Dist-USNAC 1980

United Mine Workers Of America, 1970 - A House Divided C 14 MIN
16MM FILM OPTICAL SOUND
Contrasts statements made by Tony Boyle, president of the United Mine Workers of America, with those of the anti-Boyle faction. Includes scenes of dissident miners and exposes the weaknesses of the union under his leadership two years before the rank and file rejected him.
LC NO. 79-700977
Prod-APPAL Dist-APPAL 1971

United Nations Chief Of Protocol C 28 MIN
3/4 INCH VIDEOTAPE
Focuses on the position of Chief of Protocol at the United Nations. Includes an interview with Ambassador Pedro De Churruca, United Nations protocol chief. Hosted by Marilyn Perry.
From The Marilyn's Manhatten Series.
Prod-PERRYM Dist-PERRYM

United Nations Christmas Show C 28 MIN
3/4 INCH VIDEOTAPE
Features interviews with United Nations officials. Includes dramatic presentations and a choir from the UN.
From The International Byline Series.
Prod-PERRYM Dist-PERRYM

United Nations Disaster Relief Organization C 28 MIN
3/4 INCH VIDEOTAPE
Interviews Mr Faruk Berkol, Under-Secretary-General and UNDRO Coordinator. Discusses UNDRO programs regarding a series of major disasters that had occurred around the world. Focuses on how UNDRO promotes disaster preparedness. Includes an informative film on world disasters.
From The International Byline Series.
Prod-PERRYM Dist-PERRYM

United Nations Fund For Population Activities C 28 MIN
3/4 INCH VIDEOTAPE
Interviews Dr Rafael M Salas, Under-Secretary-General of the United Nations and Executive Director of UNFPA. Covers the census in China, UNFPA's neutral approach to population policies, major contribution by United Nations member nations to UNFPA and the International Population Conference to be held in Mexico City in August of 1984. Includes a film clip on Sri Lanka.
From The International Byline Series.
Prod-PERRYM Dist-PERRYM

United Nations High Commission For Refugees C 28 MIN
3/4 INCH VIDEOTAPE
Interviews Mr Paul Hartling, United Nations High Commissioner for Refugees, who discusses the world refugee problem. Includes a film clip. Hosted by Marilyn Perry.
From The International Byline Series.
Prod-PERRYM Dist-PERRYM

United Nations In Korea B 30 MIN
16MM FILM OPTICAL SOUND H-C
A historical documentary showing how the conflict in Korea began. Includes what the United Nations did to try to prevent it and how an invading army was met by resistance of the armed forces sent by an international organization pledged to secure peace.
Prod-UN Dist-UN 1953

United Nations International Post Office C 28 MIN
3/4 INCH VIDEOTAPE
Interviews with officials from the United Nations. Focuses on the U N Post Office. Includes a film clip on U N stamps and a new post office in Austria.
From The International Byline Series.
Prod-PERRYM Dist-PERRYM

United Nations Peace-Keeping C 28 MIN
3/4 INCH VIDEOTAPE
Interviews George Sherry, United Nations Director for Special Political Affairs. Presents a film segment on peace-keeping. Hosted by Marilyn Perry.
From The International Byline Series.
Prod-PERRYM Dist-PERRYM

United Nations Relief Works Agency C 28 MIN
3/4 INCH VIDEOTAPE
Interviews Commissioner General Olof Olof Rydbeck. Discusses the problems of rebuilding the towns and cities in Lebanon. Examines some of the building projects and looks at the education of women.
From The International Byline Series.
Prod-PERRYM Dist-PERRYM

United Nations School C 28 MIN
3/4 INCH VIDEOTAPE
Interviews Mr Helmut Debatin, Chairman of the Board of Trustees for the United Nations School, Mrs Sylvia Fuhrman, Special Representative of the Secretary-General for the United Nations International School, and Mr Robert Belle-Isle, Director of the United Nations International School. Hosted by Marilyn Perry.
From The International Byline Series.
Prod-PERRYM Dist-PERRYM

United Nations Stamp Show On Environment C 28 MIN
3/4 INCH VIDEOTAPE
Interviews Mr Clayton C Timbrell, Assistant Secretary General, Office of General Services of the United Nations, and Mr Noel Brown, Director and Special Assistant to the Executive Director of UNEP. Discusses the United Nations stamp on environment. Includes a film clip on water resources.
From The International Byline Series.
Prod-PERRYM Dist-PERRYM

United Nations, New York B 13 MIN
16MM FILM OPTICAL SOUND I-H A
Tells of the designing and manufacturing of the United Nations postage stamps, first issued on October 24, 1951.
Prod-UN Dist-UN 1952

United States - Soviet Relations C
1/2 IN VIDEO CASSETTE (VHS)
Looks at the central themes and dynamics which have shaped U S - Soviet relations throughout history and continue to affect foreign policy today.
Prod-HRMC Dist-HRMC

United States Air Force In Vietnam, The C 27 MIN
16MM FILM OPTICAL SOUND
Outlines U S Air Force activities and operations in Southeast Asia since 1964. Describes personnel and equipment buildup and shows chemical, psychological and tactical air warfare.
LC NO. 74-706291
Prod-USAF Dist-USNAC 1967

United States Air Force In Vietnam, The C 28 MIN
3/4 OR 1/2 INCH VIDEO CASSETTE
Shows Air Force activities and operations in Southeast Asia beginning in 1964. Depicts personnel and equipment buildup, includes footage of chemical, psychological and tactical warfare.
Prod-IHF Dist-IHF

United States And Western Europe, The B 29 MIN
16MM FILM OPTICAL SOUND H-C
Shows informal conversations with four policy-level officers of the State Department on U S Relations with Western Europe, mentioning NATO in the mid 1960's, moves for European unity, the Common Market, and France and her allies.
LC NO. 76-707513
Prod-USDS Dist-USNAC 1966

United States Army Combat Developments Command, The - Vision To Victory C 32 MIN
16MM FILM OPTICAL SOUND
Describes the mission and organization of the U S Army Combat Developments Command, focusing on tools and techniques used to develop new concepts and equipment for the Army of the future.
LC NO. 74-706292
Prod-USA Dist-USNAC 1969

United States Arriving C 28 MIN
16MM FILM OPTICAL SOUND
Follows the visit in June, 1963, of John F Kennedy, late President of the United States, to the first fleet, Point Mugu, Nots, China Lake and the Marine Corps depot, San Diego. Presents the historical relationship between the President's fleet visit and the history and traditions of the sea service.
LC NO. 74-705876
Prod-USN Dist-USNAC 1963

United States Becomes A World Power, The C 25 MIN
16MM FILM, 3/4 OR 1/2 IN VIDEO J-C A
Examines American foreign policy and expansion, showing how dramatically these efforts were affected by the sinking of the Maine in 1898.
From The American History Series.
Prod-CRMP Dist-CRMP 1968

United States Congress, The - Of, By And For The People C 26 MIN
16MM FILM, 3/4 OR 1/2 IN VIDEO J-C
Follows two congressmen through two days of work as legislators, committee members, investigators, case workers, communicators and politicians. Examines the philosophy that has led to the evolution of Congress to its present state. Describes the specific functions of the Houses of Congress and their activities.
Prod-EBEC Dist-EBEC 1972

United States Constitution, The C 30 MIN
3/4 OR 1/2 INCH VIDEO CASSETTE C
Traces the events which led to the Constitutional Convention. Reviews the different ideologies represented and offers some conclusions about the political differences and the ways they were or were not resolved.
From The American Government 1 Series.
Prod-DALCCD Dist-DALCCD

United States Coverage Of World News C 30 MIN
3/4 OR 1/2 INCH VIDEO CASSETTE
Features Keith Fuller, president of the Associated Press, and Elmer Lower, former president of ABC News, as they examine charges that Americans are inadequately informed about international events. Hosted by Daniel Schorr.
From The Issues In World Communications, 1979 Series.
Prod-OHUTC Dist-OHUTC

United States Disciplinary Barracks, The - Our Mission, Your Future C 37 MIN
16MM FILM OPTICAL SOUND
Shows the facilities and operation of the U S Disciplinary Barracks in Ft Leavenworth, Kansas, including training, rehabilitation programs and levels of confinement.
LC NO. 74-705877
Prod-USA Dist-USNAC 1972

United States European Command C 20 MIN
16MM FILM OPTICAL SOUND A
Stresses the importance of the U S European Command. Defines the role and mission of the American Armed Forces and explains its responsibility to the NATO alliance.
LC NO. 78-700951
Prod-USDD Dist-USNAC 1974

United States Expansion - California C 16 MIN
16MM FILM, 3/4 OR 1/2 IN VIDEO I-C
Uses graphic materials and historical quotations to narrate the history of California, from its discovery by Spanish explorers to its admission to the United States.
From The United States Expansion Series.
Prod-CORF Dist-CORF 1969

United States Expansion - Florida C 13 MIN
16MM FILM, 3/4 OR 1/2 IN VIDEO J-C
Recounts the history of Florida from its discovery until its acquisition by the United States. Discusses the role of Andrew Jackson in combating the lawlessness and bringing about the annexation of Florida.
From The United States Expansion Series.
Prod-CORF Dist-CORF 1956

United States Expansion - Louisiana Purchase (2nd Ed) C 13 MIN
16MM FILM, 3/4 OR 1/2 IN VIDEO J-C
Examines the national and international issues and events which led to Thomas Jefferson's decision to purchase the Louisiana Territory.
From The United States Expansion Series.
Prod-CORF Dist-CORF 1977

United States Expansion - Northwest Territory C 13 MIN
16MM FILM, 3/4 OR 1/2 IN VIDEO J-C
Re-creates events leading to the opening of the Northwest territory. Depicts the work of the Ohio Company of Associates, the ordinances which governed the territory, and the pattern of statehood being formed.
From The United States Expansion Series.
Prod-CORF Dist-CORF 1958

United States Expansion - Oregon Country (2nd Ed) C 13 MIN
16MM FILM, 3/4 OR 1/2 IN VIDEO
Discusses the Lewis and Clarke expedition, stressing how it helped the United States establish claim to the Northwest and opened the way to settlers along the Oregon trail.
From The United States Expansion Series.
Prod-CORF Dist-CORF 1977

United States Expansion - Overseas (2nd Ed) C 14 MIN
16MM FILM, 3/4 OR 1/2 IN VIDEO J-C
Describes how the United States began expanding its territories beyond North American limits in the late 1800's. Outlines the U S involvement with Hawaii, Cuba, Puerto Rico, the Philippines, the Panama Canal and the Virgin Islands.
From The United States Expansion Series.
Prod-CORF Dist-CORF 1977

United States Expansion - Settling The West - 1853-1890 C 13 MIN
16MM FILM, 3/4 OR 1/2 IN VIDEO J-C
Explains that in the period between 1853 and 1890 the largest frontier region of the west was settled. Uses dramatized re-enactments to trace this settlement of the area which extended westward from Iowa to Missouri to the mountain ranges of California and Oregon.
From The United States Expansion Series.
Prod-CORF Dist-CORF 1960

United States Expansion - Texas And The Far Southwest (2nd Ed) C 16 MIN
16MM FILM, 3/4 OR 1/2 IN VIDEO J-C
Chronicles the events leading up to the acquisition of Texas and the far southwest by the United States.
From The United States Expansion Series.
Prod-CORF Dist-CORF 1977

United States Expansion—A Series
16MM FILM, 3/4 OR 1/2 IN VIDEO
Relates the history of the exploration and settlement of the United States.
Prod-CORF Dist-CORF

United States Expansion - California 16 MIN
United States Expansion - Florida 13 MIN
United States Expansion - Louisiana Purchase 13 MIN
United States Expansion - Northwest Territory 13 MIN
United States Expansion - Oregon Country 13 MIN
United States Expansion - Overseas (2nd Ed) 14 MIN
United States Expansion - Settling The West 13 MIN
United States Expansion - Texas And The Far 16 MIN

United States Geography—A Series
16MM FILM, 3/4 OR 1/2 IN VIDEO I-J
Deals with the physical, cultural and economic aspects of United States geography.
Prod-NGS Dist-NGS 1983

Alaska And Hawaii 025 MIN
Great Lakes States, The 025 MIN
Heartland, The 025 MIN
Lower South, The 025 MIN
Mid-Atlantic States, The 027 MIN
Mountain States, The 025 MIN
New England 023 MIN

Pacific Coast States, The 025 MIN
Southwest, The 025 MIN
Upper South, The 025 MIN

United States In The 20th Century–A Series
16MM FILM, 3/4 OR 1/2 IN VIDEO J-C
Uses newsreel footage to portray life in the United States between 1900 and 1940. Emphasizes the political events that occurred during this period.
Prod-CORF Dist-CORF

United States In The 20th Century, The -
United States In The 20th Century, The - 12 MIN
United States In The 20th Century, The - 19 MIN
United States In The 20th Century, The - 21 MIN

United States In The 20th Century, The - 1900-1912 B 12 MIN
16MM FILM, 3/4 OR 1/2 IN VIDEO J-C
Highlights U S history under the Roosevelt and Taft administrations and the election of Woodrow Wilson.
From The United States In The 20th Century Series.
Prod-CORF Dist-CORF 1974

United States In The 20th Century, The - 1912-1920 B 12 MIN
16MM FILM, 3/4 OR 1/2 IN VIDEO J-C
Highlights U S history during Woodrow Wilson's administration, through the outbreak of World War I and the rejection of the League of Nations.
From The United States In The 20th Century Series.
Prod-CORF Dist-CORF 1974

United States In The 20th Century, The - 1920-1932 B 19 MIN
16MM FILM, 3/4 OR 1/2 IN VIDEO J-C
Highlights the conservative era of the 20th century, beginning with Wilson's return from the Versailles Conference and ending with the Great Depression and new liberalism under the New Deal.
From The United States In The 20th Century Series.
Prod-CORF Dist-CORF 1967

United States In The 20th Century, The - 1932-1940 B 21 MIN
16MM FILM, 3/4 OR 1/2 IN VIDEO J-C
Presents the history of the U S from the inauguration of Franklin D Roosevelt to the eve of World War II, including the Great Depression and New Deal legislation designed to overcome it. Emphasizes events that had lasting effects on the nation, such as the Tennessee Valley Authority, the strengthening of organized labor and the growing power of the Federal government.
From The United States In The 20th Century Series.
Prod-CORF Dist-CORF 1967

United States Military Academy Cadet Mess, The C 21 MIN
3/4 OR 1/2 INCH VIDEO CASSETTE PRO
Tours the cadet mess at West Point and discusses the planning and organizational skills needed to feed 4000 people quickly and efficiently.
Prod-CULINA Dist-CULINA

United States Olympic Committee - The Struggle And Triumph C 25 MIN
3/4 INCH VIDEO CASSETTE
Describes the work of the US Olympic Committee and its purpose and programs. Highlights the committee's achievements as told through the experiences of athletes.
LC NO. 81-706236
Prod-USOC Dist-USOC Prodn-TAUPR 1980

United States Post Office, The C 6 MIN
16MM FILM, 3/4 OR 1/2 IN VIDEO P
Takes a look at the system and procedures of the U S post office.
Prod-BFA Dist-PHENIX 1970

United States Presidential Campaigning '80- What Are We Doing Wrong? C 30 MIN
3/4 OR 1/2 INCH VIDEO CASSETTE
Focuses on the strengths and weaknesses of United States presidential politicking. Analyzes the roles television and print media play in candidate coverage and voter reaction. Includes primary elections and polling procedures with emphasis on the 1980 presidential political campaign.
From The Issues In World Communications, 1980 Series.
Prod-OHUTC Dist-OHUTC

United States Strike Command, The C 20 MIN
16MM FILM OPTICAL SOUND
Examines the role of the United States Strike Command, America's composite back-up force of action-ready strength ready to deal with any type of crisis.
LC NO. 74-706293
Prod-USDD Dist-USNAC 1967

United States Supreme Court, The - Guardian Of The Constitution (2nd Ed) C 24 MIN
16MM FILM, 3/4 OR 1/2 IN VIDEO J-C
Highlights the history and landmark cases of the U S Supreme Court from its beginnings in 1789 to the 1970's. Presents Judge Luther Youngdahl explaining the uniqueness of the Supreme Court, Professor Gerald Guther discussing the power of judicial review and Senator Hubert Humphrey analyzing the role of the Court as protector of rights.
Prod-CONCPT Dist-EBEC 1973

United States Teams, The C 45 MIN
16MM FILM OPTICAL SOUND
Demonstrates the impact that private industry can have on amateur athletics, using the example of the Miller Brewing Company's support of U S national teams in boxing, track and field, cycling and skiing.
LC NO. 80-700310
Prod-MBC Dist-MBC Prodn-FARINA 1980

United States V Aaron Burr C 76 MIN
16MM FILM - 3/4 IN VIDEO
Dramatizes the Supreme Court trial of Aaron Burr and highlights the legal issues involved.
From The Equal Justice Under Law Series.
LC NO. 78-706020
Prod-USJUDC Dist-USNAC Prodn-WQED 1977

United States, The - One Out Of Many C 30 MIN
3/4 INCH VIDEO CASSETTE
See series title for descriptive statement.
From The Of Earth And Man Series.
Prod-MDCPB Dist-MDCPB

Units Of Electrical Measurement C 30 MIN
3/4 OR 1/2 INCH VIDEO CASSETTE IND
Introduces the language of electricity and basic vocabulary including ohms, volts, amperes, watts. Introduces Ohm's Law as basis for all electrical calculations.
From The Basic Electricity, DC Series.
Prod-AVIMA Dist-AVIMA

Units Of Measurement C 12 MIN
3/4 OR 1/2 INCH VIDEO CASSETTE
Covers kinds of units, length area, volume, angle, time, speed and velocity and other units of measurement.
From The Making Measurements Series.
Prod-TPCTRA Dist-TPCTRA

Unity C 30 MIN
3/4 OR 1/2 INCH VIDEO CASSETTE C
See series title for descriptive statement.
From The Writing For A Reason Series.
Prod-DALCCD Dist-DALCCD

Unity Of Nature, The, Pt 1 C 59 MIN
16MM FILM OPTICAL SOUND
Explores the sea's experience as it meets the land.
LC NO. 72-711556
Prod-CPB Dist-PBS 1971

Unity Of Nature, The, Pt 2 - The Nature Of Man And Woman C 28 MIN
16MM FILM OPTICAL SOUND
Reveals the closeness of all things in this world as discovered by a young man and woman who, while roaming the mountains, explore land called the body and the body called land. The world love is shown to encompass all things, harshness and tenderness, cruelty and consideration, apartness and togetherness.
LC NO. 76-711557
Prod-CPB Dist-PBS 1971

Unity Of Personality - Expressive Behavior B 18 MIN
16MM FILM SILENT C T
Shows the consistency of expressive movements of five individuals with very different personalities. Includes gestures, facial movements (also split portraits), handwriting responses to stimulus words and questions, handling objects, athletic activities and walking gaits. Demonstrations show similarities of expressive behavior characteristics, which relate to the 'UNITY OF PERSONALITY.'
Prod-PSUPCR Dist-PSUPCR 1946

Universal Christ C 60 MIN
3/4 OR 1/2 INCH VIDEO CASSETTE
Presents Sri Gurudev speaking on the Universal Christ present in Yoga.
Prod-IYOGA Dist-IYOGA

Universal Gravitation B 31 MIN
16MM FILM OPTICAL SOUND H-C A
Derives the law of universal gravitation by imagining a solar system of one star and one planet. The kinematics and dynamics of planetary motion are demonstrated with models. Satellite orbits are displayed using a digital computer.
From The PSSC Physics Films Series.
Prod-PSSC Dist-MLA 1961

Universal Product Code / Train Travel / Appliance Repairs C
3/4 OR 1/2 INCH VIDEO CASSETTE
Discusses the universal product code, train travel and appliance repairs.
From The Consumer Survival Series.
Prod-MDCPB Dist-MDCPB

Universal Proximal Femur Prosthesis C 20 MIN
3/4 OR 1/2 INCH VIDEO CASSETTE PRO
See series title for descriptive statement.
From The Prothesis Films Series.
Prod-WFP Dist-WFP

Universal Rhythms C 11 MIN
16MM FILM OPTICAL SOUND
Tells that harmony and motion are evident in all realms of the cosmic order. Explains that the smallest subatomic particle provides an array of motion that is comparable to movement of celestial bodies. Concludes that natural rhythms are an important link in exploring the phenomenon of periodic motion on various scales of time and space.
LC NO. 79-700334
Prod-ESPZAM Dist-EDMEDC 1979

Universal Themes In Fiction C 30 MIN
3/4 OR 1/2 INCH VIDEO CASSETTE C
See series title for descriptive statement.
From The Communicating Through Literature Series.
Prod-DALCCD Dist-DALCCD

Universal Vehicle C 11 MIN
16MM FILM, 3/4 OR 1/2 IN VIDEO P-I
Shows Boy and Grandpa experimenting with devices that will help them maneuver their wagon. Shows them creating steering and breaking mechanisms to keep it under control and constructing special wheels and paddles to transport their vehicle over water.
From The Inventive Child Series.
Prod-POLSKI Dist-EBEC 1983

Universe C 27 MIN
16MM FILM OPTICAL SOUND
Shows how scientists study the birth and death of galaxies, Earth, stars and the universe itself.
Prod-ALLFP Dist-NSTA 1977

Universe C
3/4 OR 1/2 INCH VIDEO CASSETTE
Prod-MSTVIS Dist-MSTVIS

Universe C 27 MIN
16MM FILM, 3/4 OR 1/2 IN VIDEO
Explores extremes of size and time from galaxies to subatomic particles, from cosmic events in the far-distant past to micro-cosmic events in the present that last a billionth of a second. Dramatizes a mysterious and incredibly violent universe.
Prod-NASA Dist-USNAC

Universe C 27 MIN
16MM FILM, 3/4 OR 1/2 IN VIDEO J-H
Introduces the student to the solar system, moving freely from the cosmic magnitudes of galaxies to the microcosmic and infinitesimally small events of the atoms and particles which compose it. Includes a study guide.
Prod-SCRESC Dist-MTI

Universe C 28 MIN
16MM FILM, 3/4 OR 1/2 IN VIDEO I-C A
Shows a mysterious and incredibly violent universe. Explores almost inconceivable extremes of size and time, from galaxies to subatomic particles and from cosmic events that occurred millions of years ago to microcosmic events of the present that endure only a billionth of a second.
Prod-NASA Dist-BNCHMK 1976

Universe B 28 MIN
16MM FILM, 3/4 OR 1/2 IN VIDEO I-C A
Shows Dr Donald Mac Rae, Professor of Astronomy at the University of Toronto, in a night-long vigil at the David Dunlap Observatory, as he explores the solar system. Uses animation, live photography and special effects to show the pockmarked moon, the rings of Saturn, the gaseous geysers of the sun and other galaxies.
Prod-NFBC Dist-NFBC 1960

Universe C 30 MIN
3/4 OR 1/2 INCH VIDEO CASSETTE
Presents the birth and demise of the sun and the universe within the context of vast star island galaxies contrasted with sub-atomic particles.
From The Reaching For The Stars, And Life Beyond Earth Series.
Prod-IVCH Dist-IVCH

Universe And I–A Series
J
Investigates the earth and the space sciences. Focuses on earth as a member of the interdependent universe.
Prod-KYTV Dist-AITECH 1977

Atlantis Connection, The 17 MIN
Ballad Of Ramblin' Willy, The 19 MIN
Bulletin 18 MIN
Changing Scientist, The 17 MIN
City Of Fossils 18 MIN
Freezing Point 18 MIN
Future, The 17 MIN
Gravity Drag 17 MIN
Halftime 14 MIN
I And The Universe 19 MIN
Incident On Cannon Mountain 18 MIN
Interior Motive, The 16 MIN
Jake's Gate 18 MIN
Luna The Lovely 18 MIN
Mind-Slaughter 18 MIN
Sea Search 18 MIN
Solar System, The 17 MIN
Star Salesman 17 MIN
Vectoria 16 MIN
Visit To Spectrum II, A 16 MIN

Universe From Palomar, The C 29 MIN
16MM FILM OPTICAL SOUND
Tells the story of the 200-inch Hale telescope. Provides a tour of the observatory at Mount Palomar. Describes the design of the Hale telescope, taking the viewer through the pouring, grinding, polishing, transportation and installation phases of the giant mirror. Describes the research conducted by the astronomers, including some photographs of distant stars and galaxies.
Prod-CIT Dist-CIT

Universe From Palomar, The B 30 MIN
16MM FILM OPTICAL SOUND H-C A
Presents a history of the Hale telescope at Mount Palomar and the contributions its use has made to our knowledge of the universe. Shows the construction and transportation of the 200 inch mirror. Illustrates recent discoveries with photographs taken through the telescope.
From The Spectrum Series.
LC NO. FIA68-242
Prod-NET Dist-IU 1967

Universe On A Scratchpad B 29 MIN
16MM FILM OPTICAL SOUND J-H T
A candid study of a modern astro-physicist and his methods of studying the solar system and universe. Shows the facilities of the NASA Goddard Institute for Space Studies, New York.

LC NO. FIE67-126
Prod-NASA Dist-NASA 1967

Universe, The C
3/4 OR 1/2 INCH VIDEO CASSETTE P-I
Introduces children to the wonders of the universe. Narrated by William Shatner.
Prod-CNVID Dist-KTVID

Universe, The C
1/2 IN VIDEO CASSETTE BETA/VHS
Presents a tour of the universe and its mysteries, by William Shatner.
Prod-GA Dist-GA

Universe, The - Beyond The Solar System (Spanish) C 18 MIN
16MM FILM, 3/4 OR 1/2 IN VIDEO J A
A Spanish language version of the film and videorecording The Universe - Beyond The Solar System.
Prod-EBEC Dist-EBEC 1978

Universe, The - Beyond The Solar System C 18 MIN
16MM FILM, 3/4 OR 1/2 IN VIDEO I-H
Presents a visual journey beginning with the solar system and extending into outer space. Explores the origin of the universe and discusses how it may end.
Prod-EBEC Dist-EBEC 1978

Universe, The - Flight To The Stars C 21 MIN
16MM FILM, 3/4 OR 1/2 IN VIDEO I-C A
Examines the moon, the other planets of our solar system and the stars.
Prod-AIMS Dist-AIMS 1969

Universe, The - Flight To The Stars (Norwegian) C 20 MIN
16MM FILM, 3/4 OR 1/2 IN VIDEO I-H
Creative and modern camera techniques and up to date footage are used to convey basic concepts pertaining to the universe.
Prod-CAHILL Dist-AIMS Prodn-CAHILL 1969

Universe, The - Flight To The Stars (Spanish) C 20 MIN
16MM FILM, 3/4 OR 1/2 IN VIDEO I-H
Creative and modern camera techniques and up to date footage are used to convey basic concepts pertaining to the universe.
Prod-CAHILL Dist-AIMS Prodn-CAHILL 1969

Universe, The - Man's Changing Perceptions C 29 MIN
16MM FILM OPTICAL SOUND J-C A
Takes a look at cosmological ideas from different cultures and shows the evolution these ideas have undergone. Demonstrates the way in which information gathered by astronomers today has influenced present understanding of the universe.
LC NO. 76-702106
Prod-PRESTH Dist-PRESTH 1976

University In The City, A C 16 MIN
16MM FILM OPTICAL SOUND J-C A
Shows how life at an urban university is influenced by, and inseparable from, its environment. Shows students and faculty discussing the advantages and disadvantages of city surroundings. Filmed at New York University.
From The College Profile Film Series.
LC NO. 77-711470
Prod-VISEDC Dist-VISEDC 1971

University Of Arizona - Towards New Frontiers C 24 MIN
16MM FILM OPTICAL SOUND H A
Views the rapidly expaning campus of the University of Arizona and looks into the activities of some of the scientists who have brought distinction to the university in the fields of astronomy, optics, lunar and planetary studies, environmental research and medicine.
Prod-UARIZ Dist-UARIZ 1971

University Of Chicago Round Table—A Series

Features leading scholars and public figures in discussion of controversial contemporary issues and their impact on the American public. Presents Kenneth Northcott of the University of Chicago as host of the series.
Prod-WTTWTV Dist-PUBTEL

Abortion Reform 29 MIN
Advertising In Consumer Affairs 29 MIN
Cinema 70 29 MIN
FCC, The - Television And The 70's 29 MIN
Honest Politicians Guide To Crime Control, The 29 MIN
Inner City And Mass Communications, The 29 MIN
Oh Theatre, Pt 1 29 MIN
Oh Theatre, Pt 2 29 MIN
Pill, Population And Family Planning, The 29 MIN
Politics Of Hunger In America, The 29 MIN
Revival Of Victorianism, The 29 MIN
Urban Universities And Their Responsibilities 29 MIN
What Has Happened To Political Machines 29 MIN

University Of Mexico C 3 MIN
16MM FILM OPTICAL SOUND P-I
Presents the University of Mexico.
From The Of All Things Series.
Prod-BAILYL Dist-AVED

University Of Mississippi, The C 13 MIN
16MM FILM OPTICAL SOUND
Presents an expressionistic view of the campus activities available to students at the University of Mississippi.
LC NO. 73-700772
Prod-UMISS Dist-UMISS 1972

University Of Wisconsin School Of Social Work Promotional Tape C 15 MIN
3/4 OR 1/2 INCH VIDEO CASSETTE
Describes the University of Wisconsin School of Social Work. Gives glimpses of classes and the building while the school and its programs are described.
Prod-UWISC Dist-UWISC 1977

Univerzum C 5 MIN
16MM FILM, 3/4 OR 1/2 IN VIDEO H-C A
Tells how a hero is born and how he explores the depths of the universe. Shows how he returns unnoticed in another time and place, after his moment has passed.
Prod-ZAGREB Dist-IFB 1977

Univis Division Of Itek Case History B 40 MIN
3/4 OR 1/2 INCH VIDEO CASSETTE
Shows how a manufacturer of eye glasses and frames attempts to build loyalty among wholesaling laboratories.
Prod-HBS Dist-IVCH

UNIX - An Executive Perspective C 30 MIN
3/4 OR 1/2 INCH VIDEO CASSETTE
Describes the UNIX system, its features, applications and operation. Assists users in understanding the total environment in which they are working.
Prod-COMTEG Dist-COMTEG

UNIX Administration C
3/4 OR 1/2 INCH VIDEO CASSETTE
See series title for descriptive statement.
From The UNIX And 'C'Language Training - A Full Curriculum Series.
Prod-COMTEG Dist-COMTEG

UNIX And 'C Language Training - A Full Curriculum—A Series

Presents a series on full UNIX and 'C' language curriculum training program.
Prod-COMTEG Dist-COMTEG

'C' Language Programming
Advanced 'C' Programming Under UNIX
Advanced 'C' Programming Workshop
Berkeley, UNIX Fundamentals And 'csh' Shell
Shell As A Command Language
Shell Programming
UNIX Administration
UNIX Commands
UNIX Fundamentals For Non-Programmers
UNIX Fundamentals For Programmers
UNIX Intervals
UNIX Overview
Using Advanced UNIX Commands

UNIX Fundamentals For Non-Programmers C
3/4 OR 1/2 INCH VIDEO CASSETTE
See series title for descriptive statement.
From The UNIX And 'C'Language Training - A Full Curriculum Series.
Prod-COMTEG Dist-COMTEG

UNIX Fundamentals For Programmers C
3/4 OR 1/2 INCH VIDEO CASSETTE
See series title for descriptive statement.
From The UNIX And 'C'Language Training - A Full Curriculum Series.
Prod-COMTEG Dist-COMTEG

UNIX Fundamentals—A Series

Provides what one needs to know about UNIX to fulfill his/her job tasks or provides the base skills upon which one will proceed with further UNIX training.
Prod-COMTEG Dist-COMTEG

'ed'
'ed' (Continued)
Advanced 'ed'
Advanced 'ed' (Continued)
Command Lines
Commands
Communicating With Other Users
Communicating With The System
Directory Commands
File Access Persmissions
File Name Generation
Files
I/O
More Commands
Pathnames

UNIX Internals C
3/4 OR 1/2 INCH VIDEO CASSETTE
See series title for descriptive statement.
From The UNIX And 'C'Language Training - A Full Curriculum Series.
Prod-COMTEG Dist-COMTEG

UNIX Overview C
3/4 OR 1/2 INCH VIDEO CASSETTE
See series title for descriptive statement.
From The UNIX And 'C'Language Training - A Full Curriculum Series.
Prod-COMTEG Dist-COMTEG

UNIX Overview—A Series

Offers a complete UNIX curriculum, developed after testing of content with hundreds of students in both in-house and public seminars.
Prod-COMTEG Dist-COMTEG

Commands (UNIX Overview)
Files, Data Bases, Data Communications
Introduction, An
Programmer's Workbench
Security And 'C' Language
Shell, The

UNIX—A Series
IND
Shows how to operate UNIX with more than 60 often used commands, how to get a working knowledge of most UNIX features, files and directories, shell files, pipes and tees, text editor and electronic mail. Tells how to build individual commands for UNIX repertoire.
Prod-COLOSU Dist-COLOSU

File Manipulation 030 MIN
Files And Directories, Part I 030 MIN
Files And Directories, Part II 030 MIN
Getting Started 030 MIN
Process Control 030 MIN
Shell Files, Part I 030 MIN
Shell Files, Part II 030 MIN
Text Editor, Part I 030 MIN
Text Editor, Part II 030 MIN
Wild Characters, Patterns, Pipes And Tees 030 MIN

Unknown Chaplin - A Documentary Trilogy C 3 MIN
3/4 OR 1/2 INCH VIDEO CASSETTE
Presents previously unknown footage of Charlie Chaplin in three 52 minute documentaries.
Prod-THAMES Dist-SUCBUF

Unknown Chaplin - The Mutual Period, 1916-1917 C 52 MIN
16MM FILM, 3/4 OR 1/2 IN VIDEO H-C A
Uncovers the progression of Chaplin's pioneer ideas, using fragments of his films, mostly outtakes and uncut rushes which are assembled in slate order.
From The Unknown Chaplin Series.
LC NO. 84-707279
Prod-THAMES Dist-MEDIAG 1983

Unknown Chaplin - Unshown Chaplin C 52 MIN
16MM FILM, 3/4 OR 1/2 IN VIDEO H-C A
Features a wealth of background footage screened from movies Chaplin made for fun, films he abandoned and sequences he cut from such films as City Lights and Modern Times. Shows his dance of the rolls from The Gold Rush.
From The Unknown Chaplin Series.
LC NO. 84-707282
Prod-THAMES Dist-MEDIAG 1983

Unknown Chaplin - 1918-1931 C 52 MIN
16MM FILM, 3/4 OR 1/2 IN VIDEO H-C A
Tells how Chaplin did not release his first film, How To Make Movies, which was a tour of the studio he built in 1917 as a new independent filmmaker. Includes footage and interviews about such films as The Kid, The Gold Rush and City Lights.
From The Unknown Chaplin Series.
LC NO. 84-707281
Prod-THAMES Dist-MEDIAG 1983

Unknown Chaplin—A Series
16MM FILM, 3/4 OR 1/2 IN VIDEO H-C A
Documents the results of cinema archaeologists who uncovered secret Chaplin footage - rushes, outtakes, abandoned films and home movies. Uses Chaplin's productions notes as well as interviews with his players to recreate his pioneering methods and creative process in making classic silent films.
Prod-THAMES Dist-MEDIAG 1983

Unknown Chaplin - The Mutual Period,
Unknown Chaplin - Unshown Chaplin 052 MIN
Unknown Chaplin - 1918-1931 052 MIN

Unknown Eiffel, The C 28 MIN
16MM FILM, 3/4 OR 1/2 IN VIDEO
Explores the engineering genius and accomplishments of Gustave Eiffel.
Prod-BCI Dist-FI 1975

Unknown Force C 50 MIN
16MM FILM OPTICAL SOUND
Explores and demonstrates psychic and occult phenomena, including prana, ki-power, psychokinesis and Kirlian photography.
From The Unknown Powers Series.
LC NO. 78-701406
Prod-ITFP Dist-ITFP 1978

Unknown Genius - The Savant Syndrome C 16 MIN
3/4 OR 1/2 INCH VIDEO CASSETTE H-C A
Introduces three people who have extraordinary mental talents despite being mentally retarded. Includes a gifted sculptor, a man who can tell what day of the week a given date will fall and a blind cerebral palsy victim who can play any piece of music after hearing it only once. Originally shown on the CBS program 60 Minutes.
LC NO. 84-706149
Prod-CBSNEW Dist-LAWREN 1984

Unknown Land C 28 MIN
16MM FILM OPTICAL SOUND J-C A
Covers the development of Australia's Northwest. Explains that once isolated and largely unexplored, the sparsely populated land is now being opened up by major development projects.
LC NO. 73-702260
Prod-ANAIB Dist-AUIS 1972

Unknown Powers—A Series

Prod-ITFP Dist-ITFP 1978

Unknown Force 050 MIN

Unknown Reasons C 6 MIN
16MM FILM OPTICAL SOUND H-C A

Combines animation and live-action as inks, colors and pens are taken over by the conscious, exploding in a wild fury of color and nightmarish designs.
Prod-UWFKD Dist-UWFKD

Unknown Soldiers C 58 MIN
3/4 OR 1/2 INCH VIDEO CASSETTE H-C A
Discusses the growth of importance of black soldiers through the Indian Wars and the Spanish-American War to World War I.
From The Different Drummer - Blacks In The Military Series.
LC NO. 85-700749
Prod-WNETTV Dist-FI 1983

Unknown Thirty-Six Seconds, The - Aircraft Accident Investigation C 35 MIN
16MM FILM OPTICAL SOUND
Describes the organization and mission of the Aircraft Accident Investigation board. Depicts its painstaking inspection of plane wreckage to determine possible electrical, mechanical, structural or hydraulic failure.
LC NO. 74-705878
Prod-USAF Dist-USNAC 1968

Unlikely Addicts - Middle Class Women C 29 MIN
3/4 INCH VIDEO CASSETTE
Discusses private and public addicts. Explains that some women are private addicts who attempt to keep their problem secret and who usually become dependent on alcohol and/or barbiturates.
From The Woman Series.
Prod-WNEDTV Dist-PUBTEL

Unlikely Star B 8 MIN
16MM FILM, 3/4 OR 1/2 IN VIDEO J-C A
Relates what happens when a shy young man is swallowed up by a camera and begins an odyssey into the world of celluloid that almost ends on the cutting room floor. Shows the man finally making his escape during the film's premiere when he leaps straight out from the screen.
Prod-PHENIX Dist-PHENIX 1980

Unmixed Mixed Numbers C 30 MIN
3/4 OR 1/2 INCH VIDEO CASSETTE A
Shows adult math students how mixed numbers fit into the number system and how to handle them.
From The Adult Math Series.
Prod-KYTV Dist-KYTV 1984

Unnecessary Surgery C 29 MIN
3/4 OR 1/2 INCH VIDEO CASSETTE
Examines the unnecessary surgical procedures performed in America, including the hysterectomy and tonsillectomy. Discusses sexism in the medical care field.
From The Woman Series.
Prod-WNEDTV Dist-PBS

Unnecessary Surgery - Physicians React C 29 MIN
3/4 INCH VIDEO CASSETTE
Presents two doctors discussing reports of widespread unnecessary surgery in the United States. Points out that elective and unconfirmed surgery are gray areas of medical statistics and stresses the need for clear definitions of what is and is not necessary.
From The Woman Series.
Prod-WNEDTV Dist-PUBTEL

Unorganized Manager--A Series

Teaches skills of organization, delegation and time management to improve the efficiency and effectiveness of managers and supervisors.
Prod-VIDART Dist-VISUCP

Damnation, Pt I 026 MIN
Salvation, Pt II 026 MIN

Unorganized Manager, The, Pt 1 - Damnation C 24 MIN
3/4 OR 1/2 INCH VIDEO CASSETTE A
Presents in a humorous vein important principles of good business management. Follows a bumbling manager through a typical day, a coronary and a confrontation with St. Peter, who shows him the errors of his ways.
Prod-XICOM Dist-XICOM 1983

Unorganized Manager, The, Pt 2 - Salvation C 27 MIN
3/4 OR 1/2 INCH VIDEO CASSETTE A
Presents in a humorous vein important principles of good business management. Shows a bumbling manager, with guidance from St. Peter, mend his ways and miraculously improve his business techniques.
Prod-XICOM Dist-XICOM 1983

Unpack Your Adjectives C 3 MIN
3/4 OR 1/2 INCH VIDEO CASSETTE P-I
Presents a little girl and her pet turtle unpacking adjectives from her backpack after a camping trip in order to describe the people, places and things she saw on the trip.
From The Grammar Rock Series.
Prod-ABCTV Dist-GA Prodn-SCOROC 1976

Unplanned, The C 20 MIN
16MM FILM, 3/4 OR 1/2 IN VIDEO H-C A
Uses dramatized incidents to warn industrial workers against unsafe acts which often cause serious industrial accidents. Emphasizes safety procedures which help avoid crippling and costly mishaps.
Prod-NFBC Dist-NFBC 1971

Unpleasant Feelings C 7 MIN
16MM FILM OPTICAL SOUND K-P
Helps young Mexican-American children understand that feelings of fear, disappointment and loneliness are natural and universal. Includes narration in Spanish and English.
From The Project Bilingual Series.

LC NO. 73-700625
Prod-SANISD Dist-SUTHLA 1973

Unpleasantness At Bludleigh Court C 30 MIN
3/4 OR 1/2 INCH VIDEO CASSETTE C A
Presents an adaptation of the short story Unpleasantness At Bludleigh Court by P G Wodehouse.
From The Wodehouse Playhouse Series.
Prod-BBCTV Dist-TIMLIF 1980

Unreasonable Man, The C 60 MIN
16MM FILM OPTICAL SOUND
Takes a look at today's bureaucratic institutions and how they affect the quality of man's life.
Prod-KQEDTV Dist-KQEDTV

Unreasonable Searches And Seizures C 50 MIN
3/4 OR 1/2 INCH VIDEO CASSETTE PRO
Provides a review of the fourth amendment proscription against unreasonable searches and seizures, an analysis of the exceptions to the exclusionary rule and a discussion of issues of standing to assert the defense.
From The Criminal Procedure And The Trial Advocate Series.
Prod-ABACPE Dist-ABACPE

Unremarkable Birth, An C 52 MIN
16MM FILM, 3/4 OR 1/2 IN VIDEO H-C A
Presents parents and doctors discussing less traditional methods of childbirth. Records the prepared birth of a baby and the interaction of the mother and father.
Prod-NFBC Dist-NFBC 1978

Unremitting Tenderness C 9 MIN
16MM FILM, 3/4 OR 1/2 IN VIDEO H-C A
Uses experimental techniques to show a dancer going through a series of transformations.
LC NO. 81-706835
Prod-ELDERB Dist-PHENIX 1977

Unresponsive Articulation Problem, The- Child Apraxia C 98 MIN
3/4 OR 1/2 INCH VIDEO CASSETTE
Discusses problem definition and terminology, types, diagnosis and clinical management. Includes clinical demonstrations.
Prod-PUAVC Dist-PUAVC

UNRWA C 28 MIN
3/4 INCH VIDEOTAPE
Interviews Mr Olof Rydbeck, Commissioner General of the United Nations Relief and Works Agency for Palestine refugees in the Near East. Discusses the problems and achievements of the agency during its long history. Presents clips of films about refugees.
From The International Byline Series.
Prod-PERRYM Dist-PERRYM

Unsatisfactory Work C 18 MIN
16MM FILM - 3/4 IN VIDEO
Focuses on incompetence and how supervisors can detect and correct it.
From The Preventive Discipline Series.
Prod-BNA Dist-BNA

Unsatisfactory Work (2nd Ed) C
16MM FILM - 3/4 IN VIDEO
Describes what constitutes unsatisfactory work. Shows how to find where the fault lies and how incompetency may be proved. Discusses why supervisors should check employees carefully during the probationary period and why, in many cases, discipline is not the answer.
From The Preventive Discipline (2nd Ed) Series. Unit 6
Prod-BNA Dist-BNA

Unseen Journey C 30 MIN
3/4 OR 1/2 INCH VIDEO CASSETTE
Shows how oil, brought to the surface on land and offshore, is fed through 'big inch' pipelines, barges and tankers to distant refineries.
Prod-HBS Dist-IVCH

Unseen World, The C 54 MIN
16MM FILM, 3/4 OR 1/2 IN VIDEO H-C
Uses photomicrography, rocket-mounted cameras and other photographic techniques to reveal the microscopic world of cells and ocean animals, as well as the nature of light and the planets of the solar system.
Prod-ABCTV Dist-MGHT 1970

Unseen World, The, Pt 1 - How Small Is Small C 17 MIN
16MM FILM, 3/4 OR 1/2 IN VIDEO H-C
Uses photomicrography to reveal the microscopic world of plant cells and protozoa. Shows the surface of aspirin and human hair as viewed through light-receiving and electronic instruments.
Prod-ABCTV Dist-MGHT 1970

Unseen World, The, Pt 2 - The Time Between C 14 MIN
16MM FILM, 3/4 OR 1/2 IN VIDEO H-C
Uses time lapse and slow motion photography to reveal the flick of a toad's tongue as it snares an insect, a drop of water as it splashes onto a liquid surface to form a perfect crown, the vibrations of a lightbulb filament as it approaches its glow point and blooming flowers and twisting vines in animated and accelerated motion.
Prod-ABCTV Dist-MGHT 1970

Unseen World, The, Pt 3 - Oceans Of Space C 17 MIN
16MM FILM, 3/4 OR 1/2 IN VIDEO H-C
Reveals those vast areas of the world that are hidden by barriers of water and air. Explores the seaweed forests of the ocean bottom as well as the ocean of atmosphere to the stars and far-off galaxies.
Prod-ABCTV Dist-MGHT 1970

Unsinkable Bette Davis, The B 26 MIN
16MM FILM OPTICAL SOUND
Describes major events in the life and career of Bette Davis. Illustrates her acting versatility by showing scenes from several of her films.
LC NO. FI68-288
Prod-WOLPER Dist-WOLPER 1963

Unsinkable Sea Otter, The C 25 MIN
16MM FILM, 3/4 OR 1/2 IN VIDEO I-C
A shortened version of the The Unsinkable Sea Otter. Follows Jacques Cousteau and his divers as they study the underwater life of the sea otter and examine the conditions essential for its survival. Describes reasons why the sea otter almost became extinct and examines problems caused by man and pollution.
From The Undersea World Of Jacques Cousteau Series.
Prod-METROM Dist-CF 1975

Unsinkable Sea Otter, The C 52 MIN
16MM FILM, 3/4 OR 1/2 IN VIDEO
Probes the economic factors which threaten the existence of the sea otter.
From The Undersea World Of Jacques Cousteau Series.
Prod-METROM Dist-CF 1975

Unsolicited Or Prospecting Sales Letter To Consumer B 45 MIN
2 INCH VIDEOTAPE C
See series title for descriptive statement.
From The Business Writing Series. Unit III - Persuasive Messages
Prod-CHITVC Dist-GPITVL Prodn-WTTWTV

Unsolicited Or Prospecting Sales Letter To Dealer C 45 MIN
2 INCH VIDEOTAPE C
See series title for descriptive statement.
From The Business Writing Series. Unit III - Persuasive Messages
Prod-CHITVC Dist-GPITVL Prodn-WTTWTV

Unsolved Problems - Three Dimensions, Film 2 C 21 MIN
16MM FILM OPTICAL SOUND
Presents problems in three dimensions which mathematicians cannot solve.
From The Maa General Mathematics Series.
Prod-MAA Dist-MLA

Unsolved Problems - Two Dimensions, Film 1 C 22 MIN
16MM FILM OPTICAL SOUND
Presents a number of geometric problems which mathematicians cannot solve.
From The Maa General Mathematics Series.
Prod-MAA Dist-MLA

Unspoken B 27 MIN
16MM FILM OPTICAL SOUND H-C A
Presents an allegorical love story which represents the incompatability of nature and man's technology.
LC NO. 75-701614
Prod-CSAKYA Dist-CSAKYA 1968

Unspoken Message And The Interview, The C 15 MIN
3/4 OR 1/2 INCH VIDEO CASSETTE H
Stresses the importance of non-verbal cues in a job interview.
From The Communication At Work Series.
Prod-OHSDE Dist-AITECH 1979

Unspoken Word, The B 15 MIN
2 INCH VIDEOTAPE K-P
Defines and demonstrates the gestures and movement of a pantomime. (Broadcast quality)
From The Magic Of Words Series.
Prod-GWTVAI Dist-GPITVL Prodn-WETATV

Unstable Angina - New Observations In Management C 45 MIN
3/4 OR 1/2 INCH VIDEO CASSETTE PRO
Reviews definition, prognosis, pathophysiology and therapy of unstable angina. Discusses angiographic findings and the role of spasm, platelet dynamics, prostoglandins and their inhibitors, histamine, opioids and calcium flux. Closes with Dr Bertram Pitt's discussion of therapy in light of newer pathophysiologic interpretations.
Prod-AMCARD Dist-AMCARD

Unsterile Field, The - An O R Challenge C 21 MIN
16MM FILM OPTICAL SOUND PRO
Involves the entire operating room with the exception of the 'STERILE' field. Covers problems such as filters, air exchange rate, humidity and conductive floors as well as the responsibility for mechanical performance of major equipment.
Prod-ACYDGD Dist-ACY 1966

Unsterile Field, The - An O R Challenge C 21 MIN
3/4 OR 1/2 INCH VIDEO CASSETTE PRO
Considers the entire operating room with the exception of the 'sterile' field. Covers problems such as filters, air exchange, humidity, conductive floors and the mechanical performance of major equipment.
Prod-PRIMED Dist-PRIMED

Unsuspected B 16 MIN
16MM FILM OPTICAL SOUND
Illustrates facts about the discovery of unsuspected cases of tuberculosis. Shows how community health agencies assist in the rehabilitation of patients and in aiding families of tubercular patients to solve their problems.
Prod-NTBA Dist-AMLUNG 1962

Untamed Olympics C 26 MIN
16MM FILM OPTICAL SOUND I-C A

Explains that Olympic National Park's 1400 square miles, in the extreme northwestern corner of the United States, extends across a dramatically changing landscape and includes 50 miles of rugged Pacific shoreline, rainforests and jagged granite peaks. Shows more than 50 species of plant and animal life from this area.
From The Audubon Wildlife Theatre Series.
Prod-AVEXP Dist-AVEXP

Untamed Olympics C 26 MIN
16MM FILM OPTICAL SOUND I-C A
Explores the plant and animal life of Olympic National Park, a wildlife refuge from seashore to mountain heights.
From The Audubon Wildlife Theatre Series.
LC NO. 73-703221
Prod-KEGPL Dist-AVEXP 1973

Unter Heissem Himmel B 102 MIN
16MM FILM OPTICAL SOUND
A German language film with English subtitles. Tells an adventure story of a non-commissioned skipper who becomes involved in a scheme to ship arms out of the country illegally, and who is able to take initiative to prevent the worst from happening after he realizes the seriousness of the situation.
Prod-WSTGLC Dist-WSTGLC 1936

Until I Die C 30 MIN
16MM FILM OPTICAL SOUND
Presents Dr Elizabeth Kubler-Ross and her work with terminal patients. Examines her concept of the patients' reaction to an unfavorable diagnosis as a five-state process of grieving, including denial, anger, bargaining, depression and acceptance.
Prod-AMCS Dist-AMCS 1972

Until I Die C 29 MIN
2 INCH VIDEOTAPE
See series title for descriptive statement.
From The Synergism - In Today's World Series.
Prod-WTTWTV Dist-PUBTEL

Until I Die C 30 MIN
3/4 OR 1/2 INCH VIDEO CASSETTE
Explains Dr Elisabeth Kubler-Ross' work with terminally ill patients, examining the five stages (denial, anger, bargaining, depression and acceptance) through which patients progress after they learn of their approaching death.
Prod-WTTWTV Dist-AJN

Until I Get Caught C 27 MIN
16MM FILM OPTICAL SOUND
Explores the psychological attitudes of drunk drivers, victims, judges, jurors and police. Contrasts the drunk driving problem in the United States with that of Sweden, where the problem is much less severe.
LC NO. 80-700225
Prod-NYSLG Dist-MTP Prodn-CUNIV 1980

Until I Get Caught C 20 MIN
16MM FILM, 3/4 OR 1/2 IN VIDEO H A
Discusses why more action has not been taken to stop the combination of drinking and driving. Includes interviews with a district attorney, Swedish drivers, members of a New York community action group and relatives of victims killed in DWI-related accidents.
Prod-NHTSA Dist-USNAC 1980

Until I Get Caught C 27 MIN
3/4 OR 1/2 INCH VIDEO CASSETTE J A
Features Dick Cavett as he narrates a Public Broadcasting System special on drinking and driving.
Prod-SUTHRB Dist-SUTHRB

Until I Get Caught - Excerpts C 20 MIN
16MM FILM, 3/4 OR 1/2 IN VIDEO H A
Discusses the issue of DWI in America. Features interviews with survivors of victims killed by drunken drivers. Discusses the problem and potential solutions.
Prod-USDTFH Dist-USNAC 1980

Until She Talks C 44 MIN
16MM FILM OPTICAL SOUND
Relates the true story of a young woman who chooses not to answer question which were asked illegally by a grand jury. Reveals the legal process which put her in jail.
LC NO. 81-700437
Prod-ALASSP Dist-FIRS 1981

Until We Say Good-Bye C 62 MIN
16MM FILM OPTICAL SOUND
Explores the hospice concept in its most successful forms in three English and American facilities.
LC NO. 81-700493
Prod-WJLATV Dist-WJLATV 1981

Untitled B 4 MIN
16MM FILM OPTICAL SOUND
Experimental treatment of a savage attack upon a girl. Staccato drum beats play in counterpoint to the highly formalized imagery. (A USC Cinema Student Workshop production.)
Prod-USC Dist-USC 1965

Untitled Film B 18 MIN
16MM FILM OPTICAL SOUND
Presents a documentary about a group of Tibetans living in a community in New Jersey. Shows them at prayers, eating, playing with a tape recorder, and going out for hamburgers. Intercuts the workings of a Hamburger King Restaurant with the analysis of Tibetan religious practices.
Prod-UPENN Dist-UPENN 1970

Untitled Film - A Search For Ecological Balance C 38 MIN
16MM FILM OPTICAL SOUND
Presents the views of an internationally-known ecologist, Eugene P Odum, who believes it necessary to consider a master plan for the total environment in order to maintain an ecological balance.
LC NO. 74-705706
Prod-OIPFLM Dist-RADIM 1969

Untitled Population Film, The C 12 MIN
16MM FILM, 3/4 OR 1/2 IN VIDEO I-J
Uses animation in presenting the complex problem facing national governments and international agencies of finding useful work for growing populations and for those already without jobs, while meeting the needs of economic growth.
Prod-INLAOR Dist-SF 1976

Unto Us A Child Is Born C 5 MIN
16MM FILM OPTICAL SOUND
Uses pictures and animation synchronized with measures from the 'FOR UNTO US A CHILD IS BORN' chorus of 'THE MESSIAH' to augment the expression of the music in terms of time structure, ideas and the underlying emotional intent.
LC NO. FIA68-855
Prod-USC Dist-USC Prodn-MOSTRA 1968

Untouched Land, The - Pre-Columbian America - To 1492 X 24 MIN
16MM FILM OPTICAL SOUND I-C A
Tells the story of man in America. Discusses the retreat of the glaciers, the original Indian migrations, the Norse explorers and Columbus' discovery.
From The Exploring - The Story Of America, Set 1 Series.
LC NO. FIA68-1048
Prod-NBCTV Dist-GRACUR 1968

Unusual Situation, The C 30 MIN
3/4 OR 1/2 INCH VIDEO CASSETTE
Deals with the problems of the multiple handicapped child, who requires special testing and special programs in education.
From The Hearing Screening Series.
Prod-NETCHE Dist-NETCHE 1971

Unwanted Aliens C 11 MIN
16MM FILM OPTICAL SOUND
Shows foreign insects that could be introduced into the United States in a plant-pest detection training film.
LC NO. FIE63-219
Prod-USDA Dist-USNAC 1961

Unwed Families B 44 MIN
16MM FILM OPTICAL SOUND PRO
Discusses problem of unwed families dramatizing underlying social and psychological causes of illegitima erlying social and psychological causes of illegitimacy. Describes prenatal care and hospitalization of unwed mothers and explains adoption procedures.
From The Maternity Nursing Series.
LC NO. 75-703396
Prod-VDONUR Dist-AJN Prodn-WTTWTV 1966

Unwed Mothers In Today's World C 29 MIN
3/4 INCH VIDEO CASSETTE H-C A
Features four young women discussing their experiences as unwed mothers. Emphasizes the need for sensitive counseling and sound pre-natal care.
Prod-LAWREN Dist-LAWREN

Unwelcome Guest, The C 20 MIN
16MM FILM OPTICAL SOUND
Shows how comprehensive prevention and treatment programs for helminth diseases can improve the quality of life in many nations. Discusses the commitment of Pfizer International to do research in the field of parasitic diseases.
LC NO. 78-700443
Prod-PFIZRL Dist-PFIZRL Prodn-EFFCOM 1977

Up C 15 MIN
16MM FILM, 3/4 OR 1/2 IN VIDEO I-C A
Presents an allegorical hang-gliding adventure of a young man and an eagle. Includes aerial maneuvers and soaring sequences, which lead to a thought-provoking conclusion. From the producers of the film, Solo.
Prod-PFP Dist-PFP

Up A Tree C 8 MIN
16MM FILM, 3/4 OR 1/2 IN VIDEO P-I
Shows how lumberjack Donald Duck runs into trouble when he tries to chop down the tree home of two chipmunks.
From The Three Decades Of Donald Duck Series.
Prod-DISNEY Dist-WDEMCO

Up Against The Wall Miss America C 7 MIN
16MM FILM OPTICAL SOUND
Details the attempt of womens liberation groups to disrupt the annual pageant and make boardwalk and contestant spectators more aware of the contest with its image of the 'MINDLESS WOMANHOOD.'
Prod-NEWSR Dist-NEWSR 1968

Up And Coming—A Series
H-C A
Focuses on a black family that has uprooted itself from a low income black neighborhood of San Francisco and relocated to an integrated middle-class section of the city.
Prod-KQEDTV Dist-MDCPB 1980

Cheating Cats	030 MIN
Game Plan	030 MIN
Get With It	030 MIN
Growing Pains	030 MIN
Highrise Rebounds, Part I	030 MIN
Highrise Rebounds, Part II	030 MIN
Incident At Hamilton High	030 MIN
Little Romance, A, Part I	030 MIN
Little Romance, A, Part II	030 MIN
Loss On Innocence	030 MIN
Love's Lesson Learned	030 MIN
Movin' In, Movin' On, Part I	030 MIN
Movin' In, Movin' On, Part II	030 MIN
Return Of The Kingpin	030 MIN
Righteous Rumors	030 MIN

Up And Down C 8 MIN
16MM FILM, 3/4 OR 1/2 IN VIDEO P-I
Relates the directions up and down to the student's observations of the energy of moving things.
Prod-BFA Dist-PHENIX 1971

Up And Down The Slopes C 30 MIN
3/4 OR 1/2 INCH VIDEO CASSETTE
Presents instruction in down-hill skiing techniques. Illustrates traveling around the mountain and introduces the christie or controlled skid.
From The Alpine Ski School Series.
Prod-PBS Dist-PBS 1983

Up Close And Personal C 10 MIN
16MM FILM OPTICAL SOUND
Presents National Football League players sharing their feelings after visiting United Way agencies and meeting volunteers and recipients of services.
LC NO. 81-700430
Prod-UWAMER Dist-UWAMER 1980

Up For The Cup C 15 MIN
16MM FILM OPTICAL SOUND P-J
Explains that unable to obtain tickets for the football final the 'SIX AND A HALF' gang decide to build a viewing platform.
From The Magnificent 6 And 1/2 Series.
Prod-CHILDF Dist-LUF 1972

Up Front C 27 MIN
16MM FILM, 3/4 OR 1/2 IN VIDEO
Presents a rehabilitated drug user talking to a group of young people about drugs and drug dependency. Introduces a variety of treatment facilities and points out underlying problems that lead youth to drug misuse.
Prod-LACFU Dist-IA

Up In Flames And Live! C
3/4 OR 1/2 INCH VIDEO CASSETTE IND
Shows how race car drivers walk away from fiery accidents by wearing Nomex clothing. Explains how most burn fatalities are a result of clothes igniting, and how this special clothing decreases burn-related deaths.
Prod-GPCV Dist-GPCV

Up In Smoke C 38 MIN
3/4 OR 1/2 INCH VIDEO CASSETTE J-C
Presents the history of smoking in Western society, explains the chemical makeup of tobacco and gives a description of its damaging effects on the body. Enumerates the social and personal influences on someone who is trying to decide whether or not to smoke. Provides information about how to stop smoking.
LC NO. 82-706874
Prod-GA Dist-GA 1982

Up In The Air C 29 MIN
2 INCH VIDEOTAPE
See series title for descriptive statement.
From The Observing Eye Series.
Prod-WGBHTV Dist-PUBTEL

Up Is Down C 6 MIN
16MM FILM, 3/4 OR 1/2 IN VIDEO H-C A
Presents through animation a direct treatment of some of the most central themes of intolerance, conformity and the generation gap.
Prod-GOLDSH Dist-PFP 1970

Up Pill, Down Pill C 24 MIN
16MM FILM, 3/4 OR 1/2 IN VIDEO I-H A
Relates the story of two young men who try to escape life's disappointments and frustrations with pills and of an old man who is determined to live a full life.
Prod-BFA Dist-PHENIX 1972

Up The Creek C 14 MIN
16MM FILM OPTICAL SOUND P-J
Explains that the 'SIX AND A HALF' gang are so desperate to become boat owners that they offer their services free of charge to the owner of a local boatyard in exchange for his promise of a boat.
From The Magnificent 6 And 1/2 Series.
Prod-CHILDF Dist-LUF 1972

Up The Creek C 15 MIN
16MM FILM - 3/4 IN VIDEO
Demonstrates the isolation a man feels after he batters his wife. Explores the legal consequences of his physical violence and the personal loss that he suffers.
From The Time Out Series.
LC NO. 81-707272
Prod-ODNP Dist-ODNP 1981

Up The Down Stream C 12 MIN
3/4 INCH VIDEO CASSETTE K A
Documents the natural cycle of the King Salmon as well as how humans help with hatcheries, fish ladders and transplanting.
Prod-CSDWR Dist-CALDWR

Up The Dressing Ladder - Steps To Independence C 26 MIN
3/4 INCH VIDEO CASSETTE
Demonstrates how young multiple-handicapped children can be helped to independence, including instruction in their development of skills in holding, pulling, pushing, finding and opening.
LC NO. 76-706124
Prod-USBEH Dist-USNAC 1974

Up The Ladder Down C 10 MIN
16MM FILM, 3/4 OR 1/2 IN VIDEO J-H A
Presents three vignettes dealing with marijuana, barbiturates, cocaine and heroin, showing the consequences of drug abuse.
Prod-DAVP Dist-AIMS 1976

Up The Organization C 30 MIN
16MM FILM, 3/4 OR 1/2 IN VIDEO
Presents author and businessman Robert Townsend, who discusses his views on topics, such as chief executives, personnel departments, management consultants, computers, public relations departments and business success.
Prod-BBCTV Dist-FI 1973

Up The Power Curve C 10 MIN
16MM FILM - 3/4 IN VIDEO
Demonstrates the practicality of energy conservation and the important role conservation plays in helping solve America's energy problems. Covers a variety of energy-saving ideas and points out the significant dollar savings that can be achieved when these ideas are put into practice.
LC NO. 79-706729
Prod-USFEAP Dist-USNAC 1979

Up Tight - L A Is Burning C 20 MIN
16MM FILM OPTICAL SOUND C A
Presents a psychedelic comment on the attitudes and problems of the now generation.
Prod-CFS Dist-CFS 1968

Up To Code C 18 MIN
16MM FILM, 3/4 OR 1/2 IN VIDEO
Explores the attitudinal problems encountered by many firemen when called upon to do inspection of public facilities. Discusses ways of improving attitudes and demonstrates training devices for proper, thorough inspection.
LC NO. 79-707038
Prod-PFP Dist-PFP 1979

Up To The Moon C 11 MIN
16MM FILM, 3/4 OR 1/2 IN VIDEO P
Presents an imaginative word romp with children and a gorilla on merry-go-rounds, carousels, tettertotters, swings and slides to reinforce the words up, down, walk, run, boy, girl and stop.
From The Reading And Word Play Series.
Prod-PEDF Dist-AIMS 1976

Up To The Sequoias C 8 MIN
16MM FILM OPTICAL SOUND J-C A
Shows that the sequoias on the western slopes of the Sierra Nevadas in California are some of the world's oldest living things, including trees as tall as 200 feet and some 3,000 years of age. Captures the great beauty of the region with natural sounds and extraordinary close-ups of various species of birds.
Prod-AVEXP Dist-AVEXP 1968

Up, Up And Afraid C 29 MIN
16MM FILM, 3/4 OR 1/2 IN VIDEO
Explains that for many people the fear of flying is a very real disease. Documents the many programs which help people overcome this fear.
Prod-CANBC Dist-JOU

Update - Hypertension C 37 MIN
3/4 INCH VIDEO CASSETTE PRO
Discusses history, examination and laboratory evaluation of hypertensive patient. Includes pharmacology and clinical guidelines.
Prod-AYERST Dist-AYERST

Update - Topics Of Current Concern—A Series

Presents programs from the New York City Cable TV series Eye On Dance. Discusses topics of current concern in the dance world.
Prod-ARCVID Dist-ARCVID

Dance Critic's Role, The 030 MIN
Dancers' Changing Attitudes 030 MIN
Politics And The Arts 030 MIN
Running A Dance Company 030 MIN

Update Appliances Meetings—A Series

Prod-SEARS Dist-SRCIPP 1975

Chicago 5 MIN
U S Air Force Academy 4 MIN

Update On Hypnosis In Psychiatry C 60 MIN
3/4 OR 1/2 INCH VIDEO CASSETTE
Demonstrates how the hypnotic trance is an alerting rather than a sleep experience as Dr Herbert Spiegel clarifies major misconceptions about hypnosis and uses his method of self hypnosis to treat a patient with chronic head pain. Presents his theoretical views and his clinical technique of assessing a patient.
From Hypnosis Series.
Prod-HEMUL Dist-HEMUL

Update On The Homosexualities C 60 MIN
3/4 OR 1/2 INCH VIDEO CASSETTE
Presents findings from the world's most comprehensive research on Homosexualities - A Study Of Diversity, which debunk many cultural sterotypes and myths related to homosexuals preying on children, being violent-prone, forfeiting their masculinity or feminity, or that they are pathological transvestites and transsexuals.
Prod-HEMUL Dist-HEMUL

Updated Beef Cookery C 15 MIN
3/4 OR 1/2 INCH VIDEO CASSETTE IND
Demonstrates importance of meat department personnel in having a complete knowledge of beef cookery. Covers six basic methods of beef cookery.
Prod-NLSAMB Dist-NLSAMB

Upgrading Performance Of Existing Bridge Rail Systems C 18 MIN
16MM FILM, 3/4 OR 1/2 IN VIDEO IND
Discusses retrofit concepts for upgrading various types of deficient bridge rails to provide an improved vehicle-barrier interface.
Prod-USDTFH Dist-USNAC 1983

Uphill Ride, The - A Shoplifting Fable C 13 MIN
16MM FILM, 3/4 OR 1/2 IN VIDEO P-I
Shows what happens when two boys decide to shoplift two new tires for their bikes. Shows that shoplifting can only have bad consequences.
Prod-GBHDTR Dist-LAWREN 1974

Upholstering A Dining Room Chair - Box Welted Style/Fabric To Frame Style C 60 MIN
1/2 IN VIDEO CASSETTE BETA/VHS
Details the proper way to upholster two different types of dining room chairs, and explains how to take off the old upholstering and how to measure, cut and attach the materials needed to re-make the old chair.
Prod-RMI Dist-RMI

Upholstering A Dining Room Chair - Box Welted Style / Fabric To Frame Style C 60 MIN
1/2 IN VIDEO CASSETTE BETA/VHS
Demonstrates how to upholster two different types of dining room chairs. Shows how to take off the old upholstery and how to measure, cut and attach material.
Prod-MOHOMV Dist-MOHOMV

Upholstering A Dining Room Chair - Standard Wraparound Seat Style C 60 MIN
1/2 IN VIDEO CASSETTE BETA/VHS
Demonstrates how to upholster the standard wraparound seat style dining room chair. Shows a variety of fabrics and gives step-by-step instruction.
Prod-MOHOMV Dist-MOHOMV

Upjohn Company C 19 MIN
16MM FILM OPTICAL SOUND
Traces the history of the Upjohn Company and provides an overall look at the operations of the company. Follows the development of a new medicine from discovery to usage.
LC NO. 73-700626
Prod-UPJOHN Dist-UPJOHN 1972

Upjohn Vanguard Of Medicine—A Series

Prod-UPJOHN Dist-UPJOHN

Anaerobic Infections 20 MIN
Cold-Light Endoscopy 21 MIN
Myocardial Revascularization - Vineberg 20 MIN
Obsolete Menopause, The 18 MIN
Preparatory Techniques For Gravlee Jet Washer 17 MIN
Pulmonary Complications In Shock 17 MIN

Upon This Land C 15 MIN
16MM FILM - 3/4 IN VIDEO J-C A
Discusses the quality and values of Native American culture, dealing specifically with the Cherokee Indian tribe. Examines ritual dances, sacred ceremonies and tribal activities.
LC NO. 80-706873
Prod-WDCNTV Dist-GPITVL 1979

Upper Airway Infections C 19 MIN
3/4 OR 1/2 INCH VIDEO CASSETTE
Discusses upper airway infections in children, including diagnosis, examination and management decisions and techniques.
From The Pediatric Emergency Management Series.
Prod-VTRI Dist-VTRI

Upper Back, The C 29 MIN
2 INCH VIDEOTAPE
See series title for descriptive statement.
From The Maggie And The Beautiful Machine - Backs Series.
Prod-WGBHTV Dist-PUBTEL

Upper Body Exercise C 30 MIN
3/4 OR 1/2 INCH VIDEO CASSETTE
Discusses upper body exercise.
From The Bodyworks Series.
Prod-KTXTTV Dist-MDCPB

Upper Digestive Tract, The - Eating To Live C 26 MIN
3/4 OR 1/2 INCH VIDEO CASSETTE
Looks at appetite and hunger, and observes the actions of a salivary gland, the swallowing reflex, and the powerful churning of the stomach as food is broken down and processed.
From The Living Body - An Introduction To Human Biology Series.
Prod-FOTH Dist-FOTH 1985

Upper Extremities Functional Range Of Motion—A Series
PRO
Enables the therapist to determine what range of motion needs to be increased to improve the patient's function.
Prod-HSCIC Dist-HSCIC

Elbow, Forearm, And Wrist - Pt II 011 MIN
Hand Measurement - Pt III 009 MIN
Shoulder Joint - Pt I 012 MIN

Upper Extremity - Clavicle C 20 MIN
3/4 OR 1/2 INCH VIDEO CASSETTE PRO
Emphasizes some general considerations relating shoulder problems to the support features of spinal regions and the rib cage. Demonstrates application of direct principles in both articulatory and muscle energy techniques for manipulation in acromioclavicular and sternoclavicular dysfunctions.
From The Osteopathic Examination And Manipulation Series.
Prod-MSU Dist-MSU

Upper Extremity Nerve Blocks (2nd Ed) C 14 MIN
3/4 OR 1/2 INCH VIDEO CASSETTE PRO
Covers the selection of candidates for upper extremity regional anesthesia. Describes the anatomy of the axillary area, with special emphasis upon locating the bronchial plexus. Describes and demonstrates the administration of an axillary block. Shows indications for and techniques of intravenous regional administration.
From The Anesthesiology Clerkship Series.
Prod-UMICHM Dist-UMICHM 1982

Upper Extremity Prosthetic Principles, Pt 1 C 23 MIN
16MM FILM OPTICAL SOUND
Presents highlights of prescription, fabrication, fitting and harnessing, including the criteria for acceptance of artificial arms. Emphasizes the importance of teamwork, shows preprosthetic and prosthetic training activities and describes modern devices and appliances.
Prod-USVA Dist-USVA 1952

Upper Extremity Prosthetic Principles, Pt 2 C 29 MIN
16MM FILM OPTICAL SOUND
Shows examples of research efforts resulting in a body of prosthetic principles leading to better artificial arms. Describes the functions lost at different levels of amputation and of the principles involved in their prosthetic restoration.
LC NO. FIE56-35
Prod-USVA Dist-USVA 1955

Upper Gastrointestinal Examination C 12 MIN
3/4 OR 1/2 INCH VIDEO CASSETTE PRO
Gives basic information about upper GI exam. Defines terms the patient needs to know. Explains what happens during and after exam.
Prod-HSCIC Dist-HSCIC 1983

Upper GI C
3/4 OR 1/2 INCH VIDEO CASSETTE
See series title for descriptive statement.
From The X-Ray Procedures In Layman's Terms Series.
Prod-FAIRGH Dist-FAIRGH

Upper GI Endoscopy C
3/4 OR 1/2 INCH VIDEO CASSETTE
Describes how the endoscopic procedure is used to identify and diagnose common problems in the upper digestive tract.
Prod-MIFE Dist-MIFE

Upper GI Endoscopy (Arabic) C
3/4 OR 1/2 INCH VIDEO CASSETTE
Describes how the endoscopic procedure is used to identify and diagnose common problems in the upper digestive tract.
Prod-MIFE Dist-MIFE

Upper GI Endoscopy (Spanish) C
3/4 OR 1/2 INCH VIDEO CASSETTE
Describes how the endoscopic procedure is used to identify and diagnose common problems in the upper digestive tract.
Prod-MIFE Dist-MIFE

Upper Room, The X 15 MIN
16MM FILM OPTICAL SOUND I-H T R
Jesus washes the disciples' feet after the paschal meal in the upper room. He announces that one of them will betray him. Jesus takes the bread and the wine, passes them to the disciples and offers the benediction.
From The Living Bible Series.
Prod-FAMF Dist-FAMF

Upper South, The C 25 MIN
16MM FILM, 3/4 OR 1/2 IN VIDEO I-J
Visits the state of North Carolina, Virginia, West Virginia, Kentucky and Tennessee - an area that is rich in history and mines coal, harnesses rivers, raises horses and weaves textiles.
From The United States Geography Series.
Prod-NGS Dist-NGS 1983

Uppers, Downers, All Arounders, Pt 1 - The Effects C 30 MIN
16MM FILM OPTICAL SOUND
Examines how and why the physical and emotional centers of the brain are affected by psychoactive drugs. Gives a general classification of the drugs, which are stimulants, depressants and psychedelics. Looks at the various levels of drug seeking behavior.
Prod-CINMED Dist-CINMED 1984

Upperville Show, The B 9 MIN
16MM FILM, 3/4 OR 1/2 IN VIDEO P A
Presents a documentary of the oldest horse show in America in Upperville, Virginia. Views pedigreed people and thoroughbred horses in a spring festival.
Prod-DAVT Dist-DAVT 1971

Uprooted, The C 33 MIN
3/4 INCH VIDEO CASSETTE
Presents the story of the Salvation Army refugee and relief operations in Uganda, Zambia, Thailand and Hong Kong. Filmed on location.
Prod-SALVA Dist-MTP

Ups And Downs Of Highs And Lows, The C 29 MIN
2 INCH VIDEOTAPE
Features meteorologist Frank Sechrist explaining that the forces which affect weather are pressure gradient force, Coriolis effect and friction. Includes a look at a synoptic weather chart, isobars and the weatherman when he is drawing all those highs and lows.
From The Weather Series.
Prod-WHATV Dist-PUBTEL

Ups/Downs C 24 MIN
16MM FILM, 3/4 OR 1/2 IN VIDEO J-C
Discusses the effects of amphetamines and barbiturates on the

minds and bodies of users. Explores how society fosters abuse of these sometimes useful drugs, how severe a user's dependence on them can be and what's involved in becoming free of them.
From The Drug Abuse Education Series.
Prod-CONFI Dist-EBEC

Ups, Downs, Ins, Outs C 20 MIN
16MM FILM - 3/4 IN VIDEO J
Helps students recognize the fact that pressures are an inevitable and constant part of life and to realize that there are positive methods for coping with pressure.
From The Nobody But Yourself Series.
Prod-WQED Dist-GPITVL

Upside Down And Backwards C 28 MIN
3/4 OR 1/2 INCH VIDEO CASSETTE
Presents work by video artist Joan Jonas based on two fairy tales told simultaneously.
Prod-WNETTV Dist-EAI

Upstairs Room, The C 15 MIN
3/4 OR 1/2 INCH VIDEO CASSETTE I
See series title for descriptive statement.
From The Best Of Cover To Cover 2 Series.
Prod-WETATV Dist-WETATV

Upstairs, Downstairs At The Times C 25 MIN
16MM FILM OPTICAL SOUND
Profiles Lord Roy Thompson of Fleet, who entered a newspaper office at age 50 and aspires to become a billionaire through the acquisition of hundreds of companies and some 192 newspapers, including the London Times.
LC NO. 77-702531
Prod-CTV Dist-CTV 1976

Uptake And Distribution Of Inhalation Anesthetic Agents (2nd Ed) C 23 MIN
3/4 OR 1/2 INCH VIDEO CASSETTE PRO
Describes the pharmacodynamics of administration of inhalation anesthetic agents. Covers factors influencing the alveolar anesthetic tension. Discusses the influence of the anesthetic system and various physiologic abnormalities on the development of the anesthetic state.
From The Anesthesiology Clerkship Series.
Prod-UMICHM Dist-UMICHM 1982

Upton Sinclair B 30 MIN
16MM FILM OPTICAL SOUND H
Upton Sinclair, author, socialist and reformer, expresses his desire for social justice and recalls his efforts to achieve industrial democracy, stressing his contact with the Henry Ford Empire. (Kinescope)
From The Sum And Substance Series.
LC NO. FIA67-5102
Prod-MLA Dist-MLA 1964

Upturned Face, The C 9 MIN
16MM FILM, 3/4 OR 1/2 IN VIDEO
Presents an adaptation of the short story 'THE UPTURNED FACE' by Stephen Crane which treats death with relentless honesty, protesting angrily against dying.
Prod-CHGLNG Dist-PFP 1973

Upwardly Mobile C 14 MIN
3/4 OR 1/2 INCH VIDEO CASSETTE
Explores the effects of architecture and construction on urban living. Uses visual information juxtaposed against an operatic soundtrack. An experimental film.
Prod-MEDIPR Dist-MEDIPR 1982

Upwelling Phenomenon, The C 15 MIN
16MM FILM OPTICAL SOUND C
Deals with studies of upwelling, an ocean process that covers only a thousandth of the sea surface, yet provides more than half of mankind's seafood.
From The Science In Action Series.
Prod-ALLFP Dist-COUNFI

Uranus, Neptune, And Pluto C 29 MIN
3/4 INCH VIDEO CASSETTE C A
Recounts circumstances leading to discovery of Uranus, Neptune and Pluto. Describes general physical characteristics of Uranus and Neptune.
From The Project Universe - Astronomy Series. Lesson 12
Prod-COAST Dist-CDTEL Prodn-SCCON

Urashima Taro - A Japanese Folktale C 12 MIN
16MM FILM, 3/4 OR 1/2 IN VIDEO
Uses animation to tell a Japanese folktale about a young fisherman who is rewarded for his good deed by being invited to the undersea Dragon Palace. Shows how he returns to his village and finds that he has been away for 300 years.
Prod-OKEYA Dist-BARR 1979

Urban Alternatives C 19 MIN
16MM FILM, 3/4 OR 1/2 IN VIDEO J-C A
Explores examples of what has been done to solve some of our urban problems and make our cities an environment for people to use and enjoy. Features planners who work as urban environmentalists who discuss the alternatives and their philosophy of what a city can and should be.
Prod-BARR Dist-BARR 1973

Urban Campus, The C 28 MIN
16MM FILM OPTICAL SOUND
Presents University of Pittsburgh Chancellor Wesley Posvar discussing the role of the university in a large metropolitan area with several faculty members. Interviews two students who discuss the role of higher education in their lives.
Prod-UPITTS Dist-UPITTS 1973

Urban Challenge—A Series
J-H A

Points out that behind the prosperity of big cities lies a distinct undergrowth of poverty. Uses the cities of Bangkok, Lima and New York as examples.
Prod-NYSED Dist-GPITVL 1981

City Countdown 020 MIN
Deciding A Future 020 MIN
Learning A Living 020 MIN

Urban Crisis—A Series

Prod-BROSEB Dist-BROSEB 1975

Bomb Threat - Plan, Don't Panic 015 MIN
Bunco Boys, The - And How To Beat Them 021 MIN
Cool Plates - Hot Car 019 MIN
Gaspumps And Gunmen 023 MIN
Highfire - Plan For Survival 019 MIN
Hostage Survival 025 MIN
Instant Arson - Testing Fire Bombs And 012 MIN
Intrusion Conspiracy, The 020 MIN
Kidnap - Executive Style 025 MIN
My Dad's A Cop (Captioned) 018 MIN
Senior Power And How To Use It 019 MIN
Stick Up 018 MIN
Vehicle Under Attack - Officer Survival Of 015 MIN

Urban Development, Urban Climate C 15 MIN
16MM FILM OPTICAL SOUND H-C A
Discusses how the city managers of Stuttgart improved airflow and temperature for residents, with low-budget do-it-yourself methods including how to reduce heat from city parking lots to building codes which increase the flow of cool air through the city.
Prod-WSTGLC Dist-WSTGLC

Urban Ecology - Garbage Disposal C 7 MIN
16MM FILM, 3/4 OR 1/2 IN VIDEO I-J
Explains that trash forms blemishes on the landscape and that Americans must constantly look for ways to reduce the total amount of trash.
Prod-COLLRD Dist-PHENIX 1971

Urban Education B 30 MIN
16MM FILM OPTICAL SOUND H-C
Discusses what the new goals of urban education should be, the relationship between community control of educational districts and decentralization and the new efforts needed in the area of teacher training and recruitment.
From The Conversations In Black Series.
Prod-HRAW Dist-HRAW

Urban Episodes C 9 MIN
3/4 OR 1/2 INCH VIDEO CASSETTE
Prod-EAI Dist-EAI

Urban Experience, The C 29 MIN
2 INCH VIDEOTAPE
See series title for descriptive statement.
From The Black Experience Series.
Prod-WTTWTV Dist-PUBTEL

Urban Focus—A Series

Prod-PEPSI Dist-MLA

Ask My Name 15 MIN
Generations 30 MIN
Imaginary They, An 22 MIN
My City 22 MIN

Urban Impact On Weather And Climate C 16 MIN
16MM FILM, 3/4 OR 1/2 IN VIDEO J-H
Presents a range of recent meteorological findings on the effects cities have on weather and climate causes and suggests possible solutions.
From The Environmental Sciences Series.
Prod-LCOA Dist-LCOA 1971

Urban Impact On Weather And Climate (Captioned) C 16 MIN
16MM FILM, 3/4 OR 1/2 IN VIDEO J-C A
Shows how weather and climate can be affected by the concentration of large buildings in urban environments.
Prod-LCOA Dist-LCOA 1972

Urban Indians C 20 MIN
3/4 OR 1/2 INCH VIDEO CASSETTE
Explores the problems of American Indians living in cities. Reveals the disorientation and confusion which may be experienced by Indians who leave the reservation. Portrays a member of the Oglala Sioux tribe as he struggles to overcome the drug and alcohol abuse which had comforted him.
Prod-DCTVC Dist-DCTVC

Urban Maes Amputation For Peripheral Vascular Disease, The C 12 MIN
16MM FILM OPTICAL SOUND
Demonstrates the advantages in the Urban Maes technique of below-the-knee amputation in diseases of compromised circulation. Shows the operative technique from initial incision to final stump closure and the healed stump with range of motion some weeks later. Presents several other patients who have been handled in a similar manner, with views of their stumps, ambulatory on pylon temporary and final prosthesis.
Prod-USVA Dist-USVA 1956

Urban Patterns C 16 MIN
16MM FILM, 3/4 OR 1/2 IN VIDEO H-C A
Traces the development of urban systems, past and present, and examines the dominance of a city over its surrounding area.
Prod-ANAIB Dist-SF 1971

Urban Problems C 30 MIN
3/4 OR 1/2 INCH VIDEO CASSETTE C
Discusses historical and contemporary urban problems and issues.
From The Focus On Society Series.
Prod-DALCCD Dist-DALCCD

Urban Rebellions - Prelude To Armed Struggle B 30 MIN
16MM FILM OPTICAL SOUND H-C A
Gerald Mc Worter discusses the series of events, the personalities and the organization that contributed to the ideology for revolution during the 1960's. Includes the deacons from Defense, Stokeley Carmichael, Franz Fanon, Robert F Williams and more.
From The Black History, Section 21 - Protest And Rebellion Series.
LC NO. 75-704117
Prod-WCBSTV Dist-HRAW 1969

Urban Rebellions - The Crisis From 1964-1968 B 30 MIN
16MM FILM OPTICAL SOUND H-C A
Gerald Mc Worter anaylzes the conflict between the Black community and the white society in the North during the 1960's.
From The Black History, Section 21 - Protest And Rebellion Series.
LC NO. 71-704116
Prod-WCBSTV Dist-HRAW 1969

Urban Sprawl C 22 MIN
16MM FILM OPTICAL SOUND
Points out that urban sprawl is no accident and describes the great economic pressures that cause today's zoning system to break down. Explains that what is needed is a new system which can protect natural resources and yet produce quality urban communities free from blight.
Prod-FINLYS Dist-FINLYS

Urban Sprawl Vs Planned Growth C 22 MIN
16MM FILM OPTICAL SOUND J-C A
Shows how new techniques of planning can promote orderly growth and development, thereby counteracting the natural tendency of urban sprawl which ultimately creates blighted communities. Includes scenes of the upper east branch of Brandywine Creek near Philadelphia, Pennsylvania.
LC NO. 71-702627
Prod-FINLYS Dist-FINLYS 1968

Urban Structure, The C 30 MIN
3/4 OR 1/2 INCH VIDEO CASSETTE
Explores the problems facing the architect as he designs the urban community of the future.
From The Designing The Environment Series.
Prod-NETCHE Dist-NETCHE 1971

Urban Studies—A Series

Examines the nature and function of center cities from an experimental point of view.
Prod-FOTH Dist-FOTH 1984

Aspects Of Central Place 020 MIN
Central City 020 MIN
Developing City, The 020 MIN

Urban Universities And Their Responsibilities C 29 MIN
2 INCH VIDEOTAPE
See series title for descriptive statement.
From The University Of Chicago Round Table Series.
Prod-WTTWTV Dist-PUBTEL

Urban Uses Of Land For Education, Culture And Recreation C 18 MIN
16MM FILM OPTICAL SOUND P-J
Shows ways land in a large city is used for educational, cultural and recreational purposes such as libraries, historical monuments, schools and colleges, religious buildings, museums, parks, gardens, and theaters.
LC NO. 78-712446
Prod-ACA Dist-ACA 1967

Urban Uses Of Land For Industry C 18 MIN
16MM FILM OPTICAL SOUND P-J
Presents important uses of land in a large city for many different kinds of industry. Shows how land is used for transportation facilities, large factories and special industries. Uses map-like scenes to help explain the different uses of land.
LC NO. 74-712445
Prod-ACA Dist-ACA 1967

Urban Uses Of Land In The Largest Cities Of Northern California C 18 MIN
16MM FILM OPTICAL SOUND P-J
Depicts how man makes use of land in the largest cities of northern California. Uses detailed maps and aerial photography to explain how land is utilized for residential, transportation, industrial, educational, government and recreational needs.
LC NO. 72-709726
Prod-ACA Dist-ACA 1970

Urban Youth C 30 MIN
3/4 OR 1/2 INCH VIDEO CASSETTE H-C A
Illustrates the problems of street life and runaways, prostitution, drugs and alcohol which compound other problems of young people in Maine.
From The Can I Get There From Here? Series.
Prod-MESETC Dist-UMEA 1981

Urbanissimo C 6 MIN
16MM FILM, 3/4 OR 1/2 IN VIDEO H-C
Features a humorous commentary on modern urban civilization. Deals with city growth and development.
Prod-HUBLEY Dist-TEXFLM 1968

Urbanite, The C 22 MIN
3/4 INCH VIDEO CASSETTE A
Discusses the urban experience and the need for local political

and planning control. Cites advantages of heterogeneity, cultural diversify and the variety of social worlds that exist in urban environment.
Prod-SLDTRS Dist-SLDTRS 1980

Urbanization - Structure And Function C 20 MIN
3/4 INCH VIDEO CASSETTE H-C
See series title for descriptive statement.
From The Geography For The '70's Series.
Prod-KLRNTV Dist-GPITVL

Urbanization, The Expansion Of The Ghetto B 30 MIN
16MM FILM OPTICAL SOUND H-C A
Horace Mann Bond speaks of the effects of urbanization on the education of the black child after World War II. He discusses the growth of the northern black population and the resultant defacto school segregation, the rise of black universities, and their impact on higher education for blacks.
From The Black History, Section 18 - A Period Of Transition, 1945-1954 Series.
LC NO. 75-704097
Prod-WCBSTV Dist-HRAW 1969

Urbs Mea C 11 MIN
16MM FILM OPTICAL SOUND H
A classical Latin language film. Adapted from 'ROMAN LIFE IN ANCIENT POMPEII.' Describes the economic, social, political and cultural life of the Romans who lived in ancient Pompeii. Shows scenes of the ruins of Pompeii, destroyed by Vesuvius. Tours the streets, homes, shops, temples and theatre of Pompeii.
LC NO. FIA65-292
Prod-SUEF Dist-SUTHLA 1963

Ureter In Colon Surgery, The C 19 MIN
16MM FILM OPTICAL SOUND PRO
Explains that exposure and identification of the ureter is the only sure way of preventing injury to it during resection of the colon. Demonstrates the exposure and preservation of the ureter in surgery of the colon.
Prod-ACYDGD Dist-ACY 1959

Ureteral Injury C 35 MIN
16MM FILM OPTICAL SOUND PRO
Demonstrates the operative management of surgical ureteral injuries. Demonstrates techniques for use during operation, convalescence or in a remotely post-operative period.
Prod-ACYDGD Dist-ACY 1960

Ureteral Peristaltic Activity C 21 MIN
16MM FILM OPTICAL SOUND
Demonstrates peristaltic activity in the ureter of both humans and dogs. Shows unobstructed and obstructed urine flow in the ureter and the inability of the ureter to transport urine against gravity.
LC NO. 71-705708
Prod-EATONL Dist-EATONL Prodn-AVCORP 1969

Ureteral Re-Implantation And Bladder Neck Revision C 20 MIN
16MM FILM OPTICAL SOUND PRO
Demonstrates the surgical procedure for ureteral reimplantation and bladder neck revision as it is performed transvesically. Includes a detailed step-by-step illustration of technique and prognosis and demonstrates ureteral reflux by cineradiography.
LC NO. FIA66-76
Prod-EATON Dist-EATON Prodn-AVCORP 1962

Uretero-Arachnoid Anastomosis In Treatment Of Hydrocephalus C 18 MIN
16MM FILM OPTICAL SOUND PRO
Shows the operative technique for shunting spinal fluid from the lumbar sub-arachnoid space into the ureter by means of a plastic catheter in the treatment of hydrocephalus.
Prod-ACYDGD Dist-ACY 1950

Uretero-Ileo-Neocystostomy C 15 MIN
16MM FILM OPTICAL SOUND
Demonstrates criteria for using a segment of the ileum as a replacement of the ureter and discusses the operative technique in two patients. Includes follow-up sequences.
Prod-EATONL Dist-EATONL 1964

Uretero-Ileo-Urethral Anastomosis - A Bladder Substitute C 18 MIN
16MM FILM OPTICAL SOUND
Explains that uretero-ileo-urethral anastomosis is a method of urinary diversion which may be used following total cystectomy, that this technique substitutes a segment of ileum for the normal bladder and that to this ileum are anastomosed both ureters and urethra, allowing both urinary continence and relatively normal voiding through the normal channel.
Prod-USVA Dist-USVA 1959

Uretero-Ureteral Anastamosis C 20 MIN
16MM FILM OPTICAL SOUND
Explains that, at the time of birth, this patient was found to have a mass in the right flank and a positive diagnosis of a marked hydronephrosis in a solitary kidney was made by the introduction of x-ray media through a silastic tube that was introduced into the umbilical vein. Shows that the side-to-side anastomosis was the procedure of choice and was extremely successful.
From The Surgical Correction Of Hydronephrosis, Pt 2 - Dismembering Procedures Series.
Prod-EATONL Dist-EATONL 1968

Ureterosigmoidostomy And Closure Of Exstrophy Of The Urinary Bladder C 20 MIN
16MM FILM OPTICAL SOUND PRO
Shows the authors' technique of open transcolonic ureterosigmoidostomy for urinary diversion performed on a five-year-old boy with typical exstrophy of the urinary bladder and associated epispadias as well as a large right inguinal hernia.

LC NO. 75-702239
Prod-EATONL Dist-EATONL 1974

Urethanes - The Challenge Of Change C 30 MIN
3/4 OR 1/2 INCH VIDEO CASSETTE
Reviews the commercial and industrial applications of urethane plastics. Discusses their role in conservation of natural resources.
Prod-IVCH Dist-IVCH

Urethral Catherization Of Male And Female C 17 MIN
16MM FILM OPTICAL SOUND PRO
Discusses the various purposes for, and methods of urethral catheterization and the various types of catheters. Illustrates the exact procedures for catheterization in both the male and female patient.
LC NO. FIA66-77
Prod-EATON Dist-EATON Prodn-AVCORP 1964

Urethral Catheterization C 22 MIN
16MM FILM OPTICAL SOUND PRO
Explains that urethral catheterization represents the major hospital-borne infection. Demonstrates catheterization in its relationship to anatomy and bacteriology. Shows how these techniques can significantly reduce the incidence of infection.
Prod-ACYDGD Dist-ACY 1969

Urethral Catheterization C 9 MIN
3/4 OR 1/2 INCH VIDEO CASSETTE PRO
See series title for descriptive statement.
From The Medical Skills Films Series.
Prod-WFP Dist-WFP

Urethral Meatoplasty C 10 MIN
16MM FILM OPTICAL SOUND
Illustrates an operative procedure used to permanently enlarge the urethral meatus in over 800 female patients. Discusses the symptoms associated with urethral disease based on statistics from questionnaires returned by 500 post-operative patients.
LC NO. 75-702299
Prod-EATONL Dist-EATONL 1964

Urethral Strictures C 49 MIN
16MM FILM OPTICAL SOUND PRO
Presents through a lecture, preoperative and postoperative review and operative techniques, the author's concept in the diagnosis and treatment of urethral strictures.
From The Visits In Urology Series.
LC NO. 75-702669
Prod-EATONL Dist-EATONL 1975

Urethral Suspension Using Stainless Steel Staples C 20 MIN
16MM FILM OPTICAL SOUND
Describes a simple method of urethral suspension for urinary stress incontinence. Shows how, using the vaginal approach, the fibrous tissue on each side of the upper urethra is stapled to the posterior pubic bone, thus elevating the bladder neck. Explains that this operation has been most frequently performed for recurrent urinary stress incontinence and has been well-tolerated by the patients.
LC NO. 75-702289
Prod-EATONL Dist-EATONL 1969

Urethrolysis In Girls And Urethroplasty In Women C 15 MIN
16MM FILM OPTICAL SOUND
Explains that urethroplasty is a surgical procedure in correction of a stricture of the distal segment of the urethra by lysis in girls and excision of posterior periurethral corrective tissues in women. Shows the external and internal sphincters and their relationship to the distal urethral segment. Presents surgical technique and case histories.
LC NO. 75-702290
Prod-EATONL Dist-EATONL 1969

Urethroplasty - Repair Of The Recurrent Penile Fistula C 10 MIN
16MM FILM OPTICAL SOUND
Presents a two-stage procedure to compensate for the excessive scarring and poor local vascular supply that follows a primary or secondary repair of a recurrent fistula of the anterior urethra. Presents a graphic illustration of the technique which utilizes the basic principles of the Cecil and Denis-Browne recommendations.
LC NO. 75-702280
Prod-EATONL Dist-EATONL 1969

Ureto-Ileo-Neocyctostomy C 15 MIN
16MM FILM OPTICAL SOUND PRO
Defines the rationale for using segment of the ileum as a replacement for the ureter. Demonstrates the surgical procedure in 62 year-old female patient with a bilateral ureteral occlusion due to late radiation changes with no evidence of residual carcinoma of the cervix.
LC NO. FIA66-75
Prod-EATON Dist-EATON Prodn-AVCORP 1962

Urge To Build C 27 MIN
16MM FILM, 3/4 OR 1/2 IN VIDEO H-C A
Tells about ordinary people who have decided to take the risk of planning and building their own homes.
Prod-HOOVJ Dist-DIRECT 1981

Urgent Message C 5 MIN
16MM FILM OPTICAL SOUND
Shows stockpiles of weapons in order to promote an anti-bomb message.
LC NO. 74-702772
Prod-UTORMC Dist-CANFDC 1973

Urgent Messages C 22 MIN
16MM FILM, 3/4 OR 1/2 IN VIDEO H-C A
Dispels the myths and taboos surrounding teenage suicide. Introduced by Patty Duke-Astin, this film makes the point that the two leading causes of adolescent deaths, auto accidents and suicide, may be one and the same.
Prod-LASREM Dist-MEDIAG 1983

Urinalysis - Chemical Examination Of The Urine C 12 MIN
1/2 IN VIDEO CASSETTE BETA/VHS
Explains how to perform the chemical analysis of urine.
Prod-RMI Dist-RMI

Urinalysis - Microscopic Examination Of The Urine C 9 MIN
1/2 IN VIDEO CASSETTE BETA/VHS
Explains how to perform the microscopic analysis of urine.
Prod-RMI Dist-RMI

Urinalysis - Physical Examination Of The Urine C 10 MIN
1/2 IN VIDEO CASSETTE BETA/VHS
Explains how to perform the physical analysis of urine.
Prod-RMI Dist-RMI

Urinary Calculi C 14 MIN
16MM FILM, 3/4 OR 1/2 IN VIDEO A
Provides a comprehensive picture of causes, effects and treatment of urinary stones. Illustrates anatomy, physiology and mechanics of stone formation. Outlines diagnosis, medical and surgical therapy and long term care.
Prod-PRORE Dist-PRORE

Urinary Calculi (Spanish) C 14 MIN
16MM FILM, 3/4 OR 1/2 IN VIDEO PRO
Discusses the causes, effects and treatments of urinary stones.
Prod-PRORE Dist-PRORE

Urinary Catheter Procedures C
3/4 OR 1/2 INCH VIDEO CASSETTE
Describes some commonly performed urinary catheter procedures that have proven ineffective in reducing infections and are thus no longer recommended. Illustrates measures that do reduce infection during catherization.
From The Infection Control III Series.
Prod-CONMED Dist-CONMED

Urinary Catheterization C 15 MIN
3/4 OR 1/2 INCH VIDEO CASSETTE PRO
Presents the fundamental facts about catheterization. Demonstrates equipment needed.
Prod-MEDFAC Dist-MEDFAC 1976

Urinary Diversion - The Isolated Sigmoid Conduit C 16 MIN
16MM FILM OPTICAL SOUND
Depicts the construction of an isolated sigmoid conduit. Shows that the key to this procedure is the creation of an anti-refluxing ureteral-colonic anastomosis. Points out that these conduits do not reflux, have equal resting pressures and rate of emptying compared with ileal conduits and a lower incidence of stomal problems.
LC NO. 75-702254
Prod-EATONL Dist-EATONL 1973

Urinary Incontinence In Women C
3/4 OR 1/2 INCH VIDEO CASSETTE
Describes the physioloical background of urinary incontinence. Differentiates between stress incontinence and urge incontinence. Traces the cause of each. Explains the need for tests to determine treatment alternatives.
Prod-MIFE Dist-MIFE

Urinary Retention C 19 MIN
3/4 OR 1/2 INCH VIDEO CASSETTE
Discusses urinary retention, including causes. Demonstrates techniques of evacuating the bladder, alternative approaches and precautions.
From The Emergency Management - The First 30 Minutes, Vol II Series.
Prod-VTRI Dist-VTRI

Urinary Stress Incontinence - Urethroscopy As An Aid To Surgical Treatment C 20 MIN
3/4 OR 1/2 INCH VIDEO CASSETTE PRO
Demonstrates through surgery how to correct urinary stress incontinence with the aid of the cystometer and the urethroscope.
Prod-WFP Dist-WFP

Urinary System - Pt 1 - Kidney C 39 MIN
3/4 OR 1/2 INCH VIDEO CASSETTE PRO
Describes the role, components, and functions of the kidney. Identifies the processes of urine formation, reabsorption, and secretion.
From The Histology Review Series.
Prod-HSCIC Dist-HSCIC

Urinary System - Pt 2 - Ureter Bladder, Urethra C 26 MIN
3/4 OR 1/2 INCH VIDEO CASSETTE PRO
Covers the major structural and functional characteristics of the ureter, urinary bladder, and urethra. Identifies the major histological features of the urinary passageways. Characterizes the process involved in urine transport.
From The Histology Review Series.
Prod-HSCIC Dist-HSCIC

Urinary System, The C 14 MIN
1/2 IN VIDEO CASSETTE BETA/VHS
Discusses the anatomy of the urinary tract and the purposes of urinalysis.
Prod-RMI Dist-RMI

Urinary Tract Infection C 17 MIN
16MM FILM, 3/4 OR 1/2 IN VIDEO A
Presents fact and fallacies about how infections develop. Discusses symptoms such as frequent urge to urinate, blood in

the urine and pain in the lower back. Explains medical treatment and long-term care.
Prod-PRORE Dist-PRORE

Urinary Tract Infection C 21 MIN
3/4 OR 1/2 INCH VIDEO CASSETTE PRO
Presents the magnitude of nosacomial urinary tract infection and identifies susceptible population groups. Stresses the diagnosis, treatment and prevention of urinary tract infection.
Prod-UMICHM Dist-UMICHM 1977

Urinary Tract Infection C 29 MIN
3/4 OR 1/2 INCH VIDEO CASSETTE
Describes effective methods of treating infections of the urinary tract.
From The Daniel Foster, MD Series.
Prod-KERA Dist-PBS

Urinary Tract Infection (Spanish) C 17 MIN
16MM FILM, 3/4 OR 1/2 IN VIDEO PRO
Describes the symptoms and treatment of urinary tract infections.
Prod-PRORE Dist-PRORE

Urinary Tract Infection (UTI) C 10 MIN
3/4 OR 1/2 INCH VIDEO CASSETTE
Describes common causes of UTI and necessary medical intervention. Emphasizes therapeutic techniques such as site baths, ingesting extra fluids and the critical need to take appropriate medication.
Prod-TRAINX Dist-TRAINX

Urinary Tract Infections C 32 MIN
16MM FILM OPTICAL SOUND
Presents a comprehensive approach to help recognize, diagnose and appropriately treat individuals with urinary infections. Features a working classification along with definite suggestions as to a therapeutic approach and follow-up.
LC NO. 75-702274
Prod-EATONL Dist-EATONL 1971

Urinary Tract Infections C 7 MIN
3/4 OR 1/2 INCH VIDEO CASSETTE
Focuses on the causes, symptoms and treatment for urinary tract infections. Uses illustrations to describe the area of possible infection. Encourages the patient to take responsibility for self care.
From The Take Care Of Yourself Series.
Prod-UARIZ Dist-UARIZ

Urinary Tract Infections In Girls C 20 MIN
16MM FILM OPTICAL SOUND PRO
Presents recommended diagnosis and treatment procedures of urinary tract infections in young girls, as performed at the University of Minnesota of Medicine.
LC NO. FIA66-703
Prod-EATON Dist-EATON Prodn-AVCORP 1966

Urinary Tract, The - Water C 26 MIN
3/4 OR 1/2 INCH VIDEO CASSETTE
Explains the function of water in the body and discusses the system for keeping it in balance. Covers drinking, sweating and breathing, and analyzes the urinary tract, focusing on the functioning of the kidneys.
From The Living Body - An Introduction To Human Biology Series.
Prod-FOTH Dist-FOTH 1985

Urine Collection C 15 MIN
16MM FILM OPTICAL SOUND
Depicts the proper techniques of obtaining valid urine specimens in adult males and females and in children.
LC NO. 75-702243
Prod-EATONL Dist-EATONL 1972

Urological Examination, The C 27 MIN
16MM FILM OPTICAL SOUND PRO
Points out the continuing importance of the clinical urological examination in providing the initial diagnosis upon which laboratory studies are based. Provides a step-by-step demonstration and explaination of each phase of Dr Boyarsky's technique.
LC NO. FIA66-78
Prod-EATON Dist-EATON 1965

Urology—A Series
PRO
Presents demonstrations of the equipment and procedures which can be used in the office for common urological conditions. Uses pictorial representations of each topic, instrument demonstrations and procedure demonstrations.
Prod-MSU Dist-MSU

Cystoscopy - Equipment And Procedure 030 MIN
Pre-Vasectomy Family Consultation 013 MIN
Sound For Urethral Strictures 025 MIN
Vasectomy Operative Procedure 028 MIN

Urostomy Care At Home C 13 MIN
3/4 OR 1/2 INCH VIDEO CASSETTE
Reviews important aspects of self-care, and encourages patient's confidence in his/her ability to manage the urostomy appliance. Notes program can be shown to patient prior to surgery in some cases but otherwise before discharge from the hospital.
LC NO. 79-730905
Prod-TRAINX Dist-TRAINX

Uruguay - Shark Fishing C 14 MIN
3/4 OR 1/2 INCH VIDEO CASSETTE H-C A
Presents a story of a group of men who established a small fishing village when their farms failed to yield adequate food for their families. Tells how they were successful and are able to offer hope for a better way of life for their families.
Prod-JOU Dist-JOU

Us C 20 MIN
16MM FILM OPTICAL SOUND I-C A
See series title for descriptive statement.
From The Cellar Door Cine Mites Series.
LC NO. 74-701552
Prod-CELLAR Dist-CELLAR 1972

Us And Changes C 29 MIN
16MM FILM - 3/4 IN VIDEO
Shows how to care for nature's creatures, how to conserve natural resources by recycling and how to turn a junkyard into a playground.
From The Earthkeeping Series.
Prod-WTTWTV Dist-PUBTEL

US Economic Growth - What Is The Gross National Product C 30 MIN
3/4 OR 1/2 INCH VIDEO CASSETTE C
See series title for descriptive statement.
From The Economics USA Series.
Prod-WEFA Dist-ANNCPB

USA C 47 MIN
16MM FILM OPTICAL SOUND
Presents a tour of the United States which shows it to be a land of many lands. Stresses the blending of varied cultural values into one nation by interspersing scenes of historical and geographical landmarks with those of people at work and play.
Prod-PANWA Dist-PANWA 1957

USA - Photography—A Series
16MM FILM, 3/4 OR 1/2 IN VIDEO
Looks at the lives and works of photographers Edward Weston and Dorothea Lange.
Prod-NET Dist-IU Prodn-KQEDTV 1966

Photography - Dorothea Lange - The Closer
Photography - Dorothea Lange - Under The Trees 030 MIN
Photography - The Daybooks Of Edward Weston - 030 MIN
Photography - The Daybooks Of Edward Weston - 030 MIN

USA - Seeds Of Change B 30 MIN
16MM FILM OPTICAL SOUND H-C A
Analyzes United States population trends from colonial days to the present. Focuses particularly on the baby boom era, the increasing number of senior citizens and the present and future problems to be faced in housing, rising crime, overcrowded school, unemployment and poverty.
From The Population Problem Series. No. 6
LC NO. FIA67-1519
Prod-NET Dist-IU 1967

USA Film C 17 MIN
16MM FILM, 3/4 OR 1/2 IN VIDEO H-C A
Offers a view of America by using time-lapse photography to compress a cross-country trip.
Prod-PHENIX Dist-PHENIX 1977

USA, The C 20 MIN
16MM FILM OPTICAL SOUND
A music and image tour of the United States, utilizing modern cutting and camera techniques to reveal the quality and character of the people. Includes sequences on New York, California, the Rocky Mountains and the Southwest.
LC NO. 70-711558
Prod-PANWA Dist-PANWA 1971

Usable Past, A C 60 MIN
3/4 OR 1/2 INCH VIDEO CASSETTE J-C A
Shows Alnwick Castle, whose 296 rooms have been occupied for 700 years by one of England's oldest and wealthiest families. Visits the Royal Scottish Museum in Edinburgh. Tours an estate outside London. Examines the ways institutions and individuals affect the past and the present.
From The Smithsonian World Series.
Prod-WETATV Dist-WETATV Prodn-SMITHS

USAC Champions B 30 MIN
16MM FILM OPTICAL SOUND
Shows exciting highlights from the USAC champions.
Prod-SFI Dist-SFI

USAF Aerospace 10th Anniversary C 7 MIN
16MM FILM OPTICAL SOUND
Traces the history of man's efforts to explore outer space. Discusses the overall significance of the space challenge and its present and future effect on man.
LC NO. 74-706294
Prod-USAF Dist-USNAC 1957

USAF Combat Photography - Southeast Asia C 27 MIN
3/4 OR 1/2 INCH VIDEO CASSETTE
Focuses on the advance of military photography since the Civil War. Explains the functions of combat photo groups like the 600th Photographic Squadron in Saigon. Shows air strikes filmed under enemy attack.
Prod-IHF Dist-IHF

USAF Flight Test School C 19 MIN
16MM FILM OPTICAL SOUND H-C
Describes the entrance requirements and curriculum of USAF Flight Test School at Edwards Air Force Base, California. Discusses the courses on aircraft performance data and on maneuver ability of the aircraft control system.
LC NO. FIE58-281
Prod-USDD Dist-USNAC 1957

USAF Maintenance Management Improvement Program, The B 20 MIN
16MM FILM OPTICAL SOUND A
Shows the processing of an emergency maintenance request at a typical air base to demonstrate how the maintenance management improvement program stretches the Air Force dollar and its buying power.
LC NO. FIE59-234
Prod-USDD Dist-USNAC 1958

USAF Veterinary Services C 35 MIN
16MM FILM OPTICAL SOUND C A
Portrays veterinary personnel participating in such military public health activities as food inspection, animal service, good service hygiene and sanitation, preventive medicine, nutrition and research.
Prod-KNI Dist-AMVMA

USARPAC C 29 MIN
16MM FILM OPTICAL SOUND
Shows the missions of American soldiers in the Far East.
From The Big Picture Series.
LC NO. 74-706299
Prod-USA Dist-USNAC 1968

USArt - The Gift Of Ourselves C 28 MIN
16MM FILM OPTICAL SOUND
Presents a survey of the arts in the United States for the past 200 years.
Prod-SEARS Dist-MTP Prodn-UNCMID 1975

Use And Abuse Of Diagnostic Measures In Emergencies C 15 MIN
3/4 OR 1/2 INCH VIDEO CASSETTE PRO
Considers in brief detail central venous pressure monitoring, arterial blood gas analysis and selective arteriography.
Prod-PRIMED Dist-PRIMED

Use And Abuse Of Force C 20 MIN
16MM FILM, 3/4 OR 1/2 IN VIDEO
Explores the whole phenomenon of violence in American history and the changing attitudes toward police use of force. Emphasizes that current attitudes demand an officer to use only the minimum amount of force necessary to accomplish a goal.
Prod-WORON Dist-MTI

Use And Abuse Of Intermittent Positive Pressure Breathing, The (2d Ed) C 9 MIN
3/4 OR 1/2 INCH VIDEO CASSETTE PRO
Provides information for determining when I.P.P.B. is indicated. Discusses the necessary elements in a standard prescription for I.P.P.B. including frequency, duration, pressure and medication.
Prod-UMICHM Dist-UMICHM 1974

Use And Abuse Of Interrogatories C 120 MIN
3/4 OR 1/2 INCH VIDEO CASSETTE PRO
Brings viewers up to date on how to, and how not to, use interrogatories.
Prod-CCEB Dist-ABACPE

Use And Care Of Axes And Knives C 10 MIN
16MM FILM, 3/4 OR 1/2 IN VIDEO I-H A
Shows how to select the right type of axe or knife for doing different tasks and demonstrates the correct use of each tool.
From The Survival In The Wilderness Series.
Prod-MORLAT Dist-SF 1967

Use And Care Of Basic Tools C 26 MIN
3/4 OR 1/2 INCH VIDEO CASSETTE IND
Gives a general introduction to the types of hand tools used on rigs and leases. Tells how to properly use and care for the tools.
Prod-UTEXPE Dist-UTEXPE 1973

Use And Care Of Basic Tools (Spanish) C 26 MIN
3/4 OR 1/2 INCH VIDEO CASSETTE IND
Gives a general introduction to the types of hand tools used on rigs and leases. Tells how to properly use and care for the tools.
Prod-UTEXPE Dist-UTEXPE 1973

Use And Care Of Books C 13 MIN
16MM FILM, 3/4 OR 1/2 IN VIDEO P-I
Uses cartoon animation to introduce various kinds of books, including library books and textbooks. Emphasizes ways of using, handling and protecting books.
From The School Citizenship Series.
LC NO. 79-707214
Prod-CENTRO Dist-CORF 1979

Use And Care Of Fiber Rope B 20 MIN
16MM FILM, 3/4 OR 1/2 IN VIDEO
Explains how to care for, inspect, and use fiber ropes. Compares sisal, manila and jute ropes and shows methods of splicing and eyeing. Issued in 1945 as a motion picture.
From The Shipbuilding - Rigging Series.
LC NO. 80-707055
Prod-USN Dist-USNAC 1980

Use And Care Of The Micrometer C 19 MIN
1/2 IN VIDEO CASSETTE BETA/VHS IND
See series title for descriptive statement.
From The Machine Shop - Measurement Series.
Prod-RMI Dist-RMI

Use And Care Of Wire Rope B 18 MIN
16MM FILM - 3/4 IN VIDEO
Describes the construction, use, and protective qualities of wire rope. Stresses the importance of careful handling to avoid kinks and explains seizing, the eye splice, frieze fitting, and the thimble. Issued in 1944 as a motion picture.
From The Shipbuilding Skills - Rigging Series.
LC NO. 80-707052
Prod-USN Dist-USNAC 1980

Use It In Good Health, Charlie C 27 MIN
16MM FILM, 3/4 OR 1/2 IN VIDEO J-H A
Probes problems of retirement and of the life of senior citizens. Offers suggestions for creating positive attitudes toward aging.

LC NO. 84-706041
Prod-CLYDVS Dist-AIMS 1983

Use It, Use It Up C 26 MIN
16MM FILM, 3/4 OR 1/2 IN VIDEO J-C A
Discusses products that are briefly used and then become waste. Shows how simple changes in domestic and commercial habits can have social and environmental effects.
Prod-UCEMC Dist-UCEMC 1975

Use Of A Boning Rod C 4 MIN
16MM FILM OPTICAL SOUND
Shows the importance of a boning rod in maintaining proper depth when laying a pipe.
LC NO. 76-701072
Prod-SAIT Dist-SAIT 1973

Use Of A Buret C 17 MIN
3/4 OR 1/2 INCH VIDEO CASSETTE
Examines the buret and its markings. Illustrates its cleaning, rinsing, filling and storing.
From The General Chemistry Laboratory Techniques Series.
Prod-UCEMC Dist-UCEMC

Use Of A Pipet C 14 MIN
3/4 OR 1/2 INCH VIDEO CASSETTE
Shows the volumetric pipet and its markings. Demonstrates how to manipulate it.
From The General Chemistry Laboratory Techniques Series.
Prod-UCEMC Dist-UCEMC

Use Of A Voltmeter B 38 MIN
1/2 IN VIDEO CASSETTE (BETA)
Demonstrates a procedure for setting up the multimeter (PSM-6) for use as a voltmeter. Shows how to connect the instrument into a DC circuit and how to adjust and read the meter for different values of voltage. Issued in 1970 as a motion picture.
LC NO. 79-707534
Prod-USAF Dist-USNAC 1979

Use Of Activity In The Evaluation And Treatment Process, The C
3/4 OR 1/2 INCH VIDEO CASSETTE
Shows an occupational therapist working with a group of patients in a psychiatric setting. Demonstrates the use of magazine collage as an evaluation and treatment modality. Provides several scenarios which can be used to illustrate patient pathology as well as interpersonal dynamics.
Prod-UWASH Dist-UWASH

Use Of Air Impact Cutter C 6 MIN
1/2 IN VIDEO CASSETTE BETA/VHS
Deals with auto body repair. Covers application and the use of an air impact cutter (Sioux) with upper and edging bits.
Prod-RMI Dist-RMI

Use Of Ammeter B 30 MIN
16MM FILM - 3/4 IN VIDEO
Demonstrates the procedure for setting up the multimeter for use as an ammeter. Shows the method of adjusting the meter to read values in the range of milliamperes to amperes and describes how to connect the meter in a DC circuit measure current. Issued in 1970 as a motion picture.
LC NO. 79-707530
Prod-USAF Dist-USNAC 1979

Use Of An In-Line Air File C 16 MIN
1/2 IN VIDEO CASSETTE BETA/VHS
Deals with auto body repair.
Prod-RMI Dist-RMI

Use Of Anticoagulants In Rodent Control C 11 MIN
16MM FILM OPTICAL SOUND H-C
Describes the use of various anticoagulants to kill rodents, advantages of these poisons, preparation of various baits, placement of the poisons to provide the most effective results, and precautionary measures.
LC NO. FIE61-18
Prod-USPHS Dist-USNAC 1961

Use Of Basic Layout Tools C 7 MIN
1/2 IN VIDEO CASSETTE BETA/VHS IND
See series title for descriptive statement.
From The Metal Fabrication - Hand Tool Identification, Demonstration And Applications Series.
Prod-RMI Dist-RMI

Use Of Bridging And Tracking To Overcome Apparent Resistance C 17 MIN
3/4 OR 1/2 INCH VIDEO CASSETTE
Teaches how to use bridging to change focus of therapy so client is able to understand therapist's message, explains how to use tracking to determine client's responses.
From The Multimodal Therapy Series.
Prod-RESPRC Dist-RESPRC

Use Of Chemical Agents C 22 MIN
16MM FILM, 3/4 OR 1/2 IN VIDEO
Discusses the use of various chemical agents including inert gas, tear gas or irritant gas. Examines situations in which chemical agents can be effectively used. Describes the four basic delivery systems.
Prod-WORON Dist-MTI

Use Of Computers In Complex Litigation—A Series
PRO
Explores situations in which computerized litigation support systems can assist attorneys in case preparation. Focuses on three areas - computerized litigation support systems, discovery of computer-based information and the admissibility of computer-generated evidence.
Prod-ABACPE Dist-ABACPE

Are Computerized Litigation Support Systems
Computer Evidence Law 135 MIN
Computerized Litigation Support Systems 231 MIN
Deposition Of A Computer Expert 046 MIN
Using The Computer And Preventing Its Abuse 067 MIN

Use Of Curare As A Diagnostic Test Of Myasthenia Gravis B 20 MIN
16MM FILM SILENT C T
Follows three normal individuals who have been subjected to curarization to produce artificial symptoms of myasthenia gravis. Five patients with varying degrees of true myasthenia gravis who were given from 1/10 to 1/40 of a normal dose of curare, developed marked exaggeration of the symptoms. This suggests that small doses of crare can be used as a diagnostic test in cases of myasthenia gravis.
Prod-PSUPCR Dist-PSUPCR 1944

Use Of Data Bank B 27 MIN
16MM FILM OPTICAL SOUND
See series title for descriptive statement.
From The Uses Of Media For Teaching Inquiry In The Secondary Social Studies Series.
Prod-HRAW Dist-HRAW

Use Of Disclaimers In Postmortem Planning C 54 MIN
3/4 OR 1/2 INCH VIDEO CASSETTE PRO
Provides a survey of the use of disclaimers in postmortem planning. Discusses severable property and pecuniary or fractional disclaimers.
From The Postmortem Tax Planning After ERTA Series.
Prod-ABACPE Dist-ABACPE

Use Of Dividing Head And Rotary Table C
3/4 OR 1/2 INCH VIDEO CASSETTE
See series title for descriptive statement.
From The Milling And Tool Sharpening Series.
Prod-VTRI Dist-VTRI

Use Of Dividing Head And Rotary Table C 15 MIN
3/4 OR 1/2 INCH VIDEO CASSETTE
See series title for descriptive statement.
From The Machine Technology IV - Milling Series
Prod-CAMB Dist-CAMB

Use Of Dividing Head And Rotary Table C 15 MIN
3/4 OR 1/2 INCH VIDEO CASSETTE IND
See series title for descriptive statement.
From The Machining And The Operation Of Machine Tools, Module 4 - Milling And Tool..Series.
Prod-LEIKID Dist-LEIKID

Use Of Dividing Head And Rotary Table (Spanish) C
3/4 OR 1/2 INCH VIDEO CASSETTE
See series title for descriptive statement.
From The Milling And Tool Sharpening (Spanish) Series.
Prod-VTRI Dist-VTRI

Use Of Face Milling Cutters On The Horizontal Mill C
3/4 OR 1/2 INCH VIDEO CASSETTE
See series title for descriptive statement.
From The Milling And Tool Sharpening Series.
Prod-VTRI Dist-VTRI

Use Of Face Milling Cutters On The Horizontal Mill C 15 MIN
3/4 OR 1/2 INCH VIDEO CASSETTE
See series title for descriptive statement.
From The Machine Technology IV - Milling Series
Prod-CAMB Dist-CAMB

Use Of Face Milling Cutters On The Horizontal Mill (Spanish) C
3/4 OR 1/2 INCH VIDEO CASSETTE
See series title for descriptive statement.
From The Milling And Tool Sharpening (Spanish) Series.
Prod-VTRI Dist-VTRI

Use Of Filmstrips B 27 MIN
16MM FILM OPTICAL SOUND
See series title for descriptive statement.
From The Uses Of Media For Teaching Inquiry In The Secondary Social Studies Series.
Prod-HRAW Dist-HRAW

Use Of Foam C
3/4 OR 1/2 INCH VIDEO CASSETTE IND
Demonstrates how easily foam extinguishes a diesel fire, explains how foam works, different types available, fixed and portable systems and proper technique.
From The Marine Firefighting Series. Pt 4
Prod-GPCV Dist-GPCV

Use Of Foam (Italian) C
3/4 OR 1/2 INCH VIDEO CASSETTE IND
Demonstrates how easily foam extinguishes a diesel fire, explains how foam works, different types available, fixed and portable systems and proper technique.
From The Marine Firefighting Series. Pt 4
Prod-GPCV Dist-GPCV

Use Of Foam (Korean) C
3/4 OR 1/2 INCH VIDEO CASSETTE IND
Demonstrates how easily foam extinguishes a diesel fire, explains how foam works, different types available, fixed and portable systems and proper technique.
From The Marine Firefighting Series. Pt 4
Prod-GPCV Dist-GPCV

Use Of Fossils And The Geological Time Scale C 43 MIN
3/4 OR 1/2 INCH VIDEO CASSETTE IND
See series title for descriptive statement.
From The Basic Geology Series.
Prod-GPCV Dist-GPCV

Use Of Frame Gauges C 9 MIN
1/2 IN VIDEO CASSETTE BETA/VHS
Deals with auto body repair. Explains and demonstrates the chain and strap drop type, using a Guy Chart and Buske as examples.
Prod-RMI Dist-RMI

Use Of Fully Crimpable Connectors And Crimping Tools C 26 MIN
1/2 IN VIDEO CASSETTE (BETA)
Demonstrates the use of crimping tools for replacing broken or bent pins in coaxial cable plugs. Shows how to remove defective connectors, strip wire, and crimp and install new pins. Issued in 1967 as a motion picture.
LC NO. 79-707531
Prod-USAF Dist-USNAC 1979

Use Of General Surgical Facilities By The Dental Service C 25 MIN
16MM FILM OPTICAL SOUND
Familiarizes the clinical dentist with general operating room procedures.
LC NO. 74-706302
Prod-USVA Dist-USNAC 1962

Use Of Handcuffs, The C 8 MIN
16MM FILM OPTICAL SOUND H-C
Helps police officers become familiar with the correct way to search and handcuff a suspect. Uses dramatizations to show what happens when incorrect techniques are used.
LC NO. 75-701987
Prod-MCCRNE Dist-MCCRNE 1975

Use Of Landscapes In A Sketch, The C 29 MIN
3/4 INCH VIDEO CASSETTE C A
Studies how to draw landscapes. Illustrates that the shape of the land can be as important as the growth of the land. Shows the relationship between buildings and a landscape.
From The Sketching Techniques Series. Lesson 11
Prod-COAST Dist-CDTEL

Use Of Layout Tools In Machine Technology C 15 MIN
3/4 OR 1/2 INCH VIDEO CASSETTE
See series title for descriptive statement.
From The Machine Technology II - Engine Lathe Accessories Series.
Prod-CAMB Dist-CAMB

Use Of Layout Tools In Machine Technology, The C
3/4 OR 1/2 INCH VIDEO CASSETTE
See series title for descriptive statement.
From The Basic Machine Technology Series.
Prod-VTRI Dist-VTRI

Use Of Layout Tools In Machine Technology, The (Spanish) C
3/4 OR 1/2 INCH VIDEO CASSETTE
See series title for descriptive statement.
From The Basic Machine Technology (Spanish) Series.
Prod-VTRI Dist-VTRI

Use Of Layout Tools In Machine Technology, The C 15 MIN
3/4 OR 1/2 INCH VIDEO CASSETTE IND
See series title for descriptive statement.
From The Machining And The Operation Of Machine Tools, Module 1 - Basic Machine Technology Series.
Prod-LEIKID Dist-LEIKID

Use Of Measuring Tools In Machine Technology ,The C 15 MIN
3/4 OR 1/2 INCH VIDEO CASSETTE
See series title for descriptive statement.
From The Machine Technology II - Engine Lathe Accessories Series.
Prod-CAMB Dist-CAMB

Use Of Measuring Tools In Machine Technology, The C
3/4 OR 1/2 INCH VIDEO CASSETTE
See series title for descriptive statement.
From The Basic Machine Technology Series.
Prod-VTRI Dist-VTRI

Use Of Measuring Tools In Machine Technology, The C 15 MIN
3/4 OR 1/2 INCH VIDEO CASSETTE IND
See series title for descriptive statement.
From The Machining And The Operation Of Machine Tools, Module 1 - Basic Machine Technology Series.
Prod-LEIKID Dist-LEIKID

Use Of Measuring Tools In Machine Technology, The (Spanish) C
3/4 OR 1/2 INCH VIDEO CASSETTE
See series title for descriptive statement.
From The Basic Machine Technology (Spanish) Series.
Prod-VTRI Dist-VTRI

Use Of Metal Conditioners With Lead And Plastic Fill C 15 MIN
1/2 IN VIDEO CASSETTE BETA/VHS
Deals with auto body repair. Shows the advantages and limitations of etching liquids.
Prod-RMI Dist-RMI

Use Of Motion (Verbs) To Create Impression B 30 MIN
2 INCH VIDEOTAPE J-H
Emphasizes the importance of motion in creating clearly defined mental images. (Broadcast quality)

From The English Composition Series. DESCRIPTI3(9
Prod-GRETVO Dist-GPITVL Prodn-KUHTTV

Use Of Ohmmeter B 37 MIN
16MM FILM - 1/2 IN VIDEO
Demonstrates the procedure for setting up the PSM-6 multimeter for use as an ohmmeter. Tells how to adjust the range selector switch for the most accurate reading of a resistor and stresses the precautionary steps for using the meter. Issued in 1970 as a motion picture.
LC NO. 79-707532
Prod-USAF Dist-USNAC 1979

Use Of Oscilloscope B 21 MIN
16MM FILM, 3/4 OR 1/2 IN VIDEO
Shows waveshapes, amplitudes and phase relationships on an oscilloscope screen. Shows the general operation of the oscilloscope and how to use it to find frequency and amplitude.
Prod-USAF Dist-USNAC

Use Of Overlays, The B 10 MIN
16MM FILM OPTICAL SOUND
Deals with various aspects of a civil lawsuit involving an automobile accident case. Illustrates the use of overlays in the trial.
From The Civil Advocates Series, No. 18 Series.
LC NO. 72-714026
Prod-ATLA Dist-RPATLF 1967

Use Of Picture Cards B 22 MIN
16MM FILM OPTICAL SOUND C A
Develops the use of picture cards as a teaching tool to be used in an inquiry approach to the teaching of social studies at the secondary level.
From The Uses Of Media For Teaching Inquiry In The Social Studies Series.
Prod-HRAW Dist-HRAW 1969

Use Of Plain And Side Milling Cutters On The Horizontal Milling Machine C
3/4 OR 1/2 INCH VIDEO CASSETTE
See series title for descriptive statement.
From The Milling And Tool Sharpening Series.
Prod-VTRI Dist-VTRI

Use Of Plain And Side Milling Cutters On The Horizontal Milling Machine C 15 MIN
3/4 OR 1/2 INCH VIDEO CASSETTE
See series title for descriptive statement.
From The Machine Technology IV - Milling Series
Prod-CAMB Dist-CAMB

Use Of Plain And Side Milling Cutters On The Horizontal Milling Machine C 15 MIN
3/4 OR 1/2 INCH VIDEO CASSETTE IND
See series title for descriptive statement.
From The Machining And The Operation Of Machine Tools, Module 4 - Milling And Tool..Series.
Prod-LEIKID Dist-LEIKID

Use Of Plain And Side Milling Cutters On The Horizontal Milling Machine (Spanish) C
3/4 OR 1/2 INCH VIDEO CASSETTE
See series title for descriptive statement.
From The Milling And Tool Sharpening (Spanish) Series.
Prod-VTRI Dist-VTRI

Use Of Plantar Skin In Correcting A Severe Finger Contracture, The C 15 MIN
16MM FILM OPTICAL SOUND
Shows in detail the release of a 90 degree flexion contracture at the proximal interphalangeal joint in the long finger. Illustrates immediate and long term post-operative results.
LC NO. 75-702320
Prod-EATONL Dist-EATONL 1970

Use Of Plastic Sealants In Preventive Dentistry, The C 13 MIN
3/4 OR 1/2 INCH VIDEO CASSETTE PRO
Uses typodont models to demonstrate the use of sealants to eradicate deep fissures and grooves in posterior teeth. Shows the use of two sealants, one using ultraviolet light to bring about polymerization and the other using a chemical catalyst to convert the monomer.
Prod-VADTC Dist-USNAC 1978

Use Of PNF In The Treatment Of An Adult With Limb-Girdle Muscular Dystrophy, The B 38 MIN
3/4 OR 1/2 INCH VIDEO CASSETTE
Demonstrates the various combinations of PNF strengthening techniques and patterns applied within a motor developmental framework.
Prod-BU Dist-BU

Use Of Positive Reinforcement C 49 MIN
3/4 OR 1/2 INCH VIDEO CASSETTE T
Presents six humanistic uses of reinforcement. Demonstrates some of the uses.
From The Learning And Liking It Series.
Prod-MSU Dist-MSU

Use Of Positioning And Adaptive Equipment In Management Of Disorders of Posture And Tone C
3/4 OR 1/2 INCH VIDEO CASSETTE
Demonstrates positioning and adaptive equipment used for children and adults with physical disabilities. Includes positioning in sidelying, prone, sitting and standing.
Prod-VALHAL Dist-VALHAL

Use Of Precision Tools, No. 1 C 30 MIN
2 INCH VIDEOTAPE IND
Examines a scale and shows how to read the Vernier caliper.
From The Basic Machine Shop Practices Series.
Prod-VTETV Dist-GPITVL

Use Of Precision Tools, No. 2 C 30 MIN
2 INCH VIDEOTAPE IND
Illustrates reading the micrometer and dial indicators.
From The Basic Machine Shop Practices Series.
Prod-VTETV Dist-GPITVL

Use Of Precision Tools, No. 3 C 30 MIN
2 INCH VIDEOTAPE IND
Illustrates small tools used in checking work.
From The Basic Machine Shop Practices Series.
Prod-VTETV Dist-GPITVL

Use Of Pressure-Indicating Paste During Delivery Of Dentures C 15 MIN
16MM FILM, 3/4 OR 1/2 IN VIDEO
Shows the use of pressure-indicating pastes when delivering newly made dentures to the patient.
Prod-VADTC Dist-AMDA 1970

Use Of Questions To Structure The Negotiation, The C 24 MIN
3/4 OR 1/2 INCH VIDEO CASSETTE
See series title for descriptive statement.
From The Art Of Negotiating Series.
Prod-DELTAK Dist-DELTAK

Use Of Recordings B 27 MIN
16MM FILM OPTICAL SOUND C A
Develops the use of recordings as a teaching tool to be used in an inquiry approach to the teaching of social studies at the secondary level.
From The Uses Of Media For Teaching Inquiry In The Social Studies Series.
Prod-HRAW Dist-HRAW 1969

Use Of Resonant Sections B 22 MIN
1/2 IN VIDEO CASSETTE (BETA)
Shows the use of resonant sections of transmission lines as circuit elements. Develops the lecher line oscillator and explains how a shortened quarter wavelength section of transmission line can be used as a parallel resonant circuit. Issued in 1970 as a motion picture.
LC NO. 79-707533
Prod-USAF Dist-USNAC 1979

Use Of Sealants In Preventive Dentistry, The C 13 MIN
16MM FILM OPTICAL SOUND PRO
Uses typodont models to demonstrate the use of sealants to eradicate deep fissures and grooves in posterior teeth. Shows the use of two sealants, one using ultraviolet light to bring about polymerization and the other using a chemical catalyst to convert the monomer.
LC NO. 79-700990
Prod-VADTC Dist-USNAC 1978

Use Of Sickle Scalers C 21 MIN
3/4 INCH VIDEO CASSETTE PRO
Demonstrates how to use straignt and hooked sickle scalers on anterior teeth and contra-angle scalers on posterior teeth in removal of calculus from the supragingival area.
From The Scaling Techniques Series. No. 5
LC NO. 77-706010
Prod-UTENN Dist-USNAC 1976

Use Of Side Rails C 22 MIN
16MM FILM OPTICAL SOUND
Demonstrates the need for side rails and explains how to use them safely and effectively. Shows how to handle complaints and requests of the patients.
From The Nurse's Aide, Orderly and Attendant Series.
LC NO. 75-704831
Prod-COPI Dist-COPI 1969

Use Of Side Rails C 9 MIN
3/4 INCH VIDEO CASSETTE H-C A
Demonstrates the need for side rails and explains how to use them safely and effectively. Shows how to handle complaints and requests of the patients.
From The Nurse's Aide, Orderly And Attendant Series.
Prod-COPI Dist-COPI 1969

Use Of Simulation Games B 23 MIN
16MM FILM OPTICAL SOUND C A
Develops the use of simulation games as a teaching tool to be used in the inquiry approach to the teaching of social studies at the secondary level.
From The Uses Of Media For Teaching Inquiry In The Social Studies Series.
Prod-HRAW Dist-HRAW 1969

Use Of Soldering Coppers B 8 MIN
16MM FILM, 3/4 OR 1/2 IN VIDEO
Describes the techniques of soft soldering in a sequence of operations, including proper selection and tinning of the copper, correct heating, cleaning and flexing the surfaces to be soldered and the method of transferring sufficient heat from the copper.
Prod-USN Dist-USNAC 1954

Use Of Space And Equipment, Pt 1 C 30 MIN
3/4 INCH VIDEO CASSETTE A
See series title for descriptive statement.
From The Day Care Series.
Prod-MDCPB Dist-MDCPB

Use Of Space And Equipment, Pt 2 C 30 MIN
3/4 INCH VIDEO CASSETTE A
See series title for descriptive statement.
From The Day Care Series.
Prod-MDCPB Dist-MDCPB

Use Of Split Thickness Skin Grafts In Contractures Of The Elbow, The C 10 MIN
16MM FILM OPTICAL SOUND
Demonstrates the development of a very severe soft tissue, muscular and capsular contracture at the elbow in a burned patient. Illustrates the functional and cosmetic results obtained by this procedure.
LC NO. 75-702319
Prod-EATONL Dist-EATONL 1967

Use Of Surgical Instruments C 19 MIN
16MM FILM OPTICAL SOUND PRO
Defines the various instruments and their functions in the surgical procedures. Describes a variety of basic surgical maneuvers common to practically all operations, such as cutting, dissecting, grasping with tissue forceps, clamping with hemostats, retracting and suturing.
Prod-ACYDGD Dist-ACY 1967

Use Of Synthetic Knitted Mesh In Hernia Repair, The C 27 MIN
16MM FILM OPTICAL SOUND PRO
Explains that knitted mesh made of either nylon or dacron has been used for the past two years for the repair of recurrent hernias in selected patients. Illustrates the technique of the use of this material in two patients.
Prod-ACYDGD Dist-ACY 1958

Use Of T Square And Triangles B 23 MIN
16MM FILM OPTICAL SOUND C A
Shows the correct use of T-squares and triangles.
Prod-PUAVC Dist-PUAVC 1959

Use Of The Baton - The Lamb Method C 22 MIN
16MM FILM, 3/4 OR 1/2 IN VIDEO PRO
Teaches service baton self-defense techniques based on the system developed by Arthur Lamb of the Boston Police Department.
Prod-HAR Dist-MTI Prodn-BAY 1977

Use Of The Condom Appliance For The Incontiment Patient C 9 MIN
16MM FILM OPTICAL SOUND
Presents in detail the assembly and application of the condom appliance, which provides a means whereby the incontinent male patient can be kept dry without the use of an indwelling catheter.
LC NO. 74-705886
Prod-USPHS Dist-USNAC 1966

Use Of The Condom Catheter For Incontinence C 10 MIN
3/4 OR 1/2 INCH VIDEO CASSETTE
Describes cleansing and skin preparation, use of adhesive liner and application of condom. Discusses solutions for problems with fit and skin irritation, and describes leg bag and night bag.
LC NO. 82-706232
Prod-VAMCMM Dist-USNAC 1981

Use Of The Explorer C 15 MIN
3/4 INCH VIDEO CASSETTE PRO
Demonstrates how to use an explorer stroke in the detection of calculus and caries and in examination of the texture, contour and character of tooth surfaces.
From The Scaling Techniques Series. No. 4
LC NO. 77-706012
Prod-UTENN Dist-USNAC 1976

Use Of The Face Milling Cutter On The Horizontal Mill C 15 MIN
3/4 OR 1/2 INCH VIDEO CASSETTE IND
See series title for descriptive statement.
From The Machining And The Operation Of Machine tools, Module 4 - Milling And Tool..Series.
Prod-LEIKID Dist-LEIKID

Use Of The Gracey Curet No. 07-08 C 21 MIN
3/4 INCH VIDEO CASSETTE PRO
Demonstrates how to use the gracey curet no. 07-08 in subgingival scaling and root planing. Discusses curettage which is not generally practiced by hygiene students.
From The Scaling Techniques Series. No. 6
LC NO. 77-706013
Prod-UTENN Dist-USNAC 1976

Use Of The Gracey Curet No. 11-12 C 13 MIN
3/4 INCH VIDEO CASSETTE PRO
Demonstrates how to use the gracey curet no. 11-12 in scaling mesial surfaces of posterior teeth.
From The Scaling Techniques Series. No. 7
LC NO. 77-706014
Prod-UTENN Dist-USNAC 1976

Use Of The Gracey Curet No. 13-14 C 12 MIN
3/4 INCH VIDEO CASSETTE PRO
Demonstrates how to use the gracey curet no. 13-14 in scaling distal surfaces of posterior teeth.
From The Scaling Techniques Series. No. 8
LC NO. 77-706015
Prod-UTENN Dist-USNAC 1976

Use Of The Malleable Mesh In The Reduction And Fixation Of Jaw Fractures C 11 MIN
16MM FILM OPTICAL SOUND
Demonstrates the adaptation and fixation of the mesh, used when teeth need secondary support, on a mannequin and in the operating room.
LC NO. 74-705888
Prod-USVA Dist-USNAC 1969

Use Of The Normal Value Algorithm C 50 MIN
3/4 OR 1/2 INCH VIDEO CASSETTE
Introduces evaluations using the nv algorithm, free and bound variables, conditionals, logic values.
From The Computer Languages - Pt 1 Series.
Prod-MIOT Dist-MIOT

Use Of The Oscilloscope C 30 MIN
3/4 OR 1/2 INCH VIDEO CASSETTE IND

Outlines some of the precautions and procedures to observe for successful diagnosis. Continues test procedure, covering cylinder timing, coil and condenser testing and dwell variation. Explains test procedures for secondary resistance.
From The Automotive Oscilloscope Series. Lesson 2
Prod-LEIKID Dist-LEIKID

Use Of The Periodontal Probe C 11 MIN
3/4 INCH VIDEO CASSETTE PRO
Demonstrates how to use the periodontal probe instrument in examining the shape and dimensions of the gingival sulcus and periodontal pockets.
From The Scaling Techniques Series. No. 9
LC NO. 77-706023
Prod-UTENN Dist-USNAC 1976

Use Of The Pneumatic Otoscope C 12 MIN
16MM FILM - 3/4 IN VIDEO
Demonstrates the use of the pneumatic otoscope and shows views of the human ear through the otoscope while describing conditions observed.
LC NO. 80-706409
Prod-NMAC Dist-USNAC 1978

Use Of The Polygraph In Investigations B 26 MIN
16MM FILM OPTICAL SOUND
Describes the use of the polygraph in investigations.
LC NO. 74-706303
Prod-USA Dist-USNAC 1967

Use Of The Problem In Teaching B 28 MIN
16MM FILM OPTICAL SOUND
An air university instructor employs a clever method of impressing his students with the principles and techniques of using the problem as an effective teaching aid.
LC NO. FIE58-329
Prod-USAF Dist-USNAC 1958

Use Of The Resistance Spot Welder C 13 MIN
1/2 IN VIDEO CASSETTE BETA/VHS
Deals with auto body repair.
Prod-RMI Dist-RMI

Use Of The Revocable Trust In Estate Planning, The C 150 MIN
3/4 OR 1/2 INCH VIDEO CASSETTE PRO
Discusses the pros and cons of using a revocable intervivos trust. Considers tax consequences, community property and choice of trustee.
Prod-ABACPE Dist-ABACPE

Use Of The Scribble Technique In Art Therapy As A Psychiatric Treatment Adjunct C 60 MIN
3/4 OR 1/2 INCH VIDEO CASSETTE
Demonstrates the scribble technique with a woman in her 30s as a tool to elicit repressed material and free associations for working-through. Shows how the patient is helped to make her own connections through questions rather than interpretations. Presents the step-by-step use of the scribble technique and its use as a psychotherapeutic adjunct in clincal practice.
From The Art Therapy Series.
Prod-HEMUL Dist-HEMUL

Use Of The Short Baton C 20 MIN
16MM FILM, 3/4 OR 1/2 IN VIDEO
Discusses the use of the short baton by police officers. Presents the baton as an acceptable, publicly-approved, second-level weapon. Stresses the need for such equipment in the police arsenal.
Prod-WORON Dist-MTI

Use Of The Torque Wrench C 4 MIN
16MM FILM, 3/4 OR 1/2 IN VIDEO J-C A
See series title for descriptive statement.
From The Power Mechanics Series.
Prod-THIOKL Dist-CAROUF

Use Of The Triple Beam Balance B 6 MIN
16MM FILM OPTICAL SOUND H-C
Shows the proper use of the triple beam balance in weighing chemicals. Stresses the care of the balance and the reading of the scales.
Prod-PUAVC Dist-PUAVC 1958

Use Of The Triple Beam Balance C 11 MIN
16MM FILM, 3/4 OR 1/2 IN VIDEO H-C
Shows correct tecnnique in weighing out specified amounts of solids and a specified volume of a liquid. Emphasizes careful handling of the balance and materials and accuracy in reading the weights obtained.
From The Basic Laboratory Techniques In Chemistry Series.
Prod-SCHLAT Dist-LUF

Use Of The Wire Feed Welder C 18 MIN
1/2 IN VIDEO CASSETTE BETA/VHS
Deals with auto body repair.
Prod-RMI Dist-RMI

Use Of Thickness Gauges C 10 MIN
16MM FILM, 3/4 OR 1/2 IN VIDEO J-C A
See series title for descriptive statement.
From The Power Mechanics Series.
Prod-THIOKL Dist-CAROUF

Use Of Transparencies B 27 MIN
16MM FILM OPTICAL SOUND
See series title for descriptive statement.
From The Uses Of Media For Teaching Inquiry In The Secondary Social Studies Series.
Prod-HRAW Dist-HRAW

Use Of Turning Frames B 25 MIN
16MM FILM OPTICAL SOUND
Teaches nursing personnel the clinical requirement for and proper use of turning frames.
LC NO. 74-705890
Prod-USA Dist-USNAC 1966

Use Of Visitation Logs In Permanency Planning C 15 MIN
3/4 OR 1/2 INCH VIDEO CASSETTE
Demonstrates the use of visitation logs in the coordination of visit planning and the enhancement of the working relationship of the social practitioner, natural parent and foster parent.
Prod-UWISC Dist-UWISC 1981

Use Of Voltmeter B 38 MIN
16MM FILM OPTICAL SOUND
Demonstrates the proper procedure for setting up the multimeter (PSM-6) for use of a voltmeter. Shows how to connect the instrument into a DC circuit and how to adjust and read the meter for different values of voltage. Stresses safety precautions. (Kinescope)
LC NO. 74-705891
Prod-USAF Dist-USNAC 1970

Use Of Warm Water Irrigators C 8 MIN
16MM FILM, 3/4 OR 1/2 IN VIDEO
Illustrates the proper use of the water irrigating device, both the tank type and the faucet type. Explains to the patient the benefits of water irrigation, but emphasizes that irrigation is only an additional aid to oral hygiene and does not replace proper flossing and brushing techniques.
Prod-PRORE Dist-PRORE

Use Of Your Portable Auto Syringe Pump C 26 MIN
3/4 INCH VIDEO CASSETTE
Demonstrates how to use the auto syringe pump.
Prod-UTAHTI Dist-UTAHTI

Use Your Ears C 9 MIN
16MM FILM, 3/4 OR 1/2 IN VIDEO P-I
Promotes an understanding and appreciation for the variety of sounds in everyday life, such as the sound of the police whistle, the roar of the ocean and the sound of rock and roll music.
Prod-BARR Dist-BARR Prodn-MCDOCR 1974

Use Your Ears C 15 MIN
2 INCH VIDEOTAPE P
Provides an enrichment program in the community arts area by using the sense of listening.
From The Word Magic (2nd Ed) Series.
Prod-CVETVC Dist-GPITVL

Use Your Eyes C 10 MIN
16MM FILM, 3/4 OR 1/2 IN VIDEO P-I
Shows young people exploring and discovering the wonders of a meadow and their own backyard, the details of common household items and the many elements that make up their environment. Uses close-up photography.
Prod-BARR Dist-BARR 1973

Use Your Imagination C 4 MIN
16MM FILM, 3/4 OR 1/2 IN VIDEO K-I
Emphasizes the use of imagination as a tool. Presents the imagination as a tool to making things happen and to keep from being bored.
From The Most Important Person - Creative Expression Series.
Prod-EBEC Dist-EBEC 1972

Use Your Voice To Sing C 15 MIN
3/4 OR 1/2 INCH VIDEO CASSETTE P-I
Discusses various aspects of singing.
From The Music And Me Series.
Prod-WDCNTV Dist-AITECH 1979

Used Cars - How To Find Them And Buy Them C
3/4 OR 1/2 INCH VIDEO CASSETTE
Teaches the skills of finding and evaluating used cars. Includes information on financing and insurance.
Prod-EDUACT Dist-EDUACT

Useful Knots For Boatmen C 25 MIN
16MM FILM, 3/4 OR 1/2 IN VIDEO
Discusses knots most commonly used by boat personnel.
LC NO. 80-707064
Prod-USCG Dist-USNAC 1980

Useful Propeller C 11 MIN
16MM FILM, 3/4 OR 1/2 IN VIDEO P-I
Reveals that during a hot spell, Boy fantasizes about ways to cool off, first designing a fan, then experimenting with homemade devices that make use of airpower to create suction. Shows that in the process he creates a vacuum cleaner. Develops the concept of using air pressure and vacuums to do various kinds of work.
From The Inventive Child Series.
Prod-POLSKI Dist-EBEC 1983

Useless Jug, The C 20 MIN
16MM FILM OPTICAL SOUND K-P
Relates the story of an unruly and ill-tempered jug that didn't become useful until it was broken into many pieces.
From The Animatoons Series.
LC NO. FIA68-1531
Prod-ANTONS Dist-RADTV 1968

User And The Database, The C 25 MIN
16MM FILM, 3/4 OR 1/2 IN VIDEO
Depicts the role of a database for the control and scheduling of materials, one of five databases used by a construction firm. Shows the problem of getting access to data in the field as opposed to trained personnel using equipment withing computing facilities.
Prod-OPENU Dist-MEDIAG Prodn-BBCTV 1980

User Needs And Industrial Innovation C 42 MIN
3/4 OR 1/2 INCH VIDEO CASSETTE
Discusses how to transfer an accurate understanding of user need to the manufacturer.
From The Management Of Technological Innovation Series.
Prod-MIOT Dist-MIOT

User Responsibilities In Information Management–A Series

Focuses on the user's activities in four vital areas of information management, communication, planning, implementation and ongoing support.
Prod-DELTAK Dist-DELTAK

Communicating With MIS 045 MIN
Participating In Implementation 045 MIN
Planning And Selecting High Payoff Applications 045 MIN
Supporting Ongoing Operations 045 MIN

User-Defined Data Types C 30 MIN
3/4 OR 1/2 INCH VIDEO CASSETTE H-C A
Introduces user-defined enumerated data type in Pascal. Shows examples involving assignment, loop control, CASE selectors and IF-THEN. Discusses input/output limitations, and built-in functions SUCC, PRED for manipulating enumerated data elements.
From The Pascal, Pt 1 - Beginning Pascal Series.
LC NO. 81-706049
Prod-COLOSU Dist-COLOSU 1980

User-Directed Information Systems–A Series

Provides an overview of advanced technology concepts in data processing and communications which affect the business environment. Emphasizes the need for users to understand technological advances and to participate when changes occur within data processing and communications.
Prod-DELTAK Dist-DELTAK

Changing Technology And The Role Of The User 020 MIN
Managing And Using The Data Resource 020 MIN
Network Concepts For Users 020 MIN

Users - Losers C 20 MIN
16MM FILM, 3/4 OR 1/2 IN VIDEO I-J
Tells about a boy in junior high school who tries to find acceptance at school by taking marihuana and pills. Shows an older boy, a former user, giving him the facts about narcotics and drug abuse.
Prod-DAVP Dist-AIMS 1971

Uses And Limitations Of Cost Accounting Information C 60 MIN
3/4 OR 1/2 INCH VIDEO CASSETTE C
Discusses principles of cost accounting, implicit assumptions, limitations, fixed and variable costs, and marginal and average costs, with examples.
From The Engineering Economic Analysis - A Concentrated Short Course Series.
Prod-UMAEEE Dist-AMCEE

Uses And Limitations Of Discounted Cash Flow Techniques C 60 MIN
3/4 OR 1/2 INCH VIDEO CASSETTE C
Covers projects with unequal durations, economic life, and risk and uncertainty.
From The Engineering Economic Analysis - A Concentrated Short Course Series.
Prod-UMAEEE Dist-AMCEE

Uses And Limitations Of The Rate Of Return C 60 MIN
3/4 OR 1/2 INCH VIDEO CASSETTE C
Covers calculation procedures, multiple rates of return, implicit and explicit reinvestment rates, and example problems on replacement analysis.
From The Engineering Economic Analysis - A Concentrated Short Course Series.
Prod-UMAEEE Dist-AMCEE

Uses Of Blood C 27 MIN
16MM FILM, 3/4 OR 1/2 IN VIDEO C A
Discusses the many types of research done on blood donated to Britain's National Blood Transfusion Service.
From The Perspective Series.
Prod-LONTVS Dist-STNFLD

Uses Of Control Charts C 50 MIN
3/4 OR 1/2 INCH VIDEO CASSETTE
See series title for descriptive statement.
From The Deming Video Tapes - Quality, Productivity And The Competitive...Series.
Prod-MIOT Dist-SME

Uses Of Control Charts/Advantages Of Achieving Statistical Control C
3/4 OR 1/2 INCH VIDEO CASSETTE
See series title for descriptive statement.
From The Deming Videotapes - Quality, Productivity, And Competitive...Series.
Prod-MIOT Dist-MIOT

Uses Of Light B 30 MIN
2 INCH VIDEOTAPE J
See series title for descriptive statement.
From The Investigating The World Of Science, Unit 1 - Matter And Energy Series.
Prod-MPATI Dist-GPITVL

Uses Of Media For Teaching Inquiry In The Social Studies–A Series
C A
Describes the use of three different teaching tools that can be used in the inquiry approach to the teaching of social studies at the secondary level.
Prod-HRAW Dist-HRAW 1969

Use Of Data Bank 27 MIN
Use Of Filmstrips 27 MIN
Use Of Picture Cards 22 MIN
Use Of Recordings 27 MIN
Use Of Simulation Games 23 MIN
Use Of Transparencies 27 MIN

Uses Of Motivation In Building A Championship Football Program C 27 MIN
16MM FILM, 3/4 OR 1/2 IN VIDEO T
Presents coach Joe Paterno explaining how to build a sound football program around empathy with students, parents, faculty and community. Demonstrates how to best utilize assistant coaches and how to motivate student athletes by developing pride, morale and loyalty.
From The Joe Paterno - Coaching Winning Football Series.
Prod-UNIDIM Dist-EBEC 1982

Uses Of Penicillins - Old And New B 40 MIN
16MM FILM OPTICAL SOUND PRO
Describes one observer's experiences with methicillin, oxacillin, ampicillin and cephalosporin. Discusses the use of penicillin G in gram-negative injections.
From The Boston Medical Reports Series.
LC NO. 74-705893
Prod-NMAC Dist-NMAC 1964

Uses Of Resonant Sections B 22 MIN
16MM FILM OPTICAL SOUND
Shows the use of resonant sections of transmission lines and circuit elements. Develops the Lecher line oscillator and explains how a shorted quarter wavelength section of transmission line can be used as a parallel resonant circuit. (Kinescope)
LC NO. 74-705894
Prod-USAF Dist-USNAC

Uses Of The Mouthparts Of The Orthoptera During Feeding B 8 MIN
16MM FILM OPTICAL SOUND H-C A
Uses close-ups and slow motion to show the mouthparts at work. Illustrates and explains the forms and functions of the mouthparts.
LC NO. FIA65-429
Prod-WSU Dist-WSU 1960

Usher's Syndrome - Retinitis Pigmentosa And Deafness C 20 MIN
16MM FILM, 3/4 OR 1/2 IN VIDEO PRO
Discusses progressive blindness with congenital hearing impairment, ways of diagnosing the condition, the importance of genetic counseling. Captioned or uncaptioned.
Prod-GALCO Dist-GALCO 1978

Using A Boring Bar Between Centers - Work Held On Carriage B 22 MIN
16MM FILM - 3/4 IN VIDEO
Shows how to set up a boring bar between centers of a lathe, how to clamp an irregular workpiece on a lathe carriage, how to mount, adjust and use a boring bar between centers of the lathe and how to align workpiece center with the lathe centerline. Issued in 1944 as a motion picture.
From The Machine Shop Work - Operations On The Engine Lathe Series. No. 16
LC NO. 79-707055
Prod-USOE Dist-USNAC Prodn-ATLAS 1979

Using A Boring Head C 22 MIN
1/2 IN VIDEO CASSETTE BETA/VHS IND
See series title for descriptive statement.
From The Machine Shop - Milling Machine Series.
Prod-RMI Dist-RMI

Using A Compass C 10 MIN
16MM FILM, 3/4 OR 1/2 IN VIDEO I-H A
Shows types of compasses and how to use the compass with a map. Explains how to follow a bearing, to estimate distance by tally and to use the pace system.
From The Survival In The Wilderness Series.
Prod-MORLAT Dist-SF 1967

Using A Computer C 30 MIN
3/4 OR 1/2 INCH VIDEO CASSETTE
Describes the basic components that make up computer systems. Explains these components and their interrelationships in simple terms. Examines a variety of computer systems at work in the business world.
From The Working With The Computer Series.
Prod-DELTAK Dist-DELTAK

Using A Data Base C 30 MIN
3/4 OR 1/2 INCH VIDEO CASSETTE
Describes technological advances that have and will continue to change data base use and stresses the advantages of this technology.
From The End User's Guide To Data Base Series.
Prod-DELTAK Dist-DELTAK

Using A Follower Rest B 21 MIN
16MM FILM - 3/4 IN VIDEO
Describes the follower rest and its uses. Shows how to mount a follower rest on a lathe, how to adjust the jaws of the follower rest to the work and how to lubricate the work to prevent damage to the jaws and workpiece. Issued in 1943 as a motion picture.
From The Machine Shop Work - Operations On The Engine Lathe Series. No. 15
LC NO. 79-707056
Prod-USOE Dist-USNAC Prodn-ATLAS 1979

Using A Hand Punch C 6 MIN
1/2 IN VIDEO CASSETTE BETA/VHS IND
Presents the operation and set-up for changing punches and dies in a hand punch.
Prod-RMI Dist-RMI

Using A Mathematics Laboratory Approach C 15 MIN
16MM FILM OPTICAL SOUND
Acquaints teachers with the laboratory approach by describing what labs are, why they are used, how they are organized and the kinds of activities that are valuable in the mathematics laboratory.
From The Project On Interpreting Mathematics Education Research Series.
LC NO. 74-705986
Prod-USOE Dist-USNAC 1970

Using A Pop Rivet Tool C 9 MIN
1/2 IN VIDEO CASSETTE BETA/VHS IND
Shows the basic operation of the pop rivet gun (blind rivet).
Prod-RMI Dist-RMI

Using A Portable Spray Gun B 26 MIN
16MM FILM OPTICAL SOUND
Explains how the pressure tank operates, and shows how to clean portable spray guns, adjust the paint, spray and air controls stroke while painting and use the suction type spray gun.
LC NO. FIE52-91
Prod-USOE Dist-USNAC 1945

Using A Shell End Mill B 21 MIN
16MM FILM - 3/4 IN VIDEO
Shows how the vertical milling machine differs from other milling machines. Shows how to produce a flat surface with a shell end mill and how to use the sliding head. Describes feed and speed and shows how to calculate them. Issued in 1943 as a motion picture.
From The Machine Shop Work - Operations On The Vertical Milling Machine Series. No. 1
LC NO. 79-707068
Prod-USOE Dist-USNAC Prodn-RAYBEL 1979

Using A Source, Review Of Letter Sounds - Jet Stop C 18 MIN
3/4 OR 1/2 INCH VIDEO CASSETTE J-H
See series title for descriptive statement.
From The Getting The Word Series. Unit II
Prod-SCETV Dist-AITECH 1974

Using A Spectrophotometer C 7 MIN
16MM FILM, 3/4 OR 1/2 IN VIDEO
Demonstrates the use of the spectrophotometer, an electronic laboratory instrument for measuring the concentration and absorbency of chemical compounds.
From The Basic Laboratory Techniques Series.
LC NO. 79-706042
Prod-IU Dist-IU 1978

Using A Steady Rest B 23 MIN
16MM FILM - 3/4 IN VIDEO
Describes the steady rest and its use. Shows how to spot the work for the location of the steady rest, how to mount the steady rest on the lathe and how to adjust the jaws of the rest to the work. Issued in 1943 as a motion picture.
From The Machine Shop Work - Operations On The Engine Lathe Series. No. 14
LC NO. 79-707058
Prod-USOE Dist-USNAC Prodn-ATLAS 1979

Using A Steady Rest When Boring B 21 MIN
16MM FILM - 3/4 IN VIDEO
Shows how to mount a long casting on a lathe faceplate, how to turn a true bearing spot for supporting the workpiece with a steady rest and how boring, turning, and forming operations are performed when work is supported by a steady rest. Issued in 1944 as a motion picture.
From The Machine Shop Work - Operations On The Engine Lathe Series. No. 17
LC NO. 79-707059
Prod-USOE Dist-USNAC Prodn-ATLAS 1979

Using Advanced UNIX Commands C
3/4 OR 1/2 INCH VIDEO CASSETTE
See series title for descriptive statement.
From The UNIX And 'C'Language Training - A Full Curriculum Series.
Prod-COMTEG Dist-COMTEG

Using An Analytical Balance Model H-30 C 12 MIN
1/2 IN VIDEO CASSETTE BETA/VHS
Discusses wastewater reclamation, water and wastewater technology.
Prod-RMI Dist-RMI

Using And Caring For Art Materials C 11 MIN
16MM FILM, 3/4 OR 1/2 IN VIDEO P-I
Features an animated bird describing the proper use and care of art materials.
From The School Citizenship Series.
LC NO. 79-707587
Prod-CENTRO Dist-CORF 1979

Using Bar Graphs C 14 MIN
3/4 OR 1/2 INCH VIDEO CASSETTE I
Explains how a well-labeled bar graph helps Linda's friends prove the need for a crosswalk after her bike accident. Includes an animated segment in which the King and Queen of Hearts graph tart consumption and catch the tart thief.
From The It Figures Series. No. 16
Prod-AITV Dist-AITECH Prodn-NJN 1982

Using Bread And Butterflies C 20 MIN
16MM FILM, 3/4 OR 1/2 IN VIDEO T
Demonstrates the various ways that teachers and students have used the series Bread and Butterflies as part of the curriculum. Emphasizes children's feeling and attitudes toward career development, the subject of the series.
From The Bread And Butterflies Series.
LC NO. 74-703193
Prod-AITV Dist-AITECH 1973

Using Centimeters, Meters, And Kilometers (2nd Ed) C 10 MIN
16MM FILM, 3/4 OR 1/2 IN VIDEO P
Explains centimeter, meter and kilometer units. Shows a girl and boy measuring with a metric ruler and a meter stick.
From The Let's Measure Series.
Prod-CORF Dist-CORF

Using Circuits - Application C 20 MIN
2 INCH VIDEOTAPE I
See series title for descriptive statement.
From The Exploring With Science, Unit VIII - Electricity Series.
Prod-MPATI Dist-GPITVL

Using Cleco Fasteners C 5 MIN
1/2 IN VIDEO CASSETTE BETA/VHS IND
Discusses the application of the Cleco fastener for holding a fitting or fabrication together, prior to permanent riveting.
Prod-RMI Dist-RMI

Using Community Resources C 29 MIN
3/4 OR 1/2 INCH VIDEO CASSETTE C A
Presents a teacher, who also serves as a volunteer community leader, discussing and showing examples of a range of human and institutional resources available to parents at the community level to help children and the family as a whole.
From The Focus On Children Series.
LC NO. 81-707446
Prod-IU Dist-IU 1981

Using Computer Simulations In Social Science, Science And Math C 21 MIN
3/4 OR 1/2 INCH VIDEO CASSETTE J-C A
Discusses the use of computer simulations in education, including a simulation on the lobbying process, a simulation of an automobile engine and a biology simulation on genetics.
From The New Technology In Education Series.
Prod-USDOE Dist-USNAC 1983

Using Context Clues C 30 MIN
3/4 OR 1/2 INCH VIDEO CASSETTE
See series title for descriptive statement.
From The General Reading Series.
Prod-CAMB Dist-CAMB

Using Credit Wisely C 25 MIN
3/4 OR 1/2 INCH VIDEO CASSETTE H-C A
Outlines types and sources of credit, means to evaluate loans, ways to cut interest costs and steps to developing a good credit record.
From The Money Smart - A Guide To Personal Finance Series.
Prod-SOMFIL Dist-BCNFL 1985

Using dBase II C
3/4 OR 1/2 INCH VIDEO CASSETTE
Demonstrates the use and application of the Ashton/Tate dBase II, a popular relational database program.
From The Compututor Series.
Prod-CHASCI Dist-EMBASY

Using Decimals C
3/4 OR 1/2 INCH VIDEO CASSETTE I-J A
Introduces the use of decimals. Focuses on mathematical procedures with decimals.
Prod-EDUACT Dist-EDUACT

Using DELTAK Courses—A Series

Looks at multimedia training, what it is and how it works. Explains how a student should take a DeltaVision course by focusing on the components of each of DELTAK's training formats.
Prod-DELTAK Dist-DELTAK

Selecting DeltaVision Courses 030 MIN
Taking A DeltaVision Course 030 MIN

Using Diagnosis In A Mathematics Classroom C 15 MIN
16MM FILM OPTICAL SOUND
Points out that mathematics instruction can be improved by effectively diagnosing pupil needs. Shows the use of interview inventories and a diagnostic instrument.
From The Project On Interpreting Mathematics Education Research Series.
LC NO. 74-705987
Prod-USOE Dist-USNAC 1970

Using Discovery Techniques C 30 MIN
3/4 OR 1/2 INCH VIDEO CASSETTE
See series title for descriptive statement.
From The Creating A Learning Environment Series.
Prod-NETCHE Dist-NETCHE 1975

Using Division C 14 MIN
3/4 OR 1/2 INCH VIDEO CASSETTE I
Explains that knowing when to use division helps Cliff, Roger and their classmates to a successful garage sale. Includes an animated segment in which the old woman divides her children into three shoes.
From The It Figures Series. No. 11
Prod-AITV Dist-AITECH Prodn-NJN 1982

Using Dual Shield, Flux Core Wire For Flat And Horizontal Butt Welds (MIG) C 15 MIN
3/4 OR 1/2 INCH VIDEO CASSETTE
See series title for descriptive statement.
From The Welding III - TIG and MIG (Industry) Welding series.
Prod-CAMB Dist-CAMB

Using Electricity C 20 MIN
3/4 OR 1/2 INCH VIDEO CASSETTE H-C A
See series title for descriptive statement.
From The Engineering Crafts Series.
Prod-BBCTV Dist-FI 1981

Using Electricity Safely C 15 MIN
16MM FILM - 3/4 IN VIDEO
Shows precautions to take with such things as power tools and extension cords. Discusses working conditions, overloading, temporary wiring and fire extinguishers. Describes types of injuries and what to do with a victim of electrical shock.
Prod-ALLIED Dist-BNA

Using Estimating And Approximation C 15 MIN
16MM FILM, 3/4 OR 1/2 IN VIDEO I
Shows how Vickie and David display their skills of estimation while they help weatherize the farmhouse.
From The Thinkabout Series. Estimating And Approximating
LC NO. 81-706129
Prod-EDFCEN Dist-AITECH 1979

Using Estimation C 15 MIN
3/4 OR 1/2 INCH VIDEO CASSETTE I
Utilizes a combination of realistic dramatization and animated tales to demonstrate how children can use mathematical strategies to solve problems. Shows Houston learning to use estimation to figure out how much junk food his money will buy at the fair and how much it will take to complete certain tasks.
From The It Figures Series. No. 4
LC NO. 82-707003
Prod-AITV Dist-AITECH Prodn-NJN 1982

Using Evidence C 25 MIN
3/4 OR 1/2 INCH VIDEO CASSETTE C
See series title for descriptive statement.
From The Artificial Intelligance, Pt 1 - Fundamental Concepts Series.
Prod-MIOT Dist-AMCEE

Using Evidence C 45 MIN
3/4 OR 1/2 INCH VIDEO CASSETTE PRO
Deals with strategy versus tactics, improving situation evaluation, linear evaluation, and nonlinear evaluation.
From The Artificial Intelligence - Pt 1, Fundamental Concepts Series.
Prod-MIOT Dist-MIOT

Using Fire Extinguishers C 11 MIN
3/4 OR 1/2 INCH VIDEO CASSETTE PRO
Explains fundamental principles of fighting fires and illustrates specific techniques in using fire extingusihers effectively.
LC NO. 80-731001
Prod-TRAINX Dist-TRAINX

Using Fire Extinguishers - The Right Way C 13 MIN
16MM FILM OPTICAL SOUND C A
Presents basic instruction in the proper use of fire extinguishers. Scrutinizes several demonstrations with live test fires that illustrate which extinguisher to use on each specific type of fire.
LC NO. 77-700189
Prod-NFPA Dist-NFPA 1977

Using Formulas C 12 MIN
3/4 OR 1/2 INCH VIDEO CASSETTE
Covers problem solving, length, area and volume.
From The Using Mathematics In The Plant Series.
Prod-TPCTRA Dist-TPCTRA

Using Formulas (Spanish) C 12 MIN
3/4 OR 1/2 INCH VIDEO CASSETTE
Covers problem solving, length, area and volume.
From The Using Mathematics In The Plant Series.
Prod-TPCTRA Dist-TPCTRA

Using Fractional And Rational Exponents B 28 MIN
16MM FILM OPTICAL SOUND H
Presents properties of real numbers with fractional and rational exponents. Shows methods of manipulating numbers and gives example of an exponential equation.
From The Intermediate Algebra Series.
Prod-CALVIN Dist-MLA Prodn-UNIVFI 1959

Using Fractions C 14 MIN
3/4 OR 1/2 INCH VIDEO CASSETTE I
Shows Cliff and his cabinmates at camp using their knowledge that fractions are made up of equal-sized parts to divide space, candy and a cake. Includes an animated segment in which each time Humpty Dumpty falls he breaks into equal-sized pieces.
From The It Figures Series. No. 7
Prod-AITV Dist-AITECH Prodn-NJN 1982

Using Fusible Interfacing C 3 MIN
16MM FILM SILENT J-C A
Shows how interfacing is attached to the garment by the use of steam, heat and pressure. Illustrates cutting, attaching and special effects with fusible interfacing.
From The Clothing Construction Techniques Series.
LC NO. 77-701173
Prod-IOWA Dist-IOWASP 1976

Using Gift Paper C 15 MIN
2 INCH VIDEOTAPE
See series title for descriptive statement.
From The Living Better I Series.
Prod-MAETEL Dist-PUBTEL

Using Glazing Putty C 8 MIN
1/2 IN VIDEO CASSETTE BETA/VHS
Deals with auto body work. Discusses glazing putty and its use. Shows application and sanding procedures.
Prod-RMI Dist-RMI

Using Government Agencies C 15 MIN
3/4 OR 1/2 INCH VIDEO CASSETTE H
Shows how citizens can use government agencies.
From The By The People Series.
Prod-CTI Dist-CTI

Using Grams And Kilograms (2nd Ed) C 10 MIN
16MM FILM, 3/4 OR 1/2 IN VIDEO P
Shows how to use grams and kilograms to weigh common items. Teaches basic metric weight measurement.
From The Let's Measure Series.
Prod-CORF Dist-CORF

Using Graphs, Maps And Picture Cards B 20 MIN
16MM FILM OPTICAL SOUND
See series title for descriptive statement.
From The Teaching The Slow Learner Series.
Prod-HRAW Dist-HRAW

Using Hand Stitches C 3 MIN
16MM FILM SILENT J-C A
Demonstrates hand stitches and discusses where each might be used. Shows the blind or slip stitch, catch stitch, lock stitch and buttonhole stitch.
From The Clothing Construction Techniques Series.
LC NO. 77-701180
Prod-IOWA Dist-IOWASP 1976

Using Hand Tools—A Series

Covers the most important tools used in industrial plants. Explains tools and their usage by specialty.
Prod-TPCTRA Dist-TPCTRA

Electrician's Tools	012 MIN
Hoisting And Pulling Tools	012 MIN
Masonry, Plastering, And Glazing Tools	012 MIN
Measuring Tools	012 MIN
Metalworking Tools	012 MIN
Pipefitting Tools	012 MIN
Plumbing Tools	012 MIN
Sheet Metalworking Tools	012 MIN
Woodworking Tools	012 MIN
Wrenches And Screwdrivers	012 MIN

Using Human Resources C 29 MIN
16MM FILM, 3/4 OR 1/2 IN VIDEO C T
Suggests ways of maximizing outside adult involvement in the classroom. Shows how parent volunteers, community volunteers, teachers, aides and older students may be used.
From The Teaching Children To Read Series.
Prod-MFFD Dist-FI 1975

Using Images And Things C 30 MIN
16MM FILM OPTICAL SOUND
Offers guidance on the effective utilization of the series 'IMAGES AND THINGS.' Gives examples of students and teachers involved in follow-up activities motivated by the programs.
From The Images And Things Series.
LC NO. 73-702119
Prod-NITC Dist-AITECH 1971

Using Industrial Robots C 30 MIN
3/4 OR 1/2 INCH VIDEO CASSETTE
Examines the important aspects of the industrial robot and discusses how it is being used in manufacturing today.
From The Manufacturing Automation - A Key To– Productivity Series.
Prod-DELTAK Dist-DELTAK

Using Industrial Statistics C
3/4 OR 1/2 INCH VIDEO CASSETTE
Deals with industrial statistics. Shows how to use a multi-vary chart, a scatter diagram and a component search pattern.
From The Organizational Quality Improvement Series.
Prod-BNA Dist-BNA

Using Infrared Thermography For Industrial Energy Conservation C 45 MIN
3/4 OR 1/2 INCH VIDEO CASSETTE PRO
Describes use of infrared thermography data to calculate energy conservation and the use of infrared thermography techniques in industrial heating processes.
From The Energy Auditing And Conservation Series.
LC NO. 81-706437
Prod-AMCEE Dist-AMCEE 1979

Using Legal Assistance C 15 MIN
3/4 OR 1/2 INCH VIDEO CASSETTE H
Tells how to use professional legal help. Shows how to take a case to Small Claims Court.
From The By The People Series.
Prod-CTI Dist-CTI

Using Lenses, Pt 1 - The Lens Turret B 16 MIN
16MM FILM OPTICAL SOUND
Demonstrates the four lenses usually found on a television camera lens turret by their uses in one-, twoand three-shot situations. Illustrates problems of perspective, the pitfalls of using angled lenses and techniques for smooth lens changes.
From The CETO Television Training Films Series.
Prod-CETO Dist-GPITVL

Using Lenses, Pt 2 - The Zoom And Other Lenses B 25 MIN
16MM FILM OPTICAL SOUND
Recapitulates the use of the four commonly-used turret lenses and then demonstrates narrow-angle and wide angle lenses which lie outside this range, showing some of the situations in which these special lenses are vital.
From The CETO Television Training Films Series.
Prod-CETO Dist-GPITVL

Using Lines B 15 MIN
2 INCH VIDEOTAPE P
Shows the use of lines in crayon or pencil drawings. (Broadcast quality)
From The Art Discoveries Series. Lesson 2
Prod-CVETVC Dist-GPITVL Prodn-WCVETV

Using Liquid Measure C 20 MIN
2 INCH VIDEOTAPE P
See series title for descriptive statement.
From The Mathemagic, Unit VI - Measurement Series.
Prod-WMULTV Dist-GPITVL

Using Literary Structure To Simplify Reading B 15 MIN
2 INCH VIDEOTAPE I
Explains that a finished story is determined by the structure of the story, the problem of the story, the characters, the series of episodes and the end of the story. Features selections such as Sody Sallyratus by Richard Chase and Mother Meadowlark And Brother Snake by Billy Firethunder. (Broadcast quality)
From The Bill Martin Series. No. 7
Prod-BRITED Dist-GPITVL Prodn-KQEDTV

Using Logarithm Tables B 29 MIN
16MM FILM OPTICAL SOUND H
Shows how to find the mantissa of a logarithm and a number, given its logarithm from a three place table. Illustrates interpolation and inverse interpolation in log tables. The log of a trigonometric value is found in a table and the use of a slide rule is discussed.
From The Trigonometry Series.
Prod-CALVIN Dist-MLA Prodn-UNIVFI 1959

Using Logarithms In Problems B 31 MIN
16MM FILM OPTICAL SOUND H
Defines the logarithm of a number. Shows the use of logarithms for solving problems involving powers, ratios and roots of numbers.
From The Advanced Algebra Series.
Prod-CALVIN Dist-MLA Prodn-UNIVFI 1960

Using Logarithms To Solve Equations B 28 MIN
16MM FILM OPTICAL SOUND H
Shows how to find the mantissa and antilog from logarithm tables. Includes the use of linear interpolation. Closes with examples of how to use logarithms to multiply, divide and find the roots of numbers.
From The Intermediate Algebra Series.
Prod-CALVIN Dist-MLA Prodn-UNIVFI 1959

Using Machinery Safely C 12 MIN
3/4 OR 1/2 INCH VIDEO CASSETTE
Guards against accidents when using machinery safely. Covers safety devices.
From The Protecting Your Safety And Health In the Plant Series.
Prod-TPCTRA Dist-TPCTRA

Using Machinery Safely (Spanish) C 12 MIN
3/4 OR 1/2 INCH VIDEO CASSETTE
Guards against accidents when using machinery safely. Covers safety devices.
From The Protecting Your Safety And Health In The Plant Series.
Prod-TPCTRA Dist-TPCTRA

Using Magazine Pictures In The Language Classroom C 35 MIN
3/4 INCH VIDEO CASSETTE T
Shows how a teacher using pictures cut out of magazines can demonstrate, elicit and control language in an entertaining way. Demonstrates four ways of using the pictures in a classroom.
Prod-BCACGB Dist-GPITVL 1978

Using Managerial Techniques On The Job C
3/4 OR 1/2 INCH VIDEO CASSETTE
Deals with four key skills, including using the checklist, keeping supervisor informed, doing complete staff work and getting cooperation from others.
From The Team Building For Administrative Support Staff Series.
Prod-AMA Dist-AMA

Using Maps - Measuring Distance X 11 MIN
16MM FILM, 3/4 OR 1/2 IN VIDEO P-J
Defines what a map is and shows several different ways of measuring distance. Explains what a map scale is and illustrates how it is used to measure distance on a map. Includes brief glimpses of professional map makers at their work.
Prod-EBF Dist-EBEC 1962

Using Maps - Measuring Distance (Spanish) C 11 MIN
16MM FILM, 3/4 OR 1/2 IN VIDEO P-J
Defines a map and shows several ways of measuring distance.
Prod-EBEC Dist-EBEC

Using Materials C 15 MIN
16MM FILM, 3/4 OR 1/2 IN VIDEO I-J
Explains that the family of materials known as plastics (both thermoplastic and thermosetting) can be manipulated and molded through extrusion. This is a process in which granules melt into a fluid that is shaped by pressure through dies and cooled for permanence, as well as through injection molding.
From The Craft, Design And Technology Series.
Prod-THAMES Dist-MEDIAG 1983

Using Materials C 20 MIN
3/4 OR 1/2 INCH VIDEO CASSETTE H-C A
See series title for descriptive statement.
From The Engineering Crafts Series.
Prod-BBCTV Dist-FI 1981

Using Math In Everyday Situations C
3/4 OR 1/2 INCH VIDEO CASSETTE T
Focuses on ways mathematics can be used in real situations. Discusses everyday use of computational skills, problem-solving strategies, geometric concepts and other basic skill areas.
From The Third R - Teaching Basic Mathematics Skills Series.
Prod-EPCO Dist-EDCORP

Using Mathematics C 20 MIN
2 INCH VIDEOTAPE P
See series title for descriptive statement.
From The Mathemagic, Unit VIII - Multiplication And Division Series.
Prod-WMULTV Dist-GPITVL

Using Mathematics In The Plant—A Series

Introduces mathematics basics. Examines both common fractions and decimal fractions, ratios and proportions. Covers geometry, algebra and trigonometry.
Prod-TPCTRA Dist-TPCTRA

Algebra	012 MIN
Calculators	012 MIN
Common Fractions	012 MIN
Decimal Fractions	012 MIN
Geometry	012 MIN
Powers And Roots	012 MIN
Ratios And Proportions	012 MIN
Trignometry	012 MIN
Using Formulas	012 MIN
Whole Numbers	012 MIN

Using Mathematics In The Plant—A Series (Spanish)

Introduces mathematics basics. Examines both common fractions and decimal fractions, ratios and proportions. Covers geometry, algebra and trigonometry.
Prod-TPCTRA Dist-TPCTRA

Algebra	012 MIN
Calculators	012 MIN
Common Fractions	012 MIN
Decimal Fractions	012 MIN
Geometry	012 MIN
Powers And Roots	012 MIN
Ratios And Proportions	012 MIN
Trignometry	012 MIN
Using Formulas	012 MIN
Whole Numbers	012 MIN

Using Mental Computation C 13 MIN
3/4 OR 1/2 INCH VIDEO CASSETTE I
Shows Naima and Kevin using different methods of mental addition to keep track of their sales. Includes an animated segment in which the genie shows Aladdin two ways to figure in his head how much treasure he has.
From The It Figures Series. No. 10
Prod-AITV Dist-AITECH Prodn-NJN 1982

Using Metrics C 20 MIN
3/4 INCH VIDEO CASSETTE
See series title for descriptive statement.
From The Enter - Metrics Series.
Prod-MDDE Dist-MDCPB

Using Microcomputers - An Introduction C 3 MIN
3/4 OR 1/2 INCH VIDEO CASSETTE
Introduces various applications of microcomputers in school setting.
From The Microcomputers At School Series. Program One.
Prod-EPCO Dist-EDCORP

Using Milliliters And Liters (2nd Ed) C 12 MIN
16MM FILM, 3/4 OR 1/2 IN VIDEO P
The second edition of Pints Quarts And Gallons. Shows a boy and girl following a metric recipe to make a witch's brew. Teaches liters and milliliters.
From The Let's Measure Series.
Prod-CORF Dist-CORF

Using Money C 20 MIN
2 INCH VIDEOTAPE P
See series title for descriptive statement.
From The Mathemagic, Unit VII - Money Series.
Prod-WMULTV Dist-GPITVL

Using Money Wisely C 18 MIN
16MM FILM, 3/4 OR 1/2 IN VIDEO H-C
Presents three typical families with money problems who represent a cross section of economic levels. Shows these families as they encounter, and reach solutions to their money management difficulties.
Prod-CUNA Dist-JOU Prodn-ALTSUL 1970

Using MultiPlan—A Series

Provides a foundation in how to set up a MultiPlan worksheet and use its various features. Includes screen examples and hands-on exercises.
Prod-COMTEG Dist-COMTEG

Introduction To The Worksheet
Setting Up A Worksheet
Storing, Retrieving, Printing And Advanced

Using Multiplication And Addition C 14 MIN
3/4 OR 1/2 INCH VIDEO CASSETTE I
Shows the Fourth Street Regulars learning from their candy sale and from playing miniature golf that multiplication can help with some addition problems. Includes an animated segment in which Alice uses both multiplication and addition in the Red and White Queens' problem.
From The It Figures Series. No. 13
Prod-AITV Dist-AITECH Prodn-NJN 1982

Using Networking And Bar Charting In Project Scheduling C 30 MIN
3/4 OR 1/2 INCH VIDEO CASSETTE
Shows how to use networking and bar charting in project scheduling. Includes calculating critical path and slack time.
From The Project Management Series.
Prod-ITCORP Dist-ITCORP

Using On-Line Systems C 20 MIN
3/4 OR 1/2 INCH VIDEO CASSETTE
Describes some of the things on-line systems can do for the end user, discusses on-line systems from the user's viewpoint and shows how users can work effectively with system designers. Shows how the manager of a large data processing organization was able to transfer more computer power into the hands of the users and discusses how on- line systems can cause basic changes in corporate procedures.
From The On-Line Systems Concepts For Users Series.
Prod-DELTAK Dist-DELTAK

Using Others To Save Time C 10 MIN
3/4 OR 1/2 INCH VIDEO CASSETTE
Stresses that delegation will work and will save time and in the process will develop others' abilities. Emphasizes that training is a key to saving time.
From The Management of Time Series. Module 3
Prod-RESEM Dist-RESEM

Using Oxy-Acetylene Torch For Heating Metal,- Nuts And Bolts C 15 MIN
3/4 OR 1/2 INCH VIDEO CASSETTE
See series title for descriptive statement.
From The Welding I - Basic Oxy-Acetylene Welding Series.
Prod-CAMB Dist-CAMB

Using People Sources C 15 MIN
3/4 OR 1/2 INCH VIDEO CASSETTE J
Explains how interviews can be a valuable source of information. Emphasizes the importance of planning the interview beforehand. Uses the example of a police officer interviewing an eyewitness at the scene of a crime and a girl telephoning the school superintendent to check the notes she took at their meeting.
From The In Other Words Series. Getting Ready, Pt 3
Prod-AITV Dist-AITECH Prodn-KOCETV 1983

Using Persona In Poetry C 15 MIN
1/2 INCH VIDEOTAPE I
Introduces the writing of poetry. Presents two performers/teachers who interpret several poems for a group of young children.
Prod-WHITD Dist-WHITD

Using Personal Protective Equipment C 24 MIN
3/4 OR 1/2 INCH VIDEO CASSETTE IND
Provides a detailed review of the personal protection equipment available to workers, how and why each is used, plus the foreman's responsibility.
From The Foreman's Accident Prevention Series.
Prod-GPCV Dist-GPCV

Using Poetic Structure To Simplify Reading B 15 MIN
2 INCH VIDEOTAPE I
Discusses poetic structure as a means of simplifying the reading of a story, poem or article. Features selections such as If You Should Meet A Crocodile, author unknown and Stopping By The Woods On A Snowy Evening by Robert Frost. (Broadcast quality)
From The Bill Martin Series. No. 8
Prod-BRITED Dist-GPITVL Prodn-KQEDTV

Using Political Resources C 15 MIN
3/4 OR 1/2 INCH VIDEO CASSETTE H
Suggests some resources of value in influencing political decisions.
From The By The People Series.
Prod-CTI Dist-CTI

Using Portable Fire Extinguishers The Right Way C
3/4 OR 1/2 INCH VIDEO CASSETTE
Prod-NFPA Dist-NFPA

Using Portable Power Tools (Spanish)—A Series

Explains the uses, selection, safety and care of industrial power tools, electric drills, hammers and others. Covers tool sharpening techniques for all appropriate tools.
Prod-TPCTRA Dist-TPCTRA

Circular Saws	012 MIN
Electric Drills	012 MIN
Electric Hammers	012 MIN
Electric Sanders	012 MIN
Grinders and Shears	012 MIN
Linear-Motion Saws	012 MIN
Pneumatic Drills And Hammers	012 MIN
Routers And Planes	012 MIN
Screwdrivers, Nutrunners, and Wrenches	012 MIN
Tool Sharpening	012 MIN

Using Portable Power Tools—A Series

Explains the uses, selection, safety and care of industrial power tools, electric drills, hammers and others. Covers tool sharpening techniques for all appropriate tools.
Prod-TPCTRA Dist-TPCTRA

Circular Saws	012 MIN
Electric Drills	012 MIN
Electric Hammers	012 MIN
Electric Sanders	012 MIN
Grinders And Shears	012 MIN
Linear-Motion Saws	012 MIN
Pneumatic Drills And Hammers	012 MIN
Routers And Planes	012 MIN
Screwdrivers, Nutrunners, And Wrenches	012 MIN
Tool Sharpening	012 MIN

Using Positive Discipline (Industry) C
16MM FILM, 3/4 OR 1/2 IN VIDEO A
Discusses how to use positive discipline in an industrial setting.
From The Supervisory Training (Industry) Series.
Prod-CRMP Dist-CRMP 1983

Using Positive Discipline (Office) C
16MM FILM, 3/4 OR 1/2 IN VIDEO A
Discusses how to use positive discipline in an office setting.
From The Supervisory Training (Office) Series.
Prod-CRMP Dist-CRMP 1983

Using Probability C 13 MIN
3/4 OR 1/2 INCH VIDEO CASSETTE I
Shows that in drawing straws, flipping a coin and participating in a pizza contest, Andy and his friends learn it is useful to know how to determine the likelihood of an event. Includes an animated segment in which Lancelot uses probability to discover the King's trick.
From The It Figures Series. No. 24
Prod-AITV Dist-AITECH Prodn-NJN 1982

Using Reinforcement Techniques To Manage Patient Behavior B 30 MIN
16MM FILM OPTICAL SOUND
Describes techniques of managing consequences of patient behavior in bringing about desired patient or student behavior.
From The Nursing-Cues Behavior Consequences Series. No. 3
LC NO. 76-700928
Prod-NTCN Dist-UNEBR 1973

Using Respiratory Protection C 29 MIN
3/4 OR 1/2 INCH VIDEO CASSETTE IND
Provides detailed instructions for putting on, testing and maintaining respirators and other hose-line and self-contained breathing apparatus used in industry.
From The Foreman's Accident Prevention Series.
Prod-GPCV Dist-GPCV

Using Ripples - Change And Aesthetics C 15 MIN
16MM FILM OPTICAL SOUND T
Shows teachers and children in the classroom reacting to 'RIPPLES' programs in a variety of follow-up activities. Features Dr Rose Mukerji who points out how the activities, the planning sessions and the programs' basic ideas relate to the new approach to early childhood curriculum that is the foundation of 'RIPPLES.'
From The Ripples Series.
LC NO. 73-702161
Prod-NITC Dist-AITECH 1970

Using Ripples - Values And Knowledge C 15 MIN
16MM FILM OPTICAL SOUND T
Shows teachers and children in the classroom reacting to 'RIPPLES' programs in a variety of follow-up activities. Features Dr Rose Mukerji who points out how the activities, the planning sessions and the programs' basic ideas relate to the new approach to early childhood curriculum that is the foundation of 'RIPPLES.'
From The Ripples Series.
LC NO. 73-702162
Prod-NITC Dist-AITECH 1970

Using Satellite-Based Communications C 30 MIN
3/4 OR 1/2 INCH VIDEO CASSETTE
From The Communications Satellite Systems Series. Outlines the services offered by companies marketing satellite communications systems. Discusses user responsibilities and requirements.
Prod-DELTAK Dist-DELTAK

Using Schematics And Diagrams C 12 MIN
3/4 OR 1/2 INCH VIDEO CASSETTE
Discusses using schematics and diagrams such as piping schematics, electrical, motor-starting, plant lighting diagrams, electric troubleshooting charts and hydraulic and pneumatic schematics.
From The Developing Troubleshooting Skills Series.
Prod-TPCTRA Dist-TPCTRA

Using Shapes B 15 MIN
2 INCH VIDEOTAPE P
Presents a demonstration of making constructions using shapes. (Broadcast quality)
From The Art Discoveries Series. Lesson 4
Prod-CVETVC Dist-GPITVL Prodn-WCVETV

Using Sines, Cosines And Tangents B 29 MIN
16MM FILM OPTICAL SOUND H
Reviews the definitions of the sine, cosine and tangent functions. Shows how to approach a trigonometric problem. Defines the unit circle and uses it to develop simple trigonometric identities and to show that the functions are not linear.
From The Trigonometry Series.
Prod-CALVIN Dist-MLA Prodn-UNIVFI 1959

Using Slides And Recordings B 20 MIN
16MM FILM OPTICAL SOUND
See series title for descriptive statement.
From The Teaching The Slow Learner Series.
Prod-HRAW Dist-HRAW

Using Sources Of Information C 30 MIN
3/4 OR 1/2 INCH VIDEO CASSETTE
See series title for descriptive statement.
From The Practical Reading Series.
Prod-CAMB Dist-CAMB

Using Spelling Pattern And Rhythm As Clues - Short Vowels I-I C 20 MIN
3/4 OR 1/2 INCH VIDEO CASSETTE J-H
See series title for descriptive statement.
From The Getting The Word Series. Unit III
Prod-SCETV Dist-AITECH 1974

Using Standardized Recipes C 9 MIN
16MM FILM, 3/4 OR 1/2 IN VIDEO J-C A
Shows how to properly interpret and use standardized commercial recipes with utilization of several different types of recipes.
From The Professional Food Preparation And Service Program Series.
Prod-NEM Dist-NEM 1971

Using Stimuli To Influence Behavior B 29 MIN
16MM FILM OPTICAL SOUND
See series title for descriptive statement.
From The Controlling Turnover And Absenteeism Series.
LC NO. 76-703321
Prod-EDSD Dist-EDSD

Using Swing Bass C 29 MIN
3/4 INCH VIDEO CASSETTE H A
Introduces B-flat major scale. Reviews pieces from previous programs. Begins an approach to choosing chromatic chords in playing by ear.
From The Beginning Piano - An Adult Approach Series. Lesson 26
Prod-COAST Dist-CDTEL

Using Tape Recorders In The Language Classroom C 35 MIN
3/4 INCH VIDEO CASSETTE T
Shows how teachers can use tape recorders for listening comprehension classes.
Prod-BCACGB Dist-GPITVL 1978

Using Teaching Materials C 12 MIN
3/4 OR 1/2 INCH VIDEO CASSETTE
Helps instructors establish guidelines for use and dissemination of handouts, student guides, notebooks and other teaching materials.
From The ElementsOf Effective Teaching Series.
Prod-RESEM Dist-RESEM

Using Textures B 15 MIN
2 INCH VIDEOTAPE P
Demonstrates ways students can add texture to their drawings. (Broadcast quality)
From The Art Discoveries Series. Lesson 8
Prod-CVETVC Dist-GPITVL Prodn-WCVETV

Using The Analytical Balance (Mettler) C 9 MIN
3/4 OR 1/2 INCH VIDEO CASSETTE C A
Demonstrates the use of the Mettler single pan analytical balance Model H6 to weigh an object to the nearest 0.1 mg. Emphasizes the common errrors made by beginning balance users that could result in damage to the balance or incorrect readings.
From The Chemistry - Master/Apprentice Series. Program 16
LC NO. 82-706033
Prod-CUETV Dist-CUNIV 1981

Using The Balance And Spring Scales C 20 MIN
1/2 IN VIDEO CASSETTE BETA/VHS
Demonstrates the differences between the balance and spring scales, and discusses various methods of scaling, using both the balance and spring scales.
Prod-RMI Dist-RMI

Using The Bennett Machine C 6 MIN
16MM FILM OPTICAL SOUND
Shows a mock classroom session on the use of the Bennett machine, which is used in respiratory therapy.
From The ICARE Training Series.
LC NO. 75-704051
Prod-BHME Dist-USNAC Prodn-ARHERF 1975

Using The Bunsen Burner And Working With Glass C 11 MIN
16MM FILM, 3/4 OR 1/2 IN VIDEO H-C
Demonstrates basic techniques used in working with glass tubing.
From The Basic Laboratory Techniques In Chemistry Series.
Prod-SCHLAT Dist-LUF

Using The Clues C 30 MIN
3/4 OR 1/2 INCH VIDEO CASSETTE A
See series title for descriptive statement.
From The Play Bridge Series.
Prod-KYTV Dist-KYTV 1983

Using The Computer And Preventing Its Abuse C 67 MIN
3/4 OR 1/2 INCH VIDEO CASSETTE PRO
Explores ways an attorney can use a computer to enhance a law practice. Examines the type of statistical analysis a computer expert can provide for litigation and ways to effectively present computer-generated data in a trial.
From The Use Of Computers In Complex Litigation Series.
Prod-ABACPE Dist-ABACPE

Using The Computer Terminal, Pt 1 B
16MM FILM OPTICAL SOUND
Explains how to use a computer terminal. Discusses installation, connection to the computer, and logging on.
Prod-OPENU Dist-OPENU

Using The Computer Terminal, Pt 2 B
16MM FILM OPTICAL SOUND
Explains how to use a computer terminal. Discusses installation, connection to the computer, and logging on.
Prod-OPENU Dist-OPENU

Using The Computer To Develop Writing Abilities C 27 MIN
3/4 OR 1/2 INCH VIDEO CASSETTE J-C A
Discusses what has been learned about the writing process and how the computer can be used as a tool to simplify and stimulate this process in children.
From The New Technology In Education Series.
Prod-USDOE Dist-USNAC 1983

Using The Cutoff Tool On The Lathe C
3/4 OR 1/2 INCH VIDEO CASSETTE
See series title for descriptive statement.
From The Intermediate Engine Lathe Operation Series.
Prod-VTRI Dist-VTRI

Using The Cutoff Tool On The Lathe C 15 MIN
3/4 OR 1/2 INCH VIDEO CASSETTE
See series title for descriptive statement.
From The Machine Technology III - Intermediate Engine Lathe Series.
Prod-CAMB Dist-CAMB

Using The Cutoff Tool On The Lathe C 15 MIN
3/4 OR 1/2 INCH VIDEO CASSETTE IND
See series title for descriptive statement.
From The Machining And The Operation Of Machine Tools, Module 3 - Intermediate Engine Lathe Series.
Prod-LEIKID Dist-LEIKID

Using The Cutoff Tool On The Lathe (Spanish) C
3/4 OR 1/2 INCH VIDEO CASSETTE
See series title for descriptive statement.
From The Intermediate Engine Lathe Operation (Spanish) Series.
Prod-VTRI Dist-VTRI

Using The Five You's C 37 MIN
3/4 OR 1/2 INCH VIDEO CASSETTE
Presents five types of human behavior, covering the adult, nurturing, critical, natural and adapted forms of communication behavior.
From The Super-Vision Series.
Prod-VCI Dist-DELTAK

Using The Four-Jaw Chuck C 13 MIN
1/2 IN VIDEO CASSETTE BETA/VHS IND
See series title for descriptive statement.
From The Machine Shop - Engine Lathe Series.
Prod-RMI Dist-RMI

Using The Gravity Displacement Steam Autoclave In The Biomedical Laboratory C 29 MIN
3/4 OR 1/2 INCH VIDEO CASSETTE
Demonstrates aseptic and safe procedures for preparing, processing and handling materials undergoing steam sterilization and decontamination.
LC NO. 84-706402
Prod-USDHEW Dist-USNAC 1983

Using The Gravity Displacement Steam Autoclave In The Biomedical Laboratory C 29 MIN
3/4 OR 1/2 INCH VIDEO CASSETTE PRO
Demonstrates safe and aseptic techniques and procedures for preparing, processing and handling materials undergoing steam sterilization and decontamination.
Prod-USPHS Dist-USNAC 1983

Using The Index Head C 29 MIN
1/2 IN VIDEO CASSETTE BETA/VHS IND
See series title for descriptive statement.
From The Machine Shop - Milling Machine Series.
Prod-RMI Dist-RMI

Using The Lathe To Manufacture A Spring C 15 MIN
3/4 OR 1/2 INCH VIDEO CASSETTE
See series title for descriptive statement.
From The Machine Technology III - Intermediate Engine Lathe Series.
Prod-CAMB Dist-CAMB

Using The Library C 20 MIN
3/4 OR 1/2 INCH VIDEO CASSETTE H A
Tells of resources available in the college library and how to use them. Shows how to look up a book by subject, author or title by locating it in a card catalog, on microfiche, or on a computer. Describes how to locate articles in the Reader's Guide and The New York Times Index. Deals with the reserve book area, nonprint materials and additional indexes.
From The Art Of Learning Series.
Prod-WCVETV Dist-GPITVL 1984

Using The Metric System Every Day C 20 MIN
3/4 INCH VIDEO CASSETTE J-C A
Emphasizes that the metric system is used increasingly in daily life.
From The Metric System Series.
Prod-MAETEL Dist-GPITVL 1975

Using The New ADA Exchange System For Meal Planning C 12 MIN
3/4 OR 1/2 INCH VIDEO CASSETTE
Reviews the principles of exchange diet. Reviews each exchange list with discussion and examples. Demonstrates how a diet can be created from the various lists.
Prod-MEDFAC Dist-MEDFAC 1979

Using The Normal Distribution C 20 MIN
3/4 OR 1/2 INCH VIDEO CASSETTE IND
Discusses calculation of areas under the normal curve and how applied to find percent of defective parts for a production operation. Shows comparisons for processes in and out of control, and applications for setting the mean of the process and for setting guarantees.
From The Statistics For Technicians Series.
Prod-COLOSU Dist-COLOSU

Using The Oscilloscope B 29 MIN
16MM FILM OPTICAL SOUND C A
Two teachers discuss the basic uses of the oscilloscope for calibration, timing and demonstration. They consider uses of various controls, calibration of a xenon strobe, checking the speed of a camera shutter, displaying beats between two audio oscillators and two ultrasonic oscillators, using lissajous figures to measure unknown frequencies and the use of two-axis modulation.
From The Harvard Project Physics Teacher Briefings Series. No. 11
LC NO. 71-709139
Prod-HPP Dist-HRAW 1969

Using The Pocket Calculator C 17 MIN
16MM FILM, 3/4 OR 1/2 IN VIDEO I-J
Reviews the types of pocket calculators available and gives step-by-step instructions on operating the calculator.
Prod-CENTRO Dist-CORF

Using The Pocket Calculator (Captioned) C 17 MIN
16MM FILM, 3/4 OR 1/2 IN VIDEO I-J
Reviews the types of pocket calculators that are available. Provides consumer information on buying a calculator for personal use and shows how to operate a pocket calculator.
Prod-CENTRO Dist-CORF 1978

Using The Sense Of The Sentence C 15 MIN
3/4 OR 1/2 INCH VIDEO CASSETTE J-H
See series title for descriptive statement.
From The Getting The Word Series. Unit I
Prod-SCETV Dist-AITECH 1974

Using The Shape Of The Word C 20 MIN
3/4 OR 1/2 INCH VIDEO CASSETTE J-H
See series title for descriptive statement.
From The Getting The Word Series. Unit I
Prod-SCETV Dist-AITECH 1974

Using The Shaper To Make Drawers C 14 MIN
16MM FILM, 3/4 OR 1/2 IN VIDEO J-C A
Demonstrates through the use of close-up photography the basic operations involved in using the shaper to make drawers.
From The Wood Shop - Safety And Operations Series.
Prod-EPRI Dist-AIMS 1970

Using The Shaper To Make Drawers (Spanish) C 14 MIN
16MM FILM, 3/4 OR 1/2 IN VIDEO J-C A
Demonstrates through the use of close-up photography the basic operations involved in using the shaper to make drawers.
From The Wood Shop - Safety And Operations Series.
Prod-EPRI Dist-AIMS 1970

Using The Shaper To Make Panel Doors C 16 MIN
16MM FILM, 3/4 OR 1/2 IN VIDEO J-C A
Shows step-by-step procedures for shaping and jointing stiles and rails including how to measure, how to cut sample stiles and rails to test set-ups and using a pattern and a holding jig to shape the stock.
From The Wood Shop - Safety And Operations Series.
Prod-EPRI Dist-AIMS 1971

Using The Shaper To Make Panel Doors (Spanish) C 16 MIN
16MM FILM, 3/4 OR 1/2 IN VIDEO J-C A
Shows step-by-step procedures for shaping and jointing stiles and rails, including how to measure, how to cut sample stiles and rails to test set-ups and using a pattern and a holding jig to shape the stock.
From The Wood Shop - Safety And Operations Series.
Prod-EPRI Dist-AIMS 1970

Using The Shaper To Make Raised Panels For Doors C 9 MIN
16MM FILM, 3/4 OR 1/2 IN VIDEO J-C A
Provides step-by-step instructions for producing raised panels. Explains use of tall fence and shows how to make a trial run on a practice piece. Explains how to determine the exact shape of an irregular end so that it will fit the rail.
From The Wood Shop - Safety And Operations Series.
Prod-EPRI Dist-AIMS 1971

Using The Shaper To Make Raised Panels For Doors (Spanish) C 9 MIN
16MM FILM, 3/4 OR 1/2 IN VIDEO J-C A
Provides step-by-step instructions for producing raised panels. Explains use of tall fence and shows how to make a trial run on a practice piece. Explains how to determine the exact shape of an irregular end so that it will fit the rail.
From The Wood Shop - Safety And Operations Series.
Prod-EPRI Dist-AIMS 1970

Using The Sound Of Letters C 18 MIN
3/4 OR 1/2 INCH VIDEO CASSETTE J-H
See series title for descriptive statement.
From The Getting The Word Series. Unit I
Prod-SCETV Dist-AITECH 1974

Using The Spelling Pattern Of The Word C 20 MIN
3/4 OR 1/2 INCH VIDEO CASSETTE J-H
See series title for descriptive statement.
From The Getting The Word Series. Unit I
Prod-SCETV Dist-AITECH 1974

Using The Spirometer C 25 MIN
3/4 OR 1/2 INCH VIDEO CASSETTE PRO
Explains and demonstrates the use of the spirometer, a device for measuring lung volumes and capacities.
Prod-HSCIC Dist-HSCIC 1981

Using The Steady Rest And Follower Rest On The Lathe C
3/4 OR 1/2 INCH VIDEO CASSETTE
See series title for descriptive statement.
From The Intermediate Engine Lathe Operation Series.
Prod-VTRI Dist-VTRI

Using The Steady Rest And Follower Rest On The Lathe (Spanish) C
3/4 OR 1/2 INCH VIDEO CASSETTE
See series title for descriptive statement.

From The Intermediate Engine Lathe Operation (Spanish) Series.
Prod-VTRI Dist-VTRI

Using The Steady Rest And Follower Rest To Machine On The Lathe C 15 MIN
3/4 OR 1/2 INCH VIDEO CASSETTE IND
See series title for descriptive statement.
From The Machining And The Operation Of Machine Tools, Module 3 - Intermediate Engine Lathe Series.
Prod-LEIKID Dist-LEIKID

Using The Three-Jaw Chuck C 26 MIN
1/2 IN VIDEO CASSETTE BETA/VHS IND
See series title for descriptive statement.
From The Machine Shop - Engine Lathe Series.
Prod-RMI Dist-RMI

Using The Tool Post Grinder For Grinding Lathe Centers And Other Grinding Operations C 15 MIN
3/4 OR 1/2 INCH VIDEO CASSETTE
See series title for descriptive statement.
From The Machine Technology III - Intermediate Engine Lathe Series.
Prod-CAMB Dist-CAMB

Using The Tool Post Grinder On The Lathe C
3/4 OR 1/2 INCH VIDEO CASSETTE
See series title for descriptive statement.
From The Intermediate Engine Lathe Operation Series.
Prod-VTRI Dist-VTRI

Using The Tool Post Grinder On The Lathe (Spanish) C
3/4 OR 1/2 INCH VIDEO CASSETTE
See series title for descriptive statement.
From The Intermediate Engine Lathe Operation (Spanish) Series.
Prod-VTRI Dist-VTRI

Using The Toolpost Grinder On The Lathe C 15 MIN
3/4 OR 1/2 INCH VIDEO CASSETTE IND
See series title for descriptive statement.
From The Machining And The Operation Of Machine Tools, Module 3 - Intermediate Engine Lathe series.
Prod-LEIKID Dist-LEIKID

Using The Training Day C 12 MIN
3/4 OR 1/2 INCH VIDEO CASSETTE
Helps instructors plan the best use of classroom time. Emphasizes that it is important to know when various teaching techniques are most effective.
From The Elements Of Effective Teaching Series.
Prod-RESEM Dist-RESEM

Using The Verse C 50 MIN
3/4 OR 1/2 INCH VIDEO CASSETTE
Discusses blank verse, why it is better for drama than other verse forms and how it should be read. Shows actors trying out different stresses and discovering how Shakespeare uses antithesis, short lines, end-stopped lines and pauses in the middle of a line. Uses examples from Henry V, The Winter's Tale, The Merchant Of Venice and King John.
From The Royal Shakespeare Company Series.
Prod-FOTH Dist-FOTH 1984

Using The Words Of Others C 15 MIN
3/4 OR 1/2 INCH VIDEO CASSETTE J
Shows that Jeff has overused the words of others in a report on San Francisco, without quotation marks, footnotes or a bibliography. Explains that quotations should support, not replace, a writer's ideas and should be acknowledged.
From The In Other Words Series. Giving Meaning To Messages, Pt 6
Prod-AITV Dist-AITECH Prodn-KOCETV 1983

Using The Writer's Tools C
3/4 OR 1/2 INCH VIDEO CASSETTE C
Focuses on editing, proofreading and the books which can help with these tasks. Gives instructions in using common reference books.
From The Write Course - An Introduction To College Composition Series.
Prod-DALCCD Dist-DALCCD

Using The Writer's Tools C 30 MIN
3/4 OR 1/2 INCH VIDEO CASSETTE C A
Focuses on editing, proofreading and books which can be of help with these tasks. Includes specific, practical instructions on using common reference books.
From The Write Course - An Introduction To College Composition Series.
LC NO. 85-700990
Prod-FI Dist-FI 1984

Using Time Management C 19 MIN
3/4 OR 1/2 INCH VIDEO CASSETTE
See series title for descriptive statement.
From The Time Management For Managers And Professionals Series.
Prod-DELTAK Dist-DELTAK Prodn-ONCKEW

Using Values Clarification C 30 MIN
16MM FILM, 3/4 OR 1/2 IN VIDEO A
Shows Dr Sidney Simon as he conducts a workshop in values clarification for teachers and counselors. Includes scenes of high school classes participating in values clarification exercises and interviews with students, teachers and counselors who testify to the success of this process in helping people cope with life's problems.
From The Dealing With Classroom Problems Series.
Prod-BELLDA Dist-FI 1976

Using Visicalc C
3/4 OR 1/2 INCH VIDEO CASSETTE
Shows the viewer all the basic properties and applications of the Visicalc, the electronic spreadsheet. Uses the actual screen displays on video that will be seen later on the computer.
From The Compututor Series.
Prod-CHASCI Dist-EMBASY

Using visual Aids Effectively C 30 MIN
3/4 OR 1/2 INCH VIDEO CASSETTE T
Discusses visual aids for class use. Deals with Computers and videodisc.
From The Training The Trainer Series.
Prod-ITCORP Dist-ITCORP

Using Visual Aids In Training B 14 MIN
16MM FILM - 3/4 IN VIDEO
Demonstrates the use of motion pictures and filmstrips as teaching aids. Issued in 1944 as a motion picture.
From The Problems In Supervision Series.
LC NO. 79-706517
Prod-USOE Dist-USNAC Prodn-KER 1979

Using Water Wisely C 20 MIN
16MM FILM OPTICAL SOUND PRO
Charts a series of tests on the use of fog on various types of structural fires. Shows how exposures are covered and how fires are extinguished with minimum amounts of water.
Prod-LAFIRE Dist-LAFIRE

Using WordStar C
3/4 OR 1/2 INCH VIDEO CASSETTE
Shows the use and application of the Micropro International WordStar, a popular word processing program.
From The Compututor Series.
Prod-CHASCI Dist-EMBASY

Using Your Creative Brain C 30 MIN
3/4 OR 1/2 INCH VIDEO CASSETTE J-C
Portrays the functions and differences of left and right brain thinking. Describes how to use the neglected visual and holistic power of the right brain to attain a new sense of balance and order in the thought processes.
Prod-EDDIM Dist-EDDIM

Using Your Imagination B 15 MIN
2 INCH VIDEOTAPE P
Discusses methods of communicating ideas and emotions using pantomime. (Broadcast quality)
From The Art Discoveries Series. Lesson 28
Prod-CVETVC Dist-GPITVL Prodn-WCVETV

Using Your Library C 18 MIN
3/4 INCH VIDEO CASSETTE
Introduces the great variety of materials found in libraries, including books, magazines, art, sound recordings and films. Explains the Dewey Decimal System and shows how to use the card catalog and reference books.
LC NO. 79-706405
Prod-EDDIM Dist-EDDIM 1979

Using Your Machine C
3/4 OR 1/2 INCH VIDEO CASSETTE
Gives a brief overview of computer literacy. Discusses equipment hook-up, the keyboard, major operating commands and working with printers. Shows how to write a 'BASIC' program.
From The Compututor Series.
Prod-CHASCI Dist-EMBASY

USO - Thirty Years Of Service C 28 MIN
16MM FILM OPTICAL SOUND
Takes a look at the United Service Organizations today, from San Francisco to Boston and Southeast Asia to Italy. Narrated by Bob Hope.
From The Big Picture Series.
LC NO. 75-701214
Prod-USA Dist-USNAC 1971

USO - Wherever They Go C 28 MIN
16MM FILM OPTICAL SOUND H A
A documentary account of the history and activity of the USO. Shows the entertainer, the stars and the gags, from Jolson to Hope, that have entertained service men, and the various other USO activities during its 25 years of service.
LC NO. FIE67-113
Prod-USDD Dist-USNAC 1966

Uso Correcto De Escaleras C 10 MIN
16MM FILM, 3/4 OR 1/2 IN VIDEO IND
A Spanish-language version of the motion picture Ladders And Lineman. Points out how accidents can be avoided when using a ladder. Stresses the importance of selecting the right ladder for the job, especially when electricity is involved.
Prod-EUSA Dist-IFB Prodn-KROSTR 1974

Uso De Los Triangulos Semejantes C 11 MIN
16MM FILM, 3/4 OR 1/2 IN VIDEO H
A Spanish language version of the videocassette Similar Triangles In Use. Shows how measurement of triangles is used to determine the distances between things that can't be reached. Discusses the use of the surveyor's quadrant and sextant.
Prod-IFB Dist-IFB 1961

USS Forrestal (CVA-59) B 21 MIN
16MM FILM, 3/4 OR 1/2 IN VIDEO J-H
A documentary on the construction of a modern aircraft carrier. Shows building phases from keel laying to sea trials and final commissioning.
LC NO. 82-706240
Prod-USN Dist-USNAC 1955

USS Forrestal - CVA-59 / The American Dreadnought C 50 MIN
3/4 OR 1/2 INCH VIDEO CASSETTE
Documents the construction of a U S aircraft carrier from the laying of the keel to actual sea trials and final commissions. Shows the USS New Jersey being recommissioned to join the fleet for service in Vietnam.
Prod-IHF Dist-IHF

USS Line Pipe C 9 MIN
16MM FILM OPTICAL SOUND
See series title for descriptive statement.
From The Pipe And Tubing Series.
Prod-USSC Dist-USSC

USS Mechanical And Pressure Tubing C 10 MIN
16MM FILM OPTICAL SOUND
See series title for descriptive statement.
From The Pipe And Tubing Series.
Prod-USSC Dist-USSC

USS Nautilus - Operation Sunshine C 17 MIN
16MM FILM - 3/4 IN VIDEO
Describes the events leading up to and during the actual polar passage of the USS Nautilus.
Prod-USNAC Dist-USNAC 1972

USS Nautilus - Operation Sunshine C 45 MIN
3/4 OR 1/2 INCH VIDEO CASSETTE
Documents the historic trip under the polar ice cap by the world's first nuclear submarine.
Prod-IHF Dist-IHF

USS Oil Country Goods C 11 MIN
16MM FILM OPTICAL SOUND
See series title for descriptive statement.
From The Pipe And Tubing Series.
Prod-USSC Dist-USSC

USS Rhythm—A Series
P-I
Depicts an imaginary vessel called the USS Rhythm, where crew members sing songs and introduce basic musical terms.
Prod-ARKETV Dist-AITECH 1977

America, The Beautiful 019 MIN
Animals In The Zoo 020 MIN
Autumn 019 MIN
Circus Parade 018 MIN
Dance, Indian Man 020 MIN
Deck The Halls 020 MIN
Down In The Valley 020 MIN
Dreydl Spin 020 MIN
Father, We Thank Thee For The Night 019 MIN
Five Fat Turkeys 019 MIN
Get On Board 019 MIN
Hush, Little Baby 019 MIN
Jolly Party, A 019 MIN
Kum Ba Yah 019 MIN
Lone Star Trail 018 MIN
Love Somebody 021 MIN
My Old Dan 019 MIN
Oh Susannah 019 MIN
On Halloween 020 MIN
Pick A Pumpkin 020 MIN
Review Number One 020 MIN
Review Number Two 019 MIN
Santa Claus Will Soon Be Here 019 MIN
Shepherd's Song, A 020 MIN
Shoo, Fly, Don't Bother Me 020 MIN
Sing High, Sing Low 019 MIN
Sleigh Ride 020 MIN
There Was A Crooked Man 020 MIN
Three Pirates 019 MIN
We Are Good Musicians 020 MIN
Welcome Spring 018 MIN
Yankee Doodle 019 MIN

USS Standard Pipe C 9 MIN
16MM FILM OPTICAL SOUND
See series title for descriptive statement.
From The Pipe And Tubing Series.
Prod-USSC Dist-USSC

USS Steel Sheets C 21 MIN
16MM FILM OPTICAL SOUND
Indicates that the techniques for producing steel sheets have changed considerably in the past few years and that today production is faster, bigger and more precise.
Prod-USSC Dist-USSC

USS Structural Tubing C 11 MIN
16MM FILM OPTICAL SOUND
See series title for descriptive statement.
From The Pipe And Tubing Series.
Prod-USSC Dist-USSC

Utah - Another Time Another Place C 27 MIN
16MM FILM OPTICAL SOUND
Provides a glimpse into the heritage, culture and history of Utah. Surveys its recreational and scenic opportunities.
LC NO. 79-700335
Prod-UTAPC Dist-UTAPC Prodn-HARLOV 1978

Utah, England, Taiwan, Russia, Panama C 27 MIN
16MM FILM OPTICAL SOUND P-I
Portrays a Navajo Indian from Utah, an 11-year-old Panamanian fisherman and an English animal trainer. Presents a Russian folk tale about a boy named Igor who sells magic horses to the Czar.
From The Big Blue Marble - Children Around The World Series. Program G
LC NO. 76-700646
Prod-ALVEN Dist-VITT 1975

Utamaro And His Five Women (Japanese) B 95 MIN
16MM FILM OPTICAL SOUND

Plunges the viewer into the underground world of Japan in the late 1700's, a world of brothels, drinking parties, marketplaces, intertangled love affairs and violent outbreaks of passion. Explores this period through the eyes of a placid painter, Utamaro.
Prod-NYFLMS Dist-NYFLMS 1946

Utamaro And His Five Women (Japanese) B 95 MIN
16MM FILM OPTICAL SOUND
Focuses on an 18th century Japanese printmaker and the passionate demimonde surrounding him. Directed by Kenji Mizoguchi. With English subtitles.
Prod-UNKNWN Dist-NYFLMS 1946

Uterine Aspiration In The First Trimester C 27 MIN
3/4 OR 1/2 INCH VIDEO CASSETTE PRO
Describes step-by-step uterine aspiration by means of flexible cannulas and syringe as well as by vacuum operated suction curettage.
Prod-WFP Dist-WFP

Uterine Cancer - Diagnosis And Management, Pt 1 C 20 MIN
16MM FILM OPTICAL SOUND PRO
Deals with cancer of the cervix. Demonstrates the technique of pelvic examination including cytology. Discusses etiology, symptoms, diagnosis and cone biopsy. Presents principles of treatment and end results at various stages.
Prod-AMCS Dist-AMCS 1967

Uterine Cancer - Diagnosis And Management, Pt 2 C 12 MIN
16MM FILM OPTICAL SOUND PRO
Deals with cancer of the endometrium. Presents symptoms and methods of biopsy. Demonstrates therapy, surgery and discusses indications for postoperative radiation.
Prod-AMCS Dist-AMCS 1967

Uterine Cancer - The Problem Of Early Diagnosis C 21 MIN
16MM FILM OPTICAL SOUND PRO
Illustrates the practicability of reducing deaths, from cancer of the uterus and cervix by adherence in general office practice to the routine pelvic examination of all adult women.
Prod-AMCS Dist-AMCS 1952

Utilities For Polar Regions C 180 MIN
3/4 OR 1/2 INCH VIDEO CASSETTE PRO
Discusses power, water, waste and communications.
From The Arctic Engineering Series.
Prod-UAKEN Dist-AMCEE

Utility And Process System Optimization C 35 MIN
3/4 INCH VIDEO CASSETTE C A
See series title for descriptive statement.
From The Energy Conservation In Industrial Plants Series.
LC NO. 81-706196
Prod-AMCEE Dist-AMCEE 1979

Utility Dog Obedience C 15 MIN
16MM FILM, 3/4 OR 1/2 IN VIDEO
Illustrates a variety of techniques for developing utility dog obedience.
From The Dog Obedience Training Series.
Prod-KLEINW Dist-KLEINW 1974

Utility Functions With More Than Two Attributes C 42 MIN
3/4 OR 1/2 INCH VIDEO CASSETTE
See series title for descriptive statement.
From The Decision Analysis Series.
Prod-MIOT Dist-MIOT

Utility Functions With Two Attributes C 48 MIN
3/4 OR 1/2 INCH VIDEO CASSETTE
See series title for descriptive statement.
From The Decision Analysis Series.
Prod-MIOT Dist-MIOT

Utility Rate Economics C 45 MIN
3/4 OR 1/2 INCH VIDEO CASSETTE PRO
Discusses problems associated with regulation of electric and natural gas utilities and describes past and present rate structures. Offers suggestions about long-term possibilities and problem solving.
From The Energy Auditing And Conservation Series.
LC NO. 81-706443
Prod-AMCEE Dist-AMCEE 1979

Utility Systems C
3/4 OR 1/2 INCH VIDEO CASSETTE IND
See series title for descriptive statement.
From The Drafting - Piping Familiarization Series.
Prod-GPCV Dist-GPCV

Utilizing Effective Communication B 30 MIN
16MM FILM OPTICAL SOUND C A
Reviews and reinforces basic course themes and applies the general communication theory to specific suggestions for improving communication skills.
From The Nursing - R Plus M Equals C, Relationship Plus Meaning Equals Communication Series.
LC NO. 74-700215
Prod-NTCN Dist-NTCN 1971

Utilizing Fresh Water Resources - The Columbia River C 14 MIN
16MM FILM OPTICAL SOUND J-C A
Shows how the utilization of the Columbia River for hydroelectric power, irrigation, transportation, industry and recreation constitutes a prime example of proper long-range planning with natural resources.
LC NO. FIA68-3079
Prod-NWFLMP Dist-NWFLMP 1968

Utopias C 26 MIN
16MM FILM, 3/4 OR 1/2 IN VIDEO H-C
States that the earliest Utopias date back to the 16th century and that they were seeking an ideal society. Presents the political and philosophical ideas of Utopias, and tells of some that worked.
From The Today's History Series.
Prod-JOU Dist-JOU 1984

UXB B 30 MIN
16MM FILM OPTICAL SOUND H-C
Examines the experiences and emotions of two members of a British bomb disposal unit as they dismantle a series of unexploded bombs dropped by the Nazis in World War II.
LC NO. FI67-134
Prod-GE Dist-WB 1962

V

V D Prevention C 11 MIN
3/4 OR 1/2 INCH VIDEO CASSETTE
Outlines methods of prevention and care necessary to stop infection. Discusses cleansing measures, prophylactics, preventive medications and regular VD checkups. Host-narrated by TV actress Adrienne Barbeau.
Prod-ASHA Dist-AMEDFL Prodn-AMEDFL

V D Prevention (Spanish) C 11 MIN
3/4 OR 1/2 INCH VIDEO CASSETTE
Outlines methods of prevention and care necessary to stop infection. Discusses cleansing measures, prophylactics, preventive medications and regular VD checkups. Host-narrated by TV actress Adrienne Barbeau.
Prod-ASHA Dist-AMEDFL Prodn-AMEDFL

V D Quiz C 25 MIN
3/4 OR 1/2 INCH VIDEO CASSETTE H A
Contains the most up-to-date facts, options for treatment, solutions to the pandemic of sexually transmissible diseases. Uses quiz format to encourage audience participation. Documents gonorrhea, NGU, herpes, syphillis and other venereal diseases.
Prod-ASHA Dist-AMEDFL Prodn-AMEDFL

V D Quiz (Spanish) C 25 MIN
3/4 OR 1/2 INCH VIDEO CASSETTE H A
Contains the most up-to-date facts, options for treatment, solutions to the pandemic of sexually transmissible diseases. Uses quiz format to encourage audience participation. Documents gonorrhea, NGU, herpes, syphillis and other venereal diseases.
Prod-ASHA Dist-AMEDFL Prodn-AMEDFL

V For Vigilante C 12 MIN
16MM FILM OPTICAL SOUND J-C A
Presents the story of the Mach 2 A3J vigilante 'A5). INCLUDES DRAMATIC SCENES OF STRUCTURAL 'TORTURE' testing, escape seat system firings and flight action at Columbus, Palmdale and aboard carriers.
Prod-NAA Dist-RCKWL

V Groove Open Root - 1-G Position C 15 MIN
3/4 OR 1/2 INCH VIDEO CASSETTE IND
See series title for descriptive statement.
From The Arc Welding Training Series.
Prod-AVIMA Dist-AVIMA

V Groove With Backer - 1-G Position C 15 MIN
3/4 OR 1/2 INCH VIDEO CASSETTE IND
See series title for descriptive statement.
From The Arc Welding Training Series.
Prod-AVIMA Dist-AVIMA

V Groove With Backer - 2-G Position C 15 MIN
3/4 OR 1/2 INCH VIDEO CASSETTE IND
See series title for descriptive statement.
From The Arc Welding Training Series.
Prod-AVIMA Dist-AVIMA

V Groove With Backer - 3-G Position C 15 MIN
3/4 OR 1/2 INCH VIDEO CASSETTE IND
See series title for descriptive statement.
From The Arc Welding Training Series.
Prod-AVIMA Dist-AVIMA

V Groove With Backer - 4-G Position C 15 MIN
3/4 OR 1/2 INCH VIDEO CASSETTE IND
See series title for descriptive statement.
From The Arc Welding Training Series.
Prod-AVIMA Dist-AVIMA

V Is For Voluntary Childlessness C 8 MIN
16MM FILM, 3/4 OR 1/2 IN VIDEO
Looks at reasons for having or not having children, pointing out that while, for some couples, childlessness is liberating, one-third of a million babies are born in Canada each year.
From The ABC's Of Canadian Life Series.
Prod-UTORMC Dist-UTORMC

V Sound And The Vowels, The - Long And Short U C 15 MIN
3/4 INCH VIDEO CASSETTE P
Discusses the production of the f sound and the v sound and their combination with the long and short u.
From The New Talking Shop Series.
Prod-BSPTV Dist-GPITVL 1978

V System Integration And Fabrication C
3/4 OR 1/2 INCH VIDEO CASSETTE C
Gives system design and integration, PC boards, wire-wrap, hybrids, mechanical design and guidelines.
From The Electronic Packaging Series.
Prod-UAZMIC Dist-AMCEE

V-Belts C 23 MIN
3/4 OR 1/2 INCH VIDEO CASSETTE IND
Discusses basic concept and components of V-Belts. Details advantages and disadvantages.
Prod-TAT Dist-TAT

V-Belts (Spanish) C 23 MIN
3/4 OR 1/2 INCH VIDEO CASSETTE IND
Discusses basic concept and components of V-Belts. Details advantages and disadvantages.
Prod-TAT Dist-TAT

V-Belts And V-Belt Drives C 19 MIN
16MM FILM, 3/4 OR 1/2 IN VIDEO IND
Portrays the V-belt principle as it developed from the wedge. Demonstrates their use on automobiles, machines and appliances while explaining the involvement of such forces as tension, friction and arc of contact.
From The Mechanical Power Transmission Series.
Prod-LUF Dist-LUF 1977

V-Belts Proper Care C 15 MIN
3/4 OR 1/2 INCH VIDEO CASSETTE IND
Covers installation and maintenance of V-belts and the importance of proper care. Teaches how to inspect, tension, align, store and replace V-belts.
From The Marshall Maintenance Training Programs Series. Tape 39
Prod-LEIKID Dist-LEIKID

V-Butt Joint C 3 MIN
1/2 IN VIDEO CASSETTE BETA/VHS IND
See series title for descriptive statement.
From The Welding Training (Comprehensive) - Metal Inert Gas (M I G) Welding Series.
Prod-RMI Dist-RMI

V-Butt Joint Horizontal C 2 MIN
1/2 IN VIDEO CASSETTE BETA/VHS IND
See series title for descriptive statement.
From The Welding Training (Comprehensive) - Metal Inert Gas (M I G) Welding Series.
Prod-RMI Dist-RMI

V-Butt Joint Multi-Pass C 13 MIN
1/2 IN VIDEO CASSETTE BETA/VHS IND
See series title for descriptive statement.
From The Welding Training (Comprehensive) - Basic Shielded Metal Arc Welding Series.
Prod-RMI Dist-RMI

V-2/German V-2 Rocket Tests B 29 MIN
3/4 OR 1/2 INCH VIDEO CASSETTE
Documents postwar V-2 rocket tests in the New Mexico desert.
Prod-IHF Dist-IHF

V, M, N C 15 MIN
3/4 OR 1/2 INCH VIDEO CASSETTE P
Presents techniques of handwriting, focusing on the lower case letters v, m and n.
From The Cursive Writing Series.
Prod-WHROTV Dist-GPITVL 1984

V, X, H And Y C 15 MIN
3/4 INCH VIDEO CASSETTE P
From The Writing Time Series.
Prod-WHROTV Dist-GPITVL

V, Y, Z, Q C 15 MIN
3/4 OR 1/2 INCH VIDEO CASSETTE P
Presents techniques of handwriting, focusing on the capital letters V, Y, Z and Q.
From The Cursive Writing Series.
Prod-WHROTV Dist-GPITVL 1984

VA Nursing - The Challenge Is Yours C 9 MIN
3/4 OR 1/2 INCH VIDEO CASSETTE PRO
Discusses the variety of nursing career opportunities in the Veterans Administration Nursing Service. States that the individual is responsible for managing his or her own career goals, objectives and timetable, although resources are available to enhance planning, goal setting and achievement.
Prod-VAMSLC Dist-USNAC

VA Ration Allowance As A Management Tool C 55 MIN
3/4 INCH VIDEO CASSETTE PRO
Defines terms used by the U S Veterans Administration in the operation and management of hospital food services. Features dietician Carol B Rooney explaining how food ration allowances should be applied in planning food purchases and how menu planning guides should be individualized in terms of the health care facilities and clientele.
LC NO. 77-706085
Prod-USVA Dist-USNAC 1976

Va-rice-ity - A New Look At Rice C 15 MIN
16MM FILM OPTICAL SOUND
Illustrates the growth, production and harvesting of rice. Presents recipes and highlights rice production as a significant American industry.
Prod-RICMD Dist-MTP

Vaal River Story C 19 MIN
16MM FILM OPTICAL SOUND J-C A
Explains the vital role of Vaal River in South Africa. Traces the river's course from its source in the eastern Transvaal to a point 600 miles west where it joins the Orange River.
Prod-SMUSA Dist-SMUSA

Vacances En Bretagne (Vacation In Brittany) C 15 MIN
16MM FILM OPTICAL SOUND H
A French language film. Presents the Ermonts, their children, Caroline and Victor and their friends spending their wonderful vacation in Brittany. Includes window shopping, eating at the cafe and boat rides.

From The Toute La Bande Series. No. 4
LC NO. 78-715480
Prod-SCHMAG Dist-SCHMAG 1970

Vacant Lot C 21 MIN
16MM FILM, 3/4 OR 1/2 IN VIDEO I-H
Examines the ecology of a vacant lot in a residential section.
From The Living Science Series.
Prod-IFB Dist-IFB 1961

Vacation Pena Style C 30 MIN
3/4 OR 1/2 INCH VIDEO CASSETTE
See series title for descriptive statement.
From The Que Pasa, U S A Series.
Prod-WPBTTV Dist-MDCPB

Vacation Planning C 30 MIN
3/4 OR 1/2 INCH VIDEO CASSETTE
Presents tips on vacation planning.
From The Consumer Survival Series. Recreation
Prod-MDCPB Dist-MDCPB

Vacation Safety X
16MM FILM OPTICAL SOUND
Gives tips on having vacation fun without 'OVERDOING IT' or becoming involved in an accident.
Prod-NSC Dist-NSC

Vacationing C 30 MIN
3/4 OR 1/2 INCH VIDEO CASSETTE H-C A
Presents Lawrence Solow and Sharon Neumann Solow introducing American Sign Language used by the hearing-impaired. Emphasizes signs having to do with vacationing.
From The Say It With Sign Series. Part 32
Prod-KNBCTV Dist-FI 1982

Vaccine On Trial C 60 MIN
3/4 OR 1/2 INCH VIDEO CASSETTE
Deals with the mobilization of New York's gay community to help research and test a vaccine against hepatitis B, the prime cause of fatal liver cancer.
From The Quest For The Killers Series.
Prod-PBS Dist-PBS

Vacuum Filtration C 9 MIN
3/4 OR 1/2 INCH VIDEO CASSETTE C A
Demonstrates the use of a Buchner funnel and vacuum filtration apparatus to perform a qualitative separation.
From The Chemistry - Master/Apprentice Series. Program 7
LC NO. 82-706040
Prod-CUETV Dist-CUNIV 1981

Vacuum Filtration In Gravimetric Analysis C 12 MIN
3/4 OR 1/2 INCH VIDEO CASSETTE C A
Shows how to use vacuum filtration to collect a precipitate (nickel dimethlglyoximate) in a porcelain crucible with a porous bottom. Demonstrates the techniques of quantitative transfer, decanting, washing, and testing the wash solution.
From The Chemistry - Master/Apprentice Series. Program 102
LC NO. 82-706049
Prod-CUETV Dist-CUNIV 1981

Vacuum Pump, Air Ejector, Strainer, And Trap Operations C 60 MIN
3/4 OR 1/2 INCH VIDEO CASSETTE IND
Describes the operations of a vacuum pump, air ejector, strainer and trap.
From The Equipment Operation Training Program Series.
Prod-ITCORP Dist-ITCORP

Vacuum Tubes - Bias In Triodes B 18 MIN
16MM FILM OPTICAL SOUND
Explains the term bias. Discusses fixed bias and shows the schematic of a fixed bias network. Identifies the components and gives their purpose. Traces an AC signal through the circuit. (Kinescope)
LC NO. 74-705898
Prod-USAF Dist-USNAC

Vacuum Tubes - Electron Theory And The Diode Tube B 16 MIN
16MM FILM OPTICAL SOUND J-H
The three functions of the vacuum tube in radio are explained.
LC NO. FIE52-1486
Prod-USOE Dist-USNAC 1944

Vacuum Tubes - Triode And Multi-Purpose Tubes B 14 MIN
16MM FILM OPTICAL SOUND H
Describes the triode tube as evolved from the diode tube, its structure and capacities and the circuits in which the tube functions. Indicates the functions of the grid, the grid bias, the screen and suppression grids and the multi-purpose tubes.
LC NO. FIE59-176
Prod-USA Dist-USNAC 1942

Vacuum Tubes - Triodes - Cathode Self Bias B 17 MIN
16MM FILM OPTICAL SOUND
Defines cathode self bias and shows an amplifier circuit schematic with cathode bias. Identifies the components, gives the function of the components, traces the charge and discharge paths of CK, and defines degeneration. (Kinescope)
LC NO. 74-705899
Prod-USAF Dist-USNAC

Vacuum Tubes - Triodes - Grid Leak Bias B 27 MIN
16MM FILM OPTICAL SOUND
Shows a grid-leak bias network, identifies the components that comprise the circuit and explains how the network functions. Traces the charge and discharge paths of CG and the AC signal through the circuit. (Kinescope)
LC NO. 74-705900
Prod-USAF Dist-USNAC

Vadya Vrinda B 26 MIN
16MM FILM OPTICAL SOUND H-C A
Introduces Indian music and explains the roles of the various musical instruments in the Indian orchestra.
Prod-INDIA Dist-NEDINF

Vaginal Hysterectomy C 27 MIN
16MM FILM OPTICAL SOUND PRO
Demonstrates a simplified anatomic approach to vaginal hysterectomy. Emphasizes minimizing blood loss and decreasing the time required for surgery.
Prod-ACYDGD Dist-ACY 1970

Vaginal Hysterectomy C 36 MIN
16MM FILM OPTICAL SOUND PRO
Shows the technique of vaginal hysterectomy used in the area Department of Obstetrics and Gynaecology at Oxford. Illustrates transfixion and double ligation of the pedicles following the use of clamps, together with high support of the vaginal vault, plus high anterior and posterior fascial colporrhaphy.
Prod-ACYDGD Dist-ACY 1957

Vaginal Hysterectomy And Repair C
3/4 OR 1/2 INCH VIDEO CASSETTE
Describes how physical complications resulting from childbirth often require surgical attention including vaginal hysterectomy. Discusses the problems of a prolapse, retocele and cystocele.
Prod-MIFE Dist-MIFE

Vaginal Hysterectomy For The Enlarged Uterus C 11 MIN
16MM FILM OPTICAL SOUND PRO
Demonstrates for three cases of benign myomatous uteri a simple, safe method of reducing the size of the uterus to facilitate its vaginal delivery, showing in detail each step of the procedure. Discusses indications and advantages of the vaginal approach to hysterectomy.
LC NO. 73-701952
Prod-SCPMG Dist-SQUIBB 1968

Vaginal Hysterectomy, A Simplified Technique C 28 MIN
16MM FILM OPTICAL SOUND PRO
Shows a simplified technique for the performance of vaginal hysterectomy when removal of the uterus without repair of the vagina is indicated. Explains that using this technique, hysterectomy can be accomplished vaginally in many instances in which the abdominal approach might have been done formerly.
Prod-ACYDGD Dist-ACY 1963

Vaginal Hysterectomy, Pathology Laboratory And Operation For Post-Operative Hemorrhage C 37 MIN
3/4 OR 1/2 INCH VIDEO CASSETTE
See series title for descriptive statement.
From The Gynecologic Series.
Prod-SVL Dist-SVL

Vaginal Prolapse - A Method Of Retention C 19 MIN
16MM FILM OPTICAL SOUND PRO
Uses aluminum rods and necessary equipment and anesthesia to demonstrate vaginal prolapse. (Kinescope)
Prod-CIBA Dist-AMVMA

Vaginitis C 12 MIN
16MM FILM, 3/4 OR 1/2 IN VIDEO H-C A
Describes the causes and symptoms of vaginitis. Introduces frequently-prescribed medications and demonstrates their use. Suggests ways of maintaning vaginal hygiene.
LC NO. 79-707853
Prod-CROMIE Dist-PEREN 1979

Vaginitis C 14 MIN
16MM FILM, 3/4 OR 1/2 IN VIDEO PRO
Discusses the major sources of vaginitis, its signs, symptoms, treatment and prevention.
Prod-PRORE Dist-PRORE

Vaginitis (Captioned) C 12 MIN
16MM FILM - VIDEO, ALL FORMATS
Explains bacterial, yeast and trichomonal vaginal infections. Discusses causes, symptoms, diagnosis and treatment.
Prod-CROMIE Dist-PEREN

Vagotomy And Antrectomy For Duodenal Ulcer C 23 MIN
16MM FILM OPTICAL SOUND PRO
Illustrates the technical features of both selective gastric vagotomy and truncal vagotomy combined with antral resection in definitive treatment of duodenal ulcer disease.
Prod-ACYDGD Dist-ACY 1965

Vagotomy And Pyloroplasty C 27 MIN
16MM FILM OPTICAL SOUND PRO
Discusses finney pyloroplasty, including its historical background. Demonstrates the operative techniques currently used.
Prod-ACYDGD Dist-ACY 1967

Vagotomy And Pyloroplasty For Bleeding And For Perforated Duodenal Ulcer C 25 MIN
16MM FILM OPTICAL SOUND PRO
Explains that vagotomy not only provides effective control of duodenal ulcer disease but also induces amazingly rapid healing of duodenal ulceration. Points out that pyloroplasty inherently provides a simple method for excision of perforated or bleeding anterior duodenal ulcer.
Prod-ACYDGD Dist-ACY 1963

Vagotomy And Pyloroplasty For Duodenal Ulcer C 22 MIN
16MM FILM OPTICAL SOUND PRO
Explains that vagotomy and pyloroplasty has proven to be an effective and simple method for dealing with duodenal ulcer. Shows operative technique, the operation being carried out through the abdomen.
Prod-ACYDGD Dist-ACY 1965

Vagotomy, Choice Of Drainage Sites C 24 MIN
16MM FILM OPTICAL SOUND PRO
Covers tests for completeness of vagotomy, consideration with regard to choice of gastroenterostomy, pyloroplasty or subtotal gastrectomy and technique of vagotomy and gastroenterostomy.
Prod-ACYDGD Dist-ACY 1965

Vagotomy, Pyloroplasty, And Supra-Antral Segmental Gastrectomy For Duodenal Ulcer C 34 MIN
16MM FILM OPTICAL SOUND PRO
Presents a procedure calculated to control the ulcerogenic mechanisms with maximal conservation of gastrointestinal function. Shows that adequate acid reduction is accomplished by vagotomy and subtotal resection of the acid-producing area of the stomach.
Prod-ACYDGD Dist-ACY 1956

Vagrant Woman B 8 MIN
3/4 INCH VIDEO CASSETTE
Shows police questioning an unemployed woman who has been living in her car, offering her advice and finally taking her to the Salvation Army.
From The Pittsburgh Police Series.
Prod-DOCEDR Dist-DOCEDR Prodn-MSHLLJ

Valentine C 97 MIN
3/4 OR 1/2 INCH VIDEO CASSETTE H-C A
Tells what happens when a pair of 70-year-olds in a retirement village embark on a high-spirited affair. Reveals that when the man finds that the woman has a terminal illness, he whisks her off on a romantic odyssey of fun and excitement. Stars Jack Albertson and Mary Martin.
Prod-TIMLIF Dist-TIMLIF 1982

Valentine Lane Family Practice, The C 29 MIN
16MM FILM, 3/4 OR 1/2 IN VIDEO
Looks at an approach to health care which emphasizes the treatment of the family, as well as comprehensive individual care.
Prod-DOCUA Dist-CNEMAG

Valentine Wishes C 15 MIN
3/4 OR 1/2 INCH VIDEO CASSETTE P
Demonstrates the ABA form and simple rhythms in music. Uses a Valentine theme.
From The Music Machine Series.
Prod-GPITVL Dist-GPITVL

Valentine's Day C 15 MIN
3/4 INCH VIDEO CASSETTE P
See series title for descriptive statement.
From The Celebrate Series.
Prod-KUONTV Dist-GPITVL 1978

Valentine's Second Chance C 24 MIN
16MM FILM, 3/4 OR 1/2 IN VIDEO
Tells how a 10-year-old boy helps reform the legendary safecracker Jimmy Valentine. Based on the story A Retrieved Reformation by O Henry. Originally shown on the television series ABC Weekend Specials.
LC NO. 79-707138
Prod-ABCTV Dist-MTI Prodn-ABCCIR 1978

Valentino Mystique, The B 28 MIN
16MM FILM OPTICAL SOUND
Shows Rudolph Valentino's early childhood in Italy, the fateful move to New York, and the coincidences and performances that made him a cult. Includes excerpts from such Valentino films as Passion's Playground, Alimony, An Adventuress, Stolen Moments, Eyes Of Youth, The Sheik and Blood And Sand.
From The History Of The Motion Picture Series.
Prod-KILLIS Dist-KILLIS 1972

Valerie C 15 MIN
16MM FILM, 3/4 OR 1/2 IN VIDEO J-C A
Explores some of the ideas and work of Valerie Maynard, sculptor.
Prod-PHENIX Dist-PHENIX 1975

Valerie Bettis And Pauline Koner C 30 MIN
3/4 OR 1/2 INCH VIDEO CASSETTE
Looks at the earliest days of dance on television.
From The Eye On Dance - Dance On TV And Film Series.
Prod-ARTRES Dist-ARTRES

Valerie, A Woman, An Artist, A Philosophy Of Life C 15 MIN
16MM FILM - 3/4 IN VIDEO
Documents the life and work of black sculptor Valerie Maynard. Shows her in her studio and her home in Harlem discussing her life as an artist.
Prod-BLKFMF Dist-BLKFMF

Valerie's Stained Glass Window C 25 MIN
16MM FILM, 3/4 OR 1/2 IN VIDEO I-J A
Introduces Valerie, a French girl who would like to create beautiful stained glass windows. Shows her choosing a design, selecting the colors and glass, and assembling the window.
From The World Cultures And Youth Series.
LC NO. 81-706803
Prod-SUNRIS Dist-CORF 1980

Valery And Galina Panov C 15 MIN
16MM FILM OPTICAL SOUND
Illustrates the struggle endured by Valery and Galina Panov, the former Russian ballet stars, before they were allowed to emigrate to Israel.
Prod-NBC Dist-ALDEN

Valiant Hans C 16 MIN
16MM FILM, 3/4 OR 1/2 IN VIDEO P-I
Presents an animated puppet film based on a fairy tale by the Brothers Grimm. Tells the story of Hans, a vagabond, who rescues the king's daughter from the forest where she is harassed by ghosts.
LC NO. 80-707063
Prod-NET Dist-IU 1970

Validating Pricing Strategies C
3/4 OR 1/2 INCH VIDEO CASSETTE
Introduces pricing strategies which help hospitals cope with predictable payment problems.
From The Revenues, Rates And Reimbursements Series.
Prod-TEACHM Dist-TEACHM

Valium C 7 MIN
3/4 OR 1/2 INCH VIDEO CASSETTE
Covers all the precautions your patient taking valium needs to know.
Prod-TRAINX Dist-TRAINX

Valium C 18 MIN
16MM FILM, 3/4 OR 1/2 IN VIDEO J-C A
Reports on the extensive use and abuse of Valium, the most widely used prescription drug in the world. Originally shown on the CBS television program 60 Minutes.
Prod-CBSNEW Dist-CAROUF

Valley Deep - Mountain High C 23 MIN
16MM FILM OPTICAL SOUND J-C A
Shows the attractions for skiers, bushwalkers and others of the Kosciusko National Park in the snowy mountains of Australia.
LC NO. 72-709229
Prod-ANAIB Dist-AUIS 1969

Valley Fever C 60 MIN
3/4 OR 1/2 INCH VIDEO CASSETTE PRO
Presents bacteriologic and medical aspects of coccidioidomycosis as well as new treatment methods.
LC NO. 81-706303
Prod-USVA Dist-USNAC 1980

Valley Forge C 24 MIN
16MM FILM, 3/4 OR 1/2 IN VIDEO I-C A
Re-creates the Continental Army's historic stay at Valley Forge and conveys the loyalty, dedication and fortitude of soldiers who defended the cause of American independence. Contrasts the hunger, sickness and cold endured by the patriots with the comfortable conditions enjoyed by the redcoats during the same time.
Prod-FFVF Dist-AIMS 1975

Valley Forge - No Food, No Soldier C 13 MIN
16MM FILM, 3/4 OR 1/2 IN VIDEO I-C A
Uses the authentic words of Revolutionary War soldiers to recreate the ordeal of the harsh, crucial winter of 1778. Filmed in Valley Forge National Park.
Prod-NYT Dist-CORF 1971

Valley Forge - The Battle For Survival C 16 MIN
16MM FILM, 3/4 OR 1/2 IN VIDEO J-H
Presents Valley Forge, the decisive chapter of the Revolutionary War, as seen through the eyes of a young man who was there. Shows him marching along with the other exhausted men stumbling through the snow into Valley Forge and helping in the construction of the fortifications to protect the army from British attack. Expresses the hope he feels that other men will be prepared to defend America whenever liberty is threatened.
From The Americana Series. No. 6
Prod-HANDEL Dist-HANDEL 1969

Valley Forge - The Young Spy C 24 MIN
3/4 OR 1/2 INCH VIDEO CASSETTE
Dramatizes an account of a young tory farm boy's mission to spy on George Washington's camp. Focuses on the power of the ideals that inspired the men of the Revolution.
From The Young People's Specials Series.
Prod-MULTPP Dist-MULTPP

Valley Furniture C 30 MIN
3/4 OR 1/2 INCH VIDEO CASSETTE
Presents guests who are experts in their respective fields who share tips on collecting and caring for antique valley furniture.
From The Antique Shop Series.
Prod-WVPTTV Dist-MDCPB

Valley Glaciers C 20 MIN
3/4 OR 1/2 INCH VIDEO CASSETTE
Analyzes glaciers including ice-falls, crevasses, ogives, basal sliding, the character and behavior of the ablation zone and outwash streams, and the relationship between glacier behavior, meltwater discharge and sediment loads.
From The Earth Science Series.
Prod-FOTH Dist-FOTH 1984

Valley Of The Kings, The C 29 MIN
16MM FILM, 3/4 OR 1/2 IN VIDEO
Focuses on the tombs of Ipi the workman and Kha the architect. Examines daily life in ancient Egyptian society.
From The Ancient Lives Series.
Prod-FOTH Dist-FOTH

Valley Of The Swans C 26 MIN
16MM FILM OPTICAL SOUND J-H
Views a lake sanctuary in the Kootenay Valley of British Columbia. Shows migratory birds throughout the four seasons.
LC NO. FIA64-1358
Prod-BRCOL Dist-CTFL 1964

Valley Of The Tennessee C 29 MIN
16MM FILM, 3/4 OR 1/2 IN VIDEO
Shows the need for conservation in the Tennessee River Valley, the origin of the TVA, the building of the dams and the influence of the TVA on the lives of the people in the Valley.
LC NO. 79-706479
Prod-USOWI Dist-USNAC 1979

Valley Town B 27 MIN
16MM FILM OPTICAL SOUND J-C
A study of workers displaced by automatic machinery. Traces the history of a typical American steel town of the 1920's and 30's through a boom, the depression and the war.
Prod-NYU Dist-NYU 1940

Valley, The C 28 MIN
16MM FILM OPTICAL SOUND J-C A
Explains that some pollution-sensitive organisms such as Asiatic clams and caddis fly larvae are returning to the Ohio River where they had previously been unable to live. Shows this as living proof that the river is getting cleaner.
Prod-FINLYS Dist-FINLYS

Valley, The C 28 MIN
16MM FILM OPTICAL SOUND
Describes modern water quality management programs in the Ohio Valley. Discusses some of the remaining water quality problems in the area.
LC NO. 75-700163
Prod-ORVWSC Dist-FINLYS 1974

Valleybrook Elementary School C 16 MIN
16MM FILM OPTICAL SOUND C
Presents six problem incidents which confront teachers in multi-ethnic schools. Shows how the viewers assume the role of a new teacher who is confronted and must deal with these problems.
From The Solving Multi-Ethnic Problems - A Simulation Game For School Teachers Series.
LC NO. 70-707079
Prod-UTEXIE Dist-ADL 1970

Value Clarification C 30 MIN
3/4 OR 1/2 INCH VIDEO CASSETTE T
Gives systematic approach to deciding worth and to making decisions that affect daily living.
From The Stretch Concepts For Teaching Handicapped Children Series.
Prod-HUBDSC Dist-HUBDSC

Value Clarification C 30 MIN
16MM FILM, 3/4 OR 1/2 IN VIDEO T S
Demonstrates a practical application of value clarification with a high school class.
From The Project STRETCH (Strategies To Train Regular Educators To Teach Children With...) Series. Module 3
LC NO. 80-706639
Prod-METCO Dist-HUBDSC 1980

Value Clarification And Decision Making C 30 MIN
3/4 OR 1/2 INCH VIDEO CASSETTE
See series title for descriptive statement.
From The Creating A Learning Environment Series.
Prod-NETCHE Dist-NETCHE 1975

Value Clarification In Counseling C 27 MIN
16MM FILM OPTICAL SOUND J-C A
Presents Dr Robert I Havens, professor of counselor education at the University of Wisconsin-Oshkosh, demonstrating how he would use both classroom and small group settings to help junior high school students learn the valuing process of choosing, prizing and acting by applying it to their own lives. Based on the book VALUE CLARIFICATION IN COUNSELING by Kenneth Morrison and Robert I Havens.
LC NO. 76-702381
Prod-EDMDC Dist-EDMDC Prodn-SOREND 1975

Value Engineering B 24 MIN
16MM FILM OPTICAL SOUND
Evaluates the impact of value engineering programs on cost performance. Discusses the need for incentives, savings, subcontractor participation and contractor support.
LC NO. 74-706304
Prod-USAF Dist-USNAC 1965

Value Engineering - More Ships For Less Money C 13 MIN
16MM FILM, 3/4 OR 1/2 IN VIDEO
Explains how the U S Navy's value engineering program works, enumerates its key techniques and provides examples of its results.
LC NO. 79-707983
Prod-USN Dist-USNAC Prodn-DEPICT 1979

Value Engineering - The Hundred Million Dollar Story C 28 MIN
16MM FILM OPTICAL SOUND
Tells the story of the latest Air Force economy concept - a savings of millions of dollars in aircraft and missile cost.
LC NO. FIE64-61
Prod-USAF Dist-USNAC 1963

Value Engineering—A Series
IND
Defines Value Engineering (VE) as an integrated system of techniques that maximizes return on invested assets and is most effective in terms of productivity improvement. Cites function-oriented approach as having much greater leverage on costs than traditional methods-oriented efforts. Focuses on function/cost justification and helps identify those areas offering best potential for cost reductions.
Prod-NCSU Dist-AMCEE

Case Studies, Pt 1 060 MIN
Case Studies, Pt 2 060 MIN
Cost Analysis For Value Engineering 060 MIN
Creativity 060 MIN
Execution Phase, The 060 MIN
Function Analysis System Technique (FAST) 060 MIN
Implementation Phase 060 MIN
Information Phase, The 060 MIN
Introduction To Value Engineering 060 MIN
Managing Value Engineering 060 MIN
Planning Phase, The 060 MIN
Presentation Phase, The 060 MIN
Speculation Phase, The 060 MIN
V E In Non-Hardware Applications 060 MIN

Value Of An MBA, The C 30 MIN
3/4 OR 1/2 INCH VIDEO CASSETTE
Discusses the value of the graduate degree.
From The Where The Jobs Are Series.
Prod-IVCH Dist-IVCH

Value Of Digits C 15 MIN
3/4 INCH VIDEO CASSETTE P
Explains how to express each digit in a two- or three-digit number as a single numeral. Tells how to write two numerals from two digits and six numerals from three digits. Describes how to order a list of numerals from lowest to highest.
From The Studio M Series.
Prod-WCETTV Dist-GPITVL 1979

Value Of Ongoing Direct Mail, The C 30 MIN
3/4 OR 1/2 INCH VIDEO CASSETTE
Explains the value of ongoing direct mailing.
From The Business Of Direct Mail Series.
Prod-KYTV Dist-KYTV 1983

Values C 30 MIN
3/4 OR 1/2 INCH VIDEO CASSETTE T
Presents Dr Willard M Kniep of Arizona State University instructing teachers in the strategies and skills of teaching children economics and consumer education concepts. Focuses on the topic of values by explaining it and then demonstrating specific approaches that teachers can use in their classrooms.
From The Economics Exchange Series. Program 6
LC NO. 82-706418
Prod-KAETTV Dist-GPITVL 1981

Values C 30 MIN
3/4 OR 1/2 INCH VIDEO CASSETTE C A
Begins with a values auction where such things as good marriage and leisure time are up on the block. Shows national experts discussing the importance of values clarification in life/career planning. Presents street interviews that reveal what Americans value and why.
From The Making A Living Work Series. Program 103
Prod-OHUTC Dist-OHUTC

Values - Being Friends C 9 MIN
16MM FILM, 3/4 OR 1/2 IN VIDEO I
Teaches the meaning of friendship. Shows that people may disagree but still remain friends. Emphasizes trust and helping each other.
From The Values Series.
Prod-COLLRD Dist-PHENIX 1969

Values - Being Friends (Spanish) C 9 MIN
16MM FILM, 3/4 OR 1/2 IN VIDEO I
Teaches the meaning of friendship. Shows that people may disagree but still remain friends. Emphasizes trust and helping each other.
From The Values Series.
Prod-COLLRD Dist-PHENIX 1969

Values - Cooperation C 11 MIN
16MM FILM, 3/4 OR 1/2 IN VIDEO
Applies the adage 'No man is an island unto himself,' emphasizing that no one is too young to learn this. Views Rod, Julian and John playing together, picturing them in action as they get things done and have lots of fun by cooperating with each other. Stresses the value of cooperation, whether at work, play or school.
From The Values Series.
Prod-COLLRD Dist-PHENIX

Values - Cooperation (Spanish) C 11 MIN
16MM FILM, 3/4 OR 1/2 IN VIDEO
Applies the adage 'No man is an island unto himself,' emphasizing that no one is too young to learn this. Views Rod, Julian and John playing together, picturing them in action as they get things done and have lots of fun by cooperating with each other. Stresses the value of cooperation, whether at work, play or school.
From The Values Series.
Prod-COLLRD Dist-PHENIX

Values - Playing Fair C 10 MIN
16MM FILM, 3/4 OR 1/2 IN VIDEO
Presents a class round table discussion which allows students to decide for themselves what 'playing fair' really means. Identifies various social interactions to
From The Values Series.
Prod-COLLRD Dist-PHENIX 1969

Values - Playing Fair (Spanish) C 10 MIN
16MM FILM, 3/4 OR 1/2 IN VIDEO
Presents a class round table discussion which allows students to decide for themselves what 'playing fair' really means. Identifies various social interactions to demonstrate the meaning of fair play.
From The Values Series.
Prod-COLLRD Dist-PHENIX 1969

Values - Telling The Truth C 10 MIN
16MM FILM, 3/4 OR 1/2 IN VIDEO P-I
Illustrates specific values as three boys walk home from school together. Explains that the boys pick up some stones which are left over from the cement mixer and hit Mrs Jensen's window. Concludes with Rod and Julian running away, but John stays and tells the truth.
From The Values Series.
Prod-COLLRD Dist-PHENIX 1969

Values - Telling The Truth (Spanish) C 10 MIN
16MM FILM, 3/4 OR 1/2 IN VIDEO P-I
Illustrates specific values as three boys walk home from school together. Explains that the boys pick up some stones which are left over from the cement mixer and hit Mrs Jensen's window. Concludes with Rod and Julian running away, but John stays and tells the truth.
From The Values Series.
Prod-COLLRD Dist-PHENIX 1969

Values - The Right Thing To Do C 9 MIN
16MM FILM, 3/4 OR 1/2 IN VIDEO I
Presents a dilemma in which Terry and his friends accidently cause a pile of lumber to fall on an old man, whose yard they are playing in. Shows Terry trying to decide whether to run away with the rest of his friends, or stay and help the man, in which case he may be blamed for the incident.
From The Values Series.
Prod-COLLRD Dist-PHENIX 1970

Values - The Right Thing To Do (Spanish) C 9 MIN
16MM FILM, 3/4 OR 1/2 IN VIDEO I
Presents a dilemma in which Terry and his friends accidently cause a pile of lumber to fall on an old man, whose yard they are playing in. Shows Terry trying to decide whether to run away with the rest of his friends, or stay and help the man, in which case he may be blamed for the incident.
From The Values Series.
Prod-COLLRD Dist-PHENIX 1970

Values - Understanding Others C 8 MIN
16MM FILM, 3/4 OR 1/2 IN VIDEO
Suggests how one can learn to understand other people better. Stresses that when one tries to understand how other people feel, an attitude of caring about them is created.
From The Values Series.
Prod-COLLRD Dist-PHENIX 1970

Values - Understanding Others (Spanish) C 8 MIN
16MM FILM, 3/4 OR 1/2 IN VIDEO
Suggests how one can learn to understand other people better. Stresses that when one tries to understand how other people feel, an attitude of caring about them is created.
From The Values Series.
Prod-COLLRD Dist-PHENIX 1970

Values - Understanding Others (Swedish) C 8 MIN
16MM FILM, 3/4 OR 1/2 IN VIDEO
Suggests how one can learn to understand other people better. Stresses that when one tries to understand how other people feel, an attitude of caring about them is created.
From The Values Series.
Prod-COLLRD Dist-PHENIX 1970

Values - Understanding Ourselves C 9 MIN
16MM FILM, 3/4 OR 1/2 IN VIDEO I
Uses a story of three boys to present the concept that everybody has an idea of the kind of person he is. Explains that sometimes it seems like it would be more fun to be someone else but each person, if he could really chose, would rather be himself.
From The Values Series.
Prod-COLLRD Dist-PHENIX 1969

Values - Understanding Ourselves (Spanish) C 9 MIN
16MM FILM, 3/4 OR 1/2 IN VIDEO I
Uses a story of three boys to present the concept that everybody has an idea of the kind of person he is. Explains that sometimes it seems like it would be more fun to be someone else but each person, if he could really chose, would rather be himself.
From The Values Series.
Prod-COLLRD Dist-PHENIX 1969

Values And Attitudes B 27 MIN
3/4 INCH VIDEOTAPE
See series title for descriptive statement.
From The One Strong Link Series.
Prod-CUETV Dist-CUNIV 1971

Values And Goals - A Way To Go C 29 MIN
16MM FILM, 3/4 OR 1/2 IN VIDEO H-C A
Presents the story of youth preparing to meet the world on their own terms, by their own definitions, in their own ways.
Prod-COP Dist-AIMS 1972

Values And Goals - A Way To Go (Spanish) C 29 MIN
16MM FILM, 3/4 OR 1/2 IN VIDEO H-C A
Presents the story of youth preparing to meet the world on their own terms, by their own definitions, in their own ways.
Prod-COP Dist-AIMS 1972

Values Clarification In The Classroom C 29 MIN
16MM FILM, 3/4 OR 1/2 IN VIDEO T
Shows Values Clarification teaching styles being used in an eighth grade classroom in Illinois. Includes experts who discuss how to raise issues, stimulate thinking and be nonjudgmental with positions held by students.
Prod-MFFD Dist-FI

Values For Grades K-Three—A Series
16MM FILM, 3/4 OR 1/2 IN VIDEO K-P
Prod-CF Dist-CF

Bike, The 013 MIN
Hideout, The 015 MIN
Lost Puppy 014 MIN

Values In America C
3/4 OR 1/2 INCH VIDEO CASSETTE
Introduces 'value' as a basis of choice in people's lives. Motivates an understanding and appreciation of the diversity of cultures that make up America.
Prod-CEPRO Dist-CEPRO

Values In America C 24 MIN
3/4 OR 1/2 INCH VIDEO CASSETTE J-H
Introduces values as a basis for the choices people make in their lives with emphasis on the divergence of American life.
Prod-CEPRO Dist-CEPRO

Values—A Series
16MM FILM, 3/4 OR 1/2 IN VIDEO
Prod-COLLRD Dist-PHENIX

Values - Being Friends 9 MIN
Values - Cooperation 11 MIN
Values - Playing Fair 10 MIN
Values - Telling The Truth 10 MIN
Values - The Right Thing To Do 9 MIN
Values - Understanding Others 8 MIN
Values - Understanding Ourselves 9 MIN

Valuing Assets C 30 MIN
3/4 OR 1/2 INCH VIDEO CASSETTE C
Discusses valuing assets as it applies to accounting.
From The Accounting Series. Pt 6
Prod-UMA Dist-GPITVL 1980

Valve Amintenance - Reciprocating Compressors C 60 MIN
3/4 OR 1/2 INCH VIDEO CASSETTE IND
See series title for descriptive statement.
From The Mechanical Equipment Maintenance, Module 9 - Air Compressors Series.
Prod-LEIKID Dist-LEIKID

Valve Operation C 60 MIN
3/4 OR 1/2 INCH VIDEO CASSETTE IND
Illustrates valve functions and operations. Explains how to identify and properly operate rising and non-rising gate valve stem designs.
From The Equipment Operation Training Program Series.
Prod-LEIKID Dist-LEIKID

Valve Operations C 60 MIN
3/4 OR 1/2 INCH VIDEO CASSETTE IND
Identifies valve parts and functions. Describes manual and automatic valve operation. Demonstrates safety practices and valve inspections.
From The Equipment Operation Training Program Series.
Prod-ITCORP Dist-ITCORP

Valve Spacing And Pressuring C 19 MIN
16MM FILM, 3/4 OR 1/2 IN VIDEO IND
See series title for descriptive statement.
From The Gas Lift Series.
Prod-EXXON Dist-UTEXPE

Valve Timing The 4-Cycle Engine C 8 MIN
16MM FILM, 3/4 OR 1/2 IN VIDEO J-C A
See series title for descriptive statement.
From The Power Mechanics Series.
Prod-THIOKL Dist-CAROUF

Valves C
3/4 OR 1/2 INCH VIDEO CASSETTE IND
See series title for descriptive statement.
From The Drafting - Piping Familiarization Series.
Prod-GPCV Dist-GPCV

Valves C 20 MIN
3/4 OR 1/2 INCH VIDEO CASSETTE IND
Discusses plug valves using disassembled valves. Explains pressure drop and water hammer.
Prod-TAT Dist-TAT

Valves C 240 MIN
3/4 OR 1/2 INCH VIDEO CASSETTE IND
Describes various types of valves.
From The Mechanical Equipment Maintenance Series.
Prod-ITCORP Dist-ITCORP

Valves (Spanish) C 240 MIN
3/4 OR 1/2 INCH VIDEO CASSETTE IND
Describes various types of valves.
From The Mechanical Equipment Maintenance (Spanish) Series.
Prod-ITCORP Dist-ITCORP

Valvular Incompetence And Varicose Veins C 18 MIN
16MM FILM OPTICAL SOUND PRO
Explores the fundamental pathogenesis and the importance of valvular incompetence in the production of varicose veins.
Prod-AL Dist-SCITIF 1966

Valvulotomy For Valvular Pulmonic Stenosis C 27 MIN
16MM FILM OPTICAL SOUND PRO
Explains that by brief interruption of the flow of blood into the heart under moderate hypothermia, incision can be placed in the pulmonary artery and under direct vision, complete relief of valvular obstruction in congenital pulmonic stenosis may be accomplished in a simple and precise manner.
Prod-ACYDGD Dist-ACY 1955

Vampire C 25 MIN
16MM FILM, 3/4 OR 1/2 IN VIDEO H-C A
Describes the physiology and social relationships of vampire bats.
Prod-BBCTV Dist-FI 1981

Vamps C 17 MIN
16MM FILM OPTICAL SOUND J-C
Follows volunteer firemen in West Islip, New York, through their day-to-day struggle to fight and prevent fires, and through their many other community service and rescue activities.
LC NO. 72-702091
Prod-FVINO Dist-RVINOP 1972

Vampyre C 77 MIN
16MM FILM OPTICAL SOUND
Tells a story of an ancient castle haunted by vampires and the man who tries to overcome their seemingly supernatural powers of evil.
Prod-UNKNWN Dist-FCE

Van Allen Radiation Belts, The - Exploring In Space X 17 MIN
16MM FILM, 3/4 OR 1/2 IN VIDEO J-C
Dr Van Allen and other scientists explain methods of obtaining information in space flights. Models and animation are used to relate earth, sun, magnetosphere and radiation belts. Live photography and models illustrate preparations, launching and orbit of a space vehicle designed to explore the radiation regions.
Prod-EBF Dist-EBEC 1963

Van Der Pol Equation, The B 31 MIN
3/4 OR 1/2 INCH VIDEO CASSETTE
See series title for descriptive statement.
From The Nonlinear Vibrations Series.
Prod-MIOT Dist-MIOT

Van Der Waals Forces C 29 MIN
3/4 OR 1/2 INCH VIDEO CASSETTE
See series title for descriptive statement.
From The Colloid And Surface Chemistry - Lyophobic Colloids Series.
Prod-KALMIA Dist-KALMIA

Van Der Waals Forces B 29 MIN
3/4 OR 1/2 INCH VIDEO CASSETTE PRO
See series title for descriptive statement.
From The Colloid And Surface Chemistry - Lyophobic Colloids Series.
Prod-MIOT Dist-MIOT

Van Der Waals Forces (Cont'd), Influence Of A Medium, Retardation, Lifshitz Method,... C 39 MIN
3/4 OR 1/2 INCH VIDEO CASSETTE
Discusses Van der Waals forces, influence of a medium, retardation, Lifshitz method and experiments.
From The Colloid And Surface Chemistry - Lyophobic Colloids Series.
Prod-KALMIA Dist-KALMIA

Van der Waals Forces, Influences Of A Medium, Retardation, Lifshitz Method, Experiments B 39 MIN
3/4 OR 1/2 INCH VIDEO CASSETTE PRO
See series title for descriptive statement.
From The Colloid And Surface Chemistry - Lyophobic Colloids Series.
Prod-MIOT Dist-MIOT

Van Eyck - Father Of Flemish Painting C 27 MIN
16MM FILM, 3/4 OR 1/2 IN VIDEO H-C A
Studies the personal style of the 15th-century Flemish artist, Jan Van Eyck.
Prod-IFB Dist-IFB 1974

Van Gogh C 6 MIN
16MM FILM, 3/4 OR 1/2 IN VIDEO P-I
Tells the story of Vincent van Gogh through the presentation of his major works as well as through the re-creation of settings and events in the painter's life.
Prod-CAIR Dist-PHENIX 1969

Van Gogh - A Self Portrait C 55 MIN
16MM FILM, 3/4 OR 1/2 IN VIDEO H-C A
Explores the work, life and influence of Van Gogh. Explains his brilliance and his madness.
Prod-NBC Dist-CRMP 1968

Van Gogh - A Self Portrait, Pt 1 C 26 MIN
16MM FILM, 3/4 OR 1/2 IN VIDEO J-C A
Presents the art of Vincent van Gogh and shows the places, the people and the objects affecting his tragic life.
Prod-NBC Dist-MGHT 1968

Van Gogh - A Self Portrait, Pt 2 C 29 MIN
16MM FILM, 3/4 OR 1/2 IN VIDEO J-C A
Presents the art of Vincent van Gogh and shows the places, the people and the objects affecting his tragic life.
Prod-NBC Dist-MGHT 1968

Van Pooling C 15 MIN
16MM FILM, 3/4 OR 1/2 IN VIDEO
Presents an overview of the three major types of van pooling - employer sponsored, third party sponsored and individually owned and operated. Discusses the benefits of van pooling.
Prod-USDOE Dist-USNAC

Vanadium - A Transition Element C 22 MIN
16MM FILM OPTICAL SOUND H
Explores vanadium as a typical transition element. The different oxidation states of vanadium and their colors are observed and then identified by means of a quantitative titration of vanadium (II) solution with cerium (IV) solution. Discusses the changes in vanadium in terms of ion size and charge density.
From The CHEM Study Films Series.
LC NO. FIA63-1058
Prod-CHEMS Dist-MLA 1962

Vancouver - Pacific Gateway To Canada C 12 MIN
16MM FILM OPTICAL SOUND J-H
Describes life in Vancouver. Highlights the city's climate, its many sites, its beaches, its parks and its theaters, sports events and quiet spots of greenery.
Prod-MORLAT Dist-MORLAT

Vancouver, B C C 29 MIN
16MM FILM, 3/4 OR 1/2 IN VIDEO H-C A
Takes one on a tour of Vancouver, B C, the site of the 1986 World Exposition.
Prod-SPCTRA Dist-LCOA 1985

Vandalism C 11 MIN
3/4 OR 1/2 INCH VIDEO CASSETTE I-J
Illustrates the causes of acquisitive vandalism, tactical vandalism, vindictive vandalism and play vandalism. Points out the enormous costs to society of this 'small-time offense.'
From The Cop Talk Series.
Prod-UTSBE Dist-AITECH 1981

Vandalism - Crime Or Prank C 5 MIN
16MM FILM, 3/4 OR 1/2 IN VIDEO J-C
Explores the question of whether vandalism is a crime or a prank, and whether or not an adult who witnesses such an act and recognizes one of the participants has an obligation to report the matter to either the police or the boy's parents.
Prod-HORIZN Dist-IFB 1964

Vandalism - It Is A Big Deal C 20 MIN
16MM FILM, 3/4 OR 1/2 IN VIDEO J-C A
Presents a documentary investigation into the causes, extent and consequences of vandalism. Asks audiences to examine their own attitudes as parents, potential parents and community members to this ever increasing social problem. Shows steps to be taken to control the problem.
Prod-BORTF Dist-BCNFL 1983

Vandalism - It's A Dog's Life C 12 MIN
16MM FILM, 3/4 OR 1/2 IN VIDEO P-J
Uses animation to show how a child becomes a vandal. Tells how a person's irresponsible behavior can lead to vandalizing, asks what makes a person continue to vandalize, and points out that damaging someone's property affects the instigator as well as other people.
Prod-CHRISP Dist-PHENIX 1980

Vandalism - The Mark Of Immaturity C 12 MIN
16MM FILM, 3/4 OR 1/2 IN VIDEO I-H
Shows typical scenes of vandalism and the problems they cause others and examines why children destroy property.
Prod-CAHILL Dist-AIMS 1977

Vandalism - What And Why C 12 MIN
16MM FILM, 3/4 OR 1/2 IN VIDEO I-H
Presents a group of young people discussing vandalism and what it means to them. Probes the causes of this crime and offers possible solutions.
Prod-FLMFR Dist-FLMFR

Vandalism - Why (2nd Ed) C
16MM FILM, 3/4 OR 1/2 IN VIDEO I-J
States that vandalism is one of the worst forms of destruction because it is deliberate. Points out that the large amounts of money spent to repair the damages could be used more beneficially to everyone's advantage.
Prod-HIGGIN Dist-HIGGIN 1984

Vandalism Film, The - Only You Can Stop It C 12 MIN
16MM FILM, 3/4 OR 1/2 IN VIDEO P
Tells the story of vandalism through a character known as Sneaky, a thoughtless fellow who shows no concern for the feelings, rights or privileges of others. Emphasizes cooperation and positive action that will halt destructive behavior.
Prod-SAIF Dist-BARR 1976

Vandalism Story, A - The Clubhouse C 10 MIN
16MM FILM OPTICAL SOUND P-I
Tells the story of four young boys who have made a small clubhouse. Follows the boys to a local school where they yield to peer-group pressure and throw rocks through a classroom window. Shows that three of the boys are not caught by the police and return to their clubhouse, where they are shocked to find that it too, has been vandalized.
LC NO. 74-702790
Prod-MCDOCR Dist-MCDOCR 1973

Vandals C 17 MIN
16MM FILM, 3/4 OR 1/2 IN VIDEO I-C
Tells a story about a teenage boy and girl who vandalize a construction site and their school and are caught by the police. Shows how the juvenile justice system might deal with this typical case of vandalism.
From The Under The Law, Pt 2 Series.
Prod-USNEI Dist-WDEMCO 1975

Vandals, The C 25 MIN
3/4 INCH VIDEO CASSETTE H-C
Describes the after-effects and the social causes of vandalism.
Prod-ABCTV Dist-GA

Vandenberg - Aerospace Air Force Base C 14 MIN
16MM FILM OPTICAL SOUND A
Reviews six years of progress in aerospace operations at Vandenberg Air Force Base, home of USAF'S first ballistic missile division. Depicts the training required for crews that man the missile bases.
LC NO. FIE61-62
Prod-USDD Dist-USNAC 1961

Vangrams No. 1 C 5 MIN
16MM FILM OPTICAL SOUND
Deals with an invention in camera-less film making, exposing raw film to a flashlight.
Prod-VANBKS Dist-VANBKS

Vanished Brilliance - The Universe Yesterday C 28 MIN
16MM FILM, 3/4 OR 1/2 IN VIDEO
Discusses the big bang and what it must have been like.
From The Understanding Space And Time Series.
Prod-BBCTV Dist-UCEMC 1980

Vanished Vikings, The, Pt 1 - Eric The Red C 15 MIN
16MM FILM, 3/4 OR 1/2 IN VIDEO I-C
Traces Eric the Red's travels using sagas as well as archaeological evidence to tell the story of how their settlements ceased to exist.
Prod-ALTSUL Dist-JOU 1973

Vanished Vikings, The, Pt 2 - Where Did They Go C 15 MIN
16MM FILM, 3/4 OR 1/2 IN VIDEO I-C
Introduces the leading theories about the Viking disappearances and follows leading scholars as they explain their different points of view.
Prod-ALTSUL Dist-JOU 1973

Vanishing Breed, The C 30 MIN
16MM FILM - 3/4 IN VIDEO J-C A
Explains that a balance is needed between man and the ecological order and that this can only be achieved through education.
From The Man Builds - Man Destroys Series.
Prod-UN Dist-GPITVL

Vanishing Cornwall C 54 MIN
16MM FILM, 3/4 OR 1/2 IN VIDEO I-C A
Discusses the history, legends and people of Cornwall, England.
Prod-DOUBLE Dist-SF 1968

Vanishing Heritage, A C 11 MIN
16MM FILM OPTICAL SOUND J-H
Reveals the many-sided heritage of American architecture. Explains that traditions in architecture were brought to the United States by people of many different nationalities, and that they were blended with historical styles reaching back in time to Ancient Greece and Rome to produce a culture uniquely American.
Prod-ALEF Dist-ALEF 1971

Vanishing Point C 10 MIN
3/4 OR 1/2 INCH VIDEO CASSETTE
Analogizes the metaphysics of watching a TV screen. Shows a sole viewer watching a triple screen.
From The Two Programs By Stan Vanderbeek Series.
Prod-EAI Dist-EAI

Vanishing Point - Painting And Sculpture Of Nancy Camden Witt C 10 MIN
16MM FILM OPTICAL SOUND
Looks at the paintings and sculpture of surrealist Nancy Camden Witt.
From The Virginia Artists Series.
LC NO. 78-701331
Prod-SCHDRC Dist-SCHDRC 1978

Vanishing Prairie (French)—A Series
I-H
Features prairie animals.
Prod-WDEMCO Dist-WDEMCO 1963

Buffalo, Majestic Symbol Of The Plains, The
Large Animals That Once Roamed The Plains 012 MIN
Small Animals Of The Plains (French) 015 MIN

Vanishing Prairie (German)—A Series
I-H
Features prairie animals.
Prod-WDEMCO Dist-WDEMCO 1963

Buffalo, Majestic Symbol Of The Plains, The
Large Animals That Once Roamed The Plains 012 MIN
Small Animals Of The Plains (German) 015 MIN

Vanishing Prairie (Norwegian)—A Series
I-H
Features prairie animals.
Prod-WDEMCO Dist-WDEMCO 1963

Buffalo, Majestic Symbol Of The Plains, The
Large Animals That Once Roamed The Plains 012 MIN
Pioneer Trails, Indian Lore And Bird Life Of 014 MIN
Small Animals Of The Plains (Norwegian) 015 MIN

Vanishing Prairie (Portuguese)—A Series
I-H
Features prairie animals.
Prod-WDEMCO Dist-WDEMCO 1963

Pioneer Trails, Indian Lore And Bird Life Of
Small Animals Of The Plains (Portuguese) 015 MIN

Vanishing Prairie (Swedish)—A Series
I-H
Features prairie animals.
Prod-WDEMCO Dist-WDEMCO 1963

Large Animals That Once Roamed The Plains
Small Animals Of The Plains (Swedish) 015 MIN

Vanishing Sea, The C 26 MIN
16MM FILM OPTICAL SOUND P-C A
Bob Davidson presents scenes from Utah, where the Salt Lake country touches farmlands, wetlands and industrial areas. Features many sequences, including the western grebe's mating display, family life at a muskrat hut and pelicans with their young. Shows the people of the valley, struggling to retain their quality of life by protecting the valley's wilderness.
From The Audubon Wildlife Theatre Series.
LC NO. 79-709410
Prod-KEGPL Dist-AVEXP 1969

Vanishing Stream, The C 21 MIN
3/4 OR 1/2 INCH VIDEO CASSETTE I-C A
Reports on the steams of Idaho, and presents the problem of 'man's encroachment upon his environment.' Asks the question 'How much is a stream worth?' Presents the results of a biological study conducted by the Idaho Fish and Game Department, which surveys 45 Idaho Streams.
Prod-IFGD Dist-FO

Vanishing Towns C 29 MIN
2 INCH VIDEOTAPE
Looks at the fate of the small town in America through an examination of three South Carolina towns. Includes Ft Motte, Ellenton and Cokesbury.
From The Turning Points Series.
Prod-SCETV Dist-PUBTEL

Vanishing Tribe, The C 17 MIN
16MM FILM OPTICAL SOUND H-C A
Discusses the economic, religious and social life of the Todas, who live in the 'BLUE MOUNTAINS' of South India. Explains that they are a fast dwindling tribe with a fabulous past. Highlights their customs and beliefs.
Prod-INDIA Dist-NEDINF

Vapor Compression Cycle Designs And Refrigerants C 60 MIN
3/4 OR 1/2 INCH VIDEO CASSETTE IND
Focuses on design variations and operating principles of evaporators, compressors, condensers, metering devices. Shows refrigerants, including qualities and types and auxiliary equipment.
From The Air Conditioning And Refrigeration-- Training Series.
Prod-ITCORP Dist-ITCORP

Vapor Pressure B 22 MIN
16MM FILM OPTICAL SOUND H
Explains the phenomena of evaporation and vapor pressure from considerations of kinetic theory.
From The Heat Series.
Prod-CETO Dist-GPITVL

Vapor Recovery Units - An Introduction C 19 MIN
3/4 OR 1/2 INCH VIDEO CASSETTE IND
Explains how a vapor recovery system works. Discusses the basic parts of a vapor recovery unit. Gives information on basic maintenance of the system.
Prod-UTEXPE Dist-UTEXPE 1981

Vaquero C 15 MIN
16MM FILM OPTICAL SOUND I-H
A Spanish language film. Shows the history of the Mexican cowboy and his influence upon American history. Explains that the dress, language and skills of the 'great American cowboy' are Mexican and Spanish in origin. Includes scenes of the modern vaquero, using skills that are nearly 500 years old, such as branding and roping.
LC NO. 76-700859
Prod-GARET Dist-GARET 1974

Vaquero (English) C 15 MIN
16MM FILM OPTICAL SOUND I-H
Shows the history of the Mexican cowboy and his influence upon American history. Explains that the dress, language and skills of the 'great American cowboy' are Mexican and Spanish in origin. Includes scenes of the modern vaquero, using skills that are nearly 500 years old, such as branding and roping.
LC NO. 76-700859
Prod-GARET Dist-GARET 1974

Varanger-Dora Weems Incident, The B 4 MIN
16MM FILM OPTICAL SOUND
Describes the collision of the Varanger and the Dora Weems and the causes of the accident.
LC NO. FIE52-945
Prod-USN Dist-USNAC 1943

Varia, Pt 1 C 29 MIN
2 INCH VIDEOTAPE
See series title for descriptive statement.
From The Grand Master Chess Series.
Prod-KQEDTV Dist-PUBTEL

Varia, Pt 2 C 29 MIN
2 INCH VIDEOTAPE
See series title for descriptive statement.
From The Grand Master Chess Series.
Prod-KQEDTV Dist-PUBTEL

Varia, Pt 3 C 29 MIN
2 INCH VIDEOTAPE
See series title for descriptive statement.
From The Grand Master Chess Series.
Prod-KQEDTV Dist-PUBTEL

Variable Area Light Control In X-Ray Duplication C 5 MIN
16MM FILM - 3/4 IN VIDEO
Demonstrates X-ray duplication equipment and techniques using variable area light control.
LC NO. 77-706053
Prod-NMAC Dist-USNAC 1977

Variable Metric Methods C 60 MIN
3/4 OR 1/2 INCH VIDEO CASSETTE
See series title for descriptive statement.
From The Engineering Design Optimization II Series. Pt 15
Prod-UAZMIC Dist-UAZMIC

Variable Sampling (MIL-STD-414) C 30 MIN
3/4 OR 1/2 INCH VIDEO CASSETTE
Describes the history and application of a popular variable sampling plan.
From The Quality Control Series.
Prod-MIOT Dist-MIOT

Variable Volume Hydraulic Pumps C 60 MIN
3/4 OR 1/2 INCH VIDEO CASSETTE
Discusses fixed volume and variable volume pumps. Highlights horsepower reduction and electrical checks.
From The Hydraulic Systems Series.
Prod-ITCORP Dist-ITCORP

Variables / Input Statement C 30 MIN
3/4 OR 1/2 INCH VIDEO CASSETTE J-C A
Explains variables and introduces 'let' or assignment statements, using both numeric and string variables. Discusses the impor-

tance of variable names, legal and illegal names and the reserved words which cannot be used as variable names. Introduces input statements and shows how to use more than one variable in an input statement. Emphasizes the importance of considering the user's response and providing clear instructions. Shows programs with good and poor instructions and explains how to combine print and input statements.
From The Programming For Microcomputers Series. Units 7 And 8
LC NO. 83-707125
Prod-IU Dist-IU 1983

Variables And Keyboard Input C
3/4 OR 1/2 INCH VIDEO CASSETTE
Introduces declaration of variables - Real, Integer and String. Includes READLN and formatted output.
From The PASCAL - A Modern Programming Language Series.
Prod-EDUACT Dist-EDUACT

Variables In Financial Statements C 15 MIN
3/4 OR 1/2 INCH VIDEO CASSETTE
See series title for descriptive statement.
From The Finance For Nonfinancial Managers Series.
Prod-DELTAK Dist-DELTAK

Variation - A Lesson In Reading B 26 MIN
16MM FILM OPTICAL SOUND H
Presents mathematical expressions for simple proportionalities found in the natural world--current varying with voltage, volume of a sphere varying with the cube of the radius and volume of gas at constant temperature varying inversely with pressure.
From The Intermediate Algebra Series.
Prod-CALVIN Dist-MLA Prodn-UNIVFI 1959

Variation In Living Objects B 15 MIN
2 INCH VIDEOTAPE P
See series title for descriptive statement.
From The Just Wondering Series.
Prod-EOPS Dist-GPITVL Prodn-KOACTV

Variations And Conclusion Of New Dance C 7 MIN
16MM FILM OPTICAL SOUND J-C A
Presents the concluding section of Doris Humphrey's modern dance work entitled New Dance, as reconstructed in 1972 by the Repertory Company of the American Dance Festival at Connecticut College from the choreography originally done by Doris Humphrey in 1935.
LC NO. 78-701823
Prod-ADFEST Dist-UR 1978

Variations In Normal Behavior - Brazelton Neonatal Behavioral Assessment Scale B 20 MIN
3/4 INCH VIDEOTAPE
Explains that the Neonatal Scale demonstrates three infant capabilities including the ability to start a response to disturbing events, the ability to alert and orient and the ability to control states of arousal. Contrasts performance of different infants to the same stimuli.
From The Brazelton Neonatal Behavioral Assessment Scale Films Series.
Prod-EDC Dist-EDC

Variations Of Parameters B 24 MIN
3/4 OR 1/2 INCH VIDEO CASSETTE
See series title for descriptive statement.
From The Calculus Of Differential Equations Series.
Prod-MIOT Dist-MIOT

Variations On A Cellophane Wrapper C 8 MIN
16MM FILM OPTICAL SOUND J-C A
Employs a film loop technique to produce a variety of visual images.
LC NO. 72-702588
Prod-RIMMER Dist-CANFDC 1972

Variations On A Landscape - Land And Values In Ohio C 25 MIN
16MM FILM OPTICAL SOUND
Identifies the issues concerning land use in Ohio. Includes environmentalist, localist and local/regional partnership views.
Prod-OHC Dist-HRC

Variations On A Seven Second Loop-Painting B 6 MIN
16MM FILM OPTICAL SOUND
Uses of an optical printer to show the variations involving step-printing, repetitions and optical manipulations.
Prod-SPINLB Dist-FMCOOP 1970

Variations On A Theme C 15 MIN
3/4 OR 1/2 INCH VIDEO CASSETTE
Dramatizes planning a sales event in a women's ready-to-wear shop. Shows the conflict of a cashier who is scornful of advertising and promotional themes.
From The Small Business Administration Series.
Prod-IVCH Dist-IVCH

Varicose Veins C 28 MIN
16MM FILM OPTICAL SOUND PRO
Presents the basic aspects of physiological background for the treatment of varicose veins. Demonstrates basic safeguards and the critical points of technical value.
Prod-ACYDGD Dist-ACY 1969

Varietal Meats C
3/4 INCH VIDEO CASSETTE H A
Discusses the organ meats of the animal. Shows how varietals can be the basis for flavorful and nutritious meals.
From The Matter Of Taste Series. Lesson 13
Prod-COAST Dist-CDTEL

Variety B 27 MIN
16MM FILM OPTICAL SOUND H-C
Presents this drama of human passions, which is set against a circus and vaudeville background and which contains revolutionary photographic techniques that once affected filmaking. Stars Emil Jannings.
From The History Of The Motion Picture Series.
Prod-SF Dist-KILLIS 1960

Variety C 29 MIN
2 INCH VIDEOTAPE
See series title for descriptive statement.
From The Making Things Grow III Series.
Prod-WGBHTV Dist-PUBTEL

Variety Meats C 14 MIN
2 INCH VIDEOTAPE
Introduces good tasting and low cost menus using variety meats. Discusses why variety meats are economical and how to select and store them.
From The Living Better II Series.
Prod-MAETEL Dist-PUBTEL

Variety Of Glaze Effects - Introduction To Glaze Melts C 28 MIN
2 INCH VIDEOTAPE
Features Mrs Peterson describing certain ceramic processes for her classroom at the University of Southern California. Explains a variety of glaze effects and an introduction to glaze melts.
From The Wheels, Kilns And Clay Series.
Prod-USC Dist-PUBTEL

Variety Painting, Pt 1 B 20 MIN
2 INCH VIDEOTAPE I
Describes many tools for applying paint - brushes, sponges, squeeze bottles, sticks and cotton balls.
From The For The Love Of Art Series.
Prod-GWTVAI Dist-GPITVL Prodn-WETATV

Variety Painting, Pt 2 B 20 MIN
2 INCH VIDEOTAPE I
Encourages students to experiment with different textures of paint - spray enamel, finger paint, tempera/ wheat paste and with collage effects.
From The For The Love Of Art Series.
Prod-GWTVAI Dist-GPITVL Prodn-WETATV

Variety Saw (Trim) C 43 MIN
3/4 OR 1/2 INCH VIDEO CASSETTE IND
Focuses on skill-building in operations associated with ripping, cross-cutting, grooving, mitre cutting and dadoing.
From The Furniture Manufacturing Series.
Prod-LEIKID Dist-LEIKID

Various Career Development Tracks C 19 MIN
3/4 INCH VIDEO CASSETTE PRO
Presents a panel discussion on various ladders and tracks for executive development. Features participants from the United States Civil Service, Social Security Administration and the Martin Marietta Corporation, who agree that evaluation and objectives are difficult but essential in executive training and development.
From The Executive Development And Training Issues - Government And Industry Series. Part 3
LC NO. 77-700636
Prod-USCSC Dist-USNAC 1976

Various Methods Of Fixation For The Control Of Fractured Jaws C 45 MIN
16MM FILM OPTICAL SOUND
Describes the known methods for the reduction of fractured jaw bones, including various traction methods of moving the bones and the constant fixation of splinting of bones.
LC NO. FIE58-285
Prod-USVA Dist-USVA 1958

Varnette's World - A Study Of A Young Artist C 26 MIN
16MM FILM OPTICAL SOUND
Presents Varnette Honeywood, a painter who honors her ancestral heritage while searching for alternative skills to earn a living.
LC NO. 79-701244
Prod-BLUCAP Dist-BLUCAP 1979

Varsity Show B 80 MIN
16MM FILM OPTICAL SOUND J-C A
Stars Dick Powell and Priscilla and Rosemary Lane. Presents the dance numbers created and staged by Busby Berkeley. Includes the musical numbers Have You Got Any Castles, Baby, Old King Cole, Moonlight On The Campus and Love Is In The Air Tonight.
Prod-WB Dist-UAE 1937

Vasarely (Born 1908) B 9 MIN
16MM FILM OPTICAL SOUND
Presents one of the masters of the optical illusion, Vassarely, who uses in his drawings the theme that we no longer simply believe what we see or simply see what we believe.
Prod-ROLAND Dist-ROLAND

Vascetomy Operative Procedure C 28 MIN
3/4 OR 1/2 INCH VIDEO CASSETTE PRO
See series title for descriptive statement.
From The Urology Series.
Prod-MSU Dist-MSU

Vascular Complications Of The Thoracic Outlet Syndrome C 22 MIN
16MM FILM OPTICAL SOUND PRO
Explains diagnosis and treatment of thoracic outlet syndrome using drawings to illustrate anatomy and pathophysiology. Presents X-rays and angiograms to demonstrate pathology in three patients. Shows supraclavicular approach with resection of a portion of the clavicle correcting the syndrome and its vascular complications.
LC NO. 78-700323
Prod-SCPMG Dist-SQUIBB Prodn-BURKEB 1978

Vascular--A Series

Presents a series on vascular surgery.
Prod-SVL Dist-SVL

Abdominal Aortic Endarterectomy	033 MIN
Aortic Aneurysm Review And Two Aortic	060 MIN
Carotid Endarterectomy	018 MIN
Distal Splenorenal Shunt	016 MIN
Emergency Embolectomy	008 MIN
Emergency Mesocaval Shunt	025 MIN
Femoro-Popliteal Bypass	015 MIN
Hyperalimentation I - Percutaneous	012 MIN
Insertion Of Subclavian Catbetter For	015 MIN

Vasectomia C 20 MIN
3/4 INCH VIDEO CASSETTE J-C
Presents a group of Colombian men discussing why they had vasectomies.
From The Are You Listening Series.
LC NO. 80-707407
Prod-STURTM Dist-STURTM 1972

Vasectomy B 18 MIN
16MM FILM OPTICAL SOUND H-C A
Uses live action and animated diagrams to show how doctors should proceed with vasectomy operations.
Prod-INDIA Dist-NEDINF

Vasectomy C
3/4 OR 1/2 INCH VIDEO CASSETTE
Shows how a vasectomy eliminates the risk of pregnancy and discusses the surgical procedures involved.
Prod-MIFE Dist-MIFE

Vasectomy C 5 MIN
3/4 OR 1/2 INCH VIDEO CASSETTE
Emphasizes permanency, reminds patient of physical and psychological implications. Describes how surgery interrupts seminal flow to prevent impregnation and reassures patient concerning future sexual performance.
Prod-TRAINX Dist-TRAINX

Vasectomy C 9 MIN
3/4 OR 1/2 INCH VIDEO CASSETTE
Describes normal male anatomy. Explains how a vasectomy works. Discusses possible complications.
Prod-MEDFAC Dist-MEDFAC 1972

Vasectomy C 15 MIN
16MM FILM, 3/4 OR 1/2 IN VIDEO A
Shows normal anatomy and physiology, including sperm and hormone production, erection and orgasm. Explains how a vasectomy prevents conception. Helps alleviate possible fears about loss of masculinity and sexual prowess. Gives detailed instructions for post-operative care.
Prod-PRORE Dist-PRORE

Vasectomy C 17 MIN
16MM FILM, 3/4 OR 1/2 IN VIDEO C A
Discusses the experiences of several men who sought vasectomy as a form of contraception. Observes a couple as they discuss vasectomy with their doctor and as the man undergoes the simple operation.
Prod-CF Dist-CF 1972

Vasectomy (Spanish) C
3/4 OR 1/2 INCH VIDEO CASSETTE
Shows how a vasectomy eliminates the risk of pregnancy and discusses the surgical procedures involved.
Prod-MIFE Dist-MIFE

Vasectomy (Spanish) C 15 MIN
16MM FILM, 3/4 OR 1/2 IN VIDEO PRO
Explains how a vasectomy prevents conception and helps alleviate fears about loss of masculinity and sexual prowess. Includes detailed instructions for post-operative care.
Prod-PRORE Dist-PRORE

Vasectomy (Spanish) C 17 MIN
16MM FILM, 3/4 OR 1/2 IN VIDEO C A
Uses animation to describe the male reproductive system and vasectomy surgery. Interviews men and their wives to explain their reasons for having a vasectomy and their feelings, fears and satisfactions.
Prod-CF Dist-CF 1972

Vasectomy - Male Sterilization B 29 MIN
2 INCH VIDEOTAPE
Explains a vasectomy, a simple operation to sterilize the male. Considers both the physical and possible psychological effects of this procedure.
Prod-KQEDTV Dist-PUBTEL

Vasectomy Patient Counseling C 10 MIN
16MM FILM OPTICAL SOUND
Shows a simulated interview between the physician and a couple seeking information concerning vasectomy.
LC NO. 75-702256
Prod-EATONL Dist-EATONL 1973

Vasectomy Procedures C 10 MIN
16MM FILM OPTICAL SOUND
Shows all currently employed techniques of performing vasectomy.
LC NO. 75-702255
Prod-EATONL Dist-EATONL 1973

Vasectomy Techniques C 16 MIN
3/4 OR 1/2 INCH VIDEO CASSETTE
Views each step in performing a vasectomy.
Prod-PRIMED Dist-PRIMED

Vasillis Of Athens C 15 MIN
3/4 OR 1/2 INCH VIDEO CASSETTE P

Pictures the ancient Palace of Knossis on Crete and modern Athens in Greece.
From The Other Families, Other Friends Series. Red Module - Greece
Prod-WVIZTV Dist-AITECH 1971

Vatican City C 20 MIN
3/4 OR 1/2 INCH VIDEO CASSETTE J-C A
Visits Vatican City, including St Peter's Basilica, the Sistine Chapel and the papal residence. Shows the mausoleums, Borgia apartment and the Swiss guards.
LC NO. 82-706789
Prod-AWSS Dist-AWSS 1980

Vatican, The C 18 MIN
3/4 OR 1/2 INCH VIDEO CASSETTE
Examines the functions and governmental structure of the Vatican.
Prod-UPI Dist-JOU

Vatican, The C 54 MIN
16MM FILM, 3/4 OR 1/2 IN VIDEO H-C A
Provides a tour of the Vatican, a review of its history, a display of some of its art treasures, an explanation of the Swiss Guard tradition and an audience with the late Pope John.
Prod-ABCTV Dist-MGHT 1963

Vaucherin B 32 MIN
16MM FILM OPTICAL SOUND C A
A French language film. Follows a man, alone among his books, as he meticulously tidies up his room and prepares to depart for a journey. Includes English subtitles.
Prod-UWFKD Dist-UWFKD

Vault C 12 MIN
3/4 OR 1/2 INCH VIDEO CASSETTE
Traces the relationship between a woman pole vaulter-concert cellist and a cowboy-abstract painter. Presented by Bruce and Norman Yonemoto.
Prod-ARTINC Dist-ARTINC

Vault C 12 MIN
3/4 INCH VIDEO CASSETTE
Presents a melodramatic love story by Bruce and Norman Yonemoto. A subtext of advertising, film and TV language humorously shows the power of those devices in creating personal fictions.
Prod-EAI Dist-EAI

Vaux-Le Vicomte, France C 26 MIN
16MM FILM, 3/4 OR 1/2 IN VIDEO H-C A
Used as a model for many imitators, Vaux was built as a country house by the treasurer of France, whose team of artists was commanded by King Louis XIV to build Versailles. La Fontaine's poem about the house is read.
From The Place In Europe Series.
Prod-THAMES Dist-MEDIAG 1975

VD C 26 MIN
16MM FILM OPTICAL SOUND J-C A
Presents interviews with actual patients and physicians in which symptoms and treatment are explained to dispel much of the mystery surrounding venereal diseases.
Prod-HRAW Dist-HRAW

VD C 26 MIN
16MM FILM, 3/4 OR 1/2 IN VIDEO J-H
Provides answers to the questions about syphilis and gonorrhea that students ask. Emphasizes the geometric pattern of infection and the absolute necessity of early treatment of all people who might be in contact with the diseases.
Prod-BFA Dist-PHENIX 1972

VD - A New Focus C 15 MIN
16MM FILM, 3/4 OR 1/2 IN VIDEO
Presents an entire picture of the VD problem, giving medical facts, and probing the myths and attitudes of young people concerning VD that often prevent prompt treatment.
Prod-DUNLF Dist-AMEDFL 1971

VD - A New Focus (Spanish) C 16 MIN
16MM FILM, 3/4 OR 1/2 IN VIDEO J-C
Features young people from locations throughout America who present the problems themselves and outline the answers for treating venereal disease. Describes the medical facts, the myths and the attitudes of young people that often prevent prompt treatment of VD.
Prod-AMEDFL Dist-AMEDFL

VD - A New(er) Focus C 20 MIN
16MM FILM, 3/4 OR 1/2 IN VIDEO J-H
Refers to a revised edition of 'VD-A New Focus,' which includes all of the most serious new and increasing sexually transmissible diseases. Shows symptoms and treatment, including information on herpes, one of the most serious new diseases, and is host-narrated by James Brotin and Joseph Campanella.
Prod-ASHA Dist-AMEDFL Prodn-AMEDFL

VD - Attack Plan C 14 MIN
16MM FILM, 3/4 OR 1/2 IN VIDEO
Presents an animated cartoon in which venereal disease germs plan an attack on vulnerable human beings. Helps provide a new perspective on the problems of syphilis and gonorrhea.
Prod-DISNEY Dist-WDEMCO 1973

VD - Attack Plan C 16 MIN
16MM FILM, 3/4 OR 1/2 IN VIDEO J-H
Presents a veteran germ in the contagion corps who outlines how syphilis and gonorrhea can attack man. Points out the steps which man can follow to defeat the two diseases but emphasizes the myth that keeps uninformed humans from seeking treatment.
Prod-DISNEY Dist-WDEMCO 1973

VD - It Is Your Problem C 14 MIN
3/4 OR 1/2 INCH VIDEO CASSETTE
Deals with misinformation, facts and the dangers of untreated gonorrhea and syphilis. Stresses the need for early medical care.
From The Pregnancy Prevention And Sex Hygiene Series.
LC NO. 85-700100
Prod-USA Dist-USNAC 1983

VD - Old Bugs, New Problems C 20 MIN
16MM FILM, 3/4 OR 1/2 IN VIDEO J-C A
Acquaints the viewer with the various types of sexually transmitted diseases.
Prod-HIGGIN Dist-HIGGIN 1978

VD - One, Two C 14 MIN
16MM FILM OPTICAL SOUND
States that the tracking of the source of venereal infection is as important as medical treatment. Shows why an individual infected with VD must not only seek proper medical treatment, but also cooperate with the VD contact interviewer.
LC NO. 74-706599
Prod-USN Dist-USNAC 1973

VD - Play It Safe C 14 MIN
16MM FILM, 3/4 OR 1/2 IN VIDEO J-C A
Explains, through a series of vignettes, the communicability and disease process of sexually transmitted diseases, including gonorrhea, syphilis and genital herpes. Shows how these diseases can be prevented and treated.
LC NO. 80-706825
Prod-GORKER Dist-CORF 1980

VD - Prevent It (2nd Ed) C 10 MIN
16MM FILM, 3/4 OR 1/2 IN VIDEO H A
Explains that of all communicable diseases, VD is the easiest to prevent. Discusses the ways of preventing the spread of venereal disease by using soap and water, urinating after contact, using a bacteria douche, properly employing a condom, using germ-killing medications and attending periodic physical examinations.
Prod-HIGGIN Dist-HIGGIN 1978

VD - See Your Doctor C 22 MIN
16MM FILM OPTICAL SOUND J-C A
Describes the causes, symptoms and dangers of venereal disease and emphasizes the importance of obtaining prompt medical treatment.
From The Family Life Education And Human Growth Series.
LC NO. FIA67-16
Prod-MORLAT Dist-SF 1966

VD - Self-Awareness Project—A Series
J-C
Prod-AAPHER Dist-AAHPER 1974

Next Time	12 MIN
Number 23	10 MIN
VD - Who Needs It	24 MIN

VD - The Love Bug C 15 MIN
16MM FILM, 3/4 OR 1/2 IN VIDEO J-C
Shows how to recognize the common types of sexually-transmitted diseases, how to avoid them, and what to do when one is contracted. Gives special attention to herpes simplex type 2, a rampant viral disease.
LC NO. 80-707529
Prod-WABCTV Dist-MTI 1979

VD - Truths And Consequences C 28 MIN
16MM FILM OPTICAL SOUND I-C A
Presents the prevailing myths and misinformation that have conspired to make venereal disease the epidemic it is today. Features four leading medical authorities covering their special field of practice.
LC NO. 73-702777
Prod-AVANTI Dist-MTVTM 1973

VD - Very Communicable Diseases C 19 MIN
16MM FILM, 3/4 OR 1/2 IN VIDEO J-C A
Presents the how's, why's, wherefore's and ramifications of venereal disease, syphilis and gonorrhea. Includes preventive measures.
Prod-CAHILL Dist-AIMS 1972

VD - What Is It C 18 MIN
16MM FILM, 3/4 OR 1/2 IN VIDEO J-H
Explores the concept of sexually transmissible diseases. Shows symptoms, seriousness and consequences of the various diseases, particularly of herpes simplex II, syphilis and gonorrhea. Considers prevention and treatment.
Prod-CF Dist-CF 1977

VD - Who Needs It C 24 MIN
16MM FILM OPTICAL SOUND J-C
Presents facts about venereal disease.
From The VD Self-Awareness Project Series.
LC NO. 75-702842
Prod-AAHPER Dist-AAHPER 1974

VD And Women C 17 MIN
16MM FILM, 3/4 OR 1/2 IN VIDEO H-C A
Describes the venereal diseases which sexually active women are susceptible to and the symptoms of these diseases. Shows the procedures involved in a pelvic examination. Discusses treatment for these infections and the side effects which result if a person remains untreated.
Prod-CROMIE Dist-PEREN

VD Attack Plan (French) C 14 MIN
16MM FILM, 3/4 OR 1/2 IN VIDEO I-H
Answers questions about sexually transmitted diseases. Features animation.
Prod-WDEMCO Dist-WDEMCO 1973

VD Attack Plan (French) C 16 MIN
16MM FILM, 3/4 OR 1/2 IN VIDEO I-H
Answers questions about sexually transmitted diseases. Features animation. Discusses means of prophylaxis.
Prod-WDEMCO Dist-WDEMCO 1973

VD Attack Plan (Hungarian) C 14 MIN
16MM FILM, 3/4 OR 1/2 IN VIDEO I-H
Answers questions about sexually transmitted diseases. Features animation.
Prod-WDEMCO Dist-WDEMCO 1973

VD Attack Plan (Hungarian) C 16 MIN
16MM FILM, 3/4 OR 1/2 IN VIDEO I-H
Answers questions about sexually transmitted diseases. Features animation. Discusses means of prophylaxis.
Prod-WDEMCO Dist-WDEMCO 1973

VD Attack Plan (Polish) C 14 MIN
16MM FILM, 3/4 OR 1/2 IN VIDEO I-H
Answers questions about sexually transmitted diseases. Features animation.
Prod-WDEMCO Dist-WDEMCO 1973

VD Attack Plan (Polish) C 16 MIN
16MM FILM, 3/4 OR 1/2 IN VIDEO I-H
Answers questions about sexually transmitted diseases. Features animation. Discusses means of prophylaxis.
Prod-WDEMCO Dist-WDEMCO 1973

VD Attack Plan (Portuguese) C 14 MIN
16MM FILM, 3/4 OR 1/2 IN VIDEO I-H
Answers questions about sexually transmitted diseases. Features animation.
Prod-WDEMCO Dist-WDEMCO 1973

VD Attack Plan (Portuguese) C 16 MIN
16MM FILM, 3/4 OR 1/2 IN VIDEO I-H
Answers questions about sexually transmitted diseases. Features animation. Discusses means of prophylaxis.
Prod-WDEMCO Dist-WDEMCO 1973

VD Attack Plan (Spanish) C 14 MIN
16MM FILM, 3/4 OR 1/2 IN VIDEO I-H
Answers questions about sexually transmitted diseases. Features animation.
Prod-WDEMCO Dist-WDEMCO 1973

VD Attack Plan (Spanish) C 16 MIN
16MM FILM, 3/4 OR 1/2 IN VIDEO I-H
Answers questions about sexually transmitted diseases. Features animation. Discusses means of prophylaxis.
Prod-WDEMCO Dist-WDEMCO 1973

VD Attack Plan (Swedish) C 14 MIN
16MM FILM, 3/4 OR 1/2 IN VIDEO I-H
Answers questions about sexually transmitted diseases. Features animation.
Prod-WDEMCO Dist-WDEMCO 1973

VD Attack Plan (Swedish) C 16 MIN
16MM FILM, 3/4 OR 1/2 IN VIDEO I-H
Answers questions about sexually transmitted diseases. Features animation. Discusses means of prophylaxis.
Prod-WDEMCO Dist-WDEMCO

VD Prevention C
16MM FILM OPTICAL SOUND J-C A
Reviews the symptoms of venereal disease. Emphasizes seeing a doctor for preventive advice, using condoms and telling sexual contacts about the signs of venereal disease.
LC NO. 73-703192
Prod-AMEDFL Dist-AMEDFL 1973

VD Prevention (Spanish) C 11 MIN
16MM FILM OPTICAL SOUND J-C
Outlines the methods of VD prevention showing the care necessary to stop infection. Discusses cleansing measures, prophylactics, preventative medications and VD check-ups.
Prod-AMEDFL Dist-AMEDFL

VD Questions, VD Answers C 15 MIN
16MM FILM, 3/4 OR 1/2 IN VIDEO
Describes how VD is contracted and what to do about prevention and treatment.
Prod-BFA Dist-PHENIX 1972

VD Quiz - Getting The Right Answers C 25 MIN
16MM FILM OPTICAL SOUND J-C A
Presents information on venereal disease. Discusses options for treatment and possible solutions to the epidemic.
LC NO. 77-702163
Prod-ASHA Dist-AMEDFL 1977

VD Troubles C 29 MIN
3/4 OR 1/2 INCH VIDEO CASSETTE
Features Milton Diamond, Ph D, a biologist at the University of Hawaii, discussing the difficulty of identifying, treating and controlling venereal disease.
From The Human Sexuality Series.
Prod-KHETTV Dist-PBS

VDRL Tests For Syphilis B 22 MIN
16MM FILM OPTICAL SOUND PRO
Describes the preparation of the basic antigen emulsion. Shows the procedures for the spinal fluid test and for the slide and tube flocculation tests for serum. For professional use only.
LC NO. FIE59-246
Prod-USPHS Dist-USNAC 1959

VE In Non-Hardware Applications C 60 MIN
3/4 OR 1/2 INCH VIDEO CASSETTE IND
See series title for descriptive statement.
From The Value Engineering Series.
Prod-NCSU Dist-AMCEE

VEBA's C 30 MIN
3/4 OR 1/2 INCH VIDEO CASSETTE PRO
See series title for descriptive statement.
From The Tax Reform Act Of 1984 Series.
Prod-ALIABA Dist-ALIABA

Vector Functions Of A Scalar Variable B 38 MIN
3/4 OR 1/2 INCH VIDEO CASSETTE
See series title for descriptive statement.
From The Calculus Of Several Variables - Vector--Calculus Series.
Prod-MIOT Dist-MIOT

Vector Kinematics B 16 MIN
16MM FILM OPTICAL SOUND C
Introduces velocity and acceleration vectors and shows them simultaneously for various two-dimensional motions including circular and simple harmonic.
From The PSSC Physics Films Series.
Prod-PSSC Dist-MLA 1962

Vector Q C 9 MIN
16MM FILM OPTICAL SOUND
A young hero who is taking his heroine into the autumn forest discovers that he is inextricably ensnared in physics, mathematics and nature.
LC NO. 78-711560
Prod-UMD Dist-UMD 1971

Vector Spaces B
16MM FILM OPTICAL SOUND
Defines geometric vectors and introduces the idea of a basis. Demonstrates how real vector spaces can be regarded as sets of ordered strings of numbers. Indicates the power of the vector space concept.
Prod-OPENU Dist-OPENU

Vector Spaces B 31 MIN
3/4 OR 1/2 INCH VIDEO CASSETTE
See series title for descriptive statement.
From The Calculus Of Linear Algebra Series.
Prod-MIOT Dist-MIOT

Vectoria C 16 MIN
16MM FILM, 3/4 OR 1/2 IN VIDEO J
Presents a story about a skilled pinball player and his experiences with an unusual pinball machine which demonstrates the four dimensions, including position, two-dimensional motion, three-dimensional motion and time.
From The Universe And I Series.
LC NO. 80-706488
Prod-KYTV Dist-AITECH 1977

Vectors B 12 MIN
16MM FILM, 3/4 OR 1/2 IN VIDEO
Explains vectors, changes in angle or magnitude, how vectors are plotted and how the resultant is found. Issued in 1945 as a motion picture.
From The Radio Technician Training Series.
LC NO. 78-706306
Prod-USN Dist-USNAC Prodn-CARFI 1978

Vectors C 30 MIN
16MM FILM, 3/4 OR 1/2 IN VIDEO C A
Deals with vectors which describe quantities such as displacement and velocity, expressing the laws of physics in the same way for all coordinate systems.
From The Mechanical Universe Series.
Prod-ANNCPB Dist-FI

Vectors In Polar Coordinates B 27 MIN
3/4 OR 1/2 INCH VIDEO CASSETTE
See series title for descriptive statement.
From The Calculus Of Several Variables - Vector--Calculus Series.
Prod-MIOT Dist-MIOT

VEE - A National Emergency C 11 MIN
16MM FILM OPTICAL SOUND
Shows actions to control Venezuelan equine encephalomyelitis (VEE,) the deadly horse sleeping sickness that invaded Texas in the summer of 1971 after a devastating impact on Mexico.
LC NO. 74-705904
Prod-USDA Dist-USNAC 1972

VEE - A National Emergency (Spanish) C 11 MIN
16MM FILM OPTICAL SOUND
Describes action to control the deadly horse sleeping sickness, Venezuelan equine encephalomyelitis. Depicts mass vaccination, quarantine and aerial spraying to suppress mosquitoes.
LC NO. 76-703680
Prod-USDA Dist-USNAC 1972

Vee Butt Joint C 12 MIN
1/2 IN VIDEO CASSETTE BETA/VHS IND
See series title for descriptive statement.
From The Welding Training (Comprehensive) --- Oxy-Acetylene Welding Series.
Prod-RMI Dist-RMI

Vegetable And Fruit Prints C 15 MIN
3/4 INCH VIDEO CASSETTE P
See series title for descriptive statement.
From The Is The Sky Always Blue Series.
Prod-WDCNTV Dist-GPITVL 1979

Vegetable Art 1 C 25 MIN
3/4 OR 1/2 INCH VIDEO CASSETTE PRO
Demonstrates carving techniques for making vegetables resemble flowers, including tulips from radishes and a rose from a turnip.
Prod-CULINA Dist-CULINA

Vegetable Art 2 C 12 MIN
3/4 OR 1/2 INCH VIDEO CASSETTE PRO
Presents more advanced vegetable carving techniques the chain, the fish net and the basketweave, using potatoes, rutabagas and daikon radishes.
Prod-CULINA Dist-CULINA

Vegetable Art 3 C 12 MIN
3/4 OR 1/2 INCH VIDEO CASSETTE PRO
Teaches techniques for making an exotic bouquet from common vegetables. Makes daisies from turnips, carrots and scallions, orchids from cabbages, carrots and scallions, and Hawaiian flowers from beets, carrots and young corn.
Prod-CULINA Dist-CULINA

Vegetable Art 4 C 9 MIN
3/4 OR 1/2 INCH VIDEO CASSETTE PRO
Shows how to make a rose from a celery knob, a lily and a crocus from a red onion, butterflies from zucchini, and a rose from slices of a beet, turnip or rutabaga.
Prod-CULINA Dist-CULINA

Vegetable Art 5 C 13 MIN
3/4 OR 1/2 INCH VIDEO CASSETTE PRO
Concentrates on the proper angling of the knife for precision and speed of production. A rose is carved from a beet and other exotic flowers from carrots.
Prod-CULINA Dist-CULINA

Vegetable Cuts C
3/4 OR 1/2 INCH VIDEO CASSETTE
See series title for descriptive statement.
From The Vegetable Cutting Series.
Prod-CULINA Dist-CULINA

Vegetable Cuts - Dicing C
3/4 OR 1/2 INCH VIDEO CASSETTE
See series title for descriptive statement.
From The Vegetable Cutting Series.
Prod-CULINA Dist-CULINA

Vegetable Cutting--A Series

Prod-CULINA Dist-CULINA

Mise En Place
Vegetable Cuts
Vegetable Cuts - Dicing

Vegetable Flowers C 10 MIN
3/4 OR 1/2 INCH VIDEO CASSETTE PRO
Shows how to make flowers from scallions, tomatoes, radishes and potatoes, and how to arrange them attractively.
Prod-CULINA Dist-CULINA

Vegetable Gardening C 15 MIN
16MM FILM, 3/4 OR 1/2 IN VIDEO I-C A
Shows planning, seed selection, tools, preparing the garden plot, row marking, depth of planting, thinning and other procedures connected with vegetable gardening.
From The Garden Methods Series.
Prod-PEREN Dist-PEREN

Vegetable Gardening C 55 MIN
1/2 IN VIDEO CASSETTE BETA/VHS
Explains the proper way to prepare the soil, which tools to use, the best way to water, how to fertilize, methods of controlling garden pests and diseases, when to plant and when to harvest.
Prod-RMI Dist-RMI

Vegetable Industry C 3 MIN
16MM FILM OPTICAL SOUND P-I
Discusses the vegetable industry.
From The Of All Things Series.
Prod-BAILYL Dist-AVED

Vegetable Memory C 15 MIN
3/4 OR 1/2 INCH VIDEO CASSETTE
See series title for descriptive statement.
From The Reflecting Pool Series.
Prod-EAI Dist-EAI

Vegetable Preparation C 6 MIN
3/4 OR 1/2 INCH VIDEO CASSETTE PRO
Shows how to simplify preparation of vegetables for use as crudites or in other dishes. Demonstrates the proper cleaning and handling of cauliflower, broccoli, mushrooms and potatoes, and shows how they should be cut.
Prod-CULINA Dist-CULINA

Vegetable Preparation C 10 MIN
16MM FILM, 3/4 OR 1/2 IN VIDEO J-C A
Shows how to maintain color, taste, texture and nutrition in preparing vegetables. Demonstrates proper procedures for boiling and other cooking methods, including steaming, sauteeing, deep fat frying and others. Exposes errors of overcooking, use of excessive water, delays, bad planning and harmful additives. Encourages creativity in sauces.
From The Professional Food Preparation And Service Program Series.
LC NO. 74-700408
Prod-NEM Dist-NEM 1972

Vegetable Printing, Mosaics And Drawing People C 15 MIN
3/4 INCH VIDEO CASSETTE P-I
See series title for descriptive statement.
From The Look And A Closer Look Series.
Prod-WCVETV Dist-GPITVL 1976

Vegetable Soup I--A Series
P-J
A series of 39 videocassettes. Discusses the negative, destructive effects of racial prejudice and racial isolation.
Prod-NYSED Dist-GPITVL 1975

Vegetable Soup II--A Series
P-J
A series of 39 videocassettes. Discusses the negative, destructive effects of racial prejudice and racial isolation.
Prod-NYSED Dist-GPITVL 1978

Vegetables C
3/4 INCH VIDEO CASSETTE H A
Points to the need for creativity in the preparation and serving of vegetables. Demonstrates how ordinary vegetables can be served with style.
From The Matter Of Taste Series. Lesson 5
Prod-COAST Dist-CDTEL

Vegetables - From Garden To Table C 18 MIN
16MM FILM, 3/4 OR 1/2 IN VIDEO J-C A
Demonstrates a variety of ways to cook vegetables, including baking, boiling, steaming, stir frying, and deep fat frying. Shows how to select vegetables and how to prepare them to be eaten raw.
LC NO. 81-707262
Prod-CENTRO Dist-CORF 1981

Vegetables For All Occasions C 30 MIN
3/4 OR 1/2 INCH VIDEO CASSETTE H-C
Presents fresh ideas for fresh vegetables from hors d'oeuvres to main dishes.
From The French Chef Series.
Prod-WGBH Dist-KINGFT

Vegetables For All Seasons C 10 MIN
16MM FILM, 3/4 OR 1/2 IN VIDEO J-C A
Follows vegetables from the farm to the market to the kitchen, and explains some basic tecnhiques for buying and preparing vegetables.
Prod-BARR Dist-BARR 1972

Vegetables For All Seasons (Captioned) C 10 MIN
16MM FILM - VIDEO, ALL FORMATS J-C A
Deals with basic techniques for buying and serving vegetables.
Prod-BARR Dist-BARR

Vegetables Vegetables C 3 MIN
2 INCH VIDEOTAPE
Suggests storing and preparing fresh vegetables with care. Demonstrates how to cook them briefly and suggests combining left-over vegetables with sour cream or yogurt for a good cold salad or blending them to make a cold soup.
From The Beatrice Trum Hunter's Natural Foods Series.
Prod-WGBH Dist-PUBTEL

Vegetables, Pt 1 C 29 MIN
2 INCH VIDEOTAPE
Features gourmet-humorist Justin Wilson showing ways to cook vegetables with various ingredients.
From The Cookin' Cajun Series.
Prod-MAETEL Dist-PUBTEL

Vegetables, Pt 2 C 29 MIN
2 INCH VIDEOTAPE
Features gourmet-humorist Justin Wilson showing ways to cook vegetables with various ingredients.
From The Cookin' Cajun Series.
Prod-MAETEL Dist-PUBTEL

Vegetables, Vegetables C 4 MIN
16MM FILM OPTICAL SOUND
See series title for descriptive statement.
From The Beatrice Trum Hunter's Natural Foods Series.
Prod-PUBTEL Dist-PBS 1974

Vegetarian World, The C 29 MIN
16MM FILM, 3/4 OR 1/2 IN VIDEO
Looks at the history and practice of the vegetarian lifestyle and presents archival footage of such famous vegetarians as Count Leo Tolstoy, George Bernard Shaw and Mahatma Gandhi. Traces the development of vegetarianism from its Eastern beginnings to the sophisticated vegetarian restaurants of Europe and North America. Narrated by William Shatner.
LC NO. 84-706504
Prod-KSFILM Dist-BULFRG 1983

Vegetarianism - Food For Thought C 25 MIN
3/4 OR 1/2 INCH VIDEO CASSETTE
Reports on the nutritional values of meatless diets and analyzes the reasons why people choose vegetarian diets. Shows how their regimen can save money at the market.
Prod-TRAINX Dist-TRAINX

Vegetarianism In A Nutshell C 14 MIN
3/4 OR 1/2 INCH VIDEO CASSETTE J-C A
Provides the answers to why people become vegetarians, the different types of vegetarian diets, the nutritional implications, how to plan a vegetarian diet, and the dietary precautions.
Prod-POAPLE Dist-POAPLE

Vegetation And Bathymetric Modeling C 60 MIN
3/4 OR 1/2 INCH VIDEO CASSETTE
See series title for descriptive statement.
From The Advanced Remote Sensing Techniques Series. Section I, Pt 7
Prod-UAZMIC Dist-UAZMIC

Vehicle Interaction C 21 MIN
3/4 OR 1/2 INCH VIDEO CASSETTE
Tells how to apply mental and physical skills to negotiating intersections.
From The Right Way Series.
Prod-SCETV Dist-PBS 1982

Vehicle Maintenance Story, The C 14 MIN
16MM FILM OPTICAL SOUND
Points out the value of good vehicle maintenance and the effort made by the post office to establish proper maintenance procedures.

LC NO. 74-705905
Prod-USPOST Dist-USNAC

Vehicle Safety And Maintenance Checks C 30 MIN
3/4 OR 1/2 INCH VIDEO CASSETTE
Covers the procedures for performing an extensive vehicle safety and maintenance check.
From The Keep It Running Series.
Prod-NETCHE Dist-NETCHE 1982

Vehicle Stop Tactics, Pt 1 C 20 MIN
16MM FILM, 3/4 OR 1/2 IN VIDEO
Shows safety procedures to be used when approaching a vehicle that has been required to pull off the road. Shows the safest position for the officer while writing a citation, use of emergency lights, occupant removal and arrest procedures.
Prod-BRAVO Dist-MTI

Vehicle Stop Tactics, Pt 2 C 20 MIN
16MM FILM, 3/4 OR 1/2 IN VIDEO
Shows safety procedures to be used when approaching a vehicle that has been required to pull off the road. Shows the safest position for the officer while writing a citation, use of emergency lights, occupant removal and arrest procedures.
Prod-BRAVO Dist-MTI

Vehicle Under Attack - Officer Survival Of Incendiary Ambush C 15 MIN
16MM FILM OPTICAL SOUND
Discusses police ambush and the survival of incendiary attack. Alerts law enforcement to the possibility of firebomb ambush against their vehicles. Outlines procedures, methods and tactics recommended to combat this terrorist attack.
From The Urban Crisis Series.
Prod-CPECOF Dist-BROSEB

Vehicles C 29 MIN
3/4 INCH VIDEO CASSETTE C A
Concentrates on designing several kinds of vehicles, such as cars, skateboards and wagons. Explains some of the reasoning involved in the design of vehicles.
From The Sketching Techniques Series. Lesson 27
Prod-COAST Dist-CDTEL

Vehicles C 30 MIN
3/4 OR 1/2 INCH VIDEO CASSETTE H-C A
Presents Lawrence Solow and Sharon Neumann Solow introducing American Sign Language used by the hearing-impaired. Emphasizes signs having to to do with vehicles.
From The Say It With Sign Series. Part 28
Prod-KNBCTV Dist-FI 1982

Veiled Revolution, A C 26 MIN
16MM FILM, 3/4 OR 1/2 IN VIDEO
Discusses the reasons why Egypt, which was once among the most liberal of Middle Eastern countries in regards to women's rights, is now experiencing a return to traditional Islamic women's roles.
From The Women In The Middle East Series.
Prod-ICARUS Dist-ICARUS 1982

Vejen C 22 MIN
16MM FILM, 3/4 OR 1/2 IN VIDEO J-C A
Focuses on a Buddhist priest and his acolyte as they engage in their daily activities at school, at play and at prayer.
Prod-PHTC Dist-CAROUF

Vejen (The Path) C 21 MIN
16MM FILM OPTICAL SOUND
A Danish language film. Describes the Buddhist religion with shots of Rangoon.
Prod-STATNS Dist-STATNS 1969

Vela Program - Satellite Detection System C 15 MIN
16MM FILM OPTICAL SOUND H-C A
Explains the purpose of the Vela Program. Describes the problems involved in developing satellites for detecting nuclear radiation. Illustrates the manufacturing and testing of detection systems and anticipates future developments of the Satellite Detection Program.
LC NO. FIA65-495
Prod-USAEC Dist-USNAC Prodn-SANDIA 1964

Velars And Glottals C 10 MIN
1/2 IN VIDEO CASSETTE BETA/VHS A
See series title for descriptive statement.
From The Speech Reading Materials Series.
Prod-RMI Dist-RMI

Veldt, The C 23 MIN
16MM FILM, 3/4 OR 1/2 IN VIDEO J-C A
Describes a futuristic house which can do housework, cook, and entertain. Tells how its occupants are increasingly disturbed by the images and sounds of the African veldt which appear on the playroom walls. Based on the short story The Veldt by Ray Bradbury.
Prod-WILETS Dist-BARR 1979

Velnio Nuotaka (Lithuanian) C 78 MIN
3/4 OR 1/2 INCH VIDEO CASSETTE
A Lithuanian language version of the film The Devil's Bride.
Prod-IHF Dist-IHF

Velocity And Rates C
3/4 INCH VIDEO CASSETTE
See series title for descriptive statement.
From The Calculus Series.
Prod-MDDE Dist-MDCPB

Velocity Distribution Of Atoms In A Beam B 16 MIN
16MM FILM OPTICAL SOUND H-C
Describes an experiment determing the velocity distribution of the atoms in a beam of potassium atoms.
From The College Physics Film Program Series.
LC NO. FIA68-1445
Prod-UEVA Dist-MLA 1968

Velopharyngeal Closure In Speech And Deglutition C 17 MIN
16MM FILM, 3/4 OR 1/2 IN VIDEO
Demonstrates the mechanism of velopharyngeal closure and speech in a patient who had undergone a radical right maxillectomy and orbital exenteration for carcinoma.
Prod-VADTC Dist-AMDA 1971

Velvet Roll Separator C 3 MIN
16MM FILM OPTICAL SOUND H-C A
Combines animation and live action to illustrate the mechanism for separating smooth and rough seeds to separate containers. Shows the manner and degree of separation of a sample of mixed seed.
From The Principles Of Seed Processing Series.
LC NO. 77-701160
Prod-EVERSL Dist-IOWA Prodn-IOWA 1975

Velveteen Rabbit, The C 19 MIN
16MM FILM OPTICAL SOUND
Tells a story about nursery magic which causes a toy bunny to become real.
LC NO. 75-700164
Prod-LSBPRO Dist-LSBPRO 1974

Vena Cava Bonchovascular Triad C 16 MIN
3/4 OR 1/2 INCH VIDEO CASSETTE PRO
Shows the vena cava bronchovascular triad.
Prod-WFP Dist-WFP Prodn-UKANMC

Venceremos B 20 MIN
16MM FILM OPTICAL SOUND
Examines the gap between the rich and poor sectors of Chilean society and presents a sequence on the 1970 elections in Chile.
LC NO. 74-702317
Prod-CHASKP Dist-TRIFC 1970

Vendons Ces Meubles B 13 MIN
16MM FILM OPTICAL SOUND I-H
See series title for descriptive statement.
From The Les Francais Chez Vous Series. Set II, Lesson 15
Prod-PEREN Dist-CHLTN 1967

Vendor Certification And Rating C 33 MIN
3/4 OR 1/2 INCH VIDEO CASSETTE
Describes plans used by manufacturing companies to evaluate the capabilities of vendors to produce product in conformance to delivery dates and quality requirements.
From The Quality Control Series.
Prod-MIOT Dist-MIOT

Venereal Disease C 18 MIN
3/4 OR 1/2 INCH VIDEO CASSETTE
Discusses the nature of sexually transmitted diseases. Presents basic facts about prevention, recognition and treatment.
Prod-MEDFAC Dist-MEDFAC 1981

Venereal Disease - The Hidden Epidemic C 23 MIN
16MM FILM, 3/4 OR 1/2 IN VIDEO J-H
Traces the history of venereal diseases and attitudes toward them. Examines the two major venereal diseases - gonorrhea and syphilis. Describes the symptoms and demonstrates their cycles of appearance and disappearance. Identifies the early signs of syphilis and gonorrhea and tells of the importance of getting competent medical help promptly. Emphasizes prevention and what should be done to prevent the spread of venereal disease.
Prod-EBEC Dist-EBEC 1972

Venereal Disease - The Hidden Epidemic C 30 MIN
3/4 OR 1/2 INCH VIDEO CASSETTE C A
Focuses on the recent rise in venereal diseases. Covers symptoms, tests, treatment and prevention.
From The Family Portrait - A Study Of Contemporary Lifestyles Series. Lesson 8
Prod-SCCON Dist-CDTEL

Venereal Disease - The Hidden Epidemic (Spanish) C 23 MIN
16MM FILM, 3/4 OR 1/2 IN VIDEO J-C
Presents the history of venereal diseases and attitudes towards them. Offers a clinical analysis of gonorrhea and syphilis and portrays discussions between doctors and patients in a treatment center.
Prod-EBEC Dist-EBEC

Venereal Disease - Why Do We Still Have It C 20 MIN
16MM FILM, 3/4 OR 1/2 IN VIDEO J-H A
Introduces issues of personal values, behavior and personal decision-making as they apply to sexual behavior and the threat of catching a venereal disease. Demonstrated that penicillin and antibiotics can kill the bacteria that cause gonorrhea and syphillis. Shows how VD spreads, what the symptoms are and what the long-term effects of the untreated conditions can be.
Prod-WFP Dist-PEREN Prodn-BROWN

Venereal Diseases C 17 MIN
16MM FILM, 3/4 OR 1/2 IN VIDEO
Points out that taboos surrounding venereal disease keep young people from getting proper treatment. Emphasizes the confidential nature of treatment at a clinic and shows the work of a contact investigator with patients. Portrays the examination of patients and discusses the causes, symptoms and treatment for gonorrhea and syphilis.
From The Human Sexuality Series.
Prod-WILEYJ Dist-MEDIAG 1973

Venetian Twins, The C 60 MIN
3/4 OR 1/2 INCH VIDEO CASSETTE H-C A
Explores methods of character development. Uses the play The Venetian Twins as an example.
From The Drama - Play, Performance, Perception Series. Dramatis Personae
Prod-BBCTV Dist-FI 1978

Venezia Museo All'Aperto C 13 MIN
16MM FILM, 3/4 OR 1/2 IN VIDEO H-C A
An Italian language version of the motion picture Venice. Looks at the art and architecture of Venice.
Prod-CINEVI Dist-IFB 1975

Venezuela C 14 MIN
16MM FILM, 3/4 OR 1/2 IN VIDEO I-H
Discusses Venezuela today as an extreme contrast between rich and poor. Depicts the struggle to nationalize the oil industry and shows the development of a varied industrial structure which has created more jobs and better living standards.
From The Man And His World Series.
Prod-FI Dist-FI 1970

Venezuela C 25 MIN
3/4 OR 1/2 INCH VIDEO CASSETTE H-C A
Documents the developing economy of Venezuela, which has been strengthened by oil sales, and discusses the accompanying problems.
Prod-UPI Dist-JOU

Venezuela - Children Of The Island C 26 MIN
3/4 OR 1/2 INCH VIDEO CASSETTE
Documents the life of a 13-year-old barracuda fisherman on an island off the coast of Venezuela.
From The Growing Up Young Series.
Prod-FOTH Dist-FOTH

Venezuela - Children Of The Street C 26 MIN
3/4 OR 1/2 INCH VIDEO CASSETTE
Documents the life of a 12-year-old newspaper vendor in Caracas, Venezuela.
From The Growing Up Young Series.
Prod-FOTH Dist-FOTH

Venezuela - Oil Builds A Nation C 17 MIN
16MM FILM, 3/4 OR 1/2 IN VIDEO I-H
Portrays the rapid growth, industrialization and wealth of Venezuela, with emphasis upon the importance of the vast oil resources recently discovered. Studies the problems that this rapid growth has caused. Examines future of Latin America's first modern industrial nation.
Prod-EBEC Dist-EBEC 1972

Venezuelan Adventure C 30 MIN
16MM FILM OPTICAL SOUND I-C A
Shows views of Caracas and interior Venezuela, and of the fishing and tiger hunting activities of General James H Doolittle and his companions.
LC NO. 74-702022
Prod-DAC Dist-MCDO 1966

Venezuelan Equine Encephalitis - Epidemic In Colombia C 16 MIN
16MM FILM OPTICAL SOUND
Documents two simultaneous outbreaks of Venezuelan equine encephalitis affecting both equines and humans in Colombia, South America.
LC NO. 74-705906
Prod-USPHS Dist-USNAC 1968

Venezuelan Equine Encephalitis - Epidemic In Colombia (Spanish) C 16 MIN
16MM FILM OPTICAL SOUND H-C
Documents two simultaneous outbreaks of Venezuelan equine encephalitis affecting both equines and humans in Colombia, South America.
LC NO. 74-705908
Prod-USPHS Dist-USNAC 1968

Venezuelan Prairie C 26 MIN
16MM FILM OPTICAL SOUND P A
Studies the savannah country of Central Venezuela, showing the blue-faced night herons, the scarlet ibis, vividly colored tropical birds and howler monkeys.
From The Audubon Wildlife Theatre Series.
LC NO. 71-710209
Prod-KEGPL Dist-AVEXP 1970

Vengeance Is Mine C 29 MIN
16MM FILM OPTICAL SOUND
Shows Les Merrill, a young black man, released from prison after spending three years for a crime he did not commit. Pictures him returning to the ghetto neighborhood in which he spent his boyhood, determined to find who framed him and seek vengeance. Presents his girl friend, Edith, trying to convince Les that vengeance belongs to God, and that Christians have faith that evil must be overcome with good.
LC NO. 73-701034
Prod-FAMF Dist-FAMF 1971

Vengo A Ayudarla (I Come To Help You) Program Number 3 C 20 MIN
3/4 OR 1/2 INCH VIDEO CASSETTE PRO
Presents vocabulary pertaining to time - seasons, months, days, hours. Gives language commonly used in blood tests, x-ray exams and new patient orientation.
From The Spanish For Health Professionals Series.
Prod-HSCIC Dist-HSCIC 1982

Veni-Puncture C 9 MIN
3/4 OR 1/2 INCH VIDEO CASSETTE PRO
See series title for descriptive statement.
From The Medical Skills Films Series.
Prod-WFP Dist-WFP

Veni, Vidi, Vici B 15 MIN
16MM FILM OPTICAL SOUND J-H
Discusses Caesar's campaigns in Gaul and his conquest of what

is now France, Germany and Switzerland. Shows how skillfully used 'MODERN' methods of warfare against heroic warriors with primitive weapons.
Prod-FCE Dist-FCE 1961

Venice C 13 MIN
16MM FILM, 3/4 OR 1/2 IN VIDEO H-C A
Looks at the art and architecture of Venice.
LC NO. 80-707242
Prod-CINEVI Dist-IFB 1975

Venice - The Sinking City C 11 MIN
3/4 OR 1/2 INCH VIDEO CASSETTE H-C A
Documents the damage caused by persistent flooding in Venice. Examines the work being done to prevent further disasters.
Prod-UPI Dist-JOU

Venice - Theme And Variations C 30 MIN
16MM FILM OPTICAL SOUND C A
Features Venice the way it was seen by generations of artists from the thirteenth century to the present. Portrays the city's pageantry and beauty in works of early mosaicists, engravers and painters.
Prod-FILIM Dist-RADIM 1957

Venice - Theme And Variations C 30 MIN
16MM FILM OPTICAL SOUND
Begins with sequences of Venice today and depicts the past through the eyes of a number of artists, from mosaicists of San Marco to Saul Steinberg.
Prod-IVORYJ Dist-RADIM

Venice - Themes And Variations C 20 MIN
16MM FILM OPTICAL SOUND J-C A
Depicts life in Venice from the 14th century to the 20th century. Shows the works of such artists as Bellini, Guardi, Canaletto, Carpaccio, Whistler and Saul Steinberg.
Prod-IVORYJ Dist-RADIM 1957

Venice, Etude, No. 1 C 10 MIN
16MM FILM OPTICAL SOUND
Unites the color and motion of Venice. Juxtaposes the horizontal and frontal dimensions to introduce a third plane and create a total visual experience.
Prod-HUGOI Dist-RADIM

Venipuncture C 9 MIN
3/4 OR 1/2 INCH VIDEO CASSETTE
Explains the principle of vein puncture. Demonstrates proper technique for obtaining venous sample.
Prod-MEDFAC Dist-MEDFAC 1978

Venipuncture C 10 MIN
3/4 INCH VIDEO CASSETTE PRO
Discusses venipuncture, a method of entering a vein for the purpose of injecting fluid or withdrawing blood. Demonstrates the procedure on a simulated arm and also in a clinical situation.
From The Emergency Techniques Series.
Prod-PRIMED Dist-PRIMED

Venipuncture C 16 MIN
3/4 OR 1/2 INCH VIDEO CASSETTE PRO
Describes the various equipment and techniques for performing venipunctures including methods appropriate for drawing blood samples and for starting intravenous infusions. Discusses possible complications and their resolutions.
Prod-UMICHM Dist-UMICHM 1975

Venison Sauce Piquante C 29 MIN
2 INCH VIDEOTAPE
Features gourmet-humorist Justin Wilson showing ways to cook venison with various ingredients.
From The Cookin' Cajun Series.
Prod-MAETEL Dist-PUBTEL

Venomous Creatures C 14 MIN
3/4 INCH VIDEO CASSETTE
Shows a gila monster and several kinds of snakes and insects that are potentially dangerous to man.
Prod-TUCPL Dist-GPITVL

Venomous Creatures (Spanish) C 14 MIN
3/4 INCH VIDEO CASSETTE
Shows a gila monster and several kinds of snakes and insects that are potentially dangerous to man.
Prod-TUCPL Dist-GPITVL

Venous Cannulation C 6 MIN
3/4 OR 1/2 INCH VIDEO CASSETTE PRO
Presents three types of indwelling line assemblies preferred sites for cannulation, and a step-by-step analysis of the procedure.
Prod-UWASH Dist-UWASH

Venous Cutdown C 9 MIN
16MM FILM OPTICAL SOUND
Demonstrates an approved medical procedure when entry into the circulatory system is necessary and percutaneous techniques are inadequate or inadvisable. Shows the preparation of the patient, reviews the necessary equipment and portrays the procedure in close-up detail.
From The Medical Skills Library Series.
LC NO. 73-702390
Prod-ACEPHY Dist-SUTHLA 1972

Venous Cutdown C 9 MIN
3/4 OR 1/2 INCH VIDEO CASSETTE PRO
See series title for descriptive statement.
From The Medical Skills Films Series.
Prod-WFP Dist-WFP

Venous Peripheral Vascular Disease C 28 MIN
16MM FILM OPTICAL SOUND PRO
A revised version of the 1969 motion picture Nursing Responsibilities In The Care Of Patients With Venous Peripheral Vascular Disease. Discusses the assessment of a person with peripheral venous insufficiency complicated by thrombophlebitis. Describes and demonstrates the application of moist heat and anticoagulant therapy.
LC NO. 77-703463
Prod-DENT Dist-WSU Prodn-WSU 1977

Venous Peripheral Vascular Disease C 30 MIN
16MM FILM OPTICAL SOUND PRO
A revised version of the motion picture Nursing Responsibility In The Care Of The Patient With Venous Peripheral Vascular Disease. Discusses nursing care of the patient with venous peripheral vascular disease.
From The Directions For Education In Nursing Via Technology Series.
LC NO. 77-703463
Prod-DENT Dist-WSUM Prodn-WSU 1977

Venous Peripheral Vascular Disease C 28 MIN
3/4 OR 1/2 INCH VIDEO CASSETTE
Presents the assessment of a person with peripheral venous insufficiency complicated by thrombophlebitis using the case study/problem-oriented approach. Demonstrates nursing actions related to the application of moist heat, anticoagulant therapy and preparation for care at home.
Prod-WSUN Dist-AJN

Ventilation B 25 MIN
16MM FILM OPTICAL SOUND PRO
Details the use of tools and the importance of their operations in rescue. Illustrates laddering and ventilating to accomplish the control and extinguishing of fires.
LC NO. 72-700754
Prod-LACFD Dist-FILCOM 1950

Ventilation B 25 MIN
3/4 OR 1/2 INCH VIDEO CASSETTE PRO
Details the use of tools and the importance of their operations in rescue. Illustrates laddering and ventilating to accomplish the control and extinguishing of fires.
Prod-LACFD Dist-FILCOM 1950

Ventilation C 27 MIN
16MM FILM, 3/4 OR 1/2 IN VIDEO PRO
A training film showing basic ventilation practices to use in instructing recruit fire fighters. Shows use of forcible entry equipment, proper use of hose streams for ventilating and theory of fire spread. Includes practical demonstration and blackboard discussion of ventilating techniques.
Prod-NFPA Dist-FILCOM

Ventilation C 30 MIN
3/4 OR 1/2 INCH VIDEO CASSETTE
Presents live footage covering the principles of ventilation in fire suppression. Shows how to cut holes in roofs and floors, break glass and protect against backdraft explosion.
Prod-IFSTA Dist-IFSTA

Ventilation C 56 MIN
3/4 OR 1/2 INCH VIDEO CASSETTE PRO
Shows effective fire emergency ventilation techniques for old apartments with extremely high occupancy. Describes ventilation training for use in old, multi-storied dwellings.
Prod-LACFD Dist-FILCOM

Ventilation Techniques In Lightweight Roofs C 46 MIN
3/4 OR 1/2 INCH VIDEO CASSETTE PRO
Shows ventilation of lightweight roofs under fire conditions. Gives special tips for handling fires at large commercial installations, where unbraced plywood is often a problem for roof ventilation.
Prod-LACFD Dist-FILCOM

Ventricular Aneurysm C 15 MIN
3/4 OR 1/2 INCH VIDEO CASSETTE PRO
Shows ventricular aneurysm.
Prod-WFP Dist-WFP Prodn-UKANMC

Ventricular Aneurysm Following Myocardial Infarction - Surgical Excision C 12 MIN
16MM FILM OPTICAL SOUND PRO
Shows step by step a method of surgical repair of massive left ventricular aneurysm on a 50-year-old laborer who suffered a severe anterior myocardial infarction approximately three months prior to his admission.
LC NO. FIA66-79
Prod-EATONL Dist-EATONL Prodn-AVCORP 1961

Ventricular Conduction Defects C
3/4 OR 1/2 INCH VIDEO CASSETTE PRO
Describes the anatomy of the ventricular conduction system. Shows how to determine the presence or absence of following elecrocardiographic abnormalities, alone or in combination, right bundle branch block, left bundle branch blocks left posterior hemiblock, and left anterior hemiblock.
From The Interpretation Of The Twelve Lead Electrocardiogram Series.
Prod-BRA Dist-BRA

Ventricular Conduction Disturbances C 53 MIN
3/4 OR 1/2 INCH VIDEO CASSETTE PRO
Discusses right and left bundle branch blocks. Illustrates hemiblocks and the trifascicular system.
From The Electrocardiogram Series.
Prod-HSCIC Dist-HSCIC 1982

Ventricular Defibrillation C 9 MIN
3/4 OR 1/2 INCH VIDEO CASSETTE PRO
See series title for descriptive statement.
From The Medical Skills Films Series.
Prod-WFP Dist-WFP

Ventricular System, The C 15 MIN
3/4 OR 1/2 INCH VIDEO CASSETTE PRO
Using brain specimens and diagrams, identifies the parts of the brain's ventricular system. Discusses the flow of cerebrospinal fluid within the ventricles and related pathology when applicable.
From The Neurobiology Series.
Prod-HSCIC Dist-HSCIC

Ventura, Charlene - A Leader Of Women C 30 MIN
3/4 INCH VIDEO CASSETTE
Presents Charlene Ventura, a leader of the feminist movement in Cincinnati. Discusses the movement and problems it faces.
From The Decision Makers Series.
Prod-OHC Dist-HRC

Venture Doubly Blessed C 28 MIN
16MM FILM OPTICAL SOUND R
Describes the Lay Institute for Evangelism, a program sponsored by the Campus Crusade for Christ. Reports on the program's success in evangelization in Haiti.
LC NO. 73-701573
Prod-CCFC Dist-CCFC 1972

Venture In Writing, A C 15 MIN
2 INCH VIDEOTAPE I
Uses the work of an artist as subject matter for Cinquain poetry and encourages viewers to write such poetry.
From The Images Series.
Prod-CVETVC Dist-GPITVL

Venture Into Nature C 28 MIN
16MM FILM OPTICAL SOUND
Guides the viewer through scenes which show the beauty of nature, only to discover distressing scenes of the destruction of the natural environment. Designed to promote awareness of the environmental crises.
LC NO. 75-703252
Prod-MORALL Dist-MORALL 1974

Venturer, The C 30 MIN
16MM FILM, 3/4 OR 1/2 IN VIDEO C A
See series title for descriptive statement.
From The Case Studies In Small Business Series.
Prod-UMA Dist-GPITVL 1979

Venturing - Old And New Firms C 54 MIN
3/4 OR 1/2 INCH VIDEO CASSETTE
See series title for descriptive statement.
From The Technology, Innovation, And Industrial Development Series.
Prod-MIOT Dist-MIOT

Venus And Mars And Company - The Art Of Pompeii C 45 MIN
2 INCH VIDEOTAPE
See series title for descriptive statement.
From The Humanities Series. Unit II - The World Of Myth And Legend
Prod-WTTWTV Dist-GPITVL

Venus And The Cat (Italian) C 10 MIN
16MM FILM OPTICAL SOUND H-C A
Presents an animated version of the Aesop fable about a lonely man and a cat which Venus sends him as a gift.
LC NO. 72-702042
Prod-ZAGREB Dist-RADIM 1971

Vera And The Law - Toward A More Effective System Of Justice C 39 MIN
16MM FILM OPTICAL SOUND H-C A
Examines the programs of the Vera Institute of Justice in working to reform the criminal justice system.
LC NO. 75-702970
Prod-FDF Dist-KAROL Prodn-STONEY 1975

Vera Cruz C 11 MIN
16MM FILM OPTICAL SOUND I-H A
Depicts Fortin de las Flores, the peak of Orizaba and the beach of Mocambo. Shows the flower markets from which gardenias, camelias and orchids are shipped to all parts of the world.
Prod-BARONA Dist-AVED 1958

Vera Paints Ibiza In The Sun C 20 MIN
16MM FILM, 3/4 OR 1/2 IN VIDEO J-C A
Visits the island of Ibiza off the coast of Spain with American textile designer, Vera Newmann. Shows how her sketch becomes a design for a textile print and how artists, technicians, chemists and craftsmen transmit Vera's design onto fabric.
Prod-SCHLAT Dist-LUF 1973

Verb - That's Where The Action Is C 3 MIN
3/4 OR 1/2 INCH VIDEO CASSETTE P
Shows how a little boy learns about the characteristics of verbs from a 'verb' playing the part of a super-hero.
From The Grammar Rock Series.
Prod-ABCTV Dist-GA Prodn-SCOROC 1974

Verbal Ability, Analogies, Antonyms, Sentence Completion, Lesson 2 C
3/4 OR 1/2 INCH VIDEO CASSETTE H A
See series title for descriptive statement.
From The GRE/Graduate Record Examination Series.
Prod-COMEX Dist-COMEX

Verbal And Nonverbal Congruence C 12 MIN
2 INCH VIDEOTAPE C A
Features a humanistic psychologist who, by analysis and examples, discusses verbal and nonverbal congruence in relation to effective communication.
From The Interpersonal Competence, Unit 02 - Communication Series.
Prod-MVNE Dist-TELSTR 1973

Verbal Communication (Spanish) C 28 MIN
16MM FILM, 3/4 OR 1/2 IN VIDEO H-C A
Presents some of the reasons why effective communication is

difficult, such as the ambiguity of language itself, the indirectness of speech and one's inner conflicts. Introduces processes which can be used to communicate more effectively by defusing arguments precipitated by inner conflict, by listening instead of just hearing and by using feedback to provide a two-way channel that both people can use to build on each other's ideas.
Prod-CRMP Dist-CRMP 1981

Verbal Communication - The Power Of Words C 30 MIN
16MM FILM, 3/4 OR 1/2 IN VIDEO H-C A
Uses animation, humorous vignettes and dramatized slices of organizational life to illustrate the four critical parts of every verbal exchange - the speaker, the language used, the atmosphere and the listener.
LC NO. 81-706765
Prod-CRMP Dist-CRMP 1981

Verbal Communication In The Trial C 50 MIN
3/4 OR 1/2 INCH VIDEO CASSETTE PRO
Covers matters common to all trial advocates, including avoidance of complicated language and finding the proper pace, volume and projection. Gives suggestions for solving problems that often interfere with effective communication.
From The Effective Communication In The Courtroom Series.
Prod-ABACPE Dist-ABACPE

Verbal Review, Tape 1 C 45 MIN
3/4 OR 1/2 INCH VIDEO CASSETTE H A
Introduces the verbal section of the Scholoastic Aptitude Test. Covers vocabulary, contextual clues and word analysis questions found on the SAT/ACT exam.
From The SAT/ACT Examination Video Review Series.
Prod-COMEX Dist-COMEX

Verbal Review, Tape 2 C 45 MIN
3/4 OR 1/2 INCH VIDEO CASSETTE H A
Focuses on a review of etymology, synonyms and antonyms in preparation for taking the SAT/ACT exam.
From The SAT/ACT Examination Video Review Series.
Prod-COMEX Dist-COMEX

Verbal Review, Tape 3 C 45 MIN
3/4 OR 1/2 INCH VIDEO CASSETTE H A
Focuses on analogies as presented in the SAT/ACT examination.
From The SAT/ACT Examination Video Review Series.
Prod-COMEX Dist-COMEX

Verbal Review, Tape 4 C 45 MIN
3/4 OR 1/2 INCH VIDEO CASSETTE H A
Focuses on sentence completion and reading skills as presented in the SAT/ACT exam.
From The SAT/ACT Examination Video Review Series.
Prod-COMEX Dist-COMEX

Verbal Review, Tape 5 C 45 MIN
3/4 OR 1/2 INCH VIDEO CASSETTE H A
Focuses on reading speed and finding the main ideas as they apply to the SAT/ACT exam.
From The SAT/ACT Examination Video Review Series.
Prod-COMEX Dist-COMEX

Verbal Review, Tape 6 C 45 MIN
3/4 OR 1/2 INCH VIDEO CASSETTE H A
Focuses on how to approach a reading comprehension question on the SAT/ACT examination.
From The SAT/ACT Examination Video Review Series.
Prod-COMEX Dist-COMEX

Verbal Review, Tape 7 C 45 MIN
3/4 OR 1/2 INCH VIDEO CASSETTE H A
Focuses on levels of usage, subject-verb agreement and parts of speech as tested on the SAT/ACT examination.
From The SAT/ACT Examination Video Review Series.
Prod-COMEX Dist-COMEX

Verbal Review, Tape 8 C 45 MIN
3/4 OR 1/2 INCH VIDEO CASSETTE H A
Focuses on irregular verbs and word pairs. Includes sample questions from the SAT/ACT examination.
From The SAT/ACT Examination Video Review Series.
Prod-COMEX Dist-COMEX

Verbs C 8 MIN
16MM FILM, 3/4 OR 1/2 IN VIDEO P-I
Uses a robot and two people to investigate verbs by reasoning from the behavior of a few examples to general grammatical rules.
From The Basic Grammar Series.
LC NO. 81-706575
Prod-LEVYL Dist-AIMS 1981

Verbs - Being, Action, Linking C 11 MIN
1/2 IN VIDEO CASSETTE BETA/VHS
See series title for descriptive statement.
From The English And Speech Series.
Prod-RMI Dist-RMI

Verbs And Adverbs C 9 MIN
16MM FILM, 3/4 OR 1/2 IN VIDEO P-I
Points out verbs and illustrates ways in which adding adverbs makes the verbs more expressive.
From The Wizard Of Words Series.
Prod-MGHT Dist-MGHT 1976

Verbs In Sentences C 14 MIN
16MM FILM, 3/4 OR 1/2 IN VIDEO P-I
Shows how a verb is an action word that performs important jobs in sentences. Discusses their forms, their relation to nouns and their uses.
From The Grammar Skills Series.
Prod-GLDWER Dist-JOU 1981

Verdi's Rigoletto At Verona C 115 MIN
3/4 OR 1/2 INCH VIDEO CASSETTE
Prod-MSTVIS Dist-MSTVIS

Verdict For Tomorrow X 28 MIN
16MM FILM OPTICAL SOUND H-C A
An account of the Eichmann trial, based on footage gathered during the Eichmann trial in Jerusalem, utilizes the trial as a reminder of Nazism and of persecution of the Jews rather than as a dated legal presentation. Narrated by Lowell Thomas.
Prod-CAPCBC Dist-ADL

Verdun B 29 MIN
16MM FILM OPTICAL SOUND J-C A
Shows scenes of the battle of Verdun, describing the German plan of attack and explaining the long-lasting effect the battle had on the French nation.
From The Legacy Series.
LC NO. 74-707211
Prod-NET Dist-IU 1965

Vergette Making A Pot C 9 MIN
16MM FILM, 3/4 OR 1/2 IN VIDEO J-C
Portrays the artistry of the potter and shows him at work, throwing, trimming, glazing and firing.
Prod-SILLU Dist-AIMS 1966

Vermilonectomy C 7 MIN
16MM FILM OPTICAL SOUND PRO
Demonstrates an operation to correct a recurring lesion on the lower lip by removing the lip mucosa.
LC NO. 74-705910
Prod-USA Dist-USNAC 1973

Vernier And Micrometer Scales B 10 MIN
16MM FILM OPTICAL SOUND C
Explains the principles of Vernier and micrometer scales and gives instructions for reading them.
Prod-PUAVC Dist-PUAVC 1961

Vernier Caliper C 13 MIN
3/4 OR 1/2 INCH VIDEO CASSETTE A
Shows main parts of, how to read in both inches and metric, take inside and outside measurements, and how to test measurements with a vernier caliper.
From The Metalworking - Precision Measuring Series.
Prod-VISIN Dist-VISIN

Vernier Height Gage C 13 MIN
3/4 OR 1/2 INCH VIDEO CASSETTE A
Shows main parts of Vernier height gage, Vernier principle, how to read it in both inches and metric, its use for layout and inspection, and the test on reading.
From The Metalworking - Precision Measuring Series.
Prod-VISIN Dist-VISIN

Vernier Scale And Vernier Caliper C
3/4 OR 1/2 INCH VIDEO CASSETTE
See series title for descriptive statement.
From The Basic Machine Technology Series.
Prod-VTRI Dist-VTRI

Vernier Scale And Vernier Caliper C 15 MIN
3/4 OR 1/2 INCH VIDEO CASSETTE IND
Includes inside, outside and dial calipers.
From The Machining And The Operation Of Machine Tools, Module 1 - Basic Machine technology Series.
Prod-LEIKID Dist-LEIKID

Vernier Scale And Vernier Caliper (Inside, Outside, And Dial Calipers) C 15 MIN
3/4 OR 1/2 INCH VIDEO CASSETTE
See series title for descriptive statement.
From The Machine Technology II - Engine Lathe Accessories Series.
Prod-CAMB Dist-CAMB

Vernier Scale And Vernier Caliper (Spanish) C
3/4 OR 1/2 INCH VIDEO CASSETTE
See series title for descriptive statement.
From The Basic Machine Technology (Spanish) Series.
Prod-VTRI Dist-VTRI

Veronica C 27 MIN
16MM FILM OPTICAL SOUND J-C
A cinema verite portrait of Veronica Glover, a black teenager who is president of her predominately white high school in New Haven, Conn, showing her inner struggle to maintain her identity under stress.
From The Jason Films Portrait Series.
LC NO. 75-705709
Prod-JASON Dist-JASON 1970

Veronica C 14 MIN
16MM FILM, 3/4 OR 1/2 IN VIDEO I-J
Introduces Veronica, a girl of Polish descent who lives in a multi-ethnic neighborhood in Toronto, Canada. Shows her learning traditional Polish dances at school and maintaining a strong affection for her native roots.
Prod-NFBC Dist-MEDIAG 1978

Vers Des Temps Nouveaux - Toward New Times C 52 MIN
16MM FILM OPTICAL SOUND
Explores the importance of a realistic view of death, cadavers and funeral ceremonies during the middle ages in Western Europe.
From The Le Temp Des Cathedrales Series.
Prod-FACSEA Dist-FACSEA 1979

Vers Notre Deuxieme Siecle C 30 MIN
16MM FILM OPTICAL SOUND H-C
A French version of 'THE QUALITY OF A NATION.' Celebrates Canada's 100th anniversary of confederation.
Prod-CRAF Dist-CFI

Versailles - The Lost Peace C 26 MIN
16MM FILM, 3/4 OR 1/2 IN VIDEO H-C
Shows how President Woodrow Wilson's idealistic hopes for world peace clashed at Versailles with the harsh old-world 'real-politik' of Europe, which wanted to punish Germany. Explains that the resultant punitive treaty sowed the seeds of World War II.
From The Between The Wars Series.
Prod-LNDBRG Dist-FI 1978

Versatile Machine, The C 25 MIN
16MM FILM, 3/4 OR 1/2 IN VIDEO H-C A
Introduces Richard Gomme, a victim of cerebral palsy whose life has been transformed by the addition of a microcomputer to his home. Describes all the things he is able to do despite the severity of his handicap.
From The Making The Most Of The Micro Series. Episode 1
Prod-BBCTV Dist-FI 1983

Versatility And The Variety Of Weaves Possible With The Four-Harness Loom Are... C 29 MIN
3/4 INCH VIDEO CASSETTE
Demonstrates the variety of weaves possible with the four-harness loom.
From The Your Weekly Weaver Series.
Prod-GAEDTN Dist-PUBTEL

Verse Person Singular C 60 MIN
3/4 OR 1/2 INCH VIDEO CASSETTE H-C A
Presents Richard Kiley performing some of his favorite first-person poems, including those by Lewis Carroll and some by Edgar Allen Poe.
LC NO. 84-706096
Prod-FI Dist-FI 1984

Vertebral Artery Surgery—A Series
PRO
Prod-BFLODY Dist-BFLODY Prodn-MECOM 1977

Carotid Distal Vertebral Artery Bypass For

Vertebral Fractures - Surgical Treatments B 26 MIN
16MM FILM OPTICAL SOUND PRO
Deals with vertebral fractures in the dog. Describes various methods of immobilization of the lumbar vertebrae.
Prod-AMVMA Dist-AMVMA

Vertebrates - Escaping Enemies, Protection And Adaptations C 20 MIN
2 INCH VIDEOTAPE I
See series title for descriptive statement.
From The Exploring With Science, Unit III - Animals Series.
Prod-MPATI Dist-GPITVL

Vertebrates - Fish C 15 MIN
3/4 OR 1/2 INCH VIDEO CASSETTE
Discusses the classification of various kinds of fish, explaining that scientists group animals according to characteristics such as appearance, behavior and habitat.
From The Discovering, Unit 1 - Vertebrate Animals Series.
LC NO. 79-706333
Prod-WDCNTV Dist-AITECH 1978

Vertebrates - Securing Food, Food Getting And Adaptations C 20 MIN
2 INCH VIDEOTAPE I
See series title for descriptive statement.
From The Exploring With Science, Unit III - Animals Series.
Prod-MPATI Dist-GPITVL

Vertebrates And Invertebrates In The Sea B 20 MIN
2 INCH VIDEOTAPE I
See series title for descriptive statement.
From The Science Room Series.
Prod-MCETV Dist-GPITVL Prodn-WVIZTV

Vertebrates, The - This Was The Beginning, Pt 2 (Rev) C 11 MIN
16MM FILM, 3/4 OR 1/2 IN VIDEO J-C
Provides a visual catalog in which vertebrates are grouped according to common characteristics and evolutionary sequence.
Prod-NFBC Dist-IFB

Vertical And Overhead Butt Welds With Filler Rod (Spanish) C
3/4 OR 1/2 INCH VIDEO CASSETTE
See series title for descriptive statement.
From The Oxy-Acetylene Welding (Spanish) Series.
Prod-VTRI Dist-VTRI

Vertical And Overhead Butt Welds With Filler Rod C 15 MIN
3/4 OR 1/2 INCH VIDEO CASSETTE IND
See series title for descriptive statement.
From The Welding - Oxy-Acetylene Welding Series.
Prod-ICSINT Dist-ICSINT

Vertical And Overhead Welding C 10 MIN
16MM FILM, 3/4 OR 1/2 IN VIDEO
Demonstrates mig welding techniques. Shows how to make vertical fillet and prepared butt welds and overhead fillet and prepared butt welds.
From The Welding Series.
Prod-UCC Dist-FI 1972

Vertical Bandsaws - Parts And Accessories C
3/4 OR 1/2 INCH VIDEO CASSETTE
See series title for descriptive statement.
From The Basic Machine Technology Series.
Prod-VTRI Dist-VTRI

Vertical Bandsaws - Parts And Accessories C 15 MIN
3/4 OR 1/2 INCH VIDEO CASSETTE

See series title for descriptive statement.
From The Machine Technology II - Engine Lathe Accessories Series.
Prod-CAMB Dist-CAMB

Vertical Bandsaws - Parts And Accessories (Spanish) C
3/4 OR 1/2 INCH VIDEO CASSETTE
See series title for descriptive statement.
From The Basic Machine Technology (Spanish) Series.
Prod-VTRI Dist-VTRI

Vertical Butt And Overhead Butt (MIG) Welding C 15 MIN
3/4 OR 1/2 INCH VIDEO CASSETTE
See series title for descriptive statement.
From The Welding III - TIG and MIG (Industry) Welding series.
Prod-CAMB Dist-CAMB

Vertical Butt And Overhead Butt Welds With Filler Rod C 15 MIN
3/4 OR 1/2 INCH VIDEO CASSETTE
See series title for descriptive statement.
From The Welding I - Basic Oxy-Acetylene Welding Series.
Prod-CAMB Dist-CAMB

Vertical Butt And Overhead Butt Welds With-Electric Arc C 15 MIN
3/4 OR 1/2 INCH VIDEO CASSETTE
See series title for descriptive statement.
From The Welding II - Basic Shielded Metal Arc Welding series.
Prod-CAMB Dist-CAMB

Vertical Dimension In Complete Dentures C 12 MIN
16MM FILM, 3/4 OR 1/2 IN VIDEO PRO
Demonstrates proportional and functional methods to establish a tentative vertical dimension for the edentulous patient. Emphasizes the correlation of this dimension with the centric relation.
LC NO. 80-707491
Prod-USVA Dist-USNAC 1979

Vertical Down Fillet C 6 MIN
1/2 IN VIDEO CASSETTE BETA/VHS IND
See series title for descriptive statement.
From The Welding Training (Comprehensive) - Basic Shielded Metal Arc Welding Series.
Prod-RMI Dist-RMI

Vertical File C 20 MIN
3/4 INCH VIDEO CASSETTE T
Presents information about the purposes and structure of the vertical file with emphasis on the type of materials to include in the file, their purpose and access to them.
From The Access Series.
LC NO. 76-706263
Prod-UDEN Dist-USNAC 1976

Vertical Fillet Weld E7018 Electrode C 9 MIN
1/2 IN VIDEO CASSETTE BETA/VHS IND
See series title for descriptive statement.
From The Arc Welding And MIG Welding Series.
Prod-RMI Dist-RMI

Vertical Flap Ureteropelvioplasty C 20 MIN
16MM FILM OPTICAL SOUND
Depicts a patient with a very definite extrarenal type of hydronephrosis. Explains that the pelvis was not atonic and maintained an active musculature and that the obstruction was at the ureteropelvic juncture. Describes the surgical indications for this operation.
From The Surgical Correction Of Hydronephrosis, Pt 1 - Non-Dismembering Procedures Series.
LC NO. 75-702259
Prod-EATONL Dist-EATONL 1968

Vertical Practices - Half Slave, Half Free C 44 MIN
3/4 OR 1/2 INCH VIDEO CASSETTE PRO
Discusses the economics of vertical restraints, including resale price maintenance.
From The Antitrust And Economics Series.
Prod-ABACPE Dist-ABACPE

Vertical Relation Of Occlusion By The Patient's Neuromuscular Perception C 14 MIN
16MM FILM, 3/4 OR 1/2 IN VIDEO PRO
Shows how the vertical dimension is recorded with intraoral hearing plates using the patient's memory pattern and neuromuscular perception. Follows procedures for recognizing mandibular positions which are both too high and too low, from which extreme alterations in height are made and an occlusal vertical position compatible with the neuromuscular physiology is arrived at.
LC NO. 81-707712
Prod-USVA Dist-USNAC Prodn-CONSFI 1977

Vertical Roll B 20 MIN
3/4 OR 1/2 INCH VIDEO CASSETTE
Presents repetitive, spatially and rhythmically disorienting movement of the rolling video signal.
Prod-KITCHN Dist-KITCHN

Vertical Up Butt Weld C 8 MIN
1/2 IN VIDEO CASSETTE BETA/VHS IND
See series title for descriptive statement.
From The Welding Training (Comprehensive) - Advanced Shielded Metal Arc Welding Series.
Prod-RMI Dist-RMI

Vertical Up Fillet Weld C 8 MIN
1/2 IN VIDEO CASSETTE BETA/VHS IND
See series title for descriptive statement.
From The Welding Training (Comprehensive) - Advanced Shielded Metal Arc Welding Series.
Prod-RMI Dist-RMI

Vertical Vowels And Lingua-Dentals C 10 MIN
1/2 IN VIDEO CASSETTE BETA/VHS A
See series title for descriptive statement.
From The Speech Reading Materials Series.
Prod-RMI Dist-RMI

Vertigo - A Question Of Balance C
3/4 OR 1/2 INCH VIDEO CASSETTE
Differentiates true vertigo from other forms of dizziness. Explains how it is almost always a result of some inner ear disorder. Discusses the different causes of vertigo.
Prod-MIFE Dist-MIFE

Vertigo - A Question Of Balance (Arabic) C
3/4 OR 1/2 INCH VIDEO CASSETTE
Differentiates true vertigo from other forms of dizziness. Explains how it is almost always a result of some inner ear disorder. Discusses the different causes of vertigo.
Prod-MIFE Dist-MIFE

Vertigo - Differential Diagnosis B 25 MIN
16MM FILM OPTICAL SOUND PRO
Demonstrates procedures for performing an examination of the patient with vertigo. Shows the onset of vertigo with symptoms of dizziness, loss of balance, and tinnitus. Demonstrates the Romberg and Gait tests for balance and the optokinetic, positional, and caloric tests for the measurement of nystagmus.
LC NO. FIA68-858
Prod-SKF Dist-AMEDA 1959

Very Delicate Matter, A C 30 MIN
16MM FILM, 3/4 OR 1/2 IN VIDEO H A
A shortened version of the motion picture A Very Delicate Matter. Tells the story of two teenagers whose close relationship is threatened when one contracts venereal disease and fails to inform the other. Stresses the need for infected persons to act responsibly by notifying others with whom they have had sexual contact.
Prod-HGATE Dist-LCOA 1982

Very Delicate Matter, A C 46 MIN
16MM FILM, 3/4 OR 1/2 IN VIDEO H A
Tells the story of two teenagers whose close relationship is threatened when one contracts venereal disease and fails to inform the other. Stresses the need for infected persons to act responsibly by notifying others with whom they have had sexual contact.
From The Learning To Be Human Series.
Prod-HGATE Dist-LCOA 1982

Very Enterprising Women C 15 MIN
16MM FILM, 3/4 OR 1/2 IN VIDEO
Shows women who have started their own businesses and succeeded. Presents interviews in which the women reveal what they feel is necessary to make it in the business world.
LC NO. 81-706324
Prod-SBA Dist-USNAC 1980

Very Eye Of Night, The C 15 MIN
16MM FILM OPTICAL SOUND
Highlights a celestial cinematic ballet filmed entirely in the nagative.
Prod-GROVE Dist-GROVE

Very First Easter, The C 12 MIN
16MM FILM OPTICAL SOUND
Presents a little boy telling his dog Sniffy about the events of the first Easter, how Jesus and his disciples came to Jerusalem to celebrate the Passover, the happy processional into the city, driving the merchants and the vendors out of the Temple, the Last Supper, praying in the garden, the arrest and crucifixion, the empty tomb, and Jesus forgiving Peter and telling his disciples to share the good news of God's love with all men.
Prod-FAMF Dist-FAMF 1972

Very Good Friends C 29 MIN
16MM FILM, 3/4 OR 1/2 IN VIDEO J-C A
Tells the story of 13-year-old Kate, whose younger sister is killed in a sudden accident. Describes how Kate learns to cope with the loss. Based on the book Beat The Turtle Dove by Constance Green. An ABC Afterschool Special.
Prod-TAHSEM Dist-LCOA 1977

Very Good Friends (Captioned) C 29 MIN
16MM FILM, 3/4 OR 1/2 IN VIDEO J-H A
Treats the topic of death openly and honestly. Tells story of the sudden death of an 11 year old girl.
Prod-TAHSEM Dist-LCOA

Very Important Person, A C 29 MIN
16MM FILM, 3/4 OR 1/2 IN VIDEO H-C A
Presents a dramatization about a couple whose son is disabled due to a brain injury suffered in an accident. Tells how they are fearful and unprepared to work with educators in making an individualized education plan until they turn to more experienced parents for help.
From The Giving Birth And Independence Series.
Prod-JRLLL Dist-LAWREN 1981

Very Large Scale Integration Architecture–A Series
PRO
Uses classroom format to videotape 42 lecture hours on 42 cassettes. Covers design, implementation and use of very large integrated (VLSI) technology and its impact on computer architecture. Includes VLSI processes, synthesis of simple digital structures, design process, VLSI benefits and constraints, and systems partitioning and structure for VLSI implementation.
Prod-UMAEEE Dist-AMCEE

Very Large, The, Pt 1 B 15 MIN
2 INCH VIDEOTAPE P
Shows how man extends his knowledge of the changing universe through space exploration. Explains the vastness of the universe and the motion of the planets and the moon and describes the great distances which starlight must travel to reach the earth.
From The Science Is Everywhere Series. No. 17
Prod-DETPS Dist-GPITVL

Very Large, The, Pt 2 B 15 MIN
2 INCH VIDEOTAPE P
Shows how man extends his knowledge of the changing universe through space exploration. Explains the vastness of the universe and the motion of the planets and the moon and describes the great distances which starlight must travel to reach the earth.
From The Science Is Everywhere Series. No. 18
Prod-DETPS Dist-GPITVL

Very Large, The, Pt 3 B 15 MIN
2 INCH VIDEOTAPE P
Shows how man extends his knowledge of the changing universe through space exploration. Explains the vastness of the universe and the motion of the planets and the moon and describes the great distances which starlight must travel to reach the earth.
From The Science Is Everywhere Series. No. 19
Prod-DETPS Dist-GPITVL

Very Large, The, Pt 4 B 15 MIN
2 INCH VIDEOTAPE P
Shows how man extends his knowledge of the changing universe through space exploration. Explains the vastness of the universe and the motion of the planets and the moon and describes the great distances which starlight must travel to reach the earth.
From The Science Is Everywhere Series. No. 20
Prod-DETPS Dist-GPITVL

Very Large, The, Pt 5 B 15 MIN
2 INCH VIDEOTAPE P
Shows how man extends his knowledge of the changing universe through space exploration. Explains the vastness of the universe and the motion of the planets and the moon and describes the great distances which starlight must travel to reach the earth.
From The Science Is Everywhere Series. No. 21
Prod-DETPS Dist-GPITVL

Very Merry Cricket, A C 26 MIN
3/4 INCH VIDEO CASSETTE E
Describes how a musical cricket from Connecticut takes advantage of a New York City blackout to to transform the city's discord into peace and harmony.
Prod-CJE Dist-GA

Very Perfect Woman, A C 10 MIN
16MM FILM OPTICAL SOUND
Presents the story of a beautiful woman who cannot face her husband after she has breast removal surgery.
Prod-LUTTEL Dist-LUTTEL 1979

Very Public Private Affair, A C 50 MIN
16MM FILM, 3/4 OR 1/2 IN VIDEO H-C A
Relates the love affair between millionaire publisher William Randolph Hearst and showgirl Marion Davies. Explains that Hearst leaves his family and sets up a home with her at San Simeon, an extravagant castle he built in California. Presents film stars, writers and journalists who recollect the affair.
From The Yesterday's Witness In America Series.
LC NO. 83-706522
Prod-BBCTV Dist-TIMLIF 1982

Very Remarkable Yamato Family–A Series
16MM FILM, 3/4 OR 1/2 IN VIDEO H-C A
Reports on the remarkable economic, social and political structures of Japan. Examines the culture, people, institutions, successes and problems of this complex nation.
Prod-WNETTV Dist-IU 1977

Very Remarkable Yamato Family, The, Pt 1 059 MIN
Very Remarkable Yamato Family, The, Pt 2 059 MIN

Very Remarkable Yamato Family, The, Pt 1 C 59 MIN
16MM FILM, 3/4 OR 1/2 IN VIDEO H-C A
Presents a report on the economic and social structure of Japan, as reviewed on location by journalist Bill Moyers and professor Takashi Inagaki. Includes examination of the work ethic and the need to identify with a group, the home and its structure, disappearing family farms and the fishing industry. Deals with protests over the policies of huge industries, overcrowding and pollution.
From The Very Remarkable Yamato Family Series.
LC NO. 80-706106
Prod-WNETTV Dist-IU 1977

Very Remarkable Yamato Family, The, Pt 2 C 59 MIN
16MM FILM, 3/4 OR 1/2 IN VIDEO H-C A
Presents a documentary on the social and political structure of modern Japan, as reviewed on location by journalist Bill Moyers and professor Takashi Inagaki. Includes reports on the change in family structure, individualized education, the fading image of the Emperor, women's liberation and the growing interdependence of Japan and other nations.
From The Very Remarkable Yamato Family Series.
LC NO. 80-706106
Prod-WNETTV Dist-IU 1977

Very Small, The, Pt 1 B 15 MIN
2 INCH VIDEOTAPE P
Shows how to detect molecules. Explains that the molecules of one substance may be evenly distributed through molecules of another and describes how the motion of molecules determines the state of matter.
From The Science Is Everywhere Series. No. 1
Prod-DETPS Dist-GPITVL

Very Small, The, Pt 2 B 15 MIN
2 INCH VIDEOTAPE P
Shows how to detect molecules. Explains that the molecules of one substance may be evenly distributed through molecules of another and describes how the motion of molecules determines the state of matter.
From The Science Is Everywhere Series. No. 2
Prod-DETPS Dist-GPITVL

Very Small, The, Pt 3 B 15 MIN
2 INCH VIDEOTAPE P
Shows how to detect molecules. Explains that the molecules of one substance may be evenly distributed through molecules of another and describes how the motion of molecules determines the state of matter.
From The Science Is Everywhere Series. No. 3
Prod-DETPS Dist-GPITVL

Very Special Dance, A C 20 MIN
16MM FILM OPTICAL SOUND
Focuses on the work of Anne Riordan, a dance educator of mentally and physically handicapped young adults.
Prod-KUTV Dist-NDA 1978

Very Special Day, A C 15 MIN
3/4 INCH VIDEO CASSETTE P
See series title for descriptive statement.
From The Celebrate Series.
Prod-KUONTV Dist-GPITVL 1978

Very Special Girl, A C 26 MIN
16MM FILM OPTICAL SOUND
Presents the story of Denise Anne Miller, a high school junior who won the Navy's highest award at the annual International Science and Engineering Fair. Shows her trip to the Nobel Prize ceremonies in Stockholm where she received her award from Admiral M D Van Orden, Chief of Naval Research.
LC NO. 76-702736
Prod-USN Dist-USNAC 1975

Very Special Kind Of Care, A C 18 MIN
3/4 INCH VIDEO CASSETTE PRO
See series title for descriptive statement.
From The Cancer Series. Module 5
LC NO. 81-707090
Prod-BRA Dist-BRA 1981

Very Special Man, A C 20 MIN
16MM FILM OPTICAL SOUND
Shows the importance of electronics to the Navy and opportunities available for recruits in advanced electronics.
LC NO. 74-706313
Prod-USN Dist-USNAC 1968

Very Special Place, A C 14 MIN
16MM FILM OPTICAL SOUND
Presents Anita Bryant and her husband fishing in the Florida Keys, near Marathon, in pursuit of tarpon.
Prod-FLADC Dist-FLADC

Very Special Place, A C 23 MIN
16MM FILM, 3/4 OR 1/2 IN VIDEO
Provides an opportunity to observe the value of Assateague Island National Seashore, a barrier island existing in a very fragile environment. Discusses the ecological aspects of the island.
LC NO. 81-706316
Prod-USNPS Dist-USNAC 1980

Very Special Village, A B 30 MIN
16MM FILM OPTICAL SOUND H A
Relates the story of Shaar Menashe, a village in Israel, inhabited only by people over 65. (Kinescope)
Prod-JTS Dist-NAAJS Prodn-NBCTV 1956

Very, Very, Very Best Christmas Present Of All, The C 10 MIN
16MM FILM OPTICAL SOUND
Deals with a little boy who tells his dog the story of the first Christmas. The very, very, very best Christmas present of all, explains the little boy is the gift of God's son.
Prod-SWAMD Dist-FAMF

Vesak C 20 MIN
3/4 INCH VIDEO CASSETTE H-C A
Documents the Buddhist Festival of Light which celebrates the day Buddha was born, attained enlightenment and the day he entered Nirvana.
Prod-HANMNY Dist-HANMNY 1971

Vesicle Diverticulatum C 14 MIN
16MM FILM OPTICAL SOUND PRO
Presents the surgical procedures for incision of the bladder, evacuating contents of the diverticulatum, mucosa stripping and drainage procedure, and final suturing.
Prod-LOMAM Dist-LOMAM

Vesicular Exanthema C 16 MIN
16MM FILM OPTICAL SOUND
Tells the story of the outbreak of vesicular exanthema in 1952, its rapid spread and measures taken to control it. Shows disease symptoms and depicts differential diagnostic field tests.
LC NO. FIE54-401
Prod-USDA Dist-USNAC 1954

Vessel Entry C 12 MIN
3/4 OR 1/2 INCH VIDEO CASSETTE IND
Illustrates the safety procedures that should be followed when entering any vessel or enclosed space.
From The Take Ten For Safety Series.
Prod-OLINC Dist-MTI

Vessel Rescue C 12 MIN
16MM FILM - 3/4 IN VIDEO
Points out that whenever someone enters a tank, vat, tank car or truck, or other vessel, there is always a chance of injury. Shows how to set up a vessel rescue procedure that aims to take every possibility into account. Emphasizes the importance of the standby person, describes the actions he or she should take, and delves into equipment, clothing, training and dry runs.
Prod-ALLIED Dist-BNA

Vessels And Nerves Of The Superficial Face C 12 MIN
16MM FILM, 3/4 OR 1/2 IN VIDEO C A
Focuses on the head and neck. Demonstrates the dissection of the vessels and nerves of the superficial face.
From The Guides To Dissection Series.
Prod-UCLA Dist-TEF

Vestibuloplasty With Epithelial Inlays C 19 MIN
3/4 OR 1/2 INCH VIDEO CASSETTE PRO
Shows a modified skin grafting technique for a mandibular labial vestibuloplasty and lowering of the floor of the mouth using epithelial inlays.
LC NO. 81-706310
Prod-VADTC Dist-USNAC 1980

Veteran Becomes A Farmer, The B 28 MIN
16MM FILM OPTICAL SOUND
Discusses how individuals and groups in a farm community cooperate in giving help and counsel to a veteran wishing to become a farmer.
LC NO. FIE52-316
Prod-USOE Dist-USNAC 1946

Veteran's Day C 15 MIN
3/4 INCH VIDEO CASSETTE P
See series title for descriptive statement.
From The Celebrate Series.
Prod-KUONTV Dist-GPITVL 1978

Veterans Administration - May I Help You C 29 MIN
16MM FILM OPTICAL SOUND A
Highlights the activities and functions of the Veterans Administration through visits with some of its employees.
LC NO. 78-700824
Prod-USVA Dist-USNAC 1977

Veterans Administration Extended Care Environments - Past, Present, Future C 14 MIN
3/4 INCH VIDEO CASSETTE A
Traces the history of extended medical care services and facilities in the Veterans Administration.
LC NO. 78-706082
Prod-USVA Dist-USNAC 1977

Veterinarian C 15 MIN
3/4 OR 1/2 INCH VIDEO CASSETTE I
Explains the qualifications and personal qualities required for a successful career as a veterinarian.
From The Career Awareness Series.
Prod-KLVXTV Dist-GPITVL 1973

Veterinarian C 30 MIN
1/2 IN VIDEO CASSETTE BETA/VHS
Features Dr Nora Matthews, a Cornell graduate and veterinarian who treats large and small animals in upper New York State. Describes how she helps local farmers take care of their cattle, along with her daily job of treating domestic pets.
From The American Professionals Series.
Prod-WTBS Dist-RMI

Veterinarian Looks At Functional Type, A C 22 MIN
16MM FILM OPTICAL SOUND PRO
Uses bone and marrow specimens and live animals to demonstrate the economic importance of functional type with regard to dairy cattle.
Prod-HFAA Dist-HFAA

Veterinarian Serves The Community, The C 11 MIN
16MM FILM, 3/4 OR 1/2 IN VIDEO P-I
Examines the contribution of the veterinarian to the community.
Prod-FILMSW Dist-FLMFR

Veterinarian Serves The Community, The Captioned Version) C 11 MIN
16MM FILM, 3/4 OR 1/2 IN VIDEO K-I
Introduces children to the community health services provided for their pets by the veterinarian. Shows care of all types of animals, the function and personnel of an animal hospital along with their humanitarianism.
Prod-FILMSW Dist-FLMFR 1968

Veterinary Surgeon, The - His Education, His Profession C 26 MIN
16MM FILM OPTICAL SOUND H-C
Emphasizes the training of a student of veterinary medicine in the basic and clinical sciences. Portrays areas of public service.
Prod-OMEGA Dist-AMVMA

Via Dolorosa C 10 MIN
3/4 INCH VIDEO CASSETTE
Presents a Good Friday procession in Antigua, Guatemala, as performed by the townspeople in biblical garb. Shows the Indians from the countryside observing the spectacle. Contrasts the formality of the Spanish event with the Mayan version.
Prod-OKEXNO Dist-DOCEDR

Via Dolorosa (1648 - 1705) B 14 MIN
16MM FILM OPTICAL SOUND
Shows 25 small chapels in lush meadows by a tranquil river, each one housing a life-size scene sculpted from Christ's Passion.
Prod-ROLAND Dist-ROLAND

Viajando Por Mexico Y Espana—A Series
16MM FILM, 3/4 OR 1/2 IN VIDEO
Introduces the regions, people and culture of Mexico and Spain.
Prod-EBEC Dist-EBEC

Centinelas De Silencio 019 MIN
Pablo, Un Nino De Mexico 022 MIN
Pueblo Andaluz 015 MIN
Viaje Por El Norte De Espana 015 MIN
Viaje Por El Sud De Espana 017 MIN

Viaje Por El Norte De Espana X 14 MIN
16MM FILM, 3/4 OR 1/2 IN VIDEO H-C
A Spanish language film. Presents an overview of the topography, industry and way of life in northern Spain. To be used after lesson 20 of level II, 'Emilio en Espana.'
From The Viajando Por Mexico Y Espana Series.
Prod-EBF Dist-EBEC 1966

Viaje Por El Sud De Espana C 17 MIN
16MM FILM, 3/4 OR 1/2 IN VIDEO H-C
A Spanish language film. Describes the life and culture of southern Spain. Presents scenes of Madrid, Toledo and Merida, with brief scenes of Andalucia and the Levante areas. To be used after lesson 10 of level II, 'Emilio en Espana.'
From The Viajando Por Mexico Y Espana Series.
Prod-EBF Dist-EBEC 1966

Vibe - Vanellus Vanellus (Lapwing) C 4 MIN
16MM FILM OPTICAL SOUND
Presents a description of the lapwing in his natural surroundings, accompanied by sound effects.
Prod-STATNS Dist-STATNS 1965

Vibrant Mirror Of The Sun C 10 MIN
16MM FILM, 3/4 OR 1/2 IN VIDEO
Discusses one kinetic work of Venezuelan artist Alejandro Otero Rodriguez.
LC NO. 82-707027
Prod-MOMALA Dist-MOMALA

Vibrant Mirror Of The Sun (Spanish) C 10 MIN
3/4 OR 1/2 INCH VIDEO CASSETTE
Discusses one kinetic work of Venezuelan artist Alejandro Otero Rodriguez.
Prod-MOMALA Dist-MOMALA

Vibrant Strings, Pt 1 C 16 MIN
3/4 OR 1/2 INCH VIDEO CASSETTE
See series title for descriptive statement.
From The Musical Instruments Series.
Prod-WWVUTV Dist-GPITVL

Vibrant Strings, Pt 2 C 19 MIN
3/4 OR 1/2 INCH VIDEO CASSETTE
See series title for descriptive statement.
From The Musical Instruments Series.
Prod-WWVUTV Dist-GPITVL

Vibration C 29 MIN
16MM FILM OPTICAL SOUND
Shows how destructive power brought about by vibrations can be prevented and even utilized for man's benefits. Depicts the mechanisms of vibrations caused by friction.
Prod-UNIJAP Dist-UNIJAP 1971

Vibration Analysis C 60 MIN
3/4 OR 1/2 INCH VIDEO CASSETTE IND
Goes into proper meausurement, evaluation and correction of excessive vibration.
From The Mechanical Equipment Maintenance Series.
Prod-ITCORP Dist-ITCORP

Vibration Analysis (Spanish) C 60 MIN
3/4 OR 1/2 INCH VIDEO CASSETTE IND
Deals with vibration analysis. Includes measurement, evaluation and correction.
From The Mechanical Equipment Maintenance (Spanish) Series.
Prod-ITCORP Dist-ITCORP

Vibration Control C 43 MIN
3/4 OR 1/2 INCH VIDEO CASSETTE IND
Discusses relationship between vibration and noise, vibration measurement techniques and instrumentation, criteria for machinery vibration, how to specify vibration isolation and how to specify vibration damping.
From The Industrial Noise Control, Part I - Fundamentals Series.
LC NO. 81-707500
Prod-AMCEE Dist-AMCEE 1981

Vibration Of Molecules C 11 MIN
16MM FILM OPTICAL SOUND H-C
Illustrates the motion of a molecule, the number of normal modes of a molecule, the relation between symmetry and the normal modes of vibration of methane, and the quantization of vibrational energy.
Prod-SUEF Dist-SUTHLA 1959

Vibration Of Molecules C 12 MIN
16MM FILM OPTICAL SOUND H
Shows the relationship between the structure of a molecule and its vibrational motions. Indicates the effect of molecular collision or absorption of light on molecular vibrations.
From The CHEM Study Films Series.
Prod-CHEMS Dist-MLA 1959

Vibration Problems In The Design Of Shipboard Electronic Equipment B 19 MIN
16MM FILM OPTICAL SOUND
Demonstrates how breakage can occur when equipment chassis are not protected against vibration and shock. Shows ways in which vibration can be eliminated by the use of bands, screws and braces placed in different ways on a chassis.
LC NO. FIE57-162
Prod-USN Dist-USNAC 1956

Vibration Syndrome, Pt 1 C 27 MIN
3/4 OR 1/2 INCH VIDEO CASSETTE PRO

Discusses the etiology, symptomology, assessment and treatment of Vibration Syndrome. Includes a brief introduction to the physics of vibration and an examination of different assessment techniques.
LC NO. 84-706456
Prod-USPHS Dist-USNAC 1981

Vibrations C 24 MIN
16MM FILM OPTICAL SOUND
Introduces the theory of vibrating systems and its component concepts of natural frequency, damping, transmissibility and vibration isolation. Uses examples from the automotive industry to demonstrate transmissibility problems.
Prod-BBCTV Dist-OPENU 1981

Vibrations X 14 MIN
16MM FILM, 3/4 OR 1/2 IN VIDEO I-J
Defines vibration and demonstrates how vibrations are produced and the relationship between sound and vibration. Focuses on the natural frequency of the vibrations of some objects.
Prod-EBF Dist-EBEC 1961

Vibrations C 24 MIN
16MM FILM, 3/4 OR 1/2 IN VIDEO
Introduces the theory of vibrating systems and its component concepts of natural frequency, damping, transmissibility and vibration isolation. Uses examples from the automotive industry to demonstrate transmissibility problems.
Prod-OPENU Dist-MEDIAG Prodn-BBCTV 1981

Vibrations C 60 MIN
3/4 OR 1/2 INCH VIDEO CASSETTE
Shows Swami Satchidananda speaking on Vibrations.
Prod-IYOGA Dist-IYOGA

Vibrations And Pagan Rites C 60 MIN
3/4 OR 1/2 INCH VIDEO CASSETTE J-C A
Presents flutist James Galway demonstrating how ageless and universal is the human impulse to make music and how logical and natural has been the development of Western music.
From The James Galway's Music In Time Series.
LC NO. 83-706265
Prod-POLTEL Dist-FOTH 1982

Vibrations Of Music C 24 MIN
3/4 OR 1/2 INCH VIDEO CASSETTE H-C
Uses the vibrating strings and sound board of a violin as an illustration of the physics of sound production that results in music. Reviews other instruments to show the roles of strings, air columns, plates, and membranes in the production of sound as well as music.
From The Discovering Physics Series.
Prod-BBCTV Dist-MEDIAG Prodn-OPENU 1983

Vibrato C 10 MIN
16MM FILM OPTICAL SOUND
Uses camera movement, multiple images and synchronized music to transform nature into a statement of beauty. Without narration.
LC NO. 75-700492
Prod-OAC Dist-INPAC Prodn-HAGNER 1975

Vic C 13 MIN
16MM FILM OPTICAL SOUND
Dramatizes the problems of a caretaker who has to vacate the building which has played a major part in his life.
LC NO. 76-700163
Prod-SFRASU Dist-SFRASU 1974

Vic And Tad - A Moving Portrait C 30 MIN
2 INCH VIDEOTAPE
Portrays Vic and Tad Simpson and their years of struggle to exist and endure within the framework of changing society. Shows how they adjusted to the fast pace of modern culture.
Prod-KVIETV Dist-PUBTEL

Vic Braden's Tennis For The Future—A Series

Presents Vic Braden giving instructions in the finer points of tennis, showing not only how to win more matches, but how to enjoy playing.
Prod-WGBHTV Dist-PBS 1981

Approach Shot, Spin And Service Return	029 MIN
Backhand, The	029 MIN
Conditioning	029 MIN
Lob And Drop Shot	029 MIN
Most Frequently Asked Tennis Questions	029 MIN
Overhead, The	029 MIN
Playing Doubles	029 MIN
Psychology	029 MIN
Serve, The	029 MIN
Singles Strategy, Pt 1	029 MIN
Singles Strategy, Pt 2	029 MIN
Tennis Philosophy And The Forehand Stroke	029 MIN
Volley, The	029 MIN

Vice Presidency - Adams To Ford C 15 MIN
3/4 OR 1/2 INCH VIDEO CASSETTE J-H
Examines the changing role of the Vice Presidency from John Adams to Gerald Ford.
Prod-HEARST Dist-HEARST 1974

Vicious Cycles C 7 MIN
16MM FILM, 3/4 OR 1/2 IN VIDEO I-C A
A student-produced film which spoofs commercial motorcycle movies.
Prod-CFS Dist-PFP 1969

Vicki B 10 MIN
16MM FILM OPTICAL SOUND J-C A
Tells about a girl who was born with no arms but learned to use her feet with remarkable skill through the patient training of her mother. Presents how she attended regular schools throughout her education and is now employed and engaged to be married.
LC NO. 76-701872
Prod-AUSDSS Dist-AUIS Prodn-FLMAUS 1975

Victim C 20 MIN
16MM FILM OPTICAL SOUND
Tells how a young student helps a girl who is being attacked, only to be accused of the crime himself and sent to jail.
LC NO. 80-700487
Prod-USC Dist-USC 1979

Victim Of Gravity, A C 3 MIN
3/4 OR 1/2 INCH VIDEO CASSETTE P-I
Explains the concept of gravity, describing the experiments of Galileo and Sir Isaac Newton.
From The Science Rock Series.
Prod-ABCTV Dist-GA Prodn-SCOROC 1978

Victim, The C 15 MIN
16MM FILM OPTICAL SOUND A
Presents a dramatized railcar theft. Explains the ramifications to the railroad, the shipper, the manufacturer and ultimately the consumer.
From The Cargo Security Series.
LC NO. 78-700825
Prod-USDT Dist-USNAC Prodn-TILMON 1978

Victims C 24 MIN
3/4 OR 1/2 INCH VIDEO CASSETTE A
Examines the effects of, and some means of countering, parents' violent disciplinary action toward their children. Narrated by Christina Crawford.
LC NO. 82-706396
Prod-WINTNC Dist-WINTNC 1981

Victims - Their Circumstances, Management And Legal Issues C 30 MIN
3/4 OR 1/2 INCH VIDEO CASSETTE
Discusses the context and factors in violent patient incidents. Illustrates victims as 'provocateurs' versus 'helpless', self-destructive factors and denial.
From The Management And Treatment Of The Violent Patient Series.
Prod-HEMUL Dist-HEMUL

Victims Of Crime - Once Is Enough C 29 MIN
3/4 OR 1/2 INCH VIDEO CASSETTE
Discusses whether the press should identify a crime victim's name and address. Burglary and rape victims are interviewed.
From The Inside Story Series.
Prod-PBS Dist-PBS 1981

Victims Of The Sea C 18 MIN
16MM FILM OPTICAL SOUND
Dramatizes the efforts made to rescue a diver trapped underwater. Shows the cooperation of the U S Coast Guard and the Los Angeles County lifeguards in the rescue operations.
LC NO. 77-700593
Prod-USC Dist-USC 1976

Victims, The B 50 MIN
16MM FILM OPTICAL SOUND H-C A
Dr Benjamin Spock diagnoses the causes of prejudice in children, demonstrating that adults are the cause but that they also have the power to cure it. Narrated by Pat Hingle.
LC NO. FIA67-678
Prod-ADL Dist-ADL Prodn-WEBC 1966

Victor C 11 MIN
16MM FILM OPTICAL SOUND
Presents the story of a young migrant farmworker and his struggle to maintain his share of the family workload while trying to continue his education.
LC NO. 80-700311
Prod-CHOSAN Dist-CHOSAN 1979

Victor Hugo (1802-1885) B 13 MIN
16MM FILM OPTICAL SOUND
Presents a collection of Victor Hugo's unknown drawings, many only postage stamp size and others as large as oil paintings. Filmed at the Victor Hugo House in Paris.
Prod-ROLAND Dist-ROLAND 1964

Victoria And Albert C 60 MIN
16MM FILM, 3/4 OR 1/2 IN VIDEO H-C A
Describes the family life of Queen Victoria and Prince Albert and visits Buckingham Palace. Looks at the design and construction of the Crystal Palace.
From The Royal Heritage Series.
Prod-BBCTV Dist-FI 1977

Victoria Regina C 76 MIN
3/4 OR 1/2 INCH VIDEO CASSETTE
Presents Laurence Houseman's play Victoria Regina about the fabled Queen Victoria, providing a human portrait of this queen, so troubled in her personal life and so austere in public. Stars Julie Harris, James Donald and Basil Rathbone.
Prod-FOTH Dist-FOTH 1984

Victoria, Queen And Empress C 60 MIN
16MM FILM, 3/4 OR 1/2 IN VIDEO H-C A
Reveals life at Balmoral Castle after the death of Prince Albert. Discusses the growth of communications which took place in the latter years of Victoria's realm.
From The Royal Heritage Series.
Prod-BBCTV Dist-FI 1977

Victorian Age, The C
3/4 OR 1/2 INCH VIDEO CASSETTE H
Gives literary and historical insights into key Victorian themes. Examines Victorian thought and tradition through the eyes of the writers and poets of the day, particularly Dickens. On-location photography and Victorian art are included.
Prod-GA Dist-GA

Victorian Flower Paintings C 7 MIN
16MM FILM OPTICAL SOUND C A
Presents a filmed folio of dated flower paintings which symbolically portray an unknown person passing through a temporary phase of schizophrenic illness.
LC NO. 70-711175
Prod-IPSY Dist-NYU 1968

Victorian Tapestry Workshop C 9 MIN
16MM FILM OPTICAL SOUND
Traces the making of a tapestry by a leading Australian artist.
LC NO. 80-700877
Prod-VICCOR Dist-TASCOR 1979

Victors Of The Dry Land C 58 MIN
3/4 OR 1/2 INCH VIDEO CASSETTE J-C A
Describes the characteristics that made reptiles the first successful inhabitants of dry land and shows examples of this astonishingly diverse family. Discusses the evolution of dinosaurs and the reasons for their sudden extinction.
From The Life On Earth Series. Program 7
LC NO. 82-706679
Prod-BBCTV Dist-FI 1981

Victors, The C 152 MIN
16MM FILM OPTICAL SOUND H-C A
Stars Vincent Edwards, Albert Finney and George Hamilton as part of the men and women who find themselves trapped and changed by the tragedy of war.
Prod-CPC Dist-TWYMAN

Victory At Sea B 79 MIN
16MM FILM, 3/4 OR 1/2 IN VIDEO J A
Presents significant events of World War II, including London under fire, the Pearl Harbor attack, the battle of Guadalcanal, Italian and French campaigns and the destruction of Japanese resistance in the Pacific. Musical score by Richard Rogers.
Prod-NBCTV Dist-FI 1966

Victory At Sea—A Series
16MM FILM, 3/4 OR 1/2 IN VIDEO J-H
Presents the story of World War II as it was fought on the sea, over the sea and under the sea using historical film footage.
Prod-NBCTV Dist-LUF

Battle For Leyte Gulf, The	027 MIN
Beneath The Southern Cross	027 MIN
Conquest Of Micronesia, The	027 MIN
D-Day	027 MIN
Design For Peace	027 MIN
Design For War	027 MIN
Fate Of Europe, The	027 MIN
Full Fathom Five	027 MIN
Guadalcanal	027 MIN
Killers And The Killed	027 MIN
Magnetic North	027 MIN
Mare Nostrum	027 MIN
Mediterranean Mosaic	027 MIN
Melanesian Nightmare	027 MIN
Midway Is East	027 MIN
Pacific Boils Over, The	027 MIN
Return Of The Allies	027 MIN
Rings Around Rabaul	027 MIN
Road To Mandalay, The	027 MIN
Roman Renaissance	027 MIN
Sea And Sand	027 MIN
Sealing The Breach	027 MIN
Suicide For Glory	027 MIN
Target Suribachi	027 MIN
Turkey Shoot, The	027 MIN
Two If By Sea	027 MIN

Victory At Yorktown C 12 MIN
16MM FILM - 3/4 IN VIDEO
Portrays the British surrender at Yorktown, Virginia, in 1781.
LC NO. 79-706168
Prod-USNPS Dist-USNAC 1979

Victory At Yorktown C 30 MIN
3/4 OR 1/2 INCH VIDEO CASSETTE C
See series title for descriptive statement.
From The American Story - The Beginning To
Prod-DALCCD Dist-DALCCD

Victory Division, The - 24th Infantry B 17 MIN
16MM FILM, 3/4 OR 1/2 IN VIDEO H A
Discusses the role of the 24th Infantry in the Pacific during the war.
Prod-USA Dist-USNAC 1950

Victory Garden—A Series

Demonstrates potting, planting, pruning and pest control.
Prod-WGBHTV Dist-MTI

All-American Roses	030 MIN
Bounty For The Table	030 MIN
Cutting A Bouquet	030 MIN
Flowers In Bloom	030 MIN
Good And Plenty	030 MIN
Green Thumb Needed	030 MIN
Harvest Of Things To Come	030 MIN
Herbs, Cantaloupes, Watermelon	030 MIN
Horticulture Exhibit	030 MIN
In Full Bloom	030 MIN
Landscape Artistry	030 MIN
Magnolia Gardens - Charleston	030 MIN
Native Hawaiian Plants	030 MIN
Oriental Vegetables	030 MIN
Patio Gardening	030 MIN
Peak Harvest	030 MIN
Pick Of The Crop	030 MIN
Pick The Winner	030 MIN
Preparation For Spring	030 MIN

Spring Lawn Care 030 MIN
Star Is Grown, A 030 MIN
Summer Vegetables 030 MIN
Tips From The Pros 030 MIN
Tropical Climate - Hawaii 030 MIN
Walker Gardens - Honolulu 030 MIN
Warm-Season Gardens 030 MIN

Victory Variations C 10 MIN
16MM FILM OPTICAL SOUND
Documents the reconstruction of the Victory Burlesque in Toronto.
LC NO. 77-702697
Prod-CANFDC Dist-CANFDC 1976

Vicus C 18 MIN
16MM FILM, 3/4 OR 1/2 IN VIDEO I-C A
Discusses pre-Columbian ceramics and jewelry of the Vicus culture in Peru.
LC NO. 82-707024
Prod-MOMALA Dist-MOMALA

Vicus (Spanish) C 18 MIN
16MM FILM, 3/4 OR 1/2 IN VIDEO
Discusses pre-Columbian ceramics and jewelry of the Vicus culture in Peru.
Prod-MOMALA Dist-MOMALA

Vidas En Peligro C 15 MIN
16MM FILM, 3/4 OR 1/2 IN VIDEO C A
A Spanish-language version of the motion picture Seconds Count. Emphasizes the need for speed in applying emergency resuscitation by the mouth-to-mouth method using incidents stemming from drowning and asphyxia.
From The Emergency Resuscitation (Spanish) Series.
Prod-UKMD Dist-IFB

Vidas Secas B 115 MIN
16MM FILM OPTICAL SOUND
A Portuguese language motion picture with English subtitles. Describes two years in the life of a ranch family struggling to eke out an existence in 1940's Brazil. Directed by Nelson Pereira dos Santos.
Prod-UNKNWN Dist-NYFLMS 1963

Video - A Practical Guide...And More—A Series

Presents basic videotape production techniques. Features Richard A Colla, who directed the television series, McCloud, and S Bryan Hickox, a special effects and post-production consultant and motion picture producer.
Prod-VIPUB Dist-VIPUB

Camera Techniques For Video 030 MIN
Directing Non-Professional Talent 030 MIN
Editing And Special Effects 030 MIN
Format Analysis And Writing For Video 030 MIN
Lighting Application For Video 030 MIN
Mobile Videotape Production 030 MIN
Operation And Maintenance Of A Video System 030 MIN
Preparation And Use Of Graphics 030 MIN
Producing A Videotape 030 MIN
Sets And Locations For Videotape 030 MIN
Sound Application For Video 030 MIN
What's Wrong - Troubleshooting A video System 030 MIN

Video - The New Wave C 60 MIN
3/4 OR 1/2 INCH VIDEO CASSETTE
Consists of works by 30 video artists with commentary by art critic Brian O'Doherty.
Prod-EAI Dist-EAI

Video Against Video C 30 MIN
3/4 OR 1/2 INCH VIDEO CASSETTE
Anthologizes works of Douglas Davis, innovative artist, writer and teacher, who pioneered two-way telecasting and live satellite performance.
Prod-EAI Dist-EAI

Video Amplifier B 25 MIN
16MM FILM OPTICAL SOUND
Describes the frequency range and states the function of each component of the video amplifier. Explains methods used to obtain low and high frequency response. (Kinescope)
LC NO. 74-705914
Prod-USAF Dist-USNAC

Video Amplifiers B 29 MIN
16MM FILM OPTICAL SOUND
Explains why a pentode tube is used in video amplification rather than triode tubes. Shows the schematic purpose of each of the components. (Kinescope)
LC NO. 74-705916
Prod-USAF Dist-USNAC

Video And IF Amplifiers C 30 MIN
3/4 OR 1/2 INCH VIDEO CASSETTE PRO
Discusses definition and application of wide-bandwidth amplifiers for video use and selective bandwidth amplifiers for intermediate-frequency amplifiers use. Discusses typical applications.
From The Linear And Interface Integrated Circuits, Part I - Linear Integrated Circuits Series.
Prod-TXINLC Dist-TXINLC

Video Cooking Library—A Series

Provides instruction in preparing a variety of recipes.
Prod-KARTES Dist-KARTES

Basic Bread Baker, The
Basic Italian Cuisine
Basic New Orleans Cusine
Meals For Two
One Dish Meals
Pasta, Pasta, Pasta
Seven Simple Chicken Dishes
Thanksgiving Dinner

Video Diary Of A Madman Or My Day Reflects My Mood C 83 MIN
3/4 OR 1/2 INCH VIDEO CASSETTE
Focuses on confession. Presented by Michel Auder and Michael Zwack.
Prod-ARTINC Dist-ARTINC

Video Exam Over Sterile Techniques For Oral Surgery And Periodontal Surgery... C 13 MIN
1/2 IN VIDEO CASSETTE BETA/VHS PRO
Complete title reads Video Exam Over Sterile Techniques For Oral Surgery And Periodontal Surgery Procedures. Provides an examination covering sterile techniques for oral surgery and periodontal surgery procedures.
Prod-RMI Dist-RMI

Video Feedback As A Treatment Modality For Persons With Low Back Pain C 19 MIN
3/4 INCH VIDEO CASSETTE PRO
Describes the use of videotape as a diagnostic and treatment modality for low back pain.
Prod-RICHGO Dist-RICHGO

Video For Cheerleading—A Series

Presents four programs from the Universal Cheerleaders Association. Demonstrates partner stunts, tumbling, jumps and a conditioning workout focused on flexibility and endurance. Pays special attention to spotting, safety, injury prevention and planning for group execution.
Prod-ATHI Dist-ATHI

Cheerleading Jumps 025 MIN
Conditioning For Cheerleaders 025 MIN
Partner Stunts For Cheerleading 025 MIN
Tumbling For Cheerleaders 025 MIN

Video Girls And Video Songs For Navajo Sky X 30 MIN
3/4 OR 1/2 INCH VIDEO CASSETTE
Contrasts two different cultures - the Navajo in Chinle, Arizona, and the wildly colored, accelerated images of the city.
Prod-EAI Dist-EAI

Video In Combination With Live Dance Performance C 30 MIN
3/4 OR 1/2 INCH VIDEO CASSETTE
See series title for descriptive statement.
From The Dance On Film And Television Series.
Prod-ARCVID Dist-ARCVID

Video Pioneers C 32 MIN
3/4 OR 1/2 INCH VIDEO CASSETTE
Sketches five New York artists - Vito Acconci, Richard Serra, Willoughby Sharp, Keith Sonnier and William Wegman.
Prod-ARTINC Dist-ARTINC

Video Portrait - Antonio Muntadas C 27 MIN
3/4 OR 1/2 INCH VIDEO CASSETTE
Features an interview with videomaker Antonio Muntadas. Presented by the Long Beach Museum of Art.
Prod-ARTINC Dist-ARTINC

Video Portrait - John Cage C 60 MIN
3/4 OR 1/2 INCH VIDEO CASSETTE
Portrays musician John Cage.
Prod-KITCHN Dist-KITCHN

Video Portrait - Nancy Buchanan C 25 MIN
3/4 OR 1/2 INCH VIDEO CASSETTE
Features an interview with videomaker Nancy Buchanan. Presented by the Long Beach Museum of Art.
Prod-ARTINC Dist-ARTINC

Video Portraits - Max Almy, Dara Birnbaum, David Em, Gary Hill, Bill Viola C 37 MIN
3/4 OR 1/2 INCH VIDEO CASSETTE
Portraits videomakers who discuss their work. Presented by the Long Beach Museum of Art.
Prod-ARTINC Dist-ARTINC

Video Recorders / Food Processors / Cancer C
3/4 OR 1/2 INCH VIDEO CASSETTE
Discusses the purchase of video recorders and food processors and the treatment of cancer.
From The Consumer Survival Series.
Prod-MDCPB Dist-MDCPB

Video Replay In Group Psychotherapy C 50 MIN
3/4 OR 1/2 INCH VIDEO CASSETTE
Demonstrates through instant feedback the multiple-level inconsistent and contradictory verbal and non-verbal communications which stimulate insight and working through. Allows a look at a woman who faces and is helped to work through psycho-sexual fixated material which she has not been consciously aware.
From The Family And Group Therapy Series.
Prod-HEMUL Dist-HEMUL

Video SAT Review, The C 120 MIN
1/2 IN VIDEO CASSETTE BETA/VHS H A
Offers practical advice on relaxation and concentration for those who are to take the Scholastic Aptitude Test (SAT). Discusses testtaking strategy, terminology, scoring, analogies, sentence completions and reading comprehension.
LC NO. 84-706777
Prod-DIAPRO Dist-DIAPRO 1984

Video Variations C 60 MIN
3/4 OR 1/2 INCH VIDEO CASSETTE
Presents a collaboration between WGBH, Boston, and the Boston Symphony Orchestra and eight visual artists which explores new ways of presenting symphonic music over television. Includes such artists as Nam June Paik, Jackie Classen and Douglas Davis.
Prod-WGBHTV Dist-EAI Prodn-BSO

Video Weavings C
3/4 OR 1/2 INCH VIDEO CASSETTE
Presents electronic artist Stephen Beck using a visual computer of his own design, while performing functions appropriate to images rather than numerics.
Prod-EAI Dist-EAI

Video Wine Guide, The C 90 MIN
3/4 OR 1/2 INCH VIDEO CASSETTE A
Introduces wine by visiting winemaking regions of Italy, France, Germany, California and New York State. Hosted by Dick Cavett, who demystifies the sommelier and ordering wine in a restaurant. Concludes with investing in wine, setting up a wine cellar, pronouncing wine names and selecting a cork puller.
LC NO. 83-706676
Prod-SERPRO Dist-SERPRO 1982

Video 50 C 50 MIN
3/4 OR 1/2 INCH VIDEO CASSETTE
Concocts brief, graphic vignettes lasting about 30 seconds each which are assembled in a non-narrative but rhythmically resonant sequence.
Prod-EAI Dist-EAI

Videoclinical Series—A Series
C S
Prod-WMICHU Dist-WMICHU 1972

Milisen - Articulation Testing 37 MIN
Milisen - Articulation Therapy 30 MIN

Videodance Project - Volume One—A Series

Features the dance works of recognized choreographers created specifically for television. Includes the works of Catherine Turocy, Peter Sparling and Dianne McIntyre.
Prod-ARTRES Dist-ARTRES

Etude In Free 009 MIN
Herald's Round 008 MIN
Suite Fantaisiste 009 MIN

Videodance Project, Vol 1—A Series

Presents the dance works of recognized choreographers created specifically for television.
Prod-ARCVID Dist-ARCVID

Etude In Free 008 MIN
Herald's Round 008 MIN
Suite Fantaisiste 009 MIN

Videofashion—A Series
16MM FILM, 3/4 OR 1/2 IN VIDEO H-C A
Presents four 60-minute excerpts from the major fashion shows in Paris and New York. Discusses the looks and trends for each season.
Prod-VIDFSH Dist-CRMP

Videograms B 14 MIN
3/4 OR 1/2 INCH VIDEO CASSETTE
See series title for descriptive statement.
From The Gary Hill, Part 4 Series.
Prod-EAI Dist-EAI

Videograms - Gary Hill B 14 MIN
3/4 INCH VIDEO CASSETTE A
Prod-AFA Dist-AFA 1981

Videographics (Selected Works 1972-73) C 30 MIN
3/4 OR 1/2 INCH VIDEO CASSETTE
Consists of all film/video hybrids in which video synthesized imagery figures strongly.
Prod-CANFDW Dist-CANFDW

Videosearch Behavior Skill Model—A Series

Consists of five skill models. Discusses the need for each skill, and presents a 'how not to' video segment, guidelines for using the skill, a video skill model segment showing how to use the guidelines, skill practice, and an on-the-job application. Includes a participant's workbook.
Prod-DELTAK Dist-DELTAK

Active Listening 015 MIN
Developing Ideas 016 MIN
Giving Recognition 012 MIN
Handling Conflicts 018 MIN
Providing Feedback 019 MIN

Videosearch Employment Interview—A Series

Highlights interviewing as an important management function, provides managers with a means to assess interviewing skills and practices, and discusses the interviewing process and ways to improve it. Includes an employment interview leader's guide with step-by-step instructions and a participant's workbook.
Prod-DELTAK Dist-DELTAK

Employment Interview, The - A Case Study 060 MIN
Making The Interview Work - Five Ways To 025 MIN
What's Wrong With The Interview 020 MIN

Videosearch Performance Appraisal (Case Studies)—A Series

Deals with performance appraisals, and includes concepts and

techniques based on research and experience, videotaped 'live' appraisal situations, interactive exercises, and skill practice activities. Includes dramatizations depicting good and bad interaction between supervisor and subordinate during the appraisal. Features case studies which depict an actual performance appraisal. Includes a participant's workbook and a leader's guide.
Prod-DELTAK Dist-DELTAK

Engineering 040 MIN
Finance / Control 030 MIN
Manufacturing 030 MIN
Sales / Marketing 030 MIN

Videotape-Disc-Or C 30 MIN
3/4 OR 1/2 INCH VIDEO CASSETTE T
Examines new and emerging technologies in teaching methods.
From The On And About Instruction Series.
Prod-VADE Dist-GPITVL 1983

Vielleicht Versuchen Wir's Einmal Mit Studenten C 15 MIN
16MM FILM, 3/4 OR 1/2 IN VIDEO
See series title for descriptive statement.
From The Guten Tag Wie Geht's Series. Part 14
Prod-BAYER Dist-IFB 1973

Vienna C 60 MIN
3/4 OR 1/2 INCH VIDEO CASSETTE J-C A
Presents flutist James Galway discussing the work of Mozart and Schubert, and Sir Peter Hall examining Mozart's operas.
From The James Galway's Music In Time Series.
LC NO. 83-706263
Prod-POLTEL Dist-FOTH 1982

Vienna - Stripping The Facade C 25 MIN
16MM FILM, 3/4 OR 1/2 IN VIDEO A
Portrays Vienna in the early 20th century to show what gave rise to the atonal, innovative music of Arnold Schoenberg and other modern Viennese composers. Explores the political and cultural environments which helped to shape Schoenberg's music, including achievements in the arts, architecture and literature.
From The Rise Of Modernism In Music Series.
Prod-BBCTV Dist-MEDIAG 1982

Vierundzwanzig Stunden Aus Dem Leben Einer Frau B 80 MIN
16MM FILM OPTICAL SOUND
A German language film with English subtitles. Tells the story of Helga Wanroh, a widow who moves to the Riviera, where chance brings her together with a compulsive gambler who has already tried to rid himself of his addiction and is now convinced that the only way out is death. Ends with the two sharing hope for a new beginning.
Prod-WSTGLC Dist-WSTGLC 1931

Viet Nam - Why - A Timely Report B 15 MIN
16MM FILM OPTICAL SOUND J A
Traces the history of Viet Nam from its reconstruction after the French Indo-China war to the events of the summer of 1964.
From The Screen News Digest Series. Vol 7, Issue 1
LC NO. FIA68-2101
Prod-HEARST Dist-HEARST 1964

Viet Nam Report - Focus On Indonesia B 20 MIN
16MM FILM OPTICAL SOUND
Describes the deepening crisis in Viet Nam as the Viet Cong step up their bombings and raids, and the United States retaliates with air assaults in the north. Discusses the geography and history of Indonesia, and describes her withdrawal from the United Nations.
From The Screen News Digest Series. Vol 7, Issue 8
Prod-HEARST Dist-HEARST 1965

Vietnam - A Television History—A Series
16MM FILM, 3/4 OR 1/2 IN VIDEO H-C A
Follows the events in Vietnam from the 1945 revolution against the French to the U S evacuation from Saigon in April, 1975.
Prod-WGBHTV Dist-FI 1983

America Takes Charge, 1965-1967 060 MIN
America's Mandarin, 1954-1963 060 MIN
End Of The Tunnel, 1973-1975, The 060 MIN
First Vietnam War, 1946-1954, The 060 MIN
Homefront, USA 060 MIN
LBJ Goes To War, 1964-1965 060 MIN
Legacies 060 MIN
No Neutral Ground - Cambodia And Laos 060 MIN
Peace Is At Hand 060 MIN
Roots Of War, The 060 MIN
Tet, 1968 060 MIN
Vietnamizing The War, 1969-1973 060 MIN
With America's Enemy, 1954-1967 060 MIN

Vietnam - An American Journey C 85 MIN
3/4 INCH VIDEO CASSETTE
Documents a trip down Highway One from Hanoi to Saigon in an enlightened portrait of civilian rehabilitation after a national trauma.
Prod-FIRS Dist-FIRS

Vietnam - An American Journey C 85 MIN
16MM FILM, 3/4 OR 1/2 IN VIDEO H-C A
Looks at Vietnam after the war. Includes an interview with a My Lai massacre survivor.
Prod-MCBRID Dist-FI 1979

Vietnam - An Historical Document C 56 MIN
16MM FILM, 3/4 OR 1/2 IN VIDEO J-C A
Explains the U S involvement in Vietnam and the events that led to American withdrawal.
Prod-CBSNEW Dist-CAROUF

Vietnam - Chronicle Of A War C
3/4 OR 1/2 INCH VIDEO CASSETTE
Portrays American military involvement in Vietnam as witnessed by on-the-scene, news correspondents and camera crews. Narrated by Walter Cronkite.
Prod-IHF Dist-IHF

Vietnam - Five Years After The War C 11 MIN
3/4 OR 1/2 INCH VIDEO CASSETTE H-C A
Examines society and government in Vietnam during the late 1970's.
Prod-UPI Dist-JOU

Vietnam - Images Of War C 26 MIN
3/4 OR 1/2 INCH VIDEO CASSETTE H-C A
Presents a montage of scenes which made headline news coverage during the 15 years of the Vietnam War.
Prod-UPI Dist-JOU

Vietnam - Lessons Of A Lost War C 50 MIN
3/4 OR 1/2 INCH VIDEO CASSETTE H-C A
Examines the facts and myths about the longest and most controversial war in American history. Presents facts, interpretations and film about the war's most controversial moments.
Prod-NBCNEW Dist-FI

Vietnam - Picking Up The Pieces C 60 MIN
16MM FILM OPTICAL SOUND
Takes a tour of Vietnam two years after the liberation. Reveals a nation in the throes of change, seeking to heal the social and economic wounds of war. Looks at government programs aimed at social improvement.
LC NO. 79-706203
Prod-DCTVC Dist-DCTVC 1978

Vietnam - Picking Up The Pieces C 60 MIN
3/4 INCH VIDEO CASSETTE
Tours Vietnam two years after the withdrawal of American military forces, focusing on national change.
LC NO. 79-706203
Prod-ALPERT Dist-DCTVC 1978

Vietnam - Picking Up The Pieces C 60 MIN
3/4 OR 1/2 INCH VIDEO CASSETTE
Reports Vietnam since the Americans withdrew in April, 1975. Finds the people trying to lead normal lives.
Prod-DCTVC Dist-EAI

Vietnam - The Bombing C 59 MIN
3/4 OR 1/2 INCH VIDEO CASSETTE
Tells the story of pilots, bombardiers and navigators and the air war over North Vietnam through interviews filmed between actual combat missions.
Prod-IHF Dist-IHF

Vietnam And Southeast Asia B 20 MIN
16MM FILM OPTICAL SOUND
Explains that while the U S government's direct involvement in the Vietnam war is now ten years old, the forgotten war in neighboring Laos continues. Uses an introduction in Spanish to show that our government's presence is being fought by a united front of the Laotian people.
Prod-SFN Dist-SFN

Vietnam Crucible C 29 MIN
16MM FILM OPTICAL SOUND
Reports on the American soldier's activities in Vietnam, presenting both the military and civilian situation.
From The Big Picture Series.
LC NO. 74-706314
Prod-USA Dist-USNAC 1968

Vietnam Epilogue - The End Of The Tunnel C 15 MIN
16MM FILM, 3/4 OR 1/2 IN VIDEO I-C A
Presents a chronology of United States involvement in Indo-China from the fall of Dien Bien Phu in 1954 to the Vietnam cease-fire agreement in 1973.
From The Screen News Digest Series. Vol 15, Issue 7
Prod-HEARST Dist-HEARST 1973

Vietnam Memorial C 52 MIN
3/4 OR 1/2 INCH VIDEO CASSETTE H-C A
Documents the gathering of Vietnam War Veterans and families in Washington on Veteran's Day, 1982, at which time they expressed their frustrations over bureaucracy, agent orange and public indifference.
LC NO. 84-707630
Prod-YRKWIL Dist-YRKWIL 1983

Vietnam Memorial C 58 MIN
1/2 IN VIDEO CASSETTE BETA/VHS
Describes the events of November 1982 when more than 150,000 people came to Washington DC to participate in the National Salute to Vietnam Veterans. Captures the celebration and emotion of the five-day tribute, which ended with a parade honoring the returning veterans and the dedication of the Vietnam Memorial.
From The Frontline Series.
Prod-DOCCON Dist-PBS

Vietnam Newsreel Review - 1967 C 50 MIN
3/4 OR 1/2 INCH VIDEO CASSETTE
Presents highlights of USAF military action in Vietnam in 1967 photographed by combat cameramen of the 600th Photo Squadron. Includes visits to Air Force bases by General McConnell, F-105 strikes on targets in North Vietnam, B-57 ground-support bombing, Super Sabres in action, supply drops to Khe Sanh, air-traffic controllers at Danang air base, a medical evacuation to the United States, Air Force chaplains at Cam Ranh air base and Operation ATL Buro airlift sorties.
Prod-IHF Dist-IHF

Vietnam Perspective C
16MM FILM, 3/4 OR 1/2 IN VIDEO J A
Presents an objective chronology of foreign involvement in Southeast Asia and highlights America's participation in the Vietnam War. Examines key factors from the Eisenhower Administration's commitments through the Nixon Administration's reorientation of U S-Asian policy. Includes maps and archival footage.
Prod-EBEC Dist-EBEC 1985

Vietnam Perspective C 32 MIN
16MM FILM, 3/4 OR 1/2 IN VIDEO I-C
Presents an objective chronology of foreign involvement in Southeast Asia. Highlights America's participation in the VietnamWar.
Prod-EBEC Dist-EBEC 1985

Vietnam Report C 22 MIN
3/4 OR 1/2 INCH VIDEO CASSETTE
Offers reports of Soviet correspondents on U S bombing raids over North Vietnam and the effects they are having on the people.
Prod-IHF Dist-IHF

Vietnam Report - Guardians At The Gate B 12 MIN
16MM FILM OPTICAL SOUND J-C A
Examines the history and the nature of the commitment of the United States to South Vietnam.
From The Screen News Digest Series. Vol 8, Issue 1
LC NO. 70-700508
Prod-HEARST Dist-HEARST 1965

Vietnam Requiem C 58 MIN
16MM FILM, 3/4 OR 1/2 IN VIDEO H-C A
Interviews five Vietnam veterans, all decorated war heroes who are now serving prison sentences. Relays the horrors of war and the unhappiness and bitterness felt by these heroes returning home from an unpopular war.
LC NO. 83-706625
Prod-KORTY Dist-DIRECT 1983

Vietnam Today C 18 MIN
16MM FILM, 3/4 OR 1/2 IN VIDEO I-C
Presents an overview of South Vietnam's people, heritage and progress. Points out South Vietnam's three distinct geographic areas, introduces families that live in each one and shows the traditions, challenges and changes that are part of Vietnamese life.
Prod-SIERAW Dist-AIMS 1975

Vietnam Vets - Over Here C 25 MIN
3/4 OR 1/2 INCH VIDEO CASSETTE
Points out that the Vietnam War is a fading memory, but its veterans remain a troubling presence.
Prod-WCCOTV Dist-WCCOTV 1977

Vietnam, Land Of Fire C 15 MIN
16MM FILM OPTICAL SOUND
A French language film. Documents the United States military's actions towards civilians in Vietnam, showing the war's inhumanity.
Prod-NEWSR Dist-NEWSR

Vietnam, Land Of Fire B 25 MIN
16MM FILM OPTICAL SOUND
A French language film. Shows the American invasion and attack on the civilian population. Shows the use of naplam, gas and toxic chemicals. Views bombings of schools and leprosaria. Filmed in North and South Vietnam.
Prod-UNKNWN Dist-SFN 1967

Vietnamese Cultures And Customs C 110 MIN
3/4 OR 1/2 INCH VIDEO CASSETTE
Shows a direct lecture by a U S professor on Vietnamese cultures and customs with emphasis on politics and war.
Prod-IHF Dist-IHF

Vietnamizing The War, 1969-1973 C 60 MIN
3/4 OR 1/2 INCH VIDEO CASSETTE H-C A
Describes how the U S began disinvolving itself from the war by training the South Vietnamese army to fight the battles. States that the withdrawal of U S troops resulted in hardship for the Vietnamese as the flow of goods and dollars diminished. Recalls that in the 1972 spring offensive, nearly all the casualties were Vietnamese.
From The Vietnam - A Television History Series. Episode 8
Prod-WGBHTV Dist-FI 1983

View And Do Film, No. 1 B 20 MIN
16MM FILM OPTICAL SOUND
Features three separate creative movement exercises for the elementary school student that he can watch, then get up and practice himself.
Prod-SLFP Dist-SLFP

View And Do—A Series
PRO
Presents a training series for correctional officers.
Prod-SCETV Dist-SCETV 1971

Inmate Behavior
Officer As A Source Of Change, The
Officer-Inmate Relationship
Security, Custody And Control

View From Another World C 16 MIN
16MM FILM OPTICAL SOUND C T
Uses a futuristic setting to highlight the problems of the mentally retarded and the attitudes of the public toward them. Explains the normalization or deinstitutionalization principle.
LC NO. 78-701612
Prod-UKBCR Dist-UKANS 1977

View From Below C 33 MIN
16MM FILM OPTICAL SOUND
Describes the environment of an Australian deep coal mine.

LC NO. 80-700865
Prod-IMPACT Dist-TASCOR 1978

View From Geneva B 60 MIN
16MM FILM OPTICAL SOUND
Depicts the broad spectrum of Red Cross humanitarian activities and services. Emphasizes efforts to help build the programs of newly developing Red Cross societies. Narrated by Princess Grace of Monaco.
Prod-ICRCRS Dist-AMRC Prodn-CANBC 1964

View From Mount Vernon, The B 28 MIN
16MM FILM OPTICAL SOUND J-H
A discussion with Dr Samuel Beer of Harvard University regarding the changes which have taken place in the presidency and the presidents of history who brought about those changes.
From The Government Story Series. No. 31
LC NO. 71-707213
Prod-WEBC Dist-WESTLC 1968

View From Outside, The C 3 MIN
16MM FILM OPTICAL SOUND
Shows a father giving his Marine son a 'VIEW FROM THE OUTSIDE' of Marine Corps life.
LC NO. 74-706315
Prod-USMC Dist-USNAC 1966

View From The Edge, The C 52 MIN
16MM FILM, 3/4 OR 1/2 IN VIDEO C A
Explains that Expressionism was ruined as an esthetic possibility by the horrors of World War II, when photography of the war surpassed any distortions of the body an artist could imagine. Tells how some artists struggled but lost in their attempts to maintain a mythic-religious imagery in the face of increasing secularization of 20th century life.
From The Shock Of The New Series.
Prod-BBCTV Dist-TIMLIF 1980

View From The Inside, A C 30 MIN
16MM FILM - 3/4 IN VIDEO PRO
Presents excerpts from therapy sessions in which the psychotherapist helps a patient relive her traumatic memories of child abuse.
LC NO. 79-706858
Prod-FMSP Dist-FMSP 1978

View From The People Wall - A Statement About Problem Solving And Abstract Models C 14 MIN
16MM FILM, 3/4 OR 1/2 IN VIDEO J-C
Explains the abstract models used in problem solving. Illustrates the computer's role in solving complex problems.
Prod-EAMES Dist-EBEC

View From The Top C 3 MIN
16MM FILM OPTICAL SOUND
Presents a closeup of an uncircumcised penis from manual masturbation to ejaculation.
Prod-MMRC Dist-MMRC

View From The Top C 11 MIN
16MM FILM OPTICAL SOUND PRO
Describes the functions and capabilities of the airborne warning and control system. Explains why the system is necessary to the American national defense, how it operates and how it might be used in combat situations.
LC NO. 77-702740
Prod-USAF Dist-USNAC 1977

View From The Top, The C 60 MIN
3/4 OR 1/2 INCH VIDEO CASSETTE
Stresses that successful development of a data base environment requires two types of 'views from the top,' cooperation, support and control from top management and an overall understanding of the organization's operations and resources.
From The Managing The Data Base Environment Series.
Prod-DELTAK Dist-DELTAK

View Of America From The 23rd Century, A X 21 MIN
16MM FILM, 3/4 OR 1/2 IN VIDEO H-C A
Presents John W Gardner, former Secretary of Health, Education and Welfare, who dramatizes how present American institutions might look when viewed from the perspective of the 23rd century. Shows man increasingly raging against his institutions because most have been designed to resist rather than to facilitate change. Discusses the belief that if the future does not hold destruction for our institutions they must be able to change and would-be reformers must use reason rather than destruction to achieve this end.
From The Public Broadcast Laboratory Series.
Prod-NET Dist-IU 1969

View Of Four Centuries, A C 30 MIN
3/4 INCH VIDEO CASSETTE H-C A
Offers members of the First Poetry Quartet as fictional characters from four time spans who share the love of poetry. Presents readings of the works of Donne, Milton, Gray and Thomas.
From The Anyone For Tennyson Series.
Prod-NETCHE Dist-GPITVL

View Of The Arts, A C 30 MIN
3/4 INCH VIDEO CASSETTE J-C A
Features Dr Jacob Bronowski evaluating the role of the artist. Offers a scene from his play The Face Of Violence.
From The Jacob Bronowski - 20th Century Man Series.
Prod-KPBS Dist-GPITVL 1976

View Of The Sky C 28 MIN
16MM FILM OPTICAL SOUND J-C A
Explains the historical theories of the solar system and the universe. Includes theories of Copernicus, Galileo, Newton, Einstein and others. Uses symbolic photography to illustrate these concepts and poses the question of how today's youth will envision the universe. Shows some ways in which NASA has gained new knowledge of other planets.
From The Conquest Of Space Series.
LC NO. FIE67-125
Prod-NASA Dist-NASA 1967

View Of The Sky, A C 28 MIN
16MM FILM, 3/4 OR 1/2 IN VIDEO
Explores various theories of the origin and order of the solar system, from Copernicus through Einstein, with a brief look at modern scientific exploration of space.
Prod-NASA Dist-USNAC

Viewing And Critiquing A Counseling Session B 20 MIN
3/4 OR 1/2 INCH VIDEO CASSETTE
Shows an initial interview followed by a demonstration of the social worker watching the interview and processing her internal frame of reference.
Prod-COLSTT Dist-UWISC 1982

Viewing Habits C 15 MIN
3/4 OR 1/2 INCH VIDEO CASSETTE J-H
Shows a class beginning their study of television by keeping a log of what they watch. Discusses some of their reasons for watching television and the complaints they have about their parents' TV watching rules.
From The Tuned-In Series. Lesson 1
Prod-WNETTV Dist-FI 1982

Viewpoint C 26 MIN
16MM FILM OPTICAL SOUND
Tells the story of the national forests through Bob Bray, who played Forest Ranger Corey Stuart on the Lassie TV series. Includes many striking scenes from national forests in different sections of the country.
LC NO. 74-705917
Prod-USDA Dist-USNAC 1967

Viewpoint—A Series
16MM FILM, 3/4 OR 1/2 IN VIDEO H-C A
Examines mass media from a social viewpoint, studying such topics as the role of communication in society, message mediation, and institutional structures.
Prod-THAMES Dist-MEDIAG 1975

Action	020 MIN
Believe Me	020 MIN
Communication Is Control	020 MIN
Fun Factory	020 MIN
Love Story	020 MIN
Money Talks	020 MIN
News Story	020 MIN
No Way	020 MIN
Real Thing, The	020 MIN
Show Business	020 MIN

Views Of A Decorticate Dog B 10 MIN
16MM FILM SILENT C T
Demonstrates the abnormal responses of a decorticate dog—postural and locomotional anomalies, tendency to continue locomotion once under way, lack of adaptative response to obstacles placed in its path, lack of initiative in food-getting, 'SHAM RAGE' elicited by trivial stimuli, intense resistence to impressed movements and degree of susceptibility to simple conditioning.
Prod-PSUPCR Dist-PSUPCR 1934

Views Of The Council On Economic Development C 18 MIN
3/4 OR 1/2 INCH VIDEO CASSETTE
See series title for descriptive statement.
From The Technology, Innovation, And Industrial Development Series.
Prod-MIOT Dist-MIOT

Vignette Series - Chairs B 10 MIN
16MM FILM OPTICAL SOUND T
Observes three- and four-year-olds learning, playing and talking in classroom situations. Filmed at Cambridge Neighborhood Head Start Center, Cambridge, Massachusetts.
LC NO. 70-707932
Prod-EDC Dist-EDC 1969

Vignette—A Series
T
Prod-EDS Dist-EDC 1969

Chairs	9 MIN
Injections	10 MIN
Marble Game	12 MIN
Seven Day Itch	7 MIN
Wall Washing	12 MIN
Waterplay, Pt 1	12 MIN
Waterplay, Pt 2	12 MIN

Vignettes—A Series
16MM FILM, 3/4 OR 1/2 IN VIDEO J-C A
Prod-PAULST Dist-PAULST 1973

Being Real	011 MIN
Close Feelings	011 MIN
Different With Dignity	013 MIN
Images Of God	012 MIN
Images Of The Church	012 MIN
Kinships	011 MIN
Me, Myself	012 MIN
Priorities	012 MIN
Rapport	012 MIN
Search For Faith, The	012 MIN
Walls And Windows	012 MIN

Viking C 29 MIN
16MM FILM, 3/4 OR 1/2 IN VIDEO
Presents a comprehensive look at the preparations for the Viking-Mars landing scheduled for July 4, 1976. Describes the beginning of the search for life on the Martian surface and looks at other experiments. Focuses on scientists connected with the Viking mission and explores the problems, solutions, concerns, anxieties and aspirations leading to the event.
LC NO. 82-706241
Prod-NASA Dist-USNAC 1976

Viking Ships Of Roskilde, The C 14 MIN
16MM FILM OPTICAL SOUND
Reports on the excavations made after the ships from the Viking period were found underwater in a channel in Roskilde Fjord. Explains the many problems technicians and scientists had to solve before the fragments of the wrecks could be removed for conservation.
Prod-RDCG Dist-AUDPLN

Viking Women Don't Care C 13 MIN
16MM FILM OPTICAL SOUND
Two hippies with a car load of marihuana meet a runaway bank robber in a car containing a dead body. Their confrontation satarizes the portrayal of violence in films.
LC NO. 75-703248
Prod-USC Dist-USC 1968

Vikings And Their Explorations, The C 11 MIN
16MM FILM, 3/4 OR 1/2 IN VIDEO I-H
Considers how the Viking warriors of the ninth and tenth centuries influenced the history of many nations. Discusses Leif Ericson's discovery of the North American continent. Presents a dramatization showing the homelife, manners and dress of Norsemen.
Prod-CORF Dist-CORF 1958

Vikings To The East C 10 MIN
16MM FILM OPTICAL SOUND
Portrays the Swedish Viking period, from 800-1000 A D.
Prod-ASI Dist-AUDPLN 1963

Vikings—A Series

Presents Icelander Magnus Magnusson investigating the myths and legends of the Viking culture.
Prod-KTCATV Dist-PBS 1980

Bitter Is The Wind	029 MIN
Bolt From The Blue	029 MIN
Empire Of The Northern Seas	029 MIN
England At Bay	029 MIN
From The Fury Of The Northmen	029 MIN
Halfdan Was Here	029 MIN
Hammer Of The North	029 MIN
Here King Harold Is Killed	029 MIN
Island Called Thule, An	029 MIN
Ultimate Outpost, The	029 MIN

Vikings, The - Life And Conquests X 17 MIN
16MM FILM, 3/4 OR 1/2 IN VIDEO I-H
Surveys the period of history known as the Viking Age.
Prod-EBF Dist-EBEC 1960

Villa Alegre (Spanish/English)—A Series
P-I
Uses a bilingual approach to present a curriculum dealing with human relations, natural environment, communication, energy and man-made objects.
Prod-BCTV Dist-GPITVL 1976

Villa Alegre 2001 C 30 MIN
3/4 OR 1/2 INCH VIDEO CASSETTE K-P
See series title for descriptive statement.
From The Villa Alegre Series.
Prod-BCTV Dist-MDCPB

Villa Alegre—A Series
K-P
Presents a bilingual series that features children learning how to deal with the problems of everyday life. Examines cultural traits representative of Hispanic cultures and certain aspects of American life.
Prod-BCTV Dist-MDCPB

Appetites	030 MIN
Art Is All Around Us	030 MIN
Cambios En Nuestro Mundo	030 MIN
De Las Cuevas A Las Nubes	030 MIN
El Cuerpo	030 MIN
El Idiona	030 MIN
El Mago	030 MIN
El Mundo De Las Animals	030 MIN
Farm Adventure	030 MIN
Good Morning Villa Alegre	030 MIN
Growing Up	030 MIN
Have A Little Humor	030 MIN
I Can Sing A Rainbow	030 MIN
Imaginary Friends	030 MIN
Keep An Open Mind	030 MIN
Las Invenciones	030 MIN
Love, Family In The Community	030 MIN
Measuring Up	030 MIN
Mente	030 MIN
Mitos N Leyendas Show	030 MIN
Moments Of History	030 MIN
Night Sky, The	030 MIN
Nuestras Families	030 MIN
Ocean Treasures	030 MIN
Promises, Promises	030 MIN
Putting It Together	030 MIN
Rios Del Mundo	030 MIN
Safety Week	030 MIN
Sentimientos Agradables	030 MIN
Sharing Is Caring	030 MIN
Story Time	030 MIN
Todolos Del Mundo	030 MIN
Toylandia	030 MIN
Trabago	030 MIN

Villa Alegre 2001 030 MIN
Why I Like Me 030 MIN
World Of Discoveries 030 MIN
Yo Quiero Ser 030 MIN
You Were There 030 MIN

Villa-Lobos, The Guitar, And Julian Byzantine C 26 MIN
16MM FILM, 3/4 OR 1/2 IN VIDEO J-C A
Tells how Brazilian composer Villa-Lobos (1884-1959) was inspired by Brazilian folk and popular music to write pieces he called Choros, as well as symphonies, operas, concertos, chamber music and songs. Features professional musician Julian Byzantine playing Villa-Lobos music on the guitar and commenting on his life.
From The Musical Triangle Series.
Prod-THAMES Dist-MEDIAG 1975

Village In Baltimore, A C 58 MIN
16MM FILM OPTICAL SOUND
Presents a documentary set in Baltimore's Greektown, focusing on assimilation of four Greek women into American society. Explores such issues as traditions, marriage, professional goals and views on American society.
From The Look At Greek-American Women Series.
LC NO. 81-700503
Prod-MOSESD Dist-MOSESD 1981

Village Life C 12 MIN
16MM FILM, 3/4 OR 1/2 IN VIDEO
See series title for descriptive statement.
From The Indians Of The Orinoco (Venezuela) - The Makiritare Series.
Prod-IFF Dist-IFF

Village Life C 15 MIN
16MM FILM, 3/4 OR 1/2 IN VIDEO
Illustrates the island village in the coconut groves lining the lagoon. Shows how a canoe is carved out of a whole tree that has drifted all the way from South America. Views men and women helping to build a new home, the structure of wood, the roof of thatched pandanus leaves, and the walls of braided mats of coconut leaves for air circulation.
From The Pacific Island Life Series.
Prod-IFF Dist-IFF

Village Life—A Series
16MM FILM, 3/4 OR 1/2 IN VIDEO H-C A
Describes village life in different parts of the world, joining the townspeople in their work, their play and their celebrations.
Prod-JOU Dist-JOU

Best Kept Secret, The (Western Samoa) 016 MIN
Bill, Peggy, Royal And Friends - London 016 MIN
El Pueblo (Spain) 024 MIN
I Am Fijian (Fiji) 026 MIN
Le Village, Un Village (France) 022 MIN
On Seven Hills They Built A City (Rome) 026 MIN
Samoa I Sisifo (Western Samoa) 026 MIN
Ten Times Empty (Greece) 021 MIN
Tonga Royal (Tonga) 020 MIN
Village Of The Rain Forest (Nigeria) 023 MIN

Village Of The Craftsmen, The C 23 MIN
16MM FILM, 3/4 OR 1/2 IN VIDEO
Introduces ancient Egypt at the height of its power. Looks at Tutankhamen's tomb and the lives of the people who built the tomb.
From The Ancient Lives Series.
Prod-FOTH Dist-FOTH

Village Of The Rain Forest (Nigeria) C 23 MIN
16MM FILM, 3/4 OR 1/2 IN VIDEO H-C A
Describes life in a Nigerian farming village.
From The Village Life Series.
Prod-JOU Dist-JOU 1983

Village School B 18 MIN
16MM FILM OPTICAL SOUND P-I T
Shows a primary school classroom in rural Kenya, where African children learn science in new ways by using local materials and modern methods.
LC NO. 70-712803
Prod-EDC Dist-EDC 1970

Village Singer By Mary Wilkins Freeman, The C 15 MIN
16MM FILM, 3/4 OR 1/2 IN VIDEO J-C A
Tells of the impassioned revenge of a village church vocalist directed against her successor and the congregation, and the ultimate reconciliation of all involved. Based on the short story The Village Singer by Mary Wilkins Freeman.
From The Short Story Series.
LC NO. 83-706127
Prod-IITC Dist-IU 1982

Village That Refused To Die, The B 56 MIN
3/4 OR 1/2 INCH VIDEO CASSETTE
Relates the story of a group of Chinese refugees who set up a village in South Vietnam.
Prod-IHF Dist-IHF

Village Theater In Senegal - Queen Ndate And The French Conquest C 14 MIN
16MM FILM, 3/4 OR 1/2 IN VIDEO H-C A
Presents actors, members of a rural youth association in northwestern Senegal, performing a play about the French conquest of their region in the 19th century.
Prod-IU Dist-IU 1983

Village Women In Egypt C 30 MIN
3/4 INCH VIDEO CASSETTE J-C
Presents a group of rural, tradition-bound Egyptian women talking about sex roles, family life, customs, and birth control. Reveals the conflict between traditional values and the opportunities that are becoming available to them and their children.
From The Are You Listening Series.
LC NO. 80-707408
Prod-STURTM Dist-STURTM

Village, The B 70 MIN
16MM FILM, 3/4 OR 1/2 IN VIDEO H-C A
Presents a portion of this film in Gaelic with English subtitles. Presents an intimate study of the slowpaced diurnal round of activity in Dunguin, County Kerry, one of the last Gaelic-speaking communities in Ireland. Depicts a peasant society at a time when acculturation by urban tourists was beginning.
Prod-UCLA Dist-UCEMC 1969

Village, The (Gaelic) B 70 MIN
16MM FILM OPTICAL SOUND C A
Takes a look at life in the village of Dunquin in County Kerry, Ireland. Shows the society of the village before extensive acculturation by tourists. With English subtitles.
LC NO. 76-700014
Prod-UCLA Dist-UCEMC 1969

Village, The Village, The Village, The C 36 MIN
16MM FILM, 3/4 OR 1/2 IN VIDEO H-C A
Shows how the growth of Greenwich Village in New York City has paralleled the growth of America's cities. Relates the changes that Greenwich Village has undergone to those which have taken place in America's culture and society.
Prod-COHENJ Dist-PHENIX 1977

Villages In The Sky C 13 MIN
16MM FILM OPTICAL SOUND I-J
Shows life in the high mesa villages of the Hopis. Women are shown making baskets and pottery and baking bread in outdoor adobe ovens. Portions of some of the dances conclude the film.
Prod-DAGP Dist-MLA 1952

Villains And Heroes B 15 MIN
2 INCH VIDEOTAPE K-P
Discusses action in a plot and how it must be logically resolved for each character. (Broadcast quality)
From The Magic Of Words Series.
Prod-GWTVAI Dist-GPITVL Prodn-WETATV

Villard De Honnecourt, Builder Of Cathedrals (1230-1235) C 15 MIN
16MM FILM OPTICAL SOUND
Presents a notebook of Villard de Honnecourt's life from 1230 to 1235 A D. Shows the engineer as an artist and as one of the great cathedral builders of the 12th century.
Prod-ROLAND Dist-ROLAND

Vincent Sweeney, MD And Jane Donner, PhD - How Far Can We Go? A Family's Question C 60 MIN
3/4 OR 1/2 INCH VIDEO CASSETTE PRO
Focuses on the facilitation of clear communication between a father and his eldest adolescent daughter.
From The Perceptions, Pt A - Interventions In Family Therapy Series. Vol VII, Pt A13.
Prod-BOSFAM Dist-BOSFAM

Vincent Sweeney, MD, Jane Donner, PhD, Center For The Study Of Human Systems, Chevy Chase, MD C 60 MIN
3/4 OR 1/2 INCH VIDEO CASSETTE PRO
Emphasizes the fact that two differentiated individuals make an effective co-therapy team.
From The Perceptions, Pt B - Dialogues With Family Therapists Series. Vol VII, Pt B13.
Prod-BOSFAM Dist-BOSFAM

Vincent Van Gogh C 25 MIN
16MM FILM OPTICAL SOUND J-C A
Interweaves the paintings of Van Gogh with selections from his letters to his brother Theo. Shows many of the locales associated with Van Gogh, such as the Borinage and Arles.
Prod-HULSKR Dist-CORF 1959

Vincent Van Gogh C 30 MIN
3/4 OR 1/2 INCH VIDEO CASSETTE J A
Presents various views of historians on the personal and professional life of Van Gogh, a world-famous Dutch painter.
Prod-SUTHRB Dist-SUTHRB

Vincent Van Gogh - Portrait Of A Painter C 26 MIN
3/4 INCH VIDEO CASSETTE
Describes the life and paintings of the Dutch artist Vincent Van Gogh. Emphasizes his sources of inspiration in nature. Includes paintings and drawings from many countries.
Prod-ROYNET Dist-MTP

Vintage Cars C 3 MIN
16MM FILM OPTICAL SOUND P-I
Shows vintage cars.
From The Of All Things Series.
Prod-BAILYL Dist-AVED

Vintage Cartoon Holiday Color C
3/4 OR 1/2 INCH VIDEO CASSETTE
Presents many animated cartoons made by major studios.
Prod-IHF Dist-IHF

Vintage Steam C 60 MIN
1/2 IN VIDEO CASSETTE BETA/VHS
Shows a ride on a logging Heisler steam locomotive, owned by the Roaring Camp and Big Trees Railroad.
Prod-DELUZ Dist-DELUZ 1979

Vintage, The C 7 MIN
16MM FILM OPTICAL SOUND I-C A
Shows one of Australia's major wine producing areas, the Barossa Valley in south Australia. Shows the harvesting of grapes and other stages in the production of wine.
LC NO. 74-703292
Prod-ANAIB Dist-AUIS Prodn-FILMAU 1973

Vinyl Top Repair C 18 MIN
1/2 IN VIDEO CASSETTE BETA/VHS
Deals with auto body repair. Covers the heat gun vinyl method of repair on small tears.
Prod-RMI Dist-RMI

Viola C 29 MIN
16MM FILM, 3/4 OR 1/2 IN VIDEO J-C A
Shows master craftsman Otto Erdesz creating violas considered by professional musicians as the finest made today. Follows the process from selection of the wood, through the art of its construction, to its performance in concert.
Prod-NGUZO Dist-BCNFL 1981

Violence - Just For Fun C 15 MIN
16MM FILM, 3/4 OR 1/2 IN VIDEO J-C A
Shows how Roman spectators applaud the destruction of human lives for entertainment, easily accepting violence as an enjoyable facet of 'CIVILIZED LIFE.'
From The Searching For Values - A Film Anthology Series.
Prod-LCOA Dist-LCOA 1972

Violence - The Tragic Legacy C 29 MIN
2 INCH VIDEOTAPE
See series title for descriptive statement.
From The Black Experience Series.
Prod-WTTWTV Dist-PUBTEL

Violence - Will It Ever End C 19 MIN
16MM FILM, 3/4 OR 1/2 IN VIDEO
Explores the increase of violence and asks whether the solution lies with man or with society.
Prod-DOCUA Dist-CNEMAG

Violence And Physical Restraint C 9 MIN
3/4 OR 1/2 INCH VIDEO CASSETTE PRO
Shows police working with emergency medical technicians in physically restraining a psychotic. A continuation of Psychosis - A Family Intervention.
From The Crisis Intervention Series.
Prod-SBG Dist-GPITVL 1983

Violence And The Law C 30 MIN
3/4 OR 1/2 INCH VIDEO CASSETTE H-C A
Shows former U S Attorney General Ramsey Clark and law professor-author Ernest Van Den Haag debating the effectiveness of the American system of law and justice. Highlights the question of whether the system is too lenient or severe with the criminal.
From The Ethics In America Series.
Prod-AMHUMA Dist-AMHUMA

Violence And Vandalism C
16MM FILM OPTICAL SOUND I-H A
Explains the causes of vandalism, why American cities spend millions a year clearing up the destruction caused by violence and vandalism and the alternatives to young people who feel they must destroy to be heard.
LC NO. 71-713579
Prod-DUNLF Dist-AMEDFL 1971

Violence And Vandalism C 15 MIN
16MM FILM OPTICAL SOUND J-C
Explores the problems and proposes some answers to the issue of vandalism. Points out gravity of the matter through up-to-date facts and location sites from California to New York.
LC NO. 70-713579
Prod-AMEDFL Dist-AMEDFL 1971

Violence Has No Enemies B 15 MIN
16MM FILM OPTICAL SOUND
Tells the story of three teenagers who become victims of violence in New York City.
LC NO. 77-702164
Prod-WISOT Dist-WISOT 1977

Violence In Black American Life C 60 MIN
3/4 OR 1/2 INCH VIDEO CASSETTE
See series title for descriptive statement.
From The Blacks, Blues, Black Series.
Prod-KQEDTV Dist-PBS

Violence In The Family C 30 MIN
3/4 OR 1/2 INCH VIDEO CASSETTE C A
Compares natural family conflict or agression to abnormal physical violence. Investigates the socioeconomic roots of family violence. Examines the problem of abused children.
From The Family Portrait - A Study Of Contemporary Lifestyles Series. Lesson 21
Prod-SCCON Dist-CDTEL

Violence In The Family C 44 MIN
1/2 IN VIDEO CASSETTE (VHS) J-C
Examines the causes, characteristics, and possible solutions to family violence.
LC NO. 85-703940
Prod-HRMC Dist-HRMC

Violence Sonata, No. 2 C 45 MIN
16MM FILM OPTICAL SOUND
Explores a non-verbal essay on the unconscious forces of violence in a hope for the conscious understanding of man's future to adapt or die.
Prod-VANBKS Dist-VANBKS

Violent Behavior C
3/4 OR 1/2 INCH VIDEO CASSETTE
Presents five characteristics common to individuals who exhibit violent behavior. Discusses the function of the behavioral disorder team during physical intervention.
From The Bedside Emergencies Series.
Prod-CONMED Dist-CONMED

Violent Earth, The C 52 MIN
16MM FILM, 3/4 OR 1/2 IN VIDEO

Shows French volcanologist Haroun Tazieff conducting a tour of Mt Etna in Sicily and Nyiragongo in Zaire during periods of eruption.
LC NO. 80-706373
Prod-NGS Dist-NGS 1973

Violent Universe, The B 148 MIN
16MM FILM, 3/4 OR 1/2 IN VIDEO H-C
A comprehensive report of astronomical theories, research and discoveries. Visits thirty astronomers at their observatories throughout the world as they discuss pulsars, infra-red galaxies, red giants, white dwarfs, cosmic rays and redshift. Includes a motion picture view of a quasar.
From The Public Broadcast Laboratory Series.
LC NO. 80-707091
Prod-NET Dist-IU 1969

Violent Youth - The Un-Met Challenge C 23 MIN
16MM FILM, 3/4 OR 1/2 IN VIDEO PRO
Presents various approaches to dealing with juvenile crime by examining the cases of three serious offenders who are confined to a maximum security facility for boys in Goshen, New York. Gives views of a director of an institution for serious juvenile offenders, a family court judge and a chief of police.
Prod-ALTANA Dist-MTI 1975

Violette C 123 MIN
16MM FILM OPTICAL SOUND
A French language motion picture with English subtitles. Focuses on an 18-year-old French girl who poisons her parents. Directed by Claude Chabrol.
Prod-UNKNWN Dist-NYFLMS 1978

Violin And The Viola, The C 25 MIN
3/4 INCH VIDEO CASSETTE
See series title for descriptive statement.
From The Instruments Of The Orchestra And Their Techniques Series.
Prod-UWASHP Dist-UWASHP

Violin Maker, The (In Praise Of Hands) C 12 MIN
16MM FILM, 3/4 OR 1/2 IN VIDEO I-H
Pictures, without narration, an aged craftsman at work fashioning a violin from what appears to be firewood. Shows that the old man's work reflects patience, attention to detail, a respect for both materials and tools and pride.
Prod-ZAGREB Dist-PHENIX 1972

Violin Making In Colonial America C 30 MIN
16MM FILM OPTICAL SOUND
Shows the many stages involved in making a violin with the tools and methods of 18th century craftsmen.
LC NO. 77-700006
Prod-CWMS Dist-CWMS 1976

Violin-Door B 13 MIN
16MM FILM SILENT
A character study of a deaf-mute who comes upon the farmhouse of a lonely, but over-bearing young woman.
LC NO. 77-702631
Prod-SHOWN Dist-FMCOOP 1969

Violin, The C 14 MIN
3/4 OR 1/2 INCH VIDEO CASSETTE P
Introduces the violin and visits the string section of an orchestra.
From The Stepping Into Rhythm Series.
Prod-WVIZTV Dist-AITECH

Violin, The C 25 MIN
16MM FILM, 3/4 OR 1/2 IN VIDEO J-C A
Portrays a young boy and his encounter with an old wayfarer musician. Shows the magic that can emerge when two lives touch. Presents a setting of snowy mountains and a warm cabin in which deepens the friendship.
LC NO. 73-700227
Prod-LCOA Dist-LCOA 1973

Violin, The (Spanish) C 25 MIN
16MM FILM, 3/4 OR 1/2 IN VIDEO P-C A
Tells story of a young boy and an old musician who leaves his violin with the boy.
Prod-LCOA Dist-LCOA 1973

VIP Lunch C 29 MIN
3/4 OR 1/2 INCH VIDEO CASSETTE
See series title for descriptive statement.
From The Julia Child And Company Series.
Prod-WGBHTV Dist-PBS

VIP'S C 15 MIN
3/4 INCH VIDEO CASSETTE P-I
Presents biographies of Knute Rockne, Theodore Roosevelt, the Ringling brothers and a number of well-known black Americans.
From The Can You Imagine Series.
Prod-WVIZTV Dist-GPITVL

Vir Amat C 15 MIN
16MM FILM, 3/4 OR 1/2 IN VIDEO C A
De-mythologizes homosexual relationships, showing two ordinary men in a loving relationship.
Prod-NATSF Dist-MMRC

Viracocha C 30 MIN
16MM FILM OPTICAL SOUND
Shows how Indians of pure and mixed blood interact in the Andean highlands within a near-subsistence economic system. Shows how market days and fiestas provide opportunities for the Spanish-speaking mestizos to assert their traditional social dominance over the native Indians.
From The Faces Of Change - Bolivia Series.
Prod-AUFS Dist-WHEELK

Viral Hepatitis C 30 MIN
3/4 OR 1/2 INCH VIDEO CASSETTE
Centers around three patients illustrating management problems in viral hepatitis.
Prod-ROWLAB Dist-ROWLAB

Viral Infections C
3/4 OR 1/2 INCH VIDEO CASSETTE
Discusses symptoms, diagnostic tests, management and complications of sexually transmitted diseases caused by viruses. Emphasizes the impact of herpes genitalis and the public health problems related to herpes control.
From The Sexually Transmitted Diseases Series.
Prod-CONMED Dist-CONMED

Viral, Metabolic And Etiological Studies Of ALS (Amyotrophic Lateral Sclerosis) C 30 MIN
3/4 INCH VIDEO CASSETTE PRO
Reviews research into the viral metabolic and immunological studies on the etiology and pathogenesis of amyotrophic lateral sclerosis and associated motor-neuron diseases.
LC NO. 79-707395
Prod-NINDIS Dist-USNAC 1979

Virgil Thomson, Composer C 59 MIN
16MM FILM OPTICAL SOUND
Presents a portrait of American composer Virgil Thomson. Includes selections from the composer's works.
LC NO. 81-700494
Prod-FLMAMR Dist-CANTOR 1980

Virgin Of Guadalupe, The B 111 MIN
16MM FILM OPTICAL SOUND
Portrays the vision of the virgin of Guadalupe which converted the Indian worshippers from their Aztec gods.
Prod-CATHFC Dist-TRANSW

Virginia C
3/4 OR 1/2 INCH VIDEO CASSETTE
Presents five segments about the state of Virginia, proud of its heritage and many contributions to the nation.
From The Portrait Of America Series.
Prod-TBS Dist-TBS

Virginia B 20 MIN
16MM FILM, 3/4 OR 1/2 IN VIDEO
Introduces Virginia, an elderly woman with a hearing handicap, who is presented in an oppresive interview situation on a darkened sound stage responding to muffled inquiries from a condescending young man. Shows her patience and gentleness triumphing over her interrogator.
Prod-MARBLO Dist-DIRECT 1975

Virginia Artists—A Series

Discusses the artists of Virginia.
Prod-SCHDRC Dist-SCHDRC

Vanishing Point - Painting And Sculpture Of

Virginia Blacks - A History, Pt 1 B 20 MIN
3/4 OR 1/2 INCH VIDEO CASSETTE
Prod-RCOMTV Dist-SYLWAT 1978

Virginia Blacks - A History, Pt 2 B 21 MIN
3/4 OR 1/2 INCH VIDEO CASSETTE
Prod-RCOMTV Dist-SYLWAT 1978

Virginia Hill Story, The C 77 MIN
16MM FILM, 3/4 OR 1/2 IN VIDEO H-C A
Looks at the life of Virginia Hill and her life with underground figures. Stars Dyan Cannon.
Prod-LUF Dist-LUF 1976

Virginia Law Everyone Should Know—A Series

Presents a series of discussions devoted to those aspects of the law everyone should know. Features a three-lawyer panel, all members of the legal services to the Public Committee, a division of the Young Lawyers Section Of The Virginia Bar Association. From the Syl Watkins Show.
Prod-RCOMTV Dist-SYLWAT

Accidents And Liability, Juvenile Law, And
Accidents And Liability, Juvenile Law, And 030 MIN
Domestic Relations, Contracts And Consumer 030 MIN
Domestic Relations, Contracts And Estate 030 MIN

Virginia Satir, MSW - Private Practice, California C 60 MIN
3/4 OR 1/2 INCH VIDEO CASSETTE PRO
Features family therapist Virginia Satir sharing her views of her upbringing and early experiences as a family therapist. Includes concepts about uniqueness, self-esteem and communication.
From The Perceptions, Pt B - Dialogues With Family Therapists Series. Vol I, Pt B4.
Prod-BOSFAM Dist-BOSFAM

Virginia Satir, MSW - Sisters And Parents - A Family Finds Options C 60 MIN
3/4 OR 1/2 INCH VIDEO CASSETTE PRO
Uses simple action techniques to demonstrate problem-solving in a family. Features Virginia Satir helping two sisters and their parents define their relationships.
From The Perceptions, Pt A - Interventions In Family Therapy Series. Vol I, Pt A1.
Prod-BOSFAM Dist-BOSFAM

Virginia Satir, MSW - The Light And The Dark C 60 MIN
3/4 OR 1/2 INCH VIDEO CASSETTE PRO
Interviews the family that appears in the videotape Sisters And Parents following the suicide of daughter Lisa. Consists of two tapes.
From The Perceptions, Pt A - Interventions In Family Therapy Series. Vol VIII, Pt A15.
Prod-BOSFAM Dist-BOSFAM

Virginia Silver C 30 MIN
3/4 OR 1/2 INCH VIDEO CASSETTE
Presents guests who are experts in their respective fields who share tips on collecting and caring for antique Virginia silver.
From The Antique Shop Series.
Prod-WVPTTV Dist-MDCPB

Virginia Woolf - The Moment Whole C 10 MIN
16MM FILM, 3/4 OR 1/2 IN VIDEO H-C A
Introduces the philosophy and literary style of the 20th-century writer, Virginia Woolf, by presenting visuals of the milieu in which she worked complemented by selections from 'A ROOM OF ONE'S OWN' and 'THE WAVES,' read and portrayed by Marian Seldes.
Prod-NET Dist-AIMS 1972

Virginia's Fishing Industry C 12 MIN
16MM FILM OPTICAL SOUND I-H A
Shows the importance of the fishing industry in the Chesapeake Bay. Depicts methods of catching fish.
Prod-VADE Dist-VADE 1956

Virgo I C 14 MIN
16MM FILM OPTICAL SOUND I-C A
Presents a poetic cinepoem about a young man's escape from the noise of the city to the serene environment of Big Sur.
Prod-CFS Dist-CFS 1969

Viro's Reel C 30 MIN
3/4 OR 1/2 INCH VIDEO CASSETTE
Presented by Howard Freid.
Prod-KITCHN Dist-KITCHN

Virtue Rewarded - Henry Fielding's Joseph Andrews C 45 MIN
3/4 OR 1/2 INCH VIDEO CASSETTE
Dramatizes selected incidents from Henry Fielding's novel Joseph Andrews.
From The Survey Of English Literature I Series.
Prod-MDCPB Dist-MDCPB

Viruses C 13 MIN
3/4 OR 1/2 INCH VIDEO CASSETTE J-H
A revised edition of Viruses - Threshold Of Life. Explores the nature of viruses and suggests future directions of viral research. Shows the major components of a virus, viral reproduction, transduction, latency and the roles of viral DNA and RNA.
Prod-CORF Dist-CORF

Viruses C 15 MIN
16MM FILM, 3/4 OR 1/2 IN VIDEO J-C A
Traces the discovery of viruses from the late 1800's through the advent of the electron microscope. Shows techniques for culturing viruses, describes the range of virus morphology and details two modes of virus action.
From The Inhabitants Of The Planet Earth Series.
Prod-BIOMED Dist-WARDS 1979

Viruses - The Mysterious Enemy C 39 MIN
1/2 IN VIDEO CASSETTE (VHS) I-H A
Describes viruses, their discovery, their structure, how they operate and how they can evolve, and examines some virus-caused diseases.
LC NO. 85-703881
Prod-HRMC Dist-HRMC

Visceral Angiography C 22 MIN
16MM FILM OPTICAL SOUND PRO
Discusses the proper technique and catheters for performing visceral angiography.
Prod-CORDIS Dist-CORDIS

Visceral Organ Transplants C 30 MIN
16MM FILM OPTICAL SOUND PRO
Reports developments in the field of medicine and discusses three major problems involving surgery, immunology and supply.
From The Upjohn Vanguard Of Medicine Series.
LC NO. FIA66-673
Prod-UPJOHN Dist-UPJOHN Prodn-SHNKRN 1966

Visceral Reflexes And Taste - Visceral Motor And Sensory Components C 18 MIN
16MM FILM, 3/4 OR 1/2 IN VIDEO PRO
See series title for descriptive statement.
From The Anatomical Basis Of Brain Function Series.
Prod-AVCORP Dist-TEF

Viscosity C 30 MIN
3/4 OR 1/2 INCH VIDEO CASSETTE H
Presents physics professor Jearl Walker offering graphic and unusual demonstrations exemplifying the principles of the viscosity of fluids.
From The Kinetic Karnival Of Jearl Walker. Pt 4
LC NO. 83-706118
Prod-WVIZTV Dist-GPITVL 1982

Vises, Clamps, Pliers, Screwdrivers, Wrenches C 60 MIN
3/4 OR 1/2 INCH VIDEO CASSETTE IND
See series title for descriptive statement.
From The Mechanical Maintenance Basics, Module A - Hand Tools Series.
Prod-LEIKID Dist-LEIKID

Vishnu's Maya C 30 MIN
16MM FILM, 3/4 OR 1/2 IN VIDEO H-C A
Explores the beauty of India and examines classical Hindu culture.
Prod-SARASW Dist-PHENIX 1977

Visibility - Moderate C 40 MIN
3/4 OR 1/2 INCH VIDEO CASSETTE
Presents a parody of a vacation film through Ireland. Touches upon several Irish issues, such as the sentimental mythologizing of the national past.
Prod-KITCHN Dist-KITCHN

Visible Absorption Spectrophotometry, Pt 1 - Absorbance C 30 MIN
3/4 OR 1/2 INCH VIDEO CASSETTE C A
Demonstrates the use of the Bausch and Lomb Spectronic 21 spectrophotometer and the techniques required for the quantitative and reproducible measurement of the absorbance of a solution.
From The Chemistry - Master/Apprentice Series. Program 14
LC NO. 82-706045
Prod-CUETV Dist-CUNIV 1981

Visible Absorption Spectrophotometry, Pt 2 - Concentration C 9 MIN
3/4 OR 1/2 INCH VIDEO CASSETTE C A
Uses the Spectronic 21 to directly measure the concentration of a solution using the concentration mode and the factor set button. Assumes that the viewer is familiar with the operations presented in Part 1, Program 14.
From The Chemistry - Master/Apprentice Series. Program 15
LC NO. 82-706078
Prod-CUETV Dist-CUNIV 1981

Visicalc C
3/4 OR 1/2 INCH VIDEO CASSETTE
Illustrates the overall concept of an electronic spreadsheet and the basic model-building tools of VisiCalc. Offers an introduction to the 'what if' game, split screens, inserting and deleting rows and variety of formatting options.
Prod-LANSFD Dist-ANDRST

Vision C 29 MIN
3/4 INCH VIDEO CASSETTE C A
Defines and explains vision in terms of the parts of the eye and the characteristics of light waves. Discusses handicap of blindness.
From The Understanding Human Behavior - An Introduction To Psychology Series. Lesson 8
Prod-COAST Dist-CDTEL

Vision And Movement C 60 MIN
3/4 OR 1/2 INCH VIDEO CASSETTE C A
Discusses how we perceive the world and move within it.
From The Brain, Mind And Behavior Series.
Prod-WNETTV Dist-FI

Vision For Tomorrow C 22 MIN
16MM FILM OPTICAL SOUND PRO
Shows new surgical and pharmaceutical procedures in opthalmology. Features experts in the field from Switzerland, France and the United States.
LC NO. 82-700341
Prod-MESHDO Dist-MESHDO Prodn-WOLFN 1982

Vision In Military Aviation - Sense Of Sight C 25 MIN
16MM FILM OPTICAL SOUND
Describes anatomy and physiology of the eye, including structure of the retina and functions of the rods and cones for light discrimination, dark-adaption and techniques for the relaying of rod vision. Describes how different forces and chemicals affect the eye.
LC NO. 74-705919
Prod-USN Dist-USNAC 1962

Vision In The Desert, A C 28 MIN
16MM FILM OPTICAL SOUND
Uses music and dance in order to promote the activities of the Nevada Dance Theatre.
LC NO. 74-703237
Prod-KLVXTV Dist-KLVXTV 1974

Vision Is Electric, The C 13 MIN
16MM FILM OPTICAL SOUND
Looks at the employees and activities of Mc Graw-Edison Company, a manufacturer of electrical products.
LC NO. 79-700338
Prod-MCEDCO Dist-MCEDCO Prodn-LIEB 1978

Vision Loss - Focus On Feelings C 20 MIN
3/4 INCH VIDEO CASSETTE
Discusses common fears and concerns of seven people with different types of eye problems.
Prod-ORACLE Dist-ORACLE Prodn-AFB

Vision Of Chaim Weizmann B 21 MIN
16MM FILM OPTICAL SOUND
Presents a biography of Israel's first president, incorporating the story of Zionism and the re-establishment of the Jewish people in their land.
Prod-ALDEN Dist-ALDEN

Vision Of Dr Koch, The C 22 MIN
16MM FILM, 3/4 OR 1/2 IN VIDEO I-H
Presents Dr Robert Koch, a German bacteriologist, who was the first man to prove that a single germ can cause a specific disease. Re-enacts a dramatic incident which was at first interpreted as proof that his theories were invalid, but which later led to development of vaccines and other life-saving discoveries.
From The You Are There Series.
Prod-CBSTV Dist-PHENIX 1972

Vision Of Galileo, The C 28 MIN
3/4 OR 1/2 INCH VIDEO CASSETTE I-H
Examines the findings of Galileo, the father of modern astronomy and physics.
Prod-CANBC Dist-JOU

Vision Of Juazeiro C 19 MIN
16MM FILM, 3/4 OR 1/2 IN VIDEO A
Documents the transformation of a small town in northeastern Brazil into a religious shrine under the guidance of Father Cicero, a religious and political leader in the region. Analyzes the perpetuation of his teachings through the religious festivities of pilgrims, and examines commercial and political aspects of the event. Portuguese dialog with English subtitles.
Prod-CNEMAG Dist-CNEMAG

Vision With Spatial Inversion B 18 MIN
16MM FILM SILENT C T
Follows a complete repetition of the classical experiment in which the subject wears inverting spectacles continuously for several weeks. Shows that initial difficulties in orientation, walking, eating, writing and card sorting gradually dissipate as the subject becomes accustomed to the 'UPSIDE DOWN WORLD.'
Prod-PSUPCR Dist-PSUPCR 1951

Visionaries C 30 MIN
3/4 OR 1/2 INCH VIDEO CASSETTE H-C A
Deals with American painting in the Romantic style.
From The Art America Series.
Prod-CTI Dist-CTI

Visions Of Eight C 105 MIN
16MM FILM OPTICAL SOUND J-C A
Presents eight aspects of the 1972 Olympic games in Munich, Germany. Looks at the pole-vault, decathlon, 100-meter dash, losing athletes, marathon runners, women contestants, weight-lifters and the tension of the moments before the starting gun.
LC NO. 78-701091
Prod-WOLPER Dist-CINEMV 1973

Visions Of Light - Gothic Stained Glass (1200-1300 A D) C 15 MIN
16MM FILM OPTICAL SOUND
Presents Gothic stained glass from the Middle Ages dating from 1200 to 1300 A D.
Prod-ROLAND Dist-ROLAND

Visions Of Paradise—A Series

Presents the life and work of five important American naive artistes.
Prod-SARLGT Dist-SARLGT

Angel That Stands By Me, The - Minnie Evans
Grandma's Bottle Village - The Art Of Tressa 028 MIN
Hundred And Two Mature, The Art Of Harry 029 MIN
Monument Of Chief Rolling Mountain Thunder, The 029 MIN
Possum Trot, The Life And Work Of Calvin Black 029 MIN

Visit From Captain Cook, A C 16 MIN
16MM FILM, 3/4 OR 1/2 IN VIDEO I-C A
Presents a re-enactment of Captain James Cook's stopovers on Vancouver Island's west coast during his search for the elusive 'Northwest Passage' to the Orient. Shows the importance of Captain Cook's voyages in opening up the seas to commerce and world trade. Describes the Nootke Indians and their habitats at the time of Captain Cook's visit.
LC NO. 82-706511
Prod-NFBC Dist-CRMP 1982

Visit From St Nicholas, A C 4 MIN
16MM FILM, 3/4 OR 1/2 IN VIDEO P-H
An animated story about the midnight visit of St Nicholas and his reindeer.
Prod-CORF Dist-CORF 1949

Visit Through Saturday B 14 MIN
16MM FILM OPTICAL SOUND
Features a narrative dealing with the father-son relationship. Reveals a young boy's eagerness to discover the world.
Prod-NYU Dist-NYU

Visit To A Container Port, A C 12 MIN
16MM FILM, 3/4 OR 1/2 IN VIDEO P-I
Presents a visit to a container port, showing the special machines that move containers around the terminal and onto the ship.
From The Visit To Series.
Prod-JOU Dist-JOU 1983

Visit To A County Fair, A C 11 MIN
16MM FILM, 3/4 OR 1/2 IN VIDEO P-I
Shows the sights, sounds and excitement of a country fair.
From The Visit To Series.
Prod-ALTSUL Dist-JOU 1979

Visit To A Dairy Farm, A C 12 MIN
16MM FILM, 3/4 OR 1/2 IN VIDEO P-I
Introduces a dairy farm, showing a district agricultural show and a milk factory where milk is churned into butter, made into cheese and powdered.
From The Visit To Series.
Prod-JOU Dist-JOU 1983

Visit To A Dairy Farm, A - Una Visita A Una Granja C 8 MIN
16MM FILM, 3/4 OR 1/2 IN VIDEO P-I
Shows children milking a cow, climbing trees, riding on a hay wagon and meeting farm animals. Teaches English to Spanish-speaking children.
From The Bilingual Film Series, Module 3 - Down On The Farm Series.
Prod-BRNTNO Dist-CAROUF 1973

Visit To A Honey Bee Farm, A C 10 MIN
16MM FILM, 3/4 OR 1/2 IN VIDEO P-I
Presents Gary, the beekeeper, who takes two young children on a tour of the honey bee farm. Shows the bees gathering the nectar from the blossoms and returning with it to the hive. Describes the process of collecting the honey.
From The Visit To Series.
Prod-JOU Dist-JOU 1977

Visit To A Maple Sugar Farm, A - Sugarbush C 11 MIN
16MM FILM, 3/4 OR 1/2 IN VIDEO P
Shows how maple syrup is made.
From The Visit To Series.
Prod-JOU Dist-JOU 1975

Visit To A Movie Studio, A C 14 MIN
16MM FILM, 3/4 OR 1/2 IN VIDEO P-I
Explores the world of motion pictures by focusing on the roles of actors, directors, producers, cameramen, editors and others involved in moviemaking.
From The Visit To Series.
Prod-ALTSUL Dist-JOU 1979

Visit To A Nature Center, A C 12 MIN
16MM FILM, 3/4 OR 1/2 IN VIDEO P-I
Focuses on a group of children as they visit a nature center and learn about the plant and animal life of the region.
From The Visit To Series.
Prod-ALTSUL Dist-JOU 1978

Visit To A Pacific Island Group, A - Japan B 20 MIN
2 INCH VIDEOTAPE I
Invites children to sit in a Japanese home to learn the ways and customs of these progressive people. (Broadcast quality)
From The Geography Series. Unit 4 - World Of Many People
Prod-DENVPS Dist-GPITVL Prodn-KRMATV

Visit To A Pond, A C 9 MIN
16MM FILM, 3/4 OR 1/2 IN VIDEO K-I
Shows various kinds of plants and animals found in and around a pond.
From The Visit To Series.
Prod-JOU Dist-JOU 1975

Visit To A Pond, A (Captioned) C 9 MIN
16MM FILM, 3/4 OR 1/2 IN VIDEO K-I
Shows various kinds of plants and animals found in and around a pond.
Prod-JOU Dist-JOU 1975

Visit To A Russian School B 5 MIN
16MM FILM OPTICAL SOUND
Takes viewers into a Russian school to see and hear how third grade pupils learn English.
From The Screen News Digest Series. Vol 3, Issue 4
Prod-HEARST Dist-HEARST 1960

Visit To A Sheep Farm, A C 12 MIN
16MM FILM, 3/4 OR 1/2 IN VIDEO P-I
Shows two children visiting their uncle's sheep farm and learning about the shearing of sheep and how the wool is sold.
From The Visit To Series.
LC NO. 84-707310
Prod-GFILM Dist-JOU 1982

Visit To A Theatre, A C 14 MIN
16MM FILM, 3/4 OR 1/2 IN VIDEO P-I
Takes a look at the work involved in staging a play by visiting a theater and following a production from the weeks of preparation through the opening night.
From The Visit To Series.
Prod-ALTSUL Dist-JOU 1978

Visit To A Wild Bird Island, A C 9 MIN
16MM FILM, 3/4 OR 1/2 IN VIDEO P-I
Follows a naturalist and his brothers on a visit to an island to study aquatic birds. Observes tiny chicks cut their way out of the confinement of eggs and adult birds build their nests, catch fish and return to their nests to feed the young.
From The Visit To Series.
Prod-JOU Dist-JOU 1978

Visit To An Airport, A C 12 MIN
16MM FILM, 3/4 OR 1/2 IN VIDEO P-I
Presents two children as they take a tour of an airport. Shows the kitchens, the maintenance hanger and the control tower. Describes a flight simulator where pilots are trained and discusses the care and coordination which combine to keep planes flying safely.
From The Visit To Series.
Prod-JOU Dist-JOU 1983

Visit To Apple Cider Country, A C 16 MIN
16MM FILM, 3/4 OR 1/2 IN VIDEO P-I
Shows how apple cider is made as a young city boy visits a unique, self-sustaining farm and examines the process of picking, cleaning, crushing and pressing the apples and pasteurizing and bottling the cider.
From The Visit To Series.
Prod-NELVNA Dist-JOU 1977

Visit To Aruba C 15 MIN
3/4 OR 1/2 INCH VIDEO CASSETTE P
Pictures white sand beaches and a sunken ship viewed through a glass-bottomed boat in Aruba.
From The Other Families, Other Friends Series. Blue Module - Aruba
Prod-WVIZTV Dist-AITECH 1971

Visit To EPCOT Center, A C 20 MIN
16MM FILM, 3/4 OR 1/2 IN VIDEO
Tours EPCOT center in Florida, which has exhibits of various world cultures and the world of the future.
Prod-WDEMCO Dist-WDEMCO 1982

Visit To Fra Mauro, A B 14 MIN
16MM FILM OPTICAL SOUND I-C A
Documents, from blast-off to splashdown, the flight of Apollo 14.
From The Screen News Digest Series. Vol 13, Issue 7
LC NO. 72-700571
Prod-HEARST Dist-HEARST 1971

Visit To Germany And Sweden, A C 24 MIN
16MM FILM, 3/4 OR 1/2 IN VIDEO H-C A
States that Sweden has a reputation as a leader in industrial democracy and Swedish equivalents of the British worker-director have negotiating rights. In comparison, the Germans, called information officers of the works council, serve as liaison role with no negotiating rights. British visitors criticize the European system as ineffective.

From The What About The Workers Series.
Prod-THAMES Dist-MEDIAG 1978

Visit To Good Neighbors, A B 5 MIN
16MM FILM OPTICAL SOUND
Travels with President and Mrs Kennedy of their trip to Venuzuela. Emphasizes the effort made to achieve a better understanding among the partcipants in the new Alliance for Progress in South America.
From The Screen News Digest Series. Vol 4, Issue 7
Prod-HEARST Dist-HEARST 1962

Visit To Indiana, A C 10 MIN
16MM FILM OPTICAL SOUND J-C A
Intercuts a conversation between an Indiana boy and his uncle with flashes of the boy's homelife and his family.
LC NO. 72-702288
Prod-CANCIN Dist-CANCIN

Visit To Rancho Verde, A - Una Visita Al Rancho Verde C 9 MIN
16MM FILM, 3/4 OR 1/2 IN VIDEO P-I
Shows a classroom field trip to a vegetable ranch as the children meet the ranch foreman and learn about seeds, irrigation and types of vegetables. Teaches English to Spanish-speaking children.
From The Bilingual Film Series, Module 3 - Down On The Farm Series.
Prod-BRNTNO Dist-CAROUF 1973

Visit To Snow Country, A C 9 MIN
16MM FILM, 3/4 OR 1/2 IN VIDEO P-I
Follows a young boy and his parents on a cross-country ski tour through snow-covered forests. Points out a wide variety of forest animals and shows how they survive during the winter.
From The Visit To Series.
Prod-JOU Dist-JOU 1978

Visit To Spectrum II, A C 16 MIN
16MM FILM, 3/4 OR 1/2 IN VIDEO J
Uses a story about a space laboratory of the future to introduce the electromagnetic spectrum and its effects and uses for mankind.
From The Universe And I Series.
LC NO. 80-706489
Prod-KYTV Dist-AITECH 1977

Visit To St Helens, A C 20 MIN
3/4 OR 1/2 INCH VIDEO CASSETTE
Tells the story of the eruption of Mount St Helens.
From The Nature Episodes Series.
Prod-EDIMGE Dist-EDIMGE

Visit To The Bank, A / Paddington's Patch / In And Out Of Trouble / Paddington At The Tower C 22 MIN
16MM FILM, 3/4 OR 1/2 IN VIDEO K-I
Describes Paddington's adventures at a bank. Tells how he cultivates a garden patch and tests a hammock, with alarming results. Discusses his outing to the Tower of London. Based on the books Paddington Abroad, Paddington's Garden, Paddington At The Tower and Paddington Takes The Test.
From The Paddington Bear, Series 2 Series.
LC NO. 80-707216
Prod-BONDM Dist-FLMFR Prodn-FILMF 1980

Visit To The Dentist, A / Paddington Recommended C 11 MIN
16MM FILM, 3/4 OR 1/2 IN VIDEO K-I
Describes Paddington Bear's visit to the dentist and his masquerade as a restaurant critic. Based on chapters one and six of the book Paddington Takes The Air by Michael Bond.
From The Paddington Bear, Series 1 Series.
LC NO. 80-707230
Prod-BONDM Dist-FLMFR Prodn-FILMF 1977

Visit To The Doctor, A C 30 MIN
1/2 IN VIDEO CASSETTE BETA/VHS P-J
Introduces viewers to a routine pediatric examination through visits with a young sister and brother during a regular check-up. Features Mister Rogers.
From The Mister Rogers - Conceptual Behavior Series.
Prod-BRENTM Dist-BRENTM

Visit To The Doctor, A C 30 MIN
3/4 OR 1/2 INCH VIDEO CASSETTE
Features Mister Rogers in dealing with children's uncertainties and fears about doctors and medical examinations.
From The Mister Rogers' Neighborhood Series.
Prod-FAMCOM Dist-FAMCOM

Visit To The Emergency Department, A C
3/4 OR 1/2 INCH VIDEO CASSETTE
Visits the main areas of a hospital emergency department such as triage, x-ray, suture and waiting room, while showing and explaining some of the common procedures and equipment, featuring Mister Rogers.
From The Let's Talk About The Hospital Series.
Prod-FAMCOM Dist-FAMCOM

Visit To The Emergency Department, A C 30 MIN
1/2 IN VIDEO CASSETTE BETA/VHS P-J
Visits the main areas of a hospital emergency room, such as x-ray, suture and waiting room. Shows and explains common procedures and equipment. Features Mister Rogers.
From The Mister Rogers - Health And Safety Series.
Prod-BRENTM Dist-BRENTM

Visit To The Emergency Department, A (Spanish) C
3/4 OR 1/2 INCH VIDEO CASSETTE
Visits the main areas of a hospital emergency department such as the triage, x-ray, suture and waiting room, while showing and explaining some of the common procedures and equipment. Features Mister Rogers.
From The Let's Talk About The Hospital Series.
Prod-FAMCOM Dist-FAMCOM

Visit To The Emergency Department, A (Spanish) C 30 MIN
1/2 IN VIDEO CASSETTE BETA/VHS P-J
Visits the main areas of a hospital emergency room, such as x-ray, suture and waiting room. Shows and explains common procedures and equipment. Features Mister Rogers.
From The Mister Rogers - Health And Safety Series.
Prod-BRENTM Dist-BRENTM

Visit To The John Birch Society, A C 27 MIN
16MM FILM OPTICAL SOUND A
Presents G Edward Griffin who guides a tour of the facilities of the John Birch Society, showing the headquarters in Belmont, Massachusetts and regional offices in San Marino, California. Tells about its publishing house, two magazines, four hundred book stores and reading rooms, its nationwide speakers bureau and youth program. Focuses on membership activities across the country and provides a brief bio graphical information about the founder of the organization, Robert Welch.
LC NO. 73-700816
Prod-AMMED Dist-AMMED 1972

Visit To The National Gallery Of Art, A C 27 MIN
16MM FILM OPTICAL SOUND I-C A
Tours the National Gallery of Art in Washington. Shows the work of Duccio, Tintoretto, Rembrandt, Membling, Raphael, Gerard David, Sebastian Bourdon, Castagno, Barbarini Master and many others explaining the significance of the Bible stories portrayed.
From The Human Dimension Series.
LC NO. 73-700934
Prod-GRACUR Dist-GRACUR 1972

Visit To The Sepulcher, The C 30 MIN
16MM FILM OPTICAL SOUND
Relates the Gospel story of the first Easter, including the appearance of the Archangel to the Maries at Christ's sepulcher, their discovery that the tomb is empty, the race of Peter and John to join the Maries.
Prod-TW Dist-TW

Visit To The World Of Sholom Aleichem, A, Pt 1 B 30 MIN
16MM FILM OPTICAL SOUND
Features Maurice Samuel and Mark Van Doren who discuss shtetl life as reflected in the works of Sholom Aleichem, his role as the representative of that world and one of the characters which he created—Tevya, the dairyman. Includes the reading of illustrative selections from Maurice Samuel's 'THE WORLD OF SHOLOM ALEICHEM.'
LC NO. FIA64-1182
Prod-JTS Dist-NAAJS Prodn-NBC 1960

Visit To The World Of Sholom Aleichem, A, Pt 2 B 30 MIN
16MM FILM OPTICAL SOUND
Features Maurice Samuel and Mark Van Doren who discusses Manachem Mendel, a character created by Sholom Aleichem, and the significance of the sabbath in the world of Sholom Aleichem, as well as the stories, 'THE SEAT OF THE EASTERN WALL' and 'THE JUDGEMENT OF REB YOZIFEL.' Includes selected readings from the two stories.
LC NO. FIA64-1183
Prod-JTS Dist-NAAJS Prodn-NBC 1960

Visit To The World Of The Muffins, Pt 1 C 14 MIN
2 INCH VIDEOTAPE
See series title for descriptive statement.
From The Muffinland Series.
Prod-WGTV Dist-PUBTEL

Visit To The World Of The Muffins, Pt 2 C 14 MIN
2 INCH VIDEOTAPE
See series title for descriptive statement.
From The Muffinland Series.
Prod-WGTV Dist-PUBTEL

Visit To The Zoo, A C 15 MIN
3/4 OR 1/2 INCH VIDEO CASSETTE I-J
Gives detailed information about zoo dwellers and endangered species.
From The Animals And Such Series. Module Green - Animals And Plants
Prod-WHROTV Dist-AITECH 1972

Visit To The Zoo, A - Una Visita Al Zoologico C 11 MIN
16MM FILM, 3/4 OR 1/2 IN VIDEO P-I
Shows children on a classroom field trip to the zoo as they learn places of origin of gorillas, lions, giraffes, rhinos, bears and other animals. Teaches English to Spanish-speaking children.
From The Bilingual Film Series, Module 2 - Zoo Animals Series.
Prod-BRNTNO Dist-CAROUF 1973

Visit To Tuskegee, A C 10 MIN
16MM FILM OPTICAL SOUND
Highlights the various activities and work of the VA Negro Hospital at Tuskegee. Points out that the institution has done particularly noteworthy work in malaria therapy and group therapy programs.
Prod-USVA Dist-USVA

Visit To Wild Rice Country, A C 10 MIN
16MM FILM, 3/4 OR 1/2 IN VIDEO P-I
Shows the harvesting and preparation techniques of wild rice and provides insight into the Great Lakes region. Includes a visit with the Chippewa Indians which shows that harvesting techniques have changed very little in a thousand years.
From The Visit To Series.
Prod-JOU Dist-JOU 1975

Visit To—A Series
16MM FILM, 3/4 OR 1/2 IN VIDEO P-I
Views various aspects of nature.
Prod-JOU Dist-JOU

Let's Go Out Together	013 MIN
Visit To A Container Port, A	012 MIN
Visit To A County Fair, A	011 MIN
Visit To A Dairy Farm, A	012 MIN
Visit To A Honey Bee Farm, A	010 MIN
Visit To A Maple Sugar Farm, A - Sugarbush	011 MIN
Visit To A Movie Studio, A	014 MIN
Visit To A Nature Center, A	012 MIN
Visit To A Pond, A	009 MIN
Visit To A Sheep Farm, A	012 MIN
Visit To A Theatre, A	014 MIN
Visit To A Wild Bird Island, A	009 MIN
Visit To An Airport, A	012 MIN
Visit To Apple Cider Country, A	016 MIN
Visit To Snow Country, A	009 MIN
Visit To Wild Rice Country, A	010 MIN
Visit With Farmer Joe, A	013 MIN
Visit With The Animal Doctors, A	011 MIN
Visit With The Goldminers, A	014 MIN
Visit With The Ranchers, A	016 MIN

Visit With A Jean Ayres, A C 30 MIN
3/4 INCH VIDEO CASSETTE PRO
Presents an interview with Dr A Jean Ayres about her background in occupational therapy and research. Includes a tour of her clinic and a discussion of the therapeutic equipment used there.
Prod-AOTA Dist-AOTA 1978

Visit With Beatrice Wade, A, Pt 1 C 30 MIN
3/4 INCH VIDEO CASSETTE PRO
Begins an interview with Beatrice Wade, occupational therapist.
From The Visual History Series.
Prod-AOTA Dist-AOTA 1979

Visit With Beatrice Wade, A, Pt 2 C 30 MIN
3/4 INCH VIDEO CASSETTE PRO
Concludes an interview with Beatrice Wade, occupational therapist.
From The Visual History Series.
Prod-AOTA Dist-AOTA 1979

Visit With Betty Crocker, A C 15 MIN
16MM FILM OPTICAL SOUND H A
Presents an intimate view of the Betty Crocker kitchens, their service to homemakers and philosophy of helpfulness.
Prod-GEMILL Dist-GEMILL

Visit With Bill Peet, A C 14 MIN
3/4 OR 1/2 INCH VIDEO CASSETTE P-J A
Capsulizes selected stories written by children's book author and illustrator Bill Peet and recollects their inspirations. Looks at examples of his ink-and-colored pencil drawings.
LC NO. 83-706382
Prod-HMC Dist-HMC 1983

Visit With Clare Spackman, A C 30 MIN
3/4 INCH VIDEO CASSETTE PRO
Presents an interview with Clare Spackman, occupational therapist.
From The Visual History Series.
Prod-AOTA Dist-AOTA 1979

Visit With David Macaulay, A C 25 MIN
3/4 OR 1/2 INCH VIDEO CASSETTE
Visits the studio of book illustrator and architect David Macaulay to learn how he constructs his pen-and-ink drawings. Talks about his educational and professional background.
LC NO. 83-706383
Prod-HMC Dist-HMC 1983

Visit With Don Juan In Hell, A C 22 MIN
16MM FILM, 3/4 OR 1/2 IN VIDEO H-C A
Explores the success of George Bernard Shaw's play, Don Juan In Hell. Traces the author's life with photographs and live footage and presents comments by actors and actresses concerning the play.
Prod-KROWN Dist-MCFI 1975

Visit With Dr Sidney Licht, A, Pt 1 C 30 MIN
3/4 INCH VIDEO CASSETTE PRO
Begins an interview with Dr Sidney Licht, occupational therapist.
From The Visual History Series.
Prod-AOTA Dist-AOTA 1979

Visit With Dr Sidney Licht, A, Pt 2 C 30 MIN
3/4 INCH VIDEO CASSETTE PRO
Concludes an interview with Dr Sidney Licht, occupational therapist.
From The Visual History Series.
Prod-AOTA Dist-AOTA 1979

Visit With Farmer Joe, A C 13 MIN
16MM FILM, 3/4 OR 1/2 IN VIDEO P-I
Introduces children to the world of farm animals and their products.
From The Visit To Series.
Prod-BERLET Dist-JOU 1975

Visit With Helen Willard, A C 30 MIN
3/4 INCH VIDEO CASSETTE PRO
Presents an interview with Helen Willard, occupational therapist.
From The Visual History Series.
Prod-AOTA Dist-AOTA 1979

Visit With Isaac Stern, A B 30 MIN
16MM FILM OPTICAL SOUND
Interviews Isaac Stern, concert violinist. Explores his attitudes about the United States, the American tradition, Israel and the

world in general and his feelings toward his artistry and his sense of social responsibility. (Kinescope)
Prod-JTS Dist-NAAJS Prodn-NBCTV 1962

Visit With J I Rodale, A C 15 MIN
16MM FILM, 3/4 OR 1/2 IN VIDEO J-C A
J I Rodale, pioneer organic farmer, talks about his ideas on organic farming, health and ecology.
LC NO. 82-707183
Prod-RPFD Dist-BULFRG 1972

Visit With Leland Jacobs, A C 12 MIN
16MM FILM OPTICAL SOUND
Documents a visit with a third grade class by teacher and writer Dr Leland Jacobs. Shows the expressions and reactions of the children as they listen to Dr Jacobs.
From The Access To Learning Series.
LC NO. 79-711563
Prod-OSUMPD Dist-OSUMPD 1970

Visit With Lois Duncan, A C 18 MIN
1/2 IN VIDEO CASSETTE BETA/VHS
Presents Lois Duncan, author of young adult suspense novels. Highlights her writing process.
Prod-RDAENT Dist-RDAENT

Visit With Sir John, A C 30 MIN
3/4 INCH VIDEO CASSETTE H-C A
Presents England's Poet Laureate Sir John Betjeman and the First Poetry Quartet exploring the works of 20th century English poets.
From The Anyone For Tennyson Series.
Prod-NETCHE Dist-GPITVL

Visit With The Animal Doctors, A C 11 MIN
16MM FILM, 3/4 OR 1/2 IN VIDEO P-I
Looks at the work of veterinarians.
From The Visit To Series.
Prod-JOU Dist-JOU 1980

Visit With The Goldminers, A C 14 MIN
16MM FILM, 3/4 OR 1/2 IN VIDEO P-I
Shows two children as they learn about gold mines when they visit their uncle in Alaska. Describes the different methods of mining gold and provides information on placer mines as well as underground mines. Visits operational mines, showing how they work and how the gold is processed.
From The Visit To Series.
Prod-JOU Dist-JOU 1983

Visit With The Ranchers, A C 16 MIN
16MM FILM, 3/4 OR 1/2 IN VIDEO P-I
Follows a husband and wife team of cowpunchers through a typical day on the range. Demonstrates the skills of shoeing, riding and roping as well as the veterinary skills necessary for the day-to-day care of a herd of cattle.
From The Visit To Series.
Prod-JOU Dist-JOU 1978

Visiting Teacher, The - A School Social Worker B 19 MIN
16MM FILM OPTICAL SOUND T
Tells the story of the visiting teacher by showing how she works with three children who have problems that encompass the school, home and community.
Prod-VADE Dist-VADE 1964

Visiting The Doctor C 4 MIN
16MM FILM, 3/4 OR 1/2 IN VIDEO K-I
Presents a visit to the doctor's office, where James and his pet frog learn that the doctor can do many things and be a friend as well.
From The Most Important Person - Health And Your Body Series.
Prod-EBEC Dist-EBEC 1972

Visitons La Belgique C 11 MIN
16MM FILM, 3/4 OR 1/2 IN VIDEO H-C
A French language film. Shows the sights that a Flemish boy, a Walloon boy and two French girls see while touring Belgium, including Rubens' house in Antwerp, the costumed stilt-fighters at the Namur festival, the chateau of Bouillon, the Manneken-Pis fountain and historic Grand-Place of Brussels.
From The Pays Francophones Series.
Prod-EBEC Dist-EBEC

Visitor For Christmas, A X 30 MIN
16MM FILM OPTICAL SOUND P-H T R
Aunt Hattie, an unexpected houseguest of the Thompson family during the Christmas season, decides to leave their home when she overhears an uncomplimentary telephone conversation. On her departure, the Thompsons realize they have been acting contrary to the real meaning of Christmas.
LC NO. FIA67-5760
Prod-FAMF Dist-FAMF 1967

Visitor From America B 30 MIN
16MM FILM OPTICAL SOUND
Relates the story of an American Jew's return on Passover to the old country to find a wife who will keep his home in the traditional way. Tells how he falls in love with the matchmaker's daughter but is opposed by her father, and how the rabbi adjudicates. (Kinescope)
Prod-JTS Dist-NAAJS Prodn-NBCTV 1954

Visitors Only C 30 MIN
16MM FILM OPTICAL SOUND R
Tells the story of Paul Rose, a hard-working family man who learns to see the value of regular church attendance.
Prod-GF Dist-GF

Visits In Urology—A Series
PRO
Discusses various aspects of urology.
Prod-EATONL Dist-EATONL 1975

Ectopic Ureterocele 042 MIN
Selected Surgical Approach To Testis 038 MIN
Surgery For Visical Ureteral Reflux 057 MIN
Surgery Of Upper Urinary Tract Stone Disease 039 MIN
Urethral Strictures 049 MIN

Visits With God - Two First Hand Accounts Of Near Death Experiences C 25 MIN
16MM FILM OPTICAL SOUND J-C A
Presents the accounts of two nurses who have had near-death experiences.
LC NO. 80-701404
Prod-SILO Dist-SILO 1980

Vislumbres De Madrid Y Toledo C 17 MIN
16MM FILM, 3/4 OR 1/2 IN VIDEO H-C
A Spanish language film. Views physical and artistic aspects of two Castilian cities, Madrid and Toledo.
Prod-IFB Dist-IFB 1963

Visual Aids C 26 MIN
16MM FILM OPTICAL SOUND C A
Illustrates a variety of conventional audiovisual equipment and techniques, including examples of good utilization practices. Shows the use of the chalk board, magnetic board, models, remote control slide and filmstrip projectors, the opaque projector and various graphic devices.
Prod-USN Dist-MLA 1968

Visual Aids C 27 MIN
16MM FILM - 3/4 IN VIDEO
Shows the right and wrong ways to use visual aids when making a presentation. Covers chalk boards, flannel boards, magnetic boards, charts, diagrams, models, actual products, and movie and overhead projectors.
Prod-BNA Dist-BNA

Visual Alchemy C 8 MIN
16MM FILM OPTICAL SOUND
Presents a variety of images and holographic projections in space.
LC NO. 75-704352
Prod-CANFDC Dist-CANFDC 1973

Visual And Liquid Penetrant Inspection C
3/4 OR 1/2 INCH VIDEO CASSETTE IND
Covers selection of NDT method, relationship of welding processes, discontinuities and inspection methods, visual inspection prior to, during, and after welding, liquid penetrant inspection and fluorescent penetrant method.
From The Welding Inspection And Quality Control Series.
Prod-AMCEE Dist-AMCEE

Visual Arts C 15 MIN
3/4 OR 1/2 INCH VIDEO CASSETTE K-J
See series title for descriptive statement.
From The Arts Express Series.
Prod-KYTV Dist-KYTV 1983

Visual Arts, The C 18 MIN
16MM FILM, 3/4 OR 1/2 IN VIDEO J-C
Presents an introduction to art.
From The Humanities Series.
Prod-MGHT Dist-MGHT Prodn-FALKBG 1971

Visual Arts, The, Pt 1 C 30 MIN
3/4 OR 1/2 INCH VIDEO CASSETTE H-C A
Examines the visual arts as practiced in Japan.
From The Japan - The Living Tradition Series.
Prod-UMA Dist-GPITVL 1976

Visual Arts, The, Pt 2 C 30 MIN
3/4 OR 1/2 INCH VIDEO CASSETTE H-C A
Examines the visual arts as practiced in Japan.
From The Japan - The Living Tradition Series.
Prod-UMA Dist-GPITVL 1976

Visual Clues That Help To Determine Whether A Vowel Sound Will Be Long Or Short... C 20 MIN
3/4 OR 1/2 INCH VIDEO CASSETTE J-H
Presents visual clues that help to determine whether a vowel sound will be long or short, emphasizing vowel pairs.
From The Getting The Word Series. Unit III
Prod-SCETV Dist-AITECH 1974

Visual Day Signals B 14 MIN
16MM FILM OPTICAL SOUND
Shows international day signals for ships not under command, inland day signals and various other signals.
LC NO. FIE52-939
Prod-USN Dist-USNAC 1943

Visual Detection Of Driving While Intoxicated C 10 MIN
16MM FILM, 3/4 OR 1/2 IN VIDEO H A
Illustrates 20 of the most common indicators of DWI, including drifting, weaving, erratic braking and turning, and driving off the roadway. Intended for police officers.
Prod-NHTSA Dist-USNAC 1980

Visual Distress Signals C 10 MIN
3/4 OR 1/2 INCH VIDEO CASSETTE A
Discusses the 1980 US Coast Guard visual distress signal law and requirements, safe handling, and types of visual distress signals.
Prod-USCG Dist-USNAC 1981

Visual Documents C 30 MIN
3/4 OR 1/2 INCH VIDEO CASSETTE
See series title for descriptive statement.
From The Photographic vision - All About Photography Series.
Prod-COAST Dist-CDTEL

Visual Effects - Wizardry On Film C 29 MIN
16MM FILM, 3/4 OR 1/2 IN VIDEO J-C A
Uses Mel Brooks' History Of The World, Part 1 as a backdrop to show the work of visual effects genius Albert Whitlock. Shows how Whitlock superimposes ancient Rome on a California backlot.
Prod-CF Dist-CF 1984

Visual Form Discrimination In The Cat B 11 MIN
16MM FILM SILENT C T
Cats are trained to respond positively to a triangle card in the windows of two or more food boxes. Cats trained in 'PAIRED' stimulus situation 4two boxes) transfer readily to 'UNPAIRED' situations (three or four boxes) and those trained with three or four boxes transfer to two boxes. Triangle choice remains even when stimulus sizes and figure-ground relationships are varied.
Prod-PSUPCR Dist-PSUPCR 1933

Visual Guide To Physical Examination (2nd Ed)—A Series
PRO
Demonstrates how various parts of the human body are examined by physicians.
Prod-LIP Dist-LIP Prodn-JACSTO 1981

Abdomen (2nd Ed) 011 MIN
Breast And Axillae (2nd Ed) 012 MIN
Cardiovascular - Neck Vessels And Heart (2nd 016 MIN
Cardiovascular - Peripheral Vascular (2nd Ed) 011 MIN
Eyes, Ears, And Nose (2nd Ed) 018 MIN
Female Genitalia, Anus And Rectum (2nd Ed) 020 MIN
Head, Face, Mouth, And Neck (2nd Ed) 011 MIN
Male Genitalia, Anus And Hernias (2nd Ed) 012 MIN
Musculoskeletal (2nd Ed) 017 MIN
Neurologic - Cranial Nerves And Sensory 022 MIN
Neurologic - Motor System And Reflexes (2nd Ed) 018 MIN
Thorax And Lungs (2nd Ed) 018 MIN

Visual Heritage, A C 30 MIN
3/4 OR 1/2 INCH VIDEO CASSETTE
See series title for descriptive statement.
From The Photographic Vision - All About Photography Series.
Prod-COAST Dist-CDTEL

Visual History—A Series
PRO
Presents interviews with four pioneers in the field of occupational therapy.
Prod-AOTA Dist-AOTA 1979

Visit With Beatrice Wade, A, Pt 1 030 MIN
Visit With Beatrice Wade, A, Pt 2 030 MIN
Visit With Clare Spackman, A 030 MIN
Visit With Dr Sidney Licht, A, Pt 1 030 MIN
Visit With Dr Sidney Licht, A, Pt 2 030 MIN
Visit With Helen Willard, A 030 MIN

Visual Illusions - Now You See It C 24 MIN
16MM FILM OPTICAL SOUND
Demonstrates visual illusions that can be explained, as well as some that cannot be explained by knowledge of the neurophysiology of the components of the retina and their interconnections. Shows several optical illusions that involve the phenomenon of adaptation.
Prod-BBCTV Dist-OPENU 1982

Visual Illusions - Now You See It C 24 MIN
16MM FILM, 3/4 OR 1/2 IN VIDEO
Demonstrates visual illusions that can be explained, as well as some that cannot be explained by knowledge of the neurophysiology of the components of the retina and their interconnections. Shows several optical illusions that involve the phenomenon of adaptation.
Prod-OPENU Dist-MEDIAG Prodn-BBCTV 1982

Visual Impairement, Pt 1 C 19 MIN
3/4 OR 1/2 INCH VIDEO CASSETTE PRO
Describes an organized approach for the primary care physician to take in diagnosing abnormalities of the cornea, anterior chamber, lens, vitreous cavity and retina. Discusses decreased visual acuity due to uncorrected refractive errors.
Prod-UMICHM Dist-UMICHM 1976

Visual Impairment, Pt 2 C 15 MIN
3/4 OR 1/2 INCH VIDEO CASSETTE PRO
Considers disorders occurring between the retina and brain. Discusses diagnosis of senile macular melanoma and chorioretinitis. Details causes of, and diagnostic procedures to detect, disorders of the optic nerve, including glaucoma, extraocular disorders and optic atrophy.
Prod-UMICHM Dist-UMICHM 1976

Visual Learning—A Series
T
Discusses the use of television in the classroom.
Prod-NYSED Dist-NYSED

Many Faces Of Television, The
Mechanics Of Television, The
Program Acquisition
Television In The Classroom
Towards Visual Learning

Visual Perception C 18 MIN
16MM FILM OPTICAL SOUND
Presents a display of what things appear to be when carefully laid out to be something else.
Prod-THIOKL Dist-THIOKL 1960

Visual Perception C 29 MIN
3/4 INCH VIDEO CASSETTE C A
Tells problems of man who first received sight through an operation at age 50. Shows that visual stimulation is not the same as perception and that the brain needs both innate and learned clues for interpretation.

From The Understanding Human Behavior - An Introduction To Psychology Series. Lesson 10
Prod-COAST Dist-CDTEL

Visual Perception And Failure To Learn B 20 MIN
16MM FILM, 3/4 OR 1/2 IN VIDEO T
Depicts difficulties in learning for children who have disabilities in visual perception. Demonstrates the Marianne Frostig Test and outlines a training program.
Prod-HORNE Dist-AIMS Prodn-HORNE 1970

Visual Perception And Failure To Learn (Spanish) C 20 MIN
16MM FILM, 3/4 OR 1/2 IN VIDEO T
Depicts difficulties in learning for children who have disabilities in visual perception. Demonstrates the Marianne Frostig Test and outlines a training program.
Prod-HORNE Dist-AIMS Prodn-HORNE 1970

Visual Perception Training In The Regular Classroom B 23 MIN
16MM FILM, 3/4 OR 1/2 IN VIDEO T
Demonstrates integration of training in visual perception with training in language and regular curriculum of pre-school and primary grade levels.
Prod-HORNE Dist-AIMS 1970

Visual Percption Training In The Regular Classroom (Spanish) C 23 MIN
16MM FILM, 3/4 OR 1/2 IN VIDEO T
Demonstrates integration of training in visual perception with training in language and regular curriculum of pre-school and primary grade levels.
Prod-HORNE Dist-AIMS 1970

Visual Stretches C 10 MIN
2 INCH VIDEOTAPE
See series title for descriptive statement.
From The Janaki Series.
Prod-WGBHTV Dist-PUBTEL

Visual System - The Globe C 16 MIN
16MM FILM, 3/4 OR 1/2 IN VIDEO PRO
Discusses the location, relations and functions of the structures that comprise the eyeball, including the corneoscleral coat, uveal tract, retina, lens, zonula, accommodation mechanism, posterior and anterior segments and aqueous circulation.
From The Anatomy Of The Human Eye Series.
Prod-BAYCMO Dist-TEF 1972

Visual System - The Visual Pathway C 13 MIN
16MM FILM, 3/4 OR 1/2 IN VIDEO PRO
Explains the path of visual impulses from the globe to the visual cortex, with discussion, in turn of the retina, optic nerve, optic tracts and chiasm and optic radiations.
From The Anatomy Of The Human Eye Series.
Prod-BAYCMO Dist-TEF 1972

Visualing Road C 20 MIN
3/4 OR 1/2 INCH VIDEO CASSETTE
Discusses setting goals to become an all-purpose reader.
From The Efficient Reading - Instructional Tapes Series. Tape 2
Prod-TELSTR Dist-TELSTR

Visualizacion De Un Objeto B 9 MIN
3/4 INCH VIDEO CASSETTE
A Spanish language videorecording. Explains how a blueprint is developed by pointing out how dimensions are shown by different views and how special information is indicated.
LC NO. 79-707560
Prod-USOE Dist-USNAC 1979

Visualization - A Key To Reading C 25 MIN
16MM FILM OPTICAL SOUND C A
Presents procedures for testing and developing the skill of visualization.
LC NO. 72-700947
Prod-SOUND Dist-SOUND 1972

Visualizing An Object B 9 MIN
16MM FILM - 3/4 IN VIDEO
Reading Series. Number 1 Explains how a blueprint is developed, illustrates how dimensions are shown by different views, and points out how special information is indicated on a blueprint. Issued in 1945 as a motion picture.
From The Machine Shop Work - Fundamentals Of Blueprint Reading Series.
LC NO. 79-707982
Prod-USOE Dist-USNAC Prodn-RAYBEL 1979

Visualizing An Object (Spanish) B 9 MIN
16MM FILM OPTICAL SOUND
Tells how a blueprint is developed, how dimensions are shown by different views and how various kinds of information are indicated on a blueprint.
From The Machine Shop Work Series. Fundamentals Of Blueprint Reading, No. 1
LC NO. FIE63-4
Prod-USOE Dist-USNAC 1945

Visually Handicapped In The Mainstream, The C 14 MIN
16MM FILM OPTICAL SOUND T S
Shows how teachers can help visually handicapped children learn skills necessary for mobility and independence.
From The Exceptional Learners Series.
LC NO. 79-700716
Prod-MERILC Dist-MERILC 1978

Visually Impaired, The C 30 MIN
3/4 OR 1/2 INCH VIDEO CASSETTE T
Offers an educational definition of visual impairment and identifies the common behavioral signs which may suggest visual impairment and the special material, equipment and instructional procedures which will assist the visually impaired child.

From The Promises To Keep Series. Module 7
Prod-VPISU Dist-LUF 1979

Vita Stone Working With Indians B 60 MIN
3/4 OR 1/2 INCH VIDEO CASSETTE
Presents Vita Stone, a Caucasian who has been working with Indians in Wisconsin for 20 years as she talks with Ada Deer's graduate students about being Caucasian and working with Indians.
Prod-UWISC Dist-UWISC 1978

Vital Connection, The C 17 MIN
16MM FILM OPTICAL SOUND H-C A
Presents a pictorial discussion of the economic contributions made by small-scale farming and possible steps to encourage agriculture.
LC NO. 79-700610
Prod-FENWCK Dist-FENWCK 1978

Vital Connection, The C
3/4 OR 1/2 INCH VIDEO CASSETTE
Shows a voyage of discovery into the inner space of the human brain, a visual revelation of the workings of the clusters of vital connections that manage conscious and automatic actions and reactions. Depicts tragic consequences of function breakdown and courage of doctors and patients to restore 'the vital connection'.
From The Body Human Series.
Prod-TRAINX Dist-TRAINX

Vital Force, The C 16 MIN
16MM FILM OPTICAL SOUND
Describes in simple terms how the Chicago Board of Trade functions, what a futures market is and the role the futures market plays in the world's economy.
Prod-CBT Dist-MTP

Vital Gases X 20 MIN
2 INCH VIDEOTAPE I
See series title for descriptive statement.
From The Process And Proof Series. No. 29
Prod-MCETV Dist-GPITVL Prodn-WVIZTV

Vital Key To A Better Future For Man C 10 MIN
16MM FILM OPTICAL SOUND
Examines the phosphate-producing area of Florida and explains its importance to the existence of human and animal life.
Prod-FLADC Dist-FLADC

Vital Land, The B 15 MIN
16MM FILM OPTICAL SOUND H-C A
Documents the glorious past, the scenic splendor and the modern achievements of the state of Punjab.
Prod-INDIA Dist-NEDINF

Vital Link—A Series
A
Explains and demonstrates how parents must work with teachers and schools to benefit their children. Emphasises the importance of communication between schools, homes and the community.
Prod-EDCC Dist-EDCC

College Planning
Decision Making For Careers
Drugs And Alcohol, Pt 1
Drugs And Alcohol, Pt 2
Family And The Disabled Child 030 MIN
Focus On Values - Teenage Sexuality
Focus On Values - The Age Of Adolescence
Looking For Love - Teenage Parents 029 MIN
Newcomer In School - Adventure Or Agony?
Parent-Teacher Conference
Parents And The Young Teen - A Delicate Balance
Pre-School Readiness - Foundation For Learning
Sense Of Responsibility - How It Grows
Signals Of Change - The Junior High Child 001 MIN
Signals Of Change - The Senior High Child
Single Parent Family
Testing ê What's It All About?
Today's Family - Adjusting To Change

Vital Link, The C 27 MIN
16MM FILM OPTICAL SOUND
Discusses the Parent Advisory Council of Turtle Mountain Community School in Belcourt, North Dakota. Shows how it performs its duties and meets its reponsibilities in connection with programs funded by the federal government under Title I.
LC NO. 77-700064
Prod-USBIA Dist-BAILYL Prodn-BAILYL 1976

Vital Link, The C 29 MIN
16MM FILM OPTICAL SOUND H A
Presents an overview of the world-wide tracking and data acquisition networks which the National Aeronautics and Space Administration uses to communicate between earth and manned and unmanned spacecraft.
LC NO. FIE67-129
Prod-NASA Dist-NASA 1967

Vital Link, The C 15 MIN
16MM FILM, 3/4 OR 1/2 IN VIDEO
Points out what to do and who to call in medical emergencies. Shows how anyone can become the vital link between a helpless victim and the emergency treatment needed to preserve a life.
Prod-LACFU Dist-IA

Vital Link, The C 15 MIN
3/4 OR 1/2 INCH VIDEO CASSETTE J A
Portrays how emergency medical services are designed to handle many different kinds of medical crises.
Prod-SUTHRB Dist-SUTHRB

Vital Link, The (Spanish) C 15 MIN
3/4 OR 1/2 INCH VIDEO CASSETTE J A
Portrays how emergency medical services are designed to handle many different kinds of medical crises.
Prod-SUTHRB Dist-SUTHRB

Vital Network, A C 10 MIN
3/4 OR 1/2 INCH VIDEO CASSETTE
Discusses the importance of proper telephone communication in a hospital and demonstrates proper techniques.
Prod-AHOA Dist-AHOA 1982

Vital Ocean, The C 29 MIN
16MM FILM OPTICAL SOUND
Describes the current strength of the NATO navies in the Atlantic and explains the task of SCALANT (Supreme Allied Command Atlantic) at Norfolk, Virginia, where officers from six NATO countries work together to coordinate defense plans in the North Atlantic area.
LC NO. 74-705924
Prod-NATO Dist-USNAC

Vital Sea, The C 14 MIN
16MM FILM OPTICAL SOUND
States that the U S Navy ensures free use of the sea as a means of transportation, a place for recreation and a source of food and natural resources.
LC NO. 74-706600
Prod-USN Dist-USNAC 1973

Vital Service, A C 10 MIN
16MM FILM, 3/4 OR 1/2 IN VIDEO
Introduces the Volunteer Income Tax Assistance (VITA) program, an IRS-sponsored program to train volunteers to assist low-income, non-English speaking and handicapped taxpayers with their income tax forms.
Prod-USIRS Dist-USNAC

Vital Signs C 14 MIN
3/4 OR 1/2 INCH VIDEO CASSETTE IND
Teaches recognition and evaluation of vital and diagnostic signs. Emphasizes need for association of signs to arrive at a diagnosis.
From The Emergency Medical Training Series. Lesson 20
Prod-LEIKID Dist-LEIKID

Vital Signs - Blood Pressure C 20 MIN
16MM FILM - 3/4 IN VIDEO H-C A
Discusses the terminology, equipment and techniques associated with measuring blood pressure.
From The Nurse's Aide, Orderly And Attendant Series.
LC NO. 80-707006
Prod-COPI Dist-COPI 1979

Vital Signs - How To Take Them C 14 MIN
3/4 OR 1/2 INCH VIDEO CASSETTE
Points out which are vital and diagnostic signs, the normal range for each vital sign, how a sphygomomanometer operates to measure blood pressue level and how to use vital sign information to aid diagnosis of victim.
From The Emergency Medical Training Series.
Prod-VTRI Dist-VTRI

Vital Signs - Pulse And Respiration C 17 MIN
16MM FILM - 3/4 IN VIDEO H-C A
Shows techniques for observing and measuring pulse and respiration.
From The Nurse's Aide, Orderly And Attendant Series.
LC NO. 80-707007
Prod-COPI Dist-COPI 1979

Vital Signs - Temperature C 20 MIN
16MM FILM - 3/4 IN VIDEO H-C A
Shows mercury thermometers and the steps to be taken in obtaining and recording temperature readings. Discusses indications for choosing oral, axillary or rectal thermometers.
From The Nurse's Aide, Orderly And Attendant Series.
LC NO. 80-707008
Prod-COPI Dist-COPI 1979

Vital Signs And Their Interrelation - Body Temperature, Pulse, Respiration, Blood Pressure B 32 MIN
16MM FILM OPTICAL SOUND
Discusses the physiology and inter-relationships of the respiratory, heat regulatory and circulatory systems. Shows how to find and record the vital signs-temperature, pulse, respiration and blood pressure.
From The Nursing Series.
LC NO. FIE52-412
Prod-USOE Dist-USNAC Prodn-WILLRD 1945

Vital Signs, Pt 1 - Cardinal Symptoms B 21 MIN
16MM FILM OPTICAL SOUND
Explains temperature, pulse, respiration and blood pressure by means of live action and animation, art work and sound effects. Tells how these vital signs present a picture of the condition of the body.
LC NO. FIE56-384
Prod-USN Dist-USNAC 1956

Vital Signs, Pt 2 - Taking Temperature, Pulse And Respiration B 20 MIN
16MM FILM OPTICAL SOUND
Demonstrates the techniques of taking temperature, pulse and respiration of patients with a variety of conditions. Shows equipment needed and includes sanitary procedures and charting.
LC NO. FIE56-385
Prod-USN Dist-USNAC 1956

Vital Signs, Pt 3 - Taking Blood Pressure B 11 MIN
16MM FILM OPTICAL SOUND
Explains and demonstrates the principles of taking systolic and

diastolic pressures and the procedures followed with patients. Uses sound effects to show the significant changes in pulse tone.
LC NO. FIE56-386
Prod-USN Dist-USNAC 1956

Vital Statistics C 20 MIN
16MM FILM, 3/4 OR 1/2 IN VIDEO J-H
States that all living things use energy. Everyone begins life as a single cell in which energy is consumed and new building material is added, causing growth. Discusses the validity of different methods of prediction, including a sequence showing the birth of a baby.
From The Biology - It's Life Series.
Prod-THAMES Dist-MEDIAG 1980

Vital Statistics Of A Citizen Simply Obtained B 40 MIN
3/4 OR 1/2 INCH VIDEO CASSETTE
Presented by Martha Rosler.
Prod-KITCHN Dist-KITCHN

Vital Statistics Of A Citizen, Simply Obtained C 40 MIN
3/4 INCH VIDEO CASSETTE
Shows how women come to see themselves as objects. Shows a part-by-part measurement of a woman by a white-coated examiner who is eventually joined by a chorus of three women who use whistles, bells and horns to judge whether the female subject's body complies with the arbitrary standards of physical measurement. Presents a litany of crimes against women.
Prod-WMENIF Dist-WMENIF

Vital Waterway - The Suez Canal C 14 MIN
16MM FILM OPTICAL SOUND I-C A
Examines the past and present history of the Suez Canal and its role in the Middle East. Covers the construction and history of the canal, political issues which resulted in the closing of the canal and its subsequent re-opening in 1975.
From The Screen News Digest Series. Vol 18, Issue 3
LC NO. 76-701848
Prod-HEARST Dist-HEARST 1975

Vitamin Deficiencies In Chickens And Turkeys C 23 MIN
16MM FILM OPTICAL SOUND
Presents various symptoms exhibited by chickens and turkey which are deficient in vitamins A, D, E, K, riboflavin, biotin and folicin.
Prod-COLOSU Dist-COLOSU 1975

Vitamins C 30 MIN
3/4 OR 1/2 INCH VIDEO CASSETTE
See series title for descriptive statement.
From The Food For Life Series.
Prod-MSU Dist-MSU

Vitamins - What Do They Do C 22 MIN
16MM FILM, 3/4 OR 1/2 IN VIDEO J-C A
Defines vitamins and explains how they work in the human body. Debunks myths about vitamins and points out the dangers of taking excessive amounts of vitamin supplements.
Prod-HIGGIN Dist-HIGGIN 1979

Vitamins / Vocational Schools / Homes C
3/4 OR 1/2 INCH VIDEO CASSETTE
Provides tips on selecting vocational schools and buying vitamins and homes.
From The Consumer Survival Series.
Prod-MDCPB Dist-MDCPB

Vitamins And Some Deficiency Diseases (2nd Ed) C 35 MIN
16MM FILM OPTICAL SOUND PRO
Presents vitamins A, C, D, E, K and the vitamin B complex. Demonstrates deficiencies in experimental animals, including cheilosis, scurvy, rickets, pellagra and vitamin K deficiency. Shows color rerroductions of early ocular changes due to vitamin A and riboflavin deficiencies as seen through the slit lamp and of motor disturbances in pigs suffering from pyridoxine and panothenic acid deficiencies.
Prod-ACYLLD Dist-LEDR 1955

Vitamins From Food C 20 MIN
16MM FILM, 3/4 OR 1/2 IN VIDEO I-J
Re-enacts the drama surrounding the discovery of vitamins. Features the story of Dr James Lind, curing scurvy aboard a ship in 1740, and Dr Christian Riijkman, curing beriberi in Java in 1890. Explains that the sailors and the Japanese were afflicted with vitamin deficiency diseases because of their unvaried diets. Describes their quick recuperation when foods containing the missing vitamins were included in their diet.
From The Nutrition Education Series.
Prod-PEREN Dist-PEREN 1973

Vito Acconci C 55 MIN
3/4 OR 1/2 INCH VIDEO CASSETTE
Features an interview with Vito Acconci. Presented by Kate Horsfield and Lyn Blumenthal.
Prod-ARTINC Dist-ARTINC

Vito Acconci - Association Area B 30 MIN
3/4 OR 1/2 INCH VIDEO CASSETTE
Focuses on duality.
Prod-ARTINC Dist-ARTINC

Vito Acconci - Claim Excerpts B 30 MIN
3/4 OR 1/2 INCH VIDEO CASSETTE
Features duality.
Prod-ARTINC Dist-ARTINC

Vito Acconci - Face-Off B 30 MIN
3/4 OR 1/2 INCH VIDEO CASSETTE
Highlights duality.
Prod-ARTINC Dist-ARTINC

Vito Acconci - Open Book B 10 MIN
3/4 OR 1/2 INCH VIDEO CASSETTE
Considers duality.
Prod-ARTINC Dist-ARTINC

Vito Acconci - Pryings B 20 MIN
3/4 OR 1/2 INCH VIDEO CASSETTE
Presents a silent picture. Deals with duality.
Prod-ARTINC Dist-ARTINC

Vito Acconci - The Red Tapes B 140 MIN
3/4 OR 1/2 INCH VIDEO CASSETTE
Explores duality.
Prod-ARTINC Dist-ARTINC

Vito Acconci - Turn-On B 20 MIN
3/4 OR 1/2 INCH VIDEO CASSETTE
Addresses duality.
Prod-ARTINC Dist-ARTINC

Vito Acconci - Videoviewed by Willoughby Sharp B 30 MIN
3/4 OR 1/2 INCH VIDEO CASSETTE
Presents Vito Acconci discussing his early background, poetry and artistic development.
Prod-EAI Dist-EAI

Vitrectomy - After Perforating Injury With Intraocular Foreign Body C 10 MIN
16MM FILM OPTICAL SOUND
Shows the surgical technique for vitrectomy through the pars plana. Demonstrates how the vitreous infusion suction cutter with fiber optics illumination is used to remove a non-magnet intraocular foreign body. Points out that fiber optics illumination is used as the only illumination source for the operative procedure and the photography.
LC NO. 73-702391
Prod-UMIAMI Dist-UMIAMI 1973

Vitrectomy - For Treatment Of Massive Periretinal Proliferation C 19 MIN
16MM FILM OPTICAL SOUND
Demonstrates surgical removal of the vitreous and preretinal membranes in an eye with total retinal detachment and massive periretinal proliferations. Shows how the retina is finally attached with intraocular gas and a circumferential buckle.
LC NO. 75-703547
Prod-USVA Dist-BPEI Prodn-UMIAMI 1975

Vitrectomy With Removal Of Preretinal Membranes In Diabetic Retinopathy C 15 MIN
16MM FILM OPTICAL SOUND
Demonstrates a vitrectomy with removal of clear anterior vitreous and cutting of posterior vitreous bands exerting traction on the retina. Shows how the contracting preretinal membranes are peeled off the retinal surface lacing only stumps of small proliferative stalks, pointing out that the final vision in the eye was as good as the postoperative vision.
LC NO. 74-702918
Prod-BPEI Dist-BPEI 1974

Viva La Causa C 12 MIN
16MM FILM OPTICAL SOUND
Provides a record of the making of a mural in Chicago's Chicano community and traces the mural movement back to murals done in Mexico.
Prod-KART Dist-KART 1974

Viva Las Vegas C 20 MIN
3/4 OR 1/2 INCH VIDEO CASSETTE J-C A
Takes viewers to Las Vegas to see the big hotels, gambling casinos and some of the city's finest entertainment.
LC NO. 82-706791
Prod-AWSS Dist-AWSS 1980

Viva Magritte C 20 MIN
3/4 OR 1/2 INCH VIDEO CASSETTE
Prod-EAI Dist-EAI

Viva Mexico - A Cultural Portrait C 25 MIN
16MM FILM, 3/4 OR 1/2 IN VIDEO I
Presents a cultural portrait of Mexico, including artists at work, village life, traditional Indian dances, customs, art and architecture dating back to pre-Columbian times, archeology and fiestas.
Prod-MGHT Dist-MGHT 1971

Viva San Fermin - The Bulls Of Pamplona C 48 MIN
3/4 OR 1/2 INCH VIDEO CASSETTE H-C A
Uses the importance of bullfighting to explain the Spanish concepts of machismo, honor and immortality.
LC NO. 84-706104
Prod-BOWENI Dist-FOTH 1984

Vivaldi, The Flute And James Galway C 26 MIN
16MM FILM, 3/4 OR 1/2 IN VIDEO J-C A
Presents Italian composer Antonio Vivaldi (1675-1743), who standardized the concerto grosso as a three-movement musical form and enhanced the virtuoso element in solo passages. Features professional musician James Galway playing some of Vivaldi's music on the flute.
From The Musical Triangle Series.
Prod-THAMES Dist-MEDIAG 1975

Vive Le Quebec C 14 MIN
16MM FILM OPTICAL SOUND
A French-language film which presents the many faces of Quebec, from the silent grandeur of her territory to the hustle-bustle of her city streets.
Prod-QDTFG Dist-MTP

Vive Le Tour C 19 MIN
16MM FILM OPTICAL SOUND
Depicts the marathon Tour de France bicycle race held each July, describing the speed, the collisions, the uproar, and the exploitation. Directed by Louis Malle.
Prod-UNKNWN Dist-NYFLMS 1962

Vivika Heino, Potter C 30 MIN
2 INCH VIDEOTAPE
See series title for descriptive statement.
From The World Of The American Craftsman Series.
Prod-WENHTV Dist-PUBTEL

Vivre Mieux, Demain C 10 MIN
16MM FILM, 3/4 OR 1/2 IN VIDEO I
A French language film. Describes the present and the future of industry and commerce in France. Evaluates the importance of the craftsman as well as the technician in modern France.
From The La France Contemporaine Series.
Prod-EBEC Dist-EBEC 1971

Vladimir Nabokov - LOLITA C 29 MIN
2 INCH VIDEOTAPE
Presents readings from the novel LOLITA by Vladimir Nabokov.
From The One To One Series.
Prod-WETATV Dist-PUBTEL

VLED Devices - Process And Fabrication C 30 MIN
3/4 OR 1/2 INCH VIDEO CASSETTE PRO
Gives brief summary of technology for slice processing and fabrication of visible optoelectronic devices to aid in application of these devices.
From The Optoelectronics, Part II - Optoelectronic Displays Series.
Prod-TXINLC Dist-TXINLC

VLSI - Its Impact On Your Career C 300 MIN
3/4 OR 1/2 INCH VIDEO CASSETTE PRO
Describes the technology and impact of VLSI. Covers topics such as specific application of VLSI in industry and computer graphic aspects of VLSI.
Prod-AMCEE Dist-AMCEE

VLSI Design—A Series
PRO
Uses classroom format to videotape one 1-hour and one 1 1/2 hour lectures weekly for 13 weeks and 39 cassettes. Covers IC Economics, Basic MOS Theory and MOS processing, MOS logic structures and analysis, IC design cycle, MOS layout and introduction to CAD.
Prod-USCCE Dist-AMCEE

VLSI Devices And Technology—A Series
PRO
Discusses advanced coverage of silicon VLSI device physics and fabrication technology. Concentrates on the fabrica- tion techniques used to make modern high performance ICs, and examines how these techniques impact device electrical characteristics and performance.
Prod-STITV Dist-AMCEE

VLSI Logic Design C 39 MIN
3/4 OR 1/2 INCH VIDEO CASSETTE PRO
Uses classroom format to videotape one 1-hour and one 1 1/2 hour lecture weekly for 13 weeks and 39 cassettes. Covers introduction to VLSI CAD, design hierarchy, design rules, symbolic layout language, design methodologies, logic implementation and design tools.
Prod-USCCE Dist-AMCEE

VMCJ C 15 MIN
16MM FILM OPTICAL SOUND
Presents the story of a photographic aerial reconnaissance squadron in combat.
LC NO. 74-706601
Prod-USN Dist-USNAC 1970

VME Bus, The C 60 MIN
3/4 OR 1/2 INCH VIDEO CASSETTE C
See series title for descriptive statement.
From The Microcomputer Bus Structures Series.
Prod-NEU Dist-AMCEE

Vocabulary C 6 MIN
3/4 OR 1/2 INCH VIDEO CASSETTE
See series title for descriptive statement.
From The Four Short Programs By Woody Vasulka Series.
Prod-EAI Dist-EAI

Vocabulary - Language Corner B 15 MIN
2 INCH VIDEOTAPE P
See series title for descriptive statement.
From The Language Corner Series.
Prod-CVETVC Dist-GPITVL Prodn-WCVETV

Vocabulary And Word Analogies C 120 MIN
3/4 OR 1/2 INCH VIDEO CASSETTE
See series title for descriptive statement.
From The SAT Exam Preparation Series.
Prod-KRLSOF Dist-KRLSOF 1985

Vocabulary Of Art, The C 29 MIN
2 INCH VIDEOTAPE
See series title for descriptive statement.
From The Museum Open House Series.
Prod-WGBHTV Dist-PUBTEL

Vocabulary Road C 20 MIN
3/4 OR 1/2 INCH VIDEO CASSETTE
Focuses on working with vocabulary to read better and understand more.
From The Efficient Reading - Instructional Tapes Series. Tape 3
Prod-TELSTR Dist-TELSTR

Vocabulary Skills—A Series
16MM FILM, 3/4 OR 1/2 IN VIDEO P-I
Presents vocabulary skills.
Prod-BFA Dist-PHENIX Prodn-BEAN 1976

Word Wise - Antonyms 12 MIN

Word Wise - Compound Words 10 MIN
Word Wise - Homographs 12 MIN
Word Wise - Homonyms 11 MIN
Word Wise - Prefixes 11 MIN
Word Wise - Root Words 12 MIN
Word Wise - Suffixes 12 MIN
Word Wise - Synonyms 13 MIN
Word Wise - Word Families 9 MIN

Vocal Nodules C 10 MIN
3/4 OR 1/2 INCH VIDEO CASSETTE P-I
Shows that vocal nodules can be confusing to a child because it may seem to be a punishment for shouting or getting angry. Illustrates what vocal nodules actually are and helps children find substitutes for shouting and alternative way of expressing anger.
From The Children's Medical Series.
Prod-HFDT Dist-MTI 1982

Vocal Quality Counts C 30 MIN
3/4 OR 1/2 INCH VIDEO CASSETTE
See series title for descriptive statement.
From The Your Speaking Image - When Women Talk Business Series.
Prod-WHATV Dist-DELTAK

Vocal Tract Dynamics And Stuttering Therapy C 111 MIN
3/4 OR 1/2 INCH VIDEO CASSETTE
Reviews research describing phonatory dysfunction as a component of stuttering. Emphasizes therapy techniques based on the recognition of the laryngeal components of stuttering. Includes clinical demonstrations.
Prod-PUAVC Dist-PUAVC

Vocalization And Speech In Chimpanzees B 12 MIN
16MM FILM OPTICAL SOUND C A
Shows typical chimpanzee vocalizations and demonstrates that vocal responses can be conditioned. Portrays in detail the training of a female to whisper 'MAMA,' 'PAPA' and 'CUP.'
Prod-HAYESS Dist-PSUPCR 1950

Vocational Opportunities In High School C 14 MIN
16MM FILM, 3/4 OR 1/2 IN VIDEO J-H
Offers practical suggestions in the area of vocational education for high school students. Includes a broad sampling of vocational shops and classes and points out the advantages of early exposure to different trades and fields of employment.
Prod-RUSIRV Dist-EBEC 1973

Vocational Rehabilitation In A Community Hospital C 27 MIN
16MM FILM OPTICAL SOUND C T
Discusses a vocational rehabilitation program for the disabled, using the hospital as a job training ground. Follows patients and staff through the rehabilitation process from counseling to placement.
LC NO. FIA68-860
Prod-ARHEUM Dist-CFDC Prodn-CFDC 1967

Vocational Skillfilms - Machine Shop Skills—A Series
16MM FILM, 3/4 OR 1/2 IN VIDEO IND
Presents specific machine shop skills such as the use of the engine lathe, grinding machine, and the horizontal milling machines.
Prod-RTBL Dist-RTBL 1982

Introduction To Grinding Machines 014 MIN
Introduction To Horizontal Milling Machines 014 MIN
Introduction To The Engine Lathe 014 MIN
Introduction To Vertical Millincg Machines 014 MIN
Mounting And Dressing Grinding Machines 014 MIN
Taper Turning 014 MIN

Vocational Skillfilms - Woodworking Skills—A Series
16MM FILM, 3/4 OR 1/2 IN VIDEO IND
Discusses various aspects of woodworking.
Prod-RTBL Dist-RTBL 1982

Joining Wood With Nails 014 MIN
Joining Wood With Screws 014 MIN
Measuring, Marking And Sawing Wood 014 MIN

Vocational Time Vs Management Time C 20 MIN
3/4 OR 1/2 INCH VIDEO CASSETTE
See series title for descriptive statement.
From The Time Management For Managers And Professionals Series.
Prod-DELTAK Dist-DELTAK Prodn-ONCKEW

Vocational Visions—A Series
J-H
Investigates 38 distinct career areas clustered around nine general career areas.
Prod-GA Dist-GA 1984

Agricultural Cluster 020 MIN
Business/Office Cluster 030 MIN
Communications Cluster 010 MIN
Construction Cluster 015 MIN
Health-Related Cluster 025 MIN
Personal Service Cluster 020 MIN
Repair Cluster 015 MIN
Technical/Manufacturing Cluster 1 020 MIN
Technical/Manufacturing Cluster 2 025 MIN
Transportation/Mechanical Cluster 020 MIN

Vocations In Agriculture C 15 MIN
16MM FILM, 3/4 OR 1/2 IN VIDEO J-H
Explores opportunities, requirements and rewards of specific careers in agriculture. Emphasizes need for specialized college training.
Prod-JOU Dist-JOU 1965

Vogues Of 1938 B 113 MIN
16MM FILM OPTICAL SOUND
Tells the story of the head of a famous fashion house who has two problems - financing his wife's acting ambitions and helping socialite escape an arranged marriage.
Prod-TLECUL Dist-TLECUL

Voice B 20 MIN
16MM FILM OPTICAL SOUND C A
See series title for descriptive statement.
From The All That I Am Series.
Prod-MPATI Dist-NWUFLM

Voice At Work C 29 MIN
3/4 INCH VIDEO CASSETTE
Explains how langauge and behavior work together. Shows how the different regions of sound-producing anatomy are responsible for the quality, tone and pitch of the words we hear.
From The Pike On Language Series.
Prod-UMITV Dist-UMITV 1977

Voice Box, The C 4 MIN
16MM FILM, 3/4 OR 1/2 IN VIDEO K-I
Depicts a side show barker's efforts to sell the children a 'WONDROUS' voice box. Follows as Fumble intervenes to explain that everyone already has a voice box and it works better than any that can be purchased.
From The Most Important Person - Health And Your Body Series.
Prod-EBEC Dist-EBEC 1972

Voice Cries Out, A B 29 MIN
16MM FILM OPTICAL SOUND J-C A
Pictures the sculpture and architecture of Florence, Italy. Reviews the history of the Medici family. Exposes the forces which encouraged and undermined the greatness of Florence. Discusses the Pazzi conspiracy and the influence of a Dominican monk, Savanarola.
From The Legacy Series.
LC NO. 75-707214
Prod-NET Dist-IU 1965

Voice From The Past, A C 30 MIN
3/4 OR 1/2 INCH VIDEO CASSETTE C A
Presents an adaptation of the short story A Voice From The Past by P G Wodehouse.
From The Wodehouse Playhouse Series.
Prod-BBCTV Dist-TIMLIF 1980

Voice In The Bells, The C 28 MIN
16MM FILM OPTICAL SOUND P-J
Presents the 1972 open house day at Washington Cathedral as seen through the eyes of a 12-year-old boy. Includes views of the cathedral's windows, carvings, tower and bells.
Prod-NCATHA Dist-NCATHA 1972

Voice In The City B 28 MIN
16MM FILM OPTICAL SOUND H-C A
Presents a look at district number 37 station, a county and municipal union in New York City.
LC NO. 72-703116
Prod-PFLMAS Dist-PFLMAS 1969

Voice In The Wilderness, A B 40 MIN
16MM FILM OPTICAL SOUND P-C A
Dramatizes the story of John the Baptist beginning with his birth and his early life in the desert as preparation for his ministry as forerunner to Christ.
Prod-CAFM Dist-CAFM

Voice Of Cape Cod, The C 12 MIN
3/4 OR 1/2 INCH VIDEO CASSETTE J A
Portrays turn-of-the-century Massachusetts and the occasion of the first transatlantic wireless radio transmission. Discusses the 'Father of Radio,' Guglielmo Marconi, and traces the development of radio from its beginnings to ship-to-shore and plane-to-ground transmission. Uses archival footage, vintage photos and period music.
Prod-USNPS Dist-USNAC 1984

Voice Of La Raza C 54 MIN
16MM FILM, 3/4 OR 1/2 IN VIDEO
Presents a documentary report from El Barrios of Spanish speaking America dealing with job and cultural discrimination against Spanish surnamed Americans.
Prod-EQEMOP Dist-GREAVW 1970

Voice Of The Desert, The C 22 MIN
16MM FILM, 3/4 OR 1/2 IN VIDEO I-C A
Pictures the plants and animals of the desert community in Arizona. Joseph Wood Krutch narrates. Adapted from an NBC news production.
Prod-NBCTV Dist-MGHT 1964

Voice Of The Fugitive C 28 MIN
16MM FILM, 3/4 OR 1/2 IN VIDEO I-H
Depicts a group of slaves seeking freedom in Canada in 1851. Tells how Henry Bibb's newspaper, The Voice Of The Fugitive, inspired their quest for freedom.
From The Adventures In History Series.
LC NO. 82-706170
Prod-NFBC Dist-FI 1978

Voice Of The Insect B 26 MIN
16MM FILM, 3/4 OR 1/2 IN VIDEO J-C A
Proves that insects talk to each other and explains that the nerve cells of man are fundamentally the same as those of an insect.
Prod-CBSTV Dist-CAROUF

Voice Of Those Who Are Not Here, The C 45 MIN
16MM FILM, 3/4 OR 1/2 IN VIDEO
Introduces several people who have experienced detention and torture at the hands of the special police of nations throughout the world.
Prod-RASKER Dist-FLMLIB 1982

Voice To Be Heard, A C 51 MIN
16MM FILM OPTICAL SOUND H-C A
Traces the election of members of the National Aboriginal Consultative Committee in Australia. Shows how the committee was formed to give aborigines a more direct voice in the government of Australia.
LC NO. 75-702396
Prod-FLMAUS Dist-AUIS 1975

Voice Your Choice C 10 MIN
3/4 OR 1/2 INCH VIDEO CASSETTE K-P
Points out that some methods of solving social problems are more positive than other methods.
From The Book, Look And Listen Series.
Prod-MDDE Dist-AITECH 1977

Voices From A Steeltown C 29 MIN
16MM FILM - 3/4 IN VIDEO A
Tells the story of Braddock, PA, a thriving steel mill boom town in the 1920's, now poverty-stricken and dying from the loss of its main industry. Recalls its history and documents the present through old photographs, ads and clippings, personal and family recollections and interviews with residents.
Prod-BUBAT Dist-NEWDAY

Voices From The South C 30 MIN
3/4 INCH VIDEO CASSETTE H-C A
Explores the wealth of poetry written by native Southern poets and by poets who have moved to the South. Features Ruby Dee and the First Poetry Quartet.
From The Anyone For Tennyson Series.
Prod-NETCHE Dist-GPITVL

Voices From Within C 20 MIN
16MM FILM, 3/4 OR 1/2 IN VIDEO
Examines the problems of long-term women prisoners at Bedford Hills Correction Facility. Captures the feelings and emotions, loneliness and desperation of the inmates. Discusses the effects of being separated from their families for many years.
Prod-PACSFM Dist-CNEMAG 1977

Voices In Society—A Series

Prod-TRAVLR Dist-WSTGLC 1974

How To Talk With Your Teenager About VD 28 MIN

Voices Of Blue And Grey - The Civil War C
3/4 OR 1/2 INCH VIDEO CASSETTE H
Depicts the Civil War era, its people, issues, battles and regional feelings.
Prod-GA Dist-GA

Voices Of Dance—A Series

Presents programs from the New York City Cable TV series Eye On Dance.
Prod-ARCVID Dist-ARCVID

Alexandra Danilova And Frederic Franklin 030 MIN
Change Of Attitudes Within The Ballet 030 MIN
Influences Of Bauhaus And Russian 030 MIN
Interpreting Choreographers From The 50's And 030 MIN

Voices Of Israel C 18 MIN
16MM FILM OPTICAL SOUND
Uses three generations of a family to explore Israel's past, present and future, emphasizing the nation's economic needs. Examines the cost of peace as well as the cost of settling new immigrants and establishing programs to meet the needs of the disadvantaged, aged and handicapped.
LC NO. 80-701440
Prod-UJA Dist-VISION Prodn-VISION 1979

Voices Of The Cave, The C 12 MIN
16MM FILM, 3/4 OR 1/2 IN VIDEO J A
Presents the history of Mammoth Cave in Kentucky from exploration by Indians of the Adena culture more than 4,000 years ago to its use as a mine, a hospital for tubercular patients and an underground church. Includes dramatic re-creations.
Prod-USNPS Dist-USNAC 1984

Voices On The River C 22 MIN
16MM FILM OPTICAL SOUND
Documents the history of the Minnesota River and highlights the town of St Peter, through authentic graphics, commentary and music, and interviews with two elderly local residents.
LC NO. 78-700331
Prod-MASONG Dist-MASONG 1976

Voices, Faces, Brown C 28 MIN
16MM FILM OPTICAL SOUND
Records the events in a typical academic year at Brown University.
LC NO. 79-700339
Prod-BROWNU Dist-BROWNU Prodn-SEVSEA 1978

Voici Des Fruits C 18 MIN
16MM FILM OPTICAL SOUND J A
See series title for descriptive statement.
From The En Francais, Set 1 Series.
Prod-PEREN Dist-CHLTN 1969

Voiding Dysfunction And Urinary Tract Infection C 15 MIN
16MM FILM OPTICAL SOUND
Presents actual cinefluoroscopic studies and pressure measurements obtained from patients with persistent urinary tract infection or with distal urethral stenosis. Defines the aberrations in voiding mechanisms. Describes spasm of the striated external sphincter as a functionally obstructive mechanism which can initiate or perpetuate the infection.
LC NO. 75-702286
Prod-EATONL Dist-EATONL 1970

Voila Gilbert, Le Voila B 13 MIN
16MM FILM OPTICAL SOUND I-H
See series title for descriptive statement.
From The Les Francais Chez Vous Series. Set II, Lesson 20
Prod-PEREN Dist-CHLTN 1967

Voix Et Images De France—A Series
I-C A
Prod-PEREN Dist-CHLTN

A Travers Paris 12 MIN
Au Jardin Public 8 MIN
Images De La Campagne 8 MIN
Images Du Travail 6 MIN
Je Marchais 11 MIN
La Petite Ferme 12 MIN
Le Marche 11 MIN
Le Telephone 6 MIN
Partons En Vacances 6 MIN
Un Homme Tranquille 7 MIN

Volatile Substances C 5 MIN
3/4 INCH VIDEO CASSETTE
Classifies volatile substances with regard to their psychological and physical hazards. Issued in 1971 as a motion picture.
From The Single Concept Drug Film Series.
LC NO. 80-706851
Prod-NIMH Dist-USNAC 1980

Volatiles C 10 MIN
16MM FILM, 3/4 OR 1/2 IN VIDEO
Discusses the characteristics of volatiles. Identifies the signs of use and abuse, the pharmacological and behavioral effects, and the shortand long-term dangers.
From The Drug Information Series.
Prod-MITCHG Dist-MTI 1982

Volcanic Eruptions, Pt 1 B 27 MIN
16MM FILM OPTICAL SOUND C A
Outlines means by which volcanoes are classified and illustrates volcanoes through film clips, stills and diagrams.
Prod-UTEX Dist-UTEX 1960

Volcanic Eruptions, Pt 2 B 26 MIN
16MM FILM OPTICAL SOUND C A
Illustrates the volcanian type of eruption as characterized by Paricutin and Vesuvius. Pictures the Peleean Volcano typified by Me Pelee and the lava dome of Sitkin Island. Summarizes various other kinds of volcanic eruptions.
Prod-UTEX Dist-UTEX 1960

Volcanic Landscapes, Pt 1 C 29 MIN
16MM FILM OPTICAL SOUND
Presents an examination of volcanic processes and landforms using examples from the rich landscapes of the Pacific Northwest. Suggests a source for magma and follows it to the surfaces. Studies lava flows and introduces the effect of gas-charged magma on an eruption. Views the many products and landforms produced by violent Vulcanism.
LC NO. 74-702801
Prod-MMP Dist-MMP 1973

Volcanic Landscapes, Pt 2 C 29 MIN
16MM FILM OPTICAL SOUND J-C A
Uses views of the volcanic landscapes of the Pacific Northwest in order to study special types of volcanic activity and landforms and to relate volcanism to such things as groundwater and hydrothermal activity. Shows the inevitable end of volcanoes through destruction by weathering and erosion.
LC NO. 74-702802
Prod-MMP Dist-MMP 1974

Volcanic Processes And Deposits C 51 MIN
3/4 OR 1/2 INCH VIDEO CASSETTE IND
See series title for descriptive statement.
From The Basic And Petroleum Geology For Non-Geologists - Earth's Interior...-Series
Prod-PHILLP Dist-GPCV

Volcanism B 45 MIN
2 INCH VIDEOTAPE C
See series title for descriptive statement.
From The Physical Science Series. Unit 1 - Geology
Prod-CHITVC Dist-GPITVL Prodn-WTTWTV

Volcano C 11 MIN
16MM FILM, 3/4 OR 1/2 IN VIDEO H-C A
Depicts the 1943 eruption of Paricutin, the Mexican volcano. Points out the formation of the cinder cone, the composition of the smoke column and the origin of the fumaroles and the lava flows.
Prod-UCB Dist-UCEMC 1953

Volcano C 29 MIN
2 INCH VIDEOTAPE
Shows Volcano, West Virginia in 1875 when it was reaping the benefits of the Allegheníes oil boom and possessed its own railroad line, department store and opera house. Explains that the Volcano of today is three oil tanks and a wooden shed on a dirt road.
Prod-WWVUTV Dist-PUBTEL

Volcano C 30 MIN
3/4 OR 1/2 INCH VIDEO CASSETTE P-C A
Presents spectacular footages of the eruption of Kilauea volcano in Hawaii. No narration, but musical background provided.
Prod-HNHIST Dist-HNHIST

Volcano - The Birth Of A Mountain C 24 MIN
16MM FILM, 3/4 OR 1/2 IN VIDEO J-C A
Uses film footage produced over a five-year period to document an extended Hawaiian volcanic eruption from which, in the early 1970's, a whole new mountain emerged. Reveals how the scorching lava flow covered whole forests, generated raging tornadoes and reshaped long segments of coastline during the mountain's creation.
From The Earth Science Program Series.
Prod-EBEC Dist-EBEC 1976

Volcano - The Birth Of A Mountain (Spanish) C 24 MIN
16MM FILM, 3/4 OR 1/2 IN VIDEO J-C A
A Spanish language version of the film and videorecording Volcano - The Birth Of A Mountain.
Prod-EBEC Dist-EBEC 1977

Volcano Hazards In The U S C 30 MIN
3/4 OR 1/2 INCH VIDEO CASSETTE
Prod-RCOMTV Dist-SYLWAT 1982

Volcano In The Azores C 8 MIN
16MM FILM OPTICAL SOUND J-C A
Pictures the 1957 eruption on Fayal Island. Uses animation to explain gases, viscous lava and eruption.
Prod-WSU Dist-WSU 1962

Volcano Surtsey C 26 MIN
16MM FILM OPTICAL SOUND
Shows the cycle of a volcanic eruption near Iceland on November 14, 1963. Discusses the formation of a shield volcano.
Prod-NSN Dist-GIS 1965

Volcanoes C 28 MIN
3/4 OR 1/2 INCH VIDEO CASSETTE
Explores Mount St Helens, Surtsey and Heimay, which provide an explosive backdrop for the examination of igneous activities and the creation of landforms.
From The Earth Explored Series.
Prod-BBCTV Dist-PBS

Volcanoes C 30 MIN
3/4 OR 1/2 INCH VIDEO CASSETTE C
Demonstrates the main types of volcanoes. Explores the possibility of production and avoidance of volcanic eruptions.
From The Earth, Sea And Sky Series.
Prod-DALCCD Dist-DALCCD

Volcanoes - Exploring The Restless Earth C 18 MIN
16MM FILM, 3/4 OR 1/2 IN VIDEO J
Presents scenes of the volcanic activity that formed two new islands off the coast of Iceland in the 1960's. Examines three other volcanoes and views a fourth volcano which document the destructive power of the volcanic process.
From The Earth Science Program Series.
Prod-EBEC Dist-EBEC 1973

Volcanoes - Vulcan's Forge C 18 MIN
3/4 OR 1/2 INCH VIDEO CASSETTE I
Explores the development of volcanic eruptions, shows island chains formed by volcanic activity and demonstrates uses for volcanic materials.
From The Natural Science Specials Series. Module Blue
Prod-UNPRO Dist-AITECH 1973

Volcanoes Of Hawaii B 6 MIN
16MM FILM OPTICAL SOUND
Presents excerpts from Screen News Digest Films which illustrates that Hawaii's landscape had volcanoes for shows of which Haleakala Crater, Kilauea and Mauna Loa the latter two are active volcanoes. Shows a volcano off the coast of Japan erupting from the ocean floor.
From The News Magazine Of The Screen Series. Vol 6 No. 8
Prod-PATHE Dist-HEARST 1956

Volcanoes, Earthquakes And Other Earth Movements C 17 MIN
16MM FILM, 3/4 OR 1/2 IN VIDEO J
Studies the phenomenon of plate tectonics, showing how this science can help in predicting future disasters.
From The Natural Phenomena Series.
Prod-JOU Dist-JOU Prodn-GLDWER 1981

Volga, The C 54 MIN
16MM FILM, 3/4 OR 1/2 IN VIDEO J-C A
Presents the heartland of the Soviet Union and visits the villages and cities along the banks of the Volga River. Discusses economic, social and political aspects of the country and explains the Soviet system.
LC NO. 81-706935
Prod-CBSNEW Dist-CRMP 1981

Volga, The C 59 MIN
16MM FILM, 3/4 OR 1/2 IN VIDEO
Travels along the Volga River, showing the sights of interest and visiting with the people who populate its shores. Includes visits to Lenin's birthplace, a state farm and a caviar processing plant.
LC NO. 80-706387
Prod-NGS Dist-NGS Prodn-WQED 1977

Volksfeste C 4 MIN
16MM FILM OPTICAL SOUND
From The Beginning German Films (German) Series.
Prod-MGHT Dist-CCNY

Volley, The C 29 MIN
3/4 OR 1/2 INCH VIDEO CASSETTE
Features Lew Gerrard and Don Candy giving tennis instructions, emphasizing the volley.
From The Love Tennis Series.
Prod-MDCPB Dist-MDCPB

Volley, The C 29 MIN
3/4 OR 1/2 INCH VIDEO CASSETTE
See series title for descriptive statement.
From The Vic Braden's Tennis For The Future Series.
Prod-WGBHTV Dist-PBS 1981

Volleyball - A Sport Come Of Age C 23 MIN
16MM FILM, 3/4 OR 1/2 IN VIDEO H-C A
Explains the origins of volleyball and why it has become so popular.
Prod-LEWSBS Dist-AIMS 1975

Volleyball - A Sport Come Of Age (Spanish) C 23 MIN
16MM FILM, 3/4 OR 1/2 IN VIDEO H-C A
Explains the origins of volleyball and why it has become so popular.
Prod-LEWSBS Dist-AIMS 1975

Volleyball - Dig It C 13 MIN
16MM FILM, 3/4 OR 1/2 IN VIDEO J-C
Features Kathy Gregory, volleyball expert, who discusses the skills of playing volleyball as demonstrated by a number of outstanding women players. Illustrates techniques for skillful serving, the underhand pass, recovery from the net, the set up and the spike.
Prod-BFA Dist-PHENIX 1975

Volleyball - Skills And Practice X 12 MIN
16MM FILM, 3/4 OR 1/2 IN VIDEO I-H
Uses normal and slow motion to show six specific volleyball skills and to explain the proper techniques to perfect each skill.
Prod-FA Dist-PHENIX 1967

Volleyball - Skills And Practice (Spanish) X 12 MIN
16MM FILM, 3/4 OR 1/2 IN VIDEO I-H
Uses normal and slow motion to show six specific volleyball skills and to explain the proper techniques to perfect each skill.
Prod-FA Dist-PHENIX 1967

Volleyball - The Winning Points C 17 MIN
16MM FILM OPTICAL SOUND
Explains the rules and correct officiating procedures as written by the National Federation Volleyball Rules Committee. Demonstrates such points as pre-match responsibilities of officials, player alignment, and illegal spikes.
From The National Federation Sports Films Series.
LC NO. 79-701268
Prod-NFSHSA Dist-NFSHSA Prodn-TWCF 1979

Volleyball For Boys (2nd Ed) C 13 MIN
16MM FILM, 3/4 OR 1/2 IN VIDEO I-H
Explains how actual high school volleyball teams provide an exciting in-depth study of individual and team skills of the game. Uses freeze frames and slow motion emphasizing serving, passing, setting-up, spiking and team coordination as the keys to successful competition and full enjoyment.
Prod-CORF Dist-CORF 1971

Volleyball Fundamentals C 17 MIN
16MM FILM, 3/4 OR 1/2 IN VIDEO I-J
Introduces the rules and techniques of volleyball. Includes court-positioning strategies.
Prod-ASSOCF Dist-AIMS 1979

Volleyball Today C 17 MIN
16MM FILM OPTICAL SOUND T
Provides players, coaches, officials and spectators with a detailed explanation of the rules and correct officiating procedures for volleyball.
From The National Federation Sports Films Series.
LC NO. 75-704165
Prod-NFSHSA Dist-NFSHSA 1975

Volleyball 76 C 12 MIN
16MM FILM OPTICAL SOUND H-C A
Shows the volleyball competition in the 1976 Olympics in Montreal.
Prod-CVA Dist-CVA 1977

Volleyball, The Winning Points C 17 MIN
3/4 OR 1/2 INCH VIDEO CASSETTE
Designed to provide an understanding of the rules and officiating procedures used in volleyball by focusing on such topics as play alignment, legal and illegal hits and illegal spikes.
LC NO. 79-707713
Prod-NFSHSA Dist-NFSHSA Prodn-ATHI 1978

Volt Ohmmeter Operation B 12 MIN
16MM FILM, 3/4 OR 1/2 IN VIDEO
Shows how to operate a volt ohmmeter in order to measure ohms and volts. Issued in 1944 as a motion picture.
From The Radio Technician Training Series.
LC NO. 78-706307
Prod-USN Dist-USNAC Prodn-HOLMES 1978

Volta Lake C 9 MIN
16MM FILM OPTICAL SOUND
Describes and shows the effects caused by Lake Volta, a large manmade body of water, on the food production of the country of Ghana.
LC NO. 74-701047
Prod-EDC Dist-EDC 1973

Voltage Control Equipment C
3/4 OR 1/2 INCH VIDEO CASSETTE IND
Focuses on voltage control. Demonstrates why voltage variations occur and what corrective action can be taken. Includes standards, voltage profile and regulation, network boosters and transformer traps.
From The Distribution System Operation Series. Topic 9
Prod-LEIKID Dist-LEIKID

Voltage Dividers B 21 MIN
16MM FILM, 3/4 OR 1/2 IN VIDEO
Explains and demonstrates how voltages are developed at the taps with respect to ground. Explains ground both as a reference point and current path. (Kinescope)
Prod-USAF Dist-USNAC

Voltage Dividers And Power C
3/4 OR 1/2 INCH VIDEO CASSETTE

See series title for descriptive statement.
From The Basic Electricity - DC Series.
Prod-VTRI Dist-VTRI

Voltage Dividers And Power C 30 MIN
3/4 OR 1/2 INCH VIDEO CASSETTE
Provides additional analysis involving Ohm's Law and circuit reduction techniques. Describes basic concepts for designing voltage divider circuits with plus or minus outputs. Expands basic formulas for calculating power distribution in circuits involving voltage dividers.
From The Basic Electricity And D.C. Circuits Series.
Prod-TXINLC Dist-TXINLC

Voltage Dividers With Parallel Branch Circuits C 15 MIN
3/4 OR 1/2 INCH VIDEO CASSETTE
See series title for descriptive statement.
From The Basic Electricity And D.C. Circuits, Laboratory Series.
Prod-TXINLC Dist-TXINLC

Voltage Dividers With Parallel Branch Currents C
3/4 OR 1/2 INCH VIDEO CASSETTE
See series title for descriptive statement.
From The Basic DC Circuits Series.
Prod-VTRI Dist-VTRI

Voltage Doubler B 30 MIN
16MM FILM OPTICAL SOUND
Develops, through analogy and demonstration, the theory of a voltage doubler circuit. Traces the charge and discharge paths for the capacitors, computes peak output voltage and ripple frequency and relates malfunctions in a voltage doubler circuit to the symptoms. (Kinescope)
LC NO. 74-705927
Prod-USAF Dist-USNAC

Voltage Doublers - Transistorized B 20 MIN
16MM FILM OPTICAL SOUND
Illustrates the principles of voltage doubler circuits, discusses troubleshooting procedures and shows the functions of capacitors.
LC NO. 75-703703
Prod-USAF Dist-USNAC 1967

Voltage Regulator Applications C 30 MIN
3/4 OR 1/2 INCH VIDEO CASSETTE PRO
Defines range of application of integrated circuit regulators to various voltage and current conditions. Defines and demonstrates coefficients contributing to output voltage change.
From The Linear And Interface Circuits, Part II - Interface Integrated Circuits Series.
Prod-TXINLC Dist-TXINLC

Voltage Regulators C 12 MIN
3/4 OR 1/2 INCH VIDEO CASSETTE
Covers the necessity of voltage regulators, shunt, series, IC and switching regulators.
From The Industrial Electronics - Power Supplies Series.
Prod-TPCTRA Dist-TPCTRA

Voltage Regulators B 15 MIN
16MM FILM - 3/4 IN VIDEO
Discusses the operation, use, representation and characteristic curve of zener diodes. Shows the schematic of a circuit with a zener diode and discusses its operation in the circuit. Issued in 1970 as a motion picture.
LC NO. 79-707535
Prod-USAF Dist-USNAC 1979

Voltage Regulators - Solid State B 22 MIN
16MM FILM - 3/4 IN VIDEO
Describes the principles of transistorized electronic voltage regulators. Uses schematics to show how current is controlled. Discusses differences between breakdown and zener diodes and illustrates their functions. Issued in 1967 as a motion picture.
LC NO. 79-707536
Prod-USAF Dist-USNAC 1979

Voltage, Current And Resistance C
3/4 OR 1/2 INCH VIDEO CASSETTE
See series title for descriptive statement.
From The Basic Electricity - DC Series.
Prod-VTRI Dist-VTRI

Voltage, Current And Resistance C 30 MIN
3/4 OR 1/2 INCH VIDEO CASSETTE
Analyzes voltage, current and resistance. Explains schematic diagrams. Covers resistance of a conductor, resistor color codes and voltage ratings.
From The Basic Electricity And D.C. Circuits Series.
Prod-TXINLC Dist-TXINLC

Voltaic Cell, Dry Cell And Storage Battery C 18 MIN
16MM FILM, 3/4 OR 1/2 IN VIDEO
Explains the principles of a voltaic cell, a dry cell and a storage battery.
Prod-USA Dist-USNAC

Voltaire Presents Candide - An Introduction To The Age Of Enlightenment C 34 MIN
16MM FILM, 3/4 OR 1/2 IN VIDEO H-C A
Features a dramatization of Voltaire's satiric masterpiece Candide, which provides a look at the history and culture of 18th century Western civilization. Includes Voltaire, who acts as the host, questioning the 'Age of Enlightenment' and its doctrinaire optimism and introducing the naive characters from Candide.
From The Humanities - Philosophy And Political Thought Series.
Prod-EBF Dist-EBEC

Volterra's Fishes B 37 MIN
3/4 OR 1/2 INCH VIDEO CASSETTE
See series title for descriptive statement.
From The Nonlinear Vibrations Series.
Prod-MIOT Dist-MIOT

Voltmeter And its Use, The C
3/4 OR 1/2 INCH VIDEO CASSETTE
See series title for descriptive statement.
From The Basic DC Circuits Series.
Prod-VTRI Dist-VTRI

Voltmeter And Its Use, The C 15 MIN
3/4 OR 1/2 INCH VIDEO CASSETTE
See series title for descriptive statement.
From The Basic Electricity And D.C. Circuits, Laboratory Series.
Prod-TXINLC Dist-TXINLC

Volume C 15 MIN
3/4 INCH VIDEO CASSETTE I-J
Uses special visuals in explaining how to measure the volume of a prism, a cylinder and a cone.
From The Mathways Series.
LC NO. 80-706452
Prod-STSU Dist-AITECH 1979

Volume C 27 MIN
3/4 OR 1/2 INCH VIDEO CASSETTE
Defines volume and capacity. Compares the metric system of measuring volume to the customary system. Discusses why the litre is used for measuring volume.
From The Metric Education Video Tapes For Pre And Inservice Teachers (K-8) Series.
Prod-PUAVC Dist-PUAVC

Volume C 30 MIN
3/4 INCH VIDEO CASSETTE T
Examines major metric units of volume and considers the quart-liter relationship. Depicts classroom activities involving volume measurement.
From The Measure For Measure Series.
Prod-UWISCM Dist-GPITVL 1979

Volume (Discs, Washers) C
3/4 INCH VIDEO CASSETTE
See series title for descriptive statement.
From The Calculus Series.
Prod-MDDE Dist-MDCPB

Volume (Known Cross-Section) C
3/4 INCH VIDEO CASSETTE
See series title for descriptive statement.
From The Calculus Series.
Prod-MDDE Dist-MDCPB

Volume (Shells) C
3/4 INCH VIDEO CASSETTE
See series title for descriptive statement.
From The Calculus Series.
Prod-MDDE Dist-MDCPB

Volume And Temperature C 30 MIN
3/4 OR 1/2 INCH VIDEO CASSETTE H-C A
Deals with the measurement of volume and temperature with metric units.
From The Going Metric Series.
Prod-UMA Dist-GPITVL 1977

Volume By Shells C 9 MIN
16MM FILM OPTICAL SOUND H-C
Expresses the volume of a solid of revolution as a definite integral using the method of cylindrical shells. An animated film narrated by George Leger.
From The MAA Calculus Series.
LC NO. FIA67-679
Prod-MAA Dist-MLA 1966

Volume I C 15 MIN
3/4 OR 1/2 INCH VIDEO CASSETTE I-J
Uses a detective format in a story centering around the investigation of a construction company, where the basics of volume must be learned in order to compute cubic yards of dirt and cubic yards of concrete.
From The Math Matters Series. Green Module
Prod-KRLNTV Dist-AITECH 1975

Volume II C 15 MIN
3/4 OR 1/2 INCH VIDEO CASSETTE I-J
Presents characters computing the volume of cylinders, pyramids and cones.
From The Math Matters Series. Green Module
Prod-KRLNTV Dist-AITECH 1975

Volume Of A Solid Of Revolution C 8 MIN
16MM FILM OPTICAL SOUND H-C
Presents the disc method for expressing the volume of a solid of revolution as a definite integral. An animated film narrated by George Leger.
From The MAA Calculus Series.
LC NO. FIA66-674
Prod-MAA Dist-MLA 1965

Volume Repletion In Shock C 17 MIN
3/4 INCH VIDEO CASSETTE PRO
Explains the significance of intravascular repletion in the treatment of shock. Describes the uses of central venous and pulmonary artery wedge pressures as assessments of cardiac competence during perfusion failure.
From The Shock Series. Module 5
LC NO. 80-707733
Prod-BRA Dist-BRA 1980

Volume 1 - Doc Cranshaw And The Kid - The Medicine Show C 15 MIN
16MM FILM, 3/4 OR 1/2 IN VIDEO I-J
Presents a medicine man and his grandson learning about metric measurement from residents of a Utah frontier town. Demonstrates the liter and the milliliter and examines methods for determining the volume of liquid and granular substances.
From The Measuremetric Series.
LC NO. 80-706499
Prod-AITV Dist-AITECH 1977

Volume 2 - Doc Cranshaw And The Kid - The Contest C 15 MIN
16MM FILM, 3/4 OR 1/2 IN VIDEO I-J
Presents a medicine man and his grandson demonstrating metric measurement of volume, using liters, milliliters, cubic centimeters and cubic decimeters. Includes a variety of processes for determining the volume of a rectangular solid.
From The Measuremetric Series.
LC NO. 80-706500
Prod-AITV Dist-AITECH 1977

Volume 3 - Doc Cranshaw And The Kid - The Winner C 15 MIN
16MM FILM, 3/4 OR 1/2 IN VIDEO I-J
Presents the grandson of a medicine man winning a contest by mastering metric volume measurement. Demonstrates the principle of water displacement to determine the volume of nonrectangular objects.
From The Measuremetric Series.
LC NO. 80-706501
Prod-AITV Dist-AITECH 1977

Volumetric Flask I, The C 8 MIN
3/4 OR 1/2 INCH VIDEO CASSETTE C A
Demonstrates the use of the volumetric flask in preparation of a solution of known concentration.
From The Chemistry - Master/Apprentice Series. Program 10
LC NO. 82-706038
Prod-CUETV Dist-CUNIV 1981

Volumetric Flask II C 15 MIN
3/4 OR 1/2 INCH VIDEO CASSETTE C A
Demonstrates the use of the volumetric flask in preparation of a solution of known concentration. Explains the markings on the flask, the temperature effects, and the importance of cleanliness. Also shows the preparation of solutions from solids of low solubility.
From The Chemistry - Master/Apprentice Series. Program 103
LC NO. 82-706050
Prod-CUETV Dist-CUNIV 1981

Volumetric Measurements B 9 MIN
16MM FILM OPTICAL SOUND H-C
Explains how to determine the volume of solids and liquids and demonstrates the proper use of the scales, burette and graduate cylinder.
Prod-PUAVC Dist-PUAVC 1958

Voluntary Control Of Hair Raising With Associated Autonomic Phenomena B 8 MIN
16MM FILM SILENT C T
The authors of this film discovered a man able to erect hair on the surface of the skin 'VOLUNTARILY.' Pictures show the elevation of hair on the arm and leg, accompanying 'GOOSE-FLESH,' a small amount of dilation of pupils, changes in respiration as recorded by a pneumograph, changes in the electroencephalographic record from pre-motor brain areas and other autonomic behavior.
Prod-PSUPCR Dist-PSUPCR 1938

Voluntary Tubal Sterilization C 14 MIN
16MM FILM, 3/4 OR 1/2 IN VIDEO A
Describes reproduction and how tubal sterilization prevents conception. Explains laparoscopic and ligation methods. Dispels fears of early aging, loss of sexuality and psychological changes.
Prod-PRORE Dist-PRORE

Volunteer Experience - A Patient's Perspective C 15 MIN
3/4 INCH VIDEO CASSETTE
Presents a number of patients' perspectives on the volunteer's role and the experience of being a patient at the University of Texas M D Anderson Hospital.
Prod-UTAHTI Dist-UTAHTI

Volunteer Firefighters - The Unique Breed C 18 MIN
16MM FILM, 3/4 OR 1/2 IN VIDEO A
Traces the history of volunteer firefighting from colonial times to the 1970's. Shows volunteers receiving training and presents the comments of firefighters regarding their reasons for volunteering, their duties and their emotions.
Prod-LHPRO Dist-FILCOM 1979

Volunteer Fireman, The C 19 MIN
16MM FILM OPTICAL SOUND
Shows techniques of using hand tools and back pack pumps to suppress wood fires. Includes the important work of mopping up, cleaning and storing tools, reporting and prevention follow-up.
LC NO. FIE63-220
Prod-USDA Dist-USNAC 1962

Volunteer Programs, An Agency Guide - Deciding And Planning C 45 MIN
16MM FILM, 3/4 OR 1/2 IN VIDEO
Presents the tools for creating a volunteer program and making it effective. Discusses such topics as assessment, decision-making, program planning and evaluation.
Prod-ODECA Dist-BULFRG

Volunteer Programs, An Agency Guide - Effective Management C 28 MIN
16MM FILM, 3/4 OR 1/2 IN VIDEO
Presents an effective case for borrowing techniques of effective management from the business world and applying them to volunteer programs. Covers such topics as job design, job descriptions, recruiting with targeted marketing, orientation, training and supervision.
Prod-ODECA Dist-BULFRG

Volunteer Story C 22 MIN
3/4 OR 1/2 INCH VIDEO CASSETTE J A

Explains the role of volunteers and how they serve people.
Prod-SUTHRB Dist-SUTHRB

Volunteer To Live C 30 MIN
16MM FILM OPTICAL SOUND
Shows how some churches are working with the elderly to encourage self-help projects and offer opportunities for the elderly to help others.
Prod-CBSTV Dist-CCNCC

Volunteerism C 29 MIN
3/4 OR 1/2 INCH VIDEO CASSETTE T
Visits city schools to show how a volunteer program can be designed.
From The On And About Instruction Series.
Prod-VADE Dist-GPITVL 1983

Volunteerism - Pro And Con C 29 MIN
3/4 OR 1/2 INCH VIDEO CASSETTE
Discusses both sides of the controversy over volunteerism.
From The Woman Series.
Prod-WNEDTV Dist-PBS

Volunteers C 8 MIN
16MM FILM OPTICAL SOUND
Demonstrates the structure and function of a volunteer fire company. Shows volunteers at work at when they are called to answer a false alarm.
LC NO. 80-700401
Prod-FSHRA Dist-FSHRA 1980

Volunteers C 25 MIN
3/4 OR 1/2 INCH VIDEO CASSETTE
Explores a few of the hundreds of ways that people from 14 to 100 can volunteer their services in medicine and health.
Prod-TRAINX Dist-TRAINX

Volunteers For Head Start B 7 MIN
3/4 INCH VIDEO CASSETTE
Shows that there are various opportunities for professional and non-professional service in programs of head start. Describes the work of volunteer doctors, dentists, fathers, retirees, club women, teenagers and housewives.
Prod-USNAC Dist-USNAC 1972

Volunteers In The Library C 20 MIN
3/4 INCH VIDEO CASSETTE T
Discusses five steps a library can take to develop an organized volunteer program. Touches on solutions to possible problems that could arise when using volunteers.
From The Access Series.
LC NO. 76-706264
Prod-UDEN Dist-USNAC 1976

Volunteers In Vocational Education - Four Urban Programs C 29 MIN
16MM FILM, 3/4 OR 1/2 IN VIDEO
Presents comments from community leaders from four areas about their local volunteer vocational education programs. Discusses applicable vocations, community support, recruitment techniques and student goal-setting and accomplishment.
Prod-USDED Dist-USNAC 1982

Volunteers Make The Difference C 17 MIN
3/4 OR 1/2 INCH VIDEO CASSETTE
Outlines the basics of a good library volunteer program including recruitment, selection, supervision and training.
Prod-LVN Dist-LVN

Volvox - Structure, Reproduction And Differentation In V Carteri (Hk 9 And 10) C 25 MIN
16MM FILM, 3/4 OR 1/2 IN VIDEO H-C A
Depicts the details of cellular differentiation and its control in a simple multicellular organism. Shows the form and sturcture of volvox carteri, a green, spheroidal alga and the development of asexual, male and female embryos.
LC NO. 80-707092
Prod-IU Dist-IU 1970

Volvulus Of The Sigmoid Colon C 30 MIN
16MM FILM OPTICAL SOUND PRO
Outlines the important features, the etiology, diagnosis and surgical management of volvulus of the sigmoid. Presents X-ray films of typical cases.
Prod-ACYDGD Dist-ACY 1954

Vom Mittelgebirge Bis Zu Den Alpen C 10 MIN
16MM FILM, 3/4 OR 1/2 IN VIDEO
A German language videocassette. Looks at the area of Germany containing Rothenberg, Frankfurt am Main, and Munchen. Describes the agriculture of this region.
From The German Teaching Series.
Prod-IFB Dist-IFB 1972

Vom Schwarzwald Bis Koln C 9 MIN
16MM FILM, 3/4 OR 1/2 IN VIDEO
A German language videocassette. Describes the Black Forest, Heidelberg and the Rhine, the Moselle vineyards, and the Ruhr Valley.
From The German Teaching Series.
Prod-IFB Dist-IFB 1972

Von Bodense In Die Schweiz C 4 MIN
16MM FILM OPTICAL SOUND
From The Beginning German Films (German) Series.
Prod-MGHT Dist-CCNY

Von Der Nordseekuste Bis Berlin C 9 MIN
16MM FILM, 3/4 OR 1/2 IN VIDEO
A German language videocassette. Explores the region of Germany which contains the cities of Hamburg and Berlin.
From The German Teaching Series.
Prod-IFB Dist-IFB 1972

Vor Sonnenaufgang C 104 MIN
16MM FILM OPTICAL SOUND
A German language film with English subtitles. Tells the story of the young social democrat politician Albert Loth, who studies conditions in a Silesian village that has become rich as coal is found in the region. Continues as he meets an old friend from student days, who, along with his wife, has become rich and also a drunk, and whose daughter Helene eventually falls in love with Loth. Concludes with Loth leaving Helene because she is the daughter of alcoholics, and with Helene taking her own life.
Prod-WSTGLC Dist-WSTGLC 1976

Vormittagsspuk B 7 MIN
16MM FILM OPTICAL SOUND
Presents Hans Richter's witty, cinegenic mini-classic on the universal theme of the objects' revolt, an excellent introduction to avant-garde film. Produced 1927-28.
Prod-STARRC Dist-STARRC

Vorsicht, Bremsen C 15 MIN
16MM FILM, 3/4 OR 1/2 IN VIDEO
See series title for descriptive statement.
From The Guten Tag Series. Part 21
Prod-BAYER Dist-IFB 1968

Vorticity, Pt 1 X 22 MIN
16MM FILM, 3/4 OR 1/2 IN VIDEO C
Ascher H Shapiro presents experimental demonstrations of phenomena relating to vorticity, to circulation and to the theorems of Crocco, Kelvin and Helmholtz.
From The Fluid Mechanics Series.
Prod-NCFMF Dist-EBEC Prodn-EDS 1966

Vorticity, Pt 2 X 22 MIN
16MM FILM, 3/4 OR 1/2 IN VIDEO C
Ascher H Shapiro presents experimental demonstrations of phenomena relating to vorticity, to circulation and to the theorems of Crocco, Kelvin and Helmholtz.
From The Fluid Mechanics Series.
Prod-NCFMF Dist-EBEC Prodn-EDS 1966

Vorurteile - Oder Die Not Macht Erfindersch (Prejudices - Or Necessity Is The Mother Of... C 8 MIN
3/4 INCH VIDEO CASSETTE
Complete title is Vorurteile - Oder Die Not Macht Erfindersch (Prejudices - Or Necessity Is The Mother Of Invention). Presents symbols of Western culture and industry juxtaposed with ritual objects of the Third World. Marcel Odenbach constructs with this a study of cultural hierarchies and economics, and suggests the futility of revolution.
Prod-EAI Dist-EAI

Vote - Organizing The Rural South, The B 30 MIN
16MM FILM OPTICAL SOUND H-C A
Joanne Grant discusses the evolution of the civil rights movement in the 1960's and the growth of the concept of Black Power. She explains that this period of resistance reached its peak when thousands of Blacks all over the South began to organize around the vote, which symbolized the ulimate in attaining political power.
From The Black History, Section 20 - Freedom Movement Series.
LC NO. 70-704110
Prod-WCBSTV Dist-HRAW 1969

Vote For Ira C 11 MIN
16MM FILM OPTICAL SOUND
Presents a documentary comedy which follows the exploits of Ira Bernstein, an idealistic yet inept young man running for the State Assembly of New York in 1972, reliving his past through the insights of his father.
LC NO. 76-700439
Prod-POSTMN Dist-POSTMN 1975

Vote Power C 20 MIN
16MM FILM, 3/4 OR 1/2 IN VIDEO H-C
Deals with the right to vote of the 18-year-old individual, explaining that it can make change possible. Shows such people as Julian Bond, representative from Georgia and an 18-year-old mayor in California in order to encourage young people to register and vote.
Prod-AMEDFL Dist-AMEDFL 1973

Voting C 15 MIN
3/4 OR 1/2 INCH VIDEO CASSETTE H
Demonstrates voting procedures. Looks at voting for candidates and voting on issues.
From The By The People Series.
Prod-CTI Dist-CTI

Voting At 18 C 14 MIN
16MM FILM, 3/4 OR 1/2 IN VIDEO H-C
Points out that the 26th amendment gave millions of young people a voice in important matters they feel strongly about and explains that by voting, they can make their voices heard.
Prod-CORF Dist-CORF 1972

Voting Machine, The C 20 MIN
3/4 OR 1/2 INCH VIDEO CASSETTE J-H
Shows a young person registering to vote and using an electronic voting machine. Includes a question-and-answer session between students, a professor of political science, and the chairpersons of the local Democratic and Republic parties.
From The Rights And Responsibilities Series.
Prod-WHROTV Dist-AITECH 1975

Vous, Encore Vous B 13 MIN
16MM FILM OPTICAL SOUND I-H
See series title for descriptive statement.
From The Les Francais Chez Vous Series. Set II, Lesson 19
Prod-PEREN Dist-CHLTN 1967

Vowel A, The (2nd Ed) C 13 MIN
16MM FILM, 3/4 OR 1/2 IN VIDEO P
Deals with the short and long sounds of the letter a, emphasizing the effects of the final e, the ai combination, and the ay combination at the end of a word. Presents exercises using the concepts that have been explained.
From The Reading Skills, Set 1 (2nd Ed) Series.
Prod-JOU Dist-JOU 1983

Vowel Combinations - What Are Letters For C 11 MIN
16MM FILM, 3/4 OR 1/2 IN VIDEO P-I
Shows how vowels work in the English language. Uses a story of two characters who visit a ranch and a fair to find as many vowel combinations as they can.
Prod-BFA Dist-BFA 1983

Vowel E, The (2nd Ed) C 13 MIN
16MM FILM, 3/4 OR 1/2 IN VIDEO P
Shows the major patterns of letters which give the vowel e its long and short sounds, e followed by only a consonant, e followed by a consonant and final e. Covers ee together in the middle of a word, ee and ea at the end of a word and e at the end of a word not followed by a consonant.
From The Reading Skills, Set 1 (2nd Ed) Series.
Prod-JOU Dist-JOU 1983

Vowel I, The (2nd Ed) C 13 MIN
16MM FILM, 3/4 OR 1/2 IN VIDEO P
Deals with the long and short sounds of the letter i, emphasizing the effect of the final e, the ght combination, and the final y acting like the letter i. Presents exercises using the concepts that have been explained.
From The Reading Skills, Set 1 (2nd Ed) Series.
Prod-JOU Dist-JOU 1983

Vowel O, The (2nd Ed) C 13 MIN
16MM FILM, 3/4 OR 1/2 IN VIDEO P
Shows the major patterns of letters which give the vowel o its long and short sounds, o followed by a consonant and then a final e, o followed by a consonant only, and the vowel digraph oa together. Covers o alone at the end of a word, oe at the end of a word, and the ough combination.
From The Reading Skills, Set 1 (2nd Ed) Series.
Prod-JOU Dist-JOU 1983

Vowel U, The (2nd Ed) C 13 MIN
16MM FILM, 3/4 OR 1/2 IN VIDEO P
Shows the major patterns of letters which give the vowel u its long and short sounds, u followed by a consonant and then a final e, u followed only by a consonant, and the vowel digraph ew either in the middle or at the end of a word. Covers the vowel digraph oo either in the middle or at the end of a word, and ue at the end of a word. Presents exercises using the concepts that have been explained.
From The Reading Skills, Set 1 (2nd Ed) Series.
Prod-JOU Dist-JOU 1983

Vowels - What Are Letters For (Rev Ed) C 13 MIN
16MM FILM, 3/4 OR 1/2 IN VIDEO P-I
Teaches long and short vowel sounds. Shows each letter with pictures of words using the letter in the initial position.
Prod-BEANM Dist-BFA

Vowels And Glides C 26 MIN
3/4 INCH VIDEO CASSETTE PRO
Uses live-action photography of the movements of the laryngeal and articulatory structures to illustrate the production of vowels and their movements with glide sounds. Shows the importance of resonance as a factor in speech intelligibility through samples of connected speech.
From The Articulatory Movements In The Production Of English Speech Sounds Series. Part 2
LC NO. 78-706044
Prod-USVA Dist-USNAC 1978

Vowels And Their Sounds (2nd Ed) C 12 MIN
16MM FILM, 3/4 OR 1/2 IN VIDEO P
Focuses on short and long vowel sounds and presents the steps of understanding sound-letter association. Includes scenes of children in suggested follow-up activities.
From The Reading Skills, Set 1 (2nd Ed) Series.
Prod-JOU Dist-JOU 1983

Vox Pop (The Voice Of The People) C 30 MIN
16MM FILM OPTICAL SOUND
Tells how a man is chosen as the symbol of Australian apathy and how his life undergoes upheaval as a result.
LC NO. 80-701576
Prod-TASCOR Dist-TASCOR 1979

Voyage C 8 MIN
3/4 OR 1/2 INCH VIDEO CASSETTE
Combines NASA footage of Saturn with electronically formed images to create an extraterrestrial experience.
From The TeleVisions Series.
Prod-WTV Dist-EAI

Voyage Of Charles Darwin—A Series
16MM FILM, 3/4 OR 1/2 IN VIDEO H-C A
Presents a dramatization of the five-year voyage of Charles Darwin on the H M S Beagle where he first formed his ideas on the origin of species, which 20 years later were to provoke public furor and intellectual revolution.
LC NO. 80-706462
Prod-BBCTV Dist-TIMLIF 1980

Can Any Mountain, Any Continent, Withstand	
How Wide Was The Distance Between Savage And	52 MIN
I Felt Myself Brought Within Reach Of That	52 MIN
I Was Considered A Very Ordinary Boy	52 MIN
In The Distant Future, Light Will Be Thrown	52 MIN
My Mind Was A Chaos Of Delight	52 MIN
Suppose That All Animals And All Plants Are	52 MIN

Voyage Of Charles Darwin—A Series

Dramatizes the biography of Charles Darwin.
Prod-OHC Dist-HRC

Can Any Mountains, Any Continent, Withstand	
How Wide Was The Distance Between Savage And	052 MIN
I Felt Myself Brought Within Reach Of The	052 MIN
I Was Considered A Very Ordinary Boy	052 MIN
In The Distant Future, Light Will Be Thrown	052 MIN
My Mind Was A Chaos Of Delight	052 MIN
Suppose That All Animals And All Plants Are	052 MIN

Voyage Of Discovery C 14 MIN
16MM FILM - 3/4 IN VIDEO
Uses paintings to describe the discovery of the California coast by 16th-century explorer Juan Rodriguez Cabrillo. Issued in 1969 as a motion picture.
LC NO. 79-706169
Prod-USNPS Dist-USNAC 1979

Voyage Of Dreams C 27 MIN
16MM FILM - 3/4 IN VIDEO
Documents the story of the Haitian boat people.
Prod-BLKFMF Dist-BLKFMF

Voyage Of Dreams (Captioned) C 30 MIN
16MM FILM, 3/4 OR 1/2 IN VIDEO A
Discusses the story of the Haitian boat people. Creole dialog with English subtitles.
Prod-CNEMAG Dist-CNEMAG 1983

Voyage Of Odysseus, The C 27 MIN
16MM FILM, 3/4 OR 1/2 IN VIDEO J-C A
Features Julie Harris who, as the voice of a muse, retells the voyage section of Homer's classic tale The Odyssey.
LC NO. 82-706799
Prod-CF Dist-CF 1982

Voyage Of SS Columbia - Just Short Of A Miracle C 22 MIN
16MM FILM, 3/4 OR 1/2 IN VIDEO J-C A
Looks at the development of the space shutttle Columbia and follows it on to the launch pad and into orbit with astronauts Crippen and Young. Documents the activities during the first flight through to its successful landing at Andrews Air Force Base.
Prod-ABCNEW Dist-MTI 1981

Voyage Of The Brigantine Yankee, The C 50 MIN
16MM FILM, 3/4 OR 1/2 IN VIDEO
Presents the Yankee, a two masted sailing vessel, with its captain, his wife and college-age crew. Pictures them at Pitcairn, recovering the rusty anchor of the scuttled mutiny ship.
LC NO. 80-706393
Prod-NGS Dist-NGS

Voyage Of The Elisha Kane C 15 MIN
16MM FILM OPTICAL SOUND
Follows an ocean expedition exploring the mid-Atlantic ridge and the sea floor to explain how marine geologists explore land masses beneath the sea.
LC NO. 70-705710
Prod-USNO Dist-USNPC Prodn-SUN 1969

Voyage Of The San Carlos C 18 MIN
3/4 INCH VIDEO CASSETTE I A
Documents the activities of the San Carlos, a water quality monitoring vessel, as it gathers information along the Sacramento-San Joaquin Delta.
Prod-CSDWR Dist-CALDWR

Voyage Optique B 8 MIN
16MM FILM OPTICAL SOUND H-C
A humorous collage of abstract and concrete images set to lively music.
LC NO. 75-703251
Prod-USC Dist-USC 1965

Voyage Through America, 1980 C 18 MIN
16MM FILM OPTICAL SOUND
Gives a brief history of steamboats and river travel in the United States and shows the unique vacation experience of a trip on the Delta Queen.
LC NO. 80-700402
Prod-DQSC Dist-SUNSET Prodn-SUNSET 1979

Voyage Through The Cosmos, A C 20 MIN
16MM FILM, 3/4 OR 1/2 IN VIDEO J-H
Presents a voyage on an imaginary spaceship through the distant regions of the universe, gradually approaching Earth. Shows galaxies, quasars, supernovae, red giants, yellow dwarfs, and the planets. Edited from an episode of the Cosmos series.
From The Cosmos (Edited Version) Series.
Prod-SAGANC Dist-FI Prodn-KCET 1980

Voyage To America B 12 MIN
16MM FILM OPTICAL SOUND
Portrays the contributions made by each immigrant group to the building of the United States and its democracy. Uses historical prints, archive photographs and newsreel footage to illustrate 350 years of immigration, from the early settlers to the survivors of Hitler's holocaust.
Prod-ADL Dist-ADL

Voyage To Next C 9 MIN
16MM FILM, 3/4 OR 1/2 IN VIDEO I-C A
Presents an animated film which uses the figures of Mother Earth and Father Time in order to encourage universal cooperation for a better world.
Prod-HUBLEY Dist-TEXFLM 1974

Voyage To Next C 10 MIN
16MM FILM, 3/4 OR 1/2 IN VIDEO H-C A
Presents an animated plea for world cooperation and understanding, featuring Maureen Stapleton as Mother Earth and Dizzy Gillespie as Father Time.
Prod-HUBLEY Dist-PFP

Voyage To The Arctic C 25 MIN
16MM FILM, 3/4 OR 1/2 IN VIDEO I-H A
Explores the ecological regions from British Columbia to Alaska from the vantage point of a cruise ship. Examines the land and water environments and their interrelationships.
From The Natural Environment Series.
Prod-WILFGP Dist-JOU 1977

Voyage To The Galapagos C 21 MIN
16MM FILM, 3/4 OR 1/2 IN VIDEO I-C
Takes one on a journey to the Galapagos Islands of Ecuador. Showsthe diverse flora and fauna, together with various wildlife. Musical accompaniment provided in film.
Prod-EBEC Dist-EBEC 1985

Voyage To The Ocean Of Storms C 11 MIN
16MM FILM OPTICAL SOUND I-C A
Depicts the Apollo 12 mission, including scenes of the astronauts aboard the 'YANKEE CLIPPER' and the 'INTREPID' and the moon walks of Conrad and Bean. Portrays the placement of the Apollo Lunar Experiments Package (ALSEP) on the lunar surface and the recovery of equipment from the Surveyor Three unmanned spacecraft.
Prod-NAA Dist-RCKWL

Voyage To The Planet Earth C 18 MIN
16MM FILM OPTICAL SOUND
Uses animation and live action in promoting the use of high moisture Milo grain for cattle feeding. Shows imaginary visitors to earth from another planet investigating the use of Milo.
LC NO. 72-700163
Prod-VENARD Dist-VENARD 1971

Voyage To Understanding C 56 MIN
16MM FILM - 1/2 IN VIDEO
Shows an 18-month cruise around the world by a crew of American teenagers on the 85-foot schooner Vitava.
Prod-GLNASS Dist-OFFSHR

Voyage To Understanding C 59 MIN
1/2 IN VIDEO CASSETTE BETA/VHS J-C A
Tells the story of 11 young adults, age 14 to 19, who set out to sail around the world in a refurbished schooner, a voyage which became an unparalleled adventure in seamanship, maturation and friendship recalled four years later to the accompaniment of movies shot on board.
LC NO. 84-707098
Prod-GPEF Dist-GLNASS

Voyager C 20 MIN
16MM FILM, 3/4 OR 1/2 IN VIDEO H A
Presents the flight of the Voyager and the first close-up photos of Jupiter and Saturn and their moons.
Prod-NASA Dist-USNAC 1982

Voyageurs, The C 20 MIN
16MM FILM, 3/4 OR 1/2 IN VIDEO J-H A
Documents the big business of fur-traders who drove their freighter canoes through the waterways of the wilderness. Shows how the often-hazardous trips of the voyageurs were cheered by their songs.
Prod-NFBC Dist-NFBC 1965

Vrindavan, Land Of Krishna C 23 MIN
16MM FILM OPTICAL SOUND
Depicts the lifestyles and religious observances of the inhabitants and pilgrims of Vrindavan, India, site of Lord Krishna's appearance. Features the history, art and architecture of the city and the devotion of the people who inhabit it.
Prod-ISKCON Dist-BHAKTI 1980

Vroom At The Top C 28 MIN
16MM FILM OPTICAL SOUND
Examines the racing adventures of ex-driver Roger Penske and his team's efforts in the Indianapolis 500, Monaco Grand Prix and the World 600 stock car race.
Prod-SEARS Dist-MTP

Vrooom C 17 MIN
16MM FILM, 3/4 OR 1/2 IN VIDEO J-C A
Uses a variety of cinematic devices, including stop-action, slow motion and split screen techniques in order to show some of the fun and excitement of competition drag racing.
Prod-NHRA Dist-PFP Prodn-PFP 1974

VTR - Downtown Community Television C 30 MIN
3/4 OR 1/2 INCH VIDEO CASSETTE
Gives examples of how to use video as a tool for community organizing. Includes excerpts of tapes on health education, use of mobile units, workshops, community service programs and others.
Prod-DCTVC Dist-DCTVC 1975

VTR Peter Campus C 30 MIN
3/4 OR 1/2 INCH VIDEO CASSETTE
Contains 'Three Transitions,' 'Set of Coincidence' and Peter Campus' discussion with Russell Connor.
Prod-EAI Dist-EAI

Vulnerable To Attack C 28 MIN
16MM FILM OPTICAL SOUND H-C A
Helps women learn various tactics for self-defense. Discusses physical defense, locking hardware, doors and safety strategy on streets.
LC NO. 75-701988
Prod-MCCRNE Dist-MCCRNE 1975

Vulva Self-Examination C 30 MIN
3/4 INCH VIDEO CASSETTE
Demonstrates how to perform a self-examination of the vulva.
Prod-UTAHTI Dist-UTAHTI

Vulvovaginal Problems C
3/4 OR 1/2 INCH VIDEO CASSETTE
Presents the common problems of the vulva and vagina. Discusses concepts in differential diagnosis and management of nonvenereal and venereal infections. Stresses recognition of masquerading or underlying neoplasia.
Prod-AMEDA Dist-AMEDA

Vusac - N Y C 30 MIN
3/4 INCH VIDEO CASSETTE
Presents an art video ode to TV, art, and global pop culture. Uses clay animation and image processing, and material from other tapes by Nam June Paik.
Prod-EAI Dist-EAI

W

W A Mozart C 26 MIN
16MM FILM, 3/4 OR 1/2 IN VIDEO J-C A
Features soloist Nina Milkina with the London Mozart Players for a performance of the Ninth Piano Concerto.
From The Great Composers Series.
Prod-SEABEN Dist-IFB 1974

W And X C 15 MIN
3/4 INCH VIDEO CASSETTE P
From The Writing Time Series.
Prod-WHROTV Dist-GPITVL

W C Fields Mosaic B 45 MIN
16MM FILM OPTICAL SOUND
Highlights sequences from W C Field's Paramount and Universal feature films, including The Great Mc Goryl, Big Thumb, If I Had A Million, Circus Slickers and Hurry Hurry.
Prod-CFS Dist-CFS 1975

W C Handy C 14 MIN
16MM FILM, 3/4 OR 1/2 IN VIDEO J-C A
Traces the cultural contribution of an outstanding Negro composer, W C Handy. Reflects the political, economic and sociological conditions of the American scene during the period 1890-1950. Shows the influences which directed William Christopher Handy's career
Prod-VIGNET Dist-PHENIX 1967

W E B Dubois And The Niagara Movement B 30 MIN
2 INCH VIDEOTAPE H-C A
See series title for descriptive statement.
From The Americans From Africa - A History Series. No. 23
Prod-CVETVC Dist-GPITVL Prodn-WCVETV

W Is For Wife Abuse C 8 MIN
16MM FILM, 3/4 OR 1/2 IN VIDEO
Sets the issue of wife abuse in historical context, asking why there are so few convictions for this offense and what can be done about this problem.
From The ABC's Of Canadian Life Series.
Prod-UTORMC Dist-UTORMC

W O W (Women Of The World) C 11 MIN
16MM FILM, 3/4 OR 1/2 IN VIDEO
Features an animated film without narration which presents a playfully earnest history of the world from the feminist viewpoint. Emphasizes the evolution of women's role in civilization.
Prod-WCCH Dist-PFP Prodn-HUBLEY 1975

W S Mervin C 29 MIN
3/4 INCH VIDEO CASSETTE
See series title for descriptive statement.
From The Poets Talking Series.
Prod-UMITV Dist-UMITV 1975

W Somerset Maugham C 60 MIN
3/4 OR 1/2 INCH VIDEO CASSETTE
Presents Malcolm Muggeridge discussing W Somerset Maugham. Includes the views of people who knew him and deals with what his works said about him.
From The Man Of Letters Series.
Prod-SCETV Dist-MDCPB

W Sound, The - Willie Watermelon C 15 MIN
2 INCH VIDEOTAPE P
Introduces some of the consonant sounds met in early reading. Identifies the written letter with the spoken sound.
From The Listen And Say Series.
Prod-MPATI Dist-GPITVL

W, R, S C 15 MIN
3/4 OR 1/2 INCH VIDEO CASSETTE P
Presents techniques of handwriting, focusing on the lower case letters w, r and s.
From The Cursive Writing Series.
Prod-WHROTV Dist-GPITVL 1984

Wacky Machine, The C 24 MIN
16MM FILM, 3/4 OR 1/2 IN VIDEO I
Tells how Homer Price gets his hands on Uncle Ulysses' new doughnut machine, causing it to mass produce an endless supply of doughnuts. Describes the commotion when Mrs Chambers loses her diamond ring in the batter. Originally shown on the television series ABC Weekend Specials.
Prod-ABCTV Dist-MTI 1976

Waddingtons, The - Beaulieu House C 29 MIN
3/4 INCH VIDEO CASSETTE
Presents Dana Wynter interviewing Nesbit and Sydney Waddington, tenth generation owners of Beaulieu House, one of Ireland's most beautiful estates.
From The Dana Wynter In Ireland Series.
Prod-GRIAN Dist-PUBTEL

Wages And Production C 18 MIN
16MM FILM, 3/4 OR 1/2 IN VIDEO H A
Applies demand and supply principles to labor. Shows how wage rates affect the kinds and amounts of labor services offered and the amount demanded. Presents some factors affecting wage rates.
From The People On Market Street Series.
Prod-FNDREE Dist-WDEMCO Prodn-KAHNT 1977

Waging A Campaign And Winning An Election B 20 MIN
16MM FILM OPTICAL SOUND H A
Robert Humphreys, former campaign director, Republican National Committee, shows how campaign strategy is developed.
From The Government And Public Affairs Films Series.
Prod-RSC Dist-MLA 1960

Wagner Electric Corporation C 12 MIN
16MM FILM OPTICAL SOUND
Offers a look at the Wagner Electric Corporation in order to show the flexibility of new management to the needs of the market-place.
LC NO. 77-701458
Prod-WAGNER Dist-WAGNER Prodn-ATP 1976

Wagner Ring Cycle—A Series

Offers the four operas which comprise Wagner's ring cycle.
Prod-FOTH Dist-FOTH

Das Rheingold 150 MIN
Die Walkure 245 MIN
Gotterdammerung 266 MIN
Siegfried 253 MIN

Wagons West B 14 MIN
16MM FILM OPTICAL SOUND H
Re-enacts the journey of a mule-drawn covered wagon train over the Oregon Trail, from Missouri to Oregon.
Prod-NYLI Dist-HF 1960

Wagons West C 20 MIN
16MM FILM, 3/4 OR 1/2 IN VIDEO
Traces the history of the crossing of America by using a 90-mile, 8-day tourist excursion in covered wagons to compare and contrast the experiences on the contemporary wagon train with those of the pioneers.
From The Americana Series.
Prod-HANDEL Dist-HANDEL 1977

Waika And Makiritare, The - Food Gathering C 11 MIN
16MM FILM OPTICAL SOUND J-C A
See series title for descriptive statement.
From The Indians Of The Orinoco Series.
Prod-BRYAN Dist-IFF 1972

Waika And Makiritare, The - Journey To The Makiritare C 9 MIN
16MM FILM OPTICAL SOUND J-C A
See series title for descriptive statement.
From The Indians Of The Orinoco Series.
LC NO. 72-703353
Prod-BRYAN Dist-IFF 1972

Waist Land, The - Eating Disorders C 23 MIN
16MM FILM, 3/4 OR 1/2 IN VIDEO C A
Explores the social and psychological forces behind the rapid rise of bulimia and anorexia, two eating disorders.
Prod-GANNET Dist-MTI

Waist Land, The - Why Diets Don't Work C 23 MIN
16MM FILM, 3/4 OR 1/2 IN VIDEO C A
Explores the dangerous obsession with slimness and gives tips on safe, healthy diets.
Prod-GANNET Dist-MTI

Wait 'Till We're Sixty Five C 60 MIN
3/4 INCH VIDEOTAPE J-C A
Presents a documentary that examines the aging process, the value of the elderly in our society and the importance of developing realistic attitudes about the problems of growing old. Narrated by Steve Allen and featuring interviews with Roy Rogers, Dale Evans, Molly Picon and Representative Claude Pepper.
Prod-NBCNEW Dist-ECUFLM 1981

Wait-And-Weight Method - Worksheet, Calculations And Procedures C 24 MIN
3/4 OR 1/2 INCH VIDEO CASSETTE IND
Describes filling out a kill sheet, calculations needed and using a chart to figure pump kill rate for the wait-and-weight well-killing method.
Prod-UTEXPE Dist-UTEXPE 1978

Wait, The B 18 MIN
16MM FILM OPTICAL SOUND
Presents an experimental film which presents the violent story of a confrontation between a bounty hunter and four outlaws.
LC NO. 75-700092
Prod-WESTRN Dist-WESTRN 1974

Waiter's Ball, The B 13 MIN
16MM FILM SILENT
Presents Fatty Arbuckle and Al St John in a madcap exhibition of slapstick comedy.
Prod-UNKNWN Dist-KILLIS 1914

Waiting C 7 MIN
16MM FILM OPTICAL SOUND
Describes the social, mental and physical problems of a woman suffering from kidney disease. Explains the problem of finding and keeping a job along with her many hours on a kidney machine and her eventual vocational rehabilitation.
From The Audio Visual Research Briefs Series.
LC NO. 75-702441
Prod-USRSA Dist-USNAC Prodn-DRU 1974

Waiting For A Shearwater C 17 MIN
16MM FILM OPTICAL SOUND
Shows the work of National Park rangers in keeping a balance between nature and man.
LC NO. 80-700932
Prod-TASCOR Dist-TASCOR 1979

Waiting For Fidel C 58 MIN
16MM FILM, 3/4 OR 1/2 IN VIDEO H-C A
Portrays three government and communications experts as they await a promised interview with Fidel Castro. Shows them discussing socialism and their experiences in Cuba.
Prod-NFBC Dist-NFBC 1974

Waiting For Godot B 102 MIN
16MM FILM OPTICAL SOUND H-C A
Presents Samuel Beckett's two-act tragicomedy 'WAITING FOR GODOT.'
LC NO. 72-700444
Prod-GROVE Dist-GROVE 1971

Waiting For Harry C 57 MIN
16MM FILM OPTICAL SOUND
Illustrates some of the difficulties faced by contemporary Aborigines in maintaining ancient customs, by telling the story of one funerary ceremony which is held up for lack of a needed participant.
Prod-AUSIAS Dist-UCEMC 1981

Waiting For Love (Russian) C 80 MIN
16MM FILM OPTICAL SOUND H-C A
A Russian language film with English subtitles. Presents a light-hearted romance about Rita, who plans to marry a mechanic named Gavrilov. Relates that waiting for Gavrilov at the registry, Rita is involved in a number of comical situations.
LC NO. 83-700205
Prod-MOSFLM Dist-IFEX Prodn-SOVEXP 1983

Waiting For The Go C 4 MIN
16MM FILM OPTICAL SOUND
Presents one man's dilemma while standing at a stoplight.
LC NO. 76-701391
Prod-YORKU Dist-YORKU 1975

Waiting For The Invasion - U S Citizens In Nicaragua C 27 MIN
16MM FILM OPTICAL SOUND
Presents the human side of the complex drama unfolding in Nicaragua, and approaches the situation from a novel perspective, by exploring the lives and work of the U S community residing in Managua.
Prod-ICARUS Dist-ICARUS

Waiting For The Wind C 10 MIN
3/4 OR 1/2 INCH VIDEO CASSETTE
Evokes the terror of a world completely out of personal control. Presents a tornado-like catastrophe.
Prod-KITCHN Dist-KITCHN

Waiting Game, The C 27 MIN
16MM FILM OPTICAL SOUND
A dramatization about an intelligent judge who refuses to see a doctor about his raspy throat and whose fear threatens his forthcoming marriage. Designed to motivate men to go for a cancer check-up.
From The Lifewatch Six Series.
LC NO. 70-705015
Prod-USPHS Dist-SMUSA 1969

Waiting Game, The - Control Or Confrontation C 20 MIN
3/4 OR 1/2 INCH VIDEO CASSETTE
See series title for descriptive statement.
From The Missiles Of October - A Case Study In Decision Making Series.
Prod-LCOA Dist-DELTAK

Waiting In The Wings C 60 MIN
16MM FILM, 3/4 OR 1/2 IN VIDEO C A
Describes how the bloody competition for the Roman throne intensifies and a favorable portent ushers young Claudius into the scene.
From The I, Claudius Series. Number 3
Prod-BBCTV Dist-FI 1977

Waiting Months, The (2nd Ed) C 13 MIN
3/4 OR 1/2 INCH VIDEO CASSETTE
Explains normal pregnancy. Describes physical changes. Gives some of the reasons for careful medical supervision during pregnancy.
Prod-MEDFAC Dist-MEDFAC 1981

Waiting On Tables At Sea C 14 MIN
16MM FILM OPTICAL SOUND
Provides guidelines for food service personnel aboard ships at sea, including the importance of their relationship with passengers, personal cleanliness, preparations before the meal, conduct and cleanup after the meal.
LC NO. 77-700707
Prod-USN Dist-USNAC Prodn-KOSTR 1955

Waiting Room, The C 28 MIN
16MM FILM OPTICAL SOUND
Traces the experiences of a man who is unknowingly suffering from a duodenal ulcer and does not seek medical attention until his personal and physical problems reach an advanced stage. Shows the advanced technology and treatment available for ulcers.
LC NO. 79-701310
Prod-SKF Dist-VISION Prodn-VISION 1979

Waiting Room, The C 29 MIN
16MM FILM, 3/4 OR 1/2 IN VIDEO H-C A
Discusses the pros and cons of abortion. Shows five women at an abortion clinic revealing how they feel about abortions and how the operation will affect their families and themselves.
Prod-CAROUF Dist-CAROUF

Waitress Wanted C 9 MIN
16MM FILM OPTICAL SOUND
Looks at an older man who is possessed by his love for a young woman. Tells how he confronts her with his passion and she rejects him.
LC NO. 80-700403
Prod-CYRUS Dist-CYRUS 1979

Wakaima And The Clay Man C 15 MIN
3/4 OR 1/2 INCH VIDEO CASSETTE P-I
Tells the East African tale of Wanjovu the elephant who creates a clay man to catch the thief who is stealing the crops.
From The Sixteen Tales Series.
Prod-KLCSTV Dist-AITECH

Wake Of '38 C 59 MIN
3/4 OR 1/2 INCH VIDEO CASSETTE
Documents the Great Hurricane and Tidal Wave of 1938, which killed 600 people and was the greatest natural disaster in the history of New England. Examines the effects of isolation and other long term consequences of the storm through interviews with survivors. Includes an explanation of how hurricanes are caused.
Prod-WSBETV Dist-PBS 1978

Wake Up, Charlie Churchman B 20 MIN
16MM FILM OPTICAL SOUND
Shows that, in a harrowing dream, Charlie finds himself attending God's funeral. Pictures him stealing back to the cemetery to examine the casket, and finding it empty. Concludes with Charlie's realization that it is not God who is dead, but apathetic, lethargic churchmen.
Prod-FAMF Dist-FAMF

Walbiri Fire Ceremony C 21 MIN
16MM FILM, 3/4 OR 1/2 IN VIDEO
Documents a spectacular Aboriginal ceremony, a communal ritual of penance that serves to settle disputes within the community. Shows how it culminates in a nighttime ordeal in which some of the participants are humiliated and engage in self-flagellation with burning bundles of twigs.
From The Australian Institute Of Aboriginal Studies Series.
Prod-AUSIAS Dist-UCEMC 1979

Walcott-Marciano B 30 MIN
16MM FILM OPTICAL SOUND
See series title for descriptive statement.
From The IBC Championship Fights, Series 1 Series.
Prod-SFI Dist-SFI

Walden C 10 MIN
16MM FILM, 3/4 OR 1/2 IN VIDEO H-C
Presents images which illustrate passages from Thoreau's book Walden.
Prod-LAFCAR Dist-ICARUS 1980

Waldenville I C 30 MIN
3/4 OR 1/2 INCH VIDEO CASSETTE
Shows the collective bargaining process from iniation to deadlock and the decision to use mediation.
From The Labor Relations Series.
Prod-IVCH Dist-IVCH

Waldenville I C 38 MIN
16MM FILM - 3/4 IN VIDEO
Shows the unfolding of a collective bargaining negotiation to the point of deadlock and the subsequent realization that some type of neutral third party intervention is required.
From The Out Of Conflict - Accord Series.
LC NO. 78-706118
Prod-USDL Dist-USNAC Prodn-RUDWIT 1978

Waldenville II C 30 MIN
3/4 OR 1/2 INCH VIDEO CASSETTE
Shows the mediation process and how the mediator functions after a collective bargaining deadlock.
From The Labor Relations Series.
Prod-IVCH Dist-IVCH

Waldenville II C 31 MIN
16MM FILM - 3/4 IN VIDEO
Shows the mediation process and the way in which the mediator works to assist the parties in reaching an agreement.
From The Out Of Conflict - Accord Series.
LC NO. 78-706133
Prod-USDL Dist-USNAC Prodn-RUDWIT 1978

Waldenville III C 36 MIN
16MM FILM, 3/4 OR 1/2 IN VIDEO
Presents a dramatization of collective bargaining negotiations ending in a deadlock, showing how fact finding is used as another means of reaching accord.
From The Out Of Conflict - Accord Series.
LC NO. 81-706325
Prod-USDL Dist-USNAC 1980

Waldenville Jogger C 39 MIN
16MM FILM - 3/4 IN VIDEO
Shows the arbitration of a grievance which results when a city attempts to enforce attendance rules for workers at a municipal hospital. Depicts preparations for the hearing and presentation of the case to the arbitrator.
From The Out Of Conflict, Accord Series.
LC NO. 80-706802
Prod-USDLMA Dist-USNAC Prodn-RUDWIT 1980

Walk C 16 MIN
16MM FILM OPTICAL SOUND
Attempts to re-create the feeling of the Kingston Miles for Millions Walk of 1971 and to investigate its purpose through interviews with both the walkers and organizers.
LC NO. 74-702433
Prod-QUAF Dist-QUEENU 1973

Walk C 8 MIN
16MM FILM, 3/4 OR 1/2 IN VIDEO
Uses clay figures and animation by means of modeling in presenting a story of a busy mother who sends her husband and son for a walk and the boy is carried away by a balloon on a string.
Prod-CFET Dist-PHENIX 1974

Walk - Don't Walk C 10 MIN
16MM FILM OPTICAL SOUND P-I
Discusses pedestrian safety practices for everyday situations. Includes crossing streets, the use of traffic signs and signals and becoming aware of possible dangers.
Prod-VADE Dist-VADE 1975

Walk Awhile In My Shoes C 27 MIN
16MM FILM, 3/4 OR 1/2 IN VIDEO J-C A
Explores the problems of architectural barriers and poorly designed transportation systems which make it difficult for handicapped people to get around.
Prod-NFBC Dist-NFBC 1974

Walk In C 21 MIN
16MM FILM, 3/4 OR 1/2 IN VIDEO A
Dramatizes two cases of employee theft at an industrial plant to emphasize that security is everybody's responsibility. Lists specific security guidelines.
Prod-MILLBK Dist-IFB

Walk In The Forest, A C 28 MIN
16MM FILM, 3/4 OR 1/2 IN VIDEO K-C A
Presents a documentary film on the ecological interdependence of all living things in the fir rainforests of the Pacific slope. Shows how animals, seasons, rain, fire and man work in concert.
Prod-PFP Dist-PFP Prodn-HOODR 1976

Walk In The Forest, A (French) C 28 MIN
16MM FILM, 3/4 OR 1/2 IN VIDEO K-C A
Presents a documentary film on the ecological interdependence of all living things in the fir rainforests of the Pacific slope. Shows how animals, seasons, rain, fire and man work in concert.
Prod-PFP Dist-PFP Prodn-HOODR 1976

Walk In The Forest, A (German) C 28 MIN
16MM FILM, 3/4 OR 1/2 IN VIDEO K-C A
Presents a documentary film on the ecological interdependence of all living things in the fir rainforests of the Pacific slope. Shows how animals, seasons, rain, fire and man work in concert.
Prod-PFP Dist-PFP Prodn-HOODR 1976

Walk In The Woods, A C 6 MIN
16MM FILM, 3/4 OR 1/2 IN VIDEO P-I
Presents an ecological adventure without narration to show a young boy as he explores the woods near his home, encounters some litter, and decides to do something about it.
Prod-CORF Dist-CORF 1972

Walk In The Woods, A B 15 MIN
2 INCH VIDEOTAPE P
See series title for descriptive statement.
From The Language Corner Series.
Prod-CVETVC Dist-GPITVL Prodn-WCVETV

Walk In Their Shoes - Parent-Child Communication C 24 MIN
16MM FILM OPTICAL SOUND J-C A
Tells the story of how a brother and sister find out what it is like to carry some of the responsibilities their parents have. Shows how they find that being responsible for someone's life is not easy, especially where there is opposition.
LC NO. 75-700063
Prod-BYU Dist-BYU 1968

Walk On The Moon C 15 MIN
16MM FILM, 3/4 OR 1/2 IN VIDEO J-C A
Historic documentary on the exploration of space from the pioneering flights of Dr Goodard to the lunar landing of Apollo 11.
From The Screen News Digest Series. Vol 12, Issue 1
Prod-HEARST Dist-HEARST

Walk Safe, Young America C 16 MIN
16MM FILM, 3/4 OR 1/2 IN VIDEO K-I
Presents June Lockhart as a school crossing guard pointing out pedestrian safety rules, including ways to observe traffic signs, the need to stay in crosswalks and avoid rushing into the street and the practicality of entering and leaving cars on the sidewalk side.
Prod-STNLYL Dist-PFP 1976

Walk Safely C 13 MIN
16MM FILM, 3/4 OR 1/2 IN VIDEO P
Points out the major causes of accidents to young children while crossing the street and shows correct street crossing procedures.
LC NO. 83-706566
Prod-FIESTF Dist-FIESTF 1983

Walk The First Step C 28 MIN
2 INCH VIDEOTAPE
Examines the problem of unemployment among minority groups and the success of Los Angeles' Mexican-American Opportunity Foundation (MAOF) in finding jobs for the unemployable.
From The Turning Points Series.
Prod-KCET Dist-PUBTEL

Walk Through The 20th Century With Bill Moyers--A Series

Presents Bill Moyers hosting a series of documentaries which explore the major events, personalities and mores that shaped the 20th century - the first century to be recorded on film and video tape.
Prod-CORPEL Dist-PBS 1982

America On The Road 058 MIN
Arming Of The Earth, The 058 MIN
Come To The Fairs 058 MIN
Democrat And The Dictator, The 058 MIN
Image Makers, The 058 MIN
Marshall, Texas - Marshall, Texas 090 MIN
Postwar Hopes, Cold War Fears 058 MIN
Presidents And Politics With Richard Strout 058 MIN
Reel World Of News, The 058 MIN
Second American Revolution, The, Pt 1 058 MIN
Second American Revolution, The, Pt 2 058 MIN
TR And His Times 000 MIN
Twenties, The 058 MIN
World War II - The Propaganda Battle 058 MIN

Walk Up The Hill, A C 29 MIN
16MM FILM OPTICAL SOUND
Discusses the subject of euthanasia from a Christian perspective by depicting the problems a family faces when one of its members suffers a paralyzing stroke.
LC NO. 74-700482
Prod-FAMF Dist-FAMF 1974

Walk With Me B 30 MIN
16MM FILM OPTICAL SOUND H-C A
Deals with the need to accept handicapped persons within both the life of the church and the community. Shows scenes of the Ohio Valley Goodwill Industries.
Prod-MCBM Dist-ECUFLM 1962

Walk With Me C 28 MIN
16MM FILM - VIDEO, ALL FORMATS
Deals with how children learn about sexuality from their parents. Interviews three different families. Includes a single mother, adopted children and a black family.
Prod-PPGCL Dist-PEREN

Walk Without Fear C 20 MIN
16MM FILM, 3/4 OR 1/2 IN VIDEO H-C A
Presents Chief of Police Tom Harris who addresses a local citizens' group on the growing problem of crime and the fear it breeds. Offers a number of precautionary measures which women can take to increase their peace of mind while decreasing the likelihood of their becoming a crime statistic.
Prod-DAVP Dist-AIMS 1970

Walk Your Way To Weight Control C
16MM FILM OPTICAL SOUND
Uses pedometers in order to illustrate the value of activity in weight reduction and control.
From The World Of Medicine Series.
LC NO. 75-704354
Prod-INFORP Dist-INFORP 1974

Walkabout (3rd Ed) C 25 MIN
16MM FILM OPTICAL SOUND J-C A
Shows the ancient way of life of the Aboriginals of central Australia. Includes scenes of men decorating their bodies for ceremony, the ritual of a kangaroo dance, the cooking of a kangaroo, and Aboriginal art in a cave in Ayers Rock.
LC NO. 76-700576
Prod-FLMAUS Dist-AUIS 1975

Walkaround Time C 48 MIN
3/4 INCH VIDEO CASSETTE
Presents a homage to the work of Marcel Duchamp in dance choreographed by Merce Cunningham.
Prod-CUNDAN Dist-CUNDAN

Walker Evans - His Time, His Presence, His Silence B 22 MIN
16MM FILM OPTICAL SOUND A
Presents an accumulation of individual photographic prints taken by Walker Evans.
LC NO. 73-701261
Prod-RADIM Dist-RADIM 1970

Walker Gardens - Honolulu C 30 MIN
1/2 IN VIDEO CASSETTE BETA/VHS
Explores the Walker Gardens in Honolulu and tours a Japanese-style garden. Gives tips on planting beans and celery.
From The Victory Garden Series.
Prod-WGBHTV Dist-MTI

Walker Weed, Wood Worker C 30 MIN
2 INCH VIDEOTAPE
See series title for descriptive statement.
From The World Of The American Craftsman Series.
Prod-WENHTV Dist-PUBTEL

Walkin' Blues C 15 MIN
3/4 OR 1/2 INCH VIDEO CASSETTE P
Continues the winter theme with an ice skating demonstration to 3/4 time and a song in 2/4 meter.
From The Stepping Into Rhythm Series.
Prod-WVIZTV Dist-AITECH

Walkin' On A Cloud C 52 MIN
16MM FILM OPTICAL SOUND
Tells the story of a young comedian and his mentor, an aging and forgotten vaudevillian whose alcohol problem has ruined his life.
LC NO. 80-700404
Prod-MIDSUN Dist-MIDSUN 1980

Walking C 5 MIN
16MM FILM, 3/4 OR 1/2 IN VIDEO J-C A
Uses animation without narration to depict the joys of walking. Shows that the manner of walking reflects the character of the individual.
Prod-NFBC Dist-LCOA 1970

Walking Dance For Any Number C 8 MIN
16MM FILM OPTICAL SOUND
Shows variations on a walking theme. Includes four films to be shown sinultaneously. Dance films by Elaine Summers.
Prod-EIF Dist-EIF

Walking For Physical Fitness C 11 MIN
16MM FILM, 3/4 OR 1/2 IN VIDEO H-C A
Explains that walking is one of the healthiest forms of exercise and that it can tone muscles, stimulate the heart and lungs, burn excess calories and improve mental outlook.
Prod-AF Dist-AIMS 1978

Walking For Physical Fitness (Arabic) C 11 MIN
16MM FILM, 3/4 OR 1/2 IN VIDEO H-C A
Explains that walking is one of the healthiest forms of exercise and that it can tone muscles, stimulate the heart and lungs, burn excess calories and improve mental outlook.
Prod-AF Dist-AIMS 1978

Walking Home From School C 11 MIN
16MM FILM, 3/4 OR 1/2 IN VIDEO P
Follows children on an assignment in which they must look at things very closely while walking home from school. Stresses safety in crossing streets and driveways.
Prod-AIMS Dist-AIMS 1970

Walking Home From School (Spanish) C 13 MIN
16MM FILM, 3/4 OR 1/2 IN VIDEO K-P
Stresses the concept of observing things around you and emphasizes safety.
Prod-ASSOCF Dist-AIMS Prodn-AFS 1970

Walking In A Sacred Manner - North American Indians And The Natural World C 23 MIN
16MM FILM, 3/4 OR 1/2 IN VIDEO J-C A
Explores the profound respect and appreciation of the Indians for the natural world and its importance to the physical, spiritual and psychological well-being of man. Presents photographs taken by Edward S Curtis between 1896 and 1930 combined with authentic Indian songs and commentary.
LC NO. 82-707334
Prod-CROSSS Dist-IFB 1982

Walking In The Wilderness C 20 MIN
3/4 OR 1/2 INCH VIDEO CASSETTE J-C A
Discusses walking trips as a practical alternative to motor-powered holidays. Describes pack types, shoes, clothing, food and camping gear. Includes information on pack loading, map reading, route finding, altitudes and dangerous wildlife and plants.
LC NO. 82-706792
Prod-AWSS Dist-AWSS 1981

Walking On A Miracle C 14 MIN
16MM FILM OPTICAL SOUND
Covers the design and construction of the water treatment plant at Deer Creek Lake in Ohio.
Prod-USAE Dist-MTP

Walking Safe C 10 MIN
16MM FILM, 3/4 OR 1/2 IN VIDEO K-P
Offers pedestrian safety tips.
Prod-MEDIAG Dist-MEDIAG 1978

Walking Safely To School C 18 MIN
16MM FILM OPTICAL SOUND P-I
Covers basic principles of pedestrian safety, showing both correct and incorrect examples. Follows a boy who has learned safety rules from his policeman father as he goes about helping children at school to learn safe walking habits.
LC NO. 74-702804
Prod-MMP Dist-MMP 1974

Walking Tall C 125 MIN
16MM FILM OPTICAL SOUND H A
Presents the true story of a vigilante farmer-sheriff who meets violence with violence and becomes a hero. Stars Joe Don Baker.
Prod-CROSBY Dist-TIMLIF 1973

Walking Tall Part II C 110 MIN
16MM FILM OPTICAL SOUND H A
Presents the sequel to Walking Tall. Stars Bo Svenson.
Prod-CROSBY Dist-TIMLIF 1976

Walking Tall, Final Chapter C 112 MIN
16MM FILM OPTICAL SOUND H A
Presents the sequel to Walking Tall and Walking Tall Part II. Stars Bo Svenson.
Prod-CROSBY Dist-TIMLIF 1977

Walking The Wire C 20 MIN
3/4 OR 1/2 INCH VIDEO CASSETTE
Seeks to increase employee competence by looking at responsible problem solving, decision making, and the use of power.
From The Confidence Game Series.
Prod-ERF Dist-DELTAK

Walking Through The Fire C 143 MIN
3/4 OR 1/2 INCH VIDEO CASSETTE H-C A
Chronicles Laurel Lee's real-life struggle with Hodgkin's disease.
LC NO. 80-706890
Prod-TIMLIF Dist-TIMLIF 1980

Walking To Heel C 30 MIN
3/4 OR 1/2 INCH VIDEO CASSETTE H-C A
Shows Barbara Woodhouse's method of teaching a dog to walk to heel.
From The Training Dogs The Woodhouse Way.
Prod-BBCTV Dist-FI 1982

Walking With Zuma (In Our Zoo) B 14 MIN
16MM FILM OPTICAL SOUND P-I
Tells a story about a visit to the zoo with Zuma--an orangutan designed to stimulate creative expressions.
Prod-AVED Dist-AVED 1969

Walkout That Never Was, The C 30 MIN
3/4 OR 1/2 INCH VIDEO CASSETTE H-C A
Presents a story centering on a protested school closing. Uses the story to try to reduce the minority isolation of Mexican-American students by showing the teenager as an individual, as a member of a unique cultural group and as a member of a larger complex society.
From The La Esquina (English) Series.
Prod-SWEDL Dist-GPITVL 1976

Walkover (Polish) B 77 MIN
16MM FILM OPTICAL SOUND
Follows the up-and-down life of a boxing hustler, fighting in amateur matches for beginners, throughout Poland. Underscores the feelings of alienation suffered by young people in modern society.
Prod-NYFLMS Dist-NYFLMS 1965

Wall C 1 MIN
16MM FILM OPTICAL SOUND
Uses animation to show the importance of cooperation in realizing better living conditions.
LC NO. 76-703355
Prod-CHD Dist-USCC Prodn-CREAVS 1976

Wall (Portugese) C 1 MIN
16MM FILM OPTICAL SOUND
Uses animation to show the importance of cooperation in realizing better living conditions.
LC NO. 76-703355
Prod-CHD Dist-USCC Prodn-CREAVS 1976

Wall (Spanish) C 1 MIN
16MM FILM OPTICAL SOUND
Uses animation to show the importance of cooperation in realizing better living conditions.
LC NO. 76-703355
Prod-CHD Dist-USCC Prodn-CREAVS 1976

Wall Hangings C 60 MIN
1/2 IN VIDEO CASSETTE BETA/VHS
Provides step-by-step instruction on how to utilize brooms, fans, frying pans, wicker baskets, mats and other objects to make attractive wall hangings. Features Pat Quigley.
Prod-RMI Dist-RMI

Wall Of Shame, The B 8 MIN
16MM FILM OPTICAL SOUND I-C A
Shows the wall between East Berlin and West Berlin that began August 13, 1961.
Prod-HEARST Dist-HEARST

Wall Repairs And Remodeling - Drywall And Spackle, Wainscotings C 30 MIN
1/2 IN VIDEO CASSETTE BETA/VHS
See series title for descriptive statement.
From The Wally's Workshop Series.
Prod-KARTES Dist-KARTES

Wall Street Week—A Series

Explores the investment market and analyzes economic trends and developments in down-to-earth language that takes the mystery out of money. Examines market activity and interviews guests from financial and business activities. Issued weekly.
Prod-MDCPB Dist-MDCPB

Wall To Wall C 30 MIN
2 INCH VIDEOTAPE C A
Stresses combining and coordinating a variety of wall treatments. Presents the views of designer Russell Phinder on importance of a coordinated look throughout an environment.
From The Designing Home Interiors Series. Unit 21
Prod-COAST Dist-CDTEL Prodn-RSCCD

Wall To Wall Selling C 20 MIN
16MM FILM OPTICAL SOUND
Features Orson Bean speaking to distributors of Schenley Products. Emphasizes special packaging and display techniques used during holiday seasons. Points out that wall-to-wall display of these products increases sales.
Prod-SCIND Dist-CCNY

Wall Washing B 12 MIN
16MM FILM OPTICAL SOUND T
Observes closely a group of pre-school children at Hilltop Head Start Center washing the walls and windows of their store-front school.
From The Vignette Series.
LC NO. 77-707934
Prod-EDS Dist-EDC 1968

Wall, The B 20 MIN
16MM FILM OPTICAL SOUND
Discusses radio-activity and exposes the meaning of the wall erected between East and West Berlin by the communist East Germany government in 1961.
Prod-HEARST Dist-HEARST 1962

Wall, The (Zid) C 4 MIN
16MM FILM, 3/4 OR 1/2 IN VIDEO
Presents an example of the animation coming from the Yugoslavian studios. Presents a commentary on the people user, the one who watches while others innocently do the work.
Prod-ZAGREB Dist-IFB 1966

Wallflower B 25 MIN
16MM FILM OPTICAL SOUND H-C A
Tells the story of a young man, feeling undesirable and unwanted, who decides that if he becomes a rock star he will find love and friends.
Prod-UWFKD Dist-UWFKD

Wallflower Order C 59 MIN
3/4 OR 1/2 INCH VIDEO CASSETTE
Presents a feminist women's dance theatre which incorporates theatre, music, comedy, martial arts and sign language into their work to create multi-dimensional performance pieces of strong impact.
Prod-WMENIF Dist-WMENIF

Wallpaper - Hanging Wallpaper, Steaming And Removing Wall paper C 30 MIN
1/2 IN VIDEO CASSETTE BETA/VHS
See series title for descriptive statement.
From The Wally's Workshop Series.
Prod-KARTES Dist-KARTES

Walls - Wood Paneling, Wood Paneling Over Masonry, Wainscotings, Room Dividers,... C 90 MIN
1/2 IN VIDEO CASSETTE BETA/VHS
Explains do-it-yourself procedures for the homeowner. Title continues .. Drywall And Spackle, Shelving.
From The Best Of Wally's Workshop Series.
Prod-KARTES Dist-KARTES

Walls And Bonds C 12 MIN
16MM FILM, 3/4 OR 1/2 IN VIDEO
Demonstrates different kinds of wood bonds.
From The Hand Operations - Woodworking Series.
Prod-MORLAT Dist-SF 1974

Walls And Walls C 10 MIN
16MM FILM, 3/4 OR 1/2 IN VIDEO J-C A
Traces the evolution of wall building through the ages. Discusses walls represented by prejudice and stereotypes.
Prod-NORMBP Dist-FLMFR 1973

Walls And Walls (Captioned Version) C 10 MIN
16MM FILM, 3/4 OR 1/2 IN VIDEO J-C A
Traces the evolution of wall building through the ages. Discusses walls represented by prejudice and stereotypes.
Prod-NORMBP Dist-FLMFR 1973

Walls And Walls (French) C 10 MIN
16MM FILM, 3/4 OR 1/2 IN VIDEO J-C A
Traces the evolution of wall building through the ages. Discusses walls represented by prejudice and stereotypes.
Prod-NORMBP Dist-FLMFR 1973

Walls And Windows C 12 MIN
16MM FILM, 3/4 OR 1/2 IN VIDEO J-C A
Explores values in parent-teenager communications.
From The Vignettes Series.
Prod-PAULST Dist-PAULST 1973

Walls Of Skinn B 20 MIN
16MM FILM OPTICAL SOUND
Examines 'LONELINESS' through the world of an autistic child of 11 who has spent the last seven years in a mental institution. Examines loneliness and hopelessness, as well as those who help the helpless.
Prod-UPENN Dist-UPENN 1964

Walls Of Time, The C 25 MIN
16MM FILM, 3/4 OR 1/2 IN VIDEO J-C A
Documents the history of Biblical translations in English, from Wyclif to today's new version, the Living Bible.
Prod-PFP Dist-PFP 1972

Walls We Build B 30 MIN
16MM FILM OPTICAL SOUND A
Uses a dramatization about the self-centered members of a family to point out the need for the members of a Christian family to share interests and problems.
LC NO. FIA65-1618
Prod-CONCOR Dist-CPH 1964

Wally Butts - A Great Georgian C 30 MIN
16MM FILM OPTICAL SOUND
Looks at the career of Wally Butts, the famous coach, from his birth in Milledgeville to his death on December 17, 1973. Includes such notables as Ed Sullivan and Bear Bryant. Shows footage of the famous Tarkenton to Herron pass that won the SEC Championship in 1959 and also of the 9-0 win over UCLA in the Rose Bowl. Narrated by TV celebrity and Georgia graduate Monte Markham.
From The Great Georgians Series.
Prod-WGTV Dist-WGTV 1974

Wally Butts - A Great Georgian C 60 MIN
16MM FILM OPTICAL SOUND
Looks at the career of Wally Butts, the famous coach, from his birth in Milledgeville to his death on December 17, 1973. Includes such notables as Ed Sullivan and Bear Bryant. Shows footage of the famous Tarkenton to Herron pass that won the SEC Championship in 1959 and also of the 9-0 win over UCLA in the Rose Bowl. Narrated by TV celebrity and Georgia graduate Monte Markham.
Prod-WGTV Dist-WGTV 1974

Wally's Workshop—A Series

Explains do-it-yourself procedures for the homeowner, from bathroom repairs to installing locks and adding electrical outlets.
Prod-KARTES Dist-KARTES

Alarms And Safes - Installing Burglar Alarms,
Antiques, Kits And Faking - Antique Kits, 030 MIN
Bathroom Remodeling - Ceramic Tiling, Bathtub 030 MIN
Bathroom Repairs - Toilet Repair, Copper 030 MIN
Beamed And Suspended Ceilings 030 MIN
Building Room Dividers And Shelving 030 MIN
Ceiling Ladders And Fireplaces - Ceiling 030 MIN
Decorated And Tiled Ceilings - Decorated 030 MIN
Decoupage, Framing And Matting - How To 030 MIN
Hardwood Floors - Installing Hardwood Floors, 030 MIN
Household Repairs 030 MIN
Kitchen Remodeling - Kitchen Cabinets, 030 MIN
Lamps And Electrical Outlets - Lamps And 030 MIN
Locks And Garage Door Openers - Installing 030 MIN
Maintenance And Exterior Repairs - Household 030 MIN
Murals And China Repairs - Wallpaper Murals, 030 MIN
Painting And Staining - Spray And Roller 030 MIN
Paneling - Wood Paneling, Wood Paneling Over 030 MIN
Parquet Floors And Carpet Installations 030 MIN
Refinishing Antiques - Refinishing Antiques, 030 MIN
Slate And Vinyl Floors - Slate Floors, Tile 030 MIN
Wall Repairs And Remodeling - Drywall And 030 MIN
Wallpaper - Hanging Wallpaper, Steaming And 030 MIN
Weatherizing - Fiberglass Insulation, 030 MIN

Walrus And The Carpenter, The C 6 MIN
16MM FILM, 3/4 OR 1/2 IN VIDEO
Uses animation to represent Lewis Carroll's whimsical poem in which the walrus and the carpenter entice a family of oysters to join them in their journey along the beach.
Prod-SPAMA Dist-LUF 1978

Walt Disney C 20 MIN
3/4 INCH VIDEO CASSETTE I
See series title for descriptive statement.
From The Truly American Series.
Prod-WVIZTV Dist-GPITVL 1979

Walt Whitman C 10 MIN
16MM FILM, 3/4 OR 1/2 IN VIDEO J-C
Presents both the poet and his poetry in American style by outlining the life and character of Whitman.
From The Poetry By Americans Series.
Prod-EVANSA Dist-AIMS 1972

Walt Whitman - Drum Taps B 30 MIN
2 INCH VIDEOTAPE J-H
From The Franklin To Frost Series.
Prod-GPITVL Dist-GPITVL

Walt Whitman - Poet For A New Age C 29 MIN
16MM FILM, 3/4 OR 1/2 IN VIDEO J-C
Presents a sensitive study of poet Walt Whitman - his beliefs and his conflicts with contemporaries.
From The Humanities - Poetry Series.
Prod-EBEC Dist-EBEC 1971

Walt Whitman - Song Of Myself, Pt 1 B 30 MIN
2 INCH VIDEOTAPE J-H
From The Franklin To Frost Series.
Prod-GPITVL Dist-GPITVL

Walt Whitman - Song Of Myself, Pt 2 B 30 MIN
2 INCH VIDEOTAPE J-H
From The Franklin To Frost Series.
Prod-GPITVL Dist-GPITVL

Walt Whitman - When Lilacs In The Dooryard Bloom'd B 30 MIN
2 INCH VIDEOTAPE J-H
From The Franklin To Frost Series.
Prod-GPITVL Dist-GPITVL

Walt Whitman And The Civil War C 30 MIN
3/4 INCH VIDEO CASSETTE H-C A
Takes a look at Gettysburg, scene of the Civil War's most crucial battle. Features Richard Kiley and the First Poetry Quartet reading works by Walt Whitman which center around the theme of war.
From The Anyone For Tennyson Series.
Prod-NETCHE Dist-GPITVL

Walt Whitman's 'Leaves Of Grass' C 21 MIN
16MM FILM OPTICAL SOUND J-C A
Presents the story of Walt Whitman's life, told in his own words, both prose and verse. Shows places where he lived and worked. Describes the influences which led to his writing 'LEAVES OF GRASS.'
LC NO. FIA66-1201
Prod-LINE Dist-LINE 1965

Walt Whitman's Western Journey C 15 MIN
16MM FILM OPTICAL SOUND I-C A
Traces Walt Whitman's journey across the Western prairies to the Rocky Mountains in 1879. Shows inland America through the eyes and words of a poet.
LC NO. FIA66-1202
Prod-LINE Dist-LINE 1965

Walter Cronkite Remembers And The Battle Of The Bulge B 60 MIN
1/2 IN VIDEO CASSETTE BETA/VHS
Shows Walter Cronkite reminiscing with his colleague, CBS News correspondent Charles Kuralt, about his experiences on the battlefield and in combat planes above it. Follows with the epic Battle Of The Bulge, a vicious struggle between American and German troops, which shows turned out to be the beginning of the end for the Third Reich. Concludes with a preview of future video cassettes in the series.
From The World War II With Walter Cronkite Series.
Prod-CBSNEW Dist-CBSVL

Walter Cronkite's Universe—A Series

Prod-CBSNEW Dist-MOKIN

Disappearance Of The Great Rainforest 012 MIN

Walter Fish - A Modern Adult Parable C 5 MIN
16MM FILM OPTICAL SOUND J-C A
Uses animation to present the story of a fish who finds himself on the beach and tries to get help to get back into the water. Features an interpretation of the Biblical parable of the Good Samaritan.
LC NO. 75-703013
Prod-ALBA Dist-ALBA Prodn-WITFTV 1971

Walter Gropius - His New World Home C 12 MIN
16MM FILM OPTICAL SOUND H-C A
Discusses the art and architecture of Walter Gropius, founder of the Bauhaus School. Examines the architectural innovations incorporated into Gropius's home built in Lincoln, Massachusetts in 1937.
LC NO. 75-703768
Prod-HOWRD Dist-HOWRD 1974

Walter Kerr On Theater C 26 MIN
16MM FILM, 3/4 OR 1/2 IN VIDEO H-C A
Demonstrates the joy, magic and power of the theater. Provides insight into the unique characteristics of live drama by contrasting excerpts from outstanding plays with film. Shows the range of forms and ideas possible in live theater.
Prod-IQFILM Dist-LCOA Prodn-SAUDEK 1970

Walter Verkehr - Violinist And David Renner - Pianist C 29 MIN
2 INCH VIDEOTAPE
Presents the music of violinist Walter Verkehr and pianist David Renner.
From The Young Musical Artists Series.
Prod-WKARTV Dist-PUBTEL

Walter, The Lazy Mouse C 10 MIN
16MM FILM, 3/4 OR 1/2 IN VIDEO K-I
Presents Walter, the lazy mouse who learns independently to provide for himself and to teach others.
Prod-SF Dist-SF 1972

Walzerkrieg B 93 MIN
16MM FILM OPTICAL SOUND
A German language film. Depicts the friendship of Viennese waltz composers Lanner and Strauss, which is tested when the maestros have to compete against each other in London and Vienna.
Prod-WSTGLC Dist-WSTGLC 1933

Wampanoags Of Gay Head, The C 30 MIN
3/4 INCH VIDEO CASSETTE
See series title for descriptive statement.
From The People Of The First Light Series.
Prod-WGBYTV Dist-GPITVL 1977

Wanda Gag 1893-1946 - A Minnesota Childhood C 10 MIN
3/4 OR 1/2 INCH VIDEO CASSETTE K-I
Depicts childhood of artist and author Wanda Gag. Portrays her artistic development and how she came to write her well-known children's book Millions Of Cats. Includes photographs of Gag's home and illustrations from her books.
LC NO. 84-730301
Prod-HERPRO Dist-HERPRO 1984

Wandawega Waters And Spiral 5 C 21 MIN
3/4 OR 1/2 INCH VIDEO CASSETTE
Presents startling effects which contrast between the vibrant, artificial colors and sounds of the natural environment.
Prod-EAI Dist-EAI

Wanderers, The - Paths Of Planets C 10 MIN
16MM FILM, 3/4 OR 1/2 IN VIDEO J-H
Traces the development of man's understanding of the planets and describes the observations of early Greek astronomers. Includes a discussion of Kepler's laws and the later significance of Newton's work. Includes questions and vocabulary.
Prod-BFA Dist-PHENIX Prodn-DAVFMS 1969

Wandering Through Winter C 50 MIN
16MM FILM, 3/4 OR 1/2 IN VIDEO
Describes the effects of winter throughout North America. Based on the writings of Edwin Way Teale.
From The Four Seasons Series.
Prod-DOCUA Dist-CNEMAG

Wanna See ASL Stories C 105 MIN
3/4 OR 1/2 INCH VIDEO CASSETTE S
Presents stories in sign language at all levels. Provides signed stories together with written questions and signed answers. On three tapes. Signed.
Prod-GALCO Dist-GALCO 1979

Wanted - Babies C 20 MIN
3/4 OR 1/2 INCH VIDEO CASSETTE
Explores adoption and alternatives to adoption, including surrogate mothers and 'grey market' adoptions.
Prod-WCCOTV Dist-WCCOTV 1982

Wants And Needs C 15 MIN
3/4 OR 1/2 INCH VIDEO CASSETTE P
Explains wants and needs, looks at advertising and consumerism, and explores the concept of value.
From The Common Cents Series.
Prod-KETCTV Dist-AITECH 1977

Wants And Needs C 15 MIN
3/4 OR 1/2 INCH VIDEO CASSETTE P
Uses the format of a television program to demonstrate the basic economic concept of wants and needs and the differences between them. Explains how people want and need both goods and services.
From The Pennywise Series. No. 1
LC NO. 82-706004
Prod-MAETEL Dist-GPITVL 1980

War Against Fascism, The B 30 MIN
16MM FILM OPTICAL SOUND H-C A
Dr St Clair Drake presents a study of the turmoil which surrounded Black participation in a so-called war against Fascism. He discusses the participation of blacks in World War II, the segregation policy of the army, and the records of black officers and combat units.
From The Black History, Section 17 - World War II Experience Series.
LC NO. 74-704094
Prod-WCBSTV Dist-HRAW 1969

War And Advice B 20 MIN
16MM FILM, 3/4 OR 1/2 IN VIDEO H-C
Depicts the role of the special U S forces who serve as observers and instructors for Vietnamese troops. Shows how American aid and influence reach into military, political and economic areas.
Prod-USDD Dist-USNAC 1964

War And Peace C 2 MIN
1/2 IN VIDEO CASSETTE BETA/VHS
Presents a two-cassette set of the 1956 adaptation of Leo Tolstoy's novel WAR AND PEACE. Stars Audrey Hepburn and Henry Fonda.
Prod-GA Dist-GA

War And Peace C 29 MIN
16MM FILM, 3/4 OR 1/2 IN VIDEO A
Explores problems of sibling rivalry through the dramatization of a situation in the fictional Marshall family, in which Sonny tries to make peace between two squabbling stepdaughters. Includes a brief introduction and commentary by real-life families and child development experts.
From The Footsteps Series.
LC NO. 80-707205
Prod-USDED Dist-USNAC Prodn-EDFCEN 1980

War And Peace C 60 MIN
3/4 OR 1/2 INCH VIDEO CASSETTE J-C A
Presents flutist James Galway discussing how music between the two World Wars reflected history. Includes examples from Stravinsky's Rite Of Spring, Gershwin's An American In Paris and Brecht's The Beggar's Opera.
From The James Galway's Music In Time Series.
Prod-POLTEL Dist-FOTH 1982

War At Home, The C 100 MIN
16MM FILM - 3/4 IN VIDEO J-C A
Chronicles the war that students and other anti-war dissidents waged on America's political system, military and notions of patriotism. Shows how the anti-war movement grew as a genuine people's revolt in tandem with the escalation of the war in Vietnam.
Prod-FIRS Dist-FIRS

War Between The States C
3/4 OR 1/2 INCH VIDEO CASSETTE
Prod-MSTVIS Dist-MSTVIS

War Between The Tates, The C 90 MIN
3/4 OR 1/2 INCH VIDEO CASSETTE H-C A
Reveals how the marriage of a supposedly happy couple falls apart when the husband has an affair with one of his students. Shows the ironies and complexities of the marital relationship as the children, spouses and lover adjust to their new lives. Stars Richard Crenna and Elizabeth Ashley.
LC NO. 80-706891
Prod-TIMLIF Dist-TIMLIF 1980

War Chronicles, Vols 1 And 2, The C
1/2 IN VIDEO CASSETTE BETA/VHS
Presents a two-cassette set chronicling World War II, including authentic footage shot by combat cameramen. Narrated by Patrick O'Neal.
Prod-GA Dist-GA

War Comes To America B 67 MIN
3/4 OR 1/2 INCH VIDEO CASSETTE
Treats America's reaction to the terrifying events of World War II. Observes the effects on the people of the transition from isolationism to involvement in the fight against the axis.
From The Frank Capra's 'Why We Fight' Series.
Prod-IHF Dist-IHF

War Comes To America B 67 MIN
16MM FILM - 3/4 IN VIDEO H
Reviews the history of the United States and describes the characteristics, habits and beliefs of the American people. Explains the events from 1931 to 1941 that caused the United States to enter World War II. Issued in 1945 as a motion picture.
From The Why We Fight Series.
LC NO. 79-706470
Prod-USOWI Dist-USNAC 1979

War Comes To Pearl Harbor C 26 MIN
16MM FILM, 3/4 OR 1/2 IN VIDEO H-C
Examines American diplomacy in 1941, describing the events which led to the bombing of Pearl Harbor.
From The Between The Wars Series.
Prod-LNDBRG Dist-FI 1978

War Dance C 12 MIN
16MM FILM OPTICAL SOUND I-C A
Presents a demonstration of the 'GRASS DANCE,' which was performed by Sioux warriors of proven bravery. Contrasts the slow ritualistic dance of the women with the vigorous, individualistic stepping of the warriors. Explains the symbolism of the dance steps and the traditional costume.
From The Plains Indian Culture Series.
Prod-UOKLA Dist-UOKLA 1954

War Department Film Communique No. 1 B 30 MIN
3/4 OR 1/2 INCH VIDEO CASSETTE
Presents War Department Film Communiques from 1943 including Fifth Army in Italy and With the Australians in New Guinea - Australian Footage.
Prod-IHF Dist-IHF

War Department Film Communique No. 2 B 45 MIN
3/4 OR 1/2 INCH VIDEO CASSETTE
Offers War Department Film Communiques including Hitting The Beach in Italy and Dogfight - P47s In Combat on W Front.
Prod-IHF Dist-IHF

War Department Film Communique No. 3 B 30 MIN
3/4 OR 1/2 INCH VIDEO CASSETTE
Offers War Department Film Communiques from 1944 including Capture Of Toulon And Marseilles and Operation In France And Belgium.
Prod-IHF Dist-IHF

War For Empire C 30 MIN
3/4 OR 1/2 INCH VIDEO CASSETTE C
See series title for descriptive statement.
From The American Story - The Beginning To 1877 Series.
Prod-DALCCD Dist-DALCCD

War From The Air C 57 MIN
16MM FILM OPTICAL SOUND
Discusses bombers, the development of bombing strategy and the consequences to the world since World War I.
From The Nova Series.
Prod-WGBHTV Dist-KINGFT

War From The Air C 57 MIN
3/4 OR 1/2 INCH VIDEO CASSETTE
Discusses bombers, the development of bombing strategy and the consequences to the world since World War I.
From The Nova Series.
Prod-WGBHTV Dist-PBS

War Game, The B 40 MIN
16MM FILM, 3/4 OR 1/2 IN VIDEO
Portrays, in newsreel style, the effects of a nuclear attack on Britain.
Prod-PSR Dist-PSR 1966

War Game, The B 47 MIN
3/4 OR 1/2 INCH VIDEO CASSETTE
Shows what could happen in Great Britain if it were under nuclear attack and the after-effects its survivors would suffer in a post-nuclear-war world.
Prod-IHF Dist-IHF

War Game, The B 49 MIN
16MM FILM, 3/4 OR 1/2 IN VIDEO H-C A
Enacts the carnage and destruction that would result from a thermonuclear war between the Soviet Union and England in a fictional sequence. Raises questions about the societal logic that permits the existence of thermonuclear weapons. Produced in 1966 in England.
Prod-BFI Dist-FI 1976

War In Korea B 22 MIN
16MM FILM OPTICAL SOUND H A
Presents clips from 1951-1953 screen news digest films on the Korean War, including savage fighting, peace attempts, embattled Korea, the role of the United Nations, prisoner of war exchange and finally, the truce in Korea.
From The News Magazine Of The Screen Series.
Prod-PATHE Dist-HEARST 1953

War Is Over, The C 28 MIN
16MM FILM, 3/4 OR 1/2 IN VIDEO I-H
Focuses on a returning troop ship in 1919, showing how different soldiers are reacting to this period of readjustment after the horrors of battle.
From The Adventures In History Series.
Prod-NFBC Dist-FI 1978

War Of Independence 1775-1783 B 24 MIN
3/4 INCH VIDEO CASSETTE
Presents through still pictures the general movements of the Continental Army and Navy from 1775-1783. Describes the founding Of the Navy, the battle of Valcour Island, the patriot John Paul Jones and Washington's strategy of Yorktown.
Prod-USNAC Dist-USNAC 1972

War Of The Eggs, The X 27 MIN
16MM FILM, 3/4 OR 1/2 IN VIDEO H-C A
Focuses on a case of child abuse, telling how a psychiatrist helps a young couple understand the reasons for their behavior. Stars Elizabeth Ashley, Bill Bixby and James Olson.
Prod-PAULST Dist-MEDIAG

War Of The Eggs, The (Spanish) X 27 MIN
16MM FILM, 3/4 OR 1/2 IN VIDEO H-C A
Focuses on a case of child abuse, telling how a psychiatrist helps a young couple understand the reasons for their behavior. Stars Elizabeth Ashley, Bill Bixby and James Olson.
From The Insight Series.
Prod-PAULST Dist-PAULST

War Of The Intellectuals, The C 30 MIN
3/4 INCH VIDEO CASSETTE H-C A
Presents Ben J Wattenberg, author of The Real America, and Norman Podhoretz, editor of Commentary magazine, discussing whether the American experience has been a success or a failure.
From The In Search Of The Real America Series.
Prod-WGBHTV Dist-KINGFT 1977

War Of The Worlds C
1/2 IN VIDEO CASSETTE BETA/VHS
Presents H G Wells' story of the invasion of Earth by Martians, starring Gene Barry.
Prod-GA Dist-GA

War Of The Worlds, The C 20 MIN
16MM FILM OPTICAL SOUND J-C A
Presents a melodrama about the invasion of a rural California town by seemingly invulnerable Martians. Tells of the battle between the invaders and the residents and of the invaders from the earth's bacteria.
From The American Film Genre - The Science Fiction Film Series.
LC NO. 75-702629
Prod-TWCF Dist-FI 1975

War Of 1812 C 30 MIN
3/4 OR 1/2 INCH VIDEO CASSETTE C
See series title for descriptive statement.
From The American Story - The Beginning To 1877 Series.
Prod-DALCCD Dist-DALCCD

War Of 1812 C 30 MIN
2 INCH VIDEOTAPE
Covers the rights of a neutral nation, impressment, and the failure of economic pressures to avoid the War of 1812.
From The American History I Series.
Prod-DENVPS Dist-GPITVL

War Of 1812, The C 20 MIN
3/4 INCH VIDEO CASSETTE
Presents the events leading up to the War of 1812 and the role of the U S Navy in this war. Illustrates the origins of such phrases as 'old ironsides,' 'don't give up the ship,' and 'we have met the enemy and they are ours.' Includes a sequence on the writing of the Star-Spangled Banner.
Prod-USNAC Dist-USNAC 1972

War Of 1812, The (2nd Ed) C 14 MIN
16MM FILM, 3/4 OR 1/2 IN VIDEO I-H
Reveals that when the British begin impressing American seamen, Congress declares war in 1812. Shows that stunning American land and naval victories help end the war while spurring American industry, stimulating national pride and shaping relations with Canada.
Prod-CORF Dist-CORF 1982

War On Bureaucracy - A New Way Of Looking At Organizational Development B 32 MIN
16MM FILM, 3/4 OR 1/2 IN VIDEO
Takes a look at organizational development and describes methods by which large organizations may minimize the confinement and depersonalization often experienced by their members.
From The Management Development Series.
Prod-UCLA Dist-UCEMC 1974

War Shadows C 25 MIN
3/4 OR 1/2 INCH VIDEO CASSETTE
Explores the Viet Nam war experiences of Paul Reutershan, his contact with Agent Orange, and subsequent illness and death. Reutershan was the first to bring the plight of veterans exposed to this defoliant to national attention before he died of cancer at 28 years of age.
Prod-GMPF Dist-GMPF

War Shadows C 26 MIN
3/4 OR 1/2 INCH VIDEO CASSETTE
Follows Vietnam veteran Paul Reutershan who had been exposed to Agent Orange. Records his struggle during the last six months of his life to secure the VA's recognition of cancer resulting from exposure to Agent Orange.
Prod-EAI Dist-EAI

War Story, A C 82 MIN
16MM FILM, 3/4 OR 1/2 IN VIDEO H-C A
Dramatizes life in a Japanese prisoner-of-war camp during World War II. Interweaves scenes from inside the camp with footage of the fall of Singapore and interviews survivors of the camp.
Prod-NFBC Dist-NFBC 1981

War With Mexico C 30 MIN
3/4 OR 1/2 INCH VIDEO CASSETTE C
See series title for descriptive statement.
From The American Story - The Beginning To 1877 Series.
Prod-DALCCD Dist-DALCCD

War Within, The C 60 MIN
3/4 OR 1/2 INCH VIDEO CASSETTE C A
Portrays the personal lives of six highly decorated Vietnam War veterans. Shows them as patients at the Vietnam Veterans Treatment Center in Menlo Park, California, reliving the nightmares of Vietnam by talking about them.
Prod-KRONTV Dist-FI

War Without Winners II C 29 MIN
16MM FILM, 3/4 OR 1/2 IN VIDEO
Intertwines interviews with celebrities, scientists and layman on the dangers of nuclear war. Features excerpts from a historically unprecedented nuclear effects roundtable discussion between leading American and Soviet physicians. Narrated by Paul Newman.
LC NO. 83-706909
Prod-CDINFO Dist-FI 1983

War Years And Beyond, The C 30 MIN
1 INCH VIDEOTAPE J-H
Describes the strategy for breaking down military discrimination, the Black service record of World War II, the United Nations and its impact on Black America and the administration of Harry Truman with regard to civil rights.
From The Odyssey In Black Series.
Prod-KLVXTV Dist-GPITVL

War Years, The - Fabulous 1939, Then Global Conflict C 35 MIN
16MM FILM, 3/4 OR 1/2 IN VIDEO
Shows how Hollywood used propaganda techniques to depict Germans and Japanese as totally immoral, while filling the need for symbolic heroes such as those portrayed by John Wayne.
From The Life Goes To The Movies Series. Pt 2
LC NO. 79-707674
Prod-TIMLIF Dist-TIMLIF 1976

War—A Series
C A
Focuses on the nature, consequences and future of modern warfare. Argues that war is not an outlet for natural aggression but an institution invented to settle international disputes which no longer serves its purpose. Concludes that war must be abolished and disputes settled another way to avoid World War III and the inevitable destruction of the world. Filmed in ten countries and on two oceans with cooperation of the armed forces of six nations.
Prod-NFBC Dist-FI

Anybody's Son Will Do	060 MIN
Deadly Game Of Nations, The	060 MIN
Goodbye War	060 MIN
Keeping The Old Game Alive	060 MIN
Notes On Nuclear War	060 MIN
Profession Of Arms, The	060 MIN
Road To Total War, The	060 MIN

Warao, The C 57 MIN
16MM FILM, 3/4 OR 1/2 IN VIDEO H-C A
Presents an ethnographic documentary on the Warao people, who live surrounded by water at the mouth of the Orinoco River delta in eastern Venezuela. Shows scenes of routine life, including a shaman's curing ritual and methods of conflict resolution.
LC NO. 78-701765
Prod-UCLA Dist-UCEMC 1978

Warbirds (WWII Fighters and Bombers) C 20 MIN
3/4 OR 1/2 INCH VIDEO CASSETTE J-C A
Discusses such famous World War II fighters and bombers as the Mustang, Corsair and Flying Fortress. Notes that nearly 40 years after rolling off wartime assembly lines, these fighters and bombers are still flying.
LC NO. 82-706793
Prod-AWSS Dist-AWSS 1981

Warlords Of Atlantis C 96 MIN
16MM FILM OPTICAL SOUND
Describes how a father-and-son team plumb the ocean's depth to search for the lost continent of Atlantis.
Prod-CPC Dist-TWYMAN 1978

Warm Coat, The C 14 MIN
16MM FILM OPTICAL SOUND
A documentary account of the airlifting of sea otters from the Bering Sea to Alaskan coves, an environment which will offer the animals a better chance to thrive and multiply.
LC NO. 72-704659
Prod-USAEC Dist-USNAC 1969

Warm-Blooded And Cold-Blooded Animals C 14 MIN
16MM FILM, 3/4 OR 1/2 IN VIDEO I-J
Utilizes experiments to demonstrate how environment affects the temperature of cold-blooded animals and how body coverings help warm-blooded animals keep a more constant temperature.
Prod-CORF Dist-CORF 1971

Warm-Season Gardens C 30 MIN
1/2 IN VIDEO CASSETTE BETA/VHS
Shows how to start a warm-season garden. Gives tips on growing in containers. Discusses dimension and intent of a main season bed.
From The Victory Garden Series.
Prod-WGBHTV Dist-MTI

Warm-Up And Conditioning C 30 MIN
3/4 OR 1/2 INCH VIDEO CASSETTE
See series title for descriptive statement.
From The Health And Well-Being Of Dancers Series.
Prod-ARCVID Dist-ARCVID

Warming Warning C 52 MIN
16MM FILM, 3/4 OR 1/2 IN VIDEO H-C
Analyzes a major environmental threat - the warming of the earth's climate due to increased burning of fossil fuels. Explains how the carbon dioxide content of the earth's atmosphere acts like the glass in a greenhouse resulting in warming of the global climate.
Prod-THAMES Dist-MEDIAG 1985

Warning - Breathing May Be Hazardous To Your Health C 25 MIN
3/4 OR 1/2 INCH VIDEO CASSETTE
Shows just how bad pollution really is, who is responsible and what can be done about it. Interviews Dr Joseph Boyle, specialist in internal medicine and disease of the chest and lungs, and a former member of the California State Air Resource Board, on the timely topic of pollution and its threat to mankind.
Prod-TRAINX Dist-TRAINX

Warning - Earthquake C 24 MIN
16MM FILM, 3/4 OR 1/2 IN VIDEO I-J
Presents scenes from actual earthquakes. Shows workers trying to help the injured and unharmed survivors rummaging through the debris and total destruction that surrounds them. Illustrates the devastating effects of the earthquake. Gives insights into survivors' feelings through interviews.
From The Wide World Of Adventure Series.
Prod-AVATLI Dist-EBEC 1976

Warning Arrhythmias C 22 MIN
16MM FILM OPTICAL SOUND PRO
Discusses the concept of warning arrhythmias, including a discussion of specific warning arrhythmias. Describes types, electrocardiographic patterns and treatment. Covers heart block (A-V block).
From The Intensive Coronary Care Multimedia Learning System (ICC/MMLS) Series.
LC NO. 73-701773
Prod-SUTHLA Dist-SUTHLA 1969

Warning Arrhythmias, The C 22 MIN
16MM FILM OPTICAL SOUND
Discusses the warning arrhythmias which are the precursors of more serious arrhythmias and uses animation to explain the anatomical and electrocardiographic aspects.
From The Multimedia Instructional System For Coronary Care Unit Nurses Series.
LC NO. 74-705016
Prod-HOFLAR Dist-SUTHLA Prodn-SUTHP 1969

Warning From Outer Space C 11 MIN
16MM FILM OPTICAL SOUND P-I
Space explorers find that 'OLD-FASHIONED EARTHPEOPLE' are still smoking--a habit that Z-Men made a Zeta Crime 96 million earth years ago.
Prod-PROART Dist-PROART

Warring And Roaring C
3/4 OR 1/2 INCH VIDEO CASSETTE
Prod-MSTVIS Dist-MSTVIS

Warrior C 52 MIN
3/4 OR 1/2 INCH VIDEO CASSETTE H-C A
Examines the universal experience of men who kill in time of war - preparing for it, participating in it, and reflecting on it afterward - demonstrating that no man who has experienced combat is ever quite the same again.
From The World At War Specials Series.
Prod-THAMES Dist-MEDIAG 1974

Warrior And Queen - Shakespeare C 45 MIN
2 INCH VIDEOTAPE
See series title for descriptive statement.
From The Humanities Series. Unit I - Persons, Places And Events
Prod-WTTWTV Dist-GPITVL

Warriors At Peace C 13 MIN
16MM FILM OPTICAL SOUND I-J
Presents life among the once warlike Apaches in Arizona. Shows their wealth in stock, art of basketry and the tribal tradition of the pollen blessing ceremony.
Prod-DAGP Dist-MLA 1953

Warriors Of The Wind C 52 MIN
16MM FILM OPTICAL SOUND
Looks at the Hamamatsu Kite Festival which has been held in Japan for over 400 years.
LC NO. 81-701396
Prod-SHAWBR Dist-SHAWBR 1981

Warriors' Women C 27 MIN
16MM FILM - 3/4 IN VIDEO H-C A
Explores the living situations of five Vietnam veterans and their families by interviewing wives who candidly and emotionally reveal some of the problems they have witnessed. Discusses exposure to Agent Orange and the effects of delayed stress syndrome including depression, anger, violence, unemployment and suicide.
LC NO. 81-707089
Prod-TODD Dist-TODD 1981

Wars Without Winners II C 28 MIN
16MM FILM OPTICAL SOUND
Interviews U S and Soviet experts and ordinary citizens on nuclear war and the arms race. Includes Admiral Rickover's Congressional testimony and a discussion between U S and Soviet physicians aired on Soviet and U S television.
Prod-PSR Dist-PSR 1982

Warsaw File, The C 29 MIN
3/4 OR 1/2 INCH VIDEO CASSETTE
Focuses on the continuing story of Poland and the daily problems which American correspondents face as they try to cover Polish events.
From The Ifside Story Series.
Prod-PBS Dist-PBS 1981

Warsaw, Poland C 3 MIN
16MM FILM OPTICAL SOUND P-I
Discusses the city of Warsaw in Poland.
From The Of All Things Series.
Prod-BAILYL Dist-AVED

Warship, A Society At Sea, The C 53 MIN
16MM FILM OPTICAL SOUND
Examines a ship as a model for social organization.
LC NO. 78-701580
Prod-VPISU Dist-VPISU 1978

Wartime In Washington C 30 MIN
3/4 OR 1/2 INCH VIDEO CASSETTE J-C A
Tells the story of life in the nation's capital during World War II. Includes archival footage and interviews of residents.
Prod-WETATV Dist-WETATV

Warts, Songs And Jokes B 30 MIN
3/4 INCH VIDEO CASSETTE
Discusses why jokes, songs and folk cures are a part of American folklore. Uses special staging and recordings.
From The Folklore - U S A Series.
Prod-UMITV Dist-UMITV 1967

Warty, The Toad C 13 MIN
16MM FILM, 3/4 OR 1/2 IN VIDEO P
Presents the story of Warty, the toad, who is vain about his ugliness until he learns that there are more important things than looks.
Prod-CORF Dist-CORF 1973

Was Ist Los C 15 MIN
16MM FILM, 3/4 OR 1/2 IN VIDEO
See series title for descriptive statement.
From The Guten Tag Series. Part 10
Prod-BAYER Dist-IFB 1968

Was It Something I Said C 13 MIN
16MM FILM, 3/4 OR 1/2 IN VIDEO C A
Illustrates that employees at all levels are responsible for classified information.
Prod-GLI Dist-MTI

Was It Worth Reading B 14 MIN
16MM FILM OPTICAL SOUND I-J
Discusses criteria for evaluating what is read. Presents several paragraphs to be read and judged. Lists questions on which to base the evaluation.
From The Pathways To Reading Series.
Prod-CBF Dist-AVED 1958

Was Machen Wir Jetzt C 15 MIN
16MM FILM, 3/4 OR 1/2 IN VIDEO
See series title for descriptive statement.
From The Guten Tag Series. Part 17
Prod-BAYER Dist-IFB 1968

Was Man Nicht Kann, Muss Man Eben Lernen C 15 MIN
16MM FILM, 3/4 OR 1/2 IN VIDEO
See series title for descriptive statement.
From The Guten Tag Wie Geht's Series. Part 18
Prod-BAYER Dist-IFB 1973

Was Tut Man In Dem Fall C 15 MIN
16MM FILM, 3/4 OR 1/2 IN VIDEO
See series title for descriptive statement.
From The Guten Tag Series. Part 23
Prod-BAYER Dist-IFB 1968

Wash Techniques Of Painting C 25 MIN
3/4 OR 1/2 INCH VIDEO CASSETTE H-C A
See series title for descriptive statement.
From The Paint Series. Program 6
Prod-BBCTV Dist-FI

Washing Feel Good Movie, The C 6 MIN
16MM FILM, 3/4 OR 1/2 IN VIDEO K-P
Portrays children experiencing the pleasures of getting dirty and the pleasure of being clean.
From The Feel Good - Primary Health Series.
Prod-CF Dist-CF 1974

Washington C 15 MIN
3/4 INCH VIDEO CASSETTE P
See series title for descriptive statement.
From The Celebrate Series.
Prod-KUONTV Dist-GPITVL 1978

Washington - Day One C 14 MIN
16MM FILM OPTICAL SOUND I-H
Records the inauguration of Ronald Reagan.
From The Screen News Digest Series.
LC NO. 81-701012
Prod-HEARST Dist-HEARST 1981

Washington - Time Of Triumph (1781-1783) C 22 MIN
16MM FILM OPTICAL SOUND H-C
Shows how Washington's Revolutionary Army defeats General Cornwallis' Army. Portrays how Washington, after the surrender, refused absolute power in order that democracy might work.
Prod-WOLPER Dist-FI 1974

Washington - Years Of Trial (1754-1781) C 32 MIN
16MM FILM OPTICAL SOUND H-C
Provides a more human understanding of the complex personality of Washington by stripping away much of the legendary character of the man.
Prod-WOLPER Dist-FI 1974

Washington DC - L'Enfant's Dream, Our Heritage C 21 MIN
16MM FILM, 3/4 OR 1/2 IN VIDEO I-H
Presents the story of Pierre Charles L'Enfant, the architect of Washington, DC. Tells how he planned the city and the history of the capitol. Describes how L'Enfant died in poverty never knowing that his dream was realised and that Washington today is the way he planned it.
Prod-HANDEL Dist-HANDEL 1984

Washington Irving's Spain C 50 MIN
16MM FILM, 3/4 OR 1/2 IN VIDEO
Retraces Washington Irving's stagecoach journey through Spain in the 1820's. Visits many of the places mentioned in Irving's travel accounts, including Alhambra and Madrid.
LC NO. 80-706392
Prod-NGS Dist-NGS 1966

Washington To Moscow Peacewalk - The Road To Global Sanity C 15 MIN
3/4 OR 1/2 INCH VIDEO CASSETTE
Presents the beginning of the Nuclear Freeze Campaign.
Prod-GMPF Dist-GMPF

Washington Trail, The C 25 MIN
16MM FILM, 3/4 OR 1/2 IN VIDEO H T
Traces the ancestral roots of George Washington, providing an important chapter in history as well as a valuable lesson in genealogical investigation.
Prod-TFVPRO Dist-EBEC 1983

Washington, City Of The World C 14 MIN
16MM FILM, 3/4 OR 1/2 IN VIDEO I-H
Pictures Washington, D C, showing federal buildings, national monuments and offices of the representatives of governments of other nations.
Prod-PART Dist-PHENIX 1965

Washington, D C - Symbol Of Freedom C 16 MIN
16MM FILM OPTICAL SOUND I-H
Takes the viewer on a guided tour of our nation's capital. Includes the White House and such buildings and monuments as the Library of Congress, Washington Monument and the Smithsonian Institution.
Prod-BECKLY Dist-BECKLY

Washington, DC C 3 MIN
16MM FILM OPTICAL SOUND P-I
Discusses Washington, DC.
From The Of All Things Series.
Prod-BAILYL Dist-AVED

Washington, DC C 20 MIN
16MM FILM, 3/4 OR 1/2 IN VIDEO I-H
Describes the nation's capital as more than a seat of government but as a repository of U S history and an indicator of American culture.
From The Re-discovering America Series.
Prod-COP Dist-AIMS 1973

Washington, DC C 20 MIN
16MM FILM, 3/4 OR 1/2 IN VIDEO I-C A
Tours Washington DC, the nation's capital. Shows Pierre L'Enfant's original plan and how it has been changed over the years. Emphasizes the importance of political activity to the city.
LC NO. 83-706736
Prod-NGS Dist-NGS 1983

Washington, DC - A Special City C 14 MIN
3/4 OR 1/2 INCH VIDEO CASSETTE P
Tells how Michael shows his friend Stephanie the historic sites of Washington, DC.
From The Under The Blue Umbrella Series.
Prod-SCETV Dist-AITECH 1977

Washington, DC - Story Of Our Capital C 11 MIN
16MM FILM, 3/4 OR 1/2 IN VIDEO I-H
Shows original plans of Pierre Charles L'enfant for the city of Washington. Pictures the city of today as a significant center of government and culture.
Prod-CORF Dist-CORF 1956

Washington, DC, Fancy Free C 22 MIN
16MM FILM - 3/4 IN VIDEO
Presents a montage of the variety of opportunities for the visitor in Washington, DC.
LC NO. 79-706170
Prod-USNPS Dist-USNAC Prodn-MCBRID 1979

Washington's Farewell C 15 MIN
16MM FILM, 3/4 OR 1/2 IN VIDEO J-C
Presents better-known portions of George Washington's Farewell Address. Illustrates the political context of the period through the use of original artwork and period graphics. Features William Shatner.
From The Great American Patriotic Speeches Series.
Prod-EVANSA Dist-AIMS 1973

Washinton, DC (2nd Ed) C 23 MIN
16MM FILM, 3/4 OR 1/2 IN VIDEO I-H
Reveals that from a Potomac River Swampland site, Washington, DC has become a triumph of urban engineering and architectural elegance which has continued to expand and develop for nearly two centuries.
LC NO. 83-706736
Prod-EBEC Dist-EBEC 1984

Wasp Nest, The C 20 MIN
3/4 INCH VIDEO CASSETTE
Explores the interactions between women and children as they gather food. Features the bushmen of Namibia.
From The San (Bushmen) Series.
Prod-DOCEDR Dist-DOCEDR Prodn-MRSHL

Wasps - Paper Makers Of The Summer C 10 MIN
16MM FILM, 3/4 OR 1/2 IN VIDEO I-C A
Explains that about two thousand years ago, the Chinese discovered how to make paper from wood pulp. Describes how insects have been making paper from wood pulp for about 20 million years and using it to build their homes. Examines various kinds of nests and views the growth stages of the wasps.
From The Real World Of Insects Series.
Prod-PEGASO Dist-LCOA 1973

Wasps - Paper Makers Of The Summer (Captioned) C 10 MIN
16MM FILM, 3/4 OR 1/2 IN VIDEO P-C A
Traces the development of the wasp from larva to pupa to adult. Shows how these insects chew wood, mixing it with saliva to make a pulp that hardens into durable paper.
From The Real World Of Insects Series.
Prod-PEGASO Dist-LCOA 1973

Wasps - Paper Makers Of The Summer (Spanish) C 10 MIN
16MM FILM, 3/4 OR 1/2 IN VIDEO P-C A
Traces the development of the wasp from larva to pupa to adult. Shows how these insects chew wood, mixing it with saliva to make a pulp that hardens into durable paper.
From The Real World Of Insects Series.
Prod-PEGASO Dist-LCOA 1973

Wasser Fur Canitoga B 120 MIN
16MM FILM OPTICAL SOUND
A German language film with English subtitles. Presents an adventure film about the construction of an aqueduct in Canada.
Prod-WSTGLC Dist-WSTGLC 1939

Wasser Fur Canitoga B 98 MIN
3/4 OR 1/2 INCH VIDEO CASSETTE
A German language motion picture. Portrays a drunken railroad engineer mistakenly accused of sabotaging a water conveyance for the remote town of Canitoga. Shows how he continues to work against the whiskey smugglers responsible and finally redeems himself by rescuing water-line workmen from a dynamite charge. Set in the Canadian wilderness, with music by Peter Kreuder. No subtitles.
Prod-IHF Dist-IHF

Waste C 29 MIN
3/4 OR 1/2 INCH VIDEO CASSETTE J-C A
Considers the disposal and re-use of a variety of wastes.
Prod-BULFRG Dist-BULFRG

Waste - Recycling The World C 20 MIN
16MM FILM, 3/4 OR 1/2 IN VIDEO
Discusses the value of recycling garbage.
Prod-DOCUA Dist-CNEMAG

Waste - The Penalty Of Affluence C 18 MIN
16MM FILM, 3/4 OR 1/2 IN VIDEO H-C A
Outlines the environmental hazards of improper disposal of household, commercial and industrial waste. Demonstrates sanitary landfill, composting and incineration. Emphasizes recommendations for regional planning and coordination.
Prod-WOWILF Dist-IFB 1972

Waste Disposal By Hydraulic Fracturing C 11 MIN
16MM FILM OPTICAL SOUND
Depicts the development, at Oak Ridge National Laboratory, of a process for the disposal of intermediate level radioactive wastes in underground bedded shale formations.
LC NO. 74-705933
Prod-USAEC Dist-USNAC 1966

Waste Heat Management - Energy Utilization For Profit C 26 MIN
16MM FILM, 3/4 OR 1/2 IN VIDEO A
Shows how waste heat from various industrial processes can be captured and reused to help cut industrial fuel bills and thereby increase profits while, at the same time, helping to conserve the nation's energy supply. Includes several waste heat recovery systems and techniques. Discusses how waste heat management programs have permitted industry spokesmen to maintain productivity with less fuel.
Prod-USOECE Dist-USNAC 1976

Waste Not C 15 MIN
2 INCH VIDEOTAPE
See series title for descriptive statement.
From The Making Things Work Series.
Prod-WGBHTV Dist-PUBTEL

Waste Not C 30 MIN
16MM FILM - 3/4 IN VIDEO J-C A
Offers suggestions for conserving the world's energy resources, describing low-energy technologies which can be used while alternative energy sources are being developed.
From The Man Builds - Man Destroys Series.
LC NO. 75-704152
Prod-UN Dist-GPITVL 1974

Wasted - A True Story C 24 MIN
16MM FILM, 3/4 OR 1/2 IN VIDEO I-H A
Describes how substance abuse affects not only the user, but the whole family as well. Presents a drug abuser and his sister who discuss the hurt, bewilderment and anger of family members as the abuser exhibited violent behavior toward them and a total lack of self-respect.
Prod-RINGE Dist-MTI 1983

Wasted Years, The C 28 MIN
16MM FILM, 3/4 OR 1/2 IN VIDEO J-C
Compares the penal system philosophies of Austria which has moved away from traditional closed institutions, Hungary which is experimenting with labor camps where minor offenders are not exposed to professional criminals and Denmark where open prison camps resemble holiday villages.
Prod-SF Dist-SF 1975

Wasteland - Wealth Out Of Waste C 27 MIN
16MM FILM OPTICAL SOUND
States that America's affluent society has cluttered its open spaces, fouled its streams and rivers, polluted its air, and has squandered minerals that are needed to support an expanding population and a growing economy. Discusses these problems and the steps being taken by government and the private sector to solve them.
Prod-USDIBM Dist-USDIBM

Wastewater Management - Options For Unsewered Areas C 25 MIN
16MM FILM, 3/4 OR 1/2 IN VIDEO A
Shows various options for sewage treatment used in areas where centralized treatment is too expensive and the septic tank/soil absorption system doesn't work.
Prod-UWISC Dist-USNAC 1982

Wasting Away - Understanding Anorexia Nervosa And Bulimia C
3/4 OR 1/2 INCH VIDEO CASSETTE
Uses a selection of vignettes to characterize typical anorectic and bulimic behavior. Emphasizes the psychological side of the disorders, pointing out the combinations of adolescent stresses, personality types and family/social situations that can precipitate problems.
Prod-GA Dist-GA 1984

Watch C 12 MIN
16MM FILM, 3/4 OR 1/2 IN VIDEO P-I
Presents a story involving situations that are familiar to children and raises questions about responsible behavior.
Prod-NW Dist-EBEC 1974

Watch It C 15 MIN
3/4 OR 1/2 INCH VIDEO CASSETTE J
Discusses various bicycle riding hazards and offers safety tips.
From The It's Your Move Series.
Prod-WETN Dist-AITECH 1977

Watch On Health, The B 14 MIN
16MM FILM - 3/4 IN VIDEO
Describes briefly the historic high points and current programs of the public health service.
Prod-USPHS Dist-USNAC 1972

Watch Out C 15 MIN
3/4 OR 1/2 INCH VIDEO CASSETTE P
Indicates that children have a personal responsibility for taking care of themselves. Reviews, in a humorous manner, various safety rules.
From The All About You Series.
Prod-WGBHTV Dist-AITECH Prodn-TTOIC 1975

Watch Out For My Plant C 14 MIN
16MM FILM, 3/4 OR 1/2 IN VIDEO P-J
Follows a young boy, who lives in an inner-city neighborhood, who buys a small plant to grow in the narrow patch of dirt between his house and the sidewalk.
Prod-BARR Dist-BARR 1972

Watch Out For My Plant (Spanish) C 14 MIN
16MM FILM - VIDEO, ALL FORMATS I
Tells the story of an inner-city boy trying to grow a flower in a small patch of dirt between his house and the sidewalk.
Prod-BARR Dist-BARR

Watch Out For Witchweed C 14 MIN
16MM FILM OPTICAL SOUND
Shows what is being done to control the spread of the parasitic plant witchweed and what methods of eradication have already been developed.
LC NO. FIE63-222
Prod-USDA Dist-USNAC 1963

Watch That Space—A Series
IND
Discusses confined space hazards in factories, shipbuilding and the construction industry.
Prod-AMEDFL Dist-AMEDFL 1979

Confined Space Hazards In Factories 016 MIN
Confined Space Hazards In Shipbuilding 016 MIN
Confined Space Hazards In The Construction 016 MIN

Watch Us Move B 21 MIN
16MM FILM, 3/4 OR 1/2 IN VIDEO
Documents a program of sensory integration for preschool-aged retarded children. Focuses on one aspect of their treatment, sensory integration, or the development of motor capabilities that enhance a child's ability to learn at a more complex level.
Prod-UCSNUR Dist-UCEMC 1975

Watch Word - Caution C
16MM FILM OPTICAL SOUND J-C A
Presents policewoman Pat Pocher describing crimes of personal assault against females, showing how to avoid the situations entirely and how to deal with them if they occur.
From The Community Protection And Crime Prevention Series.
LC NO. 72-701744
Prod-SUMHIL Dist-SUMHIL 1972

Watch Your Balance C 4 MIN
16MM FILM, 3/4 OR 1/2 IN VIDEO K
Introduces Fumble, who explains 'YOU NEVER REALIZE HOW IMPORTANT YOUR BALANCE IS UNTIL YOU'VE LOST IT.'
From The Most Important Person - Body Movement Series.
Prod-EBEC Dist-EBEC

Watch Your Mouth—A Series
H A
Focuses on the inappropriate language patterns used by all students and how to avoid them.
Prod-WNETTV Dist-GPITVL 1979

Watch Your Step C 6 MIN
16MM FILM OPTICAL SOUND
Discusses industrial safety and focuses on falls in the workplace.
LC NO. 80-700933
Prod-TASCOR Dist-TASCOR 1968

Watch Your Step C 11 MIN
16MM FILM OPTICAL SOUND A
Presents safe practices for railroad employees through examples of yard practices, riding cars, boarding trains, alighting from moving equipment, throwing switches, setting and releasing hand brakes and working in machine shops.
LC NO. FIA52-845
Prod-STAFER Dist-STAFER

Watchdogs Of The Treasury B 29 MIN
16MM FILM OPTICAL SOUND J-H
Discusses the relative roles of the Appropriations Committee of the House and the Senate and explains how they control government spending. Points out that appropriations are a potential source of conflict between the President and the Congress.
From The Government Story Series. No. 13
LC NO. 79-707215
Prod-WEBC Dist-WESTLC 1968

Watcher In The Woods C 25 MIN
16MM FILM, 3/4 OR 1/2 IN VIDEO I-H
Reveals that after her family moves into an old English estate, a girl is told by the caretaker of the disappearance of another young girl. Shows how the girl pieces together the solution to the mystery. Based on the novel THE WATCHER IN THE WOODS by Florence Engle Randall.
From The Film As Literature, Series 5 Series.
Prod-WDEMCO Dist-WDEMCO 1983

Watchia C 15 MIN
3/4 OR 1/2 INCH VIDEO CASSETTE P
Pictures family life on Cape Jones in Quebec.
From The Other Families, Other Friends Series. Green Module - Quebec
Prod-WVIZTV Dist-AITECH 1971

Watching A Woodcarver C 12 MIN
16MM FILM, 3/4 OR 1/2 IN VIDEO I-C A
Shows the joys of woodcarving by showing a man creating a mallard duck decoy from a block of wood. Provides a brief history of the purpose and variety of decoys.
LC NO. 82-706978
Prod-BERLET Dist-IFB 1982

Watching Animals C 12 MIN
16MM FILM, 3/4 OR 1/2 IN VIDEO P-I
Shows various kinds of animal behavior and tells how scientists learn about animals.
LC NO. 80-706252
Prod-NGS Dist-NGS 1978

Watching Birds With Roger Tory Peterson C
3/4 OR 1/2 INCH VIDEO CASSETTE
Features the spectacular sights and sounds of 52 common and backyard birds in an introduction to birdwatching with Roger Tory Peterson.
Prod-CBSC Dist-CBSC

Watching The Press/Reading Television C 10 MIN
3/4 OR 1/2 INCH VIDEO CASSETTE
Illustrates how information is trivialized by the mass media.
Prod-EAI Dist-EAI

Watching Wildlife C 26 MIN
16MM FILM OPTICAL SOUND
Looks at the various locales at which people can see wildlife, from a national park to a backyard animal feeder.
LC NO. 83-700332
Prod-STOUFP Dist-STOUFP 1982

Watching Wildlife C 26 MIN
3/4 OR 1/2 INCH VIDEO CASSETTE
Examines reasons why millions seek out wildlife. Provides facts on watching wildlife.
Prod-STOUFP Dist-STOUFP

Watchword - Caution C 27 MIN
16MM FILM, 3/4 OR 1/2 IN VIDEO J-C A
Presents policewoman Pat Parker who employs dramatized incidents to show how young girls and women can avoid crimes of personal assault.
Prod-SUMHIL Dist-AIMS 1974

Water B 11 MIN
16MM FILM OPTICAL SOUND
Explains that water is necessary to all life. Shows agricultural conditions during droughts and during floods on uncovered land. Makes the point that too much rain can be as destructive as too little rain and emphasizes the need for soil conservation practices.
LC NO. FIE52-55
Prod-USDA Dist-USNAC 1948

Water C 8 MIN
16MM FILM, 3/4 OR 1/2 IN VIDEO J-C A
Reveals a panorama of man around the world, using and enjoying the essential natural resource, because without water man cannot live. Shows how, in visuals without words, water shapes the lives of people everywhere.
Prod-IFF Dist-IFF

Water B 10 MIN
3/4 OR 1/2 INCH VIDEO CASSETTE P
Discusses the characteristics of water and its ability to change form. Includes its importance for life and survival.
From The Two For Tomorrow Series.
Prod-BEOC Dist-GPITVL

Water C 12 MIN
16MM FILM, 3/4 OR 1/2 IN VIDEO C
Demonstrates how children playing with water can have satisfying mathematical and emotional experiences as they feel water of various temperatures and depths.
From The Early Childhood Education Series.
Prod-MEDIAG Dist-MEDIAG 1976

Water C 14 MIN
16MM FILM, 3/4 OR 1/2 IN VIDEO J-C A
Discusses the possibility of a worldwide water shortage crisis and suggests solutions.
Prod-JOU Dist-JOU 1977

Water C 14 MIN
2 INCH VIDEOTAPE
Features nature photographer Jim Bones celebrating the beauty of the water.
From The Images And Memories Series.
Prod-KERA Dist-PUBTEL

Water C 15 MIN
3/4 OR 1/2 INCH VIDEO CASSETTE I
Shows the interrelation between water, the earth's surface and living things.
From The L-Four Series.
Prod-CTI Dist-CTI

Water C 15 MIN
3/4 OR 1/2 INCH VIDEO CASSETTE I-J
Demonstrates how to draw water, including underwater scenes, still water and rough waves.
From The Draw Man Series.
Prod-OCPS Dist-AITECH 1975

Water C 15 MIN
2 INCH VIDEOTAPE P-I
Shows how water has enabled people to use the land more efficiently and how the control of water has caused significant changes in agriculture, power and recreation.
From The Our Changing Community Series.
Prod-VITA Dist-GPITVL

Water C 30 MIN
3/4 OR 1/2 INCH VIDEO CASSETTE
Explores the relationship between what people know, see and do and the water around them.
From The Land And The People Series.
Prod-EKC Dist-MDCPB

Water - A Clear And Present Danger C 26 MIN
16MM FILM, 3/4 OR 1/2 IN VIDEO H-C A
Looks at the medical implications of serious ground water contamination. Shows that despite efforts to regulate it, 700 man-made chemicals have been found in drinking water, some of which are harmful.
Prod-ABCNEW Dist-MTI 1983

Water - A Cutting Edge With Time C 28 MIN
3/4 OR 1/2 INCH VIDEO CASSETTE
Deals with the science of hydrology, which comes to life on a field trip to the canyonlands of Utah and a raft ride down the Arkansas River.
From The Earth Explored Series.
Prod-BBCTV Dist-PBS

Water - A First Film C 9 MIN
16MM FILM, 3/4 OR 1/2 IN VIDEO P-I
Discusses the role played by water in the processes of life. Shows that where there is little water the land is desert. Points out that water is used to drink, to cook, to water lawns and to fight fires with.
Prod-FA Dist-PHENIX 1968

Water - A Precious Resource C 23 MIN
16MM FILM, 3/4 OR 1/2 IN VIDEO I-J A
Examines a number of topics related to water, such as where it comes from and how it is used and considers the question of whether there will be enough clean water in the future.
LC NO. 80-706266
Prod-NGS Dist-NGS 1979

Water - Coming And Going C 20 MIN
16MM FILM, 3/4 OR 1/2 IN VIDEO I
Demonstrates evaporation, condensation and precipitation of water by a series of simple, clear experiments which necessitate responses from the student, performs various experiments to explain the stages of the natural cycle of water. Shows actual examples of the water cycle in nature, including streams, clouds, fog, snow, rain and oceans. Includes multiple choice questions.
From The Science Twenty Series.
Prod-PRISM Dist-SF 1970

Water - Fluid For Life C 16 MIN
16MM FILM, 3/4 OR 1/2 IN VIDEO J-H
Documents the role played by water in the emergence and survival of life on Earth.
Prod-CORF Dist-CORF 1978

Water - Friend Or Enemy C 9 MIN
16MM FILM OPTICAL SOUND
Discusses the pollution of springs and wells, how this may be prevented and how well-water may be made safe to drink.
Prod-USIS Dist-USIS 1944

Water - Friend Or Enemy C 10 MIN
16MM FILM, 3/4 OR 1/2 IN VIDEO
Shows safe and unsafe water supplies in rural areas, sinking of wells, seepage problems, dangers and sources of contamination.
Prod-DISNEY Dist-USNAC 1946

Water - Friend Or Foe C 23 MIN
16MM FILM, 3/4 OR 1/2 IN VIDEO I-C A
Presents a series of dramatic episodes set in a variety of situations involving still and moving water. Describes basic safety rules of how to avoid accidents and how to rescue oneself and others in case of emergencies.
Prod-PFP Dist-PFP 1973

Water - Friend Or Foe (Arabic) C 23 MIN
16MM FILM, 3/4 OR 1/2 IN VIDEO I-C A
An Arabic language version of the film, Water - Friend Or Foe. Demonstrates how to prevent accidents in or around water, and how to act when accidents occur. Includes step-by-step information on what to do in common water emergencies, involving swimming, boating, fishing, and scuba diving, or being near a pond or swimming pool.
Prod-PFP Dist-PFP

Water - Lifeblood Of The West C 13 MIN
16MM FILM OPTICAL SOUND I-J
Stresses the importance of water in building the West and shows the many ways that western rivers have been harnessed by reclamation projects.
LC NO. FIA59-31
Prod-DAGP Dist-MLA 1958

Water - More Precious Than Oil C 58 MIN
3/4 OR 1/2 INCH VIDEO CASSETTE
Examines the use and abuse of water around the world. Shows how water resources must be managed on small, as well as large scales and shows the consequences for those who are unwilling or unable to manage their water resources.
LC NO. 82-706843
Prod-KTCATV Dist-PBS 1980

Water - Nebraska's Heritage C 29 MIN
16MM FILM OPTICAL SOUND H-C A
Describes the use of water in Nebraska and the extent of the supply. Illustrates the relative amounts of water used for homes, industry and agriculture. Locates geographically the sources of ground water and surface water in the state by extensive use of aerial photography.
From The Nebraska Water Resources Series.
LC NO. 74-700161
Prod-UNEBR Dist-UNL 1971

Water - Old Problems, New Approaches C 30 MIN
16MM FILM, 3/4 OR 1/2 IN VIDEO I-H
Tells the story of water shortage problems and how scientists are combatting them.
From The World We Live In Series.
Prod-TIMELI Dist-MGHT 1968

Water - The Common Necessity C 9 MIN
16MM FILM, 3/4 OR 1/2 IN VIDEO
Explains the water cycle and lists ways that water is essential to life. Raises the problem of conservation of this natural resource and points out little-known information about uses of water.
Prod-MIS Dist-MIS 1975

Water - The Effluent Society C 20 MIN
16MM FILM, 3/4 OR 1/2 IN VIDEO
Examines the availability of water and the pollution control measures necessary to maintain a constantly fresh supply.
Prod-DOCUA Dist-CNEMAG

Water - What Happens To It C 15 MIN
3/4 OR 1/2 INCH VIDEO CASSETTE I
Discusses various aspects of water.
From The Hands On, Grade 5 - Our Environment Series.
Prod-WHROTV Dist-AITECH 1975

Water - Why It Is, What It Is C 11 MIN
16MM FILM, 3/4 OR 1/2 IN VIDEO I-H
Suggests that water is one of our earth's most valuable resources and that it helps shape the earth, moderates its weather and preserves life.
Prod-MIS Dist-MIS

Water Affects The Weather C 15 MIN
3/4 OR 1/2 INCH VIDEO CASSETTE P-I
Discusses how water affects the weather.
From The Why Series.
Prod-WDCNTV Dist-AITECH 1976

Water Against Wildfire C 16 MIN
16MM FILM OPTICAL SOUND
Shows how bush fires in Australia and in all parts of the world create havoc not only in the human environment but also in the delicate balance of the natural world.
LC NO. 80-700846
Prod-VICCOR Dist-TASCOR 1978

Water Analysis C 32 MIN
3/4 OR 1/2 INCH VIDEO CASSETTE
Covers the Most Probable Numbers (MPN) and membrane filter methods for determing coloforms in finished drinking water. Includes details of each step and interpretation of MPN tables.
Prod-AMSM Dist-AVMM

Water And Dust Leak Repair C 17 MIN
1/2 IN VIDEO CASSETTE BETA/VHS
Deals with auto body repair.
Prod-RMI Dist-RMI

Water And Fire C
3/4 OR 1/2 INCH VIDEO CASSETTE IND
Demonstrates effectiveness of water for cooling a diesel oil fire. Details use of water for control purposes, hoseline team setups, proper techniques, different equipment available and hoseline tests.
From The Marine Firefighting Series. Pt 3
Prod-GPCV Dist-GPCV

Water And Fire (Italian) C
3/4 OR 1/2 INCH VIDEO CASSETTE IND
Demonstrates effectiveness of water for cooling a diesel oil fire. Details use of water for control purposes, hoseline team setups, proper techniques, different equipment available and hoseline tests.
From The Marine Firefighting Series. Pt 3
Prod-GPCV Dist-GPCV

Water And Fire (Korean) C
3/4 OR 1/2 INCH VIDEO CASSETTE IND
Demonstrates effectiveness of water for cooling a diesel oil fire. Details use of water for control purposes, hoseline team setups, proper techniques, different equipment available and hoseline tests.
From The Marine Firefighting Series. Pt 3
Prod-GPCV Dist-GPCV

Water And Life On Earth C 11 MIN
16MM FILM OPTICAL SOUND I-H
Explains the accepted theory of how water was first formed and how it is still being formed from hydrogen and oxygen. Shows the water cycle, types of clouds and methods of getting water to dry areas.
Prod-CBF Dist-AVED 1963

Water And Rain C 15 MIN
3/4 OR 1/2 INCH VIDEO CASSETTE P
Presents examples of evaporation and Myrtle shows how water recycles, while Pocus tells the story of a water droplet, and Hocus and Myrtle prepare to create a cloud.
From The Let Me See Series. No. 6
Prod-WETN Dist-AITECH Prodn-STSU 1982

Water And Spirit - A Meditation On Baptism C 5 MIN
16MM FILM OPTICAL SOUND I-C R
Presents a collection of visual images of the absence, presence and use of water in man's life. Moves from the desert to the sea, capturing dry winds, mountain streams and verdant pasture.
LC NO. 73-702537
Prod-FRACOC Dist-FRACOC 1973

Water And Wastewater Treatement Systems I—A Series
PRO
Uses classroom format to videotape one one-hour and one 1 1/2 hour lecture weekly for 13 weeks and 39 cassettes in each of two parts, I and II. Covers theory of design and operation of water and wastewater treatment systems with emphasis on chemical and physical processes.
Prod-USCCE Dist-AMCEE

Water And Wastewater Treatment Systems II—A Series
PRO
Uses classroom format to videotape one 1-hour and one 1 1/2 hour lectures weekly for 13 week and 39 cassettes in each of two parts, I and II. Covers theory of design and operation of water and wastewater treatment systems with emphasis on chemical and physical processes.
Prod-USCCE Dist-AMCEE

Water And What It Does X 11 MIN
16MM FILM, 3/4 OR 1/2 IN VIDEO P
Shows that water is composed of tiny, constantly moving particles, and that it exists in three states-solid, liquid and gas. Demonstrates dissolving, evaporation, condensation, freezing and expansion.
Prod-EBF Dist-EBEC 1962

Water And What It Does (Spanish) C 11 MIN
16MM FILM, 3/4 OR 1/2 IN VIDEO P
Explains that water is composed of tiny particles which exist in either solid, liquid or gaseous states. Demonstrates the mechanisms of dissolving, evaporation, condensation, freezing and expansion.
Prod-EBEC Dist-EBEC

Water Bikes C 24 MIN
16MM FILM OPTICAL SOUND P-I
Tells of the Chiffy Kids plan to win new bikes by winning a cross-country bicycle race aboard their old ones. Shows them outwitting a shady bicycle shop owner.
Prod-LUF Dist-LUF 1979

Water Birds C 6 MIN
16MM FILM OPTICAL SOUND P-I
Describes the characteristics of the loon, tern, heron and ring-billed gull. Discusses their habitat and breeding and migration habits. Captures the songs and calls of the birds. Uses only natural sound.
From The Birds Of America, 1, Their Songs And Sounds Series. No. 3
Prod-GIB Dist-GIB 1966

Water Birds C 32 MIN
16MM FILM, 3/4 OR 1/2 IN VIDEO I-C A
Gives glimpses into the behavior, nest building, mating and anatomical features of seaside and marshland bird life in many parts of the world.
Prod-DISNEY Dist-WDEMCO 1957

Water Birds (Afrikaans) C 32 MIN
16MM FILM, 3/4 OR 1/2 IN VIDEO I-H
Glimpses the behavior of seaside and marshland birds. Features a musical bird ballet.
Prod-WDEMCO Dist-WDEMCO 1957

Water Birds (Danish) C 32 MIN
16MM FILM, 3/4 OR 1/2 IN VIDEO I-H
Glimpses the behavior of seaside and marshland birds. Features a musical bird ballet.
Prod-WDEMCO Dist-WDEMCO 1957

Water Birds (Dutch) C 32 MIN
16MM FILM, 3/4 OR 1/2 IN VIDEO I-H
Glimpses the behavior of seaside and marshland birds. Features a musical bird ballet.
Prod-WDEMCO Dist-WDEMCO 1957

Water Birds (French) C 32 MIN
16MM FILM, 3/4 OR 1/2 IN VIDEO I-H
Glimpses the behavior of seaside and marshland birds. Features a musical bird ballet.
Prod-WDEMCO Dist-WDEMCO 1957

Water Birds (German) C 32 MIN
16MM FILM, 3/4 OR 1/2 IN VIDEO I-H
Glimpses the behavior of seaside and marshland birds. Features a musical bird ballet.
Prod-WDEMCO Dist-WDEMCO 1957

Water Birds (Italian) C 32 MIN
16MM FILM, 3/4 OR 1/2 IN VIDEO I-H
Glimpses the behavior of seaside and marshland birds. Features a musical bird ballet.
Prod-WDEMCO Dist-WDEMCO 1957

Water Birds (Portuguese) C 32 MIN
16MM FILM, 3/4 OR 1/2 IN VIDEO I-H
Glimpses the behavior of seaside and marshland birds. Features a musical bird ballet.
Prod-WDEMCO Dist-WDEMCO 1957

Water Birds (Spanish) C 32 MIN
16MM FILM, 3/4 OR 1/2 IN VIDEO I-H
Glimpses the behavior of seaside and marshland birds. Features a musical bird ballet.
Prod-WDEMCO Dist-WDEMCO 1957

Water Birds - Loon, Tern, Heron, Ring-Billed Gull C
16MM FILM OPTICAL SOUND P A
Looks at the habits and behavior of several species on the shoreline of a wilderness lake. Features the mournful cry of the loon, the graceful flight of the tern, the shrill sounds of gulls and the heron in solitude.
LC NO. FIA67-2098
Prod-GIB Dist-AVEXP

Water Birds Of The Inland C 14 MIN
16MM FILM OPTICAL SOUND J-C A
Examines bird life around a lake in inland Australia.
Prod-ANAIB Dist-AUIS 1964

Water Bugs B 30 MIN
16MM FILM OPTICAL SOUND
From The Classic Christie Comedies Series.
Prod-SFI Dist-SFI

Water California Style C 16 MIN
3/4 INCH VIDEO CASSETTE I-C A
Traces the 200-year history of water development in California. Covers water management policies, conservation, reclamation techniques and the process of planning for California's needs through the year 2000.
Prod-CSDWR Dist-CALDWR

Water Catalogue, The C 27 MIN
3/4 INCH VIDEO CASSETTE
Presents video images and original music that show the power and poetry of water and use it as a metaphor for emotional, psychological and physical conditions, by Bill Seaman.
Prod-EAI Dist-EAI

Water Chemistry And Chemical Handling Practices C 60 MIN
3/4 OR 1/2 INCH VIDEO CASSETTE IND
Deals with treatment of boiler and cooling water systems. Identifies chemicals used in water treatment. Discusses safety gear and protective clothing.
From The Equipment Operation Training Program Series.
Prod-ITCORP Dist-ITCORP

Water Crisis, The C 57 MIN
16MM FILM, 3/4 OR 1/2 IN VIDEO H-C A
Describes water problems currently being experienced by communities from the Adirondack Mountains to the American West Coast and explains that water scarcity will be the next ecology issue.
From The Nova Series.
LC NO. 81-706780
Prod-WGBHTV Dist-TIMLIF 1981

Water Cycle - Nature C 20 MIN
2 INCH VIDEOTAPE I
See series title for descriptive statement.
From The Exploring With Science, Unit V - Weather Series.
Prod-MPATI Dist-GPITVL

Water Cycle, The C 6 MIN
3/4 INCH VIDEO CASSETTE K-I
Traces the journey of water from rivers to the ocean, to clouds, rain and snow, and finally back to lakes, rivers and underground storage areas. Simplifies the water cycle so children can understand it.
Prod-CSDWR Dist-CALDWR

Water Cycle, The (Spanish) C 14 MIN
16MM FILM, 3/4 OR 1/2 IN VIDEO J-H
A Spanish language version of the film and videorecording The Water Cycle.
Prod-EBEC Dist-EBEC 1980

Water Cycle, The (2nd Ed) C 14 MIN
16MM FILM, 3/4 OR 1/2 IN VIDEO P-I
Illustrates the importance of the vast exchange of water between land, the atmosphere and the sea. Examines in detail the processes of evaporation and condensation and the effects of the water cycle on the climate and the land.
Prod-EBEC Dist-EBEC 1980

Water Dwellers, The C 15 MIN
16MM FILM OPTICAL SOUND H-C A
Studies the people who live, work or holiday along the foreshores of Broken Bay, 25 miles north of Sydney, Australia.
LC NO. FIA68-2246
Prod-ANAIB Dist-AUIS 1968

Water Farmers C 29 MIN
16MM FILM, 3/4 OR 1/2 IN VIDEO J-C A
See series title for descriptive statement.
From The Taste Of China Series.
LC NO. 84-707744
Prod-UCEMC Dist-UCEMC 1984

Water Film, The C 9 MIN
16MM FILM, 3/4 OR 1/2 IN VIDEO P
Tells a story about a curious young rabbit to introduce the concept of the water cycle.
Prod-SAIF Dist-BARR 1977

Water For A City C 13 MIN
16MM FILM OPTICAL SOUND J-C A
Shows the scale and complexity of the system to store and supply water for a large Australian city.
LC NO. 72-702251
Prod-ANAIB Dist-AUIS 1972

Water For A Thirsty World C 15 MIN
16MM FILM OPTICAL SOUND C
Tells that man's enormous demands and polluting habits threaten his limited fresh water supply which is less that one percent of all the water on earth. Explains that currently there are 1000 desalting plants in operation, producing 1,800,000,000 liters of fresh water a day. Investigates new ways of mapping ground water deposits, the more than 95 percent of fresh water that lies underground.
From The Science In Action Series.
Prod-ALLFP Dist-COUNFI

Water For Farming C 5 MIN
3/4 INCH VIDEO CASSETTE K-I
Describes agricultural water uses and how farmers conserve water.
Prod-CSDWR Dist-CALDWR

Water For Industry C 5 MIN
3/4 INCH VIDEO CASSETTE K-I
Shows cleaning and recycling of industrial water as methods for using water more efficiently. Uses foods as example of industrial process water use.
Prod-CSDWR Dist-CALDWR

Water For Jordan C 26 MIN
16MM FILM, 3/4 OR 1/2 IN VIDEO H-C
Uses animated photography to show how water can be located and stored in the desert. Traces the geology, vegetation and patterns of rainfall in Jordan Valley and explains the development of the Jordan Valley Water Project.
Prod-BBCTV Dist-MEDIAG Prodn-OPENU 1985

Water For Life C 15 MIN
16MM FILM OPTICAL SOUND
Shows the natural sources of water and demonstrates the two main systems of desalination - multi-stage flash evaporation and electrodialysis. Discusses dual-purpose plants to produce power from a nuclear reactor and at the same time to produce water, as well as the possible allocation of the costs of such a plant to water and to electricity.
Prod-UKAEA Dist-UKAEA 1967

Water For The City X 11 MIN
16MM FILM, 3/4 OR 1/2 IN VIDEO P-I
Shows that water needed by people in a city begins as rain and snow that forms rivers, lakes and underground water basins. Depicts ways this water is purified and brought into homes in the city.
Prod-FA Dist-PHENIX 1967

Water For The City (Spanish) X 11 MIN
16MM FILM, 3/4 OR 1/2 IN VIDEO P-I
Shows that water needed by people in a city begins as rain and snow that forms rivers, lakes and underground water basins. Depicts ways this water is purified and brought into homes in the city.
Prod-FA Dist-PHENIX 1967

Water From Another Time C 16 MIN
16MM FILM, 3/4 OR 1/2 IN VIDEO H-C A
Emphasizes the contributions of senior citizens to society. Features three elderly individuals in Orange County, Indiana.
LC NO. 83-706114
Prod-KANLEW Dist-KANLEW 1982

Water In The Weather C 17 MIN
16MM FILM OPTICAL SOUND P-J
Explains how the heat from the sun, the earth's atmosphere, land areas and water areas work together as weather makers. Describes the effect of sunlight on both light and dark areas, showing how it causes differences in weather. Explains the water cycle.
LC NO. FIA60-3066
Prod-ACA Dist-ACA 1960

Water Insects C 14 MIN
16MM FILM, 3/4 OR 1/2 IN VIDEO J-H
Focuses on animals that live on the surface of water or in the water.
From The Insect Series.
LC NO. 80-706709
Prod-BHA Dist-IFB 1977

Water Is So Clear That A Blind Man Could See C 30 MIN
16MM FILM, 3/4 OR 1/2 IN VIDEO J-H
Describes the plight of the Taos Indians and their home in the Blue Lake area of New Mexico, which is threatened by lumber companies. Explains that the Indian has not exploited ecology because he considers all life sacred and uses only what is necessary to him.
From The Our Vanishing Wilderness Series. No. 7
LC NO. 80-707025
Prod-NETRC Dist-IU 1970

Water Is Wet C 20 MIN
16MM FILM OPTICAL SOUND K A
Encourages singing, working with paper and colors, making up stories and acting them out, thinking and talking about things and a feeling of having done well. Suggests that the best way to bring children enjoyment is through a parent or teacher who shows enjoyment in these activities.
From The Metooshow Series.
LC NO. 77-705712
Prod-TPTP Dist-TPTP 1970

Water Its Many Voices C 20 MIN
16MM FILM OPTICAL SOUND
Shows ways to conserve water supply.
Prod-ALLISC Dist-IDEALF

Water Life To A City C 24 MIN
16MM FILM OPTICAL SOUND
Deals with the problems of water resources of Victoria, British Columbia.
LC NO. 76-701392
Prod-WILFGP Dist-WILFGP 1975

Water Masses C 24 MIN
16MM FILM, 3/4 OR 1/2 IN VIDEO
Shows how oceanographers employ technology to collect data which provides a picture of water masses. Uses animation and graphics to demonstrate methods of measuring sea water temperature and salinity.
Prod-OPENU Dist-MEDIAG Prodn-BBCTV 1979

Water Masses Of The Ocean C 45 MIN
16MM FILM OPTICAL SOUND J-H
Studies the locations and dynamic movements of the major water masses of the oceans.
LC NO. 72-700686
Prod-USN Dist-USNAC 1967

Water Means Life C 5 MIN
16MM FILM OPTICAL SOUND
Portrays the need for safe water for persons overseas who often die from the constant consumption of contaminated water.
Prod-CARE Dist-CARE

Water Means Life C 19 MIN
16MM FILM OPTICAL SOUND
Discusses the worldwide problems caused by unsafe drinking water and explains what UNICEF is doing to alleviate these problems.
LC NO. 80-700178
Prod-UNICEF Dist-UNICEF Prodn-DYP 1979

Water Means Life C 20 MIN
3/4 INCH VIDEO CASSETTE I-H
Focuses on the need for more sophisticated water systems in the countries of Tanzania, Yemen, Nepal, India, Vietnam, Guatemala and Mexico.
Prod-NYSED Dist-GPITVL 1979

Water Means Life (French) C 19 MIN
16MM FILM OPTICAL SOUND
Discusses the worldwide problems caused by unsafe drinking water and explains what UNICEF is doing to alleviate these problems.
LC NO. 80-700178
Prod-UNICEF Dist-UNICEF Prodn-DYP 1979

Water Means Life (German) C 19 MIN
16MM FILM OPTICAL SOUND
Discusses the worldwide problems caused by unsafe drinking water and explains what UNICEF is doing to alleviate these problems.
LC NO. 80-700178
Prod-UNICEF Dist-UNICEF Prodn-DYP 1979

Water Means Life (Italian) C 19 MIN
16MM FILM OPTICAL SOUND
Discusses the worldwide problems caused by unsafe drinking water and explains what UNICEF is doing to alleviate these problems.
LC NO. 80-700178
Prod-UNICEF Dist-UNICEF Prodn-DYP 1979

Water Means Life (Spanish) C 19 MIN
16MM FILM OPTICAL SOUND
Discusses the worldwide problems caused by unsafe drinking water and explains what UNICEF is doing to alleviate these problems.
LC NO. 80-700178
Prod-UNICEF Dist-UNICEF Prodn-DYP 1979

Water Movie, The C 8 MIN
16MM FILM, 3/4 OR 1/2 IN VIDEO J-C A
A visual study which presents closeup shots of the surface of a body of water moving at varying speeds, with different colored patterns created by holding objects over the water. Alternates music by William Russell with excerpts from Mozart's horn duos.
Prod-ACI Dist-AIMS 1975

Water Of Words - A Cultural Ecology Of A Small Island In Eastern Indonesia C 30 MIN
3/4 INCH VIDEO CASSETTE
Explores the poetry and ecology of the lontar (borassus) palm on the eastern Indonesian island of Roti. demonstrates tapping and cooking the juice and its transformation into syrup, beer and gin. Represents a collaboration of anthropologist James J. Fox and film makers Timothy and Patsy Asch. Available in an Indonesian language version also.
Prod-DOCEDR Dist-DOCEDR

Water People, The C 25 MIN
16MM FILM OPTICAL SOUND
Profiles the water people of Southeast Asia in Hong Kong, Macao and Thailand.
From The Eye Of The Beholder Series.
LC NO. 75-701945
Prod-RCPDF Dist-VIACOM 1972

Water Planet, The C 19 MIN
16MM FILM, 3/4 OR 1/2 IN VIDEO I-C
A shortened version of The Water Planet. Describes aspects of life aboard an underwater exploration ship. Shows the unending manual and mental labor and observes the dangers with which underwater photographers must contend.
From The Undersea World Of Jacques Cousteau Series.
Prod-METROM Dist-CF 1970

Water Planet, The C 30 MIN
3/4 OR 1/2 INCH VIDEO CASSETTE C A
Discusses the earth as a water planet, with over seventy- one percent of the earth covered by water. Explores modern theories of the origins of life.
From The Oceanus - The Marine Environment Series. Lesson 1
Prod-SCCON Dist-CDTEL

Water Planet, The C 52 MIN
16MM FILM, 3/4 OR 1/2 IN VIDEO
Recounts Jacques Cousteau's adventures aboard the Calypso.
From The Undersea World Of Jacques Cousteau Series.
Prod-METROM Dist-CF 1971

Water Plants C 15 MIN
2 INCH VIDEOTAPE K
Shows plants that live in the water having similar life activities to those plants which live on land.
From The Let's Go Sciencing, Unit III - Life Series.
Prod-DETPS Dist-GPITVL

Water Play For Teaching Young Children C 17 MIN
16MM FILM OPTICAL SOUND
Shows the value of water as a natural resource in the preschool, with children from toddler age up to age five and in settings as different as a college laboratory nursery school and an inner city day care center. Illustrates how water can provide a deeply satisfying sensory experience as well as an educational medium. Demonstrates how the staff can control and direct the use of water so that it is constructive.
Prod-VASSAR Dist-NYU

Water Pollution C 10 MIN
16MM FILM, 3/4 OR 1/2 IN VIDEO P-J
Encourages student concern about the abuse of natural resources, tracing the causes and results of water pollution. Shows how clear water becomes contaminated and useless as garbage, sewage, insecticides and industrial wastes flow into rivers, lakes and streams. Points out that science alone cannot fight the battle against pollution.
Prod-SF Dist-SF 1970

Water Pollution C 30 MIN
3/4 OR 1/2 INCH VIDEO CASSETTE C
Deals with water pollutants, their sources and their effects on wildlife and on people, as well as potential technological and economic solutions.
From The Living Environment Series.
Prod-DALCCD Dist-DALCCD

Water Pollution - A First Film C 8 MIN
16MM FILM, 3/4 OR 1/2 IN VIDEO P-I
Follows a single stream from its origin to its end in order to reveal the many different sources of pollution. Points out that individuals as well as groups can help clean up our water sources.
Prod-BEAN Dist-PHENIX 1971

Water Pollution - A First Film (French) C 8 MIN
16MM FILM, 3/4 OR 1/2 IN VIDEO P-I
Follows a single stream from its origin to its end in order to reveal the many different sources of pollution. Points out that individuals as well as groups can help clean up our water sources.
Prod-BEAN Dist-PHENIX 1971

Water Pollution - A First Film (Norwegian) C 8 MIN
16MM FILM, 3/4 OR 1/2 IN VIDEO P-I
Follows a single stream from its origin to its end in order to reveal the many different sources of pollution. Points out that individuals as well as groups can help clean up our water sources.
Prod-BEAN Dist-PHENIX 1971

Water Pollution - Can We Keep Our Water Clean C 16 MIN
16MM FILM, 3/4 OR 1/2 IN VIDEO I-J
Shows six major sources of pollution and the ways in which each contributes to the contamination of our waterways. Includes examples such as trash and garbage from individuals, fertilizers, chemicals and manure from farms, waste and oil from boats, industrial wastes and detergent effluents from factories, thermal pollution from nuclear plants and city sewage.
Prod-WER Dist-JOU 1971

Water Pollution - Can We Keep Our Water Clean (Captioned) C 16 MIN
16MM FILM, 3/4 OR 1/2 IN VIDEO I-J
Shows six major sources of pollution and the ways in which each contributes to the contamination of our waterways. Includes examples such as trash and garbage from individuals, fertilizers, chemicals and manure from farms, waste and oil from boats, industrial wastes and detergent effluents from factories, thermal pollution from nuclear plants and city sewage.
Prod-WER Dist-JOU 1971

Water Power C 15 MIN
16MM FILM OPTICAL SOUND
Presents scenes of traditional Ghana followed by scenes of people of Ghana changing their landscape and their way of life through technology. Witnesses the effects of the Volta Dam on Ghana.
LC NO. 73-702066
Prod-EDC Dist-EDC 1973

Water Power C 23 MIN
16MM FILM, 3/4 OR 1/2 IN VIDEO I-C A
Declares that man is once more turning to water as a source of energy, including the harnessing of tidal power for water-driven generators.
Prod-LUF Dist-LUF 1981

Water Power C 25 MIN
16MM FILM, 3/4 OR 1/2 IN VIDEO J-C A
Looks at the history of water power using archival footage and old photographs.
LC NO. 82-707095
Prod-LIVNGN Dist-BULFRG 1982

Water Purification, Introduction C 100 MIN
16MM FILM OPTICAL SOUND
Emphasizes the importance of disinfecting water. Explains the various sources of water and the steps required to provide a safe water supply.
LC NO. FIE54-157
Prod-USN Dist-USNAC 1953

Water Rescue C 13 MIN
3/4 INCH VIDEO CASSETTE PRO
Demonstrates the technique for rescuing a drowning person and swimming with him to shore, and for transporting him by means of the four-man carry to a beach area where he is positioned for mouth-to-mouth resuscitation. Shows the rescue procedure for lifting a drowning victim from the water into a rowboat, a canoe or onto a surfboard.
From The Rescue Procedures Series.
Prod-PRIMED Dist-PRIMED

Water Resourcefulness C 20 MIN
16MM FILM OPTICAL SOUND I-C A

Describes the accelerated water resources program of New York State. Explains how state coordination is required to provide an aggressive water conservation program consisting of federal, state and local elements. Explains examples of water resourcefulness, such as stream impoundment, drainage improvement and a wetlands preservations project.
LC NO. FIA67-684
Prod-NYSCD Dist-FINLYS Prodn-FF 1966

Water Resources C 30 MIN
3/4 OR 1/2 INCH VIDEO CASSETTE C
Probes the issues of the circulation of water through the ecosystem, the contamination of water, desalination and flood control for solutions in water management.
From The Living Environment Series.
Prod-DALCCD Dist-DALCCD

Water Resources Engineering–A Series
PRO
Uses classroom format to videotape one one-hour and one 1 1/2 hour lectures weekly for 13 weeks and 39 cassettes. Covers sediment transport, mixing and transport in surface water systems and pond reservoir hydraulics. Dicusses incipient sediment motion, sediment discharge calculations, stable channel design, hillslope erosion, environmental effects of erosion, diffusion and dispersion in water bodies, dye travel studies in streams, reservoir hydraulics and thermal discharges.
Prod-USCCE Dist-AMCEE

Water Roundup C 15 MIN
3/4 INCH VIDEO CASSETTE I-C A
Explores the California State Water Project, its many facilities and the benefits it provides Californians.
Prod-CSDWR Dist-CALDWR

Water Runs Downhill C 13 MIN
16MM FILM, 3/4 OR 1/2 IN VIDEO P-I
Presents observations and inferences about clouds, rain and running streams. Defines the terms erosion, evaporation and water cycle.
From The Scientific Fact And Fun Series.
Prod-GLDWER Dist-JOU 1980

Water Safety C 19 MIN
16MM FILM OPTICAL SOUND P-I
Tennessee Charlie gives a lesson on water safety in which he emphasizes proper handling, safety equipment and wise use of boats. He stresses safe use of swimming areas and shows rescue techniques, including the 'SHOULDER-PRESSURE ARM LIFT' method of artificial respiration.
Prod-TGAFC Dist-TGAFC

Water Safety - An Introduction C 10 MIN
16MM FILM, 3/4 OR 1/2 IN VIDEO
Illustrates a variety of ways to avoid water accidents, the right and wrong ways of helping oneself and someone else in trouble in the water and some survival floating techniques.
Prod-DELEAU Dist-PHENIX 1974

Water Safety - It's Elementary C 12 MIN
16MM FILM, 3/4 OR 1/2 IN VIDEO P-I
Attempts to promote swimming safety for young children by providing suggestions for both swimmers and nonswimmers on how to combine fun with safety.
Prod-CAHILL Dist-AIMS 1974

Water Safety - The Basics C 17 MIN
16MM FILM, 3/4 OR 1/2 IN VIDEO
Illustrates basic water safety rules and shows that knowing how to avoid dangerous situations and being aware of rescue techniques can help insure accident-free enjoyment in the water.
LC NO. 79-707216
Prod-CENTRO Dist-CORF 1979

Water Service B 11 MIN
16MM FILM OPTICAL SOUND
Illustrates the scientific and engineering methods used in the collection, storage, purification and distribution of water supplies.
Prod-USIS Dist-USIS 1945

Water Service Installation Using A Mueller B Drilling And Tapping Machine C 23 MIN
1/2 IN VIDEO CASSETTE BETA/VHS
Discusses water pipes, water supply engineering apparatus and supplies.
Prod-RMI Dist-RMI

Water Skiing C 30 MIN
1/2 IN VIDEO CASSETTE BETA/VHS
Demonstrates proper form and technique for water skiing, on one ski or two.
Prod-MOHOMV Dist-MOHOMV

Water Skiing, Acapulco C 3 MIN
16MM FILM OPTICAL SOUND P-I
Shows water skiing in Acapulco, Mexico.
From The Of All Things Series.
Prod-BAILYL Dist-AVED

Water Supply B 20 MIN
16MM FILM OPTICAL SOUND
Describes the means by which water is collected, purified and distributed to users.
Prod-USIS Dist-USIS 1951

Water Supply (2nd Ed) C 11 MIN
16MM FILM OPTICAL SOUND I-H
Shows how water for both rural and urban communities is obtained, purified and stored. Demonstrates how such devices as the rain barrel, hand-operated pump and electric pump are used. Points up the importance of the Great Lakes and the Colorado River in supplying the water needs of nearby cities.
LC NO. FIA53-197
Prod-ACA Dist-ACA 1964

Water Treatment C
3/4 OR 1/2 INCH VIDEO CASSETTE IND
Covers several aspects of water treatment such as clarifier, softener, zeolite base exchange and demineralizer.
From The Industrial Training, Module 2 - Boiler Fundamentals Series.
Prod-LEIKID Dist-LEIKID

Water Treatment Plant C
3/4 OR 1/2 INCH VIDEO CASSETTE
Visits the Akron city water treatment plant on Lake Rockwell, Portage County, Ohio. Examines the natural steam collection system and storage reservoirs. Traces the purification process from raw water to customer delivery and looks at the chemical testing procedures and EPA requirements.
From The Field Trips in Environmental Geology - Technical And Mechanical Concerns Series.
Prod-KENTSU Dist-KENTSU

Water Tricks C 13 MIN
16MM FILM OPTICAL SOUND J-C A
Presents Paul, a student, planning and carrying out an activity at a water-table. Shows how he makes use of the children's interest to show them tricks with siphons and pumps and then evaluates the activity in a discussion with his class.
From The Exploring Childhood Series.
LC NO. 76-701899
Prod-EDC Dist-EDC Prodn-FRIEDJ 1975

Water Walkers C 25 MIN
16MM FILM, 3/4 OR 1/2 IN VIDEO J-H A
Explores the miniature and unsuspected world of creatures living on the surface of ponds and streams.
LC NO. 82-707104
Prod-BBCTV Dist-FI 1981

Water Wars - The Battle Of Mono Lake C 39 MIN
3/4 OR 1/2 INCH VIDEO CASSETTE
Examines the controversies surrounding the diversion of fresh water to the city of Los Angeles from California's Mono Lake.
Prod-UCEMC Dist-UCEMC

Water-Seal Chest Drainage C 30 MIN
3/4 OR 1/2 INCH VIDEO CASSETTE
Presents a program on water-seal chest drainage. Begins with a basic review of the anatomy and physiology of the respiratory system, then explains water-seal drainage systems.
Prod-AJN Dist-AJN

Water-Solute Balance B 29 MIN
16MM FILM OPTICAL SOUND PRO
Discusses total body changes in water, protein and sodium.
From The Clinical Pathology Series.
Prod-NMAC Dist-USNAC

Water, The Plain Wonder C 9 MIN
16MM FILM, 3/4 OR 1/2 IN VIDEO
Explores some of the ways in which water shapes people's everyday lives.
From The Forest Resources Films Series.
Prod-REGIS Dist-GPITVL

Water, Water Everywhere C 15 MIN
16MM FILM OPTICAL SOUND IND
Defines cross-connections in water systems and discusses specific cases of illness which resulted from cross-connections. Describes remedial measures, such as air gaps, double check valves and vacuum breakers.
LC NO. 77-702469
Prod-LASL Dist-CS 1977

Water, Water Everywhere (Spanish) C 15 MIN
16MM FILM OPTICAL SOUND A
Defines cross-connections in water systems and discusses specific cases of illness which resulted from cross-connections. Describes remedial measures, such as air gaps, double check valves and vacuum breakers and explains their method of operation.
LC NO. 78-701187
Prod-LASL Dist-LASL 1978

Water's Edge, The, Pt 1 - The Unseen World C 28 MIN
16MM FILM, 3/4 OR 1/2 IN VIDEO C
Focuses on the interrelationships of animal and vegetable life that exist in a freshwater pond.
From The Nature Of Things Series.
Prod-CANBC Dist-FLMLIB 1978

Water's Edge, The, Pt 2 - The Silent Explosion C 28 MIN
16MM FILM, 3/4 OR 1/2 IN VIDEO C
Studies the creatures that have been lying dormant all winter in and around a freshwater pond.
From The Nature Of Things Series.
Prod-CANBC Dist-FLMLIB 1978

Water's Way C 7 MIN
16MM FILM, 3/4 OR 1/2 IN VIDEO P-I
Presents an introduction to our greatest natural resource, water. Features a little boy and a water drop who guides the boy through the basic story of water.
LC NO. 84-707088
Prod-ROMAF Dist-PHENIX 1983

Waterclock Crisis, The C 28 MIN
16MM FILM OPTICAL SOUND
Depicts the freshwater cycle in the State of Florida, documents cases of the misuse of water, presents testimony from water experts, and shows the positive contributions of various interest groups in remedying the freshwater problem.
LC NO. 79-701397
Prod-INTMCC Dist-INTMCC Prodn-FILMMA 1979

Watercolor C 15 MIN
16MM FILM, 3/4 OR 1/2 IN VIDEO I-C A
Illustrates the characteristics of watercolor as a painting medium and the many ways in which it may be used from simple pan colors to a wide palette of tube colors. Emphasizes the importance of personal vision in the development of an individual style.
From The Rediscovery - Art Media Series.
Prod-ACI Dist-AIMS 1967

Watercolor (French) C 14 MIN
16MM FILM, 3/4 OR 1/2 IN VIDEO I-C A
Presents the wide range of technical and expressive possibilities inherent in watercolor painting. Shows the use of the simplest materials as well as the more costly and professional items.
From The Rediscovery - Art Media (French) Series.
Prod-ACI Dist-AIMS 1967

Watercolor (Spanish) C 14 MIN
16MM FILM, 3/4 OR 1/2 IN VIDEO I-C A
Presents the wide range of technical and expressive possibilities inherent in watercolor painting. Shows the use of the simplest materials as well as the more costly and professional items.
From The Rediscovery - Art Media (Spanish) Series.
Prod-ACI Dist-AIMS 1967

Watercolor Painting - Imaginative Designs With Alex Ross C 20 MIN
16MM FILM, 3/4 OR 1/2 IN VIDEO
Presents Alex Ross demonstrating how he creates arresting patterns of vivid color and how he uses acrylic paint on a textured media board.
From The Watercolor Painting Series.
Prod-PERSPF Dist-CORF 1973

Watercolor Painting–A Series
16MM FILM, 3/4 OR 1/2 IN VIDEO
Shows artists in their studios or on location, as they explain how they look and plan each detail of a watercolor or an acrylic painting from start to finish.
Prod-PERSPF Dist-CORF 1973

Watercolor Painting - Abstract Designs From
Watercolor Painting - Creative Color Collage 18 MIN
Watercolor Painting - Imaginative Designs 20 MIN
Watercolor Painting - The Marine Scene With 19 MIN
Watercolor Painting - Working On Location 20 MIN
Watercolor Painting - Working With Sketches 20 MIN

Watercolor Society, The/Lou Harrison C 30 MIN
3/4 OR 1/2 INCH VIDEO CASSETTE
See series title for descriptive statement.
From The Kaleidoscope Series.
Prod-KTEHTV Dist-SCCOE

Watercolors In Action C 12 MIN
16MM FILM, 3/4 OR 1/2 IN VIDEO J-C A
Explains the method used by many contemporary watercolorists. Focuses on the method of holding the brush and the effect of its skillful manipulation on paper. Explains mixing tints, use of dry brush, neutralizing a color, laying dark values over light and obtaining color perspective and depth.
Prod-IFB Dist-IFB 1953

Waterfowl Wilderness C 26 MIN
16MM FILM OPTICAL SOUND I A
Follows the migrating flights of waterfowl through the Canadian wilderness. Examines the birds' breeding stage of life, from courting to the raising of the young in their nesting places.
From The Audubon Wildlife Theatre Series.
LC NO. 72-701986
Prod-KEGPL Dist-AVEXP 1970

Watergate - A Constitutional Crisis C 30 MIN
3/4 OR 1/2 INCH VIDEO CASSETTE C
Examines the struggle that brought into conflict all three branches of the government. Considers the questions of voting articles of impeachment, and the court states anew that not even the President is above the law.
From The American Government 1 Series.
Prod-DALCCD Dist-DALCCD

Watergate Affair, The C 29 MIN
3/4 OR 1/2 INCH VIDEO CASSETTE
Documents the Watergate scandal, which touched the highest offices in the land, caused the resignation of a President, and pushed the call for a new code of conduct and ethics by public officials.
Prod-UPI Dist-JOU

Waterground C 16 MIN
16MM FILM - 3/4 IN VIDEO H-C A
Displays the workings of the Winebarger family gristmill. Talks about its history and the social changes that have affected it.
Prod-APPAL Dist-APPAL 1977

Waterhole, The C 9 MIN
3/4 OR 1/2 INCH VIDEO CASSETTE
Depicts a day, dawn-to-dusk, at a water hole in Central Australia. Reveals changing moods as sun, wind and time trigger changes in animal life visiting the water hole.
Prod-AFTS Dist-EDMI 1984

Watering C 30 MIN
3/4 OR 1/2 INCH VIDEO CASSETTE C A
Discusses the varieties of watering techniques. Explains water movement and soil penetration.
From The Home Gardener With John Lenanton Series. Lesson 12
Prod-COAST Dist-CDTEL

Watering C 30 MIN
2 INCH VIDEOTAPE
Features Thalassa Cruso discussing different aspects of gardening. Emphasizes the watering of plants.
From The Making Things Grow I Series.
Prod-WGBHTV Dist-PUBTEL

Watering Houseplants C 30 MIN
3/4 OR 1/2 INCH VIDEO CASSETTE
Discusses the watering requirements of houseplants.
From The Even You Can Grow Houseplants Series.
Prod-WGTV Dist-MDCPB

Waterloo Farmers C 28 MIN
16MM FILM, 3/4 OR 1/2 IN VIDEO J-C A
Juxtaposes the old and new order Mennonites. Shows their differing beliefs in their methods of farming, with the old order using nonmechanized methods and the new order using modern, mechanized methods. Asks whether a compromise will have to be reached between the two groups.
LC NO. 83-706292
Prod-NFBC Dist-BULFRG 1976

Watermelon Etching And Melon Carving C 7 MIN
3/4 OR 1/2 INCH VIDEO CASSETTE PRO
Shows how to make a template to trace a pattern on a watermelon and fill the etching with cream cheese for contrast. Shows how to use masking tape as a guide for uniform zig-zag melon cuts.
Prod-CULINA Dist-CULINA

Watermelon Man C 97 MIN
16MM FILM OPTICAL SOUND
Tells how a bigoted white suburbanite turns black overnight. Stars Godfrey Cambridge.
Prod-CPC Dist-TWYMAN 1970

Watermelon Man, The C
1/2 IN VIDEO CASSETTE BETA/VHS
Presents a poignant comedy about a white bigot who turns permanently black, starring Godfrey Cambridge and Estelle Parsons.
Prod-GA Dist-GA

Watermen And Lighthouses Of The Chesapeake Bay C 13 MIN
3/4 OR 1/2 INCH VIDEO CASSETTE I-J
Serves as a supplement to a geography unit in eastern coastal states. Explains how fish and shellfish of Chesapeake Bay are caught and transported.
Prod-ENJOY Dist-ENJOY 1981

Watermen Of Chesapeake C 28 MIN
16MM FILM OPTICAL SOUND
Shows the impact which the Chesapeake Bay and its resources have exerted on a large segment of America since the early days. Portrays activities of Fishermen, America's only sail-powered oyster fleet, the Crisfield Crab Derby and a wild pony penning.
LC NO. FIE64-205
Prod-USBCF Dist-USNOAA 1964

Waterplay C 23 MIN
3/4 OR 1/2 INCH VIDEO CASSETTE C
Shows children involved in waterplay including bathtub play and water table play.
From The Learning Through Play - Modules Series. Module 3
Prod-UTORMC Dist-UTORMC 1976

Waterplay C 30 MIN
3/4 OR 1/2 INCH VIDEO CASSETTE H-C A
Discusses waterplay. Presents five illustrations, including bathtub play and water table play.
From The Learning Through Play Series.
Prod-UTORMC Dist-UTORMC 1980

Waterplay, Pt 1 B 12 MIN
16MM FILM OPTICAL SOUND T
Shows boys playing with water and such materials as funnels, basters, hoses and siphons at hilltop head start center.
From The Vignette Series.
Prod-EDS Dist-EDC 1970

Waterproof Arboreal Frog, A C 10 MIN
16MM FILM, 3/4 OR 1/2 IN VIDEO H-C A
Discusses Phyllomedusa sauvagei, a South American tree frog which lives under conditions of heat and prolonged drought by virtue of a tolerance of high temperatures, excretion of solid nitrogenous waste and a waterproof coating of wax on its skin.
From The Aspects Of Animal Behavior Series.
Prod-UCLA Dist-UCEMC 1976

Waterproofing America Or Different Strokes For Different Folks B 9 MIN
16MM FILM OPTICAL SOUND
Consists of historical footage featuring the activities and people who have made Red Cross National Aquatic and First Aid Schools a tradition over the last 50 years.
Prod-AMRC Dist-AMRC 1972

Waterproofing The Basement C 30 MIN
1/2 IN VIDEO CASSETTE BETA/VHS
Demonstrates waterproofing a basement and installing a wood stove, a free-standing chimney, windows and doors.
From The This Old House, Pt 2 - Suburban '50s Series.
Prod-WGBHTV Dist-MTI

Waters From The Mountain C 20 MIN
16MM FILM OPTICAL SOUND
Shows water supply forecasting and snow surveys. Emphasizes the need for such information and how it is used by all segments of society in the West. Traces water from snowmelt on the mountain to corps and other uses in the valley.
LC NO. 74-705934
Prod-USSCS Dist-USNAC 1964

Waters Of Kane C 11 MIN
16MM FILM OPTICAL SOUND J-C
Portrays the search for the healing waters of Kane, and the tragic fate of a creature of Milu who stalks a young warrior who invaded his land.
Prod-CINEPC Dist-CINEPC

Waters Of The Earth, The C 30 MIN
3/4 OR 1/2 INCH VIDEO CASSETTE
Describes the remarkable properties of water. Discusses the physical conditions of the sea in terms of salinity, temperature, density and pressure. Looks at water-sampling instruments and techniques used on modern research vessels.
From The Oceanus - The Marine Environment Series. Lesson 4
Prod-SCCON Dist-CDTEL

Waters Of Yosemite C 9 MIN
16MM FILM, 3/4 OR 1/2 IN VIDEO I A
Presents a poetic interpretation of running water.
From The Wilderness Series.
Prod-PFP Dist-PHENIX Prodn-ADAMS 1967

Waterskiing For Kids C 30 MIN
3/4 OR 1/2 INCH VIDEO CASSETTE
Discusses equipment, techniques and dock practice useful for teaching waterskiing to children. Includes signals, safety and crossing the wake. Stars Mike Suyderhoud.
From The Superstar Sports Tapes Series.
Prod-TRASS Dist-TRASS

Watersong C 13 MIN
16MM FILM OPTICAL SOUND
Considers the possibilities for vacationing in Missouri by showing the availability and abundance of lakes, rivers and streams within the state.
LC NO. 77-701459
Prod-MODT Dist-MODT Prodn-DMM 1977

Watertime C 5 MIN
16MM FILM OPTICAL SOUND
Presents an animated film portraying the excitement and invigoration of sailing, kayaking, canoeing and swimming.
LC NO. 77-702701
Prod-GORDND Dist-CANFDC

Waterwheel Village C 14 MIN
16MM FILM, 3/4 OR 1/2 IN VIDEO P-I
Tells how two brothers are delighted by a miniature village they find near a stream, until they learn that a girl built it. Explains how after much conflict the three finally learn to work together.
Prod-FLMFR Dist-FLMFR

Watts - Riot Or Revolt X 60 MIN
16MM FILM OPTICAL SOUND H-C A
Documents the Watts, Los Angeles, riot during the summer of 1965. Examines the situation in terms of the nationwide civil rights struggle. Presents opinions representing the Negro and the white community as it attempts to answer whether Watts was an irrational riot or a planned revolt stemming from social and economic injustice.
From The CBS Reports Series.
LC NO. FI68-308
Prod-CBSTV Dist-ADL 1965

Watts Made Out Of Thread X 26 MIN
16MM FILM, 3/4 OR 1/2 IN VIDEO J-C A
Tells how a guilt-ridden ghetto exploiter commits suicide and meets God. Stars Harold Gould, Roscoe Lee Brown and Alice Ghostley.
From The Insight Series.
Prod-PAULST Dist-PAULST

Watts Made Out Of Thread C 29 MIN
3/4 OR 1/2 INCH VIDEO CASSETTE J A
Dramatizes the story of Eddie who learns a lesson from God about honesty and admission of guilt.
Prod-SUTHRB Dist-SUTHRB

Watts Made Out Of Thread (Spanish) X 26 MIN
16MM FILM, 3/4 OR 1/2 IN VIDEO J-C A
Tells how a guilt-ridden ghetto exploiter commits suicide and meets God. Stars Harold Gould, Roscoe Lee Brown and Alice Ghostley.
From The Insight Series.
Prod-PAULST Dist-PAULST

Watts Made Out Of Thread (Spanish) C 29 MIN
3/4 OR 1/2 INCH VIDEO CASSETTE J A
Dramatizes the story of Eddie who learns a lesson from God about honesty and admission of guilt.
Prod-SUTHRB Dist-SUTHRB

Watts Tower Theatre Workshop C 28 MIN
2 INCH VIDEOTAPE
See series title for descriptive statement.
From The Synergism - In Today's World Series.
Prod-KCET Dist-PUBTEL

Watts Towers Theatre Workshop C 28 MIN
16MM FILM OPTICAL SOUND H-C A
Examines the Watts Towers Theater Workshop which consists of black teenagers from the Los Angeles Watts ghetto, and explains that its purpose is to show entertainment by, for and about people living in the ghetto.
LC NO. 70-703297
Prod-KCET Dist-IU 1969

Wattsie C 11 MIN
16MM FILM OPTICAL SOUND H-C
Focuses on the difficulties encountered by a conscientious assistant principal who is working under a likable but inefficient administrator.
Prod-OSUMPD Dist-OSUMPD 1961

Wave Jumping C 6 MIN
16MM FILM - 1/2 IN VIDEO
Shows boardsailing in Hawaii. Includes music.
Prod-OFFSHR Dist-OFFSHR

Wave Motion - Diffraction B 8 MIN
16MM FILM, 3/4 OR 1/2 IN VIDEO H-C
Demonstrates diffraction patterns formed when ripples spread beyond the barriers placed to limit wave fronts and the related patterns formed when narrow apertures and obstacles are placed in the path of a beam of light.
Prod-GATEP Dist-IFB 1971

Wave Motion - Interference B 7 MIN
16MM FILM, 3/4 OR 1/2 IN VIDEO H-C
Presents an experiment showing the true forms of interference patterns on the surface of water. Employs the Schlieren technique to explain the principles underlying the experiment.
Prod-GATEP Dist-IFB 1971

Wave Shaping And Pulse Generating C 12 MIN
3/4 OR 1/2 INCH VIDEO CASSETTE
Analyzes the output waveforms of oscillators and multivibrators. Covers pulse generators and generating pulses using oscillators and multivibrators.
From The Industrial Electronics - Oscillators And Multivibrators Series.
Prod-TPCTRA Dist-TPCTRA

Wave Velocities, Dispersion, And The B 28 MIN
16MM FILM - 3/4 IN VIDEO IND
Considers traveling waves and the way they propagate through transmission systems. Can be used in connection with lectures on phase velocity, group velocity, backward waves and dispersion. Concentrates on visualization of the concepts through animation and experiment.
Prod-NCEEF Dist-EDC 1969

Wave-Particle Duality C 22 MIN
16MM FILM, 3/4 OR 1/2 IN VIDEO H-C
Traces the development of two contrasting theories of light that also led to the discovery of the wave-like particles of matter.
Prod-BFL Dist-IFB 1974

Wave, The C 46 MIN
3/4 OR 1/2 INCH VIDEO CASSETTE
Shows a school that was brought to the brink of spiritual holocaust by a seemingly innocuous social experiment.
Prod-EMBASY Dist-EMBASY

Wave, The - A Japanese Folk Tale C 9 MIN
16MM FILM, 3/4 OR 1/2 IN VIDEO P-I
Presents the Japanese tale of how a grandfather saved the lives of the villagers from drowning by luring them to the mountain top.
Prod-FA Dist-PHENIX 1968

Waveguide Fabrication Techniques, Pt 1 C 46 MIN
3/4 OR 1/2 INCH VIDEO CASSETTE C
Discusses methods for fabricating waveguides in passive (non-light emitting) materials such as deposited thin films, ion bombardment, and ion migration, and waveguide fabrication in semiconductors such as heteroepitaxial growth of gallum aluminum arsenide.
From The Integrated Optics Series.
Prod-UDEL Dist-UDEL

Waveguide Fabrication Techniques, Pt 2 C 44 MIN
3/4 OR 1/2 INCH VIDEO CASSETTE C
Discusses proton bombarded waveguides in semiconductors, electro-optic waveguides, and methods of defining the shape of channel waveguides.
From The Integrated Optics Series.
Prod-UDEL Dist-UDEL

Waveguide Plumbing B 26 MIN
16MM FILM OPTICAL SOUND
Covers the 90 degree E and H band in rectangular waveguides by explaining the effect on the fields within the guide. Discusses twists, flexible waveguide and improper bends. (Kinescope)
LC NO. 74-705935
Prod-USAF Dist-USNAC

Waveguide To Waveguide Couplers And Modulators C 40 MIN
3/4 OR 1/2 INCH VIDEO CASSETTE C
Describes the use of closely spaced dual channel waveguides as directional couplers and electro-optic switches and modulators. Theoretical models are compared with experimental results.
From The Integrated Optics Series.
Prod-UDEL Dist-UDEL

Waveguides B 29 MIN
16MM FILM OPTICAL SOUND
Explains the inadequacy of transmission lines, other than waveguides, at microwave frequencies. Stresses factors determining the power handling capability and the frequency handling capability of waveguides. (Kinescope)
LC NO. 74-705936
Prod-USAF Dist-USNAC

Wavelines I C 11 MIN
16MM FILM OPTICAL SOUND
Presents four visual-musical compositions produced with a Moog synthesizer, an oscilloscope and acoustic sounds.
LC NO. 79-700345
Prod-MAGMUS Dist-MAGMUS 1978

Wavelines II C 8 MIN
16MM FILM OPTICAL SOUND
Contains three visual-musical compositions, produced visually with a Moog synthesizer connected to a filmed oscilloscope and musically with synthesizers and acoustic instruments.
LC NO. 80-700269
Prod-WEID Dist-WEID 1979

Waves B 24 MIN
16MM FILM OPTICAL SOUND C A
Two teachers use an overhead projector and audible sound sources to demonstrate how the ripple tank can be used to

show a variety of wave phenomena, including interference effects, the production of standing waves and the behavior of ultrasonic waves.
From The Harvard Project Physics Teacher Briefings Series. No. 13
LC NO. 74-709145
Prod-HPP Dist-HRAW 1969

Waves C 24 MIN
16MM FILM, 3/4 OR 1/2 IN VIDEO
Illustrates fundamental principles of wave motion and wave energy using a classic experiment on attenuation of storm-generated waves in the Pacific Ocean. Recaps some basic characteristics of waves in water including wave length, wave height, wave period and frequency, orbital motions of water particles and the relationships between wave energy and height.
Prod-OPENU Dist-MEDIAG Prodn-BBCTV 1979

Waves C 26 MIN
16MM FILM, 3/4 OR 1/2 IN VIDEO I-C A
Uses music, natural sounds and imaginative photography to show the natural beauty and power of the ocean.
LC NO. 80-706721
Prod-AENGUS Dist-IFB Prodn-CAREYP 1977

Waves C 30 MIN
16MM FILM, 3/4 OR 1/2 IN VIDEO C A
Shows how Newton, with an analysis of simple harmonic motion and a stroke of genius, extended mechanics to the propagation of sound.
From The Mechanical Universe Series.
Prod-ANNCPB Dist-FI

Waves And Beaches C 20 MIN
3/4 OR 1/2 INCH VIDEO CASSETTE
Discusses the shapes adopted by a beach to dissipate wave energy. Deals with the vertical profile of a beach, field measurement and sediment variability.
From The Earth Science Series.
Prod-FOTH Dist-FOTH 1984

Waves And Energy C 11 MIN
16MM FILM, 3/4 OR 1/2 IN VIDEO I-J
Shows how sound, radio, light and heat waves are made and their characteristics. Shows how waves carry energy from one plane to another and how waves are reflected.
Prod-EBF Dist-EBEC 1961

Waves And Energy (Spanish) C 11 MIN
16MM FILM, 3/4 OR 1/2 IN VIDEO I-J
A Spanish language version of the film and videorecording Waves And Energy.
Prod-EBF Dist-EBEC 1961

Waves In Fluids X 33 MIN
16MM FILM, 3/4 OR 1/2 IN VIDEO H-C
Demonstrates concepts in one-dimensional wave motion using a water channel, a flume and shock tubes. Covers particle motion in small amplitude waves, steepening and breaking of compression waves, surge waves and hydraulic jumps, sound waves and shock waves, shock diffraction and shock heating.
From The Fluid Mechanics Series.
Prod-NCFMF Dist-EBEC Prodn-EDS 1966

Waves Of Change C 29 MIN
3/4 INCH VIDEO CASSETTE
Discusses the belief that language changes through 'waves' which flow and merge.
From The Pike On Language Series.
Prod-UMITV Dist-UMITV 1977

Waves Of Change / Culture Of The Individual C 34 MIN
3/4 OR 1/2 INCH VIDEO CASSETTE
See series title for descriptive statement.
From The Focus On Change Series.
Prod-TVOTAR Dist-DELTAK

Waves Of Revolution B 30 MIN
16MM FILM OPTICAL SOUND
Presents an underground record of an historic Indian populist movement, the anti-government Bihar Movement in India, which was led by Shri Jayaprakash Narayan (JP), from March, 1974, to March, 1975.
Prod-ICARUS Dist-ICARUS 1976

Waves On Water X 16 MIN
16MM FILM, 3/4 OR 1/2 IN VIDEO I-H
Uses large experimental tanks to show that waves approaching shore bend to conform to the coastline. Presents documentary evidence proving that the seismic sea waves which crossed the Pacific Ocean in April, 1946, were directly associated with an earthquake.
From The Earth Science Program Series.
Prod-EBEC Dist-EBEC 1965

Waves On Water (Spanish) C 16 MIN
16MM FILM, 3/4 OR 1/2 IN VIDEO I-H
Explains how waves are created and demonstrates that although waves travel, the water does not move. Points out that high energy waves are created by underwater earthquakes.
Prod-EBEC Dist-EBEC

Waves, Modulation And Communication B 19 MIN
16MM FILM OPTICAL SOUND C A
Two teachers demonstrate with three different pieces of equipment--a pair of turntable oscillators, a pair of coilcapacitor circuits and a microwave generator-how modulation of a sinusoidal wave can be used to communicate information.
From The Harvard Project Physics Teacher Briefings Series. No. 19
LC NO. 78-709146
Prod-HPP Dist-HRAW 1969

Waves, Vibrations And Atoms C 10 MIN
3/4 INCH VIDEO CASSETTE
Deomstrates fundamentals of wave behavior. Relates standing wave on a guitar, drum and bell to atomic orbitals.
From The Chemistry Videotapes Series.
Prod-UMITV Dist-UMITV

Waveshaping Networks B 34 MIN
16MM FILM OPTICAL SOUND
Shows how to determine the amount of capacitor charge applied to an RC network. Discusses differentiated and integrated waves. Gives definitions for short, medium and long time constant circuits and shows how the waveforms for each circuit can be recognized. (Kinescope)
LC NO. 74-705937
Prod-USAF Dist-USNAC

Wax Grease, And Silicone Removal C 8 MIN
1/2 IN VIDEO CASSETTE BETA/VHS
Deals with auto body work. Explains the use of wax, grease and silicone removing solvent and demonstrates application procedures.
Prod-RMI Dist-RMI

Waxing And Trail Sense C 29 MIN
3/4 OR 1/2 INCH VIDEO CASSETTE
Examines the art and theory behind waxing cross country skis and provides information and tips about clothing, equipment, trail safety and how to prepare for a cross country ski trip.
From The Cross Country Ski School Series.
LC NO. 82-706435
Prod-VTETV Dist-PBS 1981

Waxing Procedure For Setting Teeth C 7 MIN
16MM FILM, 3/4 OR 1/2 IN VIDEO PRO
Discusses the waxing procedure for obtaining the anatomical contours for complete dentures. Shows the contouring of the interproximal, labial and lingual areas in the wax model. Explains the advantages of developing this form.
LC NO. 80-706797
Prod-USVA Dist-USNAC Prodn-VADTC 1980

Waxing Technique For Resin Veneered Fixed Bridge, Pt I - Coping Instruction C 7 MIN
3/4 OR 1/2 INCH VIDEO CASSETTE
Shows the technique for waxing resin veneered fixed bridges and the fabrication of resin copings to provide strength to the wax pattern and to insure uniform thickness of gold in the window area of the veneer crown.
Prod-VADTC Dist-AMDA 1975

Waxing Technique For Resin Veneered Fixed Bridge, Pt II - Anterior Bridge C 14 MIN
3/4 OR 1/2 INCH VIDEO CASSETTE
Shows the technique for waxing an anterior bridge and demonstrates the procedures for wax-up of crowns and establishing the occlusion, assuring there are no prematurities prior to spruing and investing.
Prod-VADTC Dist-AMDA 1975

Waxing Technique For Resin Veneered Fixed Bridge, Pt III - Posterior Bridge C 12 MIN
3/4 OR 1/2 INCH VIDEO CASSETTE
Shows the technique for waxing a posterior bridge and demonstrates the wax-up of crowns, developing and establishing the occlusion by performing lateral excursions on an articulator prior to spruing, investing and casting.
Prod-VADTC Dist-AMDA 1975

Waxing Technique For Resin-Veneered Fixed Bridges C 36 MIN
16MM FILM OPTICAL SOUND
Covers anterior and posterior copying construction.
LC NO. 76-701545
Prod-USVA Dist-USNAC 1975

Waxworks C 15 MIN
16MM FILM OPTICAL SOUND P-I
Reveals that when the Graham children and Alice the chimp visit the wax museum, they have an opportunity to foil a robbery.
Prod-LUF Dist-LUF 1978

Way Down East B 110 MIN
16MM FILM SILENT C A
Traces the tragic life of a poor country girl named Anna. Directed by D W Griffith.
LC NO. FIA68-2447
Prod-GFITH Dist-REELIM 1920

Way Down East B 119 MIN
16MM FILM SILENT
Portrays the story of Anna, a country girl tricked into a fake marriage by a city playboy who deserts her when she becomes pregnant. Shows her being ostracized for being an unwed mother and being forced to take refuge as a servant girl, yet finding ultimate happiness with a young man who has befriended her. Stars Lillian Gish. Directed by D W Griffith.
Prod-GFITH Dist-KILLIS 1920

Way Down East (The Rescue) B 14 MIN
16MM FILM OPTICAL SOUND J-C A
Presents an excerpt from the 1920 motion picture Way Down East. Tells how Anna gets lost in a blizzard and is swept perilously close to the edge of a waterfall. Directed by D W Griffith.
From The Film Study Extracts Series.
Prod-UNKNWN Dist-FI

Way For Diana, A C 14 MIN
16MM FILM OPTICAL SOUND
Presents a reading motivation program which shows a city girl discovering new worlds through reading in the library.
LC NO. 79-715511
Prod-MALIBU Dist-MALIBU 1972

Way I Remember It, The C 15 MIN
3/4 OR 1/2 INCH VIDEO CASSETTE J
Uses a dramatic approach to reading and understanding expository texts. Illustrates strategies for studying texts in preparing for written tests, including underlining main ideas, taking notes, visualizing, asking questions, paraphrasing, discussing and reviewing.
From The Reading For A Reason Series. No. 7
LC NO. 83-706578
Prod-WETN Dist-AITECH Prodn-GBCTP 1983

Way I See It, The C 8 MIN
16MM FILM OPTICAL SOUND
Uses animation to point out the differences in how people perceive, focusing on the themes of reading readiness, art and working together. Follows an artist and a house painter as they struggle through a see-saw battle in which each attempts to do the other's job better.
Prod-ECI Dist-ECI

Way I See It, The C 29 MIN
16MM FILM OPTICAL SOUND
Offers the pictorial views of four experienced photographers as they photograph their favorite subjects including people, backyard subjects, the action of sports and the beauty of the landscape.
Prod-EKC Dist-EKC 1983

Way I See It, The C 23 MIN
16MM FILM, 3/4 OR 1/2 IN VIDEO H-C
Presents a discussion about the influence of perceptual differences on supervisor-subordinate relations and job performance.
Prod-RTBL Dist-RTBL 1965

Way I See It, The (Dutch) C 23 MIN
16MM FILM, 3/4 OR 1/2 IN VIDEO H-C
Presents a discussion about the influence of perceptual differences on supervisor-subordinate relations and job performance.
Prod-RTBL Dist-RTBL 1965

Way In And The Way Out, The C 30 MIN
16MM FILM OPTICAL SOUND R
Examines the rise of the modern religious movement from its first flowering in the Haight-Ashbury district of San Francisco to the disillusionment of the drug culture. Focuses on a Christian community, a Billy Graham rally and a Hare Krishna ceremony.
From The Devout Young Series.
Prod-OSSHE Dist-OSSHE

Way It Can Be, The C 23 MIN
16MM FILM OPTICAL SOUND
Describes the work of the Learning Research and Development Center of the University of Pittsburgh in the field of adaptive education which strives to shape schools to fit their students rather than shaping children to fit the schools.
Prod-UPITTS Dist-UPITTS 1975

Way It Is, The C 27 MIN
16MM FILM OPTICAL SOUND
Depicts a typical day at McGill University, showing undergraduate students, researchers and part-time students engaged in their studies and other activities.
LC NO. 77-700328
Prod-MCGILU Dist-MCGILU Prodn-PFLMAS 1976

Way It Is, The B 30 MIN
16MM FILM, 3/4 OR 1/2 IN VIDEO PRO
See series title for descriptive statement.
From The Public Health Science Series. Unit III - Introduction To Epidemiology
Prod-TEXWU Dist-GPITVL Prodn-KUHTTV

Way It Is, The - After The Divorce C 24 MIN
16MM FILM, 3/4 OR 1/2 IN VIDEO I-C A
Shows how a family deals with divorce, focusing on the 12-year-old daughter who relates her experiences and feelings.
Prod-NFBC Dist-CF 1983

Way Men Behave, The C 30 MIN
3/4 INCH VIDEO CASSETTE
Features Dr Theodore Buttrey, classicist professor, as he explores the myth and reality in Herodotus' world.
From The Herodotus - Father Of History Series.
Prod-UMITV Dist-UMITV 1980

Way Of Escape C 25 MIN
16MM FILM OPTICAL SOUND C A
Tells the story of Charles, a young man from mainland China, who chose Christianity instead of communism.
Prod-CBFMS Dist-CBFMS

Way Of Life, A C 23 MIN
16MM FILM OPTICAL SOUND
Expresses some of the feelings and values of a farm family at a time when the father feels he must retire and leave the farm in order not to be in his son's way.
LC NO. 79-705454
Prod-DEERE Dist-DF Prodn-DF 1969

Way Of Life, A C 23 MIN
16MM FILM OPTICAL SOUND
Presents a collage of scenes and action revealing the history and character of Wabash College in Crawfordsville, Indiana.
LC NO. 75-703619
Prod-WABCOL Dist-STEEGP Prodn-STEEGP 1975

Way Of Life, A C 20 MIN
16MM FILM, 3/4 OR 1/2 IN VIDEO
Uses dramatic vignettes to realize safety is a way of life. Shows easily overlooked but potentially dangerous situations in automobiles, in the kitchen, canoeing, ashtrays and corrective measures to be used.
Prod-OHMPS Dist-BCNFL 1983

Way Of Life, A C 28 MIN
3/4 INCH VIDEO CASSETTE
Shows the daily activities of Henry Evaluarjuk, an Inuit carver who moved his own and two other families to a remote inlet on Baffin Island. Shows their return to a more traditional Inuit lifestyle, depending on nature for subsistence. Also available in two-inch quad and one-inch videotape.
Prod-CBCNS Dist-NAMPBC

Way Of Music, The C 60 MIN
3/4 OR 1/2 INCH VIDEO CASSETTE H-C A
Discusses different aspects of music.
From The Art Of Being Human Series.
Prod-FI Dist-FI 1978

Way Of Our Fathers, The C 33 MIN
16MM FILM, 3/4 OR 1/2 IN VIDEO J-C A
Presents members of several northern California Indian tribes, who depict unique elements of a way of life as it flourished before the imposition of a foreign culture. Explores effects of conventional white-oriented educational programs, such as destruction of Indian self-concepts and loss of cultural heritage and identity. Features native American teachers who discuss historical methods of Indian education and ways that both methods and content might be incorporated in the mainstream of American education.
Prod-HUMBLT Dist-UCEMC 1972

Way Of The Artist, The C 60 MIN
3/4 OR 1/2 INCH VIDEO CASSETTE H-C A
Discusses man as an artistic being.
From The Art Of Being Human Series.
Prod-FI Dist-FI 1978

Way Of The Dinosaur, The C 7 MIN
16MM FILM, 3/4 OR 1/2 IN VIDEO I-C A
Explores the history of energy sources. Asks whether we are going the way of the dinosaur.
Prod-LUF Dist-LUF

Way Of The Humanist C 30 MIN
3/4 OR 1/2 INCH VIDEO CASSETTE C
See series title for descriptive statement.
From The Art Of Being Human Series. Module 1
Prod-MDCC Dist-MDCC

Way Of The Nomad - Australia's Desert Aboriginals C 28 MIN
3/4 OR 1/2 INCH VIDEO CASSETTE J-C A
Shows documentary footage, recently released from a museum, made in 1963 from an expedition to remote desert areas of Central Australia. Shows how well adapted aboriginals were to survive in such an arid environment, how they were able to find adequate food and water where white explorers and prospectors perished. Views tool making, food gathering and cooking, and notes that great time and care are taken in the shaping of transportable, multipurpose utensils from tough desert trees.
Prod-EDMI Dist-EDMI 1984

Way Of The Willow, The C 30 MIN
16MM FILM, 3/4 OR 1/2 IN VIDEO J-C A
Explores the trauma, trials and tribulations of a family of Vietnamese boat people and their sponsoring family in adjusting to each other and to a whole new way of life. Concludes with a crisis which draws the two families together and establishes communications.
Prod-CATLSF Dist-BCNFL 1982

Way Of The World, The C 60 MIN
3/4 OR 1/2 INCH VIDEO CASSETTE H-C A
Discusses stylization, avantgardism, black theatre and realism in drama. Uses the play The Way Of The World as an example.
From The Drama - Play, Performance, Perception Series. Conventions Of The Theatre
Prod-BBCTV Dist-FI 1978

Way Out Of The Wilderness B 29 MIN
3/4 INCH VIDEO CASSETTE
Shows the care of retarded children at the Plymouth State Home and Training Center, where a home atmosphere is provided in preparing the children for return to the outside world. Describes what is being done to help blind and motor-handicapped children find 'a way out of the wilderness.'
Prod-USNAC Dist-USNAC 1972

Way Out West B 60 MIN
16MM FILM SILENT I A
Features Laurel and Hardy as two desert prospectors who blunder their way through a series of misadventures in the West of the 1890's.
Prod-ROACH Dist-BHAWK 1937

Way Out, A C 24 MIN
16MM FILM OPTICAL SOUND
A documentary film about the Boston State Hospital program in which chronic mental patients are integrated into community life by placing them in cooperative apartments.
LC NO. 72-701783
Prod-SQUIBB Dist-SQUIBB 1972

Way Out, A C 32 MIN
16MM FILM OPTICAL SOUND PRO
Examines the Boston State Hospital Community Residential Treatment Program for chronic mental patients. Focuses on the belief that many chronic mental patients can live useful, meaningful lives in supervised settings outside the hospital.
Prod-SQUIBB Dist-SQUIBB

Way They Live There—A Series
16MM FILM, 3/4 OR 1/2 IN VIDEO I-H
Looks at the ways of life of people living in an Egyptian village, a Ghanian fishing village and in Poland.
Prod-LUF Dist-LUF 1980

Way They Live There, The - A Ghanaian Fishing
Way They Live There, The - An Egyptian Village 018 MIN
Way They Live There, The - Poland 019 MIN

Way They Live There, The - A Ghanaian Fishing Village C 19 MIN
16MM FILM, 3/4 OR 1/2 IN VIDEO I-H
Shows everyday life in a small fishing village in Ghana as a young girl spends the day shopping in the village market, preparing the family meal, playing on the beach and sharing the excitement of the return of the fishing fleet.
From The Way They Live There Series.
Prod-LUF Dist-LUF 1980

Way They Live There, The - An Egyptian Village C 18 MIN
16MM FILM, 3/4 OR 1/2 IN VIDEO I-H
Characterizes life in a village in the Nile delta in Egypt where survival depends on local crops and livestock. Shows that the social life of the children follows centuries-old traditions.
From The Way They Live There Series.
Prod-LUF Dist-LUF 1980

Way They Live There, The - Poland C 19 MIN
16MM FILM, 3/4 OR 1/2 IN VIDEO I-H
Introduces the Popielarz family of Poland who live in an inexpensive, but small, state-owned apartment in Poland. Shows that although three-quarters of Mr Popielarz's income goes for food, his wife is part of a minority of non-working mothers.
From The Way They Live There Series.
Prod-LUF Dist-LUF 1980

Way Things Burn, The C 16 MIN
16MM FILM OPTICAL SOUND
A Japanese Language Film. Divides flame into three parts, the bright, the dark and the blue part. Points out that a flame consumes oxygen when it burns and lets out steam, carbon-dioxide, light and heat.
Prod-UNIJAP Dist-UNIJAP 1969

Way To Bridge The Distance, A C 25 MIN
3/4 OR 1/2 INCH VIDEO CASSETTE
Explores different strategies for delivering health information to rural villages, including two-way radio, mass media campaigns, satellite-linked diagnostic assistance and social marketing.
LC NO. 81-707241
Prod-USAID Dist-USNAC 1980

Way To Go, The C 11 MIN
16MM FILM OPTICAL SOUND
Traces the history of motorcycles and examines their use in the 1970's. Explains the importance of learning to ride safely.
From The Motorcycle Rider Course Series.
LC NO. 77-700195
Prod-MOSAFE Dist-MIFE Prodn-MIFE 1976

Way To Go, The C 28 MIN
16MM FILM OPTICAL SOUND A
Combines good cinematography of scenery, parks, camp sites and families with a montage of on-site comments by park officials, owners of camp sites and more elaborate recreational facilities and individuals who are sold on camping as a frequent recreation or as a way of life.
LC NO. 73-700996
Prod-RVI Dist-SFI Prodn-PILOT 1972

Way To The Capital C 15 MIN
16MM FILM OPTICAL SOUND
Discusses a youth physical fitness program.
LC NO. 74-706604
Prod-USN Dist-USNAC 1972

Way We Fight—A Series

Prod-USWD Dist-USNAC 1979

Battle Of Russia, The 067 MIN

Way We know - The Value Of Theory In Linguistic Study C 29 MIN
3/4 INCH VIDEO CASSETTE
Focuses on Kenneth Pike's theory of Tagmemics which is based on a series of components and concepts that help explain how words are arranged.
From The Pike On Language Series.
Prod-UMITV Dist-UMITV 1977

Way We Live, The C 29 MIN
16MM FILM OPTICAL SOUND J-C A
Presents four examples of urban living in the Federal Republic of Germany. Discusses government-subsidized housing programs which have been successful in reconstructing apartments and houses.
Prod-WSTGLC Dist-WSTGLC

Way We Live, The C 15 MIN
16MM FILM, 3/4 OR 1/2 IN VIDEO I-J
Pictures the range of alternative life-styles and how these are often related to career choices.
From The Bread And Butterflies Series.
LC NO. 74-703183
Prod-AITV Dist-AITECH Prodn-WNVT 1973

Way We Live, The C 25 MIN
3/4 OR 1/2 INCH VIDEO CASSETTE H A
Shows how a town and its residents contribute to keeping the crime rate low. Features interviews with residents and municipal officials in the black town of Lawnside, New Jersey.
Prod-CUETV Dist-CUNIV

Way We Were, The C 118 MIN
16MM FILM OPTICAL SOUND H-C
Tells the romantic story of an upper-crust WASP novelist and a Jewish bluestocking girl. Stars Barbara Streisand and Robert Redford. Directed by Sydney Pollack.
Prod-CPC Dist-TIMLIF 1973

Way-Out World Of Fred Feldman, The C 48 MIN
16MM FILM OPTICAL SOUND A
Describes the work of a helicopter pilot-traffic reporter. Shows reporter Fred Feldman as he reports on traffic, enjoys the beauty and grandeur of New York City from his low-flying helicopter and engages in radio repartee with his anchor man, John Gambling.
LC NO. 78-702642
Prod-CFILMC Dist-RKOGEN 1968

Wayne Cilento And Jud Alper C 30 MIN
3/4 OR 1/2 INCH VIDEO CASSETTE
Focuses on dancing in commercials.
From The Eye On Dance - Dance On TV And Film Series.
Prod-ARTRES Dist-ARTRES

Wayne Fielding - Human Skeleton C 17 MIN
3/4 OR 1/2 INCH VIDEO CASSETTE
Constructs a world through various transitions.
Prod-ARTINC Dist-ARTINC

Wayne Fielding - Motion Sickness C 6 MIN
3/4 OR 1/2 INCH VIDEO CASSETTE
Includes black and white shots.
Prod-ARTINC Dist-ARTINC

Wayne Hays Blues C
3/4 OR 1/2 INCH VIDEO CASSETTE
From The Antartica Series.
Prod-EAI Dist-EAI

Wayne Sterloff C
3/4 OR 1/2 INCH VIDEO CASSETTE
Portrays Wayne Sterloff, British Columbian filmmaker with interviews and film clips.
From The Filmmakers' Showcase Series.
Prod-CANFDW Dist-CANFDW

Wayne Thiebaud And Peter Voulkos C 30 MIN
16MM FILM OPTICAL SOUND H-C T
Contrasts the paintings and philosophy of pop artist Wayne Thiebaud with the abstract bronze sculpture of Peter Voulkos. Shows Thiebaud at work in his studio and teaching in the classroom and Boulkos working in his foundry studio. Both artists discuss their philosophy and ideas concerning teaching.
From The Creative Person Series.
LC NO. FIA68-67
Prod-NET Dist-IU 1968

Wayne's Decision C 6 MIN
16MM FILM OPTICAL SOUND J-C A
Deals with some of the complex and painful issues faced by teenage fathers.
From The Responsible Caring Series.
LC NO. 81-701350
Prod-MEMAPP Dist-MEMAPP Prodn-VISCNT 1980

Ways And The Means, The B 29 MIN
16MM FILM OPTICAL SOUND J-H
Discusses the role of Congress in raising the revenues required to run the federal government and explains the unique role of the House Ways and Means Committee in this process.
From The Government Story Series. No. 12
LC NO. 72-707216
Prod-WEBC Dist-WESTLC 1968

Ways At Wallace And Sons, The C
1/2 IN VIDEO CASSETTE BETA/VHS
Relates story of the wood construction of the ill-fated schooner John F Leavitt which went down on its maiden voyage.
Prod-MAYDYF Dist-MYSTIC 1979

Ways I Am Me, The C 20 MIN
3/4 INCH VIDEO CASSETTE I
Explains the nature of basic differences in individuals. Discusses differences in perceiving the world because of tastes and preferences.
From The People Puzzle Series.
Prod-WHROTV Dist-GPITVL

Ways In The Night (German) C 98 MIN
16MM FILM OPTICAL SOUND
Tells about the relationship between a German Army officer and a Polish countess during World War II. Includes English subtitles.
Prod-TLECUL Dist-TLECUL

Ways Of Assessing Reading Progress C 29 MIN
16MM FILM, 3/4 OR 1/2 IN VIDEO C A
Illustrates alternative means of assessing reading skills that can benefit students parents, teachers and administrators.
From The Teaching Children To Read Series.
Prod-MFFD Dist-FI 1976

Ways Of Dealing With Conflict In Organizations B 27 MIN
16MM FILM, 3/4 OR 1/2 IN VIDEO H-C A
Herbert Shepard, professor of behavioral sciences, Case Institute of Technology, analyzes three alternative methods of resolving conflict--suppression, bargaining and problem-solving.
From The Management Development Series.
Prod-UCLA Dist-UCEMC 1962

Ways Of Hearing—A Series
16MM FILM, 3/4 OR 1/2 IN VIDEO C A
Refers to hearing impaired children and the predominant approaches to teaching them language and communications skills. Applies to parents as well as educators, the film illustrates techniques used in the auditory-verbal method, the auditory-oral method, and in total communication. Discusses basics of hearing impairment and the consequences of hearing loss to a child's language development.
Prod-BCNFL Dist-BCNFL

Hearing Impairment - An Overview 016 MIN
Language Through Sight And Sound 018 MIN
Listening For Language 022 MIN

Ways Of Nature, The C 22 MIN
16MM FILM OPTICAL SOUND
Describes antibiotic processes and their effects on the environment.
LC NO. 76-702306
Prod-LILLY Dist-MTP 1976

Ways Of Our Fathers C 40 MIN
3/4 OR 1/2 INCH VIDEO CASSETTE
Focuses on improving the educational experiences of Indian children. Advocates that Indian culture is an essential part of a child's curriculum. Features elders and youths in song, dance and traditional oral history.
Prod-SHENFP Dist-SHENFP

Ways Of Seeing—A Series
16MM FILM, 3/4 OR 1/2 IN VIDEO H-C A
Considers the ways paintings are distorted by the mass media that transmits them, examines the ways in which women are portrayed in art, discusses paintings as material possessions and shows how paintings are used in advertising.
Prod-BBCTV Dist-FI 1974

Camera And Printing 25 MIN
Fine Arts And Commerce 25 MIN
Painting And Possessions 25 MIN
Women And Art 25 MIN

Ways Of The Law—A Series
H
Combines documentaries, drama, surrealism, mime and an interview with a prisoner to present a comprehensive examination of our legal system.
Prod-SCITV Dist-GPITVL 1980

Civil Law - What Really Happened 019 MIN
Contract/Consumer Law - Be Assertive 019 MIN
Criminal Procedure - Time For Not Thinking 019 MIN
Due Process - Student Rights And 019 MIN
Environmental Law 019 MIN
Family Law - Domestic Relations 019 MIN
Family Law - Juvenile Justice 019 MIN
Introduction And Overview Of Series 019 MIN
Law Enforcement - Patrol Officers 019 MIN
Law Enforcement - The Citizen's Role 019 MIN
Our Legal System 019 MIN
Reasons For Law - Le Cafe Politic 019 MIN
Sources Of Law 019 MIN
Substantive Criminal Law - Happy Here 019 MIN
Wills And Estates 019 MIN

Ways Of The Wind C 23 MIN
3/4 OR 1/2 INCH VIDEO CASSETTE J-C A
Features champion sailor Bruce Klein, a junior instructor at the Sea Cliff Yacht Club. Describes how he teaches youngsters to read cloud movements and the dark spots on the water where the stronger winds blow.
Prod-DENONN Dist-MOKIN 1983

Ways Of Water, The C 13 MIN
16MM FILM, 3/4 OR 1/2 IN VIDEO I-J
Examines undisturbed nature, explaining the different forms of water as ice, streams, dew, mist, rain, clouds and the sea. Shows the relationship between water and the forests, insects, fish, birds and other elements.
From The Earth Science Program Series.
Prod-EBEC Dist-EBEC 1971

Ways To Find Out (2nd Ed) C 11 MIN
16MM FILM, 3/4 OR 1/2 IN VIDEO P
Shows a young child experiencing the world around him
Prod-CF Dist-CF 1971

Ways To Remember C 15 MIN
3/4 OR 1/2 INCH VIDEO CASSETTE I
Tells how Cindy uses memory techniques to help her with her Tai Chi moves.
From The Thinkabout Series.
LC NO. 81-706130
Prod-OECA Dist-AITECH 1980

Ways To Solve A Problem C 15 MIN
3/4 OR 1/2 INCH VIDEO CASSETTE P
Reveals that when Molly accidentally smears paint on her brother's shirt, she is upset especially because she wore it without permission. Shows that with Sam's encouragement, she thinks of several possible solutions and finally decides to tell her mother and ask her to help wash the shirt.
From The Out And About Series.
Prod-STSU Dist-AITECH Prodn-WETN 1984

Ways To Weigh Less C 25 MIN
3/4 OR 1/2 INCH VIDEO CASSETTE
Evaluates various techniques for weight reduction, including jaw wiring, hypnosis, acupuncture, crash dieting, intestinal surgery and behavior modification.
Prod-TRAINX Dist-TRAINX

Ways With Pork C 14 MIN
2 INCH VIDEOTAPE
Identifies economical pork cuts in the retail market. Gives tips on selecting good quality pork and storing it properly. Includes recipes featuring pork.
From The Living Better II Series.
Prod-MAETEL Dist-PUBTEL

WC Fields Film Festival B 78 MIN
3/4 OR 1/2 INCH VIDEO CASSETTE
Presents WC Fields in Poolsharks, The Golf Specialist, The Dentist and The Fatal Glass Of Beer.
Prod-ADVCAS Dist-ADVCAS

WCB's Wide World Of Rescue C 10 MIN
3/4 OR 1/2 INCH VIDEO CASSETTE
Adapts the techniques of modern televison sportcasting to analyze the errors committed in an attempt to rescue several hydrogen sulphide victims.
From The Hydrogen Sulphide Safety Series.
Prod-FLMWST Dist-FLMWST

WCCO-TV On The Move - A Look To The Future C 30 MIN
3/4 OR 1/2 INCH VIDEO CASSETTE
Tours the new broadcast facilities of WCCO-TV on the day of the move to the 'new building.' Previews the news room and air control post-production unit, the satellite system and other highlights of the building that was six years in planning and construction.
Prod-WCCOTV Dist-WCCOTV

WCCO-TV On The Move - A Salute To The Past C 30 MIN
3/4 OR 1/2 INCH VIDEO CASSETTE
Explores the past 36 years of Channel 4's history. Looks at the people and technology of WCCO's past on the eve of the move to the 'new building.'
Prod-WCCOTV Dist-WCCOTV

We C 15 MIN
16MM FILM OPTICAL SOUND
Presents key findings of the 1970 census including the enormous growth of our suburbs, the continued historic movement of the population from rural to urban areas and the movement of the population towards the nation's coasts.
LC NO. 74-705938
Prod-USBC Dist-USNAC 1973

We C 29 MIN
16MM FILM OPTICAL SOUND
Explains that key findings of the 1970 census were the enormous growth of our suburbs and the continued movement of the population from rural to urban areas and towards the nation's coasts. Puts the statistics about the progress and problems of America into human terms, concentrating on the people as they work, play and relax.
LC NO. 74-705939
Prod-USBC Dist-USNAC 1973

We All Came To America C 21 MIN
16MM FILM, 3/4 OR 1/2 IN VIDEO H-C A
A shortened version of the motion picture We All Came To America. Uses archival film and photographs to document the story of people who immigrated to America.
From The American Documents (Edited) Series.
Prod-LUF Dist-LUF 1977

We All Came To America C 55 MIN
16MM FILM, 3/4 OR 1/2 IN VIDEO H-C A
Uses archival film and photographs to document the story of people who immigrated to America.
From The American Documents Series.
Prod-LUF Dist-LUF 1977

We All Have Our Reasons C 30 MIN
16MM FILM OPTICAL SOUND A
Observes a group session which is part of the recovery program at the Alcoholism Center For Women in Los Angeles, as the women share their reasons for turning to alcohol and the ways they are recovering from its destructive influence.
LC NO. 82-700342
Prod-IRIS Dist-IRIS Prodn-REST 1981

We All Need Each Other C 15 MIN
3/4 OR 1/2 INCH VIDEO CASSETTE P
Presents Dr Allhart and her friend Patience discussing the great variety of ways that people and animals help each other.
From The Dr Allhart And Patience Series.
LC NO. 81-707529
Prod-JCITV Dist-GPITVL 1979

We Are All Arab Jews In Israel C 120 MIN
16MM FILM OPTICAL SOUND
Documents the far-reaching tensions between European and Oriental Jews in Israel. Directed by Igaal Niddam.
Prod-UNKNWN Dist-NYFLMS 1977

We Are All One People C 28 MIN
16MM FILM, 3/4 OR 1/2 IN VIDEO
A shortened version of the videocassette We Are All One People. Tells how four American students travel to Israel to meet their pen pals. Tells how they participate in the customs and traditions of the people.
LC NO. 81-706451
Prod-GABOR Dist-FLMFR 1981

We Are All One People C 45 MIN
16MM FILM, 3/4 OR 1/2 IN VIDEO
Tells how four American students travel to Israel to meet their pen pals. Tells how they participate in the customs and traditions of the people.
LC NO. 81-706452
Prod-GABOR Dist-FLMFR 1981

We Are At The Controls C 17 MIN
16MM FILM OPTICAL SOUND
Identifies some causes and effects of oil pollution and appeals for individual commitment to pollution prevention.
LC NO. 78-700444
Prod-API Dist-PROCCO Prodn-PROCCO 1977

We Are Driven C 58 MIN
1/2 IN VIDEO CASSETTE BETA/VHS
Takes a probing and penetrating look into the 'darker side' of Japanese management techniques. Profiles Nissan Motors and their new anti-union auto plant in Tennessee.
From The Frontline Series.
Prod-DOCCON Dist-PBS

We Are Family C 29 MIN
3/4 OR 1/2 INCH VIDEO CASSETTE
Reveals the present state of the Hispanic community in the Twin Cities area. Looks at Hispanics and their culture, social services, economic development, education and participation in local government.
Prod-WCCOTV Dist-WCCOTV 1982

We Are Good Musicians C 20 MIN
3/4 OR 1/2 INCH VIDEO CASSETTE P-I
Studies like phrases in music. Introduces the percussion family.
From The USS Rhythm Series.
Prod-ARKETV Dist-AITECH 1977

We Are Not Alone - Myths And Realities Of Woman Abuse C 53 MIN
3/4 OR 1/2 INCH VIDEO CASSETTE
Presents an introduction to the history, sanctioning, facts and figures related to woman abuse. Confronts the reality of battered women by the grass-root response of the movement and the gains that have been made.
Prod-DACABW Dist-UWISC Prodn-UWISC 1982

We Are Of The Soil C 23 MIN
16MM FILM, 3/4 OR 1/2 IN VIDEO I-C A
Examines the processes and problems of topsoil erosion. Presents how this devastating phenomenon affects everyone and the agricultural and environmental consequences that result. Shows conservation techniques for protecting and rebuilding the soil.
Prod-ISURF Dist-IFB

We Are One C 10 MIN
16MM FILM OPTICAL SOUND
Features visuals by leading Israeli artist Pinchas Shaar and music by Issachar Miron as it dramatizes the 1975 United Jewish Appeal campaign slogan We Are One. Narrated by Melvyn Douglas.
Prod-UJA Dist-ALDEN

We Are One C 13 MIN
16MM FILM, 3/4 OR 1/2 IN VIDEO J-C A
Presents three handicapped young adults describing the difficulties that often occur when handicapped and non-handicapped individuals interact. Stresses the need for better communication.
Prod-LINCS Dist-JOU 1980

We Are One—A Series
I
Looks at pioneer life on the Great Plains in the 1880's. Features the Hanson family making a decision to leave Scandinavia for the promise of a free quarter-section of land in America. Describes their hardships and sacrifices.
Prod-NEITV Dist-GPITVL 1983

Big Decision, The 015 MIN
By The Sweat Of They Brow 015 MIN
Crisis, The 015 MIN
Getting Established 015 MIN
Getting To Nebraska 015 MIN
Heritage 015 MIN
Survival Of The Fittest 015 MIN
Those Good Old Golden Rule Days 015 MIN

We Are Ourselves C 15 MIN
3/4 OR 1/2 INCH VIDEO CASSETTE C A
Shows two thoughtful and independent women who have followed their individual desires to seek a fulfilling and creative lifestyle together.
Prod-NATSF Dist-MMRC

We Are The American Hospital Volunteers C 6 MIN
3/4 OR 1/2 INCH VIDEO CASSETTE
Reveals how to recruit new hospital volunteers and motivate current volunteers by expressing pride in their volunteer activities.
Prod-ASDVS Dist-AHOA

We Are The Church Together C
16MM FILM OPTICAL SOUND
Shows volunteers interacting with mentally impaired persons within the context of a religious education program.
Prod-TNF Dist-TNF

We Are The City C 14 MIN
16MM FILM, 3/4 OR 1/2 IN VIDEO I-C
Provides a view of city life and activities, highlighting some of the urban problems, as well as showing some of the benefits of living in the city.
Prod-CORF Dist-CORF 1972

We Are The Parcel People C 31 MIN
3/4 INCH VIDEO CASSETTE
Presents the story of the United Parcel Service from its beginnings in Seattle in 1907 through the present day. Emphasizes the company's fast, reliable service.
Prod-UPS Dist-MTP

We Are Universal B 23 MIN
16MM FILM - 3/4 IN VIDEO
Documents the art of black Americans. Shows art organizations, performances and interviews with black artists. Includes such artists as Quincy Jones, Freddie Hubbard, Nikki Giovanni and Betty Carter.
Prod-BLKFMF Dist-BLKFMF

We Are Water C 27 MIN
16MM FILM OPTICAL SOUND
Discusses problems in the use and abuse of Montana's water resources. Offers a look at the state's waterways.
From The Montana - As Science Sees It Series.
LC NO. 77-702168
Prod-CONICO Dist-CONICO 1977

We Belong To The Land C 30 MIN
16MM FILM, 3/4 OR 1/2 IN VIDEO
Shows an Indian youth spending some time with his friend Joe 'Giron, an Apache and professional range manager. Reaffirms the relationship between the Indian and the land. Explores life-styles in natural resource careers, such as forestry, game management, range management and related fields.
Prod-SHENFP Dist-SHENFP

We Build, We Fight C 22 MIN
16MM FILM OPTICAL SOUND
Tells about the Seabees from their first days of World War II to their construction and counterinsurgency activities in Vietnam. Narrated by the founder, Admiral Ben Morrell.
LC NO. 74-706316
Prod-USN Dist-USNAC 1969

We Call Them Chaplain B 11 MIN
16MM FILM OPTICAL SOUND
Explains to new recruits the role of the U S Army chaplain.
LC NO. 74-706317
Prod-USA Dist-USNAC 1967

We Call Them Killers C 16 MIN
16MM FILM, 3/4 OR 1/2 IN VIDEO I-C
Presents a close-up study of two killer whales. Features Dr Paul Spong who tells of his work with the whales, which involves trying to establish interspecies relationship and communication.
Prod-NFBC Dist-NFBC

We Came From The Valley C 28 MIN
16MM FILM OPTICAL SOUND H-C
Shows how a large aerospace firm trained and put to work in its Dallas plant several hundred unskilled Mexican-American workers from the Rio Grande Valley.
LC NO. 72-701861
Prod-VOAERO Dist-VOAERO 1971

We Came In Peace C 30 MIN
3/4 OR 1/2 INCH VIDEO CASSETTE
See series title for descriptive statement.
From The Reaching For The Stars, And Life Beyond Earth Series.
Prod-IVCH Dist-IVCH

We Came In Peace C 38 MIN
3/4 OR 1/2 INCH VIDEO CASSETTE
Spans a hundred years of space exploration, from Jules Verne to the moon landing. Shows historic pictures of triumphs and tragedies of the U S space program.
From The Reaching For The Stars, And Life Beyond Earth Series.
Prod-HBS Dist-IVCH

We Can Decide C 58 MIN
3/4 OR 1/2 INCH VIDEO CASSETTE
Looks at the use of prenatal diagnostic techniques and ethical questions resulting from their use.
From The Through The Genetic Maze Series.
Prod-PSU Dist-PBS 1982

We Can Do It C 4 MIN
16MM FILM, 3/4 OR 1/2 IN VIDEO K-I
Suggests that children try alternatives to arrive at solutions.
From The Most Important Person - Attitudes Series.
Prod-EBEC Dist-EBEC 1972

We Can Do It (Spanish) C 4 MIN
16MM FILM, 3/4 OR 1/2 IN VIDEO K-P
A Spanish language version of the film and videorecording We Can Do It.
Prod-EBEC Dist-EBEC 1972

We Can Do It Too C 15 MIN
3/4 OR 1/2 INCH VIDEO CASSETTE P
See series title for descriptive statement.
From The Strawberry Square Series.
Prod-NEITV Dist-AITECH 1982

We Can Help C 15 MIN
3/4 OR 1/2 INCH VIDEO CASSETTE
Demonstrates step-by-step procedures for documenting the declining work performance of white collar, executive-level employees and the intervention and referral process.
Prod-WHITEG Dist-WHITEG

We Can Help—A Series

Discusses social, legal and personal aspects of child abuse. Describes treatment for child abuse.
Prod-NCCAN Dist-USNAC 1979

Abusive Parents	30 MIN
Barb - Breaking The Cycle Of Child Abuse	20 MIN
Interview, The	35 MIN
Investigating Cases Of Child Abuse And Neglect	28 MIN
Medical Witness, The	35 MIN
Presenting The Case	32 MIN
Second Chance	13 MIN
Sexual Abuse - The Family	30 MIN
Working Together	30 MIN

We Can Turn The Tide C 22 MIN
16MM FILM OPTICAL SOUND
Reports on the benefits for the general economy of increased exports of farm commodities.
Prod-MTP Dist-MTP

We Can Work It Out C 29 MIN
3/4 OR 1/2 INCH VIDEO CASSETTE
See series title for descriptive statement.
From The Secretary And Management Relationship Series. No 2
Prod-VIDART Dist-VISUCP

We Can't Go On Like This C 32 MIN
16MM FILM, 3/4 OR 1/2 IN VIDEO H A
As triggers for discussion, presents vignettes portraying smokers who have recently quit or those who are considering it. Exposes the rationalizations that can become pitfalls.
Prod-NHLI Dist-USNAC 1981

We Care—A Series

Presents a series illustrating the basic skills needed by non-professional employees, such as nursing assistants, housekeepers and food service personnel, who care for patients.
Prod-VTRI Dist-VTRI

Brushing The Patient's Teeth / Care Of
Combing The Patient's Hair / How To Give A
Diabetes And Older Patient / Urine Testing
Handwashing Techniques / Vital
How To Clean A Patient's Room / How To Clean
How To Give A Partial Bed Bath / Hand And
Principles Of Body Mechanics / Moving The
Sanitation For Food Service
You Make The Difference / Food Handling And

We Choose - Scarcity And Decision Making C 15 MIN
3/4 OR 1/2 INCH VIDEO CASSETTE J-H
Reveals that when a student is injured crossing the highway, the principal of the high school threatens to restrict everyone to the school grounds during lunch hour. Shows that when the student council tries to find a better plan, they discover that reconciling conflicting goals is not easy.
From The Give And Take Series. Pt 2
LC NO. 83-706370
Prod-AITV Dist-AITECH 1982

We Decide C 20 MIN
3/4 OR 1/2 INCH VIDEO CASSETTE
Illustrates the process of social decisionmaking when a class must determine how to assign the limited number of spaces available in the school's bike rack.
From The Trade-Offs Series.
LC NO. 80-706423
Prod-AITV Dist-AITECH Prodn-KERA 1978

We Decide - Social Decision-Making C 20 MIN
16MM FILM OPTICAL SOUND I-J
Tells how a scarcity of school bicycle racks prompts a class to think of several ways the problem might be solved and then to analyze each alternative.
From The Trade-Offs Series. No. 3
LC NO. 80-700453
Prod-EDFCEN Dist-AITECH Prodn-KERA 1978

We Did It C 27 MIN
16MM FILM OPTICAL SOUND
Shows the construction of the Volkswagen of America plant, the first automobile assembly plant of a foreign manufacturer in the United States. Describes the international cooperation involved in this endeavor.
LC NO. 79-700346
Prod-VWA Dist-KAROL Prodn-MARTHN 1978

We Dig Coal - A Portrait Of Three Women C 58 MIN
16MM FILM, 3/4 OR 1/2 IN VIDEO A
Shows how, through courage, determination and persistence, Mary Louise Carson, Bernice Dombroski and Marilyn McCusker won jobs in a man's world as coal miners in Pennsylvania.
LC NO. 81-707582
Prod-SACVP Dist-CNEMAG 1981

We Discover Equivalent Fractions C 13 MIN
16MM FILM, 3/4 OR 1/2 IN VIDEO P-I
Uses animation to show how equivalent fractions are used on the number line.
Prod-CORF Dist-CORF

We Discover Fractions (2nd Ed) C 11 MIN
16MM FILM, 3/4 OR 1/2 IN VIDEO P-I
Explains the meaning of denominator and numerator and shows how the names for fractional numbers are placed on the number line.
Prod-CORF Dist-CORF

We Discover The Dictionary (2nd Ed) C 11 MIN
16MM FILM, 3/4 OR 1/2 IN VIDEO I
Explains the practical applications of the dictionary in spelling, pronunciation and word definitions. Shows the use of dictionary tabs, guide words and diacritical marks. Describes specialized dictionaries.
Prod-CORF Dist-CORF 1963

We Discover The Encyclopedia C 11 MIN
16MM FILM, 3/4 OR 1/2 IN VIDEO I
Shows children how to use the encyclopedia. Covers key word selection, alphabetical topic arrangement, guide words, sub-topic headings, pictures, charts, maps and diagrams.
Prod-CORF Dist-CORF 1971

We Do, We Do C 11 MIN
16MM FILM OPTICAL SOUND H-C
Uses a fantasized approach to explore the last minute warnings which barrage a teenage bride and groom. Pictures the young couple as they argue before a skeptical teenage jury, presenting their reasons for early marriage.
From The Marriage Series.
LC NO. 72-700512
Prod-FRACOC Dist-FRACOC 1970

We Don't Do Nothin' In Here C 14 MIN
3/4 OR 1/2 INCH VIDEO CASSETTE
Dramatizes the poetry of Ellen Turlington Jackson, which deals with the views and problems of adolescent students.
From The Poetry Alive Series.
LC NO. 79-706202
Prod-CMSS Dist-AITECH 1978

We Don't Want To Live On Our Knees C 20 MIN
3/4 OR 1/2 INCH VIDEO CASSETTE
Describes the Russian invasion of Czechoslavakia in August of 1968.
From The History In Action Series.
Prod-FOTH Dist-FOTH 1984

We Drivers C 23 MIN
16MM FILM OPTICAL SOUND A
Demonstrates safe driving practices and accident avoidance techniques.
Prod-GM Dist-GM

We Drivers (4th Ed) C 13 MIN
16MM FILM OPTICAL SOUND H-C A
Scenes from a helicopter show safe driving techniques. Driving pitfalls and their remedies are also depicted.
Prod-GM Dist-GM Prodn-HANDY 1965

We Explore Ocean Life C 11 MIN
16MM FILM, 3/4 OR 1/2 IN VIDEO P-I
Explores the coral reef and the ocean floor showing sea anemones, squids and jellyfish. Explains their dependence upon one another, how they get their food and how they protect themselves.
From The We Explore Series.
Prod-CORF Dist-CORF 1962

We Explore The Beach (2nd Ed) C 12 MIN
16MM FILM, 3/4 OR 1/2 IN VIDEO P-I
Presents marine ecology and its conservation by describing the explorations of a marine biologist and two children along the seashore.
From The We Explore Series.
Prod-CORF Dist-CORF 1977

We Explore The Desert C 10 MIN
16MM FILM, 3/4 OR 1/2 IN VIDEO P-I
On an afternoon visit to the desert, Steve and Cathy observe desert plants and how they are adapted to the desert conditions. In the desert museum, they learn about nocturnal animals. These animals are also shown in their natural habitat as night comes to the desert.
From The We Explore Series.
Prod-CORF Dist-CORF 1967

We Explore The Marsh C 11 MIN
16MM FILM, 3/4 OR 1/2 IN VIDEO P-I
Introduces the concept of marshes as wet lands. Shows some characteristic marsh plants and animals and points out some of their adaptations and interrelationships.
From The We Explore Series.
Prod-CORF Dist-CORF 1973

We Explore—A Series
16MM FILM, 3/4 OR 1/2 IN VIDEO P
Portrays children exploring various environments, including the beach, the desert, the marshlands and the ocean.
Prod-CORF Dist-CORF

We Explore Ocean Life	11 MIN
We Explore The Beach (2nd Ed)	12 MIN
We Explore The Desert	10 MIN
We Explore The Marsh	11 MIN

We Get Married Twice C 22 MIN
16MM FILM OPTICAL SOUND J-C A
Tells of a couple who first celebrated their marriage with an informal gathering of friends at their lake front cottage where the rites were performed in the living room and then had a traditional Jewish ceremony, held in order to satisfy their parents, relatives and friends who did not attend the first.
LC NO. 74-700649
Prod-WEINSM Dist-WEINSM 1973

We Go Around The Corner B 15 MIN
2 INCH VIDEOTAPE P
Shows how people everywhere live together in family groups. (Broadcast quality)
From The Around The Corner Series. No. 1
Prod-FWCETV Dist-GPITVL Prodn-WEDUTV

We Go To School (2nd Ed) C 11 MIN
16MM FILM, 3/4 OR 1/2 IN VIDEO P
Shows teachers how to help children make the normal adjustment from home to school environment. Discusses ways to foster a sense of belonging and an attitude of co-operation.
Prod-CORF Dist-CORF 1970

We Grew A Frog C 13 MIN
16MM FILM, 3/4 OR 1/2 IN VIDEO P
Shows elementary school pupils studying the development of a frog.
Prod-IFB Dist-IFB 1972

We Grow C 15 MIN
2 INCH VIDEOTAPE P
Illustrates the importance of food, water and air for the survival of humans.
From The Science Is Searching Series.
Prod-DETPS Dist-GPITVL

We Hand The Torch To You C 29 MIN
16MM FILM OPTICAL SOUND
A study of the Billy Graham Crusade in Europe, April 1970, which used the first-of-its-kind largest closed circuit TV with simultaneous translations to carry to 39 cities.
LC NO. 76-711573
Prod-WWPI Dist-WWPI 1970

We Have A Dream C 35 MIN
3/4 OR 1/2 INCH VIDEO CASSETTE
Follows three people who achieve their dreams despite severe odds. Includes stories of two handicapped persons overcoming disabilities and an adoptee locating his mother.
Prod-DCTVC Dist-DCTVC

We Have An Addict In The House C 30 MIN
16MM FILM, 3/4 OR 1/2 IN VIDEO J-C A
Uses drug abuse to provide some insight into the psychosocial causes of alienation among young adults. Provides a situation wherein the participants can explore individual and group attitudes about drugs and about intra-family relationships.
Prod-COMFON Dist-PFP 1973

We Have Met The Enemy And He Is Us C 13 MIN
16MM FILM OPTICAL SOUND J-C A
Takes a look at the problem of environmental pollution through the use of animation. Introduces the cartoon character, Pogo, who, with his friends, sets forth to find out who is responsible for pollution in the Okefenokee Swamp.
Prod-KELLYW Dist-CGWEST

We Have To Be Able To Do It Ourselves C 27 MIN
16MM FILM OPTICAL SOUND
Provides a basic overview of the activities of a community design center through the voices of people from poor and minority inner-city communities, and of personnel working in local centers to provide architectural and planning services to these communities. Explores the work of community design centers in Cleveland, New Orleans, San Francisco and Philadelphia.
LC NO. 72-700162
Prod-AIA Dist-AIA 1972

We Hold These Truths C 28 MIN
16MM FILM OPTICAL SOUND J-H A
Presents a young Negro soldier, who after visiting freedom's shrines in Washington is depressed by slum conditions into which his people are forced by race segregation, but who takes new hope from a visit to East Harlem Protestant Parish.
Prod-YALEDV Dist-YALEDV

We Hold These Truths C 29 MIN
16MM FILM OPTICAL SOUND
Helps stimulate interest in the three themes of the American revolution bicentennial celebrations heritage, horizon and festival. Shows how each of these themes is reflected in activities as varied as a health delivery system and an Afro-American Center for the Performing Arts in Boston.
LC NO. 74-700484
Prod-AMRBC Dist-AMRBC 1974

We Hold These Truths C 15 MIN
16MM FILM, 3/4 OR 1/2 IN VIDEO I-C A
Considers the ideas and ideals expressed in the Declaration of Independence.
Prod-PARACO Dist-AIMS 1975

We Know Who We Are C 28 MIN
16MM FILM OPTICAL SOUND H-C A
Presents case studies of three blind people who have overcome their disabilities through participation in a program offered by the Iowa Commission for the Blind, Orientation Center.
LC NO. 77-703472
Prod-NFB Dist-NFB 1977

We Learn About The Telephone II C 26 MIN
16MM FILM OPTICAL SOUND P-I
Presents two elementary school teachers taking a group of ten third graders of different ethnic backgrounds to the telephone company exhibit at the Museum of Science and Industry. Shows how they meet Mr Richards who guides them through the exhibits and answers their questions as the children learn basic skills in using the telephone, including how to find numbers in the phone book.
Prod-ATAT Dist-WAVE 1981

We Love You Nasty C 47 MIN
16MM FILM OPTICAL SOUND
Presents a film portrait of tennis star Ilie Nastase which has been set to music.
LC NO. 82-700137
Prod-PHILMO Dist-PHILMO 1981

We Make Anything C 15 MIN
3/4 OR 1/2 INCH VIDEO CASSETTE I
Presents John Rugg showing the mass production of bicycles and automobiles to show the importance of the assembly line in American manufacturing. Highlights the ingredients and techniques of making iron and steel. Discusses the innovations of Henry Ford and Thomas Edison.
From The American Legacy Series. Program 7
LC NO. 83-706664
Prod-KRMATV Dist-AITECH 1983

We Make Things C 20 MIN
3/4 INCH VIDEO CASSETTE I
Shows steel, automobiles, and apple pies being made. Defines technology, machinery, mass production, property, capital, labor and management.
From The Exploring Our Nation Series.
Prod-KRMATV Dist-GPITVL 1975

We Mean Business C 18 MIN
16MM FILM OPTICAL SOUND
Takes a look at PPG'S fiberglass manufacturing facilities and demonstrates the quality of product and process for potential customers.
LC NO. 75-702812
Prod-PPG Dist-PPGC Prodn-CRABRO 1975

We Need From Time To Time B 30 MIN
16MM FILM - 3/4 IN VIDEO PRO
See series title for descriptive statement.
From The Public Health Science Series. Unit III - Introduction To Epidemiology
Prod-TEXWU Dist-GPITVL Prodn-KUHTTV

We Never Left Home C 31 MIN
16MM FILM OPTICAL SOUND
Deals with the American South And Southern Living magazine. Includes scenes of various cities, resort areas and landscapes, showing how the magazine interacts with and serves its readers from Texas to the Southeast.
LC NO. 76-702214
Prod-PROFAC Dist-PROFAC Prodn-FRANKC 1976

We Only Get Paid To Win C 21 MIN
16MM FILM OPTICAL SOUND
Looks at Mark Donohue and Roger Penske, one of the most successful teams in the history of automobile racing.
Prod-GTARC Dist-GTARC

We Owe Them That Much C 20 MIN
16MM FILM OPTICAL SOUND
Deals with the mental and physical defects in rubella babies and the efforts to treat them. Supports an Oklahoma Medical Society effort to immunize a majority of Oklahoma children against rubella. Points out the results of the campaign.
Prod-WKYTV Dist-WKYTV

We Reach Beyond B 29 MIN
16MM FILM OPTICAL SOUND
Depicts the work of the Korean Red Cross.
Prod-KORRCS Dist-AMRC 1961

We Remember The Farm - Recordamos El Rancho C 6 MIN
16MM FILM, 3/4 OR 1/2 IN VIDEO P-I
Presents a follow-up review of the field trip to the dairy farm.
From The Bilingual Film Series, Module 3 - Down On The Farm Series.
Prod-BRNTNO Dist-CAROUF 1973

We See The Baby Zoo - Vemos El Zoologico Infantil C 8 MIN
16MM FILM, 3/4 OR 1/2 IN VIDEO P-I
Shows children meeting and learning how to handle smaller animals.
From The Bilingual Film Series, Module 2 - Zoo Animals Series.
Prod-BRNTNO Dist-CAROUF 1973

We Seek No Wider War B 6 MIN
16MM FILM OPTICAL SOUND
Shows how America's involvement in Vietnam deepened in 1965 with further Viet Cong attacks and U S retaliation. Defense Secretary Mc Namara emphasizes that the U S does not desire to broaden the conflict.
From The Screen News Digest Series. Vol7, Issue 8
Prod-HEARST Dist-HEARST 1965

We Serve The Public C 50 MIN
16MM FILM OPTICAL SOUND
Shows how the great service industries have grown up through the needs of more and more people living in cities. Presents the wide variety of work done by union members, indicating the improved working conditions which the union has brought about.
Prod-HREBI Dist-AFLCIO 1948

We Speak 'American' B 20 MIN
2 INCH VIDEOTAPE P
Develops an appreciation in children for their language and shows its derivation. (Broadcast quality)
From The Language Lane Series. Lesson 3
Prod-CVETVC Dist-GPITVL Prodn-WCVETV

We Speak Spanish C 30 MIN
3/4 OR 1/2 INCH VIDEO CASSETTE
See series title for descriptive statement.
From The Que Pasa, U S A Series.
Prod-WPBTTV Dist-MDCPB

We The Addicts, Pt I B 60 MIN
3/4 OR 1/2 INCH VIDEO CASSETTE
Offers comments and opinions by drug and alcohol addicts at Wisconsin's Waupun State Prison on how they started using drugs and on the lack of rehabilitation programs in and out of prison.
Prod-UWISC Dist-UWISC 1971

We The Addicts, Pt II B 60 MIN
3/4 OR 1/2 INCH VIDEO CASSETTE
Offers discussion by drug and alcohol addicts at Wisconsin's Waupun State Prison on the effects of drugs on one's personality and inconsistencies in the criminal court system in sentencing for drug related and non-drug related crimes.
Prod-UWISC Dist-UWISC 1971

We The Enemy C 26 MIN
16MM FILM OPTICAL SOUND
Presents an exposition on the environmental problems of Connecticut.
Prod-FENWCK Dist-FENWCK 1971

We The People C 15 MIN
3/4 OR 1/2 INCH VIDEO CASSETTE I-J
Looks at national governments and their functions.
From The It's All Up To You Series.
Prod-COOPED Dist-AITECH Prodn-WHATV 1978

We The People - A Freshman Comes To Washington / The Two Houses Of Congress, Pt 1 C 30 MIN
3/4 OR 1/2 INCH VIDEO CASSETTE
Introduces Congress through the eyes of a newly-elected representative.
From The Congress - We The People Series.
Prod-WETATV Dist-FI 1984

We The People - A Freshman Comes To Washington / The Two Houses Of Congress, Pt 2 C 30 MIN
3/4 OR 1/2 INCH VIDEO CASSETTE
Focuses on the U S Congress and its two Houses - the House of Representatives and the Senate.
From The Congress - We The People Series.
Prod-WETATV Dist-FI 1984

We The People - Read C 20 MIN
3/4 OR 1/2 INCH VIDEO CASSETTE
Twenty half-hour videos dealing with the fundamental os reding. Stresses basic survival skills.
Prod-CAMB Dist-CAMB

We The People - Story Of Our Federal Government C 20 MIN
16MM FILM OPTICAL SOUND
Examines the structure of the federal government of the United States and explains how it has worked for two hundred years to serve the people.
LC NO. FIA68-1821
Prod-HEARST Dist-HEARST 1968

We Tiptoed Around Whispering C 30 MIN
16MM FILM, 3/4 OR 1/2 IN VIDEO A
Presents a dramatization and documentary on what parents of deaf children experience from the birth of their child until the deafness is diagnosed.
From The Western Maryland College Series.
Prod-USBEH Dist-USNAC 1973

We Use Mammography C 1 MIN
3/4 OR 1/2 INCH VIDEO CASSETTE
Shows a radiologist stressing the safety of low dose x-rays and their effectiveness in detecting breast cancer, some- times before a lump can be felt. Concludes with message that 'Today, a tiny breast cancer is almost always curable.'
Prod-AMCS Dist-AMCS 1979

We Use The Number Line C 10 MIN
16MM FILM, 3/4 OR 1/2 IN VIDEO P
Shows a friendly artist animating a number line.
Prod-CORF Dist-CORF

We Visit A Museum C 25 MIN
2 INCH VIDEOTAPE I
Examines museum exhibits with special attention given to arrangement of the display.
From The Art Has Many Forms Series.
Prod-CVETVC Dist-GPITVL

We Visit The Post Office - Visitamos La Casa De Correos C 8 MIN
16MM FILM, 3/4 OR 1/2 IN VIDEO P-I
Shows children what happens to a letter when it is dropped in the mailbox.
From The Bilingual Film Series, Module 4 - Transportation And Community Workers Series.
Prod-BRNTNO Dist-CAROUF 1973

We Were German Jews C 58 MIN
3/4 OR 1/2 INCH VIDEO CASSETTE
Grapples with the torment of living with the legacy of the Holocaust. Shows a surviving couple confronting their past by returning to where they lived before the onslaught that claimed most of their relatives.
Prod-BLACKW Dist-BLACKW

We Were Just Too Young C 30 MIN
16MM FILM, 3/4 OR 1/2 IN VIDEO H-C A
Deals with teenage parents whose lives have been burdened by bad decisions and unrealistic expectations. Focuses on the problems of unemployment, lack of education, demands of child care and lack of freedom.
LC NO. 79-707994
Prod-MITCHG Dist-MTI 1979

We Were The Ones Who Decided C 28 MIN
16MM FILM OPTICAL SOUND
Investigates reconstruction efforts in Niger and Mali which have received encouragement from churches and organizations. Shows how both projects are affecting the lives of nomadic herdsmen who were hardest hit by the 1973 drought conditions.
LC NO. 77-702704
Prod-RTVA Dist-RTVA 1976

We Were There - But Not For Conquest C 28 MIN
16MM FILM OPTICAL SOUND
Tells the story of the U S Army Corps of Engineers in peace and war from its inception in 1775. Highlights their many contributions.
Prod-USAE Dist-MTP

We Will Freeze In The Dark C 42 MIN
16MM FILM, 3/4 OR 1/2 IN VIDEO H-C A
Shows examples of how conservation, when spurred by self-interest or economic incentive, can help solve the energy dilemma in the United States.
Prod-CAPCC Dist-MGHT 1977

We Will Not Be Beaten B 40 MIN
3/4 INCH VIDEO CASSETTE
Recounts experiences of battered women and shelter staff members. Demonstrates the incredibly difficult dilemmas that countless women face as a result of society's neglect and the economic straight-jacket in which women with children find themselves.
Prod-TRANSH Dist-WMENIF

We Will Not Do Nothing C 20 MIN
16MM FILM OPTICAL SOUND
Contrasts the effective results achieved by a branch of the League of Women Voters in San Francisco concerning the passage of a school bond issue with the frustrated attempts of a women's organization which is neither well organized nor politically involved.
LC NO. 73-702067
Prod-SFLWV Dist-SFLWV 1973

We Won't Leave You C 17 MIN
16MM FILM - 3/4 IN VIDEO J-H A
Shows how parent participation in the one-day hospitalization of their child can help make the experience more acceptable to the child.
LC NO. 79-706233
Prod-MASON Dist-DOCUFL 1975

We, The Japanese People B 25 MIN
16MM FILM OPTICAL SOUND
Shows some of the democratic changes the Japanese people have adopted since 1945.
LC NO. FIE52-2115
Prod-USA Dist-USNAC 1952

We, The People - Careers In Public Service C 13 MIN
16MM FILM OPTICAL SOUND I-H
Deals with career opportunities within government. Examines all levels of government and stresses that careers are available for people with all kinds of educational backgrounds and skills. Divides public service careers into legislation, law enforcement and the courts, transportation, social services, commercial regulation and international affairs.
From The Working Worlds Series.
LC NO. 75-701544
Prod-OLYMPS Dist-FFORIN 1974

We, The People - Story Of Our Federal Government C 20 MIN
16MM FILM OPTICAL SOUND H
Examines the federal government and explains how it has worked for almost two hundred years to serve 'WE, THE PEOPLE.'
From The Screen News Digest Series. Vol 10, Issue 6
LC NO. FIA68-1821
Prod-HEARST Dist-HEARST 1968

We, The People - The Story Of Our Federal Government B 28 MIN
16MM FILM OPTICAL SOUND H
Portrays the organization and responsibilities of the legislative, executive and judicial branches of the U S government as it is run by and for the people.
LC NO. 74-706320
Prod-USDD Dist-USNAC 1967

We'll See Tomorrow C 10 MIN
16MM FILM, 3/4 OR 1/2 IN VIDEO I-J A
Depicts those shop hazards that can cause serious eye injury, including intense light or heat, splattered liquid, flying sparks and chips of wood, cement or metal. Demonstrates the eye safety devices that can prevent these injuries from happening.
Prod-ALTSUL Dist-JOU 1971

We'll See Tomorrow (Captioned) C 10 MIN
16MM FILM, 3/4 OR 1/2 IN VIDEO I-J A
Depicts those shop hazards that can cause serious eye injury, including intense light or heat, splattered liquid, flying sparks and chips of wood, cement or metal. Demonstrates the eye safety devices that can prevent these injuries from happening.
Prod-ALTSUL Dist-JOU 1971

We're All Beautiful Here C 15 MIN
16MM FILM, 3/4 OR 1/2 IN VIDEO J-C A
Presents information on acne, showing young members of Acne Anonymous chanting, singing and shouting about acne and how it can be controlled.
Prod-KLEINW Dist-KLEINW 1976

We're All In The Driver's Seat C 15 MIN
16MM FILM, 3/4 OR 1/2 IN VIDEO
Studies the American school bus experience. Reveals facts about safety, cost, convenience and comfort.
Prod-KLEINW Dist-KLEINW

We're Counting On You C 30 MIN
3/4 OR 1/2 INCH VIDEO CASSETTE A
Discusses the role of the modern secretary, how they fit into the corporate structure, and how their jobs interact with those of their bosses.
From The Professional Skills For Secretaries Series. Pt 1
LC NO. 81-707648
Prod-TIMLIF Dist-TIMLIF 1981

We're Doing OK C 5 MIN
16MM FILM OPTICAL SOUND
Tells about a young career woman who is anxious about her aging mother living in a deteriorating neighborhood. Shows how she discovers that the neighborhood has a vitality and sense of caring which she had not been aware of at first.
LC NO. 78-701508
Prod-FRAF Dist-FRAF Prodn-TKF 1978

We're Fighting Back C 93 MIN
1/2 IN VIDEO CASSETTE BETA/VHS P A
Features story of New York City youths trying to fight crime in their neighborhood.
Prod-LCOA Dist-LCOA

We're Going Places C 15 MIN
3/4 OR 1/2 INCH VIDEO CASSETTE P
Combines looking, listening, talking, writing and reading to help establish the link between oral and written language. Presents the story Going Places by Aileen Fisher and the film Poetry For Me by Grover Film Productions.
From The I Want To Read Series.
Prod-LACOS Dist-GPITVL 1976

We're Here Now - Prostitution C 35 MIN
3/4 OR 1/2 INCH VIDEO CASSETTE
Presents seven women who talk openly about their former lives in prostitution. Discusses their struggle to return to the mainstream of society and the pressures that caused them to become prostitutes.
Prod-WIEKD Dist-FLMLIB 1984

We're In The People Business C 18 MIN
16MM FILM OPTICAL SOUND IND
Presents 15 how-to-do-it bank teller-customer vignettes on how to win customers and influence deposits.
From The Golden Triangle Teller Training Film Series.
LC NO. 76-700452
Prod-PART Dist-PART

We're In This Together - Scarcity And Economic Choice (Economics) C 15 MIN
3/4 OR 1/2 INCH VIDEO CASSETTE P
Reveals that when Kathy brags about walking home from school to save energy and money, her mother and brother point out how she doesn't always practice what she preaches.
From The Two Cents' Worth Series.
Prod-WHATV Dist-AITECH Prodn-WIEC 1976

We're No Heroes C 27 MIN
16MM FILM OPTICAL SOUND
Follows representative units of the Fire Department of the District of Columbia as they answer a variety of fire calls. Exemplifies the courage and dedication of members of the country's most dangerous profession.
LC NO. 77-700433
Prod-WMALTV Dist-WMALTV 1976

We're Not Afraid Anymore C 27 MIN
16MM FILM OPTICAL SOUND
Presents a documentary on homosexuality. Includes interviews with homosexual men and women, an attorney and a psychologist. Shows scenes of various activities of homosexuals such as church activities, a parade and protest demonstrations.
LC NO. 74-702900
Prod-PARNAS Dist-PARNAS 1974

We're Not Candy C 1 MIN
3/4 OR 1/2 INCH VIDEO CASSETTE
Features a quartet of pills singing a television spot describing their worries that a child might think they're candy and eat them.
Prod-KIDSCO Dist-KIDSCO

We're Not Drinkable C 1 MIN
3/4 OR 1/2 INCH VIDEO CASSETTE
Warns children in a television spot that bottles found under the sink are poison.
Prod-KIDSCO Dist-KIDSCO

We're Not Drinkable (Spanish) C 1 MIN
3/4 OR 1/2 INCH VIDEO CASSETTE
A Spanish language version of the television spot for children which explains that bottles usually found under the sink are poison.
Prod-KIDSCO Dist-KIDSCO

We're Number One—A Series

Prod-AMERLC Dist-AMERLC 1979

Racial Relationships 029 MIN
Sports And Business 029 MIN

We're OK C 9 MIN
16MM FILM, 3/4 OR 1/2 IN VIDEO J-C A
Uses animation to present the transactional analysis theory which explains how each individual adopts a psychological life position. States that effective interpersonal relationships result from the viewpoint that each person is an equal, expressed by the motto 'I'm OK, you're OK.'
From The Transactional Analysis Series.
Prod-BFA Dist-PHENIX 1975

We're OK (Dutch) C 9 MIN
16MM FILM, 3/4 OR 1/2 IN VIDEO J-C A
Uses animation to present the transactional analysis theory which explains how each individual adopts a psychological life position. States that effective interpersonal relationships result from the viewpoint that each person is an equal, expressed by the motto 'I'm OK, you're OK.'
From The Transactional Analysis Series.
Prod-BFA Dist-PHENIX 1975

We're OK (Swedish) C 9 MIN
16MM FILM, 3/4 OR 1/2 IN VIDEO J-C A
Uses animation to present the transactional analysis theory which explains how each individual adopts a psychological life position. States that effective interpersonal relationships result from the viewpoint that each person is an equal, expressed by the motto 'I'm OK, you're OK.'
From The Transactional Analysis Series.
Prod-BFA Dist-PHENIX 1975

We're On The Same Team, Remember C 21 MIN
16MM FILM, 3/4 OR 1/2 IN VIDEO A
Discusses the importance of teamwork, employee attitudes, internal communication and organization.
Prod-RANKAV Dist-RTBL

We're On The Same Time, Remember C 21 MIN
16MM FILM, 3/4 OR 1/2 IN VIDEO
A revised version of the videocassette Who Killed The Sale. Illustrates how an important business deal can be lost due to ineffective communication, careless talk and lack of organization.
Prod-RANKAV Dist-RTBL 1984

We're On Your Side C 24 MIN
16MM FILM OPTICAL SOUND
Documents methods of oil recovery from presumably exhausted oil fields by using new methods which are within environmental tolerances.
LC NO. 75-702761
Prod-GETTY Dist-GETTY Prodn-FAIRKS 1974

We're Spending Too Much Money C 12 MIN
3/4 OR 1/2 INCH VIDEO CASSETTE P
Eavesdrops as the Anthony family discusses how all family members have bought more than they need and can afford. Shows that all agree to spend less and help make a family budget.
From The Under The Yellow Balloon Series.
Prod-SCETV Dist-AITECH 1980

We're Taking Off C 12 MIN
16MM FILM OPTICAL SOUND
Celebrates the 25th anniversary of Honeywell's entry into the computer field by highlighting landmarks in the company's history.
LC NO. 80-700506
Prod-HONIS Dist-HONIS Prodn-GLYNG 1980

We've Come Of Age C 12 MIN
16MM FILM OPTICAL SOUND
Uses the story of an old man's efforts to urge his generation to join him in celebrating age and life in order to promote the work of the National Council of Senior Citizens.
LC NO. 74-700266
Prod-NCSCIT Dist-NCSCIT 1973

We've Come This Far C 30 MIN
16MM FILM OPTICAL SOUND
Combines cinema verite and dramatic re-creation techniques to document the true story of a black militant's battle with the courts in New Haven and Hartford, Connecticut.
LC NO. 77-701748
Prod-ROPE Dist-ROPE 1969

We've Gone Around The Corner B 15 MIN
2 INCH VIDEOTAPE P
Stresses love as the greatest of the world's needs. (Broadcast quality)
From The Around The Corner Series. No. 35
Prod-FWCETV Dist-GPITVL Prodn-WEDUTV

Weak Bullet, The C 14 MIN
3/4 OR 1/2 INCH VIDEO CASSETTE
Tells the improbable tale of a wayward bullet that wends its way from one troubled situation to another, effectively ending arguments.
Prod-EAI Dist-EAI

Weakest Link, The C 18 MIN
16MM FILM, 3/4 OR 1/2 IN VIDEO
Demonstrates safe lifting procedures for crane operators.
Prod-MILLBK Dist-IFB

Weakest Link, The - Guarding Against Head And Neck Injuries C 12 MIN
16MM FILM, 3/4 OR 1/2 IN VIDEO I-H
Deals with the importance of properly-fitted, approved football helmets and the requirement that players understand and abide by regulations against dangerous practices, such as spearing, butt blocking and face mask tackling. Explains and demonstrates correct blocking and tackling techniques.
From The Football Injury Prevention Series.
Prod-ATHI Dist-ATHI

Weaknesses Of The Flesh C 22 MIN
3/4 INCH VIDEO CASSETTE PRO
Presents Dr Michael H Brooke describing the effects of neuromuscular diseases on human bodily functions such as walking and sitting.
From The Intensive Course In Neuromuscular Diseases Series.
LC NO. 76-706129
Prod-NINDIS Dist-USNAC 1974

Wealth Out Of Wilderness B 24 MIN
16MM FILM OPTICAL SOUND I-J
Pictures the development of the major uses of California's land since the first Indian settlers.
Prod-ABCTV Dist-MLA 1963

Wealth Weapon, The C 29 MIN
3/4 OR 1/2 INCH VIDEO CASSETTE
Raises the issue of American business deals with the Soviet Union, asking whether free enterprise should help the enemies of free enterprise. Hosted by Ben Wattenberg.
From The Ben Wattenberg's 1980 Series.
Prod-WETATV Dist-PBS

Weaponeers Of The Deep C 28 MIN
16MM FILM OPTICAL SOUND
Acquaints members of selected civic organizations and personnel at Navy Recruit Training Centers with the educational and career opportunities of serving as an FBM weaponeer in the Polaris Submarine Fleet.
LC NO. 74-705940
Prod-USN Dist-USNAC 1967

Weapons Controller - Key To Effective Air Defense C 22 MIN
16MM FILM OPTICAL SOUND
Portrays the global role of weapons controller and describes career opportunities in this field.
LC NO. 74-706321
Prod-USAF Dist-USNAC 1968

Weapons In Space - National Teleconference On Space-Based Missile Defense C 28 MIN
3/4 OR 1/2 INCH VIDEO CASSETTE
Analyzes the feasibility and consequences of space-based de-

fenses. Presents four distinguished Americans who comment on these questions in a condensed version of the nationally televised two hour teleconference on space weapons in April 1984. Includes the seven-minute program Weapons in Space An Overview.
Prod-EFVP Dist-EFVP

Weapons Of The Infantry C 21 MIN
3/4 OR 1/2 INCH VIDEO CASSETTE
Describes the firing characteristics, capabilities and limitations of the weapons, M-14, M-14AI and M-16AI rifles, M-79 grenade launcher, M-60 and 50-caliber machine guns, M-72 rocket, 3.5-inch rocket launcher, 90-millimeter and 106-millimeter recoilless rifles, 50-caliber spotting gun and 81-millimeter and 4.2-inch mortars.
Prod-IHF Dist-IHF

Weapons Of The Infantry C 21 MIN
16MM FILM, 3/4 OR 1/2 IN VIDEO PRO
Shows characteristics, employment, capabilities and limitations of weapons used in the Infantry. Covers M14, M14A1 and M16A1 rifles, the M79 grenade launcher, M60 and .50 caliber machineguns, the M72 rocket, the 3.5 rocket launcher, 90 mm and 106 mm recoilless rifles, 81 mm and 4.2-inch mortars and the .50 caliber spotting gun.
LC NO. 82-706242
Prod-USA Dist-USNAC 1968

Weapons Ranges C 40 MIN
3/4 OR 1/2 INCH VIDEO CASSETTE
Shows the Strategic Air Command crews participating in actual firing exercises. Shows bombing, strafing, rocketry, shooting at air-tow targets and drones.
Prod-IHF Dist-IHF

Weapons Safety C 7 MIN
3/4 OR 1/2 INCH VIDEO CASSETTE
Demonstrates operation, malfunctions and methods of clearing malfunctions of the UZI submachine gun and the Remington model 870 shotgun.
LC NO. 81-707115
Prod-USSS Dist-USNAC 1981

Weapons Safety, Pt 5 - The M203 Grenade Launcher C 10 MIN
16MM FILM OPTICAL SOUND
Demonstrates safety precautions to be used when firing the M203 grenade launcher mounted on an M16 rifle. Shows minimum firing range and illustrates how to identify the correct ammunition.
LC NO. 80-701847
Prod-USA Dist-USNAC 1973

Weapons Safety, Pt 6 - The M18A1 Claymore Mine C 13 MIN
16MM FILM OPTICAL SOUND
Demonstrates safety precautions to be used when laying, arming, firing and disarming the Claymore antipersonnel mine.
LC NO. 80-701848
Prod-USA Dist-USNAC 1973

Wear C 32 MIN
3/4 OR 1/2 INCH VIDEO CASSETTE
Discusses wear, its definition, its place both as a cause of loss of usefulness and a process with many uses.
From The Tribology 1 - Friction, Wear, And Lubrication Series.
Prod-MIOT Dist-MIOT

Wear And Care Of Soft Contact Lenses C
3/4 OR 1/2 INCH VIDEO CASSETTE
Details the methods for cleaning, disinfecting and storing soft contact lenses.
Prod-MIFE Dist-MIFE

Wear Your Hard Hat C 8 MIN
16MM FILM, 3/4 OR 1/2 IN VIDEO IND
Details the possible injuries and disastrous consequences of not wearing protective headgear on the job. Gives a history of warrior helmets and explains the construction of a modern hard hat.
Prod-CSAO Dist-IFB

Wearing A Cast C
3/4 OR 1/2 INCH VIDEO CASSETTE
Features Mister Rogers in a program which shows how casts are applied and removed and how children can do many things for themselves even while wearing a cast.
From The Let's Talk About The Hospital Series.
Prod-FAMCOM Dist-FAMCOM

Wearing A Cast C 30 MIN
1/2 IN VIDEO CASSETTE BETA/VHS P-J
Shows how casts are applied and removed. Shows children how they can do many things for themselves even while wearing a cast. Features Mister Rogers.
From The Mister Rogers - Health And Safety Series.
Prod-BRENTM Dist-BRENTM

Wearing A Cast (Spanish) C
3/4 OR 1/2 INCH VIDEO CASSETTE
Features Mister Rogers in a program which shows how casts are applied and removed and how children can do many things for themselves even while wearing a cast.
From The Let's Talk About The Hospital Series.
Prod-FAMCOM Dist-FAMCOM

Wearing A Cast (Spanish) C 30 MIN
1/2 IN VIDEO CASSETTE BETA/VHS P-J
Shows how casts are applied and removed. Shows children how they can do many things for themselves even while wearing a cast. Features Mister Rogers.
From The Mister Rogers - Health And Safety Series.
Prod-BRENTM Dist-BRENTM

Wearing Extended Wear - Soft Contact Lenses C 11 MIN
3/4 OR 1/2 INCH VIDEO CASSETTE
Introduces the patient to the basic principles and benefits of extended wear lenses. Discusses proper technique of application, removal, hygiene and care.
Prod-TRAINX Dist-TRAINX

Wearing Soft Contact Lenses - Chemical Disinfection C 8 MIN
3/4 OR 1/2 INCH VIDEO CASSETTE
Discusses application, removal, proper hygiene and care of soft lenses.
Prod-TRAINX Dist-TRAINX

Wearing Soft Contact Lenses - Heat Disinfection C 8 MIN
3/4 OR 1/2 INCH VIDEO CASSETTE
Discusses application, removal, proper hygiene and care of soft lenses.
Prod-TRAINX Dist-TRAINX

Wearout Failure C 30 MIN
3/4 OR 1/2 INCH VIDEO CASSETTE IND
Describes use of the normal distribution for modelling wearout failure. Presents example of how to estimate the economic time to do preventative maintenance.
From The Reliability Engineering Series.
Prod-COLOSU Dist-COLOSU

Wearout Failure - Examples C 30 MIN
3/4 OR 1/2 INCH VIDEO CASSETTE IND
Contains worked-out examples of wearout failure problems to supplement previous lecture.
From The Reliability Engineering Series.
Prod-COLOSU Dist-COLOSU

Weary Pilgrimage, A C 29 MIN
3/4 INCH VIDEO CASSETTE
Discusses the aging theory proposed by David Gutman of the Psychology Department at the University of Michigan.
From The Country Of Old Men Series.
Prod-UMITV Dist-UMITV 1974

Weather C 3 MIN
3/4 OR 1/2 INCH VIDEO CASSETTE I
Explains how tornados, thunderstorms and other climatic wonders happen.
From The Science Rock Series.
Prod-ABCTV Dist-GA

Weather B 10 MIN
3/4 INCH VIDEO CASSETTE P
Explains weather as the sun, the air and the water working together.
From The Two For Tomorrow Series.
Prod-BEOC Dist-GPITVL

Weather C 15 MIN
3/4 OR 1/2 INCH VIDEO CASSETTE I
Considers how the weather influences one's life.
From The Matter And Motion Series. Module Brown
Prod-WHROTV Dist-AITECH 1973

Weather - Air In Action—A Series
16MM FILM, 3/4 OR 1/2 IN VIDEO I-H
Prod-CAHILL Dist-AIMS 1965

Fronts And Storms 11 MIN
Pressure And Humidity 10 MIN
Temperature And Wind 8 MIN

Weather - Come Rain, Come Shine C 22 MIN
16MM FILM, 3/4 OR 1/2 IN VIDEO I-H A
Discusses the global weather machine involving the interaction of sun, air and water. Shows old and new weather forecasting tools, including anemometers, barometers and satellites.
LC NO. 83-706406
Prod-NGS Dist-NGS 1983

Weather - The Water Cycle C 15 MIN
3/4 INCH VIDEO CASSETTE I
Shows that through the same volume of various elements, the same cyclical processes occur over and over with regard to vaporization and condensation.
From The Search For Science (2nd Ed.) Unit VI - Air And Weather Series.
Prod-WVIZTV Dist-GPITVL

Weather - Understanding Precipitation C 11 MIN
16MM FILM, 3/4 OR 1/2 IN VIDEO I-J
Uses live action and animation to explain the evaporation of water from the earth and its return as rain or some other form of precipitation. Explains relative humidity, dew point and basic cloud types.
Prod-CORF Dist-CORF 1962

Weather - Understanding Storms B 11 MIN
16MM FILM, 3/4 OR 1/2 IN VIDEO I-J
Shows how temperature, pressure and moisture interact to bring about the various types of storms, including thunderstorm, toronado, hurricane, blizzard and dust storm, and describes the distinguishing characteristics of each type of storm. Emphasizes the increasingly important role of meteorology and weather satellites in forecasting storms.
Prod-CORF Dist-CORF 1962

Weather - Who Votes For Rain C 20 MIN
16MM FILM, 3/4 OR 1/2 IN VIDEO
Explains how researchers are attempting to remove some of the guesswork from weather forecasting. Looks at the possibility that man might one day be able to control the weather.
Prod-DOCUA Dist-CNEMAG

Weather - Why It Changes C 10 MIN
16MM FILM, 3/4 OR 1/2 IN VIDEO I-J
Presents a simple and clear explanation of how and why changes in weather occur. Locates the air masses which govern major weather changes in North America, and shows what happens when these masses interact, forming cold fronts, warm fronts and occluded fronts.
Prod-CORF Dist-CORF 1958

Weather And Climate X 20 MIN
2 INCH VIDEOTAPE I
See series title for descriptive statement.
From The Process And Proof Series. No. 24
Prod-MCETV Dist-GPITVL Prodn-WVIZTV

Weather And Radar B 17 MIN
16MM FILM, 3/4 OR 1/2 IN VIDEO
Illustrates some of the operational values to be gained by using radar in locating and identifying weather disturbances, including cold fronts, warm fronts, thunderstorms, typhoons and hurricanes. Shows characteristic echo patterns on the planned positionindicator scope.
From The Aerology Series.
LC NO. 81-706620
Prod-USN Dist-USNAC 1954

Weather Building C 10 MIN
16MM FILM OPTICAL SOUND
Presents an experimental film depicting three-dimensional planes through positive-negative images, illuminated surfaces and video images.
LC NO. 77-702705
Prod-MCLARR Dist-CANFDC 1976

Weather Bureau - Operation C 20 MIN
2 INCH VIDEOTAPE I
See series title for descriptive statement.
From The Exploring With Science, Unit V - Weather Series.
Prod-MPATI Dist-GPITVL

Weather By Numbers C 30 MIN
16MM FILM, 3/4 OR 1/2 IN VIDEO J-C A
Shows how Dr Joseph Smagorinsky and his colleagues at the Environmental Science Services Administration experiment with mathematical equations and computers for predicting the weather.
From The Experiment Series.
Prod-NET Dist-IU 1966

Weather Cycle C 15 MIN
2 INCH VIDEOTAPE P
Correlates the weather cycle with the water cycle.
From The Science Is Searching Series.
Prod-DETPS Dist-GPITVL

Weather Does Its Thing C 28 MIN
16MM FILM, 3/4 OR 1/2 IN VIDEO J-C
Shows the ways in which scientists and meteorologists are probing the past for clues to previous climates and are using the information they find to help them make long-term climatic predictions.
Prod-UN Dist-JOU 1974

Weather Eye C 29 MIN
16MM FILM OPTICAL SOUND
Describes the duties of an aerographer's mate assigned to a duty station with the U S Naval Weather Service.
LC NO. 75-700885
Prod-USN Dist-USNAC 1974

Weather Eye For Safety C 20 MIN
3/4 OR 1/2 INCH VIDEO CASSETTE IND
Explains the procedures and equipment unique to a petroleum and petroleum product tanker. Includes special smoking restrictions, cargo hazards, compartment precautions and slip, trip and fall hazards.
Prod-TEXACO Dist-UTEXPE

Weather Eye, The C 13 MIN
16MM FILM OPTICAL SOUND H-C
Describes the design, development, and fabrication of Snap-19, a small, long-lived, radioisotope-fueled nuclear generator designed to be the auxiliary power for the nimbus weather satellite.
LC NO. 78-700857
Prod-USAEC Dist-USNAC 1969

Weather For Beginners C 10 MIN
16MM FILM, 3/4 OR 1/2 IN VIDEO P
Demonstrates concepts of weather, such as why air above land gets warmer than air above water, what causes winds, how clouds form and why it rains.
Prod-CORF Dist-CORF 1964

Weather Forecasting (2nd Ed) C 22 MIN
16MM FILM, 3/4 OR 1/2 IN VIDEO I-J
Examines the history of weather forecasting and shows the kinds of instruments and techniques used to forecast the weather.
From The Earth Science Program Series.
Prod-EBEC Dist-EBEC 1975

Weather I C 30 MIN
3/4 OR 1/2 INCH VIDEO CASSETTE H-C A
Presents Lawrence Solow and Sharon Neumann Solow introducing American Sign Language used by the hearing-impaired. Emphasizes signs that have to do with the weather.
From The Say It With Sign Series. Part 6
Prod-KNBCTV Dist-FI 1982

Weather II C 30 MIN
3/4 OR 1/2 INCH VIDEO CASSETTE H-C A
Presents Lawrence Solow and Sharon Neumann Solow introducing American Sign Language used by the hearing-impaired. Emphasizes signs that have to do with the weather.
From The Say It With Sign Series. Part 7
Prod-KNBCTV Dist-FI 1982

Weather Is Out C 15 MIN
3/4 OR 1/2 INCH VIDEO CASSETTE P
Shows the Cree culture on Cape Jones in Quebec.
From The Other Families, Other Friends Series. Green Module - Quebec
Prod-WVIZTV Dist-AITECH 1971

Weather Machine—A Series
16MM FILM, 3/4 OR 1/2 IN VIDEO H-C A
Examines the conditions that cause variations in climate around the world, the most ominous of which is the potential abrupt end to the the current interglacial period on the earth.
Prod-EDUCBC Dist-IU 1977

Weather Machine, The, Pt 1 059 MIN
Weather Machine, The, Pt 2 059 MIN

Weather Machine, Pt 1, The C 59 MIN
16MM FILM, 3/4 OR 1/2 IN VIDEO H-C A
Discusses various methods of observing climatic changes, such as examining ice layers, following global weather patterns by satellite, computer-assisted forecasting, weather modification and weather research.
From The Weather Machine Series.
LC NO. 80-706107
Prod-EDUCBC Dist-IU 1977

Weather Machine, Pt 2, The C 58 MIN
16MM FILM, 3/4 OR 1/2 IN VIDEO H-C A
Offers examples of change in global climate, including major and minor ice ages, changes in the jet stream's flow, changing solar radiation, increasing levels of carbon dioxide, droughts and inconsistent rainfall patterns.
From The Weather Machine Series.
LC NO. 80-706107
Prod-EDUCBC Dist-IU 1977

Weather Map, The C 12 MIN
16MM FILM OPTICAL SOUND J-H
Presents an explanation and interpretation of the weather map.
LC NO. FIA68-2247
Prod-ANAIB Dist-AUIS 1968

Weather Measurements X 20 MIN
2 INCH VIDEOTAPE I
See series title for descriptive statement.
From The Process And Proof Series. No. 27
Prod-MCETV Dist-GPITVL Prodn-WVIZTV

Weather Report, A C 20 MIN
3/4 INCH VIDEO CASSETTE I
Demonstrates how metric units are being used to report news and weather. Shows how such units are used in sports car racing and in measuring small objects and small volume.
From The Metric Marmalade Series.
Prod-WCVETV Dist-GPITVL 1979

Weather Satellites X 15 MIN
16MM FILM, 3/4 OR 1/2 IN VIDEO J-C
Describes how the weather satellite photographs every area of the earth at least once a day so that the information can be used in making forecasts. Explains how the satellite can observe movements of air and hurricane and tornado clouds. Uses a model satellite.
Prod-EBF Dist-EBEC 1965

Weather Science - Pierrot And Lightning And Thunder C 5 MIN
16MM FILM, 3/4 OR 1/2 IN VIDEO P
Introduces a cartoon character named Pierrot and his friends, who explain the causes of thunderstorms, thunder and lightning.
From The Weather Science Series.
Prod-CORF Dist-CORF 1979

Weather Science - Pierrot And Rain And Snow C 7 MIN
16MM FILM, 3/4 OR 1/2 IN VIDEO P
Introduces a cartoon character named Pierrot and his friends, who explain the water cycle and the causes of clouds, rain and snow.
From The Weather Science Series.
Prod-CORF Dist-CORF 1979

Weather Science - Pierrot And The Rainbow C 6 MIN
16MM FILM, 3/4 OR 1/2 IN VIDEO P
Introduces a cartoon character named Pierrot and his friends, who explain how a rainbow is formed.
From The Weather Science Series.
Prod-CORF Dist-CORF 1979

Weather Science - Pierrot And The Sun C 6 MIN
16MM FILM, 3/4 OR 1/2 IN VIDEO P
Introduces a cartoon character named Pierrot and his friends, who explain the characteristics of the sun and its effect on the earth.
From The Weather Science Series.
Prod-CORF Dist-CORF 1979

Weather Science - Pierrot And The Wind C 4 MIN
16MM FILM, 3/4 OR 1/2 IN VIDEO P
Introduces a cartoon character named Pierrot and his friends, who explain how the sun, the moving earth, mountains and bodies of water affect the movement of winds.
From The Weather Science Series.
Prod-CORF Dist-CORF 1979

Weather Science—A Series
16MM FILM, 3/4 OR 1/2 IN VIDEO P
Introduces a character named Pierrot and his friends, who discover various aspects of the weather.
Prod-CORF Dist-CORF 1979

Weather Science - Pierrot And Lightning And
Weather Science - Pierrot And Rain And Snow 007 MIN
Weather Science - Pierrot And The Rainbow 006 MIN
Weather Science - Pierrot And The Sun 006 MIN
Weather Science - Pierrot And The Wind 004 MIN

Weather Stripping C 8 MIN
3/4 INCH VIDEO CASSETTE
Describes how and why to apply weather stripping, including a discussion of insulating materials.
Prod-TUCPL Dist-GPITVL

Weather Warfare C 18 MIN
3/4 OR 1/2 INCH VIDEO CASSETTE H-C A
Discusses the potential of weather modification as an act of aggression.
Prod-CANBC Dist-JOU

Weather Watchers, The C 15 MIN
16MM FILM, 3/4 OR 1/2 IN VIDEO
Traces the development of tools used to understand weather conditions. Shows a tornado tracking mission which gathers data from aircraft satellites and radar. Shows how the data is then coordinated and analyzed by NASA scientists using computer readouts and visual images to achieve long-range severe weather forecasting.
LC NO. 81-706430
Prod-NASA Dist-USNAC Prodn-SCRESC 1977

Weather Watchers, The C 30 MIN
16MM FILM, 3/4 OR 1/2 IN VIDEO I-H
Tells the story of the baffling problems of weather watching and the possibility of eventual weather control.
From The World We Live In Series.
Prod-TIMELI Dist-MGHT 1968

Weather—A Series

Prod-WHATV Dist-PUBTEL

Climate - The Summing Up 29 MIN
Core Of The Matter, The 29 MIN
Formation Of Clouds, The 29 MIN
Hurricanes 28 MIN
Jet Streams 29 MIN
Rainmaking 29 MIN
Thunderstorm, The 29 MIN
Tornadoes 29 MIN
Ups And Downs Of Highs And Lows, The 29 MIN
What's Behind The Front 30 MIN

Weathering And Erosion C 30 MIN
3/4 OR 1/2 INCH VIDEO CASSETTE C
Shows the effects of the primary forces of weathering and erosion in such places as Bryce Canyon, the Boquillas Canyon of Big Bend, and the Gras Ventre and Madison Canyon areas of Wyoming and Montana.
From The Earth, Sea And Sky Series.
Prod-DALCCD Dist-DALCCD

Weathering And Mass-Wasting B 45 MIN
2 INCH VIDEOTAPE C
See series title for descriptive statement.
From The Physical Science Series. Unit 1 - Geology
Prod-CHITVC Dist-GPITVL Prodn-WTTWTV

Weathering Processes C 31 MIN
3/4 OR 1/2 INCH VIDEO CASSETTE IND
See series title for descriptive statement.
From The Basic And Petroleum Geology For Non-geologists - Fundamentals And...--Series.
Prod-PHILLP Dist-GPCV

Weathering, Erosion, And Unconformities C 48 MIN
3/4 OR 1/2 INCH VIDEO CASSETTE IND
See series title for descriptive statement.
From The Basic Geology Series.
Prod-GPCV Dist-GPCV

Weatherize Your Home C 19 MIN
16MM FILM, 3/4 OR 1/2 IN VIDEO J-C A
Provides step-by-step instructions on how to insulate floors, ceilings, attics, water heaters, ductwork, and windows in the interest of conserving energy.
From The Home Repairs Series.
LC NO. 80-707320
Prod-BRMFDK Dist-CORF 1980

Weatherizing - Fiberglass Insulation, Weatherstripping C 30 MIN
1/2 IN VIDEO CASSETTE BETA/VHS
See series title for descriptive statement.
From The Wally's Workshop Series.
Prod-KARTES Dist-KARTES

Weatherly Or Not C 17 MIN
16MM FILM OPTICAL SOUND
Depicts Joe Weatherly on his way to winning the 1960 Rebel Stock Car Race at the Darlington, North Carolina Raceway.
Prod-DCC Dist-DCC

Weatherman, The - A Scientist C 10 MIN
16MM FILM, 3/4 OR 1/2 IN VIDEO I
Discusses the special training required of a weatherman. Points out that most weathermen are college graduates whose training helps them understand the factors that contribute to weather changes and to be able to use a wide variety of tools to measure these factors. Tells how weathermen gather data from all over the world and prepare weather maps that help them forecast weather changes.
Prod-EVANS Dist-PHENIX 1970

Weatherman, The - Community Helper C 10 MIN
16MM FILM, 3/4 OR 1/2 IN VIDEO P-I
Describes the role the weatherman plays in the community. Describes how scientists called meteorologists use special instruments and knowledge to measure, record and predict weather. Tells how they help the farmer to know about growing conditions, the ship captain to decide the wisest course for his ship and people in all walks of life to know how to plan their day.
Prod-EVANSA Dist-PHENIX 1970

Weatherproofing C 30 MIN
3/4 OR 1/2 INCH VIDEO CASSETTE
Presents tips on weatherproofing.
From The Consumer Survival Series. Homes
Prod-MDCPB Dist-MDCPB

Weatherproofing Baca County B 6 MIN
16MM FILM OPTICAL SOUND
Depicts man's fight against drought, dust and disaster in the Great Plains. Shows how farmers and ranchers in Baca County, Colorado, through low level weed killing flights by airplanes and stubble mulching operations on the ground, protect the land against the erosive force of the wind and conserve each drop of moisture.
LC NO. FIE63-225
Prod-USDA Dist-USNAC 1963

Weave A Web Of Mystery C 15 MIN
3/4 OR 1/2 INCH VIDEO CASSETTE I
Deals with writing a mystery story.
From The Tyger, Tyger Burning Bright Series.
Prod-CTI Dist-CTI

Weave Beads C 13 MIN
3/4 OR 1/2 INCH VIDEO CASSETTE IND
See series title for descriptive statement.
From The Electric Arc Welding Series. Chapter 7
Prod-TAT Dist-TAT

Weave With Paper B 15 MIN
2 INCH VIDEOTAPE P
Develops an awareness of woven fabrics by discovering the principles of weaving through paper weaving.
From The Art Corner Series.
Prod-CVETVC Dist-GPITVL Prodn-WCVETV

Weavers Of The West C 13 MIN
16MM FILM OPTICAL SOUND I-J
The complete story of the making of the Navaho rug with some insight into the lives, habits and ceremonies of the tribe. Filmed in the Navaho country in northern Arizona and New Mexico.
Prod-DAGP Dist-MLA 1954

Weaves C 12 MIN
16MM FILM, 3/4 OR 1/2 IN VIDEO J-C
Shows various weaving processes. Depicts a weaver at her handloom and the preparation for an exhibit.
Prod-SETHNA Dist-IFB 1965

Weaving C
3/4 OR 1/2 INCH VIDEO CASSETTE
See series title for descriptive statement.
From The ITMA 1983 Review Series.
Prod-NCSU Dist-NCSU

Weaving C 14 MIN
3/4 OR 1/2 INCH VIDEO CASSETTE P-I
Discusses the art of weaving.
From The Young At Art Series.
Prod-WSKJTV Dist-AITECH 1980

Weaving C 15 MIN
16MM FILM, 3/4 OR 1/2 IN VIDEO I-C A
Illustrates the basic principle of weaving threads into cloth. Shows how even simple looms may be used creatively to produce a wide variety of effects.
From The Rediscovery - Art Media Series.
Prod-ACI Dist-AIMS 1969

Weaving C 15 MIN
3/4 OR 1/2 INCH VIDEO CASSETTE P-I
Explores weaving techniques and simple loom construction, beginning with simple paper weavings and moving on to fabric and yarn weavings.
From The Art Cart Series.
LC NO. 79-708042
Prod-WBRATV Dist-AITECH 1979

Weaving C 29 MIN
2 INCH VIDEOTAPE
See series title for descriptive statement.
From The Commonwealth Series.
Prod-WITFTV Dist-PUBTEL

Weaving (Afrikaans) C 14 MIN
16MM FILM, 3/4 OR 1/2 IN VIDEO I-C A
Demonstrates the basic principle of interlocking fibers used in weaving, then presents a variety of weaving methods.
Prod-ACI Dist-AIMS 1969

Weaving (French) C 14 MIN
16MM FILM, 3/4 OR 1/2 IN VIDEO I-C A
Demonstrates the basic principle of interlocking fibers used in weaving, then presents a variety of weaving methods.
From The Rediscovery - Art Media (French) Series.
Prod-ACI Dist-AIMS 1969

Weaving (Spanish) C 14 MIN
16MM FILM, 3/4 OR 1/2 IN VIDEO I-C A
Demonstrates the basic principle of interlocking fibers used in weaving, then presents a variety of weaving methods.
From The Rediscovery - Art Media (Spanish) Series.
Prod-ACI Dist-AIMS 1969

Weaving Cloth (Pushtu) C 9 MIN
16MM FILM, 3/4 OR 1/2 IN VIDEO
See series title for descriptive statement.

From The Mountain Peoples Of Central Asia (Afghanistan) Series.
Prod-IFF Dist-IFF

Weaving With Looms You Can Make C 16 MIN
16MM FILM, 3/4 OR 1/2 IN VIDEO J-C A
Features artist Nancy Belfer giving demonstrations of the techniques of weaving with cardboard, branch, backstrap and frame looms to make multicolored and textured materials.
From The Textile Design Series.
Prod-TETKOW Dist-AIMS 1973

Web Of Life, Endless Chain C 28 MIN
16MM FILM, 3/4 OR 1/2 IN VIDEO
Combines music and sound effects with footage of desert flora and fauna to show the interacting and interdependent chains of life in a desert ecosystem. Issued in 1972 as a motion picture.
LC NO. 79-706730
Prod-BEET Dist-USNAC Prodn-USAEC 1979

Web Of Taxes, The B 20 MIN
16MM FILM OPTICAL SOUND H A
W B Boyer, vice president and treasurer, Republic Steel Corporation, covers the problem of individual and corporate taxes and their effects on incentives and investments.
From The Government And Public Affairs Films Series.
Prod-RSC Dist-MLA 1960

Web Of Transportation, The B 15 MIN
2 INCH VIDEOTAPE P-I
See series title for descriptive statement.
From The Our Changing Community Series.
Prod-VITA Dist-GPITVL 1967

Web, The C 15 MIN
3/4 OR 1/2 INCH VIDEO CASSETTE P
See series title for descriptive statement.
From The Strawberry Square II - Take Time Series.
Prod-NEITV Dist-AITECH 1984

Webster Groves Revisited B 53 MIN
16MM FILM, 3/4 OR 1/2 IN VIDEO H-C A
Presents a sequel to the documentary Sixteen In Webster Groves. Shows how the medium of television can be a moving force for change in a community.
Prod-CBSNEW Dist-CAROUF

Wedding Bells C 15 MIN
16MM FILM OPTICAL SOUND P-I
Tells how the Graham children and Alice the chimp are almost run over on the way to a wedding and stumble into a plan to steal the wedding gifts. Reveals how Alice devises an ingenious plan to stave off disaster and alert the guests.
Prod-LUF Dist-LUF 1977

Wedding Camels, The (Turkana) C 108 MIN
16MM FILM, 3/4 OR 1/2 IN VIDEO
Shows how bridal negotiations are carried out in the Turkana culture of northwestern Kenya. Depicts a suitor for the hand of the chief's daughter who must negotiate how many camels to give her father without appearing foolish or depleting his camel herd. Presented in Turkana with English subtitles.
From The Turkana Conversations Trilogy Series.
Prod-MCDGAL Dist-UCEMC 1980

Wedding In A Persian Village C 11 MIN
16MM FILM OPTICAL SOUND I-C A
Depicts traditional marriage ceremonies of remote regions of Iran, where weddings are community events.
LC NO. 76-706445
Prod-NYU Dist-NYU 1963

Wedding In The Family, A C 22 MIN
16MM FILM OPTICAL SOUND
Presents a documentary on a family during the week before the wedding of one of the children. Focuses on issues relating to marriage, sex roles, career expectations and life choices.
LC NO. 78-700257
Prod-FRANCO Dist-NEWDAY 1977

Wedding Of Princess Margrethe, The C 32 MIN
16MM FILM OPTICAL SOUND
Covers the events preceding the wedding on June 10, 1967, of Princess Margrethe to Prince Henrick.
Prod-RDCG Dist-AUDPLN

Wedding Reception, The - The Grand Pas De Deux C 15 MIN
16MM FILM, 3/4 OR 1/2 IN VIDEO
See series title for descriptive statement.
From The Rudolf Nureyev's Film Of Don Quixote Series.
Prod-WRO Dist-SF Prodn-IARTS 1978

Weddings C 30 MIN
3/4 OR 1/2 INCH VIDEO CASSETTE
Presents tips on planning weddings.
From The Consumer Survival Series. Personal Planning
Prod-MDCPB Dist-MDCPB

Wedge - A Simple Machine C 15 MIN
3/4 OR 1/2 INCH VIDEO CASSETTE P-I
Discusses the characteristics of the wedge.
From The Why Series.
Prod-WDCNTV Dist-AITECH 1976

Wedging The Clay And Making A Pitch Pot C 28 MIN
2 INCH VIDEOTAPE
Features Mrs Peterson describing certain ceramic processes for her classroom at the University of Southern California. Demonstrates how to wedge the clay and make a pitch pot.
From The Wheels, Kilns And Clay Series.
Prod-USC Dist-PUBTEL

Wedgwood C 30 MIN
3/4 INCH VIDEO CASSETTE
See series title for descriptive statement.
From The Antiques Series.
Prod-NHMNET Dist-PUBTEL

Wediko Series - Emotionally Disturbed Children At Camp--A Series
T
Shows pioneering treatment in therapeutic camping for emotionally disturbed children.
Prod-DOCUFL Dist-DOCUFL

Beach Interview	027 MIN
Boys In Conflict	072 MIN
Bruce	026 MIN
Johnny	032 MIN
Randy	027 MIN
Troubled Campers	018 MIN

Wee Geese C 7 MIN
16MM FILM, 3/4 OR 1/2 IN VIDEO K-I
Shows the life and habits of the young Canada goose. Pictures a typical day in the life of the goslings and the adventures of one gosling who goes exploring.
Prod-ACI Dist-AIMS 1964

Wee Gillis C 19 MIN
16MM FILM, 3/4 OR 1/2 IN VIDEO P-I
Presents the story of Wee Gillis, who spends a year in the Lowlands of Scotland herding cattle with his mother's relatives and then a year in the Highlands stalking stags with his father's relatives. Tells how he finds his calling as a bagpipe player. Based on the book Wee Gillis by Munro Leaf and Robert Lawson.
Prod-CF Dist-CF 1985

Weeding The Garden C 14 MIN
16MM FILM - 3/4 IN VIDEO H-C A
Shows the Yanamamo shaman Dedeheiwa weeding his manioc garden and later being massaged and groomed by his wife as he plays with his children.
Prod-DOCEDR Dist-DOCEDR 1975

Weegee's New York C 20 MIN
16MM FILM OPTICAL SOUND H-C A
Presents a tour of New York, emphasizing the life and tempo of the metropolis and combining documentary and experimental photographic techniques.
LC NO. FIA67-1837
Prod-WEEGEE Dist-GROVE 1953

Week Full Of Saturdays, A C 17 MIN
16MM FILM OPTICAL SOUND A
Discusses the financial, residential and recreational factors of retirement. Shows the daily routines of various retired people and presents their views on retirement.
LC NO. 79-700061
Prod-ALTERC Dist-FLMLIB Prodn-DANCYN 1979

Week Of Sweet Water, A C 40 MIN
3/4 OR 1/2 INCH VIDEO CASSETTE
Documents drought conditions in the Sahel region of West Africa. Shows the building of a dam by the people of the village of Somiaga in Upper volta. Focuses on the story of one family in the village.
Prod-BBCTV Dist-DOCEDR

Weekend C 60 MIN
3/4 OR 1/2 INCH VIDEO CASSETTE J A
Reveals that the ostensibly liberal attitudes of a middle-class Anglo couple are challenged when their teenaged children invite two black school friends for the weekend.
From The Rainbow Movie Of The Week Series.
Prod-RAINTV Dist-GPITVL 1981

Weekend Athletes, The C 48 MIN
16MM FILM OPTICAL SOUND H-C A
Examines the physical fitness movement in the United States. Presents interviews with medical authorities on the values of jogging and other exercises and points out the dangers in getting too much exercise too fast.
LC NO. 77-703382
Prod-ABCTV Dist-BESTF 1977

Weekend In Vermont C 157 MIN
16MM FILM, 3/4 OR 1/2 IN VIDEO H-C A
Focuses on the prospects of democratic capitalism and the industrial West. Based on the book The Age Of Uncertainty by John Kenneth Galbraith.
From The Age Of Uncertainty Series.
LC NO. 77-701494
Prod-BBCL Dist-FI 1977

Weekend Of Champions C 29 MIN
16MM FILM OPTICAL SOUND
Films the efforts of various athletes during the Weekend of Champions in Dallas.
Prod-FELLCA Dist-FELLCA 1969

Weekend Pass B 35 MIN
16MM FILM OPTICAL SOUND H-C A
Presents a short story about a shy sailor's weekend pass in Los Angeles.
Prod-CFS Dist-CFS 1963

Weekend Sports - Fun, Not Injuries C 25 MIN
3/4 OR 1/2 INCH VIDEO CASSETTE
Features sports doctor Robert Kerlan, MD (LA Rams, Lakers, and Kings), joining tennis pro Charlie Passarel, a ski instructor, a motorcycle patrolman, and host Mario Machado for free lessons and safety tips on tennis, skiing and motorcycling.
Prod-TRAINX Dist-TRAINX

Weekend USA C 14 MIN
16MM FILM OPTICAL SOUND C A
Shows Americans enjoying weekend recreation, both indoor and outdoor, and the architect's input into recreation facilities.
Prod-AIA Dist-AIA 1973

Weekend Warriors B 11 MIN
16MM FILM OPTICAL SOUND
Features a cinematic impression of a martial arts tournament.
LC NO. 76-703817
Prod-CCAAT Dist-CCAAT 1976

Weekend, The C 16 MIN
16MM FILM OPTICAL SOUND H-C
Presents an estranged couple, who stranded together in a motel room, learn about the communication breakdown in their marriage and their need to rediscover personal identity and affirmation in the marriage relationship.
From The Marriage Series.
LC NO. 70-711574
Prod-FRACOC Dist-FRACOC 1970

Weep No More, My Lady C 24 MIN
16MM FILM, 3/4 OR 1/2 IN VIDEO
Presents an animated story about a 13-year-old boy who leads a Huck Finn-style life in the bayou country. Tells how he takes in a stray dog that brings him joy and a lesson in what it takes to become a man. Originally shown on the television series ABC Weekend Specials.
LC NO. 79-707139
Prod-ABCTV Dist-MTI Prodn-RSPRO 1979

Weetamoe B
1/2 IN VIDEO CASSETTE BETA/VHS
Shows a seldom seen look at sailing aboard a J Boat sail and boat handling and match racing in R I waters in 1934.
Prod-MYSTIC Dist-MYSTIC 1984

Weibull Failure Model C 30 MIN
3/4 OR 1/2 INCH VIDEO CASSETTE IND
Describes use of the Weibull Distribution to model failures. Plots an example on Weibull probability paper, and estimates of failure mode and characteristic life are read from the plot.
From The Reliability Engineering Series.
Prod-COLOSU Dist-COLOSU

Weibull Probability Paper--Example C 30 MIN
3/4 OR 1/2 INCH VIDEO CASSETTE IND
Contains worked-out example using Weibull probability paper to predict the characteristic life and shaping parameter for a set of sample data.
From The Reliability Engineering Series.
Prod-COLOSU Dist-COLOSU

Weighing C 22 MIN
3/4 OR 1/2 INCH VIDEO CASSETTE
Illustrates the development and principles of the balance. Examines correct weighing procedures.
From The General Chemistry Laboratory Techniques Series.
Prod-UCEMC Dist-UCEMC

Weighing And Measuring C 10 MIN
16MM FILM OPTICAL SOUND I-H
Discusses the common English system of weighing and introduces the metric system.
Prod-SF Dist-SF 1970

Weighing The Choices - Positive Approaches To Nutrition C 20 MIN
16MM FILM OPTICAL SOUND
Offers positive, practical choices for breakfast, lunch and dinner.
Prod-SPEF Dist-SPEF 1981

Weight C 15 MIN
2 INCH VIDEOTAPE K
Measures the weight of different objects.
From The Let's Go Sciencing, Unit I - Matter Series.
Prod-DETPS Dist-GPITVL

Weight C 15 MIN
3/4 INCH VIDEO CASSETTE P
Shows how to weigh an object with non-standard units and with metric units.
From The Studio M Series.
Prod-WCETTV Dist-GPITVL 1979

Weight C 20 MIN
2 INCH VIDEOTAPE P
See series title for descriptive statement.
From The Mathemagic, Unit VI - Measurement Series.
Prod-WMULTV Dist-GPITVL

Weight Control C 13 MIN
16MM FILM, 3/4 OR 1/2 IN VIDEO J-C A
Deals with the causes of obesity, how to prevent it and how to develop a lifetime program of safe and effective weight control. Notes that being overweight can shorten one's life and lead to problems such as heart disease, diabetes and high blood pressure.
From The Nutrition Series.
Prod-PRORE Dist-JOU 1975

Weight Control C 30 MIN
3/4 OR 1/2 INCH VIDEO CASSETTE
See series title for descriptive statement.
From The Food For Life Series.
Prod-MSU Dist-MSU

Weight Control (Spanish) C 13 MIN
16MM FILM, 3/4 OR 1/2 IN VIDEO J-C A
Deals with the causes of obesity, how to prevent it and how to develop a lifetime program of safe and effective weight control. Notes that being overweight can shorten one's life and lead to problems, such as heart disease, diabetes and high blood pressure.
Prod-PRORE Dist-JOU 1975

Weight Control (2nd Ed) C 9 MIN
3/4 OR 1/2 INCH VIDEO CASSETTE
Explains calories and calorie requirement. Discusses fats, protein and carbohydrates. Outlines basic principles of weight reduction.
Prod-MEDFAC Dist-MEDFAC 1981

Weight Control - Just A Step Away C 13 MIN
16MM FILM, 3/4 OR 1/2 IN VIDEO J-C A
Explains the importance of physical activity in combating obesity by showing an experiment with three groups of people, one group which dieted, one which exercised and one which did both to lose weight.
From The World Of Health Series.
Prod-INFORP Dist-SF 1975

Weight Control - Just A Step Away C 13 MIN
16MM FILM, 3/4 OR 1/2 IN VIDEO A
Tells how just an extra half hour of walking daily will burn up, in one year, the calories in 16 pounds of fat. Illustrates the value of activity in weight reduction and control.
Prod-PRORE Dist-PRORE

Weight Control / Real Estate Investments / Advertising C
3/4 OR 1/2 INCH VIDEO CASSETTE
Discusses various aspects of weight control, real estate investments and advertising.
From The Consumer Survival Series.
Prod-MDCPB Dist-MDCPB

Weight Loss B 30 MIN
3/4 OR 1/2 INCH VIDEO CASSETTE
Helps one lose weight through subliminal suggestions.
Prod-ADVCAS Dist-ADVCAS

Weight Watcher's Magazine Guide To A Healthy Lifestyle C
1/2 IN VIDEO CASSETTE BETA/VHS
Presents a guide to healthy living, including dieting tips, low-calorie recipes, exercise suggestions and more, hosted by Lynn Redgrave.
Prod-GA Dist-GA

Weight, Mass, Force, Pressure C 30 MIN
3/4 OR 1/2 INCH VIDEO CASSETTE H-C A
Explains the difference between weight and mass and tells how mass is measured in the metric system.
From The Going Metric Series.
Prod-UMA Dist-GPITVL 1977

Weight, Nutrition And Exercise During Pregnancy C 8 MIN
16MM FILM, 3/4 OR 1/2 IN VIDEO
Examines what foods a woman should eat while she is pregnant, how much weight gain is normal and safe, and what physical activities she can continue safely. Provides suggestions to improve physical comfort.
From The Prepared Childbirth And Parenting Series.
Prod-JOU Dist-JOU 1976

Weight, The C 60 MIN
16MM FILM OPTICAL SOUND
Depicts high school seniors struggling with questions of love, honor and friendship, alcohol, cruelty and war.
Prod-CAFM Dist-CAFM

Weightlifters B 11 MIN
16MM FILM OPTICAL SOUND
Documents lifestyles in a high-pressure urban environment.
LC NO. 77-702707
Prod-PEAMIL Dist-CANFDC 1972

Weights And Measures, Pt 1 - Mathematics, Grade 6 B 20 MIN
2 INCH VIDEOTAPE I
From The Mathematics, Grade 6 Series.
Prod-DENVPS Dist-GPITVL

Weights And Measures, Pt 2 - Mathematics, Grade 6 B 20 MIN
2 INCH VIDEOTAPE I
From The Mathematics, Grade 6 Series.
Prod-DENVPS Dist-GPITVL

Weimar Republic, The C 29 MIN
2 INCH VIDEOTAPE
See series title for descriptive statement.
From The Course Of Our Times I Series.
Prod-WGBHTV Dist-PUBTEL

Wein Bridge Oscillator B 21 MIN
16MM FILM OPTICAL SOUND
Explains the theory of operation of the Wein bridge vacuum tube oscillator and states the purpose of each component. Explains the action when the size of the frequency determining components is changed and gives the formula for finding the operating frequency. (Kinescope)
LC NO. 74-705941
Prod-USAF Dist-USNAC

Weird Bird C 10 MIN
3/4 OR 1/2 INCH VIDEO CASSETTE K-H
Uses animation to show a weird bird using his imagination to help him live in a society that demands conformity.
Prod-SUTHRB Dist-SUTHRB

Weird Number, The C 13 MIN
3/4 INCH VIDEO CASSETTE P
Involves the visit of the first fraction to a community of whole numbers. Tells how the 'weird number' steals a piece of cake and leads the townspeople on a merry chase.
Prod-DAVFMS Dist-GA

Weird World Of Robots, The C 18 MIN
16MM FILM, 3/4 OR 1/2 IN VIDEO J-C A
Edited version of the 1968 motion picture of the same title. Describes two types of robots, the simulators which mimic human performance and the augmentors which assist in human performance. Shows examples of several robots in action in industry and science.
From The Twenty-First Century Series.
Prod-CBSNEW Dist-MGHT 1975

Weird World Of Robots, The C 26 MIN
16MM FILM, 3/4 OR 1/2 IN VIDEO H-C
Describes two types of robots--the simulators, which mimic human performance and the augmentors, which assist in human performance. Shows examples of several robots in action in industry and science.
From The Twenty-First Century Series.
Prod-CBSNEW Dist-MGHT 1968

Welcome C 28 MIN
3/4 OR 1/2 INCH VIDEO CASSETTE
Consists of home movies sent by viewers to Old Friends - New Friends. Also features recollections of host Fred Rogers' own childhood and grandfather.
From The Old Friends - New Friends Series.
Prod-FAMCOM Dist-PBS 1981

Welcome Aboard C 11 MIN
16MM FILM, 3/4 OR 1/2 IN VIDEO P-I
Stresses the importance of children's good behavior and the practice of safety habits while riding the school bus. Illustrates disruptive behavior and the safety hazards involved.
Prod-SEGALW Dist-AIMS 1976

Welcome Aboard C 21 MIN
16MM FILM, 3/4 OR 1/2 IN VIDEO
Emphasizes the importance of new employee orientation.
LC NO. 72-701782
Prod-RTBL Dist-RTBL 1972

Welcome Aboard (Captioned) C 23 MIN
3/4 OR 1/2 INCH VIDEO CASSETTE T
Gives practical suggestions to teachers for modifying techniques to include deaf students. In classes. Signed.
Prod-GALCO Dist-GALCO

Welcome Aboard (French) C 21 MIN
16MM FILM, 3/4 OR 1/2 IN VIDEO
Emphasizes the importance of new employee orientation, of helping him to get a good start and helping him to achieve maximum productivity quickly in order to prevent excessive turnover.
Prod-RTBL Dist-RTBL 1972

Welcome Aboard (Norwegian) C 21 MIN
16MM FILM, 3/4 OR 1/2 IN VIDEO
Emphasizes the importance of new employee orientation, of helping him to get a good start and helping him to achieve maximum productivity quickly in order to prevent excessive turnover.
Prod-RTBL Dist-RTBL 1972

Welcome Aboard (Spanish) C 21 MIN
16MM FILM, 3/4 OR 1/2 IN VIDEO
Emphasizes the importance of new employee orientation, of helping him to get a good start and helping him to achieve maximum productivity quickly in order to prevent excessive turnover.
Prod-RTBL Dist-RTBL 1972

Welcome Back To School C 30 MIN
16MM FILM, 3/4 OR 1/2 IN VIDEO T
Introduces educational changes that have taken place in schools so that students will learn more. Emphasizes the professional responsibility for decision making by the adults in the classroom.
From The Aide-ing In Education Series.
Prod-SPF Dist-SPF

Welcome Back, Norman C 7 MIN
16MM FILM, 3/4 OR 1/2 IN VIDEO
Depicts a humorous tale about what befalls a weary traveler in an airport parking lot.
Prod-MTI Dist-MTI

Welcome Customer--A Series
A
Helps provide training to employees in the hospitality industry. Emphasizes pleasant and helpful relations with customers to ensure that they enjoy themselves and come back. Provides lessons for cashiers, bellmen, bartenders, restaurant service, doormen, switchboard operators, reception and maintenance.
Prod-XICOM Dist-XICOM

Have A Nice Stay 025 MIN
See You Again Soon 023 MIN

Welcome Home X 27 MIN
16MM FILM, 3/4 OR 1/2 IN VIDEO J-C A
Depicts a teenager who finally realizes that love, not aggressiveness, defines a man.
Prod-PAULST Dist-MEDIAG

Welcome Home, Stranger C 14 MIN
3/4 OR 1/2 INCH VIDEO CASSETTE A
Explains to Americans living abroad the personal reactions experienced upon returning to the United States and adjusting to American culture.
From The Going International Series.
LC NO. 84-706120
Prod-COPGRG Dist-COPGRG 1983

Welcome Mr President B 68 MIN
16MM FILM OPTICAL SOUND
Depicts President Kennedy's visit to Ireland.
Prod-CONSUI Dist-CONSUI

Welcome Spring C 18 MIN
3/4 OR 1/2 INCH VIDEO CASSETTE P-I
Distinguishes between beat and rhythm.
From The USS Rhythm Series.
Prod-ARKETV Dist-AITECH 1977

Welcome To Bangkok C 16 MIN
16MM FILM OPTICAL SOUND P-C A
Visits Bangkok, the capital of Thailand. Includes scenes of the city, temples, schools and people.
Prod-WSU Dist-WSU 1960

Welcome To Kennedy Space Center C 9 MIN
16MM FILM OPTICAL SOUND
Highlights a spaceport tour at the Kennedy Space Center in Florida.
Prod-FLADC Dist-FLADC

Welcome To Miami, Cubanos C 28 MIN
16MM FILM, 3/4 OR 1/2 IN VIDEO I-H
Shows how Mike, a high school student, has difficulty facing his Cuban heritage but must confront it and finally accept it when his cousin and his family stay at his house during their period of resettling in America.
Prod-LCOA Dist-LCOA 1981

Welcome To Our Party C 5 MIN
16MM FILM OPTICAL SOUND K-I
Portrays an insect community in puppet animation. Depicts a spirit of dance and celebration of nature.
From The Adventures In The High Grass Series.
LC NO. 74-702126
Prod-MMA Dist-MMA 1972

Welcome To Parenthood C 16 MIN
16MM FILM, 3/4 OR 1/2 IN VIDEO
Discusses the rewards and sacrifices of parenthood, presenting three young couples who describe the abrupt change in their lives after having children.
Prod-FLMLIB Dist-FLMLIB

Welcome To Spivey's Corner, N C C 17 MIN
16MM FILM, 3/4 OR 1/2 IN VIDEO
Describes life in Spivey's Corner, North Carolina, home of the National Hollerin' Contest. Interviews past hollerin' champions to explain the history and significance of this folk art.
Prod-PERSPF Dist-CORF 1978

Welcome To The Colloquium On The Bicentennial Of Medicine In The United States C 59 MIN
3/4 INCH VIDEO CASSETTE
Introduces the two-day Colloquium on the Bicentennial of Medicine in the United States. Highlights historical influences on American medicine and discusses the interplay of forces that contributed to an increase in federal support of biomedical research in the United States.
LC NO. 77-706051
Prod-NMAC Dist-USNAC 1976

Welcome To The Family C 25 MIN
16MM FILM OPTICAL SOUND
Depicts the role played by Alpha Beta Company in the lives of its employees and their families.
LC NO. 78-701332
Prod-ALPHAB Dist-SUNSET Prodn-SUNSET 1978

Welcome To The Farm C 14 MIN
3/4 OR 1/2 INCH VIDEO CASSETTE P
Shows how Uncle Estill demonstrates math's everyday usefulness.
From The Math Country Series.
Prod-KYTV Dist-AITECH 1979

Welcome To The Future - Computers In The Classroom C 28 MIN
16MM FILM, 3/4 OR 1/2 IN VIDEO T
Introduces computer literacy in the educational field including programming languages, pre-recorded software and the variety of ways computers can be used in schools. Illustrate how teachers and students can become computer literate.
From The Dealing With Social Problems In The Classroom Series.
Prod-MFFD Dist-FI 1983

Welcome To The Hospital Corps C 17 MIN
16MM FILM OPTICAL SOUND
Shows technical specialities for which hospital corps members may apply during their Navy careers and describes the training received at hospital corps schools and duty stations.
LC NO. 74-706605
Prod-USN Dist-USNAC 1972

Welcome To The USA C 13 MIN
16MM FILM OPTICAL SOUND C A
Follows immigration procedures from debarking at JFK Airport through immigrations, customs, to getting into Manhattan or making a connection to another airline.
Prod-MCDO Dist-MCDO 1970

Welcome To The Working Worlds C 17 MIN
16MM FILM OPTICAL SOUND I-J
Introduces the student to the concept of occupational clusters as a means of career exploration. Presents each of the 13 clusters in terms of its interrelated contribution to society as a whole.
From The Working Worlds Series.
Prod-OLYMPS Dist-COUNFI

Welcome To The World Of Work C 17 MIN
16MM FILM OPTICAL SOUND

Demonstrates the value of the summer work program in the Navy. Shows how supervisory training, orientation and meaningful work assignments are important to the program.
LC NO. 74-706322
Prod-USN Dist-USNAC 1970

Welcome To Yap C 58 MIN
3/4 OR 1/2 INCH VIDEO CASSETTE
Looks at the tiny island of Yap located in the south Pacific. Several years ago the United States extended aid to the country and critics claim that now it has become a welfare society whose people are abandoning their native culture.
From The World Series.
Prod-WGBHTV Dist-PBS 1980

Welcoming New Neighbors C 15 MIN
3/4 OR 1/2 INCH VIDEO CASSETTE P
Shows how to welcome new neighbors.
From The Neighborhoods Series.
Prod-NEITV Dist-GPITVL 1981

Welcoming Visitors C 15 MIN
3/4 OR 1/2 INCH VIDEO CASSETTE I
Deals with hospitality among Bedouin nomads.
From The Encounter In The Desert Series.
Prod-CTI Dist-CTI

Weld Defects - Causes And Corrections C 60 MIN
3/4 OR 1/2 INCH VIDEO CASSETTE IND
Covers weld defects and nondestructive testing.
From The Welding Training Series.
Prod-ITCORP Dist-ITCORP

Weld In Safety C 23 MIN
16MM FILM, 3/4 OR 1/2 IN VIDEO IND
Demonstrates safety measures for using gas welding or cutting equipment.
LC NO. 81-706543
Prod-STFD Dist-IFB 1980

Weld Joint Preparation And Temperature Control C
3/4 OR 1/2 INCH VIDEO CASSETTE IND
Discusses checks prior to weld joint preparation, joint preparation check, preheating and interpass heating, post weld heating and measurement of temperature.
From The Welding Inspection And Quality Control Series.
Prod-AMCEE Dist-AMCEE

Welded Beam, The, Pt A C 60 MIN
3/4 OR 1/2 INCH VIDEO CASSETTE
See series title for descriptive statement.
From The Engineering Design Optimization II Series. Pt 4
Prod-UAZMIC Dist-UAZMIC

Welded Beam, The, Pt B C 60 MIN
3/4 OR 1/2 INCH VIDEO CASSETTE
See series title for descriptive statement.
From The Engineering Design Optimization II Series. Pt 5
Prod-UAZMIC Dist-UAZMIC

Welder Certification C 19 MIN
1/2 IN VIDEO CASSETTE BETA/VHS IND
Explains and demonstrates the theory of welding, grinding, cutting and bending of weld test plates, using procedures in accordance with the American Welding Society for use of E6010 and E7018 electrodes.
Prod-RMI Dist-RMI

Welding C 13 MIN
16MM FILM, 3/4 OR 1/2 IN VIDEO H-C A
Welding equipment--setting up, lighting, shutting down, making a puddle, running a bead, adding fillerbrazing and cutting.
From The Metalwork - Hand Tools Series.
Prod-MORLAT Dist-SF 1967

Welding C 15 MIN
3/4 OR 1/2 INCH VIDEO CASSETTE
Covers steps in welding, types of welding and welding defects.
From The Manufacturing Materials And Processes Series.
Prod-GE Dist-WFVTAE

Welding - Metal Inert Gas Techniques C 13 MIN
16MM FILM, 3/4 OR 1/2 IN VIDEO H-C A
Explains the theory of MIG welding. Shows details of the equipment used and the functions of the various units, including power supplies. Demonstrates operating procedures in the making of butt and fillet welds with various metals.
From The Welding Series.
Prod-MORLAT Dist-SF 1969

Welding - MIG And TIG Welding--A Series
IND
Consists of three segments of 14 videotapes in each part, with each tape comprising 15 minutes of instruction. Amounts to a visual encyclopedia of facts and techniques of welding. Uses expert welders to promote excellence among students taking the course.
From The Welding - Shielded Metal-Arc Welding Series.
Prod-ICSINT Dist-ICSINT

Butt-Joint, T-Joint And Lap Joint With Dual
Butt-Joint, T-Joint, Lap Joint And Outside 015 MIN
Butt-Joint, T-Joint, Lap Joint And Outside 015 MIN
Multi Pass Welding With Dual Shielded 015 MIN
Safety And Equipment For Gas Shielded 015 MIN
Safety In Gas Tungsten Arc Welding 015 MIN
Selection Of Electrode, Gas, Cups, And 015 MIN
Setting Up Aluminum Wire Feed And Running 015 MIN
Setting Up And Padding Of The Inert-Gas 015 MIN
Setting Up Flux Cored Wire And Running 015 MIN
Submerged Arc Welding 015 MIN
Welding Aluminum With Inert Gas Tungsten Arc 015 MIN
Welding Mild Steel With Inert Gas Tungsten Arc 015 MIN
Welding Stainless Steel With Inert Gas 015 MIN

Welding - Oxy-Acetylene Welding--A Series
IND
Consists of three segments of 14 videotapes in each part, with each tape comprising 15 minutes of instruction. Amounts to a visual encyclopedia of facts and techniques of welding. Uses expert welders to promote excellence among students taking the course.
Prod-ICSINT Dist-ICSINT

Automatic Flame Cutting With Oxy-Acetylene 015 MIN
Brazing And Fusion Welding Of Grey Cast Iron 015 MIN
Bronze Welding In Flat And Horizontal 015 MIN
Cutting Metal With The Combustion Torch 015 MIN
Flat And Horizontal Butt Welds With Filler Rod 015 MIN
Joint Design And Welding Terms 015 MIN
Oxy-Acetylene Welding T-Joints, Lap Joints, 015 MIN
Piercing, Cutting Holes And Cutting 45 Degree 015 MIN
Puddling And Running Beads With Oxy-Acetylene 015 MIN
Set Up And Shut Down Of Oxy-Acetylene 015 MIN
Silver Brazing And Soft Soldering 015 MIN
Three Types Of Oxy-Acetylene Flames, The 015 MIN
Vertical And Overhead Butt Welds With Filler 015 MIN
Welding Equipment, Accessories And Shop Safety 015 MIN

Welding - Pipe Welding Techniques C 13 MIN
16MM FILM, 3/4 OR 1/2 IN VIDEO J A
Shows in detail the preparation of joints for arc welding and proper use of the body in making a weld. Demonstrates all the aspects of downhill and uphill welding and roll and vertical welding. Gives examples of pipe welding in industry and checking with X-rays.
From The Welding Series.
Prod-SF Dist-SF 1969

Welding - Shielded Metal-Arc Welding--A Series
IND
Consists of three segments of 14 videotapes in each part, with each tape comprising 15 minutes of instruction. Amounts to a visual encyclopedia of facts and techniques of welding. Uses expert welders to promote excellence among students taking the course.
Prod-ICSINT Dist-ICSINT

Carbon-Arc Cutting 015 MIN
Electric-Arc Power Sources And Minor 015 MIN
Electric-Arc Welding In Flat, Horizontal 015 MIN
Multi-Pass Electric-Arc Welding 015 MIN
Running Continuous Bead In Horizontal And 015 MIN
Running Continuous Beads In Vertical Up And 015 MIN
Safety In Electric-Arc Welding And Terms 015 MIN
Selection Of Electrodes For Shielded 015 MIN
Striking An Arc, Restarting The Arc And 015 MIN
T-Joint, Lap Joint, Outside Corner Joint In 015 MIN
T-Joint, Lap Joint, Outside Corner Joint In A 015 MIN
T-Joint, Lap Joint, Outside Corner Joint In A 015 MIN
T-Joint, Lap Joint, Outside Corner, Joint In 015 MIN
Welding Cast Iron In Flat Position With 015 MIN

Welding Aluminum With Inert Gas Tungsten Arc C 15 MIN
3/4 OR 1/2 INCH VIDEO CASSETTE IND
See series title for descriptive statement.
From The Welding - MIG And TIG Welding Series.
Prod-ICSINT Dist-ICSINT

Welding Aluminum With Inert Gas Tungsten Arc (Spanish) C
3/4 OR 1/2 INCH VIDEO CASSETTE
See series title for descriptive statement.
From The MIG And TIG Welding (Spanish) Series.
Prod-VTRI Dist-VTRI

Welding Aluminum With MIG And TIG C 28 MIN
16MM FILM OPTICAL SOUND J-C A
Highlights the importance of joint design cleaning and proper adjustment of welding equipment with MIG (metal inert gas) and TIG (tungsten inert gas). Includes slow motion footage of MIG and TIG.
LC NO. 76-702321
Prod-REYMC Dist-REYMC 1968

Welding And Cutting Processes, I C
3/4 OR 1/2 INCH VIDEO CASSETTE IND
Includes choosing the welding process, imperfections and discontinuities, oxyacetylene welding, brazing, arc-welding processes, SMAW, GMAW, FCAW, GTAW, SAW, stud welding, electroslag welding, thermal cutting and mechanical cutting.
From The Welding Inspection And Quality Control Series.
Prod-AMCEE Dist-AMCEE

Welding And Cutting Processes, II C
3/4 OR 1/2 INCH VIDEO CASSETTE IND
Covers electrogas welding, plasma arc welding, resistance welding, flash welding, upset welding, percussion welding, solid state welding, electron and laser beam welding, thermal welding, welding of plastics, soldering and adhesive bonding.
From The Welding Inspection And Quality Control Series.
Prod-AMCEE Dist-AMCEE

Welding And Joining Symbols C 12 MIN
3/4 OR 1/2 INCH VIDEO CASSETTE
Covers welding, joints, symbols, placement of welds, special symbols and reading welding symbols.
From The Reading Schematics And Symbols Series.
Prod-TPCTRA Dist-TPCTRA

Welding And Joining Symbols (Spanish) C 12 MIN
3/4 OR 1/2 INCH VIDEO CASSETTE
Covers welding, joints, symbols, placement of welds, special symbols and reading welding symbols.
From The Reading Schematics And Symbols Series.
Prod-TPCTRA Dist-TPCTRA

Welding Bandsaw Blades C 22 MIN
1/2 IN VIDEO CASSETTE BETA/VHS IND
See series title for descriptive statement.
From The Machine Shop - Bandsaw Series.
Prod-RMI Dist-RMI

Welding By Tape C 8 MIN
16MM FILM OPTICAL SOUND
Shows an installation used for developing automatically-controlled welding.
Prod-UKAEA Dist-UKAEA 1964

Welding Cast Iron In Flat Position With Electric Arc, Hard Facing Surfaces...(Spanish) C
3/4 OR 1/2 INCH VIDEO CASSETTE
Discusses welding cast iron in flat position and hard facing surfaces with electric arc.
From The Shielded Metal Arc Welding (Spanish) Series.
Prod-VTRI Dist-VTRI

Welding Cast Iron In Flat Position With Electric-Arc, Hard Facing Surfaces With... C 15 MIN
3/4 OR 1/2 INCH VIDEO CASSETTE IND
Discusses welding cast iron in flat position with electric-arc, hard facing surfaces with electric-arc.
From The Welding - Shielded Metal-Arc Welding Series.
Prod-ICSINT Dist-ICSINT

Welding Cast Iron In Flat Position With-Electric Arc C 15 MIN
3/4 OR 1/2 INCH VIDEO CASSETTE
See series title for descriptive statement.
From The Welding II - Basic Shielded Metal Arc Welding series.
Prod-CAMB Dist-CAMB

Welding Engineering - Principles And Applications--A Series
IND
Covers understanding and application of basic metallurgy, selecting the best welding process and material for a given application, engineering the weld and controlling the welding process and results, avoiding weld failures and minimizing costs thermal damage and distortion of weldments.
Prod-NCSU Dist-AMCEE

Welding Equipment, Accessories And Shop Safety (Spanish) C
3/4 OR 1/2 INCH VIDEO CASSETTE
See series title for descriptive statement.
From The Oxy-Acetylene Welding (Spanish) Series.
Prod-VTRI Dist-VTRI

Welding Equipment, Accessories And Shop Safety C 15 MIN
3/4 OR 1/2 INCH VIDEO CASSETTE
See series title for descriptive statement.
From The Welding I - Basic Oxy-Acetylene Welding Series.
Prod-CAMB Dist-CAMB

Welding Equipment, Accessories And Shop Safety C 15 MIN
3/4 OR 1/2 INCH VIDEO CASSETTE IND
See series title for descriptive statement.
From The Welding - Oxy-Acetylene Welding Series.
Prod-ICSINT Dist-ICSINT

Welding I - Basic Oxy-Acetylene Welding--A Series

Presents a hands-on approach to vocational training with lessons in basic oxy-acetylene welding.
Prod-CAMB Dist-CAMB

Automatic Flame Cutting With Oxy-Acetylene 015 MIN
Brazing Cast Iron With Oxy-Acetylene 015 MIN
Bronze Welding (Grazing) In Flat And 015 MIN
Cutting Round Holes And Piercing Holes With A 015 MIN
Flatt Butt And Horizontal Butt Welds With 015 MIN
Joint Design And Welding Terms 015 MIN
Pudding And Running Beads With Oxy-Acetylen e- 015 MIN
Set-up And Shut Down Of Oxy-Acetylene Welding 015 MIN
Setup Of The Combination Torch And Cutting Of 015 MIN
Silver Brazing And Soft Soldering With Oxy 015 MIN
Three Types Of Oxy-Acetylene Flames, The 015 MIN
Using Oxy-Acetylen Torch For Heating Metal, 015 MIN
Vertical Butt And Overhead Butt Welds With 015 MIN
Welding Equipment, Accessories And Shop Safety 015 MIN

Welding II - Basic Shielded Metal Arc Welding--A Series

Presents basic shielded metal arc welding with a hands-on approach to vocational training. Includes many aspects of the process in detail.
Prod-CAMB Dist-CAMB

Carbon Arc Cutting And Carbon Arc Brazing 015 MIN
Characteristics In The Use Of Electric Arc 015 MIN
Hard Facing Surfaces With Electric Arc 015 MIN
Multi Pass Electric Arc Weldin g- 015 MIN
Perform Minor Maintenance Of Welding Equipment 015 MIN
Procedures For Using Shop Equipment And Hand 015 MIN
Running Continuous Beads FLat Position 015 MIN
Safety In Electric-Arc Welding 015 MIN
Selection Of Electrodes For Arc Welding 015 MIN
Setup Electric-Arc Welding 015 MIN
T-Joint, Lap Joint, And Outside Corner Welds 015 MIN
Vertical Butt And Overhead Butt Welds With 015 MIN
Welding Cast Iron In Flat Position With 015 MIN

Welding III - TIG And MIG (Industry) Welding--A Series

Presents a hands-on approach to vocational training in welding, including equipment and safety.
Prod-CAMB Dist-CAMB

Aluminum Welding With Mig In Flat And
Equipment And Safety For Gas Tungsten Are 015 MIN
Making A T-Joint, Lap Joint And Outside 015 MIN
Making Vertical Butt, Overhead Butt Welds 015 MIN
Running Continuous Beads Flat Position, Flat 015 MIN
Running Continuous Beads Flat Position, Flat 015 MIN
Running Continuous Beads Flat Position, Flat 015 MIN
Safety And Equipment For Gas Shielded Arc 015 MIN
Selection Of Electrode, Gas, Cups And Filler 015 MIN
Selection Of Wire Type And Diameter For (MIG) 015 MIN
T-Joint, Lab Joint, Outside Corner - All 015 MIN
Using Dual Shield, Flux Core Wire For Flat 015 MIN
Vertical Butt And Overhead Butt (MIG) Welding 015 MIN

Welding Inspection And Quality Control—A Series
PRO
Provides a fundamental understanding of welding inspection and quality control.
Prod-AMCEE Dist-AMCEE

Chemical, Metallurgical And Mechanical
Codes Governing Welding Inspection 000 MIN
Eddy Current Inspection, Acoustic Emissions, 000 MIN
Magnetic Particle And Radiographic Inspection 000 MIN
Metric Systems, Welding Terms And Symbols 000 MIN
Ultrasonic Inspection 000 MIN
Visual And Liquid Penetrant Inspection 000 MIN
Weld Joint Preparation And Temperature Control 000 MIN
Welding And Cutting Process, Pt I 000 MIN
Welding And Cutting Process, Pt II 000 MIN
Welding Inspector 000 MIN
Welding Metallurgy 000 MIN
Welding Procedures And Welding Operator 000 MIN
Weldment Imperfections And Discontinuities 000 MIN

Welding Inspector C
3/4 OR 1/2 INCH VIDEO CASSETTE PRO
Describes the welding inspector, including qualifications and responsibilities.
From The Welding Inspection And Quality Control Series.
Prod-AMCEE Dist-AMCEE

Welding Machine Set-Up And Operation Miller 35 Wire Feed C 9 MIN
1/2 IN VIDEO CASSETTE BETA/VHS IND
Explains the set-up for a Miller 35 wire feed welder.
Prod-RMI Dist-RMI

Welding Metallurgy C
3/4 OR 1/2 INCH VIDEO CASSETTE PRO
Discusses welding metallurgy, including diffusion, transformation and microstructure.
From The Welding Inspection And Quality Control Series.
Prod-AMCEE Dist-AMCEE

Welding Mild Steel With Inert Gas Tungsten Arc (Spanish) C
3/4 OR 1/2 INCH VIDEO CASSETTE
See series title for descriptive statement.
From The MIG And TIG Welding (Spanish) Series.
Prod-VTRI Dist-VTRI

Welding Mild Steel With Inert Gas Tungsten Arc C 15 MIN
3/4 OR 1/2 INCH VIDEO CASSETTE IND
See series title for descriptive statement.
From The Welding - MIG And TIG Welding Series.
Prod-ICSINT Dist-ICSINT

Welding Of Carbon Steel Pipe C 37 MIN
3/4 OR 1/2 INCH VIDEO CASSETTE IND
Provides training to performance qualify to ASME code requirements using SMAW for all positions on pressure piping and vessels.
From The Advanced Welding Series
Prod-TAT Dist-TAT

Welding Of Low Alloy Steel Pipe C 34 MIN
3/4 OR 1/2 INCH VIDEO CASSETTE IND
Discusses code requirements for welding low-alloy steel pipe. Develops and proves manipulative skills through testing.
From The Advanced Arc Welding Series.
Prod-TAT Dist-TAT

Welding Of Stainless Steel Pipe C 20 MIN
3/4 OR 1/2 INCH VIDEO CASSETTE IND
Covers welding with 18 percent chrome and 8 percent nickel stainless steel pipe.
From The Advanced Arc Welding Series.
Prod-TAT Dist-TAT

Welding Procedures - Oxygen Cutting—A Series

Prod-USOE Dist-USNAC 1944

Manual Cutting A Bevel - Freehand 013 MIN
Manual Cutting A Shape - Freehand Guided 016 MIN
Manual Cutting To A Line - Freehand 021 MIN

Welding Procedures And Welding Operator Qualifications C
3/4 OR 1/2 INCH VIDEO CASSETTE IND
Discusses welding procedure specifications, joint designs, welding positions, heat input, preheat and interpass temperatures, removal of weld sections for repair, post heat treatment, prequalification procedures, welder qualification requirements, testing qualification welds and NDT requirements.
From The Welding Inspection And Quality Control Series.
Prod-AMCEE Dist-AMCEE

Welding Stainless Steel With Inert Gas Tungsten Arc (Spanish) C
3/4 OR 1/2 INCH VIDEO CASSETTE
See series title for descriptive statement.
From The MIG And TIG Welding (Spanish) Series.
Prod-VTRI Dist-VTRI

Welding Stainless Steel With Inert Gas Tungsten Arc C 15 MIN
3/4 OR 1/2 INCH VIDEO CASSETTE IND
See series title for descriptive statement.
From The Welding - MIG And TIG Welding Series.
Prod-ICSINT Dist-ICSINT

Welding Tips And Techniques C 13 MIN
3/4 OR 1/2 INCH VIDEO CASSETTE IND
See series title for descriptive statement.
From The Electric Arc Welding Series. Chapter 9
Prod-TAT Dist-TAT

Welding Training (Comprehensive) - Oxy-Acetylene Welding—A Series
IND
Contains units of basic fusion welding, brazing and flame cutting.
Prod-RMI Dist-RMI

Bevel Machine Cutting 004 MIN
Cast Iron Fusion Weld 008 MIN
Cast Iron V-Butt Bronze 011 MIN
Cutting Gauge Materials Manual 004 MIN
Hole Cutting Manual 003 MIN
Inside Corner Joint 008 MIN
Lap Weld 007 MIN
Ninety Degree Machine Cutting 004 MIN
Open Corner Joint 005 MIN
Oxy-Acetylene Equipment Set-Up And Safety 033 MIN
Plate Cutting Manual 008 MIN
Square Butt Aluminum 005 MIN
Square Butt Backhand 007 MIN
Square Butt Bronze 006 MIN
Square Butt Horizontal 006 MIN
Square Butt Joint Filler Rod 006 MIN
Square Butt Silver Bronze 004 MIN
Square Butt Vertical-Up 006 MIN
Stringer Bead 007 MIN
T Joint Aluminum Braze 005 MIN
Vee Butt Joint 012 MIN

Welding Training (Comprehensive) - Advanced Shielded Metal Arc Welding—A Series
IND
Continues Basic Arc Welding. Deals with E6010 and E7018 electrodes in the horizontal, vertical up and overhead welds.
Prod-RMI Dist-RMI

All Position Fillet Test 018 MIN
Arc Air Cutting 004 MIN
Horizontal Lap Weld 005 MIN
Horizontal V-Butt Weld 011 MIN
Overhead Fillet Weld 008 MIN
Overhead V-Butt Weld 009 MIN
Vertical Up Butt Weld 008 MIN
Vertical Up Fillet Weld 008 MIN

Welding Training (Comprehensive) - Basic Shielded Metal Arc Welding—A Series
IND
Develops manipulative welding skills, using industrial equipment, and demonstrates common types of weld joints used in welding fabrication and repair. Provides a basic understanding of arc welding, beginning with electrode classifications and progressing on to vertical down fillet welds.
Prod-RMI Dist-RMI

Arc Welding Safety 010 MIN
Butt Joint Whip 006 MIN
Electrode Identification 011 MIN
Lap Joint 004 MIN
Square Butt Joint Single-Pass 006 MIN
T Joint 012 MIN
T Joint - Multi-Pass Weave 006 MIN
T Joint - 3-Pass Stringer 007 MIN
V-Butt Joint Multi-Pass 013 MIN
Vertical Down Fillet 006 MIN

Welding Training (Comprehensive) - Metal Inert Gas (M I G) Welding—A Series
IND
Provides experience in typical welding applications, including all-position welding using base metals of mild steel, stainless steel and aluminum. Demonstrates Metal Inert Gas (M I G) welding equipment similar to industrial applications, requiring push guns for hard wires and push-pull guns for soft wires.
Prod-RMI Dist-RMI

Fillet Weld Horizontal (Aluminum) 005 MIN
Fillet Weld Overhead 002 MIN
Introduction To Flux-Cored-G M A W 009 MIN
Introduction To G M A W 010 MIN
Lap Joint V-Down 002 MIN
Multi-Pass Fillet 004 MIN
Multi-Pass Fillet Flat (Steel) 005 MIN
Multi-Pass Fillet V-Up 003 MIN
Single Pass Fillet 003 MIN
Single Pass Fillet (Vertical Down) 002 MIN
Square Butt Joint 002 MIN
Square Butt Joint Flat 002 MIN
Square Butt Joint Flat (Aluminum) 002 MIN
V-Butt Joint 003 MIN
V-Butt Joint Horizontal 002 MIN

Welding Training (Comprehensive) - Tungsten Inert Gas (T I G) Welding—A Series
IND
Contains weld exercises on aluminum and stainless metals using argon shielding gas. Discusses weld joints, made in the positions of flat, horizontal and vertical.
Prod-RMI Dist-RMI

Corner Joint A1 Open 003 MIN
Corner Weld Stainless 002 MIN
Inside Corner Joint A1 004 MIN
Introduction To T I G Welding 019 MIN
Lap Weld A1 003 MIN
Square Butt A1 002 MIN
Square Butt Joint Aluminum With Fixture 004 MIN
Square Butt Joint Stainless 004 MIN
Square Butt Joint Stainless Vertical-Up 002 MIN
Square Butt Stainless With Fixture 004 MIN

Welding Training—A Series
IND
Encompasses a comprehensive, 12-hour course in all aspects of welding. Begins with principles and metallurgy, and joint designs and symbols. Goes into general techniques and safety practices, then illustrates major techniques of cutting, brazing and other main principles of metals bonding.
Prod-ITCORP Dist-ITCORP

Brazing And Braze Welding 060 MIN
Cutting - Plasma Arc And Carbon Arc 060 MIN
General Techniques And Safety Practices 060 MIN
Joint Design And Symbols 060 MIN
Oxygen-Fuel Gas Cutting 060 MIN
Principles And Metallurgy 060 MIN
Principles And Techniques Of MIG 060 MIN
Principles Of TIG 060 MIN
Shielded Metal-Arc Structural And Pipe Welding 060 MIN
Shielded Metal-Arc Welding Principles 060 MIN
TIG Structural And Pipe Welding 060 MIN
Weld Defects - Causes And Corrections 060 MIN

Welding—A Series
16MM FILM, 3/4 OR 1/2 IN VIDEO
Prod-UCC Dist-FI 1972

Air-Acetylene Flame, The 012 MIN
Flame Cutting 011 MIN
Flame Grooving 010 MIN
Flat And Horizontal Welding 012 MIN
Fusion Welding 011 MIN
Fusion Welding Of Light Gauge Steel 010 MIN
Hard Facing 010 MIN
Heliarc (TIG) Welding Introduction To Manual 008 MIN
Heliarc Welding Of Carbon Steel Pipes 010 MIN
Oxy-Acetylene Welding And Cutting - Braze 013 MIN
Setting Up For Welding 012 MIN
Vertical And Overhead Welding 010 MIN

Weldment Imperfections And Discontinuities C
3/4 OR 1/2 INCH VIDEO CASSETTE IND
Covers classifications of discontinuities, base metal discontinuities, methods of testing and glossary of weld imperfections.
From The Welding Inspection And Quality Control Series.
Prod-AMCEE Dist-AMCEE

Welfare C 167 MIN
16MM FILM, 3/4 OR 1/2 IN VIDEO
Examines the nature and complexity of the welfare system by sequences illustrating the diversity of problems that constitute welfare, such as housing, unemployment, divorce, medical and psychiatric problems, abandoned and abused children and the elderly.
Prod-WISEF Dist-ZIPRAH

Welfare Dilemma, The C 30 MIN
3/4 OR 1/2 INCH VIDEO CASSETTE H-C A
Presents Sar A Levitan, professor of economics, and Marvin Bloom, professor of social work, exploring the strengths and weaknesses of many welfare programs. Examines whether the government is financially overextended, whether the people who really need welfare programs benefit, and what improvements are needed.
From The Ethics In America Series.
Prod-AMHUMA Dist-AMHUMA

Welfare Mothers C 28 MIN
3/4 INCH VIDEO CASSETTE J-C A
Presents women welfare recipients describing the problems of the welfare system.
From The Are You Listening Series.
LC NO. 80-707154
Prod-STURTM Dist-STURTM 1971

Welfare Revolt, The B 60 MIN
16MM FILM OPTICAL SOUND H-C A
Documents complaints of welfare recipients and their attempts to change the system by organizing local unions. Discusses the unions' goals and describes the federal government's emphasis on training programs. Shows protest marches in Cleveland and Washington, D C.
From The Net Journal Series.
LC NO. FIA68-504
Prod-NET Dist-IU 1968

Well Being Of The Organization, The C 13 MIN
3/4 OR 1/2 INCH VIDEO CASSETTE
Covers some of the symptoms of unhealthy organizations and how they get that way. Illustrates the point that office development can help solve specific organizational deficiences.
From The Organization Development Series. Module 1
Prod-RESEM Dist-RESEM

Well Completion C 40 MIN
3/4 OR 1/2 INCH VIDEO CASSETTE IND
See series title for descriptive statement.
From The Basic And Petroleum Geology For Non-Geologists - Drilling And...-Series.
Prod-PHILLP Dist-GPCV

Well Completions C 22 MIN
3/4 OR 1/2 INCH VIDEO CASSETTE IND
Covers the planning of completions, production-method operations and workover options.
Prod-UTEXPE Dist-UTEXPE 1972

Well Control Operations - Instructions On Drilling Fluids For Derrickmen C 20 MIN
3/4 OR 1/2 INCH VIDEO CASSETTE IND
Gives general instructions on drilling fluids with emphasis on density, viscosity, fluid loss, salinity, gas cutting and general procedures for increasing mud density.
Prod-UTEXPE Dist-UTEXPE 1983

Well Control Operations - Instructions On Warning Signs Of Kicks For Rotary Helpers C 23 MIN
3/4 OR 1/2 INCH VIDEO CASSETTE IND
Gives instructions on the more obvious warning signs of a kick. Includes a gain in pit volume, increase in mud return rate, hole not taking the proper amount of mud, and trip, connection and background gas changes. Designed for use by derrickmen as well as rotary helpers.
Prod-UTEXPE Dist-UTEXPE 1979

Well Control Operations - Instructions On General Well-Killing Procedures For Derrickmen C 25 MIN
3/4 OR 1/2 INCH VIDEO CASSETTE IND
Provides general instructions in the procedures for killing a well that has kicked, including the driller's method and the wait-and-weight method.
Prod-UTEXPE Dist-UTEXPE 1981

Well Control Operations - Instructions On Blowout Prevention Equipment For Rotary... C 27 MIN
3/4 OR 1/2 INCH VIDEO CASSETTE IND
Gives instructions on the purpose, operation and general maintenance of the annular blowout prevention, diverter system ram-type preventer, accumulator system, drill string inside BOP, drill string safety valve, kelly cock and adjustable choke. Designed for use by rotary helpers and derrickmen.
Prod-UTEXPE Dist-UTEXPE 1979

Well Control Operations - Instructions On OCS Training Requirements For Rotary Helpers C 6 MIN
3/4 OR 1/2 INCH VIDEO CASSETTE IND
Covers governmental regulations that are pertinent to work of rotary helpers and derrickmen on offshore drilling areas of the continental shelf of the United States.
Prod-UTEXPE Dist-UTEXPE 1979

Well In West Virginia, A C 15 MIN
16MM FILM OPTICAL SOUND
Illustrates the work and excitement of drilling for natural gas. Shows how geologists and engineers employing principles which are useful in the science class, locate the site, drill to the proper depth and penetrate through earth and rock to the gas deposits.
LC NO. 74-702680
Prod-AGA Dist-FINLYS Prodn-FINLYS 1974

Well Logging C 40 MIN
3/4 OR 1/2 INCH VIDEO CASSETTE IND
See series title for descriptive statement.
From The Petroleum Geology Series.
Prod-GPCV Dist-GPCV

Well Logging - Answers From Beneath The Ground C 23 MIN
16MM FILM, 3/4 OR 1/2 IN VIDEO IND
Explains the various well logging instruments. Describes the methods, uses and techniques of well logging.
Prod-UTEXPE Dist-UTEXPE 1978

Well Logging Fundamentals C 25 MIN
3/4 OR 1/2 INCH VIDEO CASSETTE IND
Looks at electrical, acoustic and radioactivity logging.
Prod-UTEXPE Dist-UTEXPE 1974

Well Logging Interpretation C 58 MIN
3/4 OR 1/2 INCH VIDEO CASSETTE IND
See series title for descriptive statement.
From The Basic And Petroleum Geology For Non-Geologists - Reservoirs And...--Series.
Prod-PHILLP Dist-GPCV

Well Logging Mechanics C 40 MIN
3/4 OR 1/2 INCH VIDEO CASSETTE IND
See series title for descriptive statement.
From The Basic And Petroleum Geology For Non-Geologists - Reservoirs And...--Series.
Prod-PHILLP Dist-GPCV

Well Model And Lift C 11 MIN
16MM FILM, 3/4 OR 1/2 IN VIDEO IND
See series title for descriptive statement.
From The Gas Lift Series.
Prod-EXXON Dist-UTEXPE

Well Of The Saints, The C 40 MIN
16MM FILM, 3/4 OR 1/2 IN VIDEO H-C A
Presents The Well Of The Saints by J M Synge, a traditional Irish folk drama with the satiric theme that sometimes it is better to preserve one's illusions than to face reality.
From The Humanities - Short Play Showcase Series.
Prod-EBEC Dist-EBEC 1976

Well Of The World's End, The C 27 MIN
16MM FILM, 3/4 OR 1/2 IN VIDEO
Presents the Scottish tale of a girl who is sent by her stepmother to get water from a well using a sieve. Relates that she is helped at this task by a frog who then makes many demands. Reveals that the frog then turns into a handsome prince whom she marries.
From The Storybook International Series.
Prod-JOU Dist-JOU 1982

Well Spent Life, A C 44 MIN
16MM FILM - 3/4 IN VIDEO J-C A
Captures the blues music of Mance Lipscomb, Black songster, sharecropper and sage. Visits Lipscomb in his hometown of Navasota, Texas, where he communicates his thoughts and feelings about his past and the local life and culture. Issued in 1971 as a motion picture.
LC NO. 79-707414
Prod-FLOWER Dist-FLOWER 1979

Well, The C 18 MIN
3/4 OR 1/2 INCH VIDEO CASSETTE IND
States the methods by which a well is drilled, produced and abandoned.
Prod-UTEXPE Dist-UTEXPE

Well, The - Flowing, Dead And Unloading C 13 MIN
16MM FILM, 3/4 OR 1/2 IN VIDEO IND
See series title for descriptive statement.
From The Gas Lift Series.
Prod-EXXON Dist-UTEXPE

Well, We Are Alive B 30 MIN
3/4 INCH VIDEO CASSETTE
Explores the attitudes of family, friends and society toward older people. Focuses on such issues as living on a fixed income, coping with the social services maze, physical and mental difficulties, self-image and societal emphasis on women.
Prod-WMEN Dist-WMEN

Well, Well, Well With Slim Goodbody—A Series
P
Prod-AITECH Dist-AITECH

Choosing Food Wisely	015 MIN
Cleanliness	015 MIN
Doctor/Patient Team, The	015 MIN
Emergencies And Finding Help	015 MIN
Exercise	015 MIN
First Aid And Medicine	015 MIN
Food For Energy And Growth	015 MIN
Healthy Community, The	015 MIN
Indoor Safety	015 MIN
Mental Health	015 MIN
Outside Safety	015 MIN
Senses, The	015 MIN
Sleep, Stress And Relaxation	015 MIN
Wellness	015 MIN
You Are Special	015 MIN

Wellhead Operations C 23 MIN
3/4 OR 1/2 INCH VIDEO CASSETTE IND
Introduces gas field operators to routing wellhead operations such as turning the well on or off and performing daily maintenance checks. Includes instructions on how to identify and correct common well head malfunctions such as freezes in the production line, tubing, or wellhead and fluid build-up in the wellbore.
Prod-UTEXPE Dist-UTEXPE 1981

Wellman-Lord / Allied Chemical Flue Gas Desulfurization Process C 13 MIN
16MM FILM OPTICAL SOUND
Describes the flue gas desulfurization system being demonstrated by the Environmental Protection Agency and Northern Indiana Public Services Company. Provides an overview of the sulfur dioxide problem and examines the equipment and chemistry involved in the process.
LC NO. 78-701896
Prod-USEPA Dist-USNAC Prodn-CENTF 1978

Wellmet House B 30 MIN
16MM FILM OPTICAL SOUND H-C A
Explains that the objective is not to gain conforming behavior but to help patients relate to other people in natural and unstructured ways and for the patients this means finding individual ways of expressing themselves.
From The To Save Tomorrow Series.
Prod-NET Dist-IU

Wellness C 15 MIN
3/4 OR 1/2 INCH VIDEO CASSETTE P
Tells children they're the best at taking care of themselves because they're always there. Includes a song of wellness, of being the best one can be.
From The Well, Well, Well With Slim Goodbody Series.
Prod-AITECH Dist-AITECH

Wellness In The Workplace C 24 MIN
16MM FILM, 3/4 OR 1/2 IN VIDEO PRO
Demonstrates how to strengthen a prime resource people. Features corporation executives who evaluate how employee wellness has affected company productivity and morale.
Prod-PRORE Dist-PRORE

Wellness In The Workplace C 24 MIN
3/4 OR 1/2 INCH VIDEO CASSETTE
Broadens the concept of fitness and health in the work setting. Delivers a helpful understanding of the key components of a wellness program.
From The Survival Of The Fittest Series.
Prod-SCCL Dist-HMDI

Wellness Lifestyle, The C 30 MIN
3/4 OR 1/2 INCH VIDEO CASSETTE H-C A
Presents information to help in assessing a person's health attitudes. Demonstrates a variety of techniques for handling everyday sources of stress, maintaining good working conditions and assuring proper nutrition.
From The Planning For Wellness System Series.
Prod-ABCVID Dist-MTI 1983

Wellness Revolution, The C 28 MIN
16MM FILM OPTICAL SOUND
Discusses the importance of choosing healthful lifestyles. Includes professional tips on stress management techniques, nutrition, exercises for all stages of life, available support groups and various other physical activities.
Prod-JHI Dist-MTP

Wellness-Investing In Your Health C 28 MIN
3/4 OR 1/2 INCH VIDEO CASSETTE
From The What It Means To Be Healthy Series.
Prod-RCOMTV Dist-SYLWAT 1982

Wellness, It's Not Magic C 15 MIN
3/4 OR 1/2 INCH VIDEO CASSETTE K-P
Uses puppets to explain to the overweight Wicked Witch of the Woods the importance of nutrition and exercise. Shows the four basic foods and the fun of exercising.
LC NO. 81-707650
Prod-KIDSCO Dist-KIDSCO 1981

Wells And Wellhead Equipment C 18 MIN
3/4 OR 1/2 INCH VIDEO CASSETTE IND
Introduces the well to field operators and other entry-level personnel. Teaches the basic principles of petroleum formation and accumulation, drilling and recovery procedures, casing installation and the function and assembly of a typical wellhead.
Prod-UTEXPE Dist-UTEXPE 1981

Wells, Ida B C 30 MIN
3/4 INCH VIDEO CASSETTE
Dramatizes the life of Ida B Wells, a black American who fought for the rights of blacks and women.
From The American Women - Echoes And Dreams Series.
Prod-OHC Dist-HRC

Wellsprings C 59 MIN
16MM FILM OPTICAL SOUND
Features a documentary on the importance of coastal wetlands to marine ecology as exemplified by the mangrove swamps of Florida. Shows the human side of oceanographic research with studies of scientists documenting the need to preserve coastal estuaries.
LC NO. 76-702914
Prod-WPBTTV Dist-WPBTTV 1976

Wendell Berry C 29 MIN
3/4 INCH VIDEO CASSETTE
See series title for descriptive statement.
From The Poets Talking Series.
Prod-UMITV Dist-UMITV 1975

Wendell Willkie B 26 MIN
16MM FILM, 3/4 OR 1/2 IN VIDEO H A
Uses rare actuality footage to portray the personal life and history-making deeds of Wendell Willkie.
From The Biography Series.
Prod-WOLPER Dist-SF 1965

Wendell Willkie - Of Perfect Loyalty B 15 MIN
1/2 IN VIDEO CASSETTE BETA/VHS
Tells how Wendel Willkie, Republican candidate for President of the United States, planted the seed that developed into the United Nations.
Prod-STAR Dist-STAR

Were You There?—A Series
16MM FILM, 3/4 OR 1/2 IN VIDEO
Profiles significant black Americans throughout black history in the United States.
Prod-NGUZO Dist-BCNFL 1982

Black West, The	030 MIN
Cotton Club, The	029 MIN
Facts Of Life, The	028 MIN
Oscar Micheaux, Film Pioneer	029 MIN
Portrait Of Two Artists	029 MIN
Sports Profile	029 MIN
When The Animals Talked	028 MIN

Werner Herzog Eats His Shoe C 20 MIN
16MM FILM, 3/4 OR 1/2 IN VIDEO H-C A
Documents Werner Herzog's strongly expressed belief that people must have the guts to attempt what they dream of.
Prod-BLNKL Dist-FLOWER 1980

Wernher Von Braun B 26 MIN
16MM FILM, 3/4 OR 1/2 IN VIDEO I-H
Uses rare actuality footage to portray the personal life and history-making deeds of Wernher von Braun.
From The History Makers Of The 20th Century Series.
Prod-WOLPER Dist-SF 1965

Wertheim-Meigs Hysterectomy With Pelvic Lymphadectomy C 29 MIN
16MM FILM OPTICAL SOUND PRO
Points out that this operation is the optimum choice in surgery for cancer of cervix in stages one and two-A. Stresses an extensive dissection of the para-cervical and para-vaginal tissues.
Prod-ACYDGD Dist-ACY 1970

Wes Montgomery C 30 MIN
2 INCH VIDEOTAPE
Presents the jazz music of Wes Montgomery. Features host Jim Rockwell interviewing the artist.
From The People In Jazz Series.
Prod-WTVSTV Dist-PUBTEL

WES Story, The C 14 MIN
16MM FILM OPTICAL SOUND
Shows how the Waterways Experiment Station in Mississippi grew from a small hydraulic laboratory to become the principal and most diverse research, testing and development center for Corps of Engineers research in the field of civil engineering.

LC NO. 75-700594
Prod-USAE Dist-USNAC 1969

Wesley And His Times C 15 MIN
3/4 OR 1/2 INCH VIDEO CASSETTE J-C A
Examines how the Wesleyan movement was founded and grew in England. Discusses the parallel implications between the social problems of Wesley's England and those of today. Comprises an excerpt from the motion picture John Wesley.
Prod-TRAFCO Dist-ECUFLM 1970

Wesley, Charles C 29 MIN
3/4 INCH VIDEO CASSETTE
Discusses the past, present and future of Wilberforce University and Central State University.
From The Like It Is Series.
Prod-OHC Dist-HRC

West Africa - Two Life Styles C 18 MIN
16MM FILM, 3/4 OR 1/2 IN VIDEO I-H
Compares and contrasts the life styles, occupations, recreational activities and family life of two Africans by following their daily lives.
Prod-GARJA Dist-PHENIX 1970

West African Heritage, The C 30 MIN
3/4 OR 1/2 INCH VIDEO CASSETTE J-H
Looks at the West African heritage in Black music by recounting the contributions of such artists as Alhaji Bai Konte, Dembo Konte, Hugh Masakela and the Wo'se Dance Theater.
From The From Jumpstreet Series.
Prod-WETATV Dist-GPITVL 1979

West African Instruments C 17 MIN
3/4 OR 1/2 INCH VIDEO CASSETTE
See series title for descriptive statement.
From The Musical Instruments Series.
Prod-WWVUTV Dist-GPITVL

West African Kingdoms, Life And Impact B 30 MIN
2 INCH VIDEOTAPE H-C A
See series title for descriptive statement.
From The Americans From Africa - A History Series. No. 2
Prod-CVETVC Dist-GPITVL Prodn-WCVETV

West African Panorama C 25 MIN
3/4 INCH VIDEO CASSETTE
Presents a tour through the countries of Nigeria, the People's Republic of Benin, Togo and Ghana. Shows African culture and lifestyle.
Prod-BLKFMF Dist-BLKFMF

West Bank Story, The C 58 MIN
3/4 OR 1/2 INCH VIDEO CASSETTE
Explains that since 1967, the Israelis have settled 17,000 immigrants in ninety communities on the occupied West Bank. Looks at life for both these Israeli settlers and the 7000,000 Arabs living under the military government there.
From The World Series.
LC NO. 81-707251
Prod-WGBHTV Dist-PBS 1981

West Bank, The - Whose Promised Land C 28 MIN
3/4 INCH VIDEO CASSETTE
Documents the West Bank conflict where two nationalist movements, both claiming the land, are in collision. Artist Esti Marpet argues for a compromise and sharing of the land.
Prod-EAI Dist-EAI

West Berlin - A Show Of Faith B 5 MIN
16MM FILM OPTICAL SOUND
Presents Vice President Johnson's trip to West Berlin as a message of American support to West Berlin. Shows America's determination to remain there as exemplified by the fifteen hundred U S troops that have made their way through communist East Germany to West Berlin.
From The Screen News Digest Series. Vol 4, Issue 2
Prod-HEARST Dist-HEARST 1961

West Coast Logging, Vancouver Island, 1939 B 10 MIN
16MM FILM OPTICAL SOUND
Presents a documentary produced in 1939 which shows a west coast logging operation.
LC NO. 76-703335
Prod-BCPM Dist-BCPM 1975

West Germany C 18 MIN
16MM FILM, 3/4 OR 1/2 IN VIDEO I
Depicts the life of a boy in Stade, a town in northern West Germany with strong ties to the sea. Shows him learning to sail his family's boat and attending school where his mother teaches, while his father works as a financial adviser.
From The Families Of The World Series.
Prod-NGS Dist-NGS

West Germany - New Government C 18 MIN
3/4 OR 1/2 INCH VIDEO CASSETTE H-C A
Documents the events in West Germany that led to the no-confidence vote for the coalition government of Helmut Schmidt. Provides a brief history of post World War II Germany's political parties and their maneuvers and speculation in starting new coalitions.
Prod-JOU Dist-JOU

West Germany After Adenauer C 29 MIN
2 INCH VIDEOTAPE
See series title for descriptive statement.
From The Course Of Our Times II Series.
Prod-WGBHTV Dist-PUBTEL

West Of Charles Russell, The C 53 MIN
16MM FILM, 3/4 OR 1/2 IN VIDEO J-C A
Explores the work of painter Charles Russell, who recorded the drama and color of the pioneer West.
Prod-NBCNEW Dist-FI 1970

West Of Hester Street C 58 MIN
3/4 OR 1/2 INCH VIDEO CASSETTE J-C A
Documents Jewish history during the 'Galveston Movement' at the turn of the century when Jewish immigrants were encouraged to settle in Texas. Combines theatrical interpretations and actual historical footage.
LC NO. 84-707130
Prod-MEDPRJ Dist-MEDPRJ 1984

West Point On The Hudson C 17 MIN
16MM FILM, 3/4 OR 1/2 IN VIDEO I-H
Documents the importance of West Point during the Revolutionary War and emphasizes the Academy's contribution to the development of the United States. Narrated by William Shatner.
From The Re-discovering America Series.
Prod-COP Dist-AIMS 1974

West Point Winter Knee Squad C 17 MIN
16MM FILM OPTICAL SOUND
Outlines a recovery plan designed to repair knee injuries, based on a program at the U S Military Academy to rehabilitate injured athletes to full competitive status. Traces progress of athletes who have undergone knee operations, from early orthopedic exercises with special equipment to full scale mobility tests under simulated game conditions. Emphasizes minimizing the incidence of recurring injuries.
LC NO. 75-703075
Prod-USA Dist-USNAC 1974

West Side Story C 155 MIN
16MM FILM OPTICAL SOUND
Presents a modern-day version of Romeo and Juliet against a backdrop of New York street gangs. Stars Richard Beymer and Natalie Wood.
Prod-UAA Dist-UAE 1961

West To The Mountains C 28 MIN
16MM FILM OPTICAL SOUND H
Presents a song telling Alberta's story from Wagon Train to Oil Boom, illustrated throughout by splendid photography and sung by guitar strumming Burl Ives in buckskins and sombrero.
LC NO. FIA68-1577
Prod-CTFL Dist-CTFL 1967

West Virginia State Folk Festival C 59 MIN
2 INCH VIDEOTAPE
Explains that every June in Glenville, West Virginia, a state festival is held. Traces the state's heritage of traditional Appalachian music. Includes fiddlers Ira Mullins, Lee Triplett, Delbert Hughes and Melvin Wine, fiddle and banjo contests, after-dark square dancing in the streets and a variety of performances in the Glenville State College auditorium.
Prod-WWVUTV Dist-PUBTEL

West, The - Land Of Many Faces C 13 MIN
3/4 OR 1/2 INCH VIDEO CASSETTE I
Focuses on the topography, beauty and geologic history of the five physiographic provinces that make up America's western uplands.
From The Natural Science Specials Series. Module Blue
Prod-UNPRO Dist-AITECH 1973

Westbeth C 32 MIN
3/4 INCH VIDEO CASSETTE
Presents an innovative attempt to choreograph for the camera by Merce Cunningham.
Prod-CUNDAN Dist-CUNDAN

Westcoaster C 18 MIN
16MM FILM OPTICAL SOUND
Charts the course of the Blue Water Classic yachting competition in Australia down the west coast of Tasmania from Melbourne.
LC NO. 80-700924
Prod-TASCOR Dist-TASCOR 1976

Western Civilization - Majesty And Madness—A Series
16MM FILM, 3/4 OR 1/2 IN VIDEO J-C A
Prod-INCC Dist-LCOA 1971

Bible, The - A Literary Heritage	027 MIN
Bismarck - Germany From Blood And Iron	030 MIN
Changing World Of Charles Dickens, The	028 MIN
Charlemagne - Holy Barbarian	026 MIN
Crusades, The - Saints And Sinners	028 MIN
Elizabeth - The Queen Who Shaped An Age	026 MIN
French Revolution, The - The Bastille	021 MIN
French Revolution, The - The Terror	019 MIN
Freud - The Hidden Nature Of Man	029 MIN
Galileo - The Challenge Of Reason	028 MIN
Greeks, The - In Search Of Meaning	025 MIN
Marxism - The Theory That Split A World	025 MIN
Matter of Conscience, A - Henry VIII And	030 MIN
Medieval England - The Peasant's Revolt	031 MIN
Middle Ages, The - A Wanderer's Guide To Life	027 MIN
Napoleon - The End Of A Dictator	027 MIN
Napoleon - The Making Of A Dictator	027 MIN
Newton - The Mind That Found The Future	027 MIN
Nicholas And Alexandra - Prelude To	029 MIN
Nicholas And Alexandra - The Bolshevik	026 MIN
Nicholas And Alexandra - War And The Fall Of	027 MIN
Puritan Revolution, The - Cromwell And The	033 MIN
Romans, The - Life, Laughter And Law	022 MIN
Romanticism - The Revolt Of The Spirit	024 MIN
Shakespeare - A Mirror To Man	026 MIN

Western Europe - A Community Of Nations (Rev Ed) C 21 MIN
16MM FILM - VIDEO, ALL FORMATS I-H
Looks at the nations of western Europe since World War II. Examines the ways in which these nations form a community.
Prod-SVEK Dist-BFA

Western Europe - An Introduction (2nd Ed) C 20 MIN
16MM FILM, 3/4 OR 1/2 IN VIDEO I-J
Provides an overview of the 15 nations of Western Europe. Shows Europeans creating out of their historic differences a competitive, technological society that finds unifying bonds in the Common Market and the European Parliament.
Prod-CORF Dist-CORF 1982

Western Horsemanship C 28 MIN
16MM FILM, 3/4 OR 1/2 IN VIDEO
Features Clark Bradley and Richard Shrake explaining their theory of horsemanship and illustrating individual patterns and maneuvers in both normal and slow motion.
Prod-AQHORS Dist-AQHORS 1979

Western Maryland College—A Series

Previously titled Total Communications Series. Presents information on dealing with deafness and certain related fields.
LC NO. 74-706284
Prod-USBEH Dist-USNAC 1973

Listen	30 MIN
Swan Lake - Conversations With Deaf Teenagers	15 MIN
Total Communication	15 MIN
We Tiptoed Around Whispering	30 MIN

Western Newfoundland C 27 MIN
16MM FILM OPTICAL SOUND
Describes the almost untouched beauty of Newfoundland's West coast as seen by sportsman Lee Wulff who has fished, hunted and filmed the length and breadth of this land. He takes his family and the viewer up the Trans-Canada Highway to Bonne Bay and to his own secret hideaway which will soon be opened to vacationers.
Prod-CTFL Dist-CTFL 1970

Western Pleasure - Advanced C 30 MIN
1/2 IN VIDEO CASSETTE BETA/VHS
Covers the fine points of training a pleasure horse.
From The Western Training Series.
Prod-EQVDL Dist-EQVDL

Western Pleasure - Basics C 30 MIN
1/2 IN VIDEO CASSETTE BETA/VHS
Reveals how to make pleasure horses move in a relaxed, smooth manner.
From The Western Training Series.
Prod-EQVDL Dist-EQVDL

Western Riding Clinic C 30 MIN
1/2 IN VIDEO CASSETTE BETA/VHS
Covers training and showing horses.
From The Western Training Series.
Prod-EQVDL Dist-EQVDL

Western Show C 24 MIN
3/4 OR 1/2 INCH VIDEO CASSETTE
Features bluegrass fiddling and singing, glass blowing, fencing, baton twirling and tap dancing during a visit to state high school rodeo. Shows a young boy who babysits lion cubs.
Prod-WCCOTV Dist-WCCOTV 1981

Western Training—A Series

Covers a variety of subjects with instruction by experienced horsemen.
Prod-EQVDL Dist-EQVDL

Bareback Bronc Clinic	030 MIN
Barrel Racing	030 MIN
Barrel Racing Clinic	030 MIN
Bull Riding Clinic	030 MIN
Bull Riding Clinic - Advanced	030 MIN
Calf Roping Basics	030 MIN
Calf Roping Clinic	030 MIN
Colt Training	030 MIN
Colt Training Clinic	029 MIN
Colt Training Clinic	030 MIN
Cow Cutting - Advanced	030 MIN
Cow Cutting Clinic	030 MIN
Girl Rodeo Events	030 MIN
Hackamore Magic	030 MIN
Halter Showmanship - Fitting	030 MIN
Halter Showmanship - How To Show	030 MIN
Saddle Bronc Clinic	030 MIN
Snaffle Bit Horsemanship	030 MIN
Steer Wrestling Clinic	030 MIN
Steer Wrestling Techniques	030 MIN
Team Roping Clinic	030 MIN
Western Pleasure - Advanced	030 MIN
Western Pleasure - Basics	030 MIN
Western Riding Clinic	030 MIN

Western World And Its Reaction To Genocide, The C 29 MIN
2 INCH VIDEOTAPE
See series title for descriptive statement.
From The Course Of Our Times I Series.
Prod-WGBHTV Dist-PUBTEL

Westfield Infants School B 10 MIN
16MM FILM OPTICAL SOUND T
Follows an integrated day in a British infant school. Shows ways in which an experienced teacher works with her children.
LC NO. 75-701396
Prod-EDC Dist-EDC 1974

Westinghouse In Alphabetical Order C 12 MIN
16MM FILM, 3/4 OR 1/2 IN VIDEO
Pictures some of the products of the Westinghouse company in alphabetical order.
Prod-EAMES Dist-PFP 1965

Westside Store C 23 MIN
16MM FILM, 3/4 OR 1/2 IN VIDEO I-J

Presents the economics of running a small business through a story about an ethnically mixed inner-city gang that turns from vandalism to operating its own legitimate business, a second-hand store.
LC NO. 83-706626
Prod-AMITAI Dist-BARR 1982

Westside Story, A C 27 MIN
16MM FILM OPTICAL SOUND H-C A
Features Chancellor Charles E Young and former Chancellor Franklin D Murphy narrating this chronicle of the fifty year history of UCLA.
Prod-UCLA Dist-UCLA

Westvaco Cora-Cool Case History B 60 MIN
3/4 OR 1/2 INCH VIDEO CASSETTE
Deals with the product manager concept in designing a corrugated box to ship iced poultry.
Prod-HBS Dist-IVCH

Westville, 1850 C 14 MIN
3/4 OR 1/2 INCH VIDEO CASSETTE P
Introduces family life in the 1850's, focusing on how families made the most of the things they needed.
From The Under The Blue Umbrella Series.
Prod-SCETV Dist-AITECH 1977

Westward Coal C 14 MIN
16MM FILM OPTICAL SOUND
Discusses the history of coal mining in the west and new technological advances in the industry, including all aspects of western surface mining.
Prod-AMAX Dist-MTP

Westward Expansion C
3/4 OR 1/2 INCH VIDEO CASSETTE H
Details the century-long progress to the Pacific and relates the 'pioneer spirit' to current American attitudes and beliefs. Considers the infatuation with frontier mythology.
Prod-GA Dist-GA

Westward Expansion C 25 MIN
16MM FILM, 3/4 OR 1/2 IN VIDEO J-C A
Explores the progressive settlement of the West from colonial days to the 20th century.
From The American History Series.
Prod-CRMP Dist-CRMP 1969

Westward Ho C 15 MIN
3/4 OR 1/2 INCH VIDEO CASSETTE I-J
Applies many drawing lessons to a western scene. Includes objects, figures, animals, picture design, costume and drama.
From The Draw Man Series.
Prod-OCPS Dist-AITECH 1975

Westward Movement, The - 1 - Settlers Of The Old Northwest Territory X 15 MIN
16MM FILM, 3/4 OR 1/2 IN VIDEO I-H
Describes the colonization of the old Northwest Territory during the post-revolutionary war period. Explains the political and economic effects of the provisions of the Northwest Ordinance on the movement.
Prod-EBF Dist-EBEC 1962

Westward Movement, The - 2 - Settlement Of The Mississippi Valley X 16 MIN
16MM FILM, 3/4 OR 1/2 IN VIDEO I-H
Traces development of Mississippi Valley during the early 1800's, illustrating the transformation of the area from a vast wilderness to a land of productive farms and thriving communities.
Prod-EBF Dist-EBEC 1962

Westward Movement, The - 3 - Settling Of The Great Plains X 17 MIN
16MM FILM, 3/4 OR 1/2 IN VIDEO I-H
Uses photographs, documents and illustrations to recreate the settling of the Great Plains. Includes sequences of the life of the American Cowboy, fence wars and the expansion of railroads.
Prod-EBF Dist-EBEC 1963

Westward Movement, The - 4 - Texas And The Mexican War X 18 MIN
16MM FILM, 3/4 OR 1/2 IN VIDEO I-H
Shows the Texas story against a background of expansion and growing conflict over slavery. Reveals the significance of the war with Mexico and how it has affected relations between the U S and Latin America.
Prod-EBF Dist-EBEC 1966

Westward Movement, The - 5 - The Gold Rush X 23 MIN
16MM FILM, 3/4 OR 1/2 IN VIDEO I-H
Relates how the discovery of gold at Sutter's Mill changed the history of California and the nation. Filmed in the Mother Lode country of California and Columbia Historic State Park.
Prod-EBF Dist-EBEC 1965

Westward Wagons C 24 MIN
3/4 OR 1/2 INCH VIDEO CASSETTE
Tells the story of a ten-year-old boy and his family as they cross the plains in 1870.
From The Young People's Specials Series.
Prod-MULTPP Dist-MULTPP

Wet Bush, The C 6 MIN
16MM FILM OPTICAL SOUND
Shows the variety of geographic areas in which gum trees grow.
LC NO. 80-700935
Prod-TASCOR Dist-TASCOR 1976

Wet Culture Rice C 17 MIN
16MM FILM OPTICAL SOUND
Demonstrates how Taiwan's rice farmers rely less on mechanization than on human labor to produce and harvest two crops during the annual agricultural cycle.
From The Faces Of Change - Taiwan Series.
Prod-AUFS Dist-WHEELK

Wet Earth And Warm People C 59 MIN
16MM FILM, 3/4 OR 1/2 IN VIDEO J-C
Presents a view of life in Indonesia.
Prod-NFBC Dist-NFBC 1971

Wet Look, The C 15 MIN
3/4 OR 1/2 INCH VIDEO CASSETTE
Shows how LANDSAT helps resolve water resource problems. Includes snow fall implications for water resources in western states, flood control and potential dangers of man-made lakes.
From The LANDSAT Series.
Prod-IVCH Dist-IVCH

Wet Look, The C 15 MIN
16MM FILM - 3/4 IN VIDEO PRO
Explores how the Landsat satellite helps resolve water resource problems with its remote sensing capabilities. Shows how the satellite helps hydrologists control floods and water supplies by monitoring flood plains, snow pack and potentially dangerous manmade lakes. Demonstrates its use in flood assessment and pollution control.
From The Environmental Series - Landsat - Satellite For All Seasons Series.
LC NO. 78-706015
Prod-NASA Dist-USNAC Prodn-NVETA 1977

Wet Tale, A C 11 MIN
16MM FILM, 3/4 OR 1/2 IN VIDEO K-I
Features an animated adventure of a small drop of water. Emphasizes the recycling of water on earth.
Prod-KRATKY Dist-PHENIX

Wetback Hound, The C 18 MIN
16MM FILM, 3/4 OR 1/2 IN VIDEO
Presents the story of a confused hound dog whose search for a home takes him many miles from Mexico to Arizona.
From The Animal Featurettes Series. Set 1
Prod-DISNEY Dist-WDEMCO

Wetlands - Our Natural Partners In Wastewater Management C 39 MIN
16MM FILM, 3/4 OR 1/2 IN VIDEO
Documents research in Michigan and Florida, where wetlands are being used for advanced wastewater treatment. Deals with the financial and environmental advantages of this type of treatment over dry land treatment.
LC NO. 81-706326
Prod-NSF Dist-USNAC 1980

Wetlands Problem, The C 25 MIN
3/4 OR 1/2 INCH VIDEO CASSETTE J-C
Shows the wetlands of Australia which, like Florida's Everglades, support an abundance of wildlife, including some of economic importance to man. Notes how the aborigines lived in harmony with the wetlands for centuries, but now the situation and ecology are changing by dam construction, swamp draining and clearing of wetland forests.
Prod-EDMI Dist-EDMI 1978

Wetten Ist Ehrensache C 15 MIN
16MM FILM, 3/4 OR 1/2 IN VIDEO
See series title for descriptive statement.
From The Guten Tag Wie Geht's Series. Part 2
Prod-BAYER Dist-IFB 1973

Wh Sound, The - Whoo-Oo-Oo, I Want To Go C 15 MIN
2 INCH VIDEOTAPE P
Introduces some of the consonant sounds met in early reading. Identifies the written letter with the spoken sound.
From The Listen And Say Series.
Prod-MPATI Dist-GPITVL

Whadizzit - How To Identify The Auto C 10 MIN
1/2 IN VIDEO CASSETTE BETA/VHS
Explains how to decipher the serial and identification plates on American cars.
Prod-RMI Dist-RMI

Whale Ho C 10 MIN
16MM FILM OPTICAL SOUND
Shows a camera crew in open boats with outboard motors filming the gray whale, one of the largest mammals known to man.
Prod-MERMAR Dist-TELEFM

Whale Hunters Of San Miguel C 15 MIN
3/4 OR 1/2 INCH VIDEO CASSETTE H-C A
Examines the whaling industry of San Miguel and presents the pros and cons of this ancient endeavor.
Prod-UPI Dist-JOU

Whale Of A Friend, A C 15 MIN
3/4 OR 1/2 INCH VIDEO CASSETTE P-I
Shows trainers working with dolphins and with the whale Shamu at Sea World of Ohio.
From The Explorers Unlimited Series.
Prod-WVIZTV Dist-AITECH 1971

Whale Watch C 57 MIN
16MM FILM, 3/4 OR 1/2 IN VIDEO H-C A
Observes the whales and their activities in the lagoons off the coast of central Mexico and introduces the methods used in studying and filming their behavior.
From The Nova Series.
Prod-WGBHTV Dist-TIMLIF 1982

Whales C 22 MIN
16MM FILM, 3/4 OR 1/2 IN VIDEO I-C
A shortened version of Whales. Shows Jacques Cousteau viewing an experiment with a whale at Marine World in California and conducting a series of studies with whales in the Indian Ocean.
From The Undersea World Of Jacques Cousteau Series.
Prod-METROM Dist-CF 1970

Whales C 24 MIN
VIDEODISK P-J
Presents information about whales, using still and motion pictures, narration and on-screen text. Can be used as a 24-minute presentation, as four individual six-minute lessons or as a text-and-image data base.
Prod-NGS Dist-NGS

Whales C 52 MIN
16MM FILM, 3/4 OR 1/2 IN VIDEO
Shows Jacques Cousteau touring the sea in the last surviving wooden whaling boat, viewing an experiment with a whale and conducting a series of studies of whales in the Indian Ocean.
From The Undersea World Of Jacques Cousteau Series.
Prod-METROM Dist-CF 1970

Whales - Can They Be Saved C 24 MIN
16MM FILM, 3/4 OR 1/2 IN VIDEO I-J
Shows a variety of species within the two major branches of the whale family. Identifies the whale species in danger of becoming extinct. Contrasts modern whaling techniques with those of the past. Traces the evolution of whales from land to sea. Shows how whales are trained to perform. Emphasizes the importance of saving the endangered whales.
From The Wide World Of Adventure Series.
Prod-AVATLI Dist-EBEC 1977

Whales - Close Encounters Of A Deep Kind C 23 MIN
3/4 OR 1/2 INCH VIDEO CASSETTE K-C A
Shows the intelligent humpback whale which must run the gauntlet of pirate whaling ships and killer whales to reach feeding waters.
Prod-NWLDPR Dist-NWLDPR

Whales And Whaling C 24 MIN
16MM FILM, 3/4 OR 1/2 IN VIDEO
Traces the development of the whaling industry and the subsequent overexploitation of the whale by that industry. Documents methods used to manage whale populations such as limiting catches of each species to sustainable yields.
Prod-OPENU Dist-MEDIAG Prodn-BBCTV 1979

Whales That Wouldn't Die, The C 28 MIN
16MM FILM, 3/4 OR 1/2 IN VIDEO I-C A
Uses close-up photography to depict the migration activities of the gray whale, which can ingest a ton of food a day and swim at a steady three-to-five knots a day for over 4,000 miles.
LC NO. 81-706148
Prod-KPBS Dist-CRMP 1981

Whales Weep Not C 26 MIN
16MM FILM, 3/4 OR 1/2 IN VIDEO H-C A
Looks at the underwater world of the sperm whale and the blue whale. Depicts turn-of-the-century whaling.
Prod-MTI Dist-MTI

Whales, Dolphins And Men C 52 MIN
16MM FILM, 3/4 OR 1/2 IN VIDEO H-C A
Examines and explains the extraordinary intelligence and behavior of dolphins, the smallest and most numerous members of the whale family.
LC NO. 79-707230
Prod-BBCTV Dist-FI 1973

Whaling Voyage B 23 MIN
16MM FILM OPTICAL SOUND
Shows the preparation and the voyage of a whaling ship working under sail, killing and rendering a large whale.
LC NO. 74-701048
Prod-EDC Dist-EDC 1973

What C 60 MIN
3/4 OR 1/2 INCH VIDEO CASSETTE H A
Examines various aspects of being deaf and shows how creative signing can be.
Prod-GALCO Dist-GALCO 1982

What A Difference An A Makes C 13 MIN
16MM FILM OPTICAL SOUND
Presents practical management information on the concept and methods of Large Package Hay Systems.
Prod-HESST Dist-VENARD

What A Picture - The Complete Photography Course By John Hedgecoe—A Series
H-C A
Features John Hedgecoe, Professor of Photography at London's Royal College of Art, on a variety of photographic assignments in Europe, Africa and America. Demonstrates how to explore opportunities, identify and solve problems and create special effects. Aims to develop perception, fire the imagination and teach mastery of the tools and techniques.
Prod-THREMI Dist-FI

Faces And Figures	030 MIN
Imagination And Technique	030 MIN
Landscape And Light	030 MIN
Lighting And Composition	030 MIN
Making A Picture	030 MIN
Perspectives Of Space	030 MIN
The Vital Moment	030 MIN
Travelling Light	030 MIN

What A State You're In C 15 MIN
3/4 OR 1/2 INCH VIDEO CASSETTE I-J
Concentrates on the in-between jurisdiction of state governments.
From The It's All Up To You Series.
Prod-COOPED Dist-AITECH Prodn-WHATV 1978

What A Way To Go - An Extravaganza In The Making B 26 MIN
16MM FILM OPTICAL SOUND IND

Views production problems of the set of 'WHAT A WAY TO GO.' Shows the writers, actors, costume designer and crew rehearsing and shooting.
LC NO. FI68-311
Prod-WOLPER Dist-WOLPER 1964

What A Way To Make A Living C 30 MIN
3/4 OR 1/2 INCH VIDEO CASSETTE
Provides biographies of a break dancer, a boxer, a fast-draw marksman and a turkey caller, four peculiar American success stories.
Prod-DCTVC Dist-DCTVC

What A Way To Run an Airline C 12 MIN
16MM FILM, 3/4 OR 1/2 IN VIDEO C A
Uses the success story of People Express Airlines to offer a new perspective on employee involvement in business operations.
Prod-ABCTV Dist-MTI

What A Way To Start A Day C 15 MIN
16MM FILM OPTICAL SOUND C A
A motivational film using dramatized incidents to alert workers about the importance of safety regulations on their jobs.
LC NO. 72-701862
Prod-VOAERO Dist-VOAERO 1971

What About Mom And Dad C 58 MIN
3/4 OR 1/2 INCH VIDEO CASSETTE
Deals with the problems of families facing difficult emotional and financial choices in caring for older parents whose savings have been eaten up by nursing home care, with federal programs for medical costs covering less than expected.
From The Frontline Series.
Prod-DOCCON Dist-PBS

What About Pot C 20 MIN
16MM FILM, 3/4 OR 1/2 IN VIDEO I-C A
Takes the viewer into the drug subculture. Shows how the marijuana problem develops, illustrates the differing impact of marijuana in the ghetto and in suburbia and presents a cross-section of the ideas, fears and myths that still obscure the real nature of the marijuana question. Explores the role, if any, that marijuana should have in society.
Prod-DAVP Dist-AIMS 1972

What About Reading Systems C 29 MIN
16MM FILM, 3/4 OR 1/2 IN VIDEO C A
Discusses the values and pitfalls of packaged reading systems.
From The Teaching Children To Read Series.
Prod-MFFD Dist-FI 1976

What About Thad C 9 MIN
16MM FILM OPTICAL SOUND H-C A
Considers the emotional problems of a young, lonely boy who is growing up without needed attention or acceptance from parents, teacher or friends. Allows the viewer to make judgments about ways to help the child's problems.
LC NO. 76-700917
Prod-BYU Dist-BYU 1970

What About The Russians? C 26 MIN
16MM FILM, 3/4 OR 1/2 IN VIDEO H-C A
Interviews prominent statesmen regarding the Soviet position on the nuclear arms race and other important issues affecting the nuclear field.
LC NO. 84-706140
Prod-EFVP Dist-EFVP 1983

What About The Workers--A Series
16MM FILM, 3/4 OR 1/2 IN VIDEO H-C A
Examines the participation of European workers in industry and commerce. Features factories, board rooms and union meetings to provide evidence about the practice of employee participation and industrial democracy, including the benefits of worker cooperatives.
Prod-THAMES Dist-MEDIAG 1978

Cooperatives And Company Partnership 024 MIN
Discussion On The Government White Paper 024 MIN
Industrial Democracy And The Union Way 024 MIN
Participation And The CBI Way 024 MIN
Traditional Company, The 024 MIN
Visit To Germany And Sweden, A 024 MIN

What About Timber C 20 MIN
3/4 INCH VIDEO CASSETTE I
Views the giant fir trees of Washington. Describes a timber company which believes that restoration of the forest is as important as the cutting, sorting and milling operations.
From The Exploring Our Nation Series.
Prod-KRMATV Dist-GPITVL 1975

What About Tomorrow C 20 MIN
16MM FILM, 3/4 OR 1/2 IN VIDEO
Explores the world of basic scientific research into such areas as fluorocarbons and the ozone layer, earthquake prediction, food production and laser chemistry.
Prod-NSF Dist-IU Prodn-MAYER 1978

What About Winter Driving (3rd Ed) C 11 MIN
16MM FILM OPTICAL SOUND
Illustrates safe techniques for winter driving maintenance and for starting, stopping and driving on snow-covered and ice-covered highways. Presents information on the pulling ability and stopping distances obtained with different tires.
LC NO. 75-703076
Prod-USDTFH Dist-NSC Prodn-NSC 1974

What Affects Your Hearing B 50 MIN
16MM FILM OPTICAL SOUND PRO
Demonstrates how hearing can be temporarily or permanently damaged by noise. Shows a stapedectomy and the diagnosis and correction of hearing loss due to stiffening or calcification of the tiny bones in the middle ear.
Prod-CMA Dist-LAWREN

What Am I Bid - Equal And Unequal C 14 MIN
3/4 OR 1/2 INCH VIDEO CASSETTE P
Illustrates how knowledge of sets and of equal and unequal helps at an auction.
From The Math Country Series.
Prod-KYTV Dist-AITECH 1979

What Animals Eat C 15 MIN
3/4 OR 1/2 INCH VIDEO CASSETTE I-J
Examines the feeding processes of animals, including parasites.
From The Animals And Such Series. Module Red - Life Processes
Prod-WHROTV Dist-AITECH 1972

What Animals Live In Communities B 15 MIN
2 INCH VIDEOTAPE P
Explains that many animals live together in groups.
From The Science Is Discovery Series.
Prod-DETPS Dist-GPITVL

What Are Animal Tails For C 11 MIN
16MM FILM, 3/4 OR 1/2 IN VIDEO P
Shows some interesting details about familiar animals and their tails. Combines choral speaking between children and narration.
Prod-CORF Dist-CORF 1971

What Are Families For C 15 MIN
3/4 OR 1/2 INCH VIDEO CASSETTE P
Introduces the idea that there are many different kinds of family structures in society. Suggests that members of a family depend on each other and work together to help each other.
From The All About You Series.
Prod-WGBHTV Dist-AITECH Prodn-TTOIC 1975

What Are Friends For C 47 MIN
16MM FILM, 3/4 OR 1/2 IN VIDEO I-H A
Tells a story about a 12-year-old girl who moves to California with her recently divorced mother, and comes to realize, through a friendship with another girl, that sometimes when people can not live together it is better to break apart.
From The Teenage Years Series.
LC NO. 80-706623
Prod-TAHSEM Dist-TIMLIF 1980

What Are Letters For - Consonant Blends And Combinations C 13 MIN
16MM FILM, 3/4 OR 1/2 IN VIDEO P
Prod-BFA Dist-PHENIX 1983

What Are Letters For - Initial Consonants C 12 MIN
16MM FILM, 3/4 OR 1/2 IN VIDEO P
Presents words selected from commonly used vocabulary lists and primary readers which are used orally and visually superimposed over action. Makes it clear that language and reading are fun and useful.
From The Reading Motivation Series.
Prod-BFA Dist-PHENIX 1973

What Are Letters For - Vowel Combinations C 11 MIN
16MM FILM, 3/4 OR 1/2 IN VIDEO P-I
Presents a combination of visuals and graphic demonstrations of the various vowel combinations to help children understand the ways vowels work in English.
LC NO. 84-707087
Prod-BEANM Dist-PHENIX 1983

What Are Letters For - Vowels C 12 MIN
16MM FILM, 3/4 OR 1/2 IN VIDEO P
Presents words selected from commonly used vocabulary lists and primary readers which are used orally and visually superimposed over action. Makes it clear that language and reading are fun and useful.
From The Reading Motivation Series.
Prod-BFA Dist-PHENIX 1973

What Are Man-Made Satellites Like C 20 MIN
2 INCH VIDEOTAPE I
See series title for descriptive statement.
From The Science Corner II, Unit III - Journey In Space Series.
Prod-MPATI Dist-GPITVL

What Are Planets B 15 MIN
2 INCH VIDEOTAPE P
Explains that planets are satellites of the sun.
From The Science Is Discovery Series.
Prod-DETPS Dist-GPITVL

What Are Salamanders Like C 20 MIN
2 INCH VIDEOTAPE I
See series title for descriptive statement.
From The Science Corner II, Unit I - Animals Series.
Prod-MPATI Dist-GPITVL

What Are Slips? C 12 MIN
3/4 OR 1/2 INCH VIDEO CASSETTE IND
Shows the floor hand that, although slips are simple, rugged and dependable devices, proper procedures should be followed when using them.
From The Roughneck Training Series.
Prod-UTEXPE Dist-UTEXPE 1983

What Are Some Special Forms Of Behavior B 15 MIN
2 INCH VIDEOTAPE P
Explains that many kinds of behavior are adaptations which help animals live in their environments.
From The Science Is Discovery Series.
Prod-DETPS Dist-GPITVL

What Are Spring Days Like C 20 MIN
2 INCH VIDEOTAPE I
See series title for descriptive statement.
From The Science Corner II, Unit VIII - Plants In Spring Series.
Prod-MPATI Dist-GPITVL

What Are Taxes All About C 25 MIN
16MM FILM, 3/4 OR 1/2 IN VIDEO J-H
Explains how and why tax monies are spent. Explains the functions of the Internal Revenue Service.
Prod-CBSNEW Dist-CAROUF

What Are The Characteristics Of Living Things B 15 MIN
2 INCH VIDEOTAPE P
Explains that living things grow, move, respond and reproduce.
From The Science Is Discovery Series.
Prod-DETPS Dist-GPITVL

What Are The Classifications Of Races Of Mankind C 30 MIN
2 INCH VIDEOTAPE J
From The Summer Journal, Unit 2 - You Are What You Can Do Series.
Prod-WNINTV Dist-GPITVL

What Are The Different Forms That Water Takes C 20 MIN
2 INCH VIDEOTAPE I
See series title for descriptive statement.
From The Science Corner II, Unit VII - Understanding Weather Series.
Prod-MPATI Dist-GPITVL

What Are The Humanities - General Humanities B 45 MIN
2 INCH VIDEOTAPE C
See series title for descriptive statement.
From The General Humanities Series. Unit 1 - Introduction
Prod-CHITVC Dist-GPITVL Prodn-WTTWTV

What Are The Important Parts Of A Plant C 20 MIN
2 INCH VIDEOTAPE I
See series title for descriptive statement.
From The Science Corner II, Unit VIII - Plants In Spring Series.
Prod-MPATI Dist-GPITVL

What Are The Planets Like C 20 MIN
2 INCH VIDEOTAPE I
See series title for descriptive statement.
From The Science Corner II, Unit II - The Earth In Space Series.
Prod-MPATI Dist-GPITVL

What Are The Properties Of Matter B 15 MIN
2 INCH VIDEOTAPE P
Explains that every kind of matter has its own characteristic properties.
From The Science Is Discovery Series.
Prod-DETPS Dist-GPITVL

What Are The Sounds Around You B 20 MIN
2 INCH VIDEOTAPE P
Presents the environment as one which is filled with sound. Explains that some of these sounds are made by rubbing, blowing and tapping.
From The Scienceland Series.
Prod-MPATI Dist-GPITVL

What Are The Stars Like C 20 MIN
2 INCH VIDEOTAPE I
See series title for descriptive statement.
From The Science Corner II, Unit II - The Earth In Space Series.
Prod-MPATI Dist-GPITVL

What Are They C 14 MIN
16MM FILM, 3/4 OR 1/2 IN VIDEO I
Depicts Woody and Debbie getting into a discussion of the word 'criteria.'
From The Thinkabout Series. Using Criteria
LC NO. 81-706131
Prod-KETCTV Dist-AITECH 1979

What Are They C 30 MIN
3/4 OR 1/2 INCH VIDEO CASSETTE
See series title for descriptive statement.
From The Management For The '90s - Quality Circles Series.
Prod-TELSTR Dist-DELTAK

What Are Values C 9 MIN
16MM FILM, 3/4 OR 1/2 IN VIDEO I-J
Discusses the meaning of values, explains how people learn them and describes a method for making difficult value decisions.
Prod-BFA Dist-PHENIX Prodn-MITC 1977

What Are You Anyway C 15 MIN
3/4 OR 1/2 INCH VIDEO CASSETTE
Shows that all animals are alive and growing and can move around. Explains that people are animals too with human bodies. Features Louise who points out various organs on an anatomical model and discusses the function of each.
From The All About You Series.
Prod-WGBHTV Dist-AITECH

What Are You Doing C 15 MIN
2 INCH VIDEOTAPE P
See series title for descriptive statement.
From The Avenida De Ingles Series.
Prod-SDITVA Dist-GPITVL

What Are You Made Of C 15 MIN
3/4 OR 1/2 INCH VIDEO CASSETTE P
Explains that one's body is comprised of cells and the that it grows by adding more cells. Discusses the different functions of cells.
From The All About You Series.
Prod-WGBHTV Dist-AITECH Prodn-TTOIC 1975

What Are You, Woman C 25 MIN
16MM FILM, 3/4 OR 1/2 IN VIDEO

Presents four segments, including Medea - An Aftermath, Chinese Lament, I Am A Woman Growing Old and I Wear History On My Back, each dealing with an aspect of woman's experience from a different cultural perspective.
Prod-WITTEN Dist-PHENIX 1977

What Are Your Chances B 15 MIN
2 INCH VIDEOTAPE P
See series title for descriptive statement.
From The Just Inquisitive Series. No. 29
Prod-EOPS Dist-GPITVL Prodn-KOACTV

What Black Americans Should Know About Cancer C 30 MIN
3/4 OR 1/2 INCH VIDEO CASSETTE
Prod-RCOMTV Dist-SYLWAT 1982

What Breaks Rocks C 20 MIN
2 INCH VIDEOTAPE P
See series title for descriptive statement.
From The Science Corner I, Unit II - Studying Rocks Series.
Prod-MPATI Dist-GPITVL

What Business Lawyers Need To Know About The Law Of Evidence C 120 MIN
3/4 OR 1/2 INCH VIDEO CASSETTE PRO
Advises large and small businesses on the consequences of transactions that may result in litigation.
Prod-CCEB Dist-ABACPE

What Buys More C 15 MIN
3/4 INCH VIDEO CASSETTE P
Applies simple number sentences to money problems and introduces adding with three addends.
From The Math Factory, Module VI - Money Series.
Prod-MAETEL Dist-GPITVL 1973

What Can A Frog Do B 20 MIN
2 INCH VIDEOTAPE P
Explains that the cold of Winter makes a frog go to sleep at the bottom of a pond but in the Spring it becomes active again. Shows that frogs are suited for living on land and in water.
From The Scienceland Series.
Prod-MPATI Dist-GPITVL

What Can A Guy Do C 15 MIN
16MM FILM, 3/4 OR 1/2 IN VIDEO
Discusses attitudes young men have toward birth control. Portrays high school couples and individuals in difficult circumstances, such as an unplanned pregnancy and the inability of a girlfriend to take the pill.
Prod-HEDUC Dist-CNEMAG

What Can A Guy Do C 15 MIN
16MM FILM - 3/4 IN VIDEO J-H
Uses vignettes and on-the-street interviews in offering a sampling of male attitudes and knowledge about birth control. Designed to motivate the viewer to learn the facts about sex and pregnancy from suggested reliable sources.
LC NO. 81-707098
Prod-SERIUS Dist-SERIUS 1980

What Can A Turtle Do B 20 MIN
2 INCH VIDEOTAPE P
Explains that a turtle can protect itself with its hard shell. Describes how some turtles crawl on land, some in water and some which do both.
From The Scienceland Series.
Prod-MPATI Dist-GPITVL

What Can Birds Do C 15 MIN
3/4 INCH VIDEO CASSETTE P
Studies a baby chick and a duckling to show how birds are uniquely suited for their needs.
From The Tell Me What You See Series.
Prod-WVIZTV Dist-GPITVL

What Can I Contribute C 25 MIN
16MM FILM - 3/4 IN VIDEO IND
Explains that effective organizations require team effort on the part of specialists.
From The Effective Executive Series.
Prod-BNA Dist-BNA 1968

What Can I Do C 22 MIN
16MM FILM, 3/4 OR 1/2 IN VIDEO J-C A
Tells how the average American citizen can influence ongoing social change through personal, political and social action. Includes explanations of the use of media, the impact of effective letters and the power of a single vote.
Prod-CALLFM Dist-BARR 1975

What Can I Tell You - A Portrait Of Three Generations Of Women C 55 MIN
16MM FILM - 3/4 IN VIDEO J-C A
Focuses on three generations of women from an Italian-American family, who offer anecdotes and personal perspectives on their self-images and family relationships and on such topics as marriage, children, working and independence. Depicts each woman as a unique individual who has evidenced the need to express life fully.
LC NO. 79-707651
Prod-CEPRO Dist-CEPRO 1978

What Can Magnets Do C 20 MIN
2 INCH VIDEOTAPE I
See series title for descriptive statement.
From The Science Corner II, Unit VI - Magnetism And Electricity Series.
Prod-MPATI Dist-GPITVL

What Can My Child Hear C 30 MIN
16MM FILM, 3/4 OR 1/2 IN VIDEO C A
Explains the testing process, and describes and evaluates hearing aids.
Prod-YASNYP Dist-PFP

What Can The Sun Do C 20 MIN
2 INCH VIDEOTAPE I
See series title for descriptive statement.
From The Science Corner II, Unit II - The Earth In Space Series.
Prod-MPATI Dist-GPITVL

What Can We Do With A Pumpkin C 20 MIN
2 INCH VIDEOTAPE P
See series title for descriptive statement.
From The Science Corner I, Unit I - Living Things In Autumn Series.
Prod-MPATI Dist-GPITVL

What Can We Find Out About Paper C 20 MIN
2 INCH VIDEOTAPE P
See series title for descriptive statement.
From The Science Corner I, Unit III - Looking At Things Around Us Series.
Prod-MPATI Dist-GPITVL

What Can We Learn About Butterflies And Moths C 20 MIN
2 INCH VIDEOTAPE I
See series title for descriptive statement.
From The Science Corner II, Unit I - Animals Series.
Prod-MPATI Dist-GPITVL

What Can We Learn About The Crayfish And Its Relatives C 20 MIN
2 INCH VIDEOTAPE I
See series title for descriptive statement.
From The Science Corner II, Unit I - Animals Series.
Prod-MPATI Dist-GPITVL

What Can We Learn By Looking At Rocks C 20 MIN
2 INCH VIDEOTAPE P
See series title for descriptive statement.
From The Science Corner I, Unit II - Studying Rocks Series.
Prod-MPATI Dist-GPITVL

What Can We Learn By Studying Snakes C 20 MIN
2 INCH VIDEOTAPE I
See series title for descriptive statement.
From The Science Corner II, Unit I - Animals Series.
Prod-MPATI Dist-GPITVL

What Can We See After Sunset C 20 MIN
2 INCH VIDEOTAPE I
See series title for descriptive statement.
From The Science Corner II, Unit II - The Earth In Space Series.
Prod-MPATI Dist-GPITVL

What Can You Discover In A Vacant Lot C 20 MIN
2 INCH VIDEOTAPE P
See series title for descriptive statement.
From The Science Corner I, Unit I - Living Things In Autumn Series.
Prod-MPATI Dist-GPITVL

What Can You Discover In A Wooded Area C 20 MIN
2 INCH VIDEOTAPE P
See series title for descriptive statement.
From The Science Corner I, Unit I - Living Things In Autumn Series.
Prod-MPATI Dist-GPITVL

What Can You Discover With A Magnifying Glass C 20 MIN
2 INCH VIDEOTAPE I
See series title for descriptive statement.
From The Science Corner II, Unit IV - Scientific Instruments Series.
Prod-MPATI Dist-GPITVL

What Can You Do C 26 MIN
16MM FILM OPTICAL SOUND
States that more young people from Spanish-speaking communities must aspire to careers as physicians, dentists, nurses, other health professionals and health technicians. Includes recent graduates describing how they overcame obstacles and started a career.
LC NO. 74-706606
Prod-USDHEW Dist-USNAC 1974

What Can You Do C 28 MIN
16MM FILM OPTICAL SOUND J-H A
Examines the problem of the lack of Spanish-speaking Americans in the health care fields. Presents interviews with Spanish-Americans discussing how they overcame financial obstacles, family problems and their own personal doubts.
Prod-USDHEW Dist-MTP

What Can You Do With Paper B 20 MIN
2 INCH VIDEOTAPE P-I
Conveys appreciation and understanding of paper as an art material through a demonstration of paper making in colonial Williamsburg, Virginia. Demonstrates paper sculpture so that students may express their own ideas in a three-dimensional form.
From The Art Adventures Series.
Prod-CVETVC Dist-GPITVL Prodn-WCVETV

What Can You Find C 12 MIN
16MM FILM OPTICAL SOUND K-P
Notes differences in size, shape, feel and color of similar creatures and natural objects. Illustrates seasonal change.
LC NO. FIA67-2264
Prod-LOH Dist-LOH 1966

What Can You Find In A Pond B 20 MIN
2 INCH VIDEOTAPE P
Explains that a casual visit to a pond may become an exciting adventure for those who watch, wonder and wait.
From The Scienceland Series.
Prod-MPATI Dist-GPITVL

What Can You Show Me C 29 MIN
3/4 OR 1/2 INCH VIDEO CASSETTE P-I
Tells the story of a shy but talented Chinese American boy drawn out of his shell through a class project involving puppets.
From The Bean Sprouts Series.
Prod-CTPROJ Dist-GPITVL

What Can You Show Me C 30 MIN
3/4 OR 1/2 INCH VIDEO CASSETTE
See series title for descriptive statement.
From The Bean Sprouts Series.
Prod-CTPROJ Dist-MDCPB

What Caused Agrarian Cultures C 15 MIN
3/4 INCH VIDEO CASSETTE
Shows how agrarian cultures evolved and the reasons for their development.
From The Looking Out Is In Series.
Prod-WHATV Dist-GPITVL

What Caused Industrial Complexes C 15 MIN
3/4 INCH VIDEO CASSETTE
Illustrates how industrial complexes evolved and the reasons for their development.
From The Looking Out Is In Series.
Prod-WHATV Dist-GPITVL

What Causes Current Flow - EMF B 3 MIN
16MM FILM - 3/4 IN VIDEO
Shows how an outside force is converted into an electrical force of attraction. Offers an explanation of electromotive force (EMF). Issued in 1954 as a motion picture.
From The Basic Electricity Series.
LC NO. 79-707478
Prod-USN Dist-USNAC Prodn-WPP 1979

What Causes Night And Day C 20 MIN
2 INCH VIDEOTAPE I
See series title for descriptive statement.
From The Science Corner II, Unit II - The Earth In Space Series.
Prod-MPATI Dist-GPITVL

What Causes Thunder And Lightning C 20 MIN
2 INCH VIDEOTAPE I
See series title for descriptive statement.
From The Science Corner II, Unit VII - Understanding Weather Series.
Prod-MPATI Dist-GPITVL

What Color Are You C 15 MIN
16MM FILM, 3/4 OR 1/2 IN VIDEO I
Explains why there are different races, in answer to children's questions about race. Discusses pigmentation and mutations. Describes why scientists believe all human beings derived from one common ancestor.
Prod-EBF Dist-EBEC 1967

What Color Is Skin C 9 MIN
16MM FILM, 3/4 OR 1/2 IN VIDEO K-I
Shows variations of skin coloring in the human race and explains how heredity determines skin color.
From The Who We Are Series.
LC NO. 77-701120
Prod-KORTY Dist-PFP 1977

What Color Is The Wind C 27 MIN
16MM FILM OPTICAL SOUND C A
Tells the story of twin boys, three years old, one of whom was born blind. Tells how their parents, with some professional help, are determined that the blind boy shall compete and have an opportunity no less than that of his twin brother in the sighted world.
LC NO. 74-700294
Prod-ALGRAN Dist-ALGRAN 1968

What Comes Next C 15 MIN
3/4 OR 1/2 INCH VIDEO CASSETTE P
Combines looking, listening, talking, writing and reading to help establish the link between oral and written language. Presents the story Brave Daniel by Leonore Klein.
From The I Want To Read Series.
Prod-LACOS Dist-GPITVL 1976

What Controls Current Flow - Resistance B 4 MIN
16MM FILM - 3/4 IN VIDEO H
Shows the symbol for resistance to current flow, the atomic basis for resistance in materials, and the effect of the use of a resistor in a circuit. Issued in 1954 as a motion picture.
From The Basic Electricity Series.
LC NO. 79-707479
Prod-USN Dist-USNAC Prodn-WPP 1979

What Could I Say - An Assertion Training Stimulus Program C 18 MIN
16MM FILM, 3/4 OR 1/2 IN VIDEO
Presents 20 vignettes which illustrate common situations that require assertive responses, weds professional validity with wit, charm and style.
Prod-RESPRC Dist-RESPRC

What Could You Do With A Nickel C 26 MIN
16MM FILM - 3/4 IN VIDEO J-C A
Tells the story of two hundred Black and Hispanic women in the south Bronx who formed the first domestic workers union in the history of the United States.
Prod-FIRS Dist-FIRS

What Did You Do In School Today C 35 MIN
16MM FILM OPTICAL SOUND T
Explores child-centered schooling in English informal schools. Il-

lustrates the development of curiosity and involvement with learning among children from working-class areas and describes the school's relationships with the community and parents.
LC NO. 73-703425
Prod-AGAPR Dist-AGAPR 1973

What Did You Learn In School Today B 48 MIN
16MM FILM OPTICAL SOUND H-C A
Examines, through narration by newswoman Joan Murray, the 'open-classroom,' an alternative method being used in schools in England and the United States. Interviews Lady Bridget Plowden, whose report on education altered many English classrooms. Visits North Dakota, a state changing entirely to the 'open-classroom', the Grape School in Watts, Los Angeles and a teacher-training workshop in Connecticut. Focuses on the idea of 'satellite' or 'mini' high schools in order to show changes going on in suburban schools.
Prod-WNETTV Dist-IU 1972

What Did You Read B 15 MIN
16MM FILM OPTICAL SOUND I-H
Discusses the importance of comprehension in reading. Emphasizes words, main ideas and details. Compares reading to travel. Shows how both require knowing where you're going and what you're looking for.
From The Pathways To Reading Series.
Prod-CBF Dist-AVED 1958

What Did You Say - Oral Communications C 15 MIN
16MM FILM, 3/4 OR 1/2 IN VIDEO I-J
Dramatizes the problem of poor oral communication skills and presents systematic techniques for improving oral communication skills.
LC NO. 82-707300
Prod-VITASC Dist-FLMFR

What Did You Say In School Today C 23 MIN
16MM FILM OPTICAL SOUND
Tells what is being done to help children overcome barriers to fluent speech. Portrays two speech pathologists at work in a public school, dealing with a variety of speech problems presented by children from four to 16 years of age.
LC NO. 77-700434
Prod-PCHENT Dist-PCHENT 1977

What Difference Does It Make? C 13 MIN
3/4 OR 1/2 INCH VIDEO CASSETTE
Offers a series of dramatized incidents to show how little things do make a difference. Uses a light approach to the serious matter of minutes, hours and days that are lost because of inattention to little things.
From The Production-Minded Management Series. Module 4
Prod-RESEM Dist-RESEM

What Do Farm Crops Need In Order To Grow C 20 MIN
2 INCH VIDEOTAPE I
See series title for descriptive statement.
From The Science Corner II, Unit VIII - Plants In Spring Series.
Prod-MPATI Dist-GPITVL

What Do Flowers Do - A First Film C 11 MIN
16MM FILM, 3/4 OR 1/2 IN VIDEO P-J
Describes parts of the flower, how seeds develop and how germination and growth take place.
Prod-BEAN Dist-PHENIX 1969

What Do Flowers Do - A First Film (Spanish) C 11 MIN
16MM FILM, 3/4 OR 1/2 IN VIDEO P
Describes parts of the flower, how seeds develop and how germination and growth take place.
Prod-BEAN Dist-PHENIX 1958

What Do I Do Now C 30 MIN
16MM FILM, 3/4 OR 1/2 IN VIDEO C A
Presents options for testing and treatment, education, and systems of communication.
From The Children And Deafness Series.
Prod-YASNYP Dist-PFP

What Do I Do When I See A Fire C 13 MIN
16MM FILM, 3/4 OR 1/2 IN VIDEO I-J
Deomonstrates proper responses and reactions in case of a fire. Emphasizes learning the fire department phone number, how to report a fire and the importance of getting out fast. Narrated by Sparky the Fire Dog and features puppet characters.
Prod-NFPA Dist-NFPA 1982

What Do I Know C 15 MIN
16MM FILM, 3/4 OR 1/2 IN VIDEO I
Shows characters in two problem-solving segments asking themselves what they know and need to know.
From The Thinkabout Series. Collecting Information
LC NO. 81-706132
Prod-AITV Dist-AITECH 1979

What Do I Receive For My Money C 9 MIN
16MM FILM, 3/4 OR 1/2 IN VIDEO P-J
Discusses how to find value for money, how much money a person needs, the difference between need and want, comparison shopping and bargain buying.
Prod-SF Dist-SF

What Do Plants Do - A First Film C 11 MIN
16MM FILM, 3/4 OR 1/2 IN VIDEO P-I
Points out that plants are important parts of our world, that they produce food for plants and animals, return oxygen to the air and are adapted to live almost everywhere. Tells how plants are living things that use food, grow, are sensitive and move. Shows how we use plants to make clothes and to keep us warm.
Prod-BEAN Dist-PHENIX 1971

What Do Seeds Do - A First Film C 11 MIN
16MM FILM, 3/4 OR 1/2 IN VIDEO P-J
Shows the relative size and development of various seeds.
Prod-BEAN Dist-PHENIX 1970

What Do Seeds Need In Order To Spout C 20 MIN
2 INCH VIDEOTAPE I
See series title for descriptive statement.
From The Science Corner II, Unit VIII - Plants In Spring Series.
Prod-MPATI Dist-GPITVL

What Do Seeds Need To Sprout C 11 MIN
16MM FILM, 3/4 OR 1/2 IN VIDEO P
Reveals the need for three things in order for a seed to germinate - the right temperature, water and air.
Prod-CORF Dist-CORF 1973

What Do Some Birds Do In Autumn And Winter C 20 MIN
2 INCH VIDEOTAPE P
See series title for descriptive statement.
From The Science Corner I, Unit I - Living Things In Autumn Series.
Prod-MPATI Dist-GPITVL

What Do Some Other Animals Do In Autumn And Winter C 20 MIN
2 INCH VIDEOTAPE P
See series title for descriptive statement.
From The Science Corner I, Unit I - Living Things In Autumn Series.
Prod-MPATI Dist-GPITVL

What Do They Do - Word Recognition C 30 MIN
3/4 OR 1/2 INCH VIDEO CASSETTE T
See series title for descriptive statement.
From The Teaching Early Reading Series.
Prod-CTI Dist-CTI

What Do They Eat C 5 MIN
16MM FILM, 3/4 OR 1/2 IN VIDEO P-I
Illustrates food chains and food webs commonly found in nature.
From The Wonder Walks Series.
Prod-EBEC Dist-EBEC 1971

What Do They Really Want C 20 MIN
16MM FILM - 3/4 IN VIDEO
Shows customer service people how to motivate themselves, relieve tensions and reduce frustrations. Points out that focusing on the customer needs and wants works wonders and paying attention to feelings first gives them a surprising advantage. Depicts customer service situations in a hotel and a bank. Features Dr David Scott, aeronautical research director and former astronaut, and Dru Scott.
From The Winning With Customers Series.
Prod-BNA Dist-BNA

What Do We - Cans C 4 MIN
16MM FILM, 3/4 OR 1/2 IN VIDEO I-J
Shows cans of different sizes, shapes, openings and contents taking on new dimensions as they become an instrument, a vase, a game or a telephone. Explores these and other possibilities so that children will want to try their own imaginative, creative ways of using this throw-away product.
From The Mini Movies, Unit 2 - What Do We Do Series.
Prod-MORLAT Dist-CORF 1976

What Do We - Chocolate C 4 MIN
16MM FILM, 3/4 OR 1/2 IN VIDEO I-J
Traces the chocolate bar's origins back to cocoa beans. Shows how curiosity aroused by an all-time children's favorite, the chocolate bar, results in an intriguing visit to a chocolate factory and an increased awareness of chocolate in the diet.
From The Mini Movies, Unit 2 - What Do We Do Series.
Prod-MORLAT Dist-CORF 1976

What Do We - Glass C 4 MIN
16MM FILM, 3/4 OR 1/2 IN VIDEO I-J
Discusses the uses, properties and production of glass in order to create an interest in glass and to promote an increased awareness of glass in a child's world.
From The Mini Movies, Unit 2 - What Do We Do Series.
Prod-MORLAT Dist-CORF 1976

What Do We - Shoes C 4 MIN
16MM FILM, 3/4 OR 1/2 IN VIDEO I-J
Shows how skiers, skaters, golfers and astronauts all wear shoes especially suited to their activities.
From The Mini Movies, Unit 2 - What Do We Do Series.
Prod-MORLAT Dist-CORF 1976

What Do We - Toothpicks C 4 MIN
16MM FILM, 3/4 OR 1/2 IN VIDEO I-J
Presents a colorful montage showing towering trees becoming tiny toothpicks. Depicts toothpicks in many roles from hors d'doeuvres to sculptures.
From The Mini Movies, Unit 2 - What Do We Do Series.
Prod-MORLAT Dist-CORF 1976

What Do We Do Now C 30 MIN
16MM FILM OPTICAL SOUND
Shows the difficulties faced by families in finding the right services for a handicapped child. Presents the Regional Referral System, operative in California and elsewhere, where families can learn about the needs of the handicapped and get help in meeting those needs.
LC NO. 77-700435
Prod-RSF Dist-RSF Prodn-DREW 1976

What Do We Do Now - The Need For Direction C 29 MIN
16MM FILM OPTICAL SOUND S
Discusses the problems and frustrations facing the parents of a handicapped child as they try to secure proper services for the child. Introduces Direction, a program for the handicapped in California which assesses a handicapped child's special needs and matches those needs with locally available services.
LC NO. 77-700866
Prod-USBEH Dist-USNAC 1975

What Do We Know About The Metric System C 20 MIN
3/4 INCH VIDEO CASSETTE J-C A
Reviews the first nine lessons of the Metric System series.
From The Metric System Series.
Prod-MAETEL Dist-GPITVL 1975

What Do We Look Like To Others C 10 MIN
16MM FILM, 3/4 OR 1/2 IN VIDEO H-C A
Presents seven different office situations to portray the necessity of maintaining good personal appearance, attitudes, conduct and personal habits.
Prod-SAIF Dist-BARR 1973

What Do We Mean - Culture C 20 MIN
3/4 INCH VIDEO CASSETTE I
Investigates the American way of life as a product of diverse cultural elements.
From The Exploring Our Nation Series.
Prod-KRMATV Dist-GPITVL 1975

What Do We Mean By Meaning C 30 MIN
3/4 OR 1/2 INCH VIDEO CASSETTE C
See series title for descriptive statement.
From The Language And Meaning Series.
Prod-WUSFTV Dist-GPITVL 1983

What Do We Put Under Our Streets C 20 MIN
2 INCH VIDEOTAPE P
See series title for descriptive statement.
From The Science Corner I, Unit III - Looking At Things Around Us Series.
Prod-MPATI Dist-GPITVL

What Do We See In The Sky C 10 MIN
16MM FILM, 3/4 OR 1/2 IN VIDEO P
Shows a young boy studying the sun, moon, planets, stars and constellations. He learns about their relative size, distance, light and composition.
Prod-CORF Dist-CORF 1957

What Do We Use To Make Our Streets C 20 MIN
2 INCH VIDEOTAPE P
See series title for descriptive statement.
From The Science Corner I, Unit III - Looking At Things Around Us Series.
Prod-MPATI Dist-GPITVL

What Do You Do When You See A Blind Person C 14 MIN
16MM FILM OPTICAL SOUND H-C A
Presents a light touch approach to the right and wrong ways of dealing with blind people in various situations.
LC NO. 72-700146
Prod-AFB Dist-AFB 1971

What Do You Do When You See A Blind Person C 13 MIN
16MM FILM, 3/4 OR 1/2 IN VIDEO I-C A
Shows the proper way to aid the blind.
Prod-AFB Dist-BFA

What Do You Do While You Wait C 11 MIN
16MM FILM, 3/4 OR 1/2 IN VIDEO I-J
Points out that waiting is something everyone has to do some time in their life. Shows children waiting for different things and what you can do while you wait if you use your imagination.
Prod-EBEC Dist-EBEC 1973

What Do You Do With Numbers B 15 MIN
2 INCH VIDEOTAPE I
Discusses the use of measurement and graphing. (Broadcast quality)
From The Let's Explore Science Series. No. 4
Prod-POPS Dist-GPITVL Prodn-KOAPTV

What Do You Know About Carpet C 22 MIN
16MM FILM OPTICAL SOUND
Presents information and advice from an expert on selecting carpet for the home, including tips on fibers, construction, color and style.
Prod-ACOC Dist-ACOC

What Do You Know About Computers C 30 MIN
2 INCH VIDEOTAPE J
See series title for descriptive statement.
From The Summer Journal, Unit 2 - You Are What You Can Do Series.
Prod-WNINTV Dist-GPITVL

What Do You Know About Your Teeth? C 25 MIN
3/4 OR 1/2 INCH VIDEO CASSETTE
Gives a multiple-choice and true-false fun-for-all quiz on dental health. Shows Dr David Gaynor answering and explaining important facts about dental hygience, for instance, what it means when gums bleed. Discusses fluoridation of water supply as well.
Prod-TRAINX Dist-TRAINX

What Do You Mean C 4 MIN
16MM FILM, 3/4 OR 1/2 IN VIDEO K-I
Describes Bobby's thinking as he learns that when his parents have had a 'HARD DAY,' he must treat them with more understanding.
From The Most Important Person - Getting Along With Others Series.
Prod-EBEC Dist-EBEC 1972

What Do You Mean C 30 MIN
3/4 OR 1/2 INCH VIDEO CASSETTE H-C A
Explains how words derive their meanings and the relationship between the culture and the meanings of words.

From The Principles of Human Communication Series.
Prod-UMINN Dist-GPITVL 1983

What Do You People Want C 30 MIN
16MM FILM OPTICAL SOUND
Presents an angry indictment of white oppression made by the Black Liberation Movement at a number of meetings during the turbulent events of the Black Panther party's history in 1968.
Prod-IMPACT Dist-IMPACT 1968

What Do You Say Now C 8 MIN
16MM FILM OPTICAL SOUND C A
Presents vignettes of children making statements which would elicit an adult response. Offers practice in communication and child management skills.
LC NO. 80-701592
Prod-PSUPCR Dist-PSUPCR 1980

What Do You See C 15 MIN
3/4 OR 1/2 INCH VIDEO CASSETTE P
Defines the concepts of seeing. Shows through works of art how artists see the same things from different points of view.
From The Primary Art Series.
Prod-WETATV Dist-AITECH

What Do You See C 25 MIN
2 INCH VIDEOTAPE I
Emphasizes careful observation of lines and shapes as a basis for drawing.
From The Art Has Many Forms Series.
Prod-CVETVC Dist-GPITVL

What Do You See Now, Pt 1 C 11 MIN
16MM FILM OPTICAL SOUND K-I
Shows different ideas about addition and subtraction-addition-circle, square, triangle, subtraction-circle, square, triangle, addition-rectangle, diamond, cross, subtraction-rectangle, diamond and cross.
Prod-SF Dist-SF

What Do You See Now, Pt 2 C 11 MIN
16MM FILM OPTICAL SOUND K-I
Shows different ideas about addition and subtraction-addition-circle, square, triangle, subtraction-circle, square, triangle, addition-rectangle, diamond, cross, subtraction-rectangle, diamond and cross.
Prod-SF Dist-SF

What Do You See, Nurse C 12 MIN
16MM FILM, 3/4 OR 1/2 IN VIDEO J-C A
Presents an elderly woman in a nursing home who says that people should look beyond the wrinkles and pain of old age and recognize the beauty and richness of her life.
LC NO. 80-707323
Prod-GORKER Dist-CORF 1980

What Do You See? C 6 MIN
3/4 OR 1/2 INCH VIDEO CASSETTE
Tells hospital personnel, through the thoughts of an elderly woman, how it feels to be a patient and how hospital staff affect patient care.
Prod-AHOA Dist-AHOA 1980

What Do You Think B 15 MIN
3/4 OR 1/2 INCH VIDEO CASSETTE I
Discusses the value of prediction.
From The Let's Explore Science Series.
Prod-GPITVL Dist-GPITVL

What Do You Think C 15 MIN
16MM FILM, 3/4 OR 1/2 IN VIDEO I-J
Introduces career choice as a developmental process, a continuous series of decisions about one's self and what one wants to be.
From The Whatcha Gonna Do Series.
Prod-NVETA Dist-EBEC 1974

What Do You Think You Want To Be C 4 MIN
16MM FILM, 3/4 OR 1/2 IN VIDEO K-I
Features fumble singing 'YOU CAN BE ANYTHING YOU WANT TO BE.' Observes the children visualizing the many things there are to be as an adult.
From The Most Important Person - Identity Series.
Prod-EBEC Dist-EBEC 1972

What Do You Think You Want To Be (Spanish) C 4 MIN
16MM FILM, 3/4 OR 1/2 IN VIDEO K-P
See series title for descriptive statement.
From The Most Important Person - Identity (Spanish) Series.
Prod-EBEC Dist-EBEC

What Do You Think–A Series
16MM FILM, 3/4 OR 1/2 IN VIDEO J-C
Looks at the problems of alcohol, drug and tobacco consumption in American society.
Prod-EBEC Dist-EBEC

Alcohol Problem, The - What Do You Think 018 MIN
Drug Problem, The - What Do You Think 017 MIN
Tobacco Problem, The - What Do You Think 017 MIN

What Do You Trust? C 25 MIN
3/4 OR 1/2 INCH VIDEO CASSETTE C
See series title for descriptive statement.
From The Introduction To Philosophy Series.
Prod-UDEL Dist-UDEL

What Do You Want C 27 MIN
16MM FILM OPTICAL SOUND H-C A
Points out that people with dedication can create opportunities to promote growth in towns that are dying. Explores things that some people are doing to keep their towns alive. Shows how a group of concerned local people from various walks of life come together, and begin exploring what they could do to put their community back on its feet.
LC NO. 73-700182
Prod-BANDEL Dist-BANDEL 1972

What Do You Want And I Want Some Cake, Milk, Please C 15 MIN
2 INCH VIDEOTAPE P
See series title for descriptive statement.
From The Avenida De Ingles Series.
Prod-SDITVA Dist-GPITVL

What Do You Wear To School B 15 MIN
2 INCH VIDEOTAPE P
Explains that clothing, a basic need for all people, provides comfort and protection. (Broadcast quality)
From The Around The Corner Series. No. 20
Prod-FWCETV Dist-GPITVL Prodn-WEDUTV

What Does A Fish Do B 20 MIN
2 INCH VIDEOTAPE P
Explains how the completion of work on an outdoor, artificial pool creates an interest in what it will be used for. Shows a fish and describes how it can move about, breathe and eat in water.
From The Scienceland Series.
Prod-MPATI Dist-GPITVL

What Does Fire Need To Burn C 20 MIN
2 INCH VIDEOTAPE P
See series title for descriptive statement.
From The Science Corner I, Unit IV - Protection Against The Weather Series.
Prod-MPATI Dist-GPITVL

What Does It Mean To Be A Black American C 30 MIN
2 INCH VIDEOTAPE I
Features Mrs Mildred Murphy, developer of the program on Black culture in the Berkeley Unified School District project EPOCH and representative of KQED-TV in San Francisco, who discusses the Black American.
From The That's A Good Question Series.
Prod-KGEDTV Dist-GPITVL

What Does It Mean To Be A Chinese American C 30 MIN
2 INCH VIDEOTAPE I
Features Alan Wong, executive director of the College YMCA at San Francisco State College, and Kenneth Wong, a newsman for the only paper in this country published in both Chinese and English, who discuss the Chinese Americans.
From The That's A Good Question Series.
Prod-KGEDTV Dist-GPITVL

What Does It Mean To Be A Japanese American C 30 MIN
2 INCH VIDEOTAPE I
Features Mrs Florence Yoshiware, advisory specialist in the Title TV program of the San Mateo City School District and coordinator of the Japanese American Curriculum Project in that school district, who discusses the Japanese in America.
From The That's A Good Question Series.
Prod-KGEDTV Dist-GPITVL

What Does It Mean To Be A Native American C 30 MIN
2 INCH VIDEOTAPE I
Presents David Peri, head of the Ethnic Studies Department of Sonoma State College in California, who discusses the American Indian, especially the Miwok Tribe of Northern California of which he is a member.
From The That's A Good Question Series.
Prod-KGEDTV Dist-GPITVL

What Does It Need To Grow C 29 MIN
16MM FILM, 3/4 OR 1/2 IN VIDEO
Demonstrates three major stages of cognitive development in children four to 11 years old. Reveals their concepts of the physical world as well as their religious and moral ideas.
Prod-UCEMC Dist-UCEMC

What Does Music Do C 20 MIN
16MM FILM OPTICAL SOUND I
Points out that there is no category of music that is basically good or bad, but that all of the varieties of music can be well or poorly presented. Implies that the child should not make a blanket condemnation of any type of music, but should try and judge each selection on its own merits.
From The Music Of America Series.
Prod-KQEDTV Dist-GPITVL

What Does Our Flag Mean C 11 MIN
16MM FILM, 3/4 OR 1/2 IN VIDEO P-I
Explains, through the story of a family that become naturalized American citizens, the meaning of the American flag, how it has changed through the years, how it is displayed and how one shows respect for it.
Prod-CORF Dist-CORF 1967

What Does Race Mean C 30 MIN
2 INCH VIDEOTAPE I
Shows that 'race' is a concept which is used as a convenient way of grouping people who share similiar physical traits.
From The That's A Good Question Series.
Prod-KGEDTV Dist-GPITVL

What Does The Earth Look Like From Space B 20 MIN
2 INCH VIDEOTAPE P
Explains how a trip into space is made possible when a rocket ship blasts off from earth and comes to rest on a space station.
From The Scienceland Series.
Prod-MPATI Dist-GPITVL

What Does The Wind Do C 20 MIN
2 INCH VIDEOTAPE I
See series title for descriptive statement.
From The Science Corner II, Unit VII - Understanding Weather Series.
Prod-MPATI Dist-GPITVL

What Ecologists Do C 16 MIN
16MM FILM, 3/4 OR 1/2 IN VIDEO P-J
Defines ecology and explains the role of ecologists.
Prod-CENTRO Dist-CORF

What Electricity Does In Every Electric System C 60 MIN
1 INCH VIDEOTAPE IND
Describes the elements of electricity, such as current and voltage, and what electricity does in every electric system.
From The Understanding Semiconductors Course Outline Series. No. 01
Prod-TXINLC Dist-TXINLC

What Energy Means C 15 MIN
16MM FILM, 3/4 OR 1/2 IN VIDEO P-I
Discusses the various forms of energy, the ways in which energy can be converted from one form to another, the difference between fuel and energy and the need to conserve fuels.
Prod-NGS Dist-NGS 1982

What Every Manager Needs To Know About Information Systems, Pt 1 - The Meritt Case C 25 MIN
16MM FILM - 3/4 IN VIDEO IND
Presents the most common and difficult problems in introducing information systems, particulary computer use.
From The Management Practice Series.
Prod-BNA Dist-BNA 1972

What Every Manager Needs To Know About Information Systems, Pt 2 - The Computer... C 25 MIN
16MM FILM - 3/4 IN VIDEO IND
Defines the information system and tells how to make it more effective.
From The Management Practice Series.
Prod-BNA Dist-BNA 1972

What Every Manager Needs To Know About Long-Range Planning, Pt 1 - The Merritt Case C 30 MIN
16MM FILM - 3/4 IN VIDEO IND
Shows how long-range planning must be a team effort, including an analysis of the situation, setting realistic objectives, defining strategies and alternate strategies.
From The Management Practice Series.
Prod-BNA Dist-BNA 1972

What Every Manager Needs To Know About Long-Range Planning, Pt 2 - Invent Your... C 30 MIN
16MM FILM - 3/4 IN VIDEO IND
Points out the vital benefits of long-range planning. Answers such questions as does long-range planning conflict with management intuition, what are the key elements in long-range planning and what's the payoff.
From The Management Practice Series.
Prod-BNA Dist-BNA 1972

What Every Manager Needs To Know About Marketing, Pt 1 - The Merritt Case C 30 MIN
16MM FILM - 3/4 IN VIDEO IND
Deals with the distinctions between marketing and selling, pointing out ways in which a company can improve marketing, production and delivery.
From The Management Practice Series.
LC NO. 79-708007
Prod-BNA Dist-BNA 1972

What Every Manager Needs To Know About Marketing, Pt 2 - What Business Are You... C 30 MIN
16MM FILM - 3/4 IN VIDEO IND
Discusses how to build a solid marketing plan based on behavior, competition, sales forcasts, sales organization and sales training.
From The Management Practice Series.
LC NO. 79-708007
Prod-BNA Dist-BNA 1972

What Floats On Water B 20 MIN
2 INCH VIDEOTAPE P
Explains that a bottle found floating on a nearby lake leads to an investigation of what makes some things float.
From The Scienceland Series.
Prod-MPATI Dist-GPITVL

What Foods Do We Get From The Sea C 20 MIN
2 INCH VIDEOTAPE P
See series title for descriptive statement.
From The Science Corner I, Unit VII - Obtaining And Preserving Foods Series.
Prod-MPATI Dist-GPITVL

What Games Can Families Play B 15 MIN
2 INCH VIDEOTAPE P
Explains that because of the labor saving machines of today, people have more free time for fun and the members of a family unit can cooperate in planning things that are fun. (Broadcast quality)
From The Around The Corner Series. No. 32
Prod-FWCETV Dist-GPITVL Prodn-WEDUTV

What Goes Aaaaakkkkk C 15 MIN
3/4 INCH VIDEO CASSETTE P
Shows a garage filled with dangerous chemicals. Discusses helpful and harmful aspects of medicines and chemicals. Establishes a need to discard unused portions of these when advisable or to store them safely.
From The Think Fine - Feel Fine Series.
Prod-KTCATV Dist-GPITVL

What Goes On In Scienceland B 20 MIN
2 INCH VIDEOTAPE P
Explains that a mysterious footprint initiates a series of investigations, leading to an understanding of the methods used by scientists.
From The Scienceland Series.
Prod-MPATI Dist-GPITVL

What Goes Up C 12 MIN
3/4 OR 1/2 INCH VIDEO CASSETTE
Presents a program beautifully photographed at Lake Compounce, Connecticut, for cardiovascular patients.
Prod-PRIMED Dist-PRIMED

What Good Is A Warbler C 13 MIN
16MM FILM OPTICAL SOUND P-C A
Uses the intimate family life of an endangered bird, the golden-cheeked warbler, to show what may happen when humans alter the environment. Explores the warbler's home and special needs revealing its intricate relations with other elements of the natural world. Points out that each living thing plays a role and has a value in the natural cycle.
LC NO. 75-703299
Prod-ADAMSF Dist-ADAMSF 1975

What Green Plants Reproduce By Other Means B 15 MIN
2 INCH VIDEOTAPE P
Explains that some groups of green plants reproduce by vegetative means or spores.
From The Science Is Discovery Series.
Prod-DETPS Dist-GPITVL

What Green Plants Reproduce By Seeds B 15 MIN
2 INCH VIDEOTAPE P
Explains that some groups of green plants reproduce by seeds.
From The Science Is Discovery Series.
Prod-DETPS Dist-GPITVL

What Guys Want C 16 MIN
3/4 OR 1/2 INCH VIDEO CASSETTE J-H A
Presents teenagers of diverse ethnic, racial and economic backgrounds expressing their attitudes and feelings about maleness and their male sexual behavior.
Prod-POLYMR Dist-POLYMR

What Hands Can Do C 10 MIN
16MM FILM, 3/4 OR 1/2 IN VIDEO P-I
Portrays children's hands performing all the roles in a three act play that tells of the endless variety of uses for hands.
Prod-SF Dist-SF 1967

What Happened To Harry - Back Siphonage C 20 MIN
16MM FILM OPTICAL SOUND H-C
Utilizes a comic sketch of 'HAPPY-GO-LUCKY' Harry to show dangers of back siphonage and cross-connections in plumbing systems.
Prod-OSUMPD Dist-OSUMPD 1963

What Happened To Mooretown B 19 MIN
16MM FILM OPTICAL SOUND
Shows how the major health director, president of the Neighborhood Health Council, and Public Works directors cooperate with official agencies in improving the housing, sewage disposal, vector control and general environmental sanitation of a high disease incidence neighborhood of Shreveport, Louisiana.
LC NO. 74-705943
Prod-USPHS Dist-USNAC 1965

What Happened To My Backyard Shouldn't Happen To A Dog C 11 MIN
16MM FILM OPTICAL SOUND I
Presents the concepts of good workmanship in a lighthearted manner, showing a family's backyard being drastically changed during the construction of a swimming pool.
LC NO. 78-711579
Prod-ALEF Dist-ALEF 1971

What Happened To My Paycheck C 16 MIN
16MM FILM, 3/4 OR 1/2 IN VIDEO H A
Tells about a high school student who is upset when he receives less pay than he expected because of withholding taxes. Shows him learning to fill out tax forms, visiting an IRS office, and observing the computers that check tax calculations.
LC NO. 81-706305
Prod-USIRS Dist-USNAC 1980

What Happens At A Weather Station C 20 MIN
2 INCH VIDEOTAPE I
See series title for descriptive statement.
From The Science Corner II, Unit VII - Understanding Weather Series.
Prod-MPATI Dist-GPITVL

What Happens At Night B 20 MIN
2 INCH VIDEOTAPE P
Shows how the moon and stars light up the darkness and how many animals become active at night.
From The Scienceland Series.
Prod-MPATI Dist-GPITVL

What Happens In Our High Schools C 29 MIN
16MM FILM, 3/4 OR 1/2 IN VIDEO T
Examines the essence of secondary education and looks optimistically to its future. Includes experimental learning approaches and a visit to a unique school-within-a-school program.
From The Dealing With Classroom Problems Series.
Prod-MFFD Dist-FI 1976

What Happens In Scienceland B 20 MIN
2 INCH VIDEOTAPE P
Presents an album of pictures which recalls the many places visited and the discoveries made in scienceland.
From The Scienceland Series.
Prod-MPATI Dist-GPITVL

What Happens Inside C 10 MIN
16MM FILM OPTICAL SOUND K-I
Uses animation and live action to record the growth of a fertilized mammal egg. Explains the meaning of the terms 'GESTATION,' 'UMBILICUS' and 'PLACENTA.' Shows the birth of a litter of kittens. Draws comparisons between the care of a mother cat for her kittens and of a human mother for her children. Describes the first four months of the development of a human baby inside the mother.
From The Family Life And Sex Education Series.
Prod-SF Dist-SF 1968

What Happens Inside An Egg C 20 MIN
2 INCH VIDEOTAPE P
See series title for descriptive statement.
From The Science Corner I, Unit XI - Young Animals Series.
Prod-MPATI Dist-GPITVL

What Happens Next C 18 MIN
16MM FILM, 3/4 OR 1/2 IN VIDEO IND
Dramatizes four industrial accidents and explores what should be done to protect the injured and those persons on the shop floor. Demonstrates the correct and incorrect responses to each accident.
LC NO. 81-707641
Prod-MILLBK Dist-IFB 1981

What Happens Next - Code 4 B 16 MIN
16MM FILM OPTICAL SOUND PRO
Portrays human and technical factors to be considered in organizing and training a hospital resuscitation team. Shows a program in action at the Palo Alto Hospital in California.
LC NO. FIA67-690
Prod-SKF Dist-AMEDA Prodn-LOPATN 1965

What Happens On A Freezing Day C 20 MIN
2 INCH VIDEOTAPE I
See series title for descriptive statement.
From The Science Corner II, Unit VII - Understanding Weather Series.
Prod-MPATI Dist-GPITVL

What Happens To Leaves B 20 MIN
2 INCH VIDEOTAPE P
Pictures a tree with five leaves left on a branch. Asks children what might happen to each leaf after it falls.
From The Scienceland Series.
Prod-MPATI Dist-GPITVL

What Happens To Some Furry Animals In Autumn And Winter C 20 MIN
2 INCH VIDEOTAPE P
See series title for descriptive statement.
From The Science Corner I, Unit I - Living Things In Autumn Series.
Prod-MPATI Dist-GPITVL

What Happens To Trees In Autumn C 20 MIN
2 INCH VIDEOTAPE P
See series title for descriptive statement.
From The Science Corner I, Unit I - Living Things In Autumn Series.
Prod-MPATI Dist-GPITVL

What Happens When Air Is Heated And Cooled C 15 MIN
3/4 OR 1/2 INCH VIDEO CASSETTE P-I
Discusses what happens when air is heated and cooled.
From The Why Series.
Prod-WDCNTV Dist-AITECH 1976

What Happens When Electricity Travels Through A Wire C 20 MIN
2 INCH VIDEOTAPE I
See series title for descriptive statement.
From The Science Corner II, Unit VI - Magnetism And Electricity Series.
Prod-MPATI Dist-GPITVL

What Happens When Environmental Conditions Are Altered B 15 MIN
2 INCH VIDEOTAPE P
Explains that severe environmental changes can affect changes in the plant and animal populations.
From The Science Is Discovery Series.
Prod-DETPS Dist-GPITVL

What Happens When It Works / No More Lunchsacks For Me C 29 MIN
3/4 INCH VIDEO CASSETTE
Tells how students in Stockton, California, spearheaded a successful city-wide effort to prepare for desegregation. Dramatizes a free school lunch program in Wichita, Kansas, and shows how it affected desegregation.
From The As We See It Series.
Prod-WTTWTV Dist-PUBTEL

What Happens When Things Fall Through The Air C 20 MIN
2 INCH VIDEOTAPE P
See series title for descriptive statement.
From The Science Corner I, Unit IX - Transportation Series.
Prod-MPATI Dist-GPITVL

What Happens When We Exercise C 20 MIN
2 INCH VIDEOTAPE P
See series title for descriptive statement.
From The Science Corner I, Unit V - Your Body And How It Works Series.
Prod-MPATI Dist-GPITVL

What Happens When We Mix Things With Water C 20 MIN
2 INCH VIDEOTAPE P
See series title for descriptive statement.
From The Science Corner I, Unit III - Looking At Things Around Us Series.
Prod-MPATI Dist-GPITVL

What Happens When You Go To The Hospital C 12 MIN
16MM FILM OPTICAL SOUND A
Shows young children enacting a child's recent hospitalization. Shows the roles of patient, doctor, nurse and parents, with occasional role reversal and sharing, as assumed by children and facilitates study and discussion for students and practitioners in child development, child psychology and other related disciplines.
From The Training Module On Role Enactment In Children's Play. Four
LC NO. 76-700937
Prod-UPITTS Dist-CFDC Prodn-CFDC 1974

What Happens When You're Sick C 17 MIN
16MM FILM, 3/4 OR 1/2 IN VIDEO P-I
Describes Dennis's tour through Symptom Headquarters by Selena the Symptom Sender. Explains such symptoms as fever, sneezing, upset stomach, diarrhea, bleeding, swelling and pain.
Prod-HIGGIN Dist-HIGGIN 1981

What Harvest For The Reaper B 59 MIN
16MM FILM OPTICAL SOUND H-C
Documents the experiences of a group of farmworkers who became trapped in a system that kept them perpetually in debt. Shows methods of recruitment, labor camps on Long Island and the types of work involved. Presents the opinions of growers and processors and refutes their views.
From The Net Journal Series.
LC NO. FIA68-1479
Prod-NET Dist-IU 1968

What Has Happened To Political Machines C 29 MIN
2 INCH VIDEOTAPE
See series title for descriptive statement.
From The University Of Chicago Round Table Series.
Prod-WTTWTV Dist-PUBTEL

What Have We Learned B 15 MIN
2 INCH VIDEOTAPE P
Reviews materials and make suggestions for using some of them during the summer.
From The Art Corner Series.
Prod-CVETVC Dist-GPITVL Prodn-WCVETV

What Have You Done For Yourself Lately C 20 MIN
3/4 OR 1/2 INCH VIDEO CASSETTE
Provides self-development techniques for use in achieving one's full potential. Includes a leader's guide.
Prod-DELTAK Dist-DELTAK

What Have You Done For Yourself Lately? C 15 MIN
3/4 OR 1/2 INCH VIDEO CASSETTE
Shows employees how to zero in on the priority tasks where maximum results can be achieved, helps them develop job enrichment programs for themselves and provides self-development techniques that ensure continued personal growth.
Prod-EFM Dist-EFM

What Have You Got To Lose C 30 MIN
3/4 OR 1/2 INCH VIDEO CASSETTE I-J
Shows how the Powerhouse Kids learn there are no shortcuts to losing weight.
From The Powerhouse Series.
LC NO. 83-707189
Prod-EFCVA Dist-GA 1982

What Holds You Up C 15 MIN
3/4 OR 1/2 INCH VIDEO CASSETTE P
Describes the framework of bones inside the human body. Explains that the skeleton gives the human body its shape and support and protects the vital organs.
From The All About You Series.
Prod-WGBHTV Dist-AITECH Prodn-TTOIC 1975

What I Like - Spatial Interaction (Geography) C 15 MIN
3/4 OR 1/2 INCH VIDEO CASSETTE P
Reveals that as Deron travels from his city home to his uncle's farm, he notices how the landscapes, buildings, vehicles and activities change along the way.
From The Two Cents' Worth Series.
Prod-WHATV Dist-AITECH Prodn-WIEC 1976

What If C 3 MIN
16MM FILM, 3/4 OR 1/2 IN VIDEO K-I
Presents four situations that are often difficult to cope with when they occur in real life, so that appropriate responses can be worked out in advance, or if these situations have already been met, to show why people respond the way they do. Includes a situation where a girl finds a wallet and a boy's ice cream cone is knocked out of his hand.
From The Magic Moments, Unit 1 - Let's Talk Series.
Prod-EBEC Dist-EBEC 1969

What If The Patient Has AIDS C 20 MIN
3/4 OR 1/2 INCH VIDEO CASSETTE PRO
Discusses AIDS for nurses and other professional and technical health workers who come into contact with AIDS patients. Includes 25 information booklets.
Prod-USPHS Dist-USNAC 1984

What If You Couldn't Read C 29 MIN
16MM FILM, 3/4 OR 1/2 IN VIDEO H-C A
Focuses on an illiterate fur trader who, after 40 years of being unable to read and write, has begun learning these skills with the help of a tutor. Shows how the ability to read has changed his marriage and entire life.
Prod-TODD Dist-FLMLIB 1978

What In The World Is The World Council Of Churches C 21 MIN
1/2 IN VIDEO CASSETTE (VHS) J-C A
Presents a history of the World Council of Churches from 1928

to 1982. Highlights major themes which are representative of the issues of the future. Includes worship, encounter, sharing, solidarity and expectation.
Prod-FLEMIP Dist-ECUFLM 1982

What In The World's Come Over You C 15 MIN
3/4 OR 1/2 INCH VIDEO CASSETTE I-J
Analyzes historical events as they influence present societies and act as clues to future ones.
From The It's All Up To You Series.
Prod-COOPED Dist-AITECH Prodn-WHATV 1978

What Is Communication B 30 MIN
16MM FILM OPTICAL SOUND J-C A
Defines the communication process and illustrates ways in which adolescents communicate with themselves, their peers, their parents and other adults.
From The Dial C-12-18 For Family Understanding Series.
LC NO. 74-700169
Prod-UNEBR Dist-UNEBR 1970

What Is A Bird X 17 MIN
16MM FILM, 3/4 OR 1/2 IN VIDEO H
Describes the evolutionary relationship between birds and reptiles. Shows the body structures of birds and explains how their structural characteristics help them adapt to different environments. Illustrates various patterns of behavior.
From The Biology Series. Unit 7 - Animal Classification And Physiology
Prod-EBF Dist-EBEC 1962

What Is A Bird (Spanish) C 17 MIN
16MM FILM, 3/4 OR 1/2 IN VIDEO H
Describes how the body structures of birds are adapted for flight and how birds are able to live in a wide variety of environments. Illustrates the behavior patterns of birds and the evolutionary relationships between birds and reptiles.
From The Biology (Spanish) Series. Unit 7 - Animal Classification And Physiology
Prod-EBEC Dist-EBEC

What Is A Cat C 14 MIN
16MM FILM, 3/4 OR 1/2 IN VIDEO K-H
Presents the history of the domestic cat, tracing the animal as a house pet and as a symbol of mystery and worship from ancient Egypt to the present day.
Prod-NILCOM Dist-FLMFR 1972

What Is A Cat (Captioned Version) C 14 MIN
16MM FILM, 3/4 OR 1/2 IN VIDEO K-H
Presents the history of the domestic cat, tracing the animal as a house pet and as a symbol of mystery and worship from ancient Egypt to the present day.
Prod-NILCOM Dist-FLMFR 1972

What Is A Christian B 30 MIN
16MM FILM OPTICAL SOUND H-C A R
A story concerning a hesitant Christian who is sent to four men about Christ and answers their question 'WHAT IS A CHRISTIAN.'
LC NO. 72-701662
Prod-CONCOR Dist-CPH 1956

What Is A City C 11 MIN
16MM FILM, 3/4 OR 1/2 IN VIDEO P-I
Describes the city as people living and working together, enjoying recreation and trying to solve the problems of pollution, congestion and poverty.
Prod-CORF Dist-CORF 1972

What Is A Community C 20 MIN
16MM FILM OPTICAL SOUND I
Demonstrates that plants and animals are dependent on one another, and as a result of this dependency, there is an organization or structure to nature. Points out that this organization is often referred to as a community, composed of plants and animals that live within an area with a similar environment.
From The Inherit The Earth Series.
Prod-KQEDTV Dist-GPITVL

What Is A Community B 15 MIN
2 INCH VIDEOTAPE P-I
See series title for descriptive statement.
From The Our Changing Community Series.
Prod-VITA Dist-GPITVL 1967

What Is A Community (2nd Ed) C 17 MIN
16MM FILM, 3/4 OR 1/2 IN VIDEO P-I
Defines a community as a group of people and people who live and work together to get the things they need. Lists a community's needs, functions, differences and similarities.
Prod-EBEC Dist-EBEC 1970

What Is A Computer C 20 MIN
16MM FILM, 3/4 OR 1/2 IN VIDEO H
Uses animation to explain how a computer operates. Shows how the main functions of the computer are applied to an actual problem.
Prod-EAMES Dist-EBEC

What Is A Computer Program? C 17 MIN
3/4 OR 1/2 INCH VIDEO CASSETTE A
Explains what a computer program is and details the differences between a programmer and a systems analyst. Discusses the significance of flow charts, programming specifications and programming languages.
Prod-XICOM Dist-XICOM

What Is A Computer Program? C 18 MIN
16MM FILM, 3/4 OR 1/2 IN VIDEO A
Explains the concepts of computer logic, memory and retrieval.
From The Everybody's Guide To The Computer Series.
Prod-VISUCP Dist-VISUCP 1980

What Is A Computer? C 17 MIN
16MM FILM, 3/4 OR 1/2 IN VIDEO A
Removes the myths surrounding computers. Explains the concepts of input, output and storage.
From The Everybody's Guide To The Computer Series.
Prod-VISUCP Dist-VISUCP 1980

What Is A Computer? C 18 MIN
3/4 OR 1/2 INCH VIDEO CASSETTE A
Introduces the viewer to the basic workings of the computer. Explains the connections between the central processors and the peripherals, including the printer, disk drives and video consol.
Prod-XICOM Dist-XICOM

What Is A Computer? C 30 MIN
3/4 OR 1/2 INCH VIDEO CASSETTE
Presents a nontechnical introduction to the nature of computers and the kinds of tasks they perform. Uses analogies from everyday life to explain technical concepts. Discusses a number of fears and misconceptions about computers.
From The Working With The Computer Series.
Prod-DELTAK Dist-DELTAK

What Is A Desert C 13 MIN
16MM FILM, 3/4 OR 1/2 IN VIDEO P-H
Edited from the 1953 motion picture The Living Desert. Shows how geographic factors form deserts and how winds, mountains and temperature interact to form this topography. Includes scenes of flash floods and the riddle of the rocks that move in such areas as the Great American Desert, Death Valley and the Salton Sea.
From The Living Desert Series.
Prod-DISNEY Dist-WDEMCO 1974

What Is A Desert C 20 MIN
3/4 INCH VIDEO CASSETTE I
Presents a 1500-mile photographic safari through the great American Desert from the great Sand Dunes National Monument to Monument Valley.
From The Understanding Our World, Unit II - Geography We Should Know Series.
Prod-KRMATV Dist-GPITVL

What Is A Desert (Arabic) C 13 MIN
16MM FILM, 3/4 OR 1/2 IN VIDEO I-H
Shows how geographic and weather factors such as winds, mountains and temperature create deserts.
Prod-WDEMCO Dist-WDEMCO 1974

What Is A Desert (French) C 13 MIN
16MM FILM, 3/4 OR 1/2 IN VIDEO I-H
Shows how geographic and weather factors such as winds, mountains and temperature create deserts.
From The Living Desert (French) Series.
Prod-WDEMCO Dist-WDEMCO

What Is A Family C 7 MIN
16MM FILM, 3/4 OR 1/2 IN VIDEO P
Uses animation and puppets to show that different combinations of people make a family, including single people.
From The Learning To Look Series.
Prod-MGHT Dist-MGHT 1973

What Is A Fish X 22 MIN
16MM FILM, 3/4 OR 1/2 IN VIDEO H
Illustrates the major types of fishes and shows the anatomy of a typical fish. Underwater photography shows commensalism and other types of behavior.
From The Biology Series. Unit 7 - Animal Classification And Physiology
Prod-EBF Dist-EBEC 1963

What Is A Fish (Spanish) C 22 MIN
16MM FILM, 3/4 OR 1/2 IN VIDEO H
Outlines the major types of fishes. Shows the anatomy of a typical fish and demonstrates behavior patterns in various species of fishes.
From The Biology (Spanish) Series. Unit 7 - Animal Classification And Physiology
Prod-EBEC Dist-EBEC

What Is A Food? C 30 MIN
3/4 OR 1/2 INCH VIDEO CASSETTE
See series title for descriptive statement.
From The Food For Life Series.
Prod-MSU Dist-MSU

What Is A Friend C 4 MIN
16MM FILM, 3/4 OR 1/2 IN VIDEO K-I
Explores friendship and what friends can do for each other.
From The Most Important Person - Getting Along With Others Series.
Prod-EBEC Dist-EBEC 1972

What Is A Friend C 13 MIN
16MM FILM, 3/4 OR 1/2 IN VIDEO P-I
Shows how Benny learns that to have friends he must be fair with others.
From The Learning Values With Fat Albert Series.
Prod-FLMTON Dist-CRMP 1977

What Is A Good Drawing (Neolithic - 1970 A D) C 17 MIN
16MM FILM OPTICAL SOUND
Examines the draughtman's magic over many centuries to decide what makes a drawing good, no matter what the style. Covers from the Neolothic period to 1970.
Prod-ROLAND Dist-ROLAND

What Is A Hero C 14 MIN
16MM FILM, 3/4 OR 1/2 IN VIDEO P-I
Shows how heroes can provide inspiration and guidance for young people. Looks at different kinds of heroes and the purposes they serve.
Prod-BFA Dist-BFA

What Is A Limit B
16MM FILM OPTICAL SOUND
Explains that mathematical analysis in founded on the concept of a limit. Discusses the ideas behind a limit.
Prod-OPENU Dist-OPENU

What Is A Machine C 15 MIN
3/4 OR 1/2 INCH VIDEO CASSETTE P-I
Discusses the characteristics of a machine.
From The Why Series.
Prod-WDCNTV Dist-AITECH 1976

What Is A Magazine Made Of C 20 MIN
16MM FILM OPTICAL SOUND
Shows how the Family Circle magazine comes into being each month. Depicts how the editorial features are created and how the magazine is assembled.
Prod-FAMLYC Dist-CCNY

What Is A Mammal X 14 MIN
16MM FILM, 3/4 OR 1/2 IN VIDEO H
Demonstrates the basic structural and behavioral characteristics of mammals and describes their successful adaptation to a wide variety of ecological niches. Compares reptilian and mammalian characteristics.
From The Biology Series. Unit 7 - Animal Classification And Physiology
Prod-EBF Dist-EBEC 1962

What Is A Mammal (Spanish) C 14 MIN
16MM FILM, 3/4 OR 1/2 IN VIDEO H
Demonstrates the basic structural and behavioral characteristics of mammals and describes their successful adaptation to a wide variety of ecological niches. Discusses the evolution of mammals and shows their distribution.
From The Biology (Spanish) Series. Unit 7 - Animal Classification And Physiology
Prod-EBEC Dist-EBEC

What Is A Microprocessor? C 30 MIN
3/4 OR 1/2 INCH VIDEO CASSETTE IND
Presents in four videotapes simplest architecture to get by, save costs and reduce design time. Depicts minimum hardware configuration. Demonstrates simple tasks by example.
From The Programming Microprocessors Series.
Prod-COLOSU Dist-COLOSU

What Is A Minority Group, Pt I C 30 MIN
2 INCH VIDEOTAPE I
Introduces and explains the concept of an ethnic group and reviews the ethnic history of the United States.
From The That's A Good Question Series.
Prod-KGEDTV Dist-GPITVL

What Is A Minority Group, Pt II C 30 MIN
2 INCH VIDEOTAPE I
Presents viewers with an idea of and feeling of what it means to be a newcomer in a strange country.
From The That's A Good Question Series.
Prod-KGEDTV Dist-GPITVL

What Is A Mountain C 23 MIN
16MM FILM - 3/4 IN VIDEO I-J
Highlights Mount Rainier, located in the State of Washington. Issued in 1967 as a motion picture.
LC NO. 79-706172
Prod-USNPS Dist-USNAC 1979

What Is A Muscle? C 15 MIN
3/4 OR 1/2 INCH VIDEO CASSETTE
Explains the theory of muscle contractions. Illustrates what muscle tissue is, the types of muscle, the anatomy of a typical skeletal muscle, the function of muscle and how muscle contracts.
Prod-CBSC Dist-CBSC

What Is A Neighborhood C 11 MIN
16MM FILM, 3/4 OR 1/2 IN VIDEO P
Tells what makes up a neighborhood and what neighbors can do to make a neighborhod a safer, more pleasant and more attractive place to live. Indicates the relation of the neighborhood to the larger community.
Prod-CORF Dist-CORF 1964

What Is A Painting / Realism C
3/4 OR 1/2 INCH VIDEO CASSETTE
Introduces the principles of art appreciation and explains technique, composition and personal expression. Traces realism in painting from Van Eyck to Hopper.
From The Metropolitan Museum Seminars In Art Series.
Prod-GA Dist-GA

What Is A Physician Assistant C 30 MIN
3/4 OR 1/2 INCH VIDEO CASSETTE
Prod-RCOMTV Dist-SYLWAT 1984

What Is A Policeman C 12 MIN
16MM FILM OPTICAL SOUND I-J
Discusses, for young people, the role of the policeman in society. Points out that a policeman is like other men, but that his uniform and badge make him stand out as a man who enforces the law. Explains who makes the laws, how changing times have created changes in the laws and what would happen if there were no laws.
LC NO. 70-701675
Prod-GOLDSF Dist-AVED 1969

What Is A Print C 25 MIN
3/4 OR 1/2 INCH VIDEO CASSETTE H-C A
Explains the various categories of 'print' available on the market to potential buyers, what is original and what is a reproduction. Demonstrates the making of a Turner print by the Tate Gallery in London.
From The Artist In Print Series.
Prod-BBCTV Dist-FI

What Is A Reptile X 18 MIN
16MM FILM, 3/4 OR 1/2 IN VIDEO H
Describes four orders of reptiles and discusses their physical characteristics, reproductive processes and evolutionary development. Discusses reasons for the reptile's successful evolution and survival.
From The Biology Series. Unit 7 - Animal Classification And Physiology
Prod-EBF Dist-EBEC 1961

What Is A Reptile (Spanish) C 18 MIN
16MM FILM, 3/4 OR 1/2 IN VIDEO H
Points out representatives of each of the four orders of reptiles. Describes their physical characteristics, reproductive processes and evolutionary development.
From The Biology (Spanish) Series. Unit 7 - Animal Classification And Physiology
Prod-EBEC Dist-EBEC

What Is A Set C 20 MIN
2 INCH VIDEOTAPE P
See series title for descriptive statement.
From The Mathemagic, Unit I - Place Value Series.
Prod-WMULTV Dist-GPITVL

What Is A Short Story C 14 MIN
16MM FILM, 3/4 OR 1/2 IN VIDEO J-H
Illustrates the art of the short story form, including plot, theme, motivation, characterization, mood and style. Features commentary by Clifton Fadiman.
From The Humanities - Short Story Classics Series.
Prod-EBEC Dist-EBEC 1980

What Is A String Quartet C 15 MIN
3/4 OR 1/2 INCH VIDEO CASSETTE I-H
See series title for descriptive statement.
From The Chamber Music - The String Quartet Series.
Prod-NETCHE Dist-AITECH 1977

What Is A Supervisor C 20 MIN
3/4 OR 1/2 INCH VIDEO CASSETTE
See series title for descriptive statement.
From The Effective Supervision Series.
Prod-ERF Dist-DELTAK

What Is A Teenager B 30 MIN
16MM FILM OPTICAL SOUND J-C A
Attempts to dispel some of the misconceptions about adolescence and to introduce an understanding of this stage of physical and psychological development.
From The Dial C-12-18 For Family Understanding Series.
LC NO. 74-700168
Prod-UNL Dist-UNEBR 1970

What Is A Tree C 7 MIN
16MM FILM, 3/4 OR 1/2 IN VIDEO P-I
Pictures the natural beauty of trees during the seasons and follows a young boy's developing appreciation for the value of trees.
Prod-PRECFI Dist-AIMS 1965

What Is A Word Processor? C 24 MIN
16MM FILM, 3/4 OR 1/2 IN VIDEO A
Demonstrates the ease of storage, correction, formatting, reorganizing and printing documents of a word processor.
Prod-VIDART Dist-VISUCP 1983

What Is A Word Processor? C 28 MIN
3/4 OR 1/2 INCH VIDEO CASSETTE A
Explains and demonstrates, using humorous illustrations, how a word processor works and what it can do to improve work flow. Focuses on allaying fears of the machine.
Prod-XICOM Dist-XICOM

What Is Air C 15 MIN
3/4 OR 1/2 INCH VIDEO CASSETTE P-I
Discusses the characteristics of air.
From The Why Series.
Prod-WDCNTV Dist-AITECH 1976

What Is America C 72 MIN
3/4 OR 1/2 INCH VIDEO CASSETTE C
Features economist Milton Friedman reviewing the problems and accomplishments of America. Notes that restoration of the free market is the only way the country can regain its prestige and influence.
From The Milton Friedman Speaking Series. Lecture 1
LC NO. 79-708059
Prod-HBJ Dist-HBJ Prodn-WQLN 1980

What Is An Actuary C 29 MIN
3/4 OR 1/2 INCH VIDEO CASSETTE
Prod-RCOMTV Dist-SYLWAT 1983

What Is An Agrarian Culture C 15 MIN
3/4 INCH VIDEO CASSETTE I-J
Illustrates, through example, comparative agrarian cultures.
From The Looking Out Is In Series.
Prod-WHATV Dist-GPITVL

What Is An Amphibian X 11 MIN
16MM FILM, 3/4 OR 1/2 IN VIDEO H
Illustrates the body structure and life process of amphibians and shows how they are adapted to live in water and on land.
From The Biology Series. Unit 7 - Animal Classification And Physiology
Prod-EBF Dist-EBEC 1962

What Is An Amphibian (Spanish) C 11 MIN
16MM FILM, 3/4 OR 1/2 IN VIDEO H
Examines the body and life cycle of the amphibian. Presents the development of an amphibian from egg to maturity and traces the origin and evolution of the amphibian.
From The Biology (Spanish) Series. Unit 7 - Animal Classification And Physiology
Prod-EBEC Dist-EBEC

What Is An Eclipse C 11 MIN
16MM FILM, 3/4 OR 1/2 IN VIDEO I-C A
Uses animation and three-dimensional models to show how the motion of the Moon around the Earth causes both solar and lunar eclipses.
Prod-FA Dist-PHENIX 1965

What Is An Eclipse (Spanish) C 11 MIN
16MM FILM, 3/4 OR 1/2 IN VIDEO I-C
Uses animation and three dimensional models to show how the motion of the moon around the earth causes both solar and lunar eclipses.
Prod-FA Dist-PHENIX 1965

What Is An Element C 2 MIN
16MM FILM OPTICAL SOUND
Uses animation to define the elements and their physical and chemical properties.
Prod-CUYAHO Dist-CUYAHO 1967

What Is An Industrial Complex C 15 MIN
3/4 INCH VIDEO CASSETTE I-J
Demonstrates, through example, the attributes of comparative industrial complexes.
From The Looking Out Is In Series.
Prod-WHATV Dist-GPITVL

What Is An Insect C 20 MIN
2 INCH VIDEOTAPE I
See series title for descriptive statement.
From The Science Corner II, Unit I - Animals Series.
Prod-MPATI Dist-GPITVL

What Is An Integral C 61 MIN
16MM FILM OPTICAL SOUND H-C T
Professor Edwin Hewitt proves five properties that characterize the Riemann integral. He defines averages and describes the Riesz-representation theorem, giving the construction of the weight function necessary to make the average a Stieltjes integral.
From The Maa Individual Lecturers Series. Collegiate
Prod-MAA Dist-MLA 1965

What Is Anthropology C 15 MIN
3/4 INCH VIDEO CASSETTE I-J
Explores cultural anthropology from a basic view. Explains how to distinguish 'SELF' from others.
From The Looking Out Is In Series.
Prod-WHATV Dist-GPITVL

What Is Area C 20 MIN
16MM FILM OPTICAL SOUND H-C
Defines the area of a given region as the common limit of the areas of inner and outer polygonal approximations. Uses the circle to illustrate that this definition is consistent with previous notions. An animated film narrated by Charles E Rickart.
From The MAA Calculus Series.
Prod-MAA Dist-MLA 1967

What Is Art B 15 MIN
2 INCH VIDEOTAPE P
Compares and contrasts examples of good quality art work and poor quality work. (Broadcast quality)
From The Art Discoveries Series. Lesson 27
Prod-CVETVC Dist-GPITVL Prodn-WCVETV

What Is Arthritis? C
3/4 OR 1/2 INCH VIDEO CASSETTE
Defines arthritis along with its symptoms.
Prod-MIFE Dist-MIFE

What Is Autumn C 7 MIN
16MM FILM, 3/4 OR 1/2 IN VIDEO K-I
The meaning of autumn for people, animals and plants.
From The Science Series.
Prod-MORLAT Dist-SF 1967

What Is Business C 10 MIN
16MM FILM, 3/4 OR 1/2 IN VIDEO H-C A
Acquaints the student with what a business is, how it operates, who operates it and who is responsible for making short-term decisions and overall policy. Observes the operation of a one man boutique leather shop in contrast with the operation of a large manufacturing company.
Prod-SAIF Dist-BARR 1973

What Is Cancer C 21 MIN
16MM FILM OPTICAL SOUND PRO
Explains the biology of cancer. Emphasizes the role of the nurse in early diagnosis and rehabilitation of patients who have undergone treatment. Combines scenes from operating room and clinic with animation showing how cancer begins, spreads and can be treated.
Prod-AMCS Dist-AMCS 1962

What Is Capitalism C
3/4 OR 1/2 INCH VIDEO CASSETTE H
Provides an historical perspective on the evolution of capitalist thought, from the theories of Adam Smith through concepts such as ownership of private capital and free markets based on supply and demand. Traces the history of capitalism in America.
Prod-GA Dist-GA

What Is Cerebral Palsy C 20 MIN
16MM FILM OPTICAL SOUND A
Diagrams the nature of cerebral palsy and how the brain injury affects the individual.
Prod-UCPA Dist-UCPA 1948

What Is Change B 15 MIN
2 INCH VIDEOTAPE P-I
See series title for descriptive statement.
From The Our Changing Community Series.
Prod-VITA Dist-GPITVL 1967

What Is Christmas C 10 MIN
16MM FILM, 3/4 OR 1/2 IN VIDEO K-I
Depicts the journey of Mary and Joseph, the birth of the baby Jesus and the visit by the three wise men in fairy-tale form by a young boy sharing his simple version of the nativity scene with his puppy.
Prod-FLEMRP Dist-AIMS 1972

What Is Christmas (Spanish) C 10 MIN
16MM FILM, 3/4 OR 1/2 IN VIDEO K-I
Presents the story of the Nativity as seen through the eyes of a young boy and his puppy.
Prod-FLEMRP Dist-AIMS 1972

What Is Clay C 28 MIN
2 INCH VIDEOTAPE
Features Mrs Peterson describing certain ceramic processes for her classroom at the University of Southern California. Includes the art of working with clay.
From The Wheels, Kilns And Clay Series.
Prod-USC Dist-PUBTEL

What Is Communication B 30 MIN
16MM FILM OPTICAL SOUND J-C A
Defines the communication process and illustrates ways in which adolescents communicate with themselves, their peers, their parents and other adults.
From The Dial C-12-18 For Family Understanding Series.
LC NO. 74-700169
Prod-UNEBR Dist-UNEBR 1970

What Is Communication? C 15 MIN
3/4 OR 1/2 INCH VIDEO CASSETTE K-J
See series title for descriptive statement.
From The Arts Express Series.
Prod-KYTV Dist-KYTV 1983

What Is Communism C
3/4 OR 1/2 INCH VIDEO CASSETTE H
Explains the principles, policies and history of communism, and studies various communist countries today.
Prod-GA Dist-GA

What Is Conditioning C 35 MIN
16MM FILM OPTICAL SOUND
Illustrates the importance of planning an overall conditioning program tailored to specific individual needs. Considers the cardio-pulmonary and neuro-muscular systems, body flexibility and weight control.
Prod-SC Dist-MTP 1982

What Is Conestoga C 10 MIN
16MM FILM OPTICAL SOUND
Describes the functions of Conestoga College in Kitchener, Ontario.
LC NO. 76-701494
Prod-CCAAT Dist-CCAAT 1975

What Is Corrosion C 25 MIN
3/4 OR 1/2 INCH VIDEO CASSETTE IND
Gives basic corrosion terminology and explains the mechanism of corrosion.
From The Oil Field Corrosion Series.
Prod-UTEXPE Dist-UTEXPE

What Is Culture C 15 MIN
3/4 INCH VIDEO CASSETTE I-J
Illustrates that culture is a way of life among people. Shows that the attributes of culture, such as language, religion and social organizations set humans apart from other animals.
From The Looking Out Is In Series.
Prod-WHATV Dist-GPITVL

What Is Development C 24 MIN
16MM FILM, 3/4 OR 1/2 IN VIDEO
Illustrates the three basic experimental approaches used by developmental biologists to study the component processes of growth, cell differentiation and morphogenesis of any event in an organism's development. Shows the method of direct observation as the most common and basic approach, often including the dying of selected regions of the cell.
Prod-OPENU Dist-MEDIAG Prodn-BBCTV 1982

What Is Dimension B
16MM FILM OPTICAL SOUND
Discusses vector spaces and shows how to express 'dimension' of geometric space in terms of 'vector space language.'
Prod-OPENU Dist-OPENU

What Is Discipline, Anyway C 29 MIN
16MM FILM, 3/4 OR 1/2 IN VIDEO C
Provides answers to the question, 'WHAT IS DISCIPLINE, ANYWAY,' which reveals a montage of viewpoints around the central theme of school discipline, what it is and how to achieve it within a framework of realistic, enforceable rules. Differentiates between discipline and punishment.
From The Human Relations And School Discipline Series.
Prod-MFFD Dist-FI

What Is Disease C 11 MIN
16MM FILM, 3/4 OR 1/2 IN VIDEO
Explains that disease can be caused by tiny creatures so small that they cannot be seen without a microscope, and suggests ways to protect oneself against disease. Issued in 1946 as a motion picture.
From The Health For The Americas Series.
LC NO. 80-707388
Prod-USOIAA Dist-USNAC Prodn-DISNEY 1980

What Is Disease - Unseen Enemy (Spanish) C 11 MIN
16MM FILM OPTICAL SOUND
Uses animation to show how germs and microbes cause sickness and outlines simple preventive measures.
From The Health For The Americas Series.

LC NO. FIE52-541
Prod-USIA Dist-USNAC 1945

What Is Dizziness And Why Does It Happen? C 60 MIN
3/4 OR 1/2 INCH VIDEO CASSETTE
See series title for descriptive statement.
From The Dizziness And Related Balance Disorders Series.
Prod-GSHDME Dist-GSHDME

What Is Easter C 11 MIN
16MM FILM, 3/4 OR 1/2 IN VIDEO P-I
Tells the story of the first Easter as a fairy tale.
Prod-COUNTR Dist-AIMS 1976

What Is Easter (Spanish) C 11 MIN
16MM FILM, 3/4 OR 1/2 IN VIDEO P-I
Tells the story of the first Easter as a fairy tale.
Prod-COUNTR Dist-AIMS 1976

What Is Ecology (Spanish) C 21 MIN
16MM FILM, 3/4 OR 1/2 IN VIDEO H
A Spanish language version of the film and videorecording What Is Ecology.
Prod-EBEC Dist-EBEC 1977

What Is Ecology (2nd Ed) C 21 MIN
16MM FILM, 3/4 OR 1/2 IN VIDEO H
Illustrates basic terms in the science of ecology. Features specific ecosystems and explores the ways in which plant and animal species are related to each other.
Prod-EBEC Dist-EBEC 1978

What Is Economics About C 45 MIN
3/4 OR 1/2 INCH VIDEO CASSETTE
Gives an overview of the topics which are studied in economics.
From The Economic Perspectives Series.
Prod-MDCPB Dist-MDCPB

What Is EDP Auditing C 30 MIN
3/4 OR 1/2 INCH VIDEO CASSETTE
Explains the need for Electronic Data Processing (EDP) auditing and outines the role of the EDP auditor. Discusses the relatinship of the EDP auditing function to the organization with particular emphasis on the relationship to data processing.
From The Auditing EDP Systems Series.
Prod-DELTAK Dist-DELTAK

What Is Electric Current C 14 MIN
16MM FILM, 3/4 OR 1/2 IN VIDEO I-J
Shows how electric current works. Demonstrations and charts are used to show that electric charges flow as electric current.
Prod-EBF Dist-EBEC 1961

What Is Electricity C 5 MIN
16MM FILM, 3/4 OR 1/2 IN VIDEO H-C A
Discusses electrons, protons, charges, free electrons, conducting and non-conducting materials and electron flow.
From The Basic Electricity Series.
Prod-STFD Dist-IFB 1979

What Is Emphysema? C 14 MIN
3/4 OR 1/2 INCH VIDEO CASSETTE
Describes the causes of emphysema, especially the effects of smoking on the lungs and brochi. Emphasizes the need to alter life style to control the disease.
LC NO. 71-739124
Prod-TRAINX Dist-TRAINX

What Is Emphysema? (French) C 14 MIN
3/4 OR 1/2 INCH VIDEO CASSETTE
Describes the causes of emphysema, especially the effects of smoking on the lungs and brochi. Emphasizes the need to alter life style to control the disease.
LC NO. 71-739124
Prod-TRAINX Dist-TRAINX

What Is Emphysema? (Spanish) C 14 MIN
3/4 OR 1/2 INCH VIDEO CASSETTE
Describes the causes of emphysema, especially the effects of smoking on the lungs and bronchi. Emphasizes the need to alter life style to control the disease.
LC NO. 71-7391224
Prod-TRAINX Dist-TRAINX

What Is Enculturation C 15 MIN
3/4 INCH VIDEO CASSETTE I-J
Shows how individuals learn the culture of their group from birth.
From The Looking Out Is In Series.
Prod-WHATV Dist-GPITVL

What Is Ethics? C 30 MIN
3/4 OR 1/2 INCH VIDEO CASSETTE H-C A
Defines ethics in the broad sense and discusses ethical applications in contemporary terms. A video presentation of Sidney Hooks, author of Reform And Social Justice.
From The Ethics In America Series.
Prod-AMHUMA Dist-AMHUMA

What Is Family Day Care C 28 MIN
16MM FILM, 3/4 OR 1/2 IN VIDEO
Examines family day care homes in Ithaca, New York. Shows that the quality of care does not depend upon the luxury of the setting, but rather on the talent and dedication of women serving in the day care mother role.
Prod-CUETV Dist-CUNIV 1972

What Is Fascism C
3/4 OR 1/2 INCH VIDEO CASSETTE H
Outlines the basic features of Fascist ideology and government. Details Hitler's rise to power along with the ideology and policies of the American Nazi party. Gives eyewitness accounts of the repressive measures of right-wing Latin American nations.
Prod-GA Dist-GA

What Is Fitness C
1/2 IN VIDEO CASSETTE (VHS)
Reviews the components of physical fitness and explains the benefits of fitness.
From The Dynamics Of Fitness - The Body In Action Series.
Prod-IBIS Dist-IBIS

What Is Fitness Exercise C 11 MIN
16MM FILM, 3/4 OR 1/2 IN VIDEO P
Presents the tale of a good sorceress who teaches a scrawny knight the value of physical fitness for his general health and for his knightly pursuits. Tells how he learns about the five elements of physical fitness.
From The Fitness And Me Series.
Prod-WDEMCO Dist-WDEMCO

What Is Gestalt C 24 MIN
16MM FILM, 3/4 OR 1/2 IN VIDEO H-C
Dr Frederick Perls explains the basic principles of Gestalt therapy to a group of people with one person becoming the subject for an introduction to 'AWARENESS TRAINING.'
From The Gestalt Series.
Prod-PMI Dist-FI 1969

What Is Harness Racing C 15 MIN
1/2 IN VIDEO CASSETTE BETA/VHS
Introduces harness racing. Compare gaits of trotters and pacers.
Prod-USTROT Dist-EQVDL

What Is Humanism? C 30 MIN
3/4 OR 1/2 INCH VIDEO CASSETTE J-C A
Features Corliss Lamont, author of Voice In The Wilderness, defining humanism.
From The Moral Values In Contemporary Society Series.
Prod-AMHUMA Dist-AMHUMA

What Is In A Pond B 15 MIN
2 INCH VIDEOTAPE P
Explains that every living thing must obtain from its own environment all that it needs for life.
From The Science Is Discovery Series.
Prod-DETPS Dist-GPITVL

What Is Inflation C 13 MIN
16MM FILM, 3/4 OR 1/2 IN VIDEO J-C A
Defines the concept of inflation and the options open to government in dealing with it. Reconstructs the political, social and natural factors which have given rise to the new phenomemon of stagflation.
Prod-ABCNEW Dist-PHENIX Prodn-MEDOPO 1975

What Is It Like On The Moon C 20 MIN
2 INCH VIDEOTAPE I
See series title for descriptive statement.
From The Science Corner II, Unit II - The Earth In Space Series.
Prod-MPATI Dist-GPITVL

What Is It Out There C 20 MIN
16MM FILM OPTICAL SOUND
Presents play-test instruments which test and record the response of infants to their environment. Discusses applications for helping handicapped children enrich their experiences.
Prod-CWRU Dist-CWRU 1967

What Is Judaism B 30 MIN
16MM FILM OPTICAL SOUND
Explains Jewish law and through three events in contemporary history analyzes the role of law in determining Jewish attitudes and responses to life.
Prod-ADL Dist-ADL

What Is La Raza C 30 MIN
2 INCH VIDEOTAPE I
Features Joe Coto, director of the ESEA Title III program in Alameda County, who discusses Mexican-Americans.
From The That's A Good Question Series.
Prod-KGEDTV Dist-GPITVL

What Is Leadership? C 14 MIN
3/4 OR 1/2 INCH VIDEO CASSETTE IND
Defines leadership and describes its value in the workplace. Highlights the importance of leadership in improved productivity and the relationship of leadership to effective management.
From The Man Management And Rig Management Series. Lesson 2
Prod-UTEXPE Dist-UTEXPE 1983

What Is Love B 29 MIN
16MM FILM OPTICAL SOUND
Features Indian spiritual leader Krishnamurti who discusses how we can try to discover what love is. States that in order to find the meaning of love the mind must be sensitive, energetic and free of all desire and pleasure.
From The Real Revolution - Talks By Krishnamurti Series.
LC NO. 73-703036
Prod-KQEDTV Dist-IU 1968

What Is Love C 30 MIN
1/2 IN VIDEO CASSETTE BETA/VHS P-J
Helps children understand the many facets of love. Uses an example to show that people who make each other angry can still love each other very much. Features Mister Rogers.
From The Mister Rogers - Conceptual Behavior Series.
Prod-BRENTM Dist-BRENTM

What Is Love? C 30 MIN
3/4 OR 1/2 INCH VIDEO CASSETTE
Helps children understand the many facts of love, with Mister Rogers.
From The Mister Rogers' Neighborhood Series.
Prod-FAMCOM Dist-FAMCOM

What Is M B O C 13 MIN
3/4 OR 1/2 INCH VIDEO CASSETTE
See series title for descriptive statement.
From The Practical M B O Series.
Prod-DELTAK Dist-DELTAK

What Is Managing? C 16 MIN
3/4 OR 1/2 INCH VIDEO CASSETTE
Lists the essential managerial skills, such as perception, decision-making communicating, organizing and planning what they really mean and how to tell if they are being done well.
From The Improving Managerial Skills Series.
Prod-RESEM Dist-RESEM

What Is Managment? C 23 MIN
3/4 OR 1/2 INCH VIDEO CASSETTE IND
Demonstrates the value of basic management skills such as planning, coordinating and instructing. Discusses who is responsible for developing these skills and how their absence usually results in inefficiency.
From The Man Management And Rig Management Series. Lesson 1
Prod-UTEXPE Dist-UTEXPE 1983

What Is Marketing C 15 MIN
16MM FILM, 3/4 OR 1/2 IN VIDEO
Uses animation to tell the story of Edwin, the first Iron Age marketing manager. Shows him unearthing the principles of a sound marketing operation.
Prod-RANKAV Dist-RTBL

What Is Marketing (Captioned) C 15 MIN
16MM FILM, 3/4 OR 1/2 IN VIDEO
Uses animation to tell the story of Edwin, the first Iron Age marketing manager. Shows him unearthing the principles of sound marketing operation.
Prod-RANKAV Dist-RTBL

What Is Mathematics And How Do We Teach It B 45 MIN
16MM FILM OPTICAL SOUND H-C T
Presents a panel discussion among top research mathematicians on the relation of counting circuits to group theory and other abstract mathematics. Covers the changing role of mathematics.
From The MAA Individual Lecturers Series.
LC NO. FIA66-1277
Prod-MAA Dist-MLA 1966

What Is Matter B 15 MIN
2 INCH VIDEOTAPE P
Explains that matter is anything that occupies space and has weight.
From The Science Is Discovery Series.
Prod-DETPS Dist-GPITVL

What Is Measurement - Standards C 10 MIN
16MM FILM, 3/4 OR 1/2 IN VIDEO K-J
Discusses the need for units of measurement, how our present system of units came into being and the desireability of a standard universal system like the metric system.
Prod-SF Dist-SF 1970

What Is Money C 11 MIN
16MM FILM, 3/4 OR 1/2 IN VIDEO P-J
Discusses the history of money from barter to dollar bills, how money is earned, the meaning of the parents' pay, how far a dollar goes and the real value of money.
From The Consumer Education Series.
Prod-SF Dist-SF 1970

What Is Music C 20 MIN
16MM FILM OPTICAL SOUND
Explains some of the basic concepts and terminology in music.
LC NO. 74-700697
Prod-NEA Dist-NEA 1973

What Is New C 52 MIN
16MM FILM, 3/4 OR 1/2 IN VIDEO J-C A
Looks at the work of great dance pioneers, from the Commedia dell'Arte in 17th century Italy to Martha Graham in 20th century America.
From The Magic Of Dance Series.
Prod-BBCTV Dist-TIMLIF 1980

What Is Nothing C 9 MIN
16MM FILM, 3/4 OR 1/2 IN VIDEO K-I
Explores the concept of multiple meanings and shades of meaning of a common word. Follows two young boys as they explore many ways to use the word 'NOTHING' as they search for its meaning in the dictionary and during their everyday activities.
Prod-BARR Dist-BARR 1973

What Is Ocean Water Like C 20 MIN
2 INCH VIDEOTAPE P
See series title for descriptive statement.
From The Science Corner I, Unit IX - Transportation Series.
Prod-MPATI Dist-GPITVL

What Is Organization Development? C 15 MIN
3/4 OR 1/2 INCH VIDEO CASSETTE
Examines the role of the third party as the person who gets things said that others are afraid to say, brings people together and sees to it that actions are not only planned but carried out.
From The Organization Development Series. Module 3
Prod-RESEM Dist-RESEM

What Is Past Is Prologue C 30 MIN
3/4 OR 1/2 INCH VIDEO CASSETTE C
Offers an analysis of the American prospect.
America - The Second Century Series.
Prod-DALCCD Dist-DALCCD

What Is Philosophy C 19 MIN
16MM FILM, 3/4 OR 1/2 IN VIDEO J-C A
Delineates the function of the philosopher.
Prod-FLMAUS Dist-WOMBAT

What Is Physical Fitness C 11 MIN
16MM FILM, 3/4 OR 1/2 IN VIDEO J-H
Demonstrates the elements that constitute physical fitness, including cardio-respiratory endurance, muscle strength, muscle endurance, flexibility and body composition.
From The Fitness For Living Series.
Prod-WDEMCO Dist-WDEMCO 1982

What Is Poetry C 10 MIN
16MM FILM, 3/4 OR 1/2 IN VIDEO I-H
Compares and contrasts a news report and a poem about one event, an auto wreck. Shows how the poet makes his poem an emotional experience.
Prod-FA Dist-PHENIX 1963

What Is Poetry C 30 MIN
3/4 OR 1/2 INCH VIDEO CASSETTE
Discusses poetry as an everyday language used to communicate emotion, mood and experience.
From The Engle And Poetry Series.
Prod-NETCHE Dist-NETCHE 1971

What Is Preventive Discipline C
16MM FILM - 3/4 IN VIDEO
Shows how to maintain discipline and obtain standards of performance by creating a climate in which supervisors and their people know what to expect from each other, an atmosphere that ends the vicious cycle of disruption. Presents eight things employees expect from supervisors.
From The Preventive Discipline (2nd Ed) Series. Unit 1
Prod-BNA Dist-BNA

What Is Psychology C 20 MIN
16MM FILM, 3/4 OR 1/2 IN VIDEO H-C A
Surveys the subject of psychology for high school students. Made in Australia.
Prod-FLMAUS Dist-WOMBAT 1975

What Is Psychology? C 30 MIN
3/4 OR 1/2 INCH VIDEO CASSETTE
Presents an overview, and the nature and scope of the field of Psychology. Examines the various perspectives from which psychologists look at behavior.
From The Psychology Of Human Relations Series.
Prod-MATC Dist-WFVTAE

What Is Quality? C 30 MIN
3/4 OR 1/2 INCH VIDEO CASSETTE
Discusses the interrelationships among quality of design, quality of conformance to design and quality of performance.
From The Quality Planning Series.
Prod-MIOT Dist-MIOT

What Is Rhythm C 11 MIN
16MM FILM, 3/4 OR 1/2 IN VIDEO P-J
Presents a study of rhythm by defining it in terms of beats, tempo and accents. Suggests that rhythm is not only part of music, but also part of other activities.
Prod-FA Dist-PHENIX 1966

What Is Salesmanship? C 10 MIN
3/4 OR 1/2 INCH VIDEO CASSETTE
Introduces the idea that selling can be broken down into identifiable steps, each of which, when learned, can improve selling success.
From The Basic Sales Series.
Prod-RESEM Dist-RESEM

What Is Schizophrenia C
1/2 IN VIDEO CASSETTE (VHS)
Examines the symptoms of schizophrenia. Dispels common myths. Presents major diagnostic categories. Includes examples of the paranoid, the disorganized and the catatonic types.
From The Schizophrenia - Removing The Veil Series.
Prod-IBIS Dist-IBIS

What Is Science (2nd Ed) C 11 MIN
16MM FILM, 3/4 OR 1/2 IN VIDEO I-J
Shows a class using the scientific method in determining whether an apple is alive. Illustrates the importance of observing, hypothesizing, experimenting, collecting data and reaching conclusions.
Prod-CORF Dist-CORF 1966

What Is Science - Philosophy C 20 MIN
2 INCH VIDEOTAPE I
See series title for descriptive statement.
From The Exploring With Science, Unit 1 - Introduction series.
Prod-MPATI Dist-GPITVL

What Is Sexuality? C 30 MIN
3/4 OR 1/2 INCH VIDEO CASSETTE C A
Focuses on sexuality. Gives particular attention to an analysis of culturally induced sex differences, including social and cultural role expectations and male and female sexual taboos.
From The Contemporary Health Issues Series. Lesson 5
Prod-SCCON Dist-CDTEL

What Is Socialism C
3/4 OR 1/2 INCH VIDEO CASSETTE H
Traces the formation and application of socialism. Examines the impact of 'scientific' socialism on pre-World War I thought and postwar Russia, and explores the schism between parliamentary and revolutionary socialists.
Prod-GA Dist-GA

What Is Sound C 15 MIN
3/4 OR 1/2 INCH VIDEO CASSETTE P-I
Discusses the characteristics of sound.
From The Why Series.
Prod-WDCNTV Dist-AITECH 1976

What Is Sound B 20 MIN
2 INCH VIDEOTAPE I
See series title for descriptive statement.
From The Science Room Series.
Prod-MCETV Dist-GPITVL Prodn-WVIZTV

What Is Space X 11 MIN
16MM FILM, 3/4 OR 1/2 IN VIDEO I-J
Helicopters and imaginary trips through the universe illustrate the vastness of space while experiments show presence of space in liquids and solids close at hand.
Prod-EBF Dist-EBEC 1961

What Is Space (Spanish) C 10 MIN
16MM FILM, 3/4 OR 1/2 IN VIDEO I-J
Portrays a flight by helicopter and a rocket trip through outer space in order to convey the tremendous extent of space.
Prod-EBEC Dist-EBEC

What Is Spina Bifida C 22 MIN
16MM FILM OPTICAL SOUND
Presents an introduction to the physically disabling neurological disease, spina bifida. Depicts its clinical manifestation, surgical and medical treatments possible, therapeutic exercise to prevent limb stiffness and the fitting and use of orthosis.
Prod-VASSAR Dist-NYU

What Is Spring C 7 MIN
16MM FILM, 3/4 OR 1/2 IN VIDEO P-J
The meaning of spring for people, animals and plants.
From The Science Series.
Prod-MORLAT Dist-SF 1967

What Is Summer C 7 MIN
16MM FILM, 3/4 OR 1/2 IN VIDEO P-J
The meaning of summer for people, animals and plants.
From The Science Series.
Prod-MORLAT Dist-SF 1967

What Is Teaching - What Is Learning X 23 MIN
3/4 OR 1/2 INCH VIDEO CASSETTE T
Presents contrasting attitudes and ideas about teaching and the role of the school in American society.
From The One To Grow On Series.
LC NO. 80-706186
Prod-NIMH Dist-USNAC 1979

What Is The Church X 30 MIN
16MM FILM OPTICAL SOUND
Features leaders of a local church meeting to study results of a community survey, and explore ways to minister effectively. Shows controversy developing over what the real business of the church is. Portrays the son of one of the men coming home for semester break, and bringing a college roomate, who is campus newspaper editor. Concludes with him writing an article focusing attention on the purpose of the church.
Prod-FAMF Dist-FAMF

What Is The Earth's Surface Like B 15 MIN
2 INCH VIDEOTAPE P
Explains that the earth consists of an uneven distribution of water and land surrounded by air.
From The Science Is Discovery Series.
Prod-DETPS Dist-GPITVL

What Is The Metric System C 20 MIN
3/4 INCH VIDEO CASSETTE J-C A
Explains the use of meters, liters and grams. Discusses decimal systems and precision in measurement.
From The Metric System Series.
Prod-MAETEL Dist-GPITVL 1975

What Is The Most Important Priority Of A Teacher C 28 MIN
16MM FILM OPTICAL SOUND
An updated version of the 1975 motion picture Up With Teachers. Focuses on the 'essence' of teaching and tells how teachers can rededicate themselves to the challenge at hand.
From The You Can Do It - If Series.
LC NO. 81-700094
Prod-VANDER Dist-VANDER 1980

What Is The Teacher/Student Role C 30 MIN
3/4 OR 1/2 INCH VIDEO CASSETTE T
Examines the proper teacher/student role in adult education.
From The Basic Education - Teaching The Adult Series.
Prod-MDDE Dist-MDCPB

What Is The Water Cycle B 15 MIN
2 INCH VIDEOTAPE P
Explains that there are many cycles of change in the world.
From The Science Is Discovery Series.
Prod-DETPS Dist-GPITVL

What Is This Thing Called Food C 52 MIN
16MM FILM, 3/4 OR 1/2 IN VIDEO H-C A
Examines the use of chemicals in today's food supply, with narration by Betty Furness. Shows how new food technology has served the consumer and points out a growing concern among scientists as to the possible effects of chemical additives on the human body.
Prod-NBCTV Dist-FI 1976

What Is Total Quality Control C 27 MIN
3/4 OR 1/2 INCH VIDEO CASSETTE
Gives an explanation of the characteristics and philosophy of Total Quality Control as developed in Japan, taking note of the different social backgrounds in Japan and the West.
From The Seven Steps To T Q C Promotion Series.
Prod-TOYOVS Dist-TOYOVS

What Is Weather C 15 MIN
3/4 OR 1/2 INCH VIDEO CASSETTE P-I
Discusses the causes of various weather conditions.
From The Why Series.
Prod-WDCNTV Dist-AITECH 1976

What Is Winter C 8 MIN
16MM FILM, 3/4 OR 1/2 IN VIDEO P-J
The meaning of winter for people, animals and plants.
From The Science Series.
Prod-MORLAT Dist-SF 1967

What Is Work C 20 MIN
16MM FILM OPTICAL SOUND C T
Explores the theories and concepts formulated by Dr Elliot Jacques on work measurement to determine their relevance to good labor and management relations.
LC NO. FIA68-61
Prod-SIUFP Dist-SIUFP 1966

What Is Work C 28 MIN
3/4 OR 1/2 INCH VIDEO CASSETTE
See series title for descriptive statement.
From The All About Welfare Series.
Prod-WITFTV Dist-PBS

What Is Wrong With The Welfare State C 87 MIN
3/4 OR 1/2 INCH VIDEO CASSETTE C
Presents economist Milton Friedman exploring the welfare state and discussing why it doesn't work. Concludes that voluntary cooperation and giving are preferable to welfare.
From The Milton Friedman Speaking Series. Lecture 5
LC NO. 79-708064
Prod-HBJ Dist-HBJ Prodn-WQLN 1980

What Is Your Attitude Toward Justice C 30 MIN
2 INCH VIDEOTAPE J
See series title for descriptive statement.
From The Summer Journal, Unit 4 - You Are What You Think Series.
Prod-WNINTV Dist-GPITVL

What Is Your Patient Medication Profile? C 4 MIN
3/4 OR 1/2 INCH VIDEO CASSETTE
Explains importance of patient profiles and emphasizes the pharmacist's role in protecting patients from potential problems.
Prod-TRAINX Dist-TRAINX

What Is Your Reach C 15 MIN
2 INCH VIDEOTAPE J-H
Discusses the importance of rightly selecting a career, gives guidelines to use and describes sources of information.
From The Work Is For Real Series.
Prod-STETVC Dist-GPITVL

What It Means To Be A Dentist C 13 MIN
3/4 OR 1/2 INCH VIDEO CASSETTE H-C A
Describes the main phases of dentistry such as private practice, public health, education, research, specialization and community programs. Tours several locations showing the dentist actively engaged in his daily activities.
Prod-AMDA Dist-AMDA 1976

What It Means To Be Healthy—A Series

Prod-RCOMTV Dist-SYLWAT

Body Fitness 030 MIN
Nutrition And Its Place In The Wellness Program 029 MIN
Stress And How To Live With It 029 MIN
Wellness - Investing In Your Health 028 MIN

What Johnny Can't Read C 13 MIN
16MM FILM, 3/4 OR 1/2 IN VIDEO H-C A
Focuses on a Texas housewife who has spent 18 years studying the content of textbooks and whose opinions have influenced curriculum publishing. Presents her answer to charges that she is promoting censorship. Narrated by Mike Wallace. Originally shown on the CBS television series 60 Minutes.
LC NO. 80-707722
Prod-CBSNEW Dist-CAROUF 1980

What Keeps You Alive C 15 MIN
3/4 OR 1/2 INCH VIDEO CASSETTE P
Reviews the necessities of human life. Includes food, air, water, sleep, exercise, rest, love and stimulation.
From The All About You Series.
Prod-WGBHTV Dist-AITECH Prodn-TTOIC 1975

What Kind Of Snowsuits Are There B 15 MIN
2 INCH VIDEOTAPE P
Discusses how people adapt their clothing to their environment. (Broadcast quality)
From The Around The Corner Series. No. 22
Prod-FWCETV Dist-GPITVL Prodn-WEDUTV

What Kind Of Soil Do We Need For Planting C 20 MIN
2 INCH VIDEOTAPE I
See series title for descriptive statement.
From The Science Corner II, Unit VIII - Plants In Spring Series.
Prod-MPATI Dist-GPITVL

What Kinds Of Coats Do Animals Wear B 20 MIN
2 INCH VIDEOTAPE P
Presents a visit to a pet shop to feed the animals which leads to the discovery that animals have different kinds of coverings.
From The Scienceland Series.
Prod-MPATI Dist-GPITVL

What Kinds Of Homes Do Animals Live In B 20 MIN
2 INCH VIDEOTAPE P
Shows a deserted bird's nest which leads to an investigation of different kinds of animal homes.
From The Scienceland Series.
Prod-MPATI Dist-GPITVL

What Liberty And Justice Means (2nd Ed) C 17 MIN
16MM FILM, 3/4 OR 1/2 IN VIDEO I-J
Introduces the concepts of liberty and justice. Shows how these principles affect daily life in America.
Prod-DF Dist-CF 1978

What Lights Up The Darkness B 20 MIN
2 INCH VIDEOTAPE P
Explains how a storm which extinguishes the lights in the science house leads to a rediscovery of methods of lighting of the old times and an appreciation of modern methods of lighting.
From The Scienceland Series.
Prod-MPATI Dist-GPITVL

What Living Things Can Be Found In Ponds, Rivers, Lakes And Streams C 20 MIN
2 INCH VIDEOTAPE I
See series title for descriptive statement.
From The Science Corner II, Unit IX - Exploring Our Country Series.
Prod-MPATI Dist-GPITVL

What Living Things Can Be Found In Swamps And Marshes C 20 MIN
2 INCH VIDEOTAPE I
See series title for descriptive statement.
From The Science Corner II, Unit IX - Exploring Our Country Series.
Prod-MPATI Dist-GPITVL

What Living Things Can Be Found On The Desert C 20 MIN
2 INCH VIDEOTAPE I
See series title for descriptive statement.
From The Science Corner II, Unit IX - Exploring Our Country Series.
Prod-MPATI Dist-GPITVL

What Makes A Good Negotiation C 25 MIN
16MM FILM, 3/4 OR 1/2 IN VIDEO A
Presents a lecture by Chester L Karrass defining negotiation and giving basic principles. Shows the four steps of a sample negotiation.
From The Negotiating Successfully Series. Part 1
LC NO. 79-707431
Prod-TIMLIF Dist-TIMLIF 1975

What Makes A Man Masculine C 30 MIN
2 INCH VIDEOTAPE J
See series title for descriptive statement.
From The Summer Journal, Unit 1 - You Are What You Feel Series.
Prod-WNINTV Dist-GPITVL

What Makes A Modern Army C 28 MIN
16MM FILM OPTICAL SOUND
Discusses the training and support the soldier receives to enable him to implement the four responsibilities of the modern army, namely mission, motivation, modernization and management.
From The Big Picture Series.
LC NO. 75-703706
Prod-USA Dist-USNAC 1970

What Makes A Woman Feminine C 30 MIN
2 INCH VIDEOTAPE J
See series title for descriptive statement.
From The Summer Journal, Unit 1 - You Are What You Feel Series.
Prod-WNINTV Dist-GPITVL

What Makes Air Move B 15 MIN
2 INCH VIDEOTAPE P
Explains that near large bodies of water, winds or breezes blow nearly all the time.
From The Science Is Discovery Series.
Prod-DETPS Dist-GPITVL

What Makes An Artist Famous C 25 MIN
2 INCH VIDEOTAPE I
Compares and contrasts traditional and contemporary art.
From The Art For Every Day Series.
Prod-CVETVC Dist-GPITVL

What Makes Art C 26 MIN
16MM FILM OPTICAL SOUND J-C A
Surveys the activities carried on by the department of fine art at Pennsylvania State University. Studio work includes painting, etching and woodcutting, photography, graphic design, sculpture, pottery and ceramic sculpture. Describes critiques of student work.
LC NO. 78-700712
Prod-PSU Dist-PSU 1970

What Makes Clouds X 19 MIN
16MM FILM, 3/4 OR 1/2 IN VIDEO I-H
Notes that fog and clouds are composed of droplets of water. Conducts an experiment with condensation producing fog in a bottle and concludes with an investigation of how condensation occurs in nature.
From The Earth Science Program Series.
Prod-EBEC Dist-EBEC 1965

What Makes Clouds (Spanish) C 19 MIN
16MM FILM, 3/4 OR 1/2 IN VIDEO I-H
Notes that fog and clouds are composed of droplets of water. Conducts an experiment with condensation producing fog in a bottle and concludes with an investigation of how condensation occurs in nature.
Prod-EBEC Dist-EBEC 1965

What Makes Clouds And Rain C 20 MIN
2 INCH VIDEOTAPE I
See series title for descriptive statement.
From The Science Corner II, Unit VII - Understanding Weather Series.
Prod-MPATI Dist-GPITVL

What Makes Electric Current Flow B 15 MIN
2 INCH VIDEOTAPE P
Explains that many forces can cause electricity flow.
From The Science Is Discovery Series.
Prod-DETPS Dist-GPITVL

What Makes Groups Work - Theory And Skills Of Facilitating Adult Learning Groups C 48 MIN
16MM FILM, 3/4 OR 1/2 IN VIDEO
Presents groups and group facilitators demonstrating how to effectively start groups, how to increase participants' involvement and how to handle problem situations.
Prod-ODECA Dist-BULFRG

What Makes Him Run C 12 MIN
16MM FILM OPTICAL SOUND
Presents scenes of quarter horse racing.
Prod-AQHORS Dist-AQHORS

What Makes Him Run C 23 MIN
16MM FILM, 3/4 OR 1/2 IN VIDEO
Illustrates the economical and cultural impact of quarter horse racing upon the general public, as well as upon specific geographical areas. Includes footage from major tracks around the country.
Prod-AQHORS Dist-AQHORS Prodn-JPI 1980

What Makes It Tick C 15 MIN
2 INCH VIDEOTAPE J
Shows a sixth way of developing a topic sentence by classification.
From The From Me To You...In Writing, Pt 2 Series.
Prod-DELE Dist-GPITVL

What Makes Japan Work C 11 MIN
16MM FILM, 3/4 OR 1/2 IN VIDEO
Shows Japanese workers' attitudes that influences the quality of their work, especially as relates to Buddhist concepts about life. Features Alan Watts.
Prod-HP Dist-HP

What Makes Me Different C 9 MIN
16MM FILM, 3/4 OR 1/2 IN VIDEO K-I
Demonstrates and explains differences in accents, smells and types of hair. Uses the senses of hearing, smell and sight to study human physical characteristics and differences.
From The Who We Are Series.
LC NO. 77-701121
Prod-KORTY Dist-PFP 1977

What Makes Millie Run C 16 MIN
16MM FILM OPTICAL SOUND J-H
Presents a film on aerobics for women, featuring Mildred Cooper, author of the book Aerobics For Women. Designed to motivate women to become physically fit.
Prod-BYU Dist-BYU 1977

What Makes Muscle Pull - The Structural Basis Of Contraction C 9 MIN
16MM FILM, 3/4 OR 1/2 IN VIDEO
Uses animation to clarify the relation of muscle structure to muscle function and the protein assembly to the energy flow.
From The Physiology Series.
Prod-WILEYJ Dist-MEDIAG 1972

What Makes Music C 24 MIN
16MM FILM OPTICAL SOUND J-C A
Surveys the activities carried on by the department of music at Pennsylvania State University. Shows an orchestra in rehearsal, classes at work, demonstrations of individual instruments by students and choral rehearsals.
LC NO. 78-700713
Prod-PSU Dist-PSUPCR 1970

What Makes Rain C 22 MIN
16MM FILM, 3/4 OR 1/2 IN VIDEO J-H
Considers the nature and causes of rainfall. Examines cloud formation, traces the origin of raindrops, hail, sleet and snow and shows what happens in areas where rain does not fall.
From The Earth Science Program Series.
Prod-EBEC Dist-EBEC 1975

What Makes Sally Run C 25 MIN
16MM FILM OPTICAL SOUND
Lists national and world class women athletes of the Puget Sound area while recounting the prejudice and lack of backing women's athletics have suffered in the United States.
LC NO. 74-702901
Prod-KINGSP Dist-KINGSP 1974

What Makes Sammy Spend C 20 MIN
3/4 INCH VIDEO CASSETTE J-H
Presents primary buying motives with comments from consumers on why they buy certain products.
From The Dollar Data Series.
LC NO. 81-707422
Prod-WHROTV Dist-GPITVL 1974

What Makes Static Electricity C 20 MIN
2 INCH VIDEOTAPE I
See series title for descriptive statement.
From The Science Corner II, Unit VII - Understanding Weather Series.
Prod-MPATI Dist-GPITVL

What Makes The Moon Seem To Change Its Shape C 20 MIN
2 INCH VIDEOTAPE I
See series title for descriptive statement.
From The Science Corner II, Unit II - The Earth In Space Series.
Prod-MPATI Dist-GPITVL

What Makes The Wind Blow X 16 MIN
16MM FILM, 3/4 OR 1/2 IN VIDEO I-H
Studies the causes of a typical on-shore sea breeze and a violent wind storm. Provides laboratory experiments to discover the possible causes.
From The Earth Science Program Series.
Prod-EBEC Dist-EBEC 1965

What Makes The Wind Blow (Spanish) C 16 MIN
16MM FILM, 3/4 OR 1/2 IN VIDEO I A
A Spanish language version of the film and videorecording What Makes The Wind Blow.
Prod-EBEC Dist-EBEC 1965

What Makes Theatre C 29 MIN
16MM FILM OPTICAL SOUND J-C A
Surveys the activities carried on by the department of theatre arts at Pennsylvania State University. Shows classroom demonstrations to develop expressive abilities and improve voice quality. Visits small group workshops and includes scenes from dress and technical rehearsals.
LC NO. 78-700714
Prod-PSU Dist-PSUPCR 1970

What Makes Them Run C 22 MIN
16MM FILM OPTICAL SOUND
Shows the world championship meets for orienteering held in Sweden in the summer of 1973.
LC NO. 77-702711
Prod-SILIND Dist-CRAF Prodn-CRAF 1974

What Makes Them Run C 21 MIN
16MM FILM, 3/4 OR 1/2 IN VIDEO J-C A
Explores the sport of orienteering, which requires racers to find their way through unfamiliar terrain as quickly as possible. Shows the International Orienteering Meet in Sweden.
LC NO. 81-706472
Prod-SILVAC Dist-IFB Prodn-CRAF 1976

What Makes Things Dry Up C 20 MIN
2 INCH VIDEOTAPE P
See series title for descriptive statement.
From The Science Corner I, Unit III - Looking At Things Around Us Series.
Prod-MPATI Dist-GPITVL

What Makes Water Move B 15 MIN
2 INCH VIDEOTAPE P
Explains that movements of water may be caused by an uneven distribution of heat energy.
From The Science Is Discovery Series.
Prod-DETPS Dist-GPITVL

What Makes Weather (2nd Ed) C 14 MIN
16MM FILM, 3/4 OR 1/2 IN VIDEO I-J
Uses satellite footage, animation and time-lapse photography to show the working forces that produce weather. Examines the movement of winds and air masses, and shows some of the visual clues to weather change.
From The Earth Science Program Series.
Prod-EBEC Dist-EBEC 1981

What Makes Wheels Move C 20 MIN
2 INCH VIDEOTAPE P
See series title for descriptive statement.
From The Science Corner I, Unit IX - Transportation Series.
Prod-MPATI Dist-GPITVL

What Man Shall Live And Not See Death C 57 MIN
16MM FILM, 3/4 OR 1/2 IN VIDEO H-C A
Describes various institutions which are exploring ways to deal with the dying in a realistic and compassionate manner.
Prod-WNBCTV Dist-FI 1971

What Managers Do C 30 MIN
3/4 OR 1/2 INCH VIDEO CASSETTE
Shows managers how to use planning techniques that ensure smooth operations, how to organize their department for jobs maximum productivity, organize staff in a way that matches with talent, delegate intelligently and avoid reverse delegation, motivate employees to perform to their maximum potential and select the leadership style appropriate to the situation.
Prod-EFM Dist-EFM

What Mary Jo Shared C 13 MIN
16MM FILM, 3/4 OR 1/2 IN VIDEO P
Tells the story of a little girl who overcomes her shyness and shares something unusual with her classmates. Based on the book What Mary Jo Shared by Janice May Udry.
Prod-WILETS Dist-PHENIX 1981

What Mary Jo Shared C 15 MIN
3/4 OR 1/2 INCH VIDEO CASSETTE P
Presents the children's story What Mary Jo Shared by Janice Udry.
From The Picture Book Park Series. Blue Module
Prod-WVIZTV Dist-AITECH 1974

What Mary Jo Shared / Sam, Bangs, And Moonshine C 28 MIN
1/2 IN VIDEO CASSETTE BETA/VHS
Tells about a girl who needs to find something special to bring to a sharing session at school. Based on the book by Janice May Udry. Tells of a girl who makes up a tall story that causes trouble. Based on the book by Evaline Ness.
Prod-BFA Dist-BFA

What Mary Jo Wanted C 15 MIN
16MM FILM, 3/4 OR 1/2 IN VIDEO K-P
Captures the story about a little girl who gets her wish to have a puppy and a chance to show that she can take care of it on her own, even though it isn't always easy. Based on the book of the same name by Janice May Udry.
LC NO. 83-706631
Prod-WILETS Dist-BARR 1982

What Motivates Human Behavior? C 30 MIN
3/4 OR 1/2 INCH VIDEO CASSETTE C A
Considers the various theories about the determinants of person-

ality and explores four principal theories of motivation. Shows how positive feedbacks is used to train a bear to perform a specific behavior.
From The Contemporary Health Issues Series. Lesson 2
Prod-SCCON Dist-CDTEL

What Motivates Man To Work? C 13 MIN
3/4 OR 1/2 INCH VIDEO CASSETTE
Offers suggestions for examining jobs and seeing what can be done to make them more motivating.
From The Job Enrichment Series.
Prod-RESEM Dist-RESEM

What Music Are You Like C 30 MIN
2 INCH VIDEOTAPE J
See series title for descriptive statement.
From The Summer Journal, Unit 5 - You Are What You Can Do Series.
Prod-WNINTV Dist-GPITVL

What Must I Do To Be Saved X 17 MIN
16MM FILM OPTICAL SOUND J-H T R
Presents the story of Paul who receives a call to help in Macedonia. Leads viewer into an experience of salvation through faith in Christ.
From The Book Of Acts Series.
Prod-BROADM Dist-FAMF 1957

What My Parents Didn't Tell Me C 25 MIN
3/4 OR 1/2 INCH VIDEO CASSETTE J-C A
Features a group of teenagers discussing their book, Changing Bodies, Changing Minds, which deals with the problems of puberty and sexual awareness. Discusses the learning of sex from peers and the difficulties in sharing the sexual awakening with their parents.
Prod-SIRS Dist-SIRS

What Next B
16MM FILM OPTICAL SOUND
Presents views on the probable developments in computers and computing.
Prod-OPENU Dist-OPENU

What Next C 30 MIN
3/4 OR 1/2 INCH VIDEO CASSETTE A
Reviews the main topics presented in the Bits And Bytes Series and speculates on the future of the computer in schools, workplaces and homes.
From The Bits And Bytes Series. Pt 12
Prod-TVOTAR Dist-TIMLIF 1984

What Next - Career Aspirations C 15 MIN
16MM FILM, 3/4 OR 1/2 IN VIDEO J-H
Shows how Harvey and Sam grapple with career decisions.
From The On The Level Series.
LC NO. 81-706938
Prod-EDFCEN Dist-AITECH 1980

What No Exit C 4 MIN
16MM FILM OPTICAL SOUND
Presents a texture study of pain, pathos and privacy on the frontier of urban America.
LC NO. 78-701333
Prod-KNIGN Dist-KNIGN 1978

What Now C 29 MIN
3/4 INCH VIDEO CASSETTE
Evaluates the Decision Makers Series. Describes characteristics and goals of leaders.
From The Decision Makers Series.
Prod-OHC Dist-HRC

What Now Skipper C 19 MIN
16MM FILM OPTICAL SOUND
Depicts the recommended procedures for selecting, maintaining and using marine fire extinguishers. Familiarizes the boating public with the federal requirements for fire extinguishers and their proper use on the pleasure boat.
LC NO. 74-705946
Prod-USCG Dist-USNAC 1972

What Now? C 12 MIN
3/4 OR 1/2 INCH VIDEO CASSETTE
Shows specific ways to help families during nursing home placement, including the use of family support groups, one-to-one counseling and supportive clergy.
From The Entering A Nursing Home Series.
Prod-SITH Dist-AJN

What On Earth C 10 MIN
16MM FILM, 3/4 OR 1/2 IN VIDEO I-J A
Presents an animated cartoon about Martians who visit earth and are confused about whether the prevailing and most intelligent form of life on earth is man or the automobile.
Prod-NFBC Dist-MGHT 1966

What On Earth C 15 MIN
3/4 OR 1/2 INCH VIDEO CASSETTE K-P
Discusses solids, liquids and gasses.
From The Dragons, Wagons And Wax, Set 2 Series.
Prod-CTI Dist-CTI

What On Earth C 20 MIN
3/4 INCH VIDEO CASSETTE J
Presents four earth scientists representing astronomy, meteorology, oceanography and geology. Discusses man's relationship to the Earth. Focuses on the scientific method by tracing the development of meteorology.
From The What On Earth Series.
Prod-NCSDPI Dist-GPITVL 1979

What On Earth—A Series
J
Discusses aspects of geography, meteorology, oceanography and geology.
Prod-NCSDPI Dist-GPITVL 1979

Agents Of Erosion	30 MIN
Atmosphere Yesterday And Today, The	22 MIN
Breaking Down The Rocks	30 MIN
Changing Landscape, The	30 MIN
Changing Rock	30 MIN
Climate And Our Living World	25 MIN
Clouds And Precipitation	27 MIN
Cyclonic Storms	24 MIN
Dynamic Planet, The	30 MIN
Earth In Space, The	25 MIN
Forces That Act On The Earth	24 MIN
Forecasting Tomorrow's Weather	27 MIN
Geologic Time	30 MIN
Heat And Circulation	30 MIN
Land Meets Sea	28 MIN
Land Vs Sea - The Interface	21 MIN
Location And Time	24 MIN
Man And The Sea	24 MIN
Mapping The Earth's Resources	22 MIN
Maps For Man	26 MIN
Minerals And Man	30 MIN
Nature Of Violent Storms, The	30 MIN
Our Ocean Of Air	26 MIN
Science And The Sea, Pt 1	30 MIN
Science And The Sea, Pt 2	30 MIN
Sedimentary Rocks	30 MIN
What On Earth	20 MIN
When The Earth Moves	30 MIN
Winds, Weather And Air Masses	24 MIN

What Parents Should Know About Drugs C 55 MIN
16MM FILM, 3/4 OR 1/2 IN VIDEO C A
Discusses basic facts that every parent should know about drugs by interviewing medical experts, psychiatrists, leaders of parent action groups and former young drug users. Examines new findings about the dangers of drugs and traces the four dangers of the drug-use cycle. Tells parents what signs to look for in their children which indicate drug use, what to do if their children are on drugs and where to find help.
Prod-ABCTV Dist-MTI 1981

What Persuades Whom C 30 MIN
3/4 OR 1/2 INCH VIDEO CASSETTE H-C A
See series title for descriptive statement.
From The Introduction To Technical And Business Communication Series.
Prod-UMINN Dist-GPITVL 1983

What Plants And Animals Can Be Found Along The Seashore C 20 MIN
2 INCH VIDEOTAPE I
See series title for descriptive statement.
From The Science Corner II, Unit IX - Exploring Our Country Series.
Prod-MPATI Dist-GPITVL

What Plants Need For Growth (Spanish) C 11 MIN
16MM FILM, 3/4 OR 1/2 IN VIDEO P
A Spanish language version of the film and videorecording What Plants Need For Growth.
Prod-EBEC Dist-EBEC 1982

What Plants Need For Growth (2nd Ed) C 11 MIN
16MM FILM, 3/4 OR 1/2 IN VIDEO P
Uses time-lapse photography, laboratory investigation and observation of plants in controlled environments to demonstrate the dependence of growing things on water, air, light, food and warmth. Examines agricultural practices illustrating ways in which food supply is enhanced by controlling water and plant nutrition.
LC NO. 83-706354
Prod-EBEC Dist-EBEC 1983

What Price Clean Air C 57 MIN
3/4 OR 1/2 INCH VIDEO CASSETTE
Discusses the price the American public could pay in terms of poor health and environmental damage if existing standards of the Clean Air Act are relaxed. Reveals that the auto and steel industries and Reagan administration officials charge that costs of meeting pollution standards increase industry depression and unemployment while public health and environmental groups maintain that high-sulfur coal and auto emissions cause acid rain and the deaths of thousands of lakes and streams.
Prod-PMI Dist-PMI

What Price Coal C 60 MIN
3/4 INCH VIDEO CASSETTE
Examines the 1969 Coal Mine Health and Safety Act and illustrates the problems that still remain in the 1970's, especially the fact that mines are unsafe. Explores the cost in human terms for energy.
From The Nova Series.
Prod-WGBHTV Dist-PBS 1977

What Price Confidence C 28 MIN
16MM FILM OPTICAL SOUND
Describes how the U S Army test and Evaluation Command ensures that equipment is free from defects and that it will function in any climate and on any terrain.
From The Big Picture Series.
LC NO. 75-703707
Prod-USA Dist-USNAC 1970

What Price Glory B 122 MIN
16MM FILM SILENT
Introduces Captain Flagg and Sergeant Quirt, who battle each other as vigorously as they do an opposing army, especially over the lovely but fickle Charmaine. Stars Victor McLaglen and directed by Raoul Walsh.
Prod-UNKNWN Dist-KILLIS 1926

What Price Steak C 60 MIN
3/4 OR 1/2 INCH VIDEO CASSETTE H A
Presents the economic implications of meat production, including use of grain and international demand for grain and meat. Mentions grain embargos and their effect upon producers and consumers.
Prod-CUETV Dist-CUNIV 1981

What Price Water C 35 MIN
16MM FILM OPTICAL SOUND
Details the extensive research and development program on a number of techniques which are enabling Britain to maintain her position as a leading exporter of desalination plants.
Prod-UKAEA Dist-UKAEA 1970

What Really Happened At The East Los Angeles Chicano Riot C 15 MIN
16MM FILM OPTICAL SOUND I-C A
Presents a documentary exposing the subtle biases of supposedly objective news reporting.
Prod-CFS Dist-CFS 1971

What Rocks Can We Collect C 20 MIN
2 INCH VIDEOTAPE P
See series title for descriptive statement.
From The Science Corner I, Unit II - Studying Rocks Series.
Prod-MPATI Dist-GPITVL

What Shall I Be C 8 MIN
16MM FILM, 3/4 OR 1/2 IN VIDEO P-I
Explores the fun and excitement of different occupations as the viewer follows the little hero who imagines himself in different situations.
Prod-CORF Dist-CORF 1972

What Shall It Be C 15 MIN
3/4 OR 1/2 INCH VIDEO CASSETTE P
Presents Dr Allhart and her friend Patience discussing factors to consider when choosing a pet.
From The Dr Allhart And Patience Series.
LC NO. 81-707528
Prod-JCITV Dist-GPITVL 1979

What Shall We Do About Claudius C 60 MIN
16MM FILM, 3/4 OR 1/2 IN VIDEO C A
Tells how Tiberius steps closer to power, his shadow falling on the clownish Claudius.
From The I, Claudius Series. Number 4
Prod-BBCTV Dist-FI 1977

What Shall We Do About Mother C 49 MIN
16MM FILM, 3/4 OR 1/2 IN VIDEO H-C A
Looks at the conflicts and guilt suffered by two families as they seek ways to care for their aging parents.
LC NO. 80-707726
Prod-CBSNEW Dist-CAROUF 1980

What Should I Buy C 14 MIN
3/4 OR 1/2 INCH VIDEO CASSETTE P
Reveals that Karen learns about wants and needs when she spends the $20 she receives for her birthday.
From The Under The Yellow Balloon Series.
Prod-SCETV Dist-AITECH 1980

What Should I Do C 15 MIN
16MM FILM, 3/4 OR 1/2 IN VIDEO I
Tells how three students choose different ways of gathering and collecting information.
From The Thinkabout Series. Collecting Information
LC NO. 81-706133
Prod-AITV Dist-AITECH 1979

What Should I Do (French)—A Series
P
Presents animated real-life situations and gives possible alternatives and consequences.
Prod-WDEMCO Dist-WDEMCO

Fight, The (French)	006 MIN
Game, The (French)	006 MIN
Lunch Money, The (French)	006 MIN
New Girl, The (French)	006 MIN
Project, The (French)	006 MIN

What Should I Do—A Series
16MM FILM, 3/4 OR 1/2 IN VIDEO
Prod-DISNEY Dist-WDEMCO 1970

Fight, The	6 MIN
Game, The	6 MIN
Lunch Money	6 MIN
New Girl, The	6 MIN
Project, The	6 MIN

What Should Your Business Plan Contain? C 22 MIN
16MM FILM, 3/4 OR 1/2 IN VIDEO H-C A
Notes how certain sections of business plan are essential to include, and illustrates steps to be followed in developing since effective plans reduce risks and increase potential.
From The Starting A Business Series.
Prod-SOMFIL Dist-BCNFL 1983

What Soviet Children Are Saying About Nuclear War C 22 MIN
16MM FILM, 3/4 OR 1/2 IN VIDEO
Interviews Soviet children on the subject of nuclear war. Shows a group of American doctors visiting two Soviet Pioneer camps.
Prod-EFVP Dist-EFVP

What Stories Can Rocks Tell B 20 MIN
2 INCH VIDEOTAPE P
Presents a bag of rocks to suggest how they were formed, what they are made of and how they have changed.
From The Scienceland Series.
Prod-MPATI Dist-GPITVL

What Supervisors Can Do About Planning Time C 20 MIN
3/4 OR 1/2 INCH VIDEO CASSETTE
Teaches supervisors how to conserve, ration and allocate time profitably. Dramatizes how to delegate jobs, organize work and increase planning and scheduling efficiency.
Prod-BBP Dist-BBP

What Tadoo C 18 MIN
16MM FILM, 3/4 OR 1/2 IN VIDEO P
Looks at the ways strangers entice children. Provides four basic rules for protection - say no, get away, tell someone and sometimes, yell.
From The Anti-Victimization Series.
Prod-MTI Dist-MTI

What The Decorticate Pigeon Can Do C 4 MIN
16MM FILM SILENT C
Demonstrates the various reflexes which arise in the brainstem, spinal cord, and cerebellum, using a pigeon which lacks the cerebral cortex.
From The Dukes Physiology Series.
LC NO. 75-710198
Prod-IOWA Dist-IOWA 1971

What The Earth Was Like C 15 MIN
3/4 OR 1/2 INCH VIDEO CASSETTE P-I
Discusses what the earth was like in the past.
From The Why Series.
Prod-WDCNTV Dist-AITECH 1976

What The Four Wise Monkeys Had To Say C 3 MIN
2 INCH VIDEOTAPE
Presents computer animation of shapes, colors and movements against a background of the song What The Four Wise Monkeys Had To Say, bringing a message about such everyday events as smoking, overeating, driving and the need to keep an inner equilibrium.
Prod-AMPFRI Dist-AMPFRI

What The Well Dressed Harness Horse Should Wear And Why C 10 MIN
1/2 IN VIDEO CASSETTE BETA/VHS
Explains how to dress trotters and pacers. Describes their jogging gear, points to the differences between jogging carts and sulkies.
Prod-USTROT Dist-EQVDL

What The World Dishes Out C 15 MIN
16MM FILM, 3/4 OR 1/2 IN VIDEO H-C A
Outlines some types of stressors that evoke a health-threatening response. Includes loss of self-esteem, boredom, role conflicts, excessive responsibility, lack of control and work overload. Shows specific techniques for temporarily relieving stress, such as deep breathing or meditation and gives suggestions for warding off stressors through cognitive restructuring.
From The Managing Stress Series.
Prod-CENTRO Dist-CORF 1984

What The World Needs Now Is Somebody To Listen C 30 MIN
2 INCH VIDEOTAPE J
See series title for descriptive statement.
From The Summer Journal, Unit 5 - You Are What Others See In You Series.
Prod-WNINTV Dist-GPITVL

What They Are And How They're Used C 50 MIN
3/4 OR 1/2 INCH VIDEO CASSETTE C
Covers introduction and computer parts and operation, microcomputers vs minicomputers, computer control.
From The Microcomputers - An Overview For Managers And Engineers Series.
Prod-GMIEMI Dist-AMCEE

What They Don't Know Can Hurt B 13 MIN
16MM FILM OPTICAL SOUND A
Discusses the need of knowing the right way of doing a job and for keeping a watchful eye open to correct the workers when a task is being done improperly.
From The Safety And The Foreman Series.
Prod-SARRA Dist-NSC 1956

What This Country Needs C 30 MIN
16MM FILM, 3/4 OR 1/2 IN VIDEO H-C A
Looks at America's declining productivity growth rate. Focuses on worker-management relations, the implications of changing worker attitudes, and the need for management to provide motivation.
LC NO. 81-707606
Prod-WTTWTV Dist-FI 1981

What Time Is It (2nd Ed) C 11 MIN
16MM FILM, 3/4 OR 1/2 IN VIDEO K-P
Uses animation to introduce clocks and time.
Prod-CORF Dist-CORF

What Time Is It In Tokyo C 14 MIN
16MM FILM, 3/4 OR 1/2 IN VIDEO I-J
Uses the principles pertaining to the rotation of the earth and its position in relation to the sun to develop a step-by-step logical understanding of why there are time differences around the world and how man has worked out ways of coping with them.
Prod-WER Dist-JOU 1971

What Time Is It In Tokyo (Spanish) C 14 MIN
16MM FILM, 3/4 OR 1/2 IN VIDEO I-J
Uses the principles pertaining to the rotation of the earth and its position in relation to the sun to develop a step-by-step logical understanding of why there are time differences around the world and how man has worked out ways of coping with them.
Prod-WER Dist-JOU 1971

What Time Is The Next Swan C 9 MIN
16MM FILM, 3/4 OR 1/2 IN VIDEO I-C A
Features Sarah Caldwell and the Boston Opera Company, following them through a rehearsal of an actual production.
Prod-MCFH Dist-PHENIX 1975

What Time Is Your Body C 23 MIN
16MM FILM, 3/4 OR 1/2 IN VIDEO H-C A
Contains footage of isolation experiments performed on humans to ascertain circadian rhythms and other information concerning human body rhythms.
From The Nova Series.
LC NO. 79-707248
Prod-BBCTV Dist-FI

What To Appraise C 8 MIN
3/4 OR 1/2 INCH VIDEO CASSETTE
Stresses the importance of knowing how employees perform and describes a means of evaluating what is important in a job and how to translate this into a usable form.
From The Performance Appraisal Series. Module 2
Prod-RESEM Dist-RESEM

What To Be C 18 MIN
16MM FILM OPTICAL SOUND
Presents the story of Richard, a chicano high school senior, who is having an internal struggle about his future. Explains that he is coping with the common feeling that college might not, after all, be necessary for his future development.
Prod-ELCC Dist-USC

What To Do C 15 MIN
3/4 OR 1/2 INCH VIDEO CASSETTE P
Shows how special interests may be related to career opportunities.
From The Spinning Stories Series.
Prod-MDDE Dist-AITECH 1977

What To Do At An Accident C 25 MIN
3/4 OR 1/2 INCH VIDEO CASSETTE
Shows program host Mario Machado rendering aid at a realistically recreated auto accident. Uses emergency ward doctor, policeman and fireman explaining the proper steps to be taken at the scene of an accident and demonstrating first-aid techniques.
From The Killers Series.
Prod-TRAINX Dist-TRAINX

What To Do On The Three-Day Weekend C 25 MIN
16MM FILM OPTICAL SOUND
Shows a vast collection of ways in which to spend three-day weekends, including being towed underwater behind a boat and performing a double somersault on skis. Includes views of the Grand Tetons in the clouds.
LC NO. 75-713382
Prod-JMOTOR Dist-GROENG 1970

What To Do When Someone Chokes C 15 MIN
3/4 OR 1/2 INCH VIDEO CASSETTE
Presents simple and easy-to-follow instructions and demonstrates the various ways to handle a choking victim, whether conscious or unconscious.
Prod-KGPROD Dist-FILCOM 1983

What To Do When You Need A Banker C 18 MIN
16MM FILM, 3/4 OR 1/2 IN VIDEO J-C A
Shows what happens when two young people inadvertently overdraw their checking account. Explains how to choose the correct bank and make use of all banking services.
From The What To Do Series.
LC NO. 80-707361
Prod-CORF Dist-CORF 1980

What To Do When You Need A Doctor C 20 MIN
16MM FILM, 3/4 OR 1/2 IN VIDEO J-C A
Tells how a young woman learns how to cope with the medical system after she has an accident. Explains how to find a doctor and discusses fees and services.
From The What To Do Series.
LC NO. 80-707362
Prod-CORF Dist-CORF 1980

What To Do When You Need A Lawyer C 21 MIN
16MM FILM, 3/4 OR 1/2 IN VIDEO J-C A
Shows what happens when legal services are needed, telling how to find and hire a lawyer, use small claims courts, and seek out alternatives for legal assistance.
From The What To Do Series.
LC NO. 80-707363
Prod-CORF Dist-CORF 1980

What To Do When You Need A Real Estate Agent C 21 MIN
16MM FILM, 3/4 OR 1/2 IN VIDEO J-C A
Shows a young couple finding a real estate agent and learning the process of purchasing a home.
From The What To Do Series.
LC NO. 80-707364
Prod-CORF Dist-CORF 1980

What To Do When You Need An Insurance Agent C 19 MIN
16MM FILM, 3/4 OR 1/2 IN VIDEO J-C A
Describes how to buy insurance, select an agent, and file a claim.
From The What To Do Series.
LC NO. 80-707365
Prod-CORF Dist-CORF 1980

What To Do With An Old Sock B 15 MIN
2 INCH VIDEOTAPE K-P
See series title for descriptive statement.
From The Magic Of Words Series.
Prod-GWTVAI Dist-GPITVL Prodn-WETATV

What To Do—A Series
16MM FILM, 3/4 OR 1/2 IN VIDEO J-C A
Offers consumer information on such topics as banking, real estate, medicine, insurance and law.
Prod-CORF Dist-CORF 1980

What To Do When You Need A Banker 018 MIN
What To Do When You Need A Doctor 020 MIN
What To Do When You Need A Lawyer 021 MIN
What To Do When You Need A Real Estate Agent 021 MIN
What To Do When You Need An Insurance Agent 019 MIN

What To Make Of A Wall C 30 MIN
2 INCH VIDEOTAPE C A
Introduces the importance of walls as background areas. Shows many uses of paint and wood to create interesting wall treatments.
From The Designing Home Interiors Series. Unit 19
Prod-COAST Dist-CDTEL Prodn-RSCCD

What We Are C 17 MIN
16MM FILM OPTICAL SOUND
Looks at employees of Eastman Chemical Products at work and at leisure in the communities where the plants are located.
LC NO. 80-700078
Prod-ECP Dist-ECP Prodn-PECKHM 1979

What We Have C 32 MIN
16MM FILM OPTICAL SOUND
Follows the growing relationship between a grandmother and a rebellious youth at the Teaching-Learning Communities of the Ann Arbor, Michigan, Public Schools where both elderly and young people benefit from contact with each other.
Prod-UMICH Dist-UMICH

What Will I Be Next C 30 MIN
2 INCH VIDEOTAPE J
See series title for descriptive statement.
From The Summer Journal, Unit 1 - You Are What You Feel Series.
Prod-WNINTV Dist-GPITVL

What Will I Be Tomorrow? C 14 MIN
16MM FILM, 3/4 OR 1/2 IN VIDEO I-J
Depicts the changing life of a thirteen year old son of proud, cattle-herding Masai parents in Kenya. Shows how he spends his day herding, watering, feeding, and milking the cows owned by his father, who has two wives and eight children, all living in a settlement of dried dung huts. Defines how new ways are testing traditional culture and making growing up more difficult.
From The Just One Child Series.
Prod-REYEXP Dist-BCNFL 1983

What Will I Be? C 30 MIN
3/4 INCH VIDEO CASSETTE
Examines the problems of sexism in education and its effects on children. Discusses how two teachers have been deeply involved in changing sexism in education in British Columbia.
Prod-WMENIF Dist-WMENIF

What Will I Do With My Time C 26 MIN
16MM FILM OPTICAL SOUND
Presents a series of portraits of men and women from different socio-economic and geographic backgrounds as they engage in a wide variety of professional and non-professional careers.
LC NO. 77-700595
Prod-NYLI Dist-MTP Prodn-HESJEG 1976

What Will Poor Robin Do Then C 28 MIN
16MM FILM OPTICAL SOUND
A dramatic, scientific and documentary study of rubella. Discusses the disease, the development of a vaccine and its recommended use.
LC NO. 72-706148
Prod-MESHDO Dist-SMUSA Prodn-KNIFED 1969

What Will Space Stations Be Like C 20 MIN
2 INCH VIDEOTAPE I
See series title for descriptive statement.
From The Science Corner II, Unit III - Journey In Space Series.
Prod-MPATI Dist-GPITVL

What Will The Weather Be C 11 MIN
16MM FILM, 3/4 OR 1/2 IN VIDEO I
Examines the science of weather forecasting, looking at a model of scientist's at work. Shows how they gather information, record it, study it, and draw conclusions from it.
Prod-FILMSW Dist-FLMFR

What Will We Do On Saturday C 20 MIN
16MM FILM OPTICAL SOUND I
Explains that our decreasing workday, coupled with increasing affluence, is resulting in more and more leisure time for the majority of our society. Points out that this new found leisure is creating some serious psychological and environmental problems. Stresses the fact that our society can no longer stress vocational-oriented education alone, it must also begin to educate for the use of leisure as well.
From The Inherit The Earth Series.
Prod-KQEDTV Dist-GPITVL

What Will We Do With It C 20 MIN
16MM FILM OPTICAL SOUND I
Points out that America, a nation with advanced technological abilities, a deep concern for public health and a mania for cleanliness, is about to smother in its own waste products. Explores some of the reasons behind this seeming paradox as well as methods currently used to prevent this suffocation. Discusses replacement of the concept of waste disposal with the idea of waste utilization.
From The Inherit The Earth Series.
Prod-KQEDTV Dist-GPITVL

What Will You Be When You Grow Up B 15 MIN
2 INCH VIDEOTAPE P

Explains that there are many jobs from which people can make a career choice. (Broadcast quality)
From The Around The Corner Series. No. 30
Prod-FWCETV Dist-GPITVL Prodn-WEDUTV

What Will Your New Venture Demand? C 20 MIN
16MM FILM, 3/4 OR 1/2 IN VIDEO H-C A
Challenges those planning careers to examine their strengths and interests and assess what role is best.
From The Starting A Business Series.
Prod-SOMFIL Dist-BCNFL 1983

What Would Happen If C 9 MIN
16MM FILM OPTICAL SOUND
Illustrates what would happen if everyone stole things. Stimulates oral language skills.
LC NO. 70-706883
Prod-MLA Dist-MLA 1969

What Would You Do C 8 MIN
16MM FILM OPTICAL SOUND P-I
Depicts two children at play, one black, one white. Poses problematical situations requiring active student participation and assessment of basic human values.
LC NO. 73-700632
Prod-ATLAP Dist-ATLAP 1973

What Would You Do C 20 MIN
16MM FILM OPTICAL SOUND PRO
Depicts six situations that law enforcement officers may encounter as greater numbers of handicapped persons attempt to make lives for themselves outside the confines of institutions. Discusses the needs of handicapped persons and suggests ways that police officers can meet those needs while still enforcing the law.
LC NO. 78-701613
Prod-UKBCR Dist-UKANS 1978

What Would You Do If A Robber Stuck A Gun In Your Ribs C 40 MIN
16MM FILM, 3/4 OR 1/2 IN VIDEO
Uses a question and answer session to explain what should be done during a robbery attempt.
From The National Crime And Violence Test Series.
Prod-MTI Dist-MTI

What Would You Do? C 8 MIN
3/4 OR 1/2 INCH VIDEO CASSETTE P-I
Deals with responsibility and value judgment, non-narrative.
Prod-ATLAP Dist-ATLAP

What Would You Really Do If Accosted By A Rapist C 40 MIN
16MM FILM, 3/4 OR 1/2 IN VIDEO
Uses a question and answer session to explain what to do if accosted by a rapist.
From The National Crime And Violence Test Series.
Prod-MTI Dist-MTI

What You Are Is C 60 MIN
16MM FILM, 3/4 OR 1/2 IN VIDEO C A
Presents Dr Morris Massey making observations on each generation in terms of social, political and moral events, and attitudes that affected their lives while growing up. Relates these underlying influences to the way we work, play and worship.
Prod-CBSTV Dist-FI 1983

What You Are Is Where You See C 75 MIN
3/4 OR 1/2 INCH VIDEO CASSETTE A
Shows Dr Morris Massey describing how to prepare for a better future by adopting a more flexible and realistic point of view. Focuses on positive change.
From The Massey Tapes Series.
Prod-CBSFOX Dist-CBSFOX

What You Are Is Where You Were When C 90 MIN
3/4 OR 1/2 INCH VIDEO CASSETTE A
Features Dr Morris Massey explaining how persons' individual value systems are formed through their early life experiences. Discusses imprinting, modeling and socialization.
From The Massey Tapes Series.
Prod-CBSFOX Dist-CBSFOX

What You Are Is Where You Were When C 90 MIN
16MM FILM, 3/4 OR 1/2 IN VIDEO C A
Presents Dr Morris Massey explaining his theory of how people go through self-programming periods from an early age. Discusses methods of changing this self-programming so that the person's future will be changed.
Prod-MAGVID Dist-FI 1980

What You Are Is..., Pt 1 C 30 MIN
3/4 OR 1/2 INCH VIDEO CASSETTE A
Presents Dr Morris Massey explaining how value systems are formed and how one can change his own and those of other people. Emphasizes improving communications.
From The Massey Tapes Series.
Prod-CBSFOX Dist-CBSFOX

What You Are Is..., Pt 2 C 60 MIN
3/4 OR 1/2 INCH VIDEO CASSETTE A
Presents Dr Morris Massey explaining how value systems are formed and how one can change his own and those of other people. Emphasizes improving communications.
From The Massey Tapes Series.
Prod-CBSFOX Dist-CBSFOX

What You Are Is..., Pt 3 C 30 MIN
3/4 OR 1/2 INCH VIDEO CASSETTE A
Presents Dr Morris Massey explaining how value systems are formed and how one can change his own and those of other people. Emphasizes improving communications.
From The Massey Tapes Series.
Prod-CBSFOX Dist-CBSFOX

What You Are Is'nt Necessarily What You Will Be C 60 MIN
3/4 OR 1/2 INCH VIDEO CASSETTE A
Shows Dr Morris Massey profiling two generations of Americans, traditionalists and rejectionists. Explains how the two groups attained their distinct value systems and offers a basis for bridging the generation gap.
From The Massey Tapes Series.
Prod-CBSFOX Dist-CBSFOX

What You Are Isn't Necessarily What You Will Be C 60 MIN
16MM FILM, 3/4 OR 1/2 IN VIDEO C A
Presents Dr Morris Massey profiling two unique generations within American society, the traditionalists and the rejectionists. Defines the two groups and their approaches to solving problems.
Prod-MAGVID Dist-FI 1980

What You Bring On Yourself C 15 MIN
16MM FILM, 3/4 OR 1/2 IN VIDEO H-C A
Centers on Type A personalities, the ones who drive themselves beyond normal limits. Makes a distinction between the stress response and other emotional states such as frustration or anger. Gives suggestions for lessening their stress by exercising, walking away from unreasonable situations, seeking professional help or joining groups.
From The Managing Stress Series.
Prod-CENTRO Dist-CORF 1984

What You Can Do C 30 MIN
3/4 OR 1/2 INCH VIDEO CASSETTE
Suggests ways of combatting the nine problems that may indicate a predisposition to CHD. Examines the interrelationships among obesity, exercise and elevated levels of serum cholesterol and triglyceride.
From The CHD And You Series.
Prod-NETCHE Dist-NETCHE 1976

What You Can Do, Part 2 C 30 MIN
3/4 OR 1/2 INCH VIDEO CASSETTE
Provides a detailed look at the twin problems of obesity and lack of exercise, and details only two ways of controlling weight, to decrease caloric intake through diet, and to increase caloric expenditure through increased physical activity.
From The CHD And You Series.
Prod-NETCHE Dist-NETCHE 1976

What You Don't Know - Learning About Hazardous Materials C
16MM FILM - 3/4 IN VIDEO A
Stresses joint effort by company, supervisor and workers to make the work environment safe from hazardous substance exposure.
Prod-BNA Dist-BNA 1983

What You Don't Know Can Hurt You C
3/4 OR 1/2 INCH VIDEO CASSETTE
Shows the importance for older patients in understanding their health problems and the treatments and medicines being prescribed to them.
Prod-GRANVW Dist-GRANVW

What You Just Did C 29 MIN
3/4 OR 1/2 INCH VIDEO CASSETTE I-C A
Presents visually hypnotic sequences of movement interspersed with dancers talking about improvisation, being male, touching, the give-and-take of 'contact dance' and dance as art-sport.
Prod-UCV Dist-UCV

What You Should Know About Social Security - Now C 20 MIN
3/4 OR 1/2 INCH VIDEO CASSETTE
Covers all aspects of social security, including retirement benefits, disability benefits, survivor benefits and Medicare. Includes Meidinger Guide To Social Security.
Prod-PVC Dist-DELTAK

What You Should Know About Your Pension Plan C 28 MIN
16MM FILM, 3/4 OR 1/2 IN VIDEO
Features a public affairs program in talk show format that discusses pension plans and the problems that occur with receiving benefits, and what to do about them.
Prod-USDL Dist-USNAC

What 80 Million Women Want B 55 MIN
16MM FILM SILENT J-C
Also known under the title, Eighty Million Women Want. Uses a drama featuring Emmeline Pankhurst to present the cause of women suffrage. With subtitles.
LC NO. 76-700213
Prod-FCE Dist-FCE 1974

What, Where And When - The Story Of The U S Army Supply And Maintenance Command C 27 MIN
16MM FILM OPTICAL SOUND
Describes the dual mission of the U S Army Supply and Maintenance Command to deliver supplies to the soldier and to perform fifth echelon maintenance of Army equipment.
LC NO. 74-705947
Prod-USA Dist-USNAC 1966

What'Cha Gonna Do C 11 MIN
16MM FILM - VIDEO, ALL FORMATS
Shows some simple and effective ways that children use to protect themselves from abduction. Dramatizes situations in which youngsters are approached by strangers.
Prod-PEREN Dist-PEREN

What'll I Do If C 10 MIN
16MM FILM OPTICAL SOUND H-C A
Helps bank tellers and others who handle money in dealing with a robbery situation. Stresses three simple rules which are do exactly what the robber says, make no suspicious moves while the robber is watching and get a good description of the robber.
From The Golden Triangle Teller Training Film Series.
LC NO. 75-701989
Prod-PART Dist-PART 1975

What'll It Do For Me C 22 MIN
16MM FILM OPTICAL SOUND
Demonstrates the usefulness of the UNIVAC computer, stressing capability, versatility and performance of the UNIVAC 9000 series.
Prod-SPGYRO Dist-UNIVAC 1970

What'll You Do If B 12 MIN
16MM FILM OPTICAL SOUND J-C A
Illustrates in a group of emergency situations such conditions as the brakes failing, the accelerator sticking, the car going off the pavement and the car skidding. Describes some of the dangers to be alert for in routine driving.
From The You And Your Car Series.
Prod-PART Dist-PART 1964

What's A Balanced Diet C 15 MIN
3/4 OR 1/2 INCH VIDEO CASSETTE P
Explains a balanced diet and emphasizes the importance of food choices. Features situations where children can exercise some choice over the foods they eat, namely, in the school cafeteria and at snack time.
From The Great American Eating Machine - You Series. Pt 4
LC NO. 83-706108
Prod-NJPTV Dist-GPITVL 1982

What's A Balanced Diet C 28 MIN
3/4 OR 1/2 INCH VIDEO CASSETTE J-H A
See series title for descriptive statement.
From The Food For Youth Series.
Prod-CUETV Dist-CUNIV 1975

What's A Balanced Diet C 28 MIN
16MM FILM, 3/4 OR 1/2 IN VIDEO
Defines the four basic food groups - fruits and vegetables, breads and cereals, milk and milk products, and meat, poultry and fish. Discusses how much from each group children need. Explains meat alternatives and gives the latest USDA recommendations for type A school lunches.
From The Food For Youth Series.
LC NO. 81-706398
Prod-USFNS Dist-USNAC Prodn-WGBH 1981

What's A Cop C 25 MIN
16MM FILM, 3/4 OR 1/2 IN VIDEO
Describes opinions held by the public about the police tells of problems faced by the police in doing their job.
From The Law Enforcement Education Series.
Prod-WORON Dist-MTI 1973

What's A Coward - A Drama C 15 MIN
16MM FILM OPTICAL SOUND
Shows how a young boy copes with the fears and uncertainties associated with moving from a small town to the inner city.
From The Guidance - Emotions Series.
LC NO. 74-703612
Prod-MORLAT Dist-MORLAT 1973

What's A Good Book - Selecting Books For Children C 27 MIN
16MM FILM, 3/4 OR 1/2 IN VIDEO C A
Presents librarians, authors and college professors who address the question of what constitutes a good book for children citing literary quality, incidents linking plot with life and a book's ability to fulfill a particular purpose.
Prod-PULIDO Dist-WWS Prodn-WWS 1982

What's A Heaven For C 18 MIN
16MM FILM - 3/4 IN VIDEO
Uses a collage technique to present the life of Booker T Washington. Discusses his effect upon America. Issued in 1966 as a motion picture.
LC NO. 79-706173
Prod-USNPS Dist-USNAC 1979

What's A Nice Girl Like You Doing In A Place Like This B 11 MIN
16MM FILM OPTICAL SOUND C
Presents a narrative about a young man with an hallucination. Satirizes the use of the cliche.
Prod-NYU Dist-NYU 1965

What's A Party For? C 60 MIN
3/4 OR 1/2 INCH VIDEO CASSETTE
Looks at the decline of political parties.
From The Bill Moyers' Journal Series.
Prod-WNETTV Dist-WNETTV 1976

What's Alive C 11 MIN
16MM FILM, 3/4 OR 1/2 IN VIDEO P-I
Illustrates with pictures of animals, plants, machines and chemicals how living and non-living things are alike and different. Shows that only a thing that can move, respond, change fuel into energy, reproduce and grow can be said to be alive.
Prod-FA Dist-PHENIX 1961

What's An Animal - A First Film C 17 MIN
16MM FILM, 3/4 OR 1/2 IN VIDEO P-I
Stressing that scientists categorize animals by body shape and function, this vividly photographed production showcases eight animal groups from the simple one-celled organisms to the more highly specialized vertebrates.
LC NO. 84-707157
Prod-BEAN Dist-PHENIX 1984

What's An Ergonomic C 15 MIN
16MM FILM, 3/4 OR 1/2 IN VIDEO H A

Studies ergonomics, the science that seeks to adapt work or working conditions to suit the worker. Features high-tech furnishings used by the computer society.
Prod-KLEINW Dist-KLEINW

What's Behind Behavior? C 14 MIN
3/4 OR 1/2 INCH VIDEO CASSETTE
Explains the many influences that shape a person's behavior.
From The Human Side Of Management Series.
Prod-RESEM Dist-RESEM

What's Behind The Front C 30 MIN
2 INCH VIDEOTAPE
Features meteorologist Frank Sechrist explaining how one low can cause different types of weather in different parts of the country. Relates the pressure, winds, temperature and clouds of the low to the weather.
From The Weather Series.
Prod-WHATV Dist-PUBTEL

What's Communism All About C 25 MIN
16MM FILM, 3/4 OR 1/2 IN VIDEO J-H
Presents a brief history of communism and compares communism to capitalism.
Prod-CBSNEW Dist-CAROUF

What's Cookin' C 30 MIN
16MM FILM - 3/4 IN VIDEO
Focuses on how young children acquire their food likes and dislikes, their feelings about food, and their patterns of eating. Provides some basic information about nutrition and explains how parents can help their children develop good eating habits.
From The Footsteps Series.
LC NO. 79-707639
Prod-USOE Dist-USNAC 1978

What's Cooking C 15 MIN
16MM FILM, 3/4 OR 1/2 IN VIDEO P-J
Captures the sounds, sights and spirit of five ethnic American families cooking and eating their evening meals.
LC NO. 79-708093
Prod-CF Dist-CF 1979

What's Cooking - Nutrition C 23 MIN
16MM FILM - VIDEO, ALL FORMATS
Deals with developing good eating habits in young children. Discusses attitudes toward eating, children's likes and dislikes, and some basic nutritional information.
From The Footsteps Series.
Prod-PEREN Dist-PEREN

What's Enough C 15 MIN
16MM FILM, 3/4 OR 1/2 IN VIDEO I
Explains that Bobby is sure that Eddie has stolen his bicycle until he begins to gather facts and learns the truth.
From The Thinkabout Series. Reshaping Information
LC NO. 81-706134
Prod-EDFCEN Dist-AITECH 1979

What's Expected Of Me? B 30 MIN
3/4 INCH VIDEO CASSETTE
Focuses on one year in the life of a girl named Renee. Documents the change from the 'kid's world' of sixth grade to the more grown up life of a New York City junior high school.
Prod-WMEN Dist-WMEN

What's For Breakfast C 4 MIN
16MM FILM, 3/4 OR 1/2 IN VIDEO K-I
Presents the nutritious and energy-producing foods to start the day with.
From The Most Important Person - Nutrition Series.
Prod-EBEC Dist-EBEC 1972

What's Going On Around Here C 15 MIN
3/4 OR 1/2 INCH VIDEO CASSETTE K-P
Deals with the relationship between plant and animal communities and their environment.
From The Dragons, Wagons And Wax, Set 2 Series.
Prod-CTI Dist-CTI

What's Going On With Women C 30 MIN
3/4 INCH VIDEO CASSETTE
Discusses the diversity of beliefs in the women's movement and where future feminist leaders will come from.
From The Decison Makers Series.
Prod-OHC Dist-HRC

What's Good For GM... C 55 MIN
16MM FILM OPTICAL SOUND
Offers a dramatic case study of the cost of corporate control over the vital process of urban economic development. Shows how the city of Detroit destroyed it's Poletown neighborhood in the hope of retaining a few thousand industrial jobs. Shows unions and citizen groups exploring ways to insure that their investment in reindustrialization pays off in a more stable employment base.
Prod-CBSNEW Dist-CANWRL 1981

What's Good For Me C 15 MIN
3/4 OR 1/2 INCH VIDEO CASSETTE P
Explains the body's need for a variety of foods and nutrients. Presents Mother Hubbard telling about the functions and sources of carbohydrates, fats, proteins, vitamins and minerals.
From The Great American Eating Machine - You Series. Pt 3
LC NO. 83-706107
Prod-NJPTV Dist-GPITVL 1982

What's Good To Eat (Spanish) C 17 MIN
16MM FILM - VIDEO, ALL FORMATS
Shows how the body uses nutrients and how the food groups provide necessary nutrients.
Prod-WFP Dist-PEREN

What's Good To Eat (2nd Ed) C 18 MIN
16MM FILM, 3/4 OR 1/2 IN VIDEO I-J
Shows how the four food groups give the human body the nutrition it needs. Explains how the body uses these nutrients and how the food groups provide a reliable pattern for making reasonable choices and tasty combinations.
From The Nutrition Education Series.
Prod-WFP Dist-PEREN 1978

What's Half, What's A Fourth C 15 MIN
3/4 INCH VIDEO CASSETTE P
Introduces the concepts of one-half and one-fourth.
From The Math Factory, Module V - Fractions Series.
Prod-MAETEL Dist-GPITVL 1973

What's Happened Since 'Fire' C 13 MIN
16MM FILM, 3/4 OR 1/2 IN VIDEO J-C A
Offers an update of the ABC television special Close-Up On Fire. Discusses the manufacture of flammable plastic cribs, new methods of testing urethane, and the problems of high-rise building fires.
Prod-SANDEM Dist-PHENIX 1976

What's Happening C 5 MIN
16MM FILM, 3/4 OR 1/2 IN VIDEO I
Shows five story problems, each incomplete, for children to solve.
From The Magic Moments, Unit 1 - Let's Talk Series.
Prod-EBEC Dist-EBEC 1969

What's Happening To Television B 60 MIN
16MM FILM OPTICAL SOUND H-C A
Presents a critical view of the program material which is being shown by commercial and educational TV. Includes comments by network executives, news commentators, writers, the Nielson Company President and the FCC chairman. Discusses the viewer's responsibility.
From The At Issue Series.
Prod-NET Dist-IU 1966

What's Impeachment All About C 15 MIN
16MM FILM, 3/4 OR 1/2 IN VIDEO J-H
Presents a history of the U S Constitution with an emphasis on impeachment.
Prod-CBSNEW Dist-CAROUF

What's Important C 15 MIN
16MM FILM OPTICAL SOUND I
Explains how Christie solves the mystery of Sir Gordon Grendel's death.
From The Thinkabout Series.
LC NO. 81-700161
Prod-OECA Dist-AITECH 1980

What's Important C 15 MIN
3/4 OR 1/2 INCH VIDEO CASSETTE I
Tells how Christie solves the mystery of the death of Sir Gordon Grendel. Emphasizes the necessity of judging the importance of clues.
From The Thinkabout Series. Reshaping Information
LC NO. 81-706135
Prod-TFW Dist-AITECH 1979

What's In A Book B 9 MIN
16MM FILM OPTICAL SOUND I-H
Describes the parts of a book–title page, table of contents, index, preface, foreword, introduction, chapters, footnotes, appendix, bibliography and glossary. Illustrates the design and art production involved in making a book.
From The Pathways To Reading Series.
Prod-CBF Dist-AVED 1958

What's In A Fallen Log B 20 MIN
2 INCH VIDEOTAPE P
Explains that a rotting log on the forest floor is a treasure chest full of fascinating plants and animals.
From The Scienceland Series.
Prod-MPATI Dist-GPITVL

What's In A Frame C 29 MIN
3/4 OR 1/2 INCH VIDEO CASSETTE
Explains the concepts of framing and composition and how you can use the depth-of-field control to get a good photograph.
From The Photo Show Series.
Prod-WGBHTV Dist-PBS 1981

What's In A Horn C
16MM FILM, 3/4 OR 1/2 IN VIDEO I-C A
Shows that a horn works by using valves to change pitch instead of using many horns of different tube size.
Prod-EBEC Dist-EBEC 1983

What's In A Paragraph - Besides Sentences C 15 MIN
2 INCH VIDEOTAPE J
Discusses methods of maintaining interest within a paragraph.
From The From Me To You...In Writing, Pt 1 Series
Prod-DELE Dist-GPITVL

What's In A Play C 17 MIN
16MM FILM, 3/4 OR 1/2 IN VIDEO J-C A
Analyzes a simple example of dramatic action–a conflict between a salesman and a customer–to show the structure of a play. Points out the three parts-a beginning, a climax and an ending.
Prod-FA Dist-PHENIX 1967

What's In A Rainbow C 13 MIN
16MM FILM, 3/4 OR 1/2 IN VIDEO P-I
Explains how to observe a rainbow. Discusses the techniques of building a scientific model.
From The Scientific Fact And Fun Series.
Prod-GLDWER Dist-JOU 1980

What's In A Sentence Besides Words C 15 MIN
2 INCH VIDEOTAPE J
Discusses the sentence as a complete statement.
From The From Me To You...In Writing, Pt 1 Series
Prod-DELE Dist-GPITVL

What's In A Shadow C 13 MIN
16MM FILM, 3/4 OR 1/2 IN VIDEO P-I
Relates the shadow to the idea of the Sun's position at different times of day. Shows how a knowledge of that position helps in finding directions.
From The Scientific Fact And Fun Series.
Prod-GLDWER Dist-JOU 1979

What's In A Spider Web C 13 MIN
16MM FILM, 3/4 OR 1/2 IN VIDEO P-I
Shows how a spider uses its web to capture its food, how it lays eggs and raises a family.
From The Scientific Fact And Fun Series.
Prod-GLDWER Dist-JOU 1981

What's In A Story (2nd Ed) C 12 MIN
16MM FILM, 3/4 OR 1/2 IN VIDEO I-J
Tells how pleasure and knowledge can be increased by discovering the different messages a story presents.
Prod-BFA Dist-PHENIX 1977

What's In A Word–A Series

Traces word origins as far back as they go, and tells interesting stories of the development of words. Features entymologist, Bob Smith.
Prod-KQEDTV Dist-PUBTEL

What's In An Egg C 13 MIN
16MM FILM, 3/4 OR 1/2 IN VIDEO P-I
Shows how various animals including fish, amphibians, reptiles and insects begin life within an egg.
From The Scientific Fact And Fun Series.
Prod-GLDWER Dist-JOU 1982

What's In It For Me C 27 MIN
3/4 OR 1/2 INCH VIDEO CASSETTE J-H A
See series title for descriptive statement.
From The Food For Youth Series.
Prod-CUETV Dist-CUNIV 1975

What's In It For Me C 29 MIN
16MM FILM, 3/4 OR 1/2 IN VIDEO
Tells how the Manpower Development and Training Act skills program helps a young man gain the ability and self-respect needed to get a job. Issued in 1967 as a motion picture.
From The Career Job Opportunity Film Series.
LC NO. 79-707888
Prod-USDLMA Dist-USNAC Prodn-DEROCH 1979

What's In It For Me - The Nutrients C 28 MIN
16MM FILM, 3/4 OR 1/2 IN VIDEO
Discusses the six classes of nutrients - protein, fats, carbohydrates, vitamins, minerals and water. Shows why each is important to the body, making specific reference to USDA guidelines for school lunches.
From The Food For Youth Series.
LC NO. 81-706399
Prod-USFNS Dist-USNAC Prodn-WGBH 1981

What's In It For Me?–A Series

Instructs on the use of new blood collection equipment in various phases of operation.
Prod-AMRC Dist-AMRC 1977

Central Supply 009 MIN
Mobile Unit Assistants 017 MIN
Nurses 023 MIN

What's In It For You? C 30 MIN
3/4 OR 1/2 INCH VIDEO CASSETTE
Covers the why of a systematic and ongoing performance appraisal system. Shows how appraisal systems provide organizations with meaningful data for manpower planning and development.
From The Appraisals In Action Series. Session 1
Prod-PRODEV Dist-DELTAK

What's In The Box? C 30 MIN
3/4 OR 1/2 INCH VIDEO CASSETTE T
See series title for descriptive statement.
From The Eager To Learn Series.
Prod-KTEHTV Dist-KTEHTV

What's In The Newspaper B 20 MIN
2 INCH VIDEOTAPE I-H
Explores the newspaper for content and acquaints the student with the different sections. Discusses differences and similarities and examines the skim-scan approach to reading the newspaper. (Broadcast quality)
From The Newspaper In The Classroom Series. No. 3
Prod-MOEBA Dist-GPITVL Prodn-KYNETV

What's In The Snow B 20 MIN
2 INCH VIDEOTAPE P
Reveals many clues to out-of-door events that can be found in the snow. Includes acorns, pine needles, feathers and footprints.
From The Scienceland Series.
Prod-MPATI Dist-GPITVL

What's It All About C 12 MIN
16MM FILM OPTICAL SOUND H-C
Presents a factual look at the economic consequences of competition. Shows what happens when an important product line is nearly eliminated because it no longer can compete in the market place.
Prod-GM Dist-GM

What's It All About, Harry C 29 MIN
16MM FILM OPTICAL SOUND IND
Follows a young telephone installer as he takes his kid brother along on his saturday errands. Shows how they give ratings

to the kinds of service they receive and in turn are rated on the craft jobs done the day before.
LC NO. 73-700531
Prod-ILBELL Dist-PART Prodn-PART 1970

What's Mine Is Mine B 12 MIN
16MM FILM OPTICAL SOUND
Presents a sensitive portrayal of a day in the life of a retarded child at the Rotary School for retarded children in Willowdale, Toronto, Canada.
Prod-SENCOL Dist-SENCOL

What's Mine Is Mine C 12 MIN
16MM FILM, 3/4 OR 1/2 IN VIDEO
Examines the territorial behavior of a variety of animals including lizards, gulls, prairie chickens and wolves.
From The BSCS Behavior Film Series.
Prod-BSCS Dist-PHENIX 1974

What's Missing - Missing Addends B 20 MIN
3/4 INCH VIDEO CASSETTE P
See series title for descriptive statement.
From The Let's Figure It Out Series.
Prod-WNYETV Dist-NYSED 1968

What's My Score B 20 MIN
16MM FILM OPTICAL SOUND
Demonstrates the ability of paraplegics to show their qualifications and proficiency to handle jobs in competition with non-handicapped veterans. Shows the basic steps in training a paraplegic to get around and assist himself and features other veterans with various handicaps actually on the job.
Prod-USVA Dist-USVA 1947

What's New C 15 MIN
2 INCH VIDEOTAPE I
Examines the history of communication from pre-Colonial days to the present. Explains new communication devices for the classroom and encourages students to think of future communication devices.
From The Images Series.
Prod-CVETVC Dist-GPITVL

What's New At School C 45 MIN
16MM FILM, 3/4 OR 1/2 IN VIDEO H-C A
Looks at teaching methods in primary schools, comparing the traditional desk-structured school to the open classroom school.
Prod-CBSNEW Dist-CAROUF

What's New In Solid Waste Management C 37 MIN
16MM FILM OPTICAL SOUND J A
Describes new techniques in solid waste management and shows how demonstration grants provide guidance for public works officials throughout America.
LC NO. 70-714060
Prod-USEPA Dist-FINLYS 1970

What's Nutrition C 28 MIN
3/4 OR 1/2 INCH VIDEO CASSETTE J-H A
See series title for descriptive statement.
From The Food For Youth Series.
Prod-CUETV Dist-CUNIV 1975

What's Nutrition C 29 MIN
16MM FILM, 3/4 OR 1/2 IN VIDEO
Presents a brief history of nutrition, emphasizing the importance of forming food habits for a lifetime. Stresses attitudes toward food, nutrition, and eating and how they affect the job of the school service worker.
From The Food For Youth Series.
LC NO. 81-706401
Prod-USFNS Dist-USNAC Prodn-WGBH 1981

What's Really Comin' Down C 29 MIN
2 INCH VIDEOTAPE
Focuses on teenager's views of life in suburbia, USA.
From The Turning Points Series.
Prod-NJPBA Dist-PUBTEL

What's Say C 14 MIN
16MM FILM, 3/4 OR 1/2 IN VIDEO P-I
Tells how the gang learns that a new girl in town is hard of hearing. Shows what happens when she visits a hearing specialist and discovers a new world and lots of friends.
From The Learning Values With Fat Albert Series.
Prod-FLMTON Dist-CRMP 1977

What's So Different C 15 MIN
3/4 OR 1/2 INCH VIDEO CASSETTE P
Examines the differences in environment and lifestyle in various parts of the world.
From The Spinning Stories Series.
Prod-MDDE Dist-AITECH 1977

What's So Great About Books C 14 MIN
16MM FILM OPTICAL SOUND
Deals with parents reading with their children from infancy throughout the school years to help children develop language skills, appreciate good literature and develop creative thinking.
LC NO. 78-700231
Prod-ORPULI Dist-ORPULI Prodn-CYPRES 1977

What's So Important About A Wheel (2nd Ed) C 10 MIN
16MM FILM, 3/4 OR 1/2 IN VIDEO P
Examines the many different varieties of wheels in use in our society. Traces the history of the wheel and its subsequent development from a simple wooden cart to the modern automobile, locomotive and jet aircraft.
Prod-ALTSUL Dist-JOU 1972

What's So Special About Computers? C 33 MIN
3/4 OR 1/2 INCH VIDEO CASSETTE
Illustrates many of the reasons for project failure, using the story of a company which is on the brink of financial ruin because a data processing project designed to steamline its distribution system failed to achieve its goals.
Prod-VISUCP Dist-VISUCP

What's So Special About Paper C 29 MIN
16MM FILM OPTICAL SOUND J-H
Reveals a great range of jobs, for people with almost any educational background, and shows how the paper industry is involved in such socially important work as forest conservation and water purification.
Prod-AMERPI Dist-MTP

What's That And Do You Want It And No, Thank You C 15 MIN
2 INCH VIDEOTAPE P
See series title for descriptive statement.
From The Avenida De Ingles Series.
Prod-SDITVA Dist-GPITVL

What's That And It's A C 15 MIN
2 INCH VIDEOTAPE P
See series title for descriptive statement.
From The Avenida De Ingles Series.
Prod-SDITVA Dist-GPITVL

What's That And What Do You Have C 15 MIN
2 INCH VIDEOTAPE P
See series title for descriptive statement.
From The Avenida De Ingles Series.
Prod-SDITVA Dist-GPITVL

What's The Best Business For You? C 16 MIN
16MM FILM, 3/4 OR 1/2 IN VIDEO H-C A
Provides tools for the aspiring entrepreneur in assessing a business idea, including personal considerations, possible growth, income and market share.
From The Starting A Business Series.
Prod-SOMFIL Dist-BCNFL 1982

What's The Best Word C 15 MIN
3/4 OR 1/2 INCH VIDEO CASSETTE J
Explains the importance of using the right word to convey information by telling the story of Rita who should have described the student body fund as low and not bankrupt. Shows Scott helping Jeff look up just the right word to describe his feelings for Sally Ann.
From The In Other Words Series. Giving Meaning To Messages, Pt 7
Prod-AITV Dist-AITECH Prodn-KOCETV 1983

What's The Big Idea, Ben Franklin C 15 MIN
3/4 OR 1/2 INCH VIDEO CASSETTE P
Presents librarian Phyllis Syracuse reading from the children's biography What's The Big Idea, Ben Franklin by Jean Fritz. Discusses candle and soap making.
From The Through The Pages Series. No. 7
LC NO. 82-707375
Prod-WVIZTV Dist-GPITVL 1982

What's The Danger - Drug Effects And Hazards C 30 MIN
3/4 OR 1/2 INCH VIDEO CASSETTE C A
Focuses on what is known and not known about the effects of drugs. Includes the relationships between drugs and crime, drugs and creativity and drug overdose and death.
From The Contemporary Health Issues Series. Lesson 17
Prod-SCCON Dist-CDTEL

What's The Difference Being Different? C 19 MIN
16MM FILM, 3/4 OR 1/2 IN VIDEO
Shows students and teachers participating in activities which increase feelings of self-worth and understanding of others.
Prod-RESPRC Dist-RESPRC 1977

What's The Good Of A Test X 12 MIN
16MM FILM, 3/4 OR 1/2 IN VIDEO P-I
Describes how to use tests, what tests measure and how to prepare for and take a test. Explains and illustrates composition or essay questions, objective questions and standardized tests.
Prod-JOU Dist-JOU 1965

What's The Limit C 15 MIN
16MM FILM, 3/4 OR 1/2 IN VIDEO I-J
Challenges student to evaluate themselves realistically and recognize that each person has limitations that may affect career choices and that these limitations must be accepted and dealt with positively.
From The Whatcha Gonna Do Series.
Prod-NVETA Dist-EBEC 1974

What's The Matter And My Head, Stomach, Throat Hurts C 15 MIN
2 INCH VIDEOTAPE P
See series title for descriptive statement.
From The Avenida De Ingles Series.
Prod-SDITVA Dist-GPITVL

What's The Matter With Carruthers C 15 MIN
3/4 INCH VIDEO CASSETTE P
Presents the children's story What's The Matter With Carruthers by James Marshall.
From The Tilson's Book Shop Series.
Prod-WVIZTV Dist-GPITVL 1975

What's The Meaning C 14 MIN
16MM FILM, 3/4 OR 1/2 IN VIDEO I
Tells how Alfie learns that communication involves a sender, a receiver, and information.
From The Thinkabout Series. Giving And Getting Meaning
LC NO. 81-706136
Prod-EDFCEN Dist-AITECH 1979

What's The Presidency All About C 25 MIN
16MM FILM, 3/4 OR 1/2 IN VIDEO J-H
Examines the office of the presidency and the men who have worked there. Tells how the system of checks and balances has thwarted abuses of power by the executive, legislative and judicial branches.
Prod-CBSNEW Dist-CAROUF

What's The Rule - Concepts From Algebra B 20 MIN
3/4 INCH VIDEO CASSETTE P
See series title for descriptive statement.
From The Let's Figure It Out Series.
Prod-WNYETV Dist-NYSED 1968

What's The Solution B
16MM FILM OPTICAL SOUND
Examines whether or not a system of simultaneous equations has a solution, and, if it has, whether or not it is unique.
Prod-OPENU Dist-OPENU

What's To Understand C 4 MIN
16MM FILM OPTICAL SOUND J-C A
Shows two young teenagers bitterly struggling with the apprehensions and peer pressures associated with sexuality.
From The Responsible Caring Series.
LC NO. 81-701351
Prod-MEMAPP Dist-MEMAPP Prodn-VISCNT 1980

What's Under The Hood C 29 MIN
3/4 OR 1/2 INCH VIDEO CASSETTE
See series title for descriptive statement.
From The Car Care Series.
Prod-NHMNET Dist-PBS

What's Under Your Hood (2nd Ed) C 11 MIN
16MM FILM, 3/4 OR 1/2 IN VIDEO J-C A
Uses a working model engine and animation to show how an automobile engine works.
Prod-AIMS Dist-AIMS 1967

What's Under Your Hood (2nd Ed) (Spanish) C 11 MIN
16MM FILM, 3/4 OR 1/2 IN VIDEO H-C A
Uses model engine, animation and simple narration to answer questions about the major automobile parts and how and why they do function.
Prod-PANTON Dist-AIMS 1973

What's Up Josh C 54 MIN
16MM FILM OPTICAL SOUND R
Relates the story of Tom, a student with inner conflicts who is helped by Josh Mc Dowell, Campus Crusade college representative.
Prod-GF Dist-GF

What's Up Tiger Lily C 80 MIN
16MM FILM OPTICAL SOUND
Features a Japanese spy movie re-dubbed with Woody Allen's dialogue.
Prod-UNKNWN Dist-TWYMAN 1966

What's Wrong C 13 MIN
3/4 OR 1/2 INCH VIDEO CASSETTE P
Shows how Sally questions the need for rules when she breaks one at school and her mother breaks a traffic law. Explains how she has a dream about a world without rules.
From The Under The Blue Umbrella Series.
Prod-SCETV Dist-AITECH 1977

What's Wrong - Troubleshooting A Video System C 30 MIN
3/4 OR 1/2 INCH VIDEO CASSETTE
Diagnoses many production problems and their solution through a process of observation, isolation, definition, correction and returning.
From The Video - A Practical Guide...and More Series.
Prod-VIPUB Dist-VIPUB

What's Wrong With Jonathan (Everyday Pressures) C 15 MIN
16MM FILM, 3/4 OR 1/2 IN VIDEO J
Illustrates the buildup of pressures during a difficult day. Discusses how to recognize daily pressures and how to deal with them more effectively.
From The Self Incorporated Series.
LC NO. 75-703958
Prod-AIT Dist-AITECH Prodn-UTSBE 1975

What's Wrong With Me C 16 MIN
16MM FILM, 3/4 OR 1/2 IN VIDEO I
Introduces Eddie, a victim of child abuse who is removed from his home environment and taken to a home for abused youngsters. Shows him gradually learning that the abuse he experienced was not his fault.
From The Learning Laws - Respect For Yourself, Others And The Law Series.
Prod-WDEMCO Dist-WDEMCO 1982

What's Wrong With My Child C 28 MIN
3/4 OR 1/2 INCH VIDEO CASSETTE
Examines the major signs of learning disabilities in children. Explains the learning-disabled child's difficulty in using and understanding language, poor motor coordination and short attention spans.
Prod-WQED Dist-PBS 1977

What's Wrong With Our Schools C 60 MIN
16MM FILM, 3/4 OR 1/2 IN VIDEO H-C A
Presents Dr Milton Friedman suggesting that lack of choice prevents healthy competition in education as in business and introduces his proposal for a voucher system for primary and secondary education. Offers a debate between Dr Friedman and others who both share and disagree with his views.
From The Free To Choose Series.
Prod-EBEC Dist-EBEC 1983

What's Wrong With Our Schools (Discussion) C 30 MIN
16MM FILM, 3/4 OR 1/2 IN VIDEO H-C A

Offers a debate between Dr Milton Friedman and others on the voucher system for primary and secondary education.
From The Free To Choose (Discussion) Series.
Prod-EBEC Dist-EBEC 1983

What's Wrong With Our Schools (Documentary) C 30 MIN
16MM FILM, 3/4 OR 1/2 IN VIDEO H-C A
Presents Dr Milton Friedman suggesting that lack of choice prevents healthy competition in education as in business and introduces his proposal for a voucher system for primary and secondary education.
From The Free To Choose (Documentary) Series.
Prod-EBEC Dist-EBEC 1983

What's Wrong With The Interview C 20 MIN
3/4 OR 1/2 INCH VIDEO CASSETTE
See series title for descriptive statement.
From The Videosearch Employment Interview Series.
Prod-DELTAK Dist-DELTAK

What's Your Authority C 11 MIN
16MM FILM, 3/4 OR 1/2 IN VIDEO I-J
Examines the nature of authority and prepares the child to cope with the authorities he will encounter at home, at school and in society.
Prod-EBEC Dist-EBEC 1971

What's Your Authority (Spanish) C 11 MIN
16MM FILM, 3/4 OR 1/2 IN VIDEO I-J
A Spanish language version of the film and videorecording What's Your Authority.
Prod-EBEC Dist-EBEC 1972

What's Your Bag C 16 MIN
16MM FILM, 3/4 OR 1/2 IN VIDEO H-C
Presents eight students evaluating their interests and abilities. Relates their interests and abilities to a variety of occupations within the scientific, mechanical, clerical and computational levels. Explains that these levels are found in unskilled, skilled, semiprofessional and professional occupations.
Prod-MCCRNE Dist-AIMS 1975

What's Your Excuse C 7 MIN
16MM FILM, 3/4 OR 1/2 IN VIDEO H-C A
Shows people giving excuses for their indiscretion with alcohol. Explains that it is a human quality that characterizes bad judgment with a frail excuse.
Prod-AIMS Dist-AIMS 1974

What's Your Fuel C 15 MIN
3/4 OR 1/2 INCH VIDEO CASSETTE P
Explains that just as a toy steam engine needs fuel to operate so does the human body. Illustrates how food is digested. (Broadcast quality)
From The All About You Series.
Prod-NITC Dist-AITECH Prodn-TTOIC 1975

Whatabout-A Series
J
Discusses scientific inquiry and shows how it can be applied to certain questions.
Prod-AITV Dist-AITECH 1983

Classifying In Science	015 MIN
Communicating In Science	014 MIN
Decision-Making And Science	014 MIN
Experimenting In Science	014 MIN
Hypothesizing In Science	014 MIN
Inferring In Science	014 MIN
Measuring In Science	014 MIN
Modeling In Science	014 MIN
Observing In Science	014 MIN
Predicting In Science	014 MIN
Questioning In Science	014 MIN
Recording Data In Science	014 MIN

Whatcha Gonna Do-A Series
16MM FILM, 3/4 OR 1/2 IN VIDEO I-J
Prod-NVETA Dist-EBEC 1974

Because It's Just Me	015 MIN
Getting Ready	015 MIN
Going Back	015 MIN
Let's Get To Work	020 MIN
Most Important Thing, The	015 MIN
Partners	015 MIN
Time Of Changes, A	015 MIN
Try Out	015 MIN
What Do You Think	015 MIN
What's The Limit	015 MIN

Whatever Happened To Baby Jane B 132 MIN
16MM FILM OPTICAL SOUND
Focuses on two aging actresses who live as recluses in their old mansion. Tells what happens when one woman (Joan Crawford) decides to sell the house and put her sister (Bette Davis) in an old people's home.
Prod-WB Dist-TWYMAN 1962

Whatever Happened To Childhood C 46 MIN
16MM FILM, 3/4 OR 1/2 IN VIDEO H-C T
Explains how the concept of childhood is being obliterated by early drug usage, a changing sexual morality and an indifference to criminal behavior.
LC NO. 84-706125
Prod-KCOPTV Dist-CF 1984

Whatever Happened To El Salvador C 52 MIN
3/4 OR 1/2 INCH VIDEO CASSETTE H-C A
Examines the situation in El Salvador since the elections held March 28, 1982. Includes exclusive interviews with members of the U S Special Forces training government troops, who specifically deny that they have been involved in the fighting.
Prod-NBCNEW Dist-FI 1982

Whatever Happened To Green Valley C 55 MIN
16MM FILM OPTICAL SOUND H-C A
Presents a view of Green Valley, a large government-sponsored housing project outside of Sydney, Australia, from the vantage point of its residents. Attempts to counteract unfavorable publicity and criticism from sectors of the mass media.
LC NO. 75-702397
Prod-FLMAUS Dist-AUIS 1975

Whatever Happened To Honesty C 13 MIN
16MM FILM, 3/4 OR 1/2 IN VIDEO I A
Investigates the problem of theft and its effect on the American way of life.
Prod-HIGGIN Dist-HIGGIN 1977

Whatever Happened To Lori Jean Lloyd C 28 MIN
16MM FILM, 3/4 OR 1/2 IN VIDEO J-C A
Presents a view of the life of runaway children along the back alleys of Hollywood and along New York's infamous Minnesota Strip, where they become victims of drugs, sexual exploitation, disease, fear, loneliness, deprivation and death.
From The Dealing With Social Problems In The Classroom Series.
LC NO. 81-707252
Prod-BELLDA Dist-FI 1980

Whatever Happened To Marx C 26 MIN
16MM FILM, 3/4 OR 1/2 IN VIDEO H-C
Presents the influence of Karl Marx in the Russian Revolution of 1917 and its effect on the Third World.
From The Today's History Series.
Prod-JOU Dist-JOU 1984

Whatever Happened To Mike C 12 MIN
16MM FILM - 3/4 IN VIDEO H-C A
Shows how a learning disabled youth built a full life after receiving help from his teachers. Tells how, after high school graduation, he was able to get and keep jobs and how he worked up from an unskilled laborer in a sawmill to a highly skilled worker.
LC NO. 79-706035
Prod-LAWREN Dist-LAWREN 1979

Whatever The Weather X 10 MIN
16MM FILM, 3/4 OR 1/2 IN VIDEO P
Shows how children adapt their activities to the weather.
Prod-EH Dist-EBEC Prodn-CHAPFC 1967

Whatever Your New Year's Resolutions C 1 MIN
3/4 INCH VIDEO CASSETTE
Does a take-off on the Rosie's Diner paper towel commercials. Deals with new year's resolutions.
Prod-MDPL Dist-LVN

Whats New In Diabetes Care? C 15 MIN
3/4 OR 1/2 INCH VIDEO CASSETTE S
Provides patients with information about new advancements and current research in the field of diabetes. Discusses blood glucose monitoring, insulin pumps, new oral antidiabetes medications, islet cell and pancreatic transplantation, and the use of new techniques to identify and possibly prevent Type 1 insulin dependent diabetes in certain high risk individuals. Explains how these new advancements may have an impact on the patient with diabetes in the years to come.
Prod-UMICHM Dist-UMICHM 1984

Whatsoever You Do C 8 MIN
16MM FILM, 3/4 OR 1/2 IN VIDEO
Dramatizes the plight and history of primitive people in the United States and East Africa who suffer from disease and famine. Shows the boundless faith, hope and humor which exist in people of all races and color.
Prod-PAULST Dist-PAULST

Whazzat C 10 MIN
16MM FILM, 3/4 OR 1/2 IN VIDEO P
Presents an adaptation of the East Indian folktale about six blind men who come upon an elephant and attempt to describe it. Stresses the moral that cooperating with others can achieve more than working alone.
Prod-EBEC Dist-EBEC 1975

Wheat C 22 MIN
16MM FILM, 3/4 OR 1/2 IN VIDEO
Describes wheat, from the planting of seed to the baking of bread.
Prod-KAWVAL Dist-KAWVAL

Wheat - From Field To Flower C 11 MIN
16MM FILM, 3/4 OR 1/2 IN VIDEO I-J
Outlines the major wheat-growing areas of the world and illustrates the growing, harvesting and processing of this crop.
Prod-CENTRO Dist-CORF

Wheat - Its Growth, Transportation And Marketing C 28 MIN
16MM FILM OPTICAL SOUND I-C A
Documents the history of wheat, including planting, growing and harvesting techniques, testing and grading and selling at the Kansas City Board of Trade. Shows the storage problems and elaborate railroad operations involved in moving the harvest.
From The How Does Your Garden Grow Series.
Prod-OTT Dist-STAFER 1955

Wheat Cycle C 16 MIN
16MM FILM OPTICAL SOUND
Examines farming in Afghanistan, showing the cycle of activities from the sowing to the harvesting of the wheat.
From The Faces Of Change - Afghanistan Series.
Prod-AUFS Dist-WHEELK

Wheat, White, And Cinnamon Bread C 87 MIN
1/2 INCH VIDEOTAPE
Demonstrates the basics of bread baking.
From The Baking Bread Series.
Prod-ANVICO Dist-ANVICO

Wheatstone Bridge, The C
3/4 OR 1/2 INCH VIDEO CASSETTE
See series title for descriptive statement.
From The Basic DC Circuits Series.
Prod-VTRI Dist-VTRI

Wheatstone Bridge, The C 15 MIN
3/4 OR 1/2 INCH VIDEO CASSETTE
See series title for descriptive statement.
From The Basic Electricity And D.C. Circuits, Laboratory Series.
Prod-TXINLC Dist-TXINLC

Wheeeels, No. 1 C 5 MIN
16MM FILM OPTICAL SOUND
Explores the highways and by-ways of America.
Prod-VANBKS Dist-VANBKS 1959

Wheeeels, No. 2 C 5 MIN
16MM FILM OPTICAL SOUND
Presents a fantasy farce on the car of everyday life. Depicts everything as a vehicle.
Prod-VANBKS Dist-VANBKS 1959

Wheel And Axle - An Introduction C 10 MIN
16MM FILM, 3/4 OR 1/2 IN VIDEO I-J
Explores machines of many sizes and shapes that are part of our lives. Points out that all these machines are either simple machines or combinations of simple machines. Presents experiments with different wheel and axle combinations to reveal number patterns that help us understand how simple machines work.
Prod-BFA Dist-PHENIX 1971

Wheel And Axle, The - A Simple Machine C 15 MIN
3/4 OR 1/2 INCH VIDEO CASSETTE P-I
Discusses the characteristics of the wheel and axle.
From The Why Series.
Prod-WDCNTV Dist-AITECH 1976

Wheel Bearings And Lubrication C 30 MIN
3/4 OR 1/2 INCH VIDEO CASSETTE
Explains how to lubricate the suspension and steering systems and how to inspect and service wheel bearings.
From The Keep It Running Series.
Prod-NETCHE Dist-NETCHE 1982

Wheel Is Round, A C 8 MIN
16MM FILM, 3/4 OR 1/2 IN VIDEO K-P
Introduces the youngest readers and pre-readers to words and concepts, including pictures and songs.
From The Starting To Read Series.
Prod-BURGHS Dist-AIMS 1971

Wheel Of Becoming, The C 7 MIN
3/4 OR 1/2 INCH VIDEO CASSETTE
See series title for descriptive statement.
From The Memory Surfaces And Mental Prayers Series.
Prod-EAI Dist-EAI

Wheel Of Fortune, The C 52 MIN
16MM FILM, 3/4 OR 1/2 IN VIDEO
Traces the connection between astrology, ancient Greek medical manuscripts, the need for precise measuring devices and the invention of the telescope, forged steel and interchangeable machine parts.
From The Connections Series. No. 5
LC NO. 79-706744
Prod-BBCTV Dist-TIMLIF 1979

Wheel On The Chimney C 7 MIN
16MM FILM, 3/4 OR 1/2 IN VIDEO K-P
Uses pictures, words and music from the book by Margaret Wise Brown, to tell the story of how a stork nest on cartwheels fastened to the chimneys of European farmhouses.
Prod-WWS Dist-WWS 1969

Wheel Puller C 15 MIN
3/4 OR 1/2 INCH VIDEO CASSETTE IND
Continues introduction to blueprint reading. Shows how to lay out a workpiece from a print and how to plan an effective machining sequence.
From The Blueprint Reading For Machinists Series.
Prod-LEIKID Dist-LEIKID

Wheel Puller (Intermediate) C
3/4 OR 1/2 INCH VIDEO CASSETTE
See series title for descriptive statement.
From The Blueprint Reading Series.
Prod-VTRI Dist-VTRI

Wheel Puller (Intermediate) (Spanish) C
3/4 OR 1/2 INCH VIDEO CASSETTE
See series title for descriptive statement.
From The Blueprint Reading (Spanish) Series.
Prod-VTRI Dist-VTRI

Wheelbarrow Man B 22 MIN
16MM FILM OPTICAL SOUND C A
An allegorical tale of a soldier who finds himself in purgatory and how his soul searches for an answer to what it means to die a hero.
Prod-USC Dist-UWFKD

Wheelchair Group C 21 MIN
3/4 OR 1/2 INCH VIDEO CASSETTE
Demonstrates upper torso and relaxation exercises that can be done by physically handicapped persons in their wheelchairs.
Prod-LASSWC Dist-UWISC 1979

Wheelchair Transfer C 29 MIN
3/4 INCH VIDEO CASSETTE PRO
Covers common wheelchair transfers used in the clinical care of patients. Includes a convalescent patient a weak patient and a hemiplegic patient. Demonstrates the hydraulic lifter.

From The Wheelchair Transfers Series.
Prod-PRIMED Dist-PRIMED

Wheelchair Transfers For The Paraplegic C 7 MIN
16MM FILM - 3/4 IN VIDEO
Explains and demonstrates three transfer techniques for the paraplegic patient. Issued in 1966 as a motion picture.
LC NO. 77-706093
Prod-USPHS Dist-USNAC Prodn-NMAC 1966

Wheelchair Transfers—A Series
PRO
Prod-PRIMED Dist-PRIMED

Arm Pulling - Pushing Transfer 19 MIN
Paraplegic Parient, The - Taking Off A Full 7 MIN
Paraplegic Patient, The - Putting On A Full 9 MIN
Swivel Bar Transfer For Quadriplegia 11 MIN
Wheelchair Transfer 29 MIN

Wheelchair Transport C 20 MIN
16MM FILM OPTICAL SOUND
Shows how to operate a wheelchair and transport a patient safely.
From The Nurse's Aid, Orderly And Attendant Series.
LC NO. 79-704832
Prod-COPI Dist-COPI 1969

Wheelchair Transport C 14 MIN
3/4 INCH VIDEO CASSETTE H-C A
Shows how to operate a wheelchair and transport a patient safely.
From The Nurse's Aide, Orderly And Attendant Series.
Prod-COPI Dist-COPI 1969

Wheelies C 29 MIN
16MM FILM OPTICAL SOUND P-J
Asks young people to examine their already forming attitudes toward the automobile - a major air pollutor as well as the source of many amusements. Uses animated characters to explain how the natural environment is unable to clean air that has been heavily polluted by automobiles. Presents bicycling and walking as inexpensive and nonpolluting forms of transportation.
From The Earthkeeping Series.
LC NO. 73-703397
Prod-WTTWTV Dist-IU 1973

Wheelies C 29 MIN
2 INCH VIDEOTAPE
Features an animated king and his page Alvin who experience the lure of a shiny new passion-pink car, are thoroughly impressed by a visit to an auto show and eventually realize the damage cars do to the natural self-purifying functions of the atmosphere.
From The Earthkeeping Series.
Prod-WTTWTV Dist-PUBTEL

Wheelin' Steel C 28 MIN
3/4 OR 1/2 INCH VIDEO CASSETTE
Twenty-eight minute version of the original fifty minute version of Wheelin' Steel which concentrates on the wheelchair competition itself.
Prod-UWASHP Dist-UWASHP

Wheelin' Steel C 50 MIN
3/4 OR 1/2 INCH VIDEO CASSETTE
Captures the action and emotion of the 25th National Wheelchair Games, five days of intense competition in track, field, weight-lifting, swimming, archery, table tennis and slalom.
Prod-UWASHP Dist-UWASHP

Wheels C 13 MIN
16MM FILM OPTICAL SOUND PRO
Illustrates the Kansas Neurological Institute wheelchair modification program in which wheelchairs are reconstructed and modified to meet the head and neck support, truck support, foot support and back support requirements associated with specific deformities of handicapped children.
LC NO. 75-701096
Prod-UKANBC Dist-UKANS 1974

Wheels C 15 MIN
16MM FILM OPTICAL SOUND
Features a boy who wishes for a car and gets his wish, but then finds he is too young for it.
LC NO. 76-703168
Prod-CIHIB Dist-CIHIB 1976

Wheels And Deals C 20 MIN
3/4 INCH VIDEO CASSETTE J-H
Shows a transaction between a potential buyer and a new-car salesman. Features a used-car salesman pointing out things to check before buying a used car.
From The Dollar Data Series.
LC NO. 81-707387
Prod-WHROTV Dist-GPITVL 1974

Wheels And Things - Linear Measurement B 20 MIN
3/4 INCH VIDEO CASSETTE P
See series title for descriptive statement.
From The Let's Figure It Out Series.
Prod-WNYETV Dist-NYSED 1968

Wheels And Tires C 12 MIN
16MM FILM, 3/4 OR 1/2 IN VIDEO J A
Presents information about wheels and tires, including tire construction, wheels and hubs, front wheel parts, care of tires and changing a tire.
Prod-SF Dist-SF 1968

Wheels And Tires C 30 MIN
3/4 OR 1/2 INCH VIDEO CASSETTE
Describes the functions of the various parts of the suspension and steering systems. Discusses the different types of tires and demonstrates preventive service and maintenance checks on tires.
From The Keep It Running Series.
Prod-NETCHE Dist-NETCHE 1982

Wheels Of Business C 1 MIN
16MM FILM OPTICAL SOUND H
Describes the Distributive Education Clubs Of America, showing how the free enterprise system spurs competition and how competition spurs incentive to better serve the consumer.
LC NO. 80-701273
Prod-DECA Dist-PCSI Prodn-PCSI 1980

Wheels Within Wheels C 14 MIN
16MM FILM OPTICAL SOUND H-C A
Explains the career opportunities in the trucking industry. Gives an inside view of the business.
LC NO. FIA65-431
Prod-MTRUCK Dist-WSU 1964

Wheels, Kilns And Clay—A Series

Prod-USC Dist-PUBTEL

Ancient Techniques In Clay 28 MIN
Artist Potters Make A Living Today 28 MIN
Beginning To Throw - The Bowl 28 MIN
Beginning To Throw - The Cylinder 28 MIN
Bottles, A Modification Of The Basic Cylinder 28 MIN
Building Pot Forms By Coil Methods 28 MIN
Building With Clay Slabs 28 MIN
Casting And Pressing In Molds 28 MIN
Centering And Opening The Ball 28 MIN
Ceramic Terms And Concepts 28 MIN
Clay Batches For Plastic Clay Slips 28 MIN
Clay Forms In Ancient Cultures 28 MIN
Clay Wall Treatments 28 MIN
Cliff Steward, Guest, Builds Wheel-Thrown 28 MIN
Combining Oxides To Make Glazes 28 MIN
Compotes And Attached Bases 28 MIN
Construction Of Large Pots 28 MIN
Cut And Put Together Pots From Thrown Shapes 28 MIN
Design And Decor Principles 28 MIN
Design For Mass Production 28 MIN
Dora De Larios, Guest, Builds A Slab Sculpture 28 MIN
Earthenware 28 MIN
Engobe Decorating On Bowl Forms 28 MIN
Glassblowing - Hand And Mass Production 28 MIN
Glaze Application On Bisque Ware 28 MIN
Hanging Planters, Candlesticks, Lanterns 28 MIN
Heat Treatments 28 MIN
History Of Ceramics 28 MIN
How To Mix An Engobe 28 MIN
How To Roll Coils - Preparing To Hand Build 28 MIN
How To Teach Ceramics - How To Set Up A Studio 28 MIN
Introduction - Overview Of Ceramics 27 MIN
Kiln Atmospheres And Temperatures For Glaze 28 MIN
Kilns For Firing 28 MIN
Lidded Pots 28 MIN
Loading And Firing A Bisque Kiln 28 MIN
Low Fire - Enamel On Copper 28 MIN
Mathematical Calculations Of Glaze Formulas 28 MIN
Molds And Models - How They Are Used 28 MIN
Molds And Models - Start To Finish 28 MIN
Other Uses For Ceramics 28 MIN
Potter's Wheel, The 28 MIN
Procelain 28 MIN
Raku Glaze Firing 28 MIN
Stoneware 28 MIN
Susan Peterson, Artist-Potter 28 MIN
Teapots 28 MIN
Texturing Clay 28 MIN
Throwing Pitchers, Pulling Handles 28 MIN
Trim Foot Of Thrown Bowl 28 MIN
Underglaze And Overglaze Decor 28 MIN
Variety Of Glaze Effects - Introduction To 28 MIN
Wedging The Clay And Making A Pitch Pot 28 MIN
What Is Clay 28 MIN

Wheels, Wheels, Wheels C 11 MIN
16MM FILM, 3/4 OR 1/2 IN VIDEO P-J
Explores the various forms of wheels that have contributed to our civilization, including the gears, sprockets and winches that drive everything from water wheels to computers. Teaches perceptual values in language arts as well as the value of technical accomplishment.
Prod-KINGSP Dist-PHENIX 1969

Wheelwright, The C 21 MIN
16MM FILM, 3/4 OR 1/2 IN VIDEO J-C A
Shows two methods of constructing a wheel, one traditional and one modern.
LC NO. 80-707243
Prod-BFL Dist-IFB Prodn-SMITHB 1975

When A Child Dies C 22 MIN
16MM FILM OPTICAL SOUND
Examines the experiences, feelings and needs of parents and siblings of children who have died. Uses such examples as a child killed in an auto accident, a child who died after suffering from leukemia for 18 months and a child who died as an infant in his crib.
LC NO. 79-701453
Prod-GITTFI Dist-GITTFI 1979

When A Child Enters The Hospital C 16 MIN
16MM FILM, 3/4 OR 1/2 IN VIDEO H-C A
Chronicles the hospitalization of a young girl undergoing minor surgery and shows how her mother staying with her helps.
Prod-POLYMR Dist-POLYMR 1975

When A Man's A Prince B 17 MIN
16MM FILM OPTICAL SOUND H-C
Features a slapstick comedy with added humorous commentary and a musical score.
Prod-MSENP Dist-CFS

When A Woman Fights Back C 59 MIN
3/4 OR 1/2 INCH VIDEO CASSETTE
Discusses the Yvonne Wanrow murder trial which set a legal precedent when her conviction was reversed by the Washington State Supreme Court.
Prod-KCPQTV Dist-PBS 1980

When A Word Is Worth A Thousand Pictures C 29 MIN
3/4 OR 1/2 INCH VIDEO CASSETTE T
See series title for descriptive statement.
From The Coping With Kids Series.
Prod-MFFD Dist-FI

When A Word Is Worth A Thousand Pictures C 30 MIN
3/4 OR 1/2 INCH VIDEO CASSETTE
Explains the very significant concept of encouragement. Discusses the importance of both verbal and non-verbal methods in the encouragement process.
From The Coping With Kids Series.
Prod-OHUTC Dist-OHUTC

When America Was Young C 20 MIN
2 INCH VIDEOTAPE P-I
See series title for descriptive statement.
From The Learning Our Language, Unit V - Exploring With Books Series.
Prod-MPATI Dist-GPITVL

When Are They Ready - Reading Readiness C 30 MIN
3/4 OR 1/2 INCH VIDEO CASSETTE T
See series title for descriptive statement.
From The Teaching Early Reading Series.
Prod-CTI Dist-CTI

When Chicago Was Hollywood, Pt 1 B 27 MIN
16MM FILM, 3/4 OR 1/2 IN VIDEO J-C A
Tells how Chicago was the center of the film industry from 1904 to 1915 with operations at the Selig and Essanay Studios. Interviews a cameraman, film editor and a prop man for the old companies. Uses vintage photographs, rare old films and stories about the great stars such as Chaplin.
Prod-WMAQTV Dist-TEXFLM 1967

When Chicago Was Hollywood, Pt 2 B 27 MIN
16MM FILM, 3/4 OR 1/2 IN VIDEO J-C A
Discusses the film industry in Chicago from 1915 to the closing of the studios in 1917. Tells how stars like Chaplin moved West because of the weather and better opportunities.
Prod-WMAQTV Dist-TEXFLM 1967

When Children Have Cancer C 25 MIN
3/4 OR 1/2 INCH VIDEO CASSETTE
Examines the battle against childhood cancer through profiles of past and current patients.
Prod-TRAINX Dist-TRAINX

When Comedy Was King B 81 MIN
16MM FILM, 3/4 OR 1/2 IN VIDEO
Describes the days of silent movies, presenting excerpts from comedies. Includes work by the Keystone Kops, Buster Keaton, Ben Turpin, Harry Langdon and others.
Prod-YNGSNR Dist-CAROUF

When Did You Last See Yourself On TV C 32 MIN
16MM FILM, 3/4 OR 1/2 IN VIDEO H-C A
Surveys media stereotypes of women. Presents schoolgirls, a housewife and women in television assessing what television offers and who makes the television image of women. Asks whether television reflects the changes affecting women in recent years or whether women have left television far behind.
From The Women Series.
Prod-LUF Dist-LUF 1979

When Dinosaurs Ruled The Earth C 100 MIN
16MM FILM OPTICAL SOUND
Describes the adventures of a group of Stone Age people.
Prod-WB Dist-TWYMAN 1970

When Disaster Strikes C 17 MIN
16MM FILM OPTICAL SOUND
Depicts the natural disaster operations of the Army Corps Of Engineers. Shows how they respond to disasters with personnel, equipment, technical assistance and supervision.
LC NO. 74-706325
Prod-USAE Dist-USNAC 1970

When Divorce Comes To School C 28 MIN
3/4 INCH VIDEOTAPE
Documents the successful efforts of one Massachusetts school to help students who are struggling with the breakup of their families. Demonstrates how teachers, counselors and psychologists can create a support group for children of divorce.
Prod-EDC Dist-EDC

When Fire Starts C 18 MIN
16MM FILM, 3/4 OR 1/2 IN VIDEO
Shows how employees have a vital role in preventing small fires from becoming large ones. Shows how such factors as inadequate training in immediate-response action, rapid spread, ignorance of which materials are highly flammable, inadequate equipment and training, late discovery and improper access can lead to fire disaster.
LC NO. 83-706737
Prod-MILLBK Dist-IFB 1979

When Generations Meet C 30 MIN
16MM FILM, 3/4 OR 1/2 IN VIDEO PRO
Documents role-playing sessions with teenage volunteers who express their feelings about working with the elderly.
Prod-FEIL Dist-FEIL

When Hair Came To Memphis C 54 MIN
16MM FILM OPTICAL SOUND
Portrays the various reactions of the community when the interracial rock musical Hair came to Memphis, Tennessee.
LC NO. 70-715451
Prod-SHBC Dist-SHBC 1971

When Hell Was In Session C 98 MIN
3/4 OR 1/2 INCH VIDEO CASSETTE H-C A
Tells the story of Commander Jeremiah A Denton Jr, a Navy pilot downed near Haiphong and captured by North Vietnamese regulars on July 18, 1965. Reveals that for the next seven-and-a-half years, Denton and his fellow prisoners endured torture, starvation and psychological warfare. Stars Hal Holbrook and Eva Marie Saint.
Prod-TIMLIF Dist-TIMLIF 1983

When Heroes Fall C 27 MIN
16MM FILM, 3/4 OR 1/2 IN VIDEO H-C A
Depicts what happens when a boy discovers that the father he idolizes is having an affair. Reveals the boy's anger at his father until he realizes that his mother has already forgiven her husband. Stars Panchito Gomez and Jose Perez.
From The Insight Series.
Prod-PAULST Dist-MEDIAG

When I Grow Up C 15 MIN
3/4 OR 1/2 INCH VIDEO CASSETTE P
Explores aspects of job satisfaction and offers suggestions for investigating various jobs.
From The Becoming Me, Unit 2 - Social Identity Series.
Prod-KUONTV Dist-GPITVL 1974

When I Grow Up C 18 MIN
16MM FILM, 3/4 OR 1/2 IN VIDEO H-C A
Discusses vocational choices and the ways that sex-role expectations influence the choices adults unconsciously make for children. Shows how sexual bias can affect school-aged children and explores positive ways to help children explore their future.
Prod-CAVLCD Dist-MTI 1977

When I Grow Up - Career Aspirations C 6 MIN
16MM FILM, 3/4 OR 1/2 IN VIDEO K-P
Tells the story of a group of handicapped and nonhandicapped children who dress up as the grownups they would most like to be.
From The Like You, Like Me Series.
Prod-EBEC Dist-EBEC 1977

When I Grow Up I Can Be—A Series
16MM FILM, 3/4 OR 1/2 IN VIDEO P-I
Explores a variety of different jobs within particular career clusters, as defined by the United States Office of Education. Examines well-rounded individuals, content in their private lives as well as their work.
Prod-ACI Dist-AIMS 1974

I Can Be A Builder 010 MIN
I Can Be A Community Service Worker 010 MIN
I Can Be A Food Production Worker 010 MIN
I Can Be A Hospital Worker 010 MIN
I Can Be A Mechanic 010 MIN

When I Need More Money C 9 MIN
16MM FILM, 3/4 OR 1/2 IN VIDEO I-J
Discusses living within a fixed income, the payment of bills, credit, getting a loan and installment buying.
Prod-SF Dist-SF

When I Say No, I Feel Guilty C 30 MIN
16MM FILM, 3/4 OR 1/2 IN VIDEO
Introduces Systematic Assertive Training, which tries to instill verbal assertiveness skills.
Prod-CCCD Dist-CCCD

When I'm Calling You C 16 MIN
3/4 OR 1/2 INCH VIDEO CASSETTE
Shows ways a person can offend or enrage a telephone caller before they get through to the person who can help.
Prod-VISUCP Dist-VISUCP

When I'm Calling You... C 15 MIN
3/4 OR 1/2 INCH VIDEO CASSETTE A
Shows employees how to create a favorable company image over the phone. Illustates both classic errors and exemplary techniques using light humor.
Prod-XICOM Dist-XICOM

When I'm Old Enough - Goodby B 27 MIN
16MM FILM OPTICAL SOUND
Discusses the problems faced by a young boy who drops out of high school. Emphasizes the value of proper guidance and the importance of the student's seeking this guidance.
Prod-STES Dist-SF 1962

When Illness Strikes C 29 MIN
3/4 OR 1/2 INCH VIDEO CASSETTE
Presents individuals with physical handicaps, such as paraplegia, polio, myocardial infarction, cerebral palsy and back problems, discussing their sexual abilities and concerns. Features Milton Diamond, Ph D, a biologist at the University of Hawaii.
From The Human Sexuality Series.
Prod-KHETTV Dist-PBS

When In Pain C 15 MIN
16MM FILM OPTICAL SOUND J-C A
Analyzes aspects of physical and emotional pain and examines the brain's never-ending battle with the pain of anxiety, frustration, fear, distrust and uncertainty. Gives examples of methods of alleviating pain and removing the source of pain.
LC NO. 76-703641
Prod-KARASC Dist-MALIBU 1975

When In Rome C 29 MIN
2 INCH VIDEOTAPE
See series title for descriptive statement.
From The Maggie And The Beautiful Machine - Maggie And Her Willing Accomplices Series.
Prod-WGBHTV Dist-PUBTEL

When Is A Case A Case B 30 MIN
16MM FILM - 3/4 IN VIDEO PRO
See series title for descriptive statement.
From The Public Health Science Series. Unit III - Introduction To Epidemiology
Prod-TEXWU Dist-GPITVL Prodn-KUHTTV

When Is A Function Integrable B
16MM FILM OPTICAL SOUND
Points out the difficulties involved in using the four-stage Lebesgue definition to decide whether a function is a Lebesgue integrable.
Prod-OPENU Dist-OPENU

When Is Help C 15 MIN
16MM FILM, 3/4 OR 1/2 IN VIDEO
Presents Karen, Roger and their friends who have decidedly different notions about giving and receiving help. Shows the advantages and disadvantages of their varied attitudes.
From The Inside-Out Series.
Prod-NITC Dist-AITECH

When Jenny When? C 25 MIN
3/4 OR 1/2 INCH VIDEO CASSETTE J A
Dramatizes the story of two young people who learn to accept themselves and their own sexuality. Stars Maureen McCormick.
Prod-SUTHRB Dist-SUTHRB

When Johnny Comes Marching Home C 14 MIN
3/4 OR 1/2 INCH VIDEO CASSETTE P-I
See series title for descriptive statement.
From The Ready, Sing Series.
Prod-ARKETV Dist-AITECH 1979

When Joseph Returns (Hungarian) C 92 MIN
16MM FILM OPTICAL SOUND
Follows the uneasy progress of two women awkwardly thrown together when the newlywed wife of a sailor comes to live with his mother. Directed by Zsolt Kezdi-Kovacs. With English subtitles.
Prod-UNKNWN Dist-NYFLMS 1976

When Kidneys Fail C 25 MIN
3/4 OR 1/2 INCH VIDEO CASSETTE
Notes that 50,000 people in the US are suffering from chronic renal failure and, in most areas, there are not enough facilities to take care of them. Shows what new hope is offered these people including, among other things, a mobile Belser Unit that can preserve a kidney up to three days after the death of a donor and before the transplant.
Prod-TRAINX Dist-TRAINX

When Kings Were Champagne C 30 MIN
2 INCH VIDEOTAPE
See series title for descriptive statement.
From The Koltanowski On Chess Series.
Prod-KQEDTV Dist-PUBTEL

When Knights Were Bold C 17 MIN
16MM FILM OPTICAL SOUND K-I
Tells how a member of the magnificent Six-and-A-Half gang encounters many mishaps when he is tempted to try on a suit of armor found outside a vacant house. Depicts how the gang rescues him from an aroused band of his unwitting victims.
From The Magnificent 6 And 1/2 Series.
Prod-CHILDF Dist-LUF 1970

When Life Begins C 14 MIN
16MM FILM, 3/4 OR 1/2 IN VIDEO H-C A
Looks at the development of the fetus from the earliest moments of fertilization to the time of birth.
Prod-GUIGOZ Dist-CRMP 1972

When Lilacs In The Dooryard Bloom'd C 30 MIN
2 INCH VIDEOTAPE J-H
See series title for descriptive statement.
From The From Franklin To Frost - Walt Whitman Series.
Prod-MPATI Dist-GPITVL

When Love Needs Care C 13 MIN
16MM FILM, 3/4 OR 1/2 IN VIDEO J-C A
Focuses on the medical interviews and examination of a boy and girl being examined and treated for venereal diseases. Emphasizes symptoms, treatment and prevention of venereal diseases.
Prod-SCHL Dist-PEREN 1972

When Magoo Flew C 7 MIN
16MM FILM, 3/4 OR 1/2 IN VIDEO
A reissue of the 1954 motion picture When Magoo Flew. Uses animation to tell a story in which Mr Magoo erroneously boards an airplane instead of entering a movie theater and enjoys the flight as if it were a movie.
From The Mister Magoo Series.
Prod-BOSUST Dist-CF 1978

When May Comes, We'll Move To The First Floor B 22 MIN
16MM FILM OPTICAL SOUND
A narration based on the diary of a severely involved cerebral palsied young woman is used to present the frustrations, hopes and fears that she experiences, as well as her growing anxiety regarding the health of her aging mother who cares for her.
LC NO. 78-705715
Prod-UCPA Dist-UCPA Prodn-BIVED 1969

When Parents Divorce C
1/2 IN VIDEO CASSETTE (VHS)
Shows children's reactions to divorce and examines the response of parents.
From The Daddy Doesn't Live Here Anymore - The Single-Parent Family Series.
Prod-IBIS Dist-IBIS

When Parents Grow Old C 15 MIN
16MM FILM, 3/4 OR 1/2 IN VIDEO J-C A
Tells how a young man on the verge of marriage must decide where his responsibilites lie when he is faced with the problem of a suddenly widowed father whose health is failing.
From The Searching For Values - A Film Anthology Series.
Prod-LCOA Dist-LCOA 1972

When People Care (Navajo) C 33 MIN
16MM FILM OPTICAL SOUND
Explains the role of the Parent Advisory Council of Dilcon Community School in Winslow, Arizona. Shows how the Council plans and operates programs funded by the federal government under Title I.
LC NO. 77-700065
Prod-USBIA Dist-BAILYL Prodn-BAILYL 1976

When People Move B 15 MIN
2 INCH VIDEOTAPE P-I
See series title for descriptive statement.
From The Our Changing Community Series.
Prod-VITA Dist-GPITVL 1967

When Seconds Count C 4 MIN
16MM FILM OPTICAL SOUND
Demonstrates the latest approved techniques for artificial respiration by means of mouth-to-mouth resuscitation.
LC NO. FI68-93
Prod-AMRC Dist-AMRC 1966

When Sex Means Trouble C
3/4 OR 1/2 INCH VIDEO CASSETTE J-C
Introduces the sensitive subject of sexual exploitation. Helps teens understand their own rights, learn to recognize abuse, and develop strategies for protecting themselves. Includes teacher's guide.
Prod-SUNCOM Dist-SUNCOM

When Sex Was Good, It Was Very, Very Good, When It Was Bad C 29 MIN
3/4 OR 1/2 INCH VIDEO CASSETTE
Examines the psychological and physical causes of sexual problems in adults, assesses the current state of sex therapy and offers common-sense hints for regaining sexual health.
From The Here's To Your Health Series.
Prod-KERA Dist-PBS

When Sheila Calls C 11 MIN
3/4 OR 1/2 INCH VIDEO CASSETTE
Includes brief interviews with pheresis donors, plus a non-technical explanation of why pheresis donations are necessary.
Prod-AMRC Dist-AMRC

When Shoes Eat Socks C 15 MIN
3/4 INCH VIDEO CASSETTE P
Presents the children's story When Shoes Eat Socks by Barbara Klimowicz.
From The Tilson's Book Shop Series.
Prod-WVIZTV Dist-GPITVL 1975

When Should Grownups Help B 14 MIN
16MM FILM OPTICAL SOUND C T
Shows pre-school children in various situations where they may or may not need help. Points out that adult help is necessary in order that the child succeed in projects, but that goals of speed and efficiency should not be forced.
From The Studies Of Normal Personality Development Series.
Prod-NYU Dist-NYU 1950

When Should Grownups Stop Fights B 15 MIN
16MM FILM OPTICAL SOUND C T
Shows four conflicts among two- to five-year-olds. Points out that the teacher must decide whether to intervene, thus must know her children well and must quickly size up the meaning of the conflict.
From The Studies Of Normal Personality Development Series.
Prod-NYU Dist-NYU 1950

When Songs And Legends Are Silent C 30 MIN
3/4 OR 1/2 INCH VIDEO CASSETTE
Presents ancient Russian architecture, showing masterpieces of the 11th through 13th Centuries in ancient towns such as Novgorod, Chernigov and Kiev and segments of fortress walls in Pskov and and Izborsk.
Prod-IHF Dist-IHF

When Teens Get Pregnant C 18 MIN
3/4 OR 1/2 INCH VIDEO CASSETTE
Presents girls telling about their lives before pregnancy, about their families, school, peer pressure to have sex, the reality of sex as opposed to the fantasy, the differences between their own and their partner's needs and expectations, and the fears and responsibilities introduced by a pregnancy.
Prod-POLYMR Dist-POLYMR

When The Animals Talked C 28 MIN
16MM FILM, 3/4 OR 1/2 IN VIDEO I-C A
Shows educator and folklorist William Faulkner providing fresh insight into Afro-American folklore. Illustrates how he picks up new stories on a fishing trip and reintroduces the real Brer Rabbit.
From The Were You There? Series.
LC NO. 83-706597
Prod-NGUZO Dist-BCNFL 1982

When The Blues Are Running C 22 MIN
16MM FILM OPTICAL SOUND
Shows how the medical community provides a support system for a patient and his family during the critical periods of cancer detection and treatment.
LC NO. 78-701334
Prod-AMCS Dist-AMCS Prodn-ARDENF 1977

When The Bough Breaks C 11 MIN
16MM FILM OPTICAL SOUND
Presents the story of a mother involved in child abuse as she struggles to overcome her guilt.
Prod-LUTTEL Dist-LUTTEL 1979

When The Circuit Breaks - America's Energy Crisis C 28 MIN
16MM FILM, 3/4 OR 1/2 IN VIDEO H-C A
Shows how America's energy crisis happened and what possibilities the future holds. Examines some solutions through the development of coal, oil and natural gas resources. Looks at nuclear, geothermal and solar energy, and stresses the importance of conservation.
LC NO. 79-707992
Prod-USFEAP Dist-USNAC Prodn-CONFI 1979

When The Circuit Breaks - America's Energy Crisis (Spanish) C 28 MIN
16MM FILM OPTICAL SOUND
Shows the origins and future of America's energy crisis. Examines how some solutions may be reached through the development of coal, oil and natural gas resources. Looks at nuclear, geothermal and solar energy and stresses the importance of conservation.
LC NO. 76-703441
Prod-USFEAP Dist-USNAC Prodn-CONCPT 1975

When The Earth Explodes C 22 MIN
3/4 OR 1/2 INCH VIDEO CASSETTE J-H
See series title for descriptive statement.
From The Phenomenal World Series.
Prod-EBEC Dist-EBEC 1983

When The Earth Moves C 30 MIN
3/4 INCH VIDEO CASSETTE J
Shows how folds are related to the shape of the land and explains the typical types of faults. Illustrates the results of an earthquake and demonstrates the study of seismic waves and their detection. Visits the Rockies to explore the nature of high mountains.
From The What On Earth Series.
Prod-NCSDPI Dist-GPITVL 1979

When The Honeymoon Is Over C 32 MIN
16MM FILM, 3/4 OR 1/2 IN VIDEO H-C A
Presents the personal experiences of mental and physical cruelty experienced by women of different backgrounds. Describes the treatment meted out by their husbands, the fears for their children, the efforts to stop the violence and the attempts to gain help from friends, lawyers, police and social service agencies.
From The Women Series.
Prod-LUF Dist-LUF 1979

When The Littlest Camel Knelt C 11 MIN
16MM FILM OPTICAL SOUND P-H
Tells the story of the little camel who is especially curious about kings and his journey with the wise men which leads him to a most unusual king, a baby sleeping in a stable. Describes how he kneels in adoration, as little camels do to this day.
Prod-CAFM Dist-CAFM

When The North Wind Blows C 113 MIN
16MM FILM, 3/4 OR 1/2 IN VIDEO
Depicts the experiences of an old trapper who decides to parent a Siberian tiger's cubs when it is shot by hunters. Stars Henry Brandon and Dan Haggerty.
Prod-LUF Dist-LUF 1979

When The People Awake (Captioned) C 60 MIN
16MM FILM, 3/4 OR 1/2 IN VIDEO A
Examines the attempted transition of Chile under Allende from capitalism to socialism, the development of Chile's social classes, and the tragic end of that experiment. Spanish dialog with English subtitles.
Prod-TRIFCW Dist-CNEMAG 1972

When The Rivers Run Dry C 29 MIN
16MM FILM, 3/4 OR 1/2 IN VIDEO
Presents a cultural history of water use in the semiarid Southwest, a region marked by alternating problems of drought and flood. Demonstrates how, since 300 BC, succeeding cultures have coped with water problems in unique and characteristic ways.
Prod-AROKNG Dist-UCEMC 1979

When The Snow Is Too Deep To Walk C 20 MIN
3/4 OR 1/2 INCH VIDEO CASSETTE J-C A
Discusses skiing excursions as a practical alternative to motor-powered holidays. Shows how to decide on touring skies vs snowshoes, clothing, camping gear and food. Includes information on skiing techniques, avalanches, hypothermia and telemarking.
LC NO. 82-706794
Prod-AWSS Dist-AWSS 1981

When The Unexpected Happens C 36 MIN
3/4 OR 1/2 INCH VIDEO CASSETTE
Explains that unproductive communication on the job can be avoided by the continual reinforcement of adult behavior.
From The Super-Vision Series.
LC NO. 79-706773
Prod-VCI Dist-DELTAK

When The Wind Blows B 20 MIN
16MM FILM OPTICAL SOUND
Tells how the Gang's Jackie Cooper captures a burglar. A Little Rascals film.
Prod-ROACH Dist-BHAWK 1930

When The World Stops C 23 MIN
16MM FILM OPTICAL SOUND
Discusses the basic purposes and problems of worker's compensation.
Prod-EMW Dist-EMW

When They Interfere C 30 MIN
3/4 OR 1/2 INCH VIDEO CASSETTE A
See series title for descriptive statement.
From The Play Bridge Series.
Prod-KYTV Dist-KYTV 1983

When To Double A Final Consonant Before An Ending C 20 MIN
3/4 OR 1/2 INCH VIDEO CASSETTE J-H
See series title for descriptive statement.
From The Getting The Word Series. Unit III
Prod-SCETV Dist-AITECH 1974

When To Irrigate And How Much C 26 MIN
16MM FILM OPTICAL SOUND H-C A
Describes how soil, plant and weather conditions affect irrigation timing. Explains how to determine when to irrigate and how much.
Prod-OSSHE Dist-OSSHE 1963

When Two Makes One C 20 MIN
2 INCH VIDEOTAPE P
See series title for descriptive statement.
From The Learning Our Language, Unit 2 - Dictionary Skills Series.
Prod-MPATI Dist-GPITVL

When Two Vowels Go Walking B 15 MIN
2 INCH VIDEOTAPE P
See series title for descriptive statement.
From The Listen And Say - Vowels Series.
Prod-GPITVL Dist-GPITVL

When Two Vowels Go Walking C 15 MIN
2 INCH VIDEOTAPE P
Presents the concept of a vowel digraph. Develops auditory awareness and discrimination of vowel sounds. Introduces a few common vowel generalizations which are an aid in learning to read.
From The Listen And Say Series.
Prod-MPATI Dist-GPITVL

When We Farmed With Horses C 25 MIN
16MM FILM OPTICAL SOUND
Focuses on the draft horse, around which agricultural practices of the Midwest developed in the late 19th and early 20th centuries. Comments on the evolution of equipment, seasonal activities and the combination of frustrations and pride in workmanship which characterized farming during that period.
LC NO. 79-701454
Prod-IOWA Dist-IOWA 1979

When We First Met C 30 MIN
16MM FILM, 3/4 OR 1/2 IN VIDEO J-H A
An edited version of the motion picture When We First Met. Presents a story which shows how grief can destroy a family. Based on the novel WHEN WE FIRST MET by Norma Fox Mazer.
Prod-LCOA Dist-LCOA 1984

When We First Met C 54 MIN
16MM FILM, 3/4 OR 1/2 IN VIDEO J-H A
Presents a story which shows how grief can destroy a family. Based on the novel WHEN WE FIRST MET by Norma Fox Mazer.
Prod-LCOA Dist-LCOA 1984

When Will The Birds Return C 52 MIN
16MM FILM OPTICAL SOUND J-C A
Considers conditions in Darwin, Australia, following the devastating cyclone of Christmas Day, 1974. Shows the extent of the damage, the evacuation arrangements, and the preliminary cleanup and restoration efforts.
LC NO. 76-700575
Prod-FLMAUS Dist-AUIS 1975

When Will They Realize We're Living In The Twentieth Century C 23 MIN
3/4 OR 1/2 INCH VIDEO CASSETTE
Illustrates how assumptions, actions and attitudes help to precipitate a crisis between management and labor.
Prod-VIDART Dist-VISUCP

When Will They Realize We're Living In The Twentieth Century C 24 MIN
3/4 OR 1/2 INCH VIDEO CASSETTE A
Illustrates how avoidable mistakes can lead to labor management strife. Reveals the false assumptions, hardened attitudes and provocative actions that fuel a conflict.
Prod-XICOM Dist-XICOM

When Will We Ever Learn C 60 MIN
3/4 INCH VIDEO CASSETTE
Examines the educational system in the United States as a 'partner of liberation.'
From The Liberation Series.
Prod-OHC Dist-HRC

When Winning Means No One Loses C 29 MIN
3/4 OR 1/2 INCH VIDEO CASSETTE T
See series title for descriptive statement.
From The Coping With Kids Series.
Prod-MFFD Dist-FI

When Winning Means No One Loses C 30 MIN
3/4 OR 1/2 INCH VIDEO CASSETTE
Presents methods of conflict resolution. Shows a family discussing typical problems and gives recommendations for their solution.
From The Coping With Kids Series.
Prod-OHUTC Dist-OHUTC

When You And I Were Young Maggie C 29 MIN
2 INCH VIDEOTAPE
See series title for descriptive statement.
From The Maggie And The Beautiful Machine - Shape-Up Now For Kids Series.
Prod-WGBHTV Dist-PUBTEL

When You Get Hurt C 4 MIN
16MM FILM, 3/4 OR 1/2 IN VIDEO K-I
Explains that the body will heal itself if it has the proper nutrition and rest.
From The Most Important Person - Health And Your Body Series.
Prod-EBEC Dist-EBEC 1972

When You Grow Up C 12 MIN
16MM FILM, 3/4 OR 1/2 IN VIDEO P-I
Introduces the concept of career clusters and emphasizes the interrelatedness of careers in different industries.
Prod-FILMSW Dist-FLMFR

When You Need Repairs C 15 MIN
3/4 INCH VIDEO CASSETTE P-I
Stresses the concept of a hospital as being a friendly place.
From The Can You Imagine Series.
Prod-WVIZTV Dist-GPITVL

When You Think About It C 8 MIN
16MM FILM OPTICAL SOUND
Shows the functions of the lab of International Business Machines Canada.
LC NO. 75-703443
Prod-IBM Dist-IBM 1974

When You're Alone C 15 MIN
16MM FILM, 3/4 OR 1/2 IN VIDEO
Provides tips for home and personal safety such as securing doors and windows, carrying proper ID, self-defense, nuisance calls and rape prevention.
Prod-MTI Dist-MTI 1984

When You're Smilin' C 6 MIN
16MM FILM, 3/4 OR 1/2 IN VIDEO A
Offers a montage set in motion by Louis Armstrong's song When You're Smilin' which shows that smiling is not only good for one's health but for business as well.
LC NO. 83-706112
Prod-GLDBGG Dist-LCOA 1982

When You're Waking Up C 4 MIN
16MM FILM, 3/4 OR 1/2 IN VIDEO K-I
Describes different waking scenes.
From The Most Important Person - Creative Expression Series.
Prod-EBEC Dist-EBEC 1972

When You're Young C 18 MIN
16MM FILM, 3/4 OR 1/2 IN VIDEO
Highlights the youth activities program of the American Quarter Horse Association, featuring interviews and events at the 1980 American Junior Quarter Horse Association Convention and World Championship Show.
Prod-AQHORS Dist-AQHORS

When Your Baby Needs A Doctor C 14 MIN
2 INCH VIDEOTAPE
Identifies common illnesses of newborn babies and discusses how to treat them. Demonstrates how to use, read and care for a thermometer and the proper ways to burp a baby.
From The Living Better II Series.
Prod-MAETEL Dist-PUBTEL

When Your Clothing Burns C 19 MIN
16MM FILM, 3/4 OR 1/2 IN VIDEO J-C A
Details the tremendous physical and psychological suffering caused by serious clothing burns. Provides a description of measures for prevention of igniting clothing and analyzes flammable fabrics and flame retardants.
Prod-NFPA Dist-NFPA Prodn-REPRO 1976

When Your Friend Moves Away / End-Of-The-Year Blues / Clyde's Favorite Toy C 15 MIN
3/4 OR 1/2 INCH VIDEO CASSETTE P
Presents stories presented by Muppet-like Clyde Frog presenting stories emphasizing positive self-images, feelings of optimism and self-confidence.
From The Clyde Frog Show Series.
Prod-MAETEL Dist-GPITVL 1977

When, Jenny, When C 25 MIN
16MM FILM, 3/4 OR 1/2 IN VIDEO
Tells how a teenage couple come to the realization that each is using the other and gain a new appreciation of themselves.
From The Reflections Series.
LC NO. 79-706606
Prod-PAULST Dist-PAULST 1978

Where Action Happens C 16 MIN
16MM FILM MAGNETIC SOUND K-C A S
See series title for descriptive statement.
From The PANCOM Beginning Total Communication Program For Hearing Parents Of... Series. Level 1
LC NO. 77-700504
Prod-CSDE Dist-JOYCE Prodn-CSFDF 1977

Where Airports Begin C 20 MIN
16MM FILM, 3/4 OR 1/2 IN VIDEO

Discusses how an airport can be environmentally sound, a good neighbor and an economic stimulus. Stresses the importance of planning and community interaction when building or upgrading an airport.
LC NO. 82-707229
Prod-USFAA Dist-USNAC 1976

Where Am I B 5 MIN
16MM FILM OPTICAL SOUND
Shows one of the original Mutt and Jeff cartoons with added musical score.
Prod-CFS Dist-CFS

Where Animals Live C 15 MIN
3/4 OR 1/2 INCH VIDEO CASSETTE P-I
Reveals that where animals live is sometimes determined by their physical characteristics.
From The Zoo Zoo Zoo Series.
Prod-WCETTV Dist-AITECH 1981

Where Are Living Things Found B 15 MIN
2 INCH VIDEOTAPE P
Explains that the part of the world in which an organism lives is called its environment.
From The Science Is Discovery Series.
Prod-DETPS Dist-GPITVL

Where Are My People C 28 MIN
16MM FILM - 3/4 IN VIDEO H-C A
Presents a provocative era of World War I history in the light of genocide of 1.5 million Armenians of the Middle East by the Turkish government.
Prod-ATLAP Dist-ATLAP Prodn-HAGOPN 1966

Where Are We C 14 MIN
3/4 OR 1/2 INCH VIDEO CASSETTE P
Shows how a dream, in which Donna's fairy godmother shows her how to find her way with globes, directions and maps, helps her finish her homework.
From The Under The Yellow Balloon Series.
Prod-SCETV Dist-AITECH 1980

Where Are We - Disciples/UCC C 7 MIN
3/4 OR 1/2 INCH VIDEO CASSETTE A
Presents an up-to-date status of the possible unity between the Disciples and the Church of Christ. Intended primarily for Disciples.
Prod-DCCMS Dist-ECUFLM 1980

Where Are Women Going? C 29 MIN
3/4 INCH VIDEO CASSETTE
Discusses the impact of the women's movement on employment, men, family structure and divorce rates.
From The Issue At Hand Series.
Prod-UMITV Dist-UMITV 1976

Where Are You - Where Are You Going C 24 MIN
16MM FILM, 3/4 OR 1/2 IN VIDEO
Shows a model performance appraisal from the preparatory stage to the conclusion of the interview through the story of a young manager who faces her first appraisal interview.
Prod-RTBL Dist-RTBL

Where Are You - Where Are You Going (Dutch) C 24 MIN
16MM FILM, 3/4 OR 1/2 IN VIDEO
Shows a model performance appraisal from the preparatory stage to the conclusion of the interview through the story of a young manager who faces her first appraisal interview.
Prod-RTBL Dist-RTBL

Where Are You - Where Are You Going (Norwegian) C 24 MIN
16MM FILM, 3/4 OR 1/2 IN VIDEO
Shows a model performance appraisal from the preparatory stage to the conclusion of the interview through the story of a young manager who faces her first appraisal interview.
Prod-RTBL Dist-RTBL

Where Are You - Where Are You Going (Spanish) C 24 MIN
16MM FILM, 3/4 OR 1/2 IN VIDEO
Shows a model performance appraisal from the preparatory stage to the conclusion of the interview through the story of a young manager who faces her first appraisal interview.
Prod-RTBL Dist-RTBL

Where Are You - Where Are You Going (Swedish) C 24 MIN
16MM FILM, 3/4 OR 1/2 IN VIDEO
Shows a model performance appraisal from the preparatory stage to the conclusion of the interview through the story of a young manager who faces her first appraisal interview.
Prod-RTBL Dist-RTBL

Where Are You Coming From C 14 MIN
16MM FILM, 3/4 OR 1/2 IN VIDEO I
Tells how three boys receive the same note from their math teacher and make three different assumptions about its meaning.
From The Thinkabout Series. Giving And Getting Meaning
LC NO. 81-706137
Prod-ACCESS Dist-AITECH 1979

Where Are You Going And To The Library C 15 MIN
2 INCH VIDEOTAPE P
See series title for descriptive statement.
From The Avenida De Ingles Series.
Prod-SDITVA Dist-GPITVL

Where Are You Going And To The Store, House C 15 MIN
2 INCH VIDEOTAPE P
See series title for descriptive statement.
From The Avenida De Ingles Series.
Prod-SDITVA Dist-GPITVL

Where Are You In Your Family C 4 MIN
16MM FILM, 3/4 OR 1/2 IN VIDEO K-I
Explains that whether a person in the family is the oldest or youngest, their place is very special.
From The Most Important Person - Identity Series.
Prod-EBEC Dist-EBEC 1972

Where Are You In Your Family (Spanish) C 4 MIN
16MM FILM, 3/4 OR 1/2 IN VIDEO K-P
See series title for descriptive statement.
From The Most Important Person - Identity (Spanish) Series.
Prod-EBEC Dist-EBEC

Where But The Supermarket C 29 MIN
3/4 OR 1/2 INCH VIDEO CASSETTE H-C A
Deals with alternatives to buying in the supermarket. Visits farmers' markets, a roadside stand, a neighborhood store, and a food cooperative.
From The Be A Better Shopper Series. Program 12
LC NO. 81-707312
Prod-CUETV Dist-CUNIV 1978

Where Can I Live - A Story Of Gentrification C 32 MIN
16MM FILM, 3/4 OR 1/2 IN VIDEO
Describes gentrification as a process by which an underdeveloped urban neighborhood is 'upgraded' by real estate speculation, with higher income individuals moving in and upgrading existing properties. Proceeds to document such a process in Park Slope, Brooklyn. Shows what often happens to existing residents and how they joined together to establish block associations, rent strikes and take legal action. Results were a new sense of community and purpose.
Prod-CNEMAG Dist-CNEMAG 1984

Where Can You Find Seeds Inside Your House B 20 MIN
2 INCH VIDEOTAPE P
Presents a freshly picked squash which is found to be full of seeds. Initiates a search for other foods which contain seeds.
From The Scienceland Series.
Prod-MPATI Dist-GPITVL

Where Can You Get Ideas C 25 MIN
2 INCH VIDEOTAPE I
Discusses where adult artists and other children found ideas for their art work.
From The Art Has Many Forms Series.
Prod-CVETVC Dist-GPITVL

Where Dead Men Lie C 15 MIN
16MM FILM OPTICAL SOUND H-C A
Presents a story based on a script written in 1896 by Australian literary figure, Henry Lawson. Tells of a cattle drover who dies of thirst in the desert and is later found by a search party. Follows one of the members of the party who is chosen to take the news to the drover's wife.
LC NO. 73-702493
Prod-FLMAUS Dist-AUIS 1972

Where Did Leonard Harry Go C 7 MIN
3/4 INCH VIDEO CASSETTE I-H
Tells how Leonard Harry becomes so bored with his humdrum life that he becomes a master of disguises. Shows what happens when the disguises take over and Leonard disappears.
Prod-DAVFMS Dist-GA

Where Did The Colorado Go C 59 MIN
16MM FILM, 3/4 OR 1/2 IN VIDEO H-C A
Examines suggestions by conservationists as to what should be done to save the Colorado River.
From The Nova Series.
LC NO. 79-707251
Prod-WGBHTV Dist-TIMLIF 1976

Where Did You Get That Woman C 28 MIN
16MM FILM, 3/4 OR 1/2 IN VIDEO H-C A
Describes the life of septuagenarian Joan Williams, who has worked for 20 years as a washroom attendant in a singles bar. Discusses her childhood in Oklahoma in the early 1900's, her life with a philandering husband, her widowhood, and her fresh start in Chicago.
Prod-TEXFLM Dist-TEXFLM 1983

Where Did You Get That Woman? C 28 MIN
3/4 OR 1/2 INCH VIDEO CASSETTE H-C
Reminicences by septuagenarian Joan Williams, washroom attendant in a Chicago bar for 20 years, about her life from an Oklahoma childhood to the present. Evokes history of her life span through use of sepia-toned file photographs. Comments on human life and spirit.
LC NO. 83-706335
Prod-SMTHL Dist-SMTHL 1983

Where Do Animals Live C 20 MIN
2 INCH VIDEOTAPE I
See series title for descriptive statement.
From The Science Corner II, Unit I - Animals Series.
Prod-MPATI Dist-GPITVL

Where Do Babies Come From C 29 MIN
3/4 OR 1/2 INCH VIDEO CASSETTE T
See series title for descriptive statement.
From The Coping With Kids Series.
Prod-MFFD Dist-FI

Where Do Babies Come From? C 30 MIN
3/4 OR 1/2 INCH VIDEO CASSETTE
Presents information to parents and teachers on approaches to sex education with young people which encourages more intimate relationships between parents and children. Features guest expert Dr Janice Wilson.
From The Coping With Kids Series.
Prod-OHUTC Dist-OHUTC

Where Do Evergreen Trees Come From B 20 MIN
2 INCH VIDEOTAPE P
Presents a trip to the woods and shows a place where many evergreens are growing. Includes a close examination of a pine tree revealing how it may have gotten there.
From The Scienceland Series.
Prod-MPATI Dist-GPITVL

Where Do I Belong C
16MM FILM - 3/4 IN VIDEO
Points out that responsibility for career development will depend more and more on the manager's own motivations and will involve his likes and dislikes, career goals and relationships with peers and subordinates. Shows that career development does not mean job hopping and that managers must find out what they excel in and redefine their jobs to improve themselves.
From The Managing For Tomorrow Series. Unit 5
Prod-BNA Dist-BNA

Where Do I Belong (Dutch) C
16MM FILM, 3/4 OR 1/2 IN VIDEO
Tells how to give career advice. Shows how to change employee behavior.
From The Managing For Tomorrow (Dutch) Series.
Prod-BNA Dist-BNA

Where Do I Belong (German) C
16MM FILM, 3/4 OR 1/2 IN VIDEO
Tells how to give career advice. Shows how to change employee behavior.
From The Managing For Tomorrow (German) Series.
Prod-BNA Dist-BNA

Where Do I Belong / Cuban Dropout C 29 MIN
3/4 INCH VIDEO CASSETTE
Depicts a Chicago high school student traveling to Mexico to examine his feelings of alienation from both his parents and his past culture. Demonstrates problems that Cuban immigrants to Miami face in schools trying to balance the ideas, values and languages of two different cultures.
From The As We See It Series.
Prod-WTTWTV Dist-PUBTEL

Where Do I Go From Here C 4 MIN
16MM FILM OPTICAL SOUND
Conveys the mariner's respect for the rigorous challenge of the sea and depicts a Navy career as one which offers adventure, education and travel.
LC NO. 76-701578
Prod-USN Dist-USNAC 1974

Where Do I Go From Here C 20 MIN
3/4 OR 1/2 INCH VIDEO CASSETTE
Provides a concrete, three-step process for setting objectives and creating a plan for successful career development. Includes a leader's guide.
Prod-DELTAK Dist-DELTAK

Where Do I Go From Here C 21 MIN
16MM FILM, 3/4 OR 1/2 IN VIDEO H-C A
Discusses employee review and realistic self-appraisal. Explains how workers can follow their interests and abilities, develop their skills, and choose a career direction.
From The Working Series.
Prod-JOU Dist-JOU Prodn-INCC 1980

Where Do I Go From Here? C 23 MIN
16MM FILM, 3/4 OR 1/2 IN VIDEO
Helps convince employes that they are responsible for the direction their careers take, show how the employer can supply guidance and resources to support employee goals and provides employees with the strategies for a rigorous self-development program that will help them reach their career objectives.
Prod-EFM Dist-EFM

Where Do I Live C 20 MIN
3/4 OR 1/2 INCH VIDEO CASSETTE P-I
Explores literary selections that deal with the effect of geographical, cultural and environmental settings on the way people live.
From The Once Upon A Town Series.
Prod-MDDE Dist-AITECH 1977

Where Do Jobs Come From C 20 MIN
2 INCH VIDEOTAPE J-H
Explains that jobs come from goods and services and shows the increasing proliferation of occupations in our highly specialized working world.
From The Our World Of Economics Series.
Prod-MPATI Dist-GPITVL

Where Do Jobs Come From - Derived Demand C 15 MIN
3/4 OR 1/2 INCH VIDEO CASSETTE J-H
Explains that Lindy gets the lead in the school musical, but when her mother loses her job and her brother gives up his job she is faced with some difficult decisions about finding a job. Raises questions about the job market.
From The Give And Take Series. Pt 5
LC NO. 83-706373
Prod-AITV Dist-AITECH 1982

Where Do Our Clothes Come From B 15 MIN
2 INCH VIDEOTAPE P
Explains that people make their clothing from the materials available, such as cotton, silk and wool. Describes how sewing machines and factories make it easy to buy clothes that fit. (Broadcast quality)
From The Around The Corner Series. No. 23
Prod-FWCETV Dist-GPITVL Prodn-WEDUTV

Where Do Shadows Come From B 20 MIN
2 INCH VIDEOTAPE P
Presents several objects in a shadow parade. Explains that a shadow is made when a light is stopped by an object. De-

scribes how shadows change in length and direction as the sun moves across the sky.
From The Scienceland Series.
Prod-MPATI Dist-GPITVL

Where Do Some Classroom Materials Come From C 20 MIN
2 INCH VIDEOTAPE P
See series title for descriptive statement.
From The Science Corner I, Unit III - Looking At Things Around Us Series.
Prod-MPATI Dist-GPITVL

Where Do Teenagers Come From C 47 MIN
16MM FILM, 3/4 OR 1/2 IN VIDEO I
Presents pediatrician Lendon Smith who discusses the physical and psychological aspects of adolescence. Discusses reproduction, menstruation, nocturnal emissions, mood swings, acne, the need for privacy, and other biological and emotional aspects of becoming a teenager.
From The Teenage Years Series.
Prod-DEPFRE Dist-TIMLIF 1981

Where Do The Raindrops Go B 20 MIN
2 INCH VIDEOTAPE P
Presents the end of a rainstorm which leads to a search for the water that seems to have disappeared. Explains that some rain water goes into the soil, some goes back into the air and some runs off to become a part of rivers and streams.
From The Scienceland Series.
Prod-MPATI Dist-GPITVL

Where Do They Come From - Language Development C 30 MIN
3/4 OR 1/2 INCH VIDEO CASSETTE T
See series title for descriptive statement.
From The Teaching Early Reading Series.
Prod-CTI Dist-CTI

Where Do They Go From Here - Motivating The Use Of Reading C 30 MIN
3/4 OR 1/2 INCH VIDEO CASSETTE T
See series title for descriptive statement.
From The Teaching Early Reading Series.
Prod-CTI Dist-CTI

Where Do We Get Them C 15 MIN
2 INCH VIDEOTAPE P
Discusses the origin of words.
From The Word Magic (2nd Ed) Series.
Prod-CVETVC Dist-GPITVL

Where Do We Go From Here C 33 MIN
16MM FILM OPTICAL SOUND H
Stresses that driving is the student's responsibility and offers a positive plan for improving highway safety.
From The To Get From Here To There Series.
Prod-PROART Dist-PROART

Where Do We Go From Here? C 9 MIN
3/4 INCH VIDEOTAPE
Focuses on the elderly and the families who care for them. Presents the story of a family making living arrangements for an elderly parent about to be released from the hospital. Discusses available choices for care of the elderly.
Prod-EDC Dist-EDC

Where Do You Find Them C 15 MIN
16MM FILM, 3/4 OR 1/2 IN VIDEO I
Tells how Mike and Eddie use criteria to determine who has won a soapbox-racer contest.
From The Thinkabout Series. Using Criteria
LC NO. 81-706138
Prod-KETCTV Dist-AITECH 1979

Where Do You Fit Into The Organization? C 20 MIN
3/4 OR 1/2 INCH VIDEO CASSETTE IND
Shows how first-line supervisors function inside and outside the company. Emphasizes the importance of good communication and cooperation between oil field and office.
From The Man Management And Rig Management Series. Lesson 6
Prod-UTEXPE Dist-UTEXPE 1983

Where Do You Go From Here - Installation And Follow Up Of Improvements C 16 MIN
16MM FILM OPTICAL SOUND
Shows how to conduct work simplification programs in the Army.
From The Army Work Simplication Series.
LC NO. 74-706326
Prod-USA Dist-USNAC 1973

Where Do You Live C 15 MIN
2 INCH VIDEOTAPE
Shows the differences and similarities between the city, suburb and country, and emphasizes the fact that wherever a man chooses to live is the best place for him.
From The Let's Build A City Series.
Prod-WVIZTV Dist-GPITVL

Where Do You Play If You Live In A City B 15 MIN
2 INCH VIDEOTAPE P
Explains that both cities and farms are essential to the economy. States that families living in cities have close neighbors but often do not enjoy yards or gardens. (Broadcast quality)
From The Around The Corner Series. No. 18
Prod-FWCETV Dist-GPITVL Prodn-WEDUTV

Where Does All The Money Go C 29 MIN
3/4 OR 1/2 INCH VIDEO CASSETTE H-C A
Explores how and where Americans spend their food dollar. Looks at USDA food spending plans, methods for keeping track of spending and information on how the food stamp program works.
From The Be A Better Shopper Series. Program 2
LC NO. 81-707302
Prod-CUETV Dist-CUNIV 1978

Where Does Food Come From C 15 MIN
3/4 OR 1/2 INCH VIDEO CASSETTE P
Shows how food is grown, processed and shipped to market. Provides examples of many of the people and places that maintain America's food supply.
From The Great American Eating Machine - You Series. Pt 2
LC NO. 83-706106
Prod-NJPTV Dist-GPITVL 1982

Where Does Food Come From? C
16MM FILM, 3/4 OR 1/2 IN VIDEO
Shows the origins of the foods we take for granted in a supermarket.
Prod-HIGGIN Dist-HIGGIN

Where Does Food Go C 4 MIN
16MM FILM, 3/4 OR 1/2 IN VIDEO K-I
Demonstrates the path that food takes after being eaten, featuring a rabbit chewing, a giraffe swallowing and a hippopotamus shaking his belly.
From The Most Important Person - Health And Your Body Series.
Prod-EBEC Dist-EBEC 1972

Where Does It Hurt C 90 MIN
16MM FILM OPTICAL SOUND H A
Tells the story of a profiteering hospital administrator. Black comedy starring Peter Sellers.
Prod-TIMLIF Dist-TIMLIF 1971

Where Does Life Come From C 5 MIN
16MM FILM, 3/4 OR 1/2 IN VIDEO P
Shows the growth of plants from seeds and animals from eggs.
From The Wonder Walks Series.
Prod-EBEC Dist-EBEC 1971

Where Does My Refrigerator Go From Here B 10 MIN
16MM FILM OPTICAL SOUND
Presents a look at the world of garbage, and the people who live with it all day long. Explores not only the kinds of materials that make up garbage and the route across the city it follows from pick-up to final dispositions, but also the relationships of a variety of adults and children to garbage.
Prod-UPENN Dist-UPENN 1969

Where Does The Harvest Begin C 20 MIN
16MM FILM OPTICAL SOUND
Covers in detail the four requirements that must be followed when planting to assure a profitable harvest.
Prod-ALLISC Dist-IDEALF

Where Does Your Body Get Its Energy C 20 MIN
2 INCH VIDEOTAPE P
See series title for descriptive statement.
From The Science Corner I, Unit V - Your Body And How It Works Series.
Prod-MPATI Dist-GPITVL

Where Does Your Breakfast Come From C 20 MIN
2 INCH VIDEOTAPE P
See series title for descriptive statement.
From The Science Corner I, Unit VII - Obtaining And Preserving Foods Series.
Prod-MPATI Dist-GPITVL

Where Eagles Swim C 26 MIN
16MM FILM OPTICAL SOUND P-C A
Features a search for the bald eagle, taking place in the waters and on the islands off the British Columbia coast about 350 miles north of Vancouver. Shows how the great bird flourishes in this primitive area, relatively undisturbed by man.
From The Audubon Wildlife Theatre Series.
LC NO. 72-709411
Prod-KEGPL Dist-AVEXP 1969

Where Have All The Farmers Gone C 20 MIN
16MM FILM OPTICAL SOUND I
Defines the role of agriculture and shows some of its problems. Points out that, industrialized and urbanized, Americans often forget that man biologically is an animal. Explains that through agriculture, man has modified the nature of his food web but remains dependent on the soil and the green plants growing in it for his energy.
From The Inherit The Earth Series.
Prod-KQEDTV Dist-GPITVL

Where Have All The Germans Gone C 52 MIN
16MM FILM, 3/4 OR 1/2 IN VIDEO J-C A
Tells that one-sixth of today's Americans are descended from the German immigrants who came as political and religious refugees. In 1854, half of America's immigrants were German, including teachers, writers and lawyers. The dream of a German society in America was shattered by two world wars.
From The Destination America Series.
Prod-THAMES Dist-MEDIAG 1976

Where Have We Been B 15 MIN
2 INCH VIDEOTAPE P-I
See series title for descriptive statement.
From The Our Changing Community Series.
Prod-VITA Dist-GPITVL 1967

Where Hunger Stalks C 25 MIN
16MM FILM OPTICAL SOUND H-C A
Tells the true story of P Y Singh, a young Indian boy who found a God who cares and meets human needs.
Prod-CBFMS Dist-CBFMS

Where I Want To Be C 21 MIN
16MM FILM OPTICAL SOUND
Shows the lives, goals and satisfactions of several women dentists in order to encourage more women of high school and college age to decide on a career in dentistry.
LC NO. 74-700500
Prod-ASTF Dist-MTP 1973

Where I Want To Be - The Story Of A Woman Dentist C 29 MIN
16MM FILM - 3/4 IN VIDEO
Describes career advantages for women in the field of dentistry. Emphasizes the growing need for women in the profession. Issued in 1973 as a motion picture.
LC NO. 77-706194
Prod-NIH Dist-USNAC Prodn-DURRIN 1973

Where Is Dead C 19 MIN
16MM FILM, 3/4 OR 1/2 IN VIDEO P
Tells a story about a six-year-old girl's struggle to understand her brother's sudden death, showing her relationship with the adult members of her family as they share their grief and compassion.
Prod-EBEC Dist-EBEC 1975

Where Is Dead (Captioned) C 19 MIN
16MM FILM, 3/4 OR 1/2 IN VIDEO P
Tells a story about a six-year-old girl's struggle to understand her brother's sudden death, showing her relationship with the adult members of her family as they share their grief and compassion.
Prod-EBEC Dist-EBEC 1975

Where Is He Going And To The Store, Playground C 15 MIN
2 INCH VIDEOTAPE P
See series title for descriptive statement.
From The Avenida De Ingles Series.
Prod-SDITVA Dist-GPITVL

Where Is Home For Me C 12 MIN
16MM FILM OPTICAL SOUND
Pictures Vietnamese refugees awaiting sponsorship and a chance to live in America.
LC NO. 76-700442
Prod-MRS Dist-MRS 1975

Where Is Larry C 14 MIN
3/4 OR 1/2 INCH VIDEO CASSETTE I
Discusses artificial respiration and the control of bleeding.
From The Conrad Series.
Prod-SCETV Dist-AITECH 1977

Where Is The Weather Born C 8 MIN
16MM FILM, 3/4 OR 1/2 IN VIDEO I-C A
Focuses on a team of scientists as they conduct experiments in the North Pacific in an effort to predict weather and climate.
Prod-NSF Dist-AMEDFL 1975

Where It Hurts C 29 MIN
16MM FILM OPTICAL SOUND
Examines a variety of health care delivery issues, including home care, assistant doctors, health planning and health maintenance organizations.
LC NO. 75-700707
Prod-USDHEW Dist-USNAC

Where Jesus Lived X 15 MIN
16MM FILM OPTICAL SOUND P-H T R
Explores the typical environment of the homeland of Jesus. Includes scenes related to the life of Jesus such as a carpenter at work, a synagogue school and a typical family of Galilee.
From The Land Of The Bible Series.
Prod-FAMF Dist-FAMF

Where Jesus Walked C 12 MIN
16MM FILM OPTICAL SOUND J A
Shows scenes from the Holy Lands and relates them to the Gospel accounts of Jesus' life.
Prod-CBFMS Dist-CBFMS

Where Jesus Walked C 27 MIN
16MM FILM OPTICAL SOUND J-C R
Describes the land of Palestine by using quotations from the New Testament, paintings of Jesus and scenes of the countryside where Jesus taught.
LC NO. 79-700515
Prod-BYU Dist-BYU 1978

Where Life Still Means Living C 24 MIN
16MM FILM, 3/4 OR 1/2 IN VIDEO
Describes the inner emotional world of an aged couple who are frightened by chronic illness and mental disease and suffer from feelings of rejection and helplessness. Tells about their ultimate admission to a home for the aged where rehabiliattion therapies help to lead them into a life that is meaningful.
Prod-MONTFH Dist-FEIL Prodn-FEIL 1964

Where Man Lies Buried - Field And Laboratory Treatment Of The Ancient Dead B 38 MIN
16MM FILM OPTICAL SOUND H-C A
Describes the different kinds of geological and archeological deposits where the bones of ancient man and woman are found. Shows field excavating mortuary sites and examines methods of laboratory analysis of human skeletal remains.
LC NO. 77-703196
Prod-CUNIV Dist-ITHCOL 1974

Where None Has Gone Before C 60 MIN
3/4 OR 1/2 INCH VIDEO CASSETTE J-C A
Introduces modern day pioneers. Shows pilots planning a non-stop, non-refueled flight around the world in a specially designed airplane. Interviews astronomers explaining the Hubble Space Telescope. Looks at the discovery of a new class of crustacean by a high school biology teacher.
From The Smithsonian World Series.
Prod-WETATV Dist-WETATV Prodn-SMITHS

Where Old Age Begins B 30 MIN
16MM FILM OPTICAL SOUND C
Discusses the physical impact of the aging process, the decline of function which occurs and the maintenance of health.
From The Growth And Development, The Adult Years Series.
LC NO. 76-706820
Prod-VDONUR Dist-AJN Prodn-WTTWTV 1969

Where Plants And Animals Live C 15 MIN
3/4 OR 1/2 INCH VIDEO CASSETTE I-J
Shows how life forms hibernate, migrate, or adapt in response to changing conditions within their own biomes.
From The Bioscope Series.
LC NO. 81-707583
Prod-MAETEL Dist-AITECH 1981

Where Rainbows Wait For Rain - The Chihuahuan Desert, Pt 2 C 27 MIN
16MM FILM OPTICAL SOUND
Focuses on the Chihuahuan Desert with emphasis on moisture in the desert. Reveals little-known facts and strange animals and plants adapted to a special kind of life.
LC NO. 82-700535
Prod-GRDNH Dist-ADAMSF 1982

Where Seconds Count C 12 MIN
16MM FILM OPTICAL SOUND A
Describes the public service activities of local REACT teams, such as providing emergency communications for traffic safety and performing vital communications tasks during time of disaster.
Prod-GM Dist-GM

Where Should A Squirrel Live C 11 MIN
16MM FILM, 3/4 OR 1/2 IN VIDEO P-I
Shows the experiences of a squirrel raised in a human's home and then released to its natural world.
Prod-ADAMSF Dist-BARR 1971

Where Should I Go C 15 MIN
16MM FILM, 3/4 OR 1/2 IN VIDEO I
Tells how Pete and Marty search for clues to their UFO sighting.
From The Thinkabout Series. Collecting Information
LC NO. 81-706139
Prod-AITV Dist-AITECH 1979

Where Should The Money Go C 16 MIN
16MM FILM OPTICAL SOUND
Explores allocation of funds to socially disadvantaged children and schools.
LC NO. 80-700936
Prod-TASCOR Dist-TASCOR 1976

Where The Action Is C 27 MIN
16MM FILM OPTICAL SOUND
Depicts work in today's complex technological world and shows how vocational and technical education can prepare young people through proper training, particularly at the post-secondary level, for their place in the world of work. Focuses on the problems of approximately 80 percent of the young people who do not complete college in terms of jobs, training for these jobs and their future.
LC NO. 74-706327
Prod-USOE Dist-USNAC 1967

Where The Action Is C 39 MIN
16MM FILM OPTICAL SOUND
Discusses technical details of the coal mining industry.
LC NO. 80-700866
Prod-IMPACT Dist-TASCOR 1978

Where The Cranberries Grow - An American Story C 13 MIN
16MM FILM OPTICAL SOUND
Uses historical and modern photographs to take a look at both America's and the cranberry's history. Shows how cranberries are harvested by hand and demonstrates their many uses.
LC NO. 82-700283
Prod-OSC Dist-MTP Prodn-ENVIC 1981

Where The Fish Will Be C 20 MIN
16MM FILM, 3/4 OR 1/2 IN VIDEO
Describes how the U S Fish and Wildlife Service manages fishery programs, including hatcheries, research and cooperative efforts with the states to maintain healthy fish populations.
Prod-USBSFW Dist-USNAC

Where The Future Begins - Girl Scouts C 18 MIN
16MM FILM OPTICAL SOUND
Presents scenes of Girl Scouting filmed on location at Girl Scout Councils across the nation.
Prod-GSUSA Dist-GSUSA 1979

Where The Jobs Are—A Series

Offers a series of talk shows by William J McBurney Jr on preparing for and locating jobs.
Prod-IVCH Dist-IVCH

How To Size Up The Interviewer	030 MIN
Job Outlook For Technical Graduates	030 MIN
Making Liberal Arts A Plus	030 MIN
Preparing For The Interview	030 MIN
Setting Career Goals	030 MIN
Values Of An MBA, The	030 MIN

Where The Library Dollars Are C 40 MIN
3/4 INCH VIDEO CASSETTE T
Discusses ways a small library can supplement its regular operating budget.
From The Access Series.
LC NO. 76-706265
Prod-UDEN Dist-USNAC 1976

Where The Loon Screams C 27 MIN
16MM FILM OPTICAL SOUND J-C
Tells of one of the most unusual expeditions ever assembled and its departure for the Canadian Arctic to do extensive Arctic survival studies and to search for the prehistoric musk ox.
LC NO. 76-709719
Prod-LSTI Dist-LSTI

Where The Memories Live, Pt 1 C 30 MIN
3/4 OR 1/2 INCH VIDEO CASSETTE I
Dramatizes contemporary Franco-American life. Emphasizes the theme of faith in self.
From The Franco File Series.
Prod-WENHTV Dist-GPITVL

Where The Memories Live, Pt 2 C 30 MIN
3/4 OR 1/2 INCH VIDEO CASSETTE I
Dramatizes contemporary Franco-American life. Examines the historical perspective.
From The Franco File Series.
Prod-WENHTV Dist-GPITVL

Where The River Enters The Sea C 28 MIN
16MM FILM OPTICAL SOUND
Shows how the Eskimo is emerging into modern society and looks at his culture.
Prod-STOO Dist-MTP

Where The Sewage Goes C 22 MIN
16MM FILM OPTICAL SOUND I-C A
Presents documentation of the operation of the Washington, D C Blue Plains wastewater treatment plant which is one of America's largest municipal wastewater treatment operations. Emphasizes tertiary treatment.
Prod-FINLYS Dist-FINLYS 1977

Where The Wild Things Are C 8 MIN
16MM FILM, 3/4 OR 1/2 IN VIDEO K-P
Presents an animated adaptation of the story of the same title by Maurice Sendak in which a small boy makes a visit to the land of the wild things. Tells how he tames the creatures and returns home.
Prod-WWS Dist-WWS Prodn-KRATKY 1974

Where There Is Hope C 20 MIN
16MM FILM OPTICAL SOUND
Explains that help is available for retarded children from both private and government agencies. Takes a look at some of this help, including the facilities of the John F Kennedy Institute which is associated with the Johns Hopkins Hospital in Baltimore.
LC NO. 74-706329
Prod-USSSA Dist-USNAC 1968

Where There Is Life There Is Motion - Function Of Microtubules C 25 MIN
3/4 INCH VIDEO CASSETTE C A
Documents ciliary and flagellar movement, a mechanism mediated by the microtubules in a variety of organisms.
LC NO. 80-707633
Prod-TOKYO Dist-PSUMPS 1980

Where There's A Wheel There's a Way C 19 MIN
3/4 INCH VIDEOTAPE
Addresses the physical and psychological benefits obtained by the handicapped through participation in team sports.
Prod-UNDMC Dist-UNDMC

Where There's A Will C 29 MIN
3/4 OR 1/2 INCH VIDEO CASSETTE
Shows a war veteran with artificial hands as he works at his hobby of cooking. Presents two disabled housewives demonstrating how a handicapped person can manage a home. Issued in 1969 as a motion picture.
From The To Live Again Series.
LC NO. 80-706861
Prod-USSRS Dist-USNAC 1980

Where There's Smoke C 11 MIN
16MM FILM, 3/4 OR 1/2 IN VIDEO
Describes basic steps of testing, donning, wearing and using standard breathing apparatus at live fires.
Prod-AREASX Dist-FILCOM

Where There's Smoke C 12 MIN
16MM FILM, 3/4 OR 1/2 IN VIDEO I-C A
Presents a series of brief television clips, using both live-action and animation, ridiculing the smoking habit.
Prod-CDHW Dist-NFBC 1970

Where There's Smoke Firesafety Quiz C
3/4 OR 1/2 INCH VIDEO CASSETTE
Prod-NFPA Dist-NFPA

Where Timber Wolves Call C 25 MIN
16MM FILM, 3/4 OR 1/2 IN VIDEO J-C A
Follows a Canadian wolf pack in order to detail the habits of the once-feared predators and document their contribution to the balance of nature.
Prod-TOMWLF Dist-WOMBAT

Where Time Began C 91 MIN
16MM FILM OPTICAL SOUND
Shows how a British scientist discovers the key to unlock the weird world that exists at the center of the earth.
Prod-UNKNWN Dist-TWYMAN 1978

Where To - The City And The Future C 20 MIN
2 INCH VIDEOTAPE J-H
Looks at urbanization.
From The Our World Of Economics Series.
Prod-MPATI Dist-GPITVL

Where To Begin C 30 MIN
2 INCH VIDEOTAPE C A
Introduces field of interior design and the impact it can have on the entire family. Explains psychological effects of interior design. Offers definition of interior design by professional designers and lay people.
From The Designing Home Interiors Series. Unit 1
Prod-COAST Dist-CDTEL Prodn-RSCCD

Where To Begin With Nonverbal Children C 17 MIN
16MM FILM OPTICAL SOUND C T
Follows five children through an informal screening-assessment procedure which highlights the capabilities and deficiencies of each subject in the various communication skills.
LC NO. 78-701614
Prod-UKANAV Dist-UKANS 1973

Where To Go For What You Want - Special Problems In Library Research C
3/4 OR 1/2 INCH VIDEO CASSETTE
Explores specific techniques for researching events, people and technical subjects in the library - both contemporary and historical. Highlights the benefits of such diverse reference works as Facts On File, The New York Times Index, The Reader's Guide To Periodical Literature, The Encyclopedia of American Biography and The International Encyclopedia Of Social Sciences.
Prod-CHUMAN Dist-GA

Where To Go From Here C 30 MIN
2 INCH VIDEOTAPE C A
Discusses experience and education required for would-be interior designers, how to work with an interior designer, and the future of careers in the design field.
From The Designing Home Interiors Series. Unit 30
Prod-COAST Dist-CDTEL Prodn-RSCCD

Where To Look - The Territory C 15 MIN
3/4 INCH VIDEO CASSETTE H-C A
Describes how to seek job openings.
From The Job Seeking Series.
Prod-WCETTV Dist-GPITVL 1979

Where We Live C 21 MIN
16MM FILM, 3/4 OR 1/2 IN VIDEO H-C A
Discusses the importance of the home as the most basic human environment. Explores new concepts in housing which attempt to minimize the dehumanizing realities of urban life.
From The Human Journey Series.
Prod-CTV Dist-FI 1973

Where Were You During The Battle Of The Bulge, Kid X 26 MIN
16MM FILM, 3/4 OR 1/2 IN VIDEO J-C A
Shows the parallels between a father and a son who both must decide whether to conform to society and compromise with evil or follow one's conscience and pay the price.
From The Insight Series.
Prod-PAULST Dist-PAULST

Where Were You During The Battle Of The Bulge, Kid (Spanish) X 26 MIN
16MM FILM, 3/4 OR 1/2 IN VIDEO J-C A
Shows the parallels between a father and a son who both must decide whether to conform to society and compromise with evil or follow one's conscience and pay the price.
From The Insight Series.
Prod-PAULST Dist-PAULST

Where You Are, Where You're Going C 15 MIN
16MM FILM, 3/4 OR 1/2 IN VIDEO
Stresses the importance of the small businessman keeping up-to-date records. Discusses how to begin record-keeping and to reestablish records that have been destroyed.
Prod-USSBA Dist-USNAC 1982

Where Your Money Goes C 28 MIN
16MM FILM, 3/4 OR 1/2 IN VIDEO S
Looks at the ways money may be saved or spent. Includes an explanation of payroll deductions, taxes, and the role of banks, savings and loan associations and credit unions with emphasis placed on budgeting.
From The Learning To Live On Your Own Series.
Prod-LINCS Dist-JOU 1979

Where Your Money Goes (Spanish) C 28 MIN
16MM FILM, 3/4 OR 1/2 IN VIDEO S
Looks at the ways money may be saved or spent. Includes an explanation of payroll deductions, taxes, and the role of banks, savings and loan associations and credit unions with emphasis placed on budgeting.
From The Learning To Live On Your Own Series.
Prod-LINCS Dist-JOU 1979

Where's Carlos And He's In The Hat, Bag, Box C 15 MIN
2 INCH VIDEOTAPE P
See series title for descriptive statement.
From The Avenida De Ingles Series.
Prod-SDITVA Dist-GPITVL

Where's Charlie C 12 MIN
16MM FILM OPTICAL SOUND
Introduces a new kind of resilient flooring designed to solve the problem of a skilled labor shortage.
LC NO. 77-701461
Prod-ACOC Dist-ACOC Prodn-MW 1976

Where's Danny C 16 MIN
16MM FILM, 3/4 OR 1/2 IN VIDEO
Recommends safe work procedures for interior painting contractors and their employees.
Prod-NFBTE Dist-IFB

Where's Shelley? C 13 MIN
3/4 OR 1/2 INCH VIDEO CASSETTE J-H A
Shows four children waiting in an abandoned house for Shelley

to arrive with beer and marijuana. Relates children's respective feelings about home and drugs and family and other older people who have been addicted to or involved with drugs and alcohol. Notes that by Shelley's arrival, all options had been explored, with good reasons to abstain and obvious pressures to join in.
Prod-JOHNIN Dist-EDMI 1983

Where's The Beef C 60 MIN
1/2 IN VIDEO CASSETTE BETA/VHS
Shows how to pay less for better quality meat. Explains butchering practices and marketing techniques.
Prod-MOHOMV Dist-MOHOMV

Where's The Coat, Sweater, Hat, Watch And It's On The Bed, Table, Chair, Television,... C 15 MIN
2 INCH VIDEOTAPE P
See series title for descriptive statement.
From The Avenida De Ingles Series.
Prod-SDITVA Dist-GPITVL

Where's The Trouble C 9 MIN
16MM FILM OPTICAL SOUND K-P
Teaches the concepts of front, back, top and bottom.
LC NO. 73-701038
Prod-FILMSM Dist-FILMSM 1972

Where's The Water C 14 MIN
16MM FILM, 3/4 OR 1/2 IN VIDEO IND
Examines factors which influence the delivery of water from a water tower to the scene of a fire, relating illustrations of specific principles of hydraulics to actual effects on the fire ground.
Prod-IOWAFS Dist-FILCOM 1971

Where's Tommy C 11 MIN
16MM FILM, 3/4 OR 1/2 IN VIDEO J A
Shows potential dangers surrounding an unattended child while he naps and as his mother visits a neighbor. Explains how children find things fascinating, but lack experience in juding what is harmful and what is safe.
Prod-HIGGIN Dist-HIGGIN 1974

Where's Your Loyalty C 11 MIN
16MM FILM, 3/4 OR 1/2 IN VIDEO I-J
Presents vignettes involving dilemmas of loyalty to aid children in formulating and examining their codes of living.
Prod-EBEC Dist-EBEC 1971

Where's Your Loyalty (Spanish) C 11 MIN
16MM FILM, 3/4 OR 1/2 IN VIDEO I-J
Presents vignettes involving dilemmas of loyalty to aid children in formulating and examining their codes of living.
Prod-EBEC Dist-EBEC 1971

Wherever We Find Them C 29 MIN
16MM FILM - 3/4 IN VIDEO
Enumerates the various kinds of athletic opportunities available to handicapped individuals, including racquetball, skiing, dancing, track, swimming, bowling and weight lifting. Depicts persons with all types of disabilities building strength and confidence through exercise and participation in organized competition.
LC NO. 80-706195
Prod-USVA Dist-USNAC 1979

Wherever We Lodge C 60 MIN
16MM FILM OPTICAL SOUND
Looks at the creative efforts to meet worldwide housing concerns ranging from the visionary to the common-place. Examines the concept of new towns as one possible answer to creative communities.
Prod-NBCTV Dist-CCNCC

Wherever You Are C 28 MIN
16MM FILM OPTICAL SOUND
Tells the story of an arthritis victim who cannot bring herself to seek proper medical treatment. Narrated by Henry Fonda.
LC NO. 77-702172
Prod-ARTHF Dist-MTP Prodn-KNIFED 1977

Whether To Tell The Truth B 18 MIN
16MM FILM, 3/4 OR 1/2 IN VIDEO J-C A
Tells how a young man painfully gains a sense of himself and his duty to society at the cost of losing his friends and a familiar way of life when he exposes illegal activities taking place on the docks.
From The Searching For Values - A Film Anthology Series.
Prod-LCOA Dist-LCOA 1972

Which End Do I Look In C 15 MIN
3/4 OR 1/2 INCH VIDEO CASSETTE J-H
Describes the filmmaking process. Covers planning, filming and editing.
From The Movies, Movies Series.
Prod-CTI Dist-CTI

Which Energy C 23 MIN
16MM FILM OPTICAL SOUND
Compares different energy sources by visiting field installations and research laboratories. Considers fossil fuels, nuclear fusion, fission, the breeder reactor, solar energy, wind and conservation concepts.
From The Science Of Energy Series.
LC NO. 77-700440
Prod-FINLYS Dist-FINLYS 1976

Which Is My World C 9 MIN
16MM FILM, 3/4 OR 1/2 IN VIDEO I A
Shows how greed is a major cause of environmental pollution. Tells how our demand for new things leads us to discard still usable items which lie in mounds that scar our environment. Explores the decisions and changes that may be necessary for our safe and pleasant survival.
Prod-BFA Dist-PHENIX 1971

Which Mother Is Mine C 47 MIN
16MM FILM, 3/4 OR 1/2 IN VIDEO
Tells how a young girl, after spending most of her life in foster homes, must deal with the shock of her natural mother returning to claim her. Originally shown on the television series ABC Afterschool Specials.
From The Teenage Years Series.
LC NO. 79-706815
Prod-TAHSEM Dist-TIMLIF 1979

Which Rule Wins B 28 MIN
16MM FILM OPTICAL SOUND T
Presents an unrehearsed film in which Miss Phyllis Klein teaches one of the University of Illinois Arithmetic Project topics to a class of third graders.
From The University Of Illinois Arithemtic Project Series.
LC NO. 75-702652
Prod-EDS Dist-AGAPR 1968

Which Side Are You On B
16MM FILM OPTICAL SOUND
Presents the history of the rank and file, black and white and men and women, as the hands that built America.
Prod-SFN Dist-SFN 1970

Which Way - Mapping (Geography) C 14 MIN
3/4 OR 1/2 INCH VIDEO CASSETTE P
Depicts a neighborhood treasure hunt in which two groups of children must interpret and follow simple maps to get free movie passes.
From The Two Cents' Worth Series.
Prod-WHATV Dist-AITECH Prodn-WIEC 1976

Which Way Did The Melody Go C 15 MIN
3/4 OR 1/2 INCH VIDEO CASSETTE P
Discusses musical notation.
From The Music Machine Series.
Prod-INDIPS Dist-GPITVL 1981

Which Way Is Up C 94 MIN
16MM FILM OPTICAL SOUND
Stars Richard Pryor in a triple role as a farm worker, his old father, and a hypocritical preacher.
Prod-UPCI Dist-TWYMAN 1977

Which Way Now C 28 MIN
16MM FILM OPTICAL SOUND C A
Deals with the problems facing farmers and small towns in the 70's. Discusses main choices in federal farm programs and their effects on farm incomes, taxpayers' cost and food prices.
From The Eleventh Round Series. No. 2
Prod-UNL Dist-UNEBR 1969

Which Way To The Front C 96 MIN
16MM FILM OPTICAL SOUND
Stars Jerry Lewis as a patriotic multi-billionaire who tries a variety of schemes to win World War II.
Prod-WB Dist-TWYMAN 1970

Which Way To Turn C 24 MIN
3/4 OR 1/2 INCH VIDEO CASSETTE H-C
Introduces the concept of angular momentum, which helps describe the motion of rotating physical systems in terms more complex than the theory of linear motion will allow. Uses simple examples to show the meaning of basic physics ideas.
From The Discovering Physics Series.
Prod-BBCTV Dist-MEDIAG Prodn-OPENU 1983

Which Way Wisdom C 34 MIN
16MM FILM OPTICAL SOUND
Designed to initiate discussion concerning the role of the Church in higher education. Records events and discussions as they happened on several campuses. Concludes with a chancel drama performed in a suburban church by students who speak about the problems of generational conflict.
LC NO. 70-711585
Prod-LUTHER Dist-LUTHER 1970

While I Run This Race B 29 MIN
3/4 INCH VIDEO CASSETTE
Describes the efforts of Vista volunteers in organizing a preschool program for Mexican-American migrants and helping a community of Negro farm workers conduct a clean-up campaign and obtain pure drinking water. Shows that both young and elderly persons can be useful as Vista volunteers.
Prod-USNAC Dist-USNAC 1972

While The Cat's Away C 30 MIN
3/4 OR 1/2 INCH VIDEO CASSETTE
See series title for descriptive statement.
From The Burglar-Proofing Series.
Prod-MDCPB Dist-MDCPB

While You Ride The Bus B 12 MIN
16MM FILM OPTICAL SOUND
Discusses the nonmedical New York City social improvement programs seeking volunteers. Describes their functions, locations and the ways in which prospective volunteers may offer their services.
From The Bellevue Volunteers Series.
Prod-NYU Dist-NYU

While You Were Out C 9 MIN
2 INCH VIDEOTAPE
Presents an instructional course for office employees. Presents a case study which shows how communication barriers can cause misunderstanding and confusion even with a simple business message.
From The SUCCESS, The AMA Course For Office Employees Series.
LC NO. 75-704215
Prod-AMA Dist-AMA 1972

Whiplash C 16 MIN
16MM FILM, 3/4 OR 1/2 IN VIDEO H-C A
Studies rear-end collisions at UCLA at speeds up to 55 miles per hour. Stresses safety measures to avoid these tragic accidents and their consequences.
Prod-AIMS Dist-AIMS 1968

Whiplash (Spanish) C 16 MIN
16MM FILM, 3/4 OR 1/2 IN VIDEO H A
Illustrates what happens during a rear-end collision at speeds from 10 to 55 mph. Shows how to minimize whiplash injury and safe driving practices by which rear-end collisions may be avoided.
Prod-CAHILL Dist-AIMS 1968

Whiplash And Trumpet Curves, The C 180 MIN
3/4 OR 1/2 INCH VIDEO CASSETTE PRO
Discusses one dimensional heat flow, seasonal changes, geomorphic aspects of cold regions, ice wedges and tabor ice.
From The Arctic Engineering Series.
Prod-UAKEN Dist-AMCEE

Whirling Ecstasy, The C 10 MIN
3/4 OR 1/2 INCH VIDEO CASSETTE
Presents video computer imagery inspired by Sufi poet Jala al-Din Rumi, Father of the Whirling Dervishes.
Prod-EAI Dist-EAI

Whirlwind - Bombing Germany, September 1939-1944 C 52 MIN
16MM FILM, 3/4 OR 1/2 IN VIDEO H-C A
Tells how the Allied bombing offensive in Germany left its cities in ruins at the end of the war, crippling it in its role as a major industrial power. From September 1939 through April 1944 the bombings affected both industry and civilians.
From The World At War Series.
Prod-THAMES Dist-MEDIAG 1973

Whirlwind - Bombing Germany, September, 1939 To May, 1944 C 60 MIN
16MM FILM OPTICAL SOUND H-C A
From The World At War Series.
LC NO. 76-701778
Prod-THAMES Dist-USCAN 1975

Whirlwind On Mount Egmont C 25 MIN
16MM FILM OPTICAL SOUND
Presents Japanese professional skier, Yoshiharu Fukuhara, skiing on Mount Egmont which resembles Mt Fuji. Portrays his character through his skiing and interviews.
Prod-UNIJAP Dist-UNIJAP 1969

Whirly Bird C 15 MIN
3/4 INCH VIDEO CASSETTE K-P
See series title for descriptive statement.
From The Storytime Series.
Prod-WCETTV Dist-GPITVL 1976

Whisper From Space, A C 58 MIN
16MM FILM, 3/4 OR 1/2 IN VIDEO H-C A
Explores the history of the universe. Considers whether or not the universe is expanding, the origin of the universe and the creation of various types of matter from the single element of hydrogen.
From The Nova Series.
LC NO. 79-708145
Prod-WGBHTV Dist-TIMLIF 1978

Whisperers, The B 105 MIN
16MM FILM OPTICAL SOUND J-C A
Features a perforance by British actress, Dame Edith Evans in a story of a lonely old crone who lives in a cocoon of fantasy in order to establish some meaning in her life. Directed by Bryan Forbes.
Prod-CANTOR Dist-CANTOR

Whistle For Willie C 6 MIN
16MM FILM, 3/4 OR 1/2 IN VIDEO
Tells the story of a boy who badly wants to learn to whistle so that he can call his dog. Based on the book Whistle For Willie by Ezra Jack Keats.
Prod-WWS Dist-WWS

Whistle Of The Wind C 15 MIN
16MM FILM OPTICAL SOUND
Takes a look at gliding.
LC NO. 75-704358
Prod-YORKU Dist-YORKU 1974

Whistle Signals For Approaching Steam Vessels B 17 MIN
16MM FILM OPTICAL SOUND
Shows the rules for using one, two and three blast signals, the danger signal and the bend signal in various approaching situations.
LC NO. FIE52-940
Prod-USN Dist-USNAC 1943

Whistling Smith C 27 MIN
16MM FILM, 3/4 OR 1/2 IN VIDEO J-C A
Looks at Sergeant Bernie Smith, who pounds a beat on Vancouver's skid row. Shows that he is intensely human and intensely caring.
Prod-NFBC Dist-WOMBAT

Whistling Teakettle And The Witch Of Fourth Street, The C 14 MIN
3/4 OR 1/2 INCH VIDEO CASSETTE P-I
Presents two stories, one in which Hannah's gift frightens robbers from her mother's candy store while in the other Cathy must choose between giving a daily penny to the monkey she loves or giving it to the woman she believes is a witch. Based on the books The Whistling Teakettle by Mindy Skolsky and The Witch Of Fourth Street by Myron Levoy.
From The Readit Series.
Prod-POSIMP Dist-AITECH 1982

White Archer, The / At The Mouth Of The Luckiest River C 15 MIN
3/4 OR 1/2 INCH VIDEO CASSETTE P
See series title for descriptive statement.
From The Best Of Cover To Cover 1 Series.
Prod-WETATV Dist-WETATV

White As Snow X 30 MIN
16MM FILM OPTICAL SOUND J-H T R
Tells of a young man going off to college who questions the relevance of his Christian beliefs in his new world of personal freedom, new ideas and new friends. Shows how he answers his own questions regarding the Christian faith.
LC NO. FIA65-1581
Prod-FAMF Dist-FAMF 1965

White Beach C 14 MIN
3/4 OR 1/2 INCH VIDEO CASSETTE
Documents the engineering of two collaborative performances, the Whisper Project and Freeze Frame Room For Living Room. Directed by Suzanne Lacy with Doug Smith and Eric La Brecque.
Prod-ARTINC Dist-ARTINC

White Bird - An Alternative C 26 MIN
16MM FILM, 3/4 OR 1/2 IN VIDEO H-C A
Considers the White Bird Sociomedical Aid Station an alternative health-care delivery system in Eugene, Oregon. Explains the clinic's purpose, points out the need for it and shows how it meets this need.
Prod-UCEMC Dist-UCEMC 1975

White Cloud Peaks C 22 MIN
3/4 OR 1/2 INCH VIDEO CASSETTE
Depicts the White Cloud Peaks mountain ecosystem of central Idaho via a pictorial 'journey of discovery.' Presents aerial views for general orientation and then moves in for a closer examination.
Prod-FO Dist-FO

White Collar Rip-Off, The C 52 MIN
16MM FILM, 3/4 OR 1/2 IN VIDEO J-C A
Presents a television news expose hosted by Edwin Newman which summarizes the hugely profitable white collar crimes that cost American citizens some 40 billion dollars each year. Describes the major types of crime, including employee theft, shoplifting, bribes and kickbacks, fraud and computer crimes.
Prod-FI Dist-FI 1975

White Crane Spreads Wings C 9 MIN
16MM FILM OPTICAL SOUND
Demonstrates the ancient Chinese art of T'ai Chi Chuan, which aims at complete coordination of mind and body through a system of precise physical movements.
LC NO. 77-700038
Prod-CFS Dist-CFS 1976

White Death - New Life C 26 MIN
16MM FILM, 3/4 OR 1/2 IN VIDEO H-C A
States that the changes that occurred over 10,000 years of glaciation are paralleled by tracing changes in present-day vegetation south from the Arctic to the Canadian wheat fields and maple forests. Glaciers have advanced and retreated at least four times, enabling subsequent agricultural development.
From The Botanic Man Series.
Prod-THAMES Dist-MEDIAG 1978

White Dominoes C 30 MIN
3/4 OR 1/2 INCH VIDEO CASSETTE P-I
See series title for descriptive statement.
From The Sonrisas Series.
Prod-KRLNTV Dist-MDCPB

White Dwarfs And Red Giants C 29 MIN
3/4 INCH VIDEO CASSETTE C A
Reviews properties of normal stars on the main sequence. Explains process whereby a star becomes a red giant and progresses to a white dwarf state.
From The Project Universe - Astronomy Series. Lesson 24
Prod-COAST Dist-CDTEL Prodn-SCCON

White Fang C 90 MIN
16MM FILM OPTICAL SOUND P-I
Prod-FI Dist-FI

White Heron, The C 26 MIN
16MM FILM, 3/4 OR 1/2 IN VIDEO I-H
Tells the story of a young girl who helps a hunter find a great white heron but must choose between her friendship with the hunter and her desire to save the bird.
Prod-MORRJ Dist-LCOA 1978

White House Conference On Mental Retardation C 12 MIN
16MM FILM OPTICAL SOUND
Depicts the highlights of the White House Conference on Mental Retardation held in 1963.
Prod-NMAC Dist-NMAC

White House Message - Ford 1974 C 5 MIN
16MM FILM OPTICAL SOUND
Explains inflation and its effect on United Way of America services, pointing out the increased need for giving and the ongoing need for United Way services.
LC NO. 75-700494
Prod-UWAMER Dist-UWAMER 1974

White House, The - Past And Present C 14 MIN
16MM FILM, 3/4 OR 1/2 IN VIDEO I-H
Provides a tour of many of the famous rooms of the white house, including the Blue Room, Green Room, Red Room, Oval Room and East Room. Old photos and paintings depicting former presidents and related historical events reveal the history of the White House.
Prod-CORF Dist-CORF 1960

White Lady, The C 26 MIN
16MM FILM, 3/4 OR 1/2 IN VIDEO
Dramatizes a Polish story that tells how salt mines came to be.
Prod-FOTH Dist-FOTH

White Lies C 25 MIN
16MM FILM, 3/4 OR 1/2 IN VIDEO I-J
Tells the story of 'always first' Marie-Ange and 'second place' Emma who make a solemn pact that if they both do not make the basketball team, neither will join. Their friendship is put under stress when one is selected and the other is not. Explores the relationships of teenagers.
Prod-ATLAF Dist-BCNFL 1984

White Lies (French) C 25 MIN
16MM FILM, 3/4 OR 1/2 IN VIDEO I-J
The French version of the videorecording and film White Lies.
Prod-ATLAF Dist-BCNFL 1984

White Magic, Black Magic C 20 MIN
16MM FILM, 3/4 OR 1/2 IN VIDEO J-H
Presents a witches' sabbat, including the formula for growing a living manikin and a dramatization of an episode from the Salem witch hunts. Examines the purpose and popularity of witchcraft and the occult.
From The Matter Of Fact Series.
LC NO. 74-703210
Prod-NITC Dist-AITECH Prodn-WETATV 1973

White Man Moves West, The B 30 MIN
16MM FILM OPTICAL SOUND H-C A
Sketches America's westward expansion and the problems of living in a new environment. Discusses early explorations for gold, silver and furs. Traces Spanish, French and British penetration of the Great Plains, the discovery of the Missouri River and the early trade with the Indians.
From The Great Plains Trilogy, 3 Series. Explorer And Settler - The White Man Arrives
Prod-KUONTV Dist-UNEBR 1954

White Man's Country C 28 MIN
16MM FILM, 3/4 OR 1/2 IN VIDEO
A shortened version of White Man's Country. Shows how a railroad was built through Kenya at the end of the 19th century and how the colonial ideal took root. Explains why colonists thought that Kenya should become a 'white man's country.'
From The Black Man's Land Series.
Prod-ADP Dist-FI

White Man's Country C 51 MIN
16MM FILM, 3/4 OR 1/2 IN VIDEO H-C
Presents the history of Kenya from the viewpoint of the African, through an account of the influence of the white man on Kenya. Covers the period of colonialism up through independence.
Prod-FI Dist-FI 1973

White Man's God B 30 MIN
16MM FILM OPTICAL SOUND J-C A R
A story set in the African jungles which focuses on the efforts of a missionary to overcome a native's fear and superstition and to win a soul for Christ.
LC NO. 72-701671
Prod-CONCOR Dist-CPH 1961

White Mane B
1/2 IN VIDEO CASSETTE BETA/VHS
Deals with a horse having a white mane.
Prod-EQVDL Dist-EQVDL

White Mane C 30 MIN
16MM FILM, 3/4 OR 1/2 IN VIDEO
Tells the story of a wild white stallion living in freedom, of the men who wish to capture him and break his spirit and of the boy who ultimately tames him with love.
Prod-LAM Dist-TEXFLM

White Mountains - A Cultural View, The C 14 MIN
16MM FILM OPTICAL SOUND H-C A
Examines the cultural history of New Hampshire's White Mountain region as it changed from an untrampled wilderness to a well-cultivated playground for thousands of tourists.
Prod-UNH Dist-UNH 1980

White Mountains And The City Of Gold And Lead B 20 MIN
3/4 OR 1/2 INCH VIDEO CASSETTE J-H
Presents WHITE MOUNTAINS and THE CITY OF GOLD AND LEAD by John Christopher. Tells about extraterrestial beings who have taken over most of the earth and how their plan to replace the earth's atmosphere with their own world would end the existence of the human race. Features Well Parker, an English boy, who studies to thwart the plans of the extraterrestial beings. (Broadcast quality)
From The Matter Of Fiction Series. No. 7
Prod-WETATV Dist-AITECH

White Seal, The C 26 MIN
3/4 INCH VIDEO CASSETTE E
Follows the exploits of Kotick, the white seal, as he struggles to save himself and his friends from seal hunters in the Bering Sea. Based on the story The White Seal by Rudyard Kipling. Narrated by Roddy Mc Dowall.
Prod-CJE Dist-GA

White Star Garage, The C 27 MIN
16MM FILM, 3/4 OR 1/2 IN VIDEO J-C A
Shows a young couple who are worried because they have no money to pay for the hospital so that the wife can give birth. Explains how the woman winds up giving birth in an auto repair shop. Stars Fausto Bara and Christine Avila.
From The Insight Series.
Prod-PAULST Dist-PAULST

White Water C 24 MIN
16MM FILM OPTICAL SOUND
Documents the first annual Canadian River Race.
From The Heading Out Series.
LC NO. 76-702070
Prod-CENTWO Dist-CENTWO 1975

White Water And Broke C
3/4 OR 1/2 INCH VIDEO CASSETTE IND
Includes the basic system of white water and broke, savealls, and broke.
From The Pulp And Paper Training, Module 3 - Papermaking Series.
Prod-LEIKID Dist-LEIKID

White Water Voyage C 8 MIN
16MM FILM OPTICAL SOUND
Shows the art of guiding a raft through challenging rapids.
LC NO. 78-700232
Prod-SUTHRB Dist-SUTHRB 1978

White Water, Blue Water C 14 MIN
16MM FILM OPTICAL SOUND
Concerns Canada's first school for white water kayaking and canoeing, located on the Madawaska River in northern Ontario.
LC NO. 75-704359
Prod-CANFDC Dist-CANFDC 1974

White Wilderness (Dutch)—A Series I-H
Looks at wildlife in the Arctic region.
Prod-WDEMCO Dist-WDEMCO

Arctic Region And Its Polar Bears, The (Dutch) 028 MIN
Large Animals Of The Arctic (Dutch) 022 MIN
Lemmings And Arctic Bird Life, The (Dutch) 021 MIN

White Wilderness (French)—A Series I-H
Looks at wildlife in the Arctic region.
Prod-WDEMCO Dist-WDEMCO

Arctic Region And Its Polar Bears, The (French) 028 MIN
Large Animals Of The Arctic (French) 022 MIN
Lemmings And Arctic Bird Life, The (French) 021 MIN

White Wilderness (German)—A Series I-H
Looks at wildlife in the Arctic region.
Prod-WDEMCO Dist-WDEMCO

Arctic Region And Its Polar Bears, The (German) 028 MIN
Large Animals Of The Arctic (German) 022 MIN
Lemmings And Arctic Bird Life, The (German) 021 MIN

White Wilderness (Norwegian)—A Series I-H
Looks at wildlife in the Arctic region.
Prod-WDEMCO Dist-WDEMCO

Arctic Region And Its Polar Bears, The
Large Animals Of The Arctic (Norwegian) 022 MIN
Lemmings And Arctic Bird Life, The (Norwegian) 021 MIN

White Wilderness (Portuguese)—A Series I-H
Looks at wildlife in the Arctic region.
Prod-WDEMCO Dist-WDEMCO

Arctic Region And Its Polar Bears, The
Large Animals Of The Arctic (Portuguese) 022 MIN
Lemmings And Arctic Bird Life, The (Portuguese) 021 MIN

White Wilderness (Swedish)—A Series I-H
Looks at wildlife in the Arctic region.
Prod-WDEMCO Dist-WDEMCO

Arctic Region And Its Polar Bears, The
Large Animals Of The Arctic (Swedish) 022 MIN
Lemmings And Arctic Bird Life, The (Swedish) 021 MIN

White Wilderness—A Series
16MM FILM, 3/4 OR 1/2 IN VIDEO I-C A
Prod-DISNEY Dist-WDEMCO 1964

Arctic Region And Its Polar Bears 28 MIN
Large Animals Of The Arctic 22 MIN
Lemmings And Arctic Bird Life, The 21 MIN

White-Throat C 10 MIN
16MM FILM OPTICAL SOUND
Follows a white-throated sparrow through the forest. Pictures a bullfrog, suckers, catfish, grouse, timber wolves, blue jays, sapsuckers, loons, mallards, a fox and a beaver. Uses natural sounds without narration.
From The Birds Of America, 1, Their Songs And Sounds Series. No. 1
Prod-GIB Dist-GIB 1966

Whitewater C 11 MIN
16MM FILM OPTICAL SOUND J-C A
Describes whitewater canoeing and shows slalom and down-river racing on the Nantahala River in the Smoky Mountains. Explains basic rules and shows all types of craft in actual competition.
LC NO. 72-712947
Prod-AMRC Dist-AMRC 1971

Whitewater C 30 MIN
1/2 IN VIDEO CASSETTE BETA/VHS
Talks about getting outfitted for whitewater canoeing. Features a hike and nature study a short ferry ride from San Francisco's Fisherman's Wharf.

From The Great Outdoors Series.
Prod-WGBHTV Dist-MTI

Whitewater Canoeing C 11 MIN
16MM FILM, 3/4 OR 1/2 IN VIDEO J-C
Presents the techniques for breaking into and out of a swift current while canoeing, ferry gliding across a swift current and the recovery of a second overturned canoe. Shows how to read the characteristics of rapidly moving water by its surface appearance including rapids, V's, standing waves and back eddies.
Prod-SF Dist-SF 1974

Whitewater Movies C 12 MIN
3/4 OR 1/2 INCH VIDEO CASSETTE
Consists of a number of film clips from the three films of the Whitewater series, Whitewater Primer, The Calculated Risk and Margin For Error.
Prod-AMRC Dist-AMRC

Whitewater Voyage C 8 MIN
3/4 OR 1/2 INCH VIDEO CASSETTE P A
Focuses on whitewater rafting on the Salt River. Narrated by Jay Michael.
Prod-SUTHRB Dist-SUTHRB

Whither The Mainstream C 29 MIN
3/4 OR 1/2 INCH VIDEO CASSETTE T
See series title for descriptive statement.
From The Mainstreaming The Exceptional Child Series.
Prod-MFFD Dist-FI

Whither Weather C 12 MIN
16MM FILM, 3/4 OR 1/2 IN VIDEO H-C A
Presents an animated portrayal of the effects of climate upon the world. Emphasizes the need for climate control and international cooperation to ensure the future well-being of the world.
LC NO. 77-701122
Prod-HUBLEY Dist-PFP 1977

Whitley, Joyce C 29 MIN
3/4 INCH VIDEO CASSETTE
Discusses the role and function of the urban planner in modern society.
From The Like It Is Series.
Prod-OHC Dist-HRC

Whitney Young C 20 MIN
3/4 INCH VIDEO CASSETTE I
See series title for descriptive statement.
From The Truly American Series.
Prod-WVIZTV Dist-GPITVL 1979

Whittaker 50-Man Escape Capsule C
3/4 OR 1/2 INCH VIDEO CASSETTE IND
Looks at an industry standard all rig hands most know. Covers boarding the capsule, starting the engine, how to safely launch, fire protection systems, how to operate the capsule on water and proper retrieval techniques.
From The Offshore Operations Series.
Prod-GPCV Dist-GPCV

Whittlin' C 14 MIN
16MM FILM OPTICAL SOUND
Shows the new lightweight train which the Santa Fe Railway has designed for piggyback service. Explains the concept and design of this energy-saving idea.
Prod-STAFER Dist-MTP

Whittling C 28 MIN
3/4 INCH VIDEO CASSETTE
See series title for descriptive statement.
From The Woodcarver's Workshop Series.
Prod-WOSUTV Dist-PUBTEL

Who Am I B 20 MIN
16MM FILM OPTICAL SOUND C A
See series title for descriptive statement.
From The All That I Am Series.
Prod-MPATI Dist-NWUFLM

Who Am I B 15 MIN
2 INCH VIDEOTAPE P
Shows exploring, cutting, bending and folding paper to create cut paper masks.
From The Art Corner Series.
Prod-CVETVC Dist-GPITVL Prodn-WCVETV

Who Am I C 20 MIN
3/4 OR 1/2 INCH VIDEO CASSETTE P-I
Presents literary selections that deal with self-discovery as a part of growing up.
From The Once Upon A Town Series.
Prod-MDDE Dist-AITECH 1977

Who Am I C 29 MIN
2 INCH VIDEOTAPE
See series title for descriptive statement.
From The That's Life Series.
Prod-KOAPTV Dist-PUBTEL

Who Am I C 30 MIN
2 INCH VIDEOTAPE J
See series title for descriptive statement.
From The Summer Journal, Unit 1 - You Are What You Feel Series.
Prod-WNINTV Dist-GPITVL

Who Am I - Developing Self-Concept C 15 MIN
16MM FILM, 3/4 OR 1/2 IN VIDEO J-H
Describes how Tyrone's desire to be a star saxophonist leads to problems with his schoolwork, until his employer and parents help him reach a better understanding and acceptance of himself.

From The On The Level Series.
LC NO. 80-707549
Prod-EDFCEN Dist-AITECH 1980

Who Am I - Looking At Self-Concept C
3/4 OR 1/2 INCH VIDEO CASSETTE I-J
Introduces self-concept and the many factors that shape it. Illustrates how self-concept affects everything the individual does or thinks. Helps adolescents analyze what they would like to change about themselves and how to make those changes. Includes teacher's guide.
Prod-SUNCOM Dist-SUNCOM

Who Am I - Where Are You C 20 MIN
16MM FILM OPTICAL SOUND J
Explores the need for friendship and understanding. Features Dr Gerald Edwards, educational consultant to the Center of Narcotics and Drug Abuse for the National Institute of Mental Health, who directs a group of junior high school students in an exercise to demonstrate the nature of loneliness and each individual's responsibility to reach out to the lonely person and help him feel accepted.
From The Nobody But Yourself Series.
Prod-WQED Dist-GPITVL

Who Am I This Time C
1/2 IN VIDEO CASSETTE BETA/VHS
Presents the American Playhouse production of Kurt Vonnegut's touching story about a shy young man, starring Christopher Walken and Susan Sarandon.
Prod-GA Dist-GA

Who Am I Where Are You C 20 MIN
2 INCH VIDEOTAPE J
Explores the need for friendship and understanding. Helps the viewer understand that everyone has inner thoughts, dreams and plans. Features an exercise which demonstrates the nature of loneliness and each individual's responsibility to reach out to a lonely person and help him feel accepted.
From The Nobody But Yourself Series.
Prod-WQED Dist-GPITVL

Who Are Our Leaders C 30 MIN
3/4 INCH VIDEO CASSETTE
Discusses characteristics of leadership. Introduces The Decision Makers Series.
From The Decision Makers Series.
Prod-OHC Dist-HRC

Who Are The American Jews B 30 MIN
16MM FILM OPTICAL SOUND
Surveys the diversity within the American Jewish community which is reflected by its involvement on every level of American life.
Prod-ADL Dist-ADL

Who Are The De Bolts (TV Version) C 54 MIN
16MM FILM, 3/4 OR 1/2 IN VIDEO
Focuses on the lives of Dorothy and Robert De Bolt and their 19 multiracial and handicapped children. Features Henry Winkler as host and narrator.
Prod-KORTY Dist-PFP 1979

Who Are The DeBolts - T V Version (Spanish) C 54 MIN
16MM FILM, 3/4 OR 1/2 IN VIDEO I-C A
Presents a specially edited version, hosted by Henry Winkler, of the story of the DeBolts and their 19 very special children.
Prod-KORTY Dist-PFP

Who Are The Debolts, And Where Did They Get 19 Kids C 72 MIN
16MM FILM, 3/4 OR 1/2 IN VIDEO I-C A
Focuses on the daily life of the De Bolt family and their adopted, handicapped and multiracial children.
LC NO. 79-707026
Prod-KORTY Dist-PFP 1978

Who Are The People Of America (2nd Ed) C 11 MIN
16MM FILM, 3/4 OR 1/2 IN VIDEO I-H
Compares the diversity of American citizens as immigrants and descendants of immigrants of different backgrounds with their similarities, common needs, shared aspirations and values.
Prod-CORF Dist-CORF 1975

Who Are These People C 22 MIN
16MM FILM OPTICAL SOUND
Focuses on the special educational needs of gifted children. Shows how these needs often are not met because of misidentification, inadequate programs and general apathy.
LC NO. 77-702173
Prod-GIFTAL Dist-SCOTAP Prodn-SCOTAP 1977

Who Are We - Body Talk C 4 MIN
16MM FILM, 3/4 OR 1/2 IN VIDEO P-J
Shows how arms, feet, fingers, hands and head help express ideas and feelings without ever saying a word.
From The Mini Movies, Unit 1 - Who Are We Series.
Prod-MORLAT Dist-CORF 1976

Who Are We - Hands And Feet C 4 MIN
16MM FILM, 3/4 OR 1/2 IN VIDEO P-J
Examines hands and feet in animals and humans, including walking, holding, scratching and climbing.
From The Mini Movies, Unit 1 - Who Are We Series.
Prod-MORLAT Dist-CORF 1976

Who Are We - Summertime, Wintertime C 4 MIN
16MM FILM, 3/4 OR 1/2 IN VIDEO P-J
Presents a picturesque collage of summer and winter activities.
From The Mini Movies, Unit 1 - Who Are We Series.
Prod-MORLAT Dist-CORF 1976

Who Are We - Talking C 5 MIN
16MM FILM, 3/4 OR 1/2 IN VIDEO P-J
Shows how talking with our mouths takes not only the form of words but also that of sounds, such as hmm, yuck, and tut-tut.
From The Mini Movies, Unit 1 - Who Are We Series.
Prod-MORLAT Dist-CORF 1976

Who Are We - Touching C 4 MIN
16MM FILM, 3/4 OR 1/2 IN VIDEO P-J
Describes the feel of tiny grains of sand filtering through one's fingers and other textures encountered by children as they explore nature.
From The Mini Movies, Unit 1 - Who Are We Series.
Prod-MORLAT Dist-CORF 1976

Who Are You C 9 MIN
16MM FILM, 3/4 OR 1/2 IN VIDEO P-I
Explores the concept of self-identity through a humorous animated story of a puppy who investigates his new environment in an attempt to discover his mission and identity.
Prod-WHTF Dist-FI 1976

Who Are You C 15 MIN
3/4 INCH VIDEO CASSETTE K-P
Presents an adaptation of the story What Is Big by Henry R Wing.
From The I Can Read Series.
Prod-WCETTV Dist-GPITVL 1977

Who Broke It (French) C 13 MIN
3/4 OR 1/2 INCH VIDEO CASSETTE H-C A
Features a glassmaker's studio in which a country priest's broken stained glass window is fixed.
From The En Francais Series. Part 1 - Essential Elements
Prod-MOFAFR Dist-AITECH 1970

Who Can Catch The Wind C 30 MIN
16MM FILM OPTICAL SOUND
Shows that a young man's dreams come true when he joins the Navy. Describes how he goes through boot camp training, his first sea duty and shore leave.
LC NO. 74-706607
Prod-USN Dist-USNAC 1973

Who Can Help Harry C 20 MIN
16MM FILM OPTICAL SOUND
Discusses the problem of a manager faced with unplanned organizational growth. Points out the need to apply the Army's position management program to assure sound management of civilian positions.
LC NO. 74-706331
Prod-USA Dist-USNAC 1968

Who Can I Count On - Lifelong C 30 MIN
16MM FILM, 3/4 OR 1/2 IN VIDEO C A
Discusses the ability and right of the mentally retarded to have the freedom, independence and control over their own lives accorded other members of society.
Prod-NIMR Dist-STNFLD

Who Can You Trust C 9 MIN
16MM FILM OPTICAL SOUND
Points out the dangers of children speaking to strangers.
LC NO. 80-700937
Prod-TASCOR Dist-TASCOR 1976

Who Cares C 21 MIN
16MM FILM OPTICAL SOUND C A
Describes methods and techniques for driving school buses for maximum fuel economy. Shows that proper driving can increase fuel economy by seven to eight per cent. Claims that if this goal were achieved nationwide, 50 million gallons of fuel could be saved each year.
Prod-VISUCP Dist-VISUCP 1979

Who Cares C 13 MIN
16MM FILM, 3/4 OR 1/2 IN VIDEO J-C A
Shows the conflict of an aging grandfather in the home of a family. Questions where the old man should look for comfort in his old age when his own flesh and blood don't care.
From The Family Life Education And Human Growth Series.
Prod-SF Dist-SF 1970

Who Cares C 15 MIN
3/4 OR 1/2 INCH VIDEO CASSETTE I-J
Examines the rights and responsibilities, personal involvement, and needs of citizens and how these may cause institutions to change.
From The It's All Up To You Series.
Prod-COOPED Dist-AITECH Prodn-WHATV 1978

Who Cares - About Me C 15 MIN
3/4 OR 1/2 INCH VIDEO CASSETTE I
Presents ten children selected by their peers who discuss the issues of their lives, including loneliness, boredom, failure, habits and feelings.
From The Who Cares Series.
Prod-GBCTP Dist-AITECH 1982

Who Cares - About My Habits C 15 MIN
3/4 OR 1/2 INCH VIDEO CASSETTE I
Presents ten children discussing habits, why people take drugs, why children begin alcohol or drug use, and how friendship can make a difference. Shows three girls role-playing an attempt to persuade a friend to stop drinking.
From The Who Cares Series.
Prod-GBCTP Dist-AITECH 1982

Who Cares - How We Get High Together C 15 MIN
3/4 OR 1/2 INCH VIDEO CASSETTE I
Discusses alternatives to drugs as campers build a community by working and playing together.
From The Who Cares Series.
Prod-GBCTP Dist-AITECH 1982

Who Cares - How We Survive Together C 15 MIN
3/4 OR 1/2 INCH VIDEO CASSETTE I

Shows children beginning a four-day campout by building shelters and learning about edible wild plants. Shows them gradually learning to cooperate in working together.
From The Who Cares Series.
Prod-GBCTP Dist-AITECH 1982

Who Cares - If I Drink C 15 MIN
3/4 OR 1/2 INCH VIDEO CASSETTE I
Presents ten children discussing their own decisions about alcohol. Deals with how people act when they drink too much, why people drink, how they feel and the effects alcohol has.
From The Who Cares Series.
Prod-GBCTP Dist-AITECH 1982

Who Cares - If I Have An Accident C 14 MIN
3/4 OR 1/2 INCH VIDEO CASSETTE I
Presents students in a sixth-grade classroom finding out what they could do for an injured classmate, what the Emergency Medical Services Center would do and where they can learn more about first aid.
From The Who Cares Series.
LC NO. 82-706767
Prod-GBCTP Dist-AITECH 1982

Who Cares - The Counselor's Role In The American School C 28 MIN
16MM FILM OPTICAL SOUND T
Presents a series of vignettes portraying a wide variety of actual counselor situations. Depicts the counselor's role in the education process and in the personal process of individual maturation.
LC NO. 77-702330
Prod-ASCA Dist-AACD 1973

Who Cares - What I Choose To Eat C 14 MIN
3/4 OR 1/2 INCH VIDEO CASSETTE I
Presents fifth-grade students shopping for a family of four at the supermarket and then discussing the reasons for their decisions.
From The Who Cares Series.
Prod-GBCTP Dist-AITECH 1982

Who Cares - What I Need C 15 MIN
3/4 OR 1/2 INCH VIDEO CASSETTE I
Offers a fantasy journey in which four 11-year-olds ask a wizard for feelings they need such as friendship, confidence and love from parents. Seeks to encourage openness and trust in the classroom.
From The Who Cares Series.
Prod-GBCTP Dist-AITECH 1982

Who Cares About Child Care C 33 MIN
16MM FILM, 3/4 OR 1/2 IN VIDEO H-C A
Views the importance of child care centers to a variety of parents and children and the remarkable qualities of a middle-aged child-care worker.
From The Women Series.
Prod-LUF Dist-LUF 1979

Who Cares--A Series
I
Uses an unscripted approach to the issues that affect the health and safety of young people.
Prod-GBCTP Dist-AITECH 1982

Who Cares - About Me 015 MIN
Who Cares - About My Habits 015 MIN
Who Cares - How We Get High Together 015 MIN
Who Cares - How We Survive Together 015 MIN
Who Cares - If I Drink 015 MIN
Who Cares - If I Have An Accident 014 MIN
Who Cares - What I Choose To Eat 014 MIN
Who Cares - What I Need 015 MIN

Who Cops Out C 11 MIN
16MM FILM, 3/4 OR 1/2 IN VIDEO J-H
A discussion of the question of the choices today's adolescents make when faced with the confusion and uncertainty of the teen-age years. Focusses on five adolescents who have made five different choices--a girl who may be asked to leave school, a school drop-out working at a gas station, a high school football star, a scholastic achiever and a drug user.
Prod-SMHACM Dist-IFB Prodn-MHFB 1969

Who Decides Disability C 58 MIN
3/4 OR 1/2 INCH VIDEO CASSETTE
Examines the Social Security Administration which has reviewed, over a period of two years, 775,000 disability pension cases, disqualifying over 40 percent of them from receiving benefits. Discusses on what basis the decisions are made and who decides.
From The Frontline Series.
Prod-DOCCON Dist-PBS

Who Did What To Whom C 17 MIN
16MM FILM OPTICAL SOUND H-C A
A training film for educational, religious or industrial leaders which shows how to recognize the four principles of behavior - positive reinforcement, negative reinforcement, extinction and punishment.
LC NO. 74-714963
Prod-MAGER Dist-RESPRC 1972

Who Did What To Whom - Recognizing Four Behavioral Principles In Action C 20 MIN
16MM FILM, 3/4 OR 1/2 IN VIDEO
Is directed toward the workplace. Familiarizes participants with basic principles of human behavior and gives them practice in recognizing and correcting application of these principles in their work lives.
Prod-RESPRC Dist-RESPRC

Who Discovered America C 14 MIN
16MM FILM, 3/4 OR 1/2 IN VIDEO J-C A
Presents an edited version of 'IN SEARCH OF THE LOST WORLD.' Discusses the origin of the Indians and the influence of voyagers from Africa, Asia and Europe on American culture.
Prod-FI Dist-FI 1972

Who Do I Portray To Others C 30 MIN
2 INCH VIDEOTAPE J
See series title for descriptive statement.
From The Summer Journal, Unit 5 - You Are What Others See In You Series.
Prod-WNINTV Dist-GPITVL

Who Do You Tell C 13 MIN
16MM FILM, 3/4 OR 1/2 IN VIDEO P-I
Uses animation and documentary footage in discussing various serious family problems, including sexual abuse. Describes community support systems available to help when the child's primary support system, the family, breaks down.
Prod-MITCHG Dist-MTI 1979

Who Does She Think She Is C 60 MIN
16MM FILM OPTICAL SOUND C A
Presents a candid look at novelist, singer, painter and ex-wrestler Rosalyn Drexler.
LC NO. 74-703677
Prod-NYFLMS Dist-NYFLMS 1974

Who Does What B 20 MIN
16MM FILM OPTICAL SOUND
Outlines the tasks of all involved in production of a television program.
From The CETO Television Training Films Series.
Prod-CETO Dist-GPITVL

Who Does What to What - The Work Distribution Chart C 11 MIN
16MM FILM, 3/4 OR 1/2 IN VIDEO
Explains the use of the work distribution chart as a method of observing at a glance what work is actually going on in an organization. Issued in 1972 as a motion picture.
LC NO. 80-706425
Prod-USA Dist-USNAC 1980

Who Happen To Be Gay C 23 MIN
16MM FILM, 3/4 OR 1/2 IN VIDEO A
Features six homosexuals who talk about their lifestyle and its impact upon them.
Prod-DIRECT Dist-DIRECT 1979

Who Has Touched The Sky C 8 MIN
16MM FILM, 3/4 OR 1/2 IN VIDEO
Presents scenes of Air Force activity against a background of music by the Anita Kerr Singers.
Prod-USAF Dist-USNAC 1972

Who Helps Protect Us And Our Homes B 15 MIN
2 INCH VIDEOTAPE P
Discusses the importance of services of the police and fire departments to protect life and property in a community. (Broadcast quality)
From The Around The Corner Series. No. 19
Prod-FWCETV Dist-GPITVL Prodn-WEDUTV

Who Helps Who C 27 MIN
16MM FILM, 3/4 OR 1/2 IN VIDEO
Reveals the benefits that developed countries get from providing international aid to underdeveloped nations. Shows that international aid does little more than maintain and reinforce the present domination of the underdeveloped countries by the developed ones.
From The Five Billion People Series.
Prod-LEFSP Dist-CNEMAG

Who I Am And Where I Want To Go C
3/4 OR 1/2 INCH VIDEO CASSETTE
Identifies those abilities, interests, values, personal characteristics and experiences that have important implications for choosing a job and?or career.
From The Employability Skills Series.
Prod-ILCS Dist-CAMB

Who In Me To Who In You C 26 MIN
3/4 OR 1/2 INCH VIDEO CASSETTE IND
Explains five types of behavior commonly used for communicating on the job and discusses the pros and cons of each.
From The Super-Vision Series.
LC NO. 79-706772
Prod-VCI Dist-DELTAK 1977

Who Invited Us B 60 MIN
16MM FILM, 3/4 OR 1/2 IN VIDEO H-C A
Reviews the history of United States military intervention beginning with the takeover of the Philippines and continuing through the Viet nam War. Examines motives for intervention, such as the capitalist-socialist conflict and economic reasons.
Prod-NET Dist-IU 1970

Who Is - Oscar Niemeyer C 30 MIN
16MM FILM OPTICAL SOUND H-C A
Shows how Oscar Niemeyer, a Brazilian architect who contributed to the design of the un building, designed the new city of Brasilia. Illustrates the high aesthetic impact of the new capital's buildings that avoids American and European functional emphasis. Mentions Niemeyer's disappointment in the failure of the project to produce a new, informal and unstratified society.
From The Who Is Series.
LC NO. 73-708713
Prod-NET Dist-IU 1970

Who Is - Sean Kenny C 30 MIN
16MM FILM OPTICAL SOUND H-C A
Sean Kenny, designer of the gyrotron at Montreal's Expo 67, explains the philosophies lying behind his design and architectural work. Shows how Kenny has reflected the ideas of his teacher, Frank Lloyd Wright, in his design of stage sets, especially his London Blitz, which is a new form of entertainment-architectural theater. Presents his belief that the different forms and shapes which we contact shape our work, learning and character.
From The Who Is Series.
LC NO. 70-708715
Prod-NET Dist-IU 1970

Who Is - Victor Vasarely C 30 MIN
16MM FILM OPTICAL SOUND H-C
Shows the work of the Hungarian-born artist, Victor Vasarely who is considered to be the founder of op-art and discusses his philosophy.
LC NO. 77-708714
Prod-NET Dist-IU Prodn-KING 1970

Who Is An American C 15 MIN
16MM FILM - VIDEO, ALL FORMATS K-J
Deals with prejudice. Shows Fat Albert nominating a Japanese-American student to be queen for the school's America Day, and a campaign being conducted against her.
From The Fat Albert And The Cosby Kids IV Series.
Prod-BARR Dist-BARR Prodn-FLMTON

Who Is An Artist C 25 MIN
2 INCH VIDEOTAPE I
Introduces art for every day and elements of design.
From The Art For Every Day Series.
Prod-CVETVC Dist-GPITVL

Who Is Elmer Dunaway And What Does He Want C 30 MIN
3/4 INCH VIDEO CASSETTE
Features an interview with Elmer Dunaway, statewide president, Ohio Fraternal Order of Police.
From The Decision Makers Series.
Prod-OHC Dist-HRC

Who Is Man - An Overview C 29 MIN
2 INCH VIDEOTAPE
Explains the concept of the Who Is Man series and surveys the material which will be handled in subsequent programs.
From The Who Is Man Series.
Prod-WHROTV Dist-PUBTEL

Who Is Man - Summary C 29 MIN
2 INCH VIDEOTAPE
Features Dr Puryear summing up the material presented in the Who Is Man series.
From The Who Is Man Series.
Prod-WHROTV Dist-PUBTEL

Who Is Man--A Series

Prod-WHROTV Dist-PUBTEL

Atlantis 29 MIN
Clairvoyant Frauds 29 MIN
Clairvoyants 29 MIN
Dreams 29 MIN
Edgar Cayce 29 MIN
ESP And The Artist 29 MIN
ESP Behind The Iron Curtain 29 MIN
ESP I 29 MIN
ESP II 29 MIN
Finger Reading 29 MIN
Ghost Stories 29 MIN
Gladys Davis Turner 29 MIN
Healing And Psychokinesis 29 MIN
Hypnosis 29 MIN
Meditation 29 MIN
Primitive Beliefs 29 MIN
Psychokinesis (Russia And Here) 29 MIN
Questions And Answers I 29 MIN
Questions And Answers II 29 MIN
Reincarnation 29 MIN
Research Methods And Probability 29 MIN
Sensitive, The 29 MIN
Superstitions 29 MIN
Testing Equipment And Approaches 29 MIN
Who Is Man - An Overview 29 MIN
Who Is Man - Summary 29 MIN

Who Is My Neighbor B 30 MIN
16MM FILM OPTICAL SOUND J-C
Presents the parable of the Good Samaritan--a Samaritan finds an injured man lying by the road, a victim of thieves, and takes him to an inn and arranges for his care at his own expense.
Prod-CAFM Dist-CAFM

Who Is Pulling Your Strings C 12 MIN
16MM FILM OPTICAL SOUND
Presents Ann Marie Fairchild, a ventriloquist, and her dummy Jackie, making a parallel between Ann Marie pulling Jackie's strings to control him and Jesus controlling our lives if we are willing to let him.
Prod-BROADM Dist-BROADM 1975

Who Is Sylvia C 30 MIN
16MM FILM - 3/4 IN VIDEO
Explores both the harmful and helpful aspects of television, showing how it shapes children's ideas of what the world is like, as well as their attitudes towards themselves and others. Illustrates how parents can use television to their children's benefit.
From The Footsteps Series.
LC NO. 79-707640
Prod-USOE Dist-USNAC 1978

Who Is The Real Cinderella C 19 MIN
3/4 OR 1/2 INCH VIDEO CASSETTE P
Uses puppets to illustrate variations on the Cinderella story.

From The Folk Book Series.
Prod-UWISC Dist-AITECH 1980

Who Is This Man - John Paul II In America C 28 MIN
16MM FILM OPTICAL SOUND
Reviews the verbal and nonverbal messages of Pope John Paul II during his 1979 visit to the United States.
LC NO. 80-700649
Prod-KNICOL Dist-USCC Prodn-USCC 1979

Who Is Tracy Williams B 28 MIN
16MM FILM OPTICAL SOUND C A
Focuses on the problems, frailties and strengths of Tracy Williams, an inmate of the State Correctional Institution at Muncy, Pennsylvania. Depicts prison routine. Interviews William about Muncy and her bitterness about the circumstances surrounding her confinement.
LC NO. 74-702726
Prod-PSU Dist-PSUPCR 1973

Who Is Tracy Williams B 29 MIN
2 INCH VIDEOTAPE
Explores the human and personal problems of prison life in Pennsylvania and focuses on the frailties and strengths of one inmate serving a sentence for forgery at the State Correctional Institution at Muncy, Pennsylvania.
Prod-WPSXTV Dist-PUBTEL

Who Killed Determinants B 57 MIN
16MM FILM OPTICAL SOUND
Lectures on the historical patterns of research and growth in the field of determinants, prompted by the apparent demise of determinants as an active field of research.
From The Maa Calculus Series.
Prod-MAA Dist-MLA

Who Killed Jesus Christ - The New Testament And The Facts C
2 INCH VIDEOTAPE
See series title for descriptive statement.
From The Jesus Trial Series. Program 1
LC NO. 79-706738
Prod-TVOTAR Dist-TVBUS 1979

Who Kills The Tiger C 15 MIN
16MM FILM OPTICAL SOUND H-C A
Employs the graphic arts to illustrate that man's survival is dependent upon his co-operation with his fellow men. Portrays the role of community services.
Prod-WSU Dist-WSU 1959

Who Listens C 30 MIN
3/4 OR 1/2 INCH VIDEO CASSETTE H-C A
Focuses on the constituents of good listening and ways to develop good listening habits.
From The Principles of Human Communication Series.
Prod-UMINN Dist-GPITVL 1983

Who Lives, Who Dies, Who Decides C 14 MIN
3/4 INCH VIDEO CASSETTE PRO
See series title for descriptive statement.
From The Bioethics In Nursing Practice Series. Module 4
LC NO. 81-707063
Prod-BRA Dist-BRA 1981

Who Lost A Giraffe C 10 MIN
16MM FILM, 3/4 OR 1/2 IN VIDEO K-I
Uses animation to tell the story of a small boy who discovers a rubber eraser with the imprint of a giraffe on it.
Prod-JURIST Dist-PHENIX 1975

Who Loves Amy Tonight C 25 MIN
16MM FILM, 3/4 OR 1/2 IN VIDEO J-C A
Demonstrates how a spoiled girl has always managed to manipulate her father. Shows how he decides to become firmer with her after she becomes involved in shoplifting and drug dealing. Stars Laura Dern and Tim Van Patten.
From The Reflections Series.
Prod-PAULST Dist-MEDIAG

Who Me? Make A Presentation? C 15 MIN
16MM FILM, 3/4 OR 1/2 IN VIDEO
Convinces managers that they can overcome the number one fear of most managers, public speaking. Shows managers and salespeople how to sell their ideas to peers, higher management and customers.
Prod-EFM Dist-EFM

Who Needs It C 15 MIN
3/4 OR 1/2 INCH VIDEO CASSETTE I-J
Analyzes the conditions necessary for government to function, different types of past and present governments, and the relationship between the ruler and the ruled.
From The It's All Up To You Series.
Prod-COOPED Dist-AITECH Prodn-WHATV 1978

Who Needs Math C 15 MIN
2 INCH VIDEOTAPE J-H
Explains that the ability to handle fundamental math is a real help in any job. Discusses jobs that require varying degrees of math proficiency.
From The Work Is For Real Series.
Prod-STETVC Dist-GPITVL

Who Needs Meat C 26 MIN
16MM FILM, 3/4 OR 1/2 IN VIDEO H-C A
Explains that the key to good health is balanced nutrition and tells how a vegetarian diet can be a healthful one, providing it is nutritionally balanced.
LC NO. 80-706008
Prod-WNETTV Dist-FI 1979

Who Needs Rules C 11 MIN
16MM FILM, 3/4 OR 1/2 IN VIDEO I-J
Presents a montage ranging from the simple everyday rules of getting along to more complex rules of federal law.
Prod-EBEC Dist-EBEC 1971

Who Needs Statistics? C
3/4 OR 1/2 INCH VIDEO CASSETTE IND
Discusses some of the applications of statistics and how they can be used at all management levels.
From The Statistics For Managers Series.
Prod-COLOSU Dist-COLOSU

Who Owns Schools (And What Are They Doing About It) C 34 MIN
16MM FILM OPTICAL SOUND
Discusses power and responsibility in education. Contrasts mass media portrayals of critical issues in education with the work of teachers who take their jobs seriously.
LC NO. 80-700883
Prod-CANCAE Dist-TASCOR 1979

Who Protects The Consumer C 60 MIN
16MM FILM, 3/4 OR 1/2 IN VIDEO H-C A
Presents Dr Milton Friedman contending that government regulation of industry fails to serve the best interests of consumers. Follows with a debate between Dr Friedman and others who both agree and disagree with his views.
From The Free To Choose Series.
Prod-EBEC Dist-EBEC 1983

Who Protects The Consumer C 85 MIN
3/4 OR 1/2 INCH VIDEO CASSETTE C
Features economist Milton Friedman discussing the consumer advocacy movement. Points out that international competition of free trade is perhaps the best source of protection for the consumer.
From The Milton Friedman Speaking Series. Lecture 12
LC NO. 79-708072
Prod-HBJ Dist-HBJ Prodn-WQLN 1980

Who Protects The Consumer (Discussion) C 30 MIN
16MM FILM, 3/4 OR 1/2 IN VIDEO H-C A
Offers a debate between Dr Milton Friedman and others on whether government regulation fails to serve the best interests of consumers.
From The Free To Choose (Discussion) Series.
Prod-EBEC Dist-EBEC 1983

Who Protects The Consumer (Documentary) C 30 MIN
16MM FILM, 3/4 OR 1/2 IN VIDEO H-C A
Presents Dr Milton Friedman contending that government regulation of industry fails to serve the best interests of consumers.
From The Free To Choose (Documentary) Series.
Prod-EBEC Dist-EBEC 1983

Who Protects The Worker C 60 MIN
16MM FILM, 3/4 OR 1/2 IN VIDEO H-C A
Presents Dr Milton Friedman demonstrating the ways in which a free labor market, without restrictions of trade unions, can spur business growth and create new jobs. Offers a debate between Dr Friedman and others who both agree and disagree with his views.
From The Free To Choose Series.
Prod-EBEC Dist-EBEC 1983

Who Protects The Worker C 82 MIN
3/4 OR 1/2 INCH VIDEO CASSETTE C
Records economist Milton Friedman discussing the protection of American workers. Looks at labor laws, unions, and government efforts. Concludes that the real way to protect workers is to preserve a free, competitive labor market.
From The Milton Friedman Speaking Series. Lecture 13
LC NO. 79-708073
Prod-HBJ Dist-HBJ Prodn-WQLN 1980

Who Protects The Worker (Discussion) C 30 MIN
16MM FILM, 3/4 OR 1/2 IN VIDEO H-C A
Presents a debate between Dr Milton Friedman and others on whether a free labor market, without restrictions of trade unions, can spur business growth and create new jobs.
From The Free To Choose (Discussion) Series.
Prod-EBEC Dist-EBEC 1983

Who Protects The Worker (Documentary) C 30 MIN
16MM FILM, 3/4 OR 1/2 IN VIDEO H-C A
Presents Dr Milton Friedman demonstrating the ways in which a free labor market, without restrictions of trade unions, can spur business growth and create new jobs.
From The Free To Choose (Documentary) Series.
Prod-EBEC Dist-EBEC 1983

Who Roared C 10 MIN
16MM FILM OPTICAL SOUND
Points out that everyone needs at least one thing in which they are both competent and recognized as being competent. Features a giant bird who tells the story of a boy who had been without confidence in himself but discovered that a goal and a determined effort will produce the desired results.
LC NO. 79-701649
Prod-ECI Dist-ECI

Who Runs Congress - Who Runs Congress / Varieties Of Leadership, Pt 1 C 30 MIN
3/4 OR 1/2 INCH VIDEO CASSETTE
Examines several alternative sources of leadership within Congress.
From The Congress - We The People Series.
Prod-WETATV Dist-FI 1984

Who Runs Congress - Who Runs Congress / Varieties Of Leadership, Pt 2 C 30 MIN
3/4 OR 1/2 INCH VIDEO CASSETTE
Examines several alternative sources of leadership within Congress.
From The Congress - We The People Series.
Prod-WETATV Dist-FI 1984

Who Said Today's Kids Don't Have Feelings C 15 MIN
3/4 OR 1/2 INCH VIDEO CASSETTE J-C A
See series title for descriptive statement.
From The Poetry Alive Series.
Prod-CMSS Dist-AITECH 1978

Who Says C 15 MIN
2 INCH VIDEOTAPE J
Shows a seventh way of developing a topic sentence by listing opinions.
From The From Me To You...In Writing, Pt 2 Series.
Prod-DELE Dist-GPITVL

Who Serves In Congress - A Variety Of Voices / Who Serves In Congress, Pt 1 C 30 MIN
3/4 OR 1/2 INCH VIDEO CASSETTE
Explores characteristics of the members of Congress how representative or unrepresentative they are of the American people and why they seek office.
From The Congress - We The People Series.
Prod-WETATV Dist-FI 1984

Who Serves In Congress - A Variety Of Voices / Who Serves In Congress, Pt 2 C 30 MIN
3/4 OR 1/2 INCH VIDEO CASSETTE
Explores characteristics of the members of Congress how representative or unrepresentative they are of the American people and why they seek office.
From The Congress - We The People Series.
Prod-WETATV Dist-FI 1984

Who Sets Your Standards X 30 MIN
16MM FILM OPTICAL SOUND J-H T R
The Harrison family spends a week together in an isolated mountain cabin. This becomes a time of selfexamination as they discover and evalute the pressures that influence their standards.
LC NO. FIA67-5757
Prod-FAMF Dist-FAMF 1967

Who Shall Live And Who Shall Die B 90 MIN
16MM FILM OPTICAL SOUND
Tells the story of the American response to the Holocaust. Includes interviews with government officials, Jewish leaders and concentration camp survivors combined with newsreel footage.
LC NO. 82-700289
Prod-BLULIT Dist-BLULIT 1982

Who Shot Alexander Hamilton B 60 MIN
16MM FILM, 3/4 OR 1/2 IN VIDEO
Provides an in-depth look at the Congress of the United States during a time when Congress was dealing with funding for the Vietnam War, Watergate and impeachment proceedings against President Nixon.
Prod-NEWTIM Dist-NEWTIM

Who Should Survive C 10 MIN
16MM FILM OPTICAL SOUND
Focuses on ethical questions which arise from the increasing effectiveness of modern medicine. Describes the case of a mongoloid child, who was born with an intestinal abnormality. Explains that modern medicine could correct the fatal condition, but that the parents refused permission for surgery because they did not want the mentally retarded child to live.
LC NO. 72-700488
Prod-KENJPF Dist-KENJPF 1972

Who Sold You This, Then C 22 MIN
3/4 OR 1/2 INCH VIDEO CASSETTE
Shows how to be the company's best ambassador when dealing with a customer who is unhappy.
Prod-VIDART Dist-VISUCP

Who Sold You This, Theo? C 23 MIN
3/4 OR 1/2 INCH VIDEO CASSETTE A
Highlights the role of the service representative in ensuring continued good relations between customers and businesses. Shows how service representatives can make or wreck business relationships.
Prod-XICOM Dist-XICOM

Who Speaks For Earth C 60 MIN
16MM FILM, 3/4 OR 1/2 IN VIDEO J-C A
Reviews highlights from the first 12 episodes of the Cosmos series. Weaves together the ideas of cosmic evolution, the scientific approach, history as an exemplary teacher, and the limitedness of human perception. Presents cautionary warnings about the future mankind faces as a species and as a planet. Based on the book Cosmos by Carl Sagan. Narrated by Carl Sagan.
From The Cosmos Series. Program 13
LC NO. 81-706730
Prod-KCET Dist-FI 1980

Who Spooked Rodney? C 24 MIN
3/4 OR 1/2 INCH VIDEO CASSETTE
Tells the comic story of Halloween and a young boy who allows himself to be overrun by superstition.
From The Young People's Specials Series.
Prod-MULTPP Dist-MULTPP

Who Stole The Quiet Day (2nd Ed) C 18 MIN
16MM FILM, 3/4 OR 1/2 IN VIDEO I-C A
Presents an evaluation of the noise pollution problem and how people are affected by it both physically and psychologically. Demonstrates, with the help of leading medical authorities, how loud sound destroys the nerve cells within ears and how young people can begin the deterioration process through thoughtless exposure to loud noises.
LC NO. 83-707049
Prod-HIGGIN Dist-HIGGIN 1984

Who Takes Care Of Us B 15 MIN
2 INCH VIDEOTAPE P

Describes the universal interrelationship of family members and the importance of the mother. (Broadcast quality)
From The Around The Corner Series. No. 2
Prod-FWCETV Dist-GPITVL Prodn-WEDUTV

Who Thinks Creatively C 15 MIN
2 INCH VIDEOTAPE I
Presents a problem - what should be done with a huge stone rabbit 100 feet tall and 200 feet long, the object found during construction of a super highway.
From The Images Series.
Prod-CVETVC Dist-GPITVL

Who Took The Farmer's Hat C 15 MIN
3/4 OR 1/2 INCH VIDEO CASSETTE K-P
Recounts what happens when a farmer asks the animals to help him find his old brown hat. Emphasizes the letter blend br.
From The Words And Pictures Series.
Prod-FI Dist-FI

Who Wants America Ugly C 8 MIN
16MM FILM, 3/4 OR 1/2 IN VIDEO P-I
Follows a group of school children as they examine their community and see visual pollution in ugly signs, litter, sidewalk graffiti, bad planning and poor use of open space. Shows that in their classroom, they construct a model community planned to eliminate these abuses and to bring trees and grass into the community center.
From The Caring About Our Community Series.
Prod-GORKER Dist-AIMS 1973

Who Wants To Be A Hero C 28 MIN
16MM FILM, 3/4 OR 1/2 IN VIDEO I-H
Examines involvement vs non-involvement through the story of Jason, who becomes a hero when he apprehends the thugs who mugged the school janitor. Shows that conflict and trouble set in as he and his mother are threatened when he must testify against the thugs. Based on the book Who Wants To Be A Hero by Robert E Rubinstein.
Prod-LCOA Dist-LCOA Prodn-LYONS 1981

Who Wants To Play God? C 21 MIN
3/4 OR 1/2 INCH VIDEO CASSETTE A
Teaches methods for performance review. Emphasizes positive reinforcement. Shows through a fictionalized situation the five essential elements of an effective performance interview.
Prod-AMEDIA Dist-AMEDIA

Who Wants Unions C 27 MIN
16MM FILM, 3/4 OR 1/2 IN VIDEO
Discusses the pros and cons of unions, including opposing views on why they have declined so drastically in North America. Includes the views of both labor and management.
Prod-NFBC Dist-CRMP

Who Was Jack Carrington-Smith C 22 MIN
16MM FILM OPTICAL SOUND
Presents the life and work of noted artist, teacher and Archibald Prize winner Jack Carrington-Smith. Features reminiscences by his friends and family.
LC NO. 80-700938
Prod-TASCOR Dist-TASCOR 1976

Who We Are—A Series
16MM FILM, 3/4 OR 1/2 IN VIDEO
Examines children's attitudes toward the physical and racial differences between people.
Prod-KORTY Dist-PFP

Are People All The Same	9 MIN
Is It OK To Be Me	6 MIN
What Color Is Skin	9 MIN
What Makes Me Different	9 MIN

Who Were The Ones C 7 MIN
16MM FILM, 3/4 OR 1/2 IN VIDEO H-C A
Presents an Indian's song of protest, expressive of the bitter memories of the past, still alive today. Views North American history as seen from the view of the Indians.
Prod-NFBC Dist-FI 1973

Who Will Be The Teacher C 16 MIN
16MM FILM, 3/4 OR 1/2 IN VIDEO I
Confronts the increasing problem of violence directed against teachers. Tells that in order to join a gang, Terry assaults his teacher. Shows him gradually realizing that this was really an act of cowardice and developing a new respect for his teacher.
From The Learning Laws - Respect For Yourself, Others And The Law Series.
Prod-WDEMCO Dist-WDEMCO 1982

Who Will Help You Start Your Venture? C 20 MIN
16MM FILM, 3/4 OR 1/2 IN VIDEO H-C A
Explores assistance needed by and avilable to starting business entrepreneurs. Lists help sources and presents creative methods of getting information and evaluating assistance.
From The Starting A Business Series.
Prod-SOMFIL Dist-BCNFL 1983

Who Will Your Customers Be? C 18 MIN
16MM FILM, 3/4 OR 1/2 IN VIDEO H-C A
Shows that market research clarifies the goals of a business, forming the basis for almost all other planning.
From The Starting A Business Series.
Prod-SOMFIL Dist-BCNFL 1982

Who Wins (Morality) C 15 MIN
16MM FILM, 3/4 OR 1/2 IN VIDEO J
Presents a situation in which a decision must be made concerning cheating.
From The Self Incorporated Series.
LC NO. 75-703959
Prod-AITV Dist-AITECH Prodn-NVETA 1975

Who Won World War II C 26 MIN
3/4 OR 1/2 INCH VIDEO CASSETTE H-C A
Presents distinguished American historian Stephen Ambrose, analyzing the consequences of World War II from the perspective of history, arriving at provocative conclusions regarding the effects of world leader's personalities, politics, economics and national characters.
From The World At War Specials Series.
Prod-THAMES Dist-MEDIAG 1974

Who Works At The Zoo C 15 MIN
3/4 OR 1/2 INCH VIDEO CASSETTE P-I
Outlines the varied duties of zoo workers, including the doctor and the keepers.
From The Zoo Zoo Zoo Series.
Prod-WCETTV Dist-AITECH 1981

Who-Ho-Ray, No. 1 And 2 C 20 MIN
16MM FILM OPTICAL SOUND
Deals with two studies using the analog computer as a graphic source for visual astronics and image manipulation.
Prod-VANBKS Dist-VANBKS

Who, Me C 14 MIN
16MM FILM MAGNETIC SOUND IND
Simulates situations in which store employees' carelessness or failure to follow established procedures causes loss of merchandise or discrepancies in records. Establishes the role of each employee as an error controller and an error detector.
From The Positive Shortage Prevention Series.
LC NO. 77-702198
Prod-SAUM Dist-SAUM Prodn-CALVIN 1972

Who, Me C 20 MIN
16MM FILM OPTICAL SOUND H-C
Describes the risks of cigarette smoking. Introduces fouir ex-smokers who explain how they gave up smoking. Points out the need for parents to present a good example for their children.
Prod-AUDIO Dist-AMCS 1965

Who, What And Why Of Authority, The C 29 MIN
16MM FILM, 3/4 OR 1/2 IN VIDEO
Presents a compilation of views by leading authorities on discipline regarding power, responsibility, control and rules specifically as they relate to authority, what it is, who has it and why. Explains the concept of natural authority and the conclusion that potentially, in one way or another, teachers will gain authority.
From The Human Relations And School Discipline Series.
Prod-MFFD Dist-FI

Who, What, When, Where And Why C 15 MIN
3/4 OR 1/2 INCH VIDEO CASSETTE P
Employs a magician named Amazing Alexander and his assistants to explore the use of the five W's in writing.
From The Magic Shop Series. No. 14
LC NO. 83-706159
Prod-CVETVC Dist-GPITVL Prodn-WCVETV 1982

Who'll Save Our Children C 96 MIN
3/4 OR 1/2 INCH VIDEO CASSETTE H-C A
Describes what happens when Marjory and Tommy Garver are abandoned by their parents and are literally dumped on the doorstep of the Lavers, a middle-aged, childless couple. Shows what happens when the Lavers must fight for the children when the natural parents attempt to reclaim them. Stars Shirley Jones and Len Cariou. Based on the book WHO'LL SAVE OUR CHILDREN by Rachel Maddux.
Prod-TIMLIF Dist-TIMLIF 1982

Who's Afraid Of Opera—A Series
16MM FILM, 3/4 OR 1/2 IN VIDEO J-C A
Prod-PHENIX Dist-PHENIX 1973

Barber Of Seville, The	30 MIN
Daughter Of The Regiment	30 MIN
Faust	30 MIN
La Pericole	30 MIN
La Traviata	30 MIN
Lucia Di Lammermoor	30 MIN
Mignon	30 MIN
Rigoletto	30 MIN

Who's Building Character? B 15 MIN
16MM FILM OPTICAL SOUND
Presents new understanding for parents and teachers about how the home and the school can best cooperate to instill a sense of responsibility in children.
Prod-CONCOR Dist-CPH

Who's Caring C 22 MIN
3/4 OR 1/2 INCH VIDEO CASSETTE
Studies the critical shortage of day-care facilities in the Twin Cities.
Prod-WCCOTV Dist-WCCOTV 1981

Who's Doing It? Sexual Attitudes In America C 13 MIN
3/4 OR 1/2 INCH VIDEO CASSETTE C A
Explores current sexual attitudes in America. Combines animation and live interviews with people of all ages.
Prod-MMRC Dist-MMRC

Who's First, You're Next C 29 MIN
3/4 OR 1/2 INCH VIDEO CASSETTE
Offers ideas and expert commentary on several situations encountered at the library reference desk.
Prod-BCPL Dist-LVN

Who's For Tennis C 7 MIN
16MM FILM OPTICAL SOUND J-C A
Evaluates the condition of tennis in Australia, and discusses the wide popularity of the game and its future prospects.
LC NO. 77-709230
Prod-ANAIB Dist-AUIS 1969

Who's Gonna Collect The Garbage C 44 MIN
16MM FILM - 3/4 IN VIDEO IND
Discusses the various segments of the work force, their problems and how they can be handled.
From The Managing Discontinuity Series.
Prod-BNA Dist-BNA

Who's In Charge C 15 MIN
3/4 OR 1/2 INCH VIDEO CASSETTE I-J
Discusses government as an institution established by groups of people for themselves.
From The It's All Up To You Series.
Prod-COOPED Dist-AITECH Prodn-WHATV 1978

Who's In Charge Here? C 15 MIN
16MM FILM OPTICAL SOUND
Focuses on a group of defense workers in unrehearsed conversation about their jobs, the economy and national security. Considers the relationship of military spending to national security, job security and the quality of life in the United States. Narrated by Eli Wallach.
Prod-IAM Dist-IWO 1980

Who's In Charge Of Lincoln And The Lucky Stone C 14 MIN
3/4 OR 1/2 INCH VIDEO CASSETTE P-I
Introduces two stories, the first about a man's adventures involving a sack of stolen money and the second about a lucky stone which provides good fortune for its various owners. Based on the books Who's In Charge Of Lincoln by Dale Fife and The Lucky Stone by Lucille Clifton.
From The Readit Series.
LC NO. 83-706833
Prod-POSIMP Dist-AITECH 1982

Who's In Charge? C 24 MIN
3/4 OR 1/2 INCH VIDEO CASSETTE
Focuses on the problems of a newly promoted foreman under the pressure of three challenges, communicating an unwelcome management decision, handling a breach of discipline and facing an attack on his authority.
Prod-VISUCP Dist-VISUCP

Who's In Charge? - Confrontation Handling For Supervisors And Managers C 23 MIN
3/4 OR 1/2 INCH VIDEO CASSETTE A
Shows the right way and the wrong way for a manager to handle challenges to his authority. Treats direct attacks on managerial authority, getting a group to do what it is opposed to doing and breaches of discipline.
Prod-XICOM Dist-XICOM

Who's Keeping Score - Documentary C 59 MIN
3/4 OR 1/2 INCH VIDEO CASSETTE
Discusses the minimum competency testing for reading, writing and math, and the questions and objections that have been raised. Hosted by Mike Farrell.
From The Who's Keeping Score Series.
Prod-USDHEW Dist-USNAC 1981

Who's Keeping Score - Hearing Day 1 C 59 MIN
3/4 OR 1/2 INCH VIDEO CASSETTE
Presents a summary of the first day of hearings held to discuss minimum competency testing and its benefits or harmful effects on students, curricula, teaching and public perception of educational quality. Commentary by Mike Farrell.
From The Who's Keeping Score Series.
LC NO. 82-706626
Prod-USDHEW Dist-USNAC

Who's Keeping Score - Hearing Day 2 C 59 MIN
3/4 OR 1/2 INCH VIDEO CASSETTE
Presents a summary of the second day of hearings held to discuss minimum competency testing and its benefits or harmful effects on students, curricula, teaching and public perception of educational quality. Commentary by Mike Farrell.
From The Who's Keeping Score Series.
Prod-USDHEW Dist-USNAC

Who's Keeping Score - Hearing Day 3 C 59 MIN
3/4 OR 1/2 INCH VIDEO CASSETTE
Presents a summary of the third day of hearings held to discuss minimum competency testing and its benefits or harmful effects on students, curricula, teaching and public perception of educational quality. Commentary by Mike Farrell.
From The Who's Keeping Score Series.
Prod-USDHEW Dist-USNAC

Who's Keeping Score—A Series

Discusses minimum competency testing in high schools.
Prod-USDHEW Dist-USNAC

Who's Keeping Score - Documentary	059 MIN
Who's Keeping Score - Hearing Day 1	059 MIN
Who's Keeping Score - Hearing Day 2	059 MIN
Who's Keeping Score - Hearing Day 3	059 MIN

Who's On First C 14 MIN
16MM FILM OPTICAL SOUND J-C A
Questions the stereotype of girls as non-athletic as seen through the eyes of members of a women's softball team on a nine-game winning streak.
Prod-JBFL Dist-JBFL 1975

Who's Out There C
16MM FILM, 3/4 OR 1/2 IN VIDEO
Presents Nobel Prize winning scientists who conduct an exploration of life in outer space. Narrated by Orson Welles.
Prod-DREWAS Dist-DIRECT 1973

Who's Out There C 28 MIN
16MM FILM - 3/4 IN VIDEO I
Explores the new view of extraterrestrial life now emerging from

the results of probes to the planets. Discusses the conclusion of a number of distinguished scientists that other intelligent civilizations exist in the universe. Narrated by Orson Welles.
LC NO. 77-706032
Prod-NASA Dist-USNAC Prodn-DREW 1975

Who's Out There Listening C 15 MIN
3/4 OR 1/2 INCH VIDEO CASSETTE J-H
Explains how the effectiveness of radio and television programming is determined.
From The Broadcasting Series.
Prod-CTI Dist-CTI

Who's Out There? C 30 MIN
3/4 OR 1/2 INCH VIDEO CASSETTE
Presents interviews by Orson Welles with his original 'War of Worlds' radio audience and the latest prognostications of other life within the universe.
From The Reaching For The Stars, And Life Beyond Earth Series.
Prod-IVCH Dist-IVCH

Who's Responsible C 12 MIN
16MM FILM, 3/4 OR 1/2 IN VIDEO T
Attempts to show how to recognize and eliminate negative attitudes about responsibility by telling the story of a worker who becomes a scapegoat when things go wrong at the office.
LC NO. 84-706031
Prod-VISF Dist-EBEC 1983

Who's That Knocking At My Door B 90 MIN
16MM FILM, 3/4 OR 1/2 IN VIDEO
Presents a motion picture directed by Martin Scorsese and starring Zina Bethune and Harvey Keitel.
Prod-SCOM Dist-DIRECT 1968

Who's The Cleanest C 7 MIN
16MM FILM, 3/4 OR 1/2 IN VIDEO I
Tells the story of Little Dog and his friend Kitten as they become involved with a duck playing in a mudhole and a cow with brown spots on her side.
From The Little Dog Series.
LC NO. 84-707089
Prod-KRATKY Dist-PHENIX 1983

Who's There For The Victim C 22 MIN
16MM FILM, 3/4 OR 1/2 IN VIDEO A
Demonstrates how the Rape Victim Advocates serve the special needs of the rape victim. Shows the advocates offering immediate emotional and informational support as well as interacting with medical personnel, police and family members.
Prod-WTTWTV Dist-MTI 1981

Who's To Blame C 10 MIN
16MM FILM OPTICAL SOUND I-H A
Explains the concepts of defensive driving.
From The Techniques Of Defensive Driving Film Series.
Prod-NSC Dist-NSC

Who's To Blame C 59 MIN
3/4 OR 1/2 INCH VIDEO CASSETTE
Deals with the issue of sexual abuse of children. Shows three interview sessions with a client who is seeking help with family problems. Shows the client's fears about therapy and her self-doubts in the face of problems.
From The Child Welfare Training Tapes Series.
Prod-OHIOSU Dist-UWISC 1980

Who's Who In The Ocean C 24 MIN
16MM FILM, 3/4 OR 1/2 IN VIDEO
Illustrates the diversity of organisms present in the oceans of the world by showing characteristic species of plants and animals from different habitats. Uses film taken from the Danish vessel Galathea during a 1950 round-the-world expedition to study the fauna of deep oceans.
Prod-OPENU Dist-MEDIAG Prodn-BBCTV 1979

Who's Who In The Zoo C 12 MIN
16MM FILM, 3/4 OR 1/2 IN VIDEO P-I
Introduces various careers involving zoo animal care.
Prod-CENTRO Dist-CORF

Whole Bag, The B 20 MIN
16MM FILM OPTICAL SOUND H-C A
Contrasts life patterns, attitudes and goals of America's Black and white youth.
LC NO. 78-700715
Prod-PSU Dist-PSU Prodn-HORNBG 1969

Whole Body Manual C 17 MIN
16MM FILM, 3/4 OR 1/2 IN VIDEO J-C
Uses a magazine format in presenting messages on the human body's many abilities, the four food groups and the importance of a balanced diet and physical exercise.
Prod-INST Dist-PEREN Prodn-PENWAT 1977

Whole Grains C 3 MIN
16MM FILM - 3/4 IN VIDEO
Suggests a variety of grains to use as a potato substitute, including brown rice, unpearled barley, millet, bulgar and buckwheat. Shows how they may be cooked in a variety of fluids and served as side dishes, salads and breakfast foods.
From The Beatrice Trum Hunter's Natural Foods Series.
Prod-WGBH Dist-PUBTEL 1974

Whole Lot Proud, A C 25 MIN
16MM FILM OPTICAL SOUND
Looks at the duties of park rangers who work in the rugged hills of South Dakota and the sprawling beauty of Tennessee.
Prod-USAE Dist-MTP

Whole Meal Salads C 30 MIN
1/2 IN VIDEO CASSETTE BETA/VHS
Demonstrates how to prepare whole meal salads. Includes broccoli and chicken salad, spaghetti salad with shrimp and pea salad with bacon.
From The Frugal Gourmet Series.
Prod-WTTWTV Dist-MTI

Whole New Ball Game, A C 9 MIN
16MM FILM, 3/4 OR 1/2 IN VIDEO I-J
Shows five youngsters playing tackle together to point out changes in boy-girl relationships that inevitably come with adolescence. Re-examines male-female roles in our rapidly changing society.
Prod-KINGSP Dist-PHENIX

Whole New Image, A C 15 MIN
16MM FILM, 3/4 OR 1/2 IN VIDEO H-C A
Presents information about the uniform industry, covering the relative merits of buying or renting, which uniform fabrics are best for comfort, laundering, color and shrinkage suitability, damage resistance and strength.
Prod-KLEINW Dist-KLEINW

Whole Number (Spanish) C 12 MIN
3/4 OR 1/2 INCH VIDEO CASSETTE
Covers numbers and numerals, decimal system, positive and negative numbers.
From The Using Mathematics In The Plant Series.
Prod-TPCTRA Dist-TPCTRA

Whole Numbers C 30 MIN
16MM FILM OPTICAL SOUND T
Studies whole numbers, and examines various other numeration systems. To be used following 'PRE-NUMBER IDEAS.'
From The Mathematics For Elementary School Teachers Series. No. 2
Prod-SMSG Dist-MLA 1963

Whole Numbers C 10 MIN
3/4 OR 1/2 INCH VIDEO CASSETTE IND
Explains addition, subtraction, multiplication and divisions. Includes fractions.
From The Basic Shop Math Series.
Prod-LEIKID Dist-LEIKID

Whole Numbers C 12 MIN
3/4 OR 1/2 INCH VIDEO CASSETTE
Covers numbers and numerals, decimal system, positive and negative numbers.
From The Using Mathematics In The Plant Series.
Prod-TPCTRA Dist-TPCTRA

Whole Numbers And Fractions C
3/4 OR 1/2 INCH VIDEO CASSETTE
See series title for descriptive statement.
From The Basic Shop Math Series.
Prod-VTRI Dist-VTRI

Whole Numbers And Fractions C 15 MIN
3/4 OR 1/2 INCH VIDEO CASSETTE IND
See series title for descriptive statement.
From The Basic Shop Math Series.
Prod-ICSINT Dist-ICSINT

Whole Numbers And Fractions (Spanish) C
3/4 OR 1/2 INCH VIDEO CASSETTE
See series title for descriptive statement.
From The Basic Shop Math (Spanish) Series.
Prod-VTRI Dist-VTRI

Whole Picture, The C 10 MIN
3/4 INCH VIDEO CASSETTE J-C
Tells how a local council commissions an artist to create murals in an inner city park and beside an inner city road. Shows how the artist works with unemployed and inexperienced people as assistants.
LC NO. 81-706502
Prod-SYDUN Dist-TASCOR 1980

Whole Shootin' Match, The B 108 MIN
16MM FILM - 3/4 IN VIDEO C A
Depicts the rags-to-riches-to-rags story of two 'good ole boys' from America's heartland. Delivers with keen insight, what most of us undergo in 'making it' in America.
Prod-FIRS Dist-FIRS

Whole Town's Talking, The B 86 MIN
16MM FILM OPTICAL SOUND
Relates the story of a timid little clerk who is mistaken for Public Enemy Number One. Stars Edward G Robinson, Jean Arthur and Wallace Ford. Directed by John Ford.
Prod-CPC Dist-TWYMAN 1935

Whole Truth, The C 18 MIN
3/4 INCH VIDEO CASSETTE H-C A
Centers around a man who believes he has been wrongfully ticketed for a traffic violation. Discusses aspects of justice and truth.
Prod-CHERIO Dist-GPITVL 1977

Whole World Is Watching, The C 18 MIN
16MM FILM OPTICAL SOUND H-C A
Combines sounds of rock music, excerpts from various speeches and scenes of the violence and disorder that occurred during the 1968 Democratic National Convention in Chicago to outline the major events and to characterize some of the major attitudes and forces at work there.
LC NO. 72-700399
Prod-MMA Dist-MMA 1969

Whole World Is Watching, The C 28 MIN
16MM FILM OPTICAL SOUND
Presents footage of the 1971 May Day spring offensive in Washington, D C, explores the motives of those who want to stop the work of the government and examines the response of the government.
LC NO. 71-715449
Prod-IACP Dist-IACP 1972

Whole World Is Watching, The B 55 MIN
16MM FILM OPTICAL SOUND H-C A
Discusses the question of bias in television new-casting with the help of David Brinkley, Walter Cronkite and critics such as Senator John O Pastore and John Fischer. Shows that a person who is completely objective would be a vegetable and that what is strived for is fairness, not simply objectivity. Discusses television coverage of the 1968 Democratic National Convention and the restraints upon television such as how advertising may influence what news is broadcast.
From The Public Broadcast Laboratory Series.
LC NO. 77-703087
Prod-NET Dist-IU 1969

Wholesalers And Distributors C 30 MIN
3/4 OR 1/2 INCH VIDEO CASSETTE
Covers marketing activities performed by wholesalers, the importance of merchandise selection by the wholesaler and the role of the industrial distributor.
From The Marketing Perspectives Series.
Prod-MATC Dist-WFVTAE

Wholly Cow C 11 MIN
16MM FILM OPTICAL SOUND
Uses animation and live action to illustrate how food is processed in a cow's four stomachs, how nutrients absorbed from the digestive tract are converted to milk and the role of the udder.
LC NO. 75-700165
Prod-NDC Dist-NDC Prodn-CATFSH 1975

Whose Child Is This C 28 MIN
16MM FILM, 3/4 OR 1/2 IN VIDEO H-C A
Presents a dramatization about a teacher who discovers one of her students is being physically abused by his father. Shows the legal steps which result when the teacher reports her discovery.
Prod-JRLLK Dist-LCOA Prodn-SHANDA 1979

Whose Neighborhood Is This C 20 MIN
16MM FILM, 3/4 OR 1/2 IN VIDEO
Looks at neighborhood crimes from the perspectives of the victim, the criminal and the police. Shows a variety of neighborhoods reacting to the problem.
Prod-MITCHG Dist-MTI

Whose Problem Is It C 25 MIN
16MM FILM, 3/4 OR 1/2 IN VIDEO A
Looks at the high cost which substance abuse extracts from American productivity. Deals with individual recognition of the problem, the effects of substance abuse on the individual and his job, role of the supervisor in problem identification and how friends can help bring abuse to the surface.
LC NO. 83-706913
Prod-OLINC Dist-MTI 1982

Whose Right To Bear Arms C 59 MIN
16MM FILM OPTICAL SOUND
Discusses gun control legislation and the success of lobbying efforts in the United States. Includes interviews with senators Edward Kennedy, Thomas Dodd and Roman Hruska, and with Franklin Orth, executive director of the National Rifle Association.
LC NO. 77-713329
Prod-NBCTV Dist-NBC 1967

Whose Shoes C 3 MIN
16MM FILM, 3/4 OR 1/2 IN VIDEO K-I
Presents situations involving children making decisions. Discusses alternatives and what might have happened in each instance.
From The Magic Moments, Unit 1 - Let's Talk Series.
Prod-EBEC Dist-EBEC 1969

Whose Standard English C 24 MIN
16MM FILM, 3/4 OR 1/2 IN VIDEO T
Focuses on the sensitivity and special skills required in teaching textbook English to dialect-speaking children.
Prod-GREAVW Dist-GREAVW 1975

Why C 30 MIN
3/4 OR 1/2 INCH VIDEO CASSETTE
Examines the need for a will, the realities, estate administration and mysteries of probate.
From The This Is My Will Series.
Prod-WMHTTV Dist-PBS 1983

Why A City C 15 MIN
2 INCH VIDEOTAPE
Explores the reasons why people live together and why a specific area is picked for a community.
From The Let's Build A City Series.
Prod-WVIZTV Dist-GPITVL

Why A Newspaper C 15 MIN
3/4 OR 1/2 INCH VIDEO CASSETTE J-H
Shows how newspapers meet the needs of the public.
From The Newspaper - Behind The Lines Series.
Prod-CTI Dist-CTI

Why A United Jerusalem C
16MM FILM OPTICAL SOUND
Features Teddy Kollek, the mayor of the city of Jerusalem, who tells why he is opposed to Jerusalem's internationalization and why it must never again be divided.
From The Dateline Israel, 1973 Series.
Prod-ADL Dist-ADL

Why African Heritage C 30 MIN
3/4 OR 1/2 INCH VIDEO CASSETTE C
Discusses the importance of the African heritage to black Americans.

From The Afro-American Perspectives Series.
Prod-MDDE Dist-MDCPB

Why Algorithms B
16MM FILM OPTICAL SOUND
Examines the necessity for algorithms and discusses their salient characteristics.
Prod-OPENU Dist-OPENU

Why Am I Here C 9 MIN
16MM FILM - 3/4 IN VIDEO
Tells about a man who was hospitalized for stomach problems and was referred to the dental service for an oral examination. Emphasizes the importance of early detection of cancer of the mouth. Issued in 1968 as a motion picture.
LC NO. 78-706245
Prod-USVA Dist-USNAC Prodn-DTC 1978

Why America Burns C 57 MIN
16MM FILM, 3/4 OR 1/2 IN VIDEO H-C A
Looks at why America has more fire-caused deaths than any other industrialized country. Documents how fast certain plastics catch fire, why modern high-rise buildings become towering infernos and how fire caused by cigarettes claims more than 2,000 lives annually.
From The Nova Series.
Prod-WGBHTV Dist-TIMLIF 1982

Why And How Of Standard First Aid, The B 28 MIN
16MM FILM OPTICAL SOUND
A film based on the Red Cross standard first aid course and designed to develop good safety attitudes. Describes the first aid skills used in caring for victims of accidents and sudden illness.
From The Red Cross First Aid Course. No. 1
LC NO. FIA66-798
Prod-AMRC Dist-AMRC Prodn-BYRNPR 1965

Why Animals Live Where They Do C 11 MIN
16MM FILM, 3/4 OR 1/2 IN VIDEO P
Explains how animals are suited to a particular environment by studying different animals in four envionments, woodpeckers, opossums and carpenter ants in a forest, prairie dogs, grasshoppers and meadowlarks in a grassland, lizards and snakes in a desert, and spoonbills, frogs and fish in a pond.
Prod-CORF Dist-CORF 1969

Why Appeasement C 20 MIN
16MM FILM, 3/4 OR 1/2 IN VIDEO H-C A
Describes the period in 1938 when Hitler demanded a portion of Czechoslovakia and Great Britain's Prime Minister Neville Chamberlain, eager to avoid war, gave him what he wanted. Tells how Germany absorbed all of Czechoslovakia and invaded Poland, leading to war with Britain.
From The Twentieth Century History Series.
Prod-BBCTV Dist-FI 1981

Why Appraise? C 8 MIN
3/4 OR 1/2 INCH VIDEO CASSETTE
Discusses the reasons why performance appraisal is so critical and shows that performance appraisal, when properly used, is an important and effective management tool.
From The Performance Appraisal Series. Module 1
Prod-RESEM Dist-RESEM

Why Are People Prejudiced C 30 MIN
2 INCH VIDEOTAPE I
Discusses the meaning of the concept of prejudice and shows the various ways in which prejudice can manifest itself.
From The That's A Good Question Series.
Prod-KGEDTV Dist-GPITVL

Why Are Some Houses Built On Stilts B 15 MIN
2 INCH VIDEOTAPE P
Explains the use of nearby materials when building shelters. Discusses a kind of shelter suitable for one climate is often not suitable for another. (Broadcast quality)
From The Around The Corner Series. No. 17
Prod-FWCETV Dist-GPITVL Prodn-WEDUTV

Why Are Team-Teaching And Non-Grading Important B 49 MIN
16MM FILM OPTICAL SOUND C T
Presents Dr Goodlad as he explains how team-teaching and non-grading help to bridge the gap between the problems of school organization and individual learning differences.
From The How To Provide Personalized Education In A Public School Series. No. 3
LC NO. 79-700100
Prod-SPF Dist-SPF 1966

Why Art C 29 MIN
16MM FILM OPTICAL SOUND
Studies the relationship between man and art.
LC NO. 76-703098
Prod-SBOE Dist-SBOE 1975

Why Ask Me C 30 MIN
2 INCH VIDEOTAPE I
Discusses the ethnic, sub-cultural, occupational and class differences present within the population of the United States.
From The That's A Good Question Series.
Prod-KGEDTV Dist-GPITVL

Why Bale Hay C 15 MIN
16MM FILM OPTICAL SOUND
Points out the advantages of handling hay as high moisture haylage rather than as baled hay. Presents proof of the higher nutritional value of haylage and the labor saving advantages of automating the handling and feeding of hay.
LC NO. 79-713576
Prod-VENARD Dist-VENARD 1971

Why Battery Should Always Be Clean B 6 MIN
16MM FILM OPTICAL SOUND
Demonstrates how to clean batteries to prevent engine failure. Shows how to wash with solution, wipe dry, check electrolyte level and grease terminals.
LC NO. 76-703893
Prod-USA Dist-USNAC 1955

Why Be Down When You Can Be Up C 16 MIN
16MM FILM, 3/4 OR 1/2 IN VIDEO J-H
Uses a blend of music and video techniques to present ideas on the use of marijuana by teenagers. Makes the point that there are a number of natural ways to feel good and it's up to each individual to discover what makes him happy or sad.
Prod-DANLSD Dist-MTI 1976

Why Be Physically Fit C 12 MIN
16MM FILM, 3/4 OR 1/2 IN VIDEO I
Shows how being physically fit can help a person have more energy, look better, feel better and cope with stress. Illustrates the effect physical fitness has on the heart, lungs, joints, tendons, muscular and cardio-respiratory systems.
From The Fun To Be Fit Series. Film 1
Prod-WDEMCO Dist-WDEMCO 1983

Why Bother C 15 MIN
16MM FILM, 3/4 OR 1/2 IN VIDEO I
Tells how Kelly learns that the more alternative sources she has for her report, the better.
From The Thinkabout Series. Finding Alternatives
LC NO. 81-706040
Prod-KOCETV Dist-AITECH 1979

Why Calibrate C 16 MIN
16MM FILM, 3/4 OR 1/2 IN VIDEO
Demonstrates the need for calibrating tests and monitoring equipment and shows how the U S Navy's calibration program is organized.
Prod-USN Dist-USNAC 1966

Why Can't I - Laws C 15 MIN
3/4 OR 1/2 INCH VIDEO CASSETTE P
Explains how laws protect the well-being of a community.
From The Two Cents' Worth Series.
Prod-WIEC Dist-AITECH Prodn-WHATV 1976

Why Can't I Learn C 51 MIN
16MM FILM, 3/4 OR 1/2 IN VIDEO
Explores the early symptoms of learning disabilities and the various forms of specialized instruction available to learning disabled children.
LC NO. 79-707446
Prod-MFFD Dist-FI 1979

Why Can't People Get Along And How Can A Person Not Be Prejudiced C 30 MIN
2 INCH VIDEOTAPE I
Focuses on various interpersonal relations and deals with the human problem of getting along with others of different race, color or creed.
From The That's A Good Question Series.
Prod-KGEDTV Dist-GPITVL

Why Can't You Hear Through The Noise In Your Ear C 60 MIN
16MM FILM - 3/4 IN VIDEO P A
Presents a music-rap session aimed at bringing the meaning of contemporary music into perspective for the adult generation. Elaborates on drugs, freedom to do one's own thing, the need to find excitement and meaning in life and the idea that institutions must be relevant or die.
From The Turned On Crisis Series.
Prod-WQED Dist-GPITVL

Why Communication Goes Wrong C 9 MIN
2 INCH VIDEOTAPE
Presents an instructional course for office employees. Helps identify and overcome six major barriers to successful communication. Includes a discussion of personal experiences confronting these barriers.
From The SUCCESS, The AMA Course For Office Employees Series.
LC NO. 75-704214
Prod-AMA Dist-AMA 1972

Why Competition - Market Structure C 15 MIN
3/4 OR 1/2 INCH VIDEO CASSETTE J-H
Explains that there is a monopoly on refreshments at school basketball games. Shows that Ira decides that competition will bring down prices, but finds that low prices may mean low profits. Deals with the concept of competition.
From The Give And Take Series. Pt 12
LC NO. 83-706308
Prod-AITV Dist-AITECH 1982

Why Creativity C 25 MIN
2 INCH VIDEOTAPE I
Shows creative expression in painting, sculpture, music and dramatics.
From The Art For Every Day Series.
Prod-CVETVC Dist-GPITVL

Why Did Gloria Die C 27 MIN
16MM FILM, 3/4 OR 1/2 IN VIDEO H-C A
Points out that the half-million Indians who are leaving reservations seeking a better life in the city are finding the white man's urban world alien and unfriendly. Traces the life of Gloria Curtis, a Chippewa who died of hepatitis at the age of 27, through several crises including unemployment, welfare, inadequate housing and poor medical care, in white-controlled Minneapolis, Minnesota. Features Don and Lucille Goodwin, also members of Minneapolis' Indian ghetto, who discuss how they were able to weather the painful period of adjustment from reservation to urban life.
LC NO. 80-707094
Prod-NET Dist-IU 1973

Why Did It Happen C 15 MIN
3/4 OR 1/2 INCH VIDEO CASSETTE P
Depicts the fight which ensues after school when Jason competes with Molly for Sara's friendship and attention. Shows that after knocking over a rack of books in the Library, Sam helps Molly figure out why she and Jason aren't getting along well.
From The Out And About Series.
Prod-STSU Dist-AITECH Prodn-WETN 1984

Why Did You Kiss Me Awake C 3 MIN
16MM FILM OPTICAL SOUND C A
Portrays only the initial movements of an imagined film drama, as the camera which is photographing the mirror image of a totally nude young woman is placed in a drawer, leaving us in total darkness through the rest of the film.
Prod-UWFKD Dist-UWFKD

Why Didn't Somebody Tell Me C 20 MIN
16MM FILM - 3/4 IN VIDEO
Presents the problem of bad manners in an office and discusses ways co-workers can reach a consensus on how to alert offenders. Features Hans Conreid.
Prod-BNA Dist-BNA 1980

Why Didn't You Tell Me? C 11 MIN
3/4 OR 1/2 INCH VIDEO CASSETTE C A
Shows a young women who finally gathers the courage to tell her lover that in six months together she has not had an orgasm.
Prod-MMRC Dist-MMRC

Why Discipline? C 10 MIN
3/4 OR 1/2 INCH VIDEO CASSETTE
Offers some of the reasons why discipline is necessary and what happens when it is absent from an organization. Points out some of the reasons why people don't like to discipline others and how to overcome these fears.
From The Productive Discipline Series. Module 1
Prod-RESEM Dist-RESEM

Why Do Animals Look Like They Do C 11 MIN
16MM FILM, 3/4 OR 1/2 IN VIDEO P-I
Discusses the processes of adaptation to environment and evolution of a species.
Prod-ALTSUL Dist-JOU 1978

Why Do Animals Look Like They Do (Captioned) C 11 MIN
16MM FILM, 3/4 OR 1/2 IN VIDEO P-I
Discusses the processes of adaptation to environment and evolution of a species.
Prod-ALTSUL Dist-JOU 1978

Why Do Birds Sing C 27 MIN
16MM FILM, 3/4 OR 1/2 IN VIDEO H-C A
Discusses the research that has been conducted to decipher the meaning of various types of birdsongs and to discover how fledglings learn adult birdsongs.
From The Nova Series.
LC NO. 79-707249
Prod-WGBHTV Dist-TIMLIF 1976

Why Do Boats Float C 20 MIN
2 INCH VIDEOTAPE P
See series title for descriptive statement.
From The Science Corner I, Unit IX - Transportation Series.
Prod-MPATI Dist-GPITVL

Why Do Eclipses Occur B 15 MIN
2 INCH VIDEOTAPE P
Examines specific relative positions of the sun, moon and earth which cause eclipses.
From The Science Is Discovery Series.
Prod-DETPS Dist-GPITVL

Why Do I Feel This Way - Profiles Of Depression C 48 MIN
16MM FILM, 3/4 OR 1/2 IN VIDEO H-C
Uses three case histories to illustrate the nature of depression and show its effects on individuals from all walks of life. Describes various treatments that can alleviate depression.
LC NO. 80-707530
Prod-BBINC Dist-MTI 1979

Why Do Shadows Change Outdoors C 20 MIN
2 INCH VIDEOTAPE I
See series title for descriptive statement.
From The Science Corner II, Unit II - The Earth In Space Series.
Prod-MPATI Dist-GPITVL

Why Do Temperatures Of Planets Vary B 15 MIN
2 INCH VIDEOTAPE P
Explains that the amount of solar radiation which a planet receives depends upon its distance from the sun.
From The Science Is Discovery Series.
Prod-DETPS Dist-GPITVL

Why Do Things Get In A Muddle (Come On Petunia) C 32 MIN
3/4 INCH VIDEO CASSETTE
Presents an art video based on a 'Metalogue' by Gregory Bateson. Uses reverse language, startling camerawork and a convoluted dialogue to illustrate the text. Taped by Gary Hill.
Prod-EAI Dist-EAI

Why Do We Eat C 15 MIN
3/4 OR 1/2 INCH VIDEO CASSETTE P
Establishes the relationship of food to energy, growth and well-being. Shows the need for food and how eating can be fun.
From The Great American Eating Machine - You Series. Pt 1
LC NO. 83-706105
Prod-NJPTV Dist-GPITVL 1982

Why Do We Get Sick C 30 MIN
3/4 OR 1/2 INCH VIDEO CASSETTE
Presents psychiatrist Dr George Engel in a discussion about how external events affect our internal health.
From The Here's To Your Health Series.
Prod-KERA Dist-PBS 1979

Why Do We Get Sick C 30 MIN
3/4 OR 1/2 INCH VIDEO CASSETTE
See series title for descriptive statement.
From The Here's To Your Health Series.
Prod-PBS Dist-DELTAK

Why Do We Get Sick? C 30 MIN
3/4 OR 1/2 INCH VIDEO CASSETTE C T
Shows how people react to stress. Explores the question, 'Is stress seen as a danger or a challenge for growth?' Addresses the belief that 'people seem to get sick during periods of significant multiple life changes.'
From The Here's To Your Health Series.
Prod-DALCCD Dist-DALCCD

Why Do We Need Animal Refuges C 20 MIN
2 INCH VIDEOTAPE I
See series title for descriptive statement.
From The Science Corner II, Unit IX - Exploring Our Country Series.
Prod-MPATI Dist-GPITVL

Why Do We Need Farms B 15 MIN
2 INCH VIDEOTAPE P
Describes the role of farmers in providing the food we eat. (Broadcast quality)
From The Around The Corner Series. No. 10
Prod-FWCETV Dist-GPITVL Prodn-WEDUTV

Why Do We Still Have Mountains X 20 MIN
16MM FILM, 3/4 OR 1/2 IN VIDEO I-H
Discusses the nature of mountains and the geological concepts dealing with weathering and erosion and with the formation of the earth's crust. Shows that uplift is occurring today at rates which could produce mountains in a geologically short time.
From The Earth Science Program Series.
Prod-EBEC Dist-EBEC 1964

Why Do We Still Have Mountains (Spanish) C 21 MIN
16MM FILM, 3/4 OR 1/2 IN VIDEO I-H
Discusses the nature of mountains, using natural photography and laboratory experiments.
Prod-EBEC Dist-EBEC

Why Do We Use Kitchen Tools C 20 MIN
2 INCH VIDEOTAPE P
See series title for descriptive statement.
From The Science Corner I, Unit X - Simple Machines Series.
Prod-MPATI Dist-GPITVL

Why Do We Use Mirrors C 20 MIN
2 INCH VIDEOTAPE P
See series title for descriptive statement.
From The Science Corner I, Unit VIII - Communication Series.
Prod-MPATI Dist-GPITVL

Why Do We Use Wheels C 20 MIN
2 INCH VIDEOTAPE P
See series title for descriptive statement.
From The Science Corner I, Unit IX - Transportation Series.
Prod-MPATI Dist-GPITVL

Why Do You Buy C 10 MIN
16MM FILM, 3/4 OR 1/2 IN VIDEO J-H
Uses a comical approach to focus on the emotional elements which enter into the buying decision, and shows how advertising utilizes the emotional appeals to sway purchase decisions.
Prod-ALTSUL Dist-JOU 1971

Why Do You Buy (Spanish) C 10 MIN
16MM FILM, 3/4 OR 1/2 IN VIDEO J-H
Uses a comical approach to focus on the emotional elements which enter into the buying decision, and shows how advertising utilizes the emotional appeals to sway purchase decisions.
Prod-ALTSUL Dist-JOU 1971

Why Do You Smile, Mona Lisa C 14 MIN
16MM FILM, 3/4 OR 1/2 IN VIDEO
Shows Leonardo da Vinci in his studio in Florence and explains how he got that enigmatic smile on the face of the Mona Lisa.
Prod-FLEET Dist-FI

Why Does Herr R Run Amok (German) C 87 MIN
16MM FILM OPTICAL SOUND
Presents a statement on the modern-day, bland, ordinary mass murderer. Directed by Werner Herzog. With English subtitles.
Prod-UNKNWN Dist-NYFLMS 1969

Why Does The Sun's Position Seem To Change B 15 MIN
2 INCH VIDEOTAPE P
Explains that changes in the sun's position can be measured.
From The Science Is Discovery Series.
Prod-DETPS Dist-GPITVL

Why Doesn't Somebody Ask Me C
16MM FILM - 3/4 IN VIDEO A
Uses satire to illustrate how to improve supervisory decision-making skills.
Prod-BNA Dist-BNA 1983

Why Doesn't Somebody Trust Me C
16MM FILM - 3/4 IN VIDEO A
Uses satire to illustrate how to improve supervisory decision-making skills.
Prod-BNA Dist-BNA 1983

Why Drown? C 29 MIN
3/4 OR 1/2 INCH VIDEO CASSETTE
Features an Olympic swimming champion demonstrating a life-saving technique to keep a person afloat for hours even if clothed or injured. Shows how to make water-wings out of trousers.
Prod-IHF Dist-IHF

Why Dry Corn C 14 MIN
16MM FILM OPTICAL SOUND
Uses research data from three universities to explain the advantages of feeding high moisture corn rather than dry corn to cattle.
LC NO. 76-713578
Prod-VENARD Dist-VENARD 1971

Why E C 25 MIN
16MM FILM, 3/4 OR 1/2 IN VIDEO
Explains the importance of the number 'e' in the family of functions.
Prod-OPENU Dist-MEDIAG Prodn-BBCTV 1979

Why Employees Don't Perform C 12 MIN
3/4 OR 1/2 INCH VIDEO CASSETTE
Shows supervisors that sometimes employees don't perform properly for reasons which may not suggest discipline and explores the matter of attitudes. Demonstrates that it is difficult to define 'bad' and 'good' attitudes.
From The Productive Discipline Series. Module 2
Prod-RESEM Dist-RESEM

Why Engines Are Governed B 5 MIN
16MM FILM OPTICAL SOUND
Explains that the governor in military engines limits the speed of the engine at the point where it develops maximum horsepower.
LC NO. FIE55-354
Prod-USA Dist-USNAC 1955

Why Exercise C 11 MIN
16MM FILM, 3/4 OR 1/2 IN VIDEO P
Tells the story of Knight Light who is on his way to being in top shape, but his paunchy friend needs some help. Shows how the two knights call upon all their strength and energy when they are sent to recover the king's stolen crown. Points out that exercise strengthens the heart, muscles, and other body systems, giving more energy for work and play.
From The Fitness And Me Series.
Prod-WDEMCO Dist-WDEMCO

Why Exercise (Arabic) C 14 MIN
16MM FILM, 3/4 OR 1/2 IN VIDEO J-H
Conveys ideas about the values of muscular activity. Stresses the fact that the body adapts to exercise demands and the adaptations produce increased strength, greater endurance and improved flexibility.
Prod-ASSOCF Dist-AIMS Prodn-SADLO 1965

Why Exercise (Captioned) C 14 MIN
16MM FILM, 3/4 OR 1/2 IN VIDEO J-H
Conveys ideas about the values of muscular activity. Stresses the fact that the body adapts to exercise demands and the adaptations produce increased strength, greater endurance and improved flexibility.
Prod-ASSOCF Dist-AIMS Prodn-SADLO 1965

Why Exercise (Spanish) C 14 MIN
16MM FILM, 3/4 OR 1/2 IN VIDEO J-H
Conveys ideas about the values of muscular activity. Stresses the fact that the body adapts to exercise demands and the adaptations produce increased strength, greater endurance and improved flexibility.
Prod-ASSOCF Dist-AIMS Prodn-SADLO 1965

Why Fathers Work X 14 MIN
16MM FILM, 3/4 OR 1/2 IN VIDEO P
Shows where a father goes, what he does and how his work helps his family, his community and the city. Illustrates the economic functions of the family as a community unit.
From The Social Studies Series.
Prod-EBEC Dist-EBEC 1969

Why Fathers Work (Spanish) C 14 MIN
16MM FILM, 3/4 OR 1/2 IN VIDEO P
Portrays a working father and shows where he works and what he does. Explains how the money he earns goes to buy necessities and other things for his family.
Prod-EBEC Dist-EBEC

Why Fly C 29 MIN
2 INCH VIDEOTAPE
See series title for descriptive statement.
From The Discover Flying - Just Like A Bird Series.
Prod-WKYCTV Dist-PUBTEL

Why Good Marriages Often Fail C 28 MIN
16MM FILM, 3/4 OR 1/2 IN VIDEO A
See series title for descriptive statement.
From The Care And Maintenance Of A Good Marriage Series. Program 1
Prod-UMCOM Dist-ECUFLM 1982

Why Human Relations C 29 MIN
16MM FILM, 3/4 OR 1/2 IN VIDEO C
Identifies the basic need for good human relationships in schools, re-examines goals of public education and shows how discipline and human relations are closely interwoven. Presents documentary scenes of several schools where human relationships have been consciously improved.
From The Human Relations And School Discipline Series.
Prod-MFFD Dist-FI 1974

Why I Like Me C 30 MIN
3/4 OR 1/2 INCH VIDEO CASSETTE K-P
See series title for descriptive statement.
From The Villa Alegre Series.
Prod-BCTV Dist-MDCPB

Why Is Culture Changing C 15 MIN
3/4 INCH VIDEO CASSETTE I-J
Illustrates that culture is always changing and that this process may occur slowly or in a more rapid manner. Assures that there is a degree of stability which is always protected from change.
From The Looking Out Is In Series.
Prod-WHATV Dist-GPITVL

Why Is Fruit Good For Us B 15 MIN
2 INCH VIDEOTAPE P
Discusses fruit as a valuable nutritional food. (Broadcast quality)
From The Around The Corner Series. No. 14
Prod-FWCETV Dist-GPITVL Prodn-WEDUTV

Why Is It - Beans And Seeds C 4 MIN
16MM FILM, 3/4 OR 1/2 IN VIDEO I-J
Shows how a simple can of pork and beans initiates various questions about seeds, such as whether all beans are seeds or whether all seeds are beans.
From The Mini Movies, Unit 3 - Why Is It Series.
Prod-MORLAT Dist-CORF 1976

Why Is It - Blow-Ups C 4 MIN
16MM FILM, 3/4 OR 1/2 IN VIDEO P-J
Describes air pressure in terms that are meaningful to children.
From The Mini Movies, Unit 3 - Why Is It Series.
Prod-MORLAT Dist-CORF 1976

Why Is It - Flight C 4 MIN
16MM FILM, 3/4 OR 1/2 IN VIDEO P-J
Shows natural flight such as soaring, gliding and gentle drifting. Describes man's attempts to copy the flight of birds and investigates unpowered flight.
From The Mini Movies, Unit 3 - Why Is It Series.
Prod-MORLAT Dist-CORF 1976

Why Is It - Growth C 4 MIN
16MM FILM, 3/4 OR 1/2 IN VIDEO P-J
Shows how certain changes take place as growth occurs. Uses such examples as flowers blooming and a chick hatching.
From The Mini Movies, Unit 3 - Why Is It Series.
Prod-MORLAT Dist-CORF 1976

Why Is It - On-Off C 3 MIN
16MM FILM, 3/4 OR 1/2 IN VIDEO P-J
Introduces the child to electricity by examining how electricity is used in a typical day.
From The Mini Movies, Unit 3 - Why Is It Series.
Prod-MORLAT Dist-CORF 1976

Why Is It Always Me C 14 MIN
16MM FILM, 3/4 OR 1/2 IN VIDEO I-J
Illustrates better and more effective methods for adolescents to resolve day-to-day personal problems such as conflict situations with their family or peers.
Prod-ROGRSG Dist-MTI 1983

Why Is Man A Social Animal C 15 MIN
3/4 INCH VIDEO CASSETTE I-J
Shows that culture is learned through interaction between people living or working in social organizations.
From The Looking Out Is In Series.
Prod-WHATV Dist-GPITVL

Why Is Rain Important To Us C 20 MIN
2 INCH VIDEOTAPE I
See series title for descriptive statement.
From The Science Corner II, Unit VII - Understanding Weather Series.
Prod-MPATI Dist-GPITVL

Why Is The Sky Blue C 9 MIN
3/4 OR 1/2 INCH VIDEO CASSETTE
Presented by Ilene Segalove.
Prod-KITCHN Dist-KITCHN

Why Knot—A Series
J-C A
Describes the techniques of macrame, beginning with basic knot-tying and progressing to more complex combinations of knots.
Prod-KETCTV Dist-GPITVL 1977

Clove Hitch Knot 15 MIN
Clove Hitch Patterns, Pt 1 15 MIN
Clove Hitch Patterns, Pt 2 15 MIN
Finishing Projects 15 MIN
Introductory Preview Of Series 15 MIN
Starting Your Project 15 MIN

Why Lignite C 20 MIN
16MM FILM OPTICAL SOUND
Examines the process of mining and processing lignite and explores its use as a fuel in generating electric power.
LC NO. 75-702670
Prod-STOKB Dist-STOKB 1975

Why LOTUS C 15 MIN
3/4 OR 1/2 INCH VIDEO CASSETTE
Explains why the Light Of Truth Universal Shrine (LOTUS) is being built.
Prod-IYOGA Dist-IYOGA

Why Man Creates C 25 MIN
16MM FILM, 3/4 OR 1/2 IN VIDEO K-C A
Demonstrates the nature of the creative process and the variety, richness, and importance of creative vision.
Prod-KACC Dist-PFP Prodn-BASSS 1968

Why Man Creates (German) C 25 MIN
16MM FILM, 3/4 OR 1/2 IN VIDEO I-C A

Presents a series of explorations, episodes and comments on creativity by a master of conceptual design. Uses humor and satire to explore ideas and important truths.
Prod-BASSS Dist-PFP

Why Man Creates (Italian) C 25 MIN
16MM FILM, 3/4 OR 1/2 IN VIDEO I-C A
Presents a series of explorations, episodes and comments on creativity by a master of conceptual design. Uses humor and satire to explore ideas and important truths.
Prod-BASSS Dist-PFP

Why Man Creates (Spanish) C 25 MIN
16MM FILM, 3/4 OR 1/2 IN VIDEO I-C A
Presents a series of explorations, episodes and comments on creativity by a master of conceptual design. Uses humor and satire to explore ideas and important truths.
Prod-BASSS Dist-PFP

Why Man Creates - Man, The Measure Of All Things C
3/4 OR 1/2 INCH VIDEO CASSETTE H-C
Uses great works of art and selected passages to help explain why the history of art is the history of civilization. Based on the Metropolitan Museum of Art's Centennial Exhibition, Masterpieces of Fifty Centuries.
Prod-GA Dist-GA

Why Me C 10 MIN
16MM FILM OPTICAL SOUND I-C A
Presents six short animated films made by children ages seven to 14 using cardboard, paper cutouts and clay.
LC NO. 74-701555
Prod-CELLAR Dist-CELLAR 1969

Why Me C 16 MIN
16MM FILM OPTICAL SOUND
Tells the story of an exasperated executive who blames his mistakes on his subordinates, but learns a lesson in accountability when he is visited by an angel.
LC NO. 77-702174
Prod-ITTSHE Dist-ITTSHE 1977

Why Me C 24 MIN
16MM FILM OPTICAL SOUND J-C A
Presents an exploratory documentary of a modern police force in action. Exposes the familiar Why Me syndrome experienced by police officers when confronting average citizens in the line of duty.
LC NO. 73-702084
Prod-NOMIL Dist-STSF 1973

Why Me C 10 MIN
16MM FILM, 3/4 OR 1/2 IN VIDEO
Presents an animated story in which a patient learns from his doctor that he has only a short time to live. Depicts the stages of responses to this situation, culminating with the patient's resolution to live each remaining moment to its fullest.
LC NO. 79-707040
Prod-NFBC Dist-PFP 1979

Why Me C 57 MIN
16MM FILM, 3/4 OR 1/2 IN VIDEO H-C A
Looks at the problem of breast cancer and its aftereffects. Demonstrates self-examination.
Prod-KNXT Dist-CAROUF

Why Me (A Film About Police Work) C 20 MIN
3/4 OR 1/2 INCH VIDEO CASSETTE I-C A
Discusses police work, showing how police officers go about the routines of crime prevention.
Prod-BFA Dist-BFA 1975

Why Me - An Orthopedically Handicapped Child C 7 MIN
16MM FILM, 3/4 OR 1/2 IN VIDEO K-P
Describes how a little boy with an orthopedic handicap teaches his nonhandicapped friend how to swim.
From The Like You, Like Me Series.
Prod-EBEC Dist-EBEC 1977

Why Meanings Change C 30 MIN
3/4 OR 1/2 INCH VIDEO CASSETTE C
See series title for descriptive statement.
From The Language And Meaning Series.
Prod-WUSFTV Dist-GPITVL 1983

Why Measure C 6 MIN
16MM FILM OPTICAL SOUND J-C A
Deals with the importance of measurement, moving from the ordinary experiences of life to work in the laboratory. Shows the need for and development of standards of measurement and depicts the critical relationship of measurement to science and technology.
From The Measurement Series.
LC NO. 78-700704
Prod-PSU Dist-PSU 1972

Why Men Rape C 40 MIN
16MM FILM, 3/4 OR 1/2 IN VIDEO H-C A
Presents ten rapists discussing why they committed their crimes. Offers interviews with authorities who try to present a clearer profile of the rapist. Shows interviews with mixed groups of students who discuss their sexual attitudes.
Prod-NFBC Dist-LCOA 1980

Why Microelectronics Fail C 29 MIN
2 INCH VIDEOTAPE
See series title for descriptive statement.
From The Interface Series.
Prod-KCET Dist-PUBTEL

Why Money C 20 MIN
3/4 OR 1/2 INCH VIDEO CASSETTE
Explains the function of money with a story about a young girl who tries to trade an antique lamp for a skateboard. Illustrates the usefulness of money as a medium of exchange and points out the different functions of cash, checks and credit cards.
From The Trade-Offs Series.
LC NO. 79-706334
Prod-EDFCEN Dist-AITECH 1978

Why Money - Voluntary Exchange C 20 MIN
16MM FILM OPTICAL SOUND I-J
Tells how Christina learns that using money is much more convenient than trading, and that checks as well as currency can be used as money.
From The Trade-Offs Series. No. 9
Prod-EDFCEN Dist-AITECH 1978

Why Mosquitoes Buzz In People's Ears C 10 MIN
16MM FILM, 3/4 OR 1/2 IN VIDEO K-P
Reveals that when Mosquito tells Iguana a tall tale and Iguana plugs his ears in disgust, thus sending Python down Rabbit's hole for fear of foul play, the chain reaction leads to jungle disaster. Tells how King Lion calls a meeting where all is set aright.
Prod-SCHNDL Dist-WWS 1984

Why Mothers Work C 19 MIN
16MM FILM, 3/4 OR 1/2 IN VIDEO P-I
Follows two working mothers through typical days, observing them at home and at work. Shows how families of both of the women have had to make some adjustments.
Prod-EBEC Dist-EBEC 1976

Why NATO B 26 MIN
16MM FILM OPTICAL SOUND
Tells the story of the North Atlantic Treaty Organization from its inception to its 1957 summit meeting in Paris, France.
LC NO. FIE58-372
Prod-USDD Dist-USNAC 1958

Why Not A Woman C 26 MIN
16MM FILM, 3/4 OR 1/2 IN VIDEO A
Shows women working successfully in nontraditional jobs, such as welder, carpenter and mechanic. Explores the attitudes of their male coworkers, supervisors, personnel managers and teachers. Demonstrates the wide range of job options and training available to girls and women.
LC NO. 79-708099
Prod-USETA Dist-USNAC Prodn-NORRIJ 1979

Why Not Be Beautiful C 20 MIN
16MM FILM, 3/4 OR 1/2 IN VIDEO J-C A
Explains the importance of cleanliness, good diet and exercise as prerequisites for a healthy body and a beautiful face. Shows basic facial makeup, such as the application of foundation, blush power and eye makeup. Stresses the fact that beauty is more than a pretty face, it's a way of life.
Prod-HANDEL Dist-HANDEL 1969

Why Not Sign A Union Card? C 35 MIN
3/4 OR 1/2 INCH VIDEO CASSETTE
Shows simulation of union authorization card signing campaign demonstrating organizing tactics. Attempts to prepare managers and supervisors to effectively respond and appropriately communicate to employees.
Prod-SERA Dist-SERA

Why Not Technology C 15 MIN
16MM FILM OPTICAL SOUND
Documents opportunities for women in scientific and technological fields.
LC NO. 76-701495
Prod-CNIAG Dist-CNIAG 1975

Why Not Try C 4 MIN
16MM FILM, 3/4 OR 1/2 IN VIDEO K-I
Explores a variety of things that many children may never have tried before, including sliding down a slide, finger painting and meeting someone new.
From The Most Important Person - Attitudes Series.
Prod-EBEC Dist-EBEC 1972

Why Not Try (Spanish) C 4 MIN
16MM FILM, 3/4 OR 1/2 IN VIDEO K-P
See series title for descriptive statement.
From The Most Important Person - Attitudes (Spanish) Series.
Prod-EBEC Dist-EBEC

Why Of Automation Lubrication, The C 24 MIN
16MM FILM OPTICAL SOUND J
Explains through animation the need for lubrication of automobiles and the uses of oils and greases.
Prod-AMROIL Dist-AMROIL 1952

Why Of It, The C 20 MIN
2 INCH VIDEOTAPE P
See series title for descriptive statement.
From The Learning Our Language, Unit III - Creative Writing Series.
Prod-MPATI Dist-GPITVL

Why Patients Get Angry - A Risk Management Program C
16MM FILM, 3/4 OR 1/2 IN VIDEO PRO
Discusses experiences in health care facilities which provoke anger on the part of patients. Offers suggestions to health care providers on how to handle situations which may provoke anger.
Prod-FAIRGH Dist-FAIRGH

Why People Are Scared Of Hares C 6 MIN
3/4 OR 1/2 INCH VIDEO CASSETTE P-I A
Presents a modern fable about an unusual rabbit that is not well liked by his friends because he does not conform. Describes how he finds a book and teaches himself to read, and when faced with death by a group of hunters, it is his literary skill that saves all of them.
Prod-SFSP Dist-MOKIN Prodn-TRNKAJ 1983

Why People Buy C 20 MIN
16MM FILM, 3/4 OR 1/2 IN VIDEO H-C A
Displays all types of salespeople and selling tools, including territorial representation, on-site sales, point of purchase display, radio, television, and the across-the-desk handshake.
LC NO. 81-706215
Prod-CRMP Dist-CRMP 1981

Why People Buy (Spanish) C 20 MIN
16MM FILM, 3/4 OR 1/2 IN VIDEO H-C A
Analyzes the various reasons why people purchase a product.
Prod-CRMP Dist-MGHT 1981

Why People Drink C 28 MIN
3/4 OR 1/2 INCH VIDEO CASSETTE J A
Explains rationale behind different drinking styles.
Prod-SUTHRB Dist-SUTHRB

Why People Have Special Jobs - The Man Who Made Spinning Tops C 7 MIN
16MM FILM, 3/4 OR 1/2 IN VIDEO K-P
Introduces the basic economic concept of specialization of labor. Shows how one man who made tops became a toymaker and how other fathers began to do one special job.
From The Basic Concepts In Social Studies Series.
Prod-LCOA Dist-LCOA Prodn-BOSUST 1970

Why People Smoke C 10 MIN
16MM FILM, 3/4 OR 1/2 IN VIDEO P-I
Uses animation to classify personality traits of people who smoke.
Prod-HARBER Dist-PFP 1978

Why Plant A Tree C 9 MIN
16MM FILM OPTICAL SOUND P-I
Presents the story of a little boy who uses a stick as a sword and goes about knocking shoots and branches from trees.
Prod-MLA Dist-MLA

Why Plants Grow Where They Do C 11 MIN
16MM FILM, 3/4 OR 1/2 IN VIDEO P-I
Visits an open field, woodland, desert and pond to show the reasons why certain plants grow in each area. Explains the basic needs of all plants. Pictures each type of plant community in a vivarium.
Prod-CORF Dist-CORF 1966

Why Plants Grow Where They Do (Captioned) C 11 MIN
16MM FILM, 3/4 OR 1/2 IN VIDEO P-I
Visits an open field, woodland, desert and pond to show the reasons why certain plants grow in each area. Explains the basic needs of all plants. Pictures each type of plant community in a vivarium.
Prod-CORF Dist-CORF 1966

Why Politics B 20 MIN
16MM FILM OPTICAL SOUND H A
Raymond Moley, journalist, author and political scientist, discusses our need for political information and knowledge of government.
From The Government And Public Affairs Films Series.
Prod-RSC Dist-MLA 1960

Why Politics - Interview B 15 MIN
16MM FILM OPTICAL SOUND H-C
See series title for descriptive statement.
From The Building Political Leadership Series.
LC NO. FIA68-1335
Prod-RSC Dist-MLA 1966

Why Productivity Increases As Quality Improves C
3/4 OR 1/2 INCH VIDEO CASSETTE
Outlines the 14 steps management must take to improve quality and productivity.
From The Deming Videotapes - Quality, Productivity, And Competitive...Series.
Prod-MIOT Dist-MIOT

Why Productivity Increases As Quality Improves C 50 MIN
3/4 OR 1/2 INCH VIDEO CASSETTE
See series title for descriptive statement.
From The Deming Video Tapes - Quality, Productivity And The Competitive...Series.
Prod-MIOT Dist-SME

Why Protect Animals C 15 MIN
16MM FILM OPTICAL SOUND J-C A
Shows how humane societies work effectively to protect animals through education, public action and law. Presents several case histories in their actual settings throughout America.
Prod-KLEINW Dist-KLEINW

Why Protect Animals C 15 MIN
16MM FILM, 3/4 OR 1/2 IN VIDEO J-C A
Shows how humane societies work effectively to protect animals through education, public action and law. Presents several case histories in their actual settings throughout America.
Prod-KLEINW Dist-KLEINW

Why Q A? C 60 MIN
3/4 OR 1/2 INCH VIDEO CASSETTE IND
Introduces student to quality assurance. Includes general terminology, standards and specifications. Defines differences between quality assurance and quality control.
From The Quality Assurance Series.
Prod-LEIKID Dist-LEIKID

Why Quit Quiz C 15 MIN
16MM FILM OPTICAL SOUND

Uses a quiz format to present questions which dramatize the positive health benefits of quitting cigarettes.
LC NO. 79-701125
Prod-AMCS Dist-AMCS Prodn-TAPPRO 1979

Why Rabbits Have Long Ears C 15 MIN
3/4 INCH VIDEO CASSETTE P
Features a Guatemalan folk tale.
From The Magic Carpet Series.
Prod-SDCSS Dist-GPITVL 1977

Why Read B 15 MIN
16MM FILM OPTICAL SOUND I-H
Examines some of the reasons for reading–to gain information, to prove or disprove a point, to learn how to do or make something, to satisfy curiosity, to be entertained, to recognize beauty and to gain wisdom and inspiration.
From The Pathways To Reading Series.
Prod-CBF Dist-AVED 1958

Why Read C 15 MIN
3/4 OR 1/2 INCH VIDEO CASSETTE T
Uses the adventures of a pirate and his three friends to explore the many facets of language arts. Focuses on the importance of learning to read.
From The Hidden Treasures Series. No. 6
LC NO. 82-706546
Prod-WCVETV Dist-GPITVL 1980

Why Risk A Heart Attack C 14 MIN
16MM FILM, 3/4 OR 1/2 IN VIDEO H-C A
Offers information on identifying and reducing the risk factors that lead to heart attacks.
LC NO. 79-707902
Prod-AMEDA Dist-TIMLIF Prodn-TIMLIF 1972

Why Roof Control Plans C 16 MIN
16MM FILM, 3/4 OR 1/2 IN VIDEO
Shows that the collapse of roofs and ribs in coal mines can be prevented by following an approved roof-control plan. Explains basic plans, provides examples and describes the implementation of a plan. Describes types of roof support, areas covered, types of rock strata, mining equipment and materials, roof-bolting machines and support timbers.
Prod-USDL Dist-USNAC 1981

Why Rules C 15 MIN
3/4 OR 1/2 INCH VIDEO CASSETTE J
Describes how Jeff ignores basic safety rules while bike riding and goes head over handlebars.
From The It's Your Move Series.
Prod-WETN Dist-AITECH 1977

Why Save Florence C 59 MIN
16MM FILM, 3/4 OR 1/2 IN VIDEO H A
Shows the state of affairs in Florence, Italy, following the flood of 1966 which endangered many lives and ruined thousands of priceless art treasures.
Prod-NETRC Dist-IU 1971

Why School Fire Safety? C 15 MIN
3/4 OR 1/2 INCH VIDEO CASSETTE
Shows the need for school fire safety programs.
Prod-FPF Dist-FPF

Why Seasons Change B 11 MIN
16MM FILM, 3/4 OR 1/2 IN VIDEO I-J
Uses animation to demonstrate that the yearly seasonal cycle is caused by the cyclical change in the tilt of the earth's axis relative to the sun. Explains temperature changes and seasonal differences between the Northern and Southern hemispheres.
Prod-EBF Dist-EBEC 1960

Why Seasons Change (Spanish) B 11 MIN
16MM FILM, 3/4 OR 1/2 IN VIDEO I-J
Demonstrates that the yearly seasonal changes are caused by the cyclical tilt of the Earth's axis relative to the Sun. Explains why temperatures change, why the length of the day varies and why there is a seasonal difference between the Northern and Southern hemispheres.
Prod-EBEC Dist-EBEC

Why Shoot The Teacher C 101 MIN
16MM FILM OPTICAL SOUND
Depicts a young teacher's struggle to gain respect when he arrives at a Canadian prairie town during the Great Depression.
Prod-TLECUL Dist-TLECUL

Why Should I Care? C 24 MIN
3/4 OR 1/2 INCH VIDEO CASSETTE
Stresses defensive driving concepts to motivate drivers of all types of vehicles including heavy trucks, light trucks, buses, vans and cars to conserve fuel.
Prod-VISUCP Dist-VISUCP

Why Show, The C 28 MIN
16MM FILM - 3/4 IN VIDEO P-I
Identifies the cause of various handicaps and describes how handicapped individuals adjust to their disabilities.
From The Special Delivery Series.
LC NO. 79-706884
Prod-WNVT Dist-LAWREN 1979

Why So Many Lab Tests C 24 MIN
3/4 OR 1/2 INCH VIDEO CASSETTE PRO
Explains reasons for six commonly used lab tests hemoglobin level and blood cell count, urinalysis, blood chemistry, serology, blood typing, and microbiological tests.
Prod-HSCIC Dist-HSCIC 1981

Why Space C 7 MIN
16MM FILM OPTICAL SOUND
Shows various scientific milestones which have permitted mankind to approach the age of space. Explains why we are interested in the development of military capabilities in space.

LC NO. 74-706332
Prod-USAF Dist-USNAC 1957

Why Spiders Hide In Dark Corners C 15 MIN
3/4 INCH VIDEO CASSETTE P
Presents an African folk tale.
From The Magic Carpet Series.
Prod-SDCSS Dist-GPITVL 1977

Why Stories C 15 MIN
3/4 OR 1/2 INCH VIDEO CASSETTE I-C
See series title for descriptive statement.
From The Juba Series.
Prod-WETATV Dist-WETATV

Why Study Literature? C 30 MIN
3/4 OR 1/2 INCH VIDEO CASSETTE C
See series title for descriptive statement.
From The Communicating Through Literature Series.
Prod-DALCCD Dist-DALCCD

Why Switch To Computers C 60 MIN
3/4 OR 1/2 INCH VIDEO CASSETTE IND
See series title for descriptive statement.
From The Microprocessor Fundamentals For Decision Makers Series.
Prod-NCSU Dist-AMCEE

Why The New World Was Explored C 11 MIN
16MM FILM, 3/4 OR 1/2 IN VIDEO I-H A
Discusses why so many Europeans risked their wealth and lives to explore the new world. Traces their search for a shorter, safer trade route to the East. Shows how their motives for searching changed from a search for trade routes to a search for gold, furs, forests and farm land.
Prod-FA Dist-PHENIX Prodn-FA 1968

Why The Sun And Moon Live In The Sky C 11 MIN
16MM FILM, 3/4 OR 1/2 IN VIDEO P-I
A legend of Eastern Nigeria about the sun and moon who lived on land until the sea came to visit them and the inundation forced them up into the sky.
From The Children's Storybook Theater Series.
Prod-ACI Dist-AIMS 1970

Why The Traditional Approach Fails C 30 MIN
3/4 OR 1/2 INCH VIDEO CASSETTE
Looks at why many traditional procedures put the manager on the defensive in performance reviews. Covers the first steps for attaining sound performance standards.
From The Performance Reviews That Build Commitment Series. Session 2
Prod-PRODEV Dist-DELTAK

Why The United States Did Not Abolish Slavery B 30 MIN
16MM FILM OPTICAL SOUND H-C A
Professor Staughton Lynd traces the growth of the movement to abolish the slave trade and explains why the founding fathers did not outlaw slavery.
From The Black History, Section 04 - Slave Trade And Slavery Series.
LC NO. 70-704042
Prod-WCBSTV Dist-HRAW 1969

Why Things Go Wrong C 30 MIN
16MM FILM, 3/4 OR 1/2 IN VIDEO H-C A
Presents engineer-turned-cartoonist Tim Hunkin teaming his talents to wryly expound on the the theory of why machines break down.
LC NO. 84-706266
Prod-BBCTV Dist-TEXFLM 1984

Why Us, The Lakens C 28 MIN
16MM FILM, 3/4 OR 1/2 IN VIDEO
Tells the story of a couple whose tax return is being audited. Gives an overview of IRS functions in general and shows the steps taxpayers may take when they disagree with an IRS examination decision. Narrated by Lyle Waggoner.
Prod-USIRS Dist-USNAC

Why Use Positive C 33 MIN
3/4 OR 1/2 INCH VIDEO CASSETTE T
Presents major objections to the use of reinforcement. Demonstrates the objections.
From The Learning And Liking It Series.
Prod-MSU Dist-MSU

Why Vietnam B 25 MIN
3/4 OR 1/2 INCH VIDEO CASSETTE
Relates a history of U S support in Southeast Asia, including speeches by Secretary of State Dean Rusk, Secretary of Defense Robert McNamara and President Johnson.
Prod-IHF Dist-IHF

Why Vietnam B 32 MIN
16MM FILM - 3/4 IN VIDEO
Explains U S policy on South Vietnam as stated in an address by President Lyndon B Johnson. Issued in 1965 as a motion picture.
LC NO. 79-706483
Prod-USDD Dist-USNAC 1979

Why War C 26 MIN
16MM FILM, 3/4 OR 1/2 IN VIDEO H-C
Presents rare 1925 footage from New Guinea showing tribal war. Discusses reasons for war and the role of allies. Examines the issues of Cuba, Vietnam and South America.
From The Today's History Series.
Prod-JOU Dist-JOU 1984

Why We Are The Way We Are C
3/4 OR 1/2 INCH VIDEO CASSETTE
Reveals the complexity of the human brain, common human factors, how personality and behavior are developed, the formation of individual learned needs and how to protect oneself by the development of coping and defense mechanisms.
From The Human Behavior Series.
Prod-BUSTEL Dist-BUSTEL

Why We Conserve Energy - The Witch Of The Great Black Pool C 12 MIN
16MM FILM, 3/4 OR 1/2 IN VIDEO P-I
Tells a story about the Land of the Scatterpods, where people use machines which run on Black Soup. Describes what happens when the Scatterpods must start conserving the fuel.
From The Basic Concepts In Social Studies Series.
Prod-LCOA Dist-LCOA 1978

Why We Do What We Do C 30 MIN
3/4 OR 1/2 INCH VIDEO CASSETTE
Examines the elements of motivation, expectancy-value theory of motivation, Maslow's hierarchy of needs, self-actualization, interaction of approach and avoidance motives in conflict situations.
From The Psychology Of Human Relations Series.
Prod-MATC Dist-WFVTAE

Why We Fight–A Series

Presents documentaries made between 1943 and 1945 which show battles and events in World War II. Provides information on the history of the war and the reasons for American involvement. Used the services of major Hollywood studios and Hollywood film people such as John Huston, Anatole Litvak, Robert Flaherty, William Wyler, Dimitri Tiomkin, Alfred Newman and George Stevens. Produced and directed by Frank Capra. Narrated by Walter Huston.
Prod-USOWI Dist-USNAC 1979

Battle Of Britain, The 055 MIN
Battle Of China, The 067 MIN
Divide And Conquer 060 MIN
Nazi Strike, The 041 MIN
Prelude To War 054 MIN
War Comes To America 067 MIN

Why We Have Elections - The King Of Snark (Captioned) C 9 MIN
16MM FILM, 3/4 OR 1/2 IN VIDEO P-I
Shows through storytale format that electing one person on merit is the best solution.
Prod-LCOA Dist-LCOA 1973

Why We Have Elections - The King Of Snark (Spanish) C 9 MIN
16MM FILM, 3/4 OR 1/2 IN VIDEO P-I
Shows through storytale format that electing one person on merit is the best solution.
Prod-LCOA Dist-LCOA 1973

Why We Have Elections - The Kings Of Snark C 9 MIN
16MM FILM, 3/4 OR 1/2 IN VIDEO K-P
Presents a tale set in a mythical kingdom which demonstrates the concept of holding elections to select government officials. Explains that in the land of Snark when bad King Boris dies, the citizens search for a replacement who will rule the country wisely. Explains that after several elections they choose the candidate that will serve them best.
From The Basic Concepts In Social Studies Series.
Prod-LCOA Dist-LCOA 1973

Why We Have Laws - Shiver, Gobble And Snore C 7 MIN
16MM FILM, 3/4 OR 1/2 IN VIDEO K-P
Uses animation to introduce the basic concept of laws. Concludes that no one can live peacefully without rules, and that if people help make their own laws they will usually make fair ones.
From The Basic Concepts In Social Studies Series.
Prod-LCOA Dist-LCOA Prodn-BOSUST 1970

Why We Have Laws - Shiver, Goble And Snore (Captioned) C 7 MIN
16MM FILM, 3/4 OR 1/2 IN VIDEO P-I
Notes the various laws in effect in society today.
Prod-LCOA Dist-LCOA Prodn-BOSUST 1970

Why We Have Laws - Shiver, Goble And Snore (Spanish) C 7 MIN
16MM FILM, 3/4 OR 1/2 IN VIDEO P-I
Notes the various laws in effect in society today.
Prod-LCOA Dist-LCOA Prodn-BOSUST 1970

Why We Have Laws - Shiver, Goble And Snore (Swedish) C 7 MIN
16MM FILM, 3/4 OR 1/2 IN VIDEO P-I
Notes the various laws in effect in society today.
Prod-LCOA Dist-LCOA 1970

Why We Have Taxes - The Town That Had No Policeman C 7 MIN
16MM FILM, 3/4 OR 1/2 IN VIDEO K-P
Explains how, due to the need of a policeman, everyone gives some money and the idea of taxation is born.
From The Basic Concepts In Social Studies Series.
Prod-LCOA Dist-LCOA Prodn-BOSUST 1970

Why We Have Taxes - The Town That Had No Policeman (Spanish) C 7 MIN
16MM FILM, 3/4 OR 1/2 IN VIDEO P-I
Introduces the concept of taxation and services provided by public employees for a community.
Prod-LCOA Dist-LCOA Prodn-BOSUST 1970

Why We Have Taxes - The Town That Had No Policeman (Swedish) C 7 MIN
16MM FILM, 3/4 OR 1/2 IN VIDEO P-I

Introduces the concept of taxation and services provided by public employees for a community.
Prod-LCOA Dist-LCOA Prodn-BOSUST 1970

Why We Need Doctors - No Measles, No Mumps For Me C 11 MIN
16MM FILM, 3/4 OR 1/2 IN VIDEO P
Presents an animated film in which a little boy learns about the value and importance of doctors from his grandmother, who tells him about her childhood when there were no vaccines against such illnesses as whooping cough.
From The Basic Concepts In Social Studies Series.
Prod-SPORAN Dist-LCOA 1981

Why We Need Each Other - The Animal's Picnic Day C 9 MIN
16MM FILM, 3/4 OR 1/2 IN VIDEO P
Suggests that individual differences are beneficial to all. Shows forest animals getting together for a picnic on a sunny day. Indicates that certain other animals couldn't join in because they were rejected by the picnickers for looking different. Relates how the ridiculed animals save the others. when danger is imminent.
From The Basic Concepts In Social Studies Series.
Prod-LCOA Dist-LCOA 1973

Why We Need Each Other - The Animals' Picnic Day (Captioned) C 10 MIN
16MM FILM, 3/4 OR 1/2 IN VIDEO P-I
Shows how a group of animals learn to appreciate each other after sharing in a common experience.
Prod-LCOA Dist-LCOA 1973

Why We Need Each Other - The Animals' Picnic Day (Spanish) C 10 MIN
16MM FILM, 3/4 OR 1/2 IN VIDEO P-I
Shows how a group of animals learn to appreciate each other after sharing in a common experience.
Prod-LCOA Dist-LCOA 1973

Why We Need Each Other - The Animals' Picnic Day (Swedish) C 10 MIN
16MM FILM, 3/4 OR 1/2 IN VIDEO P-I
Shows how a group of animals learn to appreciate each other after sharing in a common experience.
Prod-LCOA Dist-LCOA 1973

Why We Need Reading - The Piemaker Of Ignoramia C 11 MIN
16MM FILM, 3/4 OR 1/2 IN VIDEO P-I
Uses an animated story to present the concept that reading is the key to social mobility.
From The Basic Concepts In Social Studies Series.
Prod-LCOA Dist-LCOA 1975

Why We Need Reading - The Piemaker Of Ignoramia (Spanish) C 12 MIN
16MM FILM, 3/4 OR 1/2 IN VIDEO P-I
Shows a child why he or she needs to read and also gives some motivation to do it.
Prod-LCOA Dist-LCOA 1976

Why We Take Care Of Property - Planet Of The Tickle Bops C 12 MIN
16MM FILM, 3/4 OR 1/2 IN VIDEO P-I
Presents an animated story about two children who start damaging property for fun, until they have their own property damaged and learn that everyone is affected sooner or later when people stop caring about their surroundings.
From The Basic Concepts In Social Studies Series.
Prod-LCOA Dist-LCOA 1975

Why We Take Care Of Property - Planet Of The Ticklebops (Spanish) C 12 MIN
16MM FILM, 3/4 OR 1/2 IN VIDEO P-I
Makes the point that if you don't care about the property of other- they will not care about yours.
Prod-LCOA Dist-LCOA 1976

Why We Tell The Truth - No More Squareburgers In Straighttalk C 12 MIN
16MM FILM, 3/4 OR 1/2 IN VIDEO A
Tells a story about the inhabitants of Straighttalk, who tell the truth, until one day a spaceship lands and the Master of Lies teaches the people to lie for their own gain. Shows how they are almost doomed by their mistrust of each other until they swear to tell the truth again.
From The Basic Concepts In Social Studies Series.
Prod-IMAG Dist-LCOA 1978

Why We Use Money - The Fisherman Who Needed A Knife C 8 MIN
16MM FILM, 3/4 OR 1/2 IN VIDEO K-P
Discusses the trading a fisherman must go through in order to get a new knife. Explains how, due to the inconvenience of trading, the idea of money is born.
From The Basic Concepts In Social Studies Series.
Prod-LCOA Dist-LCOA Prodn-BOSUST 1970

Why We Use Money - The Fisherman Who Needed A Knife (Spanish) C 8 MIN
16MM FILM, 3/4 OR 1/2 IN VIDEO P-I
Makes the basic point of how money came into existence.
Prod-LCOA Dist-LCOA Prodn-BOSUST 1970

Why We Use Money - The Fisherman Who Needed A Knife (Swedish) C 8 MIN
16MM FILM, 3/4 OR 1/2 IN VIDEO P-I
Makes the basic point of how money came into existence.
Prod-LCOA Dist-LCOA Prodn-BOSUST 1970

Why Women Are Dissatisfied With Their Gynecologists C 29 MIN
3/4 INCH VIDEO CASSETTE
Discusses health care from the consumer's point of view. Maintains that women should work toward demystifying the profession of medicine and its practitioners.
From The Woman Series.
Prod-WNEDTV Dist-PUBTEL

Why Women Stay B 30 MIN
3/4 INCH VIDEO CASSETTE
Examines the complex reasons why women remain in violent homes. Challenges the prevailing attitudes that accept physical and mental violence toward women. Exposes the social structures that victimize women and contribute to their abuse.
Prod-WMEN Dist-WMEN

Why Work C 26 MIN
16MM FILM, 3/4 OR 1/2 IN VIDEO H-C
Discusses the future of work, and of the work ethic, especially in light of the considerable unemployment of the late 1970's and early 1980's.
From The Today's History Series.
Prod-JOU Dist-JOU 1984

Why Work, Pt 1 C 60 MIN
3/4 OR 1/2 INCH VIDEO CASSETTE
Explores what Bill Moyers calls 'a supreme moment of creation - labor.'
From The Bill Moyers' Journal Series.
Prod-WNETTV Dist-WNETTV 1980

Why Work, Pt 2 C 60 MIN
3/4 OR 1/2 INCH VIDEO CASSETTE
Explores what Bill Moyers calls 'a supreme moment of creation - labor.'
From The Bill Moyers' Journal Series.
Prod-WNETTV Dist-WNETTV 1980

Why Write C 30 MIN
3/4 OR 1/2 INCH VIDEO CASSETTE C A
Discusses the questions of why we write and study, and contemporary theories of the writing process.
From The Write Course - An Introduction To College Composition Series.
Prod-FI Dist-FI 1984

Why Write? C
3/4 OR 1/2 INCH VIDEO CASSETTE C
Addresses the questions of why we write and why we study writing, as well as the contemporary theories of the writing process as a whole.
From The Write Course - An Introduction To College Composition Series.
Prod-DALCCD Dist-DALCCD

Why You're You C 10 MIN
16MM FILM OPTICAL SOUND I-J
Develops the concept of individual personalities. Examines the nucleus of sperm and egg cells to show that chromosomes contain characteristics. Introduces the influence of environment and discusses the effects of physical growth on personality.
From The Family Life And Sex Education Series.
Prod-SF Dist-SF 1968

Why 55 C 15 MIN
16MM FILM OPTICAL SOUND
Dramatizes the margin of safety provided by driving at 55 miles per hour and points out that driving at 65 miles per hour does not necessarily get people to their destinations quicker. Examines the economic advantages of driving at the slower speed.
Prod-MATRIX Dist-MATRIX

Why—A Series
P-I
Focuses on life science, earth science and physical science. Shows plants and animals in different environments and discusses astronomy, machines, measurement, geology, weather and sound.
Prod-WDCNTV Dist-AITECH 1976

Air Pressure On Things	015 MIN
Animals From Different Environments	015 MIN
Different Kinds of Plants	015 MIN
Electricity Into Heat	015 MIN
Electricity Into Light	015 MIN
Electricity Into Motion	015 MIN
Flowering Plants	015 MIN
Fossils Tell The Story	015 MIN
How Do Scientists Learn About Space	015 MIN
How Do We Know	015 MIN
How Does An Electric Current Flow	015 MIN
Incliined Plane - A Simple Machine	015 MIN
Lake Community, The	015 MIN
Lawn And Vacant Lot Community, The	015 MIN
Lever - A Simple Machine	015 MIN
Light And Color	015 MIN
Light And Heat	015 MIN
Living Things And Their Environment	015 MIN
Making Work Easier	015 MIN
Measuring Distance	015 MIN
Measuring Temperature	015 MIN
Measuring Time	015 MIN
Measuring Weight	015 MIN
Moving Air Affects The Weather	015 MIN
Pulley - A Simple Machine	015 MIN
Reflected Light	015 MIN
Seashore Community, A	015 MIN
Sound And Hearing	015 MIN
Space Neighbors	015 MIN
Static Electricity	015 MIN
Stream Community, A	015 MIN
Sun And The Earth, The	015 MIN
Trees	015 MIN
Water Affects The Weather	015 MIN
Wedge - A Simple Machine	015 MIN
What Happens When Air Is Heated And Cooled	015 MIN
What Is A Machine	015 MIN
What Is Air	015 MIN
What Is Sound	015 MIN
What Is Weather	015 MIN
What The Earth Was Like	015 MIN
Wheel And Axle, The - A Simple Machine	015 MIN
Woodland Community, A	015 MIN

Why'd The Beetle Cross The Road C 8 MIN
16MM FILM, 3/4 OR 1/2 IN VIDEO I-C A
Presents a bug's-eye view of the meaning of life.
Prod-PFP Dist-PFP

Why's Of Data Processing, The B 45 MIN
2 INCH VIDEOTAPE
See series title for descriptive statement.
From The Data Processing, Unit 1 - Introduction To Data Processing Series.
Prod-GPITVL Dist-GPITVL

Wichita Now C 26 MIN
16MM FILM OPTICAL SOUND I-C A
Uses visual, sound and editing techniques with a minimum of narration to portray the city of Wichita, describing cultural activities, recreation, education industry, shopping and residential areas.
LC NO. 77-705720
Prod-SWBELL Dist-SWBELL Prodn-CENTRO 1969

Wichita 1978 Mennonite World Conference C 11 MIN
16MM FILM OPTICAL SOUND A R
Highlights events at the 1978 tenth assembly of the Mennonite World Conference held in Wichita, Kansas.
LC NO. 79-700944
Prod-MARTC Dist-EMBMC 1978

Wide Bandpass Filter Photometer C 12 MIN
3/4 OR 1/2 INCH VIDEO CASSETTE
Discusses, in detail, the characteristics of the wide bandpass filter photometer and mentions the characteristics of absorption photometers. Outlines contents of the operator's manual and demonstrates instrument calibration.
LC NO. 80-706816
Prod-CFDISC Dist-USNAC Prodn-NMAC 1979

Wide Feelings B 20 MIN
16MM FILM OPTICAL SOUND C A
See series title for descriptive statement.
From The All That I Am Series.
Prod-MPATI Dist-NWUFLM

Wide Pastures C 21 MIN
16MM FILM OPTICAL SOUND H-C A
Illustrates the introduction of modern methods to Australian wool growing.
LC NO. FIA68-1755
Prod-ANAIB Dist-AUIS 1967

Wide World Of Adventure—A Series
16MM FILM, 3/4 OR 1/2 IN VIDEO I-H
Prod-AVATLI Dist-EBEC 1977

Aggressive Impulse, The	018 MIN
Antarctica - Exploring The Frozen Continent	023 MIN
Bears - Kings Of The Wild	023 MIN
Big Cats, The - Endangered Predators	023 MIN
Bionics - Man or Machine	024 MIN
Can Primitive People Survive	024 MIN
Canines - Pets And Predators	023 MIN
Caves - The Dark Wilderness	024 MIN
Clowns - The Laugh Makers	024 MIN
Dinosaurs - The Terrible Lizards	024 MIN
Endangered Animals - Will They Survive	024 MIN
Fire - Friend And Foe	022 MIN
Great Apes, The - Fact Vs Fantasy	024 MIN
Horses	023 MIN
Insects - The Lovely And The Lethal	023 MIN
Is The Ice Age Coming	024 MIN
Jungles - The Green Oceans	023 MIN
Native American Myths	024 MIN
Occult, The - Mysteries Of The Supernatural	024 MIN
Physical Fitness - It Can Save Your Life	024 MIN
Quest For Flight	023 MIN
Racing - The Will To Win	017 MIN
Rock - The Beat Goes On	020 MIN
Sea, The - Mysteries Of The Deep	023 MIN
Shark, The - Maneater Or Myth	024 MIN
Snake, The - Villain Or Victim	024 MIN
Sun, The - Its Power And Promise	024 MIN
Television - Behind The Scenes	023 MIN
Warning - Earthquake	024 MIN
Whales - Can They Be Saved	024 MIN

Wide World Of Records C 17 MIN
3/4 OR 1/2 INCH VIDEO CASSETTE
Focuses on various aspect of servicing and supplying a drilling operation. Provides an overview of the oilfield service and supply industry with emphasis on safe operations.
From The Safety For Oilfield Contractors Series.
Prod-FLMWST Dist-FLMWST

Widening Gap, The C 30 MIN
3/4 OR 1/2 INCH VIDEO CASSETTE C A
See series title for descriptive statement.
From The Introduction To World Food Problems Series.
Prod-UMA Dist-GPITVL 1977

Widening World Of Books, The B 30 MIN
16MM FILM OPTICAL SOUND T
Illustrates how reading expands knowledge.
From The Starting Tomorrow Series. Unit 3 - Individualizing Your Reading Program
LC NO. 70-714210
Prod-EALING Dist-WALKED Prodn-MIFE 1967

Widow C 90 MIN
3/4 OR 1/2 INCH VIDEO CASSETTE H-C A
Tells of a woman slowly learning to deal with her own grief, her children's traumas and monetary worries after the death of her husband. Stars Michael Learned and Bradford Dillman. Based on the book WIDOW by Lynn Caine.
Prod-TIMLIF Dist-TIMLIF 1982

Widow, The C 102 MIN
16MM FILM, 3/4 OR 1/2 IN VIDEO H-C A
Tells of a widow's experiences with her young children after her husband dies. Reveals that as her loss and financial instability bear down on her, she loses her former values and eventually her sense of identity. Stars Michael Learned. Based on the book The Widow by Lynn Caine.
Prod-LUF Dist-LUF 1976

Widow's Lazy Daughter, The C 27 MIN
16MM FILM, 3/4 OR 1/2 IN VIDEO
Tells the Irish story of Bridget, who falls in love with a prince but is made to do various tasks of spinning, weaving and knitting by the queen before she can marry him. Relates how she is helped in her tasks by a deformed woman who asks only that she be invited to the wedding feast. Reveals that at the wedding feast, the old woman tells Bridget that she became deformed from too much weaving, spinning and knitting and that the prince forbids Bridget to ever do these tasks again.
From The Storybook International Series.
Prod-JOU Dist-JOU 1982

Widowhood C 30 MIN
3/4 INCH VIDEO CASSETTE
Examines the problems and fears of women alone in their mid-life.
From The Transitions - Caught At Midlife Series.
Prod-UMITV Dist-UMITV 1980

Widows B 41 MIN
16MM FILM OPTICAL SOUND PRO
Features several women who describe their experiences after the deaths of their husbands. Underlines the stresses of widowhood to show the needs of this group and to encourage discussion of appropriate intervention to prevent mental health problems which befall some widows and their children.
LC NO. 72-701915
Prod-MASON Dist-HMS 1972

Widows C 29 MIN
16MM FILM - 3/4 IN VIDEO J-C A
Presents a group of women discussing their emotional trauma after the deaths of their husbands.
From The Are You Listening Series.
LC NO. 80-706742
Prod-STURTM Dist-STURTM 1979

Widows B 41 MIN
3/4 OR 1/2 INCH VIDEO CASSETTE A
Deals with stresses of widowhood and single-parenthood and suggests strategies for preventive intervention.
Prod-DOCUFL Dist-DOCUFL

Wie Kann Man Berliner Luft Sichtbar Machen C 15 MIN
16MM FILM, 3/4 OR 1/2 IN VIDEO
See series title for descriptive statement.
From The Guten Tag Wie Geht's Series. Part 16
Prod-BAYER Dist-IFB 1973

Wife Among Wives, A (Turkana) C 72 MIN
16MM FILM, 3/4 OR 1/2 IN VIDEO
Investigates how the Turkana of northwestern Kenya view marriage. Shows preparation for marriage and interviews three sisters who discuss why a woman would want her husband to take a second wife and how polygamy can be a source of solidarity among women. Presented in Turkana with English subtitles.
From The Turkana Conversations Trilogy Series.
Prod-MCDGAL Dist-UCEMC 1980

Wife And Auto Trouble B 11 MIN
16MM FILM SILENT J-C A
Willie Collier, Mae Busch and the Keystone Cops star in a typical slapstick comedy in which a man is caught dining with his secretary and takes off in a model T. A silent film.
Prod-TRIS Dist-BHAWK 1916

Wife Beating C 27 MIN
16MM FILM, 3/4 OR 1/2 IN VIDEO H-C A
Examines the psychology of wife beating and the emotional and physical repercussions on women and their children.
Prod-NBC Dist-FI 1977

Wife Of Bath's Tale, The B 30 MIN
1 INCH VIDEOTAPE A
See series title for descriptive statement.
From The Canterbury Tales Series.
Prod-UMITV Dist-UMITV 1967

Wife, Writer, Warrior 1776 C 30 MIN
3/4 INCH VIDEO CASSETTE
Dramatizes three women's contributions to the Revolutionary War effort. Depicts Catherine Schuyler protecting her family. Pictures Mercy Otis Warren, a founder of the Committees of Correspondence. Tells how Deborah Sampson disguised herself in order to fight in the war.
From The American Women - Echoes And Dreams Series.
Prod-OHC Dist-HRC

Wiggle Your Ears C 20 MIN
2 INCH VIDEOTAPE P
See series title for descriptive statement.
From The Learning Our Language, Unit 1 - Listening Skills Series.
Prod-MPATI Dist-GPITVL

Wiggly Words C 15 MIN
2 INCH VIDEOTAPE J
Discusses the ambiguity of various words and how to avoid ambiguity in a composition.
From The From Me To You...In Writing, Pt 2 Series.
Prod-DELE Dist-GPITVL

Wilber C 8 MIN
16MM FILM, 3/4 OR 1/2 IN VIDEO IND
Demonstrates the many careless mistakes which can lead to accident and loss. Follows Wilber's departure for work through the morning traffic to his attempts to help others. Shows the areas in which safety precautions should be exercised.
Prod-IAPA Dist-IFB 1973

Wilberforce Pendulum M-6, The C 3 MIN
16MM FILM OPTICAL SOUND H-C
Indicates resonance between torsional vibration and translational vibration of a rigid body suspended from a helical spring. Shows energy transformations-rotational and translational, kinetic and potential.
From The Single-Concept Films In Physics Series.
Prod-OSUMPD Dist-OSUMPD 1963

Wilbur And Orville - The Air Devils C 52 MIN
16MM FILM, 3/4 OR 1/2 IN VIDEO I-C A
Presents the story of the Wright Brothers' efforts to build the first working airplane until they are rewarded for their diligence.
From The Great Americans Series.
Prod-LUF Dist-LUF 1979

Wilbur Shaw - Speed Way Star B 15 MIN
1/2 IN VIDEO CASSETTE BETA/VHS
Presents one of America's greatest race car drivers, Wilbur Shaw.
Prod-STAR Dist-STAR

Wilbur's Story C 15 MIN
16MM FILM OPTICAL SOUND P-I
An excerpt from the motion picture Charlotte's Web. Tells how a pig named Wilbur is saved from the sausage grinder by his literate friend Charlotte the spider, who schemes to save him by weaving into her web words which sing Wilbur's praises. Based on the book Charlotte's Web by E B White.
From The Peppermint Stick Selection Series.
LC NO. 77-701722
Prod-FI Dist-FI 1976

Wild America, Who Needs It C 20 MIN
16MM FILM, 3/4 OR 1/2 IN VIDEO J-H A
Creates an awareness that although we live with the conveniences and sophisticated alterations to our natural environment brought about by technology, we are still living off the land for our most basic necessities. Points out that everyone is affected by ecologically unsound practices.
LC NO. 81-706624
Prod-NAS Dist-PHENIX 1979

Wild And Tasty C 29 MIN
3/4 INCH VIDEO CASSETTE
Discusses how to identify edible wild plants and how to cook them.
From The House Botanist Series.
Prod-UMITV Dist-UMITV 1978

Wild And Wonderful Thirties, The B 28 MIN
16MM FILM OPTICAL SOUND
Examines the film industry in the 1930's, the beginning of sound, describing publicity gimmicks of the stars, films produced through the depression years, and a glimpse of the stars' lives showing their homes, cars and yachts.
From The Hollywood And The Stars Series.
LC NO. 73-702038
Prod-WOLPER Dist-WOLPER 1964

Wild And Wonderful World Of Auto Racing, The C 27 MIN
16MM FILM, 3/4 OR 1/2 IN VIDEO J-C A
Examines and compares the four major kinds of auto racing - stocks, sports, drag and Indianapolis championship cars.
Prod-RAYBEM Dist-SF Prodn-CUSTMF 1969

Wild Angels, The C 82 MIN
16MM FILM OPTICAL SOUND H A
Describes a California motorcycle gang which is run on semireligious, ritualistic, Nazi lines. Stars Peter Fonda, Nancy Sinatra and Bruce Dern in this frequently banned, social drama.
Prod-AIP Dist-TIMLIF 1966

Wild Animal Families C 11 MIN
16MM FILM, 3/4 OR 1/2 IN VIDEO K-I
Presents common North American animals in family situations, showing the care of the young by both mother and father. Animals shown in natural habitat include bison, antelope, prairie dog, bear, porcupine, elk and Canada goose.
Prod-FA Dist-PHENIX 1957

Wild Animal Families (French) C 11 MIN
16MM FILM, 3/4 OR 1/2 IN VIDEO K-I
Presents common North American animals in family situations, showing the care of the young by both mother and father. Animals shown in natural habitat include bison, antelope, prairie dog, bear, porcupine, elk and Canada goose.
Prod-FA Dist-PHENIX 1957

Wild Animal Park C 15 MIN
3/4 OR 1/2 INCH VIDEO CASSETTE P-I
Visits the San Diego Wild Animal Park to learn about an alternative type of animal keeping.
From The Explorers Unlimited Series.
Prod-WVIZTV Dist-AITECH 1971

Wild Animals C 14 MIN
3/4 OR 1/2 INCH VIDEO CASSETTE P
Shows how to draw wild animals.
From The Let's Draw Series.
Prod-KOKHTV Dist-AITECH 1976

Wild Animals C 15 MIN
3/4 OR 1/2 INCH VIDEO CASSETTE P
Presents Dr Allhart and her friend Patience visiting various large animals at the zoo, where they also see the zoo hospital and commissary.
From The Dr Allhart And Patience Series.
LC NO. 81-707530
Prod-JCITV Dist-GPITVL 1979

Wild Animals Adapt C 9 MIN
16MM FILM, 3/4 OR 1/2 IN VIDEO P-I
Shows how the physical characteristics of the bighorn sheep, the water ouzel and the squirrel provide effective adaptations in their different environments.
From The Life Science For Elementary Series.
Prod-PEDF Dist-AIMS 1976

Wild Animals Catch Fish C 9 MIN
16MM FILM, 3/4 OR 1/2 IN VIDEO P-I
Shows how several different kinds of animals and birds use diverse fishing techniques. Identifies the specialized and adaptive characteristics of each technique.
From The Life Science For Elementary Series.
Prod-PEDF Dist-AIMS 1976

Wild Animals Catch Fish (Spanish) C 9 MIN
16MM FILM, 3/4 OR 1/2 IN VIDEO P-I
Shows how several different kinds of animals and birds use diverse fishing techniques. Identifies the specialized and adoptive characteristics of each technique.
From The Life Science For Elementary Series.
Prod-PEDF Dist-AIMS 1976

Wild Animals Of Virginia C 26 MIN
16MM FILM OPTICAL SOUND P-H
Presents a survey of the mammals native to Virginia, picturing their habits and natural habitats--the chipmunk, squirrel, groundhog, beaver, muskrat, otter, mink, elk, deer, bear, grey and red fox, rabbit, opossum, bobcat, raccoon and skunk.
LC NO. FIA67-2017
Prod-VADE Dist-VADE Prodn-FPSERV 1967

Wild Animals, Pt 1 C 15 MIN
2 INCH VIDEOTAPE
See series title for descriptive statement.
From The Charlie's Pad Series.
Prod-WSIU Dist-PUBTEL

Wild Animals, Pt 2 C 15 MIN
2 INCH VIDEOTAPE
See series title for descriptive statement.
From The Charlie's Pad Series.
Prod-WSIU Dist-PUBTEL

Wild Are Free, The C 24 MIN
16MM FILM OPTICAL SOUND I-C A
Shows the game wardens in Kruger National Park as they control life among the different species of wild animals and battle droughts, forest fires and marauding poachers.
Prod-SMUSA Dist-SMUSA

Wild At The Wheel C 10 MIN
16MM FILM, 3/4 OR 1/2 IN VIDEO H-C A
Examines why people speed, showing the serious accident of a teenager who is a compulsive speeder.
Prod-AIMS Dist-AIMS 1978

Wild Babies C 26 MIN
16MM FILM, 3/4 OR 1/2 IN VIDEO
Shows wild animal youngsters learning important life-saving skills. Shows the great horned owl, toad, bull elk and other animal young.
Prod-STOUFP Dist-STOUFP 1979

Wild Bunch, The C 143 MIN
16MM FILM OPTICAL SOUND
Describes the adventures of a 1913 outlaw gang who plan one last bank robbery.
Prod-WB Dist-TWYMAN 1969

Wild But Friendly B 14 MIN
16MM FILM OPTICAL SOUND H-C A
Presents India's rich wild life as found in the sanctuaries and shows the rich variety of flora and fauna.
Prod-INDIA Dist-NEDINF

Wild Cats C 26 MIN
16MM FILM, 3/4 OR 1/2 IN VIDEO
Shows that in form and function, wild cats have reached the peak of their predatory evolution.
LC NO. 84-700166
Prod-STOUFP Dist-STOUFP 1983

Wild Characters, Patterns, Pipes And Tees C 30 MIN
3/4 OR 1/2 INCH VIDEO CASSETTE IND
Shows that command is -tr (-d,-c,-cs).
From The UNIX Series.
Prod-COLOSU Dist-COLOSU

Wild Corners Of The Great Lakes C 55 MIN
16MM FILM OPTICAL SOUND
Views wildlife and Indian relics along Lake Superior's north shore.
From The To The Wild Country Series.
LC NO. 76-701078
Prod-CANBC Dist-KEGPL 1974

Wild Dog Family, The - The Coyote C 18 MIN
16MM FILM, 3/4 OR 1/2 IN VIDEO I-H A
Presents a true story of how the coyote, a keen-witted member of nature's wild dog family, has learned to live in close proximity to his greatest enemy--man. The coyote has enlarged his

domain in spite of man's expansion of cities, industries and freeways.
Prod-DISNEY Dist-WDEMCO 1968

Wild Dogs C 26 MIN
16MM FILM OPTICAL SOUND
Looks at the social behavior of wild dogs and their role in a balanced ecosystem.
LC NO. 83-700331
Prod-STOUFP Dist-STOUFP 1982

Wild Dogs C 26 MIN
3/4 OR 1/2 INCH VIDEO CASSETTE
Profiles wild dogs in North America. Observes the behavior of the Arctic fox, endangered timber wolf and other species.
Prod-STOUFP Dist-STOUFP

Wild Duck, The C 60 MIN
3/4 OR 1/2 INCH VIDEO CASSETTE H-C A
Develops an appreciation of the playwright's craft in shaping the elements of plot, theme and character. Uses the play The Wild Duck as an example.
From The Drama - Play, Performance, Perception Series. Playwrights And Plotting
Prod-BBCTV Dist-FI 1978

Wild Duck, The C 108 MIN
3/4 OR 1/2 INCH VIDEO CASSETTE
Presents Henrik Ibsen's play The Wild Duck, which asks whether humanity can bear 'too much reality.'
From The Classic Theatre Series.
LC NO. 79-706933
Prod-BBCTV Dist-FI 1976

Wild Duck, The (German) C 106 MIN
16MM FILM OPTICAL SOUND
Describes how the family of a photographer leads a life of comfortable delusion until an old friend exposes their lies and hypocrisy. Directed by Hans W Geissendorfer. With English subtitles.
Prod-UNKNWN Dist-NYFLMS 1976

Wild Edible Plants C 17 MIN
16MM FILM, 3/4 OR 1/2 IN VIDEO
Shows how common wild plants may be harvested and used as food and stresses avoiding unknown plants that may be dangerous.
Prod-WESTWN Dist-WESTWN 1976

Wild Fire C 50 MIN
16MM FILM, 3/4 OR 1/2 IN VIDEO J-H A
Documents the tragic saga of the Wenatchee forest fire, one of the worst in history.
Prod-MGM Dist-FI 1972

Wild Foods From Wild Places C 12 MIN
16MM FILM OPTICAL SOUND J-C A
Identifies various types of edible roots, berries, seeds, nuts and greens growing in the wild.
LC NO. 79-701093
Prod-CIU Dist-CIU 1979

Wild Geese Calling C 33 MIN
16MM FILM, 3/4 OR 1/2 IN VIDEO I-H
Tells how a nine-year-old boy finds a wild Canadian gander wounded by hunters and unable to fly. Shows how he nurses the gander back to health and then must decide whether to keep it as a pet or set it free to return to its flock.
From The Animal Featurettes, Set 3 Series.
Prod-DISNEY Dist-WDEMCO 1969

Wild Goose, The B 19 MIN
16MM FILM, 3/4 OR 1/2 IN VIDEO
Presents a satiric comedy about a misanthropic old man confined in a straightlaced nursing facility. Concerns his efforts to circumvent the rules and regulations and the nurses who enforce them.
LC NO. 79-706040
Prod-CRONIN Dist-FI 1975

Wild Green Things In The City C 11 MIN
16MM FILM, 3/4 OR 1/2 IN VIDEO K-I
Shows a young girl who finds a variety of plants in neglected corners of the city and creates a flourishing garden on her rooftop.
LC NO. 81-706033
Prod-RAWMER Dist-TEXFLM 1979

Wild Highlands C 21 MIN
16MM FILM, 3/4 OR 1/2 IN VIDEO J-H
Views a wide variety of wildlife in western Scotland.
Prod-BTF Dist-IFB 1963

Wild Horses C
1/2 IN VIDEO CASSETTE BETA/VHS
Deals with wild horses.
Prod-EQVDL Dist-EQVDL

Wild Horses, Broken Wings C 30 MIN
16MM FILM, 3/4 OR 1/2 IN VIDEO H-C A
A shortened version of the motion picture Wild Horses, Broken Wings. Tells the story of Davene Bennett, who opened her home and heart to foster children of all races and ages.
Prod-VERITN Dist-LCOA 1979

Wild Horses, Broken Wings C 58 MIN
16MM FILM, 3/4 OR 1/2 IN VIDEO H-C A
Explores the life of Davene Bennett, a woman who has been a foster mother for thirty years, taking children of all ages and races into her home.
Prod-VERITN Dist-LCOA 1979

Wild In The City C
3/4 OR 1/2 INCH VIDEO CASSETTE
Looks at the intrusion of the wild raccoon into an urban environment. Follows the nightly lives of a typical urban raccoon family as they get in and out of trouble.
Prod-NWLDPR Dist-NWLDPR

Wild In The Streets C 92 MIN
16MM FILM OPTICAL SOUND H A
Tells the story of a pop singer who becomes president and launches a campaign for teenage emancipation. Social melodrama starring Shelley Winters and Chris Jones.
Prod-AIP Dist-TIMLIF 1968

Wild Indians B 29 MIN
2 INCH VIDEOTAPE K-P
See series title for descriptive statement.
From The Children's Fair Series.
Prod-WMVSTV Dist-PUBTEL

Wild Ireland C 50 MIN
3/4 OR 1/2 INCH VIDEO CASSETTE H-C A
Portrays the wildlife of Ireland showing a history of human invasion and settlement that cleared the forests, farmed the land and brought new plants and animals. Explains how the landscape is a legacy of the last Ice Age that has undergone dramatic changes. Features arctic plants beside orchids, peat-land with its own animals, birds and plants and mild marshes and estuaries feeding wintering wildfowl of Europe and North America.
Prod-BBCTV Dist-FI

Wild Lens In Algonquin, A C 55 MIN
16MM FILM OPTICAL SOUND
Takes a look at the wildlife and vegetation of Algonquin Park in Ontario, Canada.
From The To The Wild Country Series.
LC NO. 75-704360
Prod-CANBC Dist-KEGPL Prodn-KEGPL 1974

Wild Life Of India C 26 MIN
16MM FILM OPTICAL SOUND H-C A
Presents eight wild life sanctuaries in Kashmir, Uttar Pradesh, Assam, Gujaat, Mysore and Kerala in India, with their lush jungles and large varieties of flora and fauna. Includes the bird sanctuary which is frequented by birds of other countries, the Corbett National Park and the Kaziringa Sanctuary and indicates the facilities available for tourists.
Prod-INDIA Dist-NEDINF

Wild Man Of The Forest, The - The Orangutan C 23 MIN
3/4 OR 1/2 INCH VIDEO CASSETTE K-C A
Tells of an experiment which may give the orangutan a future. Shows people teaching orangutans, which have been captured, how to live in the wild.
Prod-NWLDPR Dist-NWLDPR 1982

Wild Mountain Sheep C 24 MIN
3/4 OR 1/2 INCH VIDEO CASSETTE I-H
Examines the Rocky Mountain Big Horn Sheep and the Dall Sheep of Alaska from an ecological approach which includes wildlife studies, the mountain sheep's predators such as coyotes, golden eagles and the grizzly bear, survival techniques and mating rituals.
From The Aerie Nature Series.
Prod-CEPRO Dist-CEPRO 1982

Wild One, The B 79 MIN
16MM FILM OPTICAL SOUND
Demonstrates how the lynch mob response of the townspeople is no less destructive than the wild anarchy of the cycle gangs. Stars Marlon Brando.
Prod-CPC Dist-UAE 1954

Wild Ones, The C 15 MIN
3/4 INCH VIDEO CASSETTE P-I
Looks at unusual pets, such as an eagle, mountain lion and chimp.
From The Can You Imagine Series.
Prod-WVIZTV Dist-GPITVL

Wild Pets C 29 MIN
2 INCH VIDEOTAPE
See series title for descriptive statement.
From The Observing Eye Series.
Prod-WGBHTV Dist-PUBTEL

Wild Poses B 19 MIN
16MM FILM OPTICAL SOUND
Tells what happens when Spanky's parents take him to Otto Phocus' photography studio to have his picture taken. A Little Rascals film.
Prod-ROACH Dist-BHAWK 1933

Wild River B 52 MIN
16MM FILM, 3/4 OR 1/2 IN VIDEO I-C
Shows a family exploring Idaho's Middle Fork Salmon and Salmon Rivers in rafts and kayaks and traveling the Florida everglades.
LC NO. 80-706380
Prod-PMI Dist-NGS Prodn-NGS 1970

Wild Science - Communicating With Animals C 11 MIN
16MM FILM, 3/4 OR 1/2 IN VIDEO J-H
Reports on two successful experiments that show that animals can learn language and that interspecies communication is possible. Features Morgan, a whale who helps the Navy locate submarines and guides underwater search-and-retrieve teams, and Lana, a chimpanzee who constructs sentences on a computer. Narrated by Peter Falk.
Prod-NBCTV Dist-EBEC 1976

Wild Science - Mind And Body C 10 MIN
16MM FILM, 3/4 OR 1/2 IN VIDEO J-H
Looks at the practices of mind and body regulation of the Tarahumara Indians of Central Mexico, who run distances of 200 miles nonstop, and of yoga practitioners, who control heart rate, blood flow and respiration. Demonstrates that mental and physical health are interrelated. Shows modern science's duplication of these self-regulatory processes by biofeedback training. Narrated by Peter Falk.
Prod-NBCTV Dist-EBEC

Wild Style C 83 MIN
3/4 INCH VIDEO CASSETTE
Features black story tellers known as rappers, black dancers who whirl with the speed of human tops known as breakers and the artists of graffiti, Black and Hispanic.
Prod-FIRS Dist-FIRS

Wild Swans, The C 9 MIN
16MM FILM, 3/4 OR 1/2 IN VIDEO P-I
Presents the Hans Christian Andersen story, The Wild Swans, about a young girl's devotion to her 11 brothers who have been placed under an evil spell and turned into wild swans.
From The Classic Tales Retold Series.
Prod-BFA Dist-PHENIX 1976

Wild Swans, The - A Danish Fairy Tale C 11 MIN
16MM FILM, 3/4 OR 1/2 IN VIDEO K-P
Presents the Danish fairy tale The Wild Swans. Tells the story of eleven wild swans who are really princes, bewitched by an evil queen. Shows how only their sister's hard work and devotion can return them to human form.
From The Favorite Fairy Tales And Fables Series.
Prod-CORF Dist-CORF 1980

Wild Synch C 10 MIN
16MM FILM OPTICAL SOUND
Presents an experimental film which shows how to get lip synchronization with a wind up camera and a wild tape recorder as a mother plays piano and her daughter dances.
LC NO. 74-702777
Prod-HANCXR Dist-CANFDC 1973

Wild Wings C 26 MIN
16MM FILM, 3/4 OR 1/2 IN VIDEO
Shows that America's birds come in every imaginable shape, size and color, but that they all share the awesome power of flight.
LC NO. 84-700167
Prod-STOUFP Dist-STOUFP 1983

Wild Wings C 35 MIN
16MM FILM, 3/4 OR 1/2 IN VIDEO H A
Describes a study of wildfowl by the Wildfowl Trust in England. Identifies the fowl, discusses their migration, food, and mating habits, and shows the use of blinds for observation, the taking of eggs of rare species from mothers until they are hatched, and the use of rocket-propelled nets to capture geese for banding.
Prod-BTF Dist-IFB 1967

Wild-Goose Jack C 57 MIN
3/4 OR 1/2 INCH VIDEO CASSETTE J-C A
Introduces Canadian Jack Miner who was once a skilled hunter but turned to conservation after the deaths of two of his children and his brother. Discusses Miner's contributions in the field of water fowl migration.
LC NO. 84-706505
Prod-MURPH Dist-DIRECT 1983

Wild, Wild World Of Animals–A Series
16MM FILM, 3/4 OR 1/2 IN VIDEO
Explores the lives and behavior patterns of various species of wild animals.
Prod-TIMLIF Dist-TIMLIF 1976

Cry Wolf 15 MIN
Deadly African Snakes 15 MIN
Kodiak Island 16 MIN
Octopus, The 12 MIN
Sea Turtles 13 MIN
Spider, The 18 MIN

Wildacres - The Youth Conference Story C 15 MIN
16MM FILM OPTICAL SOUND
Tells the story of the Civitan Youth Conference held in 1961. Shows the delegates and staff in action during the conference which had as its purpose the making of good citizens. Narrated by Griffin Campbell.
Prod-CVTN Dist-UNC 1961

Wildcatter C 30 MIN
16MM FILM, 3/4 OR 1/2 IN VIDEO C A
Explains how small oil and gas prospectors are playing an increasingly vital role in America's search for energy. Tells the story of one such wildcatter, Bill Brodnax of Taurus Petroleum in Louisiana, as he drills a well in hopes of the big payoff.
From The Enterprise Series.
LC NO. 81-707537
Prod-WGBHTV Dist-LCOA Prodn-DORSOL 1981

Wildebeest C 20 MIN
16MM FILM, 3/4 OR 1/2 IN VIDEO P A
Shows the white-bearded gnu, or wildebeest, in its habitat on the East African plain. Tracks the odyssey of the migrating herds and presents footage of the birth of a wildebeest.
From The Silent Safari Series.
Prod-CHE Dist-EBEC 1984

Wilder Summer, The C 33 MIN
16MM FILM, 3/4 OR 1/2 IN VIDEO I-H
An edited version of the motion picture The Wilder Summer. Presents a story set in a summer camp which attempts to show that class differences are not important. Based on the novel THE WILDER SUMMER by Stephen Krensky.
LC NO. 84-706663
Prod-LCOA Dist-LCOA 1984

Wilder Summer, The C 54 MIN
16MM FILM, 3/4 OR 1/2 IN VIDEO I-H

Presents a story set in a summer camp which attempts to show that class differences are not important. Based on the novel THE WILDER SUMMER by Stephen Krensky.
LC NO. 84-706663
Prod-LCOA Dist-LCOA 1984

Wilderness C 14 MIN
16MM FILM OPTICAL SOUND
Celebrates the American outdoors. Shares various wilderness experiences, including river running, cross-country skiing, sailing and mountaineering.
LC NO. 79-701400
Prod-FLEX Dist-FLEX 1979

Wilderness C 30 MIN
16MM FILM OPTICAL SOUND
Shows the work of the National Parks and Wildlife Service in Kosciusk National Park in Australia. Defines wilderness as a place, a park management technique and a state of mind.
LC NO. 80-700860
Prod-NSWF Dist-TASCOR 1978

Wilderness - An American Ideal C 15 MIN
16MM FILM, 3/4 OR 1/2 IN VIDEO
Presents America's changing attitudes about wild places.
Prod-WESTWN Dist-WESTWN Prodn-KEMPBJ 1975

Wilderness Below, The C 12 MIN
16MM FILM OPTICAL SOUND
Presents an impressionistic view of caving. Follows one spelunker as he explores a cavern and shows the beauty, mystery and solitude to be enjoyed in caving.
LC NO. 77-700948
Prod-INERTH Dist-IU 1977

Wilderness Dawning C 14 MIN
16MM FILM OPTICAL SOUND
Presents glimpses of animal life in Canada's northland.
From The Journal Series.
LC NO. 75-704361
Prod-FIARTS Dist-CANFDC 1973

Wilderness Nomads C 18 MIN
16MM FILM, 3/4 OR 1/2 IN VIDEO J-C A
Follows the exploits of a group of teenagers calling themselves the wilderness nomads as they make a four-week canoe trip through the northern Canadian woods.
Prod-LCOA Dist-LCOA 1976

Wilderness Road, The X 23 MIN
16MM FILM OPTICAL SOUND I-C A
Follows Daniel Boone, George Rogers Clark and other pioneers who carved out and traveled the wilderness road through Virginia and Kentucky. Describes their explorations, fight for independence and settlement of the frontier country.
Prod-VADE Dist-VADE 1953

Wilderness Trail, The C 15 MIN
3/4 INCH VIDEO CASSETTE
Takes the viewers on a pack trip into the Bridger wilderness area, Bridger National Forest, Wyoming, which is protected and kept in its natural state. Includes narration by a professional local packer.
Prod-USDA Dist-USDA 1972

Wilderness Treasure C 22 MIN
16MM FILM OPTICAL SOUND I-C A
Shows how a group of teenage boys follow the trails of the pioneers.
Prod-CAFM Dist-CAFM

Wilderness—A Series
16MM FILM, 3/4 OR 1/2 IN VIDEO J-C A
Prod-PFP Dist-PHENIX 1967

Dunes 8 MIN
Leaf 8 MIN
Waters Of Yosemite 10 MIN
Winter Geyser 7 MIN

Wildest Ride, The C 14 MIN
16MM FILM OPTICAL SOUND
Pictures Craig Breedlove in his jet-powered car, Spirit of America, as he breaks the 500-mile-per-hour land-speed record at the Bonneville Salt Flats in Utah on October 15, 1964. Includes views of the smash-up of his car following the record-setting race, showing the unharmed driver.
LC NO. FIA66-1081
Prod-GTARC Dist-GTARC Prodn-SPOTLT 1964

Wildest Show On Earth, The C 26 MIN
16MM FILM OPTICAL SOUND
Shows some of the action at the Texas Prison Rodeo, a contest in which the contestants are prison inmates.
LC NO. 74-702528
Prod-TEXDE Dist-TEXDE Prodn-MFCFP 1974

Wildflowers C 11 MIN
16MM FILM, 3/4 OR 1/2 IN VIDEO I-J
Shows several kinds of wildflowers blooming in various locations and seasons and explains that each wildflower is suited in some way to life in a particular place.
Prod-BFA Dist-PHENIX 1972

Wildflowers C 30 MIN
3/4 OR 1/2 INCH VIDEO CASSETTE
See series title for descriptive statement.
From The Roughing It Series.
Prod-KYTV Dist-KYTV 1984

Wildfowl Sanctuary C 26 MIN
16MM FILM OPTICAL SOUND I-C A
Features naturalist-photographer Bill Carrcik who is curator of the Kortwright Waterfowl Park in Guelph, Ontario, which harbors a thousand birds of more than 50 species. Observes and studies the Canada goose, black duck, pintail canvasback, redhead, the spectacular looking hooded mergaser and the rare trumpeter swan, among many others.
From The Audubon Wildlife Theatre Series.
Prod-AVEXP Dist-AVEXP

Wildlands, Our Heritage C 26 MIN
16MM FILM OPTICAL SOUND P A
Explores the moods of the wilderness and familiarizes viewers with the wild creatures of Georgian Bay. Includes scenes of white tailed deer, early summer morning mists, the gray jay and the black bear. Features close-ups of various birds.
LC NO. 79-708744
Prod-KEGPL Dist-AVEXP Prodn-KEGPL 1970

Wildlife C 24 MIN
16MM FILM OPTICAL SOUND
Shows the flora and fauna of Alberta, Canada.
From The Heading Out Series.
LC NO. 76-703337
Prod-CENTWO Dist-CENTWO 1975

Wildlife C 29 MIN
2 INCH VIDEOTAPE
See series title for descriptive statement.
From The Commonwealth Series.
Prod-WITFTV Dist-PUBTEL

Wildlife - An American Heritage C 14 MIN
3/4 OR 1/2 INCH VIDEO CASSETTE
Introduces and considers the value of America's vast and diverse wildlife resources.
Prod-WESTWN Dist-WESTWN

Wildlife By Air C 26 MIN
16MM FILM OPTICAL SOUND I-C A
Shows sequences off the shores of Maine with close-ups of plants found in New England, including the cardinal flower, Canada bead Ruby and reindeer moss. Features underwater shots, studying creatures that nature devised to balance the environment. Portrays the shallow spawning beds of many varieties of sharks and rays and examines several bizarre fish amid sea ferns and colorful stony corals off the dry Tortugas Islands.
From The Audubon Wildlife Theatre Series.
Prod-AVEXP Dist-AVEXP

Wildlife Families C 9 MIN
16MM FILM, 3/4 OR 1/2 IN VIDEO P-I
Takes a look at several kinds of wildlife families.
From The Life Science For Elementary Series.
Prod-PEDF Dist-AIMS 1976

Wildlife In A Southern Slough C 11 MIN
16MM FILM, 3/4 OR 1/2 IN VIDEO I-J
Describes animal life found in the waterways of several Southern states.
Prod-DEU Dist-IFB 1963

Wildlife In The Jungles Of Latin America C 17 MIN
16MM FILM, 3/4 OR 1/2 IN VIDEO I-J
Examines the typical animal forms of the rain forests of Latin America. Shows camouflage, methods of climbing and leaping, and the search for food.
Prod-IFB Dist-IFB 1964

Wildlife In The Managed Forest C 10 MIN
16MM FILM OPTICAL SOUND
Shows the animal and plant life in forest areas.
LC NO. 77-702720
Prod-MEPHTS Dist-MEPHTS 1976

Wildlife In The Rockies - Animal Census In Alberta C 7 MIN
16MM FILM OPTICAL SOUND
Depicts the annual spring census of animals in Bann National Park in the Rocky Mountains. Shows how the game wardens cover trail to count the animals, such as moose, bighorn sheep, elk and mountain goats.
From The News Magazine Of The Screen Series. Vol 3, Issue 2
Prod-HEARST Dist-HEARST 1960

Wildlife Island C 26 MIN
16MM FILM OPTICAL SOUND P A
Follows a class of intermediate students as they investigate a wildlife island just across the bay from the city of Toronto, Ontario.
LC NO. 76-710210
Prod-KEGPL Dist-AVEXP 1969

Wildlife Management C 30 MIN
3/4 OR 1/2 INCH VIDEO CASSETTE C
Considers attempts to manage wildlife in the environment, potential extinction of animal species, destruction of habitats and functions of state parks and wildlife protected areas.
From The Living Environment Series.
Prod-DALCCD Dist-DALCCD

Wildlife Mothers C 9 MIN
16MM FILM, 3/4 OR 1/2 IN VIDEO P-I
Shows the mothering behavior of animals in their natural habitats, concentrating on the examples of the mallard duck and the burrowing owl.
From The Life Science For Elementary Series.
Prod-PEDF Dist-AIMS 1976

Wildlife On Reprieve C 12 MIN
16MM FILM, 3/4 OR 1/2 IN VIDEO I-H A
Shows the need to protect rare, endangered species and their natural habitat.
Prod-READER Dist-MCFI

Wildlife On The Main Stem B 27 MIN
3/4 INCH VIDEO CASSETTE
Shows how an abundance of wildlife is able to live in harmony with a complex of six multi-purpose dams and resevoirs constructed by the corps of engineers on the upper Mississippi. Features the sharp tailed grouse, beaver, waterfowl, upland game and fish.
Prod-USNAC Dist-USNAC 1972

Wildlife Photographer At Work, A C 13 MIN
16MM FILM, 3/4 OR 1/2 IN VIDEO I
Features Kent Durden, naturalist-photographer, showing us the tricks of his trade. Describes how to film the tiny, distant and fast-moving animals.
Prod-PFP Dist-AIMS 1975

Wildlife Sanctuaries Of India C 26 MIN
16MM FILM OPTICAL SOUND I-C A
Portrays wildlife in four wildlife sanctuaries of India, including Kazirange, Periyar Lake, Keoladeo and the Gir forest. Shows some of the crafts and folkways of the villagers who share the vast stretches of rural India with some of the world's rarest wildlife creatures.
From The Audubon Wildlife Theatre Series.
Prod-AVEXP Dist-AVEXP

Wilf C 21 MIN
16MM FILM, 3/4 OR 1/2 IN VIDEO J-C
Presents the story of a lonely small farmer who desires to be alone and an old man who does not want to change in a changing world.
Prod-NFBC Dist-NFBC 1970

Wilkens Coffee With Puppets C 1 MIN
3/4 OR 1/2 INCH VIDEO CASSETTE
Shows a classic television commercial.
Prod-BROOKC Dist-BROOKC

Wilkinson Fundamentals B
16MM FILM OPTICAL SOUND
Presents tips on football, baseball, swimming, diving, basketball, hockey, gymnastics, track and field and other events on 25 different reels.
Prod-SFI Dist-SFI

Will C 5 MIN
16MM FILM OPTICAL SOUND
Deals with a color collage of graphics which portrays a dance.
Prod-VANBKS Dist-VANBKS

Will For Peace B 33 MIN
16MM FILM OPTICAL SOUND
Contrasts the post-war activities of the United States with Russia. Shows how the United States has worked toward peace while Russia has concentrated upon preparations for war.
LC NO. FIE52-2116
Prod-USA Dist-USNAC 1951

Will Of God C 145 MIN
3/4 OR 1/2 INCH VIDEO CASSETTE
Presents Sri Gurudev answering questions on control of the mind, bowing to the Guru, job-related problems, spontaneous acts and the Will of God.
Prod-IYOGA Dist-IYOGA

Will Of The People, The B 55 MIN
3/4 OR 1/2 INCH VIDEO CASSETTE
Recounts the story of the Spanish revolution and the rise of Franco.
Prod-IHF Dist-IHF

Will Rogers B 27 MIN
16MM FILM OPTICAL SOUND I-C A
Surveys Rogers' career from his early barnstorming days as a rodeo and vaudeville performer to his death in an airplane crash in the 1930s.
From The History Of The Motion Picture Series.
Prod-SF Dist-KILLIS 1960

Will Rogers C 20 MIN
3/4 OR 1/2 INCH VIDEO CASSETTE I
See series title for descriptive statement.
From The Truly American Series.
Prod-WVIZTV Dist-GPITVL 1979

Will Rogers B 26 MIN
16MM FILM, 3/4 OR 1/2 IN VIDEO I-H
Uses rare actuality footage to portray the personal life and history-making deeds of Will Rogers.
From The History Makers Of The 20th Century Series.
Prod-WOLPER Dist-SF 1965

Will Rogers - Champion Of The People C 52 MIN
16MM FILM, 3/4 OR 1/2 IN VIDEO J-C A
Describes the early years of Will Rogers during which he fights for law and order in his Oklahoma hometown.
From The Great Americans Series.
Prod-LUF Dist-LUF 1979

Will Rogers - The Cowboy Humorist B 15 MIN
1/2 IN VIDEO CASSETTE BETA/VHS
Tells the story of Will Rogers, who during the Depression contributed to relief in the Southwest.
Prod-STAR Dist-STAR

Will Rogers' California Ranch C 23 MIN
16MM FILM, 3/4 OR 1/2 IN VIDEO I-C A
Explores the California ranch built by cowboy comedian Will Rogers and presented to the state as a historic park.
From The American Lifestyle - Cultural Leaders Series.
Prod-COMCO Dist-AIMS 1977

Will Rogers' 1920's C 41 MIN
16MM FILM, 3/4 OR 1/2 IN VIDEO H-C A

Shows Will Rogers as a man who, more than being a beloved humorist, helped shape the attitudes of America. Uses archive materials accompanied by Will Rogers' comments to provide a visual record of some of the major events and figures of the 1920's.
Prod-OKSU Dist-CF 1976

Will The Fishing Have To Stop C 31 MIN
16MM FILM, 3/4 OR 1/2 IN VIDEO H-C A
Discusses the threat of disastrous fish shortages due to indiscriminate and unlimited ocean fishing. Proposes greater international cooperation to deal with the problem.
From The Nova Series.
LC NO. 79-707247
Prod-WGBHTV Dist-TIMLIF 1976

Will The Gator Glades Survive C 30 MIN
16MM FILM, 3/4 OR 1/2 IN VIDEO
Explores the dangers to wildlife inhabiting the Florida everglades because of man's interference with the natural water supply and his killing of alligators.
From The Our Vanishing Wilderness, No. 5 Series
LC NO. 80-707026
Prod-NETRC Dist-IU 1970

Will There Always Be An England C 24 MIN
16MM FILM, 3/4 OR 1/2 IN VIDEO H-C A
Looks at economic problems in Great Britain and suggests that during the late 1970's America is following the same path. Originally shown on the CBS television program 60 Minutes.
Prod-CBSNEW Dist-CAROUF

Will They Survive... C 24 MIN
3/4 OR 1/2 INCH VIDEO CASSETTE I-H
Shows the threat of extinction due to encroachment of human beings on North America's endangered species, such as the alligator, bald eagle, California condor, whooping crane, grizzly bear, the black-footed ferret and the peregrine falcon.
From The Aerie Nature Series.
Prod-CEPRO Dist-CEPRO 1982

Will To Be Free, The C 56 MIN
16MM FILM, 3/4 OR 1/2 IN VIDEO
Explores the origins of the ideals which inspired America's founding fathers to sign the revolutionary document they called the Declaration of Independence.
Prod-ABCNEW Dist-FI 1976

Will To Die - Right To Live C 18 MIN
3/4 OR 1/2 INCH VIDEO CASSETTE
Examines the sociological significance of euthanasia. Views death from the point of view of theology, law and medicine. Presents both positive and negative views on euthanasia.
Prod-LMP Dist-AJN

Will To Win C 25 MIN
3/4 INCH VIDEO CASSETTE
Represents a condensed version of the film Thirteen Minutes To Wait. Shows Toronto's Steve Podborski waiting 13 minutes to find out his World Cup downhill ski racing rival beat him by 28/100ths of a second. Explains how he went on to become ranked best in the world.
Prod-LAURON Dist-LAURON

Will To Win, The C 14 MIN
16MM FILM, 3/4 OR 1/2 IN VIDEO A
Outlines a five-point strategy for winning. Useful in personal, job, study or social situations.
Prod-SEVDIM Dist-SEVDIM

Will To Win, The C 15 MIN
16MM FILM, 3/4 OR 1/2 IN VIDEO J A
Presents a study of men in motion, showing auto and motorcycle racing, tobogganing, skiing, surfing and skydiving.
Prod-PFP Dist-PFP 1972

Will You Answer True? C 15 MIN
3/4 OR 1/2 INCH VIDEO CASSETTE A
Employs humor to show how to handle a customer inquiry over the telephone and turn it into a sale.
Prod-XICOM Dist-XICOM

Will You Answer True? C 16 MIN
3/4 OR 1/2 INCH VIDEO CASSETTE
Stresses the importance of having relevant information at hand, making notes and checking back on important details in handling telephone sales inquiries.
Prod-VIDART Dist-VISUCP

Will You Miss Me While I'M In The Pay Toilet B 8 MIN
16MM FILM OPTICAL SOUND
Presents a film pantomine shown through abstract images.
Prod-VANBKS Dist-VANBKS

Will You Take This Woman B 17 MIN
16MM FILM OPTICAL SOUND H-C A
A pre-marital examination reveals the presence of an ovarian cyst. Shows the surgical operation in which the benign growth is removed from the ovary.
From The Doctors At Work Series.
LC NO. FIA65-1372
Prod-CMA Dist-LAWREN Prodn-LAWREN 1963

Will Your Job Burn C 19 MIN
16MM FILM - 3/4 IN VIDEO A
Discusses the importance of industrial fire safety and demonstrates fire prevention practices.
LC NO. 77-702495
Prod-NFPA Dist-NFPA Prodn-REPRO 1977

Willa Cather's America C 60 MIN
3/4 INCH VIDEO CASSETTE J-C A
Portrays the life, work and times of American writer Willa Cather.
LC NO. 78-701145
Prod-WNETTV Dist-FOTH 1978

Willem De Kooning C 14 MIN
16MM FILM OPTICAL SOUND
A film essay on the artist Willem De Kooning, showing him as he paints and as he comments on the challenges that confront a painter with each new work. Mr De Kooning correlates his observations and solutions with the use of brush work and paint.
LC NO. FIA66-1366
Prod-FALKNA Dist-RADIM 1966

Willem De Kooning - The Painter C 13 MIN
16MM FILM OPTICAL SOUND C A
Views the painter Willem De Kooning at work on his paintings.
LC NO. 73-703075
Prod-MUSLAR Dist-MUSLAR 1964

Willi-Busch Report C 119 MIN
16MM FILM OPTICAL SOUND
A German language film with English subtitles. Tells the story of a small town newspaper publisher who realizes that he can sell more papers and enlarge his newspaper business by using sensationalism, corruption and the power of fiction, but whose initial success eventually turns to his downfall.
Prod-WSTGLC Dist-WSTGLC 1979

William C 13 MIN
16MM FILM OPTICAL SOUND K-I
Tells the story of a small boy who seeks a sense of belonging among the things of nature after facing constant, if unwitting, rejection from peers and family.
LC NO. 73-701880
Prod-FRACOC Dist-FRACOC 1972

William - From Georgia To Harlem C 15 MIN
16MM FILM, 3/4 OR 1/2 IN VIDEO P-J A
Tells the story of a black farmboy who moves to New York City with his family to stay with relatives. Shows how he learns the ways of the city from his swaggering cousin Calvin but he also teaches Calvin something about real courage.
From The Many Americans Series.
Prod-UCPAG Dist-LCOA 1971

William - From Georgia To Harlem (Captioned) C 17 MIN
16MM FILM, 3/4 OR 1/2 IN VIDEO I-J A
Follows the successful adjustment of a black youth as he moves frothe rural south to life in a New York City ghetto.
Prod-LCOA Dist-LCOA 1971

William Beaumont C 23 MIN
16MM FILM, 3/4 OR 1/2 IN VIDEO H A
Presents Professor Richard M Eakin of the Department of Zoology, University of California giving a lecture in which he impersonates William Beaumont in the words, dress and manner of his time. Recounts Beaumont's classic observations and experiments on gastric digestion, conducted through a hole in a patient's stomach.
From The Great Scientists Speak Again Series.
Prod-QUICK Dist-UCEMC 1976

William Blake C 57 MIN
16MM FILM, 3/4 OR 1/2 IN VIDEO
Presents the life and thought of William Blake. Tells how the English poet lived a visionary life, describing and painting heaven. Explains how his bizarre lifestyle kept him poor, obscure and solitary but filled his days with delight. Written and narrated by Malcolm Muggeridge.
From The Third Testament Series.
LC NO. 79-707925
Prod-CANBC Dist-TIMLIF Prodn-RAYTAF 1976

William Blake (Spanish) C 26 MIN
16MM FILM, 3/4 OR 1/2 IN VIDEO H-C A
See series title for descriptive statement.
From The Romantic Vs Classic Art (Spanish) Series.
Prod-VPSL Dist-PFP

William Boddy Reminds The FCC Of The 1934 Communications Act C 28 MIN
3/4 OR 1/2 INCH VIDEO CASSETTE
Attacks the ideology and economics of mass media. Presented by Paper Tiger Television.
Prod-ARTINC Dist-ARTINC

William Butler Yeats - The Heart Of Ireland C 30 MIN
3/4 INCH VIDEO CASSETTE H-C A
Presents actress Irene Worth as the owner of an old Irish inn who was loved by William Butler Yeats.
From The Anyone For Tennyson Series.
Prod-NETCHE Dist-GPITVL

William Christensen C 28 MIN
2 INCH VIDEOTAPE
See series title for descriptive statement.
From The Art Profile Series.
Prod-KUEDTV Dist-PUBTEL

William Cochran - Tenor C 29 MIN
2 INCH VIDEOTAPE
Presents the music of tenor William Cochran.
From The Young Musical Artists Series.
Prod-WKARTV Dist-PUBTEL

William Conway, President, Relates The Nashu Corporation's Experience To Richard Noyes C 50 MIN
3/4 OR 1/2 INCH VIDEO CASSETTE
See series title for descriptive statement.
From The Deming Video Tapes - Quality, Productivity And The Competitive...Series.
Prod-MIOT Dist-SME

William E Dillard - A Great Georgian C 30 MIN
16MM FILM OPTICAL SOUND
Features an account of the career of a man known affectionately to hundreds of railroad employees as 'Bill.' Explains that Mr Dillard began his career as a 17-year-old night ticket agent in Ellaville, Georgia, and rose to the presidency of the Central of Georgia, now owned by the Southern Railway system. Narrated by Dan Dailey.
From The Great Georgians Series.
Prod-WGTV Dist-WGTV 1973

William E Warne Power Plant, The C 6 MIN
3/4 INCH VIDEO CASSETTE A
Discusses the newest addition to the State Water Project in California, the William E Warne power plant. Covers general plant information as well as its energy efficient design.
Prod-CSDWR Dist-CALDWR

William Faulkner - A Life On Paper C 116 MIN
16MM FILM, 3/4 OR 1/2 IN VIDEO H-C A
Explores the unique talent and stormy life of William Faulkner.
LC NO. 81-707584
Prod-MAETEL Dist-FI 1980

William Faulkner's Mississippi B 49 MIN
16MM FILM, 3/4 OR 1/2 IN VIDEO J-C A
Examines the Southern heritage of William Faulkner, and explores the underlying reasons and the results of the resistance to desegregation by the people of Mississippi and of the South, as interpreted in Faulkner's writings.
Prod-METROM Dist-BNCHMK 1967

William Golding C 55 MIN
3/4 OR 1/2 INCH VIDEO CASSETTE A
Presents Nobel Prize-winning British author William Golding talking about his career and how it was influenced. Considers themes central to his novels and looks at landmarks in and around the author's native village.
LC NO. 83-707160
Prod-LONWTV Dist-FOTH 1983

William Hammond And Robert Yesselman C 30 MIN
3/4 OR 1/2 INCH VIDEO CASSETTE
Discusses running a dance company. Looks at a performance OF 'Esoterica' with Frederick Franklin. Hosted by Ted Striggles.
From The Eye On Dance - Update, Topics Of Current Concern Series.
Prod-ARTRES Dist-ARTRES

William Harvey C 19 MIN
16MM FILM, 3/4 OR 1/2 IN VIDEO H A
Presents Professor Richard Eakin of the Department of Zoology, University of California giving a lecture in which he impersonates William Harvey in the words, dress and manner of his time. Recounts Harvey's ideas regarding the heart and blood vessels and presents his concepts of pulmonary and systematic circuits, using experiments and vividly illustrated descriptions.
From The Great Scientists Speak Again Series.
Prod-QUICK Dist-UCEMC 1974

William Mayne C 16 MIN
16MM FILM OPTICAL SOUND I-J T
William Mayne, English author of stories for children, talks about his books, his childhood and the small English village where he lives.
LC NO. 77-715122
Prod-CONNF Dist-CONNF 1972

William Mc Kinley And American Imperialism C 20 MIN
16MM FILM, 3/4 OR 1/2 IN VIDEO I-C
Views the decisions President Mc Kinley had to make regarding war with Spain and the course of American imperialism. Discusses manifest destiny and colonization vs freedom.
From The Great Decisions Series.
Prod-PSP Dist-AMEDFL 1970

William Penn And The Quakers - Pennsylvania Colony (2nd Ed) C 15 MIN
16MM FILM, 3/4 OR 1/2 IN VIDEO I-H
Uses costumed reenactments and period music to recreate the settlement and development of Pennsylvania. Discusses how Penn's liberal land policies and the freedoms guaranteed by his Frame of Government produced Pennsylvania's diverse ethnic population and aided its rapid growth as a center of trade, industry and culture, and gave it a prominent role in the creation of the United States.
Prod-CORF Dist-CORF 1982

William Randolph Hearst's San Simeon C 24 MIN
16MM FILM, 3/4 OR 1/2 IN VIDEO I-C A
Features E G Marshall conducting a tour of San Simeon, the residence of tycoon William Randolph Hearst. Describes the family whose tastes are reflected in the mansion.
From The American Lifestyle - Industrialists And Inventors Series.
Prod-COMCO Dist-AIMS 1978

William S Hart B 27 MIN
16MM FILM OPTICAL SOUND H-C
Presents highlights from William S Hart's finest films, including the rush sequence from Tumbleweeds.
From The History Of The Motion Picture Series.
Prod-SF Dist-KILLIS 1960

William Shakespeare B 25 MIN
16MM FILM, 3/4 OR 1/2 IN VIDEO J-C
Recounts the life of Shakespeare from early boyhood through the years spent as a playwright and actor in London. Dramatizes scenes from Richard III, Hamlet, julius Caesar and Macbeth as they would have been performed at the Globe Theater. Produced in England.
Prod-EBF Dist-EBEC 1955

William Shakespeare - A Poet For All Times C 30 MIN
3/4 INCH VIDEO CASSETTE H-C A
Offers the First Poetry Quartet and the star of the Royal Shakespeare Company reading selections of poetry by William Shakespeare.

From The Anyone For Tennyson Series.
Prod-NETCHE Dist-GPITVL

William Shakespeare - Antony And Cleopatra C 29 MIN
2 INCH VIDEOTAPE
Presents readings from Antony And Cleopatra by William Shakespeare.
From The One To One Series.
Prod-WETATV Dist-PUBTEL

William Shakespeare - Background For His Works C 14 MIN
16MM FILM, 3/4 OR 1/2 IN VIDEO J-C
Shows the places of Shakespeare's times and the elements of English life that gave the great poet playwright his language and shaped his character. Brief episodes are given from some of his best known plays.
From The Shakespeare Series.
Prod-CORF Dist-CORF 1951

William Sloan Coffin, Jr, Religion C 29 MIN
3/4 OR 1/2 INCH VIDEO CASSETTE A
See series title for descriptive statement.
From The Quest For Peace Series.
Prod-AACD Dist-AACD 1984

William Tell B 25 MIN
16MM FILM OPTICAL SOUND J-C A
Presents the Metropolitan Opera Company's condensed version of Rossini's William Tell, with English narration.
Prod-OFF Dist-SELECT

William Tell C 11 MIN
16MM FILM, 3/4 OR 1/2 IN VIDEO P-I
Presents the legend of William Tell who must shoot an apple from his son's head to save the boy and himself. Told in an animated 12th century Swiss setting.
Prod-CORF Dist-CORF 1960

William Tell C 24 MIN
16MM FILM, 3/4 OR 1/2 IN VIDEO P-J
Presents Mr Magoo in the animated story of William Tell, who refuses to bow before a tyrant's hat and is forced to shoot an apple from his son's head in order to save his son and himself.
Prod-UPAPOA Dist-MCFI 1976

William Tell - 1965 C 27 MIN
16MM FILM OPTICAL SOUND
Highlights the William Tell interceptor competition. Focuses on preparatory training, aerial intercepts and judging and scoring details. Reviews participating teams, aircraft weapons and targets.
LC NO. 74-706333
Prod-USAF Dist-USNAC 1966

William Thomas B 28 MIN
16MM FILM OPTICAL SOUND
In a film talk before students in the Department of Cinema, USC, William Thomas lectures on the distribution and exploitation of the theatrical motion picture.
From The Theatrical Film Symposium Series.
LC NO. FIA54-139
Prod-USC Dist-USC

William Wegman - Selected Body Works B 20 MIN
3/4 OR 1/2 INCH VIDEO CASSETTE
Features a variety of works.
Prod-ARTINC Dist-ARTINC

William Wegman - Selected Works, Reel 1 B 30 MIN
3/4 OR 1/2 INCH VIDEO CASSETTE
Features a variety of works.
Prod-ARTINC Dist-ARTINC

William Wegman - Selected Works, Reel 2 B 30 MIN
3/4 OR 1/2 INCH VIDEO CASSETTE
Features a variety of works.
Prod-ARTINC Dist-ARTINC

William Wegman - Selected Works, Reel 3 B 20 MIN
3/4 OR 1/2 INCH VIDEO CASSETTE
Features a variety of works.
Prod-ARTINC Dist-ARTINC

William Wegman - Selected Works, Reel 4 B 20 MIN
3/4 OR 1/2 INCH VIDEO CASSETTE
Features a variety of works.
Prod-ARTINC Dist-ARTINC

William Wegman - Selected Works, Reel 5 B 30 MIN
3/4 OR 1/2 INCH VIDEO CASSETTE
Features a variety of works.
Prod-ARTINC Dist-ARTINC

William Whitaker C 30 MIN
16MM FILM, 3/4 OR 1/2 IN VIDEO
See series title for descriptive statement.
From The Profiles In American Art Series.
Prod-KAWVAL Dist-KAWVAL

William's Doll C 18 MIN
16MM FILM, 3/4 OR 1/2 IN VIDEO
Tells how a young boy finally gets the doll that he has been longing for when his grandfather comes for a visit. Shows the value of allowing children to grow up without false ideas about masculinity and femininity.
LC NO. 81-707553
Prod-CHIESR Dist-PHENIX

William's Doll / Dad And Me C 29 MIN
1/2 IN VIDEO CASSETTE BETA/VHS
Presents a story of a boy who wants a doll, based on the book by Charlotte Zolotow. Tells the story of a seven-year-old and his father in Dad And Me.
Prod-BFA Dist-BFA

Williams, Robert C 29 MIN
3/4 INCH VIDEO CASSETTE
Discusses how standardized tests discriminate against minorities and the poor.
From The Like It Is Series.
Prod-OHC Dist-HRC

Williamsburg - The Story Of A Patriot C 36 MIN
16MM FILM, 3/4 OR 1/2 IN VIDEO I-H A
Depicts the turbulent years just prior to the American Revolution. Shows how a Virginia planter, influenced by such persons as Washington and Jefferson, decides to support the American cause.
Prod-CWMS Dist-MGHT Prodn-PAR 1957

Williamsburg File, The C 45 MIN
16MM FILM, 3/4 OR 1/2 IN VIDEO H-C A
Explains the importance of archaeology to the 50 year restoration and subsequent discovery of Williamsburg as Virginia's colonial capital. Presents descriptions of restoration projects, including Weatherburn's tavern, the cabinetmaker's shop and America's first mental hospital.
From The Nova Series.
Prod-BBCTV Dist-CWMS 1976

Williamsburg File, The C 46 MIN
3/4 OR 1/2 INCH VIDEO CASSETTE H-C A
Explains the importance of archaeology to the 50 year restoration and subsequent discovery of Williamsburg as Virginia's colonial capital. Presents descriptions of restoration projects, including Weatherburn's tavern, the cabinetmaker's shop and America's first mental hospital.
Prod-BBCTV Dist-PBS

Williamsburg Sampler, A C 29 MIN
16MM FILM, 3/4 OR 1/2 IN VIDEO
Presents a cross section of Williamsburg's history, architecture, crafts, gardens, people and philosophy.
Prod-CWMS Dist-CWMS 1975

Willie Stargell C 28 MIN
3/4 OR 1/2 INCH VIDEO CASSETTE
Tells how as captain of the 1979 World Champion Pittburgh Pirates, Willie Stargell is a hero to his teammates and millions of fans. Fred Rogers discusses with Stargell his role as husband, father and brother.
From The Old Friends - New Friends Series.
Prod-FAMCOM Dist-PBS 1981

Willis C 29 MIN
3/4 OR 1/2 INCH VIDEO CASSETTE
Presents a classroom portrait of Willis Konick, Professor of Slavic literature at Seattle's University of Washington. Konick has been described as part actor, part scholar and a unique teacher.
Prod-KCTSTV Dist-PBS 1980

Willis Reed - Center Play, Pt 1 C 11 MIN
16MM FILM, 3/4 OR 1/2 IN VIDEO J-C
Features Willis Reed of the New York Knicks illustrating various techniques in center play. Covers shooting, the push shot, the jump shot, the hook shot, the layup and the free throw.
From The Willis Reed Basketball Series.
Prod-SCHLAT Dist-LUF 1972

Willis Reed - Center Play, Pt 2 C 12 MIN
16MM FILM, 3/4 OR 1/2 IN VIDEO J-C
Features Willis Reed of the New York Knicks illustrating various techniques in center play. Covers defensive rebounding, offensive rebounding, switching on the 'PICK' and proper training techniques.
From The Willis Reed Basketball Series.
Prod-SCHLAT Dist-LUF 1972

Willis Reed Basketball—A Series
16MM FILM, 3/4 OR 1/2 IN VIDEO J-C
Prod-SCHLAT Dist-LUF 1972

Dick Van Arsdale - Defensive Play, Pt 1 12 MIN
Dick Van Arsdale - Defensive Play, Pt 2 11 MIN
Jack Marin - Forward Play, Pt 1 12 MIN
Jack Marin - Forward Play, Pt 2 11 MIN
Jo Jo White - Offensive Guard, Pt 1 10 MIN
Jo Jo White - Offensive Guard, Pt 2 12 MIN
Willis Reed - Center Play, Pt 1 11 MIN
Willis Reed - Center Play, Pt 2 12 MIN

Willmar Eight, The C 55 MIN
3/4 INCH VIDEO CASSETTE
Tells the inspiring story of eight women bank workers in the small, mid-western town of Willmar, Minnesota, who unexpectedly find themselves in the forefront of the fight for working women's rights when they are passed over for promotion one too many times.
Prod-FIRS Dist-FIRS

Willmar 8, The C 55 MIN
16MM FILM OPTICAL SOUND A
Tells how eight women bank employees went out on strike after being passed over for promotion because they were women. Points out that they risked jobs, friends and families and that they challenged the values with which they were raised. Narrated and directed by Lee Grant.
LC NO. 80-701948
Prod-CANWRL Dist-CANWRL 1980

Willoughby, I Want You C
3/4 OR 1/2 INCH VIDEO CASSETTE
See series title for descriptive statement.
From The Fragments From Willoughby's Video Performances - Pt II Series.
Prod-EAI Dist-EAI

Willoughby, Where Are You? C
3/4 OR 1/2 INCH VIDEO CASSETTE
See series title for descriptive statement.
From The Fragments from Willoughby's Video Performances - Pt I Series.
Prod-EAI Dist-EAI

Willow Point C 15 MIN
16MM FILM, 3/4 OR 1/2 IN VIDEO J-C A
Explores fantasy, reality and obsolescence.
Prod-PHENIX Dist-PHENIX 1974

Wills C 30 MIN
3/4 OR 1/2 INCH VIDEO CASSETTE
See series title for descriptive statement.
From The Financial Management Workshops Series.
Prod-ODECA Dist-BULFRG

Wills And Estates C 19 MIN
3/4 OR 1/2 INCH VIDEO CASSETTE H
Depicts how in Purgatory, deceased individuals see the consequences of leaving or not leaving a will.
From The Ways Of The Law Series.
Prod-SCITV Dist-GPITVL 1980

Wills And Estates C 30 MIN
3/4 OR 1/2 INCH VIDEO CASSETTE
Presents tips on writing wills and planning estates.
From The Consumer Survival Series. Personal Planning
Prod-MDCPB Dist-MDCPB

Willy Mc Bean And His Flying Machine C 94 MIN
16MM FILM OPTICAL SOUND
Presents the story about Willy Mc Bean, a boy of the jet and space age, and his pal Pablo, a talking monkey. Shows their adventures through time as they encounter General Custer and Sitting Bull, King Arthur and even some cavemen. Incorporates the technique of three-dimensional figures moving against backdrops in a stop-motion photography called animagic.
Prod-RANKA Dist-TWYMAN

Wilmington B 15 MIN
16MM FILM OPTICAL SOUND
Explains how the city of Wilmington, occupied for 11 months by the National Guard after Martin Luther King's assassination, is exposed as the private domain of the Dupont family. Explains how the Dupont Corporation controls the economic and political life of Delaware.
Prod-SFN Dist-SFN

Wilson - The Road To War B 24 MIN
16MM FILM OPTICAL SOUND J-H
Shows how President Woodrow Wilson is drawn inexorably into World War I by such incidents as the sinking of the Lusitania, the resignation of the American secretary of state, the dismissal of the German ambassador and personal criticisms by both political parties. Uses excerpts from the motion picture Wilson starring Alexander Knox and Charles Coburn.
From The American Challenge Series.
Prod-TWCF Dist-FI 1975

Wilson Crisis, The - Stroke C 58 MIN
3/4 OR 1/2 INCH VIDEO CASSETTE
Documents the physical and psychological rehabilitation after a stroke. Presents narratives from the stroke victim and his son.
Prod-UMDSM Dist-UMDSM

Wilson Douglas, Fiddler C 8 MIN
16MM FILM, 3/4 OR 1/2 IN VIDEO J-C A
An excerpt from the 1975 motion picture Relations. Presents Kentucky mountain fiddler Wilson Douglas, who performs bluegrass music and discusses the excitement and emotion of this American music form.
Prod-FERTIK Dist-PHENIX 1975

Wilson Hurley C 30 MIN
16MM FILM, 3/4 OR 1/2 IN VIDEO
See series title for descriptive statement.
From The Profiles In American Art Series.
Prod-KAWVAL Dist-KAWVAL

Wilson's Creek - A Mean Fowt Fight C 14 MIN
16MM FILM, 3/4 OR 1/2 IN VIDEO I-C A
Uses the paintings and words of artist George Caleb Bingham to examine the battle at Wilson's Creek, a little-discussed but influential Civil War battle.
Prod-USNPS Dist-USNAC 1983

Win, Win C 9 MIN
3/4 OR 1/2 INCH VIDEO CASSETTE C A
Illustrates the need to develop a balance between task and people orientation.
Prod-MTI Dist-MTI

Winch Characteristics - Electric, Hydraulic And Steam B 25 MIN
16MM FILM OPTICAL SOUND
Explains characteristics, preoperation checks and preparations and operation of the two-speed steam winch, unit-type electric winch and hydraulic winch used in military stevedoring. Presents advantages and limitations of each.
LC NO. 74-705960
Prod-USA Dist-USNAC 1969

Wind C 4 MIN
16MM FILM OPTICAL SOUND
Shows how the Ontario countryside is transformed by the wind.
LC NO. 76-703100
Prod-CANFDC Dist-CANFDC 1975

Wind C 8 MIN
16MM FILM, 3/4 OR 1/2 IN VIDEO K-P
Shows sailboats gliding by, kites soaring above, and branches swaying as photography and a ballad describe the various effects of the wind. Uses simple captions in bold lettering to fa-

miliarize the beginning reader with the sound, sight and concept of short words.
From The Starting To Read Series.
Prod-ACI Dist-AIMS 1970

Wind C 9 MIN
16MM FILM, 3/4 OR 1/2 IN VIDEO K-P
Shows how a gust of wind, swirling clouds and leaves around a small boy enchant his senses and awaken kaleidoscopic visions of magical wind-borne kite and boat trips.
Prod-NFBC Dist-LCOA 1973

Wind - An Energy Alternative C 12 MIN
16MM FILM, 3/4 OR 1/2 IN VIDEO
Describes wind as an energy alternative and offers a history of its use in the United States. Focuses on developmental efforts by the U S Department of Energy. Defines various terms and concepts, including kilowatt, megawatt and utility interconnect.
LC NO. 81-706432
Prod-SERI Dist-USNAC 1980

Wind - Anemometer C 20 MIN
2 INCH VIDEOTAPE I
See series title for descriptive statement.
From The Exploring With Science, Unit V - Weather Series.
Prod-MPATI Dist-GPITVL

Wind - The Power And The Promise C 24 MIN
16MM FILM, 3/4 OR 1/2 IN VIDEO I-J
Identifies the contradictory qualities of wind, showing its solar origin, functions and usefulness as a source of energy as well as its devastating effects in the form of forest fires, hurricanes and tornadoes.
LC NO. 81-706865
Prod-EBEC Dist-EBEC 1980

Wind Across The Everglades C 93 MIN
16MM FILM OPTICAL SOUND
Tells how a young game warden pursues a gang of plumage hunters deep into Florida's Everglades.
Prod-WB Dist-TWYMAN 1958

Wind And Rain B 15 MIN
2 INCH VIDEOTAPE P
See series title for descriptive statement.
From The Children's Literature Series. No. 22
Prod-NCET Dist-GPITVL Prodn-KUONTV

Wind And The Navigator - In-Flight Analysis C 8 MIN
16MM FILM OPTICAL SOUND
Illustrates the navigator's duties while in flight, including determination of wind changes, drift causes and flight path corrections.
From The Beginning Algebra 1 Series.
LC NO. FIE58-310
Prod-USAF Dist-USNAC 1957

Wind And The Navigator - Jet Streams C 15 MIN
16MM FILM OPTICAL SOUND
Explains the high velocity wind currents called jet streams and shows how aircraft navigators save fuel and flight time through use of these forces. Discusses altitude velocity, seasonal changes, direction and turbulence.
LC NO. FIE60-342
Prod-USAF Dist-USNAC 1957

Wind And The Navigator - Pre-Flight Planning C 15 MIN
16MM FILM OPTICAL SOUND
Demonstrates how a wind flow chart, using weather data values and scales, is prepared and shows how a flight path is determined.
LC NO. FIE58-309
Prod-USAF Dist-USNAC 1957

Wind And The Navigator - Wind Theory C 15 MIN
16MM FILM OPTICAL SOUND
Discusses the theory of wind forces and patterns, pressure gradient force, pressure surfaces, coriolis force, geostrophic winds, friction and centrifugal force.
LC NO. FIE58-308
Prod-USAF Dist-USNAC 1957

Wind And The River, The B 10 MIN
16MM FILM OPTICAL SOUND I A
Captures the spirit of calm and timeless beauty of the small Himalayan country of Kashmir produces in 1950.
LC NO. FIA64-1377
Prod-PFP Dist-VIEWFI Prodn-SVENFI 1970

Wind And What It Does X 11 MIN
16MM FILM, 3/4 OR 1/2 IN VIDEO P
Uses a scientific-discovery technique to show what wind is, what it can do and how it affects man and his surroundings. Shows wind doing work and causing destruction. Includes evidence of wind action in a hurricane, tornado and sandstorm.
Prod-EBF Dist-EBEC 1963

Wind And What It Does (Spanish) C 11 MIN
16MM FILM, 3/4 OR 1/2 IN VIDEO P
Discusses the nature of wind and shows how it affects man and his surroundings.
Prod-EBEC Dist-EBEC

Wind Chill C
16MM FILM OPTICAL SOUND
Forms the preliminary basis of interdisciplinary investigation of environmental thermal stresses on man. Features concern with atmospheric heat transfer processes and physiological impact on the human body.
From The Meteorology Series.
Prod-MLA Dist-MLA 1973

Wind In The Wires C 22 MIN
16MM FILM, 3/4 OR 1/2 IN VIDEO I-C A
Sketches the development of aviation from the time of the Wright brothers to a point ten years later, when airplanes could dive, loop, spin and dance over the clouds. Narrated by James Mason.
Prod-CFDLD Dist-CORF

Wind Of Change, The C 30 MIN
16MM FILM OPTICAL SOUND C A
Pictures the delivery of the first Douglas DC-8 to Air Afrique. Points out the changes and rapid advancement taking place in the nations of West Africa.
LC NO. FIA65-519
Prod-DAC Dist-MCDO 1964

Wind Power - The Great Revival C 29 MIN
16MM FILM OPTICAL SOUND
Discusses wind energy and its storability, as well as the aesthetic considerations of windmills in large numbers. Examines the combined use of solar and wind power.
From The Energy Sources - A New Beginning Series.
Prod-UCOLO Dist-UCOLO

Wind Raiders Of The Sahara C 52 MIN
16MM FILM, 3/4 OR 1/2 IN VIDEO
Depicts the expedition of General Jean du Boucher, 20-year veteran of Sahara military service and his guide as they lead a team of international pilots across 1500 miles of the Sahara Desert by wind-driven land yacht. Illustrates the various desert peoples encountered by the expedition including the nomadic Reguibat tribes and the Imraguen fishermen on the Atlantic Coast.
LC NO. 80-706404
Prod-NGS Dist-NGS 1973

Wind Rose C 21 MIN
16MM FILM, 3/4 OR 1/2 IN VIDEO I-C A
Presents Elizabeth and Dan, walking in the woods with their five-year-old daughter, Wind Rose. Tells how the rising of the wind evokes memories in Elizabeth of the stages of her pregnancy. Emphasizes the beauty of family life.
LC NO. 84-707090
Prod-PHENIX Dist-PHENIX 1983

Wind Waves And Water Dynamics C 30 MIN
3/4 OR 1/2 INCH VIDEO CASSETTE
Looks at the movement of water particles in various kinds of waves. Describes special kinds of waves such as seiches and internal waves.
From The Oceanus - The Marine Environment Series. Lesson 13
Prod-SCCON Dist-CDTEL

Windfalls C 22 MIN
3/4 OR 1/2 INCH VIDEO CASSETTE
Features two men each telling a long story cutting into one another's. Includes fragments of a scientist's lecture on intelligence and memory.
Prod-KITCHN Dist-KITCHN

Windfalls - Matthew Geller C 21 MIN
3/4 INCH VIDEO CASSETTE
Prod-AFA Dist-AFA 1982

Windflight C 13 MIN
16MM FILM, 3/4 OR 1/2 IN VIDEO I-C A
Deals with windsurfing, the new water sport. Presents a display of physical agility and athletic artistry featuring the first 360 degree flips ever filmed, the largest windsurfing waves ever ridden, and aerial loops, jibes and freestyle performances by some of the top names in sailboarding.
Prod-PFP Dist-PFP

Windflower C 20 MIN
16MM FILM, 3/4 OR 1/2 IN VIDEO J-C A
Shows a child constructing a model hot air balloon which is magically transformed into full size and which carries him over the autumn countryside.
Prod-POBAPS Dist-LRF

Windmill Summer C 15 MIN
3/4 OR 1/2 INCH VIDEO CASSETTE I
See series title for descriptive statement.
From The Best Of Cover To Cover 2 Series.
Prod-WETATV Dist-WETATV

Windmills And Wooden Shoes C 15 MIN
3/4 OR 1/2 INCH VIDEO CASSETTE P
Presents a tour of Madurodam, a windmill and a wooden shoe factory in Holland.
From The Other Families, Other Friends Series. Red Module - Holland
Prod-WVIZTV Dist-AITECH 1971

Window C 20 MIN
16MM FILM OPTICAL SOUND
Uses both live action and animation to describe the contribution of education to business, to industry, and to the community as a whole. Stresses that taxes for education provide tangible returns for the entire society.
Prod-WSU Dist-WSU 1954

Window C 30 MIN
3/4 OR 1/2 INCH VIDEO CASSETTE
Reveals memory, not as an act, but as form. Moves script's language through memory-scapes and non-linear thinking, and selected elements are visually abstracted.
From The Doris Chase Concepts Series.
Prod-CHASED Dist-CHASED

Window Boxes C 29 MIN
2 INCH VIDEOTAPE
Features Thalassa Cruso discussing different aspects of gardening. Shows how to make flower and plant arrangements in window boxes.
From The Making Things Grow III Series.
LC NO. 80-706151
Prod-WGBHTV Dist-PUBTEL

Window Full Of Cakes, A B 20 MIN
16MM FILM OPTICAL SOUND
Tells the story of Massachusetts nursery shcools for retarded children. Depicts activities in relation to their objectives for the child.
Prod-CMHRF Dist-CMHRF

Window Of The Living Sea C 22 MIN
16MM FILM OPTICAL SOUND
Explores the educational and research activities at Miami Seaquarium. Examines the care, psychology and training of marine mammals, the collection of specimens and research carried on and the Seaquarium's philosophy of management.
LC NO. 74-702529
Prod-MIAMIS Dist-MIAMIS Prodn-TELAIR 1974

Window On The Body C 26 MIN
3/4 OR 1/2 INCH VIDEO CASSETTE
Portrays the excitement of doctors and medical scientists at the staggering implications of a new medical instrument which actually sees the body's chemistry at work.
From The Breakthroughs Series.
Prod-NOMDFI Dist-LANDMK

Window On The World—A Series

Prod-CTV Dist-CTV 1976

Britain, Who Shot The Woodcock 50 MIN
Time Of The Jackal 50 MIN

Window Problems C 15 MIN
2 INCH VIDEOTAPE
See series title for descriptive statement.
From The Making Things Work Series.
Prod-WGBHTV Dist-PUBTEL

Window Repair C 30 MIN
3/4 OR 1/2 INCH VIDEO CASSETTE
Presents the basics of window repair.
From The You Can Fixit Series.
Prod-WRJATV Dist-MDCPB

Window To The Universe C 15 MIN
16MM FILM, 3/4 OR 1/2 IN VIDEO I-C
Traces the origins and development of radio astronomy. Explains the basic parts of a radio telescope and its functions. Examines the ways in which radio astronomy has expanded the knowledge of the universe.
Prod-MIS Dist-MIS 1977

Windows C 9 MIN
3/4 OR 1/2 INCH VIDEO CASSETTE
See series title for descriptive statement.
From The Gary Hill, Part 1 Series.
Prod-EAI Dist-EAI

Windows C 30 MIN
16MM FILM, 3/4 OR 1/2 IN VIDEO
Provides basic information on repairing windows.
From The Do It Yourself Home Repairs Series.
Prod-ODECA Dist-BULFRG

Windows - An Introduction To Anesthesia C 16 MIN
16MM FILM OPTICAL SOUND
Shows what happens inside the body when anesthesia is administered during surgical complications. Illustrates reactions caused by inhaled anesthesia and by inhaled plus injected anesthesia.
LC NO. 79-700348
Prod-OHMED Dist-OHMED Prodn-RNBWP 1979

Windows In Armour C 9 MIN
16MM FILM OPTICAL SOUND
Deals with urban emotional and societal complexities. Focuses on different personal impressions of metropolitan life and the quest for feelings in the city.
LC NO. 77-702723
Prod-CANFDC Dist-CANFDC 1974

Windows In Time - Research Today For Energy Tomorrow C 29 MIN
3/4 OR 1/2 INCH VIDEO CASSETTE
Features five scientists engaged in energy research discussing contemporary research and development. Shows them at work at their labs. Illustrates both their excitement and their frustration.
Prod-EPC Dist-MTP

Windowsill Gardening C 13 MIN
16MM FILM, 3/4 OR 1/2 IN VIDEO P-C A
Shows an assortment of windowsill plants. Includes various ways of planting, development of seedlings and requirements of light and moisture. Emphasizes plants and procedures which can be used in apartments or school rooms without special equipment or facilities.
From The Green Thumb Series.
Prod-ACORN Dist-LUF

Windrifters - The Bald Eagle Story C 20 MIN
3/4 OR 1/2 INCH VIDEO CASSETTE
Tells how scientists work to reintroduce the bald eagle, an endangered species, into its former habitat.
From The Nature Episodes Series.
Prod-EDIMGE Dist-EDIMGE

Winds And Their Causes (2nd Ed) C 11 MIN
16MM FILM, 3/4 OR 1/2 IN VIDEO I-J
Pictures a glider soaring over the countryside to provide vivid evidence of moving air currents. Demonstrates that winds are created by unequal heating of air. Shows how local winds are

caused by lakes and other features, and how global winds are generated by the sun's heating effects, modified by the earth's rotation and by interaction with other winds.
Prod-CORF Dist-CORF 1967

Winds Of Change B 15 MIN
16MM FILM OPTICAL SOUND J-C A
A documentation of the transformations that have been taking place in all aspects of modern life, with particular emphasis on the implications of these changes on competitive business.
LC NO. FIA64-1081
Prod-GE Dist-GE 1963

Winds Of Change, The C 22 MIN
3/4 OR 1/2 INCH VIDEO CASSETTE J-H
See series title for descriptive statement.
From The Phenomenal World Series.
Prod-EBEC Dist-EBEC 1983

Winds, Weather And Air Masses C 24 MIN
3/4 INCH VIDEO CASSETTE J
Examines land-sea and mountain valley breezes, air temperature, altitude, precipitation and snow.
From The What On Earth Series.
Prod-NCSDPI Dist-GPITVL 1979

Windscale AGR C 28 MIN
16MM FILM OPTICAL SOUND J-C A
Illustrates the construction of the advanced gascooled reactor at Windscale, including fuel manufacture and assembly.
Prod-UKAEA Dist-UKAEA 1963

Windshield And Sideglass Types, Characteristics And Applications C 17 MIN
1/2 IN VIDEO CASSETTE BETA/VHS
Deals with auto body repair. Covers development, braking characteristics, and workability and applications of shatterproof and tempered glass.
Prod-RMI Dist-RMI

Windshield Water Leak Repair C 17 MIN
1/2 IN VIDEO CASSETTE BETA/VHS
Deals with auto body repair.
Prod-RMI Dist-RMI

Windsors, The B 26 MIN
16MM FILM OPTICAL SOUND I-C A
Uses rare actuality footage to portray the personal life and history-making deeds of the Windsors.
From The History Makers Of The 20th Century Series.
LC NO. FIA67-1432
Prod-WOLPER Dist-SF 1966

Windy Day C 9 MIN
16MM FILM, 3/4 OR 1/2 IN VIDEO H-C A
Presents a fantasy of two young girls at play on a windy day. Animation by Faith And John Hubley.
Prod-HUBLEY Dist-TEXFLM 1968

Wine - Its Selection And Enjoyment C 15 MIN
16MM FILM, 3/4 OR 1/2 IN VIDEO H-C A
Features television host Dan Resin who provides basic information about wines and gives advice on which brands to select, how much each wine should cost, how to taste wine and how to order wine at a restaurant.
Prod-KLEINW Dist-KLEINW 1978

Wine - Where The Extra Profits Are C 22 MIN
16MM FILM OPTICAL SOUND
Deals with the major aspects of building a successful wine business, concentrating specifically on the details of merchandising, stocking, selling and serving.
LC NO. 75-702762
Prod-SCHABC Dist-SCHABC Prodn-MMCON

Wine, Women And Wellness C 30 MIN
3/4 OR 1/2 INCH VIDEO CASSETTE
Explains the symptomatic differences between male and female alcoholism and chemical dependency, their impact on detection and treatment.
Prod-WHITEG Dist-WHITEG

Winemakers In France C 15 MIN
16MM FILM, 3/4 OR 1/2 IN VIDEO P-C
Describes the winemaking process from pruning the vines to the actual bottling of the wine. Tells that the traditional methods have been replaced by modern mass production methods.
From The Man And His World Series.
Prod-FI Dist-FI 1969

Winfrith Pipeline C 42 MIN
16MM FILM OPTICAL SOUND J-C A
Shows the disposal of radioactive effluent from the atomic energy establishment at Winfrith by means of a pipeline running two miles out to sea.
Prod-UKAEA Dist-UKAEA 1960

Winfrith Sghwr 100mwe C 12 MIN
16MM FILM OPTICAL SOUND
Tells the story of the steam generating heavy water reactor. Explains the design of the reactor and illustrates site construction and the manufacture and installation of the principal reactor components. Shows the loading of the fuel elements and the start-up of the completed reactor.
Prod-UKAEA Dist-UKAEA 1968

Wing Assembly - The Bow Tip B 24 MIN
16MM FILM OPTICAL SOUND
Demonstrates how to fit the bow tip strip to the leading edge strip, make the spar tip joint, install ribs, shape the bow tip, apply and glue the bow tip skins and varnish the surface.
LC NO. FIE52-286
Prod-USOE Dist-USNAC 1944

Wing Assembly - The Inboard Panel B 19 MIN
16MM FILM OPTICAL SOUND
Demonstrates how to install subassemblies in a jig, apply and glue the skins, apply and remove pressure strips, finish the outside surface and inspect the completed assembly.
Prod-USOE Dist-USNAC 1944

Wing Assembly - The Nose Section B 20 MIN
16MM FILM OPTICAL SOUND
Explains how to position the main spar in the jig, install the webbed ribs, junction ribs, regular ribs and leading edge strip, to apply and glue the skins and to finish the surface of the nose section.
LC NO. FIE52-284
Prod-USOE Dist-USNAC 1944

Wing To Wing B 50 MIN
3/4 OR 1/2 INCH VIDEO CASSETTE
Tells of the French squadron of 'Normandy-Nieman' which fought together with Soviet Pilots against the Nazis in World War II.
Prod-IHF Dist-IHF

Wing, The C 27 MIN
16MM FILM OPTICAL SOUND
Interviews men and women who work at Bitburg Air Force Base in West Germany and give their views of life in the U S Air Force and why they made the choice of military life over civilian life.
LC NO. 82-700184
Prod-VARDIR Dist-VARDIR 1981

Wingate, I Love You C 9 MIN
16MM FILM, 3/4 OR 1/2 IN VIDEO J-C A
Uses the experience of a young man running away from family discord in order to emphasize the need of people to express their love for one another.
Prod-COUNTR Dist-AIMS 1976

Winged Colt, The C 66 MIN
16MM FILM, 3/4 OR 1/2 IN VIDEO
Tells how a winged colt bridges the gap between a former movie stuntman and his bookish nephew. Based on the book The Winged Colt Of Casa Mia by Betsy Byars. Originally shown on the television series ABC Weekend Specials.
LC NO. 79-707140
Prod-ABCTV Dist-MTI Prodn-ABCCIR 1978

Winged Scourge C 10 MIN
3/4 OR 1/2 INCH VIDEO CASSETTE
Uses animation to show various methods of combatting and eliminating the anopheles mosquito. Issued in 1943 as a motion picture.
From The Health For The Americas Series.
LC NO. 80-707379
Prod-USCIAA Dist-USNAC Prodn-DISNEY 1980

Winged Victory On Foot - 43rd Infantry Division B 14 MIN
16MM FILM, 3/4 OR 1/2 IN VIDEO H A
Presents the activities of the 43rd Infantry Division in the Pacific during World War II and as occupation troops in Japan after the war.
Prod-USA Dist-USNAC 1950

Winged World C 52 MIN
16MM FILM, 3/4 OR 1/2 IN VIDEO J-C
Studies exotic birds found in different parts of the world.
LC NO. 80-706367
Prod-NGS Dist-NGS Prodn-WOLPER 1967

Wings And Things (2nd Ed) C 20 MIN
16MM FILM, 3/4 OR 1/2 IN VIDEO
Presents model airplanes and their technical creation. Analyzes the characteristics of model airplane enthusiasts.
Prod-OPUS Dist-PHENIX 1976

Wings And Wheels C 15 MIN
16MM FILM, 3/4 OR 1/2 IN VIDEO H-C A
Presents an around-the-world look at the car rental industry, emphasizing the advantages to individuals and business customers.
Prod-KLEINW Dist-KLEINW 1978

Wings For The Doctor - A Story Of The Naval Flight Surgeon C 28 MIN
16MM FILM OPTICAL SOUND
Describes training and duties of the naval flight surgeon.
LC NO. 74-706609
Prod-USN Dist-USNAC 1971

Wings For The Fleet C 29 MIN
16MM FILM, 3/4 OR 1/2 IN VIDEO
Shows United States naval aviation flight training from Aviation Officer Candidate School, to winning Navy wings and assignment to fleet operations.
Prod-USN Dist-USNAC 1982

Wings In The Grand Canyon C 14 MIN
16MM FILM OPTICAL SOUND I-C A
Shows the Grand Canyon as seen from an airplane. Includes views of Angel's Window, the Painted Desert, Hance Rapids, Holy Grail Temple, Thunder Falls, Mt Sinyala, Mooney Falls and Havasupi Falls.
LC NO. 73-701129
Prod-MMP Dist-MMP 1970

Wings Of Eagles, Wings Of Gold C 28 MIN
16MM FILM, 3/4 OR 1/2 IN VIDEO
Traces the history of naval aviation and emphasizes the importance of preserving this heritage for future generations.
LC NO. 81-706657
Prod-USN Dist-USNAC 1974

Wings Of Mercury, The C 60 MIN
3/4 OR 1/2 INCH VIDEO CASSETTE
Follows the space program from President John F Kennedy's challenge to N A S A to put a man on the moon before the end of the 1960s through successful space missions, including the Gemini program and the first space docking. Discusses the selection of America's first man in space, Mercury astronaut Alan Shephard, and the first man in space, Russian cosmonaut Yuri Gagarin.
From The Spaceflight Series.
Prod-PBS Dist-PBS

Wings Of The Army B 45 MIN
3/4 OR 1/2 INCH VIDEO CASSETTE
Shows highlights of military and civilian aviation history between the wars. Includes the first flights at Kitty Hawk, first flight across the English Channel, stunt Flyers, air-mail service and others.
Prod-IHF Dist-IHF

Wings Of The Wind C 15 MIN
16MM FILM OPTICAL SOUND
Discusses the excitement and the danger of the sport of hang gliding. Includes old photographs and films illustrating man's desire to fly.
LC NO. 76-700206
Prod-RAMFLM Dist-RAMFLM 1975

Wings Of Youth, The C 15 MIN
16MM FILM OPTICAL SOUND C A
Shows the activities carried on by the Civil Air Patrol Cadet Program and the initiation of trainees into the world of gliders, sailplanes and powered aircraft.
LC NO. FIA66-691
Prod-DAC Dist-MCDO 1965

Wings That Serve C 13 MIN
3/4 OR 1/2 INCH VIDEO CASSETTE A
Presents many facets of civil aviation from public transportation through business and private flying, and was prepared under auspices of Aviation and Space Writers Association.
Prod-FAAFL Dist-AVIMA

Wings To Alaska C 27 MIN
16MM FILM OPTICAL SOUND
Pictures the landscape of Alaska, its mountain ranges, forests and glaciers, and the people who live there-the Eskimo, the Indian and the pioneer. Emphasizes the fact that Alaska is a state with room for individual expression.
LC NO. FIA66-690
Prod-PANWA Dist-PANWA Prodn-STRAUS 1965

Wings To Germany C 29 MIN
16MM FILM OPTICAL SOUND
A tour of West Germany and Berlin showing the beauty of the Rhine and the Black Forest, the old world charm of cities such as Heidelberg and Rothenburg, the winter resorts, the fine restaurants and hotels and the Oktoberfest.
LC NO. FIA66-688
Prod-PANWA Dist-PANWA Prodn-VISION 1965

Wings To Great Britain C 28 MIN
16MM FILM OPTICAL SOUND
Presents various views of the people and interesting places in Great Britain such as the seacoast, the highlands, the lake country and London.
LC NO. FIA67-697
Prod-PANWA Dist-PANWA Prodn-STRAUS 1966

Wings To Hawaii C 30 MIN
16MM FILM OPTICAL SOUND
Pictures various aspects of life in Hawaii with emphasis on tourist resorts and attractions of the Hawaiian neighbor islands.
LC NO. FIA67-700
Prod-PANWA Dist-PANWA Prodn-FILMAU 1966

Wings To Hawaii (French) C 30 MIN
16MM FILM OPTICAL SOUND
Pictures various aspects of life in Hawaii with emphasis on tourist resorts and attractions of the Hawaiian neighbor islands.
Prod-PANWA Dist-PANWA Prodn-FILMAU 1966

Wings To Italy C 28 MIN
16MM FILM OPTICAL SOUND
Presents views of popular tourist attractions throughout Italy.
LC NO. FIA67-698
Prod-PANWA Dist-PANWA Prodn-VISION 1966

Wings To Scandinavia C 28 MIN
16MM FILM OPTICAL SOUND
Presents pictures of Norway, Sweden, Finland and Denmark during the summer and winter seasons.
Prod-PANWA Dist-PANWA

Wings To Spain C 29 MIN
16MM FILM OPTICAL SOUND
Presents a tour of Spain and its main attractions for the tourist.
Prod-PANWA Dist-PANWA

Wings To The Land Of The Maya C 20 MIN
16MM FILM OPTICAL SOUND J A
Presents the countries of Mexico, Yucatan, Guatemala and the island of Cozumel, explaining that these countries are growing in popularity yet are among the least exploited areas of Latin America. Shows scenes of typical tourist attractions, including the Mayan ruins of Chichen Itza and Uxmal and an Indian dance ceremony at Uxmal.
LC NO. FIA64-813
Prod-VISION Dist-PANWA 1963

Wings To Venezuela C 15 MIN
16MM FILM OPTICAL SOUND
Pictures small fishing villages, wind-swept mountain tops, cascading waterfalls and the thriving metropolis of Caracas to pro-

vide a view of the people and pleasures of Venezuela. Presents Venezuelan music.
LC NO. FIA68-874
Prod-PANWA Dist-PANWA Prodn-PANWA 1967

Wingtip To Canopy C 15 MIN
16MM FILM OPTICAL SOUND
Presents the Blue Angels flight team flying their A-4 Skyhawks to display the skill of the U S Navy aviator.
LC NO. 75-703127
Prod-MCDO Dist-MCDO 1975

Wingy Manone C 30 MIN
3/4 INCH VIDEO CASSETTE
Features the jazz stylings of trumpet player and singer Wingy Manone.
From The After Hours With Art Hodes Series.
Prod-FAJAZZ Dist-FAJAZZ

Winifred Wise-Anderson On Jane Addams And Hull House C 42 MIN
3/4 OR 1/2 INCH VIDEO CASSETTE
Presents a definitive biography of Jane Addams of Hull House by Winifred Wise-Anderson who worked at Hull House in Chicago while researching her book, JANE ADDAMS OF HULL HOUSE, published in 1935. Shares her personal memories of Jane Addams and the operation of Hull House.
Prod-VRL Dist-UWISC 1982

Winner Never Quits, A C 18 MIN
16MM FILM, 3/4 OR 1/2 IN VIDEO J-C A
Documents a high school football team, describing the peer group pressure and the role-playing experienced by the athletes, cheerleaders and coaches.
Prod-TARORE Dist-PHENIX 1977

Winner, The - Problem Solving, Measurement C 16 MIN
16MM FILM, 3/4 OR 1/2 IN VIDEO I
Visualizes the concept of measurement and rates, illustrates the usefulness of scale models, and demonstrates how to use a calculator to compare data and solve problems
Prod-EBEC Dist-EBEC

Winner's Circle—A Series
A
Features three gold-medal-winning Olympic athletes in different sports telling about their motivation to win. Developed for business meetings.
Prod-SFTI Dist-SFTI

Going The Distance 008 MIN
Perfect Balance, The 008 MIN
Winning Goals 008 MIN

Winners C 20 MIN
16MM FILM OPTICAL SOUND
Shows the commercial and industrial potential of New South Wales. Features ten case histories of companies which have set up successful operations there.
LC NO. 80-700861
Prod-NSWF Dist-TASCOR 1978

Winners C 24 MIN
3/4 OR 1/2 INCH VIDEO CASSETTE
Focuses on participants in the Special Olympics. Narrated by Tom Seaver.
From The Young People's Specials Series.
Prod-MULTPP Dist-MULTPP

Winners And Losers - A Worldwide Survey C 30 MIN
3/4 OR 1/2 INCH VIDEO CASSETTE
Examines the nature of manufacturing competition in terms of strategies adopted, maturity of strategies, effectiveness achieved and financial results delivered. Studies the differences between the winners and losers in the new, high-stakes competition of the 80s.
From The Successful Strategies For Manufacturing Management Series.
Prod-DELTAK Dist-DELTAK

Winners, The C 30 MIN
3/4 OR 1/2 INCH VIDEO CASSETTE P-I
See series title for descriptive statement.
From The Sonrisas Series.
Prod-KRLNTV Dist-MDCPB

Winners, The C 30 MIN
16MM FILM, 3/4 OR 1/2 IN VIDEO J-H
Shows the world of nature's most adaptable species, the insect and how they meet new threats to existence.
From The World We Live In Series.
Prod-TIMELI Dist-MGHT 1968

Winnie The Pooh And A Day For Eeyore C 26 MIN
16MM FILM, 3/4 OR 1/2 IN VIDEO K-I
Shows how Winnie the Pooh and his friends help celebrate Eeyore the donkey's birthday. Demonstrates that even though things don't go exactly as planned, Eeyore realizes it's the thought that counts.
Prod-WDEMCO Dist-WDEMCO 1983

Winnie The Pooh And The Blustery Day C 25 MIN
16MM FILM, 3/4 OR 1/2 IN VIDEO K-I
Shows what happens when Pooh visits his Thoughtful Spot and then, because of the wind, joins in some antics with Piglet.
From The Many Adventures Of Winnie The Pooh Series.
Prod-WDEMCO Dist-WDEMCO 1981

Winnie The Pooh And The Honey Tree C 26 MIN
16MM FILM, 3/4 OR 1/2 IN VIDEO K-I
Tells about Pooh's attempt to deceive the bees and about his disastrous visit to Rabbit.
From The Many Adventures Of Winnie The Pooh Series.
Prod-WDEMCO Dist-WDEMCO 1981

Winnie The Pooh And Tigger Too C 26 MIN
16MM FILM, 3/4 OR 1/2 IN VIDEO K-I
Shows that when Rabbit, Pooh and Piglet plan to unbounce Tigger, they discover they like a bouncy Tigger best.
From The Many Adventures Of Winnie The Pooh Series.
Prod-WDEMCO Dist-WDEMCO 1981

Winnie The Pooh Discovers The Seasons C 8 MIN
16MM FILM, 3/4 OR 1/2 IN VIDEO K-P
Shows Winnie The Pooh learning to use the calendar to keep track of the passage of days, weeks, months and seasons.
Prod-DISNEY Dist-WDEMCO 1982

Winning C 21 MIN
16MM FILM - 3/4 IN VIDEO
Tells how two mentally handicapped people get married and try to make a life outside the institution.
LC NO. 81-706514
Prod-VICCOR Dist-TASCOR 1980

Winning C 30 MIN
3/4 OR 1/2 INCH VIDEO CASSETTE C A
Features Conrad Leslie, Dr. Richard Sander, Francis Wolfe and others explaining the elements for successful speculation.
From The Commodities – The Professional Trader Series.
Prod-VIPUB Dist-VIPUB

Winning And Losing C 24 MIN
16MM FILM OPTICAL SOUND K-I
Reveals that Mickey and Josh are depressed because their team has lost all of its soccer games. Relates that winning a prize is very important to Boaz until he wins a prize he isn't proud of. Stresses that people are never losers in God's eyes.
From The Good Time Growing Show Series. Show 6
Prod-WHTLIN Dist-WHTLIN

Winning And Losing C 59 MIN
3/4 OR 1/2 INCH VIDEO CASSETTE C A
Focuses on what motivates young people to play high school football. Follows the DuBois Area, Pennsylvania, coach and players through their 1981 season.
Prod-PSU Dist-PSU Prodn-OCONEL 1984

Winning Battles C 8 MIN
16MM FILM, 3/4 OR 1/2 IN VIDEO
Describes a pilot program at Stanford University Children's Hospital where parents of children with cancer are actively involved in the treatment of the child and even discuss the possibility of death, while keeping up hope for the future.
Prod-FRUCTN Dist-FLMLIB 1980

Winning By Losing/The Decision C 21 MIN
3/4 OR 1/2 INCH VIDEO CASSETTE
Defines the role of 'surrender' in the recovery process of the chemically dependent and illustrates the methods that facilitate 'surrender.'
From The Caring Community - Alcoholism And Drug Abuse Series.
Prod-VTRI Dist-VTRI

Winning Combination C 20 MIN
3/4 OR 1/2 INCH VIDEO CASSETTE I
Presents dramatizations of literary works that deal with success as a combination of mind and muscle.
From The Readers' Cube Series.
Prod-MDDE Dist-AITECH 1977

Winning Combination For Cost Control, The C 11 MIN
16MM FILM - 3/4 IN VIDEO IND
A dramatization which shows the techniques used by a company supervisor to win the cooperation of his subordinates in helping to reduce waste and control costs.
From The Modern Management Series.
Prod-BNA Dist-BNA Prodn-NF 1963

Winning Combination, A C 15 MIN
16MM FILM OPTICAL SOUND
Discusses the New England Whalers hockey team of the World Hockey Association. Emphasizes the need for physical fitness, skating ability, proper equipment and teamwork.
LC NO. 75-703551
Prod-AETNA Dist-AETNA 1975

Winning Combination, The C
16MM FILM OPTICAL SOUND
Describes learning center management techniques, hardware, and business courses.
Prod-HBJ Dist-HBJ

Winning Edge, The C 10 MIN
3/4 OR 1/2 INCH VIDEO CASSETTE A
Presents Olympic hockey Coach Herb Brooks explaining his techniques for motivating his team. Discusses leadership, preparation, teamwork and taking risks.
Prod-SFTI Dist-SFTI

Winning Edge, The C 17 MIN
3/4 OR 1/2 INCH VIDEO CASSETTE
Provides an explanation of wrestling rules, covering such areas as starting position, stalling, control situations, technical violations, illegal holds and pinning situations.
LC NO. 81-707636
Prod-NFSHSA Dist-NFSHSA Prodn-NAUT 1981

Winning Goals C 8 MIN
3/4 OR 1/2 INCH VIDEO CASSETTE A
Features Mike Eruzione, captain of America's champion 1980 Olympic hockey team. Shows footage from its final victory. Emphasizes the importance of common goals and team motivation.
From The Winner's Circle Series.
Prod-SFTI Dist-SFTI

Winning Golf C
16MM FILM OPTICAL SOUND
Presents Sam Snead and Billy Casper demonstrating different techniques and styles.
Prod-SFI Dist-SFI

Winning Hand, The C 12 MIN
16MM FILM OPTICAL SOUND
Features the cast of the television show, The Odd Couple, pointing out the many benefits of purchasing bonds through the Payroll Savings Plan.
Prod-USSBD Dist-USSBD

Winning Hearts And Minds C 29 MIN
3/4 OR 1/2 INCH VIDEO CASSETTE
Explores media coverage of the Vietnam war. Presents Ben Wattenberg questioning three journalists about the realism and objectivity of war reporting. Examines the impact of television war coverage. Proposes that biased press coverage helped build public sentiment against the war and ultimately determined its outcome.
From The Ben Wattenberg's 1980 Series.
Prod-WETATV Dist-PBS

Winning Is Everything C 23 MIN
16MM FILM, 3/4 OR 1/2 IN VIDEO J-C A
Compares organized sports for children which emphasizes competition and winning at any cost with programs that provide all interested children a chance to participate.
Prod-LUF Dist-LUF 1978

Winning Isn't Everything - Improving Client Relations C 35 MIN
3/4 OR 1/2 INCH VIDEO CASSETTE PRO
Explores what clients want from their attorney. Relates the preferences of clients, as established by research studies, to practical measures which can be instituted immediately to improve client relations.
From The Managing Your Law Firm Series.
Prod-ABACPE Dist-ABACPE

Winning Job Interview, The C
1/2 IN VIDEO CASSETTE BETA/VHS H
Gives tips on job interviews for teenagers and leads them through each step of the interview process.
Prod-GA Dist-GA

Winning Linebacker, The C 60 MIN
1/2 IN VIDEO CASSETTE BETA/VHS
Covers linebacking play. Demonstrates the methods and techniques of playing the defensive backfield positions.
From The Football Fundamentals Series.
Prod-MOHOMV Dist-MOHOMV

Winning Offense, A C 57 MIN
1/2 IN VIDEO CASSETTE BETA/VHS
Shows how to create an offense for a men's basketball team. Demonstrates offensive strategy for man-to-man and zone defenses. Covers topics such as creating a lead, post play and the double stack.
From The Men's Basketball Basics Series.
Prod-MOHOMV Dist-MOHOMV

Winning Team, The B 15 MIN
2 INCH VIDEOTAPE P-I
Points out that the team formed by the cooperative patient and his dentist is the winning one. Presents the history of dentistry followed by a survey of modern dental equipment. Considers major dental problems that require the attention of an orthodontist.
From The Dental Health Series.
Prod-GPITVL Dist-GPITVL

Winning The Job Game C
3/4 OR 1/2 INCH VIDEO CASSETTE
Designed to generate behavior that will directly lead to getting a job. Stresses the need for active participation in job hunting.Shows how to organize a job search and write resumes and cover letters. Details job applications and handling references.
Prod-EDUACT Dist-EDUACT

Winning The Safari Rally C 28 MIN
16MM FILM OPTICAL SOUND
Documents the 24th running of the East African Safari Rally in Kenya in 1976 in which more than 60 cars were raced by world famous professionals, unknown bankers, farmers and businessmen during four days and three nights.
LC NO. 77-700441
Prod-KLEINW Dist-KLEINW 1976

Winning The War On Arson C 16 MIN
16MM FILM OPTICAL SOUND
Explores the problem of arson, the fastest-growing crime in the United States. Shows how the communities of Seattle, Washington, and New Haven, Connecticut, are combatting arson.
LC NO. 79-701171
Prod-AETNA Dist-AETNA 1979

Winning Way To Go C 26 MIN
16MM FILM OPTICAL SOUND
Highlights sports car racing at America's road racing and oval race courses. Illustrates the intense competition between race teams in their quest to win motor racing's top awards in the International Motor Sports Association series.
Prod-MZDAMA Dist-MTP

Winning Ways - The Rules Of Basketball C 28 MIN
16MM FILM OPTICAL SOUND I-C A
Describes rules and guidelines used in judging interscholastic and intercollegiate basketball games. Features boys' teams and girls' teams in a demonstration of rules that apply to traveling, dribble restrictions, jump ball, free throw, dunking, division lines, contact situations and officiating mechanics.
From The National Federation Sports Films Series.
LC NO. 77-700468
Prod-NFSHSA Dist-NFSHSA Prodn-CALVIN 1976

Winning With Customers—A Series
16MM FILM - 3/4 IN VIDEO
Provides information on customer service.
Prod-BNA Dist-BNA

Customer Service Is Everybody's Business 020 MIN
What Do They Really Want 020 MIN

Winning Your Wings / Wings Up B 36 MIN
3/4 OR 1/2 INCH VIDEO CASSETTE
Presents a Hollywood-Government co-production made to attract recruits into the USAF. Features Lieutenant James Stewart. Shows the intense discipline and conditioning techniques at the officer-training school in Miami to recruit officer-candidates for the Air Force. Features footage of men at the school including Mayor Glen Cove, Elmer Meadows, Robert Preston, Gilbert Roland and Clark Gable. Narrated by Clark Gable.
Prod-IHF Dist-IHF

Winslow Eaves, Sculptor C 30 MIN
2 INCH VIDEOTAPE
See series title for descriptive statement.
From The World Of The American Craftsman Series.
Prod-WENHTV Dist-PUBTEL

Winston Churchill B 10 MIN
3/4 OR 1/2 INCH VIDEO CASSETTE I A
Reviews the long and memorable career of Winston Churchill, including some of the earliest motion pictures ever made of him and scenes during World War I.
Prod-HEARST Dist-HEARST

Winston Churchill B 52 MIN
16MM FILM, 3/4 OR 1/2 IN VIDEO I-C A
Uses rare actuality footage to portray the personal life and history-making deeds of Winston Churchill.
From The History Makers Of The 20th Century Series.
Prod-WOLPER Dist-SF 1965

Winston Churchill - The Valiant Years—A Series

Prod-ABCTV Dist-SG

Alone No More 26 MIN
Be Sure You Win 26 MIN
Beginning Of The End 26 MIN
Closing The Ring 26 MIN
Combat Deepens, The 26 MIN
D-Day 26 MIN
Die Is Cast, The 26 MIN
Dunkirk 26 MIN
Final Christmas 26 MIN
French Agony, The 26 MIN
Gathering Storm, The 26 MIN
Goodbye, Mr Churchill 26 MIN
Gotterdammerung 26 MIN
Out Of The East 26 MIN
Ravens Remain, The 26 MIN
Set Europe Ablaze 26 MIN

Winston Cigarettes C 1 MIN
3/4 OR 1/2 INCH VIDEO CASSETTE
Shows a classic television commercial with animated musical notes.
Prod-BROOKC Dist-BROOKC

Winter C 8 MIN
16MM FILM, 3/4 OR 1/2 IN VIDEO J-C A
Presents the story of a bully who is done in by his own envy and love of violence.
Prod-FILBUL Dist-PHENIX 1981

Winter C 11 MIN
16MM FILM, 3/4 OR 1/2 IN VIDEO P-I
Offers a child's-eye view of winter activities.
From The Season Series.
LC NO. 80-707706
Prod-CENTRO Dist-CORF 1980

Winter C 11 MIN
16MM FILM, 3/4 OR 1/2 IN VIDEO P-I
Shows the approach of winter in a lake and explains how animals survive during the cold months.
From The Lake Of Perch Series.
LC NO. 81-706449
Prod-FISYNG Dist-CORF 1981

Winter C 11 MIN
16MM FILM, 3/4 OR 1/2 IN VIDEO
Shows that winter is as interesting as the other seasons. Studies winter weeds, abandoned nests and animal tracks and signs.
From The Many Worlds Of Nature Series.
Prod-MORALL Dist-MTI 1976

Winter C 13 MIN
16MM FILM, 3/4 OR 1/2 IN VIDEO P-I
Looks at the activities and changes common to the winter season such as the hibernation of animals and the difficult search for food by creatures which don't hibernate.
From The Four Seasons Series.
Prod-NGS Dist-NGS 1983

Winter C 15 MIN
3/4 INCH VIDEO CASSETTE P
See series title for descriptive statement.
From The Celebrate Series.
Prod-KUONTV Dist-GPITVL 1978

Winter - A Museum Experience C 15 MIN
3/4 OR 1/2 INCH VIDEO CASSETTE K-P
Features winter pictures and scenes, months of winter, and a museum visit.
From The Pass It On Series.
Prod-WKNOTV Dist-GPITVL 1983

Winter - Nature's Sights And Sounds C 14 MIN
16MM FILM, 3/4 OR 1/2 IN VIDEO P-I
Shows how winter may threaten the survival of animals and how each species has a special way to face winter.
From The Nature's Sights And Sounds Series.
Prod-MASLKS Dist-BCNFL 1984

Winter - Story Of Survival C 14 MIN
16MM FILM, 3/4 OR 1/2 IN VIDEO P-J
Studies winter and its effect on plant and animal life. Shows that some creature migrate during the Winter, some hibernate and others struggle to survive the severe times.
Prod-GATEEF Dist-AIMS 1968

Winter Bass C 8 MIN
16MM FILM OPTICAL SOUND A
Reveals the secrets of a successful fisherman in an interview with Sam Cagle. Accompanies Mr Cagle to Center Hill reservoir as he explains his techniques.
Prod-TGAFC Dist-TGAFC

Winter Birds C 5 MIN
16MM FILM OPTICAL SOUND
Shows a variety of eastern North American birds and their behavior during and just after a heavy snowfall.
LC NO. 77-702724
Prod-MEPHTS Dist-MEPHTS 1977

Winter Carnival Theme C 24 MIN
3/4 OR 1/2 INCH VIDEO CASSETTE
Features a 17-year-old athlete for all seasons, who competes in the biathlon, an event that combines cross-country skiing and sharp shooting.
Prod-WCCOTV Dist-WCCOTV 1982

Winter Comes To The City C 10 MIN
16MM FILM, 3/4 OR 1/2 IN VIDEO P
Shows a boy from the South discovering how people, plants and animals prepare for winter in Chicago.
From The Seasons In The City Series.
Prod-CORF Dist-CORF

Winter Comes To The Forest C 11 MIN
16MM FILM, 3/4 OR 1/2 IN VIDEO P
Reveals the different ways that living things adapt for surviving the winter. Shows buds containing tiny leaves, a moth cocoon, insect eggs and seeds.
From The Seasons Series.
Prod-CORF Dist-CORF 1964

Winter Days C 50 MIN
3/4 OR 1/2 INCH VIDEO CASSETTE H-C A
Portrays birds and animals in their winter struggle for survival. Shows swans from Siberia and Scandinavia, ducks from all over Europe and geese from Iceland heading south to the British Isles where the Gulf Stream provides warmth and food.
Prod-WNETTV Dist-FI Prodn-BBCTV

Winter Distress Signals C 13 MIN
16MM FILM, 3/4 OR 1/2 IN VIDEO I-H
Discusses why many of the distress methods available to the lost camper in summer time are not applicable in winter. Dramatizes the ways in which winter distress signals are employed to summon assistance.
Prod-SF Dist-SF 1968

Winter Driving C 11 MIN
16MM FILM, 3/4 OR 1/2 IN VIDEO H-C A
Discusses winter driving hazards and explores winter safety and maintenance measures.
Prod-NSC Dist-JOU 1979

Winter Driving - Keep Your Cool C 26 MIN
16MM FILM, 3/4 OR 1/2 IN VIDEO
Presents expert advice on driving on icy and snowy roads from people with lots of experience.
Prod-NFBC Dist-NFBC 1981

Winter Driving Safety - 818 - Clear And En Route C 17 MIN
16MM FILM, 3/4 OR 1/2 IN VIDEO
Follows a Michigan State Trooper as he answers accident and distress calls, illustrating common problems encountered in driving under extreme winter weather conditions.
Prod-USAF Dist-USNAC

Winter Driving Tactics C 16 MIN
16MM FILM, 3/4 OR 1/2 IN VIDEO H-C A
Demonstrates the precautions necessary when driving on icy and snowy surfaces, plus the techniques for handling slick-surface emergencies. Explains how to avoid loss of traction when climbing hills, how to avoid skids, how to practice skid recovery, how to free snow-stuck wheels, how to put on standard chains, how to read the road for hazard spots and how to winterize a car properly.
Prod-CAHILL Dist-AIMS 1975

Winter Encampment, 1779-1780 - Jockey Hollow B 12 MIN
16MM FILM - 3/4 IN VIDEO
Offers a glimpse of the 1779 winter encampment at Jockey Hollow, Morristown, New Jersey. Issued in 1972 as a motion picture.
LC NO. 79-706174
Prod-USNPS Dist-USNAC 1979

Winter Fun C 3 MIN
16MM FILM OPTICAL SOUND P-I
Gives examples of winter fun.
From The Of All Things Series.
Prod-BAILYL Dist-AVED

Winter Garden C 11 MIN
16MM FILM, 3/4 OR 1/2 IN VIDEO P-I
Reveals that as winter approaches, Boy and his friends search for a way to keep the trees and plants from freezing. Shows that Boy plans a hot water system based on the principle of solar energy. Provides insight into the means by which solar energy can be used for heating and for the generation of power.
From The Inventive Child Series.
Prod-POLSKI Dist-EBEC 1983

Winter Geyser C 7 MIN
16MM FILM, 3/4 OR 1/2 IN VIDEO P-J
Shows the end of summer and fall merging into winter. Includes scenes of streams, mud pots and geysers of Yellowstone National Park against the backdrop of snow and ice.
From The Wilderness Series.
Prod-PFP Dist-PHENIX Prodn-PFP 1968

Winter Harvest C 15 MIN
16MM FILM, 3/4 OR 1/2 IN VIDEO P-J
Focuses on the life of a farm family in a northern climate and their winter months' activities. Shows how this family's life differs from most in that it has a 300 acre timber area that provides a winter crop. Illustrates other winter activities from ice fishing and ice harvesting to skating and tobogganing.
Prod-NELVNA Dist-BCNFL 1982

Winter Heat C 28 MIN
16MM FILM OPTICAL SOUND
Presents scenes of hot dog skiing on some of the toughest slopes in America. Uses super-slow-motion photography to show every movement as the competitors somersault into space.
Prod-BARP Dist-FFORIN

Winter Ice - A First Film C 11 MIN
16MM FILM, 3/4 OR 1/2 IN VIDEO P-I
Studies the environment during the winter months when ice covers the landscape. Shows its effects on the community and its benefits on the environment. Discusses frost, snowflakes, frozen streams and lakes, icicles and the rivers and streams resulting from melted ice in the spring.
Prod-BFA Dist-PHENIX 1970

Winter Ice - A First Film (French) C 11 MIN
16MM FILM, 3/4 OR 1/2 IN VIDEO P-I
Studies the environment during the winter months when ice covers the landscape. Shows its effects on the community and its benefits on the environment. Discusses frost, snowflakes, frozen streams and lakes, icicles and the rivers and streams resulting from melted ice in the spring.
Prod-BFA Dist-PHENIX 1970

Winter Impressions C 12 MIN
16MM FILM, 3/4 OR 1/2 IN VIDEO P-I
Follows a little boy as he sets off to discover the joys of winter and finds bare trees in the woods covered with ice, a flock of sheep who stare at him curiously and other children skating on a frozen pond.
Prod-MORLAT Dist-SF 1968

Winter In Nature C 12 MIN
16MM FILM, 3/4 OR 1/2 IN VIDEO P-I
Looks at life in the natural landscape during winter.
From The Seasons In Nature Series.
Prod-FLMFR Dist-FLMFR

Winter In Stories B 20 MIN
2 INCH VIDEOTAPE I
Deals with stories that tell of winter hardships. (Broadcast quality)
From The Quest For The Best Series.
Prod-DENVPS Dist-GPITVL Prodn-KRMATV

Winter Is C 15 MIN
3/4 OR 1/2 INCH VIDEO CASSETTE P
Relates rhythm to winter experiences like shoveling snow.
From The Stepping Into Rhythm Series.
Prod-WVIZTV Dist-AITECH

Winter Is An Adventure C 11 MIN
16MM FILM, 3/4 OR 1/2 IN VIDEO P
Shows the scenes typical of winter, such as snow frosting the outdoors, winter animals appearing, and exploring a farm during the cold months.
Prod-CORF Dist-CORF

Winter Is Here (Captioned) C 9 MIN
16MM FILM, 3/4 OR 1/2 IN VIDEO P
Focuses on animal and human life during the winter and discusses winter holidays. Captioned for the hearing impaired.
Prod-BERLET Dist-IFB 1967

Winter Is Here (2nd Ed) C 11 MIN
16MM FILM, 3/4 OR 1/2 IN VIDEO P
Focuses on human and animal life during the winter and describes various holidays during this period.
From The Seasons (2nd Ed) Series.
LC NO. 80-706441
Prod-IFB Dist-IFB Prodn-BERLET 1979

Winter Landscape C 8 MIN
16MM FILM OPTICAL SOUND
Features observation of the winter scene during an ordinary day's activities.
LC NO. 77-702725
Prod-MEPHTS Dist-MEPHTS 1977

Winter Lillies C 59 MIN
3/4 OR 1/2 INCH VIDEO CASSETTE
Examines the life of Wilfred Robertson, fiddle-maker and primitive painter, who carries on the tradition of his aunt, Grandma Moses.
Prod-KITCHN Dist-KITCHN

Winter Melon C 29 MIN
2 INCH VIDEOTAPE
Features Joyce Chen showing how to adapt Chinese recipes so they can be prepared in the American kitchen and still retain the authentic flavor. Demonstrates how to prepare melon.
From The Joyce Chen Cooks Series.
Prod-WGBHTV Dist-PUBTEL

Winter Melts To Spring C 29 MIN
3/4 INCH VIDEO CASSETTE
Explores a swamp and roadside for wild plants that can be used throughout the winter for survival food.
From The Edible Wild Plants Series.
Prod-UMITV Dist-UMITV 1978

Winter Of The Witch C 25 MIN
16MM FILM, 3/4 OR 1/2 IN VIDEO P-J A
Presents a story about a young boy and his mother who move from the city into a country house which is haunted by a witch.
Prod-PARENT Dist-LCOA Prodn-TSE 1970

Winter Of The Witch (Spanish) C 25 MIN
16MM FILM, 3/4 OR 1/2 IN VIDEO P A
Tells the story of Nicky and his mother who find themselves in a spooky house with a 300-year-old witch, who eventually turns very loving and creative.
Prod-PARENT Dist-LCOA Prodn-TSE 1970

Winter On An Indian Reservation C 11 MIN
16MM FILM, 3/4 OR 1/2 IN VIDEO P-I
Provides a look into the lives of children on a forest reservation, non-narrative.
Prod-ATLAP Dist-ATLAP

Winter Park Art Festival C 12 MIN
16MM FILM OPTICAL SOUND I-C
The story of Winter Park's sidewalk art show and how it won national attention.
LC NO. FIA66-681
Prod-FDC Dist-FDC 1964

Winter Ride C 23 MIN
16MM FILM OPTICAL SOUND
Dicusses snowmobiles.
LC NO. 78-701136
Prod-ISIA Dist-MILP Prodn-MILP 1978

Winter Ride (French) C 23 MIN
16MM FILM OPTICAL SOUND
Dicusses snowmobiles.
LC NO. 78-701136
Prod-ISIA Dist-MILP Prodn-MILP 1978

Winter Safety C 14 MIN
16MM FILM, 3/4 OR 1/2 IN VIDEO P-J
Discusses the accidents that can happen to children during the winter. Demonstrates safe practices around cars, snow and ice and tells what to do if someone should fall through a frozen pond.
LC NO. 80-707550
Prod-FLMFR Dist-FLMFR 1980

Winter Signs C 13 MIN
16MM FILM, 3/4 OR 1/2 IN VIDEO I-J
Identifies various structures, marks and other signs made by insects during winter.
From The Discovering Insects Series.
Prod-MORALL Dist-MTI 1982

Winter Storm C 14 MIN
16MM FILM, 3/4 OR 1/2 IN VIDEO J-H T
Illustrates the many dangers of winter storms using the short story by Jack London, 'TO BUILD A FIRE.' Shows the depths of tragic circumstances possible during winter storms.
From The Your Chance To Live Series.
Prod-USDCPA Dist-MTI 1972

Winter Storms C 27 MIN
16MM FILM, 3/4 OR 1/2 IN VIDEO
Recounts the disastrous winter of 1978. Recalls the blizzards in New England and the Midwest, the floods and mudslides in California and the unexpected snowfalls and floods that paralyzed much of the South.
LC NO. 80-707113
Prod-USDCPA Dist-USNAC Prodn-USDA 1980

Winter Survival C 15 MIN
16MM FILM, 3/4 OR 1/2 IN VIDEO J-C A
Demonstrates how to survive outdoors in winter using the examples of a cross-country skier and a snowmobiler who find themselves stranded. Shows how knowledge means survival.
Prod-NFBC Dist-NFBC 1979

Winter Survival In The Bush C 20 MIN
16MM FILM, 3/4 OR 1/2 IN VIDEO J-C A
Through dramatic case histories and visually explicit sequences, teaches the viewer how to recognize a survival situation and how to deal with the basics of winter survival. Describes the strategies for dealing with a disabled snowmobile in isolated snowy locations.
LC NO. 82-707058
Prod-GOLDIJ Dist-BCNFL 1982

Winter Truck Driving C 19 MIN
16MM FILM OPTICAL SOUND
Illustrates safe driving techniques for drivers of commercial vehicles such as trucks and semi-trailers. Stresses preparing for winter driving runs.
Prod-NSC Dist-NSC

Winter Walking C 11 MIN
16MM FILM, 3/4 OR 1/2 IN VIDEO
Shows recommended procedures for walking in the ice and snow. Contains spectacular scenery of Vermont combined with scenes of actual tumbles.
LC NO. 82-706399
Prod-USPOST Dist-USNAC 1971

Winter Wife, The C 26 MIN
16MM FILM, 3/4 OR 1/2 IN VIDEO
Dramatizes a legend about a young Chippewa Indian who wanted above all else to be rich. Tells of his betraying his wife and being turned into an elk.
Prod-FOTH Dist-FOTH

Winter Wilderness C 30 MIN
1/2 IN VIDEO CASSETTE BETA/VHS
Explores Vermont's winter wilderness. Describes riding an elephant and searching for a tiger in Nepal.
From The Great Outdoors Series.
Prod-WGBHTV Dist-MTI

Winter Wipers C 30 MIN
1/2 IN VIDEO CASSETTE BETA/VHS
Explains how a four-stroke engine operates. Explores winter wipers. Presents a VW Jetta.
From The Last Chance Garage Series.
Prod-WGBHTV Dist-MTI

Winter Woods, The X 11 MIN
16MM FILM OPTICAL SOUND
Tennessee Charlie discusses the winter world. On a walk through the winter woods, the strange habits of the shrike, or 'BUTCHER BIRD,' are revealed.
From The World Outdoors Series. No. 12
Prod-TGAFC Dist-TGAFC

Winter World C 18 MIN
16MM FILM, 3/4 OR 1/2 IN VIDEO I-C A
Demonstrates the fundamental techniques of protection from freezing in outdoor winter conditions and details the method of sleeping in a snow cave.
From The Basic Information Film Series.
Prod-FO Dist-FO 1960

Winter World, Pt 1 C 14 MIN
2 INCH VIDEOTAPE
See series title for descriptive statement.
From The Muffinland Series.
Prod-WGTV Dist-PUBTEL

Winter World, Pt 2 C 14 MIN
2 INCH VIDEOTAPE
See series title for descriptive statement.
From The Muffinland Series.
Prod-WGTV Dist-PUBTEL

Winter's End C 10 MIN
16MM FILM, 3/4 OR 1/2 IN VIDEO I-H
Shows how animals and ecosystems in the far north of Canada are being endangered by new stresses caused by man's development of the area.
Prod-MEPHTS Dist-JOU 1973

Winter's Tale, The C 29 MIN
2 INCH VIDEOTAPE
Features Alan Levitan, associate professor of English at Brandeis University discussing The Winter's Tale by Shakespeare.
From The Feast Of Language Series.
Prod-WGBHTV Dist-PUBTEL

Winter's Tale, The C 173 MIN
3/4 OR 1/2 INCH VIDEO CASSETTE H-C A
Presents William Shakespeare's play The Winter's Tale about a king who unjustly accuses his wife of adultery. Reveals that 16 years later, their daughter, missing since infancy, is miraculously restored and reconciled with her dead mother, who is brought back to life again.
From The Shakespeare Plays Series.
LC NO. 82-707356
Prod-BBCTV Dist-TIMLIF 1981

Winter's Tale, The - Tell Us A Story B 45 MIN
2 INCH VIDEOTAPE C
See series title for descriptive statement.
From The Shakespeare Series.
Prod-CHITVC Dist-GPITVL Prodn-WTTWTV

Winter's Wildlife C 21 MIN
16MM FILM OPTICAL SOUND
Takes the viewer on a winter hike along a scenic river and through the woods to discover the wildlife that lives there during the season. Shows beaver, deer, foxes, raccoons and a territorial duel between porcupines.
LC NO. 77-702727
Prod-GIB Dist-GIB 1976

Winterdeath C 18 MIN
16MM FILM OPTICAL SOUND
Tells a story of an old man's imaginary search for a polar bear in the North woods.
LC NO. 77-700443
Prod-WECHO Dist-WECHO 1976

Wintering, Diseases, Pests C 30 MIN
3/4 OR 1/2 INCH VIDEO CASSETTE
Discusses disease symptoms, diagnosis, treatment and wintering problems. Presents methods of moving bee colonies and special practices in beekeeping.
From The Bees And Honey Series.
Prod-WGTV Dist-MDCPB

Wintersports In Sweden C 15 MIN
16MM FILM OPTICAL SOUND
Points out that Ostersund, in the center of Sweden has much to offer the tourist in the winter, including skating, sleigh riding and skiing practically on your doorstep.
Prod-SWNTO Dist-SWNTO 1962

Wipe Out Jargon C 24 MIN
3/4 OR 1/2 INCH VIDEO CASSETTE H-C A
Examines letter and report writing. Demonstrates efficient writing and principles for clear, well structured letters and reports. Includes booklets.
From The Transition Package Series.
Prod-SEVDIM Dist-SEVDIM

Wipeout B 2 MIN
16MM FILM OPTICAL SOUND
A quick succession of images synchronized with music provides impressions of life, death, war, love and hate.
LC NO. FIA67-703
Prod-USC Dist-USC 1966

Wire Rope Terminal Connections B 31 MIN
16MM FILM - 3/4 IN VIDEO
Demonstrates how to make and test such terminal connections as clips, eye splices, and metallic splices. Issued in 1944 as a motion picture.
From The Shipbuilding Skills - Rigging Series.
LC NO. 80-707053
Prod-USN Dist-USNAC 1980

Wire Sculpture C 20 MIN
16MM FILM OPTICAL SOUND J-C A
Depicts the techniques and philosophy of free-lance artist Joe Police as he constructs kinetic wire sculptures with an acetylene torch and steel wire.
Prod-UHAWAI Dist-UHAWAI 1973

Wire Sculpture C 13 MIN
16MM FILM, 3/4 OR 1/2 IN VIDEO
Shows Joe Police assembling a wire sculpture and commenting about his technique, his art form and his philosophy.
Prod-PERSPF Dist-CORF

Wire Sculpture, Crayon Batik And Figures With Rolled Paper Base C 15 MIN
3/4 INCH VIDEO CASSETTE P-I
See series title for descriptive statement.
From The Look And A Closer Look Series.
Prod-WCVETV Dist-GPITVL 1976

Wire Sizes And Voltage Drop B 13 MIN
16MM FILM - 3/4 IN VIDEO
Focuses on factors influencing the ability of conductors to carry electron flow. Discusses the measurement of wire sizes, wire area in circular mils, voltage drop and Ohm's law.
From The Electrical Work - Wiring Series. No. 4
LC NO. 79-707493
Prod-USOE Dist-USNAC Prodn-RAYBEL 1979

Wireladder Splint - The Injured Ankle C 7 MIN
3/4 OR 1/2 INCH VIDEO CASSETTE PRO
Shows the application of the wireladder splint to an injured foot and ankle, including padding, bending and securing the splint.
From The EMT Video - Group Two Series.
LC NO. 84-706501
Prod-USA Dist-USNAC 1983

Wireless Lizzie B 30 MIN
16MM FILM OPTICAL SOUND
From The Classic Christie Comedies Series.
Prod-SFI Dist-SFI

Wiring And Insulation C 30 MIN
1/2 IN VIDEO CASSETTE BETA/VHS
Discusses wiring a breezeway. Shows how to insulate the garage-turned-family-room.
From The This Old House, Pt 2 - Suburban '50s Series.
Prod-WGBHTV Dist-MTI

Wiring And One-Line Diagrams C 60 MIN
3/4 OR 1/2 INCH VIDEO CASSETTE IND
See series title for descriptive statement.
From The Electrical Maintenance Training, Module C - Electrical Print Reading Series.
Prod-LEIKID Dist-LEIKID

Wiring Old Buildings With Armored Cable B 22 MIN
16MM FILM - 3/4 IN VIDEO
Shows how to install outlet boxes, cut and strip armor from cable, attach cable to outlet boxes, run armored cable, repair openings in walls and join conductors at a ceiling outlet.
From The Electrical Work - Wiring Series. No. 4
LC NO. 79-707494
Prod-USOE Dist-USNAC Prodn-RAYBEL 1979

Wiring Telltale Panel B 17 MIN
16MM FILM OPTICAL SOUND
Explains the purpose of telltale units. Shows how to strip cable, form and lace conductors on a jig, strip the ends of conductors and put on lugs.
LC NO. FIE52-207
Prod-USOE Dist-USNAC 1945

Wiring Up The Organization C 25 MIN
3/4 OR 1/2 INCH VIDEO CASSETTE H-C A
Host Ian McNaught Davis examines how an organization's office work is affected when it provides a network that allows computers to be interconnected with a centralized data base.
From The Electronic Office Series.
LC NO. 85-700735
Prod-BBCTV Dist-FI 1984

Wiring Up The World C 25 MIN
3/4 OR 1/2 INCH VIDEO CASSETTE H-C A
Examines the implications of increasing use of electronic systems to get information between companies and between companies and their clients. Discusses the factors which have prohibited a revolutionary use of computers in offices, including human scepticism, the lack of standardization and cost.
From The Electronic Office Series.
Prod-BBCTV Dist-FI 1984

Wiring, Batteries, Coolant And Upholstery C 30 MIN
1/2 IN VIDEO CASSETTE BETA/VHS
Talks about electrical wiring and upholstery. Shows how to check the engine coolant and to recharge a dead battery. Reminisces about a 1964 Triumph Roadster.
From The Last Chance Garage Series.
Prod-WGBHTV Dist-MTI

Wisconsin Cheese For All Seasons C 25 MIN
16MM FILM OPTICAL SOUND H-C A
Shows how cheddar and other types of cheese are made and promotes the consumption of cheese by presenting it as a convenient, waste-free and nutritious food available in many flavors, shapes, and sizes and useful in a wide variety of ways. Links cheese with the ethnic groups which brought the old world formulas to America and points out that several kinds originated in Wisconsin.
LC NO. 81-700439
Prod-UWISCA Dist-UWISCA 1980

Wisconsin Cleft Palate Story, The C 36 MIN
16MM FILM OPTICAL SOUND
Discusses the problem of the cleft palate and negative influences it may have upon a child's emotional development. Describes dental and speech therapy, and gives information about correction facilities.
Prod-UWISC Dist-AJN 1955

Wisconsin Farming C 48 MIN
16MM FILM OPTICAL SOUND I-C A
Presents a survey of Wisconsin's agriculture by showing three farms situated in different parts of the State.
LC NO. 79-700106
Prod-UWISCA Dist-UWISC 1978

Wisconsin Rural Government - The Town C 16 MIN
16MM FILM OPTICAL SOUND
Provides an insight into the principle duties and problems of the town officers and the informality of procedures in a form of local government, the town, as it exists in Wisconsin.
Prod-UWISC Dist-UWISC 1964

Wisconsin, A Proud Heritage - The Menomonie People C 20 MIN
3/4 OR 1/2 INCH VIDEO CASSETTE
Presents a summary of the history of the Menomonie people, from their origins to the recent past, and then shows life of the Menomonie as it exists today.
Prod-NEWIST Dist-UWISC Prodn-WDPI 1982

Wisconsin's Central Sands C 27 MIN
16MM FILM OPTICAL SOUND
Describes how irrigation, agriculture and agricultural research changed the Wisconsin Central Sands region.
LC NO. 77-700202
Prod-UWISCA Dist-UWISCA 1976

Wisdom Has No Fear Of Death C 39 MIN
3/4 OR 1/2 INCH VIDEO CASSETTE
Presents Ram Dass lecturing on the relationship between bodily death and consciousness. Observes that if one is to work effectively with dying persons, one must first work with yourself.
From The Conscious Living/Conscious Dying - The Work Of A Lifetime Series.
Prod-ORGNLF Dist-PELICN

Wisdom Of Socrates - Plato C 45 MIN
2 INCH VIDEOTAPE
See series title for descriptive statement.
From The Humanities Series. Unit I - Persons, Places And Events
Prod-WTTWTV Dist-GPITVL

Wise Use Of Credit, The X 11 MIN
16MM FILM OPTICAL SOUND J-H
Discusses consumer credit, how it is established, the types and cost, the amount a family can afford and the circumstances under which credit should be used.
LC NO. FIA62-1676
Prod-SUEF Dist-SUTHLA 1960

Wise Use Of Drugs - A Program For Older Americans C 31 MIN
16MM FILM, 3/4 OR 1/2 IN VIDEO
Provides background information on the use of legal drugs in America and offers advice to the elderly on the use of prescription drugs. Issued in 1979 as a motion picture.
LC NO. 80-707247
Prod-NIDA Dist-USNAC 1980

Wisest Man In The World, The C 10 MIN
16MM FILM, 3/4 OR 1/2 IN VIDEO P-I
Retells old legends of the wisdom of Solomon, including visit of the Queen of Sheba and her attempts to outwit him.
From The Children's Storybook Theater Series.
Prod-TSE Dist-AIMS 1970

Wish-Phone, The C 9 MIN
16MM FILM, 3/4 OR 1/2 IN VIDEO K-P
Depicts the animated adventures of two children and their dog who receive a magic telephone which carries out their wishes.
Prod-KRATKY Dist-PHENIX 1978

Wish, The C 30 MIN
3/4 OR 1/2 INCH VIDEO CASSETTE I-H
See series title for descriptive statement.
From The Gettin' To Know Me Series.
Prod-CTI Dist-MDCPB 1979

Witch Of Blackbird Pond, The C 15 MIN
3/4 OR 1/2 INCH VIDEO CASSETTE I
Tells the story of a girl from the Carribbean in 17th century New England. From the book by Elizabeth George Speare.
From The Storybound Series.
Prod-CTI Dist-CTI

Witch Who Was Afraid Of Witches, The C 12 MIN
16MM FILM, 3/4 OR 1/2 IN VIDEO P-I
Tells the story of Wendy, a young witch who is petrified of witches, especially her two mean witch-sisters. Shows how, on Halloween, Wendy gains confidence in herself and succeeds in outwitching her two mean sisters. Adapted from the book The Witch Who Was Afraid Of Witches by Alice Low.
Prod-NOYES Dist-LCOA 1979

Witch Who Was Afraid Of Witches, The (Captioned) C 12 MIN
16MM FILM, 3/4 OR 1/2 IN VIDEO P-I
Tells the story of a little witch Wendy who does not feel up to being a witch.
Prod-NOYES Dist-LCOA 1979

Witchcraft Among The Azande C 52 MIN
3/4 OR 1/2 INCH VIDEO CASSETTE A
Focuses on the human side of the Azande tribe of the African Sudan and the deep conviction that misfortunes result from witchcraft. Follows a farmer as he seeks magical relief for an ill wife consulting oracles and by the ritual poisoning os a chicken.
From The Disappearing World Series.
LC NO. 82-707326
Prod-GRATV Dist-FLMLIB 1982

Witches Of Salem, The - The Horror And The Hope (Captioned) C 34 MIN
16MM FILM, 3/4 OR 1/2 IN VIDEO J-C A
Shows how the hysterical behavior of a few young girls set off the Salem witchcraft trials of 1692.
Prod-AZRELA Dist-LCOA 1972

Witches Of Salem, The - The Horror And The Hope (Spanish) C 34 MIN
16MM FILM, 3/4 OR 1/2 IN VIDEO J-C A
Shows how the hysterical behavior of a few young girls set off the Salem witchcraft trials of 1692.
Prod-AZRELA Dist-LCOA 1972

Witches Of Salem, The - The Horror And The Hope C 34 MIN
16MM FILM, 3/4 OR 1/2 IN VIDEO J-C A
Portrays the witchcraft trials of Salem, Massachusetts, in 1692. Attempts to give an understanding of the political, psychological and religious background of this episode in American history.
Prod-AZRELA Dist-LCOA 1972

Witches, New Fashion - Old Religion C 52 MIN
16MM FILM, 3/4 OR 1/2 IN VIDEO C A
Interviews a businessman who studies witchcraft as a hobby and a businesswoman who heads a coven about their beliefs and practices.
Prod-THAMES Dist-MEDIAG 1972

Witchy Broom, The C 15 MIN
3/4 INCH VIDEO CASSETTE P
Features the children's story The Witchy Broom by Ida De Lage.
From The Tilson's Book Shop Series.
Prod-WVIZTV Dist-GPITVL 1975

Witchy Weed, The (Captioned) C 21 MIN
16MM FILM, 3/4 OR 1/2 IN VIDEO A
Portrays the development of the tobacco industry in Brazil. Discusses the techniques, economics and problems of tobacco production. Portuguese dialog with English subtitles.
Prod-CNEMAG Dist-CNEMAG

With A Little Help From My Friends, Pt 1 C 30 MIN
3/4 OR 1/2 INCH VIDEO CASSETTE I-J
Relates how a new youth center's members are caught up in an adventure with local racketeers.
From The Powerhouse Series.
LC NO. 83-707103
Prod-EFCVA Dist-GA 1982

With A Little Help From My Friends, Pt 2 C 30 MIN
3/4 OR 1/2 INCH VIDEO CASSETTE I-J
Relates how a new youth center's members are caught up in an adventure with local racketeers.
From The Powerhouse Series.
LC NO. 83-707103
Prod-EFCVA Dist-GA 1982

With All Deliberate Speed C 59 MIN
2 INCH VIDEOTAPE
Examines the issue of school bussing in Pontiac, Michigan on all levels.
From The Syngerism - Troubled Humanity Series.
Prod-WTVSTV Dist-PUBTEL

With America's Enemy, 1954-1967 C 60 MIN
3/4 OR 1/2 INCH VIDEO CASSETTE H-C A
Contrasts the Vietnamese war by offering the views of the followers of Ho Chi Minh and their opponents, U S soldiers and POWs. Depicts the effects of growing socialization in the North and the results of U S bombing, guerilla and conventional warfare.
From The Vietnam - A Television History Series. Episode 6
Prod-WGBHTV Dist-FI 1983

With Babies And Banners - Story Of The Women's Emergency Brigade C 45 MIN
16MM FILM OPTICAL SOUND H-C A
Uses archival footage and interviews with participants to trace the role of women in the formation of the United Auto Workers. Focuses on the contributions of the Women's Emergency Brigade to the labor movement of the 1930's.
LC NO. 78-701221
Prod-WLHFP Dist-NEWDAY 1978

With Babies And Banners - The Story Of The Women's Emergency Brigade C 45 MIN
16MM FILM, 3/4 OR 1/2 IN VIDEO
Celebrates women's participation in the historic General Motors Sit-Down Strike of 1937. Portrays the transformation of wives and mothers into defiant supporters, looks at their passionate struggle and their ultimate victory.
Prod-GLGLBA Dist-CNEMAG

With Bekus In Nepal C 14 MIN
16MM FILM, 3/4 OR 1/2 IN VIDEO P-I
Looks at the life of a 13-year-old boy in Nepal.
From The World's Children Series.
Prod-ITF Dist-JOU 1980

With Bernadette In New Guinea C 13 MIN
16MM FILM, 3/4 OR 1/2 IN VIDEO P-I
Shows a young girl from Papua, New Guinea as she collects firewood and water, weeds, gardens and feeds her pigs. Shows how the men and boys of the village clear a garden, fly homemade kites, and fish and swim in the warm Pacific waters.
From The World's Children Series.
Prod-ASTRSK Dist-JOU 1981

With Claudia In Australia C 13 MIN
16MM FILM, 3/4 OR 1/2 IN VIDEO P-I
Introduces an 11-year-old who lives in North Queensland, a largely rural farming area of Australia. Tells how she learns more about her ancestors, who were rain forest aborigines, as she visits the museum and crafts co-op.
From The World's Children Series.
Prod-ASTRSK Dist-JOU 1981

With Epelli In Fiji C 13 MIN
16MM FILM, 3/4 OR 1/2 IN VIDEO P-I
Shows a young boy who lives in a small village in the South Pacific country of Fiji as he helps with the sugarcane harvest, fishes, attends school, plays soccer, and is introduced to the Kava ceremony, the ancient Fijian ritual of welcome.
From The World's Children Series.
Prod-ASTRSK Dist-JOU 1981

With Every Breath C 25 MIN
3/4 OR 1/2 INCH VIDEO CASSETTE
Covers asthma, emphysema and the effect of smoking in discussing breathing and the lungs. Uses thermography, a photographic process based on heat, to show the actual effect of smoking on the circulation of blood through the body.
Prod-TRAINX Dist-TRAINX

With Eyes Wide Open C 58 MIN
16MM FILM - VIDEO, ALL FORMATS A
Explores the life and work of handicapped artist Richard Wawro. Reveals the environments that have enabled Richard to grow and express creativity. Narrated by Richard Cactus Pryor.
Prod-CLNGEN Dist-CLNGEN 1983

With Fabric And Thread C 15 MIN
16MM FILM, 3/4 OR 1/2 IN VIDEO I-C A
Explains that creative stitchery is like painting in thread but with greater variety in texture. Explains how to select a background fabric, choose colors and types of yarn and develop a design. Demonstrates such simple stitches as the stem or outline, chain, satin, French knot and couching. Describes such techniques as punch hooking and applique. Shows the creation of a picture in applique from the first sketched design through all stages.
From The Textile Design Series.
Prod-TETKOW Dist-AIMS 1974

With Flying Colors C 55 MIN
16MM FILM OPTICAL SOUND
Presents the highlights of the 1973 horseracing season in Canada, including the Queen's visit to the Queen's Plate, Secretariat's last race in the Canadian International and Sandy Hawley's record number of wins.
LC NO. 75-701955
Prod-ONTJC Dist-VIP Prodn-INST 1974

With Gladis In Bolivia C 11 MIN
16MM FILM, 3/4 OR 1/2 IN VIDEO P-I
Focuses on a day in the life of a girl in Santa Cruz, Bolivia.
From The World's Children Series.
Prod-ITF Dist-JOU 1980

With God On Our Side C 58 MIN
16MM FILM, 3/4 OR 1/2 IN VIDEO H-C A
Explores the proliferation of the electronic church characterized by television evangelists, radio programs and drive-in churches.
LC NO. 83-706749
Prod-VONWET Dist-PHENIX 1982

With Just A Little Trust C 15 MIN
16MM FILM OPTICAL SOUND
Shows how a young, widowed Black woman is brought out of a self-pity by her mother, who urges her to trust in God and have courage in times of adversity.
From The Contemporary Family Series.
LC NO. 75-703552
Prod-FRACOC Dist-FRACOC 1975

With Michael In Kyuso, Kenya C 13 MIN
16MM FILM, 3/4 OR 1/2 IN VIDEO P-I
Introduces a boy who lives in rural Kyuso, Kenya. Shows how he must walk for an hour to get water for his thirteen brothers and sisters and how his family depends on their farmland for their livelihood.
From The World's Children Series.
Prod-ASTRSK Dist-JOU 1981

With My Red Fires C 31 MIN
16MM FILM OPTICAL SOUND
Presents an adaptation of Doris Humphrey's dance-drama With My Red Fires, performed by the professional Repertory Company of the 1972 American Dance Festival at Connecticut College.

LC NO. 78-701639
Prod-ADFEST Dist-DANCE 1978

With Nang And Nakorn In Thailand C 14 MIN
16MM FILM, 3/4 OR 1/2 IN VIDEO P-I
Introduces two children in Thailand and shows the activities of a typical day.
From The World's Children Series.
Prod-ITF Dist-JOU 1980

With Needle And Yarn B 15 MIN
2 INCH VIDEOTAPE P
Demonstrates how to thread a needle and make running stitches.
From The Art Corner Series.
Prod-CVETVC Dist-GPITVL Prodn-WCVETV

With No One To Help Us B 19 MIN
16MM FILM - 3/4 IN VIDEO
Shows how the formation of a food-buying club by a group of Newark mothers brought about a necessary change in the community.
Prod-USOEO Dist-USNAC 1972

With Oscar In Peru C 11 MIN
16MM FILM, 3/4 OR 1/2 IN VIDEO P-I
Visits 13-year-old Oscar, who lives on the Peruvian altiplano.
From The World's Children Series.
Prod-ITF Dist-JOU 1980

With Pastore In Togo C 13 MIN
16MM FILM, 3/4 OR 1/2 IN VIDEO P-I
Shows a 13-year-old boy who lives on the west coast of Africa as he attends his school where the classes are conducted in French and goes home to his house made of mud walls and thatched roof. Observes how his village people work together raising chickens and picking cotton.
From The World's Children Series.
Prod-ASTRSK Dist-JOU 1981

With Patsy In St Vincent C 13 MIN
16MM FILM, 3/4 OR 1/2 IN VIDEO P-I
Introduces 13-year-old Patsy Boyes who lives on the tiny Caribbean Island of St Vincent. Shows her going to school to learn agricultural skills, shopping with her mother, cooking dinner and reading to her young friends.
From The World's Children Series.
Prod-ASTRSK Dist-JOU 1981

With Scissors And Paste B 15 MIN
2 INCH VIDEOTAPE P
Deals with recognizing and cutting shapes.
From The Art Corner Series.
Prod-CVETVC Dist-GPITVL Prodn-WCVETV

With Six You Get Eggroll C 95 MIN
16MM FILM OPTICAL SOUND
Deals with a widow and widower who fall in love, bringing their teenagers together.
Prod-SWAMD Dist-SWANK

With Spencer In Nairobi, Kenya C 13 MIN
16MM FILM, 3/4 OR 1/2 IN VIDEO P-I
Introduces a 13-year-old boy who lives in Nairobi, Kenya and observes his life there.
From The World's Children Series.
Prod-ASTRSK Dist-JOU 1981

With Sylvia In The Philippines C 12 MIN
16MM FILM, 3/4 OR 1/2 IN VIDEO P-I
Focuses on a girl living on the island of Luzon in the Philippines.
From The World's Children Series.
Prod-ITF Dist-JOU 1980

With The Dawn B 5 MIN
16MM FILM OPTICAL SOUND H-C A
Presents a modern interpretation of Psalm 29 using a dramatization about a woman and her hospitalized husband.
From The Song Of The Ages Series.
LC NO. 73-702125
Prod-FAMLYT Dist-FAMLYT 1964

With The Grain C 29 MIN
16MM FILM OPTICAL SOUND T
Discusses the role of a supervising teacher who works with student teachers. Shows how to improve lesson plans in order to improve pupil rapport and classroom discipline and to avoid lecturing too much. Features supervising teachers having a planning conference and an evaluation session with student teachers.
Prod-WVIZTV Dist-WVIZTV

With The Marines - Chosin To Hungnam B 24 MIN
16MM FILM OPTICAL SOUND
Presents one of the most famous marches in history, the fight out of Chosin Reserve.
LC NO. FIE67-140
Prod-USMC Dist-USNAC 1951

With The Marines - Chosin To Hungnam B 58 MIN
3/4 OR 1/2 INCH VIDEO CASSETTE
Relates the surprise onslaught by Chinese Communists around Chosin reservoir in Korea and the U S Marines fight back to Hungnam beachhead, where they embarked upon history's most successful evacuation.
Prod-IHF Dist-IHF

With The Marines At Tarawa C 20 MIN
3/4 OR 1/2 INCH VIDEO CASSETTE
Highlights the American troops fight to the death with the Japanese. Includes the initial naval bombardment of the tiny Pacific island of Tarawa.
Prod-IHF Dist-IHF

With Their Eyes On The Stars C 24 MIN
16MM FILM OPTICAL SOUND
Uses folk music to underscore the historic importance of the lunar mission.
Prod-NAA Dist-RCKWL

With Their Eyes Upon The Stars C 20 MIN
16MM FILM OPTICAL SOUND
Shows the pioneer spirit applied to the 1960's space age.
Prod-WB Dist-THIOKL 1964

With These Hands C 10 MIN
16MM FILM OPTICAL SOUND
Presents a series of scenes of people fixing things, such as automobiles, telephones, appliances, clocks and shoes, with musical accompaniment and little narration.
LC NO. 78-700387
Prod-GM Dist-SANDYC Prodn-SANDYC 1977

With These Hands C 22 MIN
16MM FILM OPTICAL SOUND
Examines ways to reduce hand injuries sustained in outside industrial use.
Prod-USSC Dist-USSC

With These Hands C 53 MIN
16MM FILM, 3/4 OR 1/2 IN VIDEO H-C A
Presents eight American artisans discussing why they do what they do and how they came to do it. Includes potters Toshiko Takaezu and Paul Soldner, sculptors Peter Voulkos, Harry Nohr, Clayton Bailey and J B Blunk, fiber artist Dorian Zachai and glass blower James Tanner.
LC NO. 80-706901
Prod-WILSND Dist-TIMLIF 1979

With Yau Kai In Hong Kong C 13 MIN
16MM FILM, 3/4 OR 1/2 IN VIDEO P-I
Visits a boy living in Hong Kong.
From The World's Children Series.
Prod-ITF Dist-JOU 1980

Withdrawal Symptoms C 30 MIN
3/4 OR 1/2 INCH VIDEO CASSETTE
Explains the concept of aggregate demand and aggregate supply. Shows what happens when demand is not the same as supply.
From The Money Puzzle - The World Of Macroeconomics Series. Module 7
Prod-MDCC Dist-MDCC

Withdrawing Medication From A Vial C 17 MIN
3/4 OR 1/2 INCH VIDEO CASSETTE PRO
Discusses locating sites for imtramuscular medications. Shows how to administer intramuscular medications.
From The Basic Nursing Skills Series. Tape 15
Prod-MDCC Dist-MDCC

Withdrawing Medication From A Vial, Locating Sites For Intra-Muscular Medications C 17 MIN
3/4 OR 1/2 INCH VIDEO CASSETTE PRO
See series title for descriptive statement.
From The Basic Nursing Skills Series.
Prod-BRA Dist-BRA

Withdrawn Client, The C 30 MIN
16MM FILM - 3/4 IN VIDEO PRO
Presents course instructors Grayce Sills and Doreen James Wise discussing assessment of the withdrawn client's behavior and intervention and evaluation as aspects of nursing care. Depicts clients exhibiting mild to severe withdrawal.
LC NO. 77-700133
Prod-AJN Dist-AJN Prodn-WGNCP 1977

Withdrawn Patient - Implications For The Nurse-Patient Relationship, The B 44 MIN
16MM FILM OPTICAL SOUND PRO
Discusses the significance of the nurse-patient relationship in working with a withdrawn patient toward his eventual rehabilitation.
From The Nursing In Psychiatry Series.
LC NO. 72-703442
Prod-VDONUR Dist-AJN Prodn-WTTWTV 1968

Withdrawn Patient, The B 44 MIN
16MM FILM OPTICAL SOUND PRO
Describes behaviors that typify the withdrawn patient and discusses the implications that those behavior hold for understanding current mental function and causative factors.
From The Nursing In Psychiatry Series.
LC NO. 79-703441
Prod-VDONUR Dist-AJN Prodn-WTTWTV 1968

Withdrawn Patient, The B 20 MIN
3/4 OR 1/2 INCH VIDEO CASSETTE
Discusses how to help patients overcome the withdrawn state. Deals with how the feelings of mental health specialists may add to the patients' problems, such as withdrawing from the patient when the patient rejects the counselor.
From The Basic Therapeutic Approaches To Abnormal Behaviors Series.
Prod-SCDMH Dist-UWISC 1979

Within A Lifetime C 30 MIN
16MM FILM OPTICAL SOUND
Informs about Safeway Stores worldwide operations, presenting some of the company's history as well as its current trends. Emphasizes the diversity and spirit of Safeway employees.
LC NO. 82-700319
Prod-SAFEWS Dist-SAFEWS 1981

Within A Lifetime (German) C 30 MIN
16MM FILM OPTICAL SOUND
Informs about Safeway Stores worldwide operations, presenting some of the company's history as well as its current trends. Emphasizes the diversity and spirit of Safeway employees.
Prod-SAFEWS Dist-SAFEWS 1981

Within America--A Series
J-C A
Looks at the lives of individuals and families in the Native-American culture, the Spanish-American culture, the Irish-American culture and the Italian-American culture.
Prod-CEPRO Dist-CEPRO

Crow Dog's Paradise	028 MIN
Land Of Heart's Desire, The	029 MIN
Luisa Torres	043 MIN
What Can I Tell You - A Portrait Of Three	055 MIN

Within And Without C 9 MIN
16MM FILM OPTICAL SOUND
Presents sculptress Marilynn Stewart discussing her technique and outlook. Shows some of her work.
LC NO. 76-703169
Prod-GOLNDA Dist-GOLNDA 1974

Within Normal Limits C 23 MIN
16MM FILM, 3/4 OR 1/2 IN VIDEO
Examines the strengths and weakness of diagnostic tests and encourages realistic expectations from the results. Analyzes the referral process, where initiators often do not know whether the specific test they are requesting will provide the needed answers. Shows how parents and teachers may have different views of the testing process than doctors.
Prod-MTI Dist-MTI

Within Our Power C 60 MIN
3/4 OR 1/2 INCH VIDEO CASSETTE
Reports on alternative energy sources, featuring a citizen's energy program in Franklin County, Massachusetts, a conversation with Hazel Henderson, author and economist, and an interview with Congressman Richard Ottinger on federal funding for energy projects.
From The Bill Moyers' Journal Series.
Prod-WNETTV Dist-WNETTV 1980

Within Our Reach C 17 MIN
16MM FILM OPTICAL SOUND
Shows what steps are necessary to receive grant funds and describes what individuals can do to ensure cleaner water. Documents the actions of the city officials and citizens of Parsippany-Troy Hills, New Jersey, to clean up its wastewater.
LC NO. 76-702722
Prod-USEPA Dist-USNAC Prodn-MCBRID 1976

Within The Circle C 12 MIN
16MM FILM OPTICAL SOUND
Deals with the production of Israeli coins. Shows how excavations of ancient coins inspire the use of ancient art motifs on the current coins of Israel.
Prod-ALDEN Dist-ALDEN

Within The Town B 25 MIN
16MM FILM OPTICAL SOUND
Shows the planning and development of the Veterans Administration Volunteer Service Program in VA hospitals throughout the country. Discusses the indoctrination and utilization of volunteers at the hospital level explains the urgent need of the volunteer service to supplement the VA hospital program.
Prod-USVA Dist-USVA 1952

Within This Decade - America In Space C 29 MIN
16MM FILM OPTICAL SOUND
Traces the principal accomplishments of NASA in aeronautics and space research from 1959 until the eve of the first lunar landing. Places emphasis on the progressives experience gained on each manned Apollo mission.
LC NO. 74-705963
Prod-NASAMS Dist-NASLBJ 1969

Within This Decade - America In Space C 29 MIN
3/4 OR 1/2 INCH VIDEO CASSETTE
Reviews major accomplishments in NASA research from 1959 through preparations for the first manned lunar landing, focusing on the manned space flight. Issued in 1969 as a motion picture.
LC NO. 80-707164
Prod-NASA Dist-USNAC 1980

Within This Earth C 12 MIN
16MM FILM OPTICAL SOUND I-H
Presents ways of using modern equipment and technology to obtain the resources within the earth.
Prod-VA Dist-MTP 1978

Without Saying A Word C 4 MIN
16MM FILM, 3/4 OR 1/2 IN VIDEO K-I
Describes nodding, shrugging and staring as ways of saying a lot without saying a word.
From The Most Important Person - Creative Expression Series.
Prod-EBEC Dist-EBEC 1972

Without Warning C 27 MIN
16MM FILM OPTICAL SOUND
Describes the dangers of high blood pressure and illustrates what happens, using an example of a busy man who is struck down without warning while preparing a display for a flower show.
Prod-CIBA Dist-MTP

Without Words C 20 MIN
3/4 OR 1/2 INCH VIDEO CASSETTE I
Focuses on images without words in art and music.
From The Readers' Cube Series.
Prod-MDDE Dist-AITECH 1977

Witness C 6 MIN
16MM FILM MAGNETIC SOUND J-C R
Presents practical implications of Christian love.
From The Christian Encounter Series,
LC NO. 72-700559
Prod-FRACOC Dist-FRACOC 1969

Witness Before A King X 17 MIN
16MM FILM OPTICAL SOUND J-H T R
Presents the adventures of Paul to encourage Christians to keep fresh in their hearts the meaning of their conversion.
From The Book Of Acts Series.
Prod-BROADM Dist-FAMF 1957

Witness Examination C 97 MIN
3/4 OR 1/2 INCH VIDEO CASSETTE PRO
See series title for descriptive statement.
From The James Jean Trial Advocacy Series.
Prod-ABACPE Dist-ABACPE

Witness Preparation For The Grand Jury C 175 MIN
3/4 OR 1/2 INCH VIDEO CASSETTE PRO
Critiques the methodology used in preparing witnesses for testimony before a grand jury. Examines government policy regarding the granting of immunity.
From The Representing A Client Before A Grand Jury Series.
Prod-ABACPE Dist-ABACPE

Witness To The American Experience C 30 MIN
3/4 OR 1/2 INCH VIDEO CASSETTE J-H
Focuses on the use of the photograph as historical data.
From The Developing Image Series.
Prod-CTI Dist-CTI

Witness To The Holocaust—A Series
16MM FILM, 3/4 OR 1/2 IN VIDEO J-C A
Documents the horror of the Holocaust by interviewing survivors who provide narration to documentary footage and photographs.
Prod-HORECE Dist-CNEMAG 1983

Deportations 019 MIN
Final Solution, The 019 MIN
Ghetto Life 019 MIN
Liberation 019 MIN
Reflections 017 MIN
Resistance 017 MIN
Rise Of The Nazis 020 MIN

Witness, The C 24 MIN
16MM FILM OPTICAL SOUND
Presents a drama in which a detective story writer finds himself confronted with real criminals in the dark streets of the city.
LC NO. 77-702176
Prod-MARTG Dist-MARTG 1977

Witness, The C 14 MIN
16MM FILM, 3/4 OR 1/2 IN VIDEO J-C A
Presents an open-ended film about a boy who witnesses a classmate assaulting an elderly lady. Shows how out of fear of the larger boy he does not report the incident to the police, but ponders the situation and outcome.
Prod-VITASC Dist-FLMFR 1976

Witness, The (Captioned Version) C 14 MIN
16MM FILM, 3/4 OR 1/2 IN VIDEO J-C A
Presents an open-ended film about a boy who witnesses a classmate assaulting an elderly lady. Shows how out of fear of the larger boy he does not report the incident to the police, but ponders the situation and outcome.
Prod-VITASC Dist-FLMFR 1976

Witwatersrand Basin, The C 30 MIN
3/4 OR 1/2 INCH VIDEO CASSETTE
Shows detailed geological history of development of the lower Proterozoic basin and deposition of the famous gold- and uranium-bearing quartz-pebble conglomerates.
Prod-EDMI Dist-EDMI 1982

Wives And Mothers C 29 MIN
3/4 INCH VIDEO CASSETTE
Looks at the benefits available to women who are eligible under their husband's account. Discusses benefits to widows, dependent children and divorced spouses.
From The Her Social Security Series.
Prod-UMITV Dist-UMITV 1977

Wives Of Alcoholics C 29 MIN
3/4 INCH VIDEO CASSETTE
Interviews two women married to alcoholics. Tells how alcoholism nearly destroyed their marriage and how they and their husbands successfully sought help.
From The Woman Series.
Prod-WNEDTV Dist-PUBTEL

Wives' Tale, A C 73 MIN
16MM FILM, 3/4 OR 1/2 IN VIDEO H-C A
Introduces the wives of striking Canadian miners and shows how participation in the strike transformed their lives. Shows how the women sponsored community suppers, set up clothing depots and thrift shops, undertook fund-raising, organized a city-wide Christmas party for 10,000 and even staged a mock trial for INCO, a multinational corporation.
LC NO. 84-707174
Prod-CNEMAG Dist-CNEMAG

Wizard Of Earthsea, A C 15 MIN
3/4 OR 1/2 INCH VIDEO CASSETTE I
See series title for descriptive statement.
From The Best Of Cover To Cover 2 Series.
Prod-WETATV Dist-WETATV

Wizard Of No, The C 19 MIN
16MM FILM, 3/4 OR 1/2 IN VIDEO P-I
Shows how young Billy learns after smoking a cigarette that his inability to say no to his friends stems from his self-esteem.
Prod-MTI Dist-MTI

Wizard Of Waukesha, The C 58 MIN
16MM FILM, 3/4 OR 1/2 IN VIDEO
Deals with jazz guitarist Les Paul's career as a musician, performer and inventor in the field of music recording.
Prod-STRAY Dist-DIRECT 1979

Wizard Of Waukesha, The C 59 MIN
3/4 INCH VIDEO CASSETTE
Pays tribute to Les Paul whose development of the electric guitar and multi-track recording revolutionized popular music.
Prod-FIRS Dist-FIRS

Wizard Of Words—A Series
16MM FILM, 3/4 OR 1/2 IN VIDEO P-I
Combines information about various parts of speech with comic situations.
Prod-MGHT Dist-MGHT 1976

Nouns And Adjectives 9 MIN
Prepositions 10 MIN
Verbs And Adverbs 9 MIN

Wizard Who Spat On The Floor, The - Thomas Alva Edison C 41 MIN
16MM FILM, 3/4 OR 1/2 IN VIDEO I-C A
A shortened version of the videotape The Wizard Who Spat On The Floor - Thomas Alva Edison. Examines the life and work of the American inventor Thomas Edison. Shows some of his inventions, such as the light bulb, fluoroscope and the phonograph and traces his work in his last years in which his experimentation proved to be less successful.
From The Nova Series.
LC NO. 79-707903
Prod-BBCTV Dist-TIMLIF 1974

Wizard, The C 8 MIN
16MM FILM, 3/4 OR 1/2 IN VIDEO P-I
Presents a story about a small town wizard who misapplies his magical powers by casting spells on his neighbors. Shows how he discovers that the negative use of imagination leads to loneliness and that by channeling his imagination to creative ends he can be fulfilled and admired.
Prod-PAJON Dist-TEXFLM 1975

Wizard, The C 8 MIN
16MM FILM - 1/2 IN VIDEO, VHS
Presents a lighthearted story about learning to be content with yourself. Relates the story of a mouse who visits the Wizard because he is tired of being a mouse, and who, after considering the possible personae promised by a mysterious potion, decides that, while being himself has its problems, at least he knows what to expect.
Prod-WIZPRO Dist-WWS

Wizard, The C 15 MIN
3/4 INCH VIDEO CASSETTE K-P
Presents an adaptation of the story The Wizard by Bill Martin Jr.
From The I Can Read Series.
Prod-WCETTV Dist-GPITVL 1977

Wizard's Son, The C 10 MIN
16MM FILM, 3/4 OR 1/2 IN VIDEO
Presents an animated story about a proud and talented wizard who insists that his young son follow in his magical footsteps. Reveals that after a near disaster in which the boy turns the family pig into a rampaging colossus, the father decides to to allow his son to follow his own desires.
LC NO. 81-707007
Prod-CANEJ Dist-PHENIX 1981

Wizardry With Wood C 25 MIN
16MM FILM OPTICAL SOUND
Shows that wood is a material of great possibilities and indispensable to our existence.
Prod-SIS Dist-SIS 1963

Wizdom Beats The Blahs C 20 MIN
3/4 OR 1/2 INCH VIDEO CASSETTE P
Emphasizes the necessity of choosing a nutritious, well-balanced diet that includes a variety of foods and the importance of reading container labels to determine the nutritive value of the food.
Prod-BCSBIT Dist-GPITVL 1982

Wo Ist Meine Breiftasche C 15 MIN
16MM FILM, 3/4 OR 1/2 IN VIDEO
See series title for descriptive statement.
From The Guten Tag Series. Part 9
Prod-BAYER Dist-IFB 1968

Wobblies, The C 89 MIN
16MM FILM - 3/4 IN VIDEO H-C A
Chronicles the Industrial Workers of the World, known as Wobblies, combining rare newsreel footage, interviews with former members, propaganda cartoons and songs from the period.
Prod-FIRS Dist-FIRS 1981

Wodehouse Playhouse—A Series
16MM FILM, 3/4 OR 1/2 IN VIDEO C A
Presents adaptations of 20 short stories by P G Wodehouse.
Prod-BBCTV Dist-TIMLIF 1980

Anselm Gets His Chance 030 MIN
Big Business 030 MIN
Code Of The Mulliners, The 030 MIN
Editor Regrets, The 030 MIN
Feet Of Clay 030 MIN
Luck Of The Stiffhams, The 030 MIN
Mr Potter Takes A Rest Cure 030 MIN
Mulliner's Buck-U-Uppo 030 MIN
Nodder, The 030 MIN
Portrait Of A Disciplinarian 030 MIN
Rise Of The Minna Nordstrom, The 030 MIN
Rodney Fails To Qualify 030 MIN
Romance At Droitwich Spa 030 MIN
Smile That Wins, The 030 MIN
Strychnine In The Soup 030 MIN
Tangled Hearts 030 MIN
Trouble Down At Studleigh 030 MIN
Truth About George, The 030 MIN
Unpleasantness At Bludleigh Court 030 MIN
Voice From The Past, A 030 MIN

Woe That Is In Marriage - The Wife Of Bath And The Nun's Priest's Tale C 45 MIN
3/4 OR 1/2 INCH VIDEO CASSETTE
Analyzes the marriages depicted in The Wife of Bath and The Nun's Priest's Tales.
From The Survey Of English Literature I Series.
Prod-MDCPB Dist-MDCPB

Wolf C 22 MIN
16MM FILM, 3/4 OR 1/2 IN VIDEO P-I
Explores the world of the much-maligned and unjustifiably-feared wolf and tells a new version of the story of Little Red Riding Hood. Visits a resettled pack of wolves in northern Michigan and discusses this animals' highly sophisticated communication network. Hosted by Hal Linden.
From The Animals, Animals, Animals Series.
Prod-ABCNEW Dist-MEDIAG 1977

Wolf And The Seven Kids, The C 10 MIN
16MM FILM, 3/4 OR 1/2 IN VIDEO P-I
Presents an animated folktale of a wolf who tricks seven young goats into opening their door and eats all but one. Shows how Mother Goat finds the wolf, cuts open his stomach to free the kids and fills his stomach with stones.
Prod-GREATT Dist-EBEC 1978

Wolf And The Whitetail, The C 26 MIN
16MM FILM, 3/4 OR 1/2 IN VIDEO
Follows both the deer and the wolf through their age of innocence into maturity, into winter when they assume their traditional adult roles as predator and prey.
Prod-STOUFP Dist-STOUFP 1979

Wolf Pack C 20 MIN
16MM FILM, 3/4 OR 1/2 IN VIDEO I-C A
Focuses on the life cycle and social structure of a wolf pack during one year in northern Canada.
Prod-CWSO Dist-NFBC Prodn-NFBC 1976

Wolf Pack - U-Boats In The Atlantic, 1939 To 1944 C 60 MIN
16MM FILM OPTICAL SOUND H-C A
From The World At War Series.
LC NO. 76-701778
Prod-THAMES Dist-USCAN 1975

Wolf Pack - U-Boats In The Atlantic, 1939-1944 C 52 MIN
16MM FILM, 3/4 OR 1/2 IN VIDEO H-C A
Shows how German submarines, called U-boats, nearly wiped out Allied shipping in the Atlantic, bringing deadly havoc by attacking in groups. Britain's lack of coordination facilitated their success. The battle of the Atlantic ended with the virtual extermination of German submarines.
From The World At War Series.
Prod-THAMES Dist-MEDIAG 1973

Wolf Trap C 28 MIN
16MM FILM - 3/4 IN VIDEO
Presents a view of the Wolf Trap Farm Park for the Performing Arts in Virginia. Highlights performances and recreational uses of the park.
LC NO. 79-706175
Prod-USNPS Dist-USNAC Prodn-EQINOX 1979

Wolves And Coyotes Of The Rockies C 15 MIN
16MM FILM, 3/4 OR 1/2 IN VIDEO K-J
Illustrates in documentary style the story of the remaining wolves and coyotes, the wild dogs, that inhabit the last great wilderness areas in the Rockies. Cites how numerous moose and elk provide abundant food supplies for predators such as wolves. Shows a pack of wolves bringing down a moose, and how a new wolf pack is formed.
From The North American Species Series.
Prod-KARVF Dist-BCNFL 1983

Wolves And The Wolfmen C 52 MIN
16MM FILM, 3/4 OR 1/2 IN VIDEO K-J
A documentary about naturalists fighting to save the rapidly vanishing species - wolves.
Prod-MGM Dist-FI 1971

Wolves Of Willoughby Chase, The C 15 MIN
3/4 OR 1/2 INCH VIDEO CASSETTE I
See series title for descriptive statement.
From The Best Of Cover To Cover 2 Series.
Prod-WETATV Dist-WETATV

Woman - The Question Of Self-Concept C 28 MIN
16MM FILM, 3/4 OR 1/2 IN VIDEO
Looks at the causes and effects of the many changes in woman's role definitions.
From The Inner Woman Series.
Prod-WXYZTV Dist-CRMP 1977

Woman - Who Is Me C 10 MIN
16MM FILM OPTICAL SOUND H-C A
Uses animation to explore how men and women see each other and themselves.
LC NO. 78-700647
Prod-TRICPS Dist-SERIUS 1977

Woman - Who Is Me? C 11 MIN
3/4 OR 1/2 INCH VIDEO CASSETTE C A
Explores the persistence of myths about women and men by comparing classical mythology, biblical themes, Renaissance and 19th century art with pop art and other contemporary images.
Prod-MMRC Dist-MMRC

Woman As Painter C 29 MIN
2 INCH VIDEOTAPE

Examines the often overlooked feminine artist and presents a look at woman as the subject-ornament at the central field of the painter's vision. Studies in detail the American impressionists Mary Cassatt and Berthe Morisot and briefly covers a number of other artists.
From The Synergism - Profiles, People Series.
Prod-MAETEL Dist-PUBTEL

Woman At The Well X 15 MIN
16MM FILM OPTICAL SOUND I-H T R
Jesus and the disciples go through Samaria. Jesus talks with the woman of Sychar at Jacob's well and tells her of the spiritual living water. She goes back to her village and tells the people she has found the Christ.
From The Living Bible Series.
Prod-FAMF Dist-FAMF

Woman Candidate, Running For Office Is A Victory C 13 MIN
16MM FILM OPTICAL SOUND
Features Flora Crater being interviewed at her home where she discusses how she decided to run for the office of Lieutenant Governor of Virginia and how she set up her campaign. Follows her as she travels through the state meeting people and discussing the issues. Explains why women should become involved in politics and how to produce social change.
LC NO. 75-700341
Prod-BLURIG Dist-BLURIG 1974

Woman In Green B 70 MIN
16MM FILM OPTICAL SOUND
Describes how Sherlock Holmes matches wits against the evil Professor Moriarity in a case that involves the deaths of several attractive girls. Stars Nigel Bruce and Basil Rathbone.
Prod-UNKNWN Dist-NAFVC 1945

Woman In Question, The C 16 MIN
16MM FILM OPTICAL SOUND H-C A
Describes the efforts of three communities to conduct intensive uterine cancer education and case-finding programs.
Prod-AMCS Dist-AMCS

Woman In Sports, Get Up, Get Out, Get Going, The C 30 MIN
16MM FILM, 3/4 OR 1/2 IN VIDEO P-C A
Motivates women to exercise. Looks at meditation, competition, concentration, coordination and cooperation.
Prod-KLEINW Dist-KLEINW

Woman In Sports, Records, Rewards, Heroines, The C 30 MIN
16MM FILM, 3/4 OR 1/2 IN VIDEO P-C A
Documents the evolution of women in sports. Shows women excelling in swimming, basketball, golf, gymnastics, skating, skiing, auto racing, tennis and softball.
Prod-KLEINW Dist-KLEINW

Woman In Sports, Reflections Of The Champions, The C 30 MIN
16MM FILM, 3/4 OR 1/2 IN VIDEO P-C A
Observes special moments in the lives of great women athletes including Janet Guthrie at the racetracks and Diane Kallian at softball practice.
Prod-KLEINW Dist-KLEINW

Woman In Sports, The, Pt 1 C 30 MIN
16MM FILM, 3/4 OR 1/2 IN VIDEO J-C A
Shows a young woman who resolves to start her own exercise regimen.
Prod-KLEINW Dist-KLEINW 1980

Woman In Sports, The, Pt 2 C 30 MIN
16MM FILM, 3/4 OR 1/2 IN VIDEO J-C A
Provides a look at famous female athletes competing in swimming, basketball, tennis and other sports.
Prod-KLEINW Dist-KLEINW 1980

Woman In Sports, The, Pt 3 C 30 MIN
16MM FILM, 3/4 OR 1/2 IN VIDEO J-C A
Shows great moments in the lives of such women as Janet Guthrie and Cathy Rigby.
Prod-KLEINW Dist-KLEINW 1980

Woman Is C 12 MIN
16MM FILM, 3/4 OR 1/2 IN VIDEO
Uses a series of photographic stills in order to illustrate the history and character of the roles that women occupy in society.
Prod-SILLU Dist-PHENIX 1973

Woman On The Moon (German) B 115 MIN
3/4 OR 1/2 INCH VIDEO CASSETTE
Shows a group of people embark on a journey to the moon. Directed by Fritz Lang.
Prod-IHF Dist-IHF

Woman Rebel, The C 59 MIN
16MM FILM OPTICAL SOUND H-C A
Dramatizes the life and work of Margaret Sanger, who was responsible for gaining social and political acceptance for the concept of bith control. Features actress Piper Laurie.
From The Nova Series.
Prod-WGBHTV Dist-KINGFT 1977

Woman Rebel, The C 59 MIN
3/4 INCH VIDEO CASSETTE H-C A
Dramatizes the life and work of Margaret Sanger, who was responsible for gaining social and political acceptance for the concept of birth control. Features actress Piper Laurie.
From The Nova Series.
Prod-WGBHTV Dist-PBS 1977

Woman Talk–A Series
16MM FILM, 3/4 OR 1/2 IN VIDEO H-C A
Presents a health care education series which gives a clear understanding of the often complex issues in gynecology and obstetrics.
Prod-CORF Dist-CORF 1983

Abortion	014 MIN
Birth Control	020 MIN
Breast-Feeding	017 MIN
Childbirth	017 MIN
Feminine Hygiene	017 MIN
Fertility Investigation	017 MIN
Menopause	019 MIN
Operative Procedures	017 MIN
Post-Natal Care	014 MIN
Pre-Natal Care	015 MIN
Preventive Health Care	020 MIN
Sex Education	018 MIN
Your First Gynecological Examination	017 MIN

Woman To Remember, A B 30 MIN
16MM FILM OPTICAL SOUND J-C A
Depicts the story of Miriam, a vain and selfish woman who loses her wealth and social position by a trick of fate. Shows how she is forced to live in the poorest section of town and how she comes face to face with Jesus.
Prod-CAFM Dist-CAFM

Woman To Woman C 48 MIN
16MM FILM OPTICAL SOUND
Interviews women in a variety of occupations and explores the nature of women's work. Includes an historical perspective of women's work roles through the decades.
Prod-DETD Dist-DETD 1975

Woman Wrote A Letter B 14 MIN
16MM FILM OPTICAL SOUND P-C A
Traces the development of the American National Red Cross since its organization by Clara Barton in 1881. Describes its achievements in the field of disaster and war relief and its peacetime activities such as the nurses aide and gray lady programs, the teaching of first aid and swimming, and the collection of blood.
LC NO. FI56-256
Prod-AREDC Dist-AMRC 1956

Woman–A Series

Deals with the concerns of women, covering social, economic, political and personal issues.
Prod-WNEDTV Dist-PUBTEL

Affirmative Action In Business	029 MIN
Age Is A Woman's Issue	029 MIN
Age Is Becoming	029 MIN
Battered Wives	029 MIN
Breast Cancer Controversies	029 MIN
Changing Motherhood	029 MIN
Concerns Of American Indian Women	029 MIN
Consciousness Raising Groups	029 MIN
Contemporary Women Poets	029 MIN
Conversation With Florynce Kennedy, A	029 MIN
Conversation With Lotte Jacobi, A	029 MIN
Conversation With Simone De Beauvoir, A	060 MIN
DES Daughters And Sons, Pt 1	029 MIN
DES Daughters And Sons, Pt 2	029 MIN
Divorce Insurance	029 MIN
Elsa Dorfman - Impressions	029 MIN
Engineered Foods - What Are They	029 MIN
Equal Rights Amendment, Pt 2	029 MIN
Female Sexuality, Pt 1	029 MIN
Female Sexuality, Pt 2	029 MIN
Feminist Therapy	029 MIN
Food Additives - Helpful Or Harmful, Pt 2	029 MIN
Great Pretenders, The - The New Foods	029 MIN
How To Start Your Own Business, Pt 1	029 MIN
How To Start Your Own Business, Pt 2	029 MIN
Judy Chicago On Feminist Art	029 MIN
Lois Gould On Women Writers	029 MIN
Masculine, Feminine And Androgyny	029 MIN
Mental Health Care For Women, Pt 1	029 MIN
Money And The Single Woman	029 MIN
Myth Of The Happy Child, The	029 MIN
New Image For Black Women	029 MIN
New Image For Nurses, Pt 1	029 MIN
New Image For Nurses, Pt 2	029 MIN
New Mental Health Care - One Patient's View	029 MIN
New Roles For Women In Sports	029 MIN
One Woman's Divorce	029 MIN
Picking Up The Pieces - One Widow Speaks	029 MIN
Rape, Pt 1	029 MIN
Rape, Pt 2	029 MIN
Remarrieds, The	029 MIN
Sex Bias In Education, Pt 1	029 MIN
Sex Bias In Education, Pt 2	029 MIN
Sex Therapy, Pt 1	029 MIN
Sex Therapy, Pt 2	029 MIN
Sexual Abuse Of Children	029 MIN
Sexual Harassment On The Job	029 MIN
Toys For Children	029 MIN
Two Earner Family, The	029 MIN
Two-Profession Marriage, The	029 MIN
Unnecessary Surgery	029 MIN
Volunteerism - Pro And Con	029 MIN
Women And Depression	029 MIN
Women And Heart Attacks, Pt 1	029 MIN
Women And Heart Attacks, Pt 2	029 MIN
Women And Success	029 MIN
Women In Prison, Pt 1	029 MIN
Women In Prison, Pt 2	029 MIN
Women In Transition	029 MIN
Women Workers	029 MIN
Women's Health Care - A History	029 MIN
Women's Image - Down The Tube	029 MIN
Women's Pages	029 MIN
Write On, Women Playwrights	029 MIN

Woman-Child C 15 MIN
16MM FILM, 3/4 OR 1/2 IN VIDEO
Looks at some of the consequences of adolescent pregnancy through the eyes of six teenagers.
Prod-NFMD Dist-NFMD 1982

Woman, A Family, A C 108 MIN
16MM FILM OPTICAL SOUND J A
Offers a personal study of life in the People's Republic of China using direct cinema techniques and dubbed conversations. Shows scenes of the daily routines of a young factory worker living in the suburbs as contrasted with scenes of bustling Peking streets. Emphasizes how the cultural revolution has positively affected living conditions, men's and women's roles and work relationships.
From The How Yukong Moved The Mountains Series.
LC NO. 80-700575
Prod-CAPI Dist-CINPER 1978

Woman's Hospital C 20 MIN
3/4 OR 1/2 INCH VIDEO CASSETTE J A
Orients expectant mothers toward what they can expect from hospital staff before and during childbirth.
Prod-SUTHRB Dist-SUTHRB

Woman's Place C 23 MIN
16MM FILM, 3/4 OR 1/2 IN VIDEO
Deals with the role of women in ancient Egypt.
From The Ancient Lives Series.
Prod-FOTH Dist-FOTH

Woman's Place C 52 MIN
3/4 INCH VIDEO CASSETTE H-C
Examines the traditional role of women in American society and shows how that role is changing. Narrated by Bess Myerson.
Prod-ABCTV Dist-GA

Woman's Place Is In The House, A C 30 MIN
16MM FILM, 3/4 OR 1/2 IN VIDEO
Profiles Massachusetts State Representative Elaine Noble at work, in a discussion with her constituents and at home.
Prod-WGBHTV Dist-TEXFLM 1977

Woman's Place, A C 25 MIN
16MM FILM, 3/4 OR 1/2 IN VIDEO
Pays tribute to noted women of the past and points out that a woman's place is everyplace. Narrated by Julie Harris.
Prod-CCCD Dist-CCCD

Woman's Touch, A C 20 MIN
16MM FILM, 3/4 OR 1/2 IN VIDEO J-C
Edited from the motion picture The Battle Of The Sexes. Tells a story about the difficulties which arise when a woman with progressive business ideas tries to work with a man whose manufacturing firm is operated according to his less modern views. Focuses on the conflict between individual efficiency and the systemization of machines.
From The Patterns Series.
Prod-SF Dist-SF 1977

Woman's Work, A C 20 MIN
16MM FILM OPTICAL SOUND
Investigates the wage gap between men and women. Interviews working women, lawyers and union leaders in order to provide insight into this subject, emphasizing the problem in Canada.
LC NO. 77-702728
Prod-CANFDC Dist-CANFDC 1976

Womanpower - A Woman's Place Is C 28 MIN
16MM FILM, 3/4 OR 1/2 IN VIDEO J-C A
Addresses the problem of revising rigid social patterns of sexism and promotes women's rights. Shows a Swedish family in which the wife works in heavy industry and the children attend schools teaching new ideas about roles. Encourages men to participate in child rearing with an example of the work of a male nurse.
From The Womanpower Series.
Prod-UN Dist-SF 1976

Womanpower - Equality And Development C 28 MIN
16MM FILM, 3/4 OR 1/2 IN VIDEO J-C A
Shows delegates to a preconference for International Women's Year, 1975, convening at the United Nations. Reports on the status of women in their respective countries, revealing remarkably similar conditions. Illustrates issues discussed by a visit to Tunisia.
From The Womanpower Series.
Prod-UN Dist-SF 1976

Womanpower - The Hidden Asset C 17 MIN
16MM FILM, 3/4 OR 1/2 IN VIDEO J-C A
Shows why the integration of women in the national economy affects a nation's overall development. Focuses on the way in which women of Sri Lanka have attempted to change the traditional system which discounts their contribution to the national economy.
From The Womanpower Series.
Prod-UN Dist-SF 1976

Womanpower - The People's Choice C 28 MIN
16MM FILM, 3/4 OR 1/2 IN VIDEO J-C A
Promotes equality between the sexes with an example of the struggle of three women running for election to political office in Colombia, a country where women were given the right to vote in 1957.
From The Womanpower Series.
Prod-UN Dist-SF 1976

Womanpower–A Series
3/4 OR 1/2 INCH VIDEO CASSETTE
Discusses women's rights.
Prod-UN Dist-SF

Womanpower - A Woman's Place Is	28 MIN

Womanpower - Equality And Development 28 MIN
Womanpower - The Hidden Asset 17 MIN
Womanpower - The People's Choice 28 MIN

Women C 13 MIN
3/4 OR 1/2 INCH VIDEO CASSETTE C A
Shows women naked, dressed, laughing, crying, contemporary, ancient, passive. Deals with women's feelings about other women.
Prod-NATSF Dist-MMRC

Women C 28 MIN
3/4 INCH VIDEO CASSETTE I-C A
Presents a group of women describing their common concerns and the changes that will advance the cause of women's equality. Stresses the need to avoid stereotypical roles for women or men.
From The Are You Listening Series.
LC NO. 80-707155
Prod-STURTM Dist-STURTM 1971

Women - The Hand That Cradles The Rock C 20 MIN
16MM FILM, 3/4 OR 1/2 IN VIDEO
Presents advocates of women's liberation, as well as women satisfied with their traditional roles.
Prod-DOCUA Dist-CNEMAG

Women - Up The Career Ladder B 30 MIN
16MM FILM OPTICAL SOUND A
Presents a tool for administrators, personnel managers and consultants for use in implementing affirmative action programs for women. Provides an honest and revealing portrayal of women's experiences in preparation for career mobility.
LC NO. 73-701884
Prod-UCLA Dist-UCLA 1972

Women Abuse - Alcohol And Other Drug Abuse Connections C 30 MIN
3/4 OR 1/2 INCH VIDEO CASSETTE
Explores the relationship between chemical abuse and the continuing cycles of abuse by a review of the research and a discussion of the dynamics that work to maintain the destructive patterns.
Prod-DACABW Dist-UWISC Prodn-VRL 1982

Women And Alcohol - Through The Drinking Glass C 28 MIN
16MM FILM - 3/4 IN VIDEO H-C A
Focuses on the lives of four recovering alcoholic women, contrasting their drinking habits with those of a group of teenagers who still find drinking fun. Probes the social and psychological factors which affect women's use of and dependence on alcohol. Narrated by Carol Burnett.
LC NO. 80-706109
Prod-FMSP Dist-FMSP 1979

Women And Art C 25 MIN
16MM FILM, 3/4 OR 1/2 IN VIDEO H-C A
Presents art critic John Berger, who discusses whether paintings and media celebrate or exploit women.
From The Ways Of Seeing Series.
Prod-BBCTV Dist-FI 1974

Women And Children In China C 29 MIN
3/4 INCH VIDEO CASSETTE
Describes the Chinese law, passed after the 1949 revolution, which made husbands and wives equal, abolished arranged marriages, and permitted women to divorce.
From The Woman Series.
Prod-WNEDTV Dist-PUBTEL

Women And Creativity C 29 MIN
3/4 OR 1/2 INCH VIDEO CASSETTE H-C A
Presents Bill Moyers interviewing three women about the choices between a life of creativity and raising a family. Features artist Judy Chicago, Bernie Lasseau, a rural artist, and best-selling novelist Mary Gordon.
From The Creativity With Bill Moyers Series.
Prod-CORPEL Dist-PBS 1982

Women And Depression C 29 MIN
3/4 OR 1/2 INCH VIDEO CASSETTE
Discusses a study of 40 acutely depressed women and tells how they responded to treatment. Analyzes the relationship between depression and family problems and explains how proper treatment has helped women cope.
From The Woman Series.
Prod-WNEDTV Dist-PBS

Women And Drugs C 14 MIN
3/4 OR 1/2 INCH VIDEO CASSETTE
Examines one woman's experience with tranquilizers and describes the extent of the present situation as well as factors contributing to it.
Prod-ARFO Dist-ARFO 1979

Women And Heart Attacks, Pt 1 C 29 MIN
3/4 OR 1/2 INCH VIDEO CASSETTE
Explains why women are vulnerable to heart attacks and outlines common risk factors in women.
From The Woman Series.
Prod-WNEDTV Dist-PBS

Women And Heart Attacks, Pt 2 C 29 MIN
3/4 OR 1/2 INCH VIDEO CASSETTE
Explores the effects of birth control pills, physical activity, diet, smoking, alcohol, sex and health education on the incidence of heart attacks among women.
From The Woman Series.
Prod-WNEDTV Dist-PBS

Women And Insurance C 29 MIN
3/4 INCH VIDEO CASSETTE
Discusses sex discrimination in insurance.
From The Woman Series.
Prod-WNEDTV Dist-PUBTEL

Women And Insurance - The Industry Responds C 29 MIN
3/4 INCH VIDEO CASSETTE
Features representatives of the insurance industry answering charges of discrimination against women.
From The Woman Series.
Prod-WNEDTV Dist-PUBTEL

Women And Power In The Nuclear Age C 30 MIN
3/4 OR 1/2 INCH VIDEO CASSETTE
Features Dr Helen Caldicott, a leading figure in the anti-nuclear movement, discussing grassroots tactics for anti-nuclear activity. Recalls her early reactions to the potential horrors of nuclear warfare and her long-term committment to fighting nuclear war technology.
Prod-HIHOPE Dist-WMENIF

Women And Sexuality - A Century Of Change C 36 MIN
16MM FILM OPTICAL SOUND A
Uses selected art reproductions and four unusually articulate and astute modern professional women to express the current state of feminine sexuality.
LC NO. 83-700505
Prod-KLUGDP Dist-ALTANA 1983

Women And Society C 26 MIN
16MM FILM, 3/4 OR 1/2 IN VIDEO H-C
Explores the true picture of women in history, and looks at social history, including women in everyday life. Shows film clips of unconscious female stereotyping.
From The Today's History Series.
Prod-JOU Dist-JOU 1984

Women And Sports - Basketball C 11 MIN
16MM FILM OPTICAL SOUND
Features highlights from a women's basketball tournament and interviews with players and coaches.
LC NO. 78-701411
Prod-COCA Dist-COCA Prodn-BORDEN 1977

Women And Sports - Gymnastics C 15 MIN
16MM FILM OPTICAL SOUND
Shows performances in a national women's gymnastics competition. Presents training sessions, comments from coaches and slow-motion scenes of performances.
LC NO. 77-702179
Prod-COCA Dist-COCA Prodn-BOR 1977

Women And Sports - Volleyball C 13 MIN
16MM FILM OPTICAL SOUND
Combines highlights from the National Invitational Volleyball Tournament, practice sessions with the University of Southern California volleyball team, and tips from top players to give a comprehensive view of collegiate women's volleyball.
LC NO. 78-701412
Prod-COCA Dist-COCA Prodn-BORDEN 1978

Women And Success C 29 MIN
3/4 OR 1/2 INCH VIDEO CASSETTE
Talks about women's attitudes toward success.
From The Woman Series.
Prod-WNEDTV Dist-PBS

Women And Taxes C 29 MIN
3/4 INCH VIDEO CASSETTE
Explains changes in federal tax laws that have made tax credits available for child care expenses. Discusses the differences that filing status can make in the amount of due tax and looks at changes in estate laws.
From The Woman Series.
Prod-WNEDTV Dist-PUBTEL

Women At Arms—A Series
16MM FILM, 3/4 OR 1/2 IN VIDEO H-C A
Visits military facilities which serve as training grounds for a new generation of military women. Includes candid interviews with enthusiastic women trainees and established women officers.
Prod-BBCTV Dist-FI 1983

As Deadly As The Male 050 MIN
Catch 36-24-36 050 MIN
Irresistable Force, The 050 MIN

Women At Work C 35 MIN
3/4 INCH VIDEO CASSETTE A
Discusses the role conflicts of women in business. Emphasizes voluntarism and involvement rather than challenging men employees.
LC NO. 80-706692
Prod-CSULA Dist-CSULA 1980

Women At Work - Change, Choice, Challenge C 19 MIN
16MM FILM, 3/4 OR 1/2 IN VIDEO H-C A
Shows women at work in both traditional and non-traditional women's occupations in business, professions and industry. Shows how many women continue to find satisfaction in traditional activities, while others are taking advantage of new openings in previously male-only fields.
Prod-EBEC Dist-EBEC

Women At Work - Employment Discrimination B 30 MIN
3/4 INCH VIDEO CASSETTE
Examines employment discrimination against women in both traditional and non-traditional jobs. Focuses on legal remedies for such discrimination, the comparable value of jobs, employment opportunities for women in skilled trades and affirmative action groups.
Prod-SEAFEM Dist-WMENIF

Women Business Owners C 28 MIN
3/4 INCH VIDEO CASSETTE J-C A
Features a group of women entrepreneurs talking about the rewards of a business career, as well as the motivations, doubts, guilts and surprises they found along the way.
From The Are You Listening Series.
LC NO. 80-707156
Prod-STURTM Dist-STURTM 1977

Women Candidates C 35 MIN
3/4 OR 1/2 INCH VIDEO CASSETTE A
Focuses on avoiding illegal questions while interviewing women candidates for a job.
From The Interview - EEO Compliance Series. Pt 1
Prod-XICOM Dist-XICOM

Women Composers C 30 MIN
3/4 INCH VIDEO CASSETTE
Presents classical women composers from the middle ages to modern times, and the social barriers which have prevented women from devoting their time to musical pursuits. Includes examples of modern women composers.
Prod-WMENIF Dist-WMENIF

Women Do Know About Mechanics (French) C 14 MIN
3/4 OR 1/2 INCH VIDEO CASSETTE H-C A
Involves a housewife whose car and vacuum cleaner break down and a woman engineer at the Center of Nuclear Studies at Saday.
From The En Francais Series. Part 1 - Essential Elements
Prod-MOFAFR Dist-AITECH 1970

Women Emerging - Comparing Cultural Expectations B 27 MIN
16MM FILM, 3/4 OR 1/2 IN VIDEO
Documents the experiences of a multicultural women's class in Agora, an experimental school associated with Berkeley High School in California. Presents four days, each separated by intervals of five weeks, from one semester in 1974.
From The Sex Role Stereotyping In Schools Series.
Prod-FWLERD Dist-UCEMC 1975

Women Get The Vote, The B 27 MIN
16MM FILM, 3/4 OR 1/2 IN VIDEO J-C
Traces the campaign of the suffragettes from the meeting in Seneca Falls to discuss the rights of women to the passage of the Susan B Anthony amendment to the Constitution in 1919.
From The Twentieth Century Series.
Prod-CBSNEW Dist-MGHT 1962

Women Gold Medalists C 50 MIN
16MM FILM OPTICAL SOUND
Presents a television special from the CTV program Olympiad which gives tribute to women athletes who gained fame in various Olympic competitions for their winning performances.
LC NO. 77-702545
Prod-CTV Dist-CTV 1976

Women In A Changing World C 48 MIN
16MM FILM OPTICAL SOUND
Presents women from Bolivia, Afghanistan, northern Kenya and the China Coast who express their concern over fundamental rights and human dignity.
Prod-AUFS Dist-WHEELK

Women In America C 30 MIN
3/4 OR 1/2 INCH VIDEO CASSETTE C
Shows Bella Abzug and Phyllis Schlafly debating the Equal Rights Amendment, while other women discuss their changing status.
America - The Second Century Series.
Prod-DALCCD Dist-DALCCD

Women In Business C 24 MIN
16MM FILM OPTICAL SOUND H-C A
Introduces career women, including owners and operators of an auto leasing firm, a commodities broker and a clothing designer.
LC NO. 80-700576
Prod-LSBPRO Dist-LSBPRO 1980

Women In China C 27 MIN
16MM FILM OPTICAL SOUND
Introduces several aspects of the change in status of women since the founding of the People's Republic Of China. Focuses on changing work roles of both men and women, child care as it supports these roles and the use of education to transform ideas.
LC NO. 79-700852
Prod-OPEN Dist-EDC 1978

Women In Communications C 15 MIN
16MM FILM, 3/4 OR 1/2 IN VIDEO J-C
Features three women discussing how they entered their professions, what special problems a woman has in each field and how each job relates to the other.
Prod-BFA Dist-PHENIX 1975

Women In Danger C 29 MIN
3/4 OR 1/2 INCH VIDEO CASSETTE
Presents critics Roger Ebert and Gene Siskel taking a look at a recent trend in American movies, reversal of the traditional sexual stereotypes of men, women and romance.
From The Sneak Previews Series.
Prod-WTTWTV Dist-PBS 1981

Women In Management C 28 MIN
16MM FILM - 3/4 IN VIDEO J-C A
Presents women in management discussing the problems of operating within preordained hierarchies and by men's rules. Focuses on the fear of success that inhibits many women, the difficulty of getting equal compensation, the sacrifices required to advance professionally, and the fears that men have of strong, successful women.
From The Are You Listening Series.
LC NO. 80-707158
Prod-STURTM Dist-STURTM 1974

Women In Management - Threat Or Opportunity C 30 MIN
16MM FILM, 3/4 OR 1/2 IN VIDEO H-C A
Examines the effects of the women's liberation movement on several different organizations and shows the many ways leaders are dealing with these effects.
Prod-CRMP Dist-CRMP 1975

Women In Management - Threat Or Opportunity (Spanish) C 30 MIN
16MM FILM, 3/4 OR 1/2 IN VIDEO H-C A
Examines the stereotypes commonly associated with women in business. Shows how a program at Weyerhaeuser Lumber Company has helped men and women deal with the new relationships caused by Affirmative Action programs and the new role for women.
From The Behavior In Business Film Series.
Prod-CRMP Dist-CRMP 1975

Women In Medicine, Goals For Today And Tomorrow B 50 MIN
3/4 INCH VIDEO CASSETTE
Highlights a regional conference on women in medicine sponsored by the Women's Medical Association of New York City. Addresses the problems encountered by women both in the health professions and as consumers of health services.
Prod-WMANY Dist-WMEN

Women In Middle Management C 28 MIN
16MM FILM - 3/4 IN VIDEO J-C A
Introduces some women who have worked their way from entry level positions to the realm of middle management.
From The Are You Listening Series.
LC NO. 80-707157
Prod-STURTM Dist-STURTM 1974

Women In Policing C 29 MIN
3/4 INCH VIDEO CASSETTE
Focuses on the dramatic increase in policewomen and discusses the problems women still face in entering police careers.
From The Woman Series.
Prod-WNEDTV Dist-PUBTEL

Women In Politics C 14 MIN
16MM FILM, 3/4 OR 1/2 IN VIDEO I-H
Examines the rise of women in politics from 1848 to 1980.
From The Screen News Digest Series.
Prod-HEARST Dist-HEARST 1981

Women In Prison C 54 MIN
16MM FILM, 3/4 OR 1/2 IN VIDEO H-C A
Documents the treatment given to most women sent to prison, emphasizing the process of dehumanization. Describes an alternative prison project in Iowa.
Prod-ABCNEW Dist-CAROUF

Women In Prison, Pt 1 C 29 MIN
3/4 OR 1/2 INCH VIDEO CASSETTE
Focuses on life in a women's prison.
From The Woman Series.
Prod-WNEDTV Dist-PBS

Women In Prison, Pt 2 C 29 MIN
3/4 OR 1/2 INCH VIDEO CASSETTE
Explores some of the realities of life in a women's prison.
From The Woman Series.
Prod-WNEDTV Dist-PBS

Women In Sports C 26 MIN
16MM FILM, 3/4 OR 1/2 IN VIDEO J-C A
A shortened version of the motion picture Women In Sports. Reviews the history of women in sports and examines the status of women athletes and women's athletics. Narrated by James Michener.
From The Sports In America Series.
LC NO. 82-706488
Prod-EMLEN Dist-PFP Prodn-CAPPY 1980

Women In Sports C 27 MIN
16MM FILM - 3/4 IN VIDEO
Depicts women's growing involvement in strenuous, competitive sports in recent years. Includes marathon runs, hockey, racketball and tennis. Close captioned.
Prod-SRCCPD Dist-MTP

Women In Sports C 58 MIN
16MM FILM, 3/4 OR 1/2 IN VIDEO J-C A
Reviews the history of women in sports and examines the status of women athletes and women's athletics. Narrated by James Michener.
From The Sports In America Series.
Prod-EMLEN Dist-PFP Prodn-CAPPY 1980

Women In Sports - An Informal History C 28 MIN
16MM FILM OPTICAL SOUND
Surveys the participation of women in sports from classical time to the 1970's. Discusses the prejudice against physically active women, the growing awareness of women's rights as sports particpants and the new enthusiasm of women for sports.
LC NO. 77-700445
Prod-KLUGDP Dist-ALTANA 1976

Women In The City (New York 1880-1920, Indianapolis 1880-1920) C 30 MIN
3/4 OR 1/2 INCH VIDEO CASSETTE J-C A
Presents the story of two non-urban women who confront the process of urbanization when they move to the city. Portrays one woman from a small midwestern family farm who moves to Indianapolis, and one woman from a small Eastern European Jewish settlement who moves to New York City.
From The American City Series.
Prod-WNETTV Dist-FI 1982

Women In The Corporation - On A Par, Not A Pedestal C 26 MIN
16MM FILM, 3/4 OR 1/2 IN VIDEO
Describes the affirmative action program at Connecticut General Insurance Company.
From The Human Resources And Organizational Behavior Series.
Prod-DOCUA Dist-CNEMAG

Women In The Middle East—A Series
16MM FILM, 3/4 OR 1/2 IN VIDEO
Looks at the status of women in Egypt and in Lebanon.
Prod-ICARUS Dist-ICARUS 1982

Price Of Change, The	026 MIN
Veiled Revolution, A	026 MIN
Women Under Seige	026 MIN

Women In The NDP C 28 MIN
3/4 INCH VIDEO CASSETTE
Presents two long-time associates of the New Democratic Party (Canada) Eileen Sufrin and Olga Nunn, discussing the contributions of women to the party's history.
Prod-WMENIF Dist-WMENIF

Women In The Trades B 25 MIN
3/4 INCH VIDEO CASSETTE
Looks at the Pre-Trades Program for Women in Winnipeg, which is designed to introduce women to different trades and give them basic skills and experience in entering and working within male-dominated jobs.
Prod-WMENIF Dist-WMENIF

Women In The Work Place C 20 MIN
3/4 OR 1/2 INCH VIDEO CASSETTE
Explains the twelve basic behaviors of the troubled female employee.
Prod-WHITEG Dist-WHITEG

Women In Trades C 57 MIN
3/4 INCH VIDEO CASSETTE
Shows women from eight different skilled trades demonstrating their jobs, talking about different aspects of their work and commenting on some of the advantages and disadvantages of employment in their trades.
Prod-SASWT Dist-WMENIF

Women In Transition C 29 MIN
3/4 OR 1/2 INCH VIDEO CASSETTE
Describes the services of the group called Women In Transition, which provides discussion support groups and paralegal advice for women going through separation and divorce.
From The Woman Series.
Prod-WNEDTV Dist-PBS

Women In Your Life Is You, The - Women's Sexuality C 33 MIN
16MM FILM, 3/4 OR 1/2 IN VIDEO H-C A
Explores the sexual experiences of four women, including a lesbian couple, to answer questions about what goes wrong with sexual relationships and what can be done to develop satisfying contact with partners.
From The Women Series.
Prod-LUF Dist-LUF 1979

Women Inside C 60 MIN
16MM FILM, 3/4 OR 1/2 IN VIDEO C A
Examines life within a women's prison. Includes the comments of the inmates and wardens.
From The Bill Moyers' Journal Series.
Prod-WNETTV Dist-IU 1980

Women Like Us C 52 MIN
16MM FILM, 3/4 OR 1/2 IN VIDEO H-C A
Looks at three women who exemplify some of the options open to women, including a working wife and mother, a single working woman, and a homemaker.
Prod-NBC Dist-FI 1979

Women Make Movies C 58 MIN
3/4 OR 1/2 INCH VIDEO CASSETTE
Illustrates life from various perspectives of the physically disabled using dramatizations performed by five variously handicapped women. Portrays day-to-day problems faced by the blind, the hearing impaired, the arthritic and those confined to wheelchairs, including attitudes of the nonhandicapped in their dealings with handicapped.
LC NO. 84-707095
Prod-WMEN Dist-WMEN 1982

Women Make The Difference C 28 MIN
16MM FILM OPTICAL SOUND
Looks at 25 years of Community Improvement Projects including crime reduction efforts, protecting the elderly and welcoming soldiers.
Prod-SEARS Dist-MTP

Women Of Hodson, The C 30 MIN
16MM FILM, 3/4 OR 1/2 IN VIDEO H-C A
Introduces elderly women of the Hodson Senior Citizen Center in the Bronx, NY, who use improvisational theater to portray their life stories and establish a rapport with one another and their audience.
LC NO. 81-707570
Prod-DEANJ Dist-FLMLIB 1980

Women Of Neve Ur, The C 29 MIN
16MM FILM OPTICAL SOUND
Depicts the courage of Israeli women who live in the Kibbutz of Neve Ur and the lack of hostility toward those who have sworn to destroy them.
Prod-NET Dist-ADL

Women Of Russia C 11 MIN
16MM FILM, 3/4 OR 1/2 IN VIDEO J-H
See series title for descriptive statement.
From The Russia Today Series.
Prod-IFF Dist-IFF 1968

Women Of The Toubou C 25 MIN
16MM FILM, 3/4 OR 1/2 IN VIDEO H-C A
Presents a documentary on the African tribe known as the Toubou. Explains that the tribe revolves around a strong matriarchy but is extremely protective of their fragilely beautiful, but strong, enduring, graceful women.
Prod-PHENIX Dist-PHENIX 1973

Women Of The Western Reserve - Women's Suffrage In Northeastern Ohio In The Late... C 43 MIN
16MM FILM OPTICAL SOUND
Complete title reads The Women Of The Western Reserve - Women's Suffrage In Northeastern Ohio In The Late 1800's. Dramatizes the women's suffrage movement in northeastern Ohio. Discusses whether law changes public opinion or if public opinion is stronger than law.
Prod-OHC Dist-HRC

Women On Orgasm C 15 MIN
16MM FILM OPTICAL SOUND A
Offers information on sex and orgasm. Includes a simulation of a pre-orgasmic women's group, scenes of intercourse and comments by older women on orgasm.
LC NO. 76-701198
Prod-DUIPA Dist-MMRC 1974

Women On The March, Pt 1 C 29 MIN
16MM FILM, 3/4 OR 1/2 IN VIDEO J-C A
Shows the struggle of women for equal rights from the beginning of the suffragette movement in England to World War I. Includes footage dating back to the Victorian Era.
Prod-NFBC Dist-NFBC 1958

Women On The March, Pt 2 C 29 MIN
16MM FILM, 3/4 OR 1/2 IN VIDEO J-C A
Depicts the struggle of women for equal rights from World War I to the present. Shows how women of the United States, Canada and Europe have achieved status in world councils, politics and many professions.
Prod-NFBC Dist-NFBC 1958

Women Studies C 30 MIN
3/4 INCH VIDEO CASSETTE
Discusses women's studies courses and the problems of teaching and studying such a topic.
Prod-WMENIF Dist-WMENIF

Women Take Back The Night B 17 MIN
3/4 OR 1/2 INCH VIDEO CASSETTE A
Tells how, united by their common fears and anger, 5,000 women gathered in Minneapolis on August 14, 1979, to protest female victimization. Shows how the women pool their skills and presence in a significant social and political event, which includes an integrated program of music, poetry, speeches, demonstrations in the martial arts, and testimony of those who have suffered and survived criminal assault.
LC NO. 81-706192
Prod-IBIS Dist-UCV 1980

Women Talking B 80 MIN
16MM FILM OPTICAL SOUND
Features conversations with leading personalities in the forefront of the Women's Liberation Movement. Seeks to bring an understanding of the vital problem confronting society by relating experiences that contribute to a greater awareness of the social oppression of women.
Prod-WLIBCC Dist-IMPACT 1971

Women Under Fire C 20 MIN
3/4 OR 1/2 INCH VIDEO CASSETTE H-C A
Tells how the Madison, Wisconsin Fire Department hired women as firefighters. Describes the physical strength, technical expertise and tricks-of-the-trade needed to become a firefighter.
Prod-FILCOM Dist-FILCOM

Women Under Siege C 26 MIN
16MM FILM, 3/4 OR 1/2 IN VIDEO
Documents the crucial role women play in Rashadiyah, Southern Lebanon, a town which is home to 14,000 Palestinian refugees. Shows the women playing the roles of mothers, teachers, political organizers, farm laborers and fighters.
From The Women In The Middle East Series.
Prod-ICARUS Dist-ICARUS 1982

Women Up In Arms B 29 MIN
16MM FILM, 3/4 OR 1/2 IN VIDEO
Views the women's place in the Moslem society in a study of a seventeen-year-old Tunisian girl who dances to Beatles' records, her mother who removed her veil seven years before, and her grandmother who maintains the old, traditional ways.
Prod-UN Dist-MGHT 1966

Women Who Didn't Have An Abortion C 28 MIN
16MM FILM - 3/4 IN VIDEO H-C
Presents several women of different backgrounds discussing their reasons for deciding against an abortion. Touches on the emotional, moral, religious, social, political and practical aspects of this difficult personal question.
From The Are You Listening Series.
LC NO. 80-707159
Prod-STURTM Dist-STURTM 1977

Women Who Have Had An Abortion C 28 MIN
16MM FILM - 3/4 IN VIDEO H-C
Describes the experiences of women who have had abortions. Discusses their relationships with doctors, postoperational depression, family relations, and moral quandries. Emphasizes the importance of counselling as an adjunct to having an abortion.
From The Are You Listening Series.

LC NO. 80-707160
Prod-STURTM Dist-STURTM 1972

Women With A Message C 20 MIN
16MM FILM OPTICAL SOUND
Depicts training and career opportunities in the field of telecommunications for officers and enlisted women in the U S Navy.
LC NO. 74-706610
Prod-USN Dist-USNAC 1973

Women Within Two Cultures C 30 MIN
3/4 INCH VIDEO CASSETTE
Looks at the situation of the British Columbia West Coast Indian woman and the early white pioneer woman from a white but feminist perspective.
Prod-WMENIF Dist-WMENIF

Women Workers C 29 MIN
3/4 OR 1/2 INCH VIDEO CASSETTE
Suggests that there is a changing consciousness among office workers who are banding together for better wages and job conditions.
From The Woman Series.
Prod-WNEDTV Dist-PBS

Women—A Series
16MM FILM, 3/4 OR 1/2 IN VIDEO H-C A
Looks at various issues concerning women including mental and physical cruelty by their husbands, depression among married women, sexuality, child care and media representations of women.
Prod-LUF Dist-LUF 1979

Marriage - Is It A Health Hazard 030 MIN
When Did You Last See Yourself On TV 032 MIN
When The Honeymoon Is Over 032 MIN
Who Cares About Child Care 033 MIN
Women In Your Life Is You, The - Women's 033 MIN

Women, Amen C 15 MIN
16MM FILM, 3/4 OR 1/2 IN VIDEO A
Explores the role of women in the church and the responsibilities of the church in ministering to women. Looks at three women involved in church activities. Includes a biblical scholar, a mother and a woman who seeks ordination into the ministry.
Prod-UMCOM Dist-ECUFLM 1974

Women, Birth Control And Nutrition C 15 MIN
16MM FILM, 3/4 OR 1/2 IN VIDEO H-C A
Discusses the fact that certain birth control methods deplete the female body of vitamins it needs and what women can do about it.
Prod-CINIMA Dist-PEREN

Women, Children And War C 12 MIN
16MM FILM OPTICAL SOUND
Examines the impact of the Yom Kippur War on the women and children of Israel.
Prod-UJA Dist-ALDEN

Women, Drugs And Alcohol C 21 MIN
16MM FILM, 3/4 OR 1/2 IN VIDEO A
Looks at the use of alcohol and prescription drugs among women. Narrated by Jessica Walter.
LC NO. 81-707270
Prod-MITCHG Dist-MTI 1980

Women, Money And Power C 29 MIN
3/4 INCH VIDEO CASSETTE
Discusses the need for women to educate themselves about the nature of the American economic system before they can attain real power.
From The Woman Series.
Prod-WNEDTV Dist-PUBTEL

Women, Work And Babies - Can America Cope C 49 MIN
3/4 OR 1/2 INCH VIDEO CASSETTE H-C A
Presents interviews with working parents, researchers, authors, business people, professors and politicians on the subject of working mothers. Shows scenes from family homes, day-care centers, classrooms and the work place. Examines re-definition of mother-father roles and the absence of support for single parents. Considers the effect of working parents on children.
Prod-NBCTV Dist-FI

Women's Basketball - Defense C 6 MIN
16MM FILM, 3/4 OR 1/2 IN VIDEO J-C
Presents basketball coach Pat Head exploring every phase of defense skills which must be mastered to become an effective defensive team player.
From The Women's Championship Basketball Series.
Prod-ATHI Dist-ATHI 1981

Women's Astrology C 29 MIN
3/4 INCH VIDEO CASSETTE
Looks at the negativism found in the traditional interpretation of astrology for women. Comments on the appeal of astrology and how it influences its adherents.
From The Woman Series.
Prod-WNEDTV Dist-PUBTEL

Women's Banks And Credit Unions C 29 MIN
3/4 INCH VIDEO CASSETTE
Describes the foundation of women's banks and credit unions.
From The Woman Series.
Prod-WNEDTV Dist-PUBTEL

Women's Basketball - Jump Ball C 15 MIN
16MM FILM, 3/4 OR 1/2 IN VIDEO J-C
Provides incentive and motivation for women who play and enjoy basketball. Stresses the importance of practice and determination in developing the basic skills of the game and shows how togetherness between teammates and coach can make the difference in winning or losing.
Prod-BFA Dist-PHENIX Prodn-DOBROF 1976

Women's Basketball - Offense C 6 MIN
16MM FILM, 3/4 OR 1/2 IN VIDEO J-C
Presents U S Olympic Coach Billie Moore and her UCLA champions showing the basic offensive plays for winners.
From The Women's Championship Basketball Series.
Prod-ATHI Dist-ATHI 1981

Women's Basketball, Pt 1 C 15 MIN
16MM FILM, 3/4 OR 1/2 IN VIDEO J-C
Demonstrates drills for improving techniques in ball handling, dribbling, passing and shooting different types of basket shots.
Prod-LRDKNG Dist-MCFI 1977

Women's Basketball, Pt 2 C 15 MIN
16MM FILM, 3/4 OR 1/2 IN VIDEO J-C
Demonstrates competitive basketball shots, including lay-up, underhanded lay-up, reverse lay-up, one hander and jump shot.
Prod-LRDKNG Dist-MCFI 1977

Women's Championship Basketball—A Series
16MM FILM, 3/4 OR 1/2 IN VIDEO J-C
Deals with various aspects of women's basketball, including shooting, defense, offense, team drill and body conditioning.
Prod-ATHI Dist-ATHI 1981

Women's Basketball - Body Conditioning 006 MIN
Women's Basketball - Defense 006 MIN
Women's Basketball - Offense 006 MIN
Women's Basketball - Shooting 006 MIN
Women's Basketball - Team Drills 006 MIN

Women's Coalition For The Third Century C 29 MIN
3/4 INCH VIDEO CASSETTE
Explains the objectives of the Women's Coalition for the Third Century, which intends to bring together national organizations to identify practical movements for change.
From The Woman Series.
Prod-WNEDTV Dist-PUBTEL

Women's Films, The B 45 MIN
16MM FILM OPTICAL SOUND
Presents the story of the poor and working women who talk about the oppression they have felt in their homes, on the job and in society. Explains how women are struggling for their liberation on all fronts.
Prod-SFN Dist-SFN 1970

Women's Golf Has Come A Long Way C 15 MIN
16MM FILM OPTICAL SOUND
Shows women learning to play golf.
Prod-NGF Dist-NGF

Women's Golf With Patty Sheehan C 60 MIN
1/2 IN VIDEO CASSETTE BETA/VHS
Presents neuromuscular training using Patty Sheehan as the model for an improved golf game. Includes four audiocassettes and personal training guide.
Prod-SYBVIS Dist-SYBVIS

Women's Health - A Question Of Survival C 49 MIN
16MM FILM, 3/4 OR 1/2 IN VIDEO H-C A
Investigates the questionable health care women may receive, including the administering of potentially dangerous drugs to pregnant women, questionable mastectomies and hysterectomies, and unproven birth control methods. Discusses the disinterest of doctors, drug manufacturers and government regulators.
Prod-ABCTV Dist-CRMP 1977

Women's Health Care - A History C 29 MIN
3/4 OR 1/2 INCH VIDEO CASSETTE
Discusses the history of women's involvement in the health care field.
From The Woman Series.
Prod-WNEDTV Dist-PBS

Women's Image - Down The Tube C 29 MIN
3/4 OR 1/2 INCH VIDEO CASSETTE
States that women have a ridiculous television image, citing commercials as the biggest offenders. Explains that consumers have some redress through the Federal Trade Commission and their own selective buying.
From The Woman Series.
Prod-WNEDTV Dist-PBS

Women's Issues C 22 MIN
16MM FILM, 3/4 OR 1/2 IN VIDEO A
Presents 14 vignettes demonstrating how various women's issues could be handled including sexual harassment, unequal treatment on the job, receiving the dummy treatment from mechanics, being excluded from the husband's business travel and experiencing the to-work-or-not-to-work dilemma.
Prod-MTI Dist-MTI

Women's Issues - Sexuality—A Series

Deals with women's sexuality.
Prod-DAVFMS Dist-DAVFMS

Five Women, Five Births 029 MIN
Reaching Orgasm 017 MIN
Sharing Orgasm - Communicating Your Sexual 010 MIN

Women's Liberation, Sexuality, And The Family C 30 MIN
3/4 OR 1/2 INCH VIDEO CASSETTE H-C A
Shows Sol Gordon, director of the Institute for Family Research and Education at Syracuse University, and Jim and Andrea Fordham, authors of The Assault On The Sexes, debating the benefits of women's liberation and changes in sexual attitudes and practices.
From The Ethics In America Series.
Prod-AMHUMA Dist-AMHUMA

Women's Olamal, The - The Organization Of A Masai Fertility Ceremony C 110 MIN
3/4 OR 1/2 INCH VIDEO CASSETTE
Follows the events that led up to a controversial ceremony in Loita, Kenya to bless the women in order to increase their ability to have children. Examines some of the tensions between men and women in Masai society. Interviews women involved in the ceremony.
Prod-BBCTV Dist-DOCEDR

Women's Pages C 29 MIN
3/4 OR 1/2 INCH VIDEO CASSETTE
Asks whether women's pages are the pioneers in positive coverage of various lifestyles or dumping grounds for engagement pictures and advertising. Gives a brief history of women's pages and the kinds of style and content changes that occurred between 1969 and 1973.
From The Woman Series.
Prod-WNEDTV Dist-PBS

Women's Prejudice Film, The C 19 MIN
16MM FILM, 3/4 OR 1/2 IN VIDEO I-C A
Examines questionable concepts along with alternative viewpoints that stimulate men and women to re-appraise current attitudes concerning equality. Explores many myths and cliches.
Prod-SAIF Dist-BARR 1974

Women's Rally For Action - March 22, 1976 C 29 MIN
3/4 INCH VIDEO CASSETTE
Documents the massive mobilization effort of British Columbia feminists to pressure the newly elected Social Credit government to change its policies affecting women.
Prod-WMENIF Dist-WMENIF

Women's Rights C 30 MIN
3/4 OR 1/2 INCH VIDEO CASSETTE C
Follows women's struggle for equality from its beginnings in America to the 1977 IWY conference in Houston. Reviews some of the early women's meetings, the public's reaction to the 'suffragettes' and the pros and cons of ERA.
From The American Government 2 Series.
Prod-DALCCD Dist-DALCCD

Women's Rights In The U S - An Informal History C 27 MIN
16MM FILM OPTICAL SOUND H-C A
Surveys the conditions and movements which brought about changes in the status of women, such as the frontier, abolition, the Civil War, industrialization and suffragettism. Explores attitudes toward marriage, employment, fashion, education and women's 'proper place' in society.
LC NO. 73-702668
Prod-KLUGDP Dist-ALTANA 1973

Women's Service To The Nation B 10 MIN
16MM FILM OPTICAL SOUND
Discusses the contributions of American women to the national welfare from colonial times to the 20th century.
LC NO. 75-703078
Prod-USA Dist-USNAC 1964

Women's Service To The Nation - Summary And Conclusion C 8 MIN
16MM FILM OPTICAL SOUND
Describes contributions of America's women to the nation from pioneer days to the 20th century. Recalls their courage and self-sacrifice during times of war and their progressive efforts in times of peace. Emphasizes the expanded role of women in the Armed Forces and in industrial, professional and governmental areas.
LC NO. 75-703077
Prod-USA Dist-USNAC 1968

Women's Studies C 29 MIN
3/4 INCH VIDEO CASSETTE
Discusses the increase in women's studies courses offered at American colleges and universities.
From The Woman Series.
Prod-WNEDTV Dist-PUBTEL

Women's Suffrage Movement In Canada, The C 23 MIN
3/4 INCH VIDEO CASSETTE
Examines the Women's Suffrage Movement, the women who were active at the time and some of the most controversial issues. Draws parallels between the feminist movement today and the roots in the early feminist and suffrage movements.
Prod-WMENIF Dist-WMENIF

Women's Track And Field—A Series

Demonstrates techniques and training for the events in women's track and field. Includes slow motion and stop frame photography.
Prod-MOHOMV Dist-MOHOMV

Conditioning 033 MIN
Discus / Shot Put 039 MIN
High Jump 023 MIN
Javelin 053 MIN
Long Jump 046 MIN
Middle Distance Running 042 MIN
Sprints, Hurdles And Relays 048 MIN
Talent Search 060 MIN

Women's World Of Golf - Betsy Rawls B 20 MIN
16MM FILM OPTICAL SOUND
From The Women's World Of Golf Series.
Prod-SFI Dist-SFI

Women's World Of Golf - Mickey Wright B 20 MIN
16MM FILM OPTICAL SOUND

See series title for descriptive statement.
From The Women's World Of Golf Series.
Prod-SFI Dist-SFI

Women's World Of Golf - Patty Berg B 20 MIN
16MM FILM OPTICAL SOUND
From The Women's World Of Golf Series.
Prod-SFI Dist-SFI

Women's World Of Golf—A Series

Shows highlights of the pros in action.
Prod-SFI Dist-SFI

Women's World Of Golf - Betsy Rawls 20 MIN
Women's World Of Golf - Mickey Wright 20 MIN
Women's World Of Golf - Patty Berg 20 MIN

Won Ton C 29 MIN
2 INCH VIDEOTAPE
Features Joyce Chen showing how to adapt Chinese recipes so that they can be prepared in the American kitchen and still retain the authentic flavor. Demonstrates how to prepare won ton.
From The Joyce Chen Cooks Series.
Prod-WGBHTV Dist-PUBTEL

Wonder C 2 MIN
16MM FILM OPTICAL SOUND I-H A R
Creates a mood for discussion, thought, prayer or meditation on the gifts people take for granted.
From The Meditation Series.
LC NO. 80-700753
Prod-IKONOG Dist-IKONOG 1974

Wonder B 5 MIN
16MM FILM OPTICAL SOUND P-C A
Inspired by Psalm 8 of the Bible. Pictures the beauty of nature as seen through the eyes of a two-year-old girl, and studies the child as the greatest of all wonders.
From The Song Of The Ages Series.
LC NO. 75-702120
Prod-FAMLYT Dist-FAMLYT 1965

Wonder Baby C 3 MIN
3/4 OR 1/2 INCH VIDEO CASSETTE P-I
Features the animated superhero Wonder Gram in a discussion of metric measurement.
From The Metric Marvels Series.
Prod-NBCTV Dist-GA 1978

Wonder Bar B 84 MIN
16MM FILM OPTICAL SOUND J-C A
Stars Dick Powell, Al Jolson and Kay Francis. Presents the dance numbers created and staged by Busby Berkeley, including the musical numbers Going To Heaven On A Mule, Why Do I Dream Those Dreams, Don't Say Goodnight, Wonder Bar and Vive La France.
Prod-WB Dist-UAE 1934

Wonder Dog C 8 MIN
16MM FILM, 3/4 OR 1/2 IN VIDEO
Shows Pluto trying to impress his girlfriend by impersonating a circus dog. Demonstrates that the feats he must perform prove trickier than he expected.
From The Tales Of Pluto Series.
Prod-DISNEY Dist-WDEMCO

Wonder Factory C 10 MIN
16MM FILM OPTICAL SOUND
A French language film. Discusses how the leadership of the French Communist Party is aligned with the power structure and does not serve the needs of the people.
Prod-NEWSR Dist-NEWSR

Wonder Gram C 3 MIN
3/4 OR 1/2 INCH VIDEO CASSETTE P-I
Tells how Wonder Gram foils a gang of snack thieves and demonstrates the multiples of metric weight.
From The Metric Marvels Series.
Prod-NBCTV Dist-GA 1978

Wonder Of Dolphins, The C 11 MIN
16MM FILM, 3/4 OR 1/2 IN VIDEO
Discusses the dolphin, one of nature's most incredible creatures.
LC NO. 80-706826
Prod-WIESEM Dist-CORF

Wonder Of Drag Racing, The C 13 MIN
16MM FILM OPTICAL SOUND
Depicts the excitement, complexity and intense competition of drag racing as experienced by one participant.
LC NO. 73-702400
Prod-PTRSEN Dist-PTRSEN 1973

Wonder Of Form, The C 30 MIN
3/4 OR 1/2 INCH VIDEO CASSETTE C
See series title for descriptive statement.
From The Art Of Being Human Series. Module 15
Prod-MDCC Dist-MDCC

Wonder Of Insects' Colors And Figures C 19 MIN
16MM FILM OPTICAL SOUND
Explains that insects possess various devices for protecting themselves from the outside world and describes how they adapt themselves to different circumstances.
Prod-TOEI Dist-UNIJAP 1970

Wonder Of Our Body (2nd Ed) C 13 MIN
16MM FILM, 3/4 OR 1/2 IN VIDEO I-J
Introduces the human body. Reveals the skeleton, the body's lubricating system, the hand, the brain, the eye, the ear and the heart as part of the intricate design that has gone into making the human body.
Prod-MIS Dist-MIS 1976

Wonder Of Work C 10 MIN
16MM FILM OPTICAL SOUND
Deals with the subject of occupational therapy and important developments in treating disabilities which result from disease and accidents.
Prod-IREFL Dist-IREFL

Wonder Walks—A Series
16MM FILM, 3/4 OR 1/2 IN VIDEO
Invites children to investigate the world around them. Presents insects, animals, the effects of rain and sun, the 'HOW' and 'WHERE' of life and the way things look up close.
Prod-EBEC Dist-EBEC

Bending And Reflecting Sunlight 7 MIN
How Do They Move 6 MIN
Let's Find Life 8 MIN
Some Friendly Insects 5 MIN
Time For Rain, A 8 MIN
Time For Sun, A 6 MIN
What Do They Eat 5 MIN
Where Does Life Come From 6 MIN
World Of Up Close, The 9 MIN

Wonder World C 25 MIN
16MM FILM OPTICAL SOUND
Searches for the secret of the life of antibiotic bacteria and how staphylococci acquire antibiotic-resistance. Shows how bacterial-genes act and how to deal with antibiotic-resistive bacteria.
Prod-UNIJAP Dist-UNIJAP 1972

Wonderama Of The Arts—A Series
I
Presents an overview of the arts, including drama, art, music, dance and pantomime.
Prod-WBRATV Dist-GPITVL 1979

Artistic Adventure On Planet Wek 20 MIN
Circle, Pt 1 20 MIN
Circle, Pt 2 20 MIN
Creative Investigation 20 MIN
Magic And Motion 20 MIN
Math Show, The 20 MIN
Muscle Of Imagination 20 MIN
Proud Girl And Bold Eagle 20 MIN
Rushcape 20 MIN
Tailor And The Weaver, The 20 MIN

Wonderful Baby C 30 MIN
3/4 OR 1/2 INCH VIDEO CASSETTE H-C A
Presents Lawrence Solow and Sharon Neumann Solow introducing American Sign Language used by the hearing-impaired. Emphasizes signs that have to do with a new baby in the family.
From The Say It With Sign Series. Part 9
Prod-KNBCTV Dist-FI 1982

Wonderful Bird Was The Pelican, A C 26 MIN
16MM FILM, 3/4 OR 1/2 IN VIDEO
Shows the effects of DDT in the diet of the brown pelican, once common along the coast of California.
Prod-UPA Dist-MCFI 1975

Wonderful Construction, A C 15 MIN
16MM FILM OPTICAL SOUND
Celebrates as creative artists the men who build buildings, comparing them to the men in Leger's painting 'LES CONSTRUCTEURS.'
LC NO. 72-702454
Prod-RADIM Dist-RADIM

Wonderful Crook, The (French) C 112 MIN
16MM FILM OPTICAL SOUND
Describes a modern Robin Hood's double life and loves. Directed by Claude Goretta. With English subtitles.
Prod-UNKNWN Dist-NYFLMS 1975

Wonderful Day C 14 MIN
3/4 OR 1/2 INCH VIDEO CASSETTE P-I
See series title for descriptive statement.
From The Ready, Sing Series.
Prod-ARKETV Dist-AITECH 1979

Wonderful Flight To The Mushroom Planet, The C 15 MIN
3/4 OR 1/2 INCH VIDEO CASSETTE I
Tells a story of two boys who discover the secret of a doomed planet. From the book by Elinor Cameron.
From The Book Bird Series.
Prod-CTI Dist-CTI

Wonderful Lollypop Rooster, The C 8 MIN
16MM FILM, 3/4 OR 1/2 IN VIDEO P
Presents the nonnarrated story of a mysterious organ grinder who gives the children of a colorless village lollypops. Reveals that one of the lollypops is shaped like a rooster and has magic powers.
Prod-SF Dist-SF 1972

Wonderful Walking Stick, The - A Bulgarian Folk Tale C 10 MIN
16MM FILM, 3/4 OR 1/2 IN VIDEO P-I
Tells the tale of a magic stick that by a mere touch changes anger into laughter.
From The Folk Tales From Around The World Series.
Prod-FILBUL Dist-SF 1980

Wonderful Weather Machine, The C 13 MIN
16MM FILM, 3/4 OR 1/2 IN VIDEO P-J
Describes how gravity, water, land, air and the sun all act together to create different weather conditions. Explains how the tilt of the earth determines whether it's summer or winter. Reveals how clouds, rain, wind and snow are generated and the causes of thunderstorms, tornadoes and hurricanes.
LC NO. 83-706757
Prod-LEARN Dist-BARR 1983

Wonderful Winter Haven C 15 MIN
16MM FILM OPTICAL SOUND
Explores Lakeland, the citrus center of Florida.
Prod-FLADC Dist-FLADC

Wonderful Womenfolk C 19 MIN
3/4 OR 1/2 INCH VIDEO CASSETTE P
See series title for descriptive statement.
From The Folk Book Series.
Prod-UWISC Dist-AITECH 1980

Wonderful Word And Wordless Story Wagon, The C 10 MIN
3/4 OR 1/2 INCH VIDEO CASSETTE K-P
Focuses on the ability to respond to language games with one word, a phrase or complete sentence stories.
From The Book, Look And Listen Series.
Prod-MDDE Dist-AITECH 1977

Wonderful World Of Adventure C 32 MIN
16MM FILM OPTICAL SOUND
Views the floats, bands and horses of the floral festival and parade held in Pasadena, California, on New year's Day, 1968.
LC NO. FIA68-627
Prod-TRA Dist-TRA 1968

Wonderful World Of Water Sports C 15 MIN
16MM FILM OPTICAL SOUND
Features the wide variety of water sports available to the enthusiast in Florida.
Prod-FLADC Dist-FLADC

Wondering C 15 MIN
3/4 OR 1/2 INCH VIDEO CASSETTE P-I
See series title for descriptive statement.
From The Ready, Sing Series.
Prod-ARKETV Dist-AITECH 1979

Wondering About Air C 13 MIN
16MM FILM OPTICAL SOUND P
Presents a lesson about air. Uses the setting of three clowns on a beach. Shows motion of a hat, balloon and kite moving in the air.
LC NO. 85-703265
Prod-EBEC Dist-EBEC 1986

Wondering About Light C 10 MIN
16MM FILM OPTICAL SOUND P
Learn about light from the four children playing hide and seek and from the girl who enters the garage.
LC NO. 85-703266
Prod-EBEC Dist-EBEC 1986

Wonders In A Country Stream (2nd Ed) C 12 MIN
16MM FILM, 3/4 OR 1/2 IN VIDEO K-I
Shows children near a stream discovering tadpoles, frogs, damsel flies, newts, a turtle and water striders.
Prod-CF Dist-CF 1977

Wonders In Your Own Backyard (2nd Ed) C 11 MIN
16MM FILM, 3/4 OR 1/2 IN VIDEO K-I
Discusses close and early observation. Shows a group of children finding a snail, sow bug, grasshopper, earthworm, spider, caterpillar and inchworm in their backyard.
Prod-CF Dist-CF 1977

Wonders Of Florida C 3 MIN
16MM FILM OPTICAL SOUND P-I
Shows some of the wonders of the state of Florida.
From The Of All Things Series.
Prod-BAILYL Dist-AVED

Wonders Of Growing Plants (2nd Ed) C 11 MIN
16MM FILM, 3/4 OR 1/2 IN VIDEO P-I
Uses time-lapse photography to present plant reproduction, showing that plants grow not only from seeds, but also from stems, roots and leaves.
Prod-CF Dist-CF 1975

Wonders Of Wilderness C 21 MIN
3/4 INCH VIDEO CASSETTE
Portrays the frustration and tension of living and working in crowded urban areas. Suggests a trail riding vacation into one of the forest service wilderness areas.
Prod-USDA Dist-USDA 1972

Wondrous Complexity, A C 29 MIN
3/4 INCH VIDEO CASSETTE
Discusses the numerous analytical tools used by the operations engineer to aid handling of complex systems.
From The Future Without Shock Series.
Prod-UMITV Dist-UMITV 1976

Wondrous World Of Sight, The C 28 MIN
1 INCH VIDEOTAPE
Explores the amazing role the eye plays in life. Gives some helpful suggestions in addition to a detailed description of its fantastic performance.
Prod-MURINE Dist-MTP

Wood C 12 MIN
3/4 OR 1/2 INCH VIDEO CASSETTE
Covers properties of wood, grades, defects, measuring, choosing wood, preservation and uses.
From The Working With Nonmetals In The Plant Series.
Prod-TPCTRA Dist-TPCTRA

Wood - A Masterpiece Of Creation C 28 MIN
16MM FILM, 3/4 OR 1/2 IN VIDEO H-C
Examines the structure of wood.
Prod-HARL Dist-IFB 1966

Wood And Glass C 29 MIN
2 INCH VIDEOTAPE
Provides a glimpse of Hawaiian craftsmen working with wood and glass.
From The Directions In Design Series.
Prod-HETV Dist-PUBTEL

Wood And Wooden Objects C 29 MIN
3/4 INCH VIDEO CASSETTE C A
Focuses on wood grain as a natural art element. Teaches how to draw some wooden objects such as a table, box, or stool, and how to draw grain on the wood to add to its appearance.
From The Sketching Techniques Series. Lesson 20
Prod-COAST Dist-CDTEL

Wood Bending - A New Twist C 13 MIN
16MM FILM, 3/4 OR 1/2 IN VIDEO H-C
Shows the new process of bending wood by using anhydrous ammonia.
Prod-SUNY Dist-IFB 1969

Wood Chip Mulch For Erosion Control C 13 MIN
16MM FILM OPTICAL SOUND
Demonstrates how wood chip mulch provides a solution to erosion during and after highway construction. Shows that air and water pollution can be controlled and a natural resource put to use instead of being wasted or burned.
LC NO. 74-705965
Prod-USDTFH Dist-USNAC 1972

Wood Finishes C 14 MIN
16MM FILM, 3/4 OR 1/2 IN VIDEO H-C A
Stains, shellac, varnish, lacquer, wax and oil for use on wood.
From The Hand Tools For Wood Working Series, No. 10.
Prod-MORLAT Dist-SF 1967

Wood Heat C 28 MIN
16MM FILM, 3/4 OR 1/2 IN VIDEO A
Provides information on wood-burning stoves.
From The Home Energy Conservation Series.
LC NO. 81-706764
Prod-RPFD Dist-BULFRG 1980

Wood Is Too Good To Burn C 29 MIN
3/4 OR 1/2 INCH VIDEO CASSETTE
Explains how, in the face of rising materials' costs and resource depletion, timber offers a renewable and versatile alternative to plastics and fibers in the making of many products.
LC NO. 82-706621
Prod-WETN Dist-PBS 1980

Wood Joints C 13 MIN
16MM FILM, 3/4 OR 1/2 IN VIDEO J-C A
Joining wood--butt, rabbet, dado and groove, dowel and half lap joints.
From The Hand Tools For Wood Working Series.
Prod-MORLAT Dist-SF 1967

Wood Lathe, The C 17 MIN
1/2 IN VIDEO CASSETTE BETA/VHS IND
See series title for descriptive statement.
From The Woodworking Power Tools Series.
Prod-RMI Dist-RMI

Wood Plastic - A New Dimension C 12 MIN
16MM FILM, 3/4 OR 1/2 IN VIDEO H-C
Demonstrates the use of the catalyst heat system in making wood plastic. Shows how the usual disadvantages of wood are minimized by this process and presents a commercial use for the new material.
Prod-HOLTMB Dist-IFB 1969

Wood Preservation - Control Of Marine Organisms C 21 MIN
16MM FILM OPTICAL SOUND
Describes corrective measures for effective control of damage by marine organisms to wood.
LC NO. FIE61-135
Prod-USN Dist-USNAC 1959

Wood Preservation - Control Of Wood Destroying Organisms C 24 MIN
16MM FILM OPTICAL SOUND
Outlines methods which can be employed to control wood destroying organisms.
LC NO. FIE57-33
Prod-USN Dist-USNAC 1959

Wood Preservation - Effects Of Marine Organisms C 20 MIN
16MM FILM OPTICAL SOUND
Shows the habits, characteristics and economic significance of marine organisms in waterfront structures.
LC NO. FIE61-134
Prod-USN Dist-USNAC 1959

Wood Preservation - Inspection For Wood Destroying Organisms C 18 MIN
16MM FILM OPTICAL SOUND
Describes problems faced by the navy in maintaining its wooden structures.
LC NO. FIE57-34
Prod-USN Dist-USNAC 1959

Wood Sculptor C 6 MIN
16MM FILM, 3/4 OR 1/2 IN VIDEO I-C A
Follows sculptor Nick Edmunds through the creation of a massive wood sculpture.
Prod-MCFH Dist-PHENIX 1975

Wood Shell, The C 31 MIN
16MM FILM OPTICAL SOUND
Depicts the carpentry construction of a home. Illustrates architectural plans, the installation of wood sills, girders, floor joists, stud walls, framing of ceiling joists and roof rafters, and plywood sheathing of walls and roof. Shows the daily progress on a residential building site and the basic steps and procedures in wood frame construction.
From The House Construction Series.
LC NO. 81-700821
Prod-COPRO Dist-COPRO 1980

Wood Shop - Safety And Operations—A Series
16MM FILM, 3/4 OR 1/2 IN VIDEO J-C A
Prod-EPRI Dist-AIMS Prodn-EPRI 1970

Center Guiding Of Drawers 010 MIN
Safety And Operation Of Faceplate Turning, Pt 1 008 MIN
Safety And Operation Of Faceplate Turning, Pt 2 012 MIN
Safety Demonstration On The Band Saw 014 MIN
Safety Demonstration On The Jointer 012 MIN
Safety Demonstration On The Radial Saw 012 MIN
Safety Demonstration On The Single Surface 016 MIN
Safety Demonstration On The Table Saw, Pt 1 011 MIN
Safety Demonstration On The Table Saw, Pt 2 009 MIN
Safety Demonstration On The Wood Lathe 011 MIN
Safety Demonstration On The Wood Shaper, Pt 1 011 MIN
Safety Demonstration On The Wood Shaper, Pt 2 009 MIN
Using The Shaper To Make Drawers 014 MIN
Using The Shaper To Make Panel Doors 016 MIN
Using The Shaper to Make Raised Panels For 009 MIN

Wood Turning X 10 MIN
16MM FILM OPTICAL SOUND J-C A
Hugh Baird, industrial arts instructor for the Los Angeles school system, demonstrates the technique of wood turning, using one of the new multiple unit power tools.
Prod-ALLMOR Dist-AVED 1957

Wood—A Series
H-C A
Prod-NCDCC Dist-MOKIN

Choosing And Cutting Firewood 025 MIN
Fireplaces And Woodstoves 024 MIN

Wood, Pt. 1 C
3/4 OR 1/2 INCH VIDEO CASSETTE IND
Covers types of wood, wood structure and wood characteristics.
From The Pulp And Paper Training, Module 1 - Kraft Pulping Series.
Prod-LEIKID Dist-LEIKID

Wood, Woodyard And Pulping C
3/4 OR 1/2 INCH VIDEO CASSETTE IND
Covers wood, wood preparation, chipping and pulping methods.
From The Pulp And Paper Training, Module 1 - Kraft Pulping Series.
Prod-LEIKID Dist-LEIKID

Woodblock Mandala - The World Of Shiko Munkata C 30 MIN
16MM FILM OPTICAL SOUND H-C A
Explains the process of Japanese woodblock prints.
From The Japanese Woodblock Series.
Prod-NHK Dist-FI 1973

Woodcarver's Workshop—A Series

Features woodcarver Mike Gaber and friends explaining and demonstrating woodcarving techniques. Looks at whittling, toolmaking, finishing techniques, carving in the round, decoy carving, and different artistic styles.
Prod-WOSUTV Dist-PUBTEL

Decoy Carving 028 MIN
Finishing Techniques 028 MIN
Relief Carving 029 MIN
Review 029 MIN
Sculpture In The Round 028 MIN
Tools Of The Trade 030 MIN
Whittling 028 MIN

Woodcutter And The Magic Tree, The - A North African Folk Tale C 7 MIN
16MM FILM, 3/4 OR 1/2 IN VIDEO K-I
Presents an animated story about a poor woodcutter who spares an ancient tree and is rewarded with a magic platter that constantly replenishes itself with food.
From The Folk Tales From Around The World Series.
Prod-ADPF Dist-SF 1980

Woodcutters Of The Deep South C 90 MIN
16MM FILM OPTICAL SOUND
Shows how poor black and white working people of the deep South are trying to overcome the forces of racism among themselves to organize into a cooperative association to dispel the bonds of their economic captors - the paper and the pulpwood companies. Features interviews with the men directly involved in the formation of this group, the Gulf-Coast Pulpwood Association.
Prod-ROGOSN Dist-IMPACT 1973

Wooden Box - Made By Steaming And Bending C 34 MIN
16MM FILM, 3/4 OR 1/2 IN VIDEO
Shows the construction of a traditional cedar, pegged box by a chief of the Kwakiutl Indians of British Columbia. Describes the felling of a cedar tree and the cutting, steaming, bending and assembling of the box.
From The American Indian Series.
Prod-UCEMC Dist-UCEMC 1962

Wooden Lullaby B 7 MIN
16MM FILM OPTICAL SOUND H-C A
Presents a short vignette about a whorish mother, her lonely son and his wooden rocking horse.
Prod-CFS Dist-CFS 1964

Wooden Overcoat, The C 14 MIN
16MM FILM OPTICAL SOUND
Shows that a container having six-inch-thick shells of fir plywood will adequately protect the inner metal container of radioactive material. Shows the development and testing of the wooden containers as well as how they are made.
LC NO. 74-705967
Prod-USAEC Dist-USNAC 1965

Wooden Ships and Men Of Iron C 14 MIN
16MM FILM, 3/4 OR 1/2 IN VIDEO J A
Portrays the Cape Cod whaling industry through archival footage of ships under sail, harpooners on the attack and shipwrecks. Presents the US Livesaving Service in action rescuing victims of these shipwrecks.
Prod-USNPS Dist-USNAC 1984

Wooden Shoe (Clog) Study C 24 MIN
3/4 OR 1/2 INCH VIDEO CASSETTE PRO
Demonstrates the improvement in walking ability exhibited by multiple sclerosis patients wearing wooden clogs with a special ankle strap.
LC NO. 80-707598
Prod-USVA Dist-USNAC 1980

Woodland Community, A C 15 MIN
3/4 OR 1/2 INCH VIDEO CASSETTE P-I
Discusses the living things found in a forest.
From The Why Series.
Prod-WDCNTV Dist-AITECH 1976

Woodland Indians Of Early America (2nd Ed) C 10 MIN
16MM FILM, 3/4 OR 1/2 IN VIDEO P
Shows a Chippewa family preparing for winter, each member doing his or her special job.
LC NO. 80-707370
Prod-CORF Dist-CORF 1980

Woodlands, The C 28 MIN
16MM FILM OPTICAL SOUND C A
Emphasizes planning and initial reconnaissance that form the early part of work in any reservoir project. All the stages of the project, through final publications are included. Covers the stories of two reservoir projects--the Allegheny Reservoir, a public flood control project in northwestern Pennsylvania, and the Gaston Reservoir, a private power project in North Carolina.
From The Spadework For History Series.
Prod-UTEX Dist-UTEX 1964

Woodlawn Sisterhood C 28 MIN
16MM FILM - 3/4 IN VIDEO J-C
Offers a primer on do-it-yourself community organization as delivered by the women who created their own organization on the south side of Chicago.
From The Are You Listening Series.
LC NO. 80-707161
Prod-STURTM Dist-STURTM 1972

Woodpecker Gets Ready For Winter, The C 9 MIN
16MM FILM, 3/4 OR 1/2 IN VIDEO P-I
Reveals the unique manner in which the el carpentero woodpecker stores acorns for winter. Shows the interrelationship between animals and plants of the forest.
Prod-MIS Dist-MIS 1958

Woodpeckers C 3 MIN
16MM FILM OPTICAL SOUND P-I
Discusses the birds known as woodpeckers.
From The Of All Things Series.
Prod-BAILYL Dist-AVED

Woodrow Cornett - Letcher County Butcher C 10 MIN
16MM FILM - 3/4 IN VIDEO H-C A
Portrays Woodrow Cornett, a butcher, as he performs his master craft of hog butchering in the mountain custom.
Prod-APPAL Dist-APPAL 1971

Woodrow Wilson B 20 MIN
2 INCH VIDEOTAPE I
See series title for descriptive statement.
From The Americans All Series.
Prod-DENVPS Dist-GPITVL Prodn-KRMATV

Woodrow Wilson B 51 MIN
16MM FILM, 3/4 OR 1/2 IN VIDEO I-H
Dramatizes the controversy surrounding President Woodrow Wilson's nomination of Louis Brandeis, a Jew, to the Supreme Court. Shows how Wilson braved religious prejudice and political opposition to defend Brandeis. Based on book Profiles In Courage by John F Kennedy.
From The Profiles In Courage Series.
LC NO. 83-706548
Prod-SAUDEK Dist-SSSSV 1965

Woodrow Wilson - Peace And War And The Professor President C 23 MIN
16MM FILM, 3/4 OR 1/2 IN VIDEO J-C A
Present mementoes of Woodrow Wilson's distinguished and inspiring career.
From The American Lifestyles - U S Presidents Series.
LC NO. 84-706111
Prod-COMCO Dist-AIMS 1984

Woodrow Wilson - The Fight For A League Of Nations C 20 MIN
16MM FILM, 3/4 OR 1/2 IN VIDEO I-C
Focuses on the problem Woodrow Wilson had in making his dream of a new League of Nations into a reality. Presents facts and asks the viewer to decide whether or not he would have voted for the League.
From The Great Decisions Series.
Prod-PSP Dist-AMEDFL 1970

Woodrow Wilson And The Treaties C 29 MIN
2 INCH VIDEOTAPE

See series title for descriptive statement.
From The Course Of Our Times I Series.
Prod-WGBHTV Dist-PUBTEL

Woodrow Wilson, Pt 1 C 25 MIN
16MM FILM OPTICAL SOUND I-C A
Portrays Woodrow Wilson standing by his nomination of Louis D Brandeis to the U S Supreme Court despite widespread religious prejudice against Brandeis.
From The Profiles In Courage Series.
Prod-SAUDEK Dist-SSSSV 1965

Woodrow Wilson, Pt 2 C 25 MIN
16MM FILM OPTICAL SOUND I-C A
Portrays Woodrow Wilson standing by his nomination of Louis D Brandeis to the U S Supreme Court despite widespread religious prejudice against Brandeis.
From The Profiles In Courage Series.
Prod-SAUDEK Dist-SSSSV 1965

Woods-Review B 13 MIN
16MM FILM OPTICAL SOUND
Highlights of Byron Nelson's professional career with Jimmy Demaret giving a lesson on the use of irons and woods.
Prod-SFI Dist-SFI

Woodstove Wisdom C 15 MIN
16MM FILM, 3/4 OR 1/2 IN VIDEO
Presents Ezra Winter, a Maine backwoodsman and volunteer fire fighter, who tells about his newsletter, Woodstove Wisdom, which offers advice on solid fuel safety. Relates answers to the questions his readers commonly ask about buying, installing and maintaining woodstoves.
Prod-NFPA Dist-NFPA 1981

Woodwind Family, The C 15 MIN
3/4 OR 1/2 INCH VIDEO CASSETTE P
Teaches recognition of woodwind musical instruments.
From The Music Machine Series.
Prod-GPITVL Dist-GPITVL

Woodwind Family, The C 15 MIN
3/4 OR 1/2 INCH VIDEO CASSETTE I
Demonstrates the flute, oboe, clarinet and bassoon. Features a woodwind ensemble which plays various works.
From The Music And Me Series.
LC NO. 80-706871
Prod-WDCNTV Dist-AITECH 1979

Woodwinds And Dance C 10 MIN
16MM FILM, 3/4 OR 1/2 IN VIDEO P-H
See series title for descriptive statement.
From The Indians Of The Orinoco (Venezuela) - The Makiritare Series.
Prod-IFF Dist-IFF

Woodwinds In Multiples B 29 MIN
2 INCH VIDEOTAPE
See series title for descriptive statement.
From The American Band Goes Symphonic Series.
Prod-WGTV Dist-PUBTEL

Woodworking - Trees To Lumber C 10 MIN
1/2 IN VIDEO CASSETTE BETA/VHS IND
Shows the processes involved in woodworking, from logging to lumber.
Prod-RMI Dist-RMI

Woodworking Lathe - Face Plate Turning C 13 MIN
16MM FILM, 3/4 OR 1/2 IN VIDEO J-C A
Presents five concepts dealing with the woodworking lathe - face plate turning--mounting the face plate, mounting work on the face plate, setting up, turning to diameter and finishing edge to shape. The projector may be stopped after each concept.
From The Woodwork - Machine Tools Series.
Prod-SF Dist-SF 1967

Woodworking Lathe - Spindle Turning C 13 MIN
16MM FILM, 3/4 OR 1/2 IN VIDEO J-C A
Presents six concepts dealing with the woodworking lathe - spindle turning--parts, cutting tools, centering stock, mounting the work, rough turning, and cutting curves, grooves and shoulders. The projector may be stopped after each concept.
From The Woodwork - Machine Tools Series.
Prod-MORLAT Dist-SF 1967

Woodworking Power Tools--A Series
IND
Deals with woodworking and construction tools.
Prod-RMI Dist-RMI

Band, Jig And Saber Saws	018 MIN
Circular Saws	019 MIN
Drilling Machines	015 MIN
Planing Machines	015 MIN
Router And Shaper	014 MIN
Sanding Machines	013 MIN
Wood Lathe, The	017 MIN

Woodworking Tools C 12 MIN
3/4 OR 1/2 INCH VIDEO CASSETTE
Covers woodworking tools such as handsaws, crosscut saws, ripsaws, special purpose saws, planes, scrapers, drills and others.
From The Using Hand Tools Series.
Prod-TPCTRA Dist-TPCTRA

Woodworking Tools C 30 MIN
3/4 OR 1/2 INCH VIDEO CASSETTE
Presents guests who are experts in their respective fields who share tips on collecting and caring for antique woodworking tools.
From The Antique Shop Series.
Prod-WVPTTV Dist-MDCPB

Woodworking Tools (Spanish) C 12 MIN
3/4 OR 1/2 INCH VIDEO CASSETTE
Covers woodworking tools such as handsaws, crosscut saws, ripsaws, special purpose saws, planes, scrapers, drills and others.
From The Using Hand Tools Series.
Prod-TPCTRA Dist-TPCTRA

Woodworking--A Series

Presents advice by an English craftsman on woodworking.
Prod-ANVICO Dist-ANVICO

Basic Tools	088 MIN
Doretails	080 MIN
Finishing And Polishing	080 MIN
Hinging, Clamping And Screwing	074 MIN
Mortice And Tenon-Dados	056 MIN
Preparation Of Surfaces (Plaining)	063 MIN
Sharpening-Inlaying And Detailing	086 MIN

Woodworking--A Series
A
Tells how to use basic woodworking techniques.
Prod-VISIN Dist-VISIN

Creative Sculpturing For Everyone, Pt 1	013 MIN
Creative Sculpturing For Everyone, Pt 2	013 MIN
Dovetail Fixture, The	013 MIN
How To Hang A Door	013 MIN
How To Use Chisels And Gouges	013 MIN
How To Use Hammers	013 MIN
How To Use Hand Boring Tools	013 MIN
How To Use Measuring Tools	013 MIN
How To Use Planes	013 MIN
How To Use Saws	013 MIN
Router, The	013 MIN

Woody Allen - An American Comedy C 33 MIN
3/4 INCH VIDEO CASSETTE J-C A
Presents Woody Allen talking about his life and work as a writer, dramatist and filmmaker and discusses his creative sources, theoretical approaches and working methods. Shows scenes from some of his major films, including Take The Money And Run, Sleeper, Love And Death and Annie Hall.
LC NO. 77-701974
Prod-FOTH Dist-FOTH 1977

Woody Guthrie C 52 MIN
3/4 OR 1/2 INCH VIDEO CASSETTE
Features a solo performance by Pete Seeger in which he sings some of the hundreds of songs composed by Woody Guthrie. Includes film and photos of Woody.
From The Rainbow Quest Series.
Prod-SEEGER Dist-CWATER

Woody Vasulka - Artifacts C 23 MIN
3/4 OR 1/2 INCH VIDEO CASSETTE
Presented by Woody Vasulka.
Prod-ARTINC Dist-ARTINC

Woody Vasulka - The Commission C 45 MIN
3/4 OR 1/2 INCH VIDEO CASSETTE
Employs an operatic form to tell the story of a 19th century commission offered to the violinist Niccolo Paganini.
Prod-ARTINC Dist-ARTINC

Wool In Australia C 19 MIN
16MM FILM, 3/4 OR 1/2 IN VIDEO P-C
Describes life in an isolated area of Australia and the living conditions of a family who raise sheep. Tells how the sheep are sheared, the wool is sorted, graded, baled and shipped to a market in Melbourne or Sydney to be auctioned to buyers from all over the world.
From The Man And His World Series.
Prod-FI Dist-FI 1969

Woonspe (Education And The Sioux) C 28 MIN
3/4 INCH VIDEO CASSETTE
Discusses the problems of Native American education. Examines the history and pros and cons of the four school systems available - BIA boarding schools, public schools, tribal contract schools and mission schools. Also available in two-inch quad and one-inch videotape.
Prod-SDETV Dist-NAMPBC

Word Analysis Skills C 20 MIN
16MM FILM, 3/4 OR 1/2 IN VIDEO T
Focuses on literacy instruction techniques involving the development of word analysis skills to facilitate reading fluency and comprehension. Includes the use of formal diagnostic procedures to determine the student's instructional needs and a case study of a man who is seeking to improve his reading skills.
From The Literacy Instructor Training Series.
LC NO. 80-706062
Prod-IU Dist-IU 1978

Word Arithmetic C 20 MIN
2 INCH VIDEOTAPE P
See series title for descriptive statement.
From The Learning Our Language, Unit IV - Speaking And Spelling Series.
Prod-MPATI Dist-GPITVL

Word Elements C 11 MIN
3/4 OR 1/2 INCH VIDEO CASSETTE
See series title for descriptive statement.
From The Better Spelling Series. Lesson 3A
Prod-TELSTR Dist-DELTAK

Word Families / Compound Words C 19 MIN
1/2 IN VIDEO CASSETTE BETA/VHS
Teaches basic vocabulary skills. Uses stories and visuals to show how words are formed.
Prod-BFA Dist-BFA

Word Feathers--A Series
P
A series of 32 videocassettes. Emphasizes skills for beginning readers, offering information on consonants and vowels, word sounds, compound words, word endings, poetry, and other topics.
Prod-KYTV Dist-AITECH 1979

Word From Our Sponsor C 4 MIN
16MM FILM OPTICAL SOUND H-C A
Presents the role of the television commercial in modern love life.
Prod-UWFKD Dist-UWFKD

Word Gets Around C 18 MIN
16MM FILM OPTICAL SOUND
Follows three Maryknoll missionaries over a 24-hour period as they visit an isolated village in northern Nicaragua.
LC NO. 75-700496
Prod-MARYFA Dist-MARYFA Prodn-NOWAKA 1974

Word Grouping Road C 20 MIN
3/4 OR 1/2 INCH VIDEO CASSETTE
Demonstrates how to read groups of words to help structure the author's main idea.
From The Efficient Reading - Instructional Tapes Series. Tape 9
Prod-TELSTR Dist-TELSTR

Word Is Out C 45 MIN
16MM FILM OPTICAL SOUND
A shortened version of the motion picture Word Is Out. Chronicles what it's like to be a homosexual. Presents interviews with gay men and lesbians of various life-styles, races, ages, and socio-economic backgrounds.
Prod-UNKNWN Dist-NYFLMS 1978

Word Is Out C 130 MIN
16MM FILM OPTICAL SOUND
Chronicles what it's like to be a homosexual. Presents interviews with gay men and lesbians of various life-styles, races, ages, and socio-economic backgrounds.
Prod-UNKNWN Dist-NYFLMS 1978

Word Magic (2nd Ed)--A Series
P
Prod-CVETVC Dist-GPITVL

Act It Out	15 MIN
All By Yourself	15 MIN
Big Brother Telephone	15 MIN
Book Fair, The	15 MIN
Dance-A-Story	15 MIN
Do Animals Communicate	15 MIN
Do You Have A Hobby	15 MIN
Famous People	15 MIN
Gift For You, A	15 MIN
Good Sentence, A	15 MIN
Let's Look Back	15 MIN
Look And See	15 MIN
Marionettes	15 MIN
Mind Your Manners	15 MIN
Occupational Communication	15 MIN
Off To See The Dentist	15 MIN
Poetry For You	15 MIN
Puppets Are Fun	15 MIN
Share To Communicate	15 MIN
Story Starters	15 MIN
Trip Through Imagination, A	15 MIN
Use Your Ears	15 MIN
Where Do We Get Them	15 MIN
Words, Words, Words	15 MIN
Writing A Letter	15 MIN
Writing A Story	15 MIN
Your Body Speaks	15 MIN
Your Face Speaks	15 MIN
Your Voice Speaks	15 MIN
Your Voice, Your Eyes, Your Story	15 MIN

Word Order, The Pause And The Importance Of Meaning C 15 MIN
3/4 OR 1/2 INCH VIDEO CASSETTE
Discusses the use and implications of altered or unusual work sequences, double entendres, timing of words, pauses and accentuations.
From The Treatment Of The Borderline Patient Series.
Prod-HEMUL Dist-HEMUL

Word Origins C 15 MIN
2 INCH VIDEOTAPE I
Relates the stories behind names, phrases and other words and examines Greek and Latin root words.
From The Images Series.
Prod-CVETVC Dist-GPITVL

Word Parade, The B 20 MIN
2 INCH VIDEOTAPE P
Explores the beauty and variety in the English language. (Broadcast quality)
From The Language Lane Series. Lesson 7
Prod-CVETVC Dist-GPITVL Prodn-WCVETV

Word Play C 15 MIN
3/4 OR 1/2 INCH VIDEO CASSETTE P
See series title for descriptive statement.
From The Strawberry Square II - Take Time Series.
Prod-NEITV Dist-AITECH 1984

Word Power - Vocabulary Building--A Series

Presents a program for building word skills, increasing ability to read more rapidly and with more word knowledge, leading to successful writing and speaking, and encouraging faster learning, more productive work and clearer thinking. Includes a pre-test and a post-test, Tachistoscope exercises, a student

workbook and study guide, a student word power game and a student text.
Prod-TELSTR Dist-DELTAK

Be Brief 030 MIN
Be Concrete 030 MIN
Be Lively 030 MIN
Be Orderly 030 MIN
Be Personal 030 MIN
Be Poetic 030 MIN
Be Simple 030 MIN
Be Tactful 030 MIN

Word Power Workouts, Tape 1 C 30 MIN
3/4 OR 1/2 INCH VIDEO CASSETTE
Focuses on increasing fluency through working with antonyms. Shows tachistoscopic flashes of 20 digits with the shutter speed set at one tenths of a second.
From The Efficient Reading - Expediter Tapes Series.
Prod-TELSTR Dist-TELSTR

Word Power Workouts, Tape 10 C 30 MIN
3/4 OR 1/2 INCH VIDEO CASSETTE
Focuses on the LDE Formula for word power workouts. Uses geometric forms as perception promoters.
From The Efficient Reading - Expediter Tapes Series.
Prod-TELSTR Dist-TELSTR

Word Power Workouts, Tape 11 C 30 MIN
3/4 OR 1/2 INCH VIDEO CASSETTE
Studies roots of words in order to increase word power. Looks at span developers as perception promoters.
From The Efficient Reading - Expediter Tapes Series.
Prod-TELSTR Dist-TELSTR

Word Power Workouts, Tape 12 C 30 MIN
3/4 OR 1/2 INCH VIDEO CASSETTE
Focuses on word suffixes in order to increase word power and speed. Uses digits at 1/100 a second for perception promoters.
From The Efficient Reading - Expediter Tapes Series.
Prod-TELSTR Dist-TELSTR

Word Power Workouts, Tape 2 C 30 MIN
3/4 OR 1/2 INCH VIDEO CASSETTE
Discusses how to increase fluency through working with synonyms. Shows how to look at words in phrase groups to increase speed.
From The Efficient Reading - Expediter Tapes Series.
Prod-TELSTR Dist-TELSTR

Word Power Workouts, Tape 3 C 30 MIN
3/4 OR 1/2 INCH VIDEO CASSETTE
Shows how to increase word power by use of contextual clues. Discusses geometric forms.
From The Efficient Reading - Expediter Tapes Series.
Prod-TELSTR Dist-TELSTR

Word Power Workouts, Tape 4 C 30 MIN
3/4 OR 1/2 INCH VIDEO CASSETTE
Focuses on understanding the word-meaning in a sentence. Looks at digits as perception promoters.
From The Efficient Reading - Expediter Tapes Series.
Prod-TELSTR Dist-TELSTR

Word Power Workouts, Tape 5 C 30 MIN
3/4 OR 1/2 INCH VIDEO CASSETTE
Covers finding the right meaning when reading. Looks at span developers, or spreading out what the eye takes in, as perception promoters.
From The Efficient Reading - Expediter Tapes Series.
Prod-TELSTR Dist-TELSTR

Word Power Workouts, Tape 6 C 30 MIN
3/4 OR 1/2 INCH VIDEO CASSETTE
Discusses how to use the context of a passage for comprehension. Presents sentences as perception promoters.
From The Efficient Reading - Expediter Tapes Series.
Prod-TELSTR Dist-TELSTR

Word Power Workouts, Tape 7 C 30 MIN
3/4 OR 1/2 INCH VIDEO CASSETTE
Focuses on word parts, how to look for meaning and the prefix 'ex.' Covers digits as perception promoters.
From The Efficient Reading - Expediter Tapes Series.
Prod-TELSTR Dist-TELSTR

Word Power Workouts, Tape 8 C 30 MIN
3/4 OR 1/2 INCH VIDEO CASSETTE
Focuses on the prefix 'pre-.' Looks at span developers as perception promoters.
From The Efficient Reading - Expediter Tapes Series.
Prod-TELSTR Dist-TELSTR

Word Power Workouts, Tape 9 C 30 MIN
3/4 OR 1/2 INCH VIDEO CASSETTE
Uses the prefix 'de' to improve word power. Studies how to read complete sentences for speed.
From The Efficient Reading - Expediter Tapes Series.
Prod-TELSTR Dist-TELSTR

Word Processing C
16MM FILM OPTICAL SOUND
Introduces vital concepts and skills required in word processing, describes on-the-job settings, and contains personal statements, which convey the excitement and challenge of the word processing environment. Takes a close look at the equipment of a word processing center, and shows how a central dictating system works.
Prod-HBJ Dist-HBJ

Word Processing - Communication And Technology C
3/4 OR 1/2 INCH VIDEO CASSETTE
Discusses word processing and computer use.
From The Computer Literacy/Computer Language Series.
Prod-LIBFSC Dist-LIBFSC

Word Processing - With Microcomputers C
3/4 OR 1/2 INCH VIDEO CASSETTE
Presents the possibilities for doing word processing with microcomputers.
Prod-LIBFSC Dist-LIBFSC

Word Processing In Office Systems C 30 MIN
3/4 OR 1/2 INCH VIDEO CASSETTE H-C A
Discusses the application of computer technology to the production of written communications needed by business and industry. Compares the different types of word processing equipment in terms of display and output methods, storage and access methods, and text editing and formatting capabilities. Discusses the factors affecting successful implementation of a system and looks at some future applications of computer technology to office systems.
From The Making It Count Series.
LC NO. 80-707582
Prod-BCSC Dist-BCSC 1980

Word Processing On Your Microcomputer - From Keyboard To Printout C
3/4 OR 1/2 INCH VIDEO CASSETTE
Familiarizes with the general applications and techniques of word processing programs. Explores several common editing commands and the interrelationship between word processors and dictionary, mail-merge and communications software.
Prod-GA Dist-GA 1984

Word Selection To Identify Sensory Impressions B 30 MIN
2 INCH VIDEOTAPE J-H
Gives practice in selecting words that best convey sensory impressions. (Broadcast quality)
From The English Composition Series. Description
Prod-GRETVO Dist-GPITVL Prodn-KUHTTV

Word Shop—A Series
P
Deals with developing language skills. Focuses on such skills as listening, interpreting, visualizing, speaking, reading, dramatizing, illustrating and writing. Features host John Robbins and his puppets.
Prod-WETATV Dist-WETATV

Action In Stories 015 MIN
Books About Animals 015 MIN
Books About Fantasy 015 MIN
Books About People 015 MIN
Books About Places 015 MIN
Books That Answer Questions 015 MIN
Character Playing 015 MIN
Characters In Stories 015 MIN
Comic Strips 015 MIN
Fantasy Stories 015 MIN
Folk Tales 015 MIN
Making A Book 015 MIN
Mystery Books 015 MIN
Mystery Stories 015 MIN
News Stories 015 MIN
Nonsense And Made-Up Words In Poetry 015 MIN
Playwrights 015 MIN
Poems As Descriptions 015 MIN
Poems As Rhythm 015 MIN
Poems As Sounds 015 MIN
Poems As Stories 015 MIN
Poets 015 MIN
Scene Playing 015 MIN
Setting In Stories 015 MIN
Signs 015 MIN
Story Maker 015 MIN
Story Playing 015 MIN
Story Telling 015 MIN
Structure In Stories 015 MIN
Tall Tales 015 MIN

Word Strategy C
3/4 OR 1/2 INCH VIDEO CASSETTE C
Shows common abuses of words with a continuation of a previous lesson.
From The Write Course - An Introduction To College Composition Series.
Prod-DALCCD Dist-DALCCD

Word Strategy C 30 MIN
3/4 OR 1/2 INCH VIDEO CASSETTE C A
Emphasizes common abuses of words.
From The Write Course - An Introduction To College Composition Series.
Prod-FI Dist-FI 1984

Word Surprises C 20 MIN
2 INCH VIDEOTAPE P
See series title for descriptive statement.
From The Learning Our Language, Unit IV - Speaking And Spelling Series.
Prod-MPATI Dist-GPITVL

Word To The Wise, A C 11 MIN
3/4 OR 1/2 INCH VIDEO CASSETTE H-C A
Addresses consumer questions such as how to choose a dentist, how to reduce dental bills and how to buy oral health products.
Prod-AMDA Dist-AMDA 1980

Word To The Wise, A C 14 MIN
16MM FILM - 3/4 IN VIDEO
Treats common consumer questions related to dentistry, including how to choose a dentist, how to reduce bills, how to handle disagreements with a dentist and what oral health products to buy. Close-captioned.
Prod-AMDA Dist-MTP

Word Weaving - The Art Of Story Telling C 25 MIN
3/4 OR 1/2 INCH VIDEO CASSETTE
Follows a teacher as she learns techniques for story telling. Observes her telling stories to elementary students.
Prod-PUBEYE Dist-UCEMC

Word Wise - Antonyms C 12 MIN
16MM FILM, 3/4 OR 1/2 IN VIDEO P-I
Tells the story of the search for the missing Professor Updown in the Antonyms, where all the animals talk in antonyms.
From The Vocabulary Skills Series.
Prod-BFA Dist-PHENIX Prodn-BEAN 1977

Word Wise - Compound Words C 10 MIN
16MM FILM, 3/4 OR 1/2 IN VIDEO P-I
Uses the story of a canoe trip to teach the concept of compound words.
From The Vocabulary Skills Series.
Prod-BFA Dist-PHENIX Prodn-BEAN 1976

Word Wise - Homographs C 12 MIN
16MM FILM, 3/4 OR 1/2 IN VIDEO P-I
Tells the story of Joey Patterson, by who seeks a solution to an attack on Australia by words that are spelled alike but have different meanings, called homographs.
From The Vocabulary Skills Series.
Prod-BFA Dist-PHENIX Prodn-BEAN 1977

Word Wise - Homonyms C 11 MIN
16MM FILM, 3/4 OR 1/2 IN VIDEO P-I
Tells the story of Daisy Daring, who finds a book of secret homonym passwords that if used correctly will lead her to the sunken city of Homonym Bay. Includes Caribbean scenery and underwater photography.
From The Vocabulary Skills Series.
Prod-BFA Dist-PHENIX Prodn-BEAN 1977

Word Wise - Prefixes C 11 MIN
16MM FILM, 3/4 OR 1/2 IN VIDEO P-I
Presents 15 prefixes in a story of a forgetful secret service agent who forgets the secret code, a prefix he must use to identify himself to his fellow agent.
From The Vocabulary Skills Series.
Prod-BFA Dist-PHENIX Prodn-BEAN 1976

Word Wise - Root Words C 12 MIN
16MM FILM, 3/4 OR 1/2 IN VIDEO P-I
Follows the adventures of a spaceman disguised as an Earthling as he attempts to learn about root or base words. Presents 20 root or base words, forming more than 44 different words.
From The Vocabulary Skills Series.
Prod-BFA Dist-PHENIX Prodn-BEAN 1976

Word Wise - Suffixes C 12 MIN
16MM FILM, 3/4 OR 1/2 IN VIDEO P-I
Tells the Great Suffix Mystery about what happens when all the suffixes disappear from our language. Presents 13 suffixes and basic rules for affixing them to words.
From The Vocabulary Skills Series.
Prod-BFA Dist-PHENIX Prodn-BEAN 1976

Word Wise - Synonyms C 13 MIN
16MM FILM, 3/4 OR 1/2 IN VIDEO P-I
Tells the story of Colonel Daring and his search for Lord and Lady Synonym to find out how the Synonym diamond is like a synonym.
From The Vocabulary Skills Series.
Prod-BFA Dist-PHENIX Prodn-BEAN 1977

Word Wise - Word Families C 9 MIN
16MM FILM, 3/4 OR 1/2 IN VIDEO P-I
Introduces the concept of families of words which have the same ending letters. Provides an understanding of how words are put together and offers aids in rapid word recognition.
From The Vocabulary Skills Series.
Prod-BFA Dist-PHENIX Prodn-BEAN 1976

Wordless Books C 30 MIN
1/2 IN VIDEO CASSETTE BETA/VHS K-I
See series title for descriptive statement.
From The Jump Over The Moon - Sharing Literature With Young Children Series.
Prod-HRAW Dist-HRAW

Wordly Wise C 14 MIN
16MM FILM, 3/4 OR 1/2 IN VIDEO P
Focuses on the many ways in which life is made up of words.
From The Serendipity Series.
Prod-MGHT Dist-MGHT 1976

Words B 10 MIN
16MM FILM OPTICAL SOUND I-H
Stresses the importance of understanding words and gives ways to develop a wider vocabulary.
From The Cues To Reading Series.
Prod-CBF Dist-AVED 1958

Words C 10 MIN
3/4 OR 1/2 INCH VIDEO CASSETTE
See series title for descriptive statement.
From The Janaki Series.
Prod-WGBHTV Dist-PUBTEL

Words C 14 MIN
16MM FILM, 3/4 OR 1/2 IN VIDEO K-I
Shows children working with a teacher and making letters and words with their bodies, brainstorming words for alliterative sentences, pantomiming words, using words as inspirations for stories, composing cinquains and visiting a printer to have their cinquain realized in type.
From The Joy Of Writing Series.
Prod-CF Dist-CF 1977

Words - They Come And Go C 30 MIN
3/4 OR 1/2 INCH VIDEO CASSETTE C

See series title for descriptive statement.
From The Language And Meaning Series.
Prod-WUSFTV Dist-GPITVL 1983

Words About Herbs C 29 MIN
3/4 INCH VIDEO CASSETTE
Shows how to plant, maintain and use an herb garden.
From The House Botanist Series.
Prod-UMITV Dist-UMITV 1978

Words And Ideas C 6 MIN
16MM FILM OPTICAL SOUND K-I
Outlines several familiar objects, producing circles, to encourage the learning of the relationship between geometric shapes and concrete objects.
Prod-SF Dist-SF 1968

Words And Labels B 23 MIN
16MM FILM OPTICAL SOUND
Points out that one important aspect of television communications is the written word and that there are many techniques for showing printing and writing on the screen. Considers the best method generally available, particularly from the viewpoints of the presenter and director.
From The CETO Television Training Films Series.
Prod-CETO Dist-GPITVL

Words And Meaning C
3/4 OR 1/2 INCH VIDEO CASSETTE C
Supplies a heightened awareness of words as a stylistic device and an increased sense of the finer points of style.
From The Write Course - An Introduction To College Composition Series.
Prod-DALCCD Dist-DALCCD

Words And Meanings C 30 MIN
3/4 OR 1/2 INCH VIDEO CASSETTE C A
Emphasizes a heightened awareness of style.
From The Write Course - An Introduction To College Composition Series.
Prod-FI Dist-FI 1984

Words And More Words C 15 MIN
3/4 OR 1/2 INCH VIDEO CASSETTE T
Uses the adventures of a pirate and his three friends to explore the many facets of language arts. Focuses on verbs and adverbs, and shows what they are and how they are used in oral and written expression.
From The Hidden Treasures Series. No. 15
LC NO. 82-706555
Prod-WCVETV Dist-GPITVL 1980

Words And Music B 15 MIN
2 INCH VIDEOTAPE K-P
Emphasizes that the song has carefully chosen words which, set to music, convey a thought, a meaning and a moment of pleasure through both participation and listening. (Broadcast quality)
From The Magic Of Words Series.
Prod-GWTVAI Dist-GPITVL Prodn-WETATV

Words And Music C 29 MIN
3/4 INCH VIDEO CASSETTE
Discusses the importance of the right word fitting the write sounds.
From The Song Writer Series.
Prod-UMITV Dist-UMITV 1977

Words And Pictures—A Series
16MM FILM, 3/4 OR 1/2 IN VIDEO K-P
Presents fairy tales designed to improve reading and vocabulary skills.
Prod-FI Dist-FI

Frog And Toad Together 015 MIN
I Am Better Than You 015 MIN
Letter, The 015 MIN
Little Girl And The Tiny Doll, The 015 MIN
Monkey And The Crocodile, The 015 MIN
Too Much Noise 015 MIN
Who Took The Farmer's Noise 015 MIN

Words And Place—A Series

Captures the complex oral traditions of the Southwestern American Indian. Explores the mythology and rituals of the Indian universe where words and place possess symbolic and time honored significance.
Prod-CWATER Dist-CWATER

By This Song I Walk - Navajo Song 025 MIN
Conversation With Vine Deloria, Jr, A 029 MIN
Iisaw - Hopi Coyote Stories 018 MIN
Natwaniwa - A Hopi Philosophical Statement 027 MIN
Origin Of The Crown Dance - An Apache 040 MIN
Running On The Edge Of The Rainbow - Laguna 028 MIN
Seyewailo - The Flower World 051 MIN
Songs Of My Hunter Heart - Laguna Songs And 034 MIN

Words And Symbols C 19 MIN
3/4 OR 1/2 INCH VIDEO CASSETTE J-H
Shows students in everyday situations where their problems can be solved by using mathematics. Key words are identified which will enable students to decide which operation to use in order to solve a given problem.
From The Reading Approach To Math Series.
Prod-WNVT Dist-GPITVL 1979

Words And Their Meaning B 32 MIN
16MM FILM OPTICAL SOUND H T
Shows the deficiencies of word-for-word translation. Discusses how the meanings of words change with usage. Demonstrates in a French class for English speakers how words are taught in meaningful contexts and how ranges of meanings are developed appropriately.
From The Principles And Methods Of Teaching A Second Language Series.
Prod-MLAA Dist-IU Prodn-RAY 1962

Words Are Important C 15 MIN
2 INCH VIDEOTAPE I
Examines the dictionary and its features. Shows a copy of Samuel Johnson's dictionary.
From The Images Series.
Prod-CVETVC Dist-GPITVL

Words Make The Difference C 20 MIN
2 INCH VIDEOTAPE P
See series title for descriptive statement.
From The Learning Our Language, Unit 1 - Listening Skills Series.
Prod-MPATI Dist-GPITVL

Words Of Fire C 20 MIN
3/4 OR 1/2 INCH VIDEO CASSETTE H-C A
Offers dramatizations of the words of Samuel Adams, Thomas Paine, Patrick Henry, James Rivington and Benjamin Franklin, as well as from the Declaration of Independence and the Constitution.
From The American Literature Series.
LC NO. 83-706250
Prod-AUBU Dist-AITECH 1983

Words Of Life, People Of Rivers C 30 MIN
3/4 INCH VIDEO CASSETTE
Discusses the value of land and water to the Indian.
From The Real People Series.
Prod-KSPSTV Dist-GPITVL 1976

Words Of Love C 5 MIN
3/4 OR 1/2 INCH VIDEO CASSETTE C A
Looks into heterosexual bedrooms and provides a quick and delightful show-and-tell-lesson on anatomy and sexual activity.
Prod-MMRC Dist-MMRC

Words Of The Language C
3/4 OR 1/2 INCH VIDEO CASSETTE
Defines identifier and data type, identifying the two categories of data types in 'C' language. Describes the difference between literal and symbolic constants and the categories of key words in a 'C' language program.
From The 'C' Language Programming Series.
Prod-COMTEG Dist-COMTEG

Words That Work C 30 MIN
3/4 OR 1/2 INCH VIDEO CASSETTE
See series title for descriptive statement.
From The Your Speaking Image - When Women Talk Business Series.
Prod-WHATV Dist-DELTAK

Words Words Words C 10 MIN
16MM FILM OPTICAL SOUND K
Illustrates language, communication and association of letter sounds with words as seen through the eyes of an animated boy.
From The Amazing Life Game Theater Series.
LC NO. 72-701741
Prod-HMC Dist-HMC 1971

Words 1 C 30 MIN
3/4 OR 1/2 INCH VIDEO CASSETTE C
See series title for descriptive statement.
From The Writing For A Reason Series.
Prod-DALCCD Dist-DALCCD

Words 2 C 30 MIN
3/4 OR 1/2 INCH VIDEO CASSETTE C
See series title for descriptive statement.
From The Writing For A Reason Series.
Prod-DALCCD Dist-DALCCD

Words, Words, Words C 15 MIN
2 INCH VIDEOTAPE P
Provides an enrichment program in the communitive arts area utilizing words.
From The Word Magic (2nd Ed) Series.
Prod-CVETVC Dist-GPITVL

Words, Words, Words C 15 MIN
3/4 OR 1/2 INCH VIDEO CASSETTE I
Introduces writing as a building process and investigates words as tools for individual expression.
From The Zebra Wings Series.
Prod-NITC Dist-AITECH Prodn-MAETEL 1975

Words, Words, Words C 30 MIN
3/4 OR 1/2 INCH VIDEO CASSETTE T
Uses interviews and candid classroom scenes to show how innovative teachers are employing word recognition and vocabulary-building exercises to help children learn to read.
From The Reading Is Power Series. No. 4
LC NO. 81-707519
Prod-NYCBED Dist-GPITVL 1981

Wordsmith—A Series
I
focuses on standard vocabulary development, incorporating terms from specialized vocabularies and from foreign languages and slang.
Prod-NITC Dist-AITECH Prodn-KLCSTV 1975

Module Blue - Body I 15 MIN
Module Blue - Body II 15 MIN
Module Blue - Fire 15 MIN
Module Blue - Looking 15 MIN
Module Blue - Sound 15 MIN
Module Brown - Leading 15 MIN
Module Brown - Nature 15 MIN
Module Brown - Position 15 MIN
Module Brown - Transportation I 15 MIN
Module Brown - Transportation II 15 MIN
Module Green - Numbers I 15 MIN
Module Green - Numbers II 15 MIN
Module Green - Numbers III 15 MIN
Module Green - Walk And Run 15 MIN
Module Green - Water 15 MIN
Module Orange - Communication 15 MIN
Module Orange - Connection 15 MIN
Module Orange - Measure And Metrics 15 MIN
Module Orange - Relatives 15 MIN
Module Orange - Twist And Turn 15 MIN
Module Red - Animals I 15 MIN
Module Red - Animals II 15 MIN
Module Red - Cutting 15 MIN
Module Red - Serendipity 15 MIN
Module Red - Time 15 MIN
Module Yellow - Food 15 MIN
Module Yellow - Form 15 MIN
Module Yellow - Potpourri 15 MIN
Module Yellow - Size 15 MIN
Module Yellow - Talking 15 MIN

Wordstar C
3/4 OR 1/2 INCH VIDEO CASSETTE
Illustrates the overall concept of word processing and the basic text editing function of WordStar. Shows how to open a document file, set margins and tabs, find and replace and do general text editing. Shows how to mark, copy, move and delete blocks of text, or paragraphs.
Prod-LANSFD Dist-ANDRST

Wordsworth's Lake Country - Image Of Man And Nature C 20 MIN
16MM FILM OPTICAL SOUND J-C
Presents scenes of Dove Cottage, Duddon Valley, Cokermouth, Grasmere and Lakeland scenery in the England lake country and portrays the influence of these settings on Wordsworth as a romantic poet.
LC NO. 75-713540
Prod-PERFET Dist-PERFET 1971

Wordworks, The, Pt 01 C 11 MIN
16MM FILM OPTICAL SOUND P
Uses animation and live action to present lessons for the beginning reader. Focuses on beginning letter-sound associations for F, M, B, T, N and D, as well as the high-frequency words 'a' and 'to.'
LC NO. 74-703086
Prod-ALGC Dist-HMC 1974

Wordworks, The, Pt 02 C 10 MIN
16MM FILM OPTICAL SOUND P
Uses animation and live action to present lessons for the beginning reader. Focuses on beginning letter-sound associations for P, W, C and S, and high-frequency words, such as 'is,' 'go,' 'I' and 'in.'
LC NO. 74-703087
Prod-ALGC Dist-HMC 1974

Wordworks, The, Pt 03 C 11 MIN
16MM FILM OPTICAL SOUND P
Uses animation and live action to present lessons for the beginning reader. Focuses on beginning letter-sound associations for L, R, Y, Wh, H and K, and the high-frequency words 'he,' 'we,' 'on,' 'will' and 'not.'
LC NO. 74-703088
Prod-ALGC Dist-HMC 1974

Wordworks, The, Pt 04 C 10 MIN
16MM FILM OPTICAL SOUND P
Uses animation and live action to present lessons for the beginning reader. Focuses on beginning letter-sound associations for V and the clusters Ch, Th and Sh, as well as the high-frequency words 'the,' 'and' and 'you.'
LC NO. 74-703090
Prod-ALGC Dist-HMC 1974

Wordworks, The, Pt 05 C 10 MIN
16MM FILM OPTICAL SOUND P
Uses animation and live action to present lessons for the beginning reader. Focuses on letter-sound associations for words ending in Z, S and ing, the clusters st and tr, the phonograms at and an, and examples of the comma to show address.
LC NO. 74-703091
Prod-ALGC Dist-HMC 1974

Wordworks, The, Pt 06 C 9 MIN
16MM FILM OPTICAL SOUND P
Uses animation and live action to present lessons for 'ay,' 'ee,' 'oa,' and for the use of C to attain an S sound. Explains using Y as a vowel and discusses words with more than one meaning.
LC NO. 74-703092
Prod-ALGC Dist-HMC 1974

Wordworks, The, Pt 07 C 9 MIN
16MM FILM OPTICAL SOUND P
Uses animation and live action to present lessons for the beginning reader. Focuses on compound words, 'all' and 'ake' sounds, words ending in 'er' and verbs ending in 'ed.'
LC NO. 74-703093
Prod-ALGC Dist-HMC 1974

Wordworks, The, Pt 08 C 10 MIN
16MM FILM OPTICAL SOUND P
Uses animation and live action to present lessons for the beginning reader. Focuses on sound association for 'oo,' the word endings 'en' and 'ly,' the clusters Bl and Br and the phonograms 'et' and 'old.'
LC NO. 74-703094
Prod-ALGC Dist-HMC 1974

Wordworks, The, Pt 09 C 10 MIN
16MM FILM OPTICAL SOUND P
Uses animation and live action to present lessons for the beginning reader. Focuses on sound association for A, 'ee' and G, the prefixes 'be' and A, and the common syllables 'un' and 'ful.'
LC NO. 74-703095
Prod-ALGC Dist-HMC 1974

Wordworks, The, Pt 10 C 10 MIN
16MM FILM OPTICAL SOUND P
Uses animation and live action to present lessons for the beginning reader. Focuses on sound association for I, O, U, Kn and mb, the clusters Qu and Squ, words with more than one meaning, and following directions.
LC NO. 74-703096
Prod-ALGC Dist-HMC 1974

Work C 15 MIN
2 INCH VIDEOTAPE P
Shows how the rate of doing work is determined by the rate the energy is transferred.
From The Science Is Searching Series.
Prod-DETPS Dist-GPITVL

Work C 15 MIN
3/4 OR 1/2 INCH VIDEO CASSETTE K-P
Deals with French-American culture. Focuses on the theme of pride in work.
From The La Bonne Aventure Series.
Prod-MPBN Dist-GPITVL

Work C 30 MIN
3/4 INCH VIDEO CASSETTE
Discusses work-related problems that may occur at mid-life.
From The Transitions - Caught At Midlife Series.
Prod-UMITV Dist-UMITV 1980

Work - Coping With The Twenty Hour Week C 20 MIN
16MM FILM, 3/4 OR 1/2 IN VIDEO
Predicts that in the future work will be redefined and work weeks will be shorter. Explains that new priorities will be needed to cope with this situation.
Prod-DOCUA Dist-CNEMAG

Work - Don't Let Your Attitude Intrude—A Series
H T
Shows the putting together of programs telling how to seek employment, and group discussions on employment techniques. Includes a musical, skits and a documentary.
Prod-USDL Dist-USNAC

Work - Don't Let Your Attitude Intrude
Work - Don't Let Your Attitude Intrude 018 MIN
Work - Don't Let Your Attitude Intrude (Skits) 021 MIN

Work - Don't Let Your Attitude Intrude (Musical) C 40 MIN
3/4 OR 1/2 INCH VIDEO CASSETTE H T
Presents a musical that shows how to seek employment.
From The Work - Don't Let Your Attitude Intrude Series.
Prod-USDL Dist-USNAC

Work - Don't Let Your Attitude Intrude (Documentary) C 18 MIN
3/4 OR 1/2 INCH VIDEO CASSETTE
Presents a documentary explaining what is involved in putting together a program telling how to seek employment and right and wrong job-seeking techniques.
From The Work - Don't Let Your Attitude Intrude Series.
Prod-USDL Dist-USNAC

Work - Don't Let Your Attitude Intrude (Skits) C 21 MIN
3/4 OR 1/2 INCH VIDEO CASSETTE H T
Shows skits that tell how to seek employment and use group discussions to determine the right and wrong job-seeking techniques.
From The Work - Don't Let Your Attitude Intrude Series.
Prod-USDL Dist-USNAC

Work - The New Discipline C 24 MIN
16MM FILM, 3/4 OR 1/2 IN VIDEO
Employs location filming in modern factories, workshops and museums to illustrate the social history of work. Uses a case study of the continuing struggle of the metal working and engineering trades in England begun in the late 19th and early 20th centuries and continuing to the 1980s.
Prod-OPENU Dist-MEDIAG Prodn-BBCTV 1981

Work And Energy B 45 MIN
2 INCH VIDEOTAPE C
See series title for descriptive statement.
From The Physical Science Series. Unit 4 - Motion, Work And Energy
Prod-CHITVC Dist-GPITVL Prodn-WTTWTV

Work And Fulfillment C 59 MIN
3/4 OR 1/2 INCH VIDEO CASSETTE H-C A
Discusses what the American Dream means to the old and the young. Examines changing values about work, money, education, business and success.
From The Young And Old - Reaching Out Series.
LC NO. 80-707181
Prod-CRFI Dist-PBS 1979

Work And Retirement C 21 MIN
16MM FILM - 3/4 IN VIDEO
Looks at historical achievement of a society that can afford retirement for its workers. Discusses the importance for some older citizens to continue working.
From The Aging In The Future Series.
Prod-UMICH Dist-UMITV 1981

Work And You - Do You Know What You Want C 18 MIN
16MM FILM, 3/4 OR 1/2 IN VIDEO H-C A
Explores the reasons people must work and points out that career decisions should be based on careful and thoughtful investigation. Illustrates the factors to be considered when choosing a career.
From The Work And You Series.
Prod-SAIF Dist-BARR 1976

Work And You—A Series
16MM FILM, 3/4 OR 1/2 IN VIDEO J-C
Discusses the various factors which young people must consider when making decisions about employment.
Prod-SAIF Dist-BARR

I Want To Work For Your Company 011 MIN
Interview Film, The 021 MIN
What Is Business 010 MIN
Work And You 018 MIN
Work Prejudice Film, The 013 MIN
Your New Job 010 MIN

Work By Ante Bozanich C 31 MIN
3/4 OR 1/2 INCH VIDEO CASSETTE
Presents work by Yugoslavian born video artist Ante Bozanich.
Prod-EAI Dist-EAI

Work Communications C 19 MIN
3/4 OR 1/2 INCH VIDEO CASSETTE H
Tells how Roland can't get along with his foreman and then becomes a foreman himself. Shows that he is a terrible boss until he begins working on his communication skills.
From The Jobs - Seeking, Finding, Keeping Series.
Prod-MSDOE Dist-AITECH 1980

Work Crisis, The C 30 MIN
16MM FILM OPTICAL SOUND J-H T R
Documentary study of the effects of technological development on work and leisure. Explores the biblical meaning of work and the necessity of dignity of the individual in an increasingly automated work world.
LC NO. FIA67-5756
Prod-FAMF Dist-FAMF 1967

Work Environment C 19 MIN
3/4 OR 1/2 INCH VIDEO CASSETTE H
Presents people from many kinds of work talking about their jobs, the importance of on-the-job surroundings, and the need for new workers to be realistic about what they expect in their jobs.
From The Jobs - Seeking, Finding, Keeping Series.
Prod-MSDOE Dist-AITECH 1980

Work Ethic, The C 30 MIN
3/4 OR 1/2 INCH VIDEO CASSETTE C
Discusses the Protestant Ethic. Examines affluence, alienation, individualism, hedonism and other variables.
From The Focus On Society Series.
Prod-DALCCD Dist-DALCCD

Work Execution C 30 MIN
3/4 OR 1/2 INCH VIDEO CASSETTE
Considers work execution. Focuses on job assignment, communication, supervision and overtime.
From The Maintenance Management Series.
Prod-ITCORP Dist-ITCORP

Work Hardening C 10 MIN
1/2 IN VIDEO CASSETTE BETA/VHS
Deals with auto body repair. Defines and demonstrates work hardening.
Prod-RMI Dist-RMI

Work Is For Real—A Series
A
Informs students of the various types of jobs available in today's changing work world and develops student interest in obtaining details about some particular career that seems to fit individual interest and aptitude. Promotes honest self-appraisals and gives special attention to those students who won't be seeking a four-year college degree.
Prod-STETVC Dist-GPITVL

Agriculturally Speaking 15 MIN
And Loot To Boot 15 MIN
Art For The Artist's Sake 15 MIN
Backup Group, The 15 MIN
Brush, Chisel And Curtain 15 MIN
Computer The Future 15 MIN
D E Develops 'Know-How' 15 MIN
Do You Dig You 15 MIN
Double Future For You, A 15 MIN
For The 'People-Minded' 15 MIN
Information Interpreters, The 15 MIN
Lovers Of Language 15 MIN
Man, The Manager 15 MIN
Math For Us Moderns 15 MIN
Medical Mystery Tours, Pt 1 15 MIN
Medical Mystery Tours, Pt 2 15 MIN
Medical Mystery Tours, Pt 3 15 MIN
Music Makers And Miscellaneous 15 MIN
No Unskilled 'I' In Industry 15 MIN
Professional Scientists 15 MIN
Public Service - Federal 15 MIN
Public Service - State And Local 15 MIN
Science Technicians 15 MIN
Science Unlimited 15 MIN
Serve Your Nation 15 MIN
Society-Serving Skills 15 MIN
Storytellers, The 15 MIN
There Is No 'Nothing' Job 15 MIN
What Is Your Reach 15 MIN
Who Needs Math 15 MIN

Work Means C 15 MIN
16MM FILM, 3/4 OR 1/2 IN VIDEO I-J
Examines a variety of attitudes toward work and explores the significance that work has for the development of individuals and society. Shows how a junior high school reporter learns through interviews that work means different things to different people.
From The Bread And Butterflies Series.
LC NO. 74-703175
Prod-AITV Dist-AITECH Prodn-UTSBE 1974

Work Measurement C 30 MIN
3/4 OR 1/2 INCH VIDEO CASSETTE
See series title for descriptive statement.
From The Effective Supervision Series.
Prod-ERF Dist-DELTAK

Work Measurement Works B 23 MIN
16MM FILM, 3/4 OR 1/2 IN VIDEO
Illustrates work measurement in four areas, improving work methods, scheduling and controlling work, determining productivity and forecasting resource requirements.
Prod-USA Dist-USNAC 1969

Work Methods C 30 MIN
3/4 OR 1/2 INCH VIDEO CASSETTE
See series title for descriptive statement.
From The Effective Supervision Series.
Prod-ERF Dist-DELTAK

Work Of Gomis C 47 MIN
3/4 INCH VIDEO CASSETTE C A
Documents a healing ceremony in Sri Lanka utilizing dance, theater and decorations made of clay, flowers and leaves.
Prod-HANMNY Dist-HANMNY 1972

Work Of Love, A C 21 MIN
16MM FILM OPTICAL SOUND J-C A
Deals with the experiences of campers and counselors at the Texas Lions Camp for Crippled Children.
LC NO. 77-701860
Prod-CASTOP Dist-TEXLCC 1976

Work Of Love, The - A M Sullivan, Poet C 26 MIN
16MM FILM OPTICAL SOUND
Presents the poetry of A M Sullivan.
LC NO. 80-700182
Prod-GUINEA Dist-GUINEA 1979

Work Of Rivers, The C 3 MIN
16MM FILM OPTICAL SOUND P-I
Shows the work of rivers.
From The Of All Things Series.
Prod-BAILYL Dist-AVED

Work Of The Goethe Institute In Germany, The C 5 MIN
16MM FILM, 3/4 OR 1/2 IN VIDEO
Describes the function of the Goethe Institute in Germany, which aims at fostering appreciation of the German language and culture.
From The European Studies - Germany Series. Part 26
Prod-BAYER Dist-IFB 1973

Work Of The Heart X 19 MIN
16MM FILM, 3/4 OR 1/2 IN VIDEO H-C A
Provides close-ups of the structure and functions of the heart and operating rooms, cardiac laboratories, heart models and photomicroscopy. Includes a view of the mitral valve in a living heart and open chest sequences of living hearts in a human body and a laboratory animal. Shows operating procedures to correct certain cardiovascular defects and mentions heart transplants.
From The Biology Series. Unit 8 - Human Physiology
Prod-EBEC Dist-EBEC 1968

Work Of The Heart (Spanish) C 19 MIN
16MM FILM, 3/4 OR 1/2 IN VIDEO H
Provides close-ups of the structure and function of the heart.
From The Biology (Spanish) Series. Unit 8 - Human Physiology
Prod-EBEC Dist-EBEC

Work Of The Kidneys, The (2nd Ed) C 20 MIN
16MM FILM, 3/4 OR 1/2 IN VIDEO H-C
Demonstrates the essential work of the kidneys in maintaining the fluid environment body cells must have. Examines the kidneys' major structures and the function of each.
From The Biology Series. Unit 8 - Human Physiology
Prod-EBEC Dist-EBEC 1972

Work Of The Kidneys, The (2nd Ed) (Captioned) C 20 MIN
16MM FILM, 3/4 OR 1/2 IN VIDEO H-C
Demonstrates the essential work of the kidneys in maintaining the fluid environment body cells must have. Examines the kidneys' major structures and the function of each.
Prod-EBEC Dist-EBEC 1972

Work Of The Kidneys, The (2nd Ed) (Spanish) C 20 MIN
16MM FILM, 3/4 OR 1/2 IN VIDEO H-C
Demonstrates the essential work of the kidneys in maintaining the fluid environment body cells must have. Examines the kidney's major structures and the function of each.
From The Biology Series. Unit 8 - Human Physiology
Prod-EBEC Dist-EBEC 1972

Work Of The Wind And Running Water C 19 MIN
16MM FILM, 3/4 OR 1/2 IN VIDEO J-H
Explains and illustrates the processes involved in the geologic work of wind and running water and their effects on landforms.
Prod-WILEYJ Dist-MEDIAG 1970

Work Or Play C 5 MIN
16MM FILM OPTICAL SOUND
Discusses hobbies and their relaxing effects. Stimulates oral language skills.

LC NO. 74-706884
Prod-DBA Dist-MLA 1969

Work Performance Rating X 27 MIN
16MM FILM OPTICAL SOUND IND
Shows time-study personnel in action under simulated shop conditions measuring 40 operations from ten basic categories common in many industrial organizations.
LC NO. 72-701863
Prod-VOAERO Dist-VOAERO 1968

Work Planning And Scheduling C 30 MIN
3/4 OR 1/2 INCH VIDEO CASSETTE PRO
Suggests some approaches for work planning and scheduling that are practiced during the discussion period following the session.
From The You - The Supervisor Series.
Prod-PRODEV Dist-DELTAK

Work Prejudice Film, The C 13 MIN
16MM FILM, 3/4 OR 1/2 IN VIDEO I-C A
Investigates the work world as it relates to sterotypes, attitudes and opportunities. Explores preconceived misconceptions. Presents statistics to indicate that women are succeeding in business and that a variety of ethnic groups are achieving in a broad assortment of jobs, crafts and professions.
Prod-SAIF Dist-BARR 1974

Work Procedures For a Derrickman C
3/4 OR 1/2 INCH VIDEO CASSETTE IND
Discusses derrickman's duties in the derrick and in the pump room. Looks at safe work procedures for handling drill pipe during tripping operations. Details pump room equipment and maintenance procedures.
From The Working Offshore Series.
Prod-GPCV Dist-GPCV

Work Procedures For A Roustabout C
3/4 OR 1/2 INCH VIDEO CASSETTE IND
Looks at a roustabout's life in terms of personal safety equipment and responsibilities, housekeeping procedures, painting procedures and safety, assisting the crane operator, working with slings and hitches, crane communica- tion and safety, and unloading crews and workboats.
From The Working Offshore Series.
Prod-GPCV Dist-GPCV

Work Songs B 29 MIN
3/4 INCH VIDEO CASSETTE
Surveys the old work songs, chanties and chain gang songs by using guitar and field recordings from the Library of Congress.
From The Folklore - U S A Series.
Prod-UMITV Dist-UMITV 1967

Work Songs - Sea Chanties C 20 MIN
16MM FILM OPTICAL SOUND I
Emphasizes the sea chanty and conveys the basic concept that work songs make the job seem lighter becasue they buoy up the spirits of the worker and supply him with a rhythm to work by. Contrasts the cultured life of the cities and the chamber music of the time with the hearty life and song of the men on the ships, in the fields and in the wilderness. Features Ed Ellison and John Jacob Niles.
From The Music Of America Series.
Prod-KQEDTV Dist-GPITVL

Work Supervisor, The C 8 MIN
16MM FILM, 3/4 OR 1/2 IN VIDEO
Depicts a variety of actual work and training situations where Neighborhood Youth Corps supervisors teach trainees. Issued in 1970 as a motion picture.
From The Career Job Opportunity Film Series.
LC NO. 79-707889
Prod-USDLMA Dist-USNAC Prodn-DEROCH 1979

Work World - Vocational Reading Resource Kit, Pt 1 C
3/4 OR 1/2 INCH VIDEO CASSETTE J-H
Gives information about job hunting and keeping a job. Reinforces vocabulary. Includes getting a job, how to fill out forms, and on-the-job behavior.
Prod-EDUACT Dist-EDUACT

Work World - Vocational Reading Resource Kit, Pt 2 C
3/4 OR 1/2 INCH VIDEO CASSETTE J-H
Gives information about job hunting and keeping a job. Reinforces vocabulary skills. Includes strategies for developing appropriate on-the-job behavior.
Prod-EDUACT Dist-EDUACT

Work, Bike And Eat B 45 MIN
16MM FILM OPTICAL SOUND
Presents the adventures of a man as he copes with shoplifters, family dinners, beer fights, hush puppy stories, infantile bikers, brief encounters and calisthenics.
LC NO. 77-702730
Prod-CANFDC Dist-CANFDC 1972

Work, Energy And Friction B 15 MIN
2 INCH VIDEOTAPE P
See series title for descriptive statement.
From The Just Curious Series. No. 27
Prod-EOPS Dist-GPITVL Prodn-KOACTV

Work, Income, And Your Career C 30 MIN
3/4 OR 1/2 INCH VIDEO CASSETTE C A
Discusses the factors that affect career choices and the ability to advance in a profession or trade. Explores salary considerations, fringe benefits, and laws and regulations that protect the worker.
From The Personal Finance Series. Lesson 2
Prod-SCCON Dist-CDTEL

Work, Pt 1 C
3/4 INCH VIDEO CASSETTE
See series title for descriptive statement.
From The Calculus Series.
Prod-MDDE Dist-MDCPB

Work, Pt 2 C
3/4 INCH VIDEO CASSETTE
See series title for descriptive statement.
From The Calculus Series.
Prod-MDDE Dist-MDCPB

Work, Work, Work C 59 MIN
3/4 OR 1/2 INCH VIDEO CASSETTE
Examines the concept of work from ancient times to the 20th century. Discusses the work ethic and introduces individual workers who explore their feelings about their jobs.
Prod-NJPBA Dist-PBS

Work, Work, Work - Income C 15 MIN
3/4 OR 1/2 INCH VIDEO CASSETTE P
Explores the gap between income and the expenses of life.
From The Two Cents' Worth Series.
Prod-WIEC Dist-AITECH Prodn-WHATV 1976

Workable Way, The C 19 MIN
16MM FILM OPTICAL SOUND
Demonstrates the action taken by a group of Virginia and North Carolina farmers in solving local labor problems. Told in first person and by narration. Describes the background planning of a youth work center, putting the plan into effect and some of the final results.
LC NO. 74-711594
Prod-VAEC Dist-VAEC 1971

Worker To Worker C 29 MIN
16MM FILM OPTICAL SOUND
Tells the stories of Americans who know their rights are more that words on paper, they are rights to be used for protection on the job. Gives case histories and is narrated by Studs Terkel.
Prod-DURRIN Dist-DURRIN

Worker's Lib C 30 MIN
3/4 INCH VIDEO CASSETTE H-C A
Challenges the assumption that work in America is boring, servile and meaningless and suggests that in fact workers have never had it so good as in America in 1976. Features George Meany and Richard Goodwin.
From The In Search Of The Real America Series.
Prod-WGBHTV Dist-KINGFT 1977

Workers Comp Connection, The C 30 MIN
16MM FILM OPTICAL SOUND
Focuses on the physician's key role in the worker's compensation system and attempts to promote closer teamwork among physicians, insurers, employers and others working within the system.
Prod-EMW Dist-EMW

Workers Depend On Each Other C 10 MIN
16MM FILM, 3/4 OR 1/2 IN VIDEO P
Presents the workers necessary to make a doll house to show their dependence on one another.
Prod-CORF Dist-CORF 1973

Workers In Tropical Medicine - Calista E Causey, D Sc C 60 MIN
3/4 OR 1/2 INCH VIDEO CASSETTE
Presents a biographical interview with Dr Calista E Causey, who recalls her years of research working with a field team in Brazil and later in Ibadam, Nigeria, which led to the discovery of many virus/vector/host relationships of significance to man.
LC NO. 81-707187
Prod-NMAC Dist-USNAC 1979

Workers Of Our Community (2nd Ed) C 12 MIN
16MM FILM, 3/4 OR 1/2 IN VIDEO P
The second edition of Helpers In Our Community. Shows jobs and services essential to the efficient working of a community.
Prod-CORF Dist-CORF

Workers Who Come To Our House (2nd Ed) C 10 MIN
16MM FILM, 3/4 OR 1/2 IN VIDEO P
The second edition of Helpers Who Come To Our House. Shows workers who do such jobs as repairing telephones, reading meters and collecting garbage.
Prod-CORF Dist-CORF

Workers' Compensation - It Should Be Your Right C 12 MIN
16MM FILM OPTICAL SOUND
Explains the process of claiming for workers' compensation in Australia. Follows the case of Spiros Tripos, a Greek migrant who speaks little English. Shows how he has an accident at work and has difficulty in following the correct procedure for lodging his claim. Re-enacts the procedure Spiros should have taken to lodge his claim and gain benefit.
Prod-NSWF Dist-TASCOR 1978

Working C 57 MIN
16MM FILM, 3/4 OR 1/2 IN VIDEO H-C A
Looks at China's industrial workers, focusing on those in the cities of Datong. Views Datong's two main industries, coal mining and railways. Introduces a young woman who wanted to be writer, but stoically accepts the State's decision that she should train to become a welder.
From The Heart Of The Dragon Series. Pt 6
Prod-ASH Dist-TIMLIF 1984

Working C 90 MIN
3/4 OR 1/2 INCH VIDEO CASSETTE H-C A
Offers a musical which explores the world of work using actual interview responses which reveal the attitudes, aspirations and aggravations of people on the job. Based on the book Working by Studs Terkel.

LC NO. 83-706567
Prod-WNETTV Dist-FI 1982

Working - Soviet Style C 27 MIN
16MM FILM, 3/4 OR 1/2 IN VIDEO J-C A
Examines the role of workers and natural resources in the development of the Soviet economy. Studies the interrelationships of government, management and trade unions and examines a coal mine, a refrigerator factory, a timber processing plant and dock workers on the Odessa waterfront.
From The Soviet Style Series.
LC NO. 84-707069
Prod-JOU Dist-JOU 1982

Working Against The Force Of Gravity C 15 MIN
2 INCH VIDEOTAPE P
Illustrates energy that must be used to do work against the force of gravity.
From The Science Is Searching Series.
Prod-DETPS Dist-GPITVL

Working Artist–A Series

Focuses on seven artists and their individual activities.
Prod-MARXHA Dist-MARXS

Carole Morisseau And The Detroit City Dance	
Gerhardt Knodel - An Artist And His Work	013 MIN
Jim Pallas - Electronic Sculptor	012 MIN
John Glick - An Artist And His Work	009 MIN
John Voelker (Alias Robert Traver) - Anatomy	020 MIN
Lavinia Moyer And The Attic Theater	022 MIN
Michael Hall - Sculptor	010 MIN

Working Artists–A Series

Examines via film portraits the creative process through which working artists develop finished pieces.
Prod-SWARR Dist-LRF

Working At The Car Wash Blues C 15 MIN
3/4 INCH VIDEO CASSETTE H
Looks at various jobs and features counselers and educators commenting about the relationship between work and self-fulfillment.
From The Success In The Job Market Series.
LC NO. 80-706454
Prod-KUONTV Dist-GPITVL 1980

Working Class Women C 29 MIN
3/4 INCH VIDEO CASSETTE
Looks at the role of the working woman. Cites conditioning, culture mores and the lack of communication among women as factors contributing to the voicelessness of working class women.
From The Woman Series.
Prod-WNEDTV Dist-PUBTEL

Working Couples - Urban And Family Life C 28 MIN
16MM FILM, 3/4 OR 1/2 IN VIDEO H-C A
Deals with the pressures of urban life in Japan. Focuses on a typical middle-income couple and what their life is like on a day-to-day basis.
From The Human Face Of Japan Series.
LC NO. 82-707156
Prod-FLMAUS Dist-LCOA 1982

Working Cow Horse C 25 MIN
16MM FILM, 3/4 OR 1/2 IN VIDEO
Discusses the origination of the working cow horse and its training.
Prod-AQHORS Dist-AQHORS

Working Effectively With Different Managerial Styles C
3/4 OR 1/2 INCH VIDEO CASSETTE
Helps employees to work more productively with their own supervision and with other managers. Shows how three different types deal with a variety of work situations.
From The Team Building For Administrative Support Staff Series.
Prod-AMA Dist-AMA

Working For A Living - Job Skills For The Real World C 48 MIN
3/4 OR 1/2 INCH VIDEO CASSETTE J-H
Provides an inside look at a variety of entry-level jobs, and shows how to transfer the skills learned in school to new environments. Discusses job dissatisfaction and how to leave a job gracefully.
LC NO. 81-706153
Prod-GA Dist-GA 1981

Working For And With Others - Economic Security C 20 MIN
2 INCH VIDEOTAPE J-H
Discusses the kinds of risks faced in the economic world and how individuals and society can insure them selves against such risks.
From The Our World Of Economics Series.
Prod-MPATI Dist-GPITVL

Working For And With Others - Taxes C 20 MIN
2 INCH VIDEOTAPE J-H
Deals with the kinds of taxes there are, who pays taxes and how they are spent.
From The Our World Of Economics Series.
Prod-MPATI Dist-GPITVL

Working For The Lord C 52 MIN
16MM FILM, 3/4 OR 1/2 IN VIDEO J-H A
Analyzes religious societies which originated because of dissatisfaction with greater society and survived by vigorous enterprise and commerce.

From The American Documents Series.
Prod-LUF Dist-LUF 1976

Working For The U S A B 14 MIN
16MM FILM OPTICAL SOUND
Tells of Federal Civil Service employment. Includes how positions are obtained, wage scales, opportunities for advancement and fringe benefits.
LC NO. FIE57-151
Prod-USA Dist-USNAC 1957

Working For The United States C 25 MIN
16MM FILM - 3/4 IN VIDEO H A
Presents the new or prospective civil service employee with information on the executive branch and its relation to the other branches of the U S Government. Discusses the role of the federal employee in the political system and the work of the federal workforce.
From The Working For The United States Series.
LC NO. 77-706028
Prod-USCSC Dist-USNAC Prodn-LOUISP 1976

Working For The United States—A Series
H A
Discusses all information pertinent to the new civil service employee, including information regarding benefits, employment rights, on-job performance, the merit system and pay systems.
Prod-USCSC Dist-USNAC Prodn-LOUISP 1976

Benefits You Earn 16 MIN
Road Ahead, The 17 MIN
Working For The United States 25 MIN
You And The Merit System 15 MIN
Your Rights And Responsibilities 17 MIN

Working Forest, The C 24 MIN
16MM FILM OPTICAL SOUND
Explains lumber forestation, location and types of trees and describes tree farm concept. Gives details of planning, cutting, transportation of the lumber.
Prod-UPR Dist-UPR 1969

Working In Communications And Media C 20 MIN
16MM FILM, 3/4 OR 1/2 IN VIDEO I-C A
Takes a look at the duties of a photojournalist, a film editor, a television engineer and a telephone installer.
From The Working Series.
LC NO. 82-707288
Prod-NICKWA Dist-LCOA 1982

Working In Food Services C 21 MIN
16MM FILM, 3/4 OR 1/2 IN VIDEO I-C A
Looks at the duties of a restaurant manager, a baker and a meat wrapper.
From The Working Series.
LC NO. 82-707281
Prod-NICKWA Dist-LCOA 1982

Working In Marketing And Distribution C 22 MIN
16MM FILM, 3/4 OR 1/2 IN VIDEO I-C A
Looks at the duties of a clothing buyer, a window display designer, a graphic artist and a toy designer.
From The Working Series.
LC NO. 82-707283
Prod-NICKWA Dist-LCOA 1982

Working In Science C 20 MIN
16MM FILM, 3/4 OR 1/2 IN VIDEO I-C A
Introduces the duties of a mechanical engineer, a computer scientist, an industrial engineer and a physicist.
From The Working Series.
Prod-NICKWA Dist-LCOA 1982

Working In The Integrated Classroom C 29 MIN
16MM FILM, 3/4 OR 1/2 IN VIDEO T
Examines the dynamics of the integrated classroom environment. Shows practical options for promoting positive intergroup relations in a climate which encourages academic achievement and individual self-esteem. Covers dealing with both student and teacher expectations, grouping strategies which avoid resegregation, parent and peer influence, and the place of extracurricular activities in a successful integration program.
From The Survival Skills For The Classroom Teacher Series.
Prod-MFFD Dist-FI

Working In Transportation C 21 MIN
16MM FILM, 3/4 OR 1/2 IN VIDEO I-C A
Looks at the duties of a fishing boat captain, an auto repair shop owner, a construction equipment operator, an air traffic controller and a truck driver.
From The Working Series.
LC NO. 82-707282
Prod-NICKWA Dist-LCOA 1982

Working In Washington C 13 MIN
3/4 OR 1/2 INCH VIDEO CASSETTE P
Shows Joanne visiting Washington where Dad has just begun to work and learning about the presidency, seeing laws being made and explained, and visiting famous monuments and the Smithsonian Institution.
From The Under The Yellow Balloon Series.
Prod-SCETV Dist-AITECH 1980

Working In Watercolor C 18 MIN
16MM FILM, 3/4 OR 1/2 IN VIDEO J-C
Presents basic tools and materials and demonstrates novel and new manipulations of water color. Stimulates students to use water color in an individual and personal style.
Prod-IFB Dist-IFB 1959

Working In Wax C 13 MIN
3/4 OR 1/2 INCH VIDEO CASSETTE
Offers a behind-the-scenes look at London's Wax Museum, where the famous and the infamous stand side by side.
Prod-UPI Dist-JOU

Working It Out C 18 MIN
16MM FILM OPTICAL SOUND
Provides information on the Comprehensive Employment and Training Act (CETA), which provides federal money to fund jobs in private industry. Shows what happens when three people try the CETA program.
LC NO. 78-700400
Prod-MGMO Dist-MGMO Prodn-FILMA 1977

Working It Out C 29 MIN
16MM FILM - 3/4 IN VIDEO PRO
Discusses problems accompanying a neurologically disabled patient's admission to a rehabilitation hospital, including aphasia, differences in reactions of patients with left and right hemiplegia and difficulties encountered by family members.
From The Neurologically Disabled Patient, Pt 2 - Nursing During The Rehabilitative... Series.
LC NO. 77-700612
Prod-AJN Dist-AJN Prodn-TVPC 1977

Working Model Of The Thorax C 3 MIN
16MM FILM SILENT C
Uses a bell, jar and balloon model to illustrate the role of the chest cavity and diaphragm in normal respiration, pneumothorax, the return of blood to the heart, and regurgitation in ruminants.
From The Dukes Physiology Series.
LC NO. 77-710185
Prod-IOWA Dist-IOWA 1971

Working More Effectively With People C 10 MIN
3/4 OR 1/2 INCH VIDEO CASSETTE
Discusses why and how an effective supervisor can change unacceptable employee attitudes and behavior to acceptable ones. Emphasizes that it is important for the employee to see problems as their own as well as the organization's.
From The Human Side Of Management Series.
Prod-RESEM Dist-RESEM

Working Mother, The C 28 MIN
16MM FILM OPTICAL SOUND A
Describes how mothers can have fun with their children. Shows different game experiences possible at various locations.
From The Look At Me Series. No. 2
LC NO. 77-700464
Prod-PARLTF Dist-USNAC 1975

Working Mother, The C 28 MIN
16MM FILM, 3/4 OR 1/2 IN VIDEO
See series title for descriptive statement.
From The Look At Me Series.
Prod-PEREN Dist-PEREN

Working Of Magnesium, The B 27 MIN
16MM FILM OPTICAL SOUND
Portrays the correct technique for matching, forming, arc and spot welding, riveting, chemical treating and painting of magnesium alloys.
LC NO. FIA55-1029
Prod-DCC Dist-DCC 1953

Working Offshore—A Series
IND
Illustrates oil field trainers demonstrating techniques on rigs recognized as teachers in offshore safety. Covers roustabout work procedures, making a connection on the drill string, safe use of drill pipe tongs, the trip into the hole and out of the hole, and work procedures for a derrickman.
Prod-GPCV Dist-GPCV

Making A Connection
Safe Use Of Drill Pipe Tongs
Trip Into The Hole
Trip Out Of The Hole
Work Procedures For A Derrickman
Work Procedures For A Roustabout

Working On Working C 29 MIN
16MM FILM, 3/4 OR 1/2 IN VIDEO T
Focuses on the mainstreaming of handicapped students in vocational education programs.
LC NO. 80-707206
Prod-USDED Dist-USNAC 1979

Working Out An Epistemology C 36 MIN
3/4 OR 1/2 INCH VIDEO CASSETTE C
See series title for descriptive statement.
From The Artificial Intelligence, Pt 1 - Fundamental Concepts Series.
Prod-MIOT Dist-AMCEE

Working Out An Epistemology C 45 MIN
3/4 OR 1/2 INCH VIDEO CASSETTE PRO
Discusses role of natural constraints in solving perception problems, coping with thousands of possibilities, increased constraint, and illustration.
From The Artificial Intelligence - Pt 1, Fundamental Concepts Series.
Prod-MIOT Dist-MIOT

Working Outdoors C 20 MIN
16MM FILM, 3/4 OR 1/2 IN VIDEO I-C A
Introduces the duties of a tree surgeon, a zoo tour guide and a trash collector.
From The Working Series.
Prod-NICKWA Dist-LCOA 1982

Working River C 59 MIN
16MM FILM OPTICAL SOUND
Provides a modern history of the Ohio River as told by the people who live and work on it including a towboat crew, a retired river captain and a homesteading author/artist.
Prod-LNGRDL Dist-UPITTS 1982

Working Safely C 12 MIN
3/4 OR 1/2 INCH VIDEO CASSETTE
Emphasizes working safely in the plant in clean, safe areas and in a wide variety of locations and conditions.
From The Protecting Your Safety And Health In the Plant Series.
Prod-TPCTRA Dist-TPCTRA

Working Safely (Spanish) C 12 MIN
3/4 OR 1/2 INCH VIDEO CASSETTE
Emphasizes working safely in the plant in clean, safe areas and in a wide variety of locations and conditions.
From The Protecting Your Safety And Health In The Plant Series.
Prod-TPCTRA Dist-TPCTRA

Working Safely With Scaffolds C 19 MIN
3/4 OR 1/2 INCH VIDEO CASSETTE IND
Describes and demonstrates correct safety procedures for working with scaffolds, how to build a scaffold according to safety regulations, and how to safely work the scaffold.
From The Safety Action For Employees Series.
Prod-GPCV Dist-GPCV

Working Safely With Unibolt Couplings C 15 MIN
3/4 OR 1/2 INCH VIDEO CASSETTE IND
Explains safe and proper procedures to use when changing out a choke housed in a unibolt coupling.
Prod-UTEXPE Dist-UTEXPE 1983

Working Solution, A C 15 MIN
16MM FILM, 3/4 OR 1/2 IN VIDEO H-C A
Provides information on temporary help companies, showing how they organize part-time work for people. Discusses how to get temporary or part-time employment.
Prod-KLEINW Dist-KLEINW

Working Solution, The C 27 MIN
3/4 OR 1/2 INCH VIDEO CASSETTE IND
Studies the effects of on-the-job injuries. Explores the cost to the company, the emotional and physical cost to the worker, and the role of supervisor in the return to work program.
Prod-FLMEDS Dist-FLMEDS

Working The Double Shift C 20 MIN
3/4 OR 1/2 INCH VIDEO CASSETTE
Projects images from the home which conflict with mass media 'home life.' Presented by Lisa Steele and Kim Tomczak.
Prod-ARTINC Dist-ARTINC

Working Through College B 20 MIN
16MM FILM OPTICAL SOUND
Tells the story of a college student and the assistance provided him by a student employment adviser in finding a job which helps meet his expenses and enables him to acquire practical experience in the field he has chosen as a career.
LC NO. FIE52-2117
Prod-USA Dist-USNAC 1954

Working Through Depression And Releasing Anger C 90 MIN
3/4 OR 1/2 INCH VIDEO CASSETTE A
See series title for descriptive statement.
From The Growing Through Loss - A Howard Clinebell Resource Series. Session 4
Prod-UMCOM Dist-ECUFLM 1982

Working Together C 20 MIN
16MM FILM OPTICAL SOUND
Shows how the cooperative effort of the hospital and nursing home is beneficial to the hospital, the nursing home and the patient.
LC NO. FIE63-108
Prod-USPHS Dist-USNAC 1962

Working Together C 12 MIN
16MM FILM, 3/4 OR 1/2 IN VIDEO J-H
Stresses that cooperation is an important part of the office and its work. Dramatizes a hectic day in a typing pool where Linda realizes the necessity of working together.
From The Careers In The Office Series.
Prod-EBEC Dist-EBEC 1970

Working Together C 16 MIN
3/4 OR 1/2 INCH VIDEO CASSETTE
See series title for descriptive statement.
From The Funny Business Series.
Prod-LCOA Dist-DELTAK

Working Together C 19 MIN
3/4 OR 1/2 INCH VIDEO CASSETTE
Examines specialization and division of labor as a means of increasing productivity. Uses the example of a group of students working together washing cars.
From The Trade-Offs Series.
LC NO. 80-706424
Prod-AITV Dist-AITECH Prodn-OECA 1978

Working Together C 30 MIN
16MM FILM - 3/4 IN VIDEO PRO
Stresses the importance of cooperation between various agencies and disciplines in the handling of child abuse cases.
From The We Can Help Series.
LC NO. 79-706249
Prod-NCCAN Dist-USNAC 1979

Working Together (Spanish) C 12 MIN
16MM FILM, 3/4 OR 1/2 IN VIDEO J-H
Presents a case study demonstrating the necessity of cooperation in an office. Shows how Linda, a member of a typing pool, discovers a rewarding way to tackle an unforeseen and difficult job.
Prod-EBEC Dist-EBEC

Working Together - Government As A Producer C 20 MIN
2 INCH VIDEOTAPE J-H

Discusses how governments use resources to produce public services, such as flood control, education and highways.
From The Our World Of Economics Series.
Prod-MPATI Dist-GPITVL

Working Together - Government As A Rulemaker C 20 MIN
2 INCH VIDEOTAPE J-H
Introduces the idea of government regulation of big labor.
From The Our World Of Economics Series.
Prod-MPATI Dist-GPITVL

Working Together - Protecting The Consumer C 20 MIN
2 INCH VIDEOTAPE J-H
Shows how governments help consumers make wise choices.
From The Our World Of Economics Series.
Prod-MPATI Dist-GPITVL

Working Together - Specialization C 20 MIN
16MM FILM OPTICAL SOUND I-J
Shows how Maury, Eddie and Diane learn that they can save valuable time on Saturdays if they specialize and work together to wash their fathers' cars. Points out some of the disadvantages of specialization.
From The Trade-Offs Series. No. 6
LC NO. 80-700454
Prod-EDFCEN Dist-AITECH 1978

Working Together For Action–A Series

Presents a series on working together for action. Depicts a senior center in trouble because of lack of membership. Shows how a group working together brings new life to the center.
Prod-SYRCU Dist-UWISC

Deciding What To Do, Pt 2 025 MIN
Starting To Work Together, Pt 1 020 MIN
Taking Action, Pt 3 015 MIN

Working Together Series, The C 19 MIN
16MM FILM, 3/4 OR 1/2 IN VIDEO A
Presents six comic aspects of the difficulties encountered by group leaders and participants in meetings.
Prod-SEVDIM Dist-SEVDIM

Working Unit, The C 30 MIN
3/4 OR 1/2 INCH VIDEO CASSETTE C A
Looks at the practical steps involved in creating a working organizational structure and examines certain key organizational concepts such as unity of command and span of control. Explores various types of organizational structures.
From The Business Management Series. Lesson 9
Prod-SCCON Dist-SCCON

Working With Animals C 11 MIN
16MM FILM, 3/4 OR 1/2 IN VIDEO P-I
Shows how Audrey takes her dog to its training lessons and learns that the lessons involve training for her too. Introduces Manuel and Patrick who work at a Texas Zoo.
From The Zoom Series.
Prod-WGBHTV Dist-FI

Working With Animals C 20 MIN
16MM FILM, 3/4 OR 1/2 IN VIDEO I-C A
Introduces the duties of a dairy farmer, a horse trainer, a zoo keeper, a dog groomer and a vet.
From The Working Series.
Prod-NICKWA Dist-LCOA 1982

Working With Chains C 5 MIN
3/4 OR 1/2 INCH VIDEO CASSETTE IND
Looks at chain inspection and discusses possible causes for damages. Identifies and stresses safe working procedures.
From The Steel Making Series.
Prod-LEIKID Dist-LEIKID

Working With Einstein C 60 MIN
3/4 INCH VIDEO CASSETTE
Presents men who worked with Albert Einstein. Illustrates his philosophies and methods of working.
Prod-OHC Dist-HRC

Working With Groups B 30 MIN
3/4 INCH VIDEOTAPE
See series title for descriptive statement.
From The One Strong Link Series.
Prod-CUETV Dist-CUNIV 1971

Working With Groups - A Behavioral Approach C 60 MIN
3/4 OR 1/2 INCH VIDEO CASSETTE
Gives an overview of the various types of group work. Outlines operant role modeling, communication and problem solving groups. Covers model target, interest groups, cross age tutoring and group desensitization.
Prod-UWISC Dist-UWISC 1979

Working With Lead C 14 MIN
3/4 OR 1/2 INCH VIDEO CASSETTE IND
Discusses special safety precautions when working with lead. Examines the use of respirators in detail.
From The Steel Making Series.
Prod-LEIKID Dist-LEIKID

Working With Metals In The Plant–A Series

Introduces metals, metallurgy, and metalworking. Discusses the properties of metals. Examines industrial manufacturing processes.
Prod-TPCTRA Dist-TPCTRA

Aluminum 012 MIN
Copper 012 MIN
Heat Treatment 012 MIN
Introduction To Metals 012 MIN
Iron And Steel 012 MIN
Lead, Nickel, Tin And Zinc 012 MIN
Magnesium And Titanium 012 MIN
Manufacturing Processes 012 MIN
Properties Of Metals 012 MIN
Standard Steels 012 MIN

Working With Modern School Mathematics X 20 MIN
16MM FILM OPTICAL SOUND
Lelon Capps gives an overview of the content and objectives of the text entitled 'MODERN SCHOOL MATHEMATICS, STRUCTURE AND USE' and explains how to use the teacher's annotated edition of the text.
From The Duncan - Modern School Math Films Series.
LC NO. 72-701740
Prod-HMC Dist-HMC 1971

Working With Nebraska's Water C 29 MIN
16MM FILM OPTICAL SOUND H-C A
Describes current water-management practices in Nebraska and the problems encountered. Discusses three manageable reservoirs of water - the soil moisture reservoirs, stream reservoirs and groundwater reservoirs. Shows these reservoirs in relation to water use.
From The Nebraska Water Resources Series.
LC NO. 74-700163
Prod-UNL Dist-UNEBR 1971

Working With Nonmetals In The Plant–A Series

Introduces nonmetal materials and explains how to classify them. Covers plastic, rubber and wood. Examines construction insulating materials and their uses.
Prod-TPCTRA Dist-TPCTRA

Adhesives 012 MIN
Carbon 012 MIN
Construction Materials 012 MIN
Industrial Chemicals 012 MIN
Insulating Materials 012 MIN
Introduction To Nonmetals 012 MIN
Paints And Coatings 012 MIN
Plastics 012 MIN
Rubber 012 MIN
Wood 012 MIN

Working With Offshore Cranes C
3/4 OR 1/2 INCH VIDEO CASSETTE IND
Familiarizes new operator with work procedures and specific job responsibilities associated with electric and hydraulic cranes. Discusses crane components, how load requirements are determined, wire ropes and slings and how to properly secure a load. Looks at lift planning, the personnel basket, hand signals, maintenance and safety.
From The Offshore Operations Series.
Prod-GPCV Dist-GPCV

Working With Other People C 12 MIN
3/4 OR 1/2 INCH VIDEO CASSETTE
Discusses communicating with people, human behavior, aids to communicating, being tactful while working with other people, working with older people, dealing with responsibilities and differences of opinion.
From The Developing Troubleshooting Skills Series.
Prod-TPCTRA Dist-TPCTRA

Working With Other Supervisors B 8 MIN
3/4 INCH VIDEO CASSETTE
Shows the importance of working harmoniously with other people on the job. Issued in 1944 as a motion picture.
From The Problems In Supervision Series.
LC NO. 79-706454
Prod-USOE Dist-USNAC Prodn-MODART 1979

Working With Others C
3/4 OR 1/2 INCH VIDEO CASSETTE
Shows how to improve teamwork throughout an organization by sensitizing participants to the problems and pressures faced by both managers and co-workers. Dramatizes the operating realities of the modern manager.
From The Team Building For Administrative Support Staff Series.
Prod-AMA Dist-AMA

Working With Others C 10 MIN
16MM FILM, 3/4 OR 1/2 IN VIDEO P
An open-end approach to four situation-type episodes involving respect for other races, the opposite sex, the handicapped and 'becoming involved.'
From The Guidance For Primary Grades Series. No. 3
Prod-CAHILL Dist-AIMS 1969

Working With Others C 30 MIN
3/4 OR 1/2 INCH VIDEO CASSETTE A
Explains that interpersonal skills make a secretary's workday easier and more pleasant and contribute to the good will and good public relations of the organization itself. Urges the proofreading of typewritten correspondence and the use of a dictionary to check spelling and usage.
From The Professional Skills For Secretaries Series. Pt 3
LC NO. 81-707648
Prod-TIMLIF Dist-TIMLIF 1981

Working With People B 30 MIN
16MM FILM OPTICAL SOUND
Discusses the way people become supervisors and relates some of the common mistakes made by supervisors who are inexperienced or untrained.
From The Success In Supervision Series.
LC NO. 74-706339
Prod-WETATV Dist-USNAC 1965

Working With Positive And Negative Exponents B 30 MIN
16MM FILM OPTICAL SOUND H
Discusses rules for manipulating numbers with positive exponents. Shows that negative exponents equal reciprocals with a corresponding positive power. Gives examples to illustrate the rules.
Prod-CALVIN Dist-MLA Prodn-UNIVFI 1959

Working With Radiation - And Protecting The Unborn C 24 MIN
16MM FILM OPTICAL SOUND
Deals with the effects of ionizing radiation on workers in medical, university, governmental and industrial facilities. Includes discussion of mutagenetic effects and the necessity of avoiding excessive exposure, especially for pregnant women.
LC NO. 79-701199
Prod-RADIAM Dist-RADIAM Prodn-JHMI 1979

Working With Scale C 11 MIN
16MM FILM, 3/4 OR 1/2 IN VIDEO I-J
Introduces the concepts and practical uses of scale. Compares a scale model car to the fullsize car and explains methods of writing scale. Shows other examples of the use of the scale–the laying out of a floor plan from a scale drawing, and finding locations on a map after measuring the distances by interpretation of the map scale.
Prod-BOUNDY Dist-PHENIX Prodn-BOUNDY 1969

Working With The Beginning Teacher - Teaching Story Analysis–A Series

Demonstrates an effective framework for the productive supervision of the beginning teacher.
Prod-SPF Dist-SPF

Instructional Conference 029 MIN
Lesson And Analysis 029 MIN

Working With The Beginning Teacher - Teaching Division With Decimal Remainders–A Series

Demonstrates an effective framework for the productive supervision of the beginning teacher.
Prod-SPF Dist-SPF

Instructional Conference 029 MIN
Lesson And Analysis 029 MIN

Working With The Computer–A Series

Introduces the world of computers to individuals in the business world who have little or no computer background. Uses analogies and everyday language. Explains the nature of electronic data processing (EDP) and the reasons for using computer systems in business.
Prod-DELTAK Dist-DELTAK

Computer And Your Job, The 030 MIN
Using A Computer 030 MIN
What Is A Computer? 030 MIN

Working With The Current Balance B 19 MIN
16MM FILM OPTICAL SOUND C A
A teacher discusses with his students the uses of the current balance, ways to avoid some of the problems associated with its adjustment and use, and the steps needed to convert current balance measurements into a useful result to determine the strength of the earth's magnetic field.
From The Harvard Project Physics Teacher Briefings Series. No. 16
LC NO. 77-709151
Prod-HPP Dist-HRAW 1969

Working With The System C 93 MIN
3/4 INCH VIDEO CASSETTE C A
Describes how social workers can better work with the professionals both within and outside their own agencies.
From The Skills Of Helping Series. Program 3
LC NO. 80-707460
Prod-MCGILU Dist-SYRCU 1980

Working With Trigonometric Identities B 29 MIN
16MM FILM OPTICAL SOUND H
Reviews the fundamental trigonometric identities and shows techniques of manipulating them, such as working on only one side of the identity, watching the form of the terms and checking results. Develops geometric illustrations of the identities on the unit circle and shows alternate proofs of the identities.
From The Trigonometry Series.
Prod-CALVIN Dist-MLA Prodn-UNIVFI 1959

Working With Troubled Employees C 28 MIN
16MM FILM - 3/4 IN VIDEO IND
Illustrates two common types of troubled behavior in employees, the depressed employee and the overly aggressive employee. Gives guidelines on how to distinguish emotional troubles from behavior associated with disciplinary action or low morale. Outlines the supervisor's role in dealing with troubled employees.
From The Advanced Supervision Series.
Prod-BNA Dist-BNA 1973

Working Woman, The C 29 MIN
3/4 INCH VIDEO CASSETTE
Discusses importance of Social Security benefits for the working woman.
From The Her Social Security Series.
Prod-UMITV Dist-UMITV 1977

Working Women C 25 MIN
3/4 OR 1/2 INCH VIDEO CASSETTE
Looks at some of the underlying causes of why most women are still employed in what is called 'women's work,' work with less pay, less chance for advancement and subtle and not so subtle discrimination.
Prod-WCCOTV Dist-WCCOTV 1979

Working Women—A Series

Focuses on women in the work force and offers insights on how to juggle career and family. Covers such topics as IRAs, timing careers and owning a business. Issued weekly.
Prod-MDCPB Dist-MDCPB

Working Worlds—A Series
I-H
Presents 13 pertinent and practical films covering all basic occupational areas.
Prod-OLYMPS Dist-COUNFI 1974

At Your Service - Careers In Business And
Culture And Conscience - Careers In Education 13 MIN
Earth People - Careers In Natural Resources 13 MIN
First Step, The - Careers In Construction 13 MIN
Foodmakers, The - Careers In Agribusiness And 13 MIN
Good Time People - Careers In Hospitality And 13 MIN
Helping Hands - Careers In Health 13 MIN
Marketeers, The - Careers In Marketing 13 MIN
On The Move - Careers In Transportation 13 MIN
Organizers, The - Careers In Business Office 13 MIN
People And Things - Careers In Manufacturing 13 MIN
People To People - Careers In Communications 13 MIN
We, The People - Careers In Public Service 13 MIN

Working—A Series
16MM FILM, 3/4 OR 1/2 IN VIDEO H-C A
Examines various aspects of working, including interviews, training, office conduct, evaluations and career planning.
Prod-JOU Dist-JOU Prodn-INCC 1980

Decision Making 020 MIN
Doing Your Eight 020 MIN
Rules Of The Game 019 MIN
Where Do I Go From Here 021 MIN

Working—A Series
16MM FILM, 3/4 OR 1/2 IN VIDEO I-C A
Discusses job opportunities in the mass media, food services, marketing and distribution, and transportation.
Prod-NICKWA Dist-LCOA 1982

Working In Communications And Media 019 MIN
Working In Food Services 021 MIN
Working In Marketing And Distribution 022 MIN
Working In Science 020 MIN
Working In Transportation 021 MIN
Working Outdoors 020 MIN
Working With Animals 020 MIN

Workmanship Myth, The C 18 MIN
16MM FILM OPTICAL SOUND
Documents the quality of American workmanship in the making of automotive and other products. Use photography taken on location in Japan, South America, West Germany and elsewhere.
LC NO. 76-702920
Prod-CMD Dist-MTP Prodn-SANDYB 1976

Workout C 30 MIN
16MM FILM, 3/4 OR 1/2 IN VIDEO H-C A
Describes the attempt of the Gloria Stevens women's fitness chain to revitalize the company by attracting younger customers.
From The Enterprise Series.
Prod-MTI Dist-MTI

Workout C 30 MIN
3/4 OR 1/2 INCH VIDEO CASSETTE H-C A
Discusses the six-billion dollars a year business of health clubs and exercise salons. Features the Gloria Stevens chain of salons which has fallen on hard times and struggles to find a formula for survival.
From The Enterprise III Series.
Prod-WGBHTV Dist-KINGFT

Workout C 90 MIN
1/2 IN VIDEO CASSETTE (VHS)
Provides a complete workout by Jane Fonda for beginning and advanced people in two parts. Provides tips for having a good workout.
Prod-KARLVI Dist-KARLVI

Workout Challenge C 90 MIN
1/2 IN VIDEO CASSETTE BETA/VHS
Presents a program for advanced exercisers. Includes 20 minutes of advanced aerobics.
Prod-GA Dist-GA

Workout Challenge C 90 MIN
1/2 IN VIDEO CASSETTE (VHS)
Shows a vigorous exercise class, led by Jane Fonda designed to build strength, develop flexibility and increase endurance. Presents instruction and advice for experienced athletes and dancers.
Prod-KARLVI Dist-KARLVI

Workover Fluids C 19 MIN
3/4 OR 1/2 INCH VIDEO CASSETTE IND
Defines workover fluids and points out the many factors that must be considered in the selection of a good workover fluid.
Prod-UTEXPE Dist-UTEXPE 1975

Workplace Hustle, The C 30 MIN
16MM FILM, 3/4 OR 1/2 IN VIDEO A
Explores the issue of sexual harassment of women in the workplace. Features Lin Farley, an expert on the topic, and actor Ed Asner.
LC NO. 81-707434
Prod-CLRKCO Dist-MTI 1980

Works For Broadcast B 4 MIN
3/4 INCH VIDEO CASSETTE
Presents a series of video spots designed to confront the audience, aired as commercial breaks on local television.
From The James Byrne - Five Works 1974-79 Series.
Prod-EAI Dist-EAI

Works Of Calder C 20 MIN
16MM FILM OPTICAL SOUND
Interprets Calder's mobiles. Rhythmical sequences suggest parallels between familiar forms and movements in nature and the movements of the artist's works.
Prod-MERB Dist-MOMA 1950

Workshop For Peace C 23 MIN
16MM FILM, 3/4 OR 1/2 IN VIDEO I-H
Presents a pictorial study of the United Nations describing its varied activities in the maintenance of peace. Introduces the variety of organizations and activities that make up the structure and function of the United Nations.
Prod-UN Dist-JOU 1975

Workshop With Martin Booth, A C 30 MIN
3/4 OR 1/2 INCH VIDEO CASSETTE
Uses an ancient Spanish coin forged from Aztec gold as the focus for a discussion of the poet as myth-maker. Reveals bits and pieces of the coin's history as the students compose, contemplating the personal history of the coin and its various owners. Focuses on the history of the object and the description of images from the past.
From The Booth And Bly - Poets Series.
Prod-NETCHE Dist-NETCHE 1978

Workshop With Robert Bly, A C 30 MIN
3/4 OR 1/2 INCH VIDEO CASSETTE
Uses an old, gnarled tree stump as a prop and the five senses to discover a new writing experience. Focuses on strong, sensory descriptions of the stump, including word selection, points of view and images.
From The Booth And Bly - Poets Series.
Prod-NETCHE Dist-NETCHE 1978

World According To Nicholas—A Series
16MM FILM, 3/4 OR 1/2 IN VIDEO P-J
Presents stories dealing with topics viewed from a child's viewpoint. Deals with such matters as divorce, fear, helping one another and the value of school.
Prod-LUF Dist-LUF 1980

Comes In All Colors, Shapes And Sizes 025 MIN
Fraidy Cats 024 MIN
Just Like Me 026 MIN
Magic Man 024 MIN

World After Nuclear War, The - The Nuclear Winter C 28 MIN
3/4 OR 1/2 INCH VIDEO CASSETTE
Reveals that the use of a small fraction of the world's nuclear arsenal would have such devastating climatic consequences that civilization as we know it would be destroyed and the human species would probably become extinct. From the conference on the Long Term World Wide Biological Consequences of nuclear war.
Prod-EFVP Dist-EFVP 1984

World And Basic Facts, The C 12 MIN
16MM FILM OPTICAL SOUND P-J
Depicts education as a building process starting with a child's blank mind which, as it acquires a few basic facts, triggers a quest for more information. Explains basic facts about the origin of the earth and its geography.
Prod-AVED Dist-AVED 1963

World Around Us—A Series
16MM FILM, 3/4 OR 1/2 IN VIDEO
Prod-ICARUS Dist-ICARUS 1979

Taureg 046 MIN

World Around Us, The C 25 MIN
16MM FILM, 3/4 OR 1/2 IN VIDEO I-H
Identifies the subject of ecology, or environmental biology, and defines its limits and relationships with other life sciences. Discusses the interdependence of living things.
From The Smithsonian Series.
Prod-NBCTV Dist-MGHT 1967

World At War B 45 MIN
3/4 OR 1/2 INCH VIDEO CASSETTE
Traces the trend toward war during the decade 1931-1941, showing the events in Asia and Europe from the Japanese invasion of Manchuria to the bombing of Pearl Harbor.
Prod-IHF Dist-IHF

World At War Specials—A Series
16MM FILM, 3/4 OR 1/2 IN VIDEO H-C A
Presents in-depth examinations of specific aspects of the Second World War. Based on archive film and research in eighteen countries in addition to interviews and location footage.
Prod-THAMES Dist-MEDIAG 1974

Final Solution, The - Auschwitz 208 MIN
Hitler's Germany 156 MIN
Secretary To Hitler 026 MIN
Two Deaths Of Adolph Hitler, The 052 MIN
Warrior 052 MIN
Who Won World War II 026 MIN

World At War—A Series
16MM FILM, 3/4 OR 1/2 IN VIDEO H-C A
Presents a series about World War II, focusing on what it meant to its generation and to individual soldiers of America, Japan, England, Russia, France and Germany.
Prod-THAMES Dist-MEDIAG 1973

Alone - May 1940-May 1941 052 MIN
Banzai - Japan, 1931-1942 052 MIN
Barbarossa - June-December 1941 052 MIN
Bomb, The - February-September 1945 052 MIN
Desert, The - North Africa, 1940-1943 052 MIN
Distant War - September 1939-May 1940 052 MIN
France Falls - May-June 1940 052 MIN
Genocide - 1941-1945 052 MIN
Home Fires - Britain, 1940-1941 052 MIN
Inside The Reich - Germany, 1940-1944 052 MIN
It's A Lovely Day Tomorrow - Burma, 052 MIN
Japan, 1941-1945 052 MIN
Morning - June-August 1944 052 MIN
Nemesis - Germany, February-May 1945 052 MIN
New Germany, A - 1933-1939 052 MIN
Occupation - Holland, 1940-1944 052 MIN
On Our Way - U S A, 1939-1942 052 MIN
Pacific, February 1942-1945 052 MIN
Pincers - August 1944-March 1945 052 MIN
Reckoning - 1945 And After 052 MIN
Red Star - The Soviet Union, 1941-1943 052 MIN
Remember 052 MIN
Stalingrad - June 1942-1943 052 MIN
Tough Old Gut - Italy, November 052 MIN
Whirlwind - Bombing Germany, September 052 MIN
Wolf Pack - U-Boats In The Atlantic, 052 MIN

World At War, The B 44 MIN
16MM FILM, 3/4 OR 1/2 IN VIDEO
Traces the trend toward war during the decade of 1931-1941, showing the events in Asia and Europe from the Japanese invasion of Manchuria in 1931 to the bombing of Pearl Harbor. Issued in 1943 as a motion picture.
LC NO. 79-706464
Prod-USOWI Dist-USNAC 1979

World At Your Feet, The C 15 MIN
16MM FILM, 3/4 OR 1/2 IN VIDEO J-C A
Features carpet stylist Lee Kolker who presents information on buying and using carpet. Discusses design, construction, color, resilience, wear, stain resistance, soil resistance, texture retention, cleaning, cost, fire safety, backing and function.
Prod-KLEINW Dist-KLEINW

World At Your Fingertips, A C 15 MIN
16MM FILM, 3/4 OR 1/2 IN VIDEO J-C A
Features the workings of the book club relationship.
Prod-KLEINW Dist-KLEINW

World Beneath The Sea C 29 MIN
16MM FILM OPTICAL SOUND
Tells the story of man's search for oil off the coasts of the United States. Illustrates the history of offshore drilling and explains how industry has learned to produce oil efficiently and safely in deep water.
Prod-EXXON Dist-EXXON 1973

World Beneath The Sea C 23 MIN
16MM FILM, 3/4 OR 1/2 IN VIDEO I-C A
Explores the world of life beneath the sea and among reefs. Features the camouflage, predation, aggression and mimicry used as protection and survival mechanisms within this ecological system.
Prod-DUTCHE Dist-AIMS 1976

World Beneath The Sea (Spanish) C 23 MIN
16MM FILM, 3/4 OR 1/2 IN VIDEO I-C A
Explores the world of life beneath the sea and among reefs. Features the camouflage, predation, aggression and minicry used as protection and survival mechanisms within this ecological system.
Prod-DUTCHE Dist-AIMS 1976

World Between, The C 26 MIN
16MM FILM, 3/4 OR 1/2 IN VIDEO
Dramatizes an Ojibway Indian legend that begins in The Path Of Souls. Tells, in this second part, of a man journeying between the land of the living and the dead to search for his wife. Continues in The Path Of Life.
Prod-FOTH Dist-FOTH

World Beyond Death C 52 MIN
16MM FILM OPTICAL SOUND
Explores life-after-death experiences, including mediumship, ectoplasm, spirit entities, hypnotic regression and mind over matter. Features Will Geer and Dr Elizabeth Kubler-Ross.
From The Fourth Dimension Series.
LC NO. 79-700408
Prod-INTTFP Dist-INTTFP 1978

World Car Is Born, The C 26 MIN
16MM FILM, 3/4 OR 1/2 IN VIDEO
Presents the story of a new automobile, built because American industry has responded to the ever-changing energy environment, rising costs, consumer needs and preferences. Covers four years of planning, development engineering, testing and manufacturing of engines, transmissions, suspension and interior and other parts of a motor car.
Prod-FORDFL Dist-FORDFL

World City - An Artist's Report C 17 MIN
16MM FILM, 3/4 OR 1/2 IN VIDEO H-C A
Shows how artist-reporter Franklin McMahon captures the sights and sounds of cities in the United States, Europe, South America and the Far East.
Prod-PHENIX Dist-PHENIX 1978

World Cultures And Youth—A Series
16MM FILM, 3/4 OR 1/2 IN VIDEO I-J A
Introduces children of 13 cultures who tell about their hobbies, lifestyles and future plans.
Prod-SUNRIS Dist-CORF 1980

Amy The Photographer 025 MIN
Francesco The Potter 025 MIN

Gopal's Golden Pendant 025 MIN
Hasan The Carpetweaver 025 MIN
Jafar's Blue Tiles 025 MIN
Julia The Gourdcarver 025 MIN
Lee's Parasol 025 MIN
Ming-Oi The Magician 025 MIN
Serama's Mask 025 MIN
Slima The Dhowmaker 025 MIN
Steffan The Violinmaker 025 MIN
Valerie's Stained Glass Window 025 MIN
Yoshiko The Papermaker 025 MIN

World Exchange—A Series

Prod-VIDVER Dist-DIRECT

Third Coast, The 055 MIN

World Feminists C 29 MIN
3/4 INCH VIDEO CASSETTE J-C
Presents an international group of feminists exploring some of the primary issues facing women. Discusses the need for collaboration among all women, the role of male feminists, and the ways in which the women's movement is transforming societies.
From The Are You Listening Series.
LC NO. 80-707409
Prod-STURTM Dist-STURTM 1980

World From One Point Of View, The C
3/4 INCH VIDEO CASSETTE
Describes growth and development of a child from 34 to 35 months.
From The Growth And Development - A Chronicle Of Four Children Series. Series 8
Prod-JUETHO Dist-LIP

World From One Point Of View, The - Gregory, 34 Months C 6 MIN
16MM FILM OPTICAL SOUND
See series title for descriptive statement.
From The Growth And Development - A Chronicle Of Four Children Series. Series 8
LC NO. 78-700689
Prod-JUETHO Dist-LIP Prodn-CONCOM 1976

World From One Point Of View, The - Joseph, 35 Months C 7 MIN
16MM FILM OPTICAL SOUND
See series title for descriptive statement.
From The Growth And Development - A Chronicle Of Four Children Series. Series 8
LC NO. 78-700689
Prod-JUETHO Dist-LIP Prodn-CONCOM 1976

World From One Point Of View, The - Melissa, 34 Months C 6 MIN
16MM FILM OPTICAL SOUND
See series title for descriptive statement.
From The Growth And Development - A Chronicle Of Four Children Series. Series 8
LC NO. 78-700689
Prod-JUETHO Dist-LIP Prodn-CONCOM 1976

World From One Point Of View, The - Terra, 35 Months C 6 MIN
16MM FILM OPTICAL SOUND
See series title for descriptive statement.
From The Growth And Development - A Chronicle Of Four Children Series. Series 8
LC NO. 78-700689
Prod-JUETHO Dist-LIP Prodn-CONCOM 1976

World Health C 10 MIN
16MM FILM OPTICAL SOUND J-H
Introduces the concept of environmental health to stimulate discussions about the implications of world health problems in the modern context. Details the nature and achievements of the World Health Organization (WHO.) Discusses structure and staff training, population and birth control, international drug standards, food, pesticides, pollution and sewage. Illustrates the need for a new approach to international cooperation.
From The Problems Of World Order Series.
LC NO. 73-703430
Prod-VISNEW Dist-AGAPR 1972

World Health Organization C 28 MIN
3/4 INCH VIDEOTAPE
Interviews a senior information officer at the World Health Organization of the United Nations and a diabetes specialist from a Boston clinic. Presents a film clip on the last known case of smallpox.
From The International Byline Series.
Prod-PERRYM Dist-PERRYM

World Health Organization At Work B 10 MIN
16MM FILM OPTICAL SOUND H-C A
Shows the assistance given Turkey in the fight against tuberculosis by getting up a model demonstration and training center for Turkish doctors. Depicts attempts to control rabies by inoculating dogs in Israel and Mexico and other countries of the world.
Prod-UN Dist-UN 1952

World Hunger - Who Will Survive C 90 MIN
3/4 INCH VIDEO CASSETTE
Focuses on the world food crisis, questioning whether nations are equipped to deal with the problem of rocketing population combined with static and even faltering food production. Uses the nations of Niger, Columbia and India as case studies. Narrated by Bill Moyers.
Prod-CPT Dist-PUBTEL

World In A Marsh C 22 MIN
16MM FILM, 3/4 OR 1/2 IN VIDEO J-C
Shows a variety of life forms which inhabit a marsh, such as insects, amphibious creatures and birds, and records their activities.
Prod-NFBC Dist-MGHT 1968

World In A Schoolroom B 17 MIN
16MM FILM OPTICAL SOUND
Portrays citizens demonstrating their skills in the classroom so that students may see the application of the principles and techniques taught in school.
LC NO. FIE52-2118
Prod-USA Dist-USNAC Prodn-IMPS 1951

World In The Camera, The C 22 MIN
16MM FILM, 3/4 OR 1/2 IN VIDEO
Explores the influence of George Eastman on the history of photography.
From The Screen News Digest Series. Volume 23, Issues 1 And 2
Prod-HEARST Dist-HEARST 1980

World Is A Bank, The C 9 MIN
16MM FILM, 3/4 OR 1/2 IN VIDEO P-I
Explores some of the ways we can safeguard our wealth of natural resources so that we can enjoy them for many more years.
Prod-BFA Dist-PHENIX 1972

World Is A Stage, The C 13 MIN
16MM FILM, 3/4 OR 1/2 IN VIDEO
Interviews two creative teenagers, one a member of a children's dance theater and the other a member of a clown club.
From The Zoom Series.
Prod-WGBHTV Dist-FI 1978

World Is Born, A C 20 MIN
16MM FILM, 3/4 OR 1/2 IN VIDEO I-C A
Pictures the 'RITES OF SPRING' sequence from the 1940 feature film 'FANTASIA' which depicts the birth of the earth and the first living creatures to inhabit it.
Prod-DISNEY Dist-WDEMCO 1955

World Is Built, A B 30 MIN
16MM FILM OPTICAL SOUND H-C A
Tells how the seas have advanced and withdrawn through the ages. Illustrates how the world scene changed as mountains were built and how life began in the plains of Central North Ameria.
From The Great Plains Trilogy, 1 Series. In The Beginning - The Primitive Man
Prod-KUONTV Dist-UNEBR 1954

World Is My Habitat, The C 20 MIN
16MM FILM, 3/4 OR 1/2 IN VIDEO J-H
Tells how Earth is a complex biological system in which the lives of all animals and plants are interconnected all over the world. Each small habitat is always a part of a larger habitat that supports life and all life is dependent on other life.
From The Biology - It's Life Series.
Prod-THAMES Dist-MEDIAG 1980

World Is One, The C 28 MIN
1 INCH VIDEOTAPE
Presents events and performances at the 1964 Innsbruck-Tokyo Olympic Games--Billy Mills' victory in the 10,000 metre race, Fred Hansen's pole vault triumph and Don Schollander's swimming achievements.
Prod-AMDAS Dist-MTP

World Leaders—A Series
J-C A
Presents biographies of world leaders. Includes both documentary and dramatic portraits.
Prod-CORF Dist-CORF

Alfred Nobel - The Merchant Of Death 027 MIN
Churchill And British History (1874-1918) 029 MIN
Churchill And British History (1919-1965) 032 MIN
Marie Curie - A Love Story 032 MIN
Martin Luther King Jr - The Assassin Years 026 MIN
Queen Victoria And British History (1837-1901) 028 MIN
Roosevelt And U S History (1882-1929) 028 MIN
Roosevelt And U S History (1930-1945) 032 MIN
Stalin And Russian History (1879-1927) 029 MIN
Stalin And Russian History (1928-1953) 031 MIN
Theodore Roosevelt - Cowboy In The White House 029 MIN

World Medicine - Disease Recognition C 17 MIN
16MM FILM OPTICAL SOUND
Describes signs, symptoms and laboratory findings on virus borne Japanese B encephalitis.
LC NO. 74-706611
Prod-USN Dist-USNAC 1965

World Needs Help, The C 20 MIN
16MM FILM OPTICAL SOUND I-C A
See series title for descriptive statement.
From The Cellar Door Cine Mites Series.
LC NO. 74-701552
Prod-CELLAR Dist-CELLAR 1972

World Of 'Hip Hop,' The - Rapping, Break Dancing And Electric Boogie C 30 MIN
3/4 OR 1/2 INCH VIDEO CASSETTE
See series title for descriptive statement.
From The Popular Culture In Dance Series.
Prod-ARCVID Dist-ARCVID

World Of A Primitive Painter, The C 20 MIN
16MM FILM, 3/4 OR 1/2 IN VIDEO
Examines the work of Jose Antonio Velasquez, a Honduran primitive painter, placing his art against the background of the mining town in which he lives and works.
LC NO. 82-707025
Prod-OOAS Dist-MOMALA

World Of A Primitive Painter, The (Spanish) C 20 MIN
16MM FILM, 3/4 OR 1/2 IN VIDEO
Examines the work of Jose Antonio Velasquez, a Honduran primitive painter, placing his art against the background of the mining town in which he lives and works.
Prod-OOAS Dist-MOMALA

World Of Andrew Wyeth C 26 MIN
16MM FILM, 3/4 OR 1/2 IN VIDEO I-C
Covers the significant facts in Andrew Wyeth's life, especially the influence of his father, N C Wyeth, the well-known illustrator. Explores more than 35 paintings, giving both an overall impression of each canvas and a close look at specific details of Wyeth's technique.
Prod-ABCTV Dist-IFB 1968

World Of Apu, The (The Honeymoon) B 14 MIN
16MM FILM OPTICAL SOUND J-C A
Presents an excerpt from the 1959 motion picture The World Of Apu. Tells how Apu and his wife set up a household in Apu's tiny tenement apartment. Directed by Satyajit Ray.
From The Film Study Extracts Series.
Prod-UNKNWN Dist-FI

World Of Archery, The C 30 MIN
16MM FILM OPTICAL SOUND
Introduces archery and distinguistes between the different types--tournament, hunting and fishing archery.
LC NO. FIA68-2708
Prod-AMARCH Dist-AMARCH 1968

World Of Care In Brewing, A C 20 MIN
16MM FILM OPTICAL SOUND
Presents the history of beermaking, with emphasis on the complex and quality-conscious process of brewing.
LC NO. 77-700446
Prod-SCHLTZ Dist-SCHLTZ Prodn-SWANSP 1976

World Of Carl Sandburg, The (2nd Ed) C 59 MIN
16MM FILM, 3/4 OR 1/2 IN VIDEO J-C A
Presents a portrait of the American writer, Carl Sandburg and a look, through his eyes, at America and its people.
Prod-KROLL Dist-PHENIX 1976

World Of Change, World Of Promise C 22 MIN
16MM FILM OPTICAL SOUND
Shows the different goals and activities of members of the World Association of Girl Guides and Girl Scouts. Visits troops of Girl Guides and Girl Scouts in various parts of the world and shows them teaching reading and hygiene, practicing first aid, preserving traditional customs and acquiring income-producing skills.
LC NO. 79-701694
Prod-WAGGGS Dist-GSUSA Prodn-CINEMK 1979

World Of Children B 29 MIN
3/4 INCH VIDEO CASSETTE
Discusses the games, rhymes and chants of children. Features a group of nine-year-olds demonstrating some favorites.
From The Folklore - U S A Series.
Prod-UMITV Dist-UMITV 1967

World Of Comic Books, The C 16 MIN
16MM FILM, 3/4 OR 1/2 IN VIDEO J-C A
Examines the highly competitive world of comic book publishing and briefly chronicles the development of comic book art and writing. Shows the devotion of comic book fans and collectors at a comics convention.
Prod-MEDLIM Dist-LUF 1980

World Of Cooking—A Series
16MM FILM, 3/4 OR 1/2 IN VIDEO J-C A
Describes the foods of several countries.
Prod-SCRESC Dist-MTI

Brazil - A Bahian Menu 028 MIN
Finland - A Karelian Menu 028 MIN
France - An Alpine Menu 028 MIN
Germany - A Southern Menu 028 MIN
Hong Kong - A Cantonese Menu 028 MIN
India - A Northern Menu 028 MIN
Italy - A Venetian Menu 028 MIN
Japan - A Banquet Menu 028 MIN
Mexico - A Family-Style Menu 028 MIN
Netherlands, The - A Traditional Menu 028 MIN
Spain - A Catalonian Menu 028 MIN

World Of Cousteau, The C 28 MIN
16MM FILM OPTICAL SOUND J-C A
Shows that the sea is a source of natural resources as the earth's resources are being depleted and the population continues to grow.
Prod-AETNA Dist-AETNA 1967

World Of Credit, A C 12 MIN
16MM FILM OPTICAL SOUND
Looks at Dun and Bradstreet's information gathering and disseminating operations. Includes actual reporter interviews, filmed throughout the United States. Points out the importance of credit to the American economy.
LC NO. 81-701404
Prod-DBI Dist-MTP Prodn-SECOM 1981

World Of CRS, The - People First C 24 MIN
16MM FILM - 3/4 IN VIDEO
Looks at the humanitarian efforts of Catholic Relief Services in five of the seventy-five countries in which it works. The countries are Thailand, Egypt, Kenya, Colombia and Costa Rica. Emphasises long-term development assistance.
Prod-CATHRS Dist-MTP

World Of Darkness, The C 25 MIN
16MM FILM, 3/4 OR 1/2 IN VIDEO
A shortened version of the 1973 motion picture Strange Creature

Of The Night. Uses night-vision camera devices in presenting studies of bats, owls, hyenas and sightless cave-dwelling fish during their nighttime activities.
LC NO. 80-706303
Prod-NGS Dist-NGS 1973

World Of David Rockefeller, The, Pt 1 C 60 MIN
3/4 OR 1/2 INCH VIDEO CASSETTE
Looks at the power and influence of David Rockefeller. Shows Bill Moyers as he accompanies Rockefeller on a whirlwind trip through five European countries.
From The Bill Moyers' Journal Series.
Prod-WNETTV Dist-WNETTV

World Of David Rockefeller, The, Pt 2 C 60 MIN
3/4 OR 1/2 INCH VIDEO CASSETTE
Looks at the power and influence of David Rockefeller. Shows Bill Moyers as he accompanies Rockefeller on a whirlwind trip through five European countries.
From The Bill Moyers' Journal Series.
Prod-WNETTV Dist-WNETTV

World Of Deaf-Blind Children, The - Growing Up C 29 MIN
16MM FILM OPTICAL SOUND
Shows programs for deaf-blind children at the Perkins School for the Blind. Covers career education, skills for home life and mobility skills.
LC NO. 76-702950
Prod-PERKNS Dist-CAMPF Prodn-CAMPF 1975

World Of Deaf-Blind Children, The - How They Communicate C 29 MIN
16MM FILM OPTICAL SOUND
Shows how the educational programs at the Perkins School for the Blind can help deaf-blind children learn to deal with the world around them.
LC NO. 74-702530
Prod-PERKNS Dist-CAMPF 1974

World Of Difference, A C 9 MIN
16MM FILM OPTICAL SOUND C A
Explains the signs of child abuse, including descriptions of the typical abused child, the typical abusive parent and the external circumstances that may provoke the parent to violence or willful neglect. Provides a legal definition of child abuse and neglect and explains what may happen to an abusive family if a report is made against them.
From The Child Abuse And Neglect Series.
LC NO. 78-701591
Prod-UKANS Dist-UKANS 1977

World Of Difference, A C 27 MIN
16MM FILM OPTICAL SOUND
Helps motivate distributor prospects for amway corporation, a maker of household products and cosmetics.
LC NO. 74-700496
Prod-AMWAY Dist-AMWAY 1973

World Of Difference, A - B F Skinner And The Good Life C 58 MIN
16MM FILM, 3/4 OR 1/2 IN VIDEO C A
Traces the life of behavioral psychologist B F Skinner, who believes that environment alone molds behavior. Visits Twin Oaks, a rural cooperative where Skinner's theories were put into practice.
From The Nova Series.
Prod-WGBHTV Dist-TIMLIF 1979

World Of Discoveries C 30 MIN
3/4 OR 1/2 INCH VIDEO CASSETTE K-P
See series title for descriptive statement.
From The Villa Alegre Series.
Prod-BCTV Dist-MDCPB

World Of Dreams, The C
1/2 IN VIDEO CASSETTE (VHS)
Deals with research on dreams. Compares Freud's theories to those of modern physiological psychologists.
From The Theater Of The Night - The Science Of Sleep And Dreams Series.
Prod-IBIS Dist-IBIS

World Of Dredging C 18 MIN
16MM FILM, 3/4 OR 1/2 IN VIDEO
Shows how the Corps of Engineers on its own and in cooperation with the private dredging industry maintains our waterways and harbors.
Prod-USAE Dist-USNAC

World Of Emily Dickinson, The C 30 MIN
3/4 INCH VIDEO CASSETTE H-C A
Features Claire Bloom as Emily Dickinson, the shy 19th century poet who seldom left her room. Offers selections from Dickinson's work.
From The Anyone For Tennyson Series.
Prod-NETCHE Dist-GPITVL

World Of Energy, A C 28 MIN
16MM FILM OPTICAL SOUND J-H
Portrays major developments and turning points in the history of energy production. Talks about protection of the environment, resource recovery, the role of transportation and efficient use of energy.
From The Energy - An Overview Series.
Prod-CENTRO Dist-CONPOW

World Of Energy, A - The Breeder Reactor C 13 MIN
16MM FILM OPTICAL SOUND
Uses a tour of the 1982 World's Fair to show international advancements in breeder reactor technology. Presents Dr Alvin Weinberg explaining what the breeder means to Americans. Closes with President Reagan calling for the development of safe nuclear energy.
Prod-MTP Dist-MTP

World Of Enrico Fermi, The B 46 MIN
16MM FILM OPTICAL SOUND H-C
A documentary which portrays the life and work of the nearly contemporary physicist, Enrico Fermi, whose work helped to transform not only physics and the style of doing research, but even the course of history itself.
LC NO. 75-706154
Prod-HPP Dist-HRAW 1970

World Of F Scott Fitzgerald—A Series
C
Brings to life the Jazz Age of the Twenties and the Great Depression of the Thirties in eight one-hour programs. Includes a documentary of the period and a dramatization of a Fitzgerald short story. Designed as a complete instructional system for a three hour undergraduate American Literature course.
Prod-DALCCD Dist-DALCCD

Death Of Heroism, The	060 MIN
End Of An Era, The	060 MIN
Golden Boom, The	060 MIN
He Called It The Jazz Age	060 MIN
Last And Lucky	060 MIN
Last Novelist, The	060 MIN
Most Famous Forgotten Writer In America, The	060 MIN
Spoiled Priest, The	060 MIN

World Of Feelings, The C 28 MIN
16MM FILM OPTICAL SOUND
Uses a series of discussions with children to explore their likes, dislikes and fears.
From The Many Worlds Of Childhood Series.
LC NO. 74-701320
Prod-OECA Dist-OECA 1972

World Of Ford, The C 30 MIN
16MM FILM, 3/4 OR 1/2 IN VIDEO
Relates the story of the Ford Motor Company, within the context of an American dream come true.
Prod-FORDFL Dist-FORDFL

World Of Franklin And Jefferson, The C 28 MIN
16MM FILM, 3/4 OR 1/2 IN VIDEO J-C A
Traces the interlocking careers of Benjamin Franklin and Thomas Jefferson. Presents the background and accomplishments of these two men.
Prod-EAMES Dist-PFP 1976

World Of Hare Krishna, The C 34 MIN
16MM FILM OPTICAL SOUND
Studies the International Society for Krishna Consciousness.
Prod-ISKCON Dist-BHAKTI 1982

World Of Health—A Series
3/4 OR 1/2 INCH VIDEO CASSETTE J-C A
Prod-INFORP Dist-SF 1975

Birth Control - Five Effective Methods	10 MIN
Cholesterol - Eat Your Heart Out	14 MIN
Common Cold, The	9 MIN
Fad Diet Circus	15 MIN
Physical Fitness - The New Perspective	10 MIN
Run For Your Life	15 MIN
Snacking - Garbage In Your Gut	15 MIN
Stress	16 MIN
Weight Control - Just A Step Away	13 MIN

World Of I T W, The C 2 MIN
16MM FILM OPTICAL SOUND
An industry management-oriented film which shows how the world has changed in the past thirty-five years and indicates the changes that will occur in the next thirty-five years.
LC NO. 72-700330
Prod-ITW Dist-ITW 1971

World Of Illusion C 28 MIN
16MM FILM OPTICAL SOUND J-C A
Portrays the difference between the world of illusion and the world of reality. Features Mr Kole, one of the foremost inventors of magical effects, who displays his talent in mystifying his audience with a series of illusions.
LC NO. 73-701568
Prod-CCFC Dist-CCFC 1970

World Of Insects, The C 20 MIN
16MM FILM, 3/4 OR 1/2 IN VIDEO J-C A
Enumerates the major anatomical parts of the insect, identifies various distinguishing characteristics, and describes the stages of complete and incomplete metamorphosis. Explains how insect numbers are kept in check and evaluates the advantages and disadvantages of biological pest control and chemical spraying.
LC NO. 79-707892
Prod-NGS Dist-NGS 1979

World Of Islam—A Series

Analyzes the Islamic religion and shows how it affects the lives of its followers.
Prod-FOTH Dist-FOTH 1984

Five Pillars Of Islam, The	030 MIN
Islam Today	030 MIN
Islamic Art	030 MIN
Islamic City, The	030 MIN
Islamic Science And Technology	030 MIN
Orient / Occident	030 MIN

World Of Jacques-Yves Cousteau C 53 MIN
16MM FILM, 3/4 OR 1/2 IN VIDEO J A
Records the day-by-day events in the lives of six aquanauts who pioneered an inner space expedition 328 feet below the surface of the Mediterranean for 27 days.
LC NO. 80-706372
Prod-NGS Dist-NGS 1966

World Of Jai-Alai C 14 MIN
16MM FILM OPTICAL SOUND
Gives a brief history of the sport of jai-alai from its origins in the Basque region to the game played in the United States in the 1970's. Culminates with the first American amateur to become a professional world champion.
LC NO. 80-700312
Prod-WJAIAL Dist-FLADC Prodn-CINEST 1979

World Of Jesus Christ, The C 42 MIN
16MM FILM, 3/4 OR 1/2 IN VIDEO J-C
Retells the story of the life of Christ and shows how biblical events have inspired paintings by various artists. Features music that has sprung from the Christian tradition.
Prod-ABCNEW Dist-MTI 1978

World Of Light - A Portrait Of May Sarton C 30 MIN
16MM FILM OPTICAL SOUND H-C A
Follows the activities of writer May Sarton at her home in Maine as she explores her life and works. Features Sarton discussing her creative process, presenting her views and experiences on solitude, aging, the woman writer, discipline, integrity and relationships, and reading from her poetry and novels.
Prod-ISHTAR Dist-ISHTAR

World Of Little Things (2nd Ed) C 16 MIN
16MM FILM, 3/4 OR 1/2 IN VIDEO I-H
Introduces the microscopic world. Shows examples of the amoeba, volvox, paramecium and didinium. Studies the structure and nature of marine life, such as flatworms, medusa and protozoans. Shows algae and diatoms in relation to their variety and usefulness to man.
Prod-MIS Dist-MIS 1976

World Of Living Things, The C 15 MIN
3/4 OR 1/2 INCH VIDEO CASSETTE I-J
Describes some of the remarkable features of living organisms. Focuses on seed dispersal mechanisms, plants that defend themselves, and plants that attack and kill animals for food. Offers information on jellyfish, army ants, dolphins and anacondas.
From The Bioscope Series.
LC NO. 81-707651
Prod-MAETEL Dist-AITECH 1981

World Of Mark Twain, The C
3/4 OR 1/2 INCH VIDEO CASSETTE H-C
Shows how Mark Twain's boyhood, journalistic and riverboat experiences formed his writings, and presents excerpts from his fiction, essays and letters.
Prod-GA Dist-GA

World Of Martin Luther, The B 30 MIN
16MM FILM OPTICAL SOUND I-C A
Re-creates in Luther's own words his work, life and era. Retraces Luther's footsteps from St Peter's Church in Eisleben, where he was baptized, to the very room where he died.
LC NO. 72-701664
Prod-LUTHER Dist-CPH 1966

World Of Medicine—A Series

Prod-INFORP Dist-INFORP 1974

Walk Your Way To Weight Control

World Of Molecules (2nd Ed) C 12 MIN
16MM FILM, 3/4 OR 1/2 IN VIDEO I
Explores molecules, using children's experiments to illustrate their size, their behavior in solid, liquid and gaseous forms and their changes of state.
Prod-CF Dist-CF 1977

World Of Molecules (2nd Ed) (Captioned) C 12 MIN
16MM FILM, 3/4 OR 1/2 IN VIDEO I
Explores molecules, using children's experiments to illustrate their size, their behavior in solid, liquid and gaseous forms and their changes of state.
Prod-CF Dist-CF 1977

World Of Mother Teresa, The C 58 MIN
16MM FILM, 3/4 OR 1/2 IN VIDEO H-C A
Tells how Mother Teresa, without assistance from church or state, formed her own Order to work with the poorest of the poor. Explains how she inspires people to deal with abject poverty.
LC NO. 81-707325
Prod-MGM Dist-FI 1981

World Of Motion C 27 MIN
16MM FILM OPTICAL SOUND
Presents a kaleidoscopic chronicle of the past history and present world-wide operations of the General Motors Corporation.
LC NO. 73-701878
Prod-GM Dist-GM 1973

World Of Muffins C 14 MIN
2 INCH VIDEOTAPE
See series title for descriptive statement.
From The Muffinland Series.
Prod-WGTV Dist-PUBTEL

World Of Music—A Series
16MM FILM, 3/4 OR 1/2 IN VIDEO
Prod-NET Dist-IU

Music Lesson, The	30 MIN
Music Of Shakespeare's Time	30 MIN
Philadelphia Woodwind Quintet, The	30 MIN
Renaissance Band, The	30 MIN
Secular Music Of The Renaissance - Josquin	30 MIN

World Of Numbers, The C 28 MIN
16MM FILM OPTICAL SOUND R

Compares such developments as the laser beam, computers that draw and talk, and the scientific machinery that controls navigation with the claims of Jesus Christ.
Prod-OUTRCH Dist-OUTRCH

World Of Paul Delvaux, The (French) C 12 MIN
16MM FILM OPTICAL SOUND
Pictures the dream world through poetry and music.
Prod-GROVE Dist-GROVE

World Of People, The C 28 MIN
16MM FILM OPTICAL SOUND
Describes the development of the child from birth to age four.
From The Many Worlds Of Childhood Series.
LC NO. 74-701322
Prod-OECA Dist-OECA 1972

World Of Piri Thomas, The X 60 MIN
16MM FILM, 3/4 OR 1/2 IN VIDEO H-C A
Piri Thomas, a painter, poet, author, ex-con and ex-junkie, describes the life of a puerto Rican in the Spanish Harlem ghetto in New York City.
LC NO. 80-707105
Prod-NETRC Dist-IU 1968

World Of Plant And Animal Communities, The C 13 MIN
16MM FILM, 3/4 OR 1/2 IN VIDEO P-I
Shows how living things depend on one another for food and shelter in forests, deserts, oceans and grasslands. Stresses the importance of food chains in a community and the interrelationship between people, plants and animals in the food chains of the human community.
Prod-EBEC Dist-EBEC 1981

World Of Polo, A C 56 MIN
1/2 IN VIDEO CASSETTE BETA/VHS
Covers the history of polo and modern polo events.
Prod-ROLEX Dist-EQVDL

World Of Print, The C 18 MIN
16MM FILM, 3/4 OR 1/2 IN VIDEO H-C A
Presents a short history of printing from early Chinese woodblocks through the Gutenberg press to linotype machines. Illustrates printing methods and discusses the wide variety of knowledge and skills needed in printing and allied industries.
LC NO. 80-706579
Prod-MOOREN Dist-IFB 1979

World Of Real-Time, The C 15 MIN
16MM FILM OPTICAL SOUND
Describes SITA, an organization dealing with interline communications for major airlines, Kesko, a shopping chain in Finland and Lockheed, and a manufacturer in Georgia, showing how they use the various capabilities of UNIVAC real-time systems.
Prod-SPGYRO Dist-UNIVAC 1969

World Of Rembrandt, The B 30 MIN
16MM FILM OPTICAL SOUND H-C A
A documentary filmed in Amsterdam. Presents some of the masterpieces of the Dutch artist, Rembrandt Van Rijn, including many of his portraits. Also shows Amsterdam's historic Spanish Portugese Synagogue and deals with the history of the Jews in Holland. (Kinescope)
From The Eternal Light Series.
LC NO. 77-700976
Prod-JTS Dist-NAAJS 1968

World Of Semiconductors, The C 38 MIN
16MM FILM, 3/4 OR 1/2 IN VIDEO J-H
Describes the electrical properties of semiconductor materials, the effect of adding various controlled impurities, and the ways in which semiconductors can be used for rectification or as amplifiers.
Prod-AEIND Dist-IFB 1964

World Of Sholom Aleichem B 30 MIN
16MM FILM OPTICAL SOUND
Brings to life some of the folk characters in the East-European town of Kasrilevka, created by Sholom Aleichem. A companion film to 'VISIT TO THE WORLD OF SHOLOM ALEICHEM.' Based on the book of the same title. (Kinescope)
Prod-JTS Dist-NAAJS Prodn-NBCTV 1952

World Of Strawberry Shortcake, The C 24 MIN
16MM FILM OPTICAL SOUND K-I
Uses animation to present a story about Strawberry Shortcake. Shows how her surprise birthday party is spoiled and the valley where she lives is flooded because of the Peculiar Purple Pieman's evil doings with a fantastic watering can. Tells how a special birthday wish that the Sun grants to Strawberry Shortcake turns everything right and converts the Purple Pieman into a friend.
Prod-CORF Dist-CORF 1982

World Of The American Craftsman—A Series

Presents a series of five programs offering a visual portrait of five new Hampshire craftsmen.
Prod-WENHTV Dist-PUBTEL

Barbara Scarponi, Jewelry And Metal Worker	30 MIN
Dorothy Young, Weaver	30 MIN
Vivika Heino, Potter	30 MIN
Walker Weed, Wood Worker	30 MIN
Winslow Eaves, Sculptor	30 MIN

World Of The Beaver, The C 32 MIN
16MM FILM, 3/4 OR 1/2 IN VIDEO P-C
A shortened version of the film The World Of The Beaver. Shows the world of the small furry conservationist, the beaver, who engineered many of the waterways of our continent and who is an industrious, intelligent, social creature who benefits most of the animals around him, including man. Presents the life cycle of the beaver with emphasis on the beaver's ecological role and the excellent example which he presents to mankind. Narrated by Henry Fonda.
Prod-CBSTV Dist-PHENIX Prodn-ANGLIA 1969

World Of The Dark Crystal, The C 55 MIN
16MM FILM, 3/4 OR 1/2 IN VIDEO
Shows us the evolution of the story, sets and characters of the motion picture The Dark Crystal, from conception to the work of the same puppeteers who work with the Muppets.
Prod-HENASS Dist-FLMLIB 1982

World Of The Diving Spider, The C 12 MIN
16MM FILM, 3/4 OR 1/2 IN VIDEO J-H
Studies the 'diving spider' (argyoneta aquatica), an air-breathing member of the animal kingdom that lives its entire life under water. Reveals the spider's habits and life-cycle, from the creation of its mobile air supply and its bubble-chamber submarine house to its food hunting techniques, mating, birth of its young and its death.
Prod-AIMS Dist-AIMS 1977

World Of The Forest, Pt 1 C 14 MIN
2 INCH VIDEOTAPE
See series title for descriptive statement.
From The Muffinland Series.
Prod-WGTV Dist-PUBTEL

World Of The Forest, Pt 2 C 14 MIN
2 INCH VIDEOTAPE
See series title for descriptive statement.
From The Muffinland Series.
Prod-WGTV Dist-PUBTEL

World Of The Future, The C 19 MIN
16MM FILM, 3/4 OR 1/2 IN VIDEO
Interviews author Alvin Toffler, who explains that in a society exploding with change it becomes difficult for people to maintain their equilibrium. Suggests that society, rather than the individual, will be the effective cushion against the phenomenon of future shock.
Prod-DOCUA Dist-CNEMAG

World Of The Microscope, The C 12 MIN
16MM FILM OPTICAL SOUND P-J
Explains the principles and use of the microscope by relating the instrument to things familiar to the student—light from the sun and a magnifying glass. Uses line drawings and live action.
LC NO. FIA67-706
Prod-STNFRD Dist-BAL 1966

World Of The Scarlet Letter And Its Structure, The C 30 MIN
2 INCH VIDEOTAPE J-H
Presents the novel THE SCARLET LETTER by Nathaniel Hawthorne.
From The From Franklin To Frost - Nathaniel Hawthorne Series.
Prod-MPATI Dist-GPITVL

World Of The Sea C 27 MIN
16MM FILM OPTICAL SOUND
Shows the development of new diving techniques and systems which will enable divers to live and work in the sea for extended periods of time.
LC NO. 74-706612
Prod-USN Dist-USNAC 1973

World Of The Seance C 30 MIN
16MM FILM OPTICAL SOUND R
Reveals how people are tricked into believing they are communicating with the dead during a seance.
Prod-GF Dist-GF

World Of Things, The C 28 MIN
16MM FILM OPTICAL SOUND
Shows children learning about their world through everyday things.
From The Many Worlds Of Childhood Series.
LC NO. 74-701323
Prod-OECA Dist-OECA 1972

World Of U S Holsteins, The C 19 MIN
16MM FILM OPTICAL SOUND
Shows all the details concerning the exporting of U S Holsteins to other countries.
Prod-HFAA Dist-HFAA

World Of U S Holsteins, The (Portuguese) C 19 MIN
16MM FILM OPTICAL SOUND
Shows all the details concerning the exporting of U S Holsteins to other countries.
Prod-HFAA Dist-HFAA

World Of U S Holsteins, The (Spanish) C 19 MIN
16MM FILM OPTICAL SOUND
Shows all the details concerning the exporting of U S Holsteins to other countries.
Prod-HFAA Dist-HFAA

World Of Up Close, The C 9 MIN
16MM FILM, 3/4 OR 1/2 IN VIDEO P-I
Views commonly seen objects in extra close-up range.
From The Wonder Walks Series.
Prod-EBEC Dist-EBEC 1971

World Of Vatican II, An Artist's Report, The C 30 MIN
16MM FILM, 3/4 OR 1/2 IN VIDEO J-C A
Presents artist-reporter Franklin Mc Mahon discussing the Vatican Councils and its world-wide implications. Includes paintings and drawings made by the artists in Rome, Japan, India and the United States.
From The Artists As A Reporter Series.
Prod-ROCSS Dist-PHENIX 1967

World Of William Shakespeare—A Series
16MM FILM, 3/4 OR 1/2 IN VIDEO
Describes the life and times of William Shakespeare and presents adaptations of several of his plays.
Prod-NGS Dist-NGS 1978

Fair Is Foul, And Foul Is Fair	020 MIN
Hamlet	035 MIN
Macbeth	036 MIN
Romeo And Juliet	036 MIN
Shakespeare Of Stratford And London	032 MIN
Star-Crossed Love	020 MIN
Time Is Out Of Joint, The	020 MIN

World Of Work C 19 MIN
3/4 OR 1/2 INCH VIDEO CASSETTE H
Profiles three young people who aren't sure what they want to do with their lives but who agree that they should seek careers by choice, not chance.
From The Jobs - Seeking, Finding, Keeping Series.
Prod-MSDOE Dist-AITECH 1980

World Of Work C 30 MIN
3/4 OR 1/2 INCH VIDEO CASSETTE C A
Focuses on working women and transferable skills. Shows several women talking about their experiences as working mothers. Examines the need for changes in the world of work as the needs of the work force change. Includes such ideas as flextime.
From The Making A Living Work Series. Program 105
Prod-OHUTC Dist-OHUTC

World Of Work—A Series
16MM FILM, 3/4 OR 1/2 IN VIDEO I-H
Looks at the duties and responsibilities of various professions including veterinarians, paramedics and interns.
Prod-EBEC Dist-EBEC 1972

Country Vet	012 MIN
Intern - A Long Year	020 MIN
Newspaper Story (2nd Ed)	027 MIN
Rescue Squad	014 MIN
Space Exploration - A Team Effort	024 MIN
Tugboat Captain	014 MIN
TV News - Behind The Scenes	027 MIN

World Of Work, The C 14 MIN
16MM FILM OPTICAL SOUND J-H
Divides the world of work into major categories and shows selected occupations in each. Examines all possibilities. Suggests how to go about each. Considers both the satisfaction people derive from work and the relationship between their own talent, interests and values and the requirements of major career fields.
From The Library Of Career Counseling Films Series.
LC NO. 74-702068
Prod-COUNFI Dist-COUNFI Prodn-LOPATN 1974

World Of Work, The - Intercultural Aspects C 15 MIN
16MM FILM OPTICAL SOUND
Discusses how employees affect others, how to bridge cultural gaps and the importance of punctuality and reliability.
From The Job Hunt Game Series. Show 5
Prod-ICVT Dist-ICVT 1982

World Outside, The B 31 MIN
16MM FILM OPTICAL SOUND C A
Illustrates some central concepts of therapy with severely emotionally disturbed children. Filmed at the Marianne Frostig School of Educational Therapy in Los Angeles.
LC NO. FIA65-1588
Prod-SLFP Dist-SLFP 1963

World Outside, The C 34 MIN
16MM FILM OPTICAL SOUND H
Discusses street and highway design with stress on necessary improvements.
From The To Get From Here To There Series.
Prod-PROART Dist-PROART

World Peace Is A Local Issue C 20 MIN
16MM FILM, 3/4 OR 1/2 IN VIDEO
Documents a textbook example of democracy at its best, the grassroots impact of the citizenry upon units of government. Shows how an aroused citizenry in California espoused their views in a prolonged presentation to a City council and got support for a resolution endorsing a Soviet/American Bilateral Nuclear Weapons freeze.
Prod-FADMND Dist-CNEMAG 1984

World Population C 4 MIN
16MM FILM, 3/4 OR 1/2 IN VIDEO J-C A
Condenses 200 years of world population growth with statistical accuracy and stresses the importance of population control as fundamental to the solution of environmental crisis.
Prod-PERSPF Dist-CORF 1973

World Population, 1000 B C - 1965 A D C 4 MIN
16MM FILM OPTICAL SOUND
Uses an animated population record on a dymaxion air ocean world map to trace the growth of the world's population from the year 1,000 B C to 1965 A D.
LC NO. FIA67-707
Prod-SILLU Dist-SIUFP 1965

World Society, A C 29 MIN
3/4 INCH VIDEO CASSETTE
Looks at political, cultural and value dimensions of technology. Discusses the importing of technology by developing nations.
From The On To Tomorrow Series.
Prod-UMITV Dist-UMITV 1976

World Streets And Avenues C 20 MIN
3/4 INCH VIDEO CASSETTE I

Discusses latitude and longitude with host John Rugg.
From The Understanding Our World, Unit I - Tools We Use Series.
Prod-KRMATV Dist-GPITVL

World To Perceive, A - Perception B 29 MIN
16MM FILM, 3/4 OR 1/2 IN VIDEO H-C A
Discusses basic theories and methods for investigating perception. Explains the role of perception in handling and processing information from the environment and the way in which our personalities affect our perception.
From The Focus On Behavior Series.
Prod-NET Dist-IU 1963

World Today, The - Listening To The Earth C 30 MIN
3/4 INCH VIDEO CASSETTE
See series title for descriptive statement.
From The Of Earth And Man Series.
Prod-MDCPB Dist-MDCPB

World Tomorrow, The - Possibilities And Impossibilities C 30 MIN
3/4 INCH VIDEO CASSETTE
See series title for descriptive statement.
From The Of Earth And Man Series.
Prod-MDCPB Dist-MDCPB

World Tour C 90 MIN
3/4 OR 1/2 INCH VIDEO CASSETTE
Documents Swami Satchidananda's 1970 World Service Tour. Portrays Sri Gurudev's life of dedication to humanity.
Prod-IYOGA Dist-IYOGA

World Trade And Regional Trading Groups C 20 MIN
3/4 INCH VIDEO CASSETTE H-C
See series title for descriptive statement.
From The Geography For The '70's Series.
Prod-KLRNTV Dist-GPITVL

World Trade And US Jobs C 30 MIN
3/4 OR 1/2 INCH VIDEO CASSETTE
Gives a true case history in documentary style of Caterpillar's multinational operations showing the benefits of free world trade.
Prod-IVCH Dist-IVCH

World Tree, The - A Scandinavian Creation Myth C 10 MIN
16MM FILM, 3/4 OR 1/2 IN VIDEO J-C A
Depicts the beginning of the world according to a Scandinavian creation myth. Using animation, it shows opposing forces of fire and ice, frost giant and ice cow, trolls and the most important Scandinavian Gods. Covers how the Gods created the earth, mountains, rivers, the sky, grass, animals and plants, and dividing time into night and day. Concludes with gods transforming two trees into man and woman and, finally, bringing a world tree into being to form a bridge between the gods and the universe they had created.
Prod-NOITA Dist-IFF 1977

World Turned Upside Down, The C 52 MIN
16MM FILM OPTICAL SOUND H-C
Continuation of the film Washington - Time Of Triumph. Follows Washington to provide a view of General Cornwallis' surrender to Washington. Portrays how Washington, after the surrender, refused absolute power in order that democracy might work.
From The American Heritage Series.
Prod-WOLPER Dist-FI 1974

World Turned Upside Down, The C 15 MIN
16MM FILM, 3/4 OR 1/2 IN VIDEO I
Follows British and American soldiers during the Revolutionary War. Re-creates battle scenes in New York and Virginia.
From The American Scrapbook Series.
Prod-WVIZTV Dist-GPITVL 1977

World Upside Down, The C 30 MIN
3/4 OR 1/2 INCH VIDEO CASSETTE A
Tells what is happening to the Disciples' ministries overseas. Looks at the Church in Zaire. Stresses the values of church and scriptures.
Prod-DCCMS Dist-ECUFLM 1982

World War I C 25 MIN
16MM FILM, 3/4 OR 1/2 IN VIDEO H-C A
Discusses factors influencing America's entry into World War I, as well as her contributions to the Allied victory and role in the peace settlement.
From The American History Series.
Prod-CRMP Dist-CRMP 1969

World War I C 30 MIN
1 INCH VIDEOTAPE J-H
Explains the influence of the Wilson administration on the Black situation, the role of Blacks in the war, causes and effects of military discrimination, the service record of Blacks in France, postwar conditions and their psychological effects on the nation's racial climate.
From The Odyssey In Black Series.
Prod-KLVXTV Dist-GPITVL

World War I C 30 MIN
2 INCH VIDEOTAPE
Examines Wilson's efforts to avoid the war and his ultimate attempt to make it a moral crusade.
From The American History II Series.
Prod-KRMATV Dist-GPITVL

World War I (Historically Speaking) C 30 MIN
3/4 OR 1/2 INCH VIDEO CASSETTE H
Looks at the general causes of World War I and the assassination of Archduke Ferdinand. Reveals the permanent changes it caused in European life.
From The Historically Speaking Series. Part 19
Prod-KRMATV Dist-AITECH 1983

World War I (2nd Ed)—A Series
J-C
Looks at the causes of World War I, the battles and the leaders. Examines the failure of the treaty of Versailles.
Prod-CORF Dist-CORF

Background Tensions (2nd Ed) 013 MIN
Fighting On Two Fronts (2nd Ed) 018 MIN
Politics Of Peacemaking, The (2nd Ed) 014 MIN

World War I - A Documentary On The Role Of The U S A B 28 MIN
16MM FILM, 3/4 OR 1/2 IN VIDEO J-C
Describes the events which led the United States into war, the course of the war and Wilson's role at the peace conference.
Prod-EBF Dist-EBEC 1957

World War I - A Documentary On The Role Of The U S A (Spanish) B 28 MIN
16MM FILM, 3/4 OR 1/2 IN VIDEO J-C
Describes the events which led the United States into the First World War. Examines the course of the war and Woodrow Wilson's role at the peace conference.
Prod-EBEC Dist-EBEC

World War I - Here And 'Over There' B 28 MIN
16MM FILM SILENT H A
Presents 'Oregon's finest' in training and on the parade ground, combined with U S Army Signal Corps footage which was unreleased at the time of WW I.
Prod-OREGHS Dist-OREGHS

World War I Overseas Fliers Reunion C 12 MIN
16MM FILM OPTICAL SOUND
Reviews exploits of America's first fighter pilots as World War I airmen hold their first reunion at USAF Museum at Wright-Patterson AFB. Features presentation of awards and excerpts of speeches.
LC NO. 74-705970
Prod-USAF Dist-USNAC 1962

World War I—A Series
16MM FILM, 3/4 OR 1/2 IN VIDEO H-C
Studies the events of the First World War.
Prod-CBSTV Dist-FI 1967

Assassination At Sarajevo 016 MIN
Day The Guns Stopped Firing, The - 1918 018 MIN
Doomed Dynasties Of Europe 016 MIN
Home Front, 1917-1919 017 MIN
Revolution In Russia, 1917 019 MIN
Sinking Of The Lusitania, The 017 MIN
Soviet Union - Civil War And Allied 017 MIN
U S Neutrality, 1914-1917 017 MIN

World War II C 30 MIN
3/4 OR 1/2 INCH VIDEO CASSETTE H
Shows how the Western policy of appeasement failed to prevent aggression by Axis nations. Views the persecution of the Jews, the war itself and its results.
From The Historically Speaking Series. Part 22
Prod-KRMATV Dist-AITECH 1983

World War II - Background C 30 MIN
2 INCH VIDEOTAPE
Concerns the rise of fascism in Italy and Germany and war in Europe. Includes scenes of Hitler and the Munich Conference.
From The American History II Series.
Prod-KRMATV Dist-GPITVL

World War II - GI Diary—A Series
16MM FILM, 3/4 OR 1/2 IN VIDEO H-C A
Looks at the events of World War II by documenting the human drama of the American GIs who were actually in the foxholes.
Prod-TIMLIF Dist-TIMLIF 1980

Americans In Paris 030 MIN
Anzio To Rome 030 MIN
Battle For Saipan, The 030 MIN
Big Ben 030 MIN
Bulge, The 030 MIN
D-Day - One Bad Day In June 030 MIN
Desert War 030 MIN
Double Strike, The - Air Force Raids On 030 MIN
Flying Fortress, The 030 MIN
GI Christmas 030 MIN
Hell In The Arctic 030 MIN
Iwo Jima - Eight Square Miles Of Hell 030 MIN
Kamikaze - Flower Of Death 030 MIN
Last Barrier, The - Crossing The Rhine 030 MIN
Medal Of Honor 030 MIN
Midway 030 MIN
Nightmare At San Pietro 030 MIN
Okinawa - At The Emperor's Doorstep 030 MIN
Peleliu - The Killing Ground 030 MIN
Return To The Philippines 030 MIN
Road To Berlin 030 MIN
Savage Road To China 030 MIN
Sicily - The Yanks Are Coming 030 MIN
Target - Tokyo 030 MIN
Toughest Target, The 030 MIN

World War II - Prologue, U S A B 29 MIN
16MM FILM, 3/4 OR 1/2 IN VIDEO J-C
Reviews the events that led the U S into the war, showing the different stages of public opinion as events in Europe took place. Follows the conflict of World War II from Japan's invasion of Manchuria to the bombing of Pearl Harbor and the entry of the U S.
Prod-EBF Dist-EBEC 1956

World War II - Prologue, U S A (Spanish) C 29 MIN
16MM FILM, 3/4 OR 1/2 IN VIDEO J-C
Reviews the historic events which led the United States into World War II. Traces the conflict from Japan's invasion of Manchuria to the bombing of Pearl Harbor.
Prod-EBEC Dist-EBEC

World War II - The Propaganda Battle C 58 MIN
3/4 OR 1/2 INCH VIDEO CASSETTE
Describes how World War II saw two motion picture experts from Germany and the United States battle to make films that would inspire and instill the desire to win the war. Features filmmakers Frank Capra of the United States and Fritz Hippler of Germany.
From The Walk Through The 20th Century With Bill Moyers Series.
Prod-CORPEL Dist-PBS 1982

World War II - U S Involvement C 30 MIN
2 INCH VIDEOTAPE
Discusses the arguments over Pearl Harbor. Includes a summary of the U S war effort and an analysis of the decision to drop the atomic bomb.
From The American History II Series.
Prod-KRMATV Dist-GPITVL

World War II In The Pacific C 15 MIN
3/4 OR 1/2 INCH VIDEO CASSETTE PRO
Portrays Japan's rise as an industrial power from the opening of foreign trade to expansionism and defeat in WWII. Uses seldom seen WWII photographs. Looks at modern Japan.
Prod-USNPS Dist-USNAC 1984

World War II With Walter Cronkite—A Series

Illustrates the terrors, the tensions, the triumphs and tragedies of World War II. Uses actual film footage culled from the newsreel companies, US Signal Corps and many archives from around the world, and was produced by CBS News and narrated by Walter Cronkite.
Prod-CBSNEW Dist-CBSVL

World War II—A Series
J-C A
Uses documentary footage that chronicles global events from 1919 to 1945. Shows the conditions that bred totalitarianism and led to World War II. Examines the impact of technology on modern war.
Prod-CORF Dist-CORF 1985

Expanding Conflict, The (1940-1941) 012 MIN
Fragile Peace, A (1918-1929) 011 MIN
Inevitable War, The (1939-1940) 013 MIN
Roots Of Aggression, The (1929-1939) 014 MIN
World At War, A (1942-1945) 016 MIN

World War One C 28 MIN
16MM FILM OPTICAL SOUND
Describes Ohio's response to World War I. Covers events leading to the war, the war itself, and the period immediately following the war.
From The Glory And The Dream - Ohio's Response To War Series.
Prod-OHC Dist-HRC

World War Two C 25 MIN
16MM FILM OPTICAL SOUND
Describes Ohio's reaction to World War II. Discusses conscientious objectors, war protests and prisioners of war.
From The Glory And The Dream - Ohio's Response To War Series.
Prod-OHC Dist-HRC

World War 1 C 30 MIN
3/4 OR 1/2 INCH VIDEO CASSETTE C
Analyzes U S involvement in World War 1.
America - The Second Century Series.
Prod-DALCCD Dist-DALCCD

World War 2 C 30 MIN
3/4 OR 1/2 INCH VIDEO CASSETTE C
Shows how the U S, the super nation with the super weapon, emerged from World War II with a responsibility to help reshape the postwar world.
America - The Second Century Series.
Prod-DALCCD Dist-DALCCD

World War, Garveyism And Negro Cultural Renaissance B 30 MIN
2 INCH VIDEOTAPE H-C A
See series title for descriptive statement.
From The Americans From Africa - A History Series. No. 25
Prod-CVETVC Dist-GPITVL Prodn-WCVETV

World Was All Before Them, The C 30 MIN
3/4 OR 1/2 INCH VIDEO CASSETTE C
See series title for descriptive statement.
From The Art Of Being Human Series. Module 15
Prod-MDCC Dist-MDCC

World Was Once Very Different, The B 15 MIN
2 INCH VIDEOTAPE P
Discusses Indian artifacts and fossils from prehistoric times to show how forms of life have changed on earth. (Broadcast quality)
From The Land And Sea Series.
Prod-TTOIC Dist-GPITVL Prodn-WCVETV

World Was There, The C 28 MIN
16MM FILM, 3/4 OR 1/2 IN VIDEO
Shows how the news media of the world covered the manned space launches of NASA's Project Mercury. Covers the flights of astronauts Shepard, Grissom, Glenn, Carpenter, Schirra and Cooper. Narrated by Alexander Scourby. Issued in 1975 as a motion picture.
LC NO. 80-707384
Prod-NASA Dist-USNAC 1980

World We Live In–A Series
16MM FILM, 3/4 OR 1/2 IN VIDEO
Presents a variety of topics in the area of science, exploration and psychology designed for both entertainment purposes as well as educational.
Prod-TIMELI Dist-MGHT

Animal War, Animal Peace	30 MIN
Antarctica - Because It's There	29 MIN
Child Watchers, The	30 MIN
Dam Builders, The	30 MIN
Life In Parched Lands	30 MIN
Questions Of Time	30 MIN
Riddle Of Heredity	30 MIN
Sun Watchers, The	30 MIN
Survival In The Sea	30 MIN
Water - Old Problems, New Approaches	30 MIN
Weather Watchers, The	30 MIN
Winners, The	30 MIN

World We Live In, The C 15 MIN
3/4 OR 1/2 INCH VIDEO CASSETTE K-J
See series title for descriptive statement.
From The Arts Express Series.
Prod-KYTV Dist-KYTV 1983

World Within C 27 MIN
16MM FILM, 3/4 OR 1/2 IN VIDEO
Shows how parasitism is found among plants and animals. Examines how parasites differ from other organisms that live together symbiotically. Reveals how parasites follow a birth-to-death cycle.
Prod-UCEMC Dist-UCEMC

World Within A World - The Maximum Containment Laboratory C 5 MIN
3/4 OR 1/2 INCH VIDEO CASSETTE
Describes the need for and construction of a modular laboratory. Longer version issued in 1978.
LC NO. 80-706767
Prod-CFDISC Dist-USNAC 1979

World Within A World - The Maximum Containment Laboratory C 24 MIN
16MM FILM - 3/4 IN VIDEO
Describes principles and procedures used to safely operate a class IV laboratory which handles virulent viruses and hazardous DNA.
LC NO. 78-706145
Prod-CFDISC Dist-USNAC 1978

World Within A World, A C 10 MIN
16MM FILM OPTICAL SOUND
Depicts the function of duty-free shops and seastores around the world.
LC NO. 79-701314
Prod-PHILMO Dist-PHILMO 1979

World Within World C 52 MIN
16MM FILM, 3/4 OR 1/2 IN VIDEO J-C A
Explores the world within the atom and traces the history of men and ideas that have made 20th-century physics.
From The Ascent Of Man Series. No. 10
LC NO. 79-707236
Prod-BBCTV Dist-TIMLIF 1973

World Within World (Spanish) C 52 MIN
16MM FILM OPTICAL SOUND H-C A
Explores the world within the atom and traces the history of men and ideas that have made 20th-century physics.
From The Ascent Of Man Series.
Prod-BBCTV Dist-TIMLIF 1973

World Within Worlds C 23 MIN
16MM FILM, 3/4 OR 1/2 IN VIDEO H-C A
Shows how different photographic techniques, such as microphotography, time-lapse photography, Kirlian photography, and ultraviolet photography, can overcome obstacles of size and time and depict things that were previously invisible.
LC NO. 81-706832
Prod-NGS Dist-NGS 1981

World Within, The C
3/4 INCH VIDEO CASSETTE
Describes growth and development of a child from 27 to 28 months.
From The Growth And Development - A Chronicle Of Four Children Series. Series 7
Prod-JUETHO Dist-LIP

World Within, The - Gregory, 27 Months C 7 MIN
16MM FILM OPTICAL SOUND
See series title for descriptive statement.
From The Growth And Development - A Chronicle Of Four Children Series. Series 7
Prod-JUETHO Dist-LIP Prodn-CONCOM 1976

World Within, The - Joseph, 28 Months C 7 MIN
16MM FILM OPTICAL SOUND
See series title for descriptive statement.
From The Growth And Development - A Chronicle Of Four Children Series. Series 7
LC NO. 78-700688
Prod-JUETHO Dist-LIP Prodn-CONCOM 1976

World Within, The - Melissa, 27 Months C 7 MIN
16MM FILM OPTICAL SOUND
See series title for descriptive statement.
From The Growth And Development - A Chronicle Of Four Children Series. Series 7
LC NO. 78-700688
Prod-JUETHO Dist-LIP Prodn-CONCOM 1976

World Within, The - Terra, 28 Months C 7 MIN
16MM FILM OPTICAL SOUND
See series title for descriptive statement.
From The Growth And Development - A Chronicle Of Four Children Series. Series 7
LC NO. 78-700688
Prod-JUETHO Dist-LIP Prodn-CONCOM 1976

World Without Sun C 8 MIN
16MM FILM OPTICAL SOUND
Presents an abridged version of a segment from The Undersea World Of Jacques Cousteau. Analyzes life beneath the Red Sea.
Prod-TIMLIF Dist-TIMLIF 1982

World Without Sun C 93 MIN
16MM FILM OPTICAL SOUND
Illustrates Cousteau and his divers testing themselves and a new underwater vehicle by remaining submerged for a month.
Prod-CPC Dist-TWYMAN 1964

World–A Series
H-C A
Presents a series of international documentaries.
Prod-WGBHTV Dist-PBS

Australia - The Lucky Country	058 MIN
Bogota, One Day	090 MIN
Chinese Way, The	079 MIN
Death Of A Princess	118 MIN
Frank Terpil - Confessions Of A Dangerous Man	118 MIN
Getting Elected In Papua, New Guinea	058 MIN
Inside Europe - F-16, The Arms Sale Of The	058 MIN
Inside Europe - Italy, Chain Reaction	058 MIN
Inside Europe - The Shirt Of Your Back	058 MIN
La Mal Vie - Algerian Migrants	058 MIN
Nguba Connection, The	058 MIN
No More Mountains - The Story Of The Hmong	058 MIN
Red Army	058 MIN
Return To Poland	058 MIN
Sweden, Waiting For The Spring	058 MIN
Welcome To Yap	058 MIN
West Bank Story, The	058 MIN
Yulya's Diary	058 MIN

World-Wide Fallout From Nuclear Weapons C 41 MIN
16MM FILM, 3/4 OR 1/2 IN VIDEO
Explains what is and is not known about the long-term consequences of world-wide fallout. Discusses only the fallout on which a substantial amount of information is available, to correct any factually unsupported statements which may have been issued.
Prod-USDD Dist-USNAC

World-Wide Naval Operations In Peace And War - 1815-1860 C 23 MIN
16MM FILM OPTICAL SOUND
Describes contributions to naval science, such as the development of steam power, and the navy's role in protecting American citizens and promoting trade.
From The History Of The United States Navy.
Prod-USN Dist-USNAC Prodn-CAS 1956

World, The Flesh And Jimmy Jones, The B 13 MIN
16MM FILM OPTICAL SOUND
Reviews the life of one of America's 600,000 cerebral palsied from the day the diagnosis was made through the therapies, special education and vocational training through the frustrating period of job-seeking.
Prod-UCPA Dist-UCPA

World's Children–A Series
16MM FILM, 3/4 OR 1/2 IN VIDEO P-I
Introduces children from around the world.
Prod-ITF Dist-JOU 1980

With Bekus In Nepal	014 MIN
With Bernadette In New Guinea	013 MIN
With Claudia In Australia	013 MIN
With Epelli In Fiji	013 MIN
With Gladis In Bolivia	011 MIN
With Michael In Kyuso, Kenya	013 MIN
With Nang And Nakorn In Thailand	014 MIN
With Oscar In Peru	011 MIN
With Pastore In Togo	013 MIN
With Patsy In St Vincent	013 MIN
With Spencer In Nairobi, Kenya	013 MIN
With Sylvia In The Philippines	012 MIN
With Yau Kai In Hong Kong	013 MIN

World's Columbia Exposition, The C 30 MIN
3/4 OR 1/2 INCH VIDEO CASSETTE H-C A
Deals with the Columbia Exposition and with architecture in the early 1900's.
From The Art America Series.
Prod-CTI Dist-CTI

World's Favorite Prune, The C 22 MIN
16MM FILM OPTICAL SOUND
Presents the story of prunes from their development in 1860 to the present and traces the development of the prune industry. Looks at the cultivation, harvest and processing of prunes.
LC NO. 82-700113
Prod-MTP Dist-MTP 1982

World's Greatest Freak Show, The C 11 MIN
3/4 INCH VIDEO CASSETTE P
Tells how a magician presents a freak show and learns that the wildly applauding audience is as deformed as his three 'freaks.' Examines the nature of beauty and selfish vanity.
From The Desire To Read Series.
Prod-BOSUST Dist-GA

World's Greatest Photography Course, The C
1/2 IN VIDEO CASSETTE BETA/VHS H
Gives a hands-on introduction to photography. Offers demonstrations and professional tips on all the basics by photographer Lief Ericksenn.
Prod-GA Dist-GA

World's Largest Nest, The - The Sociable Weaverbird C 9 MIN
16MM FILM, 3/4 OR 1/2 IN VIDEO I-C A
Examines the colonial nest of the sociable weaverbird of southern Africa, including the details of nest structure, the variety of nest configurations, the process of nest building and the ecological contributions of the nest to the success of the bird in the Kalahari Desert.
From The Aspects Of Animal Behavior Series.
Prod-UCLA Dist-UCEMC 1976

World's Largest TV Studio, The B 60 MIN
3/4 OR 1/2 INCH VIDEO CASSETTE
Documents the 1972 Democratic National Convention in Miami Beach. Includes behind the scenes with McGovern forces.
Prod-TOPTV Dist-EAI

World's Most Versatile Horse, The C 13 MIN
16MM FILM, 3/4 OR 1/2 IN VIDEO
Features some of the quarter horse breed's finest individuals cutting, roping, reining and barrel racing.
Prod-AQHORS Dist-AQHORS

World's Still Young, The B 5 MIN
16MM FILM OPTICAL SOUND
Presents a montage of international scenes leading to a review of world-wide production facilities of the Levi Strauss Organization, followed by marketing differences between various countries. Includes views of children around the world wearing Levis.
LC NO. 73-702401
Prod-LEVI Dist-LEVI 1972

World's Winter Strawberry Capital C 14 MIN
16MM FILM OPTICAL SOUND
Highlights the Hillsborough County Fair and Florida Strawberry Festival.
Prod-FLADC Dist-FLADC

Worlds Apart B 16 MIN
16MM FILM OPTICAL SOUND T
Explains the techniques devised by the institute for developmental studies to bridge the gap between the world of the ghetto and the world of textbooks. Shows how to develop a sense of self-esteem and how to teach concept formation and language in a pre-kindergarten class.
LC NO. FIA68-577
Prod-NYUIDS Dist-ADL Prodn-ADL 1967

Worlds Apart C 96 MIN
16MM FILM OPTICAL SOUND
Tells the story of Captain Paul Matthews, an army doctor, whose battlefield surgery won decorations for bravery including a Purple Heart. Wounded in action, he was forced to return to the United States, where he renews an acquaintance with Denise Henley, a college classmate whose rise to stardom in show business came while Paul was in combat. Paul's dedication to Christ soon brings them into conflict.
LC NO. FIA68-880
Prod-YOUTH Dist-GF 1967

Worlds Apart C 55 MIN
16MM FILM, 3/4 OR 1/2 IN VIDEO H-C A
Visits Aldabra Island in the Indian Ocean to visit giant tortoises that have reached their zenith in a hostile landscape of jagged coral rock where survival may mean eating your neighbor.
From The Living Planet Series. Pt 10
Prod-BBCTV Dist-TIMLIF 1984

Worlds Apart–A Series
16MM FILM, 3/4 OR 1/2 IN VIDEO
Reports on different communities around the world, each relatively isolated. Shows that each is in danger of losing its identity due to increasing pressures from the outside.
Prod-BBCTV Dist-FI 1982

Connemara Family, A	055 MIN
Muria, The	055 MIN
Panare, The - Scenes From The Frontier	060 MIN
Raj Gonds	055 MIN
South-East Nuba, The	060 MIN

Worlds Of Martha Schlamme, The B 30 MIN
16MM FILM OPTICAL SOUND H-C A
Miss Schlamme, folk singer, presents selections in Yiddish, Hebrew, English and German. (Kinescope)
From The Eternal Light Series.
LC NO. 70-700958
Prod-JTS Dist-NAAJS 1966

Worlds Within, The C 29 MIN
16MM FILM OPTICAL SOUND
A nontechnical description of the design, construction and use of the Stanford linear accelerator. Presents a background account on its development and a discussion on the theory of its operation and the problems encountered in its construction and use. Examines the fabrication and testing of a two-mile long copper tube through which atomic particles will be fired, and of high-power radio tubes, called klystrons, which are used to project electrons down the tube. Compares various methods of projecting particles of minute dimensions.
LC NO. FIE64-185
Prod-STNFRD Dist-EDUC 1963

Worldwide Competition C 30 MIN
3/4 OR 1/2 INCH VIDEO CASSETTE
Describes the six major groups in the information industry. Identifies the challenges faced by each industry group and explains how these challenges, if not met, provide competitive opportunities for other firms.

From The Information Industry - Strategic Planning Considerations Series.
Prod-DELTAK Dist-DELTAK

Worms - Flat, Round And Segmented C 16 MIN
16MM FILM, 3/4 OR 1/2 IN VIDEO H-C
Emphasizes regeneration and tropism in flatworms, parasitism in roundworms and evolutionary advances of segmented worms.
From The Major Phyla Series.
Prod-CORF Dist-CORF 1970

Worms - The Annelida X 13 MIN
16MM FILM, 3/4 OR 1/2 IN VIDEO J-C
A study of the four classes of annelid worms showing their structure, distinguishing characteristics, behavior and habitats. Shows the various ways in which annelids move, breathe, gather food and reproduce. Explains how the earthworm contributes to the conservation of the soil.
Prod-EBF Dist-EBEC 1955

Worms To Wings C 13 MIN
16MM FILM, 3/4 OR 1/2 IN VIDEO P-H
Shows the metamorphic process of the anise swallowtail butterfly in its entirety.
Prod-MIS Dist-MIS 1955

Worried Man C 30 MIN
3/4 OR 1/2 INCH VIDEO CASSETTE H-C A
Shows how to master various banjo fingering exercises and presents the song Worried Man.
From The Bluegrass Banjo (Level One) Series.
Prod-OWL Dist-GPITVL 1980

Worry - I'm In Big Trouble Now C 12 MIN
3/4 INCH VIDEO CASSETTE I-J
Tells what happens when Billy is entrusted with the care of his little brother and his brother disappears into the woods.
Prod-GA Dist-GA

Worship Of Nature, The C 52 MIN
16MM FILM, 3/4 OR 1/2 IN VIDEO J-C A
Surveys the development of Western civilization during the late 1700's and the 1800's as characterized by a romantic belief in the divinity of nature and as evidenced in the work of Rousseau, Goethe and Wordsworth and in the paintings of Constable, Casper David Friederich and William Turner.
From The Civilisation Series. No. 11
LC NO. 79-707051
Prod-BBCTV Dist-FI 1970

Worst Child Killer, The B 9 MIN
16MM FILM OPTICAL SOUND PRO
Presents a visit to a hospital, a doctor's office and a poison information center to warn of common accidents and hazards that affect children, such as bicycle-auto collisions, knocking pots off stoves and investigating medicine chests.
From The Doctors At Work Series.
Prod-CMA Dist-LAWREN Prodn-LAWREN

Worst Winter Of The Century B 5 MIN
16MM FILM OPTICAL SOUND
Tells the story of the coldest winter of the twentieth century which assaulted most of the world with unprecedented cold weather. Shows that man may be able to forecast and prepare for all kinds of weather but he cannot yet control it.
From The Screen News Digest Series. Vol 5, Issue 8
Prod-HEARST Dist-HEARST 1963

Worth A Thousand Words C 18 MIN
16MM FILM OPTICAL SOUND
Explains the uses of automated computer graphical output and describes a system developed at the Culham Laboratory for achieving it. Includes a number of examples of computer-produced cine output, drawn from the fields of astronomy, geometry and plasma physics.
Prod-UKAEA Dist-UKAEA 1968

Worth Of A Child C 22 MIN
16MM FILM OPTICAL SOUND
Features a young woman who has made a friend of a mentally handicapped person. Shows how she goes on to become a teacher of the mentally and physically handicapped.
LC NO. 77-702180
Prod-BYU Dist-BYU 1977

Worth Of Waste, The C 18 MIN
16MM FILM OPTICAL SOUND
Examines the efforts of industry and government to reclaim and re-use much of the material previously considered junk.
Prod-GM Dist-GM

Worth The Effort C 16 MIN
16MM FILM OPTICAL SOUND
Presents three examples of how the Grace Corporation, a large chemical corporation, has spent over $350 million insuring minimal impact of their activity on the environment.
LC NO. 81-701213
Prod-GRACE Dist-GRACE Prodn-VISION 1981

Worth Waiting For B 28 MIN
16MM FILM OPTICAL SOUND J-H A
Describes the problems that arose for a high school couple when they decided to become engaged .
Prod-BYU Dist-CAMPF 1962

Worthington - The New Eden C 29 MIN
3/4 INCH VIDEO CASSETTE
Describes the settling of Worthington, Ohio, in 1803.
Prod-OHC Dist-HRC

Worthington - The Virtuous Society In Transition C 29 MIN
3/4 INCH VIDEO CASSETTE
Discusses the economic, cultural, religious, social, educational and political life of the town of Worthington, Ohio, from 1803 to the mid-century.
Prod-OHC Dist-HRC

Worthy Destination, A C
1/2 IN VIDEO CASSETTE BETA/VHS
Deals with setting and achieving goals, Focuses on developing positive attitudes, creating opportunities and planning.
Prod-NIGCON Dist-NIGCON

Woton's Wake B 32 MIN
16MM FILM OPTICAL SOUND H-C
Features a new experimental film which combines the sardonic humor of James Broughton's 'THE PLEASURE GARDEN' with the mysterioso of 'THE STRANGER LEFT NO CARD.'
Prod-DEPALB Dist-CFS

Would An Example Help C 15 MIN
3/4 OR 1/2 INCH VIDEO CASSETTE J
Explains the importance of following form and language by telling the story of Ricky, whose first play confuses the cast because the language is inappropriate and the script isn't typed in the usual way. Shows that before writing to the editor, Darlene checks the form, language and organization of letters that have made it into print.
From The In Other Words Series. Organizing Ideas, Pt 5
Prod-AITV Dist-AITECH Prodn-KOCETV 1983

Would You Believe C 15 MIN
3/4 INCH VIDEO CASSETTE P-I
Looks at the world of fantasy.
From The Can You Imagine Series.
Prod-WVIZTV Dist-GPITVL

Would You Bet Your Life C 17 MIN
16MM FILM, 3/4 OR 1/2 IN VIDEO IND
Compares bets to the chances taken when an electrical lineman does not heed the safety rules. Presents linemen who have had accidents who tell how the accident occurred.
Prod-EUSA Dist-IFB

Would You Like To Make A Book B 15 MIN
2 INCH VIDEOTAPE P
Demonstrates manipulating paper to achieve a simple four-page book to decorate with drawings or prints.
From The Art Corner Series.
Prod-CVETVC Dist-GPITVL Prodn-WCVETV

Wouldn't It Be Nice C 15 MIN
16MM FILM, 3/4 OR 1/2 IN VIDEO P-C A
Informs about the methodology and mechanism of catalog purchasing that make it a successful process.
Prod-KLEINW Dist-KLEINW

Wound Healing By Primary Intention C 27 MIN
16MM FILM OPTICAL SOUND
Shows the critical differences between healing by secondary and primary intention.
LC NO. 75-703130
Prod-BAYUCM Dist-MMAMC 1975

Wound Healing I(By Secondary Intention) C 27 MIN
3/4 INCH VIDEO CASSETTE PRO
Visualizes by animation the six processes involved in wound healing when tissue heals without approximation.
Prod-MMAMC Dist-MMAMC

Wound Healing II(By Primary Intention) C 23 MIN
3/4 INCH VIDEO CASSETTE PRO
Combines animation and live action to discuss the six phases of healing when sutures or wound closure strips are used to approximate tissue.
Prod-MMAMC Dist-MMAMC

Wound Rotor Controllers B 17 MIN
16MM FILM - 3/4 IN VIDEO
Demonstrates the principles of the wound rotor motor and shows the operation of a faceplate controller, drum-type nonreversing controllers, drum-type reversing controllers and automatic magnetic starter for a wound rotor motor.
From The Electrical Work - Motor Control Series. No. 4
LC NO. 79-707498
Prod-USOE Dist-USNAC Prodn-CALVCO 1979

Wounded Knee Affair, The C 17 MIN
3/4 OR 1/2 INCH VIDEO CASSETTE H-C A
Describes the 1973 protest at Wounded Knee, South Dakota, during which American Indians tried to draw international attention to the problems facing their culture.
Prod-UPI Dist-JOU

Wounds C 20 MIN
3/4 INCH VIDEO CASSETTE
Identifies general types of injuries, describing basic principles of emergency care. Shows the anatomy and physiology of the skin and the result of injury to the skin. Recommends emergency care techniques for wounds.
From The Medical Legal Component Film Series.
LC NO. 74-706527
Prod-KYDHPS Dist-USNAC Prodn-UKY 1974

Wounds And Bleeding C 30 MIN
3/4 OR 1/2 INCH VIDEO CASSETTE
Shows how to recognize 'life threatening situations' and how to treat punctures, abrasions, incisions and lacerations.
From The First Aid In The Classroom Series.
Prod-NETCHE Dist-NETCHE 1973

Woven Gardens C 52 MIN
16MM FILM, 3/4 OR 1/2 IN VIDEO
Examines the woven rugs of the Qashqa tribe of Iran and explains how the rugs are made, what functions they serve and the significance of the traditional symbols used in their design.
From The Tribal Eye Series.
LC NO. 79-707120
Prod-BBCTV Dist-TIMLIF 1976

Woven Hangings C 25 MIN
3/4 OR 1/2 INCH VIDEO CASSETTE J-C A
Portrays innovation in weaving today. Demonstrates the shaft-switching technique which makes possible the complex design on the rugs of series consultant Peter Collingwood. Includes Ann Sutton talking about her own work, and looks at the range and variety of woven hangings.
From The Craft Of The Weaver Series.
Prod-BBCTV Dist-FI 1983

Woyzeck C 82 MIN
16MM FILM OPTICAL SOUND
A German language motion picture with English subtitles. Depicts the tragedy of an ordinary man's headlong plunge into madness and murder. Directed by Werner Herzog.
Prod-UNKNWN Dist-NYFLMS 1978

Woyzeck C 60 MIN
3/4 OR 1/2 INCH VIDEO CASSETTE H-C A
Explores methods of character development. Uses the play Woyzeck as an example.
From The Drama - Play, Performance, Perception Series. Dramatis Personae
Prod-BBCTV Dist-FI 1978

Wrap It Up C 15 MIN
2 INCH VIDEOTAPE
See series title for descriptive statement.
From The Umbrella Series.
Prod-KETCTV Dist-PUBTEL

Wrapping A Permanent Wave (On A Mannequin) C
3/4 OR 1/2 INCH VIDEO CASSETTE
Explains the relationship of rod size to block size. Shows how hair is held while wrapping, the application of end papers, proper wrapping technique and the fastening of bands to avoid breakage and indentations. Illustrates wrong procedures relative to the above. Demonstrates how the comb is used to protect the scalp during styling with a hot brush.
From The Lessons On A Mannequin Series, Lesson IV.
Prod-MPCEDP Dist-MPCEDP 1984

Wrapping It Up C 29 MIN
3/4 INCH VIDEO CASSETTE H A
Reviews the Beethoven and Kabalevsky pieces. Gives suggestions regarding newly acquired piano playing skills.
From The Beginning Piano - An Adult Approach Series. Lesson 30
Prod-COAST Dist-CDTEL

Wrappings C 15 MIN
2 INCH VIDEOTAPE
See series title for descriptive statement.
From The Making Things Work Series.
Prod-WGBHTV Dist-PUBTEL

Wrappings And Trappings C 20 MIN
16MM FILM, 3/4 OR 1/2 IN VIDEO
Shows how people in various cultures have made and used costumes, masks and headdress for ceremonies and other special occasions. Considers how a person can use clothing to create a special image of himself and how clothing can effect behavior.
From The Images And Things Series.
LC NO. 73-702116
Prod-NITC Dist-AITECH 1971

Wraps C 11 MIN
16MM FILM OPTICAL SOUND
Discusses the versatility of aluminum wrap and describes its artistic and scientific uses.
LC NO. 79-700349
Prod-REYMC Dist-MTP Prodn-FILMCI 1978

Wreck Of The New York Subway, The B 17 MIN
16MM FILM OPTICAL SOUND
Explains how fares increase, conditions become more perilous and how subway workers and riders organize to educate the public about municipal corruption and cynicism.
Prod-SFN Dist-SFN

Wreck Raisers C 45 MIN
16MM FILM OPTICAL SOUND P-I
Presents Tom and his pals attempting to raise a wrecked boat in order to prove they aren't to blame for its destruction.
Prod-LUF Dist-LUF

Wrenches B 19 MIN
16MM FILM OPTICAL SOUND
Explains the uses and advantages of various wrenches and shows the damage which may result from incorrect and dangerous practices in using them.
Prod-USA Dist-USNAC 1943

Wrenches C 14 MIN
16MM FILM, 3/4 OR 1/2 IN VIDEO
Illustrates the versatilities and practicalities of a variety of wrenches.
From The Hand Operations - Woodworking Series.
Prod-MORLAT Dist-SF 1974

Wrenches B 19 MIN
16MM FILM, 3/4 OR 1/2 IN VIDEO
Explains the uses and advantages of various wrenches and shows the damage which can result from improper usage. Issued in 1943 as a motion picture.
From The Care And Use Of Hand Tools Series. Number 1
LC NO. 80-706604
Prod-USWD Dist-USNAC 1980

Wrenches And Screwdrivers C 12 MIN
3/4 OR 1/2 INCH VIDEO CASSETTE
Covers the use, kinds and care of different wrenches and screwdrivers.
From The Using Hand Tools Series.
Prod-TPCTRA Dist-TPCTRA

Wrenches And Screwdrivers (Spanish) C 12 MIN
3/4 OR 1/2 INCH VIDEO CASSETTE
Covers the use, kinds and care of different wrenches and screwdrivers.
From The Using Hand Tools Series.
Prod-TPCTRA Dist-TPCTRA

Wrestling B 13 MIN
16MM FILM OPTICAL SOUND
National AAU champion Danny Hodge wrestles according to amateur rules.
Prod-SFI Dist-SFI

Wrestling Fundamentals C 11 MIN
16MM FILM, 3/4 OR 1/2 IN VIDEO J-H
Explains that good wrestling requires a series of moves and counter-moves and the basic ones are, the take downs, double leg, single leg, arm drag and whip over, the escapes, sit out and roll out, the reverses, switch short switch and side roll, and the pin holds, bar arm and half nelson, and the cradle.
Prod-RICH Dist-PHENIX 1969

Wrestling Fundamentals (Spanish) C 11 MIN
16MM FILM, 3/4 OR 1/2 IN VIDEO J-H
Explains that good wrestling requires a series of moves and counter-moves and the basic ones are, the take downs, double leg, single leg, arm drag and whip over, the escapes, sit out and roll out, the reverses, switch short switch and side roll, and the pin holds, bar arm and half nelson, and the cradle.
Prod-RICH Dist-PHENIX 1969

Wrestling Today C 17 MIN
16MM FILM OPTICAL SOUND J-C
Discusses the rules of interscholastic wrestling. Illustrates the decisions of officials and shows the bases for these decisions.
LC NO. 74-703506
Prod-NFSHSA Dist-NFSHSA 1973

Wrestling—A Series
16MM FILM, 3/4 OR 1/2 IN VIDEO
Discusses the techniques used in wrestling.
Prod-ATHI Dist-ATHI 1976

Fundamentals Of Wrestling 019 MIN
Pinning Combinations 020 MIN
Rides And Escapes 022 MIN
Takedown Techniques 022 MIN

Wright Brothers - Wings Over Kitty Hawk B 15 MIN
1/2 IN VIDEO CASSETTE BETA/VHS
Reviews the first airplane flight of the Wright Brothers in 1903. Covers aviation's progress during the next 50 years.
Prod-STAR Dist-STAR

Wright Morris C 29 MIN
16MM FILM, 3/4 OR 1/2 IN VIDEO
Presents an interview with author Wright Morris.
From The Writer In America Series.
Prod-PERSPF Dist-CORF

Wrinkle In Time, A C 15 MIN
3/4 OR 1/2 INCH VIDEO CASSETTE I
Presents a science fiction story about the adventures of a girl and her family. From the book by Madeline L'Engle.
From The Storybound Series.
Prod-CTI Dist-CTI

Wrinkles C 29 MIN
3/4 INCH VIDEO CASSETTE C A
Demonstrates two different kinds of wrinkles used in drawing, those in fabric and skin.
From The Sketching Techniques Series. Lesson 28
Prod-COAST Dist-CDTEL

Write A Poem - Share Your Feelings C 15 MIN
16MM FILM - VIDEO, ALL FORMATS K-J
Presents a Fat Albert cartoon about a boy who writes poems, and the gang learning about poetry.
From The Fat Albert And The Cosby Kids IV Series.
Prod-BARR Dist-BARR Prodn-FLMTON

Write Channel, The, Pt 01 C 15 MIN
3/4 OR 1/2 INCH VIDEO CASSETTE P-I
Discusses the use of 'and' for compound subjects, objects and verbs. Points out the need to start a sentence with a capital letter and end a statement with a period.
Prod-MAETEL Dist-AITECH 1979

Write Channel, The, Pt 02 C 14 MIN
3/4 OR 1/2 INCH VIDEO CASSETTE P-I
Explains adjective modification and looks at the correct use of the period and capital letter.
Prod-MAETEL Dist-AITECH 1979

Write Channel, The, Pt 03 C 14 MIN
3/4 OR 1/2 INCH VIDEO CASSETTE P-I
Describes the use of conjunctions 'and' and 'but' in a compound sentence and focuses on the comma.
Prod-MAETEL Dist-AITECH 1979

Write Channel, The, Pt 04 C 15 MIN
3/4 OR 1/2 INCH VIDEO CASSETTE P-I
Tells how to add when, where and how information to a base sentence. Describes the capitalization of the days and months and the use of a comma between the day and the year.
Prod-MAETEL Dist-AITECH 1979

Write Channel, The, Pt 05 C 15 MIN
3/4 OR 1/2 INCH VIDEO CASSETTE P-I
Discusses the addition of adjective clauses introduced by 'who' or 'that' to a base sentence. Considers the use of the question mark and the exclamation point.
Prod-MAETEL Dist-AITECH 1979

Write Channel, The, Pt 06 C 14 MIN
3/4 OR 1/2 INCH VIDEO CASSETTE P-I
Focuses on the use of the prepositional phrase introduced by 'with.' Describes the use of a comma after an introductory 'yes' or 'no.'
Prod-MAETEL Dist-AITECH 1979

Write Channel, The, Pt 07 C 15 MIN
3/4 OR 1/2 INCH VIDEO CASSETTE P-I
Examines the addition of prepositional phrases to a base sentence. Tells how to capitalize the name of a city or a state and discusses the use of a comma between a city and a state.
Prod-MAETEL Dist-AITECH 1979

Write Channel, The, Pt 08 C 15 MIN
3/4 OR 1/2 INCH VIDEO CASSETTE P-I
Exemplifies the variety of sentence types and emphasizes the need to choose the one that best expresses an idea. Discusses the use of a capital letter to begin a person's name and the use of a comma to separate a series of adjectives.
Prod-MAETEL Dist-AITECH 1979

Write Channel, The, Pt 09 C 15 MIN
3/4 OR 1/2 INCH VIDEO CASSETTE P-I
Focuses on the use of the subordinating conjunctions 'when,' 'after' and 'before.' Explains the capitalization of 'I.'
Prod-MAETEL Dist-AITECH 1979

Write Channel, The, Pt 10 C 14 MIN
3/4 OR 1/2 INCH VIDEO CASSETTE P-I
Describes the use of the subordinating conjunctions 'because,' 'although' and 'if.' Explores the use of the apostrophe in a contraction.
Prod-MAETEL Dist-AITECH 1979

Write Channel, The, Pt 11 C 15 MIN
3/4 OR 1/2 INCH VIDEO CASSETTE P-I
Looks at the use of infinitives and participial phrases, as well as the use of the apostrophe in possessives.
Prod-MAETEL Dist-AITECH 1979

Write Channel, The, Pt 12 C 15 MIN
3/4 OR 1/2 INCH VIDEO CASSETTE P-I
Discusses the use of appositives and the use of commas to set off an appositive.
Prod-MAETEL Dist-AITECH 1979

Write Channel, The, Pt 13 C 15 MIN
3/4 OR 1/2 INCH VIDEO CASSETTE P-I
Explains the use of commas and the conjunction 'and' in a series of phrases or clauses.
Prod-MAETEL Dist-AITECH 1979

Write Channel, The, Pt 14 C 15 MIN
3/4 OR 1/2 INCH VIDEO CASSETTE P-I
Describes the use of 'that' in a noun clause. Offers information on the capitalization and underlining of a book title.
Prod-MAETEL Dist-AITECH 1979

Write Channel, The, Pt 15 C 15 MIN
3/4 OR 1/2 INCH VIDEO CASSETTE P-I
Reviews sentence combining techniques, capitalization, and punctuation rules.
Prod-MAETEL Dist-AITECH 1979

Write Course - An Introduction To College Composition—A Series
C A
Presents contemporary scholarship on the teaching of composition as a process. Contains real-life adaptations of the writing process at work. Addresses the needs of non-traditional students.
Prod-FI Dist-FI 1984

Argumentation 030 MIN
Audience And Style 030 MIN
Audience, The 030 MIN
Beginning And Ending 030 MIN
Beginning, The 030 MIN
Definition 030 MIN
Developing Form 030 MIN
Discovering Ideas 030 MIN
Discovering The Library 030 MIN
Drama Of Thinking, The 030 MIN
Essay Test, The 030 MIN
Narration And Description 030 MIN
New Directions 030 MIN
Paragraph Patterns 030 MIN
Process And Analysis 030 MIN
Report And Proposal Writing 030 MIN
Revision Strategies 030 MIN
Sentence Patterns 030 MIN
Sentence Strategy 030 MIN
Sharpening The Focus 030 MIN
Structuring The Topic 030 MIN
Style 030 MIN
Using The Writer's Tools 030 MIN
Why Write 030 MIN
Word Strategy 030 MIN
Words And Meanings 030 MIN
Writing A Research Paper 030 MIN
Writing About Books 030 MIN
Writing At Work 030 MIN
Writing Process, The 030 MIN

Write Course - An Introduction To College Composition—A Series
C
Focuses on the writing process as a whole. Discusses pre-writing, drafting, revising and editing. Incorporates the changes in teaching composition made over the last decade. Helps students develop individual writing skills that will prepare them for writing assignments in the academic environment and most career fields.
Prod-DALCCD Dist-DALCCD

Argumentation
Audience And Style
Audience, The
Beginning And Ending
Beginning, The
Definition
Developing Form
Discovering Ideas
Discovering The Library
Drama Of Thinking, The
Essay Test, The
Narration and Description
New Directions
Paragraph Patterns
Process And Analysis
Report And Proposal Writing
Revision Strategies
Sentence Patterns
Sentence Strategy
Sharpening The Focus
Structuring The Topic
Style
Using The Writer's Tools
Why Write?
Word Strategy
Words And Meaning
Writing A Research Paper
Writing About Books
Writing At Work
Writing Process

Write In Water C 10 MIN
16MM FILM OPTICAL SOUND
Presents nature's forms as they are reflected by the flux of the landscape over the changing seasonal periods.
Prod-DAVISJ Dist-RADIM

Write It Right C 15 MIN
3/4 OR 1/2 INCH VIDEO CASSETTE T
Uses the adventures of a pirate and his three friends to explore the many facets of language arts. Focuses on observation and organization in writing a story, including the determination of who, what, when, which and why.
From The Hidden Treasures Series. No. 7
LC NO. 82-706547
Prod-WCVETV Dist-GPITVL 1980

Write It Right - It All Starts With Paragraphs C 55 MIN
3/4 OR 1/2 INCH VIDEO CASSETTE J-H
Uses a step-by-step approach to describe the essentials of paragraph writing. Stresses the importance of considering audience and purpose, and of narrowing one's subject. Demonstrates proper paragraph construction.
LC NO. 83-707019
Prod-CHUMAN Dist-GA 1983

Write Move, The C 24 MIN
16MM FILM OPTICAL SOUND
Presents several situations which demonstrate the need for basic writing skills. Explains that four facets of good writing are mechanics, organization, vocabulary and expression.
LC NO. 78-700235
Prod-BYU Dist-BYU 1977

Write On C 14 MIN
16MM FILM, 3/4 OR 1/2 IN VIDEO P
Considers the activity of writing as a part of communication.
From The Serendipity Series.
Prod-MGHT Dist-MGHT 1976

Write On, Set 1—A Series
J-H
Provides instruction in grammar, usage, punctuation and writing, using a humorous and dramatic format. Covers such areas as word choice and the correct use of words, sentence structure, pronoun reference and comma rules.
Prod-CTI Dist-CTI

Bard, The 005 MIN
Calling Dr Kent 005 MIN
Captain Kent 005 MIN
Cinderella Newton 005 MIN
Comma Kid, The 005 MIN
Comrades X And B 005 MIN
Dracula's Defeat 005 MIN
Escaped Convict, The 005 MIN
Foolish Suitor, The 005 MIN
Fragment Fred 005 MIN
Goodbye, Cruel World 005 MIN
Henry Chan 005 MIN
Irma Faust 005 MIN
King Kane 005 MIN
La Bellicosa 005 MIN
Lucretia 005 MIN
Mad Bomber, The 005 MIN
Making Of Flaws, The 005 MIN
Miss Grouse 005 MIN
Miss Newton's Trial 005 MIN
Paolo Carbonara 005 MIN
Peter Berton 005 MIN
Reginald Parse 005 MIN
Rhubarb Power 005 MIN
Robber's Guide, The 005 MIN
Slick Stagger 005 MIN
Spice Of Life, The 005 MIN
Stocky Mariano 005 MIN

UFO, The 005 MIN
You Bet Your Life 005 MIN

Write On, Set 2–A Series
J-H
Demonstrates the methods of clear and correct writing. Covers diction, sentence style, and the development of the paragraph and the essay. Uses a humorous and dramatic format.
Prod-CTI Dist-CTI

Almost Dangerous Game, The 005 MIN
Beau Jest 005 MIN
Case Of The Missing Editor, The 005 MIN
Critical Lapse, A 005 MIN
Curses, Foiled Again 005 MIN
Devil And Henry Kent, The 005 MIN
Dream On 005 MIN
Dream Weaving 005 MIN
Dreamer, The 005 MIN
Gone With The Paragraph 005 MIN
Happy Daze 005 MIN
Henry Kent, Tycoon 005 MIN
Henry's Angels 005 MIN
I, Henry 005 MIN
Jungle Madness 005 MIN
Leo Claws 005 MIN
MacHenry 005 MIN
Night Before, The 005 MIN
Old Man And The Paragraph, The 005 MIN
Perchance To Dream 005 MIN
Pharaoh's Daughter, The 005 MIN
Revengers, The 005 MIN
Rocking Horse Writer, The 005 MIN
Scarlet Pen Pal, The 005 MIN
Scribbling Beauty, Pt 1 005 MIN
Scribbling Beauty, Pt 2 005 MIN
Show Business 005 MIN
SOS, An 005 MIN
Their Finest Paragraph 005 MIN
Transition Trek 005 MIN

Write On, Women Playwrights C 29 MIN
3/4 OR 1/2 INCH VIDEO CASSETTE
Features playwright Myrna Lamb discussing the attitudes of women playwrights in general.
From The Woman Series.
Prod-WNEDTV Dist-PBS

Write Stories About Daydreams B 15 MIN
2 INCH VIDEOTAPE P
See series title for descriptive statement.
From The Language Corner Series.
Prod-CVETVC Dist-GPITVL

Write Your Own Ticket C 14 MIN
16MM FILM, 3/4 OR 1/2 IN VIDEO A
Outlines strategy for setting and achieving goals. Relates to career planning, relationships, and health and fitness.
Prod-SEVDIM Dist-SEVDIM

Writer In America–A Series
16MM FILM, 3/4 OR 1/2 IN VIDEO
Presents interviews with eight American authors. Focuses on the source of their ideas, the influence of their physical surroundings, and their attitudes toward writing.
Prod-PERSPF Dist-CORF

Eudora Welty 29 MIN
Janet Flanner 29 MIN
John Gardner 29 MIN
Muriel Rukeyser 28 MIN
Robert Duncan 29 MIN
Ross Mac Donald 29 MIN
Toni Morrison 28 MIN
Wright Morris 29 MIN

Writer's Block C 7 MIN
16MM FILM, 3/4 OR 1/2 IN VIDEO
Presents a single-take closeup of a typewriter ribbon and rolled up paper to show the problems of writer's block. Features false starts, crossings out, and new beginnings.
Prod-PERSPF Dist-CORF

Writer's Plan Road C 20 MIN
3/4 OR 1/2 INCH VIDEO CASSETTE
Shows how to understand the writer's style and key word signs in order to get the whole picture.
From The Efficient Reading - Instructional Tapes Series. Tape 11
Prod-TELSTR Dist-TELSTR

Writer's Tools C 15 MIN
3/4 OR 1/2 INCH VIDEO CASSETTE I
Illustrates the steps in writing a report or article. Emphasizes the importance of research and creative organization and presentation of non-fiction material.
From The Zebra Wings Series.
Prod-NITC Dist-AITECH Prodn-MAETEL 1975

Writers - John Updike B 30 MIN
16MM FILM, 3/4 OR 1/2 IN VIDEO H-C A
Presents interviews with John Updike during which he discusses some of the beliefs, concepts and attitudes which have influenced his novels. Shows him in and about his home at Ipswich, Mass. He reads selections from several of his short stories, accompanied by scenes which depict the things described.
Prod-NET Dist-IU 1966

Writers - Philip Roth B 30 MIN
16MM FILM OPTICAL SOUND H-C A
A conversation between writer Philip Roth and Jerre Mangione, novelist and professor of English at the University of Pennsylvania, during which Roth discusses his stories and plays and explains the covert and ostensible meanings of his works. Discusses the relationship of his work to that of Saul Bellow and Roth's reactions to critics' reviews.
From The USA Series.
Prod-NET Dist-IU 1966

Writers - Science Fiction B 30 MIN
16MM FILM OPTICAL SOUND H-C A
Presents a discussion of science fiction by a panel of writers, a scientist and an English professor which includes both historical and future perspectives and definitions of science fiction.
From The USA Series.
Prod-NET Dist-IU 1966

Writers And Artists Of The New Era B 30 MIN
16MM FILM OPTICAL SOUND H-C A
Professor E A Toppin discusses the accomplishments of Blacks, including Paul Laurence Dunbar, Charles Chesnutt, Edward Bannister, and Edmonia Lewis-in the arts and other fields prior to World War I, pointing out that most of their works were imitative of whites and showed no Black heritage.
From The Black History, Section 11 - W E B Dubois And The New Century Series.
LC NO. 70-704074
Prod-WCBSTV Dist-HRAW 1969

Writers On Writing C 20 MIN
3/4 OR 1/2 INCH VIDEO CASSETTE H-C A
Presents seven of American's finest contemporary authors discussing their lives, sources of inspiration and writing methods. Includes Catherine Drinker Bowen and James Houston.
Prod-DAVFMS Dist-DAVFMS

Writers On Writing–A Series

Presents seven American writers discussing their lives, their sources of inspiration and their writing methods.
Prod-DAVFMS Dist-DAVFMS

Catherine Drinker Bowen - Other People's Lives 017 MIN
Ernest Gaines - Blood Lines In Ink 016 MIN
James Houston - The Vision Beyond The Mask 018 MIN
Jessamyn West - My Hand, My Pen 017 MIN
Joe Gores - A Penny A Word 020 MIN
Ross Macdonald - In The First Person 023 MIN
Walter D Edmonds - The Presence Of The Past 018 MIN

Writing C 29 MIN
3/4 OR 1/2 INCH VIDEO CASSETTE
Focuses on the role the teacher assumes when guiding students to write. Explains how the teacher can create an environment conducive to writing by removing obstacles to writing and by providing reinforcing stimuli.
From The Teaching Writing - A Process Approach Series.
Prod-MSITV Dist-PBS 1982

Writing - An Interview With Irving Stone C 19 MIN
16MM FILM, 3/4 OR 1/2 IN VIDEO H-C A
Interviews novelist Irving Stone and his wife, Jean, who discuss Stone's writings and speak on the functions of a writer, the hard work and perseverance which professional writing entails and the problems involved in transforming books into screenplays.
Prod-CORF Dist-CORF 1978

Writing - Cursive Capital Letters A-M C 30 MIN
3/4 OR 1/2 INCH VIDEO CASSETTE
See series title for descriptive statement.
From The Printing And Writing Series.
Prod-KITTLC Dist-KITTLC

Writing - Cursive Capital Letters N-Z C 30 MIN
3/4 OR 1/2 INCH VIDEO CASSETTE
See series title for descriptive statement.
From The Printing And Writing Series.
Prod-KITTLC Dist-KITTLC

Writing - Cursive Small Letters a-m C 30 MIN
3/4 OR 1/2 INCH VIDEO CASSETTE
See series title for descriptive statement.
From The Printing And Writing Series.
Prod-KITTLC Dist-KITTLC

Writing - Cursive Small Letters n-z C 30 MIN
3/4 OR 1/2 INCH VIDEO CASSETTE
See series title for descriptive statement.
From The Printing And Writing Series.
Prod-KITTLC Dist-KITTLC

Writing - Everyman's Art C 28 MIN
16MM FILM OPTICAL SOUND
Discusses the mechanical age and electronic pen making, inks and inkwells, the problems of portability, the arrival of the fountain pen, modern pen making, modern calligraphy and the alphabet of the future.
From The Alphabet - The Story Of Writing Series.
Prod-CFDLD Dist-FILAUD 1982

Writing - Plain And Fancy C 9 MIN
16MM FILM, 3/4 OR 1/2 IN VIDEO I-C A
Looks at the development of writing including the introduction of capital letters by the ancient Romans, the standardization of the print manuscript alphabet by Charlemagne and the refinement of writing into a distinctive cursive flow by Renaissance Italians.
Prod-PEREZ Dist-WDEMCO 1981

Writing - Who Needs It C 15 MIN
2 INCH VIDEOTAPE J
Outlines the history of writing and introuuces the remainder of the series.
Prod-DELE Dist-GPITVL

Writing A Good Paragraph C 11 MIN
16MM FILM, 3/4 OR 1/2 IN VIDEO J-H
Uses live action and still photography to show how to develop paragraphs logically according to time, space or contrast. Suggests the use of transitions to connect ideas smoothly.
Prod-CORF Dist-CORF 1963

Writing A Letter C 15 MIN
2 INCH VIDEOTAPE P
Provides an opportunity to communicate through letterwriting.
From The Word Magic (2nd Ed) Series.
Prod-CVETVC Dist-GPITVL

Writing A Research Paper C
3/4 OR 1/2 INCH VIDEO CASSETTE C
Extablishes an understanding about writing a research paper by explaining the nature of the research paper and the steps necessary to produce it.
From The Write Course - An Introduction To College Composition Series.
Prod-DALCCD Dist-DALCCD

Writing A Research Paper C 7 MIN
3/4 OR 1/2 INCH VIDEO CASSETTE
Teaches the basic steps of writing a research paper. Includes choosing a topic, outlining, footnotes, typing, and proofreading.
From The Library Skills Tapes Series.
Prod-MDCC Dist-MDCC

Writing A Research Paper C 30 MIN
3/4 OR 1/2 INCH VIDEO CASSETTE C A
Explains the nature of the research paper and the steps required to produce it.
From The Write Course - An Introduction To College Composition Series.
LC NO. 85-700909
Prod-FI Dist-FI 1984

Writing A Story C 15 MIN
2 INCH VIDEOTAPE P
Provides an enrichment program in the communitive arts area by allowing each child to write an original story.
From The Word Magic (2nd Ed) Series.
Prod-CVETVC Dist-GPITVL

Writing About Books C
3/4 OR 1/2 INCH VIDEO CASSETTE C
Encourages students to go beyond summary and changes commonly held misconceptions about book reviews.
From The Write Course - An Introduction To College Composition Series.
Prod-DALCCD Dist-DALCCD

Writing About Books C 30 MIN
3/4 OR 1/2 INCH VIDEO CASSETTE C A
Discusses commonly held misconceptions about book reviews and encourages students to go beyond summary.
From The Write Course - An Introduction To College Composition Series.
Prod-FI Dist-FI 1984

Writing About Drama C 30 MIN
3/4 OR 1/2 INCH VIDEO CASSETTE C
See series title for descriptive statement.
From The Communicating Through Literature Series.
Prod-DALCCD Dist-DALCCD

Writing About Fiction C 30 MIN
3/4 OR 1/2 INCH VIDEO CASSETTE C
See series title for descriptive statement.
From The Communicating Through Literature Series.
Prod-DALCCD Dist-DALCCD

Writing About Film C 30 MIN
3/4 OR 1/2 INCH VIDEO CASSETTE C
See series title for descriptive statement.
From The Communicating Through Literature Series.
Prod-DALCCD Dist-DALCCD

Writing About Literature C 30 MIN
3/4 OR 1/2 INCH VIDEO CASSETTE C
See series title for descriptive statement.
From The Communicating Through Literature Series.
Prod-DALCCD Dist-DALCCD

Writing About Poetry C 30 MIN
3/4 OR 1/2 INCH VIDEO CASSETTE C
See series title for descriptive statement.
From The Communicating Through Literature Series.
Prod-DALCCD Dist-DALCCD

Writing About You B 20 MIN
2 INCH VIDEOTAPE P
Introduces the term 'autobiography' and presents it so that children will be motivated to write their own. (Broadcast quality)
From The Language Lane Series. Lesson 25
Prod-CVETVC Dist-GPITVL Prodn-WCVETV

Writing And Editing B 55 MIN
3/4 OR 1/2 INCH VIDEO CASSETTE IND
See series title for descriptive statement.
From The Technical And Professional Writing For Industry, Government And Business Series.
Prod-UMICE Dist-AMCEE

Writing And Speaking (French) C 14 MIN
3/4 OR 1/2 INCH VIDEO CASSETTE H-C A
Shows two feuding neighbors and a sequence at the French Space Telecommunications Center at Pleumeur-Bodou in Brittany.
From The En Francais Series. Part 1 - Essential Elements
Prod-MOFAFR Dist-AITECH 1970

Writing At Work C
3/4 OR 1/2 INCH VIDEO CASSETTE C
Integrates a practical approach to the writing of common forms

of business communications with information from current research on successful business writers.
From The Write Course - An Introduction To College Composition Series.
Prod-DALCCD Dist-DALCCD

Writing At Work C 30 MIN
3/4 OR 1/2 INCH VIDEO CASSETTE C A
Discusses the writing of common forms of business communications, integrated with information from current research on business writers.
From The Write Course - An Introduction To College Composition Series.
Prod-FI Dist-FI 1984

Writing Behavioral Objectives C 25 MIN
3/4 OR 1/2 INCH VIDEO CASSETTE
Centers around the formulation of objectives in patient education. Points out points to remember when writing objectives and explains and examines three domains of behavioral objectives, including cognitive, affective and psychomotor.
From The How To Of Patient Education Series.
Prod-FAIRGH Dist-FAIRGH

Writing Better Business Letters (2nd Ed) C 11 MIN
16MM FILM, 3/4 OR 1/2 IN VIDEO J-C
Examines the business letters of three students to illustrate important aspects of form, content, style and tone that help make business letters more effective.
Prod-CORF Dist-CORF 1973

Writing Challenging Specific Objectives C 30 MIN
3/4 OR 1/2 INCH VIDEO CASSETTE
Defines and examines specific objectives. Shows the relationship of job descriptions, performance standards, specific objectives and corporate goals.
From The Performance Reviews That Build Commitment Series.
Prod-PRODEV Dist-DELTAK

Writing Clearly C 30 MIN
3/4 OR 1/2 INCH VIDEO CASSETTE
Deals with writing clearly as part of improving business writing skills.
From The Business Of Better Writing Series.
Prod-KYTV Dist-KYTV 1983

Writing Compilers C 30 MIN
3/4 OR 1/2 INCH VIDEO CASSETTE H-C A
Tells more about parsing activities within compilers. Shows Pascal code representation for common syntax diagram constructs. Illustrates an example code generation for a simple Pascal program.
From The Pascal, Pt 3 - Advanced Pascal Series.
LC NO. 81-706049
Prod-COLOSU Dist-COLOSU 1980

Writing Concisely C 30 MIN
3/4 OR 1/2 INCH VIDEO CASSETTE
Deals with writing concisely as part of improving business writing skills.
From The Business Of Better Writing Series.
Prod-KYTV Dist-KYTV 1983

Writing Correctly C 30 MIN
3/4 OR 1/2 INCH VIDEO CASSETTE
Deals with writing correctly as part of improving business writing skills.
From The Business Of Better Writing Series.
Prod-KYTV Dist-KYTV 1983

Writing For A Reason—A Series
C
Focuses on the basic writing skills needed for writing in college and in most entry level careers. Covers the high points about the way language functions historically, socially and psychologically.
Prod-DALCCD Dist-DALCCD

Beginning, The	030 MIN
Coherence	030 MIN
Completeness	030 MIN
Dictionary, The	030 MIN
English Language, The - A Brief History	030 MIN
Epistomology And Logic	030 MIN
Essay Test, The	030 MIN
Essay, The	030 MIN
Evaluative Essay, The	030 MIN
Fallacies	030 MIN
Language Options	030 MIN
Letter Of Application, The	030 MIN
Nature Of Communication, The	030 MIN
Order	030 MIN
Paper Of Analysis, The	030 MIN
Paper Of Classification, The	030 MIN
Paper Of Comparison, The	030 MIN
Paper Of Definition, The	030 MIN
Paragraph, The	030 MIN
Persuasive Paper, The	030 MIN
Readiness - Audience And Persona	030 MIN
Report, The	030 MIN
Sentence 1, The	030 MIN
Sentence 2, The	030 MIN
Special Paragraphs - Conclusions And	030 MIN
Special Paragraphs - Introduction	030 MIN
Style	030 MIN
Unity	030 MIN
Words 1	030 MIN
Words 2	030 MIN

Writing For Others C 30 MIN
3/4 OR 1/2 INCH VIDEO CASSETTE H-C A
See series title for descriptive statement.
From The Introduction To Technical And Business Communication Series.
Prod-UMINN Dist-GPITVL 1983

Writing For Results C 30 MIN
3/4 OR 1/2 INCH VIDEO CASSETTE C A
Discusses effective and ineffective writing and analyzes the cost of writing in business, emphasizing that effective writing saves time and money and usually gets results. Focuses on organization of ideas and use of effective language. Hosted by Ed Asner.
From The Effective Writing For Executives Series.
LC NO. 80-707288
Prod-TIMLIF Dist-TIMLIF 1980

Writing For The Modern Harp C 30 MIN
3/4 OR 1/2 INCH VIDEO CASSETTE C T
Demonstrates fingering, visual location of strings and tactile relationships, advance finger placement, pedal slides, the glissando and the arpeggiated chord. Explores the harp's capability for special effects. Offers some general advice for the harp composer.
From The Sounds They Make Series.
Prod-OHUTC Dist-OHUTC

Writing For The Pedal Harp C 45 MIN
3/4 OR 1/2 INCH VIDEO CASSETTE
Presents step-by-step demonstration of harp notation and technique. Shows 135 examples of harp notation that the American Harp Society would like to standardize. Gives the notation and demonstration on the screen simultaneously.
Prod-OHUTC Dist-OHUTC

Writing For Work—A Series
16MM FILM, 3/4 OR 1/2 IN VIDEO A
Emphasizes the writing skills employees should have to succeed in the work environment. Hosted by Cicely Tyson.
Prod-TIMLIF Dist-TIMLIF 1981

Complete Sentences	030 MIN
First Drafts	030 MIN
Organizing Ideas	030 MIN
Revising And Editing	030 MIN
Tools Of Writing	030 MIN
Writing For Your Reader	030 MIN
Writing Paragraphs	030 MIN

Writing For Your Reader C 30 MIN
3/4 OR 1/2 INCH VIDEO CASSETTE A
Presents basic writing skills for office workers, emphasizing the importance of clearly stating the purpose of the communication and knowing as much as possible about the who will be reading the letter, memo or report. Points out that tone and style can play a significant part in the success or failure of any communication. Hosted by Cicely Tyson.
From The Writing For Work Series. Pt 4
LC NO. 81-706737
Prod-TIMLIF Dist-TIMLIF 1981

Writing For Yourself C 30 MIN
3/4 OR 1/2 INCH VIDEO CASSETTE H-C A
See series title for descriptive statement.
From The Introduction To Technical And Business Communication Series.
Prod-UMINN Dist-GPITVL 1983

Writing Instructional Objectives Using Task Analysis Data C 50 MIN
3/4 OR 1/2 INCH VIDEO CASSETTE IND
See series title for descriptive statement.
From The Task Analysis And Job Instructor Training Series.
Prod-NCSU Dist-AMCEE

Writing Interestingly C 30 MIN
3/4 OR 1/2 INCH VIDEO CASSETTE
Deals with writing interestingly as part of improving business writing skills.
From The Business Of Better Writing Series.
Prod-KYTV Dist-KYTV 1983

Writing It Down C 29 MIN
3/4 INCH VIDEO CASSETTE
Shows composer Jerry Bilik as he sets a poem to music.
From The Music Shop Series.
Prod-UMITV Dist-UMITV 1974

Writing Letters That Get Results C 28 MIN
16MM FILM, 3/4 OR 1/2 IN VIDEO H-C A
Explains how to write letters that create interest, present facts and stimulate action. Features Waldo J Marra, correspondence consultant, discussing the principles and techniques of writing effective business letters.
LC NO. FIA67-5712
Prod-RTBL Dist-RTBL 1967

Writing Letters That Get Results (Dutch) C 28 MIN
16MM FILM, 3/4 OR 1/2 IN VIDEO H A S
Explains how to write letters that create interest, present facts and stimulate action. Features Waldo J Marra, correspondence consultant, discussing the principles and techniques of writing effective business letters.
Prod-RTBL Dist-RTBL 1967

Writing Number Sentences C 15 MIN
3/4 INCH VIDEO CASSETTE P
Presents the language and symbolism of addition and subtraction.
From The Math Factory, Module IV - Problem Solving Series.
Prod-MAETEL Dist-GPITVL 1973

Writing On An Interesting And Complete Thought B 15 MIN
2 INCH VIDEOTAPE P
See series title for descriptive statement.
From The Language Corner Series.
Prod-CVETVC Dist-GPITVL Prodn-WCVETV

Writing On The Wall, The C 50 MIN
16MM FILM, 3/4 OR 1/2 IN VIDEO
Explores the relationship between crime and architecture, considering the question of whether modern skyscraper living is responsible for the rising crime rate.
From The Horizon Series.
LC NO. 79-707910
Prod-BBCTV Dist-TIMLIF 1978

Writing Paragraphs C 30 MIN
3/4 OR 1/2 INCH VIDEO CASSETTE A
Presents basic writing skills for office workers, emphasizing how paragraphs are structured, their aim and ways to create smooth transitions between sentences. Hosted by Cicely Tyson.
From The Writing For Work Series. Pt 3
LC NO. 81-706736
Prod-TIMLIF Dist-TIMLIF 1981

Writing Persuasively C 30 MIN
3/4 OR 1/2 INCH VIDEO CASSETTE
Deals with writing persuasively as part of improving business writing skills.
From The Business Of Better Writing Series.
Prod-KYTV Dist-KYTV 1983

Writing Plain Letters B 5 MIN
16MM FILM OPTICAL SOUND
Shows the administrator of veterans affairs who explains the purpose and advantages of the information gained in the plain letters (4-S) course and gives his personal views on the value of short, simple, strong and sincere letter writing.
Prod-USVA Dist-USVA 1958

Writing Poetry C 30 MIN
3/4 OR 1/2 INCH VIDEO CASSETTE
Describes the process of writing poetry as making ordinary words do things they were never intended to do.
From The Engle And Poetry Series.
Prod-NETCHE Dist-NETCHE 1971

Writing Position Descriptions - A Helping Hand C 22 MIN
3/4 OR 1/2 INCH VIDEO CASSETTE A
Discusses the skills required for writing good position descriptions. Emphasizes interaction between supervisor, employe-eand personnel specialist. Describes how good position descriptions facilitate the personnel and managements process.
From The Position Management Series.
Prod-USOPMA Dist-USNAC 1984

Writing Principles C 30 MIN
3/4 OR 1/2 INCH VIDEO CASSETTE
Deals with bettering writing principles as part of improving business writing skills.
From The Business Of Better Writing Series.
Prod-KYTV Dist-KYTV 1983

Writing Process, The C
3/4 OR 1/2 INCH VIDEO CASSETTE C
Studies how to be a successful writer by providing current research information. Clarifies concepts about the writing process.
From The Write Course - An Introduction To College Composition Series.
Prod-DALCCD Dist-DALCCD

Writing Process, The C 28 MIN
3/4 OR 1/2 INCH VIDEO CASSETTE T
See series title for descriptive statement.
From The Next Steps With Computers In The Classroom Series.
Prod-PBS Dist-PBS

Writing Process, The C 30 MIN
3/4 OR 1/2 INCH VIDEO CASSETTE C A
Discusses how to be a successful writer. Clarifies concepts about the writing process.
From The Write Course - An Introduction To College Composition Series.
Prod-FI Dist-FI 1984

Writing Process, The - An Overview C 29 MIN
3/4 OR 1/2 INCH VIDEO CASSETTE
Introduces writing as an extension of speaking, emphasizing the five interdependent stages of writing - diagnosis, prewriting, writing, rewriting and evaluation.
From The Teaching Writing - A Process Approach Series.
Prod-MSITV Dist-PBS 1982

Writing Program, The C 20 MIN
3/4 OR 1/2 INCH VIDEO CASSETTE
Illustrates rules which are keys to good writing. Focuses on longer written communications, especially report writing, proposal writing and long letters.
Prod-MELROS Dist-VISUCP

Writing Reviews C 15 MIN
3/4 OR 1/2 INCH VIDEO CASSETTE J-H
Presents a student-produced television program which includes a sitcom with an original theme song, a commercial for a student body office candidate, a news report, a commercial, a documentary about student's with unusual jobs and a slightly censored sports report.
From The Tuned-In Series. Lesson 9
Prod-WNETTV Dist-FI 1982

Writing Says It All C 24 MIN
16MM FILM, 3/4 OR 1/2 IN VIDEO I
Shows a young boy learning, through a journal writing assignment, that he can understand himself better if he spells out his thoughts and feelings.
Prod-BARR Dist-BARR 1982

Writing Skills - Kindergarten Starting Points C 15 MIN
3/4 OR 1/2 INCH VIDEO CASSETTE T
Shows kindergarten authors engaged in a variety of language ex-

periences including beginning reading and writing. Stresses writing stages.
From The Young Writer's Workshop Series.
Prod-BCNFL Dist-BCNFL 1986

Writing Skills - Reluctant Writers C 15 MIN
3/4 OR 1/2 INCH VIDEO CASSETTE T
Demonstrates that student understanding of punctuation is enhanced when learned in context.
From The Young Writer's Workshop Series.
Prod-BCNFL Dist-BCNFL 1986

Writing Skills - The Final Touch - Editing, Rewriting And Polishing C
3/4 OR 1/2 INCH VIDEO CASSETTE H-C
Stresses the need for clear, direct and concise communication and gives pointers on achieving it through consideration of the structure of the composition as a whole, then each paragraph, and finally the polishing of sentences and words.
Prod-GA Dist-GA

Writing Skills - The Stages Of Writing C 15 MIN
3/4 OR 1/2 INCH VIDEO CASSETTE T
Deals with six key stages of the writing process prewriting, drafting, editing, proofreading, publishing and presenting.
From The Young Writer's Workshop Series.
Prod-BCNFL Dist-BCNFL 1986

Writing Skills - The Writing Process C 15 MIN
3/4 OR 1/2 INCH VIDEO CASSETTE
Shows three teachers working together to help students develop a sense of belonging to a school language family. Includes working on writing projects and grammar.
From The Young Writer's Workshop Series.
Prod-BCNFL Dist-BCNFL 1986

Writing Skills - Young Authors C 15 MIN
3/4 OR 1/2 INCH VIDEO CASSETTE T
Follows students through the writing process. Gives audience feedback. Deals with students on first and sixth grade level.
From The Young Writer's Workshop Series.
Prod-BCNFL Dist-BCNFL 1986

Writing Skills - Young Editors C 15 MIN
3/4 OR 1/2 INCH VIDEO CASSETTE T
Shows students workshopping and editing their work and the work of fellow students.
From The Young Writer's Workshop Series.
Prod-BCNFL Dist-BCNFL 1986

Writing Skills - Young Poets C 15 MIN
3/4 OR 1/2 INCH VIDEO CASSETTE T
Observes a fourth grade class involved in a writer's workshop. Includes narrowing poem topic, brainstorming prewriting, editing and final draft.
From The Young Writer's Workshop Series.
Prod-BCNFL Dist-BCNFL 1986

Writing Skills—A Series
16MM FILM, 3/4 OR 1/2 IN VIDEO P-I
Teaches basic techniques and elements of writing.
Prod-BEAN Dist-PHENIX 1978

Capitalization With Ralph And Stanley 012 MIN
Paragraphs With Ralph And Stanley 014 MIN
Punctuation With Ralph And Stanley 014 MIN
Sentences With Ralph And Stanley 015 MIN

Writing The Letter C 30 MIN
3/4 OR 1/2 INCH VIDEO CASSETTE
Deals with writing letters as part of improving business writing skills.
From The Business Of Better Writing Series.
Prod-KYTV Dist-KYTV 1983

Writing The Report C 30 MIN
3/4 OR 1/2 INCH VIDEO CASSETTE
Deals with writing business reports as part of improving business writing skills.
From The Business Of Better Writing Series.
Prod-KYTV Dist-KYTV 1983

Writing Time—A Series
P
Prod-WHROTV Dist-GPITVL

A, C And E 015 MIN
Cane Stroke - H And K 015 MIN
Continuous Ovals - S And R 015 MIN
Double-Curve Connecting Stroke And F 015 MIN
G, Q, A And D 015 MIN
G, S And L 015 MIN
I, U And W 015 MIN
Introduction Of Cursive Writing - Paper, 015 MIN
J And I 015 MIN
J And P 015 MIN
L, T And E 015 MIN
N And M 015 MIN
Names Of The Months, The - January 015 MIN
Numbers - 0 Through Nine 015 MIN
O And C 015 MIN
O And D 015 MIN
P, R And B 015 MIN
Q, U And V 015 MIN
Rainbow Stroke - B And K 015 MIN
Review 'Cane' Letters And I And J 015 MIN
Review Of All Capital Letters 015 MIN
Review Of All 13 Lower Case Letters 015 MIN
Review Of Writing Position And The Last 015 MIN
Review Of Writing Position, Indirect And 015 MIN
Rocker Curve - I And U 015 MIN
T And E 015 MIN
T And F 015 MIN
V, X, H And Y 015 MIN
W And X 015 MIN
Y And Z 015 MIN
Z, N And M 015 MIN

Writing To Different Executive Levels. C 30 MIN
3/4 OR 1/2 INCH VIDEO CASSETTE
Shows how to write to different executive levels when using direct mail.
From The Business Of Direct Mail Series.
Prod-KYTV Dist-KYTV 1983

Writing Well - Paragraphs C 16 MIN
16MM FILM, 3/4 OR 1/2 IN VIDEO I
Explains topic sentences and paragraph organization and unity. Illustrates various sentence constructions.
From The Writing Well Series.
Prod-CF Dist-CF

Writing Well - Planning C 8 MIN
16MM FILM, 3/4 OR 1/2 IN VIDEO I
Spells out how to gather and develop ideas before starting to write. Tells how a girl first clusters her possible general choices and then makes another cluster to develop the details in her chosen subject.
From The Writing Well Series.
Prod-CF Dist-CF 1985

Writing Well - Sentences C 14 MIN
16MM FILM, 3/4 OR 1/2 IN VIDEO I
Demonstrates run-on and choppy sentences. Involves sentence combining. Stresses using descriptive words.
From The Writing Well Series.
Prod-CF Dist-CF

Writing Well - Sharing C 11 MIN
16MM FILM, 3/4 OR 1/2 IN VIDEO I
Shows the post-writing process of sharing writing in a small group. Tells how positive comments and constructive criticism help each writer to rewrite.
From The Writing Well Series.
Prod-CF Dist-CF 1985

Writings Of The Nazi Holocaust B 60 MIN
16MM FILM OPTICAL SOUND
Ernest Pawel, critic and novelist analyzes the literary merits of the writings during the Nazi holocaust and interprets its relevance today.
Prod-ADL Dist-ADL

Written Communication C 28 MIN
16MM FILM OPTICAL SOUND A
Presents basic techniques for communication using letters, forms, memos and reports.
From The You In Public Service Series.
LC NO. 77-700970
Prod-USOE Dist-USNAC 1977

Written Language C 15 MIN
2 INCH VIDEOTAPE I
Traces the history of written language and demonstrates cuneiform letters and other symbols of years passed.
From The Images Series.
Prod-CVETVC Dist-GPITVL

Written Language C 30 MIN
3/4 OR 1/2 INCH VIDEO CASSETTE A
Demonstrates how young children can be introduced to written language and books through simple family activities and specially planned trips.
From The Rainbow Road Series. Pt 3
LC NO. 82-707395
Prod-KAIDTV Dist-GPITVL 1982

Written Language Disabilities C 30 MIN
3/4 OR 1/2 INCH VIDEO CASSETTE C A
Discusses specific written language disorders in children.
From The Characteristics Of Learning Disabilities Series.
Prod-WCVETV Dist-FI 1976

Written Word, The C 20 MIN
3/4 OR 1/2 INCH VIDEO CASSETTE H A
Deals with the preparation of written assignments. Defines different types of short papers and demonstrates a step-by-step method of preparing a term paper.
From The Art Of Learning Series.
Prod-WCVETV Dist-GPITVL 1984

Written Word, The C 30 MIN
3/4 OR 1/2 INCH VIDEO CASSETTE
See series title for descriptive statement.
From The Language - Thinking, Writing, Communicating Series.
Prod-MDCPB Dist-MDCPB

Wrong Again B 24 MIN
16MM FILM SILENT
Presents a comedy in which two boys confuse the painting 'BLUE BOY' with a horse of the same name.
LC NO. 73-713143
Prod-ROACH Dist-BHAWK 1960

Wrong Box, The C 105 MIN
16MM FILM OPTICAL SOUND J-C A
Stars John Mills and Ralph Richardson as elderly heirs, involved in a winner-take-all kind of insurance whereby the sole survivor inherits the total fortune.
Prod-CPC Dist-TIMLIF

Wrong Kid B 4 MIN
3/4 INCH VIDEO CASSETTE
Shows the police questioning the wrong youth as they search for a suspect.
From The Pittsburgh Police Series.
Prod-DOCEDR Dist-DOCEDR Prodn-MSHLLJ

Wrong Man, The B 105 MIN
16MM FILM OPTICAL SOUND
Stars Henry Fonda as a man who is arrested and convicted for a crime he did not commit.
Prod-WB Dist-TWYMAN 1956

Wrong Stuff, The - American Architecture C 13 MIN
16MM FILM, 3/4 OR 1/2 IN VIDEO H-C A
Introduces social critic Tom Wolfe who examines current styles of American architecture and finds it bland.
LC NO. 83-706404
Prod-CBSNEW Dist-CAROUF 1982

Wrong Way Kid—A Series
16MM FILM, 3/4 OR 1/2 IN VIDEO J-H
Uses children's stories to point out that growing up, at any age, is a process of change and learning. Shows that the turmoil young people may feel is normal and that there are ways to deal with these feelings.
Prod-BOSUST Dist-CF 1983

Hardlucky 011 MIN
I'm Not Oscar's Friend Anymore 007 MIN
Martha Ann And The Mother Store 007 MIN
Someone New 004 MIN

Wrong Way Kid, The C 42 MIN
16MM FILM, 3/4 OR 1/2 IN VIDEO J-H
Uses children's stories to point out that growing up, at any age, is a process of change and learning. Shows that the turmoil young people may feel is normal and that there are ways to deal with these feelings.
LC NO. 83-707024
Prod-BOSUST Dist-CF 1983

Wu Shu C 10 MIN
16MM FILM OPTICAL SOUND
Shows the ancient Chinese discipline of physical training as studied by a group of American students under the direction of a dedicated Chinese teacher of martial arts.
LC NO. 80-700314
Prod-WHITNM Dist-WHITNM 1980

Wunder Des Fliegens (German) B 80 MIN
3/4 OR 1/2 INCH VIDEO CASSETTE
A German language film. Incorporates world-famous stunt pilot Ernst Udet's famous flight-routine footage.
Prod-IHF Dist-IHF

Wunderbar C 20 MIN
16MM FILM OPTICAL SOUND
Promotes the Kitchener-Waterloo Octoberfest.
LC NO. 76-703820
Prod-CCAAT Dist-CCAAT 1975

Wuthering Heights B 104 MIN
16MM FILM OPTICAL SOUND
Stars Merle Oberon as the headstrong Cathy, who traps the brooding Heathcliffe (Laurence Olivier) with her love and then cruelly rejects him. Directed by William Wyler.
Prod-UNKNWN Dist-TWYMAN 1939

Wuxing People's Commune C 57 MIN
16MM FILM, 3/4 OR 1/2 IN VIDEO H-C A
Deals with daily life in a rural Chinese commune, touching on the political and social organization of this unique institution.
Prod-NFBC Dist-NFBC 1980

Wuxing People's Commune C 59 MIN
3/4 INCH VIDEO CASSETTE
Reveals how peasants on an agricultural commune in North China farm their land and organize themselves. Illustrates the importance of work and its dignity according to an old man shown bringing in the wheat harvest of 1978.
Prod-NFBC Dist-DOCEDR

Wyeth Phenomenon, The C 26 MIN
16MM FILM, 3/4 OR 1/2 IN VIDEO H-C A
Displays more than forty of Wyeth's paintings which provide an in-depth study of the famous artist. His paintings have a large amount of detail and his subjects are the people and places he knows best.
Prod-CBSTV Dist-PHENIX 1967

Wyeth Story, The C 40 MIN
16MM FILM OPTICAL SOUND I-C A
Traces a company from its origins before the Civil War to its current complex structure. Portrays its activities around the world. Shows the workings of research, manufacturing, quality control, distribution and marketing, indicating how modern medicines evolve.
Prod-WYETH Dist-WYLAB 1966

Wyman-Gordon - The Problem Solvers C 24 MIN
16MM FILM OPTICAL SOUND
Promotes the capabilities of the Wyman-Gordon Co in producing high quality forgings for the gas turbine, nuclear power and airframe industries.
LC NO. 75-701597
Prod-WYMGOR Dist-WYMGOR Prodn-URBNIM 1975

Wynken, Blynken And Nod B 4 MIN
16MM FILM, 3/4 OR 1/2 IN VIDEO K-P
Uses the pictures and text of the poem by Eugene Field to tell the story about Wynken, Blynken and Nod.
Prod-WWS Dist-WWS 1971

Wynn Bullock - Photographer C 24 MIN
16MM FILM, 3/4 OR 1/2 IN VIDEO H-C A
Presents photographer Wynn Bullock commenting on his work and demonstrating unusual photographic techniques. Includes views of some of his photographs and scenes of the artist with his family.
Prod-TYSONT Dist-PHENIX 1978

Wyoming - The Awakening Giant C 28 MIN
16MM FILM OPTICAL SOUND I-C A
Depicts Wyoming as a state with great industrial and natural resource potential. Spotlights the scenic beauty of the state as well.
Prod-UPR Dist-PCF

Wyoming Connection C 19 MIN
16MM FILM OPTICAL SOUND
Shows the construction effort made to supply natural gas from a new field by reusing part of an existing oil pipeline and adding to it.
LC NO. 80-701316
Prod-CITSER Dist-CITSER Prodn-CENTEF 1979

X

X - Et C 17 MIN
16MM FILM OPTICAL SOUND
Points out that Sven Erixon is one of Sweden's best known artists. Features the artist in his studio and conducts a tour through his paintings into his special world.
Prod-ASI Dist-AUDPLN 1963

X - The Man With The X-Ray Eyes C 80 MIN
16MM FILM OPTICAL SOUND
Features Ray Milland as a crusading opthamologist who tests a special sight-improvement serum on himself and acquires x-ray vision.
Prod-AIP Dist-TWYMAN 1963

X P B Z Q Keys B 30 MIN
2 INCH VIDEOTAPE
From The Typewriting, Unit 1 - Keyboard Control Series.
Prod-GPITVL Dist-GPITVL

X-Ray Examinations - A Guide To Good Practice C 15 MIN
16MM FILM OPTICAL SOUND PRO
Examines the proper procedures and safe practices which help reduce the potential hazards of radiation in x-ray examinations.
Prod-SQUIBB Dist-SQUIBB

X-Ray Inspection B 21 MIN
16MM FILM - 3/4 IN VIDEO
Discusses the use of radiographs in industry, including generation of X-rays in the X-ray tube, the wave nature of X-rays, procedures in making radiographs, and interpretation of radiographs for locating defects in metals. Issued in 1944 as a motion picture.
From The Engineering Series.
LC NO. 79-706444
Prod-USOE Dist-USNAC Prodn-AUDIO 1979

X-Ray Procedures In Layman's Terms—A Series

Explains x-ray procedures in layman's terms, pointing out that millions of diagnostic radiology procedures are performed each year. Answers questions about the safety of the radioactive compound that is injected, swallowed or inhaled and the equipment used.
Prod-FAIRGH Dist-FAIRGH

Abdominal Ultrasound
Barium Enema
Bone Scan
Brain Scan
Cardiac Stress Test And Imaging
Cholecystogram
CT Scan
Diagnostic Radiology
IVP
Liver Scan
Lung Ventilation Scan
Mammography
Nuclear Medicine
Pelvic Ultrasound
Thyroid Uptake And Scan
Ultrasound And The CT Scanner
Upper GI

X-Ray Spectroscopy - The Inside Story C 26 MIN
16MM FILM - 3/4 IN VIDEO J-C
Explains how and why the spectroscope is used to study x-ray beams. Describes how specially grown crystals are used to diffuse the beam in the spectrometer, isolate a single wavelength, scan the spectrum and record its characteristics.
Prod-NASA Dist-USNAC 1968

X-Ray Technician C 15 MIN
16MM FILM, 3/4 OR 1/2 IN VIDEO I
From The Career Awareness Series.
Prod-KLVXTV Dist-GPITVL

X-Ray, Ultrasound And Thermography In Diagnosis C 22 MIN
16MM FILM OPTICAL SOUND PRO
Demonstrates for physicians the potential of three electronic diagnostic techniques. Reveals the movement of a twelve-week-old human fetus as it was recorded with ultrasound. Explains the significant advantages of thermography in mass screening for early breast cancer and shows examples of color thermography.
From The Upjohn Vanguard Of Medicine Series.
LC NO. 76-705728
Prod-UPJOHN Dist-UPJOHN Prodn-SHNKRN 1969

X-Rays - How Safe C 28 MIN
16MM FILM OPTICAL SOUND
Discusses reduction of unnecessary radiation exposure to the public from diagnostic radiology. Describes the federal standard for the manufacture of x-ray systems as a major contribution in reducing unnecessary radiation exposure to patients and operators.
From The Consultation Series.
LC NO. 75-702444
Prod-USBRH Dist-USNAC 1974

X-Rays And Energy Levels C 24 MIN
3/4 OR 1/2 INCH VIDEO CASSETTE H-C
Documents the discovery of X-rays and its implications for the newly emerging quantum theory.
From The Discovering Physics Series.
Prod-BBCTV Dist-MEDIAG Prodn-OPENU 1983

X-15 - Man Into Space C 8 MIN
16MM FILM OPTICAL SOUND J-C A
Shows an X-15 rocket plane being carried aloft by a B-52 bomber and its actual 'drop.' Uses graphic animation to take the viewer along as the X-15 climbs to a height of more than 100 miles above the earth.
Prod-IBM Dist-IBM

X-15 Story, The C 27 MIN
16MM FILM OPTICAL SOUND I-C A
Documents the development and flight testing of the X-15.
Prod-NAA Dist-RCKWL

X-17 Story, The C 14 MIN
16MM FILM OPTICAL SOUND
Traces the development of the X-17, a three-stage test missile designed to solve the re-entry problem.
LC NO. FIE59-235
Prod-USDD Dist-USNAC 1958

X, Y, Z C 15 MIN
3/4 OR 1/2 INCH VIDEO CASSETTE P
Presents techniques of handwriting, focusing on the lower case letters x, y and z.
From The Cursive Writing Series.
Prod-WHROTV Dist-GPITVL 1984

Xala (French) C 123 MIN
16MM FILM OPTICAL SOUND
An English subtitle version of the French language film. Discusses the supposed myth of African independence as black African leaders adopt white colonial policies. Shows the sometimes unfortunate blending of the French and Senegalese cultures in the central character.
Prod-NYFLMS Dist-NYFLMS 1974

Xala (Wolof) C 123 MIN
16MM FILM OPTICAL SOUND
Discusses the supposed myth of African independence as black African leaders adopt white colonial policies. Shows the sometimes unfortunate blending of the French and Senegalese cultures in the central character.
Prod-NYFLMS Dist-NYFLMS 1974

Xavieria On Campus B 12 MIN
16MM FILM OPTICAL SOUND
Documents a visit by Xavieria Hollander to the campus of Niagara College.
LC NO. 76-701498
Prod-CNIAG Dist-CNIAG 1975

XB-70 Phase One C 13 MIN
16MM FILM OPTICAL SOUND I-C A
Tells the story of the engineering development of the XB-70.
Prod-NAA Dist-RCKWL

XB-70A Roll-Out C 10 MIN
16MM FILM OPTICAL SOUND I-C A
Presents the unveiling of the USAF XB-70A at the NAA-PALMDALE facility in May, 1964.
Prod-NAA Dist-RCKWL

Xenon Tetraflouride C 5 MIN
16MM FILM OPTICAL SOUND C A
Shows the preparation of xenon tetrafluoride, the tests to verify its nature and prospects of producing similar compounds.
LC NO. FIE63-195
Prod-ANL Dist-USERD 1962

Xenon Tetrafluoride C 6 MIN
16MM FILM OPTICAL SOUND
Explains that XEF is an 'IMPOSSIBLE' compound involving a supposedly inert element—xenon—with fluorine. Tells how their recently discovered reaction has led to experiments yielding other compounds such as XEF2 (produced under ultraviolet light) and experiments with radon and fluorine. Provides science with new insight into the nature of chemical bonding.
Prod-USAEC Dist-USNAC 1962

Xerox Report, A C 45 MIN
16MM FILM OPTICAL SOUND
Provides insight and understanding into the complex strategy that is guiding the Xerox Corporation toward the close of the century as told through the unscripted reflections of the key people who created and experienced it.
LC NO. 80-701308
Prod-XEROX Dist-GITTFI Prodn-GITTFI 1980

Xerox Sales Training B 40 MIN
3/4 OR 1/2 INCH VIDEO CASSETTE
Deals with career development of salesmen with emphasis on basic skills such as probing, effective listening and systems analysis.
Prod-HBS Dist-IVCH

Xian C 58 MIN
16MM FILM, 3/4 OR 1/2 IN VIDEO J-C A
Explores the Chinese urban experience, past and present. Focuses on the historical sites, scenery and culture in Xian, China, and observes the activities of its modern residents.
From The Cities In China Series.
LC NO. 82-706430
Prod-YUNGLI Dist-UCEMC 1981

Xinbu Energy Story, The (Cantonese)—A Series
J-C A
Documents the various aspects of the Xinbu biogas and solar energy system. Includes an overview of the entire energy cycle of the village, a description of the operation of a communal biogas digester, and the process of building a home digester. In Cantonese with English transcripts.
Prod-STURTM Dist-STURTM 1981

XTX - Expect The Unexpected C
16MM FILM - 3/4 IN VIDEO A
Alerts workers to prepare for the unexpected by illustrating the potential for accidents in everyday activities at work and at home.
Prod-BNA Dist-BNA 1983

XVII-3 - Get The Facts C 20 MIN
16MM FILM OPTICAL SOUND
Presents two grievances in which the Postal Union representatives solve the problem according to the Postal Manual and union contract, pointing out that one grievance is resolved at the local level while the second requires arbitration.
LC NO. 74-702681
Prod-NALC Dist-NALC Prodn-PARA 1974

Y

Y And Z C 15 MIN
3/4 INCH VIDEO CASSETTE P
From The Writing Time Series.
Prod-WHROTV Dist-GPITVL

Y Consonant Sound, The C 15 MIN
3/4 INCH VIDEO CASSETTE P
Discusses the sound of the y consonant.
From The New Talking Shop Series.
Prod-BSPTV Dist-GPITVL 1978

Y E S Inc—A Series
J-H
Focuses upon a community employment skills training center, Youth Employment Skills, Inc, located in an inner-city, ethnically-mixed neighborhood. The primary purpose of the center is to help teenagers foster an awareness of their own interests, to develop skills and then relate these to career options.
Prod-KCET Dist-GPITVL 1983

All The Difference 030 MIN
Nature's Rhythms 030 MIN
Neighborhood Drums 030 MIN
Time For Myself 030 MIN
Top Of The Line 030 MIN

Y-Riders, The C 14 MIN
16MM FILM OPTICAL SOUND
Traces the history of the Y-Rider Program designed to fight drug abuse among teenagers. Features interviews with the young program directors.
LC NO. 76-713472
Prod-AHONDA Dist-AHONDA 1970

Ya Vamos—A Series
J-C A
Prod-JOSHUA Dist-HRAW 1969

A Chapultepec 14 MIN
A Mexico 15 MIN
A Toledo 17 MIN
Al Desfile 14 MIN
Al Escorial 14 MIN

Yachting In The Thirties B
1/2 IN VIDEO CASSETTE BETA/VHS
Presents four short sailing programs, including Dorade-A Most Significant Yacht, Yankee Cruise To England, Brilliant In The Thirties, and The Last J-Boat Race.
Prod-MYSTIC Dist-MYSTIC 1983

Yahoo C 28 MIN
16MM FILM OPTICAL SOUND
Follows two ski instructors, Dave Wheeler and Ted Mc Coy, on the freewheeling hot dog circuit. Shows how they use their winnings to finance a trip to the spectacular Caribou Mountains in Canada for helicopter skiing in untracked powder. Features Jeff Jobe flying his hand kite at Snowbird, Utah, and depicts a hot dog contest at Aspen, Colorado.
Prod-BARP Dist-FFORIN

Yakuza, The C 112 MIN
16MM FILM OPTICAL SOUND
Tells how Robert Mitchum takes a martial arts expert to Tokyo to save Brian Keith from Japanese gangs.
Prod-WB Dist-TWYMAN 1975

Yalta B 26 MIN
16MM FILM OPTICAL SOUND
Uses documentary footage to describe the Yalta Conference of February, 1945, where Churchill, Roosevelt and Stalin discussed final military moves against Germany and the structure of the proposed United Nations. Based on the book 'THE SECOND WORLD WAR' by Winston S Churchill.
From The Winston Churchill - The Valiant Years Series. No. 23
LC NO. FI67-2121
Prod-ABCTV Dist-SG 1961

Yanamamo - A Multidisciplinary Study C 45 MIN
3/4 INCH VIDEO CASSETTE

Illustrates anthropological field techniques used by researchers from the University of Michigan in collaboration with their Venezuelan colleagues as they studied the Yanamamo Tribe. Features the tragedy of measles deaths among the tribe in 1968.
Prod-DOCEDR Dist-DOCEDR

Yang-Xun The Peasant Painter C 25 MIN
16MM FILM, 3/4 OR 1/2 IN VIDEO J-C A
Introduces Yang-Xun, a Chinese boy who wants to be skilled in the style of art known as peasant painting. Shows how he gets advice from his aunt, an accomplished peasant painter, on how to put feeling in his painting. Depicts Yang-Xun putting the advice to use when he is taken on a field trip to sketch a bridge.
From The World Cultures And Youth Series.
Prod-SUNRIS Dist-CORF 1981

Yangju Sandae Nori - Masked Drama Of Korea C 33 MIN
16MM FILM OPTICAL SOUND J-C A
Describes the masked drama of Korea, which probably derived from old Buddhist morality plays, and explains how it has evolved into a folk drama consisting of a number of short acts using stock characters.
From The Ethnic Music And Dance Series.
LC NO. 72-700264
Prod-UWASH Dist-UWASHP 1971

Yanis And His Dream C 20 MIN
16MM FILM, 3/4 OR 1/2 IN VIDEO I-J
Tells a story about a Greek peasant boy who was bound by tradition to be a farmer, but wanted to be a fisherman.
Prod-BARR Dist-BARR 1980

Yanis And His Dream (Captioned) C 20 MIN
16MM FILM - VIDEO, ALL FORMATS I
Tells the story of a peasant boy on the Greek island of Corfu who goes against tradition to become a fisherman rather than a farmer.
Prod-BARR Dist-BARR

Yankee Calling C 29 MIN
16MM FILM OPTICAL SOUND
Recalls the history of Yankee craftsmen, inventors and peddlers who made Connecticut into a manufacturing state during the period from the end of the revolution to the start of the Civil War.
Prod-FENWCK Dist-FENWCK

Yankee Clipper B 27 MIN
16MM FILM OPTICAL SOUND
Presents William Boyd in a film about early clipperships. Features a typhoon, a mutiny and a race between British and American ships for China tea trade.
From The History Of The Motion Picture Series.
Prod-SF Dist-KILLIS 1960

Yankee Craftsman C 18 MIN
16MM FILM, 3/4 OR 1/2 IN VIDEO
A documentary film about a man who has spent his life making furniture in the old way with old tools in his own shop. Contrasts the furniture maker's life-style and his product with that of a modern factory worker on the production line.
Prod-CHAPWW Dist-JOU 1972

Yankee Do C 28 MIN
16MM FILM OPTICAL SOUND
Illustrates the importance of the attack carrier as the backbone of the fast carrier task force as seen through the eyes of a Canadian naval aviator. Shows how the men of the navy maintain and operate these carriers.
LC NO. FIE62-49
Prod-USN Dist-USNAC 1962

Yankee Doodle C 10 MIN
16MM FILM, 3/4 OR 1/2 IN VIDEO
Travels with Yankee Doodle as he goes to town riding on a pony. Presents a pictorial representation of the Revolutionary era in American history.
Prod-WWS Dist-WWS 1976

Yankee Doodle C 19 MIN
3/4 OR 1/2 INCH VIDEO CASSETTE P-I
Presents a patriotic song and introduces the brass family.
From The USS Rhythm Series.
Prod-ARKETV Dist-AITECH 1977

Yankee Doodle Cricket C 26 MIN
3/4 INCH VIDEO CASSETTE P
Presents an animated tale about how the course of American Independence was directly influenced by a cat, a mouse and a cricket.
Prod-CJE Dist-GA

Yankee Doodle Dandy B 126 MIN
16MM FILM OPTICAL SOUND I-C
Stars James Cagney as America's great patriot and composer, George M Cohan.
Prod-WB Dist-UAE 1942

Yankee Go Home - Communist Propaganda B 45 MIN
3/4 OR 1/2 INCH VIDEO CASSETTE
Features George V Allen, the first director of the United States Information Agency, explaining the purpose of his organization and the ways he hopes to counter anti-American propaganda in the popular media, especially motion pictures. Examines various Soviet documentary and feature films, including segments from an International Youth Festival in Moscow Stadium, Meeting On The Elbe, The Partisan and The Forty First.
Prod-IHF Dist-IHF

Yankee Painter - The Work Of Winslow Homer (Rev Ed) C 27 MIN
16MM FILM, 3/4 OR 1/2 IN VIDEO H-C A
Presents drawings, watercolors and oils of Winslow Homer to show the progress of his career, his artistic development and the breadth of his interests.
LC NO. 81-706474
Prod-UARIZ Dist-IFB 1976

Yankee Sails Across Europe C 51 MIN
16MM FILM, 3/4 OR 1/2 IN VIDEO
Presents the Brigantine Yankee taking a captain and his wife through Western Europe on an interconnected series of rivers and canals in Western Europe. Shows the varied coastline.
LC NO. 80-706394
Prod-NGS Dist-NGS 1967

Yankee Years, The C 58 MIN
3/4 OR 1/2 INCH VIDEO CASSETTE A
Looks at the turbulent years from the Spanish-American War in 1898 to the 1950s when U S preeminence in Central America was never successfully challenged. Covers the building of the Panama Canal, the early Marine occupation of Nicaragua and the Cold War crisis in Guatemala in 1954 which resulted in the CIA's first 'covert' war in the region.
From The Crisis In Central America Series.
Prod-WGBHTV Dist-FI

Yankees At Bat, The C 15 MIN
16MM FILM, 3/4 OR 1/2 IN VIDEO J-C
Yankee players, such as Mickey Mantle, Elston Howard and Roger Maris, talk about their approach to various facets of baseball.
Prod-MOKIN Dist-MOKIN 1965

Yanki No C
16MM FILM, 3/4 OR 1/2 IN VIDEO
Looks at people who are in political and social turmoil in Latin America.
Prod-DREWAS Dist-DIRECT 1960

Yanks Are Coming, The C 52 MIN
16MM FILM OPTICAL SOUND H-C
Tells of a world plunging from peace into a catastrophic war, World War I.
Prod-WOLPER Dist-FI 1974

Yanomamo - A Multidisciplinary Study C 45 MIN
16MM FILM, 3/4 OR 1/2 IN VIDEO
Describes the field techniques and findings of teams from such disciplines as human genetics, anthropology, epidemiology, dentistry, linguistics and medicine as they conduct a biological-anthropological study of the jungles.
Prod-USAEC Dist-USNAC

Yanomamo Indians - Moonblood C 14 MIN
16MM FILM OPTICAL SOUND
Features a Yanomamo headman explaining creation and accounting for the human capacity for violence.
From The Yanomamo Series.
LC NO. 76-702852
Prod-DOCEDR Dist-DOCEDR 1975

Yanomamo—A Series
H-C A
Examines Indian life in Venezuela.
Prod-DOCEDR Dist-DOCEDR 1975

Arrow Game	7 MIN
Ax Fight, The	30 MIN
Bride Service	10 MIN
Children's Magical Death	8 MIN
Climbing The Peach Palm	9 MIN
Father Washes His Children, A	13 MIN
Feast, The	29 MIN
Firewood	10 MIN
Magical Death	28 MIN
Man And His Wife Make A Hammock, A	9 MIN
Man Called Bee, A - Studying The Yanomamo	40 MIN
Myth Of Naro As Told By Dedeheiwa	22 MIN
Myth Of Naro As Told By Kaobawa	22 MIN
New Tribes Mission	12 MIN
Ocamo Is My Town	22 MIN
Tapir Distribution	15 MIN
Tug Of War	9 MIN
Weeding The Garden	14 MIN
Yanomamo Indians - Moonblood	14 MIN

Yantra C 7 MIN
16MM FILM OPTICAL SOUND H-C
Designed to stimulate a greater awareness of cosmic, temporal and psychological order.
Prod-WHITNY Dist-CFS

Yarn Preparation For Weaving And Warp Knitting C
3/4 OR 1/2 INCH VIDEO CASSETTE
See series title for descriptive statement.
From The ITMA 1983 Review Series.
Prod-NCSU Dist-NCSU

Yawn Wave Theory C 20 MIN
16MM FILM OPTICAL SOUND
Presents a humorous insight into the various levels of consciousness in a young man who tries to stay awake for 48 hours.
LC NO. 76-703102
Prod-SHERCL Dist-CFDEVC 1976

Yea, Verily B 13 MIN
16MM FILM OPTICAL SOUND
Presents an irreverent parody of Catholicism.
Prod-NYU Dist-NYU

Yeah You Right C 29 MIN
3/4 OR 1/2 INCH VIDEO CASSETTE A
Discusses the language and idioms of the residents of New Orleans.
Prod-CNAM Dist-CNEMAG 1984

Year In Review - 1974 C 28 MIN
3/4 OR 1/2 INCH VIDEO CASSETTE H-C A
Presents highlights of the final Nixon White House days and a review of the events just prior to his resignation. Includes an overview of accelerated Middle East tensions, the OPEC influenced international economic crisis and the violent changes in many governments.
Prod-JOU Dist-JOU

Year In Review - 1975 C 50 MIN
3/4 OR 1/2 INCH VIDEO CASSETTE H-C A
Presents the major news event of 1975, the final withdrawal of all United States personnel from Vietnam. Shows footage of those final days and the fall of Hanoi. Captures a year of international terrorism and continued armed hostilities in the Middle East.
Prod-JOU Dist-JOU

Year In Review - 1976 C 28 MIN
3/4 OR 1/2 INCH VIDEO CASSETTE H-C A
States that the United States elected a president while she celebrated 200 years of independence. Describes how Africa struggled in many civil wars and political upheavals while Lebanon became embroiled in her own war and Middle East tensions focused on it. Tells how many changes in European governments occurred as China lost her leaders, Mao and Chairman Chou En Lai. Features the many technological advances of the year.
Prod-JOU Dist-JOU

Year In Review - 1977 C 28 MIN
3/4 OR 1/2 INCH VIDEO CASSETTE H-C A
Tells that this was the year Jimmy Carter was sworn in as the 39th President of the United States. Shows that tensions continued in the Middle East though signs of hope emerged when Anwar El Sadat visited Israel and addressed the Knesset, the first Egyptian president ever to do so. Recounts the strife and political upheavals that plagued Africa.
Prod-JOU Dist-JOU

Year In Review - 1978 C 28 MIN
3/4 OR 1/2 INCH VIDEO CASSETTE H-C A
This year is best remembered as one of hope for peace in the Middle East as Carter, Begin and Sadat participated in the historic summit meeting at Camp David. Tells how instability continued in Central America and Africa as terrorism swept the international scene. The year ended on a happy note as Louise Joy Brown, the first test-tube baby was born in London.
Prod-JOU Dist-JOU

Year In Review - 1980 C 28 MIN
3/4 OR 1/2 INCH VIDEO CASSETTE
Presents a capsulized summary of the key events of the year. Focuses on those stories that have the greatest impact on the world. Covers those changes and milestones that have occurred in religion, politics, science and sports. Reports the events and charts the trends of a year that is a most significant one in the world's history.
Prod-JOU Dist-JOU

Year In Review - 1982 C 50 MIN
3/4 OR 1/2 INCH VIDEO CASSETTE H-C A
Reports that late in the year Leonid Brezhnev died after 18 years as leader of the Soviet Union. Describes how conflict in the Middle East escalated as Israel invaded Lebanon and international support for the Israelis began to waiver. Presents the Falklands crisis, the anti-nuclear weapons movement and Central American instability. Shows also the headline news in science, sports, politics and religion.
Prod-JOU Dist-JOU

Year In Review - 1983 C 50 MIN
3/4 OR 1/2 INCH VIDEO CASSETTE H-C A
Shows the year beginning with continued protests over armaments, instability in Central America, United States presidential candidates from the Democratic Party making themselves known and Republicans awaiting a decision from Ronald Reagan. Presents international headlines, background for the upcoming Olympic Games, as well as news in science.
Prod-JOU Dist-JOU

Year Of Birth B 28 MIN
16MM FILM OPTICAL SOUND
Depicts facts of pregnancy, delivery and the first year of life. Shows research being done at the National Institute of Neurological Diseases and Blindness for prevention and control of cerebral palsy and other neurological diseases in infants.
LC NO. FIE63-109
Prod-USPHS Dist-USNAC Prodn-NF 1958

Year Of Change - 1932 B 17 MIN
3/4 OR 1/2 INCH VIDEO CASSETTE
Reviews prohibition, Adolf Hitler's rise and world threat, the ominous signs inherent in the Olympics, the optimism associated with the remarkable flight of Amelia Earhart and the election of Franklin D. Roosevelt.
Prod-KINGFT Dist-KINGFT

Year Of Fulfillment, A C 23 MIN
16MM FILM OPTICAL SOUND
Summarizes events and progress in the Manned Space Flight Program between the late 1950's and early 1969.
Prod-NASA Dist-NASA

Year Of The Big Surprise, The C 27 MIN
16MM FILM OPTICAL SOUND J-C A
Highlights the 1965 professional baseball season featuring team and individual performances of the New York Giants.
LC NO. FIA68-1411
Prod-NFL Dist-NFL 1966

Year Of The Buffalo C 25 MIN
16MM FILM OPTICAL SOUND H-C A
Follows Fred Bear to Portuguese East Africa where he stalks the wily cape buffalo, rated by experienced hunters as one of the most dangerous beasts of the African bush Includes scenes

of Fred as he battles spectacular tiger fish in the hippo-infested Save River.
Prod-GFS Dist-GFS

Year Of The Dragon, The C 24 MIN
3/4 OR 1/2 INCH VIDEO CASSETTE
Tells of an orphaned Chinese boy's involvement in the building of the Transcontinental Railroad in nineteenth century America.
From The Young People's Specials Series.
Prod-MULTPP Dist-MULTPP

Year Of The Hyena, The C 25 MIN
16MM FILM, 3/4 OR 1/2 IN VIDEO
Documents a time of decay and change in ancient Egypt.
From The Ancient Lives Series.
Prod-FOTH Dist-FOTH

Year Of The Jeep, The B 20 MIN
3/4 OR 1/2 INCH VIDEO CASSETTE J-H
Presents YEAR OF THE JEEP by Keith Robertson. Concerns two boys who find a jeep and restore it to running order. Tells that when the owner wants the jeep back to sell at a public auction, the boys try to earn money to buy it. Gives their money-bearing adventures which include capturing and selling bats to a biologist and assisting in the arrest of a gang of thieves. (Broadcast quality)
From The Matter Of Fiction Series. No. 11
Prod-WETATV Dist-AITECH

Year Of The Wildebeest, The C 55 MIN
16MM FILM - 1/2 IN VIDEO, VHS J-C
Shows the epic 2,000 mile migration of one million wildebeests across Tanzania in search of grass and water during the dry summer months. Shows how the herd is thinned by the predators through whose territory the herd passes.
Prod-ROOTA Dist-BNCHMK 1976

Year Of 53 Weeks, The - USAF Supersonic Pilot Training C 37 MIN
16MM FILM OPTICAL SOUND
Describes day-to-day experiences of an Air Force ROTC graduate enrolled in the Air Training Command's 53 week supersonic pilot training program. Focuses on the program's academic, flying, military and physical training courses.
LC NO. 74-706340
Prod-USAF Dist-USNAC 1966

Year One C 25 MIN
3/4 OR 1/2 INCH VIDEO CASSETTE
Shows Dr Richard Koch of Children's Hospital demonstrating physical and mental development in the first year of life, with nine guests ranging in age from two weeks to twelve months. Has pediatrician Carter Wright explaining common health problems in infancy.
Prod-TRAINX Dist-TRAINX

Year They Discovered People, The C 14 MIN
16MM FILM OPTICAL SOUND
Presents a documentary on employee attitudes within the Western Electric Company over the past 50 years, indicating advances and opportunities which have resulted. Features recollections of participants in the Hawthorne Studies of the 1920's, film footage, photographs and re-creations of factory conditions.
LC NO. 75-700338
Prod-WESTEC Dist-MTP Prodn-APPOLO 1974

Year Times Changed, The C 27 MIN
16MM FILM OPTICAL SOUND
Uses still photographs, archival footage, and animation to document the nature of America during the years 1900 to 1910. Highlights events and inventions which made this period a turning point in the history and development of the United States.
LC NO. 79-700351
Prod-PENN Dist-MTP Prodn-LEBO 1978

Year Towards Tomorrow, A B 29 MIN
16MM FILM - 3/4 IN VIDEO
Describes the difficulties and the satisfactions which three Vista volunteers experience. Relates the experiences of two girls on a Navajo reservation in Arizona and an ex-navy volunteer in the slums of Atlanta.
Prod-USVIST Dist-USNAC Prodn-SUN 1972

Yearling, The C
1/2 IN VIDEO CASSETTE BETA/VHS
Presents Marjorie Kinnan Rawlings' story of a young boy and his adopted fawn, starring Gregory Peck and Jane Wyman.
Prod-GA Dist-GA

Yearnings Versus Earnings C 20 MIN
3/4 INCH VIDEO CASSETTE J-H
Presents examples of how goals, values and attitudes influence the use of income or personal resources and how to reduce the problem of unlimited wants and limited resources.
From The Dollar Data Series.
LC NO. 81-707345
Prod-WHROTV Dist-GPITVL 1974

Years Ahead, The C 30 MIN
16MM FILM OPTICAL SOUND
Provides biographical sketches of six senior citizens who have confronted various problems in the later years and have found constructive and satisfying solutions.
LC NO. 80-701492
Prod-CPTEL Dist-CPTEL 1980

Years In Review - The Thirties—A Series
C
Presents year by year coverage of the major international news events of the 1930's. Uses period footage gathered by Hearst Metronome News.
Prod-KRAUS Dist-KRAUS Prodn-AMSLFM 1975

Years In Review - The Thirties, 1930 7 MIN
Years In Review - The Thirties, 1931 7 MIN
Years In Review - The Thirties, 1932 8 MIN
Years In Review - The Thirties, 1933 9 MIN
Years In Review - The Thirties, 1934 8 MIN
Years In Review - The Thirties, 1935 9 MIN
Years In Review - The Thirties, 1936 9 MIN
Years In Review - The Thirties, 1937 10 MIN
Years In Review - The Thirties, 1938 10 MIN
Years In Review - The Thirties, 1939 7 MIN

Years In Review - The Thirties, 1930 B 7 MIN
16MM FILM MAGNETIC SOUND C
See series title for descriptive statement.
From The Years In Review - The Thirties Series.
LC NO. 75-703312
Prod-KRAUS Dist-KRAUS Prodn-AMSLFM 1975

Years In Review - The Thirties, 1931 B 7 MIN
16MM FILM MAGNETIC SOUND C
See series title for descriptive statement.
From The Years In Review - The Thirties Series.
LC NO. 75-703313
Prod-KRAUS Dist-KRAUS Prodn-AMSLFM 1975

Years In Review - The Thirties, 1932 B 8 MIN
16MM FILM MAGNETIC SOUND C
See series title for descriptive statement.
From The Years In Review - The Thirties Series.
LC NO. 75-703314
Prod-KRAUS Dist-KRAUS Prodn-AMSLFM 1975

Years In Review - The Thirties, 1933 B 9 MIN
16MM FILM MAGNETIC SOUND C
See series title for descriptive statement.
From The Years In Review - The Thirties Series.
LC NO. 75-703315
Prod-KRAUS Dist-KRAUS Prodn-AMSLFM 1975

Years In Review - The Thirties, 1934 B 8 MIN
16MM FILM MAGNETIC SOUND C
See series title for descriptive statement.
From The Years In Review - The Thirties Series.
LC NO. 75-703316
Prod-KRAUS Dist-KRAUS Prodn-AMSLFM 1975

Years In Review - The Thirties, 1935 B 9 MIN
16MM FILM MAGNETIC SOUND C
See series title for descriptive statement.
From The Years In Review - The Thirties Series.
LC NO. 75-703317
Prod-KRAUS Dist-KRAUS Prodn-AMSLFM 1975

Years In Review - The Thirties, 1936 B 9 MIN
16MM FILM MAGNETIC SOUND C
See series title for descriptive statement.
From The Years In Review - The Thirties Series.
LC NO. 75-703318
Prod-KRAUS Dist-KRAUS Prodn-AMSLFM 1975

Years In Review - The Thirties, 1937 B 10 MIN
16MM FILM MAGNETIC SOUND C
See series title for descriptive statement.
From The Years In Review - The Thirties Series.
LC NO. 75-703319
Prod-KRAUS Dist-KRAUS Prodn-AMSLFM 1975

Years In Review - The Thirties, 1938 B 10 MIN
16MM FILM MAGNETIC SOUND C
See series title for descriptive statement.
From The Years In Review - The Thirties Series.
LC NO. 75-703320
Prod-KRAUS Dist-KRAUS Prodn-AMSLFM 1975

Years In Review - The Thirties, 1939 B 7 MIN
16MM FILM MAGNETIC SOUND C
See series title for descriptive statement.
From The Years In Review - The Thirties Series.
LC NO. 75-703321
Prod-KRAUS Dist-KRAUS Prodn-AMSLFM 1975

Years Of Change—A Series
16MM FILM, 3/4 OR 1/2 IN VIDEO J-C A
Looks at government, politics, foreign affairs and culture in America in 1968.
Prod-CORPEL Dist-PHENIX 1979

America In 1968, Pt 1 - World Affairs 20 MIN
America In 1968, Pt 2 - Government And 22 MIN
America In 1968, Pt 3 - People And Culture 20 MIN

Years Of Crisis, The C 30 MIN
1 INCH VIDEOTAPE J-H
Describes contributions made by Blacks in early America—the Abolitionist Movement and the underground railroad, Jim Crow legislation and the Black Colonization Movement.
From The Odyssey In Black Series.
Prod-KLVXTV Dist-GPITVL

Years Of Destiny B 21 MIN
16MM FILM OPTICAL SOUND
Tells why and how a Jewish state rose again, independent, in our day. Presents the record of the struggle for that independence and its results.
Prod-ALDEN Dist-ALDEN

Years Of Reconstruction, The - 1865-1877 C 25 MIN
16MM FILM, 3/4 OR 1/2 IN VIDEO J-C A
Examines economic, social and political problems still unsettled after the Civil War, as well as attempts by North and South to reach a reasonable peace.
From The American History Series.
Prod-CRMP Dist-CRMP 1969

Years 1904-1914, The - The Drums Begin To Roll, Pt 1 C 26 MIN
3/4 OR 1/2 INCH VIDEO CASSETTE H-C A
Special two-part version of the film and videorecording The Years 1904-1914 - The Drums Begin To Roll.
From The Europe - The Mighty Continent Series.
Prod-BBCTV Dist-TIMLIF 1976

Years 1904-1914, The - The Drums Begin To Roll, Pt 2 C 26 MIN
3/4 OR 1/2 INCH VIDEO CASSETTE H-C A
Special two-part version of the film and videorecording The Years 1904-1914 - The Drums Begin To Roll.
From The Europe - The Mighty Continent Series.
Prod-BBCTV Dist-TIMLIF 1976

Years 1904-1914, The - The Drums Begin To Roll C 52 MIN
16MM FILM - 1/2 IN VIDEO
Analyzes the European events and conditions that set the stage for World War I. Discusses the Russian defeat in the Russo-Japanese War, which convinced Asians, Africans and Indians that Europe was not invincible and which inspired confidence in Germany.
From The Europe, The Mighty Continent Series. No. 4
LC NO. 79-707419
Prod-BBCTV Dist-TIMLIF 1976

Yeast Dough Shaping Made Easy C 15 MIN
16MM FILM OPTICAL SOUND J-H A
Shows techniques for making dinner rolls, cinnamon buns, sticky buns, coffee cakes and foreign specialties from two basic, simple doughs.
Prod-FLSMNY Dist-MTP

Yeats Country C 18 MIN
16MM FILM, 3/4 OR 1/2 IN VIDEO H-C
Combines the sights of Western Ireland with the poetry of William Butler Yeats.
Prod-AENGUS Dist-IFB 1965

Yellow Ball Cache, The C 18 MIN
16MM FILM OPTICAL SOUND P-H
Presents a demonstration of the creativity and skill of children, ages 5 to 15, as observed in their work in the planning and production of 13 short animated films which they created using cut-out techniques. Features instructor Yvonne Andersen.
LC NO. FIA67-5040
Prod-YELLOW Dist-YELLOW 1965

Yellow Box, The C 30 MIN
16MM FILM, 3/4 OR 1/2 IN VIDEO
Shows three managers confronted by a salesman offering a new product to analyze three different management styles and the strength and weaknesses of each.
Prod-MILLBK Dist-IFB

Yellow Pages Commercial C 1 MIN
3/4 OR 1/2 INCH VIDEO CASSETTE
Shows a classic animated television commercial.
Prod-BROOKC Dist-BROOKC

Yellow Rain C 29 MIN
3/4 OR 1/2 INCH VIDEO CASSETTE
Considers the fact that the alleged use of 'yellow rain', a poisonous substance used in chemical-biological warfare is a major story of critical international importance that has received spotty media coverage.
From The Inside Story Series.
Prod-PBS Dist-PBS 1981

Yellow School Bus, The C 10 MIN
16MM FILM, 3/4 OR 1/2 IN VIDEO P-I
Illustrates basic safety practices on school buses. Demonstrates emergency exit techniques and stresses the need for calmness.
Prod-FLMFR Dist-FLMFR

Yellow Slippers C 45 MIN
16MM FILM, 3/4 OR 1/2 IN VIDEO P-J
Dramatizes the story of an orphan boy, apprenticed to a sculptor, who witnesses a church robbery by a mysterious pilgrim, is kidnapped and trained by the robber after his release from jail, and is finally rescued.
From The CBS Children's Film Festival Series.
Prod-WRLDP Dist-MGHT 1969

Yellow Submarine, The C 85 MIN
16MM FILM OPTICAL SOUND
Presents the animated story of how Pepperland is saved from the evil Blue Meanies when the Beatles arrive in a yellow submarine.
Prod-KINGFT Dist-TWYMAN 1968

Yellow Wallpaper By Charlotte Perkins Gilman, The C 15 MIN
16MM FILM, 3/4 OR 1/2 IN VIDEO J-C A
Presents a tale of a woman's gradual mental breakdown as a result of confinement and denial of her creative energies by her husband and doctors. Based on the short story The Yellow Wallpaper by Charlotte Perkins Gilman.
From The Short Story Series.
LC NO. 83-706126
Prod-IITC Dist-IU 1982

Yellow-Headed Blackbird C 3 MIN
16MM FILM OPTICAL SOUND P-I
Discusses the bird known as the yellow-headed blackbird.
From The Of All Things Series.
Prod-BAILYL Dist-AVED

Yellowstone C 3 MIN
16MM FILM OPTICAL SOUND P-I
Shows Yellowstone National Park in the state of Wyoming.

From The Of All Things Series.
Prod-BAILYL Dist-AVED

Yellowstone - The Living Sculpture C 9 MIN
3/4 INCH VIDEO CASSETTE
Highlights Yellowstone National Park as a living sculpture, showing how ground water seeps through subsurface ducts to trigger natural phenomena such as bubbling mud pots, hot springs and geysers. Uses animation to demonstrate how these phenomena operate. Issued in 1972 as a motion picture.
LC NO. 79-706176
Prod-USNPS Dist-USNAC Prodn-FROST 1979

Yellowstone Adventure C 15 MIN
16MM FILM OPTICAL SOUND
Shows rare shooper swans, bears, osprey with fish in its tallons in Yellow stone Park.
Prod-SFI Dist-SFI

Yellowstone Concerto, The C 32 MIN
16MM FILM OPTICAL SOUND
Follows the course of the Yellowstone River from its many mountain tributaries. Shows the diversity of life which depends on the river and makes a plea for future preservation.
LC NO. 77-702181
Prod-MDFG Dist-MDFG 1977

Yellowstone Cubs C 47 MIN
16MM FILM, 3/4 OR 1/2 IN VIDEO
Presents the adventures of two mischievous bear cubs as they blaze a hilarious trail through Yellowstone National Park after they become separated from their mother.
From The Animal Featurettes Series. Set 2
Prod-DISNEY Dist-WDEMCO 1967

Yellowstone In Winter C 27 MIN
16MM FILM, 3/4 OR 1/2 IN VIDEO I-C A
Offers views of Yellowstone National Park during the winter season. Shows the fall courting prances of male elk and bighorn sheep and the desperate food foraging of buffalo, deer and elk during the winter.
LC NO. 83-706355
Prod-BAYERW Dist-EBEC 1983

Yellowstone National Park C 19 MIN
16MM FILM, 3/4 OR 1/2 IN VIDEO
Describes Yellowstone National park, where animals roam with freedom and dignity.
Prod-KAWVAL Dist-KAWVAL

Yellowstone, The Living Sculpture C 9 MIN
16MM FILM OPTICAL SOUND A
Shows how ground water seeps through subsurface ducts to trigger such natural phenomena as bubbling mud pots, hot springs and geysers. Uses animation to demonstrate how these phenomena operate.
LC NO. 77-703162
Prod-USNPS Dist-USNAC Prodn-FROST 1972

Yemen C 30 MIN
3/4 INCH VIDEO CASSETTE I-J
Focuses on two teenagers from the Yemen Arab Republic.
From The Teenagers Of The World Series.
Prod-UNICEF Dist-GPITVL 1978

Yemen - Land Of Suffering C 20 MIN
16MM FILM OPTICAL SOUND
Focuses on one of the most adventurous actions ever undertaken by the International Committee of the Red Cross, relief for the Yemeni victims of civil strife.
Prod-ICRCRS Dist-AMRC 1964

Yemen Arab Republic C 28 MIN
3/4 INCH VIDEOTAPE
Interviews Ambassador Ahmed Al-Haddad, permanent representative to the United Nations. Includes a film clip on the architecture of Yemen. Hosted by Marilyn Perry.
From The International Byline Series.
Prod-PERRYM Dist-PERRYM

Yen For Harmony, A - Japanese Managers Try Their Style In North America C 26 MIN
16MM FILM, 3/4 OR 1/2 IN VIDEO
Investigates the aspects of Japanese management which effect productivity in organizations.
From The Human Resources And Organizational Behavior Series.
Prod-DOCUA Dist-CNEMAG

Yes X 54 MIN
16MM FILM OPTICAL SOUND
Presents a surrealistic tale of a teenage girl nearing break-down in a room peopled by a TV set. Shows other teens who wander in and hallucinatory images.
Prod-NWRTVF Dist-NWUFLM

YES C 26 MIN
3/4 OR 1/2 INCH VIDEO CASSETTE
Celebrates the inherent unity of mankind and documents All Faith's Day at Satchidananda Ashram-Yogaville.
Prod-IYOGA Dist-IYOGA

Yes And No C 7 MIN
3/4 INCH VIDEO CASSETTE I-H
Stresses the importance of self-discipline by describing the kingdom of Yesland, where people can do anything they want.
Prod-DAVFMS Dist-GA

Yes Is A Growing Word C 12 MIN
16MM FILM OPTICAL SOUND T
Presents an in-service teacher training film which shows programs developed at the Far West Laboratory for Educational Research and Development.
LC NO. 76-701860
Prod-FWLERD Dist-FWLERD 1972

Yes Ma'am C 48 MIN
16MM FILM, 3/4 OR 1/2 IN VIDEO H-C A
Presents a study of black domestics employed in the stately, old houses of New Orleans. Shows how old-timers resent those newcomers who work only for money and not for pride in their work and the care of the family, while younger household workers feel exploited and are offended by the 'mammy' role they are expected to play as part of their job.
Prod-FLMLIB Dist-FLMLIB 1982

Yes We Can B 31 MIN
3/4 INCH VIDEO CASSETTE
Shows six women speaking of the difficulties they encounter, the changes they hope for and the growth and self-worth brought about by their pursuit of traditionally 'masculine' trades.
Prod-VIDFEM Dist-WMENIF

Yes You Can C 28 MIN
16MM FILM OPTICAL SOUND J-C A
Explains how people can pinpoint areas in their lives they would like to change, and suggests how to carry out these changes.
From The You Can Do It - If Series.
LC NO. 81-700095
Prod-VANDER Dist-VANDER 1980

Yes, But B 30 MIN
16MM FILM OPTICAL SOUND A
Shows how a white chief engineer and his newly-appointed negro research assistant learn to recognize the proper approach to the problems of race relations.
LC NO. FIA65-1617
Prod-CPH Dist-CPH 1964

Yes, I Can C 13 MIN
3/4 OR 1/2 INCH VIDEO CASSETTE P
Tells how six-year-old Tommy gains self confidence when he finds that he has his own abilities to contribute to the family.
From The Under The Blue Umbrella Series.
Prod-SCETV Dist-AITECH 1977

Yes, I Can C 15 MIN
16MM FILM, 3/4 OR 1/2 IN VIDEO I
Presents David who insists that he is ready to go out on his own for an overnight stay at summer camp at the age of nine. Shows what happens when he gets his chance, but comes up against problems he hadn't counted on. Considers the limits of independent actions and recognizes the prudence of thorough preparation.
From The Inside-Out Series.
Prod-NITC Dist-AITECH 1973

Yes, No - Stop, Go C 13 MIN
16MM FILM, 3/4 OR 1/2 IN VIDEO K-P
Offers a visual interpretation of the words yes, no, stop and go. Helps the child relate the sights and sounds of the words to reading the words.
Prod-EVANSA Dist-AIMS 1971

Yes, Virginia, There Is A Santa Claus C 25 MIN
16MM FILM OPTICAL SOUND P-I
Presents the story of eight-year-old Virginia O'Hanlan and her attempt to find out if there really is a Santa Claus. Shows how she tried several sources before finally getting an answer from the editor of the New York Sun.
LC NO. 76-701135
Prod-WOLPER Dist-FI 1975

Yes, You Can Make A Difference C 15 MIN
16MM FILM OPTICAL SOUND
Demonstrates that performance coaching is, or should be, a part of every manager's day-to-day responsibilities. Emphasizes skills development.
Prod-EFM Dist-EFM

Yesterday And Today B
3/4 OR 1/2 INCH VIDEO CASSETTE
Presents a skillful argument of National Socialism with film clips contrasting the new prosperity under Nazi rule compared with an earlier Weimar Republican Germany inflicted with economic depression and unemployment.
From The Pre-War German Featurettes Series.
Prod-IHF Dist-IHF

Yesterday And Today—A Series
16MM FILM, 3/4 OR 1/2 IN VIDEO I-C A
Presents studies of Americans who have resisted the lure of technological society and who live and work much as their ancestors did 200 years ago.
Prod-ACI Dist-AIMS

Birch Canoe Builder, The	22 MIN
Cider Maker	18 MIN
Grist Miller	18 MIN
Maple Sugar Farmer, The	29 MIN

Yesterday Lives Again C 14 MIN
16MM FILM OPTICAL SOUND
Recaptures the day-to-day world of our ancestors at the Oldest Store Museum in St Augustine, Florida.
Prod-FLADC Dist-FLADC

Yesterday The Coyote Sang, Pt 1 B 30 MIN
16MM FILM OPTICAL SOUND I-C A
Describes the 'GREAT AMERICAN COWBOY,' focusing on cattle drives and their leaders.
From The Glory Trail Series.
LC NO. FIA66-975
Prod-NET Dist-IU 1965

Yesterday The Coyote Sang, Pt 2 B 30 MIN
16MM FILM OPTICAL SOUND I-C A
Discusses the cattleman's economic troubles and his chief enigma—the incoming farmer with his plows, wire fences and sod homes.
From The Glory Trail Series.
LC NO. FIA66-974
Prod-NET Dist-IU 1965

Yesterday, Today - The Netsilik Eskimo C 57 MIN
16MM FILM - 3/4 IN VIDEO
Examines one day in the life of a Netsilik family in a government village ten years after settlement in Pelly Bay, Canada. Shows that the inter-dependency and specialization of modern living have replaced the self-sufficiency of traditional Eskimo family life.
Prod-EDC Dist-EDC

Yesterday, Tomorrow And You C 52 MIN
16MM FILM, 3/4 OR 1/2 IN VIDEO H-C A
Illustrates the common factors that make for change and discusses whether they will continue operating in the future, and if so, will human beings recognize them. Examines the extent to which people have become increasingly incapable of understanding how change occurs. Looks ahead to the need for radical change in the availability and use of information in the future, if people are to remain in control of their destinies.
From The Connections Series.
LC NO. 79-706749
Prod-BBCTV Dist-TIMLIF 1979

Yesterday's Farm C 20 MIN
16MM FILM OPTICAL SOUND
Discusses the need to preserve the farm heritage.
LC NO. 76-702579
Prod-ATKINS Dist-HRAWC 1974

Yesterday's Farm C 17 MIN
16MM FILM, 3/4 OR 1/2 IN VIDEO P-J
Points out that the old farms that spread across North America are rich sources of information about our past, showing the ruggedness of life, the trials of the movement westward, the values that were held by early settlers and the hopes and ambitions of generations.
Prod-BFA Dist-PHENIX 1972

Yesterday's Heroes C 23 MIN
3/4 OR 1/2 INCH VIDEO CASSETTE
Focuses on the wild descendants of the animals that helped build the continent of Australia, such as horses, donkeys and camels.
Prod-NWLDPR Dist-NWLDPR

Yesterday's Wings C 20 MIN
3/4 OR 1/2 INCH VIDEO CASSETTE J-C A
Discusses vintage aircraft, including Curtiss, Waco, Ryan and Beechcraft, among others.
LC NO. 82-706795
Prod-AWSS Dist-AWSS 1981

Yesterday's Witness - A Tribute To The American Newsreel C 52 MIN
16MM FILM, 3/4 OR 1/2 IN VIDEO
Presents the history of the American newsreel, as told by the men who made them.
Prod-BLACKW Dist-BLACKW 1976

Yesterday's Witness In America—A Series
16MM FILM, 3/4 OR 1/2 IN VIDEO H-C A
Uses firsthand accounts, rare film footage and period photographs to analyze such historical incidents as the affair between William Randolph Hearst and Marion Davies, the Colorado Gold Rush of 1891, the internment of the Japanese during World War II and the women's suffrage movement.
Prod-BBCTV Dist-TIMLIF 1982

Gold Rush At Cripple Creek	050 MIN
Long March Of The Suffragists, The	050 MIN
Question Of Loyalty, A	050 MIN
Very Public Private Affair, A	050 MIN

Yesteryear Bloopers B 45 MIN
3/4 OR 1/2 INCH VIDEO CASSETTE A
Presents outtakes and mistakes made by actors and actresses of the '30s and '40s. Includes Jimmy Cagney, Errol Flynn, Bette Davis and Ronald Reagan.
Prod-ADVCAS Dist-ADVCAS

Yet C 2 MIN
16MM FILM OPTICAL SOUND
Presents a short film-fillum.
Prod-VANBKS Dist-VANBKS

Yetta Bernhard, MA - Conflict Resolution With A Couple C 60 MIN
3/4 OR 1/2 INCH VIDEO CASSETTE PRO
Illustrates the concepts outlined in Yetta Bernhard's book, Self Care. Includes an interview with a reconstituted family. Discusses communication and contracts with family members.
From The Perceptions, Pt A - Interventions In Family Therapy Series. Vol VI, Pt A12.
Prod-BOSFAM Dist-BOSFAM

Yetta Bernhard, MA, Private Practice, Los Angeles, California C 60 MIN
3/4 OR 1/2 INCH VIDEO CASSETTE PRO
Traces the evolution of a school teacher to a family therapist who combines the experiences of her family of origin and her marriage.
From The Perceptions, Pt B - Dialogues With Family Therapists Series. Vol VI, Pt B12.
Prod-BOSFAM Dist-BOSFAM

Yevtushenko - A Poet's Journey C 29 MIN
3/4 OR 1/2 INCH VIDEO CASSETTE J-C T
An account of Yevtushenko's travels around the world, his working methods in his moscow apartment, the Siberia of his youth and his conversations with friends and admirers. Includes sequences of the poet reading his works in Russian, over which English interpretations are imposed.
Prod-MANTLH Dist-FOTH 1970

Yield - Research To Reality C 17 MIN
16MM FILM OPTICAL SOUND
Shows how hybrid corn is developed at Dekalb AgResearch and the factors involved in developing these plants.
Prod-MTP Dist-MTP

Yin Hsien C 9 MIN
16MM FILM, 3/4 OR 1/2 IN VIDEO
Uses an image synthesizer to create abstract moving forms from live action. Presents a Chinese master of the martial art of T'ai chi chu'uan and transforms him into kinetic figures, mists and hieroglyphs.
Prod-WHIT Dist-PFP 1975

Yin-Yang C 5 MIN
16MM FILM OPTICAL SOUND H-C A
Presents a psychedelic time-painting, using positive, negative and black light illuminated alternating frames.
Prod-CFS Dist-CFS 1969

Yippie B 15 MIN
16MM FILM OPTICAL SOUND
Shows a spaced-out view of what took place in the streets of Chicago during the 1968 Democratic Convention.
Prod-SFN Dist-SFN

Yippie Film C 15 MIN
16MM FILM OPTICAL SOUND
Views what took place in the streets of Chicago during the 1968 Democratic Convention. Records original songs by the Fugs, Phil Ochs, Lawrence Welk, Wolf Lowenthal and Rennie Davis.
Prod-NEWSR Dist-NEWSR 1968

Yo Contemplare Su Gloria C 55 MIN
16MM FILM OPTICAL SOUND J-C A
A Spanish version of 'I BEHELD HIS GLORY.' A Roman centurion describes events which led up to the death of Jesus and tells about His crucifixion, resurrection and appearance to Thomas.
Prod-CAFM Dist-CAFM 1965

Yo Me Recuerdo B 13 MIN
16MM FILM OPTICAL SOUND
Presents a day in the life of a Tucson, Arizona, shoeshine boy.
LC NO. 78-701581
Prod-RUBIOA Dist-RUBIOA 1978

Yo Quiero Ser C 30 MIN
3/4 OR 1/2 INCH VIDEO CASSETTE K-P
See series title for descriptive statement.
From The Villa Alegre Series.
Prod-BCTV Dist-MDCPB

Yo Soy Chicano (Captioned) C 60 MIN
16MM FILM, 3/4 OR 1/2 IN VIDEO A
Portrays the Chicano experience from its roots in the Pre-Columbian past to current Mexican-American struggles. Spanish dialog with English subtitles and narration.
Prod-CNEMAG Dist-CNEMAG

Yo Soy Chicano (English) C 59 MIN
16MM FILM OPTICAL SOUND H-C A
Portrays the Chicano experience, from its roots in pre-Columbian history to the present, by actors who recreate key events in Mexican history and through interviews with Chicano leaders.
LC NO. 73-700537
Prod-KCET Dist-IU 1972

Yo Soy Pablo Neruda (English) C 29 MIN
3/4 OR 1/2 INCH VIDEO CASSETTE
Shows Chilean author Pablo Neruda in his native habitat on the fierce rocky shores of Isla Negra, in the flea market of Santiago surrounded by a world of entrancing everyday objects and in the streets of Chile's capital.
Prod-FOTH Dist-FOTH 1984

Yo-Yo And A Physical Fitness Program, A C 8 MIN
16MM FILM OPTICAL SOUND K-P
Follows Crystal as she tries to break the yo-yo record only to realize she is out of shape and needs to start on a physical fitness program.
From The Crystal Tipps And Alistair Series.
LC NO. 73-700454
Prod-BBCTV Dist-VEDO 1972

Yoga For Health B 11 MIN
16MM FILM OPTICAL SOUND H-C A
Introduces the time-honored science of yoga and shows how certain 'ASANAS,' if practiced correctly, can help to build up physical health, mental alertness and stamina.
Prod-INDIA Dist-NEDINF

Yoga For Riders C 40 MIN
1/2 IN VIDEO CASSETTE BETA/VHS
Deals with yoga for horse riders. Teaches hip and lower back stretching to loosen and strengthen the pelvic area.
Prod-MHRSMP Dist-EQVDL

Yoga In Daily Life C 30 MIN
3/4 OR 1/2 INCH VIDEO CASSETTE
Presents Sri Gurudev speaking on Yoga in daily life.
Prod-IYOGA Dist-IYOGA

Yogic Approach To Happiness And Healing, The C 120 MIN
3/4 OR 1/2 INCH VIDEO CASSETTE
Shows Sri Gurudev speaking to the Johns Hopkins University faculty and student body emphasizing that he is a skilled Naturopath. Depicts him speaking on laughter, health, breathing, selflessness and Yoga in action.
Prod-IYOGA Dist-IYOGA

Yogurt C 3 MIN
16MM FILM - 3/4 IN VIDEO
Demonstrates a simple method for making yogurt at home. Shows the three steps involved, heating the milk, culturing it with a bit of completed yogurt and incubating it long enough for the process of fermentation to happen and the liquid to thicken. Suggests saving a bit of yogurt to use as a culture in the next batch.
From The Beatrice Trum Hunter's Natural Foods Series.
Prod-WGBH Dist-PUBTEL 1974

Yogurt And Cheese, Make Your Own C 30 MIN
1/2 IN VIDEO CASSETTE BETA/VHS
Shows how to make yogurt without special equipment. Demonstrates making a cheese spread, yogurt sauce and yogurt balls in garlic oil.
From The Frugal Gourmet Series.
Prod-WTTWTV Dist-MTI

Yohannes The Silversmith C 25 MIN
16MM FILM, 3/4 OR 1/2 IN VIDEO J-C A
Introduces an Ethiopian who is working to become a master silversmith.
From The World Cultures And Youth Series.
Prod-SUNRIS Dist-CORF 1981

Yojimbo C 111 MIN
1/2 IN VIDEO CASSETTE (BETA)
Tells how a hired sword fights with various feuding factions in 1860 Japan.
Prod-UNKNWN Dist-VIDIM 1962

Yojimbo (Japanese) B 110 MIN
3/4 OR 1/2 INCH VIDEO CASSETTE
Presents the conflict of one man against many. Directed by Akira Kurosawa and featuring Toshiro Mifune.
Prod-IHF Dist-IHF

Yokneam C 50 MIN
16MM FILM OPTICAL SOUND H-C A
Takes a look at the election process as lived out in a small town called Yokneam near Haifa. Present local party members who explain how they recruit new voters and describe the process by which people get involved with a particular party.
Prod-NJWB Dist-NJWB 1981

Yonder Come Day C 26 MIN
16MM FILM, 3/4 OR 1/2 IN VIDEO H-C A
Illustrates slave culture by presenting the songs and words of Bessie Jones, a 72-year-old folk singer. Communicates the defiance and dignity of black people bereft of all material ties with their African homeland.
Prod-CAPCC Dist-CRMP 1976

Yonge Street B 7 MIN
16MM FILM OPTICAL SOUND
Presents scenes of Toronto's Yonge Street, from Bloor Street south to the lake.
LC NO. 77-702732
Prod-CANFDC Dist-CANFDC 1972

Yoo Hoo, I'm A Bird C 28 MIN
1 INCH VIDEOTAPE
Shows winter in Colorado, including skiing.
Prod-UAL Dist-MTP

Yorick's Skull - Gallows Humor In Hamlet C 45 MIN
3/4 OR 1/2 INCH VIDEO CASSETTE
Looks at gallows humour in Shakespeare's work Hamlet.
From The Survey Of English Literature I Series.
Prod-MDCPB Dist-MDCPB

York C 30 MIN
3/4 INCH VIDEO CASSETTE
Focuses on the life of York, the Black servant of Lieutenant William Clark, who accompanied the Lewis and Clark expedition which reached the Pacific Ocean in Novenber, 1805. Tells how due to his active role in the success of the expedition, York was given his freedom upon the party's return to Missouri in 1806.
From The South By Northwest Series.
Prod-KWSU Dist-GPITVL

Yorktown - The World Turned Upside Down C 13 MIN
16MM FILM, 3/4 OR 1/2 IN VIDEO J-C A
Re-creates the events and atmosphere of the victory of the French and American forces over the British army on October 19, 1781. Shows the battleground and surrounding landscape at Yorktown.
Prod-TERF Dist-CORF 1971

Yosemite C 3 MIN
16MM FILM OPTICAL SOUND P-I
Shows Yosemite National Park in the state of California.
From The Of All Things Series.
Prod-BAILYL Dist-AVED

Yosemite B 10 MIN
16MM FILM OPTICAL SOUND
Presents a scenic tour of Yosemite National Park in California and explains, using maps, models and animated drawings, the three major geologic changes in the Yosemite Valley.
Prod-USNPS Dist-USNPS

Yosemite C 48 MIN
16MM FILM OPTICAL SOUND
Depicts scenes from Yosemite National Park, including Sentinel Peak, Half Dome, Cathedral Spires, El Capitan and Mirror Lake, and explains the three major geologic changes in the Yosemite Valley.
LC NO. FIE54-257
Prod-USNPS Dist-USNPS 1954

Yosemite National Park (2nd Ed) C 17 MIN
16MM FILM, 3/4 OR 1/2 IN VIDEO I-C A
Pictures the scenic beauty and wildlife of Yosemite National Park through the changing seasons. Explains the geological development of Yosemite Valley and surrounding terrain and shows views of the Sierra Nevada Mountains, Half Dome, El Capitan, Merced River, Yosemite Falls and the sequoias.
Prod-HOE Dist-MCFI 1973

Yoshiko Chuma, Yves Musard And Jack Waters C 30 MIN
3/4 OR 1/2 INCH VIDEO CASSETTE
Discusses counter-culture dance at the clubs and alternate locations of New York. Hosted by Celia Ipiotis.
From The Eye On Dance - Dance And The Plastic Arts Series.
Prod-ARTRES Dist-ARTRES

Yoshiko The Papermaker C 25 MIN
16MM FILM, 3/4 OR 1/2 IN VIDEO I-J A
Introduces a young Japanese girl named Yoshiko who is learning the ancient art of papermaking from a local master. Shows her making a paper panel from a kozo tree and designing a bamboo forest to adorn it.
From The World Cultures And Youth Series.
Prod-SUNRIS Dist-CORF 1980

You C 4 MIN
16MM FILM, 3/4 OR 1/2 IN VIDEO
Suggests that adults would be happier and would have richer lives if they recaptured the imagination and curiousity characteristic of children.
Prod-CCCD Dist-CCCD 1979

You C 17 MIN
16MM FILM, 3/4 OR 1/2 IN VIDEO P-I
Examines the concept of empathy in human relations by telling how two young brothers begin to explore each other's feelings and viewpoints.
Prod-PHENIX Dist-CORF

You C 20 MIN
16MM FILM - 3/4 IN VIDEO J
Introduces two main elements, the behavioral and the factual. Shows the behavioral element of self-identity through special film effects, explaining that each person is a composite of many personalities and the search for self-identification is continuous throughout life. Places drug use in its proper historical perspective.
From The Nobody But Yourself Series.
Prod-WQED Dist-GPITVL

You (Parents) Are Special—A Series

Presents 10-minute dialogues with children and parents as Fred Rogers explores topics of concern to families.
Prod-FAMCOM Dist-FAMCOM

Discipline	010 MIN
Divorce	010 MIN
Friends Who Fight	010 MIN
Imaginary Friends	010 MIN
Moving	010 MIN
Nurturing Creativity	010 MIN
School Experiences	010 MIN
Set Of Eight	010 MIN
Siblings	010 MIN

You (Spanish) C 17 MIN
16MM FILM, 3/4 OR 1/2 IN VIDEO P-I
Examines the concept of empathy in human relations by telling how two young brothers begin to explore each other's feelings and viewpoints.
Prod-PHENIX Dist-CORF

You - And Your Ears C 8 MIN
16MM FILM, 3/4 OR 1/2 IN VIDEO P-J
Jiminy Cricket explains the structure of the ear and shows how sound waves affect the ear.
From The This Is You - Health Series.
Prod-DISNEY Dist-WDEMCO 1957

You - And Your Eyes C 8 MIN
16MM FILM, 3/4 OR 1/2 IN VIDEO P-J
Jiminy Cricket explains the structure and anatomy of the eye by comparing it with a camera. Stresses the safety features designed by nature to protect the eyes and the rules for care of the eyes.
From The This Is You - Health Series.
Prod-DISNEY Dist-WDEMCO 1958

You - And Your Five Senses C 8 MIN
16MM FILM, 3/4 OR 1/2 IN VIDEO P-J
Discusses man's five senses. Explains that some are more highly developed than others and that man compensates accordingly.
From The This Is You - Health Series.
Prod-DISNEY Dist-WDEMCO 1956

You - And Your Food C 8 MIN
16MM FILM, 3/4 OR 1/2 IN VIDEO P-J
Jiminy Cricket stresses the value of foods which are necessary to good health. Uses the analogy of the construction of an automobile to point out that proper foods must be eaten to build the body, to supply energy and to maintain the body in good condition.
From The This Is You - Health Series.
Prod-DISNEY Dist-WDEMCO 1959

You - And Your Sense Of Smell And Taste C 8 MIN
16MM FILM, 3/4 OR 1/2 IN VIDEO P-J
Jiminy Cricket explains the senses of smell and taste in humans as compared to other animals. He shows how these two senses act together.
From The This Is You - Health Series.
Prod-DISNEY Dist-WDEMCO 1963

You - And Your Sense Of Touch C 8 MIN
16MM FILM, 3/4 OR 1/2 IN VIDEO P-J

Jiminy Cricket explains the importance of the sense of touch, the four sensations involved and their effects.
From The This Is You - Health Series.
Prod-DISNEY Dist-WDEMCO 1962

You - Poor Kids Can Learn C 29 MIN
2 INCH VIDEOTAPE
Presents a study of the various services of the Department of Health, Education and Welfare. Discusses educational opportunities which are available for needy children.
From The You Series.
Prod-WRCTV Dist-PUBTEL

You - The Human Animal C 8 MIN
16MM FILM, 3/4 OR 1/2 IN VIDEO P-J
Discusses the differences between the human animal and other animals, emphasizing ability to think.
From The This Is You - Health Series.
Prod-DISNEY Dist-WDEMCO 1957

You - The Living Machine C 8 MIN
16MM FILM, 3/4 OR 1/2 IN VIDEO P-J
Jiminy Cricket shows the difference between a living machine and a manufactured machine. He explains how to take care of the body and shows the functions of the digestive and circulatory systems.
From The This Is You - Health Series.
Prod-DISNEY Dist-WDEMCO 1959

You - The Supervisor - Introduction C 30 MIN
3/4 OR 1/2 INCH VIDEO CASSETTE
Shows a newly promoted supervisor trying to handle his job. Discusses the common concerns of supervisors and the anxieties they experience on the job. Introduces the concept of promotion depression.
From The You - The Supervisor Series.
Prod-PRODEV Dist-DELTAK

You - The Supervisor—A Series
PRO
Presents a program to increase the student's ability to get results and build a more productive team, and covers scheduling, planning and delegating more effectively, interviewing correctly, becoming a better listener and establishing the proper environment for a new employee, and providing proper orientation and job training for the new employee, among other key topics. Addresses first line supervisors, those new to the job and those with some experience. Includes a participant's guide and a discussion leader's guide.
Prod-PRODEV Dist-DELTAK 1974

Building A Productive Climate 030 MIN
Counseling And Coaching 030 MIN
Interviewing And Selecting 030 MIN
Leadership And Growth 030 MIN
Orientation And Training 030 MIN
Performance Reviews That Get Results 030 MIN
Work Planning And Scheduling 030 MIN
You - The Supervisor - Introduction 030 MIN

You Always Have The Nicest Parties C 18 MIN
16MM FILM OPTICAL SOUND
Shows how a young couple plans a party featuring gourmet recipes that are prepared ahead of time in Temper-ware by Lenox, are refrigerated and are then heated just before the party.
LC NO. 74-702904
Prod-LENOXC Dist-LENOXC Prodn-MUYMAD 1974

You And Addiction C 29 MIN
2 INCH VIDEOTAPE
Presents a study of the various services of the Department of Health, Education and Welfare. Includes a discussion on addicts.
From The You Series.
Prod-WRCTV Dist-PUBTEL

You And Alcohol C 29 MIN
2 INCH VIDEOTAPE
Presents a study of the various services of the Department of Health, Education and Welfare. Includes a discussion of alcohol.
From The You Series.
Prod-WRCTV Dist-PUBTEL

You And Disaster C 29 MIN
2 INCH VIDEOTAPE
Presents a study of the various services of the Department of Health, Education and Welfare.
From The You Series.
Prod-WRCTV Dist-PUBTEL

You And Drugs C 29 MIN
2 INCH VIDEOTAPE
Presents a study of the various services of the Department of Health, Education and Welfare. Includes a discussion on drugs.
From The You Series.
Prod-WRCTV Dist-PUBTEL

You And Family Health C 29 MIN
2 INCH VIDEOTAPE
Presents a study of the various services of the Department of Health, Education and Welfare. Emphasizes the family health services which are available.
From The You Series.
Prod-WRCTV Dist-PUBTEL

You And Kentucky Justice C 60 MIN
3/4 OR 1/2 INCH VIDEO CASSETTE
Contains a question-answer self-test on jury duty, the Kentucky court system, and humorous stories on historic area justice, lawyers, and magistrates.
Prod-EASTKU Dist-EASTKU

You And M-Das (Multispectral Data Analysis System) C 15 MIN
16MM FILM OPTICAL SOUND
Demonstrates the use of data from Earth scanners on the LANDSAT satellite. Shows how computer analysis and categorization can be used with color video displays in order to depict Earth resources and features in detail. Emphasizes the system's great versatility in the fields of agriculture, land-use planning, oil exploration and pollution control.
LC NO. 76-700448
Prod-CYBRN Dist-CYBRN 1975

You And M-Das (Multispectral Data Analysis System (Arabic) C 15 MIN
16MM FILM OPTICAL SOUND
Demonstrates the use of data from Earth scanners on the LANDSAT satellite. Shows how computer analysis and categorization can be used with color video displays in order to depict Earth resources and features in detail. Emphasizes the system's great versatility in the fields of agriculture, land-use planning, oil exploration and pollution control.
LC NO. 76-700448
Prod-CYBRN Dist-CYBRN 1975

You And M-Das (Multispectral Data Analysis System (Spanish) C 15 MIN
16MM FILM OPTICAL SOUND
Demonstrates the use of data from Earth scanners on the LANDSAT satellite. Shows how computer analysis and categorization can be used with color video displays in order to depict Earth resources and features in detail. Emphasizes the system's great versatility in the fields of agriculture, land-use planning, oil exploration and pollution control.
LC NO. 76-700448
Prod-CYBRN Dist-CYBRN 1975

You And Manana C 29 MIN
2 INCH VIDEOTAPE
Presents a study of the various services of the Department of Health, Education and Welfare.
From The You Series.
Prod-WRCTV Dist-PUBTEL

You And Me C 30 MIN
16MM FILM, 3/4 OR 1/2 IN VIDEO J-C
Discusses careers in engineering, showing some of America's largest engineering projects and some of the nation's foremost mechanical engineers. Presents noted engineers who reveal how they prepared themselves for their careers while still in school and how that training paid off.
Prod-KLEINW Dist-KLEINW

You And Mental Retardation C 29 MIN
2 INCH VIDEOTAPE
Shows how the Department of Health, Education and Welfare is becoming increasingly concerned with mental retardation.
From The You Series.
Prod-WRCTV Dist-PUBTEL

You And Mobility C 29 MIN
2 INCH VIDEOTAPE
Presents a study of the various services of the Department of Health, Education and Welfare.
From The You Series.
Prod-WRCTV Dist-PUBTEL

You And Mr Rat C 29 MIN
2 INCH VIDEOTAPE
Presents a study of the various services of the Department of Health, Education and Welfare. Shows various techniques of rat extermination.
From The You Series.
Prod-WRCTV Dist-PUBTEL

You And Office Safety C 9 MIN
3/4 INCH VIDEO CASSETTE H-C A
Illustrates how easy it is to avoid most office accidents. Shows that safety in the office can be assured by using a little common sense, by thinking ahead and by considering the consequences of one's actions.
Prod-ACAMC Dist-GA

You And Only You C 14 MIN
16MM FILM OPTICAL SOUND I-C A
Demonstrates the social and economic value of forest land by showing the dependency of the American way of life upon the forest. Emphasizes methods and needs of reforestation.
LC NO. 72-701109
Prod-VADE Dist-VADE 1972

You And Quackery C 29 MIN
2 INCH VIDEOTAPE
Presents a study of the various services of the Department of Health, Education and Welfare.
From The You Series.
Prod-WRCTV Dist-PUBTEL

You And Returning Veterans C 29 MIN
2 INCH VIDEOTAPE
Presents a study of the various services of the Department of Health, Education and Welfare. Includes a discussion on veterans who are returning home.
From The You Series.
Prod-WRCTV Dist-PUBTEL

You And Rx Learning C 29 MIN
2 INCH VIDEOTAPE
Presents a study of the various services of the Department of Health, Education and Welfare.
From The You Series.
Prod-WRCTV Dist-PUBTEL

You And Services C 29 MIN
2 INCH VIDEOTAPE
Presents a study of the services of the Department of Health, Education and Welfare.
From The You Series.
Prod-WRCTV Dist-PUBTEL

You And Surplus Property C 29 MIN
2 INCH VIDEOTAPE
Presents a study of the various services of the Department of Health, Education and Welfare. Includes a discussion of property.
From The You Series.
Prod-WRCTV Dist-PUBTEL

You And The Computer C 9 MIN
16MM FILM OPTICAL SOUND I-C
Uses live action and animated art to show the issuance of a paycheck, a basic function of a computer.
LC NO. 79-704300
Prod-GE Dist-GE 1969

You And The Delinquents C 29 MIN
2 INCH VIDEOTAPE
Presents a study of the various services of the Department of Health, Education and Welfare. Includes a discussion of delinquents.
From The You Series.
Prod-WRCTV Dist-PUBTEL

You And The Drivotrainer System C 20 MIN
16MM FILM OPTICAL SOUND
Introduces the Drivotrainer System. Includes elementary procedures such as readying cars for either manual or automatic shift. Shows the correct use of several control devices. Designed for use with the Aetna Drivotrainer System.
From The New Aetna Drivotrainer Film Series. No. 1
LC NO. FI67-867
Prod-AETNA Dist-AETNA 1964

You And The Future C
3/4 OR 1/2 INCH VIDEO CASSETTE
Explains the traditional types of jobs in business data processing and discusses the job responsibilities of the systems analyst. Outlines the duties of a typical computer center operations manager.
From The Computers At Work Series.
Prod-COMTEG Dist-COMTEG

You And The Handicapped C 29 MIN
2 INCH VIDEOTAPE
Presents a study of the various services of the Department of Health, Education and Welfare. Includes a discussion of the handicapped.
From The You Series.
Prod-WRCTV Dist-PUBTEL

You And The Law C 17 MIN
16MM FILM OPTICAL SOUND H-C A
Creates an understanding of the rights and duties of citizens and police officers. Discusses probable cause, search and seizure, warrants, arrest procedures and juvenile and adult court procedures.
LC NO. 75-701990
Prod-MCCRNE Dist-MCCRNE 1974

You And The Law C 29 MIN
16MM FILM, 3/4 OR 1/2 IN VIDEO H-C A
Dramatizes various types of practical legal problems which deaf persons may encounter, including job discrimination, consumer rights violations and civil actions. Explains how and where a deaf person can find help to protect his rights under the law. With captions.
Prod-LINCS Dist-JOU 1978

You And The Law (Captioned) C 16 MIN
16MM FILM OPTICAL SOUND A
Uses four different stories that bring up a different legal issue - job discrimination, consumer rights, landlord-tenant disagreements, and criminal law. Discusses importance of reading and understanding legal papers before signing them.
Prod-GALCO Dist-GALCO 1976

You And The Law (Captioned) C 29 MIN
16MM FILM, 3/4 OR 1/2 IN VIDEO H-C A
Dramatizes various types of practical legal problems which deaf persons may encounter, including job discrimination, consumer rights violations and civil actions. Explains how and where a deaf person can find help to protect his rights under the law.
Prod-LINCS Dist-JOU 1978

You And The Merit System C 15 MIN
16MM FILM - 3/4 IN VIDEO H A
Presents the new or prospective civil service employee with information on the federal merit principles, probationary period, career status, pay systems, classification systems and equal employment opportunities.
From The Working For The United States Series.
LC NO. 77-706029
Prod-USCSC Dist-USNAC Prodn-LOUISP 1976

You And The Pap Test C 29 MIN
2 INCH VIDEOTAPE
Presents a study of the various services of the Department of Health, Education and Welfare. Explains how the pap test is used as a safeguard against cancer and other abnormalities.
From The You Series.
Prod-WRCTV Dist-PUBTEL

You And The Police - Victim Or Witness Of A Crime (Captioned) C 37 MIN
3/4 OR 1/2 INCH VIDEO CASSETTE S
Shows deaf persons what they are to do if they are victims or witnesses of crime. Urges deaf person to give the police as much help as possible. Signed.
Prod-NCLD Dist-GALCO 1978

You And The Question Mark Kids C 29 MIN
2 INCH VIDEOTAPE
Presents a study of the various services of the Department of Health, Education and Welfare.

From The You Series.
Prod-WRCTV Dist-PUBTEL

You And The Red Schoolhouse C 29 MIN
2 INCH VIDEOTAPE
Presents a study of the various services of the Department of Health, Education and Welfare. Discusses educational opportunities which are available.
From The You Series.
Prod-WRCTV Dist-PUBTEL

You And The Road Children C 29 MIN
2 INCH VIDEOTAPE
Presents a study of the various services of the Department of Health, Education and Welfare.
From The You Series.
Prod-WRCTV Dist-PUBTEL

You And The Telephone C 21 MIN
16MM FILM OPTICAL SOUND IND
Points out the six basic guidelines that can produce top telephone performance. Suggests that every phone call is another chance to build that respect and trust which can attract and hold customers.
From The Golden Triangle Teller Training Series.
LC NO. 76-700453
Prod-PART Dist-PART

You And Traffic Safety C 60 MIN
3/4 OR 1/2 INCH VIDEO CASSETTE
Presents a question-answer traffic safety self-test with film illustrations on Kentucky driving law.
Prod-EASTKU Dist-EASTKU

You And What You Do It With C
16MM FILM - 3/4 IN VIDEO A
Presents five accident victims who are given a second chance after learning how to treat their machinery or equipment with respect. Shows how to care for equipment and heed any warning signals it gives.
Prod-BNA Dist-BNA 1983

You And When It Matters C 29 MIN
2 INCH VIDEOTAPE
Presents a study of the various services of the Department of Health, Education and Welfare.
From The You Series.
Prod-WRCTV Dist-PUBTEL

You And Women's Lib C 29 MIN
2 INCH VIDEOTAPE
Presents a study of the Department of Health, Education and Welfare. Includes a discussion on the Women's Liberation Movement.
From The You Series.
Prod-WRCTV Dist-PUBTEL

You And Your Aging Parents C 59 MIN
3/4 OR 1/2 INCH VIDEO CASSETTE A
Discusses some of the myths and describes stresses associated with growing old. Addresses the challenges of those who must raise their own children while caring for their aging parents.
Prod-USPHS Dist-USNAC 1985

You And Your Baby Come Home C 18 MIN
16MM FILM OPTICAL SOUND H-C A
Emphasizes the new mother's needs for sleep, rest, proper exercise and correct diet. Uses a baby boy and a baby girl in demonstrations of handling, bathing, bottle and breast feeding, and preparation for sleep.
LC NO. FIA66-1185
Prod-MORLAT Dist-SF 1960

You And Your Breath C 29 MIN
2 INCH VIDEOTAPE
Presents a study of the various services of the Department of Health, Education and Welfare.
From The You Series.
Prod-WRCTV Dist-PUBTEL

You And Your Customers C 15 MIN
3/4 OR 1/2 INCH VIDEO CASSETTE
Dramatizes retailer's problems with customer relations.
From The Small Business Administration Series.
Prod-IVCH Dist-IVCH

You and Your Ears (Arabic) C 8 MIN
16MM FILM, 3/4 OR 1/2 IN VIDEO P
Explains the structure of the ear. Provides rules for ear care and safety.
From The This Is You (Arabic) Series.
Prod-WDEMCO Dist-WDEMCO 1957

You And Your Ears (Dutch) C 8 MIN
16MM FILM, 3/4 OR 1/2 IN VIDEO P
Explains the structure of the ear. Provides rules for ear care and safety.
From The This Is You (Dutch) Series.
Prod-WDEMCO Dist-WDEMCO 1957

You And Your Ears (French) C 8 MIN
16MM FILM, 3/4 OR 1/2 IN VIDEO P
Explains the structure of the ear. Provides rules for ear care and safety.
From The This Is You (French) Series.
Prod-WDEMCO Dist-WDEMCO 1957

You And Your Ears (Spanish) C 8 MIN
16MM FILM, 3/4 OR 1/2 IN VIDEO P
Explains the structure of the ear. Provides rules for ear care and safety.
From The This Is You (Spanish) Series.
Prod-WDEMCO Dist-WDEMCO 1957

You And Your Ears (Thai) C 8 MIN
16MM FILM, 3/4 OR 1/2 IN VIDEO P
Explains the structure of the ear. Provides rules for ear care and safety.
From The This Is You (Thai) Series.
Prod-WDEMCO Dist-WDEMCO 1957

You And Your Eyes (Arabic) C 8 MIN
16MM FILM, 3/4 OR 1/2 IN VIDEO P
Explains eye structure and function. Provides rules for eye safety and care.
From The This Is You (Arabic) Series.
Prod-WDEMCO Dist-WDEMCO 1958

You And Your Eyes (Dutch) C 8 MIN
16MM FILM, 3/4 OR 1/2 IN VIDEO P
Explains eye structure and function. Provides rules for eye safety and care.
From The This Is You (Dutch) Series.
Prod-WDEMCO Dist-WDEMCO 1958

You And Your Eyes (French) C 8 MIN
16MM FILM, 3/4 OR 1/2 IN VIDEO P
Explains eye structure and function. Provides rules for eye safety and care.
From The This Is You (French) Series.
Prod-WDEMCO Dist-WDEMCO 1958

You And Your Eyes (Spanish) C 8 MIN
16MM FILM, 3/4 OR 1/2 IN VIDEO P
Explains eye structure and function. Provides rules for eye safety and care.
From The This Is You (Spanish) Series.
Prod-WDEMCO Dist-WDEMCO 1958

You And Your Eyes (Thai) C 8 MIN
16MM FILM, 3/4 OR 1/2 IN VIDEO P
Explains eye structure and function. Provides rules for eye safety and care.
From The This Is You (Thai) Series.
Prod-WDEMCO Dist-WDEMCO 1958

You And Your Feelings C 15 MIN
3/4 OR 1/2 INCH VIDEO CASSETTE P
Explains emotions and discusses consideration of the feelings of other people. Indicates that as children grow up their feelings grow up too. Introduces a character puppet named Muggsy. (Broadcast quality)
From The All About You Series.
Prod-NITC Dist-AITECH Prodn-TTOIC 1975

You And Your Five Senses (Arabic) C 8 MIN
16MM FILM, 3/4 OR 1/2 IN VIDEO P
Compares the responses of humans and other animals to stimuli.
From The This Is You (Arabic) Series.
Prod-WDEMCO Dist-WDEMCO 1956

You And Your Five Senses (French) C 8 MIN
16MM FILM, 3/4 OR 1/2 IN VIDEO P
Compares the responses of humans and other animals to stimuli.
From The This Is You (French) Series.
Prod-WDEMCO Dist-WDEMCO 1956

You And Your Five Senses (Spanish) C 8 MIN
16MM FILM, 3/4 OR 1/2 IN VIDEO P
Compares the responses of humans and other animals to stimuli.
From The This Is You (Spanish) Series.
Prod-WDEMCO Dist-WDEMCO 1956

You And Your Food (Arabic) C 8 MIN
16MM FILM, 3/4 OR 1/2 IN VIDEO P
Explains the role a balanced diet plays in maintaining health.
From The This Is You (Arabic) Series.
Prod-WDEMCO Dist-WDEMCO 1959

You And Your Food (Dutch) C 8 MIN
16MM FILM, 3/4 OR 1/2 IN VIDEO P
Explains the role a balanced diet plays in maintaining health.
From The This Is You (Dutch) Series.
Prod-WDEMCO Dist-WDEMCO 1959

You And Your Food (French) C 8 MIN
16MM FILM, 3/4 OR 1/2 IN VIDEO P
Explains the role a balanced diet plays in maintaining health.
From The This Is You (French) Series.
Prod-WDEMCO Dist-WDEMCO 1959

You And Your Food (Hungarian) C 8 MIN
16MM FILM, 3/4 OR 1/2 IN VIDEO P
Explains the role a balanced diet plays in maintaining health.
Prod-WDEMCO Dist-WDEMCO 1959

You And Your Food (Spanish) C 8 MIN
16MM FILM, 3/4 OR 1/2 IN VIDEO P
Explains the role a balanced diet plays in maintaining health.
From The This Is You (Spanish) Series.
Prod-WDEMCO Dist-WDEMCO 1959

You And Your Food (Thai) C 8 MIN
16MM FILM, 3/4 OR 1/2 IN VIDEO P
Explains the role a balanced diet plays in maintaining health.
From The This Is You (Thai) Series.
Prod-WDEMCO Dist-WDEMCO 1959

You And Your Heritage C 29 MIN
2 INCH VIDEOTAPE
Presents a study of the various services of the Department of Health, Education and Welfare.
From The You Series.
Prod-WRCTV Dist-PUBTEL

You And Your Parents - Making It Through The Tough Years C
3/4 OR 1/2 INCH VIDEO CASSETTE I-J
Helps aid in understanding and coping with tensions in parent-child relationships that accompany the years from ages eleven to fourteen.
Prod-SUNCOM Dist-SUNCOM

You And Your Personal Computer—A Series

Explains what a personal computer is and what it can do for the user.
Prod-VISUCP Dist-VISUCP

Machine At Work 014 MIN
Machine, The 012 MIN

You And Your Sense Of Smell And Taste (Arabic) C 8 MIN
16MM FILM, 3/4 OR 1/2 IN VIDEO P
Shows the relationship between aroma and taste. Explains how the senses of smell and taste contribute to daily enjoyment and safety.
From The This Is You (Arabic) Series.
Prod-WDEMCO Dist-WDEMCO

You And Your Sense Of Touch (Arabic) C 8 MIN
16MM FILM, 3/4 OR 1/2 IN VIDEO P
Explains the function and importance of touch.
From The This Is You (Arabic) Series.
Prod-WDEMCO Dist-WDEMCO 1962

You And Your Sense Of Touch (French) C 8 MIN
16MM FILM, 3/4 OR 1/2 IN VIDEO P
Explains the function and importance of touch.
From The This Is You (French) Series.
Prod-WDEMCO Dist-WDEMCO 1962

You And Yours C 20 MIN
3/4 OR 1/2 INCH VIDEO CASSETTE
Tells about preventing fires, burns and clothing fires, baby sitters, home fire detection systems, escape planning and what to do if fire strikes.
Prod-FPF Dist-FPF

You Are A - Do Your Own Thing - Using Imagine That C 22 MIN
3/4 OR 1/2 INCH VIDEO CASSETTE T
Introduces the Imagine That Series and explains how teachers can use its multisensory approach to help children develop mind-body coordination.
From The Imagine That Series. Program 15
Prod-WBRATV Dist-GPITVL 1981

You Are A Band Member C 15 MIN
3/4 OR 1/2 INCH VIDEO CASSETTE P
Uses a multisensory approach to help children develop mind-body coordination. Integrates an imaginary theme with indoor classroom activities and calisthenics.
From The Imagine That Series. Program 12
Prod-WBRATV Dist-GPITVL 1981

You Are A Dancer C 15 MIN
3/4 OR 1/2 INCH VIDEO CASSETTE P
Uses a multisensory approach to help children develop mind-body coordination. Integrates an imaginary theme with indoor classroom activities and calisthenics.
From The Imagine That Series. Program 14
Prod-WBRATV Dist-GPITVL 1981

You Are A Happy Farmer C 15 MIN
3/4 OR 1/2 INCH VIDEO CASSETTE P
Uses a multisensory approach to help children develop mind-body coordination. Integrates an imaginary theme with indoor classroom activities and calisthenics.
From The Imagine That Series. Program 13
Prod-WBRATV Dist-GPITVL 1981

You Are A Skeleton C 15 MIN
3/4 OR 1/2 INCH VIDEO CASSETTE P
Uses a multisensory approach to help children develop mind-body coordination, focusing on the body and the identification of its parts. Integrates an imaginary theme with indoor classroom activities and calisthenics.
From The Imagine That Series. Program 11
LC NO. 82-706437
Prod-WBRATV Dist-GPITVL 1981

You Are A Zoo Animal C 15 MIN
3/4 OR 1/2 INCH VIDEO CASSETTE P
Uses a multisensory approach to help children develop mind-body coordination, focusing on gross motor movements and spatial awareness. Integrates an imaginary zoo theme with the use of rhythmic music, pantomime, and indoor classroom activities and calisthenics.
From The Imagine That Series. Program 7
LC NO. 82-706473
Prod-WBRATV Dist-GPITVL 1981

You Are Changing C 15 MIN
16MM FILM OPTICAL SOUND
Portrays the attitudes and concerns of a group of students as they research and film a class assignment on how they feel about the physical and emotional changes that take place as they enter puberty.
LC NO. 74-700487
Prod-WSTGLF Dist-WSTGLC 1972

You Are In Outer Space C 15 MIN
3/4 OR 1/2 INCH VIDEO CASSETTE P
Uses a multisensory approach to help children develop mind-body coordination, focusing on gross motor activities such as skipping, walking, hopping and running, along with rhythmical movements and pantomimes. Integrates an outer space theme with indoor classroom activities and calisthenics.
From The Imagine That Series. Program 10
LC NO. 82-706438
Prod-WBRATV Dist-GPITVL 1981

You Are In The Computer C 60 MIN
3/4 OR 1/2 INCH VIDEO CASSETTE
Examines computerized information systems and the issue of privacy.
From The Frontline Series.
Prod-DOCCON Dist-PBS

You Are Not Alone C 27 MIN
16MM FILM - 3/4 IN VIDEO
Explores the physical and emotional aspects of grief after the sudden death of an infant, and assures parents that the death was not their fault. Discusses problems which may arise with a spouse, siblings, in-laws and friends.
From The Sudden Infant Death Syndrome Series.
LC NO. 79-706257
Prod-USHSA Dist-USNAC Prodn-NOWAKA 1979

You Are Not Alone C 29 MIN
2 INCH VIDEOTAPE
See series title for descriptive statement.
From The That's Life Series.
Prod-KOAPTV Dist-PUBTEL

You Are Not Alone (Danish) C 92 MIN
16MM FILM, 3/4 OR 1/2 IN VIDEO
A Danish-language film with English subtitles. Explores the boundaries of friendship and love within a private boys school in Copenhagen where a headmaster's inability to cope with his students leads to their rebellion.
Prod-AWARD Dist-IFEX 1980

You Are Old, Father William C 50 MIN
16MM FILM, 3/4 OR 1/2 IN VIDEO C A
Looks at what happens to the body and the mind as people age. Pinpoints what goes wrong in the brain when senility occurs.
LC NO. 82-706854
Prod-BBCTV Dist-FI 1981

You Are Someone Else C 15 MIN
3/4 OR 1/2 INCH VIDEO CASSETTE P
Uses a multisensory approach to help children develop mind-body coordination, focusing on the identification and movement of specific body parts, the development of spatial awareness and experience of movement through mirror imaging with a partner. Integrates an imaginary theme with the use of rhythmic music, pantomime and indoor classroom activities and calisthenics.
From The Imagine That Series. Program 1
LC NO. 82-706467
Prod-WBRATV Dist-GPITVL 1981

You Are Something Else C 15 MIN
3/4 OR 1/2 INCH VIDEO CASSETTE P
Uses a multisensory approach to help children develop mind-body coordination, focusing on axial movements, basic locomotor experiences and the movement of the body to form floor designs. Integrates an imaginary theme with the use of rhythmic music, pantomime, and indoor classroom activities and calisthenics.
From The Imagine That Series. Program 3
LC NO. 82-706469
Prod-WBRATV Dist-GPITVL 1981

You Are Somewhere Else C 15 MIN
3/4 OR 1/2 INCH VIDEO CASSETTE P
Uses a multisensory approach to help children develop mind-body coordination, focusing on hand-eye coordination, rhythmical movements, and the demonstration of creative shapes with the body. Integrates an imaginary theme with the use of rhythmic music, pantomime, and indoor classroom activities and calisthenics.
From The Imagine That Series. Program 4
LC NO. 82-706470
Prod-WBRATV Dist-GPITVL 1981

You Are Special C 13 MIN
16MM FILM, 3/4 OR 1/2 IN VIDEO K-P S
Presents Mr Rogers discussing uniqueness and differences, including differences relating to handicaps.
From The I Am, I Can, I Will, Level I Series.
LC NO. 80-706539
Prod-FAMCOM Dist-HUBDSC 1979

You Are Special C 15 MIN
3/4 OR 1/2 INCH VIDEO CASSETTE P
Features song 'You Are Special.' Explains how everyone is different in looks, thoughts, feelings and abilities. Teaches children how to improve their self-image by learning more about themselves.
From The Well, Well, Well With Slim Goodbody Series.
Prod-AITECH Dist-AITECH

You Are The Game - Sexual Harassment On Campus C 59 MIN
3/4 OR 1/2 INCH VIDEO CASSETTE C A
Dramatizes the situation of two college women students who have experienced different forms of sexual harassment from male professors.
Prod-IU Dist-IU 1985

You Are The Teacher C 13 MIN
16MM FILM OPTICAL SOUND PRO
Demonstrates the practical application of audio-visual devices and tools in a teaching situation. Shows several methods of incorporating teaching tools into programs which supplement in-service training.
Prod-ACYDGD Dist-ACY 1969

You Are There - With Your Fair Share C 15 MIN
16MM FILM OPTICAL SOUND
Demonstrates the many ways in which money donated to the Heart of America United Fund campaign is used to help people.
LC NO. FIA66-702
Prod-HAUFC Dist-HAUFC Prodn-CALVIN

You Are There–A Series
16MM FILM, 3/4 OR 1/2 IN VIDEO I-H
Prod-CBSTV Dist-PHENIX 1972

Columbus And Isabella 22 MIN
Fall Of Troy, The 22 MIN
Galileo And His Universe 22 MIN
Harriet Tubman And The Underground Railroad 22 MIN
Lewis And Clark At The Great Divide 22 MIN
Mystery Of Amelia Earhart, The 22 MIN
Nomination Of Abraham Lincoln, The 22 MIN
Ordeal Of A President 22 MIN
Paul Revere's Ride 22 MIN
Record Ride From The Pony Express, The 22 MIN
Siege Of The Alamo, The 22 MIN
Torment Of Joan Of Arc, The 22 MIN
Treason Of Benedict Arnold, The 22 MIN
Trial Of Susan B Anthony, The 22 MIN
Vision Of Dr Robert Koch, The 22 MIN

You As A Manager C 30 MIN
3/4 OR 1/2 INCH VIDEO CASSETTE C A
Discusses skills that are important to success. Suggests ways in which prospective and working managers can improve their performance.
From The Business Management Series. Lesson 3
Prod-SCCON Dist-SCCON

You Be The Judge C 13 MIN
16MM FILM, 3/4 OR 1/2 IN VIDEO I-J
Uses a stop-projector technique to present three cases involving juveniles in order to give the viewer an opportunity to witness the events and discuss possible decisions by the judge.
Prod-CAHILL Dist-AIMS 1972

You Be The Judge C 15 MIN
3/4 OR 1/2 INCH VIDEO CASSETTE I
Tells how Tom is found guilty of endangering himself on the street and is sentenced by the judge of a very strange court.
From The It's Your Move Series.
Prod-WETN Dist-AITECH 1977

You Belong C 15 MIN
16MM FILM, 3/4 OR 1/2 IN VIDEO I
Explores the vital connections between human beings and their surroundings. Stresses the increase of a sense of responsibility which all people must feel for the environment.
From The Inside-Out Series.
Prod-NITC Dist-AITECH 1973

You Bet - They Wynn Dollars C 26 MIN
16MM FILM OPTICAL SOUND
Takes a look at the gambling industry, focusing on a rural bingo parlor in Maryland and a large Las Vegas casino, both owned and operated by the Wynn brothers.
LC NO. 80-701448
Prod-WJLATV Dist-WJLATV 1979

You Bet My Life C 15 MIN
16MM FILM OPTICAL SOUND IND
Demonstrates the importance of production cleanliness. Shows that because one assemblyman failed to retrieve a dropped rivet, a pilot was killed and a multi-million dollar airplane was destroyed. Emphasizes that only the worker's constant attention can ensure a quality product free of potentially dangerous manufacturing scraps.
LC NO. 72-701860
Prod-VOAERO Dist-VOAERO

You Bet Your Burger C 30 MIN
3/4 OR 1/2 INCH VIDEO CASSETTE P-I
See series title for descriptive statement.
From The Sonrisas Series.
Prod-KRLNTV Dist-MDCPB

You Bet Your Life C 5 MIN
3/4 OR 1/2 INCH VIDEO CASSETTE J-H
Teaches correct word usage. Explains 'Already' and 'All ready' and 'Further' and 'Farther'.
From The Write On, Set 1 Series.
Prod-CTI Dist-CTI

You Bet Your Life C 13 MIN
16MM FILM, 3/4 OR 1/2 IN VIDEO H-C A
Looks at the problem of compulsive gambling and discusses a treatment method used at the Miami Veterans Administration Medical Center. Narrated by Sharon Lovejoy.
Prod-CBSNEW Dist-CAROUF

You Bet Your Life C 60 MIN
3/4 OR 1/2 INCH VIDEO CASSETTE
Features two great episodes of the comedy TV series starring Groucho Marx.
Prod-IHF Dist-IHF

You Bring Your Lunch, I'll Bring Mine C 13 MIN
16MM FILM, 3/4 OR 1/2 IN VIDEO K-P
Explores the ideas about differences in people and points out that individual characteristics are to be appreciated. Visits a playground where everyone is having fun, demonstrating self-expression of emotions, and physical activity.
From The Growing Up With Sandy Offenheim Series.
LC NO. 82-707059
Prod-PLAYTM Dist-BCNFL 1982

You Call That Art C 29 MIN
3/4 INCH VIDEO CASSETTE H-C A
Surveys different approaches to contemporary art, with examples drawn from exhibits at Chicago's Museum of Contemporary Art.
LC NO. 80-707183
Prod-WTTWTV Dist-PUBTEL 1978

You Can C 28 MIN
16MM FILM, 3/4 OR 1/2 IN VIDEO
Features a summer marine biology program for disabled youths. High school students are shown discovering marine biology, ways of communicating and good times at the beach. These students have disabilities such as blindness, hearing impairments and paralysis.
Prod-USNOAA Dist-USNAC

You Can Compose A Dance, Pt 1 B 10 MIN
16MM FILM OPTICAL SOUND P-I
Illustrates how young children can create their own dances. Shows how to start with an idea.
Prod-WINTER Dist-SLFP 1970

You Can Compose A Dance, Pt 2 B 10 MIN
16MM FILM OPTICAL SOUND P-I
Illustrates how young children can create their own dances. Shows dance structure.
Prod-WINTER Dist-SLFP 1970

You Can Count On Computers C 30 MIN
16MM FILM, 3/4 OR 1/2 IN VIDEO I-H
Presents various types and uses of computer software, especially educational programs, such as games which teach math or science skills, and speed reading programs. Demonstrates simple computer programming.
From The Mr Microchip Series.
Prod-JOU Dist-JOU

You Can Do Anything C 15 MIN
3/4 OR 1/2 INCH VIDEO CASSETTE P
Uses a multisensory approach to help children develop mind-body coordination, focusing on simple stunts, spatial awareness and creative stunt combinations. Integrates an imaginary theme with the use of rhythmic music, pantomime, and indoor classroom activities and calisthenics.
From The Imagine That Series. Program 6
LC NO. 82-706472
Prod-WBRATV Dist-GPITVL 1981

You Can Do It - If–A Series

Discusses aspects of motivation and success.
Prod-VANDER Dist-VANDER 1980

Accept And Excel 028 MIN
Acquiring Greatness 028 MIN
All Successful People Have It 028 MIN
Detour - A Challenge 028 MIN
If You Don't - Who Will 028 MIN
Surprises Of Failure Can Lead To The 028 MIN
Try It, They'll Like It 028 MIN
What Is The Most Important Priority Of A 028 MIN
Yes You Can 028 MIN
You Decide 028 MIN

You Can Do Something About Acne C 16 MIN
16MM FILM, 3/4 OR 1/2 IN VIDEO J-H
Outlines the physiological reasons for acne and offers health care suggestions.
Prod-WHITEP Dist-AIMS 1973

You Can Fixit–A Series

Presents home repair experts Thomas Dabbs and Jordy Johnson showing how do-it-yourself home repairs and additions can be easy and inexpensive.
Prod-WRJATV Dist-MDCPB

Chairs And Other Furniture 030 MIN
Counter Tops 030 MIN
Dead Bolts 030 MIN
Doors And Windows 030 MIN
Electrical Outlets 030 MIN
Faucets 030 MIN
Floor Cover 030 MIN
Hot Water Time Switch 030 MIN
Lighting 030 MIN
Sheet Rock 030 MIN
Tool Box I, The 030 MIN
Tool Box II, The 030 MIN
Window Repair 030 MIN

You Can Fly C 4 MIN
16MM FILM, 3/4 OR 1/2 IN VIDEO
Uses a comic character to dispel the notion that only a special breed of person can fly a plane. Shows some of the basic maneuvers of flying through aerial photography.
Prod-NASM Dist-USNAC

You Can Handle It B 10 MIN
16MM FILM OPTICAL SOUND
Combines cartoons and real-life action to demonstrate safe material handling methods.
Prod-NSC Dist-NSC

You Can Have All Of The Numbers All Of The Time B
16MM FILM OPTICAL SOUND
Demonstrates how set theory can be used to set up natural numbers and arithmetic. Pays special attention to the recursion theorem and to comparing recursion with induction.
Prod-OPENU Dist-OPENU

You Can Hear Again B 30 MIN
16MM FILM OPTICAL SOUND
Presents the story of Harry Walker and his recognition and conquest of defective hearing with the aid of the VA Aural Rehabilitation Program. Shows how he was finally forced to admit his defective hearing to himself and how the VA program restored him to normal living.
Prod-USVA Dist-USVA 1949

You Can Help C 15 MIN
16MM FILM OPTICAL SOUND J-C

Describes careers in property and liability insurance.
Prod-III Dist-III 1973

You Can Help - Throw It Here C 30 MIN
16MM FILM - 3/4 IN VIDEO J-C A
Takes a look at the worldwide problem of trash, junk, garbage and litter. Shows how one family handles waste disposal. Pictures the Wentworths cutting their garbage in half by putting such vegetable matter as lettuce, egg shells, coffee grounds, grapefruit and banana peels into a compost, removing labels from and cleaning bottles and cans, flattening the cans and collecting both for recycling, along with newspapers.
From The Man Builds - Man Destroys Series.
Prod-UN Dist-GPITVL 1971

You Can If You Want C 28 MIN
16MM FILM OPTICAL SOUND
Explores the career opportunities available to women as seen by a woman attending night school programs.
From The Education Showcase Series.
LC NO. 74-701326
Prod-OECA Dist-OECA 1972

You Can Lead A Horse To Water C 28 MIN
3/4 OR 1/2 INCH VIDEO CASSETTE A
Shows supervisors how to increase employee productivity. Designed to compliment existing management techniques in a variety of organizational settings.
Prod-AMEDIA Dist-AMEDIA

You Can Learn A Lot From A Lobster - The Family Puppet Interview C 28 MIN
3/4 OR 1/2 INCH VIDEO CASSETTE
Shows how the Family Puppet Interview technique is useful in facilitating communication and interaction among family members in therapy. Shows a typical interview session with a family of four. Demonstrates the four parts of the Family Puppet Interview, including selection, planning, presentation and discussion.
Prod-PSU Dist-PSU

You Can Make It If You Try C 15 MIN
16MM FILM, 3/4 OR 1/2 IN VIDEO P-J
Tells how Thurman teaches the gang how to study and how the gang helps Thurman learn athletic skills.
From The Fat Albert And The Cosby Kids Series III Series.
Prod-BARR Dist-BARR Prodn-FLMTON 1979

You Can Remember C 15 MIN
16MM FILM, 3/4 OR 1/2 IN VIDEO I
Describes the memory techniques of grouping and picturing.
From The Thinkabout Series. Finding Alternatives
LC NO. 81-706040
Prod-KOCETV Dist-AITECH 1979

You Can See Tomorrow C 24 MIN
16MM FILM - 3/4 IN VIDEO
Demonstrates how parents, teachers and health professionals can work together to observe, detect and prevent health problems in the early elementary school years. Filmed in classrooms around the country.
Prod-MLIC Dist-MTP

You Can Speak Well C 13 MIN
3/4 OR 1/2 INCH VIDEO CASSETTE
Stresses the importance of being able to speak well and offers four practical rules to improve speaking ability.
From The Effective Speaking Series.
Prod-RESEM Dist-RESEM

You Can Stop Rubella C 29 MIN
2 INCH VIDEOTAPE
Presents a study of the various services of the Department of Health, Education and Welfare. Shows how it is attempting to put a stop to rubella epidemics.
From The You Series.
Prod-WRCTV Dist-PUBTEL

You Can Surpass Yourself C 28 MIN
16MM FILM OPTICAL SOUND I-C A
Presents Dr Eden Ryl, who examines the learning process and the forces and strategies that render people more teachable.
LC NO. 77-703333
Prod-RAMIC Dist-RAMIC Prodn-RAMIC 1975

You Can Take It With You B 15 MIN
16MM FILM OPTICAL SOUND
Tells a humorous story of the worker who won't leave the plant after a series of nerve-shattering accidents at home.
Prod-NSC Dist-NSC

You Can Use It Now C 20 MIN
3/4 INCH VIDEO CASSETTE J-C A
Points out that the metric system can be used in daily life. Reviews the content of the Metric System series.
From The Metric System Series.
Prod-MAETEL Dist-GPITVL 1975

You Can't Always Get What You Want C 30 MIN
3/4 OR 1/2 INCH VIDEO CASSETTE
Explains the law of demand and the law of supply.
From The Money Puzzle - The World Of Macroeconomics Series. Module 2
Prod-MDCC Dist-MDCC

You Can't Be Too Careful C 20 MIN
16MM FILM, 3/4 OR 1/2 IN VIDEO
Uses flashback sequences to show the dangers in rehabilitating older buildings. Uses the example of a worker who was working on an older building where the electricity had been supposedly cut off.
Prod-NFBTE Dist-IFB

You Can't Bite Back C 10 MIN
16MM FILM OPTICAL SOUND
Shows the employee the most effective way to handle neighborhood dogs. Points out that dogs have various personalities and the tactics that are useful when each type of dog is encountered.
LC NO. 74-705980
Prod-USPOST Dist-USNAC 1969

You Can't Buy Friendship X 15 MIN
16MM FILM OPTICAL SOUND P-I R
Tells of a boy visiting his cousins in another city who learns that winning friends involves Christian attitudes of respect.
From The Our Children Series.
Prod-FAMF Dist-FAMF

You Can't Buy Health C 27 MIN
16MM FILM OPTICAL SOUND
Tells how corporations, government, other organizations and other individuals can help contain health costs. Interviews physicians and directors of fitness programs that give practical ideas for health promotion and cost containment.
Prod-NABSP Dist-NABSP

You Can't Catch It C 40 MIN
16MM FILM OPTICAL SOUND
Portrays the experience of two sickle cell anemia victims in an attempt to clarify many misconceptions about the incurable disease which afflicts blacks. Presents a modern dance sequence to dramatize how sickle cell anemia is inherited.
LC NO. 73-702069
Prod-EDC Dist-EDC 1973

You Can't Get There From Here B 30 MIN
16MM FILM OPTICAL SOUND I-C A
Traces the growth of transportation and communication methods and their influence upon the West.
From The Glory Trail Series. No. 2
LC NO. FIA66-1238
Prod-NET Dist-IU 1965

You Can't Lick Stamps In China C 30 MIN
3/4 OR 1/2 INCH VIDEO CASSETTE
Presents old friends relating stories of their trip to China.
Prod-EAI Dist-EAI

You Can't Shift The Blame C 16 MIN
16MM FILM - 3/4 IN VIDEO IND
Explores some of the dangers faced by crane drivers.
LC NO. 81-706515
Prod-TASCOR Dist-TASCOR 1981

You Can't Take It With You B 127 MIN
16MM FILM OPTICAL SOUND I-C A
Stars James Stewart as the young man who wants to marry the daughter of a family of eccentrics.
Prod-CPC Dist-TIMLIF 1938

You Choose - Scarcity And Personal Decision Making C 15 MIN
3/4 OR 1/2 INCH VIDEO CASSETTE J-H
Reveals that when Lily and her friend decide to earn money by painting an apartment, they must allocate their time and money. Shows Lily's father demonstrating a five-step decision-making model that helps them.
From The Give And Take Series. Pt 1
LC NO. 83-706369
Prod-AITV Dist-AITECH 1982

You Decide C 28 MIN
16MM FILM OPTICAL SOUND J-C A
Explains that accomplishment comes from persistence.
From The You Can Do It - If Series.
LC NO. 81-700096
Prod-VANDER Dist-VANDER 1980

You Discovered Something New C 15 MIN
3/4 OR 1/2 INCH VIDEO CASSETTE P
Uses a multisensory approach to help children develop mind-body coordination, focusing on movement experiences using newspaper and the development of small muscle skills and hand-eye coordination. Integrates an imaginary theme with the use of rhythmic music, pantomime, and indoor classroom activities and calisthenics.
From The Imagine That Series. Program 2
LC NO. 82-706468
Prod-WBRATV Dist-GPITVL 1981

You Got The Same Thing, Aincha C 17 MIN
3/4 OR 1/2 INCH VIDEO CASSETTE
Focuses on an urban school in which students and teachers alike experience the frustrations of teaching and learning in an environment marked by change. Issued in 1974 as a motion picture.
From The Social Seminar Series.
LC NO. 80-707340
Prod-NIMH Dist-USNAC 1980

You Got What C 23 MIN
16MM FILM OPTICAL SOUND J-C A
Presents graphic sequences on the development of venereal diseases, describes the confidential treatment that is provided by clinics and stresses the importance of naming one's sexual contacts.
LC NO. 75-711597
Prod-CINIKA Dist-FRAF 1970

You Gotta Think About It C 21 MIN
16MM FILM OPTICAL SOUND
Discusses the need for serious thought in making necessary decisions in life.
LC NO. 74-706613
Prod-USN Dist-USNAC 1973

You Have A Choice, Pt 1 C 25 MIN
3/4 OR 1/2 INCH VIDEO CASSETTE J A
Shows right and left brain research used in the prevention of teenage alcohol and drug abuse. Discusses peer pressure.
Prod-GOLDTO Dist-SUTHRB

You Have A Choice, Pt 2 C 25 MIN
3/4 OR 1/2 INCH VIDEO CASSETTE J A
Shows right and left brain research used in the prevention of teenage alcohol and drug abuse. Discusses peer pressure.
Prod-GOLDTO Dist-SUTHRB

You Have A Favorite Partner C 15 MIN
3/4 OR 1/2 INCH VIDEO CASSETTE P
Uses a multisensory approach to help children develop mind-body coordination, focusing on partner activities and basic locomotor activities. Integrates an imaginary theme with the use of rhythmic music, pantomime, and indoor classroom activities and calisthenics.
From The Imagine That Series. Program 8
LC NO. 82-706474
Prod-WBRATV Dist-GPITVL 1981

You Have A Job Offer - Now What C 13 MIN
3/4 OR 1/2 INCH VIDEO CASSETTE H A
Shows Marcie and Diane considering the pros and cons of a sales job each has been offered. Explains gross and net pay and common deductions. Presents Joe and his wife Gail reviewing their deductions to understand his paycheck.
From The Making It Work Series.
Prod-ERF Dist-AITECH 1983

You Have A Little Friend C 15 MIN
3/4 OR 1/2 INCH VIDEO CASSETTE P
Uses a multisensory approach to help children develop mind-body coordination, focusing on simple exercise patterns, gross motor movements and the development of listening skills. Integrates an imaginary theme of friendship with the use of rhythmic music, pantomime, and indoor classroom activities and calisthenics.
From The Imagine That Series. Program 9
LC NO. 82-706475
Prod-WBRATV Dist-GPITVL 1981

You Have Got The Power C 27 MIN
16MM FILM, 3/4 OR 1/2 IN VIDEO
Demonstrates the nature of the rehabilitation process, both physical and psychological, for the bone cancer amputee. Shows the experiences of five individuals and the impact of amputation upon their lives.
Prod-STNFLD Dist-STNFLD

You Have More Power Than You Think C 25 MIN
16MM FILM, 3/4 OR 1/2 IN VIDEO A
Presents a lecture by Chester L Karrass explaining the use of power in negotiating, showing the sources of power, the illusions of power and the techniques of power.
From The Negotiating Successfully Series. Part 3
LC NO. 79-707431
Prod-TIMLIF Dist-TIMLIF 1975

You Have Rights C 30 MIN
3/4 INCH VIDEO CASSETTE J-C A
Tells how some consumers have complained to companies and have gotten results. Tells about the various mechanisms through which a consumer can achieve redress.
LC NO. 81-707318
Prod-NYSED Dist-GPITVL 1979

You Have Something To Offer C 14 MIN
16MM FILM, 3/4 OR 1/2 IN VIDEO P-I
Shows how Duane's handicap limits his sporting abilities until he finds his particular skill.
From The Learning Values With Fat Albert Series.
Prod-FLMTON Dist-CRMP 1977

You Have Struck A Rock C 28 MIN
16MM FILM OPTICAL SOUND
Recounts the experiences of women who took the lead in mobilizing mass opposition to apartheid during the 1950s when the South African regime attempted to extend the hated pass system to them.
Prod-MAYDEB Dist-CANWRL 1981

You Haven't Changed A Bit C 15 MIN
16MM FILM OPTICAL SOUND H-C
Presents a dramatization about a young couple who after a quarrel take separate vacations at their parents' homes, showing how they learn that their real identity lies in their relationship with each other.
From The Marriage Series.
LC NO. 72-700515
Prod-FRACOC Dist-FRACOC 1970

You Hide Me B 20 MIN
16MM FILM, 3/4 OR 1/2 IN VIDEO C A
Analyzes the policy of European colonial regimes which, in establishing their rule, wiped out all traces of African civilization, religion, language and art.
Prod-TRIFCW Dist-CNEMAG 1973

You In Japan B 19 MIN
16MM FILM OPTICAL SOUND
Tours major Japanese cities and scenic rural areas. Describes the cultural, social and religious background of Japan. Explains her political, military and economic structure.
LC NO. FIE56-323
Prod-USDD Dist-USNAC 1956

You In OPD C 22 MIN
16MM FILM OPTICAL SOUND
Shows how to develop techniques for an effective relationship between staff and patients in the outpatient department.
LC NO. 74-706342
Prod-USN Dist-USNAC 1969

You In Public Service—A Series
A
Explains what public service is, the types of public service jobs and how to obtain them. Includes the different skills needed and practical tips for self-improvement.
Prod-USOE Dist-USNAC 1977

Applying For A Public Service Job	28 MIN
Basic Record Keeping	28 MIN
Basic Report Writing	28 MIN
Good Grooming	28 MIN
Interviewing Skills	28 MIN
Introduction - You In Public Service	28 MIN
Oral Communication	28 MIN
Person-To-Person Relationships	28 MIN
Techniques Of Decision Making	28 MIN
Written Communication	28 MIN

You Irresistible You C 11 MIN
16MM FILM, 3/4 OR 1/2 IN VIDEO J-C A
Features comedian Marshall Efron as he points out that an increasing number of men are willing to pay high prices for furnishings and cosmetics which promise to make them irresistible to the opposite sex. spotlights suntan lotions, stereos, waterbeds and various grooming aids.
Prod-WNETTV Dist-BNCHMK 1972

You Just Love Your Children C 12 MIN
16MM FILM OPTICAL SOUND
Presents two short studies of homosexuals as parents.
LC NO. 79-701126
Prod-TEMPLU Dist-TEMPLU Prodn-JALU 1979

You Light Up My Life C 90 MIN
16MM FILM OPTICAL SOUND
Tells how a young singer-songwriter beats all the odds to make it to the top of the charts.
Prod-CPC Dist-TWYMAN 1977

You Look Ridiculous Said The Rhinocerus To The Hippopotamus C 15 MIN
3/4 OR 1/2 INCH VIDEO CASSETTE P
See series title for descriptive statement.
From The Magic Pages Series.
Prod-KLVXTV Dist-AITECH 1976

You Made Some Other Noise C 15 MIN
3/4 OR 1/2 INCH VIDEO CASSETTE P
Uses a multisensory approach to help children develop mind-body coordination, focusing on gross and small motor movements and the development of listening skills. Integrates an imaginary theme with the use of rhythmic music, pantomime, and indoor classroom activities and calisthenics.
From The Imagine That Series. Program 5
LC NO. 82-706471
Prod-WBRATV Dist-GPITVL 1981

You Make Me Sick C 30 MIN
3/4 OR 1/2 INCH VIDEO CASSETTE I-J
Shows how the Powerhouse Kids race the clock to find the source of a deadly illness.
From The Powerhouse Series.
LC NO. 83-707181
Prod-EFCVA Dist-GA 1982

You Make The Difference C 9 MIN
3/4 OR 1/2 INCH VIDEO CASSETTE
Introduces library circulation assistants and their job. Emphasizes a good public service attitude.
Prod-BCPL Dist-LVN

You Make The Difference / Food Handling And You / Safety In Housekeeping C
3/4 OR 1/2 INCH VIDEO CASSETTE
Portrays the role of the health care employee as it relates to the care and well-being of a patient. Emphasizes the importance of cleanliness, shows the importance of being safety conscious.
From The 'We Care' Series. Pt. 1
Prod-VTRI Dist-VTRI

You Meant What C 15 MIN
3/4 OR 1/2 INCH VIDEO CASSETTE H
Discusses the difference between clarity and ambiguity and considers the problems of misconstrued meaning.
From The Communication At Work Series.
Prod-OHSDE Dist-AITECH 1979

You Must Take It With You C 14 MIN
16MM FILM OPTICAL SOUND
Traces the need for creating artificial environment not only in aircraft but also in space vehicles. Describes the environment on earth and explains how it is reproduced in pressurized aircraft and space vehicles.
Prod-GARET Dist-GARET Prodn-ARCO 1964

You Need To Know—A Series
IND
Shows rig personnel the proper maintenance procedures for Continental Emsco equipment to keep it running better and longer.
Prod-UTEXPE Dist-UTEXPE 1981

Drawworks	024 MIN
F-FA Mud Pumps	055 MIN
FB Mud Pumps	047 MIN
Mechanical Compounds	008 MIN
Swivels, Blocks, Rotaries	025 MIN

You Never Miss The Water C 15 MIN
16MM FILM, 3/4 OR 1/2 IN VIDEO J-C A
Tells how to reduce water usage in the home and thus save on water bills while at the same time helping to preserve the environment.
Prod-KLEINW Dist-KLEINW 1978

You Only Live Once C 11 MIN
16MM FILM OPTICAL SOUND
Shows the difference between a professional driver and the complacent driver, and demonstrates driving errors and correct procedures.
LC NO. 70-714166
Prod-USPOST Dist-USPOST 1971

You Owe It To Yourself C 23 MIN
16MM FILM OPTICAL SOUND PRO
Explains benefits made available to servicemen by the US government whether they remain in the service or are discharged.
LC NO. FIE68-70
Prod-VA Dist-USVA 1968

You Owe It To Yourself—A Series

Discusses money management, using a game show format to introduce techniques for handling personal finance. Covers budgeting, credit, insurance, investments and estate planning.
Prod-WITFTV Dist-PUBTEL

Banking And Savings Institutions	029 MIN
Budgeting	029 MIN
Credit	028 MIN
Estate Planning	029 MIN
Health Insurance	029 MIN
Housing For Family Needs	029 MIN
Investments And Risk Capital	024 MIN
Life Insurance	029 MIN
Property And Liability Insurance	029 MIN
Social Security	030 MIN

You Pack Your Own Chute C 30 MIN
16MM FILM - 3/4 IN VIDEO
Shows cinema verite coverage of the first parachute jump into the ocean by Eden Ryl. Uses this jump as a symbol, with discussion and illustrative vignettes, to show how to recognize and overcome unrealistic fears.
From The Eden Ryl Behavioral Series.
Prod-RAMIC Dist-RAMIC 1972

You Pack Your Own Chute (Portuguese) C 30 MIN
16MM FILM OPTICAL SOUND
Shows cinema verite coverage of the first parachute jump into the ocean by Eden Ryl. Uses this jump as a symbol with discussion and illustrative vignettes, to show how to recognize and overcome the unrealistic fears which inhibit so many people in their daily lives.
LC NO. 73-702404
Prod-RAMIC Dist-RAMIC 1972

You Pack Your Own Chute (Spanish) C 30 MIN
16MM FILM OPTICAL SOUND
Shows cinema verite coverage of the first parachute jump into the ocean by Eden Ryl. Uses this jump as a symbol with discussion and illustrative vignettes, to show how to recognize and overcome the unrealistic fears which inhibit so many people in their daily lives.
LC NO. 73-702404
Prod-RAMIC Dist-RAMIC 1972

You Really Shouldn't Do That C 15 MIN
3/4 OR 1/2 INCH VIDEO CASSETTE T
Uses the adventures of a pirate and his three friends to explore the many facets of language arts. Shows what can happen in 'shouldn't do' situations, focusing on their use in oral and written expression.
From The Hidden Treasures Series. No. 14
LC NO. 82-706554
Prod-WCVETV Dist-GPITVL 1980

You Run For Your Life C 14 MIN
16MM FILM OPTICAL SOUND
Shows the components necessary to create good running shoes for running as well as other sports.
Prod-MTP Dist-MTP

You See I've Had A Life C 32 MIN
16MM FILM OPTICAL SOUND J-C
Presents Paul Hendricks, a teenager who has leukemia.
LC NO. 73-700635
Prod-TEMPLU Dist-TEMPLU 1972

You See What You Say - An Introduction To Latin Prepositions C 13 MIN
16MM FILM, 3/4 OR 1/2 IN VIDEO H-C
Uses animation to introduce the Latin prepositions ab, ad, de, in and ex, and illustrates their correct usage.
LC NO. 80-706722
Prod-VPISU Dist-IFB 1979

You Sell Shoes C 15 MIN
16MM FILM OPTICAL SOUND
Demonstrates techniques for selling shoes to customers of various ages, sizes and lifestyles.
LC NO. 78-700322
Prod-USSHOE Dist-USSHOE Prodn-BRAINS 1978

You Too Can Make A Map C 16 MIN
16MM FILM, 3/4 OR 1/2 IN VIDEO I-J
Demonstrates how to make a topographical map. Shows how to interpret legends and symbols on maps.
Prod-CYPRES Dist-CF

You Touched Me C 24 MIN
16MM FILM OPTICAL SOUND A
Explores a volunteer program providing recreation for the mentally retarded.
Prod-OMNIFS Dist-OMNIFS

You Want To Be A Volunteer B 8 MIN
16MM FILM OPTICAL SOUND
Instructs new volunteers in the correct grooming, behavior and attitude necessary for effective service.
From The Bellevue Volunteers Series.
Prod-NYU Dist-NYU

You Wasn't Loitering B 15 MIN
3/4 INCH VIDEO CASSETTE
Treats the problem of 'loitering' in sequences showing police warning youths, administrators discussing loitering laws, officers being insulted and youths being arrested.
From The Pittsburgh Police Series.
Prod-DOCEDR Dist-DOCEDR Prodn-MSHLLJ

You Were Never Lovelier B 18 MIN
16MM FILM OPTICAL SOUND
An abridged version of the motion picture You Were Never Lovelier. Relates how a hotel tycoon tries to keep his daughter happy with fake romance but that the plan backfires when real love blossoms.
Prod-TIMLIF Dist-TIMLIF 1982

You Were Never Lovelier B 97 MIN
16MM FILM OPTICAL SOUND
Features a music comedy starring Fred Astaire and Rita Hayworth.
Prod-CPC Dist-TWYMAN 1942

You Were There C 30 MIN
3/4 OR 1/2 INCH VIDEO CASSETTE K-P
See series title for descriptive statement.
From The Villa Alegre Series.
Prod-BCTV Dist-MDCPB

You Would If You Loved Me - Making Decisions About Sex C 31 MIN
3/4 OR 1/2 INCH VIDEO CASSETTE I-H
Deals with the sexual pressures of modern society, discussing the consequences of early pregnancy and venereal disease, and the effect of peer pressure. Stresses the importance of getting accurate information about sexual behavior and emphasizes the need for strong personal values.
LC NO. 81-706154
Prod-GA Dist-GA 1981

You—A Series

Prod-WRCTV Dist-PUBTEL

You - Poor Kids Learn	29 MIN
You And Addiction	29 MIN
You And Alcohol	29 MIN
You And Disaster	29 MIN
You And Drugs	29 MIN
You And Family Health	29 MIN
You And Manana	29 MIN
You And Mental Retardation	29 MIN
You And Mobility	29 MIN
You And Mr Rat	29 MIN
You And Quackery	29 MIN
You And Returning Veterans	29 MIN
You And Rx Learning	29 MIN
You And Services	29 MIN
You And Surplus Property	29 MIN
You And The Delinquents	29 MIN
You And The Handicapped	29 MIN
You And The Pap Test	29 MIN
You And The Question Mark Kids	29 MIN
You And The Red Schoolhouse	29 MIN
You And The Road Children	29 MIN
You And When It Matters	29 MIN
You And Women's Lib	29 MIN
You And Your Breath	29 MIN
You And Your Heritage	29 MIN
You Can Stop Rubella	29 MIN

You, Me, And Technology—A Series
J-H
Discusses the various ways in which technology affects human civilization.
Prod-TEMPLU Dist-AITECH Prodn-NJN 1983

Decisions, Decisions, Decisions	020 MIN
Living With Technology	020 MIN

You, The Human Animal (Arabic) C 8 MIN
16MM FILM, 3/4 OR 1/2 IN VIDEO P
Theorizes that the uniqueness of human beings stems from highly developed intelligence, language skills and the ability to reason and to adapt.
From The This Is You (Arabic) Series.
Prod-WDEMCO Dist-WDEMCO 1957

You, The Human Animal (French) C 8 MIN
16MM FILM, 3/4 OR 1/2 IN VIDEO P
Theorizes that the uniqueness of human beings stems from highly developed intelligence, language skills and the ability to reason and to adapt.
From The This Is You (French) Series.
Prod-WDEMCO Dist-WDEMCO 1957

You, The Human Animal (Spanish) C 8 MIN
16MM FILM, 3/4 OR 1/2 IN VIDEO P
Theorizes that the uniqueness of human beings stems from highly developed intelligence, language skills and the ability to reason and to adapt.
From The This Is You (Spanish) Series.
Prod-WDEMCO Dist-WDEMCO 1957

You, The Law, And Criminals C 60 MIN
3/4 OR 1/2 INCH VIDEO CASSETTE
Explores ways citizens can aid themselves and the police in dealing with crime. Deals with burglary precautions and the Kentucky Uniform And Crime Reporting System.
Prod-EASTKU Dist-EASTKU

You, The Living Machine (Arabic) C 8 MIN
16MM FILM, 3/4 OR 1/2 IN VIDEO P

Demonstrates how the body converts food into energy. Discusses body maintenance and repair.
From The This Is You (Arabic) Series.
Prod-WDEMCO Dist-WDEMCO 1959

You, The Living Machine (French) C 8 MIN
16MM FILM, 3/4 OR 1/2 IN VIDEO P
Demonstrates how the body converts food into energy. Discusses body maintenance and repair.
From The This Is You (French) Series.
Prod-WDEMCO Dist-WDEMCO 1959

You, You, Unique C 15 MIN
2 INCH VIDEOTAPE J
Stresses the importance of individuality of style in compositions.
From The From Me To You...In Writing, Pt 2 Series.
Prod-DELE Dist-GPITVL

You, Yourself, Incorporated C 24 MIN
16MM FILM - 3/4 IN VIDEO PRO
Joe uses seriousness and humor to demonstrate the only real development is self-development. Explains that every motivated man can do more than he thinks he can and that motivated men make progress and profits.
Prod-BNA Dist-BNA 1969

You'll Find It In The Library C 13 MIN
16MM FILM, 3/4 OR 1/2 IN VIDEO I
Demonstrates how to find books in a library by title, author and subject matter.
Prod-CORF Dist-CORF 1966

You'll Soon Get The Hang Of It C 24 MIN
3/4 OR 1/2 INCH VIDEO CASSETTE A
Humorously presents the major mistakes most people make in training new recruits. Discusses both how to organize training to fit the basic ways people learn and when to use different motivational techniques at different stages of training.
Prod-XICOM Dist-XICOM

You'll Soon Get The Hang Of It C 29 MIN
16MM FILM, 3/4 OR 1/2 IN VIDEO A
Uses a variety of situations, manual, clerical and technical to show the two aspects of one-on-one training.
Prod-VIDART Dist-VISUCP 1982

You're A Big Boy Now C 96 MIN
16MM FILM OPTICAL SOUND
Tells how an innocent library worker falls in love with a man-hating go-go dancer and then hits the road to find maturity.
Prod-WB Dist-TWYMAN 1967

You're Being Asked C 25 MIN
3/4 OR 1/2 INCH VIDEO CASSETTE
Shows blood donors and recipients telling why giving blood is important, because ten pints of blood are used every minute in the US, 16,000 pints per day, to save lives of people threatened by illness or injury.
Prod-TRAINX Dist-TRAINX

You're Coming Along Fine C 23 MIN
16MM FILM, 3/4 OR 1/2 IN VIDEO H-C A
Examines a manager's problems in appraising employee work, discussing employee achievement with higher management and explaining unsatisfactory work to the employees themselves.
LC NO. FIA68-2709
Prod-RTBL Dist-RTBL 1968

You're Coming Along Fine (Dutch) C 23 MIN
16MM FILM, 3/4 OR 1/2 IN VIDEO H-C A
Examines a manager's problem in appraising employee work, discussing employee achievement with higher management and explaining unsatisfactory work to the employees themselves.
Prod-RTBL Dist-RTBL 1968

You're Coming Along Fine (French) C 23 MIN
16MM FILM, 3/4 OR 1/2 IN VIDEO H-C A
Examines a manager's problem in appraising employee work, discussing employee achievement with higher management and explaining unsatisfactory work to the employees themselves.
Prod-RTBL Dist-RTBL 1968

You're Coming Along Fine (German) C 23 MIN
16MM FILM, 3/4 OR 1/2 IN VIDEO H-C A
Examines a manager's problem in appraising employee work, discussing employee achievement with higher management and explaining unsatisfactory work to the employees themselves.
Prod-RTBL Dist-RTBL 1968

You're Coming Along Fine (Norwegian) C 23 MIN
16MM FILM, 3/4 OR 1/2 IN VIDEO H-C A
Examines a manager's problem in appraising employee work, discussing employee achievement with higher management and explaining unsatisfactory work to the employees themselves.
Prod-RTBL Dist-RTBL 1968

You're Coming Along Fine (Portuguese) C 23 MIN
16MM FILM, 3/4 OR 1/2 IN VIDEO H-C A
Examines a manager's problems in appraising employee work, discussing employee achievement with higher management and explaining unsatisfactory work to employees themselves.
Prod-RTBL Dist-RTBL 1968

You're Coming Along Fine (Swedish) C 23 MIN
16MM FILM, 3/4 OR 1/2 IN VIDEO H-C A
Examines a manager's problem in appraising employee work, discussing employee achievement with higher management and explaining unsatisfactory work to the employees themselves.
Prod-RTBL Dist-RTBL 1968

You're Costing Me Money C 15 MIN
3/4 OR 1/2 INCH VIDEO CASSETTE H
Explores the principles of on-the-job persuasion, including saving face, considering the other person, establishing a common ground, and avoiding name-calling.
From The Communication At Work Series.
Prod-OHSDE Dist-AITECH 1979

You're Eating For Two C 20 MIN
16MM FILM, 3/4 OR 1/2 IN VIDEO H-C A
Discusses the importance of nourishment during pregnancy for both the mother and the baby. Shows the consequences of poor nutrition on the unborn baby.
Prod-NFBC Dist-PEREN

You're Gonna Have To Get Big To Be Heard C 16 MIN
16MM FILM OPTICAL SOUND
Shows how the National Federation of Independent Business speaks for over 400,000 independent businesses around the United States and how the NFIB is lobbying in Washington to create legislation favorable to small businesses.
LC NO. 76-703172
Prod-NFIB Dist-NFIB Prodn-FURMAN 1976

You're Growing Up With Dr Joyce Brothers C 12 MIN
1/2 IN VIDEO CASSETTE BETA/VHS
Presents six articulate adolescent girls, who discuss growing up with psychologist Dr Joyce Brothers, including topics such as menstruation, other physical changes, and relationships with boys, friends and family.
Prod-WSTGLC Dist-WSTGLC

You're In Charge B 12 MIN
16MM FILM OPTICAL SOUND
Rules for safe, successful baby sitting. Shows both a girl and a boy in situations with children.
From The Secondary School Safety Series.
Prod-NSC Dist-NSC 1955

You're It C 15 MIN
16MM FILM, 3/4 OR 1/2 IN VIDEO K-P
Examines, with a group of children, some paintings, showing the children how to learn to 'feel' with the eyes. Suggests that the children try to become part of the painting.
From The Ripples Series.
LC NO. 73-702159
Prod-NITC Dist-AITECH 1970

You're Nobody Till Somebody Loves You B 12 MIN
16MM FILM OPTICAL SOUND
Documents the marriage of Timothy Leary to a model. By D A Pennebaker.
Prod-PENNAS Dist-PENNAS

You're Not Alone With Herpes C
16MM FILM, 3/4 OR 1/2 IN VIDEO H-C A
Discusses various aspects of herpes, including the definition of the Herpes virus, related diseases, transmission of the disease, initial attack and ways of keeping the virus under control.
Prod-SKYLTE Dist-PEREN 1983

You're Not Communicating C 20 MIN
16MM FILM, 3/4 OR 1/2 IN VIDEO J-H
Demonstrates how to think and express oneself clearly, choose the right time for communication, understand and use verbal and nonverbal feedback, tailor the message to the listener's level of knowledge and be honest about one's own feelings.
Prod-BARR Dist-BARR 1980

You're Not Communicating (Spanish) C 20 MIN
16MM FILM - VIDEO, ALL FORMATS J-C A
Demonstrates the basic rules of effective communication.
Prod-CALLFM Dist-BARR

You're Not Listening C 32 MIN
16MM FILM OPTICAL SOUND
Shows how a young second-grade teacher with a problem child in her class comes to learn and recognize aspects of brain dysfunction which are afflicting the boy.
LC NO. 76-702309
Prod-CIBA Dist-MTP Prodn-TELTRO 1976

You're Not Listening C 21 MIN
16MM FILM, 3/4 OR 1/2 IN VIDEO J-C A
Uses humorous vignettes to illustrate techniques for building listening skills. Points out that listening is a complex skill which requires specific training and practice.
Prod-BARR Dist-BARR Prodn-CALLFM 1978

You're Not Listening (Spanish) C 21 MIN
16MM FILM - VIDEO, ALL FORMATS J-C A
Illustrates techniques for building seven basic listening skills.
Prod-CALLFM Dist-BARR

You're Not There Yet C 32 MIN
16MM FILM OPTICAL SOUND C A
Follows one man with a drinking problem through his day as he gradually becomes aware of, and at the same time denies, his drinking problem.
LC NO. 79-701855
Prod-LENWAY Dist-FILCOM 1978

You're Only Old Once C 60 MIN
3/4 OR 1/2 INCH VIDEO CASSETTE
Attempts to dispel some of the myths about aging through an examination of the issues and concerns of Minnesota's large and active population of senior citizens. Gives insight into the loneliness and hardship that often dominate old age.
Prod-WCCOTV Dist-WCCOTV 1979

You're The Doctor - Prevention C 30 MIN
3/4 OR 1/2 INCH VIDEO CASSETTE
Tells how the 'lifestyle' disease brought on by abuse of the body can be avoided through preventive maintenance by the individual. Discusses the dangers of smoking, the importance of moderation in drinking alcohol and the need for adequate sleep. Explains the merits of a well balanced diet and discusses how people are led astray by television commercials and the importance of the right kind of exercise.
Prod-FAIRGH Dist-FAIRGH

You're The Judge C 18 MIN
1 INCH VIDEOTAPE
Uses an unusual cooking contest to emphasize the fun of mean preparation and pride of accomplishment. Covers many essential elements of mean preparation including baking and frying.
Prod-PROGAM Dist-MTP

You're The Key Man B 10 MIN
16MM FILM OPTICAL SOUND
Shows how a foreman's decision to become active in the safety program paid off.
From The Key Man Series.
Prod-NSC Dist-NSC

You're Under Arrest C 15 MIN
16MM FILM, 3/4 OR 1/2 IN VIDEO
Provides a close-up look at America's drunk driving problem, with a special focus on efforts aimed at toughening and enforcing drunk driving laws. Shows how alcohol seriously impairs the reflexes, judgment and control of drivers behind the wheel. Witnesses the procedure law enforcement officers follow after pulling over individuals suspected of being under the influence. Originally shown on the CBS program 60 Minutes.
Prod-CBSNEW Dist-MTI

You're Why We're Here C 25 MIN
16MM FILM OPTICAL SOUND
Introduces the physical structure and academic attractions of Cuyahoga Community College, Metro campus. Describes the academic programs, student services and registration processes at Cuyahoga Community College.
Prod-CUYAHO Dist-CUYAHO 1971

You've Come A Long Way, Maybe? C 55 MIN
3/4 OR 1/2 INCH VIDEO CASSETTE J-C A
Explores the issue of comparable worth, focusing on women and their role in the U S work force. Includes comments of women, their supporters and detractors, attorneys, and policy-making executives, who voice their opinions about the validity of comparable worth claims as opposed to need to let supply and demand or the market determine salaries.
From The Moore Report Series.
LC NO. 82-707399
Prod-WCCOTV Dist-IU 1981

You've Come A Long Way, Rene C 22 MIN
16MM FILM, 3/4 OR 1/2 IN VIDEO I-J
Reveals that Rene has to decide whether to stick with her goal of becoming a championship runner or become one of the crowd and start smoking. Encourages young people to resist peer pressure and advertising and to make their own decisions about smoking.
LC NO. 83-706245
Prod-HAMRL Dist-BARR 1983

You've Got To Be Up C 15 MIN
16MM FILM OPTICAL SOUND
Takes a look at the game of bowls.
LC NO. 80-700939
Prod-TASCOR Dist-TASCOR 1976

You've Sold Me, Mrs Marlowe C 9 MIN
16MM FILM OPTICAL SOUND H A
Emphasizes the importance of making the most of each contact with each customer and describes the necessary requirements for making a sale completely successful.
From The People Sell People Series.
Prod-SAUM Dist-MLA 1965

Young Alcoholic, The - A Family Dilemma C 30 MIN
16MM FILM, 3/4 OR 1/2 IN VIDEO
Focuses on the intervention process as the major step toward treating minors addicted to alcohol and helping their families. Examines the physical and emotional effects of chemical dependency, explores the dynamics occuring in families beset by this problem and shows why typical reactions often backfire.
Prod-CBSNEW Dist-MTI

Young And Just Beginning C 29 MIN
16MM FILM OPTICAL SOUND
Features the work of a ten-year-old gymnast, examining her summer training and her prospects for the 1980 Olympics.
LC NO. 76-701499
Prod-OVTNF Dist-OVTNF 1975

Young And Old - Reaching Out - Work And Fulfillment C 60 MIN
3/4 OR 1/2 INCH VIDEO CASSETTE
Deals with the American Dream and what it means to the old and the young. Discusses changing values about work, money, education, business and success. Features Senator Sam Ervin and George Willing, the man who scaled New York's World Trade Center. Brings together young adults and the elderly from diverse backgrounds to share life experiences.
Prod-PBS Dist-DELTAK

Young And Old - Reaching Out—A Series

Brings together adults and elderly people from diverse backgrounds to share life experiences. Touches on such subjects as love, work and loneliness.
Prod-CRFI Dist-PBS

Love And Loneliness 059 MIN
Raising Children 059 MIN
Work And Fulfillment 059 MIN

Young Art, The - Children Make Their Own Films C 16 MIN
16MM FILM OPTICAL SOUND
Demonstrates how to set up and run a filmmaking class for young students. Shows students developing their ideas, such as shooting, splicing and editing film, and discussing their results. Includes scenes from student films.
LC NO. 73-714116
Prod-VANNOS Dist-VANREN 1971

Young At Art C 29 MIN
3/4 OR 1/2 INCH VIDEO CASSETTE H-C A
Explores the creativity of self-discovery exhibited by students at New York City's High School of Performing Arts in the classroom, rehearsals and in performance.
From The Creativity With Bill Moyers Series.
Prod-CORPEL Dist-PBS 1982

Young At Art - Introduction C 14 MIN
3/4 OR 1/2 INCH VIDEO CASSETTE P-I
Introduces the Young At Art Series.
From The Young At Art Series.
Prod-WSKJTV Dist-AITECH 1980

Young At Art—A Series
P-I
Explores the use of line, shape, color, texture and space in art. Presents a variety of classroom art activities.
Prod-WSKJTV Dist-AITECH 1980

Aquarium Classroom 015 MIN
Clay Figures 015 MIN
Combed Patterns 015 MIN
Crayon And Paint Thinner 015 MIN
Crayon And Tempera Resist 015 MIN
Cubist Flips 015 MIN
Discovering Design 015 MIN
Environmental Art 015 MIN
Foil And String Relief 015 MIN
Found Object Masks 015 MIN
Innertube Prints 015 MIN
Line Prints 015 MIN
Look At Lines 015 MIN
Magic Of Color 015 MIN
Moon Creatures 015 MIN
Name Designs 015 MIN
Near And Far 015 MIN
Op Art 015 MIN
Paint Engravings 015 MIN
Paper Sculpture Animals 015 MIN
Papier-Mache Birds 015 MIN
Pop Art 015 MIN
Prehistoric Magic 015 MIN
Snap Art 015 MIN
Super Bugs 015 MIN
Super Realists 015 MIN
Tempera As Watercolor 015 MIN
Textile Art 015 MIN
Weaving 015 MIN
Young At Art - Introduction 015 MIN

Young Audiences/Muralist C 30 MIN
3/4 OR 1/2 INCH VIDEO CASSETTE
See series title for descriptive statement.
From The Kaleidoscope Series.
Prod-KTEHTV Dist-SCCOE

Young Bullfighters, The C 45 MIN
16MM FILM OPTICAL SOUND
Presents the story of two young men, one Mexican and one American, who train to become toreadors. Shows how the bulls are raised and selected and also other people involved in the bullfights.
Prod-SCORPO Dist-FILCOM 1970

Young Caesar B 11 MIN
16MM FILM OPTICAL SOUND J-H
A Latin classic for classroom use.
Prod-FCE Dist-FCE

Young Champions, The C 30 MIN
16MM FILM, 3/4 OR 1/2 IN VIDEO
Depicts the World Youth Soccer Championships held in Tokyo, Japan.
Prod-COCA Dist-AMEDFL Prodn-AMEDFL 1980

Young Champions, The (French) C 30 MIN
16MM FILM, 3/4 OR 1/2 IN VIDEO
Depicts the World Youth Soccer Championships held in Tokyo, Japan.
Prod-COCA Dist-AMEDFL Prodn-AMEDFL 1980

Young Champions, The (Japanese) C 30 MIN
16MM FILM, 3/4 OR 1/2 IN VIDEO
Depicts the World Youth Soccer Championships held in Tokyo, Japan.
Prod-COCA Dist-AMEDFL Prodn-AMEDFL 1980

Young Champions, The (Spanish) C 30 MIN
16MM FILM, 3/4 OR 1/2 IN VIDEO
Depicts the World Youth Soccer Championships held in Tokyo, Japan.
Prod-COCA Dist-AMEDFL Prodn-AMEDFL 1980

Young Chemists - In Transition C 28 MIN
16MM FILM OPTICAL SOUND C
Presents young industrial chemists offering their views on the transition from the academic to the industrial community, while company recruiters describe what they look for in young chemists. Offers suggestions about job hunting in industrial fields.
LC NO. 79-701627
Prod-AMCHEM Dist-AMCHEM 1979

Young Child Is, A C 30 MIN
16MM FILM, 3/4 OR 1/2 IN VIDEO A
Shows infant and pre-school children in the process of learning.
Prod-EDIMP Dist-LAWREN 1983

Young Children In Brief Separation—A Series

Discusses situations in which children have been separated from their parents for brief periods.
Prod-TVKI Dist-NYU Prodn-ROBJJ

Jane - Aged 17 Months In Fostercare For 10 Days 037 MIN
John, 17 Months - 9 Days In A Residential 045 MIN
Thomas, Aged Two Years And Four Months- 038 MIN

Young Children On The Kibbutz B 26 MIN
16MM FILM OPTICAL SOUND
Describes the life of four-year-old children on an Israeli kibbutz. Shows how they are trained in groups and live in quarters separated from their parents.
From The Exploring Childhood Series.
LC NO. 73-702071
Prod-EDC Dist-EDC 1973

Young Children With Special Needs C 14 MIN
16MM FILM - 3/4 IN VIDEO A S
Looks at the importance of early intervention, showing preschoolers in home- and center-based programs for handicapped children. Correlated with the book Behavior Of Exceptional Children.
LC NO. 79-706533
Prod-MERILC Dist-MERILC 1978

Young Children With Special Needs - Conceptual Development C 30 MIN
3/4 INCH VIDEO CASSETTE
Deals with the importance of sequential instruction and methods used to facilitate concept development in the developmentally disabled child.
LC NO. 79-706215
Prod-VACOMU Dist-MERILC 1978

Young Children With Special Needs - Social And Emotional Development, No. 11 C 30 MIN
3/4 INCH VIDEO CASSETTE PRO
Deals with the development of the mental health of the developmentally disabled child. Covers differences in techniques needed to encourage growth in various settings such as home, foster home, institution.
LC NO. 79-706217
Prod-MERILC Dist-MERILC 1978

Young Children With Special Needs, No. 01 - Introduction C 30 MIN
3/4 INCH VIDEO CASSETTE
Deals with the identification of young children with developmental disabilities.
LC NO. 79-706207
Prod-VACOMU Dist-MERILC 1978

Young Children With Special Needs, No. 02 - Children At High Risk C 30 MIN
3/4 INCH VIDEO CASSETTE
Deals with the child with developmental disabilities, including the rationale for early identification and intervention, procedures for securing services and the child's right to an education.
LC NO. 79-706208
Prod-VACOMU Dist-MERILC 1978

Young Children With Special Needs, No. 03 - Who Can Help C 30 MIN
3/4 INCH VIDEO CASSETTE
Introduces the types of professionals who deal with children with developmental disabilities, including pediatricians, nurses, physical and occupational therapists, language pathologists, psychologists, psychiatrists, social workers and child development specialists.
Prod-VACOMU Dist-MERILC 1978

Young Children With Special Needs, No. 04 - Assessment, Diagnosis, Remediation C 30 MIN
3/4 INCH VIDEO CASSETTE
Discusses the use of developmental scales and the information provided by ancillary professionals to determine the educational requirements of the child with developmental disabilities.
LC NO. 79-706210
Prod-VACOMU Dist-MERILC 1978

Young Children With Special Needs, No. 05 - Community Resources C 30 MIN
3/4 INCH VIDEO CASSETTE
Describes the home as the first school for children with developmental disabilities and surveys possible and existing facilities, telling how facilities can be improved to provide quality services for these children.
LC NO. 79-706211
Prod-VACOMU Dist-MERILC 1978

Young Children With Special Needs, No. 06 - How Do Children Learn C 30 MIN
3/4 INCH VIDEO CASSETTE
Deals with the ways in which all children acquire knowledge, skills and attitudes and examines barriers to learning, effects of early learning and readiness for learning.
LC NO. 79-706212
Prod-VACOMU Dist-MERILC 1978

Young Children With Special Needs, No. 07 - Motor Skills C 30 MIN
3/4 INCH VIDEO CASSETTE
Focuses on both gross and fine motor skills and ways of working with the developmentally disabled child to facilitate development in these areas.
LC NO. 79-706213
Prod-VACOMU Dist-MERILC 1978

Young Children With Special Needs, No. 08 - Language And Verbal Skills C 30 MIN
3/4 INCH VIDEO CASSETTE
Distinguishes between receptive and expressive language in the developmentally disabled child. Focuses on inner language and aspects of nonverbal language.
LC NO. 79-706214
Prod-VACOMU Dist-MERILC 1978

Young Children With Special Needs, No. 10 - Self-Help Skills C 30 MIN
3/4 INCH VIDEO CASSETTE
Deals with self-help skills for the developmentally disabled child, including self-feedings, dressing and toilet training. Demonstrates homemade aids for facilitating self-feeding.
LC NO. 79-706216
Prod-VACOMU Dist-MERILC 1978

Young Children With Special Needs, No. 12 - Child's Play C 30 MIN
3/4 INCH VIDEO CASSETTE
Deals with the relationship between play and development for the developmentally disabled child and focuses on various attitudinal issues.
LC NO. 79-706219
Prod-VACOMU Dist-MERILC 1978

Young Children With Special Needs, No. 13 C 30 MIN
3/4 OR 1/2 INCH VIDEO CASSETTE PRO
Deals with a variety of considerations with a developmentally disabled child, including nutrition and hygiene, the child's role in the family and concern for the siblings and other family members. Points out differences in the family life of the institutionalized child.
LC NO. 79-706220
Prod-VACOMU Dist-MERILC Prodn-VARC 1978

Young Children With Special Needs, No. 14 - Health, Safety, Nutrition C 30 MIN
3/4 INCH VIDEO CASSETTE
Deals with practices that are appropriate in the health care and safety of all young children but especially important for handicapped children because of their special needs.
LC NO. 79-706221
Prod-VACOMU Dist-MERILC 1978

Young Children With Special Needs, No. 15 - Review C 30 MIN
3/4 INCH VIDEO CASSETTE
Reviews and summarizes the Young Children With Special Needs programs dealing with the developmentally disabled child.
LC NO. 79-706222
Prod-VACOMU Dist-MERILC 1978

Young Conqueror, The C 60 MIN
3/4 OR 1/2 INCH VIDEO CASSETTE C A
Follows Alexander's ascendancy to the throne after his father's assassination. Shows that against formidable obstacles, the young conqueror emerges victorious in his military campaign and begins his lifelong quest to conquer the world.
From The Search For Alexander The Great Series. Pt 2
LC NO. 82-707381
Prod-TIMLIF Dist-TIMLIF 1981

Young Dillinger B 102 MIN
16MM FILM OPTICAL SOUND H-C A
Focuses on John Dillinger's younger years and on the influences at work which led him into a life of crime.
Prod-CINEWO Dist-CINEWO 1965

Young Fingers On A Typewriter - A New Concept In Learning B 36 MIN
16MM FILM, 3/4 OR 1/2 IN VIDEO
Demonstrates a typewriter's ability to develop general learning processes. Shows how beginning typewriter activities are turned into exercises for developing language skills of spelling, reading and writing as well as powers of concentration, memory and visual imagery.
Prod-PETITG Dist-UCEMC 1975

Young Goodman Brown C 30 MIN
16MM FILM, 3/4 OR 1/2 IN VIDEO H-C A
Probes the heart and captures the complexities and ambiguities in Hawthorne's story of man's involvement with hidden evil.
Prod-PFP Dist-PFP 1973

Young Japanese Women C 29 MIN
3/4 OR 1/2 INCH VIDEO CASSETTE H-C A
Shows Japanese women in their 20s and 30s discussing issues of concern to them, such as marriage, careers, children and the uniquely Japanese concept of daughter-in-law.
From The Are You Listening Series.
LC NO. 84-706131
Prod-STURTM Dist-STURTM 1983

Young Japanese Women (Japanese) C 29 MIN
3/4 OR 1/2 INCH VIDEO CASSETTE H-C A
Shows Japanese women in their 20s and 30s discussing issues of concern to them, such as marriage, careers, children and the uniquely Japanese concept of daughter-in-law.
From The Are You Listening Series.
LC NO. 84-706131
Prod-STURTM Dist-STURTM 1983

Young Job Seekers—A Series
H-C A
Presents information and job-finding skills to young job seekers.
Prod-SEVDIM Dist-SEVDIM

Answering Questions 010 MIN

Improving Performance 010 MIN
Preparation 008 MIN
Presentation 008 MIN
Showing Initiative 010 MIN
Your First Job Interview 010 MIN

Young Lady And The Cellist, The - La Demoiselle Et La Violoncelliste C 10 MIN
16MM FILM, 3/4 OR 1/2 IN VIDEO J-C
Presents an animated tale about a musician who, inspired by the sight of the sea, improvises a concerto on his cello, only to provoke a wild storm which sweeps away a lovely girl.
LC NO. 77-701540
Prod-LESFG Dist-TEXFLM 1977

Young Life - A Commitment C 28 MIN
16MM FILM OPTICAL SOUND
Shows how a nonsectarian Christian organization, Young Life, communicates and carries on its work with youth.
LC NO. 73-702406
Prod-YLC Dist-YLC 1973

Young Lion, The C 60 MIN
3/4 OR 1/2 INCH VIDEO CASSETTE C A
Introduces Alexander the Great as a young boy when he begins his Spartan training. Shows him learning the power of knowledge from Aristotle and the power of the lance from his father, King Philip.
From The Search For Alexander The Great Series. Pt 1
LC NO. 82-707380
Prod-TIMLIF Dist-TIMLIF 1981

Young Man And Death C 16 MIN
16MM FILM OPTICAL SOUND H-C A
Dramatizes in dance the story of a young man's encounter with death.
LC NO. 76-701273
Prod-MACM Dist-FI 1976

Young Marriage - When's The Big Day C 14 MIN
16MM FILM, 3/4 OR 1/2 IN VIDEO J-H
Shows how, prior to their own marriage, Dorie and Alan visit friends who have been married for a year.
From The Conflict And Awareness Series.
Prod-CRMP Dist-CRMP 1975

Young Musical Artists—A Series

Offers viewers a wide range of music from the renaissance to the present. Features young professional musicians.
Prod-WMSBTV Dist-PUBTEL 1969

Anne Elgar - Soprano 29 MIN
Arthur Thompson - Baritone 29 MIN
Blanca Uribe - Pianist 29 MIN
Jeffry And Roland Marlowe - Duo-Pianists 29 MIN
Jessy Norman - Soprano 29 MIN
Joseph Kalichstein - Pianist 29 MIN
Nerine Barrett - Pianist 29 MIN
New York Trio Da Camera 29 MIN
Nicolai Neilsen - Guitarist 29 MIN
Ralph Votapek - Pianist 29 MIN
Trio - Easley Blackwood 29 MIN
Walter Verdehr - Violinist And David Renner - 29 MIN
William Cochran - Tenor 29 MIN

Young People Can Do Anything C 16 MIN
16MM FILM, 3/4 OR 1/2 IN VIDEO
Shows how two young people helped raise money for the establishment of a performing arts center for talented Black students as well as talented White students. Stimulates discussion about images of minority groups, career guidance, problems of the disadvantaged and schools.
From The Six To Remember Series.
Prod-AMEDFL Dist-AMEDFL 1973

Young People In Sports C 15 MIN
16MM FILM, 3/4 OR 1/2 IN VIDEO J-H
Describes the importance of sports for young people. Points out that sports teaches about competition, about defeat as well as victory, about making decisions and living with them, about goals and aspirations, and about good relationships with family, friends, competitors and coaches.
LC NO. 82-706660
Prod-KLEINW Dist-KLEINW 1981

Young People's Specials—A Series

Presents stories or documentaries for children.
Prod-MULTPP Dist-MULTPP 1979

All About Dogs 024 MIN
Atomic Legs 024 MIN
Boy Who Couldn't Lose, The 024 MIN
Championship, The 024 MIN
Edison Adventurers, The 024 MIN
Goin Along 024 MIN
Grandma Didn't Wave Back 024 MIN
Just Another Stupid Kid 024 MIN
My Special World 024 MIN
Navajo Moon 024 MIN
PR 024 MIN
Skater, The 024 MIN
Winners 024 MIN

Young Perch, The C 13 MIN
16MM FILM, 3/4 OR 1/2 IN VIDEO P-I
Describes the life cycle of fish, focusing on perch.
From The Lake Of Perch Series.
LC NO. 81-706450
Prod-FISYNG Dist-CORF 1981

Young Puppeteers Of South Vietnam B 20 MIN
16MM FILM OPTICAL SOUND
Explains how teenagers in the NLF liberated areas of Vietnam, armed with puppets made from scraps of war material, perform puppet plays for the local children while our planes 'SEARCH AND DESTROY.' Shows a view of the war even more powerful than images of atrocities.
Prod-SFN Dist-SFN

Young Sam Gompers B 30 MIN
16MM FILM OPTICAL SOUND
Presents the early life of Samuel Gompers. Tells of his job as a cigar maker, his role in the cigar makers union and his participation in the American Federation of Labor. (Kinescope)
Prod-JTS Dist-NAAJS Prodn-NBCTV 1961

Young Single Parents C 30 MIN
3/4 OR 1/2 INCH VIDEO CASSETTE H-C A
Asks how teenage mothers survive and who helps them.
From The Can I Get There From Here? Series.
Prod-MESETC Dist-UMEA 1981

Young Torless B 85 MIN
16MM FILM OPTICAL SOUND
Displays the violence and confused sensuality of adolescence under a repressive educational system. Explores the question of individual guilt and the possible roots of totalitarianism.
Prod-UNKNWN Dist-NYFLMS 1966

Young Uruguay B 17 MIN
16MM FILM OPTICAL SOUND
Portrays the young people of Uruguay at home, play and school. Emphasizes progressive steps being made in education. Includes scenes of primary schools, special classes for children from families whose histories show tuberculosis, rural schools, athletics in secondary schools and music education.
LC NO. FIE52-716
Prod-UWF Dist-USOIAA 1943

Young Veterans Program, The C 24 MIN
3/4 OR 1/2 INCH VIDEO CASSETTE PRO
Describes a specialized in-patient psychiatric unit for Vietnam veterans, established at the VAMC, Northport, NY, in 1975.
LC NO. 82-706315
Prod-VAMCNY Dist-USNAC 1982

Young Vote, The - Power, Politics And Participation C 15 MIN
16MM FILM, 3/4 OR 1/2 IN VIDEO J-C
Raises questions about attitudes and values relating to voting, politics and the democratic process itself. Examines disillusionment, apathy, commitment, involvement and idealism.
Prod-BFA Dist-PHENIX 1972

Young Women In Sports C 16 MIN
16MM FILM, 3/4 OR 1/2 IN VIDEO I-C A
Examines the attitudes of four young women athletes about strength, competition and themselves as women and as athletes.
Prod-SILSHA Dist-PHENIX 1974

Young Wonders, Inc C 29 MIN
3/4 OR 1/2 INCH VIDEO CASSETTE
Shows 35 students from a Manhattan public school who formed an opera company, the Young Wonders Inc, and then wrote, produced and performed their own opera with the help of the Metropolitan Opera Guild. Shows the opera performance.
Prod-MOG Dist-MOG Prodn-EQINOX 1983

Young Writer's Workshop—A Series
T
Stresses a process-oriented approach to teaching writing in elementary grades. Includes leader's manual and participant's manual.
Prod-BCNFL Dist-BCNFL

Writing Skills - Kindergarten Starting Points 015 MIN
Writing Skills - Reluctant Writer 015 MIN
Writing Skills - The Stages Of Writing 015 MIN
Writing Skills - The Writing Process 015 MIN
Writing Skills - Young Authors 015 MIN
Writing Skills - Young Editors 015 MIN
Writing Skills - Young Poets 015 MIN

Young, Single And Pregnant C 18 MIN
16MM FILM, 3/4 OR 1/2 IN VIDEO J-C A
Shows four young women who reflect on their experiences since becoming pregnant as teenagers. Presents the different solutions, including adoption, abortion, marriage and single parenthood.
LC NO. 73-703141
Prod-SCHL Dist-PEREN 1973

Young, Single And Pregnant - A New Perspective C 48 MIN
3/4 OR 1/2 INCH VIDEO CASSETTE J-C
Presents several case histories which illustrate common problems and questions that attend any teenage pregnancy. Describes reliable birth control methods, examines the complex decisions that must be made by the mother and father-to-be, and offers reliable sources of assistance and guidance for pregnant teenagers.
LC NO. 81-706756
Prod-GA Dist-GA 1982

Younger Brother C 19 MIN
16MM FILM OPTICAL SOUND J-H A
Presents the story of Jiro, one of the many lost and puzzled second sons in modern Japan, and the struggle he has to make a place for himself and to find a faith to replace the old order.
Prod-YALEDV Dist-YALEDV

Your Air Force C 18 MIN
16MM FILM OPTICAL SOUND
Presents a panorama of the major Air Force commands and their contributions to the USAF team.
LC NO. 74-706345
Prod-USAF Dist-USNAC 1966

Your Air Weather Service C 30 MIN
16MM FILM OPTICAL SOUND
Pictures the operation of Air Weather Service (AWS). Portrays the AWS control center at SAC command post where worldwide weather conditions are gathered, computer-processed and transmitted to subordinate weather units.
LC NO. 74-706346
Prod-USDD Dist-USNAC 1962

Your Appearance After A Mastectomy C 10 MIN
3/4 OR 1/2 INCH VIDEO CASSETTE
Explains and provides concrete information on how a mastectomy patient looks as attractive after her surgery as she did before. Shows clothing that is suitable in the hospital and during early recovery, and describes various breast prostheses. Emphasizes that after recovery the woman can still dress appropriately for any activity.
Prod-TRAINX Dist-TRAINX

Your Apple Computer - A User's Guide C
3/4 OR 1/2 INCH VIDEO CASSETTE
Clarifies important Apple functions and hardware including keyboards, CRTs, disk drives, printers and modems. Shows how the disk operating system works.
Prod-GA Dist-GA

Your Army Reports, No. 12 C 29 MIN
16MM FILM OPTICAL SOUND
Shows General Harold K Johnson, Army Chief of Staff, speaking at the annual convention of the Association of the United States Army. Shows Vietnamese civilians working with the United States Army and describes the work of the Army combat photographer.
From The Big Picture Series.
LC NO. 74-706347
Prod-USA Dist-USNAC 1967

Your Army Reports, No. 13 C 29 MIN
16MM FILM OPTICAL SOUND
Shows General Harold K Johnson, Army Chief of Staff, decorating Warrant Officer Jerome R Daley for gallantry in action. Pictures Army combat photographers moving forward with the first Cavalry Division and Vietnamese troops during an amphibious landing and search for Viet Cong. Depicts the mission of harbor pilots in the port of Qui Nhon.
From The Big Picture Series.
LC NO. 74-706348
Prod-USA Dist-USNAC 1967

Your Army Reports, No. 14 C 29 MIN
16MM FILM OPTICAL SOUND
Features training activities of the 205th Infantry Brigade of the U S Army Reserve as it prepares to meet its mission in defense of America.
From The Big Picture Series.
LC NO. 74-706349
Prod-USA Dist-USNAC 1967

Your Attitude Is Showing C 19 MIN
16MM FILM, 3/4 OR 1/2 IN VIDEO J-C A
Presents short vignettes which show how attitudes can affect individual and team job performance. Illustrates a correlation between positive attitudes and increased production.
Prod-BOSUST Dist-CF 1979

Your Baby Well Born - Steps To A Healthy Pregnancy C 10 MIN
3/4 OR 1/2 INCH VIDEO CASSETTE H-C A
Identifies maternal behaviors and characteristics know to increase the risk of low birth rate, neurological abnormality and/or perinatal death. Gives recommendations for reducing risks.
Prod-UARIZ Dist-UARIZ

Your Baby With A Congenital Heart Defect C 29 MIN
3/4 OR 1/2 INCH VIDEO CASSETTE A
Designed for parents of infants with congenital heart defects. Shows families relating their feelings and experiences resulting from caring for their infants with a heart defect.
Prod-UMICHM Dist-UMICHM 1981

Your Baby's First Days C
3/4 OR 1/2 INCH VIDEO CASSETTE
Uses close-ups of various newborn infants to explain normal appearance, behavior and development. Presents information on caring for both the physical and emotional needs of new infants.
Prod-MIFE Dist-MIFE

Your Baby's First Days C 21 MIN
16MM FILM, 3/4 OR 1/2 IN VIDEO H-C A
Presents childbirth education with emphasis on the difficult tasks, for the inexperienced, of holding, nursing and bathing a baby.
LC NO. 81-707013
Prod-POLYMR Dist-POLYMR 1980

Your Beautiful Lawn C 48 MIN
1/2 IN VIDEO CASSETTE BETA/VHS
Shows how to seed and maintain a lawn. Includes topics such as liming and moss control, raking and thatching.
From The Lawn And Garden Series.
Prod-MOHOMV Dist-MOHOMV

Your Beautiful Roses C 56 MIN
1/2 IN VIDEO CASSETTE BETA/VHS
Explains the differences between different kinds of roses. Tells how to grow climbing and tree roses. Includes fertilization and insect control.
From The Lawn And Garden Series.
Prod-MOHOMV Dist-MOHOMV

Your Behavior Affects Results C 27 MIN
3/4 OR 1/2 INCH VIDEO CASSETTE IND
Defines types of behavior and applies these to the relationship between supervisor and employee.
From The Super-Vision Series.
LC NO. 79-706770
Prod-VCI Dist-DELTAK 1977

Your Bicycle And You C 13 MIN
16MM FILM OPTICAL SOUND P-J
Gives rules of the road for cyclists and compares these rules with automobile rules. 'FIVE DON'TS FOR BIKE SAFTY' Point out dangerous bike riding practices that lead to accidents and injuries.
Prod-CARSON Dist-MLA 1962

Your Birthday Suit C 15 MIN
3/4 OR 1/2 INCH VIDEO CASSETTE
Introduces the concept that skin is a living organ which protects one's body from germs and puts one in touch with the world. Explains the scientific basis for differences in skin color.
From The All About You Series.
Prod-WGBHTV Dist-AITECH Prodn-TTOIC

Your Body And Its Parts X 12 MIN
16MM FILM, 3/4 OR 1/2 IN VIDEO P
Provides an overview of human physiology, showing that body parts working together to do a job form a system. Introduces muscular, respiratory, circulatory, skeletal and nervous systems.
From The Basic Life Science Series.
Prod-EBF Dist-EBEC 1964

Your Body And Its Parts (Spanish) C 12 MIN
16MM FILM, 3/4 OR 1/2 IN VIDEO P
Introduces the five systems of the human body, describing the muscles, the respiratory system, circulation, the skeleton and the nervous system. Demonstrates the interdependence between these systems.
Prod-EBEC Dist-EBEC

Your Body Repairs And Maintains Itself C 10 MIN
16MM FILM, 3/4 OR 1/2 IN VIDEO I-J
Shows how the body maintains itself by replacing skin cells and blood cells and by producing antibodies and how it repairs itself by producing scar tissue and by replacing broken bone.
Prod-CORF Dist-CORF 1966

Your Body Speaks C 15 MIN
2 INCH VIDEOTAPE P
Provides an enrichment program in the communitive arts area by doing pantomimes.
From The Word Magic (2nd Ed) Series.
Prod-CVETVC Dist-GPITVL

Your Breast Biopsy C 9 MIN
3/4 OR 1/2 INCH VIDEO CASSETTE
Suggests program should be viewed by women who must have a breast biopsy, and provides details of what the woman can expect when admitted to the hospital.
LC NO. 79-730753
Prod-TRAINX Dist-TRAINX

Your Busy Brain C 15 MIN
3/4 OR 1/2 INCH VIDEO CASSETTE P
Presents a diagram of the brain and nerve network which shows that the brain is like a control center, receiving and sending messages all the time. Explains that the brain is able to store information. Describes the functions of specialized cells.
From The All About You Series.
Prod-WGBHTV Dist-AITECH Prodn-TTOIC 1975

Your Cancer Diet C 13 MIN
3/4 OR 1/2 INCH VIDEO CASSETTE
Helps the cancer patient understand the importance of minimizing weight loss during therapy, and recommends ways of increasing calories and protein in the diet. Suggests ways to overcome eating problems that may occur during cancer treatments.
From The Patient Education Programs - Clinical Diet Series.
Prod-POAPLE Dist-POAPLE

Your Car And Clean Air C 13 MIN
16MM FILM OPTICAL SOUND
Presents the report of the automobile manufacturers association and the American petroleum Institute's work aimed at removing automobiles from the list of air polluters.
Prod-GM Dist-GM 1970

Your Car In Motion C 10 MIN
16MM FILM, 3/4 OR 1/2 IN VIDEO
See series title for descriptive statement.
From The Driving Tips Series.
Prod-FORDFL Dist-FORDFL

Your Career As A Secretary C 27 MIN
16MM FILM OPTICAL SOUND J-H
Shows classwork in typing, shorthand, bookkeeping, business law and arithmetic, and points out that the modern high school offers more complete training for a job in the secretarial field than in any other.
Prod-WFPC Dist-MLA 1954

Your Career As An Electronics Technician C 27 MIN
16MM FILM OPTICAL SOUND J-H
Shows how interest in physics, electricity and shop, an ability to make precise measurements and a facility with tools are advantageous for an electronics career. Gives suggestions for training after high school.
Prod-WFPC Dist-MLA 1954

Your Career In Aeronautical Engineering C 27 MIN
16MM FILM OPTICAL SOUND J-H
Explorers careers in aeronautical engineering, including the importance of mathematics, highlights of college course material and scenes from industry showing graduate application of technical training.
From The Your Career Series.
LC NO. 73-701179
Prod-RARIG Dist-MLA 1962

Your Career In Architecture C 27 MIN
16MM FILM OPTICAL SOUND H
Reviews the education needed for a career as an architect. Includes a view of the five-year college course and the three-year apprentice period.
From The Your Career Series.
LC NO. 78-701180
Prod-RARIG Dist-MLA 1962

Your Career In Elementary Teaching C 27 MIN
16MM FILM OPTICAL SOUND J-H
Describes the personal attributes and preparation necessary for elementary school teachers–ability to understand people, broad academic background and good teaching skills. Illustrates practice teaching, and tells what a graduate may expect in job-seeking.
Prod-WFPC Dist-MLA 1954

Your Career In Forestry C 27 MIN
16MM FILM OPTICAL SOUND J-H
Tells why college schools of forestry require good preparation in English, math, botany and physics. Illustrates the application of forestry skills in both private and public employment.
Prod-WFPC Dist-MLA 1954

Your Career In Hotel Management C 27 MIN
16MM FILM OPTICAL SOUND H
Reviews the education recommended for a career in hotel management. Surveys preparatory courses and shows many of the career opportunities available to a person trained in this field.
From The Your Career Series.
LC NO. 79-701183
Prod-RARIG Dist-MLA 1962

Your Career In Journalism C 27 MIN
16MM FILM OPTICAL SOUND H
Reviews the liberal arts education recommended for a career in journalism. Presents a view of beginning jobs in reporting and describes some specialized jobs.
From The Your Career Series.
LC NO. 71-701181
Prod-RARIG Dist-MLA 1962

Your Career In Law (2nd Ed) C 27 MIN
16MM FILM OPTICAL SOUND H
Stresses reading comprehension and capacity, love for words and respect for truth as the mark of the future lawyer. A mock trial in a law school illustrates professional study of torts, contracts, property rights and other aspects of the law.
From The Your Career Series.
Prod-RARIG Dist-MLA 1962

Your Career In Meteorology C 27 MIN
16MM FILM OPTICAL SOUND H
Reviews the education necessary for a career in the field of meteorology. Describes preparatory courses and shows various areas of specialization within each field.
From The Your Career Series.
LC NO. 72-701184
Prod-RARIG Dist-MLA 1962

Your Career In Nursing C 27 MIN
16MM FILM OPTICAL SOUND J-H
Examines both avenues to a nursing degree–college training and hospital apprenticeship. Explores specialization in specific fields and explains the importance of a background of science in high school.
Prod-WFPC Dist-MLA 1954

Your Career In Printing C 27 MIN
16MM FILM OPTICAL SOUND J-H
High school student becomes interested in the industry while working with a printer to publish his school paper. He sees the importance of high school courses in art and photography in relation to printing. Six separate, but related, skilled trades in the industry are named.
Prod-WFPC Dist-MLA 1954

Your Career, J Kenneth Lund C
3/4 OR 1/2 INCH VIDEO CASSETTE PRO
See series title for descriptive statement.
From The Management Skills Series.
Prod-AMCEE Dist-AMCEE

Your Chance To Live–A Series
16MM FILM, 3/4 OR 1/2 IN VIDEO J-H T
Explores aspects of natural and man-made disasters.
Prod-USDCPA Dist-MTI 1972

Earthquake 014 MIN
Flood 014 MIN
Forest Fire 014 MIN
Heat Wave 014 MIN
Hurricane 014 MIN
Pollution 014 MIN
Tornado 014 MIN
Winter Storm 014 MIN

Your Child And Diabetes C 23 MIN
3/4 OR 1/2 INCH VIDEO CASSETTE
Provides an understanding of diabetes, its cases and how it will affect the family's lifestyle. Prepares parents to provide the guidance, encouragement, and direction that the child requires.
LC NO. 83-730081
Prod-TRAINX Dist-TRAINX

Your Child And Diabetes (Spanish) C 23 MIN
3/4 OR 1/2 INCH VIDEO CASSETTE
Provides an understanding of diabetes, its cases and how it will affect the family's lifestyle. Prepares parents to provide the guidance, encouragement, and direction that the child requires.
LC NO. 83-730081
Prod-TRAINX Dist-TRAINX

Your Child Has A Fever C 15 MIN
16MM FILM, 3/4 OR 1/2 IN VIDEO A
Demonstrates how to recognize a fever, use a thermometer and reduce a fever. Indicates when to call a doctor.
Prod-CF Dist-CF

Your Child's First Few Steps C 15 MIN
16MM FILM, 3/4 OR 1/2 IN VIDEO J-C A
Explores infant footwear. Discusses the walking process.
Prod-KLEINW Dist-KLEINW

Your Child's Growth And Development C 10 MIN
16MM FILM, 3/4 OR 1/2 IN VIDEO PRO
A revised edition of Growth And Development/Toilet Training. Describes the basic elements vital to a child's growth and social progress and provides guidelines for toilet training using positive reinforcement.
Prod-PRORE Dist-PRORE

Your Child's Safety C 10 MIN
16MM FILM OPTICAL SOUND
Provides education and motivation for parents, especially new mothers, regarding child care and accident prevention, as part of an audiovisual system of learning.
LC NO. 79-711598
Prod-ROCOM Dist-SUTHLA 1971

Your Children Come Back To You B 27 MIN
16MM FILM OPTICAL SOUND
Tells the story of Tovi, a little black girl caught between European and African values within her own family.
Prod-BLKFMF Dist-BLKFMF

Your Choice - Decision-Making (Anthropology-Sociology) C 15 MIN
3/4 OR 1/2 INCH VIDEO CASSETTE P
Reveals that Pat decides to go hiking alone rather than help his family set up camp. Shows that when he does not return, a search party is organized.
From The Two Cents' Worth Series.
Prod-WHATV Dist-AITECH Prodn-WIEC 1976

Your Church And The Mentally Retarded C 20 MIN
16MM FILM OPTICAL SOUND
Prod-BROADM Dist-BROADM 1977

Your Clothing Can Burn (2nd Ed) C 16 MIN
16MM FILM, 3/4 OR 1/2 IN VIDEO I A
Presents laboratory demonstrations showing burning characteristics of various fabrics. Describes what to do if clothes catch on fire.
Prod-HIGGIN Dist-HIGGIN 1981

Your Communication Skills - Listening C 11 MIN
16MM FILM, 3/4 OR 1/2 IN VIDEO I-J
Points out that listening is as important for communication as speaking, and shows some of the listening skills that can help improve communication.
Prod-CORF Dist-CORF 1969

Your Complete Denture C 10 MIN
16MM FILM OPTICAL SOUND P-H
Provides the patient having a new complete denture, with methods for adjusting to appearance, speech, eating and other activities. Uses animation to portray the problems of a denture in the mouth and shows the proper care and cleaning of the denture.
From The Dental Health Series.
LC NO. 75-700037
Prod-MIFE Dist-MIFE 1973

Your Congressman At Work B 22 MIN
16MM FILM - 3/4 IN VIDEO
Presents a typical day in the life of a member of Congress. Urges all members of the armed forces to become familiar with the issues and candidates in forthcoming elections and to vote.
Prod-USDD Dist-USNAC Prodn-USA 1956

Your Contact Lens Procedures - Hard Lens C 7 MIN
3/4 OR 1/2 INCH VIDEO CASSETTE
Instructs patient on proper technique of application and removal of contact lenses. Discusses proper hygiene and care.
Prod-TRAINX Dist-TRAINX

Your Coronary Care Diet C 11 MIN
3/4 OR 1/2 INCH VIDEO CASSETTE
Discusses the restrictions on sodium, saturated fats and cholesterol in the coronary care diet. Talks about the significance of dietary fiber and the importance of achieving and maintaining one's ideal body weight.
From The Patient Education Programs - Clinical Diet Series.
Prod-POAPLE Dist-POAPLE

Your Credit Is Good - A Film About Paying Later (Captioned) C 15 MIN
16MM FILM, 3/4 OR 1/2 IN VIDEO J-C
Demonstrates in a series of dramatic vignettes, that the lure of extended credit can hold many hazards for the unwary consumer.
Prod-ALTSUL Dist-JOU 1972

Your Credit Is Good - A Film About Paying Later C 15 MIN
16MM FILM, 3/4 OR 1/2 IN VIDEO J-C
Demonstrates in a series of dramatic vignettes, that the lure of

extended credit can hold many hazards for the unwary consumer.
Prod-ALTSUL Dist-JOU 1972

Your Credit Is Good, Unfortunately C 10 MIN
16MM FILM, 3/4 OR 1/2 IN VIDEO I-H A
Warns against fraudulent credit practices which can leave credit buyers with enormous monthly payments.
From The Consumer Fraud Series.
Prod-PART Dist-PFP 1976

Your Dental X-Ray Exam C 8 MIN
16MM FILM, 3/4 OR 1/2 IN VIDEO
Helps answer patients' questions and concerns about the necessity and safety of dental radiographic procedures. Emphasizes the important information that can be gained from X-rays, as well as the ways modern safety standards have minimized patient exposure and risk.
Prod-PRORE Dist-PRORE

Your Diet - Carbohydrates C 12 MIN
16MM FILM, 3/4 OR 1/2 IN VIDEO J-C A
Explains the various forms of carbohydrates and the roles they play in one's diet. Tells of some good sources of carbohydrates.
From The Your Diet Series.
Prod-ALTSUL Dist-JOU 1982

Your Diet - Exercise C 12 MIN
16MM FILM, 3/4 OR 1/2 IN VIDEO J-C A
Looks at various forms of exercise and recreation and their effects on health. Emphasizes that people of all ages need daily exercise for healthy bodies and minds.
From The Your Diet Series.
Prod-ALTSUL Dist-JOU 1982

Your Diet - Fats C 12 MIN
16MM FILM, 3/4 OR 1/2 IN VIDEO J-C A
Looks at the effects of the overconsumption of fats and offers alternative foods to help reduce intake of fats while still maintaining the proper amount of proteins in the daily diet.
From The Your Diet Series.
Prod-ALTSUL Dist-JOU 1982

Your Diet - Fiber C 12 MIN
16MM FILM, 3/4 OR 1/2 IN VIDEO J-C A
Examines what fiber is and the role it play's in one's diet. Tells how fast foods have caused the fiber content in diets to decrease and what diseases and conditions are attributed to lack of fiber. Names some good sources of fiber.
From The Your Diet Series.
Prod-ALTSUL Dist-JOU 1982

Your Diet - Salt And Hypertension C 13 MIN
16MM FILM OPTICAL SOUND
Presents a history of salt as a seasoning and preservative. Discusses why modern food processing methods and trends in eating habits have contributed to the prevalence of salt in the American diet, and uncovers the link between sodium and hypertension. Explains dietary changes needed to reduce the risk of heart disease.
Prod-ADA Dist-ADA

Your Diet - Salt And Hypertension C 13 MIN
16MM FILM, 3/4 OR 1/2 IN VIDEO J-C A
Defines hypertension, describes how it affects the heart and examines the correlation between salt intake and the incidence of hypertension. Explains which individuals, either through hereditary factors, stress, body conditions, or diet, are most prone to hypertension and heart disease.
From The Your Diet Series.
Prod-ALTSUL Dist-JOU 1978

Your Diet - Water C 10 MIN
16MM FILM, 3/4 OR 1/2 IN VIDEO J-H A
Discusses the importance of water in people's diets.
From The Your Diet Series.
Prod-ALTSUL Dist-JOU 1981

Your Diet—A Series
16MM FILM, 3/4 OR 1/2 IN VIDEO
Provides information on how specific foods and lifestyles affect health. Presents instructions on avoiding or correcting poor health habits.
Prod-JOU Dist-JOU

Calories - Enough Is Enough (2nd Ed) 010 MIN
Food Labeling - Understanding What You Eat 013 MIN
Snacks Count Too (2nd Ed) 012 MIN
Your Diet - Carbohydrates 012 MIN
Your Diet - Exercise 012 MIN
Your Diet - Fats 012 MIN
Your Diet - Fiber 012 MIN
Your Diet - Salt And Hypertension 013 MIN
Your Diet - Water 010 MIN

Your Driving Habits B 15 MIN
16MM FILM OPTICAL SOUND
Shows the elements of good driving. Demonstrates how to start the engine, use the clutch, shift gears and use the brakes. Explains how to drive under hazardous conditions.
LC NO. FIE52-315
Prod-USOE Dist-USNAC Prodn-HANDY 1945

Your Ear - What Can Go Wrong C 55 MIN
3/4 OR 1/2 INCH VIDEO CASSETTE PRO
Discusses the mechanism of hearing, the causes of hearing impairment and the medical and surgical treatment of otologic problems.
Prod-HOUSEI Dist-HOUSEI

Your Ear And Noise C 50 MIN
3/4 OR 1/2 INCH VIDEO CASSETTE PRO
Discusses the concepts of industrial noise and its effect on hearing. Presents controls and methods of determining harmful industrial noise levels.
Prod-HOUSEI Dist-HOUSEI

Your Ears X 6 MIN
16MM FILM, 3/4 OR 1/2 IN VIDEO P
Children discover their dependence on ears for hearing. Animation is used to show the function of the ear, explaining what happens when sound enters it. Good health habits are stressed.
Prod-EBF Dist-EBEC 1964

Your Ears (Spanish) C 6 MIN
16MM FILM, 3/4 OR 1/2 IN VIDEO P
Explains the functions of the human ear and stresses good health habits relating to the ear. Illustrates what happens when sound enters the ear.
Prod-EBEC Dist-EBEC

Your Environment Is The Earth C 12 MIN
16MM FILM, 3/4 OR 1/2 IN VIDEO I-J
Takes the viewer on a journey from the polar ice caps to the Northern Tundra, from the forests of the temperate zone to tropical jungles and from outer space to the ocean depths in order to demonstrate that our environment is our surroundings.
Prod-WER Dist-JOU 1969

Your Erroneous Zones C 97 MIN
3/4 OR 1/2 INCH VIDEO CASSETTE A
Presents Wayne Dyer, psychologist and author, discussing how to avoid such unhealthy behavioral patterns as guilt, anger, anxiety and insecurity. Based upon his book Your Erroneous Zones.
Prod-CBSFOX Dist-CBSFOX

Your Erroneous Zones C 97 MIN
16MM FILM, 3/4 OR 1/2 IN VIDEO C A
Features psychologist Wayne Dyer explaining his approach to managing stress and building self-worth.
Prod-FI Dist-FI

Your Ever Well Wisher C 57 MIN
16MM FILM OPTICAL SOUND
Presents a biography of His Divine Grace A C Bhaktivedanta Swami from his childhood days in Calcutta through his glorious achievements as the founder and leader of the Hare Krishna movement.
Prod-ISKCON Dist-BHAKTI 1983

Your Exercises After A Mastectomy C 10 MIN
3/4 OR 1/2 INCH VIDEO CASSETTE
Recommends program to be viewed on second or third postoperative day by the woman who has had a mastectomy. Reviews the physical therapy that will help the woman return to her normal activities as soon as possible after her operation. Describes passive exercises and nature of normal recovery, and concludes with demonstrations of the five different exercises frequently prescribed.
Prod-TRAINX Dist-TRAINX

Your Eyes X 7 MIN
16MM FILM, 3/4 OR 1/2 IN VIDEO P
Children demonstrate their dependence on their eyes. Simple animation is used to show how the eye works, and ways to care for eyes are stressed.
Prod-EBF Dist-EBEC 1964

Your Eyes (Spanish) C 7 MIN
16MM FILM, 3/4 OR 1/2 IN VIDEO P
Demonstrates ways in which man depends on his eyes. Shows how the eye works and illustrates good eye care.
Prod-EBEC Dist-EBEC

Your Face Speaks C 15 MIN
2 INCH VIDEOTAPE P
Provides an enrichment program in the communitive arts area by using facial expressions.
From The Word Magic (2nd Ed) Series.
Prod-CVETVC Dist-GPITVL

Your Feet's Too Big C 3 MIN
16MM FILM, 3/4 OR 1/2 IN VIDEO I A
Features story of a monkey who rejects an amorous elephant because of his large feet.
Prod-MTOLP Dist-MTOLP 1984

Your Fire Service C 20 MIN
3/4 OR 1/2 INCH VIDEO CASSETTE
Shows people in their communities what it costs to run a fire department, risks firefighters take and other fire department public information.
Prod-FPF Dist-FPF

Your Fireman B 12 MIN
16MM FILM OPTICAL SOUND I-C A
Depicts the jobs of a fire department other than putting out fires. Includes rescue work, fire inspection and prevention programs, maintaining equipment and continuous education of firemen.
Prod-RVIERA Dist-RVIERA 1953

Your First Gynecological Examination C 17 MIN
16MM FILM, 3/4 OR 1/2 IN VIDEO H-C A
Gives a brief animated explanation of the female internal and external genitalia, and follows Jenny through her first gynecological visit. Details the initial consultation, breast examination and pap smear and the importance of each procedure is stated. Special attention is given to the necessity for frank, honest communication between doctor and patient.
From The Woman Talk Series.
Prod-CORF Dist-CORF 1983

Your First Job Interview C 10 MIN
3/4 OR 1/2 INCH VIDEO CASSETTE H-C A
Presents the candidates for the same job. Shows interviews and comments of interviewer.
From The Young Job Seekers Series.
Prod-SEVDIM Dist-SEVDIM

Your First Pony C
1/2 IN VIDEO CASSETTE BETA/VHS
See series title for descriptive statement.
From The Captain Mark Phillips Horsemanship Training Series.
Prod-EQVDL Dist-EQVDL

Your First Six Years C 10 MIN
16MM FILM OPTICAL SOUND K-J
Considers the development of abilities, emotions and self-expression during the first six years of life. Shows changing attitudes and expanding roles of children of different ages at play, in school and in their relationship to their parents. Emphasizes the role of the parents in the development of young children.
From The Family Life And Sex Education Series.
Prod-SF Dist-SF 1968

Your Food X 7 MIN
16MM FILM, 3/4 OR 1/2 IN VIDEO P
Shows what happens to food when it enters the digestive system, and relates this system to other body systems. Presents examples of a balanced diet.
From The Basic Life Science Series.
Prod-EBF Dist-EBEC 1964

Your Food Allergies C 7 MIN
3/4 OR 1/2 INCH VIDEO CASSETTE
Explains what food allergy is and how it acts. Presents a method for finding causes of food allergy through a food diary.
Prod-MEDFAC Dist-MEDFAC 1978

Your Friend The Forest - Save It Or Destroy It (Spanish) C 6 MIN
16MM FILM, 3/4 OR 1/2 IN VIDEO P-I
Uses animation to demonstrate the importance of preventing forest fires.
Prod-EBEC Dist-EBEC

Your Friend The Forest - Save It Or Destroy It C 6 MIN
16MM FILM, 3/4 OR 1/2 IN VIDEO P-I
An animated cartoon story demonstrates the importance of preventing forest fires.
Prod-EBF Dist-EBEC 1954

Your Friend The Water - Clean Or Dirty C 6 MIN
16MM FILM, 3/4 OR 1/2 IN VIDEO P-I
An animated cartoon of a little boy who learns the factors behind a good supply of pure water, as well as the conditions which produce dirty, polluted water.
Prod-EBF Dist-EBEC 1954

Your Future In Art - A Career For The 80's C 22 MIN
16MM FILM OPTICAL SOUND
Focuses on a group of commercial artists, photographers and interior designers working at their jobs in various cities and describing opportunities, responsibilities and achievements in their respective fields. Shows the skills and training essential for a career in commercial art.
Prod-MTP Dist-MTP

Your Future Is Now--A Series B 60 MIN
2 INCH VIDEOTAPE
Covers the major subject matter areas and skills of a high school education.
Prod-GPITVL Dist-GPITVL

Your Guardian Angel C 15 MIN
16MM FILM, 3/4 OR 1/2 IN VIDEO IND
Reviews the characteristics of 600-volt lines and illustrates basic safety techniques in handling them.
LC NO. 82-707028
Prod-IAPA Dist-IFB 1974

Your Guardian Angel (Spanish) C 15 MIN
16MM FILM, 3/4 OR 1/2 IN VIDEO IND
Reviews the characteristics of 600-volt lines and illustrates basic safety techniques in handling them.
Prod-IAPA Dist-IFB 1974

Your Health Care After A Mastecomy C 11 MIN
3/4 OR 1/2 INCH VIDEO CASSETTE
Describes some precautions which can contribute to a woman's health care after a mastectomy. Discusses precautions to help the patient avoid injury and infection of the infected hand and arm, followed by a demonstration of breast self-examination. Stresses follow-up therapy and follow-up physician visits.
LC NO. 79-730753
Prod-TRAINX Dist-TRAINX

Your Heart - The Mighty Muscle C 15 MIN
3/4 OR 1/2 INCH VIDEO CASSETTE P
Utilizes an X-ray, siphon pump and heart model to describe the functions of the heart and blood and to show how blood is circulated through the body.
From The All About You Series.
Prod-WGBHTV Dist-AITECH Prodn-TTOIC 1975

Your Hemodiolysis Therapy C 9 MIN
3/4 OR 1/2 INCH VIDEO CASSETTE
Introduces hemodialysis therapy with overview of normal kidney function, followed by explanation of purpose and function of the artificial kidney. Emphasizes patient's participatory role in his health care and gives guidelines to apply to one's own treatment. Focuses attention on scheduling of treatment sessions, care of the circulatory access site and diet modification.
LC NO. 80-730458
Prod-TRAINX Dist-TRAINX

Your Hero Heart C 15 MIN
3/4 OR 1/2 INCH VIDEO CASSETTE K-P
See series title for descriptive statement.

From The Cardio Series.
Prod-NCSDPI Dist-PCATEL

Your Home Beautiful C 15 MIN
16MM FILM, 3/4 OR 1/2 IN VIDEO J-C A
Presents a talking house which personifies the modern, American, single-family home and how it is decorated. Provides information on home buying and decorating.
Prod-KLEINW Dist-KLEINW 1975

Your House In Order C 18 MIN
16MM FILM, 3/4 OR 1/2 IN VIDEO
Shows how industrial accidents can be the result of poor housekeeping and sloppiness. Uses the examples of a reckless forklift operator, a careless maintenance man, two workers unloading pipe without looking, a lathe operator who doesn't clean up the scrap and other workers leaving tools and trucks in dangerous places.
LC NO. 83-706828
Prod-MILLBK Dist-IFB

Your Image C 25 MIN
2 INCH VIDEOTAPE I
Describes material to be covered in the images series and notes the overall aim of the series is to Foster effective expression.
From The Images Series.
Prod-CVETVC Dist-GPITVL

Your Image - Make It Work For You C 17 MIN
16MM FILM, 3/4 OR 1/2 IN VIDEO H-C A
Explores how grooming, dress, verbal communication and body language come together to create an image of a person in the minds of others.
Prod-BARR Dist-BARR 1983

Your Image - Making It Work For You (Captioned) C 17 MIN
16MM FILM - VIDEO, ALL FORMATS
Deals with ways to improve personal image. Explores areas such as grooming, body language and work performance.
Prod-BARR Dist-BARR

Your IPPB Therapy C 12 MIN
3/4 OR 1/2 INCH VIDEO CASSETTE
Illustrates the techniques of Intermittent Positive Pressure Breathing. Presents an IPPB therapy machine and shows its use. Notes that patient must be instructed in his role during treatment and need of cooperation.
LC NO. 73-732792
Prod-TRAINX Dist-TRAINX

Your Job C 20 MIN
3/4 OR 1/2 INCH VIDEO CASSETTE
Shows what to do in case of fire at the job site. Illustrates the value of fire protection equipment.
Prod-FPF Dist-FPF

Your Job - Applying For It C 14 MIN
16MM FILM, 3/4 OR 1/2 IN VIDEO H-C A
Uses interviews with workers of varying ages and education to show that the way to apply for a job and get it is by following a planned procedure which includes getting enough good leads, sticking with it, selling oneself and making the most of what one has.
From The Your Job Series.
Prod-CORF Dist-CORF 1968

Your Job - Finding The Right One C 14 MIN
16MM FILM, 3/4 OR 1/2 IN VIDEO H-C A
Shows how young people can locate jobs suited to their needs and abilities. Shows how to organize a plan of action that will get the 'RIGHT' job.
From The Your Job Series.
Prod-CORF Dist-CORF 1968

Your Job - Fitting In C 16 MIN
16MM FILM, 3/4 OR 1/2 IN VIDEO H-C A
Examines two situations wherein an employee is fired for doing 'TOO LITTLE' and another is fired for trying to do 'TOO MUCH.' Challenges the viewer to decide how he would respond to each situation.
From The Your Job Series.
Prod-CORF Dist-CORF 1968

Your Job - Getting Ahead C 16 MIN
16MM FILM, 3/4 OR 1/2 IN VIDEO H-C A
Interviews experienced workers at their jobs, and gives tips on getting ahead. Discusses questions about changing jobs, recognizing dead-end jobs, picking areas for advancement and planning for additional education.
From The Your Job Series.
Prod-CORF Dist-CORF 1968

Your Job - Good Work Habits C 14 MIN
16MM FILM, 3/4 OR 1/2 IN VIDEO H-C A
Interviews two high school graduates on their first full-time jobs regarding their opinions about good work habits. Shows that working steadily, concentration, and planning ahead can lead to promotions, raises and/or other benefits.
From The Your Job Series.
Prod-CORF Dist-CORF 1968

Your Job - You And Your Boss C 16 MIN
16MM FILM, 3/4 OR 1/2 IN VIDEO H-C A
Discusses the qualifications of leadership and many of the employee qualities that the leader seeks in those who work under his supervision. Stresses the need for mutual understanding.
From The Your Job Series.
Prod-CORF Dist-CORF 1968

Your Job In Germany B 15 MIN
16MM FILM, 3/4 OR 1/2 IN VIDEO
Presents a film made for American occupation troops to discourage fraternization with our former enemies. Unlike earlier Frank Capra films that blamed the war on German leaders, this film condemned the German people as a whole. Considered one of the most bitter and angry films to be made during the war.
Prod-USAPS Dist-USNAC 1982

Your Job In Germany / Our Job In Japan B 32 MIN
3/4 OR 1/2 INCH VIDEO CASSETTE
Promotes anti-German sentiments intended to discourage American occupation troops from fraternizing with their former enemies, made shortly before Germany's surrender. Blames World War II on the 'inherent belligerism' of Germans. Portrays Japanese as victims of cynical leaders who filled their minds with thoughts of world conquest. Suggests that these ideas must be changed so Japan can join the community of peaceful nations.
Prod-IHF Dist-IHF

Your Job—A Series
16MM FILM, 3/4 OR 1/2 IN VIDEO H-C A
Presents interviews with people at their work in order to explain how to get and keep a job.
Prod-CORF Dist-CORF 1968

Your Job - Applying For It	14 MIN
Your Job - Finding The Right One	14 MIN
Your Job - Fitting In	15 MIN
Your Job - Getting Ahead	16 MIN
Your Job - Good Work Habits	14 MIN
Your Job - You And Your Boss	16 MIN

Your Last Chance X 30 MIN
16MM FILM OPTICAL SOUND J-H T R
Motivates church members to be alert to the needs of others.
LC NO. FIA67-5754
Prod-FAMF Dist-FAMF 1967

Your Life And The Pill C 13 MIN
16MM FILM OPTICAL SOUND
Considers some of the common questions about reproductive physiology and oral contraception.
LC NO. 76-700207
Prod-WYLAB Dist-WYLAB Prodn-INTERM 1975

Your Life And The Pill (French) C 13 MIN
16MM FILM OPTICAL SOUND
Considers some of the common questions about reproductive physiology and oral contraception.
LC NO. 76-700207
Prod-WYLAB Dist-WYLAB Prodn-INTERM 1975

Your Life And The Pill (Spanish) C 13 MIN
16MM FILM OPTICAL SOUND
Considers some of the common questions about reproductive physiology and oral contraception.
LC NO. 76-700207
Prod-WYLAB Dist-WYLAB Prodn-INTERM 1975

Your Money Matters—A Series
H-C A
Covers all the current topics on consumer finance and investments.
Prod-FILMID Dist-FILMID

ABC'S Of Life Insurance	025 MIN
Best Investments For The Small Saver	025 MIN
Creative Financing	025 MIN
Especially For Women	025 MIN
Evaluating Employee Benefits	025 MIN
Investments For Seniors	025 MIN
Money Management In Troubled Times	025 MIN
Old And New Investments	025 MIN
Planning Your Estate	025 MIN
Practical Tax Shelters, Pt I	025 MIN
Practical Tax Shelters, Pt II	025 MIN
Pre-Retirement Planning	025 MIN
Real Estate Investments	025 MIN
Stock Strategies For Individuals	025 MIN
Things You Should Know About Your Financial	025 MIN

Your Money Or Your Life C 14 MIN
16MM FILM, 3/4 OR 1/2 IN VIDEO
Reports on the types of investments corporations are making to protect themselves. Discusses ways to minimize the risk of being kidnapped.
Prod-CBSNEW Dist-MTI

Your Money Or Your Life C 45 MIN
16MM FILM, 3/4 OR 1/2 IN VIDEO
Presents an illuminating and provocative story about urban crime in America and how the resulting atmosphere of fear that pervades cities encourages racial antagonism. Shows two examples supporting such views. Counters with an alternative viewpoint of a black Mugger/Philosopher/Economist who compares mugging to the American economic system and justifies his actions as a means of redistributing wealth.
Prod-CNEMAG Dist-CNEMAG 1984

Your Money Or Your Life C 45 MIN
3/4 OR 1/2 INCH VIDEO CASSETTE
Addresses the problems of America today and approaches them in a totally American way.
Prod-EAI Dist-EAI

Your Mouth C 16 MIN
16MM FILM, 3/4 OR 1/2 IN VIDEO I-C
Examines many aspects of the development of the human mouth from babyhood to maturity. Describes the growth of temporary and permanent teeth, the function of gums, tongue, lips, muscles, nerves and peridontal membrance, the attack of tooth enamel by bacteria and acids and the importance of saliva as a protector. Discusses the part played by the mouth in more complex activities, such as taste, smell and speech.
Prod-LEVER Dist-PHENIX 1972

Your Move C 22 MIN
16MM FILM, 3/4 OR 1/2 IN VIDEO
Presents myths and taboos which have prevented women from enjoying competitive and recreational sports. Shows a variety of sports activities and encourages girls and women to move and enjoy physical activity.
Prod-NFBC Dist-FI 1976

Your Move C 25 MIN
16MM FILM, 3/4 OR 1/2 IN VIDEO J-C A
Presents a fictional story of a young couple struggling with sex roles in contemporary family life. Focuses on the professional as well as personal issues confronting dual-career couples. Points out the pitfalls that can ensnare marriages when one partner sacrifices a successful career for the sake of the other.
From The New Partnerships Series.
LC NO. 83-706615
Prod-BERKS Dist-UCEMC 1982

Your New Baby (2nd Ed) C 19 MIN
3/4 OR 1/2 INCH VIDEO CASSETTE
Presents details of caring for a new baby during the first few weeks after birth. Describes basic materials which will be needed. Discusses common problems such as diaper rash, fever and feeding problems.
Prod-MEDFAC Dist-MEDFAC 1981

Your New Job C 10 MIN
16MM FILM, 3/4 OR 1/2 IN VIDEO H-C A
Depicts the excitement, nervousness and apprehension of young men and women on the first day of their employment. Follows young employees from the first minute to the conclusion of their first day.
From The Work And You Series.
Prod-SAIF Dist-BARR 1973

Your Next Two Years C 14 MIN
16MM FILM OPTICAL SOUND
Introduces Queensborough Community College by describing the college's academic, athletic and cultural programs. Presents faculty and students who explain what attracted them to the college.
LC NO. 78-701455
Prod-QUEECC Dist-QUEECC Prodn-HF 1977

Your Own Place C 21 MIN
16MM FILM, 3/4 OR 1/2 IN VIDEO H-C
Discusses the responsibilities of maintaining a residence.
From The Making It On Your Own Series.
Prod-BARR Dist-BARR 1979

Your Own Place (Captioned) C 21 MIN
16MM FILM - VIDEO, ALL FORMATS J-C
Shows two young men getting their own apartment and learning about all the responsibilities involved in being on their own.
Prod-BARR Dist-BARR

Your Own Worst Enemy C 26 MIN
3/4 OR 1/2 INCH VIDEO CASSETTE J A
Gives an overview of stress and how it manifests itself in people's lives. Demonstrates ways of dealing with stress.
Prod-SUTHRB Dist-SUTHRB

Your Own Worst Enemy - Stress C 24 MIN
16MM FILM, 3/4 OR 1/2 IN VIDEO H-C A
Documents the stories of individuals who have suffered the debilitating effects of stress and have taken steps against it, including counseling, recreation, religion, acupuncture, biofeedback, meditation and other Eastern spiritual and physical exercises.
Prod-FIVSON Dist-CF 1976

Your Pelvic And Breast Examination C 12 MIN
16MM FILM, 3/4 OR 1/2 IN VIDEO J-C A
Provides a step-by-step description and explanation of the routine pelvic and breast examination. Emphasizes the importance of breast self-examination and of a regular check-up, including a pap smear.
LC NO. 75-704180
Prod-CROMIE Dist-PEREN 1975

Your Pelvic Examination C 7 MIN
3/4 OR 1/2 INCH VIDEO CASSETTE
Describes reason for doing a pelvic examination. Explains the PAP test.
Prod-MEDFAC Dist-MEDFAC 1977

Your Peritoneal Dialysis Therapy C 9 MIN
3/4 OR 1/2 INCH VIDEO CASSETTE
Introduces peritoneal dialysis with overview of normal kidney function and explanation of peritoneal dialysis. Emphasizes patient's participatory role in his health care and demonstrates guidelines he can apply to his own treatment. Focuses attention to scheduling of treatment sessions, care of the peritoneal catheter and diet modifications.
LC NO. 80-730459
Prod-TRAINX Dist-TRAINX

Your Permit To Drive C 14 MIN
16MM FILM OPTICAL SOUND H
Emphasizes the privileges and responsibilities of a driver's license.
Prod-GM Dist-GM Prodn-GM 1969

Your Personal Affairs Officer B 22 MIN
16MM FILM OPTICAL SOUND
Depicts how the personal affairs officer assists servicemen and their families during illness, accident or death, acts as counselor in insurance and retirement planning, assists in oversea transfer preparations, coordinates saving bonds campaigns and briefs new personnel.
LC NO. FIE63-279
Prod-USDD Dist-USNAC 1962

Your Personal Appearance C 10 MIN
16MM FILM, 3/4 OR 1/2 IN VIDEO

Illustrates principles for dressing appropriately for different business situations, for different kinds of jobs and for different cultures. Emphasizes the importance of first impressions and discusses proper fit and dressing economically as well as tastefully.
From The Communications And Selling Program Series.
Prod-NEM Dist-NEM 1977

Your Personal Appearance (Spanish) C 10 MIN
16MM FILM, 3/4 OR 1/2 IN VIDEO
Addresses the impact of the first impression and how to dress to make sure it is the right impression. Illustrates timeless principles of dress.
From The Communications And Selling Program (Spanish) Series.
Prod-NEM Dist-NEM

Your Personal Health History C 6 MIN
3/4 OR 1/2 INCH VIDEO CASSETTE
Emphasizes patient's responsibility to provide complete and accurate information and cites importance and reason for accurate healthy history.
Prod-TRAINX Dist-TRAINX

Your Pet - Forty Million BC B 30 MIN
16MM FILM OPTICAL SOUND H-C A
Traces the evolution of dogs and cats from primitive stages to domestication by man. Views the flesh-eating relatives of household pets.
From The Great Plains Trilogy, 1 Series. In The Beginning - The Primitive Man
Prod-KUONTV Dist-UNEBR 1954

Your Place In The Nuclear Age C 26 MIN
16MM FILM OPTICAL SOUND J-C A
Pictures the professional environment of a career employee in nuclear science or engineering. Covers the three major employment areas--contractors' laboratories of the United States Atomic Energy Commission, commerical nuclear industries and colleges and universities.
From The Careers In Nuclear Science And Nuclear Engineering Series.
LC NO. 74-706770
Prod-USAEC Dist-USERD Prodn-USAPS 1970

Your Place In Time C 21 MIN
16MM FILM OPTICAL SOUND
Offers a profile of Confederation College and Thunder Bay, Ontario.
LC NO. 75-704365
Prod-CONCOL Dist-CONCOL 1974

Your Police (2nd Ed) B 11 MIN
16MM FILM OPTICAL SOUND I-C A
Presents information about the police department and its services to citizens.
Prod-RVIERA Dist-RVIERA 1957

Your Prescription And Generic Drugs C 4 MIN
3/4 OR 1/2 INCH VIDEO CASSETTE
Explains pharmacist's role in selecting drug products, including use of generics and economic considerations.
Prod-TRAINX Dist-TRAINX

Your Price Is Right - Sell It C 30 MIN
16MM FILM, 3/4 OR 1/2 IN VIDEO
Features Joe Batten who uses his tough-minded approach to convince salesmen that their price is right. demonstrates a classic technique salesmen can use to overcome even the most stubborn price resistance.
Prod-DARTNL Dist-DARTNL

Your Protection Against Disease X 8 MIN
16MM FILM, 3/4 OR 1/2 IN VIDEO P
Shows how germs spread disease, how the body has certain means of controlling microorganisms that enter the body and how good health habits prevent disease.
Prod-EBF Dist-EBEC 1964

Your Protection Against Disease (Spanish) C 8 MIN
16MM FILM, 3/4 OR 1/2 IN VIDEO P
Shows some of the ways in which germs spread disease, as well as examples of health habits to prevent disease. Describes how the body controls the microorganisms entering it.
Prod-EBEC Dist-EBEC

Your Renal Diet C 9 MIN
3/4 OR 1/2 INCH VIDEO CASSETTE
Presents the dietary restrictions imposed by kidney failure and considers the complications of not following the special renal diet. Discusses the key nutrients, including protein, sodium, and potassium and emphasizes calorie fluid intakes.
From The Patient Education Programs - Clinical Diet Series.
Prod-POAPLE Dist-POAPLE

Your Right To A Hearing C 10 MIN
16MM FILM, 3/4 OR 1/2 IN VIDEO J-C A
Stresses the debtor's right to a hearing before such creditor actions are taken as repossession and garnishment of wages. Illustrates the hearing of an 18-year-old unable to pay off a purchase. Points out the pressures and confusion of sales techniques, the responsibilities inherent in the new legal status of the 18-year old and the help he is given at the hearing by a young attorney from the neighborhood legal services.
From The Consumer Education Series.
Prod-FLMFR Dist-FLMFR 1972

Your Right To A Hearing (Captioned Version) C 10 MIN
16MM FILM, 3/4 OR 1/2 IN VIDEO J-C A
Stresses the debtor's right to a hearing before such creditor actions are taken as repossession and garnishment of wages. Illustrates the hearing of an 18-year-old unable to pay off a purchase. Points out the pressures and confusion of sales techniques, the responsibilities inherent in the new legal status of the 18-year-old and the help he is given at the hearing by a young attorney from the neighborhood legal services.
From The Consumer Education Series.
Prod-FLMFR Dist-FLMFR 1972

Your Right To A Hearing (Spanish) C 10 MIN
16MM FILM, 3/4 OR 1/2 IN VIDEO J-C A
Presents the case of a 19-year-old boy who is unable to pay off a purchase. Stresses a debtor's right to a hearing before such creditor actions as repossession and garnishment of wages are taken.
Prod-FLMFR Dist-FLMFR 1972

Your Rights And Responsibilities C 17 MIN
16MM FILM - 3/4 IN VIDEO H A
Presents the new or prospective civil service employee with information on employee conduct, grievance procedures, Equal Employment Opportunity complaints, adverse actions, reduction in force (RIF), privacy, political activity, unions and safety.
From The Working For The United States Series.
LC NO. 77-706030
Prod-USCSC Dist-USNAC Prodn-LOUISP 1976

Your Safety Systems C 10 MIN
16MM FILM, 3/4 OR 1/2 IN VIDEO P-J
Presents rules of the road for pedestrians and bicyclists. Shows how youngsters in the course of a typical day use a number of their safety systems to handle correctly the traffic situations they meet.
Prod-DAVP Dist-AIMS 1973

Your School Safety Patrol (2nd Ed) C 17 MIN
16MM FILM OPTICAL SOUND P-I
Presents guidelines for the organization and safe operation of school safety patrol programs designed to protect children as they travel to and from school.
Prod-AAAFTS Dist-AAAFTS 1975

Your Self-Image C 8 MIN
16MM FILM OPTICAL SOUND P-J
Presents James, a small boy, who is continually rejected by others with whom he seeks to play. Shows James opening a closet door and seeing mirror man, a superman-type hero in charge of telling people about self-image. Concludes with James and mirror man flying through the star-lit sky, gazing down upon examples of people succeeding and failing, retaining their self-images through the various situations.
LC NO. 79-701650
Prod-ECI Dist-ECI

Your Self-Images C 30 MIN
3/4 OR 1/2 INCH VIDEO CASSETTE
See series title for descriptive statement.
From The Personal Development And Professional Growth - Mike McCaffrey's Focus Seminar Series.
Prod-DELTAK Dist-DELTAK

Your Share In Space C 30 MIN
3/4 OR 1/2 INCH VIDEO CASSETTE
See series title for descriptive statement.
From The History Of Space Travel Series.
Prod-NASAC Dist-MDCPB

Your Share In Tomorrow C 27 MIN
1 INCH VIDEOTAPE
Presents a historical pageant of America's growth, picturing the role of investors and the New York Stock Exchange. Explains stock transactions, the function of brokers and how everyone can share in America's boundless future.
Prod-ARMCO Dist-MTP

Your Silent Partner C 52 MIN
16MM FILM OPTICAL SOUND I-C A
Creates public awareness of organized crime and its impact on society. Features the chief of the Organized Crime Division of the Michigan Attorney-General's Office answering questions regarding mutual numbers rackets, the effect of the two dollar bet, illicit narcotics, sports and off-track betting, police corruption, loan sharking, infiltration into legitimate businesses and other related topics.
LC NO. 73-702809
Prod-MOCJP Dist-MOCJP 1972

Your Skin Problem - Let's Face It C 30 MIN
3/4 INCH VIDEO CASSETTE
See series title for descriptive statement.
From The Ounce Of Prevention Series.
Prod-CFDC Dist-CFDC

Your Sleep And Rest X 6 MIN
16MM FILM, 3/4 OR 1/2 IN VIDEO P
Uses animation to show important body processes. Emphasizes the need for body cells to replenish their energy and building materials and to eliminate wastes which accumulate. Shows the part played by the circulatory system in this process.
From The Basic Life Science Series.
Prod-EBF Dist-EBEC 1964

Your Sleep And Rest (Spanish) C 6 MIN
16MM FILM, 3/4 OR 1/2 IN VIDEO P
Describes how the body requires sleep and rest. Emphasizes the need for the body cells to replenish their energy and eliminate wastes.
Prod-EBEC Dist-EBEC

Your Softlens Contact Lens Procedures C 9 MIN
3/4 OR 1/2 INCH VIDEO CASSETTE
Provides instructions for application and removal of B and L Softlens with emphasis placed on proper hygiene and care.
Prod-TRAINX Dist-TRAINX

Your Speaking Image - When Women Talk Business--A Series

Presents a program for women who want to build more successful communication skills, and addresses key topics, including successful attitudes and speaking behaviors, improving vocal quality and articulation, choosing language that best serves professional needs and avoiding self-defeating communication habits. Includes a training and self-improvement guide.
Prod-WHATV Dist-DELTAK

Finding Your Public Voice	030 MIN
Interactions That Count	030 MIN
Sounds Of Success	030 MIN
Vocal Quality Counts	030 MIN
Words That Work	030 MIN
Your Vocal Assets	030 MIN

Your Spelling Profile C 7 MIN
3/4 OR 1/2 INCH VIDEO CASSETTE
See series title for descriptive statement.
From The Better Spelling Series.
Prod-TELSTR Dist-DELTAK

Your Stake In The Political Process C 15 MIN
3/4 OR 1/2 INCH VIDEO CASSETTE H
Deals with the ways political events and conditions affect the life of the individual.
From The By The People Series.
Prod-CTI Dist-CTI

Your Stay In The Hospital C 10 MIN
16MM FILM, 3/4 OR 1/2 IN VIDEO
Clarifies the role of the hospital in modern medical care. Discusses reasons for hospital charges, emphasizes the importance of following hospital routine and procedures, and answers many questions asked by patients.
Prod-PRORE Dist-PRORE

Your Stay In The Hospital (Spanish) C 10 MIN
16MM FILM, 3/4 OR 1/2 IN VIDEO
Clarifies the role of the hospital in modern medical care. Discusses reasons for hospital charges, emphasizes the importance of following hospital routine and procedures, and answers many questions asked by patients.
Prod-PRORE Dist-PRORE

Your Sterling Heritage C 27 MIN
16MM FILM OPTICAL SOUND
Tells the story of how Sterling designs are developed, including many of the manufacturing steps. Presents a historical background of many famous Sterling patterns.
Prod-REEBAR Dist-MTP

Your Study Skills - Doing An Assignment C 11 MIN
16MM FILM, 3/4 OR 1/2 IN VIDEO I-J
Presents steps to follow in doing an assignment--make sure you understand, be a self-starter and have a plan.
From The Your Study Skills Series.
Prod-CORF Dist-CORF 1970

Your Study Skills - How To Use A Textbook C 14 MIN
16MM FILM, 3/4 OR 1/2 IN VIDEO I-J
Demonstrates the effective use of a table of contents, a glossary, illustrations and other special clues in textbooks when previewing a book, reading for details and reviewing.
From The Your Study Skills Series.
Prod-CORF Dist-CORF 1970

Your Study Skills - Taking Notes From Reading C 11 MIN
16MM FILM, 3/4 OR 1/2 IN VIDEO I-J
Uses fast paced examples to show how notes act as a record when a book is not available, help you read, organize ideas and remember what you've read.
From The Your Study Skills Series.
Prod-CORF Dist-CORF 1970

Your Study Skills - Taking Tests C 11 MIN
16MM FILM, 3/4 OR 1/2 IN VIDEO I-J
Introduces basic methods for approaching essay and objective tests with an episode in which a newspaper columnist helps students to estimate test time, stick to the point, follow instructions and deal with multiple choice, essay and true-false questions.
Prod-CORF Dist-CORF 1977

Your Study Skills - Using Reference Materials C 14 MIN
16MM FILM, 3/4 OR 1/2 IN VIDEO I-J
Introduces many types of reference materials, shows how to find information in them, and presents detailed information on the use of dictionaries, encyclopedias and almanacs.
From The Your Study Skills Series.
Prod-CORF Dist-CORF 1970

Your Study Skills--A Series
16MM FILM, 3/4 OR 1/2 IN VIDEO I-J
Presents steps in developing effective study skills. Covers the use of textbooks, reference materials and pictures and discusses how to do an assignment, take notes from reading and review for and take tests.
Prod-CORF Dist-CORF

Your Study Skills - Doing An Assignment	11 MIN
Your Study Skills - How To Use A Textbook	14 MIN
Your Study Skills - Learning From Pictures	14 MIN
Your Study Skills - Reviewing For A Test	11 MIN
Your Study Skills - Taking Notes From Reading	11 MIN
Your Study Skills - Taking Tests	11 MIN
Your Study Skills - Using Reference Materials	14 MIN

Your Teeth X 6 MIN
16MM FILM, 3/4 OR 1/2 IN VIDEO P
Uses animation to show how the first teeth form and are replaced by larger, permanent teeth. Shows the way decay can start, and stresses the importance of good dental habits and good food.
Prod-EBF Dist-EBEC 1964

Your Teeth (Spanish) C 6 MIN
16MM FILM, 3/4 OR 1/2 IN VIDEO P
Points out how first teeth are formed, how teeth serve different purposes, how decay starts and how to protect teeth.
Prod-EBEC Dist-EBEC

Your Town C 25 MIN
16MM FILM, 3/4 OR 1/2 IN VIDEO I-C A
Describes how a small town in New Hampshire is divided in the townspeoples' opinions as to whether to allow an electronics plant to locate in their town or to preserve the rural quality of their lives.
LC NO. 84-706562
Prod-CINEWO Dist-PHENIX 1984

Your Turn In The Box C 17 MIN
16MM FILM, 3/4 OR 1/2 IN VIDEO J-C A
Features baseball player Hank Aaron demonstrating the proper methods for hitting a baseball. Suggests the need for discipline and the desire to succeed.
Prod-LRDKNG Dist-MCFI 1971

Your Turn On The Court, Film 1 - The Serve And Volley C 16 MIN
16MM FILM, 3/4 OR 1/2 IN VIDEO J-C A
Presents Ken Stuart demonstrating the fundamentals of the serve and volley in tennis.
Prod-LRDKNG Dist-MCFI 1978

Your Turn On The Court, Film 2 - The Ground Strokes C 22 MIN
16MM FILM, 3/4 OR 1/2 IN VIDEO J-C A
Demonstrates the fundamentals of the tennis forehand and backhand ground strokes, including proper grips, footwork, racquet position, swing, ball contact and follow through.
Prod-LRDKNG Dist-MCFI 1978

Your Turn, My Turn (French) C 101 MIN
16MM FILM OPTICAL SOUND
Focuses on two veterans of unhappy marriages who pursue an affair in the face of hostile children, unpleasant spouses, and troublesome new moralities. Directed by Francois Leterrier. With English subtitles.
Prod-UNKNWN Dist-NYFLMS 1978

Your Two Cents Worth C 11 MIN
16MM FILM OPTICAL SOUND J-C A
Shows highlights of the first decade of man in space, which was financed by just two cents out of every tax dollar. Enumerates some of the resulting benefits to mankind and describes our future goals in space.
Prod-NAA Dist-RCKWL

Your Ulcer Diet C 9 MIN
3/4 OR 1/2 INCH VIDEO CASSETTE
Discusses an ulcer diet intended for the patient who needs to be treated for pectic ulcer disease.
From The Patient Education Programs - Clinical Diet Series.
Prod-POAPLE Dist-POAPLE

Your Union C 25 MIN
16MM FILM OPTICAL SOUND
Educates new and current members of the largest local group in the painters union on how to protect their job security and improve their standard of living. Explains how the union is administered, the structure of the union, the apprenticeship program and the benefits which evolve from union membership.
Prod-PDP Dist-AFLCIO 1964

Your Upper Body C 10 MIN
2 INCH VIDEOTAPE
See series title for descriptive statement.
From The Janaki Series.
Prod-WGBHTV Dist-PUBTEL

Your Vision, Your Life C 25 MIN
16MM FILM OPTICAL SOUND
Presents the full scope of optometric care with dramatic vignettes ranging from how the profession serves the child with a vision problem that interferes with learning to the older person with a potentially blinding disease.
Prod-AOA Dist-MTP 1982

Your Vocal Assets C 30 MIN
3/4 OR 1/2 INCH VIDEO CASSETTE
See series title for descriptive statement.
From The Your Speaking Image - When Women Talk Business Series.
Prod-WHATV Dist-DELTAK

Your Voice And Its Speech Helpers C 15 MIN
16MM FILM OPTICAL SOUND J-C
Explains the uses of the vocal cords and its speech helpers, tongue, mouth, teeth, hard and soft palate, lips and nasal cavity. Shows several experiments that students can do to further understand their voice and its speech helpers.
LC NO. 70-712444
Prod-ACA Dist-ACA 1970

Your Voice Is A Gift B 20 MIN
2 INCH VIDEOTAPE P
Stresses the importance of good voice quality in communicating. (Broadcast quality)
From The Language Lane Series. Lesson 2
Prod-CVETVC Dist-GPITVL Prodn-WCVETV

Your Voice Speaks C 15 MIN
2 INCH VIDEOTAPE P
Provides an enrichment program in the communitive arts area by using vocal expressions.
From The Word Magic (2nd Ed) Series.
Prod-CVETVC Dist-GPITVL

Your Voice, Your Eyes, Your Story C 15 MIN
2 INCH VIDEOTAPE P
Provides an enrichment program in the communitive arts area through oral reading and listening.
From The Word Magic (2nd Ed) Series.
Prod-CVETVC Dist-GPITVL

Your Vote Counts - State And Local Government C
3/4 OR 1/2 INCH VIDEO CASSETTE H
Outlines the structures and functions of state, county and city government. Discusses urban and suburban problems, and the facts and values of real local political disputes.
Prod-GA Dist-GA

Your Way Or Mine C 17 MIN
16MM FILM, 3/4 OR 1/2 IN VIDEO
Dramatizes a grievance incident, from the employee's point of view as well as from the supervisor's point of view.
Prod-USDL Dist-USNAC 1981

Your Way Out C 17 MIN
16MM FILM, 3/4 OR 1/2 IN VIDEO
Shows when, where and how to use the fire shelter tent for forest firefighters in danger of being surrounded or overtaken by fire.
LC NO. 82-706236
Prod-USDA Dist-USNAC 1967

Your Weekly Weaver—A Series

Demonstrates a variety of looms and weaves for making tapestries, scarves, shawls, and fabric for upholstery and pillows.
Prod-GAEDTN Dist-PUBTEL

Ancient Art Of Tablet Weaving (Also Called 029 MIN
Frame Looms And How To Build, Buy Or Find 029 MIN
Introduction To A Small Lap Loom Called The 029 MIN
Introduction To The Four-Harness Loom, An - 029 MIN
Rigid Heddle Looms And How To Warp Them For 029 MIN
Versatility And The Variety Of Weaves 029 MIN

Your Weight Reduction Diet C 12 MIN
3/4 OR 1/2 INCH VIDEO CASSETTE
Discusses how a weight reduction diet reduces the health risks of obesity by urging the overweight patient to become involved in a comprehensive program, including calorie counting, behavior modification, and increased physical activity.
From The Patient Education Programs - Clinical Diet Series.
Prod-POAPLE Dist-POAPLE

Your Will And Estate C 25 MIN
3/4 OR 1/2 INCH VIDEO CASSETTE H-C A
Focuses on estate planning. Covers what should be included in a will and who should be chosen as executors and guardians. Includes trust funds and revisions.
From The Money Smart - A Guide To Personal Finance Series.
Prod-SOMFIL Dist-BCNFL 1985

Yours For A Song C 22 MIN
16MM FILM OPTICAL SOUND P-H
Shows a backyard bird sanctuary established to attract migrating and resident birds throughout the year. Explains that birds are attracted to yards and gardens if they are provided with food, water and shelter. Includes views of 24 different species of birds.
Prod-WILCOX Dist-FENWCK 1954

Yours Truly C 15 MIN
3/4 OR 1/2 INCH VIDEO CASSETTE P
Employs a magician named Amazing Alexander and his assistants to explore letter writing.
From The Magic Shop Series. No. 12
LC NO. 83-706157
Prod-CVETVC Dist-GPITVL Prodn-WCVETV 1982

Yours Truly, Andrea G Stern C 38 MIN
16MM FILM, 3/4 OR 1/2 IN VIDEO J-C A
Dramatizes some common problems of single-parent families in a story about the conflicts that arise between a young girl, her mother and her mother's live-in lover.
Prod-SEIDS Dist-PHENIX 1979

Yours, Mine And Ours X 11 MIN
16MM FILM, 3/4 OR 1/2 IN VIDEO P
Shows seven episodes at school in which the problems of ownership and responsibility are depicted. At the end of each episode the film may be stopped and the class asked to formulate solutions to the situation.
Prod-EH Dist-EBEC 1967

Youth And Music In Detroit C 24 MIN
16MM FILM OPTICAL SOUND H-C A
Depicts the music department activities of a Detroit high school. Various choral, instrumental and dance groups are shown.
Prod-WSU Dist-WSU 1956

Youth And The Man Of Property B 7 MIN
3/4 INCH VIDEO CASSETTE
Documents a police call to intervene between a suburban couple and a youth who has harrassed them.
From The Pittsburgh Police Series.
Prod-DOCEDR Dist-DOCEDR Prodn-MSHLLJ

Youth Communications C 36 MIN
16MM FILM OPTICAL SOUND
Uses illustrations from the pre-1970 era to emphasize the more important general youth communications patterns that continue to this day. Developed to assist in understanding the drug problem and to close the understanding gap that exists between adults and today's youthful media audience.
LC NO. 74-705984
Prod-USDD Dist-USNAC 1969

Youth Drug Scene, The C 30 MIN
16MM FILM OPTICAL SOUND J-H
Shows that Mark has overcome his three year addiction to drugs because he has found a personal relationship with Jesus Christ. Discusses the risks and dangers of drug experimentation.
Prod-FAMF Dist-FAMF

Youth Gives A Damn C 25 MIN
3/4 OR 1/2 INCH VIDEO CASSETTE
Tells about VD pollution, sex education, drugs, filmed at YGAD camp, which was simultaneously a mountain retreat, health learn-in, weekend rap session, and if not quite a bridge, at least a rope ladder across that so- called chasm, the 'generation gap'.
Prod-TRAINX Dist-TRAINX

Youth Lifeskills—A Series

Addresses the myriad of problems confronting today's adolescents. Concentrates on pertinent issues which determine the development of a healthy individual.
Prod-SCCL Dist-HMDI

Career Planning 016 MIN
Making It Young 028 MIN
Productivity And Performance By Alex K 024 MIN
Streetproofing 028 MIN
Understanding Adolescence 022 MIN
Youth Stress 024 MIN

Youth Sports - Is Winning Everything C 28 MIN
16MM FILM OPTICAL SOUND A
Explains that many sports coaches ignore a child's emotional needs and physical limitations, often disregarding the recreational value of sports.
LC NO. 80-701873
Prod-COXBAR Dist-COXBAR 1980

Youth Stress C 24 MIN
16MM FILM - VIDEO, ALL FORMATS
Presents experts in the field of adolescent psychology discussing insights into stress concepts. Hosted by Don Francks.
From The Youth Lifeskills Series.
Prod-SCCL Dist-PEREN

Youth Terror - The View From Behind The Gun C 48 MIN
16MM FILM, 3/4 OR 1/2 IN VIDEO J-C A
Views teenage crime.
Prod-ABCTV Dist-MGHT 1978

Youth Terror - The View From Behind The Gun, Pt 1 C 29 MIN
16MM FILM, 3/4 OR 1/2 IN VIDEO J-C A
Offers a view of teenage crime.
Prod-ABCTV Dist-MGHT 1978

Youth Terror - The View From Behind The Gun, Pt 2 C 19 MIN
16MM FILM, 3/4 OR 1/2 IN VIDEO J-C A
Offers a view of teenage crime.
Prod-ABCTV Dist-MGHT 1978

Youth To Maturity C 29 MIN
16MM FILM, 3/4 OR 1/2 IN VIDEO J-C A
Portrays the evolution of the United States from a small, weak nation into a world power. Covers Admiral Perry's trip to Japan, Civil War diplomacy, the Spanish-American War, the Philippines expedition, the construction of the Panama Canal and the U S role as international peacemaker in the Portsmouth negotiations, the Algeciras Conference and the two Hague Conferences.
From The History Of U S Foreign Relations Series.
Prod-USDS Dist-MTI 1972

Youth Who Wanted To Shiver, The C 9 MIN
16MM FILM, 3/4 OR 1/2 IN VIDEO K-I
Presents an animated adaptation of the classic fairy tale by the Brothers Grimm, about a young boy who sets out into the world to learn how to fear and shiver.
From The Grimm's Fairy Tales Series.
Prod-BOSUST Dist-CF 1978

Youth Who Wanted To Shiver, The (Spanish) C 9 MIN
16MM FILM, 3/4 OR 1/2 IN VIDEO P-J
Recounts how the fearless Jack learns to shiver.
From The Grimm's Fairy Tale (Spanish) Series.
Prod-BOSUST Dist-CF

Youth, Maturity, Old Age, Death C 8 MIN
16MM FILM, 3/4 OR 1/2 IN VIDEO J-C
Features Marcel Marceau presenting symbolically the cycle of life.
From The Humanities - The Performing Arts, Art Of Silence, Pantomimes With Marcel Marceau Series.
Prod-EBEC Dist-EBEC 1975

Youth's Finest Hour C 20 MIN
16MM FILM OPTICAL SOUND
Shows the opportunities of a young athlete to learn and then apply the 'LANGUAGE OF VICTORY.'
Prod-FELLCA Dist-FELLCA

Youthful David, The C 45 MIN
2 INCH VIDEOTAPE
See series title for descriptive statement.
From The Humanities Series. Unit I - Persons, Places And Events
Prod-WTTWTV Dist-GPITVL

Yoyo Man C 12 MIN
16MM FILM - 3/4 IN VIDEO
Presents Nemo Concepcion, Duncan Yoyo demonstrator, explaining his philosophy and describing his career which began during the Great Depression. Demonstrates various yoyo tricks.
Prod-DOCEDR Dist-DOCEDR 1978

Yrs Truly C 26 MIN
16MM FILM OPTICAL SOUND
Presents the value of keeping schools open all year. Features Senator Charles Percy who describes the need and outlines the values inherent in this way of looking to the future educational system. Interviews administrators and teachers in three areas of the United States where schools have been operating on a year-round basis - Prince William County Schools in Virginia, the San Diego School District and the Valley View School District in Romeoville, Illinois.
LC NO. 73-702403
Prod-GOLDSH Dist-GOLDSH 1973

Yucatan Ruins C 15 MIN
16MM FILM OPTICAL SOUND J-C A
Pictures Merida, Capital of Yucatan, and Chichen-Itza, America's Egypt. Shows fields where the game Pelota was played, the observatory, pyramids and the Temple.
Prod-BARONA Dist-AVED 1957

Yucatec Maya, The - A Case Study In Marriage C 30 MIN
3/4 INCH VIDEO CASSETTE C A
Explores characteristics of an extended family in an agricultural society. Describes pressures on the traditional extended family to change.
From The Faces Of Culture - Studies In Cultural Anthropology Series. Lesson 10
Prod-COAST Dist-CDTEL Prodn-HRAW

Yugoslav Farm Family C 12 MIN
16MM FILM OPTICAL SOUND P-H
Pictures farmers of the Dalmation Coast, who must struggle with a harsh land and an oppressive government. No narration is used, but a musical score based on Yugoslav folk melodies is provided.
From The How We Live Series.
LC NO. FIA66-1855
Prod-IFF Dist-IFF 1964

Yugoslav, Pt 1 C 29 MIN
2 INCH VIDEOTAPE
See series title for descriptive statement.
From The Grand Master Chess Series.
Prod-KQEDTV Dist-PUBTEL

Yugoslav, Pt 2 C 29 MIN
2 INCH VIDEOTAPE
See series title for descriptive statement.
From The Grand Master Chess Series.
Prod-KQEDTV Dist-PUBTEL

Yugoslavia C 20 MIN
16MM FILM OPTICAL SOUND I-C A
Highlights the various groups of people who live in Yugoslavia. Depicts how shy, isolated cultures have survived invasion in fortified mountain cities.
Prod-WIANCK Dist-AVED 1963

Yugoslavia C 28 MIN
16MM FILM OPTICAL SOUND C A
Tours Yugoslavia's historic and scenic areas, including views of the Adriatic coast, the Roman Coliseum at Pula, the inland parks and the Dubrovnik Music FestiVal.
LC NO. 72-702166
Prod-MCDO Dist-MCDO 1972

Yugoslavia C 18 MIN
16MM FILM, 3/4 OR 1/2 IN VIDEO I
Presents a girl in the city of Bor in southern Yugoslavia, where the parents work in a huge copper manufacturing plant. Features a class trip and a visit to her grandparents' farm revealing a lot about her life and her country.
From The Families Of The World Series.
Prod-NGS Dist-NGS

Yugoslavia C 27 MIN
16MM FILM, 3/4 OR 1/2 IN VIDEO J-C A
Prod-IFF Dist-IFF 1962

Yugoslavia C 28 MIN
3/4 INCH VIDEOTAPE
Features interviews with several representatives from Yugoslavia. Includes a film on the Sava Center in Belgrade and on the country of Yugoslavia. Hosted by Marilyn Perry.
From The Marilyn's Manhatten Series.
Prod-PERRYM Dist-PERRYM

Yugoslavia - Land Of Contrasts C 27 MIN
16MM FILM OPTICAL SOUND J-C A
Depicts 26 cities and towns in Yugoslavia and points out the contrasts in people, traditions, customs, history, art and architecture of each.
LC NO. FIA66-1683
Prod-BAILYL Dist-AVED 1965

Yugoslavia - Life After Tito C 15 MIN
3/4 OR 1/2 INCH VIDEO CASSETTE H-C A
Discusses the post-Tito era in Yugoslavia, focusing on politics, people, economy and life style.
Prod-UPI Dist-JOU

Yugoslavian Coastline C 14 MIN
16MM FILM, 3/4 OR 1/2 IN VIDEO P-C
Describes life in the towns along the Adriatic Sea. Contrasts the old face of the city with narrow streets, stone houses and market places with produce and fish displayed with a modernized area which has a fish-canning factory and bauxite mine.
From The Man And His World Series.
Prod-PMI Dist-FI 1969

Yukon Jake B 21 MIN
16MM FILM SILENT
Presents a comedy about the complications that arise when Sheriff Cylone Bill tries to capture Yukon jake.
LC NO. 70-713142
Prod-SENN Dist-BHAWK 1960

Yukon Passage C 59 MIN
16MM FILM, 3/4 OR 1/2 IN VIDEO
Presents a documentary about four young men who retrace the passage of oldtime prospectors to the gold-rich Klondike during the period 1897-1898.
LC NO. 80-706402
Prod-NGS Dist-NGS 1977

Yukon Territory, The C 15 MIN
16MM FILM, 3/4 OR 1/2 IN VIDEO I-H A
Presents different ecological regions of the Yukon Territory, from the ice fields to the vast, treeless plains, and describes the animals native to each area.
From The Natural Environment Series.
Prod-WILFGP Dist-JOU 1977

Yule Rules C 15 MIN
16MM FILM OPTICAL SOUND C
Parodies safety films by looking at a typical suburban family and the many risks involved in trying to enjoy a typical suburban Christmas. Explores the hazards of sending Christmas cards, cuddling under the mistletoe, giving gifts and eating Christmas dinner.
LC NO. 81-700484
Prod-NYUFL Dist-RWLNSJ 1981

Yuletide Reflections - Vietnam C 16 MIN
16MM FILM OPTICAL SOUND
Describes impressions of the chief of Navy chaplains concerning the war in Vietnam.
LC NO. 74-706350
Prod-USN Dist-USNAC 1968

Yulya's Diary C 60 MIN
16MM FILM OPTICAL SOUND
Presents a partially-dramatized documentary which tells the story of the poet Yulya Voznesenskaya and the artists, writers and musicians whose work is unofficial and unrecognized in the Soviet Union.
From The World Series.
LC NO. 80-700315
Prod-WGBHTV Dist-KINGFT 1980

Yulya's Diary C 60 MIN
3/4 OR 1/2 INCH VIDEO CASSETTE
Presents a partially-dramatized documentary which tells the story of the poet Yulya Voznesenskaya and the artists, writers and musicians whose work is unofficial and unrecognized in the Soviet Union.
From The World Series.
Prod-WGBHTV Dist-PBS 1980

Yuri Schmidt Show C 30 MIN
3/4 OR 1/2 INCH VIDEO CASSETTE
Presents basically crazy cooks Larry Bly and Laban Johnson who offer recipes, cooking and shopping tips.
From The Cookin' Cheap Series.
Prod-WBRATV Dist-MDCPB

Z

Z Is For Zoo C 8 MIN
16MM FILM, 3/4 OR 1/2 IN VIDEO K-P
Describes various activities performed by animals in a zoo and spells out the action words.
From The Starting To Read Series.
Prod-ACI Dist-AIMS 1970

Z Sound, The C 15 MIN
3/4 INCH VIDEO CASSETTE P
Examines the proper production of the z sound and discusses the various ways the z sound is spelled.
From The New Talking Shop Series.
Prod-BSPTV Dist-GPITVL 1978

Z-Transform Properties C 56 MIN
3/4 OR 1/2 INCH VIDEO CASSETTE PRO
See series title for descriptive statement.
From The Digital Signal Processing Series.
Prod-GPCV Dist-GPCV

Z-Transform Properties C 56 MIN
3/4 OR 1/2 INCH VIDEO CASSETTE
See series title for descriptive statement.
From The Digital Signal Processing - An Introduction Series.
Prod-MIOT Dist-MIOT

Z-Transform, The C 51 MIN
3/4 OR 1/2 INCH VIDEO CASSETTE PRO
See series title for descriptive statement.
From The Digital Signal Processing Series.
Prod-GPCV Dist-GPCV

Z-Transform, The C 51 MIN
3/4 OR 1/2 INCH VIDEO CASSETTE
Discusses the relationship between the Fourier transform and the z-transform, region of convergence for z-transforms and the relationship among region of convergence, causality and stability.
From The Digital Signal Processing - An Introduction Series.
Prod-MIOT Dist-MIOT

Z, N And M C 15 MIN
3/4 INCH VIDEO CASSETTE P
From The Writing Time Series.
Prod-WHROTV Dist-GPITVL

Zaa, The Little White Camel C 25 MIN
16MM FILM OPTICAL SOUND
Explains the escape of Zaa, a baby camel, from a camel merchant, reflecting the terrain of an arid land and the daily living habits of the Islamic people.
Prod-BELLNY Dist-RADIM

Zack And The Magic Factory C 50 MIN
16MM FILM, 3/4 OR 1/2 IN VIDEO I
Reveals that when Zack visits his eccentric aunt one summer, he discovers her magic factory is deeply in debt and in danger of take-over by her arch-enemy. Shows Zack becoming a hero when he stages a magic show to raise money to save the factory.
Prod-ABCLR Dist-MTI 1983

Zaire - Health Care C 30 MIN
3/4 OR 1/2 INCH VIDEO CASSETTE H-C A
Examines Zaire's great need for basic programs that will promote the health and nutrition of its people, especially rural children.
From The Life In The Developing World Series. Pt 3
LC NO. 83-706077
Prod-UNICEF Dist-GPITVL Prodn-NHK 1982

Zale Dalen C
3/4 OR 1/2 INCH VIDEO CASSETTE
Portrays Zale Dalen, British Columbian filmmaker with interviews and film clips.
From The Filmmakers' Showcase Series.
Prod-CANFDW Dist-CANFDW

Zalman P Usiskin C
3/4 OR 1/2 INCH VIDEO CASSETTE
Focuses on the way mathematics can be used in real situations. Illustrates ways in which computational skills and other basic skills can be used in a wide range of everyday situations.
From The Third R - Teaching Basic Mathematics Skills Series.
Prod-EDCPUB Dist-EDCPUB

Zambezi Express, The C 60 MIN
16MM FILM, 3/4 OR 1/2 IN VIDEO J-H A
Travels with historian Michael Woods aboard the Blue Train, the most luxurious train in the world, from Cape Town, South Africa to Victoria Falls. Traverses the wilderness area of the Karoo, the diamond fields of Kimberly and the gold city of Johannesberg.
Prod-BBCTV Dist-FI 1981

Zambia C 28 MIN
3/4 INCH VIDEOTAPE
Interviews Mr. Muuka L M Muchimba, tourist officer of Zambia for North America. Presents film clips on the Zambia National Parks, Victoria Falls and safaris.
From The International Byline Series.
Prod-PERRYM Dist-PERRYM

Zambia C 30 MIN
3/4 INCH VIDEO CASSETTE I-J
Shows the life of the Mapili family in Zambia.
From The Families Of The World Series.
Prod-UNICEF Dist-GPITVL 1974

Zambia (Marilyn's Manhattan) C 28 MIN
3/4 INCH VIDEOTAPE
Interviews Ambassador Gwendoline Chomba Konie. Includes a film clip on Zambia. Hosted by Marilyn Perry.
From The Marilyn's Manhatten Series.
Prod-PERRYM Dist-PERRYM

Zambia/Namibia C 28 MIN
3/4 INCH VIDEOTAPE
Interviews Ambassador Paul Lusaka, permanent representative of Zambia to the United Nations and president of the United Nations Council for Namibia. Includes a film clip. Hosted by Marilyn Perry.
From The International Byline Series.
Prod-PERRYM Dist-PERRYM

Zany Fiancee, The C 11 MIN
16MM FILM, 3/4 OR 1/2 IN VIDEO I-C
Chronicles the ceaseless misfortunes of a would-be bridegroom who experiences a change of heart concerning his bad luck when he observes that his misadventures may have prevented him from getting in even deeper trouble.
Prod-PHENIX Dist-PHENIX 1981

Zap C 10 MIN
16MM FILM OPTICAL SOUND
Tells the story of how a young hero in a park loses his girl, but wins her back when he finds a shrinking machine that falls out of a flying saucer.
LC NO. 77-702309
Prod-LBRD Dist-LBRD 1975

Zap - Static Awareness C 20 MIN
16MM FILM, 3/4 OR 1/2 IN VIDEO
Discusses the nature and generation of static electricity and the hazard which it presents to electronic equipment. Shows how an electrostatic charge acccumulates on people and nonconducting materials. Demonstrates precautions for minimizing this hazard.
LC NO. 81-706341
Prod-USN Dist-USNAC 1978

Zarabanda—A Series
16MM FILM, 3/4 OR 1/2 IN VIDEO
A Spanish language series. Uses the adventures of a young Spanish man contending with romance, jobs, strange places and people in order to present lessons in beginning conversational Spanish. Features 25 lessons, each 25 minutes in length.
LC NO. 79-707912
Prod-BBCTV Dist-FI

Zarethan C 30 MIN
16MM FILM OPTICAL SOUND I-C A
Presents the ancient city of Zarethan, inhabited as early as 3000

B C during the early Bronze Age. Takes great step back into the exploration of mankind's past.
From The Human Dimension Series.
Prod-GRACUR Dist-GRACUR

Zax, The C 5 MIN
16MM FILM, 3/4 OR 1/2 IN VIDEO
Deals with stubbornness and the inability to change. Presents an animated cartoon about the North-going zax and the South-going zax, who meet and quarrel with one another on their journeys, each stubbornly refusing to let the other pass.
From The Dr Seuss On The Loose Series.
Prod-CBSTV Dist-PHENIX Prodn-DEPFRE 1974

Zayre Credit Story, The C 12 MIN
16MM FILM OPTICAL SOUND
Discusses the success of private enterprise in terms of the availability of consumer goods and services on credit. Encourages Zayre employees to promote the use of Zayre credit cards.
LC NO. 74-702668
Prod-ZAYRE Dist-ZAYRE Prodn-INF 1969

Zazie (French) C 85 MIN
16MM FILM OPTICAL SOUND
Tells of Zazie, a foul-mouthed cynic, age 11, who comes to Paris for a weekend with her uncle, a female impersonator. Points out that nobody is quite like what they seem to be.
Prod-NYFLMS Dist-NYFLMS 1960

Zbigniew In Love C 4 MIN
16MM FILM OPTICAL SOUND H-C A
Uses animation and experimental techniques to tell the story of Zbigniew, who enjoys creating shadow figures. Shows how he becomes absorbed in the fantasy of a shapely female who assumes a reality for him, only to turn him into a shadowy substance that disappears.
LC NO. 80-700720
Prod-LIBBYE Dist-CFS 1979

Zea C 6 MIN
16MM FILM, 3/4 OR 1/2 IN VIDEO
Zeros in on a blimp-shaped object whose orange-rust skin becomes coated with a clear fluid. Scans around the increasingly changing pellet until the kernel bursts open in a cloud of white.
LC NO. 82-706962
Prod-NFBC Dist-NFBC 1981

Zebra C 10 MIN
16MM FILM, 3/4 OR 1/2 IN VIDEO I-H
Describes the physical characteristics of the zebra, and tells of its mode of life. Shows how zebras wander in large herds, constantly in search of food and water and alert to predatory animals, especially the lion. Explains how they rely on birds for warnings of danger.
From The Silent Safari Series.
Prod-EBEC Dist-EBEC 1972

Zebra Wings—A Series
I
Presents a creative writing course. Includes instruction in various styles of writing, including humor, fiction, persuasive writing, folk tales, autobiography, drama and poetry.
Prod-NITC Dist-AITECH Prodn-MAETEL 1975

Advertising	15 MIN
Humor I	15 MIN
Humor II	15 MIN
Journal	15 MIN
Myths And Fables	15 MIN
Newspaper Writing	15 MIN
Persuasive Writing	15 MIN
Plays	15 MIN
Poetry I	15 MIN
Poetry II	15 MIN
Script Writing	15 MIN
Short Story I	15 MIN
Short Story II	15 MIN
Words, Words, Words	15 MIN
Writer's Tools	15 MIN

Zebras C 10 MIN
16MM FILM, 3/4 OR 1/2 IN VIDEO K-I
Uses animation to tell the story of two zebras who misplace one of their stripes and prance through various adventures before they recover it.
Prod-CHOICE Dist-TEXFLM 1973

Zeca C 19 MIN
16MM FILM, 3/4 OR 1/2 IN VIDEO H-C A
Traces the professional, social and family life of Zeca, a cowherder from the northeast of Brazil.
Prod-SLUIZR Dist-PHENIX 1974

Zen And Now C 14 MIN
16MM FILM, 3/4 OR 1/2 IN VIDEO H-C
Presents meditation as a counter to the compulsion to be constantly active. Features Alan Watts.
Prod-HP Dist-HP 1969

Zen Archer, The C 11 MIN
3/4 INCH VIDEO CASSETTE H A
Captures a Japanese woman's exercise in the art of Zen archery. Shows her executing the ordered, ancient procedures utilized by Samurai warriors. Contrasts the silence surrounding the ceremonial practice with the woman's journey home, which takes her through the clamor of traffic and hurrying commuters, past video arcades and the sounds of rock music. Without narration.
Prod-MOBIUS Dist-MOBIUS 1982

Zen Master C 3 MIN
16MM FILM OPTICAL SOUND J-C A
Shows Zen Buddhist master Roshi Joshu Sasaki doing everyday chores and conducting Zen meditation.
LC NO. 79-700701
Prod-IA Dist-IA 1966

Zen Mountain Center C 45 MIN
2 INCH VIDEOTAPE
Explores Zen life and teaching at the Tassajara Zen monastery. Attempts to suggest the new range of sensations and quality at participation of the Zen mountain center, the only Zen monastery in America.
Prod-KQEDTV Dist-PUBTEL

Zenana, A - Scenes And Recollections C 36 MIN
3/4 INCH VIDEO CASSETTE
Unfolds, through songs, dances and memories of palace women, life in the most secluded section of the palace at Dhrangadra in northern India. Filmed by Roger Sandall and Jayasinhji Jhala.
Prod-DOCEDR Dist-DOCEDR

Zerda's Children C 53 MIN
16MM FILM, 3/4 OR 1/2 IN VIDEO H-C A
Focuses on the life of Sixto Ramon Zerda, a modern-day peasant in Argentina. Shows how his serfdom to his employer, his lack of protected rights, his poverty and his hope for his children are common to the majority of rural families living in South America, Asia and Africa.
Prod-PRELJ Dist-PHENIX 1978

Zero - Something For Nothing C 8 MIN
3/4 INCH VIDEO CASSETTE P
Shows how a 'mathemagician' demonstrates the property of zero in the operations of addition and multiplication.
Prod-DAVFMS Dist-GA

Zero Defects - Right The First Time C 22 MIN
16MM FILM - 3/4 IN VIDEO
Describes the purpose of the zero defects program emphasizing responsibility of each individual to do his job right the first time. Depicts how errors result from inadequare equipment and wrong attitudes.
Prod-USAF Dist-USNAC 1972

Zero Defects - The Personal Commitment To Economy, Readiness And Effectiveness B 32 MIN
16MM FILM OPTICAL SOUND
Explains the zero defects program and relates its benefits to national defense, industrial cooperation, improved production and worker motivation.
LC NO. 74-706351
Prod-USAF Dist-USNAC 1965

Zero Defects For The Air Force B 28 MIN
16MM FILM OPTICAL SOUND
Presents a panel discussion explaining the value of the zero defects program to the Air Force and contractor personnel. Stresses perfection in the production of complex weapon systems.
LC NO. 75-703737
Prod-USAF Dist-USNAC 1965

Zero Draft B 14 MIN
16MM FILM, 3/4 OR 1/2 IN VIDEO I-C A
Examines military conscription in the United States from the Civil War to the modern volunteer army.
From The Screen News Digest Series. Vol 15, Issue 8
Prod-HEARST Dist-HEARST 1973

Zero For Conduct (The Dormitory Revolt) B 10 MIN
16MM FILM OPTICAL SOUND J-C A
Presents an excerpt from the 1959 motion picture Zero For Conduct. Depicts the revolt in the dormitory, including the famed pillow fight. Directed by Jean Vigo.
From The Film Study Extracts Series.
Prod-UNKNWN Dist-FI

Zero G C 50 MIN
16MM FILM, 3/4 OR 1/2 IN VIDEO C A
Shows how Skylab astronauts have coped with life in space. Points out that Skylab's medical experiments have discovered disappearing body fluids, dissolving bones, deformed blood cells, and hormone imbalance.
Prod-BBCTV Dist-FI 1981

Zero Hour C 20 MIN
16MM FILM, 3/4 OR 1/2 IN VIDEO I-C
Presents a story about a girl and her friends who play a game called 'Invasion.' Shows how the girl's mother becomes alarmed when she discovers that the invasion is to come from outer space, and she begins to wonder what will happen at zero hour.
Prod-WILETS Dist-BARR 1978

Zero In C 10 MIN
16MM FILM OPTICAL SOUND
Strives to motivate workers toward plant and factory safety by showing a series of fabricated hazards. Gives a review of normal plant safety methods. Shows how the individual workers can prevent accidents by paying attention to everyday hazards.
LC NO. 72-701068
Prod-NSC Dist-NSC 1971

Zero In On Safety C 10 MIN
16MM FILM OPTICAL SOUND
Dramatizes major causes of industrial accidents and gives an organized plan to be followed by companies or departments in order to improve safety records. Features Howard W Pyle, President of the National Safety Council.
LC NO. 72-711599
Prod-NSC Dist-NSC 1970

Zero Point In Measuring C 30 MIN
3/4 OR 1/2 INCH VIDEO CASSETTE
See series title for descriptive statement.
From The Infinity Factory Series.
Prod-EDFCEN Dist-MDCPB

Zero Power Reactor 3 (ZPR-3) C 10 MIN
16MM FILM OPTICAL SOUND
Illustrates the ZPR-3 operating method to study fuel configurations and their effect upon critical assembly, particularly operation and current applications in the Argonne National Laboratory's fast reactor program.
LC NO. FIE63-194
Prod-USAEC Dist-USNAC 1958

Zero Waste In Railroad Fueling C 27 MIN
16MM FILM OPTICAL SOUND IND
Presents an industrial training film that explores basic causes of diesel fuel waste. Shows ways of preventing and reducing oil leaks and spills, covers all types of high-speed automatic railroad fueling equipment and several types of manual fueling operations.
LC NO. 76-703961
Prod-SUNOIL Dist-VCI Prodn-VCI 1976

Zero-G C 15 MIN
16MM FILM, 3/4 OR 1/2 IN VIDEO
Presents a tour of the Skylab spacecraft and an introduction to its laboratory which is effectively free from the Earth's gravitational field. Explains the dynamics of the Earth's orbit and the meaning of the term zero-g. Issued in 1975 as a motion picture.
From The Skylab Science Demonstrations Series.
LC NO. 80-706411
Prod-NASA Dist-USNAC Prodn-AVCORP 1980

Zero, One And Rational Numbers B 45 MIN
2 INCH VIDEOTAPE H-C
See series title for descriptive statement.
From The Fundamentals Of Mathematics Series. Unit 2 - Introduction To Arithmetic.
Prod-CHITVC Dist-GPITVL Prodn-WTTWTV

Zero, The Troublemaker C 11 MIN
16MM FILM, 3/4 OR 1/2 IN VIDEO P
Explains the many uses of zero in addition and subtraction.
Prod-CORF Dist-CORF

Zest For Living, A C 29 MIN
2 INCH VIDEOTAPE
See series title for descriptive statement.
From The That's Life Series.
Prod-KOAPTV Dist-PUBTEL

Zeus, By Jove C 60 MIN
16MM FILM, 3/4 OR 1/2 IN VIDEO C A
Tells how Claudius is drawn perilously closer to power as his mad nephew Caligula proclaims himself a deity equal to Zeus.
From The I, Claudius Series. Number 9
Prod-BBCTV Dist-FI 1977

ZH Sound, The C 15 MIN
3/4 INCH VIDEO CASSETTE P
Explains that the ZH sound is spelled in a variety of ways.
From The New Talking Shop Series.
Prod-BSPTV Dist-GPITVL 1978

Ziehl-Neelsen Staining Procedure C 6 MIN
3/4 OR 1/2 INCH VIDEO CASSETTE
Demonstrates the various steps in the Ziehl-Neelsen staining procedure.
LC NO. 80-706598
Prod-CFDISC Dist-USNAC 1979

Ziel In Den Wolken B 101 MIN
3/4 OR 1/2 INCH VIDEO CASSETTE
A German language motion picture. Presents a drama about a young cavalry officer trying to convince his superiors of the role of aircraft in army reconnaissance, in the pioneer age of aviation in Germany. Shows how he leaves the military to pursue aviation development independently, forsaking the conservative old order to realize a progressive ideal without support from his contemporaries. No subtitles.
Prod-IHF Dist-IHF

Zigzag C 7 MIN
16MM FILM OPTICAL SOUND
Creates an abstract experiment on film using the colors and movement of neon advertising signs at night. Expresses the frenzied pace of our modern cities.
Prod-STAHER Dist-RADIM

Zikkaron C 6 MIN
16MM FILM, 3/4 OR 1/2 IN VIDEO
An allegorical film in which ephemeral images depict the cycle of life. Without narration.
Prod-NFBC Dist-IFB 1971

Zimbabwe - The New Struggle C 58 MIN
1/2 IN VIDEO CASSETTE BETA/VHS
Deals with the most compelling aspects of Zimbabwe's current political, social, and economic development, which include social and economic development in Matabeleland, the 'dissident' problem in Matabeleland, and the debate over Zimbabwe's possible future as a Marxist one-party state. Includes interviews with Prime Minister Mugabe, opposition leader Joseph Nkomo, Mozambican President Samora Machel and many people at the grass roots level.
Prod-ICARUS Dist-ICARUS

Zip Code - The Swing Six C 13 MIN
16MM FILM OPTICAL SOUND
Shows the need for ZIP code and how ZIP code works.
LC NO. 74-705986
Prod-USPOST Dist-USNAC

Zipper Applications C 28 MIN
3/4 OR 1/2 INCH VIDEO CASSETTE C A

Covers applying a lapped zipper (open and closed seam methods), hand stitching a lapped zipper, applying an exposed zipper, and applying a fly front zipper.
From The Clothing Construction Techniques Series.
Prod-IOWASP Dist-IOWASP

Zipper Installation C 29 MIN
2 INCH VIDEOTAPE
Features Mrs Ruth Hickman demonstrating how to install a zipper.
From The Sewing Skills - Tailoring Series.
Prod-KRMATV Dist-PUBTEL

Zipper Special, The C 29 MIN
2 INCH VIDEOTAPE
See series title for descriptive statement.
From The Designing Women Series.
Prod-WKYCTV Dist-PUBTEL

Zippers C 5 MIN
16MM FILM, 3/4 OR 1/2 IN VIDEO K-C A
See series title for descriptive statement.
From The How It's Made Series.
Prod-HOLIA Dist-LUF

Zlateh The Goat C 20 MIN
16MM FILM, 3/4 OR 1/2 IN VIDEO I-J
Presents a jewish folk tale by the Yiddish author, Isaac Bashevis Singer, about village life in pre-war Poland. Tells a deceptively simple story about a goat taken by its owner's son to be sold to the town butcher. Reveals the ecological balance that exists throughout nature and which links man to all living things.
Prod-WWS Dist-WWS

Zodiak C 9 MIN
16MM FILM OPTICAL SOUND
Presents a rhythmic fantasy created by the metamorphosis of images with drumbeats.
LC NO. 74-701328
Prod-DORAYA Dist-CANFDC 1972

Zollinger-Ellison Syndrome C 23 MIN
3/4 OR 1/2 INCH VIDEO CASSETTE PRO
Discusses Zollinger-Ellison Syndrome.
Prod-WFP Dist-WFP Prodn-UKANMC

Zonal Centrifuge, The C 6 MIN
16MM FILM OPTICAL SOUND H-C A
Explains that one of the most powerful tools of the molecular biologist is the zonal ultracentrifuge, and that its improved separation capabilities are playing an ever-increasing vital role in the fractionation of cell constituents and the purification of vaccines.
Prod-USAEC Dist-USERD 1971

Zonal Ultracentrifuge, The C 6 MIN
16MM FILM OPTICAL SOUND PRO
Explains that in man's continuing attack on human diseases, molecular biologists have begun to employ new zonal ultracentrifuges capable of rapid fractionization of large volumes of cell constituents.
LC NO. 78-714197
Prod-ANL Dist-USNAC 1971

Zontendijk's Method Of Feasible Directions C 60 MIN
3/4 OR 1/2 INCH VIDEO CASSETTE
See series title for descriptive statement.
From The Engineering Design Optimization II Series. Pt 26
Prod-UAZMIC Dist-UAZMIC

Zoo B 12 MIN
16MM FILM, 3/4 OR 1/2 IN VIDEO I-C A
Presents a visual essay on the comic characters at the zoo, including those on both sides of the bars. Filmed in Holland.
Prod-HA Dist-PFP 1975

Zoo C 15 MIN
3/4 OR 1/2 INCH VIDEO CASSETTE P
Presents the children's stories May I Bring A Friend by Beatrice De Regniers and Zoo, Where Are You by Ann Mc Govern.
From The Picture Book Park Series. Brown Module
Prod-WVIZTV Dist-AITECH 1974

Zoo C 22 MIN
16MM FILM, 3/4 OR 1/2 IN VIDEO
Takes a look at the behind-the-scenes activity at the National Zoological Park in Washington, D C. Shows how the animals are fed and doctored and how the Zoo conducts research in the areas of animal behavior and reproduction.
Prod-FNZOO Dist-AIMS Prodn-NVETA 1974

Zoo And You, The C 14 MIN
16MM FILM OPTICAL SOUND
Shows zoo animals and describes the operations of a zoo and its importance in our increasingly urbanized society.
Prod-NFBC Dist-CTFL 1970

Zoo Animals - Mammals, Pt 1 C 11 MIN
16MM FILM OPTICAL SOUND K-J
Provides a 'behind the scenes' look at the San Diego Zoo. Explains how animals are placed in a setting similar to their natural habitat and how they are fed and cared for. Features a kinkajou, panda, elephants, baby lions, Bengal tigers and sea lions.
LC NO. FIA58-327
Prod-ACA Dist-ACA 1957

Zoo Animals - Mammals, Pt 2 C 11 MIN
16MM FILM OPTICAL SOUND K-J
Shows how several mammals live and are cared for at the San Diego Zoo. Features the axis deer, eland, zebras, kangaroos, bears and a chimpanzee. Discusses the role of a zoo doctor.
LC NO. FIA58-328
Prod-ACA Dist-ACA 1957

Zoo Animals Behind The Scenes C 14 MIN
16MM FILM, 3/4 OR 1/2 IN VIDEO P-I
Shows the needs of zoo animals, telling how zoo workers prepare various foods for different animals, provide proper surroundings and necessary medical care. Relates this care to facts about the animals.
Prod-CORF Dist-CORF 1971

Zoo Animals In Rhyme C 11 MIN
16MM FILM, 3/4 OR 1/2 IN VIDEO P
Presents rhymes telling about zoo animals such as the lion, monkey, elephant, kangaroo, giraffe and bear.
Prod-CORF Dist-CORF 1965

Zoo Animals In The Wild C 10 MIN
16MM FILM, 3/4 OR 1/2 IN VIDEO P-I
Discusses the natural habitats of North American mammals using footage of the animals in the zoo intercut with scenes of the same animals in their natural environments.
LC NO. 80-706182
Prod-BERLET Dist-IFB 1979

Zoo Animals In The Wild—A Series
16MM FILM, 3/4 OR 1/2 IN VIDEO K-P
Describes the lifestyles of various animals, such as apes, elephants, crocodiles, beavers, pelicans, giant turtles and monkeys.
Prod-CORF Dist-CORF 1981

Apes	005 MIN
Baboons	007 MIN
Bears	006 MIN
Beavers	006 MIN
Crocodiles	006 MIN
Elephants	005 MIN
Giant Turtles	005 MIN
Lions And Tigers	006 MIN
Monkeys	005 MIN
Ostriches	005 MIN
Pelicans	006 MIN
Rhinos And Hippos	006 MIN

Zoo Babies C 15 MIN
3/4 OR 1/2 INCH VIDEO CASSETTE P-I
Views the various amounts of care which the babies of different species receive. Reveals that snakes, ducklings and goslings need little mothering while robins, alpacas, lions, gorillas and humans need lots of care.
From The Zoo Zoo Zoo Series.
Prod-WCETTV Dist-AITECH 1981

Zoo Babies (2nd Ed) C 8 MIN
16MM FILM, 3/4 OR 1/2 IN VIDEO K-P
Describes zoo babies and their relationships to their parents. Observes monkeys, gnus, kudus, peacocks, alligators and bears.
Prod-CORF Dist-CORF 1978

Zoo Babies - Large And Small C 11 MIN
16MM FILM, 3/4 OR 1/2 IN VIDEO P-I
Views some of the baby animals which can be found in zoos including bears, antelopes, zebras, giraffes, elephants and monkeys. Shows animals being fed at the children's zoo.
Prod-DEU Dist-MCFI

Zoo Baby Animals X 11 MIN
16MM FILM, 3/4 OR 1/2 IN VIDEO P
Gives a behind-the-scenes look at the zoo to see how baby animals are fed and cared for by their keepers. Shows children's zoo sections at the Lincoln Park and Brookfield Zoos of Chicago.
Prod-EBF Dist-EBEC 1961

Zoo Families (2nd Ed) C 9 MIN
16MM FILM, 3/4 OR 1/2 IN VIDEO P
Shows a group of children visiting a zoo, where they learn to recognize some of the animals and understand their ways of behaving.
Prod-BFA Dist-PHENIX 1977

Zoo Keepers C 29 MIN
16MM FILM, 3/4 OR 1/2 IN VIDEO J-H A
Describes behind-the-scenes activities at Chicago's Lincoln Park Zoo.
LC NO. 82-706266
Prod-LINCPK Dist-FI 1981

Zoo Time C 17 MIN
16MM FILM OPTICAL SOUND P-I
Describes how Mr and Mrs Graham convince the children that Alice the chimp should be returned to the zoo. Explains how Alice escapes, taking four other chimps with her.
Prod-LUF Dist-LUF 1977

Zoo Zoo Zoo—A Series
P-I
Offers close-up views of many different zoo animals.
Prod-WCETTV Dist-AITECH 1981

All About Ears	015 MIN
All About Eyes	015 MIN
All About Feet	015 MIN
All About Tails	015 MIN
Animal Costumes	015 MIN
Animal Defenses	015 MIN
Animal Groups	015 MIN
Animal Homes	015 MIN
Do Animals Talk	015 MIN
How And What Animals Eat	015 MIN
How Animals Help Each Other	015 MIN
How Animals Move	015 MIN
Importance Of Predators, The	015 MIN
Where Animals Live	015 MIN
Who Works At The Zoo	015 MIN
Zoo Babies	015 MIN

Zoo, The C 6 MIN
16MM FILM, 3/4 OR 1/2 IN VIDEO P-I
Portrays the varied personalities of animals at the zoo.
Prod-KINGSP Dist-PHENIX 1971

Zoo, The (2nd Ed) C 11 MIN
16MM FILM, 3/4 OR 1/2 IN VIDEO K-I
Features the Brookfield Zoo near Chicago, pointing out the pleasures, pastimes and purposes of a zoo. Looks at the animals' habitats, the necessary jobs humans perform, and special sights, such as the Children's Zoo and animal shows. Emphasizes the importance of zoos in conserving and protecting endangered species.
Prod-EBEC Dist-EBEC Prodn-WITTYC 1979

Zoo's-Eye View, A - Dawn To Dark C 11 MIN
16MM FILM, 3/4 OR 1/2 IN VIDEO P
Depicts the drama of a typical day at the zoo.
Prod-EBEC Dist-EBEC 1973

Zooful Of Poetry, A C 30 MIN
3/4 INCH VIDEO CASSETTE H-C A
Presents the first Poetry Quartet reading poems about animals while visiting the San Diego Zoo.
From The Anyone For Tennyson Series.
Prod-NETCHE Dist-GPITVL

Zoom In On Video C 15 MIN
3/4 OR 1/2 INCH VIDEO CASSETTE H-C A
Demonstrates techniques of video production.
Prod-SEVDIM Dist-SEVDIM

Zoom—A Series
16MM FILM, 3/4 OR 1/2 IN VIDEO P-I
Offers views of children from a variety of backgrounds, locations and ethnic groups who are involved in various activities.
Prod-WGBHTV Dist-FI

Alone In The Family	13 MIN
Animal Partners	13 MIN
Best I Can, The	12 MIN
Country Families	13 MIN
Everybody Likes Jazz	10 MIN
Experiments In Design	9 MIN
Fancy Footwork	9 MIN
Fast-Talking Jobs	11 MIN
Finding My Way	8 MIN
First It Seemed Kinda Strange	6 MIN
Foot-Stompin Music	12 MIN
For Love Or Money	12 MIN
From Generation To Generation	11 MIN
I'm On The Waltons	7 MIN
In Business For Myself	10 MIN
It's Harder For Patrick	7 MIN
Messages By Hand	8 MIN
More Than A Snapshot	10 MIN
My Family Business	12 MIN
Nobody Treats Me Different	8 MIN
On Stage And Screen	10 MIN
Rooted In The Past	13 MIN
They Call Me Pele	8 MIN
Working With Animals	11 MIN
Working With My Dad	9 MIN

Zooms On Self-Similar Figures C 8 MIN
16MM FILM, 3/4 OR 1/2 IN VIDEO
See series title for descriptive statement.
From The Topology Short Films Series.
LC NO. 81-706249
Prod-NSF Dist-IFB 1979

Zoos Of The World C 52 MIN
16MM FILM, 3/4 OR 1/2 IN VIDEO I-C A
Travels around the globe to some of the best zoos, which are striving to fill a new role that relates directly to environmental education.
LC NO. 80-706362
Prod-NGS Dist-NGS 1970

Zoot Sims Quartet C 29 MIN
16MM FILM - 1/2 IN VIDEO
See series title for descriptive statement.
From The Jazz On Stage Series.
Prod-RHPSDY Dist-RHPSDY

Zu Spat, Zu Spat C 15 MIN
16MM FILM, 3/4 OR 1/2 IN VIDEO
See series title for descriptive statement.
From The Guten Tag Series. Part 5
Prod-BAYER Dist-IFB 1968

Zubin And The IPO C 59 MIN
3/4 INCH VIDEO CASSETTE
Discusses the history of the Israel Philharmonic Orchestra. Focuses on its place in the musical world and on its relationship with conductor Zubin Mehta. Presents interviews with Mehta, other well-known musicians, and members of the orchestra.
LC NO. 83-707098
Prod-ADL Dist-ADL

Zubin Mehta - Commitment And Fulfillment As A Way Of Life C 22 MIN
16MM FILM OPTICAL SOUND J-C A
Shows musician and conductor Zubin Mehta conducting the Los Angeles Philharmonic Orchestra and presents a discussion by Mehta on the need for fulfillment and commitment to a goal.
From The Search Of Zubin Mehta Series.
LC NO. 78-700996
Prod-ESMRDA Dist-ESMRDA 1978

Zubin Mehta - If You Are Going To Lead, Lead C 36 MIN
16MM FILM OPTICAL SOUND J-C A
Presents musician and conductor Zubin Mehta, who talks about the need for an orchestra conductor to be a strong, resourceful

leader and about the demands that conducting make upon his life. Shows Mehta leading the Los Angeles Philharmonic Orchestra in excerpts from music by Beethoven, Mahler and others.
From The Search Of Zubin Mehta Series.
LC NO. 78-700997
Prod-ESMRDA Dist-ESMRDA 1978

Zubin Mehta And His Masters - Piatigorsky And Rubinstein C 29 MIN
16MM FILM OPTICAL SOUND J-C A
Interviews musician and conductor Zubin Mehta, who reveals how Gregor Piatigorsky, Arthur Rubinstein and others have influenced his life. Includes footage showing the interaction between Mehta, Piatigorsky and Rubenstein, as well as portions of a concert conducted by Mehta.
From The Search Of Zubin Mehta Series.
LC NO. 78-700994
Prod-ESMRDA Dist-ESMRDA 1978

Zubin Mehta Rocks The Gospel C 21 MIN
16MM FILM OPTICAL SOUND J-C A
Shows musician and conductor Zubin Mehta as he conducts the rock gospel music of the Inter-Denominational Gospel Choir.
From The Search Of Zubin Mehta Series.
LC NO. 78-700998
Prod-ESMRDA Dist-ESMRDA 1978

Zucker Aus Ruben C 5 MIN
16MM FILM, 3/4 OR 1/2 IN VIDEO H-C A
A German-language version of the motion picture Sugar From Beets. Describes the processes involved in obtaining sugar from beets.
From The European Studies - Germany (German) Series.
Prod-MFAFRG Dist-IFB Prodn-BAYER 1973

Zuckerandl C 15 MIN
16MM FILM, 3/4 OR 1/2 IN VIDEO H-C A
Presents a satire on an essay by Robert M Hutchins. Focuses on the fictitious philosopher Alexander Zucherandl, who expounds the view that the anesthetized life is the best life.
LC NO. 77-701738
Prod-HUBLEY Dist-TEXFLM 1976

Zulu C 138 MIN
16MM FILM OPTICAL SOUND
Tells the stirring story of the battle of Rorke's Drift and the handful of men who defended the mission station against 4,000 Zulu warriors during the British conquest of Zululand in 1879. Stars Stanley Baker, Jack Hawkins and Ulla Jacobsson.
Prod-AVCEP Dist-TWYMAN

Zurich C 3 MIN
16MM FILM OPTICAL SOUND P-I
Discusses the city of Zurich in Switzerland.
From The Of All Things Series.
Prod-BAILYL Dist-AVED

Zydrasis Horizontas (Lithuanian) B 70 MIN
3/4 OR 1/2 INCH VIDEO CASSETTE
Relates a popular children's adventure story. Presents the Lithuanian film studio's first independently-produced feature film.
Prod-IHF Dist-IHF

THE FREE LIBRARY OF PHILADELPHIA
3 2222 05283 0223